D0990269

The AMERICAN RACING MANUAL

•

2005 EDITION

ISBN: 1-9329109-7-2
Library of Congress Control Number: 2004118361

All statistical information subsequent to July 22, 1998, provided by Equibase Company LLC. Pedigree and sales information provided by The Jockey Club Information Systems, Inc.

Published by
Daily Racing Form Press
100 Broadway, 7th Floor
New York, NY 10005

Acknowledgements

It would be impossible to put out a book like the 2005 American Racing Manual, the authoritative source of data and statistics on its subject, without vital contributions from many individuals both within the Daily Racing Form and from racing organizations throughout the world.

Special thanks go to Graphics Editor William K. Scurry Jr.; Jeff Frank and Pete Shewchuk, for preparation of the chart pages; Chuck Kuehhas; Steve Davidowitz, for his contribution to the handicapping section; and writers Jay Privman (U.S.); Bill Tallon (Canada); Alan Shuback (foreign); Glenye Cain (breeding and sales); Daniel Kim and Noel Michaels. Thanks in particular are due to Vice President Irwin Cohen, a constant champion and supporter of the American Racing Manual since its hardcover return in 2000.

No less important are the endless contributions from outside organizations, to whom the Daily Racing Form is indebted.

Sincerest thanks, once again, go to Alan Marzelli, Chairman of Equibase Company LLC, and the President of The Jockey Club, who continues his strong personal support to the project; Christopher Scherf, Executive Vice President of Thoroughbred Racing Associations and Secretary of Equibase; and Carl Hamilton, Chairman and President of The Jockey Club Information Servies. Special mention also goes to Connie Brannen, Operations Manager at Equibase and liaison to this project, for her tireless contributions for the fifth straight year.

Thanks are due to Breeders' Cup Limited and its Media Relations Director Jim Gluckson; the Thoroughbred Racing Associations' Karen Darling; the Breeders' Cup's McKay Smith; The Jockey Club's Janet Olson and John Cooney; the National Thoroughbred Racing Association's Peggy Hendershot and Carol Paulick; and Andrew Schweigardt of the Thoroughbred Owners and Breeders Association, all of whom provided timely material on behalf of their organizations. Thanks also to contributing writers Andrew Beyer and Joe Clancy; photographer Cindy Pierson-Dulay and the Mid-Atlantic Thoroughbred; and Bill Christine and the Los Angeles Times for their generous contributions. Particular thanks go to the many individuals at racing tracks across the United States and Canada who contributed updates on their facilities for the Track Directory section.

In the end, however, the greatest thanks go out to the racing industry professionals and racing fans who will make use of this book in their research endeavors.

Paula Welch Prather
Editor, American Racing Manual

Acknowledgements

Foreword

Long after other similar sports encyclopedias have come and gone, the American Racing Manual continues to serve and entertain fans of the Thoroughbred and members of the racing industry. Now in its 110th year, the Manual continues to grow and change according to the need of its readers. The most notable addition to this year's ARM is the expansion of the handicapping section. This and future editions will carry excerpts from handicapping books in the DRF Press library. A chapter from Brad Free's "Handicapping 101," a basic guide for the everyday horseplayer, is featured this year. The stakes history section has been enhanced once again, this year adding histories of major Canadian graded stakes and classics. The popularity of handicapping contests has grown rapidly in the past few years, and in response the section covering the tournaments leading up to and including the National Handicapping Championship has received an upgrade. These changes, and the many others that have been made in the six years since the Manual was returned to its unabridged print form, help to maintain the ARM's legacy as the prime statistical resource for the Thoroughbred sport.

Irwin Cohen
Vice President/Senior Editor
DRF

Index

C

E

F

Gallery of Champions

Ghostzapper ....Horse of the Year
.....................Older Male
Declan's Moon ......2-Year-Old Male
Sweet Catomine ......2-Year-Old Filly
Smarty Jones ....3-Year-Old Male
Ashado ....3-Year-Old Filly
Azeri ....Older Female
Kitten's Joy ....Grass Horse, Male
Ouija Board ....Grass Horse, Female
Speightstown ....Sprinter
Hirapour ....Steeplechase

Older Male
Horse of the Year

Frank Stronach

Robert Frankel

GHOSTZAPPER, 2000

Br: Adena Springs (Ky.)

		Vice Regent
	Deputy Minister	
		Mint Copy
Awesome Again 1994		
		Blushing Groom
	Primal Force	
		Prime Prospect
		In Reality
	Relaunch	
		Foggy Note
Baby Zip 1991		
		Tri Jet
	Thirty Zip	
		Sailaway

Ghostzapper
Own: Stronach Stables

B. h. 5 (Apr)
Sire: Awesome Again (Deputy Minister) $125,000
Dam: Baby Zip (Relaunch)
Br: Adena Springs (Ky)
Tr: Frankel Robert J(0 0 0 0 .00) 2004:(491 135 .27)

Life	10	8	0	1	$2,996,120	128	D.Fst	8	6	0	1	$2,849,120	124
2004	4	4	0	0	$2,590,000	128	Wet(419)	2	2	0	0	$147,000	128
2003	4	3	0	1	$378,400	116	Turf(282)	0	0	0	0	$0	–
	0	0	0	0	$0	–	Dst(0)	0	0	0	0	$0	–

30Oct04–9LS	fst	1¼	:47 1:11¹ 1:35¹ 1:59	3↑BCClasic-G1	**124**	1	1½	1½	1¹	1²	1³	Castellano J J	L126 b	*2.50	–	–	Ghostzapper126³	Roses inMay126⁴	PleasantlyPerfect126¾	Drew clear late	13
11Sep04–10Bel	fst	1⅛	:45³ 1:08³ 1:33¹ 1:46¹	3↑Woodward-G1	**114**	3	3nk	2½	2hd	2hd	1nk	Castellano J J	L126 b	*.40	100–	15	*Ghostzapper*126nk	*SaintLiam*126⁹¼	BowmansBnd126⁷¼	Carried out, bumped	7
21Aug04–9Mth	sly	1⅛	:45⁴ 1:09³ 1:35¹ 1:47³	3↑IselnBCH-G3	**128**	3	21½	21½	2½	1²	110¾	Castellano J J	L120 b	*.40	103–	16	*Ghostzpper*120¹⁰¾	Prsidntilffir117²1¼	Zoffingr115no	Drew out,hand ridden	4
4Jly04–9Bel	fst	7f	:22² :44³ 1:08¹ 1:20²	3↑TomFoolH-G2	**120**	3	2	3²	2hd	14½	14¼	Castellano J J	L119 b	*1.35	98–	13	*Ghostzpper*119⁴¼	Aggdn114³½	UnforgettbleMx114½	4 wide move, hand ride	4

2–Year–Old Male

Victor Espinoza

Ron Ellis

DECLAN'S MOON, 2002

Br: Brice Ridgely (Md)

		Seattle Slew
	A.P. Indy	
		Weekend Surprise
Malibu Moon 1997		
		Mr. Prospector
	Macoumba	
		Maximova
		Conquistador Cielo
	Norquestor	
		Linda North
Vee Vee Star 1996		
		Somethingfabulous
	Fabulous Vee	
		Mrs. Vee Vee

Declan's Moon
Own: Jay Em Ess Stable

Dk. b or b. g. 3 (Feb) EASSEP03 $125,000
Sire: Malibu Moon (A.P. Indy) $17,500
Dam: Vee Vee Star (Norquestor)
Br: Brice Ridgely (Md)
Tr: Ellis Ronald W(0 0 0 0 .00) 2004:(121 24 .20)

Life	4	4	0	0	$507,300	107	**D.Fst**	4 4 0 0	$507,300 107
2004	4	4	0	0	$507,300	107	**Wet(349)**	0 0 0 0	$0 –
2003	0	M	0	0	$0	–	**Turf(303)**	0 0 0 0	$0 –
	0	0	0	0	$0	–	**Dst(0)**	0 0 0 0	$0 –

18Dec04–8Hol fst $1\frac{1}{16}$:23^{2} :46 1:10 1:41^{3} HolFut-G1 **96** 3 2^{1} 2$\frac{1}{2}$ 1^{hd} 1^{1} 1^{1} Espinoza V LB121 *1.20 93–11 Declan's Moon121^{1} Giacomo121^{no} Wilko121^{2} Bid,led,held gamely 7

20Nov04–8Hol fst 7f :21^{4} :44^{1} 1:08^{2} 1:21^{3} HolPrevu-G3 **98** 5 5 3^{2} 3^{1} 1$\frac{1}{2}$ 1^{2} Espinoza V LB122 *.40 94–11 *Declan's Moon*122^{2} Bushwacker114^{hd} Seize theDay117^{2} 3wd bid,ridden out 8

8Sep04–8Dmr fst 7f :22^{1} :44^{3} 1:08^{4} 1:21^{1} DmrFut-G2 **107** 1 3 2$3\frac{1}{2}$ 2^{4} 2$\frac{1}{2}$ 1^{nk} Espinoza V LB116 6.20 96–11 *DeclansMoon*116^{nk} *RomanRuler*120$9\frac{1}{2}$ *SwissLad*116^{4} Bid btwn,brushed,game 4

31Jly04–3Dmr fst $5\frac{1}{2}$f :22 :45^{1} :57^{2} 1:03^{3} Md Sp Wt 49k **87** 1 2 1^{hd} 1^{hd} 1^{1} 1^{5} Flores D R LB118 14.70 97–09 *Declan's Moon*118^{5} Currency Trader118^{2} Cashmula118$\frac{1}{2}$ Inside, ridden out 7

Julio Canani

Corey Nakatani

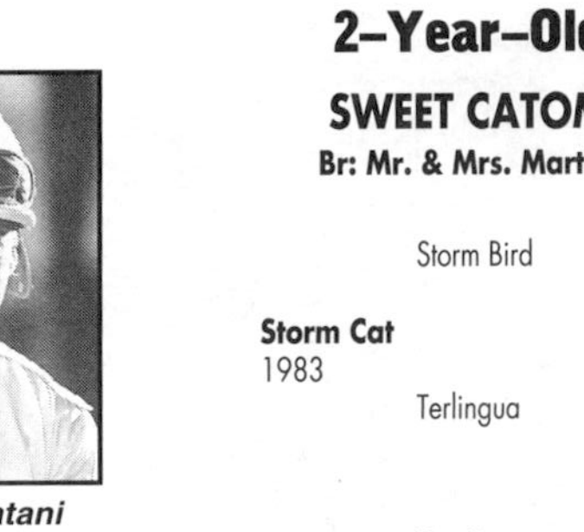

2–Year–Old Female

SWEET CATOMINE, 2002

Br: Mr. & Mrs. Martin J. Wygod (Ky)

Storm Cat 1983	Storm Bird	Northern Dancer
		South Ocean
	Terlingua	Secretariat
		Crimson Saint
Sweet Life 1996	Kris S.	Roberto
		Sharp Queen
	Symbolically	Flying Paster
		Hail to the Queen

Sweet Catomine
Own: Wygod Mr. and Mrs. Martin J

B. f. 3 (Feb)
Sire: Storm Cat (Storm Bird) $500,000
Dam: Sweet Life (Kris S.)
Br: Mr. & Mrs. Martin J. Wygod (Ky)
Tr: Canani Julio C(0 0 0 0 .00) 2004:(186 42 .23)

Life	4	3	1	0	$799,800	102	**D.Fst**	4	3	1	0	$799,800	102
2004	4	3	1	0	$799,800	102	**Wet(430)**	0	0	0	0	$0	–
2003	0	M	0	0	$0	–	**Turf(376)**	0	0	0	0	$0	–
	0	0	0	0	$0	–	**Dst(0)**	0	0	0	0	$0	–

30Oct04–3LS fst $1\frac{1}{16}$:22⁴ :46² 1:10³ 1:41³ ⒻBCJuvFil-G1 **102** 9 7$5\frac{1}{2}$ 7$4\frac{1}{4}$ 7$1\frac{3}{4}$ 2hd 1$3\frac{3}{4}$ Nakatani C S L119 b *2.30 94–02 SweetCatomine119$3\frac{3}{4}$ Blletto119$1\frac{1}{4}$ *RunwyModel*119$\frac{3}{4}$ Blocked 5/16,checked 12

20Oct04–9SA fst $1\frac{1}{16}$:23 :46⁴ 1:11¹ 1:42⁴ ⒻOakLeaf-G2 **91** 9 7$2\frac{3}{4}$ 6⁶ 5$2\frac{1}{4}$ 1$2\frac{1}{2}$ 1⁴ Nakatani C S LB119 b 2.00 91–08 *SweetCatomine*119⁴ *SplendidBlended*119$2\frac{1}{2}$ Memorette119⁴ 4wd surge,clear 9

28Aug04–8Dmr fst 7f :22 :44² 1:10² 1:24 ⒻDmrDeb-G1 **76** 7 9 9$6\frac{1}{4}$ 7$8\frac{1}{4}$ 3³ 1$\frac{3}{4}$ Espinoza V LB114 b *1.60e 82–13 *SwtCtomin*114$\frac{3}{4}$ SouvnirGift120$1\frac{1}{2}$ HlloLucky116$2\frac{1}{2}$ Hopd brk,5w,nailed foe 9

31Jly04–1Dmr fst $5\frac{1}{2}$f :22¹ :45¹ :57⁴ 1:04² ⒻMd Sp Wt 50k **64** 9 3 4$2\frac{3}{4}$ 4$2\frac{1}{2}$ 3$3\frac{1}{2}$ 2⁵ Flores D R LB118 b 5.70 88–09 She's Salty118⁵ *Sweet Catomine*118nk Wild Humor118$\frac{1}{2}$ 5wd,3wd,late 2nd 9

3–Year–Old Male

Stewart Elliott

John Servis

SMARTY JONES, 2001

Br: Someday Farm (Pa)

		Mr. Prospector
	Gone West	
		Secrettame
Elusive Quality 1993		
		Hero's Honor
	Touch of Greatness	
		Ivory Wand
		In Reality
	Smile	
		Sunny Smile
I'll Get Along 1992		
		Foolish Pleasure
	Dont Worry Bout Me	
		Stolen Base

Smarty Jones
Own: Someday Farm

Ch. c. 4 (Feb)
Sire: Elusive Quality (Gone West) $100,000
Dam: I'll Get Along (Smile)
Br: Someday Farm (Pa)
Tr: Servis John C(0 0 0 0 .00) 2004:(284 68 .24)

Life	9	8	1	0	$7,613,155	118	D.Fst	7	6	1	0	$1,128,355	118
2004	7	6	1	0	$7,563,535	118	Wet(343)	2	2	0	0	$6,484,800	107
2003	2	2	0	0	$49,620	105	Turf(276)	0	0	0	0	$0	–
	0	0	0	0	$0	–	Dst(0)	0	0	0	0	$0	–

5Jun04-11Bel fst 1½ :48³ 1:11³ 2:00² 2:27² Belmont-G1 **100** 9 3¹ 1½ 13½ 11½ 2¹ Elliott S L126 f *.35 94–10 *Birdstone*126¹ Smarty Jones126⁸ Royal Assault126³ Vied, clear, gamely 9
15May04-12Pim fst 1 3/16 :47¹ 1:11² 1:36² 1:55² Preakness-G1 **118** 6 21½ 22½ 2¹ 1⁵ 111½ Elliott S L126 f *.70 100–13 SmrtyJons126 11½ RockHrdTn126² Eddington126hd 3-4w,angled in,driving 10
1May04-10CD sly 1¼ :46³ 1:11⁴ 1:37¹ 2:04 KyDerby-G1 **107** 13 42½ 21½ 2hd 1hd 12¾ Elliott S L126 f *4.10 79–21 *Smarty Jones*126 2¾ Lion Heart126 3¼ Imperialism126² Stalked,bid,clear 18
10Apr04-9OP my 1⅛ :46⁴ 1:11³ 1:36⁴ 1:49² ArkDerby-G2 **107** 11 2½ 2½ 1hd 1³ 11½ Elliott S 122 f *1.00 91–17 *Smarty Jones*122 1½ Borrego118 1½ Pro Prado122 3½ Cleared at will,drivng 11
20Mar04-10OP fst 1 1/16 :23² :47³ 1:12 1:42 Rebel200k **108** 7 2¹ 2¹ 2½ 1¹ 13¼ Elliott S 122 f 3.50 100–16 *Smarty Jones*122 3¼ Purge117 3¾ Pro Prado117 3¾ Kicked strongly clear 9
28Feb04-9OP fst 1 :22⁴ :45⁴ 1:11¹ 1:37² Southwest100k **95** 6 21½ 22½ 2hd 1² 1¾ Elliott S 122 f *.50 97–18 *SmrtyJons*122¾ *TwoDownAtomtc*112½ ProPrd117 7¼ Chased,took over,drvng 9
3Jan04-8Aqu fst 1⁷⁰ ⊡ :23¹ :47 1:11³ 1:41² CountFleet81k **97** 7 3¹ 3¹ 2hd 1½ 1⁵ Elliott S 116 f *.40 91–21 *Smarty Jones*11 5 Risky Trick116⁶ Mr. Spock116½ Stumbled start, 3 wide 7

Eibar Coa

Todd Pletcher

3–Year–Old Female

ASHADO, 2001

Br: Aaron U. Jones & Marie D. Jones (Ky.)

		Hail to Reason
	Halo	
		Cosmah
Saint Ballado 1989		
		Herbager
	Ballade	
		Miss Swapsco
		Northern Dancer
	Mari's Book	
		Mari Her
Goulash 1993		
		Blushing Groom
	Wise Bride	
		Wising Up

Ashado
Own: Starlight Stables LLC Saylor, Paul an

Dk. b or b. f. 4 (Feb) KEESEP02 $170,000
Sire: Saint Ballado (Halo) $125,000
Dam: Goulash (Mari's Book)
Br: Aaron U. Jones & Marie D. Jones (Ky)
Tr: Pletcher Todd A(0 0 0 0 .00) 2004:(948 240 .25)

Life	14	9	3	2	$2,870,440	106
2004	8	5	2	1	$2,259,640	106
2003	6	4	1	1	$610,800	95
	0	0	0	0	$0	-

D.Fst	8	4	3	1	$985,000	103
Wet(364)	6	5	0	1	$1,885,440	106
Turf(306)	0	0	0	0	$0	-
Dst(0)	0	0	0	0	$0	-

Date/Race	Cond	Dist	Fractions	Race	Fig	PP	St	1C	2C	Str	Fin	Jockey	Wt	Odds	Comp	Top Finishers	Comment	Fld
30Oct04-2LS	gd	1⅛	:463 1:102 1:352 1:481	3↑ⒻBCDistaf-G1	102	1	31	52	41½	1½	11¼	Velazquez J R	L119	*2.00	108-02	Ashado1191¼ StormFlagFlying123nk StellrJyne1191½	Blocked 1/4,steadied	11
20Oct04-9Pha	fst	1 1/16	:234 :473 1:111 1:413	ⒻCotillnH-G2	103	5	21½	21	2½	1½	12¾	Coa E M	L124	*.20	107-13	Ashado1242¾ Ender'sSister1173½ MyLordship1151¼	When ready,drew clear	7
21Aug04-10Sar	sly	1¼	:471 1:112 1:362 2:023	ⒻAlabama-G1	103	5	3½	3nk	1hd	2hd	33	Velazquez J R	L121	*.60	91-18	SocietySelection1212½ StellarJyne121½ Ashdo1215¼	Vied 3 wide, weakened	8
24Jly04-8Bel	my	1¼	:483 1:122 1:363 2:022	ⒻCCAOaks-G1	106	4	2½	2½	11½	15	14½	Velazquez J R	L121	*.75	85-22	Ashado1214½ StellarJayne1217½ MagicIllusion1214	Drew clear when asked	6
26Jun04-9Bel	fst	1⅛	:47 1:104 1:352 1:48	ⒻMthrGoos-G1	96	4	1hd	2hd	1hd	2½	22½	Velazquez J R	L121	*.90	88-11	Stellar Jayne1212½ Ashado1211¾ Island Sand1215	Stayed on for place	6
30Apr04-10CD	my	1⅛	:46 1:094 1:363 1:504	ⒻKyOaks-G1	102	1	33½	24½	24	2hd	11¼	Velazquez J R	L121	*2.30	83-17	Ashado1211¼ IslandSand1211¾ MadcapEscapde1211¼	Moved 4w,stiff drive	11
3Apr04-9Kee	fst	1 1/16	:24 :472 1:112 1:442	ⒻAshland-G1	97	1	31	32	32	22½	2½	Velasquez C	L123	1.70	89-14	Madcap Escapade118½ Ashado1234 Last Song1203	Ck 1st turn,4w bid	4
6Mar04-9FG	fst	1 1/16	:234 :473 1:121 1:43	ⒻFGOaks-G2	94	1	32	32½	31½	12½	13¾	Velasquez C	L121	*1.10	95-10	Ashado1213¾ Victory U. S. A.1211¼ Shadow Cast121½	3-w bid, clear,driving	6

D. Wayne Lukas

Pat Day

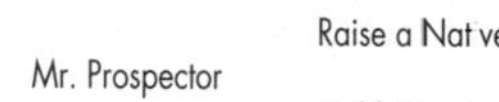

Older Female

AZERI, 1998

Br: Allen E. Paulson (Ky.)

		Raise a Native
	Mr. Prospector	
		Gold Digger
Jade Hunter 1984		
		Pharly
	Jadana	
		Janina
		Lorenzaccio
	Ahonoora	
		Helen Nichols
Zodiac Miss 1989		
		Try My Best
	Capricornia	
		Franconia

Azeri
Own: Allen E. Paulson Living Trust

Ch. m. 7 (May)
Sire: Jade Hunter (Mr. Prospector) $10,000
Dam: Zodiac Miss*Aus (Ahonoora*GB)
Br: Allen E. Paulson (Ky)
Tr: Lukas D. W(0 0 0 0 .00) 2004:(577 67 .12)

Life	24	17	4	0	$4,079,820	112	D.Fst	23 16 4 0	$3,039,820 112
2004	8	3	2	0	$1,035,000	112	Wet(329)	1 1 0 0	$1,040,000 111
2003	5	4	1	0	$817,080	109	Turf(272)	0 0 0 0	$0 –
	0	0	0	0	$0	–	Dst(0)	0 0 0 0	$0 –

Date/Race	Cond	Dist	Fractions	Race	Speed	PP	St	1C	2C	Str	Fin	Jockey	Med/Wt	Odds	Pace	Top Finishers	Comment	Fld
30Oct04-9LS	fst	1¼	:47 1:11¹ 1:35¹ 1:59	3↑BCClasic-G1	**109**	3	3¹	4²	7³½	5⁵½	5⁹¾	Day P	L123	15.20	- -	Ghostzpper126≡ RosesinMy126⁴ PlesntlyPerfect126¾	Broke slow, rail trip	13
10Oct04-8Kee	fst	1⅛	:46⁴ 1:11³ 1:37 1:49³	3↑ⒻSpinster-G1	**108**	1	2¹½	2¹½	2hd	1hd	1³	Day P	L123	*.40	93- 12	Azeri123³ Tamweel123½ Mayo On the Side123³¾	3-4w,mild hand urging	7
27Aug04-9Sar	fst	1¼	:46¹ 1:09³ 1:35⁴ 2:03³	3↑ⒻPrsnlEnH-G1	**97**	2	2¹½	2hd	1¹½	2hd	2¹¼	Day P	L122	*.60	88- 11	StormFlagFlying116¹¼ *Azeri*122½ Nevermore114⁴½	Stalked fast pace game	5
1Aug04-9Sar	fst	1⅛	:47³ 1:10⁴ 1:35 1:47⁴	3↑ⒻGoFWandH-G1	**106**	5	1¹½	1½	1½	1hd	1¹¾	Day P	L120	2.95	96- 14	Azeri120¹¾ *Sightseek*122² *Storm Flag Flying*117⁷	Pace, resolute, clear	5
19Jun04-9Bel	fst	1$\frac{1}{16}$	:23¹ :45³ 1:10 1:41²	3↑ⒻOPhippsH-G1	**78**	1	1½	1hd	2½	4¹⁰	4¹¹¾	Day P	L123	*.80	81- 20	Sightseek120³¼ Storm Flag Flying117⁶½ Passing Shot116²	Set pace, tired	4
31May04-9Bel	fst	1	:23² :46 1:10 1:35²	3↑MtropltH-G1	**103**	3	3²½	3½	5¹¼	6²¾	8⁶¾	Day P	L117	5.80	77- 34	PicoCntrl119¾ BowmnsBnd114²¼ StrongHop119¹½	Close up inside, empty	9
1May04-8CD	fst	7f	:22² :45 1:09³ 1:22³	4↑ⒻHmnaDstH-G1	**99**	2	4	2¹	2¹½	2hd	2hd	Smith M E	L125	*.70	89- 06	Mayo On the Side114hd Azeri125⁷¼ Randaroo121nk	Bid btwn,game rail	4
3Apr04-9OP	fst	1$\frac{1}{16}$	:23¹ :46³ 1:10⁴ 1:41¹	4↑ⒻAplBlsmH-G1	**112**	1	1¹	1½	1¹½	1²½	1¹½	Smith M E	L123	2.00	104- 09	Azeri123¹½ ⒹWild Spirit119¹¾ Star Parade114⁷¼	Pace off rail, driving	6

Turf Male

Dale Romans

Kenneth Ramsey

KITTEN'S JOY, 2001

Br: Kenneth L. Ramsey & Sarah K. Ramsey (Ky)

El Prado 1989	Sadler's Wells	Northern Dancer
		Fairy Bridge
	Lady Capulet	Sir Ivor
		Cap and Bells
Kitten's First 1991	Lear Fan	Roberto
		Wac
	That's My Hon	L'Enjoleur
		One Lane

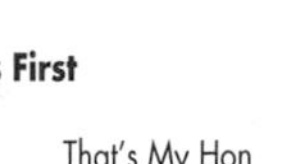

Kitten's Joy
Own: Ramsey Kenneth L. and Sarah K

Ch. c. 4 (May)
Sire: El Prado*Ire (Sadler's Wells) $100,000
Dam: Kitten's First (Lear Fan)
Br: Kenneth L. Ramsey & Sarah K. Ramsey (Ky)
Tr: Romans Dale L(0 0 0 0 .00) 2004:(580 109 .19)

Life	12	8	3	0	$1,705,911	114	**D.Fst**	2	0	1	0	$10,550	74
2004	8	6	2	0	$1,625,796	114	**Wet(346)**	0	0	0	0	$0	–
2003	4	2	1	0	$80,115	86	**Turf(325)**	10	8	2	0	$1,695,361	114
	0	0	0	0	$0	–	**Dst(0)**	0	0	0	0	$0	–

Date/Race	Cond	Dist	Fractions	Race	Fig	PP	St	1C	2C	Str	Fin	Jockey	Wt	Odds		Top finishers	Comment	Fld
30Oct04–8LS	yl	1½	Ⓣ:49 1:134 2:04 2:293	3↑BCTurf-G1	**108**	4	37	32½	32	31½	21¾	Velazquez J R	L121	*.70	121–07	BettrTlkNow1261¾ KittnsJoy1211 Powrscourt1262¼	Inside move, 2nd best	8
2Oct04–9Bel	yl	1½	Ⓣ:504 1:171 2:071 2:294	3↑TfClscIv-G1	**114**	5	42½	41¾	21½	1hd	12½	Velazquez J R	L121	2.40	72–22	Kitten's Joy1212½ Magistretti126¾ Tycoon1213	Strong when set down	7
14Aug04–11AP	fm	1¼	Ⓣ:463 1:11 1:351 1:593	Secretar-G1	**113**	1	611	610	52¾	1½	13¼	Bailey J D	L123	*.90	113 –	*KittensJoy*1233¼ GreekSun1211¼ MoscowBallet1191	5w, vigorous hand ride	7
10Jly04–9Cnl	fm	1¼	Ⓣ:471 1:112 1:364 2:011	VaDby-G3	**108**	2	616	413	33½	1½	12¾	Prado E S	L117	1.70	99–16	*Kitten'sJoy*1172¾ *ArtieSchiller*1174¾ *PrinceArch*11912¾	4wd move,drifted out	8
12Jun04–5CD	yl	1⅛	Ⓣ:49 1:134 1:381 1:503	JfrsnCup-G3	**101**	8	85	64	41	1hd	2hd	Bailey J D	L122	*.70	80–25	PrncArch120hd *KttnsJoy*1224¾ CoolCondctor1161¼	5w,bid,clear,outgamed	9
30Apr04–9CD	gd	1 1/16	Ⓣ:243 :492 1:131 1:431	AmerTurf-G3	**93**	4	93¾	82¾	42½	1½	12½	Bailey J D	L123	*1.10	88–11	Kitten's Joy1232½ *Prince Arch*123½ Capo1172¼	Bmp gate,6w,driving	9
21Feb04–11GP	fm	1⅛	Ⓣ:494 1:133 1:371 1:483	PalmBch-G3	**91**	1	43½	43	52½	3½	11¾	Bailey J D	L122	*.60e	92–06	*Kitten's Joy*1221¾ Prince Arch118nk Pa Pa Da118¾	Angled out, clear	12
1Jan04–9Crc	fm	1⅛	Ⓣ:471 1:112 1:351 1:464	+ TrpPkDby-G3	**91**	9	43	64½	41½	1hd	14½	Bailey J D	L119	3.60	95–08	*KittensJoy*1194½ BrodwyView112nk SoverignHonor117hd	3wd bid,drew off	11

Turf Female

Lord Derby

Kieren Fallon

OUIJA BOARD, 2001

Br: Stanley Estate and Stud Co. (GB)

Sire / Dam	Grandsire / Granddam	Great-grandparents
Cape Cross 1994	Green Desert	Danzig
		Foreign Courier
	Park Appeal	Ahonoorc
		Balidaress
Selection Board 1982	Welsh Pageant	Tudor Melody
		Picture Light
	Ouija	Silly Season
		Samanda

Ouija Board (GB)
Own: Lord Derby

B. f. 4 (Mar)
Sire: Cape Cross*Ire (Green Desert) $67,835
Dam: Selection Board*GB (Welsh Pageant*Fr)
Br: Stanley Estate and Stud Co (GB)
Tr: Dunlop Edward(0 0 0 0 .00) 2004:(1 1 1.00)

Life	8	5	0	3	$1,671,768	10[illegible]	D.Fst	0	0	0	0	$0	–
2004	5	4	0	1	$1,659,958	10[illegible]	Wet(280*)	0	0	0	0	$0	–
2003	3	1	0	2	$11,810	–	Turf(263*)	8	5	0	3	$1,671,768	108
	0	0	0	0	$0	–	Dst(0)	0	0	0	0	$0	–

300ct04–6LS yl 1⅜ Ⓣ :52²1:18² 1:42¹2:18¹ 3↑ⒻBCF&MTrf-G1 **108** 5 5⁵½ 4³½ 4³ 2ʰᵈ 1¹½ Fallon K L118 *.90 98–07 Ouija Board11[illegible]1½ Film Maker123ⁿᵏ Wonder Again123²¾ Drew off late 12

30ct04 Longchamp (Fr) gd *1½ Ⓣ RH 2:25 3↑ Prix de l'Arc de Triomphe-G1 Stk 1986000 3¹½ Murtagh J P 120 9.00 Bago123½ Che[illegible]ry Mix123¹ *Ouija Board*120² 19
Timeform rating: 124+ *Rated in 14th,lacked room 2f out,sharp late run into 3rd*

18Jly04 Curragh (Ire) gf 1½ Ⓣ RH 2:28¹ ⒻIrish Oaks-G1 Stk 498000 1¹ Fallon K 126 *.57 Ouija Board12[illegible]1 Punctilious126¾ Hazarista126⁷ 7
Timeform rating: 116+ *Dwelt,rated in 5th,led 1-1/2f out,handily.AllTooBeautiful4th*

4Jun04 Epsom (GB) gd 1½ Ⓣ LH 2:35² ⒻEnglish Oaks-G1 Stk 644000 1⁷ Fallon K 126 3.50 *Ouija Board*126 All Too Beautiful126³½ *Punctilious*1261½ 7
Timeform rating: 124 *Dwelt,rated in 6th,led 2f out,surged clear.Necklace4th*

2May04 Newmarket (GB) gd 1¼ Ⓣ Str 2:02⁴ ⒻPretty Polly Stakes (Listed) Stk 53300 1⁶ Fallon K 120 *2.00 *Ouija Board*120[illegible] Sahool120½ Rave Reviews1201¼ 9
Timeform rating: 116+ *Rated in 5th,led over 1f out,ridden clear*

Sprinter

Eugene Melnyk

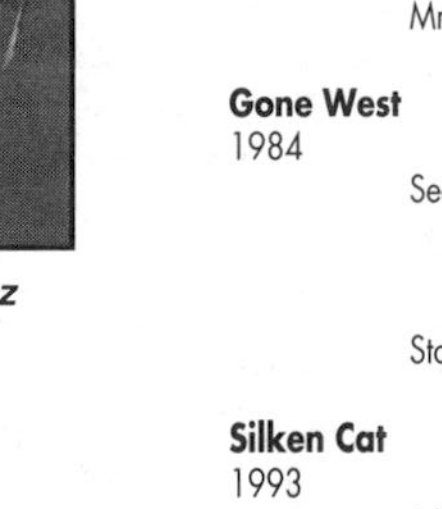

John Velazquez

SPEIGHTSTOWN, 1998

Br: Aaron U. Jones & Marie D. Jones (Ky)

Gone West 1984	Mr. Prospector	Raise a Native
		Gold Digger
	Secrettame	Secretariat
		Tamerett
Silken Cat 1993	Storm Cat	Storm Bird
		Terlingua
	Silken Doll	Chieftain
		Insilca

Speightstown
Own: Melnyk Eugene and Laura

Ch. h. 7 (Feb)
Sire: Gone West (Mr. Prospector) $150,000
Dam: Silken Cat (Storm Cat)
Br: Aaron U. Jones & Marie Jones (Ky)
Tr: Pletcher Todd A(0 0 0 0 .00) 2004:(948 240 .25)

Life	16	10	2	2	$1,258,256	117
2004	6	5	0	1	$1,045,556	117
2003	2	1	1	0	$56,020	105
	0	0	0	0	$0	–

D.Fst	13	8	1	2	$1,064,600	117
Wet(409)	3	2	1	0	$193,656	116
Turf(329)	0	0	0	0	$0	–
Dst(0)	0	0	0	0	$0	–

Date/Race	Cond	Dist	Fractions	Race	Spd	PP	St	1C	2C	Str	Fin	Jockey	Wt	Odds	Pace	Top Finishers	Comment	Fld
30Oct04–5LS	fst	6f	:21^1 :43^2 :55^2 1:08	3↑BCSprint-G1	**112**	2	8	4$1\frac{1}{2}$	3^1	1$1\frac{1}{2}$	1$1\frac{1}{4}$	Velazquez J R	L126	3.70	100– 04	Speightstown126$1\frac{1}{4}$ Kela126$\frac{3}{4}$ My Cousin Matt126$\frac{1}{2}$	Rail trip,edged clear	13
2Oct04–8Bel	fst	6f	:22^3 :45^3 :57^1 1:09^3	3↑Vosburgh-G1	**102**	2	2	1$\frac{1}{2}$	2^{hd}	2$\frac{1}{2}$	3$4\frac{1}{2}$	Velazquez J R	L124	*.80	86– 22	Pico Central124^4 Voodoo124$\frac{1}{2}$ *Speightstown*124^{hd}	Bobbled start, between	5
14Aug04–7Sar	fst	6f	:22 :44^2 :55^4 1:08	3↑AGVndbtH-G2	**117**	2	5	1^{hd}	2^{hd}	1$2\frac{1}{2}$	1$1\frac{1}{2}$	Velazquez J R	L120	*.90	102– 12	Spghtstown120$1\frac{1}{2}$ ClockStoppr115$1\frac{1}{2}$ GtrsNBrs118^2	Vied inside, kept busy	6
5Jun04–7Bel	fst	6f	:21^2 :43^3 :55^1 1:08	3↑TrNthBCH-G2	**115**	3	1	2$2\frac{1}{2}$	1$\frac{1}{2}$	1$1\frac{1}{2}$	1$1\frac{1}{2}$	Velazquez J R	L119	*1.80	99– 07	*Speightstown*119$1\frac{1}{2}$ Cat Genius116$1\frac{3}{4}$ *Pohave*117^{nk}	When roused, driving	9
1May04–5CD	gd	7f	:22^2 :45^1 1:08^4 1:21^1	4↑CDH-G2	**116**	1	3	1^1	1^1	1$2\frac{1}{2}$	1$3\frac{1}{2}$	Velazquez J R	L115	5.40	96– 06	*Speightstown*115$3\frac{1}{2}$ McCannsMojve117^2 Publiction116^2	Speed,inside,clear	7
27Mar04–11GP	fst	7f	:22^1 :44^4 1:09 1:22	3↑ArtaxH100k	**106**	1	1	1^{hd}	1^{hd}	1$3\frac{1}{2}$	1$4\frac{1}{2}$	Coa E M	L116	*3.20	92– 16	*Speightstown*116$4\frac{1}{2}$ *PrttyWild*111no WckyforLov115$3\frac{1}{4}$	Dueled rail, drew off	9

Steeplechase

Matt McCarron

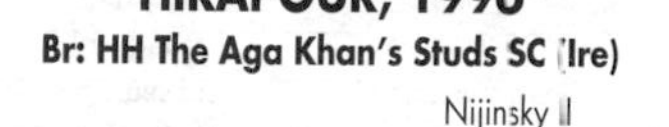

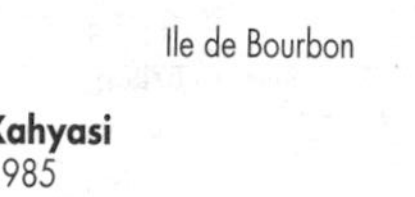

Paul Fout

HIRAPOUR, 1996

Br: HH The Aga Khan's Studs SC (Ire)

		Nijinsky II
	Ile de Bourbon	
		Roseliere
Kahyasi 1985		
		Blushing Groom
	Kadissya	
		Kalkeen
		Nishapour
	Mouktar	
		Molitva
Himaya 1988		
		Hethersett
	Highest Hopes	
		Verdura

Hirapour (Ire)
Own: Eldon Farm LLC

B. g. 8 (Apr)
Sire: Kahyasi (Ile de Bourbon) $8,140
Dam: Himaya*Ire (Mouktar)
Br: His Highness the Aga Khans Studs S. C. (Ire)
Tr: Fout Paul D(0 0 0 0 .00) 2004:(95 16 .17)

Life	32	13	5	2	$373,401	–						
Jumps	13	8	3	1	$320,292	–						
2004	4	2	2	0	$199,625	–	Wet	0	0	0	0	$0 –
2003	10	7	1	1	$128,167	–	Turf	19	5	2	1	$53,109 –

Date/Race	Trk	Dist	Surface	Time	Race		PP	Start	Calls				Fin	Jockey	Wt	Odds			Top Finishers	Comment	Fld
21Nov04–7Cam	fm	2¾	Hurdles	5:04^{3}	4↑ColonlCp-G1	–	4	6^{24}	4^{18}	4^{2}	1^{hd}		$1^{2\frac{3}{4}}$	McCarron M O	L156	-	-	-	Hirapour$156^{2\frac{3}{4}}$ Preemptive Strike156^{5} Sur La Tete156^{9}	Settled, stiff drive	7
23Oct04–5FH	fm	2⅝	Hurdles	5:06^{4}	4↑BrCupStp-G1	–	2	$7^{6\frac{1}{2}}$	$7^{7\frac{1}{2}}$	4^{4}	$2^{1\frac{1}{2}}$		$2^{1\frac{1}{2}}$	McCarron M O	L156	-	-	-	McDynamo156 $\frac{1}{2}$ *Hirapour*$156^{\frac{1}{2}}$ Sur La Tete$156^{15\frac{1}{2}}$	Loomed, finished well	7
16Apr04–8Kee	fm	2½	Hurdles	4:41^{2}	4↑RylChsHd-G1	–	1	6^{9}	6^{7}	$4^{1\frac{1}{4}}$	2^{hd}		$1^{1\frac{3}{4}}$	Chipperfield C	L148	*1.20	-	-	Hirapour$148^{1\frac{3}{4}}$ Preemptive Strike150^{7} *Dancewel*142^{1}	Driving,clear	8
27Mar04–6Cam	fm	2⅜	Hurdles	4:23	4↑Crl1Crln-G3	–	3	6^{5}	$3^{5\frac{1}{2}}$	$2^{1\frac{1}{2}}$	1^{1}		$2^{\frac{3}{4}}$	Chipperfield C	L146	-	-	-	PreemptiveStrike$146^{\frac{3}{4}}$ *Hirpour*146^{7} *AlSkywlkr*158^{12}	Led strch, outfinished	6

Past Divisional Champions

Year	2-Year-Old Male	2-Year-Old Filly	3-Year-Old Male	3-Year-Old Filly	Handicap Horse	Handicap Mare	Grass Horse	Sprinter	Steeplechase	Horse of the Year
1936	Pompoon		Granville		Discovery			Myrtlewood	Bushranger	Granville
1937	Menow		War Admiral		Seabiscuit				Jungle King	War Admiral
1938	El Chico	Inscoelda	Stagehand		Seabiscuit	Marica				Seabiscuit
1939	Bimelech	Now What	Challedon	Unerring	Kayak II	Lady Maryland				Challedon
1940	Our Boots	Level Best	Bimelech		Challedon	War Plumage				Challedon
1941	Alsab	Petrify	Whirlaway	Painted Veil	Mioland	Fairy Chant			Speculate	Whirlaway
1942	Count Fleet	Askmenow	Alsab	Vagrancy	Whirlaway	Vagrancy			Elkridge	Whirlaway
1943	Platter	Duranza	Count Fleet	Stefanita	Market Wise	Mar-Kell			Brother Jones	Count Fleet
					Devil Diver					
1944	Pavot	Busher	By Jimminy	Twilight Tear	Devil Diver	Twilight Tear			Rouge Dragon	Twilight Tear
1945	Star Pilot	Beaugay	Fighting Step	Busher	Stymie	Busher			Mercator	Busher
1946	Double Jay	First Flight	Assault	Bridal Flower	Armed	Gallorette			Elkridge	Assault
1947	Citation	Bewitch	Phalanx	But Why Not	Armed	But Why Not		Polynesian	War Battle	Armed
1948	Blue Peter	Myrtle Charm	Citation	Miss Request	Citation	Conniver		Coaltown	American Way	Citation
1949	Hill Prince	Bed o' Roses	Capot	Two Lea	Coaltown	Bewitch		Delegate	Trough Hill	Capot
				Wistful				Royal Governor		
1950	Battlefield	Aunt Jinny	Hill Prince	Next Move	Noor	Two Lea		Sheilas Reward	Oedipus	Hill Prince
1951	Tom Fool	Rose Jet	Counterpoint	Kiss Me Kate	Hill Prince	Bed o' Roses		Sheilas Reward	Oedipus	Counterpoint
1952	Native Dancer	Sweet Patootie	One Count	Real Delight*	Crafty Admiral	Real Delight		Tea-Maker	Jam*	One Count
1953	Porterhouse	Evening Out	Native Dancer	Grecian Queen	Tom Fool	Sickle's Image	Iceberg II	Tom Fool	The Mast	Tom Fool
1954	Nashua	High Voltage	High Gun	Parlo*	Native Dancer	Parlo	Stan	White Skies	King Commander	Native Dancer
1955	Needles	Doubledogdare*	Nashua	Misty Morn	High Gun	Misty Morn*	St. Vincent	Berseem	Neji	Nashua
1956	Barbizon	Leallah*	Needles	Doubledogdare	Swaps	Blue Sparkler	Career Boy	Decathlon	Shipboard	Swaps
1957	Nadir*	Idun	Bold Ruler	Bayou	Dedicate	Pucker Up	Round Table	Decathlon	Neji	Bold Ruler
1958	First Landing	Quill	Tim Tam	Idun	Round Table	Bornastar	Round Table	Bold Ruler	Neji	Round Table
1959	Warfare	My Dear Girl	Sword Dancer	Royal Native*	Sword Dancer*	Tempted	Round Table	Intentionally	Ancestor	Sword Dancer
1960	Hail to Reason	Bowl of Flowers	Kelso	Berlo	Bald Eagle	Royal Native			Benguala	Kelso
1961	Crimson Satan	Cicada	Carry Back	Bowl of Flowers	Kelso	Airmans Guide	T.V. Lark		Peal	Kelso
1962	Never Bend	Smart Deb	Jaipur	Cicada	Kelso	Primonetta			Barnabys Bluff	Kelso
1963	Hurry to Market	Tosmah*	Chateaugay	Lamb Chop	Kelso	Cicada	Mongo		Amber Diver	Kelso
1964	Bold Lad	Queen Empress	Northern Dancer	Tosmah*	Kelso	Tosmah			Bon Nouvel	Kelso
1965	Buckpasser	Moccasin	Tom Rolfe	What a Treat	Roman Brother	Old Hat	Parka	Affectionately	Bon Nouvel	Roman Brother*
1966	Successor	Regal Gleam	Buckpasser	Lady Pitt	Buckpasser*	Open Fire*	Assagai	Impressive	Mako*	Buckpasser
1967	Vitriolic	Queen of the Stage	Damascus	Furl Sail	Damascus	Straight Deal	Fort Marcy	Dr. Fager	Quick Pitch	Damascus
1968	Top Knight	Gallant Bloom	Stage Door Johnny	Dark Mirage	Dr. Fager	Gamely	Dr. Fager	Dr. Fager	Bon Nouvel	Dr. Fager
1969	Silent Screen	Fast Attack*	Arts and Letters	Gallant Bloom	Arts and Letters*	Gallant Bloom*	Hawaii	Ta Wee	L'Escargot	Arts and Letters
1970	Hoist the Flag	Forward Gal	Personality	Office Queen*	Fort Marcy*	Shuvee	Fort Marcy	Ta Wee	Top Bid	Fort Marcy

Fillies voted Best 2-Year-Old: Beaugay (1945); First Flight (1946); Idun (1957)

Fillies voted Best 3-Year-Old: Twilight Tear (1944); Busher (1945); Dark Mirage (1968)

Eclipse Award Winners

Year	2-Year-Old Male	2-Year-Old Filly	3-Year-Old Male	3-Year-Old Filly	Handicap Horse	Handicap Mare	Grass Horse	Sprinter	Steeplechase	Horse of the Year
1971	Riva Ridge	Numbered Account	Canonero II	Turkish Trousers	Ack Ack	Shuvee	Run the Gauntlet	Ack Ack	Shadow Brook	Ack Ack
1972	Secretariat	La Prevoyante	Key to the Mint	Susan's Girl	Autobiography	Typecast	Cougar II	Chou Croute	Soothsayer	Secretariat
1973	Protagonist	Talking Picture	Secretariat	Desert Vixen	Riva Ridge	Susan's Girl	Secretariat	Shecky Greene	Athenian Idol	Secretariat
1974	Foolish Pleasure	Ruffian	Little Current	Chris Evert	Forego	Desert Vixen	Dahlia	Forego	Gran Kan	Forego
1975	Honest Pleasure	Dearly Precious	Wajima	Ruffian	Forego	Susan's Girl	Snow Knight	Gallant Bob	Life's Illusion	Forego
1976	Seattle Slew	Sensational	Bold Forbes	Revidere	Forego	Proud Delta	Youth	My Juliet	Straight and True	Forego
1977	Affirmed	Lakeville Miss	Seattle Slew	Our Mims	Forego	Cascapedia	Johnny D.	What a Summer	Cafe Prince	Seattle Slew
1978	Spectacular Bid	Candy Eclair It's in the Air	Affirmed	Tempest Queen	Seattle Slew	Late Bloomer	Mac Diarmida	Dr. Patches J.O. Tobin	Cafe Prince	Affirmed
1979	Rockhill Native	Smart Angle	Spectacular Bid	Davona Dale	Affirmed	Waya	Bowl Game (M) Trillion (F)	Star de Naskra	Martie's Anger	Affirmed
1980	Lord Avie	Heavenly Cause	Temperence Hill	Genuine Risk	Spectacular Bid	Glorious Song	John Henry (M) Just a Game II (F)	Plugged Nickle	Zaccio	Spectacular Bid
1981	Deputy Minister	Before Dawn	Pleasant Colony	Wayward Lass	John Henry	Relaxing	John Henry (M) De La Rose (F)	Guilty Conscience	Zaccio	John Henry
1982	Roving Boy	Landaluce	Conquistador Cielo	Christmas Past	Lemhi Gold	Track Robbery	Perrault (M) April Run (F)	Gold Beauty	Zaccio	Conq'st'dorCielo
1983	Devil's Bag	Althea	Slew o' Gold	Heartlight No. One	Bates Motel	Ambassador of Luck	John Henry (M) All Along (F)	Chinook Pass	Flatterer	All Along
1984	Chief's Crown	Outstandingly	Swale	Life's Magic	Slew o' Gold	Princess Rooney	John Henry (M) Royal Heroine (F)	Eillo	Flatterer	John Henry
1985	Tasso	Family Style	Spend a Buck	Mom's Command	Vanlandingham	Life's Magic	Cozzene (M) Pebbles (F)	Precisionist	Flatterer	Spend a Buck
1986	Capote	Brave Raj	Snow Chief	Tiffany Lass	Turkoman	Lady's Secret	Manila (M) Estrapade (F)	Smile	Flatterer	Lady's Secret
1987	Forty Niner	Epitome	Alysheba	Sacahuista	Ferdinand	North Sider	Theatrical (M) Miesque (F)	Groovy	Inlander	Ferdinand
1988	Easy Goer	Open Mind	Risen Star	Winning Colors	Alysheba	Personal Ensign	Sunshine Forever (M) Miesque (F)	Gulch	Jimmy Lorenzo	Alysheba
1989	Rhythm	Go for Wand	Sunday Silence	Open Mind	Blushing John	Bayakoa	Steinlen (M) Brown Bess (F)	Safely Kept	Highland Bud	Sunday Silence
1990	Fly So Free	Meadow Star	Unbridled	Go for Wand	Criminal Type	Bayakoa	Itsallgreektome (M) Laugh and Be Merry (F)	Housebuster	Morley Street	Criminal Type
1991	Arazi	Pleasant Stage	Hansel	Dance Smartly	Black Tie Affair	Queena	Tight Spot (M) Miss Alleged (F)	Housebuster	Morley Street	Black Tie Affair

Year	2-Year-Old Male	2-Year-Old Filly	3-Year-Old Male	3-Year-Old Filly	Handicap Horse	Handicap Mare	Grass Horse	Sprinter	Steeplechase	Horse of the Year
1992	Gilded Time	Eliza	A.P. Indy	Saratoga Dew	Pleasant Tap	Paseana	Sky Classic (M) Flawlessly (F)	Rubiano	Lonesome Glory	A.P. Indy
1993	Dehere	Phone Chatter	Prairie Bayou	Hollywood Wildcat	Bertrando	Paseana	Kotashaan (M) Flawlessly (F)	Cardmania	Lonesome Glory	Kotashaan
1994	Timber Country	Flanders	Holy Bull	Heavenly Prize	The Wicked North	Sky Beauty	Paradise Creek (M) Hatoof (F)	Cherokee Run	Warm Spell	Holy Bull
1995	Maria's Mon	Golden Attraction	Thunder Gulch	Serena's Song	Cigar	Inside Information	Northern Spur (M) Possibly Perfect (F)	Not Surprising	Lonesome Glory	Cigar
1996	Boston Harbor	Storm Song	Skip Away	Yanks Music	Cigar	Jewel Princess	Singspiel (M) Wandesta (F)	Lit de Justice	Coreggio	Cigar
1997	Favorite Trick	Countess Diana	Silver Charm	Ajina	Skip Away	Hidden Lake	Chief Bearhart (M) Ryafan (F)	Smoke Glacken	Lonesome Glory	Favorite Trick
1998	Answer Lively	Silverbulletday	Real Quiet	Banshee Breeze	Skip Away	Escena	Buck's Boy (M) Fiji (F)	Reraise	Flat Top	Skip Away
1999	Anees	Chilukki	Charismatic	Silverbulletday	Victory Gallop	Beautiful Pleasure	Daylami (M) Soaring Softly (F)	Artax	Lonesome Glory	Charismatic
2000	Macho Uno	Caressing	Tiznow	Surfside	Lemon Drop Kid	Riboletta	Kalanisi (M) Perfect Sting (F)	Kona Gold	All Gong	Tiznow
2001	Johannesburg	Tempera	Point Given	Xtra Heat	Tiznow	Gourmet Girl	Fantastic Light (M) Banks Hill (F)	Squirtle Squirt	Pompeyo	Point Given
2002	Vindication	Storm Flag Flying	War Emblem	Farda Amiga	Left Bank	Azeri	High Chaparral (M) Golden Apples (F)	Orientate	Flat Top	Azeri
2003	Action This Day	Halfbridled	Funny Cide	Bird Town	Mineshaft	Azeri	High Chaparral (M) Islington (F)	Aldebaran	McDynamo	Mineshaft
2004	Declan's Moon	Sweet Catomine	Smarty Jones	Ashado	Ghostzapper	Azeri	Kitten's Joy (M) Ouija Board (F)	Speightstown	Hirapour	Ghostzapper

*-Thoroughbred Racing Associations made alternate selection (listed below)

1952	Next Move-Handicap Mare	1966	Bold Bidder-Handicap Horse
1952	Oedipus-Steeplechase	1966	Summer Scandal-Handicap Mare
1954	Lavender Hill-Handicap Mare	1966	Tuscalee-Steeplechase
1955	Nasrina-2-Year-Old Filly	1967	Buckpasser-Handicap Horse
1955	Parlo-Handicap Mare	1967	Gamely-3-Year-Old Filly
1956	Romanita-2-Year-Old Filly	1968	Process Shot-2-Year-Old Filly
1957	Jewel's Reward-2-Year-Old Male	1968	Fort Marcy-Grass Horse
1959	Silver Spoon-3-Year-Old Filly	1969	Tudor Queen-2-Year-Old Filly
1959	Round Table-Handicap Horse	1969	Nodouble-Handicap Horse
1963	Castle Forbes-2-Year-Old Filly	1969	Gamely-Handicap Mare
1964	Old Hat-Handicap Mare	1970	Fanfreluche-3-Year-Old Filly
1965	Moccasin-Horse of the Year	1970	Nodouble-Handicap Horse

Previous Eclipse Award Winners

Year	Jockey
1971	Laffit Pincay Jr.
1972	Braulio Baeza
1973	Laffit Pincay Jr.
1974	Laffit Pincay Jr.
1975	Braulio Baeza
1976	Sandy Hawley
1977	Steve Cauthen
1978	Darrel McHargue
1979	Laffit Pincay Jr.
1980	Chris McCarron
1981	William Shoemaker
1982	Angel Cordero Jr.
1983	Angel Cordero Jr.
1984	Pat Day
1985	Laffit Pincay Jr.
1986	Pat Day
1987	Pat Day
1988	Jose Santos
1989	Kent Desormeaux
1990	Craig Perret
1991	Pat Day
1992	Kent Desormeaux
1993	Mike Smith
1994	Mike Smith
1995	Jerry Bailey
1996	Jerry Bailey
1997	Jerry Bailey
1998	Gary Stevens
1999	Jorge Chavez
2000	Jerry Bailey
2001	Jerry Bailey
2002	Jerry Bailey
2003	Jerry Bailey
2004	John Velazquez

Year	Trainer
1971	Charles Whittingham
1972	Lucien Laurin
1973	H. Allen Jerkens
1974	Sherill Ward
1975	Steve DiMauro
1976	Lazaro Barrera
1977	Lazaro Barrera
1978	Lazaro Barrera
1979	Lazaro Barrera
1980	Bud Delp
1981	Ron McAnally
1982	Charles Whittingham
1983	Woody Stephens
1984	Jack Van Berg
1985	D. Wayne Lukas
1986	D. Wayne Lukas
1987	D. Wayne Lukas
1988	Shug McGaughey
1989	Charles Whittingham
1990	Carl Nafzger
1991	Ron McAnally
1992	Ron McAnally
1993	Robert Frankel
1994	D. Wayne Lukas
1995	William I. Mott
1996	William I. Mott
1997	Bob Baffert
1998	Bob Baffert
1999	Bob Baffert
2000	Robert Frankel
2001	Robert Frankel
2002	Robert Frankel
2003	Robert Frankel
2004	Todd Pletcher

Year	Apprentice Jockey
1971	Gene St. Leon
1972	Thomas Wallis
1973	Steve Valdez
1974	Chris McCarron
1975	Jimmy Edwards
1976	George Martens
1977	Steve Cauthen
1978	Ron Franklin
1979	Cash Asmussen
1980	Frank Lovato Jr.
1981	Richard Migliore
1982	Alberto Delgado
1983	Declan Murphy
1984	Wesley Ward
1985	Art Madrid Jr.
1986	Allen Stacy
1987	Kent Desormeaux
1988	Steve Capanas
1989	Michael Luzzi
1990	Mark Johnston
1991	Mickey Walls
1992	Rosemary Homeister Jr.
1993	Juan Umana
1994	Dale Beckner
1995	Ramon Perez
1996	Neil Poznansky
1997	Roberto Rosado Philip Teator (tie)
1998	Shaun Bridgmohan
1999	Ariel Smith
2000	Tyler Baze
2001	Jeremy Rose
2002	Ryan Fogelsonger
2003	Eddie Castro
2004	Brian Hernandez Jr

Year	Owner-Breeder
1971	Paul Mellon
1972	Meadow Stable
1973	Meadow Stable

Year	Owner
1971	Mr./Mrs. E.E. Fogelson
1974	Dan Lasater
1975	Dan Lasater
1976	Dan Lasater
1977	Maxwell Gluck
1978	Harbor View Farm
1979	Harbor View Farm
1980	Mr./Mrs. B. Firestone
1981	Dotsam Stable
1982	Viola Sommer
1983	John Franks
1984	John Franks
1985	Mr. and Mrs. Eugene Klein
1986	Mr. and Mrs. Eugene Klein
1987	Mr. and Mrs. Eugene Klein
1988	Ogden Phipps
1989	Ogden Phipps
1990	Frances Genter
1991	Sam-Son Farms
1992	Juddmonte Farms
1993	John Franks
1994	John Franks
1995	Allen Paulson
1996	Allen Paulson
1997	Carolyn Hine
1998	Frank Stronach
1999	Frank Stronach
2000	Frank Stronach
2001	Richard Englander
2002	Richard Englander
2003	Juddmonte Farms
2004	Kenneth and Sarah Ramsey

Year	Breeder
1974	John W. Galbreath
1975	Fred W. Hooper
1976	Nelson Bunker Hunt
1977	E.P. Taylor
1978	Harbor View Farm
1979	Claiborne Farm
1980	Mrs. Henry D. Paxson
1981	Golden Chance Farm
1982	Fred W. Hooper
1983	E.P. Taylor
1984	Claiborne Farm
1985	Nelson Bunker Hunt
1986	Paul Mellon
1987	Nelson Bunker Hunt
1988	Ogden Phipps
1989	North Ridge Farm
1990	Calumet Farm
1991	Mr./Mrs. John C. Mabee
1992	William S. Farish
1993	Allen Paulson
1994	William T. Young
1995	Juddmonte Farms
1996	Farnsworth Farms
1997	Mr./Mrs. John C. Mabee
1998	Mr./ Mrs. John C. Mabee
1999	William S. Farish
2000	Frank Stronach
2001	Juddmonte Farms
2002	Juddmonte Farms
2003	Juddmonte Farms
2004	Adena Springs

Year	Award of Merit
1976	Jack Dreyfus
1977	Steve Cauthen
1978	Ogden Mills Phipps
1979	Frank E. Kilroe
1980	John D. Shapiro
1981	William Shoemaker
1984	John Gaines

1985 Keene Daingerfield
1986 Herman Cohen
1987 J.B. Faulconer
1988 John Forsythe
1989 Michael Sandler
1990 Warner L. Jones
1991 Fred W. Hooper
1992 Joe Hirsch
Robert P. Strub
1993 Paul Mellon
1994 Alfred G. Vanderbilt
1995 James E. "Ted Bassett III
1996 Allen Paulson
1997 Bob and Beverly Lewis
1998 D. G. Van Clief Jr.
2000 Jim McKay
2001 Pete Pedersen
Harry Mangurian
2002 Ogden Phipps
Howard Battle
2003 Richard Duchossois
2004 Oaklawn Park and Cella Family

Special Award

1971 Robert J. Kleberg
1974 Charles Hatton
1976 William Shoemaker
1980 John T. Landry
Pierre E. Bellocq
1984 C.V. Whitney
1985 Arlington Park
1987 Anheuser-Busch
1988 Edward DeBartolo Sr.
1989 Richard L Duchossois
1994 Edward Arcaro
John Longden
1995 Russell Baze
1998 Oak Tree Racing Association
1999 Laffit Pincay Jr.
2000 John Hettinger
2001 Sheikh Mohammed bin Rashid al Maktoum
2004 Dale Baird

Outstanding Achievement

1971 Charles Engelhard
(posthumously)
1972 Arthur B. Hancock Jr.
(posthumously)

Man of the Year

1972 John W. Galbreath
1973 Edward P. Taylor
1974 William L. McKnight
1975 John A. Morris

Outstanding Newspaper Writing

1971 Scott Young, Toronto Telegram
1972 Phil Ranallo, Buffalo Courier Express
1973 Red Smith, The New York Times
1974 William H. Rudy, New York Post
1975 Bob Harding, Newark Star-Ledger
1976 Edwin Pope, Miami Herald
1977 Skip Bayless, Los Angeles Times
1978 Joe Hirsch, Daily Racing Form
1979 Billy Reed, Louisville Courier-Journal
1980 Maryjean Wall, Lexington Herald
1981 Dave Kindred, Washington Post
1982 Edwin Pope, Miami Herald
1983 Dave Koerner, Louisville Times
1984 Bill Christine, Los Angeles Times
Eddie Donnally, Dallas Morning News
1985 Paul Moran, Newsday
1986 Edwin Pope, Miami Herald
1987 Tim Layden, Capital Newspapers
1988 Billy Reed, Lexington Herald-Leader
1989 Ronnie Virgets, Gambit
1990 Paul Moran, Newsday
1992 James Wallace, Seattle Post Intelligencer
1993 Jennie Rees, Louisville Courier-Journal
1994 Mike Downey, Los Angeles Times
1995 Stephanie Diaz, Riverside Press-Enterprise
1996 Tom Keyser, The Baltimore Sun
1997 Maryjean Wall, Lexington Herald-Leader
1998 Tom Keyser, The Baltimore Sun
1999 Maryjean Wall, Lexington Herald-Leader

Outstanding Magazine Writing

1971 Bill Surface, Reader's Digest
1972 Edward L. Bowen, The Blood-Horse
1973 Pete Axthelm, Newsweek
1974 Chet Hagen, Spur
1975 Frank Deford, Sports Illustrated
1976 Whitney Tower, Classic
1977 Whitney Tower, Classic
1978 Bill Nack, Sports Illustrated
1979 William Leggett, Sports Illustrated
1980 Clive Gammon, Sports Illustrated
1981 Joseph P. Pons Jr., The Blood-Horse
1982 Jay Hovdey, Horsemen's Journal
1983 Arnold Kirkpatrick, Keeneland
1984 Frank Deford, Sports Illustrated
1985 Bill Mooney, Thoroughbred Record
1986 Bill Nack, Sports Illustrated
1987 Jack Mann, Spur
1988 Jennie Rees, Sunday Magazine, Louisville
Courier-Journal
1989 Bill Nack, Sports Illustrated
1990 Bill Nack, Sports Illustrated
1992 Joseph P. Pons Jr., The Blood-Horse
1993 Stephanie Diaz, The Backstretch
1994 Jay Hovdey, The Blood-Horse
1995 Award vacated
1996 Don Clippinger, Mid-Atlantic Thoroughbred
1997 Bill Heller, The Backstretch
1998 Laura Hillenbrand, American Heritage
1999 Tom Keyser, Breeders' Cup Souvenir Magazine

Outstanding News Writing

1991 Bill Nack, Sports Illustrated

Outstanding Feature Writing

1991 Bill Nack, Sports Illustrated

Outstanding News/Commentary
2000 Jay Hovdey, Daily Racing Form
2001 Janet Patton, Lexington Herald-Leader
2002 Joe Drape, The New York Times
2003 Jay Hovdey, Daily Racing Form
2004 Bill Christine, Los Angeles Times

Outstanding Feature/Enterprise
2000 Mary Simon, Thoroughbred Times
2001 Laura Hillenbrand, Equus
2002 John Jeremiah Sullivan, Harper's
2003 William Nack, GQ
2004 Mike Jensen, Philadelphia Enquirer

Photography Achievement
1971 Art Rogers, Los Angeles Times
1972 Bob Coglianese, New York Racing Times
1973 Harry Leder, United Press International
1974 Michael Burns, Ontario Jockey Club
1975 John Pineda, Miami Herald
1976 John J. Vasile, Covina (Cal.) Sentinel
1977 John Walther, Miami Herald
1978 Douglas Lees, Fauquier Democrat
1979 Skip Ball, Maryland Horse
1980 Bob Coglianese, New York Racing Assn.
1981 Tony Baker, River Downs
1982 Kay Coyte, Horsemen's Journal
1983 Rayetta Burr, Paddock
1984 Bill Straus, Breeders' Cup Ltd.
1985 Kim Pratt, Garden State Park
1986 Janice Wilkman, Los Angeles Times
1987 Dan Farrell, New York Daily News
1988 Ben Van Hook, Louisville Courier-Journal
1989 Ron Cortes, Philadelphia Inquirer
1990 Michael Cartee, California Thoroughbred
1991 Rayetta Burr, Benoit and Associates
1992 Barbara Livingston, The Blood-Horse
1993 Michael Burns, Ontario Jockey Club
1994 Tony Leonard
1995 Michael J. Marten
1996 Skip Dickstein
1997 Jean Raftery Russell
1998 Ryan Haynes, Northlands Park
1999 Michael J. Marten
2000 Dave Landry
2001 Barbara Livingston
2002 Michael Clevenger, Louisville Courier-Journal
2003 Frank Anderson, Thoroughbred Times
2004 Cindy Pierson Dulay, Mid-Atlantic Thoroughbred

Local Television Achievement
1975 Cawood Ledford, WHAS, Louisville
1976 NYRA-OTB Race of the Week
1977 Jane Chastain, KABC, Los Angeles
1978 Cawood Ledford, WHAS, Louisville
1979 Dave Johnson, ON-TV
1980 WCAU, Philadelphia
1981 WHAS, Louisville
1982 ON-TV, Los Angeles
1983 Cawood Ledford Productions
1984 NYRA/Cinema Mistral
1985 Oak Tree Racing Association
1986 Louisiana Downs
1987 Arlington Park
1988 Joseph Kwong. KCET-TV, Los Angeles
1989 Chris Thomas, WFLA-TV, Tampa
1990 Philip von Borries, WKPC-TV, Louisville
1991 WABC-TV, New York
1992 Rick Cushing, WKPC-TV, Louisville
1993 Stephen Sadis, KBTC, Tacoma
1994 Ronnie Virgets, WNXO, New Orleans
1995 JCM Productions, New York
1996 Kenny Rice, WTVQ-TV, Lexington
1997 Brian Blessing, Ontario Jockey Club
1998 Jeff Lifson, WHAS-TV, Louisville
1999 Fox Sports West 2 – The Best of Santa Anita
2000 Maryland Jockey Club, WMAR, Baltimore
2001 Steve Crump, WTVI-TV, Charlotte, NC
2002 Bryan Krantz, Fox SportsNet Southwest
2003 G.D. Hieronymus, WKYT-27, Lexington
2004 Dan Foos, WAVE 3, Louisville

National Television Achievement
1971 Burt Bacharach, CBS
1972 Chuck Milton, Tony Verna, CBS
1973 Chuck Milton, Tony Verna, CBS
1974 Pen Densham, John Watson, Insight Productions
1975 CBS
1976 CBS
1977 Jack Whitaker, CBS
1978 Roger Murphy, Public Broadcasting Service
1979 Don Ohlmeyer, NBC
1980 ABC
1981 Canadian Broadcasting Corporation
1982 ESPN
1983 CBS
1984 NBC
1985 CBS
1986 ABC
1987 ABC
1988 Thoroughbred Sports, Racing Across America
1989 ABC Sports
1990 ABC Sports
1991 CBS News, Sunday Morning with Charles Kuralt
1992 ABC Sports
1993 E.S. Lamoreaux III, CBS News, Sunday Morning with Charles Kuralt
1994 ABC's Wide World of Sports
1995 ABC's Wide World of Sports
1996 NBC Sports
1997 E.S. Lamoreaux III, CBS News, Sunday Morning with Charles Kuralt
1998 E.S. Lamoreaux III, CBS News, Sunday Morning with Charles Kuralt
1999 Live Racing – ABC Sports, Belmont coverage
Feature – ESPN, Sports Century's 50 Greatest Athletes
2000 ABC Sports, Kentucky Derby coverage
2001 NBC, Breeders' Cup coverage

Live Racing
2002 David Michaels, NBC Sports, Preakness Stakes
2003 David Michaels, NBC Sports, Preakness Stakes
2004 David Michaels, NBC Sports, Belmont Stakes

National Television Feature
2000 Paul Hutchinson, ABC Sports
2001 Mark Shapiro and Jim Cohen, ESPN, Sports Century Top 50 and Beyond
2002 Alexander Piper, NBC Sports
2003 Dora Militaru and Craig Deleval, MSNBC
Joan Ciampi, ESPN2
2004 Fritz Mitchell, ESPN

Audio/Multi-Media Internet
2002 Shelby Whitfield, Premiere Radio Networks
2003 Hannan/Stauffer, KSPN ESPN
Mark Miller, WBAL
2004 Shelby Whitfield, Premiere Radio Networks

Film Achievement
1972 Joseph Burnham

Radio Achievement
1971 Win Elliot
1976 Win Elliot
1978 Ted Patterson, WBAL, Baltimore
1979 Dick Woolley, WITH, Baltimore
1981 WBAL, Baltimore
1982 ABC Radio Network
1983 Tom Davis, WCBM, Baltimore
1984 WBAL, Baltimore
1985 Bob Lauder, WHAS, Louisville
1986 ABC Radio Network
1987 Bob Lauder, WHAS, Louisville
1988 John Asher, WAVG, Louisville
1989 John Asher, WAVG, Louisville
1990 John Asher, WHAS, Louisville
1991 Julia McEvoy, National Public Radio
1992 John Asher, WHAS, Louisville
1993 Tom Leach, WVLK, Lexington
1994 John Asher, WHAS, Louisville
1995 Vic Stauffer, KKAR, Omaha
1996 Robin Dawson, CJCL, Toronto
1997 John Patti, WBAL, Baltimore
1998 No award presented
1999 Tom Leach, WVLK, Lexington
2000 Premiere Radio
2001 Mark Miller, WBAL, Baltimore

2004 ECLIPSE AWARD

OUTSTANDING NEWS/COMMENTARY

BY BILL CHRISTINE, LOS ANGELES TIMES

"Getting Lost in a Legend - Kayak II is ignored in 'Seabiscuit' movie, but jockeys' relatives say the horse might have been held back from winning the 1940 Big 'Cap."

(Originally published in Los Angeles Times, Dec. 24, 2003. Copyright Los Angeles Times, Dec. 2003.)

The best-selling book about Seabiscuit, the Golden Globe-nominated movie based on the book, and the recently released DVD based on the movie all poignantly document the wonder horse's rise from ne'er-do-well to champion.

But where's Kayak II?

Ignored by the writers and filmmakers responsible for the Seabiscuit phenomenon, Kayak II, more than half a century later, remains a source of intrigue and controversy.

He was a stablemate of Seabiscuit, and many think a horse good enough to have won the 1940 Santa Anita Handicap, the race that successfully capped Seabiscuit's incredible career.

The 1940 Big 'Cap has long been a flash point among racing buffs and historians. The Kayak II camp has said that its horse might have won if jockey Leon "Buddy" Haas apparently hadn't been content to finish second. Seabiscuit's supporters – and his trainer, the late Tom Smith – have argued that their horse was clearly the best.

Now relatives of two of the jockeys closely connected to the controversial finish of that race have fueled the theory that Haas, following orders from owner Charles S. Howard, didn't ride Kayak II vigorously to the wire, guaranteeing that Seabiscuit would win.

Howard owned both horses, and had won the 1939 Big 'Cap with Kayak II, but Seabiscuit was his favorite, and he desperately wanted the 7-year-old veteran to win the race that had previously eluded him. A victory in a $100,000 race would enhance Seabiscuit's value as a stallion. In 1940, the horses were coupled in the betting, which meant that bettors backing the Howard entry cashed their tickets regardless of which horse won.

Johnny Bucalo, a nephew of Johnny Adams, the Hall of Fame rider who had ridden Kayak II to victory in the 1939 Santa Anita Handicap, said that his uncle turned down the mount for the 1940 running of the race because he always rode to win and didn't want to follow Howard's Seabiscuit-must-win instructions.

Biggie Haas Walker, Buddy Haas' sister, has said that her brother told her several times that he was under orders from Howard to let Seabiscuit win.

Laura Hillenbrand, who wrote "Seabiscuit: An American Legend," the book that was developed into the movie, "Seabiscuit," said she was aware of the post-race gossip, but chose to leave it out.

The recently released Seabiscuit DVD, which includes the movie and a lot of historical background on a second disc, does not mention Kayak II's role in the 1940 race. The movie doesn't even acknowledge that Kayak II ran in the race.

In 1940, when $100,000 was a small fortune, Seabiscuit was trying for the third time to win the so-called "hundred-grander." When Adams, one of the best riders of his era, reportedly refused the mount on Kayak II, he was left without a horse in the race. Seabiscuit, in the last race of his storied career, beat his stablemate by an estimated 1 1/2 lengths.

Adams won 3,270 races. He retired in

1958, was voted into the Racing Hall of Fame in 1965 and died in 1995. Bucalo, a familiar Southern California racetrack figure and the off-track betting manager of the Barona Valley Ranch Resort and Casino near San Diego, recently recalled what his uncle had told him about the 1940 Big 'Cap.

"John said that he could have ridden Kayak," Bucalo said. "He was asked to ride the horse. But [Howard] didn't want Kayak to win if it would prevent Seabiscuit from winning, and my uncle was told that. My uncle told me he couldn't have ridden Kayak, or any horse, under those conditions. He turned down the mount."

Bucalo's story about his uncle seems the strongest indication that Howard wanted Kayak II to win the Santa Anita Handicap only if Seabiscuit couldn't. All of the principals – Howard, Haas, Smith and Seabiscuit's jockey, Red Pollard -- are dead. Smith trained Kayak II as well as Seabiscuit.

At the time, Howard and the others discounted the rumors that Kayak II was restrained from running his best, although Haas, two days after the race, cryptically said, "I had the best horse in the race."

Was Haas dancing around the fact that Howard, as he had apparently asked of Johnny Adams, had requested that Kayak II not get in Seabiscuit's way?

Smith tried to cold-water the speculation at the time, saying, "Kayak never saw the day he could beat Seabiscuit when Seabiscuit was at his best."

Ralph Shaffer, professor emeritus in history at Cal Poly Pomona, has written about the 1940 Santa Anita Handicap. Several months ago, he contacted Haas' sister and asked her about the race.

"My brother said many times that C.S. Howard had instructed him to let Seabiscuit win," Biggie Haas Walker, who is in her 80s, told Shaffer. "I'm from the generation that if your boss tells you to throw a letter on the floor, you do it. If Mr. Howard told [Buddy] to do it, he did, and I heard Buddy say more than once that those were his instructions. I still vividly remember the race and how Buddy handled it."

Walker did not respond to requests from The Times for an interview.

Author Hillenbrand said, "In the four years I spent researching, I came to the conclusion that the idea that Kayak was robbed of the race simply isn't very plausible. It was rumored that Haas told friends just after the race that he could have won, but I was unable to find any quotes to support the rumor."

Haas, though, didn't whip Kayak II through the stretch. The third-place horse, Whichcee, couldn't hold the lead and finished a length behind Kayak. The Daily Racing Form's chart footnotes, written shortly after the race was over, said:

"Seabiscuit, close to the pace from the start, was urged forward and out of trouble when it seemed as if he might be in close quarters nearing the first turn, then came on to catch Whichcee entering the final eighth [of a mile] and was going in his best form to the finish. Kayak II, slow to get going, ran a sensational race to make a very strong move in the backstretch and might have been closer to the winner had he been vigorously ridden in the last sixteenth."

The chart indicates that Seabiscuit won by half a length, but photos of the finish show that the margin was greater. Eventually, in Seabiscuit's career past-performance lines, the margin was changed to a more realistic 1 1/2 lengths.

What isn't open to conjecture is that Seabiscuit, carrying 130 pounds to Kayak II's 129, ran 1 1/4 miles in 2:01 1/5, a Santa Anita record and one of the fastest clockings ever for that distance. Only two horses had run faster at 1 1/4 miles, Whisk Broom II and Sarazen, and Whisk Broom's time had been questioned because of a possible timer malfunction.

Some veteran horsemen, including the retired trainer, Farrell Jones, say that Kayak II would not have been able to pass Seabiscuit, no matter how much Haas encouraged his horse. But Ernest Gardetto, who was 20 when the race was run, embraces the theory that Kayak II wasn't given a fair chance.

"I was a devoted racetrack aficionado in 1940," Gardetto said. "I was standing along the home stretch, within 100 feet of the finish line, with hundreds of other fans.... A feeling of doubt pervaded the area. Kayak's jockey [Haas] had let up. I am not a Seabiscuit detractor. I loved Seabiscuit. But Kayak was also a hell of a horse."

The across-the-board payoffs on the Howard-Smith entry were $3.40, $2.80 and $2.60. Under racing rules of the day, an owner could "declare to win" if he ran a multiple entry, and before the race Joe Hernandez, the track announcer at Santa Anita, announced to the crowd of 68,526 that Howard had "declared to win" with Seabiscuit.

Haas was riding Kayak II for the first time, and rode him only once more, in the Argentine-bred's final race, a second-place finish at Santa Anita in January of 1941.

Seabiscuit earned $86,650 in the 1940 Big 'Cap and Kayak collected $20,000. By prerace agreement, their jockeys, Pollard and Haas, split their commissions, which came to about $5,300 apiece.

Adams rode Kayak II twice after the 1940 Santa Anita Handicap, winning the Sunset Handicap with him at 131 pounds at Hollywood Park. Overall, Adams won four times and had one second with Kayak II in seven tries.

Seabiscuit, who was voted into the Hall of Fame in 1958, had been injured and didn't run when Kayak II won the Santa Anita Handicap, under 110 pounds, in 1939.

Kayak II's chances of being enshrined in Saratoga Springs, N.Y., are remote. He won 14 of 26 starts, including the Hollywood Gold Cup, the Santa Anita Handicap and five other stakes. But he would have needed a second win in the Big 'Cap to have a chance with the voters. Whether he was afforded the best opportunity to do that remains an argument for the ages.

Eclipse Award-winning photograph

By Cindy Pierson Dulay, Mid-Atlantic Thoroughbred

Alphabetical Listing of North American Champions and Leading Sires and Broodmares

Horse	YOB	Title	Year
A.P. Indy	1989	Horse of the year	1992
A.P. Indy	1989	Champion 3-year-old colt	1992
A.P. Indy	1989	Leading sire	2003
A.P. Indy	1989	Among the leading sires	2001
A.P. Indy	1989	Among the leading sires	2000
A.P. Indy	1989	Among the leading sires	2004
Ace Card	1942	Broodmare of the year	1952
Ack Ack	1966	Horse of the year	1971
Ack Ack	1966	Champion sprinter	1971
Ack Ack	1966	Champion older horse	1971
Action This Day	2001	Champion 2-year-old colt	2003
Advising Anna	1930	Champion handicap mare	1934
Affectionately	1960	Champion 2-year-old filly	1962
Affectionately	1960	Champion sprinter	1965
Affectionately	1960	Champion older mare	1965
Affirmed	1975	Horse of the year	1978
Affirmed	1975	Horse of the year	1979
Affirmed	1975	Champion 2-year-old colt	1977
Affirmed	1975	Champion 3-year-old colt	1978
Affirmed	1975	Champion older horse	1979
Affirmed	1975	Among the leading bm sires	2003
Affirmed	1975	Among the leading bm sires	2004
Affirmed	1975	Triple Crown	1978
Afleet	1984	Among the leading sires	1996
Afleet	1984	Among the leading sires	1997
Ahoy	1960	Champion sprinter	1964
Airmans Guide	1957	Champion older mare	1961
Ajina	1994	Champion 3-year-old filly	1997
Alcibiades	1927	Champion 2-year-old filly	1929
Alcibiades	1927	Champion 3-year-old filly	1930
Aldebaran	1998	Champion sprinter	2003
All Along (FR)	1979	Horse of the year	1983
All Along (FR)	1979	Champion grass mare	1983
All Beautiful	1959	Broodmare of the year	1969
All Gong (GB)	1994	Champion steeplechaser	2000
Alleged	1974	Among the leading bm sires	2003
Alpenstock III	1936	Broodmare of the year	1951
Alsab	1939	Champion 2-year-old colt	1941
Alsab	1939	Champion 3-year-old colt	1942
Althea	1981	Champion 2-year-old filly	1983
Alydar	1975	Leading sire	1990
Alydar	1975	Among the leading sires	1986
Alydar	1975	Among the leading sires	1987
Alydar	1975	Among the leading sires	1988
Alydar	1975	Among the leading sires	1989
Alydar	1975	Among the leading sires	1992
Alydar	1975	Among the leading bm sires	1997
Alydar	1975	Among the leading bm sires	1999
Alydar	1975	Among the leading bm sires	2000
Alysheba	1984	Horse of the year	1988
Alysheba	1984	Champion 3-year-old colt	1987
Alysheba	1984	Champion older horse	1988
Ambassador of Luck	1979	Champion older mare	1983
Amber Diver	1954	Champion steeplechaser	1963
Ambiorix	1946	Leading sire	1961
American Flag	1922	Champion 3-year-old colt	1925
American Way	1942	Champion steeplechaser	1948
Ancestor	1949	Champion steeplechaser	1959
Anees	1997	Champion 2-year-old colt	1999
Anita Peabody	1925	Champion 2-year-old filly	1927
Anne Campbell	1973	Broodmare of the year	1999
Answer Lively	1996	Champion 2-year-old colt	1998
Apogee	1934	Champion 2-year-old filly	1936
April Run (IRE)	1978	Champion grass mare	1982
Arazi	1989	Champion 2-year-old colt	1991
Armed	1941	Horse of the year	1947
Armed	1941	Champion handicap horse	1946
Armed	1941	Champion handicap horse	1947
Artax	1995	Champion sprinter	1999
Arts and Letters	1966	Horse of the year	1969
Arts and Letters	1966	Champion 3-year-old colt	1969
Arts and Letters	1966	Champion older horse	1969
Ashado	2001	Champion 3-year-old filly	2004
Askmenow	1940	Champion 2-year-old filly	1942
Assagai	1963	Champion grass horse	1966
Assault	1943	Horse of the year	1946
Assault	1943	Champion 3-year-old colt	1946
Assault	1943	Triple Crown	1946
Athenian Idol	1968	Champion steeplechaser	1973
Aunt Jinny	1948	Champion 2-year-old filly	1950
Autobiography	1968	Champion older horse	1972
Azeri	1998	Horse of the year	2002
Azeri	1998	Champion older mare	2002
Azeri	1998	Champion older mare	2003
Azeri	1998	Champion older mare	2004
Baba Kenny	1928	Champion 2-year-old filly	1930
Bald Eagle	1955	Champion older horse	1960
Balladier	1932	Champion 2-year-old colt	1934
Banja Luka	1968	Broodmare of the year	1987
Banks Hill (GB)	1998	Champion grass mare	2001
Banshee Breeze	1995	Champion 3-year-old filly	1998
Barbizon	1954	Champion 2-year-old colt	1956
Barn Swallow	1930	Champion 3-year-old filly	1933
Barnabys Bluff	1958	Champion steeplechaser	1962
Bateau	1925	Champion 3-year-old filly	1928
Bateau	1925	Champion handicap mare	1929
Bates Motel	1979	Champion older horse	1983
Battlefield	1948	Champion 2-year-old colt	1950
Bayakoa (ARG)	1984	Champion older mare	1989
Bayakoa (ARG)	1984	Champion older mare	1990
Bayou	1954	Champion 3-year-old filly	1957
Bazaar	1931	Champion 2-year-old filly	1933
Bazaar	1931	Champion 3-year-old filly	1934
Beaugay	1943	Champion 2-year-old filly	1945
Beautiful Pleasure	1995	Champion older mare	1999
Bed o' Roses	1947	Champion 2-year-old filly	1949
Bed o' Roses	1947	Champion older mare	1951
Before Dawn	1979	Champion 2-year-old filly	1981
Belle Jeep	1949	Broodmare of the year	1957
Benguala	1954	Champion steeplechaser	1960
Berlo	1957	Champion 3-year-old filly	1960
Berseem	1950	Champion sprinter	1955
Bertrando	1989	Champion older horse	1993
Best in Show	1965	Broodmare of the year	1982
Bewitch	1945	Champion 2-year-old filly	1947
Bewitch	1945	Champion older mare	1949
Big Pebble	1936	Champion handicap horse	1941
Bimelech	1937	Champion 2-year-old colt	1939
Bimelech	1937	Champion 3-year-old colt	1940
Bird Town	2000	Champion 3-year-old filly	2003
Black Helen	1932	Champion 3-year-old filly	1935
Black Maria	1923	Champion 3-year-old filly	1926
Black Maria	1923	Champion handicap mare	1927
Black Maria	1923	Champion handicap mare	1928
Black Tie Affair (IRE)	1986	Horse of the year	1991
Black Tie Affair (IRE)	1986	Champion older horse	1991
Blenheim II	1927	Leading sire	1941
Bloodroot	1932	Broodmare of the year	1946

Horse	YOB	Title	Year
Blue Larkspur	1926	Horse of the year	1929
Blue Larkspur	1926	Champion 3-year-old colt	1929
Blue Larkspur	1926	Champion handicap horse	1930
Blue Peter	1946	Champion 2-year-old colt	1948
Blue Sparkler	1952	Champion older mare	1956
Blushing Groom (FR)	1974	Among the leading bm sires	1998
Blushing John	1985	Champion older horse	1989
Bold Bidder	1962	Champion older horse	1966
Bold Forbes	1973	Champion 3-year-old colt	1976
Bold Lad	1962	Champion 2-year-old	1964
Bold Liz	1970	2nd highweighted filly	1972
Bold Ruler	1954	Horse of the year	1957
Bold Ruler	1954	Champion 3-year-old colt	1957
Bold Ruler	1954	Champion sprinter	1958
Bold Ruler	1954	Leading sire	1963
Bold Ruler	1954	Leading sire	1964
Bold Ruler	1954	Leading sire	1965
Bold Ruler	1954	Leading sire	1966
Bold Ruler	1954	Leading sire	1967
Bold Ruler	1954	Leading sire	1968
Bold Ruler	1954	Leading sire	1969
Bold Ruler	1954	Leading sire	1973
Bold Venture	1933	Champion 3-year-old colt	1936
Bon Nouvel	1960	Champion steeplechaser	1964
Bon Nouvel	1960	Champion steeplechaser	1965
Bon Nouvel	1960	Champion steeplechaser	1968
Bornastar	1953	Champion older mare	1958
Boston Harbor	1994	Champion 2-year-old colt	1996
Bowl Game	1974	Champion grass horse	1979
Bowl of Flowers	1958	Champion 2-year-old filly	1960
Bowl of Flowers	1958	Champion 3-year-old filly	1961
Brave Raj	1984	Champion 2-year-old filly	1986
Bridal Flower	1943	Champion 3-year-old filly	1946
Broad Brush	1983	Leading sire	1994
Broad Brush	1983	Among the leading sires	1999
Broomstick	1901	Leading broodmare sire	1932
Broomstick	1901	Leading broodmare sire	1933
Brother Jones	1936	Champion steeplechaser	1943
Brown Bess	1982	Champion grass mare	1989
Buckaroo	1975	Leading sire	1985
Buckpasser	1963	Horse of the year	1966
Buckpasser	1963	Champion 2-year-old colt	1965
Buckpasser	1963	Champion 3-year-old colt	1966
Buckpasser	1963	Champion older horse	1966
Buckpasser	1963	Champion older horse	1967
Buckpasser	1963	Leading broodmare sire	1983
Buckpasser	1963	Leading broodmare sire	1984
Buckpasser	1963	Leading broodmare sire	1988
Buckpasser	1963	Leading broodmare sire	1989
Buck's Boy	1993	Champion grass horse	1998
Bull Dog	1927	Leading sire	1943
Bull Dog	1927	Leading broodmare sire	1953
Bull Dog	1927	Leading broodmare sire	1954
Bull Dog	1927	Leading broodmare sire	1956
Bull Lea	1935	Leading sire	1947
Bull Lea	1935	Leading sire	1948
Bull Lea	1935	Leading sire	1949
Bull Lea	1935	Leading sire	1952
Bull Lea	1935	Leading sire	1953
Bull Lea	1935	Leading broodmare sire	1958
Bull Lea	1935	Leading broodmare sire	1959
Bull Lea	1935	Leading broodmare sire	1960
Bull Lea	1935	Leading broodmare sire	1961
Burgoo King	1929	Champion 3-year-old colt	1932
Burning Blaze	1929	Champion 2-year-old colt	1931
Busher	1942	Horse of the year	1945
Busher	1942	Champion 2-year-old filly	1944

Horse	YOB	Title	Year
Busher	1942	Champion 3-year-old filly	1945
Busher	1942	Champion handicap mare	1945
Bushranger	1930	Champion steeplechaser	1936
But Why Not	1944	Champion 3-year-old filly	1947
But Why Not	1944	Champion handicap mare	1947
By Jimminy	1941	Champion 3-year-old colt	1944
Cafe Prince	1970	Champion steeplechaser	1977
Cafe Prince	1970	Champion steeplechaser	1978
Candy Eclair	1976	Champion 2-year-old filly	1978
Canonero II	1968	Champion 3-year-old colt	1971
Capot	1946	Horse of the year	1949
Capot	1946	Champion 3-year-old colt	1949
Capote	1984	Champion 2-year-old colt	1986
Capote	1984	Among the leading sires	1996
Cardmania	1986	Champion sprinter	1993
Career Boy	1953	Champion grass horse	1956
Careful	1918	Champion 2-year-old filly	1920
Careful	1918	Champion handicap mare	1922
Caressing	1998	Champion 2-year-old filly	2000
Carry Back	1958	Champion 3-year-old colt	1961
Cascapedia	1973	Champion older mare	1977
Castle Forbes	1961	Champion 2-year-old filly	1963
Cavalcade	1931	Horse of the year	1934
Cavalcade	1931	Champion 2-year-old colt	1933
Cavalcade	1931	Champion 3-year-old colt	1934
Celt	1905	Leading sire	1921
Celt	1905	Leading broodmare sire	1930
Chacolet	1918	Champion handicap mare	1923
Chacolet	1918	Champion handicap mare	1924
Challedon	1936	Horse of the year	1939
Challedon	1936	Horse of the year	1940
Challedon	1936	Champion 3-year-old	1939
Challedon	1936	Champion handicap horse	1940
Challenger II	1927	Leading sire	1939
Chance Play	1923	Horse of the year	1927
Chance Play	1923	Champion handicap horse	1927
Chance Play	1923	Leading sire	1935
Chance Play	1923	Leading sire	1944
Charismatic	1996	Horse of the year	1999
Charismatic	1996	Champion 3-year-old colt	1999
Chateaugay	1960	Champion 3-year-old colt	1963
Chatterton	1919	Leading sire	1932
Cherokee Run	1990	Champion sprinter	1994
Chicle	1913	Leading sire	1929
Chicle	1913	Leading broodmare sire	1942
Chief Bearhart	1993	Champion grass horse	1997
Chief's Crown	1982	Champion 2-year-old colt	1984
Chilukki	1997	Champion 2-year-old filly	1999
Chinook Pass	1979	Champion sprinter	1983
Chou Croute	1968	Champion sprinter	1972
Chris Evert	1971	Champion 3-year-old filly	1974
Chris Evert	1971	Filly Triple Crown	1974
Christmas Past	1979	Champion 3-year-old filly	1982
Cicada	1959	Champion 2-year-old filly	1961
Cicada	1959	Champion 3-year-old filly	1962
Cicada	1959	Champion older mare	1963
Cigar	1990	Horse of the year	1995
Cigar	1990	Horse of the year	1996
Cigar	1990	Champion older horse	1995
Cigar	1990	Champion older horse	1996
Citation	1945	Horse of the year	1948
Citation	1945	Champion 2-year-old colt	1947
Citation	1945	Champion 3-year-old colt	1948
Citation	1945	Champion older horse	1948
Citation	1945	Champion older horse	1951
Citation	1945	Triple Crown	1948
Cleopatra	1917	Champion 3-year-old filly	1920

Horse	YOB	Title	Year
Coaltown	1945	Horse of the year	1949
Coaltown	1945	Champion sprinter	1948
Coaltown	1945	Champion older horse	1949
Conniver	1944	Champion older mare	1948
Conquistador Cielo	1979	Horse of the year	1982
Conquistador Cielo	1979	Champion 3-year-old colt	1982
Constancy	1917	Champion 2-year-old filly	1919
Correggio (IRE)	1991	Champion steeplechaser	1996
Cosmah	1953	Broodmare of the year	1974
Cougar II	1966	Champion grass horse	1972
Count Fleet	1940	Horse of the year	1943
Count Fleet	1940	Champion 2-year-old colt	1942
Count Fleet	1940	Champion 3-year-old colt	1943
Count Fleet	1940	Leading sire	1951
Count Fleet	1940	Leading broodmare sire	1963
Count Fleet	1940	Triple Crown	1943
Counterpoint	1948	Horse of the year	1951
Counterpoint	1948	Champion 3-year-old colt	1951
Countess Diana	1995	Champion 2-year-old filly	1997
Courtly Dee	1968	Broodmare of the year	1983
Cox's Ridge	1974	Among the leading bm sires	2002
Cozzene	1980	Champion grass horse	1985
Cozzene	1980	Leading sire	1996
Crafty Admiral	1948	Champion older horse	1952
Crafty Admiral	1948	Leading broodmare sire	1978
Crafty Prospector	1979	Among the leading sires	1997
Criminal Type	1985	Horse of the year	1990
Criminal Type	1985	Champion older horse	1990
Crimson Satan	1959	Champion 2-year-old colt	1961
Crusader	1923	Horse of the year	1926
Crusader	1923	Champion 3-year-old colt	1926
Cudgel	1914	Champion handicap horse	1919
Current	1926	Champion 2-year-old filly	1928
Dahlia	1970	Champion grass horse	1974
Damascus	1964	Horse of the year	1967
Damascus	1964	Champion 3-year-old colt	1967
Damascus	1964	Champion handicap horse	1967
Dance Smartly	1988	Champion 3-year-old filly	1991
Danzig	1977	Leading sire	1991
Danzig	1977	Leading sire	1992
Danzig	1977	Leading sire	1993
Danzig	1977	Among the leading sires	1985
Danzig	1977	Among the leading sires	1986
Danzig	1977	Among the leading sires	1994
Danzig	1977	Among the leading bm sires	2001
Danzig	1977	Among the leading bm sires	2000
Dark Mirage	1965	Champion 3-year-old filly	1968
Dark Mirage	1965	Filly Triple Crown	1968
Dark Vintage	1956	2nd highweighted filly	1958
Darshaan (GB)	1981	Among the leading bm sires	2002
Davona Dale	1976	Champion 3-year-old filly	1979
Davona Dale	1976	Filly Triple Crown	1979
Dawn Play	1934	Champion 3-year-old filly	1937
Daylami (IRE)	1994	Champion grass horse	1999
De La Rose	1978	Champion grass mare	1981
Dearly Precious	1973	Champion 2-year-old filly	1975
Decathlon	1953	Champion sprinter	1956
Decathlon	1953	Champion sprinter	1957
Declan's Moon	2002	Champion 2-year-old colt	2004
Dedicate	1952	Champion older horse	1957
Dehere	1991	Champion 2-year-old colt	1993
Dehere	1991	Among the leading sires	2002
Delegate	1944	Champion sprinter	1949
Delta	1952	Broodmare of the year	1968
Deputy Minister	1979	Champion 2-year-old colt	1981
Deputy Minister	1979	Leading sire	1997
Deputy Minister	1979	Leading sire	1998
Deputy Minister	1979	Among the leading sires	1996
Deputy Minister	1979	Among the leading bm sires	2002
Deputy Minister	1979	Among the leading bm sires	2003
Deputy Minister	1979	Among the leading bm sires	2004
Desert Vixen	1970	Champion 3-year-old filly	1973
Desert Vixen	1970	Champion older mare	1974
Devil Diver	1939	Champion handicap horse	1943
Devil Diver	1939	Champion handicap horse	1944
Devil's Bag	1981	Champion 2-year-old colt	1983
Diavolo	1925	Champion handicap horse	1929
Dice	1925	Champion 2-year-old colt	1927
Discovery	1931	Horse of the year	1935
Discovery	1931	Champion handicap horse	1935
Discovery	1931	Champion handicap horse	1936
Dixieland Band	1980	Leading broodmare sire	2004
Dixieland Band	1980	Among the leading sires	1993
Dixieland Band	1980	Among the leading sires	1999
Dixieland Band	1980	Among the leading bm sires	2001
Double Jay	1944	Champion 2-year-old colt	1946
Double Jay	1944	Leading broodmare sire	1971
Double Jay	1944	Leading broodmare sire	1975
Double Jay	1944	Leading broodmare sire	1977
Double Jay	1944	Leading broodmare sire	1981
Doubledogdare	1953	Champion 2-year-old filly	1955
Doubledogdare	1953	Champion 3-year-old filly	1956
Dr. Fager	1964	Horse of the year	1968
Dr. Fager	1964	Champion sprinter	1967
Dr. Fager	1964	Champion sprinter	1968
Dr. Fager	1964	Champion grass horse	1968
Dr. Fager	1964	Champion older horse	1968
Dr. Fager	1964	Leading sire	1977
Dr. Patches	1974	Champion sprinter	1978
Dunce Cap II	1960	Broodmare of the year	1985
Durazna	1941	Champion 2-year-old filly	1943
Dynaformer	1985	Among the leading sires	2001
Dynaformer	1985	Among the leading sires	2002
Dynaformer	1985	Among the leading sires	2003
Easter Stockings	1925	Champion 3-year-old filly	1928
Easy Goer	1986	Champion 2-year-old colt	1988
Easy Lass	1940	Broodmare of the year	1949
Edith Cavell	1923	Champion 3-year-old filly	1926
Education	1944	Champion 2-year-old colt	1946
Eillo	1980	Champion sprinter	1984
El Chico	1936	Champion 2-year-old colt	1938
El Prado (IRE)	1989	Leading sire	2002
El Prado (IRE)	1989	Among the leading sires	2003
El Prado (IRE)	1989	Among the leading sires	2004
Eliza	1990	Champion 2-year-old filly	1992
Elkridge	1938	Champion steeplechaser	1942
Elkridge	1938	Champion steeplechaser	1946
Elusive Quality	1993	Leading sire	2004
Emotion	1919	Champion 3-year-old filly	1922
Epinard	1920	Champion handicap horse	1924
Epitome	1985	Champion 2-year-old filly	1987
Equipoise	1928	Horse of the year	1932
Equipoise	1928	Horse of the year	1933
Equipoise	1928	Champion 2-year-old colt	1930
Equipoise	1928	Champion handicap horse	1932
Equipoise	1928	Champion handicap horse	1933
Equipoise	1928	Champion handicap horse	1934
Equipoise	1928	Leading sire	1942
Escena	1993	Champion older mare	1998
Esposa	1932	Champion handicap mare	1937
Esposa	1932	Champion handicap mare	1938
Estrapade	1980	Champion grass mare	1986
Evening Out	1951	Champion 2-year-old filly	1953
Exclusive Native	1965	Leading sire	1978
Exclusive Native	1965	Leading sire	1979
Exterminator	1915	Horse of the year	1922

Horse	YOB	Title	Year
Exterminator	1915	Champion handicap horse	1920
Exterminator	1915	Champion handicap horse	1921
Exterminator	1915	Champion handicap horse	1922
Fair Play	1905	Leading sire	1920
Fair Play	1905	Leading sire	1924
Fair Play	1905	Leading sire	1927
Fair Play	1905	Leading broodmare sire	1931
Fair Play	1905	Leading broodmare sire	1934
Fair Play	1905	Leading broodmare sire	1938
Fair Star	1924	Champion 2-year-old filly	1926
Faireno	1929	Champion 3-year-old colt	1932
Fairy Chant	1937	Champion 3-year-old filly	1940
Fairy Chant	1937	Champion handicap mare	1941
Fall Aspen	1976	Broodmare of the year	1994
Family Style	1983	Champion 2-year-old filly	1985
Fanfreluche	1967	Champion 3-year-old filly	1970
Fantastic Light	1996	Champion grass horse	2001
Farda Amiga	1999	Champion 3-year-old filly	2002
Fast Attack	1967	Champion 2-year-old filly	1969
Favorite Trick	1995	Horse of the year	1997
Favorite Trick	1995	Champion 2-year-old colt	1997
Ferdinand	1983	Horse of the year	1987
Ferdinand	1983	Champion older horse	1987
Fighting Step	1942	Champion 3-year-old colt	1945
Fiji (GB)	1994	Champion grass mare	1998
First Flight	1944	Champion 2-year-old filly	1946
First Landing	1956	Champion 2-year-old colt	1958
Flanders	1992	Champion 2-year-old filly	1994
Flat Top	1993	Champion steeplechaser	2002
Flat Top	1993	Champion steeplechaser	1998
Flatterer	1979	Champion steeplechaser	1983
Flatterer	1979	Champion steeplechaser	1984
Flatterer	1979	Champion steeplechaser	1985
Flatterer	1979	Champion steeplechaser	1986
Flawlessly	1988	Champion grass mare	1992
Flawlessly	1988	Champion grass mare	1993
Florence Nightingale	1922	Champion 3-year-old filly	1925
Fluvanna	1921	Champion 2-year-old filly	1923
Fly So Free	1988	Champion 2-year-old colt	1990
Fly So Free	1988	Among the leading sires	2001
Foolish Pleasure	1972	Champion 2-year-old colt	1974
Forego	1970	Horse of the year	1974
Forego	1970	Horse of the year	1975
Forego	1970	Horse of the year	1976
Forego	1970	Champion sprinter	1974
Forego	1970	Champion older horse	1974
Forego	1970	Champion older horse	1975
Forego	1970	Champion older horse	1976
Forego	1970	Champion older horse	1977
Forever Yours	1933	Champion 2-year-old filly	1935
Fort Marcy	1964	Horse of the year	1970
Fort Marcy	1964	Champion grass horse	1967
Fort Marcy	1964	Champion grass horse	1970
Fort Marcy	1964	Champion older horse	1970
Forty Niner	1985	Champion 2-year-old colt	1987
Forty Niner	1985	Among the leading sires	1996
Forward Gal	1968	Champion 2-year-old filly	1970
Forward Pass	1965	Champion 3-year-old colt	1968
Friar's Carse	1923	Champion 2-year-old filly	1925
Funny Cide	2000	Champion 3-year-old colt	2003
Furl Sail	1964	Champion 3-year-old filly	1967
Gaga	1942	Broodmare of the year	1953
Gallant Bloom	1966	Champion 2-year-old filly	1968
Gallant Bloom	1966	Champion 3-year-old filly	1968
Gallant Bloom	1966	Champion handicap mare	1969
Gallant Bob	1972	Champion sprinter	1975
Gallant Fox	1927	Horse of the year	1930
Gallant Fox	1927	Champion 3-year-old colt	1930
Gallant Fox	1927	Triple Crown	1930
Gallorette	1942	Champion handicap mare	1946
Gamely	1964	Champion 3-year-old filly	1967
Gamely	1964	Champion older mare	1968
Gamely	1964	Champion older mare	1969
Gazala II	1964	Broodmare of the year	1976
Genuine Risk	1977	Champion 3-year-old filly	1980
Ghostzapper	2000	Horse of the year	2004
Ghostzapper	2000	Champion older horse	2004
Gilded Time	1990	Champion 2-year-old colt	1992
Glorious Song	1976	Champion older mare	1980
Glowing Tribute	1973	Broodmare of the year	1993
Go for Wand	1987	Champion 2-year-old filly	1989
Go for Wand	1987	Champion 3-year-old filly	1990
Gold Beauty	1979	Champion sprinter	1982
Golden Apples (IRE)	1998	Champion grass mare	2002
Golden Attraction	1993	Champion 2-year-old filly	1995
Gourmet Girl	1995	Champion older mare	2001
Gran Kan	1966	Champion steeplechaser	1974
Granville	1933	Horse of the year	1936
Granville	1933	Champion 3-year-old colt	1936
Graustark	1963	Among the leading bm sires	1993
Grecian Banner	1974	Broodmare of the year	1988
Grecian Queen	1950	Champion 3-year-old filly	1953
Grey Dawn II	1962	Leading broodmare sire	1990
Grey Lag	1918	Horse of the year	1921
Grey Lag	1918	Champion 3-year-old colt	1921
Grey Lag	1918	Champion handicap horse	1922
Grey Lag	1918	Champion handicap horse	1923
Groovy	1983	Champion sprinter	1987
Guilty Conscience	1976	Champion sprinter	1981
Gulch	1984	Champion sprinter	1988
Hail to Reason	1958	Champion 2-year-old colt	1960
Hail to Reason	1958	Leading sire	1970
Halfbridled	2001	Champion 2-year-old filly	2003
Halo	1969	Leading sire	1983
Halo	1969	Leading sire	1989
Halo	1969	Among the leading bm sires	2002
Handcuff	1935	Champion 3-year-old filly	1938
Hansel	1988	Champion 3-year-old colt	1991
Happy Gal	1930	Champion 2-year-old filly	1932
Hasty Queen II	1963	Broodmare of the year	1984
Hasty Road	1951	Champion 2-year-old colt	1953
Hatoof	1989	Champion grass mare	1994
Hawaii	1964	Champion grass horse	1969
Head Play	1930	Champion 3-year-old colt	1933
Heartlight No. One	1980	Champion 3-year-old filly	1983
Heavenly Cause	1978	Champion 2-year-old filly	1980
Heavenly Prize	1991	Champion 3-year-old filly	1994
Heliopolis	1936	Leading sire	1950
Heliopolis	1936	Leading sire	1954
Hidden Lake	1993	Champion older mare	1997
High Chaparral (IRE)	1999	Champion grass horse	2002
High Chaparral (IRE)	1999	Champion grass horse	2003
High Fleet	1933	Champion 3-year-old filly	1936
High Gun	1951	Champion 3-year-old colt	1954
High Gun	1951	Champion older horse	1955
High Strung	1926	Champion 2-year-old colt	1928
High Time	1916	Leading sire	1928
High Time	1916	Leading broodmare sire	1936
High Time	1916	Leading broodmare sire	1940
High Voltage	1952	Champion 2-year-old filly	1954
High Voltage	1952	Champion 3-year-old filly	1955
Highland Bud	1985	Champion steeplechaser	1989
Hildene	1938	Broodmare of the year	1950
Hill Prince	1947	Horse of the year	1950
Hill Prince	1947	Champion 2-year-old colt	1949
Hill Prince	1947	Champion 3-year-old colt	1950

Horse	YOB	Title	Year
Hill Prince	1947	Champion older horse	1951
Hirapour (IRE)	1996	Champion steeplechaser	2004
His Majesty	1968	Leading sire	1982
Hoist the Flag	1968	Champion 2-year-old colt	1970
Hoist the Flag	1968	Leading broodmare sire	1987
Hollywood Wildcat	1990	Champion 3-year-old filly	1993
Holy Bull	1991	Horse of the year	1994
Holy Bull	1991	Champion 3-year-old colt	1994
Honest Pleasure	1973	Champion 2-year-old colt	1975
Housebuster	1987	Champion sprinter	1990
Housebuster	1987	Champion sprinter	1991
Hurry to Market	1961	Champion 2-year-old colt	1963
Iberia	1954	Broodmare of the year	1971
Iceberg II	1948	Champion grass horse	1953
Idun	1955	Champion 2-year-old filly	1957
Idun	1955	Champion 3-year-old filly	1958
Impressive	1963	Champion sprinter	1966
In Memoriam	1920	Champion 3-year-old colt	1923
In Neon	1982	Broodmare of the year	1998
Inlander (GB)	1981	Champion steeplechaser	1987
Inscoelda	1936	Champion 2-year-old filly	1938
Inside Information	1991	Champion older mare	1995
Intentionally	1956	Champion sprinter	1959
Iron Reward	1946	Broodmare of the year	1955
Islington (IRE)	1999	Champion grass mare	2003
It's in the Air	1976	Champion 2-year-old filly	1978
Itsallgreektome	1987	Champion grass horse	1990
J. O. Tobin	1974	Champion sprinter	1978
Jacola	1935	Champion 2-year-old filly	1937
Jaipur	1959	Champion 3-year-old colt	1962
Jam	1947	Champion steeplechaser	1952
Jamestown	1928	Champion 2-year-old colt	1930
Jewel Princess	1992	Champion older mare	1996
Jewel's Reward	1955	Champion 2-year-old colt	1957
Jimmy Lorenzo (GB)	1982	Champion steeplechaser	1988
Johannesburg	1999	Champion 2-year-old colt	2001
John Henry	1975	Horse of the year	1981
John Henry	1975	Horse of the year	1984
John Henry	1975	Champion grass horse	1980
John Henry	1975	Champion grass horse	1981
John Henry	1975	Champion grass horse	1983
John Henry	1975	Champion grass horse	1984
John Henry	1975	Champion older horse	1981
Johnny D.	1974	Champion grass horse	1977
Juliets Nurse	1948	Broodmare of the year	1966
Jungle King	1930	Champion steeplechaser	1937
Just a Game (IRE)	1976	Champion grass mare	1980
Kalanisi (IRE)	1996	Champion grass horse	2000
Kamar	1976	Broodmare of the year	1990
Kayak II	1935	Champion handicap horse	1939
Kelso	1957	Horse of the year	1960
Kelso	1957	Horse of the year	1961
Kelso	1957	Horse of the year	1962
Kelso	1957	Horse of the year	1963
Kelso	1957	Horse of the year	1964
Kelso	1957	Champion 3-year-old colt	1960
Kelso	1957	Champion older horse	1961
Kelso	1957	Champion older horse	1962
Kelso	1957	Champion older horse	1963
Kelso	1957	Champion older horse	1964
Kerala	1958	Broodmare of the year	1967
Key Bridge	1959	Broodmare of the year	1980
Key to the Mint	1969	Champion 3-year-old colt	1972
King Commander	1949	Champion steeplechaser	1954
Kiss Me Kate	1948	Champion 3-year-old filly	1951
Kitten's Joy	2001	Champion grass horse	2004
Knight's Daughter	1941	Broodmare of the year	1959
Kona Gold	1994	Champion sprinter	2000
Kotashaan (FR)	1988	Horse of the year	1993
Kotashaan (FR)	1988	Champion grass horse	1993
Kris S.	1977	Among the leading sires	2003
Kris S.	1977	Among the leading sires	1993
La Prevoyante	1970	Champion 2-year-old filly	1972
Lady Broadcast	1926	Champion handicap mare	1930
Lady Maryland	1934	Champion handicap mare	1939
Lady Pitt	1963	Champion 3-year-old filly	1966
Lady's Secret	1982	Horse of the year	1986
Lady's Secret	1982	Champion older mare	1986
Ladysman	1930	Champion 2-year-old colt	1932
Lakeville Miss	1975	Champion 2-year-old filly	1977
Lamb Chop	1960	Champion 3-year-old filly	1963
Landaluce	1980	Champion 2-year-old filly	1982
Langfuhr	1992	Among the leading sires	2003
Late Bloomer	1974	Champion older mare	1978
Late Date	1929	Champion handicap mare	1935
Laugh and Be Merry	1985	Champion grass mare	1990
Lavender Hill	1949	Champion older mare	1954
Leallah	1954	Champion 2-year-old filly	1956
Left Bank	1997	Champion older horse	2002
Lemhi Gold	1978	Champion older horse	1982
Lemon Drop Kid	1996	Champion older horse	2000
L'Escargot	1963	Champion steeplechaser	1969
Levee	1953	Broodmare of the year	1970
Level Best	1938	Champion 2-year-old filly	1940
Life's Illusion	1971	Champion steeplechaser	1975
Life's Magic	1981	Champion 3-year-old filly	1984
Life's Magic	1981	Champion older mare	1985
Lit de Justice	1990	Champion sprinter	1996
Little Current	1971	Champion 3-year-old colt	1974
Lonesome Glory	1988	Champion steeplechaser	1992
Lonesome Glory	1988	Champion steeplechaser	1993
Lonesome Glory	1988	Champion steeplechaser	1995
Lonesome Glory	1988	Champion steeplechaser	1997
Lonesome Glory	1988	Champion steeplechaser	1999
Lord Avie	1978	Champion 2-year-old colt	1980
Lyphard	1969	Leading sire	1986
Mac Diarmida	1975	Champion grass horse	1978
Macho Uno	1998	Champion 2-year-old colt	2000
Mad Hatter	1916	Champion handicap horse	1921
Mahmoud	1933	Leading sire	1946
Mahmoud	1933	Leading broodmare sire	1957
Maid At Arms	1922	Champion 3-year-old filly	1925
Maid of Flight	1951	Broodmare of the year	1964
Mako	1960	Champion steeplechaser	1966
Man o' War	1917	Horse of the year	1920
Man o' War	1917	Champion 2-year-old colt	1919
Man o' War	1917	Champion 3-year-old colt	1920
Man o' War	1917	Leading sire	1926
Manila	1983	Champion grass horse	1986
Maria's Mon	1993	Champion 2-year-old colt	1995
Marica	1933	Champion handicap mare	1938
Mar-Kell	1939	Champion handicap mare	1943
Market Wise	1938	Champion handicap horse	1943
Martie's Anger	1975	Champion steeplechaser	1979
Master Charlie	1922	Champion 2-year-old colt	1924
Mata Hari	1931	Champion 2-year-old filly	1933
Mata Hari	1931	Champion 3-year-old filly	1934
Maud Muller	1922	Champion 2-year-old filly	1924
McDynamo	1997	Champion steeplechaser	2003
McGee	1900	Leading sire	1922
Meadow Star	1988	Champion 2-year-old filly	1990
Menow	1935	Champion 2-year-old colt	1937
Mercator	1939	Champion steeplechaser	1945
Miesque	1984	Champion grass mare	1987
Miesque	1984	Champion grass mare	1988
Mike Hall	1924	Champion handicap horse	1928

Horse	YOB	Title	Year
Milkmaid	1916	Champion 3-year-old filly	1919
Milkmaid	1916	Champion handicap mare	1920
Mineshaft	1999	Horse of the year	2003
Mineshaft	1999	Champion older horse	2003
Mioland	1937	Champion handicap horse	1941
Mira Femme	1964	Champion 2-year-old filly	1966
Miss Alleged	1987	Champion grass mare	1991
Miss Disco	1944	Broodmare of the year	1958
Miss Jemima	1917	Champion 2-year-old filly	1919
Miss Request	1945	Champion 3-year-old filly	1948
Misty Morn	1952	Champion 3-year-old filly	1955
Misty Morn	1952	Champion older mare	1955
Misty Morn	1952	Broodmare of the year	1963
Miswaki	1978	Among the leading bm sires	1999
Moccasin	1963	Horse of the year	1965
Moccasin	1963	Champion 2-year-old filly	1965
Moment of Truth II	1959	Broodmare of the year	1972
Mom's Command	1982	Champion 3-year-old filly	1985
Mom's Command	1982	Filly Triple Crown	1985
Mongo	1959	Champion grass horse	1963
Morley Street	1984	Champion steeplechaser	1990
Morley Street	1984	Champion steeplechaser	1991
Morvich	1919	Champion 2-year-old colt	1921
Mother Goose	1922	Champion 2-year-old filly	1924
Mr. Prospector	1970	Leading sire	1987
Mr. Prospector	1970	Leading sire	1988
Mr. Prospector	1970	Leading broodmare sire	2001
Mr. Prospector	1970	Leading broodmare sire	2002
Mr. Prospector	1970	Leading broodmare sire	2003
Mr. Prospector	1970	Leading broodmare sire	1997
Mr. Prospector	1970	Leading broodmare sire	1998
Mr. Prospector	1970	Leading broodmare sire	1999
Mr. Prospector	1970	Leading broodmare sire	2000
Mr. Prospector	1970	Among the leading sires	1980
Mr. Prospector	1970	Among the leading sires	1981
Mr. Prospector	1970	Among the leading sires	1982
Mr. Prospector	1970	Among the leading sires	1984
Mr. Prospector	1970	Among the leading sires	1989
Mr. Prospector	1970	Among the leading sires	1990
Mr. Prospector	1970	Among the leading sires	1991
Mr. Prospector	1970	Among the leading sires	1993
Mr. Prospector	1970	Among the leading sires	2000
Mr. Prospector	1970	Among the leading bm sires	1990
Mr. Prospector	1970	Among the leading bm sires	1993
Mr. Prospector	1970	Among the leading bm sires	1994
Mr. Prospector	1970	Among the leading bm sires	1995
Mr. Prospector	1970	Among the leading bm sires	1996
Mr. Prospector	1970	Among the leading bm sires	2004
My Dear	1917	Champion handicap mare	1921
My Dear Girl	1957	Champion 2-year-old filly	1959
My Juliet	1972	Champion sprinter	1976
Myrtle Charm	1946	Champion 2-year-old filly	1948
Myrtlewood	1932	Champion sprinter	1936
Myrtlewood	1932	Champion handicap mare	1936
Nadir	1955	Champion 2-year-old colt	1957
Nail	1953	Champion 2-year-old colt	1955
Nashua	1952	Horse of the year	1955
Nashua	1952	Champion 2-year-old colt	1954
Nashua	1952	Champion 3-year-old colt	1955
Nasrina	1953	Champion 2-year-old filly	1955
Nasrullah	1940	Leading sire	1955
Nasrullah	1940	Leading sire	1956
Nasrullah	1940	Leading sire	1959
Nasrullah	1940	Leading sire	1960
Nasrullah	1940	Leading sire	1962
Natashka	1963	Broodmare of the year	1981
Native Dancer	1950	Horse of the year	1952
Native Dancer	1950	Horse of the year	1954
Native Dancer	1950	Champion 2-year-old colt	1952
Native Dancer	1950	Champion 3-year-old colt	1953
Native Dancer	1950	Champion older horse	1954
Needles	1953	Champion 2-year-old colt	1955
Needles	1953	Champion 3-year-old colt	1956
Neji	1950	Champion steeplechaser	1955
Neji	1950	Champion steeplechaser	1957
Neji	1950	Champion steeplechaser	1958
Nellie Flag	1932	Champion 2-year-old filly	1934
Nellie Morse	1921	Champion 3-year-old filly	1924
Never Bend	1960	Champion 2-year-old colt	1962
Next Move	1947	Champion 3-year-old filly	1950
Next Move	1947	Champion older mare	1952
Nijinsky II	1967	Leading broodmare sire	1993
Nijinsky II	1967	Leading broodmare sire	1994
Nijinsky II	1967	Among the leading bm sires	2001
Nijinsky II	1967	Among the leading bm sires	1996
Nijinsky II	1967	Among the leading bm sires	1998
Nijinsky II	1967	Among the leading bm sires	1999
Nijinsky II	1967	Among the leading bm sires	2000
Nimba	1924	Champion 3-year-old filly	1927
Nodouble	1965	Champion older horse	1969
Nodouble	1965	Champion older horse	1970
Nodouble	1965	Leading sire	1981
Noor	1945	Champion older horse	1950
North Sider	1982	Champion older mare	1987
Northern Dancer	1961	Champion 3-year-old colt	1964
Northern Dancer	1961	Leading sire	1971
Northern Dancer	1961	Leading broodmare sire	1991
Northern Spur (IRE)	1991	Champion grass horse	1995
Northern Sunset (IRE)	1977	Broodmare of the year	1995
Not Surprising	1990	Champion sprinter	1995
Now What	1937	Champion 2-year-old filly	1939
Numbered Account	1969	Champion 2-year-old filly	1971
Nureyev	1977	Among the leading bm sires	2003
Occupy	1941	Champion 2-year-old colt	1943
Oedipus	1946	Champion steeplechaser	1950
Oedipus	1946	Champion steeplechaser	1951
Oedipus	1946	Champion steeplechaser	1952
Office Queen	1967	Champion 3-year-old filly	1970
Oil Capitol	1947	Champion 2-year-old colt	1949
Old Hat	1959	Champion older mare	1964
Old Hat	1959	Champion older mare	1965
Olympia	1946	Leading broodmare sire	1974
Omaha	1932	Champion 3-year-old colt	1935
Omaha	1932	Triple Crown	1935
One Count	1949	Horse of the year	1952
One Count	1949	Champion 3-year-old colt	1952
Open Fire	1961	Champion older mare	1966
Open Mind	1986	Champion 2-year-old filly	1988
Open Mind	1986	Champion 3-year-old filly	1989
Open Mind	1986	Filly Triple Crown	1989
Orientate	1998	Champion sprinter	2002
Ouija Board (GB)	2001	Champion grass mare	2004
Our Boots	1938	Champion 2-year-old colt	1940
Our Mims	1974	Champion 3-year-old filly	1977
Our Page	1940	Broodmare of the year	1948
Outstandingly	1982	Champion 2-year-old filly	1984
Painted Veil	1938	Champion 3-year-old filly	1941
Palace Music	1981	Leading sire	1995
Paradise Creek	1989	Champion grass horse	1994
Parka	1958	Champion grass horse	1965
Parlo	1951	Champion 3-year-old filly	1954
Parlo	1951	Champion older mare	1954
Parlo	1951	Champion older mare	1955
Paseana (ARG)	1987	Champion older mare	1992
Paseana (ARG)	1987	Champion older mare	1993
Pavot	1942	Champion 2-year-old colt	1944

Horse	YOB	Title	Year
Peal	1956	Champion steeplechaser	1961
Pebbles (GB)	1981	Champion grass mare	1985
Perfect Sting	1996	Champion grass mare	2000
Perrault (GB)	1977	Champion grass horse	1982
Personal Ensign	1984	Champion older mare	1988
Personal Ensign	1984	Broodmare of the year	1996
Personality	1967	Horse of the year	1970
Personality	1967	Champion 3-year-old colt	1970
Petrify	1939	Champion 2-year-old filly	1941
Phalanx	1944	Champion 3-year-old colt	1947
Phone Chatter	1991	Champion 2-year-old filly	1993
Platter	1941	Champion 2-year-old colt	1943
Pleasant Colony	1978	Champion 3-year-old colt	1981
Pleasant Stage	1989	Champion 2-year-old filly	1991
Pleasant Tap	1987	Champion older horse	1992
Plugged Nickle	1977	Champion sprinter	1980
Pocahontas	1955	Broodmare of the year	1965
Point Given	1998	Horse of the year	2001
Point Given	1998	Champion 3-year-old colt	2001
Polynesian	1942	Champion sprinter	1947
Pompey	1923	Champion 2-year-old colt	1925
Pompeyo (CHI)	1994	Champion steeplechaser	2001
Pompoon	1934	Champion 2-year-old colt	1936
Porterhouse	1951	Champion 2-year-old colt	1953
Possibly Perfect	1990	Champion grass mare	1995
Potheen	1928	Broodmare of the year	1947
Prairie Bayou	1990	Champion 3-year-old colt	1993
Precisionist	1981	Champion sprinter	1985
Primonetta	1958	Champion older mare	1962
Primonetta	1958	Broodmare of the year	1978
Prince John	1953	Leading broodmare sire	1979
Prince John	1953	Leading broodmare sire	1980
Prince John	1953	Leading broodmare sire	1982
Prince John	1953	Leading broodmare sire	1986
Princequillo	1940	Leading sire	1957
Princequillo	1940	Leading sire	1958
Princequillo	1940	Leading broodmare sire	1966
Princequillo	1940	Leading broodmare sire	1967
Princequillo	1940	Leading broodmare sire	1968
Princequillo	1940	Leading broodmare sire	1969
Princequillo	1940	Leading broodmare sire	1970
Princequillo	1940	Leading broodmare sire	1972
Princequillo	1940	Leading broodmare sire	1973
Princequillo	1940	Leading broodmare sire	1976
Princess Doreen	1921	Champion 3-year-old filly	1924
Princess Doreen	1921	Champion handicap mare	1925
Princess Doreen	1921	Champion handicap mare	1926
Princess Rooney	1980	Champion older mare	1984
Private Account	1976	Among the leading sires	1993
Process Shot	1966	Champion 2-year-old filly	1968
Protagonist	1971	Champion 2-year-old colt	1973
Proud Delta	1972	Champion older mare	1976
Prudery	1918	Champion 2-year-old filly	1920
Prudery	1918	Champion 3-year-old filly	1921
Pucker Up	1953	Champion older mare	1957
Queen Empress	1962	Champion 2-year-old filly	1964
Queen of the Stage	1965	Champion 2-year-old filly	1967
Queena	1986	Champion older mare	1991
Quick Pitch	1960	Champion steeplechaser	1967
Quill	1956	Champion 2-year-old filly	1958
Rahy	1985	Among the leading sires	2001
Rahy	1985	Among the leading sires	2000
Raise a Native	1961	Champion 2-year-old colt	1963
Raja Baba	1968	Leading sire	1980
Real Delight	1949	Champion 3-year-old filly	1952
Real Delight	1949	Champion older mare	1952
Real Quiet	1995	Champion 3-year-old colt	1998
Regal Gleam	1964	Champion 2-year-old filly	1966
Reigh Count	1925	Horse of the year	1928
Reigh Count	1925	Champion 2-year-old colt	1927
Reigh Count	1925	Champion 3-year-old colt	1928
Relaunch	1976	Among the leading bm sires	2004
Relaxing	1976	Champion older mare	1981
Relaxing	1976	Broodmare of the year	1989
Reraise	1995	Champion sprinter	1998
Revidere	1973	Champion 3-year-old filly	1976
Rhythm	1987	Champion 2-year-old colt	1989
Riboletta (BRZ)	1995	Champion older mare	2000
Ridan	1959	Champion 2-year-old colt	1961
Risen Star	1985	Champion 3-year-old colt	1988
Riva Ridge	1969	Champion 2-year-old colt	1971
Riva Ridge	1969	Champion older horse	1973
Riverman	1969	Among the leading bm sires	1997
Roberto	1969	Among the leading bm sires	1993
Rockhill Native	1977	Champion 2-year-old colt	1979
Roman	1937	Leading broodmare sire	1965
Roman Brother	1961	Horse of the year	1965
Roman Brother	1961	Champion older horse	1965
Romanita	1954	Champion 2-year-old filly	1956
Rose Jet	1949	Champion 2-year-old filly	1951
Rose of Sharon	1926	Champion 3-year-old filly	1929
Rouge Dragon	1938	Champion steeplechaser	1944
Round Table	1954	Horse of the year	1958
Round Table	1954	Champion grass horse	1957
Round Table	1954	Champion grass horse	1958
Round Table	1954	Champion grass horse	1959
Round Table	1954	Champion older horse	1958
Round Table	1954	Champion older horse	1959
Round Table	1954	Leading sire	1972
Roving Boy	1980	Champion 2-year-old colt	1982
Royal Governor	1944	Champion sprinter	1949
Royal Heroine (IRE)	1980	Champion grass mare	1984
Royal Native	1956	Champion 3-year-old filly	1959
Royal Native	1956	Champion older mare	1960
Rubiano	1987	Champion sprinter	1992
Ruffian	1972	Champion 2-year-old filly	1974
Ruffian	1972	Champion 3-year-old filly	1975
Ruffian	1972	Filly Triple Crown	1975
Run the Gantlet	1968	Champion grass horse	1971
Ryafan	1994	Champion grass mare	1997
Sacahuista	1984	Champion 3-year-old filly	1987
Safely Kept	1986	Champion sprinter	1989
Saint Ballado	1989	Among the leading sires	2004
Sally's Alley	1920	Champion 2-year-old filly	1922
Saratoga Dew	1989	Champion 3-year-old filly	1992
Sarazen	1921	Horse of the year	1924
Sarazen	1921	Horse of the year	1925
Sarazen	1921	Champion 3-year-old colt	1924
Sarazen	1921	Champion handicap horse	1925
Sarazen	1921	Champion handicap horse	1926
Scapa Flow	1924	Champion 2-year-old colt	1926
Seabiscuit	1933	Horse of the year	1938
Seabiscuit	1933	Champion handicap horse	1937
Seabiscuit	1933	Champion handicap horse	1938
Seattle Slew	1974	Horse of the year	1977
Seattle Slew	1974	Champion 2-year-old colt	1976
Seattle Slew	1974	Champion 3-year-old colt	1977
Seattle Slew	1974	Champion older horse	1978
Seattle Slew	1974	Leading sire	1984
Seattle Slew	1974	Leading broodmare sire	1995
Seattle Slew	1974	Leading broodmare sire	1996
Seattle Slew	1974	Among the leading sires	1986
Seattle Slew	1974	Among the leading sires	1989
Seattle Slew	1974	Among the leading sires	1992
Seattle Slew	1974	Among the leading bm sires	1998
Seattle Slew	1974	Triple Crown	1977

Horse	Foaled	Honor	Year
Secretariat	1970	Horse of the year	1972
Secretariat	1970	Horse of the year	1973
Secretariat	1970	Champion 2-year-old colt	1972
Secretariat	1970	Champion 3-year-old colt	1973
Secretariat	1970	Champion grass horse	1973
Secretariat	1970	Leading broodmare sire	1992
Secretariat	1970	Among the leading bm sires	1996
Secretariat	1970	Among the leading bm sires	1997
Secretariat	1970	Triple Crown	1973
Seeking the Gold	1985	Among the leading sires	2000
Sensational	1974	Champion 2-year-old filly	1976
Serena's Song	1992	Champion 3-year-old filly	1995
Shadow Brook	1964	Champion steeplechaser	1971
Shannon II	1941	Champion handicap horse	1948
Shecky Greene	1970	Champion sprinter	1973
Sheilas Reward	1947	Champion sprinter	1950
Sheilas Reward	1947	Champion sprinter	1951
Shenanigans	1963	Broodmare of the year	1975
Shipboard	1950	Champion steeplechaser	1956
Shuvee	1966	Champion older mare	1970
Shuvee	1966	Champion older mare	1971
Shuvee	1966	Filly Triple Crown	1971
Siama	1947	Broodmare of the year	1960
Sickle	1924	Leading sire	1936
Sickle	1924	Leading sire	1938
Sickle's Image	1948	Champion older mare	1953
Silent Screen	1967	Champion 2-year-old colt	1969
Silver Buck	1978	Among the leading sires	1998
Silver Charm	1994	Champion 3-year-old colt	1997
Silver Deputy	1985	Among the leading sires	1998
Silver Deputy	1985	Among the leading sires	1999
Silver Spoon	1956	Champion 3-year-old filly	1959
Silverbulletday	1996	Champion 2-year-old filly	1998
Silverbulletday	1996	Champion 3-year-old filly	1999
Singspiel (IRE)	1992	Champion grass horse	1996
Sir Barton	1916	Horse of the year	1919
Sir Barton	1916	Champion 3-year-old colt	1919
Sir Barton	1916	Triple Crown	1919
Sir Gallahad III	1920	Leading sire	1930
Sir Gallahad III	1920	Leading sire	1933
Sir Gallahad III	1920	Leading sire	1934
Sir Gallahad III	1920	Leading sire	1940
Sir Gallahad III	1920	Leading broodmare sire	1939
Sir Gallahad III	1920	Leading broodmare sire	1943
Sir Gallahad III	1920	Leading broodmare sire	1944
Sir Gallahad III	1920	Leading broodmare sire	1945
Sir Gallahad III	1920	Leading broodmare sire	1946
Sir Gallahad III	1920	Leading broodmare sire	1947
Sir Gallahad III	1920	Leading broodmare sire	1948
Sir Gallahad III	1920	Leading broodmare sire	1949
Sir Gallahad III	1920	Leading broodmare sire	1950
Sir Gallahad III	1920	Leading broodmare sire	1951
Sir Gallahad III	1920	Leading broodmare sire	1952
Sir Gallahad III	1920	Leading broodmare sire	1955
Skip Away	1993	Horse of the year	1998
Skip Away	1993	Champion 3-year-old colt	1996
Skip Away	1993	Champion older horse	1997
Skip Away	1993	Champion older horse	1998
Skip Trial	1982	Among the leading sires	1997
Sky Beauty	1990	Champion older mare	1994
Sky Beauty	1990	Filly Triple Crown	1993
Sky Classic	1987	Champion grass horse	1992
Slew o' Gold	1980	Champion 3-year-old colt	1983
Slew o' Gold	1980	Champion older horse	1984
Slightly Dangerous	1979	Broodmare of the year	1997
Smart Angle	1977	Champion 2-year-old filly	1979
Smart Deb	1960	Champion 2-year-old filly	1962
Smartaire	1962	Broodmare of the year	1979
Smarty Jones	2001	Champion 3-year-old colt	2004
Smile	1982	Champion sprinter	1986
Smoke Glacken	1994	Champion sprinter	1997
Snow Chief	1983	Champion 3-year-old colt	1986
Snow Knight	1971	Champion grass horse	1975
Snowflake	1927	Champion 3-year-old filly	1930
Soaring Softly	1995	Champion grass mare	1999
Social Outcast	1950	Champion handicap horse	1955
Some Pomp	1931	Champion handicap mare	1935
Somethingroyal	1952	Broodmare of the year	1973
Soothsayer	1967	Champion steeplechaser	1972
Speak John	1958	Leading broodmare sire	1985
Spectacular Bid	1976	Horse of the year	1980
Spectacular Bid	1976	Champion 2-year-old colt	1978
Spectacular Bid	1976	Champion 3-year-old colt	1979
Spectacular Bid	1976	Champion older horse	1980
Speculate	1936	Champion steeplechaser	1941
Speightstown	1998	Champion sprinter	2004
Spend a Buck	1982	Horse of the year	1985
Spend a Buck	1982	Champion 3-year-old colt	1985
Squirtle Squirt	1998	Champion sprinter	2001
St. Germans	1921	Leading sire	1931
St. James	1921	Champion 2-year-old colt	1923
St. Vincent	1951	Champion grass horse	1955
Stage Door Johnny	1965	Champion 3-year-old colt	1968
Stagehand	1935	Champion 3-year-old colt	1938
Stan	1950	Champion grass horse	1954
Star de Naskra	1975	Champion sprinter	1979
Star Pilot	1943	Champion 2-year-old colt	1945
Star Shoot	1898	Leading sire	1919
Star Shoot	1898	Leading broodmare sire	1924
Star Shoot	1898	Leading broodmare sire	1925
Star Shoot	1898	Leading broodmare sire	1926
Star Shoot	1898	Leading broodmare sire	1928
Star Shoot	1898	Leading broodmare sire	1929
Startle	1919	Champion 2-year-old filly	1921
Stefanita	1940	Champion 3-year-old filly	1943
Steinlen (GB)	1983	Champion grass horse	1989
Storm Cat	1983	Leading sire	1999
Storm Cat	1983	Leading sire	2000
Storm Cat	1983	Among the leading sires	2002
Storm Cat	1983	Among the leading sires	1997
Storm Cat	1983	Among the leading sires	2004
Storm Flag Flying	2000	Champion 2-year-old filly	2002
Storm Song	1994	Champion 2-year-old filly	1996
Straight and True	1970	Champion steeplechaser	1976
Straight Deal	1962	Champion older mare	1967
Strawberry Road (AUS)	1979	Among the leading sires	1998
Striking	1947	Broodmare of the year	1961
Stymie	1941	Champion handicap horse	1945
Successor	1964	Champion 2-year-old	1966
Summer Scandal	1962	Champion older mare	1966
Sun Beau	1925	Champion handicap horse	1929
Sun Beau	1925	Champion handicap horse	1930
Sun Beau	1925	Champion handicap horse	1931
Sun Briar	1915	Champion handicap horse	1919
Sunday Silence	1986	Horse of the year	1989
Sunday Silence	1986	Champion 3-year-old colt	1989
Sunshine Forever	1985	Champion grass horse	1988
Surfside	1997	Champion 3-year-old filly	2000
Susan's Girl	1969	Champion 3-year-old filly	1972
Susan's Girl	1969	Champion older mare	1973
Susan's Girl	1969	Champion older mare	1975
Swale	1981	Champion 3-year-old colt	1984
Swaps	1952	Horse of the year	1956
Swaps	1952	Champion older horse	1956
Sweep	1907	Leading sire	1925
Sweep	1907	Leading broodmare sire	1937

Sweep	1907	Leading broodmare sire	1941
Sweet Catomine	2002	Champion 2-year-old filly	2004
Sweet Patootie	1950	Champion 2-year-old filly	1952
Sweet Tooth	1965	Broodmare of the year	1977
Swoon	1942	Broodmare of the year	1956
Sword Dancer	1956	Horse of the year	1959
Sword Dancer	1956	Champion 3-year-old colt	1959
Sword Dancer	1956	Champion older horse	1959
T. V. Lark	1957	Champion grass horse	1961
T. V. Lark	1957	Leading sire	1974
Ta Wee	1966	Champion sprinter	1969
Ta Wee	1966	Champion sprinter	1970
Talking Picture	1971	Champion 2-year-old filly	1973
Tambour	1928	Champion 3-year-old filly	1931
Tambour	1928	Champion handicap mare	1933
Tasso	1983	Champion 2-year-old colt	1985
Tea-Maker	1943	Champion sprinter	1952
Tempera	1999	Champion 2-year-old filly	2001
Temperence Hill	1977	Champion 3-year-old colt	1980
Tempest Queen	1975	Champion 3-year-old filly	1978
Tempted	1955	Champion older mare	1959
The Finn	1912	Leading sire	1923
The Mast	1947	Champion steeplechaser	1953
The Porter	1915	Leading sire	1937
The Wicked North	1989	Champion older horse	1994
Theatrical (IRE)	1982	Champion grass horse	1987
Thunder Gulch	1992	Champion 3-year-old colt	1995
Thunder Gulch	1992	Leading sire	2001
Tiffany Lass	1983	Champion 3-year-old filly	1986
Tight Spot	1987	Champion grass horse	1991
Tim Tam	1955	Champion 3-year-old colt	1958
Timber Country	1992	Champion 2-year-old colt	1994
Tintagel	1933	Champion 2-year-old colt	1935
Tiznow	1997	Horse of the year	2000
Tiznow	1997	Champion 3-year-old colt	2000
Tiznow	1997	Champion older horse	2001
Toll Booth	1971	Broodmare of the year	1991
Tom Fool	1949	Horse of the year	1953
Tom Fool	1949	Champion 2-year-old colt	1951
Tom Fool	1949	Champion sprinter	1953
Tom Fool	1949	Champion older horse	1953
Tom Rolfe	1962	Champion 3-year-old colt	1965
Too Bald	1964	Broodmare of the year	1986
Top Bid	1964	Champion steeplechaser	1970
Top Flight	1929	Champion 2-year-old filly	1931
Top Flight	1929	Champion 3-year-old filly	1932
Top Knight	1966	Champion 2-year-old colt	1968
Tosmah	1961	Champion 2-year-old filly	1963
Tosmah	1961	Champion 3-year-old filly	1964
Tosmah	1961	Champion older mare	1964
Track Medal	1950	Broodmare of the year	1962
Track Robbery	1976	Champion older mare	1982
Traffic Court	1938	Broodmare of the year	1954
Tred Avon	1928	Champion handicap mare	1932
Trillion	1974	Champion grass mare	1979
Trough Hill	1942	Champion steeplechaser	1949
Tryster	1918	Champion 2-year-old colt	1920
Tudor Queen	1967	Champion 2-year-old filly	1969
Turbo Jet II	1960	Champion grass horse	1964
Turkish Trousers	1968	Champion 3-year-old filly	1971
Turkoman	1982	Champion older horse	1986
Tuscalee	1960	Champion steeplechaser	1966
Twenty Grand	1928	Horse of the year	1931
Twenty Grand	1928	Champion 3-year-old colt	1931
Twilight Tear	1941	Horse of the year	1944
Twilight Tear	1941	Champion 2-year-old filly	1943
Twilight Tear	1941	Champion 3-year-old filly	1944
Twilight Tear	1941	Champion handicap mare	1944
Two Lea	1946	Champion 3-year-old filly	1949
Two Lea	1946	Champion older mare	1950
Typecast	1966	Champion older mare	1972
Unbridled	1987	Champion 3-year-old colt	1990
Unbridled	1987	Among the leading sires	1999
Unerring	1936	Champion 3-year-old filly	1939
Untidy	1920	Champion 3-year-old filly	1923
Vagrancy	1939	Champion 3-year-old filly	1942
Vagrancy	1939	Champion handicap mare	1942
Valenciennes	1927	Champion handicap mare	1931
Vanlandingham	1981	Champion older horse	1985
Vexatious	1916	Champion 3-year-old filly	1919
Vice Regent	1967	Among the leading bm sires	2001
Vice Regent	1967	Among the leading bm sires	1993
Vice Regent	1967	Among the leading bm sires	1996
Vice Regent	1967	Among the leading bm sires	1998
Vice Regent	1967	Among the leading bm sires	1999
Vice Regent	1967	Among the leading bm sires	2000
Victory Gallop	1995	Champion older horse	1999
Vindication	2000	Champion 2-year-old colt	2002
Vitriolic	1965	Champion 2-year-old colt	1967
Wajima	1972	Champion 3-year-old colt	1975
Wandesta (GB)	1991	Champion grass mare	1996
War Admiral	1934	Horse of the year	1937
War Admiral	1934	Champion 3-year-old colt	1937
War Admiral	1934	Leading sire	1945
War Admiral	1934	Leading broodmare sire	1962
War Admiral	1934	Leading broodmare sire	1964
War Admiral	1934	Triple Crown	1937
War Battle	1941	Champion steeplechaser	1947
War Emblem	1999	Champion 3-year-old colt	2002
War Plumage	1936	Champion 3-year-old filly	1939
War Plumage	1936	Champion handicap mare	1940
Warfare	1957	Champion 2-year-old colt	1959
Warm Spell	1988	Champion steeplechaser	1994
Waya (FR)	1974	Champion older mare	1979
Wayward Lass	1978	Champion 3-year-old filly	1981
Weekend Surprise	1980	Broodmare of the year	1992
What a Pleasure	1965	Leading sire	1975
What a Pleasure	1965	Leading sire	1976
What a Summer	1973	Champion sprinter	1977
What a Treat	1962	Champion 3-year-old filly	1965
Whichone	1927	Champion 2-year-old colt	1929
Whirlaway	1938	Horse of the year	1941
Whirlaway	1938	Horse of the year	1942
Whirlaway	1938	Champion 2-year-old colt	1940
Whirlaway	1938	Champion 3-year-old colt	1941
Whirlaway	1938	Champion handicap horse	1942
Whirlaway	1938	Triple Crown	1941
Whiskaway	1919	Champion 3-year-old colt	1922
Whiskery	1924	Champion 3-year-old colt	1927
White Skies	1949	Champion sprinter	1954
Wild Again	1980	Among the leading sires	2002
Wild Again	1980	Among the leading sires	1997
Winning Colors	1985	Champion 3-year-old filly	1988
Wise Counsellor	1921	Champion 2-year-old colt	1923
Wistful	1946	Champion 3-year-old filly	1949
Wrack	1909	Leading broodmare sire	1935
Xtra Heat	1998	Champion 3-year-old filly	2001
Yanks Music	1993	Champion 3-year-old filly	1996
Youth	1973	Champion grass horse	1976
Zaccio	1976	Champion steeplechaser	1980
Zaccio	1976	Champion steeplechaser	1981
Zaccio	1976	Champion steeplechaser	1982
Zev	1920	Horse of the year	1923
Zev	1920	Champion 2-year-old colt	1922
Zev	1920	Champion 3-year-old colt	1923

2004 SOVEREIGN RESULTS WITH POINT TOTALS

Horse of the Year
Soaring Free 239
A Bit O'Gold 182
One for Rose 30

2-year-old filly
Simply Lovely 200
South Bay Cove 145
Higher World 119

2-year-old colt/gelding
Wholelottabourbon 221
Dance With Ravens 114
Moonshine Justice 101

3-year-old filly
Eye of the Sphynx 226
Blonde Executive 132
Regal Red 60

3-year-old colt/gelding
A Bit O'Gold 290
Niigon 129
Organ Grinder 80

Older filly or mare
One for Rose 278
Winter Garden 107
Brass in Pocket 46

Older colt, horse or gelding
Mobil 246
Mark One 100
Norfolk Knight 75

Turf filly or mare
Inish Glora 185
Classic Stamp 159
Hour of Justice 67

Turf colt, horse or gelding
Soaring Free 286
Slew Valley 68
Shoal Water 56

Sprinter
Blonde Executive 109
Winter Garden 101
Chris's Bad Boy 68

Jockey
Todd Kabel 294
Patrick Husbands 86
Quincy Welch 41

Apprentice jockey
Corey Fraser 259
Shannon Beauregard ... 102
Jillian Scharfstein 80

Trainer
Bob Tiller 211
Mark Frostad 159
Sid Attard 111

Owner
Sam-Son Farm 240
Stronach Stable 148
Eugene & Laura Melnyk. 36

Breeder
Sam-Son Farm 261
Adena Springs 105
Gustav Schickedanz..... 51

Broodmare
Annasan 193
Queen of Egypt 101
Native Rights 89

Canadian Horse of the Year

1951	Bull Page
1952	Canadiana
1953	King Maple
1954	Queen's Own
1955	Ace Marine
1956	Canadian Champ
1957	Hartney
1958	Nearctic
1959	Wonder Where
1960	Victoria Park
1961	Hidden Treasure
1962	Crafty Lace
1963	Canebora
1964	Northern Dancer
1965	George Royal
1966	Victorian Era
1967	He's A Smoothie
1968	Viceregal
1969	Jumpin Josephine
1970	Fanfreluche
1971	Lauries Dancer
1972	La Prevoyante
1973	Kennedy Road
1974	L' Enjoleur
1975	L' Enjoleur
1976	Norcliffe
1977	L' Alezane
1978	Overskate
1979	Overskate
1980	Glorious Song
1981	Deputy Minister
1982	Frost King
1983	Travelling Victor
1984	Dauphin Fabuleux
1985	Imperial Choice
1986	Ruling Angel
1987	Afleet
1988	Play the King
1989	With Approval
1990	Izvestia
1991	Dance Smartly
1992	Benburb
1993	Peteski
1994	Alywow
1995	Peaks and Valleys
1996	Mt. Sassafras
1997	Chief Bearhart
1998	Chief Bearhart
1999	Thornfield
2000	Quiet Resolve
2001	Win City
2002	Wake at Noon
2003	Wando
2004	Soaring Free

2004 Sovereign Awards

By Bill Tallon

Soaring Free, winner of Woodbine's Grade 1 Atto Mile and undefeated in five starts in his homeland in 2004, was honored as Canada's Horse of the Year at the 30th annual Sovereign Awards ceremony in Toronto on Dec. 17.

A total of 76 voters participated in the Sovereign Awards balloting, naming their three top choices in each category with points assigned on a 4-2-1 basis. Horses must have started at least three times in Canada by Nov. 28 to be eligible for consideration.

Soaring Free was the only Grade 1 winner among this year's Sovereign Award finalists. The $1 million Atto Mile is one of three such events on the Canadian calendar, with all three being run over Woodbine's turf course.

Sulamani came over from England to win the $1.5 million Canadian International while Commercante shipped up from New York to take the $750,000 E.P. Taylor Stakes.

Soaring Free, a 5-year-old gelding owned and bred by Sam-Son Farm, also was voted outstanding turf male and outpointed A Bit O'Gold, who was a handy winner of the 3-year-old colt or gelding award, in a fairly close Horse of the Year vote.

Both Soaring Free and A Bit O' Gold, who is owned by The Two Bit Racing Stable and trained by Catherine Day Phillips, earned more than $1 million this year.

A Bit O'Gold finished second behind Niigon in Woodbine's $1 million Queen's Plate, which is the first leg of the Canadian Triple Crown, but swept the balance of the series with victories in Fort Erie's Prince of Wales and Woodbine's Breeders' Stakes.

Soaring Free's coronation capped a big night for Sam-Son Farm, which was a runaway winner in the owner and breeder categories and also campaigned Eye of the Sphynx, who was voted champion 3-year-old filly.

The breeder award was the fifth straight and seventh overall but the first in the owner category since 2001 for Sam-Son, which now has captured that award eight times.

Todd Kabel, Soaring Free's regular rider, was close to being a unanimous choice in the outstanding jockey balloting.

Kabel, who captured 36 stakes races at Woodbine this year to equal the Ontario record set by the late Avelino Gomez in 1966, was the meet's runaway leader in both races and money won. The award was the second straight and fifth overall, including one as champion apprentice, for Kabel.

This year's outstanding apprentice award went to Corey Fraser, who led his category in both races and money won at Woodbine in his first full campaign.

Mark Frostad, Sam-Son Farm's private trainer, was the runner-up in his category behind Bob Tiller, who was named outstanding trainer for the second straight year and third time in the past four seasons.

Tiller registered 15 stakes wins this year with three coming courtesy of Simply Lovely, who is owned by Rocco Marcello and was honored as champion 2-year-old filly.

Sid Attard, Woodbine's leading trainer in races won, was the other finalist in his category. Attard's runners included One for Rose, owned by Tucci Stable, who repeated in the older filly/mare division and was the third Horse of the Year finalist.

The closest vote of the evening came in the sprinter category, with Blonde Executive prevailing over Winter Garden.

Owned and bred by Bruno Brothers Farm and trained by Radlie Loney, Blonde Executive also was the runner-up in the 3-year-old filly balloting.

Winter Garden, owned by Frank DiGiulio Jr. and trained by Bob Tiller, was a dual runner-up, also finishing second in the older filly/mare vote.

The female turf horse award was hotly contested, as expected. Inish Glora, owned by Bob Costigan and trained by Mac Benson, prevailed in the category for the second straight year with Classic Stamp a solid runner-up.

The 2-year-old colt or gelding award also had been billed as being up for grabs but went to Wholelottabourbon by a convincing margin.

Wholelottabourbon is owned by M.A.D. Racing Stable in partnership with Martha Gonzalez, whose husband, Nick Gonzalez, is the trainer.

The older male award went to Mobil, a multiple stakes winner for owner/breeder Gustav Schickedanz and trainer Mike Keogh.

Annasan, dam of A Bit O'Gold, was honored as outstanding broodmare, which is a lifetime achievement award.

Awards also were presented in four media categories, with the winners determined by the votes of panels of judges.

Dave Landry was the recipient of the outstanding photograph award and the Woodbine Entertainment Group was honored in the film/video/broadcast category.

Paul Wiecek was the recipient of the newspaper article award and Darryl Kaplan was the feature story winner.

Alphabetical Listing of Canadian Champions and Leading Sires and Broodmares

Horse	YOB	Title	Year
A Fleets Dancer	1995	Champion older horse	2001
A Bit O'Gold	2001	Champion 3-year-old colt	2004
Ada Prospect	1981	Champion 2-year-old filly	1983
Added Edge	2000	Champion 2-year-old colt	2002
Afleet	1984	Horse of the year	1987
Afleet	1984	Champion 3-year-old colt	1987
Aim n Fire	1960	Champion 2-year-old	1962
Allan Blue	1977	Champion 2-year-old	1979
Almoner	1967	Champion 3-year-old colt	1970
Alydeed	1989	Leading sire	2001
Alywow	1991	Horse of the year	1994
Alywow	1991	Champion 3-year-old filly	1994
Alywow	1991	Champion grass horse	1994
Amber Sherry	1966	Champion 2-year-old filly	1968
Amelia Bearhart	1983	Broodmare of the year	1996
Annasan	1994	Broodmare of the year	2004
Apelia	1989	Champion sprinter	1993
Archers Bay	1995	Champion 3-year-old colt	1998
Archers Bay	1995	Among the leading sires	2004
Arctic Blizzard	1965	Champion 2-year-old	1967
Arctic Vixen	1978	Broodmare of the year	1987
Ascot Knight	1984	Among the leading sires	2001
Ascot Knight	1984	Among the leading sires	2002
Ascot Knight	1984	Among the leading sires	1997
Ascot Knight	1984	Among the leading sires	1998
Ascot Knight	1984	Among the leading sires	1999
Avant's Gold	1987	Champion older mare	1991
Avowal	1979	Champion 3-year-old filly	1982
Avowal	1979	Champion sprinter	1982
Balaklair	1960	2nd highweighted filly	1963
Ballade	1972	Broodmare of the year	1992
Basqueian	1991	Champion older horse	1995
Bayford	1978	Champion 2-year-old	1980
Belle Geste	1968	Champion handicap mare	1972
Ben Fab	1977	Champion 3-year-old	1980
Ben Fab	1977	Champion grass horse	1981
Benburb	1989	Horse of the year	1992
Benburb	1989	Champion 3-year-old colt	1992
Bessarabian	1982	Champion older mare	1986
Blonde Executive	2001	Champion sprinter	2004
Blue Finn	1984	Champion 2-year-old colt	1986
Blushing Katy	1986	Champion 3-year-old filly	1989
Bold Debra	1981	Broodmare of the year	1993
Bold Executive	1984	Leading sire	2003
Bold Executive	1984	Leading sire	2004
Bold Executive	1984	Among the leading sires	2001
Bold Executive	1984	Among the leading sires	2002
Bold Executive	1984	Among the leading sires	1998
Bold Executive	1984	Among the leading sires	1999
Bold Ruckus	1976	Leading sire	1997
Bold Ruckus	1976	Leading sire	1998
Bold Ruckus	1976	Leading sire	1999
Bold Ruckus	1976	Among the leading sires	2001
Bold Ruritana	1990	Champion grass mare	1995
Bold Ruritana	1990	Champion older mare	1995
Bolulight	1988	Champion 3-year-old	1991
Bompago	1980	Champion 3-year-old colt	1983
Bounding Away	1981	Champion grass horse	1984
Brave Front	1963	Champion 2-year-old filly	1965
Bruce's Mill	1991	Champion 3-year-old	1994
Brusque	2000	Champion 2-year-old filly	2002
Buckys Solution	1989	Champion 2-year-old filly	1991
Bye and Near	1963	Champion handicap horse	1969
Bye Bye Paris	1973	Champion 3-year-old filly	1976
Canadian Factor	1980	Champion older horse	1984
Candle Bright	1980	Champion 2-year-old filly	1982
Canebora	1960	Horse of the year	1963
Canebora	1960	Champion 3-year-old	1963
Canebora	1960	Triple Crown	1963
Carotene	1983	Champion 3-year-old filly	1986
Carotene	1983	Champion grass horse	1986
Carotene	1983	Champion grass horse	1987
Carotene	1983	Champion grass horse	1988
Carotene	1983	Champion grass mare	1988
Carotene	1983	Champion older mare	1987
Carotene	1983	Champion older mare	1988
Cash Deposit	1994	Champion 2-year-old colt	1996
Catch the Ring	1997	Champion 3-year-old filly	2000
Cesca	1960	Champion 2-year-old filly	1962
Cesca	1960	Champion 3-year-old filly	1963
Charlie Barley	1986	Champion grass horse	1989
Charming Sassafras	1985	Broodmare of the year	1997
Chief Bearhart	1993	Horse of the year	1997
Chief Bearhart	1993	Horse of the year	1998
Chief Bearhart	1993	Champion grass horse	1996
Chief Bearhart	1993	Champion grass horse	1997
Chief Bearhart	1993	Champion grass horse	1998
Chief Bearhart	1993	Champion older horse	1997
Choperion	1959	2nd highweighted	1962
Chopinina	1998	Champion grass mare	2002
Choral Group	1979	Champion 2-year-old filly	1981
Christy's Mount	1973	Champion older mare	1978
Ciboulette	1961	2nd highweighted filly	1963
Claim	1985	Among the leading sires	1997
Classy 'n Smart	1981	Champion 3-year-old filly	1984
Classy 'n Smart	1981	Broodmare of the year	1991
Colorful Vices	1993	Champion grass mare	1998
Come in Dad	1970	Champion 3-year-old	1973
Comet Shine	1991	Champion 2-year-old colt	1993
Connie Pat	1968	Champion handicap mare	1973
Cool Reception	1964	Champion 2-year-old	1966
Cotton Carnival	1994	Champion 3-year-old filly	1997
Coup d'Etat	1957	Champion older mare	1962
Court Royal	1959	Champion older mare	1963
Cozzene's Prince	1987	Champion older horse	1993
Crafty Lace	1959	Horse of the year	1962
Crafty Lace	1959	Champion 3-year-old	1962
Cryptocloser	1994	Champion 3-year-old colt	1997
Dance Act	1966	Champion handicap horse	1970
Dance Act	1966	Champion handicap horse	1971
Dance for Donna	1989	Champion older mare	1993
Dance in Time	1974	Champion 3-year-old	1977
Dance Smartly	1988	Horse of the year	1991
Dance Smartly	1988	Champion 2-year-old filly	1990
Dance Smartly	1988	Champion 3-year-old filly	1991
Dance Smartly	1988	Broodmare of the year	2001
Dance Smartly	1988	Triple Crown	1991
Dance to Market	1967	Champion 2-year-old	1969
Dancethruthedawn	1998	Champion 3-year-old filly	2001
Dauphin Fabuleux	1982	Horse of the year	1984
Dauphin Fabuleux	1982	Champion 2-year-old colt	1984
Dawn Deluxe	1969	Champion 2-year-old filly	1971
Dawson's Legacy	1995	Champion 2-year-old colt	1997
Deceit Dancer	1982	Champion 2-year-old filly	1984
Decidedly	1959	Champion older horse	1963
Deputy Inxs	1991	Champion sprinter	1998
Deputy Inxs	1991	Champion sprinter	1999
Deputy Inxs	1991	Champion older horse	1999
Deputy Jane West	1990	Champion 2-year-old filly	1992
Deputy Jane West	1990	Champion 3-year-old filly	1993
Deputy Minister	1979	Horse of the year	1981
Deputy Minister	1979	Champion 2-year-old colt	1981
Dianne's Lady	1974	Highweighted filly	1978
Diapason	1980	Champion sprinter	1984
Diva's Debut	1986	Champion older mare	1990
Doris White	1966	Broodmare of the year	1977
Double Ripple	1965	Highweighted filly	1969
Dr. Giddings	1960	2nd highweighted	1963
Driving Home	1977	Champion older horse	1981
El Bandido	1957	Champion older horse	1962
Eternal Search	1978	Champion sprinter	1981
Eternal Search	1978	Champion older mare	1982

Horse	YOB	Title	Year
Eternal Search	1978	Champion older mare	1983
Etimota	1960	2nd highweighted filly	1962
Exciting Story	1997	Champion 2-year-old colt	1999
Eye of the Sphynx	2001	Champion 3-year-old filly	2004
Famous Road	1961	Champion 2-year-old filly	1963
Fanfreluche	1967	Horse of the year	1970
Fanfreluche	1967	Champion 3-year-old filly	1970
Fanfreluche	1967	Broodmare of the year	1978
Fantasy Lake	1996	Champion 2-year-old filly	1998
First Class Gal	1988	Broodmare of the year	2002
Fitz's Fancy	1962	Broodmare of the year	1979
Flaming Page	1959	Champion 3-year-old filly	1962
Fleet Courage	1972	Broodmare of the year	1998
Foxy Parent	1967	Champion 2-year-old filly	1969
Fraud Squad	1979	Champion sprinter	1983
Free At Last	1989	Champion 2-year-old colt	1991
Free Vacation	1996	Champion grass mare	1999
Friendly Ways	1968	Broodmare of the year	1984
Frost King	1978	Horse of the year	1982
Frost King	1978	Champion 3-year-old colt	1981
Frost King	1978	Champion grass horse	1982
Frost King	1978	Champion older horse	1982
Gandria	1996	Champion 3-year-old filly	1999
Gentleman Conn	1969	Champion 2-year-old colt	1971
George Royal	1961	Horse of the year	1965
Giboulee	1974	Champion older horse	1978
Ginger Gold	1999	Champion 2-year-old filly	2001
Glanmire	1990	Champion sprinter	1997
Glorious Song	1976	Horse of the year	1980
Glorious Song	1976	Champion older mare	1980
Glorious Song	1976	Champion older mare	1981
Glory Hill	1960	Champion 3-year-old filly	1963
Golden Choice	1983	Champion 3-year-old	1986
Gomtuu	1993	Champion 2-year-old colt	1995
Good Old Mort	1962	Champion 2-year-old	1964
Great Gladiator	1977	Among the leading sires	1998
Great Gladiator	1977	Among the leading sires	1999
Grey Classic	1983	Champion 2-year-old colt	1985
Hangin Round	1970	Broodmare of the year	1980
Happy Victory	1969	Champion 3-year-old filly	1972
Hasten To Add	1990	Champion grass horse	1995
Heliotrope	1995	Champion grass mare	2000
Hello Seattle	1997	Champion 2-year-old filly	1999
Henry Tudor	1969	Champion older horse	1974
Hero's Love	1988	Champion grass horse	1993
He's a Smoothie	1963	Horse of the year	1967
He's a Smoothie	1963	Champion 3-year-old	1966
He's a Smoothie	1963	Champion handicap horse	1967
He's a Smoothie	1963	Champion handicap horse	1968
Highland Legacy	1998	Champion 2-year-old colt	2000
Hometown News	1965	Champion 3-year-old filly	1968
Honky Tonk Tune	1992	Champion 2-year-old filly	1994
Hope for a Breeze	1989	Champion 3-year-old filly	1992
Ice Water	1963	Champion handicap mare	1968
Imperial Choice	1982	Horse of the year	1985
Imperial Choice	1982	Champion 3-year-old colt	1985
Imperial Choice	1982	Champion grass horse	1985
Inish Glora	1998	Champion grass mare	2003
Inish Glora	1998	Champion grass mare	2004
Izvestia	1987	Horse of the year	1990
Izvestia	1987	Champion 3-year-old colt	1990
Izvestia	1987	Champion grass horse	1990
Izvestia	1987	Triple Crown	1990
Judiths Wild Rush	2001	Champion 2-year-old colt	2003
Jumpin Joseph	1966	Horse of the year	1969
Jumpin Joseph	1966	Champion 3-year-old colt	1969
Kamar	1976	Champion 3-year-old filly	1979
Kennedy Road	1968	Horse of the year	1973
Kennedy Road	1968	Champion 2-year-old	1970
Kennedy Road	1968	Champion handicap horse	1972
Kennedy Road	1968	Champion handicap horse	1973
Kerensa	1963	Champion 3-year-old filly	1966
Key to the Moon	1981	Champion 3-year-old colt	1984
King Corrie	1988	Champion sprinter	1991
King Corrie	1988	Champion sprinter	1992
King Ruckus	1990	Champion sprinter	1994
King Ruckus	1990	Champion older horse	1994
Kingsbridge	1980	Champion grass horse	1983
Kirby's Song	1995	Champion 3-year-old filly	1998
Kiridashi	1992	Among the leading sires	2004
Kiss a Native	1997	Champion 3-year-old colt	2000
La Lorgnette	1982	Champion 3-year-old filly	1985
La Prevoyante	1970	Horse of the year	1972
La Prevoyante	1970	Champion 2-year-old filly	1972
La Prevoyante	1970	Champion older mare	1974
La Voyageuse	1975	Champion 3-year-old filly	1978
La Voyageuse	1975	Champion sprinter	1980
La Voyageuse	1975	Champion older mare	1979
Lady Shari	1999	Champion 3-year-old filly	2002
Lake Country	1981	Champion older mare	1985
L'Alezane	1975	Horse of the year	1977
L'Alezane	1975	Champion 2-year-old	1977
Langfuhr	1992	Champion sprinter	1996
Larkwhistle	1994	Champion 2-year-old filly	1996
Lauries Dancer	1968	Horse of the year	1971
Lauries Dancer	1968	Champion 3-year-old filly	1971
Le Cinquieme Essai	1999	Champion 3-year-old colt	2002
Legarto	1986	Champion 2-year-old filly	1988
L'Enjoleur	1972	Horse of the year	1974
L'Enjoleur	1972	Horse of the year	1975
L'Enjoleur	1972	Champion 2-year-old colt	1974
L'Enjoleur	1972	Champion 3-year-old colt	1975
Let's Go Blue	1981	Champion older horse	1986
Liz's Pride	1976	Champion 2-year-old filly	1978
Lord Durham	1971	Champion 2-year-old	1973
Loudrangle	1974	Broodmare of the year	1986
Lubicon	1987	Champion 3-year-old filly	1990
Magic Code	1995	Champion older mare	1999
Maudlin	1978	Among the leading sires	1999
Medaille d'Or	1976	Champion 2-year-old	1978
Mercedes Won	1986	Champion 2-year-old colt	1988
Minsky	1968	Champion 3-year-old	1971
Mobil	2000	Champion older horse	2004
Momigi	1972	Champion 3-year-old filly	1975
Momigi	1972	Champion grass horse	1977
Momigi	1972	Champion handicap mare	1976
Mountain Angel	1997	Champion older mare	2001
Mr. Epperson	1995	Champion sprinter	2001
Mr. Hot Shot	1985	Champion sprinter	1989
Mt. Sassafras	1992	Horse of the year	1996
Mt. Sassafras	1992	Champion older horse	1996
My Vintage Port	2001	Champion 2-year-old filly	2003
Native Flower	1968	Broodmare of the year	1981
New Connection	1981	Champion sprinter	1986
Nice Dancer	1969	Champion 3-year-old colt	1972
No Class	1974	Broodmare of the year	1985
Norcliffe	1973	Horse of the year	1976
Norcliffe	1973	Champion 3-year-old	1976
Norcliffe	1973	Champion handicap horse	1977
Northern Blossom	1980	Champion 3-year-old filly	1983
Northern Dancer	1961	Horse of the year	1964
Northern Dancer	1961	Champion 2-year-old colt	1963
Northern Minx	1963	Broodmare of the year	1976
Northern Queen	1962	Champion 3-year-old filly	1965
Northernette	1974	Champion 2-year-old filly	1976
Northernette	1974	Champion 3-year-old filly	1977
Not Too Shy	1966	Champion 3-year-old filly	1969
Not Too Shy	1966	Champion handicap mare	1970
Not Too Shy	1966	Champion handicap mare	1971
Numerous Times	1997	Champion grass horse	2001
One for Rose	1999	Champion older mare	2003
One for Rose	1999	Champion older mare	2004
One From Heaven	1984	Champion 3-year-old filly	1987
One Way Love	1995	Champion sprinter	2000
One Way Love	1995	Champion older horse	2000
Overskate	1975	Horse of the year	1978
Overskate	1975	Horse of the year	1979
Overskate	1975	Champion 2-year-old colt	1977
Overskate	1975	Champion 3-year-old colt	1978
Overskate	1975	Champion grass horse	1978

Horse	YOB	Title	Year
Overskate	1975	Champion grass horse	1979
Overskate	1975	Champion grass horse	1980
Overskate	1975	Champion older horse	1979
Overskate	1975	Champion older horse	1980
Par Excellance	1977	Champion 2-year-old filly	1979
Par Excellance	1977	Champion 3-year-old filly	1980
Passing Mood	1978	Broodmare of the year	1989
Peaks and Valleys	1992	Horse of the year	1995
Peaks and Valleys	1992	Champion 3-year-old colt	1995
Pennyhill Park	1990	Champion older mare	1994
Perfect Soul (IRE)	1998	Champion grass horse	2003
Peteski	1990	Horse of the year	1993
Peteski	1990	Champion 3-year-old colt	1993
Peteski	1990	Triple Crown	1993
Phantom Light	1999	Champion older horse	2003
Phoenix Factor	1985	Champion 2-year-old filly	1987
Pine Point	1964	Champion 3-year-old	1967
Play the King	1983	Horse of the year	1988
Play the King	1983	Champion sprinter	1987
Play the King	1983	Champion sprinter	1988
Play the King	1983	Champion older horse	1987
Play the King	1983	Champion older horse	1988
Poetically	1998	Champion 2-year-old filly	2000
Polite Lady	1977	Broodmare of the year	1988
Portcullis	1999	Champion grass horse	2002
Primaly	1995	Champion 2-year-old filly	1997
Primarily	1988	Broodmare of the year	2000
Prince Avatar	1981	Champion 2-year-old	1983
Proper Evidence	1985	Champion older mare	1989
Proud Tobin	1973	Champion 2-year-old colt	1975
Queen Louie	1968	Champion 2-year-old filly	1970
Quiet Resolve	1995	Horse of the year	2000
Quiet Resolve	1995	Champion grass horse	2000
Radiant Ring	1988	Broodmare of the year	2003
Rainbow Connection	1978	Champion 2-year-old filly	1980
Rainbow Connection	1978	Champion 3-year-old filly	1981
Rainbow Connection	1978	Broodmare of the year	1994
Rainbows for Life	1988	Champion 2-year-old colt	1990
Rainbows for Life	1988	Champion grass horse	1992
Rainbows for Life	1988	Champion older horse	1992
Ramblin Road	1961	2nd highweighted	1963
Rare Friends	1999	Champion 2-year-old colt	2001
Rash Move	1971	Champion handicap horse	1975
Reasonable Wife	1968	Broodmare of the year	1975
Reasonable Win	1972	Champion handicap mare	1977
Regal Classic	1985	Champion 2-year-old colt	1987
Regal Classic	1985	Among the leading sires	1997
Regal Intention	1985	Champion 3-year-old colt	1988
Riddell's Creek	1996	Champion 2-year-old colt	1998
Rouletabille	1965	Champion 3-year-old	1968
Royal Tara	1961	Highweighted filly	1964
Royal Tara	1961	Highweighted older mare	1965
Ruling Angel	1984	Horse of the year	1986
Ruling Angel	1984	Champion 2-year-old filly	1986
Runaway Groom	1979	Champion 3-year-old colt	1982
Rushton's Corsair	1971	Champion 3-year-old	1974
Ruthie's Run	1972	Champion 2-year-old filly	1974
Santa Amelia	1993	Champion older mare	1998
Saoirse	1996	Champion older mare	2000
Scotzanna	1992	Champion 3-year-old filly	1995
Scotzanna	1992	Champion sprinter	1995
Sea Regent	1977	Broodmare of the year	1995
Seraphic	1973	Champion 2-year-old filly	1975
Sharpening Up	1983	Broodmare of the year	1999
Shy Spirit	1975	Broodmare of the year	1990
Silent Fleet	1993	Champion 3-year-old filly	1996
Silken Cat	1993	Champion 2-year-old filly	1995
Simply Lovely	2002	Champion 2-year-old filly	2004
Sintrillium	1978	Champion older mare	1984
Sky Classic	1987	Champion 2-year-old colt	1989
Sky Classic	1987	Champion grass horse	1991
Sky Classic	1987	Champion older horse	1991
Small Promises	1998	Champion older mare	2002
Soaring Free	1999	Horse of the year	2004
Soaring Free	1999	Champion sprinter	2003
Soaring Free	1999	Champion grass horse	2004
Sonny Says Quick	1968	Highweighted filly	1970
Sound Reason	1974	Champion 2-year-old	1976
Sound Stage	1960	2nd highweighted	1962
Speedy Lament	1961	Champion older mare	1966
Square Angel	1970	Champion 3-year-old filly	1973
Stage Flite	1983	Champion 2-year-old filly	1985
Steady Growth	1976	Champion 3-year-old	1979
Steady Power	1984	Champion older horse	1989
Summer Mood	1981	Champion sprinter	1985
Sunny's Halo	1980	Champion 2-year-old	1982
Sweetest Thing	1998	Champion grass mare	2001
Talkin Man	1992	Champion 2-year-old	1994
Tejabo	1985	Among the leading sires	2002
Ten Gold Pots	1981	Champion older horse	1985
Term Limits	1991	Champion 2-year-old filly	1993
Terremoto	1991	Champion older horse	1998
Tethra	1992	Among the leading sires	2003
The Axe II	1958	Champion grass horse	1963
Thornfield	1994	Horse of the year	1999
Thornfield	1994	Champion grass horse	1999
Tilt My Halo	1985	Champion 3-year-old filly	1988
Titled Hero	1963	Champion 2-year-old	1965
Titled Hero	1963	Champion 3-year-old	1966
Too Late Now	2000	Champion 3-year-old filly	2003
Travelling Victor	1979	Horse of the year	1983
Travelling Victor	1979	Champion older horse	1983
Trudie Tudor	1971	Champion 2-year-old filly	1973
Trudie Tudor	1971	Champion 3-year-old filly	1974
Truth of It All	1990	Champion 2-year-old colt	1992
Twist the Snow	1986	Champion sprinter	1990
Twist the Snow	1986	Champion older horse	1990
Two Rings	1970	Broodmare of the year	1983
Vase	1959	2nd highweighted filly	1962
Vice Regent	1967	Among the leading sires	1997
Vice Regent	1967	Among the leading sires	1998
Viceregal	1966	Horse of the year	1968
Viceregal	1966	Champion 2-year-old colt	1968
Victor Cooley	1993	Champion 3-year-old colt	1996
Victorian Era	1962	Horse of the year	1966
Victorian Era	1962	Champion handicap horse	1966
Victorian Prince	1970	Champion grass horse	1976
Victorian Prince	1970	Champion older horse	1976
Victorian Queen	1971	Champion grass horse	1975
Victorian Queen	1971	Champion handicap mare	1975
Vying Victor	1989	Among the leading sires	2002
Vying Victor	1989	Among the leading sires	2003
Vying Victor	1989	Among the leading sires	2004
Wake At Noon	1997	Horse of the year	2002
Wake At Noon	1997	Champion sprinter	2002
Wake At Noon	1997	Champion older horse	2002
Wando	2000	Horse of the year	2003
Wando	2000	Champion 3-year-old colt	2003
Wando	2000	Triple Crown	2003
War Deputy	1991	Leading sire	2002
War Deputy	1991	Among the leading sires	2001
War Deputy	1991	Among the leading sires	2003
Wavering Girl	1987	Champion 2-year-old filly	1989
Whiskey Wisdom	1993	Among the leading sires	2003
Whiskey Wisdom	1993	Among the leading sires	2004
Wholelottabourbon	2002	Champion 2-year-old colt	2004
Wilderness Song	1988	Champion older mare	1992
Win City	1998	Horse of the year	2001
Win City	1998	Champion 3-year-old colt	2001
Windsharp	1991	Champion grass mare	1996
Windsharp	1991	Champion older mare	1996
With Approval	1986	Horse of the year	1989
With Approval	1986	Champion 3-year-old	1989
With Approval	1986	Triple Crown	1989
Woodcarver	1996	Champion 3-year-old colt	1999
Woolloomooloo	1992	Champion grass mare	1997
Woolloomooloo	1992	Champion older mare	1997
Yonnie Girl	1966	Broodmare of the year	1982
Zaca Spirit	1970	Champion 2-year-old	1972

Past Performances
of
Great Horses of the 20th Century

☆

Affirmed
Buckpasser
Cigar
Citation
Colin
Count fleet
Damascus
Dr. Fager
Equipoise
Exterminator
Forego
Holy Bull
John Henry
Kelso

Lady's Secret
Man o' War
Nashua
Native Dancer
Personal Ensign
Ruffian
Seabiscuit
Seattle Slew
Secretariat
Shuvee
Skip Away
Spectacular Bid
Swaps
Tom Fool
Twilight Tear

Past Performances of Great Horses of the 20th Century

Affirmed

ch. c. 1975, by Exclusive Native (Raise a Native)–Won't Tell You, by Crafty Admiral — Lifetime record: 29 22 5 1 $2,393,818

Own.– Harbor View Farm

Br.– Harbor View Farm (Fla)

Tr.– Lazaro S. Barrera

6Oct79- 8Bel fst 1½ :49 1:131 2:022 2:272 3↑ J C Gold Cup-G1 3 2 1½ 1hd 1½ 1¾ Pincay L Jr 126 *.60 83-21 Affirmed126¾Spectacular Bid1213Coastal12131 Driving 4
22Sep79- 8Bel sly 1¼ :473 1:114 1:361 2:013 3↑ Woodward-G1 2 2 24 1½ 13 12½ Pincay L Jr 126 *.40 92-15 Affirmed1262½Coastal1203¾Czaravich1208½ Ridden out 5
29Aug79- 0Bel sly 1 :222 :45 1:092 1:34 3↑ Alw 30000 3 1 1½ 11 12 16 Pincay L Jr 122 - 98-15 Affirmed1226Island Sultan11514Prefontaine117 Ridden out 3
No wagering. Exhibition race run between 7th and 8th races
24Jun79- 8Hol fst 1¼ :453 1:093 1:341 1:582 3↑ Hol Gold Cup-G1 1 2 1hd 1hd 1hd 1¾ Pincay L Jr 132 *.30 99-13 Affirmed132¾Sirlad1204Text1195 Driving 10
20May79- 8Hol fst 1 1/16 :222 :444 1:091 1:411 3↑ Californian-G1 2 1 11 11 12 15 Pincay L Jr 130 *.30 89-16 Affirmed1305Syncopate1144Harry's Love117¾ Driving 8
4Mar79- 8SA fst 1¼ :462 1:101 1:341 1:583 4↑ S Anita H-G1 3 2 21 11½ 14 14½ Pincay L Jr 128 *1.30 103-09 Affirmed1284½Tiller1273[DH]PaintedWagon115 Speed to spare 8
4Feb79- 8SA gd 1¼ :47 1:104 1:353 2:01 C H Strub-G1 8 2 31 11 12 110 Pincay L Jr 126 *.90 91-17 Affirmed12610Johnny's Image1154Quip1157 Handily 9
20Jan79- 8SA gd 1⅛ :453 1:093 1:35 1:48 San Fernando-G2 4 3 49½ 57½ 33½ 22¾ Cauthen S 126 *.50 88-14 Radar Ahead1232¾Affirmed126nkLittle Reb1204 Drifted out 8
7Jan79- 8SA fst 7f :222 :45 1:083 1:21 Malibu-G2 2 1 32 32½ 32½ 32¼ Cauthen S 126 *.30 96-13 LittleReb1202¼RadarAhed123hdAffrmd1263 Hemmed in to str 5
14Oct78- 8Bel sly 1½ :451 1:092 2:014 2:271 3↑ J C Gold Cup-G1 2 2 2hd 37 415 518¾ Cauthen S 121 2.20e 65-13 Exceller126noSeattle Slew12614Great Contractor1264¾ 6
Saddle slipped
16Sep78- 8Bel fst 1⅛ :47 1:101 1:333 1:454 3↑ Marlboro Cup H-G1 1 2 22½ 22½ 23 23 Cauthen S 124 *.50 95-12 SeattleSlew1283Affirmed1245NastyandBold1184 No excuse 6
19Aug78- 8Sar fst 1¼ :48 1:113 1:364 2:02 Travers-G1 3 2 2hd 11½ 12 11¾ Pincay L Jr 126 *.70 91-14 [D]Affirmed1261¾Alydar1263¾NastyandBold12615 Came over 4
Disqualified and placed second
8Aug78- 8Sar gd 1⅛ :463 1:101 1:35 1:474 Jim Dandy-G3 4 2 28 27 24 1½ Cauthen S 128 *.05 96-04 Affirmed128½SensitivePrince11920Addison1146½ Going away 5
10Jun78- 8Bel fst 1½ :50 1:14 2:013 2:264 Belmont-G1 3 1 11 1hd 1hd 1hd Cauthen S 126 *.60 86-11 Affirmed126hdAlydar12613Darby Creek Road1267¾ Driving 5
20May78- 8Pim fst 1 3/16 :473 1:114 1:361 1:542 Preakness-G1 6 2 11 11 1½ 1nk Cauthen S 126 *.50 98-12 Affirmed126nkAlydar1267½Believe It1262½ Brisk handling 7
6May78- 8CD fst 1¼ :453 1:104 1:354 2:011 Ky Derby-G1 2 2 35½ 2hd 12 11½ Cauthen S 126 1.80 91-12 Affirmed1261½Alydar1261¼Believe It1264¼ Fully extended 11
16Apr78- 8Hol fst 1⅛ :45 1:092 1:35 1:481 Hol Derby-G1 2 1 1hd 11 12½ 12 Cauthen S 122 *.30 91-17 Affirmed1222Think Snow1223Radar Ahead1222 Driving 9
2Apr78- 8SA fst 1⅛ :454 1:094 1:353 1:48 S Anita Derby-G1 7 2 11 11½ 13½ 18 Pincay L Jr 120 *.30 92-16 Affirmed1208Balzac1201Think Snow1202½ Handily 12
18Mar78- 8SA fst 1 1/16 :241 :482 1:12 1:423 San Felipe-G2 4 2 21 2hd 1hd 12 Cauthen S 126 *.30 89-17 Affirmed1262Chance Dancer1176Tampoy1181½ Driving 6
8Mar78- 6SA fst 6½f :213 :442 1:09 1:153 Alw 30000 4 1 43½ 11½ 14 15 Cauthen S 124 *.20 92-16 Affirmed1245Spotted Charger114½Don F.114hd Easily 5
29Oct77- 8Lrl fst 1 1/16 :24 :484 1:133 1:441 Lrl Futurity-G1 3 2 21 2hd 1hd 1nk Cauthen S 122 1.40 92-27 Affirmed122nkAlydar12210StardeNskr12227 Long,hard drive 4
15Oct77- 6Bel my 1 :242 :481 1:122 1:363 Champagne-G1 5 3 32 1hd 1½ 21¼ Cauthen S 122 *1.20 84-17 Alydar1221¼Affirmed1221¼Darby Creek Road1221½ 2nd best 6
10Sep77- 8Bel gd 7f :233 :463 1:094 1:213 Futurity-G1 2 2 2½ 1hd 2hd 1no Cauthen S 122 *1.20 94-10 Affirmed122noAlydar12211NastyandBold122hd Strong drive 5
27Aug77- 8Sar fst 6½f :224 :451 1:091 1:152 Hopeful-G1 4 1 32 2hd 1hd 1½ Cauthen S 122 2.30 98-11 Affirmed122½Alydar1222½RegalandRoyal122hd Good handling 5
17Aug77- 8Sar fst 6f :214 :443 1:093 Sanford-G2 3 2 35½ 43 2½ 12¾ Cauthen S 124 *1.30 92-15 Affirmed1242¾TltUp122hdJtDplomcy124nk Driving,very wide 6
23Jly77- 5Hol fst 6f :213 :442 :562 1:091 Juv Champ (Div 1) 104k 6 3 1hd 1½ 14 17 Pincay L Jr 122 *.40 93-15 Affirmed1227He's Dewan1226Esops Foibles122¾ Easily 8
6Jly77- 8Bel fst 5½f :222 :454 :572 1:033 Great American 36k 1 1 11 2hd 21½ 23½ Cordero A Jr 122 4.60 93-16 Alydar1173½Affirmed1222Going Investor1224 No match 7
15Jun77- 8Bel fst 5½f :222 :453 :582 1:05 ©Youthful 37k 1 1 2½ 2½ 1hd 1nk Cordero A Jr 119 3.40 90-17 Affirmed119nkWood Native119½Sensitive Nose1192½ Driving 11
24May77- 4Bel fst 5½f :23 :472 :593 1:06 Md Sp Wt 10 1 1½ 11½ 12 14½ Gonzalez B 117 14.30 85-21 Affirmed1174½Innocuous1223½Gymnast1222 Ridden out 10

Past Performances of Great Horses of the 20th Century

Buckpasser

b. c. 1963, by Tom Fool (Menow)–Busanda, by War Admiral

Lifetime record: 31 25 4 1 $1,462,014

Own.– O. Phipps
Br.– Ogden Phipps (Ky)
Tr.– E.A. Neloy

Date	Track / Dist	Fractions	Age	Race	PP	St	1st	2nd	Str	Fin	Jockey	Wt	Eqp	Odds	Speed	Top finishers	Comment	Field
30Sep67- 7Aqu	fst 1¼	:45^1 1:09^1 1:35^3 2:00^3	3↑	Woodward 107k	6	6	6^{14}	3^{3}½	3^8	2^{10}	Baeza B	126	b	*1.60e	85-15	Damascus120^{10}Buckpasser126½Dr. Fager120^{13}	Good try	6
22Jly67- 7Aqu	fst 1¼	:46^2 1:09^4 1:34^2 2:00^1	3↑	Brooklyn H 106k	3	3	3^3	2^3	2^5	2^8	Baeza B	136	b	*.70	89-11	Handsome Boy116^{8}Buckpassr136^{4}½Mr. Right113^{3}½	No excuse	5
4Jly67- 7Aqu	fst 1¼	:47^4 1:11^4 1:36^3 2:02^1	3↑	Suburban H 109k	1	5	6^5	4^4	4^4	1½	Baeza B	133	b	*.50	87-17	Buckpasser133½RingTwice111^{2}½Yondr109^{1}½	Up final strides	7
17Jun67- 7Aqu	hd 1⅝Ⓣ	2:41^2	3↑	Bowling Green H 55k	3	4	4^{7}½	4^{6}½	3^5	3^{4}½	Baeza B	135	b	*.40e	82-13	Poker112^{1}½Assagai127Buckpasser135½	Failed to respond	5
30May67- 7Aqu	fst 1	:23^2 :45^4 1:10 1:34^3	3↑	Metropolitan H 109k	5	3	3^2	3^{4}½	2^1	1^{1}¼	Baeza B	130	b	*.30	95-13	Buckpasser130^{1}¼Yonder108^{4}½Impressive113^1	Scored easily	6
14Jan67- 8SA	fst 1⅛	:46^2 1:10^3 1:35^4 1:48^1		San Fernando 56k	3	3	3^{7}½	4^{4}½	3^{2}½	1^{1}½	Baeza B	124	b	*.30	91-12	Buckpasser124^{1}½Fleet Host121¾Pretens118^{hd}	With authority	6
31Dec66- 6SA	fst 7f	:22^3 :45^1 1:09^3 1:22		Malibu 29k	2	9	7^{6}½	5^{4}½	2^1	1¾	Baeza B	126	b	*.40	93-15	Buckpasser126¾Drin121^{1}KingsFvor117^{1}½	Slow start,driving	9
29Oct66- 7Aqu	fst 2	:49^4 2:33^3 3:26^1	3↑	J C Gold Cup 110k	1	4	4^{4}½	1^{hd}	1^1	1^{1}¾	Baeza B	119	b	*.30e	65-21	Buckpasser119^{1}¾Niarchos124½O'Hara124^8	Drew out handling	7
19Oct66- 7Aqu	sly 1⅝	:49^2 1:42^3 2:07^1 2:44^1		Lawrence Realizatn 54k	4	5	4^{4}½	3^{3}½	3^{2}½	1^{2}½	Baeza B	126	b	*.20e	84-19	Buckpasser126^{2}½Ring Twice116½Poker116^{12}	Going away	5
1Oct66- 7Aqu	sly 1¼	:47 1:11^4 1:37^3 2:02^4	3↑	Woodward 112k	4	6	6^{4}½	3^{1}½	1^{hd}	1¾	Baeza B	121	b	*.90e	84-24	Buckpasser121¾Royal Gunner126¾Buffle121^5	Ridden out	9
20Aug66- 6Sar	fst 1¼	:47^2 1:11^2 1:36^2 2:01^3		Travers 82k	6	5	5^{12}	4^{3}½	2^1	1¾	Baeza B	126	b	*.30e	100-10	Buckpssr126¾Ambrod123^{3}½Buffl120^{no}	Under strong handling	6
6Aug66- 8AP	fst 1⅛	:46^4 1:10^3 1:35^4 1:47		American Derby 129k	9	5	5^{9}½	6^8	4^2	1^{nk}	Baeza B	128	b	*.60e	101-09	Buckpasser128^{nk}Jolly Jet116^{1}Advocator116^3	Driving	9
23Jly66- 7Aqu	fst 1¼	:48^3 1:12^2 1:36^4 2:01^4	3↑	Brooklyn H 107k	2	2	2^{2}½	2^{1}½	1^{hd}	1^{hd}	Baeza B	120	b	*.60	89-16	Buckpasser120^{hd}Buffle113^{5}Pluck113^2	Faltered,came again	5
9Jly66- 8AP	fst 1⅛	:47^3 1:11^2 1:36^3 1:49^1		Chicagoan 103k	3	3	3^3	2½	1^{hd}	1¾	Baeza B	123	b	*.30	90-18	Buckpasser123¾Whisper Jet114^{nk}Abe's Hope116^7	Mild drive	5
25Jun66- 8AP	fst 1	:22^1 :43^3 1:06^4 1:32^3		Arl Classic H 108k	4	6	7^9	5^9	3^4	1¾	Baeza B	125	b	*.70e	103-04	Buckpasser125^{1}¾CremeDelaCreme123¾HeJr.116^{nk}	Ridden out	8
18Jun66- 8Del	fst 1⅛	:46^3 1:10 1:36^4 1:49^2		Leonard Richards 41k	2	4	4^7	4^{8}½	2^{hd}	1¾	Baeza B	126	b	*.30e	90-14	Buckpasser126¾Buffle114¾Deck Hand114^4	Under hand urging	6
4Jun66- 6Aqu	fst 6f	:22^2 :45^1 1:09^1	3↑	Alw 8500	5	3	2^2	1^{hd}	1^{hd}	1^2	Baeza B	115	b	*.40	97-14	Buckpasser115^{2}Tim'sStingry115^{2}Undrstudy121^{nk}	Mild drive	7
3Mar66- 0Hia	fst 1⅛	:46^2 1:10^4 1:36^3 1:50		Flamingo 136k	4	3	3^4	3^2	2½	1no	Shoemaker W	122	b	-	85-18	Buckpasser122^{no}Abe'sHope122^{2}¼BlueSkyer122^{2}½	Came again	9
	Run between 7th and 8th races. No wagering																	
23Feb66- 8Hia	fst 1⅛	:45^2 1:09 1:34^3 1:47^4		Everglades 30k	6	2	2^3	2^1	2^{hd}	1^{hd}	Shoemaker W	122	b	*.20e	96-12	Buckpasser122^{hd}Stupendous115¾Abe's Hope115^4	Swerved	8
14Feb66- 0Hia	fst 7f	:22^4 :45 1:08^4 1:21^4		Alw 5000	1	5	5^{14}	5^{12}	4^6	2^{4}½	Shoemaker W	124	b	-e	95-13	Impressive122^{4}½Buckpasser124^{1}½Stupendous113^{nk}	Rallied	5
	Exhibition race run between 7th and 8th races. No wagering;Previously trained by W.C. Winfrey																	
16Oct65- 7Aqu	fst 1	:22^3 :45^3 1:10^4 1:36^2		Champagne 223k	1	7	5^{4}½	5^{4}½	1½	1^4	Baeza B	122	b	*.90e	86-20	Buckpasser122^{4}Our Michael122½Advocator122^{1}½	Easily	9
25Sep65- 7Aqu	gd 6½f	:23 :46^2 1:10^4 1:17^1		Futurity 151k	7	6	4^{1}¾	2^1	2^1	2½	Baeza B	122	b	*.70	93-20	PricelessGem119½Buckpassr122^{10}ⒹAdvoctor122^3	No excuse	9
11Sep65- 8AP	fst 7f	:22^3 :45^2 1:10^2 1:23		Arl-Wash Futurity 335k	8	8	6^{6}½	5^{6}¼	1^4	1½	Baeza B	122	b	*.80	92-15	Buckpasser122½Fathers Image122^{2}Flame Tree122^{no}	Driving	10
28Aug65- 6Sar	fst 6½f	:22 :44^4 1:09^3 1:16		Hopeful 110k	7	7	4^{2}½	3^{1}½	3^{nk}	1^{2}½	Baeza B	122	b	*.30e	98-08	Buckpasser122^{2}½Impressive122¾Indulto122^{2}½	Going away	7
7Aug65- 8Mth	fst 6f	:22 :45 1:10^3		Sapling 112k	1	7	6^{3}¾	3^{3}½	3^3	1½	Baeza B	122	b	1.90	89-21	Buckpasser122½Quinta122^{1}½OurMichael122^5	Left at post,up	7
30Jly65- 7Mth	fst 5½f	:22^1 :45^4 1:04		Alw 5000	3	5	4^2	3^3	1^1	1^7	Baeza B	122	b	*.90	97-19	Buckpasser122^{7}Model Fool116¾Gary Dear119^3	Drew far out	6
7Jly65- 7Aqu	fst 5½f	:22^1 :45 :57^2 1:03^4		Tremont 34k	3	6	6^{6}½	4^{2}½	2½	1^{nk}	Baeza B	118	b	*.70	94-13	Buckpasser118^{nk}SpringDouble118^{2}½Hospitalty118^{no}	Driving	6
28Jun65- 7Aqu	fst 5½f	:22^2 :45^2 :53 1:04^3		©National Stallion 32k	3	5	5^9	4^7	3^4	1^5	Baeza B	122	b	*1.00	90-15	[DH]Hospitality117[DH]Buckpassr122^{5}KentuckyKn117^{no}	Just up	6
8Jun65- 6Aqu	fst 5½f	:22^3 :46^1 :53^3 1:05		Alw 5500	7	5	5^5	5^{2}½	2½	1^{1}½	Baeza B	122		*1.90	88-21	Buckpassr122^{1}½KentuckyKin122^{2}½BanderaBeau119^4	Driving	9
29May65- 3Aqu	sly 5f	:23 :47^1 1:00		©Md Sp Wt	7	5	4^3	4^2	2½	1^2	Baeza B	122		*1.25	85-20	Buckpasser122^{2}Exhibitionist122^{2}½Clique122^4	Easy score	8
13May65- 4Aqu	fst 5½f	:23^1 :48^2 1:00^3 1:07		©Md Sp Wt	8	10	6^6	5^7	5^5	4^{1}¼	Baeza B	122		5.30	77-26	LonelyGambler122½HndsmeBy122^{no}MaskofPlay117¾	Greenly	10

Past Performances of Great Horses of the 20th Century

Cigar

b. c. 1990, by Palace Music (The Minstrel)–Solar Slew, by Seattle Slew — Lifetime record: 33 19 4 5 $9,999,815

Own.– Allen E. Paulson
Br.– Allen E. Paulson (Md)
Tr.– William I. Mott

26Oct96-10WO fst 1¼ :462 1:104 1:352 2:01 3↑ B C Classic-G1 7 7 85¾ 5¾ 41 3nk Bailey JD L 126 *.65 106-02 AlphabetSoup126noLouisQuatorze121hdCigar126½ 5-wide bid 13
5Oct96-10Bel fst 1¼ :473 1:112 1:354 2:003 3↑ JC Gold Cup-G1 6 3 34½ 31½ 31 2hd Bailey JD L 126 *.20 94-10 SkipAway121hdCigr1262LousQutorz1211 Drifted,outfinished 6
14Sep96- 8Bel fst 1⅛ :461 1:102 1:343 1:47 3↑ Woodward-G1 4 4 42½ 31 11½ 14 Bailey JD L 126 *.35 95-10 Cigar1264L'Carriere126½Golden Larch126¾ Ridden out 5
10Aug96- 6Dmr fst 1¼ :454 1:091 1:333 1:594 3↑ Pacific Classic-G1 4 2 21 1hd 2½ 23½ Bailey JD LB 124 *.10 94-07 Dare and Go1243½Cigar1247Siphon1248 Led,outfinished 6
13Jly96-10AP fst 1⅛ :464 1:101 1:353 1:481 3↑ Citation Challnge 1075k 10 7 63 31½ 1½ 13½ Bailey JD L 130 *.30 103-16 Cigar1303½Dramatic Gold118nkEltish1182 Ridden out,wide 10
1Jun96-10Suf fst 1⅛ :454 1:101 1:361 1:493 3↑ Mass H 500k 3 4 34 12 14 12¼ Bailey JD LB 130 *.10 95-08 Cigar1302¼PersonalMerit11110Prolanzr112nk 3 path,easily 6
27Mar96 ♦ NadAlSheba(Dub) fst *1¼LH 2:034 4↑ Dubai World Cup Stk4000000 1½ Bailey JD 124 - Cigar124½Soul of the Matter1248¾L'Carriere1243½ 11
5th after 1f,bid 4f out,led 2f out,dueled 1½f out,prevailed
10Feb96-10GP fst 1⅛ :464 1:104 1:353 1:49 3↑ Donn H-G1 1 3 32 2hd 13 12 Bailey JD L 128 *.20 92-12 Cigar1282Wekiva Springs1174Heavenly Prize1153 8
Six wide top str,easily best
28Oct95- 8Bel my 1¼ :481 1:121 1:353 1:592 3↑ B C Classic-G1 10 3 31 11½ 12 12½ Bailey JD L 126 *.70 97-08 Cgr1262½L'Crrr1261UnccountdFor126¾ Four wide bid,driving 11
7Oct95-10Bel wf 1¼ :48 1:112 1:36 2:011 3↑ JC Gold Cup-G1 6 3 31½ 2½ 12 11 Bailey JD L 126 *.35 88-14 Cigar1261Unaccounted For1269¾Star Standard1212 7
Carried 7 wide,gamely
16Sep95- 9Bel fst 1⅛ :454 1:093 1:334 1:47 3↑ Woodward-G1 5 3 34 2½ 13½ 12¾ Bailey JD L 126 *.10 97-09 Cigar1262¾Star Standard1213Golden Larch126¾ Under wraps 6
2Jly95- 6Hol fst 1¼ :453 1:092 1:34 1:592 3↑ Hol Gold Cup H-G1 1 4 42 11 13 13½ Bailey JD LB 126 *.90 103-04 Cigar1263½Tinners Way118hdTossofthecoin118½ 8
4 wide ½,strong handling
3Jun95-10Suf fst 1⅛ :471 1:102 1:351 1:483 3↑ Mass H 750k 6 4 33 2½ 13½ 14 Bailey JD LB 124 *.20 110-05 Cigar1244Poor but Honest1075½Double Calvados113nk 6
Rated 3w,mild urging
13May95-10Pim fst 1 3/16 :48 1:112 1:351 1:533 4↑ Pim Special H-G1 1 1 11½ 11½ 15 12¼ Bailey JD L 122 *.40 106-02 Cigar1222¼Devil His Due1212¾Concern1214½ Ridden out 6
15Apr95- 9OP fst 1⅛ :462 1:104 1:352 1:471 4↑ Oaklawn H-G1 4 4 45 41½ 1hd 12½ Bailey JD L 120 *1.70 103-13 Cigar1202½Silver Goblin1194Concern1221 7
Bumped,hit by opponent's whip,driving
5Mar95- 9GP fst 1¼ :472 1:114 1:364 2:024 3↑ Gulf Park H-G1 9 4 45 1hd 15 17½ Bailey JD L 118 *.50 88-19 Cigar1187½Pride of Burkaan1141Mahogany Hall1132 11
Six wide bkstr,six wide top str,ridden out
11Feb95- 9GP fst 1⅛ :462 1:103 1:363 1:493 3↑ Donn H-G1 4 1 12 1hd 1½ 15½ Bailey JD L 115 4.00 89-13 Cigar1155½Primitive Hall1121½Bonus Money1123½ 9
Five wide top str,drifted out,driving
22Jan95-10GP fst 1 1/16 :231 :464 1:112 1:431 4↑ Alw 33000 5 1 1hd 11 11½ 12 Bailey JD L 122 *.50 92-13 Cigar1222Upping the Ante1198¾Chasin Gold1221 8
Crowded,bumped start,driving
26Nov94- 8Aqu fst 1 :223 :454 1:111 1:36 3↑ NYRA Mile-G1 6 4 42 11½ 17 17 Bailey JD 111 8.90 88-28 Cigar1117DevilHisDue1242½PunchLine1121 Wide,ridden out 12
28Oct94- 6Aqu fst 1 :222 :443 1:094 1:353 3↑ Alw 34000 6 2 12 13 16 18 Smith ME 117 3.50 90-23 Cigar1178Golden Plover1193½Gulliviegold1092 Handily 6
7Oct94- 8Bel fm 1 1/16 Ⓣ :232 :463 1:104 1:412 3↑ Alw 36000 2 4 35 2½ 34½ 38½ Krone JA 117 3.40 80-15 UnaccountdFor1142½SameOldWish1196Cgr117½ Flattened out 6
16Sep94- 7Bel fm 1 Ⓣ :23 :452 1:083 1:33 3↑ Alw 34000 10 8 77¼ 45 66¾ 78½ Bailey JD 117 *1.90 89-13 Jido1082½BrmudaCedr1142LimtdWr1132 Wide,flattened out 11
8Aug94- 1Sar fm 1⅛ Ⓣ :472 1:12 1:363 1:483 3↑ Alw 34000 1 4 43½ 42 3½ 33 Smith ME 117 3.20 89-11 MyMogul1191½NextEndvr1191½Cgr117nk Lacked room stretch 8
8Jly94- 7Bel fm 1 1/16 Ⓣ :243 :482 1:123 1:43 3↑ Alw 34000 5 2 1hd 2hd 43 49 Smith ME 117 *1.70 72-16 DancingHuntr117½Compdr1173I'mVryIrsh1115½ Dueled,tired 5
Previously trained by Alex Hassinger Jr
20Nov93- 6Hol fm 1⅛ Ⓣ :461 1:102 1:341 1:464 Hol Derby-G1 9 4 55 41¼ 64½ 1114½ Valnzuela PA LB 122 24.80 76-08 ExplsiveRed1221¼JeuneHomm122nkErlofBrkng122½ Wide trip 14
5Nov93- 8SA fm 1⅛ Ⓣ :48 1:121 1:36 1:48 Volante H-G3 4 3 43 32½ 21½ 22 Valnzuela PA LB 118 7.70 77-21 EasternMemories1132Cigar118nkSnkEys120½ Bid,outfinished 9
25Sep93- 5BM fm 1 1/16 Ⓣ :23 :453 1:10 1:413 Ascot H-G3 1 5 44 41¼ 12 3½ Valnzuela PA LB 117 4.10 102-03 Siebe115nkNonproductiveasset114hdCigar1172¼ Held well 11
3Sep93- 8Dmr fm 1 Ⓣ :224 :47 1:11 1:35 3↑ Alw 40000 4 2 21½ 21 2hd 2½ McCarron CJ LB 115 3.30 95-04 Kingdom of Spain119½Cigar115½Saturnino1173 Sharp effort 6
18Aug93- 5Dmr fm 1 1/16 Ⓣ :231 :472 1:111 1:414 3↑ Alw 36000 5 4 53½ 43½ 3nk 12¾ McCarron CJ LB 115 *1.90 97-04 Cigr1152¾OurMotionGrantd122hdTheBerklyMn1142¼ Driving 10

Past Performances of Great Horses of the 20th Century

Date/Race	Cond	Dist	Fractions	Race	Calls	Jockey	Wt	Odds	Speed	Top three finishers	Comment	Field
12Jun93-10Hol	gd	1 1/16Ⓣ	:231 :48 1:113 1:412	Alw 39000	10 7 73 42 31½ 31¾	Valnzuela PA	LB 117	2.90	87-11	Nonprddctvast115½ Tos ofthcn1191¼Cigar1172¾	4 wide stretch	10
23May93-9Hol	fm	1 1/16Ⓣ	:232 :471 1:103 1:411	Alw 39000	11 3 31 2½ 11½ 41¾	Valnzuela PA	L 117	3.80	88-10	Fleasedontexplain117½Stately Warrior115½Fleet Wizard115¾	Weakened a bit	12
9May93-3Hol	fst	6f	:22 :443 :564 1:092	Md Sp Wt	3 6 21 1½ 13 12¼	Valenzuela PA	117	5.20	93-11	Cigr1172¼GoldnSlwpy115½FmousFn115hd	Off slowly,driving	6
21Feb93-6SA	gd	6f	:214 :452 :58 1:104	Md Sp Wt	9 7 65½ 65¼ 68 713	Valenzuela PA	118	5.10	70-18	Demigod118nkCardiac1132[D]SirHutch1182½	Wide backstretch	9

Citation

b. c. 1945, by Bull Lea (Bull Dog)–Hydroplane II, by Hyperion

Own.– Calumet Farm

Br.– Calumet Farm (Ky)

Tr.– H.A. Jones

Lifetime record: 45 32 10 2 $1,085,760

Date/Race	Cond	Dist	Fractions	Race	Calls	Jockey	Wt	Odds	Speed	Top three finishers	Comment	Field
14Jly51-7Hol	fst	1¼	:464 1:103 2:01	3↑ Hol Gold Cup 137k	10 6 33 12 13 14	Brooks S	120 w	*.35e	94-10	Citation1204Bewitch108noBe Fleet1221	Ridden out	10
4Jly51-7Hol	fst	1⅛	:464 1:11 1:36 1:482	3↑ American H 56k	5 5 52½ 4nk 2hd 1½	Brooks S	123 w	*.75e	98-07	Citation123½Bewitch1062¾Sturdy One112¾	Driving	8
14Jun51-7Hol	fst	1	:232 :463 1:104 1:354	4↑ Handicap 15000	3 3 31 1hd 1½ 1½	Brooks S	120 w	*.95	98-10	Citation120½Be Fleet1223¾Sturdy One110½	Driving	5
30May51-7Hol	fst	1 1/16	:222 :45 1:101 1:42	3↑ Argonaut H 30k	6 5 59½ 44 24 23	Smith FA	121 w	*.45e	95-08	Be Fleet1183Citation121nkSturdy One111½	Closed well	10
11May51-7Hol	fst	6f	:221 :452 :573 1:10	3↑ Premiere H 18k	3 8 86½ 96¼ 84 52¾	Brooks S	120 w	*1.15	93-12	SpecilTouch122nkMnyunk1141¼BullrghJr.1101	Closed ground	10
26Apr51-8BM	fst	6f	:223 :453 1:094	3↑ Alw 3000	2 5 55 43½ 33 32¼	Brooks S	120 w	*.60	97-10	Pancho Supreme1181¼A Lark1181Citation1203½	No excuse	5
18Apr51-8BM	fst	6f	:223 :453 1:094	4↑ Alw 3250	4 3 46 43½ 32 31	Brooks S	120 w	*.55	98-13	A Lark109noPancho Supreme1201Citation1202¼	Good effort	6
24Jun50-8GG	fst	1¼	:451 1:091 1:34 1:581	3↑ Golden Gate H 57k	3 2 313 37 34 23	Brooks S	126 w	1.20	105-12	Noor1273Citation12610On Trust1032½	No excuse	5
17Jun50-8GG	fst	1⅛	:463 1:093 1:344 1:464	3↑ Forty-Niners H 10k	3 2 21½ 1hd 1hd 2nk	Brooks S	128 w	*.50	104-08	Noor123nkCitation1283Roman In1112	Outgamed	5
3Jun50-8GG	fst	1	:221 :441 1:073 1:333	3↑ GG Mile H 23k	6 2 22 2½ 1hd 1¾	Brooks S	128 w	*.60	104-08	Citation128¾Bolero1235On Trust116nk	Driving	6
17May50-7GG	fst	6f	:22 :442 1:082	4↑ Alw 4000	4 5 55 52¾ 21½ 2¾	Glisson G	120 w	*.25	99-10	Roman In120¾Citation1201¼Blue Border1173	Forced wide	6
4Mar50-7SA	fst	1¾	:474 2:023 2:271 2:524	3↑ S Juan Capistrano H 64k	8 4 2hd 1hd 1hd 2no	Brooks S	130 w	*.60	127-06	Noor117noCitation13013⁄2Mocopo107hd	Just failed	8
25Feb50-7SA	fst	1¼	:462 1:11 1:351 2:00	3↑ S Anita H 135k	5 7 64 32½ 32 21¼	Arcaro E	132 w	*.35e	105-11	Noor1101¼Citation1321Two Lea113nk	Close quarters	11
11Feb50-7SA	gd	1⅛	:471 1:113 1:372 1:501	3↑ San Antonio H 60k	7 4 35 22 2½ 21	Arcaro E	130 w	*.45e	91-17	Ponder1281Citation130Noor114¾	Forced wide	9
26Jan50-7SA	fst	6f	:223 :46 1:104	4↑ Handicap 6000	4 1 42¼ 31½ 2hd 2nk	Brooks S	130 w	*.25	93-15	Miche114nkCitation130½Huon Kid107½	Close quarters	6
11Jan50-4SA	sly	6f	:223 :461 1:112	4↑ Alw 5000	3 4 33 31½ 3nk 11½	Brooks S	124 w	*.15	90-19	Citation1241½Bold Gallant112nkRoman In1163½	Drew away	4
11Dec48-7Tan	gd	1¼	:48 1:13 1:373 2:024	3↑ Tanforan H 54k	2 2 1½ 11½ 13½ 15	Arcaro E	123 w	*.05	103-12	Citation1235Stepfather1102½See-tee-see1172	Easily best	7
3Dec48-7Tan	my	6f	:231 :463 1:12	Alw 5000	4 5 21½ 2hd 11½ 11½	Arcaro E	126 w	*.10	95-23	Citation1261½Bold Gallant1122Barsard1095	In hand	5
29Oct48-6Pim	fst	1 3/16	:504 1:152 1:421 1:594	3↑ Pim Spl 10k	1 1 1 1 1 1	Arcaro E	120 w		83-11	Citation120	Breezing	1
Walkover												
16Oct48-7Bel	fst	1⅝	:48 1:331 2:034 2:424	3↑ Gold Cup 111k	8 3 33 12 14 12	Arcaro E	119 w	*.15	90-19	Citation1192Phalanx1225Carolyn A.1232½	In hand	9
Geldings not eligible												
2Oct48-6Bel	fst	2	:48 2:234 2:562 3:213	3↑ J C Gold Cup 108k	7 1 15 18 18 17	Arcaro E	117 w	*.30	96-09	Citation1177Phalanx12112Beauchef124hd	Easily	7
Geldings not eligible												
29Sep48-6Bel	fst	1	:224 :452 1:101 1:36	3↑ Sysonby Mile 29k	6 4 46 12 12 13	Arcaro E	119 w	*.10e	94-14	Citation1193First Flight123nkCoaltown1194	Eased up	6
28Aug48-7Was	fst	1¼	:462 1:10 1:353 2:013	American Derby 88k	1 1 21½ 11½ 1hd 11	Arcaro E	126 w	*.10e	95-10	Citation1261Free America1181Volcanic1182	Driving	5
21Aug48-4Was	fst	6f	:223 :45 1:104	Alw 4000	4 3 22 21 11 12½	Pierson NL	120 w	*.20	93-09	Citation1202½King Rhymer1141¼Speculation1176½	Easily	4
5Jly48-7AP	fst	1⅛	:464 1:104 1:354 1:491	3↑ Stars & Stripes H 56k	6 5 53½ 3½ 11½ 12	Arcaro E	119 w	*.30e	100-07	Citation1192Eternal Reward116nkPellicle106hd	Driving	9
12Jun48-6Bel	fst	1½	:482 1:123 2:023 2:281	Belmont 117k	1 1 1hd 14 15 18	Arcaro E	126 w	*.20	97-10	Citation1268Better Self126½Escadru1265	Much the best	8
Geldings not eligible												
29May48-6GS	fst	1¼	:47 1:113 1:36 2:03	Jersey 61k	4 4 1hd 13 18 111	Arcaro E	126 w	*.10	108-11	Citation12611Macbeth 14¾[D]Bovard114¾	Eased up	5
15May48-6Pim	hy	1 3/16	:502 1:16 1:43 2:022	Preakness 134k	4 1 11½ 12 12½ 15½	Arcaro E	126 w	*.10	70-43	Citation1265½Vulcan's Forge1263½Bovard126nk	Galloping	4

Past Performances of Great Horses of the 20th Century

Date-Race	Cond. Dist.	Fractions	Race	PP	St	1st	2nd	Str	Fin	Jockey	Wt	Eq	Odds	Speed	Top Finishers	Comment
	Previously trained by B.A. Jones															
1May48-7CD	sly $1\frac14$	$:46^3$ $1:11^2$ 1:38 $2:05^2$	Ky Derby 111k	1	2	2^6	$2^{\frac12}$	1^2	$1^{3\frac12}$	Arcaro E	126	w	*.40e	80-22	Citation$126^{3\frac12}$Coaltown126^3My Request$126^{1\frac12}$	Drew away 6
27Apr48-5CD	fst 1	:23 :46 $1:10^3$ $1:37^2$	Derby Trial 12k	2	2	$2^{\frac12}$	1^2	$1^{1\frac12}$	$1^{1\frac14}$	Arcaro E	118	w	*.10	92-23	Citation$118^{1\frac14}$Escadru$118^{\frac12}$Eagle Look110^{20}	Easily 4
	Previously trained by H.A. Jones															
17Apr48-6HdG	gd $1\frac{1}{16}$	:24 $:48^3$ $1:13^2$ $1:45^4$	Chesapeake 29k	4	3	3^1	1^1	1^3	$1^{4\frac12}$	Arcaro E	122	w	*.20	84-16	Citation$122^{4\frac12}$Bovard119^5Dr. Almac119^6	Easily 4
12Apr48-6HdG	my 6f	$:23^3$:47	$1:12^2$	Chesapeake Trial 12k	6	1	$4^{1\frac34}$	$4^{1\frac12}$	2^2	2^1	Arcaro E	126	w	*.30	88-27	Saggy122^1Citation126^4Dr. Almac$122^{1\frac12}$	Carried wide 6
28Feb48-6Hia	fst $1\frac18$	$:46^2$ $1:10^3$ $1:35^4$ $1:48^4$	Flamingo 62k	4	4	1^{hd}	1^{hd}	1^3	1^6	Snider A	126	w	*.20	97-09	Citation126^6Big Dial118^4Saggy122^1	Easily 7
18Feb48-6Hia	fst $1\frac18$	$:45^4$ 1:10 $1:35^2$ 1:49	Everglades H 10k	1	2	2^3	$1^{\frac12}$	1^1	1^1	Snider A	126	w	*.15	96-11	Citation126^1Hypnos109^4Silverling112	Easily 3
11Feb48-6Hia	fst 7f	$:23^2$:46 $1:10^1$ 1:23	3↑ Seminole H 12k	8	2	2^{hd}	2^{hd}	1^{hd}	1^1	Snider A	112	w	*.40e	97-16	Citation112^1Delegate123^{nk}Armed128^2	Drew out 9
2Feb48-6Hia	fst 6f	$:22^3$ $:45^4$ $1:10^2$	3↑ Alw 5000	2	7	2^{hd}	2^{hd}	1^{hd}	1^1	Snider A	113	w	*.20e	96-10	Citation113^1Kitchen Police$110^{1\frac34}$Say Blue$107^{1\frac12}$	Handily 7
8Nov47-5Pim	my $1\frac{1}{16}$	$:23^4$ $:48^3$ 1:14 $1:48^4$	Pim Futurity 48k	4	2	$3^{1\frac12}$	2^{hd}	$1^{\frac12}$	$1^{1\frac12}$	Dodson D	119	w	*.40	74-41	Citation$119^{1\frac12}$Better Self119^8Ace Admiral122^2	Ridden out 5
4Oct47-4Bel	fst $6\frac12$f-W	$:22^1$ $:44^4$ $1:09^2$ $1:15^4$	Futurity 106k	14	4		$3^{1\frac12}$	1^3	1^3	Snider A	122	w	*.85e	93-10	Citation122^3Whirling Fox114^{nk}Bewitch123^1	Easily 14
	Geldings not eligible															
30Sep47-4Bel	fst 6f-WC	$:23^3$ $:45^3$ 1:11	Futurity Trial 10k	2	9		7^1	$6^{1\frac14}$	1^1	Snider A	116	w	2.10	86-16	Citation116^1Gasparilla116^{nk}Up Beat116^{hd}	Drew away 14
16Aug47-6Was	fst 6f	$:22^3$:45 $1:10^2$	Was Futurity 78k	5	3	4^4	4^7	3^6	2^1	Brooks S	118	w	*.20e	97-07	Bewitch119^1Citation118^{hd}Free America118^2	Good effort 10
30Jly47-7Was	fst 6f	$:22^4$ $:45^3$ $1:10^3$	Elementary 24k	10	5	$2^{1\frac12}$	$1^{\frac12}$	1^1	1^2	Dodson D	122	w	*1.40	97-07	Citation122^2Salmagundi110^{no}Billings113^{nk}	Going away 10
24Jly47-5AP	fst 5f	$:22^3$ $:45^3$:58	Alw 4000	2	4	4^2	$4^{3\frac12}$	3^2	$1^{\frac12}$	Dodson D	117	w	2.20	102-12	Citation$117^{\frac12}$Kandy Comfort$114^{1\frac12}$Queen Hairan114^2	Driving 8
21May47-5HdG	gd 5f	:23 $:46^4$ $:59^1$	Alw 3500	1	4	2^2	2^3	2^2	$1^{1\frac34}$	Snider A	119	w	*.40	99-18	Citation$119^{1\frac34}$Little Tony113^8Grand Entry116^3	Going away 6
3May47-4Pim	fst 5f	$:23^1$ $:48^1$ $1:01^1$	Alw 3500	1	1	1^1	1^{hd}	$1^{\frac12}$	$1^{3\frac12}$	Snider A	119	w	*1.00	95-19	Citation$119^{3\frac12}$Newsweekly119^1Still Champ119^{nk}	Going away 6
22Apr47-3HdG	sl $4\frac12$f	:23 $:48^2$ $:54^2$	©Md Sp Wt	2	2		3^5	3^3	$1^{\frac12}$	Snider A	120	w	*1.60	93-07	Citation$120^{\frac12}$Sunday Beau120^{nk}Brass Band120^{no}	Driving 11

Past Performances of Great Horses of the 20th Century

Colin

b. c. 1905, by Commando (Domino)–Pastorella, by Springfield — **Lifetime record: 15 15 0 0 $180,912**

Own.– J.R. Keene
Br.– James R. Keene (Ky)
Tr.– J. Rowe

20Jun08- 4She fst 1¼ :47 1:11^3 1:38 2:04 Tidal 20k 3 1 1^2 1$^{1\frac{1}{2}}$ 1^3 1^2 Notter 126 w *.20 103-06 Colin126^{2}Dorante126 Stamin121^8 Bore out,tiring slightly 4
30May08- 3Bel sly 1⅜ Belmont 25k 2 - 1$^{1\frac{1}{2}}$ 1^{hd} Notter 126 w *.50 - - Colin126^{hd}Fair Play126^{15}King James126^{10} Eased up 4
Driving rainstorm,no time taken
23May08- 4Bel hy 1 :24 :48 1:14 1:41 Withers 14k 2 1 1^3 1^3 1^4 1^2 Notter 126 w *.40 82-19 Colin126^{2}Fair Play126$^{\frac{3}{4}}$King James126^8 Eased up 6
16Oct07- 3Bel fst 7f-Str 1:23 Champagne 7.2k 2 1 1^3 1^4 1^5 1^6 Miller W 122 w *.14 103-06 Colin122^{6}Stamina119 Drawing away 2
7Oct07- 2Bel fst 6f-Str 1:12 ©Matron 10k 3 1 2^4 1^5 1^4 1^3 Miller W 129 w *.14 90-11 Colin129^{3}Fair Play122^{4}Royal Tourist119$^{\frac{1}{2}}$ Easing up 4
30Sep07- 4Bri my 6f :24^2 :47^4 1:12^3 ©Produce (2nd half) 12k 1 1 1$^{1\frac{1}{2}}$ 1^4 1^4 1^5 Miller W 125 w *.25 96-13 Colin125^{5}Fair Play119^{hd}Royal Tourist119^{20} Eased up 4
7Sep07- 3She fst 7f-FC 1:24^4 Flatbush 10k 6 1 1$^{1\frac{1}{2}}$ 1$^{1\frac{1}{2}}$ 1^3 1^3 Miller W 120 w *.35e 100-00 Colin120^{3}Celt105^{5}Bar None105$^{1\frac{1}{2}}$ Hard held 7
31Aug07- 4She fst 6f-FC 1:11^1 Futurity 28k 5 1 2^1 2^2 1$^{\frac{1}{2}}$ 1$^{1\frac{1}{2}}$ Miller W 125 w *.33 97-03 Coln125$^{1\frac{1}{2}}$BrNon117^{1}Chpultpc117$^{1\frac{1}{2}}$ Blocked,as rider pleased 8
14Aug07- 3Sar fst 6f :24^1 :48^2 1:13 Grand Union Hotel 10k 3 4 2^{hd} 2^{hd} 1^{hd} 1^2 Miller W 127 w *.13e 95-05 Colin127^{2}Jim Gaffney112^{3}Ben Fleet117^1 Hard held 6
10Aug07- 3Sar fst 6f :23^3 :47 :58^2 1:12 Sar Spl 9.5k 2 2 1^{hd} 1^{hd} 1^1 1^1 Miller W 122 w *.40 100-04 Colin122^{1}Uncle122 Decisively 2
27Jly07- 4Bri fst 6f :23^2 :47^1 1:12^1 Brighton Junior 15k 2 2 1$^{\frac{1}{2}}$ 1$^{1\frac{1}{2}}$ 1$^{1\frac{1}{2}}$ 1$^{1\frac{1}{2}}$ Miller W 127 w *.65 99-06 Coln127$^{1\frac{1}{2}}$Chpultpc12^{6}BrNon112$^{\frac{1}{2}}$ Repelled stretch challenge 8
29Jun07- 3She sl 6f-FC 1:12^2 Great Trial 25k 7 2 2^1 1^1 1^2 1^2 Miller W 129 w *2.60e 91-09 Colin129^{2}Meelick122$^{\frac{1}{2}}$Monopolist122$^{1\frac{1}{2}}$ Mild restraint 14
5Jun07- 3Bel my 5½f-Str 1:06^3 Eclipse 9.2k 6 2 1^{nk} 1^{hd} 1^{hd} 1^{hd} Mountain 125 w *.60 94-07 Colin125^{hd}Beaucoup117^{10}WvCrst117^5 Under pressure,gamely 6
1Jun07- 3Bel fst 5f-Str :58 National Stallion 10k 3 1 1$^{1\frac{1}{2}}$ 1$^{1\frac{1}{2}}$ 1^2 1^3 Miller W 122 w *.75 102-00 Colin122^{3}Bar None11^{4}Ben Fleet122^{hd} Never threatened 6
29May07- 2Bel gd 5f-Str 1:01 Md Sp Wt 10 1 1^2 1^3 1^2 1^2 Miller W 110 w *1.20 87-17 Colin110^{2}Bar None11^{8}Harcourt110$^{1\frac{1}{2}}$ Easily 23

Count Fleet

br. c. 1940, by Reigh Count (Sunreigh)–Quickly, by Haste — **Lifetime record: 21 16 4 1 $250,300**

Own.– Mrs J. Hertz
Br.– Mrs John D. Hertz (Ky)
Tr.– G.D. Cameron

5Jun43- 6Bel fst 1½ :48 1:12^3 2:03^3 2:28^1 Belmont 42k 2 1 1^8 1^{20} 1^{20} 1^{25} Longden J 126wb *.05 97-12 CountFleet126^{25}FairyManhurst126$^{\frac{3}{4}}$Deseronto126 Galloping 3
Geldings not eligible
22May43- 6Bel my 1 :23 :46^2 1:10^3 1:36 Withers 17k 2 1 1$^{1\frac{1}{2}}$ 1^3 1^2 1^5 Longden J 126wb *.05 94-21 Count Fleet126^{5}Slide Rule126^{12}Tip-Toe126 Wide,easily 3
Geldings not eligible
8May43- 6Pim gd 1$\frac{3}{16}$:47^2 1:11^4 1:38^1 1:57^2 Preakness 60k 2 1 1^4 1^4 1^5 1^8 Longden J 126wb *.15 95-15 Count Fleet126^{8}Blue Swords126^{5}Vincentive126^{20} Easily 4
1May43- 7CD fst 1¼ :46^3 1:12^3 1:37^3 2:04 Ky Derby 72k 5 1 1^{hd} 1^2 1^2 1^3 Longden J 126wb *.40 87-12 Count Fleet126^{3}Blue Swords126^{6}Slide Rule126^6 Handily 10
17Apr43- 5Jam fst 1$\frac{1}{16}$:23^2 :46^4 1:11^2 1:43 Wood Mem 28k 4 1 1^4 1^4 1^4 1$^{3\frac{1}{2}}$ Longden J 126wb *.25 98-06 Count Fleet126$^{3\frac{1}{2}}$Blue Swords126^{7}Twoses121^2 Much the best 8
13Apr43- 5Jam sly 1 70 :23^4 :47^2 1:12^4 1:42^4 Alw 3000 8 4 3$^{1\frac{1}{2}}$ 2^2 2^{hd} 1$^{3\frac{1}{2}}$ Longden J 122wb *.15 90-19 CountFlt122$^{3\frac{1}{2}}$Bossut 13^{5}Towsr113^{hd} Forced wide first turn 8
10Nov42- 6Pim gd 1$\frac{1}{16}$:23^1 :47^3 1:12 1:44^4 Walden 12k 3 1 1^8 1^{15} 1^{25} 1^{30} Longden J 122 w *.10 94-14 Count Fleet122^{30}Uncle Billies113^{15}Rough Doc113^1 Easily 4
31Oct42- 6Pim fst 1$\frac{1}{16}$:23^1 :45^2 1:11 1:43^3 Pim Futurity 34k 3 2 2^{hd} 1$^{\frac{1}{2}}$ 1^3 1^5 Longden J 119wb 1.25 100-06 Count Fleet119^{5}Occupation122^{4}Vincentive122 3
Geldings not eligible
20Oct42- 5Jam fst 1 70 :23^4 :47^3 1:13 1:44 Alw 5000 5 5 1^{hd} 1^4 1^5 1^6 Longden J 122wb *.25 84-16 Count Fleet122^{6}Towser116$^{2\frac{1}{2}}$Jack S.L.113^3 Easily 8
10Oct42- 5Bel fst 1 :23^1 :46 1:10 1:34^4 Champagne 12k 8 1 1^2 1^3 1^3 1^6 Longden J 116wb *1.05 101-07 Count Fleet116^{6}Blue Swords119^{7}Attendant110^1 Easily 8
3Oct42- 4Bel fst 6½f-W :22^2 :44^3 1:08^3 1:15^1 Futurity 69k 7 9 2^2 3^4 3^4 3^5 Longden J 119wb *1.55 91-04 Occupation126^{5}Askmenow116^{hd}Count Fleet119$^{1\frac{1}{2}}$ Gamely 10
Geldings not eligible

Past Performances of Great Horses of the 20th Century

Date-Race	Cond/Dist	Fractions	Race	PP	St	1st	2nd	Str	Fin	Jockey	Wt	Odds	Fig	Top Three	Comment	Strs
24Sep42-6Bel	fst 6f-WC	:23 :461 1:103	Alw 2000	9	12	51¾	53	21	12½	Longden J	122wb	*1.40	94-06	CountFleet1222½BullsEye111nkJackS.L.111hd	Swerved start	13
15Sep42-5Aqu	fst 6f	:224 :462 1:12	Alw 2500	2	1	21½	33	31	1nk	Longden J	118wb	*.70	92-12	CntFlt118nkVrySnooty1124NoondySun1121½	Bumped,driving	10
15Aug42-6Was	fst 6f	:222 :454 1:12	Wash Park Futurity 68k	11	9	75	54¼	22	2nk	Longden J	117wb	4.80	91-12	Occupation122nkCntFleet1175BluSwords117hd	Wide,bumped	11
11Aug42-6Was	gd 6f	:23 :463 1:13	Alw 1800	6	5	3½	2½	1½	1nk	Longden J	119wb	*.50	86-20	CountFleet119nkBlueSwords1084Hygrohour1223	Forced wide	9
22Jly42-5Emp	fst 5¾f	:232 :463 1:074	Wakefield 6.8k	4	1	31¼	11	12	14	Longden J	116wb	*.65	98-10	CountFleet1164Rurales1132GoldShower1229	Speed to spare	4
15Jly42-5Emp	fst 5¾f	:23 :454 1:08	©East View 7.1k	6	5	52	21½	22	21	Longden J	116wb	*.50	96-09	Gold Shower1161Count Fleet1167Rurales1122	Gamely	6
4Jly42-4Emp	fst 5½f	:23 :462 :592 1:054	Alw 2000	5	5	53¾	42½	11	15	Longden J	111wb	*1.15	97-07	Count Fleet1115Samhar1143Bullpen114hd	Drew away easily	6
19Jun42-3Aqu	fst 5½f	:23 :471 1:06	©Md Sp Wt	8	6	3¾	2½	3½	14	Longden J	116wb	*.75	97-08	CountFleet1164SewrdBound1161Crst116nk	Bore out str turn	10
15Jun42-5Aqu	fst 5½f	:23 :473 1:061	Md Sp Wt	9	8	63	44½	22	21½	Longden J	116wb	*1.35	94-12	Supermont1161½Count Fleet1163Quiz116nk	Trouble early	14
1Jun42-5Bel	fst 5f-WC	:572	©Md Sp Wt	13	5	3½	3½	32½	21½	Longden J	116wb	4.10	91-07	DoveShoot1161½CountFlet116noSuprmont116nk	Swerved start	16

Damascus

b. c. 1964, by Sword Dancer (Sunglow)–Kerala, by My Babu

Lifetime record: 32 21 7 3 $1,176,781

Own.– Mrs Edith W. Bancroft
Br.– Mrs Thomas Bancroft (Ky)
Tr.– F.Y. Whiteley Jr

Date-Race	Cond/Dist	Fractions	Race	PP	St	1st	2nd	Str	Fin	Jockey	Wt	Odds	Fig	Top Three	Comment	Strs
26Oct68-7Bel	gd 2	:502 2:313 3:224	3↑ J C Gold Cup 109k	1	3	48	612	624	637	Adams L	124	*1.30	48-16	QuickenTree1241¼FunnyFllow1193½Chmpon1193	Bowed tendon	6
28Sep68-7Bel	fst 1¼	:472 1:113 1:37 2:03	3↑ Woodward 106k	3	2	1hd	1hd	1hd	2no	Baeza B	126	*.10	85-16	Mr. Right126noDamascus1267Grace Born12616	Just failed	4
14Sep68-9Det	fst 1⅛	:471 1:111 1:361 1:49	3↑ Mich 1⅛ H 123k	1	9	1014	79½	66¾	22¾	Baeza B	133	*.30e	93-19	Nodouble1112¾Dmscs133hdMstyRun1092¼	Very wide stretch	12
2Sep68-7Aqu	fst 1⅛	:47 1:11 1:354 1:482	3↑ Aqueduct 108k	4	3	35	33	2½	11½	Baeza B	134	*.40	94-13	Damascus1341½More Scents1148Fort Drum1143	Going away	6
10Aug68-8Del	fst 1 1/16	:24 :484 1:123 1:433	3↑ W Du Pont H 53k	4	5	31	2hd	1hd	12	Baeza B	134	*.20	91-20	Damascus1342BigRockCandy113¾CharlesElliott11010	Driving	5
20Jly68-7Aqu	fst 1¼	:454 1:092 1:343 1:591	3↑ Brooklyn H 109k	2	5	511	2½	1½	12½	Ycaza M	130	1.40e	102-13	Damascus1302½Dr. Fager1353Mr. Right114hd	Won going away	7
13Jly68-8Mth	fst 1¼	:48 1:121 1:371 2:03	3↑ AL Haskell H 111k	6	6	68	33	21	31½	Ycaza M	131	*.60	85-16	BoldHour1161¼Mr.Rght114nkDmscus1315	Stumbled after start	8
4Jly68-7Aqu	fst 1¼	:482 1:11 1:343 1:593	3↑ Suburban H 107k	1	2	2½	2hd	22	35	Ycaza M	133	1.40	95-11	Dr. Fager1322Bold Hour1163Damascus1333½	Failed to rally	5
17Jun68-5Del	fst 1 70	:234 :473 1:114 1:402	4↑ Alw 10000	3	3	24	2hd	11	13¾	Ycaza M	124	*.10	98-16	Damascus1243¾LighttheFuse1196ClassicWork120nk	Handily	5
10Feb68-8SA	sl 1¼	:482 1:131 1:382 2:04	C H Strub 118k	1	5	57	1½	1hd	2hd	Turcotte R	126	*.20	78-22	Most Host114hdDamscs12610Ruken117½	Gave way gradually	6
20Jan68-6SA	fst 1⅛	:49 1:13 1:371 1:484	San Fernando 56k	4	2	2½	1hd	11	12	Shoemaker W	126	*.10	88-12	Damascs1262Most Host113hdRuken1204½	Won drawing clear	6
6Jan68-8SA	fst 7f	:223 :45 1:09 1:211	Malibu 45k	4	1	32½	3½	1½	12½	Shoemaker W	126	*.40	97-15	Damascus1262½Rising Market120nkRuken1231	Handily	8
11Nov67-7Lrl	fm 1½Ⓣ	:491 1:14 2:03 2:27	3↑ D C Int'l 150k	2	4	43½	3½	2hd	2no	Shoemaker W	120	*.60	84-13	FortMarcy120noDmascus1202½TobinBronze1272½	Just failed	9
28Oct67-7Aqu	fst 2	:494 2:302 2:554 3:201	3↑ J C Gold Cup 106k	1	2	22	2hd	14	14½	Shoemaker W	119	*.30	95-12	Dmascus1194½HandsomBoy1247½Successr1196½	Handy score	4
30Sep67-7Aqu	fst 1¼	:451 1:091 1:353 2:003	3↑ Woodward 107k	5	5	512	1½	15	110	Shoemaker W	120	1.80e	95-15	Damascus12010Buckpasser126½Dr. Fager12013	Easy score	6
4Sep67-7Aqu	fst 1⅛	:482 1:121 1:361 1:481	3↑ Aqueduct 106k	3	3	34	32	1hd	12	Shoemaker W	125	*.30	95-14	Damascus1252Ring Twice119½Straight Deal1166	Handily	5
19Aug67-6Sar	sly 1¼	:454 1:11 1:364 2:013	Travers 80k	4	3	316	16	110	122	Shoemaker W	126	*.20	100-10	Damascus12622Reason to Hail1207Tumiga1175	Won eased up	4
5Aug67-8AP	fst 1⅛	:46 1:101 1:343 1:464	American Derby 120k	2	6	612	66¼	14	17	Shoemaker W	126	*.80	101-16	Damascus1267InReality1203FavorableTurn1121½	Ridden out	7
15Jly67-7Aqu	sly 1¼	:473 1:12 1:374 2:03	Dwyer H 83k	6	9	912	21	1hd	1¾	Shoemaker W	128	*.50	83-18	Damascus128¾FavorableTurn1122½BlastingChrg116hd	Driving	9
8Jly67-8Del	fst 1 1/16	:234 :471 1:104 1:421	3↑ W Du Pont Jr H 54k	4	5	58	43	21	2no	Shoemaker W	121	*.20	98-12	Exceedingly113noDamascus1214Flag Raiser1145	Hung	5
17Jun67-8Del	fst 1⅛	:47 1:113 1:37 1:491	Leonard Richards 41k	4	4	32½	1½	1hd	13¼	Turcotte R	126	*.10	91-13	Damascus1263¼Misty Cloud1191½Favorable Turn1192½	Easily	6
3Jun67-8Aqu	fst 1½	:47 1:122 2:023 2:284	Belmont 148k	1	6	59½	31	2hd	12½	Shoemaker W	126	*.80	87-15	Dmascus1262½CoolReception126½GentlmanJams1261	In hand	9
20May67-8Pim	fst 1 3/16	:462 1:104 1:364 1:551	Preakness 194k	2	9	811	86	13½	12¼	Shoemaker W	126	*1.80e	97-11	Damascus1262¼In Reality1264Proud Clarion126¾	Ridden out	10
6May67-7CD	fst 1¼	:463 1:104 1:36 2:003	Ky Derby 162k	2	6	44	41½	32	34	Shoemaker W	126	*1.70	93-07	ProudClarion1261BarbsDelight1263Damascus1261¼	Bid,hung	14
22Apr67-7Aqu	fst 1⅛	:462 1:104 1:363 1:493	Wood Memorial 112k	4	3	45	42	11	16	Shoemaker W	126	*.70	88-16	Damascus1266Gala Performance1263Dawn Glory1261½	Easily	9
15Apr67-7Aqu	fst 1	:233 :461 1:102 1:351	Gotham 57k	9	2	23	2hd	1hd	2½	Shoemaker W	122	*1.30	91-14	Dr. Fager122½Damascus1225Reason to Hail1147	Game try	9

Past Performances of Great Horses of the 20th Century

Date/Race	Cond/Dist	Fractions	Race							Jockey	Wt	Odds	Speed	Top Finishers	Comment	Field
25Mar67-7Aqu	my 7f	:224 :464 1:124 1:254	Bay Shore 28k	1 4	46	45½	22	12½		Shoemaker W	115	2.40	77-35	Damascus1152½Disciplinarian1171½Nhoc'sBullt1103	Driving	7
11Mar67-7Pim	fst 6f	:233 :472 1:121	Alw 5000	8 3	31½	42	53¼	1hd		Shuk N	122	*.60	89-16	Dmascus122hdSolar Bomb1221½Last Cry119½	Bumped late,up	8
30Nov66-7Aqu	gd 1	:231 :46 1:112 1:37	Remsen 30k	2 3	2hd	32	4¾	11½		Shoemaker W	117	*1.30	83-22	Damascus1171½NativeGuile117½ReflectedGlory119¾	Driving	14
29Oct66-3Lrl	fst 7f	:224 :462 1:121 1:251	©Alw 4000	2 1	1½	12	19	112		Shoemaker W	119	*.40	93-16	Damascus11912Jaxer1153½Roman Away1172½	Scored in hand	7
12Oct66-5Aqu	fst 7f	:23 :462 1:12 1:243	©Md Sp Wt	8 1	11	11	14	18		Shoemaker W	122	*.30	83-18	Damascus1228Winslow Homer1225Gun Mount1221	Easily	14
28Sep66-4Aqu	fst 7f	:223 :46 1:113 1:243	©Md Sp Wt	11 9	76	77½	32½	22½		Shoemaker W	122	*2.60	80-19	Comprador1222½Damascus122¾Air Rights1221	Game try	14

Dr. Fager

b. c. 1964, by Rough'n Tumble (Free for All)–Aspidistra, by Better Self — **Lifetime record: 22 18 2 1 $1,002,642**

Own.– Tartan Stable
Br.– Tartan Farms (Fla)
Tr.– John A. Nerud

Date/Race	Cond/Dist	Fractions	Race	PP St	1st	2nd	Str	Fin	Jockey	Wt	Odds	Speed	Top Finishers	Comment	Field
2Nov68-7Aqu	fst 7f	:221 :434 1:074 1:201	3↑ Vosburgh H 57k	3 4	1hd	1hd	13	16	Baeza B	139	*.30	105-12	Dr.Fager1396Kissin'George1276JmJ.125hd	Under mild drive	7
11Sep68-8Atl	fm 1 3/16 (T)	:484 1:123 1:364 1:551	3↑ U Nations H 100k	6 1	1hd	2hd	1hd	1nk	Baeza B	134	*.80	94-10	Dr Fgr134nkAdvocator1121¼FortMrcy1181¼	Under stiff drive	9
24Aug68-8AP	fst 1	:224 :44 1:073 1:321	3↑ Washington Park H 112k	9 6	2hd	1½	13	110	Baeza B	134	*.30	102-10	Dr. Fager13410Racing Room1161½Info1121	Easily best	10
3Aug68-6Sar	fst 1⅛	:471 1:113 1:363 1:484	3↑ Whitney 53k	2 1	1½	13	13	18	Baeza B	132	*.05	97-12	Dr. Fager1328Spoon Bait1141Fort Drum11415	Much the best	4
20Jly68-7Aqu	fst 1¼	:454 1:092 1:343 1:591	3↑ Brooklyn H 109k	3 2	21½	1½	2½	22½	Baeza B	135	*.60	99-13	Damascus1302½Dr.Fager1353Mr.Right114hd	Rank early going	7
4Jly68-7Aqu	fst 1¼	:482 1:11 1:343 1:593	3↑ Suburban H 107k	3 1	1½	1hd	12	12	Baeza B	132	*.80	100-11	Dr.Fager1322BoldHour1163Damascus1333½	Under mild drive	5
18May68-8Hol	fst 1 1/16	:222 :45 1:083 1:404	3↑ Californian 119k	11 4	2½	1½	14	13	Baeza B	130	*1.20	91-13	Dr. Fager1303Gamely1161Rising Market1211½	Much the best	14
4May68-7Aqu	fst 7f	:222 :45 1:084 1:212	3↑ Roseben H 54k	5 1	1½	11	13	13	Rotz JL	130	*.20	99-17	Dr. Fager1303Tumiga1213Diplomat Way121¾	Won eased up	5
7Nov67-7Aqu	fst 7f	:222 :451 1:093 1:213	3↑ Vosburgh H 57k	6 8	52½	2hd	1hd	14½	Baeza B	128	*.20e	98-16	Dr. Fager1284½Jim J.1151½R. Thomas1223	Wide,easily best	9
21Oct67-8Haw	fst 1¼	:461 1:101 1:351 2:011	3↑ Haw Gold Cup H 121k	1 1	1½	1hd	11½	12½	Baeza B	123	*.30	90-12	Dr.Fagr1232½WhispJt1141¼Pontmnow1081¼	Without urging	7
30Sep67-7Aqu	fst 1¼	:451 1:091 1:353 2:003	3↑ Woodward 107k	2 1	1hd	2½	25	310½	Boland W	120	1.80	84-15	Damascus12010Buckpasser126½Dr. Fager12013	Faltered	6
2Sep67-8Rkm	fst 1¼	:463 1:11 1:351 1:594	NH Sweep Classic 255k	1 1	1½	2hd	2hd	11¼	Baeza B	120	*.20	115-17	Dr.Fager1201¼InReality1269BarbsDelight1152¾	Mild drive	5
15Jly67-9Rkm	fst 1⅛	:462 1:101 1:353 1:481	Rkm Spl 85k	5 1	16½	13½	13½	14¼	Baeza B	124	*.10	105-15	Dr.Fager1244¼ReasontoHail1214¾JackofAllTrds1128¼	Easily	7
24Jun67-8AP	sly 1	:224 :45 1:102 1:36	AP Classic 106k	1 3	3nk	13	16	110	Baeza B	120	*.40	83-25	Dr.Fagr12010LightningOrphan1161¾DiplomatWay1187	Easily	6
30May67-7GS	fst 1⅛	:47 1:103 1:353 1:48	Jersey Derby 119k	4 1	1½	12	13	16½	Ycaza M	126	*.30	97-14	[D]Dr.Fager1266½InReality1268AirRghts12612	Crowded field	4
	Disqualified and placed fourth														
13May67-7Aqu	fst 1	:223 :441 1:08 1:334	Withers 58k	8 4	21	2hd	11½	16	Baeza B	126	*.80	99-16	Dr. Fager1266Tumiga1265Reason to Hail1265	Easy score	8
15Apr67-7Aqu	fst 1	:233 :461 1:102 1:351	Gotham 57k	5 4	33	3nk	2hd	1½	Ycaza M	122	*1.30e	92-14	Dr. Fager122½Damascus1225Reason to Hail1147	Driving	9
15Oct66-7Aqu	fst 1	:222 :444 1:092 1:35	Champagne 208k	7 4	3½	1hd	13	21	Shoemaker W	122	*1.00	92-14	Successor1221Dr. Fager1224Proviso1224	Rank early,failed	10
5Oct66-7Aqu	gd 7f	:224 :46 1:113 1:244	Cowdin 88k	1 10	31	32	21½	1¾	Shoemaker W	117	*.80	82-22	Dr.Fager117¾InRlty1171½Succssor1172½	Slow start,driving	10
10Sep66-8Atl	fst 7f	:223 :452 1:103 1:231	World's Playground 28k	3 6	1hd	1½	14	112	Ycaza M	115	*.90	87-24	Dr. Fager11512Glengary1153½Pointsman115hd	Much the best	11
13Aug66-4Sar	fst 6f	:223 :462 1:102	Alw 5500	5 5	21½	22	12	18	Hidalgo D5	117	*.90	96-09	Dr. Fager1178Bandera Road1172Quaker City1152	Easily	8
15Jly66-3Aqu	fst 5½f	:224 :464 :59 1:05	©Md Sp Wt	8 8	83	21	11½	17	Hidalgo D5	117	10.30	88-20	Dr. Fager1177Lift Off1224Rising Market122½	Easily best	11

Past Performances of Great Horses of the 20th Century

Equipoise

ch. c. 1928, by Pennant (Peter Pan)–Swinging, by Broomstick — **Lifetime record: 51 29 10 4 $338,610**

Own.– C.V. Whitney
Br.– H.P. Whitney (Ky)
Tr.– T.J. Healey

Date	Cond	Dist	Fractions/Time	Race	Running line	Jockey	Wt	Odds	Sp-Var	Top three	Comment	Field
23Feb35- 6SA	fst	1¼	:45 1:10 1:36 2:02^{1}	3↑ S Anita H 125k	19 12 12^{13} 12^{13} 7$^{4\frac{1}{4}}$ 7$^{7\frac{1}{2}}$	Workman R	130wb	*1.70e	- -	Azucar117^{2}Ladysman117^{1}Time Supply118^{2}		20
	Off slowly,close quarters											
18Feb35- 5SA	fst	1$\frac{1}{16}$	:24 :47^{3} 1:12 1:43^{2}	3↑ Handicap 1200	4 3 3$^{1\frac{1}{2}}$ 3^{1} 1^{hd} 1^{1}	Workman R	125wb	*.60	- -	[D]Equipos125^{1}TwntyGrnd116^{3}Srd105$^{1\frac{1}{2}}$	Bumped rival,bore in	5
	Disqualified											
13Feb35- 5SA	fst	1	:23 :46^{3} 1:10^{2} 1:36^{3}	3↑ Handicap 1000	5 5 4^{5} 3^{3} 3$^{\frac{1}{2}}$ 2^{1}	Workman R	128wb	*.30	- -	Sweping Light109^{1}Equipoise128^{nk}Ted Clark111$^{1\frac{1}{2}}$	Impeded	8
6Nov34- 3Bel	sly	1¼	:49^{3} 1:14^{3} 1:40^{4} 2:06^{3}	3↑ Whitney Trophy H 5.5k	5 1 5^{1} 2$^{1\frac{1}{2}}$ 2^{hd} 1$^{1\frac{1}{2}}$	Workman R	128wb	*.55	67-23	Equipoise128$^{1\frac{1}{2}}$Faireno122^{2}Mr. Khayyam120^{4}	Ridden out	6
31Oct34- 6Nar	fst	6f	:23 :45^{3} 1:10^{4}	3↑ Invitation 5.1k	5 2 4$^{5\frac{1}{2}}$ 4$^{4\frac{1}{2}}$ 4$^{3\frac{3}{4}}$ 3$^{\frac{1}{2}}$	Workman R	130wb	*.45	100-07	Okapi130$^{\frac{1}{2}}$All Forlorn127^{no}Equipoise130^{hd}	Closed fast	5
30May34- 5Bel	fst	1¼	:47^{1} 1:12 1:37^{1} 2:02^{3}	3↑ Suburban H 7.4k	1 4 5$^{3\frac{1}{4}}$ 3$^{1\frac{1}{4}}$ 2$^{\frac{1}{2}}$ 2no	Robertson A	134wb	*.50	87-16	Ladysman114^{no}Equipoise134^{10}War Glory115$^{1\frac{1}{2}}$	Just missed	8
19May34- 4Bel	fst	1	:23^{3} :47 1:11^{2} 1:37	3↑ Metropolitan H 4.3k	6 8 8$^{2\frac{3}{4}}$ 4$^{\frac{1}{2}}$ 1^{hd} 1^{2}	Workman R	132wb	*.70	90-15	[D]Equipoise132^{2}Mr.Khyym119^{1}SunArchr106^{5}	Swerved stretch	9
	Disqualified											
5May34- 5Pim	fst	1$\frac{3}{16}$	:48^{3} 1:14 1:40 2:01^{4}	3↑ Dixie H 5.9k	4 1 2^{nk} 2$^{\frac{1}{2}}$ 1^{4} 1$^{1\frac{1}{2}}$	Workman R	130wb	*.10	81-19	Equipoise130$^{1\frac{1}{2}}$Chatmoss110^{3}Flaming Mamie102^{7}	Easily	4
21Apr34- 5HdG	fst	1$\frac{1}{16}$	:23^{2} :47^{2} 1:12^{2} 1:44^{2}	3↑ Philadelphia H 8.4k	4 4 3$^{2\frac{1}{2}}$ 2^{1} 1$^{1\frac{1}{2}}$ 1^{1}	Workman R	130wb	*.50	98-08	Equipoise130^{1}Springsteel117^{4}Larranaga113^{6}	In hand	5
30Sep33- 5HdG	fst	1⅛	:48 1:11^{4} 1:37^{1} 1:49^{4}	3↑ Havre de Grace H 11k	1 4 4^{2} 3$^{1\frac{1}{2}}$ 2^{1} 2^{1}	Workman R	132wb	*1.60	100-09	Osculator104^{1}Equipoise132$^{1\frac{1}{2}}$Mate110$^{1\frac{1}{2}}$	Closed well	9
16Sep33- 5Bel	my	2	:50 2:34^{1} 3:25^{1}	3↑ J C Gold Cup 8.1k	1 2 2$^{1\frac{1}{2}}$ 2^{1} 3$^{1\frac{1}{4}}$ 3^{12}	Workman R	125wb	*.45	71-16	Dark Secret125^{4}Gusto125^{8}Equipoise125^{7}	No excuses	4
2Sep33- 5Sar	fst	1¾	:52 2:09^{2} 2:34^{4} 3:00	3↑ Sar Cup 6.9k	3 2 2$^{1\frac{1}{2}}$ 2^{1} 1^{1} 1$^{1\frac{1}{2}}$	Workman R	126 w	*.12	75-14	Equipoise126$^{1\frac{1}{2}}$Gusto126^{8}Keep Out118	Going away	3
24Aug33- 6Haw	fst	1¼	:48^{3} 1:13^{2} 1:38^{3} 2:02^{4}	3↑ Haw Gold Cup 27k	3 1 3^{3} 2$^{\frac{1}{2}}$ 1^{hd} 1^{2}	Workman R	126wb	*.18	94-14	Equipoise126^{2}GallantSir126$^{1\frac{1}{2}}$Mr.Khayyam117$^{1\frac{1}{2}}$	Going away	5
3Aug33- 5Sar	fst	1	:24^{2} :48 1:13^{3} 1:39	3↑ Wilson 3.3k	3 3 3$^{1\frac{3}{4}}$ 3^{nk} 1^{hd} 1^{3}	Workman R	126wb	*.20	86-15	Equipoise126^{3}Tambour106^{2}Mate111^{3}	Eased up	5
22Jly33- 6AP	fst	1¼	:47^{1} 1:11^{4} 1:37 2:02^{3}	3↑ Arlington H 12k	4 5 4^{2} 3$^{1\frac{1}{2}}$ 2^{nk} 1$^{1\frac{1}{2}}$	Workman R	135wb	*.75	96-13	Equipoise135$^{1\frac{1}{2}}$Watch Him106^{5}Gallant Sir125^{no}	Going away	7
7Jun33- 4Bel	fst	1¼	:47 1:11^{1} 1:36 2:02	3↑ Suburban H 8.9k	7 2 4$^{3\frac{1}{2}}$ 2$^{1\frac{1}{2}}$ 2^{hd} 1^{2}	Workman R	132wb	*.40	90-18	Equipoise132^{2}Osculator107^{6}Apprentice112^{nk}	Eased up	7
3Jun33- 5Bel	fst	1	:23^{2} :46^{4} 1:11^{4} 1:37^{2}	3↑ Metropolitan H 5.8k	7 5 3^{2} 2$^{\frac{1}{2}}$ 1^{1} 1^{4}	Workman R	128wb	*.90	88-15	Equipoise128^{4}Okapi102^{1}Scotch Gold106^{1}	Eased up	10
22Apr33- 5HdG	fst	1$\frac{1}{16}$	:23^{2} :47^{2} 1:12 1:44^{3}	3↑ Philadelphia H 8.9k	1 5 4^{3} 4$^{1\frac{1}{4}}$ 1^{2} 1$^{1\frac{1}{2}}$	Workman R	128wb	*.90	99-05	Equipoise128$^{1\frac{1}{2}}$Tred Avon112^{2}Osculator105^{1}	Won easily	8
	Previously trained by F. Hopkins											
29Oct32- 5Lrl	gd	1¼	:48 1:13^{4} 1:39^{3} 2:05^{3}	3↑ Washington H 18k	6 4 8^{6} 2^{1} 2$^{\frac{1}{2}}$ 2^{hd}	Workman R	129wb	*1.10	82-25	Tred Avon112^{hd}Equipoise129^{no}Mate112^{6}	Finished fast	9
15Oct32- 5Lrl	fst	1	:23^{3} :47^{3} 1:13 1:37^{1}	2↑ Laurel 7.1k	1 7 5^{4} 4$^{1\frac{1}{2}}$ 3$^{\frac{1}{2}}$ 3$^{1\frac{1}{2}}$	Workman R	126wb	*.70	100-11	Jack High118^{no}Gallant Sir108$^{1\frac{1}{2}}$Equipoise126^{3}	No excuse	7
1Oct32- 5HdG	fst	1⅛	:46^{1} 1:11 1:36^{4} 1:50^{1}	3↑ H de Grace Cup H 26k	4 6 3$^{4\frac{1}{2}}$ 2$^{\frac{1}{2}}$ 1$^{1\frac{1}{2}}$ 1^{1}	Workman R	128wb	*1.05	99-06	Equipoise128^{1}Gallant Sir107^{3}Tred Avon110^{3}	Handily	13
24Sep32- 3HdG	gd	6f	:23 :46^{4} 1:12	3↑ Handicap 1500	3 5 5^{4} 5$^{3\frac{1}{2}}$ 5$^{8\frac{1}{2}}$ 5^{9}	Workman R	129wb	*.65	86-08	Pairbypair107$^{\frac{1}{2}}$Jack High123$^{1\frac{1}{2}}$Con Amore112^{5}	Dull effort	5
13Aug32- 5Sar	fst	1¼	:50 1:14^{2} 1:40 2:05^{3}	3↑ Whitney 6.9k	2 1 1$^{1\frac{1}{2}}$ 1^{4} 1^{4} 1^{3}	Workman R	126wb	*.14	81-16	Equipoise126^{3}Gusto117^{8}Rocky News116	Easily	3
6Aug32- 5Sar	fst	1	:23^{3} :46^{2} 1:11^{3} 1:38^{1}	3↑ Wilson 7.8k	2 3 3$^{2\frac{1}{4}}$ 3^{1} 1^{1} 1^{2}	Workman R	126wb	*.13	90-11	Equipoise126^{2}Blind Bowboy121^{6}Pompeius113	Easily	3
23Jly32- 6AP	fst	1¼	:48 1:13 1:37^{2} 2:02^{1}	3↑ Arlington H 27k	3 4 3$^{2\frac{1}{2}}$ 2$^{\frac{1}{2}}$ 2^{hd} 2^{nk}	Workman R	134wb	*.82	98-08	Plucky Play111^{nk}Equipoise134^{6}Pittsburgher105^{3}	Hard try	6
9Jly32- 6AP	fst	1¼	:48^{2} 1:13^{1} 1:37 2:02^{4}	3↑ Arl Gold Cup 24k	3 1 2$^{1\frac{1}{2}}$ 1$^{2\frac{1}{2}}$ 1^{5} 1^{4}	Workman R	126wb	*.24	95-04	Equipoise126^{4}Gusto114$^{3\frac{1}{2}}$Mate126	Easily	3
4Jly32- 5AP	hy	1⅛	:49^{2} 1:15 1:41^{2} 1:54^{4}	3↑ Stars & Stripes H 27k	1 2 1^{hd} 1^{hd} 1^{3} 1$^{\frac{3}{4}}$	Workman R	129wb	*.34	73-31	Equipoise129$^{\frac{3}{4}}$Tred Avon107^{5}Dr. Freeland110^{3}	Easily	6
30Jun32- 5AP	fst	1	:23^{1} :46 1:09^{1} 1:34^{2}	3↑ Handicap 1450	1 2 2$^{1\frac{1}{2}}$ 2$^{1\frac{1}{2}}$ 2^{1} 1^{3}	Workman R	128wb	*.90	106-02	Equipoise128^{3}Jamestown118$^{3\frac{1}{2}}$Spanish Play106	Easily	3
21May32- 4Bel	fst	1	:22^{4} :46^{2} 1:10^{2} 1:37	3↑ Metropolitan H 9k	6 5 3$^{3\frac{1}{4}}$ 2$^{1\frac{1}{2}}$ 2^{hd} 1$^{2\frac{1}{2}}$	Workman R	127 w	*.60	90-15	Equipoise127$^{2\frac{1}{2}}$Sun Meadow118$^{1\frac{1}{2}}$Mate128^{4}	Easily	7
12May32- 4Bel	fst	6f-WC	1:09^{3}	3↑ Toboggan H 8.2k	10 6 2^{1} 1^{hd} 1^{1}	Workman R	129wb	*1.00	99-02	Equipoise129^{1}Ironclad108$^{1\frac{1}{2}}$Helianthus110^{4}	Handily	10
16Apr32- 5HdG	fst	6f	:23^{2} :47^{2} 1:12^{2}	3↑ Harford H 13k	9 5 7$^{2\frac{1}{4}}$ 4$^{1\frac{1}{2}}$ 1$^{1\frac{1}{2}}$ 1^{3}	Workman R	128wb	*.55	93-16	Equipoise128^{3}Happy Scot106.5^{hd}Evening105^{1}	Easily	12
13Apr32- 4Bow	fst	5f	:23^{1} :46 :59^{2}	3↑ Handicap 1400	7 2 5$^{1\frac{3}{4}}$ 3$^{1\frac{1}{2}}$ 2^{nk} 1$^{\frac{1}{2}}$	Workman R	126wb	*1.40	109-14	Equipoise126$^{\frac{1}{2}}$Hygro112$^{\frac{1}{2}}$Brandon Mint104^{6}	Drew out	7
9May31- 5Pim	fst	1$\frac{3}{16}$	:48^{3} 1:13^{2} 1:38^{3} 1:59	Preakness 58k	2 7 6$^{3\frac{1}{4}}$ 6$^{2\frac{1}{4}}$ 4$^{1\frac{3}{4}}$ 4$^{2\frac{3}{4}}$	Workman R	126wb	1.95	94-10	Mate126$^{1\frac{1}{2}}$Twenty Grand126^{nk}Ladder126^{1}	Impeded early	7
	Geldings not eligible											
25Apr31- 5HdG	fst	1$\frac{1}{16}$	:24 :48^{3} 1:14^{3} 1:46^{4}	Cheseapeake 13k	6 6 6$^{4\frac{1}{4}}$ 6$^{2\frac{1}{4}}$ 6^{11} 6$^{13\frac{1}{2}}$	Robertson A	122wb	*.15	74-13	Anchors Aweigh114^{no}Soll Gills114^{3}Levante112^{1}	Distressed	6

Past Performances of Great Horses of the 20th Century

13Apr31- 4HdG fst 6f :231 :47 1:113 Alw 1400 4 1 21 2½ 1½ 12½ Robertson A 123wb *.25 97-14 Equipoise1232½Pa■etian1084DarkHero1083 Outclassed field 5
5Nov30- 5Pim my 1 1/16 :234 :482 1:142 1:483 Pim Futurity 58k 2 8 87½ 54¾ 22 1½ Workman R 119wb *.95 79-26 Equipoise119½TwentyGrand119nkMat1194 Driving,great rush 8
Geldings not eligible;Previously owned by H.P. Whitney
16Oct30- 5CD fst 1 :231 :464 1:111 1:36 Ky Jockey Club 31k 4 2 2½ 12 2hd 2no Workman R 122wb *.76 101-13 Twenty Grand122n Equipoise12210Knight's Call1225 7
Going best at end
4Oct30- 3Aqu fst 1 :233 :473 1:13 1:38 Jr Champion 9.8k 4 5 53¼ 31¾ 21 21 Workman R 122wb *.20 89-15 Twenty Grand1111Equipoise1223Ormesby1168 Driving 7
27Sep30- 5HdG fst 6f :224 :463 1:122 Eastern Shore H 31k 2 8 52 2½ 11 15 Workman R 126wb *.60e 93-12 Equipoise1265Don Leon119½Magnifico110hd Closed fast 15
13Sep30- 4Bel fst *7f-WC 1:203 Futurity 114k 7 6 2nk 32 2hd Workman R 130wb 3.60 92-11 Jamestown130hdEquipoise1303Mate1221 Driving,interfered 15
Geldings not eligible
6Sep30- 4Bel fst *7f-WC 1:214 Champagne 7.6k 9 6 2½ 1hd 2hd Workman R 132 w *1.20 86-15 Mate119hdEquipoise1323Sunny Lassie1135 Driving,faltered 10
9Aug30- 4Sar fst 6f :23 :46 1:112 Sar Spl 14k 1 4 21½ 21½ 21½ 22½ Workman R 122wb *.70 92-09 Jamestown1222½Equipoise1228SunMedow1222 Not good enough 4
21Jun30- 3Aqu fst 5f 1:001 Great American 16k 3 1 11 12 12 Workman R 130wb *.45e 86-15 Equipos1302Polydorus1154Hlnthus1152½ Cleverly,mild drive 7
7Jun30- 3Bel fst 5f-WC :593 National Stallion 26k 7 4 21 13 16 Workman R 122wb *.40e 82-20 Equipoise1226Polycorus1222Baba Kenny119hd Easily 8
27May30- 4Bel gd 5f-WC :59 Juvenile 17k 1 4 34 31½ 1nk Workman R 125wb *.40e 85-24 Equipoise125nkHappy Scot122½Panasette1146 Driving 7
17May30- 3Bel sl 4½f-WC :523 Keene Mem 8.6k 2 2 3½ 2hd 12 Workman R 122wb *.60 92-13 Equipoise1222Happy Scot1228Avaricious1172 Easily 5
10May30- 3Jam fst 5f :231 :47 :591 Youthful 11k 1 2 4¾ 1nk 11 14 Workman R 117wb 3.50 97-14 DEquipoise1174Vander Pool1254Chouette1254 Drew away 8
Disqualified for impeding runner-up
2May30- 5Pim fst 4½f :223 :47 :534 Pim Nursery 7.6k 2 2 - - - - Workman R 122 w *1.65 - - Happy Scot1224Up1125St. Agnes1191 8
Stumbled after start,lost rider
23Apr30- 5HdG fst 4½f :23 :463 :53 Aberdeen 15k 7 9 55¼ 32¼ 34 Robertson A 122 w 4.25e 96-05 Vander Pool1221Up1173Equipoise1221½ Driving,closed well 10
15Apr30- 2HdG fst 4½f :233 481 :542 Alw 1200 1 2 1½ 11½ 11½ Robertson A 118 w *.90 93-07 Equipoise1181½Schooner1123Uncle Sam1121 Driving 15
7Apr30- 3Bow hy 4f :232 :481 Alw 1200 8 4 1hd 1nk 14 Robertson A 111 w *2.15 92-08 Equipoise1114Glidelia1103Dry Dock112hd Won easily 11

Exterminator

ch. g. 1915, by McGee (White Knight)–Fair Empress, by Jim Gore **Lifetime record: 99 50 17 17 $252,996**
Own.– W.S. Kilmer
Br.– F.D. Knight (Ky)
Tr.– H. McDaniel

21Jun24- 5Dor gd 1 1/16 :232 :474 1:132 1:47 3↑ Queen's Hotel H 3k 4 3 31¼ 3¾ 42½ 35½ Wallace J 113 w *1.30 84-13 SpotCash1282½Forest Lor1033Extrmntor113nk Pulled up lame 5
7Jun24- 6BB gd 1 :232 :473 1:132 1:394 3↑ Alw 1000 1 4 21½ 21 22 11 Wallace J 111 w 1.85 90-14 Exterminator1111Golden Rule1134Opperman1116 Handily 5
1May24- 6Pim fst 1 :242 :483 1:13 1:383 3↑ Handicap 2000 4 5 42½ 55¼ 46¼ 310½ Johnson A 126 w 4.80 84-11 Martingale120½Spicn Spn10610Extrmntor1261 Always outrun 6
19Apr24- 5HdG hy 1 1/16 :232 :482 1:153 1:492 3↑ Philadelphia H 5.1k 6 5 65½ 63 56¾ 58¼ Johnson A 125 w *1.20e 69-25 SpotCash111hdFlintStone118nkNewHampshire1124 No mishap 6
17Apr24- 5HdG fst 1 70 :244 :49 1:14 1:44 3↑ Alw 2000 2 2 21½ 1hd 1hd 1½ Walls P 107 w *.50 92-11 Exterminator107½GoldenSpher103½SttngSun10615 Ridden out 5
30Mar24- 6Tij fst 1¼ :474 1:124 1:39 2:052 3↑ Coffroth H 51k 11 7 65¾ 54¼ 53 41½ Johnson A 130 w *1.60e 97-14 Runstar123noOsprey113noCherryTree1171½ Challenged,tired 18
17Feb24- 4Tij fst 1 70 :241 :483 1:133 1:443 4↑ Alw 700 4 2 2¾ 21 11 11 Johnson A 113 w *.30 83-12 Extermintor1131Suprargo1161VnPtrck1011 Gentle hand ride 5
Previously trained by W. Shields
28Apr23- 5HdG my 1 70 :242 :493 1:143 1:452 3↑ Handicap 2500 3 4 31½ 21 2½ 2no Johnson A 132 w *1.10 85-21 Chickvl101noExtrmntr1321PulJons10810 Getting to winner 5
21Apr23- 5HdG fst 1 1/16 :24 :43 1:123 1:454 3↑ Philadelphia H 5.1k 2 4 53½ 42¼ 2¾ 1nk McAtee L 129 w *.80 95-10 Exterminator129nkPaul Jones1092Fair Phantom107nk Gamely 6
16Apr23- 4HdG my 6f :24 :49 1:15 3↑ Harford H 5.1k 4 5 64 62¾ 42½ 31¼ Sande E 132 w 3.70 80-32 Blazes106nkCareful11[illegible]Exterminator1326 Finished fast 8
Previously trained by E. Wayland
11Nov22- 4Pim fst 2¼ :50 2:34 3:04 3:532 3↑ Pim Cup H 10k 5 2 2hd 46 418 331½ Marineli B 126 w *.65 66-13 CaptanAlcock1061½PulJons9930Extrmntor126100 Forced pace 5
28Oct22- 5Lrl fst 1¼ :47 1:122 1:382 2:044 3↑ Washington H 28k 8 5 54 44½ 45 43½ Johnson A 132 w *.90 82-17 Oceanic104½Lucky Hour1202Paragon II1211 Finished fast 8

Past Performances of Great Horses of the 20th Century

21Oct22-5Lrl	fst	1	:24^4 :49 1:14 1:40	2↑ Laurel 13k	1	5	5^3	4^2	3^{1½}	1^{2½}	Johnson A	132	w	2.25	88-15	Extermintor132^{2½}[D]PrgonII125^{1½}Trystr123^{hd}	Won easing up	8
14Oct22-4Lrl	fst	6f	:23 :47 1:12^4	3↑ Handicap 2000	8	2	8^{6¾}	6^{4½}	6^5	4^{1½}	Johnson A	133	w	*2.25	92-16	CalamityJane113^{hd}OnWatch124^{1}TipptyWtcht112^{½}	Steady gain	8
30Sep22-5Haw	fst	1¼	:51^4 1:18^3 1:45^1 2:10	Special	-	1	1	1	1	1	Johnson A	126	w	-	73-19	Exterminator126	Good run	1
	Race against time																	
20Sep22-5OW	fst	1¼	:46^3 1:11^3 1:38^2 2:05^1	3↑ Toronto Aut Cup H 16k	5	5	5^{3¼}	4^{2½}	3^{½}	1^{1½}	Johnson A	132	w	*.80	95-09	Exterminator132^{1½}Guy102^{hd}BitofWhit100^1	Rated,going away	8
31Aug22-4Sar	gd	1¾	:50 2:10 2:35 3:00^2	3↑ Sar Cup 8.3k	1	1	1^1	1^1	1^1	1^{nk}	Johnson A	126	w	1.40	80-18	Exterminatr126^{nk}MdHttr126^{12}BonHomm126	Outstayed rivals	3
1Aug22-4Sar	fst	1¼	:48^1 1:12^3 1:38 2:03^1	3↑ Saratoga H 9.2k	1	4	5^2	5^{3½}	5^7	5^{10¼}	Johnson A	137	w	5.00	83-09	Grey Lag130^{½}Bon Homme109^{1¼}Prudery114^6	Hard ridden	5
4Jly22-5Lat	gd	1½	:48^2 1:12^2 2:04^1 2:30^2	3↑ Independence H 18k	2	4	4^{4½}	5^{9½}	6^8	6^{12}	Johnson A	140	w	*.90	84-14	Firebrand116^{3}Devastation102^{6}Minto II116^1		8
	Appeared in distress after mile																	
16Jun22-4Aqu	fst	1⅛	:47^3 1:12^3 1:37 1:50	3↑ Brooklyn H 9.8k	2	3	3^2	2^{½}	2^{hd}	1^{hd}	Johnson A	135	w	1.50	95-10	Exterminator135^{hd}GreyLag126^{4}PollyAnn103^{hd}	Strong finish	5
13Jun22-4Bel	fst	1$\frac{1}{16}$	:23^4 :48 1:13^1 1:44	3↑ Handicap 1635	5	4	2^{1½}	2^2	1^1	1^{1½}	Johnson A	135	w	1.40	96-12	Exterminator135^{1½}Mad Hatter128^{6}Devastation102^{nk}	Rated	6
5Jun22-4Bel	gd	1⅛	:47 1:12^2 1:38^2 1:52^2	3↑ Handicap 1470	2	1	1no	1^{½}	1^{½}	1^{½}	Johnson A	133	w	*.07	83-11	Exterminator133^{½}Be Frank107	Won hard held	2
27May22-5CD	sl	1¼	:48 1:12^2 1:38^2 2:04^2	3↑ Kentucky H 12k	1	2	2^{hd}	1^1	1^{1½}	1^{1½}	Johnson A	138	w	*.45	94-15	Exterminator138^{1½}Firebrand119^{5}Blarney Stone95^8	Easily	4
20May22-5CD	fst	1⅛	:47^1 1:12 1:37 1:50	3↑ Clark H 13k	5	4	5^{1½}	2^{nk}	1^{½}	1^{1½}	Johnson A	133	w	*.60	99-10	Exterminator133^{1½}Lady Madcap111^{1}Rouleau107^4	Drew away	9
6May22-6Pim	sl	1$\frac{1}{16}$	:24^3 :49^3 1:14 1:45^4	3↑ Pim Spring H 5.6k	3	2	2^1	1^{nk}	1^{hd}	1^{hd}	Johnson A	133	w	*.75	97-18	Exterminator133^{hd}Boniface125^{10}Registrar102^2	Hard drive	7
22Apr22-5HdG	fst	1$\frac{1}{16}$	:24^4 :48^3 1:14^1 1:45	3↑ Philadelphia H 5.5k	2	2	3^{1¼}	3^{1½}	2^{hd}	2no	Johnson A	133	w	*.65	99-09	Boniface122^{no}Exterminator133^{6}BungaBuck110^{nk}	Cut off ⅜	6
15Apr22-4HdG	hy	6f	:23^4 :48^1 1:14^1	3↑ Harford H 5.2k	7	4	6^{4½}	4^3	4^2	1^1	Johnson A	132	wb	4.95	85-24	Exterminator132^{1}Billy Kelly132^{1}Dexterous102^1	Going away	12
	Previously trained by W. Knapp																	
12Nov21-5Pim	hy	2¼	:55 2:46^2 3:12 4:08^1	3↑ Pim Cup H 9.8k	1	1	1^{½}	1^{½}	1^{hd}	1^{hd}	Johnson A	126	w	*.70	--	Exterminator126^{hd}Boniface121^{20}Lady Emmeline96	Held on	3
29Oct21-5Lxt	fst	1½	:50^2 1:16^1 2:07 2:31^3	3↑ Lex Cup H 6.2k	5	3	3^3	2^3	3^{2½}	3^{6½}	Johnson A	135	w	*.80	84-10	Firbrnd118^{1½}UntdVrd105^{5}Extrmntor135^2	Tired under impost	5
22Oct21-4Lrl	fst	1¼	:47^1 1:12 1:38^2 2:04^2	3↑ Handicap 2038	6	3	3^7	3^4	2^{nk}	1^1	Johnson A	132	w	*1.65	88-14	Exterminator132^{1}My Dear115^{1½}Bygone Days96^{1½}	Driving	6
8Oct21-4Lrl	sly	1½	:48^3 1:14^1 2:06 2:35	3↑ Annapolis H 12k	6	4	1^{hd}	2^1	3^3	3^{8½}	Kelsay W	135	w	*2.15	64-23	ThePorter120^{2½}MyDer114^{6}Extrmntr135^{1½}	Eased when beaten	8
24Sep21-5OW	fst	1¼	:48 1:13^2 1:38^3 2:05^1	3↑ Toronto Aut Cup H 7.9k	6	4	4^{3½}	2^{½}	1^{½}	1^{nk}	Kelsay W	137	w	*1.40	95-12	Exterminator137^{nk}My Dear117^{2}Golden Sphere106^1	Gamely	9
16Sep21-4Bel	fst	2	:49^3 2:35^2 3:02 3:29^1	3↑ Autumn Gold Cup H 5.7k	2	2	1^{hd}	1^1	1^3	1^6	Kelsay W	130	w	*.33	63-19	Exterminator130^{6}Bellsolar104	In a canter	2
31Aug21-4Sar	sl	1¾	:55^4 2:13^2 2:39^3 3:04^3	3↑ Sar Cup 4.5k	-	1	1	1	1	1	Kelsay W	126	w	-	59-22	Exterminator126	Galloped	1
	Walkover																	
27Aug21-4Sar	fst	1$\frac{3}{16}$	:47^2 1:11^4 1:37^3 1:57^2	3↑ Merchants & Cits H 8.7k	6	5	5^{1¾}	2^1	1^{½}	1^1	Kelsay W	130	w	6.00	91-10	Exterminator130^{1}MadHattr132^{¾}Bllsolr104^{hd}	Outside,gamely	7
	Previously trained by F. Curtis																	
12Jly21-4Wnr	fst	1⅛	:47^1 1:12 1:38^2 1:51^2	3↑ Frontier H 12k	7	4	5^{1¾}	3^{2½}	3^{1½}	3^2	Simpson R	132	w	4.20	97-07	BestPal119^{1½}IrishKiss108^{½}Extrmntor132^8	Closed with rush	8
9Jly21-5Lat	fst	1$\frac{3}{16}$	:47^3 1:12^2 1:37^3 1:56^1	3↑ Daniel Boone H 14k	7	4	2^1	1^{½}	2^{1½}	3^2	Haynes E	135	w	2.20	100-08	Best Pal119^{1}La Rablee106^{1}Exterminator135^6		8
	Cut off by winner fina ⅛																	
4Jly21-5Lat	fst	1½	:49^3 1:14^1 2:05^2 2:30^1	3↑ Independence H 19k	5	3	3^2	2^1	1^{½}	1^1	Haynes E	130	w	*.55	97-07	Exterminator130^{1}Woodtrap111^{1½}La Rablee108^6	Handily	7
	Previously trained by W. McDaniel																	
17Jun21-4Aqu	gd	1⅛	:46^2 1:11 1:35^2 1:49^4	3↑ Brooklyn H 9.8k	10	7	7^4	4^{2½}	4^{2½}	3^3	Ensor L	129	w	4.00	94-08	GreyLag112^{1½}JohnP.Grier124^{1½}Extrmntor129^1	Inside,gamely	11
4Jun21-4Bel	fst	1¼	:47^3 1:12 1:36^1 2:02^1	3↑ Suburban H 11k	8	5	5^{8½}	5^{9½}	5^{9½}	5^{8¾}	Johnson A	133	w	*1.20	80-09	Audacious120^{¾}MadHattr130^{6}SennngsPrk110^{no}	Always outrun	8
21May21-4Jam	fst	1⅛	:48 1:12^3 1:37^2 1:50	3↑ Long Beach H 5.8k	3	2	2^{1½}	1^{hd}	1^{½}	1^{¾}	Johnson A	130	w	*1.00	106-03	Exterminator130^{¾}Mad Hatter130^{5}Cirrus128^7	Drew clear	4
14May21-4Jam	my	1$\frac{1}{16}$	:23^3 :48^1 1:14 1:47^1	3↑ Excelsior H 10k	1	5	5^3	4^{2½}	3^{1½}	2^1	Johnson A	129	w	3.60	89-15	Blazes118^{1}Exterminator129^{6}Naturalist126^{¾}	Slow late gain	7
7May21-4Jam	fst	1$\frac{1}{16}$	:23^3 :47^2 1:12 1:45	3↑ Kings County H 6.1k	3	3	4^{4½}	3^5	2^5	2^3	Haynes E	129	w	2.20	98-08	MadHatter124^{3}Extrmintr129^{3}YllowHnd110^{1½}	Closed gamely	5
12Nov20-4Pim	fst	2¼	:47^2 2:32^1 2:58^3 3:53	3↑ Pim Cup H 10k	2	3	2^1	1^1	1^{½}	1no	Ensor L	126	w	*.75	20--	Exterminator126^{no}Bonifc114^{10}PulJons110.5^6	Rated,all out	7
8Nov20-4Pim	fst	1½	:48^3 1:14^2 2:05^1 2:31^3	3↑ Bowie H 11k	3	7	7^{3½}	5^{3½}	6^{3¾}	5^{3½}	Fairbrother C	135	w	2.80	94-08	Mad Hatter120^{no}Boniface122^{1½}The Porter128^{no}	In a pocket	9
20Oct20-5OW	hy	2¼	:51^3 2:39^3 3:09^4 4:04^4	3↑ Ont Jockey Club Cup 7.7k	1	1	2^2	2^2	1^{nk}	1^{1¼}	Fairbrother C	134	w	*.15	49-26	Exterminator134^{1¼}Bondage110^{6}St. Germain90^{1½}	Easily	4
25Sep20-5OW	fst	1¼	:48^2 1:13^3 1:39^4 2:04^2	3↑ Toronto Aut Cup 7.8k	4	2	1^1	1^1	1^{½}	1^{hd}	Fairbrother C	132	w	*.25	99-10	Exterminator132^{hd}My Dear92^{12}Bondage108^1	Driving	5
	Previously trained by J.S. Healey																	

Past Performances of Great Horses of the 20th Century

15Sep20-4Bel	fst	2	:48^2 2:29^3 3:21^4	3↑ Autumn Gold Cup 6.3k	2	3	$3^{2½}$	3^{2}	$2^{½}$	1^{hd}	Fairbrother C	128	w	*.70	--	Exterminator128^{hd}Damask98^{2½}Cleopatra105	Rated,driving	3
31Aug20-4Sar	sl	1¾	:50^2 2:04^3 2:29^4 2:56^2	3↑ Sar Cup 5.6k	2	1	1^{1}	$1^{1½}$	1^{3}	1^{6}	Fairbrother C	126	w	*.55	108-12	Exterminator126^{6}Cleopatra111	Easily	2
28Aug20-4Wnr	fst	1 1/16	:23 :47^2 1:12 1:44^3	3↑ George Hendrie H 8.6k	4	3	$3^{1½}$	$3^{1¼}$	$2^{½}$	1^{1}	Fairbrother C	131	w	*1.15	98-09	Exterminator131^{1}Wildair114^{3}My Dear95^{hd}	Rated,going away	6
21Aug20-4Wnr	sl	1⅛	:48 1:13^2 1:38^4 1:51^1	3↑ Wnr Jockey Club H 11k	1	3	$2^{1½}$	$2^{1½}$	2^{nk}	$1^{1¼}$	Fairbrother C	125	w	2.50	100-17	Exterminator125^{1¼}Wildair110^{10}Boniface130^{nk}	Drew away	7
14Aug20-4Sar	gd	1⅛	:48^4 1:14 1:40^2 1:53^1	3↑ Champlain H 4.1k	1	4	2^{1}	$3^{1½}$	$1^{½}$	$2^{1½}$	Schuttinger A	128	w	*2.20	82-13	Gnome109^{1½}Extrminatr128^{1}MadHatter117^{5}	Inside,no match	7
2Aug20-4Sar	fst	1¼	:47^4 1:11 1:36 2:01^4	3↑ Saratoga H 6.7k	3	5	$5^{4¼}$	$2^{1½}$	$2^{2½}$	2^{2}	Schuttinger A	126	w	7.00	100-06	SirBarton129^{2}Exterminator126^{3}Wildair115^{3}	Gamely,no match	5
14Jly20-4Wnr	hy	1⅛	:49^2 1:18^2 1:47 2:01^1	3↑ Frontier H 12k	5	3	4^{4}	2^{2}	$3^{2½}$	$3^{2½}$	Davies T	127	w	*1.25	47-48	Slippery Elm109^{½}The Porter129^{2}Exterminator127^{5}	Tired	8
3Jly20-4Aqu	my	1⅛	:48^1 1:12^4 1:37^3 1:50^1	3↑ Brookdale H 4.2k	2	3	$3^{½}$	2^{1}	$2^{½}$	$1^{1½}$	Schuttinger A	129	w	2.00	96-11	Exterminator129^{1½}Cirrus123^{4}Gladiator112^{6}	Hard ridden	4
29Jun20-4Aqu	fst	1 1/16	:23^3 :46^2 1:11 1:44	3↑ Handicap 1290	3	3	3^{4}	3^{3}	3^{1}	$1^{¾}$	Schuttinger A	126	w	3.00	101-18	Exterminator126^{¾}Naturalist120^{½}Wildair114^{12}	Drew away	5
24Jun20-4Aqu	fst	1⅛	:47 1:11 1:36^3 1:50	3↑ Brooklyn H 7.3k	7	7	7^{5}	7^{6}	4^{6}	$4^{8¼}$	Schuttinger A	124	w	6.00	89-09	Cirrus108^{hd}Boniface122^{8}Mad Hatter115^{hd}	Steadily	7
19Jun20-4Jam	gd	1⅛	:47^4 1:13 1:38^2 1:51^1	3↑ Long Beach H 4k	2	3	$1^{½}$	1^{1}	1^{1}	1^{1}	Schuttinger A	119	w	2.20	102-06	Exterminator119^{1}Cirrus109^{8}Naturalist120^{3}	Handily	5
5Jun20-4Bel	my	1¼	:52 1:16^3 1:43^2 2:09^3	3↑ Suburban H 7.8k	5	5	$5^{8½}$	$4^{6½}$	4^{7}	3^{6}	Rice T	123	w	*2.20	46-30	Paul Jones106^{hd}Boniface115^{6}Exterminator123^{½}	Game try	5
29May20-5Bel	fst	1 1/16	:24^2 :48 1:13 1:44^3	3↑ Handicap 1605	4	3	$2^{1½}$	3^{1}	$1^{½}$	2^{nk}	Davies T	128	w	*2.00	97-10	Alibi107^{nk}Exterminator128^{2}Sea Mint98^{no}	Led,tired	5
Previously trained by H. McDaniel																		
13Nov19-4Pim	hy	2¼	:52^3 2:50 3:18^2 4:13	3↑ Pim Cup H 4.9k	1	1	2^{2}	1^{4}	1^{2}	1^{4}	Kummer C	121	w	*1.00	--	Extrminatr121^{4}Royce Rools105^{8½}Woodtrp102^{3}	Won easing up	3
8Nov19-4Pim	fst	1½	:49^3 1:15 2:07^2 2:33^4	3↑ Bowie H 10k	5	3	$5^{2¾}$	$5^{5½}$	5^{11}	$5^{13½}$	Kummer C	128	w	2.90	73-11	Royce Rools107^{1½}Cudgel131^{4}Mad Hatter113^{2}	Quit badly	5
18Oct19-5Lat	hy	2¼	:54 2:50 3:18^4 4:17	3↑ Lat Cup 8.7k	4	3	1^{1}	2^{hd}	$2^{1½}$	2^{2}	Knapp W	134	w	*.45	--	Be Frank122^{2}Exterminator134^{20}Legal105^{20}	Tired	4
11Oct19-4Lrl	fst	1½	:47^3 1:13 2:03^3 2:29^3	3↑ Annapolis H 8.3k	3	3	$3^{4½}$	2^{1}	$2^{1½}$	2^{hd}	Knapp W	128	w	2.05	107-06	Thunderclp108^{hd}Extmntor128^{3}Cudgl132^{1}	Getting to winner	5
3Oct19-3Lrl	fst	1 1/16	:24^2 :49 1:15^3 1:46^1	3↑ Alw 1200	2	1	1^{1}	1^{hd}	$1^{½}$	1^{nk}	Knapp W	120	w	*.05	86-15	Exterminator120^{nk}Orestes120^{10}Douglass S.113	Hard ridden	3
27Sep19-5HdG	fst	1⅛	:47^1 1:12^2 1:37^3 1:50	3↑ Havre de Grace H 10k	5	6	$6^{4¾}$	$4^{¾}$	$4^{1¾}$	$2^{½}$	Knapp W	126	w	10.50	105-05	Cudgel129^{½}Extrmntr126^{no}SrBrton124^{2}	Impeded,game finish	8
22Sep19-5HdG	fst	1 1/16	:24 :48 1:13 1:45	3↑ Purse 2527	1	2	2^{2}	$2^{1½}$	2^{1}	$1^{¾}$	Schuttinger A	124	w	5.05	100-11	Exterminator124^{¾}Cudgel129^{1}Slippery Elm99^{3}	Gamely	5
11Sep19-4HdG	my	1 70	:25 :49 1:14^3 1:45	3↑ Harford County H 5.4k	4	2	$3^{½}$	2^{3}	2^{4}	2^{4}	Schuttinger A	125	w	*.35	83-25	The Porter121^{4}Exterminator125^{8}Slippery Elm103^{3}	No match	5
30Aug19-4Sar	sl	1¾	:48 2:07 2:32 2:58	3↑ Sar Cup 6.3k	3	1	$1^{1½}$	1^{2}	$1^{½}$	$1^{1½}$	Schuttinger A	126	w	2.50	100-14	Extrmntr126^{1½}Purchase116^{50}ThTrump116	Challenged,drew away	3
23Aug19-4Sar	fst	1 3/16	:48^4 1:13^3 1:37^2 1:57^2	3↑ Merchants & Cits H 3.4k	1	1	1^{1}	$2^{½}$	$3^{2½}$	3^{3}	Loftus J	126	w	*1.10e	90-08	Cudgel132^{1}Star Master122^{2}Exterminator126^{1½}	No menace	5
9Aug19-4Sar	fst	1⅛	:48 1:12^3 1:37^1 1:50	3↑ Champlain H 3.4k	6	4	$4^{2¼}$	3^{1}	2^{1}	2^{1}	Loftus J	120	w	*.90e	106-09	SunBriar128^{1}Extermntor120^{½}Hollstr115^{1½}	Not hard ridden	6
5Aug19-4Sar	fst	1	:23^2 :46^2 1:11^2 1:36^1	3↑ Delaware H 3.4k	6	5	$4^{4½}$	3^{4}	$3^{3½}$	3^{1}	Loftus J	121	w	*1.20e	99-08	FairyWand107^{hd}SunBriar128^{1}Exterminator121^{½}	Fast finish	8
14Jun19-4Jam	fst	1 1/16	:24^4 :48^2 1:13 1:45^2	3↑ Excelsior H 4.8k	8	5	$4^{4½}$	$4^{5½}$	6^{8}	$5^{3¾}$	Loftus J	124	w	8.00	96-07	Naturalist122^{1}Star Master119^{1}Boniface108^{nk}	No threat	8
7Jun19-4Bel	fst	1¼	:46^3 1:11^3 1:38 2:02^1	3↑ Suburban H 6.7k	1	4	$5^{7½}$	$7^{5¼}$	$7^{6¾}$	$5^{5¼}$	Rice T	128	w	5.00	84-16	Corn Tassel108^{nk}Sweep On108^{1½}Boniface107^{3}	Outrun	8
24May19-5CD	hy	1¼	:48^2 1:14^3 1:42 2:10^2	3↑ Kentucky H 14k	1	4	$1^{½}$	1^{hd}	1^{hd}	3^{1}	Morys J	134	w	*2.15	64-31	Midway122^{1}Beaverkill108^{no}Exterminator134^{2}	Gamely	7
22May19-6CD	my	1	:25 :50 1:15^3 1:42^3	3↑ Handicap 1660	4	1	$1^{1½}$	1^{2}	$1^{1½}$	1^{5}	Morys J	134	w	*.60	74-39	Exterminator134^{5}Flyaway97^{nk}Drastic112^{10}	Ridden out	4
15May19-4CD	fst	1	:25 :49^3 1:14^3 1:39^1	3↑ Alw 1800	4	1	$1^{½}$	1^{1}	2^{hd}	2no	Morys J	115	w	*.20	91-11	Under Fire103^{no}Exterminator115^{1½}Bribed Voter108^{8}		4
Tight restraint,tired																		
8May19-4Lxt	my	1¼	:49^3 1:15^2 1:42 2:07^3	3↑ Camden H 2.5k	1	1	1^{1}	1^{1}	1^{1}	1^{1}	Morys J	132	w	*.35	81-28	Exterminator132^{1}Midway118	Drawing away	2
1May19-4Lxt	hy	1 1/16	:24^3 :49^1 1:16 1:50^2	3↑ Ben Ali H 2.9k	4	3	$2^{1½}$	$2^{1½}$	$1^{1½}$	1^{3}	Morys J	124	w	*.60	70-33	Exterminator124^{3}AmericanAc99^{6}Mdwy120^{hd}	As rider pleased	5
31Mar19-4OP	fst	6f	:23^3 :48 1:12^4	3↑ Handicap 800	3	1	$3^{1½}$	3^{2}	1^{hd}	$1^{1½}$	Haynes E	123	w	*1.00	96-09	Extrmntor123^{1½}UltmThul114^{1½}A.N.Akn107^{2}	As rider pleased	6
22Mar19-4OP	fst	1 70	:24^2 :48 1:13 1:43^2	3↑ Handicap 800	2	2	$2^{½}$	$1^{1½}$	$1^{1½}$	1^{3}	Schuttinger A	126	w	*.80	109-09	Exterminator126^{3}Lucky B.111^{1½}Drastic111^{3}	Won eased up	4
28Nov18-5Lat	my	1 1/16	:24^3 :49^3 1:15^3 1:50^3	2↑ Handicap 2090	2	4	$3^{½}$	1^{2}	1^{4}	$1^{2½}$	Loftus J	126	w	*.85	64-37	Exterminator126^{2½}Drastic104^{6}WrMchn109^{5}	As rider pleased	8
23Nov18-5Lat	hy	2¼	:54 2:43^3 3:11 4:06^3	3↑ Lat Cup H 8.9k	6	6	$1^{1½}$	1^{1}	1^{hd}	1no	Loftus J	121	w	*1.25	--	Exterminator121^{no}Beaverkill110^{5}Moscowa115^{3}	Gamely	6
12Nov18-4Pim	fst	1½	:49 1:14^2 2:04^3 2:31^1	3↑ Bowie H 12k	4	5	$1^{½}$	2^{4}	2^{2}	$3^{1¼}$	Loftus J	120	w	6.85	102-06	GeorgeSmith130^{¾}OmarKhayyam115^{½}Extrmntr120^{6}	Resolutely	15
6Nov18-4Pim	fst	1¼	:49^2 1:14^1 1:39^3 2:05^3	Pim Autumn H 5.4k	2	2	1^{hd}	2^{hd}	1^{1}	$1^{½}$	Ensor L	118	w	3.20	99-09	Extrmntor118^{½}Forground107^{nk}ThPortr127^{6}	Outstayed rivals	5
31Oct18-4Lrl	hy	1⅛	:50 1:16 1:41^4 1:54^2	3↑ National H 3k	1	1	1^{nk}	1^{nk}	1^{nk}	2^{hd}	Knapp W	117	w	1.75	76-25	Midway117^{hd}Exterminator117^{20}Tombolo98	Wide	3
26Oct18-6Lrl	fst	1⅛	:49 1:14^1 1:39^3 1:52^1	Ellicott City H 2.5k	5	1	1^{nk}	1^{3}	$1^{1½}$	$1^{2½}$	Knapp W	113	w	*.30	87-08	Extermintor113^{2½}Aurum104.5^{1½}RdSox105.5^{nk}	Never extended	5
12Oct18-5Lrl	gd	1⅛	:49 1:14^3 1:40^2 1:51^2	3↑ Washington H 2.5k	3	1	$1^{¾}$	2^{2}	3^{2}	$3^{3½}$	Knapp W	114	w	3.15	87-13	Midway111.5^{2}Cudgel130^{1½}Exterminator113.5^{1½}	Tired badly	4

Past Performances of Great Horses of the 20th Century

8Oct18- 4Lrl fst 1 1/16 :231 :464 1:124 1:441 Carrollton H 1.9k 4 1 1nk 1½ 1½ 1hd Knapp W 118 w 12.70 96-11 Exterminator118hdThe Porter1265Sunny Slope1304 Gamely 4
4Oct18- 4Lrl fst 1 1/16 :24 :481 1:15 1:461 3↑ Alw 1408 4 1 12 11½ 11 11 Kummer C 103 w *.65 86-11 Exterminator1031Franklin1122John I. Day100no Ridden out 4
30Aug18- 4Sar hy 1¼ :501 1:171 1:451 2:122 3↑ Handicap 1313 4 2 22 42½ 47 39½ Knapp W 115 w *2.20 48-34 Ticket1061½Bondage1068Extermntr1151½ Impeded by winner 5
17Aug18- 4Sar fst 1¼ :49 1:133 1:382 2:031 Travers 10k 2 2 44½ 47 48 412 Schuttinger A 123 w *1.10e 92-05 Sun Briar120hdJohren1266War Cloud1266 Outrun 4
3Aug18- 4Sar fst 1 3/16 :483 1:132 1:383 1:563 Kenner 4k 3 2 32½ 33 31¾ 22 Knapp W 129 w 5.00 105-02 Enfilade1142Exterminator129nkTippityWitcht1235 Game try 5
22Jun18- 5Lat fst 1½ :494 1:142 2:063 2:33 Lat Derby 12k 5 4 42½ 35½ 31½ 22 Knapp W 124 w 8.75 85-11 Johren1272Exterminator124½Frecuttr1228 Hard ridden late 6
25May18- 4BPT fst 1 3↑ Turf and Field H .7k - - 21 Knapp W 122 *.45 - - Kilts II1261Exterminator1221Square Dealer1262 Driving 6
No time taken
11May18- 5CD my 1¼ :491 1:161 1:433 2:104 Ky Derby 18k 5 5 42½ 1hd 2hd 11 Knapp W 114 w 29.60 63-25 Exterminator1141Escoba1178Viva America1134 Saved ground 8
Previously owned and trained by J.C. Milam
26Jly17- 2Knw fst 5½f :233 :473 1:004 1:071 Alw 800 3 7 64¾ 45 66¾ 4½ Morys J 112 w *1.55 102-00 MissBryn112noOwnRoeO'Neil104½Salvstr112no Finished fast 11
17Jly17- 3Wnr hy 5½f :244 :51 1:052 1:13 Alw 800 2 6 43½ 3nk 13 11 Kelsay W 105 w 7.85 63-41 Exterminator1051Fern Handley1031Lady Eileen1103 Handily 6
14Jly17- 2Wnr gd 5f :23 :473 1:011 Alw 800 11 3 48 79¾ 49 410 Morys J 105 w 14.35 84-18 Jack Hare Jr.1111High Cost1153Viva America1156 Bumped 11
30Jun17- 1Lat fst 6f :233 :483 1:144 Md Sp Wt 2 2 12 12 11½ 13 Morys J 109 w 5.20 81-12 Exterminator1093Mistress Polly1091Quito112½ Easily 12

Forego

b. g. 1970, by Forli (Aristophanes)–Lady Golconda, by Hasty Road **Lifetime record: 57 34 9 7 $1,938,957**
Own.– Lazy F Ranch
Br.– Lazy F Ranch (Ky)
Tr.– Frank Y. Whiteley Jr

4Jly78- 8Bel sly 1¼ :483 1:123 1:37 2:014 3↑ Suburban H-G1 3 5 43½ 68½ 611 514 Shoemaker W 132 *.90 89-13 Upper Nile1131½Nearly on Time1092¼Great Contractor1143 6
Tired after ¾
19Jun78- 8Bel fst 7f :233 :462 1:094 1:213 3↑ Alw 25000 4 4 41½ 31½ 31½ 1nk Shoemaker W 122 *.30 94-12 Forego122nkDr. Patches1227Gabe Benzur1152 Ridden out 4
17Sep77- 8Bel sly 1⅛ :453 1:101 1:352 1:48 3↑ Woodward H-G1 3 8 79½ 44 4¾ 11½ Shoemaker W 133 *1.90 87-18 Forego1331½SilverSeries114nkGrtContrctor115nk Ridden out 10
6Aug77- 8Sar sly 1⅛ :463 1:103 1:361 1:492 3↑ Whitney H-G2 7 6 712 716 716 718 Shoemaker W 136 *.80 70-16 Nearly on Time1034½American History1124¾Dancing Gun112¾ 7
Disliked going
23Jly77- 8Bel fst 1½ :49 1:124 2:023 2:261 3↑ Brooklyn H-G1 12 6 2hd 21½ 25 211 Shoemaker W 137 *.70 78-17 GreatContractr11211Forego137nkAmrcnHstory112¾ Held 2nd 13
4Jly77- 8Bel fst 1¼ :472 1:113 1:373 2:03 3↑ Suburban H-G1 4 3 36½ 45 42 2nk Shoemaker W 138 *.30 84-16 QuietLittleTable114nkForego138nkNearlyonTm104¾ Bore out 6
13Jun77- 8Bel fst 1⅛ :471 1:111 1:354 1:481 3↑ Nassau County H-G3 3 5 54 51¼ 4¾ 1½ Shoemaker W 136 *.05 86-21 Forego136½Co Host110nkNorcliffe117½ Easily 7
30May77- 8Bel fst 1 :23 :451 1:101 1:344 3↑ Metropolitan H-G1 10 10 1014 86½ 2hd 12 Shoemaker W 133 *.50 94-14 Forego1332Co Host1112Full Out1151½ Handily 12
23May77- 6Bel fst 7f :242 :47 1:11 1:224 4↑ Alw 25000 2 3 31 32 2hd 1½ Shoemaker W 122 *.05 88-17 Forego122½Dance Spell1147Sawbones1092 Ridden out 5
2Oct76- 8Bel sly 1¼ :472 1:104 1:35 2:00 3↑ Marlboro Cup H-G1 10 4 86¼ 67½ 44 1hd Shoemaker W 137 *1.10 99-11 Forego137hdHonestPleasure1191FthrHogn1102¾ Wide,just up 11
18Sep76- 8Bel fst 1⅛ :453 1:091 1:332 1:454 3↑ Woodward H-G1 2 7 76 76½ 42½ 11¼ Shoemaker W 135 *1.10 98-10 Forgo1351¼DanceSpell1152¾[DH]HonstPleasur121 Ridden out 10
21Aug76- 8Mth fst 1¼ :472 1:112 1:354 2:003 3↑ AL Haskell H-G1 7 5 33 22 21 31 Vasquez J 136 *.60 98-12 Hatchet Man1121Intrepid Hero119hdForego1366 Forced wide 8
24Jly76- 8Aqu fst 1¼ :464 1:111 1:362 2:011 3↑ Brooklyn H-G1 4 6 68½ 21½ 2hd 12 Gustines H 134 *.70 90-14 Forego1342LordRebeau1144½FoolishPleasur126no Ridden out 8
5Jly76- 8Aqu fst 1 3/16 :474 1:112 1:361 1:552 3↑ Suburban H-G1 2 3 32½ 21½ 31½ 2no Gustines H 134 *.40 85-15 Foolish Pleasure125noForego134noLord Rebeau1164¼ Gamely 4
13Jun76- 8Bel fst 1⅛ :472 1:112 1:362 1:483 3↑ Nassau County H-G3 1 4 42½ 32 1hd 12¾ Vasquez J 132 *.80 84-22 Forego1322¾El Pitirre1152¾Hatchet Man1142 Easily 5
31May76- 8Bel fst 1 :231 :453 1:092 1:344 3↑ Metropolitan H-G1 4 5 54½ 44 41½ 1hd Gustines H 130 *1.10 94-16 Forego130hdMaster Derby1261¼Lord Rebeau1192¼ 6
Sluggish,just up
20May76- 8Bel fst 7f :234 :464 1:10 1:22 4↑ Alw 25000 2 2 41½ 3½ 1hd 11¼ Gustines H 126 *.30 92-18 Forego1261¼Wishing Stone1196½Tiempazo III119½ Easily 4
Previously trained by S.W. Ward

Past Performances of Great Horses of the 20th Century

Date/Track	Cond	Dist	Fractions	Race	PP	St	1st	2nd	Str	Fin	Jockey	Wt	Odds	Sp-Var	Company Line	Comment	Field
27Sep75- 8Bel	fst	1½	:493 1:132 2:023 2:271	3↑ Woodward-G1	6	3	3½	1hd	1hd	11¾	Gustines H	126	*.90	84-19	Forego1261¾Wajima11911Group Plan126¾	Drew clear	6
13Sep75- 8Bel	fst	1¼	:472 1:104 1:352 2:00	3↑ Marlboro Cup Inv'l H-G1	3	7	76	32	1hd	2hd	Gustines H	129	*1.40	99-11	Wajima119hdForego1297½Ancient Title126¾	Bore out,missed	7
1Sep75- 8Bel	fst	1⅛	:452 1:09 1:341 1:471	3↑ Governor-G1	8	8	710	88¾	54½	42¾	Gustines H	134	*2.00	88-18	Wajima115hdFoolishPleasure1252AncntTtl130¾	Wide stretch	10
19Jly75- 8Bel	fst	1½	:484 1:132 2:024 2:274	3↑ Suburban H-G1	3	6	69½	42½	3½	1hd	Gustines H	134	*.60	81-18	Forego134hdArbees Boy1182¼Loud1147	Just up	7
4Jly75- 8Bel	fst	1¼	:463 1:101 1:344 1:594	3↑ Brooklyn H-G1	2	5	412	31½	1hd	11½	Gustines H	132	*.70	101-07	Frgo1321½MonetryPrncpl109noStopthMusc1215¾	Ridden out	8
26May75- 8Aqu	fst	1	:231 :453 1:084 1:333	3↑ Metropolitan H-G1	3	7	75¼	64¾	34	31	Gustines H	136	*.90	97-11	GoldandMyrrh121¾StoptheMusic124nkForego1363½	Rallied	7
17May75- 8Aqu	fst	7f	:223 :444 1:091 1:213	3↑ Carter H-G2	5	10	811	87¾	22	1hd	Gustines H	134	*.90	93-11	Forego134hdStop the Music1232½Orders1141¼	Brisk drive	10
15Feb75- 9Hia	fst	1¼	:463 1:102 1:35 2:014	3↑ Widener H-G1	5	9	813	45½	1hd	11¼	Gustines H	131	*.70	89-11	Forego1311¼Hat Full1111¼Gold and Myrrh115nk	Ridden out	9
1Feb75- 9Hia	fst	1⅛	:47 1:103 1:343 1:471	3↑ Seminole H-G2	5	8	85	32	2½	1¾	Gustines H	129	*.80	96-09	Forego129¾Mr. Door1151Lord Rebeau1152½	Ridden out	8
9Nov74- 8Aqu	fst	2	:493 2:304 2:56 3:211	3↑ J C Gold Cup-G1	2	8	42½	1hd	12½	12½	Gustines H	124	*.70	90-15	Forego1242½Copte124¾Group Plan1243¼	Ridden out	8
19Oct74- 8Aqu	fst	7f	:223 :452 1:094 1:213	3↑ Vosburgh H-G2	4	10	99½	77½	21	13½	Gustines H	131	*2.20	93-10	Forgo1313½StoptheMusic118noPrinceDantn1191¾	Ridden out	12
28Sep74- 8Bel	fst	1½	:49 1:132 2:022 2:272	3↑ Woodward-G1	5	10	1017	84¼	42	1nk	Gustines H	126	*2.30	83-13	Forego126nkArbees Boy1261¾Group Plan1262½	Driving	11
14Sep74- 8Bel	sly	1⅛	:46 1:102 1:343 1:463	3↑ Marlboro Cup H 250k	2	9	810	72¾	34½	34	Gustines H	126	2.70	90-12	Big Spruce1202¾Arbees Boy1191¼Forego126½	No final rally	10
2Sep74- 8Bel	fst	1⅛	:452 1:092 1:34 1:461	3↑ Governor-G1	10	8	812	65	57	45¼	Gustines H	128	*1.60	91-09	Big Spruce1182½Arbees Boy1211½Plunk1211¼	Wide	10
20Jly74- 8Aqu	fst	1¼	:472 1:111 1:361 2:012	3↑ Suburban H-G1	6	6	512	46½	44½	31½	Gustines H	131	*1.40	87-12	True Knight1271½Plunk114hdForego1312½	Rallied	10
4Jly74- 8Aqu	fst	1 3/16	:463 1:102 1:354 1:544	3↑ Brooklyn H-G1	6	6	615	48	2hd	1¾	Gustines H	129	*.40	88-14	Forego129¾BillyComeLately1142ArbeesBoy1166	Ridden out	7
26Jun74- 8Aqu	fst	7f	:223 :444 1:084 1:211	3↑ Nassau County H-G3	2	6	612	612	56½	2½	Gustines H	132	*.70	94-10	Timeless Moment112½Forego132½North Sea1142½	Fast finish	6
27May74- 8Bel	fst	1	:222 :443 1:09 1:342	3↑ Metropolitan H-G1	2	6	47½	2hd	11½	22	Gustines H	134	*1.30	94-11	Arbees Boy1122Forego134½Timeless Moment109hd	Gamely	8
18May74- 8Bel	fst	7f	:221 :45 1:092 1:221	3↑ Carter H-G2	7	8	89	63½	11½	12¼	Gustines H	129	*1.40	91-13	Forego1292¼Mr.Prospector1241TimelessMoment1132¾	Easily	8
23Mar74- 9Hia	fst	1¼	:471 1:11 1:354 2:011	3↑ Widener H-G1	5	5	58½	1½	11½	11	Gustines H	129	*.80	92-12	Forego1291True Knight1242Play the Field114no	Driving	7
23Feb74- 9GP	fst	1¼	:464 1:104 1:354 1:594	3↑ Gulf Park H-G2	2	4	413	22	1hd	1½	Gustines H	127	1.40	98-14	Forego127½True Knight1236Golden Don1183	Ridden out	6
9Feb74- 9GP	fst	1⅛	:471 1:112 1:362 1:483	3↑ Donn H-G3	2	4	35	32½	21	1no	Gustines H	125	*.70	91-19	Forego125noTrue Knight123½Proud and Bold122nk	Just up	5
8Dec73- 8Aqu	fst	1⅛	:454 1:10 1:35 1:471	Discovery H-G3	6	5	37	34	11½	1¾	Gustines H	127	*.60	100-13	Forego127¾MyGallant1225[D]KeytotheKingdom1131	Driving	7
24Nov73- 8Aqu	fst	1 3/16	:462 1:11 1:36 1:543	Roamer H-G2	9	4	514	32½	13	15	Gustines H	123	*2.10	89-13	Forego1235My Gallant1212½Twice a Prince1141	Handily	10
10Nov73- 6Aqu	fst	7f	:233 :463 1:102 1:223	3↑ Alw 12000	2	5	35½	36	34	34	Gustines H	122	*.90	84-22	North Sea1152¾Tap the Tree1141¼Forego1223½	Evenly	5
20Oct73- 8Aqu	fst	1	:233 :46 1:094 1:34	Jerome H-G2	7	6	63½	32½	2hd	2hd	Gustines H	124	2.20	87-14	Step Nicely118hdForego1243Linda's Chief1261¾	Gamely	10
8Oct73- 5Bel	fst	1	:234 :461 1:093 1:333	3↑ Alw 20000	3	3	31	1½	12½	15½	Gustines H	120	*1.60	100-07	Forego1205½Rule by Reason114noRoyal Owl12010	Ridden out	5
15Sep73- 8Bel	fst	1 1/16	:232 :462 1:102 1:402	Alw 20000	6	4	41½	1hd	13	12½	Gustines H	116	2.10	101-07	Forego1162½Arbees Boy1132Matinee Idol1133	Driving	8
1Sep73- 4Bel	fst	7f	:214 :442 1:091 1:221	Alw 20000	1	6	49½	25	13	1hd	Gustines H	113	*.60	91-10	Forego113hdCutlass113¾Jazziness116nk	Driving	6
24Aug73- 5Sar	fst	7f	:224 :451 1:083 1:21	3↑ Alw 12000	5	4	56½	56	47½	37¼	Anderson P	116	*.60	95-10	Prove Out1126½Cutlass109¾Forego1161¼	No excuse	6
9Jun73- 7Bel	fst	1 1/16	:232 :46 1:101 1:404	Alw 20000	4	5	53¼	12	17	19	Gustines H	111	*1.00	99-05	Forego1119AdaptivePace114noIllberightbck114no	Ridden out	10
30May73- 7Bel	fst	1	:231 :45 1:091 1:344	Withers-G2	3	5	56	45	43½	35	Anderson P	126	8.00	93-17	Lnda'sChief1263StoptheMusc1262Forgo126½	Between horses	6
5May73- 9CD	fst	1¼	:472 1:114 1:361 1:592	Ky Derby-G1	9	9	912	66	46½	411	Anderson P	126	28.60	92-10	Secretariat1262½Sham1268OurNative126½	Hit rail far turn	13
26Apr73- 6Kee	fst	1⅛	:463 1:11 1:37 1:493	Blue Grass-G1	5	6	611	52½	52¾	55	Anderson P	117	*2.60	84-18	My Gallant117hdOur Native1233½[DH]Warbucks117	No rally	9
31Mar73- 9GP	fst	1⅛	:471 1:102 1:342 1:472	Florida Derby-G1	6	4	56	33	23	23	Anderson P	118	*2.30	94-06	Royal and Regal1222Forego1181¼Restless Jet122hd	Gamely	8
24Mar73- 3GP	fst	7f	:221 :444 1:092 1:213	Alw 6500	1	8	65	53	11	12	Anderson P	119	*.30	96-12	Forego1192Cades Cove114noMalicious Music1143½	Driving	8
7Mar73- 9GP	fst	7f	:221 :443 1:082 1:204	Hutcheson-G3	1	7	56¾	37	24	23¼	Anderson P	116	2.40	97-10	Shecky Greene1223¼Forego1169Leo's Pisces1124½		7
			Away sluggishly														
10Feb73- 4Hia	fst	6f	:214 :452 1:094	Alw 6500	5	4	45½	32½	11	12½	Anderson P	122	*.60	95-18	Forego1222½Borage1152½Paternity1174	Easily	8
29Jan73- 1Hia	fst	6f	:222 :46 1:102	©Md Sp Wt	4	1	22	1hd	1½	18	Anderson P	122	*1.30	92-16	Forego1228Jonata122nkBarclay Jet122½	Easily	11
17Jan73- 1Hia	fst	7f	:232 :461 1:11 1:233	©Md Sp Wt	9	11	97¼	89	79½	47	Anderson P	122	10.30	82-04	BuffaloLark1223¾TwoHarbrs1222CommandrLiz1221¼	Bumped	12

Past Performances of Great Horses of the 20th Century

Holy Bull

gr. c. 1991, by Great Above (Minnesota Mac)–Sharon Brown, by Al Hattab — Lifetime record: 16 13 0 0 $2,481,760

Own.– Warren A. Croll Jr
Br.– Pelican Stable (Fla)
Tr.– Warren A. Croll Jr

11Feb95- 9GP fst 1⅛ :46^2 1:10^3 1:36^3 1:49^3 3↑ Donn H-G1 9 2 2^2 — — — Smith ME 127 *.30 -- Cigar115^{5½}Primitive Hall112^{1½}Bonus Money112^{3½} 9
Pulled up 5½ furlong pole,lame left front
22Jan95- 9GP fst 7f :22^3 :45^1 1:09^3 1:22 3↑ Olympic H 100k 5 3 2^1 2^{hd} 1^{1½} 1^{2½} Smith ME 126 *.40 93-15 Holy Bull126^{2½}Birdonthewire119^{2¾}Patton115^{¾} 6
Raced well out in the track early,six wide top str,ridden out
17Sep94- 8Bel fst 1⅛ :46^2 1:10^2 1:34^3 1:46^4 3↑ Woodward-G1 5 2 2^1 1^{½} 1^3 1^5 Smith ME 121 *.90 97-10 Holy Bull121^{5}Devil His Due126^{1½}Colonial Affair126^{3½} 8
Bump brk,ridden out
20Aug94- 7Sar wf 1¼ :46^1 1:10^2 1:35^4 2:02 Travers-G1 1 2 2^{hd} 1^4 1^{1½} 1^{nk} Smith ME 126 *.80 94-06 Holy Bull126^{nk}Concern126^{17}Tabasco Cat126^1 Hard drive 5
31Jly94-10Mth fst 1⅛ :47^2 1:11^2 1:35^4 1:48^1 Haskell Inv H-G1 3 1 1^2 1^{2½} 1^{1½} 1^{1¾} Smith ME 126 *.20 93-07 Holy Bull126^{1¾}Meadow Flight118^{1¾}Concern118^1 Ridden out 6
3Jly94- 8Bel fst 1$\frac{1}{16}$:22^2 :45^1 1:09^2 1:41 Dwyer-G2 1 1 1^1 1^{1½} 1^3 1^{6¾} Smith ME 124 *.30 97-14 Holy Bull124^{6¾}Twining122^{5}Bay Street Star119^9 Handily 4
30May94- 8Bel fst 1 :22^4 :45 1:09^2 1:33^4 3↑ Metropolitan H-G1 6 1 1^1 1^{½} 1^{2½} 1^{5½} Smith ME 112 *1.00 94-09 HolyBull112^{5½}CherokeeRun118^{no}DevilHisDue122^2 Driving 10
7May94- 8CD sly 1¼ :47^1 1:11^4 1:37^3 2:03^3 Kentucky Derby-G1 4 6 5^{3½} 9^9 12^{12} 12^{18¼} Smith ME 126 *2.20 76-06 Go for Gin126^{2}Strodes Creek126^{2½}Blumin Affair126^{¾} 14
Off slow,in tight start,tired badly
16Apr94- 9Kee fst 1⅛ :47^4 1:12^3 1:37^4 1:50 Blue Grass-G2 1 1 1^3 1^2 1^{1½} 1^{3½} Smith ME 121 *.60 84-26 Holy Bull121^{3½}Valiant Nature121^{5}Mahogany Hall121^{2¼} 7
Sharp,ridden out
12Mar94-10GP fst 1⅛ :46 1:10 1:34^4 1:47^2 Florida Derby-G1 6 1 1^{2½} 1^{2½} 1^5 1^{5¾} Smith ME 122 2.70 100-06 HolyBull122^{5¾}RidetheRails122^{no}Halo'sImag122^1 Ridden out 14
19Feb94- 9GP gd 1$\frac{1}{16}$:22^4 :45^3 1:10^2 1:44^3 Fountain of Youth-G2 4 1 1^{½} 2^1 6^8 6^{24¼} Smith ME 119 *1.30 63-19 Dehere119^{¾}GoforGin119^{1¼}RidetheRails117^{3¾} Stopped badly 6
30Jan94- 9GP fst 7f :21^3 :44 1:08^1 1:21^1 Hutcheson-G2 1 4 1^{1½} 1^{1½} 2^{½} 1^{¾} Smith ME 122 *.50 97-11 Holy Bull122^{¾}Patton113^{3}You and I119^3 5
Broke inward start,raced well off rail,ridden out
23Oct93-11Crc fst 1$\frac{1}{16}$:23 :46^2 1:11^3 1:46^1 Ⓡ In Reality 400k 9 1 1^{1½} 1^2 1^4 1^{7½} Smith ME 120 *.50 88-12 HolyBull120^{7½}RusticLight120^{1}ForwardtoLd120^{1½} Ridden out 12
18Sep93- 6Bel sly 7f :22^2 :45^3 1:10^1 1:23^1 Futurity-G1 2 1 1^1 1^1 1^{2½} 1^{½} Smith ME 122 3.10 87-14 Holy Bull122^{½}Dehere122^{5}Prenup122^8 All out 6
2Sep93- 7Bel fst 6½f :22 :44^1 1:09^4 1:17 Alw 28000 3 1 1^{½} 1^{hd} 1^{2½} 1^7 Smith ME 119 *.90 88-15 Holy Bull119^{7}Goodbye Doeny117^{3}End Sweep119^{½} Ridden out 6
Previously owned by Targan Stable
14Aug93- 7Mth fst 5½f :21^3 :44^4 :57^1 1:03^4 Md Sp Wt 1 3 1^1 1^{1½} 1^{1½} 1^{2½} Rivera L Jr 118 *1.10 95-17 Holy Bull118^{2½}Palance118^{7½}Hold My Tongue118^9 Driving 9

John Henry

b. g. 1975, by Ole Bob Bowers (Prince Blessed)–Once Double, by Double Jay — Lifetime record: 83 39 15 9 $6,597,947

Own.– Dotsam Stable
Br.– Golden Chance Farm Inc (Ky)
Tr.– Ronald McAnally

13Oct84- 8Med fm 1⅜Ⓣ :46^4 1:11 1:35^1 2:13 3↑ Ballantine H 900k 4 8 8^9 5^{3½} 3^{1½} 1^{2¾} McCarron CJ 126 *.60 100-06 JohnHnry126^{2¾}Who'sforDinner115^{hd}Win120^1 Came out,clear 12
22Sep84- 8Bel fm 1½Ⓣ :48^4 1:13 2:01^3 2:25^1 3↑ Turf Classic-G1 4 1 1^{1½} 1^{½} 1^{½} 1^{nk} McCarron CJ 126 *1.00 98-10 JohnHnry126^{nk}Win126^{4}Majesty'sPrnc126^{hd} Strong handling 6
26Aug84- 9AP fm 1¼Ⓣ :48^2 1:12^2 1:37^2 2:01^2 3↑ Bud Arl Million-G1 6 4 3^{1½} 3^2 1^{hd} 1^{1¾} McCarron CJ 126 *1.10 87-15 JohnHenry126^{1¾}RoyalHeroine122^{3}GatodelSol126^{no} Drew out 12
23Jly84- 8Hol fm 1½Ⓣ :47^1 1:10^3 1:59^4 2:24^4 3↑ Sunset H-G1 7 5 4^7 3^2 2^1 1^1 McCarron CJ 126 *1.20 96-08 JhnHnry126^{1}LoadtheCannons118^{1½}PairofDeuces113^{nk} Driving 9
24Jun84- 8Hol fst 1¼ :47 1:10 1:35 2:00^2 3↑ Hol Gold Cup H-G1 4 4 4^{3½} 3^2 3^2 2^2 McCarron CJ 125 2.60 87-20 DesertWine122^{2}JohnHnry125^{1½}Sari'sDreamer114^{nk} Game try 8
28May84- 8Hol fm 1½Ⓣ :49 1:12^3 2:01^1 2:25 3↑ Hol Inv'l H-G1 1 2 3^{1½} 3^{1½} 3^{nk} 1^{½} McCarron CJ 126 *.80 95-08 JohnHnry126^{½}GalantVert116^{2¾}LoadtheCannons120^{1¼} Driving 9
6May84- 8GG fm 1⅜Ⓣ :47^2 1:12 1:35^4 2:13 3↑ Golden Gate H-G3 6 3 3^{4½} 2^2 1^{½} 1^2 McCarron CJ 125 *.50 103-09 John Henry125^{2}Silveyville117^{6}Lucence116^6 Slow st.,clear 6

Past Performances of Great Horses of the 20th Century

Date/Race	Cond	Dist	Fractions	Age	Race	PP	St	1st call	2nd call	Str	Fin	Jockey	Wt	Odds	Speed	Top Finishers	Comment	Field
1Apr84- 8SA	fm	1½Ⓣ	:482 1:132 2:022 2:264	3↑	San Luis Rey-G1	4	2	21	1½	2½	3¾	McCarron CJ	126	1.60	80-17	Interco126nkGato del Sol126½John Henry1263½	Weakened	10
4Mar84- 8SA	fst	1¼	:453 1:10 1:35 2:003	4↑	S Anita H-G1	10	7	76¼	45	56	58	McCarron CJ	127	*2.40	78-17	Interco1212¾Journey at Sea1171½Gato del Sol1171¾		12
	Stumble after start																	
11Dec83- 8Hol	gd	1⅜Ⓣ	:494 1:153 1:40 2:163	3↑	Hol Turf Cup-G1	4	2	22½	1½	2hd	1½	McCarron CJ	126	*1.50	72-27	John Henry126½Zalataia1231½Palikaraki1261¼	Came again	12
13Nov83- 8SA	gd	1½Ⓣ	:472 1:131 2:034 2:291	3↑	Oak Tree Inv'l-G1	2	5	31	43½	31	2½	McCarron CJ	126	*.80	68-31	Zalataia123½JohnHnry1261½LoadthCnnons1223½	Held gamely	9
15Oct83- 8Bel	fst	1½	:48 1:123 2:01 2:261	3↑	J C Gold Cup-G1	7	6	53	45	55	56¾	McCarron CJ	126	2.90	82-14	Slew o'Gold1213Highland Blade126nkBounding Basque1211½		11
	Weakened																	
28Aug83- 9AP	gd	1¼Ⓣ	:503 1:154 1:413 2:042	3↑	Arl Million-G1	13	3	21	2½	2½	2nk	McCarron CJ	126	*1.40	72-28	Tolomeo118nkJohnHenry126½Nijinsky'sSecret1262	Sharp try	14
4Jly83- 8Hol	fm	1⅛Ⓣ	:49 1:13 1:363 1:482	3↑	American H-G2	1	3	33	21½	2½	11¼	McCarron CJ	127	2.10	88-12	JohnHenry1271¼PrinceFlorimund120½Tonzarun114no	Driving	8
28Nov82♦Tokyo(Jpn)	fm	*1½ⓉLH	2:27	3↑	Japan Cup-G1 Stk801000						138	Shoemaker W	126	*.90		Half Iced121nkAll Along117nkApril Run1211	Prominent to stretch	15
13Nov82- 6Med	gd	1¼	:473 1:121 1:37 2:012	3↑	Med Cup H-G2	2	5	37½	44¼	35½	35¾	Shoemaker W	129	*1.10	89-15	Mehmet1181¼ThirtyEightPcs1134½JhnHnry1294½	Lacked a bid	9
31Oct82- 8SA	fm	1½Ⓣ	:472 1:103 1:593 2:24	3↑	Oak Tree Inv'l-G1	6	4	44	21½	2½	12½	Shoemaker W	126	1.40	95-05	John Henry1262½Craelius1221½Regalberto1262	Drew clear	7
17Oct82- 8SA	fm	1¼Ⓣ	:471 1:11 1:343 1:583	3↑	C F Burke H-G2	6	3	31½	42	42¾	41½	Shoemaker W	129	*.30	92-06	Mehmet117hdCraelius1141½It's the One124no	Evenly	7
28Mar82- 8SA	fm	1½Ⓣ	:462 1:102 2:00 2:24	4↑	San Luis Rey-G1	3	3	33	33	43½	34¾	Shoemaker W	126	*.50	90-05	Perrault1263¼Exploded1261½John Henry126no	Evenly	5
7Mar82- 8SA	fst	1¼	:45 1:09 1:342 1:59	4↑	S Anita H-G1	9	8	913	51¼	2½	2no	Shoemaker W	130	*1.30	94-07	ⒹPerrault126noJhnHenry1303¼It'stheOne123nk	Impeded end	11
	Placed first by disqualification																	
6Dec81- 8Hol	fm	1½Ⓣ	:49 1:13 2:03 2:264	3↑	Hol Turf Cup 550k	5	1	12	11	3½	42	Shoemaker W	126	*.40	84-11	Providential II126nkQueen to Conquer1231½Goldiko126nk		10
	Weakened;Previously trained by Victor J. Nickerson																	
8Nov81- 8SA	fm	1½Ⓣ	:472 1:102 1:593 2:232	3↑	Oak Tree Inv'l-G1	4	3	1½	1½	2hd	1nk	Shoemaker W	126	*.40	98-02	John Henry126nkSpence Bay1264½The Bart126no	Driving	7
10Oct81- 8Bel	fst	1½	:48 1:123 2:021 2:282	3↑	J C Gold Cup-G1	8	5	42½	21	11½	1hd	Shoemaker W	126	*3.10	78-14	JohnHenry126hdPeatMoss126¾Relaxing123hd	Bore in,driving	11
	Previously trained by Ronald McAnally																	
30Aug81- 6AP	sf	1¼Ⓣ	:501 1:153 1:422 2:073	3↑	Arl Million 1000k	12	8	86½	56	31	1no	Shoemaker W	126	*1.10e	- -	John Henry126noThe Bart1262¼Madam Gay117½	Just up	12
	Previously trained by Victor J. Nickerson																	
11Jly81- 8Bel	fm	1½Ⓣ	:494 1:142 2:03 2:264	3↑	Sword Dancer-G3	3	3	31½	11	11½	13½	Shoemaker W	126	*.30	90-13	JohnHnry1263½PassingZone1261¾PeatMoss1261¾	Ridden out	5
	Previously trained by Ronald McAnally																	
14Jun81- 8Hol	fst	1¼	:453 1:093 1:344 2:002	3↑	Hol Gold Cup H-G1	7	7	66¼	65¾	46½	42¾	Pincay L Jr	130	*1.20	86-16	ⒹCaterman120hdEleven Stitches1222½Super Moment117nk		10
	Wide late																	
17May81- 8Hol	fm	1½Ⓣ	:511 1:151 2:04 2:274	3↑	Hol Inv'l H-G1	5	2	2½	2½	1½	1¾	Pincay L Jr	130	*.40	81-12	John Henry130¾Caterman122hdGalaxy Libra118nk	Driving	7
29Mar81- 8SA	fm	1½Ⓣ	:46 1:104 2:00 2:251	4↑	San Luis Rey-G1	1	2	21½	22	1hd	12¼	Pincay L Jr	126	*.20	89-11	John Henry1262¼Obraztsovy1261½Fiestero126hd	Easily	6
8Mar81- 8SA	fst	1¼	:452 1:092 1:341 1:592	4↑	S Anita H-G1	3	7	65¼	22	1hd	11	Pincay L Jr	128	1.90	92-11	John Henry1281King Go Go1171¼Exploded115no	Driving	11
16Feb81- 8SA	fm	1½Ⓣ	:474 1:113 1:59 2:24	4↑	San Luis Obispo H-G2	4	1	11	11	12½	11½	Pincay L Jr	127	*.50	95-05	John Henry1271½Galaxy Libra1195½Zor1151½	Ridden out	6
16Nov80- 8SA	fm	1½Ⓣ	:454 1:101 1:582 2:232	3↑	Oak Tree Inv-G1	6	5	56½	66¾	37½	11½	Pincay L Jr	126	*1.50	98-02	John Henry1261½Balzac126½Bold Tropic126nk	Drew clear	10
	Previously trained by Victor J. Nickerson																	
25Oct80- 8Aqu	sf	1½Ⓣ	:514 1:192 2:13 2:393	3↑	Turf Classic-G1	4	1	12	23	25	38	Pincay L Jr	126	*2.00	35-57	Anifa1233Golden Act1265John Henry126nk	Weakened	8
4Oct80- 8Bel	fst	1½	:494 1:15 2:051 2:301	3↑	J C Gold Cup-G1	3	2	21	2½	23	25½	Cordero A Jr	126	*.70	63-19	Temperence Hill1215½John Henry1262Ivory Hunter1263¼		7
	Best of others																	
7Sep80- 8Bel	fm	1¼Ⓣ	:483 1:122 1:362 1:592	3↑	Brighton Beach H-G3	5	1	1hd	11½	11½	1nk	Cordero A Jr	125	*.40	97-15	John Henry125nkPremier Ministre1174Match the Hatch1133		5
	Driving																	
12Jly80- 8Bel	fm	1½Ⓣ	:47 1:111 2:01 2:251	3↑	Sword Dancer 161k	2	2	21	1½	2hd	21¼	McHargue DG	126	*.80	97-15	Tiller1261¼John Henry1265Sten12612	Gamely	4
14Jun80- 8Bel	fm	1⅜Ⓣ	:473 1:113 1:352 2:131	3↑	Bowling Green H-G2	3	1	1½	1hd	1½	2nk	McHargue DG	128	*1.80	96-15	Sten117nkJohn Henry1281Lyphard's Wish120nk	Brushed	9
	Previously trained by Ronald McAnally																	
26May80- 8Hol	fm	1½Ⓣ	:483 1:123 2:012 2:252	3↑	Hol Inv'l H-G1	4	1	14	12½	1½	1nk	McHargue DG	128	*.90	93-09	John Henry128nkBalzac1201½Go West Young Man1172½		10
	Fully extended																	

Past Performances of Great Horses of the 20th Century

Date/Race	Track/Dist	Fractions	Race	PP St	1st	2nd	Str	Fin	Jockey	Wt	Eq	Odds	Figs	Top Finishers	Comment
6Apr80- 8SA	fm *1¾Ⓣ	:46 1:594 2:464	4↑ S Juan Capistrano H-G1	3 1	12	11½	12	11¼	McHargue DG	126		*2.20	93-08	John Henry1261¼Fiestero114nkThe Very One113hd	Driving 11
16Mar80- 8SA	fm 1½Ⓣ	:464 1:104 1:592 2:23	4↑ San Luis Rey-G1	3 2	21	2½	2½	1½	McHargue DG	126		6.90	100-00	John Henry1261½Relaunch126noSilver Eagle126no	Drew out 7
23Feb80-10Hia	fm 1½Ⓣ	2:292	3↑ Hia Turf Cup H-G2	10 2	31½	11	11½	1½	McHargue DG	122		2.30	84-22	JohnHenry122½DancingMaster1135IvoryHunter111hd	Driving 10
20Jan80- 8SA	fst 1¼	:47 1:113 1:364 2:013	4↑ San Marcos H-G3	2 1	11½	11	11	12½	McHargue DG	124		*.80	85-17	John Henry1242½El Fantastico1132¼Commemorativo110nk	5
	Handily														
1Jan80- 8SA	gd 1⅛Ⓣ	:48 1:121 1:371 1:494	4↑ San Gabriel H-G3	4 2	22	21½	2½	1hd	McHargue DG	123		*1.70	78-22	John Henry123hdSmasher1115As de Copas1173	Driving 9
8Dec79- 8BM	fm 1⅛Ⓣ	:471 1:111 1:363 1:493	3↑ Bay Meadows H 114k	7 5	44½	83¾	1hd	21¼	McHargue DG	123		2.70	103-00	Leonotis1181¼John Henry1234Capt. Don117½	Held on 14
5Nov79- 8SA	fm 1⅛Ⓣ	:461 1:102 1:352 1:48	3↑ HP Russell H (Div 2) 45k	5 2	11	11	12	13¼	McHargue DG	122		*.70	87-15	JohnHenry1223¼Rusty Canyon114hdLeonotis1172	Ridden out 8
14Oct79- 8SA	fm 1¼Ⓣ	:454 1:10 1:343 1:591	3↑ C F Burke H-G2	5 3	21½	1hd	1hd	21¼	McHargue DG	118		3.40	90-09	Silver Eagle1151¼John Henry118½Shagbark1181¼	Gamely 9
	Previously trained by Victor J. Nickerson														
10Sep79- 7Bel	fm 1$\frac{1}{16}$Ⓣ	:24 :47 1:11 1:414	3↑ Alw 30000	2 1	13	11½	12	12	Santiago A	117		1.90	87-17	John Henry1172Silent Cal117½Waya119no	Ridden out 4
22Aug79- 7Sar	fm 1⅛Ⓣ	:462 1:111 1:343 1:462	3↑ Alw 27000	3 1	11½	11½	11½	12½	Santiago A	115		*1.40	95-13	John Henry1152½Told114¾Poison Ivory1224	Driving 7
29Jly79- 7Pen	sly 1$\frac{1}{16}$	:232 :471 1:114 1:443	3↑ Capital City H 33k	7 5	41½	31	41¼	42	Santiago A	113		2.30	81-23	Horatius118nkTanthem1121½Shy Jester115nk	Hung 7
14Jly79- 8Bel	fm 1$\frac{1}{16}$Ⓣ	:233 :47 1:104 1:413	3↑ Sword Dancer 57k	2 1	2hd	21	22	22½	Santiago A	119		5.70	85-11	Darby Creek Road1192½John Henry1194Poison Ivory1191¾	8
	Best of others														
6Jly79- 6Atl	fm 1$\frac{1}{16}$Ⓣ	:23 :462 1:102 1:411	3↑ Sunrise H 35k	2 2	21½	1½	1hd	22¼	McCauley WH	111		*1.50	98-09	Chati1182¼John Henry111½Fed Funds1154	Tired 11
24Jun79-10Suf	fst 1⅛	:453 1:10 1:36 1:483	3↑ Mass H-G3	9 4	68¾	84¼	96	108½	Borden DA	108		6.90	89-21	Island Sultan110¾Western Front113½Quiet Jay1161½	Tired 13
5Jun79- 8Mth	fst 1	:232 :47 1:114 1:373	4↑ Alw 18000	1 3	2hd	13	18	114	McCauley WH	119		*.90	85-23	John Henry11914Thou Fool119noM.A.'s Date1131¾	Driving 7
26May79- 6Mth	fst 6f	:22 :443 1:104	4↑ Alw 16000	4 4	53½	41¾	21½	2½	McCauley WH	117		6.90	85-19	ReallyandTruly117½JohnHnry1171¼Kintla'sFolly1153	Gamely 7
	Previously trained by Robert A. Donato														
29Oct78- 6Pen	fm 1$\frac{1}{16}$Ⓣ	1:412	Chcltetwn H (Div 2) 22k	5 2	21	1½	12	11	Broussard R	124		*.70	--	John Henry1241Scythian Gold1166½Berlin's Burning1122	7
	Ridden out														
15Oct78- 5SA	fm 1¼Ⓣ	:453 1:094 1:342 1:59	3↑ C F Burke H (Div 1)-G2	2 1	1hd	1hd	44	65	Baltazar C	117		2.80	87-08	Star of Erin II113noImproviser1152¾Mr. Redoy1181¼	Tired 9
8Oct78- 8SA	fm 1⅛Ⓣ	:46 1:102 1:351 1:474	Volante H-G3	6 4	42	41	31½	3½	Baltazar C	122		*2.30	87-12	WaysideStation117noAprilAxe120½JohnHenry1222	In close 11
16Sep78- 8AP	gd 1$\frac{1}{16}$Ⓣ	:241 :484 1:131 1:454	Round Table H-G3	6 1	11	13	18	112	Amy J	121		*.50	80-30	JhnHnry12112GordieH.109noBringtheMoney111no	Ridden out 9
9Sep78- 5Bel	fm 7fⓉ	:232 :46 1:093 1:22	3↑ Alw 21000	1 1	11½	11½	11	11½	Amy J	113		3.60	94-09	John Henry1131½Gab Bag1174Proud Arion1171¼	Hard ridden 8
18Aug78- 7Sar	fm 1$\frac{1}{16}$Ⓣ	:251 :49 1:12 1:41	3↑ Alw 23000	7 2	2½	2hd	44	47¼	Amy J	112		5.10	85-08	Blue Baron1172¼Quip1141Stir the Embers1194	Weakened 8
8Aug78- 7Sar	gd 7f	:223 :444 1:081 1:202	3↑ Alw 23000	2 2	31½	24	38	514	Santiago A	113		2.90	89-04	DarbyCreekRoad11311Liberal117¾GoldenReserve117¾	Tired 6
29Jly78- 8Bel	fm 1$\frac{1}{16}$Ⓣ	:233 :46 1:103 1:41	Lexington H-G2	5 1	12½	12	11	2hd	Santiago A	112		5.90	91-11	Mac Diarmida126hdJohn Henry1124¼Ashikaga110hd	Gamely 9
19Jly78- 8Bel	fm 1Ⓣ	:24 :473 1:104 1:351	Hill Prince H 37k	5 1	2hd	2hd	2½	21½	Santiago A	111		3.60	92-12	DarbyCreekRd1211½JhnHnry1112ScythianGold1116	Gamely 9
1Jly78- 8Mth	fm 1$\frac{1}{16}$Ⓣ	:232 :47 1:11 1:432	Lamplighter H-G3	4 2	2hd	1hd	1½	3½	Santiago A	112		*1.50	83-16	North Course112nkHoratius114nkJohnHenry112no	Weakened 9
25Jun78- 6Bel	hd 1$\frac{1}{16}$Ⓣ	:232 :47 1:102 1:411	3↑ Alw 18000	2 5	62½	52	42	1nk	Santiago A	112		3.40	90-07	John Henry112nkTurn of Coin1171¾Valinsky1171¾	Driving 9
1Jun78- 7Bel	fm 1$\frac{1}{16}$Ⓣ	:231 :47 1:11 1:413	Clm 35000	1 2	21	1½	17	114	Santiago A	117		3.30	88-12	JhnHnry11714ContinentalCousin117¾CptnPeter1132¼	Driving 10
21May78- 2Aqu	fst 6f	:224 :471 1:123	Clm 25000	4 4	32½	1½	11	12½	Santiago A	117		12.30	80-27	John Henry1172½Please See Me1171½Orfanik115nk	Driving 9
	Previously owned and trained by H. Snowden Jr														
11Apr78- 7Kee	fst 6f	:22 :45 :59 1:093	Alw 8500	4 4	47½	46	48½	49½	McKnight J	113		6.40	84-15	Johnny Blade1074½Schottis112½Jester Beau1154½	No mishap 6
	Previously owned by D. Lingo & C. Madere; previously trained by Phil Marino														
22Mar78- 9FG	fst 6f	:23 :47 1:12	Clm 25000	7 6	78	89	64¾	34	Copling D	114		25.10	81-16	Kim's Red1142Bunny Wag1122John Henry1141	Rallied 9
22Feb78- 9FG	fst 6f	:223 :463 1:113	Clm 20000	11 2	98¾	98¾	1015	1020	Elmer D	112	b	19.10	67-19	AdriaticEditions1144Bladesville113½Kim'sRed1141	Outrun 11
15Feb78- 6FG	fst 6f	:22 :462 1:113	Clm 25000	5 5	85¼	61¼	63¾	66¼	Guajardo A	112	b	4.90	81-19	MercrCounty1121½Gen'sLTroy1121AdrtcEdtons1141	No mishap 8
4Feb78- 6FG	fst 1 40	:252 :493 1:151 1:43	Alw 7500	2 9	84¾	83½	53¼	55¾	Guajardo A	112		17.10	72-23	HogTown114¾TrafficWarning114hdSmokePole1092½	No mishap 10
23Jan78- 8FG	gd 1 40	:241 :473 1:131 1:424	Alw 7500	7 4	42¾	52¾	86¾	86½	Guajardo A	112		22.20	72-24	CabriniGreen117½DayTimeTudor1121As in Elbow112no	Tired 9
31Dec77- 9FG	fst 6f	:22 :46 1:121	Sugar Bowl H 50k	4 12	127¾	127½	1210	1114	McKnight J	113		16.80	70-21	CabriniGreen122½CouponRate113¾SpecialHonr1101¼	Outrun12

Past Performances of Great Horses of the 20th Century

17Dec77- 6FG gd 6f :223 :472 1:122 ©Alw 7000 1 6 64¼ 62¾ 53¾ 31¼ McKnight J 113 7.90 82-18 CabriniGreen1201¼CouponRate113hdJohnHenry113hd Rallied 12
3Dec77- 8FG fst 6f :222 :462 1:114 Alw 7000 1 7 75¾ 54 51¾ 43½ McKnight J 120 8.70 82-19 DragonTamer1171½TrafficWarnng1171¼HogTwn117¾ Rallied 11
19Nov77- 9FG fst 6f :221 :464 1:124 ©Sthrern Hospitality 19k 8 12 105 63¼ 64¼ 59 Guajardo A 122 9.60 72-22 CbrniGreen1144MajesticSpiral1122½HogTown112hd Late bid 12
5Sep77-11EvD sly 6f :232 :47 1:01 1:142 Lafayette Futurity 86k 1 6 45 32½ 1hd Guajardo A 120 5.10 79-26 JohnHenry120hdLilLizaJayne1171SoundNote1203½ Driving 12
25Aug77- 7EvD gd 6f :223 :462 1:002 1:13 Sp Wt 2700 8 5 33 32 2½ Guajardo A 120 4.10 85-21 Note to Mame117½John Henry1203Tudor Luck117hd 9
6Aug77- 7EvD sly 5f :224 :483 1:001 Alw 2400 4 9 54½ 1hd 13 Guajardo A 120 3.00 82-19 John Henry1203Motor Dude1201½Bell's Chief1174 Driving 12
29Jly77- 8JnD fst *6f :233 :473 1:02 1:152 Handicap 7500 9 9 - - - - Munster L 102 3.90 - - RunLikeHeck1191CapGardnr1072HarktheLedr1102 Lost rider 9
2Jly77- 6JnD sly 5f :23 :481 1:011 Alw 4500 2 5 42 33 23 Spiehler G 116 *2.60 81-19 KindaNughty1133JhnHnry1161MossBluffKd1152 Bid,weakened 7
7Jun77- 8JnD fst 4f :22 :471 Alw 3500 4 6 59 55½ 31 Spiehler G 120 14.60 89-11 DancngMeadw109¾DancingJudge120nkJhnHnry1201 Rallied 8
20May77- 1JnD fst 4f :23 :481 Md Sp Wt 1 7 54½ 34 1no Spiehler G 120 1.70 85-15 JhnHnry120noYouSexyThing1172Ricky'sChoice112¾ Driving 8

Kelso

dkbbr. g. 1957, by Your Host (Alibhai)–Maid of Flight, by Count Fleet

Lifetime record: 63 39 12 2 $1,977,896

Own.– Bohemia Stable
Br.– Mrs Richard C. duPont (Ky)
Tr.– C.H. Hanford

2Mar66- 9Hia fst 6f :222 :444 1:10 4↑ Alw 10000 8 3 87¾ 89¾ 77¾ 44½ Boland W 113 3.30 89-13 DavusII119hdTimeTested1191CountryFrind1133½ Closed well 8
22Sep65- 7Aqu fst 1¼ :473 1:12 1:364 2:024 3↑ Stymie H 27k 6 4 45½ 1½ 16 18 Valenzuela I 128 *.30 84-17 Kelso1288[D]O'Har107[?]Ky.Ponr110¾ With complete authority 6
6Sep65- 7Aqu fst 1⅛ :481 1:121 1:363 1:49 3↑ Aqueduct 108k 7 5 510 56 48 49 Valenzuela I 130 *1.00 82-14 Malicious1163Pluck1[?]noRmnBrothr1216 Lacked any response 7
7Aug65- 6Sar fst 1⅛ :471 1:111 1:364 1:494 4↑ Whitney 54k 3 4 44 45 22½ 1no Valenzuela I 130 *1.20 96-08 Kelso130noMalicious1146PiaStar127nk Up in final strides 5
24Jly65- 7Aqu fst 1¼ :47 1:102 1:35 2:003 3↑ Brooklyn H 107k 1 5 56½ 43½ 33½ 34 Valenzuela I 132 *1.20 91-10 PiaStar1212RomnBrothr1212Kelso1321½ Hung under impost 5
10Jly65- 8Del fst 1 1/16 :241 :482 1:122 1:422 3↑ Diamond State H 21k 2 2 21½ 2½ 1½ 13¼ Valenzuela I 130 *.30 97-13 Kelso1303¼Kilmoray1093Big Brigade114no Going away 4
29Jun65- 8Mth fst 6f :222 :454 1:111 4↑ Alw 5000 8 3 56 86¾ 54¼ 3½ Boland W 122 *.50 85-23 Cachto117noCommunqu122½Klso122hd Showed strong late bid 8
11Nov64- 7Lrl hd 1½Ⓣ :464 1:102 2:00 2:234 3↑ D C Int'l 150k 5 2 24 1½ 13 14½ Valenzuela I 126 *1.20 112-00 Kelso1264½Gun Bow1269Aniline1223½ Drew out handily 8
31Oct64- 7Aqu fst 2 :484 2:533 3:191 3↑ J C Gold Cup 108k 2 5 43 11½ 14 15½ Valenzuela I 124 *.45 101-14 Kelso1245½Roman Brother1196Quadrangle11916 Easy score 6
3Oct64- 7Aqu gd 1¼ :481 1:121 1:371 2:022 3↑ Woodward 108k 3 2 21½ 2hd 1hd 2no Valenzuela I 126 *.95 86-22 Gun Bow126noKelso1264Quadrangle12125 Bore in slightly 5
7Sep64- 7Aqu fst 1⅛ :463 1:104 1:353 1:483 3↑ Aqueduct 107k 3 2 25 21½ 1½ 1¾ Valenzuela I 128 2.20 98-16 Klso128¾GnBow1286Sadm1194½ Responded to strong urging 5
27Aug64- 7Sar hd 1⅛Ⓣ 1:463 3↑ Alw 9500 4 2 22½ 2hd 1½ 12½ Valenzuela I 118 *.30 102-00 Klso1182½Knghtsborc1161½RockyThumb1205 Scored in hand 8
25Jly64- 7Aqu fst 1¼ :461 1:101 1:35 1:593 3↑ Brooklyn H 110k 5 6 69 58½ 610 514 Valenzuela I 130 *.85 88-12 GnBow12212OldnTimes122noSunriseFlght113hd Bumped gate 8
18Jly64- 8Mth fst 1¼ :451 1:101 1:353 2:014 3↑ Monmouth H 107k 1 5 56 43¼ 3½ 2nk Valenzuela I 130 *.60 93-17 Mngo127nkKlso1304½GunBow12418 Hung through late stages 5
4Jly64- 7Aqu fst 1¼ :472 1:112 1:364 2:014 3↑ Suburban H 110k 6 4 34 32 31½ 2hd Valenzuela I 131 *1.35 91-17 Iron Peg116hdKelso1314Olden Times128¾ Getting to winner 8
25Jun64- 7Aqu fst 1⅛ :483 1:124 1:371 1:50 3↑ Handicap 15000 5 4 43½ 21½ 11½ 11¼ Valenzuela I 136 *.55 91-15 Kelso1361¼TropicalBreeze114½SunrisFlght12110 Mild drive 5
6Jun64- 8Hol fst 1 1/16 :224 :461 1:102 1:413 3↑ Californian 115k 3 5 65 75¼ 78¾ 68 Valenzuela I 127 *1.40 79-14 Mustard Plaster1111[?]Mr. Consistency1231½ColordoKing1232½ 10
Impeded
23May64- 8Hol fst 7f :214 :44 1:084 1:212 3↑ Los Angeles H 55k 9 1 713 98½ 913 89¼ Valenzuela I 130 *1.70 84-13 Cyrano124hdQuitaDude1142Admiral's Voyag121no Dull effort 9
11Nov63- 7Lrl fm 1½Ⓣ :483 1:133 2:033 2:272 3↑ D C Int'l 150k 8 4 41½ 21 2½ 2½ Valenzuela I 126 *.50 93-14 Mongo126½Klso12612Nyrcos1223 Sluggish start,game effort 10
19Oct63- 7Aqu fst 2 :482 2:30 2:551 3:22 3↑ J C Gold Cup 108k 1 4 2hd 12 16 14 Valenzuela I 124 *.15 87-14 Kelso1244Guadalcanal1245Garwol1243½ Speed in reserve 7
28Sep63- 7Aqu fst 1¼ :473 1:114 1:362 2:004 3↑ Woodward 108k 2 3 34 2½ 1½ 13½ Valenzuela I 126 *.25 96-13 Kelso1263½NeverBend1201½CrimsonSatn1266 Speed to spare 5
2Sep63- 7Aqu fst 1⅛ :49 1:124 1:371 1:494 3↑ Aqueduct 110k 7 3 41½ 31 12 15½ Valenzuela I 134 *.70 92-17 Kelso1345½CrimsonSatan129hdGrwol115no Under mild urging 8
3Aug63- 6Sar fst 1⅛ :48 1:12 1:372 1:502 4↑ Whitney 55k 2 4 42½ 42½ 11 12½ Valenzuela I 130 *.35 93-14 Kelso1302½Saidam111[?]1Sunrise County117hd Easily the best 7
4Jly63- 7Aqu fst 1¼ :484 1:131 1:381 2:014 3↑ Suburban H 108k 7 3 33 31½ 11½ 11¼ Valenzuela I 133 *.45 91-13 Kelso1331¼Saidam111[?]1½Garwol1121 Retained a safe margin 7
19Jun63- 7Aqu fst 1⅛ :474 1:113 1:36 1:484 3↑ Nassau County 27k 3 3 31½ 31 12 11½ Valenzuela I 132 *.30 97-07 Kelso1321½Lnvn114noPolyld1143 Cleverly rated,easy score 5

Past Performances of Great Horses of the 20th Century

```
23Mar63- 8Bow fst 1 1/16 :242 :481 1:12 1:43 3↑ J B Campbell H 109k 5 5 44½ 33 21½ 1¾ Valenzuela I 131 *.80 98-15 Kelso131¾Crimson Satan124hdGushing Wind1166 Hard drive 6
16Mar63- 8GP fst 1¼ :482 1:121 1:372 2:031 3↑ Gulf Park H 110k 2 2 1½ 12 12 13¼ Valenzuela I 130 *.20 83-20 Kelso1303¼Sensitivo1129Jay Fox113½ Speed in reserve 6
23Feb63- 7Hia fst 1¼ :483 1:122 1:364 2:014 3↑ Widener H 128k 5 3 54½ 42½ 23 22¼ Valenzuela I 131 *.45 87-18 Beau Purple1252¼Kelso1313Heroshogala1104 Best of others 9
9Feb63- 7Hia fst 1⅛ :462 1:104 1:354 1:484 3↑ Seminole H 58k 1 4 47½ 42 12 12¾ Valenzuela I 128 2.35 91-19 Kelso1282¾Ridan1292½Senstvo1153½ Rallied wide,drew away 6
30Jan63- 8Hia fst 7f :233 :46 1:101 1:224 3↑ Palm Beach H 29k 4 2 2hd 32 43½ 45½ Valenzuela I 128 2.45 89-16 Ridan1273¾Jaipur127¾MerryRulr1171 Broke in stride,tired 5
1Dec62- 8GS fst 1½ :493 1:15 2:051 2:301 3↑ Gov's Plate 54k 2 1 1hd 13 13 15 Valenzuela I 129 *.40 105-20 Kelso1295Bass Clef1175Polylad1178 Drew away with ease 5
12Nov62- 7Lrl sf 1½Ⓣ :471 1:112 2:031 2:281 3↑ D C Int'l 125k 3 2 2hd 11 1hd 21½ Valenzuela I 126 2.10 88-20 MatchII1281½Kelso1264½CarryBack1265 Easily best of rest 13
27Oct62- 7Bel sf 1½Ⓣ 2:283 3↑ Man o' War 114k 12 5 43 21½ 22 22 Valenzuela I 126 *1.05 101-11 BeauPurple1262Klso1266½ThAxII1261¼ Finished very gamely 12
20Oct62- 7Bel fst 2 :483 2:282 2:532 3:194 3↑ J C Gold Cup 108k 3 2 32 12 18 110 Valenzuela I 124 *.25 103-08 Kelso12410Guadalcanal1242Nickel Boy1241½ Easily best 6
29Sep62- 7Aqu gd 1¼ :471 1:113 1:37 2:031 3↑ Woodward 115k 5 3 38½ 13 13 14½ Valenzuela I 126 *.90 84-17 Kelso1264½Jaipur1206½Guadlcnl1261½ Won as rider pleased 8
19Sep62- 7Aqu fst 1¼ :48 1:12 1:362 2:004 3↑ Stymie H 29k 2 3 34½ 11½ 13 12½ Valenzuela I 128 *1.25 96-14 Klso1282½Plyld114hdTutnkhmn110hd With complete authority 11
8Sep62- 7Atl fm 1 1/16Ⓣ 1:431 3↑ Alw 6000 2 1 2hd 11½ 1½ 41¾ Pierce D 113 *.40 93-05 CalltheWitness113nkArtMarket113hdWindySands1131½ Tired 7
22Aug62- 6Sar fm 1 1/16Ⓣ 1:414 3↑ Alw 5000 3 4 41¾ 2½ 1½ 11½ Valenzuela I 124 *.25 97-03 Kelso1241½CalltheWitness1175FountainHill1172 Mild drive 7
14Jly62- 8Mth fst 1¼ :46 1:10 1:344 2:002 3↑ Monmouth H 109k 5 4 45½ 44 42½ 23 Shoemaker W 130 *.80 101-14 Carry Back1243Kelso130¾Beau Purple117½ In close turn 6
4Jly62- 7Aqu fst 1¼ :484 1:124 1:363 2:003 3↑ Suburban H 105k 4 3 36 22 22 22½ Shoemaker W 132 *.65 100-08 BeauPurpl1152½Klso1323½Grwol1091¼ Couldn't reach winner 4
16Jun62- 3Bel fst 1 :241 :472 1:113 1:353 3↑ Alw 7500 2 4 42 22 2hd 12¼ Shoemaker W 117 *.25 96-14 Klso1172¼Grwol1153½RosNt117½ Rated early,drew out easily 6
30May62- 7Aqu fst 1 :221 :44 1:08 1:333 3↑ Metropolitan H 111k 2 6 69 56½ 510 68¼ Shoemaker W 133 *.60 92-08 CarryBack1232½MerryRuler120½RullahRed1114½ Dull effort 9
11Nov61- 7Lrl fm 1½Ⓣ :483 2:013 2:261 3↑ D C Int'l 100k 6 1 1½ 1hd 2hd 2¾ Arcaro E 126 *.40 108-01 T.V.Lrk126¾Klso12612Prnupcl12610 Made very sharp effort 8
21Oct61- 7Aqu fst 2 :494 2:35 3:004 3:254 3↑ J C Gold Cup 105k 3 2 22 13 14 15 Arcaro E 124 *.10 68-25 Kelso1245Hillsborough1248Peace Isle12430 Easily best 4
30Sep61- 7Bel fst 1¼ :461 1:10 1:344 2:00 3↑ Woodward 109k 5 3 21½ 2hd 13 18 Arcaro E 126 *.50 100-13 Kelso1268Divine Comedy126½Carry Back120nk Much the best 5
4Sep61- 8AP gd 1 :224 :452 1:093 1:343 3↑ Wash Park H 120k 8 9 106½ 67 47 45¾ Arcaro E 132 *.70 94-08 ChiefofChiefs1124¾TalentShow110nkRunforNurse112¾Boxed 11
22Jly61- 7Aqu fst 1¼ :462 1:101 1:36 2:013 3↑ Brooklyn H 112k 7 4 316 35½ 31½ 11¼ Arcaro E 136 *.50 98-10 Klso1361¼DvnComdy118noYorky122hd Under strong handling 10
4Jly61- 7Aqu fst 1¼ :482 1:122 1:373 2:02 3↑ Suburban H 111k 7 4 43½ 3nk 12 15 Arcaro E 133 *.60 96-13 Kelso1335NickelBoy112nkTalentShow110hd Speed in reserve 10
17Jun61- 7Bel fst 1⅛ :454 1:102 1:351 1:48 4↑ Whitney 56k 5 3 33½ 11 2hd 2hd Arcaro E 130 *.45 96-12 DOur Hope111hdKelso1305Reinzi114hd Roughed repeatedly 7
Placed first through disqualification
30May61- 7Aqu fst 1 :23 :46 1:102 1:353 3↑ Metropolitan H 114k 9 8 85¼ 76¼ 44 1nk Arcaro E 130 *1.05 90-16 Kelso130nkAllHands1173SweetWillim1084 Altered course,up 10
19May61- 7Aqu fst 7f :23 :461 1:11 1:24 4↑ Alw 10000 7 6 54½ 31½ 2hd 11½ Arcaro E 124 *.35 90-17 Kelso1241½Gyro115nkLongGoneJohn121½ Drew out with ease 8
29Oct60- 7Aqu sly 2 :472 2:29 2:54 3:192 3↑ J C Gold Cup 109k 8 3 313 2½ 11 13½ Arcaro E 119 *.80 114-16 Kelso1193½Don Poggio12410Bald Eagle12415 Speed to spare 8
15Oct60- 8Haw my 1¼ :464 1:113 1:364 2:02 3↑ Haw Gold Cup H 144k 4 6 41½ 12 13 16 Arcaro E 117 *2.20 86-21 Kelso1176Heroshogala119½On-and-On1221¾ Speed to spare 9
28Sep60- 7Bel fst 1⅝ :472 1:372 2:021 2:404 Lawrence Realizatn 56k 1 4 42½ 11 14 14½ Arcaro E 120 *.50 100-14 Kelso1204½Tompion1231½ToothandNal1165½ Speed in reserve 8
14Sep60- 7Aqu fst 1⅛ :463 1:102 1:354 1:482 Discovery H 28k 2 6 43½ 42 1½ 11¼ Arcaro E 124 *1.20 102-14 Kelso1241¼CarelssJohn1161½CountAmbr116½ Swerved,driving 8
3Sep60- 7Aqu fst 1 :223 :452 1:10 1:344 Jerome H 59k 7 9 95¼ 53 32½ 1hd Arcaro E 121 2.65 94-13 Kelso121hdCarelessJohn1162½FourLan1192½ Long,hard drive 13
3Aug60- 7Mth fst 1 1/16 :224 :46 1:093 1:411 Choice 56k 7 2 21 11 16 17 Hartack W 114 3.90 99-18 Klso1147CarelessJohn114¾CountAmber1143½ Speed to spare 8
23Jly60- 8AP fst 1 :223 :452 1:103 1:361 Arl Classic 135k 5 10 75¼ 97¾ 77½ 87½ Brooks S 117 3.90 81-13 T.V. Lark120¾John William1232½Venetian Way1231 Dull try 12
16Jly60- 5Aqu fst 1 :23 :451 1:09 1:341 Alw 4500 4 1 1½ 13 110 112 Blum W 117 *1.30 97-10 Kelso11712DoubleDly120noAugustSun109nk As rider pleased 8
22Jun60- 5Mth fst 6f :214 :45 1:10 Alw 4500 6 3 43½ 31 13 110 Hartack W 117 *1.00 92-12 Kelso11710Burnt Clover1172½Gordian Knot1171½ Ridden out 8
Previously trained by J.M. Lee
23Sep59- 3Atl fst 7f :22 :442 1:093 1:23 ©Alw 3600 3 5 2hd 1hd 2hd 2¾ Blum W 117 *1.90 87-11 WindySands117¾Klso1172WeGuarantee1172½ Made good try 8
14Sep59- 4Atl fst 6f :231 :462 1:112 ©Alw 3400 6 4 42¼ 42½ 43½ 21½ Block J 117 4.40 86-18 DressUp1201½Kelso1171¾DuskyRam117nk Rallied for placing 7
4Sep59- 2Atl gd 6f :232 :471 1:134 ©Md Sp Wt 7 8 72¼ 66 45 11¼ Block J 120 6.00 76-23 Kelso1201¼Crafty Master120¾Adapt1201 Under a hard drive 12
```

Past Performances of Great Horses of the 20th Century

Lady's Secret

gr. f. 1982, by Secretariat (Bold Ruler)–Great Lady M., by Icecapade
Own.– Mr. and Mrs. Eugene V. Klein
Br.– R.H. Spreen (Okla)
Tr.– D. Wayne Lukas

Lifetime record: 45 25 9 3 $3,021,425

Date	Cond	Dist	Fractions	Age	Race	PP	St	1c	2c	Str	Fin	Jockey	Wt	Odds	Spd	Top three finishers	Comment	Fld
10Aug87-1Sar	sly	1⅛	:47^1 1:11^3 1:36^1 1:49^2	3↑	Alw 45000	2	0	-	-	-	-	McCarron CJ	117	*.30	--	Kamakura115^{11}The Watcher122^{2¼}Jack of Clubs119^{2½}	Bolted	5
21Jly87-8Mth	fst	1$\frac{1}{16}$	:23^1 :46^2 1:11 1:43^2	3↑	ⒻAlw 25000	1	2	1^{½}	1^{3½}	1^{9}	1^{7}	McCarron CJ	119	*.10	88-18	Lady'sSecret119^{7}BriefRemarks115^{nk}ShaknBy115^{¾}	Easy score	6
4Jly87-10Mth	fst	1$\frac{1}{16}$	:23^1 :46^1 1:10 1:42	3↑	ⒻMolly Pitcher H-G2	3	2	2^{1½}	2^{½}	2^{hd}	2^{2}	McCarron CJ	125	*.30	93-10	ReelEasy112^{2}Lady'sSecret125^{¾}Cattonc117^{nk}	Best of others	8
13Jun87-8Mth	sly	6f	:22^2 :44^4 1:09^4	3↑	ⒻAlw 25000	5	1	2^{hd}	1^{½}	1^{1}	1^{3½}	Cordero A Jr	122	*.30	91-14	Lady'sSecret122^{3½}Nick'sNag115^{6}BriefRmrks115^8	Ridden out	5
14Mar87-10GP	fst	1⅛	:46^2 1:11 1:36^1 1:48^4	3↑	Donn H-G2	2	1	1^{2}	4^{3}	6^{18}	6^{32½}	Day P	120	*.80	55-18	LittleBoldJohn111^{no}SkipTrl118^{6}WsTms117^{4½}	Fin. after½	7
1Nov86-5SA	fst	1¼	:46^1 1:10 1:34^4 2:01^1	3↑	ⒻBC Distaff-G1	5	1	1^{4}	1^{4}	1^{4}	1^{2½}	Day P	123	*.50	83-13	Lady's Secret123^{2½}Fran's Valentine123^{2}Outstandingly123^{¾}		8
	Ridden out																	
12Oct86-8Bel	fst	1¼	:46^1 1:10 1:35^2 2:01^3	3↑	ⒻBeldame-G1	4	1	1^{5}	1^{1}	1^{½}	1^{½}	Day P	123	*.05	90-13	Lady's Secret123^{½}Coup de Fusil123^{1¾}Classy Cathy118^{23½}		4
	Drifted,ridden out																	
21Sep86-8Bel	fst	1⅛	:45^4 1:09^3 1:34^1 1:46^4	3↑	ⒻRuffian H-G1	5	2	1^{½}	1^{3½}	1^{6}	1^{8}	Day P	129	*.50	93-12	Lady's Secret129^{8}Steal a Kiss109^{2¼}Endear119^6	Handily	6
6Sep86-8Bel	fst	1	:23^1 :45^4 1:09^4 1:33^2	3↑	ⒻMaskette-G1	5	1	1^{1}	1^{1½}	1^{4½}	1^{7}	Day P	125	*.30	98-10	Lady's Secret125^{7}Steal a Kiss109^{1¾}Endear120^{no}	Handily	6
30Aug86-8Bel	fst	1⅛	:45^3 1:09^2 1:33^4 1:46	3↑	Woodward-G1	4	1	1^{1½}	1^{2½}	2^{hd}	2^{4¾}	Cordero A Jr	121	1.40e	92-14	Precisionist126^{4¾}Lady'sScrt121^{5½}PrsonlFlg110^{5¾}	2nd best	5
16Aug86-9Mth	sly	1⅛	:46^4 1:10^3 1:35^3 1:48^4	3↑	Iselin H-G1	1	1	1^{1½}	1^{hd}	1^{hd}	3^{3½}	Day P	120	*1.20	86-16	Roo Art117^{2¼}Precisionist125^{1¼}Lady's Secret120^6	Gave way	5
2Aug86-8Sar	sly	1⅛	:46^3 1:10^4 1:36^3 1:49^4	3↑	Whitney H-G1	2	1	1^{2½}	1^{3}	1^{2½}	1^{4½}	Day P	119	*1.30e	86-22	Lady's Secret119^{4½}Ends Well116^{3¼}Fuzzy110^{nk}	Ridden out	7
5Jly86-9Mth	fst	1$\frac{1}{16}$	:23 :46 1:09^1 1:41^1	3↑	ⒻMolly Pitcher H-G2	4	1	1^{½}	1^{½}	1^{3½}	1^{6¼}	Day P	126	*.20	99-13	Lady's Secret126^{6¼}Chaldea114^{2¼}Key Witness112^{1½}	Easily	8
8Jun86-8Bel	my	1⅛	:44^4 1:09^4 1:35^3 1:48^3	3↑	ⒻHempstead H-G1	4	2	1^{hd}	1^{hd}	2^{2½}	2^{6}	Day P	128	*.40	78-16	Endear115^{6}Lady's Secret128^{1½}Ride Sally124^{13}	2nd best	5
26May86-8Bel	fst	1	:23^2 :45^4 1:09^1 1:33^3	3↑	Metropolitan H-G1	4	1	2^{hd}	1^{hd}	1^{½}	3^{1¼}	Day P	120	5.30	96-11	Garthorn124^{1¼}LoveThatMac117^{no}Lady'sSecrt120^{nk}	Held well	8
17May86-8Bel	fst	1$\frac{1}{16}$	:23^3 :46^1 1:10^1 1:41^4	3↑	ⒻShuvee H-G1	3	1	1^{1}	1^{1}	1^{3}	1^{3½}	Day P	126	*.70	93-15	Lady's Secret126^{3½}Endear115^{6¼}Ride Sally125^1	Easy score	6
16Apr86-9OP	fst	1$\frac{1}{16}$	:23^1 :45^4 1:10^1 1:40^2	4↑	ⒻApple Blossom H-G1	4	1	1^{3}	1^{hd}	2^{½}	2^{nk}	Velasquez J	127	*.40	99-16	LoveSmitten119^{nk}Lady'sSecret127^{6}Sefa'sBeauty122^6	Failed	7
23Feb86-8SA	fst	1⅛	:46^2 1:10 1:34^3 1:47	4↑	ⒻS Margarita H-G1	1	1	1^{1½}	1^{1}	1^{1½}	1^{2¾}	Velasquez J	125	*1.60	94-11	Lady'sSecret125^{2¾}Johnica120^{1¼}DontstopThemusc122^2	Easily	9
9Feb86-8SA	fst	1⅛	:46^4 1:11 1:36^3 1:49^4		ⒻLa Canada-G1	3	1	1^{½}	1^{1½}	1^{1½}	1^{1¼}	McCarron CJ	126	*.50	80-16	Lady'sSecret126^{1¼}Shywing119^{4}NorthSider118^{1¾}	Hard ridden	6
18Jan86-8SA	fst	1$\frac{1}{16}$	:22^2 :45^2 1:09^3 1:41^4		ⒻEl Encino-G3	8	3	1^{½}	1^{3}	1^{2½}	1^{2}	McCarron CJ	124	*.80	92-12	Ldy'sScrt124^{2}Shywng119^{4}ShrpAscnt119^{nk}	Lugged into stretch	10
27Dec85-8SA	fst	7f	:22^2 :45 1:09^3 1:22^2		ⒻLa Brea-G3	1	3	1^{hd}	1^{½}	2^{hd}	2^{½}	McCarron CJ	124	*.80	87-16	SavannahSlew119^{½}Lady'sScret124^{3}AmbraRidge114^{2½}	Gamely	7
	Previously owned by E.V. Klein																	
2Nov85-5Aqu	fst	1¼	:46^4 1:11^2 1:36^4 2:02	3↑	ⒻBC Distaff-G1	1	1	1^{4}	1^{1}	2^{1½}	2^{6¼}	Velasquez J	119	*.40e	80-10	Life's Magic123^{6¼}Lady's Secret119^{3}Dontstop Themusic123^{1¼}		7
	Ducked out start																	
13Oct85-8Bel	fst	1¼	:45^4 1:10^2 1:36 2:03^3	3↑	ⒻBeldame-G1	4	1	1^{½}	1^{2}	1^{3}	1^{2}	Velasquez J	118	*.60	80-19	Lady'sSecret118^{2}Isayso123^{2¾}KamikazeRick118^{2¼}	Ridden out	5
22Sep85-8Bel	fst	1⅛	:46^2 1:09^4 1:34^3 1:47^2	3↑	ⒻRuffian H-G1	3	1	1^{1½}	1^{4}	1^{5}	1^{4}	Velasquez J	116	*.30e	90-17	Lady's Secret116^{4}Isayso115^{2¼}Sintrillium118^{hd}	Ridden out	6
7Sep85-8Bel	fst	1	:22^2 :44^4 1:09^1 1:34^4	3↑	ⒻMaskette-G1	6	1	1^{½}	1^{1}	1^{4}	1^{5½}	Velasquez J	111	*1.00e	91-14	Lady's Secret111^{5½}Dowery117^{no}Mrs. Revere117^{¾}	Ridden out	8
9Aug85-8Sar	fst	7f	:21^4 :44^1 1:09^1 1:22^3	3↑	ⒻBallerina-G2	4	3	2^{1½}	2^{hd}	1^{½}	1no	MacBeth D	117	*.90e	89-19	Lady'sSecret117^{no}Mrs.Revere116^{2¾}SolarHalo116^{¾}	Driving	9
1Aug85-8Sar	gd	7f	:22^1 :44^4 1:09 1:21^3		ⒻTest-G2	9	1	4^{2½}	3^{1½}	1^{hd}	1^{2}	Velasquez J	121	10.10	94-13	Lady'sScrt121^{2}Mom'sCommand124^{nk}MjstcFolly118^{½}	Driving	10
6Jly85-6Bel	fst	6f	:22 :45^1 1:11^1	3↑	ⒻThe Rose 54k	6	1	3^{2}	3^{nk}	1^{2}	1^{4¾}	Velasquez J	116	*.40	86-20	Lady'sScrt116^{4¾}FoolishIntentions115^{¾}ProudClarioness115^{nk}		6
	Ridden out																	
22Jun85-9Mth	fst	6f	:22^1 :44^3 1:09^3	3↑	ⒻRegret H 49k	6	1	1^{1½}	1^{1½}	1^{2½}	1^{3½}	Antley CW	114	*.40	92-16	Lady'sSecret114^{3½}FurashFolly118^{2}Nck'sNg120^{2½}	Ridden out	6
26May85-5Bel	fst	6f	:22^2 :44^4 1:09		ⒻBowl of Flowers 55k	6	1	1^{½}	1^{hd}	1^{4}	1^{7}	Velasquez J	121	*.50	97-13	Lady'sSecret121^{7}RideSally114^{nk}IndinRomnc114^3	Ridden out	7
11May85-8Bel	fst	7f	:22 :44^3 1:09^1 1:22^1		ⒻComely-G3	1	4	4^{3}	4^{5}	4^{7½}	4^{11}	Cordero A Jr	121	6.30	80-12	Mom'sCommnd121^{4½}MajestcFolly113^{1¾}ClocksScrt121^{4¾}	Tired	9
28Apr85-8Aqu	fst	6f	:22^2 :45^1 1:10		ⒻPrioress-G3	5	1	2^{1}	2^{1½}	2^{1½}	2^{1¼}	Velasquez J	118	*1.30	90-21	ClocksSecret115^{1¼}Lady'sSecret118^{5}RideSally112^2	Gamely	8
16Apr85-9OP	fst	6f	:21^4 :45 1:10		ⒻPrima Donna 76k	7	2	3^{2½}	3^{½}	1^{1½}	1^{5}	Velasquez J	123	*.80	90-18	Lady'sSecret123^{5}TakeMyPictur123^{2}Lt.A.J.112^{1¾}	Ridden out	9
23Feb85-8GG	fst	6f	:21^3 :44^2 :57^3 1:10		ⒻVallejo 43k	1	3	1^{½}	1^{½}	1^{hd}	2^{1½}	Baze RA	122	1.90	87-16	SavannahSlew114^{1½}Lady'sScrt122^{6}SprtdMdm114^{3½}	Game try	7

Past Performances of Great Horses of the 20th Century

30Jan85- 8SA fst 7f :22^{1} :44^{4} 1:09^{4} 1:23^{2} ⒻS Ynez-G3 6 1 2^{hd} 1^{hd} 2^{hd} 5$3\frac{3}{4}$ Valenzuela PA 122 7.40 79-17 Wising Up119¾Rascal Lass122^{2}Reigning Countess119¾ Hung 9
12Jan85- 8BM fst 6f :22^{2} :44^{4} :57^{2} 1:10^{1} Determine 44k 7 1 2½ 1^{hd} 2^{hd} 2^{nk} Baze RA 115 *1.10 88-21 Bedside Promise113^{nk}Lady'sScrt115 1½[D]SantaRosaPrince115^{no} 8
Gamely
5Jan85- 8BM fst 6f :22^{2} :45 :57^{3} 1:10 ⒻHail Hilarious 43k 5 3 3 1½ 1^{hd} 1^{3} 1^{4} Baze RA 120 *.70 89-16 Lady's Secret120^{4}Missadoon112^{5}Bloomer Miss115^{no} 7
Bumped start,wide into str
9Nov84- 9Hol fst 6f :22^{1} :45^{3} :58 1:11^{1} ⒻMoccasin 61k 8 1 1^{hd} 2½ 1½ 1½ McCarron CJ 120 *1.90 -- Lady's Secret120½Neshia113^{1}Lotta Blue117^{3} Driving 9
20Oct84- 8SA fst 1 1/16 :22^{4} :45^{4} 1:10^{2} 1:42^{3} ⒻOak Leaf-G1 6 1 1^{3} 1½ 3^{6} 5 16¼ Sibille R 115 7.10 72-13 FolkArt117 4½Pirate'sGlow115 6½WaywardPirate115 3½ Tired 6
8Oct84- 8SA fst 7f :22 :44^{3} 1:10^{1} 1:23^{3} ⒻAnoakia-G3 11 1 1 2½ 1 3½ 1^{2} 3^{hd} Black K 120 6.10e 82-16 WaywardPirate120^{hd}Prt'sGlow117^{no}Ldy'sScrt120 1¼ Weakened 11
8Aug84- 8Dmr fst 6f :22 :45^{1} :58 1:11^{1} ⒻJunior Miss 53k 3 1 2^{hd} 1^{hd} 2 2½ 4^{6} Valenzuela PA 122 3.00e 76-21 Doon's Baby117 2½Fiesta Lady117^{3}Trunk117½ Weakened 6
23Jly84- 3Hol fst 6f :21^{4} :44^{3} :57^{2} 1:11 Ⓕ[R]Wavy Waves 46k 5 1 1½ 1^{2} 1^{2} 1 1½ Valenzuela PA 117 2.20 82-18 Lady's Secret117 1½Full o Wisdom115½Neshia117 2¼ Driving 6
7Jly84- 8Hol fst 6f :21^{3} :44^{4} :57^{1} 1:10 ⒻLandaluce-G3 13 1 2^{hd} 2 2½ 2^{5} 4^{9} Valenzuela PA 116 21.40e 78-18 WindowSeat114 6½RaiseaProspctor119^{1}FulloWsdom114 1½ Tired 13
2Jly84- 8Bel fst 5½f :21^{4} :45^{4} :58^{3} 1:05^{1} ⒻAstoria 75k 4 3 1^{hd} 1^{hd} 2^{1} 5 5½ Cordero A Jr 112 2.60 83-15 Faster Than Fast110^{3}Something113½Queen Breeze112 1½ 9
Pace between horses
21May84- 4Bel fst 5f :22^{1} :45^{4} :58^{4} ⒻMd Sp Wt 1 3 1 1½ 1 1½ 1 1½ 1 1½• Cordero A Jr 117 *1.40 93-09 [DH]Lady'sScrt117[DH]Bonnie's Axe117 1½Launching Shot117 2¼ 8
Drifted out

Man o' War

ch. c. 1917, by Fair Play (Hastings)–Mahubah, by Rock Sand **Lifetime record: 21 20 1 0 $249,465**
Own.– S.D. Riddle
Br.– August Belmont (Ky)
Tr.– L. Feustel

12Oct20- 4Knw fst 1¼ :46^{2} 1:11^{4} 1:37^{2} 2:03 3↑ Ken Park Gold Cup 75k 2 1 1^{2} 1^{5} 1^{6} 1^{7} Kummer C 120 w *.05 132-03 Man o' War120^{7}Sir Barton126 Never extended 2
18Sep20- 5HdG fst 1 1/16 :23 :47^{3} 1:11^{3} 1:44^{4} Potomac H 10k 4 1 1 1½ 1^{1} 1 1½ 1 1½ Kummer C 138 w *.15 101-16 Man o' War138 1½Wildair108 15Blazes104.5^{2} Easing late 4
11Sep20- 4Bel fst 1½ :49^{3} 1:14^{1} 2:03^{2} 2:28^{4} 3↑ Jockey Club 6.8k 2 1 1^{5} 1^{8} 1^{12} 1^{15} Kummer C 118 w *.01 117-02 Man o' War118 15Damask118 Under a pull 2
4Sep20- 4Bel fst 1⅝ :47^{4} 1:38^{2} 2:03^{3} 2:40^{4} Lawrence Realizatn 16k 2 1 1^{20} 1^{30} 1^{50} 1^{100} Kummer C 126 w *.01 134-00 Man o' War126 100Hoodwink116 Restrained at end 2
21Aug20- 4Sar fst 1¼ :46^{3} 1:10 1:35^{3} 2:01^{4} Travers 12k 1 1 1^{2} 1^{4} 1^{4} 1 2½ Schuttinger A 129 w *.22 102-08 Mano'War129 2½Upset123^{7}JohnP.Grier115 Restrained in str 3
7Aug20- 4Sar fst 1 3/16 :48^{1} 1:12^{4} 1:37^{4} 1:56^{3} Miller 5.7k 2 1 1 1½ 1^{3} 1^{4} 1^{6} Sande E 131 w *.03 97-09 Mano'War131^{6}Donnacona119^{4}KingAlbert114 Never extended 3
10Jly20- 4Aqu fst 1⅛ :46 1:09^{3} 1:36 1:49^{1} Dwyer 5.5k 1 1 1^{hd} 1^{hd} 1½ 1 1½ Kummer C 126 w *.20 101-08 Man o' War126 1½John P. Grier108 Hard ridden,drew away 2
22Jun20- 4Jam gd 1 :25^{3} :49 1:14^{1} 1:41^{3} Stuyvesant H 4.5k 1 1 1^{4} 1^{7} 1^{8} 1^{8} Kummer C 135 w *.01 86-13 Man o' War135^{8}Yellow Hand103 Eased final ⅛ 2
12Jun20- 4Bel fst 1⅜ 2:14^{1} Belmont 9.2k 1 1 1^{2} 1^{7} 1^{12} 1^{20} Kummer C 126 w *.04 116-10 Man o' War126 20Donnacona126 Taken up final 1/16 2
29May20- 4Bel fst 1 :24 :47^{1} 1:11 1:35^{4} Withers 5.8k 2 1 1 1½ 1^{2} 1^{2} 1^{2} Kummer C 118 w *.14 104-10 Man o' War118^{2}Wildair118 12David Harum118 Won under pull 3
18May20- 4Pim fst 1⅛ :47^{3} 1:12^{2} 1:38^{1} 1:51^{3} Preakness 29k 7 1 1 1½ 1^{4} 1^{2} 1 1½ Kummer C 126 w *.80 97-10 Man o' War126 1½Upset122^{5}Wildair114^{5} Speed in reserve 9
13Sep19- 3Bel fst 6f-Str 1:11^{3} Futurity 31k 8 2 3 1½ 1½ 1^{2} 1 2½ Loftus J 127 w *.50 85-21 Mano'War127 2½JohnP.Grier117^{4}Dominiqu122^{nk} Won easing up 10
30Aug19- 3Sar sl 6f :23 :47 1:13 Hopeful 29k 3 4 2^{2} 2^{1} 1^{5} 1^{4} Loftus J 130 w *.45 87-14 Man o' War130^{4}Cleopatra112^{4}Constancy124^{2} Easily 8
23Aug19- 3Sar fst 6f :22^{3} :46^{2} 1:12 Grand Union Hotel 9.8k 2 3 1^{hd} 1^{3} 1^{3} 1^{1} Loftus J 130 w *.55 92-08 Man o' War130^{1}Upset125^{4}Blazes122½ Eased final 16th 10
13Aug19- 4Sar fst 6f :23^{1} :46^{4} 1:11^{1} Sanford Memorial 4.9k 6 5 4 1½ 3^{2} 3 1½ 2½ Loftus J 130 w *.55 95-09 Upst115½Mno'Wr130^{3}GoldnBroom130^{2} Slow start,gaining 7
2Aug19- 3Sar fst 6f :23 :47^{1} 1:12^{2} U S Hotel 9.8k 8 1 1^{3} 1^{3} 1^{4} 1^{2} Loftus J 130 w *.90 90-13 Man o' War130^{2}Upset115^{1}Homely112^{1} Eased final 16th 10
5Jly19- 3Aqu fst 6f :23^{3} :47^{2} 1:13 Tremont 5.8k 2 2 1^{1} 1^{1} 1 1½ 1^{1} Loftus J 130 w *.10 90-12 Man o' War130^{1}Ralco115^{20}Ace of Aces112 Never extended 3
23Jun19- 3Aqu fst 5f 1:01^{3} Hudson 3.4k 2 1 1½ 1^{1} 1^{1} 1 1½ Loftus J 130 w *.10e 83-12 Mano'War130 1½VioletTip109^{4}Shoal115^{12} Broke thru barrier 5
21Jun19- 3Jam gd 5½f :23^{1} :47^{3} 1:00^{1} 1:06^{3} Youthful 4.8k 4 3 1^{1} 1^{2} 1^{4} 1 2½ Loftus J 120 w *.50 92-09 Mno'War120 2½OnWtch108^{2}LdyBrumml105^{10} Easing final 16th 4
9Jun19- 4Bel sl 5½f-Str 1:05^{3} Keene Mem 5.2k 3 2 2½ 3¾ 3^{1} 1^{3} Loftus J 115 w *.70 91-17 Man o' War115^{3}On Watch115½Anniversary115^{4} Drew away 6
6Jun19- 6Bel fst 5f-Str :59 Md Sp Wt 7 1 2^{nk} 2½ 1^{3} 1^{6} Loftus J 115 w *.60 83-18 Man o' War115^{6}Retrieve112½Neddam115^{4}
Easily 7

Past Performances of Great Horses of the 20th Century

Nashua

b. c. 1952, by Nasrullah (Nearco)–Segula, by Johnstown
Own.–Leslie Combs II
Br.– Belair Stud Inc (Ky)
Tr.– J. Fitzsimmons

Lifetime record: 30 22 4 1 $1,288,565

Date/Race	Cond	Dist	Fractions	Race	PP	St	1C	2C	Str	Fin	Jockey	Wt	Odds	Fig	Company	Comment	Field
13Oct56-6Bel	fst	2	:491 2:282 2:541 3:202	3↑ J C Gold Cup 54k	1	1	1½	2hd	11½	12¼	Arcaro E	124wb	*.75	102-09	Nashua1242¼Rily1191¾ hrdBrothr1194	Kept to strong drive	7
29Sep56-7Bel	gd	1¼	:47 1:112 1:371 2:03	3↑ Woodward 80k	1	2	1hd	3nk	31½	22½	Arcaro E	126wb	*.30	82-12	Mister Gus1262½Nashua126½Jet Action12620	No excuse	4
14Jly56-6Mth	my	1¼	:46 1:11 1:364 2:024	3↑ Monmouth H 114k	7	1	14	14	14	13½	Arcaro E	129wb	*.30	92-20	Nashua1293½Mr. First 105Mielleux1071	Speed in reserve	8
4Jly56-7Bel	fst	1¼	:463 1:101 1:35 2:004	3↑ Suburban H 83k	4	2	2hd	2hd	2½	11¼	Arcaro E	128wb	*1.20	96-10	Nashua1281¼Dedicat1 12¼Subhdr1125	Well rated,going away	8
30Jun56-7Bel	fst	7f	:221 :452 1:102 1:231	3↑ Carter H 58k	3	6	44½	65	62¾	73½	Arcaro E	130 w	*1.10	90-12	Red Hannigan1141½Switch On119½Artismo111¾	Well up,hung	10
30May56-7Bel	fst	1	:224 :451 1:094 1:35	3↑ Metropolitan H 55k	7	1	32½	42½	53	4¾	Arcaro E	130 w	*.65	98-09	Midaftrnoon111hdSwtchOn113½Fnd116nk	Came again too late	7
19May56-7GS	fst	1⅛	:463 1:111 1:362 1:491	3↑ Camden H 33k	4	1	11	1½	11	12	Arcaro E	129 w	*.40	91-10	Nashua1292Fisherman1201½Mielleux1102	Very handy score	5
5May56-7Jam	fst	1⅛	:49 1:13 1:38 1:503	3↑ Grey Lag H 55k	6	3	2hd	1hd	1hd	1hd	Atkinson T	128 w	*.95	93-17	Nashua128hdFind118hdFisherman1201¾	Almost fell at start	7
17Mar56-8GP	fst	1¼	:47 1:113 1:36 2:003	3↑ Gulf Park H 112k	6	5	43½	53¼	56	57	Arcaro E	129 w	*.70	89-08	Sailor1191¾Mielleux1101Find116¾	Wide both turns,tired	7
18Feb56-8Hia	fst	1¼	:463 1:104 1:353 2:02	3↑ Widener H 129k	9	3	41¾	2½	2hd	1hd	Arcaro E	127 w	*.40	95-11	Nashua127hdSocilOut st121hdSlor119nk	Under strong drive	9
	Previously owned by Belair Stud																
15Oct55-6Bel	sly	2	:494 2:321 2:583 3:244	3↑ J C Gold Cup 79k	3	2	1½	11	13½	15	Arcaro E	119 w	*.25	80-14	Nashua1195Thinking Cap11915Mark's Puzzle1198	Easy score	5
24Sep55-6Bel	sly	1⅛	:451 1:101 1:36 1:491	3↑ Sysonby 106k	5	1	41½	3nk	22	31¾	Arcaro E	121 w	*.65	91-10	HighGun126hdJetActr1261¾Nshu1213½	Weakened when urged	5
31Aug55-7Was	gd	1¼	:46 1:102 1:373 2:041	WP Match 100k	1	1	1½	11½	12	16½	Arcaro E	126 w	1.20	81-17	Nashua1266½Swaps126	Drew far out to handy score	2
16Jly55-7AP	fst	1	:231 :453 1:093 1:351	Arl Classic 148k	2	2	22	24	21	1½	Arcaro E	126 w	*.30	96-10	Nashua126½Traffic Judge1201¼Impromptu1204	Under a drive	7
2Jly55-0Aqu	fst	1¼	:493 1:134 1:382 2:034	Dwyer 55k	3	1	1½	11½	11½	15	Arcaro E	126 w	-	88-15	Nashua1265Saratoga12240Mainlander114	Easing up late	3
	Run as special event with no wagering																
11Jun55-6Bel	fst	1½	:49 1:133 2:042 2:29	Belmont 119k	5	2	1hd	12½	16	19	Arcaro E	126 w	*.15	93-12	Nashua1269Blazing Count1265½Portersville1266	A romp	8
	Geldings not eligible																
28May55-7Pim	fst	1 3/16	:471 1:11 1:353 1:543	Preakness 116k	5	4	42½	2hd	1hd	11	Arcaro E	126 w	*.30	106-08	Nashua1261Saratoga1267TrafficJudg126nk	Rated,mild drive	8
7May55-7CD	fst	1¼	:472 1:122 1:37 2:014	Ky Derby 152k	5	3	31	2½	2½	21½	Arcaro E	126 w	*1.30	95-12	Swaps1261½Nashua1266½Summer Tan1264	Good bid,no excuse	10
23Apr55-6Jam	fst	1⅛	:471 1:111 1:363 1:503	Wood Memorial 111k	4	2	21½	22	21½	1nk	Atkinson T	126 w	1.10	93-17	Nashua126nkSummer Tan12625Simmy1266	Sensational score	5
26Mar55-7GP	sly	1⅛	:463 1:122 1:391 1:531	Fla Derby 148k	1	5	56½	22½	2½	1nk	Arcaro E	122 w	*.95	73-26	Nashua122nkBlueLem1132¼FirstCabin1131	Unruly,hard urged	9
26Feb55-7Hia	fst	1⅛	:462 1:113 1:371 1:493	Flamingo 141k	2	2	1hd	1hd	1hd	11½	Arcaro E	122 w	*.70	88-12	Nashua1221½Saratoga1224½CupMan1227	Drifted out in drive	12
21Feb55-0Hia	fst	1 1/16	:231 :47 1:114 1:441	Alw 7500	2	2	3nk	2hd	1½	11½	Arcaro E	126wb	-	94-11	Nshua1261½Munchausen1172HappyMemries1142½	Unruly late	4
	Special event run between 2nd and 3rd races - No wagering																
9Oct54-6Bel	fst	6½f-W	:222 :451 1:092 1:153	Futurity 112k	6	4		21	1½	1hd	Arcaro E	122wb	*.65	94-06	Nshua122hdSummrTan122¾RoylCoinage1227	Held on gamely	7
	Geldings not eligible																
1Oct54-6Bel	fst	6f-WC	:22 :442 1:081	Sp Wt 10000	4	2		4¾	2hd	11	Arcaro E	118wb	*1.05	100-00	Nashua1181Royal Coinage1185Pyrenees1181½	Clever score	7
21Sep54-6Aqu	fst	6½f	:223 :451 1:092 1:16	Cowdin 30k	9	1	2hd	4¾	41½	21½	Arcaro E	124wb	*1.25	101-12	SummerTn1201½Nshua124¾Bunny'sBabe1201½	Mildly impeded	10
28Aug54-6Sar	fst	6½f	:23 :464 1:111 1:174	Hopeful 78k	4	1	1½	1hd	11	1nk	Arcaro E	122wb	*.55e	96-18	Nashua122nkSummrTan1221½Pyrens1221½	Well rated,held on	8
21Aug54-4Sar	fst	6f	:23 :463 :592 1:122	Grand Union Hotel 27k	5	2	23	1hd	12	11¾	Arcaro E	122 w	2.75e	86-17	Nashua1221¾Pyrens1152½ModlAc1143½	Won in clever fashion	6
19May54-7GS	fst	5f	:221 :454 :583	Cherry Hill 20k	3	5	2½	22	21½	2nk	Higley J	119 w	3.80	98-13	RoyalNote122nkNashua1195Menolen1191½	Unruly all the way	11
12May54-6Bel	fst	5f-WC	:221 :453 :58	Juvenile 15k	1	2		1hd	2½	1½	Arcaro E	117 w	3.00e	89-18	Nshua117½SummerTn1228Lugh1172	Scored under clever ride	8
5May54-4Bel	fst	4½f-W	:222 :462 :523	©Md Sp Wt	14	9		81½	11½	13	Higley J	118 w	8.50e	86-14	Nashua1183Retract118½Danger Quest118no	Won in hand	21

Past Performances of Great Horses of the 20th Century

Native Dancer gr. c. 1950, by Polynesian (Unbreakable)–Geisha, by Discovery

Lifetime record: 22 21 1 0 $785,240

Own.– A.G. Vanderbilt
Br.– Alfred G. Vanderbilt (Ky)
Tr.– W.C. Winfrey

16Aug54-0Sar	sly 7f	:23^3 :47^2 1:12 1:24^4	3↑ Handicap 5025	2	3	2^{2½}	2^2	1^8	1^9	Guerin E	137	w	-	91-19	Native Dancer137^{9}First Glance119^{4½}Gigantic107	Easily 3
15May54-6Bel	fst 1	:23^1 :46 1:10^1 1:35^1	3↑ Metropolitan H 39k	3	8	7^{7¾}	5^7	2^{3½}	1^{nk}	Guerin E	130	w	*.25	98-11	Native Dancer130^{nk}Straight Face117^{6}Jamie K.110^2	Just up 9
7May54-6Bel	fst 6f	:22^4 :46^3 1:11^4	3↑ Alw 15000	4	3	4^2	3^1	1^2	1^{1¼}	Guerin E	126	w	*.15	90-15	Native Dancer126^{1¼}Laffango121^{nk}Impasse114^{nk}	Easily best 7
22Aug53-7Was	fst 1⅛	:46^2 1:10^3 1:35^2 1:48^2	American Derby 112k	4	7	7^{11}	4^{5½}	4^{1¾}	1^2	Arcaro E	128	w	*.20e	99-11	NativeDancr128^{2}Landlocked120^{1¼}PrecousSton114^3	Drew out 8
15Aug53-6Sar	fst 1¼	:49^4 1:14 1:39^3 2:05^3	Travers 27k	1	3	3^1	2^{1½}	1^1	1^{5½}	Guerin E	126	w	*.05	80-20	NativeDancer126^{5½}Dictar120^{2½}GuardianII114^1	Easily best 5
	Geldings not eligible															
18Jly53-7AP	hy 1	:23^2 :47^1 1:11^4 1:38	Arl Classic 154k	4	6	6^7	3^4	1^3	1^9	Guerin E	126	w	*.70	82-25	NativeDancer126^{9}SirMango120^{hd}VanCrosby120^2	Easily best 8
4Jly53-6Aqu	fst 1¼	:49^4 1:14 1:39^2 2:05^1	Dwyer 56k	3	4	3^{3½}	1^{1½}	1^{2½}	1^{1¾}	Guerin E	126	w	*.05	81-17	NativeDancer126^{1¾}[D]Dictar114^{2}GuardnII114^4	Much the best 5
13Jun53-6Bel	fst 1½	:50^1 1:15 2:04^1 2:28^3	Belmont 118k	5	4	3^{2½}	2^{hd}	1^{hd}	1^{nk}	Guerin E	126	w	*.45	95-11	NativeDancr126^{nk}JamieK.126^{10}RoylByGm126^{4½}	Held gamely 6
	Geldings not eligible															
23May53-7Pim	fst 1 3/16	:47 1:11^4 1:38^2 1:57^4	Preakness 113k	4	3	3^3	2^{hd}	1^{hd}	1^{nk}	Guerin E	126	w	*.20	91-19	NativeDancer126^{nk}JamieK.126^{6}RoyalBayGem126^2	Hard drive 7
16May53-6Bel	fst 1	:23^4 :47^1 1:11^3 1:36^1	Withers 32k	3	2	2^{½}	1^{½}	1^{2½}	1^4	Guerin E	126	w	*.05	93-12	Native Dancer126^{4}Invigorator126^{2½}Real Brother126	Easily 3
	Geldings not eligible															
2May53-7CD	fst 1¼	:47^4 1:12^1 1:36^3 2:02	Ky Derby 118k	6	8	4^{2½}	4^{2½}	2^{1½}	2^{hd}	Guerin E	126	w	*.70e	97-09	DarkStar126^{hd}NativeDancer126^{5}Invgortor126^2	Roughed,wide 11
25Apr53-6Jam	fst 1⅛	:50 1:13^3 1:37^1 1:50^3	Wood Memorial 123k	4	2	3^1	2^{hd}	1^{½}	1^{4½}	Guerin E	126	w	*.10e	93-12	NativeDancer126^{4½}TahitianKing126^{hd}Invigortor126^3	Easily 7
	Geldings not eligible															
18Apr53-6Jam	fst 1 1/16	:24^2 :49 1:13^4 1:44^1	Gotham (Div 1) 35k	8	4	6^{2¾}	4^{1¼}	2^{hd}	1^2	Guerin E	120	w	*.15	91-10	NatveDancr120^{2}MagicLmp120^{3}Sckl'sSound120^{1¼}	Ridden out 9
22Oct52-6Jam	fst 1 1/16	:24^2 :48 1:12^3 1:44^1	©East View 56k	1	4	4^6	3^3	1^{½}	1^{1½}	Guerin E	122	w	*.20	91-15	Native Dancer122^{1½}Laffango122^{9}Teds Jeep122^{1½}	Ridden out 6
	Geldings not eligible															
27Sep52-6Bel	fst 6½f-W	:21^4 :44^2 1:08^2 1:14^2	Futurity 107k	8	6		5^4	2^{½}	1^{2¼}	Guerin E	122	w	*.35	100-05	NativeDancer122^{2¼}TahitianKing122^{4}DarkStr122^3	Ridden out 10
	Geldings not eligible															
22Sep52-5Bel	fst 6f-WC	:22 :44^3 1:09^3	Sp Wt 5000	6	6		5^3	1^2	1^{1¼}	Guerin E	118	w	*.40	93-07	NativeDancer118^{1¼}TahitianKing118^{2¼}Reprimnd118^{hd}	In hand 8
30Aug52-6Sar	fst 6½f	:23^3 :48 1:12^3 1:18^4	Hopeful 62k	4	1	6^{2¾}	5^{2½}	2^{hd}	1^2	Guerin E	122	w	*.25	91-19	Native Dancer122^{2}Tiger Skin122^{2}Platan122^1	Handily 7
23Aug52-4Sar	fst 6f	:22^4 :46^2 1:11^1	Grand Union Hotel 20k	1	2	3^1	1^{½}	1^{1½}	1^{3½}	Guerin E	126	w	*.55	92-17	NativeDancer126^{3½}Laffango122^{2½}TahitianKing122^{5½}	In hand 5
16Aug52-4Sar	sly 6f	:23^1 :46^4 1:13^1	Sar Spl 17k	4	2	4^{2½}	4^2	1^1	1^{3½}	Guerin E	122	w	*.70	82-22	NativeDancr122^{3½}DocWalkr122^{4}SouthPont122^{3½}	Ridden out 8
4Aug52-6Sar	fst 5½f	:23^1 :47 :59^3 1:06	Flash 10k	6	4	3^1	3^1	1^{½}	1^{2¼}	Guerin E	122	w	*.80	87-20	Native Dancer122^{2¼}Tiger Skin114^{2}Bradley122^{no}	Easily 7
23Apr52-6Jam	fst 5f	:22^3 :46^3 :59^2	©Youthful 14k	4	2	2^1	2^{hd}	1^3	1^6	Guerin E	117	w	*.90	93-19	NativeDancr117^{6}Tribe122^{1½}[DH]Mr.Mdnght117^1	Much the best 12
19Apr52-2Jam	fst 5f	:23 :47 :59^3	Md Sp Wt	9	7	4^2	4^2	1^{½}	1^{4½}	Guerin E	118	w	*1.40	92-16	Native Dancer118^{4½}Putney118^{nk}Khan118^{hd}	Drew out easily 9

Past Performances of Great Horses of the 20th Century

Personal Ensign

b. f. 1984, by Private Account (Damascus)–Grecian Banner, by Hoist the Flag — **Lifetime record: 13 13 0 0 $1,679,880**

Own.– Ogden Phipps
Br.– Ogden Phipps (Ky)
Tr.– Claude McGaughey III

5Nov88- 6CD my 1⅛ :474 1:12 1:381 1:52 3↑ ⒻBC Distaff-G1 6 6 58½ 58 34 1no Romero RP 123 *.50 82-20 Personal Ensign123noWinning Colors119½Goodbye Halo1195 9
Tight early,just up
16Oct88- 8Bel fst 1¼ :481 1:12 1:362 2:011 3↑ ⒻBeldame-G1 1 3 22 2hd 12 15½ Romero RP 123 *.10 92-16 PersorlEnsign1235½ClassicCrown118½ShmSy1187 Ridden out 5
10Sep88- 8Bel fst 1 :224 :451 1:09 1:341 3↑ ⒻMaskette-G1 2 3 36 22 2hd 1¾ Romero RP 123 *.30 94-14 PersonalEnsgn123¾WinningColrs1185¼ShmSy11511¼ Driving 4
6Aug88- 8Sar sly 1⅛ :472 1:113 1:353 1:474 3↑ Whitney H-G1 3 3 33 21 1hd 11½ Romero RP 117 *.80 96-12 PersonalEnsign1171½Gulch12417King'sSwan123 Brisk urging 3
4Jly88-10Mth fst 1 1/16 :24 :472 1:104 1:414 3↑ ⒻMolly Pitcher H-G2 5 3 23 2½ 12½ 18 Romero RP 125 *.40 96-14 Personal Ensign1258Grecian Flight1197Le L'Argent1171 5
Bumped,forced wide
11Jun88- 7Bel fst 1⅛ :471 1:112 1:353 1:473 3↑ ⒻHempstead H-G1 5 3 31½ 31 14 17 Romero RP 123 *.40 89-13 PersonlEnsgn1237HometwnQun1092ClbbrGrl118nk Ridden out 5
15May88- 8Bel fst 1 1/16 :23 :453 1:10 1:413 3↑ ⒻShuvee H-G1 5 3 33 2hd 1½ 11¾ Romero RP 121 *.70 94-15 Personal Ensign1211¾Clabber Girl1183¼Bishop's Delight1112¾ 6
Driving
18Oct87- 8Bel fst 1¼ :493 1:134 1:382 2:042 3↑ ⒻBeldame-G1 8 2 2½ 13 14 12¼ Romero RP 118 1.30 76-23 PersnlEnsgn1182¼CoundFusl1232½SlntTurn1183¾ Drew clear 10
10Oct87- 5Bel fst 1 :223 :454 1:102 1:363 ⒻRare Perfume-G2 2 3 11 15 15 14¾ Romero RP 115 *.80 82-22 PrsnlEnsign1154¾OneFromHevn1183¾KyBd1181½ Ridden out 9
24Sep87- 5Bel fst 1 :233 :464 1:113 1:361 3↑ ⒻAlw 33000 5 2 12½ 13 15 17¾ Romero RP 113 *.20 84-20 PersonalEnsign1137¾WithaTwist117nkRosaMay1176 Handily 5
6Sep87- 5Bel fst 7f :232 :462 1:103 1:231 3↑ ⒻAlw 31000 3 5 43 1hd 11½ 13¾ Bailey JD 113 *.70 86-19 PersonalEnsign1133¾ChicShirine1131¼WithTwst117½ Handily 6
13Oct86- 8Bel fst 1 :232 :46 1:101 1:362 ⒻFrizette-G1 2 2 2½ 2hd 1hd 1hd Romero RP 119 *.30 83-16 PersonalEnsign119hdCollins1195½FlyingKatuna119 Driving 3
28Sep86- 6Bel my 7f :231 :453 1:103 1:224 ⒻMd Sp Wt 5 7 22½ 11½ 17 112¾ Romero RP 117 *.90 88-15 Personal Ensign11712Graceful Darby1172¾Nastique1171½ 7
Hesitated start,clear

Ruffian

dkbbr. f. 1972, by Reviewer (Bold Ruler)–Shenanigans, by Native Dancer — **Lifetime record: 11 10 0 0 $313,429**

Own.– Locust Hill Farm
Br.– Mr & Mrs Stuart S. Janney Jr (Ky)
Tr.– F.Y. Whiteley Jr

6Jly75- 8Bel fst 1¼ :443 1:083 1:352 2:024 Match Race 350k 1 1 - - - - Vasquez J 121 *.40 -- Foolish Pleasure126 Broke down 2
21Jun75- 8Bel fst 1½ :49 1:132 2:031 2:274 ⒻC C A Oaks-G1 5 1 14 11½ 13 12¾ Vasquez J 121 *.05 81-12 Ruffn1212¾EqulChng 219LtMLngr1212¼ Confidently ridden 7
31May75- 8Aqu fst 1⅛ :473 1:113 1:353 1:474 ⒻMother Goose-G1 6 1 11¾ 12 18 113½ Vasquez J 121 *.10 96-07 Rffian12113½SweetOldGirl1212SunandSnow1212½ Easy score 7
10May75- 8Aqu fst 1 :232 :453 1:093 1:342 ⒻAcorn-G1 3 1 11 13 17 18¼ Vasquez J 121 *.10 94-08 Ruffian1218¼Somethingregal121noGallantTrial1211 In hand 7
30Apr75- 8Aqu fst 7f :224 :45 1:084 1:211 ⒻComely-G3 3 5 11 11½ 16 17¾ Vasquez J 113 *.05 95-16 Ruffian1137¾AuntJin 132½PointnTm1132 Slow start,handily 5
14Apr75- 8Aqu fst 6f :23 :454 1:092 ⒻAlw 20000 2 3 11 1½ 12 14¾ Vasquez J 122 *.10 96-17 Ruffian1224¾SirIvor'sSorrow113hdChannelette1132 Easily 5
23Aug74- 8Sar fst 6f :221 :444 1:083 ⒻSpinaway-G1 2 1 12 13 17 112¾ Bracciale V Jr 120 *.20 97-10 Ruffian12012¾LaughingBridge1201½ScottshMlody1205 Easily 4
27Jly74- 8Mth fst 6f :213 :441 1:09 ⒻSorority-G1 3 3 1½ 1hd 1½ 12¼ Vasquez J 119 *.30 95-15 Ruffian1192¼Hot n Nasty11922Stream Across1194 Driving 4
10Jly74- 8Aqu fst 5½f :214 :442 :562 1:024 ⒻAstoria-G3 2 2 11 13 16 19 Bracciale V Jr 118 *.10 99-15 Ruffian1189Laughing Bridge11512Our Dancing Girl1153¼ 4
Speed to spare
12Jun74- 8Bel fst 5½f :222 :451 :57 1:03 ⒻFashion-G3 3 4 11½ 11½ 14 16¾ Vasquez J 117 *.40 100-12 Ruffian1176¾Copernica11713Jan Verzal117nk Ridden out 6
22May74- 3Bel fst 5½f :221 :45 :57 1:03 ⒻMd Sp Wt 9 8 13 15 18 115 Vasquez J 116 4.20 100-15 Ruffian11615Suzest1 35Garden Quad116½ Ridden out 10

Past Performances of Great Horses of the 20th Century

Seabiscuit

b. c. 1933, by Hard Tack (Man o' War)–Swing On, by Whisk Broom II
Own.– C.S. Howard
Br.– Wheatley Stable (Ky)
Tr.– T. Smith

Lifetime record: 89 33 15 13 $437,730

2Mar40-6SA	fst 1$\frac{1}{4}$	:47^1 1:11^1 1:36 2:01^1	3↑ S Anita H 121k	12 5	2^1	2^{hd}	1^{hd}	$1^{1\frac{1}{2}}$	Pollard J	130wb	*.70e	101-11	Seabiscuit130$^{1\frac{1}{2}}$Kayak II129^{1}Whichcee114$^{1\frac{1}{2}}$	13
	Avoided trouble first turn													
24Feb40-6SA	fst 1$\frac{1}{16}$	:23^1 :46^4 1:11^1 1:42^2	3↑ S Antonio H 13k	10 5	$2^{\frac{1}{2}}$	$2^{\frac{1}{2}}$	$1^{\frac{1}{2}}$	$1^{2\frac{1}{2}}$	Pollard J	124wb	*1.70e	100-07	Seabiscuit124$^{2\frac{1}{2}}$Kayak II128$^{\frac{1}{2}}$Viscounty110^4	Much best 13
17Feb40-6SA	fst 7f	:22^3 :45^3 1:10^3 1:23^2	3↑ San Carlos H 12k	1 2	9^4	$8^{5\frac{1}{4}}$	6^9	$6^{6\frac{3}{4}}$	Pollard J	127wb	*.80e	88-14	Specify115$^{1\frac{1}{4}}$Lassator105^{hd}Viscounty109^3	Close quarters 11
9Feb40-6SA	fst 7f	:22^4 :45^4 1:10^3 1:23	4↑ Handicap 2000	2 5	$5^{2\frac{1}{4}}$	$6^{3\frac{3}{4}}$	$4^{3\frac{1}{4}}$	3^3	Pollard J	128wb	*1.00	94-13	Heelfly118^{1}Sun Egret115^{2}Seabiscuit128^3	Close quarters 8
14Feb39-6SA	fst 1	:22^3 :45^3 1:10^2 1:35^3	4↑ Alw 1900	1 3	2^{nk}	2^3	2^3	$2^{2\frac{1}{4}}$	Woolf G	128wb	*.20	99-06	Today104$^{2\frac{1}{4}}$Seabiscuit128^{6}Marica113	Went lame 3
1Nov38-6Pim	fst 1$\frac{3}{16}$	:47^3 1:11^4 1:36^4 1:56^3	3↑ Pim Spl 15k	2 1	1^1	1no	$1^{\frac{1}{2}}$	1^4	Woolf G	120wb	2.20	101-08	Seabiscuit120^{4}War Admiral120	Driving,best 2
15Oct38-5Lrl	fst 1	:23^1 :47^2 1:12^1 1:37	2↑ Laurel 10k	6 8	$6^{3\frac{1}{2}}$	$4^{1\frac{1}{4}}$	$2^{1\frac{1}{2}}$	$2^{2\frac{1}{2}}$	Woolf G	126wsb	*.60	98-12	Jacola102$^{2\frac{1}{2}}$Seabiscuit126^{3}The Chief116^4	Second best 12
28Sep38-5HdG	fst 1$\frac{1}{8}$	:47^2 1:12^2 1:37^2 1:50	3↑ Havre de Grace H 11k	6 5	$3^{2\frac{1}{2}}$	$2^{\frac{1}{2}}$	1^1	$1^{2\frac{1}{2}}$	Woolf G	128wb	*.55	99-16	Seabiscuit128$^{2\frac{1}{2}}$Savage Beauty103^{1}Menow120$^{1\frac{1}{2}}$	Going away 8
20Sep38-5Bel	my 1$\frac{1}{2}$	:49 1:14 2:05^1 2:31	3↑ Manhattan H 6k	4 1	$5^{2\frac{3}{4}}$	$5^{3\frac{1}{2}}$	$3^{4\frac{1}{4}}$	3^3	Woolf G	128wb	*1.20	85-12	Isolater108^{hd}Regal Lily108^{3}Seabiscuit128^{10}	Forced wide 5
12Aug38-5Dmr	fst 1$\frac{1}{8}$	:46^2 1:10^4 1:36^1 1:49	3↑ Match Race 25k	1 2	2^{hd}	1^{hd}	1^{hd}	1no	Woolf G	130wb	-	124-02	Seabiscuit130^{no}Ligaroti115	Driving 2
16Jly38-7Hol	fst 1$\frac{1}{4}$	:47^1 1:11^2 1:37^3 2:03^4	3↑ Hol Gold Cup 55k	7 8	9^{12}	4^8	2^4	$1^{1\frac{1}{2}}$	Woolf G	133wb	*.70	- -	Seabiscuit133$^{1\frac{1}{2}}$Specify109^{no}Whichcee114^5	Going away 10
4Jly38-6AP	sl 1$\frac{1}{8}$	:48^4 1:14^3 1:41 1:54^1	3↑ Stars & Stripes H 12k	10 7	$9^{7\frac{3}{4}}$	6^7	$4^{2\frac{1}{2}}$	$2^{3\frac{1}{2}}$	Woolf G	130wb	*.90	72-30	WarMinstrel107$^{3\frac{1}{2}}$Seabiscut130$^{\frac{1}{2}}$Arb'sArrow111^4	Closed fast 10
16Apr38-7BM	fst 1$\frac{1}{8}$	:47^4 1:11^4 1:37 1:49	3↑ Bay Meadows H 16k	7 2	2^1	2^{hd}	1^1	1^3	Woolf G	133wb	*.20e	107-10	Seabiscuit133^{3}Gosum113$^{1\frac{3}{4}}$Today112^{no}	Going away 7
27Mar38-8AC	fst 1$\frac{1}{8}$	:47 1:11^4 1:37 1:50^2	3↑ Agua Caliente H 13k	1 1	$1^{\frac{1}{2}}$	$1^{1\frac{1}{2}}$	1^3	1^2	Rich'son N	130wb	*.30	97-13	Seabiscuit130^{2}Gray Jack103^{hd}Little Nymph98$^{4\frac{1}{2}}$	Eased up 8
5Mar38-6SA	fst 1$\frac{1}{4}$	:46^1 1:11^1 1:36^4 2:01^3	3↑ S Anita H 126k	12 14	$12^{7\frac{1}{2}}$	1^{hd}	1^{hd}	2no	Woolf G	130wb	*1.90	103-12	Stagehand100^{no}Seabisct130^{6}Pmpoon120^2	Impeded,game try 18
26Feb38-6SA	fst 1$\frac{1}{8}$	:47 1:11^3 1:37^1 1:50	3↑ San Antonio H 9.2k	5 5	4^6	$4^{2\frac{1}{2}}$	$3^{\frac{1}{2}}$	2no	Workman R	130wb	*.40e	94-12	Aneroid118^{no}Seabiscuit130$^{1\frac{1}{2}}$IndianBroom108^{hd}	Just missed 13
11Nov37-6Pim	fst 1$\frac{5}{8}$	:50^1 1:41 2:06^2 2:45^1	3↑ Bowie H 12k	8 3	$5^{2\frac{3}{4}}$	$4^{1\frac{1}{4}}$	1^{hd}	2no	Pollard J	130wb	*1.25	107-11	Esposa115^{no}Seabiscuit130$^{1\frac{1}{4}}$Burning Star114^1	Game try 8
5Nov37-5Pim	fst 1$\frac{3}{16}$	:47 1:11^3 1:37 1:57^2	3↑ Riggs H 12k	11 4	$5^{5\frac{1}{2}}$	$4^{\frac{3}{4}}$	$1^{\frac{1}{2}}$	1^{nk}	Pollard J	130wb	*.40e	103-11	Seabiscuit130^{nk}BurningStar114$^{\frac{3}{4}}$CaballroII116$^{\frac{1}{2}}$	Hard drive 11
	Previously owned by Mrs C.S. Howard													
16Oct37-5Lrl	fst 1	:24 :47^1 1:12^1 1:37^2	2↑ Laurel 9.6k	7 3	2^{hd}	2^{nk}	1^{hd}	$1^{1\frac{1}{2}}$●	Pollard J	126wb	*.70	99-14	[DH]Seabiscuit126[DH]Heelfly114$^{1\frac{1}{2}}$Deliberator116^1	Gamely 7
12Oct37-5Jam	fst 1$\frac{1}{16}$	:24 :48 1:12^4 1:44^4	3↑ Continental H 12k	2 1	1^{hd}	1^{nk}	1^2	1^5	Pollard J	130wb	*.80	89-20	Seabiscuit130^{5}Caballero II117^{2}Moon Side112^1	Easily 12
11Sep37-5Nar	sly 1$\frac{3}{16}$	:47^3 1:12 1:38 1:57	3↑ Nar Spl H 33k	5 4	$4^{6\frac{1}{2}}$	$2^{1\frac{1}{2}}$	$3^{3\frac{1}{2}}$	$3^{2\frac{1}{2}}$	Pollard J	132wb	*.85	87-16	Calumet Dick115^{1}Snark117$^{1\frac{1}{2}}$Seabiscuit132^4	Weakened 6
7Aug37-5Suf	fst 1$\frac{1}{8}$	:47 1:11 1:36 1:49	3↑ Mass H 70k	3 3	$2^{2\frac{1}{2}}$	2^1	1^{nk}	1^1	Pollard J	130wb	*1.00	102-06	Seabiscuit130^{1}CaballeroII108^{1}FairKnghtss108$^{2\frac{1}{2}}$	Drove out 13
24Jly37-5Emp	fst 1$\frac{1}{16}$	:23^3 :47^2 1:11^3 1:44^1	3↑ Yonkers H 10k	2 2	2^2	1^{hd}	$1^{1\frac{1}{2}}$	1^4	Pollard J	129wb	*1.00	102-12	Seabiscuit129^{4}Jesting108^{3}Corinto109^3	Going away 6
10Jly37-5Emp	fst 1$\frac{3}{16}$	:48 1:12 1:38^2 1:58^3	3↑ Butler H 25k	1 2	$1^{\frac{1}{2}}$	$1^{\frac{1}{2}}$	$1^{1\frac{1}{2}}$	$1^{1\frac{1}{2}}$	Pollard J	126wb	*.90	98-08	Seabiscuit126$^{1\frac{1}{2}}$Thorson107^{3}Corinto109^1	Driving,best 6
26Jun37-5Aqu	fst 1$\frac{1}{8}$	:47 1:11^2 1:37 1:50^1	3↑ Brooklyn H 25k	1 1	1^1	$1^{\frac{1}{2}}$	1^{hd}	1no	Pollard J	122wb	3.20	90-14	Seabiscuit122^{no}Aneroid122^{5}Memory Book114^3	Hard drive 9
22May37-7BM	fst 1$\frac{1}{16}$	:24 :47^3 1:11 1:44^3	3↑ Bay Meadows H 11k	8 2	2^{nk}	2^1	$1^{\frac{1}{2}}$	$1^{1\frac{1}{4}}$	Pollard J	127wb	*.10e	87-15	Seabiscuit127$^{1\frac{1}{4}}$Exhibit105^{no}Watersplash103^1	Going away 8
17Apr37-6Tan	fst 1$\frac{1}{8}$	:45^2 1:10^3 1:36 1:48^4	3↑ Marchbank H 11k	7 1	1^5	1^2	1^4	1^3	Pollard J	124wb	*.40	94-08	Seabiscuit124^{3}Grand Manitou110^{hd}Sobriety109^5	Easily 7
6Mar37-6SA	fst 1$\frac{1}{8}$	:46^3 1:11 1:36^1 1:48^4	3↑ S Juan Capistrano H 12k	2 2	$2^{1\frac{1}{2}}$	2^{hd}	1^4	1^7	Pollard J	120wb	*1.50	103-08	Seabiscuit120^{7}GrandManitou108$^{\frac{3}{4}}$SpecialAgent116^{nk}	Easily 10
27Feb37-6SA	gd 1$\frac{1}{4}$	:45^4 1:10^4 1:36^4 2:02^4	3↑ S Anita H 125k	3 9	$4^{4\frac{1}{2}}$	$4^{1\frac{1}{2}}$	1^{hd}	2no	Pollard J	114wb	6.40	97-13	Rosemont124^{no}Seabiscuit114^{1}Indian Broom116$^{2\frac{1}{2}}$	Nosed out 18
20Feb37-6SA	fst 1$\frac{1}{8}$	:46^4 1:11 1:37^2 1:50^1	3↑ San Antonio H 9.4k	11 14	$12^{8\frac{3}{4}}$	$12^{9\frac{1}{4}}$	$9^{8\frac{3}{4}}$	$5^{3\frac{3}{4}}$	Pollard J	115wb	2.30	92-11	Rosemnt122$^{\frac{3}{4}}$StarShadow106$^{\frac{1}{2}}$SpecialAgent117^1	Forced wide 16
9Feb37-6SA	fst 7f	:22^4 :45^2 1:10^4 1:23^1	4↑ Handicap 1545	5 1	$1^{\frac{1}{2}}$	1^1	$1^{\frac{1}{2}}$	$1^{4\frac{1}{2}}$	Pollard J	112wb	3.20	96-13	Seabiscuit112$^{4\frac{1}{2}}$Sir Emerson104^{nk}Time Supply118^5	Easily 6
12Dec36-7BM	fst 1$\frac{3}{16}$	:47 1:11^2 1:36^4 1:55^4	2↑ World's Fair H 11k	4 3	1^5	1^3	1^3	1^5	Pollard J	113wb	*1.10	- -	Seabiscuit113^{5}Wildland101$^{2\frac{1}{2}}$GiantKiller107$^{1\frac{1}{2}}$	Easily best 7
28Nov36-7BM	fst 1	:23^2 :46^4 1:11^2 1:36	2↑ Bay Bridge H 2.7k	6 8	$5^{1\frac{3}{4}}$	2^2	1^{hd}	1^5	Pollard J	116wb	*2.20	106-07	Seabiscuit116^{5}Uppermost114$^{\frac{1}{2}}$Velociter107^{nk}	Eased up 8
31Oct36-4Emp	fst 1$\frac{1}{8}$	:49^1 1:14 1:39^2 1:52	3↑ Yorktown H 6.5k	7 6	5^4	$6^{6\frac{1}{2}}$	$3^{3\frac{1}{2}}$	$3^{1\frac{3}{4}}$	Pollard J	119wb	8.00	93-11	Thorson112^{nk}Piccolo107$^{1\frac{1}{2}}$Seabiscuit119^3	Closed fast 8
24Oct36-4Emp	fst 1 70	:23^3 :47^3 1:12^1 1:44	3↑ Scarsdale H 7.3k	2 7	$8^{4\frac{3}{4}}$	$8^{8\frac{3}{4}}$	$6^{3\frac{3}{4}}$	1no	Pollard J	116wb	12.00e	90-13	Seabiscuit116^{no}Jesting112^{hd}Piccolo105.5^3	Just up 11
17Oct36-6RD	my 1$\frac{1}{16}$	:26 :51 1:18 1:56^2	3↑ East Hills H 2.7k	4 2	2^2	2^4	2^3	$3^{2\frac{1}{2}}$	Pollard J	116wb	3.20	29-59	MuchoGusto111$^{1\frac{1}{2}}$SafeandSound103^{1}Sebscut116$^{2\frac{1}{2}}$	Closed well 6
3Oct36-5RD	fst 1$\frac{1}{16}$	:23^2 :46^4 1:11^3 1:44	3↑ Western Hills H 2.8k	7 4	$5^{2\frac{1}{4}}$	$5^{3\frac{1}{2}}$	$4^{3\frac{1}{2}}$	$3^{1\frac{1}{2}}$	Pollard J	116wb	4.90	92-16	Marynell100$^{\frac{1}{2}}$Cristate108^{1}Seabiscuit116^1	Closed fast 8

Past Performances of Great Horses of the 20th Century

Date	Cond/Dist	Fractions	Race	Running line	Jockey	Wt	Odds	Fig	Company line	Comment
26Sep36-6Det	fst 1 1/16	:243 :483 1:13 1:442	3↑ Hendrie H 2.8k	2 2 2½ 11 12 14	Pollard J	115wb	2.10	98-12	Seabiscuit1154Cristate1142½Safe and Sound1083	Easily 6
19Sep36-6Det	fst 1 1/16	:243 :483 1:133 1:46	3↑ De La Salle H 2.8k	7 1 11 31 63½ 63¾	Pollard J	115wb	*1.60	86-13	Cristate106hdProfessor Paul105hdParadisical1091½	Quit 8
7Sep36-6Det	fst 1⅛	:47 1:12 1:38 1:504	3↑ Governor's H 5.6k	12 3 2hd 2hd 1½ 1nk	Pollard J	109wb	4.90	96-13	Seabiscuit109nkProfessor Paul991½Azucar1123	Driving 12
2Sep36-6Det	sl 1 70	:243 :484 1:14 1:44	3↑ Handicap 1200	3 1 1hd 41¼ 31 3½	Pollard J	114wb	3.90	89-18	ProfessorPaul104noSafeandSound102½Seabsct1142½	Impeded 8
22Aug36-6Det	fst 1 1/16	:24 :47 1:113 1:432	3↑ Motor City H 5.7k	3 1 33 78 65 44¼	Pollard J	110wb	13.20	99-08	Myrtlewood1223Professor Paul95nkCristate1061	Tired 11
Previously owned by Wheatley Stable; previously trained by J. Fitzsimmons										
10Aug36-6Sar	gd 1⅛	:482 1:132 1:401 1:54	3↑ Handicap 1070	1 1 12 12 13 14	Stout J	112wb	*.90	80-17	Seabiscuit1124Treford110	Easily 2
3Aug36-5Sar	fst 1	:242 :481 1:124 1:382	3↑ Mohawk Claiming 6k	1 1 11½ 11 13 16	Stout J	109wb	4.00	89-15	Seabiscuit1096Ann O'Ruley1122Balkan Land1092	Easily 7
25Jly36-5Suf	fst 1⅛	:473 1:122 1:381 1:511	Miles Standish H 3k	1 2 24 31¾ 33½ 44¼	Kopel F	115wb	5.90	87-08	Kearsarge99nkTatterdemalion113.54BrownTop109no	Faltered 7
29Jun36-4Suf	fst 6f	:224 :453 1:114	Alw 1000	2 8 64¾ 62¾ 34 11½	Knott K	115wb	12.60	96-11	Seabiscuit1151½Deliberate115½Liberal1153	Handily 12
24Jun36-5Suf	sl 6f	:234 :48 1:134	Commonwealth H 3.2k	6 13 128 1212 109¼ 1010¾	Kopel F	115wb	29.40	75-21	PartySpirit107nkIndomitable1054SpeedtoSpare114½	Outrun 13
1Jun36-5Bel	fst 1 1/16	:24 :474 1:13 1:45	3↑ Handicap 1240	5 6 67¼ 65½ 65 66¼	Hanford I	112wb	*1.60e	80-16	Gallant Prince1161½Brown Twig114hdGillie114nk	Stumbled 6
27May36-5Rkm	sly 1	:234 :473 1:132 1:411	New Hampshire H 4k	9 11 129 129½ 129 129½	Kopel F	116wb	8.40	71-16	Faust103noGallant Gay110.5noParty Spirit1112	Outrun 15
18May36-5Nar	fst 1 1/16	:234 :472 1:123 1:441	Alw 1200	7 1 11 1hd 1½ 13	Kopel F	111wb	2.60	96-11	Seabiscuit1113Piccolo1063Swamp Angel1113½	Easily 7
13May36-5Nar	fst 1 1/16	:234 :472 1:123 1:444	Providence H 3.8k	8 1 12½ 21 31¼ 42½	Kopel F	115wb	4.20	90-13	Tugboat Frank1102Piccolo108noGallant Gay109½	No excuse 8
8May36-4Jam	fst 6f	:231 :47 1:12	Alw 1000	4 6 77 77¾ 53½ 42¾	Stout J	113wb	*2.40	89-14	Gleeman1101½Wha Hae1131Stubbs116nk	Finished fast 7
23Apr36-4Jam	fst 6f	:233 :471 1:121	Handicap 1220	4 4 48 47½ 33½ 37	Hanford I	120wb	*.50	84-17	Goldeneye1053Chancer1054Seabiscuit1203	No excuse 4
18Apr36-3Jam	fst 6f	:224 :462 1:12	Alw 1000	1 1 22 25 21½ 21½	Hanford I	105wb	5.00	90-13	Tintagel1181½Seabiscuit1054Hollyrood1188	Good effort 5
11Nov35-6Pim	my 1 1/16	:24 :491 1:143 1:494	Walden H 11k	10 7 108¾ 1012 915 66	Kopel F	108wb	14.45	65-27	Ned Reigh116½Challephen107hdWise Duke112½	No excuse 10
26Oct35-5Nar	fst 6f	:223 :451 1:111	Pawtucket H 6k	4 4 43½ 44 43¾ 2½	Stout J	117wb	*1.35	95-10	Clocks111½Seabiscuit1171½Crossbow II1211	Finished fast 5
23Oct35-5Emp	fst 5¾f	:23 :47 1:084	Ardsley H 3.7k	4 3 2hd 2hd 11 13	Kopel F	112wb	4.00	95-13	Seabiscuit1123Neap1172Wha Hae115½	Easily 6
16Oct35-5Agm	fst 6f	:234 :46 1:112	Springfield H 2.8k	8 1 12 11½ 11 11	Stout J	109wb	8.00	- -	Seabiscuit1091Bright Plumage117hdInfidox1171½	Ridden out 8
2Oct35-4Suf	fst 6f	:231 :462 1:121	Constitution H 9.2k	10 10 95½ 107 108¼ 1010	Woolf G	115wb	21.30	84-08	Infidox110nkClocks110nkSparta109½	Outrun 10
21Sep35-3Jam	fst 6f	:233 :464 1:12	Remsen H 4.7k	2 11 1115 1014 912 97¾	Horn F	112wb	7.00e	84-12	The Fighter122noTeufel1122Postage Due1241½	Off slowly 11
14Sep35-4HdG	fst 6f	:232 :474 1:13	Eastern Shore H 14k	6 7 85¼ 92½ 64½ 41½	Rosengarten C	112wb	38.50e	86-11	Postage Due117½Wise Duke115noMaerial1201	Forced wide 14
9Sep35-6Aqu	fst 6f	:233 :48 1:131	Alw 1000	4 4 11 11½ 12 13	Kopel F	115wb	12.00	88-13	Seabiscuit1153Count Morse1095Dark Wizard1122	Easily 8
4Sep35-3Aqu	sly 6f	:232 :473 1:122	Alw 1000	5 3 46¾ 45½ 54½ 36	Kopel F	110wb	10.00	86-10	PhantomFox106noPullman1146Seabiscuit110nk	Finished well 7
2Sep35-3Aqu	fst 6f	:241 :49 1:12	Babylon H 4.2k	5 6 511 67 67¾ 612	Horn F	112wb	1.50e	82-09	NedReigh116noSpeedtoSpare115noGranville1145	No excuse 6
26Aug35-4Sar	fst 6f	:23 :47 1:12	Alw 1000	5 8 812 86¼ 66 68½	Horn F	112wb	25.00	83-10	BoldVenture1151½GrandSlam1223Valvctorn1152	Dropped back 9
14Aug35-5Sar	gd 5½f	:231 :473 1:071	Alw 1000	11 13 1313 139¼ 106½ 95¼	Gilbert J	112wb	6.00e	82-14	Maerial1181Lovely Girl1042Speed109no	Off slowly 13
27Jly35-6Suf	fst 6f	:233 :463 1:122	Bay State 3.7k	4 6 31¼ 52¼ 32½ 43	Stout J	123wb	13.60	- -	BlackHighbrow1113NouveauRiche108noSt.Lous108no	Faltered 7
22Jly35-3Suf	fst 6f	:231 :454 1:112	Alw 1000	5 5 21 2½ 22½ 21½	Stout J	115wb	*1.70	- -	Black Highbrow1151½Seabiscuit1158Nedvive112½	Gamely 5
15Jly35-5Suf	fst 6f	:232 :472 1:131	Mayflower 3k	4 8 52¼ 42¼ 62½ 44	Horn F	123wb	15.00	- -	Maerial1232Jair111½Tugboat Frank1111½	No excuse 9
4Jly35-5Nar	fst 5f	:223 :46 :593	Old Colony 6.7k	3 4 42 45 44¾ 52½	Stout J	117wb	*1.40	101-07	BrightandEarly1141Swashbuckler114½Chllphn1121	No excuse 6
26Jun35-5Nar	fst 5f	:223 :454 :593	Watch Hill Claiming 5k	6 5 2½ 11½ 11 12	Horn F	108wb	*1.70	104-08	Seabiscuit1082Infidox1081Zowie1022	Easily 8
22Jun35-2Nar	fst 5f	:231 :464 1:003	Alw 1000	9 5 1½ 12 11½ 12	Stout J	110wb	*2.55	99-12	Seabiscuit1102Ned Reigh1102½Tugboat Frank1151½	Easily 9
11Jun35-1Rkm	hy 5f	:234 :49 1:02	Md Sp Wt	3 8 1½ 21½ 24 26	Stout J	116wb	*.60	78-18	Jubilee Jim1166Seabiscuit1162½Sky Pirate1162	Gamely 8
8Jun35-4Rkm	fst 5f	:231 :462 :594	Juvenile H 5.7k	2 8 74¼ 65 31¾ 31¼	Stout J	103wb	30.20	94-12	WinterSport1051PostageDue124nkSeabiscut103½	Good effort 12
1Jun35-1Rkm	fst 5f	:23 :461 1:011	Md Sp Wt	5 7 21 21½ 23 23	Stout J	116wb	7.75	85-14	Swashbuckler1163Seabiscuit1161½Sobriety1163	Good effort 12
28May35-1Rkm	fst 5f	:232 :474 1:011	Md Sp Wt	2 11 98¼ 97¾ 34½ 42½	Stout J	116wb	*2.05	85-11	SandyMack1161½Browbeatn1131TugboatFrnk116hd	Closed gap 11
21May35-2Rkm	fst 5f	:231 :473 1:004	Alw 800	7 9 76¼ 87½ 31¼ 3nk	Stout J	106wb	9.85	90-13	Microbe114nkBlackMistress111noSeabiscut1061	Closed fast 9
4May35-1Jam	fst 5f	:233 :472 1:002	Md Sp Wt	2 2 57½ 55¼ 64½ 68	Burke JH	115wb	2.00e	83-11	Pullman1151½Knowing115½Royal Fox1155	Shuffled 8
1May35-4Jam	fst 5f	:231 :473 1:01	Alw 1000	4 6 69¼ 56½ 53¾ 2½	Horn F	110wb	10.00	87-15	Galsac116½Seabiscuit110noTransitLady110no	Finished fast 6

Past Performances of Great Horses of the 20th Century

Date-Race	Cond	Dist	Fractions				Class	PP	St	Call 1	Call 2	Call 3	Fin	Jockey	Wt	Odds	Speed-Var	Top Finishers	Comment	Field
Previously trained by G. Tappen																				
25Apr35- 2HdG	fst	4½f	:232	:473		:542	Clm 4000	5	2		51¾	44½	4½	Workman R	114wb	3.50	92-07	Cherry Stone115noHiatus110hdProsy113½	Finished fast	11
22Apr35- 2HdG	fst	4½f	:232	:473		:542	Clm 2500	6	7		89¼	47½	33½	Peters M	116wb	11.95	89-07	Hiatus113½Deliberate1143Seabiscuit1161½	Close quarters	13
13Apr35- 3Bow	my	4f	:234			:492	Md Sp Wt	8	7		712	66¼	35½	Horn F	115wb	7.35	80-13	ParaguayTea1122½PatseyBegone1123Sebscut1151½	Off slowly	9
10Apr35- 4Bow	my	4f	:233			:492	Alw 800	9	10		911	97¾	87¼	Horn F	110wb	30.35	79-15	VictoriousAnn112hdWinterSport1151½Ste.Louise1121	Outrun	12
4Apr35- 1Bow	sl	4f	:24			:493	©Md Sp Wt	1	1		58½	35½	21½	Horn F	115wb	3.80	83-15	Borsa1151½Seabiscuit1153Green Mist1151	Finished gamely	8
Previously trained by V. Mara																				
8Mar35- 1Hia	fst	3f				:344	Alw 1000	12	10			63¼	43½	Horn F	113wb	4.50f	--	VctorousAnn1102WllwWood113hdTwoEdgd1131½	Finished fast	14
5Mar35- 1Hia	fst	3f				:343	Alw 800	8	8			83¾	85	Horn F	109wb	49.50	--	James City1191½Grand Slam108nkBright Light114hd	Impeded	13
27Feb35- 1Hia	fst	3f				:341	Clm 2500	2	1			73¾	63	Horn F	108 w	11.35	--	Black Bess100noTransit110noEdri1051½	No excuse	11
22Jan35- 2Hia	fst	3f				:351	Clm 2500	10	6			53¾	22	Stout J	110	9.50	--	ClappingJane1072Seabiscuit110hdSpart107nk	Finished fast	12
19Jan35- 1Hia	fst	3f				:343	Alw 1000	5	6			55¾	44½	Stout J	110	16.85e	--	Wha Hae1131Wise Duke1103Blue Donna107½	Good effort	10

Seattle Slew

dkbbr. c. 1974, by Bold Reasoning (Boldnesian)–My Charmer, by Poker

Lifetime record: 17 14 2 0 $1,208,726

Own.– Tayhill Stable
Br.– B.S. Castleman (Ky)
Tr.– Douglas Peterson

Date-Race	Cond	Dist	Fractions				Class	PP	St	Call 1	Call 2	Call 3	Fin	Jockey	Wt	Odds	Speed-Var	Top Finishers	Comment	Field
11Nov78- 8Aqu	fst	1⅛	:464	1:10	1:342	1:472	3↑ Stuyvesant H-G3	1	1	11½	13	13	13¼	Cordero A Jr	134	*.10	98-12	SeattleSlew1343¼JumpingHill1152¾WisePhlp113½	Ridden out	5
14Oct78- 8Bel	sly	1½	:451	1:092	2:014	2:271	3↑ J C Gold Cup-G1	1	1	1hd	1hd	2½	2no	Cordero A Jr	126	*.60	84-13	Exceller126noSeattleSlew12614GrtContrctor1264¾	Bore out	6
30Sep78- 8Bel	fst	1¼	:473	1:104	1:351	2:00	3↑ Woodward-G1	5	1	12	12½	12½	14	Cordero A Jr	126	*.30	109-12	SeattleSlew1264Exceller1266¾It'sFreezng126no	Ridden out	5
16Sep78- 8Bel	fst	1⅛	:47	1:101	1:333	1:454	3↑ Marlboro Cup H-G1	4	1	12½	12½	13	13	Cordero A Jr	128	2.10	98-12	Seattle Slew1283Affirmed1245Nasty and Bold1184	Driving	6
Previously owned by Karen L. Taylor																				
5Sep78- 6Med	fst	1⅛	:46	1:094	1:35	1:48	3↑ Paterson H-G3	10	1	13½	11½	1½	2nk	Cruguet J	128	*.20	93-13	Dr.Patches114nkSeattleSlew1282¼It'sFrzng1125	Drifted in	10
12Aug78- 7Sar	sly	7f	:22	:444	1:091	1:213	3↑ Alw 25000	5	2	11	15	14	16	Cruguet J	119	*.10	97-18	SeattleSlew1196ProudBirdie1152¾CapitalIdea11516	Handily	5
14May78- 7Aqu	sly	7f	:224	:453	1:101	1:224	4↑ Alw 25000	3	3	2½	11½	17	18¼	Cruguet J	122	*.10	87-26	SeattleSlew1228¼ProudArion1191¼Capult'sSong1155	Handily	6
Previously trained by William Turner Jr																				
3Jly77- 8Hol	fst	1¼	:452	1:091	1:333	1:583	Swaps-G1	2	2	32	36	411	416	Cruguet J	126	*.20	82-11	J.O. Tobin1208Affiliate117noText1208	Steadied,bore in	7
11Jun77- 8Bel	my	1½	:482	1:14	2:034	2:293	Belmont-G1	5	1	1½	14	13½	14	Cruguet J	126	*.40	72-17	SeattleSlw1264RunDstyRun1262Sanhedrn1262¼	Handy score	8
21May77- 8Pim	fst	1 3/16	:453	1:094	1:344	1:542	Preakness-G1	8	2	1hd	2½	13	11½	Cruguet J	126	*.40	98-10	Seattle Slew1261½Iron Constitution1262Run Dusty Run1261¼		9
Drew clear																				
7May77- 8CD	fst	1¼	:454	1:103	1:36	2:021	Ky Derby-G1	4	2	2hd	1hd	13	11¾	Cruguet J	126	*.50	86-12	SeattleSlew1261¾RunDstyRn126nkSanhdrn1263¼	Ridden out	15
23Apr77- 8Aqu	fst	1⅛	:474	1:121	1:363	1:493	Wood Memorial-G1	6	1	1hd	11½	16	13¼	Cruguet J	126	*.10	87-13	Seattle Slew1263¼Sanhedrin1264½Catalan126hd	Handily	7
26Mar77- 9Hia	fst	1⅛	:451	1:09	1:34	1:472	Flamingo-G1	4	1	11½	16	16	14	Cruguet J	122	*.20	95-15	SeattleSlew1224Gboul122nkFortPrvl1224½	Speed in reserve	13
9Mar77- 9Hia	fst	7f	:221	:44	1:08	1:203	Alw 7000	2	6	1hd	12	14	19	Cruguet J	117	*.10	102-10	SeattleSlw1179WhitRammr1223½SmashingNatv1192½	Easily	8
16Oct76- 8Bel	fst	1	:232	:46	1:10	1:342	Champagne-G1	3	1	12	12	13	19¾	Cruguet J	122	*1.30	96-13	SeattleSlw1229¾FortheMoment1221¼SltoRom1223	Easy score	10
5Oct76- 7Bel	fst	7f	:223	:454	1:092	1:22	Alw 11000	1	8	11½	11	13	13½	Cruguet J	122	*.40	92-13	SeattleSlew1223½CruiseonIn1196Lancer'sPrid1172¼	Handily	8
20Sep76- 5Bel	fst	6f	:222	:452		1:101	Md Sp Wt	8	10	1½	12	15	15	Cruguet J	122	*2.60	91-12	Seattle Slew1225Proud Arion122½Prince Andrew1222	Easily	12

Past Performances of Great Horses of the 20th Century

Secretariat

ch. c. 1970, by Bold Ruler (Nasrullah)–Somethingroyal, by Princequillo — Lifetime record: 21 16 3 1 $1,316,808

Own.– Meadow Stable
Br.– Meadow Stud Inc (Va)
Tr.– L. Laurin

28Oct73-8WO	fm 1⅝Ⓣ	:472 1:373 2:414 3↑	Can Int'l-G2	12 2	21½ 15 112	16½	Maple E	117	b	*.20	96-04	Secretariat1176½BigSpruce1261½GoldenDon117¾	Ridden out	12
8Oct73-7Bel	fm 1½Ⓣ	:47 1:113 2:00 2:244 3↑	Man o' War-G1	3 1	13 11½ 13	15	Turcotte R	121	b	*.50	103-01	Secretariat1215Tentam1267½Big Spruce126½	Ridden out	7
29Sep73-7Bel	sly 1½	:50 1:132 2:014 2:254 3↑	Woodward-G1	5 2	2½ 1hd 21½	24½	Turcotte R	119	b	*.30	86-15	ProveOut1264½Secretariat11911CougarII126½	Best of rest	5
15Sep73-7Bel	fst 1⅛	:453 1:091 1:33 1:452 3↑	Marl Cup Inv'l H 250k	7 5	51¼ 3½ 12	13½	Turcotte R	124	b	*.40e	104-07	Secretariat1243½RivaRidge1272Cougar II1266½	Ridden out	7
4Aug73-7Sar	fst 1⅛	:474 1:11 1:36 1:491 3↑	Whitney H-G2	3 4	31 2½ 2hd	21	Turcotte R	119	b	*.10	94-15	Onion1191Secretariat119½Rule by Reason1192	Weakened	5
30Jun73-8AP	fst 1⅛	:48 1:111 1:35 1:47	Invitational 125k	4 1	13 12½ 16	19	Turcotte R	126	b	*.05	99-17	Secretariat1269My Gallant120nkOur Native12017	Easily	4
9Jun73-8Bel	fst 1½	:461 1:094 1:59 2:24	Belmont-G1	1 1	1hd 120 128	131	Turcotte R	126	b	*.10	113-05	Secretariat12631TwiceaPrince126½MyGllnt12613	Ridden out	5
19May73-8Pim	fst 1 3/16	:481 1:112 1:353 1:542	Preakness-G1	3 4	1½ 12½ 12½	12½	Turcotte R	126	b	*.30	98-13	Secretariat1262½Sham1268Our Native1261	Handily	6
	Daily Racing Form time 1:53 2/5													
5May73-9CD	fst 1¼	:472 1:114 1:361 1:592	Ky Derby-G1	10 11	69½ 2½ 1½	12½	Turcotte R	126	b	*1.50e	103-10	Secretariat1262½Sham1268Our Native126½	Handily	13
21Apr73-7Aqu	fst 1⅛	:481 1:121 1:364 1:494	Wood Memorial-G1	6 7	66 55½ 45½	34	Turcotte R	126	b	*.30e	83-17	Angle Light126hdSham1264Secretariat126½	Wide,hung	8
7Apr73-7Aqu	fst 1	:231 :451 1:083 1:332	Gotham-G2	3 3	1hd 12 1½	13	Turcotte R	126	b	*.10	100-08	Secretariat1263ChampagneCharl11710Flush117 2½	Ridden out	6
17Mar73-7Aqu	sly 7f	:221 :444 1:10 1:231	Bay Shore-G3	4 5	56 53 1hd	14½	Turcotte R	126	b	*.20	85-17	Secretarit1264½ChmpgnChrl1182½Impcunous126no	Mild drive	6
18Nov72-8GS	fst 1 1/16	:241 :472 1:12 1:442	Garden State 298k	6 6	46¼ 33 11½	13½	Turcotte R	122	b	*.10e	83-23	Secretariat1223½Angle Light122½Step Nicely122¾	Handily	6
28Oct72-7Lrl	sly 1 1/16	:224 :454 1:112 1:424	Lrl Futurity 133k	5 6	510 53 15	18	Turcotte R	122	b	*.10e	99-14	Secretariat1228Stop the Music1228Angle Light1221	Easily	6
14Oct72-7Bel	fst 1	:224 :451 1:094 1:35	Champagne 146k	4 11	98½ 53½ 1½	12	Turcotte R	122	b	*.70e	97-12	DSecretariat1222StoptheMusic1222StepNicly1221½	Bore in	12
	Disqualified and placed second													
16Sep72-7Bel	fst 6½f	:223 :453 1:10 1:162	Futurity 144k	4 5	65½ 53½ 12	11¾	Turcotte R	122	b	*.20	98-09	Secretariat1221¾StoptheMusic1225SwiftCourr1222½	Handily	7
26Aug72-7Sar	fst 6½f	:224 :463 1:094 1:161	Hopeful 86k	8 8	96½ 1hd 14	15	Turcotte R	121	b	*.30	97-12	Secretariat1215Flight toGlory121nkStopthMusc1212	Handily	9
16Aug72-7Sar	fst 6f	:224 :461 1:10	Sanford 27k	2 5	54 41 1½	13	Turcotte R	121	b	1.50	96-14	Secretariat1213Lnd'sChf1216NorthstrDncr1213½	Ridden out	5
31Jly72-4Sar	fst 6f	:231 :462 1:104	Alw 9000	4 7	73¾ 3½ 1hd	11½	Turcotte R	118	b	*.40	92-13	Secretariat1181½Rust Miron1187Joe Iz1182½	Ridden out	7
15Jly72-4Aqu	fst 6f	:221 :452 1:103	©Md Sp Wt	8 11	66½ 43 1½	16	Feliciano P5	113	b	*1.30	90-14	Secretariat1136Master Achiever118¾Be on It1184	Handily	11
4Jly72-2Aqu	fst 5½f	:222 :461 :584 1:05	©Md Sp Wt	2 11	107 108¾ 75½	41¼	Feliciano P5	113	b	*3.10	87-11	Herbull118nkMaster Achiever1181Fleet 'n Royal118no		12
	Impeded,rallied													

Shuvee

ch. f. 1966, by Nashua (Nasrullah)–Levee, by Hill Prince — Lifetime record: 44 16 10 6 $890,445

Own.– Mrs. Whitney Stone
Br.– W. Stone (Va)
Tr.– W.C. Freeman

30Oct71-7Aqu	fst 2	:482 2:30 2:552 3:202 3↑	J C Gold Cup 111k	6 4	2½ 11½ 15	17	Velasquez J	121		*1.30	94-16	Shuvee1217Paraje1242Loud1248	Ridden out	7
11Oct71-8Atl	gd 1 3/16	:482 1:113 1:364 1:564 3↑	ⒻMatchmaker 50k	6 5	45½ 56½ 31	4¾	Turcotte R	118		*1.30	91-12	Deceit113hdSea Saga114hdDouble Delta125½	No excuse	8
2Oct71-7Bel	fst 1¼	:461 1:10 1:35 2:002 3↑	Woodward 113k	7 4	510 69 69	69	Turcotte R	123		3.70	89-13	DCougarII1265WestCoastScout121nkTinajero121no	No threat	10
11Sep71-7Bel	sly 1⅛	:453 1:093 1:351 1:483 3↑	ⒻBeldame 82k	2 6	46½ 26 24	2½	Baeza B	123		*.70	90-12	Double Delta123½Shuvee12310Cathy Honey1231½	Second best	7
23Aug71-7Sar	fst 1⅛	:50 1:141 1:382 1:503 3↑	ⒻDiana H 44k	5 3	31½ 21 21	1nk	Turcotte R	128		*1.10	88-11	Shuvee128nkDouble Delta1265½Cathy Honey116nk	Hard drive	5
7Aug71-7Sar	fst 1⅛	:473 1:114 1:364 1:492 3↑	Whitney 60k	13 9	108¼ 116¼ 66	33	Turcotte R	116		*4.10	91-11	Protanto117hdPeace Corps1143Shuvee116nk	Rallied wide	14
22May71-7Aqu	fst 1⅛	:471 1:122 1:37 1:493 3↑	ⒻTop Flight H 53k	5 3	31½ 1½ 11	1¾	Turcotte R	127		*.70e	88-17	Shuvee127¾Cathy Honey1181¼Office Queen1277	Driving	5
28Apr71-7Aqu	fst 1	:232 :464 1:113 1:364 3↑	ⒻBed o' Roses H 32k	2 4	42½ 42 21½	22	Turcotte R	127		*.60	81-23	Office Queen1252Shuvee1273Royal Fillet1103½	Gamely	6
15Apr71-7Aqu	fst 6f	:23 :462 1:103 3↑	Alw 20000	6 1	53½ 67 68	25	Baeza B	116		*1.50e	85-25	SummerAir1195Shuvee116nkPrimeVenture1211½	Finished well	9
31Oct70-7Aqu	fst 2	:503 2:302 2:554 3:213 3↑	J C Gold Cup 108k	4 1	1½ 1hd 12½	12	Turcotte R	121		2.90	88-16	Shuvee1212Loud1194Hydrologist1243¾	Mild urging	5

Past Performances of Great Horses of the 20th Century

Date	Cond	Dist	Fractions	Age	Race	PP St	1C	2C	Str	Fin	Jockey	Wt	Eqp	Odds	Figs	Top finishers	Comment	Field
3Oct70-7Bel	fst	1¼	:46^{2} 1:10^{1} 1:35^{3} 2:01^{4}	3↑	Woodward 109k	2 4	4^{6}	4^{1½}	5^{5½}	5^{7¾}	Turcotte R	123		7.70	83-08	Personality121^{nk}[DH]Hydrologst126[DH]Twogundn126^{4½}	Hit rail	7
12Sep70-7Bel	fst	1⅛	:45^{4} 1:10 1:35^{1} 1:48	3↑	ⒻBeldame 83k	2 2	2^{5}	2^{3}	1^{1}	1^{1}	Turcotte R	123		*1.30e	94-14	Shuvee123^{1}Obeah123^{1¼}Cold Comfort118^{2½}	Brisk drive	7
24Aug70-7Sar	sly	1⅛	:46^{4} 1:11^{2} 1:37^{1} 1:49^{3}	3↑	ⒻDiana H 49k	4 6	7^{6¾}	4^{3}	2^{1}	1no	Turcotte R	120		3.50	93-15	Shuvee120^{no}Dark Emerald109^{4}Native Partner112^{1}	Driving	12
8Jly70-8Mth	fst	1$\frac{1}{16}$	:23^{2} :46^{3} 1:11^{1} 1:44	3↑	ⒻMolly Pitcher 44k	4 3	5^{8¼}	6^{7½}	6^{6½}	5^{6}	Baeza B	123		*.70	79-13	DoubleRipple112^{¾}WhataDream115^{1}Deb'sDarlng114^{4}	No excuse	9
10Jun70-7Bel	fst	7f	:22^{2} :45^{2} 1:10^{2} 1:23^{4}	3↑	ⒻVagrancy H 28k	2 4	5^{11}	6^{11}	6^{11}	5^{10}	Baeza B	123		2.00	78-15	Process Shot127^{2½}Powder Mountain104^{¾}Native Partner110^{6}		6
	No response																	
23May70-7Aqu	fst	1⅛	:48^{1} 1:11^{4} 1:36^{2} 1:48^{3}	3↑	ⒻTop Flight H 57k	2 1	1^{hd}	1^{½}	1^{½}	1^{4}	Baeza B	120		2.40	93-13	Shuvee120^{4}Singing Rain122^{7}Swiss Cheese110^{¾}	Handily	10
2May70-8Pim	fst	1$\frac{1}{16}$	:23^{3} :46^{4} 1:11 1:43^{3}	3↑	ⒻGallorette H 32k	5 6	6^{7}	5^{6½}	2^{7}	2^{8}	Davidson J	122		*1.20	84-13	SingingRain119^{8}Shuvee122^{3½}MissFallRiver109^{1½}	No excuse	7
25Apr70-8Aqu	fst	1	:24 :46^{4} 1:11 1:35^{2}	3↑	Alw 15000	6 5	7^{5¼}	5^{3}	4^{2}	4^{3¼}	Davidson J	113		*3.30	87-18	GleamingSword116^{1¾}ShiningSword118^{1½}Bromtr120^{hd}	No rally	9
8Apr70-7Aqu	fst	7f	:23 :45^{2} 1:10 1:22^{4}	3↑	ⒻDistaff H 27k	2 5	5^{10}	5^{12}	6^{13}	6^{15}	Davidson J	123		7.50	72-20	ProcessShot126^{1¾}TaWee134^{2}DedctdtoSu115^{hd}	Never a factor	6
27Nov69-7Aqu	fst	1⅛	:49^{2} 1:13^{4} 1:38^{1} 1:50	3↑	ⒻFirenze H 56k	1 1	2^{½}	4^{2}	2^{1}	2^{¾}	Davidson J	122		*1.40	85-19	Amerigo Lady121^{¾}Shuvee122^{1½}Obeah120^{½}	Finished willingly	8
11Nov69-7Aqu	gd	1¼	:47^{3} 1:12^{1} 1:38 2:03	3↑	ⒻLadies H 58k	7 3	6^{12}	4^{3}	3^{½}	1^{1¼}	Davidson J	117		*2.80	81-22	Shuvee117^{1¼}AmerigoLady121^{1¼}Obeh121^{2½}	Blocked,hard drive	11
1Nov69-7Aqu	fst	7f	:22^{1} :44^{2} 1:08^{3} 1:21^{3}	3↑	Vosburgh H 58k	3 10	11^{9}	10^{12}	8^{5½}	6^{1¾}	Turcotte R	114		14.90	91-13	TaWee123^{hd}[DH]PluckyLucky116[DH]RisingMarket120^{½}	Late bid	11
13Sep69-7Bel	fst	1⅛	:46^{2} 1:10^{3} 1:36 1:49^{1}	3↑	ⒻBeldame 81k	3 4	4^{8½}	4^{6}	3^{7}	3^{6½}	Davidson J	118		3.00	83-16	Gamely123^{3}Amerigo Lady123^{3½}Shuvee118^{2}	Finished willing	5
30Aug69-7Bel	fst	1⅛	:46^{2} 1:10^{2} 1:35^{2} 1:49		ⒻGazelle H 53k	1 5	5^{7}	5^{6½}	4^{7}	3^{6½}	Davidson J	127		*1.10	84-12	Gallant Bloom127^{3½}Pit Bunny116^{3}Shuvee127^{1½}	No excuse	5
9Aug69-6Sar	gd	1¼	:48^{3} 1:13^{1} 1:39^{2} 2:06^{2}		ⒻAlabama 54k	2 4	4^{6}	3^{1½}	1^{1½}	1^{4}	Davidson J	124		*1.00	76-15	Shuvee124^{4}PitBunny114^{½}HailtoPatsy118^{2}	Easily the best	5
26Jly69-8Del	gd	1⅛	:46^{4} 1:12^{2} 1:38^{4} 1:51^{1}		ⒻDel Oaks 59k	7 5	6^{8½}	5^{6½}	4^{11}	4^{17}	Davidson J	121		1.60	64-23	[D]PitBunny112^{1¼}GallantBloom121^{12}WhitXmss111^{3¼}	No excuse	7
12Jly69-7Lib	fst	1$\frac{1}{16}$	:23^{1} :47 1:10^{4} 1:43^{1}		ⒻCotillion H 55k	3 6	5^{4¾}	5^{3¼}	3^{½}	1^{nk}	Davidson J	124		*.40	- -	Shuvee124^{nk}Class Is Out113^{3}Secret Verdict114^{2}	Just up	7
21Jun69-7Bel	fst	1¼	:46^{2} 1:10^{3} 1:36^{3} 2:03^{1}		ⒻC C A Oaks 119k	4 5	5^{11}	4^{4½}	1^{hd}	1^{3}	Davidson J	121		*.30	84-17	Shuvee121^{3}Hail to Patsy121^{1½}Secret Verdict121^{1½}	Easily	7
31May69-7Aqu	fst	1⅛	:47^{4} 1:12^{3} 1:38 1:50^{1}		ⒻMother Goose 87k	1 4	5^{11}	5^{5½}	2^{2}	1^{2½}	Davidson J	121		*1.10	85-17	Shuvee121^{2½}HailtoPatsy121^{2½}RestlssTorndo121^{4}	Ridden out	6
17May69-7Aqu	fst	1	:22^{3} :44^{3} 1:09^{1} 1:35^{3}		ⒻAcorn 59k	7 5	5^{8½}	3^{6}	2^{hd}	1^{¾}	Davidson J	121		*.80	89-14	Shuvee121^{¾}Hail to Patsy121^{3}Big Advance121^{nk}	Mild drive	9
7May69-7Aqu	fst	7f	:22^{2} :45^{1} 1:09^{2} 1:22^{3}		ⒻComely 28k	3 6	6^{6}	4^{5}	2^{3}	2^{hd}	Davidson J	121		2.90	88-13	TaWee118^{hd}Shuvee121^{5}HastyHitter118^{hd}	Getting to winner	6
9Nov68-8GS	sl	1$\frac{1}{16}$	:23 :47^{4} 1:13 1:45^{4}		ⒻGardenia 183k	5 7	5^{2½}	2^{hd}	2^{1½}	2^{1¼}	Davidson J	119		*1.00	75-28	Gallant Bloom119^{1¼}Shuvee119^{15}Let's Be Gay119^{nk}	Game try	7
26Oct68-0Lrl	fst	1$\frac{1}{16}$	:23 :46^{3} 1:12^{3} 1:44^{4}		ⒻSelima 108k	4 5	4^{7}	2^{3½}	2^{hd}	1^{nk}	Turcotte R	122		-	93-17	Shuvee122^{nk}Process Shot119^{6}Queen's Double119^{40}	Driving	5
	Exhibition race run between 7th and 8th races-No wagering.																	
5Oct68-7Bel	fst	1	:23 :46^{3} 1:11^{2} 1:37		ⒻFrizette 130k	7 8	9^{9½}	7^{6}	2^{3}	1^{nk}	Davidson J	119		4.50e	89-13	Shuvee119^{nk}Gallant Bloom119^{3}Dihela119^{4}	Up final strides	11
23Sep68-7Bel	fst	7f	:22^{3} :46 1:10^{4} 1:24^{1}		ⒻAstarita (Div 2) 23k	3 6	5^{6½}	6^{5½}	7^{4¾}	3^{1¼}	Davidson J	112		10.80	85-17	Dihela112^{1}Imbibe116^{nk}Shuvee112^{2}	Found stride late	8
14Sep68-4Aqu	fst	6f	:22^{3} :46^{1} 1:11^{4}		ⒻAlw 7000	3 10	10^{7½}	9^{7}	6^{4¼}	2^{1¼}	Davidson J	119		*2.70	83-14	Gunite108^{1¼}Shuvee119^{¾}Plane119^{hd}	In close,rallied	12
30Aug68-6Aqu	fst	6f	:22^{2} :46 1:11^{2}		ⒻAlw 12000	1 7	7^{11}	6^{9½}	2^{5}	2^{3}	Baeza B	114		6.40	83-20	Gallant Bloom106^{3}Shuvee114^{3}Prefer116^{1}	Finished strongly	7
20Aug68-5Sar	fst	6f	:22^{1} :46^{2} 1:11^{4}		ⒻMd Sp Wt	13 11	9^{8}	9^{8¼}	2^{½}	1^{4}	Baeza B	119		3.70	89-09	Shuvee119^{4}Table D'Hote119^{½}Ambranded119^{2½}	Easily best	14
13Aug68-5Sar	fst	5½f	:22^{1} :45^{4} :57^{3} 1:04		ⒻMd Sp Wt	4 7	8^{7¼}	10^{12}	6^{13}	5^{12}	Gustines H	119		4.20	85-11	Ta Wee119^{6}Drip Spring119^{2}Socializing119^{2½}	No mishap	12
3Aug68-1Sar	fst	5½f	:22^{4} :47^{1} :59^{2} 1:05^{4}		ⒻMd Sp Wt	7 4	4^{1½}	5^{2¾}	3^{1½}	3^{1½}	Baeza B	119	b	*1.40	86-12	Pashamin119^{no}Elizabeth'sDancer116^{1½}Shuvee119^{5}	No mishap	10
25Jly68-5Aqu	gd	5½f	:22^{2} :46^{2} :58^{4} 1:05^{1}		ⒻMd Sp Wt	8 8	6^{3½}	7^{4¾}	3^{3½}	2^{3}	Baeza B	119	b	*2.50	84-18	French Bread119^{3}Shuvee119^{4}Keep a Secret119^{1}	Rallied	9
5Jun68-4Bel	fst	5½f	:23^{1} :47 :59^{1} 1:05^{3}		ⒻMd Sp Wt	9 8	5^{2}	5^{2}	4^{3½}	3^{5¾}	Davidson J	119	b	*1.70	87-15	Golden Or119^{¾}Go to Bed119^{5}Shuvee119^{¾}	Raced wide late	10
22May68-4Bel	fst	5½f	:23 :46^{2} :58^{4} 1:05^{2}		ⒻMd Sp Wt	4 7	3^{4}	3^{3}	4^{5}	4^{2¼}	Davidson J	119		*2.50	92-14	Fillypasser119^{hd}Foolish Miss119^{nk}Tudor Home119^{2}	Hung	10
8May68-4Aqu	fst	5f	:22^{2} :46^{1} :59		ⒻMd Sp Wt	5 8	8^{7¾}	6^{9½}	5^{6½}	4^{7¾}	Davidson J	119		*1.90	82-11	Gunite119^{4}Miss Georgene119^{¾}Most Welcome119^{3}	No threat	10

Past Performances of Great Horses of the 20th Century

Skip Away

gr/ro. c. 1993, by Skip Trial (Bailjumper)–Ingot Way, by Diplomat Way — Lifetime record: 38 18 10 6 $9,616,360

Own.– Carolyn H. Hine
Br.– Anna Marie Barnhart (Fla)
Tr.– Hubert Hine

Date/Race	Cond/Dist	Fractions	Race	PP St 1/4 1/2 Str Fin	Jockey	M/Wt	Odds	Speed	Top finishers	Comment	Field
7Nov98-10CD	fst 1¼	:473 1:12 1:371 2:02	3↑ B C Classic-G1	6 3 21 4¾ 63¼ 64	Bailey JD	L 126 b	*1.90	91-07	AwesomeAgn126¾Slvr Chrm126nkSwain126no	Pressed,empty	10
10Oct98-10Bel	sly 1¼	:462 1:093 1:341 2:003	3↑ JC Gold Cup-G1	4 1 2hd 22 34 310¼	Bailey JD	L 126 b	*.35	81-14	Wagon Limit1265½Gentlemen1264¾Skip Away1264		6
	Dueled outside,faded										
19Sep98-9Bel	fst 1⅛	:452 1:09 1:341 1:474	3↑ Woodward-G1	2 2 1½ 11 12 11¾	Bailey JD	L 126 b	*1.10	91-18	Skip Away1261¾Gentlemen1266RunningStag1269		5
	About his business										
30Aug98-11Mth	fst 1⅛	:463 1:10 1:344 1:471	3↑ P H Iselin H-G2	4 3 2hd 11 1hd 1no	Bailey JD	L 131 b	*.05	102-09	Skip Away131noStormin Fever1139Testafly1142¾	Driving	7
28Jun98-7Hol	fst 1¼	:462 1:093 1:34 2:00	3↑ Hol Gold Cup-G1	2 1 11 1hd 11 11¾	Bailey JD	LB 124 b	*.40	95-05	Skip Away1241¾Puerto Madero1241Gentlemen1243		8
	Gamely kicked clear										
30May98-9Suf	fst 1⅛	:462 1:101 1:344 1:471	3↑ Mass H-G3	1 1 12½ 12 13½ 14¼	Bailey JD	L 130 b	*.30	103-07	Skip Away1304¼Puerto Madero1164¾K.J.'s Appeal1134		5
	2 path,ridden out										
9May98-7Pim	gd 1 3/16	:47 1:112 1:354 1:541	3↑ Pim Special H-G1	4 1 13 12½ 13 13¼	Bailey JD	L 128 b	*.20	94-16	Skip Away1283¼Precocity115nkHot Brush113¾	Driving	5
28Feb98-10GP	fst 1¼	:463 1:101 1:351 2:031	3↑ Gulf Park H-G1	2 2 21 12½ 13 12¼	Bailey JD	L 127 b	*.10	95-16	Skip Away1272¼Unruled1121¾Behrens1141¼	Driving,clear	6
7Feb98-10GP	fst 1⅛	:463 1:104 1:362 1:50	3↑ Donn H-G1	3 2 31½ 1hd 13 12¾	Bailey JD	L 126 b	*.40	87-24	SkipAway1262¾Unruled1121½SirBr113nk	3-wide bid,hand ride	10
8Nov97-8Hol	fst 1¼	:461 1:093 1:334 1:59	3↑ B C Classic-G1	1 3 31 14 15 16	Smith ME	L 126 b	*1.80	102-06	Skip Away1266DeputyCommnder123¾[D]Whiskey Wisdom1263		9
	Much best,driving										
18Oct97-9Bel	wf 1¼	:47 1:10 1:334 1:584	3↑ J C Gold Cup-G1	1 2 2½ 11 16 16½	Bailey JD	L 126 b	1.45	103-04	Skip Away1266½Instant Friendship12610Wagon Limit121¾		7
	Contested pace,gamely										
20Sep97-9Bel	fst 1⅛	:471 1:111 1:35 1:472	3↑ Woodward-G1	2 1 2hd 32½ 33½ 25½	Sellers SJ	L 126 b	1.35	87-15	FormalGold1265½SkpAwy126nkWll'sWy12640	Game,2nd best	5
23Aug97-9Mth	fst 1 1/16	:224 :452 1:09 1:401	3↑ PH Iselin H-G2	1 4 44 32½ 25 25¼	Sellers SJ	L 124 b	*.90	101-07	Formal Gold1215¼Skip Away1242½Distorted Humor1156		4
	3-wide bid,2nd best										
2Aug97-8Sar	fst 1⅛	:47 1:104 1:352 1:481	3↑ Whitney H-G1	2 3 32½ 31½ 33 36½	Sellers SJ	L 125 b	*1.10	88-25	Will's Way117noFormal Gold1206½Skip Away1259½		6
	Lacked response										
4Jly97-9Bel	fst 1¼	:472 1:12 1:371 2:021	3↑ Suburban H-G2	1 2 3½ 31½ 3½ 11½	Sellers SJ	L 122 b	*1.00	86-23	Skip Away1221½Will's Way116¾Formal Gold12015		6
	Shuffled back ½ pl,awaited room turn,determinedly										
31May97-11Suf	fst 1⅛	:471 1:104 1:351 1:474	3↑ Mass H-G3	3 2 2½ 1hd 1hd 1hd	Sellers SJ	L 119 b	*.70	104-01	SkpAwy119hdFormlGold1143½Wll'sWy1142¼	2 wide,long drive	6
10May97-9Pim	fst 1 3/16	:463 1:10 1:343 1:53	3↑ Pim Spl H-G1	8 4 42½ 32 21½ 2½	Sellers SJ	L 119 b	3.30	101-17	Gentlemen122½Skip Away1196½Tejano Run1148		8
	Three wide both turns,gamely										
20Apr97-7LS	fst 1	:232 :461 1:093 1:342	3↑ Texas Mile 250k	5 6 52½ 43½ 34 37½	Sellers SJ	L 11 b	*.60	--	Isitingood1233Spiritbound1164½Skip Away1162½		7
	5 wide first turn,empty drive										
1Mar97-10GP	fst 1¼	:46 1:104 1:354 2:021	3↑ Gulf Park H-G1	2 2 21 2hd 2hd 22¼	Sellers SJ	L 122 b	*.40	89-19	Mt. Sassafras1132¼Skip Away122nkTejano Run1142	Gamely	6
8Feb97-10GP	fst 1⅛	:47 1:104 1:35 1:472	3↑ Donn H-G1	7 2 21 21½ 22 21¼	Sellers SJ	L 123 b	*.70	99-04	Formal Gold1131¼Skip Away1236Mecke120hd	Rallied 3 path	10
5Oct96-10Bel	fst 1¼	:473 1:112 1:354 2:003	3↑ J C Gold Cup-G1	4 2 2½ 2½ 11 1hd	Sellers SJ	L 121 b	5.80	94-10	Skip Away121hdCigar 1262Louis Quatorze1211	Hard drive	6
15Sep96-9WO	fst 1⅛	:464 1:103 1:36 1:49	WO Million-G1	1 5 55 53¼ 1hd 14	Sellers SJ	L 126 b	*1.15	101-09	SkipAwy1264VictorCooley119noStephanotis1193½	Drew away	7
24Aug96-7Sar	fst 1¼	:461 1:103 1:361 2:022	Travers-G1	3 4 32 31 31½ 31¾	Santos JA	L 126 b	*1.45	95-03	Will's Way126¾Louis Quatorze1261Skip Away1263½		7
	In tight ¾ pl,wide turn										
4Aug96-10Mth	fst 1⅛	:461 1:094 1:342 1:473	Haskell Inv'l H-G1	2 4 43 3½ 3½ 11	Santos JA	L 124 b	*.60	103-01	Skip Away1241Dr. Caton1151Victory Speech1214½	Driving	7
23Jun96-14Tdn	fst 1⅛	:461 1:104 1:353 1:474	Ohio Derby-G2	10 5 52 1½ 13 13½	Santos JA	LB 122 b	*.70	103-08	Skip Away1223½Victory Speech1189¼Clash by Night118nk		10
	Widened,brisk hand ride										
8Jun96-9Bel	fst 1½	:464 1:104 2:02 2:284	Belmont-G1	13 6 2hd 11½ 1½ 21	Santos JA	L 126 b	8.00	89-13	Editor'sNote1261SkipAwy1264MyFlg1216	Long drive,gamely	14

Past Performances of Great Horses of the 20th Century

18May96-10Pim fst 1 3/16 :461 1:094 1:342 1:532 Preakness-G1 11 2 22 2½ 2½ 2¼ Sellers SJ L 126 b 3.30 98-10 Louis Quatorze1263¼Skip Away1263Editor's Note1262½ 12
Bid far turn,2nd best
4May96-8CD fst 1¼ :46 1:103 1:35 2:01 Ky Derby-G1 16 5 64½ 108¾ 1319 1216¾ Sellers SJ L 126 b 7.70 84-04 Grindstone126noCavonnr1263½PrncofThvs126nk 5 wide tired 19
13Apr96-9Kee wf 1⅛ :462 1:101 1:344 1:471 Blue Grass-G2 5 2 1hd 1½ 14½ 16 Sellers SJ L 121 b 4.60 98-10 Skip Away1216Louis Quatorze1211½Editor's Note1213 7
Dueled,driving clear impressivey
16Mar96-10GP fst 1⅛ :462 1:094 1:343 1:474 Florida Derby-G1 3 5 46½ 46½ 24 36¼ Sellers SJ L 122 b 7.90 92-07 Unbridled's Song1225¾Editor's Note122½Skip Away1222¼ 9
Seven wide top stretch,weakened
10Feb96-8GP fst 1 1/16 :233 :474 1:114 1:441 Alw 26000 4 5 31½ 11 17 112 Sellers SJ L 117 b *1.10 87-12 Skip Away11712Hedge120noNatural Selection1201½ 12
Crowded,bumped turn,five wide final turn,driving
10Jan96-1GP fst 1 1/16 :23 :463 1:114 1:454 Alw 26000 1 4 54 58 528 - Bailey JD 117 *.40 - - Blushing Jim1171½HedMinistr1171¼Night Runner1177¾ 5
Eased str in distress
25Nov95-7Bel fst 1⅛ :471 1:114 1:373 1:501 Remsen-G2 1 5 42½ 32 1hd 2nk Bailey JD 112 2.30 89-09 Tropcool112nkSkpAwy1122CrftyFrnd1133 Yielded grudgingly 11
29Oct95-7Bel fst 1 :223 :461 1:113 1:37 Cowdin-G2 7 3 31 2½ 2hd 2no Wilson R 122 5.30 78-19 Gator Dancer122noSkip Away1223In Contention1224¾ 8
Lost bob,gamely
6Oct95-9Med fst 1⊗ :23 :463 1:104 1:371 World Appeal 40k 10 6 62½ 34½ 36 33¼ Wilson R 115 1.80 87-10 SpicyFact1153¼PlayItAgnStn117noSkpAwy1159 Even finish 10
16Aug95-5Mth fst 1 :24 :474 1:13 1:39 Md Sp Wt 2 3 23 11½ 19 112¼ Wilson R 118 *.80 83-17 SkpAwy11812ClashbyNight1187½DarnThatErc1134¼ Drew off 8
9Jly95-9Mth fm 5f(T) :22 :451 :572 Gilded Time 33k 4 7 77½ 66½ 45 21½ Marquez CH Jr 112 5.00 85-13 ColdSnap1181½SkipAway1121Cobb'sCreek1211¾ Closed well 7
16Jun95-5Mth fst 5f :22 :462 :584 Md Sp Wt 2 10 87½ 79½ 59 48¾ Marquez CH Jr 118 *.80e 81-18 ColdSnap1134¼Foolspruce1182BeauCoup1182½ Broke slowly 10

Spectacular Bid

gr. c. 1976, by Bold Bidder (Bold Ruler)–Spectacular, by Promised Land
Lifetime record: 30 26 2 1 $2,781,608
Own.– Hawksworth Farm
Br.– Mmes Gilmour & Jason (Ky)
Tr.– Grover G. Delp

20Sep80-0Bel fst 1¼ :502 1:141 1:381 2:022 3↑ Woodward-G1 1 1 1 1 1 1 Shoemaker W 126 88-21 Spectacular Bid126 In hand 1
Walkover,run between 7th and 8th race - Walkover,no wagering
16Aug80-9Mth fst 1⅛ :464 1:111 1:353 1:48 3↑ AL Haskell H-G1 5 7 65½ 5¾ 1½ 11¾ Shoemaker W 132 *.10 95-15 SpectcularBd1321¾Glorious Song1171¼The Cool Virginian1124 8
Ridden out
19Jly80-8AP fst 1⅛ :461 1:094 1:34 1:461 3↑ Wash Park-G3 4 4 44 2hd 14 110 Shoemaker W 130 *.05 103-17 SpectacularBid13010HoldYourTrcks1198Archtct1191½ Easily 6
8Jun80-8Hol fst 1⅛ :45 1:084 1:331 1:454 3↑ Californian-G1 3 3 31½ 11 16 14¼ Shoemaker W 130 *.05 103-05 SpectaculrBid1304¼PaintKng1153¾CroBmbno1188 Easy score 7
18May80-8Hol fst 1 1/16 :223 :452 1:084 1:402 3↑ Mervyn LeRoy H-G2 1 5 42 2hd 13½ 17 Shoemaker W 132 *.20 93-18 SpectaculrBd1327Peregrintor119¾Beau'sEgl1212 Ridden out 6
2Mar80-8SA sly 1¼ :483 1:122 1:364 2:003 4↑ S Anita H-G1 5 2 22½ 1hd 12½ 15 Shoemaker W 130 *.30 90-18 SpctaclarBid1305FlyingPstr1238Beau'sEgl12214 Ridden out 5
3Feb80-8SA fst 1¼ :443 1:082 1:324 1:574 C H Strub-G1 3 4 29 2hd 13 13¼ Shoemaker W 126 *.30 104-08 SpectacularBid1263¼FlyingPaster1219Vldz122½ Handy score 4
19Jan80-8SA gd 1⅛ :462 1:11 1:353 1:48 San Fernando-G2 1 3 33½ 1hd 1½ 11½ Shoemaker W 126 *.05 89-19 SpectacularBid1261½FlyngPstr12615Rlunch12033 Drew clear 4
5Jan80-8SA fst 7f :221 :442 1:08 1:20 Malibu-G2 3 4 52½ 41 1½ 15 Shoemaker W 126 *.30 103-10 SpectacularBid1265FlyingPastr1231½Ros'sSvll117no Easily 5
18Oct79-6Med fst 1¼ :474 1:12 1:362 2:011 3↑ Med Cup H-G2 1 3 33 1½ 11½ 13 Shoemaker W 126 *.10 102-14 Spectacular Bid1263Smarten120hdValdez12111 Drew out 5
6Oct79-8Bel fst 1½ :49 1:131 2:022 2:272 3↑ J C Gold Cup-G1 2 3 2½ 31 2½ 2¾ Shoemaker W 121 1.40 82-21 Affirmed126¾Spectacular Bid1213Coastal12131 Gamely 4
8Sep79-8Bel fst 1⅛ :472 1:11 1:341 1:463 3↑ Marlboro Cup H-G1 5 3 1hd 1½ 13 15 Shoemaker W 124 *.50 94-17 SpectacularBid1245GenrlAssmbly1201¼Costl122½ Ridden out 6
26Aug79-7Del gd 1 1/16 :23 :463 1:111 1:413 Alw 18000 3 3 21½ 16 112 117 Shoemaker W 122 *.05 101-14 SpectacularBd12217ArmadaStrik1127NotSoProud1126 Easily 5
9Jun79-8Bel fst 1½ :473 1:111 2:022 2:283 Belmont-G1 3 2 2½ 13 2½ 33½ Franklin RJ 126 *.30 73-17 Coastal1263¼Golden Act126nkSpectacular Bid1269½ Tired 8
19May79-8Pim gd 1 3/16 :464 1:103 1:35 1:541 Preakness-G1 2 4 45 1hd 16 15½ Franklin RJ 126 *.10 99-09 SpctacularBd1265½GoldenAct1264ScrnKng1261½ Ridden out 5
5May79-8CD fst 1¼ :472 1:122 1:373 2:022 Ky Derby-G1 3 7 610 2hd 11½ 12¾ Franklin RJ 126 *.60 85-14 SpectacularBid1262¾GnrlAssmbly1263GoldnAct1261¾ Driving 10

Past Performances of Great Horses of the 20th Century

Date/Race	Cond/Dist	Fractions	Race	PP	St	1C	2C	Str	Fin	Jockey	Wt	Odds	Speed-Track	Top Finishers	Field
26Apr79-7Kee	fst 1⅛	:463 1:103 1:361 1:50	Blue Grass-G1	4	4	1hd	12	15½	17	Franklin RJ	121	*.05	87-20	Spectacular Bid1217Lot o' Gold1218Bishop's Choice12110	4
	Easily best														
24Mar79-10Hia	fst 1⅛	:46 1:093 1:351 1:482	Flamingo-G1	8	3	1½	18	110	112	Franklin RJ	122	*.05	90-16	Spectacular Bid12212Strike the Min1183Sir Ivor Again122hd	8
	Ridden out														
6Mar79-11GP	fst 1⅛	:474 1:114 1:363 1:484	Florida Derby-G1	5	5	47½	3½	11½	14½	Franklin RJ	122	*.05	90-14	Spectacular Bid1224½Lot o' Gold122¾Fantasy 'n Reality1223	7
	Four wide,clear														
19Feb79-9GP	fst 1 1/16	:24 :472 1:104 1:411	Fountain of Youth-G3	2	3	1hd	13	14	18½	Franklin RJ	122	*.10	95-12	Spectacular Bid1228½Lot o'Gold1171Bishop's Choice1221	6
	Ridden out														
7Feb79-9GP	fst 7f	:224 :444 1:084 1:212	Hutcheson 28k	1	2	2hd	22	13	13¾	Franklin RJ	122	*.05	97-22	SpectcularBid1223¾Lot o' Gold1147½Northern Prospect1143½	4
	In hand														
11Nov78-8Key	fst 1 1/16	:224 :462 1:103 1:42	Heritage-G2	6	5	55	1hd	13	16	Franklin RJ	122	*.10	94-13	SpctacularBid1226SunWatcher1123¼TerrfcSon117no Handily	7
28Oct78-8Lrl	fst 1 1/16	:234 :464 1:11 1:413	Lrl Futurity-G1	2	1	11½	1½	14	18½	Franklin RJ	122	*.90	105-14	SpectacularBd1228½General Assembly12212Clever Trick1223½	4
	Driving														
19Oct78-6Med	fst 1 1/16	:232 :462 1:111 1:431	Young America-G1	5	3	2hd	2½	2hd	1nk	Velasquez J	122	*.30	95-14	SpectclrBid122nkStrikeYourColrs119hdInstrumntLanding1134	9
	Driving														
8Oct78-8Bel	fst 1	:231 :46 1:101 1:344	Champagne-G1	1	2	11	12½	14	12¾	Velasquez J	122	2.40	94-19	SpectclrBid1222¾GeneralAssembly1225½Crest of theWave122¾	6
	Ridden out														
23Sep78-8Atl	gd 7f	:22 :443 1:09 1:204	World's Playground-G3	3	3	1½	12	16	115	Franklin RJ	114	5.20	93-25	SpctaculrBid11415CrstofthWv1241¼GrotonHgh118½ Driving	7
20Aug78-9Del	fst 6f	:222 :46 :58 1:104	Dover 34k	2	4	43	53¾	44	22½	Franklin RJ	112	*1.00	88-13	StrikeYourColors1122½SpectacularBid1125½Spy Charger1221	7
	2nd best														
2Aug78-8Mth	sly 5½f	:224 :461 :59 1:044	Tyro (Div 2) 27k	6	8	816	812	610	46¾	Franklin RJ	118	*1.70	86-22	GrotonHigh1222½GreatBoon116nkOurGry1164 Very wide early	8
22Jly78-5Pim	fst 5½f	:223 :461 :581 1:041	Alw 6500	3	4	31	1hd	13	18	Franklin RJ5	115	*.30	100-17	SpectacularBid1158SilentNative1209DoublePrd1141 Driving	5
30Jun78-3Pim	fst 5½f	:223 :463 :582 1:043	Md Sp Wt	5	4	1½	11½	12½	13¼	Franklin RJ5	115	6.30	93-15	Spectacular Bid1153¼Strike Your Colors1204Instant Love1124	11
	Drew out														

Swaps

ch. c. 1952, by Khaled (Hyperion)–Iron Reward, by Beau Pere

Lifetime record: 25 19 2 2 $848,900

Own.– R.C. Ellsworth
Br.– Rex C. Ellsworth (Cal)
Tr.– M.A. Tenney

Date/Race	Cond/Dist	Fractions	Race	PP	St	1C	2C	Str	Fin	Jockey	Wt	Eqp	Odds	Speed-Track	Top Finishers	Comment	Field
3Sep56-8Was	fst 1	:221 :441 1:074 1:332	3↑ Wash Park H 142k	5	3	22	1½	13	12	Shoemaker W	130	w	*.40	102-13	Swaps1302Summer Tan1152Sea o Erin1123	Well in hand late	6
25Aug56-8Was	fm 1 3/16 (T)	:47 1:103 1:362 1:55	3↑ Arch Ward Mem H 54k	7	2	3½	2hd	31	76¼	Shoemaker W	130	w	*.30	92-02	Mahan1141½SirTribal1161¾PrincMorv113hd	Well up,no excuse	8
25Jly56-7Hol	fst 1⅝	:463 1:361 2:003 2:381	3↑ Sunset H 110k	5	1	11½	11½	16	14¼	Shoemaker W	130	w	*.10	112-08	Swaps1304¼Honeys Alibi1081Blue Volt1083	Eased up late	9
14Jly56-8Hol	fst 1¼	:452 1:09 1:331 1:583	3↑ Hol Gold Cup H 162k	3	1	22	1hd	14	12	Shoemaker W	130	w	*.15	105-05	Swaps1302MisterGus 1171¼Porterhouse1192¼	Eased at finish	7
4Jly56-8Hol	fst 1⅛	:462 1:092 1:34 1:464	3↑ American H 103k	3	3	34½	3nk	13	11¾	Shoemaker W	130	w	*.20	100-12	Swaps1301¾MstrGus1116BobbyBrocto1158	Eased final stages	5
23Jun56-7Hol	fst 1 1/16	:231 :46 1:09 1:39	3↑ Inglewood H 52k	5	3	21½	1hd	13	12¾	Shoemaker W	130	w	*.30	107-06	Swaps1302¾MisterGus1152BobbyBrocto1217	Eased final 16th	7
9Jun56-7Hol	fst 1	:222 :451 1:084 1:331	3↑ Argonaut H 52k	1	1	11	1½	12	11¼	Shoemaker W	128	w	*.20	108-07	Swaps1281¼Bobby Brocato1236Porterhouse1192¾	In hand	6
26May56-7Hol	fst 1 1/16	:23 :453 1:092 1:404	3↑ Californian 109k	6	4	21½	1½	13	2hd	Shoemaker W	127	w	*.35	98-11	Porterhse118hdSwaps1275MistrGus1181¾	Eased by mistake	6
14Apr56-7GP	fst 1 70	:23 :453 1:092 1:393	3↑ Broward H 25k	4	2	22	11½	13	12¼	Shoemaker W	130	w	*.30	105-09	Swaps1302¼Gldr1055OurGob114no	Never to a drive,eased up	8
17Feb56-7SA	fst 1 1/16	:224 :462 1:103 1:43	4↑ Handicap 15000	7	4	42	1hd	1hd	11¾	Shoemaker W	127	w	*.70	89-15	Swaps1271¾Bobby Brocato124nkArrogate1159	Strong finish	7
31Aug55-7Was	gd 1¼	:46 1:102 1:373 2:041	WP Match 100k	2	2	21	21½	22	26½	Shoemaker W	126	w	*.30	74-17	Nashua1266½Swaps12	Wide on stretch turn,tired,swerved	2
20Aug55-7Was	fm 1 3/16 (T)	:472 1:114 1:354 1:543	American Derby 146k	5	1	11	11½	13	11	Shoemaker W	126	w	*.20	101-05	Swaps1261Traffic Judge1194Parador1131½	Very handy score	6
9Jly55-7Hol	fst 1¼	:463 1:102 1:344 2:003	Westerner 57k	1	1	11½	12	110	16	Shoemaker W	126	w	*.05	96-11	Swaps1266Fabulous Vegas1171Jean's Joe1203½	Eased up	5
11Jun55-7Hol	fst 1 1/16	:231 :46 1:10 1:402	3↑ Californian 109k	1	1	22	21	11	11¼	Erb D	115	w	*.65	103-06	Swaps1151¼Detrmine 26½MistrGus1173	In hand throughout	6

Past Performances of Great Horses of the 20th Century

Date/Race	Cond	Dist	Fractions				Race	PP	St	1st	2nd	Str	Fin	Jockey	Wt	Eq	Odds	Speed	Top finishers	Comment	Field
30May55- 6Hol	fst	1	:222	:452	1:101	1:35	©Will Rogers 27k	3	3	2½	1hd	13	112	Shoemaker W	126	w	*.15e	100-07	Swaps12612Bequeath122noMr.Sullivan1183	Drew out in hand	6
7May55- 7CD	fst	1¼	:472	1:122	1:37	2:014	Ky Derby 152k	8	1	11	1½	1½	11½	Shoemaker W	126	w	2.80	98-12	Swps1261½Nshua1266½SummrTn1264	Drew clear when urged	10
30Apr55- 6CD	fst	6f	:23	:462		1:101	Alw 5000	1	3	12½	12	14	18½	Shoemaker W	123	w	*.30	99-13	Swaps1238½TrimDestiny115¾Styrunnr1104½	Speed in reserve	5
19Feb55- 7SA	fst	1⅛	:454	1:103	1:37	1:50	SA Derby 137k	12	3	31	13	11	1½	Longden J	118	w	3.60e	91-14	Swaps118½Jean'sJoe1183½BlueRuler1183	Went wide,driving	14
19Jan55- 7SA	my	7f	:214	:45	1:103	1:24	San Vicente 22k	1	5	56½	21	12	13½	Shoemaker W	116	w	4.40e	83-25	Swaps1163½Trentonian120hdJean'sJoe1146	Speed in reserve	8
30Dec54- 6SA	fst	6f	:221	:451		1:10	Alw 6000	5	5	2hd	21	2hd	1no	Shoemaker W	118	w	5.25	95-11	Swaps118noBeau Busher1131¾Battle Dance118½	Strong drive	12
8Jly54- 6Hol	fst	5½f	:221	:453	:581	1:044	©CS Howard 29k	1	5	63½	65¼	58	58¾	Burton J	118	w	9.95e	85-12	ColonlMack114¾Mr.Sullivan1221BackHo1181	Showed nothing	6
22Jun54- 7Hol	fst	5f	:221	:454		:582	©Haggin 24k	9	7	83¾	73	31½	32	Burton J	122	w	6.40e	92-13	Mr. Sullivan114½Back Hoe1221½Swaps1221¾	Good effort	10
10Jun54- 7Hol	fst	5f	:221	:46		:582	©June Juv 16k	5	5	42½	32	1½	12½	Burton J	116	w	4.70	94-10	Swaps1162½Trentonian1192Noir116nk	Drew out	7
3Jun54- 7Hol	fst	5f	:221	:452		:58	Westchester 16k	2	5	42½	53½	51¾	32¼	Burton J	116	w	7.25	94-11	Back Hoe1191¼Trentonian1191Swaps116½	Failed to rally	7
20May54- 2Hol	fst	5f	:222	:454		:582	©Md Sp Wt	9	5	2hd	2hd	1hd	13	Burton J	120	w	12.60	94-12	Swaps1203Irish Cheer1203½Battle Dance1201½	Won handily	11

Tom Fool

b. c. 1949, by Menow (Pharamond II)–Gaga, by Bull Dog **Lifetime record: 30 21 7 1 $570,165**

Own.– Greentree Stable
Br.– Duval A. Headley (Ky)
Tr.– J.M. Gaver

Date/Race	Cond	Dist	Fractions				Race	PP	St	1st	2nd	Str	Fin	Jockey	Wt	Eq	Odds	Speed	Top finishers	Comment	Field
24Oct53- 7Pim	fst	1 3/16	:474	1:114	1:371	1:554	3↑ Pim Spl 50k	1	1	13	15	16	18	Atkinson T	126	w	-	101-20	Tom Fool1268Navy Page120noAlerted126	Much the best	3
	No wagering																				
26Sep53- 6Bel	fst	1	:231	:461	1:11	1:364	3↑ Sysonby 54k	2	1	11	12½	16	13	Atkinson T	126	w	-	90-15	Tom Fool1263Alerted126½Grecian Queen116	Under restraint	3
	No wagering																				
8Aug53- 7Sar	fst	1¼	:49	1:13	1:382	2:052	3↑ Whitney 27k	1	2	22	12	14	13½	Atkinson T	126	w	-	81-20	Tom Fool1263½Combat Boots114	Very much the best	2
	No wagering																				
4Aug53- 6Sar	fst	1	:232	:462	1:111	1:371	3↑ Wilson 16k	1	1	11	12½	16	18	Atkinson T	126	w	-	91-17	Tom Fool1268Indian Land117	No competition here	2
	No wagering																				
11Jly53- 6Aqu	fst	1¼	:483	1:132	1:38	2:042	3↑ Brooklyn H 56k	3	2	2hd	13½	13	11½	Atkinson T	136	w	*.25	85-13	Tom Fool1361½Golden Gloves1107High Scud109no	Easing up	5
27Jun53- 6Aqu	fst	7f	:22	:443	1:092	1:22	3↑ Carter H 59k	5	5	56	45	21½	12	Atkinson T	135	w	*.65	100-09	Tom Fool1352Squared Away1222¼Eatontown1131¼	Easily best	9
30May53- 6Bel	fst	1¼	:471	1:11	1:353	2:003	3↑ Suburban H 58k	1	1	13	13	11	1no	Atkinson T	128	w	*2.05	97-17	Tom Fool128noRoyal Vale1247Cold Command1142	Hard drive	7
23May53- 6Bel	gd	1	:223	:46	1:111	1:354	3↑ Metropolitan H 36k	3	2	22½	1½	11½	1½	Atkinson T	130	w	*.50	95-13	Tom Fool130½Royal Vale1278½Intent1251½	Driving,bore in	7
19May53- 6Bel	fst	6f	:223	:462		1:113	3↑ Joe Palmer H 15k	4	3	21½	2hd	12½	11½	Atkinson T	130	w	*.70	91-27	Tom Fool1301½Tea-Maker1141½Dark Peter121¾	Eased up	7
25Apr53- 5Jam	fst	5½f	:23	:461	:582	1:041	3↑ Handicap 7560	1	1	33	33½	2½	12½	Atkinson T	128	w	*.95	97-12	Tom Fool1282½Do Report1162¼Earmarked1143	Ridden out	5
8Nov52- 6Jam	fst	1 3/16	:47	1:112	1:381	1:58	Empire City H 55k	4	1	1½	1hd	1½	1hd	Atkinson T	128	w	*.65	86-23	Tom Fool128hdMarcador1092Roaring Bull1051½	Hard drive	8
1Nov52- 6Jam	fst	1⅛	:484	1:13	1:374	1:501	3↑ Westchester H 56k	3	2	31	31	2½	2no	Atkinson T	125	w	*1.75	95-18	Battlefield123noTomFool1251Alerted1251¼	Blocked,gaining	9
18Oct52- 6Jam	fst	1⅛	:471	1:11	1:354	1:492	3↑ Grey Lag H 60k	10	2	1hd	2hd	1hd	1no	Atkinson T	119	wb	*1.40e	99-16	Tom Fool119noBattlefield118nkAlerted1211¼	Hard drive	11
11Oct52- 6Jam	fst	1 3/16	:472	1:11	1:361	1:554	Roamer H 47k	7	5	42	31½	21	22	Atkinson T	126	w	*.75	95-14	Quiet Step1112Tom Fool1261Risque Rouge105¾	No excuse	9
30Sep52- 6Bel	fst	1	:232	:463	1:114	1:362	3↑ Sysonby H 15k	7	3	31½	3½	12	11¼	Atkinson T	126	w	*1.10	92-18	Tom Fool1261¼Alerted1183Greek Ship1181¼	Easily	8
17Sep52- 6Bel	fst	1	:232	:471	1:122	1:37	Jerome H 24k	5	2	21½	21½	14	17	Atkinson T	120	w	2.80	89-26	Tom Fool1207Marcador111nkMark-Ye-Well1301½	Hard drive	10
16Aug52- 6Sar	sly	1¼	:493	1:144	1:401	2:072	Travers 23k	4	1	11	11½	21	34	Atkinson T	114	w	*1.55	67-22	OneCount1263Armageddon1231TomFl114¾	Wide,weakened	8
	Geldings not eligible																				
11Aug52- 6Sar	sl	1⅛	:482	1:13	1:383	1:532	Alw 5000	3	2	21	2½	1hd	2no	Atkinson T	117	w	*.80	83-22	CountFlame117noTomFool117½GoldnGloves117½	Just missed	7
5Aug52- 6Sar	sly	1	:232	:47	1:123	1:392	3↑ Wilson 16k	1	3	37	22	12	14½	Atkinson T	106	w	*.25e	80-25	TomFool1064½NorthernStar1201ColonyDate1148	Drew clear	4
14Jly52- 6AP	fst	7f	:232	:452	1:10	1:223	Alw 6000	4	1	2hd	31	33½	44	Atkinson T	124	w	*.90	93-11	High Scud118½Mark-Ye-Well118½Eljay1183	Weakened	5
26Jun52- 6Aqu	fst	6f	:223	:462		1:103	Rippey H 10k	3	4	41½	52¾	2hd	2hd	Atkinson T	126	w	*1.00	99-15	Hitex120hdTom Fool1262Duke Fanelli1022	Hung	8
19Apr52- 6Jam	fst	1⅛	:48	1:12	1:383	1:522	Wood Memorial 63k	2	1	2hd	22½	1hd	2nk	Atkinson T	126	w	*1.65	84-16	Master Fiddle126nkTom Fool126½Pintor126½	Just failed	14

Past Performances of Great Horses of the 20th Century

7Apr52- 6Jam fst 6f :232 :464 1:121 Alw 10000 1 5 1½ 1hd 11 1nk Atkinson T 120 w *.80 86-20 Tom Fool120nkPrimate117nkCousin1202 Won cleverly 6
24Oct51- 6Jam sly 1 1/16 :242 :48 1:131 1:451 ©East View 53k 4 3 45½ 42 1hd 1nk Atkinson T 122 w *.65 86-15 Tom Fool122nkPut Out122nkRisque Rouge122¾ Hard drive 6
6Oct51- 6Bel fst 6½f-W :221 :451 1:101 1:171 Futurity 111k 7 4 41¼ 1nk 11¾ Atkinson T 122 w 5.75 86-14 Tom Fool1221¾Primate1221Jet's Date122hd Driving 10
Geldings not eligible
1Oct51- 5Bel fst 6f-WC :223 :45 1:092 Sp Wt 5000 3 1 31½ 31½ 24 Atkinson T 118 w *1.90 90-11 Hill Gail1184Tom Fool118nkBaybrook1182 Bothered early 16
1Sep51- 6Sar gd 6½f :233 :472 1:123 1:191 Hopeful 62k 2 4 31 1hd 1hd 21¼ Atkinson T 122 w *.75e 88-20 Cousin1221¼Tom Fool122nkHannibal12212 No excuse 6
25Aug51- 4Sar fst 6f :224 :463 1:114 Grand Union Hotel 21k 4 3 32 32 1hd 11 Atkinson T 122 w 2.05 89-16 Tom Fool1221Cousin126¾Jet Master1261¼ Driving 5
20Aug51- 6Sar fst 6f :231 :47 1:123 Sanford 11k 6 3 21 21 1½ 12¼ Atkinson T 113 w *.90 85-18 Tom Fool1132¼First Refusal1163½Secant1082½ Easily 8
13Aug51- 5Sar fst 5½f :232 :47 :593 1:062 ©Md Sp Wt 8 7 52 43½ 11 14 Atkinson T 118 w *2.00 85-17 Tom Fool1184Handsome Teddy1181Warpath1181 Easily 12

Twilight Tear

b. f. 1941, by Bull Lea (Bull Dog)–Lady Lark, by Blue Larkspur
Own.– Calumet Farm
Br.– Calumet Farm (Ky)
Tr.– B.A. Jones

Lifetime ecord: 24 18 2 2 $202,165

28Aug45- 6Was fst 6f :221 :452 1:102 3↑ Alw 5000 3 1 21½ 24 47½ - Dodson D 117 w 1.80 -- FightingDon1103Occupy1165MyTetRambler1111½ Bled,eased 5
1Nov44- 7Pim fst 1 3/16 :481 1:122 1:372 1:563 3↑ Pim Spl 25k 2 1 13 14 14 16 Dodson D 117 w *.65 99-12 Twilight Tear1176Devil Diver12610Megogo120 Galloping 3
21Oct44- 6Lrl my 1¼ :481 1:14 1:414 2:083 Maryland H 16k 4 1 11 23 46½ 415½ Dodson D 130 w *.15e 51-40 Dare Me1097Miss Keeneland1102½Aera1066 Quit badly 6
12Oct44- 6Lrl fst 1⅛ :472 1:123 1:40 1:531 3↑ ⒻQueen Isabella H 11k 4 1 16 16 15 15 Dodson D 126 w *.15e 82-23 Twilight Tear1265Good Morning1182Legend Bearer1083½ 8
Never extended
2Oct44- 5Bel fst 5½f-W :224 :452 1:032 3↑ ⒻHandicap 3480 3 1 2hd 1½ 12½ Arcaro E 126 w *.40e 97-08 Twilight Tear1262½Tellmenow118¾Cocopet1145 5
Bore out,impeded runner-up str
8Aug44- 6Bel fst 1¼ :471 1:112 1:372 2:033 ⒻAlabama 23k 1 1 1½ 11 11½ 2¾ Haas L 126 w *.05 81-14 Vienna114¾Twilight Tear1265Thread o' Gold1171¼ Faltered 4
22Jly44- 6Was fst 1¼ :48 1:12 1:372 2:033 Classic 79k 1 1 11 12 13 12 Haas L 114 w *.10e 92-08 TwlghtTr1142OldKntuck1194½Pnsv1265 Saved ground,handily 5
17Jly44- 3Was fst 1 :233 :471 1:112 1:361 Alw 5000 2 1 12 12 13 11¼ Haas L 117 w -e 97-11 Twilight Tear1171¼Pensive1222Appleknocker1101 Easily 4
Nonwagering event
6Jly44- 6Was fst 7f :23 :453 1:093 1:223 Skokie H 11k 5 2 11 12 13 11½ Haas L 121 w *.30e 103-10 TwilightTear1211½Sirde1142½ChallengM1065 Speed to spare 7
28Jun44- 6Was fst 6f :222 :453 1:103 ⒻPrincess Doreen 11k 1 2 21 22½ 2hd 11½ McCreary C 121 w *.40 98-09 TwilightTear1211½BelSong1106HrrtSu114nk Altered course 6
27May44- 6Bel gd 1⅜ :481 1:133 1:40 2:21 ⒻC C A Oaks 17k 1 1 12 13 13 14 McCreary C 121 w *.10 66-27 Twilight Tear1214Dare Me1213Plucky Maud1212 Easily 6
17May44- 6Bel fst 1 :233 :464 1:112 1:37 ⒻAcorn 14k 9 4 42 21 11½ 12½ McCreary C 121 w *.20 83-13 TwilightTear1212½Whirlabout1216Evrgt1211 Speed to spare 10
10May44- 6Pim fst 1 1/16 :234 :48 1:123 1:451 ⒻPim Oaks 18k 5 1 11½ 11 11½ 13 McCreary C 121 w *.30 92-19 Twilight Tear1213Plucky Maud1213Everget1215 In hand 5
3May44- 6Pim fst 6f :221 :453 1:113 Rennert H 7k 10 3 22 2½ 13 11½ McCreary C 118 w *.40e 95-17 TwilightTear1181½Glcc1083IdlGft112.52 As rider pleased 10
25Apr44- 6Pim sl 6f :224 :474 1:14 Alw 4000 3 2 2hd 11 1½ 11¼ McCreary C 117 w *.50e 83-35 TwilightTear1171¼GrampsImage1145Jmm1146Rated,drew away 5
17Mar44- 5TrP sly 6f :221 :453 1:122 ⒻAlw 1800 5 3 37 36½ 2¼ 13 McCreary C 118 w *.30 88-29 Twilight Tear1183Lassie Sue1201½Cuban Bomb1062 Handily 7
10Mar44- 6TrP fst 6f :23 :464 1:114 Alw 1800 7 1 11 11 14 12 McCreary C 117 w *.25 91-16 Twilight Tear1172Comenow1192½Surrogate122nk Easily 7
29Feb44- 6Hia fst 6f :23 :462 1:121 3↑ Leap Year H 5k 4 5 42¼ 3½ 31 32 Smith FA 101 w 9.00 86-23 Mettlesome1161Adulator1121Twilight Tear101hd Held well 8
8Nov43- 6Pim sly 1 70 :241 :49 1:153 1:472 ⒻAlw 5000 4 1 15 12 11 12¼ Thompson B 120 w *.50e 74-28 Twilight Tear1202¼Miss Keeneland1208Red Wonder11110 5
Speed in reserve
27Oct43- 6Pim my 1 1/16 :234 :481 1:14 1:482 ⒻSelima 24k 5 3 11 11½ 1nk 21 Thompson B 119 w *1.20e 75-27 MissKeeneland1111TwilightTear1191½Whrlbout1226 No match 8
20Oct43- 5Pim fst 1 70 :241 :49 1:143 1:454 ⒻAlw 2500 6 1 11½ 12 11 12 Thompson B 115 w *.40e 82-21 TwilightTear1152MissKenlnd1096MyMlch1061 Speed to spare 6
16Oct43- 7Pim sly 6f :23 :481 1:153 ⒻAlw 2500 1 4 1nk 2hd 2hd 32½ Smith FA 117 w *1.05e 72-21 Red Wonder111noCountess Wise1142½Twilight Tear117nk 8
Used in pace,lost ground
3Jly43- 6Was fst 6f :224 :464 1:131 ⒻArl Lassie 34k 3 6 22 22 13 12½ Jemas N 113 w *1.00e 85-14 TwilightTear1132½MissKeeneland1132MusicHall1104 Easily 15
25Jun43- 1Was fst 5½f :224 :473 1:003 1:073 ⒻMd Sp Wt 6 5 68½ 45 21 1¾ Eads W 115 w *1.60 87-17 Twilight Tear115¾Letmenow1151Durazna1153 12
Slow into stride,drawing clear

2004 RACING IN REVIEW

BY JAY PRIVMAN

The year 2004 - like the Carolinas, the Dakotas and Korea - was divided into two distinct halves. The first half, which encompassed the Triple Crown, belonged to Smarty Jones. He picked up where Funny Cide left off the previous spring and provided even greater highs and - because of the anticipation that the longest Triple Crown drought in history would finally end - an even more crushing low. But he last raced on June 5, then was subsequently retired. His racing career lasted seven months.

Exactly 29 days after the Belmont, on July 4, Ghostzapper won the Tom Fool at Belmont Park. The second half had started, and it belonged to him. Ghostzapper won two more stakes before a dazzling, runaway victory against the best Breeders' Cup Classic field ever assembled. His campaign lasted less than four months.

Smarty Jones and Ghostzapper never met on the racetrack, but they were the two most prominent candidates for Horse of the Year. In the end, Eclipse Award voters went for the horse they considered the better racehorse, not the most popular, and made Ghostzapper the 2004 Horse of the Year. He also was named champion older horse, and Frank Stronach, who bred and owned Ghostzapper, was voted champion breeder. Smarty Jones was named champion 3-year-old colt.

Smarty Jones may have prepped during the winter in Arkansas, but he belonged to

Ghostzapper s season began in early July, nearly a month after Smarty Jones career finale in the Belmont in June, and concluded with a definitive victory in the Breeders Cup Classic.

Philadelphia. Smarty Jones was bred in Pennsylvania. Owners Roy and Pat Chapman, trainer John Servis and jockey Stewart Elliott all were based out of Philadelphia Park, the utilitarian track lovingly referred to as The Pha, where Smarty Jones began his career. Smarty Jones returned in the spring as a conquering hero after capturing the Kentucky Derby.

The city's rabid sports fans, accustomed to the annual disappointments of the Phillies, Flyers, 76ers and Eagles, went wild over Smarty Jones. He was a prominent topic on sports talk shows. Thousands of fans came to watch him gallop - gallop! - at The Pha. They made pilgrimages to both the Preakness Stakes and Belmont Stakes to cheer their hometown boy, and others packed The Pha to watch those races on television. Sure, they could have watched the race at home, but they wanted to be a part of something special.

So did the record crowd of 120,139 that attended the Belmont Stakes. No horse had swept the Triple Crown since Affirmed in 1978. Smarty Jones was the sixth horse in the last eight years, and the third horse in consecutive years, to head to the Belmont with a chance to become the 12th Triple Crown winner. A quarter-mile from the finish, Smarty Jones had the lead, and the noise was deafening. Then the building went eerily silent. To paraphrase the old question about a tree falling in the woods, if a horse going for the Triple Crown gets beat in the final 100 yards and 120,000 people don't make a sound, did he really lose?

Sadly, for those who came to see history, yes. But Smarty Jones's loss left open the chance for someone to come along and overtake him for Horse of the Year.

Trainer Bobby Frankel always believed Ghostzapper would handle two turns, but the colt was such a good sprinter, he didn't get his chance until his eighth lifetime start. All Ghostzapper did was earn the biggest Beyer Speed Figure of the year, a 128, in Monmouth's Iselin Handicap.

Unlike Smarty Jones, there was nothing romantic about Ghostzapper. Frankel has been one of the sport's leaders for two decades, and Stronach, a native of Austria who deals with horsepower that has both four legs and four-wheel drive, is one of the world's wealthiest men. But purists were captivated by Ghostzapper's sheer brilliance. He might not have been the feel-good story of the year, but his performances were sublime.

The Breeders' Cup Classic, run for the first time in Texas at Lone Star Park, attracted a star-studded field that included Pleasantly Perfect, the winner of the Dubai World Cup; Birdstone, the conqueror of Smarty Jones in the Belmont and subsequent winner of the Travers; the mare Azeri, the 2002 Horse of the Year, and Roses in May, who had won all five of his previous starts in 2004.

Ghostzapper left them all gasping for air, romping by three lengths while covering the final quarter-mile of a 1 1/4-mile race in 23.64 seconds. That's a turn of foot that harkens back to Spectacular Bid and Secretariat.

Smarty Jones and Ghostzapper might both one day wind up in the Hall of Fame. If they make it, they would join the 2004 inductees, the horses Bowl of Flowers, Flawlessly and Skip Away, trainer Shug McGaughey, and jockeys Kent Desormeaux and Jimmy Winkfield.

Jockeys were in the news all year long. John Velazquez, who won his first Eclipse Award as champion jockey, set a single-season record for wins at Saratoga, but there were horrific tragedies - such as the death of Mike Rowland, and paralyzing injury to Gary Birzer - that led to contentious dealings both within the Jockeys' Guild itself, and between the Guild and racetracks, most notably at Churchill Downs, where 14 jockeys refused to ride because of insurance concerns. Shane Sellers retired, as did Ray Sibille, Patti Cooksey, and Rosemary Homeister Jr., and Julie Krone all but did. Rick Wilson was forced to retire after a nasty accident at Pimlico. The best young rider was Midwest-based Brian Hernandez Jr., who was voted champion apprentice jockey.

Todd Pletcher, the trainer for whom Velazquez rode first call, continued his steady ascent up the national standings and finally landed atop the money-won list, propelled by Breeders' Cup victories by Ashado in the Distaff and Speightstown in the Sprint. That helped bring Pletcher his first Eclipse Award as champion trainer. But Pletcher was not the only trainer who had an outstanding year.

Steve Asmussen obliterated the 28-year-old record for victories in a year held by Jack Van Berg. He went past Van Berg's 496 in November and finished with 555. Frankel, who has set his bar impossibly high, nearly reached it again, with 13 Grade 1 wins, twice as many as anybody else. And Servis did a masterful job not only with Smarty Jones, but also the undefeated Rockport Harbor, who won the Nashua and Remsen for 2-year-olds.

Tim Smith left the National Thoroughbred Racing Association. His expected coronation as the president of the New York Racing Association was aborted, however. Charlie Hayward, the former president of Daily Racing Form, got the top paying job. A month earlier, Barry Schwartz stepped down from his unpaid job as chairman.

Churchill Downs bought Fair Grounds, the biggest family-run track in the country. Magna Entertainment knocked down Gulfstream and rebuilt the racing surfaces to rave reviews but continued to bleed money. The company did, however, manage to get its HRTV on Dish Network, putting it on equal footing there with TVG.

Several icons of the sport passed, most notably Hall of Fame trainer P.G. Johnson, and owners Robert Sangster and W.T. Young. The outstanding sires Deputy Minister, Private Account and Storm Bird also died.

Racetracks continued to lobby with state and local governments to be put on equal footing with other forms of gaming. There was headway made on that front in Florida and Oklahoma, but the biggest stride was made in Pennsylvania, where approval was given for slots that will help fund purses. That might prove to be Smarty Jones's most significant, long-term achievement.

Here's a look back at the racing year 2004, division by division:

THREE-YEAR-OLD MALES

Smarty Jones earned a $5 million bonus from Oaklawn Park for sweeping that track's Rebel Stakes and Arkansas Derby, as well as the Kentucky Derby. When he subsequently won the Preakness, Smarty Jones was 8-for-8. But a demanding middle half-mile in the Belmont softened him up just enough to get run down by Birdstone. In a show of how popular Smarty Jones had become, Birdstone's co-owner, Marylou Whitney, apologized for beating him. Two months later, on a dark and stormy afternoon, Birdstone won the Travers. Had he upset older horses in the Breeders' Cup Classic, Birdstone could have been both champion 3-year-old colt and Horse of the Year, but he finished seventh, more than 12 lengths behind Ghostzapper. Nick Zito, who trained Birdstone, also won the Blue Grass with The Cliff's Edge, who ran second to Birdstone in the Travers. Most of the division's best had abbreviated campaigns, or were retired by the end of the year, including Santa Anita Derby winner Castledale, Florida Derby winner Friends Lake, and Haskell winner Lion Heart.

OLDER MALES

The two best horses in training in early 2004, Pleasantly Perfect and Medaglia d'Oro, went halfway around the world and thrilled an international audience with a memorable duel in Dubai. Pleasantly Perfect returned home and, after a freshening and a prep race, won the Pacific Classic, his third Grade 1 victory at 1 1/4 miles in less than 10 months. Southern Image began the year on a roll, taking the Sunshine Millions Classic, Santa Anita Handicap and Pimlico Special, then lost a narrow decision to Colonial Colony in the Stephen Foster. Roses in May re-rallied bravely to capture the Whitney during a five-race win streak. Frequent runner-up Total Impact jumped up and won the Hollywood Gold Cup. Funny Cide and Peace Rules, two graduates of the Triple Crown class of 2003, raced at a high level all year, with Funny Cide taking the Jockey Club Gold Cup and Peace Rules the Suburban. It was a strong division, but no one was stronger than Ghostzapper.

OLDER FILLY OR MARE

In 2003, Azeri dominated in the West, Sightseek in the East, but they never met.

Their duels in 2004 were among the highlights of the year. At the end of 2003, Azeri was so sour she refused to train. Trainer Laura de Seroux did not like the look of a tendon, and recommended she be retired. Michael Paulson, who manages the Allen Paulson Living Trust that owns Azeri, put her back in training after a two-month recuperation and transferred her to trainer D. Wayne Lukas. In her first start for Lukas, Azeri won the Apple Blossom Handicap for an unprecedented third straight year. Paulson's desire to race Azeri against males found her taking on the boys, without success, in both the Metropolitan Handicap and Breeders' Cup Classic. But she won two other Grade 1 races, the Go for Wand and Spinster, and split two decisions with Sightseek. In the Ogden Phipps, Sightseek trounced Azeri, but Azeri avenged that setback in the Go for Wand. At year's end, Azeri won this division's Eclipse Award for the third straight year. Sightseek, who fought unsoundness problems all year, bounced back from the Go for Wand defeat to take the Ruffian and Beldame. Storm Flag Flying mixed it up with Azeri and Sightseek all year and upset Azeri in the Personal Ensign. In California, Star Parade won the Santa Maria and Milady, Adoration took the Santa Margarita, Island Fashion the Santa Monica and Victory Encounter the Vanity.

3-YEAR-OLD FILLIES

Ashado was no match for Halfbridled in the 2003 Breeders' Cup Juvenile Fillies, but while Halfbridled failed to train on in 2004, Ashado rose to the top of the charts and was named champion. Ashado won the Kentucky

Kentucky Derby and Preakness winner Smarty Jones (right) has the lead in the stretch of the Belmont but is unable to hold off the late run of Birdstone, who would go on to win by a length.

Oaks and Coaching Club American Oaks, then defeated older fillies and mares in the Breeders' Cup Distaff. Society Selection got hot at Saratoga, taking the Test and Alabama. But for a troubled trip Society Selection also could have won the Acorn, which went to Kentucky Oaks runner-up Island Sand. The speedy Madcap Escapade burst onto the scene with four straight victories, including the Ashland against Ashado. She was hurt in the Kentucky Oaks, as were A.P. Adventure, the Las Virgenes winner, and Silent Sighs, the Santa Anita Oaks winner. Hard-knocking Stellar Jayne upset Ashado in the Mother Goose, was second in the CCA Oaks and Alabama, won the Gazelle, and was third in the Breeders' Cup Distaff. Friendly Michelle took the Prioress.

MALE TURF HORSE

Kitten's Joy, the Secretariat winner, emerged from a talented group of 3-year-olds to soundly defeat older runners in the Turf Classic, but he was stunned by Better Talk Now in the Breeders' Cup Turf. Still, his overall record made him the logical choice as this division's champion. In addition to the Turf, Better Talk Now scored an upset in the Sword Dancer in the summer. Kicken Kris bypassed the Sword Dancer to take a shot at the Arlington Million, in which he got kissed in when Powerscourt was disqualified from victory. Singletary, owned by a bunch of fun-loving thirtysomethings from California, won the Breeders' Cup Mile. Designed for Luck captured the Shoemaker, and Leroidesanimaux the Citation, Hollywood Park's Grade 1 races for middle-distance runners. Canada's favorite son, Soaring Free, scored a popular victory in the Atto Mile. Magistretti emerged from a thicket of horses with a dazzling turn of foot in the Man O' War. Meteor Storm, the best long-distance horse in California, headed east and took the Manhattan. Other major winners included Good Reward (Hollywood Derby), Nothing to Lose (Shadwell), Request for Parole (United Nations), Sabiango (Whittingham) and Special Ring (Eddie Read). Ken and Sarah Ramsey, who campaigned Kitten's Joy, Nothing to Lose, and the top older horse Roses in May, won the Eclipse Award as champion owner.

FEMALE TURF HORSE

Ouija Board, the top filly in Europe, scored a workmanlike victory in her lone United States outing, the Breeders' Cup Filly and Mare Turf, but that was enough to get her the division's championship. Another European, Crimson Palace, took the Beverly D. Riskaverse, the Beverly D. runner-up, returned to win the Flower Bowl. The best middle-distance runner might have been Intercontinental, who captured the Matriarch. Her trainer, Frankel, also trained Grade 1 winners Light Jig (Yellow Ribbon), Commercante (E.P. Taylor) and the tiny but mighty Megahertz. Ticker Tape could only finish third against older runners in the Matriarch, but she won the Queen Elizabeth II and American Oaks, and lost a heartbreaker in the Del Mar Oaks. Wonder Again crushed Intercontinental on a yielding course in the Diana. Musical Chimes captured the Mabee and beat the boys in the Oak Tree Mile. Other major winners included Amorama (Del Mar Oaks), Lucifer's Stone (Garden City) and Noches de Rosa (Gamely).

2-YEAR-OLD COLTS

Declan's Moon bypassed the Breeders' Cup Juvenile but nailed down the Eclipse Award by beating Breeders' Cup winner Wilko and Champagne Stakes winner Proud Accolade in a pivotal Hollywood Futurity. Earlier in the summer, Declan's Moon outdueled Roman Ruler in a thrilling Del Mar Futurity. Afleet Alex tenaciously prevailed on a sloppy track in the Hopeful, then lost narrowly in the Champagne and Breeders' Cup. Consolidator couldn't handle Afleet Alex at Saratoga but later won the Breeders' Futurity. Rockport Harbor defeated Galloping Grocer in a gripping battle of the unbeatens in the Remsen.

2-YEAR-OLD FILLIES

Sweet Catomine overcame a troubled trip by swiftly accelerating past her rivals in the Breeders' Cup Juvenile Fillies, in which she defeated the winners of the Frizette (Balletto), Alcibiades (Runway Model), and Matron (Sense of Style). The big, rangy filly also took the Del Mar Debutante and Oak Leaf. She towered, literally and figuratively, over the division, and received 273 out of a possible 274 votes as the Eclipse Award winner.

SPRINTER

Ghostzapper's lone sprint, in the Tom Fool, was outstanding. So too were the year-long exploits of Pico Central and Speightstown. Pico Central left his California base to win the Carter, Met Mile and Vosburgh, the latter in his lone head-to-head meeting with Speightstown. The Vosburgh was the only setback for Speightstown, who returned to win the Breeders' Cup Sprint; Pico Central passed the Breeders' Cup because of a stiff supplementary fee. Lion Tamer, like Speightstown trained by Pletcher, then upset Pico Central in the Cigar Mile. It was a difficult choice, but Eclipse Award voters opted for Speightstown. Kela, the Breeders' Cup runner-up, upset Pico Central in the Pat O'Brien, which completed a sweep of Del Mar's major stakes, including the Bing Crosby. Pohave, the Crosby runner-up, took the Triple Bend. Wildcat Heir was the longshot winner of the DeFrancis, defeating Forego winner Midas Eyes. Our New Recruit went halfway around the world and won the Dubai Golden Shaheen. Pomeroy rallied to win the King's Bishop. Champali and the mare Ema Bovary were the stars of Calder's Summit of Speed. The best female sprinter on the East Coast was Lady Tak, who won the Ballerina.

STEEPLECHASER

The popular McDynamo returned from a lengthy layoff to win the Breeders' Cup Steeplechase, but he was no match for Hirapour in the Colonial Cup, and that weighed strongly with voters, who gave Hirapour the championship. Two other well-regarded veterans, Praise the Prince and Tres Touche, were the stars of the summer at Saratoga.

The Year in Sales and Breeding

By Glenye Cain

As in the racing world, thoroughbred breeding's top story in 2004 was Smarty Jones. The Elusive Quality colt validated every small breeder's dream when he won the 2004 Kentucky Derby and Preakness for Roy and Pat Chapman, who had bred and raced their own stock from their small Someday Farm in Pennsylvania, mainly competing in Philadelphia and the Mid-Atlantic.

The tale of the "backyard-bred" runner and his modest breeders and owners captivated the general public and created a mania for the colt. But the story got even more interesting for Thoroughbred breeding insiders in early summer as major farms began jockeying for the right to stand the popular runner. Before his Triple Crown attempt in the Belmont, the Chapmans had arranged interviews in Philadelphia for farm officials. They followed up by visiting central Kentucky to tour the farms still in the running as the price escalated beyond $35 million. The Chapmans and their suitors didn't discuss negotiations publicly, but bloodstock players followed the secretive process day to day as well as they could, gossiping daily on where the couple had last been seen and which farm appeared to have the momentum. Even Smarty Jones's loss to Birdstone in the Belmont didn't dent his appeal, and at the end of June the winning stud farm got the nod: Robert and Blythe Clay's Three Chimneys nursery in Midway, Ky., inked a deal reportedly worth about $39 million. Though not as large as the reported $60 million total syndication value Coolmore put on Fusaichi Pegasus in 2000 or the $40 million for Shareef Dancer in 1983, the Smarty Jones syndication was one of the largest in Thoroughbred history.

Three Chimneys got Smarty Jones in an innovative deal that stretched the boundaries of usual syndication to 60 shares. The Chapmans kept half of those, with Three Chimneys acquiring the remaining 30, of which it sold 20 shares for $650,000 each. By August, the farm reported that all of those shares were sold out.

To get Smarty Jones, Three Chimneys agreed to several terms the Chapmans had set out: that the colt not shuttle, that his book not be excessively large (Three Chimneys has contractually limited the horse's book to 110 mares), that he be available to his fans, and that the Chapmans determine his racing plans at 4. As it happened, much to the dismay and anger of many racing fans, the colt was retired in August due to what veterinarians described as racing- and training-related bruising of all four cannon bones. Smarty Jones paraded one last time for his Philadelphia Park faithful on Aug. 14, then headed for Three Chimneys.

By the end of the year, before he had covered a single mare, Smarty Jones already had changed the face of Three Chimneys. In keeping with its fan-friendly promise, the farm hired a full-time tour director and began expanding its parking area to accommodate tour buses. At the close of 2004, the farm estimated it was leading 175 visitors, on average, through the stallion barn each week.

The Smarty story rippled through other facets of the bloodstock world. In November, his dam, the 12-year-old Smile mare I'll Get Along, sold at Fasig-Tipton Kentucky's November breeding stock sale in a televised event. Carrying a full sibling to the Derby and Preakness winner, she brought $5 million from Olin Gentry of Gaines-Gentry Thoroughbreds. John and Susan Sykes, who own CloverLeaf Farms II in Florida, sold the mare. Their farm manager, Brent Fernung, had bought her for them when the Chapmans dispersed their stock at the 2001 Keeneland November auction. Her cost then: $130,000. Fernung responded to the $5 million sale with relief, revealing that he had advised Sykes to turn down a $3.5 million deal for the mare just before Smarty Jones lost the Belmont.

Before selling at Fasig-Tipton, I'll Get Along survived one of the year's other big stories: the series of three hurricanes - Ivan, Jeanne, and Frances - that hit Florida between August and November, wreaking havoc on central Florida horse farms.

Smarty Jones was the dominant personality of the year, but he was not the biggest issue. Ethics in bloodstock transactions became front-page news in Thoroughbred trade publications when prominent buyer Satish Sanan boycotted the summer select yearling auctions over what he felt were unethical business practices by agents and auction houses. His public airing of concerns about dual agency and other practices led the Thoroughbred Owners and Breeders Association to form a sales integrity task force. And in December, after four months of study, the 22-member panel released a recommended code of ethics for public and private horse sales. The code was a mixed result for Sanan, who had served on the panel. It encouraged more disclosure of clients' identities and of equine veterinary information, but it did not set out any penalties for violations, and panelists acknowledged that they had little legal leverage to require auction houses or agents to reveal the actual identities of agents' clients in a transaction.

The code's shortcomings in that area were immediately made apparent when Keeneland president Nick Nicholson, at the code's unveiling, declined to reveal the buyer of a sale-record $8 million colt at the 2004 Keeneland September auction.

The $8 million sale was one of the year's strangest incidents. During bidding for the Lane's End, agency's chestnut Storm Cat - Welcome Surprise colt, Coolmore chief John Magnier found himself outgunned by an inconspicuous-looking Japanese trainer named Hideyuki Mori, who was just a few feet away from Magnier and bidding while on his cell phone. When the hammer fell, Mori signed for the colt and then bolted for cover, declining to name his client. Flamboyant Japanese entrepreneur Fusao Sekiguchi, who campaigned 2000 Derby winner Fusaichi Pegasus, was a leading suspect and even admitted the purchase before his entourage, led by his daughter-in-law, began denying that claim. At year's end, the colt was known to be in training at the McKathan brothers' Florida training center, but his owner's identity was still officially a mystery, though it was generally assumed in racing circles to be Sekiguchi.

The $8 million colt served to remind the

commercial breeding community of Storm Cat's dominance, and of W. T. Young's faith in the stallion. Young, who died in January of 2004, built a breeding empire on Storm Cat. Young's death of a heart attack at age 85 prompted a flood of memories about his contributions to the sport. A Lexington, Ky., businessman and philanthropist, Young developed Overbrook Farm in to a showplace and believed in Storm Cat strongly enough that he gave away seasons to the stallion when the horse proved unpopular in his initial year at stud.

Young, who also bred and campaigned 1996 Kentucky Derby winner Grindstone, was also well known for his long association with Hall of Fame trainer D. Wayne Lukas, a relationship that Lukas believed had been a "stabilizing force."

"I have a tendency to get a little opinionated and go off the deep end every once in a while, and he was a stabilizer against that," Lukas said after Young's death. "I don't think there's another person who could have had more influence on my career and in my life in general than Bill Young did."

Young's runners included champions Timber Country, Flanders, Golden Attraction, Boston Harbor, and Surfside; classic winners Grindstone, Tabasco Cat, and Editor's Note; and Breeders' Cup Classic winner Cat Thief, among others.

Another major death was that of Robert Sangster, who helped found the powerful Coolmore operation, which has grown since the 1970s into the single most powerful commercial breeding entity in the world. Sangster, 67, died in April of pancreatic cancer. He had bred and raced more than 100 Group or Grade 1 winners but was perhaps best remembered by the public as the man who, in partnership, bought the yearling Seattle Dancer for $13.1 million, still a world-record auction price, at Keeneland's 1985 July sale.

The Thoroughbred market in 2004 hit record heights, starting with the early spring juvenile sales. Fusao Sekiguchi paid a world-record $4.5 million for Fusaichi Samurai at Fasig-Tipton's Calder auction, Keeneland's April sale featured a sale-record $3.3 million Pulpit colt, and the Ocala Breeders' Sales Company's Calder vendue saw a sale-record $1.6 million Wild Rush colt. At Barretts, a $2 million Awesome Again filly set a world mark for a juvenile filly at the Barretts March auction.

The yearling sales were also bullish, and Keeneland September's record $8 million colt helped it to become the world's richest auction with $324 million in gross receipts.

In sire rankings for 2004, Smarty Jones's sire Elusive Quality led all North American sires by progeny earnings, beating out El Prado by a little less than $1 million. The year's top freshman sire was Successful Appeal; juvenile sire was Storm Cat; and broodmare sire was Dixieland Band.

Though he ended the year as the eighth-ranked general sire (and second-leading third crop sire), Awesome Again scored a notable triumph in the Breeders' Cup as the sire of two winners: Classic winner Ghostzapper, who also was named Horse of the Year, and Juvenile winner Wilko. Awesome Again stands at Frank Stronach's Adena Springs Farm, which received an Eclipse Award as 2004's leading breeder.

PROFILES OF TOP HORSES OF 2004

BY MIKE WATCHMAKER

2-Year-Old Colts and Geldings

Declan's Moon

This gelding was perfect in four starts, defeated the Breeders' Cup Juvenile winner in what all agreed was the definitive race for his category and led a division that inspired as much skepticism as optimism...impressed winning at first asking, and in light of that, he was a bigger surprise than he should have been when he recorded a 6-1 upset over the 1-5 Roman Ruler in the Del Mar Futurity second time out...won the Del Mar Futurity on the square, simply outfighting Roman Ruler in the late stages...was purposely withheld from the Breeders' Cup Juvenile, partly because his connections wanted to give him plenty of recovery time after having to run fast enough to earn a Beyer Speed Figure of 107 in the Del Mar Futurity and partly because his connections felt passing that race would benefit his future development...that decision could not have worked out better, as his late-season goal of the Hollywood Futurity evolved into the race with the most divisional championship implications...prepped for the Hollywood Futurity with a comfortable win in the Hollywood Prevue...had to work harder in the Hollywood Futurity, his first venture around two turns, than some expected, and his final time was good for only a moderate Beyer Figure of 96...at the same time, he easily handled Champagne Stakes winner Proud Accolade and beat upset Breeders' Cup Juvenile winner Wilko back to third.

Afleet Alex

The victim of bad racing luck, and perhaps questionable rides, in two very critical races...could have easily won all six of his starts and been unanimously recognized as the leader of his division...had traffic trouble when second, beaten a half-length, in the Champagne Stakes, his first career defeat...was probably best in the Breeders' Cup Juvenile...was last of eight early in the Juvenile, farther back than he ever had been before, and made a sustained, five-wide rally to reach the front in midstretch but was run down late by Wilko...with it all, he was beaten less than a length finishing second...began his career with two sensational, double-digit victories at Delaware Park and then crushed a big group of intriguing prospects in the Sanford Stakes...looked beaten at 3-5 in deep stretch of the Hopeful but surged late despite ducking out sharply to prevail.

Fusaichi Sumurai

Raced only once but added some much-needed pizzazz to a division that lacked truly compelling figures...was no secret even well before he made his first public appearance...was purchased for a record $4.5 million as a 2-year-old in training in February by Fusao Sekiguchi, who raced his sire, Fusaichi Pegasus...he then was turned over to trainer Neil Drysdale, who trained Fusaichi Pegasus to win the 2000 Kentucky Derby...weeks before he made his first start, he was as low as 20-1 in 2005 Kentucky Derby future book betting in some Las Vegas racebooks...finally made his first start in mid December...despite being far from cranked up, he toyed with his opponents, finished powerfully and won in the manner of a colt with vast potential.

Wilko

He came from England unheralded and engineered the biggest upset of Breeders' Cup Day, coming again on the outside after appearing beaten in upper stretch to win the Breeders' Cup Juvenile at 28-1...he was that price in a Juvenile field of only eight because he had won only two of 10 starts in England, both novice stakes at Yarmouth, although he did hit the board in two Group 2 events and one Group 3 race...given the nature of his Juvenile upset and the trouble encountered in that race by Afleet Alex, he went into the Hollywood Futurity with the responsibility of proving he wasn't a fluke...could not keep step with Declan's Moon in the stretch of the Hollywood Futurity but still ran creditably to be beaten one length finishing third...is clearly more effective on dirt than he was on turf in England, which is logical considering he is by Breeders' Cup Classic winner Awesome Again.

2-Year-Old Fillies

Sweet Catomine

Along with Ghostzapper and Smarty Jones, she totally dominated her division...the intriguing thing is, she did so at a time when her running style, manner, and the large frame she has yet to grow into suggests she hasn't even come close to her peak...after finishing second in an abbreviated sprint in her career debut and then getting her first win with a last-to-first rally in the Grade 1 Del Mar Debutante, she really signaled she was a force to deal with in her third start, the Oak Leaf...looking like a natural in her first attempt at two turns, she made a wide sustained run from well back and maintained her momentum after getting the lead in upper stretch to score with complete authority...that Oak Leaf performance made her the favorite in the Breeders' Cup Juvenile Fillies, in which she was even better...despite being stopped in traffic nearing the stretch, she still managed to romp over her 11 opponents...notably, her final time in the Juvenile Fillies was 44 hundredths of a second faster than her male counterparts required to complete the same distance in the Breeders' Cup Juvenile.

Balletto

Never worse than second in five starts, like Sweet Catomine, she blossomed when given the opportunity to race at longer distances...was bred in the United Arab Emirates and is a Darley Stable homebred...no match for Sweet Catomine in the Juvenile Fillies and fortunate to be second instead of third, this was the only time Balletto was really outrun...won the first two starts of her career at sprint distances but in slow final times...demonstrated dramatic improvement when stretched out to a mile in the Matron Stakes in her third start, rallying to finish a sharp second to Sense of Style, who won the Spinaway in her prior start and who, at the time, was the top 2-year-old filly in the east...affirmed her affinity for distance with a next-to-last to first rally in the Frizette.

Runway Model

By far the most active of the prominent 2-year-old fillies of 2004, she started 10 times from late April through late November...was just another face in the crowd with a maiden win through her first four starts but began to come to hand after the confidence gained from a fast allowance score at River Downs in August...she competed in nothing but stakes from that point and ran well in each...following seconds in the Bassinet and Arlington-Washington Lassie, she edged a solid and deep field in the Alcibiades...she may have won that race by just a head at 17-1, but that doesn't do justice to the fact that she did so with a wide rally from far back over Keeneland, which is notoriously tilted toward inside runners with speed...finished third in the Breeders' Cup Juvenile Fillies but certainly would have been second to Sweet Catomine, and ahead of Balletto, had she not been shut off twice during the stretch run...completed her campaign with a victory in the Golden Rod, which was only the third time in her career she was sent off the favorite.

Splendid Blended

A very capable performer who went three for four on the season...at the same time, she is an excellent measure of just how good Sweet Catomine is...won the first start of her career in a common gallop, and as a result, was actually favored over Sweet Catomine in the Oak Leaf despite the latter's victory in the Del Mar Debutante...was clearly no match for Sweet Catomine in the Oak Leaf, although she was easily second best...passed on the Breeders' Cup Juvenile Fillies, and another meeting with Sweet Catomine, to make a late-season run at the Hollywood Starlet...cruised at 1-10 in an allowance prep for the Starlet and proved best in the Starlet itself, besting Sharp Lisa, who previously was a narrowly beaten second to Runway Model in the Alcibiades but who finished sixth in the Breeders' Cup after a tough, outside draw.

3-Year-Old Colts and Geldings

Smarty Jones

By far and away the best 3-year-old of 2004, and with the way he captured the public's imagination and help move thoroughbred racing into the mainstream media during his gallant bid for the Triple Crown, many regard him as the horse who did more for the sport than any other in many years...despite going three for three at 2, he began the year in relative obscurity and did not advance his profile much with a workmanlike score in the Southwest in his first start of the season...he really began to gain notice with a drubbing of the highly regarded Purge in the Rebel Stakes...completed a perfect stay at Oaklawn Park with a decisive victory in the Arkansas Derby, a score that proved to be important because it gave him the graded stakes earnings to assure a berth in the Kentucky Derby...was flawless in extremely wet conditions in the Kentucky Derby, establishing forward early position through a quick opening half-mile, and then having the stamina his pedigree did not promise to draw away in the final furlongs...was positively electrifying in the Preakness, blowing his field away through the stretch to rack up an 11 1-2 length victory in time fast enough to earn an excellent Beyer Speed Figure of 118...he was 2-5 in the Belmont Stakes to become the first Triple Crown winner since Affirmed in 1978...was comfortable through a moderate opening half-mile, but was then goaded (and allowed by jockey Stewart Elliott) into running the fastest middle half-mile in the history of the Belmont, which had been run only 135 times before...still had a clear lead with an eighth of a mile to go but understandably ran out of gas and was caught by Birdstone...along with Spectacular Bid in

1979, he was the most worthy horse to be denied the Triple Crown in the Belmont...some racing fans were alienated when, with his owners already having a lucrative stud contract in hand, he was retired in late summer.

Birdstone

Winner of the Champagne at 2, this small colt did not develop much physically into his 3-year-old year, which meant his light constitution made it difficult for him to maintain a regular racing schedule...nevertheless, he did turn into something of a big race specialist...began his season with an easy allowance win but never ran a step as the odds-on favorite in the subsequent Lane's End over a track that was sealed just before race time...went on to the Kentucky Derby anyway and turned in another dull effort, finishing eighth...after skipping the Preakness, he returned to the scene of his Champagne win in the Belmont Stakes and capitalized on a perfect trip to spring a 36-1 upset and become the only horse to ever defeat Smarty Jones...by this point, trainer Nick Zito determined this colt did his best with plenty of time between starts, which explains why he did not have a prep before competing in the Travers...in surreal conditions due to the onset of a powerful summer storm, he came from off the pace and pulled away late to win as much the best...went into the Breeders' Cup Classic without a prep off a similar layoff and was in position with a victory to steal the 3-year-old championship from Smarty Jones and lay claim to Horse of the Year honors...never mounted a threat, however, finishing a distant seventh, which raised the question of whether 2004's best 3-year-olds were really comparable to the year's best older horses...retired soon after the Classic.

Kitten's Joy

Three-year-old turf specialists are not often mentioned in the same breath with the top 3-year-old main track performers, but here is a legitimate exception as the 2004 3-year-old division lacked real depth, and he had an outstanding campaign on turf...in fact, he was so good, he ranked as the best turf horse of any age in 2004...won the Tropical Park Derby, the Palm Beach, the Crown Royal American Turf, and the Virginia Derby, and was beaten a head in the Jefferson Cup, in his first five starts of the year...however, he signaled he was a force in the Secretariat Stakes on the Arlington Million undercard...not only did he come from way back to win the Secretariat with great style, he did so in faster time than the Arlington Million at the same distance was run in two races earlier...even more impressive winning the Turf Classic, running his final quarter-mile in that 1 1-2 mile race in a little more than 22 seconds, which is brilliant under optimal circumstances and even more so over the yielding ground he caught that day...that decisive victory made him the only prominent 3-year-old of 2004 to have won a meaningful race over older opponents...was the shortest priced favorite on Breeders' Cup Day but had a troubled trip and also seemed to have trouble with the footing and settled for second...remains in training for 2005, although he has since undergone knee surgery.

Lion Heart

Had plenty of talent but may have been stifled by some distance limitations that were apparent when he faced top company...sustained tough beats when second in his first two starts of the year (his first two career losses), getting nailed in the San Rafael after contesting a fast pace and getting caught late in the Blue Grass while racing wide on the rail-favoring Keeneland surface...gave Smarty Jones a battle to deep stretch of the Kentucky Derby before settling for second, finishing ahead of 16 opponents...the Preakness looked like a replay in the early stages, with him leading Smarty Jones again, but when Smarty Jones broke that race open so explosively, he lost heart and faded to fourth...returned from a freshening with victories in the Long Branch Breeders' Cup and Haskell Invitational and was sent off the favorite in the Travers as a result...was on an easy lead in the Travers but went wrong in the race and was retired the next day.

3-Year-Old Fillies

Ashado

A gem of consistency from early March until the end of October in a division that saw many of the leading lights of the early months sidelined by injury and a new wave of challengers emerge in the summer...then again, she was very reliable at 2, when she won four of six starts, including three stakes, and was never worse than third...never worse than third in her eight 2004 starts and among her five victories, clear-cut decisions in the Fair Grounds Oaks, the Kentucky Oaks and the Coaching Club American Oaks gave her a leg up on command of her division...avenged a narrow defeat to early-season threat Madcap Escapade in the Ashland by beating her back to third in the Kentucky Oaks...avenged a second to Stellar Jayne in the Mother Goose by beating that opponent in the CCA Oaks...and, she avenged a loss to Society Selection and Stellar Jayne when third in the Alabama by beating them both, as well as Storm Flag Flying, Island Fashion, and other older opponents in the Breeders' Cup Distaff, which she won despite some trouble at the top of the stretch...remains in training in 2005.

Society Selection

After winning the Frizette at 2, she was expected to be a major player in her division in 2004...yet, despite a victory in the Comely in April, seconds in the Acorn and Bonnie Miss and a third in the Davona Dale suggested she wasn't making the progress expected of her...that all changed when she got Lasix at Saratoga as she crushed a talented field of sprinters in the seven-furlong Test Stakes and then successfully stretched out to 1 1-4 miles in the Alabama to soundly defeat Stellar Jayne and Ashado to complete a Grade 1 stakes double at that meeting...she proved her sudden emergence was not merely due to an affinity for Saratoga (which she does have) when she followed with a fine second to Sightseek in the Beldame...as a stretch runner, she was severely compromised by the slow pace the top-class Sightseek controlled, but she ran on well

to be beaten less than three lengths while finishing ahead of Storm Flag Flying...was well backed in the Breeders' Cup Distaff but was dull, just as she was when she unsuccessfully traveled for the 2003 Breeders' Cup Juvenile Fillies at Santa Anita...also to remain in training in 2005.

Stellar Jayne

Certainly the most active of the most prominent 3-year-old fillies of 2004, she never looked destined for this list after six ineffective stakes attempts at the beginning of her campaign...that all changed in June in the Dogwood Breeders' Cup Stakes...after competing in Grade 1 events in three of her prior four starts, she found the easier company in the Dogwood more to her liking and won going away...that did wonders for her confidence, as she came right back to spring a 29-1 surprise on Ashado in the Mother Goose...she proved that was no fluke with game seconds in the CCA Oaks and Alabama, a win over the improving Daydreaming in the Gazelle Handicap and a troubled trip third in the Indiana Breeders' Cup Oaks...her best performance, however, may have been her third in the Breeders' Cup Distaff...poorly drawn on the outside in a field of 11, she trailed early, made a very wide, sustained rally and was beaten only 1 1-2 lengths for it all...sold for $3.6 million at the Keeneland November breeding stock sale, she is now a member of the Dubai based Godolphin Racing and is scheduled to return to this country for a campaign the second half of 2005.

Ouija Board

She made only one start in the United States and that on turf, but her victory in the Breeders' Cup Filly and Mare Turf as a 3-year-old over a high-class field of older opponents means she merits inclusion on this list...her Breeders' Cup victory was no surprise, as she was 4-5 off dominating wins in the English and Irish Oaks and an outstanding third, beaten only 1 1-2 lengths, against Europe's best males, 3-years-old and older, in the Arc de Triomphe...sat comfortably off a very slow early pace in the Filly and Mare Turf and powered clear in the final furlong despite giving the impression that she was not comfortable with either the footing or the setting...the 108 Beyer Speed Figure she earned in her Breeders' Cup win was higher than the career-best Beyers so far earned by Ashado, Society Selection and Stellar Jayne.

Older Males

Ghostzapper

Was simply the best horse to set foot on an American race track in 2004 and may well have been the best horse seen in this country in several years...required only four starts from July to October to prove it...overwhelmed an uncommonly deep field in the Breeders' Cup Classic, humbling, among others, five opponents – Roses in May, Pleasantly Perfect, Azeri, Birdstone and Funny Cide – who with a victory would have laid strong claim to Horse of the Year honors...the 124 Beyer Speed Figure he earned in his front-running Classic victory was easily the highest of all the winning Beyer Figures in the Classic published in this manual dating back to 1990...began his 4-year-old season with an easy victory in the seven-furlong Tom Fool Stakes, for which he received a Beyer Figure of 120, which was the highest of the year in North America in races under a mile...was then sent beyond seven furlongs for the first time in his career in the 1 1-8 mile Iselin Breeders' Cup Handicap and responded with a near 11-length romp in the slop, earning a Beyer of 128, which was the highest assigned in any type of race over any surface in 2004...between the Iselin and Breeders' Cup, he demonstrated he could handle a battle as well, prevailing in the Woodward after a near race-long battle with Saint Liam, who also carried him out severely through the stretch run...the 128 Beyer he earned in the Iselin and the 124 Beyer he received in the Classic were the two best Beyers assigned in all of 2004...remains in training in 2005.

Pleasantly Perfect

The 2003 Breeders' Cup Classic winner was the top older horse in the country until the late-season emergence of Ghostzapper...set an ambitious early-season goal of the Dubai World Cup and prepped for it with a decisive victory in the San Antonio...succeeded in Dubai, catching fellow American invader Medaglia d'Oro in the late stages, while leaving highly fancied local hope Victory Moon five lengths farther back in third...after being given plenty of time to recover from his arduous journey, he was upset in the San Diego Handicap in his first start back in this country, uncharacteristically failing to hold on to a clear stretch lead...that gave rise to the suspicion that he fell victim to the Dubai World Cup effect that has found so many American horses rendered ineffective after competing in that race, though he did rebound in his next start to win the Pacific Classic, albeit with a slightly less-than-vintage performance...his closing style was up against it in the Classic at Lone Star, where the short stretch and track surface combine for a natural tilt toward horses with speed...was also compromised in the Classic by a wide trip...nevertheless, he failed to mount a serious threat and was beaten seven lengths finishing third in what proved to be his career finale.

Roses in May

Like Ghostzapper, he brought a perfect 2004 record into the Breeders' Cup Classic...although no match for Ghostzapper in that race, was very game chasing him around the track and proving easily second best in a strong field...despite his win in the Cornhusker Breeders' Cup Handicap in his third start of the year, he became a national name after a memorable effort in the Whitney Handicap...after disputing a blistering early pace in the nine-furlong Whitney that saw fractions of 22.64 seconds, 45.25 and 1:08.92, and then being collared by Perfect Drift in midstretch, he would not capitulate and prevailed by a nose in a truly courageous performance...a draining race like that would have soured the subsequent

form of many horses, but he showed substance by coming back to gallop in the Kentucky Cup Classic Handicap and with his big Breeders' Cup try...also remains in training in 2005.

Medaglia d'Oro

Started only twice in 2004, but that's all this multiple Grade 1 winner required to again demonstrate brilliance and prove he was near the top of his class...began his 5-year-old campaign in the Donn Handicap and won with total authority, by nearly five lengths, over Seattle Fitz and Funny Cide, who would each go on to important stakes victories later in the year...the Donn proved to be his prep for the Dubai World Cup...if the Dubai Cup were at 1 1-8 miles, a distance at which he may have been superior to Pleasantly Perfect, he would have won...instead, the Dubai Cup is at about 1 1-4 miles, and he was caught by Pleasantly Perfect in the last 100 yards...was retired in the spring, unfortunately joining a long list of American horses who never raced again, or never regained their form, after competing in that event.

Older Fillies and Mares

Azeri

The 2002 Horse of the Year and divisional champion in 2002 and 2003 went from being an inch away from retirement at the start of 2004 to leader of her division again…was kept in training by owner Michael Paulson despite concerns over a tendon held by previous trainer Laura De Seroux and was turned over to Hall of Fame trainer D. Wayne Lukas, for whom she ran some of the best races of her accomplished career…began her 6-year-old campaign with a victory in the Apple

Blossom Handicap for the third straight year…that was her first start for Lukas, and she earned a career-best Beyer Speed Figure of 112…then lost her next three starts but with extenuating circumstances: was beaten a head in the Humana Distaff Handicap by Mayo on the Side while conceding that opponent 11 pounds, finished eighth of nine when pitted against males in the Metropolitan Handicap, and then uncharacteristically failed to be competitive when back in with members of her own sex in the Ogden Phipps Handicap…those last two defeats came at Belmont Park, and her non-effort in the Phipps gives weight to the belief that she could not handle the unique surface of that track…regained top form at Saratoga, beating back Sightseek in a battle between the two best older females in the country in the Go for Wand Handicap and running a winning race in defeat in the Personal Ensign Handicap…moved prematurely into a fast pace in the 1 1-4 mile Personal Ensign and was caught late by Storm Flag Flying…rebounded to win the Spinster decisively, showing for the first time in more than a year a willingness to rate effectively off the early lead…would have been a heavy favorite to win another Breeders' Cup Distaff, a race she won in 2002, but was instead placed against males again in the Classic…faded in the Classic to be a well-beaten fifth in what turned out to be the last start of a Hall of Fame career.

Sightseek

A top class performer who was absolutely championship-worthy, but she had the misfortune of being a contemporary of Azeri's…after turning in a dull fourth to kick off her season in the Santa Monica Handicap over a Santa Anita surface she never enjoyed success over, she was sent east…she romped in the Rampart Handicap, flopped in the slop in the Louisville Breeders' Cup Handicap and then completed her career with four straight strong performances…won the Ogden Phipps Handicap in a common gallop, leaving Azeri nearly 12 lengths back in fourth and last, although in fairness, Azeri clearly did not show up on a surface she could not handle…both she and Azeri brought it to the table in the Go for Wand and she gave Azeri all she could handle until the final furlong, when the reigning champ proved too much…came back to win the Ruffian Handicap by a double digit margin…her connections stuck to their guns, ruled out a Breeders' Cup appearance from her and made the Beldame at her beloved Belmont Park (she completed her career having won all six of her starts there) her final start…she again won easily, prompting such a display of emotion from her Hall of Fame trainer Bobby Frankel that it was clear that, with all the important horses he has trained, this one had a special place in his heart.

Storm Flag Flying

She never really fulfilled the great promise she offered when she was an undefeated 2-year-old filly champion in 2002, and she was never a true match for Azeri and Sightseek, but she came back with an honest 4-year-old campaign that erased the bad taste of her brief and forgettable 3-year-old season...won the Shuvee Handicap in her third start of the year and then moved up to face the best in the final five starts of her career...couldn't dent Sightseek when easily second best in the Ogden Phipps, or Azeri and Sightseek when third in the Go For Wand but was rewarded for her persistence in the Personal Ensign who, interestingly, is her granddam...she capitalized on Azeri prematurely moving into a strong pace, and the fact that the 1 1-4 mile distance may have been just beyond Azeri's reach, and she outgamed Azeri in the final furlong to win clear...she encountered the other sign of the coin when third to Sightseek in the Beldame as she was compromised by a slow early pace...concluded her career with a second in the Breeders' Cup Distaff that was a fine effort considering she was one of just a few deep closers in the Breeders' Cup races on the Lone Star main track to be close at the finish.

Island Fashion

Had a most unconventional campaign but showed on her day that she definitely belonged near the top of her division...she left Sightseek back in fourth when she began 2004 with a victory in the Santa Monica, and then stretched out from 7 furlongs to 1 1-4 miles to face males in the Santa Anita Handicap...she was an outstanding second in the Big Cap, beaten only a little more than a length by Southern Image, who came back to win the Pimlico Special and who almost certainly would have ranked among the top four in the older male division had he been able to stay healthy...did not fire her best shot when a distant fourth behind Azeri in the Apple Blossom...what to do after a race like that? Why, go to Japan, of course...she was sent to Tokyo for the Yasuda Kinen in June, run over a surface, turf, that she had but one previous unsuccessful start over...she wound up 16th of 18 and was not seen again until October...won the Lady's Secret Breeders' Cup Handicap in her comeback, basically on class as she was not wound tight for that race...followed with a deceptively good effort in the Breeders' Cup Distaff, finishing fifth, beaten less than five lengths, after middle moving and racing wide...went back to the turf for her final start as a 4-year-old, finishing fourth in the Matriarch.

Turf Males

Kitten's Joy

Became the first American-raced 3-year-old to be voted turf champion since Sunshine Forever in 1988 and the first turf champion to have not won the Breeders' Cup Turf since Singspiel in 1996...was also the only prominent 3-year-old of 2004 to have won a major race against older opponents...despite the obvious importance of the Breeders' Cup Turf in the division, he turned in the division's definitive performance winning the Turf Classic Invitational...in the stretch, he blew past an opponent in Magistretti who was immensely impressive visually winning the Man o' War in his prior start to win going away...he went his final quarter mile in the 1 1-2 mile Turf Classic in a sensational 22.20 seconds...making that even more awesome is the Turf Classic was over a deep course labeled yielding...won the Tropical Park Derby, Palm Beach, Crown Royal American Turf, Virginia Derby and was headed in the Jefferson Cup in his first five starts of the year but emerged as a force in the Secretariat on the Arlington Million undercard...dominated the Secretariat and won in faster final time than a top-class field of older international horses completed the same distance in the Arlington Million itself...went off the shortest-priced favorite on the Breeders' Cup card when bet down to 3-5 in the Turf...finished second after a troubled trip and after also appearing uncomfortable with the footing...has since undergone knee surgery but remains in training for 2005.

Powerscourt

Was a notch below top class in his home base in Europe and completed his season in disappointing fashion in Asia but required only two starts in this country to clearly demonstrate he was one of the best in his division here...lost both of his starts in this country but one was on disqualification, both could have been attributed to questionable rides, and a case can be made that he should have won both...made his first American start in the Arlington Million...he stormed from far off the pace with a bold burst into the stretch and sustained his momentum to finish first by daylight...in a controversial decision, however, he was disqualified and placed fourth for lugging in through the stretch...he did lug in, and horses did check behind him in his wake, but there was no question he was the best horse as that race was run...after a sharp third back home in the Irish Champion Stakes, he returned for the Breeders' Cup Turf and was accorded a good chance against the heavily favored Kitten's Joy, going off the clear-cut second choice in the betting...he was, by any measure, the victim of a ridiculous ride...spotted the field a big head start after a poor break and then made a premature rush to the lead despite there being more than a half-mile to go...still fought gamely after being spent imprudently and finished third.

Singletary

Truly a miler as all of his six 2004 starts came at that distance and capped a deliberate campaign that had the Breeders' Cup Mile as its ultimate goal with a 16-1 upset in that event...made his starts in pairs with designed breaks in between...indicated he belonged in the discussion of top American turf milers by finishing ahead of 12 opponents when a narrowly beaten second in the Frank Kilroe Handicap in March...later won the San Francisco Mile Breeders' Cup Handicap and finished second in the Shoemaker Breeders' Cup Mile to Designed for Luck, who was subsequently injured...following another freshening, he returned in the Oak Tree Breeders' Cup Mile, California's premier prep for the Breeders' Cup Mile...he was the 3-2 favorite but was beaten two noses after losing considerable ground...enjoyed good fortune in the Breeders' Cup, picking his way through between horses essentially unstopped...he prevailed over Antonius Pius, and 2003 Breeders' Cup Mile winner Six Perfections, neither of whom had nearly as good a trips as he did...remains in training in 2005.

Better Talk Now

Won only two of eight starts on the year, but this gelding saved those winning efforts for very big spots: the Breeders' Cup Turf and the Sword Dancer Invitational...was 27-1 in the Breeders' Cup Turf and yet wasn't even the biggest Breeders' Cup upsetter...that distinction went to Wilko, who took the Breeders' Cup Juvenile at 28-1...came from far off the early pace in the Turf and was good enough to capitalize on Kitten's Joy's trouble and Powerscourt's premature move to win going away...he employed the same style at the same 1 1-2 mile distance over the same type of yielding course to win the Sword Dancer...in fairness, the Sword Dancer had a depleted field as the richer Arlington Million, run on the same day, attracted the bigger names...also finished second in the Bowling Green...the only time all year he was favored was in his final start of the year, the Hollywood Turf Cup...in the hopes of winning that event, he was attempting to build a stronger case for a divisional championship...after being closer to a very slow pace than usual, however, he faded to finish sixth.

Turf Fillies and Mares

Ouija Board

In a division that lacked a clear-cut leader all season, she won the race that has evolved into the one that, within a divisional context, has perhaps the greatest impact in determining a champion, the Breeders' Cup Filly and Mare Turf...was the second lowest-priced favorite on the Breeders' Cup card next to Kitten's Joy in the Turf and was the heaviest favorite to win a 2004 Breeders' Cup race...earned such support with a series of brilliant performances in her home base of Europe, including decisive victories in the English and Irish Oaks and an outstanding third in the Arc de Triomphe as a 3-year-old filly against Europe's finest older males...seemed slightly below that form in the Breeders' Cup...speculation is she either regressed from her taxing effort in the Arc less than four weeks earlier, did not care for the configuration of the Lone Star turf course or did not fancy the yielding going...she nevertheless managed to rally effectively from midpack despite an extremely slow pace and proved clearly best through the final furlong.

Six Perfections

Sensational winning the 2003 Breeders' Cup Mile as a 3-year-old filly, she did not win in four starts in 2004, including her one American outing, and yet still belongs in the discussion of the year's top female turf performers...came from France to defend her title in the Breeders' Cup Mile amid talk that she wasn't as sharp as she was a year before...even though she did not win in the Mile, she demonstrated she was as good as ever...was in the midst of launching a bold rally nearing the stretch of the Mile, only to have the hole she was going for close suddenly...at the time of her trouble, she was moving in company with, and just as well as, eventual Mile winner Singletary...she managed to regroup after losing all momentum and passed four horses in the final furlong to finish third...in light of the fact she was beaten only two lengths, a case could be made that she would have won the Mile were it not for her bad racing luck.

Wonder Again

Was for a time during the summer the top-ranked female turf specialist in the nation and is the only American-based runner on this list...dominated the New York Handicap in her second start of the season in July, signaling a return to her Grade 1-winning form as a 3-year-old in 2002...was even more impressive romping in the subsequent Diana Handicap to shoot to the top of her class...could have built an imposing case for a divisional championship regardless of what were to happen in the Breeders' Cup with a win in the Flower Bowl Invitational...she was odds-on to do so but picked a bad time to deliver a flat performance...after being closer to the pace than she prefers, even an extremely slow early pace, she weakened in the stretch and finished sixth...despite being known as a poor shipper, she ventured to the Breeders' Cup Filly and Mare Turf and encountered the other extreme, being much farther back early than she had been in 18 prior career starts...she was also compromised by dawdling fractions but turned in a winning effort, rallying past eight opponents to finish third, beaten less than two lengths by Ouija Board, who enjoyed a better trip...remains in training for 2005.

Crimson Palace

Like Ouija Board and Six Perfections, she required only one appearance in America to prove she was among the best in her division...was intended to have more action but was forced to miss the Flower Bowl due to injury and was retired after failing to recover in time to have sufficient training for the Breeders' Cup...a close fourth against males in the Group 1 Dubai Duty Free and a Group 3 victory at York earned her the right to come to America for the Beverly D., an important international event on the Arlington Million undercard...benefiting from a perfect ride by Frankie Dettori, she was placed close to a pokey early pace, which put her in a position to prevail after a hotly contested stretch run...her Beverly D. victory was made to look even better when runner up Riskaverse came back to upset Wonder Again in the Flower Bowl.

Sprinters

Pico Central

In the minds of many, he was the best sprinter of 2004 but not in the minds of the majority of Eclipse Award voters, who gave that award to Speightstown...came from his native Brazil and won five of seven starts...his only two losses came the only two times he was favored...he was odds-on in both losses, third-place finishes in the Pat O'Brien Breeders' Cup Handicap and in the Cigar Mile, and both occurred after he was caught inside in early speed duels...after winning the San Carlos in March, he made the first of three successful trips from his base in California to New York and won the Carter Handicap in April...he traveled again in May and took the Metropolitan Handicap...in October, he made the Vosburgh Stakes his third Grade 1 victory of the year with an overwhelming, four lengths score...the Vosburgh was the only time he faced Speightstown, his chief rival for the sprint title, and he left him 4 1-2 lengths behind in third...after the Vosburgh, the decision was made to not supplement him to the $1 million Breeders' Cup Sprint at a cost of $200,000...that choice was understandable; not only was it a poor gamble, but in defeating Speightstown in the Vosburgh, he seemed to do all he had to in order to clinch his division...apparently, the decision to pass the Breeders' Cup, coupled with Speightstown's Sprint victory, and his subsequent loss in the Cigar Mile changed the atmosphere...remains in training for 2005.

Speightstown

After a career that had been marred by many gaps due to injury, he was finally able to put together a strong campaign at age 6 of six stakes starts...he won all but one of them and retired with a championship...commanded attention right from the start of his season with lopsided victories in the Artax and Churchill Downs handicaps...continued like clockwork with decisive victories in the True North Breeders' Cup and Alfred G. Vanderbilt handicaps...the Vanderbilt may have been the high point of his year, as after he disputed a very fast early pace, he still managed to draw away from a strong field and post a final time fast enough to earn a Beyer Speed Figure of 117...as a result of his Vanderbilt performance, he was 4-5 against Pico Central in the Vosburgh...he did bobble leaving the gate, and his connections insist he did not handle an unusually deep and cuppy track...was back on his game in the Breeders' Cup Sprint, successfully coming from a little farther back than he ever had before...depending on your perspective, his victory in the Sprint either confirmed that he did not run his race in the Vosburgh or was extremely flattering to Pico Central.

Ghostzapper

Duly rewarded for his exploits at 1 1-4 miles in the Breeders' Cup Classic and at 1 1-8 miles in the Woodward and Iselin, it should not be overlooked that it took only one race to demonstrate that he was also one of the best sprinters of 2004...his only sprint start came in his first start of the year, the Tom Fool Handicap in July, which happened to be his first outing since his overwhelming victory in 2003 Vosburgh Stakes...faced a modest field in the Tom Fool, but it wasn't who he beat, it was how he did it...he gained two lengths to challenge for the lead through a second quarter run in 22.25 seconds, and opened up a 4 1-2 length lead through a third quarter in 23.47...despite not being asked for his best, he maintained his advantage and completed the seven furlongs in a near-track record for Belmont Park of 1:20.42...that final time earned him a Beyer Figure of 120, which was the highest Beyer assigned all year in all races under a mile...the 128 Beyer he earned winning the Iselin, and the 124 Beyer he earned winning the Breeders' Cup Classic were the two highest Beyers in all North American races in 2004...although the "trifecta" didn't quite happen for him, the last Horse of the Year and Handicap champion to win the sprint title in the same year was Forego in 1974.

Kela

This deep closer rode a three-race hot streak into mention as one of the more prominent sprinters of the year...he began the year in rocky fashion, with only a win in the Texas Mile from his first five starts of 2004, and he ended it a bit rough, too, with a fourth as the favorite in the Vernon O. Underwood...he got on a roll at Del Mar with an upset victory in the Bing Crosby Breeders' Cup Handicap and bettered that with an emphatic upset over Pico Central in the Pat O'Brien...as if to prove he didn't suddenly become a horse for a course, he turned in another high quality effort in the Breeders' Cup Sprint...with his running style, he was up against it in the Sprint at Lone Star, a track that is not only naturally speed favoring, but also has a comparatively short stretch, which is not of much help to big finishers...he nevertheless came tantalizingly close...he came very wide into the stretch while launching a rally from 10th and finished second, beaten a diminishing 1 1-4 lengths...he remains in training in 2005.

2004 Obituary of the Turf

OWNERS AND BREEDERS

Date	Name	Age	Location	Cause
Jan. 12	W.T. Young	85	Gulfstream, FL	Heart attack
Jan. 13	Mary Lou Heleringer	76		
Jan. 24	Susan Hundley	62	Versailles, KY	Cancer
Jan. 31	Jay Weiss	76	Bal Harbour, FL	
Feb. 1	Doug Cameron	87	Toronto	
Feb. 11	Al Carpenito	60	Holmdel, NJ	
Feb. 18	Chris Thomas	55		Cancer
Feb. 22	Einar Paul Robsham	75	Boston, MA	
Mar. 16	Pat O'Neill	69		Heart attack
Mar. 23	Russell Reineman	86	Chicago, IL	
Apr. 7	Robert Sangster	67	London, England	Pancreatic cancer
Apr. 7	Wilhelmine Waller	90		
May 25	Mary Kay Johnson	79	Roslyn, NY	Heart attack
June 13	Morley Engelson	69	Hollywood, CA	Homicide
June 17	Ruth Claflin	64	Rockdale, TX	Car accident
July 13	R.V. Argante	91		
Aug. 30	William G. Clark Sr.	80	Lexington, KY	Diabetes
Oct. 24	Dominic Marotta	74	Michigan	
Nov. 11	Rick Littrell	50	Lexington, KY	Blood clot

TRAINERS

Date	Name	Age	Location	Cause
Jan. 4	David Schmidt	46	Ontario	Kicked by horse
Jan. 8	Joe Catanese	72		Long illness
Jan. 13	J.R. Smith	68	Chicago	Pancreatic cancer
Jan. 22	Tony Basile	82	Hollywood, FL	Pneumonia
Jan. 23	Leland Anderson	78		Emphysema
Feb	Jerome Leon	54	Montana	Skiing accident
Feb. 2	Gene Hargrove	78	Fayre, OK	Cancer
Feb. 7	Chris Bukowiecki	51	Wellington, FL	Suicide
Feb. 25	John Russell	67	Del Mar, CA	
Feb. 29	Richard O'Connell	54		Blood disease
Mar. 26	Victor Nickerson	75	Smithtown, NY	
April	Wally Dunn	92	Arcadia, CA	
Apr. 4	Paul Cooper	92		
June 4	Peter Fortay	56		Kidney illness
July 5	Patrick Myer	61		Stroke
July 19	Woody Sedlacek	85	Ocala, FL	Cancer
Aug. 2	Louis Meittinis	61	Westbury, NY	Heart attack
Aug. 6	Phil Johnson	78	Rockville Centre, NY	Cancer
Aug. 29	George Krikorian Sr.	89	Vista, CA	Cancer
Sept. 2	Edward I. Kelly	83	Brooksville, FL	

Sept. 19	Martin Wansborough	50		
Nov. 21	Doug Peterson	53	Los Angeles, CA	
Dec. 29	Willie Belmonte	38	Charles Town, WV	Cancer
Dec. 27	Sylvia Bishop	84	Ranson, WV	Illness

JOCKEYS

Date	Name	Age	Location	Cause
Jan. 3	Bob Edens	81	Aiken, SC	
Jan. 13	Dave Penna	46	Victoria, BC	
Jan. 18	Mike Ewing	58	Daytona Beach, FL	
Jan. 20	Mel Lewis	88		
Jan. 23	Gil Robillard	80	Barrie, Ontario	
Feb. 9	Mike Rowland	41	Cincinnati, OH	Racing accident
Feb. 21	Jay Northcutt	61	Ocala, FL	Cancer
Apr. 5	Fred Winter	77		
Sept. 26	Dean Kutz	48	Lexington, KY	Cancer
Nov. 12	Frank Adams	77	Southern Pines, N.C.	
Nov. 19	Joey Cuffari	71		Heart complications
Dec. 5	Robert Gaffglione	68	Ft. Lauderdale, FL	Parkinson's

OTHERS CONNECTED WITH THE TURF

Date	Name	Age	Location	Cause
Jan. 7	Hannah Blumenthal	52	New York	Training accident
Jan. 7	Richard Becker	82		
Jan. 9	Donald Levinson	91		
Jan. 10	Alex Kahn	94	Los Angeles	
Jan. 19	John W. Rooney	78		
Jan. 21	Tommy Scott	83		
Jan. 27	Kevin Goemmer	48		Heart attack
Jan. 28	Valerie Hinson	49	Germantown, TN	Cancer
Jan. 29	Frank E. Tours Jr.	76	Ojai, CA	
Feb. 2	Jerry Nielsen	69	Darien, CT	Heart attack
Feb. 8	Joss Collins	56	England	Liver cancer
Feb. 13	Ray Gambone Sr.	56		Cancer
Feb. 18	Don Lee	82	Omaha, NE	
Feb. 28	Bud Baedeker	90	New York, NY	
Mar. 6	Charles DiRocco	69	Las Vegas, NV	Pneumonia
Mar. 6	Thomas Clark	61		Cancer
Mar. 7	Dana Broccoli	82		
Mar. 7	Jane Engelhard	86		
Mar. 8	Drexel Engel	79	Columbus, NE	
Mar. 22	Fritz Engel	71	Clarks, NE	
Apr. 2	Bruce Davis	72		
Apr. 18	Christopher Elser	20	Baltimore, MD	
Apr. 20	Terry Pion	65		
Apr. 26	James McGrath	76		
Apr. 29	Chuck Badone	67	Phoenix, AZ	Esophagus cancer
May 14	Danny Hutt	55	Louisville, KY	Heart attack
May 22	Gary Henson	60	Renton, WA	
May 25	George Buckham	82	Del Mar, CA	
June 16	Dale Duspiva	53	San Mateo, CA	Brain tumor
July 5	Ray Rogers	87	Santa Anita, CA	Heart attack
July 23	Vikki Kitchingman	34		Cancer
Sept. 1	Lou Mondello	81	Long Island, NY	

Sept. 14	Dilip Amarsingh	31	Mineola, NY	Homicide
Oct. 7	Desmond Wickham	35	Hallandale Beach, FL	
Oct. 13	Larry Boyle	68	Council Bluffs, IA	
Oct. 21	Elwood D. Heironimus	83	Charles Town, WV	
Oct. 25	William Reed	83	Long Island, NY	Alzheimer's
Nov. 4	James Binger	88	Ocala, FL	
Nov. 22	Tony Pellegrino	64	Lone Grove, OK	
Dec. 1	Anthony Hemmerick	75	Hollywood, FL	Stomach aneurysm
Dec. 15	Ed Devine	78	New Jersey	Heart arrhythmia
Dec. 31	Joe Durso	80	Stony Brook, NY	Cancer

HORSES

Date	Horse	Age	Location	Cause
Jan. 3	Petrograd	35		
Jan. 14	Withallprobability	16		Laminitis
Jan. 30	Angel Fever	14	Paris, KY	Paddock Accident
Jan. 31	With Ability	6	Union, VA	Fracture
Feb. 7	Toby's Success		Delta Downs	Heart Attack
Feb. 14	Razyana	23	Juddmonte Farm	
Feb. 19	Be My Guest	30	Ocala, FL	
March	Jair du Cocher	7	Les Mathes, France	Euthanized
March	Hyde Park	7	Louisville, KY	Barn fire
Mar. 4	Booklet	5	Midway, KY	Euthanized
Mar. 6	Tabasco Cat	13	Japan	Heart failure
Mar. 7	She's Zealous	4		Euthanized
Mar. 15	Evil Elaine	20	Lexington, KY	Euthanized
Mar. 22	Rowdy Angel	25	Goshen, KY	Natural causes
Mar. 23	Wynn Dot Comma	3	Miami, FL	Euthanized
Mar. 23	Excellent Meeting	8	Lexington, KY	
Mar. 27	Puffy Shirt	4		Euthanized
Mar. 31	Stalwart	25	Midway, KY	Euthanized
Apr. 2	Miss Snowflake	26	Paris, KY	
Apr. 19	Centaine	23	New Zealand	
Apr. 20	Carlos Folly	17	Georgetown, KY	Ruptured cecum
Apr. 25	Irish River	28	Lexington, KY	
Apr. 28	Persian Punch	11		Ruptured aorta
May	Devious Boy	4		Virus
May 2	Private Emblem			Euthanized
May 3	Chic Shirine	20	Lexington, KY	
June	Puzzlement	5	Florida	Tendon infection
June	Machiavellian	17		Laminitis
June	Soud	6		Heart attack
June	Smolderin Heart	9	Arkansas	
June 5	Clever Trick	28		
June 17	Wavering Monarch	25	Midway, KY	Euthanized
June 26	Multiplication	3	Belmont, NY	Heart attack
July 2	Sky Beauty	14	Paris, KY	Euthanized
July 5	Sound of Gold	6	Houston, TX	
July 19	Free House	10	Bonsall, CA	Head injury
July 24	Boomzeeboom	3		Euthanized
July 30	Awesome Drive	3	Oklahoma	Euthanized
Aug. 1	American Son	4	Del Mar, CA	Euthanized
Aug. 1	Wixoe Express	5	Del Mar, CA	Euthanized
Aug. 3	Dollar Bill	6	Lexington, KY	
Aug. 5	Glowing Tribute	31	Lexington, KY	Colic

Aug. 8	Exclusive Ribot	32	Decatur, TX	Heart failure
Aug. 10	Quick Nip	5	Albany, CA	Euthanized
Aug. 13	Sugar and Spice	27	Paris, KY	Natural causes
Aug. 20	Katies	23	Nicholasville, KY	Euthanized
Sept. 1	Atswhatimtalknbout	4	San Luis Rey, CA	Euthanized
Sept. 5	Castle Gandolfo	5	Chile	Neck injury
Sept. 10	Deputy Minister	25	Columbus, OH	Heart failure
Oct. 12	Bates Motel	25	Lexington, KY	Euthanized
Nov. 8	Flying Continental	18	Coalinga, CA	
Nov. 12	Epitome	19	Lexington, KY	Ruptured artery
Nov. 25	Private Account	28	Paris, KY	Natural causes
Nov. 26	Blitey	28	Claiborne Farm, KY	Euthanized
Dec. 3	Storm Bird	26	Versailles, KY	Euthanized
Dec. 10	Prospector's Music	25	Washington, OK	Ruptured cecum
Dec. 10	Cherokee Colony	19	Davis, CA	
Dec. 11	Northern Taste	33	Hokkaido, Japan	Natural causes
Dec. 14	Eastern Echo	16	Woodbine, MD	Heart attack
Dec. 16	Miswaki	26	Lexington, KY	
Dec. 24	Carson City	17	Lexington, KY	

–Compiled by Daniel Kim

Experimental Free Handicap Weights

Highweight 2-Year-Olds in Annual Experimentals

Year	Horse	Weight
1933	First Minstrel	126
1935	Red Rain	126
1936	Brooklyn	126
1937	Menow	126
1938	El Chico	126
1939	Bimelech	130
1940	Whirlaway	126
1941	Alsab	130
1942	Count Fleet	132
1943	Pukka Gin	126
1944	Pavot	126
	Free for All	126
1945	Lord Boswell	126
1946	Cosmic Bomb	126
	First Flight	126
	Double Jay	126
1947	Citation	126
1948	Blue Peter	126
1949	Middleground	126
1950	Uncle Miltie	126
1951	Tom Fool	126
1952	Native Dancer	130
1953	Porterhouse	126
	Turn-to	126
1954	Summer Tan	128
1955	Career Boy	126
1956	Barbizon	126
1957	Jewel's Reward	126
1958	First Landing	126
1959	Warfare	126
1960	Hail to Reason	126
1961	Crimson Satan	126
1962	Never Bend	126
1963	Raise a Native	126
1964	Bold Lad	130
1965	Buckpasser	126
1966	Successor	126
1967	Vitriolic	126
1968	Top Knight	126
1969	Silent Screen	128
1970	Hoist the Flag	126
1971	Riva Ridge	126
1972	Secretariat	129
1973	Protagonist	126
1974	Foolish Pleasure	127
1975	Honest Pleasure	126
1976	Seattle Slew	126
1977	Affirmed	126
1978	Spectacular Bid	126
1979	Rockhill Native	126
1980	Lord Avie	126
1981	Deputy Minister	126
	Timely Writer	126
1982	Copelan	126
	Roving Boy	126
1983	Devil's Bag	128
1984	Chief's Crown	126
1985	Ogygian	126
	Tasso	126
	I'm Splendid (f)	123
1986	Capote	126
	Brave Raj (f)	123
1987	Forty Niner	126
	Epitome (f)	123
	All Over (f)	123
1988	Easy Goer	126
	Open Mind (f)	123
1989	Rhythm	126
	Go for Wand (f)	123
1990	Fly So Free	126
	Meadow Star (f)	123
1991	Arazi	130
	Pleasant Stage (f)	123
1992	Gilded Time	126
	Eliza (f)	123
1993	Brocco	126
	Dehere	126
	Phone Chatter (f)	123
1994	Timber Country	126
	Flanders (f)	124
1995	Maria's Mon	126
	Unbridled's Song	126
	My Flag (f)	123
1996	Boston Harbor	126
	Storm Song (f)	124
1997	Favorite Trick	128
	Countess Diana (f)	125
1998	Answer Lively	126
	Silverbulletday (f)	123
1999	Anees	126
	Cash Run (f)	123
	Chilukki (f)	123
	Surfside (f)	123
2000	Macho Uno	126
	Caressing (f)	123
2001	Johannesburg	126
	Tempera	123
2002	Vindication	126
	Storm Flag Flying (f)	123
2003	Action This Day	126
	Cuvee	126
	Ruler's Court	126
	Halfbridled (f)	124
2004	Declan's Moon	126
	Wilko	126
	Sweet Catomine (f)	124

Experimental Handicap for 2-Year-Olds in 2004

In 2004, for the second straight year, more than one male shared highweight on the Experimental Handicap while one filly was rated far above her peers. Breeders' Cup Juvenile winner Wilko, and Declan's Moon, who beat Wilko in the Hollywood Futurity, were top rated among the males, while Breeders' Cup Juvenile Fillies winner Sweet Catomine received the highest weighting among fillies. The Experimental Free Handicap annually is published in Daily Racing Form and is compiled by a panel of racing secretaries based on 2-year-old form projected in a hypothetical 1 1/16-mile race on the dirt in the spring of their 3-year-old seasons.

Declan's Moon and Wilko were each assigned 126 pounds, the standard weight for a leading 2-year-old colt or gelding, while Sweet Catomine was assigned 124 pounds, a pound higher than par for fillies.

The participating racing secretaries for the 2004 Experimental were Mike Lakow of NYRA, Frank Gabriel Jr. of Arlington Park and Tom Robbins of Del Mar Turf Club. A total of 87 colts and geldings were rated along with 66 fillies.

COLTS and GELDINGS

Wgt.	Horse	Color	Sire	State	Breeder
126	Declan's Moon	dk b/br	Malibu Moon	MD	Brice Ridgely
	Wilko	ch	Awesome Again	KY	Ro Parra
124	Afleet Alex	b	Northern Afleet	FL	John Martin Silvertand
	Roman Ruler	dk b/br	Fusaichi Pegasus	KY	Needham/Betz, Liberation Fm & Ashford Stud
123	Proud Accolade	dk b/br	Yes It's True	FL	Marion G. Montanari
	Sun King	dk b/br	Charismatic	KY	Cambridge Farm & James Daniel Conway
122	Giacomo	gr/ro	Holy Bull	KY	Mr. & Mrs. J. S. Moss
	Rockport Harbor	gr/ro	Unbridled's Song	KY	Heiligbrodt Racing Stable & Taylor Made Farm, Inc.
121	Devils Disciple	dk b/br	Devil His Due	FL	Earl Pierpont
120	Consolidator	ch	Storm Cat	KY	Pacelco S.A.
119	Galloping Grocer	ch	A. P Jet	NY	Robert D. Rosenthal & Estate of Ira Waldbaum
118	Southern Africa	dk b/br	Cape Town	KY	Hassan Ahamdi & Michael Anderson
117	Chandtrue	b	Yes It's True	FL	W. E. Waltrip
116	Flamenco	ch	Dance Master	FL	Moloney & Thompson
	Park Avenue Ball	ch	Citidancer	NJ	C. J. Hesse, Inc.
115	Dubleo	dk b/br	Southern Halo	KY	Anzac LLC
	Greater Good	b	Intidab	KY	A. Lakin & Sons, Inc.
114	Crown Point	b	Honor Grades	KY	Albert Coppola
	Lunarpal	b	Successful Appeal	FL	L. William Heiligbrodt
	Primal Storm	b	Storm Boot	KY	Everest Stables Inc.
113	Actxecutive	ch	Noactor	FL	Randy Mills
	Defer	b	Danzig	KY	Ogden Mills Phipps
	Straight Line	dk b/br	Boundary	KY	R. Alex Rankin & Louis Wright
	Texcess	b	In Excess (IRE)	CA	Ron E. Gomez
112	Boston Glory	ch	Boston Harbor	KY	Tom Clark
111	Better Than Bonds	b	Sweetsouthernsaint	FL	L. Riley Mangum
	Drum Major	dk b/br	Dynaformer	KY	Roger W. Clark
	Elusive Chris	ch	Elusive Quality	KY	James T. Hines Jr.

WGT	HORSE	COLOR	SIRE	STATE	BREEDER
	Leaving On My Mind	b	Valid Expectations	TX	George A. Wolff
	Patriot Act	dk b/br	A.P. Indy	KY	W. S. Farish
	Seattles Best Joe	b	Personable Joe	WA	Frank Reynolds
	Seize the Day	dk b/br	Montbrook	FL	J. Michael O'Farrell, Jr.
	Storm Surge	dk b/br	Storm Cat	KY	Overbrook Farm
110	Bellamy Road	dk b/br	Concerto	FL	Dianne D. Cotter
	Boggy Creek	dk b/br	Menifee	KY	Diane Waldron
	Cajun Pepper	dk b/br	Barricade	CO	Harry L. Veruchi
	Closing Argument	b	Successful Appeal	FL	France Weiner & Irwin J. Weiner
	Evil Minister	ch	Deputy Minister	KY	ClassicStar, LLC
	Gold Joy	ch	Joyeux Danseur	NY	Chasemedaly Farm
	Wallstreet Scandal	ch	Mt. Livermore	OH	Langoom Farm, Inc. & Eutrophia Farm
109	D. D. Best	dk b/br	Yes It's True	FL	Bent Oak Farm
	Cin Cin	dk b/br	Precocity	FL	John Franks
	Funk	b	Unbridled's Song	KY	Formal Gold LLC
	Magoo's Magic	dk b/br	Awesome Again	KY	The Allen E. Paulson Living Trust
	Three Hour Nap	b	Afternoon Deelites	KY	Frank A. Penn Jr. & D. Flannigan
108	Anthony J.	b	Tiger Ridge	FL	Mrs. Helen M. Napolitano
	Bushwacker	b	Outflanker	FL	Starship Stables
	Littlebitofzip	dk b/br	Littlebitlively	FL	John Franks
	Sunny Sky (FR)	ch	Septieme Ciel	FR	Franck Benillouche
	Tadreeb	b	Theatrical (IRE)	KY	Fittocks Stud
107	G P's Black Knight	b	Tiger Ridge	FL	Tony & Dawn Bowling
	Rey de Cafe	ch	Kingmambo	KY	G. Watts Humphrey Jr.
106	Chips Are Down	dk b/br	Distorted Humor	KY	Charles Nuckols Jr. & Sons
	D'court's Speed	gr/ro	Doneraile Court	KY	Establo P. R. Speed
	Killenaule	dk b/br	Fusaichi Pegasus	KY	High Creek Farm
	Maximus C	b	Coronado's Quest	KY	Shortleaf Stable
	Wild Desert	b	Wild Rush	ON	Windways Farm Limited
	Winsomemoneyhoney	dk b/br	Spinning World	KY	Jeanne Sheets
105	Cherokee Chase	dk b/br	Rizzi	FL	Stride Rite Racing Stable, Inc.
	City Code	b	Carson City	KY	Pin Oak Stud, LLC
	Doctor Voodoo	dk b/br	Petionville	KY	Joel Kligman
	Major League	b	Magic Cat	TX	Sandstone Farms, LLC
	Rush Bay	b	Cozzene	KY	Phoebe Ann Mueller, Trust
	Winning Expression	dk b/br	Western Expression	NY	Flying Zee Stables
104	Diamond Isle	dk b/br	Gilded Time	KY	Mike S. Sloan
	Hal's Image	dk b/br	Halo's Image	FL	Harold Rose
	Magna Graduate	dk b/br	Honor Grades	KY	Nicole Zitani & Ramon Rangel
	Positive Prize	dk b/br	Prized	KY	Donna Moore
	Ready Ruler	dk b/br	More Than Ready	KY	Vinery, LLC

WGT	HORSE	COLOR	SIRE	STATE	BREEDER
	Smooth Bid	gr/ro	Rubiano	MD	Margaret Addis
	Spanish Chestnut	ch	Horse Chestnut (SAF)	FL	Don Graham & Ocala Oaks
103	Rubialedo	gr/ro	Rubiano	KY	Lewis A. Hall Jr.
	Scipion	b	A.P. Indy	KY	Payson Stud Inc.
	Smoke Warning	b	Smoke Glacken	KY	Sidney Brown
	Upscaled	b	Sir Cat	KY	Walter B. Mills
102	Malanato	ch	Malagra	LA	Danny M. Brown & Donna B. Brown
	My Parade	b	Parade Ground	KY	W. S. Farish, James D. Conway & Marietta Conway
	Silver Haze	dk b/br	Silver Deputy	KY	Foxfield
101	Chattahoochee War	b	War Chant	KY	Edmund J. Loder
	Dusty Minister	gr/ro	Open Forum	FL	Irma Stein
	Elusive Thunder	ch	Thunder Gulch	KY	Hopewell Investments LLC
	Social Probation	gr/ro	Jules	KY	Chris Cahill & Kirt Cahill
	Woody's Apache	dk b/br	Cryptoclearance	KY	Jim D. Tilton Jr.
100	Favorite Minit	b	Favorite Trick	LA	Brittlyn Stable, Inc., M. Benoit & E. Benoit
	Fusaichi Rock Star	gr/ro	Wild Wonder	FL	Hannahill Farm Inc.
	Reno Bob	b	Miesque's Son	KY	Eaglestone Farm Inc.
	Storm Creek Rising	b	Storm Creek	KY	Aaron U. Jones & Marie D. Jones

FILLIES

Wgt.	Horse	Color	Sire	State	Breeder
124	Sweet Catomine	b	Storm Cat	KY	Mr. & Mrs. Martin J. Wygod
117	Balletto (UAE)	ch	Timber Country	UAE	Darley
	Sense of Style	b	Thunder Gulch	KY	Twelve Oaks Stud
	Splendid Blended	ch	Unbridled's Song	FL	Peter Vegso Racing Stable
115	Ready's Gal	ch	More Than Ready	KY	R. Alex Rankin & Louis Wright
114	Inspiring	ch	Golden Missile	KY	Timothy Thornton, Meg Buckley & Mike Buckley
	Runway Model	dk b/br	Petionville	KY	Everest Stables, Inc.
	Souvenir Gift	b	Souvenir Copy	KY	Mrs. John C. Mabee
113	Sharp Lisa	ch	Dixieland Band	KY	WinStar Farm, LLC
	Sis City	b	Slew City Slew	KY	Heiligbrodt Racing Stable
112	In the Gold	ch	Golden Missile	KY	Whitewood Stable, Inc.
111	Classic Elegance	b	Carson City	KY	Brereton C. Jones
	Dance Away Capote	gr/ro	Capote	KY	Mt. Brilliant Farm LLC
	Paddy's Daisy	ch	King of Kings (IRE)	KY	Stonehaven Farm
	Play With Fire	dk b/br	Boundary	KY	Claiborne Farm
110	Melhor Ainda	b	Pulpit	KY	Jayeff B Stables & Reynolds Bell Jr.
	Punch Appeal	b	Successful Appeal	FL	Rosebrook Farms LLC

109	Broadway Gold	dk b/br	Seeking the Gold	KY	Madeleine Paulson, W. S. Farish & Skara Glen Stables
	Culinary	gr/ro	El Amante	KY	Diana Snowden & Guy B. Snowden
	Louvain (IRE)	b	Sinndar (IRE)	IRE	Twelve Oaks Stud Establishment
	Northern Mischief	dk b/br	Yankee Victor	KY	Sequel 2000
	Toll Taker	b	Bernstein	IL	Lothenbach Stables, Inc.
108	Chocolate Brown	dk b/br	Lion Hearted	NJ	Dennis A. Drazin
	Enduring Will	dk b/br	Arch	KY	Michael Rainier
	Hello Lucky	b	Lucky Lionel	FL	Adena Springs
	Short Route	ch	Mud Route	CA	Herrick Racing LLC
107	Conveyor's Angel	dk b/br	Conveyor	FL	Debra Backlinie & Bill Backlinie
	Megascape	dk b/br	Cape Canaveral	NY	Sez Who Thoroughbreds
	Summer Raven	b	Summer Squall	KY	Mt. Brilliant Farm LLC
106	Buzz Song	dk b/br	Unbridled's Song	KY	Kings Way Farm Inc. & Paraneck Stallions, Inc.
	Culture Clash	dk b/br	Petionville	KY	Everest Stables, Inc.
	Hear Us Roar	b	Lion Hearted	MD	Rosalee C. Davison
	Memorette	dk b/br	Memo (CHI)	CA	Oak Tree Farm
	Take a Check	gr/ro	Touch Gold	MD	Robert E. Meyerhoff
105	Double D Appeal	b	Successful Appeal	FL	McKathan Farms
	Kota	b	Indian Charlie	FL	Circle M Farms
	Queens Plaza	dk b/br	Forestry	KY	Classic Thoroughbreds XIV
104	Angel Trumpet	dk b/br	Cape Canaveral	KY	Dreabon Copeland
	Bella Banissa	b	Good and Tough	KY	Thomas/Lakin/Kintz
	Im a Dixie Girl	dk b/br	Dixie Union	KY	Wakefield Farm
	No Bull Baby	b	Indian Charlie	KY	Hal Earnhardt
	Royal Copenhagen (FR)	dk b/br	Inchinor (GB)	FR	Eric Puerari & Har. Des Capucines
103	Aspen Tree	ch	Holy Bull	KY	Ellen B. Kill Kelley
	Dansetta Light	dk b/br	Colony Light	FL	J D Farms
	Jill Robin L	b	Precocity	FL	John Franks
	K. D.'s Shady Lady	gr/ro	Maria's Mon	KY	Anna Steele Oliver
	La Maitresse (IRE)	b	Desert King (IRE)	IRE	Kildare Racing Syndicate
	Limited Entry	b	Carson City	KY	Two Sisters Stable
	My Miss Storm Cat	dk b/br	Sea of Secrets	KY	Bob Austin
	Smuggler	b	Unbridled	KY	Ogden Mills Phipps
102	Berbatim	dk b/br	Bernstein	KY	Douglas S. Arnold & W. E. Zemer Jr.
	Leona's Knight	b	Suave Prospect	FL	Rose Family Stables Ltd.
	Paragon Queen	ch	Lord Carson	KY	Russ Fisher
	Running Bobcats	b	Running Stag	FL	Adena Springs
	Secrets Galore	b	Honour and Glory	KY	Heiligbrodt Racing Stables
	She's a Jewel	b	Successful Appeal	FL	Moloney & Thompson
101	Gotta Rush	b	Wild Rush	KY	Inwood Farms & Andrew Savas

	Lady Glade	b	Straight Man	FL	L. William Heiligbrodt
	Ninadivina	dk b/br	Cape Town	KY	Patchen Wilkes Farm, LLC
	Salute	b	Unbridled	KY	Phipps Stable
	Winning Season	ch	Lemon Drop Kid	KY	Marvin Delfiner & Fred Seitz
100	Darn That Girl	gr/ro	Darn That Alarm	FL	Shannon Fredrick
	Malika's Gold	dk b/br	Gold Case	FL	Haras de la Pomme
	Miss Matched	dk b/br	Formal Gold	KY	John Gallo & William Perry
	Western Princess	ch	Gone West	KY	Manganaro, LLC
	Wild Chick	b	Forest Wildcat	FL	New Farm

North American Ratings Committee

The North American Ratings Committee rates thoroughbreds that take part in North American stakes events. In 2004, the NARC consisted of Frank Gabriel, Jr., of Arlington Park; Chris Evans of Woodbine Entertainment; Michael Lakow of the New York Racing Association; Thomas Robbins of Del Mar Thoroughbred Club; and Martin Panza of Hollywood Park.

Every thoroughbred which competed in a non-restricted stakes race with a purse value of $75,000 or above in North America from 10/27/2003 through 10/31/2004 was eligible to be rated on its best performance. The ratings are based on the SMILE (Sprint, Mile, Intermediate, Long, Extended) distance categories utilized by the World Thoroughbred Racehorse Rankings. NARC ratings include the following distance breakdowns:

	DIRT	TURF
S	Less than 8 furlongs	Less than 7.5 furlongs
M	8 furlongs or more, and less than 9.5 furlongs	7.5 furlongs or more, and less than 9.5 furlongs
I	9.5 furlongs or more, and less than 11 furlongs	Same as Dirt
L	Greater than 11 furlongs	Same as Dirt

NARC Ratings supplied by The Jockey Club Information Systems, Inc (TJCIS), on behalf of TJCIS, Thoroughbred Owners and Breeder's Association and Breeders' Cup.

North American Ratings Committee Annual Leaders since 2000 (separated by age, category and surface)

3-Year-Olds

Year	Horse	Rating
	Sprint Dirt	
2000	Caller One	121
	Dixie Union	121
	More Than Ready	121
	Trippi	121
2001	Squirtle Squirt	125
2002	Thunderello	121
2003	Cajun Beat	120
2004	Bwana Charlie	114
	Sprint Turf	
2000	Squall City (f)	112
2001	None	
2002	None	
2003	King Robyn	112
2004	None	
	Mile Dirt	
2000	Fusaichi Pegasus	123
2001	Point Given	124
2002	Harlan's Holiday	123
	Medaglia d'Oro	123
	War Emblem	123
2003	Empire Maker	120
	Peace Rules	120
2004	Smarty Jones	118
	Mile Turf	
2000	War Chant	123
2001	Affluent (f)	119
	Voodoo Dancer (f)	119
2002	Rock of Gibraltar	122
2003	Six Perfections (f)	117
2004	Antonius Pius	117

Year	Horse	Rating
	Intermediate Dirt	
2000	Fusaichi Pegasus	127
2001	Point Given	127
2002	War Emblem	124
2003	Funny Cide	122
2004	Smarty Jones	128
	Intermediate Turf	
2000	King Cugat	120
2001	Banks Hill (f)	124
2002	Islington (f)	120
2003	L'Ancresse (f)	119
2004	Kitten's Joy	119
	Long Dirt	
2000	Commendable	121
2001	Point Given	128
2002	Sarava	122
2003	Empire Maker	122
2004	Birdstone	120
	Long Turf	
2000	Ciro	119
2001	Milan	125
2002	High Chaparral	125
2003	Kicken Kris	111
2004	Kitten's Joy	122

4-Year-Olds & Up

Year	Horse	Rating
	Sprint Dirt	
2000	Kona Gold	126
2001	Kona Gold	128
2002	Orientate	123
2003	Aldebaran	121
	Congaree	121
2004	Pico Central	123
	Sprint Turf	
2000	El Cielo	116
2001	Hallowed Dreams (f)	114
	Swept Overboard	114
2002	Sarafan	116
2003	Heat Haze (f)	111
	Joe's Son Joey	111
	Morluc	111
	Speak in Passing	111
2004	Cajun Beat	114
	Mile Dirt	
2000	Riboletta (f)	128
2001	Albert the Great	122
2001	Lido Palace	122
2002	Azeri (f)	125
2003	Mineshaft	127
2004	Ghostzapper	123
	Mile Turf	
2000	Affirmed Success	122
	Dansili	122
	Ladies Din	122
	North East Bound	122
	Silic	122
2001	Val Royal	124
2002	Domedriver	123
2003	Candy Ride	122
	Good Journey	122
2004	Singletary	118

Year	Horse	Rating
	Intermediate Dirt	
2000	General Challenge	124
	Lemon Drop Kid	124
2001	Sakhee	127
	Tiznow	127
2002	Volponi	125
2003	Candy Ride	127
2004	Ghostzapper	130
	Intermediate Turf	
2000	Chester House	122
2001	Silvano	123
2002	Astra (f)	122
	Beat Hollow	122
	Golden Apples (f)	122
	Starine (f)	122
2003	Storming Home	121
2004	Powerscourt	120
	Long Dirt	
	No performances in races originally carded for the dirt.	
	Long Turf	
2000	Kalanisi	123
	Perfect Sting (f)	123
2001	Fantastic Light	127
2002	With Anticipation	123
2003	High Chaparral	127
	Johar	127
2004	Better Talk Now	121

2004 United States Thoroughbred Ratings

Top Performances of 2004 by 2-Year-Olds, 3-Year-Olds and 4-Year-Olds and Upward, rated by the North American Ratings Committee

2-Year-Olds – Ratings of 105 or Greater

Horse	S	A	Fin	Date	Trk	Stakes Race and Grade	Cat	R
Sweet Catomine	F	2	1	10/30	LS	Breeders' Cup Juvenile Fillies S.-G1	M	120
Declan's Moon	G	2	1	12/18	HOL	Hollywood Futurity-G1	M	119
Wilko	C	2	1	10/30	LS	Bessemer Trust Breeders' Cup Juvenile S.-G1	M	119
Afleet Alex	C	2	1	08/21	SAR	Hopeful S.-G1	S	117
Roman Ruler	C	2	1	08/15	DMR	Best Pal S.-G2	S	117
Roman Ruler	C	2	2	09/08	DMR	Del Mar Futurity-G2	S	117
Afleet Alex	C	2	2	10/30	LS	Bessemer Trust Breeders' Cup Juvenile S.-G1	M	117
Proud Accolade	C	2	1	10/09	BEL	Champagne S.-G1	M	116
Sun King	C	2	3	10/30	LS	Bessemer Trust Breeders' Cup Juvenile S.-G1	M	116
Giacomo	C	2	2	12/18	HOL	Hollywood Futurity-G1	M	115
Rockport Harbor	C	2	1	11/02	AQU	Nashua S.-G3	M	115
Devils Disciple	G	2	2	08/21	SAR	Hopeful S.-G1	S	114
Balletto (UAE)	F	2	1	10/09	BEL	Frizette S.-G1	M	113
Sense of Style	F	2	1	08/20	SAR	Spinaway S.-G2	S	113
Consolidator	C	2	4	10/30	LS	Bessemer Trust Breeders' Cup Juvenile S.-G1	M	113
Splendid Blended	F	2	1	12/19	HOL	Hollywood Starlet S.-G1	M	113
Galloping Grocer	G	2	2	11/27	AQU	Remsen S.-G2	M	112
Ready's Gal	F	2	2	10/09	BEL	Frizette S.-G1	M	111
Southern Africa	C	2	4	12/18	HOL	Hollywood Futurity-G1	M	111
Chandtrue	C	2	1	07/17	HOL	Hollywood Juvenile Championship S.-G3	S	110
Inspiring	F	2	1	08/07	DMR	Sorrento S.-G3	S	110
Souvenir Gift	F	2	2	08/28	DMR	Del Mar Debutante S.-G1	S	110
Runway Model	F	2	1	11/27	CD	Golden Rod S.-G2	M	110
Park Avenue Ball	C	2	1	09/19	BEL	Futurity S.-G2	M	109
Flamenco	C	2	3	08/21	SAR	Hopeful S.-G1	S	109
Sis City	F	2	3	10/09	BEL	Frizette S.-G1	M	109
Sis City	F	2	1	11/27	AQU	Demoiselle S.-G2	M	109
Flamenco	C	2	1	10/17	BEL	Cowdin S.-GL	S	109
Sharp Lisa	F	2	2	12/19	HOL	Hollywood Starlet S.-G1	M	109
Dubleo	C	2	1	11/27	HOL	Generous S.-G3	MT	108
Greater Good	C	2	1	11/27	CD	Kentucky Jockey Club S.-G2	M	108
In the Gold	F	2	3	10/08	KEE	Darley Alcibiades S.-G2	M	108
Classic Elegance	F	2	1	07/28	SAR	Schuylerville S.-G2	S	107
Paddy's Daisy	F	2	1	11/26	HOL	Miesque S.-G3	MT	107
Crown Point	C	2	1	10/24	BEL	Pilgrim S.-GL	MT	107
Dance Away Capote	F	2	4	10/08	KEE	Darley Alcibiades S.-G2	M	107
Lunarpal	C	2	1	07/05	CD	Bashford Manor S.-G3	S	107
Play With Fire	F	2	3	09/19	BEL	Matron S.-G1	M	107
Primal Storm	C	2	1	06/04	BEL	Flash S.-G3	S	107
Melhor Ainda	F	2	1	10/24	BEL	Miss Grillo S.-GL	MT	106
Texcess	G	2	1	12/04	DED	Boyd Gaming's Delta Jackpot S.-GL	M	106
Actxecutive	C	2	2	07/17	HOL	Hollywood Juvenile Championship S.-G3	S	106
Defer	C	2	1	11/20	PIM	Laurel Futurity-G3	M	106
Punch Appeal	F	2	1	12/04	DED	Boyd Gaming's Delta Princess S.-GL	M	106
Straight Line	C	2	1	11/06	CD	Iroquois S.-G3	M	106
Broadway Gold	F	2	1	06/27	BEL	Astoria S.-GL	S	105
Culinary	F	2	1	09/19	AP	Arlington-Washington Lassie S.-G3	M	105
Louvain (IRE)	F	2	1	11/26	HOL	Miesque S.-G3	MT	105
Toll Taker	F	2	1	10/17	BEL	Astarita S.-G3	S	105
Boston Glory	C	2	2	10/03	SA	Norfolk S.-G2	M	105
Northern Mischief	F	2	3	12/19	HOL	Hollywood Starlet S.-G1	M	105

3-Year-Olds – Ratings of 112 or Greater

Horse	S	A	Fin	Date	Trk	Stakes Race and Grade	Cat	R
Smarty Jones	C	3	1	05/15	PIM	Preakness S.-G1	I	128
Kitten's Joy	C	3	1	10/02	BEL	Joe Hirsch Turf Classic Invitational S.-G1	LT	122
Birdstone	C	3	1	06/05	BEL	Belmont S.-G1	L	120
Birdstone	C	3	1	08/28	SAR	Travers S.-G1	I	120
Ouija Board (GB)	F	3	1	10/30	LS	VO5 Breeders' Cup Filly & Mare Turf S.-G1	LT	118
Antonius Pius	C	3	2	10/30	LS	NetJets Breeders' Cup Mile S.-G1	MT	117
Ashado	F	3	1	10/30	LS	Breeders' Cup Distaff Presented By Nextel S.-G1	M	117
Lion Heart	C	3	2	05/01	CD	Kentucky Derby-G1	I	117
Tycoon (GB)	C	3	3	10/02	BEL	Joe Hirsch Turf Classic Invitational S.-G1	LT	116
Read the Footnotes	C	3	1	02/14	GP	Fountain of Youth S.-G2	M	115
Society Selection	F	3	1	08/21	SAR	Alabama S.-G1	I	115
Artie Schiller	C	3	1	08/09	SAR	National Museum of Racing Hall of Fame H.-G2	MT	115
Artie Schiller	C	3	1	09/26	BEL	Jamaica H.-G2	MT	115
Purge	C	3	1	08/08	SAR	Jim Dandy S.-G2	M	115
The Cliff's Edge	C	3	2	08/28	SAR	Travers S.-G1	I	115
The Cliff's Edge	C	3	1	04/10	KEE	Toyota Blue Grass S.-G1	M	115
Love of Money	C	3	1	09/06	PHA	Pennsylvania Derby-G2	M	114
Ticker Tape (GB)	F	3	1	07/03	HOL	American Oaks-G1	IT	114
Action This Day	C	3	4	02/08	SA	Sham S.-GL	M	114
Bwana Charlie	C	3	4	10/30	LS	Breeders' Cup Sprint S.-G1	S	114
Island Sand	F	3	1	06/04	BEL	Acorn S.-G1	M	114
Medallist	C	3	1	07/11	BEL	Dwyer S.-G2	M	114
Silent Sighs	F	3	1	03/13	SA	Santa Anita Oaks-G1	M	114
Castledale (IRE)	C	3	1	04/03	SA	Santa Anita Derby-G1	M	114
Wimbledon	C	3	1	03/07	FG	Louisiana Derby-G2	M	114
Rock Hard Ten	C	3	1	07/10	HOL	Swaps Breeders' Cup S.-G2	M	114
Good Reward	C	3	1	11/28	HOL	Hollywood Derby-G1	IT	113
Friends Lake	C	3	1	03/13	GP	Florida Derby-G1	M	113
Madcap Escapade	F	3	1	03/13	GP	Stonerside Forward Gal S.-G2	S	113
Quintons Gold Rush	C	3	1	04/17	KEE	Coolmore Lexington S.-G2	M	113
St Averil	C	3	2	03/14	SA	San Felipe S.-G2	M	113
Stellar Jayne	F	3	3	10/30	LS	Breeders' Cup Distaff Presented By Nextel S.-G1	M	113
Stellar Jayne	F	3	1	06/26	BEL	Mother Goose S.-G1	M	113
Tapit	C	3	1	04/10	AQU	Wood Memorial S.-G1	M	113
Greek Sun	C	3	1	10/17	SA	Oak Tree Derby-G2	MT	113
Blackdoun (FR)	C	3	1	09/06	DMR	Del Mar Derby-G2	MT	113
Stellar Jayne	F	3	1	09/11	BEL	Gazelle H.-G1	M	113
Dance in the Mood (Jpn)	F	3	2	07/03	HOL	American Oaks-G1	IT	112
Imperialism	C	3	1	03/06	SA	San Rafael S.-G2	M	112
Lucifer's Stone	F	3	1	09/12	BEL	Garden City Breeders' Cup H.-G1	MT	112
Fast and Furious (Fr)	C	3	2	11/28	HOL	Hollywood Derby-G1	IT	112
Second of June	C	3	2	02/14	GP	Fountain of Youth S.-G2	M	112
Yearly Report	F	3	1	07/17	DEL	Delaware Oaks-G2	M	112
Amorama (FR)	F	3	1	08/21	DMR	Del Mar Oaks-G1	MT	112
Eddington	C	3	3	04/10	AQU	Wood Memorial S.-G1	M	112
Fire Slam	C	3	1	05/08	CD	Matt Winn S.-GL	S	112
Fire Slam	C	3	1	06/05	BEL	Riva Ridge Breeders' Cup S.-G2	S	112
Hollywood Story	F	3	2	02/15	SA	Las Virgenes S.-G1	M	112
House of Fortune	F	3	1	06/12	HOL	Hollywood Breeders' Cup Oaks-G2	M	112
Imperialism	C	3	3	05/01	CD	Kentucky Derby-G1	I	112
Master David	C	3	2	04/10	AQU	Wood Memorial S.-G1	M	112
Prince Arch	C	3	1	06/12	CD	Jefferson Cup S.-G3	MT	112
Pro Prado	C	3	3	04/10	OP	Arkansas Derby-G2	M	112
Victory U. S. A.	F	3	1	04/08	KEE	Stonerside Beaumont S.-G2	S	112
Wynn Dot Comma	C	3	1	03/13	GP	Swale S.-G3	S	112
Brass Hat	G	3	1	10/02	HOO	Indiana Derby-G2	M	112
Eurosilver	C	3	2	03/13	GP	Swale S.-G3	S	112
Limehouse	C	3	1	02/14	GP	Hutcheson S.-G2	S	112
Second of June	C	3	1	01/17	GP	Holy Bull S.-G3	M	112
Three Valleys	C	3	3	11/27	HOL	Citation H.-G1	MT	112
Commentator	G	3	1	10/14	KEE	Perryville S.-GL	S	112
Mass Media	C	3	1	10/31	AQU	Sport Page H.-G3	S	112

4-Year-Olds & Upward – Ratings of 115 or Greater

Horse	S	A	Fin	Date	Trk	Stakes Race and Grade	Cat	R
Ghostzapper	C	4	1	10/30	LS	Breeders' Cup Classic Powered By Dodge S.-G1	I	130
Roses in May	C	4	2	10/30	LS	Breeders' Cup Classic Powered By Dodge S.-G1	I	124
Pico Central (BRZ)	C	5	1	10/02	BEL	Vosburgh S.-G1	S	123
Medaglia d'Oro	C	5	1	02/07	GP	Donn H.-G1	M	122
Pleasantly Perfect	C	6	1	01/31	SA	San Antonio H.-G2	M	122
Southern Image	C	4	1	05/14	PIM	Pimlico Special H.-G1	I	122
Southern Image	C	4	2	06/12	CD	Stephen Foster H.-G1	M	122
Speightstown	C	6	1	08/14	SAR	Alfred G. Vanderbilt H.-G2	S	122
Speightstown	C	6	1	10/30	LS	Breeders' Cup Sprint S.-G1	S	122
Better Talk Now	G	5	1	10/30	LS	John Deere Breeders' Cup Turf S.-G1	LT	121
Powerscourt (GB)	C	4	4	08/14	AP	Arlington Million S.-G1	IT	120
Peace Rules	C	4	1	02/29	FG	New Orleans H.-G2	M	119
Peace Rules	C	4	1	07/03	BEL	Suburban H.-G1	I	119
Perfect Drift	G	5	2	08/07	SAR	Whitney H.-G1	M	119
Perfect Drift	G	5	2	08/22	DMR	Pacific Classic S.-G1	I	119
Saint Liam	C	4	2	09/11	BEL	Woodward S.-G1	M	119
Azeri	F	6	1	08/01	SAR	Go for Wand H.-G1	M	118
Azeri	F	6	1	04/03	OP	Apple Blossom H.-G1	M	118
Kela	C	6	2	10/30	LS	Breeders' Cup Sprint S.-G1	S	118
Kela	C	6	1	08/15	DMR	Pat O'Brien Breeders' Cup H.-G2	S	118
Midas Eyes	C	4	1	09/04	SAR	Forego H.-G1	S	118
Sightseek	F	5	1	10/09	BEL	Beldame S.-G1	M	118
Singletary	C	4	1	10/30	LS	NetJets Breeders' Cup Mile S.-G1	MT	118
Sightseek	F	5	1	09/19	BEL	Ruffian H.-G1	M	118
Kicken Kris	C	4	1	08/14	AP	Arlington Million S.-G1	IT	117
Magistretti	C	4	2	10/02	BEL	Joe Hirsch Turf Classic Invitational S.-G1	LT	117
Special Ring	G	7	1	07/25	DMR	Eddie Read H.-G1	MT	117
Total Impact (CHI)	C	6	3	08/22	DMR	Pacific Classic S.-G1	I	117
Adoration	F	5	1	03/14	SA	Santa Margarita Invitational H.-G1	M	116
Bayamo (IRE)	G	5	1	07/04	HOL	American H.-G2	MT	116
Adoration	F	5	1	09/04	AP	Arlington Matron H.-G3	M	116
Bayamo (IRE)	G	5	2	07/25	DMR	Eddie Read H.-G1	MT	116
Funny Cide	G	4	3	07/03	BEL	Suburban H.-G1	I	116
Funny Cide	G	4	1	10/02	BEL	Jockey Club Gold Cup S.-G1	I	116
Meteor Storm (GB)	C	5	1	06/05	BEL	Manhattan H.-G1	IT	116
Mr O'Brien (IRE)	G	5	2	07/03	MTH	United Nations S.-G1	LT	116
Mr O'Brien (IRE)	G	5	1	10/09	BEL	Kelso Breeders' Cup H.-G2	MT	116
Stroll	C	4	1	05/01	CD	Woodford Reserve Turf Classic S.-G1	MT	116
Strong Hope	C	4	2	04/10	AQU	Carter H.-G1	S	116
Nothing to Lose	C	4	1	10/09	KEE	Shadwell Turf Mile S.-G1	MT	115
Bluesthestandard	G	7	1	02/01	SA	Palos Verdes H.-G2	S	115
Designed for Luck	G	7	1	05/31	HOL	Shoemaker Breeders' Cup Mile S.-G1	MT	115
Dynever	C	4	1	04/03	SA	San Bernardino H.-G3	M	115
Evening Attire	G	6	1	08/22	SAR	Saratoga Breeders' Cup H.-G2	I	115
Film Maker	F	4	2	10/30	LS	VO5 Breeders' Cup Filly & Mare Turf S.-G1	LT	115
Intercontinental (GB)	F	4	1	11/28	HOL	Matriarch S.-G1	MT	115
Island Fashion	F	4	1	01/25	SA	Santa Monica H.-G1	S	115
Island Fashion	F	4	2	03/06	SA	Santa Anita H.-G1	I	115
Midway Road	C	4	2	05/14	PIM	Pimlico Special H.-G1	I	115
My Cousin Matt	G	5	3	10/30	LS	Breeders' Cup Sprint S.-G1	S	115
Pohave	G	6	2	10/10	SA	Ancient Title Breeders' Cup H.-G1	S	115
Request for Parole	C	5	2	08/14	SAR	Sword Dancer Invitational H.-G1	LT	115
Request for Parole	C	5	1	07/03	MTH	United Nations S.-G1	LT	115
Sabiango (GER)	C	6	1	06/12	HOL	Charles Whittingham Memorial H.-G1	IT	115
Star Over the Bay	G	6	1	10/03	SA	Clement L. Hirsch Mem Turf Championship S.-G1	IT	115
Sweet Return (GB)	C	4	1	03/06	SA	Frank E. Kilroe Mile H.-G2	MT	115
Sweet Return (GB)	C	4	3	07/25	DMR	Eddie Read H.-G1	MT	115
Ten Most Wanted	C	4	1	04/17	HAW	National Jockey Club H.-G3	M	115
Wonder Again	F	5	3	10/30	LS	VO5 Breeders' Cup Filly & Mare Turf S.-G1	LT	115
Wonder Again	F	5	6	10/02	BEL	Flower Bowl Invitational S.-G1	IT	115
Ema Bovary (CHI)	F	5	1	07/10	CRC	Princess Rooney H.-G2	S	115
Even the Score	C	6	1	06/12	HOL	Californian S.-G2	M	115
Wonder Again	F	5	1	07/31	SAR	Diana H.-G1	MT	115
Lundy's Liability (Brz)	C	4	1	10/02	SA	Goodwood Breeders' Cup H.-G2	M	115
Sweet Return (GB)	C	4	1	01/19	SA	San Marcos S.-G2	IT	115

2004 Graded Stakes Ratings

Graded stakes events of 2004, with their North American Ratings Committee (NARC) Race Rating

A GLEAM INVITATIONAL H. (107.0)
ACK ACK H. (106.3)
ACORN S. (111.0)
ADENA STALLIONS' MISS PREAKNESS S. (102.8)
ADIRONDACK S. (105.3)
AEGON TURF SPRINT S. (105.0)
AFFECTIONATELY H. (96.0)
AFFIRMED H. (104.0)
ALABAMA S. (110.8)
ALFRED G. VANDERBILT H. (115.5)
ALL ALONG BREEDERS' CUP S. (107.5)
AMERICAN DERBY (106.8)
AMERICAN H. (105.5)
AMERICAN OAKS (110.3)
AMSTERDAM S. (111.3)
ANCIENT TITLE BREEDERS' CUP H. (112.8)
ANNE ARUNDEL S. (100.5)
APPLE BLOSSOM H. (113.8)
APPLETON H. (107.8)
AQUEDUCT H. (103.8)
ARCADIA H. (106.3)
ARGENT DIXIE S. (113.0)
ARGENT MORTGAGE S. (108.5)
ARISTIDES BREEDERS' CUP H. (105.5)
ARKANSAS DERBY (115.0)
ARLINGTON BREEDERS' CUP OAKS (97.0)
ARLINGTON CLASSIC S. (103.3)
ARLINGTON H. (109.8)
ARLINGTON MATRON H. (110.3)
ARLINGTON MILLION S. (116.3)
ARLINGTON-WASH BREEDERS' CUP FUTURITY (93.5)
ARLINGTON-WASH LASSIE S. (101.0)
ASHLAND S. (108.8)
ASTARITA S. (99.8)
ATHENIA H. (106.0)
AZALEA BREEDERS' CUP S. (92.0)
BALDWIN S. (103.8)
BALLERINA H. (110.3)
BALLSTON SPA BREEDERS' CUP H. (107.8)
BARBARA FRITCHIE H. (104.3)
BASHFORD MANOR S. (101.5)
BAY MEADOWS BREEDER'S CUP H. (102.5)
BAY MEADOWS BREEDERS' CUP SPRINT H. (102.5)
BAY MEADOWS DERBY (102.5)
BAY SHORE S. (102.3)
BAYAKOA H. (110.0)
BAYOU BREEDERS' CUP H. (104.8)
BEAUGAY H. (106.5)
BED O' ROSES BREEDERS' CUP H. (109.8)
BELDAME S. (112.8)
BELMONT BREEDERS' CUP H. (109.8)
BELMONT S. (114.5)
BEN ALI S. (99.8)
BERKELEY BREEDERS' CUP H. (103.0)
BERNARD BARUCH H. (109.0)
BESSEMER TRUST BREEDERS' CUP JUV (117.5)
BEST PAL S. (90.8)
BEVERLY D. S. (113.3)
BEVERLY HILLS H. (109.5)
BEWITCH S. (107.0)
BING CROSBY BREEDERS' CUP H. (111.5)
BLACK-EYED SUSAN S. (104.3)
BOILING SPRINGS S. (107.8)
BOLD RULER H. (105.0)
BONNIE MISS S. (105.0)
BOWLING GREEN H. (109.8)
BREEDERS' CUP CLASSIC POWERED BY DODGE (122.5)
BREEDERS' CUP DISTAFF PRESENTED BY NEXTEL (114.5)
BREEDERS' CUP JUVENILE FILLIES (113.3)
BREEDERS' CUP SPRINT (118.3)
BROOKLYN H. (111.3)
BROWN BESS H. (103.3)
BUENA VISTA H. (106.8)
CALDER DERBY (106.0)
CALIFORNIAN S. (112.0)
CANADIAN TURF H. (91.3)
CARDINAL H. (111.0)
CARLETON F. BURKE H. (109.0)
CARRY BACK S. (109.3)
CARTER H. (114.3)
CHAMPAGNE S. (114.8)
CHAPOSA SPRINGS H. (98.8)
CHARLES WHITTINGHAM MEMORIAL H. (114.0)
CHICAGO BREEDERS' CUP H. (102.0)
CHURCHILL DOWNS DISTAFF H. (109.0)
CHURCHILL DOWNS H. (113.8)
CICADA S. (99.5)
CIGAR MILE H. (114.3)
CINEMA BREEDERS' CUP H. (106.5)
CITATION H. (113.5)
CLARK H. (112.8)
CLEMENT L. HIRSCH H. (112.0)
CLEMENT L. HIRSCH MEM TURF CHAMP S. (114.0)
CLIFF HANGER H. (104.5)
COACHING CLUB AMERICAN OAKS (103.5)
COMELY S. (105.8)
COMMONWEALTH BREEDERS' CUP S. (108.3)
COOLMORE LEXINGTON S. (109.8)
COTILLION H. (107.5)
COUNT FLEET SPRINT H. (106.3)
CROWN ROYAL AMERICAN TURF S. (105.8)
DAHLIA H. (110.0)
DARLEY ALCIBIADES S. (109.3)
DAVONA DALE S. (109.0)
DEBUTANTE S. (103.3)
DEL MAR BREEDERS' CUP H. (110.5)
DEL MAR DEBUTANTE S. (108.5)
DEL MAR DERBY (111.3)
DEL MAR FUTURITY (101.0)
DEL MAR H. (111.5)
DEL MAR OAKS (111.0)
DELAWARE H. (104.0)
DELAWARE OAKS (105.8)
DEMOISELLE S. (109.0)
DEPUTY MINISTER H. (109.8)
DERBY TRIAL S. (101.8)
DESERT STORMER H. (101.0)
DIANA H. (112.3)

DISCOVERY H. (102.5)
DISTAFF BREEDERS' CUP H. (100.8)
DOGWOOD BREEDERS' CUP S. (102.8)
DONALD LEVINE MEMORIAL H. (102.8)
DONN H. (116.3)
DWYER S. (112.0)
EARLY TIMES MINT JULEP H. (108.0)
EATONTOWN H. (103.5)
EDDIE READ H. (115.0)
EL CAMINO REAL DERBY (103.5)
EL CONEJO H. (102.5)
EL ENCINO S. (107.0)
ELKHORN S. (107.5)
ENDINE H. (102.3)
ESSEX H. (105.3)
EXCELSIOR BREEDERS' CUP H. (107.3)
FAIR GROUNDS OAKS (109.0)
FALL HIGHWEIGHT H. (104.3)
FALLS CITY H. (109.3)
FANTASY S. (111.0)
FAYETTE S. (110.5)
FIFTH SEASON S. (103.5)
FIRECRACKER BREEDERS' CUP H. (112.0)
FIRST FLIGHT H. (99.8)
FIRST LADY H. (107.0)
FLASH S. (103.3)
FLEUR DE LIS H. (112.0)
FLORAL PARK H. (101.3)
FLORIDA DERBY (114.3)
FLOWER BOWL INVITATIONAL S. (113.5)
FOREGO H. (113.8)
FORT MARCY H. (106.0)
FOUNTAIN OF YOUTH S. (104.5)
FOURSTARDAVE H. (112.3)
FRANK E. KILROE MILE H. (116.0)
FRANK J. DE FRANCIS MEMORIAL DASH S. (109.8)
FRED W. HOOPER H. (105.5)
FRIZETTE S. (109.3)
FUTURITY S. (102.8)
GALLANT BLOOM H. (108.3)
GALLORETTE H. (107.5)
GAMELY BREEDERS' CUP H. (111.0)
GARDEN CITY BREEDERS' CUP S. (110.8)
GARDENIA H. (106.5)
GAZELLE H. (108.8)
GENERAL GEORGE H. (107.8)
GENEROUS S. (104.3)
GENUINE RISK H. (105.0)
GLENS FALLS H. (108.6)
GLENS FALLS H. (108.6)
GO FOR WAND H. (114.8)
GOLDEN GATE BREEDERS' CUP H. (104.8)
GOLDEN GATE DERBY (100.0)
GOLDEN ROD S. (106.8)
GOODWOOD BREEDERS' CUP H. (110.0)
GOTHAM S. (105.0)
GRAVESEND H. (109.3)
GULFSTREAM PARK BREEDERS' CUP H. (113.3)
GULFSTREAM PARK H. (106.5)
HAL'S HOPE H. (101.0)
HANSHIN CUP H. (106.3)
HASKELL INVITATIONAL H. (111.8)
HAWTHORNE DERBY (100.8)
HAWTHORNE GOLD CUP H. (109.5)
HAWTHORNE H. (103.8)
HERECOMESTHEBRIDE S. (106.3)
HILL PRINCE S. (106.0)
HILLSBOROUGH S. (105.8)
HOLLYWOOD BREEDERS' CUP OAKS (108.0)
HOLLYWOOD DERBY (113.3)
HOLLYWOOD FUTURITY (107.8)
HOLLYWOOD GOLD CUP S. (111.5)
HOLLYWOOD JUVENILE CHAMPIONSHIP S. (94.0)
HOLLYWOOD STARLET S. (107.0)
HOLLYWOOD TURF CUP S. (110.8)
HOLLYWOOD TURF EXPRESS H. (107.0)
HOLY BULL S. (106.5)
HONEY FOX H. (106.3)
HONEYMOON BREEDERS' CUP H. (109.5)
HONORABLE MISS H. (106.3)
HOPEFUL S. (113.3)
HUMANA DISTAFF H. (104.0)
HUTCHESON S. (108.5)
ILLINOIS DERBY (107.8)
INDIANA BREEDERS' CUP OAKS (106.5)
INDIANA DERBY (111.5)
INGLEWOOD H. (111.3)
IOWA OAKS (97.3)
IROQUOIS S. (100.8)
JACK DANIEL'S HOLLYWOOD PREVUE S. (106.3)
JAIPUR H. (106.3)
JAMAICA H. (103.3)
JEFFERSON CUP S. (109.3)
JENNY WILEY S. (111.5)
JEROME H. (102.8)
JERSEY DERBY (104.5)
JERSEY SHORE BREEDERS' CUP S. (96.0)
JIM DANDY S. (114.5)
JOCKEY CLUB GOLD CUP (115.3)
JOE HIRSCH TURF CLASSIC INVITATIONAL S. (116.5)
JOHN C. MABEE H. (111.0)
JOHN DEERE BREEDERS' CUP TURF (118.8)
JUST A GAME BREEDERS' CUP H. (113.0)
KELSO BREEDERS' CUP H. (113.8)
KENT BREEDERS' CUP S. (107.3)
KENTUCKY BREEDERS' CUP S. (96.0)
KENTUCKY CUP CLASSIC H. (109.3)
KENTUCKY CUP JUVENILE S. (91.8)
KENTUCKY CUP SPRINT S. (99.8)
KENTUCKY CUP TURF H. (105.3)
KENTUCKY DERBY (119.8)
KENTUCKY JOCKEY CLUB S. (105.3)
KENTUCKY OAKS (114.5)
KING'S BISHOP S. (111.3)
KNICKERBOCKER H. (105.0)
LA BREA S. (111.3)
LA CANADA S. (109.3)
LA JOLLA H. (108.8)
LA PREVOYANTE H. (110.5)
LA TROIENNE S. (104.8)
LADIES H. (99.8)
LADY'S SECRET BREEDERS' CUP H. (110.8)
LAFAYETTE S. (92.5)
LAKE GEORGE S. (109.3)
LAKE PLACID H. (108.3)
LANDALUCE S. (101.0)

LANE'S END BREEDERS' FUTURITY (105.8)
LANE'S END S. (105.8)
LAS CIENEGAS H. (106.5)
LAS FLORES H. (102.3)
LAS PALMAS H. (105.8)
LAS VIRGENES S. (111.5)
LAUREL FUTURITY (101.3)
LAWRENCE REALIZATION S. (98.0)
LAZARO BARRERA MEMORIAL S. (100.8)
LECOMTE S. (105.0)
LEONARD RICHARDS S. (107.8)
LEXINGTON S. (104.5)
LOCUST GROVE H. (106.5)
LONE STAR PARK H. (106.5)
LONG BRANCH BREEDERS' CUP S. (108.3)
LONG ISLAND H. (109.8)
LONGACRES MILE H. (101.5)
LOS ANGELES TIMES H. (108.3)
LOUISIANA DERBY (111.3)
LOUISVILLE BREEDERS' CUP H. (111.5)
LOUISVILLE H. (107.8)
MAC DIARMIDA H. (106.8)
MAKER'S MARK MILE S. (113.8)
MALIBU S. (113.8)
MAN O' WAR S. (116.5)
MANHATTAN H. (115.0)
MARTHA WASHINGTON BREEDERS' CUP S. (102.5)
MARYLAND BREEDERS' CUP H. (104.5)
MASSACHUSETTS H. (111.8)
MATCHMAKER S. (106.0)
MATRIARCH S. (115.0)
MATRON S. (107.0)
MEADOWLANDS BREEDERS' CUP S. (111.8)
MEMORIAL DAY H. (104.5)
MERVIN H. MUNIZ JR. MEMORIAL H. (112.3)
MERVYN LEROY H. (111.8)
METROPOLITAN H. (116.8)
MIAMI MILE BREEDERS' CUP H. (103.3)
MIESQUE S. (104.3)
MILADY BREEDERS' CUP H. (109.0)
MILLER GENUINE DRAFT CRADLE S. (96.8)
MODESTY H. (108.3)
MOLLY PITCHER BREEDERS' CUP H. (109.8)
MONMOUTH BREEDERS' CUP OAKS (105.0)
MONROVIA H. (107.0)
MORVICH H. (107.5)
MOTHER GOOSE S. (114.0)
MR. PROSPECTOR H. (109.0)
MRS. REVERE S. (110.5)
MY CHARMER H. (106.5)
NASHUA S. (103.8)
NASSAU COUNTY BREEDERS' CUP S. (92.5)
NATIONAL JOCKEY CLUB H. (98.8)
NATIONAL MUSEUM OF RACING HALL OF FAME H. (107.3)
NATIVE DIVER H. (107.0)
NETJETS BREEDERS' CUP MILE (117.3)
NEW ORLEANS H. (116.3)
NEW YORK H. (111.0)
NEXT MOVE H. (102.0)
NOBLE DAMSEL H. (108.0)
NORFOLK S. (94.0)
NORTHERN DANCER S. (104.8)
OAK LEAF S. (108.3)
OAK TREE BREEDERS' CUP MILE S. (114.5)
OAK TREE DERBY (111.3)
OAKLAWN BREEDERS' CUP S. (106.3)
OAKLAWN H. (113.0)
OCEANPORT H. (106.3)
OGDEN PHIPPS H. (115.0)
OHIO DERBY (110.0)
OKLAHOMA DERBY (103.8)
ORCHID H. (109.5)
OVERBROOK SPINSTER S. (112.3)
PACIFIC CLASSIC S. (118.0)
PALM BEACH S. (108.3)
PALOMAR BREEDERS' CUP H. (110.0)
PALOS VERDES H. (108.5)
PAN AMERICAN H. (109.5)
PAT O'BRIEN BREEDERS' CUP H. (113.3)
PEBBLES S. (106.5)
PEGASUS S. (108.3)
PENNSYLVANIA DERBY (112.5)
PERSONAL ENSIGN H. (112.8)
PETER PAN S. (112.5)
PHILIP H. ISELIN BREEDERS' CUP H. (94.3)
PHOENIX BREEDERS' CUP S. (111.0)
PIMLICO BREEDERS' CUP DISTAFF H. (105.0)
PIMLICO SPECIAL H. (115.8)
POKER H. (111.0)
POTRERO GRANDE BREEDERS' CUP H. (110.3)
PRMCORNHUSKER BREEDERS' CUP H. (114.0)
PREAKNESS S. (116.8)
PRINCESS ROONEY H. (113.5)
PRIORESS S. (109.0)
PUCKER UP S. (107.8)
QUEEN ELIZABETH II CHALLENGE CUP S. (111.0)
QUEENS COUNTY H. (106.0)
RAILBIRD S. (103.0)
RAMPART H. (110.3)
RANCHO BERNARDO H. (106.5)
RAVEN RUN S. (106.3)
RAZORBACK H. (106.5)
RED BANK H. (106.3)
RED SMITH H. (111.0)
REGRET S. (104.3)
REMSEN S. (103.5)
RICHTER SCALE BREEDERS' CUP SPRINT CHAMPIONSHIP H. (108.0)
RISEN STAR S. (106.3)
RIVA RIDGE BREEDERS' CUP S. (105.5)
RIVER CITY H. (108.0)
ROBERT F. CAREY MEMORIAL H. (103.3)
ROYAL HEROINE S. (108.8)
RUFFIAN H. (110.3)
SABIN H. (111.3)
SAFELY KEPT BREEDERS' CUP S. (101.8)
SALVATOR MILE H. (103.0)
SAN ANTONIO H. (112.3)
SAN BERNARDINO H. (114.0)
SAN CARLOS H. (117.8)
SAN CLEMENTE H. (107.0)
SAN DIEGO H. (112.8)
SAN FELIPE S. (110.5)
SAN FERNANDO BREEDERS' CUP S. (110.0)
SAN FRANCISCO BREEDERS' CUP MILE H. (107.8)
SAN GABRIEL H. (108.8)

SAN GORGONIO H. (108.8)
SAN JUAN CAPISTRANO INVITATIONAL H. (111.8)
SAN LUIS OBISPO H. (112.3)
SAN LUIS REY H. (112.3)
SAN MARCOS S. (109.8)
SAN MIGUEL S. (99.0)
SAN PASQUAL H. (110.3)
SAN RAFAEL S. (113.5)
SAN SIMEON H. (100.5)
SAN VICENTE S. (105.0)
SANDS POINT S. (108.5)
SANFORD S. (111.5)
SANTA ANA H. (109.8)
SANTA ANITA DERBY (113.8)
SANTA ANITA H. (114.3)
SANTA ANITA OAKS (112.5)
SANTA BARBARA H. (105.5)
SANTA CATALINA S. (110.5)
SANTA MARGARITA INVITATIONAL H. (112.0)
SANTA MARIA H. (111.3)
SANTA MONICA H. (108.5)
SANTA YNEZ S. (104.0)
SANTA YSABEL S. (108.0)
SAPLING S. (103.8)
SARANAC H. (102.8)
SARATOGA BREEDERS' CUP H. (112.5)
SARATOGA SPECIAL S. (107.0)
SCHUYLERVILLE S. (102.0)
SEABISCUIT BREEDERS' CUP H. (102.8)
SECRETARIAT S. (111.5)
SENATOR KEN MADDY H. (107.3)
SENORITA S. (108.3)
SHADWELL TURF MILE S. (114.0)
SHAKERTOWN S. (106.5)
SHEEPSHEAD BAY H. (109.8)
SHIRLEY JONES H. (104.8)
SHOEMAKER BREEDERS' CUP MILE S. (116.0)
SHUVEE H. (106.5)
SILVERBULLETDAY S. (101.0)
SIXTY SAILS H. (104.0)
SKIP AWAY H. (109.5)
SMILE SPRINT H. (111.5)
SORRENTO S. (104.8)
SPECTACULAR BID S. (103.3)
SPEND A BUCK H. (102.8)
SPINAWAY S. (108.0)
SPORT PAGE H. (111.3)
STARS AND STRIPES BREEDERS' CUP TURF H. (108.3)
STEPHEN FOSTER H. (118.3)
STONERSIDE BEAUMONT S. (99.0)
STONERSIDE FORWARD GAL S. (98.0)
STRUB S. (110.5)
STUYVESANT H. (106.3)
SUBURBAN H. (115.3)
SUNSET H. (109.5)
SUPER DERBY (111.0)
SWALE S. (106.3)
SWAPS BREEDERS' CUP S. (108.0)
SWORD DANCER INVITATIONAL S. (114.5)
SYCAMORE BREEDERS' CUP S. (107.0)
TAMPA BAY DERBY (108.3)
TEMPTED S. (97.5)
TEST S. (110.3)
TEXAS MILE S. (108.8)
THE VERY ONE H. (105.8)
THOROUGHBRED CLUB OF AMERICA S. (105.0)
TOBOGGAN H. (108.0)
TOM FOOL H. (108.8)
TOP FLIGHT H. (104.8)
TOYOTA BLUE GRASS S. (114.0)
TRANSYLVANIA S. (103.8)
TRAVERS S. (116.0)
TRIPLE BEND BREEDERS' CUP INV'L H. (112.0)
TROPICAL PARK DERBY (109.8)
TROPICAL TURF H. (106.8)
TRUE NORTH BREEDERS' CUP H. (114.0)
TURFWAY BREEDERS' CUP S. (107.3)
TURFWAY PARK FALL CHAMPIONSHIP S. (105.5)
TURNBACK THE ALARM H. (104.8)
UNITED NATIONS S. (114.8)
V05 BREEDERS' CUP FILLY & MARE TURF (114.8)
VAGRANCY H. (106.0)
VALLEY STREAM S. (98.0)
VALLEY VIEW S. (102.5)
VANITY H. (111.0)
VERNON O. UNDERWOOD S. (108.8)
VIOLET H. (107.3)
VIRGINIA DERBY (104.0)
VOSBURGH S. (117.5)
W. L. MCKNIGHT H. (111.0)
WALMAC LONE STAR DERBY (109.3)
WASHINGTON PARK H. (109.8)
WEST VIRGINIA DERBY (109.3)
WESTCHESTER H. (106.8)
WHIRLAWAY H. (108.5)
WHITNEY H. (117.8)
WILL ROGERS S. (104.8)
WILLIAM DONALD SCHAEFER H. (102.8)
WILSHIRE H. (111.3)
WINSTAR DISTAFF H. (109.0)
WINSTAR GALAXY S. (110.0)
WITHERS S. (109.0)
WOOD MEMORIAL S. (112.0)
WOODFORD RESERVE TURF CLASSIC S. (115.0)
WOODWARD S. (115.5)
YELLOW RIBBON S. (108.5)
YERBA BUENA BREEDERS' CUP H. (103.3)

Thoroughbred Racing Hall of Fame

Mailing Address and Phone

National Museum of Racing and Hall of Fame
191 Union Avenue
Saratoga Springs, NY 12866-3566
Phone: (518) 584-0400
Fax: (518) 584-4574
Email: nmrinfo@racingmuseum.net Website: www.racingmuseum.org

Location and Directions

The National Museum of Racing and Hall of Fame is located in Saratoga Springs, New York, across from the historic Saratoga Race Course, the oldest operating track in the country.

To get to the National Museum of Racing and Hall of Fame, take exit 14 from I-87 (the Northway) to Saratoga Springs. Proceed 1 1/2 miles into town, taking Union Avenue. The Museum is located on the right hand side at the corner of Union Avenue and Ludlow Street.

Hours

Monday-Saturday — 10:00 a.m. to 4:00 p.m.
Sunday — 12.00 p.m. to 4:00 p.m.
During the Race Meet, the Museum is open daily from 9:00 a.m. to 5:00 p.m. The Museum is closed New Year's Day, Easter, Thanksgiving, and Christmas.

Admission Fees

$7.00 adults, $5.00 students and senior citizens; members and children under 5 are free. Group rates available; call (518) 584-0400, ext. 120.

Mission

The mission of the Official National Thoroughbred Racing Hall of Fame is to honor the achievements of those horses, jockeys, and trainers whose records and reputations have withstood the difficult test of time.

Brief History

The National Museum of Racing was incorporated in historic Saratoga Springs, New York, in 1950. In 1955 the Museum moved to its present site on Union Avenue, and the Hall of Fame was created to recognize and honor deserving horses, jockeys, and trainers.

Over the years the selection process and criteria have been fine-tuned, but the Hall of Fame remains devoted to the original three categories.

As of Hall of Fame Day 2004, members include 171 Thoroughbreds, 84 jockeys, and 78 trainers.

The Nomination and Induction Process

The Hall of Fame Nomination and Induction process has undergone significant changes. Please refer to the National Museum of Racing and Hall of Fame's web site for further details.

2004 Hall of Fame Inductees

Male Horse

SKIP AWAY

Gray or roan colt foaled in 1993.
By Skip Trial - Ingot Way, by Diplomat Way
Breeder: Anna Marie Barnhart
Owner: Carolyn H. Hine
Trainer: Hubert "Sonny" Hine

RACE RECORD

YEAR	AGE	ST.	1ST	2ND	3RD	EARNED
1995	2	6	1	3	1	$88,080
1996	3	12	6	2	2	2,699,280
1997	4	11	4	5	2	4,089,000
1998	5	9	7	0	1	2,740,000
Total		**38**	**18**	**10**	**6**	**$9,616,000**

A horse of remarkable consistency and durability, Skip Away was a champion at 3, 4 and 5, earning Horse of the Year honors in his last season of racing. He retired as the second-leading earner in history, behind only Cigar, whom he had defeated as a 3-year-old in the Jockey Club Gold Cup. At the time of his retirement, his time of 1:59.16 in winning the Breeders' Cup Classic of 1997 was a stakes record as was the winning margin of six lengths. Among his other career highlights was a nine-race winning streak, commencing in late 1997 with his second consecutive Jockey Club Gold Cup victory. A throwback to another era, Skip Away took part in 34 stakes events in his career and was unplaced in only two of them: both times he ran at Churchill Downs. Aside from disappointing efforts in the 1996 Kentucky Derby and the 1998 Breeders' Cup Classic in his career finale at the Louisville site, the well-traveled horse handled nearly everything else, winning important races in Canada and eight states. His trainer, Hubert "Sonny" Hine, entered the Hall of Fame posthumously in 2003.

Female Horse

FLAWLESSLY

Bay filly foaled in 1988.
By Affirmed - La Confidence, by Nijinsky II
Breeder: Harbor View Farm
Owner: Harbor View Farm
Trainers: Richard Dutrow, Charles Whittingham

RACE RECORD

YEAR	AGE	ST.	1ST	2ND	3RD	EARNED
1990	2	7	3	0	1	188,286
1991	3	7	5	1	0	452,550
1992	4	5	3	2	0	696,500
1993	5	5	4	0	0	886,700
1994	6	4	1	1	2	348,500
Total		**28**	**16**	**4**	**3**	**$2,572,536**

After a primarily dirt-based campaign in New York and New Jersey at 2 and early in her 3-year-old season, highlighted by a pair of Grade 3 wins and a third in the Frizette, Flawlessly was sent to California where she blossomed with a full-time switch to the turf. Winner of five of six starts at 3, including the Grade 1 Matriarch against her elders, Flawlessly went on to champion turf female honors at 4 and 5 and remained a credible force at 6. Unplaced just once in 21 turf starts - a ninth after a troubled trip in the Breeders' Cup Mile in her only start against males - Flawlessly virtually owned filly and mare turf racing in California in the early 1990s, winning the then-Grade 1 Beverly Hills twice and Ramona Handicap and Matriarch three consecutive times each. Flawlessly died in 2002 without producing a notable runner.

Jockey

KENT DESORMEAUX
Riding Career: 1986-Present
Mounts: 22,605
Winners: 4,477
Winning Percentage: 19.8% *(Note: Statistics through Jan. 19, 2005)*

Achievements

* Rode winners of the Kentucky Derby, Preakness, Breeders' Cup Turf, Sprint
* Twice times honored with an Eclipse Award as leading jockey (1989 and 1992)
* Won Eclipse Award as leading apprentice (1987)
* Annual leader, races won (1987, 1988, 1989); record of 598 wins, set in 1989, still stands
* Annual leader, money won (1992)

Classic and Breeders' Cup Races Won

Kentucky Derby: Real Quiet, Fusaichi Pegasus
Preakness: Real Quiet
Breeders' Cup Turf: Kotashaan
Breeders' Cup Sprint: Desert Stormer

Other Significant Mounts

Best Pal, Fiji, Possibly Perfect, Safely Kept, The Wicked North

Kent Desormeaux was born on Feb. 27, 1970, in Louisiana and rode his first winner in July 1986 at Evangeline Downs. After moving to Maryland early in his career, he proved to be an immediate sensation, earning recognition as the nation's leading apprentice rider in 1987, the first of three straight years of leading the list of riders by races won. In 1989, he won 598 races, breaking the previous record of 546 wins in one season set in 1974 by Chris McCarron. The record still stands. Early in 1990, Desormeaux moved to California and experienced some success but also suffered a serious accident in 1992 and saw his fortunes slip somewhat through the mid-1990s. Classic success was yet to come, however, first in 1998 in the form of Real Quiet, whom Desormeaux had been riding regularly since his the colt's 2-year-old season, and then Fusaichi Pegasus two years later.

Trainer

CLAUDE R. "SHUG" MCGAUGHEY

Champions

Easy Goer (1988 2-year-old colt or gelding), Heavenly Prize (1994 3-year-old filly) Inside Information (1995 older filly or mare), Personal Ensign (1988 older filly or mare), Queena (1991 older filly or mare), Rhythm (1989 2-year-old colt or gelding), Vanlandingham (1985 older male)

Major achievements

* Trained eight Breeders' Cup winners (Dancing Spree, 1989 Sprint; Inside Information, 1995 Distaff; Lure, 1992-1993 Mile; My Flag, 1995 Juvenile Fillies; Personal Ensign, 1988 Distaff; Rhythm, 1989 Juvenile; Storm Flag Flying, 2002 Juvenile Fillies).
* Trained Belmont winner Easy Goer.
* Trained undefeated champion Personal Ensign.
* Saddled winners of five graded stakes events on one day at Belmont

Claude "Shug" McGaughey saddled his first winner at Rockingham Park in 1976 and had his first big star with Loblolly Stable's Vanlandingham, who earned a championship as top older horse of 1985. Hired shortly thereafter by Ogden Phipps, McGaughey saddled Grade 1 winners like Personal Ensign and Polish Navy for the Phipps family in 1986 and went on to become associated with a galaxy of stars for the Phippses in subsequent years. McGaughey also has developed major winners for a variety of other stables, such as Lure for Claiborne Farm and Coronado's Quest for Stuart Janney III.

Historic Horse

BOWL OF FLOWERS

Chestnut filly foaled in 1958.
By Sailor - Flower Bowl, by Alibhai
Breeder: Brookmeade Stable
Owner: Brookmeade Stable
Trainer: Elliott Burch

RACE RECORD

YEAR	AGE	ST.	1ST	2ND	3RD	EARNED
1960	2	8	6	2	0	198,706
1961	3	8	4	1	4	199,798
Total		**16**	**10**	**3**	**3**	**$398,504**

A divisional champion both seasons she raced, Bowl of Flowers had consistent, if somewhat limited, campaign that saw her win some of the greatest prizes available to 2- and 3-year-old fillies of the day. After winning two of her first three starts in the spring of her 2-year-old year, she was away until the fall, returning to win the rich Gardenia Stakes after several prep races and concluding the season with a victory in the Frizette. Her late-running style inspired expectations of classic ability, which she lived up to by winning the Coaching Club American Oaks at 3, following up a win in the Acorn and a narrow loss in the Mother Goose. A distant third-place Alabama effort behind main divisional rival Primonetta momentarily dimmed her chances at a repeat championship, but a victory in the Spinster over Primonetta and top older mare Airmans Guide sealed her case. She closed her season and, as it turned out, her career losing by inches in the Roamer Handicap behinid Belmont winner Sherluck and Hitting Away. Never the soundest individual, Bowl of Flowers was troubled occasionally by bothersome ankles and was retired after a sesamoid injury. A daughter of a major stakes winner and a half-sister to full brothers Graustark and His Majesty, Bowl of Flowers failed to produce any runners of great significance, though her son Whiskey Road did sire major stallion Strawberry Road.

Historic Jockey

JIMMY WINKFIELD
Riding Career: 1898-1930
Winners: More than 2,500

Achievements

* Rode back-to-back winners of the Kentucky Derby
* Won numerous important races in Eastern Europe

American Classic Races Won

Kentucky Derby: His Eminence
Kentucky Derby: Alan-a-Dale

Jimmy Winkfield was born in 1882 and rode his first race at Hawthorne in 1898. Unable to ride for a year after causing a four-horse pileup in his first ride, he returned to win for the first time in 1899 and rapidly achieved success in the Midwest - then considered "western" racing. Finishing third in his first Kentucky Derby ride in 1900, Winkfield returned to win the race in 1901 with His Eminence and in 1902 with Alan-a-Dale, becoming only the second jockey to win back-to-back runnings of the event. An attempt to win a third straight failed when he finished second in 1902. By 1904, Winkfield was riding in Eastern Europe, one of many American jockeys who left the United States during a troubled time in racing history. After a successful career in the East, Winkfield had to leave because of the Russian revolution and wound up his career riding in Paris. After his riding career ended, Winkfield turned to training, both in France and later in the United States. He died in France in 1974.

Horses

Horse	Year Elected	Year Foaled	Horse	Year Elected	Year Foaled
A.P. Indy	2000	1989	Easy Goer	1997	1986
Ack Ack	1986	1966	Eight Thirty	1994	1936
Affectionately	1989	1960	Elkridge	1966	1938
Affirmed	1980	1975	Emperor of Norfolk	1988	1885
All Along	1990	1979	Equipoise	1957	1928
Alsab	1976	1939	Exceller	1999	1973
Alydar	1989	1975	Exterminator	1957	1915
Alysheba	1993	1984	Fair Play	1956	1905
American Eclipse	1970	1814	Fairmount	1985	1921
Armed	1963	1941	Fashion	1980	1837
Artful	1956	1902	Firenze	1981	1884
Arts and Letters	1994	1966	Flawlessly	2004	1988
Assault	1964	1943	Flatterer	1994	1979
Battleship	1969	1927	Foolish Pleasure	1995	1972
Bayakoa	1998	1984	Forego	1979	1970
Bed o'Roses	1976	1947	Fort Marcy	1998	1964
Beldame	1956	1901	Gallant Bloom	1977	1966
Ben Brush	1955	1893	Gallant Fox	1957	1927
Bewitch	1977	1945	Gallant Man	1987	1954
Bimelech	1990	1937	Gallorette	1962	1942
Black Gold	1989	1921	Gamely	1980	1964
Black Helen	1991	1932	Genuine Risk	1986	1977
Blue Larkspur	1957	1926	Go For Wand	1996	1987
Bold 'n Determined	1997	1977	Good and Plenty	1956	1900
Bold Ruler	1973	1954	Granville	1997	1933
Bon Nouvel	1976	1960	Grey Lag	1957	1918
Boston	1955	1833	Gun Bow	1999	1960
Bowl of Flowers	2004	1958	Hamburg	1986	1895
Broomstick	1956	1901	Hanover	1955	1884
Buckpasser	1970	1963	Henry of Navarre	1985	1891
Busher	1964	1942	Hill Prince	1991	1947
Bushranger	1967	1930	Hindoo	1955	1878
Cafe Prince	1985	1970	Holy Bull	2001	1991
Carry Back	1975	1958	Imp	1965	1894
Cavalcade	1993	1931	Jay Trump	1971	1957
Challedon	1977	1936	John Henry	1990	1975
Chris Evert	1988	1971	Johnstown	1992	1936
Cicada	1967	1959	Jolly Roger	1965	1922
Cigar	2002	1990	Kelso	1967	1957
Citation	1959	1945	Kentucky	1983	1861
Coaltown	1983	1945	Kingston	1955	1884
Colin	1956	1905	L'Escargot	1977	1963
Commando	1956	1898	La Prevoyante	1995	1970
Count Fleet	1961	1940	Lady's Secret	1992	1982
Crusader	1995	1923	Lexington	1955	1850
Dahlia	1981	1970	Longfellow	1971	1867
Damascus	1974	1964	Luke Blackburn	1956	1877
Dance Smartly	2003	1988	Majestic Prince	1988	1966
Dark Mirage	1974	1965	Man o 'War	1957	1917
Davona Dale	1985	1976	Maskette	2001	1906
Desert Vixen	1979	1970	Miesque	1999	1984
Devil Diver	1980	1939	Miss Woodford	1967	1880
Discovery	1969	1931	Myrtlewood	1979	1932
Domino	1955	1891	Nashua	1965	1952
Dr. Fager	1971	1964	Native Dancer	1963	1950

Horses

Horse	Year Elected	Year Foaled	Horse	Year Elected	Year Foaled
Native Diver	1978	1959	Serena's Song	2002	1992
Needles	2000	1953	Shuvee	1975	1966
Neji	1966	1950	Silver Spoon	1978	1956
Northern Dancer	1976	1961	Sir Archy	1955	1805
Oedipus	1978	1946	Sir Barton	1957	1916
Old Rosebud	1968	1911	Skip Away	2004	1993
Omaha	1965	1932	Slew o' Gold	1992	1980
Pan Zareta	1972	1910	Spectacular Bid	1982	1976
Parole	1984	1873	Stymie	1975	1941
Paseana	2001	1987	Sun Beau	1996	1925
Personal Ensign	1993	1984	Sunday Silence	1996	1986
Peter Pan	1956	1904	Susan's Girl	1976	1969
Precisionist	2003	1981	Swaps	1966	1952
Princess Doreen	1982	1921	Sword Dancer	1977	1956
Princess Rooney	1991	1980	Sysonby	1956	1902
Real Delight	1987	1949	Ta Wee	1994	1966
Regret	1957	1912	Ten Broeck	1982	1872
Reigh Count	1978	1925	Tim Tam	1985	1955
Riva Ridge	1998	1969	Tom Fool	1960	1949
Roamer	1981	1911	Top Flight	1966	1929
Roseben	1956	1901	Tosmah	1984	1961
Round Table	1972	1954	Twenty Grand	1957	1928
Ruffian	1976	1972	Twilight Tear	1963	1941
Ruthless	1975	1864	Two Lea	1982	1946
Salvator	1955	1886	War Admiral	1958	1934
Sarazen	1957	1921	Whirlaway	1959	1938
Seabiscuit	1958	1933	Whisk Broom II	1979	1907
Searching	1978	1952	Winning Colors	2000	1985
Seattle Slew	1981	1974	Zaccio	1990	1976
Secretariat	1974	1970	Zev	1983	1920

Jockeys

Jockey	Year Inducted	Jockey	Year Inducted
John Adams	1965	John Eric Longden	1958
Frank D. Adams	1970	Daniel A. Maher	1955
Joe Aitcheson , Jr	1978	J. Linus McAtee	1956
G. Edward Arcaro	1958	Chris McCarron	1989
Ted F. Atkinson	1957	Conn McCreary	1975
Braulio Baeza	1976	Rigan McKinney	1968
Jerry Bailey	1995	James McLaughlin	1955
George Barbee	1996	Walter Miller	1955
Caroll K. Bassett	1972	Isaac B. Murphy	1955
Russell Baze	1999	Ralph Neves	1960
Walter Blum	1987	Joe Notter	1963
George Bostwick	1968	Winfield O'Conner	1956
Sam Boulmetis , Sr.	1973	Frank O'Neill	1956
Steve Brooks	1963	George M. Odom	1955
Don Brumfield	1996	Ivan H. Parke	1978
Thomas H. Burns	1983	Gilbert W. Patrick	1970
James H. Butwell	1984	Laffit Pincay Jr.	1975
J. Dallett Byers	1967	Samuel Purdy	1970
Steve Cauthen	1994	John Reiff	1956
Frank Coltiletti	1970	Alfred Robertson	1971
Angel Cordero , Jr.	1988	John L. Rotz	1983
Robert H. Crawford	1973	Earl Sande	1955
Pat Day	1991	Carroll H. Shilling	1970
Eddie Delahoussaye	1993	William Shoemaker	1958
Kent Desormeaux	2004	Willie Simms	1977
Lavelle Ensor	1962	Tod Sloan	1955
Laverne Fator	1955	Mike Smith	2003
Earlie Fires	2001	Alfred P. Smithwick	1973
Jerry Fishback	1992	Gary Stevens	1997
Mack Garner	1969	James Stout	1968
Edward Garrison	1955	Fred Taral	1955
Avelino Gomez	1982	Bayard Tuckerman Jr.	1973
Henry F. Griffin	1956	Ron Turcotte	1979
O. Eric Guerin	1972	Nash Turner	1955
William J. Hartack	1959	Robert N. Ussery	1980
Sandy Hawley	1992	Jacinto Vasquez	1998
Albert Johnson	1971	Jorge Velasquez	1990
William J. Knapp	1969	Jack Westrope	2002
Julie Krone	2000	Jimmy Winkfield	2004
Clarence Kummer	1972	George M. Woolf	1955
Charles Kurtsinger	1967	Raymond Workman	1956
John P. Loftus	1959	Manuel Ycaza	1977

Trainers

Trainer	Year Inducted
Lazaro S. Barrera	1979
H. Guy Bedwell	1971
Edward D. Brown	1984
J. Elliott Burch	1980
Preston M. Burch	1963
William P. Burch	1955
Fred Burlew	1973
Frank E. Childs	1968
Henry S. Clark	1982
W. Burling Cocks	1985
James P. Conway	1996
Warren A. Croll , Jr.	1994
Grover G. Delp	2002
Neil D. Drysdale	2000
William Duke	1956
Louis Feustel	1964
James Fitzsimmons	1958
Robert Frankel	1995
John M. Gaver Sr.	1966
Thomas J. Healey	1955
Samuel C. Hildreth	1955
Hubert "Sonny" Hine	2003
Maximilian Hirsch	1959
William J. Hirsch	1982
Thomas Hitchcock	1973
Hollie Hughes	1973
John J. Hyland	1956
Hirsch Jacobs	1958
H. Allen Jerkens	1975
Philip G. Johnson	1997
William R. Johnson	1986
LeRoy Jolley	1987
Benjamin A. Jones	1958
Horace A. Jones	1959
A. Jack Joyner	1955
Thomas J. Kelly	1993
Lucien Laurin	1977
J. Howard Lewis	1969
D. Wayne Lukas	1999

Trainer	Year Inducted
Horatio A. Luro	1980
John E. Madden	1983
James W. Maloney	1989
Richard Mandella	2001
Frank Martin	1981
Ron McAnally	1990
Henry McDaniel	1956
Claude "Shug" McGaughey	2004
MacKenzie Miller	1987
William Molter	1960
William I. Mott	1998
W. F. Mulholland	1967
Edward A. Neloy	1983
John A. Nerud	1972
Burley Parke	1986
Angel Penna	1988
Jacob Pincus	1988
John W. Rogers	1955
James G. Rowe Sr.	1955
Flint S. Schulhofer	1992
Jonathan Sheppard	1990
Robert A. Smith	1976
D. M. Smithwick	1971
Woodford Stephens	1976
Mesh Tenney	1991
Henry J. Thompson	1969
Harry Trotsek	1984
Jack C. Van Berg	1985
Marion Van Berg	1970
Sylvester Veitch	1977
R. W. Walden	1970
Michael G. Walsh	1997
Sherrill W. Ward	1978
Frank Whiteley Jr	1978
Charles Whittingham	1974
Ansel Williamson	1998
G. Carey Winfrey	1975
William C. Winfrey	1971

Richest Stakes Races in North America in 2004

Race Name	Date	Race	Winning Horse	Jockey	Track	Earnings	Purse
Kentucky Derby-G1 *	1-May	10	Smarty Jones	Elliott, S.	CD	$5,884,800	$1,000,000
Breeders' Cup Classic (Dodge)-G1	30-Oct	9	Ghostzapper	Castellano, J.	LS	2,080,000	4,000,000
Breeders' Cup Distaff (NexTel)-G1	30-Oct	2	Ashado	Velazquez, J.R.	LS	1,040,000	2,000,000
John Deere Breeders' Cup Turf-G1	30-Oct	8	Better Talk Now	Dominguez, R.A.	LS	1,040,000	2,000,000
NetJets Breeders' Cup Mile-G1	30-Oct	4	Singletary	Flores, D.R.	LS	873,600	1,500,000
Pattison Canadian International S.-G1	24-Oct	9	Sulamani (IRE)	Dettori, L.	WO	900,000	1,500,000
Bessemer Trust BC Juvenile-G1	30-Oct	7	Wilko	Dettori, L.	LS	780,000	1,500,000
VO5 BC Filly & Mare Turf-G1	30-Oct	6	Ouija Board (GB)	Fallon, K.	LS	733,200	1,000,000
Breeders' Cup Sprint-G1	30-Oct	5	Speightstown	Velazquez, J.R.	LS	551,200	1,000,000
Breeders' Cup Juvenile Fillies-G1	30-Oct	3	Sweet Catomine	Nakatani, C.S.	LS	520,000	1,000,000
Belmont S.-G1	5-Jun	11	Birdstone	Prado, E.S.	BEL	600,000	1,000,000
Travers S.-G1	28-Aug	11	Birdstone	Prado, E.S.	SAR	600,000	1,000,000
Pacific Classic S.-G1	22-Aug	8	Pleasantly Perfect	Bailey, J.D.	DMR	600,000	1,000,000
Haskell Invitational H.-G1	8-Aug	13	Lion Heart	Bravo, J.	MTH	600,000	1,000,000
Jockey Club Gold Cup-G1	2-Oct	10	Funny Cide	Santos, J.A.	BEL	600,000	1,000,000
Arlington Million S.-G1	14-Aug	9	Kicken Kris	Desormeaux, K.J.	AP	600,000	1,000,000
Florida Derby-G1	13-Mar	9	Friends Lake	Migliore, R.	GP	600,000	1,000,000
Queen's Plate S.	27-Jun	9	Niigon	Landry, R.C.	WO	600,000	1,000,000
Preakness S.-G1	15-May	12	Smarty Jones	Elliott, S.	PIM	650,000	1,000,000
Arkansas Derby-G2	10-Apr	9	Smarty Jones	Elliott, S.	OP	600,000	1,000,000
Atto Mile S.-G1	19-Sep	9	Soaring Free	Kabel, T.	WO	600,000	1,000,000
Barretts/CTBA Classic S.	24-Jan	6	Southern Image	Espinoza, V.	SA	550,000	1,000,000
Santa Anita H.-G1	6-Mar	10	Southern Image	Espinoza, V.	SA	600,000	1,000,000
Boyd Gaming's Delta Jackpot S.	4-Dec	8	Texcess	Espinoza, V.	DED	600,000	1,000,000
Stephen Foster H.-G1	12-Jun	9	Colonial Colony	Bejarano, R.	CD	502,665	750,000
Delaware H.-G2	18-Jul	10	Summer Wind Dancer	Espinoza, V.	DEL	450,000	750,000
Metropolitan H.-G1	31-May	9	Pico Central (BRZ)	Solis, A.O.	BEL	450,000	750,000
Alabama S.-G1	21-Aug	10	Society Selection	Velasquez, C.H.	SAR	450,000	750,000
Flower Bowl Invitational S.-G1	2-Oct	7	Riskaverse	Velasquez, C.H.	BEL	450,000	750,000
United Nations S.-G1	3-Jul	10	Request for Parole	Prado, E.S.	MTH	450,000	750,000
Whitney H.-G1	7-Aug	9	Roses in May	Prado, E.S.	SAR	450,000	750,000
Hawthorne Gold Cup H.-G2	2-Oct	7	Freefourinternet	Kuntzweiler, G.	HAW	450,000	750,000
Beldame S.-G1	9-Oct	9	Sightseek	Castellano, J.	BEL	450,000	750,000
Joe Hirsch Turf Classic Inv'l S.-G1	2-Oct	9	Kitten's Joy	Velazquez, J.R.	BEL	450,000	750,000
E. P. Taylor S.-G1	24-Oct	6	Commercante (FR)	Velazquez, J.R.	WO	450,000	750,000
Santa Anita Derby-G1	3-Apr	8	Castledale (IRE)	Valdivia, Jr., J.	SA	450,000	750,000
American Oaks-G1	3-Jul	6	Ticker Tape (GB)	Desormeaux, K.J.	HOL	450,000	750,000
Beverly D. S.-G1	14-Aug	8	Crimson Palace (SAF)	Dettori, L.	AP	450,000	750,000
Hollywood Gold Cup S.-G1	10-Jul	9	Total Impact (CHI)	Smith, M.E.	HOL	450,000	750,000
Wood Memorial S.-G1	10-Apr	8	Tapit	Dominguez, R.A.	AQU	450,000	750,000
Pennsylvania Derby-G2	6-Sep	10	Love of Money	Albarado, R.	PHA	418,500	750,000
Toyota Blue Grass S.-G1	10-Apr	9	The Cliff's Edge	Sellers, S.J.	KEE	465,000	750,000
Louisiana Derby-G2	7-Mar	9	Wimbledon	Santiago, J.	FG	360,000	600,000
West Virginia Derby-G3	7-Aug	8	Sir Shackleton	Bejarano, R.	MNR	363,000	600,000
Shadwell Turf Mile S.-G1	9-Oct	8	Nothing to Lose	Albarado, R.	KEE	372,000	600,000
Kentucky Oaks-G1	30-Apr	10	Ashado	Velazquez, J.R.	CD	354,640	500,000
Clark H.-G2	26-Nov	11	Saint Liam	Prado, E.S.	CD	345,960	500,000
Indiana Derby-G2	2-Oct	9	Brass Hat	Martinez, W.	HOO	306,780	500,000
Delaware Oaks-G2	17-Jul	8	Yearly Report	Bailey, J.D.	DEL	300,000	500,000
Frizette S.-G1	9-Oct	6	Balletto (UAE)	Nakatani, C.S.	BEL	300,000	500,000
Goodwood Breeders' Cup H.-G2	2-Oct	8	Lundy's Liability (BRZ)	Flores, D.R.	SA	300,000	500,000
WinStar Galaxy S.-G2	10-Oct	6	Stay Forever	Castro, E.	KEE	310,000	500,000

Race Name	Date	Race	Winning Horse	Jockey	Track	Earnings	Purse
Virginia Derby-G3	10-Jul	9	Kitten's Joy	Prado, E.S.	CNL	300,000	500,000
Diana H.-G1	31-Jul	7	Wonder Again	Prado, E.S.	SAR	300,000	500,000
Massachusetts H.-G2	19-Jun	10	Offlee Wild	Prado, E.S.	SUF	300,000	500,000
Man o' War S.-G1	11-Sep	9	Magistretti	Prado, E.S.	BEL	300,000	500,000
Ocala Breeders' Sales Distaff S.	24-Jan	9	Secret Request	Coa, E.	GP	275,000	500,000
Illinois Derby-G2	3-Apr	7	Pollard's Vision	Coa, E.	HAW	300,000	500,000
Super Derby-G2	25-Sep	10	Fantasticat	Melancon, G.	LAD	300,000	500,000
Woodward S.-G1	11-Sep	10	Ghostzapper	Castellano, J.	BEL	300,000	500,000
Oaklawn H.-G2	3-Apr	11	Peace Rules	Bailey, J.D.	OP	300,000	500,000
New Orleans H.-G2	29-Feb	9	Peace Rules	Bailey, J.D.	FG	300,000	500,000
Smile Sprint H.-G3	10-Jul	10	Champali	Bailey, J.D.	CRC	294,000	500,000
Hollywood Derby-G1	28-Nov	9	Good Reward	Bailey, J.D.	HOL	300,000	500,000
Suburban H.-G1	3-Jul	7	Peace Rules	Bailey, J.D.	BEL	300,000	500,000
Matriarch S.-G1	28-Nov	7	Intercontinental (GB)	Bailey, J.D.	HOL	300,000	500,000
Donn H.-G1	7-Feb	10	Medaglia d'Oro	Bailey, J.D.	GP	300,000	500,000
Meadowlands Breeders' Cup S.-G2	8-Oct	7	Balto Star	Velazquez, J.R.	MED	300,000	500,000
Jim Dandy S.-G2	8-Aug	9	Purge	Velazquez, J.R.	SAR	300,000	500,000
Coaching Club American Oaks-G1	24-Jul	8	Ashado	Velazquez, J.R.	BEL	300,000	500,000
Champagne S.-G1	9-Oct	7	Proud Accolade	Velazquez, J.R.	BEL	300,000	500,000
John Deere Filly and MareTurf S.	24-Jan	5	Valentine Dancer	Court, J.K.	SA	275,000	500,000
Prince of Wales S.	18-Jul	9	A Bit O'Gold	Jones, J.C.	FE	300,000	500,000
Breeders' S.	8-Aug	9	A Bit O'Gold	Jones, J.C.	WO	300,000	500,000
Queen Elizabeth II Challenge Cup S.-G1	16-Oct	8	Ticker Tape (GB)	Desormeaux, K.J.	KEE	310,000	500,000
Apple Blossom H.-G1	3-Apr	9	Azeri	Smith, M.E.	OP	300,000	500,000
Overbrook Spinster S.-G1	10-Oct	8	Azeri	Day, P.	KEE	310,000	500,000
Lane's End S.-G2	20-Mar	8	Sinister G	Toscano, P.R.	TP	300,000	500,000
Lane's End Breeders' Futurity-G1	9-Oct	7	Consolidator	Bejarano, R.	KEE	310,000	500,000
Sword Dancer Invitational S.-G1	14-Aug	8	Better Talk Now	Dominguez, R.A.	SAR	300,000	500,000
Yellow Ribbon S.-G1	2-Oct	4	Light Jig (GB)	Douglas, R.R.	SA	300,000	500,000
Ashland S.-G1	3-Apr	9	Madcap Escapade	Douglas, R.R.	KEE	310,000	500,000
Franks Farm Turf S.	24-Jan	10	Proud Man	Douglas, R.R.	GP	275,000	500,000
WinStar Derby	28-Mar	8	Hi Teck Man	Jaime, R.	SUN	270,000	500,000
Mervin H. Muniz Jr. Memorial H.-G2	21-Mar	8	Mystery Giver	Albarado, R.	FG	300,000	500,000
Princess Rooney H.-G2	10-Jul	11	Ema Bovary (CHI)	Gonzalez, R.M.	CRC	294,000	500,000
Labatt Woodbine Oaks	13-Jun	8	Eye of the Sphynx	Kabel, T.	WO	300,000	500,000
Vosburgh S.-G1	2-Oct	8	Pico Central (BRZ)	Espinoza, V.	BEL	300,000	500,000
Pimlico Special H.-G1	14-May	11	Southern Image	Espinoza, V.	PIM	300,000	500,000
Shoemaker Breeders' Cup Mile S.-G1	31-May	7	Designed for Luck	Valenzuela, P.A.	HOL	282,000	350,000
Woodford Reserve Turf Classic S.-G1	1-May	9	Stroll	Bailey, J.D.	CD	281,418	400,000
Hollywood Futurity-G1	18-Dec	8	Declan's Moon	Espinoza, V.	HOL	267,900	449,500
Fleur de Lis H.-G2	12-Jun	8	Adoration	Espinoza, V.	CD	272,304	400,000
Swaps Breeders' Cup S.-G2	10-Jul	7	Rock Hard Ten	Nakatani, C.S.	HOL	252,780	400,000
Gamely Breeders' Cup H.-G1	31-May	2	Noches De Rosa (CHI)	Smith, M.E.	HOL	187,500	350,000
Indiana Breeders' Cup Oaks-G3	1-Oct	9	Daydreaming	Velazquez, J.R.	HOO	243,780	400,000
Del Mar Derby-G2	6-Sep	8	Blackdoun (FR)	Nakatani, C.S.	DMR	240,000	400,000
Florida Stallion In Reality S.	23-Oct	12	B. B. Best	Castro, E.	CRC	240,000	400,000
Secretariat S.-G1	14-Aug	11	Kitten's Joy	Bailey, J.D.	AP	240,000	400,000
Personal Ensign H.-G1	27-Aug	9	Storm Flag Flying	Velazquez, J.R.	SAR	240,000	400,000
Citation H.-G1	27-Nov	7	Leroidesanimaux (Brz)	Court, J.K.	HOL	240,000	400,000
Manhattan H.-G1	5-Jun	10	Meteor Storm (GB)	Valdivia, Jr., J.	BEL	240,000	400,000
John C. Mabee H.-G1	24-Jul	6	Musical Chimes	Desormeaux, K.J.	DMR	240,000	400,000
Florida Stallion My Dear Girl S.	23-Oct	11	Aclassysassylassy	Aguilar, M.	CRC	240,000	400,000
Darley Alcibiades S.-G2	8-Oct	9	Runway Model	Bejarano, R.	KEE	248,000	400,000
Eddie Read H.-G1	25-Jul	8	Special Ring	Espinoza, V.	DMR	240,000	400,000

Race Name	Date	Race	Winning Horse	Jockey	Track	Earnings	Purse
Hollywood Starlet S.-G1	19-Dec	8	Splendid Blended	Desormeaux, K.J.	HOL	233,400	380,000
Ohio Derby-G2	12-Jun	14	Brass Hat	Martinez, W.	TDN	210,000	350,000
British Columbia Derby-G3	26-Sep	8	Flamethrowintexan	Frazier, R.	HST	191,400	250,000
Jim Murray Memorial H.	8-May	7	Rhythm Mad (FR)	Solis, A.O.	HOL	210,000	350,000
Carter H.-G1	10-Apr	9	Pico Central (BRZ)	Solis, A.O.	AQU	210,000	350,000
Kelso Breeders' Cup H.-G2	9-Oct	8	Mr O'Brien (IRE)	Coa, E.	BEL	150,000	350,000
Washington Park H.-G2	31-Jul	8	Eye of the Tiger	Razo, Jr., E.	AP	210,000	350,000
Frank E. Kilroe Mile H.-G2	6-Mar	9	Sweet Return (GB)	Stevens, G.L.	SA	210,000	350,000
Kentucky Cup Classic H.-G2	18-Sep	11	Roses in May	Velazquez, J.R.	TP	221,500	350,000
Cigar Mile H.-G1	27-Nov	9	Lion Tamer	Santos, J.A.	AQU	210,000	350,000
Charles Whittingham Memorial H.-G1	12-Jun	3	Sabiango (GER)	Baze, T.	HOL	210,000	350,000
Chinese Cultural Centre S.-G2	25-Jul	8	Shoal Water	Kabel, T.	WO	199,980	300,000
Canadian H.-G2	19-Sep	6	Classic Stamp	Husbands, P.	WO	198,300	250,000
Louisville Breeders' Cup H.-G2	30-Apr	8	Lead Story	Borel, C.H.	CD	202,740	300,000
Falls City H.-G2	25-Nov	10	Halory Leigh	Martin, Jr., E.M.	CD	201,624	300,000
Coolmore Lexington S.-G2	17-Apr	9	Quintons Gold Rush	Bailey, J.D.	KEE	201,500	325,000
King Edward Breeders' Cup H.-G2	19-Jun	8	Slew Valley	McAleney, J.	WO	194,580	300,000
Niagara Breeders' Cup H.-G2	6-Sep	8	Strut the Stage	Kabel, T.	WO	194,400	300,000
Nassau S.-G3	5-Jun	8	Inish Glora	Kabel, T.	WO	193,350	250,000
Carry Back S.-G3	10-Jul	9	Weigelia	Toribio, Jr., A.	CRC	177,000	300,000
Molly Pitcher Breeders' Cup H.-G2	4-Jul	10	La Reason	Lopez, C.C.	MTH	180,000	300,000
NEXTEL Filly and Mare Sprint S.	24-Jan	4	Mooji Moo	Nakatani, C.S.	SA	165,000	300,000
Fair Grounds Oaks-G2	6-Mar	9	Ashado	Velasquez, C.H.	FG	180,000	300,000
Texas Mile S.-G3	24-Apr	8	Kela	Nuesch, D.C.	LS	175,000	300,000
Del Mar Oaks-G1	21-Aug	3	Amorama (FR)	Flores, D.R.	DMR	180,000	300,000
Santa Anita Oaks-G1	13-Mar	8	Silent Sighs	Flores, D.R.	SA	180,000	300,000
Pegasus S.-G3	1-Oct	7	Pies Prospect	Prado, E.S.	MED	180,000	300,000
Matron S.-G1	19-Sep	8	Sense of Style	Prado, E.S.	BEL	180,000	300,000
Futurity S.-G2	19-Sep	7	Park Avenue Ball	Castellano, J.	BEL	180,000	300,000
Ogden Phipps H.-G1	19-Jun	9	Sightseek	Bailey, J.D.	BEL	180,000	300,000
Gulfstream Park H.-G2	3-Apr	9	Jackpot	Bravo, J.	GP	180,000	300,000
Ruffian H.-G1	19-Sep	9	Sightseek	Velazquez, J.R.	BEL	180,000	300,000
Clement L. Hirsch H.-G2	8-Aug	8	Miss Loren (ARG)	Court, J.K.	DMR	180,000	300,000
Garden City Breeders' Cup S.-G1	12-Sep	9	Lucifer's Stone	Santos, J.A.	BEL	180,000	300,000
Strub S.-G2	7-Feb	9	Domestic Dispute	Desormeaux, K.J.	SA	180,000	300,000
Prairie Meadows Cornhusker BC H.-G3	3-Jul	9	Roses in May	Guidry, M.	PRM	180,000	300,000
Padua Stables Sprint S.	24-Jan	8	Shake You Down	Luzzi, M.J.	GP	165,000	300,000
Santa Margarita Invitational H.-G1	14-Mar	8	Adoration	Smith, M.E.	SA	180,000	300,000
Lone Star Park H.-G3	31-May	9	Yessirgeneralsir	Figueroa, O.	LS	180,000	300,000
West Virginia Breeders' Classic S.	9-Oct	7	A Huevo	Dominguez, R.A.	CT	135,000	300,000
Mother Goose S.-G1	26-Jun	9	Stellar Jayne	Albarado, R.	BEL	180,000	300,000
Azalea Breeders' Cup S.-G3	10-Jul	8	Dazzle Me	Sellers, S.J.	CRC	176,000	300,000
Frank J. De Francis Mem Dash S.-G1	20-Nov	10	Wildcat Heir	Elliott, S.	PIM	180,000	300,000
Triple Bend Breeders' Cup Inv'l H.-G1	3-Jul	9	Pohave	Espinoza, V.	HOL	180,000	300,000
Firecracker Breeders' Cup H.-G2	3-Jul	8	Quantum Merit	Sellers, S.J.	CD	178,405	250,000
Nearctic H.-G2	24-Oct	3	I Thee Wed	McAleney, J.	WO	169,650	250,000
Humana Distaff H.-G1	1-May	8	Mayo On the Side	Day, P.	CD	174,375	250,000
Mazarine Breeders' Cup S.-G2	3-Oct	9	Higher World	Husbands, P.	WO	167,250	175,000
Summer S.-G2	19-Sep	3	Dubleo	Nakatani, C.S.	WO	166,650	250,000
Sky Classic H.-G2	2-Oct	8	Colorful Judgement	Callaghan, S.	WO	165,150	250,000
Selene S.-G2	23-May	8	Eye of the Sphynx	Kabel, T.	WO	165,000	250,000
Phoenix Breeders' Cup S.-G3	8-Oct	7	Champali	Bejarano, R.	KEE	168,175	250,000
Commonwealth Breeders' Cup S.-G2	10-Apr	5	Lion Tamer	Smith, M.E.	KEE	167,555	250,000
Grey Breeders' Cup S.-G2	11-Oct	8	Dance With Ravens	Kabel, T.	WO	162,000	175,000

Race Name	Date	Race	Winning Horse	Jockey	Track	Earnings	Purse
WinStar/Sunland Park Oaks	27-Mar	8	Speedy Falcon	Jaime, R.	SUN	156,900	250,000
Milady Breeders' Cup H.-G1	11-Jul	8	Star Parade (ARG)	Espinoza, V.	HOL	125,670	250,000
Kent Breeders' Cup S.-G3	26-Jun	8	Timo	Migliore, R.	DEL	150,000	250,000
Leonard Richards S.-G3	18-Jul	9	Pollard's Vision	Bailey, J.D.	DEL	150,000	250,000
Vanity H.-G1	9-May	8	Victory Encounter	Solis, A.O.	HOL	150,000	250,000
Ancient Title Breeders' Cup H.-G1	10-Oct	8	Pt's Grey Eagle	Bisono, A.	SA	120,000	250,000
Snow Chief S.	24-Apr	9	Cheiron	Solis, A.O.	HOL	150,000	250,000
Las Virgenes S.-G1	15-Feb	8	A. P. Adventure	Solis, A.O.	SA	150,000	250,000
San Antonio H.-G2	31-Jan	8	Pleasantly Perfect	Solis, A.O.	SA	150,000	250,000
Arlington H.-G3	24-Jul	7	Senor Swinger	Blanc, B.	AP	150,000	250,000
Sixty Sails H.-G3	24-Apr	8	Allspice	Emigh, C.A.	HAW	150,000	250,000
Prioress S.-G1	3-Jul	8	Friendly Michelle	Nakatani, C.S.	BEL	150,000	250,000
California Cup Classic H.	16-Oct	8	Cozy Guy	Nakatani, C.S.	SA	150,000	250,000
Saratoga Breeders' Cup H.-G2	22-Aug	9	Evening Attire	Velasquez, C.H.	SAR	150,000	250,000
National Jockey Club H.-G3	17-Apr	8	Ten Most Wanted	Flores, D.R.	HAW	150,000	250,000
Ocala Stud Oaks	24-Jan	7	Silent Sighs	Flores, D.R.	GP	137,500	250,000
Californian S.-G2	12-Jun	9	Even the Score	Flores, D.R.	HOL	150,000	250,000
Boyd Gaming's Delta Princess S.	4-Dec	6	Punch Appeal	Meche, D.J.	DED	150,000	250,000
Gulfstream Park Breeders' Cup H.-G1	22-Feb	11	Hard Buck (BRZ)	Prado, E.S.	GP	90,000	250,000
Forego H.-G1	4-Sep	8	Midas Eyes	Prado, E.S.	SAR	150,000	250,000
Spinaway S.-G2	20-Aug	8	Sense of Style	Prado, E.S.	SAR	150,000	250,000
New York Stallion S.	4-Aug	8	Chowder's First	Prado, E.S.	SAR	150,000	250,000
Test S.-G1	31-Jul	8	Society Selection	Prado, E.S.	SAR	150,000	250,000
New York H.-G2	5-Jul	9	Wonder Again	Prado, E.S.	BEL	150,000	250,000
King's Bishop S.-G1	28-Aug	10	Pomeroy	Prado, E.S.	SAR	150,000	250,000
Cotillion H.-G2	2-Oct	9	Ashado	Coa, E.	PHA	150,000	250,000
Princess Elizabeth S.	23-Oct	8	Victorious Ami	Ramsammy, E.	WO	150,000	250,000
Malibu S.-G1	26-Dec	8	Rock Hard Ten	Stevens, G.L.	SA	150,000	250,000
Hollywood Turf Cup S.-G1	4-Dec	7	Pellegrino (BRZ)	Stevens, G.L.	HOL	150,000	250,000
Coronation Futurity	13-Nov	8	Ablo	Olguin, G.	WO	150,000	250,000
Canadian Derby-G3	28-Aug	9	Organ Grinder	McAleney, J.	NP	157,500	250,000
San Felipe S.-G2	14-Mar	5	Preachinatthebar	Santiago, J.	SA	150,000	250,000
Empire Classic H.	23-Oct	10	Spite the Devil	Castellano, J.	BEL	150,000	250,000
Hopeful S.-G1	21-Aug	9	Afleet Alex	Rose, J.	SAR	150,000	250,000
Ballerina H.-G1	29-Aug	9	Lady Tak	Bailey, J.D.	SAR	150,000	250,000
Fountain of Youth S.-G2	14-Feb	11	Read the Footnotes	Bailey, J.D.	GP	150,000	250,000
Stonerside Beaumont S.-G2	8-Apr	8	Victory U. S. A.	Bailey, J.D.	KEE	155,000	250,000
Just a Game Breeders' Cup H.-G2	5-Jun	8	Intercontinental (GB)	Bailey, J.D.	BEL	150,000	250,000
New York Stallion Statue of Liberty S.	5-Aug	8	So Sweet a Cat	Velazquez, J.R.	SAR	150,000	250,000
Walmac Lone Star Derby-G3	29-Oct	7	Pollard's Vision	Velazquez, J.R.	LS	150,000	250,000
Wonder Where S.	1-Aug	8	My Vintage Port	Jones, J.C.	WO	150,000	250,000
San Juan Capistrano Invitational H.-G2	18-Apr	9	Meteor Storm (GB)	Valdivia, Jr., J.	SA	150,000	250,000
Hawthorne Derby-G3	16-Oct	8	Cool Conductor	Santos, J.A.	HAW	150,000	250,000
Santa Monica H.-G1	25-Jan	8	Island Fashion	Desormeaux, K.J.	SA	150,000	250,000
NATC Dash S.	24-Jan	3	Saint Afleet	Desormeaux, K.J.	SA	137,500	250,000
Oak Tree Breeders' Cup Mile S.-G2	9-Oct	9	Musical Chimes	Desormeaux, K.J.	SA	150,000	250,000
Lady's Secret Breeders' Cup H.-G2	3-Oct	6	Island Fashion	John, K.	SA	150,000	250,000
Aventura S.	3-Apr	11	Kaufy Mate	Cruz, M.R.	GP	150,000	250,000
La Brea S.-G1	27-Dec	8	Alphabet Kisses	Smith, M.E.	SA	150,000	250,000
Go for Wand H.-G1	1-Aug	9	Azeri	Day, P.	SAR	150,000	250,000
American Derby-G2	24-Jul	5	Simple Exchange (IRE)	Smullen, P.	AP	150,000	250,000
Tampa Bay Derby-G3	14-Mar	11	Limehouse	Day, P.	TAM	150,000	250,000
Labatt Bison City S.	4-Jul	8	Touchnow	Husbands, P.	FE	150,000	250,000
West Virginia Breeders' Classic S.	9-Oct	6	Original Gold	Dominguez, R.A.	CT	112,500	250,000

Race Name	Date	Race	Winning Horse	Jockey	Track	Earnings	Purse
Brooklyn H.-G2	12-Jun	7	Seattle Fitz (ARG)	Migliore, R.	BEL	150,000	250,000
Gazelle H.-G1	11-Sep	8	Stellar Jayne	Albarado, R.	BEL	150,000	250,000
Longacres Mile H.-G3	22-Aug	7	Adreamisborn	Baze, R.A.	EMD	137,500	250,000
Iowa Derby	2-Jul	7	Swingforthefences	Bridgmohan, S.	PRM	150,000	250,000
Cup and Saucer S.	17-Oct	8	Slew's Saga	Bahen, S.R.	WO	150,000	250,000
Acorn S.-G1	4-Jun	10	Island Sand	Thompson, T.J.	BEL	150,000	250,000
Del Mar H.-G2	29-Aug	8	Star Over the Bay	Baze, T.	DMR	150,000	250,000
Bing Crosby Breeders' Cup H.-G1	25-Jul	2	Kela	Baze, T.	DMR	150,000	250,000
C.L. Hirsch Mem Turf Championship S.-G1	3-Oct	5	Star Over the Bay	Baze, T.	SA	150,000	250,000
Del Mar Futurity-G2	8-Sep	8	Declan's Moon	Espinoza, V.	DMR	150,000	250,000
Del Mar Breeders' Cup H.-G2	5-Sep	8	Supah Blitz	Espinoza, V.	DMR	150,000	250,000
Del Mar Debutante S.-G1	28-Aug	8	Sweet Catomine	Espinoza, V.	DMR	150,000	250,000
San Diego H.-G2	1-Aug	8	Choctaw Nation	Espinoza, V.	DMR	150,000	250,000
Santa Maria H.-G1	16-Feb	8	Star Parade (ARG)	Espinoza, V.	SA	150,000	250,000
Maple Leaf S.-G3	13-Nov	6	One for Rose	Ramsammy, E.	WO	141,510	175,000
Northern Dancer S.-G3	12-Jun	6	Suave	Bejarano, R.	CD	144,088	200,000
Churchill Downs Distaff H.-G2	7-Nov	10	Halory Leigh	Perret, C.	CD	142,848	200,000
Natalma S.-G3	12-Sep	8	Fearless Flyer (IRE)	Ramsammy, E.	WO	106,380	150,000
Jefferson Cup S.-G3	12-Jun	5	Prince Arch	Blanc, B.	CD	140,244	200,000
Raven Run S.-G2	15-Oct	9	Josh's Madelyn	Shepherd, J.	KEE	139,004	200,000
San Fernando Breeders' Cup S.-G2	10-Jan	8	During	Flores, D.R.	SA	134,280	200,000
Kentucky Jockey Club S.-G2	27-Nov	11	Greater Good	McKee, J.	CD	138,384	200,000
John B. Connally Breeders' Cup Turf H.	10-Apr	7	Warleigh	Beasley, J.	HOU	133,200	200,000
Regret S.-G3	12-Jun	7	Sister Star	Blanc, B.	CD	137,516	200,000
Churchill Downs H.-G2	1-May	5	Speightstown	Velazquez, J.R.	CD	137,516	200,000
Scotts Highlander H.-G3	27-Jun	4	Soaring Free	Kabel, T.	WO	131,400	200,000
Royal North H.-G3	2-Aug	8	Hour of Justice	Kabel, T.	WO	100,530	150,000
New York Breeders' Futurity	6-Sep	9	Caribbean Cruiser	Yang, C.C.	FL	130,415	217,359
Dominion Day H.-G3	1-Jul	8	Mobil	Kabel, T.	WO	130,320	200,000
Golden Rod S.-G2	27-Nov	9	Runway Model	Martin, Jr., E.M.	CD	133,548	200,000
Ballston Spa Breeders' Cup H.-G3	30-Aug	8	Ocean Drive	Velazquez, J.R.	SAR	128,400	200,000
Bessarabian H.-G3	28-Nov	8	Miss Grindstone	Sabourin, R.B.	WO	97,650	150,000
Dance Smartly H.-G3	17-Jul	4	Mona Rose	Da Silva, E.R.	WO	133,844	150,000
True North Breeders' Cup H.-G2	5-Jun	7	Speightstown	Velazquez, J.R.	BEL	126,840	200,000
Potrero Grande Breeders' Cup H.-G2	28-Mar	8	McCann's Mojave	Valdivia, Jr., J.	SA	66,840	200,000
George C. Hendrie H.-G3	16-May	8	Winter Garden	Clark, D.	WO	96,750	150,000
Duchess S.-G3	21-Aug	8	Blonde Executive	Dos Ramos, R.A.	WO	126,390	150,000
Belmont Breeders' Cup H.-G2	18-Sep	8	Senor Swinger	Prado, E.S.	BEL	124,380	200,000
Miller Genuine Draft Cradle S.-G3	6-Sep	13	Bellamy Road	Castellano, Jr., A.	RD	120,000	200,000
NATC Futurity	4-Sep	8	Closing Argument	Castillo, Jr., H.	DEL	120,984	250,000
Endine H.-G3	11-Sep	8	Ebony Breeze	Castillo, Jr., H.	DEL	120,000	200,000
NATC Sorority Futurity	4-Sep	7	Swither	Gryder, A.T.	DEL	120,000	250,000
Caesar Rodney H.	16-Oct	8	B. A. Way	Castellano, Jr., A.	DEL	120,000	200,000
Santa Barbara H.-G2	17-Apr	9	Megahertz (GB)	Solis, A.O.	SA	120,000	200,000
La Canada S.-G2	14-Feb	8	Cat Fighter	Solis, A.O.	SA	120,000	200,000
Fantasy S.-G2	9-Apr	10	House of Fortune	Solis, A.O.	OP	120,000	200,000
Beverly Hills H.-G2	27-Jun	8	Light Jig (GB)	Solis, A.O.	HOL	120,000	200,000
Kentucky Cup Turf H.-G3	25-Sep	14	Sabiango (GER)	Blanc, B.	KD	124,000	200,000
Oaklawn Breeders' Cup S.-G3	13-Mar	10	Golden Sonata	Marquez, Jr., C.H.	OP	120,000	200,000
El Camino Real Derby-G3	13-Mar	7	Kilgowan	Rollins, C.J.	GG	110,000	200,000
Maryland Breeders' Cup H.-G3	15-May	11	Gators N Bears	Lopez, C.C.	PIM	120,000	200,000
James B. Moseley Breeders' Cup H.	19-Jun	9	Gators N Bears	Lopez, C.C.	SUF	120,000	200,000
Monmouth Breeders' Cup Oaks-G2	15-Aug	10	Capeside Lady	DeCarlo, C.P.	MTH	120,000	200,000
Oak Leaf S.-G2	2-Oct	9	Sweet Catomine	Nakatani, C.S.	SA	120,000	200,000

Race Name	Date	Race	Winning Horse	Jockey	Track	Earnings	Purse
Melair S.	24-Apr	3	Yearly Report	Nakatani, C.S.	HOL	120,000	200,000
Norfolk S.-G2	3-Oct	7	Roman Ruler	Nakatani, C.S.	SA	120,000	200,000
Elmer Heubeck Distaff H.	13-Nov	7	Hopelessly Devoted	Velasquez, C.H.	CRC	120,000	200,000
Calder Oaks	23-Oct	7	Hopelessly Devoted	Velasquez, C.H.	CRC	120,000	200,000
Pin Oak Stud USA S.	31-May	10	No Place Like It	Martin, Jr., E.M.	LS	120,000	200,000
Bonnie Miss S.-G2	6-Mar	8	Last Song	Prado, E.S.	GP	120,000	200,000
General George H.-G2	16-Feb	9	Well Fancied	Prado, E.S.	LRL	120,000	200,000
Maker's Mark Mile S.-G2	9-Apr	9	Perfect Soul (IRE)	Prado, E.S.	KEE	124,000	200,000
All Along Breeders' Cup S.-G3	10-Jul	8	Film Maker	Prado, E.S.	CNL	120,000	200,000
Orchid H.-G2	21-Mar	11	Meridiana (GER)	Prado, E.S.	GP	120,000	200,000
La Prevoyante H.-G2	18-Dec	9	Arvada (GB)	Prado, E.S.	CRC	120,000	200,000
Calder Derby-G3	23-Oct	10	Eddington	Coa, E.	CRC	120,000	200,000
Arlington-Washington BC Futurity-G3	19-Sep	6	Three Hour Nap	Razo, Jr., E.	AP	120,000	200,000
Philip H. Iselin Breeders' Cup H.-G3	21-Aug	9	Ghostzapper	Castellano, J.	MTH	120,000	200,000
Gotham S.-G3	20-Mar	7	Saratoga County	Castellano, J.	AQU	120,000	200,000
W. L. McKnight H.-G2	18-Dec	11	Dreadnaught	Samyn, J.	CRC	120,000	200,000
Black-Eyed Susan S.-G2	14-May	10	Yearly Report	Bailey, J.D.	PIM	120,000	200,000
Nassau County Breeders' Cup S.-G2	8-May	8	Bending Strings	Bailey, J.D.	BEL	120,000	200,000
Carl G. Rose Classic H.	13-Nov	10	Supah Blitz	Bailey, J.D.	CRC	120,000	200,000
Rampart H.-G2	14-Mar	6	Sightseek	Bailey, J.D.	GP	120,000	200,000
Richter Scale BC Sprint Championship H. G2	6-Mar	11	Lion Tamer	Velazquez, J.R.	GP	120,000	200,000
Peter Pan S.-G2	22-May	8	Purge	Velazquez, J.R.	BEL	120,000	200,000
Shuvee H.-G2	15-May	8	Storm Flag Flying	Velazquez, J.R.	BEL	120,000	200,000
Fourstardave H.-G2	28-Aug	9	Nothing to Lose	Velazquez, J.R.	SAR	120,000	200,000
Alfred G. Vanderbilt H.-G2	14-Aug	7	Speightstown	Velazquez, J.R.	SAR	120,000	200,000
Demoiselle S.-G2	27-Nov	7	Sis City	Velazquez, J.R.	AQU	120,000	200,000
Palomar Breeders' Cup H.-G2	4-Sep	7	Etoile Montante	Valdivia, Jr., J.	DMR	120,000	200,000
Excelsior Breeders' Cup H.-G3	3-Apr	8	Funny Cide	Santos, J.A.	AQU	120,000	200,000
San Luis Rey H.-G2	20-Mar	9	Meteor Storm (GB)	Valdivia, Jr., J.	SA	120,000	200,000
Pucker Up S.-G3	18-Sep	9	Ticker Tape (GB)	Desormeaux, K.J.	AP	120,000	200,000
Gardenia H.-G3	7-Aug	10	Angela's Love	Guidry, M.	ELP	120,000	200,000
Dallas Turf Cup H.	19-Jun	9	Maysville Slew	Berry, M.C.	LS	120,000	200,000
Violet H.-G3	22-Oct	8	Changing World	Fragoso, P.	MED	120,000	200,000
Pan American H.-G2	20-Mar	6	Quest Star	Day, P.	GP	120,000	200,000
Riva Ridge Breeders' Cup S.-G2	5-Jun	9	Fire Slam	Day, P.	BEL	120,000	200,000
Argent Dixie S.-G2	15-May	10	Mr O'Brien (IRE)	Dominguez, R.A.	PIM	120,000	200,000
Stars and Stripes BC Turf H.-G3	4-Jul	7	Ballingarry (IRE)	Douglas, R.R.	AP	120,000	200,000
Arlington Classic S.-G2	3-Jul	9	Toasted	Douglas, R.R.	AP	120,000	200,000
Jamaica H.-G2	26-Sep	9	Artie Schiller	Migliore, R.	BEL	120,000	200,000
Cliff Hanger H.-G3	15-Oct	8	Dr. Kashnikow	Migliore, R.	MED	120,000	200,000
Barbara Fritchie H.-G2	14-Feb	9	Bear Fan	Fogelsonger, R.	LRL	120,000	200,000
Virginia Oaks	10-Jul	7	Art Fan	Fogelsonger, R.	CNL	120,000	200,000
WinStar Distaff H.-G3	31-May	8	Academic Angel	Sellers, S.J.	LS	120,000	200,000
Louisiana Premier Night Championship S.	7-Feb	8	Spritely Walker	Sellers, S.J.	DED	120,000	200,000
Remsen S.-G2	27-Nov	8	Rockport Harbor	Elliott, S.	AQU	120,000	200,000
Rebel S.	20-Mar	10	Smarty Jones	Elliott, S.	OP	120,000	200,000
Maryland Million Classic S.	9-Oct	11	Presidentialaffair	Elliott, S.	PIM	110,000	200,000
Pat O'Brien Breeders' Cup H.-G2	15-Aug	8	Kela	Baze, T.	DMR	120,000	200,000
San Rafael S.-G2	6-Mar	7	Imperialism	Espinoza, V.	SA	120,000	200,000
San Luis Obispo H.-G2	16-Feb	9	Puerto Banus	Espinoza, V.	SA	120,000	200,000

* Earnings include $5,000,000 bonus

Snapshot Facts: There were 318 North American stakes worth $200,000 or more in 2004 of which 89 were worth 500,000 or more and 24 were worth $1 million or more.

Leading Money-Winning Horses in 2004

Horse	Age	Sex	Sts	1st	2d	3d	Won
Smarty Jones *	3	C	7	6	1	0	$7,563,535
Pleasantly Perfect	6	H	5	3	1	1	4,840,000
Dance in the Mood (JPN)	3	F	9	3	3	0	2,866,978
Ghostzapper	4	C	4	4	0	0	2,590,000
Ashado	3	F	8	5	2	1	2,259,640
Roses in May	4	C	6	5	1	0	1,723,277
Ouija Board (GB)	3	F	5	4	0	1	1,659,958
Kitten's Joy	3	C	8	6	2	0	1,625,796
Southern Image	4	C	4	3	1	0	1,612,150
Sulamani (IRE)	5	H	5	2	1	1	1,611,523
Lundy's Liability (BRZ)	4	C	5	2	1	0	1,542,500
Medaglia d'Oro	5	H	2	1	1	0	1,500,000
Better Talk Now	5	G	8	2	2	0	1,407,000
Polish Summer (GB)	7	H	7	2	0	0	1,316,120
Our New Recruit	5	H	5	2	0	1	1,265,795
Birdstone	3	C	6	3	0	0	1,236,600
Singletary	4	C	6	3	2	1	1,192,910
Personal Rush	3	C	8	4	0	1	1,165,761
Ticker Tape (GB)	3	F	10	5	3	1	1,159,075
Epalo (GER)	5	H	5	2	2	1	1,141,228
Pico Central (BRZ)	5	H	7	5	0	2	1,139,000
Soaring Free	5	G	8	6	0	0	1,113,862
Lion Heart	3	C	7	2	3	0	1,080,000
Funny Cide	4	G	10	3	2	3	1,075,100
A Bit O'Gold	3	G	7	4	3	0	1,060,790
Speightstown	6	H	6	5	0	1	1,045,556
Azeri	6	M	8	3	2	0	1,035,000
Peace Rules	4	C	6	3	0	0	1,024,288
Pollard's Vision	3	C	11	4	4	1	1,022,020
Sightseek	5	M	7	4	1	0	1,011,350
The Cliff's Edge	3	C	8	1	4	2	1,010,000
Stellar Jayne	3	F	13	3	2	3	992,169
Total Impact (CHI)	6	H	11	1	5	2	988,390
Storm Flag Flying	4	F	8	3	2	3	963,248
Perfect Drift	5	G	9	0	5	2	947,595
Wilko	2	C	12	3	2	5	934,074
Society Selection	3	F	9	3	3	1	929,700
Powerscourt (GB)	4	C	9	1	2	2	903,837
Niigon	3	C	9	2	2	1	864,610
Hard Buck (BRZ)	5	H	6	1	3	0	840,526
Sweet Catomine	2	F	4	3	1	0	799,800
Rock Hard Ten	3	C	8	4	1	1	790,380
Yearly Report	3	F	7	5	1	0	787,500
Magistretti	4	C	7	1	2	0	782,981
Request for Parole	5	H	10	3	2	0	757,100
Kicken Kris	4	C	6	2	0	1	727,000
Texcess	2	G	4	3	1	0	725,427
Riskaverse	5	M	6	1	2	0	717,472
Kela	6	H	9	3	1	0	710,212
Eye of the Sphynx	3	F	7	4	2	0	688,340
Afleet Alex	2	C	6	4	2	0	680,800
Nothing to Lose	4	C	9	2	3	1	643,200
Crimson Palace (SAF)	5	M	5	3	0	0	637,731
Champali	4	C	8	4	1	1	634,398
Commercante (FR)	4	F	4	2	1	0	630,000
Moscow Burning	4	F	11	2	4	2	627,970
Brass Hat	3	G	9	3	4	0	624,430
Saint Liam	4	C	5	2	2	1	618,760
Island Fashion	4	F	7	2	1	0	615,000
Balletto (UAE)	2	F	5	3	2	0	614,000
Friends Lake	3	C	4	1	0	1	611,800
Wonder Again	5	M	5	2	0	1	611,767
Colonial Colony	6	H	9	1	1	1	607,625
Adoration	5	M	5	3	1	0	607,304
Eddington	3	C	11	3	2	4	605,360
Summer Wind Dancer	4	F	7	2	2	1	598,905
Intercontinental (GB)	4	F	6	4	1	0	592,386
Lion Tamer	4	C	9	5	1	0	592,380
Stay Forever	7	M	7	4	1	0	581,946
Runway Model	2	F	10	4	2	2	580,598
Sir Shackleton	3	C	9	4	1	1	566,105
Purge	3	C	8	3	1	0	562,734
Imperialism	3	C	9	2	1	2	542,000
Madcap Escapade	3	F	5	4	0	1	536,400
Punctilious (GB)	3	F	6	2	2	1	534,199
Meteor Storm (GB)	5	H	6	3	0	1	529,800
Freefourinternet	6	H	9	2	1	0	527,693
Newfoundland	4	C	9	2	3	1	523,750
Ema Bovary (CHI)	5	M	5	4	1	0	521,780
Mr O'Brien (IRE)	5	G	9	3	1	1	514,050
Declan's Moon	2	G	4	4	0	0	507,300
Ocean Drive	4	F	11	4	3	3	505,900
Hopelessly Devoted	3	F	14	6	4	0	499,260
Aclassysassylassy	2	F	7	5	2	0	498,800
Bear Fan	5	M	6	4	1	1	496,180
Bending Strings	3	F	13	3	5	0	495,150
Light Jig (GB)	4	F	7	4	1	0	494,800
Star Over the Bay	6	G	9	5	1	0	493,960
Love of Money	3	C	5	3	1	0	491,500
One for Rose	5	M	8	4	2	0	489,832
Star Parade (ARG)	5	M	6	2	2	1	483,670
Daydreaming	3	F	8	5	1	1	483,180
Alke	4	C	3	2	1	0	482,800
Consolidator	2	C	7	2	1	1	480,260
Simonas (IRE)	5	G	8	3	1	0	479,639
Tapit	3	C	4	1	0	0	477,500
Pies Prospect	3	C	14	4	1	2	473,865
Film Maker	4	F	6	1	2	1	470,430
Mystery Giver	6	G	6	2	1	1	470,390
Artie Schiller	3	C	8	5	1	0	467,578
Antonius Pius	3	C	9	0	1	2	460,158
Borrego	3	C	8	0	5	0	452,190
Pohave	6	G	8	3	3	2	450,740
Castledale (IRE)	3	C	3	1	0	0	450,000
Suave	3	C	11	2	2	2	448,328
Weigelia	3	C	12	4	3	3	447,790
Supah Blitz	4	C	13	2	5	2	446,280
Sweet Return (GB)	4	C	7	2	1	1	446,180
Good Reward	3	C	8	3	1	2	444,353
Blackdoun (FR)	3	C	9	4	2	1	440,864
Mobil	4	C	8	3	2	0	440,213
Lady Tak	4	F	7	4	1	1	439,412
Bowman's Band	6	H	12	0	3	5	439,334
Musical Chimes	4	F	7	2	1	0	438,300
Leroidesanimaux (BRZ)	4	C	6	5	0	0	436,860
Halory Leigh	4	F	10	3	1	1	434,634
Inish Glora	6	M	5	3	2	0	433,730
Fire Slam	3	C	9	4	2	0	427,381
Classic Stamp	4	F	8	2	2	3	425,043
Closing Argument	2	C	5	2	2	1	421,984
Evening Attire	6	G	11	1	6	0	420,040
Fantasticat	3	C	14	3	4	2	418,400
Senor Swinger	4	C	10	4	0	1	418,178
Organ Grinder	3	C	8	4	2	2	414,813
Blonde Executive	3	F	6	5	0	0	414,263
Domestic Dispute	4	C	7	1	2	0	413,428
Wimbledon	3	C	4	2	1	0	412,400
Balto Star	6	G	5	1	1	1	410,834
Prince Arch	3	C	9	4	3	1	405,946
Mayo On the Side	5	M	12	2	2	3	405,241
Seattle Fitz (ARG)	5	H	7	3	1	0	404,810
Mustanfar	3	C	11	3	3	1	394,716
Little Jim (ARG)	4	C	5	1	1	2	393,510
Island Sand	3	F	7	2	2	1	391,937
Perfect Soul (IRE)	6	H	6	1	2	0	391,549
Whipper	3	C	6	2	1	0	389,850
Punch Appeal	2	F	9	6	0	1	389,840

Horse	Age	Sex	Sts	1st	2d	3d	Won
Swingforthefences	3	C	9	2	2	2	385,745
Stage Player	5	G	12	8	2	1	383,645
My Vintage Port	3	F	9	2	1	4	383,302
Mark One	5	G	10	3	3	1	378,988
Rocky Gulch	3	G	10	6	1	1	377,179
Midway Road	4	C	8	4	1	0	372,015
Brass in Pocket	5	M	9	4	2	0	371,038
Sense of Style	2	F	5	3	0	0	369,000
Flamethrowintexan	3	G	11	7	1	1	368,813
Sonic West	5	G	10	2	2	2	367,813
Limehouse	3	C	5	2	0	1	367,000
Olmodavor	5	H	6	1	2	1	367,000
House of Fortune	3	F	7	3	2	0	364,875
Proud Accolade	2	C	5	3	0	0	364,130
Dubleo	2	C	9	6	1	1	360,899
B. B. Best	2	C	7	4	0	1	360,710
Six Perfections (FR)	4	F	4	0	2	1	359,635
Gators N Bears	4	C	8	3	1	2	357,910
Lucifer's Stone	3	F	6	4	1	0	357,147
Secret Request	4	F	6	3	1	0	355,250
Winter Garden	4	F	6	4	2	0	353,460
Slew Valley	7	H	9	3	1	1	353,360
Bwana Charlie	3	C	10	4	2	2	349,690
Stroll	4	C	5	1	1	0	348,524
Tamweel	4	F	10	3	3	1	348,240
Even the Score	6	H	4	2	0	2	343,272
Sinister G	3	C	8	2	1	0	342,466
Etoile Montante	4	F	6	2	2	1	340,149
Norfolk Knight	5	G	13	4	0	4	338,923
Susan's Angel	3	F	12	3	4	2	338,540
Shoal Water	4	G	5	2	1	1	336,414
Friendly Michelle	3	F	7	3	0	2	335,754
Offlee Wild	4	C	4	2	1	0	335,640
Sabiango (GER)	6	H	4	2	0	0	334,000
Brian Boru (GB)	4	C	9	1	2	1	331,104
La Reason	4	F	11	3	0	2	331,080
Roman Ruler	2	C	5	3	1	0	330,800
Bare Necessities	5	M	9	1	3	3	328,970
Roar Emotion	4	F	11	2	2	3	328,652
Silver Tree	4	C	10	3	2	2	328,060
Splendid Blended	2	F	4	3	1	0	327,400
Touchnow	3	F	9	2	2	0	327,283
Alphabet Kisses	3	F	9	5	2	1	326,910
Cajun Beat	4	G	6	2	1	0	326,800
Tycoon (GB)	3	C	5	0	0	3	325,494
Cozy Guy	3	G	10	5	2	1	324,504
Megahertz (GB)	5	M	6	2	2	0	322,500
Quintons Gold Rush	3	C	9	3	0	0	322,235
Mona Rose	4	F	8	4	0	0	319,439
Ender's Sister	3	F	7	2	3	1	317,580
Silent Sighs	3	F	3	2	0	0	317,500
Toasted	3	C	6	2	2	1	315,680
I Thee Wed	4	G	8	4	0	2	314,337
Proud Man	6	H	5	1	0	1	313,334
My Snookie's Boy	3	C	12	4	3	1	312,766
A to the Z	4	G	10	3	3	1	312,612
My Trusty Cat	4	F	10	3	3	0	311,290
Designed for Luck	7	G	4	1	1	0	311,180
Dream of Summer	5	M	4	4	0	0	309,000
During	4	C	9	1	1	3	307,614
Diamond Green (FR)	3	C	7	0	4	1	306,046
Wildcat Heir	4	C	7	4	2	0	305,860
Twisted Wit	3	G	8	3	2	0	305,223
Chance Dance	4	F	14	7	3	3	303,125
Flamenco	2	C	6	4	1	1	303,085
Board Elligible	4	F	15	5	4	0	302,921
Millennium Dragon (GB)	5	H	8	1	5	0	302,520
West Virginia	3	C	7	2	2	0	302,345
Choctaw Nation	4	G	6	5	0	0	301,800
Royal Assault	3	C	10	2	1	3	301,501
Leaving On My Mind	2	G	13	5	2	3	299,873
Rhythm Mad (FR)	4	C	4	2	1	0	299,600
Hi Teck Man	3	C	4	2	0	1	298,875
Cool Conductor	3	C	9	2	1	3	298,295
Eye of the Tiger	4	C	8	2	1	1	296,450
Pomeroy	3	C	5	2	2	0	296,250
Gygistar	5	G	12	1	1	3	295,320
He Loves Me	3	F	10	5	0	1	295,000
Financingavailable	3	F	10	4	2	2	294,151
Cheiron	3	C	9	3	1	0	293,822
Clock Stopper	4	G	8	1	3	2	292,725
Medallist	3	C	10	4	1	1	291,375
Burst of Fire	3	G	11	4	2	2	290,765
Simply Lovely	2	F	5	3	1	0	288,240
Miss Loren (ARG)	6	M	7	1	1	2	288,032
Hollywood Story	3	F	7	1	1	2	287,105
Valentine Dancer	4	F	3	1	0	0	287,000
Wholelottabourbon	2	G	5	4	1	0	286,230
Torrestrella (IRE)	3	F	6	3	0	0	285,488
Emerald Earrings	3	F	9	5	4	0	285,406
Presidentialaffair	5	G	8	3	4	0	285,040
Lunarpal	2	C	5	4	0	0	284,677
Moonshine Justice	2	C	4	3	0	0	283,914
Sis City	2	F	7	3	0	2	282,980
Humaita (GER)	4	F	9	4	2	0	281,440
Quantum Merit	5	G	3	3	0	0	280,585
Cologny	4	F	15	7	4	2	280,408
Danieltown	3	G	16	7	4	1	279,361
Shake You Down	6	G	6	3	0	0	278,604
Park Avenue Ball	2	C	5	3	1	0	278,600
Yessirgeneralsir	4	G	7	2	0	1	278,250
Colorful Judgement	4	G	5	2	1	0	277,602
Western Hemisphere	3	F	9	3	3	1	274,465
Victory Encounter	4	F	7	2	1	0	274,287
B. A. Way	4	C	10	5	1	1	273,561
Just in Case Jimmy	3	G	11	3	0	1	272,825
Britt's Jules	3	G	11	3	2	4	272,500
Bayamo (IRE)	5	G	5	2	2	0	272,400
Miss Grindstone	5	M	8	5	0	2	271,985
Destiny Calls	4	F	8	6	1	0	271,670
Dreadnaught	4	G	10	3	4	0	271,243
Greek Sun	3	C	4	2	1	0	270,802
Warleigh	6	H	9	2	1	1	269,200
Areyoutalkintome	3	G	11	4	5	1	268,352
A. P. Adventure	3	F	5	2	0	2	268,080
Shadow Cast	3	F	12	4	1	4	267,480
Dazzle Me	3	F	6	4	0	0	266,276
Capeside Lady	3	F	7	2	1	2	266,220
Katdogawn (GB)	4	F	9	1	3	2	264,158
Aggadan	5	H	10	4	3	1	263,371
Victory U. S. A.	3	F	5	1	1	1	263,267
The Lady's Groom	4	C	10	2	3	2	262,520
Cyber Slew	4	F	14	5	1	3	262,215
Chris's Bad Boy	7	G	7	3	2	0	261,480
Put Me In	4	F	9	5	1	1	261,222
Pellegrino (BRZ)	5	H	9	3	2	2	260,060
Song of the Sword	3	C	10	4	2	1	258,600
Midas Eyes	4	C	5	2	1	0	258,600
Smok'n Frolic	5	M	8	1	3	1	258,220
Placid Star	3	F	7	6	1	0	258,100
Adreamisborn	5	G	10	5	2	2	257,740
Amorama (FR)	3	F	8	1	1	2	257,683
Aud	4	F	9	2	3	0	257,578
Cryptograph	3	C	10	4	1	2	257,398
Spite the Devil	4	G	9	3	0	1	256,922
Sugar Punch	3	F	6	6	0	0	256,920
South Bay Cove	2	F	4	3	0	0	256,897
Noches De Rosa (CHI)	6	M	7	1	1	1	256,600

Horse	Age	Sex	Sts	1st	2d	3d	Won
Shaconage	4	F	11	2	1	3	256,340
Ebony Breeze	4	F	9	2	3	1	255,360
Black Bart	5	G	13	6	1	1	254,720
Dynever	4	C	7	1	3	0	254,694
Last Song	3	F	11	3	1	2	254,253
Millfleet	3	G	12	3	1	4	253,371
Timo	3	C	6	2	1	1	253,308
Spooky Mulder	6	G	17	7	5	0	253,275
Silver Bid	6	G	8	6	1	0	252,520
Arvada (GB)	4	F	7	3	2	1	251,700
Expect Will	2	C	10	6	2	0	251,496
Sweet Problem	3	F	10	4	2	1	249,205
Classic Endeavor	6	H	15	5	2	0	248,798
G P Fleet	4	G	11	4	3	1	247,786
Happy Ticket	3	F	7	7	0	0	247,260
Laura's Lucky Boy	3	C	9	3	2	1	246,730
Market Garden	4	F	16	4	4	5	246,658
Twilight Road	7	G	9	3	3	0	246,500
Misty Sixes	6	M	8	3	3	1	246,074
Josh's Madelyn	3	F	9	6	1	0	245,172
So Sweet a Cat	3	F	8	5	1	0	244,890
Sun King	2	C	4	1	0	2	244,850
Master David	3	C	8	1	1	2	244,640
Royally Chosen	6	M	8	2	1	1	244,500
Hour of Justice	4	F	5	3	0	2	243,953
Daddy Cool	6	G	7	5	1	0	243,358
Bronze Abe	5	M	10	4	1	3	241,900
Pie N Burger	6	G	10	3	4	1	241,200
Zakocity	3	C	14	3	3	3	240,967
Coach Jimi Lee	4	G	12	3	4	1	240,618
Witt Ante	4	G	11	4	2	2	240,600
Vespone (IRE)	4	C	7	0	4	0	240,073
Special Ring	7	G	3	1	0	0	240,000
Seducer's Song	3	F	8	4	1	1	239,760
Velvet Snow	3	F	10	3	2	0	238,629
Quest Star	5	H	10	2	0	0	238,035
Saratoga County	3	C	12	2	3	1	237,390
Le Cinquieme Essai	5	G	6	3	2	1	237,004
Seek Gold	4	G	9	2	3	1	236,780
Royal Regalia	6	G	4	2	0	2	236,200
Lead Story	5	M	3	1	0	2	235,740
Slim Dusty	5	G	12	4	2	3	233,553
Herculated	4	G	6	3	1	0	233,200
Lord Langfuhr	4	C	15	6	5	1	231,328
Meridiana (GER)	4	F	5	3	0	1	231,308
Strut the Stage	6	H	4	1	0	1	231,063
Lava Man	3	G	13	3	6	1	230,008
Silver Ticket	3	G	6	2	1	2	229,100
Muir Beach	3	F	16	7	5	1	228,710
Excess Summer	4	G	6	1	1	2	228,200
Caribbean Cruiser	2	C	4	3	0	0	228,140
Greater Good	2	C	5	3	0	1	226,275
Feline Story	3	F	9	2	4	2	224,985
Angela's Love	4	F	9	3	0	2	224,795
Personal Legend	4	F	8	3	2	1	224,330
Dance With Ravens	2	C	3	1	1	1	223,820
Abbondanza	3	C	11	4	2	1	223,305
Yougottawanna	5	G	11	5	3	1	223,008
Bedanken	5	M	8	3	0	1	222,555
Chowder's First	3	C	8	3	0	1	222,328
Teton Forest	3	C	8	3	2	0	222,000
Western Ransom	3	F	7	4	2	0	221,860
Elusive Diva	3	F	9	3	1	2	221,470
Value Plus	3	C	5	1	1	0	220,900
Clever Electrician	5	H	10	5	1	3	220,870
Molto Vita	4	F	8	3	2	0	220,730
My Pal Lana	4	F	9	3	2	0	220,075
Sister Swank	3	F	9	2	2	3	219,679
Krz Ruckus	7	G	9	4	1	1	219,351
Don Six	4	C	11	4	1	2	218,733
Tangle (IRE)	4	F	7	2	1	3	218,669
Built Up	6	G	13	3	2	2	217,195
Redoubled Miss	5	M	12	2	4	0	216,890
Icy Atlantic	3	C	9	3	3	1	216,720
Umpateedle	5	M	13	5	4	2	216,160
Mubtaker	7	H	3	1	0	0	215,103
Kaufy Mate	3	C	4	2	0	0	215,000
Canadian Frontier	5	H	8	5	0	0	214,962
Loving (BRZ)	8	G	10	5	1	1	214,400
Ole Faunty	5	G	5	2	1	0	214,240
Scooter Roach	5	G	12	2	3	3	213,827
Anthony J.	2	R	5	1	1	1	213,630
Higher World	2	F	4	2	1	0	213,210
Green Team	5	G	9	2	3	1	212,625
Souvenir Gift	2	F	5	3	2	0	211,760
Cat Genius	4	C	9	2	3	1	211,280
Flashy Anna	3	F	11	4	2	0	210,773
Slew's Saga	2	C	6	2	1	0	210,603
Academic Angel	5	M	7	3	0	2	210,520
Rockport Harbor	2	C	4	4	0	0	210,300
Raylene	4	F	9	4	2	2	210,134
Gin and Sin	4	G	9	4	3	0	210,125
Read the Footnotes	3	C	3	1	0	0	210,000
Sur La Tete	6	G	7	3	1	3	209,310
Speedy Falcon	3	F	5	2	0	1	209,112
Var	5	H	5	3	1	0	209,038
Maysville Slew	8	G	14	3	2	0	208,440
My Cousin Matt	5	G	8	1	0	2	208,200
Consecrate	3	G	14	1	4	4	207,904
Gold Storm	4	G	8	3	1	2	207,300
Spritely Walker	4	C	5	3	1	1	206,900
Courageous Act	3	C	11	2	3	3	206,521
Cat Fighter	4	F	5	1	1	3	206,060
Surging River	4	C	7	2	0	1	204,907
Host (CHI)	4	C	6	2	2	2	204,480
Friel's for Real	4	F	6	5	1	0	204,450
Classic Elegance	2	F	6	3	0	1	204,006
Mooji Moo	5	M	5	1	2	0	203,500
Wildwood Royal	4	F	11	5	3	1	203,100
Synco Peach	4	F	8	6	1	0	202,940
Silver Impulse	2	F	7	2	2	3	202,662
River Belle (GB)	3	F	4	2	0	2	202,613
Irish Colony	4	G	16	4	4	4	202,310
May Gator	5	M	13	3	3	2	201,115
Electrical Carlita	4	F	17	6	5	0	200,795
Broadway View	3	C	10	3	2	0	200,213

* Includes $5,000,000 bonus

Horses with at least one North American start and earnings of $200,000 or more in 2004.

There were 31 horses with earnings of at least 1 million.

Annual Leading Money Winners Since 1902

Year	Horse	Age	Strs	1st	2d	3d	Earnings
1902	Major Daingerfield	3	7	4	2	1	$57,685
1903	Africander	3	15	8	3	1	70,810
1904	Delhi	3	10	6	2	0	75,225
1905	Sysonby	3	9	9	0	0	144,380
1906	Accountant	3	13	9	1	1	131,705
1907	Colin	2	12	12	0	0	131,705
1908	Sir Martin	2	13	8	4	0	78,590
1909	Joe Madden	3	15	5	9	1	44,905
1910	Novelty	2	16	11	2	2	72,630
1911	Worth	2	13	10	1	0	16,645
1912	Star Charter	4	17	6	2	5	14,655
1913	Old Rosebud	2	14	12	2	0	19,057
1914	Roamer	3	16	12	1	2	29,105
1915	Borrow	7	9	4	1	1	20,195
1916	Campfire	2	9	6	2	0	49,735
1917	Sun Briar	2	9	5	1	2	59,505
1918	Eternal	2	8	6	1	0	56,173
1919	Sir Barton	3	13	8	3	2	88,250
1920	Man o' War	3	11	11	0	0	166,140
1921	Morvich	2	11	11	0	0	115,234
1922	Pillory	3	7	4	1	1	95,654
1923	Zev	3	14	12	1	0	272,008
1924	Sarazen	3	12	8	1	1	95,640
1925	Pompey	2	10	7	2	0	121,630
1926	Crusader	3	15	9	4	0	166,033
1927	Anita Peabody	2	7	6	0	1	111,905
1928	High Strung	2	6	5	0	0	153,590
1929	Blue Larkspur	3	6	4	1	0	153,450
1930	Gallant Fox	3	10	9	1	0	308,275
1931	Gallant Flight	2	7	7	0	0	219,000
1932	Gusto	3	16	4	3	2	145,940
1933	Singing Wood	2	9	3	2	2	88,050
1934	Cavalcade	3	7	6	1	0	111,235
1935	Omaha	3	9	6	1	2	142,255
1936	Granville	3	11	7	3	0	110,295
1937	Seabiscuit	4	15	11	2	2	168,580
1938	Stagehand	3	15	8	2	3	189,710
1939	Challedon	3	15	9	2	3	184,535
1940	Bimelech	3	7	4	2	1	110,005
1941	Whirlaway	3	20	13	5	2	272,386
1942	Shut Out	3	12	8	2	0	238,872
1943	Count Fleet	3	6	6	0	0	174,055
1944	Pavot	3	8	8	0	0	179,040
1945	Busher	3	13	10	2	1	273,735
1946	Assault	3	15	8	2	3	424,195
1947	Armed	6	17	11	4	1	376,325
1948	Citation	3	20	19	1	0	709,470
1949	Ponder	3	21	9	5	2	321,825
1950	Noor	5	12	7	4	1	346,940
1951	Counterpoint	3	15	7	2	1	250,525
1952	Crafty Admiral	4	16	9	4	1	277,225
1953	Native Dancer	3	10	9	1	0	513,425
1954	Determine	3	15	10	3	2	328,700
1955	Nashua	3	12	10	1	1	752,550
1956	Needles	3	8	4	2	0	445,850
1957	Round Table	3	22	15	1	3	600,383
1958	Round Table	4	20	14	4	0	662,780
1959	Sword Dancer	3	13	8	4	0	537,004
1960	Bally Ache	3	15	10	3	1	445,045
1961	Carry Back	3	16	9	1	3	565,349
1962	Never Bend	2	10	7	1	2	402,969
1963	Candy Spots	3	12	7	2	1	604,481
1964	Gun Bow	4	16	8	4	2	580,100
1965	Buckpasser	2	11	9	1	0	568,096
1966	Buckpasser	3	14	13	1	0	669,078
1967	Damascus	3	16	12	3	1	817,941
1968	Forward Pass	3	13	7	2	0	546,674
1969	Arts and Letters	3	14	8	5	1	555,604
1970	Personality	3	18	8	2	1	444,049
1971	Riva Ridge	2	9	7	0	0	503,263
1972	Droll Role	4	19	7	3	4	471,633
1973	Secretariat	3	12	9	2	1	860,404
1974	Chris Evert (f)	3	8	5	1	2	551,063
1975	Foolish Pleasure	3	11	5	4	1	716,278
1976	Forego	6	8	6	1	1	401,701
1977	Seattle Slew	3	7	6	0	0	641,370
1978	Affirmed	3	11	8	2	0	901,541
1979	Spectacular Bid	3	12	10	1	1	1,279,334
1980	Temperance Hill	3	17	8	3	1	1,130,452
1981	John Henry	6	10	8	0	0	1,798,030
1982	*Perrault	5	8	4	1	2	1,197,400
1983	*All Along (f)	4	7	4	1	1	2,138,963
1984	Slew o' Gold	4	6	5	1	0	2,627,944
1985	Spend a Buck	3	7	5	1	1	3,552,704
1986	Snow Chief	3	9	6	1	1	1,875,200
1987	Alysheba	3	10	3	3	1	2,511,156
1988	Alysheba	4	9	7	1	0	3,808,600
1989	Sunday Silence	3	9	7	2	0	4,578,454
1990	Unbridled	3	11	4	3	2	3,718,149
1991	Dance Smartly (f)	3	8	8	0	0	2,876,821
1992	A.P. Indy	3	7	5	0	1	2,622,560
1993	Kotashaan	5	10	6	3	0	2,619,014
1994	Paradise Creek	5	11	8	2	1	2,620,283
1995	Cigar	5	10	10	0	0	4,819,800
1996	Cigar	6	8	5	2	1	4,910,000
1997	Skip Away	4	11	4	5	2	4,089,000
1998	Silver Charm	4	9	6	2	0	4,696,506
1999	Almutawakel	4	5	1	1	1	3,290,000
2000	Fantastic Light	4	9	3	2	1	4,524,423
2001	Captain Steve	4	6	2	1	1	4,210,200
2002	Street Cry	4	4	3	1	0	4,323,777
2003	Moon Ballad	4	6	2	0	0	3,719,798
2004	Smarty Jones	3	7	6	1	0	7,563,535

Leading Horses in 2004 – Races Won

Horse	Age	Sex	Sts	1st	2d	3d	Won
Gran Rojo *	6	H	19	11	2	0	$63,384
Flamanteguille *	3	C	22	10	5	2	66,558
Triangulo *	4	G	20	10	4	1	62,078
Creating a Ruckus *	4	G	23	10	2	4	43,211
Diligent Gambler	3	C	15	9	2	3	196,400
Out of Pride	5	M	14	9	2	1	105,837
Kipper's an Angel	5	G	16	9	2	2	100,790
Warrior's Dance	4	G	16	9	1	0	78,800
Time to Be Sassy	5	G	19	9	1	1	65,420
Runaway Boy *	4	C	22	9	4	3	50,686
Tender Offer (IRE)	7	H	12	9	0	0	24,345
Stage Player	5	G	12	8	2	1	383,645
Hispanica *	4	F	12	8	1	3	157,720
Triano *	2	C	11	8	2	1	146,640
Dusty's Lil Book *	5	M	12	8	1	2	135,118
Aly's Leader	7	M	13	8	4	1	86,115
Chisholm	7	G	12	8	0	1	85,886
Mr Mag	5	G	17	8	3	1	65,356
Jimmy Jones	7	G	14	8	2	0	59,253
Roxana Milagros *	5	M	19	8	6	2	55,232
Ricachona *	4	F	18	8	5	4	47,442
Migwaki	8	G	10	8	0	1	46,276
Lee Gage	4	F	20	8	3	2	44,500
Sunshine Boy *	7	H	12	8	1	2	38,825
The Joist *	4	F	25	8	1	1	37,518
Co Twining Niner	5	G	16	8	0	0	33,484
Private Approval *	3	C	13	8	1	2	31,566
Son of Mariah	6	G	21	8	1	3	29,029
Miner's Surprise	4	G	14	8	1	0	24,646
Mr. Melcap	5	G	16	8	3	0	24,478
Flamethrowintexan	3	G	11	7	1	1	368,813
Chance Dance	4	F	14	7	3	3	303,125
Cologny	4	F	15	7	4	2	280,408
Danieltown	3	G	16	7	4	1	279,361
Spooky Mulder	6	G	17	7	5	0	253,275
Happy Ticket	3	F	7	7	0	0	247,260
Muir Beach	3	F	16	7	5	1	228,710
Ninety Nine Jack	5	G	12	7	3	0	173,821
Zarb's Dahar	4	G	11	7	0	1	157,835
My Man George	4	G	15	7	3	1	155,369
Rize	8	G	13	7	3	2	152,160
Heroic Sight	6	G	15	7	1	3	145,370
Special Concerto *	3	F	11	7	2	2	135,700
The Niner Account	6	G	15	7	4	3	133,610
Divac *	3	C	9	7	0	1	127,812
Cumby Texas	4	C	14	7	4	1	127,780
Smooth Lover	5	G	22	7	3	1	126,750
Proud Tears	4	F	12	7	1	0	122,555
Lone Traveler	6	G	16	7	1	2	119,362
Milky Way Guy	6	G	14	7	2	1	115,600
Cayenne Red	3	G	11	7	2	1	113,458
Fatal Caper	4	F	16	7	2	3	110,474
Good as Silver	3	F	13	7	1	2	108,916
Taint It the Truth	5	H	13	7	0	1	100,124
Joann Jr	3	F	14	7	0	1	100,000
Swim Easy	4	C	13	7	4	0	89,045
Real Special	7	G	15	7	4	1	85,529
Home Deed	6	M	20	7	2	6	84,705
Assaggini	5	M	11	7	1	1	83,975
Regal Watch	4	G	17	7	2	5	82,415
Transcendent	5	G	16	7	1	1	82,394
Gimme the Willys	6	M	11	7	2	1	82,000
Jackie's Hope	4	F	16	7	1	1	79,037
Mister Riley	4	G	22	7	5	7	78,700
Hook Call (BRZ)	9	G	11	7	0	2	78,120
Vantage Star	3	F	19	7	3	1	73,065
Rough Draft	7	G	11	7	2	1	71,025
Karakorum Dixie	4	G	9	7	1	1	69,200
Sea Power	4	C	19	7	1	0	68,920
War County Road	6	G	21	7	5	2	66,487
Violanda	5	M	14	7	0	2	62,575
Senfully Easy	5	M	10	7	1	2	62,335
Gentleman Jerry	5	G	14	7	3	1	51,700
Lord Albion	6	G	19	7	4	0	50,038
Dancing Poet *	5	H	24	7	9	3	47,830
Buzz Cat	7	G	14	7	3	1	44,015
Damaso S *	4	G	15	7	3	1	43,648
Baby Book	5	M	14	7	5	1	43,634
I'm Confederate	4	G	14	7	1	1	42,128
Paola Ines *	4	F	18	7	5	2	41,658
Miss Silvette *	3	F	20	7	4	1	41,382
Chief Cahill	4	G	14	7	1	3	41,000
Yankee Ruler	8	G	15	7	3	1	40,969
Forge Away	6	G	16	7	2	1	40,590
Herpotofgold	4	F	20	7	4	1	40,492
Kens Dancer	6	H	14	7	1	0	38,566
Lady Berkley *	6	M	18	7	7	0	38,184
Bo. Palomas *	4	F	21	7	3	3	36,968
Rainkona *	4	F	20	7	3	5	36,816
Wild Mayi *	3	F	14	7	1	1	36,630
Over the Summit *	4	G	18	7	4	3	35,997
Mr. Roland C *	3	C	17	7	2	3	34,598
Knines Dream	9	G	16	7	4	0	34,294
Cabreo	7	G	17	7	2	5	31,133
Smarty Jones **	3	C	7	6	1	0	7,563,535
Kitten's Joy	3	C	8	6	2	0	1,625,796
Soaring Free	5	G	8	6	0	0	1,113,862
Hopelessly Devoted	3	F	14	6	4	0	499,260
Punch Appeal	2	F	9	6	0	1	389,840
Rocky Gulch	3	G	10	6	1	1	377,179
Dubleo	2	C	9	6	1	1	360,899
Destiny Calls	4	F	8	6	1	0	271,670
Placid Star	3	F	7	6	1	0	258,100
Sugar Punch	3	F	6	6	0	0	256,920
Black Bart	5	G	13	6	1	1	254,720
Silver Bid	6	G	8	6	1	0	252,520
Expect Will	2	C	10	6	2	0	251,496
Josh's Madelyn	3	F	9	6	1	0	245,172
Lord Langfuhr	4	C	15	6	5	1	231,328
Synco Peach	4	F	8	6	1	0	202,940
Electrical Carlita	4	F	17	6	5	0	200,795
Marwood	4	F	11	6	2	0	197,400
Demon Warlock	4	C	11	6	2	2	192,990
We All Love Aleyna	3	G	14	6	1	1	188,020
Catboat	3	F	12	6	3	1	184,598
Long Term Success	5	G	13	6	5	2	177,750
Deputy Country	6	H	10	6	0	0	171,250

Horse	Age	Sex	Sts	1st	2d	3d	Won
Twist and Pop	5	M	10	6	3	0	167,440
Eleusis	3	F	7	6	1	0	165,801
Banished Lover	6	M	12	6	2	0	164,753
Charming Socialite	3	G	18	6	4	2	152,210
Mr. Amano	4	G	13	6	2	1	150,670
Beyond Brilliant	6	G	12	6	2	0	149,828
Whenthedoveflies	4	F	8	6	1	0	139,160
Cheyenne Breeze	5	G	11	6	2	0	134,204
Lost Bride	3	F	12	6	0	1	133,785
Stonewood	3	G	14	6	1	3	129,005
Garrett's Girl	3	F	13	6	4	1	128,610
Outstanding Lady *	3	F	12	6	4	0	116,592
Formal and Fancy	4	F	15	6	2	2	116,400
Dorst	3	G	15	6	2	2	116,300
Vaca City Flyer	3	F	9	6	2	1	116,280
Abbi's Choice	6	G	14	6	1	0	113,642
Firststatedeposit	6	G	11	6	2	1	112,800
Late Expectations	3	G	23	6	1	6	111,661
Lethal Grande	5	G	15	6	3	2	111,367
Ben's Reflection	4	G	9	6	0	3	109,880
September Dawn	3	F	10	6	0	1	108,242
Actuary's Son	6	G	14	6	2	2	106,222
S. Cherry Legacy	3	G	16	6	2	2	105,897
Leon's Bull	2	C	7	6	0	0	101,714
My Limit	3	F	12	6	0	0	101,660
Gators Get	6	G	16	6	2	2	95,149
Momoney Moe	5	G	9	6	0	0	94,950
Countryfide	4	F	11	6	1	1	93,730
Credit Gal	6	M	16	6	3	0	93,475
Improvised	4	F	8	6	1	0	92,057
Tour of the Rose	7	M	15	6	3	2	91,568
Raise the Heat	4	G	12	6	2	2	91,213
Top of the News	6	G	17	6	4	3	90,600
Sweet Time	5	M	10	6	0	2	90,455
Cocoa Latte	3	G	11	6	2	1	89,680
Ceez the Minute	3	G	9	6	0	1	89,077
Concisely	4	G	18	6	3	1	88,433
Wicklow Highlands	8	H	16	6	2	1	88,110
Piedra Peak Lad	7	G	10	6	0	1	85,776
Wimauma Mama	6	M	13	6	0	0	85,263
Victory Prospect	5	M	15	6	4	2	84,879
Rupert's Rose Morn	5	G	20	6	4	2	84,649
Searchfor Diamonds	5	M	20	6	0	5	83,478
Clever Coed	6	M	8	6	1	0	83,085
Ciano Country	3	G	14	6	1	0	82,272
Very Clever	3	G	14	6	2	0	81,397
Speedy Tiffany	3	F	13	6	1	2	80,214
I Love Racing	4	G	16	6	5	2	80,206
Blazing Countess	4	F	14	6	0	3	80,176
Chicago's Girl	4	F	14	6	3	1	77,108
Lady Loot	4	F	10	6	1	0	76,020
Char's Bob'n Robin	5	G	14	6	2	1	74,937
Givemethreedimes	6	G	13	6	3	0	74,845
Bailey's Yodeler	3	G	13	6	4	2	74,150
Pine Brook	4	G	14	6	3	0	71,399
Long Star	5	H	11	6	1	1	67,904
Bird Key	4	F	13	6	0	3	65,794
Rose of Etbauer	3	F	18	6	2	1	64,390
Luckymata	4	C	14	6	2	3	62,605
Fancy M. D.	5	G	15	6	5	1	62,555
Sunshine Bear	5	G	17	6	3	4	62,383
Dr. Tony	4	G	13	6	1	2	60,749
Savvy Girl	4	F	16	6	0	3	60,662
Four Cards Too	5	G	10	6	1	1	60,325
Super Cherokee	3	C	16	6	1	5	59,583
Phone the Diva	4	F	14	6	1	1	59,057
Private American	3	C	17	6	3	3	58,280
Producer	6	G	16	6	0	3	57,285
Thebigbrushoff	4	G	16	6	3	3	56,005
Smart Agenda	5	G	13	6	2	1	55,165
Southern Legacy	4	C	15	6	2	1	54,500
Song Dancer	6	H	15	6	2	1	53,321
Fortunate One	6	G	14	6	0	0	53,320
Fiesty Jones	3	F	6	6	0	0	52,200
River Monster	5	H	25	6	5	4	51,823
Lunar Bounty	5	G	13	6	3	1	50,455
In C C's Honor	10	G	14	6	2	0	49,948
Hacan (ARG)	6	H	19	6	2	2	49,180
Airtiteanni	3	F	14	6	1	2	48,800
Chiquitina *	3	F	21	6	4	1	48,369
Timber	4	G	13	6	1	2	48,135
No Strings	4	G	16	6	1	1	47,995
Oro Viejo *	5	H	28	6	4	7	47,955
How Say You	3	C	12	6	1	1	47,775
V'ville Lady	4	F	9	6	2	0	47,500
Terciaria *	5	M	21	6	5	6	46,666
Zadar	6	G	9	6	0	0	46,333
Rich March	6	G	21	6	3	3	46,098
We Danced Anyway	4	F	12	6	1	1	45,757
Gotta Ballado	6	G	16	6	4	1	45,516
Valle de Coamo *	3	F	19	6	5	4	45,418
Our Revival	4	F	10	6	1	0	44,370
Way West Dolly	4	F	14	6	0	3	44,343
Smokester's Pride	4	F	15	6	3	1	43,950
Privateer (ARG)	6	H	19	6	3	4	43,884
Pyrite Dash	4	G	19	6	3	0	43,708
Dance Winner	3	F	20	6	1	5	43,515
Thisbucksforyou	5	M	16	6	4	3	43,046
Drown the Sorrows	4	F	17	6	3	4	42,553
Broadway Buzz	4	C	18	6	4	3	42,006
Royalette	4	F	15	6	1	2	41,920
Corona Del Hielo	3	F	10	6	1	1	41,722
Luz A. *	4	F	20	6	5	3	40,930
Here Comes Baby	5	G	16	6	0	3	40,888
La Violetera *	3	F	15	6	2	2	40,742
Army Hero	4	G	19	6	2	3	40,162
Gatemoney *	6	H	20	6	6	4	40,150
Limary's Girl *	4	F	25	6	3	9	39,058
Classic Habit *	4	F	16	6	6	2	38,654
Jaycue *	4	F	21	6	4	6	37,682
Carrizales *	3	C	16	6	4	4	37,439
Beaudazzler	8	G	13	6	1	1	37,200
Quick Trend	3	G	13	6	0	2	36,249
Jenny's Gold	6	G	10	6	2	0	35,815
J. R. Honor	6	G	16	6	2	2	35,417
Dra. Wilma Cotto *	3	F	20	6	4	3	35,221
Gallero *	5	H	19	6	4	2	35,216
P. R. Queen *	3	F	18	6	4	3	35,006

Horse	Age	Sex	Sts	1st	2d	3d	Won
Thunzarr	7	G	15	6	2	0	34,930
Fantastic Blitzz *	3	F	22	6	3	3	34,885
Wavering Chief	5	G	20	6	1	4	34,734
Kid Russell	4	G	17	6	1	1	33,352
P R Sensation *	6	H	17	6	1	3	33,208
Home a Winner	10	G	16	6	2	1	33,112
Fever Don *	4	G	18	6	1	3	33,108
Iztla	3	F	10	6	0	0	33,017
Convexity	4	G	16	6	4	1	32,697
That Smith Girl	5	M	17	6	3	2	32,510
Formal Salute *	6	G	14	6	2	1	32,493
Forbidden Queen *	3	F	19	6	2	4	31,751
Formerly Diablo *	7	H	22	6	5	4	30,864
Uno Passer	4	G	17	6	1	0	30,605
Racey Stacey	9	M	10	6	2	1	30,015
Red Seattle	8	G	13	6	1	3	29,940
Bliss Landing	4	G	15	6	2	1	29,558
Legal Thief	7	G	14	6	1	3	29,199
Rules of the Game	4	C	14	6	1	3	29,197
Second Shift	4	F	15	6	0	2	28,463
Count Centavos	6	G	12	6	0	3	28,215
Viento Recio *	3	C	14	6	3	1	27,614
Intuitive Miss	5	M	18	6	3	1	27,440
Longingly *	3	F	20	6	2	1	26,820
Secret Compliance	5	M	11	6	2	2	26,731
Vibod	5	G	12	6	0	0	26,340
Crafty Wac	4	F	16	6	3	0	26,286
Johnnies Wagon	6	G	9	6	0	0	26,275
Like Flying	5	M	14	6	1	1	25,275
Whiz Alone *	5	H	13	6	2	1	24,777
Wickedsisofthewest	4	F	18	6	4	1	24,743
Dark Magic	6	G	12	6	1	3	24,107
Dylans Secret	4	G	15	6	0	2	23,511
Hazzari	3	C	11	6	0	2	22,870
Irish Pal	6	G	17	6	0	2	21,220
Bold Passer	7	G	9	6	0	0	19,965
The Lord Is Eager	6	G	16	6	1	4	19,709
Peggys' Girl	3	F	16	6	1	1	18,347
Slick Sand	5	G	7	6	0	0	17,980
Desert Master	4	G	13	6	0	1	16,638
Baldjim	8	G	15	6	3	2	11,290
Harbour Axe	3	C	16	6	1	0	10,027
Cee'z the Dream	4	F	9	6	0	0	9,460

* Raced exclusively in Puerto Rico.

** Earnings include a $5,000,000 bonus.

There were 278 horses that won six or more races in North America in 2004. Canadian Horse of the Year Soaring Free, Eclipse Award-winning 3-year-old male Smarty Jones and champion turf male Kitten's Joy, also a 3-year-old, each won six races in 2004.

Annual Leading Winner of Races Since 1975

Year	Horse	Age	St	1st	2d	3d	Earnings	Year	Horse	Age	St	1st	2d	3d	Earnings
1975	Gallant Bob	3	18	14	1	2	$273,388	1987	Navajo Family	6	17	12	1	1	31,107
1975	Up Alone	4	24	14	6	3	58,585	1988	Gene	5	24	16	3	2	54,590
1976	T.V. Vixen	3	16	13	2	0	315,424	1989	Just Like Lace	3	18	13	0	2	140,417
1976	Nickel C.	7	28	13	3	7	33,778	1989	Immunity	5	18	13	2	0	49,205
1977	Jiva Cool It	5	23	12	5	4	77,462	1990	Jilsie's Gigalo	6	26	17	5	1	78,885
1978	Albert the Consort	8	31	15	3	6	46,416	1991	The King's Sloop	3	24	14	2	2	114,128
1979	American Moon	5	19	12	0	0	28,782	1991	Sweet Sachet	5	21	14	0	1	65,615
1979	Little Chuck	7	25	12	1	1	18,050	1992	Speedy Crossing	5	18	14	1	0	38,591
1980	Sunny Lee	7	29	13	1	2	17,360	1993	Inspector Moomaw	6	19	12	1	3	52,209
1981	Antiquarian	6	27	13	5	5	38,196	1994	Belle's Ruckus	9	20	16	0	1	59,068
1982	Lunamor	4	24	13	2	1	86,916	1995	Bandit Bomber	4	13	11	0	0	104,275
1982	City Fair	4	23	13	4	1	46,420	1995	Time to Cope	4	18	11	2	0	91,740
1982	Rollar Ring	6	27	13	3	1	26,917	1996	Tragedy	5	24	11	7	2	111,172
1983	Expressive Dock	2	12	11	0	1	231,001	1996	Meine Empress	7	18	11	3	2	42,822
1983	Diamond Road	7	25	11	4	5	66,900	1997	Maybe Jack	4	23	13	1	4	137,220
1983	Navy Days	5	15	11	3	1	21,960	1998	Aunt Ping	4	23	11	6	3	131,993
1984	Paumatuck	4	34	13	7	4	56,568	1999	Ben's Quixote	5	19	10	3	0	88,919
1984	Rapid Robber	5	17	13	3	1	34,210	1999	Raise a Count	4	18	10	2	0	70,546
1985	Billy the Best	6	24	13	6	2	111,884	2000	Bricola	3	14	12	2	0	462,330
1985	Fastway Home	8	30	13	4	4	58,549	2000	Difficult Doll	4	26	12	1	4	83,900
1985	Olga M.	4	28	13	3	2	50,311	2000	Governors Ego	5	21	12	1	3	78,470
1986	Moxeytown	9	29	14	7	4	74,506	2001	La Mistica	4	16	13	3	0	180,176
1987	Chilcoton Blaze	7	15	12	0	1	221,810	2002	La Policlinica	4	15	12	3	0	71,222
1987	Power Rule	4	24	12	3	1	45,795	2003	D' Wildcat Speed	3	12	12	0	0	290,815
1987	Center Stage Anne	4	21	12	3	2	40,100	2004	Gran Rojo	6	19	11	2	0	63,384

Leading North American Stakes Earners in 2004

Horse	Stakes Starts	1st	2nd	3rds	Stakes Earnings
Smarty Jones	7	6	1	0	*$7,563,535
Ghostzapper	4	4	0	0	2,590,000
Ashado	8	5	2	1	2,259,640
Roses in May	4	3	1	0	1,651,500
Kitten's Joy	8	6	2	0	1,625,796
Southern Image	4	3	1	0	1,612,150
Better Talk Now	8	2	2	0	1,407,000
Pleasantly Perfect	4	2	1	1	1,240,000
Birdstone	5	2	0	0	1,215,000
Singletary	6	3	2	1	1,192,910
Ticker Tape (GB)	10	5	3	1	1,159,075
Pico Central (BRZ)	6	4	0	2	1,103,000
Lion Heart	7	2	3	0	1,080,000
Soaring Free	7	5	0	0	1,066,762
A Bit O'Gold	7	4	3	0	1,060,790
Funny Cide	9	2	2	3	1,047,500
Speightstown	6	5	0	1	1,045,556
Azeri	8	3	2	0	1,035,000
Peace Rules	6	3	0	0	1,024,288
Sightseek	7	4	1	0	1,011,350
The Cliff's Edge	8	1	4	2	1,010,000
Pollard's Vision	9	3	3	1	995,500
Stellar Jayne	13	3	2	3	992,169
Perfect Drift	9	0	5	2	947,595
Storm Flag Flying	7	2	2	3	935,648
Society Selection	9	3	3	1	929,700
Sulamani (IRE)	1	1	0	0	900,000
Wilko	2	1	0	1	833,580
Niigon	5	1	2	1	825,150
Total Impact (CHI)	10	1	5	2	793,430
Sweet Catomine	3	3	0	0	790,000
Yearly Report	7	5	1	0	787,500
Magistretti	4	1	2	0	764,000
Ouija Board (GB)	1	1	0	0	733,200
Rock Hard Ten	6	2	1	1	732,780
Request for Parole	9	2	2	0	729,500
Kicken Kris	6	2	0	1	727,000
Riskaverse	6	1	2	0	717,472
Kela	9	3	1	0	710,212
Texcess	3	2	1	0	695,007
Eye of the Sphynx	6	3	2	0	662,920
Afleet Alex	4	2	2	0	640,000
Nothing to Lose	8	2	2	1	632,000
Moscow Burning	11	2	4	2	627,970
Island Fashion	6	2	1	0	615,000
Friends Lake	4	1	0	1	611,800
Wonder Again	5	2	0	1	611,767
Adoration	5	3	1	0	607,304
Brass Hat	6	3	1	0	606,690
Colonial Colony	7	1	1	0	602,265
Commercante (FR)	3	1	1	0	600,000
Summer Wind Dancer	7	2	2	1	598,905
Saint Liam	4	1	2	1	595,960
Champali	6	3	0	1	579,208
Lion Tamer	8	4	1	0	569,580
Balletto (UAE)	3	1	2	0	560,000
Eddington	8	1	1	4	560,000
Stay Forever	6	3	1	0	554,346
Intercontinental (GB)	5	3	1	0	553,386
Purge	7	2	1	0	542,334
Imperialism	9	2	1	2	542,000
Runway Model	6	2	2	1	531,548
Freefourinternet	9	2	1	0	527,693
Newfoundland	9	2	3	1	523,750
Meteor Storm (GB)	5	3	0	0	522,000
Ema Bovary (CHI)	5	4	1	0	521,780
Madcap Escapade	4	3	0	1	517,200
Mr O'Brien (IRE)	8	3	1	1	513,000
Sir Shackleton	6	2	0	1	507,374
Ocean Drive	10	4	3	2	500,380
Bear Fan	6	4	1	1	496,180
Bending Strings	13	3	5	0	495,150
Star Parade (ARG)	6	2	2	1	483,670
Aclassysassylassy	6	4	2	0	480,000
Declan's Moon	3	3	0	0	477,900
Tapit	4	1	0	0	477,500
One for Rose	7	4	1	0	473,092
Film Maker	6	1	2	1	470,430
Mystery Giver	6	2	1	1	470,390
Borrego	8	0	5	0	452,190
Consolidator	5	1	1	1	450,750
Crimson Palace (SAF)	1	1	0	0	450,000
Castledale (IRE)	3	1	0	0	450,000
Sweet Return (GB)	7	2	1	1	446,180
Weigelia	11	4	2	3	440,590
Mobil	8	3	2	0	440,213
Artie Schiller	7	4	1	0	439,978
Bowman's Band	12	0	3	5	439,334
Hopelessly Devoted	7	3	2	0	438,000
Pies Prospect	10	3	0	2	434,065
Star Over the Bay	5	3	1	0	430,000
Love of Money	2	1	0	0	428,500
Musical Chimes	6	2	0	0	427,500
Fire Slam	9	4	2	0	427,381
Suave	7	1	2	1	423,508
Evening Attire	11	1	6	0	420,040
Light Jig (GB)	4	2	0	0	420,000
Supah Blitz	9	2	2	2	418,000
Balto Star	5	1	1	1	410,834
Pohave	6	2	2	2	409,140
Lady Tak	6	3	1	1	408,412
Good Reward	6	2	1	1	406,842
Mayo On the Side	12	2	2	3	405,241
Seattle Fitz (ARG)	7	3	1	0	404,810
Daydreaming	5	2	1	1	403,980
Halory Leigh	9	2	1	1	397,736
Closing Argument	4	1	2	1	394,984
Island Sand	7	2	2	1	391,937
Perfect Soul (IRE)	6	1	2	0	391,549
Prince Arch	7	3	3	1	385,346
My Vintage Port	9	2	1	4	383,302
Inish Glora	4	2	2	0	381,890
Blackdoun (FR)	5	3	0	0	381,270
Senor Swinger	9	3	0	1	377,913
Rocky Gulch	9	6	1	1	375,567
Wimbledon	2	1	0	0	375,000
Punch Appeal	7	5	0	0	373,390
Blonde Executive	5	4	0	0	372,263
Mustanfar	9	2	3	0	369,516
Sonic West	10	2	2	2	367,813
Limehouse	5	2	0	1	367,000
Olmodavor	6	1	2	1	367,000
Leroidesanimaux (BRZ)	3	3	0	0	366,540
House of Fortune	7	3	2	0	364,875
Swingforthefences	7	1	1	2	359,225
Gators N Bears	8	3	1	2	357,910
Secret Request	6	3	1	0	355,250
Fantasticat	7	1	2	0	348,800
Stroll	5	1	1	0	348,524
Classic Stamp	5	1	0	3	344,823
Even the Score	4	2	0	2	343,272
Sense of Style	4	2	0	0	342,000
B. B. Best	6	3	0	1	341,910
Etoile Montante	6	2	2	1	340,149
Lucifer's Stone	5	3	1	0	336,747
Antonius Pius	1	0	1	0	336,000
Friendly Michelle	7	3	0	2	335,754
Sabiango (GER)	4	2	0	0	334,000
Midway Road	6	3	1	0	333,975
Slew Valley	8	2	1	1	329,360

Horse	Stks Starts	1st	2nd	3rd	Stks Earnings
Bare Necessities	9	1	3	3	328,970
Megahertz (GB)	6	2	2	0	322,500
Ender's Sister	7	2	3	1	317,580
Silent Sighs	3	2	0	0	317,500
Toasted	6	2	2	1	315,680
Dubleo	6	4	1	0	315,279
Bwana Charlie	8	2	2	2	314,890
Proud Man	5	1	0	1	313,334
Designed for Luck	4	1	1	0	311,180
Mark One	7	2	2	1	309,948
Proud Accolade	3	1	0	0	308,930
Winter Garden	5	3	2	0	307,800
Sinister G	6	1	0	0	306,866
Organ Grinder	4	2	2	0	306,555
La Reason	9	2	0	1	306,480
Roar Emotion	10	1	2	3	305,852
Roman Ruler	4	2	1	0	305,000
Millennium Dragon (GB)	8	1	5	0	302,520
West Virginia	7	2	2	0	302,345
Offlee Wild	2	1	0	0	300,000
Lundy's Liability (BRZ)	2	1	0	0	300,000
Medaglia d'Oro	1	1	0	0	300,000
Simonas (IRE)	1	0	1	0	300,000
Pomeroy	5	2	2	0	296,250
Gygistar	12	1	1	3	295,320
He Loves Me	10	5	0	1	295,000
Domestic Dispute	6	1	2	0	293,428
Miss Loren (ARG)	7	1	1	2	288,032
During	8	1	1	3	287,614
Hollywood Story	7	1	1	2	287,105
Valentine Dancer	3	1	0	0	287,000
Touchnow	6	1	2	0	286,525
Leaving On My Mind	9	4	1	2	285,543
Brass in Pocket	5	3	0	0	284,287
Shoal Water	3	1	1	1	282,924
Hi Teck Man	3	1	0	1	282,795
Susan's Angel	7	2	2	1	282,580
Moonshine Justice	3	3	0	0	280,386
Flamenco	5	3	1	1	277,285
My Trusty Cat	8	2	2	0	276,930
Simply Lovely	4	3	0	0	276,840
Tamweel	4	1	2	0	275,440
Flamethrowintexan	4	2	1	1	274,650
Victory Encounter	7	2	1	0	274,287
A to the Z	6	2	1	1	273,696
Splendid Blended	2	1	1	0	273,400
Britt's Jules	11	3	2	4	272,500
Royal Assault	7	1	0	2	272,101
Silver Tree	8	1	2	2	271,660
Greek Sun	4	2	1	0	270,802
Dream of Summer	3	3	0	0	270,000
Powerscourt (GB)	2	0	0	1	270,000
Warleigh	9	2	1	1	269,200
A. P. Adventure	5	2	0	2	268,080
Presidentialaffair	6	3	2	0	267,940
Capeside Lady	7	2	1	2	266,220
Katdogawn (GB)	9	1	3	2	264,158
Victory U. S. A.	5	1	1	1	263,267

Horse	Stks Starts	1st	2nd	3rd	Stks Earnings
Sis City	4	2	0	1	263,000
Cool Conductor	7	1	1	2	262,150
Yessirgeneralsir	6	1	0	1	260,250
Medallist	6	3	0	0	260,015
Rhythm Mad (FR)	2	1	1	0	260,000
Lunarpal	4	3	0	0	259,257
Shake You Down	5	2	0	0	258,654
Quintons Gold Rush	7	1	0	0	258,500
Smok'n Frolic	8	1	3	1	258,220
Amorama (FR)	8	1	1	2	257,683
Aud	9	2	3	0	257,578
Twisted Wit	6	2	2	0	257,280
Dynever	7	1	3	0	254,694
Timo	6	2	1	1	253,308
Humaita (GER)	6	3	1	0	253,220
Noches De Rosa (CHI)	6	1	1	1	252,700
Eye of the Tiger	5	1	0	1	251,750
Park Avenue Ball	4	2	1	0	251,000
Wholelottabourbon	4	3	1	0	250,050
Clock Stopper	6	0	3	2	250,125
Quantum Merit	2	2	0	0	246,985
Wildcat Heir	4	2	1	0	246,850
Black Bart	12	5	1	1	245,720
Master David	8	1	1	2	244,640
Shaconage	8	2	0	2	244,560
Royally Chosen	8	2	1	1	244,500
Ebony Breeze	8	2	2	1	241,960
Bronze Abe	10	4	1	3	241,900
Bayamo (IRE)	4	1	2	0	240,000
Special Ring	3	1	0	0	240,000
Lead Story	3	1	0	2	235,740
Mona Rose	6	2	0	0	235,439
Twilight Road	7	3	2	0	235,000
The Lady's Groom	8	1	2	2	232,500
Strut the Stage	4	1	0	1	231,063
Colorful Judgement	3	1	1	0	229,950
My Snookie's Boy	4	0	2	0	228,234
Midas Eyes	4	1	1	0	228,000
Cajun Beat	5	2	1	0	226,800
Norfolk Knight	9	2	0	3	225,138
Cheiron	6	1	1	0	223,866
Pie N Burger	9	2	4	1	222,000
South Bay Cove	3	2	0	0	221,617
Dreadnaught	3	2	1	0	221,400
Bedanken	7	3	0	1	220,875
Spite the Devil	4	2	0	0	220,612
Expect Will	7	3	2	0	220,596
Misty Sixes	7	2	3	1	220,274
Cryptograph	8	2	1	2	218,398
Alphabet Kisses	5	2	1	1	218,150
Put Me In	8	4	1	1	217,827
Dance With Ravens	2	1	1	0	217,550

* Includes $5,000,000 bonus

Snapshot Facts: Smarty Jones earned a $5 million bonus for sweeping the Rebel Stakes and Arkansas Derby at Oaklawn Park and the Kentucky Derby at Churchill Downs. It was the largest bonus in North American racing history.

Top Money–Winning Turf Runners in North America in 2004

Horse	Age	Sex	St	1st	2d	3d	Earnings
Kitten's Joy	3	C	8	6	2	0	$1,625,796
Better Talk Now	5	G	8	2	2	0	1,407,000
Singletary	4	C	6	3	2	1	1,192,910
Ticker Tape (GB)	3	F	10	5	3	1	1,159,075
Soaring Free	5	G	7	6	0	0	1,113,862
Sulamani (IRE)	5	H	1	1	0	0	900,000
Magistretti	4	C	4	1	2	0	764,000
Request for Parole	5	H	10	3	2	0	757,100
Ouija Board (GB)	3	F	1	1	0	0	733,200
Kicken Kris	4	C	6	2	0	1	727,000
Riskaverse	5	M	6	1	2	0	717,472
Nothing to Lose	4	C	9	2	3	1	643,200
Commercante (FR)	4	F	4	2	1	0	630,000
Moscow Burning	4	F	11	2	4	2	627,970
Wonder Again	5	M	5	2	0	1	611,767
Intercontinental (GB)	4	F	6	4	1	0	592,386
Stay Forever	7	M	7	4	1	0	581,946
Meteor Storm (GB)	5	H	6	3	0	1	529,800
Mr O'Brien (IRE)	5	G	7	3	1	1	510,000
Ocean Drive	4	F	11	4	3	3	505,900
Light Jig (GB)	4	F	7	4	1	0	494,800
Star Over the Bay	6	G	8	5	1	0	491,560
Film Maker	4	F	6	1	2	1	470,430
Mystery Giver	6	G	6	2	1	1	470,390
Artie Schiller	3	C	7	5	1	0	463,600
Crimson Palace (SAF)	5	M	1	1	0	0	450,000
Sweet Return (GB)	4	C	7	2	1	1	446,180
Good Reward	3	C	8	3	1	2	444,353
Musical Chimes	4	F	7	2	1	0	438,300
Leroidesanimaux (BRZ)	4	C	6	5	0	0	436,860
Inish Glora	6	M	5	3	2	0	433,730
Classic Stamp	4	F	8	2	2	3	425,043
Senor Swinger	4	C	9	4	0	1	418,178
Prince Arch	3	C	9	4	3	1	405,946
Perfect Soul (IRE)	6	H	6	1	2	0	391,549
Blackdoun (FR)	3	C	5	3	0	0	381,270
Lucifer's Stone	3	F	6	4	1	0	357,147
Slew Valley	7	H	9	3	1	1	353,360
Stage Player	5	G	9	7	1	1	348,530
Stroll	4	C	5	1	1	0	348,524
Etoile Montante	4	F	6	2	2	1	340,149
Shoal Water	4	G	5	2	1	1	336,414
Antonius Pius	3	C	1	0	1	0	336,000
Sabiango (GER)	6	H	4	2	0	0	334,000
Silver Tree	4	C	10	3	2	2	328,060
Megahertz (GB)	5	M	6	2	2	0	322,500
Mona Rose	4	F	8	4	0	0	319,439
Toasted	3	C	5	2	2	1	315,680
Proud Man	6	H	5	1	0	1	313,334
Designed for Luck	7	G	4	1	1	0	311,180
A Bit O'Gold	3	G	1	1	0	0	300,000
Simonas (IRE)	5	G	1	0	1	0	300,000
Rhythm Mad (FR)	4	C	4	2	1	0	299,600
Cool Conductor	3	C	9	2	1	3	298,295
Dubleo	2	C	5	4	1	0	296,910
Millennium Dragon (GB)	5	H	7	1	4	0	282,520
Mustanfar	3	C	7	2	2	0	282,016
Humaita (GER)	4	F	9	4	2	0	281,440
Quantum Merit	5	G	3	3	0	0	280,585
Colorful Judgement	4	G	5	2	1	0	277,602
Valentine Dancer	4	F	2	1	0	0	275,000
Bayamo (IRE)	5	G	5	2	2	0	272,400
Greek Sun	3	C	4	2	1	0	270,802
Powerscourt (GB)	4	C	2	0	0	1	270,000
Warleigh	6	H	9	2	1	1	269,200
Katdogawn (GB)	4	F	9	1	3	2	264,158
Dreadnaught	4	G	7	3	2	0	264,043
Pellegrino (BRZ)	5	H	9	3	2	2	260,060
Aud	4	F	9	2	3	0	257,578
Noches De Rosa (CHI)	6	M	7	1	1	1	256,600
B. A. Way	4	C	8	4	1	1	254,041
Timo	3	C	6	2	1	1	253,308
Amorama (FR)	3	F	7	1	1	2	252,683
Arvada (GB)	4	F	7	3	2	1	251,700
Shaconage	4	F	10	2	0	3	249,120
Laura's Lucky Boy	3	C	9	3	2	1	246,730
Hour of Justice	4	F	5	3	0	2	243,953
Special Ring	7	G	3	1	0	0	240,000
Royal Regalia	6	G	4	2	0	2	236,200
Herculated	4	G	6	3	1	0	233,200
Meridiana (GER)	4	F	5	3	0	1	231,308
Strut the Stage	6	H	4	1	0	1	231,063
Black Bart	5	G	10	5	1	0	229,511
Silver Ticket	3	G	5	2	1	2	229,100
Velvet Snow	3	F	8	3	1	0	228,855
Burst of Fire	3	G	6	2	2	1	226,966
A to the Z	4	G	5	1	2	1	225,280
Bedanken	5	M	8	3	0	1	222,555
Seducer's Song	3	F	5	3	1	0	216,400
I Thee Wed	4	G	4	2	0	0	215,010
My Pal Lana	4	F	8	3	1	0	205,135
Surging River	4	C	7	2	0	1	204,907
Western Ransom	3	F	6	3	2	0	203,860
River Belle (GB)	3	F	4	2	0	2	202,613
Epalo (GER)	5	H	2	0	1	1	200,000
Sarafan	7	G	6	1	3	0	198,400
Ballingarry (IRE)	5	H	7	1	0	2	197,074
Madeira Mist (IRE)	5	M	8	3	2	2	195,520
Where We Left Off (GB)	4	F	7	4	2	0	194,480
Market Garden	4	F	13	3	4	3	194,392
Quest Star	5	H	9	2	0	0	193,035
Tangle (IRE)	4	F	5	2	1	2	190,480
Host (CHI)	4	C	5	2	2	1	189,480
Geronimo (CHI)	5	G	10	3	3	1	187,987
Heyahohowdy	5	M	8	1	4	1	186,067
Paddy's Daisy	2	F	5	4	0	0	186,050
Six Perfections (FR)	4	F	1	0	0	1	184,800
King's Drama (IRE)	4	G	5	2	0	1	184,600
Mambo Slew	3	F	8	2	2	0	183,820
Cayoke (FR)	7	H	8	3	2	2	183,780
Icy Atlantic	3	C	7	2	2	1	183,120
Sister Star	3	F	3	2	1	0	182,381
G P Fleet	4	G	7	2	2	1	182,126
May Gator	5	M	11	3	2	2	179,315
Sabellina	3	F	7	4	1	0	179,005
With Patience	5	M	9	3	2	2	178,750
Test the Waters	5	M	6	3	1	1	177,870
Janeian (NZ)	6	M	6	2	2	0	177,820
Mobil	4	C	4	1	1	0	177,773
Gulch Approval	4	G	6	3	0	1	177,638
Msbaileyscream	6	M	11	4	1	2	177,084

Horse	Age	Sex	St	1st	2d	3d	Earnings
Le Cinquieme Essai	5	G	5	2	2	1	177,004
Nicole's Dream	4	F	9	4	3	0	175,821
Silverfoot	4	G	8	4	0	1	175,793
Wire Bound	3	G	8	4	0	0	173,500
Black Rock Road	3	F	4	3	0	0	173,040
Lennyfromalibu	5	G	6	2	2	1	172,639
Chance Dance	4	F	9	4	2	2	171,625
On the Bus	4	F	7	3	1	1	171,220
Dyna Da Wyna	4	F	6	4	0	1	171,183
Spotlight (GB)	3	F	4	2	1	0	170,800
Kabul	4	F	7	3	2	0	170,615
Burning Roma	6	H	6	2	1	1	170,163
Simple Exchange (IRE)	3	C	2	1	0	0	170,000
Changing World	4	F	4	2	0	1	168,500
Brian Boru (GB)	4	C	1	0	0	1	165,000
Running Free	3	G	8	4	2	1	164,428
Fun House	5	M	9	1	3	2	163,476
Fortunate Damsel	3	F	7	3	0	2	163,394
Gin and Sin	4	G	8	3	3	0	163,250
King of Happiness	5	H	8	2	1	2	161,802
Miss Vegas (IRE)	3	F	3	2	1	0	161,160
Emerald Earrings	3	F	4	2	2	0	161,126
Glick	8	H	7	3	2	0	160,960
Skate Away	5	G	5	1	2	1	160,400
Lady of the Future	6	M	8	2	2	1	160,141
My Vintage Port	3	F	3	1	0	0	159,936
Honor in War	5	H	7	0	1	2	159,261
Maysville Slew	8	G	5	2	1	0	158,800
Blonde Executive	3	F	2	2	0	0	158,250
Magnificent Val	5	M	7	4	3	0	156,800
Dedication (FR)	5	M	7	2	2	0	156,660
Dalavin	3	G	5	3	0	0	155,205
Jinny's Gold	3	F	8	2	1	3	153,044
Whilly (IRE)	3	C	5	2	0	1	150,439
Slew's Saga	2	C	1	1	0	0	150,000
Punctilious (GB)	3	F	1	0	1	0	150,000
Dance in the Mood (JPN)	3	F	1	0	1	0	150,000
Sweet Win	3	F	6	2	0	2	149,220
Cloudy's Knight	4	G	10	4	2	1	148,155
Irish Colonial	5	H	9	1	0	5	148,150
No Place Like It	3	G	5	3	0	1	147,800
Final Prophecy	5	H	10	3	2	0	147,784
Noisette	4	F	7	2	3	0	147,764
Art Fan	3	F	7	1	1	1	147,105
Mocha Queen	3	F	10	4	2	1	146,648
Archers Bow	3	C	5	2	1	0	145,080
Special Matter	6	G	8	2	0	1	144,400
Major Rhythm	5	G	7	3	0	2	144,318
Formal Miss	4	F	12	4	2	0	144,250
Sand Springs	4	F	7	1	1	1	143,756
Fade to Blue	8	G	13	4	3	1	143,652
L'Oiseau d'Argent	5	G	9	4	1	1	142,960
Western Hemisphere	3	F	5	1	2	0	142,785
Mr. Sulu	6	G	8	4	0	1	140,456
Snowdrops (GB)	4	F	6	3	2	0	140,281
Barancella (FR)	3	F	2	0	2	0	140,000
Penny's Fortune	3	F	7	3	2	0	139,073
Puerto Banus	5	H	6	1	0	0	139,000
Rainbows for Luck	3	G	6	2	1	1	138,873
Beret	5	M	7	3	0	0	138,086
Uraib (IRE)	4	F	9	3	1	1	137,440
Melody of Colors	5	M	9	3	3	2	137,360
Gunning For	3	G	9	4	0	2	137,330
Belleski	5	M	4	3	0	0	136,567
In Hand	4	G	10	3	1	0	136,517
Rochester	8	G	8	0	3	1	136,450
Shaunavon	3	F	7	4	0	0	136,320
Coney Kitty (IRE)	6	M	9	2	1	2	136,145
Certifiably Crazy	4	G	9	1	5	1	135,729
Inesperado (FR)	5	H	6	1	4	1	135,270
Mogador	4	C	8	3	4	0	134,820
Hotstufanthensome	4	G	9	4	2	0	134,800
Epicentre	5	H	4	2	0	0	134,125
Statement	6	H	9	2	1	0	133,846
Dell Place	5	G	9	3	1	2	133,840
Golden Commander	4	G	8	2	1	3	133,149
Alternate	5	M	7	1	1	2	133,092
Continental Red	8	G	6	0	2	2	132,800
The Toast of Troy	4	F	11	3	3	2	132,600
Rosharon	5	M	8	3	0	1	132,378
Hard Buck (BRZ)	5	H	3	1	1	0	132,180
Sweet Frippery	6	M	12	3	3	3	132,166
Dr. Kashnikow	7	G	6	1	1	0	132,080
Ocean Silk	4	F	11	2	2	2	131,740
Whenthedoveflies	4	F	7	6	0	0	131,160
Skywalker Red	4	G	9	3	0	3	130,828
Sister Swank	3	F	5	2	0	2	130,264
Super Strut	4	G	7	3	1	0	129,974
Broadway View	3	C	4	1	1	0	129,513
Legal Logic	4	G	11	2	6	0	129,280
Theater R. N.	4	F	3	2	0	0	129,000
Very Vegas	3	F	5	2	2	1	128,760
Finery	4	F	7	2	2	0	127,920
Personal Legend	4	F	6	2	1	1	127,910
F J's Pace	9	G	9	4	0	3	127,554
Slew's Prince	4	C	10	3	0	2	127,278
Literacy	4	F	12	2	1	3	126,018
R Obsession	3	F	6	3	1	0	125,700
Lovely Rafaela	3	F	6	1	1	0	125,535
High Court (BRZ)	4	F	6	1	2	1	125,410
Financingavailable	3	F	7	1	2	2	124,501
Cherylville Slew	5	M	8	4	0	0	123,400
Scooter Roach	5	G	5	1	1	1	123,180
Megantic	6	H	5	2	0	1	122,640
Ninebanks	6	G	5	2	1	0	122,550
Missme	5	G	8	2	0	2	122,305
Prince Prado	4	C	8	3	1	1	121,923
Royal Price (GER)	4	C	8	3	0	2	121,840
Passionate Bird	5	M	7	3	1	1	121,688
Lost Bride	3	F	8	5	0	1	121,370
Sheer Enchantment	3	F	8	1	4	1	120,810
Any for Love (ARG)	6	M	6	3	0	1	120,747
P. J.'s Paulie Boy	6	H	9	2	1	3	120,690
Ivan Jay Perry	8	G	9	3	1	1	120,327
Eddington	3	C	1	1	0	0	120,000
Hopelessly Devoted	3	F	1	1	0	0	120,000
Academic Angel	5	M	3	1	0	0	120,000

The above list contains only the performance records of horses that raced on the grass in North America in 2004. It does not include earnings outside North America.

Leading Money-Winning Horses by Division in 2004

2-Year-Olds

Horse	Sex	St	1st	2d	3d	Earnings
Wilko	C	12	3	2	5	$934,074
Sweet Catomine	F	4	3	1	0	799,800
Texcess	G	4	3	1	0	725,427
Afleet Alex	C	6	4	2	0	680,800
Balletto (UAE)	F	5	3	2	0	614,000
Runway Model	F	10	4	2	2	580,598
Declan's Moon	G	4	4	0	0	507,300
Aclassysassylassy	F	7	5	2	0	498,800
Consolidator	C	7	2	1	1	480,260
Closing Argument	C	5	2	2	1	421,984
Punch Appeal	F	9	6	0	1	389,840
Sense of Style	F	5	3	0	0	369,000
Proud Accolade	C	5	3	0	0	364,130
Dubleo	C	9	6	1	1	360,899
B. B. Best	C	7	4	0	1	360,710
Roman Ruler	C	5	3	1	0	330,800
Splendid Blended	F	4	3	1	0	327,400
Flamenco	C	6	4	1	1	303,085
Leaving On My Mind	G	13	5	2	3	299,873
Simply Lovely	F	5	3	1	0	288,240
Wholelottabourbon	G	5	4	1	0	286,230
Lunarpal	C	5	4	0	0	284,677
Moonshine Justice	C	4	3	0	0	283,914
Sis City	F	7	3	0	2	282,980
Park Avenue Ball	C	5	3	1	0	278,600
South Bay Cove	F	4	3	0	0	256,897
Expect Will	C	10	6	2	0	251,496
Sun King	C	4	1	0	2	244,850
Caribbean Cruiser	C	4	3	0	0	228,140
Greater Good	C	5	3	0	1	226,275
Dance With Ravens	C	3	1	1	1	223,820
Anthony J.	R	5	1	1	1	213,630
Higher World	F	4	2	1	0	213,210
Souvenir Gift	F	5	3	2	0	211,760
Slew's Saga	C	6	2	1	0	210,603
Rockport Harbor	C	4	4	0	0	210,300
Classic Elegance	F	6	3	0	1	204,006
Silver Impulse	F	7	2	2	3	202,662
Enough Is Enough	C	5	2	1	1	199,410
Killenaule	C	9	4	3	2	198,540
Storm Surge	C	7	4	1	0	192,770
Ablo	C	4	2	0	0	191,040
Victorious Ami	F	4	1	2	0	188,600
Paddy's Daisy	F	6	4	0	0	186,336
Chandtrue	C	4	4	0	0	182,970
Berdelia	F	8	2	1	2	173,248
Sharp Lisa	F	4	1	2	0	171,600
Summer Raven	F	7	2	2	1	168,910
Straight Line	C	6	3	1	0	166,312
Coastal Fortress	F	6	2	1	1	165,309

2-Year-Old Fillies

Horse	St	1st	2d	3d	Earnings
Sweet Catomine	4	3	1	0	$799,800
Balletto (UAE)	5	3	2	0	614,000
Runway Model	10	4	2	2	580,598
Aclassysassylassy	7	5	2	0	498,800
Punch Appeal	9	6	0	1	389,840
Sense of Style	5	3	0	0	369,000
Splendid Blended	4	3	1	0	327,400
Simply Lovely	5	3	1	0	288,240
Sis City	7	3	0	2	282,980
South Bay Cove	4	3	0	0	256,897
Higher World	4	2	1	0	213,210
Souvenir Gift	5	3	2	0	211,760
Classic Elegance	6	3	0	1	204,006
Silver Impulse	7	2	2	3	202,662
Victorious Ami	4	1	2	0	188,600
Paddy's Daisy	6	4	0	0	186,336
Berdelia	8	2	1	2	173,248
Sharp Lisa	4	1	2	0	171,600
Summer Raven	7	2	2	1	168,910
Coastal Fortress	6	2	1	1	165,309
Dansetta Light	9	4	1	0	165,080
Megascape	5	3	0	1	161,740
Memorette	6	2	1	1	158,325
Foolininthemeadow	5	4	0	1	155,987
Ready's Gal	3	2	1	0	155,200
Im a Dixie Girl	9	3	1	1	150,200
Angel Trumpet	8	3	3	1	146,456
Hello Lucky	7	3	0	2	142,140
Dancehall Deelites	7	1	2	3	140,002
Kota	7	2	2	3	139,450

3-Year-Olds

Horse	Sex	St	1st	2d	3d	Earnings
Smarty Jones *	C	7	6	1	0	$7,563,535
Dance in the Mood (JPN)	F	9	3	3	0	2,866,978
Ashado	F	8	5	2	1	2,259,640
Ouija Board (GB)	F	5	4	0	1	1,659,958
Kitten's Joy	C	8	6	2	0	1,625,796
Birdstone	C	6	3	0	0	1,236,600
Personal Rush	C	8	4	0	1	1,165,761
Ticker Tape (GB)	F	10	5	3	1	1,159,075
Lion Heart	C	7	2	3	0	1,080,000
A Bit O'Gold	G	7	4	3	0	1,060,790
Pollard's Vision	C	11	4	4	1	1,022,020
The Cliff's Edge	C	8	1	4	2	1,010,000
Stellar Jayne	F	13	3	2	3	992,169
Society Selection	F	9	3	3	1	929,700
Niigon	C	9	2	2	1	864,610
Rock Hard Ten	C	8	4	1	1	790,380
Yearly Report	F	7	5	1	0	787,500
Eye of the Sphynx	F	7	4	2	0	688,340
Brass Hat	G	9	3	4	0	624,430
Friends Lake	C	4	1	0	1	611,800
Eddington	C	11	3	2	4	605,360
Sir Shackleton	C	9	4	1	1	566,105
Purge	C	8	3	1	0	562,734
Imperialism	C	9	2	1	2	542,000
Madcap Escapade	F	5	4	0	1	536,400
Punctilious (GB)	F	6	2	2	1	534,199
Hopelessly Devoted	F	14	6	4	0	499,260
Bending Strings	F	13	3	5	0	495,150
Love of Money	C	5	3	1	0	491,500
Daydreaming	F	8	5	1	1	483,180
Tapit	C	4	1	0	0	477,500
Pies Prospect	C	14	4	1	2	473,865
Artie Schiller	C	8	5	1	0	467,578
Antonius Pius	C	9	0	1	2	460,158
Borrego	C	8	0	5	0	452,190
Castledale (IRE)	C	3	1	0	0	450,000
Suave	C	11	2	2	2	448,328
Weigelia	C	12	4	3	3	447,790
Good Reward	C	8	3	1	2	444,353
Blackdoun (FR)	C	9	4	2	1	440,864
Fire Slam	C	9	4	2	0	427,381
Fantasticat	C	14	3	4	2	418,400
Organ Grinder	C	8	4	2	2	414,813
Blonde Executive	F	6	5	0	0	414,263
Wimbledon	C	4	2	1	0	412,400
Prince Arch	C	9	4	3	1	405,946
Mustanfar	C	11	3	3	1	394,716
Island Sand	F	7	2	2	1	391,937
Whipper	C	6	2	1	0	389,850
Swingforthefences	C	9	2	2	2	385,745

* Includes $5,000,000 bonus

3-Year-Old Fillies

Horse	St	1st	2d	3d	Earnings
Dance in the Mood (JPN)	9	3	3	0	$2,866,978
Ashado	8	5	2	1	2,259,640
Ouija Board (GB)	5	4	0	1	1,659,958
Ticker Tape (GB)	10	5	3	1	1,159,075
Stellar Jayne	13	3	2	3	992,169
Society Selection	9	3	3	1	929,700
Yearly Report	7	5	1	0	787,500
Eye of the Sphynx	7	4	2	0	688,340
Madcap Escapade	5	4	0	1	536,400
Punctilious (GB)	6	2	2	1	534,199
Hopelessly Devoted	14	6	4	0	499,260
Bending Strings	13	3	5	0	495,150
Daydreaming	8	5	1	1	483,180
Blonde Executive	6	5	0	0	414,263
Island Sand	7	2	2	1	391,937
My Vintage Port	9	2	1	4	383,302
House of Fortune	7	3	2	0	364,875
Lucifer's Stone	6	4	1	0	357,147
Susan's Angel	12	3	4	2	338,540
Friendly Michelle	7	3	0	2	335,754
Touchnow	9	2	2	0	327,283
Alphabet Kisses	9	5	2	1	326,910
Ender's Sister	7	2	3	1	317,580
Silent Sighs	3	2	0	0	317,500
He Loves Me	10	5	0	1	295,000
Financingavailable	10	4	2	2	294,151
Hollywood Story	7	1	1	2	287,105
Torrestrella (IRE)	6	3	0	0	285,488
Emerald Earrings	9	5	4	0	285,406

4-Year-Olds

Horse	Sex	Starts	1st	2d	3d	Earnings
Ghostzapper	C	4	4	0	0	$2,590,000
Roses in May	C	6	5	1	0	1,723,277
Southern Image	C	4	3	1	0	1,612,150
Lundy's Liability (BRZ)	C	5	2	1	0	1,542,500
Singletary	C	6	3	2	1	1,192,910
Funny Cide	G	10	3	2	3	1,075,100
Peace Rules	C	6	3	0	0	1,024,288
Storm Flag Flying	F	8	3	2	3	963,248
Powerscourt (GB)	C	9	1	2	2	903,837
Magistretti	C	7	1	2	0	782,981
Kicken Kris	C	6	2	0	1	727,000
Nothing to Lose	C	9	2	3	1	643,200
Champali	C	8	4	1	1	634,398
Commercante (FR)	F	4	2	1	0	630,000
Moscow Burning	F	11	2	4	2	627,970
Saint Liam	C	5	2	2	1	618,760
Island Fashion	F	7	2	1	0	615,000
Summer Wind Dancer	F	7	2	2	1	598,905
Intercontinental (GB)	F	6	4	1	0	592,386
Lion Tamer	C	9	5	1	0	592,380
Newfoundland	C	9	2	3	1	523,750
Ocean Drive	F	11	4	3	3	505,900
Light Jig (GB)	F	7	4	1	0	494,800
Alke	C	3	2	1	0	482,800
Film Maker	F	6	1	2	1	470,430
Supah Blitz	C	13	2	5	2	446,280
Sweet Return (GB)	C	7	2	1	1	446,180
Mobil	C	8	3	2	0	440,213
Lady Tak	F	7	4	1	1	439,412
Musical Chimes	F	7	2	1	0	438,300
Leroidesanimaux (BRZ)	C	6	5	0	0	436,860
Halory Leigh	F	10	3	1	1	434,634
Classic Stamp	F	8	2	2	3	425,043
Senor Swinger	C	10	4	0	1	418,178
Domestic Dispute	C	7	1	2	0	413,428
Little Jim (ARG)	C	5	1	1	2	393,510
Midway Road	C	8	4	1	0	372,015
Six Perfections (FR)	F	4	0	2	1	359,635

Horse	Age	Sex	Starts	1st	2d	3d	Won
Gators N Bears		C	8	3	1	2	357,910
Secret Request		F	6	3	1	0	355,250
Winter Garden		F	6	4	2	0	353,460
Stroll		C	5	1	1	0	348,524
Tamweel		F	10	3	3	1	348,240
Etoile Montante		F	6	2	2	1	340,149
Shoal Water		G	5	2	1	1	336,414
Offlee Wild		C	4	2	1	0	335,640
Brian Boru (GB)		C	9	1	2	1	331,104
La Reason		F	11	3	0	2	331,080
Roar Emotion		F	11	2	2	3	328,652
Silver Tree		C	10	3	2	2	328,060

5-Year-Olds and Up

Horse	Age	Sex	St	1st	2d	3d	Earnings
Pleasantly Perfect	6	H	5	3	1	1	$4,840,000
Sulamani (IRE)	5	H	5	2	1	1	1,611,523
Medaglia d'Oro	5	H	2	1	1	0	1,500,000
Better Talk Now	5	G	8	2	2	0	1,407,000
Polish Summer (GB)	7	H	7	2	0	0	1,316,120
Our New Recruit	5	H	5	2	0	1	1,265,795
Epalo (GER)	5	H	5	2	2	1	1,141,228
Pico Central (BRZ)	5	H	7	5	0	2	1,139,000
Soaring Free	5	G	8	6	0	0	1,113,862
Speightstown	6	H	6	5	0	1	1,045,556
Azeri	6	M	8	3	2	0	1,035,000
Sightseek	5	M	7	4	1	0	1,011,350
Total Impact (CHI)	6	H	11	1	5	2	988,390
Perfect Drift	5	G	9	0	5	2	947,595
Hard Buck (BRZ)	5	H	6	1	3	0	840,526
Request for Parole	5	H	10	3	2	0	757,100
Riskaverse	5	M	6	1	2	0	717,472
Kela	6	H	9	3	1	0	710,212
Crimson Palace (SAF)	5	M	5	3	0	0	637,731
Wonder Again	5	M	5	2	0	1	611,767
Colonial Colony	6	H	9	1	1	1	607,625
Adoration	5	M	5	3	1	0	607,304
Stay Forever	7	M	7	4	1	0	581,946
Meteor Storm (GB)	5	H	6	3	0	1	529,800
Freefourinternet	6	H	9	2	1	0	527,693
Ema Bovary (CHI)	5	M	5	4	1	0	521,780
Mr O'Brien (IRE)	5	G	9	3	1	1	514,050
Bear Fan	5	M	6	4	1	1	496,180
Star Over the Bay	6	G	9	5	1	0	493,960
One for Rose	5	M	8	4	2	0	489,832
Star Parade (ARG)	5	M	6	2	2	1	483,670
Simonas (IRE)	5	G	8	3	1	0	479,639
Mystery Giver	6	G	6	2	1	1	470,390
Pohave	6	G	8	3	3	2	450,740
Bowman's Band	6	H	12	0	3	5	439,334
Inish Glora	6	M	5	3	2	0	433,730
Evening Attire	6	G	11	1	6	0	420,040
Balto Star	6	G	5	1	1	1	410,834
Mayo On the Side	5	M	12	2	2	3	405,241
Seattle Fitz (ARG)	5	H	7	3	1	0	404,810
Perfect Soul (IRE)	6	H	6	1	2	0	391,549
Stage Player	5	G	12	8	2	1	383,645
Mark One	5	G	10	3	3	1	378,988
Brass in Pocket	5	M	9	4	2	0	371,038
Sonic West	5	G	10	2	2	2	367,813
Olmodavor	5	H	6	1	2	1	367,000
Slew Valley	7	H	9	3	1	1	353,360
Even the Score	6	H	4	2	0	2	343,272
Norfolk Knight	5	G	13	4	0	4	338,923
Sabiango (GER)	6	H	4	2	0	0	334,000

Annual Leaders by Age

2-Year-Olds

Year	Horse	Earnings	Year	Horse	Earnings	Year	Horse	Earnings
1876	Leonard	$8,450	1919	Man o' War	83,325	1962	Never Bend	402,969
1877	Duke of Magenta	9,987	1920	Tryster	49,925	1963	Castle Forbes	237,690
1878	Harold	9,250	1921	Morvich	115,234	1964	Sadair	498,217
1879	Sensation	19,670	1922	Sally's Alley	94,847	1965	Buckpasser	568,096
1880	Spinaway	16,100	1923	St. James	89,385	1966	Successor	441,404
1881	Onondaga	17,690	1924	Master Charlie	95,525	1967	Vitriolic	429,896
1882	George Kinney	17,370	1925	Pompey	121,630	1968	Top Knight	325,954
1883	General Harding	16,635	1926	Fair Star	88,960	1969	Silent Screen	397,966
1884	Wanda	35,475	1927	Anita Peabody	111,905	1970	Limit to Reason	319,055
1885	Ban Fox	22,840	1928	High Strung	153,590	1971	Riva Ridge	503,263
1886	Tremont	39,135	1929	Whichone	136,455	1972	Secretariat	456,404
1887	Emperor of Norfolk	37,020	1930	Equipoise	156,835	1973	Protagonist	200,527
1888	Proctor Knott	69,780	1931	Top Flight	219,000	1974	L'Enjoleur	285,865
1889	Chaos	63,550	1932	Ladysman	111,435	1975	Honest Pleasure	370,227
1890	Potomac	78,460	1933	Singing Wood	88,050	1976	Royal Ski	309,704
1891	His Highness	106,900	1934	Chance Sun	83,985	1977	Affirmed	343,477
1892	Morello	55,260	1935	Tintagel	75,100	1978	Spectacular Bid	384.484
1893	Domino	170,890	1936	Pompoon	82,260	1979	Smart Angle	359,717
1894	The Butterflies	50,410	1937	Menow	65,825	1980	Lord Avie	439,240
1895	Requital	58,615	1938	El Chico	84,100	1981	Stalwart	528,595
1896	Ogden	58,855	1939	Bimelech	135,090	1982	Roving Boy	800,425
1897	L'Alouette	42,290	1940	Whirlaway	77,275	1983	Fali Time	748,829
1898	Jean Beraud	65,357	1941	Alsab	110,600	1984	Chief's Crown	920,890
1899	Mesmerist	49,152	1942	Occupation	192,355	1985	Snow Chief	935,740
1900	Commando	40,862	1943	Occupy	112,949	1986	Brave Raj	933,650
1901	Blue Girl	64,105	1944	Pavot	179,040	1987	Tejano	1,177,189
1902	Savable	46,100	1945	Star Pilot	165,385	1988	Open Mind	724,064
1903	Hamburg Belle	47,125	1946	Education	164,473	1989	Grand Canyon	1,019,540
1904	Artful	57,805	1947	Bewitch	213,675	1990	Best Pal	1,026,195
1905	Burgomaster	39,500	1948	Blue Peter	189,185	1991	Pleasant Stage	687,240
1906	Electioneer	53,701	1949	Bed o' Roses	199,200	1992	Mountain Cat	1,460,627
1907	Colin	131,007	1950	Battlefield	198,677	1993	Brocco	653,550
1908	Sir Martin	78,590	1951	Tom Fool	155,960	1994	Timber Country	928,590
1909	Sweep	41,323	1952	Native Dancer	230,495	1995	Golden Attraction	675,587
1910	Novelty	72,630	1953	Hasty Road	277,132	1996	Boston Harbor	1,928,605
1911	Worth	72,630	1954	Summer Tan	230,421	1997	Favorite Trick	1,231,998
1912	Helios	12,524	1955	Nail	239,930	1998	Silverbulletday	1,114,110
1913	Old Rosebud	19,057	1956	Greek Game	214,805	1999	Chilukki	762,723
1914	Regret	17,390	1957	Jewel's Reward	349,642	2000	Macho Uno	768,803
1915	Dominant	18,495	1958	First Landing	396,460	2001	Johannesburg	1,002,893
1916	Campfire	49,735	1959	Warfare	394,610	2002	Storm Flag Flying	967,000
1917	Sun Briar	59,505	1960	Hail to Reason	428,434	2003	Halfbridled	849,400
1918	Eternal	56,137	1961	Cicada	384,676	2004	Wilko	934,074

2-Year-Old Fillies

Year	Horse	Earnings	Year	Horse	Earnings	Year	Horse	Earnings
1901	Blue Girl	$64,105	1917	Rosie o' Grady	9,800	1933	Mata Hari	55,364
1902	Eugenia Burch	23,330	1918	Elfin Queen	15,936	1934	Nellie Flag	57,240
1903	Hamburg Belle	47,125	1919	Miss Jemima	20,055	1935	Forever Yours	34,165
1904	Artful	57,805	1920	Step Lightly	40,471	1936	Apogee	35,940
1905	Perverse	23,990	1921	Startle	47,970	1937	Jacola	31,715
1906	Court Dress	31,094	1922	Sally's Alley	94,847	1938	Dinner Date	33,950
1907	Stamina	29,265	1923	Anna Marrone II	21,061	1939	Now What	36,245
1908	Maskette	53,140	1924	Mother Goose	72,775	1940	Valdina Myth	41,625
1909	Ocean Bound	12,545	1925	Taps	20,250	1941	Petrify	41,085
1910	Bashti	27,235	1926	Fair Star	88,960	1942	Askmenow	39,510
1911	Moisant	8,010	1927	Anita Peabody	111,905	1943	Bee Mac	44,900
1912	Gowell	7,812	1928	Current	50,501	1944	Busher	60,300
1913	Southern Maid	8,373	1929	Khara	34,017	1945	Beaugay	105,910
1914	Regret	17,390	1930	Baba Kenny	28,750	1946	First Flight	134,965
1915	Pleione	5,915	1931	Top Flight	219,000	1947	Bewitch	213,675
1916	America	7,064	1932	Swivel	71,755	1948	Alsab's Day	66,970

Year	Horse	Earnings
1949	Bed o' Roses	199,200
1950	Aunt Jinny	78,370
1951	Rose Jet	132,285
1952	Fulvous	111,375
1953	Queen Hopeful	169,534
1954	High Voltage	167,825
1955	Nasrina	152,625
1956	Leallah	129,240
1957	Idun	220,995
1958	Quill	144,692
1959	My Dear Girl	185,622
1960	Bowl of Flowers	198,706
1961	Cicada	384,676
1962	Affectionately	216,357
1963	Castle Forbes	237,690
1964	Queen Empress	319,262
1965	Moccasin	319,731
1966	Mira Femme	229,525
1967	Queen of the Stage	289,275
1968	Gallant Bloom	231,400
1969	Tudor Queen	150,004
1970	Forward Gal	268,194
1971	Numbered Account	446,594
1972	La Prevoyante	417,109
1973	Talking Picture	158,939
1974	Hot n Nasty	172,562
1975	Optimistic Gal	356,477
1976	Sensational	218,710
1977	L'Alezane	254,390
1978	Terlingua	271,596
1979	Smart Angle	359,717
1980	Heavenly Cause	269,819
1981	Skillful Joy	411,312
1982	Fabulous Notion	378,368
1983	Althea	582,630
1984	Outstandingly	867,872
1985	Family Style	805,809
1986	Brave Raj	933,650
1987	Epitome	534,805
1988	Open Mind	724,064
1989	Go for Wand	548,390
1990	Meadow Star	992,250
1991	Pleasant Stage	687,240
1992	Eliza	808,000
1993	Phone Chatter	753,500
1994	Flanders	805,000
1995	Golden Attraction	675,587
1996	Storm Song	898,205
1997	Countess Diana	1,019,785
1998	Silverbulletday	1,114,110
1999	Chilukki	762,723
2000	Caressing	690,642
2001	Tempera	670,240
2002	Storm Flag Flying	967,000
2003	Halfbridled	849,400
2004	Sweet Catomine	799,800

3-Year-Olds

Year	Horse	Earnings
1903	Africander	$70,810
1904	Delhi	75,225
1905	Sysonby	144,380
1906	Accountant	83,750
1907	Peter Pan	86,790
1908	Fair Play	70,215
1909	Joe Madden	44,905
1910	Sweep	22,625
1911	Governor Grey	15,051
1912	The Manager	12,270
1913	Ten Point	12,840
1914	Roamer	29,105
1915	The Finn	17,985
1916	Dodge	26,410
1917	Omar Khayyam	49,070
1918	Johren	49,156
1919	Sir Barton	88,250
1920	Man o' War	166,140
1921	Grey Lag	62,596
1922	Pillory	95,651
1923	Zev	272,008
1924	Sarazen	95,610
1925	American Flag	68,350
1926	Crusader	166,033
1927	Sir Harry	86,842
1928	Victorian	126,750
1929	Blue Larkspur	153,450
1930	Gallant Fox	308,275
1931	Twenty Grand	218,545
1932	Gusto	145,940
1933	Inlander	57,430
1934	Cavalcade	111,235
1935	Omaha	142,255
1936	Granville	110,295
1937	War Admiral	166,500
1938	Stagehand	189,710
1939	Challedon	184,535
1940	Bimelech	110,005
1941	Whirlaway	272,386
1942	Shut Out	238,972
1943	Count Fleet	174,055
1944	Twilight Tear (f)	165,555
1945	Busher (f)	273,735
1946	Assault	424,195
1947	Phalanx	269,250
1948	Citation	709,470
1949	Ponder	321,825
1950	Hill Prince	314,265
1951	Counterpoint	250,525
1952	Mark Ye-Well	268,745
1953	Native Dancer	513,425
1954	Determine	328,700
1955	Nashua	752,550
1956	Needles	440,850
1957	Round Table	600,383
1958	Tim Tam	467,200
1959	Sword Dancer	537,004
1960	Bally Ache	455,045
1961	Carry Back	565,349
1962	Jaipur	395,437
1963	Candy Spots	604,481
1964	Northern Dancer	490,171
1965	Tom Rolfe	444,901
1966	Buckpasser	669,078
1967	Damascus	817,941
1968	Forward Pass	449,074
1969	Arts and Letters	555,604
1970	Personality	444,049
1971	Jim French	320,291
1972	Riva Ridge	395,632
1973	Secretariat	860,404
1974	Chris Evert (f)	551,063
1975	Foolish Pleasure	716,278
1976	Bold Forbes	460,286
1977	Seattle Slew	641,370
1978	Affirmed	901,541
1979	Spectacular Bid	1,279,334
1980	Temperence Hill	1,130,452
1981	Pleasant Colony	877,415
1982	Gato Del Sol	588,779
1983	Sunny's Halo	1,011,962
1984	Gate Dancer	1,136,525
1985	Spend a Buck	3,552,704
1986	Snow Chief	1,875,200
1987	Alysheba	2,511,156
1988	Seeking the Gold	2,145,620
1989	Sunday Silence	4,578,454
1990	Unbridled	3,718,149
1991	Dance Smartly (f)	2,876,821
1992	A.P. Indy	2,622,560
1993	Sea Hero	2,484,190
1994	Concern	2,541,670
1995	Thunder Gulch	2,644,080
1996	Skip Away	2,699,280
1997	Silver Charm	1,638,750
1998	Victory Gallop	1,981,720
1999	Cat Thief	3,020,500
2000	Tiznow	3,445,950
2001	Point Given	3,350,000
2002	War Emblem	3,455,000
2003	Wando	2,017,323
2004	Smarty Jones	7,563,535

4-Year-Olds

Year	Horse	Earnings
1903	Waterboy	$50,775
1904	Irish Lad	29,150
1905	Beldame	26,850
1906	Dandelion	26,850
1907	Nealon	44,890
1908	Ballot	55,915
1909	King James	38,253
1910	Olambala	22,815
1911	Follie Levy	9,324
1912	Star Charter	14,655
1913	Rudolfo	14,450
1914	Robert Bradley	10,345
1915	Hodge	16,928
1916	Ed Crump	16,351
1917	King Gorin	15,575
1918	Cudgel	33,826
1919	Exterminator	26,402
1920	Citrus	25,193

Year	Horse	Earnings
1921	Yellow Hand	42,271
1922	Firebrand	39,110
1923	Rebuke	31,800
1924	Spot Cash	46,420
1925	Princess Doreen (f)	69,220
1926	Peanuts	41,450
1927	Chance Play	86,800
1928	Crystal Peanut	97,200
1929	Diavolo	87,190
1930	Blue Larkspur	51,650
1931	Plucky Play	86,725
1932	Equipoise	101,375
1933	Larranga	47,240
1934	Clarify	15,115
1935	Discovery	102,545
1936	Roman Soldier	42,145
1937	Seabiscuit	168,580
1938	War Admiral	90,840
1939	Kayak II	170,875
1940	Eight Thirty	81,450
1941	Mioland	123,520
1942	Whirlaway	211.250
1943	Thumbs Up	97,100
1944	Happy Issue	118,500
1945	Stymie	225,375
1946	Gallorette (f)	159,160
1947	Assault	181,925
1948	On Trust	196,950
1949	Coaltown	276,125
1950	Ponder	219,050
1951	County Delight	170,985
1952	Crafty Admiral	277,225
1953	Tom Fool	256,355
1954	Rejected	276,800
1955	Helioscope	225,250
1956	Swaps	409,400
1957	Pucker Up	229,235
1958	Round Table	662,780
1959	Hillsdale	502,090
1960	Dotted Swiss	296,900
1961	Kelso	425,965
1962	Carry Back	319,177
1963	Crimson Satan	383,355
1964	Gun Bow	580,100
1965	Hill Rise	318,365
1966	Bold Bidder	360,092
1967	Pretense	431,850
1968	Dr. Fager	460,110
1969	Nodouble	454,240
1970	Shuvee (f)	201,852
1971	Twice Worthy	179,520
1972	Droll Role	471,633
1973	Susan's Girl (f)	340,496
1974	Forego	545,086
1975	Snow Knight	286,435
1976	King Pellinore	463,390
1977	Crystal Water	564,627
1978	Seattle Slew	473,006
1979	Affirmed	1,148,800
1980	Spectacular Bid	1,117,790
1981	Eleven Stitched	644,125
1982	Lemhi Gold	1,066,375
1983	All Along (f)	2,138,963
1984	Slew o' Gold	2,627,944
1985	Gate Dancer	1,229,720
1986	Lady's Secret (f)	1,871,053
1987	Ferdinand	2,185,150
1988	Alysheba	3,808,600
1989	Blushing John	1,232,030
1990	Flying Continental	1,096,700
1991	Farma Way	2,598,350
1992	Fraise	1,534,720
1993	Bertrando	2,217,800
1994	Cherokee Run	943,690
1995	Northern Spur	1,265,000
1996	Singspiel	2,721,987
1997	Skip Away	4,089,000
1998	Silver Charm	4,696,506
1999	Almutawakel	3,290,000
2000	Fantastic Light	4,524,423
2001	Captain Steve	4,201,200
2002	Street Cry	4,323,777
2003	Moon Ballad	3,719,798
2004	Ghostzapper	2,590,000

5-Year-Olds or Older

Year	Horse	Age	Erngs
1903	Land of Clover	5	$16,040
1904	Colonial Girl	5	49,635
1905	Proper	5	20,125
1906	Go Between	5	38,255
1907	Glorifier	5	21,800
1908	Dandelion	6	9,300
1909	Jack Atkin	5	10,820
1910	Jack Atkin	6	15,965
1911	Plate Glass	5	13,165
1912	High Private	6	12,046
1913	Donald McDonal	7	16,080
1914	Buckthorn	5	11,175
1915	Borrow	7	20,195
1916	Short Grass	8	16,395
1917	Old Rosebud	6	31,720
1918	Roamer	7	21,950
1919	Midway	5	22,065
1920	Exterminator	5	52,405
1921	Exterminator	6	56,827
1922	Exterminator	7	71,075
1923	Chacolet	5	73,970
1924	Runstar	5	44,550
1925	Atherstone	5	58,025
1926	Sarazen	5	42,970
1927	Jolly Roger	5	63,075
1928	Jolly Roger	6	45,950
1929	Golden Prince	5	121,600
1930	Sun Beau	5	105,005
1931	Mike Hall	7	112,975
1932	Phar Lap	6	50,050
1933	Equipoise	5	55,760
1934	Falreno	5	27,160
1935	Azucar	7	117,950
1936	Top Row	5	106,600
1937	Rosemont	5	97,525
1938	Seabiscuit	5	130,395
1939	Whichee	5	35,950
1940	Seabiscuit	7	96,850
1941	Big Pebble	5	159,437
1942	Marriage	6	59,600
1943	Marriage	7	88,875
1944	First Fiddle	5	124,105
1945	First Fiddle	6	129,965
1946	Armed	5	288,725
1947	Armed	6	376,325
1948	Shannon II	7	211,610
1949	Donor	5	99,075
1950	Noor	5	346,940
1951	Moonrush	5	221,050
1952	Two Lea		174,550
1953	Royal Vale	5	215,825
1954	Pet Bully	6	240,375
1955	Social Outcast	5	390,775
1956	Bobby Brocato	5	298,800
1957	Dedicate	5	259,500
1958	Swoon's Son	5	201,700
1959	Round Table	5	413,380
1960	Bald Eagle	5	396,085
1961	Whodunit	6	142,260
1962	Prove It	5	348,750
1963	Kelso	6	569,762
1964	Kelso	7	311,660
1965	Native Diver	6	241,650
1966	Native Diver	7	205,750
1967	Straight Deal	5	302,270
1968	Politely	5	317,473
1969	Hawaii	5	279,280
1970	Fort Marcy	6	388,537
1971	Cougar II	7	416,022
1972	Typecast	6	366,387
1973	Cougar II	7	356,344
1974	True Knight	5	359,495
1975	Royal Glint	5	487,110
1976	Forego	6	491,701
1977	Forego	7	268,740
1978	Exceller	5	879,790
1979	Bowl Game	5	585,738
1980	John Henry	5	925,217
1981	John Henry	6	1,798,030
1982	Perrault	5	1,197,400
1983	Sangue (f)	5	764,600
1984	John Henry	9	2,336,650
1985	Bounding Basque	5	678,360
1986	Precisionist	5	1,262,560
1987	Theatrical	5	2,235,500
1988	Great Communicator	5	2,017,950
1989	Steinlen	6	1,521,378
1990	Criminal Type	5	2,270,290
1991	Black Tie Affair	5	2,483,540
1992	Pleasant Tap	5	1,959,914
1993	Kotashaan	5	2,619,014
1994	Paradise Creek	5	2,620,283
1995	Cigar	5	4,819,800
1996	Cigar	6	4,910,000
1997	Gentlemen	5	2,125,300
1998	Swain	6	2,260,526
1999	Daylami	5	3,488,217
2000	Behrens	6	1,786,500
2001	Fantastic Light	5	3,634,859
2002	Sarafan	5	2,039,765
2003	Falbrav	5	3,013,845
2004	Pleasantly Perfect	6	4,840,000

Annual Leading Money Winning Stakes Performers

Year	Horse	Events Won	Stakes Earnings
1930	Gallant Fox	9	$304,275
1931	Top Flight	7	219,000
1932	Gusto	3	145,190
1933	Singing Wood	1	86,800
1934	Cavalcade	5	110,535
1935	Omaha	5	141,425
1936	Granville	6	109,445
1937	Seabiscuit	10	167,455
1938	Stagehand	5	186,810
1939	Challedon	9	184,535
1940	Bimelech	4	110,005
1941	Whirlaway	9	267,486
1942	Shut Out	6	234,837
1943	Count Fleet	5	172,105
1944	Pavot	7	177,390
1945	Busher	9	277,235
1946	Assault	8	424,195
1947	Armed	11	375,025
1948	Citation	17	703,620
1949	Ponder	6	314,775
1950	Noor	6	343,190
1951	Counterpoint	6	248,800
1952	Crafty Admiral	6	269,250
1953	Native Dancer	9	513,425
1954	Determine	10	328,700
1955	Nashua	9	747,675
1956	Needles	4	438,850
1957	Round Table	12	593,883
1958	Round Table	11	656,030
1959	Sword Dancer	6	531,479
1960	Bally Ache	6	441,345
1961	Carry Back	7	556,874
1962	Jaipur	6	395,437
1963	Candy Spots	6	598,981
1964	Gun Bow	8	580,100
1965	Buckpasser	6	558,331
1966	Buckpasser	12	662,553
1967	Damascus	11	814,691
1968	Forward Pass	7	546,674
1969	Arts and Letters	8	555,054
1970	Personality	5	427,549
1971	Riva Ridge	5	492,763
1972	Droll Role	6	462,973
1973	Secretariat	9	860,404
1974	Forego	8	545,086
1975	Foolish Pleasure	4	706,678
1976	Forego	5	476,701
1977	Seattle Slew	5	637,170
1978	Affirmed	7	885,041
1979	Spectacular Bid	9	1,268,534
1980	Spectacular Bid	9	1,117,790
1981	John Henry	8	1,798,030
1982	Perrault	4	1,197,400
1983	All Along	3	1,813,630
1984	Slew O' Gold	4	2,606,344
1985	Spend A Buck	5	3,552,704
1986	Snow Chief	6	1,875,200
1987	Alysheba	3	2,508,906
1988	Alysheba	7	3,808,600
1989	Sunday Silence	6	4,560,854
1990	Unbridled	3	3,704,049
1991	Dance Smartly	8	2,876,821
1992	A. P. Indy	5	2,622,560
1993	Kotashaan	6	2,619,014
1994	Concern	2	2,523,070
1995	Cigar	9	4,800,000
1996	Skip Away	5	2,683,420
1997	Skip Away	4	4,089,000
1998	Awesome Again	5	3,818,090
1999	Cat Thief	2	3,020,500
2000	Fantastic Light	3	4,524,423
2001	Captain Steve	2	4,201,200
2002	War Emblem	4	3,428,000
2003	Pleasantly Perfect	2	2,470,000
2004	Smarty Jones	6	7,563,535

All–Time Leading Money Earners ($1 million minimum)

Horse	Sex	Born	Sts	1st	2d	3d	Earnings
Cigar	H	1990	33	19	4	5	$9,999,815
Skip Away	H	1993	38	18	10	6	9,616,360
Fantastic Light	H	1996	25	12	5	3	8,486,957
Pleasantly Perfect	H	1998	18	9	3	2	7,789,880
Smarty Jones	C	2001	9	8	1	0	7,613,155
Silver Charm	H	1994	24	12	7	2	6,944,369
Captain Steve	H	1997	25	9	3	7	6,828,356
Alysheba	H	1984	26	11	8	2	6,679,242
John Henry	G	1975	83	39	15	9	6,591,860
Tiznow	H	1997	15	8	4	2	6,427,830
Singspiel (IRE)	H	1992	20	9	8	0	5,952,825
Falbrav (IRE)	H	1998	26	13	5	5	5,825,517
Medaglia d'Oro	H	1999	17	8	7	0	5,754,720
Best Pal	G	1988	47	18	11	4	5,668,245
Taiki Blizzard	H	1991	23	6	8	2	5,523,549
High Chaparral (IRE)	H	1999	13	10	1	2	5,331,231
Sulamani (IRE)	H	1999	17	9	3	1	5,252,368
Street Cry (IRE)	H	1998	12	5	6	1	5,150,837
Preeminence (JPN)	M	1997	50	13	9	7	5,042,956
Jim and Tonic (FR)	G	1994	39	13	13	4	4,975,807
Sunday Silence	H	1986	14	9	5	0	4,968,554
Easy Goer	H	1986	20	14	5	1	4,873,770
Daylami (IRE)	H	1994	21	11	3	4	4,614,762
Behrens	H	1994	27	9	8	3	4,563,500
Unbridled	H	1987	24	8	6	6	4,489,475
Awesome Again	H	1994	12	9	0	2	4,374,590
Moon Ballad (IRE)	H	1999	14	5	3	1	4,364,791
Spend a Buck	H	1982	15	10	3	2	4,220,689
Pilsudski (IRE)	H	1992	22	10	6	2	4,080,297
Azeri	M	1998	24	17	4	0	4,079,820
Creme Fraiche	G	1982	64	17	12	13	4,024,727
Seeking the Pearl	M	1994	21	8	2	3	4,021,716
Point Given	H	1998	13	9	3	0	3,968,500
Cat Thief	H	1996	30	4	9	8	3,951,012
Devil His Due	H	1989	41	11	12	3	3,920,405
Sandpit (BRZ)	H	1989	40	14	11	6	3,812,597
Swain (IRE)	H	1992	22	10	4	6	3,797,566
Ferdinand	H	1983	29	8	9	6	3,777,978
Almutawakel (GB)	H	1995	19	4	4	1	3,643,021
Harlan's Holiday	H	1999	22	9	6	1	3,632,664
Gentlemen (ARG)	H	1992	24	13	4	2	3,608,558
Spain	M	1997	35	9	9	7	3,540,542
Slew o' Gold	H	1980	21	12	5	1	3,533,534
Victory Gallop	H	1995	17	9	5	1	3,505,895
War Emblem	H	1999	13	7	0	0	3,491,000
Precisionist	H	1981	46	20	10	4	3,485,398
Strike the Gold	H	1988	31	6	8	5	3,457,026
Lando (GER)	H	1990	24	10	3	1	3,438,727
Paradise Creek	H	1989	25	14	7	1	3,401,416
Snow Chief	H	1983	24	13	3	5	3,383,210
Chief Bearhart	H	1993	26	12	5	3	3,381,557
Cryptoclearance	H	1984	44	12	10	7	3,376,327
Black Tie Affair (IRE)	H	1986	45	18	9	6	3,370,694
Agnes World	H	1995	20	8	6	1	3,365,680
Sky Classic	H	1987	29	15	6	1	3,320,398
Paseana (ARG)	M	1987	36	19	10	2	3,317,427
Bet Twice	H	1984	26	10	6	4	3,308,599
Steinlen (GB)	H	1983	45	20	10	7	3,297,169
Serena's Song	M	1992	38	18	11	3	3,283,388
Real Quiet	H	1995	20	6	5	6	3,271,802
Awad	H	1990	70	14	10	11	3,270,131
Congaree	H	1998	25	12	2	4	3,267,490
Dance Smartly	M	1988	17	12	2	3	3,263,835
Paolini (GER)	H	1997	28	5	6	4	3,253,469
Sakhee	H	1997	14	8	3	1	3,253,253
Lemon Drop Kid	H	1996	24	10	3	3	3,245,370
Caller One	G	1997	21	10	3	3	3,190,000
Volponi	H	1998	31	7	12	5	3,187,232
Bertrando	H	1989	24	9	6	2	3,185,610
Free House	H	1994	22	9	5	3	3,178,971
Montjeu (IRE)	H	1996	16	11	2	0	3,178,177
Funny Cide	G	2000	21	8	4	5	3,174,485
Perfect Drift	G	1999	27	9	8	3	3,168,963
Siphon (BRZ)	H	1991	25	12	6	2	3,136,428
Gulch	H	1984	32	13	8	4	3,095,521
Silverbulletday	M	1996	23	15	3	1	3,093,207
Peace Rules	C	2000	19	9	2	2	3,084,278
Concern	H	1991	30	7	7	11	3,079,350
Giant's Causeway	H	1997	13	9	4	0	3,078,989
Lady's Secret	M	1982	45	25	9	3	3,021,325
Albert the Great	H	1997	22	8	6	4	3,012,490
Ghostzapper	C	2000	10	8	0	1	2,996,120
Alphabet Soup	H	1991	24	10	3	6	2,990,270
A.P. Indy	H	1989	11	8	0	1	2,979,815
Escena	M	1993	29	11	9	3	2,962,639
Theatrical (IRE)	H	1982	22	10	4	2	2,940,036
Hansel	H	1988	14	7	2	3	2,936,586
Dance in the Mood (JPN)	F	2001	10	4	3	0	2,931,889
Sea Hero	H	1990	24	6	3	4	2,929,869
Great Communicator	H	1983	56	14	10	7	2,922,615
Thunder Gulch	H	1992	16	9	2	2	2,915,086
Farma Way	H	1987	23	8	5	1	2,897,175
Milwaukee Brew	H	1997	24	8	4	5	2,879,612
General Challenge	G	1996	21	9	3	1	2,877,178
Ashado	F	2001	14	9	3	2	2,870,440
With Approval	H	1986	23	13	5	1	2,863,540
Bayakoa (ARG)	M	1984	39	21	9	0	2,861,701
Rough Habit (NZ)	G	1986	66	28	16	7	2,861,579
Marquetry	H	1987	36	10	9	4	2,857,886
Budroyale	G	1993	52	17	12	2	2,840,810
Kotashaan (FR)	H	1988	22	10	5	2	2,812,114
Banshee Breeze	M	1995	18	10	5	2	2,784,798
Spectacular Bid	H	1976	30	26	2	1	2,781,608
Symboli Rudolf (JPN)	H	1981	16	13	1	1	2,764,980
Buck's Boy	G	1993	30	16	5	2	2,750,148
Beautiful Pleasure	M	1995	25	10	5	2	2,734,078
Forty Niner	H	1985	19	11	5	0	2,726,000
Pleasant Tap	H	1987	32	9	9	5	2,721,169
Lido Palace (CHI)	H	1997	23	11	7	2	2,705,865
Izvestia	H	1987	21	11	2	2	2,702,527
Manila	H	1983	18	12	5	0	2,692,799
With Anticipation	G	1995	48	15	9	8	2,660,543
Broad Brush	H	1983	27	14	5	5	2,656,793
Trinycarol (VEN)	M	1979	29	18	3	1	2,644,392
Fraise	H	1988	34	10	5	6	2,613,105
Sarafan	G	1997	44	10	12	4	2,588,671
Flawlessly	M	1988	28	16	4	3	2,572,536
Dramatic Gold	G	1991	39	9	13	6	2,567,630
Wando	C	2000	19	11	2	1	2,543,229
Sir Bear	G	1993	71	19	12	14	2,538,422

Horse	Sex	Born	Sts	1st	2d	3d	Earnings
Let's Elope (NZ)	M	1987	26	11	0	5	2,528,902
Lure	H	1989	25	14	8	0	2,515,289
Gate Dancer	H	1981	28	7	8	7	2,501,705
Holy Bull	H	1991	16	13	0	0	2,481,760
Take Charge Lady	M	1999	22	11	7	0	2,480,377
Mecke	H	1992	40	12	7	9	2,470,550
Golden Pheasant	H	1986	22	7	4	3	2,453,958
Marlin	H	1993	26	9	3	5	2,448,880
Sightseek	M	1999	20	12	5	0	2,445,216
Affirmed	H	1975	29	22	5	1	2,393,818
Xtra Heat	M	1998	35	26	5	2	2,389,635
Malek (CHI)	H	1993	23	10	7	2	2,382,623
Heritage of Gold	M	1995	28	16	2	4	2,381,762
Evening Attire	G	1998	39	11	12	3	2,373,010
Balto Star	G	1998	38	12	7	3	2,363,780
Criminal Type	H	1985	24	10	5	3	2,351,274
Tabasco Cat	H	1991	18	8	3	2	2,347,671
Quiet Resolve	G	1995	31	10	6	4	2,346,768
Bien Bien	H	1989	26	9	8	1	2,331,875
Fly So Free	H	1988	33	12	5	3	2,330,954
Silvano (GER)	H	1996	18	7	2	2	2,321,024
Triptych	M	1982	41	14	5	11	2,318,946
Star of Cozzene	H	1988	38	14	8	5	2,308,923
Seeking the Gold	H	1985	15	8	6	0	2,307,000
Soul of the Matter	H	1991	16	7	4	2	2,302,818
Kona Gold	G	1994	30	14	7	2	2,293,384
Skimming	H	1996	20	8	5	1	2,286,601
Affirmed Success	G	1994	42	17	10	6	2,285,315
Mineshaft	H	1999	18	10	3	1	2,283,402
Yankee Affair	H	1982	55	22	14	8	2,282,156
Polish Summer (GB)	H	1997	27	6	10	0	2,277,871
Prized	H	1986	17	9	2	3	2,262,555
Festin (ARG)	H	1986	24	9	4	4	2,256,295
Pine Bluff	H	1989	13	6	1	3	2,255,884
Life's Magic	M	1981	32	8	11	6	2,255,218
Galileo (IRE)	H	1998	8	6	1	0	2,245,373
Skywalker	H	1982	20	8	3	3	2,226,750
Waquoit	H	1983	30	19	4	3	2,225,360
Wild Again	H	1980	28	8	7	4	2,204,829
Perfect Sting	M	1996	21	14	3	0	2,202,042
Proud Truth	H	1982	21	10	4	0	2,198,895
Golden Missile	H	1995	25	7	7	4	2,194,510
Safely Kept	M	1986	31	24	2	3	2,194,206
Chief's Crown	H	1982	21	12	3	3	2,191,168
Twilight Agenda	H	1986	32	13	5	4	2,174,529
Nostalgia's Star	H	1982	59	9	17	13	2,154,827
Kalanisi (IRE)	H	1996	11	6	4	1	2,148,836
Turkoman	H	1982	22	8	8	3	2,146,924
Caitano (GB)	H	1994	44	9	6	7	2,137,459
All Along (FR)	M	1979	21	9	4	2	2,125,828
Daliapour (IRE)	H	1996	26	7	3	3	2,123,763
Val's Prince	G	1992	52	13	12	5	2,118,785
You	M	1999	23	9	8	2	2,101,353
Say Florida Sandy	H	1994	98	33	17	12	2,085,408
Lost Code	H	1984	27	15	5	2	2,085,396
Sunshine Forever	H	1985	23	8	6	3	2,084,800
Hernando (FR)	H	1990	20	7	4	1	2,081,978
Majesty's Prince	H	1979	43	12	10	10	2,077,796
Phoenix Reach (IRE)	C	2000	10	4	1	1	2,075,669
Miesque	M	1984	16	12	3	1	2,070,163

Horse	Sex	Born	Sts	1st	2d	3d	Earnings
Louis Quatorze	H	1993	18	7	5	1	2,054,434
Adoration	M	1999	20	8	3	1	2,051,160
Coronado's Quest	H	1995	17	10	2	0	2,046,190
Charismatic	H	1996	17	5	2	4	2,038,064
Sharp Cat	M	1994	22	15	3	0	2,032,575
Risen Star	H	1985	11	8	2	1	2,029,845
Essence of Dubai	H	1999	13	5	1	2	2,001,058
Itsallgreektome	G	1987	29	8	10	2	1,994,618
Fusaichi Pegasus	H	1997	9	6	2	0	1,994,400
Empire Maker	C	2000	8	4	3	1	1,985,800
Arcangues	H	1988	19	6	2	2	1,981,423
Kelso	G	1957	63	39	12	2	1,977,896
Ladies Din	G	1995	37	12	6	6	1,966,754
Aptitude	H	1997	15	5	4	2	1,965,410
Guided Tour	G	1996	31	12	8	1	1,964,253
Little Bold John	G	1982	105	38	16	14	1,956,406
Storm Flag Flying	F	2000	14	7	3	3	1,951,828
Chester House	H	1995	21	6	4	4	1,944,545
Greinton (GB)	H	1981	22	10	8	0	1,943,605
Forego	G	1970	57	34	9	7	1,938,957
Estrapade	M	1980	30	12	5	5	1,937,142
Boston Harbor	H	1994	8	6	1	0	1,934,605
Pay the Butler	H	1984	40	5	5	5	1,934,140
Da Hoss	G	1992	20	12	5	2	1,931,558
King's Swan	H	1980	107	31	19	18	1,924,845
Soaring Free	G	1999	22	13	3	0	1,917,544
Java Gold	H	1984	15	9	3	1	1,908,832
Deputy Commander	H	1994	13	4	3	2	1,906,640
Jewel Princess	M	1992	29	13	4	7	1,904,060
Rock of Gibraltar (IRE)	H	1999	13	10	2	0	1,888,048
Royal Anthem	H	1995	12	6	3	1	1,876,876
High-Rise (IRE)	H	1995	13	5	2	2	1,871,726
Missionary Ridge (GB)	H	1987	42	8	5	8	1,864,498
Subotica (FR)	H	1988	15	6	4	1	1,856,255
Surfside	M	1997	15	8	3	2	1,852,987
Macho Uno	H	1998	14	6	1	3	1,851,803
Tinners Way	H	1990	27	7	6	4	1,846,546
Open Mind	M	1986	19	12	2	2	1,844,372
Summer Squall	H	1987	20	13	4	0	1,844,282
Southern Image	C	2000	8	6	1	1	1,843,750
Hatoof	M	1989	21	9	4	1	1,841,070
Skip Trial	H	1982	38	16	7	2	1,837,451
Came Home	H	1999	12	9	0	0	1,835,940
Precocity	H	1994	33	9	7	5	1,835,798
Native Desert	G	1993	74	21	13	17	1,828,177
Heavenly Prize	M	1991	18	9	6	3	1,825,940
Ruhlmann	H	1985	27	10	3	4	1,824,154
Gander	G	1996	60	15	10	9	1,824,011
Banks Hill (GB)	M	1998	15	5	5	3	1,824,008
Lu Ravi	M	1995	26	11	8	3	1,819,781
Flying Continental	H	1986	51	12	15	10	1,815,938
Beat Hollow (GB)	H	1997	12	7	2	2	1,814,481
Six Perfections (FR)	F	2000	14	6	6	1	1,811,179
Sea Cadet	H	1988	29	10	6	5	1,807,150
Mutafaweq	H	1996	19	7	1	3	1,800,800
Big Jag	G	1993	30	13	5	3	1,800,329
Redattore (BRZ)	H	1995	32	15	2	6	1,799,883
Roses in May	C	2000	11	7	3	0	1,795,187
Quest for Fame (GB)	H	1987	19	5	4	4	1,790,417
Tout Charmant	M	1996	29	9	9	1	1,781,879

Horse	Sex	Born	Sts	1st	2d	3d	Earnings
Unbridled Elaine	M	1998	11	6	2	1	1,770,740
El Senor	H	1984	44	12	7	5	1,769,215
Express Tour	H	1998	14	5	1	1	1,767,515
User Friendly (GB)	M	1989	16	8	1	2	1,764,938
Miss Alleged	M	1987	15	5	4	3	1,757,342
Round Table	H	1954	66	43	8	5	1,749,869
Better Talk Now	G	1999	25	8	5	2	1,744,437
Denon	H	1998	22	6	4	3	1,744,025
Dear Doctor (FR)	H	1987	32	8	7	4	1,742,671
Ballingarry (IRE)	H	1999	23	6	1	6	1,741,049
Aldebaran	H	1998	25	8	12	3	1,739,186
In Excess (IRE)	H	1987	25	11	2	3	1,736,733
Grey Memo	H	1997	54	8	4	10	1,736,683
Spinning World	H	1993	14	8	3	1	1,734,477
Good Journey	H	1996	16	7	5	3	1,733,058
Menifee	H	1996	11	5	4	1	1,732,000
Hawksley Hill (IRE)	G	1993	46	14	12	6	1,730,922
Island Fashion	F	2000	17	6	2	0	1,727,970
Frisk Me Now	H	1994	36	12	5	6	1,727,707
Favorite Trick	H	1995	16	12	0	1	1,726,793
L'Carriere	G	1991	23	8	4	3	1,726,175
Monarchos	H	1998	10	4	1	3	1,720,830
Ten Most Wanted	C	2000	13	5	3	1	1,718,460
Riskaverse	M	1999	27	8	6	4	1,717,706
Orientate	H	1998	19	10	3	0	1,716,950
Geri	H	1992	19	9	4	3	1,707,980
Goodbye Halo	M	1985	24	11	5	4	1,706,702
Kitten's Joy	C	2001	12	8	3	0	1,705,911
Fleetstreet Dancer	G	1998	25	5	7	3	1,704,806
Urban Sea	M	1989	23	8	4	3	1,704,553
Yagli	H	1993	27	10	6	3	1,702,121
Proper Reality	H	1985	19	10	3	1	1,701,650
Flag Down	H	1990	43	11	11	8	1,699,711
Borgia (GER)	M	1994	22	6	7	2	1,697,771
Defensive Play	H	1987	26	6	4	5	1,688,631
Artax	H	1995	25	7	9	3	1,685,840
Forbidden Apple	H	1995	31	8	6	9	1,680,640
Pistols and Roses	H	1989	44	10	4	6	1,680,506
Touch Gold	H	1994	15	6	3	1	1,679,907
Personal Ensign	M	1984	13	13	0	0	1,679,880
Odalea (ARG)	M	1986	21	8	7	2	1,674,812
Exceller	H	1973	33	15	5	6	1,674,587
Starine (FR)	M	1997	33	10	12	1	1,674,491
Snurge (IRE)	H	1987	30	7	10	5	1,674,441
Golden Apples (IRE)	M	1998	16	6	6	2	1,672,583
Ouija Board (GB)	F	2001	8	5	0	3	1,671,768
Opening Verse	H	1986	30	10	7	2	1,669,357
Simply Majestic	H	1984	44	18	4	7	1,667,713
Smile	H	1982	27	14	4	3	1,664,027
Running Stag	H	1994	40	7	11	2	1,663,227
Tranquility Lake	M	1995	27	11	7	3	1,662,390
Keeper Hill	M	1995	21	4	7	5	1,661,281
Include	H	1997	20	10	1	4	1,659,560
Strawberry Road (AUS)	H	1979	50	21	7	9	1,655,678
Touch of the Blues (FR)	H	1997	35	8	6	5	1,655,358
River Keen (IRE)	H	1992	42	11	5	5	1,642,385
Inside Information	M	1991	17	14	1	2	1,641,806
Fourstardave	G	1985	100	21	18	16	1,636,737
Colonial Affair	H	1990	20	7	4	3	1,635,228
Ibn Bey (GB)	H	1984	28	10	3	4	1,626,059
Golan (IRE)	H	1998	11	4	2	1	1,623,376
Desert Wine	H	1980	25	8	8	3	1,618,043
Kissin Kris	H	1990	35	4	8	5	1,616,936
Valley Crossing	H	1988	48	8	13	8	1,616,490
Sultry Song	H	1988	23	9	3	5	1,616,276
Northern Spur (IRE)	H	1991	15	6	4	3	1,614,425
Hawk Wing	H	1999	12	5	5	0	1,610,604
Dancethruthedawn	M	1998	16	7	2	3	1,609,643
Dare and Go	H	1991	22	7	7	5	1,608,972
Very Subtle	M	1984	29	12	6	4	1,608,360
Wake At Noon	H	1997	51	19	7	6	1,601,829
Editor's Note	H	1993	31	6	4	3	1,601,394
Tikkanen	H	1991	17	4	2	3	1,599,335
Fourstars Allstar	H	1988	59	14	14	9	1,596,760
Rhythm	H	1987	20	6	3	4	1,592,532
Peaks and Valleys	H	1992	16	9	3	2	1,589,270
Total Impact (CHI)	H	1998	22	5	8	2	1,586,778
Swale	H	1981	14	9	2	2	1,583,660
Judge Angelucci	H	1983	22	10	4	2	1,582,535
Happyanunoit (NZ)	M	1995	21	9	6	2	1,582,118
Fastness (IRE)	H	1990	24	9	6	1	1,581,165
Birdstone	C	2001	9	5	0	0	1,575,600
River Verdon (IRE)	G	1987	26	16	4	2	1,574,735
John's Call	G	1991	40	16	11	3	1,571,267
Temperence Hill	H	1977	31	11	4	2	1,567,650
Tight Spot	H	1987	21	12	3	1	1,566,100
In the Wings (GB)	H	1986	11	7	1	0	1,562,335
Timber Country	H	1992	12	5	1	4	1,560,400
My Flag	M	1993	20	6	3	4	1,557,057
Fly Till Dawn	H	1986	27	10	5	4	1,556,525
Riboletta (BRZ)	M	1995	28	13	3	3	1,555,103
Lundy's Liability (BRZ)	C	2000	7	4	1	0	1,553,930
Islington (IRE)	M	1999	15	6	0	4	1,553,043
Blushing John	H	1985	19	9	1	2	1,548,081
Brave Act (GB)	H	1994	27	13	6	2	1,546,269
Lively One	H	1985	36	9	7	5	1,544,100
Annus Mirabilis (FR)	H	1992	30	9	7	6	1,541,938
Family Style	M	1983	35	10	8	7	1,537,118
Storming Home (GB)	H	1998	24	8	4	3	1,536,704
Perrault (GB)	H	1977	25	9	5	5	1,536,103
Smok'n Frolic	M	1999	33	9	8	2	1,534,720
Formal Gold	H	1993	16	8	4	1	1,533,600
Cherokee Run	H	1990	28	13	5	5	1,531,818
Ipi Tombe (ZIM)	M	1998	14	12	2	0	1,529,799
Perfect Soul (IRE)	H	1998	21	7	5	1	1,527,764
Winning Colors	M	1985	19	8	3	1	1,526,837
Gold Mover	M	1998	31	13	9	5	1,523,010
Wekiva Springs	H	1991	21	10	4	2	1,512,575
Dispersal	H	1986	22	12	3	2	1,511,137
Hawkster	H	1986	23	6	3	4	1,510,942
Mobil	C	2000	23	11	5	1	1,507,924
Ecton Park	H	1996	23	6	4	6	1,503,825
Cardmania	G	1986	76	16	12	20	1,503,780
Music Merci	G	1986	35	12	7	4	1,500,710
Burning Roma	H	1998	36	13	5	7	1,500,200
Affluent	M	1998	23	8	5	4	1,497,651
Strut the Stage	H	1998	23	10	2	3	1,496,986
Johar	H	1999	16	6	4	2	1,494,496
Polar Expedition	G	1991	49	20	5	7	1,491,071
Dahlia	M	1970	48	15	3	7	1,489,105

Horse	Sex	Born	Sts	1st	2d	3d	Earnings
Dr Devious (IRE)	H	1989	15	6	4	0	1,484,230
Wilderness Song	M	1988	37	15	12	2	1,482,033
Megahertz (GB)	M	1999	28	10	5	5	1,481,594
Mountain Cat	H	1990	11	6	2	0	1,478,901
Kooyonga (IRE)	M	1988	18	9	4	1	1,476,193
Mi Selecto	H	1985	40	9	7	9	1,475,762
Tates Creek	M	1998	17	11	3	0	1,471,674
Our New Recruit	H	1999	19	6	7	2	1,470,915
Ski Paradise	M	1990	20	6	8	1	1,470,588
Dancing Spree	H	1985	35	10	6	9	1,470,484
Indian Skimmer	M	1984	16	10	1	3	1,469,299
Super Diamond	H	1980	37	16	5	5	1,469,233
Labeeb (GB)	H	1992	20	8	3	4	1,464,950
Buckpasser	H	1963	31	25	4	1	1,462,014
Halo America	M	1990	40	15	8	2	1,460,992
Carnegie (IRE)	H	1991	13	7	1	1	1,458,787
Raging Fever	M	1998	26	11	7	3	1,458,198
Regal Classic	H	1985	27	8	8	3	1,456,584
Olympio	H	1988	17	9	4	0	1,456,315
Equalize	H	1982	43	13	9	8	1,455,298
Men's Exclusive	G	1993	48	11	16	4	1,451,126
Prairie Bayou	G	1990	12	7	3	0	1,450,621
Soviet Line (IRE)	G	1990	48	16	8	6	1,450,130
Bet On Sunshine	G	1992	47	22	7	10	1,449,882
Summer Colony	M	1998	24	10	5	1	1,448,930
Memories of Silver	M	1993	19	9	3	5	1,448,715
Twice the Vice	M	1991	23	12	6	1	1,447,064
Meadow Star	M	1988	20	11	1	2	1,445,740
Singletary	C	2000	16	6	5	2	1,439,732
Dream Well (FR)	H	1995	14	4	4	4	1,139,441
Lil E. Tee	H	1989	13	7	4	1	1,437,506
Dancing Brave	H	1983	10	8	1	0	1,435,434
Hollywood Wildcat	M	1990	21	12	3	3	1,432,160
Noverre	H	1998	21	5	7	4	1,429,344
Falcon Flight (FR)	H	1996	20	5	2	3	1,428,849
Tejano	H	1985	21	5	6	3	1,428,177
Voodoo Dancer	M	1998	21	11	4	2	1,427,952
Talloires	H	1990	28	5	8	3	1,423,949
Silic (FR)	H	1995	15	8	2	0	1,422,299
Slew of Damascus	G	1988	48	16	9	8	1,420,350
Surfers Paradise (NZ)	G	1987	57	17	5	0	1,419,964
Pebbles (GB)	M	1981	15	8	4	0	1,419,632
Epalo (GER)	H	1999	21	8	8	2	1,419,259
Imperial Gesture	M	1999	11	6	2	1	1,419,140
Outstandingly	M	1982	28	10	4	3	1,412,206
Vanlandingham	H	1981	19	10	3	3	1,409,476
Win	G	1980	44	14	10	3	1,408,980
Dynever	C	2000	16	4	6	1	1,408,714
Sayyedati (GB)	M	1990	22	6	5	3	1,408,616
Best of the Rest	H	1995	32	16	8	2	1,407,796
Cutlass Reality	H	1982	66	14	12	9	1,405,660
Left Bank	H	1997	24	14	2	0	1,402,806
Excellent Meeting	M	1996	20	8	5	3	1,402,396
Peeping Tom	G	1997	49	14	7	9	1,398,547
Lit de Justice	H	1990	36	10	8	6	1,397,649
Opera House (GB)	H	1988	18	8	4	3	1,397,456
Timboroa (GB)	H	1996	25	10	3	3	1,397,228
Honor Glide	H	1994	38	11	5	2	1,397,187
Lion Heart	C	2001	10	5	3	0	1,390,800
Jostle	M	1997	20	8	5	2	1,389,932
Clever Trevor	G	1986	30	15	5	2	1,388,841
Mutamam (GB)	H	1995	21	11	2	1	1,388,410
Apple Tree (FR)	H	1989	26	7	4	5	1,388,260
Solar Splendor	G	1987	42	11	3	6	1,386,468
Wild Rush	H	1994	16	8	0	3	1,386,302
Mt. Sassafras	G	1992	47	8	7	14	1,382,985
Go for Gin	H	1991	19	5	7	2	1,380,866
Astra	M	1996	16	11	1	2	1,378,424
Possibly Perfect	M	1990	18	11	2	4	1,377,634
State City	H	1999	17	6	0	3	1,375,993
Fran's Valentine	M	1982	34	13	4	5	1,375,465
Go for Wand	M	1987	13	10	2	0	1,373,338
Trempolino	H	1984	11	4	3	3	1,369,233
Sunny Sunrise	G	1987	63	18	12	9	1,367,268
North East Bound	G	1996	50	12	7	3	1,363,228
Puerto Madero (CHI)	H	1994	24	11	3	2	1,361,626
Tank's Prospect	H	1982	14	5	2	2	1,355,645
Rodrigo de Triano	H	1989	13	9	0	0	1,354,192
Track Barron	H	1981	21	12	3	1	1,353,674
Refuse To Bend (IRE)	C	2000	15	7	0	1	1,350,034
Different (ARG)	M	1992	19	9	3	5	1,349,802
Rhythm Band	G	1996	18	5	2	2	1,349,066
Honor Medal	H	1981	87	19	13	19	1,347,073
Groovy	H	1983	26	12	4	1	1,346,956
Ibero (ARG)	H	1987	34	10	7	4	1,345,199
Princess Rooney	M	1980	21	17	2	1	1,343,339
Ryafan	M	1994	10	7	1	0	1,342,142
Gato Del Sol	H	1979	39	7	9	7	1,340,107
In the Groove (GB)	M	1987	21	7	4	4	1,336,783
Sky Beauty	M	1990	21	15	2	2	1,336,000
Dixie Dot Com	H	1995	23	8	6	1	1,332,775
Halling	H	1991	18	12	1	0	1,332,651
Tuzla (FR)	M	1994	26	12	6	1	1,332,587
Hap	H	1996	20	10	2	2	1,329,210
Ajina	M	1994	17	7	3	2	1,327,915
Kicken Kris	C	2000	19	6	3	3	1,326,600
Lonesome Glory	G	1988	44	24	5	6	1,325,868
Savinio	G	1990	48	11	11	8	1,321,860
Victor Cooley	G	1993	39	13	12	3	1,320,475
Grecian Flight	M	1984	40	21	6	3	1,320,215
Unshaded	G	1997	20	6	3	3	1,318,492
Lassigny	H	1991	28	8	2	5	1,318,371
Secretariat	H	1970	21	16	3	1	1,316,808
Bowman's Band	H	1998	34	7	11	6	1,315,774
Richman	H	1988	33	14	5	5	1,314,360
Alphabatim	H	1981	22	7	3	5	1,313,175
Unbridled's Song	H	1993	12	5	4	0	1,311,800
Manistique	M	1995	15	11	1	1	1,311,800
Concerto	H	1994	21	10	4	2	1,308,118
Tappiano	M	1984	34	17	2	4	1,305,522
Littlebitlively	H	1994	33	10	9	5	1,303,343
Brown Bess	M	1982	36	16	8	6	1,300,920
Sacahuista	M	1984	21	6	7	2	1,298,842
Elloluv	F	2000	16	5	3	2	1,297,075
Lazy Lode (ARG)	H	1994	29	8	4	6	1,296,740
Misil	H	1988	36	14	8	3	1,296,417
King Cugat	H	1997	16	7	7	1	1,293,782
Windsharp	M	1991	29	11	7	3	1,293,075
A Bit O'Gold	G	2001	11	7	3	0	1,290,819
Western Pride	H	1998	32	10	4	1	1,289,929

Horse	Sex	Born	Sts	1st	2d	3d	Earnings
Victory Speech	H	1993	27	9	2	5	1,289,020
Nashua	H	1952	30	22	4	1	1,288,565
Peteski	H	1990	11	7	2	1	1,287,866
Exchange	M	1988	30	15	7	4	1,287,795
Carotene	M	1983	41	12	8	5	1,287,232
Raintrap (GB)	H	1990	28	9	4	2	1,283,707
Silveyville	H	1978	56	19	11	8	1,282,880
Farda Amiga	M	1999	8	4	1	0	1,282,302
Petite Ile (IRE)	M	1986	14	6	3	4	1,281,665
Shake You Down	G	1998	42	17	6	4	1,277,164
Saumarez (GB)	H	1987	9	5	1	0	1,275,719
Althea	M	1981	15	8	4	0	1,275,255
Frankly Perfect	H	1985	22	6	6	4	1,272,957
Sangue (IRE)	M	1978	30	13	6	3	1,272,086
Shine Again	M	1997	34	14	10	7	1,271,840
Pleasant Breeze	G	1995	36	10	8	6	1,271,680
Versailles Treaty	M	1988	20	9	9	2	1,271,154
Soaring Softly	M	1995	16	9	1	3	1,270,433
Cozzene's Prince	G	1987	68	16	10	10	1,270,057
Scott's Scoundrel	H	1992	50	22	4	8	1,270,052
Ticker Tape (GB)	F	2001	18	7	6	2	1,267,426
Diplomatic Jet	H	1992	51	9	5	9	1,267,202
One Dreamer	M	1988	25	12	6	2	1,266,067
Chief Honcho	H	1987	34	10	6	3	1,265,719
The Cliff's Edge	C	2001	13	4	5	2	1,265,258
Magistretti	C	2000	16	4	6	0	1,264,117
Allez France	M	1970	21	13	3	1	1,262,801
Bienamado	H	1996	16	8	3	0	1,261,089
Personal Flag	H	1983	24	8	4	4	1,258,924
Speightstown	H	1998	16	10	2	2	1,258,256
Glitter Woman	M	1994	23	10	9	3	1,256,805
Society Selection	F	2001	12	5	3	1	1,256,700
Bounding Basque	H	1980	40	10	4	6	1,256,258
Repent	H	1999	10	5	3	1	1,255,660
Gourmet Girl	M	1995	33	9	7	10	1,255,373
Stephan's Odyssey	H	1982	16	6	4	1	1,255,328
Wandesta (GB)	M	1991	21	7	3	5	1,255,145
Cavonnier	G	1993	23	8	3	2	1,254,165
Rubiano	H	1987	28	13	6	1	1,252,817
Ancient Title	H	1970	57	24	11	9	1,252,791
Susan's Girl	M	1969	63	29	14	11	1,251,668
Al Mamoon	H	1981	32	11	7	3	1,249,906
Sunny's Halo	H	1980	20	9	3	2	1,247,791
Friendly Lover	H	1988	66	22	13	12	1,247,670
Private Terms	H	1985	17	12	0	0	1,243,947
Irish Prize	G	1996	28	10	4	2	1,242,364
Desert Waves	G	1990	63	15	9	6	1,241,295
Carry Back	H	1958	62	21	11	11	1,241,165
Candid Glen	G	1997	40	11	10	6	1,239,330
Kudos	G	1997	24	7	5	4	1,238,935
Personal Rush	C	2001	10	5	0	1	1,234,820
Nuclear Debate	G	1995	52	11	8	10	1,234,054
Erins Isle (IRE)	H	1978	33	9	9	3	1,233,889
Dixie Union	H	1997	12	7	3	0	1,233,190
Lite Light	M	1988	26	8	4	4	1,231,596
Earl of Barking (IRE)	H	1990	37	9	3	10	1,230,519
Sheikh Albadou (GB)	H	1988	15	6	4	1	1,229,702
Housebuster	H	1987	22	15	3	1	1,229,696
Royal Heroine (IRE)	M	1980	21	10	4	2	1,229,449
Fit for a Queen	M	1986	51	13	14	9	1,226,429
Zoffany	H	1980	36	15	10	2	1,225,569
Dollar Bill	H	1998	22	4	5	5	1,225,546
Real Connection	M	1991	72	7	14	7	1,225,018
Grindstone	H	1993	6	3	2	0	1,224,510
Classic Cat	H	1995	20	6	3	5	1,221,300
Subordination	H	1994	21	11	3	1	1,221,068
Irish Linnet	M	1988	62	19	16	10	1,220,180
Isitingood	H	1991	24	11	3	4	1,219,430
Gaily Magnum	G	1993	24	8	2	2	1,218,578
Jolie's Halo	H	1987	20	8	0	2	1,218,120
Foolish Pleasure	H	1972	26	16	4	3	1,216,705
Arazi	H	1989	14	9	1	1	1,212,351
Fieldy (IRE)	M	1983	54	19	9	8	1,212,168
Stalwars	H	1985	79	17	17	8	1,211,556
Leger Cat (ARG)	H	1986	53	16	5	7	1,211,402
Primal	G	1985	45	17	11	7	1,209,530
Ten Keys	H	1984	54	21	8	4	1,209,211
Brian Boru (GB)	C	2000	18	4	4	3	1,209,054
Seattle Slew	H	1974	17	14	2	0	1,208,726
Tasso	H	1983	23	9	4	4	1,207,884
Tomisue's Delight	M	1994	20	7	5	4	1,207,537
Dahar	H	1981	29	7	6	4	1,207,286
Lottsa Talc	M	1990	65	21	10	12	1,206,248
Thornfield	G	1994	19	6	1	3	1,206,074
Atticus	H	1992	18	7	3	1	1,205,933
Wallenda	H	1990	33	7	5	5	1,205,929
Request for Parole	H	1999	34	9	7	3	1,205,892
Volochine (IRE)	H	1991	45	8	12	9	1,205,580
Honour and Glory	H	1993	17	6	5	2	1,202,942
Kiridashi	H	1992	44	14	9	8	1,201,981
Chilukki	M	1997	17	11	3	0	1,201,828
Powerscourt (GB)	C	2000	17	4	5	3	1,200,917
License Fee	M	1995	43	16	7	6	1,200,416
Kostroma (IRE)	M	1986	26	12	2	3	1,200,088
Yavana's Pace (IRE)	G	1992	74	16	14	11	1,199,409
Nasr El Arab	H	1985	16	6	2	2	1,198,585
Dushyantor	H	1993	20	5	5	2	1,197,570
Frost King	H	1978	55	27	10	3	1,196,954
My Big Boy	G	1983	50	10	12	10	1,196,102
Anet	H	1994	19	8	5	0	1,189,873
Barathea (IRE)	H	1990	16	5	4	0	1,189,181
Val Royal (FR)	H	1996	12	7	2	0	1,186,687
Blazing Sword	G	1994	45	11	7	7	1,184,055
Heat Haze (GB)	M	1999	14	7	2	2	1,183,696
Pico Central (BRZ)	H	1999	15	9	0	3	1,183,145
April Run (IRE)	M	1978	18	8	2	4	1,182,819
The Wicked North	H	1989	17	8	4	1	1,180,750
Continental Red	G	1996	64	7	14	13	1,180,358
Ridgewood Pearl (GB)	M	1992	8	6	1	1	1,179,301
Damascus	H	1964	32	21	7	3	1,176,781
King Glorious	H	1986	9	8	1	0	1,175,650
Maxzene	M	1993	23	11	5	0	1,175,259
Cougar II	H	1966	50	20	7	17	1,172,625
Homebuilder	H	1984	60	11	11	17	1,172,153
Ezzoud (IRE)	H	1989	22	6	5	2	1,171,885
Sefa's Beauty	M	1979	52	25	7	8	1,171,628
Gorgeous	M	1986	14	8	4	1	1,171,370
Mystic Lady	M	1998	27	10	8	2	1,170,390
Cetewayo	H	1994	37	11	5	4	1,170,258
High Yield	H	1997	14	4	4	3	1,170,196

Horse	Sex	Born	Sts	1st	2d	3d	Earnings
Cacoethes	H	1986	14	4	3	3	1,169,064
River Bay	H	1993	20	8	3	3	1,167,970
Tejano Run	H	1992	21	8	4	6	1,166,842
Slew City Slew	H	1984	42	11	10	6	1,166,296
Mystery Giver	G	1998	33	11	7	2	1,165,900
Educated Risk	M	1990	23	11	6	4	1,163,717
Red Bullet	H	1997	14	6	2	2	1,161,920
Chorwon	G	1993	44	13	7	8	1,161,795
Luthier Fever	H	1991	25	6	5	6	1,160,852
Benburb	G	1989	22	7	2	4	1,159,949
Cajun Beat	G	2000	17	7	3	0	1,159,100
Bonapaw	G	1996	48	18	7	4	1,158,752
Kelly Kip	H	1994	31	15	3	4	1,157,142
Early Pioneer	G	1995	33	9	9	5	1,156,815
Lady Tak	F	2000	18	10	4	1	1,155,682
Empress Club (ARG)	M	1988	26	16	2	1	1,155,235
Videogenic	M	1982	73	20	9	10	1,154,360
Flying Pidgeon	H	1981	56	12	9	13	1,154,337
King's Theatre (IRE)	H	1991	19	5	3	4	1,154,329
Present Value	H	1984	42	15	5	3	1,153,853
Dernier Empereur	H	1990	30	8	5	4	1,152,425
Bourbon Belle	M	1995	40	16	11	5	1,152,223
Pine Tree Lane	M	1982	38	19	4	4	1,150,561
High Brite	H	1984	45	15	7	9	1,150,519
Lazy Slusan	M	1995	47	12	7	10	1,150,410
Nite Dreamer	H	1995	37	5	10	6	1,149,788
Sir Beaufort	H	1987	34	10	10	4	1,149,130
Graeme Hall	H	1997	22	7	7	1	1,147,441
Brass in Pocket	M	1999	24	14	3	2	1,146,023
Maltese Superb	M	1997	35	4	7	4	1,145,491
Island Whirl	H	1978	34	11	6	6	1,144,010
Dimitrova	F	2000	14	4	2	1	1,142,696
Volga (IRE)	M	1998	19	7	5	2	1,141,759
Drum Taps	H	1986	31	15	5	2	1,140,788
Bold Ruritana	M	1990	44	14	10	6	1,140,163
Richter Scale	H	1994	25	12	2	0	1,139,958
Swept Overboard	H	1997	20	8	5	3	1,137,767
Mr Purple	H	1992	21	6	3	5	1,133,538
Tenpins	H	1998	17	9	3	2	1,133,449
Shantou	H	1993	14	6	2	4	1,132,399
Steady Power	G	1984	70	13	19	9	1,132,197
Helmsman	H	1992	22	6	7	3	1,132,142
Lemhi Gold	H	1978	22	8	3	1	1,131,355
War Chant	H	1997	7	5	1	0	1,130,600
Manndar (IRE)	H	1996	20	4	6	3	1,128,835
Western Playboy	H	1986	45	8	7	7	1,128,449
Lashkari (GB)	H	1981	13	5	2	2	1,127,658
Flying Paster	H	1976	27	13	7	2	1,127,460
Strategic Choice	H	1991	33	5	5	5	1,126,735
North Sider	M	1982	36	15	7	5	1,126,400
On the Line	H	1984	37	14	7	2	1,125,810
Ela Athena (GB)	M	1996	17	3	7	2	1,125,252
Pleasant Variety	H	1984	58	8	10	11	1,123,783
Star Standard	H	1992	25	7	4	3	1,121,512
Polish Navy	H	1984	12	7	1	3	1,118,076
Countess Diana	M	1995	14	7	2	0	1,117,185
Timarida (IRE)	M	1992	16	10	2	2	1,116,186
Sky Jack	G	1996	18	10	2	2	1,115,127
Temperate Sil	H	1984	19	6	2	1	1,113,775
Colonial Waters	M	1985	32	6	12	3	1,112,847
Not Surprising	G	1990	61	23	4	5	1,112,301
Squirtle Squirt	H	1998	16	8	4	0	1,112,220
Wonder Again	M	1999	19	7	2	3	1,111,682
Riva Ridge	H	1969	30	17	3	1	1,111,497
Stellar Jayne	F	2001	18	6	2	3	1,111,244
Single Empire (IRE)	H	1994	23	5	5	3	1,110,889
Top Corsage	M	1983	53	15	7	9	1,110,028
Fort Marcy	G	1964	75	21	18	14	1,109,791
Kiss a Native	G	1997	40	14	5	3	1,109,022
Dispute	M	1990	19	9	4	4	1,106,907
Rainbows for Life	H	1988	36	15	5	3	1,105,926
The Very One	M	1975	71	22	12	9	1,104,623
Public Purse	H	1994	14	7	1	4	1,103,324
Celtic Arms (FR)	H	1991	23	5	2	3	1,102,806
Flute	M	1998	8	4	3	0	1,101,504
Elmhurst	G	1990	51	9	11	6	1,100,567
Recoup the Cash	G	1990	74	23	6	3	1,098,920
Track Robbery	M	1976	59	22	12	7	1,098,537
Hal's Hope	H	1997	33	9	5	3	1,098,422
Sabin	M	1980	25	18	0	2	1,098,341
The Tin Man	G	1998	21	7	4	2	1,097,860
Full Moon Madness	G	1995	46	15	11	12	1,097,805
Eliza	M	1990	12	5	2	2	1,095,316
Event of the Year	H	1995	9	5	2	1	1,095,200
Basqueian	G	1991	37	13	10	2	1,094,767
Thirty Six Red	H	1987	20	4	3	5	1,094,310
Kazzia (GER)	M	1999	7	5	0	0	1,094,206
Mr Ross	G	1995	44	18	6	10	1,091,046
Fruits of Love	H	1995	23	5	3	5	1,089,543
Parose	G	1994	92	21	22	15	1,089,156
Freedom Cry (GB)	H	1991	12	5	5	0	1,089,080
Mercedes Won	H	1986	52	12	7	12	1,087,435
Citation	H	1945	45	32	10	2	1,085,760
Judy's Red Shoes	M	1983	83	25	13	12	1,085,668
Clear Mandate	M	1992	31	10	6	4	1,085,588
Silver Goblin	G	1991	26	16	4	3	1,083,895
Regal Intention	H	1985	41	14	7	10	1,083,103
Prowl (AUS)	G	1995	22	5	2	2	1,082,344
Mandy's Gold	M	1998	24	11	4	6	1,081,744
Yes It's True	H	1996	22	11	2	3	1,080,700
Dave's Friend	H	1975	76	35	16	8	1,079,915
Tobougg (IRE)	H	1998	12	3	2	2	1,079,901
Mr. Epperson	G	1995	70	19	11	12	1,079,851
Dumaani	H	1991	26	7	3	3	1,079,098
De Roche	G	1986	28	5	8	7	1,078,200
State Shinto	H	1996	38	9	7	2	1,078,174
Pollard's Vision	C	2001	17	5	5	3	1,075,311
Bien Nicole	M	1998	26	12	8	2	1,074,620
Champali	C	2000	22	11	2	4	1,073,794
Hard Buck (BRZ)	H	1999	19	9	5	0	1,073,674
Silver Ending	H	1987	37	8	1	9	1,073,420
Hopeful Word	H	1981	43	10	12	3	1,073,051
Interco	H	1980	21	10	4	3	1,070,688
Corporate Report	H	1988	10	3	5	0	1,067,908
Taylor's Special	H	1981	41	21	7	2	1,065,805
Ginger Gold	M	1999	25	7	6	2	1,065,448
Megan's Interco	G	1989	36	16	11	0	1,062,465
Bare Necessities	M	1999	26	8	4	7	1,062,251
Afternoon Deelites	H	1992	12	7	3	0	1,061,193
Critical Eye	M	1997	38	14	4	3	1,060,984

Horse	Sex	Born	Sts	1st	2d	3d	Earnings
Two Item Limit	M	1998	28	7	3	5	1,060,585
White Muzzle (GB)	H	1990	17	6	3	2	1,060,443
Mysterious Affair	M	1997	37	12	9	6	1,059,971
Beau Genius	H	1985	42	19	7	4	1,055,600
Excessivepleasure	G	2000	16	5	5	1	1,054,970
Secret Status	M	1997	19	8	3	4	1,053,705
Colstar	M	1996	18	11	2	1	1,053,056
Tap to Music	M	1995	21	6	4	4	1,052,526
Capades	M	1986	27	11	9	2	1,051,006
Hodges Bay	G	1985	51	7	15	3	1,050,363
Freefourinternet	H	1998	34	8	3	6	1,050,275
Alpride (IRE)	M	1991	26	11	4	4	1,048,270
Thunder Rumble	H	1989	19	8	0	1	1,047,552
One for Rose	M	1999	22	12	4	2	1,047,243
Maysville Slew	G	1996	69	17	11	7	1,046,409
Salem Drive	H	1982	46	13	7	10	1,046,065
Morluc	H	1996	40	11	9	5	1,045,758
Kalookan Queen	M	1996	25	11	8	4	1,044,474
Echo Eddie	G	1997	28	10	7	3	1,044,354
Starrer	M	1998	20	6	5	3	1,043,033
Algenib (ARG)	H	1987	21	7	5	2	1,042,299
Fit to Fight	H	1979	26	14	3	3	1,042,075
Southjet	H	1983	30	5	7	2	1,040,483
Crafty Shaw	H	1998	42	15	7	7	1,040,440
Zoman	H	1987	24	7	5	3	1,040,372
Krz Ruckus	G	1997	39	15	8	4	1,040,036
Bolshoi Boy	G	1983	58	16	7	8	1,039,702
Silent Eskimo	M	1995	31	9	4	9	1,039,485
Jameela	M	1976	58	27	15	6	1,038,704
It's the One	H	1978	28	9	7	9	1,038,444
West by West	H	1989	30	10	3	7	1,038,123
Troyanos (BRZ)	H	1985	13	10	1	1	1,038,083
Vivace	M	1993	40	20	4	6	1,037,671
Lite the Fuse	H	1991	21	9	4	6	1,036,882
A Fleets Dancer	H	1995	45	12	6	8	1,036,649
Urgent Request (IRE)	H	1990	25	7	4	1	1,035,339
Queen Alexandra	M	1982	46	19	8	5	1,034,144
Fali Time	H	1981	15	5	4	2	1,033,179
Bessarabian	M	1982	37	18	5	4	1,032,640
Vision and Verse	H	1996	21	4	3	5	1,030,330
Janet (GB)	M	1997	27	8	4	6	1,027,237
Native Diver	H	1959	81	37	7	12	1,026,500
More Than Ready	H	1997	17	7	4	1	1,026,229
Sure Shot Biscuit	G	1996	54	23	10	11	1,025,480
Del Mar Dennis	G	1990	26	10	1	4	1,023,373
Heatherten	M	1979	53	21	7	4	1,022,699
J J'sdream	M	1993	40	13	11	7	1,022,217
Hever Golf Rose (GB)	M	1991	66	17	11	10	1,020,328
Storm Song	M	1994	12	4	1	2	1,020,050
Grand Canyon	H	1987	8	4	3	0	1,019,540
Stephen Got Even	H	1996	11	5	1	1	1,019,200
Corwyn Bay (IRE)	H	1986	15	6	4	0	1,018,749
Urbane	M	1992	18	8	4	4	1,018,568
Riviera (FR)	H	1994	21	10	4	3	1,018,535
Super Moment	H	1977	47	10	8	5	1,017,940
Sewickley	H	1985	32	11	9	4	1,017,517
My Own Business (VEN)	H	1997	50	37	5	1	1,016,908
Spook Express (SAF)	M	1994	22	11	2	3	1,016,744
Captain Bodgit	H	1994	12	7	1	4	1,014,849
Johannesburg	H	1999	10	7	1	0	1,014,585
Letthebighossroll	G	1988	60	18	14	6	1,014,377
Alwuhush	H	1985	22	5	4	7	1,012,423
Antespend	M	1993	24	10	4	2	1,011,954
Roo Art	H	1982	27	10	4	5	1,011,723
Kela	H	1998	25	8	6	0	1,011,527
Miss Oceana	M	1981	19	11	6	1	1,010,385
Forty Niner Days	G	1987	45	9	9	3	1,009,625
Kurofune Mystery	M	1990	21	6	5	4	1,009,342
Mubtaker	H	1997	20	9	6	3	1,007,998
Down the Aisle	H	1993	21	9	5	5	1,007,988
Dream Supreme	M	1997	16	9	2	2	1,007,680
Clabber Girl	M	1983	39	8	12	6	1,006,261
Kiri's Clown	H	1989	62	16	6	8	1,005,469
Rivlia	H	1982	41	9	2	8	1,005,041
Lost Mountain	H	1988	36	5	6	8	1,004,939
Royal Glint	H	1970	52	21	9	4	1,004,816
Glorious Song	M	1976	34	17	9	1	1,004,534
Fighting Fit	H	1979	49	14	7	8	1,004,174
Brocco	H	1991	8	4	2	0	1,003,550
Dr. Fager	H	1964	22	18	2	1	1,002,642
Danzig Connection	H	1983	17	6	5	4	1,002,620
Annoconnor	M	1984	29	12	7	5	1,002,420
Forever Silver	H	1985	47	8	9	9	1,001,974
Brian's Time	H	1985	21	5	2	6	1,001,269
Exbourne	H	1986	14	8	5	1	1,000,198

This section includes all horses with at least $1 million in career earnings that had at least one start in North America. It includes any foreign earnings and bonus money awarded for racing performance that was reported to *Daily Racing Form*.

Lifetime Leaders – Races Won

Kingston, a brown horse by Spendthrift - Kapanga, by Victorious, holds the record of most wins in North American racing. He won 89 of his 138 starts and was unplaced only four times in his racing career, which extended from 1886 to 1894.

Kingston was bred at James R. Keene's Spendthrift Stud, near Lexington, Ky. He was sold as a yearling to E.V. Snedeker and J.F. Cushman for $2,200. He raced as a 2-year-old in Snedeker's colors. In July 1887, he was purchased by the Dwyer brothers for $12,500 and raced in their red and blue silks until the parnership was dissolved in November 1890, when he was acquired by Michael F. Dwyer for $30,000. He raced for the latter until he retired, perfectly sound, in 1894. During his career, Kingston reigned as America's leading money winner for a time but was displaced from that spot prior to his retirement by Domino, who amassed more in just over three months as a 2-year-old in 1893 than had then-9-year-old Kingston in his entire career to that point.

Thoroughbreds on record who won the most number of races in North America during their careers are listed below:

Horse	YOB	Sts	1st	2d	3d	Won
Kingston	1884	138	89	33	12	$138,917
Little Minch	1880	222	85	40	39	58,225
King Crab	1885	310	85	63	52	55,682
Hiblaze	1935	396	78	72	51	31,597
Tippity Witchet	1915	266	78	52	42	88,241
Pan Zareta	1910	151	76	31	21	39,082
Raceland	1885	130	70	25	12	116,391
Badge	1885	167	70	47	27	73,253
Care Free	1918	227	67	36	35	59,873
Shot One	1941	360	65	65	68	29,982
Worthowning	1935	333	63	61	64	41,760
Banquet	1887	166	62	42	23	118,535
Seth's Hope	1924	327	62	51	50	74,341
Imp	1894	171	62	35	29	70,119
Leochares	1910	175	62	47	28	68,867
Ed R.	1948	248	62	49	35	63,552
Vantime	1939	295	62	65	36	46,290
Mucho Gusto	1932	216	61	32	36	101,880
Irene's Bob	1929	237	61	37	30	58,010
Brandon Prince	1929	280	61	36	47	47,207
Shuchor	1936	261	61	49	36	33,607
Vantryst	1936	334	61	78	48	31,971
Lewis A. D.	1947	212	60	50	27	65,482
George de Mar	1922	333	60	54	64	69,091

Horses with at least 40 wins in North America or Canada who raced in 1950 or later are listed below:

Horse	YOB	Sex	Sts	1st	2d	3d	Won
Hiblaze	1935	H	396	78	72	51	$31,597
Shot One	1941	G	360	65	65	68	29,982
Worthowning	1935	G	333	63	61	64	41,760
Ed R.	1948	G	248	62	49	35	63,552
Vantime	1939	G	295	62	65	36	46,290
Shuchor	1936	G	261	61	49	36	33,607
Vantryst	1936	H	334	61	78	48	31,971
Lewis A. D.	1947	H	212	60	50	27	65,482
Charlie Boy	1955	H	241	58	45	35	207,642
Golden Arrow	1961	H	176	58	25	22	167,264
Columcille	1948	H	182	57	30	30	89,665
End of Street	1963	H	202	57	40	30	67,686
Tommy Whelan	1936	G	233	55	34	23	33,279
Argos	1937	G	215	54	40	27	37,507
Crying for More	1965	H	192	53	32	29	183,685
Bee Golly	1942	M	183	53	34	26	54,544
Post War Style	1941	M	179	53	26	23	52,600
Port Conway Lane	1969	H	242	52	39	36	431,593
Agrarian-U	1942	G	236	52	36	34	199,345
Fleet Argo	1947	G	243	52	37	38	149,000
Billy Brier	1953	G	231	52	27	33	83,168
Float Away	1936	G	265	52	43	41	61,365
Air Patrol	1941	H	146	51	33	17	163,100
Sagely	1970	H	124	51	23	11	116,196
Blenweed	1938	G	202	51	35	25	105,415
Dr. Johnson	1940	H	256	51	44	27	54,422
Time to Bid	1975	H	179	50	33	35	241,247
Big Devil	1963	H	237	50	42	34	222,715
Go Lite	1960	H	211	50	28	27	96,938
Brownskin	1946	H	224	50	41	36	77,913
Misty Eye	1938	M	220	50	26	40	25,236
Candle Wood	1949	H	253	49	53	37	171,127
Ahba's Bull	1949	H	157	49	22	22	97,057
Imahead	1955	H	246	49	46	30	69,884
Win Man	1985	G	178	48	38	23	416,316
Dot the T.	1972	H	261	48	33	31	227,033
Bayou Teche	1961	G	281	48	35	43	107,577
Apple	1958	G	195	48	27	20	102,385
Flyingphere	1961	G	213	48	41	25	85,683
Bill Pac	1951	H	272	48	42	37	73,374
Waco Scamp	1950	H	226	48	33	21	64,647
Youville	1939	G	275	48	28	49	51,326
See D.	1942	H	260	48	41	32	48,890
Thos	1938	H	255	48	38	43	43,884
Lexington Park	1967	G	209	47	35	29	357,861
Grand Wizard	1956	G	220	47	35	36	222,312
Montana Winds	1967	H	191	47	29	15	202,535
Maxwell G.	1961	H	234	47	52	37	181,420
Master Red	1950	G	217	47	44	23	109,684
Bee Lee Tee	1947	H	270	47	51	46	104,805
Aquanotte	1960	H	142	47	29	18	80,603
Gary's Star	1954	H	210	47	37	23	72,105
Annette G.	1951	M	237	47	47	25	68,932
Cain's Abel	1956	H	102	47	24	12	58,267
Gourmet	1937	G	177	47	22	21	53,400
Pooch	1948	H	209	47	38	26	48,505
Algasir	1946	G	165	46	39	24	210,250
Amberope	1968	H	153	46	26	13	197,085
Perennial	1967	G	216	46	52	31	137,010
War Marshal	1953	H	227	46	33	41	120,259
Bold Scholar	1956	H	141	46	27	22	101,752
Legate	1949	H	260	46	39	57	99,915
Silver Fir	1963	H	165	46	20	18	79,347
Nirgo	1955	G	273	46	39	33	63,987
Dakota Bill	1952	H	170	46	29	27	39,215
Jilsie's Gigalo	1984	G	136	45	28	22	315,456
Guy	1974	H	161	45	25	13	281,085
Dot's Imp	1966	H	138	45	34	14	265,112
Dobi's Knight	1971	G	219	45	28	22	178,996
War Allies	1942	G	182	45	38	24	141,313
Sailawayin	1967	G	172	45	36	19	138,917
Tidy Sum	1943	H	149	45	21	23	116,271
Happy Monday	1965	H	157	45	22	15	115,008
Roman Spy	1951	H	229	45	26	23	106,462
Acerullah	1970	H	219	44	33	39	186,214
Vet's Boy	1950	H	177	44	22	20	122,230

Horse	Age	Sex	Sts	1st	2d	3d	Won
Title Gain	1958	G	171	44	21	24	106,086
Station Master	1968	H	185	44	28	36	95,496
Arrc Flash	1960	G	205	44	38	31	91,451
Ogham	1941	G	198	44	24	28	73,815
Navy	1936	H	202	44	34	21	65,345
Betty's Bobby	1937	G	224	44	30	29	60,655
Brown Pirate	1949	H	167	44	22	15	56,214
Irish Wash	1942	H	180	44	32	18	51,269
Javalina	1950	H	168	44	25	31	49,664
Half Nelson	1954	G	147	44	23	14	47,203
Slamming Slam	1948	G	201	44	30	24	44,465
Jack Rubens	1939	G	207	44	36	23	38,255
Prince A. A.	1950	G	192	44	30	33	34,495
Grand Lady	1937	M	287	44	47	54	27,406
Chronology	1935	G	301	44	41	46	14,632
Round Table	1954	H	66	43	8	5	1,749,869
Kintla's Folly	1972	G	130	43	25	21	397,761
Damage Control	1965	H	168	43	27	21	250,364
Alhambra Son	1964	H	160	43	17	16	244,032
Git	1967	H	203	43	44	34	191,423
Alexis	1942	G	253	43	56	45	183,404
Norman Prince	1974	H	161	43	37	15	169,947
Rob Bob	1957	H	261	43	31	38	166,716
Chrystal Gail	1973	M	137	43	25	20	154,910
Flying Hitch	1972	H	125	43	27	13	124,352
Fleet Charge	1952	G	226	43	32	27	115,192
Mister Snow Man	1959	G	310	43	37	36	104,074
Till's Jeff	1963	H	163	43	27	32	101,880
Quien Es	1938	G	126	43	26	16	89,136
Bolo Tie	1940	G	252	43	48	32	77,062
Lindsey-Jan	1965	H	208	43	36	27	68,958
Leaping Moose	1941	G	205	43	33	26	55,067
Vinum	1937	H	264	43	29	30	53,990
Golden Grip	1950	H	180	43	32	24	45,870
Happy's First	1954	H	250	43	32	34	42,985
Swear Off	1947	G	246	43	36	31	41,964
Brown Blizzard	1939	G	190	43	26	32	25,755
Michaelmas	1935	G	245	43	31	28	24,231
Opelika	1936	H	215	43	45	48	22,850
English Dancer	1967	G	172	42	41	21	208,239
Appease Not	1946	G	314	42	44	46	122,802
Missouri Brave	1972	H	137	42	22	12	116,717
Cheju	1962	G	185	42	28	23	114,040
Johnathen J. S.	1970	H	191	42	26	28	111,594
Sky Light	1955	H	176	42	30	25	111,577
Three Larks	1969	H	154	42	32	18	111,339
Bee's Little Man	1961	H	315	42	32	31	108,675
Turkson	1954	H	228	42	49	33	105,477
A Roman Dragon	1967	H	157	42	25	17	101,266
Cross Ring	1948	H	161	42	33	26	83,605
Halterman	1962	H	173	42	22	25	79,760
Phantom Heels	1942	H	206	42	28	23	73,642
Lawless Miss	1943	M	111	42	22	13	67,415
Ormazd	1952	G	118	42	20	8	63,677
Flyfosta	1951	H	178	42	26	20	56,864
Walloon	1941	G	243	42	40	35	56,320
Boss Bennie	1948	G	187	42	32	28	51,530
Free Valley	1943	H	89	42	18	7	37,695
Ready Standard	1947	H	245	42	25	27	35,401
Virden	1950	M	162	42	22	28	34,911
Copin	1937	H	323	42	40	53	27,926
Slaver	1941	G	252	42	47	32	26,357
Glenpool	1935	G	223	42	40	32	25,185
Scotch Dot	1942	M	247	42	41	31	13,332
Armed	1941	G	81	41	20	10	817,475
Lancer's Pride	1974	G	217	41	28	32	294,903
Rose's Gem	1954	H	125	41	34	12	230,964
Victory Beauty	1956	H	184	41	18	28	223,716
Moxeytown	1977	H	116	41	20	19	216,652
Mandingo	1948	G	208	41	29	29	177,662
Flaming Folly	1970	G	207	41	34	24	164,410
Flying Weather	1943	H	226	41	43	31	145,164
Boca Ratony	1988	G	139	41	18	15	133,715
Ariel Beau	1967	H	229	41	34	26	118,183

Horse	Age	Sex	Sts	1st	2d	3d	Won
Gerowa	1963	G	203	41	32	25	112,630
Mighty Master	1939	G	203	41	37	31	111,021
Diamond in the Sky	1968	G	203	41	37	26	110,482
Night Final	1960	H	238	41	32	26	107,537
Scholarship	1942	G	192	41	22	21	104,460
Loons Buster	1968	G	159	41	25	18	97,990
Air Flight	1948	H	261	41	43	44	95,870
Trico	1953	H	198	41	25	25	88,675
Hypostyle	1945	G	225	41	37	20	85,833
Navy Coach	1966	H	129	41	14	8	69,899
Bell's Range	1954	G	274	41	44	39	65,100
Prince Bonanza	1955	H	137	41	27	17	65,026
Prince Ivan	1956	H	164	41	28	23	62,198
Slipton Fell	1960	H	180	41	17	37	60,303
High Nail	1963	H	112	41	13	12	59,700
Mr. Edgor	1956	H	209	41	25	29	58,235
Little Welch	1955	H	220	41	44	32	55,884
Alfios	1940	G	204	41	27	25	54,390
Turntable	1938	G	278	41	33	32	53,920
Fort Garry	1943	G	173	41	27	18	50,052
Plitshon	1960	H	219	41	41	39	49,700
Cosmo Lea	1953	H	204	41	31	23	49,272
Port o' Fogo	1958	H	119	41	23	15	46,688
Heliolater	1952	H	201	41	26	38	43,632
Galafre	1949	H	153	41	31	16	27,246
Jubilo	1936	H	238	41	42	43	26,575
Soldiers Call	1936	G	226	41	37	23	25,370
Last Don B.	1987	G	104	40	31	18	471,461
Creme de La Fete	1976	G	151	40	27	16	460,350
Noble But Nasty	1981	G	200	40	44	27	325,588
Hereford Man	1978	H	165	40	29	21	308,286
Kiss and Run	1968	H	144	40	23	22	295,681
Sawmill Run	1988	G	160	40	30	9	253,744
Best Boy's Jade	1989	G	175	40	14	24	223,983
Navy Admiral	1962	H	194	40	37	34	219,303
Untangle	1970	G	229	40	45	27	179,819
Hi Billee	1948	G	172	40	38	25	160,520
Laran	1944	G	194	40	33	29	138,037
Wild Wink	1969	H	275	40	48	53	129,004
Beau Sock	1969	H	132	40	27	16	124,910
Toeless Tom	1968	G	197	40	32	19	118,243
Dobi Pay	1971	H	136	40	19	24	118,188
Our Holiday	1953	H	204	40	39	30	117,626
Conty Bay	1949	H	188	40	21	28	117,255
First Refusal	1949	H	209	40	36	33	106,720
Full Steam Ahead	1966	H	216	40	36	25	105,568
Seebit	1947	G	123	40	26	13	104,195
Sloop	1959	H	213	40	29	31	93,706
Family Trouble	1965	H	240	40	31	38	90,891
Traveler	1945	H	172	40	31	20	86,925
Dermagh	1957	G	222	40	40	31	79,252
One Only	1939	G	252	40	42	39	78,345
Hi-Sag	1953	H	158	40	23	17	71,752
Ducat	1951	G	205	40	32	17	70,031
Kantar Run	1938	G	265	40	37	39	67,070
Eagle Speed	1946	G	284	40	47	41	66,337
Layaway	1939	G	213	40	41	22	65,742
Andy Johnson	1951	G	160	40	16	16	63,658
Birchwood	1955	G	153	40	19	10	59,046
Austin Venn	1956	G	224	40	27	33	56,444
Crafty Charger	1966	G	163	40	15	21	50,074
Herby B. Good	1964	H	151	40	20	26	49,000
Naomi	1950	M	231	40	33	31	47,015
Miss Boston	1947	M	148	40	22	20	44,990
Firey Isle	1951	H	149	40	37	21	43,872
Bow to You	1945	H	108	40	14	14	42,080
Deep Current	1954	H	164	40	29	19	41,690
Mister Buckle	1957	G	160	40	24	21	36,170
Victory Play	1940	M	192	40	30	22	34,715
Copper Buster	1950	G	179	40	31	31	32,294
Salesman	1957	H	141	40	17	13	31,798
Khayyam's Kid	1942	G	212	40	35	30	26,755
Whirling Dust	1947	H	196	40	25	25	21,320

Top Beyer Speed Figures

By Andrew Beyer

As he compiled a perfect record in four starts during 2004, Ghostzapper did more than earn an Eclipse Award as the Horse of the Year. He established himself as the fastest American Thoroughbred in many, many years.

When the Bobby Frankel-trained colt captured the Iselin Handicap at Monmouth Park, he earned a Beyer Speed Figure of 128—the highest number recorded since these ratings were incorporated into Daily Racing Form's past performances in 1992.

At the time, some skeptics questioned the accuracy of the figure. Ghostzapper had not yet established himself as a major star in the sport, and he had accomplished the feat over a sloppy track in a four-horse field.

While the team that creates the Beyer Speed Figures sometimes harbors its own doubts about big figures earned under unusual circumstances, we had no doubts about the accuracy of that lofty number. Ghostzapper's main rival at Monmouth was the mud-loving Presidentialaffair, who had won his previous two starts with figures of 110 and 112. In the Iselin, Presidentialaffair ran his usual strong race, earning a figure of 110, and to overpower him by more than 10 lengths Ghostzapper had to run a 128. The figure made sense, and it surpassed the 126s earned by a trio of stakes stars in 1997: Formal Gold, Will's Way and Gentlemen.

Ultimately it was Ghostzapper himself who verified the legitimacy of his historic speed figure. When he completed his season by leading all the way to win the Breeders' Cup Classic at Lone Star Park, he earned another spectacular number, a 124, surpassing every Breeders' Cup performance since 1992. (He equaled Sunday Silence's 124 in the 1989 Classic, before the Beyer Speed Figures had been introduced in the DRF.)

Ghostzapper accomplished another extraordinary achievement in 2004 as well. He started his 4-year-old campaign by winning the seven-furlong Tom Fool Handicap at Belmont and earned a figure of 120 with his victory. He is the only horse to have led both the lists of the fastest sprinters and the fastest distance runners.

At the end of the 2004 racing year, there was considerable debate about whether Ghostzapper or Smarty Jones deserved the sport's top honor. Smarty Jones' pursuit of the Triple Crown had certainly been the most compelling story of the year, and Smarty Jones' runaway victory in the Preakness was one of the most impressive by any 3-year-old in recent years. But from the standpoint of sheer speed, there was no comparison between the two. While Ghostzapper had earned figures of 120 or more in three of his four races, Smarty Jones topped 110 only once—with his 118 at Pimlico. There seems little doubt that Smarty Jones would have run faster races if his career had lasted longer, but it is questionable if he could have been a match for the horse who earned the best Beyer Speed Figure since 1992.

When the Beyer Speed Figures were incorporated into Daily Racing Form past performances, their principal purpose was to aid bettors in everyday handicapping by answering the question, "Who is faster than whom?" But by providing an objective measurement of horses' ability, the numbers also made possible the comparison of horses from different generations. (American breeders recognize the importance of such a measurement; advertisements for stallions now regularly cite the top Beyer Speed Figures that a racehorse has earned.)

From 1992 to 2003, the top performer in American racing, from the standpoint of figures, was a horse who never earned a single championship or the acclaim he deserved. In 1997, as a 4-year-old, Formal Gold recorded Beyer Speed Figures of 126, 124 and 125—three of the eight highest numbers earned between 1992 and 2003. The fastest sprinter during this period was Artax; although he was an in-and-outer for much of his career, he recorded figures of 124, 123 and 123 in his championship season of 1997. But since the publication of the Beyer Speed Figures, no horse can match the combination of speed, versatility and consistency that Ghostzapper displayed in 2004.

2-year-olds, 1996

Beyer No.	Horse	Track	Date
108	THISNEARLYWASMINE	SA	10/23/1996
107	KELLY KIP	SAR	07/26/1996
106	IN EXCESSIVE BULL	SA	10/23/1996
104	KELLY KIP	BEL	06/ 21/1996
104	HOLZMEISTER	HAW	11/ 17/1996
103	IN C C'S HONOR	LRL	12/ 21/1996
102	DIXIE FLAG (F)	AQU	11/ 24/1996
101	GOLD CASE	FG	12/ 30/1996
101	IN EXCESSIVE BULL	SA	10/05/1996
101	MUD ROUTE	HOL	02/15/1996
101	IN EXCESSIVE BULL	HOL	11/10/1996
101	ORDWAY	BEL	10/05/1996
101	CAPTAIN BODGIT	LRL	11/02/1996

Several of the highest figures of the year belonged to In Excessive Bull and Kelly Kip, neither of which took part in the Juvenile, won by divisional champion Boston Harbor. Boston Harbor's lone defeat of 1996 came in the Sanford, won by Kelly Kip.

2-year-olds, 1997

Beyer No.	Horse	Track	Date
108	ORVILLE N WILBUR'S	HOL	11/07/1997
108	ORVILLE N WILBUR'S	HOL	12/11/1997
105	CORONADO'S QUEST	AQU	10/26/1997
103	RODEO	BEL	09/07/1997
102	GRAND SLAM	BEL	10/18/1997
102	REAL QUIET	HOL	12/14/1997
101	LIQUID GOLD	SA	12/28/1997
101	LIL'S LAD	BEL	10/18/1997
101	FAVORITE TRICK	HOL	11/08/1997
100	STAR OF BROADWAY	CD	11/28/1997
100	BOURBON BELLE (F)	KEE	10/08/1997
100	UNREAL MADNESS	MED	12/05/1997
100	BOURBON BELLE (F)	TP	12/06/1997
100	ALLEN'S OOP	HOL	11/15/1997
100	SOUVENIR COPY	SA	10/19/1997
100	ARTAX	HOL	12/14/1997
100	FAVORITE TRICK	KEE	10/18/1997

Favorite Trick was the unbeaten 2-year-old champion and 1997 Horse of the Year..

2-year-olds, 1998

Beyer No.	Horse	Track	Date
107	OLYMPIC CHARMER (F)	SA	12/28/1998
105	BET ME BEST	FG	12/12/1998
104	LONG DISTANCE (F)	AQU	11/15/1998
104	SILVERBULLETDAY (F)	CD	11/28/1998
103	SHAMROCK'S PICK	BEL	10/10/1998
103	BET ME BEST	LAD	11/07/1998
102	ARRESTED DREAMS (F)	FG	11/29/1998
102	SWEEP BACK	HOL	12/12/1998
101	LOVESME LEGEND (F)	PRM	09/06/1998
101	INCURABLE OPTIMIST	HOL	11/28/1998
101	SILVERBULLETDAY (F)	CD	11/07/1998
101	EXPLOIT	CD	11/28/1998
101	EXCELLENT MEETING (F)	HOL	12/13/1998

Silverbulletday won the Breeders' Cup Juvenile Fillies and was champion 2-year-old filly as well as the 3-year-old filly champion in 1999. Answer Lively, who doesn't appear on this list, won the Breeders' Cup Juvenile and was champion 2-year-old in 1998.

2-year-olds, 1999

Beyer No.	Horse	Track	Date
110	HOOK AND LADDER	HOL	11/28/1999
109	CHILUKKI (F)	CD	04/28/1999
106	FOREST CAMP	DMR	09/08/1999
105	MORE THAN READY	BEL	07/04/1999
105	MORE THAN READY	SAR	07/29/1999
105	CAPTAIN STEVE	CD	11/27/1999
104	PERSONAL FIRST	TP	12/26/1999
104	DIXIE UNION	SA	10/10/1999
103	LITTLEEXPECTATIONS	FG	11/27/1999
103	JOOPY DOOPY	SA	10/22/1999
103	FOREST CAMP	SA	10/10/1999

More Than Ready, the only 2-year-old with two top-rated figures on this list, won his first five starts but lost the Futurity and Champagne and skipped the Breeders' Cup Juvenile, won by divisional champion Anees. Chilukki, the champion 2-year-old filly, won several graded stakes before finishing second to Cash Run in the Breeders' Cup Juvenile Fillies.

2-year-olds, 2000

Beyer No.	Horse	Track	Date
105	FLAME THROWER	SA	10/07/2000
105	STREET CRY	SA	10/07/2000
104	PROUD TOWER	SA	12/30/2000
103	FLAME THROWER	DMR	09/13/2000
103	STREET CRY	DMR	09/13/2000
101	RAGING FEVER (F)	SAR	08/14/2000
101	UNBRIDLED ELAINE (F)	CD	11/03/2000
101	POINT GIVEN	HOL	12/16/2000
101	PROUD TOWER	SA	10/28/2000
100	LASERSPORT	TP	12/09/2000
100	SILK CONCORDE (F)	CRC	08/26/2000
100	I'MADRIFTER	GG	12/26/2000

Flame Thrower was undefeated until a disappointing showing in the Breeders' Cup Juvenile, won by divisional champion Macho Uno by a nose over Point Given. Likewise, Raging Fever was undefeated until a similarly poor performance behind Caressing in the Juvenile Fillies.

2-year-olds, 2001

Beyer No.	Horse	Track	Date
108	CAME HOME	SAR	09/01/2001
107	ROMAN DANCER	SA	10/20/2001
107	WERBLIN	SA	12/26/2001
107	YOU (F)	SAR	08/13/2001
107	TEMPERA (F)	BEL	10/27/2001
106	CASHEL CASTLE	HOO	11/24/2001
106	OFFICER	DMR	08/15/2001
106	CASHIER'S DREAM (F)	SAR	08/13/2001
105	FOREST HEIRESS (F)	AQU	11/18/2001
105	CAME HOME	HOL	07/15/2001

Tempera, the eventual 2-year-old filly champ, earned the highest route figure with a 107 in the Breeders' Cup Juvenile Fillies, eight points higher than Johannesburg's performance in the Juvenile.

2-year-olds, 2002

Beyer No.	Horse	Track	Date
110	TRUST N LUCK	CRC	12/14/2002
105	D'S BERTRANDO	GG	11/09/2002
104	RANDAROO (F)	AQU	11/24/2002
103	LADY TAK (F)	CD	11/29/2002
103	SCRIMSHAW	SA	12/26/2002
103	ZAYED	SA	12/26/2002
103	POINT CLEAR (F)	SA	12/28/2002
103	FUNNY CIDE	BEL	09/29/2002
103	SKY MESA	KEE	08/31/2002
102	ZAVATA	BEL	06/29/2002
102	SIBERLAND	DMR	08/18/2002
102	WHYWHYWHY	BEL	09/15/2002

Trust N Luck's victory in the What a Pleasure at Calder was one of the top Beyer Figures on record for a 2-year-old. Sky Mesa was a fast juvenile, but was forced to scratch from the Breeders' Cup because of injury.

2-year-olds, 2003

Beyer No.	Horse	Track	Date
105	FOREST MUSIC (F)	LRL	10/08/2003
105	SMARTY JONES	PHA	11/22/2003
105	READ THE FOOTNOTES	AQU	11/29/2003
105	SILENT SIGHS (F)	SA	12/27/2003
103	CUVEE	SAR	08/13/2003
103	LION HEART	HOL	11/15/2003
103	JUDITHS WILD RUSH	WO	11/15/2003
103	WILDCAT SHOES	FG	12/28/2003
102	RULER'S COURT	SA	10/05/2003
101	CACTUS RIDGE	CBY	07/12/2003
101	CUVEE	BEL	09/14/2003
101	THE CLIFF'S EDGE	CD	11/2/2003

Cuvee won four of six starts but finished last in the Breeders' Cup Juvenile as the favorite. Many top 2-year-olds bypassed the Breeders' Cup, including Read the Footnotes, Lion Heart and Ruler's Court.

2-year-olds, 2004

Beyer No.	Horse	Track	Date
109	LOST IN THE FOG	TUP	12/26/2004
107	DECLAN'S MOON	DMR	09/08/2004
106	ROMAN RULER	DMR	09/08/2004
103	DEVILS DISCIPLE	CRC	07/25/2004
103	ROMAN RULER	DMR	08/15/2004
102	DILIGENT PROSPECT	HOL	05/30/2004
102	AFLEET ALEX	SAR	07/29/2004
102	SWEET CATOMINE (F)	LS	10/30/2004
102	LOST IN THE FOG	GG	11/14/2004
102	ROCKPORT HARBOR	AQU	11/27/2004
102	GALLOPING GROCER	AQU	11/27/2004
102	GOING WILD	SA	12/26/2004

Neither Lost in the Fog nor divisional champion Declan's Moon took part in the Breeders' Cup Juvenile. Roman Ruler, favored in the Juvenile, was unplaced in the event. Champion filly Sweet Catomine won the Juvenile Fillies in faster time than the Juvenile.

2-year-olds, 1996-2004

Beyer No.	Horse	Track	Date
110	TRUST N LUCK	CRC	12/14/2002
110	HOOK AND LADDER	HOL	11/28/1999
109	LOST IN THE FOG	TUP	12/26/2004
109	CHILUKKI (F)	CD	04/28/1999
108	ORVILLE N WILBUR'S	HOL	11/07/1997
108	ORVILLE N WILBUR'S	HOL	12/11/1997
108	THISNEARLYWASMINE	SA	10/23/1996
108	CAME HOME	SAR	09/01/2001
107	DECLAN'S MOON	DMR	09/08/2004
107	ROMAN DANCER	SA	10/20/2001
107	WERBLIN	SA	12/26/2001
107	YOU (F)	SAR	08/13/2001
107	TEMPERA (F)	BEL	10/27/2001
107	KELLY KIP	SAR	07/26/1996
107	OLYMPIC CHARMER (F)	SA	12/28/1998
106	ROMAN RULER	DMR	09/08/2004
106	FOREST CAMP	DMR	09/08/1999
106	CASHEL CASTLE	HOO	11/24/2001
106	OFFICER	DMR	08/15/2001
106	CASHIER'S DREAM (F)	SAR	08/13/2001

3-year-olds, 1996

Beyer No.	Horse	Track	Date
119	LOUIS QUATORZE	SAR	08/04/1996
119	WILL'S WAY	SAR	08/04/1996
118	HONOUR AND GLORY	SAR	08/08/1996
115	SKIP AWAY	BEL	10/05/1996
115	LOUIS QUATORZE	WO	10/26/1996
114	CAPOTE BELLE (F)	BEL	06/23/1996
114	UNBRIDLED'S SONG	GP	03/16/1996
114	DEVIL'S HONOR	PHA	09/02/1996
114	WILL'S WAY	SAR	08/24/1996
113	ELUSIVE QUALITY	SAR	08/24/1996
113	HONOUR AND GLORY	SAR	08/24/1996
113	VALID ROMEO	CRC	09/28/1996
113	SKIP AWAY	KEE	04/13/1996
113	SKIP AWAY	MTH	08/04/1996
113	FORMAL GOLD	PHA	09/02/1996
113	LOUIS QUATORZE	SAR	08/24/1996

Skip Away, winner of several Grade-1 stakes, was voted top 3 year old despite not winning a Triple Crown event. Louis Quatorze won the Preakness, while Will's Way beat both in winning the Travers.

3-year-olds, 1997

Beyer No.	Horse	Track	Date
120	KELLY KIP	SAR	08/23/1997
118	BEHRENS	MED	09/20/1997
118	CAPTAIN BODGIT	PIM	05/17/1997
118	FREE HOUSE	PIM	05/17/1997
118	SILVER CHARM	PIM	05/17/1997
117	SMOKE GLACKEN	MTH	06/28/1997
116	TOUCH GOLD	PIM	05/17/1997
115	FREE HOUSE	HOL	07/20/1997
115	CAPTAIN BODGIT	CD	05/03/1997
115	SILVER CHARM	CD	05/03/1997

Silver Charm won the Kentucky Derby and Preakness and was second to Touch Gold in the Belmont Stakes. Captain Bodgit was second in the Derby and third behind Silver Charm and Free House in the Preakness. Silver Charm was voted champion 3-year-old. Smoke Glacken, champion sprinter.

3-year-olds, 1998

Beyer No.	Horse	Track	Date
121	ROCK AND ROLL	BEL	06/13/1998
119	RERAISE	TP	09/26/1998
116	LIMIT OUT	AQU	04/11/1998
116	CORONADO'S QUEST	AQU	04/11/1998
116	OLD TRIESTE	HOL	07/19/1998
116	RERAISE	HOL	07/04/1998
115	BANSHEE BREEZE (F)	KEE	10/17/1998
114	GOOD AND TOUGH	BEL	06/14/1998
114	DICE DANCER	AQU	05/02/1998
114	EVENT OF THE YEAR	TP	03/29/1998
114	VICTORY GALLOP	CD	11/07/1998

Reraise, the only 3-year-old of 1998 to have two top-rated figures on this list, won the Breeders' Cup Sprint and was the champion sprinter. Victory Gallop won the Belmont Stakes over Derby-Preakness winner Real Quiet, who was voted champion 3-year-old colt; Banshee Breeze was voted champion 3-year-old filly.

3-year-olds, 1999

Beyer No.	Horse	Track	Date
119	SUCCESSFUL APPEAL	TP	09/25/1999
119	GENERAL CHALLENGE	DMR	08/29/1999
118	YES IT'S TRUE	PIM	05/15/1999
118	GENERAL CHALLENGE	SA	10/16/1999
118	CAT THIEF	GP	11/06/1999
117	ECTON PARK	LAD	10/02/1999
116	FORESTRY	SAR	08/28/1999
115	TEXAS GLITTER	GP	01/03/1999
115	SILVERBULLETDAY (F)	SAR	08/21/1999
114	FORESTRY	GP	11/06/1999
114	SUCCESSFUL APPEAL	GP	11/06/1999
114	LOVE THAT RED	SA	10/30/1999
114	HIDDEN CITY	SAR	08/01/1999
114	DAVID	AQU	12/18/1999
114	STEPHEN GOT EVEN	BEL	09/18/1999
114	MENIFEE	LAD	10/02/1999

Silverbulletday, a champion at 2, repeated as a champion at 3. Not appearing on this list is Charismatic, voted Horse of the Year, who won the Kentucky Derby and Preakness and was third in the Belmont while injured. Lemon Drop Kid won the Belmont and the Travers. Cat Thief won the Breeders' Cup Classic.

3-Year-Olds, 2000

Beyer No.	Horse	Track	Date
121	CONCERNED MINISTER	FG	12/03/2000
119	TIZNOW	SA	10/15/2000
119	ALBERT THE GREAT	BEL	10/14/2000
118	CAPTAIN STEVE	SA	10/15/2000
117	CALLER ONE	TP	09/16/2000
116	CALLER ONE	CRC	07/15/2000
116	CALLER ONE	HOL	05/29/2000
116	SURFSIDE (F)	CD	11/24/2000
116	CAPTAIN STEVE	TP	09/16/2000
116	TIZNOW	CD	11/04/2000
116	GIANT'S CAUSEWAY	CD	11/04/2000

Tiznow, 2000 Horse of the Year, scored his top figure in the Goodwood Handicap against older horses, then followed up with a victory in the Breeders' Cup Classic. Caller One was the top 3-year-old sprinter, with his best race coming in the Kentucky Cup Sprint.

3-Year-Olds, 2001

Beyer No.	Horse	Track	Date
120	XTRA HEAT (F)	DEL	09/29/2001
119	SQUIRTLE SQUIRT	BEL	10/27/2001
118	XTRA HEAT (F)	BEL	10/27/2001
117	XTRA HEAT (F)	DEL	09/08/2001
117	SQUIRTLE SQUIRT	BEL	09/22/2001
117	POINT GIVEN	SAR	08/25/2001
116	MONARCHOS	CD	05/05/2001
116	MILAN	BEL	10/27/2001
114	HE'S A KNOCKOUT	LRL	11/22/2001
114	BURNING ROMA	DEL	06/172001
114	MILLENNIUM WIND	KEE	04/14/2001
114	POINT GIVEN	BEL	06/09/2001

Xtra Heat, a sprinting filly, turned in several of the top performances in the division. Her runner-up effort in the Breeders' Cup Sprint, in which she set a heavily pressured pace before succumbing to eventual sprint champion Squirtle Squirt, enabled her to win the 3-year-old filly title.

3-Year-Olds, 2002

Beyer No.	Horse	Track	Date
120	MEDAGLIA D'ORO	SAR	08/04/2002
116	CAME HOME	DMR	08/25/2002
114	WAR EMBLEM	CD	05/04/2002
113	THUNDERELLO	AP	10/26/2002
113	GYGISTAR	SAR	08/24/2002
113	MEDAGLIA D'ORO	SAR	08/24/2002
112	MIGHTY DAVID	HOL	06/10/2002
112	SAINT MARDEN	BEL	09/19/2002
112	IMPERIAL GESTURE (F)	BEL	09/07/2002
112	WAR EMBLEM	SPT	04/06/2002
112	WAR EMBLEM	MTH	08/04/2002
112	REPENT	SAR	08/24/2002

Medaglia d'Oro posted two of the fastest figures of the year in the Jim Dandy (120) and Travers (113) at Saratoga. War Emblem, who was named champion, won the Kentucky Derby off the highest-rated prep race, the Illinois Derby, in which he earned a 112 Beyer.

3-Year-Olds, 2003

Beyer No.	Horse	Track	Date
120	CAJUN BEAT	SA	10/25/2003
116	GHOSTZAPPER	BEL	09/27/2003
116	DYNEVER	SA	10/25/2003
115	KAFWAIN	SA	02/01/2003
114	FUNNY CIDE	PIM	05/17/2003
114	SOTO	MNR	08/09/2003
114	DYNEVER	MNR	08/09/2003
113	QAIS	SAR	08/30/2003
113	CAJUN BEAT	TP	09/13/2003
112	ZAVATA	SAR	08/02/2003
112	TEN MOST WANTED	SAR	08/23/2003

Champion Funny Cide's Preakness ranks among the fastest 3-year-old performances of 2003, but Breeders' Cup third Dynever is the only routing 3-year-old with two top-rated performances. Breeders' Cup Sprint winner Cajun Beat ranked among the best sprinters in the nation.

3-Year-Olds, 2004

Beyer No.	Horse	Track	Date
118	SMARTY JONES	PIM	05/15/2004
115	MASS MEDIA	AQU	10/31/2004
114	KITTEN'S JOY	BEL	10/02/2004
113	READ THE FOOTNOTES	GP	02/14/2004
113	SECOND OFJUNE	GP	02/14/2004
113	KITTEN'S JOY	AP	08/14/2004
113	TRICKY DEVIL	KEE	10/08/2004
113	MEDALLIST	CRC	12/18/2004
112	MEDALLIST	BEL	07/11/2004
112	LOVE OF MONEY	PHA	09/06/2004
112	COMMENTATOR	CD	11/25/2004

Champion Smarty Jones' Preakness was the fastest 3-year-old performance of 2004, but turf champion Kitten's Joy, along with Medallist, had two top-rated performances.

3-year-olds, 1996-2004

Beyer No.	Horse	Track	Date
121	CONCERNED MINISTER	FG	12/03/2000
121	ROCK AND ROLL	BEL	06/13/1998
120	CAJUN BEAT	SA	10/25/2003
120	MEDAGLIA D'ORO	SAR	08/04/2002
120	XTRA HEAT (F)	DEL	09/29/2001
120	KELLY KIP	SAR	08/23/1997
119	TIZNOW	SA	10/15/2000
119	ALBERT THE GREAT	BEL	10/14/2000
119	SUCCESSFUL APPEAL	TP	09/25/1999
119	RERAISE	TP	09/26/1998
119	GENERAL CHALLENGE	DMR	08/29/1999
118	SMARTY JONES	PIM	05/15/2004
118	XTRA HEAT (F)	BEL	10/27/2001
118	CAPTAIN STEVE	SA	10/15/2000
118	YES IT'S TRUE	PIM	05/15/1999
118	GENERAL CHALLENGE	SA	10/16/1999
118	BEHRENS	MED	09/20/1997
118	CAPTAIN BODGIT	PIM	05/17/1997
118	FREE HOUSE	PIM	05/17/1997
118	SILVER CHARM	PIM	05/17/1997

Sprints, 1996

Beyer No.	Horse	Track	Date
123	PROSPECT BAY	SAR	08/08/1996
118	HONOUR AND GLORY	SAR	08/08/1996
118	MEADOW MONSTER	LRL	02/19/1996
117	MEADOW MONSTER	GP	01/03/1996
117	LITE THE FUSE	LRL	07/20/1996
117	MEADOW MONSTER	LRL	07/20/1996
117	FOREST WILDCAT	PIM	09/15/1996
116	SPLENDID SPRINTER	AQU	01/06/1996
116	LITE THE FUSE	AQU	04/14/1996
116	ABAGINONE	SA	04/06/1996
116	CONSTANT ESCORT	CRC	09/28/1996
116	SMART STRIKE	WO	07/07/1996

Meadow Monster had several of the fastest figures among sprinters and Prospect Bay turned in the division's highest-rated performance of the year in winning the A Phenomenon, but neither took part in the Breeders' Cup Sprint, won by divisional champion Lit de Justice.

Sprint, 1997

Beyer No.	Horse	Track	Date
122	ELUSIVE QUALITY	GP	02/21/1997
120	KELLY KIP	SAR	08/23/1997
118	DISTORTED HUMOR	CD	06/04/1997
118	WILD ESCAPADE	CD	06/04/1997
118	UNBRIDLED'S SONG	GP	01/19/1997
117	MEN'S EXCLUSIVE	HOL	05/26/1997
117	SMOKE GLACKEN	MTH	06/28/1997
116	BUNKER HILL ROAD	OP	01/24/1997
115	APPEALING SKIER	GP	03/16/1997
115	PUNCH LINE	GP	03/16/1997

Elmhurst, who did not make this list, won the Breeders' Cup Sprint. Smoke Glacken was voted Eclipse Award Champion.

Sprints, 1998

Beyer No.	Horse	Track	Date
123	ELUSIVE QUALITY	GP	02/05/1998
121	KELLY KIP	AQU	04/11/1998
120	AFFIRMED SUCCESS	SAR	09/07/1998
119	KELLY KIP	LRL	07/18/1998
119	RERAISE	TP	09/26/1998
119	AFFIRMED SUCCESS	BEL	09/26/1998
118	SON OF A PISTOL	DMR	07/26/1998
118	WAGON LIMIT	AQU	04/04/1998
118	WILD RUSH	BEL	05/25/1998
117	DISTORTED HUMOR	CD	05/02/1998
117	ORIGINAL GRAY	LRL	03/04/1998

Reraise won the Breeders' Cup Sprint and was voted champion sprinter.

Sprints, 1999

Beyer No.	Horse	Track	Date
124	ARTAX	GP	11/06/1999
123	ARTAX	BEL	10/16/1999
123	KONA GOLD	GP	11/06/1999
123	ARTAX	AQU	05/02/1999
121	LEXICON	DMR	08/08/1999
120	KELLY KIP	AQU	04/10/1999
120	LEXICON	SA	10/17/1999
120	INTIDAB	SAR	08/11/1999
119	SUCCESSFUL APPEAL	TP	09/25/1999
118	YES IT'S TRUE	PIM	05/15/1999
118	MAZEL TRICK	HOL	06/27/1999

Sprint champion Artax broke Dr. Fager's track record for 7 furlongs at Aqueduct in May, Groovy's 6-furlong track record at Belmont Park in October and equaled Mr. Prospector's track record for six furlongs while winning the Breeders' Cup Sprint at Gulfstream Park in November.

Sprints, 2000

Beyer No.	Horse	Track	Date
119	KONA GOLD	SA	04/08/2000
118	KONA GOLD	DMR	07/29/2000
117	KONA GOLD	SA	10/14/2000
117	CALLER ONE	TP	09/16/2000
116	CALLER ONE	CRC	07/15/2000
116	LOVE THAT RED	DMR	07/29/2000
116	FIVE STAR DAY	KEE	10/14/2000
116	DELAWARE TOWNSHIP	MTH	08/27/2000
116	CALLER ONE	HOL	05/29/2000
116	CROWNING MEETING	EMD	09/10/2000

Kona Gold dominated the sprint ranks in 2000 winning all but one start. He set a track and stakes record in winning the Breeders' Cup Sprint at Churchill Downs.

Sprints, 2001

Beyer No.	Horse	Track	Date
121	SWEPT OVERBOARD	SA	10/06/2001
120	XTRA HEAT (F)	DEL	09/29/2001
119	SQUIRTLE SQUIRT	BEL	10/27/2001
119	KONA GOLD	DMR	07/22/2001
119	BONAPAW	OP	04/12/2001
119	EL CORREDOR	DMR	08/12/2001
118	XTRA HEAT (F)	BEL	10/27/2001
118	EXPLICIT	GP	03/12/2001
118	LEFT BANK	BEL	09/22/2001
118	LEFT BANK	AQU	11/24/2001

Squirtle Squirt defeated top 3-year-olds in the King's Bishop and ran second to top Grade 1 older horses in the Vosburgh before clinching the sprint title with a half-length victory over Xtra Heat in the Breeders' Cup Sprint.

Sprints, 2002

Beyer No.	Horse	Track	Date
122	SWEPT OVERBOARD	BEL	05/27/2002
121	LEFT BANK	BEL	07/04/2002
120	SLIDER	KEE	04/20/2002
120	CONGAREE	AQU	11/30/2002
117	SNOW RIDGE	SA	01/27/2002
116	BONAPAW	FG	01/12/2002
116	MOUNTAIN GENERAL	FG	11/28/2002
116	ORIENTATE	SAR	09/01/2002
115	ORIENTATE	CRC	07/15/2002
115	ORIENTATE	CD	06/29/2002
115	THERE'S ZEALOUS	AP	08/17/2002
115	REBA'S GOLD	SA	02/09/2002

Orientate came on late to dominate the division, but Swept Overboard, in the Metropolitan Mile, and Left Bank, in the Tom Fool, posted the biggest numbers of the year.

Sprints, 2003

Beyer No.	Horse	Track	Date
122	ALDEBARAN	SAR	08/31/2003
121	SHAKE YOU DOWN	CRC	07/12/2003
120	CAJUN BEAT	SA	10/25/2003
120	CONGAREE	AQU	11/29/2003
118	SHAKE YOU DOWN	AQU	04/11/2003
118	SHAKE YOU DOWN	AQU	04/26/2003
117	CAPTAIN SQUIRE	SA	01/25/2003
117	AVANZADO	SA	01/26/2003
117	SMOOTH JAZZ	KEE	04/13/2003
117	PRIVATE HORDE	SAR	08/10/2003
117	YANKEE GENTLEMAN	DMR	09/06/2003

Shake You Down , third in the Breeders' Cup Sprint, owned the three of the highest figures, but divisional champion Aldebaran rated highest of all with his Forego Handicap victory. Versatile Congaree had high figures at both short and long distances.

Sprints, 2004

Beyer No.	Horse	Track	Date
120	GHOSTZAPPER	BEL	07/04/2004
117	SPEIGHTSTOWN	SAR	08/14/2004
116	PICO CENTRAL	AQU	04/10/2004
116	SPEIGHTSTOWN	CD	05/01/2004
116	PICO CENTRAL	BEL	05/31/2004
116	KELA	DMR	08/15/2004
115	BOWMAN'S BAND	BEL	05/31/2004
115	SPEIGHTSTOWN	BEL	06/05/2004
115	MASS MEDIA	AQU	10/31/2004

Breeders' Cup Sprint winner and divisional champion Speightstown had three top-rated performances in 2004, but the highest sprint figure awarded in 2004 ironically went to subsequent Breeders' Cup Classic winner and Horse of the Year Ghostzapper. Pico Central beat Speightstown in their only meeting.

Sprints, 1992-2004

Beyer No.	Horse	Track	Date
124	ARTAX	GP	11/06/1999
123	ARTAX	BEL	10/16/1999
123	KONA GOLD	GP	11/06/1999
123	PROSPECT BAY	SAR	08/08/1996
123	ARTAX	AQU	05/02/1999
123	ELUSIVE QUALITY	GP	02/05/1998
122	ALDEBARAN	SAR	08/31/2003
122	SWEPT OVERBOARD	BEL	05/27/2002
122	ELUSIVE QUALITY	GP	02/21/1997
122	HOLY BULL	BEL	05/30/1994
121	SHAKE YOU DOWN	CRC	07/12/2003
121	LEFT BANK	BEL	07/04/2002
121	LEXICON	DMR	08/08/1999
121	KELLY KIP	AQU	04/11/1998
121	IMTOOCOOL	PIM	05/05/1995
121	SWEPT OVERBOARD	SA	10/06/2001
120	GHOSTZAPPER	BEL	07/04/2004
120	CAJUN BEAT	SA	10/25/2003
120	CONGAREE	AQU	11/29/2003
120	KELLY KIP	AQU	04/10/1999
120	XTRA HEAT (F)	DEL	09/29/2001
120	LEXICON	SA	10/17/1999
120	INTIDAB	SAR	08/11/1999
120	LUCKY FOREVER	HOL	05/20/1995
120	KELLY KIP	SAR	08/23/1997
120	NOT SURPRISING	SAR	08/23/1995
120	AFFIRMED SUCCESS	SAR	09/07/1998

Races More Than 1 Mile, 1996

Beyer No.	Horse	Track	Date
120	KIRIDASHI	WO	08/17/1996
119	LOUIS QUATORZE	SAR	08/04/1996
119	WILL'S WAY	SAR	08/04/1996
118	GENTLEMEN	HOL	12/22/1996
117	CIGAR	AP	07/13/1996
117	CIGAR	GP	02/10/1996
117	SIPHON	HOL	06/30/1996
116	SIPHON	HOL	05/04/1996
116	CIGAR	BEL	09/14/1996
116	JEWEL PRINCESS (F)	HOL	07/21/1996
116	GERI	OP	04/06/1996
116	DARE AND GO	DMR	08/10/1996
116	GERI	HOL	6/30/1996
116	L'CARRIERE	SAR	08/25/1996

Cigar's 16-race winning streak that began in 1994 ended when he was defeated by Dare and Go in the 1996 Pacific Classic, at Del Mar, August 25. Cigar was voted Horse of the Year for the 2nd consecutive season.

Races More Than 1 Mile, 1997

Beyer No.	Horse	Track	Date
126	FORMAL GOLD	SAR	08/02/1997
126	WILL'S WAY	SAR	08/02/1997
126	GENTLEMEN	PIM	05/10/1997
125	FORMAL GOLD	BEL	09/20/1997
125	SKIP AWAY	PIM	05/10/1997
124	FORMAL GOLD	MTH	08/23/1997
123	TEJANO RUN	HIA	03/22/1997
122	FORMAL GOLD	SUF	05/31/1997
122	SKIP AWAY	SUF	05/31/1997
121	ORMSBY	AQU	04/26/1997
121	GENTLEMEN	DMR	08/09/1997
121	GENTLEMEN	HOL	06/29/1997

Many of the highest Beyer Figures since 1992 were scored by the top routers on this list. Skip Away won the Breeders' Cup Classic and was champion older horse.

Races More Than 1 Mile, 1998

Beyer No.	Horse	Track	Date
123	SILVER CHARM	TP	09/26/1998
123	WILD RUSH	TP	09/26/1998
121	ROCK AND ROLL	BEL	06/13/1998
121	SKIP AWAY	SUF	05/30/1998
119	SKIP AWAY	BEL	09/19/1998
119	SHARP CAT (F)	BEL	10/10/1998
119	MOSSFLOWER (F)	BEL	06/20/1998
118	AWESOME AGAIN	CD	06/13/1998
118	SKIP AWAY	PIM	05/09/1998
117	FREE HOUSE	DMR	08/15/1998
117	SKIP AWAY	HOL	06/28/1998

Awesome Again won the Breeders' Cup Classic, but Skip Away was voted Horse of the Year for several excellent performances.

Races More Than 1 Mile, 1999

Beyer No.	Horse	Track	Date
119	GENERAL CHALLENGE	DMR	08/29/1999
119	FREE HOUSE	SA	03/06/1999
118	MAZEL TRICK	DMR	08/07/1999
118	RUNNING STAG	BEL	06/12/1999
118	VICTORY GALLOP	CD	06/12/1999
118	OLD TRIESTE	HOL	05/29/1999
118	BUDROYALE	SA	10/16/1999
118	GENERAL CHALLENGE	SA	10/16/1999
118	CAT THIEF	GP	11/06/1999
118	EVENT OF THE YEAR	SA	03/06/1999
118	SILVER CHARM	SA	03/06/1999

Victory Gallop, who didn't take part in the Breeders' Cup Classic, was elected champion of this evenly matched division.

Races More Than 1 Mile, 2000

Beyer No.	Horse	Track	Date
122	SKY JACK	SA	12/03/2000
121	CONCERNED MINISTER	FG	12/03/2000
120	STEPHEN GOT EVEN	GP	02/05/2000
119	GOLDEN MISSILE	GP	02/05/2000
119	TIZNOW	SA	10/15/2000
119	ALBERT THE GREAT	BEL	10/14/2000
118	CAPTAIN STEVE	SA	10/15/2000
118	LEMON DROP KID	SAR	08/06/2000
118	SKIMMING	DMR	08/26/2000
117	FORTY ONE CARATS	CRC	07/09/2000
117	RUNNING STAG	SUF	06/03/2000
117	GENERAL CHALLENGE	SA	03/04/2000

Sky Jack and Concerned Minister individually came up big in relatively obscure races to score the two highest Beyer Figures of the season. Stephen Got Even rated a 120 in the Donn Handicap, but subsequently was injured and retired.

Races More Than 1 Mile, 2001

Beyer No.	Horse	Track	Date
123	APTITUDE	BEL	10/06/2001
119	ALBERT THE GREAT	BEL	07/01/2001
119	SKIMMING	DMR	08/19/2001
118	EUCHRE	PRM	07/07/2001
117	GUIDED TOUR	CD	06/16/2001
117	INCLUDE	SUF	06/02/2001
117	ALBERT THE GREAT	PIM	05/12/2001
117	INCLUDE	PIM	05/12/2001
117	GUIDED TOUR	AP	07/21/2001
117	TIZNOW	BEL	10/27/2001
117	SAKHEE	BEL	10/27/2001
117	TIZNOW	SA	03/03/2001
117	POINT GIVEN	SAR	08/25/2001

Tiznow won his second straight Breeders' Cup Classic, defeating Arc winner Sakhee in a courageous performance. Aptitude, an also-ran in the Classic, scored the year's highest Beyer Figure with a stunning 10-length score in the Jockey Club Gold Cup.

Races More Than 1 Mile, 2002

Beyer No.	Horse	Track	Date
121	LEFT BANK	SAR	08/03/2002
120	MEDAGLIA D'ORO	SAR	08/04/2002
119	MIZZEN MAST	SA	02/02/2002
119	LIDO PALACE	SAR	08/03/2002
119	STREET CRY	SAR	08/03/2002
118	STREET CRY	CD	06/15/2002
118	MILWAUKEE BREW	SA	03/02/2002
116	PLEASANTLY PERFECT	SA	10/06/2002
116	MACHO UNO	SAR	08/03/2002
116	VOLPONI	AP	10/26/2002
116	CAME HOME	DMR	08/25/2002

Left Bank turned the rare trick of posting 120-plus Beyers going short and long. Volponi, winner of the Breeders' Cup Classic, scored 110-plus Beyers on both the dirt and turf.

Races More Than 1 Mile, 2003

Beyer No.	Horse	Track	Date
123	CANDY RIDE	DMR	08/24/2003
119	MEDAGLIA D'ORO	SA	02/01/2003
119	PLEASANTLY PERFECT	SA	10/25/2003
118	CONGAREE	SA	02/02/2003
118	MINESHAFT	PIM	05/16/2003
118	MEDAGLIA D'ORO	DMR	08/24/2003
117	PERFECT DRIFT	CD	06/14/2003
117	MINESHAFT	CD	06/14/2003
117	MINESHAFT	BEL	09/06/2003
117	MEDAGLIA D'ORO	SA	10/25/2003

Champion Mineshaft turned in three of the fastest route performances of the year, as did Medaglia d'Oro. Congaree had high figures both routing and sprinting. The best figure of the season was turned in by Candy Ride, in defeating Medaglia d'Oro in the Pacific Classic.

Races More Than 1 Mile, 2004

Beyer No.	Horse	Track	Date
128	GHOSTZAPPER	MTH	08/21/2004
124	GHOSTZAPPER	LS	10/30/2004
123	MIDWAY ROAD	KEE	04/22/2004
119	ROSES IN MAY	LS	10/30/2004
118	SOUTHERN IMAGE	PIM	05/14/2004
118	SMARTY JONES	PIM	05/15/2004
117	MEDAGLIA D'ORO	GP	02/07/2004
116	MIDWAY ROAD	PIM	05/14/2004
114	ROSES IN MAY	SAR	08/07/2004
114	PERFECT DRIFT	SAR	08/07/2004
114	EVENING ATTIRE	SAR	08/22/2004
114	GHOSTZAPPER	BEL	09/11/2004
114	SAINT LIAM	BEL	09/11/2004

Champion Ghostzapper had not just the highest figure of the season, but the highest figure of the last 12 years, and all three of his route starts resulted in superior figures. Midway Road and Roses in May also recorded multiple fast times. Medaglia d'Oro, who had only two starts in 2004, is the only horse to have a figure of 117 or above in a dirt route in both 2003 and 2004.

Races More Than 1 Mile, 1992-2004

Beyer No.	Horse	Track	Date
128	GHOSTZAPPER	MTH	08/21/2004
126	FORMAL GOLD	SAR	08/02/1997
126	WILL'S WAY	SAR	08/02/1997
126	GENTLEMEN	PIM	05/10/1997
125	BERTRANDO	BEL	09/18/1993
125	FORMAL GOLD	BEL	09/20/1997
125	SKIP AWAY	PIM	05/10/1997
124	GHOSTZAPPER	LS	10/30/2004
124	FORMAL GOLD	MTH	08/23/1997
123	MIDWAY ROAD	KEE	04/22/2004
123	CANDY RIDE	DMR	08/24/2003
123	APTITUDE	BEL	10/06/2001
123	TEJANO RUN	HIA	03/22/1997
123	SILVER CHARM	TP	09/26/1998
123	WILD RUSH	TP	09/26/1998
123	BEST PAL	SA	03/07/1992
122	SKY JACK	SA	12/03/2000

122	FORMAL GOLD	SUF	05/31/1997
122	SKIP AWAY	SUF	05/31/1997
121	LEFT BANK	SAR	08/03/2002
121	CONCERNED MINISTER	FG	12/03/2000
121	ROCK AND ROLL	BEL	06/13/1998
121	ORMSBY	AQU	04/26/1997
121	BEST PAL	OP	04/11/1992
121	CRAFTY CASH*	OP	04/11/1992
121	CIGAR	OP	04/15/1995
121	BEST PAL	SA	01/18/1992
121	SKIP AWAY	SUF	05/30/1998
121	GENTLEMEN	DMR	08/09/1997
121	GENTLEMEN	HOL	06/29/1997

The top three Beyer Speed Figures and seven of the top 10, were earned in 1997. Formal Gold earned three of the top 10 Beyer Figures himself.

Turf, 1996

Beyer No.	Horse	Track	Date
118	FASTNESS	DMR	08/04/1996
117	SMOOTH RUNNER	DMR	08/04/1996
115	SINGSPIEL	WO	09/29/1996
115	PILSUDSKI	WO	10/26/1996
114	DA HOSS	WO	10/26/1996
114	TALLOIRES	HOL	07/21/1996
113	SINGSPIEL	WO	10/26/1996
112	URGENT REQUEST	SA	10/05/1996
112	KIRIDASHI	WO	09/29/1996
112	FASTNESS	HOL	05/12/1996
112	AURIETTE (F)	HOL	06/09/1996
112	SANDPIT	HOL	05/27/1996
112	BROADWAY FLYER	SAR	08/10/1996

Singspiel was second to European invader Pilsudski in the Breeders' Cup Turf at Woodbine and was voted champion turf horse of 1996.

Turf, 1997

Beyer No.	Horse	Track	Date
115	ATTICUS	SA	03/01/1997
114	SPINNING WORLD	HOL	11/08/1997
113	RIVER FLYER	BM	02/15/1997
112	LUCKY COIN	BEL	09/20/1997
112	LUCKY COIN	BEL	10/18/1997
112	CHIEF BEARHART	WO	09/28/1997
111	ISITINGOOD	SA	02/05/1997
111	INFLUENT	ATL	06/28/1997
111	GERI	BEL	06/14/1997
111	CHIEF BEARHART	WO	10/19/1997

Chief Bearhart won the Breeders' Cup Turf at Hollywood Park and was voted Eclipse Award champion. Atticus set a world record when he earned his 115 Beyer Figure over a blazingly fast turf course at Santa Anita.

Turf, 1998

Beyer No.	Horse	Track	Date
114	JIM AND TONIC	WO	09/20/1998
114	LABEEB	WO	09/20/1998
113	DA HOSS	CD	11/07/1998
113	HAWKSLEY HILL	CD	11/07/1998
112	ELUSIVE QUALITY	BEL	07/04/1998
112	FANTASTIC FELLOW	HOL	04/26/1998
112	JOYEUX DANSEUR	CD	05/02/1998
112	JOYEUX DANSEUR	FG	02/07/1998
112	JOYEUX DANSEUR	FG	03/29/1998
112	BUCK'S BOY	BEL	10/10/1998

Da Hoss, winner of the 1996 Mile at Woodbine, scored his second victory in that Breeders' Cup race after missing the 1997 Mile and racing only once in 1998. Buck's Boy won the Breeders' Cup Turf and was voted champion turf horse.

Turf, 1999

Beyer No.	Horse	Track	Date
118	DAYLAMI	GP	11/06/1999
113	BRAVE ACT	HOL	05/16/1999
113	ROYAL ANTHEM	GP	11/06/1999
112	CRYSTAL HEARTED	DMR	07/30/1999
112	TRANQUILITY LAKE (F)	HOL	06/06/1999
111	HAWKSLEY HILL	SA	03/06/1999
111	LORD SMITH	SA	03/06/1999
111	SUPER QUERCUS	HOL	11/28/1999
110	MIDDLESEX DRIVE	BEL	10/16/1999
110	SILIC	GP	11/06/1999
110	GARBU	GP	03/13/1999
110	BUCK'S BOY	WO	09/10/1999
110	LAZY LODE	HOL	06/26/1999
110	VAL'S PRINCE	BEL	09/11/1999
110	YAGLI	GP	02/06/1999
110	BUCK'S BOY	GP	11/06/1999
110	LAZY LODE	HOL	12/04/1999

European Horse of the Year, Daylami, owned by Dubai based Godolphin stables, won the Breeders' Cup Turf and was voted champion turf horse in North America. Silic won the Breeders' Cup Mile.

Turf, 2000

Beyer No.	Horse	Track	Date
112	JOHN'S CALL	SAR	08/12/2000
110	SILIC	HOL	06/18/2000
110	FEDERAL TRIAL	GP	02/19/2000
110	CHESTER HOUSE	AP	08/19/2000
110	ROYAL ANTHEM	GP	02/12/2000
110	KALANISI	CD	11/04/2000
109	FULL MOON MADNESS	HOL	12/22/2000
109	TEXAS GLITTER	HOL	12/22/2000
109	FORBIDDEN APPLE	BEL	10/08/2000
109	LADIES DIN	HOL	06/18/2000
109	SPINDRIFT	AQU	05/06/2000
109	LADIES DIN	DMR	07/30/2000
109	TOUT CHARMANT (F)	HOL	11/26/2000
109	TRANQUILITY LAKE (F)	HOL	11/26/2000
109	BRAVE ACT	SA	01/01/2000
109	NATIVE DESERT	SA	01/01/2000
109	JOHN'S CALL	BEL	10/07/2000
109	JOHN'S CALL	CD	11/04/2000
109	QUIET RESOLVE	CD	11/04/2000
109	MUTAMAM	CD	11/04/2000

The 9-year-old John's Call recorded the highest figure of the year, going wire to wire to win the Sword Dancer at Saratoga. Many of the division's stars, including Silic, Chester House and Royal Anthem, were derailed by injury.

Turf, 2001

Beyer No.	Horse	Track	Date
118	SILVANO	AP	08/18/2001
117	FANTASTIC LIGHT	BEL	10/27/2001
116	MILAN	BEL	10/27/2001
114	VAL ROYAL	BEL	10/27/2001
114	KING CUGAT	BEL	07/07/2001
113	SLEW VALLEY	BEL	07/07/2001
112	YARALINO	GG	02/04/2001
112	BANKS HILL (F)	BEL	10/27/2001
111	SPEAK IN PASSING	HOL	11/23/2001
111	SWEPT OVERBOARD	HOL	11/23/2001
111	EL CIELO	SA	11/05/2001
111	EL CIELO	SA	01/04/2001

German-bred Silvano turned in a very impressive performance on a soggy Arlington turf course in the Million. Fantastic Light, who defeated many of the top turf horses in Europe, clinched a title in North America with a victory in the Breeders' Cup Turf over another European, the 3-year-old Milan.

Turf, 2002

Beyer No.	Horse	Track	Date
113	DOMEDRIVER	AP	10/26/2002
113	GOOD JOURNEY	AP	10/26/2002
111	ROCK OF GIBRALTAR	AP	10/26/2002
111	LADIES DIN	HOL	05/27/2002
111	BEAT HOLLOW	BEL	06/08/2002
111	HIGH CHAPARRAL	AP	10/26/2002
111	BALLINGARRY	WO	09/29/2002
110	BLU AIR FORCE	HOL	06/19/2002
110	VOLPONI	BEL	07/05/2002
110	SPECIAL RING	HOL	07/07/2002
110	DEL MAR SHOW	SAR	07/26/2002
110	WITH ANTICIPATION	MTH	07/06/2002

The Europeans dominated turf racing in North America once again, as Domedriver and High Chaparral took the Breeders' Cup Mile and Turf, respectively.

Turf, 2003

Beyer No.	Horse	Track	Date
112	STORMING HOME	HOL	05/10/2003
112	JOHAR	SA	10/25/2003
112	HIGH CHAPARRAL	SA	10/25/2003
112	FALBRAV	SA	10/25/2003
111	THE TIN MAN	SA	02/15/2003
111	REDATTORE	HOL	05/26/2003
111	SPECIAL RING	DMR	07/27/2003
110	HONOR IN WAR	CD	05/03/2003
110	BALTO STAR	MTH	07/05/2003
110	TRADEMARK	SAR	07/25/2003
110	LUNAR SOVEREIGN	BEL	09/06/2003
110	SULAMANI	BEL	09/27/2003

There was a four-way tie for the top figure in turf racing in 2003, shared in part by the dead-heat Breeders' Cup Turf winners, Johar and High Chaparral; Falbrav, who was beaten just a head in the Turf; and Storming Home.

Turf, 2004

Beyer No.	Horse	Track	Date
115	SULAMANI	WO	10/24/2004
114	KITTEN'S JOY	BEL	10/02/2004
113	KITTEN'S JOY	AP	08/14/2004
112	SIMONAS	WO	10/24/2004
112	LEROIDESANIMAUX	HOL	11/27/2004
111	LEROIDESANIMAUX	HOL	05/01/2004
111	MAGISTRETTI	BEL	09/11/2004
111	NOTHING TO LOSE	KEE	10/09/2004
111	LEROIDESANIMAUX	SA	10/30/2004
111	BETTER TALK NOW	LS	10/30/2004
111	A TO THE Z	HOL	11/27/2004

Canadian International winner Sulamani had the fastest turf performance of 2004, but divisional champion Kitten's Joy the next two fastest races. Leroidesanimaux had three top-rated performances of 2004.

Turf, 1992-2004

Beyer No.	Horse	Track	Date
118	FASTNESS	DMR	08/04/1996
118	DAYLAMI	GP	11/06/1999
118	SILVANO	AP	08/18/2001
117	FANTASTIC LIGHT	BEL	10/27/2001
117	MEGAN'S INTERCO	HOL	05/22/1994
117	SMOOTH RUNNER	DMR	08/04/1996
117	STAR OF COZZENE	ATL	06/27/1993
117	PARADISE CREEK	BEL	06/11/1994
117	STAR OF COZZENE	BEL	09/18/1993
116	MILAN	BEL	10/27/2001
116	STAR OF COZZENE	BEL	06/06/1993
115	SULAMANI	WO	10/24/2004
115	ROTSALUCK	SA	11/05/1994
115	FURIOUSLY	HOL	05/22/1994
115	ATTICUS	SA	03/01/1997
115	LURE	ATL	06/27/1993
115	STAR OF COZZENE	AP	08/29/1993
115	SINGSPIEL	WO	09/29/1996
115	PILSUDSKI	WO	10/26/1996
114	KITTEN'S JOY	BEL	10/02/2004
114	PEMBROKE	HOL	07/15/1995
114	RIDGEWOOD PEARL (F)	BEL	10/28/1995
114	SPINNING WORLD	HOL	11/08/1997
114	DA HOSS	WO	10/26/1996
114	JIM AND TONIC	WO	09/20/1998
114	LABEEB	WO	09/20/1998
114	AWAD	AP	08/27/1995
114	LURE	BEL	06/06/1993
114	PARADISE CREEK	LRL	10/15/1994
114	FREEDOM CRY	BEL	10/28/1995
114	NORTHERN SPUR	BEL	10/28/1995
114	TALLOIRES	HOL	07/21/1996

Graded Stakes

2004 Graded Stakes Charts

Past Performances for Graded Stakes Winners

Graded Stakes Chart Index

NINTH RACE
Calder
JANUARY 1, 2004

1⅛ MILES. (Turf Chute) (1.444) TROPICAL PARK DERBY Grade III. Purse $100,000 FOR THREE YEAR OLDS (FOALS OF 2001). By subscription of $100 each which shall accompany the nomination, $1,000 to pass the entry box and an additional $1,000 to start. The owner of the winner to receive $60,000, $20,000 to second, $11,000 to third, $6,000to fourth and $3,000 to fifth. Weight: 122 lbs. Non-winners of $35,000 twice at a mile or over allowed 3 lbs.; $30,000 at a mile or over, 5 lbs.; $15,000 at a mile or over other than Maiden or Claiming, 7 lbs.; a race other than Maiden or Claiming, 10 lbs. Graded placed horses of equal weights preferred. A trophy will be presented to the winning Owner. Closed Wednesday, November 17, 2003 with (26) nominations.

Value of Race: $100,000 Winner $60,000; second $20,000; third $11,000; fourth $6,000; fifth $3,000. Mutuel Pool $400,844.00 Exacta Pool $314,979.00 Trifecta Pool $234,026.00 Superfecta Pool $76,356.00

Last Raced	Horse	M/Eqt.	A.	Wt	PP	St	¼	½	¾	Str	Fin	Jockey	Odds $1
16Nov03 7CD1	Kitten's Joy	L	3	119	9	5	4½	61½	4hd	1hd	14½	Bailey J D	3.60
13Dec03 6Crc4	Broadway View	L b	3	112	1	2	31	2½	21	3hd	2nk	Castro E	35.60
13Dec03 6Crc1	Soverign Honor	L b	3	117	5	1	11	11½	1½	21½	3hd	Cruz M R	29.50
29Nov03 8Aqu10	Milestone Victory	L	3	114	6	11	5hd	5½	3hd	41½	41	Luzzi M J	9.60
29Nov03 11Crc2	Imperialism	L b	3	115	8	9	11	91	71	5hd	5nk	Velazquez J R	4.90
29Nov03 11CD4	Commendation	L	3	119	11	10	91½	11	8hd	6hd	6nk	Velasquez C H	3.70
23Nov03 7CD1	Up Anchor	L	3	117	10	8	101	10½	103	93	7nk	Lanerie C J	20.20
29Nov03 11Crc1	Timo	L b	3	122	7	7	81	81	6½	7½	8½	Coa E	1.90
1Dec03 8Crc1	Potomac Chase	L b	3	115	2	3	21	41½	5½	81½	97¾	Karamanos H	45.60
23Nov03 7CD2	Wasabi Cat	L	3	113	3	4	7½	7hd	91½	1014	1024½	Blanc B	14.30
27Nov03 11Crc5	Global Arena	bf	3	112	4	6	6½	3½	11	11	11	Matutes L	158.90

OFF AT 3:54 Start Good For All But MILESTONE VICTORY, TIMO. Won driving. Course firm.
TIME :232, :471, 1:112, 1:351, 1:464 (:23.40, :47.36, 1:11.46, 1:35.38, 1:46.95)

$2 Mutuel Prices:

10 – KITTEN'S JOY	9.20	6.40	5.80
1 – BROADWAY VIEW		26.60	13.80
5 – SOVERIGN HONOR			16.20

$2 EXACTA 10–1 PAID $234.00 $2 TRIFECTA 10–1–5 PAID $4,166.80
$2 SUPERFECTA 10–1–5–6 PAID $55,739.80

Ch. c, (May), by El Prado-Ire – Kitten's First , by Lear Fan . Trainer Romans Dale. Bred by Kenneth L Ramsey & Sarah K Ramsey (Ky).

KITTEN'S JOY rated just off the pace toward the outside, took aim three wide entering the stretch, dueled onto the eighth pole then drew off under a moderate drive. BROADWAY VIEW rated close in the three path, lacked room on the final turn, gave chase into the stretch then endured a long drive for place. SOVERIGN HONOR rated the pace from the inside, drew clear entering the stretch then leveled out the final furlong. MILESTONE VICTORY lunged at the start, steadied into the first turn, rated off the pace inside, bid from the top of the stretch and finished evenly inside. IMPERIALISM rated off the pace toward the outside, came widest through the final turn and finished evenly outside. COMMENDATION steadied on the first turn, rated back toward mid track, bid through the final turn, lacked room approaching the eighth pole then leveled out the remainder. UP ANCHOR saved ground early, angled out into the lane and offered no rally. TIMO stumbled at the start and never factored. POTOMAC CHASE gave chase in mid track then weakened. WASABI CAT was outrun. GLOBAL ARENA ran out into the opening turn then faded after half.

Owners– 1, Ramsey Kenneth L and Sarah K; 2, Sacks Sidney; 3, Chin James; 4, TYB Stable; 5, R G Torrone; 6, Courtlandt Farms; 7, Ralls and Foster LLC; 8, C K Woods Stable; 9, W Harrison; 10, Dooley Thomas M; 11, Raising Dust Stable

Trainers– 1, Romans Dale L; 2, Procino Gerald; 3, Pinchin Jose; 4, Brennan Niall J; 5, Salinas Angel C; 6, Motion H Graham; 7, McGee Paul J; 8, Badgett William Jr; 9, Blengs Vincent L; 10, McPeek Kenneth G; 11, Malek Raja

Scratched– Cool Conductor (29Nov03 11Crc3)

$2 Pick Three (4–6–10) Paid $2,976.20 ; Pick Three Pool $29,371 .

EIGHTH RACE
Santa Anita
JANUARY 1, 2004

5½ FURLONGS. (1.013) EL CONEJO H. Grade III. Purse $100,000 A HANDICAP FOR FOUR-YEAR-OLDS AND UPWARD. By subscription of $100 each to accompany the nomination. $1,000 additional to start with $100,000 added. The added money and all fees to be divided 60% to the winner, 20% to second, 12% to third, 6% to fourthand 2% to fifth. A trophy will be presented to the owner of the winner. Nominations Closed Tuesday, December 23rd, 2003 with 16.

Value of Race: $107,600 Winner $64,560; second $21,520; third $12,912; fourth $6,456; fifth $2,152. Mutuel Pool $374,589.00 Exacta Pool $201,503.00 Quinella Pool $21,053.00 Trifecta Pool $190,750.00 Superfecta Pool $82,875.00

Last Raced	Horse	M/Eqt.	A.	Wt	PP	St	¼	⅜	Str	Fin	Jockey	Odds $1
6Dec03 3GG1	Boston Common	LB	5	117	4	1	46	32	2½	1nk	Stevens G L	4.80
8Nov03 6SA2	Summer Service	LB b	4	112	5	6	52	5½	42	21½	Smith M E	3.60
28Nov03 9Hol1	King Robyn	LB	4	119	1	3	1hd	1½	11	32½	Solis A O	1.40
13Dec03 11Crc1	Hasty Kris	LB b	7	116	6	4	6	6	5½	43	Desormeaux K J	7.30
26Jly03 6Dmr9	Giovannetti	LB	5	114	3	2	21	22½	32	51	Sorenson D	25.30
5Jly03 4Hol1	Casas Caballo	LB	4	115	2	5	3½	42½	6	6	Valenzuela P A	3.40

OFF AT 4:08 Start Good . Won driving. Track fast.
TIME :211, :434, :554, 1:021 (:21.27, :43.83, :55.87, 1:02.35)

$2 Mutuel Prices:

6 – BOSTON COMMON	11.60	5.00	3.40
7 – SUMMER SERVICE		4.60	3.20
2 – KING ROBYN			2.80

$1 EXACTA 6–7 PAID $26.80 $2 QUINELLA 6–7 PAID $31.80
$1 TRIFECTA 6–7–2 PAID $84.80 $1 SUPERFECTA 6–7–2–9 PAID $275.00

B. g, (Apr), by Boston Harbor – Especially , by Mr. Prospector . Trainer Mullins Jeff. Bred by Overbrook Farm (Ky).

BOSTON COMMON stalked outside a rival or off the rail, bid three deep into the stretch, gained a short lead while lugging in outside KING ROBYN past midstretch and held gamely under left handed urging. SUMMER SERVICE bobbled slightly at the start, settled off the rail, also came three deep into the stretch and closed willingly to just miss. KING ROBYN went up inside to duel for the lead, inched away nearing midstretch, fought back when headed but could not match the top pair late while best of the rest. HASTY KRIS unhurried off the rail early, angled in leaving the backstretch, went outside a rival into the stretch, came out in upper stretch and lacked the needed rally. GIOVANNETTI had speed between horses then dueled outside a rival to upper stretch and weakened in the final furlong. CASAS CABALLO also had speed between horses then stalked a bit off the rail, angled to the fence leaving the backstretch, fell back some on the turn and weakened.

Owners– 1, Englander Richard A; 2, Valente Roddy J; 3, Cornejo Racing Inc; 4, C R K Stable; 5, Schiappa Bernard C; 6, House Michael

Trainers– 1, Mullins Jeff; 2, Spawr William; 3, Mullins Jeff; 4, Sadler John W; 5, Monteleone Frank J; 6, Mitchell Mike R

Scratched– Rojo Toro (22Mar03 6SA 5) , Grimm (06Dec03 8TuP1) , Avanzado (ARG) (27Nov03 7Hol5)

$2 Daily Double (8–6) Paid $65.00 ; Daily Double Pool $42,331 .
$1 Pick Three (1–8–6) Paid $1,080.30 ; Pick Three Pool $69,028 .

NINTH RACE
Gulfstream
JANUARY 3, 2004

1 1/16 MILES. (1.40[1]) HAL'S HOPE H. Grade III. Purse $100,000 FOR THREE YEAR OLDS AND UPWARD. By subscription of $100 each, which shall accompany the nomination, $1,000 to pass the entry box and $1,000 additional to start, with $100,000 guaranteed. The owner of the winner to receive $60,000; $20,000 to second, $11,000 to third, $6,000 to fourth and $3,000 to fifth. WEIGHTS: Friday, December 26, 2003. Starters to be named through the entry box by the usual time of closing. Trophy to winning Owner. This race will be limited to 14 Starters, with Also Eligibles. (HighWeights on the scale Preferred).

Value of Race: $100,000 Winner $60,000; second $20,000; third $11,000; fourth $6,000; fifth $3,000. Mutuel Pool $499,429.00 Exacta Pool $321,178.00 Trifecta Pool $236,812.00 Superfecta Pool $73,968.00

Last Raced	Horse	M/Eqt.	A.	Wt	PP	St	1/4	1/2	3/4	Str	Fin	Jockey	Odds $1
6Sep03 9Bel3	Puzzlement	L b	5	116	4	4	7	7	62	21½	1nk	Chavez J F	2.70
29Nov03 9Aqu4	Bowman's Band	L	6	118	3	2	4hd	52	3½	12½	28	Dominguez R A	2.10
27Nov03 7Aqu1	Stockholder	L b	4	114	6	7	52	3hd	41½	41½	32	Bailey J D	2.30
11Nov03 8Aqu3	Gander	L	8	115	1	1	3½	4½	52	5½	4nk	Santos J A	4.40
12Nov03 8CD1	Senor Amigo	L	4	108	7	5	2½	21	2½	32½	56¼	Castro E	14.80
6Dec03 7Crc2	Vinemeister	L	5	115	2	3	11½	11½	1½	63	64	Velez J A Jr	45.40
26Oct03 9CD4	Woodmoon	L bf	6	113	5	6	64	63½	7	7	7	Coa E	33.10

OFF AT 4:40 Start Good. Won driving. Track fast.

TIME :23[3], :47[2], 1:11[2], 1:36, 1:42[1] (:23.74, :47.40, 1:11.52, 1:36.12, 1:42.39)

$2 Mutuel Prices:

5 – PUZZLEMENT	7.40	3.40	2.40
3 – BOWMAN'S BAND		3.40	2.60
9 – STOCKHOLDER			2.40

$1 EXACTA 5–3 PAID $10.60 $1 TRIFECTA 5–3–9 PAID $27.80
$1 SUPERFECTA 5–3–9–1 PAID $42.20

B. h, (Jan), by Pine Bluff – Taine , by Sir Ivor . Trainer Jerkens H Allen. Bred by J V Shields Jr (Fla).

PUZZLEMENT, unhurriedly early, rallied outside through the final turn, advanced steadily toward the front and edged ahead the final strides. BOWMAN'S BAND rated off the pace toward the outside, advanced to the lead in the four path nearing the quarter pole, drew clear entering the stretch, was kept to steady pressure but outfinished in the final strides. STOCKHOLDER lunged at the start, rated off the pace toward the outside, was held in check from the quarter pole to the top of the stretch then bid to finish evenly for show. GANDER rated off the pace inside, lacked room leaving the quarter pole, eased out into the lane and finished evenly. SENOR AMIGO rated just off the pace in the three path, contested between rivals on the final turn, dropped back on the rail entering the stretch then faded. VINEMEISTER was quickly in front rating the pace just off the rail, contested inside through the final turn, steadied leaving the quarter pole then gave way. WOODMOON raced unhurriedly toward the outside then had no rally.

Owners– 1, Shields Joseph V Jr; 2, Schwartz Martin S; 3, Dapple Stable LLC; 4, Catsas Thoroughbreds LLC; 5, Howard William O; 6, Travin Stables; 7, Pabst Henry E

Trainers– 1, Jerkens H Allen; 2, Jerkens H Allen; 3, Mott William I; 4, Terranova II John P; 5, Duke Caleb; 6, Seewald Alan S; 7, O'Callaghan Niall M

Scratched– Well Fancied (29Nov03 9Aqu5) , New York Hero (20Dec03 11Crc4) , Cool N Collective (15Nov03 8Hoo2)

$1 Pick Three (7–7–5) Paid $46.40 ; Pick Three Pool $63,750 .

TENTH RACE
Gulfstream
JANUARY 3, 2004

6 FURLONGS. (1.07[4]) MR. PROSPECTOR H. Grade III. Purse $100,000 FOR THREE YEAR OLDS AND UPWARD. By subscription of $100 each, which shall accompany the nomination, $1,000 to pass the entry box and $1,000 additional to start, with $100,000 guaranteed. The owner of the winner to receive $60,000; $20,000 to second, $11,000 to third, $6,000 to fourth and $3,000 to fith. Weights: Friday, December 26, 2003. Starters to be named through the entry box by the usual time of closing. Trophy to winning Owner. This race will be limited to 14 Starters, with Also Eligibles. (HighWeights on the scale Preferred).

Value of Race: $100,000 Winner $60,000; second $20,000; third $11,000; fourth $6,000; fifth $3,000. Mutuel Pool $370,614.00 Exacta Pool $234,509.00 Trifecta Pool $169,274.00 Superfecta Pool $49,611.00

Last Raced	Horse	M/Eqt.	A.	Wt	PP	St	1/4	1/2	Str	Fin	Jockey	Odds $1
25Oct03 5SA1	Cajun Beat	L b	4	121	6	2	1hd	1hd	11½	11½	Velasquez C H	0.80
27Sep03 7Bel4	Gygistar	L	5	118	4	3	2½	4½	43	2¾	Bailey J D	2.30
27Nov03 8CD1	Deer Lake	L	5	115	2	5	51½	2hd	2½	33	Prado E S	10.70
29Nov03 9Aqu7	Voodoo	L b	6	115	3	4	31	31	31½	42¾	Chavez J F	5.40
13Dec03 11Crc2	Wake At Noon	L bf	7	116	5	1	4½	51½	5½	51¾	Karamanos H	17.90
4Dec03 8Aqu3	Multiple Choice	L b	6	115	1	6	6	6	6	6	Douglas R R	20.00

OFF AT 5:10 Start Good. Won driving. Track fast.

TIME :22[1], :44[4], :56[3], 1:09 (:22.30, :44.98, :56.62, 1:09.06)

$2 Mutuel Prices:

6 – CAJUN BEAT	3.60	2.40	2.10
4 – GYGISTAR		2.80	2.10
2 – DEER LAKE			2.10

$1 EXACTA 6–4 PAID $4.30 $1 TRIFECTA 6–4–2 PAID $14.60
$1 SUPERFECTA 6–4–2–3 PAID $26.90

Dk. b or br. g, (Mar), by Grand Slam – Beckys Shirt , by Cure the Blues . Trainer Margolis Stephen R. Bred by John T L Jones Jr & H Smoot Fahlgren (Ky).

CAJUN BEAT hustled up outside to take the early lead, maintained a slight advantage through the turn, drew clear entering the stretch, responded willingly to upper stretch pressure then finished the final furlong with a hand ride. GYGISTAR rated with the pace just off the rail, dropped back angling four wide to make his bid nearing the quarter pole then advanced steadily to finish second while gaining on the winner. DEER LAKE rated off the pace toward the outside, advanced to near even terms at the quarter pole, dueled close to midstretch then reluctantly yielded the final sixteenth. VOODOO rated close to the early pace inside, gave chase while apprehensively ridden into the turn, had aim entering the stretch then faded the final furlong. WAKE AT NOON chased the pace toward mid track then faded on the turn. MULTIPLE CHOICE showed no early speed and no rally.

Owners– 1, John & Joseph Iracane & Padua Stable; 2, Evans Edward P; 3, Fugitte Steve; 4, Moore Susan and John; 5, Schickedanz Bruno; 6, Blum Peter E

Trainers– 1, Margolis Stephen R; 2, Hennig Mark A; 3, Simon Charles; 4, Jerkens James A; 5, Collazo Henry; 6, Jerkens James A

$1 Pick Three (7–5–6) Paid $55.80 ; Pick Three Pool $39,497 .

ELEVENTH RACE
Gulfstream
JANUARY 3, 2004

$1\frac{1}{16}$ MILES. (Turf) (1.39^{1}) HONEY FOX H. Grade III. Purse $100,000 FOR FILLIES AND MARES, THREE YEARS OLD AND UPWARD. By subscription of $100 each, which shall accompany the nomination, $1,000 to pass the entry box and $1,000 additional to start, with $100,000 guaranteed. The owner of the winner to receive $60,000; $20,000 to second, $11,000 to third, $6,000 to fourth and $3,000 to fifth. Weights: Friday. December 26, 2003. Starters to be named through the entry box by the usual time of closing. Trophy to winning Owner. This race will be limited to 12 Starters, with AlsoEligibles. (High Weights on the scale Preferred). In the event this stake race is taken off the turf, it may be subject to downgrading upon review by the Graded Stakes Committee.

Value of Race: $100,000 Winner $60,000; second $20,000; third $11,000; fourth $6,000; fifth $3,000. Mutuel Pool $406,739.00 Exacta Pool $316,400.00 Trifecta Pool $255,175.00 Superfecta Pool $105,282.00

Last Raced	Horse	M/Eqt.	A.	Wt	PP	St	¼	½	¾	Str	Fin	Jockey	Odds $1
22Nov03 ^{9}CD^{6}	Delmonico Cat	L	5	116	6	8	6^{hd}	7^{hd}	$7^{1\frac{1}{2}}$	5^{1}	$1^{\frac{1}{2}}$	Bailey J D	4.90
8Nov03 ^{9}Aqu^{3}	Coney Kitty-Ire	L f	6	115	7	6	$4^{\frac{1}{2}}$	$4^{\frac{1}{2}}$	3^{hd}	3^{hd}	2^{nk}	Velasquez C H	5.90
14Dec03 ^{5}Crc^{2}	Madeira Mist-Ire	L	5	117	1	1	5^{1}	5^{hd}	5^{1}	$2^{\frac{1}{2}}$	3^{nk}	Prado E S	3.20
28Nov03 ^{10}CD^{4}	May Gator	L b	5	113	8	5	1^{hd}	$1^{1\frac{1}{2}}$	$1^{\frac{1}{2}}$	$1^{\frac{1}{2}}$	4^{1}	Chavez J F	34.40
6Dec03 ^{9}Crc^{2}	SomethingVentured	L b	5	117	5	7	8^{1}	$8^{1\frac{1}{2}}$	9^{3}	$8^{\frac{1}{2}}$	5^{1}	Velazquez J R	2.40
20Dec03 ^{8}Crc^{4}	Gal O Gal	L	4	115	10	9	9^{2}	9^{3}	8^{hd}	$9^{1\frac{1}{2}}$	6^{1}	Karamanos H	9.20
7Dec03 ^{9}Crc^{3}	Paga-Arg	L	7	113	4	4	$2^{1\frac{1}{2}}$	3^{1}	$4^{1\frac{1}{2}}$	4^{1}	$7^{1\frac{3}{4}}$	Coa E	8.30
13Oct03 ^{7}Bel^{2}	Katzen	L	5	114	3	3	$7^{\frac{1}{2}}$	6^{1}	$6^{\frac{1}{2}}$	6^{hd}	$8^{1\frac{1}{2}}$	Santos J A	15.90
19Jly03 ^{8}Del^{8}	Virgin Voyage	L bf	4	114	9	10	10	10	10	10	$9^{1\frac{1}{2}}$	Beckner D V	79.50
6Dec03 ^{9}Crc^{5}	Love Sting	L b	4	114	2	2	3^{hd}	2^{1}	$2^{1\frac{1}{2}}$	$7^{\frac{1}{2}}$	10	Bain G W	29.60

OFF AT 5:40 Start Good . Won driving. Course firm.

TIME :23^{4}, :48^{1}, 1:12, 1:35^{2}, 1:41^{1} (:23.84, :48.30, 1:12.02, 1:35.58, 1:41.30)

$2 Mutuel Prices:				
	8 – DELMONICO CAT	11.80	5.80	4.40
	9 – CONEY KITTY–IRE		6.00	4.00
	1 – MADEIRA MIST–IRE			3.60

$1 EXACTA 8–9 PAID $37.80 $1 TRIFECTA 8–9–1 PAID $140.60
$1 SUPERFECTA 8–9–1–10 PAID $2,322.30

Dk. b or br. m, (Feb), by Storm Cat – Glass Ceiling , by Pirate's Bounty . Trainer Mott William I. Bred by Mr & Mrs Martin J Wygod (Ky).

DELMONICO CAT rated back toward mid track, eased out rallying entering the stretch then edged ahead through the final yards. CONEY KITTY (IRE) rated off the pace in mid track, came five wide through the final turn, took aim midstretch then dueled gamely for place while outfinished for the win. MADEIRA MIST (IRE) rated back inside, eased out entering the stretch, lacked room through the upper stretch, bid inside to a short brief lead in late stretch then outfinished the final yards. MAY GATOR rated the pace angling toward the hedge, moved briefly clear entering the stretch, dueled gamely from the furlong pole but was outfinished in the final yards. SOMETHING VENTURED, unhurriedly in mid track, came slightly out into the stretch and finished evenly. GAL O GAL raced outside, bid widest on the final turn and finished evenly. PAGA (ARG) was rank steadying early on, rated close inside, dueled to midstretch then faded. KATZEN lacked room inside on the final turn then gave way. VIRGIN VOYAGE never factored. LOVE STING rated just off the pace and off the hedge, took aim in the three path of the final turn then faded abruptly.

Owners– 1, Wygod Mr and Mrs Martin J; 2, Willima Betz Steve Humphrey & Arthur Seelbinder; 3, Skymarc Farm Inc; 4, Klein Richard Bertram and Elaine; 5, Wiemer Irvin and McLane John; 6, Hugel Max; 7, Hubbard R D and Allred Edward C; 8, Marcia & Philip Cohen & Steve Klesaris; 9, Paraneck Stable; 10, Emerald Pastures Corp Inc

Trainers– 1, Mott William I; 2, Toner James J; 3, Clement Christophe; 4, Flint Steven B; 5, Pletcher Todd A; 6, Blengs Vincent L; 7, Hennig Mark A; 8, Klesaris Steve B; 9, Pedersen Jennifer; 10, Gutierrez Rosie

Scratched– Miss Terrible (ARG) (03Aug03 ^{8}Sar^{6}) , Delta Princess (17Oct03 ^{7}Med^{4})

$2 Daily Double (6–8) Paid $25.20 ; Daily Double Pool $132,288 .
$1 Pick Three (5–6–8) Paid $52.50 ; Pick Three Pool $256,059 .
$1 Pick Four (7–5–6–8) Paid $302.40 ; Pick Four Pool $121,352 .
$2 Pick Six (10–7–7–5–6–8) 6 Correct Paid $4,143.00 .
$2 Pick Six (10–7–7–5–6–8) 5 Correct Paid $40.60 ; Pick Six Pool $20,715 .

Gulfstream Park Attendance: 21,501 Mutuel Pool: $2,169,788.00 ITW Mutuel Pool: $482,325.00 ISW Mutuel Pool: $8,031,016.00

SEVENTH RACE
Santa Anita
JANUARY 3, 2004

$1\frac{1}{16}$ MILES. (1.39) SAN PASQUAL H. Grade II. Purse $150,000 A HANDICAP FOR FOUR-YEAR-OLDS AND UPWARD. By subscription of $150 each to accompany the nomination.$1,500 additional to start, with $150,000 guaranteed, of which $90,000 to first, $30,000 to second, $18,000 to third, $9,000 to fourth and $3,000 to fifth.A trophy will be presented to the owner of the winner. Nominations Closed, Friday, December 26th, 2003 with 12.

Value of Race: $150,000 Winner $90,000; second $30,000; third $18,000; fourth $9,000; fifth $3,000. Mutuel Pool $519,745.00 Exacta Pool $291,775.00 Quinella Pool $29,840.00 Trifecta Pool $343,303.00

Last Raced	Horse	M/Eqt.	A.	Wt	PP	St	¼	½	¾	Str	Fin	Jockey	Odds $1
28Nov03 ^{7}GG^{1}	Star Cross-Arg	LB b	7	113	3	5	5^{hd}	5^{hd}	$4^{\frac{1}{2}}$	2^{2}	$1^{\frac{1}{2}}$	Espinoza V	8.70
6Dec03 ^{8}Hol^{2}	Nose The Trade-GB	LB	6	115	2	3	2^{hd}	$2^{\frac{1}{2}}$	$2^{2\frac{1}{2}}$	1^{2}	2^{3}	Valenzuela P A	3.70
6Dec03 ^{8}Hol^{1}	Olmodavor	LB	5	118	4	6	6^{2}	6^{3}	$6^{3\frac{1}{2}}$	3^{hd}	$3^{2\frac{1}{2}}$	Solis A O	1.50
21Aug03 ^{3}Dmr^{1}	Gift of the Eagle	LB b	6	114	1	1	4^{2}	$4^{\frac{1}{2}}$	3^{hd}	4^{hd}	4^{6}	Baze T	26.00
6Dec03 ^{8}Hol^{5}	Total Impact-Chi	LB	6	116	6	4	3^{1}	$3^{1\frac{1}{2}}$	$5^{1\frac{1}{2}}$	6^{5}	$5^{2\frac{1}{2}}$	Smith M E	2.40
13Dec03 ^{8}Hol^{5}	Hot Market	LB b	6	116	5	2	1^{1}	$1^{\frac{1}{2}}$	1^{hd}	$5^{2\frac{1}{2}}$	6^{6}	Flores D R	8.30
7Sep03 YOR^{18}	Sharp Breeze	LB	4	114	7	7	7	7	7	7	7	Sterling L J Jr	28.70

OFF AT 3:41 Start Good . Won driving. Track fast.

TIME :22^{4}, :45^{4}, 1:09^{3}, 1:35^{2}, 1:42^{1} (:22.80, :45.84, 1:09.69, 1:35.40, 1:42.22)

$2 Mutuel Prices:				
	3 – **STAR CROSS-ARG**	19.40	7.60	3.40
	2 – **NOSE THE TRADE-GB**		5.20	3.00
	4 – **OLMODAVOR**			2.40

$1 EXACTA 3–2 PAID $45.10 $2 QUINELLA 2–3 PAID $42.60
$1 TRIFECTA 3–2–4 PAID $126.10

Ch. h, (Sep), by Southern Halo – Other Star , by Logical . Trainer Vienna Darrell. Bred by La Quebrada (Arg).

STAR CROSS (ARG) pulled early, drifted out a bit into the first turn, chased off the rail, went between horses leaving the backstretch was in a bit tight early on the second turn, continued between foes on that bend, angled out three deep into the stretch and rallied under left handed urging to wear down the runner-up late. NOSE THE TRADE (GB) stalked between horses then bid between foes on the backstretch, battled outside HOT MARKET into and on the second turn, took a short lead nearing the quarter pole, inched away and angled to the inside into the stretch and held on well but was caught late. OLMODAVOR floated out into the first turn, chased outside, came four wide into the stretch and picked up the show. GIFT OF THE EAGLE was in a good position stalking the pace inside, came around a rival into the stretch, split foes in midstretch and lacked the needed late kick. TOTAL IMPACT (CHI) stalked outside then bid three deep on the backstretch, dropped back on the second turn and weakened. HOT MARKET sped to the early lead and angled in, dueled inside on the backstretch and second turn and weakened. SHARP BREEZE off a bit slowly, pulled his way along off the rail then angled in, came out on the second turn and was outrun.

Owners– 1, E A Ranches; 2, Tanaka Gary A; 3, Wertheimer and Frere; 4, Bell Lance and Krikorian George; 5, Al Kabeer Sultan Mohammed Saud and Bridport S A; 6, Harris Farms Inc and Antonsen Per; 7, MacDonald or Sky Chase Farms

Trainers– 1, Vienna Darrell; 2, Frankel Robert J; 3, Mandella Richard E; 4, Shirreffs John A; 5, De Seroux Laura; 6, Lewis Craig A; 7, Puhich Michael

---

$2 Daily Double (8–3) Paid $630.40 ; Daily Double Pool $31,991 .
$1 Pick Three (3–8–3) Paid $2,720.10 ; Pick Three Pool $105,644 .

NINTH RACE
Gulfstream
JANUARY 4, 2004

1 MILE. (Turf) (1.31^{2}) APPLETON H. Grade III. Purse $150,000 FOR THREE YEAR OLDS AND UPWARD. By subscription of $150 each, which shall accompany the nomination, $1,500 to pass the entry box and $1,500 additional to start, with $150,000 guaranteed. The owner of the winner to receive $90,000; $30,000 to second, $16,500 to third, $9,000 to fourth and $4,500 to fifth. Weights: Friday, December 26, 2003. Starters to be named through the entry box by the usual time of closing. Trophy to winning Owner. This race will be limited to 12 Starters, with Also Eligibles. (High Weights on the scale Preferred) In the event this stake race is taken off the turf, it may be subject to downgrading upon review by the Graded Stakes Committee. Closed Monday, December 22, 2003 with (36) nominations.

Value of Race: $150,000 Winner $90,000; second $30,000; third $16,500; fourth $9,000; fifth $4,500. Mutuel Pool $369,220.00 Exacta Pool $260,534.00 Trifecta Pool $191,058.00 Superfecta Pool $68,267.00

Last Raced	Horse	M/Eqt.	A.	Wt	PP	St	¼	½	¾	Str	Fin	Jockey	Odds $1
6Dec03 ^{11}Crc^{2}	MillnnumDrgon-GB	L	5	116	7	9	1^{1}	1^{1}	$1^{\frac{1}{2}}$	$1^{1\frac{1}{2}}$	$1^{1\frac{1}{4}}$	Migliore R	4.10
6Dec03 ^{11}Crc^{1}	Political Attack	L b	5	118	10	7	2^{hd}	2^{1}	2^{1}	$2^{2\frac{1}{2}}$	2^{4}	Douglas R R	7.80
15Nov03 ^{5}Crc^{3}	Proud Man	L b	6	116	4	4	5^{hd}	5^{hd}	6^{1}	$6^{\frac{1}{2}}$	3^{nk}	Prado E S	3.50
6Dec03 ^{11}Crc^{8}	French Charmer	L b	5	117	1	1	$11^{2\frac{1}{2}}$	11^{3}	11^{hd}	$10^{1\frac{1}{2}}$	4no	Decarlo C P	11.10
15Jun03 ^{8}AP^{2}	Miesque's Approval	L	5	117	9	8	$7^{1\frac{1}{2}}$	7^{1}	$3^{\frac{1}{2}}$	4^{1}	$5^{\frac{1}{2}}$	Bailey J D	4.30
5Oct03 ^{4}Kee^{1}	Remind	L	4	115	2	2	9^{2}	9^{2}	8^{hd}	7^{hd}	6^{nk}	Velasquez C	9.80
15Nov03 ^{5}Crc^{5}	Military Man	L	5	113	11	10	$8^{\frac{1}{2}}$	8^{hd}	9^{1}	9^{hd}	7^{hd}	Castro E	107.50
20Dec03 ^{11}Crc^{4}	New York Hero	L b	4	114	6	6	$3^{1\frac{1}{2}}$	3^{1}	$4^{\frac{1}{2}}$	3^{hd}	$8^{1\frac{3}{4}}$	Santos J A	11.30
15Nov03 ^{5}Crc^{1}	Stormy Roman	L	5	114	5	5	$4^{\frac{1}{2}}$	4^{hd}	5^{hd}	8^{hd}	9^{hd}	Aguilar M	15.60
6Dec03 ^{11}Crc^{3}	Sforza-FR	L	5	115	3	3	6^{hd}	$6^{\frac{1}{2}}$	$7^{\frac{1}{2}}$	5^{hd}	$10^{\frac{1}{2}}$	Karamanos H A	27.70
1Nov03 ^{8}Haw^{2}	Al's Dearly Bred	L b	7	116	8	12	12	12	12	11^{3}	$11^{3\frac{1}{4}}$	Coa E M	19.30
1Sep03 ^{5}Crc^{4}	Supah Blitz	L b	4	113	12	11	$10^{\frac{1}{2}}$	10^{hd}	$10^{\frac{1}{2}}$	12	12	Velazquez J R	17.80

OFF AT 4:40 Start Good For All But REMIND. Won driving. Course firm.

TIME :24, :49, 1:11^{4}, 1:34^{2} (:24.19, :49.00, 1:11.88, 1:34.40)

$2 Mutuel Prices:				
	9 – **MILLENNIUM DRAGON-GB**	10.20	6.40	3.80
	12 – **POLITICAL ATTACK**		8.40	4.20
	6 – **PROUD MAN**			3.40

$1 EXACTA 9–12 PAID $44.00 $1 TRIFECTA 9–12–6 PAID $211.60
$1 SUPERFECTA 9–12–6–1 PAID $1,969.20

B. h, (Jan), by Mark of Esteem-Ire – Feather Bride-Ire , by Groom Dancer . Trainer McLaughlin Kiaran P. Bred by Elsdon Farms (GB).

MILLENNIUM DRAGON (GB) rated the pace on the hedge, felt stiff pressure from the top of the stretch and held on well with steady handling. POLITICAL ATTACK rated close in the three path, appeared to take a bad step approaching the final turn, drew close nearing the quarter pole then finished well while not threatening the winner. PROUD MAN rated off the pace toward mid track, was steadied briefly entering the final turn, in tight through the turn, eased out for room in midstretch and finished well. FRENCH CHARMER, unhurriedly off the hedge, was eased out entering the lane and made a mild bid. MIESQUE'S APPROVAL rated back outside and finished evenly. REMIND stumbled at the start and never factored. MILITARY MAN rated back outside then finished evenly. NEW YORK HERO rated just off the pace inside, lacked room on the hedge through the final turn then weakened in the stretch. STORMY ROMAN rated off the pace toward mid track, was checked toward the outside into the final turn then empty in the stretch. SFORZA (FR) rated back on the hedge, was roughed lacking room through the final turn and lost all chance. AL'S DEARLY BRED raced unhurriedly outside and offered no rally. SUPAH BLITZ never factored.

Owners– 1, Darley Stable; 2, Erdenheim Farm; 3, Double R Stable Kaufman Robert and Weiss Stephen; 4, Double S Stable Avanzino Kenneth and Sullivan Joseph; 5, Live Oak Plantation; 6, Claiborne Farm; 7, Muench David L and Block Roger; 8, Paraneck Stable; 9, Croley Thomas L; 10, Eaton John and Laymon Steve; 11, Castro John; 12, Bee Bee Stables Inc and Tortora Jacqueline

Trainers– 1, McLaughlin Kiaran P; 2, Matz Michael R; 3, Clement Christophe; 4, Benson Harry; 5, Mott William I; 6, Mott William I; 7, Muench David L; 8, Pedersen Jennifer; 9, Hills Timothy A; 10, Picou James E; 11, Robertson Hugh H; 12, Tortora Emanuel

Scratched– Justification (27Nov03 ^{3}Aqu^{2}) , Newfoundland (29Oct03 ^{8}Aqu^{5}) , Everything to Gain (21Nov03 ^{9}CD ^{1})

$1 Pick Three (7–10–9) Paid $166.30 ; Pick Three Pool $42,214 .

SIXTH RACE
Santa Anita
JANUARY 4, 2004

1 1/16 MILES. (1.39) SANTA YSABEL S. Grade III. Purse $100,000 FOR FILLIES, THREE YEARS OLD. By subscription of $100 each to accompany the nomination. $1,000 additional to start, with $100,000 added. The added money and all fees to be divided 60% to the winner, 20% to second, 12% to third, 6% to fourth and 2% tofifth. 120 lbs. Winners of a race of $200,000 to carry 3 lbs., additional; non-winners of $55,000 at one mile or over allowed 3 lbs.; of such a race any distance, 5 lbs.; of $20,000 at one mile or over or $30,000 any distance, 7 lbs. (Maiden and Claiming races not considered). A trophy will be presented to the owner of the winner. Nominations closed Friday, December 26, 2003 with 8.

Value of Race: $106,800 Winner $64,080; second $21,360; third $12,816; fourth $6,408; fifth $2,136. Mutuel Pool $390,637.00 Exacta Pool $218,664.00 Quinella Pool $20,148.00 Trifecta Pool $230,817.00

Last Raced	Horse	M/Eqt.	A.	Wt	PP	St	1/4	1/2	3/4	Str	Fin	Jockey	Odds $1
30Oct03 1SA1	A. P. Adventure	LB	3	115	3	6	6	4 1/2	3hd	31	13 1/2	Solis A O	0.90
5Dec03 6DeD1	Salty Romance	B	3	120	6	3	12	11 1/2	11 1/2	12 1/2	2 1/2	Smith M E	2.80
22Nov03 3GG1	Wildwood Flower	LB	3	115	1	1	21 1/2	21 1/2	21 1/2	21 1/2	3 1/2	Valenzuela P A	4.70
29Nov03 10CD8	Stellar Jayne	LB	3	120	4	2	5hd	6	6	4 1/2	42	Espinoza V	9.00
23Oct03 8Kee4	Penny's Fortune	LB	3	117	2	5	41 1/2	54	5hd	53 1/2	56	Nakatani C S	10.20
15Nov03 3Crc1	Super G I	LB	3	116	5	4	31	3hd	41 1/2	6	6	Stevens G L	20.30

OFF AT 3:10 Start Good. Won driving. Track fast.

TIME :23[1], :46[4], 1:11[1], 1:37[3], 1:44[1] (:23.26, :46.89, 1:11.34, 1:37.63, 1:44.27)

$2 Mutuel Prices:

3 – A. P. ADVENTURE	3.80	2.40	2.20
6 – SALTY ROMANCE		3.00	2.40
1 – WILDWOOD FLOWER			2.60

$1 EXACTA 3–6 PAID $5.10 $2 QUINELLA 3–6 PAID $6.40
$1 TRIFECTA 3–6–1 PAID $10.90

B. f, (Jan), by A.P. Indy – Nataliano, by Fappiano. Trainer Dollase Wallace. Bred by Lazy E Ranch Inc (Ky).

A. P. ADVENTURE broke a bit slowly and was squeezed, went up outside on the first turn then stalked three deep, came four wide into the stretch and rallied late under steady urging to collar the runner-up in deep stretch and won clear. SALTY ROMANCE sped to the early lead outside a rival, set the pace off the rail, opened up into the stretch, then drifted out and shortened stride late but held second. WILDWOOD FLOWER stalked the pace a just off the rail, came out a bit wide into the stretch, angled inward in deep stretch and could not catch the pacesetter but held third. STELLAR JAYNE chased outside a rival early then dropped back off the rail on the backstretch, moved up outside on the second turn and five wide into the stretch, drifted in some in the drive and was edged for the show. PENNY'S FORTUNE saved ground chasing the pace, went around a rival leaving the second turn, regained the rail in the stretch and lacked the needed rally. SUPER G I three deep into the first turn, angled in outside a rival, stalked between horses on the backstretch and inside on the second turn and weakened.

Owners– 1, Lewis Robert B and Beverly J; 2, Flying Zee Stable; 3, Gunther John D; 4, Spenthrift Farm LLC Cole Kidder Et Al; 5, Lester Howard and Mary; 6, Bongo Racing Stable or Turrell

Trainers– 1, Dollase Wallace A; 2, Biancone Patrick L; 3, Hollendorfer Jerry; 4, Lukas D Wayne; 5, Sahadi Jenine; 6, Mandella Gary

$2 Daily Double (1–3) Paid $157.60 ; Daily Double Pool $25,698 .
$1 Pick Three (2–1–3) Paid $155.70 ; Pick Three Pool $91,928 .

THIRD RACE
Golden Gate
JANUARY 10, 2004

1 1/16 MILES. (1.39[2]) GOLDEN GATE DERBY Grade III. Purse $100,000 FOR THREE-YEAR-OLDS. By subscription of $100 each to accompany the nomination or by supplementary nomination of $2,000 by time of entry. $500 to pass the entry box and $500 additional to start with $100,000 Guaranteed of which $55,000 to the winner, $20,000 to second, $15,000 to third, $7,500 to fourth and $2,500 to fifth. Weight, 120 lbs. A trophy will be presented to the owner of the winner. CLOSED THURSDAY, JANUARY 1,2004 WITH 12 NOMINATIONS.

Value of Race: $100,000 Winner $55,000; second $20,000; third $15,000; fourth $7,500; fifth $2,500. Mutuel Pool $155,414.00 Exacta Pool $106,492.00 Quinella Pool $11,438.00

Last Raced	Horse	M/Eqt.	A.	Wt	PP	St	1/4	1/2	3/4	Str	Fin	Jockey	Odds $1
13Dec03 7GG1	Skipaslew	LB b	3	120	5	5	33 1/2	34	33	1 1/2	12	Saint-Martin E	1.00
13Dec03 7GG3	O. K. Mikie	LB b	3	120	1	4	4hd	4hd	42 1/2	4 1/2	2hd	Lopez A D	7.10
4Dec03 3GG1	Bensquito	LB b	3	120	2	3	5	5	5	5	31 1/2	Perez M A	8.30
29Dec03 1SA3	Gwaihir-Ire	LB b	3	120	3	2	21	21	21	31	41	Rollins C J	4.40
13Dec03 2GG1	Dixieland Heater	LB f	3	120	4	1	1 1/2	1 1/2	1hd	2hd	5	Radke K	2.40

OFF AT 1:49 Start Good. Won driving. Track wet fast.

TIME :22[4], :46[2], 1:10[1], 1:35[1], 1:41[4] (:22.96, :46.41, 1:10.25, 1:35.35, 1:41.84)

$2 Mutuel Prices:

5 – SKIPASLEW	4.00	3.00	2.20
1 – O. K. MIKIE		5.00	2.80
2 – BENSQUITO			3.00

$1 EXACTA 5–1 PAID $7.90 $2 QUINELLA 1–5 PAID $11.60

Ch. c, (Mar), by Skip Away – Slew Be, by Seattle Slew. Trainer O'Neill Doug. Bred by Morgan's Ford Farm & Skip Away LLC (Va).

SKIPASLEW stalked the leaders to the second turn, responded when asked and rallied to the lead three wide, took the lead in mid stretch then edged away under steady urging. O. K. MIKIE was allowed to settle, commenced a bid into the second turn, was forced to circle rivals and swung five wide into the stretch, looked a factor to mid stretch then could not impact the winner and just held off BENSQUITO for second. BENSQUITO had no speed, saved ground and was asked for run on the second turn, rallied to the stretch, was blocked behind rivals and had to wait in mid stretch then shifted out and came on late but just missed the place. GWAIHIR (IRE) attended the pace from the rail for six furlongs, was asked for his best and remained a factor to mid stretch but weakened in the final sixteenth. DIXIELAND HEATER dueled for the lead outside of GWAIHIR(IRE) to the second turn, also responded to the stretch but also weakened late.

Owners– 1, The Merv Griffin Ranch Co; 2, Lo Charles; 3, Mastrocinque Mastrocinque and Raygoza; 4, Kirkwood Al and Saundra S; 5, Debruycker Lloyd Glassman Richard Hollendorfer Jerry and Todaro George

Trainers– 1, O'Neill Doug; 2, McArthur Jerry; 3, Miyadi Steven; 4, Lewis Craig A; 5, Hollendorfer Jerry

$2 Daily Double (2–5) Paid $45.80 ; Daily Double Pool $11,645 .
$1 Pick Three (4/6–2–5) Paid $32.10 ; Pick Three Pool $32,310 .

EIGHTH RACE
Gulfstream
JANUARY 10, 2004

6 FURLONGS. (1.07^4) SPECTACULAR BID S. Grade III. Purse $100,000 FOR THREE YEAR OLDS. By subscription of $100 each, which shall accompany the nomination, $1,000 to pass the entry box and $1,000 additional to start, with $100,000 guaranteed. The owner of the winner to receive $60,000, $20,000 to second, $11,000 to third, $6,000 to fourth, and $3,000 to fifth. Supplemental nominations may be made on Thursday, January 8, 2004 at a fee of $3,000, which includes entry and start fees. Weight: 122 lbs. Non-winners of $50,000 twice allowed 2 lbs.;$40,000 once or $25,000 twiceallowed 4 lbs., $35,000 once or two races other than maiden or claiming, 6 lbs. Trophy to winning owner. Closed Monday, December 29, 2003 with (15) nominations.

Value of Race: $100,000 Winner $60,000; second $20,000; third $11,000; fourth $6,000; fifth $3,000. Mutuel Pool $509,054.00 Exacta Pool $361,899.00 Trifecta Pool $237,838.00 Superfecta Pool $61,911.00

Last Raced	Horse	M/Eqt.	A.	Wt	PP	St	¼	½	Str	Fin	Jockey	Odds $1
15Nov03 ^{10}Crc^{2}	Wynn Dot Comma	L	3	120	4	2	6$^{1\frac{1}{2}}$	5^{hd}	4$^{2\frac{1}{2}}$	1$^{1\frac{1}{4}}$	Bravo J	1.70
26Sep03 ^{3}Bel^{2}	Saratoga County	L bf	3	116	5	6	3^{hd}	2$^{\frac{1}{2}}$	3$^{\frac{1}{2}}$	2$^{\frac{3}{4}}$	Velazquez J R	3.60
15Nov03 ^{6}Lrl^{3}	Ghost Mountain	L b	3	120	2	1	4^{1}	4^{hd}	2^{1}	3$^{\frac{1}{2}}$	Prado E S	4.80
16Nov03 ^{8}Aqu^{2}	Smokume		3	120	3	5	2$^{\frac{1}{2}}$	1^{hd}	1^{hd}	4$^{5\frac{1}{2}}$	Uske S^{7}	4.30
13Dec03 ^{7}Lrl^{1}	Excellent Band	L	3	120	7	4	7	7	5$^{2\frac{1}{2}}$	5$^{7\frac{3}{4}}$	Vega H	4.20
27Dec03 ^{6}Crc^{1}	Fortunate Buy	L	3	116	1	7	1$^{1\frac{1}{2}}$	3$^{\frac{1}{2}}$	6^{2}	6$^{3\frac{3}{4}}$	Santos J A	34.10
13Dec03 ^{10}Tam^{14}	Heart of Jules	L f	3	116	6	3	5^{hd}	6$^{1\frac{1}{2}}$	7	7	Castro E	41.00

OFF AT 4:10 Start Good . Won driving. Track fast.

TIME :22^2, :45^4, :58^1, 1:10^3 (:22.47, :45.97, :58.28, 1:10.60)

$2 Mutuel Prices:				
	4 – WYNN DOT COMMA	5.40	3.20	2.40
	5 – SARATOGA COUNTY		3.80	3.60
	2 – GHOST MOUNTAIN			3.40

$1 EXACTA 4–5 PAID $11.10 $1 TRIFECTA 4–5–2 PAID $41.60
$1 SUPERFECTA 4–5–2–3 PAID $103.10

Ch. c, (May), by Struggler–GB – I Like Punch , by Two Punch . Trainer Wolfson Martin D. Bred by T Wynn Jolley & Harry Hoglander (Fla).

WYNN DOT COMMA taken in hand to track the pace, eased outside the leaders in the stretch, rallied under pressure to take over at the sixteenth pole and edged away. SARATOGA COUNTY chased the pace three wide, was floated out by SMOKUME at the top of the stretch, then continued on with good courage to be up for the place while being outfinished by the winner. GHOST MOUNTAIN tracked the pace along the inside, came around the tiring FORTUNATE BUY on the turn, rallied along the rail to reach near even terms for command in midstretch, then gave way in the final sixteenth. SMOKUME chased the pace, moved to gain a slim lead on the turn, then drifted out at the top of the stretch, was straightened away, maintained a slim advantage to the sixteenth pole and weakened. EXCELLENT BAND was no factor after being outrun early. FORTUNATE BUY broke to the inside at the start, showed speed along the inside to past midway of the turn and faltered. HEART OF JULES raced four wide on the turn and faded.

Owners– 1, Cherry Martin L; 2, Pollard Evelyn M; 3, La Penta Robert V; 4, Hobeau Farm; 5, R N R Stable; 6, Runnin Horse Farm Inc; 7, Denise & Nathan Fisler & D & R Chaslon

Trainers– 1, Wolfson Martin D; 2, Weaver George; 3, Zito Nicholas P; 4, Jerkens H Allen; 5, Testerman Valora A; 6, Pointer Norman R; 7, Green Donna

$1 Pick Three (8–9–4) Paid $2,263.40 ; Pick Three Pool $93,366 .

THIRD RACE
Santa Anita
JANUARY 10, 2004

1⅛ MILES. (Turf) (1.43^4) SAN GORGONIO H. Grade II. Purse $150,000 FOR FILLIES AND MARES FOUR YEARS OLD AND UPWARD. By subscription of $150 each to accompany the nomination or by supplementary nomination of $3,000 by Sunday, January 4. $500 to pass the entry box and $1,000 additional to start, with $150,000 guaranteed,ofwhich $90,000 to first, $30,000 to second, $18,000 to third, $9,000 to fourth, and $3,000 to fifth. Weights Tuesday, January 6. High weights preferred. Starters to be named through the entry box by the closing time of entries. A trophy will be presentedto the owner of the winner. (Rail at 15 feet). Closed with 13 Nominations. (Rail at 15 feet).

Value of Race: $147,000 Winner $90,000; second $30,000; third $18,000; fourth $9,000. Mutuel Pool $358,505.00 Exacta Pool $200,651.00 Quinella Pool $19,499.00

Last Raced	Horse	M/Eqt.	A.	Wt	PP	St	¼	½	¾	Str	Fin	Jockey	Odds $1
25Oct03 ^{6}SA^{5}	Megahertz-GB	LB	5	119	2	1	4	4	4	2$^{\frac{1}{2}}$	1^{1}	Solis A O	0.60
30Nov03 ^{6}Hol^{7}	GardenintheRin-FR	LB	7	116	4	2	1^{1}	1^{1}	1$^{\frac{1}{2}}$	1$^{1\frac{1}{2}}$	2$^{1\frac{1}{2}}$	Stevens G L	2.70
22Nov03 ^{9}CD^{3}	Firth of Lorne-Ire	LB	5	116	3	3	2$^{\frac{1}{2}}$	2^{hd}	2^{1}	3^{hd}	3^{hd}	Flores D R	11.80
30Nov03 ^{6}Hol^{8}	Mer de Corail-Ire	L	5	115	1	4	3^{1}	3^{1}	3^{hd}	4	4	Smith M E	3.00

OFF AT 1:34 Start Good . Won driving. Course firm.

TIME :25^2, :51, 1:14^3, 1:37^4, 1:49^2 (:25.51, :51.08, 1:14.79, 1:37.86, 1:49.51)

$2 Mutuel Prices:				
	3 – MEGAHERTZ–GB	3.20	2.10	—
	5 – GARDEN IN THE RAIN–FR		2.10	—
	4 – FIRTH OF LORNE–IRE		—	—

$1 EXACTA 3–5 PAID $3.40 $2 QUINELLA 3–5 PAID $4.40

Ch. m, (May), by Pivotal–GB – Heavenly Ray , by Rahy . Trainer Frankel Robert. Bred by Cheveley Park Stud Ltd (GB).

MEGAHERTZ (GB) close up stalking the pace outside a rival or a bit off the rail, went outside a foe into and on the second turn, came three deep into the stretch, rallied under some urging to gain the lead nearing the sixteenth pole, tried to lug in a bit but proved best under good handling. GARDEN IN THE RAIN (FR) pulled her way to the front, angled in nearing the first turn, set the pace inside, dueled inside a rival when headed on the backstretch, regained the advantage into the second turn, inched away on that turn and continued willingly but could not match the winner. FIRTH OF LORNE (IRE) off a bit slowly, pulled her way along to stalk the pace outside a rival, bid outside the runner-up and took a short lead on the backstretch, dueled outside that one into and early on the second turn, dropped back a bit on that turn and lacked the needed response in the stretch. MER DE CORAIL (IRE) broke slowly, pulled under a hold along the inside stalking the pace, inched forward leaving the backstretch, was in a bit tight into the second turn, remained inside and was outfinished.

Owners– 1, Bello Michael; 2, Englander Richard A; 3, Darley Stable; 4, Magnier Susan

Trainers– 1, Frankel Robert J; 2, Mullins Jeff; 3, Harty Eoln G; 4, Biancone Patrick L

Scratched– Tropical Blossom (29Nov03 ^{7}GG ^{1})

$2 Daily Double (3–3) Paid $32.40 ; Daily Double Pool $32,748 .
$1 Pick Three (7–3–2/3) Paid $136.90 ; Pick Three Pool $116,701 .

EIGHTH RACE
Santa Anita
JANUARY 10, 2004

$1\frac{1}{16}$ MILES. (1.39) SAN FERNANDO BREEDERS' CUP S. Grade II. Purse $200,000 (includes $100,000 BC – Breeders' Cup) FOR FOUR-YEAR-OLDS. By subscription of $200 each to accompany the nomination or by supplementary nomination of $4,000 by time of entry. $2,000 additional to start, with $100,000 added, and an additional $100,000 from Breeders' Cup Fund for cup nomineesonly. The host association's added monies and fees to be divided 60% to the winner, 20% to second, 12% to third, 6% to fourth and 2% to fifth. Breeders' Cup fund monies also correspondingly divided provided a Breeders' Cup nominee has finished in an awardedposition. Any Breeders' Cup fund monies not awarded will revert to the fund. 122 lbs. Non-winners of $100,000 twice at one mile or over in 2003–2004 allowed 2 lbs.; of such a race in 2003–2004 or $60,000 any distance since December 25, 4 lbs.; of a raceof $50,000 since July 1, 6 lbs. Starters to be named through the entry box by the closing time of entires with preference given to Breeders' Cup nominees only of equal racing quality or weight assignment (respective of sex and weight for age). A trophy will be presented to the owner of the winner. A trophy will be presented to the owner of the winner. Closed with 20 Nominations.

Value of Race: $221,800 Winner $134,280; second $44,760; third $26,856; fourth $13,428; fifth $2,476. Mutuel Pool $543,456.00 Exacta Pool $303,189.00 Quinella Pool $28,354.00 Trifecta Pool $311,199.00 Superfecta Pool $109,042.00

Last Raced	Horse	M/Eqt.	A.	Wt	PP	St	¼	½	¾	Str	Fin	Jockey	Odds $1
28Nov03 ^{11}CD^{13}	During	LB b	4	120	3	3	$2^{1\frac{1}{2}}$	2^{1}	$2^{1\frac{1}{2}}$	2^{hd}	1^{1}	Flores D R	4.00
26Dec03 ^{8}SA^{11}	Toccet	LB b	4	116	9	5	3^{hd}	$3^{1\frac{1}{2}}$	$3^{2\frac{1}{2}}$	$3^{1\frac{1}{2}}$	2^{1}	Espinoza V	8.80
29Nov03 ^{8}Hol^{1}	Touch the Wire	LB b	4	117	7	8	9^{1}	10	7^{hd}	1^{1}	3^{2}	Nakatani C S	9.80
26Dec03 ^{8}SA^{6}	Domestic Dispute	LB	4	116	6	6	7^{hd}	8^{3}	$8^{1\frac{1}{2}}$	5^{1}	4^{2}	Solis A O	4.80
18May03 ^{6}CD^{4}	Spensive	LB b	4	116	10	10	10	$9^{\frac{1}{2}}$	$9^{3\frac{1}{2}}$	7^{5}	5^{2}	Stevens G L	11.90
30Nov03 ^{9}Hol^{12}	Senor Swinger	LB b	4	120	5	7	$6^{\frac{1}{2}}$	7^{1}	$4^{\frac{1}{2}}$	$6^{\frac{1}{2}}$	$6^{2\frac{1}{2}}$	Ramsammy E	9.40
16Nov03 ^{8}RP^{2}	Excessivepleasure	LB b	4	122	1	1	$1^{\frac{1}{2}}$	1^{hd}	1^{hd}	4^{hd}	7^{13}	Court J K	6.60
20Dec03 ^{6}Hol^{1}	Anziyan Royalty	LB b	4	116	8	9	$8^{4\frac{1}{2}}$	6^{1}	6^{hd}	$8^{\frac{1}{2}}$	8^{8}	Valdivia J Jr	4.20
26Dec03 ^{8}SA^{5}	Watchem Smokey	LB	4	118	2	2	5^{2}	4^{hd}	5^{1}	9^{3}	9^{2}	Desormeaux K J	8.50
30Nov03 ^{8}Hol^{1}	Ender's Shadow	LB bf	4	116	4	4	4^{hd}	5^{hd}	10	10	10	Smith M E	54.60

OFF AT 4:08 Start Good . Won driving. Track fast.

TIME :22^{2}, :45^{2}, 1:09^{1}, 1:35, 1:41^{3} (:22.51, :45.57, 1:09.33, 1:35.01, 1:41.63)

$2 Mutuel Prices:

3 – DURING	10.00	5.60	4.20
9 – TOCCET		10.00	7.60
7 – TOUCH THE WIRE			8.80

$1 EXACTA 3–9 PAID $44.00 $2 QUINELLA 3–9 PAID $51.20
$1 TRIFECTA 3–9–7 PAID $520.70 $1 SUPERFECTA 3–9–7–6 PAID $2,024.10

Dk. b or br. c, (Feb), by Cherokee Run – Blading Saddle , by Blade . Trainer Baffert Bob. Bred by Gulf States Racing Stables II (Ky).

DURING between horses early, dueled outside a rival, put a head in front into the stretch, came back at TOUCH THE WIRE between horses in deep stretch to regain the lead and proved best under urging. TOCCET four wide into the first turn, stalked three deep, bid outside between calls on the backstretch, continued close up off the rail into and on the second turn and into the stretch and went willingly to the wire. TOUCH THE WIRE in tight early, angled in and saved ground off the pace, moved up inside on the second turn, slipped through along the rail to gain the lead in upper stretch and weakened late but held third. DOMESTIC DISPUTE in tight between foes early, chased between horses then a bit off the rail, waited off heels early on the second turn, came out into the stretch and bested the others. SPENSIVE angled in and settled off the rail then outside a rival, came out four wide into the stretch and improved position. SENOR SWINGER bumped in tight between horses early, angled in and pulled his way along to stalk the pace toward the inside, came out on the second turn, waited behind foes in upper stretch and lacked the needed rally. EXCESSIVEPLEASURE sped to the early lead, dueled inside the winner to the stretch and weakened. ANZIYAN ROYALTY in tight between horses early, stalked three deep, dropped back leaving the second turn, came six wide into the stretch and gave way. WATCHEM SMOKEY stalked inside then a bit off the rail, was between horses into the second turn, came out five wide into the stretch and also gave way. ENDER'S SHADOW in tight early, chased between horses, dropped back into the second turn and had nothing left.

Owners– 1, McIngvale James; 2, Borislow Daniel M; 3, Creel Allan Lanni J Terrance and Schiappa Bernard C; 4, Bienstock Dave and Winner Charles; 5, Watson and Weitman Performances LLC; 6, Lewis Robert B and Beverly J; 7, Leatherman Lee and Ty; 8, Cafarchia Nick; 9, Gann Edmund A; 10, Green Lantern Stables LLC

Trainers– 1, Baffert Bob; 2, Scanlan John F; 3, Dollase Craig; 4, Gallagher Patrick; 5, Baffert Bob; 6, Baffert Bob; 7, O'Neill Doug; 8, Dollase Craig; 9, Frankel Robert J; 10, Sahadi Jenine

---

$2 Daily Double (11–3) Paid $103.00 ; Daily Double Pool $45,642 .
$1 Pick Three (14–11–3) Paid $196.20 ; Pick Three Pool $95,654 .

TENTH RACE
Gulfstream
JANUARY 11, 2004

6 FURLONGS. (1.07^{4}) FIRST LADY H. Grade III. Purse $100,000 FOR FILLIES AND MARES, THREE YEARS OLD AND UPWARD. By subscription of $100 each, which shall accompany the nomination, $1,000 to pass the entry box and $1,000 additional to start, with $100,000 guaranteed. The owner of the winner to receive $60,000; $20,000 to second, $11,000 to third, $6,000 to fourth and $3,000 to fifth. Trophy to winning Owner. Closed Monday, December 29, 2003 with (23) nominations.

Value of Race: $100,000 Winner $60,000; second $20,000; third $11,000; fourth $6,000; fifth $3,000. Mutuel Pool $327,257.00 Exacta Pool $217,371.00 Trifecta Pool $213,417.00 Superfecta Pool $74,721.00

Last Raced	Horse	M/Eqt.	A.	Wt	PP	St	¼	½	Str	Fin	Jockey	Odds $1
5Oct03 ^{9}Bel^{1}	Harmony Lodge	L	6	119	3	5	3^{1}	$3^{1\frac{1}{2}}$	$1^{3\frac{1}{2}}$	$1^{1\frac{3}{4}}$	Migliore R	1.60
5Oct03 ^{9}Bel^{2}	House Party		4	118	1	9	8^{1}	8^{4}	$2^{\frac{1}{2}}$	$2^{\frac{1}{2}}$	Santos J A	1.70
27Nov03 ^{10}CD^{2}	Mayo On the Side	L bf	5	115	2	8	9	9	7^{hd}	3^{2}	Velez J A Jr	33.20
16Nov03 ^{8}WO^{3}	Mille Feville	L	5	114	7	4	5^{hd}	$6^{1\frac{1}{2}}$	$3^{\frac{1}{2}}$	4no	Velasquez C H	53.60
13Dec03 ^{10}Crc^{8}	Belle Artiste	L	6	114	5	6	7^{5}	$7^{\frac{1}{2}}$	6^{1}	$5^{3\frac{3}{4}}$	Prado E S	54.70
4Oct03 ^{8}Med^{1}	Cupid Season	L	4	113	9	1	4^{1}	$4^{1\frac{1}{2}}$	4^{hd}	6no	Velazquez J R	11.60
22Nov03 ^{4}CD^{1}	Double Scoop	L f	4	114	4	7	6^{2}	5^{hd}	8^{3}	$7^{4\frac{3}{4}}$	Bailey J D	4.40
25Oct03 ^{4}Bel^{6}	Follow Me Home	L b	4	112	8	3	2^{1}	$2^{\frac{1}{2}}$	5^{1}	$8^{6\frac{3}{4}}$	Chavez J F	36.30
13Dec03 ^{10}Crc^{2}	Holy Bubbette	L	4	114	6	2	$1^{\frac{1}{2}}$	1^{hd}	9	9	Coa E	11.10

OFF AT 5:11 Start Good. Won driving. Track fast.
TIME :21^{4}, :44^{4}, :57, 1:09^{3} (:21.87, :44.91, :57.08, 1:09.64)

$2 Mutuel Prices:			
3 – HARMONY LODGE	5.20	3.20	2.80
1 – HOUSE PARTY		3.00	2.80
2 – MAYO ON THE SIDE			8.60

$1 EXACTA 3–1 PAID $5.90 $1 TRIFECTA 3–1–2 PAID $45.50
$1 SUPERFECTA 3–1–2–8 PAID $118.30

Ch. m, (Mar), by Hennessy – Win Crafty Lady, by Crafty Prospector. Trainer Pletcher Todd A. Bred by Sabine Stables (Ky).

HARMONY LODGE stalked the pace, angled three wide on the turn, rallied to open a clear advantage in midstretch, then was under pressure to remain clear to the wire. HOUSE PARTY unhurried after breaking slowly, angled out for the stretch run and rallied for the place while unable to catch the winner. MAYO ON THE SIDE outrun early, swung out for the stretch run and finished full of run for the show. MILLE FEVILLE rated off the pace, advanced between horses to reach contention in midstretch but had no late response. BELLE ARTISTE failed to menace. CUPID SEASON chased the leaders three wide around the turn and gave way. DOUBLE SCOOP saved ground and tired. FOLLOW ME HOME forced the pace outside HOLY BUBBETTE to nearing the stretch and faltered. HOLY BUBBETTE set the pace under pressure along the inside, then faded in the drive.

Owners– 1, Melnyk Eugene and Laura; 2, Shields Joseph V Jr; 3, Lothenbach Stables Inc; 4, Haras Santa Maria de Araras; 5, Peace John H; 6, Antonini Guerino; 7, Humphrey G Watts Jr; 8, Braunsdorf Robert and Levine Robert; 9, Elam Katherine

Trainers– 1, Pletcher Todd A; 2, Jerkens H Allen; 3, Nafzger Carl A; 4, Attfield Roger L; 5, Weaver George; 6, Iwinski Allen; 7, Arnold George R II; 8, Levine Robert L; 9, Fawkes David

Scratched– Big Cheque (28Nov03 ^{2}WO ^{1}), Awesome Charm (07Nov03 ^{8}Lrl^{1})

$1 Pick Three (1–7–3/6/11) Paid $129.00 ; Pick Three Pool $34,694 .

SEVENTH RACE
Santa Anita
JANUARY 11, 2004

6 FURLONGS. (1.07^{1}) SAN MIGUEL S. Grade III. Purse $100,000 FOR THREE–YEAR–OLDS. By subscription of $100 each to accompany the nomination or by supplementary nomination of $2,000 by time of entry. $1,000 additional to start, with $100,000 added. The added money and all fees to be divided 60% to the winner, 20% tosecond, 12% to third, 6% to fourth and 2% to fifth. 121 lbs. Non–winners of a race of $50,000 or two of $30,000 allowed 3 lbs.; of a race of $35,000 since July 23 or $25,000 at any time, 5 lbs.; of a race other than Maiden of Claiming, 7 lbs. (Claiming races not considered). Starters to be named through the entry box by the closing time of entries. A trophy will be presented to the owner of the winner. Closed with 11 nominations.

Value of Race: $108,100 Winner $64,860; second $21,620; third $12,972; fourth $6,486; fifth $2,162. Mutuel Pool $381,824.00 Exacta Pool $201,262.00 Quinella Pool $24,176.00 Trifecta Pool $241,383.00

Last Raced	Horse	M/Eqt.	A.	Wt	PP	St	¼	½	Str	Fin	Jockey	Odds $1
26Dec03 ^{1}SA^{1}	Hosco	LB b	3	118	1	3	1^{1}	$1^{\frac{1}{2}}$	$1^{1\frac{1}{2}}$	1^{1}	Baze T	4.00
20Dec03 ^{3}Hol^{1}	Roi Charmant	LB	3	117	2	4	3^{hd}	2^{hd}	2^{2}	2^{3}	Nakatani C S	4.40
15Nov03 ^{10}CD^{1}	Gethsemani	LB	3	116	5	7	6^{2}	5^{2}	4^{hd}	3^{hd}	Stevens G L	12.70
7Dec03 ^{6}Hol^{1}	Last Minute Detail	LB	3	114	4	5	5^{hd}	6^{3}	$6^{3\frac{1}{2}}$	4^{3}	Espinoza V	3.30
22Nov03 ^{3}GG^{4}	Hot Weekend	LB	3	116	7	2	$2^{1\frac{1}{2}}$	$3^{\frac{1}{2}}$	$3^{1\frac{1}{2}}$	5^{5}	Valenzuela P A	16.90
13Dec03 ^{7}GG^{2}	The Herc	LB	3	121	6	1	$4^{3\frac{1}{2}}$	$4^{2\frac{1}{2}}$	$5^{1\frac{1}{2}}$	6^{nk}	Desormeaux K J	1.60
14Jun03 ^{2}CPR^{1}	Laditude	LB f	3	116	3	6	7	7	7	7	Solis A O	13.80

OFF AT 3:38 Start Good. Won driving. Track fast.
TIME :21, :43^{4}, :56, 1:09^{1} (:21.03, :43.80, :56.09, 1:09.36)

$2 Mutuel Prices:			
1 – HOSCO	10.00	5.20	3.80
2 – ROI CHARMANT		6.40	4.60
5 – GETHSEMANI			5.40

$1 EXACTA 1–2 PAID $20.60 $2 QUINELLA 1–2 PAID $24.20
$1 TRIFECTA 1–2–5 PAID $166.90

Dk. b or br. c, (Mar), by Honour and Glory – Cucina Cucina, by Carson City. Trainer O'Neill Doug. Bred by Northwest Farms (Ky).

HOSCO sent inside to gain the lead, inched away on the backstretch, responded when challenged a bit off the rail leaving the turn, inched away again in the stretch and held on gamely under urging. ROI CHARMANT taken off the inside early to stalk the pace, bid three deep on the turn and into the stretch, could not match the winner in the final furlong but was clearly second best. GETHSEMANI allowed to settle off the rail on the backstretch and turn, came out into the stretch and edged a rival for third. LAST MINUTE DETAIL chased off the rail on the backstretch, angled in for the turn, came out into the stretch and just missed the show. HOT WEEKEND stalked outside on the backstretch and between foes into and on the turn and weakened in the stretch. THE HERC had good early speed and stalked off the rail on the backstretch, angled to the inside for the turn, dropped back into the stretch and also weakened. LADITUDE allowed to settle off the pace away from the inside, came out into the stretch and did not rally.

Owners– 1, Rodriguez Lorraine and Rod; 2, Sens Du Cheval Farm; 3, Hancock III Stonerside Stable LLC; 4, Little Jerry D; 5, Soares Michael and Suarez Pablo; 6, I S Longo Living Trust; 7, Bello & Lenner

Trainers– 1, O'Neill Doug; 2, Robbins Jay M; 3, Lukas D Wayne; 4, Chatlos Donald Jr; 5, O'Neill Doug; 6, Stute Gary; 7, Bray Simon

$2 Daily Double (3–1) Paid $62.40 ; Daily Double Pool $25,374 .
$1 Pick Three (1–3–1) Paid $234.20 ; Pick Three Pool $82,451 .

FOURTH RACE
Aqueduct
JANUARY 17, 2004

$1\frac{1}{16}$ MILES. (1.41) AQUEDUCT H. Grade III. Purse $100,000 (plus $10,100 Other Sources) INNER DIRT. A HANDICAP FOR THREE YEAR OLDS AND UPWARD. By subscription of $100 each, which should accompany the nomination; $500 to pass the entry box; $500 to start, with $100,000 added. The added money and all fees to be divided 60% to the winner, 20% to second, 10% to third, 5% to fourth, 3% to fifth and 2% to be divided equally among the remaining finishers. A trophy will be presented to he winning owner. Closed Saturday, January 3, 2004 with 16 Nomination.

Value of Race: $110,100 Winner $66,060; second $22,020; third $11,010; fourth $5,505; fifth $3,303; sixth $735; seventh $735; eighth $732. Mutuel Pool $456,578.00 Exacta Pool $468,128.00 Quinella Pool $37,137.00 Trifecta Pool $321,373.00

Last Raced	Horse	M/Eqt.	A.	Wt	PP	St	¼	½	¾	Str	Fin	Jockey	Odds $1
13Dec03 ^{8}Aqu^{3}	Seattle Fitz-Arg	L	5	114	8	6	4^{hd}	$2^{3\frac{1}{2}}$	2^{5}	1^{hd}	1no	Gryder A T	2.70
13Dec03 ^{8}Aqu^{2}	Evening Attire	L b	6	122	4	7	8	$5^{\frac{1}{2}}$	$4^{\frac{1}{2}}$	3^{7}	$2^{1\frac{1}{4}}$	Bridgmohan S	0.90
28Dec03 ^{8}Aqu^{2}	Rogue Agent	L b	5	112	6	5	$1^{1\frac{1}{2}}$	$1^{1\frac{1}{2}}$	$1^{\frac{1}{2}}$	$2^{2\frac{1}{2}}$	$3^{8\frac{3}{4}}$	Arroyo N Jr	30.50
2Jan04 ^{8}Aqu^{3}	Lord Ofthe Thunder	L bf	5	113	3	1	7^{hd}	8	$6^{1\frac{1}{2}}$	5^{hd}	4^{2}	Castellano J	16.60
17Dec03 ^{7}Aqu^{1}	Boston Park	L b	4	113	5	4	3^{6}	$3^{\frac{1}{2}}$	3^{hd}	4^{2}	$5^{3\frac{3}{4}}$	Cotto P L Jr	27.75
2Jan04 ^{8}Aqu^{5}	Peekskill	L b	5	111	1	2	$5^{1\frac{1}{2}}$	6^{hd}	$7^{4\frac{1}{2}}$	7^{8}	6^{1}	Chavez J F	15.20
2Jan04 ^{8}Aqu^{1}	Abreeze	L	9	116	7	8	$2^{\frac{1}{2}}$	$4^{1\frac{1}{2}}$	5^{3}	6^{1}	$7^{14\frac{1}{4}}$	Luzzi M J	9.10
2Jan04 ^{8}Aqu^{2}	Classic Endeavor	L f	6	114	2	3	$6^{1\frac{1}{2}}$	$7^{2\frac{1}{2}}$	8	8	8	Lopez C C	10.00

OFF AT 1:49 Start Good . Won driving. Track fast.

TIME :22^{4}, :46, 1:10^{1}, 1:35^{2}, 1:42 (:22.93, :46.19, 1:10.25, 1:35.58, 1:42.13)

$2 Mutuel Prices:

8 – SEATTLE FITZ-ARG	7.40	3.30	2.70
5 – EVENING ATTIRE		2.40	2.20
6 – ROGUE AGENT			4.60

$2 EXACTA 8–5 PAID $14.60 $2 QUINELLA 5–8 PAID $5.90
$2 TRIFECTA 8–5–6 PAID $154.50

Dk. b or br. h, (Oct), by Fitzcarraldo-Arg – Hug a Slew , by Seattle Slew . Trainer McLaughlin Kiaran P. Bred by Firmamento (Arg).

SEATTLE FITZ (ARG) was in hand early on, advanced outside on the backstretch, responded when roused, dug in gamely in the stretch and prevailed under a drive. EVENING ATTIRE was outrun early, rallied three wide on the second and finished gamely outside, just missing. ROGUE AGENT quickly opened a clear lead, set the pace along the inside and dug in gamely on the rail in the stretch. LORD OFTHE THUNDER was outrun early, raced three wide on the second turn and had no rally. BOSTON PARK showed speed along the inside, was steadied nearing the first turn, chased the pace and tired in the stretch. PEEKSKILL raced inside and had no response when roused. ABREEZE chased the pace while between rivals and tired. CLASSIC ENDEAVOR tired.

Owners– 1, West Point Stable; 2, Mary Grant Thomas J Kelly and Joseph M Grant; 3, My Goose Stable Oringer Jay Fein Scott and Parrotta Gene; 4, Paraneck Stable; 5, Overbrook Farm William T Young Jr; 6, Morino Gregory A; 7, Rotella John; 8, Schwartz Herbert T and Carol A

Trainers– 1, McLaughlin Kiaran P; 2, Kelly Patrick J; 3, Brice Michael; 4, Pedersen Jennifer; 5, Lukas D Wayne; 6, LaBoccetta Frank Jr; 7, Lake Scott A; 8, Schwartz Scott M

Scratched– Big Country (19Dec03 ^{7}Aqu^{1})

$2 Pick Three (3–2–8) Paid $172.50 ; Pick Three Pool $95,483 .

NINTH RACE
Aqueduct
JANUARY 17, 2004

$1\frac{1}{16}$ MILES. (1.41) AFFECTIONATELY H. Grade III. Purse $100,000 (plus $9,600 Other Sources) INNER DIRT. A HANDICAP FOR FILLIES AND MARES THREE YEARS OLD AND UPWARD. By subscription of $100 each, which should accompany the nomination; $500 to pass the entry box; $500 to start, with $100,000 added. The added money and all fees to be divided 60% tothe winner, 20% to second, 10% to third, 5% to fourth, 3% to fifth and 2% divided equally among the remaining finishers. A trophy will be presented to the winning owner. Closed Saturday, December 27, 2003 with 16 Nominations.

Value of Race: $109,600 Winner $65,760; second $21,920; third $10,960; fourth $5,480; fifth $3,288; sixth $732; seventh $732; eighth $728. Mutuel Pool $522,683.00 Exacta Pool $419,457.00 Trifecta Pool $313,004.00

Last Raced	Horse	M/Eqt.	A.	Wt	PP	St	¼	½	¾	Str	Fin	Jockey	Odds $1
2Nov03 ^{7}Del^{1}	Austin's Mom	L	4	112	6	6	5^{1}	$6^{\frac{1}{2}}$	7^{3}	$3^{\frac{1}{2}}$	$1^{5\frac{1}{2}}$	Fragoso P	11.50
11Dec03 ^{8}Aqu^{1}	Golden Damsel	L b	4	114	4	3	1^{7}	1^{6}	$1^{\frac{1}{2}}$	$1^{\frac{1}{2}}$	2^{1}	Gryder A T	4.10
20Dec03 ^{8}Aqu^{6}	Consort Music	L	5	114	1	8	8	8	6^{hd}	$5^{1\frac{1}{2}}$	$3^{\frac{3}{4}}$	Pimentel J	57.25
7Dec03 ^{9}Lrl^{1}	Cruise Along	L b	6	115	2	7	$7^{3\frac{1}{2}}$	3^{hd}	$2^{\frac{1}{2}}$	2^{2}	$4^{2\frac{3}{4}}$	Luzzi M J	2.60
20Dec03 ^{8}Aqu^{2}	Queen's Triomphe	L	5	114	5	2	$2^{\frac{1}{2}}$	$2^{\frac{1}{2}}$	$3^{4\frac{1}{2}}$	$4^{\frac{1}{2}}$	$5^{6\frac{1}{4}}$	Espinoza J L	4.70
30Nov03 ^{8}Aqu^{2}	Message Red		5	116	8	4	$6^{\frac{1}{2}}$	$7^{1\frac{1}{2}}$	$5^{\frac{1}{2}}$	6^{6}	$6^{11\frac{1}{4}}$	Castellano J	2.05
26Nov03 ^{8}WO^{2}	Dancen in the Sun	L f	6	112	3	1	$3^{2\frac{1}{2}}$	4^{2}	4^{hd}	7^{7}	$7^{4\frac{1}{4}}$	Arroyo N Jr	29.00
16Apr03 ^{6}Aqu^{4}	Green Jeans	L	5	114	7	5	4^{hd}	5^{hd}	8	8	8	Lopez C C	14.30

OFF AT 4:07 Start Good . Won driving. Track fast.

TIME :23^{1}, :47^{4}, 1:12^{3}, 1:37^{4}, 1:44 (:23.31, :47.82, 1:12.67, 1:37.98, 1:44.02)

$2 Mutuel Prices:

6 – AUSTIN'S MOM	25.00	10.40	8.30
4 – GOLDEN DAMSEL		5.80	5.10
1 – CONSORT MUSIC			17.40

$2 EXACTA 6–4 PAID $141.00 $2 TRIFECTA 6–4–1 PAID $3,029.00

Dk. b or br. f, (Feb), by Sefapiano – Precious Brenda , by Habitonia . Trainer Iwinski Allen. Bred by Sefa's Farm (Ky).

AUSTIN'S MOM was rated along inside, came wide into the stretch, responded when roused, surged to the front leaving the eighth pole and was going away late, driving. GOLDEN DAMSEL quickly opened a clear lead, set the pace, dug in determinedly in the stretch but had no answer for the winner while holding on for the place award. CONSORT MUSIC was outrun early, rallied four wide on the second turn and finished well outside. CRUISE ALONG was outrun early, rallied three wide on the second turn and tired in the final furlong. QUEEN'S TRIOMPHE raced close up inside, put in a run along the rail on the second turn and had nothing left for the stretch drive. MESSAGE RED was outrun early, raced three wide on both turns and had no rally. DANCEN IN THE SUN raced inside and tired after three quarters. GREEN JEANS tired after showing brief speed.

Owners– 1, Friedman Len Nilsen Jan and Keifetz Brom; 2, Our Canterbury Stables; 3, Evans Edward P; 4, Bender Sondra D; 5, Kelly Gregory W and Stephen P; 6, Robbins Lansdon B; 7, Gibbs Sandra and Gerald; 8, Richards Althea D

Trainers– 1, Iwinski Allen; 2, Contessa Gary C; 3, Hennig Mark A; 4, Murray Lawrence E; 5, Bush Thomas M; 6, Jerkens James A; 7, Contessa Gary C; 8, Turner William H Jr

TENTH RACE
Gulfstream
JANUARY 17, 2004

1 1/16 MILES. (1.40[1]) HOLY BULL S. Grade III. Purse $100,000 FOR THREE YEAR OLDS. By subscription of $100 each, which shall accompany the nomination, $1,000 to pass the entry box and $1,000 additional to start, with $100,000 guaranteed. The owner of the winner to receive $60,000; $20,000 to second, $11,000 to third, $6,000 to fourth and $3,000 to fifth. Supplemental nominations may be made on WEDNESDAY, January 14, 2004 at a fee of $3,000, which includes entry and start fees. Weight: 122 lbs. Non-winners of $50,000 at a mile or over, allowed, 2 lbs.; $50,000 at anydistance or $35,000 at a mile or over, 4 lbs.; $30,000 at any distance or $25,000 at a mile or over, 6 lbs. Horses finishing first, second or third in the Holy Bull Stakes will automatically be nominated to the Florida Derby. Trophy to winning Owner. Closed Wednesday, January 7, 2004 with (8) nominations. Includes (160) nominations from the Florida Derby which closed Wednesday, November 12, 2003.

Value of Race: $100,000 Winner $60,000; second $20,000; third $11,000; fourth $6,000; fifth $3,000. Mutuel Pool $696,994.00 Exacta Pool $460,197.00 Trifecta Pool $358,019.00 Superfecta Pool $110,736.00

Last Raced	Horse	M/Eqt.	A.	Wt	PP	St	¼	½	¾	Str	Fin	Jockey	Odds $1
13Dec03 9Crc1	Second of June	L f	3	122	5	5	41	2½	21½	11½	12¾	Velasquez C H	2.80
13Dec03 9Crc3	Silver Wagon	L	3	120	3	3	3hd	4½	31	23½	210	Bailey J D	1.60
18Oct03 5Bel1	Friends Lake	L	3	122	4	6	5½	6hd	51½	41½	3½	Migliore R	3.20
29Nov03 8Aqu6	El Prado Rob	L	3	118	2	2	1hd	1½	1hd	33	44¾	Prado E S	7.70
15Nov03 8WO2	Smoocher	L	3	122	9	9	7hd	5hd	7½	51½	52¼	Santos J A	9.40
10Dec03 6TP1	Tap Dancing Mauk	L	3	116	6	8	9	71¼	6hd	82¼	61¼	Perret C	24.20
20Dec03 10Crc1	Hitthegroundrunnin	L	3	116	7	4	6hd	84	88	6hd	71¼	Toscano P R	81.20
17Oct03 8Hip1	Caiman		3	116	8	7	8½	9	9	9	83	Boulanger G	75.70
15Nov03 7Hou4	Seneca Summer	L	3	120	1	1	2½	31	4½	72½	9	Coa E	34.40

OFF AT 5:13 Start Good . Won driving. Track fast.

TIME :24, :48[1], 1:12[2], 1:36[3], 1:43 (:24.01, :48.22, 1:12.44, 1:36.78, 1:43.00)

$2 Mutuel Prices:				
	6 – SECOND OF JUNE	7.60	3.20	2.60
	4 – SILVER WAGON		3.00	2.60
	5 – FRIENDS LAKE			3.00

$1 EXACTA 6–4 PAID $9.10 $1 TRIFECTA 6–4–5 PAID $22.90
$1 SUPERFECTA 6–4–5–2 PAID $72.00

Dk. b or br. c, (Jun), by Louis Quatorze – Whow , by Spectacular Bid . Trainer Cesare William. Bred by Lambholm & E Felcher (Fla).

SECOND OF JUNE raced with the leaders four wide around the first turn, prompted the pace outside EL PRADO ROB, moved to gain command from that rival three wide on the far turn, then drew clear through the final eighth under urging. SILVER WAGON up close early, eased off the leaders leaving the first turn, made a run four wide on the far turn to reach the attending position, then drifted to the rail when struck right handed approaching the eighth pole and couldn't stay with the winner while clearly second best. FRIENDS LAKE rated off the pace, raced in contention three wide around the far turn, then couldn't keep pace with the top ones in the drive while up for the show. EL PRADO ROB set the pace along the inside into the far turn and gave way. SMOOCHER reserved off the pace, raced four wide on the far turn and tired. TAP DANCING MAUK raced in contention into the far turn and faltered.. HITTHEGROUNDRUNNIN allowed to settle early, faded leaving the far turn. CAIMAN was through after a half mile. SENECA SUMMER chased the pace along the inside into the far turn and stopped.

Owners– 1, Cesare Barbara; 2, Buckram Oak Farm; 3, Broman Mary R and Chester Sr; 4, La Penta Robert V; 5, Franks Farms; 6, Mauk 1 Racing Stable; 7, Van Worp Judson; 8, Achar Victor; 9, Puglisi Stables

Trainers– 1, Cesare William J; 2, Ziadie Ralph; 3, Kimmel John C; 4, Zito Nicholas P; 5, Bell David R; 6, Romans Dale L; 7, Croft Barry N; 8, Medina Angel M; 9, Klesaris Steve B

Scratched– Hopefortheroses (21Dec03 7Crc1)

$1 Pick Three (2–4–6) Paid $243.80 .
$1 Pick Three (2–4–3) Paid $49.60 ; Pick Three Pool $43,784 .

SEVENTH RACE
Santa Anita
JANUARY 17, 2004

$1\frac{1}{16}$ MILES. (1.39) SANTA CATALINA S. Grade II. Purse $150,000 FOR THREE-YEAR-OLDS. By subscription of $150 each to accompany the nomination or by supplementary nomination of $3,000 by time of entry. $1,500 additional to start, with $150,000 guaranteed of which $90,000 to first, $30,000 to second, $18,000 to third,$9,000 to fourth and $3,000 to fifth. 120 lbs. Winners of a race of $200,000 to carry 3 lbs. additional; non-winners of $55,000 at one mile or over allowed 3 lbs.; of such a race any distance, 5 lbs.; of $20,000 at one mile or over or $30,000 at any distance, 7 lbs. (Maiden and Claiming races not considered.) Starters to be named through the entry box by the closing time of entries. A trophy will be presented to the owner of the winner. Closed with 16 Nominations.

Value of Race: $150,000 Winner $90,000; second $30,000; third $18,000; fourth $9,000; fifth $3,000. Mutuel Pool $659,812.00 Exacta Pool $382,308.00 Quinella Pool $36,526.00 Trifecta Pool $404,722.00 Superfecta Pool $143,706.00

Last Raced	Horse	M/Eqt.	A.	Wt	PP	St	¼	½	¾	Str	Fin	Jockey	Odds $1
20Dec03 ^{4}Hol^{2}	St Averil	LB b	3	113	8	7	4^{2}	5^{hd}	$3^{1\frac{1}{2}}$	3^{3}	$1^{1\frac{1}{2}}$	Baze T	2.20
29Nov03 ^{5}Hol^{3}	Lucky Pulpit	LB bf	3	115	6	3	$3^{1\frac{1}{2}}$	3^{1}	$2^{1\frac{1}{2}}$	$1^{\frac{1}{2}}$	2^{2}	Valenzuela P A	18.80
29Nov03 ^{8}Aqu^{2}	Master David	LB	3	113	7	9	7^{hd}	$6^{\frac{1}{2}}$	5^{2}	$6^{2\frac{1}{2}}$	3^{hd}	Velazquez J R	1.30
17Dec03 ^{5}Hol^{1}	Preachinatthebar	LB b	3	116	3	5	5^{hd}	8^{3}	6^{hd}	4^{hd}	4^{hd}	Flores D R	8.20
13Dec03 ^{7}GG^{4}	Harvard Avenue	LB	3	115	4	4	6^{hd}	$4^{\frac{1}{2}}$	$7^{1\frac{1}{2}}$	$5^{\frac{1}{2}}$	5^{nk}	Solis A O	26.60
5Dec03 ^{8}DeD^{3}	Perfect Moon	LB b	3	117	5	2	1^{hd}	$2^{\frac{1}{2}}$	1^{hd}	2^{1}	6^{4}	Espinoza V	6.60
20Dec03 ^{4}Hol^{3}	That's an Outrage	LB b	3	116	2	6	9	9	9	7^{2}	7^{3}	Stevens G L	9.80
19Dec03 ^{1}Hol^{2}	Mambo Train	LB b	3	115	9	8	8^{3}	7^{1}	$8^{\frac{1}{2}}$	$8^{3\frac{1}{2}}$	8^{12}	Valdivia J Jr	88.50
29Nov03 ^{11}CD^{6}	Saltire	LB b	3	113	1	1	2^{hd}	1^{hd}	4^{hd}	9	9	Ramsammy E	85.40

OFF AT 3:38 Start Good . Won driving. Track fast.

TIME :22^{3}, :45^{3}, 1:09^{4}, 1:34^{4}, 1:41^{3} (:22.75, :45.61, 1:09.81, 1:34.93, 1:41.62)

$2 Mutuel Prices:				
	8 – ST AVERIL	6.40	4.20	2.80
	6 – LUCKY PULPIT		11.40	5.60
	7 – MASTER DAVID			2.80

$1 EXACTA 8–6 PAID $47.00 $2 QUINELLA 6–8 PAID $63.40

$1 TRIFECTA 8–6–7 PAID $112.00 $1 SUPERFECTA 8–6–7–3 PAID $610.10

Dk. b or br. c, (Mar), by Saint Ballado – Avie's Fancy , by Lord Avie . Trainer Becerra Rafael. Bred by Gunsmith Stables (Ky).

ST AVERIL four wide into the first turn, stalked off the rail then three deep leaving the backstretch and on the second and into the stretch, bid three wide, gained the lead past midstretch and inched clear under some urging. LUCKY PULPIT dueled three deep then outside a rival on the second turn, took the lead into the stretch, fought back between horses in midstretch but could not match the winner late. MASTER DAVID off a bit slowly, chased between horses then outside a rival on the second turn, came three deep into the stretch and split horses at the wire for the show. PREACHINATTHEBAR saved ground chasing the pace, split rivals on the second turn, came four wide into the stretch and closed willingly outside. HARVARD AVENUE stalked between horses then a bit off the rail leaving the backstretch, steadied off heels nearing midway on the second turn, went around a rival into the stretch and put in a late bid at third. PERFECT MOON dueled between horses then inside on the second turn, fought back in the stretch but weakened late. THAT'S AN OUTRAGE saved ground off the pace, came out into the stretch and passed a pair of tiring rivals. MAMBO TRAIN five wide into the first turn, stalked four wide on the backstretch, dropped back outside on the second turn and weakened. SALTIRE pulled early and was in a bit tight into the first turn, dueled inside, dropped back on the second turn and gave way.

Owners– 1, Fulton Stan E; 2, Williams Mr and Mrs Larry D; 3, Georgica Stable Mack & Rosen; 4, Pegram Michael E; 5, Ron Crockett Inc; 6, Royce S Jaime Racing Stable Inc; 7, Bull Stick Stables LLC and Mercedes Stables LLC; 8, Everest Stables Inc; 9, Atkins Clinton C

Trainers– 1, Becerra Rafael; 2, Sise Clifford W Jr; 3, Frankel Robert J; 4, Baffert Bob; 5, O'Neill Doug; 6, O'Neill Doug; 7, Puhich Michael; 8, Polanco Marcelo; 9, Lukas D Wayne

---

$2 Daily Double (3–8) Paid $77.80 ; Daily Double Pool $45,483 .

$1 Pick Three (7–3–8) Paid $174.60 ; Pick Three Pool $105,054 .

SEVENTH RACE
Santa Anita
JANUARY 18, 2004

1$\frac{1}{16}$ MILES. (1.39) EL ENCINO S. Grade II. Purse $150,000 FOR FILLIES, FOUR YEARS OLD. By subscription of $150 each to accompany the nomination or by supplementary nomination of $3,000 by time of entry, $1,500 additional to start, with $150,000 guaranteed, of which $90,000 to first, $30,000 to second, $18,000tothird, $9,000 to fourth and $3,000 to fifth. 122 lbs. Non-winners of $100,000 twice at one mile or over in 2003–2004, allowed 3 lbs.; of such a race in 2003–2004 or $60,000 any distance since October 1, 5 lbs.; of $35,000 at any distance at any time,7 lbs. (Maiden and claiming races not considered). Starters to be named through the entry box by the closing time of entries. A trophy will be presented to the owner of the winner. Closed with 10 nominations.

Value of Race: $150,000 Winner $90,000; second $30,000; third $18,000; fourth $9,000; fifth $3,000. Mutuel Pool $480,188.00 Exacta Pool $284,841.00 Quinella Pool $29,263.00 Trifecta Pool $321,683.00

Last Raced	Horse	M/Eqt.	A.	Wt	PP	St	¼	½	¾	Str	Fin	Jockey	Odds $1
7Sep03 ^{8}Dmr^{1}	Victory Encounter	LB	4	117	4	6	6^{4}	$6^{3\frac{1}{2}}$	5^{hd}	$1^{\frac{1}{2}}$	$1^{1\frac{1}{4}}$	Smith M E	3.40
20Dec03 ^{9}Hol^{2}	Personal Legend	LB b	4	115	7	7	7	7	7	4^{hd}	$2^{\frac{1}{2}}$	Solis A O	2.20
5Dec03 ^{7}Hol^{1}	Cat Fighter	LB b	4	115	5	4	$3^{3\frac{1}{2}}$	$3^{1\frac{1}{2}}$	2^{1}	$2^{1\frac{1}{2}}$	$3^{\frac{1}{2}}$	Fogelsonger R	13.90
27Dec03 ^{7}SA^{4}	Hope Rises	LB	4	116	3	2	$4^{1\frac{1}{2}}$	$5^{2\frac{1}{2}}$	$4^{1\frac{1}{2}}$	$5^{\frac{1}{2}}$	4^{3}	Flores D R	4.80
14Dec03 ^{6}Hol^{1}	Sea Jewel	LB b	4	115	2	3	$5^{1\frac{1}{2}}$	4^{hd}	3^{1}	6^{5}	$5^{2\frac{1}{2}}$	Valenzuela P A	5.60
27Dec03 ^{7}SA^{8}	Gone Exclusive	LB	4	116	6	5	2^{2}	$2^{1\frac{1}{2}}$	1^{hd}	3^{hd}	$6^{9\frac{1}{2}}$	Stevens G L	13.10
23Nov03 ^{8}Hol^{10}	Voodoo's Sister	LB b	4	115	1	1	1^{1}	$1^{1\frac{1}{2}}$	6^{2}	7	7	Valdivia J Jr	4.10

OFF AT 3:40 Start Good. Won driving. Track fast.
TIME :22^{3}, :46, 1:10^{2}, 1:36, 1:42^{2} (:22.69, :46.04, 1:10.50, 1:36.03, 1:42.52)

$2 Mutuel Prices:			
4 – VICTORY ENCOUNTER	8.80	3.60	3.60
7 – PERSONAL LEGEND		3.20	2.80
5 – CAT FIGHTER			6.00

$1 EXACTA 4–7 PAID $13.20 $2 QUINELLA 4–7 PAID $12.60
$1 TRIFECTA 4–7–5 PAID $99.80

B. f, (Mar), by Victory Speech – Marvelous Moment, by Raise a Native. Trainer Sadler John W. Bred by Helen Smith (Ky).

VICTORY ENCOUNTER chased a bit off the rail, moved up outside on the second turn and four wide into the stretch, gained the advantage outside foes in midstretch and gamely prevailed under urging. PERSONAL LEGEND unhurried and angled in early, saved ground off the pace, came out on the second turn, also swung four wide into the stretch and finished willingly for second. CAT FIGHTER bobbled slightly just after the start, was between rivals early then angled in to stalk the pace, split foes leaving the backstretch, bid three deep on the second turn, took the lead outside a rival past midway on that bend, fought back between foes in midstretch and was outfinished. HOPE RISES pulled a bit early, chased just off the inside, went outside a rival on the second turn, waited momentarily then split horses in midstretch, bid along the rail and also went on well to the end. SEA JEWEL also pulled early, drifted out into the first turn, chased outside, went up four wide into the second turn, continued three deep into the stretch and weakened. GONE EXCLUSIVE four wide early, prompted the pace outside a rival then stalked off the rail, bid between horses into the second turn, dueled inside on that turn and into the stretch but weakened in the final furlong. VOODOO'S SISTER sped to the early lead, set the pace inside, dropped back once headed into the second turn and gave way.

Owners– 1, Mankiewicz Tom; 2, Gann Edmund A; 3, The Thoroughbred Corporation; 4, Jay Em Ess Stable; 5, Moss Mr and Mrs Jerome S; 6, Milch David S; 7, Everest Stables Inc

Trainers– 1, Sadler John W; 2, Frankel Robert J; 3, Baffert Bob; 4, Ellis Ronald W; 5, Shirreffs John A; 6, Vienna Darrell; 7, Polanco Marcelo

Scratched– Island Fashion (27Dec03 ^{7}SA ^{1})

$2 Daily Double (4–4) Paid $41.00; Daily Double Pool $34,051.
$1 Pick Three (5–4–4) Paid $81.70; Pick Three Pool $88,324.

FIFTH RACE
Santa Anita
JANUARY 19, 2004

7 FURLONGS. (1.20) SANTA YNEZ S. Grade II. Purse $150,000 FOR FILLIES, THREE YEARS OLDS. By subscription of $150 each to accompany the nomination or by supplementary nomination of $3,000 by time of entry. $1,500 additional to start, with $150,000 guaranteed, of which $90,000 to first, $30,000 to second, $18,000 to third, $9,000 to fourth and $3,000 to fifth. 121 lbs. Winners of $50,000 twice to carry 2 lbs. additional. Non-winners of two races of $40,000 or one of $60,000 at any time allowed 3 lbs.; of two of $20,000 or one of $30,000 at any time, 5 lbs.; of arace of $20,000, 7 lbs. (Maiden and Claiming races not considered). Starters to be named through the entry box by the closing time of entries. A trophy will be presented to the owner of the winner. Closed with 15 Nominations.

Value of Race: $150,000 Winner $90,000; second $30,000; third $18,000; fourth $9,000; fifth $3,000. Mutuel Pool $449,119.00 Exacta Pool $258,992.00 Quinella Pool $23,394.00 Trifecta Pool $249,325.00 Superfecta Pool $96,090.00

Last Raced	Horse	M/Eqt.	A.	Wt	PP	St	¼	½	Str	Fin	Jockey	Odds $1
27Dec03 ^{3}SA^{2}	Yearly Report	LB	3	114	3	6	4^{hd}	$2^{\frac{1}{2}}$	1^{hd}	1^{4}	Bailey J D	2.10
21Dec03 ^{9}Hol^{3}	House of Fortune	LB	3	121	7	2	2^{1}	4^{hd}	$3^{2\frac{1}{2}}$	$2^{4\frac{1}{2}}$	Solis A O	4.30
28Nov03 ^{4}Hol^{1}	Papa to Kinzie	LB	3	115	2	3	1^{1}	1^{1}	2^{2}	3^{3}	Valenzuela P A	8.60
12Dec03 ^{3}GG^{1}	Bending Strings	LB	3	114	8	1	3^{hd}	5^{3}	5^{4}	4^{2}	Espinoza V	16.50
21Dec03 ^{9}Hol^{2}	Rahy Dolly	LB b	3	115	1	4	$5^{1\frac{1}{2}}$	3^{hd}	4^{hd}	5^{3}	Valdivia J Jr	2.00
11Aug03 ^{8}Sar^{1}	Whoopi Cat	L	3	121	6	8	6^{hd}	$7^{3\frac{1}{2}}$	6^{hd}	6^{1}	Smith M E	6.10
20Dec03 ^{8}Hol^{1}	Nandu	LB	3	114	5	5	$7^{\frac{1}{2}}$	$6^{\frac{1}{2}}$	7^{12}	7^{20}	Stevens G L	27.70
21Dec03 ^{6}Hol^{1}	Cardinalli	LB	3	116	4	7	8	8	8	8	Flores D R	66.50

OFF AT 2:36 Start Good. Won driving. Track fast.
TIME :22, :44^{1}, 1:08^{2}, 1:21 (:22.03, :44.28, 1:08.59, 1:21.11)

$2 Mutuel Prices:			
3 – YEARLY REPORT	6.20	3.00	2.60
10 – HOUSE OF FORTUNE		4.00	2.80
2 – PAPA TO KINZIE			4.60

$1 EXACTA 3–10 PAID $12.50 $2 QUINELLA 3–10 PAID $11.80
$1 TRIFECTA 3–10–2 PAID $82.70 $1 SUPERFECTA 3–10–2–11 PAID $462.00

B. f, (Jan), by General Meeting – Fiscal Year, by Half a Year. Trainer Baffert Bob. Bred by Mr & Mrs John C Mabee (Cal).

YEARLY REPORT stalked between horses on the backstretch and into the turn, continued outside a rival leaving the turn, bid alongside the pacesetter and took a short lead in midstretch, then drew clear under left handed urging. HOUSE OF FORTUNE had good early speed outside then stalked three deep between horses on the backstretch, remained three wide on the turn and into the stretch and was second best. PAPA TO KINZIE sped between horses to the early lead, set the pace a bit off the rail and weakened in the final furlong but saved the show. BENDING STRINGS stalked outside then four wide leaving the backstretch and on the turn and into the stretch and weakened. RAHY DOLLY pulled her way up inside to stalk the pace on the backstretch and turn, dropped back into the stretch and also weakened. WHOOPI CAT wide early, angled in outside a rival leaving he backstretch and on the turn, came out into the stretch and did not rally. NANDU pulled between horses chasing the early pace, angled in for the turn, came out into the stretch and could not summon the necessary response. CARDINALLI angled in and chased inside, dropped back nearing the turn and gave way.

Owners– 1, Golden Eagle Farm; 2, Zetcher Arnold; 3, Always Believe Inc; 4, Gunther John D; 5, Fulton Stan E; 6, Smith Derrick and Tabor Michael; 7, King Edward Racing Stable; 8, Finney Albert and Taylor Mickey and Karen LLC

Trainers– 1, Baffert Bob; 2, McAnally Ronald L; 3, Jones Martin F; 4, Hollendorfer Jerry; 5, Becerra Rafael; 6, Biancone Patrick L; 7, Jones Martin F; 8, French Neil

Scratched– Church Editor (27Dec03 ^{8}GG ^{3}), Silent Sighs (27Dec03 ^{3}SA ^{1}), Renaissance Lady (27Dec03 ^{8}GG ^{4})

$2 Daily Double (5–3) Paid $33.60; Daily Double Pool $35,955.
$1 Pick Three (1–5–3) Paid $64.30; Pick Three Pool $74,134.

EIGHTH RACE
Santa Anita
JANUARY 19, 2004

$1\frac{1}{4}$ MILES. (Turf) (1.57^{2}) SAN MARCOS S. Grade II. Purse $150,000 FOR FOUR-YEAR-OLDS AND UPWARD. By subscription of $150 each to accompany the nomination or by supplementary nomination of $3,000 by time of entry. $1,500 additional to start, with $90,000 guaranteed, of which $90,000 to first, $30,000 to second, $18,000to third, $9,000 to fourth and $3,000 to fifth. 122 lbs. Non-winners of $200,000 or $90,000 twice at a mile or over since July 1 allowed 3 lbs.; non-winners of $90,000 at a mile or over since July 1, 5 lbs.; of such a race since January 15, 7 lbs. Startersto be named through the entry box by the closing time of entries. A trophy will be presented to the owner of the winner. Closed with 18 Nominations. (Rail at 8 feet).

Value of Race: $150,000 Winner $90,000; second $30,000; third $18,000; fourth $9,000; fifth $3,000. Mutuel Pool $463,808.00 Exacta Pool $265,175.00 Quinella Pool $26,016.00 Trifecta Pool $279,648.00 Superfecta Pool $115,160.00

Last Raced	Horse	M/Eqt.	A.	Wt	PP	¼	½	¾	1	Str	Fin	Jockey	Odds $1
30Nov03 ^{9}Hol^{1}	Sweet Return-GB	LB	4	121	9	$1^{\frac{1}{2}}$	1^{1}	1^{1}	1^{1}	1^{1}	$1^{\frac{1}{2}}$	Stevens G L	6.90
21Feb03 ^{9}GP^{1}	Nothing to Lose	LB b	4	116	5	3^{1}	$3^{1\frac{1}{2}}$	2^{hd}	$3^{1\frac{1}{2}}$	2^{hd}	$2^{1\frac{1}{2}}$	Bailey J D	4.80
28Dec03 ^{8}SA^{6}	Blue Steller-Ire	LB	6	116	2	2^{1}	$2^{\frac{1}{2}}$	$3^{\frac{1}{2}}$	2^{hd}	3^{1}	$3^{\frac{1}{2}}$	Valenzuela P A	6.00
9Aug03 ^{9}Sar^{6}	Puerto Banus	LB b	5	120	6	8^{1}	$8^{2\frac{1}{2}}$	7^{1}	$4^{\frac{1}{2}}$	4^{2}	$4^{1\frac{1}{2}}$	Espinoza V	a- 3.40
16Nov03 ^{9}CD^{5}	Sharbayan-Ire	LB b	6	116	7	9	9	9	9	6^{1}	5^{1}	Valdivia J Jr	7.70
30Nov03 ^{9}Hol^{2}	Fairly Ransom	LB	4	118	8	$5^{1\frac{1}{2}}$	5^{2}	5^{hd}	$8^{\frac{1}{2}}$	8^{3}	6^{hd}	Solis A	1.70
3Aug03 ^{16}GVA^{9}	GenedeCampeo-Brz	LB	5	116	3	6^{hd}	$7^{\frac{1}{2}}$	8^{hd}	7^{hd}	5^{hd}	$7^{\frac{1}{2}}$	Berrio O A	34.30
30Nov03 ^{9}Hol^{9}	Californian-GB	LB	4	116	1	$4^{\frac{1}{2}}$	4^{hd}	$6^{1\frac{1}{2}}$	5^{1}	7^{hd}	8^{6}	Desormeaux K J	a- 3.40
29Dec03 ^{7}SA^{4}	Hecandigit	LB b	5	116	4	$7^{1\frac{1}{2}}$	6^{hd}	4^{1}	6^{1}	9	9	Garcia M S	56.60

a-Coupled: Puerto Banus and Californian-GB.

OFF AT 4:08 Start Good . Won driving. Course firm.

TIME :23^{3}, :47^{4}, 1:12^{1}, 1:35^{3}, 1:58^{4} (:23.72, :47.98, 1:12.26, 1:35.76, 1:58.82)

$2 Mutuel Prices:				
	8 – SWEET RETURN-GB.................	15.80	7.20	4.20
	5 – NOTHING TO LOSE.................		6.60	5.20
	2 – BLUE STELLER-IRE................			5.60

$1 EXACTA 8–5 PAID $44.70 $2 QUINELLA 5–8 PAID $46.20
$1 TRIFECTA 8–5–2 PAID $294.80 $1 SUPERFECTA 8–5–2–1 PAID $910.10

Ch. c, (Mar), by Elmaamul – Sweet Revival-GB , by Claude Monet . Trainer McAnally Ronald. Bred by C S Tateson (GB).

SWEET RETURN (GB) wide on the hill, angled in outside a rival on the early lead in the stretch the first time, inched away, was well rated on a short advantage a bit off the rail, came out a bit into the stretch and held on gamely under urging. NOTHING TO LOSE angled in and stalked the pace outside a rival, came three deep into the stretch and continued willingly but could not catch the winner. BLUE STELLER (IRE) prompted the early pace inside the winner, stalked that one along the rail the rest of the way and could not offer the necessary late kick. PUERTO BANUS settled off the rail, went up three deep leaving the backstretch and four wide on the second turn and into the stretch and just missed the show. SHARBAYAN (IRE) squeezed a bit at the start, raced unhurried inside then outside a rival into and on the second turn, split horses in midstretch and improved position. FAIRLY RANSOM kept wide on the hill, angled in and stalked outside a rival then between horses on the backstretch, was in tight into the second turn then shuffled back some, swung five wide into the stretch and lacked the needed rally. GENE DE CAMPEAO (BRZ) pulled between horses then hopped on the dirt crossing, angled in and tugged his way along inside chasing the pace and did not rally. CALIFORNIAN (GB) stalked the pace along the inside, came out on the second turn and three deep into the stretch and weakened. HECANDIGIT pulled between horses down the hill, chased outside a rival then three deep, dropped back between foes on the second turn, came four wide into the stretch and also weakened.

Owners– 1, Red Oak Stable; 2, Ramsey Kenneth L and Sarah K; 3, Amerman Racing Stables LLC; 4, Noctis Stable Papiano Neil and Taub Steve; 5, Iron County Farms Inc and Miller Trust; 6, Zetcher Arnold; 7, Bandeirantes Stable; 8, Noctis Stable Papiano Neil and Taub Steve; 9, Thomas Paula and Thomas Racing

Trainers– 1, McAnally Ronald; 2, Frankel Robert; 3, Frankel Robert; 4, Mulhall Kristin; 5, Dollase Wallace; 6, McAnally Ronald; 7, Avila A C; 8, Mulhall Kristin; 9, Stute Warren

---

$2 Daily Double (5–8) Paid $162.60 ; Daily Double Pool $35,979 .
$1 Pick Three (4–5–8) Paid $193.20 ; Pick Three Pool $74,561 .

NINTH RACE
Fair Grounds
JANUARY 24, 2004

1 MILE. (1.35^{4}) LECOMTE S. Grade III. Purse $100,000 GUARANTEED. For Three Year Olds. (Louisiana Derby early bird nominees automatically subscribed). $100,000 Guaranteed of which $60,000 to the winner; $20,000 to second; $11,000 to third; $6,000 to fourth; $3,000 to fifth. Weight: 122 lbs. Non-winnersof $36,000 allowed 3 lbs.; $25,000, 5 lbs.; $20,000, 8 lbs. (Maiden and claiming races not considered). THE OWNER OF THE WINNER TO RECEIVE A TROPHY. Closed Friday, January 16, 2004, with 9 nominations.

Value of Race: $100,000 Winner $60,000; second $20,000; third $11,000; fourth $6,000; fifth $3,000. Mutuel Pool $219,694.00 Exacta Pool $115,068.00 Quinella Pool $10,659.00 Trifecta Pool $95,381.00 Superfecta Pool $27,963.00

Last Raced	Horse	M/Eqt.	A.	Wt	PP	St	¼	½	¾	Str	Fin	Jockey	Odds $1
5Dec03 ^{8}DeD^{2}	Fire Slam	L	3	119	3	2	2^{1}	$2^{1\frac{1}{2}}$	$2^{1\frac{1}{2}}$	$1^{1\frac{1}{2}}$	1^{2}	Sellers S J	1.70
7Dec03 ^{9}TP^{1}	Shadowland	L	3	118	6	5	4^{hd}	4^{1}	3^{hd}	$2^{\frac{1}{2}}$	$2^{1\frac{1}{2}}$	Martin E M Jr	7.70
28Dec03 ^{9}FG^{2}	TwoDownAutomtic	L b	3	117	7	1	1^{1}	$1^{\frac{1}{2}}$	1^{hd}	3^{2}	$3^{2\frac{1}{2}}$	Lovato F Jr	7.20
10Jan04 ^{9}FG^{3}	Bogangles	L f	3	119	1	3	$6^{2\frac{1}{2}}$	6^{3}	5^{1}	5^{3}	4^{nk}	Lanerie C J	18.50
15Nov03 ^{6}Lrl^{2}	Polish Rifle	L	3	122	4	6	5^{3}	3^{hd}	4^{3}	4^{1}	5^{hd}	Albarado R J	1.00
14Dec03 ^{7}FG^{1}	America Alive	L b	3	117	5	7	7	7	7	$6^{\frac{1}{2}}$	$6^{6\frac{1}{4}}$	Borel C H	25.00
20Dec03 ^{8}Haw^{8}	Jaguar Friend	L	3	122	2	4	$3^{\frac{1}{2}}$	$5^{4\frac{1}{2}}$	6^{7}	7	7	Melancon G	49.00

OFF AT 4:16 Start Good . Won driving. Track fast.

TIME :24^{3}, :48^{4}, 1:13^{4}, 1:38^{2} (:24.65, :48.93, 1:13.92, 1:38.48)

$2 Mutuel Prices:				
	3 – FIRE SLAM.........................	5.40	3.60	3.20
	6 – SHADOWLAND........................		4.80	3.60
	7 – TWO DOWN AUTOMATIC................			4.20

$2 EXACTA 3–6 PAID $40.80 $2 QUINELLA 3–6 PAID $34.80
$2 TRIFECTA 3–6–7 PAID $178.60 $2 SUPERFECTA 3–6–7–1 PAID $1,048.60

B. c, (Jan), by Grand Slam – Miss Firefly , by Salt Lake . Trainer Carroll David. Bred by Julie Jones Mogge (Ky).

FIRE SLAM stalked TWO DOWN AUTOMATIC around the first turn, collared that one midway down the backstretch, dueled for the lead around the second turn, surged clear in upper stretch and proved best while kept to the task. SHADOWLAND reserved off the rail while out sprinted, moved up around the second turn, loomed a threat and while no match for the winner was game for second. TWO DOWN AUTOMATIC broke alertly, sprinted clear to the rail around the first turn, was collared by FIRE SLAM midway down the backstretch, dueled with that one around the second turn, was headed before mid stretch and faded. BOGANGLES devoid speed, raced off the rail down the backstretch, moved up nearing the drive then lacked the needed rally. POLISH RIFLE between foes early, was restrained down the backstretch, had no response when asked. AMERICA ALIVE well back until the drive, showed late interest. JAGUAR FRIEND forwardly placed along the inside, faded before the drive.

Owners– 1, Fulton Stan E; 2, Team Valor Stables LLC; 3, Dapple Stable LLC; 4, Mahler Ken; 5, Heiligbrodt RacStb& Stonerside Stb LLC LWHeiligbrodtR& JMcNair; 6, Mill House; 7, Jaguar on The Run Stable

Trainers– 1, Carroll David; 2, Nicks Ralph E; 3, Asmussen Steven M; 4, Kenneally Eddie; 5, Asmussen Steven M; 6, Howard Neil J; 7, Springer Frank R

$2 Pick Three (1–8–3) Paid $444.60 ; Pick Three Pool $16,604 .

TENTH RACE
Gulfstream
JANUARY 25, 2004

1⅜ MILES. (Turf) (2.10^{3}) MAC DIARMIDA H. Grade III. Purse $100,000 FOR THREE YEAR OLDS AND UPWARD. By subscription of $100 each, which shall accompany the nomination, $1,000 to pass the entry box and $1,000 additonal to start, with $100,000 guaranteed. The owner of the winner to receive $60,000; $20,000 to second, $11,000 to third, $6,000 to fourth and $3,000 to fifth. Trophy to winning owner. This race will be limited to 12 Starters, with Also Eligibles. (High Weights on the scale Preferred.) In the event this stake is taken off the turf, it may be subject to downgrading upon review of the Graded Stakes Committee. Closed, Wednesday, January 14, 2004 with (24) nominations.

Value of Race: $100,000 Winner $60,000; second $20,000; third $11,000; fourth $6,000; fifth $3,000. Mutuel Pool $457,613.00 Exacta Pool $323,019.00 Trifecta Pool $253,983.00 Superfecta Pool $84,397.00

Last Raced	Horse	M/Eqt.	A.	Wt	PP	¼	½	¾	1	Str	Fin	Jockey	Odds $1
11Jan04 ^{8}GP^{1}	Request for Parole	L	5	115	7	9^{2}	7^{1}	7^{1}	8^{hd}	2^{1}	$1^{1½}$	Santos J A	3.20
30Nov03 ^{10}Tok^{13}	Slew Valley	L	7	117	1	1^{hd}	$1^{½}$	$1^{½}$	1^{1}	$1^{1½}$	$2^{¾}$	Chavez J F	7.50
27Dec03 ^{11}Crc^{4}	Sir Brian's Sword	L	6	113	6	7^{1}	8^{1}	$9^{½}$	11^{1}	$3^{1½}$	$3^{3¼}$	Bravo J	8.40
30Nov03 ^{9}WO^{5}	Mark One	L b	5	114	8	3^{hd}	$4^{1½}$	$4^{½}$	$4^{½}$	4^{1}	$4^{¾}$	Coa E M	20.70
4Jan04 ^{9}GP^{10}	Sforza-FR	L	5	114	4	5^{1}	$5^{½}$	6^{hd}	$7^{½}$	$5^{1½}$	$5^{½}$	Velasquez C	12.80
22Oct03 ^{9}Kee^{3}	In Hand	L f	4	112	9	12	11^{1}	11^{1}	10^{1}	11^{12}	6^{nk}	Perret C	25.30
20Oct03 ^{8}Del^{3}	Spanish Spur-GB	L	6	112	5	10^{2}	$10^{1½}$	$10^{½}$	9^{hd}	8^{1}	7^{hd}	Douglas R R	23.20
22Nov03 ^{8}Aqu^{2}	Macaw-Ire	L bf	5	117	2	$11^{½}$	12	12	12	10^{hd}	8^{nk}	Bridgmohan S X	2.00
3Jan04 ^{9}GP^{4}	Gander	L	8	117	10	4^{1}	3^{hd}	3^{1}	$3^{½}$	7^{hd}	$9^{1½}$	Velazquez J R	9.60
11Jan04 ^{8}GP^{9}	Bicentennial	L b	6	112	11	6^{1}	$6^{½}$	$5^{1½}$	5^{hd}	$6^{½}$	10^{nk}	Prado E S	44.20
27Dec03 ^{11}Crc^{5}	Prodigus-Brz	L	5	114	3	$8^{½}$	9^{1}	$8^{½}$	$6^{½}$	9^{1}	$11^{19½}$	Cruz M R	20.60
23Dec03 ^{10}Crc^{1}	Office Ghost	L bf	4	112	12	2^{1}	2^{hd}	2^{hd}	2^{1}	12	12	Garcia J A	29.70

OFF AT 5:10 Start Good. Won driving. Course firm.

TIME :24^{2}, :48^{3}, 1:13^{2}, 1:37, 2:01^{1}, 2:12^{2} (:24.41, :48.73, 1:13.42, 1:37.15, 2:01.23, 2:12.58)

$2 Mutuel Prices:				
	8 – REQUEST FOR PAROLE	8.40	4.80	4.20
	1 – SLEW VALLEY		9.60	6.00
	7 – SIR BRIAN'S SWORD			6.20

$1 EXACTA 8–1 PAID $30.80 $1 TRIFECTA 8–1–7 PAID $180.80
$1 SUPERFECTA 8–1–7–9 PAID $3,164.80

Dk. b or br. h, (Feb), by Judge T C – Madison's Quest, by Deputy Minister. Trainer Hough Stanley M. Bred by Robert H Roberts & Bea Roberts (Ky).

REQUEST FOR PAROLE rated off the pace, steadied in traffic on the final turn, made a run along the inside to reach contention, eased outside SLEW VALLEY in the stretch and rallied to draw clear. SLEW VALLEY set the pace along the hedge into the stretch, then couldn't stay with the winner late while holding the place. SIR BRIAN'S SWORD allowed to settle, was saving ground when steadied in traffic on the final turn, recovered and rallied along the hedge to prove best of the rest. MARK ONE tracked the pace along the inside, then angled out for the drive and weakened. SFORZA (FR) reserved along the inside after being steadied racing into the first turn, angled out for the stretch run and tired. IN HAND unhurried early, raced four wide on the final turn and passed tired rivals. SPANISH SPUR (GB) failed to menace. MACAW (IRE) outrun early, steadied to avoid running up on rivals entering the stretch and failed to be a factor. GANDER stalked the pace three wide into the final turn and tired. BICENTENNIAL raced in striking position into the stretch and faltered. PRODIGUS (BRZ) checked racing into the first turn, moved into contention four wide on the final turn and faded. OFFICE GHOST prompted the pace outside SLEW VALLEY for a mile, stopped and was eased in the final eighth.

Owners– 1, Knighton Jeri and Sam; 2, Rich Meadow Farm; 3, Jeb Racing Stable Inc; 4, Stronach Stable; 5, Eaton John and Laymon Steve; 6, Shining Armour Stb GW Humphrey Jr & B Klatsky; 7, Augustin Stable; 8, Melillo George and Sandra; 9, Gatsas Thoroughbreds LLC; 10, Ryan Mary; 11, Late Night Stables LLC; 12, Sessa Ralph C

Trainers– 1, Hough Stanley M; 2, Sciacca Gary; 3, Clement Christophe; 4, Vella Daniel J; 5, Picou James E; 6, Oliver Philip J; 7, Sheppard Jonathan E; 8, Tagg Barclay; 9, Terranova John P II; 10, Weaver George; 11, McPeek Kenneth G; 12, Musgrave Shawn

Scratched– Newfoundland (29Oct03 ^{8}Aqu^{5})

$1 Pick Three (5–5–8) Paid $98.20 ; Pick Three Pool $39,653 .

EIGHTH RACE
Santa Anita
JANUARY 25, 2004

7 FURLONGS. (1.20) SANTA MONICA H. Grade I. Purse $250,000 FOR FILLIES AND MARES FOUR YEARS OLD AND UPWARD. By subscription of $200 each to accompany the nomination or by supplementary nomination of $5,000 by Sunday, January 18. $2,000 additional to start, with $250,000 guaranteed, of which $150,000 to first, $50,000 to second, $30,000 to third, $15,000 to fourth and $5,000 to fifth. Weights Monday, January 19. Starters to be named through the entry box by the closing time of entries. A trophy will be presented to the owner of the winner. Closed with 10 Nominations.

Value of Race: $250,000 Winner $150,000; second $50,000; third $30,000; fourth $15,000; fifth $5,000. Mutuel Pool $469,675.00 Exacta Pool $210,853.00 Quinella Pool $21,838.00 Trifecta Pool $286,119.00

Last Raced	Horse	M/Eqt.	A.	Wt	PP	St	¼	½	Str	Fin	Jockey	Odds $1
27Dec03 ^{7}SA^{1}	Island Fashion	LB b	4	120	4	5	4^{1}	$3^{½}$	$2^{1½}$	$1^{¾}$	Desormeaux K J	1.50
27Dec03 ^{7}SA^{3}	Buffythecenterfold	LB	4	114	1	4	2^{3}	1^{hd}	1^{1}	$2^{½}$	Garcia M S	16.10
25Oct03 ^{2}SA^{3}	Got Koko	LB b	5	119	6	6	6	6	$5^{1½}$	$3^{3½}$	Solis A	2.90
25Oct03 ^{2}SA^{4}	Sightseek	LB	5	122	2	3	5^{5}	$5^{4½}$	4^{2}	$4^{5½}$	Bailey J D	1.20
3Jan04 ^{3}GG^{4}	Princess V.	LB	4	115	5	1	1^{hd}	2^{2}	3^{hd}	5^{2}	Smith M E	31.70
31Dec03 ^{8}SA^{3}	Sparkling Ava	LB b	5	109	3	2	3^{hd}	$4^{1½}$	6	6	Martinez F F	71.50

OFF AT 4:11 Start Good. Won driving. Track fast.

TIME :21^{4}, :44, 1:08^{2}, 1:21^{1} (:21.98, :44.04, 1:08.53, 1:21.37)

$2 Mutuel Prices:				
	5 – ISLAND FASHION	5.00	3.40	2.40
	1 – BUFFYTHECENTERFOLD		6.80	3.00
	7 – GOT KOKO			2.60

$1 EXACTA 5–1 PAID $12.60 $2 QUINELLA 1–5 PAID $25.40
$1 TRIFECTA 5–1–7 PAID $37.10

Gr/ro. f, (Mar), by Petionville – Danzigs Fashion, by A Native Danzig. Trainer Polanco Marcelo. Bred by Everest Stables Inc (Ky).

ISLAND FASHION chased outside on the backstretch and turn, came three deep leaving the turn and a bit wider into the stretch, gained the lead outside the runner-up past midstretch and proved best under left handed urging. BUFFYTHECENTERFOLD sent inside early, dueled along the rail, came off the fence and inched away into the stretch, fought back inside the winner but could not quite match that one late. GOT KOKO unhurried well off the rail early, angled in some for the turn, swung wide into the stretch and finished well. SIGHTSEEK stalked inside on the backstretch, came out nearing the turn and continued outside a rival, then lacked the needed late kick toward the rail in the stretch. PRINCESS V. sped to the early lead then dueled outside a rival, dropped back some into the stretch and weakened. SPARKLING AVA close up stalking the pace off the rail, angled in for the turn and also weakened.

Owners– 1, Everest Stables Inc; 2, Brian Allen A and Stronach Stables; 3, Headley Aase and Leung Paul; 4, Juddmonte Farms Inc; 5, Porter Ken V; 6, Schwartz Barry K

Trainers– 1, Polanco Marcelo; 2, Stute Melvin F; 3, Headley Bruce; 4, Frankel Robert; 5, French Neil; 6, Inda Eduardo

Scratched– Star Parade (ARG) (07Dec03 ^{8}Hol^{1})

$2 Daily Double (8–5) Paid $217.20 ; Daily Double Pool $45,893 .
$1 Pick Three (5/9/10/11–8–5) Paid $134.10 ; Pick Three Pool $71,741 .

THIRD RACE
Golden Gate
JANUARY 31, 2004

$1\frac{1}{16}$ MILES. (Turf Chute) (1.41^{1}) BROWN BESS H. Grade III. Purse $100,000 FOR FILLIES AND MARES FOUR YEARS OLD AND UPWARD. By subscription of $100 each to accompany the nomination or by supplementary nomination of $2,000 by Noon, January 25, 2004. $500 to pass the entry box and $500 additional to start, with $100,000 Guaranteedof which $55,000 to the winner, $20,000 to second, $15,000 to third, $7,500 to fourth and $2,500 to fifth. A trophy will be presented to the owner of the winner. High weights preferred. (Four Year Olds allowed 1 lb.). CLOSED THURSDAY, JANUARY 22,2004WITH 32 NOMINATIONS.

Value of Race: $100,000 Winner $55,000; second $20,000; third $15,000; fourth $7,500; fifth $2,500. Mutuel Pool $358,581.00 Exacta Pool $239,133.00 Quinella Pool $17,821.00 Trifecta Pool $223,334.00 Superfecta Pool $70,164.00

Last Raced	Horse	M/Eqt.	A.	Wt	PP	St	¼	½	¾	Str	Fin	Jockey	Odds $1
15Oct03 ^{2}SA^{2}	Red Rioja-Ire	LB	5	117	7	11	7^{hd}	7^{1}	$7^{\frac{1}{2}}$	$4^{\frac{1}{2}}$	1^{1}	Saint-Martin E	1.20
3Jan04 ^{7}GG^{2}	Hooked On Niners	LB f	5	117	9	7	9^{2}	9^{2}	8^{1}	5^{2}	$2^{1\frac{1}{4}}$	Baze R A	5.30
3Jan04 ^{7}GG^{1}	A B Noodle	LB	5	116	4	3	3^{2}	3^{2}	2^{2}	$1^{2\frac{1}{2}}$	3^{1}	Gonzalez R M	5.90
8Jan04 ^{7}SA^{2}	Drew Away	LB	5	116	11	10	10^{1}	10^{3}	10^{3}	$6^{1\frac{1}{2}}$	$4^{1\frac{1}{2}}$	Rollins C J	22.50
15Nov03 ^{8}Haw^{10}	Hippogator	LB b	4	115	5	2	$2^{1\frac{1}{2}}$	2^{1}	3^{1}	2^{hd}	$5^{1\frac{1}{2}}$	Carr D	48.30
9Jan04 ^{7}SA^{1}	Abbey Bridge	LB b	6	116	6	9	$4^{\frac{1}{2}}$	4^{1}	4^{hd}	3^{hd}	6^{1}	Radke K	6.30
3Jan04 ^{7}GG^{3}	Frisco Belle	LB b	4	116	10	4	5^{1}	$5^{1\frac{1}{2}}$	5^{hd}	$7^{1\frac{1}{2}}$	7^{1}	Castro J M	20.30
13Dec03 ^{5}Hol^{4}	Ilha Grande	LB	5	115	1	5	$8^{1\frac{1}{2}}$	8^{hd}	9^{hd}	8^{hd}	8^{1}	Duran F	10.80
19Dec03 ^{4}GG^{1}	Lady's Mantle-Ire	LB f	4	117	3	6	11	11	11	10^{3}	9^{4}	Mercado P	43.90
7Dec03 ^{8}Hol^{5}	Keys to the Heart	LB	5	115	8	8	6^{2}	6^{1}	6^{1}	9^{2}	$10^{2\frac{1}{2}}$	Puglisi I	20.20
31Dec03 ^{8}SA^{6}	Just Bill Me	LB f	4	115	2	1	$1^{1\frac{1}{2}}$	1^{2}	1^{hd}	11	11	Warren R J Jr	27.50

OFF AT 1:49 Start Good For All But DREW AWAY. Won driving. Course soft.

TIME :23^{2}, :48^{1}, 1:12^{4}, 1:38^{3}, 1:46 (:23.44, :48.22, 1:12.98, 1:38.77, 1:46.01)

$2 Mutuel Prices:

7 – RED RIOJA–IRE	4.40	3.00	2.40
9 – HOOKED ON NINERS		4.40	3.20
4 – A B NOODLE			3.40

$1 EXACTA 7–9 PAID $10.70 $2 QUINELLA 7–9 PAID $13.80
$1 TRIFECTA 7–9–4 PAID $41.90 $1 SUPERFECTA 7–9–4–11 PAID $491.20

B. m, (Mar), by King's Theatre–Ire – Foreign Relation–Ire , by Distant Relative–Ire . Trainer Cecil B D A. Bred by Dr Karen Monica Sanderson (Ire).

RED RIOJA (IRE) raced unhurried for a half, took closer attendance on the second turn, found room between horses and rallied to the stretch, was caught in traffic, waited and angled inside of HIPPOGATOR in upper stretch then closed strongly to take the lead and edged away late. HOOKED ON NINERS had no speed, commenced a bid into the second turn, was fanned four wide to the stretch then closed willingly in the final furlong. A B NOODLE stalked the leaders to the half, responded and took the lead into the stretch, edged clear to mid stretch then could not stall the top two. DREW AWAY dwelt at the start and was left about four lengths, lagged to the second turn, came two wide to the stretch then closed well but was outrun by HOOKED ON NINERS to the line. HIPPOGATOR pressed the pace to the second turn, responded gamely to the stretch and only weakened late. ABBEY BRIDGE never far back to the half, was asked for run into the second turn, came through traffic to the stretch but weakened in the drive. FRISCO BELLE was three wide to the backstretch, stalked the leaders to the half, got fanned five wide to the stretch and lacked a late response. ILHA GRANDE saved ground throughout but could not make an impact. LADY'S MANTLE (IRE) had no speed and was not a factor. KEYS TO THE HEART was allowed to settle to the half, responded when asked for speed on the second turn, loomed briefly to the stretch then was tiring and had to check off the winner's heels in upper stretch and gave out. JUST BILL ME set the pace to the second turn but stopped thereafter.

Owners– 1, Sanderson Dr Karen; 2, Langbein Trust Morey Jr Robinson and Sandall; 3, Amity and Bench; 4, M-2 Stable LLC; 5, Blanchard Bob Maser Tom and Todaro George; 6, Robertson Sanford R; 7, Aleo Harry J; 8, Old Friends Inc; 9, Leotti Thomas; 10, Nichols Thomas L; 11, Franks Farms

Trainers– 1, Cecil B D A; 2, Morey William J Jr; 3, Jenda Charles J; 4, Greely C Beau; 5, Hollendorfer Jerry; 6, Walsh Kathy; 7, Gilchrist Greg; 8, Lobo Paulo H; 9, Delia William; 10, Greely C Beau; 11, Hollendorfer Jerry

---

$2 Daily Double (3–7) Paid $27.20 ; Daily Double Pool $17,062 .
$1 Pick Three (7–3–7) Paid $57.00 ; Pick Three Pool $35,693 .

EIGHTH RACE
Gulfstream
JANUARY 31, 2004

$1\frac{1}{16}$ MILES. (1.40^{1}) CANADIAN TURF H. Purse $100,000 FOR THREE YEAR OLDS AND UPWARD. By subscription of $100 each, which shall accompany the nomination, $1,000 to pass the entry box and $1,000 additional to start, with $100,000 guaranteed. The owner of the winner to receive $60,000, $20,000 to second, $11,000 to third, $6,000 to fourth and $3,000 to fifth. Trophy to winning Owner. In the event this stake is taken off the turf, it may be subject to downgrading upon review of the Graded Stakes Committee. Closed Wednesday, January 21, 2004 with (24) nominations.(ORIGINALLY SCHEDULED FOR TURF).

Value of Race: $100,000 Winner $60,000; second $20,000; third $11,000; fourth $6,000; fifth $3,000. Mutuel Pool $381,106.00 Exacta Pool $251,836.00 Trifecta Pool $166,447.00 Superfecta Pool $41,013.00

Last Raced	Horse	M/Eqt.	A.	Wt	PP	St	¼	½	¾	Str	Fin	Jockey	Odds $1
29Oct03 ^{8}Aqu^{5}	Newfoundland	L b	4	115	4	6	5^{4}	$4^{1\frac{1}{2}}$	2^{2}	2^{2}	1^{nk}	Velazquez J R	2.70
4Jan04 ^{9}GP^{1}	MillnnumDrgon-GB	L	5	118	6	5	2^{2}	$1^{\frac{1}{2}}$	$1^{\frac{1}{2}}$	1^{1}	$2^{8\frac{1}{2}}$	Migliore R	2.00
10Jan04 ^{9}GP^{1}	Everything to Gain	L	5	113	3	2	6	6	$5^{\frac{1}{2}}$	$3^{3\frac{1}{2}}$	$3^{5\frac{1}{4}}$	Santos J A	10.80
16Nov03 ^{9}CD^{1}	Hard Buck-Brz	L	5	119	2	3	1^{hd}	$2^{\frac{1}{2}}$	$3^{1\frac{1}{2}}$	$4^{3\frac{1}{2}}$	$4^{9\frac{3}{4}}$	Prado E S	3.70
10Jan04 ^{10}GP^{4}	Justification	L	7	115	5	4	3^{hd}	$3^{\frac{1}{2}}$	4^{hd}	$5^{\frac{1}{2}}$	5^{11}	Chavez J F	6.80
18Dec03 ^{10}Crc^{1}	Light Night		5	112	1	1	$4^{\frac{1}{2}}$	$5^{3\frac{1}{2}}$	6	6	6	Velasquez C	5.40

OFF AT 4:10 Start Good . Won driving. Track sloppy.

TIME :23^{3}, :47^{1}, 1:11^{4}, 1:38^{1}, 1:44^{4} (:23.74, :47.26, 1:11.93, 1:38.25, 1:44.90)

$2 Mutuel Prices:

5 – NEWFOUNDLAND	7.40	3.40	3.00
9 – MILLENNIUM DRAGON–GB		3.40	3.20
3 – EVERYTHING TO GAIN			4.00

$1 EXACTA 5–9 PAID $11.60 $1 TRIFECTA 5–9–3 PAID $71.30
$1 SUPERFECTA 5–9–3–2 PAID $136.10

Ch. c, (Feb), by Storm Cat – Clear Mandate , by Deputy Minister . Trainer Pletcher Todd A. Bred by G Watts Humphrey (Ky).

NEWFOUNDLAND hit the gate at the start, moved up to stalk the pace three wide, then wore down MILLENNIUM DRAGON to be just up at the wire while being floated out by that rival through the stretch. MILLENNIUM DRAGON (GB) showed speed off the rail, then drifted out through the stretch run and just failed to last. EVERYTHING TO GAIN unhurried early, advanced into contention three wide on the far turn but couldn't keep pace with the top ones in the drive. HARD BUCK (BRZ) showed speed along the inside to nearing the far turn and tired. JUSTIFICATION chased the pace off the rail into the far turn and faltered. LIGHT NIGHT saved ground and was through early.

Owners– 1, Sumaya Us Stables; 2, Darley Stable; 3, Ramsey Kenneth L and Sarah K; 4, Team Victory I; 5, Shields Joseph V Jr; 6, Lambholm Stable

Trainers– 1, Pletcher Todd A; 2, McLaughlin Kiaran P; 3, Romans Dale; 4, McPeek Kenneth G; 5, Jerkens H Allen; 6, Lerman Roy S

Scratched– Steadfast and True (03Jan04 ^{8}GP ^{1}) , Remind (04Jan04 ^{9}GP ^{6}) , French Charmer (04Jan04 ^{9}GP ^{4})

$1 Pick Three (12–4–5) Paid $110.30 ; Pick Three Pool $44,004 .

ELEVENTH RACE
Gulfstream
JANUARY 31, 2004

1⅛ MILES. (1.46^{2}) SUWANNEE RIVER H. Purse $100,000 FOR FILLIES AND MARES, THREE YEAR OLDS AND UPWARD. By subsciption of $100 each, which shall accompany the nomination, $1,000 to pass the entry box and $1,000 additional to start, with $100,000 guaranteed. The owner of the winner to receive $60,000; $20,000 to second, $11,000 to third, $6,000 to fourth and $3,000 to fifth. Trophy to winning Owner. In the event this stake is taken off the turf, it may be subject to downgrading upon review of the Graded Stakes Committee. Closed Wednesday, January 21, 2004with (28) nominations.(ORIGINALLY SCHEDULED FOR TURF).

Value of Race: $100,000 Winner $60,000; second $20,000; third $11,000; fourth $6,000; fifth $3,000. Mutuel Pool $223,494.00 Exacta Pool $127,725.00 Trifecta Pool $59,817.00 Superfecta Pool $20,307.00

Last Raced	Horse	M/Eqt.	A.	Wt	PP	St	¼	½	¾	Str	Fin	Jockey	Odds $1
28Dec03 ^{6}Crc^{1}	Wishful Splendor	L f	5	114	3	2	2^{hd}	$3^{2\frac{1}{2}}$	$2^{\frac{1}{2}}$	1^{1}	$1^{1\frac{1}{4}}$	Santos J A	7.60
3Jan04 ^{11}GP^{4}	May Gator	L b	5	113	1	1	1^{1}	1^{2}	1^{1}	2^{1}	$2^{2\frac{1}{4}}$	Chavez J F	1.40
19Nov03 ^{9}CD^{1}	Mymich	L b	4	113	4	3	4^{2}	4^{hd}	5	$3^{4\frac{1}{2}}$	$3^{3\frac{3}{4}}$	Blanc B	4.50
22Nov03 ^{9}CD^{8}	San Dare	L	6	115	2	5	5	5	$4^{\frac{1}{2}}$	4^{6}	4^{21}	Guidry M	4.50
14Dec03 ^{5}Crc^{1}	Young Star	L	5	114	5	4	$3^{\frac{1}{2}}$	2^{hd}	3^{1}	5	5	Douglas R R	2.40

OFF AT 5:35 Start Good . Won driving. Track sloppy.

TIME :24^{2}, :50^{1}, 1:15^{4}, 1:41^{3}, 1:54^{4} (:24.42, :50.28, 1:15.84, 1:41.61, 1:54.86)

$2 Mutuel Prices:

	Win	Place	Show
9 – WISHFUL SPLENDOR	17.20	5.20	2.80
2 – MAY GATOR		3.20	2.60
10 – MYMICH			3.00

$1 EXACTA 9–2 PAID $22.00 $1 TRIFECTA 9–2–10 PAID $82.70
$1 SUPERFECTA 9–2–10–5 PAID $141.00

Ch. m, (Feb), by Smart Strike – Kaylem Ho , by Salem . Trainer Russo Sal. Bred by JMJ Stables Corp (Ky).

WISHFUL SPLENDOR stalked the pace along the inside, rallied inside MAY GATOR to take over at the top of the stretch, then was fully extended to prevail. MAY GATOR set the pace three wide, was outmoved by the winner entering the stretch but continued with good courage to hold the place. MYMICH reserved early, advanced along the rail to loom a threat entering the stretch but had no late response. SAN DARE unhurried early, moved into contention three wide on the far turn, then tired in the drive. YOUNG STAR stalked the pace into the far turn, faded and was eased in the final eighth.

Owners– 1, Manganaro John H Jr; 2, Klein Richard Bertram and Elaine; 3, Willmott Stables Inc; 4, Mounts David G; 5, Live Oak Plantation

Trainers– 1, Russo Sal; 2, Flint Steve; 3, Reinstedler Anthony; 4, Hiles Rick; 5, Mott William I

Scratched– Changing World (20Dec03 ^{8}Crc^{1}) , New Economy (27Dec03 ^{9}Crc^{6}) , Madeira Mist (IRE) (03Jan04 ^{11}GP ^{3}) , Mystery Itself (19Dec03 ^{9}Crc^{1}) , Approach (GB) (07Jan04 ^{7}GP ^{1}) , Sixty Seconds (NZ) (27Dec03 ^{9}Crc^{5}) , Something Ventured (03Jan04 ^{11}GP ^{5})

$1 Pick Three (9–2–9) Paid $535.50 ; Pick Three Pool $20,084 .

EIGHTH RACE
Santa Anita
JANUARY 31, 2004

1⅛ MILES. (1.45^{4}) SAN ANTONIO H. Grade II. Purse $250,000 FOR FOUR-YEAR-OLDS AND UPWARD. By subscription of $250 each to accompany the nomination or by supplementary nomination of $5,000 by Sunday, January 25. $2,500 additional to start, with $250,000 guaranteed, of which $150,000 to first, $50,000 to second, $30,000 to third, $15,000 to fourth and $5,000 to fifth. Weights Tuesday, January 27. Starters to be named through the entry box by the closing time of entries. A trophy will be presented to the owner of the winner. Closed with 9 Nominations and 1 Supplementary Nomination (Toccet).

Value of Race: $245,000 Winner $150,000; second $50,000; third $30,000; fourth $15,000. Mutuel Pool $531,309.00 Exacta Pool $387,050.00 Quinella Pool $33,674.00

Last Raced	Horse	M/Eqt.	A.	Wt	PP	St	¼	½	¾	Str	Fin	Jockey	Odds $1
25Oct03 ^{9}SA^{1}	Pleasantly Perfect	LB b	6	121	4	4	4	4	2^{hd}	1^{1}	1^{4}	Solis A	1.90
3Jan04 ^{7}SA^{1}	Star Cross-Arg	LB b	7	114	2	2	2^{1}	$1^{\frac{1}{2}}$	3^{hd}	3^{3}	2^{nk}	Espinoza V	10.80
29Nov03 ^{11}Tok^{1}	Fleetstreet Dancer	LB bf	6	116	1	1	$1^{\frac{1}{2}}$	3^{1}	1^{hd}	2^{1}	3^{4}	Court J K	11.90
29Nov03 ^{9}Aqu^{1}	Congaree	LB	6	124	3	3	3^{hd}	2^{hd}	4	4	4	Bailey J D	0.40

OFF AT 4:08 Start Good . Won driving. Track fast.

TIME :23, :46^{3}, 1:10, 1:34^{3}, 1:47^{1} (:23.05, :46.60, 1:10.10, 1:34.64, 1:47.25)

$2 Mutuel Prices:

	Win	Place	Show
4 – PLEASANTLY PERFECT	5.80	6.00	—
2 – STAR CROSS–ARG		10.00	—
1 – FLEETSTREET DANCER		—	—

$1 EXACTA 4–2 PAID $15.30 $2 QUINELLA 2–4 PAID $21.00

B. h, (Apr), by Pleasant Colony – Regal State , by Affirmed . Trainer Mandella Richard. Bred by Clovelly Farms (Ky).

PLEASANTLY PERFECT angled in off the rail stalking the pace nearing the first turn, pulled a bit on the backstretch, went up four wide into and on the second turn, gained a short lead a quarter mile out, came in a bit into the stretch, inched away in the drive and pulled clear under a couple taps of the whip and a strong hand ride while drifting inward. STAR CROSS (ARG) drifted out into the first turn, dueled outside a rival then between horses, fought back between foes on the second turn, was in a bit tight behind the winner into the stretch, was no match for that one in the lane but game for second. FLEETSTREET DANCER had good early speed and dueled inside, regained the advantage into the second turn, fought back on that turn and into the stretch and was edged late for the place. CONGAREE floated out a bit into the first turn, went up three deep to duel for command, battled three wide between horses into the second turn, dropped back leaving that turn and weakened.

Owners– 1, Diamond A Racing Corporation; 2, E A Ranches; 3, Leatherman Lee and Ty; 4, Stonerside Stable LLC

Trainers– 1, Mandella Richard; 2, Vienna Darrell; 3, O'Neill Doug; 4, Baffert Bob

Scratched– Nose The Trade (GB) (03Jan04 ^{7}SA ^{2})

$2 Daily Double (8–4) Paid $19.40 ; Daily Double Pool $51,649 .
$1 Pick Three (5–8–4) Paid $53.60 ; Pick Three Pool $81,251 .

EIGHTH RACE
Fair Grounds
FEBRUARY 1, 2004

$1\frac{1}{16}$ MILES. (1.42) WHIRLAWAY H. Grade III. Purse $100,000 FOR FOUR YEAR OLDS AND UPWARD. $100,000 Guaranteed of which $60,000 to the winner; $20,000 to second; $11,000 to third; $6,000 to fourth; $3,000 to fifth. Failure to draw into the race will cancel all fees. THE OWNER OF THE WINNER TO RECEIVE A TROPHY.Closed Saturday, January 24, 2004, with 18 nominations.

Value of Race: $100,000 Winner $60,000; second $20,000; third $11,000; fourth $6,000; fifth $3,000. Mutuel Pool $238,639.00 Exacta Pool $145,198.00 Quinella Pool $11,680.00 Superfecta Pool $40,184.00 Trifecta Pool $120,064.00

Last Raced	Horse	M/Eqt.	A.	Wt	PP	St	¼	½	¾	Str	Fin	Jockey	Odds $1
3Jan04 ^{7}SA^{3}	Olmodavor	L	5	121	9	9	6^{2}	$8^{2\frac{1}{2}}$	$5^{\frac{1}{2}}$	2^{1}	$1^{\frac{3}{4}}$	Lanerie C J	1.50
2Jan04 ^{9}FG^{1}	Spanish Empire	L	4	118	2	2	2^{2}	2^{2}	1^{1}	$1^{\frac{1}{2}}$	$2^{2\frac{1}{4}}$	Martin E M Jr	2.40
6Dec03 ^{9}FG^{5}	Almuhathir	L	6	114	7	8	9	9	9	6^{1}	$3^{\frac{1}{2}}$	Melancon L	30.30
2Jan04 ^{9}FG^{4}	Kodema	L f	5	114	8	5	4^{2}	4^{4}	3^{1}	3^{2}	$4^{\frac{3}{4}}$	Martinez J R Jr	22.20
3Jan04 ^{7}SA^{5}	Total Impact-Chi	L	6	118	1	3	3^{1}	$3^{\frac{1}{2}}$	4^{3}	7^{2}	5^{hd}	Sellers S J	6.90
14Dec03 ^{9}FG^{2}	Classic Par	L	6	118	4	4	7^{hd}	7^{hd}	8^{1}	$5^{\frac{1}{2}}$	$6^{6\frac{1}{2}}$	Bourque C C	33.80
28Nov03 ^{11}CD^{7}	M B Sea	L b	5	117	5	6	8^{hd}	6^{1}	6^{1}	$4^{\frac{1}{2}}$	7^{2}	Albarado R J	7.60
27Dec03 ^{9}FG^{4}	G. W.'s Skippie	L	4	116	6	7	$5^{\frac{1}{2}}$	5^{2}	$7^{2\frac{1}{2}}$	$8^{2\frac{1}{2}}$	$8^{1\frac{3}{4}}$	Lovato F Jr	20.90
11Jan04 ^{9}FG^{3}	El Ruller	L	4	117	3	1	$1^{\frac{1}{2}}$	$1^{\frac{1}{2}}$	$2^{1\frac{1}{2}}$	9	9	Borel C H	6.50

OFF AT 2:52 Start Good . Won driving. Track fast.

TIME :24^{2}, :47^{2}, 1:11^{4}, 1:38^{2}, 1:45^{2} (:24.53, :47.54, 1:11.99, 1:38.57, 1:45.59)

$2 Mutuel Prices:

9 – OLMODAVOR	5.00	3.00	2.80
2 – SPANISH EMPIRE		3.00	2.60
7 – ALMUHATHIR			5.60

$2 EXACTA 9–2 PAID $19.60 $2 QUINELLA 2–9 PAID $12.60
$2 SUPERFECTA 9–2–7–8 PAID $1,944.20 $2 TRIFECTA 9–2–7 PAID $225.40

B. h, (Apr), by A.P. Indy – Corrazona , by El Gran Senor . Trainer Mandella Richard. Bred by Wertheimer et Frere (Ky).

OLMODAVOR off last, settled off the rail while unhurried, was asked for run entering the second turn, rallied four wide approaching the drive, loomed outside SPANISH EMPIRE and proved best under strong handling. SPANISH EMPIRE forward early, eased out nearing the first turn to collar EL RULLER around the turn, prompted the pace outside that one until midway around the second turn, gained the clear advantage for the drive and then fought back when challenged but was out kicked to the wire. ALMUHATHIR raced in the back until approaching the drive, swung widest and closed willingly. KODEMA never far back, ranged up three wide for the drive and then failed to sustain his bid. TOTAL IMPACT (CHI) raced close up from early on, came inside in the drive and lacked a finish. CLASSIC PAR raced inside until the drive, angled out and could make little impact. M B SEA between foes until the second turn, moved up and then faded. G. W.'S SKIPPIE reserved, had no response. EL RULLER broke alertly, moved to the rail to set the pace and then faltered once headed.

Owners– 1, Wertheimer & Frere A&GWertheimer & CHeilbronn; 2, Jubilee Stable Cherry Martin L and Twin Creeks Farm; 3, Shadwell Stable; 4, Farfellow Farms Ltd; 5, Bridport S A & Sultan Al Kabeer Lilianna Solari; 6, Centaur Farms Inc; 7, Bruder Michael J; 8, Warren Glen C; 9, Warren Jr Mr and Mrs William K

Trainers– 1, Mandella Richard; 2, Asmussen Steven M; 3, Peitz Daniel C; 4, Carroll David; 5, De Seroux Laura; 6, Scherer Merrill R; 7, Romans Dale; 8, Leggio Andrew Jr; 9, Amoss Thomas

---

$2 Pick Three (2–7–9) Paid $971.20 ; Pick Three Pool $15,541 .
$2 Pick Six (6–4–7–2–7–9) 5 Correct Paid $59.60 ; Pick Six Pool $3,053 ; Carryover Pool $3,687.

SEVENTH RACE
Santa Anita
FEBRUARY 1, 2004

6 FURLONGS. (1.07^{1}) PALOS VERDES H. Grade II. Purse $150,000 FOR FOUR-YEAR-OLDS AND UPWARD. By subscription of $150 each to accompany the nomination or by supplementary nomination of $3,000 by Sunday, January 25. $1,500 additional to start, with $150,000 guaranteed, of which $90,000 to first, $30,000 to second, $18,000 to third, $9,000 to fourth and $3,000 to fifth. Weights Tuesday, January 27. Starters to be named through the entry box by the closing time of entries. A trophy will be presented to the owner of the winner. Closed with 13 Nominations.

Value of Race: $150,000 Winner $90,000; second $30,000; third $18,000; fourth $9,000; fifth $3,000. Mutuel Pool $463,982.00 Exacta Pool $241,017.00 Quinella Pool $24,113.00 Trifecta Pool $231,806.00 Superfecta Pool $93,753.00

Last Raced	Horse	M/Eqt.	A.	Wt	PP	St	¼	½	Str	Fin	Jockey	Odds $1
25Oct03 ^{5}SA^{2}	Bluesthestandard	LB	7	117	7	1	4^{hd}	2^{hd}	$2^{2\frac{1}{2}}$	1^{1}	Smith M E	1.80
26Dec03 ^{8}SA^{2}	Marino Marini	LB	4	115	5	4	2^{1}	$1^{\frac{1}{2}}$	1^{hd}	2^{4}	Baze T C	4.20
27Nov03 ^{7}Hol^{2}	Our New Recruit	LB	5	114	3	5	$6^{3\frac{1}{2}}$	$5^{1\frac{1}{2}}$	$3^{1\frac{1}{2}}$	$3^{\frac{1}{2}}$	Ramsammy E	18.10
1Jan04 ^{8}SA^{1}	Boston Common	LB	5	117	4	3	5^{2}	6^{2}	$4^{\frac{1}{2}}$	4^{1}	Stevens G L	4.80
29Nov03 ^{9}Hol^{6}	Captain Squire	LB	5	117	1	6	7	7	7	5^{3}	Solis A	4.10
26Dec03 ^{4}SA^{1}	Tough Game	LB bf	5	115	2	7	3^{hd}	$4^{\frac{1}{2}}$	6^{1}	6^{7}	Espinoza V	3.90
1Jan04 ^{8}SA^{5}	Giovannetti	LB	5	112	6	2	1^{hd}	$3^{1\frac{1}{2}}$	$5^{\frac{1}{2}}$	7	Sorenson D	41.20

OFF AT 2:06 Start Good . Won driving. Track fast.

TIME :21, :43^{2}, :55^{2}, 1:08 (:21.08, :43.58, :55.56, 1:08.13)

$2 Mutuel Prices:

8 – BLUESTHESTANDARD	5.60	3.00	2.20
6 – MARINO MARINI		4.40	2.80
4 – OUR NEW RECRUIT			3.80

$1 EXACTA 8–6 PAID $11.80 $2 QUINELLA 6–8 PAID $12.00
$1 TRIFECTA 8–6–4 PAID $93.20 $1 SUPERFECTA 8–6–4–5 PAID $384.20

B. g, (Apr), by American Standard – Bob's Blue , by Bob's Dusty . Trainer West Ted H. Bred by Terry Brown (Ga).

BLUESTHESTANDARD stalked five wide then four wide on the backstretch and three deep into the turn, bid three wide leaving the turn, gained a short lead under some left handed urging past the eighth pole, drifted out a bit but proved best under good handling. MARINO MARINI moved up between horses on the backstretch, dueled outside a rival, took the lead between foes leaving the turn, fought back inside the winner and continued willingly but was second best. OUR NEW RECRUIT between horses early, chased off the rail, advanced outside on the turn and four wide into the stretch and held third. BOSTON COMMON chased between rivals on the backstretch and off the rail on the turn, came out into the stretch and just missed the show. CAPTAIN SQUIRE stalked inside then steadied in tight on the backstretch, saved ground off the pace, came out on the turn and four wide into the stretch and lacked the needed rally. TOUGH GAME between horses early, angled in on the backstretch, stalked inside, came out into the stretch and weakened. GIOVANNETTI had good early speed off the rail, dueled inside the runner-up, angled to the rail on the turn, dropped back nearing the stretch and had little left for the drive.

Owners– 1, Sengara Jeffrey; 2, Rancho San Miguel; 3, C R K Stable; 4, Englander Richard A; 5, Bone Robert D and Diener Jeffrey S; 6, Noctis Stable Papiano Neil and Taub Steve; 7, Schiappa Bernard C

Trainers– 1, West Ted H; 2, O'Neill Doug; 3, Sadler John W; 4, Mullins Jeff; 5, Mullins Jeff; 6, Mulhall Kristin; 7, Monteleone Frank J

Scratched– Summer Service (01Jan04 ^{8}SA ^{2})

$2 Daily Double (9–8) Paid $133.00 ; Daily Double Pool $47,502 .
$1 Pick Three (4–9–1/8) Paid $254.80 ; Pick Three Pool $72,471 .

EIGHTH RACE
Gulfstream
FEBRUARY 7, 2004

1 1/16 MILES. (1.40[1]) 17TH RUNNING OF THE DAVONA DALE. Grade II. Purse $150,000 FOR FILLIES, THREE YEARS OLD. By subscription of $150 each, which shall accompany the nomination, $1,500 to pass the entry box and $1,500 additional to start, with $150,000 guaranteed. The owner of the winner to receive $90,000, $30,000 to second, $16,500to third, $9,000 to fourth and $4,500 to fifth. Supplemental nominations may be made on Thursday, February 5, 2004 at a fee of $4,000, which includes entry and start fees. Weight: 121 lbs. Non-winners of $50,000 once at a mile or over, allowed, 2 lbs.; $40,000 once at any distance or $30,000 at a mile or over, 4 lbs.; $25,000 once at any distance or $20,000 at a mile or over, 6 lbs. Trophy to winning Owner. Closed Wednesday, January 28,2004 with (14) nominations.

Value of Race: $150,000 Winner $90,000; second $30,000; third $16,500; fourth $9,000; fifth $4,500. Mutuel Pool $638,012.00 Exacta Pool $444,175.00 Trifecta Pool $313,170.00 Superfecta Pool $85,756.00

Last Raced	Horse	M/Eqt.	A.	Wt	PP	St	¼	½	¾	Str	Fin	Jockey	Odds $1
4Jan04 4SA1	Miss Coronado	L	3	117	1	1	1¹	1½	1hd	1½	1hd	Velasquez C	8.40
9Jan04 7GP1	Eye Dazzler	L	3	115	5	7	5½	5½	5¹	4½	2nk	Velazquez J R	4.80
25Oct03 3SA10	Society Selection		3	121	2	3	3hd	41½	3¹	3¹	3nk	Bailey J D	0.80
19Jan04 8GP1	Last Song	L f	3	117	7	5	4²	2hd	2½	2½	45¼	Prado E S	2.60
13Dec03 12Crc2	Marina de Chavon	L b	3	121	4	2	2¹	31½	4hd	5⁵	52¼	Santos J A	35.40
1Nov03 8Del2	From Away	L	3	119	6	6	6²	6⁷	6¹⁰	6¹⁰	617¾	Day P	16.00
29Nov03 8Crc12	Pick of the Pack	L b	3	117	3	4	7	7	7	7	7	Chavez J F	74.10

OFF AT 4:12 Start Good. Won driving. Track fast.

TIME :24², :49, 1:14, 1:38², 1:44³ (:24.48, :49.13, 1:14.11, 1:38.47, 1:44.62)

$2 Mutuel Prices:				
	1 – MISS CORONADO	18.80	8.60	3.60
	5 – EYE DAZZLER		6.00	3.00
	2 – SOCIETY SELECTION			2.20

$1 EXACTA 1–5 PAID $56.20 $1 TRIFECTA 1–5–2 PAID $133.90
$1 SUPERFECTA 1–5–2–7 PAID $249.20

Dk. b or br. f, (May), by Coronado's Quest – Miss Caerleona-Fr , by Caerleon . Trainer Frankel Robert. Bred by Stonerside Stable (Ky).

MISS CORONADO set the pace along the rail, responded when challenged in the stretch and was fully extended to last over EYE DAZZLER. The latter, off slowly, was rated off the pace, angled four wide on the far turn and rallied along the outside to just miss. SOCIETY SELECTION taken in hand to track the pace, made a run three wide on the far turn to reach the leaders, then didn't do enough late. LAST SONG stalked the pace, made a run at the winner between horses through the stretch and hung. MARINA DE CHAVON chased the winner into the far turn and tired. FROM AWAY reserved into the far turn, faltered in the drive. PICK OF THE PACK steadied in the early going and again along the inside on the first turn, then was outrun.

Owners– 1, Stonerside Stable LLC; 2, Lewis Lee; 3, Cowan Marjorie and Irving M; 4, Buckram Oak Farm; 5, Establo Madoca; 6, Erdenheim Farm; 7, Durst Lillian and Murray

Trainers– 1, Frankel Robert; 2, Hennig Mark; 3, Jerkens H Allen; 4, Nafzger Carl A; 5, Catanese Joseph C III; 6, Matz Michael R; 7, Plesa Edward

$1 Pick Three (6 1–1) Paid $206.90 ; Pick Three Pool $76,606 .
$1 Consolation Pick 3 (6–3/4/7/9–1) Paid $26.70 .

TENTH RACE
Gulfstream
FEBRUARY 7, 2004

1⅛ MILES. (1.46²) 46TH RUNNING OF THE DONN HANDICAP. Grade I. Purse $500,000 FOR THREE YEAR OLDS AND UPWARD. By subscription of $500 each, will shall accompany the nomination, $5,000 to pass the entry box and $5,000 additional to start, with $500,000 guaranteed. The owner of the winner to receive $300,000, $95,000 to second, $50,000 to third, $30,000 to fourth, $15,000 to fifth and 10,000 to sixth. Trophy to winning Owner. Closed Wednesday, January 28, 2004 with (15) nominations.

Value of Race: $500,000 Winner $300,000; second $95,000; third $50,000; fourth $30,000; fifth $15,000; sixth $10,000. Mutuel Pool $1,140,319.00 Exacta Pool $665,893.00 Trifecta Pool $544,129.00 Superfecta Pool $159,075.00

Last Raced	Horse	M/Eqt.	A.	Wt	PP	St	¼	½	¾	Str	Fin	Jockey	Odds $1
25Oct03 9SA2	Medaglia d'Oro	L	5	122	3	1	2³	2½	2¹	1³	14¾	Bailey J D	0.60
17Jan04 4Aqu1	Seattle Fitz-Arg	L	5	113	7	5	5⁶	5⁹	5⁶	2¹	23¾	Velazquez J R	9.80
10Jan04 10GP1	Funny Cide	L	4	119	5	6	31½	3¹	3hd	34½	3⁴	Santos J A	3.00
3Jan04 9GP1	Puzzlement	L b	5	115	2	3	7³	7³	7²	5hd	41½	Chavez J F	7.80
24Jan04 6SA3	The Judge Sez Who	L	5	114	8	8	6⁴	6³	62½	6⁴	54¼	Velasquez C	88.90
13Dec03 8Aqu5	Country Be Gold	L	7	114	1	4	8	8	8	71½	6¾	Douglas R R	105.60
27Dec03 12Crc1	Predawn Raid	L b	5	114	4	2	1hd	1½	1½	4³	74½	Coa E M	74.40
3Jan04 9GP2	Bowman's Band	L	6	116	6	7	4hd	4½	4¹	8	8	Dominguez R A	11.10

OFF AT 5:10 Start Good. Won ridden out. Track fast.

TIME :23¹, :47¹, 1:11, 1:35³, 1:47³ (:23.31, :47.24, 1:11.15, 1:35.60, 1:47.68)

$2 Mutuel Prices:				
	3 – MEDAGLIA D'ORO	3.20	2.40	2.10
	7 – SEATTLE FITZ–ARG		5.40	2.10
	5 – FUNNY CIDE			2.10

$1 EXACTA 3–7 PAID $7.50 $1 TRIFECTA 3–7–5 PAID $24.90
$1 SUPERFECTA 3–7–5–2 PAID $62.70

Dk. b or br. h, (Apr), by El Prado-Ire – Cappucino Bay , by Bailjumper . Trainer Frankel Robert. Bred by Albert Bell & Joyce Bell (Ky).

MEDAGLIA D'ORO showed speed inside PREDAWN RAID, was eased back off the lead when caught in tight inside that rival on the first turn, stalked the pace, rallied to gain command midway of the far turn, then drew away through the stretch while being ridden out. SEATTLE FITZ (ARG) reserved off the pace, angled four wide on the far turn and closed to prove second best while unable to stay with the winner. FUNNY CIDE taken in hand to track the pace three wide, made a run to loom a threat midway of the far turn, then tired in the drive. PUZZLEMENT unhurried early, passed tired rivals without threatening. THE JUDGE SEZ WHO allowed to settle, was never a factor. COUNTRY BE GOLD was outrun. PREDAWN RAID showed speed outside MEDAGLIA D'ORO, angled over to the inside when that rival took back leaving the first turn, made the pace along the inside, then was bumped from behind by BOWMAN'S BAND midway of the far turn, steadied and faltered. BOWMAN'S BAND rated off the pace, was attempting to rally along the rail when he bumped soundly with PREDAWN RAID on the far turn, then clipped heels, stumbled and faded. There was a stewards inquiry into the incident on the far turn. No action was taken.

Owners– 1, Gann Edmund A; 2, West Point Stable; 3, Sackatoga Stable; 4, Shields Joseph V Jr; 5, Sez Who Racing; 6, Seinfeld Barry and Dodson Elizabeth K; 7, Mount Joy Stables Inc; 8, Schwartz Martin S

Trainers– 1, Frankel Robert; 2, McLaughlin Kiaran P; 3, Tagg Barclay; 4, Jerkens H Allen; 5, Wolfson Milton W; 6, Nobles Reynaldo H; 7, Stutts Bennie F Jr; 8, Jerkens H Allen

$1 Pick Three (1–4–3) Paid $39.80 ; Pick Three Pool $99,444 .

ELEVENTH RACE
Gulfstream
FEBRUARY 7, 2004

$6\frac{1}{2}$ FURLONGS. (1.15) 15TH RUNNING OF THE DEPUTY MINISTER HANDICAP. Grade III. Purse $100,000 FOR THREE YEAR OLDS AND UPWARD. By subscription of $100 each, which shall accompany the nomination, $1,000 to pass the entry and $1,000 additional to start, with $100,000 guaranteed. The owner of the winner to receive $60,000; $20,000 to second, $11,000tothird, $6,000 to fourth and $3,000 to fifth. Trophy to winning Owner. Closed Wednesday, January 28, 2004 with (14) nominations.

Value of Race: $100,000 Winner $60,000; second $20,000; third $11,000; fourth $6,000; fifth $3,000. Mutuel Pool $504,949.00 Exacta Pool $348,739.00 Trifecta Pool $263,122.00 Superfecta Pool $66,656.00

Last Raced	Horse	M/Eqt.	A.	Wt	PP	St	¼	½	Str	Fin	Jockey	Odds $1
8Jan04 ^{8}GP^{1}	Alke	L	4	112	5	3	2^{hd}	$2^{1\frac{1}{2}}$	1^{hd}	$1^{2\frac{1}{2}}$	Velazquez J R	4.40
3Jan04 ^{10}GP^{1}	Cajun Beat	L b	4	123	4	1	$1^{\frac{1}{2}}$	1^{hd}	$2^{2\frac{1}{2}}$	$2^{1\frac{1}{4}}$	Velasquez C	0.90
12Dec03 ^{7}Haw^{1}	Coach Jimi Lee	L	4	115	3	2	$3^{1\frac{1}{2}}$	5^{hd}	$3^{1\frac{1}{2}}$	$3^{2\frac{1}{4}}$	Day P	12.90
3Jan04 ^{10}GP^{2}	Gygistar	L	5	118	1	6	5^{hd}	4^{hd}	$4^{2\frac{1}{2}}$	4^{5}	Bailey J D	3.50
3Jan04 ^{7}GP^{1}	Buju	L f	4	114	2	7	4^{hd}	6^{hd}	6^{3}	5^{nk}	Santos J A	10.10
21Jun03 ^{13}Suf^{3}	True Direction	L b	5	116	6	5	6^{hd}	3^{hd}	5^{hd}	6^{4}	Dominguez R A	14.00
10Jan04 ^{10}GP^{2}	American Style	L	5	113	7	4	7	7	7	7	Prado E S	40.50

OFF AT 5:40 Start Good . Won driving. Track fast.

TIME :23, :46, 1:09^{3}, 1:15^{4} (:23.04, :46.05, 1:09.64, 1:15.80)

$2 Mutuel Prices:

5 – ALKE	10.80	4.60	3.00
4 – CAJUN BEAT		2.60	2.20
3 – COACH JIMI LEE			3.60

$1 EXACTA 5–4 PAID $13.10 $1 TRIFECTA 5–4–3 PAID $94.40
$1 SUPERFECTA 5–4–3–1 PAID $306.60

Dk. b or br. c, (May), by Grand Slam – Pasampsi , by Crow–Fr . Trainer Pletcher Todd A. Bred by White Fox Farm (Ky).

ALKE vied for the lead outside CAJUN BEAT to inside the eighth pole, then edged away under pressure. CAJUN BEAT vied for the lead along the inside, then couldn't stay with the winner late while holding the place. COACH JIMI LEE chased the pace duel three wide into the stretch, weakened and outfinished the others for the show. GYGISTAR steadied to avoid running up on the leaders racing down the backstretch, chased the pace into the stretch and tired. BUJU off slowly, steadied off rivals heels racing down the backstretch, chased the leaders three wide around the turn and gave way. TRUE DIRECTION chased the pace four wide around the turn and faltered. AMERICAN STYLE raced five wide on the turn and faded.

Owners– 1, English Kenneth D and Braun Alan; 2, Padua Stable & John & Joseph Iracane; 3, Battaglia Lee and Divito James P; 4, Evans Edward P; 5, Triple F Stable; 6, Binn Morton and Marisol; 7, Buckram Oak Farm

Trainers– 1, Pletcher Todd A; 2, Margolis Stephen R; 3, DiVito James P; 4, Hennig Mark; 5, Jerkens H Allen; 6, Morales Carlos J; 7, Zito Nicholas P

$1 Pick Three (4–3–5) Paid $26.80 ; Pick Three Pool $62,205 .

THIRD RACE
Santa Anita
FEBRUARY 7, 2004

7 FURLONGS. (1.20) 63RD RUNNING OF THE SAN VICENTE. GRADE II Grade II. Purse $150,000 FOR THREE–YEAR–OLDS. By subscription of $150 each to accompany the nomination or by supplementary nomination of $3,000 by time of entry. $1,500 additional to start, with $150,000 guaranteed, of which $90,000 to first, $30,000 to second, $18,000 to third,$9,000 to fourth, and $3,000 to fifth. 123 lbs. Non–winners of two races of $60,000 allowed 3 lbs., of one of $60,000 at any time, 5 lbs.; of a race of $40,000 since December 25 or two races of $25,000 at any time, 7 lbs. (Maiden and Claiming races notconsidered). Starters to be named through the entry box by the closing time of entries. A trophy will be presented to the owner of the winner. Closed with 17 Nominations.

Value of Race: $150,000 Winner $90,000; second $30,000; third $18,000; fourth $9,000; fifth $3,000. Mutuel Pool $438,812.00 Exacta Pool $252,701.00 Quinella Pool $28,796.00 Trifecta Pool $256,331.00

Last Raced	Horse	M/Eqt.	A.	Wt	PP	St	¼	½	Str	Fin	Jockey	Odds $1
1Jan04 ^{9}Crc^{5}	Imperialism	LB b	3	116	1	6	6	6	$4^{\frac{1}{2}}$	$1^{1\frac{1}{4}}$	Espinoza V	14.10
11Jan04 ^{7}SA^{1}	Hosco	LB b	3	120	6	1	$1^{\frac{1}{2}}$	1^{1}	1^{1}	2^{hd}	Baze T C	1.10
5Dec03 ^{8}DeD^{7}	Consecrate	LB b	3	116	5	4	2^{1}	2^{hd}	2^{hd}	3^{1}	Desormeaux K J	10.20
8Jan04 ^{5}SA^{1}	Wimplestiltskin	LB b	3	116	4	2	$4^{2\frac{1}{2}}$	$4^{\frac{1}{2}}$	5^{1}	4^{1}	Valdivia J Jr	51.00
3Jan04 ^{4}SA^{1}	Teton Forest	LB b	3	116	3	3	3^{hd}	3^{2}	$3^{1\frac{1}{2}}$	5^{2}	Flores D R	1.30
25Jan04 ^{4}SA^{1}	Number Juan	LB	3	116	2	5	5^{6}	5^{4}	6	6	Stevens G L	8.20

OFF AT 1:03 Start Good . Won driving. Track fast.

TIME :22^{2}, :44^{3}, 1:09^{1}, 1:22^{1} (:22.44, :44.77, 1:09.34, 1:22.34)

$2 Mutuel Prices:

1 – IMPERIALISM	30.20	7.20	3.60
6 – HOSCO		3.00	2.40
5 – CONSECRATE			3.20

$1 EXACTA 1–6 PAID $33.30 $2 QUINELLA 1–6 PAID $20.60
$1 TRIFECTA 1–6–5 PAID $161.40

Gr/ro. c, (Apr), by Langfuhr – Bodhavista , by Pass the Tab . Trainer Mulhall Kristin. Bred by Farnsworth Farms (Ky).

IMPERIALISM broke in a bit, was taken off the rail and raced unhurried on the backstretch, began to move up on the turn, came four wide into the stretch, rallied under some left handed urging, lugged inward through the final furlong, gained the lead past midstretch and proved best under a late hold. HOSCO sped to the early lead, set the pace off the rail, angled in on the turn, could not hold off the winner but gamely saved the place. CONSECRATE prompted the pace outside the runner-up, stalked outside a rival on the turn, bid again past midstretch and was edged for second. WIMPLESTILTSKIN stalked the pace between horses then outside a rival, came three deep into the stretch and was outfinished. TETON FOREST close up stalking the pace inside, waited off heels in upper stretch, was boxed in along the rail in midstretch and lacked a late bid. NUMBER JUAN saved ground chasing the pace, came out into the stretch and did not rally.

Owners– 1, Taub Steve; 2, Rodriguez Lorraine and Rod; 3, McIngvale James; 4, Everest Stables Inc; 5, Hughes B Wayne; 6, Pegram Michael E

Trainers– 1, Mulhall Kristin; 2, O'Neill Doug; 3, Baffert Bob; 4, Polanco Marcelo; 5, Baffert Bob; 6, Puhich Michael

$2 Daily Double (1–1) Paid $421.40 ; Daily Double Pool $30,369 .
$1 Pick Three (3–1–1) Paid $3,157.20 ; Pick Three Pool $114,707 .

NINTH RACE
Santa Anita
FEBRUARY 7, 2004

1⅛ MILES. (1.45^{4}) 57TH RUNNING OF THE STRUB. Grade II. Purse $300,000 FOR FOUR-YEAR-OLDS. By subscription of $300 each to accompany the nomination. Supplementary nominations may be made at time of entry, by payment of $6,000. All horses shall pay $1,000 to pass the entry box and $2,000 additional to start, with $400,000guaranteed, of which $180,000 guaranteed to the winner, $60,000 to second, $36,000 to third, $18,000 to fourth and $6,000 to fifth; Weight: 123 lbs. Non-winners of $200,000 twice or $300,000 once at one mile or over since May 1, 2003 allowed 2 lbs.; of sucha race of $200,000 since then or $100,000 any distance since December 25, 2003, 4 lbs.; of $100,000 at one mile or over in 2003-2004 or $60,000 any distance since July 1, 2003, 6 lbs. Starters to be named through the entry box by the closing time ofentries. A trophy will be presented to the owner of the winner. Closed with 19 Nominations.

Value of Race: $300,000 Winner $180,000; second $60,000; third $36,000; fourth $18,000; fifth $6,000. Mutuel Pool $875,135.00 Exacta Pool $480,422.00 Quinella Pool $39,524.00 Trifecta Pool $454,635.00 Superfecta Pool $167,665.00

Last Raced	Horse	M/Eqt.	A.	Wt	PP	St	¼	½	¾	Str	Fin	Jockey	Odds $1
10Jan04 ^{8}SA^{4}	Domestic Dispute	LB	4	117	7	9	4^{hd}	5^{hd}	$6\frac{1}{2}$	$7\frac{1}{2}$	1^{nk}	Desormeaux K J	14.30
10Jan04 ^{8}SA^{1}	During	LB b	4	121	11	7	$5\frac{1}{2}$	4^{1}	4^{1}	5^{2}	$2\frac{3}{4}$	Flores D R	5.50
26Dec03 ^{3}SA^{1}	Buckland Manor	LB	4	117	6	2	$1\frac{1}{2}$	$2\frac{1}{2}$	2^{1}	$1^{1\frac{1}{2}}$	$3\frac{1}{2}$	Nakatani C S	5.20
26Dec03 ^{8}SA^{3}	Midas Eyes	LB	4	119	10	10	$7\frac{1}{2}$	7^{1}	$7\frac{1}{2}$	6^{hd}	$4\frac{1}{2}$	Solis A	2.80
14Jan04 ^{8}GP^{1}	Formal Attire	LB b	4	117	5	4	8^{1}	8^{1}	$8^{2\frac{1}{2}}$	$9^{1\frac{1}{2}}$	$5\frac{1}{2}$	Smith M E	25.10
15Jan04 ^{4}GG^{4}	Eye of the Tiger	LB	4	117	9	8	6^{1}	3^{hd}	3^{hd}	$2\frac{1}{2}$	6^{1}	Espinoza V	12.30
17Jan04 ^{8}SA^{1}	Saint Buddy	LB b	4	117	1	1	3^{1}	6^{hd}	5^{hd}	3^{hd}	$7^{1\frac{1}{2}}$	Baze T C	30.40
10Jan04 ^{8}SA^{2}	Toccet	LB b	4	117	2	5	$9^{1\frac{1}{2}}$	$10^{3\frac{1}{2}}$	9^{hd}	10^{1}	8no	Albarado R J	6.70
1Jan04 ^{3}SA^{1}	Mud Shark	LB b	4	117	3	11	11	11	11	11	9^{hd}	Santiago Javier	41.30
26Dec03 ^{8}SA^{9}	Buddy Gil	LB	4	119	4	3	$10^{2\frac{1}{2}}$	$9\frac{1}{2}$	10^{3}	$8^{1\frac{1}{2}}$	10^{hd}	Stevens G L	3.50
10Jan04 ^{8}SA^{8}	Anziyan Royalty	LB b	4	117	8	6	$2\frac{1}{2}$	1^{hd}	1^{hd}	4^{hd}	11	Valdivia J Jr	35.90

OFF AT 4:19 Start Good . Won driving. Track fast.

TIME :22^{1}, :45^{4}, 1:10^{1}, 1:35^{4}, 1:49 (:22.35, :45.83, 1:10.35, 1:35.87, 1:49.08)

$2 Mutuel Prices:				
	7 – DOMESTIC DISPUTE	**30.60**	**10.40**	**5.40**
	11 – DURING		**6.40**	**4.20**
	6 – BUCKLAND MANOR			**4.60**

$1 EXACTA 7-11 PAID $95.50 $2 QUINELLA 7-11 PAID $81.00
$1 TRIFECTA 7-11-6 PAID $972.80 $1 SUPERFECTA 7-11-6-10 PAID $3,717.50

Ch. c, (Mar), by Unbridled's Song – Majestical Moment , by Magesterial . Trainer Gallagher Patrick. Bred by Gary Garber (Ky).

DOMESTIC DISPUTE stalked between horses, waited behind rivals leaving the second turn and into the stretch, was blocked off heels in midstretch, came out and rallied under urging to get up late. DURING close up stalking the pace four wide to the stretch, rallied to a slim advantage in deep stretch and just failed to hold off the winner. BUCKLAND MANOR had good early speed between foes then angled in and dueled inside, inched away in the stretch, fought back gamely along the rail and held third. MIDAS EYES chased five wide then four wide on the backstretch, continued five wide on the second turn and into the stretch and finished with interest. FORMAL ATTIRE pulled early and was in a bit tight into the first turn, chased off the rail then between horses into and on the second turn, came out five wide into the stretch and could not summon the necessary late kick. EYE OF THE TIGER stalked three deep between horses, loomed a threat into the stretch but was outfinished. SAINT BUDDY tracked the leaders along the inside, awaited room into the stretch, was blocked along the rail and steadied in midstretch and again in deep stretch and could not recover. TOCCET in a bit tight into the first turn, saved ground chasing the pace, continued inside and lacked the needed rally. MUD SHARK unhurried a bit off the rail early, came out in the stretch and was not a threat. BUDDY GIL pulled early and steadied hard off heels into the first turn, chased outside a rival then between foes, continued outside a rival on the second turn, found the inside in the stretch and could not summon the necessary response. ANZIYAN ROYALTY had good early speed three deep then dueled outside a rival, battled between foes leaving the second turn and weakened in the stretch.

Owners– 1, Bienstock Dave and Winner Charles; 2, McIngvale James; 3, McCaffery Trudy and Toffan John A; 4, Gann Edmund A; 5, Flying Zee Stable; 6, Gunther John D; 7, Fulton Stan E; 8, Borislow Daniel M; 9, Jacobs and Pegram; 10, Billingsley Creek Ranch Desperado Stables Inc and Merrill Stables et al; 11, Cafarchia Nick

Trainers– 1, Gallagher Patrick; 2, Baffert Bob; 3, Gonzalez J Paco; 4, Frankel Robert; 5, Serpe Philip M; 6, Hollendorfer Jerry; 7, Becerra Rafael; 8, Scanlan John F; 9, Baffert Bob; 10, Mullins Jeff; 11, Dollase Craig

$2 Daily Double (11-7) Paid $284.40 ; Daily Double Pool $62,748 .
$1 Pick Three (7-11-7) Paid $1,437.10 ; Pick Three Pool $104,430 .

ELEVENTH RACE
Gulfstream
FEBRUARY 8, 2004

7 FURLONGS. (1.20) 26TH RUNNING OF THE SHIRLEY JONES HANDICAP. Grade III. Purse $100,000 FOR FILLIES AND MARES, THREE YEAR OLDS AND UPWARD. By subscription of $100 each, which shall accompany the nomination, $1,000 to pass the entry box and $1,000 additional to start, with $100,000 guaranteed. The owner of the winner to receive $60,000; $20,000 to second, $11,000 to third, $6,000 to fourth and $3,000 to fifth. Weights: Saturday, January 31, 2004. Trophy to winning Owner. Closed Wednesday, January 28, 2004 with (17) nominations.

Value of Race: $100,000 Winner $60,000; second $20,000; third $11,000; fourth $6,000; fifth $3,000. Mutuel Pool $505,368.00 Exacta Pool $339,062.00 Trifecta Pool $277,765.00 Superfecta Pool $93,450.00

Last Raced	Horse	M/Eqt.	A.	Wt	PP	St	¼	½	Str	Fin	Jockey	Odds $1
27Dec03 ^{7}SA^{2}	Randaroo	L	4	118	5	2	1^{hd}	1^{½}	12^{½}	17^{¼}	Velazquez J R	1.80
11Jan04 ^{10}GP^{1}	Harmony Lodge	L	6	121	8	1	21^{½}	2^{3}	22^{½}	2^{¾}	Migliore R	1.20
30Nov03 ^{9}TP^{1}	Halory Leigh	L	4	114	6	5	7^{hd}	72^{½}	4^{½}	32^{½}	Perret C	13.20
11Jan04 ^{10}GP^{3}	Mayo On the Side	L bf	5	115	2	8	8	8	8	4^{½}	Velez J A Jr	12.80
11Jan04 ^{9}GP^{2}	Honeymooner	L f	5	111	3	6	4^{1}	3^{hd}	31^{½}	5^{hd}	Castro E	82.70
23Nov03 ^{4}CD^{1}	Nannycam	L	4	112	7	4	6^{1}	6^{hd}	7^{1}	63^{¼}	Day P	17.70
11Jan04 ^{9}GP^{1}	Kitty Knight	L	4	113	4	3	3^{½}	41^{½}	6^{1}	7^{½}	Samyn J L	24.90
30Nov03 ^{6}Hol^{3}	Dedication-FR	L	5	114	1	7	5^{2}	5^{1}	5^{1}	8	Prado E S	6.20

OFF AT 5:42 Start Good . Won driving. Track fast.

TIME :22^{2}, :44^{4}, 1:08^{4}, 1:21^{2} (:22.43, :44.90, 1:08.87, 1:21.42)

$2 Mutuel Prices:			
5 – RANDAROO	5.60	2.80	2.60
8 – HARMONY LODGE		2.40	2.20
6 – HALORY LEIGH			3.80

$1 EXACTA 5–8 PAID $6.00 $1 TRIFECTA 5–8–6 PAID $26.60
$1 SUPERFECTA 5–8–6–2 PAID $74.00

B. f, (Feb), by Gold Case – Validated , by Valid Appeal . Trainer McLaughlin Kiaran P. Bred by Dennis Drazin (Ky).

RANDAROO showed speed off the rail, then drew away through the stretch under urging. HARMONY LODGE prompted the pace three wide into the stretch, then was no match for the winner while holding the place. HALORY LEIGH unhurried early, raced three wide on the turn and closed to gain the show. MAYO ON THE SIDE outrun early, swung wide for the stretch run and passed tired rivals. HONEYMOONER chased the leaders along the inside into the stretch and gave way. NANNYCAM was outrun. KITTY KNIGHT chased the pace, raced three wide on the turn and tired. DEDICATION (FR) rated in striking position off the pace, faltered in the drive.

Owners– 1, Allen Joseph; 2, Melnyk Eugene and Laura; 3, Jerry Crawford Matt Gannon & Charlie Grask; 4, Lothenbach Stables Inc; 5, Paul Derek K; 6, Oxley John C; 7, Bohemia Stable; 8, Head Mrs Alec

Trainers– 1, McLaughlin Kiaran P; 2, Pletcher Todd A; 3, Romans Dale; 4, Nafzger Carl A; 5, Green N; 6, Ward John T Jr; 7, Jerkens H Allen; 8, Clement Christophe

$1 Pick Three (12–8–5) Paid $41.00 ; Pick Three Pool $27,608 .

NINTH RACE
Fair Grounds
FEBRUARY 14, 2004

1$\frac{1}{16}$ MILES. (1.42) 23RD RUNNING OF THE SILVERBULLETDAY. Grade II. Purse $150,000 FOR THREE YEAR OLD FILLIES. $150,000 of which $90,000 to the winner; $30,000 to second; $16,500 to third; $9,000 to fourth; $4,500 to fifth. Weight: 122 lbs. Non–winners of $36,000, allowed 3 lbs.; $25,000, 5 lbs.(Maiden and claiming races not considered); two races other than maiden or claiming since November 16, 8 lbs.; $15,000 other than maiden or claiming since December 16, 10 lbs. THE OWNER OF THE WINNER TO RECEIVE A TROPHY. Closed Friday, February 6, 2004, with 14 nominations.

Value of Race: $150,000 Winner $90,000; second $30,000; third $16,500; fourth $9,000; fifth $4,500. Mutuel Pool $244,931.00 Exacta Pool $129,491.00 Quinella Pool $11,695.00 Trifecta Pool $101,106.00 Superfecta Pool $25,946.00

Last Raced	Horse	M/Eqt.	A.	Wt	PP	St	¼	½	¾	Str	Fin	Jockey	Odds $1
18Jan04 ^{7}FG^{1}	Shadow Cast	L b	3	116	4	4	4^{½}	4^{hd}	5^{1}	2^{1}	1^{¾}	Albarado R J	2.90
19Jan04 ^{8}GP^{2}	Quick Temper	L	3	113	1	3	1^{1}	21^{½}	2^{½}	1^{½}	2^{4}	Melancon L	4.00
25Jan04 ^{9}FG^{4}	Sister Swank	L	3	117	3	2	31^{½}	1^{½}	1^{hd}	3^{2}	33^{¾}	Sellers S J	5.30
25Jan04 ^{9}FG^{2}	Josie G.	L	3	118	5	5	5^{2}	51^{½}	4^{hd}	51^{½}	44^{¼}	Martin E M Jr	3.20
23Jan04 ^{8}OP^{2}	Movant	L	3	122	2	1	2^{1}	3^{hd}	31^{½}	4^{½}	5^{nk}	Borel C H	2.20
25Jan04 ^{9}FG^{3}	Love Power	L	3	117	6	6	6	6	6	6	6	Melancon G	15.10

OFF AT 4:19 Start Good . Won driving. Track sloppy.

TIME :24, :48^{2}, 1:14^{1}, 1:40, 1:46^{4} (:24.01, :48.48, 1:14.39, 1:40.19, 1:46.82)

$2 Mutuel Prices:			
4 – SHADOW CAST	7.80	4.40	2.60
1 – QUICK TEMPER		5.00	3.00
3 – SISTER SWANK			2.40

$2 EXACTA 4–1 PAID $40.40 $2 QUINELLA 1–4 PAID $21.80
$2 TRIFECTA 4–1–3 PAID $192.40 $2 SUPERFECTA 4–1–3–5 PAID $540.00

Ch. f, (Mar), by Smart Strike – Daily Special , by Dayjur . Trainer Howard Neil J. Bred by William S Farish Jr (Ky).

SHADOW CAST reserved early, raced between foes approaching the second turn, angled outside the leaders entering the drive, bid for the lead in mid stretch and prevailed in the final yards. QUICK TEMPER got clear early from the inside entering the first turn, drifted out just after reaching the backstretch, was straightened to race close up just outside SISTER SWANK down the backstretch and around the second turn, gained the edge nearing mid stretch and then did not have enough late. SISTER SWANK under stout restraint early, bid inside QUICK TEMPER after entering the backstretch, gained the edge, responded when headed and then lasted for the show. JOSIE G. crossed to the inside entering the first turn, remained inside while advancing, moved out nearing the drive and had no final kick. MOVANT held the early lead, was forced out by QUICK TEMPER entering the backstretch, settled off the leaders while remaining off the rail, loomed three wide before the drive, drifted out and faded. LOVE POWER trailed from early on, advanced outside around the second turn and then was no factor.

Owners– 1, Farish William S Jr; 2, Stanley Mark H; 3, Heiligbrodt Racing Stable; 4, England Greg L; 5, Griffin Richard E; 6, Zitani Nicole and Rangel Ramon

Trainers– 1, Howard Neil J; 2, O'Callaghan Niall M; 3, Asmussen Steven M; 4, Calhoun William Bret; 5, Amoss Thomas; 6, Barnett Bobby C

Scratched– He Loves Me (25Jan04 ^{9}FG ^{6})

$2 Pick Three (5–1–4) Paid $57.40 ; Pick Three Pool $10,236 .

TENTH RACE
Gulfstream
FEBRUARY 14, 2004

7 FURLONGS. (1.20) 51ST RUNNING OF THE HUTCHESON. Grade II. Purse $150,000 FOR THREE YEAR OLDS. By subscription of $150 each, which shall accompany the nomination, $1,500 to pass the entry box and $1,500 additional to start. Supplemental nominations may be made on Thursday, February 12, 2004 at a fee of $4,000, which includes entry and start fees. Weight: 122 lbs. Non-winners of $50,000 once, allowed 2 lbs,; $40,000 once anytime or $30,000 in 2004, 4 lbs.; $25,000 once or two races other than Maiden or Claiming, 6 lbs. Horses finishing first, second or third in the Hutcheson Stakes will automatically be nominated to the Florida Derby. Closed Wednesday, February 4, 2004 with (16) nominations. Early Bird Florida Derby Nominations closed on Wednesday, November 12, 2003 with 160 nominations.

Value of Race: $150,000 Winner $90,000; second $30,000; third $16,500; fourth $9,000; fifth $4,500. Mutuel Pool $819,770.00 Exacta Pool $642,027.00 Trifecta Pool $457,987.00 Superfecta Pool $122,277.00

Last Raced	Horse	M/Eqt.	A.	Wt	PP	St	¼	½	Str	Fin	Jockey	Odds $1
4Oct03 ^{6}Kee^{3}	Limehouse	L	3	122	1	2	6^{1}	$4^{\frac{1}{2}}$	2^{2}	$1^{2\frac{1}{4}}$	Velazquez J R	4.20
9Aug03 ^{10}Mth^{2}	Deputy Storm	L	3	118	5	5	1^{1}	1^{1}	1^{2}	$2^{1\frac{3}{4}}$	Bailey J D	8.50
10Jan04 ^{8}GP^{2}	Saratoga County	L bf	3	116	3	10	10	$9^{3\frac{1}{2}}$	6^{hd}	$3^{\frac{3}{4}}$	Coa E M	13.70
10Jan04 ^{8}GP^{1}	Wynn Dot Comma	L	3	122	6	6	4^{hd}	$5^{\frac{1}{2}}$	5^{2}	$4^{3\frac{3}{4}}$	Bravo J	2.30
25Jan04 ^{5}GP^{2}	Weigelia	L	3	116	2	9	8^{hd}	7^{2}	7^{3}	$5^{2\frac{1}{4}}$	Penalba C	51.70
7Jan04 ^{8}GP^{1}	Blushing Indian	L	3	116	7	7	$9^{4\frac{1}{2}}$	$8^{3\frac{1}{2}}$	8^{3}	6^{hd}	Santos J A	2.70
17Jan04 ^{10}Tam^{3}	Bourbon N Blues	L b	3	116	9	8	$3^{\frac{1}{2}}$	$3^{\frac{1}{2}}$	4^{hd}	7^{2}	Garcia J A	138.90
24Jan04 ^{4}GP^{1}	Harbour Gate	L	3	116	4	1	2^{1}	$2^{\frac{1}{2}}$	$3^{1\frac{1}{2}}$	$8^{8\frac{1}{4}}$	Velasquez C	9.30
10Jan04 ^{8}GP^{3}	Ghost Mountain	L b	3	118	8	3	5^{1}	6^{2}	9^{9}	9^{11}	Prado E S	9.80
10Jan04 ^{9}FG^{2}	Bachelor Blues	L	3	122	10	4	7^{1}	10	10	10	Day P	28.90

OFF AT 5:13 Start Good . Won driving. Track fast.

TIME :21^{3}, :43^{3}, 1:08^{4}, 1:22^{1} (:21.68, :43.73, 1:08.96, 1:22.23)

$2 Mutuel Prices:

2 – LIMEHOUSE	10.40	5.80	4.00
6 – DEPUTY STORM		10.00	6.60
4 – SARATOGA COUNTY			9.60

$1 EXACTA 2–6 PAID $39.50 $1 TRIFECTA 2–6–4 PAID $287.40
$1 SUPERFECTA 2–6–4–7 PAID $1,030.40

Ch. c, (Feb), by Grand Slam – Dixieland Blues , by Dixieland Band . Trainer Pletcher Todd A. Bred by Cheryl A Curtin (Fla).

LIMEHOUSE reserved racing along the inside, eased out and rallied to catch DEPUTY STORM at the sixteenth pole, then drew clear. DEPUTY STORM set the pace along the inside to the sixteenth pole, then couldn't stay with the winner while holding the place. SARATOGA COUNTY hit the gate at the start, then checked soon after, saved ground around the turn, swung wide for the stretch run and closed well to be up for the show. WYNN DOT COMMA tracked the pace, lacked room leaving the turn, angled out and had no late response. WEIGELIA failed to menace after breaking slowly. BLUSHING INDIAN unhurried early, raced five wide on the turn and was not a factor. BOURBON N BLUES off slowly, chased the pace three wide around the turn and tired. HARBOUR GATE chased the pacesetter into the stretch and faltered. GHOST MOUNTAIN up close early, raced four wide on the turn and faded. BACHELOR BLUES was through early.

Owners– 1, Dogwood Stable; 2, Spence James C; 3, Pollard Evelyn M; 4, Cherry Martin L; 5, Balsamo Joseph J; 6, Pacella William Rizza Joseph and Schwed Ronald; 7, Jacks or Better Farm Inc; 8, McDonnell Francis C; 9, La Penta Robert V; 10, Schettine William C

Trainers– 1, Pletcher Todd A; 2, Pletcher Todd A; 3, Weaver George; 4, Wolfson Martin D; 5, Azpurua Manuel J; 6, Romans Dale; 7, Hatchett James; 8, Handy George R; 9, Zito Nicholas P; 10, Carroll Josie

Scratched– Silver Rapt (21Jan04 ^{8}GP ^{1})

$1 Pick Three (7–2–2) Paid $71.80 ; Pick Three Pool $90,289 .

ELEVENTH RACE
Gulfstream
FEBRUARY 14, 2004

1$\frac{1}{16}$ MILES. (1.40^{1}) 58TH RUNNING OF THE FOUNTAIN OF YOUTH. Grade II. Purse $250,000 FOR THREE YEAR OLDS. By subscription of $250 each which shall accompany the nomination, $2,000 to pass the entry box and $2,000 additional to start. Weight: 122 lbs. Non-winners of $75,000 once at a mile or over, allowed, 2 lbs.; $50,000 once at any distance or $30,000 at a mile or over, 4 lbs.; $30,000 at any distance or $24,000 twice at a mile or over, 6 lbs. Horses finishing first, second or third in the Fountain of Youth Stakes will automatically be nominated to the Florida Derby. Trophy to winning Owner. Closed Wednesday, February 4 2004 with (8) nominations. Early Bird Florida Derby Nominations Closed on Wednesday, November 12, 2003 with 160 nominations.

Value of Race: $250,000 Winner $150,000; second $50,000; third $27,500; fourth $15,000; fifth $7,500. Mutuel Pool $1,034,656.00 Exacta Pool $583,794.00 Trifecta Pool $484,686.00 Superfecta Pool $157,116.00

Last Raced	Horse	M/Eqt.	A.	Wt	PP	St	¼	½	¾	Str	Fin	Jockey	Odds $1
29Nov03 ^{8}Aqu^{1}	Read the Footnotes	L	3	122	8	7	$3^{\frac{1}{2}}$	$3^{1\frac{1}{2}}$	2^{2}	2^{5}	1^{nk}	Bailey J D	2.10
17Jan04 ^{10}GP^{1}	Second of June	L f	3	120	7	6	2^{1}	$2^{\frac{1}{2}}$	1^{1}	$1^{\frac{1}{2}}$	$2^{7\frac{1}{2}}$	Velasquez C	1.50
17Jan04 ^{10}GP^{2}	Silver Wagon	L b	3	120	6	8	5^{hd}	6^{3}	6^{2}	3^{2}	$3^{5\frac{1}{2}}$	Santos J A	5.20
17Jan04 ^{10}GP^{4}	El Prado Rob	L	3	120	3	3	$7^{2\frac{1}{2}}$	5^{hd}	$3^{\frac{1}{2}}$	$4^{1\frac{1}{2}}$	$4^{1\frac{1}{2}}$	Prado E S	19.90
15Nov03 ^{10}Crc^{1}	Sir Oscar	b	3	122	1	1	$4^{1\frac{1}{2}}$	$4^{\frac{1}{2}}$	4^{1}	$5^{1\frac{1}{2}}$	5^{nk}	Garcia J A	5.20
1Jan04 ^{9}Crc^{2}	Broadway View	L b	3	116	4	4	$6^{\frac{1}{2}}$	7^{3}	7^{6}	7^{3}	$6^{\frac{3}{4}}$	Douglas R R	61.50
25Jan04 ^{5}GP^{1}	Frisky Spider	L	3	116	2	2	$1^{1\frac{1}{2}}$	$1^{\frac{1}{2}}$	5^{1}	6^{1}	$7^{2\frac{1}{4}}$	King E L Jr	14.70
25Jan04 ^{5}GP^{4}	Hopefortheroses	L b	3	116	5	5	8	8	8	8	8	Aguilar M	75.30

OFF AT 5:44 Start Good . Won driving. Track fast.

TIME :23^{4}, :47^{3}, 1:11^{1}, 1:36, 1:42^{3} (:23.97, :47.70, 1:11.21, 1:36.16, 1:42.71)

$2 Mutuel Prices:

8 – READ THE FOOTNOTES	6.20	3.20	2.20
7 – SECOND OF JUNE		2.60	2.20
6 – SILVER WAGON			2.60

$1 EXACTA 8–7 PAID $6.80 $1 TRIFECTA 8–7–6 PAID $17.10
$1 SUPERFECTA 8–7–6–3 PAID $79.10

B. c, (Apr), by Smoke Glacken – Baydon Belle , by Al Nasr–Fr . Trainer Violette Richard A Jr. Bred by Lawrence Goichman (NY).

READ THE FOOTNOTES stalked the pace three wide to the top of the stretch, then wore down SECOND OF JUNE in a long drive to be up at the wire. SECOND OF JUNE stalked the pace off the rail, moved to gain a slim lead outside FRISKY SPIDER leaving the backstretch, continued on gamely when challenged in the drive and just failed to last. SILVER WAGON reserved early, raced four wide on the far turn, angled in entering the stretch and closed to gain the show while unable to keep pace with the top ones. EL PRADO ROB was knocked into BROADWAY VIEW and steadied at the start, advanced off the rail to loom a threat on the far turn, then tired. SIR OSCAR tracked the pace three wide into the far turn and faltered. BROADWAY VIEW bumped at the start, saved ground and failed to be a factor. FRISKY SPIDER broke out and bumped with EL PRADO at the start, quickly moved to the fore, made the pace along the inside to nearing the far turn, then was fading when steadied inside SILVER WAGON leaving the far turn. HOPEFORTHEROSES trailed.

Owners– 1, Klaravich Stables Inc; 2, Cesare Barbara; 3, Buckram Oak Farm; 4, La Penta Robert V; 5, International Fair Play Inc; 6, Sacks Sidney; 7, Dender Carol R and Friedman Martin; 8, Rose Family Stable

Trainers– 1, Violette Richard A Jr; 2, Cesare William; 3, Ziadie Ralph; 4, Zito Nicholas P; 5, Azpurua Manuel J; 6, Procino Gerald M; 7, Durso Robert J; 8, Rose Barry R

$1 Pick Three (2–2–8) Paid $78.60 ; Pick Three Pool $77,972 .
$2 Pick Five (8–2–8–12–8) Paid $8,574.40 ; Pick Five Pool $571,628 .

NINTH RACE
Laurel
FEBRUARY 14, 2004

7 FURLONGS. (1.21^{2}) 51ST RUNNING OF THE BARBARA FRITCHIE HANDICAP. Grade II. Purse $200,000 A HANDICAP FOR FILLIES AND MARES, THREE-YEARS-OLD AND UPWARD. By free subscription. $1000 to pass the entry box. $1000 additional to start. Weights Sunday, February 8, 2004. Preference to high weights on the scale. Closed Wednesday, January 28, 2004 with27 nominations.

Value of Race: $200,000 Winner $120,000; second $40,000; third $22,000; fourth $12,000; fifth $6,000. Mutuel Pool $332,771.00 Exacta Pool $254,220.00 Superfecta Pool $57,297.00 Trifecta Pool $194,672.00

Last Raced	Horse	M/Eqt.	A.	Wt	PP	St	¼	½	Str	Fin	Jockey	Odds $1
24Jan04 ^{4}SA^{3}	Bear Fan	L f	5	116	6	5	5^{1}	2^{1}	1^{3}	1^{1}	Fogelsonger R	1.10
17Jan04 ^{8}Lrl^{3}	Gazillion	L f	5	116	3	7	6^{hd}	4^{hd}	4^{2}	$2^{1\frac{1}{2}}$	Dominguez R A	3.20
17Jan04 ^{8}Lrl^{1}	Bronze Abe	L f	5	117	4	3	$3^{\frac{1}{2}}$	3^{3}	3^{hd}	$3^{1\frac{1}{4}}$	Rodriguez E D	4.90
22Jan04 ^{8}Aqu^{1}	Jester Rahab	L f	5	112	8	2	8^{hd}	5^{hd}	5^{5}	$4^{3\frac{3}{4}}$	Luzzi M J	10.00
31Jan04 ^{9}Aqu^{3}	Balmy	L bf	5	115	2	4	2^{hd}	1^{hd}	2^{1}	5^{nk}	Elliott S	12.40
19Jan04 ^{8}Lrl^{1}	Wallop	L f	4	109	1	9	1^{hd}	7^{hd}	7^{2}	$6^{\frac{3}{4}}$	Acosta J D	64.70
31Jan04 ^{9}Lrl^{1}	City Fire	L b	4	114	9	1	4^{hd}	$6^{2\frac{1}{2}}$	6^{hd}	$7^{1\frac{1}{4}}$	Wilson R	13.10
24Jan04 ^{7}Lrl^{7}	Pleasant Note	L bf	6	111	5	6	7^{1}	9	$8^{1\frac{1}{2}}$	$8^{\frac{1}{2}}$	Panell D	119.20
7Dec03 ^{9}Lrl^{2}	Shiny Sheet	L b	6	118	7	8	9	8^{1}	9	9	Rose J	9.50

OFF AT 4:55 Start Good . Won driving. Track fast.

TIME :23^{2}, :46^{2}, 1:10^{3}, 1:23^{2} (:23.43, :46.41, 1:10.73, 1:23.55)

$2 Mutuel Prices:

8 – BEAR FAN	4.20	2.60	2.20
4 – GAZILLION		3.00	2.40
5 – BRONZE ABE			2.60

$2 EXACTA 8–4 PAID $13.60 $1 SUPERFECTA 8–4–5–10 PAID $65.40
$2 TRIFECTA 8–4–5 PAID $38.20

B. m, (Mar), by Pine Bluff – Shezalong , by Shimatoree . Trainer Ward Wesley A. Bred by Wesley Ward (Cal).

BEAR FAN prompted the pace four wide under some rating, drew on even terms mid turn, took a short lead entering the stretch, opened a clear advantage when roused in upper stretch then held sway under a drive. GAZILLION was taken to rate in a forward position, split rivals leaving the sixteenth marker, angled to the inside and finished gamely. BRONZE ABE dueled early three wide between rivals chased the leaders around the turn, came four wide for the drive and continued willingly to the finish. JESTER RAHAB , wide early, moved up between rivals leaving three furlong pole, swung out in upper stretch, made a run leaving the eighth pole then flattened out late. BALMY dueled two wide between rivals the opening quarter, took command into the turn, battled on even terms inside of the winner to the quarter pole then gave way in the final eighth. WALLOP , fractious in the starting gate, broke a step slow, was sent up inside to take a short early lead, dueled briefly, eased back entering the turn, dropped further back on the turn, angled out and finished with mild interest. CITY FIRE was an early presence five wide, dropped back off the pace leaving the three furlong marker and failed to recover. PLEASANT NOTE raced under rating along the inside into the turn, angled out some but lacked a late response. SHINY SHEET , bumped at the break, raced wide in the drive and failed to respond.

Owners– 1, Fan Peter and Ward Wesley; 2, Kessler Lucy C; 3, Bayard Samuel; 4, Weatherwatch Farm and Valente Roddy; 5, Fox Hill Farms Inc; 6, Childs and Childs Stable; 7, Gill Michael J; 8, O'Brien Mary T; 9, Rathbun Mrs Henry T

Trainers– 1, Ward Wesley A; 2, Smith Hamilton A; 3, Delp Grover G; 4, Levine Bruce N; 5, Servis John C; 6, Barr Donald H; 7, Shuman Mark; 8, Grove Christopher W; 9, Hadry Charles J

Scratched– River Cruise (13Dec03 ^{8}Lrl^{4}) , Worldly Pleasure (24Jan04 ^{7}Lrl^{1}) , Bamba (17Jan04 ^{8}Lrl^{2})

$2 Daily Double (3–8) Paid $60.00 ; Daily Double Pool $34,456 .

EIGHTH RACE
Santa Anita
FEBRUARY 14, 2004

1⅛ MILES. (1.45^{4}) 30TH RUNNING OF THE LA CANADA. Grade II. Purse $200,000 FOR FILLIES, FOUR YEARS OLD. By subscription of $200 each to accompany the nomination or by supplementary nomination of $4,000 by time of entry. $2,000 additional to start, with $200,000 guaranteed, of which $120,000 to first, $40,000 to second, $24,000to third, $12,000 to fourth and $4,000 to fifth. 121 lbs. Non–winners of $100,000 twice at one mile or over in 2003–2004 or $90,000 once at a mile or over in 2004 allowed 3 lbs.; of such a race of $60,000 in 2003–2004, 5 lbs.; of such a race of $40,000or$60,000 any distance at any time, 7 lbs. Starters to be named through the entry box by the closing time of entries. A trophy will be presented to the owner of the winner. Closed with 8 Nominations.

Value of Race: $200,000 Winner $120,000; second $40,000; third $24,000; fourth $12,000; fifth $4,000. Mutuel Pool $577,728.00 Exacta Pool $322,237.00 Quinella Pool $33,975.00 Trifecta Pool $386,477.00

Last Raced	Horse	M/Eqt.	A.	Wt	PP	St	¼	½	¾	Str	Fin	Jockey	Odds $1
18Jan04 ^{7}SA^{3}	Cat Fighter	LB b	4	115	3	3	$1^{\frac{1}{2}}$	1^{hd}	$1^{\frac{1}{2}}$	$2^{\frac{1}{2}}$	1^{hd}	Solis A	a- 3.40
24Jan04 ^{5}SA^{4}	Fencelineneighbor	LB b	4	116	7	4	3^{hd}	3^{1}	$3^{1\frac{1}{2}}$	1^{1}	2^{nk}	Espinoza V	8.30
16Jan04 ^{6}SA^{1}	Tangle-Ire	LB	4	116	4	1	2^{1}	2^{1}	2^{hd}	3^{hd}	3^{2}	Desormeaux K J	9.70
24Jan04 ^{5}SA^{1}	Valentine Dancer	LB b	4	121	8	5	5^{2}	4^{hd}	$4^{\frac{1}{2}}$	$4^{1\frac{1}{2}}$	$4^{\frac{1}{2}}$	Flores D R	2.60
24Jan04 ^{5}SA^{3}	Bartok's Blithe	LB	4	118	5	7	6^{4}	$6^{2\frac{1}{2}}$	$6^{2\frac{1}{2}}$	6^{hd}	$5^{\frac{1}{2}}$	Santiago Javier	13.00
24Jan04 ^{5}SA^{10}	Atlantic Ocean	LB	4	118	2	2	4^{1}	$5^{3\frac{1}{2}}$	$5^{2\frac{1}{2}}$	5^{1}	6^{1}	Baze T C	a- 3.40
18Jan04 ^{7}SA^{5}	Sea Jewel	LB b	4	117	6	8	7^{hd}	$7^{1\frac{1}{2}}$	$7^{2\frac{1}{2}}$	7^{6}	7^{24}	Nakatani C S	13.20
18Jan04 ^{7}SA^{1}	Victory Encounter	LB	4	121	1	6	8	8	8	8	8	Smith M E	1.90

a–Coupled: Cat Fighter and Atlantic Ocean.

OFF AT 4:09 Start Good . Won driving. Track fast.

TIME :22^{4}, :46^{3}, 1:11, 1:36^{4}, 1:50^{2} (:22.99, :46.79, 1:11.08, 1:36.82, 1:50.41)

$2 Mutuel Prices:

1A– CAT FIGHTER(a–entry)	8.80	5.80	3.80
6 – FENCELINENEIGHBOR		7.20	4.20
3 – TANGLE–IRE			6.20

$1 EXACTA 1–6 PAID $37.30 $2 QUINELLA 1–6 PAID $41.80
$1 TRIFECTA 1–6–3 PAID $279.40

Dk. b or br. f, (Mar), by Storm Cat – Strategic Maneuver , by Cryptoclearance . Trainer Baffert Bob. Bred by Brushwood Stable (Ky).

CAT FIGHTER sped to the early lead and angled in, dueled inside, responded when passed in the stretch and came back on gamely under urging to prove narrowly best. FENCELINENEIGHBOR stalked the pace outside a rival then off the rail, bid three deep into and on the second turn and into the stretch, gained the advantage in upper stretch, inched away in midstretch and just held second between foes late. TANGLE (IRE) prompted the pace outside the winner then between horses into and on the second turn and into the stretch, had the runner-up get away in midstretch then also came back on three deep late. VALENTINE DANCER stalked outside a rival, came out four wide into the stretch and could not summon the necessary late kick. BARTOK'S BLITHE allowed to settle off the rail, came four wide into the stretch and lacked the needed rally. ATLANTIC OCEAN close up stalking the pace inside, came out into the stretch and weakened. SEA JEWEL chased a bit off the rail, angled to the inside in deep stretch and also lacked the necessary response. VICTORY ENCOUNTER unhurried inside early, dropped farther back on the second turn, came out a bit into the stretch and was eased in the final furlong.

Owners– 1, The Thoroughbred Corporation; 2, Amerman Racing Stables LLC; 3, Reddam J Paul; 4, Kirkwood Al and Saundra S; 5, 5C Racing Stable LLC; 6, The Thoroughbred Corporation; 7, Moss Mr and Mrs Jerome S; 8, Mankiewicz Tom

Trainers– 1, Baffert Bob; 2, Machowsky Michael; 3, Dollase Craig; 4, Lewis Craig A; 5, Gutierrez Jorge; 6, Baffert Bob; 7, Shirreffs John; 8, Sadler John W

$2 Daily Double (3–1) Paid $30.00 ; Daily Double Pool $30,703 .
$1 Pick Three (6–3–1) Paid $25.90 ; Pick Three Pool $78,855 .

NINTH RACE
Fair Grounds
FEBRUARY 15, 2004

$1\frac{1}{16}$ MILES. (1.42) 32ND RUNNING OF THE RISEN STAR. Grade III. Purse $150,000 FOR THREE YEAR OLDS. $150,000 Guaranteed of which $90,000 to the winner; $30,000 to second; $16,500 to third; $9,000 to fourth; $4,500 to fifth. Weight: 122 lbs. Non–winners of $36,000, allowed 3 lbs.; $25,000, 5 lbs.; $20,000, 8 lbs. (Maiden and claiming races not considered). THE OWNER OF THE WINNER TO RECEIVE A TROPHY. Closed Saturday, February 7, 2004, with 11 nominations (Louisiana Derby early bird nominees automatically subscribed).

Value of Race: $150,000 Winner $90,000; second $30,000; third $16,500; fourth $9,000; fifth $4,500. Mutuel Pool $263,764.00 Exacta Pool $145,146.00 Quinella Pool $10,462.00 Trifecta Pool $126,268.00 Superfecta Pool $37,046.00

Last Raced	Horse	M/Eqt.	A.	Wt	PP	St	¼	½	¾	Str	Fin	Jockey	Odds $1
2Jan04 ^{7}FG^{1}	Gradepoint	L	3	116	1	3	6	6	6	4^{5}	$1\frac{1}{2}$	Albarado R J	1.90
5Dec03 ^{8}DeD^{1}	Mr. Jester	L	3	122	2	4	$5^{1\frac{1}{2}}$	$5^{3\frac{1}{2}}$	4^{1}	$2^{\frac{1}{2}}$	2^{1}	Chapa R	1.10
17Jan04 ^{9}FG^{4}	Nightlifeatbigblue	L	3	118	4	2	$1^{1\frac{1}{2}}$	1^{3}	$1^{3\frac{1}{2}}$	3^{1}	$3^{1\frac{1}{4}}$	Martin E M Jr	13.50
24Jan04 ^{9}FG^{5}	Polish Rifle	L	3	122	6	5	2^{1}	2^{2}	$2^{2\frac{1}{2}}$	1^{1}	$4^{8\frac{1}{4}}$	Sellers S J	2.90
18Jan04 ^{6}SA^{3}	Oneverycoolcat	L f	3	116	5	6	$4^{1\frac{1}{2}}$	$4^{\frac{1}{2}}$	5^{2}	$5^{1\frac{1}{2}}$	5^{nk}	Lanerie C J	14.70
2Feb04 ^{9}FG^{6}	Assault Commander	L	3	118	3	1	$3^{\frac{1}{2}}$	3^{1}	3^{hd}	6	6	Smith V L	85.40

OFF AT 4:16 Start Good . Won driving. Track fast.

TIME :24^{2}, :48^{1}, 1:13^{2}, 1:38^{4}, 1:45^{1} (:24.45, :48.37, 1:13.45, 1:38.92, 1:45.36)

$2 Mutuel Prices:				
	1 – GRADEPOINT	5.80	2.60	2.10
	2 – MR. JESTER		2.40	2.10
	4 – NIGHTLIFEATBIGBLUE			2.10

$2 EXACTA 1–2 PAID $12.80 $2 QUINELLA 1–2 PAID $4.80
$2 TRIFECTA 1–2–4 PAID $44.20 $2 SUPERFECTA 1–2–4–6 PAID $72.80

Dk. b or br. c, (May), by A.P. Indy – Class Kris , by Kris S. . Trainer Howard Neil J. Bred by W S Farish & H Greg Goodman (Ky).

GRADEPOINT unhurried until nearing the second turn, was asked for run midway around the turn, came inside approaching the drive, angled out turning for home, switched out to rally outside the leaders and proved best under strong handling. MR. JESTER in tight from along the inside entering the first turn, steadied when ASSAULT COMMANDER came in a bit, settled along the rail, advanced after entering the second turn, moved out to rally before the drive, rallied outside but was out kicked by the winner. NIGHTLIFEATBIGBLUE sprinted clear and to the rail approaching the first turn, set the pace until upper stretch, got overtaken by POLISH RIFLE a furlong out, fought back from the rail and was game for third. POLISH RIFLE reserved off NIGHTLIFEATBIGBLUE until midway around the second turn, was asked for run nearing the drive, raged up outside the leader in upper stretch, took over and then faltered inside the final sixteenth. ONEVERYCOOLCAT settled off the rail, was no real threat. ASSAULT COMMANDER came in a bit entering the first run, raced forward for six furlongs and then gave way.

Owners– 1, Mount Brilliant Stable LLC and Farish William; 2, Biggs Kaaren J; 3, Gray Mr and Mrs Fletcher; 4, Heiligbrodt Racing Stable and Stonerside Stable LLC; 5, Vreeland James and Young Candace M; 6, Wall John R

Trainers– 1, Howard Neil J; 2, Wren Steve; 3, Barnett Bobby C; 4, Asmussen Steven M; 5, Sauque Alex; 6, Bailey Isaac L

Scratched– Shiloh Bound (10Jan04 ^{9}FG ^{1})

$2 Pick Three (7–1–1) Paid $249.80 ; Pick Three Pool $10,825 .

ELEVENTH RACE
Gulfstream
FEBRUARY 15, 2004

$1\frac{1}{16}$ MILES. (1.40^{1}) 14TH RUNNING OF THE SABIN HANDICAP. Grade III. Purse $100,000 FOR FILLIES AND MARES, THREE YEARS OLD AND UPWARD. By subscription of $100 each, which shall accompany the nomination, $1,000 to pass the entry box and $1,000 additional to start, with $100,000 guaranteed. The owner of the winner to receive $60,000; $20,000 to second, $11,000 to third, $8,000 to fourth and $3,000 to fifth. Weights: Saturday, February 7, 2004. Trophy to winning Owner. Closed Wednesday, February 4, 2004 with (17) nominations.

Value of Race: $100,000 Winner $60,000; second $20,000; third $11,000; fourth $6,000; fifth $3,000. Mutuel Pool $473,110.00 Exacta Pool $339,114.00 Trifecta Pool $284,240.00 Superfecta Pool $84,110.00

Last Raced	Horse	M/Eqt.	A.	Wt	PP	St	¼	½	¾	Str	Fin	Jockey	Odds $1
15Jan04 ^{8}GP^{1}	Roar Emotion	L	4	116	6	6	$2^{1\frac{1}{2}}$	$2^{1\frac{1}{2}}$	2^{2}	1^{4}	$1^{5\frac{1}{2}}$	Velazquez J R	2.20
28Jan04 ^{7}GP^{2}	Nonsuch Bay	L	5	115	3	5	4^{hd}	$5^{1\frac{1}{2}}$	3^{hd}	2^{hd}	$2^{\frac{3}{4}}$	Velasquez C	7.50
27Nov03 ^{10}CD^{1}	Lead Story	L	5	119	9	9	9	9	9	4^{4}	$3^{1\frac{3}{4}}$	Borel C H	7.40
24Jan04 ^{9}GP^{6}	Ivanavinalot	L f	4	114	5	3	1^{1}	1^{hd}	1^{hd}	3^{2}	$4^{2\frac{1}{4}}$	Scocca D	32.80
24Jan04 ^{9}GP^{1}	Secret Request	L	4	114	7	8	7^{1}	8^{4}	$7^{1\frac{1}{2}}$	7^{4}	$5^{2\frac{3}{4}}$	Coa E M	22.60
11Jan04 ^{9}GP^{3}	Final Round	L	4	114	4	4	$6^{1\frac{1}{2}}$	3^{hd}	$4^{1\frac{1}{2}}$	5^{hd}	$6^{2\frac{1}{4}}$	Day P	9.90
24Jan04 ^{9}GP^{2}	Smok'n Frolic	L b	5	117	1	1	3^{hd}	4^{1}	6^{1}	6^{hd}	$7^{3\frac{1}{2}}$	Bailey J D	2.00
27Dec03 ^{10}Crc^{2}	Grab Bag	L f	5	111	8	7	$8^{2\frac{1}{2}}$	7^{hd}	8^{hd}	9	$8^{1\frac{1}{4}}$	Chavez J F	36.50
4Oct03 ^{9}Bel^{7}	Passing Shot	L	5	117	2	2	5^{hd}	6^{4}	5^{1}	$8^{3\frac{1}{2}}$	9	Santos J A	8.00

OFF AT 5:41 Start Good . Won driving. Track fast.

TIME :23^{4}, :47^{3}, 1:11^{4}, 1:36^{3}, 1:43^{1} (:23.93, :47.66, 1:11.98, 1:36.79, 1:43.32)

$2 Mutuel Prices:				
	6 – ROAR EMOTION	6.40	4.40	3.40
	3 – NONSUCH BAY		6.40	4.20
	9 – LEAD STORY			4.20

$1 EXACTA 6–3 PAID $20.30 $1 TRIFECTA 6–3–9 PAID $106.00
$1 SUPERFECTA 6–3–9–5 PAID $1,577.00

Dk. b or br. f, (Mar), by Roar – Emotional Outburst , by Capote . Trainer McLaughlin Kiaran P. Bred by Brenda Jones (Ky).

ROAR EMOTION vied for the lead outside IVANAVINALOT into the stretch, then drew off under pressure. NONSUCH BAY reserved racing along the inside, angled out at the top of the stretch and closed to be up for the place. LEAD STORY outrun early, saved ground and closed along the rail to gain the show. IVANAVINALOT vied for the lead along the inside into the stretch and gave way. SECRET REQUEST failed to menace. FINAL ROUND bumped and forced out on the first turn, moved up to chase the pace three wide to nearing the stretch and tired. SMOK'N FROLIC bore out and bumped with PASSING SHOT after being checked in behind IVANAVINALOT entering the first turn, tracked the pace to the far turn and faltered. GRAB BAG unhurried after being forced out and steadied on the first turn, attempted to bolt on the far turn, then was no factor after being straightened away. PASSING SHOT was knocked into FINAL ROUND and steadied on the first turn, raced in contention three wide into the far turn and faded.

Owners– 1, Allen Joseph; 2, Thorn Stable; 3, Miles A Stevens Jr; 4, Campbell Gilbert G; 5, J D Farms; 6, Humphrey G Watts Jr; 7, Dogwood Stable; 8, Waring Racing LLC; 9, Shields Joseph V Jr

Trainers– 1, McLaughlin Kiaran P; 2, Alexander Frank A; 3, Nafzger Carl A; 4, O'Connell Kathleen; 5, Brownlee David R; 6, Arnold George R II; 7, Pletcher Todd A; 8, Skiffington Thomas J; 9, Jerkens H Allen

Scratched– Pampered Princess (28Jan04 ^{7}GP ^{1})

$1 Pick Three (12–3–6) Paid $37.00 ; Pick Three Pool $45,688 .

EIGHTH RACE
Santa Anita
FEBRUARY 15, 2004

1 MILE. (1.33^{2}) 22ND RUNNING OF THE LAS VIRGENES. Grade I. Purse $250,000 FOR FILLIES, THREE YEARS OLD. By subscription of $200 each to accompany the nomination or by supplementary nomination of $5,000 by time of entry. Closed with 1. $2,500 additional to start, with $250,000 guaranteed, of which $150,000 to first, $50,000 tosecond, $30,000 to third, $15,000 to fourth and $5,000 to fifth. 122 lbs. Non-winners of $70,000 twice or $50,000 three times allowed 2 lbs.; of $50,000 twice since December 25 or one of $70,000 at any time, 4 lbs.; of a race of $50,000 since December25or two of $30,000 at any time, 6 lbs. (Maiden and claiming races not considered). A Trophy will be presented to the owner of the winner. Nominations Closed Thursday, February 5th, 2004 with 13.

Value of Race: $250,000 Winner $150,000; second $50,000; third $30,000; fourth $15,000; fifth $5,000. Mutuel Pool $607,602.00 Exacta Pool $318,371.00 Quinella Pool $30,191.00 Trifecta Pool $345,473.00 Superfecta Pool $146,214.00

Last Raced	Horse	M/Eqt.	A.	Wt	PP	St	1/4	1/2	3/4	Str	Fin	Jockey	Odds $1
4Jan04 6SA1	A. P. Adventure	LB	3	118	1	7	6^{hd}	$5^{2\frac{1}{2}}$	4^{hd}	$4^{1\frac{1}{2}}$	$1^{\frac{1}{2}}$	Solis A	1.10
21Dec03 9Hol1	Hollywood Story	LB b	3	120	5	5	$4^{\frac{1}{2}}$	$4^{\frac{1}{2}}$	$5^{2\frac{1}{2}}$	$3^{\frac{1}{2}}$	$2^{2\frac{1}{2}}$	Espinoza V	2.30
31Dec03 7SA1	Friendly Michelle	LB b	3	116	2	2	$1^{\frac{1}{2}}$	1^{hd}	$1^{\frac{1}{2}}$	$1^{1\frac{1}{2}}$	3^{1}	Baze T C	20.40
14Jan04 7SA6	Stellar Jayne	LB b	3	118	8	8	8	8	$6^{\frac{1}{2}}$	6^{1}	4^{3}	Santiago Javier	45.30
19Jan04 5SA6	Whoopi Cat	LB	3	120	7	4	$3^{2\frac{1}{2}}$	$3^{2\frac{1}{2}}$	$3^{1\frac{1}{2}}$	$5^{1\frac{1}{2}}$	$5^{\frac{1}{2}}$	Smith M E	34.70
19Jan04 5SA5	Rahy Dolly	LB b	3	116	4	1	$2^{1\frac{1}{2}}$	2^{1}	2^{2}	2^{hd}	6no	Valdivia J Jr	6.10
25Oct03 3SA7	Class Above	LB	3	116	6	6	$7^{1\frac{1}{2}}$	6^{1}	7^{4}	7^{3}	7^{3}	Flores D R	4.50
31Jan04 2SA1	Mme. Espionage	B	3	116	3	3	5^{1}	7^{hd}	8	8	8	Pedroza M A	81.80

OFF AT 4:08 Start Good. Won driving. Track fast.

TIME :22^{3}, :46, 1:10^{2}, 1:23^{2}, 1:36^{2} (:22.78, :46.17, 1:10.57, 1:23.45, 1:36.50)

$2 Mutuel Prices:

2 – A. P. ADVENTURE	4.20	2.60	2.40
6 – HOLLYWOOD STORY		2.80	2.60
3 – FRIENDLY MICHELLE			5.00

$1 EXACTA 2–6 PAID $6.00 $2 QUINELLA 2–6 PAID $6.20
$1 TRIFECTA 2–6–3 PAID $41.20 $1 SUPERFECTA 2–6–3–9 PAID $247.70

B. f, (Jan), by A.P. Indy – Nataliano, by Fappiano. Trainer Dollase Wallace. Bred by Lazy E Ranch Inc (Ky).

A. P. ADVENTURE a bit slow to begin, settled just off the inside, began to advance leaving the backstretch, continued between horses leaving the second turn and into the stretch, then split rivals with a bid to gain the lead in deep stretch and proved best under urging. HOLLYWOOD STORY stalked the dueling leaders off the rail, bid three deep into the stretch, was even with the winner in deep stretch and continued willingly but could not quite match that one late. FRIENDLY MICHELLE had good early speed and set a pressured pace inside, inched clear into the stretch, fought back in deep stretch and weakened some late but held third. STELLAR JAYNE off a bit slowly, settled just off the rail, split rivals leaving the backstretch, angled in on the second turn, came out in upper stretch and bested the rest. WHOOPI CAT stalked the pace off the rail, angled in on the second turn and weakened in the stretch. RAHY DOLLY forced the pace outside a rival until nearing the stretch and also weakened. CLASS ABOVE allowed to settle three deep then outside, angled in outside a rival on the second turn, came out some in upper stretch and did not rally. MME. ESPIONAGE angled in and saved ground chasing the pace, dropped back on the backstretch, came out on the second turn and gave way.

Owners– 1, Lewis Robert B and Beverly J; 2, Krikorian George; 3, Friendly Ed; 4, Spenthrift Farm LLC Cole Nancy Kidder Chuck et al; 5, Smith Derrick and Tabor Michael; 6, Fulton Stan E; 7, Padua Stable; 8, Coles Diana Padilla Robert and Saip Jack

Trainers– 1, Dollase Wallace; 2, Shirreffs John; 3, Baffert Bob; 4, Lukas D Wayne; 5, Biancone Patrick L; 6, Becerra Rafael; 7, Baffert Bob; 8, Saip Jack

Scratched– Wildwood Flower (04Jan04 6SA 3)

$2 Daily Double (7–2) Paid $14.00 ; Daily Double Pool $58,394 .
$1 Pick Three (7–7–1/2) Paid $29.50 ; Pick Three Pool $81,385 .
$2 Consolation Daily Double (7–1) Paid $7.60 .

EIGHTH RACE
Santa Anita
FEBRUARY 16, 2004

1$\frac{1}{16}$ MILES. (1.39) 62ND RUNNING OF THE SANTA MARIA HANDICAP. Grade I. Purse $250,000 FOR FILLIES AND MARES FOUR YEARS OLD AND UPWARD. By subscription of $200 each to accompany the nomination or by supplementary nomination of $5,000 by Sunday, February 8. $2,500 additional to start, with $250,000 guaranteed, of which $150,000 to first, $50,000 to second, $30,00 to third, $15,000 to fourth and $5,000 to fifth. Weights Tuesday, February 10. Starters to be named through the entry box by the closing time of entries. A trophy will be presented to the owner of the winner. Closed with 8 Nominations.

Value of Race: $250,000 Winner $150,000; second $50,000; third $30,000; fourth $15,000; fifth $5,000. Mutuel Pool $428,754.00 Exacta Pool $214,304.00 Quinella Pool $23,796.00 Trifecta Pool $249,198.00

Last Raced	Horse	M/Eqt.	A.	Wt	PP	St	1/4	1/2	3/4	Str	Fin	Jockey	Odds $1
7Dec03 8Hol1	Star Parade-Arg	LB	5	114	6	2	1^{1}	$1^{1\frac{1}{2}}$	$1^{1\frac{1}{2}}$	$1^{1\frac{1}{2}}$	1^{hd}	Espinoza V	1.20
16Jan04 7SA1	Bare Necessities	LB	5	118	2	4	4^{1}	$5^{1\frac{1}{2}}$	3^{2}	$3^{\frac{1}{2}}$	2^{2}	Valdivia J Jr	2.50
16Jan04 7SA3	La Tour-Chi	LB	5	115	4	5	6	4^{hd}	4^{1}	4^{4}	3^{2}	Solis A	14.50
7Dec03 8Hol2	Adoration	LB	5	120	5	3	$2^{1\frac{1}{2}}$	$2^{1\frac{1}{2}}$	$2^{1\frac{1}{2}}$	2^{hd}	4^{6}	Smith M E	2.30
23Dec03 10Nag2	Preeminence-Jpn	B f	7	117	1	1	$3^{2\frac{1}{2}}$	$3^{2\frac{1}{2}}$	$5^{3\frac{1}{2}}$	5^{6}	5^{13}	Nakatani C S	13.50
16Jan04 7SA2	Angel Gift	LB	6	116	3	6	5^{hd}	6	6	6	6	Stevens G L	26.10

OFF AT 4:07 Start Good. Won driving. Track fast.

TIME :22^{2}, :46, 1:10^{2}, 1:36^{4}, 1:43^{4} (:22.59, :46.00, 1:10.52, 1:36.87, 1:43.87)

$2 Mutuel Prices:

7 – STAR PARADE–ARG	4.40	2.60	2.40
2 – BARE NECESSITIES		3.00	2.40
5 – LA TOUR–CHI			3.40

$1 EXACTA 7–2 PAID $5.70 $2 QUINELLA 2–7 PAID $7.00
$1 TRIFECTA 7–2–5 PAID $38.00

Dk. b or br. m, (Oct), by Parade Marshal – Clerical Etoile–Arg, by The Watcher. Trainer Vienna Darrell. Bred by Firmamento (Arg).

STAR PARADE (ARG) pulled her way to the front outside a rival and angled in, set the pace a bit off the rail, inched clear on the backstretch, remained clear on the second turn and into the stretch and held on gamely under steady urging. BARE NECESSITIES between horses early, was floated out into the first turn, angled in and stalked a bit off the rail, moved up on the second turn, came out three deep into the stretch and closed gamely. LA TOUR (CHI) fanned five wide into the first turn, angled in and chased three deep then outside a rival, found the rail leaving the second turn, bid inside in the stretch and bested the others, then stumbled after the wire, unseated the rider and was vanned off. ADORATION angled to the inside early then stalked the winner off the rail, remained a threat in midstretch but weakened in the final furlong. PREEMINENCE (JPN) drifted out into the first turn, stalked off the rail, angled in and dropped back on the second turn and also weakened. ANGEL GIFT fanned four wide into the first turn, angled in and chased inside, dropped back on the second turn and gave way.

Owners– 1, Tanaka Gary A; 2, Iron County Farms Inc; 3, Hunt Nelson B; 4, Amerman Racing Stables LLC; 5, Ito Yoshiyuki; 6, Delahoussaye Enterprises Strauss Richard C and Williford Roberta

Trainers– 1, Vienna Darrell; 2, Dollase Wallace; 3, McAnally Ronald; 4, Hofmans David; 5, De Seroux Laura; 6, Gallagher Patrick

Scratched– Island Fashion (25Jan04 8SA 1)

$2 Daily Double (7–7) Paid $15.00 ; Daily Double Pool $39,255 .
$1 Pick Three (10–7–4/7) Paid $94.80 ; Pick Three Pool $102,716 .

NINTH RACE
Santa Anita
FEBRUARY 16, 2004

1½ MILES. (Turf) (2.22⁴) 37TH RUNNING OF THE SAN LUIS OBISPO HANDICAP. Grade II. Purse $200,000 FOR FOUR-YEAR-OLDS AND UPWARD. By subscription of $200 each to accompany the nomination or by supplementary nomination of $4,000 by Sunday, February 8. $2,000 additional to start, with $200,000 guaranteed,of which $120,000 to first, $40,000 to second, $24,000 to third, $12,000 to fourth and $4,000 to fifth. Weights Tuesday, February 10. High weights preferred. Starters to be named through the entry box by the closing time of entries. A trophy will be presented to the owner of the winner. Closed with 16Nominations.

Value of Race: $200,000 Winner $120,000; second $40,000; third $24,000; fourth $12,000; fifth $4,000. Mutuel Pool $529,256.00 Exacta Pool $280,273.00 Quinella Pool $26,853.00 Trifecta Pool $299,344.00 Superfecta Pool $130,615.00

Last Raced	Horse	M/Eqt.	A.	Wt	PP	¼	½	1	1¼	Str	Fin	Jockey	Odds $1
19Jan04 8SA4	Puerto Banus	LB b	5	115	2	8hd	8½	81	81½	6½	1nk	Espinoza V	3.90
27Dec03 11Crc2	Continuously	LB	5	116	12	9hd	91	91½	5hd	5hd	2hd	Desormeaux K J	3.40
24Jan04 6SA6	Continental Red	LB	8	117	7	3½	3½	3hd	41½	4hd	3no	Nakatani C S	11.40
8Jan04 2SA3	Meteor Storm-GB	LB	5	116	1	11	11	1hd	1hd	12	4nk	Valdivia J Jr	14.50
22Nov03 8Hol7	Labirinto	LB	6	115	9	101	112½	112	112	9hd	5½	Baze T C	14.70
19Jan04 8SA6	Fairly Ransom	LB	4	115	8	111½	10½	10hd	9hd	102½	61	Solis A	5.50
27Dec03 11Crc8	Runaway Dancer	LB	5	115	11	12	12	12	12	12	7½	Smith M E	11.70
24Oct03 8SA5	Researched-Ire	LB	5	116	4	21	21	22	22½	21	8no	Stevens G L	4.40
24Jan04 10GP5	Bourbon County	LB b	5	115	10	51½	52	51	71	81	9½	Jauregui L H	58.20
19Jan04 8SA7	GenedeCampeo-Brz	LB	5	114	6	71½	71	6hd	6hd	111	10½	Berrio O A	58.10
10Jan04 8SA6	Senor Swinger	LB b	4	113	3	6½	6½	7½	101½	7hd	111	Santiago Javier	12.90
24Jan04 10GP8	Adminniestrator	LB	7	116	5	41	41	41½	3hd	3hd	12	Flores D R	33.80

OFF AT 4:39 Start Good . Won driving. Course firm.

TIME :25², :49⁴, 1:15, 1:40⁴, 2:04⁴, 2:28 (:25.51, :49.83, 1:15.15, 1:40.90, 2:04.90, 2:28.00)

$2 Mutuel Prices:				
	2 – PUERTO BANUS	9.80	5.60	4.00
	12 – CONTINUOUSLY		4.20	2.80
	7 – CONTINENTAL RED			5.40

$1 EXACTA 2–12 PAID $18.40 $2 QUINELLA 2–12 PAID $19.00
$1 TRIFECTA 2–12–7 PAID $131.40 $1 SUPERFECTA 2–12–7–1 PAID $1,271.40

Ch. h, (Feb), by Supremo – Drina , by Regal and Royal . Trainer Mulhall Kristin. Bred by The Thoroughbred Corporation (Ky).

PUERTO BANUS chased inside then between horses on the backstretch, split rivals on the second turn, came out four wide into the stretch and rallied gamely between foes to prove narrowly best. CONTINUOUSLY chased outside a rival, moved up three deep on the second turn, came five wide into the stretch and closed gamely. CONTINENTAL RED stalked outside, bid three deep into the stretch and also rallied between foes in a game try. METEOR STORM (GB) set a pressured but moderate pace inside, dueled along the rail into and on the second turn, kicked clear Into the stretch and held on gamely until the late stages. LABIRINTO settled outside a rival, came out four wide on the second turn and seven wide into the stretch and closed willingly. FAIRLY RANSOM angled in and saved ground off the pace, came out into the second turn, was in tight off heels nearing midway on that bend, circled six wide into the stretch and finished well. RUNAWAY DANCER off a bit slowly, settled just off the inside, came out In upper stretch and found his best stride late. RESEARCHED (IRE) forced the pace outside a rival, drifted out a bit into the stretch and weakened. BOURBON COUNTY chased outside a rival, angled in for the second turn, was blocked into the stretch, split rivals in midstretch, squeezed through tight quarters and was bumped late. GENE DE CAMPEAO (BRZ) chased outside a rival, came out on the second turn, was fanned five wide and steadied when squeezed between foes into the stretch, drifted in through the drive and weakened. SENOR SWINGER saved ground chasing the pace, dropped back some on the second turn, got through inside in upper stretch, then was in tight and bumped into the rail in deep stretch. ADMINNIESTRATOR 'bobbled a bit at the start, stalked the pace inside, dropped back past midstretch, then was bumped in tight late and weakened.

Owners– 1, Noctis Stable Papiano Neil and Taub Steve; 2, Khaled Saud b; 3, Fitzpatrick Sharon M; 4, Jarvis Michael Margolis Gary and Smole Ken et al; 5, Mio Jean P; 6, Zetcher Arnold; 7, R L Stables; 8, Tanaka Gary A; 9, Stathatos Damon; 10, Bandeirantes Stable; 11, Lewis Robert B and Beverly J; 12, Gill Michael J

Trainers– 1, Mulhall Kristin; 2, Frankel Robert; 3, Jory Ian P D; 4, Dollase Wallace; 5, Powell Leonard; 6, McAnally Ronald; 7, Hendricks Dan L; 8, Cecil B D A; 9, Whittingham Michael C; 10, Avila A C; 11, Baffert Bob; 12, Canani Nick

$2 Daily Double (7–2) Paid $25.40 ; Daily Double Pool $59,803 .
$1 Pick Three (7–4/7–2) Paid $43.40 ; Pick Three Pool $106,107 .

NINTH RACE
Laurel
FEBRUARY 16, 2004

7 FURLONGS. (1.21^{2}) 29TH RUNNING OF THE GENERAL GEORGE HANDICAP. Grade II. Purse $200,000 A HANDICAP FOR THREE-YEAR-OLDS AND UPWARD. By free subscription. $1000 to pass the entry box. $1000 additional to start with $200,000 Guaranteed, of which 60% to the winner, 20% to second, 11% to third, 6% to fourth, and 3% to fifth. Supplemental nominations of $2000 each will be accepted by Saturday, February 7, 2004 with all other fees due as noted. Weights Sunday, February 8, 2004. Preference to high weights on the scale. Starters to be named through the entry box by the usual timeof closing. Trophy tothe owner of the winner. Closed Wednesday, January 28, 2004.

Value of Race: $200,000 Winner $120,000; second $40,000; third $22,000; fourth $12,000; fifth $6,000. Mutuel Pool $343,401.00 Exacta Pool $269,811.00 Trifecta Pool $199,771.00 Superfecta Pool $61,546.00

Last Raced	Horse	M/Eqt.	A.	Wt	PP	St	¼	½	Str	Fin	Jockey	Odds $1
29Nov03 ^{9}Aqu^{5}	Well Fancied	L	6	115	6	1	1^{1}	1^{1}	1^{1}	1^{1}	Prado E S	3.00
13Dec03 ^{8}Aqu^{4}	Unforgettable Max	L	4	114	2	8	9	8^{hd}	3^{hd}	$2^{\frac{3}{4}}$	Dominguez R A	15.00
24Jan04 ^{8}Lrl^{1}	Gators N Bears	L bf	4	116	4	4	3^{hd}	3^{hd}	$4^{1\frac{1}{2}}$	3^{hd}	Wilson R	9.30
24Jan04 ^{8}Aqu^{1}	Peeping Tom	L bf	7	117	1	9	8^{hd}	9	$5^{\frac{1}{2}}$	$4^{\frac{1}{2}}$	Smith A E	8.90
23Jan04 ^{9}FG^{1}	Badge of Silver	L	4	117	8	3	$2^{\frac{1}{2}}$	$2^{\frac{1}{2}}$	$2^{1\frac{1}{2}}$	5^{1}	Albarado R J	0.70
24Jan04 ^{8}Aqu^{5}	Way to the Top	L f	6	115	5	6	$6^{3\frac{1}{2}}$	5^{hd}	8^{3}	$6^{1\frac{1}{2}}$	Luzzi M J	13.10
24Jan04 ^{8}Lrl^{2}	My Good Trick	L b	5	114	3	7	7^{2}	6^{1}	$6^{\frac{1}{2}}$	7no	Castellano A Jr	a- 22.70
31Jan04 ^{8}Lrl^{1}	Out of Fashion	L b	8	114	7	5	4^{2}	$4^{2\frac{1}{2}}$	7^{hd}	$8^{3\frac{3}{4}}$	Rose J	a- 22.70
24Jan04 ^{10}TP^{2}	Founding Chairman	L	4	112	9	2	$5^{\frac{1}{2}}$	7^{hd}	9	9	Bejarano R	53.20

a-Coupled: My Good Trick and Out of Fashion.

OFF AT 4:37 Start Good . Won driving. Track fast.

TIME :22^{3}, :45^{2}, 1:10, 1:22^{2} (:22.71, :45.58, 1:10.19, 1:22.49)

$2 Mutuel Prices:

6 – WELL FANCIED	8.00	4.80	5.60
3 – UNFORGETTABLE MAX		12.80	13.00
4 – GATORS N BEARS			8.00

$2 EXACTA 6-3 PAID $74.80 $2 TRIFECTA 6-3-4 PAID $399.20
$1 SUPERFECTA 6-3-4-2 PAID $1,904.00

B. g, (Mar), by Prosper Fager – Patty's Fancy Tric , by Tricky Creek . Trainer Dutrow Richard E Jr. Bred by Seymour Cohn (NY).

WELL FANCIED broke on top, set a rated pace in the two path, took pressure from BADGE OF SILVER entering the lane, edged away from that one leaving the eighth pole and held sway under a drive. UNFORGETTABLE MAX , unhurried early while off the rail, angled out early turn, advanced five wide entering the lane and finished gamely. GATORS N BEARS , forwardly placed towards the inside, continued willingly and saved the show. PEEPING TOM , outrun early while saving ground, moved closer leaving the three furlong marker, swung out six wide for the drive and closed gamely. BADGE OF SILVER prompted the pace three wide, tried the winner entering the lane, battled to mid stretch then faded. WAY TO THE TOP saved ground throughout and came up empty. MY GOOD TRICK angled out entering the turn, steadily advanced four wide mid turn, raced between rivals in mid stretch but had no late response. OUT OF FASHION raced prominently between rivals to the head of the lane then gradually weakened in the drive. FOUNDING CHAIRMAN , fractious in the gate, raced three wide in a forward position to the turn, dropped back on the turn and could not recover.

Owners– 1, Hoffman J S and F and Goldfarb S; 2, Dweck Raymond; 3, Nechamkin Leo S II; 4, Flatbird Stable; 5, Ramsey Kenneth L and Sarah K; 6, Valente Roddy J; 7, Gill Michael J; 8, Gill Michael J; 9, Glasscock C E and Ray Brad

Trainers– 1, Dutrow Richard E Jr; 2, Perkins Ben W Jr; 3, Nechamkin Leo S II; 4, Reynolds Patrick L; 5, Werner Ronny; 6, Levine Bruce N; 7, Schoenthal Phil; 8, Shuman Mark; 9, Mackey Wayne

$2 Daily Double (7–6) Paid $51.80 ; Daily Double Pool $42,705 .

Laurel Park Attendance: Unavailable Mutuel Pool: $.00

NINTH RACE
Oaklawn
FEBRUARY 21, 2004

1$\frac{1}{16}$ MILES. (1.40^{1}) 56TH RUNNING OF THE ESSEX HANDICAP. Purse $100,000 FOUR YEAR OLDS AND UPWARD No nomination fee. $500 to pass the entry box and $1000 additional to start. Weights to be announced Sunday, February 15. In Handicap Stakes starting preference will be given to heavyweights. Closed Friday, February 13, 2004 with25 nominees.

Value of Race: $100,000 Winner $60,000; second $20,000; third $10,000; fourth $5,000; fifth $3,000; sixth $2,000. Mutuel Pool $350,915.00 Exacta Pool $245,532.00 Trifecta Pool $260,064.00

Last Raced	Horse	M/Eqt.	A.	Wt	PP	St	¼	½	¾	Str	Fin	Jockey	Odds $1
17Jan04 ^{7}Hou^{4}	Private Emblem	L f	5	113	2	1	$2^{1\frac{1}{2}}$	2^{2}	2^{1}	1^{hd}	$1^{1\frac{1}{4}}$	Doocy T T	8.70
25Oct03 ^{11}SA^{1}	Pie N Burger	L b	6	118	1	8	$1^{\frac{1}{2}}$	$1^{\frac{1}{2}}$	1^{hd}	2^{4}	2^{4}	Theriot H J II	1.20
1Feb04 ^{9}OP^{1}	Crafty Shaw	L	6	118	3	7	3^{hd}	3^{2}	3^{2}	3^{2}	3^{hd}	Perret C	2.40
1Feb04 ^{9}OP^{2}	Docent	L bf	6	116	4	4	4^{2}	$4^{3\frac{1}{2}}$	4^{2}	$5^{\frac{1}{2}}$	$4^{1\frac{1}{2}}$	Lopez J	4.30
1Feb04 ^{9}OP^{3}	Missme	L b	5	113	7	3	5^{1}	$5^{1\frac{1}{2}}$	5^{hd}	4^{hd}	$5^{1\frac{3}{4}}$	McKee J	11.70
17Jan04 ^{7}Hou^{3}	Dusty Spike	L f	5	115	8	5	8	8	$7^{1\frac{1}{2}}$	$6^{2\frac{1}{2}}$	$6^{\frac{1}{2}}$	Quinonez L S	19.60
24Jan04 ^{8}OP^{4}	Crowned King	L	4	117	6	2	6^{hd}	$6^{\frac{1}{2}}$	8	8	7^{nk}	Rennie C R	25.00
11Feb04 ^{8}OP^{1}	Morning Merry	L	4	112	5	6	7^{1}	$7^{\frac{1}{2}}$	$6^{\frac{1}{2}}$	7^{hd}	8	Noll C S	52.20

OFF AT 5:18 Start Good . Won driving. Track fast.

TIME :24^{1}, :48, 1:13, 1:37^{2}, 1:43^{3} (:24.32, :48.18, 1:13.05, 1:37.49, 1:43.66)

$2 Mutuel Prices:

2 – PRIVATE EMBLEM	19.40	7.20	3.60
1 – PIE N BURGER		3.80	2.60
3 – CRAFTY SHAW			2.60

$2 EXACTA 2-1 PAID $56.00 $2 TRIFECTA 2-1-3 PAID $151.60

Dk. b or br. h, (Mar), by Our Emblem – Merion Miss , by Halo . Trainer Asmussen Steven M. Bred by Berkshire Stud and Oak Cliff Stable (NY).

PRIVATE EMBLEM away well, pressured leader outside that one, breather into the far turn, asked drive, outkicked foe to wire. PIE N BURGER away a bit slow, recovered to narrowly set the pace inside, continued to set the pace into the far turn after some soft fractions, could not match the winner in the drive, well clear of the others. CRAFTY SHAW broke his gate doors just prior to the rest of the field start, fell back in a bit of a tangle, regathered, prompted leaders, narrowly held the show spot. DOCENT evenly paced throughout, lacked a winning bid. MISSME raced in some traffic well off the leaders second turn, evenly stretch. DUSTY SPIKE far back for six furlongs, came five wide turning for home, managed little gain. CROWNED KING failed to fire. MORNING MERRY never involved.

Owners– 1, Cassels James and Zollars Bob; 2, Kagele Brothers Inc and Bailey James A; 3, Cella Charles J; 4, Arlene R Daney LLC; 5, Whippoorwill Farm Inc; 6, Deiter Raymond W; 7, McKeever Racing Stable LLC; 8, Orion Stables

Trainers– 1, Asmussen Steven M; 2, Norman Cole; 3, Vestal Peter M; 4, Ritchey Tim F; 5, Whiting Lynn S; 6, Lee Mark; 7, McKeever Billy C Jr; 8, McCoy James B

$2 Pick Three (11–10–2) Paid $2,737.80 ; Pick Three Pool $24,259 .

ELEVENTH RACE
Gulfstream
FEBRUARY 21, 2004

1⅛ MILES. (Turf) (1.45^{3}) 18TH RUNNING OF THE PALM BEACH. Grade III. Purse $100,000 FOR THREE YEAR OLDS. By subscription of $100 each, which shall accompany the nomination, $1,000 to pass the entry box and $1,000 additional to start. Supplemental nominations may be made on Thursday, February 19, 2004 at a fee of $3,000, which includes entry and start fees. Weight: 122 lbs. Non-winners of $50,000 at a mile or over on the turf, allowed, 2 lbs.;$40,000 at any distance or $30,000 at a mile or over, 4 lbs.; $24,000 at any distance or $18,000 at a mile or over, 6 lbs.Trophy to winning owner. This race will be limited to 12 Starters, with Also Eligibles. (High Weights Prferred). (Total lifetime earnings will be used to determine the order of preference of horses with equal weight). Closed Wednesday, February 11, 2004 with (30) nominations.

Value of Race: $100,000 Winner $60,000; second $20,000; third $11,000; fourth $6,000; fifth $3,000. Mutuel Pool $524,809.00 Exacta Pool $382,625.00 Trifecta Pool $311,668.00 Superfecta Pool $108,390.00

Last Raced	Horse	M/Eqt.	A.	Wt	PP	St	¼	½	¾	Str	Fin	Jockey	Odds $1
1Jan04 ^{9}Crc^{1}	Kitten's Joy	L	3	122	1	1	4^{1}	4^{1}	$5^{\frac{1}{2}}$	3^{2}	$1^{1\frac{3}{4}}$	Bailey J D	a- 0.60
17Jan04 ^{8}GP^{1}	Prince Arch	L b	3	118	3	8	$9^{1\frac{1}{2}}$	8^{1}	$9^{1\frac{1}{2}}$	$9^{1\frac{1}{2}}$	2^{nk}	Blanc B	37.10
17Jan04 ^{8}GP^{3}	Pa Pa Da	L	3	118	10	5	5^{1}	$5^{\frac{1}{2}}$	$4^{\frac{1}{2}}$	1^{hd}	$3^{\frac{3}{4}}$	Coa E M	16.10
9Nov03 ^{9}CD^{8}	Master William	L b	3	122	8	10	$10^{3\frac{1}{2}}$	9^{hd}	$8^{\frac{1}{2}}$	4^{hd}	4^{hd}	Prado E S	a- 0.60
18Jan04 ^{10}GP^{3}	Commendation	L	3	122	2	2	6^{1}	6^{hd}	$6^{\frac{1}{2}}$	$5^{\frac{1}{2}}$	5^{hd}	Velazquez J R	5.00
24Jan04 ^{3}GP^{1}	Mustanfar	L b	3	118	6	9	$7^{1\frac{1}{2}}$	$7^{2\frac{1}{2}}$	$7^{1\frac{1}{2}}$	6^{hd}	$6^{\frac{3}{4}}$	Santos J A	7.40
7Jan04 ^{9}GP^{1}	Pincay	L	3	118	4	11	11^{1}	11^{2}	12	8^{hd}	$7^{1\frac{1}{2}}$	Bravo J	25.20
1Jan04 ^{9}Crc^{3}	Soverign Honor	L b	3	116	5	12	12	12	10^{1}	10^{hd}	$8^{\frac{1}{2}}$	Cruz M R	30.10
1Jan04 ^{11}Crc^{1}	Gin Rummy Champ	L	3	116	11	4	2^{1}	$2^{2\frac{1}{2}}$	$2^{1\frac{1}{2}}$	$2^{\frac{1}{2}}$	$9^{1\frac{3}{4}}$	Decarlo C P	44.90
18Jan04 ^{10}GP^{6}	America America	L	3	115	9	7	8^{hd}	10^{4}	$11^{1\frac{1}{2}}$	11^{3}	$10^{2\frac{1}{2}}$	Douglas R R	66.40
26Dec03 ^{9}Crc^{1}	Gold Shield	L b	3	116	12	6	$1^{1\frac{1}{2}}$	1^{hd}	1^{hd}	7^{1}	$11^{3\frac{1}{2}}$	Chavez J F	35.80
17Dec03 ^{8}Aqu^{1}	West Virginia	L	3	120	7	3	3^{1}	$3^{\frac{1}{2}}$	$3^{\frac{1}{2}}$	12	12	Velasquez C	17.40

a–Coupled: Kitten's Joy and Master William.

OFF AT 5:45 Start Good . Won driving. Course firm.

TIME :24^{2}, :49^{4}, 1:13^{3}, 1:37^{1}, 1:48^{3} (:24.45, :49.95, 1:13.66, 1:37.39, 1.40.70)

$2 Mutuel Prices:			
1 – KITTEN'S JOY(a–entry)	3.20	2.40	2.20
3 – PRINCE ARCH		13.40	6.80
11 – PA PA DA			5.40

$1 EXACTA 1–3 PAID $25.90 $1 TRIFECTA 1–3–11 PAID $191.40
$1 SUPERFECTA 1–3–11–2 PAID $789.20

Ch. c, (May), by El Prado-Ire – Kitten's First , by Lear Fan . Trainer Romans Dale. Bred by Kenneth L Ramsey & Sarah K Ramsey (Ky).

KITTEN'S JOY moved out a bit along the backstretch, raced in good position for six furlongs, saved ground through the turn, angled out approaching the stretch then unleashed a strong late run to win going away. PRINCE ARCH was unhurried for six furlongs, gained three wide on the turn, angled seven wide entering the stretch and finished strongly to best the others. PA PA DA lodged a bid three wide on the turn, surged to the front in midstretch then yielded in the final seventy yards. MASTER WILLIAM raced far back to the turn, advanced along the inside entering the stretch and rallied belatedly between horses. COMMENDATION raced between horses on the turn, swung seven wide in upper stretch then closed late from outside. MUSTANFAR raced evenly while five wide on the turn then rallied mildly. PINCAY raced well back to the turn and rallied belatedly. SOVERIGN HONOR steadied while being pinched back at the start and failed to threaten thereafter. GIN RUMMY CHAMP forced the pace from outside into upper stretch and tired. AMERICA AMERICA failed to threaten while saving ground. GOLD SHIELD was used up setting the early pace. WEST VIRGINIA chased in the two path for six furlongs and faded.

Owners– 1, Ramsey Kenneth L and Sarah K; 2, Cottrell Raymond H Sr; 3, Behrendt John T and Theresa E; 4, Ramsey Kenneth L and Sarah K; 5, Courtlandt Farms; 6, Shadwell Stable; 7, Young Joyce B; 8, Chin James; 9, Harris J Robert Jr; 10, Cameron Express Inc; 11, Fore Hearts Stable and Muro F; 12, Donald S Zuckerman & Mary Roberta

Trainers– 1, Romans Dale; 2, McPeek Kenneth G; 3, Donk David; 4, Dickinson Michael W; 5, Motion H Graham; 6, McLaughlin Kiaran P; 7, Tagg Barclay; 8, Pinchin Jose; 9, Gomez Frank; 10, Mourier Franck; 11, Calascibetta Joseph; 12, Pletcher Todd A

Scratched– Tap Day (18Jan04 ^{10}GP ^{1}) , Tales of Glory (05Dec03 ^{8}DeD^{8}) , Paper Man (07Jan04 ^{8}GP ^{9}) , Inducement (21Jan04 ^{9}GP ^{6})

$1 Pick Three (9–10–1) Paid $34.00 ; Pick Three Pool $56,015 .
$2 Pick Five (7–10–2–1–1) Paid $8,960.00 ; Pick Five Pool $608,823 .

EIGHTH RACE
Santa Anita
FEBRUARY 21, 2004

1 MILE. (Turf) (1.31^{4}) 17TH RUNNING OF THE BUENA VISTA HANDICAP. Grade II. Purse $150,000 FOR FILLIES AND MARES, FOUR YEARS OLD AND UPWARD. By subscription of $150 each to accompany the nomination or by supplementary nomination of $3,000 by Sunday, February 15. $1,500 additional to start, with $150,000 guaranteed, with $90,000 to first, $30,00 to second, $18,000 to third, $9,000 to fouth, and $3,000 to fifth. Weights Tuesday, Monday, February 16. High weights preferred. Starters to be named through the entry box by the closing time of entries. A trophy will be presented to the owner of thewinner. (Rail at 8 feet). Closed with 16 Nominations.

Value of Race: $150,000 Winner $90,000; second $30,000; third $18,000; fourth $9,000; fifth $3,000. Mutuel Pool $546,009.00 Exacta Pool $319,667.00 Quinella Pool $30,866.00 Trifecta Pool $400,592.00

Last Raced	Horse	M/Eqt.	A.	Wt	PP	St	¼	½	¾	Str	Fin	Jockey	Odds $1
28Jan04 ^{7}SA^{3}	Fun House	LB	5	116	5	3	4^{1}	4^{1}	$3^{1\frac{1}{2}}$	$2^{\frac{1}{2}}$	$1^{2\frac{3}{4}}$	Stevens G L	11.00
20Dec03 ^{9}Hol^{1}	Katdogawn-GB	LB	4	117	2	6	7	7	5^{1}	$4^{2\frac{1}{2}}$	$2^{\frac{1}{2}}$	Smith M E	3.90
28Jan04 ^{7}SA^{1}	Fudge Fatale	LB	4	116	3	2	$2^{1\frac{1}{2}}$	$2^{1\frac{1}{2}}$	$2^{2\frac{1}{2}}$	$1^{1\frac{1}{2}}$	$3^{\frac{1}{2}}$	Valdivia J Jr	17.30
18Jan04 ^{7}SA^{2}	Personal Legend	LB b	4	115	7	5	6^{hd}	6^{hd}	7	5^{1}	$4^{\frac{1}{2}}$	Solis A	2.10
30Nov03 ^{6}Hol^{13}	Maiden Tower-GB	LB	4	118	1	1	$1^{1\frac{1}{2}}$	1^{1}	1^{hd}	3^{2}	5^{4}	Flores D R	1.40
16Jan04 ^{7}SA^{4}	Southern Oasis	LB	6	114	6	4	$3^{1\frac{1}{2}}$	3^{1}	4^{hd}	6^{2}	6^{2}	Baze T C	9.90
31Jan04 ^{3}GG^{4}	Drew Away	LB	5	113	4	7	5^{hd}	5^{hd}	$6^{\frac{1}{2}}$	7	7	Espinoza V	28.20

OFF AT 4:08 Start Good . Won driving. Course good.

TIME :23^{2}, :47^{3}, 1:12, 1:24, 1:36 (:23.50, :47.75, 1:12.07, 1:24.06, 1:36.13)

$2 Mutuel Prices:

5 – FUN HOUSE	24.00	8.60	5.00
2 – KATDOGAWN–GB		5.40	3.40
3 – FUDGE FATALE			6.20

$1 EXACTA 5–2 PAID $45.60 $2 QUINELLA 2–5 PAID $42.80
$1 TRIFECTA 5–2–3 PAID $454.10

B. m, (Feb), by Prized – Bistra , by Classic Go Go . Trainer McAnally Ronald. Bred by Verne H Winchell (Ky).

FUN HOUSE angled in and stalked inside, came out into the stretch, rallied to the front under urging a sixteenth out and pulled clear. KATDOGAWN (GB) off a bit slowly, settled along the inside chasing the pace, came out in midstretch and gained the place late. FUDGE FATALE stalked the pace off the rail, bid outside MAIDEN TOWER on the second turn, put a head in front nearing the stretch, inched away toward the inside and just held third. PERSONAL LEGEND three deep early, chased between horses or outside a rival, angled in leaving the second turn, came out again in midstretch and found her best stride late. MAIDEN TOWER (GB) took the early lead and set the pace inside, dueled along the rail on the second turn but weakened in the stretch. SOUTHERN OASIS bobbled at the start, stalked off the rail then between horses on the second turn and also weakened in the lane, then did not return to be unsaddled and was vanned off. DREW AWAY off a bit slowly, chased three deep then outside a rival, continued three wide leaving the backstretch and on the second turn and had little left for the stretch.

Owners– 1, Winchell Thoroughbreds LLC; 2, Cuchna John R Jim Ford Inc and Pearson Daron; 3, Greely John J III; 4, Gann Edmund A; 5, Darley Stable; 6, Whitham Janis R; 7, M-2 Stable LLC

Trainers– 1, McAnally Ronald; 2, Cassidy James; 3, Greely C Beau; 4, Frankel Robert; 5, Harty Eoin; 6, McAnally Ronald; 7, Greely C Beau

$2 Daily Double (5–5) Paid $145.60 ; Daily Double Pool $44,974 .
$1 Pick Three (5–5–5) Paid $335.00 ; Pick Three Pool $68,420 .

ELEVENTH RACE
Gulfstream
FEBRUARY 22, 2004

1⅜ MILES. (Turf) (2.10^{3}) 19TH RUNNING OF THE GULFSTREAM PARK BREEDERS' CUP HANDICAP. Grade I. Purse $250,000 (includes $100,000 BC – Breeders' Cup) FOR THREE YEAR OLDS AND UPWARD. (Includes $100,000 from Breeders' Cup Fund for Cup nominees only). By subscription of $250 each, which shall accompany the nomination, $2,000 to pass the entry box and $2,000 additional to start, with $150,000 guaranteed. The host association monies to be divided, 60% to the owner of the winner, 20% to second, 11% to third, 6% to fourth and 3% to fifth. Breeders' Cup Fund monies not awarded will revert back to the fund. Weight: Sunday, February 15, 2004. This race will notbe divided. Trophy to winning Owner given by Breeders' Cup, Ltd. (High Weights on the scale Preferred). In the event this stake is taken off the turf, it may be subject to downgrading upon review by the Graded Stakes Committee. Closed Thursday, February12, 2004 with (20) nominations.

Value of Race: $190,000 Winner $90,000; second $50,000; third $27,500; fourth $15,000; fifth $7,500. Mutuel Pool $649,022.00 Exacta Pool $418,382.00 Trifecta Pool $360,061.00 Superfecta Pool $113,817.00

Last Raced	Horse	M/Eqt.	A.	Wt	PP	¼	½	¾	1	Str	Fin	Jockey	Odds $1
31Jan04 ^{8}GP^{4}	Hard Buck-Brz	L	5	117	6	$5^{1\frac{1}{2}}$	$4^{\frac{1}{2}}$	$4^{\frac{1}{2}}$	4^{1}	$4^{1\frac{1}{2}}$	1^{hd}	Prado E S	11.50
27Dec03 ^{11}Crc^{1}	Balto Star	L	6	122	7	1^{1}	1^{1}	$1^{1\frac{1}{2}}$	1^{2}	$1^{1\frac{1}{2}}$	$2^{\frac{1}{2}}$	Velazquez J R	2.30
30Nov03 ^{9}Hol^{3}	Kicken Kris	L	4	118	2	4^{hd}	5^{1}	5^{1}	$5^{1\frac{1}{2}}$	5^{hd}	3^{1}	Castellano J J	4.70
25Jan04 ^{10}GP^{1}	Request for Parole	L	5	116	1	6^{1}	$6^{1\frac{1}{2}}$	6^{1}	$7^{1\frac{1}{2}}$	$6^{2\frac{1}{2}}$	4^{nk}	Santos J A	2.80
28Nov03 ^{11}CD^{9}	Quest Star	L b	5	115	5	$3^{\frac{1}{2}}$	$3^{\frac{1}{2}}$	$3^{1\frac{1}{2}}$	3^{1}	2^{hd}	$5^{1\frac{1}{2}}$	Day P	15.40
25Jan04 ^{10}GP^{2}	Slew Valley	L	7	117	8	$2^{\frac{1}{2}}$	$2^{1\frac{1}{2}}$	$2^{\frac{1}{2}}$	$2^{\frac{1}{2}}$	3^{hd}	$6^{1\frac{1}{4}}$	Chavez J F	21.90
24Jan04 ^{10}GP^{11}	Man From Wicklow	L bf	7	118	3	8	8	8	8	7^{1}	$7^{3\frac{3}{4}}$	Bailey J D	4.20
24Jan04 ^{10}GP^{4}	Magic Mecke	L	4	114	4	$7^{2\frac{1}{2}}$	$7^{\frac{1}{2}}$	7^{hd}	6^{hd}	8	8	Coa E M	13.50

OFF AT 5:44 Start Good . Won driving. Course firm.

TIME :24^{1}, :48^{4}, 1:36^{1}, 2:11^{2} (:24.33, :48.87, 1:36.23, 2:11.56)

$2 Mutuel Prices:

6 – HARD BUCK–BRZ	25.00	9.60	6.60
7 – BALTO STAR		4.40	3.20
2 – KICKEN KRIS			3.40

$1 EXACTA 6–7 PAID $54.50 $1 TRIFECTA 6–7–2 PAID $263.20
$1 SUPERFECTA 6–7–2–1 PAID $889.10

Dk. b or br. h, (Nov), by Spend a Buck – Social Secret , by Secreto . Trainer McPeek Kenneth G. Bred by Haras Old Friends (Brz).

HARD BUCK (BRZ) tracked the pace, raced three wide on the final turn, then rallied under pressure to be up in the final strides. BALTO STAR quickly moved to the fore, made the pace along the hedge into the stretch and just failed to last. KICKEN KRIS rated off the pace, lacked room leaving the final turn, angled out and was gaining on the top ones at the finish. REQUEST FOR PAROLE reserved off the pace after being steadied along the inside entering the first turn, angled out and closed with a mild rally. QUEST STAR stalked the pace along the hedge into the stretch but couldn't gain late. SLEW VALLEY stalked the pace into the stretch and weakened. MAN FROM WICKLOW unhurried early, lacked a late response. MAGIC MECKE was not a factor.

Owners– 1, Team Victory I; 2, Anstu Stables Inc; 3, Brushwood Stable; 4, Knighton Jeri and Sam; 5, Mansell Stables LLC; 6, Rich Meadow Farm; 7, Violette Richard A Jr; 8, Trilogy Stables

Trainers– 1, McPeek Kenneth G; 2, Pletcher Todd A; 3, Matz Michael R; 4, Hough Stanley M; 5, Walden W Elliott; 6, Sciacca Gary; 7, Violette Richard A Jr; 8, Plesa Edward Jr

$1 Pick Three (1–6–6) Paid $576.30 ; Pick Three Pool $59,793 .

EIGHTH RACE
Santa Anita
FEBRUARY 22, 2004

6 FURLONGS. (1.07¹) 52ND RUNNING OF THE LAS FLORES HANDICAP. Grade III. Purse $100,000 FOR FILLIES AND MARES FOUR YEARS OLD AND UPWARD. By subscription of $100 each to accompany the nomination or by supplementary nomination of $2,000 by Sunday, February 15 and $1,000 additional to start, with $100,000 added. The added money and all fees tobe divided 60% to first, 20% to second, 12% to third, 6% to fourth and 2% to fifth. Weights Monday, February 16. Starters to be named through the entry box by the closing time of entries. A trophy will be presented to the owner of the winner. Closed with 13 nominations.

Value of Race: $107,300 Winner $64,380; second $21,460; third $12,876; fourth $6,438; fifth $2,146. Mutuel Pool $389,518.00 Exacta Pool $243,471.00 Quinella Pool $24,821.00 Trifecta Pool $272,374.00

Last Raced	Horse	M/Eqt.	A.	Wt	PP	St	1/4	1/2	Str	Fin	Jockey	Odds $1
24Jan04 8GG1	Ema Bovary-Chi	LB	5	121	2	3	5hd	43	11½	13¾	Gonzalez R M	1.40
25Jan04 8SA2	Buffythecenterfold	LB	4	117	4	5	2hd	3½	2½	21	Garcia M S	1.20
10Aug03 3Dmr1	Coconut Girl	LB f	5	113	1	4	31	2hd	31½	35	Espinoza V	10.70
24Jan04 4SA6	Icantgoforthat	LB b	5	115	6	2	11	1½	45	44	Baze T C	7.50
5Jun03 4LP2	Sarasota-Arg	LB	4	115	3	6	6	6	6	5hd	Smith M E	10.70
24Jan04 4SA3	Channing Way	LB	6	116	5	1	4hd	5hd	5hd	6	Corbett G W	21.40

OFF AT 4:14 Start Good. Won driving. Track wet fast.
TIME :21¹, :43⁴, :55³, 1:08 (:21.29, :43.81, :55.77, 1:08.02)

$2 Mutuel Prices:

2 – EMA BOVARY-CHI	4.80	2.60	2.20
4 – BUFFYTHECENTERFOLD		2.60	2.20
1 – COCONUT GIRL			3.00

$1 EXACTA 2–4 PAID $5.00 $2 QUINELLA 2–4 PAID $4.20
$1 TRIFECTA 2–4–1 PAID $20.00

B. m, (Oct), by Edgy Diplomat – Coqueta , by Domineau . Trainer Ross Larry. Bred by Haras San Patricio (Chi).

EMA BOVARY (CHI) between horses early, stalked inside, was in a bit tight leaving the backstretch, came out for room on the turn, ranged up four wide leaving the turn and into the stretch, gained the lead in upper stretch, drifted in a bit but pulled clear under some urging and steady handling. BUFFYTHECENTERFOLD also between rivals early, stalked outside a foe, bid three deep between horses leaving the turn and into the stretch but could not match the winner. COCONUT GIRL close up tracking the leader inside, bid along the rail leaving the turn and into the stretch and bested the others. ICANTGOFORTHAT sped to the early lead outside, angled in and set the pace off the rail, battled between horses leaving the turn and into the stretch, was crowded between foes nearing midstretch and weakened. SARASOTA (ARG) in a bit tight early, pulled her way between horses chasing the pace, angled in on the turn and also weakened. CHANNING WAY lunged a bit at the start but broke on top, stalked three deep on the backstretch, dropped back off the rail on the turn and had little left for the stretch.

Owners– 1, Beal Richard T and Ramsey Lana; 2, Brian Allen A and Stronach Stables; 3, Jpf Investments I LLC; 4, Broberg Andy and Knapp Palmer; 5, Alesia Bran Jam Stables and Royalty Stable et al; 6, Becker Lawrence G

Trainers– 1, Ross Larry; 2, Stute Melvin F; 3, Aguirre Paul G; 4, Knapp Steve; 5, Eurton Peter; 6, Morgan Dan

Scratched– Annabelly (15Jan04 3SA 1)

$2 Daily Double (10–2) Paid $23.60 ; Daily Double Pool $39,446 .
$1 Pick Three (1–5/8/10–2) Paid $54.90 ; Pick Three Pool $60,738 .

NINTH RACE
Fair Grounds
FEBRUARY 28, 2004

ABOUT 1⅛ MILES. (Turf) (1.46⁴) 38TH RUNNING OF THE BAYOU BREEDERS' CUP HANDICAP. Grade III. Purse $125,000 (includes $50,000 BC – Breeders' Cup) FOR FILLIES AND MARES, FOUR YEAR OLDS AND UPWARD. With $75,000 and an additional $50,000 from the Breeders' Cup Fund for cup nominees only. The host association's money to be divided 60% to the winner; 20% to second; 11% to third; 6% to fourth; 3% tofifth. Breeders' Cup monies also correspondingly divided providing a Breeders' Cup nominee has finished in an awarded position. Any Breeders' Cup monies not awarded will revert back to the Fund. THE OWNER OF THE WINNER TO RECEIVE A TROPHY. Closed Friday, February 20, 2004, with 18 nominations. (If deemed inadvisable by management to run this race over the turf course, it will be run on the main track at One Mile and 1/8) (Rail at 15 feet).

Value of Race: $113,500 Winner $75,000; second $15,000; third $13,750; fourth $7,500; fifth $2,250. Mutuel Pool $299,360.00 Exacta Pool $190,963.00 Quinella Pool $15,414.00 Trifecta Pool $167,676.00 Superfecta Pool $38,769.00

Last Raced	Horse	M/Eqt.	A.	Wt	PP	St	1/4	1/2	3/4	Str	Fin	Jockey	Odds $1
26Dec03 9FG1	Bedanken	L f	5	121	3	6	41	41	4hd	11½	11¾	Pettinger D R	1.50
30Jan04 9FG1	Due to Win Again	L b	6	118	10	1	6hd	72½	61½	51	2no	Martin E M Jr	11.70
8Feb04 8Lrl2	Lady Linda	L b	6	115	9	2	81½	92	82	71½	31¼	Borel C H	10.40
1Feb04 7FG3	Mexican Moonlight	L	4	114	5	4	12	13	11½	21	4hd	Perrodin E J	36.00
26Dec03 9FG2	Flager-Arg	L	5	117	2	8	72½	6hd	71	41	51¾	Sellers S J	6.20
20Dec03 9FG2	Baie-FR	L	4	118	7	9	10	10	10	82	6hd	Albarado R J	3.30
11Jan04 7FG1	Float and Sting	L	5	114	8	3	22	21½	2½	3½	7nk	Melancon L	70.30
10Jan04 3SA3	Firth of Lorne-Ire	L	5	117	4	10	51	51½	5½	61½	82½	Melancon G	4.00
23Feb04 8FG3	No Other Like You	L b	4	110	6	5	3½	31½	31½	93	93¼	Martinez J R Jr	70.50
11Jan04 7FG4	Dynamic Lady	L b	5	117	1	7	9½	8hd	9hd	10	10	Lovato F Jr	53.70

OFF AT 4:19 Start Good. Won driving. Course firm.
TIME :24³, :50¹, 1:15, 1:40¹, 1:52³ (:24.71, :50.31, 1:15.18, 1:40.34, 1:52.74)

$2 Mutuel Prices:

4 – BEDANKEN	5.00	3.60	3.00
11 – DUE TO WIN AGAIN		9.00	6.60
10 – LADY LINDA			4.80

$2 EXACTA 4–11 PAID $40.60 $2 QUINELLA 4–11 PAID $35.40
$2 TRIFECTA 4–11–10 PAID $307.00 $2 SUPERFECTA 4–11–10–6 PAID $6,014.40

Gr/ro. m, (Feb), by Geri – Danka , by Strawberry Road–Aus . Trainer Von Hemel Donnie K. Bred by Pin Oak Stud LLC (Ky).

BEDANKEN settled along the inside from early on, advanced midway around the second turn, slipped through inside MEXICAN MOONLIGHT approaching the drive, took over command in upper stretch and proved best under mild encouragement late. DUE TO WIN AGAIN wide early, eased in a bit approaching the first turn, was restrained down the backstretch while a bit off the rail, swung out entering the drive and was gaining late. LADY LINDA reserved off the rail, continued wide to rally and got up for the show. MEXICAN MOONLIGHT set the pace off the inside, got displaced turning for home and gave way grudgingly. FLAGER (ARG) raced inside and had no rally. BAIE (FR) raced in the back until the drive and was no real threat. FLOAT AND STING forward for six furlongs, weakened. FIRTH OF LORNE (IRE) reserved, had no kick between foes in the lane. NO OTHER LIKE YOU forwardly placed while widest until the drive, gave way. DYNAMIC LADY showed little.

Owners– 1, Pin Oak Stable LLC; 2, Scarberry Howard and Penny; 3, Domino Stud of Lexington LLC; 4, Pass Taggart Racing; 5, Stony Oak Farm LLC; 6, 6 C Stable LLC; 7, Polk Jr Hiram and Richardson J David; 8, Darley Stable; 9, Clifton Beth H; 10, C K Woods Stable

Trainers– 1, Von Hemel Donnie K; 2, Scarberry Howard; 3, Eppler Mary E; 4, Murphy Paul H; 5, Barnett Bobby C; 6, Frostad Mark; 7, Barnett Bobby C; 8, Harty Eoin; 9, Kessinger Burk Jr; 10, Badgett William Jr

Scratched– Titia (24Jan04 8FG 2)

$2 Pick Three (8–3–4) Paid $160.80 ; Pick Three Pool $16,739 .

EIGHTH RACE
Gulfstream
FEBRUARY 28, 2004

1⅛ MILES. (Turf) (1.45^{3}) 19TH RUNNING OF THE HERECOMESTHEBRIDE. Grade III. Purse $100,000 FOR FILLIES, THREE YEARS OLD. By subscription of $100 each, which shall accompany the nomination, $1,000 to pass the entry box and $1,000 additional to start, with $100,000 guaranteed. The owner of the winner will receive $60,000; $20,000 to second, $11,000 to third, $6,000 to fourth and $3,000 to fifth. Supplemental nominations may be made on Thursday, February 26, 2004 at a fee of $3,000, which includes entry and start fees. Weight: 121 lbs. Non-winners of $50,000 at a mile or over on the turf, allowed2 lbs.; $40,000 at any distance or $30,000 at a mile or over, 4 lbs.; $24,000 at any distance or $18,000 at a mile or over, 6 lbs. Trophy to winning Owner. This race will be limited to 12 Starters, with Also Eligibles. (High Weights Preferred). (Total lifetime earnings will be used to determine the order of preference of horses with equal weight). In the event this stake race is taken off the turf, it may be subject to downgrading upon review by the Graded Stakes Committee. Closed Wednesday February18, 2004 with (25) nominations. (Rail at 10 feet).

Value of Race: $100,000 Winner $60,000; second $20,000; third $11,000; fourth $6,000; fifth $3,000. Mutuel Pool $667,051.00 Exacta Pool $512,692.00 Trifecta Pool $353,166.00 Superfecta Pool $108,411.00

Last Raced	Horse	M/Eqt.	A.	Wt	PP	St	¼	½	¾	Str	Fin	Jockey	Odds $1
14Jan04 ^{7}GP^{1}	Lucifer's Stone	L b	3	117	1	8	8^{hd}	9^{1}	$7^{\frac{1}{2}}$	2^{hd}	$1^{\frac{1}{2}}$	Santos J A	3.70
3Jan04 ^{7}FG^{1}	Dynamia	L	3	115	12	6	5^{hd}	5^{hd}	5^{1}	$4^{\frac{1}{2}}$	$2^{\frac{3}{4}}$	Bailey J D	2.70
6Feb04 ^{4}GP^{1}	Honey Ryder	L b	3	117	11	7	$7^{1\frac{1}{2}}$	7^{hd}	6^{hd}	6^{hd}	$3^{1\frac{1}{4}}$	Prado E S	17.70
22Jan04 ^{9}GP^{1}	Minge Cove	L	3	117	8	10	$11^{3\frac{1}{2}}$	$11^{3\frac{1}{2}}$	11^{hd}	$8^{\frac{1}{2}}$	$4^{1\frac{1}{4}}$	Decarlo C P	21.30
9Feb04 ^{6}GP^{2}	Vous	L	3	121	7	11	10^{1}	$10^{\frac{1}{2}}$	$10^{1\frac{1}{2}}$	10^{1}	5^{hd}	Bravo J	8.00
9Feb04 ^{6}GP^{1}	Last Waltz	L b	3	117	2	3	4^{hd}	$4^{\frac{1}{2}}$	4^{hd}	$7^{\frac{1}{2}}$	$6^{\frac{3}{4}}$	Velazquez J R	8.20
9Feb04 ^{6}GP^{3}	Cold Wynnter	L	3	115	10	4	$3^{\frac{1}{2}}$	$3^{\frac{1}{2}}$	$3^{\frac{1}{2}}$	3^{hd}	$7^{1\frac{1}{2}}$	Velasquez C	24.70
1Jan04 ^{6}Crc^{4}	Pink Champagne	L	3	121	9	5	$2^{\frac{1}{2}}$	2^{1}	2^{1}	1^{hd}	$8^{\frac{1}{2}}$	Day P	7.60
6Feb04 ^{4}GP^{3}	Cute Connie	L	3	115	3	12	12	12	12	12	9^{1}	Penalba C	105.50
1Jan04 ^{6}Crc^{1}	Bobbie Use	L	3	121	6	9	$9^{\frac{1}{2}}$	8^{hd}	$8^{\frac{1}{2}}$	9^{2}	$10^{\frac{1}{2}}$	Coa E M	6.70
21Feb04 ^{11}GP^{10}	America America	L	3	119	5	1	$6^{\frac{1}{2}}$	$6^{1\frac{1}{2}}$	$9^{\frac{1}{2}}$	$11^{\frac{1}{2}}$	$11^{3\frac{3}{4}}$	Blanc B	49.70
29Nov03 ^{8}Crc^{3}	Chelsea's Pearl	L	3	115	4	2	$1^{\frac{1}{2}}$	$1^{\frac{1}{2}}$	$1^{\frac{1}{2}}$	5^{1}	12	Douglas R R	13.60

OFF AT4:12 Start Good . Won driving. Course firm.

TIME :24^{2}, :50, 1:15^{3}, 1:40^{4}, 1:52^{3} (:24.51, :50.09, 1:15.64, 1:40.90, 1:52.78)

$2 Mutuel Prices:

1 – LUCIFER'S STONE	9.40	4.40	3.40
13 – DYNAMIA		4.40	3.80
12 – HONEY RYDER			6.60

$1 EXACTA 1–13 PAID $24.20 $1 TRIFECTA 1–13–12 PAID $230.70
$1 SUPERFECTA 1–13–12–8 PAID $5,420.50

B. f, (Mar), by Horse Chestnut–Saf – Ladue , by Demons Begone . Trainer Rice Linda. Bred by Mega Stable (Ky).

LUCIFER'S STONE reserved along the hedge after hitting the gate at the start, steadied waiting for room on the far turn, slipped through inside CHELSEA'S PEARL to gain a slim lead in midstretch, then was fully extended to prevail. DYNAMIA tracked the pace three wide, made a run four wide around the far turn to reach near even terms for command in midstretch and continued on gamely while being edged to the wire. HONEY RYDER reserved in striking position off the pace, came between horses on the far turn, angled to the outside for racing room in the stretch and closed to be up for the show. MINGE COVE unhurried while saving ground, steadied in behind LUCIFER'S STONE on the far turn, eased out to come between rivals in the stretch and finished willingly. VOUS steadied in traffic on the first turn, raced four wide on the far turn and improved her position in the drive without threatening. LAST WALTZ stalked the pace along the hedge into the stretch and weakened. COLD WYNNTER chased the pace three wide, made a run to reach even terms for command in midstretch, then tired. PINK CHAMPAGNE prompted the pace outside CHELSEA'S PEARL, moved to gain a slim lead in midstretch, then faltered. CUTE CONNIE off slowly, raced five wide on the far turn and was not a factor. BOBBIE USE allowed to settle, made a run five wide on the far turn to reach contention racing into the stretch, then gave way. AMERICA AMERICA rated off the pace, steadied in traffic on the far turn and failed to recover. CHELSEA'S PEARL set the pace along the inside, came of the hedge for the stretch run and faded.

Owners– 1, Team Solaris Stable; 2, Chandler John A; 3, Glencrest Farm LLC; 4, Double S Wachtel Friedman and Iwinski; 5, Tee-N-Jay Farm; 6, Ramsey Kenneth L and Sarah K; 7, Live Oak Plantation; 8, Starview Stable; 9, Ford Homestead Centre Ltd; 10, Goldfarb Sanford J; 11, Cameron Express Inc; 12, Meahjohn Zamin R

Trainers– 1, Rice Linda; 2, Dickinson Michael W; 3, Pletcher Todd A; 4, Iwinski Allen; 5, Hills Timothy A; 6, Romans Dale; 7, Mott William I; 8, Kimmel John C; 9, Nazareth John A; 10, Dutrow Richard E Jr; 11, Mourier Franck; 12, Collazo Henry

Scratched– Really American (08Feb04 ^{5}GP ^{1}) , Irish Melody (25Jan04 ^{6}GP ^{1})

$1 Pick Three (6–2–1) Paid $107.80 ; Pick Three Pool $81,435 .

ELEVENTH RACE
Gulfstream
FEBRUARY 28, 2004

1⅜ MILES. (Turf) (2.10^{3}) 16TH RUNNING OF THE VERY ONE HANDICAP. Grade III. Purse $100,000 FOR FILLIES AND MARES, THREE YEAR OLDS AND UPWARD. By subscription of $100 each, which shall accompany the nomination, $1,000 to pass the entry box and $1,000 additional to start, with $100,000 guaranteed. The owner of the winner to receive $60,000; $20,000 to second, $11,000 to third, $6,000 to fourth and $3,000 to fifth. Trophy to winning Owner. This race will be limited to 12 Starters, with Also Eligibles. (High Weights on the scale Preferred). In the event this stake is taken off the turf, it may besubject to downgrading upon review by the Graded Stakes Committee. Closed Wednesday February 18, 2004 with (25) nominations. (Rail at 10 feet).

Value of Race: $100,000 Winner $60,000; second $20,000; third $11,000; fourth $6,000; fifth $3,000. Mutuel Pool $634,670.00 Exacta Pool $455,633.00 Trifecta Pool $336,848.00 Superfecta Pool $129,058.00

Last Raced	Horse	M/Eqt.		A.	Wt	PP	¼	½	¾	1	Str	Fin	Jockey	Odds $1
16Jan04 ^{8}GP^{1}	Binya-Ger	L		5	114	8	2^{2}	$2^{1\frac{1}{2}}$	$2^{1\frac{1}{2}}$	2^{2}	$1^{2\frac{1}{2}}$	$1^{2\frac{1}{2}}$	Velazquez J R	2.10
19Oct03 ^{8}Kee^{2}	Ocean Silk	L		4	115	6	4^{1}	4^{2}	3^{hd}	$3^{\frac{1}{2}}$	3^{hd}	$2^{\frac{1}{2}}$	Day P	2.90
11Feb04 ^{3}GP^{1}	Boana-Ger	L		6	114	2	8^{1}	8^{hd}	$8^{1\frac{1}{2}}$	$5^{1\frac{1}{2}}$	2^{hd}	$3^{\frac{3}{4}}$	Douglas R R	12.70
24Jan04 ^{5}SA^{5}	Lost Appeal	L	b	6	114	4	$11^{1\frac{1}{2}}$	10^{1}	$9^{\frac{1}{2}}$	11^{2}	$5^{1\frac{1}{2}}$	4^{hd}	Bailey J D	6.00
20Dec03 ^{8}Aqu^{1}	Savedbythelight	L	b	4	115	10	$9^{\frac{1}{2}}$	9^{hd}	10^{hd}	7^{hd}	6^{hd}	$5^{\frac{1}{2}}$	Migliore R	18.40
31Jan04 ^{11}GP^{4}	San Dare	L		6	114	11	12	12	12	12	11^{2}	6^{nk}	Velasquez C	14.80
31Jan04 ^{11}GP^{2}	May Gator	L	b	5	114	7	1^{1}	$1^{1\frac{1}{2}}$	1^{1}	$1^{1\frac{1}{2}}$	4^{1}	$7^{\frac{3}{4}}$	Chavez J F	38.90
6Feb04 ^{9}GP^{1}	Stay Forever	L	b	7	114	1	10^{1}	11^{2}	$11^{2\frac{1}{2}}$	10^{hd}	9^{hd}	8^{nk}	Santos J A	6.20
6Feb04 ^{7}GP^{1}	Sun Brightia	L		4	113	12	5^{1}	5^{1}	6^{1}	9^{1}	$10^{1\frac{1}{2}}$	9^{1}	Blanc B	15.00
5Feb04 ^{5}GP^{5}	New Dreams-Brz	L		5	117	9	6^{1}	$6^{\frac{1}{2}}$	$5^{\frac{1}{2}}$	$8^{\frac{1}{2}}$	$8^{1\frac{1}{2}}$	$10^{1\frac{3}{4}}$	Mota A	55.10
31Jan04 ^{11}GP^{3}	Mymich	L	b	4	115	5	3^{hd}	3^{hd}	4^{3}	4^{1}	$7^{1\frac{1}{2}}$	$11^{2\frac{3}{4}}$	Guidry M	50.60
24Jan04 ^{9}Tam^{9}	Dick's Chick	L		5	115	3	$7^{\frac{1}{2}}$	$7^{1\frac{1}{2}}$	$7^{\frac{1}{2}}$	$6^{\frac{1}{2}}$	12	12	Court J K	106.50

OFF AT 5:45 Start Good. Won driving. Course firm.

TIME :25^{3}, :51, 1:17^{2}, 1:42^{3}, 2:07^{3}, 2:19^{3} (:25.65, :51.13, 1:17.59, 1:42.65, 2:07.67, 2:19.65)

$2 Mutuel Prices

8 – BINYA-GER	6.20	3.40	2.80
6 – OCEAN SILK		3.60	2.80
2 – BOANA-GER			5.00

$1 EXACTA 8–6 PAID $12.00 $1 TRIFECTA 8–6–2 PAID $62.50
$1 SUPERFECTA 8–6–2–4 PAID $223.00

Ch. m, (Mar), by Royal Solo–Ire – Beaconaire , by Vaguely Noble . Trainer McLaughlin Kiaran P. Bred by Gestut Hof Iserneichen (Ger).

BINYA (GER) stalked the pace, moved to take over leaving the final turn and drew clear under urging. OCEAN SILK tracked the pace, moved into contention three wide on the final turn but couldn't gain on the winner late while up for the place. BOANA (GER) taken in hand while saving ground, angled out four wide on the final turn and made a run to loom a threat in the stretch but didn't do enough late. LOST APPEAL unhurried for a mile, advanced along the hedge around the final turn to reach contention, was forced to alter course outside MAY GATOR in midstretch and couldn't sustain her bid. SAVEDBYTHELIGHT allowed to settle, improved her position in the drive without threatening. SAN DARE outrun early, swung out for the stretch run and passed tired rivals. MAY GATOR set the pace along the inside to nearing the stretch and gave way. STAY FOREVER raced four wide on the final turn and failed to be a factor. SUN BRIGHTIA raced in striking position for six furlongs and faltered. NEW DREAMS (BRZ) saved ground and tired. MYMICH tracked the pace along the hedge into the stretch and faded. DICK'S CHICK in good position, raced four wide on the final turn and came up empty.

Owners– 1, Allen Joseph; 2, Sangster Robert E; 3, Tanaka Gary A; 4, Poston Bill and Vicki; 5, Mack Earle I; 6, Mounts David G; 7, Klein Richard Bertram and Elaine; 8, Santa Cruz Ranch Inc; 9, Kobayashi Masashi; 10, Estrela Energia Stable; 11, Willmott Stables Inc; 12, McGinn Dave

Trainers– 1, McLaughlin Kiaran P; 2, Byrne Patrick B; 3, Attfield Roger L; 4, Edwards Oliver S; 5, Violette Richard A Jr; 6, Hiles Rick; 7, Flint Steve; 8, Wolfson Martin D; 9, Gothard Akiko; 10, McPeek Kenneth G; 11, Reinstedler Anthony; 12, Shapoff Alan W

Scratched– Madeira Mist (IRE) (10Feb04 ^{8}Tam^{1}), Gal O Gal (10Feb04 ^{8}Tam^{7}), Aztec Pearl (13Feb04 ^{8}GP ^{2}), Victory Snit (07Jan04 ^{7}GP ^{10})

$1 Pick Three (6–7–8) Paid $320.10 ; Pick Three Pool $53,217 .
$2 Pick Five (8–7–4–6–8) Paid $205,703.00 ; Pick Five Pool $538,636 .

EIGHTH RACE
Santa Anita
FEBRUARY 28, 2004

ABOUT 6½ FURLONGS. (Turf) (1.11) 37TH RUNNING OF THE BALDWIN. Grade III. Purse $100,000 FOR THREE-YEAR-OLDS. By subscription of $100 each to accompany the nomination or by supplementary nomination of $2,000 by time of entry. $250 to pass the entry box and $750 additional to start, with $100,000 added. The added money and all fees to be divided 60% to first, 20% to second, 12% to third, 6% to fourth and 2% to fifth. 122 lbs. Non-winners of a race of $60,000 allowed 3 lbs.; of a race of $40,000 since December 25, 5 lbs.; of a race other than Maiden or Claiming since then or $25,000 at any time, 8 lbs. (Maiden and Claiming races not considered). Starters to be named through the entry box by the closing tme of entries. A trophy will be presented to the owner of the winner. (Rail at 15 feet). Closed with 25 nominations.

Value of Race: $113,350 Winner $68,010; second $22,670; third $13,602; fourth $6,801; fifth $2,267. Mutuel Pool $603,400.00 Exacta Pool $351,757.00 Quinella Pool $33,292.00 Trifecta Pool $347,324.00 Superfecta Pool $148,029.00

Last Raced	Horse	M/Eqt.	A.	Wt	PP	St	¼	½	Str	Fin	Jockey	Odds $1
26Oct03 ^{5}Del^{1}	Seattle Borders	LB	3	114	2	5	$4^{1}\frac{1}{2}$	5^{1}	3^{2}	1^{1}	Solis A	5.30
30Jly03 ^{7}Dmr^{2}	Stalking Tiger	LB bf	3	117	9	2	$3\frac{1}{2}$	$1\frac{1}{2}$	$2^{1}\frac{1}{2}$	$2\frac{1}{2}$	Almeida G F	11.80
31Jan04 ^{7}SA^{3}	Jungle Prince	LB b	3	114	10	1	1^{hd}	3^{2}	1^{hd}	$3\frac{1}{2}$	Espinoza V	5.00
24Jan04 ^{3}SA^{1}	Saint Afleet	LB b	3	122	3	8	6^{hd}	$6^{1}\frac{1}{2}$	4^{1}	$4^{1}\frac{1}{2}$	Desormeaux K J	1.70
18Jan04 ^{5}SA^{4}	Matt Blanc-Ire	LB	3	114	1	10	10	$8^{1}\frac{1}{2}$	5^{hd}	5^{hd}	Pedroza M A	20.80
18Jan04 ^{8}TuP^{7}	Rush Into Heaven	LB	3	117	5	6	8^{1}	10	$8^{1}\frac{1}{2}$	6^{1}	Baze T C	32.20
25Aug03 NC^{7}	MoulindMougns-Ire	LB	3	114	8	9	$9^{1}\frac{1}{2}$	7^{1}	$6\frac{1}{2}$	7^{3}	Stevens G L	12.50
31Jan04 ^{9}SA^{1}	Trois Villes	LB b	3	114	7	4	2^{hd}	2^{hd}	$7^{2}\frac{1}{2}$	8^{3}	Ruis M	28.50
10Jan04 ^{3}GG^{4}	Gwaihir-Ire	LB	3	122	6	7	7^{3}	9^{2}	10	$9\frac{1}{2}$	Flores D R	6.10
24Jan04 ^{3}SA^{4}	Don'tsellmeshort	LB	3	122	4	3	5^{1}	4^{hd}	9^{1}	10	Smith M E	9.70

OFF AT 4:09 Start Good . Won driving. Course good.

TIME :22^{1}, :44^{4}, 1:07^{4}, 1:14 (:22.36, :44.84, 1:07.91, 1:14.09)

$2 Mutuel Prices:

3 – SEATTLE BORDERS	12.60	7.80	5.20
10 – STALKING TIGER		10.60	6.40
11 – JUNGLE PRINCE			4.00

$1 EXACTA 3–10 PAID $90.30 $2 QUINELLA 3–10 PAID $104.40
$1 TRIFECTA 3–10–11 PAID $475.50 $1 SUPERFECTA 3–10–11–4 PAID $1,495.60

B. c, (Feb), by Western Borders – Assets On Ice , by Seattle Dancer . Trainer Frankel Robert. Bred by CaroLin Stables Inc (Fla).

SEATTLE BORDERS prompted the early pace inside then stalked along the rail down the hill, came out into the stretch and rallied to the front under urging three deep in late stretch to prove best. STALKING TIGER pulled his way to the early lead then dueled between horses, battled along the inside down the hill, fought back in the stretch, could not match the winner late but held second. JUNGLE PRINCE cut the corner at the right hand curve then dueled four wide, battled three deep down the hill and into the stretch, fought back to a short lead outside the runner-up in midstretch and continued willingly between the top pair late. SAINT AFLEET stalked off the rail then three deep leaving the hill, was floated far wide on the dirt crossing but finished well. MATT BLANC (IRE) broke slowly, saved ground off the pace, came out into the stretch, split rivals in midstretch and put in a late bid. RUSH INTO HEAVEN between horses early, dropped back down the hill, angled in, came out in the stretch and improved position. MOULIN DE MOUGINS (IRE) bumped at the start, chased off the rail then inside down the hill and lacked the needed rally. TROIS VILLES bumped at the start, went up to duel for the lead between horses, dropped back nearing the dirt and weakened. GWAIHIR (IRE) between horses early, cut the corner at the right hand curve then chased outside, fell back leaving the hill and also weakened. DON'TSELLMESHORT stalked the pace off the rail, drifted far wide on the dirt crossing, then hopped back onto the turf and had little left. Rail on hill at zero.

Owners– 1, Gann Edmund A; 2, Davis John Milch David and Rocchio Al; 3, Burk Jack D Sciarra Joseph A Zamarripa Robert et al; 4, Waranch Ronald C; 5, Gill Michael J; 6, Wood Jason; 7, Jim Ford Inc Pearson Daron and Sweesy Jack; 8, Everest Stables Inc; 9, Kirkwood Al and Saundra S; 10, Peacock Cecil N

Trainers– 1, Frankel Robert; 2, Aguirre Paul G; 3, Garcia Juan; 4, Dollase Craig; 5, Canani Nick; 6, O'Neill Doug; 7, Cassidy James; 8, Polanco Marcelo; 9, Lewis Craig A; 10, Hendricks Dan L

Scratched– Wimplestiltskin (07Feb04 ^{3}SA ^{4}) , Teton Forest (07Feb04 ^{3}SA ^{5}) , Roi Charmant (31Jan04 ^{3}SA ^{3}) , Minister Eric (25Oct03 ^{7}SA ^{2})

$2 Daily Double (5–3) Paid $52.00 ; Daily Double Pool $41,757 .
$1 Pick Three (6–5–3) Paid $315.60 ; Pick Three Pool $71,961 .

NINTH RACE
Fair Grounds
FEBRUARY 29, 2004

1⅛ MILES. (1.48) 79TH RUNNING OF THE NEW ORLEANS HANDICAP. Grade II. Purse $500,000 FOR FOUR YEAR OLDS AND UPWARD. $500,000 Guaranteed of which $300,000 to the winner; $100,000 to second; $55,000 to third; $30,000 to fourth; $15,000 to fifth. THE OWNER OF THE WINNER TO RECEIVE A TROPHY. Closed Saturday, February 21, 2004, with 22 nominations.

Value of Race: $500,000 Winner $300,000; second $100,000; third $55,000; fourth $30,000; fifth $15,000. Mutuel Pool $1,025,017.00 Exacta Pool $504,334.00 Quinella Pool $31,431.00 Trifecta Pool $415,109.00 Superfecta Pool $127,222.00

Last Raced	Horse	M/Eqt.	A.	Wt	PP	St	¼	½	¾	Str	Fin	Jockey	Odds $1
24Jan04 ^{6}SA^{4}	Peace Rules	L	4	119	5	2	1^{2}	1^{2}	1^{1}	1^{hd}	1^{hd}	Bailey J D	3.60
18Jan04 ^{6}GP^{1}	Saint Liam	L	4	114	4	3	$2^{\frac{1}{2}}$	2^{1}	2^{1}	2^{3}	$2^{2\frac{3}{4}}$	Prado E S	5.60
7Feb04 ^{10}GP^{3}	Funny Cide	L	4	118	2	4	$3^{1\frac{1}{2}}$	$3^{\frac{1}{2}}$	$3^{1\frac{1}{2}}$	4^{5}	$3^{1\frac{1}{4}}$	Santos J A	5.40
7Feb04 ^{10}GP^{2}	Seattle Fitz-Arg	L	5	115	1	5	4^{hd}	$4^{1\frac{1}{2}}$	4^{3}	3^{hd}	$4^{5\frac{3}{4}}$	Velazquez J R	*2.60
25Oct03 ^{9}SA^{8}	Ten Most Wanted	L b	4	120	8	1	7^{2}	$7^{3\frac{1}{2}}$	6^{2}	$5^{2\frac{1}{2}}$	$5^{2\frac{3}{4}}$	Day P	2.60
17Jan04 ^{7}Hou^{1}	Sir Cherokee	L	4	115	6	7	5^{hd}	5^{hd}	8	7^{2}	$6^{2\frac{1}{2}}$	Thompson T J	11.70
1Feb04 ^{8}FG^{2}	Spanish Empire	L	4	118	3	6	6^{2}	$6^{\frac{1}{2}}$	5^{hd}	$6^{1\frac{1}{2}}$	$7^{\frac{3}{4}}$	Martin E M Jr	21.30
2Jan04 ^{9}FG^{3}	Comic Truth	L b	4	116	7	8	8	8	$7^{2\frac{1}{2}}$	8	8	Albarado R J	59.30

***–Actual Betting Favorite.**

OFF AT 4:47 Start Good . Won driving. Track fast.

TIME :23^{3}, :47, 1:10^{2}, 1:35^{2}, 1:48^{3} (:23.60, :47.06, 1:10.56, 1:35.48, 1:48.61)

$2 Mutuel Prices:				
	5 – PEACE RULES	9.20	4.60	3.60
	4 – SAINT LIAM		6.20	5.00
	2 – FUNNY CIDE			4.60

$2 EXACTA 5–4 PAID $77.80 $2 QUINELLA 4–5 PAID $44.00
$2 TRIFECTA 5–4–2 PAID $520.60 $2 SUPERFECTA 5–4–2–1 PAID $1,551.40

Ch. c, (Apr), by Jules – Hold to Fashion , by Hold Your Peace . Trainer Frankel Robert. Bred by Newchance Farm (Fla).

PEACE RULES vied outside SAINT LIAM in the early going, eased to the inside entering the first turn, set the pace until approaching the final furlong, responded when collared and headed between calls, fought back under strong handling and proved best. SAINT LIAM vied inside PEACE RULES before the first turn, eased in inside that one, switched out when that one eased to the inside, stalked the leader until the drive, bid outside PEACE RULES a furlong out, gained the lead between calls and then was out kicked late. FUNNY CIDE bumped with SPANISH EMPIRE nearing the first turn, settled off the rail while in reserve down the backstretch, moved up midway around the second turn and while no match for the top two was game for third. SEATTLE FITZ (ARG) settled along the inside, advanced around the second turn and then lacked the final kick. TEN MOST WANTED four wide early, was carried out by SIR CHEROKEE entering the first turn, recovered, moved to the inside down the backstretch, continued inside when asked but had no response. SIR CHEROKEE between foes approaching the first turn, was steered out off SAINT LIAM'S heels entering the turn carrying TEN MOST WANTED out, raced forward until the second turn and faded. SPANISH EMPIRE bumped with FUNNY CIDE entering the first turn, was unhurried just after and was no real threat. COMIC TRUTH trailed early and was no factor. FOLLOWING A STEWARDS INQUIRY INTO THE FIRST TURN AND STRETCH RUN AND A CLAIM OF FOUL BY THE RIDER OF SAINT LIAM AGAINST PEACE RULES RIDER, THE STEWARDS DEEMED NO CHANGES NECESSARY.

Owners– 1, Gann Edmund A; 2, Warren Jr Mr and Mrs William K; 3, Sackatoga Stable JKnowlton AWilliams DMahan et al; 4, West Point Thoroughbreds LLC; 5, Chisholm James Jarvis Michael Reddam J Paul et al; 6, Domino Stud of Lexington LLC; 7, Jubilee Stable Cherry Martin L and Twin Creeks Farm; 8, Buckram Oak Farm Mahmoud Fustok

Trainers– 1, Frankel Robert; 2, Dutrow Richard E Jr; 3, Tagg Barclay; 4, McLaughlin Kiaran P; 5, Dollase Wallace; 6, Tomlinson Michael A; 7, Asmussen Steven M; 8, Daly Patrick J

$2 Pick Three (5–1–5) Paid $121.80 ; Pick Three Pool $49,704 .

NINTH RACE
Fair Grounds
MARCH 6, 2004

1$\frac{1}{16}$ MILES. (1.42) 39TH RUNNING OF THE FAIR GROUNDS OAKS Grade II. Purse $300,000 FOR THREE YEAR OLD FILLIES. By subscription of $100 each; $2,000 to enter; $2,000 additional to start. $300,000 Guaranteed of which $180,000 to the winner; $60,000 to second; $33,000 to third; $18,000 to fourth; and $9,000 to fifth. Weight: 121 lbs. THE OWNER OF THE WINNER TO RECEIVE A TROPHY. Closed Friday, February 27, 2004, with 20 nominations.

Value of Race: $300,000 Winner $180,000; second $60,000; third $33,000; fourth $18,000; fifth $9,000. Mutuel Pool $341,071.00 Exacta Pool $196,785.00 Quinella Pool $13,489.00 Trifecta Pool $144,425.00 Superfecta Pool $41,896.00

Last Raced	Horse	M/Eqt.	A.	Wt	PP	St	¼	½	¾	Str	Fin	Jockey	Odds $1
29Nov03 ^{7}Aqu^{1}	Ashado	L	3	121	1	1	3^{1}	3^{1}	$3^{1\frac{1}{2}}$	$1^{2\frac{1}{2}}$	$1^{3\frac{3}{4}}$	Velasquez C	1.10
21Dec03 ^{9}Hol^{4}	Victory U. S. A.	L	3	121	5	2	2^{1}	2^{1}	$2^{\frac{1}{2}}$	2^{hd}	$2^{1\frac{1}{4}}$	Lanerie C J	3.30
14Feb04 ^{9}FG^{1}	Shadow Cast	L b	3	121	2	3	$5^{1\frac{1}{2}}$	4^{hd}	$5^{1\frac{1}{2}}$	5^{2}	$3^{\frac{1}{2}}$	Albarado R J	5.70
13Feb04 ^{9}FG^{1}	Steady Course	L	3	121	6	6	6	6	6	$3^{1\frac{1}{2}}$	$4^{1\frac{1}{2}}$	Sellers S J	2.60
14Feb04 ^{9}FG^{2}	Quick Temper	L	3	121	3	4	1^{1}	$1^{1\frac{1}{2}}$	1^{1}	4^{1}	$5^{\frac{1}{2}}$	Melancon L	19.60
8Feb04 ^{8}GG^{2}	Bending Strings	L	3	121	4	5	4^{1}	$5^{1\frac{1}{2}}$	$4^{\frac{1}{2}}$	6	6	Martin E M Jr	27.30

OFF AT 4:25 Start Good . Won driving. Track fast.

TIME :23^{4}, :47^{3}, 1:12^{1}, 1:36^{3}, 1:43 (:23.91, :47.78, 1:12.34, 1:36.61, 1:43.07)

$2 Mutuel Prices:				
	1 – ASHADO	4.20	2.60	2.20
	5 – VICTORY U. S. A.		3.40	2.40
	2 – SHADOW CAST			2.60

$2 EXACTA 1–5 PAID $13.20 $2 QUINELLA 1–5 PAID $8.40
$2 TRIFECTA 1–5–2 PAID $35.80 $2 SUPERFECTA 1–5–2–6 PAID $54.60

Dk. b or br. f, (Feb), by Saint Ballado – Goulash , by Mari's Book . Trainer Pletcher Todd A. Bred by Aaron U Jones & Marie D Jones (Ky).

ASHADO broke alertly, drifted out a bit just after the break, was reserved along the inside until midway down the backstretch, moved out three wide before the second turn, ranged up before the drive to bid three wide, surged clear approaching mid stretch and proved best while kept to the task. VICTORY U. S. A. forward while three wide early, eased in a bit around the first turn to stalk QUICK TEMPER down the backstretch, loomed up outside that one in upper stretch and while no match for the winner was game for second. SHADOW CAST steadied off ASHADO just after the break, settled along the inside until entering the drive, was asked for run in upper stretch, eased out a bit and closed willingly to get up for the show. STEADY COURSE three wide early, raced four wide early down the backstretch, eased in a bit approaching the second turn, split foes while advancing for the drive, angled out in upper stretch and then hung. QUICK TEMPER vied for the early lead, got clear around the first turn, set the pace until upper stretch, was overtaken and faltered along the rail. BENDING STRINGS between foes early, was unhurried while racing four wide down the backstretch, continued four wide around the second turn and faded once turning for home.

Owners– 1, Starlight Stb LLC P Saylor J Martin Jack Wolf; 2, Van Meter Thomas F II; 3, Farish William S Jr; 4, Overbrook Farm; 5, Stanley Mark H; 6, Gunther John D

Trainers– 1, Pletcher Todd A; 2, Baffert Bob; 3, Howard Neil J; 4, Stewart Dallas; 5, O'Callaghan Niall M; 6, Hollendorfer Jerry

$2 Pick Three (2–10–1) Paid $98.80 ; Pick Three Pool $10,937 .

EIGHTH RACE
Gulfstream
MARCH 6, 2004

1⅛ MILES. (1.46^{2}) 34TH RUNNING OF THE BONNIE MISS. Grade II. Purse $200,000 FOR FILLIES, THREE YEARS OLD. By subscription of $200 each, which shall accompany the nomination, $2,000 to pass the entry box and $2,000 additional to start, with $200,000 guaranteed. The owner of the winner to receive $120,000, $40,000 to second, $22,000 to third, $12,000 to fourth and $6,000 fifth. Supplemental nominations may be made on Thursday, March 4, 2004 at a fee of $6,000, which includes entry and start fees. Weight: 122 lbs. Non–winners of $50,000 twice at a mile or over, allowed 2 lbs.; $50,000 once at a mile or over anytime or $35,000 at any distance in 2004, 4 lbs.; $30,000 at any distance or $25,000 at a mile or over, 6 lbs. Trophy to winning Owner. Closed Wednesday, February 25,2004 with (13) nominations. Supplemental nominee: Marina deChavon.

Value of Race: $200,000 Winner $120,000; second $40,000; third $22,000; fourth $12,000; fifth $6,000. Mutuel Pool $390,303.00 Exacta Pool $231,817.00 Trifecta Pool $121,463.00 Superfecta Pool $56,140.00

Last Raced	Horse	M/Eqt.	A.	Wt	PP	St	¼	½	¾	Str	Fin	Jockey	Odds $1
7Feb04 8GP4	Last Song	L	3	118	5	5	4hd	2hd	2½	1hd	12	Prado E S	3.10
7Feb04 8GP3	Society Selection		3	120	4	4	11½	1½	1½	26	24¾	Bailey J D	0.50
7Feb04 3GP1	Rare Gift	L	3	116	3	3	31	33½	34	32½	37	Day P	3.50
7Feb04 8GP5	Marina de Chavon	L b	3	120	2	2	5	41½	42	44½	47¾	Santos J A	27.30
14Feb04 8GP4	Journey Fever		3	120	1	1	2hd	5	5	5	5	Guidry M	27.30

OFF AT 4:13 Start Good. Won driving. Track fast.

TIME :23^{2}, :47^{3}, 1:11^{3}, 1:37, 1:50^{3} (:23.54, :47.77, 1:11.64, 1:37.09, 1:50.60)

$2 Mutuel Prices:

5 – LAST SONG	8.20	2.60	2.10
4 – SOCIETY SELECTION		2.20	2.10
3 – RARE GIFT			2.10

$1 EXACTA 5–4 PAID $6.30 $1 TRIFECTA 5–4–3 PAID $11.50
$1 SUPERFECTA 5–4–3–2 PAID $23.90

B. f, (Mar), by Unbridled's Song – Queen of Spirit, by Deputy Minister. Trainer Nafzger Carl A. Bred by Katalpa Farm (Ky).

LAST SONG stalked the pace three wide, made a run to reach even terms for command outside SOCIETY SELECTION midway of the far turn, then dueled with that rival to nearing the sixteenth pole and edged away. SOCIETY SELECTION outran JOURNEY FEVER to gain the lead on the first turn, made the pace along the inside into the far turn, responded when challenged by LAST SONG, dueled for command to inside the eighth pole, then couldn't stay with the winner while clearly second best. RARE GIFT chased the pace off the rail into the far turn and tired. MARINA DE CHAVON rated off the pace after being steadied to avoid running up on rivals on the first turn, faltered in the drive. JOURNEY FEVER was through early.

Owners– 1, Buckram Oak Farm; 2, Cowan Marjorie and Irving M; 3, Bolton George Dipietro David and Honour Roger; 4, Establo Madoca; 5, Carroll Justin and Stefanie

Trainers– 1, Nafzger Carl A; 2, Jerkens H Allen; 3, Kimmel John C; 4, Catanese Joseph C III; 5, Vanier Harvey L

$1 Pick Three (3–1–5) Paid $27.80 ; Pick Three Pool $83,827 .

ELEVENTH RACE
Gulfstream
MARCH 6, 2004

7 FURLONGS. (1.20) 2ND RUNNING OF THE RICHTER SCALE BREEDERS' CUP SPRINT CHAMPIONSHIP HANDICAP. Grade II. Purse $200,000 (includes $100,000 BC – Breeders' Cup) FOR THREE YEAR OLDS AND UPWARD. By subscription of $200 each which shall accompany the nomination, $1,500 to pass the entry box and $1,500 additional to start, with $100,000 guaranteed and an additional $100,000 from the Breeders' Cup Fund for cup nominees only. The host association monies to be divided 60% to the owner of the winner; 20% to second, 11% to third, 6% to fourth and 3% to fifth. Breeders' Cup Fund monies not awarded will revert back to the fund. Trophy to winning Owner given by Breeders' Cup, Ltd. (High Weights Preferred). Closed Wednesday, February 25, 2004 with (17) nominations.

Value of Race: $200,000 Winner $120,000; second $40,000; third $22,000; fourth $12,000; fifth $6,000. Mutuel Pool $577,508.00 Exacta Pool $352,823.00 Trifecta Pool $268,883.00 Superfecta Pool $78,983.00

Last Raced	Horse	M/Eqt.	A.	Wt	PP	St	¼	½	Str	Fin	Jockey	Odds $1
28Jan04 8GP1	Lion Tamer	L	4	116	7	3	4½	31	3½	1¾	Velazquez J R	1.60
7Feb04 11GP3	Coach Jimi Lee	L	4	115	2	4	3½	4½	2hd	2½	Day P	4.90
31Jan04 9OP2	Wacky for Love	L b	4	114	4	5	2½	21	1hd	3hd	Santos J A	58.70
7Feb04 11GP4	Gygistar	L	5	117	6	2	6hd	62	52½	43½	Bailey J D	2.80
24Jan04 8GP3	Valid Video	L	4	118	1	6	7	7	7	5hd	Bravo J	2.60
7Feb04 11GP6	True Direction	L b	5	114	5	1	11½	1hd	41½	6nk	Coa E M	19.70
3Jan04 10GP6	Multiple Choice	L b	6	113	3	7	51½	51	6½	7	Chavez J F	28.00

OFF AT 5:47 Start Good. Won driving. Track fast.

TIME :22, :44^{1}, 1:08^{3}, 1:21^{2} (:22.12, :44.38, 1:08.78, 1:21.52)

$2 Mutuel Prices:

7 – LION TAMER	5.20	3.40	2.60
2 – COACH JIMI LEE		4.60	3.20
4 – WACKY FOR LOVE			7.20

$1 EXACTA 7–2 PAID $14.70 $1 TRIFECTA 7–2–4 PAID $168.00
$1 SUPERFECTA 7–2–4–6 PAID $643.80

Ch. c, (Feb), by Will's Way – Tippecanoe Creek, by Olympio. Trainer Pletcher Todd A. Bred by Paul Smith (Ky).

LION TAMER chased the pace three wide around the turn, rallied to gain a slim lead inside the eighth pole, then was fully extended to prevail. COACH JIMI LEE chased the pace along the rail, slipped through inside TRUE DIRECTION to reach even terms for command in midstretch but was outgamed to the wire. WACKY FOR LOVE chased the pace, moved to gain a slim lead leaving the turn, then gave way grudgingly in the final seventy yards. GYGISTAR reserved early, raced three wide on the turn, angled to the outside for the drive and gaining slowly at the finish. VALID VIDEO unhurried early, swung wide for the stretch run and failed to threaten. TRUE DIRECTION showed speed along the inside, responded when headed leaving the turn, then tired in the final eighth. MULTIPLE CHOICE reserved in striking position off the pace, faltered in the drive.

Owners– 1, Tabor Michael B; 2, Battaglia Lee and Divito James P; 3, Hammer Time Stable LLC; 4, Evans Edward P; 5, Fehsenfeld Mac; 6, Binn Morton and Marisol; 7, Blum Peter E

Trainers– 1, Pletcher Todd A; 2, DiVito James P; 3, Sirota Keith; 4, Hennig Mark; 5, Manning Dennis J; 6, Morales Carlos J; 7, Jerkens James A

$1 Pick Three (3–2–7) Paid $126.20 ; Pick Three Pool $57,909 .
$1 Pick Three (3–6–7) Paid $28.70 .
$2 Pick Five (6–2/6–5–2–7) Paid $4,657.60 ; Pick Five Pool $615,046 .

SEVENTH RACE
Santa Anita
MARCH 6, 2004

1 MILE. (1.33^{2}) 24TH RUNNING OF THE SAN RAFAEL. Grade II. Purse $200,000 FOR THREE-YEAR-OLDS. By subscription of $200 each to accompany the nomination or by supplementary nomination of $4,000 by time of entry. $2,000 additional to start with $200,000 guaranteed, of which $120,000 to first, $40,000 to second, $24,000 to third,$12,000 to fourth and $4,000 to fifth. *Early bird nominees to the 2004 Santa Anita Derby (Closing Date Thursday, December 11, 2003) are automatically eligible to the San Rafael Stakes with all fees waived. Weight: 121 lbs. Non-winners of $70,000 at one mile or over allowed 3 lbs.; of a race of $40,000 at any distance, 6 lbs. Starters to be named through the entry box by the closing time of entries. A trophy will be presented to the owner of the winner. Closed with 138 earlybird nominations and 10 regular nominations.

Value of Race: $200,000 Winner $120,000; second $40,000; third $24,000; fourth $12,000; fifth $4,000. Mutuel Pool $984,299.00 Exacta Pool $558,874.00 Quinella Pool $46,737.00 Trifecta Pool $549,620.00 Superfecta Pool $183,376.00

Last Raced	Horse	M/Eqt.	A.	Wt	PP	St	¼	½	¾	Str	Fin	Jockey	Odds $1
7Feb04 3SA1	Imperialism	LB b	3	118	3	9	10	10	7hd	4½	1nk	Espinoza V	7.40
20Dec03 4Hol1	Lion Heart	B	3	121	7	3	3hd	1hd	1½	11½	24½	Smith M E	1.00
7Feb04 3SA3	Consecrate	LB b	3	115	8	10	8hd	8hd	61	62½	31	Santiago Javier	44.30
18Jan04 6SA1	Quintons Gold Rush	LB	3	116	9	7	5hd	3hd	3½	31	41	Nakatani C S	4.80
7Feb04 3SA2	Hosco	LB b	3	118	6	1	1½	21½	21	2½	51½	Baze T C	20.90
29Nov03 5Hol1	Castledale-Ire	LB	3	118	5	2	72	71	51	51½	64	Flores D R	11.00
7Feb04 3SA4	Wimplestiltskin	LB b	3	115	1	4	2hd	51	92	81½	71	Valdivia J Jr	55.50
17Jan04 7SA2	Lucky Pulpit	LB bf	3	115	4	6	61	61	8½	91½	83	Desormeaux K J	6.60
23Jan04 4SA1	Spellbinder	LB b	3	116	10	8	92½	94½	10	10	9hd	Solis A	12.40
30Aug03 8Sar6	Hasslefree	LB b	3	116	2	5	41	4½	41½	7hd	10	Stevens G L	45.00

OFF AT 3:13 Start Good. Won driving. Track fast.

TIME :22^{3}, :45^{3}, 1:10, 1:23, 1:36 (:22.67, :45.71, 1:10.10, 1:23.05, 1:36.11)

$2 Mutuel Prices:

3 – IMPERIALISM	16.80	5.40	4.20
7 – LION HEART		3.00	3.00
8 – CONSECRATE			8.80

$1 EXACTA 3–7 PAID $24.60 $2 QUINELLA 3–7 PAID $17.00
$1 TRIFECTA 3–7–8 PAID $455.00 $1 SUPERFECTA 3–7–8–10 PAID $2,061.50

Gr/ro. c, (Apr), by Langfuhr – Bodhavista, by Pass the Tab. Trainer Mulhall Kristin. Bred by Farnsworth Farms (Ky).

IMPERIALISM unhurried along the inside early, came out on the second turn, circled five wide into the stretch and rallied gamely under urging to get up late. LION HEART four wide on the first turn, dueled outside then alongside a rival on the backstretch, was three deep leaving the second turn, inched clear in the stretch and just failed to hold off the winner. CONSECRATE bumped at the start, was between horses early then chased off the rail, came out on the second turn and four wide into the stretch and gained the show. QUINTONS GOLD RUSH four wide on the first turn, stalked outside, ranged up four wide leaving the second turn but lacked the needed late kick. HOSCO had good early speed three deep, angled in and dueled a bit off the rail, was between horses leaving the second turn, continued inside the runner-up and weakened. CASTLEDALE (IRE) four wide into the first turn, angled in and stalked a bit off the rail, came outside a rival into the stretch and did not rally. WIMPLESTILTSKIN broke out a bit, forced then stalked the pace inside, dropped back on the second turn and weakened. LUCKY PULPIT between horses early, chased off the rail, went four wide on the second turn and six wide into the stretch and also weakened. SPELLBINDER settled three deep on the first turn then outside a rival, went four wide on the second turn and did not rally. HASSLEFREE crowded at the start, pulled his way between horses stalking the pace, bid inside nearing the quarter pole, then dropped back and had little left for the stretch.

Owners– 1, Taub Steve; 2, Smith Derrick and Tabor Michael; 3, McIngvale James; 4, Manoogian Padua Stables & Riches; 5, Rodriguez Lorraine and Rod; 6, Lyons Frank and Knee Greg; 7, Everest Stables Inc; 8, Williams Mr and Mrs Larry D; 9, Moss Mr and Mrs Jerome S; 10, Lewis Robert B and Beverly J

Trainers– 1, Mulhall Kristin; 2, Biancone Patrick L; 3, Baffert Bob; 4, Mitchell Mike; 5, O'Neill Doug; 6, Mullins Jeff; 7, Polanco Marcelo; 8, Sise Clifford Jr; 9, Mandella Richard; 10, Lukas D Wayne

Scratched– Toasted (23Aug03 1409DEA3), Lipan (22Feb04 6SA 1)

$1 Pick Three (4–2/5–3) Paid $525.20 ; Pick Three Pool $109,883 .
$2 Daily Double (2–3) Paid $77.80 ; Daily Double Pool $47,635 .

NINTH RACE
Santa Anita
MARCH 6, 2004

1 MILE. (Turf) (1.31^{4}) 4TH RUNNING OF THE FRANK E. KILROE MILE HANDICAP. Grade II. Purse $350,000 FOR FOUR-YEAR-OLDS AND UPWARD. By subscription of $350 each to accompany the nomination or by supplementary nomination of $7,000 by 12 noon Saturday, February 28. $4,000 additional to start, with $350,000 guaranteed, of which $210,000 to first, $70,000 tosecond, $42,000 to third, $21,000 to fourth, and $7,000 to fifth. Weights Saturday, February 28. Starters to be named through the entry box by the closing time of entries. High weights preferred. A trophy will be presented to the owner of the winner. Closed with 24 nominations.

Value of Race: $350,000 Winner $210,000; second $70,000; third $42,000; fourth $21,000; fifth $7,000. Mutuel Pool $903,126.00 Exacta Pool $487,633.00 Quinella Pool $44,625.00 Trifecta Pool $457,822.00 Superfecta Pool $168,130.00

Last Raced	Horse	M/Eqt.	A.	Wt	PP	St	¼	½	¾	Str	Fin	Jockey	Odds $1
19Jan04 ^{8}SA^{1}	Sweet Return-GB	LB	4	119	14	10	7^{1}	7^{1}	7^{1}	2^{hd}	$1^{\frac{1}{2}}$	Stevens G L	9.80
11Feb04 ^{7}SA^{1}	Singletary	LB	4	117	5	6	$6^{2\frac{1}{2}}$	6^{3}	5^{hd}	$3^{\frac{1}{2}}$	2^{2}	Valdivia J Jr	6.90
11Feb04 ^{7}SA^{2}	Inesperado-FR	LB	5	116	3	7	8^{1}	9^{hd}	$9^{1\frac{1}{2}}$	7^{1}	$3^{\frac{1}{2}}$	Desormeaux K J	5.80
30Nov03 ^{10}Tok^{17}	Sarafan	LB	7	119	9	12	12^{2}	$12^{2\frac{1}{2}}$	10^{2}	$8^{\frac{1}{2}}$	4^{nk}	Espinoza V	9.40
11Feb04 ^{7}SA^{7}	Designed for Luck	LB b	7	118	11	5	5^{1}	$5^{\frac{1}{2}}$	6^{hd}	1^{hd}	5no	Baze T C	9.10
7Feb04 ^{9}SA^{3}	Buckland Manor	LB	4	116	4	2	$2^{\frac{1}{2}}$	$2^{\frac{1}{2}}$	$3^{\frac{1}{2}}$	4^{hd}	$6^{\frac{1}{2}}$	Nakatani C S	3.30
11Feb04 ^{7}SA^{3}	Apache Wings	LB	6	116	2	3	4^{2}	4^{2}	2^{hd}	$5^{1\frac{1}{2}}$	$7^{\frac{1}{2}}$	Puglisi I	34.60
15Feb04 ^{7}SA^{4}	NeedwoodBlde-GB	LB	6	113	7	9	11^{1}	$11^{1\frac{1}{2}}$	$13^{1\frac{1}{2}}$	10^{1}	8no	Santiago Javier	27.60
11Feb04 ^{7}SA^{4}	Statement	LB	6	116	10	11	$10^{2\frac{1}{2}}$	$8^{\frac{1}{2}}$	$8^{1\frac{1}{2}}$	$9^{1\frac{1}{2}}$	9^{2}	Flores D R	32.60
7Feb04 ^{7}TuP^{1}	Irish Warrior	LB	6	118	1	8	13^{3}	13^{hd}	14	13^{1}	10no	Solis A	4.30
11Feb04 ^{7}SA^{5}	Geronimo-Chi	LB b	5	117	6	4	3^{1}	3^{hd}	4^{1}	11^{1}	$11^{\frac{1}{2}}$	Saint-Martin E	45.10
22Jan04 ^{7}SA^{1}	Golden Dragon-GB	LB b	6	113	13	13	14	14	11^{hd}	12^{hd}	12no	Ramsammy E	14.20
7Feb04 ^{7}GG^{1}	Wixoe Express-Ire	LB f	5	114	8	14	9^{hd}	$10^{3\frac{1}{2}}$	$12^{\frac{1}{2}}$	14	13^{2}	Garcia M S	56.90
7Feb04 ^{7}TuP^{3}	Rock N Rosh	LB	4	112	12	1	$12^{\frac{1}{2}}$	1^{5}	1^{3}	6^{hd}	14	Sorenson D	87.20

OFF AT 4:17 Start Good For All But WIXOE EXPRESS (IRE). Won driving. Course firm.

TIME :22^{4}, :45^{2}, 1:09^{4}, 1:22, 1:33^{4} (:22.84, :45.55, 1:09.84, 1:22.10, 1:33.87)

$2 Mutuel Prices:			
14 – SWEET RETURN–GB	21.60	10.00	6.20
5 – SINGLETARY		9.00	5.80
3 – INESPERADO–FR			5.20

$1 EXACTA 14–5 PAID $114.70 $2 QUINELLA 5–14 PAID $113.80

$1 TRIFECTA 14–5–3 PAID $729.40 $1 SUPERFECTA 14–5–3–9 PAID $5,591.70

Ch. c, (Mar), by Elmaamul – Sweet Revival-GB , by Claude Monet . Trainer McAnally Ronald. Bred by C S Tateson (GB).

SWEET RETURN (GB) angled in and chased outside, swung five wide into the stretch, rallied to a short lead outside foes past midstretch and gamely prevailed under urging. SINGLETARY between horses early, chased a bit off the rail on the backstretch and toward the inside on the second turn, waited off heels on that bend, swung four wide into the stretch, bid between horses in midstretch, then continued gamely to the wire inside the winner. INESPERADO (FR) saved ground off the pace, came off the rail on the second turn and into the stretch, was in behind foes in midstretch, came out and just got third between horses late. SARAFAN unhurried outside a rival then off the rail, came out into the stretch and again in upper stretch and found his best stride late. DESIGNED FOR LUCK four wide into the first turn, angled in and chased off the rail, moved up outside on the second turn and four wide into the stretch, gained a short lead between foes nearing midstretch and was outfinished. BUCKLAND MANOR stalked between horses then outside a rival, was between horses again leaving the second turn and lacked the needed response. APACHE WINGS stalked the leader along the inside to the stretch and weakened. NEEDWOOD BLADE (GB) angled in and saved ground off the pace, came out leaving the second turn and five wide into the stretch and could not offer the needed late kick. STATEMENT settled outside a rival chasing the leaders, continued inside on the second turn and did not rally. IRISH WARRIOR unhurried inside then off the rail on the backstretch, swung five wide into the stretch and was not a threat. GERONIMO (CHI) stalked three deep then outside a rival, continued three wide leaving the second turn and weakened. GOLDEN DRAGON (GB) angled in and saved ground off the pace, remained toward the inside in the stretch and was not a factor. WIXOE EXPRESS (IRE) hopped in the air at the start, chased three deep, came four wide into the stretch and weakened. ROCK N ROSH sped to the early lead and angled in, set the pace inside, opened up on the backstretch, continued inside in the stretch and also weakened.

Owners– 1, Red Oak Stable; 2, Little Red Feather Racing; 3, 3 Plus U Stable; 4, Tanaka Gary A; 5, Wilson David W and Holly F; 6, McCaffery Trudy and Toffan John A; 7, Henton Hitbound Stable and Turrell; 8, Vreeland James R; 9, Bienstock Papiano Winner Et Al; 10, Coleman John Dasaro George Thompson James et al; 11, Buster Jr William C Hays and Surfside Equine et al; 12, Cobra Farm Inc; 13, Pottinger Piers; 14, Jones Kimberly M and Schiappa Sonja

Trainers– 1, McAnally Ronald; 2, Chatlos Donald Jr; 3, Frankel Robert; 4, Drysdale Neil; 5, Cerin Vladimir; 6, Gonzalez J Paco; 7, Breuer Denise E; 8, Walsh Kathy; 9, Mulhall Kristin; 10, Dollase Wallace; 11, Machowsky Michael; 12, Puype Mike; 13, Drysdale Neil; 14, Monteleone Frank J

$1 Pick Three (3–10–14) Paid $604.70 ; Pick Three Pool $168,190 .
$2 Daily Double (10–14) Paid $134.00 ; Daily Double Pool $54,757 .

TENTH RACE
Santa Anita
MARCH 6, 2004

$1\frac{1}{4}$ MILES. (1.57^{4}) 67TH RUNNING OF THE SANTA ANITA HANDICAP. Grade I. Purse $1,000,000 FOR FOUR-YEAR-OLDS AND UPWARD. By subscription of $300 each to accompany the nomination or by supplementary nomination of $20,000 by 12 noon Saturday, February 28. $2,500 to pass the entry box and $7,500 to start with $1,000,000 guaranteed, of which $600,000 to first, $200,000 to second, $120,000 to third, $60,00 to fourth and $20,000 to fifth. Weights Saturday, February 28. Starters to be named through the entry box by the closing time of entries. The field will be limited to 14 starters. Preference shall be given to the high weights based upon the weight assignments, adjusted for the sex allowance. Total earnings in 2003–2004 will be used in determining the preference of horses with equally assigned weights. No horse shall be assigned more than 126 lbs.Trophies will be presented to the winning owner, breeder, trainer, and jockey. Closed with 21 nominations.

Value of Race: $1,000,000 Winner $600,000; second $200,000; third $120,000; fourth $60,000; fifth $20,000. Mutuel Pool $1,031,982.00 Exacta Pool $493,934.00 Quinella Pool $46,567.00 Trifecta Pool $512,401.00 Superfecta Pool $190,653.00

Last Raced	Horse	M/Eqt.	A.	Wt	PP	¼	½	¾	1	Str	Fin	Jockey	Odds $1
24Jan04 ^{6}SA^{1}	Southern Image	LB	4	118	2	3^{1}	$4\frac{1}{2}$	$3\frac{1}{2}$	$1^{1\frac{1}{2}}$	$1^{1\frac{1}{2}}$	$1^{1\frac{1}{4}}$	Espinoza V	1.00
25Jan04 ^{8}SA^{1}	Island Fashion	LB b	4	115	4	$5\frac{1}{2}$	5^{2}	5^{2}	4^{hd}	$2\frac{1}{2}$	$2^{2\frac{1}{4}}$	Desormeaux K J	6.70
7Feb04 ^{9}SA^{7}	Saint Buddy	LB b	4	111	1	6^{1}	$6^{1\frac{1}{2}}$	$6^{2\frac{1}{2}}$	$5^{1\frac{1}{2}}$	$3^{2\frac{1}{2}}$	3^{4}	Baze T C	13.50
1Feb04 ^{8}FG^{1}	Olmodavor	LB	5	119	7	8	7^{2}	7^{hd}	7^{4}	6^{1}	4^{2}	Smith M E	4.60
7Feb04 ^{9}SA^{8}	Toccet	LB b	4	113	6	1^{hd}	1^{hd}	1^{hd}	6^{2}	7^{6}	5^{3}	Ramsammy E	23.50
7Feb04 ^{9}SA^{10}	Buddy Gil	LB	4	117	8	$4\frac{1}{2}$	3^{hd}	4^{1}	3^{hd}	$4\frac{1}{2}$	$6^{1\frac{1}{2}}$	Stevens G L	6.70
31Jan04 ^{6}SA^{1}	Royal Place	LB	4	114	3	2^{hd}	2^{1}	2^{hd}	$2\frac{1}{2}$	5^{hd}	7^{6}	Valdivia J Jr	43.50
31Jan04 ^{8}SA^{2}	Star Cross-Arg	LB b	7	116	5	7^{1}	8	8	8	8	8	Nakatani C S	6.90

OFF AT 4:48 Start Good . Won driving. Track fast.

TIME :23, :46^{1}, 1:10^{1}, 1:35^{1}, 2:01^{3} (:23.04, :46.30, 1:10.34, 1:35.37, 2:01.64)

$2 Mutuel Prices:			
2 – SOUTHERN IMAGE	4.00	3.00	2.40
4 – ISLAND FASHION		4.80	3.60
1 – SAINT BUDDY			4.80

$1 EXACTA 2–4 PAID $12.00 $2 QUINELLA 2–4 PAID $16.60
$1 TRIFECTA 2–4–1 PAID $94.90 $1 SUPERFECTA 2–4–1–8 PAID $209.30

Dk. b or br. c, (Apr), by Halo's Image — Pleasant Dixie , by Dixieland Band . Trainer Machowsky Michael. Bred by Arthur I Appleton (Fla).

SOUTHERN IMAGE forced or stalked the pace inside, took the lead into the second turn, inched away leaving that turn and held on gamely under urging. ISLAND FASHION stalked the pace between rivals, bid four wide leaving the second turn and three deep into the stretch and continued willingly but could not catch the winner. SAINT BUDDY chased inside then came off the rail into the backstretch, ranged up five wide leaving the second turn and four wide into the stretch and bested the others. OLMODAVOR settled off the rail chasing the pace, came out into the stretch and lacked the needed rally. TOCCET had good early speed four wide then set a pressured pace three deep, dropped back on the second turn and weakened. BUDDY GIL close up stalking the pace three deep, bid four wide into the second turn, continued between horses leaving that turn, angled in outside a rival into the stretch and also weakened. ROYAL PLACE had good early speed and dueled between horses or just off the rail, was between foes again into the second turn, angled in behind the winner leaving that turn and had little left for the stretch. STAR CROSS (ARG) allowed to settle off the rail, chased outside on the backstretch, continued off the inside on the second turn, came wide into the stretch and was not a factor.

Owners– 1, Blahut Stables LLC or Kagele Bros or Tepper Et Al; 2, Everest Stables Inc; 3, Fulton Stan E; 4, Wertheimer and Frere; 5, Borislow Daniel M; 6, Billingsley Creek Ranch Desperado Stables Inc and Merrill Stables et al; 7, Sangara K K; 8, E A Ranches

Trainers– 1, Machowsky Michael; 2, Polanco Marcelo; 3, Becerra Rafael; 4, Mandella Richard; 5, Scanlan John F; 6, Mullins Jeff; 7, Becerra Rafael; 8, Vienna Darrell

Scratched– Pleasantly Perfect (31Jan04 ^{8}SA ^{1})

$1 Pick Three (10–14–2/5) Paid $122.10 ; Pick Three Pool $139,062 .
$2 Daily Double (14–2) Paid $70.80 ; Daily Double Pool $81,195 .
$1 Place Pick All (10–OF–10) Paid $6,757.10 ; Place Pick All Pool $33,862 .

NINTH RACE
Fair Grounds
MARCH 7, 2004

$1\frac{1}{16}$ MILES. (1.42) 92ND RUNNING OF THE LOUISIANA DERBY. Grade II. Purse $600,000 FOR THREE YEAR OLDS. The guaranteed purse will be divided as follows: $360,000 to first; $120,000 to second; $66,000 to third; $36,000 to fourth; $18,000 to fifth. Weight: Colts and Geldings, 122 lbs.; Fillies, 117 lbs. THE OWNER OF THE WINNER TO RECEIVE A TROPHY. Closed Saturday, February 28, 2004, with 8 nominations and 105 Early Bird nominations.

Value of Race: $600,000 Winner $360,000; second $120,000; third $66,000; fourth $36,000; fifth $18,000. Mutuel Pool $882,177.00 Exacta Pool $514,565.00 Quinella Pool $35,284.00 Trifecta Pool $440,787.00 Superfecta Pool $139,507.00

Last Raced	Horse	M/Eqt.	A.	Wt	PP	St	¼	½	¾	Str	Fin	Jockey	Odds $1
8Feb04 ^{1}SA^{1}	Wimbledon	L	3	122	3	9	8^{1}	7^{hd}	$6^{\frac{1}{2}}$	2^{1}	$1^{2\frac{1}{4}}$	Santiago Javier	7.20
8Feb04 ^{8}SA^{2}	Borrego	L b	3	122	1	2	10^{3}	10^{2}	$9^{2\frac{1}{2}}$	4^{1}	2^{hd}	Espinoza V	5.50
8Feb04 ^{9}GP^{1}	Pollard's Vision	L	3	122	7	4	4^{2}	$4^{1\frac{1}{2}}$	3^{1}	$1^{1\frac{1}{2}}$	$3^{\frac{3}{4}}$	Velazquez J R	6.50
15Feb04 ^{6}FG^{1}	Breakaway	L b	3	122	2	1	1^{1}	1^{1}	1^{1}	$6^{2\frac{1}{2}}$	$4^{5\frac{1}{4}}$	Borel C H	a- 2.30
24Jan04 ^{9}FG^{1}	Fire Slam	L	3	122	10	6	$2^{\frac{1}{2}}$	2^{1}	$2^{2\frac{1}{2}}$	$3^{\frac{1}{2}}$	5^{nk}	Sellers S J	3.20
15Nov03 ^{10}Crc^{3}	Stolen Time	L b	3	122	5	8	6^{3}	$6^{2\frac{1}{2}}$	$5^{1\frac{1}{2}}$	5^{1}	$6^{\frac{3}{4}}$	Velasquez C	16.50
24Jan04 ^{9}FG^{2}	Shadowland	L	3	122	6	3	$5^{\frac{1}{2}}$	5^{1}	4^{1}	$9^{3\frac{1}{2}}$	$7^{1\frac{1}{2}}$	Day P	20.40
15Feb04 ^{9}FG^{1}	Gradepoint	L	3	122	9	11	9^{2}	9^{1}	8^{1}	7^{2}	8^{4}	Albarado R J	a- 2.30
14Feb04 ^{9}GP^{2}	Shaniko	L	3	122	4	10	7^{2}	8^{3}	$7^{\frac{1}{2}}$	$8^{\frac{1}{2}}$	$9^{14\frac{1}{4}}$	Bailey J D	10.40
5Feb04 ^{5}Aqu^{1}	Indian War Dance	L b	3	122	8	5	$1^{\frac{1}{2}}$	1^{1}	1^{hd}	10^{8}	$10^{15\frac{1}{2}}$	Prado E S	17.40
15Feb04 ^{9}FG^{3}	Nightlifeatbigblue	L	3	122	11	7	$3^{3\frac{1}{2}}$	3^{3}	10^{1}	11	11	Martin E M Jr	58.60

a-Coupled: Breakaway and Gradepoint.

OFF AT 4:21 Start Good. Won driving. Track fast.

TIME :22^{2}, :45^{1}, 1:10^{3}, 1:36^{1}, 1:42^{3} (:22.48, :45.27, 1:10.65, 1:36.29, 1:42.71)

$2 Mutuel Prices:

3 – WIMBLEDON	16.40	8.40	6.60
2 – BORREGO		6.00	5.40
7 – POLLARD'S VISION			7.20

$2 EXACTA 3–2 PAID $110.00 $2 QUINELLA 2–3 PAID $64.40
$2 TRIFECTA 3–2–7 PAID $680.80 $2 SUPERFECTA 3–2–7–1 PAID $1,919.80

Gr/ro. c, (Feb), by Wild Rush – Strawberry Clover, by Darn That Alarm. Trainer Baffert Bob. Bred by Sabine Stables (Ky).

WIMBLEDON settled along the inside until before the second turn, advanced nearing the drive, angled out four wide turning for home, rallied to bid outside POLLARD'S VISION inside the furlong marker, gained the edge and won going away. BORREGO back early, settled off the rail down the backstretch, was asked for run entering the second turn, circled foes before the drive, swung out eight wide for the drive, closed willingly and got up for second. POLLARD'S VISION settled off the early leaders, was put to pressure midway around the second turn, bid three wide for the drive, took over outside FIRE SLAM in upper stretch, was challenged inside the furlong grounds and weakened late after being headed. BREAKAWAY trailed until the second turn, advanced from the inside approaching the drive, angled out around foes in upper stretch, dropped back to the inside for the drive then lacked the needed finish. FIRE SLAM forced the pace outside INDIAN WAR DANCE from early on, ranged up outside that one entering the second turn, gained the lead between calls just before the drive, got headed by POLLARED'S VISION and faltered once reaching mid stretch. STOLEN TIME reserved off the rail, rallied mid track and lacked a late kick. SHADOWLAND moved to the rail before the first turn, advanced approaching the drive, lacked room inside INDIAN WAR DANCE entering the drive and then lacked a response when clear. GRADEPOINT settled off the rail, was asked for run entering the second turn, split foes approaching the drive, angled out and was no real threat. SHANIKO devoid speed, raced wide down the backstretch and around the second turn while outrun. INDIAN WAR DANCE angled quickly to the rail to set the pace, was headed nearing the drive and stopped. NIGHTLIFEATBIGBLUE prompted the pace three wide until the second turn and stopped abruptly.

Owners– 1, McIngvale James; 2, Ralls & Foster LLC BScott JKelly et al R Ralls & D Foster; 3, Edgewood Farm; 4, Farish William S; 5, Fulton Stan E; 6, Estate of Jeanne G Vance; 7, Team Valor Stables LLC; 8, William S Farish & Mt Brilliant Stable Llc H Greg Goodman; 9, Jones Aaron U and Marie D; 10, Sanford Goldfarb William Vidro Ira Davis; 11, Gray Mr and Mrs Fletcher

Trainers– 1, Baffert Bob; 2, Greely C Beau; 3, Pletcher Todd A; 4, Howard Neil J; 5, Carroll David; 6, Mott William I; 7, Nicks Ralph E; 8, Howard Neil J; 9, Pletcher Todd A; 10, Dutrow Richard E Jr; 11, Barnett Bobby C

$2 Pick Three (8–4–3) Paid $635.80; Pick Three Pool $32,218.

EIGHTH RACE
Santa Anita
MARCH 7, 2004

7 FURLONGS. (1.20) 66TH RUNNING OF THE SAN CARLOS HANDICAP. Grade II. Purse $150,000 FOR FOUR-YEAR-OLDS AND UPWARD. By subscription of $150 each to accompany the nomination or by supplementary nomination of $3,000 by Sunday, February 29. $1,500 additional to start, with $150,000 guaranteed, of which $90,000 to first, $30,000 to second, $18,000 to third, $9,000 to fourth and $3,000 to fifth. Weights Tuesday, March 2. Starters to be named through the entry box by the closing time of entries. A trophy will be presented to the owner of the winner. Closed with 17 Nominations.

Value of Race: $150,000 Winner $90,000; second $30,000; third $18,000; fourth $9,000; fifth $3,000. Mutuel Pool $629,912.00 Exacta Pool $370,867.00 Quinella Pool $37,085.00 Trifecta Pool $381,286.00 Superfecta Pool $153,799.00

Last Raced	Horse	M/Eqt.	A.	Wt	PP	St	¼	½	Str	Fin	Jockey	Odds $1
25Jan04 7SA1	Pico Central-Brz	LB	5	116	5	2	1½	1½	12½	12	Flores D R	43.20
5Jly03 8Hol2	Publication	LB b	5	116	10	9	10	10	7½	22	Desormeaux K J	5.00
16Feb04 7SA2	Pohave	LB	6	112	7	1	51	51	3½	31	Court J K	15.20
17Aug03 8Dmr6	Kela	LB b	6	117	6	8	81½	8hd	8hd	41	Nakatani C S	27.60
22Feb04 5SA2	Eye of the Tiger	LB	4	116	8	10	93½	94	92½	5½	Stevens G L	12.90
24Jan04 9SA1	Casas Caballo	LB	4	115	2	4	21	3½	4hd	6nk	Valdivia J Jr	10.00
1Feb04 7SA1	Bluesthestandard	LB	7	119	1	7	64	64	51½	72½	Smith M E	1.60
1Feb04 7SA5	Captain Squire	LB	5	116	3	5	3½	2hd	2hd	8hd	Solis A	6.20
25Oct03 11SA5	Taste of Paradise	LB	5	113	9	3	72	71½	6hd	93	Ruis M	62.70
1Feb04 7SA2	Marino Marini	LB	4	115	4	6	4½	4½	10	10	Baze T C	4.00

OFF AT 4:11 Start Good. Won driving. Track fast.

TIME :22^{1}, :44, 1:08^{2}, 1:21 (:22.24, :44.06, 1:08.58, 1:21.16)

$2 Mutuel Prices:				
	6 – PICO CENTRAL–BRZ	88.40	29.60	11.80
	12 – PUBLICATION		6.40	4.80
	9 – POHAVE			7.00

$1 EXACTA 6–12 PAID $332.90 $2 QUINELLA 6–12 PAID $239.60
$1 TRIFECTA 6–12–9 PAID $4,410.70 $1 SUPERFECTA 6–12–9–8 PAID $61,381.10

Dk. b or br. h, (Oct), by Spend a Buck – Sheila Purple, by Purple Mountain. Trainer Lobo Paulo H. Bred by Haras Fronteira PAP (Brz).

PICO CENTRAL (BRZ) had good early speed and dueled outside a rival then between horses into the turn, slipped away a bit off the rail leaving the bend, kicked clear in the stretch and held under urging. PUBLICATION unhurried off the rail on the backstretch, angled in for the turn, came out into the stretch, swung out from behind rivals in upper stretch and closed fast. POHAVE stalked the pace four wide then bid five wide into the turn, had the rider lose the whip five wide into the stretch but held the show. KELA settled a bit off the rail, came out on the turn, split horses into the stretch, waited briefly then went between foes in mid and deep stretch and was outkicked. EYE OF THE TIGER unhurried off the rail, angled in some on the backstretch, came three deep into the stretch and improved position. CASAS CABALLO prompted the pace inside on the backstretch and into the turn, stalked along the rail on the bend and weakened. BLUESTHESTANDARD chased inside, came out leaving the turn, was between horses in midstretch and lacked the needed response. CAPTAIN SQUIRE stalked the early pace off the rail then bid between horses three deep leaving the backstretch and into the turn, came three wide into the stretch and weakened. TASTE OF PARADISE settled off the rail, angled in leaving the backstretch, rode the rail on the turn, lacked room off heels into the stretch and could not summon the necessary response. MARINO MARINI stalked between horses then bid four wide between foes into the turn, continued four wide into the stretch and weakened.

Owners– 1, Garlipp Christina; 2, Mercedes Stables LLC; 3, Kagele Brothers Inc Leatherman Ty and Leib Mark A; 4, Manoogian Jay; 5, Gunther John D; 6, House Michael; 7, Sengara Jeffrey; 8, Bone Robert D and Diener Jeffrey S; 9, Bloom David B; 10, Rancho San Miguel

Trainers– 1, Lobo Paulo H; 2, Cerin Vladimir; 3, O'Neill Doug; 4, Mitchell Mike; 5, Hollendorfer Jerry; 6, Mitchell Mike; 7, West Ted H; 8, Mullins Jeff; 9, Robbins Jay M; 10, O'Neill Doug

Scratched– Amerindio (ARG) (02Jan04 2SA 1), Question (ARG) (11Oct03 8SI 1)

$2 Daily Double (8–6) Paid $491.40; Daily Double Pool $45,868.
$1 Pick Three (3–8–6) Paid $1,458.20; Pick Three Pool $91,346.

EIGHTH RACE
Aqueduct
MARCH 13, 2004

7 FURLONGS. (1.20) 111TH RUNNING OF THE TOBOGGAN HANDICAP. Grade III. Purse $100,000 (Up To $19400 NYSBFOA)FOR THREE YEAR OLDS AND UPWARD. By subscription of $100 each, which should accompany the nomination; $500 to pass the entry box; $500 to start, with $100,000 added. The added money and all fees to be divided 60% to the winner, 20% tosecond, 10% to third, 5% to fourth, 3% to fifth and 2% divided equally among the remaining finishers. A trophy will be presented to the winning owner. Closed Saturday, February 28, 2004 with 22 nominations.

Value of Race: $112,200 Winner $67,320; second $22,440; third $11,220; fourth $5,610; fifth $3,366; sixth $449; seventh $449; eighth $449; ninth $449; tenth $448. Mutuel Pool $651,562.00 Exacta Pool $516,355.00 Trifecta Pool $381,815.00

Last Raced	Horse	M/Eqt.	A.	Wt	PP	St	¼	½	Str	Fin	Jockey	Odds $1
16Feb04 9Lrl1	Well Fancied	L	6	118	7	4	2½	2½	1hd	12	Coa E M	1.50
16Feb04 9Lrl3	Gators N Bears	L bf	4	115	8	2	31	31½	31½	2nk	Lopez C C	11.80
24Jan04 8Aqu2	Don Six	L	4	113	2	7	12½	12½	2½	31¾	Bridgmohan S X	12.80
14Feb04 4Aqu1	Black Silk-GB	L f	8	112	9	3	5hd	5hd	4½	4¾	Arroyo N Jr	50.75
16Feb04 9Lrl4	Peeping Tom	L bf	7	117	3	9	10	8½	7½	5nk	Smith A E	7.10
13Feb04 8Aqu1	New York Hero	L bf	4	114	10	1	4hd	41½	6½	6no	Gryder A T	5.40
16Feb04 9Lrl2	Unforgettable Max	L b	4	115	6	8	7hd	6hd	910	7nk	Luzzi M J	4.10
15Feb04 8Aqu1	Papua	L bf	5	114	1	10	91	10	8hd	8½	Fragoso P	14.40
25Feb04 5Aqu3	Super Fuse	L b	4	114	4	5	62½	72	5½	98½	Dunkelberger T L	45.50
14Feb04 7GP2	Roaring Fever	L b	4	113	5	6	8½	9½	10	10	Pimentel J	24.50

OFF AT 4:17 Start Good. Won driving. Track fast.

TIME :22^{2}, :45, 1:09^{2}, 1:22 (:22.52, :45.17, 1:09.43, 1:22.06)

$2 Mutuel Prices:				
	7 – WELL FANCIED	5.00	3.30	3.10
	8 – GATORS N BEARS		8.40	4.90
	2 – DON SIX			6.20

$2 EXACTA 7–8 PAID $46.00 $2 TRIFECTA 7–8–2 PAID $366.00

B. g, (Mar), by Prosper Fager – Patty's Fancy Tric, by Tricky Creek. Trainer Dutrow Richard E Jr. Bred by Seymour Cohn (NY).

WELL FANCIED raced with the pace from the outside while in hand, responded when roused and drew clear under a drive. GATORS N BEARS chased the pace while three wide and finished gamely outside. DON SIX soon opened a clear lead, set the pace and weakened along the inside in the final furlong. BLACK SILK (GB) raced close up while between rivals and finished well. PEEPING TOM was outrun early, raced wide on the turn, altered course to the inside in upper stretch and lacked a rally. NEW YORK HERO chased the pace while three wide and had no response when roused. UNFORGETTABLE MAX raced three wide and had no response when roused. PAPUA was outrun early, raced inside and had no rally. SUPER FUSE stumbled at the start, raced inside and tired in the stretch. ROARING FEVER was outrun early, raced between rivals and tired.

Owners– 1, Goldfarb Sanford J Hoffman Stewart Fleisig Jonathan; 2, Nechamkin II Leo S; 3, Generazio Patricia A; 4, Fustok Salah M; 5, Flatbird Stable; 6, Paraneck Stable; 7, Dweck Raymond; 8, Schwartz Barry K; 9, Tom Marski; 10, Evans Edward P

Trainers– 1, Dutrow Richard E Jr; 2, Nechamkin Leo S II; 3, Generazio Frank Jr; 4, LaFavers Laurie; 5, Reynolds Patrick L; 6, Pedersen Jennifer; 7, Perkins Ben W Jr; 8, Hushion Michael E; 9, Ciardullo Richard Jr; 10, Hennig Mark

SEVENTH RACE
Golden Gate
MARCH 13, 2004

1 1/16 MILES. (1.39^{2}) 25TH RUNNING OF THE EL CAMINO REAL DERBY. Grade III. Purse $200,000 FOR THREE-YEAR-OLDS. By subscription of $200 each to accompany the nomination or by supplementary nominaiton of $4,000 by time of entry. $1,000 to pass the entry box and $1,000 additional to start with $200,000 Guaranteed, of which $110,000 to the winner,$40,000 to second, $30,000 to third, $15,000 to fourth and $5,000 to fifth. Weight, 120 lbs. Non-winners of $75,000 at one mile or over allowed 3 lbs; $50,000 allowed 5 lbs. (Maiden, claiming and starter races not considered). A trophy will be presentedto the owner of the winner. High weights preferred. Closed Thursday, March 4, 2004 with 33 nominations.

Value of Race: $200,000 Winner $110,000; second $35,000; second $35,000; fourth $15,000; fifth $5,000. Mutuel Pool $456,554.00 Exacta Pool $241,718.00 Quinella Pool $21,260.00 Trifecta Pool $232,053.00 Superfecta Pool $68,937.00

Last Raced	Horse	M/Eqt.	A.	Wt	PP	St	¼	½	¾	Str	Fin	Jockey	Odds $1
8Feb04 ^{8}GG^{4}	Kilgowan	LB b	3	116	4	5	6^{1}	7^{hd}	6^{1}	6½	1½	Rollins C J	26.90
21Feb04 ^{2}SA^{2}	DH Capitano	LB b	3	116	2	4	2^{2½}	1^{hd}	2^{1}	1½	2	Valdivia J Jr	6.30
28Feb04 ^{8}SA^{1}	DH Seattle Borders	LB	3	117	10	2	3^{hd}	3^{1}	3^{1½}	3^{2}	2^{hd}	Desormeaux K J	1.90
8Feb04 ^{8}GG^{1}	O. K. Mikie	LB b	3	116	6	10	10	9^{2}	8½	4½	4^{1½}	Lopez A D	9.20
4Jan04 ^{6}SA^{3}	Wildwood Flower	LB	3	115	5	1	1½	2^{1}	1^{hd}	2^{1}	5^{1}	Radke K	8.10
18Jan04 ^{5}SA^{8}	Totally Platinum	LB b	3	117	3	8	4^{hd}	5^{2½}	5^{1½}	5½	6^{hd}	Steiner J J	18.40
10Jan04 ^{3}GG^{1}	Skipaslew	LB b	3	120	7	6	5^{2}	4^{hd}	4^{hd}	7^{4}	7^{7}	Saint-Martin E	2.10
22Feb04 ^{6}SA^{1}	Lipan	LB	3	116	9	3	7^{1}	6^{hd}	9^{8}	8^{1}	8^{1}	Baze R A	20.30
21Feb04 ^{2}GG^{4}	Tacky	LB	3	116	1	9	9^{2½}	10	10	10	9^{1}	Rodriguez M	78.70
21Feb04 ^{2}GG^{1}	Trevanian	LB	3	116	8	7	8^{4}	8^{6}	7^{1}	9^{1}	10	Carr D	28.40

DH-Dead Heat.

OFF AT 4:01 Start Good. Won driving. Track fast.
TIME :23, :46^{4}, 1:11, 1:37, 1:43^{4} (:23.13, :46.91, 1:11.08, 1:37.06, 1:43.87)

$2 Mutuel Prices:

4 – KILGOWAN	55.80	15.20	9.20
2 – DH CAPITANO		4.00	4.60
10 – DH SEATTLE BORDERS		3.00	3.80

$1 EXACTA 4–10 PAID $61.70 $1 EXACTA 4–2 PAID $93.30
$2 QUINELLA 2–4 PAID $75.60 $2 QUINELLA 4–10 PAID $43.00
$1 TRIFECTA 4–10–2 PAID $753.00 $1 TRIFECTA 4–2–10 PAID $899.00
$1 SUPERFECTA 4–10–2–6 PAID $2,751.30
$1 SUPERFECTA 4–2–10–6 PAID $3,438.90

Gr/ro. c, (Mar), by Smoke Glacken – Port Roberto, by Dynaformer. Trainer Arterburn Lonnie. Bred by Ann Marie Farm (Ky).

KILGOWAN broke cleanly but was permitted to lag early while racing just off the rail, moved a bit closer three wide on the second turn, responded in the upper stretch but was bumped off stride nearing the furlong pole by SKIPASLEW, recovered and came back on gamely from the extreme outside and was up in the late stages. CAPITANO alternated on the lead outside WILDWOOD FLOWER throughout and continued gamely in the lane to just miss. SEATTLE BORDERS stalked the dueling leaders three wide throughout and finished willingly to just miss. O. K. MIKIE broke a bit slow and was permitted to lag far back to the second turn, quickly reached contention two wide into the lane, shifted outside SEATTLE BORDERS at the furlong pole and continue to close from between horses late. WILDWOOD FLOWER broke alertly to take command into the first turn, alternated on the lead with CAPITANO to mid stretch and gradually slackened. TOTALLY PLATINUM stalked the leaders from the rail to the stretch but lacked the needed response. SKIPASLEW was permitted to settle early three wide to the backstretch, remained out on the second turn, drifted out nearing the furlong pole and bumped solidly with the winner, recovered but lacked the needed response. LIPAN raced wide throughout and failed to threaten. TACKY was void of early speed and never reached serious contention. TREVANIAN raced forwardly placed but five wide to the backstretch, continued wide on the second turn and came up empty.

Owners– 1, Ann Marie Farm; 2, Mr & Mrs Meguerditchian; 3, Gann Edmund A; 4, Lo Charles; 5, Gunther John D; 6, Chess Phil; 7, The Merv Griffin Ranch Co; 8, Gill Michael J; 9, Bell Joyce; 10, Car-Den Racing Stable

Trainers– 1, Arterburn Lonnie; 2, Bell Thomas R II; 3, Frankel Robert; 4, McArthur Jerry; 5, Hollendorfer Jerry; 6, Baffert Bob; 7, O'Neill Doug; 8, Canani Nick; 9, Peery Chuck; 10, Patterson Dennis M

$2 Daily Double (10–4) Paid $2,246.00 ; Daily Double Pool $9,849 .
$1 Pick Three (7–10–ALL) Paid $804.50 ; Pick Three Pool $31,247 .
$1 Pick Three (7–ALL–4) Paid $804.50 .
$1 Pick Three (ALL–10–4) Paid $804.50 .

FOURTH RACE
Gulfstream
MARCH 13, 2004

7 FURLONGS. (1.20) 24TH RUNNING OF THE STONERSIDE FORWARD GAL. Grade II. Purse $150,000 FOR FILLIES, THREE YEAR OLDS. By subscription of $100 each, which shall accompany the nomination, $1,500 to pass the entry box and $1,500 additional to start, with $150,000 guaranteed. The owner of the winner to receive $90,000; $30,000 to second, $16,500to third, $9,000 to fourth and $4,500 to fifth. Weight: 121 lbs. Non-winners of $50,000 once allowed, 2 lbs.; $40,000 once anytime or $30,000 in 2004, 4 lbs.; $25,000 once or two races other than Maiden of Claiming, 6 lbs. . Trophy to winning Owner. Closed Wednesday, March 3, 2004 with (16) nominations.

Value of Race: $150,000 Winner $90,000; second $30,000; third $16,500; fourth $9,000; fifth $4,500. Mutuel Pool $1,071,997.00 Exacta Pool $263,003.00 Trifecta Pool $172,150.00

Last Raced	Horse	M/Eqt.	A.	Wt	PP	St	¼	½	Str	Fin	Jockey	Odds $1
14Feb04 ^{8}GP^{1}	Madcap Escapade	L	3	121	2	5	1^{1½}	1^{1½}	1^{7}	1^{4¾}	Bailey J D	0.20
29Nov03 ^{7}Aqu^{2}	La Reina	L	3	121	4	3	4^{3½}	3^{1}	2^{1½}	2^{2¼}	Velazquez J R	3.50
15Feb04 ^{9}GP^{1}	Frenchglen	L	3	115	3	1	3^{hd}	4^{6}	3½	3^{2¼}	Day P	18.80
6Mar04 ^{8}GP^{5}	Journey Fever		3	121	1	4	5	5	5	4^{4¼}	Diego I V	60.40
24Jan04 ^{7}GP^{2}	Wacky Patty	L b	3	121	5	2	2^{2}	2^{1½}	4^{2½}	5	Velasquez C	11.80

OFF AT 1:31 Start Good. Won handily. Track fast.
TIME :21^{4}, :44^{3}, 1:09^{1}, 1:22^{4} (:21.85, :44.61, 1:09.26, 1:22.97)

$2 Mutuel Prices:

3 – MADCAP ESCAPADE	2.40	2.10	2.10
4 – LA REINA		2.20	2.10
1A – FRENCHGLEN			2.10

$1 EXACTA 3–4 PAID $2.30 $1 TRIFECTA 3–4–1 PAID $5.40

B. f, (May), by Hennessy – Sassy Pants, by Saratoga Six. Trainer Brothers Frank L. Bred by Needham/ Betz Thoroughbreds & James &Blackburn (Ky).

MADCAP ESCAPADE off a step slowly, quickly moved to the fore, made the pace along the inside, then drew away leaving the turn and remained well clear to the wire while in hand. LA REINA allowed to settle, raced three wide on the turn and closed to gain the place while no threat to the winner. FRENCHGLEN tracked the pace along the inside into the turn, then couldn't keep pace with the top ones in the drive. JOURNEY FEVER was outrun. WACKY PATTY chased the winner into the stretch and faltered.

Owners– 1, Lunsford Bruce; 2, Hamilton Emory A; 3, Jones Aaron U and Marie D; 4, Carroll Justin and Stefanie; 5, Turf Express Inc Debruycker and Jacobson

Trainers– 1, Brothers Frank L; 2, McGaughey III Claude R; 3, Pletcher Todd A; 4, Vanier Harvey L; 5, Asmussen Steven M

Scratched– Irish Melody (25Jan04 ^{6}GP ^{1})

$1 Pick Three (5–5–3) Paid $6.20 ; Pick Three Pool $100,652 .

NINTH RACE
Gulfstream
MARCH 13, 2004

1⅛ MILES. (1.46^{2}) 53RD RUNNING OF THE FLORIDA DERBY. Grade I. Purse $1,000,000 FOR THREE YEAR OLDS. By subscription of $3,000 each, which shall accompany the nomination, $6,000 to pass the entry box and $6,000 additional to start, with $1,000,000 guaranteed. The owner of the winner to receive $600,000; $190,000 to second, $100,000tothird, $60,000 to fourth, $30,000 to fifth and $20,000 to sixth. WEIGHT: 122 lbs. Horses finishing first, second or third in the Holy Bull Stakes, Hutcheson Stakes, and/or the Fountain of Youth Stakes, will automatically be nominated to the Florida Derby. Early bird nominations to the Florida Derby series closed on Wednesday, November 12, 2003 with 160 nominations. Florida Derby Trophy to the winning Owner. Closed Wednesday, March 3, 2004 with 162 nominations.

Value of Race: $1,000,000 Winner $600,000; second $190,000; third $100,000; fourth $60,000; fifth $30,000; sixth $20,000. Mutuel Pool $1,909,691.00 Exacta Pool $1,133,843.00 Trifecta Pool $976,401.00 Superfecta Pool $276,369.00

Last Raced	Horse	M/Eqt.	A.	Wt	PP	St	¼	½	¾	Str	Fin	Jockey	Odds $1
17Jan04 ^{10}GP^{3}	Friends Lake	L	3	122	2	2	4^{hd}	$6^{2\frac{1}{2}}$	6^{1}	$3^{\frac{1}{2}}$	$1^{\frac{3}{4}}$	Migliore R	37.40
14Feb04 ^{6}GP^{1}	Value Plus	L	3	122	8	8	$2^{1\frac{1}{2}}$	$2^{\frac{1}{2}}$	1^{hd}	$1^{\frac{1}{2}}$	$2^{\frac{3}{4}}$	Velazquez J R	3.80
21Feb04 ^{10}Tam^{2}	The Cliff's Edge	L	3	122	1	1	8^{hd}	$8^{3\frac{1}{2}}$	7^{1}	$4^{1\frac{1}{2}}$	$3^{2\frac{1}{2}}$	Sellers S J	5.20
14Feb04 ^{11}GP^{1}	Read the Footnotes	L	3	122	3	3	$3^{1\frac{1}{2}}$	$3^{\frac{1}{2}}$	2^{1}	$2^{2\frac{1}{2}}$	4no	Bailey J D	1.00
14Feb04 ^{1}GP^{5}	Farnum Alley	L	3	122	5	4	$9^{1\frac{1}{2}}$	9^{2}	9^{6}	$6^{\frac{1}{2}}$	$5^{1\frac{3}{4}}$	Day P	58.40
15Nov03 ^{6}Lrl^{1}	Tapit	L f	3	122	4	5	$5^{\frac{1}{2}}$	$4^{\frac{1}{2}}$	5^{2}	5^{3}	$6^{1\frac{1}{2}}$	Prado E S	5.60
14Feb04 ^{1}GP^{4}	Smoocher	L b	3	122	10	9	7^{4}	$7^{2\frac{1}{2}}$	8^{3}	$7^{2\frac{1}{2}}$	$7^{6\frac{1}{4}}$	Santos J A	71.20
14Feb04 ^{11}GP^{5}	Sir Oscar	L b	3	122	6	6	$6^{1\frac{1}{2}}$	5^{3}	$4^{\frac{1}{2}}$	$8^{2\frac{1}{2}}$	8^{1}	Garcia J A	12.10
14Feb04 ^{11}GP^{7}	Frisky Spider	L b	3	122	9	7	$1^{1\frac{1}{2}}$	1^{4}	$3^{\frac{1}{2}}$	9^{2}	$9^{1\frac{3}{4}}$	King E L Jr	62.50
25Feb04 ^{7}GP^{2}	Notorious Rogue	L b	3	122	7	10	10	10	10	10	10	Bravo J	40.70

OFF AT 4:22 Start Good. Won driving. Track fast.

TIME :23^{2}, :47, 1:11^{2}, 1:37^{3}, 1:51^{1} (:23.44, :47.05, 1:11.54, 1:37.60, 1:51.38)

$2 Mutuel Prices:				
	2 – FRIENDS LAKE	76.80	24.80	12.20
	8 – VALUE PLUS		6.40	5.00
	1 – THE CLIFF'S EDGE			4.80

$1 EXACTA 2–8 PAID $221.50 $1 TRIFECTA 2–8–1 PAID $1,052.10
$1 SUPERFECTA 2–8–1–3 PAID $3,004.00

Ch. c, (Apr), by A.P. Indy – Antespend, by Spend a Buck. Trainer Kimmel John C. Bred by Chester Broman & Mary R Broman (NY).

FRIENDS LAKE reserved along the inside around the first turn, eased off the rail entering the backstretch, swung out four wide on the far turn, then rallied under pressure to catch VALUE PLUS just inside the seventy yard pole and prevailed. VALUE PLUS stalked the pace three wide, moved up to reach even terms for command on the far turn, vied for the lead outside READ THE FOOTNOTES into the stretch, edged away from that rival approaching the sixteenth pole but couldn't resist the winner late. THE CLIFF'S EDGE fractious in the gate, broke to the inside, was steadied slightly entering the first turn, saved ground while advancing into contention around the far turn, bumped with TAPIT in early stretch, eased out finished willingly for the show. READ THE FOOTNOTES angled in soon after the start to stalk the pace along the rail, slipped through to reach even terms for command on the far turn, vied for the lead inside VALUE PLUS to nearing the sixteenth pole and gave way. FARNUM ALLEY unhurried early, swung wide for the stretch run and gained ground late without threatening. TAPIT tracked the pace three wide, was caught in tight on the far turn, was still in contention when he bumped with THE CLIFF'S EDGE in early stretch and tired. SMOOCHER allowed to settle, raced four wide and had no response when set down for the drive. SIR OSCAR tracked the leader four wide into the far turn and faltered. FRISKY SPIDER hustled to get the lead, sprinted clear while racing off the rail down the backstretch, made the pace into the far turn and faded. NOTORIOUS ROGUE trailed.

Owners– 1, Broman Sr Chester and Mary; 2, Jones Aaron U and Marie D; 3, La Penta Robert V; 4, Klaravich Stables Inc; 5, Melnyk Eugene and Laura; 6, Winchell Thoroughbreds LLC; 7, Franks Farms; 8, International Fair Play Inc; 9, Dender Carol R and Friedman Martin; 10, Lewis Lee

Trainers– 1, Kimmel John C; 2, Pletcher Todd A; 3, Zito Nicholas P; 4, Violette Richard A Jr; 5, Reinstedler Anthony; 6, Dickinson Michael W; 7, Bell David R; 8, Wolfson Martin D; 9, Durso Robert J; 10, Hennig Mark

---

$1 Pick Three (7–9–2) Paid $1,840.40 ; Pick Three Pool $154,140 .

TENTH RACE
Gulfstream
MARCH 13, 2004

7 FURLONGS. (1.20) 19TH RUNNING OF THE SWALE. Grade III. Purse $150,000 FOR THREE YEAR OLDS. By subscription of $150 each, which shall accompany the nomination, $1,500 to pass the entry box and $1,500 additional to start, with $150,000 guaranteed. The owner of the winner to receive $90,000; $30,000 to second, $16,500 to third, $9,000 to fourth and $4,500 to fifth. Weight: 122 lbs. Non–winners of $50,000 twice allowed, 2 lbs.; $50,000 once anytime or $30,000 twice in 2004, 4 lbs.; $30,000 in 2004 or two races other than Maiden or Claiming, 6 lbs. Trophy to the winning Owner. Closed Wednesday, March 3, 2004 with (7) nomintations.

Value of Race: $150,000 Winner $90,000; second $30,000; third $16,500; fourth $9,000; fifth $4,500. Mutuel Pool $879,018.00 Exacta Pool $451,430.00 Trifecta Pool $260,067.00 Superfecta Pool $79,022.00

Last Raced	Horse	M/Eqt.	A.	Wt	PP	St	¼	½	Str	Fin	Jockey	Odds $1
14Feb04 ^{10}GP^{4}	Wynn Dot Comma	L	3	120	2	4	$2^{1\frac{1}{2}}$	2^{2}	$1^{1\frac{1}{2}}$	1^{hd}	Prado E S	4.00
4Feb04 ^{3}GP^{1}	Eurosilver	L	3	120	5	2	3^{2}	3^{2}	3^{3}	$2^{4\frac{1}{4}}$	Castellano J J	1.10
4Oct03 ^{7}Bel^{3}	DashboardDrummer	L	3	120	4	1	$4^{2\frac{1}{2}}$	4^{5}	4^{5}	3^{1}	Dominguez R A	14.30
25Oct03 ^{7}SA^{3}	Chapel Royal	L	3	122	1	5	$1^{\frac{1}{2}}$	1^{hd}	2^{hd}	$4^{4\frac{1}{2}}$	Velazquez J R	1.30
14Feb04 ^{1}GP^{3}	Caiman	L	3	116	3	3	5	5	5	5	Boulanger G	51.00

OFF AT 5:00 Start Good. Won driving. Track fast.

TIME :22, :44^{3}, 1:09^{2}, 1:22^{4} (:22.18, :44.64, 1:09.40, 1:22.87)

$2 Mutuel Prices:				
	3 – WYNN DOT COMMA	10.00	3.00	2.10
	6 – EUROSILVER		2.40	2.10
	5 – DASHBOARD DRUMMER			2.10

$1 EXACTA 3–6 PAID $9.70 $1 TRIFECTA 3–6–5 PAID $47.40
$1 SUPERFECTA 3–6–5–1 PAID $72.60

Ch. c, (May), by Struggler–GB – I Like Punch, by Two Punch. Trainer Wolfson Martin D. Bred by T Wynn Jolley & Harry Hoglander (Fla).

WYNN DOT COMMA forced the pace outside CHAPEL ROYAL, moved to gain a slim lead outside that rival midway of the turn, drew clear in the stretch, then just lasted over. EUROSILVER stalked the pace off the rail into the stretch, then rallied to just miss. DASHBOARD DRUMMER rated off the pace, angled out in the stretch, then closed to be up for the show while unable to gain on the winner late and his rider lost his whip inside the sixteenth pole. CHAPEL ROYAL showed speed along the inside, then faltered in the drive. CAIMAN was outrun.

Owners– 1, Cherry Martin L; 2, Buckram Oak Farm; 3, Double S Stable Preferred Pals Stables & E Wachtel; 4, Smith Derrick and Tabor Michael; 5, Achar Victor

Trainers– 1, Wolfson Martin D; 2, Zito Nicholas P; 3, Iwinski Allen; 4, Pletcher Todd A; 5, Medina Angel M

Scratched– Saratoga County (14Feb04 ^{10}GP^{3})

$1 Pick Three (9–2–3) Paid $947.40 ; Pick Three Pool $156,336 .

THIRTEENTH RACE
Gulfstream
MARCH 13, 2004

$1\frac{1}{16}$ MILES. (1.40^{1}) 18TH RUNNING OF THE SKIP AWAY HANDICAP. Grade III. Purse $100,000 FOR THREE YEAR OLDS AND UPWARD. By subscription of $100 each, which shall accompany the nomination, $1,000 to pass the entry box and $1,000 additional to start, with $100,000 guaranteed. The owner of the winner to receive $60,000; $20,000 to second, $11,000 to third, $6,000 to fourth and $3,000 to fifth. Weights: Saturday, March 6, 2004. Trophy to winning Owner. Closed Wednesday, March 3,2004 with (18) nominations.

Value of Race: $100,000 Winner $60,000; second $20,000; third $11,000; fourth $6,000; fifth $3,000. Mutuel Pool $589,540.00 Exacta Pool $383,616.00 Trifecta Pool $296,186.00 Superfecta Pool $110,600.00

Last Raced	Horse	M/Eqt.	A.	Wt	PP	St	¼	½	¾	Str	Fin	Jockey	Odds $1
31Jan04 $^{8}GP^{1}$	Newfoundland	L b	4	116	6	5	4^{hd}	3^{hd}	$3^{1\frac{1}{2}}$	1^{1}	$1^{\frac{1}{2}}$	Velazquez J R	6.00
27Feb04 $^{9}GP^{2}$	Supah Blitz	L b	4	114	4	6	7^{2}	7^{3}	7^{1}	$5^{2\frac{1}{2}}$	$2^{2\frac{1}{4}}$	Velasquez C	14.70
7Feb04 $^{10}GP^{8}$	Bowman's Band	L	6	117	1	2	$5^{1\frac{1}{2}}$	$5^{\frac{1}{2}}$	4^{hd}	4^{hd}	$3^{4\frac{1}{4}}$	Dominguez R A	1.40
27Oct03 $^{7}Crc^{5}$	Super Frolic	L f	4	114	5	4	$2^{1\frac{1}{2}}$	2^{1}	$2^{\frac{1}{2}}$	2^{hd}	$4^{2\frac{1}{2}}$	Santos J A	96.30
9Feb04 $^{8}GP^{1}$	Christine's Outlaw	L f	4	113	2	1	$1^{\frac{1}{2}}$	$1^{\frac{1}{2}}$	1^{hd}	$3^{\frac{1}{2}}$	5^{nk}	Prado E S	4.90
15Feb04 $^{10}GP^{1}$	Bourbonnais-Ire	L	4	114	9	10	$6^{\frac{1}{2}}$	6^{1}	5^{hd}	6^{2}	6^{1}	Bailey J D	2.90
7Feb04 $^{10}GP^{6}$	Country Be Gold	L	7	115	3	3	$9^{1\frac{1}{2}}$	10	10	$8^{2\frac{1}{2}}$	$7^{\frac{3}{4}}$	Douglas R R	56.20
9Feb04 $^{5}GP^{2}$	Offlee Wild	L	4	114	8	8	$8^{1\frac{1}{2}}$	9^{1}	8^{1}	7^{hd}	$8^{1\frac{1}{2}}$	Guidry M	12.70
27Feb04 $^{9}GP^{1}$	Whos Crying Now	L bf	4	115	10	7	3^{hd}	4^{1}	$6^{1\frac{1}{2}}$	9^{3}	$9^{10\frac{3}{4}}$	Bravo J	70.50
27Feb04 $^{9}GP^{3}$	M B Sea	L b	5	116	7	9	10	$8^{\frac{1}{2}}$	$9^{\frac{1}{2}}$	10	10	Perret C	34.40

OFF AT 6:26 Start Good . Won driving. Track fast.

TIME :24, :48^{1}, 1:12, 1:37, 1:43^{1} (:24.05, :48.27, 1:12.06, 1:37.01, 1:43.26)

$2 Mutuel Prices:			
6 – NEWFOUNDLAND	14.00	7.20	3.80
4 – SUPAH BLITZ		14.80	5.60
1 – BOWMAN'S BAND			3.00

$1 EXACTA 6–4 PAID $64.70 $1 TRIFECTA 6–4–1 PAID $215.40
$1 SUPERFECTA 6–4–1–5 PAID $8,295.00

Ch. c, (Feb), by Storm Cat – Clear Mandate , by Deputy Minister . Trainer Pletcher Todd A. Bred by G Watts Humphrey (Ky).

NEWFOUNDLAND stalked the pace three wide, rallied to take over at the top of the stretch, then responded when challenged at the sixteenth pole and was all out to prevail. SUPAH BLITZ reserved early, angled out for the stretch run, rallied to reach NEWFOUNDLAND at the sixteenth pole but was outgamed to the wire. BOWMAN'S BAND well placed racing along the inside, was forced to wait for room in behind the leaders leaving the far turn, made a run inside NEWFOUNDLAND to loom a threat inside the eighth pole, then weakened. SUPER FROLIC forced the pace outside CHRISTINE'S OUTLAW to the top of the stretch and tired. CHRISTINE'S OUTLAW set the pace under pressure along the inside to the top of the stretch and gave way. BOURBONNAIS (IRE) off slowly, raced in striking position three wide into the stretch and faltered. COUNTRY BE GOLD saved ground and failed to threaten. OFFLEE WILD allowed to settle, raced three wide on the far turn and was not a factor. WHOS CRYING NOW chased the leaders four wide into the far turn and faded. M B SEA was outrun while racing four wide.

Owners– 1, Sumaya Us Stables; 2, Bee Bee Stables Inc and Tortora Jacqueline; 3, Schwartz Martin S; 4, Stride Rite Racing Stable Inc; 5, RC Hill Stable; 6, Darley Stable; 7, Seinfeld Barry and Dodson Elizabeth K; 8, Azalea Stables LLC; 9, Lewis James R Jr; 10, Bruder Michael J

Trainers– 1, Pletcher Todd A; 2, Tortora Emanuel; 3, Jerkens H Allen; 4, Wolfson Milton W; 5, Weaver George; 6, Albertrani Thomas; 7, Nobles Reynaldo H; 8, Smith Thomas V; 9, Tortora Emanuel; 10, Romans Dale

---

$2 Daily Double (3–6) Paid $54.40 ; Daily Double Pool $169,004 .
$1 Pick Three (2–3–6) Paid $72.50 ; Pick Three Pool $130,212 .
$1 Pick Four (3–2–3–6) Paid $594.70 ; Pick Four Pool $205,948 .
$2 Pick Six (9–2–3–2–3–6) 5 Correct Paid $825.60 ; Pick Six Pool $94,964 ; Carryover Pool $79,909.

Gulfstream Park Attendance: 25,505 Mutuel Pool: $4,488,463.00 ITW Mutuel Pool: $1,198,414.00 ISW Mutuel Pool: $17,339,023.00

TENTH RACE
Oaklawn
MARCH 13, 2004

1 1/16 MILES. (1.40¹) 18TH RUNNING OF THE OAKLAWN BREEDERS' CUP. Purse $200,000 (includes $100,000 BC – Breeders' Cup) FILLIES AND MARES, THREE YEAR OLDS AND UPWARD. No nomination fee, original nominators paying $1,000 to pass the entry box and $2,000 additional to start. Supplementary nominations may be made by closing time of entries at a fee of $10,000 which qualifiesto start with $100,000 Guaranteed and an additional $100,000 from the Breeders' Cup Fund for CUP ELIGIBLES ONLY. Breeders' Cup Fund monies also correspondingly divided providing a Breeders' Cup nominee has finished in an award position. Any Breeders' CupFund monies not awarded will revert back to the Fund. Three Year Olds: WEIGHT 114 lbs.; OLDER 122 lbs. Non-winnersof $60,000 twice at a mile or over since October 13, 2003 allowed 3 lbs.; $50,000 once at a mile or over since October 13, 2003, allowed 5 lbs.; $30,000 at a mile or over in 2004 allowed 7 lbs.; $25,000 at any distance in 2004, allowed 9 lbs.

Value of Race: $200,000 Winner $120,000; second $40,000; third $20,000; fourth $10,000; fifth $6,000; sixth $4,000. Mutuel Pool $303,296.00 Exacta Pool $193,520.00 Trifecta Pool $198,559.00

Last Raced	Horse	M/Eqt.	A.	Wt	PP	St	¼	½	¾	Str	Fin	Jockey	Odds $1
21Feb04 9FG6	Golden Sonata	L	5	117	8	10	10	10	10	61½	11¾	Marquez C H Jr	29.30
12Feb04 7SA1	Keys to the Heart	L	5	117	6	8	84½	6½	61½	42	2¾	Thompson T J	8.10
8Feb04 11GP4	Mayo On the Side	L bf	5	113	2	3	5½	4½	51½	1hd	3½	Doocy T T	3.90
21Feb04 9FG1	Spectacular Lisa	L b	4	119	4	7	31	32½	1hd	2½	41¾	Albarado R J	0.90
14Feb04 9OP2	There Runs Hattie	L b	5	113	7	6	6hd	7½	83½	5½	51½	McKee J	25.80
29Feb04 9OP1	Small Promises	L b	6	113	1	4	1hd	1hd	3hd	3½	6nk	Chapa R	24.40
19Feb04 9OP1	My Trusty Cat	L bf	4	113	3	2	2½	21½	2hd	71½	74½	Shepherd J	5.20
29Feb04 9OP3	La Reason	L f	4	114	10	5	41	5½	4hd	86	81½	Johnson J M	62.30
14Feb04 9OP1	Drexel Monorail	L	5	117	9	1	73	86	7½	91½	9¾	Theriot H J II	12.30
21Feb04 9FG5	Took Out	L	5	115	5	9	96½	98	92½	10	10	Pettinger D R	54.90

OFF AT 5:24 Start Good . Won driving. Track fast.

TIME :23, :46⁴, 1:12, 1:38, 1:44¹ (:23.19, :46.90, 1:12.14, 1:38.06, 1:44.32)

$2 Mutuel Prices:				
	8 – GOLDEN SONATA	60.60	24.40	9.60
	6 – KEYS TO THE HEART		8.60	6.00
	2 – MAYO ON THE SIDE			3.80

$2 EXACTA 8–6 PAID $629.00 $2 TRIFECTA 8–6–2 PAID $3,524.80

Dk. b or br. m, (Feb), by Mr. Prospector – Elissa Beethoven-GB , by Royal Academy . Trainer Nicks Morris G. Bred by James C Spence (Ky).

GOLDEN SONATA far back for six furlongs, swung to the far outside for the drive, full of run to be in time down the middle part of the strip. KEYS TO THE HEART back early, raced in the second flight into the stretch, waited briefly midstretch in traffic, no match winner, second best. MAYO ON THE SIDE forwardly placed, came four wide to challenge in the second turn, showed the way past the furlong marker, could not contain the top two. SPECTACULAR LISA forwardly placed, vied three wide in the second turn, not enough in the late going. THERE RUNS HATTIE behind the pace along the inside, improved late while continuing up the rail. SMALL PROMISES set or forced the pace inside, weakened. MY TRUSTY CAT contested the pace while between foes, faltered. LA REASON five wide in the first turn, ranged up again to be five wide in the second turn, gave way in the drive. DREXEL MONORAIL failed to menace. TOOK OUT was never involved.

Owners– 1, Spence James C; 2, Nichols Thomas L; 3, Lothenbach Stables Inc Robert L Lothenbach; 4, Green River Farms Gary S Logsdon; 5, Markwell Steve and Froedge Samuel; 6, West Wind Farm; 7, Pollard Carl F; 8, K and K Racing Stable LLC; 9, Stoneway Farm LLC; 10, Scarberry Howard and Penny

Trainers– 1, Nicks Morris G; 2, Greely C Beau; 3, Nafzger Carl A; 4, Stidham Michael; 5, Huffman William G; 6, Flint Bernard S; 7, Vance David R; 8, Vance David R; 9, Flint Bernard S; 10, Scarberry Howard

$2 Pick Three (12–1/4–8) Paid $2,411.40 ; Pick Three Pool $24,421 .

EIGHTH RACE
Santa Anita
MARCH 13, 2004

1 1/16 MILES. (1.39) 65TH RUNNING OF THE SANTA ANITA OAKS. Grade I. Purse $300,000 FOR FILLIES, THREE YEARS OLD. By subscription of $300 each to accompany the nomination or by supplementary nomination of $6,000 by time of entry. $3,000 additional to start, with $300,000 guaranteed, of which $180,000 to first, $60,000 to second, $36,000to third, $18,000 to fourth and $6,000 to fifth. 117 lbs. Starters to be named through the entry box by the closing time of entries. A trophy will be presented to the owner of the winner. The winner of the 2004 Santa Anita Oaks will be automatically eligible to the 2004 Santa Anita Derby with no fees. Should the winner have paid nomination fees to the Santa Anita Derby, those fees will be refunded only if the winner starts in the Santa Anita Derby. Closed with 14 nominations.

Value of Race: $300,000 Winner $180,000; second $60,000; third $36,000; fourth $18,000; fifth $6,000. Mutuel Pool $678,633.00 Exacta Pool $342,030.00 Quinella Pool $29,117.00 Trifecta Pool $362,466.00 Superfecta Pool $143,521.00

Last Raced	Horse	M/Eqt.	A.	Wt	PP	St	¼	½	¾	Str	Fin	Jockey	Odds $1
24Jan04 7GP1	Silent Sighs	LB b	3	117	3	3	21	21½	21½	12	11½	Flores D R	6.70
25Oct03 3SA1	Halfbridled	LB	3	117	1	1	31	4hd	4½	21	21½	Stevens G L	0.50
15Feb04 8SA1	A. P. Adventure	LB	3	117	5	5	4½	31	51	4hd	3½	Solis A	3.30
15Feb04 8SA2	Hollywood Story	LB b	3	117	4	2	51	51½	3hd	31	42	Espinoza V	7.50
15Feb04 8SA4	Stellar Jayne	LB b	3	117	7	6	7	7	61½	54	58½	Santiago Javier	34.60
30Jan04 4SA1	Vencedora Amiga	LB b	3	117	6	7	61½	6½	7	7	68	Pedroza M A	40.20
4Jan04 6SA2	Salty Romance	B	3	117	2	4	11½	11	1hd	61	7	Smith M E	36.60

OFF AT 4:19 Start Good . Won driving. Track fast.

TIME :22⁴, :46², 1:10⁴, 1:36, 1:42⁴ (:22.98, :46.49, 1:10.82, 1:36.12, 1:42.84)

$2 Mutuel Prices:				
	4 – SILENT SIGHS	15.40	5.20	2.40
	1 – HALFBRIDLED		2.60	2.10
	6 – A. P. ADVENTURE			2.20

$1 EXACTA 4–1 PAID $16.40 $2 QUINELLA 1–4 PAID $9.60
$1 TRIFECTA 4–1–6 PAID $42.40 $1 SUPERFECTA 4–1–6–5 PAID $88.50

Dk. b or br. f, (Mar), by Benchmark – Quiet Romance , by Bertrando . Trainer Canani Julio C. Bred by Mr & Mrs Martin J Wygod (Cal).

SILENT SIGHS stalked outside a rival then off the rail, bid alongside the pacesetter on the second turn and gained the lead, inched clear while drifting out some into the stretch, then drifted in through the drive but held gamely under some urging. HALFBRIDLED stalked inside then a bit off the rail, split rivals into the stretch, could not catch the winner but continued willingly for the place. A. P. ADVENTURE a bit wide into the first turn, stalked outside a rival, continued between horses on the second turn, was shuffled back some leaving that turn, found the inside in midstretch and gained the show. HOLLYWOOD STORY angled in approaching the first turn then came out into the backstretch, chased outside a foe, went three deep into and on the second turn and into the stretch and was edged for third. STELLAR JAYNE wide into the first turn, settled off the inside, went four wide into the stretch and lacked the needed rally. VENCEDORA AMIGA angled in and was unhurried along the inside, saved ground off the pace, came out into the stretch and was not a threat. SALTY ROMANCE sped between horses to the early lead, set the pace inside, dueled inside the winner on the second turn and gave way in the stretch.

Owners– 1, Wygod Mr and Mrs Martin J; 2, Wertheimer and Frere; 3, Lewis Robert B and Beverly J; 4, Krikorian George; 5, Spenthrift Farm LLC Cole Nancy Kidder Chuck et al; 6, Old Friends Inc and Winner Silk Inc; 7, Flying Zee Stable

Trainers– 1, Canani Julio C; 2, Mandella Richard; 3, Dollase Wallace; 4, Shirreffs John; 5, Lukas D Wayne; 6, Lobo Paulo H; 7, Biancone Patrick L

Scratched– Miss Coronado (07Feb04 8GP 1)

$2 Daily Double (13–4) Paid $132.80 ; Daily Double Pool $50,185 .
$1 Pick Three (2–13–4) Paid $1,665.70 ; Pick Three Pool $112,690 .

EIGHTH RACE
Aqueduct
MARCH 14, 2004

1⅛ MILES. (1.47) 30TH RUNNING OF THE NEXT MOVE HANDICAP. Grade III. Purse $100,000 (Up to $19,400 NYSBFOA). FOR FILLIES AND MARES THREE YEARS OLD AND UPWARD . By subscription of $100 each, which should accompany the nomination; $500 to pass the entry box; $500 to start, with $100,000 added. The added money and all fees to be divided 60%to the winner, 20% to second, 10% to third, 5% to fourth, 3% to fifth and 2% divided equally among the remaining finishers. A trophy will be presented to the winning owner. Closed Saturday, February 28, 2004 with 14 Nominations.

Value of Race: $108,400 Winner $65,040; second $21,680; third $10,840; fourth $5,420; fifth $3,252; sixth $1,084; seventh $1,084. Mutuel Pool $356,643.00 Exacta Pool $320,914.00 Trifecta Pool $252,447.00

Last Raced	Horse	M/Eqt.	A.	Wt	PP	St	¼	½	¾	Str	Fin	Jockey	Odds $1
15Feb04 ^{11}GP^{7}	Smok'n Frolic	L b	5	119	5	4	$5^{1\frac{1}{2}}$	3^{1}	$2^{1\frac{1}{2}}$	1^{6}	$1^{6\frac{1}{2}}$	Migliore R	0.80
22Feb04 ^{8}Lrl^{1}	Stake	L	4	112	1	2	2^{hd}	2^{hd}	$3^{\frac{1}{2}}$	$2^{1\frac{1}{2}}$	2no	Bridgmohan S X	6.50
16Feb04 ^{8}Aqu^{2}	U K Trick	L bf	4	110	7	7	7	7	7	6^{7}	3^{nk}	Cotto P L Jr	8.90
15Feb04 ^{11}GP^{9}	Passing Shot	L	5	118	4	6	4^{hd}	4^{hd}	$5^{3\frac{1}{2}}$	5^{1}	$4^{\frac{1}{2}}$	Chavez J F	3.10
4Mar04 ^{8}Aqu^{2}	Virgin Voyage	L bf	4	112	3	3	6^{6}	$5^{1\frac{1}{2}}$	4^{3}	$4^{\frac{1}{2}}$	5^{6}	Arroyo N Jr	17.10
16Feb04 ^{5}Aqu^{1}	Our Tune	L	4	113	6	5	$1^{1\frac{1}{2}}$	$1^{1\frac{1}{2}}$	$1^{\frac{1}{2}}$	$3^{1\frac{1}{2}}$	$6^{4\frac{1}{4}}$	Luzzi M J	17.80
16Feb04 ^{8}Aqu^{6}	Green Jeans	L	5	112	2	1	3^{hd}	6^{10}	6^{7}	7	7	Castellano J J	31.00

OFF AT 4:20 Start Good . Won driving. Track fast.

TIME :23^{3}, :47, 1:11^{1}, 1:37^{2}, 1:51^{2} (:23.74, :47.12, 1:11.27, 1:37.40, 1:51.55)

$2 Mutuel Prices:			
5 – SMOK'N FROLIC	3.60	2.50	2.10
1 – STAKE		3.90	3.20
7 – U K TRICK			2.60

$2 EXACTA 5–1 PAID $19.60 $2 TRIFECTA 5–1–7 PAID $78.00

Gr/ro. m, (Apr), by Smoke Glacken – Cherokyfrolicflash , by Green Dancer . Trainer Pletcher Todd A. Bred by Cherokee Farms Inc (Fla).

SMOK'N FROLIC stumbled at the start, raced four wide on the first turn, rallied three wide on the second turn, drew away when roused and was kept to a drive to the wire. STAKE stumbled at the start, raced close up early while in hand, rallied three wide approaching the stretch, was no match for the winner and continued on to hold the place. U K TRICK ducked out at the start, dropped back early, raced inside and finished well on the rail. PASSING SHOT bobbled at the start, raced three wide on the first turn and lacked a rally. VIRGIN VOYAGE stumbled at the start, raced inside and had no response when roused. OUR TUNE was hustled out to a clear lead, set the pace and tired in the stretch. GREEN JEANS tired after showing brief speed.

Owners– 1, Dogwood Stable; 2, Dor-Sea Stable Desert Green Stable and Raiche Timothy; 3, Rising Graph Stable and Sturgill Richard A; 4, Shields Joseph V Jr; 5, Paraneck Stable; 6, Our Sugar Bear Stable; 7, Richards Althea D

Trainers– 1, Pletcher Todd A; 2, Barker Edward R; 3, Hushion Michael E; 4, Jerkens H Allen; 5, Pedersen Jennifer; 6, Brice Michael; 7, Turner William H Jr

---

SEVENTH RACE
Golden Gate
MARCH 14, 2004

1⅛ MILES. (Turf) (1.47^{3}) 58TH RUNNING OF THE GOLDEN GATE BREEDERS' CUP HANDICAP. Grade III. Purse $125,000 (includes $50,000 BC – Breeders' Cup) FOR THREE-YEAR-OLDS AND UPWARD. By subscription of $75 each to accompany the nomination or by supplementary nomination of $2,000 by Noon, Sunday, March 7, 2004. $375 to pass the entry box and $375 additional to start (Additional $50,000 from Breeders' CupFund for Breeders' Cup eligibles only). This race will not be divided. Closed Thursday, March 4, 2004 with 15 nominations.

Value of Race: $90,000 Winner $41,250; second $25,000; third $11,250; fourth $9,375; fifth $3,125. Mutuel Pool $273,466.00 Exacta Pool $134,927.00 Quinella Pool $13,580.00 Trifecta Pool $152,935.00 Superfecta Pool $63,483.00

Last Raced	Horse	M/Eqt.	A.	Wt	PP	St	¼	½	¾	Str	Fin	Jockey	Odds $1
11Feb04 ^{3}SA^{3}	Tronare-Chi	LB b	6	115	4	2	3^{2}	3^{5}	3^{2}	1^{hd}	1^{1}	Gonzalez R M	10.70
19Feb04 ^{7}SA^{1}	Soud	LB f	6	118	5	3	2^{2}	1^{hd}	1^{1}	$2^{2\frac{1}{2}}$	2^{2}	Desormeaux K J	1.70
7Feb04 ^{7}GG^{2}	Aly Bubba	LB	5	116	2	7	5^{1}	5^{1}	4^{hd}	$3^{1\frac{1}{2}}$	3no	Castro J M	21.70
20Feb04 ^{7}SA^{2}	Gent	LB	5	118	6	9	7^{hd}	8^{4}	8^{8}	5^{2}	4^{hd}	Saint-Martin E	5.30
20Feb04 ^{7}SA^{1}	Epicentre	LB	5	121	3	4	6^{hd}	$6^{\frac{1}{2}}$	6^{hd}	4^{1}	$5^{1\frac{1}{2}}$	Baze R A	1.90
28Feb04 ^{8}GG^{2}	Gold Ruckus	LB bf	6	116	7	1	4^{1}	4^{hd}	7^{2}	$6^{1\frac{1}{2}}$	6^{4}	Radke K	18.50
8Feb04 ^{3}GG^{8}	Lucayan Indian-Ire	LB bf	9	115	9	6	8^{1}	9	9	9	7^{6}	Rodriguez M	71.10
22Jan04 ^{7}SA^{8}	Mananan McLir	LB b	5	115	1	8	9	7^{2}	5^{1}	7^{4}	8^{5}	Warren R J Jr	8.90
28Feb04 ^{8}GG^{4}	Bring HomeThegold	LB	6	115	8	5	1^{hd}	2^{2}	2^{hd}	8^{2}	9	Carr D	39.50

OFF AT 4:03 Start Good . Won driving. Course firm.

TIME :24, :47^{3}, 1:11^{3}, 1:36, 1:48^{2} (:24.06, :47.62, 1:11.74, 1:36.17, 1:48.48)

$2 Mutuel Prices:			
4 – TRONARE–CHI	23.40	8.80	5.20
5 – SOUD		3.20	2.80
2 – ALY BUBBA			7.60

$1 EXACTA 4–5 PAID $44.10 $2 QUINELLA 4–5 PAID $29.40
$1 TRIFECTA 4–5–2 PAID $474.90 $1 SUPERFECTA 4–5–2–6 PAID $2,682.00

Ch. h, (Jul), by Stuka – Pijama Party , by Manos de Piedra . Trainer Mulhall Kristin. Bred by Haras Don Alberto (Chi).

TRONARE (CHI) broke alertly then settled just off the dueling leaders in the opening half, advanced three wide into the second turn to offer his bid, got to terms with SOUJD in the upper stretch, engaged in a prolonged duel and gradually proved best. SOUD dueled early from the inside with BRING HOME THEGOLD, disposed of that rival into the second turn but was quickly challenged by TRONARE, resisted that rival gamely deep into the stretch then gave way grudgingly. ALY BUBBA was permitted to settle from the inside early, advanced gradually into the second turn, saved ground to the stretch to loom a bold factor at the head of the lane, finished steadily but lacked the needed response. GENT raced unhurried to the second turn, was forced to rally five wide into the lane and closed a gap late. EPICENTRE settled early, commenced his bid four wide on the second turn and finished steadily but was never a serious factor. GOLD RUCKUS raced unhurried early, advanced behind a wall of horses on the second turn, found room in the lane but could not reach the leaders. LUCAYAN INDIAN (IRE) lagged far back to the stretch then could not threaten. MANANAN MCLIR settled early, offered his bid three wide and between horses on the final turn but came up empty in the lane. BRING HOME THEGOLD prompted the pace two wide to the second turn then had nothing left.

Owners– 1, Noctis Stable Papiano Neil and Taub Steve; 2, Shadwell Farm LLC; 3, Daehling Ives Marek et al; 4, Bell Stanley J and Rita; 5, Juddmonte Farms Inc; 6, Franks Farms; 7, Zinent John; 8, Horizon Stable Jarvis and Margolis et al; 9, Craig Sidney H and Jenny

Trainers– 1, Mulhall Kristin; 2, Drysdale Neil; 3, Evans Holly; 4, Inda Eduardo; 5, Frankel Robert; 6, Hollendorfer Jerry; 7, Dempsey Robert S; 8, Dollase Wallace; 9, Hollendorfer Jerry

---

$2 Daily Double (4–4) Paid $1,364.20 ; Daily Double Pool $12,819 .
$1 Pick Three (2–4–4) Paid $3,656.60 ; Pick Three Pool $27,487 .

SIXTH RACE
Gulfstream
MARCH 14, 2004

1⅛ MILES. (1.46²) 25TH RUNNING OF THE RAMPART HANDICAP. Grade II. Purse $200,000 FOR FILLIES AND MARES, THREE YEARS OLD AND UPWARD. By subscription of $200 each, which shall accompany the nomination, $2,000 to pass the entry box and $2,000 additional to start, with $200,000 guaranteed. The owner of the winner to receive $120,000; $40,000 to second, $22,000 to third, $12,000 to fourth and $6,000 to fifth. Weights: Saturday, March 6, 2004. Trophy to winning Owner. Closed Thursday, March 4, 2004 with (12) nominations.

Value of Race: $194,000 Winner $120,000; second $40,000; third $22,000; fourth $12,000. Mutuel Pool $239,632.00 Exacta Pool $216,817.00

Last Raced	Horse	M/Eqt.	A.	Wt	PP	St	¼	½	¾	Str	Fin	Jockey	Odds $1
25Jan04 8SA4	Sightseek	L	5	121	3	2	2²½	2⁶½	2¹²	1⁶	1⁷½	Bailey J D	0.50
26Feb04 8GP2	Redoubled Miss	L bf	5	113	4	4	3¹½	3⁵	3²	3¹½	2²	Coa E M	20.60
15Feb04 11GP3	Lead Story	L	5	117	2	3	4	4	4	4	3⁹	Borel C H	9.70
15Feb04 11GP1	Roar Emotion	L	4	118	1	1	1¹½	1¹	1hd	2hd	4	Velazquez J R	1.50

OFF AT 3:13 Start Good. Won easily. Track fast.

TIME :24³, :48², 1:11⁴, 1:37², 1:51 (:24.70, :48.46, 1:11.81, 1:37.51, 1:51.07)

$2 Mutuel Prices:				
	3 – SIGHTSEEK	3.00	2.60	—
	4 – REDOUBLED MISS		5.40	—
	2 – LEAD STORY		—	—

$1 EXACTA 3–4 PAID $16.30

Ch. m, (Feb), by Distant View – Viviana , by Nureyev . Trainer Frankel Robert. Bred by Juddmonte Farms Inc (Ky).

SIGHTSEEK taken in hand to stalk the pacesetter, moved to gain command approaching the quarter pole, then drew off while well in hand. REDOUBLED MISS unhurried early, saved ground to nearing the stretch, angled out and gained the place while no match for the winner. LEAD STORY failed to menace after being outrun early. ROAR EMOTION set the pace along the inside into the far turn, then had nothing left for the drive.

Owners– 1, Juddmonte Farms Inc; 2, Centaur Farms Inc; 3, Miles A Stevens Jr; 4, Allen Joseph

Trainers– 1, Frankel Robert; 2, Spatz Ronald B; 3, Nafzger Carl A; 4, McLaughlin Kiaran P

$1 Pick Three (1–4–3) Paid $40.70 ; Pick Three Pool $56,847 .

NINTH RACE
Oaklawn
MARCH 14, 2004

1 1/16 MILES. (1.40¹) 45TH RUNNING OF THE RAZORBACK HANDICAP. Grade III. Purse $100,000 FOUR YEAR OLDS AND UPWARD. No nomination fee. $500 to pass the entry box and $1,000 additional to start, with $100,000 Guaranteed of which $60,000 to the Owner of the winner, $20,000 to second, $10,000 to third, $5,000 to fourth, $3,000 to fifth and $2,000 to sixth. Weights to be announced Sunday, March 7. In Handicap Stakes starting preference will be given to highweights. (See reverse side for additional starting limitation information). Starters to be named through the entry box by the usual time of closing. The Owner of the winner to receive a trophy.

Value of Race: $100,000 Winner $60,000; second $20,000; third $10,000; fourth $5,000; fifth $3,000; sixth $2,000. Mutuel Pool $309,183.00 Exacta Pool $157,020.00 Trifecta Pool $174,771.00

Last Raced	Horse	M/Eqt.	A.	Wt	PP	St	¼	½	¾	Str	Fin	Jockey	Odds $1
13Dec03 10TP2	Sonic West	L b	5	113	2	4	4½	3½	3³½	1¹	1²¾	Martinez W	7.40
21Feb04 9OP3	Crafty Shaw	L	6	117	3	2	2¹½	2²½	1hd	3²½	2hd	Perret C	3.40
21Feb04 9OP2	Pie N Burger	L b	6	119	1	1	1½	1hd	2½	2hd	3²	Theriot H J II	0.60
21Feb04 9OP6	Dusty Spike	L f	5	115	4	5	5⁴½	5⁴	4½	4⁴	4²	Berry M C	23.50
21Feb04 6OP5	Maysville Slew	L f	8	112	5	6	6¹	6¹	6½	6⁴½	5²	Noll C S	44.00
8Nov03 8WO1	No Comprende	L b	6	116	6	7	7	7	7	5hd	6⁷¼	Marquez C H Jr	10.20
21Feb04 9OP4	Docent	L bf	6	115	7	3	3¹	4³½	5⁴	7	7	Pettinger D R	9.10

OFF AT 5:28 Start Good. Won driving. Track fast.

TIME :23⁴, :47², 1:11⁴, 1:37¹, 1:43² (:23.91, :47.46, 1:11.99, 1:37.21, 1:43.56)

$2 Mutuel Prices:				
	3 – SONIC WEST	16.80	8.80	2.20
	5 – CRAFTY SHAW		5.40	2.20
	2 – PIE N BURGER			2.20

$2 EXACTA 3–5 PAID $72.20 $2 TRIFECTA 3–5–2 PAID $156.20

B. g, (Feb), by West by West – Contumellous , by Northern Baby . Trainer Van Berg Thomas L. Bred by Richard Lake (Ky).

SONIC WEST stalked the leaders, ranged up to challenge on the outside turning for home, set down when straightened for home, drew clear. CRAFTY SHAW dueled up front off the inside, proved no match for the winner, game for the place while off the inside. PIE N BURGER broke sharp, set the pace while in hand closest to the inside, asked for a bit of some run turning for home, outfinished for the place. DUSTY SPIKE allowed to settle, mild advance toward the inside into the stretch, finished evenly. MAYSVILLE SLEW evenly pace, not a threat. NO COMPRENDE last away, trailed early, failed to fire. DOCENT forwardly placed early, faded.

Owners– 1, Stone Spire LLC Nelson E Clemmens et al; 2, Cella Charles J; 3, Kagele Brothers Inc; 4, Deiter Raymond W; 5, Trout C R; 6, Clarity Stables Dennis & Deborah Brown; 7, Arlene R Daney LLC

Trainers– 1, Van Berg Thomas L; 2, Vestal Peter M; 3, Norman Cole; 4, Lee Mark; 5, Trout C R; 6, Smith James J; 7, Ritchey Tim F

Scratched– Fourth Floor (21Feb04 6OP 2) , Cowboy Stuff (04Feb04 8OP 1)

$2 Pick Three (1–2–3) Paid $440.80 ; Pick Three Pool $14,510 .

FIFTH RACE
Santa Anita
MARCH 14, 2004

$1\frac{1}{16}$ MILES. (1.39) 67TH RUNNING OF THE SAN FELIPE. Grade II. Purse $250,000 FOR THREE-YEAR-OLDS. By subscription of $250 each to accompany the nomination or by supplementary nomination of $5,000 by time of entry. $2,500 additional to start, with $250,000 guaranteed, of which $150,000 to first, $50,000 to second, $30,000 to third,$15,000 to fourth and $5,000 to fifth. *Early bird nominees to the 2004 Santa Anita Derby (Closing Date Thursday, December 11) are automatically eligible to the San Felipe Stakes with all fees waived. 122 lbs. Non-winners of $60,000 twice at one mile orover at any time or one such race since December 25 allowed 3 lbs.; of $50,000 at any distance, 6 lbs. Starters to be named through the entry box by the closing time fo entries. A trophy will be presented to the owner of the winner. Closed with 138 original and 9 regular nominations..

Value of Race: $250,000 Winner $150,000; second $50,000; third $30,000; fourth $15,000; fifth $5,000. Mutuel Pool $924,098.00 Exacta Pool $483,401.00 Quinella Pool $46,622.00 Trifecta Pool $478,193.00 Superfecta Pool $194,660.00

Last Raced	Horse	M/Eqt.	A.	Wt	PP	St	¼	½	¾	Str	Fin	Jockey	Odds $1
8Feb04 ^{8}SA^{3}	Preachinatthebar	LB b	3	116	6	3	$3^{1\frac{1}{2}}$	$2^{2\frac{1}{2}}$	1^{hd}	$1^{1\frac{1}{2}}$	1no	Santiago Javier	8.60
17Jan04 ^{7}SA^{1}	St Averil	LB b	3	122	7	4	$5^{2\frac{1}{2}}$	$4^{\frac{1}{2}}$	3^{1}	$2^{1\frac{1}{2}}$	$2^{4\frac{1}{2}}$	Baze T C	1.30
17Jan04 ^{7}SA^{5}	Harvard Avenue	LB	3	116	8	5	$7^{2\frac{1}{2}}$	7^{2}	$7^{2\frac{1}{2}}$	6^{1}	3^{1}	Court J K	19.70
20Feb04 ^{6}SA^{1}	Cheiron	LB	3	116	2	7	$6^{\frac{1}{2}}$	6^{1}	$5^{\frac{1}{2}}$	4^{1}	4^{2}	Espinoza V	10.20
31Jan04 ^{3}SA^{1}	Last Minute Detail	LB	3	117	5	2	$2^{\frac{1}{2}}$	3^{1}	4^{1}	5^{hd}	5^{1}	Nakatani C S	15.50
21Feb04 ^{2}SA^{1}	Odds On	LB b	3	116	4	6	$1^{1\frac{1}{2}}$	$1^{1\frac{1}{2}}$	2^{2}	$3^{1\frac{1}{2}}$	6^{1}	Solis A	8.00
8Feb04 ^{8}SA^{4}	Action This Day	LB	3	119	3	1	4^{hd}	5^{1}	6^{1}	$7^{\frac{1}{2}}$	$7^{1\frac{1}{2}}$	Flores D R	2.60
23Aug03 DEA^{3}	Toasted	LB	3	116	9	9	8	8	8	8	8	Stevens G L	21.20
12Feb04 ^{3}SA^{2}	Laditude	LB	3	116	1	8		—	—	—	—	Smith M E	60.90

OFF AT 2:46 Start Good For All But LADITUDE. Won driving. Track fast.

TIME :23^{1}, :46^{4}, 1:11, 1:36^{1}, 1:42^{4} (:23.39, :46.82, 1:11.10, 1:36.38, 1:42.87)

$2 Mutuel Prices:

6 – PREACHINATTHEBAR	19.20	6.60	4.60
8 – ST AVERIL		3.20	2.80
9 – HARVARD AVENUE			5.20

$1 EXACTA 6–8 PAID $25.10 $2 QUINELLA 6–8 PAID $18.60
$1 TRIFECTA 6–8–9 PAID $249.40 $1 SUPERFECTA 6–8–9–2 PAID $1,203.80

Gr/ro. c, (Feb), by Silver Charm – Holy Nola, by Silver Deputy. Trainer Baffert Bob. Bred by Michael Pegram (Ky).

PREACHINATTHEBAR stalked three deep on the first turn then off the rail on the backstretch, bid outside the pacesetter to take a short lead on the second turn, inched clear in the stretch and held on gamely under left handed urging. ST AVERIL four wide on the first turn, chased outside on the backstretch and second turn, ranged up three deep into the stretch and closed willingly to just miss. HARVARD AVENUE angled in and settled outside a rival, continued just off the inside leaving the backstretch and outside a foe on the second turn, came out into the stretch and gained the show late. CHEIRON chased inside then a bit off the rail, went outside a rival into and on the second turn and three deep into the stretch and lacked the needed rally. LAST MINUTE DETAIL stalked the leader just off the inside, angled in on the second turn, came out into the stretch and weakened. ODDS ON sped between horses to the early lead, set the pace inside, fought back inside the winner on the second turn but weakened in the stretch. ACTION THIS DAY pulled his way along inside to stalk the pace, came a bit off the rail on the second turn, angled out some into the stretch and also weakened. TOASTED broke a bit slowly and awkwardly, was climbing early, settled off the rail, angled in leaving the second turn and did not rally. LADITUDE stumbled a step out of the gate and lost the rider. The stewards held an inquiry into the start and determined LADITUDE stumbled of his own accord.

Owners– 1, Pegram Michael E; 2, Fulton Stan E; 3, Ron Crockett Inc; 4, Noctis Stable Papiano Neil and Taub Steve; 5, Little Racing Stables & Murphy; 6, McIngvale James; 7, Hughes B Wayne; 8, Port Sidney L and Trust 720270; 9, Bello Michael and Lenner Tom

Trainers– 1, Baffert Bob; 2, Becerra Rafael; 3, O'Neill Doug; 4, Mulhall Kristin; 5, Chatlos Donald Jr; 6, Baffert Bob; 7, Mandella Richard; 8, De Seroux Laura; 9, Bray Simon

Scratched– Rush Into Heaven (28Feb04 ^{8}SA ^{6}), Boss Nass (07Mar04 ^{4}SA ^{1})

$2 Daily Double (7–6) Paid $81.80 ; Daily Double Pool $40,719 .
$1 Pick Three (4–7–6) Paid $300.30 ; Pick Three Pool $97,090 .

EIGHTH RACE
Santa Anita
MARCH 14, 2004

1⅛ MILES. (1.45^{4}) 67TH RUNNING OF THE SANTA MARGARITA INVITATIONAL HANDICAP. Grade I. Purse $300,000 FOR FILLIES AND MARES FOUR YEARS OLD AND UPWARD. By invitation, with no nomination or starting fees. The winner to receive $180,000, with $60,000 to second, $36,000 to third, $18,000 to fourth and $6,000 to fifth.. A trophy will be presented to the ownerof the winner.

Value of Race: $300,000 Winner $180,000; second $60,000; third $36,000; fourth $18,000; fifth $6,000. Mutuel Pool $441,895.00 Exacta Pool $267,028.00 Quinella Pool $27,887.00

Last Raced	Horse	M/Eqt.	A.	Wt	PP	St	¼	½	¾	Str	Fin	Jockey	Odds $1
16Feb04 ^{8}SA^{4}	Adoration	LB	5	118	5	4	2^{1}	$2^{2\frac{1}{2}}$	2^{2}	1^{1}	1^{2}	Smith M E	a- 2.30
16Feb04 ^{8}SA^{1}	Star Parade-Arg	LB	5	115	2	1	1^{1}	1^{2}	1^{1}	$2^{2\frac{1}{2}}$	2^{hd}	Espinoza V	2.10
16Feb04 ^{8}SA^{2}	Bare Necessities	LB	5	118	4	3	$4^{2\frac{1}{2}}$	$4^{2\frac{1}{2}}$	3^{hd}	$3^{2\frac{1}{2}}$	3^{2}	Valdivia J Jr	1.60
16Feb04 ^{8}SA^{3}	La Tour-Chi	LB	5	115	3	5	5	5	5	4^{1}	$4^{8\frac{1}{2}}$	Solis A	4.00
14Feb04 ^{8}SA^{2}	Fencelineneighbor	LB	4	114	1	2	$3^{3\frac{1}{2}}$	3^{2}	$4^{4\frac{1}{2}}$	5	5	Baze T C	a- 2.30

a–Coupled: Adoration and Fencelineneighbor.

OFF AT 4:21 Start Good . Won driving. Track fast.

TIME :23^{1}, :46^{3}, 1:11, 1:35^{4}, 1:48^{4} (:23.20, :46.76, 1:11.07, 1:35.88, 1:48.85)

$2 Mutuel Prices:

1A– ADORATION(a-entry)	6.60	3.60	—
2 – STAR PARADE–ARG		3.60	—
4 – BARE NECESSITIES		—	—

$1 EXACTA 1–2 PAID $8.90 $2 QUINELLA 1–2 PAID $8.40

B. m, (Apr), by Honor Grades – Sewing Lady, by Key to the Mint. Trainer Hofmans David. Bred by Lucy G Bassett (Ky).

ADORATION stalked the pace off the rail, bid outside the runner-up into the stretch, took the lead and inched clear and proved best under some urging and good handling. STAR PARADE (ARG) pulled her way to the front and angled in, set the pace along the inside, kicked clear on the backstretch, inched away again when the winner loomed into the second turn, continued along the inside, could not match the winner in the stretch but gamely held second. BARE NECESSITIES angled in and chased inside, came a bit off the rail on the second turn, angled out into the stretch and just missed the place. LA TOUR (CHI) angled in and saved ground on the first turn, chased off the rail on the backstretch, angled in again on the second turn, swung out into the stretch and lacked the needed rally. FENCELINENEIGHBOR pulled her way along inside to stalk the pace, came off the rail into the backstretch, continued outside a rival, went three deep into the stretch and weakened.

Owners– 1, Amerman Racing Stables LLC; 2, Tanaka Gary A; 3, Iron County Farms Inc; 4, Hunt Nelson B; 5, Amerman Racing Stables LLC

Trainers– 1, Hofmans David; 2, Vienna Darrell; 3, Dollase Wallace; 4, McAnally Ronald; 5, Machowsky Michael

Scratched– Sweetshew (23Jan04 ^{3}SA ^{1})

$2 Daily Double (9–1) Paid $144.40 ; Daily Double Pool $33,206 .
$1 Pick Three (8/10/11–9–1) Paid $127.00 ; Pick Three Pool $73,389 .

TENTH RACE
Tampa Bay
MARCH 14, 2004

ABOUT 1⅛ MILES. (Turf) (1.47^4) 6TH RUNNING OF THE HILLSBOROUGH. Grade III. Purse $100,000 FOR FILLIES AND MARES FOUR YEARS OLD AND UPWARD. By subscription of $100 each which should accompany the nomination, $400 to pass the entry box and $500 additional to start with $100,000 guaranteed. With 60% to the winner, 20% to second, 10% to third, 5%to fourth, 3% to fifth and 2% to sixth. Weight 122 lbs. Non-winners of a Sweepstakes on the turf at one mile or over in 2004, 2 lbs.; $50,000 at one mile or over since November 30, 2003, 4 lbs.; $25,000 once or $15,000 twice at any distance since then, 6lbs. (Maiden, Claiming and starter races not considered in estimating weight allowances) Starters and riders to be named through the entry box by the usual time of closing. This field will be limited to twelve starters. In the event more than twelve passthrough the entry box, the twelve starters will be determined with preference given to those that have accumulated the highest turf earnings in 2003–04. In addition, no same owner entry may start, regardless of earnings, to the exclusion of a singleentry. For those that enter and are eliminated under these conditions, the nomination and entry fees will be refunded.

Value of Race: $100,000 Winner $60,000; second $20,000; third $10,000; fourth $5,000; fifth $3,000; sixth $2,000. Mutuel Pool $248,609.00 Exacta Pool $160,112.00 Trifecta Pool $131,974.00 Superfecta Pool $36,541.00

Last Raced	Horse	M/Eqt.	A.	Wt	PP	St	¼	½	¾	Str	Fin	Jockey	Odds $1
10Feb04 ^{8}Tam^{3}	Coney Kitty-Ire	L f	6	116	3	2	7½	6^{1½}	6½	4^{1}	1^{nk}	Santos J A	2.90
10Feb04 ^{8}Tam^{1}	Madeira Mist-Ire	L	5	122	6	3	4^{hd}	4½	4^{1}	3½	2^{nk}	Prado E S	2.70
19Oct03 ^{8}Kee^{4}	Alternate	L b	5	116	8	7	6^{1½}	5^{1½}	5½	5^{1½}	3^{3½}	Velasquez C	6.60
10Feb04 ^{8}Tam^{5}	Strait From Texas	L	5	116	9	5	1^{hd}	2½	2^{1½}	2½	4½	Castanon J L	9.90
10Feb04 ^{8}Tam^{12}	Lady Bi Bi	L	5	116	10	6	5^{hd}	7½	9½	6^{2}	5^{nk}	Buckley P R	54.90
28Jan04 ^{7}SA^{6}	Star Vega-GB	L	4	116	1	10	12	10½	7^{1}	7^{1}	6^{nk}	Ramsammy E	8.30
6Mar04 ^{6}Tam^{4}	Kimster	L b	5	116	4	9	11^{1½}	11^{2}	8½	8^{1}	7^{1}	Woolsey R W	45.10
10Feb04 ^{8}Tam^{2}	SomethingVentured	L b	5	116	5	8	9^{1½}	8^{hd}	10^{1}	9^{1}	8½	Day P	3.30
10Feb04 ^{8}Tam^{10}	Love Sting	L b	4	116	7	4	2^{hd}	1^{1½}	1^{1}	1½	9^{2}	Mata F	54.40
10Feb04 ^{8}Tam^{6}	Chef's Choice	L	6	116	2	1	10^{hd}	1^{2}	1^{1½}	1^{1½}	10^{nk}	Pompell T L	38.50
10Feb04 ^{8}Tam^{9}	Brandala		6	116	11	12	8^{1}	9^{1}	12	12	11^{nk}	Castillo O O	49.00
20Dec03 ^{8}Aqu^{5}	Caught in the Rain	L	5	117	12	11	3^{1½}	3^{1}	3½	10^{1}	12	Warner T	10.70

OFF AT 4:48 Start Good . Won driving. Course firm.

TIME :24^3, :49, 1:12^4, 1:37, 1:48^4 (:24.71, :49.07, 1:12.80, 1:37.09, 1:48.83)

$2 Mutuel Prices:			
3 – CONEY KITTY-IRE	7.80	3.60	3.20
6 – MADEIRA MIST-IRE		3.20	2.60
8 – ALTERNATE			4.40

$2 EXACTA 3–6 PAID $23.80 $2 TRIFECTA 3–6–8 PAID $119.60
$2 SUPERFECTA 3–6–8–9 PAID $370.80

Ch. m, (Apr), by Lycius – Auntie Maureen-Ire , by Roi Danzig . Trainer Toner James J. Bred by Tony Doyle (Ire).

CONEY KITTY (IRE) unhurried early, advanced in traffic through the second turn, split rivals while rallying in the furlong grounds then was all out to prevail late after coming out and pushing out both MADEIRA MIST and ALTERNATE late. MADEIRA MIST (IRE) stalked inside for seven furlongs, angled out three wide out of the second turn to loom boldly a furlong out then just missed after being brushed and pushed out late. ALTERNATE was stoutly rated for seven furlongs, bid outside the top two five wide out of the second turn then just hung late after also being carried out late. STRAIT FROM TEXAS chased from the outset, bid outside the leader after seven furlongs,drew even in the furlong grounds then weakened late. LADY BI BI was well placed much of the way but failed to gain. STAR VEGA (GB) passed tiring rivals. KIMSTER failed to menace. SOMETHING VENTURED was no factor. LOVE STING set a moderate pace to mid stretch then faded. CHEF'S CHOICE was no factor. BRANDALA showed little. CAUGHT IN THE RAIN stopped. There was a stewards inquiry and claim of foul by the rider of MEDEIRA MIST against the winner for interference in the stretch but the results were allowed to stand as is.

Owners– 1, Betz William J Humphrey Steve and Seelbinder Arthur; 2, Skymarc Farm Inc; 3, Pin Oak Stable LLC; 4, J and J Investments; 5, Tri County Stables; 6, Cuchna John R Jim Ford Inc and Pearson Daron; 7, Joyce Daniel L Jr; 8, Wiemer Irvin and McLane John; 9, Emerald Pastures Corp Inc; 10, Amato Stefanie; 11, Sorin Stables; 12, Heiligbrodt Racing Stable and New Walter L

Trainers– 1, Toner James J; 2, Clement Christophe; 3, Motion H Graham; 4, Michael James A; 5, Alexander Bruce F; 6, Cassidy James; 7, Kielty Donald E; 8, Pletcher Todd A; 9, Connelly Ronald Rex; 10, Rice Don; 11, Walsh Timothy; 12, Brinkman Brett

Scratched– Rizzi Girl (06Mar04 ^{6}Tam^{1}) , Raise Her Flag (02Mar04 ^{7}Tam^{1})

$2 Pick Four (2/3–1/5–1–3) Paid $89.40 ; Pick Four Pool $28,090 .

ELEVENTH RACE
Tampa Bay
MARCH 14, 2004

1 1/16 MILES. (1.43^{2}) 24TH RUNNING OF THE TAMPA BAY DERBY. Grade III. Purse $250,000 FOR THREE YEAR OLDS. By subscription of $100 each which should accompany the nomination, $1,000 to pass the entry box and $1,500 additional to start with $250,000 guaranteed. With 60% to the winner, 20% to second, 10% to third, 5% to fourth, 3% to fifthand 2% to sixth. Weight 122 lbs. Non–winners of a Sweepstakes at one mile or over in 2004, 2 lbs.; $50,000 twice at one mile or over other than maiden or claiming, 4 lbs.; $50,000 once or $25,000 twice at any distance other than maiden or claiming, 6 lbs. Closed February 29, 2004 with 44 nominations.

Value of Race: $250,000 Winner $150,000; second $50,000; third $25,000; fourth $12,500; fifth $7,500; sixth $5,000. Mutuel Pool $431,675.00 Exacta Pool $273,179.00 Trifecta Pool $252,745.00 Superfecta Pool $79,910.00

Last Raced	Horse	M/Eqt.	A.	Wt	PP	St	¼	½	¾	Str	Fin	Jockey	Odds $1
14Feb04 ^{10}GP^{1}	Limehouse	L	3	118	1	2	2½	4^{1}	5^{1}	3½	1^{nk}	Day P	0.90
21Feb04 ^{11}GP^{6}	Mustanfar	L b	3	116	3	8	8	6^{hd}	4^{hd}	5½	2^{1}	Judice J C	7.00
14Feb04 ^{9}GP^{1}	Swingforthefences	L	3	116	6	5	3½	2^{hd}	2½	2^{1}	$3^{1\frac{3}{4}}$	Prado E S	2.10
21Feb04 ^{10}Tam^{3}	Zakocity	L b	3	116	7	7	7^{hd}	7½	6^{hd}	4½	$4^{1\frac{3}{4}}$	Santos J A	9.00
21Feb04 ^{10}Tam^{1}	Kaufy Mate	L b	3	122	2	3	5^{1}	5^{hd}	7^{1}	$6^{1\frac{1}{2}}$	$5^{1\frac{3}{4}}$	Zimmerman R	10.90
14Feb04 ^{4}GP^{1}	Very Formal M. D.	L	3	118	5	1	$1^{1\frac{1}{2}}$	1^{1}	1½	1½	6^{hd}	Husbands P	27.10
29Nov03 ^{11}Crc^{5}	Tap Dancer	L	3	116	4	6	6½	8	8	7^{15}	$7^{26\frac{3}{4}}$	Houghton T D	23.70
21Feb04 ^{10}Tam^{4}	Misguided Left	L b	3	116	8	4	4^{1}	3½	3½	8	8	Castanon J L	66.40

OFF AT 5:21 Start Good . Won driving. Track fast.

TIME :23^{3}, :47^{3}, 1:11^{4}, 1:37^{1}, 1:43^{4} (:23.69, :47.78, 1:11.90, 1:37.35, 1:43.99)

$2 Mutuel Prices:

1 – LIMEHOUSE	3.80	2.60	2.20
3 – MUSTANFAR		4.20	2.40
6 – SWINGFORTHEFENCES			2.40

$2 EXACTA 1–3 PAID $21.40 $2 TRIFECTA 1–3–6 PAID $50.20
$2 SUPERFECTA 1–3–6–7 PAID $117.80

Ch. c, (Feb), by Grand Slam – Dixieland Blues , by Dixieland Band . Trainer Pletcher Todd A. Bred by Cheryl A Curtin (Fla).

LIMEHOUSE was never far back, angled off the rail four wide out of the second turn then responded to strong left hand pressure to be up in the closing strides. MUSTANFAR made one move up the rail to the quarter pole, dropped back a bit out of the second turn then came on again inside to draw even for the lead in the final 40 yards before just hanging late. SWINGFORTHEFENCES was never far back, bid out of the second turn to draw even for the lead leaving the furlong marker then also just hung late. ZAKOCITY was stoutly rated for five furlongs, looped four wide out of the turn to be in striking distance a furlong out but weakened late. KAUFY MATE chased for five furlongs, dropped back and angled to the inside then got through to be in striking distance a furlong out but weakened. VERY FORMAL M. D. set a quick pace to mid stretch then faltered. TAP DANCER failed to menace. MISGUIDED LEFT bid three wide after five furlongs then stopped.

Owners– 1, Dogwood Stable; 2, Shadwell Stable; 3, Klaravich Stables Inc; 4, Franks Farms; 5, Kaufman Gregory; 6, Schickedanz Bruno; 7, Campbell Gilbert G; 8, Sainer Joel W

Trainers– 1, Pletcher Todd A; 2, McLaughlin Kiaran P; 3, Violette Richard A Jr; 4, Wolfson Martin D; 5, Ziadie Kirk; 6, Collazo Henry; 7, O'Connell Kathleen; 8, Braddy J David

$2 Daily Double (3–1) Paid $18.80 ; Daily Double Pool $22,455 .
$2 Pick Three (1–3–1) Paid $48.40 ; Pick Three Pool $34,505 .

SEVENTH RACE
Aqueduct
MARCH 20, 2004

1 MILE. (1.32^{2}) 52ND RUNNING OF THE GOTHAM. Grade III. Purse $200,000 (Up to $34,800 NYSBFOA) FOR THREE YEAR OLDS. By subscription of $200 each, which should accompany the nomination; $1,000 to pass the entry box; $1,000 to start. The purse to be divided 60% to the winner, 20% to second, 10% to third, 5% to fourth, 3% to fifth and 2% divided equally among the remaining finishers. 123 lbs. Non–winners of $150,000; or $45,000 twice other than restricted stakes allowed 3 lbs.; $50,000; or $30,000 in 2004, 5 lbs.; three races other than maiden or claiming, 7 lbs. A trophy will be presented to thewinning owner. Closed Saturday, March 6, 2004 with 36 Nominations.

Value of Race: $200,000 Winner $120,000; second $40,000; third $20,000; fourth $10,000; fifth $6,000; sixth $1,334; seventh $1,334; eighth $1,332. Mutuel Pool $933,664.00 Exacta Pool $693,414.00 Trifecta Pool $512,689.00

Last Raced	Horse	M/Eqt.	A.	Wt	PP	St	¼	½	¾	Str	Fin	Jockey	Odds $1
14Feb04 ^{10}GP^{3}	Saratoga County	L bf	3	116	5	2	5^{hd}	5½	3^{hd}	1½	$1^{2\frac{1}{4}}$	Castellano J J	4.70
13Sep03 ^{10}TP^{3}	Pomeroy	b	3	116	4	4	2½	2½	1½	$2^{2\frac{1}{2}}$	2¾	Smith M E	9.20
28Feb04 ^{1}GP^{1}	Eddington	L b	3	116	2	8	7½	7^{hd}	5½	4^{2}	$3^{5\frac{1}{4}}$	Prado E S	1.35
14Feb04 ^{10}GP^{2}	Deputy Storm	L	3	116	1	5	1½	1½	$2^{1\frac{1}{2}}$	3½	4½	Chavez J F	8.00
21Feb04 ^{9}Aqu^{1}	Redskin Warrior	L f	3	120	6	3	3^{hd}	3½	4^{1}	5^{3}	5^{2}	Migliore R	2.75
22Feb04 ^{6}Aqu^{2}	Rockhewn	L	3	116	7	6	8	8	$7^{1\frac{1}{2}}$	$6^{3\frac{1}{2}}$	$6^{8\frac{3}{4}}$	Molina V H	61.25
7Feb04 ^{9}Aqu^{3}	Quick Action	L	3	120	8	1	4½	$6^{2\frac{1}{2}}$	$6^{2\frac{1}{2}}$	$7^{3\frac{1}{2}}$	7^{4}	Bridgmohan S X	15.00
22Feb04 ^{6}Aqu^{1}	War's Prospect	L b	3	116	3	7	$6^{3\frac{1}{2}}$	4^{hd}	8	8	8	Santana D	71.50

OFF AT 3:57 Start Good . Won driving. Track good.

TIME :21^{4}, :43^{3}, 1:08, 1:35^{2} (:21.88, :43.67, 1:08.03, 1:35.53)

$2 Mutuel Prices:

5 – SARATOGA COUNTY	11.40	6.10	3.20
4 – POMEROY		9.20	4.40
2 – EDDINGTON			2.50

$2 EXACTA 5–4 PAID $93.50 $2 TRIFECTA 5–4–2 PAID $287.50

B. c, (Mar), by Valid Expectations – Grub's Dancer , by Grub . Trainer Weaver George. Bred by Round Table LLC (Ky).

SARATOGA COUNTY raced close up between rivals while in hand, advanced inside on the turn, came wide into the stretch, dug in determinedly when roused and drew clear late under a drive. POMEROY pressed the pace from the outside, earned a short lead turning for home then dug in gamely on the rail in the stretch. EDDINGTON was bumped after the start, dropped back early, split rivals on the turn, came wide into the stretch and finished well outside. DEPUTY STORM was hustled to the front, set a rapid pace along the inside and tired in the final furlong. REDSKIN WARRIOR chased the pace while three wide and had no response when roused. ROCKHEWN was outrun early, raced wide throughout and had no rally. QUICK ACTION raced close up while three wide and tired after three quarters. WAR'S PROSPECT was bumped after the start, stumbled, showed brief speed along the inside and tired.

Owners– 1, Pollard Evelyn M; 2, Tabor Michael B Smith Derrick; 3, Willmott Stables Inc; 4, Spence James C; 5, Paraneck Stable; 6, Dirienzo Orlando; 7, Overbrook Farm; 8, W A and R Stable

Trainers– 1, Weaver George; 2, Biancone Patrick L; 3, Hennig Mark; 4, Pletcher Todd A; 5, Pedersen Jennifer; 6, Reid Robert E Jr; 7, Lukas D Wayne; 8, Anderson William D

$2 Daily Double (3–5) Paid $140.50 ; Daily Double Pool $147,219 .
$2 Pick Three (4–3–5) Paid $1,011.00 ; Pick Three Pool $78,902 .

NINTH RACE
Aqueduct
MARCH 20, 2004

7 FURLONGS. (1.20) 12TH RUNNING OF THE CICADA. Grade III. Purse $100,000 (Up to $19,400 NYSBFOA) FOR FILLIES THREE YEARS OLD. By subscription of $100 each, which should accompany the nomination; $500 to pass the entry box; $500 to start, with $100,000 added. The added money and all fees to be divided 60% to the winner, 20% tosecond, 10% to third, 5% to fourth, 3% to fifth and 2% divided equally among the remaining finishers. Weight 122 lbs. Non-winners of $35,000 in 2004 other than restricted stake allowed 2 lbs.; three races other than maiden or claiming, 4 lbs.; two racesother than maiden or claiming, 6 lbs. A trophy will be presented to the winning owner. Closed Saturday, March 6, 2004 with 26 Nominations.

Value of Race: $109,100 Winner $65,460; second $21,820; third $10,910; fourth $5,455; fifth $3,273; sixth $2,182. Mutuel Pool $424,013.00 Exacta Pool $357,090.00 Trifecta Pool $237,490.00

Last Raced	Horse	M/Eqt.	A.	Wt	PP	St	¼	½	Str	Fin	Jockey	Odds $1
14Feb04 9Aqu2	Bohemian Lady	L	3	116	3	2	2½	2½	15½	16½	Prado E S	1.55
15Feb04 8SA5	Whoopi Cat	L	3	116	4	3	3½	45½	22	24¾	Smith M E	1.10
14Feb04 9Aqu3	Baldomera	L b	3	122	1	6	6	6	6	3nk	Vega H	8.00
12Dec03 8Aqu5	Whirlwind Charlott	L b	3	116	6	1	43	3hd	3hd	4nk	Molina V H	34.00
20Nov03 3Aqu1	Freeroll	L	3	116	5	4	51	5½	51½	51¼	Castellano J J	9.50
26Feb04 8Aqu2	She's a Mugs	L	3	116	2	5	11	1½	42½	6	Gryder A T	14.10

OFF AT 4:56 Start Good. Won driving. Track good.
TIME :22, :443, 1:094, 1:231 (:22.07, :44.67, 1:09.97, 1:23.22)

$2 Mutuel Prices:				
	3 – BOHEMIAN LADY	5.10	2.90	2.40
	4 – WHOOPI CAT		2.80	2.40
	1 – BALDOMERA			2.80

$2 EXACTA 3–4 PAID $9.10 $2 TRIFECTA 3–4–1 PAID $25.60

B. f, (Feb), by Carson City – Weekend in Indy, by A.P. Indy. Trainer Pletcher Todd A. Bred by WinStar Farm LLC (Ky).

BOHEMIAN LADY raced with the pace from the outside while in hand, took over when asked for run, drew well clear and widened while being kept to the task to the wire. WHOOPI CAT was hustled along early, chased the pace along the inside, was no match for the winner and was clearly best of the others. BALDOMERA was outrun along the inside early, came wide for the drive and lacked a rally. WHIRLWIND CHARLOTT raced close up outside, put in a three wide run nearing the stretch and tired in the drive. FREEROLL had no response when roused. SHE'S A MUGS set the pace along the inside and tired in the stretch.

Owners– 1, Padua Stable; 2, Tabor Michael B Smith Derrick; 3, Hidden Lane Farms Inc; 4, Classic Star Stable LLC; 5, Brodsky Alan; 6, Lucky Shamrock Stable

Trainers– 1, Pletcher Todd A; 2, Biancone Patrick L; 3, Preciado Guadalupe; 4, Dowd John F; 5, Hennig Mark; 6, Zito Nicholas P

Scratched– Among My Souvenirs (14Feb04 9Aqu1)

SIXTH RACE
Gulfstream
MARCH 20, 2004

1½ MILES. (Turf) (2.23) 43RD RUNNING OF THE PAN AMERICAN HANDICAP. Grade II. Purse $200,000 FOR THREE YEAR OLDS AND UPWARD. By subscription of $200 each, which shall accompany the nomination, $2,000 to pass the entry box and $2,000 additional to start, with $200,000 guaranteed. The owner of the winner to receive $120,000; $40,000 to second, $22,000 to third, $12,000 to fourth and $6,000 to fifth. Trophy to winning Owner. In the event this stake is taken off the turf, it may be subject to downgrading upon review of the Graded Stakes Committee. Closed Wednesday, March 10, 2004 with (20) nominations.

Value of Race: $200,000 Winner $120,000; second $40,000; third $22,000; fourth $12,000; fifth $6,000. Mutuel Pool $445,815.00 Exacta Pool $311,730.00 Trifecta Pool $211,707.00 Superfecta Pool $65,253.00

Last Raced	Horse	M/Eqt.	A.	Wt	PP	¼	½	1	1¼	Str	Fin	Jockey	Odds $1
22Feb04 11GP5	Quest Star	L b	5	114	3	2½	2½	21½	11	13	1½	Day P	1.70
22Feb04 11GP4	Request for Parole	L	5	115	5	51	4½	4½	62	3½	21¾	Santos J A	1.40
6Mar04 10GP1	Megantic	L	6	112	1	7	7	62½	31	21	32½	Bravo J	20.90
21Feb04 9GP5	Believe I Can Fly	L b	5	111	4	6hd	6½	7	7	7	4no	Arango L E	a- 14.60
30Jan04 9GP1	Charge	L	4	113	6	31	3½	3½	4hd	62	51¼	Samyn J L	7.40
22Feb04 5GP1	Jocy Blueeyes	L b	4	114	2	4hd	5½	5½	5hd	5hd	62	Coa E M	a- 14.60
22Feb04 11GP7	Man From Wicklow	L bf	7	117	7	11½	11½	1hd	2hd	4½	7	Landry R C	4.50

a–Coupled: Believe I Can Fly and Joey Blueeyes.

OFF AT 3:13 Start Good. Won driving. Course firm.
TIME :241, :50, 1:153, 1:403, 2:262 (:24.34, :50.13, 1:15.68, 1:40.78, 2:26.46)

$2 Mutuel Prices:				
	3 – QUEST STAR	5.40	2.60	2.20
	4 – REQUEST FOR PAROLE		2.60	2.20
	2 – MEGANTIC			3.60

$1 EXACTA 3–4 PAID $4.80 $1 TRIFECTA 3–4–2 PAID $36.10
$1 SUPERFECTA 3–4–2–1 PAID $95.30

Dk. b or br. h, (May), by Broad Brush – Tinaca, by Manila. Trainer Walden W Elliott. Bred by John Messara (Ky).

QUEST STAR tracked the pace along the hedge, slipped through inside MAN FROM WICKLOW on the clubhouse turn to prompt the pace, took over from that rival entering the far turn and opened a clear lead, then was fully extended to last over. REQUEST FOR PAROLE reserved off the pace, raced three wide on the final turn and was gaining on the winner at the finish. MEGANTIC steadied entering the first turn, then steadied again on the clubhouse turn, moved up quickly to reach contention three wide on the final turn but couldn't sustain his bid. BELIEVE I CAN FLY failed to menace. CHARGE stalked the leaders into the final turn and gave way. JOEY BLUEEYES reserved off the pace, saved ground and tired in the drive. MAN FROM WICKLOW quickly moved to the fore, made the pace along the hedge to the final turn and faltered.

Owners– 1, Mansell Stables LLC; 2, Knighton Jeri and Sam; 3, Runnin Horse Farm Inc; 4, Happy Valley Stables; 5, Whitney Wheelock; 6, Happy Valley Stables; 7, Violette Richard A Jr

Trainers– 1, Walden W Elliott; 2, Hough Stanley M; 3, Pointer Norman R; 4, Collazo Henry; 5, McGaughey III Claude R; 6, Collazo Henry; 7, Violette Richard A Jr

---

$1 Pick Three (5–1–3) Paid $39.00 ; Pick Three Pool $61,210 .

NINTH RACE
Santa Anita
MARCH 20, 2004

1½ MILES. (Turf) ($2:22^4$) 53RD RUNNING OF THE SAN LUIS REY HANDICAP. Grade II. Purse $200,000 FOR FOUR-YEAR-OLDS AND UPWARD. By subscription of $200 each to accompany the nomination or by supplementary nomination of $4,000 by Sunday, March 14. $2,000 additional to start, with $200,000 guaranteed, of which $120,000 to first, $40,000 to second, $24,000 to third, $12,000 to fourth and $4,000 to fifth. Weights Tuesday, March 16. Starters to be named through the entry box by the closing time of entries. High weights preferred. A trophy will be presented to the owner of the winner. Closed with 17 nominations. (Rail at 8 feet).

Value of Race: $200,000 Winner $120,000; second $40,000; third $24,000; fourth $12,000; fifth $4,000. Mutuel Pool $598,337.00 Exacta Pool $308,252.00 Quinella Pool $28,934.00 Trifecta Pool $311,947.00 Superfecta Pool $127,897.00

Last Raced	Horse	M/Eqt.	A.	Wt	PP	¼	½	1	1¼	Str	Fin	Jockey	Odds $1
16Feb04 ^{9}SA^4	Meteor Storm-GB	LB	5	115	5	$4^{1\frac{1}{2}}$	$4^{1\frac{1}{2}}$	$4^{1\frac{1}{2}}$	4^1	$2^{1\frac{1}{2}}$	1^{nk}	Valdivia J Jr	7.80
16Feb04 ^{9}SA^5	Labirinto	LB	6	114	7	9^{10}	9^{10}	9^{10}	$8^{1\frac{1}{2}}$	5^{hd}	$2^{\frac{3}{4}}$	Santiago Javier	4.00
16Feb04 ^{9}SA^{10}	GenedeCampeo-Brz	LB f	5	114	8	3^3	$3^{3\frac{1}{2}}$	3^2	$2^{\frac{1}{2}}$	1^{hd}	$3^{\frac{3}{4}}$	Berrio O A	33.00
16Feb04 ^{9}SA^7	Runaway Dancer	LB b	5	115	3	7^{hd}	$8^{1\frac{1}{2}}$	7^{hd}	6^{hd}	6^3	4^{hd}	Solis A	5.10
16Feb04 ^{9}SA^1	Puerto Banus	LB b	5	116	9	8^2	$7^{\frac{1}{2}}$	$6^{\frac{1}{2}}$	5^1	$3^{1\frac{1}{2}}$	5^4	Espinoza V	2.80
24Jan04 ^{6}SA^7	White Buck	LB b	4	117	4	6^1	6^1	8^1	9^{12}	7^{hd}	$6^{\frac{1}{2}}$	Nakatani C S	16.10
6Mar04 ^{10}SA^5	Toccet	LB b	4	114	2	$1^{1\frac{1}{2}}$	1^1	1^1	1^{hd}	4^{hd}	$7^{\frac{1}{2}}$	Pedroza M A	18.80
24Jan04 ^{10}GP^3	Special Matter	LB b	6	114	6	5^2	$5^{\frac{1}{2}}$	5^1	$7^{1\frac{1}{2}}$	$8^{\frac{1}{2}}$	8^4	Baze T C	9.70
11Feb04 ^{7}SA^8	Asong for Billy	LB	5	117	1	$2^{1\frac{1}{2}}$	2^1	2^2	$3^{1\frac{1}{2}}$	9^{15}	9^{11}	Saint-Martin E	17.20
16Feb04 ^{9}SA^3	Continental Red	LB	8	116	10	10	10	10	10	10	10	Stevens G L	5.20

OFF AT 4:39 Start Good For All But CONTINENTAL RED. Won driving. Course firm.

TIME $:23^1$, $:47^1$, 1:12, $1:37^4$, 2:02, 2:26 (:23.31, :47.32, 1:12.09, 1:37.88, 2:02.18, 2:26.03)

$2 Mutuel Prices:				
	6 – METEOR STORM–GB	**17.60**	**8.80**	**6.80**
	8 – LABIRINTO		**6.40**	**4.80**
	9 – GENE DE CAMPEAO–BRZ			**15.80**

$1 EXACTA 6–8 PAID $53.80 $2 QUINELLA 6–8 PAID $50.60
$1 TRIFECTA 6–8–9 PAID $1,174.50 $1 SUPERFECTA 6–8–9–4 PAID $3,926.40

B. h, (Apr), by Bigstone–Ire – Hunt the Sun–GB , by Rainbow Quest . Trainer Dollase Wallace. Bred by Juddmonte Farms (GB).

METEOR STORM (GB) content to stalk leaders while leading second pack and saving ground, advanced around final bend, angled out and three wide into the lane, collared foe passing sixteenth marker and held late under urging. LABIRINTO reserved well off pace while saving ground, came off fence then regained the rail on the final bend, later angled out in upper stretch, split foes through the drive and was getting to the winner nearing the wire. GENE DE CAMPEAO (BRZ) drifted out crossing the dirt, content to track leaders a bit off the rail, advanced and challenged three deep, edged away in upper stretch, angled in some but could not stave off rivals late. RUNAWAY DANCER settled off the pace while saving ground to the final turn, shifted out, moved up three wide into the lane, came out further and finished with flourish from the outside. PUERTO BANUS reserved outside foe early, later three wide to the last bend, then four wide into the stretch but lacked the needed late response. WHITE BUCK settled from the inside and hugged to the rail to the stretch, came out a bit, split foes and improved placing. TOCCET stepped to the front and dictated the fractions under snug hold, continued inside, resisted briefly on final turn but then weakened. SPECIAL MATTER settled off the leaders and off the fence, raced outside eventual winner in middle stages, later swung out for room entering the stretch and failed to menace. ASONG FOR BILLY stalked the pacesetter to the final turn, bid between rivals early on that bend but failed to sustain effort and weakened. CONTINENTAL RED went to his knees at the break, fell far back in the early stages, then continued to trail throughout.

Owners– 1, Jarvis Michael Margolis Gary and Smole Ken et al; 2, Mio Jean P; 3, Bandeirantes Stable; 4, R L Stables; 5, Noctis Stable Papiano Neil and Taub Steve; 6, Manoogian Jay; 7, Borislow Daniel M; 8, Elder Nancy and McClintock Janice and George et al; 9, Wongs Stable Inc; 10, Fitzpatrick Sharon M

Trainers– 1, Dollase Wallace; 2, Powell Leonard; 3, Avila A C; 4, Hendricks Dan L; 5, Mulhall Kristin; 6, Mitchell Mike; 7, Scanlan John F; 8, Becerra Rafael; 9, O'Neill Doug; 10, Jory Ian P D

Scratched– Researched (IRE) (16Feb04 ^{9}SA ^{8})

$2 Daily Double (4–6) Paid $55.00 ; Daily Double Pool $37,412 .
$1 Pick Three (8–4–6) Paid $584.60 ; Pick Three Pool $81,304 .

EIGHTH RACE

Turfway Park

MARCH 20, 2004

1⅛ MILES. (1.46^{3}) 33RD RUNNING OF THE LANE'S END. Grade II. Purse $500,000 FOR THREE-YEAR-OLDS. Colts and Geldings, 121 lbs.; Fillies, 116 lbs. By subscription of $300, $2,500 to enter and $2,500 additional to start. Supplementary nominations may be made at the time of entry March 18, 2004 by payment of $30,000 each (includes entry and starting fees). The maximum number of starters will be twelve. In the event more than twelve pass the entry box, the starters will be determined with preference given to Graded/Group Stakes winners in order (I-II-III), Stakes winners, then highestcareer earnings. Subscription fees may be paid with subscription or at a later date when invoiced. All nominees will be required to pay entry and starting fees, (including subscription fee) prior to the running of the race. Closed February 18, 2004 with147 nominations.

Value of Race: $500,000 Winner $300,000; second $100,000; third $50,000; fourth $25,000; fifth $15,000; sixth $10,000. Mutuel Pool $790,458.00 Exacta Pool $503,547.00 Trifecta Pool $465,237.00 Superfecta Pool $136,985.00

Last Raced	Horse	M/Eqt.	A.	Wt	PP	St	¼	½	¾	Str	Fin	Jockey	Odds $1
5Mar04 ^{8}Aqu^{2}	Sinister G	L	3	121	11	5	$1^{1\frac{1}{2}}$	1^{1}	1^{hd}	1^{1}	$1^{1\frac{1}{2}}$	Toscano P R	16.40
29Feb04 ^{7}TP^{1}	Tricky Taboo	L f	3	121	9	10	7^{1}	7^{2}	6^{2}	3^{4}	$2^{\frac{3}{4}}$	D'Amico A J	54.60
28Feb04 ^{10}TP^{2}	Little Matth Man	L b	3	121	10	11	11	10^{4}	9^{2}	4^{2}	3^{1}	Fragoso P	10.80
17Jan04 ^{7}SA^{7}	That's an Outrage	L b	3	121	2	6	$6^{\frac{1}{2}}$	5^{hd}	$2^{1\frac{1}{2}}$	$2^{1\frac{1}{2}}$	$4^{7\frac{1}{2}}$	Albarado R J	18.80
14Feb04 ^{1}GP^{1}	Birdstone	L	3	121	1	1	5^{hd}	6^{hd}	5^{1}	5^{5}	$5^{1\frac{1}{4}}$	Bailey J D	0.60
6Mar04 ^{7}SA^{10}	Hasslefree	L b	3	121	6	9	9^{3}	9^{7}	8^{1}	$7^{\frac{1}{2}}$	$6^{1\frac{3}{4}}$	Court J K	37.70
28Feb04 ^{10}TP^{4}	Tap Dancing Mauk	L	3	121	5	8	$10^{\frac{1}{2}}$	11	11	9^{3}	$7^{1\frac{3}{4}}$	Zuniga J E	95.90
7Mar04 ^{9}FG^{6}	Stolen Time	L b	3	121	4	2	$3^{\frac{1}{2}}$	2^{hd}	3^{hd}	6^{hd}	8^{nk}	Velasquez C	7.20
15Feb04 ^{5}FG^{1}	New Element	L b	3	121	8	4	$4^{\frac{1}{2}}$	$3^{\frac{1}{2}}$	$7^{1\frac{1}{2}}$	$8^{2\frac{1}{2}}$	$9^{5\frac{1}{4}}$	Guidry M	60.00
14Feb04 ^{4}SA^{1}	Hippocrates	L	3	121	3	7	8^{hd}	8^{hd}	10^{3}	11	10^{3}	Flores D R	16.10
28Feb04 ^{10}TP^{1}	Silver Minister	L	3	121	7	3	$2^{\frac{1}{2}}$	4^{1}	4^{hd}	10^{1}	11	Bejarano R	5.50

OFF AT 4:17 Start Good. Won driving. Track fast.

TIME :23^{1}, :47^{1}, 1:11^{2}, 1:37^{1}, 1:50^{3} (:23.35, :47.33, 1:11.46, 1:37.24, 1:50.71)

$2 Mutuel Prices:			
11 – SINISTER G.	34.80	14.20	8.00
9 – TRICKY TABOO.		33.60	13.00
10 – LITTLE MATTH MAN.			5.80

$2 EXACTA 11-9 PAID $1,176.00 $2 TRIFECTA 11-9-10 PAID $14,811.60
$2 SUPERFECTA 11-9-10-2 PAID $106,848.20

Dk. b or br. c, (Feb), by Matty G – Sinister Punch, by Two Punch. Trainer Toscano John T Jr. Bred by Devonia Stud Inc (Fla).

SINISTER G sprinted clear and angled in, set the pace in the two path, responded willingly when challenged by THAT'S AN OURRAGE entering the second turn, raced that one into defeat in midstretch and drew clear under steady urging. TRICKY TABOO five wide on the first turn when within striking distance, moved closer four wide on the backstretch, continued in that path on the second turn and rallied willingly to be up for the place. LITTLE MATTH MAN far back early three wide, moved in a bit, advanced inside into the second turn, moved out three wide with three furlongs to go, came a path wider approaching the stretch and finished fast on the outside. THAT'S AN OUTRAGE steadied in the initial furlong when in tight, dropped back, angled out three wide on the first turn, moved to the outside on the backstretch, moved up quickly five wide into the second turn to challenge, stayed on well to midstretch and weakened late. BIRDSTONE steadied in the initial furlong, steadied again in traffic entering the first turn, recovered to race forwardly, saved ground when making a mild gain after six furlongs but tired in the drive. HASSLEFREE bumped at the start, was outsprinted early three wide then was no threat. TAP DANCING MAUK roughed at the start, was far back for a half and could not menace. STOLEN TIME swerved out at the start, was straightened to be forwardly placed three wide, held on well for six furlongs and faded. NEW ELEMENT close up early four wide, made a run at the leaders four wide entering the second turn but faded in the final three furlongs. HIPPOCRATES reserved off the inside, gave way. SILVER MINISTER closest to the pace along the inside, stopped.

Owners– 1, Toscano III John T Corrado Kim and Carlat Yamile; 2, Oak Haven Farm; 3, Papandrea Vincent; 4, Bull Stick Stables LLC and Mercedes Stables LLC; 5, Marylou Whitney Stables; 6, Lewis Robert B and Beverly J; 7, Mauk 1 Racing Stable; 8, Estate of Jeanne G Vance Robert K Smith; 9, Select Stable; 10, Robertson Sanford R; 11, Lloyd Madison Farms LLC

Trainers– 1, Toscano John T Jr; 2, Frederick Edward; 3, Ciresa Martin E; 4, Puhich Michael; 5, Zito Nicholas P; 6, Lukas D Wayne; 7, Mauk Fletcher; 8, Mott William I; 9, Werner Ronny; 10, Walsh Kathy; 11, Foley Gregory D

$2 Pick Three (7-7-11) Paid $8,399.00 ; Pick Three Pool $37,688 .
$2 Daily Double (7-11) Paid $913.20 ; Daily Double Pool $24,587 .

EIGHTH RACE
Fair Grounds
MARCH 21, 2004

ABOUT 1⅛ MILES. (Turf) (1.48^{1}) 13TH RUNNING OF THE MERVIN H. MUNIZ JR. MEMORIAL HANDICAP. Grade II. Purse $500,000 FOR FOUR YEAR OLDS AND UPWARD. $500,000 Guaranteed of which $300,000 to the winner; $100,000 to second; $55,000 to third; $30,000 to fourth; $15,000 to fifth. THE OWNER OF THE WINNER TO RECEIVE A TROPHY. Closed Friday, March 12, 2004, with 18 nominations. (If deemed inadvisable by management to run this race over the turf course, it will be run on the main track at One Mile and 1/8).

Value of Race: $500,000 Winner $300,000; second $100,000; third $55,000; fourth $30,000; fifth $15,000. Mutuel Pool $463,100.00 Exacta Pool $271,109.00 Quinella Pool $20,742.00 Trifecta Pool $226,217.00 Superfecta Pool $77,519.00

Last Raced	Horse	M/Eqt.	A.	Wt	PP	St	¼	½	¾	Str	Fin	Jockey	Odds $1
31Jan04 ^{9}FG^{1}	Mystery Giver	L	6	120	10	3	8½	9^{1}	9^{1}	4^{hd}	1¾	Albarado R J	15.00
28Feb04 ^{7}FG^{1}	Herculated	L	4	116	7	7	4^{1½}	4^{1}	4^{1½}	3^{1½}	2½	Lovato F Jr	13.30
24Feb04 ^{9}FG^{2}	Skate Away	L	5	117	2	8	6^{1}	5½	2^{1}	1^{2½}	3^{1}	Melancon G	13.20
29Feb04 ^{2}SA^{1}	Burning Sun	L f	5	116	3	9	9^{4}	8^{2½}	6^{hd}	6^{1}	4^{nk}	Solis A	3.30
24Jan04 ^{10}GP^{1}	Proud Man	L b	6	118	9	2	5^{hd}	6^{2}	7^{1}	7^{2}	5^{nk}	Douglas R R	6.80
19Jan04 ^{8}SA^{2}	Nothing to Lose	L b	4	118	4	6	3^{hd}	3^{2}	5^{hd}	5½	6^{1}	Desormeaux K J	4.30
20Feb04 ^{9}GP^{1}	Willard Straight	L	4	116	6	10	10	10	10	9^{1}	7^{nk}	Chavez J F	21.30
21Feb04 ^{9}GP^{1}	Silver Tree	L	4	118	1	5	2½	1^{hd}	3^{hd}	2½	8^{4½}	Bailey J D	2.30
4Jan04 ^{9}GP^{2}	Political Attack	L bf	5	118	8	1	1^{1}	2^{1½}	1^{hd}	8^{1}	9^{nk}	Martin E M Jr	10.50
24Feb04 ^{9}FG^{1}	Majestic Thief	L b	5	117	5	4	7^{1½}	7^{hd}	8^{1}	10	10	Sellers S J	32.80

OFF AT 4:03 Start Good . Won driving. Course firm.

TIME :24^{1}, :49, 1:12^{2}, 1:36^{1}, 1:48^{1} (:24.28, :49.01, 1:12.59, 1:36.23, 1:48.29)

(New Course Record)

$2 Mutuel Prices:

10 – MYSTERY GIVER	32.00	13.20	7.80
7 – HERCULATED		14.00	11.20
2 – SKATE AWAY			8.80

$2 EXACTA 10–7 PAID $241.00 $2 QUINELLA 7–10 PAID $130.80
$2 TRIFECTA 10–7–2 PAID $1,895.60 $2 SUPERFECTA 10–7–2–3 PAID $14,534.80

B. g, (Apr), by Dynaformer – Ioya , by Naskra . Trainer Scherer Richard R. Bred by David Block & Patricia Block (Ill).

MYSTERY GIVER settled off the rail, moved up a bit approaching the drive, rallied between foes nearing mid stretch, closed determinedly and was along in time while setting a new course record. HERCULATED parked wide early, eased inward after reaching the backstretch, advanced around the second turn, came inside turning for home, switched outside SKATE AWAY before the final sixteenth, tried hard and just missed. SKATE AWAY restrained along the inside early, made a quick move inside POLITICAL ATTACK entering the second turn, surged clear turning for home then was no match late. BURNING SUN allowed to settle from the inside, remained inside for the drive, closed willingly but lacked the needed finish. PROUD MAN settled between foes, lacked the needed response. NOTHING TO LOSE restrained off the leaders early, settled while wide down the backstretch, swung out for the drive and then had no final kick. WILLARD STRAIGHT trailed until the drive and improved position along the inside. SILVER TREE restrained from the inside early, eased outside to move up outside POLITICAL ATTACK before the backstretch, gained the edge completing a half, was overtaken before the second turn and then faltered once reaching mid stretch. POLITICAL ATTACK set the pace while off the rail, got headed midway down the backstretch, regained the lead around the second turn, got displaced and then weakened. MAJESTIC THIEF was always outrun.

Owners– 1, Team Block; 2, Oak Crest Farm; 3, Robinson J Mack; 4, Juddmonte Farms Inc; 5, Robert Kaufman Roger & Stephen Weiss; 6, Ramsey Kenneth L and Sarah K; 7, Goichman Lawrence; 8, Vegso Racing Stable Peter Vegso; 9, Erdenheim Farm; 10, Freeman Walt Rudd Mason and McClinton Don

Trainers– 1, Scherer Richard R; 2, Stidham Michael; 3, Trosclair Jeff; 4, Frankel Robert; 5, Clement Christophe; 6, Frankel Robert; 7, Pletcher Todd A; 8, Mott William I; 9, Matz Michael R; 10, Bindner Walter M Jr

---

$2 Pick Three (2–7–10) Paid $4,593.20 ; Pick Three Pool $15,311 .
$2 Pick Six (4–6–9–2–7–10) 3 Correct Paid $22.60 ; Pick Six Pool $2,213 ; Carryover Pool $1,161.

ELEVENTH RACE
Gulfstream
MARCH 21, 2004

$1\frac{1}{2}$ MILES. (Turf) (2.23) 41ST RUNNING OF THE ORCHID HANDICAP. Grade II. Purse $200,000 FOR FILLIES AND MARES, THREE YEARS OLD AND UPWARD. By subscription of $200 each, which shall accompany the nomination, $2,000 to pass the entry box and $2,000 additional to start, with $200,000 guaranteed. The owner of the winner to receive $120,000; $40,000 to second, $22,000 to third, $12,000 to fourth and $6,000 to fifth. Weights: Sunday, March 14,2004. Trophy to winning Owner. In the event this stake is taken off the turf, it may be suject to downgrading upon review of the Graded Stakes Committee. Closed Wednesday, March 10, 2004 with (19) nominations.

Value of Race: $200,000 Winner $120,000; second $40,000; third $22,000; fourth $12,000; fifth $6,000. Mutuel Pool $444,635.00 Exacta Pool $303,719.00 Trifecta Pool $236,231.00 Superfecta Pool $74,449.00

Last Raced	Horse	M/Eqt.	A.	Wt	PP	¼	½	1	1¼	Str	Fin	Jockey	Odds $1
5Mar04 ^{9}GP^1	Meridiana-Ger	L	4	114	7	1^1	1^1	1^{hd}	1^1	1^2	$1^{1\frac{1}{4}}$	Prado E S	7.40
28Feb04 ^{11}GP^5	Savedbythelight	L b	4	114	5	$4^{1\frac{1}{2}}$	$3^{\frac{1}{2}}$	$3^{\frac{1}{2}}$	$3^{1\frac{1}{2}}$	2^1	$2^{\frac{1}{2}}$	Velazquez J R	10.90
11Feb04 ^{3}GP^2	Miss Hellie	L	5	114	8	10	10	10	10	7^{hd}	3^{nk}	Santos J A	24.80
28Feb04 ^{11}GP^3	Boana-Ger	L	6	114	1	$7^{2\frac{1}{2}}$	7^2	6^1	7^1	$6^{\frac{1}{2}}$	4^{nk}	Blanc B	11.70
15Feb04 ^{3}SA^2	Moscow Burning	L	4	115	6	5^{hd}	$5^{\frac{1}{2}}$	$5^{1\frac{1}{2}}$	$5^{1\frac{1}{2}}$	5^{hd}	5^{nk}	Ramsammy E	4.20
27Dec03 ^{9}Crc^{11}	Spice Island	L b	5	119	3	3^{hd}	4^1	$4^{1\frac{1}{2}}$	4^{hd}	$3^{\frac{1}{2}}$	$6^{1\frac{3}{4}}$	Ferrer J C	3.60
5Mar04 ^{9}GP^4	Gal O Gal	L	4	114	2	8^{hd}	9^2	8^2	6^{hd}	8^2	$7^{1\frac{3}{4}}$	Decarlo C P	46.60
28Feb04 ^{11}GP^2	Ocean Silk	L	4	115	10	2^1	$2^{\frac{1}{2}}$	2^1	$2^{\frac{1}{2}}$	4^{hd}	8^1	Day P	2.40
28Feb04 ^{11}GP^4	Lost Appeal	L b	6	114	9	$9^{2\frac{1}{2}}$	8^{hd}	9^2	$9^{\frac{1}{2}}$	9^2	$9^{1\frac{3}{4}}$	Coa E M	13.60
28Feb04 ^{11}GP^6	San Dare	L	6	114	4	6^{hd}	6^{hd}	7^1	8^{hd}	10	10	Velasquez C	12.40

OFF AT 5:43 Start Good . Won driving. Course firm.

TIME :25^3, :51, 1:15^1, 1:39^3, 2:03^1, 2:26^4 (:25.64, :51.08, 1:15.34, 1:39.69, 2:03.35, 2:26.99)

$2 Mutuel Prices:

7 – MERIDIANA–GER	16.80	8.20	6.60
5 – SAVEDBYTHELIGHT		12.20	9.00
8 – MISS HELLIE			11.20

$1 EXACTA 7–5 PAID $84.50 $1 TRIFECTA 7–5–8 PAID $1,221.80
$1 SUPERFECTA 7–5–8 1 PAID $9,308.10

Ch. f, (May), by Lomitas–GB – Monbijou , by Dashing Blade . Trainer Clement Christophe. Bred by Gestut Etzean (Ger).

MERIDIANA (GER) well handled while making the pace along the hedge, increased her advantage in midstretch, then was fully extended to prevail. SAVEDBYTHELIGHT stalked the pace three wide into the stretch and continued on with good courage to gain the place while unable to get to the winner. MISS HELLIE outrun early, split rivals in the stretch and rallied to be up for the show. BOANA (GER) steadied in behind rivals racing into the first turn, was reserved off the pace into the far turn, swung out for the stretch run and closed with a mild rally. MOSCOW BURNING taken in hand to track the pace, raced in contention into the stretch and didn't do enough late. SPICE ISLAND well placed while saving ground into the stretch, lacked a rally. GAL O GAL bobbled soon after the start, was unhurried while saving ground into the final turn and failed to threaten. OCEAN SILK stalked the pace, made a run at the winner racing down the backstretch and into the final turn, then tired. LOST APPEAL failed to menace. SAN DARE allowed to settle after being rank in the run to the first turn, faltered leaving the final turn.

Owners– 1, Kelly Jon and Sarah; 2, Mack Earle I; 3, Hamilton Emory A; 4, Tanaka Gary A; 5, J Mariani M Nentwig & D Van Kempen; 6, Denlea Park Ltd; 7, Hugel Max; 8, Sangster Robert F; 9, Poston Bill and Vicki; 10, Mounts David G

Trainers– 1, Clement Christophe; 2, Violette Richard A Jr; 3, McGaughey III Claude R; 4, Attfield Roger L; 5, Cassidy James; 6, Pregman John S Jr; 7, Blengs Vincent L; 8, Byrne Patrick B; 9, Edwards Oliver S; 10, Hiles Rick

$1 Pick Three (2–1–7) Paid $395.90 ; Pick Three Pool $33,161 .

EIGHTH RACE
Aqueduct
MARCH 27, 2004

7 FURLONGS. (1.20) 51ST RUNNING OF THE DISTAFF BREEDERS' CUP HANDICAP. Grade II. Purse $150,000 (includes $50,000 BC – Breeders' Cup) FOR FILLIES AND MARES THREE YEARS OLD AND UPWARD. By subscription of $100 each, which should accompany the nomination $500 to pass the entry box; $500 to start, with $100,000 added and an additional $50,000 from the Breeders' Cup Fund for cup nominees only. The NYRA added money and all fees to be divided 60% to the winner, 20% to second, 10% to third, 5% to fourth, 3% to fifth and 2% divided equally among the remaining finishers. Breeders' Cup Fund monies also correspondingly divided, provided a Breeders'Cup nominee has finished in an award position. Any Breeders' Cup fund monies not awarded will revert back to the Fund. Trophy to winning owner given by Breeders' Cup Ltd. Closed Saturday, March 13,2004 with 14 Nominations.

Value of Race: $147,900 Winner $93,240; second $31,188; third $15,648; fourth $7,824. Mutuel Pool $344,670.00 Exacta Pool $329,494.00

Last Raced	Horse	M/Eqt.	A.	Wt	PP	St	¼	½	Str	Fin	Jockey	Odds $1
8Feb04 ^{11}GP^1	Randaroo	L	4	121	4	1	$1^{\frac{1}{2}}$	$1^{\frac{1}{2}}$	1^3	$1^{3\frac{1}{2}}$	Migliore R	0.45
22Feb04 ^{8}Aqu^3	Chirimoya	L f	5	110	3	2	$3^{\frac{1}{2}}$	$2^{1\frac{1}{2}}$	$2^{3\frac{1}{2}}$	$2^{2\frac{1}{4}}$	Cotto P L Jr	23.50
26Feb04 ^{8}GP^1	Storm Flag Flying	L	4	118	2	3	2^{hd}	3^{hd}	3^3	$3^{11\frac{1}{4}}$	Prado E S	2.10
22Feb04 ^{8}Aqu^1	Fit Performer	L f	7	115	1	4	4	4	4	4	Pimentel J	6.80

OFF AT 4:20 Start Good . Won ridden out. Track fast.

TIME :22^4, :46^1, 1:10, 1:22^3 (:22.81, :46.35, 1:10.17, 1:22.64)

$2 Mutuel Prices:

4 – RANDAROO	2.90	2.30	—
3 – CHIRIMOYA		5.40	—
2 – STORM FLAG FLYING		—	—

$2 EXACTA 4–3 PAID $24.00

B. f, (Feb), by Gold Case – Validated , by Valid Appeal . Trainer McLaughlin Kiaran P. Bred by Dennis Drazin (Ky).

RANDAROO quickly showed in front, set the pace while well in hand, drew away when asked for run and was wrapped up nearing the wire, winning with speed to spare. CHIRIMOYA was hustled outside, chased the pace, proved no match for the winner and continued on gamely to earn the place award. STORM FLAG FLYING raced close up inside, dropped back on the turn and had no response when roused. FIT PERFORMER was rated along early, came wide for the drive and tired.

Owners– 1, Allen Joseph; 2, Rising Graph Stable; 3, Phipps Ogden Mills et al; 4, Steel Your Face Stables

Trainers– 1, McLaughlin Kiaran P; 2, Hushion Michael E; 3, McGaughey III Claude R; 4, Dutrow Richard E Jr

SEVENTH RACE
Golden Gate
MARCH 27, 2004

1 MILE. (1.33) 53RD RUNNING OF THE BERKELEY BREEDERS' CUP HANDICAP. Grade III. Purse $100,000 (includes $25,000 BC – Breeders' Cup) FOR THREE-YEAR-OLDS AND UPWARD. By subscription of $75 each to accompany the nomination or by supplementary nomination of $1,500 by Noon, Sunday March 21, 2004. $375 to pass the entry box and $375 additional to start, with $75,000 Guaranteed and an additional $25,000 from Breeders' Cup Fund for Breeders' Cup eligibles only. The host association's monies to be divided 55% to the winner, 20% to second, 15% to third, 7.5% to fourth and 2.5% to fifth. Breeders' Cup monies also correspondingly divided providing a Breeders' Cup nominee has finished in an awarded position. Any Breeders's Cup Fund monies not awarded will revert back to the Fund. This race will not be divided. The starters will be determined at that time with preference given to Breeders' Cup nominees only of equal racing quality or weight assignment (respective of sex and weight for age). Preference to Non-Breeders' Cup nominees follow the same stipulation. A trophy will be presented to the owner of the winner by Breeders' Cup Ltd. Closed Thursday, March 18, 2004 with 11 nominations.

Value of Race: $94,375 Winner $55,000; second $15,000; third $15,000; fourth $7,500; fifth $1,875. Mutuel Pool $277,336.00 Exacta Pool $147,959.00 Quinella Pool $15,178.00 Trifecta Pool $140,436.00

Last Raced	Horse	M/Eqt.	A.	Wt	PP	St	¼	½	¾	Str	Fin	Jockey	Odds $1
4Feb04 ^{6}SA^{1}	Snorter	LB b	4	116	1	2	$3^{1\frac{1}{2}}$	$3^{\frac{1}{2}}$	3^{hd}	3^{hd}	1^{1}	Baze R A	2.00
28Feb04 ^{3}GG^{1}	Yougottawanna	LB bf	5	116	2	3	1^{1}	1^{1}	$1^{\frac{1}{2}}$	1^{hd}	2^{nk}	Carr D	2.20
7Mar04 ^{8}SA^{9}	Taste of Paradise	LB	5	116	5	4	2^{hd}	2^{1}	2^{hd}	2^{hd}	3^{hd}	Lovato A J	3.40
14Mar04 ^{7}GG^{6}	Gold Ruckus	LB bf	6	116	3	5	5	4^{hd}	4^{2}	$4^{2\frac{1}{2}}$	$4^{1\frac{1}{2}}$	Radke K	6.40
28Feb04 ^{8}GG^{1}	Jets Fan	LB	4	116	4	1	$4^{\frac{1}{2}}$	5	5	5	5	Castro J M	4.10

OFF AT 3:53 Start Good . Won driving. Track fast.

TIME :22^{4}, :46, 1:09^{4}, 1:21^{3}, 1:33^{4} (:22.88, :46.14, 1:09.87, 1:21.78, 1:33.92)

$2 Mutuel Prices:

2 – SNORTER	6.00	3.40	2.40
3 – YOUGOTTAWANNA		3.60	2.80
6 – TASTE OF PARADISE			2.80

$1 EXACTA 2–3 PAID $9.30 $2 QUINELLA 2–3 PAID $11.40
$1 TRIFECTA 2–3–6 PAID $26.20

B. c, (Jan), by Awesome Again – Retiro Park , by Meadowlake . Trainer Frankel Robert. Bred by John Toffan & Trudy McCaffery (Ky).

SNORTER broke alertly and tracked the pace from the inside under patient handling, remained inside when called upon near the quarter pole, came through a bit tight quarters at the three sixteenths, challenged leaving the furlong pole and gradually proved best. YOUGOTTAWANNA set all of the pace from just off the rail, turned back repeated challenges to mid stretch but could not hold the winner late in a game try. TASTE OF PARADISE broke a bit outward but quickly raced up outside and prompted the pace three wide, offered his best bid into the lane but slackened in the late stages. GOLD RUCKUS took back early but was always within striking distance, advanced to challenge four wide on the second turn then lacked the needed late response. JETS FAN was never far back while racing just outside the winner to the second turn, could not keep up into the lane, swung to the outside but could make little impact

Owners– 1, Gary and Mary West Stables Inc; 2, Kenton Michael Martin John F and O'Connor Patrick; 3, Bloom David B; 4, Franks Farms; 5, Sumja Brent

Trainers– 1, Frankel Robert; 2, Martin John F; 3, Robbins Jay M; 4, Hollendorfer Jerry; 5, Sumja Brent

Scratched– Wolfwithintegrity (19Mar04 ^{7}SA ^{4})

$2 Daily Double (8–2) Paid $33.80 ; Daily Double Pool $9,606 .
$1 Pick Three (4–8–2) Paid $100.50 ; Pick Three Pool $28,347 .

NINTH RACE
Santa Anita
MARCH 27, 2004

1⅛ MILES. (Turf) (1.43^{4}) 37TH RUNNING OF THE SANTA ANA HANDICAP. Grade II. Purse $150,000 FOR FILLIES AND MARES FOUR YEARS OLD AND UPWARD. By subscription of $150 each to accompany the nomination or by supplementary nomination by Sunday, March 21. $500 to pass the entry box and $1,000 additional to start, of which $150,000 guaranteed, with $90,000 to first, $30,000 to second, $18,000 to third, $9,000 to fourth, $3,000 to fifth. Weights Tuesday, March 23. High weights preferred. Starters to be named through the entry box by the closing time of entries. A trophy will be presented to the ownerofthe winner. (Rail at 8 feet). Closed with 11 nominations.

Value of Race: $150,000; Winner $90,000; second $30,000; third $18,000; fourth $9,000; fifth $3,000. Mutuel Pool $475,120.00 Exacta Pool $274,781.00 Quinella Pool $22,516.00 Trifecta Pool $279,287.00 Superfecta Pool $121,471.00

Last Raced	Horse	M/Eqt.	A.	Wt	PP	St	¼	½	¾	Str	Fin	Jockey	Odds $1
10Jan04 ^{3}SA^{1}	[D]Megahertz-GB	LB	5	120	4	6	6^{hd}	7	7	$1^{1\frac{1}{2}}$	1^{1}	Espinoza V	0.70
21Feb04 ^{8}SA^{2}	Katdogawn-GB	LB	4	117	2	5	5^{2}	$5^{\frac{1}{2}}$	5^{hd}	3^{hd}	$2^{1\frac{1}{2}}$	Smith M E	5.30
21Feb04 ^{8}SA^{1}	Fun House	LB	5	118	5	2	3^{hd}	$3^{\frac{1}{2}}$	3^{hd}	2^{hd}	$3^{1\frac{1}{2}}$	Valdivia J Jr	8.00
13Aug03 ^{7}Dmr^{1}	Arabic Song-Ire	LB	5	117	7	1	4^{2}	$4^{\frac{1}{2}}$	$4^{1\frac{1}{2}}$	5^{1}	4no	Nakatani C S	12.00
4Mar04 ^{4}SA^{1}	Mandela-Ger	LB	4	113	6	7	7	6^{hd}	6^{hd}	$6^{1\frac{1}{2}}$	$5^{2\frac{1}{2}}$	Santiago Javier	6.00
13Feb04 ^{4}SA^{3}	Go On Baby	LB	6	113	1	4	1^{1}	1^{1}	$1^{\frac{1}{2}}$	4^{hd}	$6^{2\frac{1}{2}}$	Baze T C	12.70
23Jan04 ^{3}SA^{1}	Sweetshew	LB	5	109	3	3	2^{2}	2^{1}	$2^{1\frac{1}{2}}$	7	7	Martinez F F	23.80

[D] – Megahertz-GB disqualified and placed 7th

OFF AT 4:40 Start Good . Won driving. Course firm.

TIME :23^{4}, :47^{4}, 1:12, 1:35^{2}, 1:47^{1} (:23.94, :47.98, 1:12.00, 1:35.43, 1:47.36)

$2 Mutuel Prices:

2 – KATDOGAWN-GB	12.60	5.60	4.80
6 – FUN HOUSE		7.20	5.80
8 – ARABIC SONG-IRE			7.40

$1 EXACTA 2–6 PAID $36.40 $2 QUINELLA 2–6 PAID $34.20
$1 TRIFECTA 2–6–8 PAID $217.90 $1 SUPERFECTA 2–6–8–7 PAID $881.40

B. f, (Feb), by Bahhare – Trempkate , by Trempolino . Trainer Cassidy James. Bred by Mrs W H Gibson Fleming (GB).

MEGAHERTZ (GB) content to settle off the pace while a bit off the rail, launched rally early on final bend, split foes, swung out, advanced five wide into the lane, surged to front, then swerved inward passing midstretch, continued to lug inward to the rail and held under urging. KATDOGAWN (GB) chased while saving ground to the second bend, blocked and awaited room behind wall of rivals entering the stretch, angled to the fence and finished full of run. FUN HOUSE well placed from the inside, continued to save ground well into the second turn, bid between rivals entering the lane and finished very willingly. ARABIC SONG (IRE) chased while outside foe into the backstretch, angled out around final bend, caught four wide into the stretch, forced to steady sharply off heels of MEGAHERTZ in midstretch, then recovered and gained a minor award. MANDELA (GER) unhurried while on three wide path to the stretch, angled in some in upper stretch and finished with interest. GO ON BABY stepped to the front, dictated he fractions to the final bend, resisted briefly from the inside but weakened through the drive. SWEETSHEW stalked the pacesetter while outside that rival to second bend, moved alongside that foe, battled three wide and between foes into the lane, dropped back slightly, then forced to steady sharply off heels of ARABIC SONG and lost all momentum. Following a stewards' inquiry into the incident in the stretch, MEGAHERTZ was disqualified and placed last for coming in sharply and causing ARABIC SONG to steady, who in turn caused SWEETSHEW to steady.

Owners– 1, Bello Michael; 2, Cuchna John R Jim Ford Inc and Pearson Daron; 3, Winchell Thoroughbreds LLC; 4, Speelman Anthony; 5, Tanaka Gary A; 6, Shah Stables; 7, DeBruycker Lloyd

Trainers– 1, Frankel Robert; 2, Cassidy James; 3, McAnally Ronald; 4, Drysdale Neil; 5, Frankel Robert; 6, O'Neill Doug; 7, Bray Simon

Scratched– Noches De Rosa (CHI) (24May03 ^{7}BM ^{2})

$2 Daily Double (3–2) Paid $47.20 ; Daily Double Pool $44,892 .
$1 Pick Three (1–3–2) Paid $175.30 ; Pick Three Pool $91,180 .

EIGHTH RACE
Santa Anita
MARCH 28, 2004

6½ FURLONGS. (1.13³) 22ND RUNNING OF THE POTRERO GRANDE BREEDERS' CUP HANDICAP. Grade II. Purse $200,000 (includes $100,000 BC - Breeders' Cup) FOR FOUR-YEAR-OLDS AND UPWARD. By subscription of $200 each, which shall accompany the nomination or by supplmenentary nomination of $4,000 by Sunday, March 21. $2,000 additional to start, with $100,000 added and an additional $100,000 from Breeders' CupFund for Cup nominees only. The host assiociation's added monies and fees to be divided 60% to the winner, 20% to second, 12% to third, 6% to fourth, 2% to fifth. Breeders' Cup Fund monies also correspondingly divided provided a Breeder's Cup nominee hasfinished in an awarded position. Any Breeders' Cup Fund monies not awarded will revert to the fund. Weights Tuesday, March 23. This race will not be divided. The starters will be determined at entry time with preference given to Breeders' Cup nomineesonlyof equal racing quality or weight assignment (respective of sex and weight for age). A trophy will be presented to the owner of the winner. Closed with 7 nominations.

Value of Race: $122,488 Winner $66,840; second $42,280; third $13,368. Mutuel Pool $430,911.00 Exacta Pool $326,922.00 Quinella Pool $31,438.00

Last Raced	Horse	M/Eqt.	A.	Wt	PP	St	¼	½	Str	Fin	Jockey	Odds $1
14Feb04 3SA1	McCann's Mojave	LB	4	116	2	5	2hd	1hd	2 2½	1 1¾	Valdivia J Jr	6.90
21Feb04 7SA1	Unfurl the Flag	LB b	4	114	3	1	1hd	21	1hd	2 1¾	Baze T C	3.40
7Mar04 8SA7	Bluesthestandard	LB	7	118	1	2	3hd	3½	3	3	Smith M E	0.80
10Jan04 8SA9	Watchem Smokey	LB	4	115	4	4	5	5	—	—	Espinoza V	7.10
7Mar04 8SA6	Casas Caballo	LB	4	114	5	3	4 1½	4 1½	—	—	Pedroza M A	4.70

OFF AT 4:11 Start Good. Won driving. Track fast.
TIME :21⁴, :44¹, 1:08⁴, 1:15³ (:21.88, :44.30, 1:08.89, 1:15.60)

$2 Mutuel Prices:				
	2 – MCCANN'S MOJAVE	15.80	6.00	2.60
	3 – UNFURL THE FLAG		3.80	2.40
	1 – BLUESTHESTANDARD			2.20

$1 EXACTA 2–3 PAID $28.80 $2 QUINELLA 2–3 PAID $23.80

B. c, (Feb), by Memo-Chi - Joni U. Bar , by Nordic Prince . Trainer Dorfman Leonard. Bred by Alix Nikki Hunt & Mike Willman (Cal).

MCCANN'S MOJAVE sent up and forced the pace from between rivals, battled inside UNFUL THE FLAG entering the stretch, forged to front inside eighth marker then edged away under steady right hand urging while drifting out slightly in deep stretch. UNFURL THE FLAG contested pace while three deep early, then outside the winner around the bend and into the stretch, could not match that rival in the final eighth, but safely held the place. BLUESTHESTANDARD dueled in early stages from along the fence, dropped back slightly into and around the bend, shifted to the outside and could not make any late impact. WATCHEM SMOKEY content to settle off the early leaders from well off the rail, continued a bit wide leaving the backstretch, then plowed into the fallen horse midway on the turn, unseating the rider. CASAS CABALLO was off smartly but taken off the leaders, stalked the leading trio from off the rail, remained bit wide and broke down midway on the turn. Following a stewards' inquiry into the incident on the turn there was no change.

Owners– 1, Hunt Alix Nikke and Willman Mike; 2, Ailshie Gaylord Harris Tom and Rose Bruce et al; 3, Sengara Jeffrey; 4, Gann Edmund A; 5, House Michael

Trainers– 1, Dorfman Leonard; 2, Bernstein David; 3, West Ted H; 4, Frankel Robert; 5, Mitchell Mike

$2 Daily Double (3–2) Paid $514.20 ; Daily Double Pool $44,130 .
$1 Pick Three (10–3–2) Paid $1,229.50 ; Pick Three Pool $75,481 .

NINTH RACE
Keeneland
APRIL 2, 2004

1 MILE. (Turf) (1.33^{3}) 16TH RUNNING OF THE TRANSYLVANIA. Grade III. Purse $100,000 FOR THREE YEAR OLDS. By subscription of $100 each, which should accompany the nomination; $1,000 to enter and start with $100,000 added, of which 62% of all monies to the owner of the winner, 20% to second, 10% to third, 5% to fourth and 3% to fifth. Weeight 123 lbs. Non-winners of $45,000 twice at a mile or over on the turf allowed 3 lbs.; $45,000 at a mile or over on the turf, 5 lbs.; $30,000 twice at a mile or over, 7 lbs. The maximum number of starters for the Transylvania will be limited to ten wiith two also eligibles. In the event that more than ten pass the entry box, the ten starters will be determined at that time with preference by condition eligibility, beginning with graded stakes winners. Starters to be named through the entry box by thee usual time of closing. A gold julep cup will be presented to the owner of the winner. Closed Wednesday, March 24, 2004 with 24 nominations. Keeneland Course. (Rail at 15 feet).

Value of Race: $113,400 Winner $70,308; second $22,680; third $11,340; fourth $5,670; fifth $3,402. Mutuel Pool $372,490.00 Exacta Pool $267,596.00 Trifecta Pool $243,525.00 Superfecta Pool $83,198.00 Quinella Pool $9,755.00

Last Raced	Horse	M/Eqt.	A.	Wt	PP	St	¼	½	¾	Str	Fin	Jockey	Odds $1
1Jan04 ^{9}Crc^{8}	Timo	L b	3	123	1	1	3^{hd}	3^{1}	2^{hd}	2^{hd}	$1^{\frac{3}{4}}$	Prado E S	2.30
18Feb04 ^{9}GP^{1}	Mr. J. T. L.	L b	3	116	4	3	$1^{1\frac{1}{2}}$	$1^{1\frac{1}{2}}$	$1^{1\frac{1}{2}}$	$1^{1\frac{1}{2}}$	2^{nk}	Bejarano R	26.00
13Mar04 ^{2}FG^{2}	America Alive	L b	3	116	6	7	7^{hd}	8^{3}	$8^{3\frac{1}{2}}$	5^{hd}	3^{nk}	Albarado R J	11.80
10Mar04 ^{6}GP^{1}	Grand Heritage	L	3	116	2	5	5^{hd}	$6^{1\frac{1}{2}}$	6^{1}	4^{2}	4^{nk}	Day P	2.80
21Feb04 ^{11}GP^{5}	Commendation	L	3	120	5	6	$6^{2\frac{1}{2}}$	5^{1}	4^{hd}	$3^{1\frac{1}{2}}$	$5^{5\frac{3}{4}}$	Velazquez J R	1.90
1Nov03 ^{6}WO^{3}	Dynafire	L	3	116	7	2	$2^{\frac{1}{2}}$	2^{hd}	3^{1}	6^{2}	6^{nk}	Perret C	9.10
13Mar04 ^{2}FG^{1}	Exploited Storm	L	3	116	8	4	4^{1}	4^{hd}	$5^{\frac{1}{2}}$	7^{2}	7^{7}	Melancon L	15.30
19Feb04 ^{9}Hou^{3}	Captain Prudent	L b	3	117	9	8	8^{4}	7^{hd}	7^{2}	8^{2}	$8^{\frac{3}{4}}$	Sellers S J	60.90
13Mar04 ^{9}TP^{1}	Lost in Transit	L b	3	116	3	9	9	9	9	9	9	Velasquez C	102.00

OFF AT 5:15 Start Good. Won driving. Course firm.

TIME :23^{1}, :47^{1}, 1:12^{1}, 1:24^{1}, 1:36^{2} (:23.30, :47.39, 1:12.31, 1:24.34, 1:36.52)

$2 Mutuel Prices:

1 – TIMO	6.60	4.60	3.40
4 – MR. J. T. L.		20.00	11.20
6 – AMERICA ALIVE			7.00

$2 EXACTA 1–4 PAID $140.40 $2 TRIFECTA 1–4–6 PAID $1,264.40
$2 SUPERFECTA 1–4–6–2 PAID $8,985.20 $2 QUINELLA 1–4 PAID $100.00

Gr/ro. c, (Mar), by El Prado-Ire – Elocat's Burglar, by Criminal Type. Trainer Badgett William Jr. Bred by CK Woods Stables Inc (Ky).

TIMO, nicely placed near the inside under light rating from early on, eased out four wide entering the stretch, was bumped for a stride or two by COMMENDATION about the furlong grounds, then was ridden hard to prevail. MR. J. T. L. leaned in early and bumped with LOST IN TRANSIT, moved to the fore soon after, raced three or four wide while showing the way, managed a clear lead into the final furlong but couldn't contain the winner's surge. AMERICA ALIVE, unhurried early, worked his way inward, saved ground for nearly six furlongs, came out seven wide to commence a sweeping run into the stretch and was going well at the end. GRAND HERITAGE came out at the break bumping with LOST IN TRANSIT, settled inside, raced within easy striking distance, worked his way out four abreast in the final sixteenth but couldn't muster the needed response. COMMENDATION, never far back, raced under light restraint four wide, edged closer to the inside on the far turn, came out and bumped soundly with TIMO at the furlong grounds and was empty late. DYNAFIRE went up early to force the pace four or five wide, continued forwardly to the stretch and weakened. EXPLOITED STORM stalked the leaders five wide to the stretch and came up empty. CAPTAIN PRUDENT settled four wide early and failed to seriously menace. LOST IN TRANSIT, bumped from both sides soon after the start and checked in tight quarters, never was prominent.

Owners– 1, C K Woods Stable; 2, Werner W Canino M Magliocco J and Attfield R; 3, Mill House; 4, Mrs Bertram R Firestone; 5, Courtlandt Farms; 6, Allard Cam; 7, Stony Oak Farm LLC; 8, Plemmons Jim H; 9, Zapp Billy and Kinmon Keith

Trainers– 1, Badgett William Jr; 2, Attfield Roger L; 3, Howard Neil J; 4, Mott William I; 5, Motion H Graham; 6, Attfield Roger L; 7, Barnett Bobby C; 8, Mayo Larry A; 9, Kinmon Keith

Scratched– Bachelor Blues (10Mar04 ^{6}GP ^{7}), Ballado Breeze (29Feb04 ^{8}GP ^{4})

$2 Pick Three (5–5–1) Paid $478.40 ; Pick Three Pool $57,601 .
$1 Pick Four (8/9–5–5–1) Paid $1,081.80 ; Pick Four Pool $77,471 .

EIGHTH RACE
Aqueduct
APRIL 3, 2004

1⅛ MILES. (1.47) 96TH RUNNING OF THE EXCELSIOR BREEDERS' CUP HANDICAP. Grade III. Purse $200,000 (includes $50,000 BC – Breeders' Cup) BY SUBSCRIPTION OF $150 EACH, WHICH SHOULD ACCOMPANY THE NOMINATION; $750 TO PASS THE ENTRY BOX; $750 TO START. The NYRA purse to be divided 60% to the winner, 20% to second, 10% to third, 5% to fourth, 3% to fifth and 2% divided equally among the remainiing finishers. Breeders' Cup Fund monies also correspondingly divided, provided a Breeders' Cup nominee has finished in an award position. Any Breeders' Cup Fund monies not awarded will revert back to the Fund. Trophy to the winning owner given by the Breeeders' Cup Ltd. Closed Saturday, March 20, 2004 with 21 Nominations.

Value of Race: $196,000 Winner $120,000; second $40,000; third $20,000; fourth $10,000; fifth $6,000. Mutuel Pool $646,282.00 Exacta Pool $515,346.00 Trifecta Pool $262,465.00

Last Raced	Horse	M/Eqt.	A.	Wt	PP	St	¼	½	¾	Str	Fin	Jockey	Odds $1
29Feb04 ^{9}FG^{3}	Funny Cide	L	4	120	3	2	2^{1}	2^{1}	$2^{1\frac{1}{2}}$	1^{2}	$1^{\frac{1}{2}}$	Santos J A	1.30
14Feb04 ^{8}Lrl^{2}	Evening Attire	L b	6	119	2	5	5	5	5	$2^{2\frac{1}{2}}$	2^{8}	Bridgmohan S X	1.45
23Feb04 ^{8}GP^{2}	Host-Chi	L	4	114	5	4	$1^{1\frac{1}{2}}$	$1^{\frac{1}{2}}$	1^{hd}	$3^{1\frac{1}{2}}$	3^{nk}	Luzzi M J	4.70
6Mar04 ^{8}Aqu^{1}	Ground Storm	L bf	8	115	4	3	$3^{\frac{1}{2}}$	3^{hd}	3^{hd}	$4^{\frac{1}{2}}$	$4^{3\frac{1}{2}}$	Castellano J J	8.00
20Feb04 ^{6}Aqu^{1}	Loving-Brz	L b	8	113	1	1	$4^{1\frac{1}{2}}$	4^{hd}	4^{hd}	5	5	Espinoza J L	21.80

OFF AT 4:20 Start Good. Won driving. Track muddy.

TIME :23^{4}, :48, 1:12, 1:36^{4}, 1:49^{2} (:23.85, :48.10, 1:12.17, 1:36.87, 1:49.57)

$2 Mutuel Prices:

3 – FUNNY CIDE	4.60	2.60	2.10
2 – EVENING ATTIRE		2.50	2.10
6 – HOST-CHI			2.60

$2 EXACTA 3–2 PAID $7.20 $2 TRIFECTA 3–2–6 PAID $21.20

Ch. g, (Apr), by Distorted Humor – Belle's Good Cide, by Slewacide. Trainer Tagg Barclay. Bred by Win Star Farm LLC (NY).

FUNNY CIDE came away well, showed good speed while in hand, let HOST (CHI) make the pace for the opening three quarters, took over from that rival when asked, drew clear into the stretch then dug in gamely and held off EVENING ATTIRE under a steady drive. EVENING ATTIRE was rated along while between rivals, came wide for the drive, responded when roused in upper stretch and finished gamely outside but could not get by the winner. HOST (CHI) showed in front soon after the start, set the pace along the inside, could not stay with the winner into the stretch and tired in the final furlong. GROUND STORM was hard ridden while three wide and tired in the stretch. LOVING (BRZ) raced inside and had no response when roused.

Owners– 1, Sackatoga Stable; 2, Grant Mary and Joseph and Kelly Thomas J; 3, Melnyk Eugene and Laura; 4, Centennial Farms; 5, Goldfarb Sanford Roach Lawrence Ketcham John and Carney Christopher L

Trainers– 1, Tagg Barclay; 2, Kelly Patrick J; 3, Pletcher Todd A; 4, Mott William I; 5, Dutrow Richard E Jr

Scratched– Snake Mountain (18Mar04 ^{8}Aqu^{5})

NINTH RACE
Gulfstream
APRIL 3, 2004

1¼ MILES. (1.59) 59TH RUNNING OF THE GULFSTREAM PARK HANDICAP. Grade II. Purse $300,000 FOR THREE YEAR OLDS AND UPWARD. By subscription of $200 each, which shall accompany the nomination, $3,000 to pass the entry box and $3,000 additional to start, with $300,000 guaranteed. The owner of the winner to receive $180,000; $60,000 to second, $33,,000 to third, $18,000 to fourth and $9,000 to fifth. Trophy to winning Owner. Closed Wednesday, March 24, 2004 with 17 nominations.

Value of Race: $300,000 Winner $180,000; second $60,000; third $33,000; fourth $18,000; fifth $9,000. Mutuel Pool $472,993.00 Exacta Pool $304,586.00 Trifecta Pool $231,944.00 Superfecta Pool $69,055.00

Last Raced	Horse	M/Eqt.	A.	Wt	PP	¼	½	¾	1	Str	Fin	Jockey	Odds $1
28Feb04 ^{9}GP^{2}	Jackpot	L b	6	113	2	$5^{4\frac{1}{2}}$	4^{3}	4^{7}	3^{1}	2^{hd}	1^{2}	Bravo J	17.10
13Mar04 ^{13}GP^{1}	Newfoundland	L b	4	116	3	$2^{\frac{1}{2}}$	$2^{1\frac{1}{2}}$	$2^{1\frac{1}{2}}$	2^{1}	3^{4}	2^{1}	Chavez J F	1.90
6Mar04 ^{10}Tam^{4}	The Lady's Groom	L bf	4	113	6	$1^{\frac{1}{2}}$	1^{2}	$1^{2\frac{1}{2}}$	$1^{1\frac{1}{2}}$	$1^{2\frac{1}{2}}$	$3^{1\frac{3}{4}}$	King E L Jr	16.70
6Mar04 ^{10}Tam^{5}	The Judge Sez Who	L	5	114	5	$4^{\frac{1}{2}}$	5^{5}	5^{1}	5^{2}	4^{1}	4^{3}	Boulanger G	26.10
9Feb04 ^{5}GP^{3}	Indy Dancer	L	4	113	1	6	6	6	6	6	$5^{6\frac{3}{4}}$	Mojica R Jr	9.10
29Feb04 ^{9}FG^{4}	Seattle Fitz-Arg	L	5	115	4	$3^{\frac{1}{2}}$	3^{1}	3^{hd}	4^{3}	5^{2}	6	Gryder A T	0.70

OFF AT 4:42 Start Good . Won driving. Track fast.

TIME :23^{3}, :47^{2}, 1:11^{2}, 1:36^{2}, 2:02^{4} (:23.76, :47.56, 1:11.52, 1:36.48, 2:02.80)

$2 Mutuel Prices:				
	3 – JACKPOT	36.20	9.80	19.60
	4 – NEWFOUNDLAND		3.80	9.00
	7 – THE LADY'S GROOM			20.40

$1 EXACTA 3–4 PAID $52.70 $1 TRIFECTA 3–4–7 PAID $289.90
$1 SUPERFECTA 3–4–7–6 PAID $1,479.70

Ch. h, (Mar), by Seeking the Gold – Frolic , by Cox's Ridge . Trainer McGaughey III Claude R. Bred by Cynthia Phipps (Ky).

JACKPOT rated off the pace, moved into contention three wide on the far turn, then rallied to catch THE LADY'S GROOM at the sixteenth pole and edged away. NEWFOUNDLAND taken in hand to stalk the pace, responded to pressure in the drive and wore down THE LADY'S GROOM for the place while being outfinished by the winner. THE LADY'S GROOM moved up soon after the start gain the lead, set the pace along the inside to the sixteenth pole and weakened. THE JUDGE SEZ WHO unhurried while saving ground, swung out for the stretch run and failed to threaten. INDY DANCER was never a factor. SEATTLE FITZ (ARG) stalked the pace along the inside into the far turn and faltered.

Owners– 1, Phipps Cynthia; 2, Sumaya Us Stables; 3, Murphy John D Sr; 4, Sez Who Racing; 5, Wertheimer and Frere; 6, West Point Stable

Trainers– 1, McGaughey III Claude R; 2, Pletcher Todd A; 3, Gorham Michael E; 4, Wolfson Milton W; 5, Pletcher Todd A; 6, McLaughlin Kiaran P

Scratched– Gran Cesare (ARG) (06Mar04 ^{10}Tam^{6})

$1 Pick Three (9–2–3) Paid $333.40 ; Pick Three Pool $49,606 .

SEVENTH RACE
Hawthorne
APRIL 3, 2004

1⅛ MILES. (1.46^{3}) 47TH RUNNING OF THE ILLINOIS DERBY. Grade II. Purse $500,000 Guaranteed. FOR THREE YEAR OLDS. By subscription of $100 each Early Bird nomination made by February 4, 2004, or $500 each, which shall accompany the nomination made by Friday, March 19, 2004, $2,500 to pass the entry box, $2,500 additional to start. With$500,000 Guaranteed, of which 60 percent to the winner, 20 percent to second, 11 percent to third, 6 percent to fourth, 3 percent to fifth. Weight 122 lbs. Winners of $100,000 at a mile or over in 2004 to carry 2 lbs. Non–winners of $75,000 at a mile orover in 2004 allowed, 2 lbs.; of such a race at anytime, 4 lbs.; of $50,000 at a mile or over at any time, 6 lbs.; of $30,000 at a mile or over at any time, 8 lbs. (Maiden and claiming . Early Nominations Closed February 4, 2004 with 105 ($100 Fee). Latenominations closed March 19, 2004 with 10 ($500 Fee).

Value of Race: $500,000 Winner $300,000; second $100,000; third $55,000; fourth $30,000; fifth $15,000. Mutuel Pool $931,678.00 Exacta Pool $590,966.00 Trifecta Pool $513,762.00 Superfecta Pool $129,338.00

Last Raced	Horse	M/Eqt.	A.	Wt	PP	St	¼	½	¾	Str	Fin	Jockey	Odds $1
7Mar04 ^{9}FG^{3}	Pollard's Vision	L	3	114	2	2	$1^{1\frac{1}{2}}$	$1^{1\frac{1}{2}}$	1^{1}	1^{2}	$1^{2\frac{3}{4}}$	Coa E M	1.70
5Mar04 ^{8}Aqu^{1}	Song of the Sword	L bf	3	116	5	7	$6^{1\frac{1}{2}}$	5^{1}	2^{hd}	2^{3}	$2^{2\frac{3}{4}}$	Migliore R	3.40
13Mar04 ^{7}GP^{1}	Suave	L b	3	114	4	1	$4^{\frac{1}{2}}$	6^{1}	$5^{1\frac{1}{2}}$	3^{3}	$3^{8\frac{1}{2}}$	Bejarano R	4.50
13Mar04 ^{7}GG^{4}	O. K. Mikie	L b	3	116	9	10	11	11	11	$7^{\frac{1}{2}}$	4^{1}	Radke K	12.10
13Mar04 ^{7}GG^{7}	Skipaslew	L b	3	118	3	4	$3^{\frac{1}{2}}$	2^{hd}	$4^{\frac{1}{2}}$	4^{hd}	5^{nk}	Saint-Martin E	12.10
13Mar04 ^{7}GG^{1}	Kilgowan	L b	3	124	1	3	7^{hd}	7^{hd}	8^{2}	$6^{\frac{1}{2}}$	$6^{3\frac{1}{2}}$	Rollins C J	18.30
28Feb04 ^{10}OP^{1}	Pure American	L	3	114	8	6	5^{hd}	$4^{1\frac{1}{2}}$	3^{hd}	5^{2}	$7^{1\frac{1}{4}}$	Kuntzweiler G	10.90
14Mar04 ^{1}Haw^{2}	Dancefortyniner		3	114	7	11	10^{6}	$9^{\frac{1}{2}}$	9^{hd}	8^{1}	8^{2}	Montalvo C	105.20
14Mar04 ^{1}Haw^{1}	Chrome Soldier	L	3	115	6	5	2^{hd}	3^{hd}	$6^{\frac{1}{2}}$	9^{6}	9^{12}	Sterling L J Jr	69.80
13Mar04 ^{9}GP^{5}	Farnum Alley	L	3	116	10	8	$8^{1\frac{1}{2}}$	$8^{1\frac{1}{2}}$	$7^{1\frac{1}{2}}$	10^{15}	$10^{16\frac{1}{4}}$	Razo E Jr	11.70
28Feb04 ^{10}TP^{3}	White MountainBoy	L b	3	118	11	9	9^{1}	10^{6}	10^{4}	11	11	Castellano A Jr	19.10

OFF AT 4:25 Start Good For All But DANCEFORTYNINER. Won driving. Track fast.

TIME :23^{4}, :47^{4}, 1:12^{3}, 1:37^{4}, 1:50^{4} (:23.99, :47.94, 1:12.73, 1:37.83, 1:50.80)

$2 Mutuel Prices:				
	2 – POLLARD'S VISION	5.40	3.60	2.80
	5 – SONG OF THE SWORD		3.80	3.20
	4 – SUAVE			3.60

$2 EXACTA 2–5 PAID $20.20 $2 TRIFECTA 2–5–4 PAID $66.40
$2 SUPERFECTA 2–5–4–9 PAID $402.40

Dk. b or br. c, (Jan), by Carson City – Etats Unis , by Dixieland Band . Trainer Pletcher Todd A. Bred by Charles A Smith (Ky).

POLLARD'S VISION sprinted clear soon after the start, set the pace in hand while saving ground along the backstretch, shook loose leaving the far turn, dug in when challenged in upper stretch, shook off SONG OF THE SWORD leaving the furlong marker then edged away under strong left hand encouragement. SONG OF THE SWORD steadied in tight between horses approaching the first turn, raced in good position along the backstretch, moved out to launch his bid on the far turn, rapidly closed the gap while three wide to threaten nearing the quarter pole, made a run outside the winner to challenge in upper stretch but couldn't stay with that one through the final eighth. SUAVE settled just off the early pace, swung out entering the backstretch, raced in the middle of the pack while well off the rail for six furlongs, closed the gap while four wide on the turn, moved into contention from outside at the top of the stretch then lacked a strong closing bid. O. K. MIKIE was outrun for six furlongs, raced far back to the turn, swung six wide at the top of the stretch then improved his position with a late run in the middle of the track. SKIPASLEW raced in good position through the opening half, raced just behind the leaders while saving ground to the turn, dropped back in upper stretch and steadily tired thereafter. KILGOWAN steadied along the inside on the first turn, raced in midpack while three wide along the backstretch, angled, four wide while gaining slightly on the turn then lacked a strong closing response. PURE AMERICAN stalked the leaders while four wide along the backstretch, continued wide while just off the pace on the turn, drifted out in upper stretch then raced erratically while tiring in the la lane. DANCEFORTYNINER broke in the air at the start and was never closed thereafter while saving ground throughout. CHROME SOLDIER prompted the pace between horses for six furlongs and faded. FARNUM ALLEY failed to mount a serious rally while five wide throughout. WHITE MOUNTAIN BOY was never a factor and faltered badly in the stretch.

Owners– 1, Edgewood Farm; 2, Paraneck Stable; 3, Jay Em Ess Stable; 4, Lo Charles; 5, The Merv Griffin Ranch Co; 6, Ann Marie Farm; 7, Kirkwood Al and Saundra S; 8, Allen Irene; 9, Anderson Robert L; 10, Melnyk Eugene and Laura; 11, Gill Michael J

Trainers– 1, Pletcher Todd A; 2, Pedersen Jennifer; 3, McGee Paul J; 4, McArthur Jerry; 5, O'Neill Doug; 6, Arterburn Lonnie; 7, Forster Grant T; 8, Cole Eddie A; 9, Gore Terrel; 10, Reinstedler Anthony; 11, Schoenthal Phil

$2 Pick Three (3–2–2) Paid $733.20 ; Pick Three Pool $14,149 .

NINTH RACE
Keeneland
APRIL 3, 2004

$1\frac{1}{16}$ MILES. (1.40^{4}) 67TH RUNNING OF THE ASHLAND. Grade I. Purse $500,000 FOR FILLIES THREE YEARS OLD. By subscription of $250 each, which should accompany the nomination; $5,000 to enter and start, with $500,000 guaranteed, of which $310,000 to the owner of the winner, $100,000 to second, $50,000 to third, $25,000 to fourthand $15,000 to fifth. Weight: 123 lbs. Non-winners of $60,000 twice at a mile or over allowed 3 lbs.; $60,000 at a mile or over, 5 lbs.; $45,000 twice at any distance, 7 lbs. Starters to named through the entry box by the usual time of closing. Aggold julep cup will be presented to the owner of the winner. A silver julep cup will be presented to the winning trainer and jockey. No supplementary nominations. Closed Wednesday, February 18, 2004 with 73 nominations.

Value of Race: $485,000 Winner $310,000; second $100,000; third $50,000; fourth $25,000. Mutuel Pool $504,826.00 Exacta Pool $283,448.00 Trifecta Pool $77,623.00 Quinella Pool $8,194.00

Last Raced	Horse	M/Eqt.	A.	Wt	PP	St	¼	½	¾	Str	Fin	Jockey	Odds $1
13Mar04 ^{4}GP^{1}	Madcap Escapade	L	3	118	2	2	1^{1}	$1^{1\frac{1}{2}}$	$1^{1\frac{1}{2}}$	$1^{2\frac{1}{2}}$	$1^{\frac{1}{2}}$	Douglas R R	0.70
6Mar04 ^{9}FG^{1}	Ashado	L	3	123	1	4	$3^{2\frac{1}{2}}$	$3^{3\frac{1}{2}}$	$3^{2\frac{1}{2}}$	$2^{3\frac{1}{2}}$	2^{4}	Velasquez C	1.70
6Mar04 ^{8}GP^{1}	Last Song	L	3	120	4	1	4	4	4	4	3^{3}	Albarado R J	8.50
13Mar04 ^{4}GP^{2}	La Reina	L	3	120	3	3	2^{hd}	$2^{\frac{1}{2}}$	$2^{\frac{1}{2}}$	$3^{1\frac{1}{2}}$	4	Velazquez J R	5.30

OFF AT 5:15 Start Good . Won driving. Track fast.

TIME :24, :47^{2}, 1:11^{2}, 1:37^{2}, 1:44^{2} (:24.03, :47.50, 1:11.46, 1:37.49, 1:44.55)

$2 Mutuel Prices:

3 – MADCAP ESCAPADE	3.40	2.20	—
2 – ASHADO		2.60	—
5 – LAST SONG		—	—

$2 EXACTA 3–2 PAID $5.40 $2 TRIFECTA 3–2–5 PAID $7.80
$2 QUINELLA 2–3 PAID $3.40

B. f, (May), by Hennessy – Sassy Pants , by Saratoga Six . Trainer Brothers Frank L. Bred by Needham/ Betz Thoroughbreds & James &Blackburn (Ky).

MADCAP ESCAPADE drifted in after the start while gaining the lead, made the pace in the two path under a rating hold, was asked for a bit more speed entering the far turn, settled into the stretch with a clear advantage, was roused with the whip four times on the right side, then, after the rider switched to the left side, nine more times to hold sway. ASHADO, never far back, was checked in behind the winner midway on first turn, continued near the inside until the stretch, eased out four wide for the drive and finished with good courage to prove easily second best. LAST SONG, away in good order, quickly settled, angled near the inside, saved ground most of the way and couldn't offer a serious late response. LA REINA went up early to press the winner three or four wide, continued in closest attendance to MADCAP ESCAPDE until the five-sixteenths pole and faltered.

Owners– 1, Lunsford Bruce; 2, Starlight Stables Jack Wolf Paul Saylor and John Martin; 3, Buckram Oak Farm; 4, Hamilton Emory A

Trainers– 1, Brothers Frank L; 2, Pletcher Todd A; 3, Nafzger Carl A; 4, McGaughey III Claude R

Scratched– Halfbridled (13Mar04 ^{8}SA ^{2})

$2 Pick Three (5–9/11–1/3) Paid $91.40 ; Pick Three Pool $60,308 .
$2 Pick Four (3–5–9/11–1/3) Paid $356.00 ; Pick Four Pool $72,973 .

NINTH RACE
Oaklawn
APRIL 3, 2004

$1\frac{1}{16}$ MILES. (1.40^{1}) 39TH RUNNING OF THE APPLE BLOSSOM HANDICAP. Grade I. Purse $500,000 FILLIES AND MARES, FOUR YEAR OLDS AND UPWARD. By subscritpion of $200 each, which shall accompany the nomination, $3,500 to pass the entry box and $5,000 additional to start, with $500,000 Guaranteed of which $300,000 to the Owner of the winner, $100,000 to second, $50,000 to third, $25,000 to fourth, $15,000 to fifth and $10,000 to sixth. Weights to be announced Friday, March 26. In Handicap Stakes starting preference will be given to heavyweights. (See reverse side for additional starting limitatiion information). Starters to be named through the entry box by the usual time of closing. The Owner of the winner to receive a trophy. Nominatons Closed Saturday, March 20, 2004 with 12 Nominees.

Value of Race: $500,000 Winner $300,000; second $100,000; third $50,000; fourth $25,000; fifth $15,000; sixth $10,000. Mutuel Pool $749,150.00 Exacta Pool $337,530.00 Trifecta Pool $292,981.00

Last Raced	Horse	M/Eqt.	A.	Wt	PP	St	¼	½	¾	Str	Fin	Jockey	Odds $1
28Sep03 ^{6}SA^{2}	Azeri	L	6	123	1	4	1^{1}	$1^{\frac{1}{2}}$	$1^{1\frac{1}{2}}$	$1^{2\frac{1}{2}}$	$1^{1\frac{1}{2}}$	Smith M E	2.00
13Sep03 ^{9}Bel^{1}	Wild Spirit-Chi	L	5	119	2	5	$4^{1\frac{1}{2}}$	5^{8}	$4^{2\frac{1}{2}}$	$2^{\frac{1}{2}}$	$2^{1\frac{3}{4}}$	Bailey J D	1.50
14Mar04 ^{8}SA^{2}	Star Parade-Arg	L	5	114	3	6	$2^{2\frac{1}{2}}$	2^{3}	$2^{\frac{1}{2}}$	3^{5}	$3^{7\frac{1}{4}}$	McKee J	10.50
6Mar04 ^{10}SA^{2}	Island Fashion	L b	4	118	5	2	$3^{\frac{1}{2}}$	3^{3}	3^{hd}	4^{3}	4^{2}	Desormeaux K J	1.80
13Mar04 ^{10}OP^{2}	Keys to the Heart	L	5	111	4	3	5^{8}	4^{1}	5^{8}	$5^{4\frac{1}{2}}$	5^{3}	Prado E S	46.70
13Mar04 ^{10}OP^{1}	Golden Sonata	L	5	114	6	1	6	6	6	6	6	Marquez C H Jr	34.20

OFF AT 5:05 Start Good . Won driving. Track fast.

TIME :23^{1}, :46^{3}, 1:10^{4}, 1:35, 1:41^{1} (:23.29, :46.71, 1:10.99, 1:35.19, 1:41.24)

$2 Mutuel Prices:

1 – AZERI	6.00	3.20	2.20
2 – WILD SPIRIT–CHI		2.80	2.20
3 – STAR PARADE–ARG			2.60

$2 EXACTA 1–2 PAID $16.40 $2 TRIFECTA 1–2–3 PAID $60.00

Ch. m, (May), by Jade Hunter – Zodiac Miss–Aus , by Ahonoora–GB . Trainer Lukas D Wayne. Bred by Allen E Paulson (Ky).

AZERI took control soon after the start while off the inside into the first turn, controlled a moderate pace, shook clear again second turn, maintained a comfortable advantage down the lane under steady handling. WILD SPIRIT (CHI) unhurried early, moved closer along the inside late in the second turn, angled out abruptly turning for home to soundly bump STAR PARADE who in turn bothered ISLAND FASHION, asked for her best, no match late. FOLLOWING A STEWARDS' INQUIRY AND A CLAIM OF FOUL BY THE RIDER OF STAR PARADE AGAINST WILD SPIRIT FOR INTERFERENCE ENTERING THE STRETCH, THE RESULT WAS ALLOWED TO STAND. STAR PARADE (ARG) closest to the winner, moved a bit closer into the far turn, soundly bumped by the runner up exiting the final turn, could not keep up with that one for the runner up spot the final furlong. ISLAND FASHION within striking distance well off the rail, bothered when STAR PARADE came out due to a bump from WILD SPIRIT into the stretch, came up empty in the late going. KEYS TO THE HEART went singularly paced, no threat. GOLDEN SONATA fell back to trail by a wide margin after the start, remained back, little late gain.

Owners– 1, Allen E Paulson Living Trust J Michael Paulson; 2, Sumaya Us Stables Oussama Aboughazale; 3, Tanaka Gary A; 4, Everest Stables Inc Jeffrey Lynn Nielsen; 5, Nichols Thomas L; 6, Spence James C

Trainers– 1, Lukas D Wayne; 2, Frankel Robert; 3, Vienna Darrell; 4, Polanco Marcelo; 5, Greely C Beau; 6, Nicks Morris G

$2 Pick Three (3–3/5/6–1) Paid $192.80 ; Pick Three Pool $27,589 .

THIRD RACE
Santa Anita
APRIL 3, 2004

1⅛ MILES. (Turf) (1.43^{4}) 45TH RUNNING OF THE ARCADIA HANDICAP. Grade II. Purse $150,000 FOR FOUR-YEAR-OLDS AND UPWARD. By subscription of $150 each to accompany the nomination or by supplenemtary nomination of $3,000 by Sunday, March 28. $1,500 additional to start, with $150,000 guaranteed, of which $90,000 to first, $30,000 to second, $18,0000 to third, $9,000 to fourth and $3,000 to fifth. Weights Tuesday, March 30. High weights preferred. Starters to be named through the entry box by the closing time of entries. A trophy will be presented to the owner of the winner. Closed with 13 nominations.

Value of Race: $150,000 Winner $90,000; second $30,000; third $18,000; fourth $9,000; fifth $3,000. Mutuel Pool $551,615.00 Exacta Pool $313,265.00 Quinella Pool $32,023.00 Trifecta Pool $278,883.00 Superfecta Pool $84,625.00

Last Raced	Horse	M/Eqt.	A.	Wt	PP	St	¼	½	¾	Str	Fin	Jockey	Odds $1
17Oct03 ML^{4}	Diplomatic Bag	LB	4	116	5	4	2^{1}	$3^{2\frac{1}{2}}$	$3^{1\frac{1}{2}}$	$3^{\frac{1}{2}}$	$1^{\frac{3}{4}}$	Flores D R	4.10
6Mar04 ^{9}SA^{9}	Statement	LB	6	114	1	3	$3^{1\frac{1}{2}}$	2^{hd}	$2^{1\frac{1}{2}}$	1^{hd}	2^{2}	Santiago Javier	6.00
23Mar03 ^{8}FG^{4}	Seinne-Chi	LB	7	115	3	1	4^{hd}	$4^{\frac{1}{2}}$	5^{hd}	$5^{1\frac{1}{2}}$	3^{1}	Espinoza V	7.60
31Aug03 ^{8}Dmr^{4}	Ballingarry-Ire	LB	5	118	6	6	7	7	7	6^{2}	$4^{1\frac{1}{2}}$	Valdivia J Jr	7.80
14Mar04 ^{7}GG^{2}	Soud	LB f	6	116	7	5	$1^{1\frac{1}{2}}$	$1^{1\frac{1}{2}}$	1^{1}	$2^{1\frac{1}{2}}$	5^{hd}	Baze T C	1.60
14Jun03 ^{3}Hol^{6}	Gigli-Brz	LB	6	117	2	2	$5^{1\frac{1}{2}}$	5^{1}	4^{hd}	4^{1}	6^{1}	Nakatani C S	6.20
16Feb04 ^{9}SA^{8}	Researched-Ire	LB	5	115	4	7	$6^{\frac{1}{2}}$	6^{2}	6^{2}	7	7	Ramsammy E	8.30

OFF AT 1:02 Start Good . Won driving. Course firm.

TIME :24^{1}, :48^{3}, 1:12^{3}, 1:36^{1}, 1:47^{4} (:24.27, :48.69, 1:12.71, 1:36.36, 1:47.90)

$2 Mutuel Prices:				
	6 – DIPLOMATIC BAG	10.20	5.60	4.20
	2 – STATEMENT		7.40	4.60
	4 – SEINNE-CHI			5.00

$1 EXACTA 6–2 PAID $35.60 $2 QUINELLA 2–6 PAID $40.00
$1 TRIFECTA 6–2–4 PAID $180.50 $1 SUPERFECTA 6–2–4–7 PAID $964.70

B. c, (Feb), by Devil's Bag – Louis d'Or , by Mr. Prospector . Trainer Frankel Robert. Bred by Juddmonte Farms Inc (Ky).

DIPLOMATIC BAG angled in and pulled his way along inside stalking the pace, continued a bit off the rail on the backstretch and second turn, came out into the stretch and rallied gamely under a strong hand ride to prove best. STATEMENT stalked the leader a bit off the inside then outside the winner, bid outside the former on the second turn, gained a short lead in upper stretch, inched away past midstretch but could not hold off the winner. SEINNE (CHI) chased outside a rival then between foes into and on the second turn, came out three deep into the stretch and picked up the show. BALLINGARRY (IRE) unhurried outside a rival then a bit off the inside, split horses in deep stretch and improved position. SOUD took the early lead and angled in, set the pace inside, dueled along the rail on the second turn and until past midstretch and weakened late. GIGLI (BRZ) was in a good position chasing outside a rival then along the inside on the backstretch and second turn, continued inside in the stretch and lacked a rally. RESEARCHED (IRE) off a bit slowly, settled outside a rival, went three deep into and on the second turn and into the stretch and failed to menace.

Owners– 1, Juddmonte Farms Inc; 2, Bienstock & Winner Stables Mandabach & Papiano; 3, Hunt Nelson B; 4, Port Trust Naify Marsha and San Gabriel Investments; 5, Shadwell Farm LLC; 6, T N T Stud; 7, Tanaka Gary A

Trainers– 1, Frankel Robert; 2, Mulhall Kristin; 3, McAnally Ronald; 4, De Seroux Laura; 5, Drysdale Neil; 6, Frankel Robert; 7, Cecil B D A

Scratched– Toccet (20Mar04 ^{9}SA ^{7})

$1 Pick Three (2–4–6) Paid $20.80 ; Pick Three Pool $149,187 .
$2 Daily Double (4–6) Paid $13.60 ; Daily Double Pool $35,446 .

ELEVENTH RACE
Oaklawn
APRIL 3, 2004

1⅛ MILES. (1.46^{3}) 58TH RUNNING OF THE OAKLAWN HANDICAP. Grade II. Purse $500,000 FOUR YEAR OLDS AND UPWARD. By subscription of $200 each which shall accompany the nomination. $3,500 to pass the entry box and $5,000 additional to start, with $500,000 guaranteed of which $300,000 to the Owner of the winner, $100,000 to second, $50,0000 to third, $25,000 to fourth, $15,000 to fifth and $10,000 to sixth. Weights to be announced Thursday, March 25. In Handicap Stakes starting preference will be given to heavyweights. (See reverse side for additional starting limitation information). Starters to be named through the entry box by the usual time of closing. The Owner of the winner to receive a trophy. Nominations Closed Saturday, March 20, 2004 with 17 Nominees.

Value of Race: $500,000 Winner $300,000; second $100,000; third $50,000; fourth $25,000; fifth $15,000; sixth $10,000. Mutuel Pool $609,670.00 Exacta Pool $323,120.00 Trifecta Pool $259,060.00

Last Raced	Horse	M/Eqt.	A.	Wt	PP	St	¼	½	¾	Str	Fin	Jockey	Odds $1
29Feb04 ^{9}FG^{1}	Peace Rules	L	4	120	3	1	$2^{8\frac{1}{2}}$	2^{10}	$2^{4\frac{1}{2}}$	$1^{1\frac{1}{2}}$	1^{2}	Bailey J D	0.80
14Feb04 ^{8}Lrl^{1}	Ole Faunty	L	5	116	6	4	3^{3}	$5^{2\frac{1}{2}}$	$5^{2\frac{1}{2}}$	$3^{1\frac{1}{2}}$	2^{nk}	Smith M E	8.90
29Feb04 ^{9}FG^{2}	Saint Liam	L	4	114	2	2	1^{1}	$1^{\frac{1}{2}}$	1^{hd}	2^{hd}	$3^{2\frac{1}{4}}$	Prado E S	1.90
14Mar04 ^{9}OP^{1}	Sonic West	L b	5	112	1	6	$4^{\frac{1}{2}}$	3^{hd}	3^{1}	4^{3}	$4^{1\frac{1}{2}}$	Martinez W	22.80
29Feb04 ^{9}FG^{6}	Sir Cherokee	L	4	113	5	5	6	$4^{\frac{1}{2}}$	$4^{\frac{1}{2}}$	$5^{\frac{1}{2}}$	5^{2}	Thompson T J	7.80
21Feb04 ^{9}OP^{1}	Private Emblem	L f	5	113	4	3	5^{1}	6	6	6	6	Doocy T T	11.20

OFF AT 6:07 Start Good . Won driving. Track fast.

TIME :22^{1}, :45^{2}, 1:09^{3}, 1:35^{2}, 1:48^{1} (:22.20, :45.46, 1:09.62, 1:35.59, 1:48.26)

$2 Mutuel Prices:				
	3 – PEACE RULES	3.60	3.00	2.20
	6 – OLE FAUNTY		5.20	2.80
	2 – SAINT LIAM			2.40

$2 EXACTA 3–6 PAID $27.20 $2 TRIFECTA 3–6–2 PAID $50.20

Ch. c, (Apr), by Jules – Hold to Fashion , by Hold Your Peace . Trainer Frankel Robert. Bred by Newchance Farm (Fla).

PEACE RULES hooked up on the front end furthest from the rail, quick splits while comfortably in hand, shook off the other speed when straightened for home, plenty left late. OLE FAUNTY well back while racing outside, steady advance into the stretch, attempted to go in then out under a spirited right handed whip stretch, game for place while not a threat to the winner. SAINT LIAM dueled quick closest to but certainly not on the rail, fell off the winner nearing the furlong marker, moved out, outfinished for the place. SONIC WEST moved a bit closer turning for home, roused, came off the rail, came up empty in the late going. SIR CHEROKEE lacked speed, roused turning for home, failed to respond. PRIVATE EMBLEM saved ground to no avail.

Owners– 1, Gann Edmund A; 2, Thomas Van Meter II & Doug Hendrickson; 3, Mr and Mrs William K Warren Jr; 4, Stone Spire LLC; 5, Domino Stud of Lexington LLC Kenneth T Jones; 6, Cassels James and Zollars Bob

Trainers– 1, Frankel Robert; 2, Walden W Elliott; 3, Dutrow Richard E Jr; 4, Van Berg Thomas L; 5, Tomlinson Michael A; 6, Asmussen Steven M

$2 Pick Three (1–6–3) Paid $96.20 ; Pick Three Pool $80,462 .
$2 Daily Double (1–3) Paid $21.20 ; Daily Double Pool $47,738 .

EIGHTH RACE

Santa Anita

APRIL 3, 2004

1⅛ MILES. (1.45^4) 67TH RUNNING OF THE SANTA ANITA DERBY. Grade I. Purse $750,000 FOR THREE-YEAR-OLDS. By subscription of $250 each to accompany the nomination (Early Bird) on or before December 11, 2003. Early Bird nominees to the Santa Anita Derby are automatically eligible to both the San Rafael and San Felipe Stakes with nominationn and starting fees waived to those two stakes. Late nominations close Saturday, March 20, 2004 by payment of $2,500 each. Supplementary nominations are due at time of entry, by payment of $15,000. All horses shall pay $7,500 to start, with $750,000 guaraanteed, of which $450,000 to first, $150,000 to second, $90,000 to third, $45,000 to fourth and $15,000 to fifth. 122 lbs. Starters to be named through the entry box by the closing time of entries. A trophy will be presented to the owner of the winner. Closed Dec. 11, 2003 with 137 original nominations. March. 20, 2004 with 5 late nominations.

Value of Race: $750,000 Winner $450,000; third $90,000; second $150,000; fourth $45,000; fifth $15,000. Mutuel Pool $2,075,308.00 Exacta Pool $934,344.00 Quinella Pool $73,114.00 Trifecta Pool $904,354.00

Last Raced	Horse	M/Eqt.	A.	Wt	PP	St	¼	½	¾	Str	Fin	Jockey	Odds $1
6Mar04 $^7SA^6$	Castledale-Ire	LB	3	122	4	4	$6^{1\frac{1}{2}}$	6^3	$5^{1\frac{1}{2}}$	3^{hd}	1^{hd}	Valdivia J Jr	30.00
3Mar04 $^2SA^1$	[D]Rock Hard Ten	LB	3	122	6	5	3^{hd}	3^{hd}	4^2	2^1	2^2	Flores D R	3.00
6Mar04 $^7SA^1$	Imperialism	LB b	3	122	1	3	7	7	7	$4^{2\frac{1}{2}}$	3^1	Espinoza V	4.70
6Mar04 $^7SA^4$	Quintons Gold Rush	LB	3	122	5	1	$2^{2\frac{1}{2}}$	1^{hd}	2^{hd}	1^{hd}	$4^{6\frac{1}{2}}$	Nakatani C S	7.00
7Mar04 $^9FG^1$	Wimbledon	LB	3	122	3	7	4^1	4^2	$3^{\frac{1}{2}}$	$5^{2\frac{1}{2}}$	5^1	Santiago Javier	2.60
14Mar04 $^5SA^2$	St Averil	LB b	3	122	7	6	$5^{\frac{1}{2}}$	5^{hd}	$6^{\frac{1}{2}}$	7	6^1	Baze T C	2.20
6Mar04 $^7SA^8$	Lucky Pulpit	LB bf	3	122	2	2	$1^{\frac{1}{2}}$	$2^{2\frac{1}{2}}$	1^{hd}	6^{hd}	7	Court J K	33.60

[D] – Rock Hard Ten disqualified and placed 3rd

OFF AT 3:47 Start Good . Won driving. Track fast.

TIME :22^4, :46^4, 1:11, 1:36^2, 1:49^1 (:22.87, :46.84, 1:11.11, 1:36.45, 1:49.24)

$2 Mutuel Prices:				
	4 – CASTLEDALE-IRE	62.00	17.00	5.60
	1 – IMPERIALISM		5.80	3.80
	6 – ROCK HARD TEN			4.00

$1 EXACTA 4–1 PAID $157.40 $2 QUINELLA 1–4 PAID $115.60

$1 TRIFECTA 4–1–6 PAID $815.60

B. c, (Apr), by Peintre Celebre – Louju , by Silver Hawk . Trainer Mullins Jeff. Bred by Gigginstown House Stud (Ire).

CASTLEDALE (IRE) pulled early, chased a bit off the rail, went outside a rival on the second turn, swung widest into the stretch, had the rider lose the whip nearing midstretch, then rallied under strong handling while drifting in to get up late. ROCK HARD TEN three deep into the first turn, stalked outside, went up four wide with a bid leaving the backstretch and on the second turn and into the stretch, put a head in front past the eighth pole, drifted in under right handed pressure in deep stretch, brushed with the winner and held on gamely but was caught late. IMPERIALISM came a bit off the rail on the first turn and settled off the pace, moved up inside on the second turn, went around LUCKY PULPIT nearing the stretch, bid along the rail in the lane, steadied sharply in tight a sixteenth out and could not offer the necessary late kick. QUINTONS GOLD RUSH had good early speed and dueled outside a rival, regained the advantage on the second turn, fought back off the rail into the stretch and between foes past midstretch and weakened. WIMBLEDON a half step slow to begin, stalked a bit off the rail, came out on the backstretch and bid three deep between foes into and on the second turn and into the stretch and weakened. ST AVERIL four wide into the first turn, chased outside, dropped back into and on the second turn and also weakened. LUCKY PULPIT dueled inside, put a head back in front into the second turn, dropped back leaving that turn, steadied into the stretch and had little left. Following a stewards' inquiry, ROCK HARD TEN was disqualified and placed third for interference in deep stretch. A claim of foul by the rider of ROCK HARD TEN against the winner was not allowed by the stewards, who ruled both runners contributed to the light contact between them.

Owners– 1, Lyons Frank and Knee Greg; 2, Mercedes Stables LLC and Paulson; 3, Taub Steve; 4, Manoogian & Padua Stables; 5, McIngvale James; 6, Fulton Stan E; 7, Williams Mr and Mrs Larry D

Trainers– 1, Mullins Jeff; 2, Orman Jason; 3, Mulhall Kristin; 4, Mitchell Mike; 5, Baffert Bob; 6, Becerra Rafael; 7, Sise Clifford Jr

$1 Pick Three (8–6–4) Paid $479.70 ; Pick Three Pool $138,842 .
$2 Daily Double (6–4) Paid $228.00 ; Daily Double Pool $61,033 .
$2 Pick Five (3–2–4–12–4) Paid $80,836.60 ; Pick Five Pool $621,821 .

TENTH RACE
Santa Anita
APRIL 3, 2004

1⅛ MILES. (1.45^{4}) 48TH RUNNING OF THE SAN BERNARDINO HANDICAP. Grade III. Purse $100,000 FOR FOUR-YEAR-OLS AND UPWARD. By subscription of $100 each to accompany the nomination or by supplementary nomination of $2,000 by Sunday, March 28. $1,000 additional to start with $100,000 guaranteed, of which $60,000 to first, $20,000 to second, $12,000 to third, $6,000 to fourth and $2,000 to fifth. Weights: Tuesday, March 30. High weights preferred. Starters to be named through the entry box by the usual time of closing. A trophy will be presented tot he owner of the winner. Closed with 16 nominations.

Value of Race: $110,600 Winner $66,360; second $22,120; third $13,272; fourth $6,636; fifth $2,212. Mutuel Pool $565,145.00 Exacta Pool $335,195.00 Quinella Pool $29,756.00 Trifecta Pool $396,599.00

Last Raced	Horse	M/Eqt.	A.	Wt	PP	St	¼	½	¾	Str	Fin	Jockey	Odds $1
25Oct03 ^{9}SA^{3}	Dynever	LB	4	117	1	5	4^{hd}	$4^{\frac{1}{2}}$	$3^{\frac{1}{2}}$	$1^{\frac{1}{2}}$	$1^{4\frac{1}{2}}$	Nakatani C S	0.60
13Mar04 ^{6}SA^{2}	Total Impact-Chi	LB b	6	116	5	2	$2^{2\frac{1}{2}}$	$2^{2\frac{1}{2}}$	2^{2}	2^{hd}	2^{2}	Valdivia J Jr	14.40
13Sep03 ^{11}TP^{4}	Even the Score	LB b	6	116	3	3	5^{hd}	5^{2}	$5^{2\frac{1}{2}}$	$4^{2\frac{1}{2}}$	3^{2}	Flores D R	14.80
13Mar04 ^{6}SA^{1}	Ender's Shadow	LB bf	4	114	4	1	$1^{1\frac{1}{2}}$	1^{3}	$1^{\frac{1}{2}}$	$3^{1\frac{1}{2}}$	$4^{\frac{1}{2}}$	Ruis M	11.00
7Mar04 ^{8}SA^{4}	Kela	LB b	6	114	7	7	7	7	7	7	5^{1}	Baze T C	6.20
6Mar04 ^{10}SA^{8}	Star Cross-Arg	LB b	7	114	2	4	$3^{\frac{1}{2}}$	3^{1}	4^{1}	5^{1}	6^{2}	Espinoza V	4.70
22Feb04 ^{5}SA^{1}	Calkins Road	LB f	5	114	6	6	$6^{1\frac{1}{2}}$	$6^{2\frac{1}{2}}$	6^{hd}	6^{hd}	7	Santiago Javier	16.20

OFF AT 4:57 Start Good . Won ridden out. Track fast.

TIME :23^{3}, :47^{1}, 1:11^{2}, 1:35^{4}, 1:48 (:23.74, :47.31, 1:11.57, 1:35.88, 1:48.07)

$2 Mutuel Prices:			
1 – DYNEVER	3.20	2.80	2.40
5 – TOTAL IMPACT-CHI		8.00	4.40
3 – EVEN THE SCORE			4.00

$1 EXACTA 1–5 PAID $14.60 $2 QUINELLA 1–5 PAID $23.80
$1 TRIFECTA 1–5–3 PAID $85.30

Dk. b or br. c, (Mar), by Dynaformer – Flamboyance , by Zilzal . Trainer Clement Christophe. Bred by Catherine Wills (Ky).

DYNEVER chased inside, moved up along the rail leaving the backstretch came out on the second turn, bid three deep nearing the stretch, gained the advantage in upper stretch and drew clear under a brisk hand ride. TOTAL IMPACT (CHI) stalked the pace off the rail, bid outside a rival into the second turn and between horses leaving that turn, could not match the winner in the lane but was clearly second best. EVEN THE SCORE pulled between horses early, went three deep into the first turn, chased outside, tried to go between foes leaving the backstretch but was in a bit tight into the second turn, continued just off the rail and bested the others. ENDER'S SHADOW sped to the early lead, set the pace inside, dueled along the rail into and on the second turn and into the stretch, then weakened in the final furlong. KELA unhurried off the inside early, came widest into the stretch and was not a threat. STAR CROSS (ARG) pulled his way along between horses early, stalked outside a rival or a bit off the rail, swung four wide into the stretch and weakened. CALKINS ROAD three deep into the first turn, chased between rivals then off the rail, angled in on the second turn, came out into the stretch and lacked a further response.

Owners– 1, Karches & Wills; 2, Al Kabeer Sultan Mohammed Saud and Bridport S A; 3, Parra Rosendo G; 4, Green Lantern Stables LLC; 5, Manoogian Jay; 6, E A Ranches; 7, Shapiro Mr and Mrs Thomas A

Trainers– 1, Clement Christophe; 2, De Seroux Laura; 3, Cerin Vladimir; 4, Sahadi Jenine; 5, Mitchell Mike; 6, Vienna Darrell; 7, Shirreffs John

$1 Pick Three (4–7–1) Paid $283.70 ; Pick Three Pool $126,539 .
$2 Daily Double (7–1) Paid $14.60 ; Daily Double Pool $52,783 .
$1 Place Pick All (10–OF–10) Paid $3,546.70 ; Place Pick All Pool $44,434 .

EIGHTH RACE
Keeneland
APRIL 4, 2004

7 FURLONGS. (1.20^{1}) 67TH RUNNING OF THE LAFAYETTE. Grade III. Purse $100,000 FOR THREE YEAR OLDS. By subscription of $100 each, which should accompany the nomination; $1,000 to enter and start with $100,000 added, of which 62% of all monies to the owner of the winner, 20% to second, 10% to third, 5% to fourth and 3% to fifth. Weeight 123 lbs. Non-winners of $60,000 twice allowed 3 lbs.; $45,000 twice, 5 lbs.; $30,000 twice, 7 lbs. Starters to be named through the entry box by the usual time of closing. A gold julep cup will be presented to the owner of the winner. Closed Wednesday, March 24, 2004 with 25 nominations.

Value of Race: $109,500 Winner $67,890; second $21,900; third $10,950; fourth $5,475; fifth $3,285. Mutuel Pool $312,520.00 Exacta Pool $191,542.00 Trifecta Pool $146,321.00 Superfecta Pool $30,330.00 Quinella Pool $7,315.00

Last Raced	Horse	M/Eqt.	A.	Wt	PP	St	¼	½	Str	Fin	Jockey	Odds $1
6Mar04 ^{7}FG^{1}	Bwana Charlie	L	3	117	3	2	$2^{\frac{1}{2}}$	2^{3}	$1^{1\frac{1}{2}}$	$1^{3\frac{1}{4}}$	Sellers S J	2.30
20Mar04 ^{7}Aqu^{7}	Quick Action	L	3	116	4	1	3^{hd}	1^{hd}	2^{4}	2^{7}	Day P	4.40
20Mar04 ^{7}TP^{2}	Tales of Glory	L	3	116	1	6	$1^{\frac{1}{2}}$	3^{1}	3^{1}	3^{3}	Bailey J D	2.10
28Feb04 ^{12}GP^{1}	Call Me Shane	L	3	116	5	5	6	6	$5^{2\frac{1}{2}}$	4^{2}	Prado E S	4.60
11Oct03 ^{11}Crc^{3}	Perpetual Peace	L f	3	116	6	4	$5^{2\frac{1}{2}}$	4^{1}	4^{hd}	$5^{\frac{1}{2}}$	Albarado R J	10.70
20Mar04 ^{10}TP^{3}	Wulpe	L	3	116	2	3	$4^{2\frac{1}{2}}$	5^{2}	6	6	Velazquez J R	6.50

OFF AT 4:45 Start Good . Won driving. Track fast.

TIME :21^{3}, :44, 1:10, 1:24^{3} (:21.68, :44.08, 1:10.17, 1:24.73)

$2 Mutuel Prices:			
3 – BWANA CHARLIE	6.60	3.60	2.60
4 – QUICK ACTION		5.20	3.00
1 – TALES OF GLORY			2.60

$2 EXACTA 3–4 PAID $41.60 $2 TRIFECTA 3–4–1 PAID $109.80
$2 SUPERFECTA 3–4–1–5 PAID $254.40 $2 QUINELLA 3–4 PAID $19.20

B. c, (Mar), by Indian Charlie – Shahalo , by Halo . Trainer Asmussen Steven M. Bred by E & D Enterprises (Ky).

BWANA CHARLIE, forwardly placed between foes from the outset, gained a narrow lead leaving the backstretch, was headed briefly from the outside just prior to going a half by QUICK ACTION, regained the edge soon after, shook off that rival, drifted out briefly at the eighth pole, then, when straightened away, widened a bit under steady right-handed encouragement. QUICK ACTION broke in front, eased back outside of TALES OF GLORY and BWANA CHARLIE, inched to challenge midway on the turn, briefly put his head in front of the winner, lost the advantage back to BWANA CHARLIE soon after and couldn't keep pace as second best. TALES OF GLORY, off a half-step slow, rushed to the front after a furlong, lost the lead to the winner concluding the backstretch and weakened gradually after a half. CALL ME SHANE came out at the break bumping lightly with PERPETUAL PEACE, raced five or six wide most of the way and wasn't a threat while improving position. PERPETUAL PEACE, lightly bumped at the start by CALL ME SHANE, was five wide early, edged in slightly on the turn, was again four wide for the stretch run and came up empty. WULPE, well placed near the inside between foes during the early stages, remained near the inside and was finished approaching the stretch.

Owners– 1, Heiligbrodt Racing Stable; 2, Overbrook Farm; 3, Smith Derrick and Tabor Michael; 4, McNulty John W; 5, Ramsey Kenneth L and Sarah K; 6, Starlight Stable LLC Jack Wolf and John Rose

Trainers– 1, Asmussen Steven M; 2, Lukas D Wayne; 3, Pletcher Todd A; 4, O'Callaghan Niall M; 5, Werner Ronny; 6, Pletcher Todd A

Scratched– Risky Trick (28Feb04 ^{10}TP ^{9})

$2 Pick Three (3–1–3) Paid $56.40 ; Pick Three Pool $33,229 .

EIGHTH RACE

Santa Anita

APRIL 4, 2004

ABOUT $6\frac{1}{2}$ FURLONGS. (Turf) (1.11) 30TH RUNNING OF THE LAS CIENEGAS HANDICAP. Grade III. Purse $100,000 DOWNHILL TURF FOR FILLIES AND MARES FOUR YEARS OLD AND UPWARD. By subscription of $100 each to accompany the nomination or by supplementary nomination of $2,000 by Sunday, March 28. $1,000 additional to start, with $100,000 added. The added money and allfees to be divided 60% to the winner, 20% to second, 12% to third, 6% to fourth and 2% to fifth. Weights Tuesday, March 30. Starters to be named through the entry box by the closing time of entries. A trophy will be presented to the owner of the winner.Closed with 18 nominations.

Value of Race: $112,800 Winner $67,680; second $22,560; third $13,536; fourth $6,768; fifth $2,256. Mutuel Pool $476,209.00 Exacta Pool $267,133.00 Quinella Pool $29,584.00 Trifecta Pool $294,013.00 Superfecta Pool $123,175.00

Last Raced	Horse	M/Eqt.	A.	Wt	PP	St	¼	½	Str	Fin	Jockey	Odds $1
30Nov03 ^{6}Hol^{11}	Etoile Montante	LB	4	121	1	7	2^{hd}	$4^{1\frac{1}{2}}$	1^{hd}	$1^{\frac{1}{2}}$	Santiago Javier	1.20
13Mar04 ^{11}GP^{1}	Dedication-FR	LB	5	118	6	5	7^{1}	5^{hd}	$4^{1\frac{1}{2}}$	$2^{\frac{3}{4}}$	Nakatani C S	2.70
23Jan04 ^{5}SA^{1}	Any for Love-Arg	LB	6	115	7	1	$4^{1\frac{1}{2}}$	$3^{\frac{1}{2}}$	$3^{\frac{1}{2}}$	$3^{\frac{1}{2}}$	Espinoza V	12.10
28Jan04 ^{7}SA^{2}	Polygreen-FR	LB	5	116	9	2	9	9	6^{2}	4^{1}	Solis A	6.50
5Mar04 ^{7}SA^{2}	Notting Hill-Brz	LB	5	114	4	6	5^{hd}	6^{hd}	5^{hd}	5^{1}	Baze T C	9.20
27Dec03 ^{6}ROH^{6}	How Funny-Aus	LB b	4	113	5	9	8^{1}	8^{hd}	9	6^{2}	Ruis M	24.80
31Jly03 ^{7}Dmr^{2}	Little Treasure-FR	LB	5	117	2	8	$3^{\frac{1}{2}}$	2^{hd}	2^{hd}	7^{3}	Valdivia J Jr	20.90
21Feb04 ^{8}SA^{3}	Fudge Fatale	LB	4	116	8	3	$6^{\frac{1}{2}}$	7^{1}	7^{1}	$8^{4\frac{1}{2}}$	Flores D R	18.10
6Oct02 Tip^{8}	Petite Histoire-Ire	LB	4	116	3	4	1^{1}	$1^{1\frac{1}{2}}$	8^{hd}	9	Desormeaux K J	29.90

OFF AT 4:08 Start Good . Won driving. Course firm.

TIME :22, :44^{1}, 1:07^{1}, 1:13^{1} (:22.07, :44.32, 1:07.32, 1:13.32)

$2 Mutuel Prices:

2 – ETOILE MONTANTE	4.40	3.60	2.80
7 – DEDICATION-FR		3.40	2.60
8 – ANY FOR LOVE-ARG			4.00

$1 EXACTA 2–7 PAID $6.30 $2 QUINELLA 2–7 PAID $7.00
$1 TRIFECTA 2–7–8 PAID $53.00 $1 SUPERFECTA 2–7–8–1 PAID $140.80

Ch. f, (Feb), by Miswaki – Willstar , by Nureyev . Trainer Frankel Robert. Bred by Juddmonte Farms Inc (Ky).

ETOILE MONTANTE stalked the pace inside down the hill, bid along the rail in the stretch to gain a short lead and held on gamely under urging. DEDICATION (FR) chased off the rail then between horses down the hill, came three deep into the stretch and waited briefly, split rivals with a bid and continued gamely to the wire. ANY FOR LOVE (ARG) stalked three deep, came four wide into the stretch, bid four across the course in midstretch and also went on willingly to the end. POLYGREEN (FR) angled left in the early going and chased outside a rival down the hill, came out on the dirt and four wide into the stretch and put in a late bid. NOTTING HILL (BRZ) pulled early, stalked off the rail, awaited room off heels in upper stretch, got through but could not quite summon the needed late response. HOW FUNNY (AUS) allowed to settle off the rail, swung out in upper stretch and had a mild bid. LITTLE TREASURE (FR) close up stalking the pace between horses, bid between foes in the stretch but weakened in the final furlong. FUDGE FATALE cut the corner at the right hand curve then stalked four and three wide, came four wide into the stretch and weakened. PETITE HISTOIRE (IRE) sped to the early lead, set the pace a bit off the rail, was between horses into the stretch and also weakened. Rail on hill at zero.

Owners– 1, Juddmonte Farms Inc; 2, Head Ghislaine; 3, Diamond A Racing and North Wales LLC; 4, Wertheimer and Frere; 5, Green Lantern Stables LLC and Barber Gary; 6, O'Connor David; 7, Port Trust Naify Marsha and San Gabriel Investments; 8, Greely John J III; 9, Wilson David W and Holly F

Trainers– 1, Frankel Robert; 2, Clement Christophe; 3, Mandella Richard; 4, Mandella Richard; 5, Sahadi Jenine; 6, Cardenas Ruben; 7, De Seroux Laura; 8, Greely C Beau; 9, Cerin Vladimir

Scratched– Stormica (10Mar04 ^{6}SA ^{1})

$2 Daily Double (5–2) Paid $17.60 ; Daily Double Pool $55,629 .
$1 Pick Three (10–5–2) Paid $73.50 ; Pick Three Pool $85,030 .

NINTH RACE

Oaklawn

APRIL 7, 2004

$1\frac{1}{16}$ MILES. (1.40^{1}) 17TH RUNNING OF THE FIFTH SEASON. Grade III. Purse $100,000 FOUR YEAR OLDS AND UPWARD. No nomination fee. $500 to pass the entry box and $1,000 additional to start, with $100,000 Guaranteed of which $60,000 to the Owner of the winner, $20,000 to second, $10,000 to third, $5,000 to fourth, $3,000 to fifth and $2,,000 to sixth. WEIGHTS: 122 lbs. Non-winners of $50,000 since November 7, allowed 3 lbs.; $35,000 since January 7, allowed 5 lbs.; $18,000 since February 7, 2004, allowed 7 lbs.; $15,000 since January 7, 2004 allowed 9 lbs. (Maiden and Claiming racess not considered). In Allowance Stakes starting preference will be given to horses that have accumulated the highest earnings, excluding money won in restricted races (See reverse side for additional starting limitation information). Starters to be nameed through the entry box by the usual time of closing. The Owner of the winner to receive a trophy. Nominations closed Saturday, March 20, 2004 with 37 nominees.

Value of Race: $100,000 Winner $60,000; second $20,000; third $10,000; fourth $5,000; fifth $3,000; sixth $2,000. Mutuel Pool $211,133.00 Exacta Pool $155,013.00 Trifecta Pool $169,873.00

Last Raced	Horse	M/Eqt.	A.	Wt	PP	St	¼	½	¾	Str	Fin	Jockey	Odds $1
29Feb04 ^{9}FG^{7}	Spanish Empire	L	4	118	7	2	$3^{\frac{1}{2}}$	$3^{1\frac{1}{2}}$	2^{1}	$1^{\frac{1}{2}}$	1^{1}	Martin E M Jr	*1.80
14Mar04 ^{9}OP^{2}	Crafty Shaw	L	6	122	1	7	1^{1}	$1^{\frac{1}{2}}$	1^{hd}	$3^{2\frac{1}{2}}$	2^{nk}	Doocy T T	1.80
14Mar04 ^{9}OP^{6}	No Comprende	L b	6	122	4	4	$4^{1\frac{1}{2}}$	$4^{1\frac{1}{2}}$	3^{1}	2^{hd}	3^{2}	Martinez W	17.60
20Mar04 ^{9}OP^{1}	Missme	L b	5	117	8	6	5^{3}	5^{4}	5^{4}	4^{3}	4^{1}	Meche L J	29.30
13Mar04 ^{10}TP^{1}	Ask the Lord	L	7	118	6	3	$7^{1\frac{1}{2}}$	6^{hd}	$6^{2\frac{1}{2}}$	6^{2}	5^{hd}	Theriot H J II	8.10
21Feb04 ^{6}OP^{1}	River Mountain Rd	L b	4	117	5	5	8	8	8	$5^{\frac{1}{2}}$	$6^{5\frac{3}{4}}$	McKee J	7.10
20Mar04 ^{9}OP^{2}	Gimmeawink	L	4	115	3	1	$2^{2\frac{1}{2}}$	2^{hd}	4^{hd}	7^{10}	7^{8}	Pettinger D R	6.00
21Mar04 ^{8}OP^{1}	Go Legs Go	L b	5	117	2	8	$6^{\frac{1}{2}}$	$7^{\frac{1}{2}}$	$7^{\frac{1}{2}}$	8	8	Marquez C H Jr	21.00

***–Actual Betting Favorite.**

OFF AT 5:22 Start Good . Won driving. Track fast.

TIME :23, :46^{2}, 1:10^{3}, 1:36, 1:42^{2} (:23.17, :46.58, 1:10.72, 1:36.04, 1:42.50)

$2 Mutuel Prices:

7 – SPANISH EMPIRE	5.60	3.20	2.60
1 – CRAFTY SHAW		3.40	2.80
4 – NO COMPRENDE			5.20

$2 EXACTA 7–1 PAID $14.80 $2 TRIFECTA 7–1–4 PAID $94.20

Dk. b or br. c, (May), by Pleasant Colony – La Paz , by Hold Your Peace . Trainer Asmussen Steven M. Bred by John R Gaines Thoroughbreds & Twin &Creeks Farm (Ky).

SPANISH EMPIRE prompted the early pace three wide, vied on the outside into the far turn, put a head in front turning for home, proved determined in the drive. CRAFTY SHAW showed the way along the inside through some moderate splits, displaced turning for home, came back for the place while continuing inside. NO COMPRENDE hard rated along the inside for five furlongs, fell back a bit into the far turn, moved out, challenged three wide upper stretch, hung late, outfinished for the place. MISSME rated behind the pace, loomed outside turning for home, failed to follow through. ASK THE LORD failed to seriously menace. RIVER MOUNTAIN RD lacked a significant rally. GIMMEAWINK pressed pace, gave way. GO LEGS GO was finished early.

Owners– 1, Jubilee Stable Cherry Martin L and Twin Creeks Farm; 2, Cella Charles J; 3, Clarity Stables; 4, Whippoorwill Farm Inc; 5, L T B Inc and Williams R A; 6, Rosenblum Harry T; 7, Wienkowitz Walter; 8, Eberts Don

Trainers– 1, Asmussen Steven M; 2, Vestal Peter M; 3, Smith James J; 4, Whiting Lynn S; 5, Flint Bernard S; 6, Holthus Robert E; 7, Ritchey Tim F; 8, Nicks Morris G

$2 Pick Three (1–4–7) Paid $91.00 ; Pick Three Pool $15,513 .

EIGHTH RACE
Keeneland
APRIL 8, 2004

ABOUT 7 FURLONGS. (1.24³) 19TH RUNNING OF THE STONERSIDE BEAUMONT. Grade II. Purse $250,000 FOR FILLIES THREE YEARS OLD. By subscription of $250 each, which should accompany the nomination; $2,500 to enter and start with $250,000 guaranteed, of which $155,000 to the owner of the winner, $50,000 to second, $25,000 to third, $12,500 to fourth andd $7,500 to fifth. Weight 123 lbs. Non–winners of a Grade I allowed 3 lbs.; Grade II, 5 lbs.; a sweepstakes, 7 lbs. Starters to be named through the entry box by the usual time of closing. A gold julep cup will be presented to the owner of the winner.Closed Wednesday, March 24, 2004 with 39 nominations. Beard Course.

Value of Race: $250,000 Winner $155,000; second $50,000; third $25,000; fourth $12,500; fifth $7,500. Mutuel Pool $318,353.00 Exacta Pool $192,477.00 Trifecta Pool $190,710.00 Superfecta Pool $74,219.00 Quinella Pool $6,125.00

Last Raced	Horse	M/Eqt.	A.	Wt	PP	St	¼	½	Str	Fin	Jockey	Odds $1
6Mar04 9FG2	Victory U. S. A.	L	3	118	6	3	5hd	5hd	11½	18¼	Bailey J D	2.80
13Mar04 8SA2	Halfbridled	L	3	123	4	5	8	8	3½	21½	Solis A	0.40
13Mar04 7GG5	Wildwood Flower	L	3	118	7	2	31½	31	21½	31¾	Day P	9.80
26Feb04 9OP1	Ktestormedthebird	L b	3	116	2	7	62	4½	5hd	42	Albarado R J	14.50
14Feb04 9FG5	Movant	L	3	118	3	4	2hd	2hd	64	54½	Borel C H	50.90
21Mar04 8SA3	Very Vegas	L	3	118	8	1	11½	11½	4hd	63¼	Sterling L J Jr	31.50
11Mar04 9OP1	She's a Rebel Too	L f	3	116	1	6	4hd	62	72	77¾	Shepherd J	42.60
14Feb04 8GP2	Sweet Vision	L	3	116	5	8	74	72	8	8	Chavez J F	30.20

OFF AT 4:45 Start Good . Won driving. Track fast.
TIME :21⁴, :44², 1:10³, 1:27 (:21.83, :44.51, 1:10.68, 1:27.06)

$2 Mutuel Prices:				
	6 – VICTORY U. S. A.	7.60	2.40	2.10
	4 – HALFBRIDLED		2.10	2.10
	8 – WILDWOOD FLOWER			2.10

$2 EXACTA 6–4 PAID $14.20 $2 TRIFECTA 6–4–8 PAID $46.60
$2 SUPERFECTA 6–4–8–2 PAID $185.40 $2 QUINELLA 4–6 PAID $3.80

Ch. f, (Feb), by Victory Gallop – Fordyce , by Cox's Ridge . Trainer Baffert Bob. Bred by George Brunacini (Ky)

VICTORY U. S. A. settled nicely under light rating four or five wide, remained in that position on the track while edging closer approaching the stretch, swept to the front leaving the three-sixteenths pole, was roused seven times with the whip on the right side and finished under hand urging as much the best. HALFBRIDLED, outrun on the backstretch and five or six wide, attempted to drift out through much of the turn while continuing well off the inside, advanced six or seven wide at the quarter-mile ground, remained well off the fence for the drive and bested the others while not a threat to the winner. WILDWOOD FLOWER tracked the pace from early on while four wide, was with the winner while just inside that one when straightened for the drive but came up empty. KATESTORMEDTHEBIRD, within striking distance near the inside to the stretch, angled five wide for the drive but flattened out. MOVANT, forwardly placed along the inside from early on, lacked room nearing the final quarter, eased out a bit when straightened for the drive and tired. VERY VEGAS sprinted clear soon after the start, worked her way in three wide, made the pace until the upper stretch and faltered. SHE'S A REBEL TOO raced inside and tired gradually upon going a half. SWEET VISION, outsprinted early, was five wide on the backstretch, attempted to drift out midway of the turn and never menaced.

Owners– 1, Van Meter Thomas F II; 2, Wertheimer Farm LLC; 3, Gunther John D; 4, Rafter L Stables; 5, Griffin Richard E; 6, Everest Stables Inc; 7, Langford Michael; 8, Sovereign Stable Matt Gatsas and Gatsas Stables Mike Gatsas

Trainers– 1, Baffert Bob; 2, Mandella Richard; 3, McLaughlin Kiaran P; 4, Lukas D Wayne; 5, Amoss Thomas; 6, Polanco Marcelo; 7, Vance David R; 8, Terranova John P II

Scratched– Thisgirldontlaugh (20Mar04 3TP 1)

$2 Pick Three (8/9/14–4–6) Paid $113.80 ; Pick Three Pool $41,999 .

TENTH RACE
Oaklawn
APRIL 8, 2004

6 FURLONGS. (1.07⁴) 31ST RUNNING OF THE COUNT FLEET SPRINT HANDICAP. Grade III. Purse $150,000 FOUR YEAR OLDS AND UPWARD. By subscription of $100 each, which shall accompany the nomination, $1,000 to pass the entry box and $1,500 additional to start, with $150,000 Guaranteed of which $90,000 to the Owner of the winner, $30,000 to second, $15,000 tto third, $7,500 to fourth, $4,500 to fifth and $3,000 to sixth. Weights to be announced Thursday, April 1. In Handicap Stakes starting preference will be given to heavyweights. (See reverse side for additional starting limitation information). Starters to be named through the entry box by the usual time of closing. Nominations Closed Saturday, March 20, 2004 with 17 Nominees.

Value of Race: $150,000 Winner $90,000; second $30,000; third $15,000; fourth $7,500; fifth $4,500; sixth $3,000. Mutuel Pool $241,930.00 Exacta Pool $147,191.00 Trifecta Pool $130,351.00

Last Raced	Horse	M/Eqt.	A.	Wt	PP	St	¼	½	Str	Fin	Jockey	Odds $1
21Mar04 10OP5	Shake You Down	L bf	6	121	6	5	12	11½	12½	1hd	Dominguez R A	1.40
7Mar04 6OP2	Where's the Ring	L bf	5	115	4	1	4½	31	2½	21¼	Pettinger D R	23.20
14Mar04 9FG3	Aloha Bold	L	6	114	5	3	51	4hd	41½	3nk	Meche L J	11.60
21Mar04 10OP1	Skeet	L	4	116	1	6	6	6	3hd	42¾	McKee J	1.90
3Oct03 7Kee8	Beau's Town	L	6	118	3	2	3½	5½	6	51	Theriot H J II	2.90
19Mar04 2OP1	Was My Case	L	4	112	2	4	2½	2hd	51½	6	Chapa R	9.80

OFF AT 6:00 Start Good . Won driving. Track fast.
TIME :21⁴, :44³, :56³, 1:09¹ (:21.80, :44.60, :56.67, 1:09.27)

$2 Mutuel Prices:				
	7 – SHAKE YOU DOWN	4.00	3.80	2.80
	5 – WHERE'S THE RING		9.20	4.20
	6 – ALOHA BOLD			3.20

$2 EXACTA 7–5 PAID $64.40 $2 TRIFECTA 7–5–6 PAID $282.40

Ch. g, (Apr), by Montbrook – Mauvin Gway , by Rajab . Trainer Lake Scott A. Bred by Ocala Stud Farm (Fla).

SHAKE YOU DOWN outbroke by everyone but SKEET, quickly ranged up to clear off the inside, daylight into the turn, continued to looked comfortable while maintaining a daylight advantage through the turn, roused for the drive, enough left late. WHERE'S THE RING off the pace for a half three wide, moved a bit closer exiting the turn, brushed with WAS MY CASE into the stretch, set down with a left handed stick nearing the furlong marker, finished willingly to miss. ALOHA BOLD unhurried for a half, four wide late in the turn, modest gain while continuing widest of all. SKEET off slow to spot the field two lengths, moved up, traffic into the turn, waited behind horses when the real running started at the head of the lane, dropped inside with less than a furlong remaining, not enough late. BEAU'S TOWN within striking distance between foes, came up empty in the drive. WAS MY CASE closest to the winner early, brushed while racing toward the inside and tiring entering the stretch, continued to back up.

Owners– 1, Cole Robert L Jr; 2, Pin Oak Stable LLC; 3, Cooper Michael E; 4, Fly Racing LLC; 5, Hulkewicz David J; 6, Rand Jeff S

Trainers– 1, Lake Scott A; 2, Von Hemel Donnie K; 3, Hawley Wesley; 4, Holthus Robert E; 5, Norman Cole; 6, Brennan Terry J

Scratched– That Tat (21Mar04 10OP 2)

$2 Pick Three (3–6–4/7) Paid $89.40 ; Pick Three Pool $28,407 .

EIGHTH RACE
Aqueduct
APRIL 9, 2004

1 MILE. (1.32^{2}) 55TH RUNNING OF THE COMELY. Grade III. Purse $100,000 FOR FILLIES THREE YEARS OLD. By subscription of $100 each, which should accompany the nomination; $500 to pass the entry box; $500 to start, with $100,000 added. The added money and all fees to be divided 60% to the winner, 20% to second, 10% to third, 5%% to fourth, 3% to fifth and 2% divided equally among the remaining finishers. 122 lbs. Non-winners of $60,000 other than restricted stake; or $30,000 twice in 2004 allowed 2 lbs.; $30,000 at a mile or over in 2004, 4 lbs.; $30,000; or three races other tthan maiden or claiming, 6 lbs. A trophy will be presented to the winning owner. Closed Saturday, March 27, 2004 with 35 nominations.

Value of Race: $112,000 Winner $67,200; second $22,400; third $11,200; fourth $5,600; fifth $3,360; sixth $747; seventh $747; eighth $746. Mutuel Pool $422,929.00 Exacta Pool $366,419.00 Trifecta Pool $279,546.00

Last Raced	Horse	M/Eqt.	A.	Wt	PP	St	¼	½	¾	Str	Fin	Jockey	Odds $1
6Mar04 ^{8}GP^{2}	Society Selection		3	122	5	5	7$1\frac{1}{2}$	8	$2\frac{1}{2}$	$1\frac{1}{2}$	1^{3}	Chavez J F	1.65
6Mar04 ^{9}FG^{6}	Bending Strings	L	3	116	6	2	$2\frac{1}{2}$	2$1\frac{1}{2}$	1$1\frac{1}{2}$	2^{6}	2$2\frac{3}{4}$	Luzzi M J	10.40
1Mar04 ^{8}GP^{1}	Daydreaming	L	3	116	2	7	$5\frac{1}{2}$	6^{1}	5$2\frac{1}{2}$	3$1\frac{1}{2}$	3$8\frac{1}{2}$	Castellano J J	6.50
20Mar04 ^{9}Aqu^{3}	Baldomera	L b	3	118	7	1	8	$7\frac{1}{2}$	$4\frac{1}{2}$	4$2\frac{1}{2}$	4^{nk}	Vega H	48.00
28Feb04 ^{8}Aqu^{4}	Please Take Me Out	L	3	118	1	6	4$1\frac{1}{2}$	5^{hd}	$7\frac{1}{2}$	$5\frac{1}{2}$	5$6\frac{1}{4}$	Gryder A T	42.75
18Mar04 ^{7}Aqu^{1}	Two Bayou	L	3	116	4	4	1^{hd}	$1\frac{1}{2}$	3^{hd}	6^{6}	6$1\frac{1}{2}$	Cotto P L Jr	19.70
14Mar04 ^{4}GP^{1}	Irish Melody	L	3	116	3	8	$3\frac{1}{2}$	3^{hd}	8	7^{2}	7$5\frac{1}{2}$	Velazquez J R	1.75
5Mar04 ^{9}FG^{1}	A Lulu Ofa Menifee	L b	3	116	8	3	6$2\frac{1}{2}$	4^{hd}	$6\frac{1}{2}$	8	8	Santos J A	7.30

OFF AT 4:20 Start Good. Won ridden out. Track fast.

TIME :22^{4}, :45^{3}, 1:10^{4}, 1:35^{4} (:22.96, :45.76, 1:10.86, 1:35.89)

$2 Mutuel Prices:

6 – SOCIETY SELECTION	5.30	3.30	3.40
7 – BENDING STRINGS		7.40	6.50
3 – DAYDREAMING			5.20

$2 EXACTA 6–7 PAID $36.40 $2 TRIFECTA 6–7–3 PAID $151.50

B. f, (Apr), by Coronado's Quest – Love That Jazz, by Dixieland Band. Trainer Jerkens H Allen. Bred by Marjorie Cowan & Irving Cowan (Ky).

SOCIETY SELECTION was outrun early, was steadied along the inside on the turn, angled out, swept five wide approaching the stretch, collared BENDING STRINGS nearing the eighth pole and drew clear from that rival under a confident hand ride. BENDING STRINGS pressed the pace from the outside, drew clear on the turn, was no match for the winner in the stretch but stayed on gamely to be second best. DAYDREAMING was hustled along between rivals, rallied three wide into the stretch and finished well outside. BALDOMERA was outrun early, put in a four wide run on the turn and tired in the stretch. PLEASE TAKE ME OUT was hustled along inside, chased the pace, angled out into the stretch and had no rally. TWO BAYOU was hustled to the front, set the pace along the inside and tired in the stretch. IRISH MELODY was hustled along between rivals, chased the pace for a half mile and tired. A LULU OFA MENIFEE raced in hand outside early, put in a three wide run on the turn and tired after three quarters.

Owners– 1, Cowan Irving M Majorie Cowan; 2, Gunther John D; 3, Phipps Ogden M; 4, Hidden Lane Farms Inc; 5, Perez Robert; 6, Flatbird Stable; 7, Jones Aaron U and Marie D; 8, Lael Stables

Trainers– 1, Jerkens H Allen; 2, McLaughlin Kiaran P; 3, McGaughey III Claude R; 4, Preciado Guadalupe; 5, Callejas Alfredo; 6, Reynolds Patrick L; 7, Pletcher Todd A; 8, Tagg Barclay

Scratched– Rare Gift (06Mar04 ^{8}GP ^{3})

TENTH RACE
Oaklawn
APRIL 9, 2004

1$\frac{1}{16}$ MILES. (1.40^{1}) 32ND RUNNING OF THE FANTASY. Grade II. Purse $200,000 FILLIES, THREE YEAR OLDS. By subscription of $100 each, which shall accompany the nomination, original nominators paying $2,000 to pass the entry box and $2,000 additional to start. Supplementary nominations may be made by the closing time of entries att a fee of $15,000 which qualifies to start, with $200,000 Guaranteed of which $120,000 to the Owner of the winner, $40,000 to second, $20,000 to third, $10,000 to fourth, $6,000 to fifth and $4,000 to sixth. WEIGHTS: 121 lbs. Non-winners of a sweepstaakes allowed 4 lbs. In Allowance Stakes starting preference will be given to horses that have accumulated the highest earnings, excluding money won in restricted races (See reverse side for additional starting limitation information). Starters to be nammed through the entry box by the usual time of closing. The Owner of the winner to receive a trophy. Nominations closed Saturday, March 20, 2004 with 37 nominees.

Value of Race: $200,000 Winner $120,000; second $40,000; third $20,000; fourth $10,000; fifth $6,000; sixth $4,000. Mutuel Pool $412,303.00 Exacta Pool $257,287.00 Trifecta Pool $298,574.00

Last Raced	Horse	M/Eqt.	A.	Wt	PP	St	¼	½	¾	Str	Fin	Jockey	Odds $1
6Mar04 ^{3}GG^{1}	House of Fortune	L	3	121	1	3	5^{1}	4^{1}	4^{2}	$1\frac{1}{2}$	1$1\frac{3}{4}$	Solis A	0.70
25Jan04 ^{8}Aqu^{1}	Island Sand	L b	3	121	11	2	$2\frac{1}{2}$	2$1\frac{1}{2}$	1^{hd}	2$2\frac{1}{2}$	2^{4}	Thompson T J	8.40
13Mar04 ^{8}SA^{5}	Stellar Jayne	L b	3	121	9	7	9^{2}	10^{2}	$8\frac{1}{2}$	$4\frac{1}{2}$	3$2\frac{1}{4}$	McKee J	10.10
10Mar04 ^{2}SA^{1}	Elusive Diva	L	3	117	3	5	3$1\frac{1}{2}$	$3\frac{1}{2}$	3$1\frac{1}{2}$	$6\frac{1}{2}$	4^{hd}	Valdivia J Jr	29.90
6Mar04 ^{9}FG^{3}	Shadow Cast	L b	3	121	6	11	10^{hd}	9^{hd}	9^{3}	7$3\frac{1}{2}$	5^{nk}	Borel C H	7.50
6Mar04 ^{10}OP^{1}	Yoursmineours	L	3	121	8	1	1^{hd}	1^{hd}	2$1\frac{1}{2}$	3$3\frac{1}{2}$	6^{nk}	Pettinger D R	33.80
6Mar04 ^{10}OP^{2}	Stephan's Angel	L f	3	121	4	6	$8\frac{1}{2}$	$7\frac{1}{2}$	$6\frac{1}{2}$	5^{hd}	7^{2}	Elliott S	51.30
7Feb04 ^{8}GP^{1}	Miss Coronado	L	3	121	5	8	$4\frac{1}{2}$	5^{1}	5$1\frac{1}{2}$	8^{1}	$8\frac{1}{2}$	Velasquez C	4.50
7Mar04 ^{8}OP^{1}	Platinum Ballet	L	3	117	10	10	11	11	$10\frac{1}{2}$	9^{4}	9$4\frac{1}{4}$	Martinez W	53.10
20Mar04 ^{9}TP^{5}	Slewpy's Storm	L f	3	121	2	4	7$2\frac{1}{2}$	8^{2}	7^{hd}	10^{20}	10^{18}	D'Amico A J	50.20
25Mar04 ^{2}OP^{1}	True Blonde Beauty	L b	3	118	7	9	$6\frac{1}{2}$	6^{1}	11	11	11	Theriot H J II	68.00

OFF AT 6:01 Start Good. Won driving. Track fast.

TIME :23^{1}, :46^{3}, 1:11, 1:36^{1}, 1:42^{3} (:23.25, :46.79, 1:11.15, 1:36.28, 1:42.62)

$2 Mutuel Prices:

1 – HOUSE OF FORTUNE	3.40	3.20	2.60
11 – ISLAND SAND		5.20	3.80
9 – STELLAR JAYNE			3.60

$2 EXACTA 1–11 PAID $30.60 $2 TRIFECTA 1–11–9 PAID $177.20

Dk. b or br. f, (Mar), by Free House – So Fortunate, by Garthorn. Trainer McAnally Ronald. Bred by John Treasure (Cal).

HOUSE OF FORTUNE away in good order, steadied behind the pace while saving all the ground, moved a bit closer into the far turn while continuing under confident handling, angled out when asked turning for home, came out bit nearing the furlong marker, drove clear. ISLAND SAND asked a bit into the first turn, dueled through a lively pace off the inside, put a head in front in the second turn, dropped to the inside when challenged and disposing of the other speed when straightened for home, clearly second best. STELLAR JAYNE lacked early foot, steady gain well off the rail, came five wide turning for home, finished willingly for the show. ELUSIVE DIVA forwardly placed early, firmly in hand in traffic first turn, continued within striking distance, roused into the stretch, empty. SHADOW CAST in tight and rank past the wire the first time, raced far back, modest late run up the rail. YOURSMINEOURS broke sharp, dueled inside through some quick fractions, gave way. STEPHAN'S ANGEL saved ground to no avail. MISS CORONADO broke out, raced in traffic early, faded after six furlongs. PLATINUM BALLET trailed outside, moved closer to the inside second turn, did not make an impact. SLEWPY'S STORM fractious saddling, finished early. TRUE BLONDE BEAUTY stopped after a half, finished far back.

Owners– 1, Arnold Zetcher LLC Arnold Zetcher; 2, B A Man Inc James L Osborne; 3, Spendthrift Farm LLC N Cole C Kidder & N Strong Kenneth B Kline; 4, John W & Doris Konecny & Allen & Susan Branch; 5, Farish William S Jr; 6, Burnstein Stan and Nelson Jim E; 7, Fox Hill Farms Inc; 8, Stonerside Stable LLC; 9, Sanders Wayne R; 10, Oak Haven Farm; 11, Jayaraman Kalarikkal K and Vilasini D

Trainers– 1, McAnally Ronald; 2, Jones J Larry; 3, Lukas D Wayne; 4, Glatt Mark; 5, Howard Neil J; 6, Von Hemel Donnie K; 7, Servis John C; 8, Frankel Robert; 9, Von Hemel Donnie K; 10, Frederick Edward; 11, Norman Cole

---

$2 Pick Three (2/3/6/7/10–2–1) Paid $47.40 ; Pick Three Pool $25,927.

NINTH RACE
Keeneland
APRIL 9, 2004

1 MILE. (Turf) (1.33^{2}) 16TH RUNNING OF THE MAKER'S MARK MILE. Grade II. Purse $200,000 FOR FOUR YEAR OLDS AND UPWARD. By subscription of $200 each, which should accompany the nomination; $2,000 to enter and start with $200,000 guaranteed, of which $124,000 to the owner of the winner, $40,000 to second, $20,000 to third, $10,000 to fourthand $6,000 to fifth. Weight 123 lbs. Non-winners of Grade I or II stakes on the turf since October 4, allowed 3 lbs.; $60,000 twice on the turf since August 1, 5 lbs.; $45,000 twice on the turf since July 4, 7 lbs. Starters to be named through the enntry box by usual time of closing. A gold julep cup will be presented to the owner of the winner. Closed Wednesday, March 31, 2004 with 29 nominations. Haggin Course.

Value of Race: $200,000 Winner $124,000; second $40,000; third $20,000; fourth $10,000; fifth $6,000. Mutuel Pool $622,897.00 Exacta Pool $404,493.00 Trifecta Pool $333,053.00 Superfecta Pool $110,246.00 Quinella Pool $16,016.00

Last Raced	Horse	M/Eqt.	A.	Wt	PP	St	¼	½	¾	Str	Fin	Jockey	Odds $1
25Oct03 ^{4}SA^{9}	Perfect Soul-Ire	L b	6	116	7	9	7½	7^{2}	7^{1}	4^{1½}	1½	Prado E S	3.40
6Mar04 ^{10}Tam^{3}	Burning Roma	L	6	116	3	2	3^{1}	3^{hd}	2½	2^{1}	2^{hd}	Castanon J L	18.90
28Feb04 ^{7}FG^{2}	Royal Spy	L	6	116	2	1	1^{1}	1^{1}	1½	1^{1½}	3^{1}	Albarado R J	12.60
15Mar04 ^{8}GP^{3}	Honor in War	L	5	116	8	5	8^{1½}	8^{1}	8^{1}	5½	4½	Flores D R	4.60
11Oct03 ^{12}Crc^{1}	Stroll	L	4	120	6	10	4½	4^{1½}	4^{1}	3^{2}	5^{nk}	Bailey J D	3.10
31Jan04 ^{8}GP^{2}	MillnnumDrgon-GB	L	5	116	4	3	6^{1½}	6½	6½	6^{3}	6^{4}	Migliore R	7.50
7Feb04 ^{7}TuP^{5}	Freefourinternet	L	6	116	1	7	10	10	10	10	7^{nk}	Perret C	26.30
25Oct03 ^{9}SA^{6}	Perfect Drift	L	5	116	5	4	5½	5½	5½	7½	8^{3¼}	Day P	3.80
6Mar04 ^{9}SA^{8}	NeedwoodBlde-GB	L	6	116	9	8	9^{15}	9^{15}	9^{12}	9^{2}	9^{2¾}	Santiago Javier	23.30
24Jan04 ^{10}GP^{2}	Hear No Evil	L bf	4	116	10	6	2^{2½}	2^{2½}	3^{hd}	8½	10	Garcia J A	35.50

OFF AT 5:16 Start Good . Won driving. Course firm.

TIME :23, :45^{1}, 1:09, 1:21, 1:33^{2} (:23.03, :45.29, 1:09.13, 1:21.06, 1:33.54)

(New Course Record)

$2 Mutuel Prices:

7 – PERFECT SOUL–IRE	8.80	5.40	4.00
3 – BURNING ROMA		11.60	9.00
2 – ROYAL SPY			8.00

$2 EXACTA 7–3 PAID $113.60 $2 TRIFECTA 7–3–2 PAID $1,306.40
$2 SUPERFECTA 7–3–2–8 PAID $8,504.60 $2 QUINELLA 3–7 PAID $91.60

B. h, (Apr), by Sadler's Wells – Ball Chairman , by Secretariat . Trainer Attfield Roger L. Bred by C Fipke (Ire).

PERFECT SOUL (IRE), reserved between rivals four wide from early on, was asked for his best leaving the five-sixteenths pole, maneuvered out six wide when straightened for the drive, then was hard ridden to prevail in course record time. BURNING ROMA, well placed from the outset while lightly rated three or four wide, moved between rivals entering the stretch, loomed boldly through the drive, then was outfinished when bumped for several strides about 50 yards from the finish by ROYAL SPY and carried out a bit by that one. ROYAL SPY moved to the fore inside, went along under careful handling, made the pace into deep stretch and couldn't last while coming out approaching the wire and bumping with BURNING ROMA. HONOR IN WAR followed the leaders five or six wide from early on, moved outside the winner to be eight wide when straightened for the drive and offered a mild gain. STROLL angled in behind the leaders early, saved ground most of the way, raced prominently near the rail into the final furlong and flattened out when the test came. MILLENNIUM DRAGON (GB) settled two wide, raced within easy striking distance, eased out between rivals four or five wide for the drive but couldn't muster the needed response. FREEFOURINTERNET, badly outrun to the stretch, was near the inside for the drive and improved position while not a threat. PERFECT DRIFT, within easy striking distance while following the leaders four or five wide, eased out between foes six or seven wide in the upper stretch and never menaced. NEEDWOOD BLADE (GB) was outrun. HEAR NO EVIL bobbled sharply soon after the start, was hustled along soon after to go after front-running ROYAL SPY five wide, held on well until nearing the final quarter and steadily weakened.

Owners– 1, Fipke Charles E; 2, Queen Harold L; 3, Jayaraman Kalarikkal K and Vilasini D; 4, 3rd Turn Stables LLC; 5, Claiborne Farm; 6, Darley Stable; 7, EquiraceCom LLC; 8, Stonecrest Farm; 9, Vreeland James R; 10, Jacks or Better Farm Inc

Trainers– 1, Attfield Roger L; 2, Giglio Heather A; 3, Amoss Thomas; 4, McGee Paul J; 5, Mott William I; 6, McLaughlin Kiaran P; 7, Scott Joan; 8, Johnson Murray W; 9, Walsh Kathy; 10, Hatchett James

$2 Pick Three (6–5/6/9–7) Paid $81.20 ; Pick Three Pool $68,198 .
$2 Pick Four (10–6–5/6/9–7) Paid $375.40 ; Pick Four Pool $87,614 .

SEVENTH RACE
Aqueduct
APRIL 10, 2004

7 FURLONGS. (1.20) 45TH RUNNING OF THE BAY SHORE. Grade III. Purse $150,000 (UP TO $21,900 NYSBFOA) FOR THREE YEAR OLDS. By subscription of $150 each, which should accompany the nomination; $750 to pass the entry box; $750 to start. The purse to be divided 60% to the winner, 20% to second, 10% to third, 5% to fourth, 3% to fifthand 2% divided equally among the remaining finishers. 123 lbs. Non-winners of $100,000; or $50,000 twice allowed 3 lbs.; $60,000; or $35,000 in 2004, 5 lbs.; $30,000; or three races other than maiden or claiming, 7 lbs. A trophy will be presented to thewinning owner. Closed Saturday, March 27,2004 with 24 Nominations.

Value of Race: $150,000 Winner $90,000; second $30,000; third $15,000; fourth $7,500; fifth $4,500; sixth $1,000; seventh $1,000; eighth $1,000. Mutuel Pool $729,729.00 Exacta Pool $589,731.00 Trifecta Pool $399,353.00

Last Raced	Horse	M/Eqt.	A.	Wt	PP	St	¼	½	Str	Fin	Jockey	Odds $1
13Mar04 ^{2}GP^{1}	Forest Danger	L	3	116	2	5	1^{hd}	$1^{\frac{1}{2}}$	1^{6}	$1^{7\frac{1}{2}}$	Velazquez J R	1.10
20Mar04 ^{7}Lrl^{1}	Abbondanza	L f	3	116	1	7	$5^{1\frac{1}{2}}$	3^{hd}	3^{6}	$2^{3\frac{1}{2}}$	Dominguez R A	8.00
7Mar04 ^{9}FG^{10}	Indian War Dance	L b	3	116	6	3	2^{hd}	$2^{2\frac{1}{2}}$	2^{hd}	$3^{2\frac{1}{2}}$	Coa E M	31.00
21Feb04 ^{9}Aqu^{4}	Smokume	L	3	118	4	8	$7^{1\frac{1}{2}}$	7^{8}	$4^{\frac{1}{2}}$	4^{3}	Uske S	5.30
17Mar04 ^{7}Aqu^{2}	American Comedy	L	3	116	3	4	$3^{\frac{1}{2}}$	5^{6}	$5^{3\frac{1}{2}}$	5^{1}	Castellano J J	26.00
5Dec03 ^{8}DeD^{9}	Judiths Wild Rush	L b	3	118	7	1	$6^{5\frac{1}{2}}$	6^{2}	7^{6}	6^{3}	Luzzi M J	8.10
14Mar04 ^{5}SA^{5}	Last Minute Detail	L	3	116	5	6	8	8	8	$7^{1\frac{3}{4}}$	Solis A	4.50
20Mar04 ^{7}Aqu^{6}	Rockhewn	L b	3	116	8	2	$4^{\frac{1}{2}}$	$4^{\frac{1}{2}}$	$6^{\frac{1}{2}}$	8	Bailey J D	14.20

OFF AT 3:52 Start Good . Won driving. Track fast.

TIME :22^{1}, :44^{1}, 1:08^{1}, 1:20^{3} (:22.39, :44.39, 1:08.27, 1:20.67)

$2 Mutuel Prices:			
2 – FOREST DANGER	4.20	3.10	2.60
1 – ABBONDANZA		6.10	4.80
6 – INDIAN WAR DANCE			9.30

$2 EXACTA 2–1 PAID $24.40 $2 TRIFECTA 2–1–6 PAID $304.00

B. c, (Feb), by Forestry – Starry Ice , by Ice Age . Trainer Pletcher Todd A. Bred by Barbara Jean Dutton & Jerry Dutton (Ky).

FOREST DANGER quickly showed in front, set the pace along the inside while in hand, responded when roused in upper stretch, drew away and widened under a drive. ABBONDANZA raced close up inside while in hand, dug in gamely when roused but could not get to the winner while clearly best of the others. INDIAN WAR DANCE pressed the pace while between rivals and tired in the final furlong. SMOKUME was outrun along the inside early, altered course to the outside in upper stretch and had no rally. AMERICAN COMEDY chased the pace while between rivals and was finished early. JUDITHS WILD RUSH raced close up early and had no response when roused. LAST MINUTE DETAIL hit the gate at the start, dropped back early and had no rally. ROCKHEWN chased the pace while three wide and tired after a half mile.

Owners– 1, Jones Aaron U and Marie D; 2, Aldie Germania Farms Inc; 3, Goldfarb Sanford J Vidro William Davis Ira; 4, Hobeau Farm; 5, Berens Fred Garazi Solomon and Muhtar Glenda; 6, Tenenbaum Harvey; 7, Little Jerry D Kenneth E Murphy; 8, Dirienzo Orlando

Trainers– 1, Pletcher Todd A; 2, Tullock Timothy Jr; 3, Dutrow Richard E Jr; 4, Jerkens H Allen; 5, Iwinski Allen; 6, Fairlie Scott H; 7, Chatlos Donald Jr; 8, Reid Robert E Jr

$2 Pick Three (2–1–2) Paid $30.00 ; Pick Three Pool $98,380 .
$2 Daily Double (1–2) Paid $16.40 ; Daily Double Pool $114,949 .

EIGHTH RACE
Aqueduct
APRIL 10, 2004

1⅛ MILES. (1.47) 80TH RUNNING OF THE WOOD MEMORIAL. Grade I. Purse $750,000 (UP TO $65,500 NYSBFOA) FOR THREE YEAR OLDS. By subscription of $750 each, which should accompany the nomination; $3,500 to pass the entry box; $4,000 to start. The purse to be divided 60% to the winner, 20% to second, 10% to third, 5% to fourth 3% to fifth and 2% divided equally among the remaining finishers. 123 lbs. Trophies will be presented to the winning owner, trainer and jockey. A bonus of $100,000 (which will follow the horse) to the trainer of the horse which wins both The Wood Memorial and TheKentucky Derby. Closed Saturday, March 27, 2004 with 39 Nominations.

Value of Race: $750,000 Winner $450,000; second $150,000; third $75,000; fourth $37,500; fifth $22,500; sixth $2,500; seventh $2,500; eighth $2,500; ninth $2,500; tenth $2,500; eleventh $2,500. Mutuel Pool $1,758,562.00 Exacta Pool $1,094,620.00 Superfecta Pool $100,630.00 Trifecta Pool $828,677.00

Last Raced	Horse	M/Eqt.	A.	Wt	PP	St	¼	½	¾	Str	Fin	Jockey	Odds $1
13Mar04 ^{9}GP^{6}	Tapit	L f	3	123	2	11	11	$9^{\frac{1}{2}}$	$7^{1\frac{1}{2}}$	2^{hd}	$1^{\frac{1}{2}}$	Dominguez R A	5.30
8Feb04 ^{8}SA^{1}	Master David	L f	3	123	5	7	4^{hd}	5^{3}	5^{hd}	3^{hd}	2no	Solis A	3.75
20Mar04 ^{7}Aqu^{3}	Eddington	L b	3	123	8	6	5^{2}	4^{hd}	3^{hd}	$4^{5\frac{1}{2}}$	$3^{1\frac{1}{2}}$	Bailey J D	3.20
14Mar04 ^{11}Tam^{3}	Swingforthefences	L	3	123	4	2	$6^{1\frac{1}{2}}$	$6^{2\frac{1}{2}}$	6^{2}	$1^{\frac{1}{2}}$	$4^{4\frac{1}{4}}$	Bridgmohan S X	10.40
13Mar04 ^{7}GP^{2}	Royal Assault	L	3	123	1	10	7^{hd}	7^{hd}	$8^{2\frac{1}{2}}$	$6^{4\frac{1}{2}}$	5^{2}	Castellano J J	42.25
13Mar04 ^{9}GP^{2}	Value Plus	L	3	123	6	4	$2^{\frac{1}{2}}$	1^{hd}	1^{hd}	5^{hd}	$6^{2\frac{1}{2}}$	Velazquez J R	2.85
20Mar04 ^{8}TP^{3}	Little Matth Man	L b	3	123	7	5	9^{hd}	11	$9^{\frac{1}{2}}$	8^{7}	$7^{5\frac{1}{4}}$	Fragoso P	20.40
12Mar04 ^{7}Aqu^{2}	Cuba	L bf	3	123	11	9	3^{1}	$3^{\frac{1}{2}}$	$4^{1\frac{1}{2}}$	7^{2}	8^{8}	Gryder A T	86.50
28Mar04 ^{8}Sun^{2}	Consecrate	L	3	123	3	1	$8^{2\frac{1}{2}}$	$8^{1\frac{1}{2}}$	$10^{\frac{1}{2}}$	$9^{1\frac{1}{2}}$	9^{4}	Chavez J F	14.40
20Mar04 ^{8}TP^{1}	Sinister G	L	3	123	9	3	$1^{\frac{1}{2}}$	$2^{1\frac{1}{2}}$	2^{hd}	11	$10^{5\frac{1}{4}}$	Toscano P R	17.90
12Mar04 ^{7}Aqu^{1}	Hornshope	L	3	123	10	8	$10^{2\frac{1}{2}}$	10^{hd}	11	$10^{\frac{1}{2}}$	11	Luzzi M J	70.00

OFF AT 4:21 Start Good . Won driving. Track fast.

TIME :23^{3}, :47, 1:11^{2}, 1:37, 1:49^{3} (:23.74, :47.12, 1:11.40, 1:37.03, 1:49.70)

$2 Mutuel Prices:			
2 – TAPIT	12.60	6.60	4.80
5 – MASTER DAVID		5.10	3.30
8 – EDDINGTON			3.50

$2 EXACTA 2–5 PAID $66.50 $2 SUPERFECTA 2–5–8–4 PAID $1,317.00
$2 TRIFECTA 2–5–8 PAID $223.50

Gr/ro. c, (Feb), by Pulpit – Tap Your Heels , by Unbridled . Trainer Dickinson Michael W. Bred by Oldenburg Farms LLC (Ky).

TAPIT was taken back after the start, advanced outside while in hand, closed four wide on the second turn, responded to left handed pressure once straightened away for the drive, dug in gamely and prevailed after a long drive. MASTER DAVID raced close up along the inside while in hand, saved ground, got through on the rail in upper stretch and dug in gamely to the wire, getting the nod over EDDINGTON for the place. EDDINGTON raced close up outside, rallied three wide on the second turn and stayed on gamely in the stretch. SWINGFORTHEFENCES was taken in hand early, raced outside, advanced four wide on the second turn, rallied to earn a short lead nearing the eighth pole and weakened in the final furlong. ROYAL ASSAULT stumbled at the start, was rated inside, advanced inside nearing the stretch, came wide for the drive and lacked a rally. VALUE PLUS contested the pace along the rail and was finished turning for home. LITTLE MATTH MAN was outrun early, came wide into the stretch and had no rally. CUBA chased the pace while three wide throughout and tired after three quarters. CONSECRATE dropped back early, raced wide and had no response when roused. SINISTER G contested the pace while between rivals and tired after the opening three quarters. HORNSHOPE raced outside and tired.

Owners– 1, Winchell Ronald; 2, Georgica Stable Mack Stephan Star Crown Stable; 3, Willmott Stables Inc; 4, Klaravich Stables Inc; 5, Farmer Tracy; 6, Jones Aaron U and Marie D; 7, Papandrea Vincent; 8, Allard Cam; 9, McIngvale James; 10, Toscano III John T Corrado Kim Carlat Yamile Toscano Robert; 11, Ahern Timothy

Trainers– 1, Dickinson Michael W; 2, Frankel Robert; 3, Hennig Mark; 4, Violette Richard A Jr; 5, Zito Nicholas P; 6, Pletcher Todd A; 7, Ciresa Martin E; 8, Bush Thomas M; 9, Baffert Bob; 10, Toscano John T Jr; 11, Daggett Michael H

$2 Pick Three (1–2–2) Paid $109.00 ; Pick Three Pool $170,364 .

NINTH RACE
Aqueduct
APRIL 10, 2004

7 FURLONGS. (1.20) 104TH RUNNING OF THE CARTER HANDICAP. Grade I. Purse $350,000 (UP TO $45,900 NYSBFOA) A HANDICAP FOR THREE YEAR OLDS AND UPWARD. By subscription of $350 each, which should accompany the nomination; $1,500 to pass the entry box; $2,000 to start. The purse to be divided 60% to the winner, 20% to second, 10% to third,5% to fourth, 3% to fifth and 2% divided equally among the remaining finishers. Trophies will be presented to the winning owner, trainer and jockey. Closed Saturday, March 27, 2004 with 22 Nominations.

Value of Race: $350,000 Winner $210,000; second $70,000; third $35,000; fourth $17,500; fifth $10,500; sixth $1,750; seventh $1,750; eighth $1,750; ninth $1,750. Mutuel Pool $902,337.00 Exacta Pool $663,389.00 Trifecta Pool $548,931.00

Last Raced	Horse	M/Eqt.	A.	Wt	PP	St	¼	½	Str	Fin	Jockey	Odds $1
7Mar04 ^{8}SA^{1}	Pico Central-Brz	L	5	117	3	5	2½	1½	2^{6}	11¼	Solis A	4.30
10Mar04 ^{8}GP^{1}	Strong Hope	L	4	119	8	3	31½	3^{5}	1^{hd}	2^{2}	Velazquez J R	0.85
7Mar04 ^{8}SA^{5}	Eye of the Tiger	L	4	114	2	9	7^{1}	7½	52½	3¾	Luzzi M J	26.50
6Mar04 ^{11}GP^{4}	Gygistar	L	5	115	4	6	6^{hd}	61½	3½	44¾	Fragoso P	12.30
28Mar04 ^{8}Aqu^{1}	Super Fuse	L b	4	112	1	8	9	9	7½	51¾	Chavez J F	25.75
13Mar04 ^{8}Aqu^{3}	Don Six	L	4	112	6	4	1^{hd}	2^{hd}	4^{hd}	6^{hd}	Bridgmohan S X	37.75
2Apr04 ^{8}Aqu^{3}	Peeping Tom	L bf	7	114	9	1	82½	83½	8½	71¾	Smith A E	22.60
13Mar04 ^{8}Aqu^{1}	Well Fancied	L	6	116	7	2	4½	4^{hd}	6^{1}	87½	Coa E M	4.50
12Mar04 ^{8}Aqu^{1}	Secret Run	L b	4	112	5	7	5^{7}	54½	9	9	Arroyo N Jr	24.50

OFF AT 4:53 Start Good . Won driving. Track fast.
TIME :21^{3}, :43^{2}, 1:07^{2}, 1:20^{1} (:21.77, :43.50, 1:07.52, 1:20.22)

$2 Mutuel Prices:

3 – PICO CENTRAL–BRZ	10.60	4.20	3.30
9 – STRONG HOPE		2.80	2.40
2 – EYE OF THE TIGER			6.00

$2 EXACTA 3–9 PAID $27.40 $2 TRIFECTA 3–9–2 PAID $276.00

Dk. b or br. h, (Oct), by Spend a Buck – Sheila Purple , by Purple Mountain . Trainer Lobo Paulo H. Bred by Haras Fronteira PAP (Brz).

PICO CENTRAL (BRZ) contested the pace along the inside, dug in resolutely in the stretch and came again on the rail to get the job done. STRONG HOPE contested the pace while three wide, earned a short lead in the stretch and weakened in the final furlong. EYE OF THE TIGER was outrun early, raced inside, rallied nearing the stretch and finished gamely on the rail. GYGISTAR was outrun early, advanced outside on the turn, rallied four wide into the stretch and finished well outside. SUPER FUSE was outrun early, raced inside and had no response when roused. DON SIX contested the pace while between rivals and tired in the stretch. PEEPING TOM was outrun early, raced three wide and had no rally. WELL FANCIED chased the pace from the outside and tired in the stretch. SECRET RUN chased the pace along the inside, came wide into the stretch and tired.

Owners– 1, Tanaka Gary A; 2, Melnyk Eugene and Laura; 3, Gunther John D; 4, Evans Edward P; 5, Alpha One Stable; 6, Generazio Patricia A; 7, Flatbird Stable; 8, Goldfarb Sanford J Hoffman Stewart Flesig Jonathan A; 9, Chapman Laz K Wexler Avers and Stiegal Michael

Trainers– 1, Lobo Paulo H; 2, Pletcher Todd A; 3, McLaughlin Kiaran P; 4, Hennig Mark; 5, Ciardullo Richard Jr; 6, Generazio Frank Jr; 7, Reynolds Patrick L; 8, Dutrow Richard F Jr; 9, Laboccetta Frank Jr

Scratched– Badge of Silver (16Feb04 ^{9}Lrl^{5})

$2 Daily Double (2–3) Paid $62.50 ; Daily Double Pool $160,761 .

FIFTH RACE
Keeneland
APRIL 10, 2004

7 FURLONGS. (1.20^{1}) 18TH RUNNING OF THE COMMONWEALTH BREEDERS' CUP. Grade II. Purse $250,000 (includes $100,000 BC – Breeders' Cup) FOR THREE YEAR OLDS AND UPWARD. By subscription of $250 each, which should accompany the nomination, $2,500 to enter and start with $150,000 added and an additional $100,000 from the Breeders' Cup Fund for Cup eligibles only. Keeneland Association addedmonies and all fees to be divided 62% to the owner of the winner, 20% to second, 10% to third, 5% to fourth and 3% to fifth. Breeders' Cup Fund monies also correspondingly divided providing a Breeders' Cup nominee has finished in an awarded position. Any Breeders' Cup monies not awarded will revert back to the fund. Weights: Three year olds, 116 lbs.; Older 124 lbs. Non–winners of a Grade I stakes since October 25 allowed 2 lbs.; a Grade II since September 1, 4 lbs.; $45,000 twice since July 4, 6 lbs. Starters to be named through the entry box by the usual time of closing. A Breeders' Cup trophy and gold julep cup will be presented to the owner of the winner. Closed Wednesday, March 31,2004 with 21 nominations.

Value of Race: $250,250 Winner $167,555; second $34,050; third $27,025; fourth $13,513; fifth $8,107. Mutuel Pool $286,214.00 Exacta Pool $382,375.00 Trifecta Pool $273,660.00 Superfecta Pool $56,260.00 Quinella Pool $17,789.00

Last Raced	Horse	M/Eqt.	A.	Wt	PP	St	¼	½	Str	Fin	Jockey	Odds $1
6Mar04 ^{11}GP^{1}	Lion Tamer	L	4	122	4	5	52½	54½	32½	1¾	Smith M E	1.40
10Mar04 ^{9}TP^{1}	Private Horde	L bf	5	120	5	3	2^{hd}	21½	2½	2½	Lumpkins J	4.50
7Mar04 ^{8}SA^{10}	Marino Marini	L	4	118	1	1	1½	1^{hd}	1^{hd}	32¼	Flores D R	1.70
23Aug03 ^{10}Sar^{10}	Scrimshaw	L b	4	118	3	2	31½	41½	4½	4^{2}	Prado E S	12.10
13Mar04 ^{13}GP^{5}	Christine's Outlaw	L b	4	118	6	4	4½	3½	55½	513¾	Albarado R J	6.70
21Mar04 ^{10}OP^{3}	Saint Waki	L	4	118	2	6	6	6	6	6	Perret C	27.00

OFF AT 3:15 Start Good . Won driving. Track fast.
TIME :22^{3}, :45^{1}, 1:09^{3}, 1:23 (:22.63, :45.20, 1:09.78, 1:23.14)

$2 Mutuel Prices:

4 – LION TAMER	4.80	2.80	2.20
5 – PRIVATE HORDE		3.60	2.40
1 – MARINO MARINI			2.40

$2 EXACTA 4–5 PAID $15.20 $2 TRIFECTA 4–5–1 PAID $35.20
$2 SUPERFECTA 4–5–1–3 PAID $73.20 $2 QUINELLA 4–5 PAID $9.20

Ch. c, (Feb), by Will's Way – Tippecanoe Creek , by Olympio . Trainer Pletcher Todd A. Bred by Paul Smith (Ky).

LION TAMER settled three or four wide when outsprinted early, remained four abreast while advancing on the turn, came out a bit farther on the track when straightened for the drive, was soundly shaken up with the whip on the left side, then, after the rider switched his stick to the right hand, continued under strong encouragement to prevail. PRIVATE HORDE broke a bit awkwardly, moved up soon after to press front-running MARINO MARINI five wide, edged in on the turn, gained a brief, slim lead about the sixteenth pole but couldn't withstand LION TAMER'S surge. MARINO MARINI gained the lead at the start, raced four wide early while managing a slight advantage, edged in two wide on the turn, lost the lead to PRIVATE HORDE a sixteenth out and held on stubbornly the remainder. SCRIMSHAW, well placed inside from early on, continued inside into the lane, eased out four wide for the final sixteenth but couldn't muster a further response. CHRISTINE'S OUTLAW tracked the leaders four or five wide on the backstretch, edged in a bit around the turn while within easy striking distance, came out again to race five wide in the drive but was empty. SAINT WAKI, sluggish to begin, raced four wide, came out six abreast into the lane but never menaced.

Owners– 1, Tabor Michael B; 2, Tucker Billy R; 3, Rancho San Miguel Tom Clark; 4, Lewis Robert B and Beverly J; 5, R C Hill Stable Raymond and Christine Hill; 6, Carey Thomas M

Trainers– 1, Pletcher Todd A; 2, Cain Joe; 3, O'Neill Doug; 4, Lukas D Wayne; 5, Weaver George; 6, Vestal Peter M

$2 Pick Three (1–6–4) Paid $95.00 ; Pick Three Pool $49,514 .
$2 Pick Four (1/2/5–1–6–4) Paid $225.20 ; Pick Four Pool $57,979 .

SEVENTH RACE
Keeneland
APRIL 10, 2004

$5\frac{1}{2}$ FURLONGS. (Turf) (1.01^{3}) 9TH RUNNING OF THE SHAKERTOWN. Grade III. Purse $100,000 FOR THREE YEAR OLDS AND UPWARD. By subscription of $100 each, which should accompany the nomination; $1,000 to enter and start with $100,000 added of which 62% of all monies to the owner of the winner, 20% to second, 10% to third, 5% to fourth and 3% too fifth. Weights: Three year olds, 116 lbs.; older 123 lbs. Non-winners of $45,000 twice on the turf since October 3 allowed 3 lbs.; a sweepstakes on the turf in 2003–2004, 5 lbs. The maximum number of starters for the Shakertown will be limited to twelve. In the event that more than twelve pass the entry box, the twelve starters will be determined at that time with preference given by condition eligibility, beginning with graded stakes winners. Starters to be named through the entry box by the ussual time of closing. A gold julep cup will be presented to the owner of the winner. Closed Wednesday, March 31, 2004 with 31 nominations.

Value of Race: $115,100 Winner $71,362; second $23,020; third $11,510; fourth $5,755; fifth $3,453. Mutuel Pool $535,387.00 Exacta Pool $358,736.00 Trifecta Pool $296,028.00 Superfecta Pool $85,221.00 Quinella Pool $14,616.00

Last Raced	Horse	M/Eqt.	A.	Wt	PP	St	¼	⅜	Str	Fin	Jockey	Odds $1
25Oct03 ^{4}SA^{5}	Soaring Free	L	5	120	4	2	2^{hd}	1^{hd}	1^{hd}	$1^{1\frac{1}{2}}$	Sellers S J	0.70
6Nov03 ^{8}CD^{4}	Chosen Chief	L b	5	118	2	3	1^{hd}	3^{2}	2^{2}	$2^{\frac{1}{2}}$	Butler D P	34.00
27Nov03 ^{6}CD^{1}	Banned in Boston	L	4	118	10	1	8^{hd}	6^{2}	6^{3}	$3^{\frac{1}{2}}$	Blanc B	29.50
12Mar04 ^{9}FG^{1}	Cat Singer	L	4	118	7	5	3^{2}	2^{hd}	$3^{1\frac{1}{2}}$	4^{nk}	Albarado R J	5.70
7Mar04 ^{10}GP^{4}	Day Trader	L b	5	118	12	7	4^{hd}	4^{1}	4^{1}	$5^{2\frac{1}{4}}$	Prado E S	22.60
20Mar04 ^{8}FG^{7}	Red Lightning	L b	6	118	8	6	$6^{\frac{1}{2}}$	5^{hd}	5^{2}	$6^{\frac{1}{2}}$	Graham J	66.70
12Mar04 ^{4}SA^{2}	Abderian-Ire	L	7	118	6	12	11^{1}	11^{2}	8^{hd}	$7^{\frac{3}{4}}$	Santiago Javier	7.20
20Feb04 ^{9}GP^{2}	Fiscally Speaking	L f	5	120	9	9	$10^{1\frac{1}{2}}$	9^{hd}	$9^{\frac{1}{2}}$	$8^{\frac{1}{2}}$	Santos J A	10.90
22Mar04 ^{4}GP^{1}	Blakelock	L	4	118	11	8	9^{2}	7^{2}	7^{hd}	9^{nk}	Smith M E	16.10
21Feb04 ^{9}TP^{2}	Doc D	L	5	118	1	10	$7^{\frac{1}{2}}$	10^{1}	10^{hd}	10^{hd}	Bejarano R	15.60
9Mar03 ^{9}FG^{7}	Prince Alphie	L bf	4	120	3	11	12	12	12	$11^{2\frac{1}{2}}$	Perret C	34.30
20Jly03 ^{9}EIP^{10}	AirbourneCommand	L f	9	118	5	4	5^{hd}	8^{1}	11^{2}	12	Flores D R	67.50

OFF AT 4:16 Start Good . Won driving. Course firm.

TIME :21^{2}, :44, :55^{3}, 1:01^{3} (:21.54, :44.09, :55.64, 1:01.78)

(New Course Record)

$2 Mutuel Prices:

4 – SOARING FREE	3.40	3.20	2.80
2 – CHOSEN CHIEF		20.00	12.00
10 – BANNED IN BOSTON			10.40

$2 EXACTA 4–2 PAID $66.40 $2 TRIFECTA 4–2–10 PAID $1,220.20
$2 SUPERFECTA 4–2–10–7 PAID $5,522.20 $2 QUINELLA 2–4 PAID $57.40

Dk. b or br. g, (Jan), by Smart Strike – Dancing With Wings , by Danzig . Trainer Frostad Mark. Bred by Sam–Son Farm (Ont–C).

SOARING FREE bumped after the start by PRINCE ALPHIE and briefly in front, raced between foes while vying for the advantage, inched to the fore on the turn, was briefly headed from the inside in the upper stretch by CHOSEN CHIEF, regained the advantage, then edged clear late under strong handling. CHOSEN CHIEF drifted out at the start bumping with PRINCE ALPHIE, moved up inside to gained a slight edge before going a quarter, was headed by the winner on the turn, came again to reach the front briefly in the upper stretch, then couldn't match strides with SOARING FREE late as second best. BANNED IN BOSTON broke sharply, quickly settled, raced in behind horses on the turn, came out eight wide for the drive and was gaining late. CAT SINGER went up to force the pace early while three abreast, battled on about even terms until leaving the quarter-mile ground and weakened. DAY TRADER gained a striking position early while working his way in five wide, remained prominent off the inside into the final furlong and flattened out. RED LIGHTNING, within striking distance, edged in behind the leaders on the turn, continued three wide into the stretch and was empty the last eighth. ABDERIAN (IRE), five or six wide on the backstretch while outrun, came out 10 wide for the stretch run and improved position while unable menace. FISCALLY SPEAKING never reached contention. BLAKELOCK, six wide much of the way, tired in the drive. DOC D, checked along the inside at the half-mile ground, weakened soon after. PRINCE ALPHIE came out at the start bumping the winner, was bumped soon after by CHOSEN CHIEF when that one came out, then never reached contention. AIRBOURNE COMMAND, checked behind horses leaving the backstretch, weakened soon after.

Owners– 1, Sam-Son Farms; 2, Lynch Emmy; 3, Hubbard R D; 4, Sugar Jr Joe and Daniels Eugene; 5, Overbrook Farm; 6, Maas Phillip S; 7, Englander Richard A; 8, Whitham Janis R; 9, Stillmeadow Farm Inc Michael Duffy; 10, Rooker John W; 11, Schettine William C; 12, Saland Richard

Trainers– 1, Frostad Mark; 2, Porter Ron; 3, Hennig John K; 4, Gabriel Toni; 5, Lukas D Wayne; 6, Thornbury Jeffrey D; 7, Mullins Jeff; 8, Nafzger Carl A; 9, Weaver George; 10, Reed Eric R; 11, Carroll Josie; 12, Saland Richard

Scratched– Mr. Krisley (08Nov03 ^{8}CD ^{2}) , Punch (29Jan04 ^{8}TP ^{1})

$2 Pick Three (4–2–4/13/14) Paid $72.20 ; Pick Three Pool $80,394 .

NINTH RACE
Keeneland
APRIL 10, 2004

1⅛ MILES. (1.46^{4}) 80TH RUNNING OF THE TOYOTA BLUE GRASS. Grade I. Purse $750,000 FOR THREE YEAR OLDS. By subscription of $300 each, which should accompany the nomination; $7,500 to enter and start, with $750,000 guaranteed, of which $465,000 to the owner of the winner, $150,000 to second, $75,000 to third, $37,500 to fourth and $22,500 to fifth. Weights: Colts and geldings, 123 lbs.; Fillies, 118 lbs. A gold julep cup will be presented to the owner of the winner. A silver julep cup will be presented to the winning trainer and jockey. No supplementary nominations. Closed Wednesdday, February 18, 2004 with 157 nominations.

Value of Race: $750,000 Winner $465,000; second $150,000; third $75,000; fourth $37,500; fifth $22,500. Mutuel Pool $1,586,193.00 Exacta Pool $906,526.00 Trifecta Pool $750,324.00 Superfecta Pool $203,440.00 Quinella Pool $27,996.00

Last Raced	Horse	M/Eqt.	A.	Wt	PP	St	¼	½	¾	Str	Fin	Jockey	Odds $1
13Mar04 ^{9}GP^{3}	The Cliff's Edge	L	3	123	2	5	7^{2}	$7^{1\frac{1}{2}}$	$6^{\frac{1}{2}}$	$2^{1\frac{1}{2}}$	$1^{\frac{1}{2}}$	Sellers S J	5.70
6Mar04 ^{7}SA^{2}	Lion Heart		3	123	5	2	2^{hd}	1^{1}	$1^{2\frac{1}{2}}$	1^{1}	2^{6}	Smith M E	0.90
14Mar04 ^{11}Tam^{1}	Limehouse	L	3	123	3	1	1^{hd}	2^{1}	2^{1}	$3^{2\frac{1}{2}}$	$3^{3\frac{3}{4}}$	Santos J A	6.30
14Mar04 ^{11}Tam^{2}	Mustanfar	L b	3	123	6	4	4^{6}	$4^{1\frac{1}{2}}$	3^{hd}	$4^{2\frac{1}{2}}$	$4^{1\frac{3}{4}}$	Migliore R	10.60
7Mar04 ^{9}FG^{4}	Breakaway	L b	3	123	8	7	8	8	8	5^{hd}	$5^{1\frac{1}{2}}$	Albarado R J	14.70
14Mar04 ^{5}SA^{7}	Action This Day	L	3	123	1	6	5^{1}	$6^{2\frac{1}{2}}$	7^{1}	6^{8}	6^{17}	Flores D R	10.30
14Mar04 ^{5}SA^{1}	Preachinatthebar	L b	3	123	7	3	3^{2}	$3^{1\frac{1}{2}}$	$4^{1\frac{1}{2}}$	7^{2}	$7^{4\frac{1}{2}}$	Santiago Javier	5.80
20Mar04 ^{8}TP^{4}	That's an Outrage	L b	3	123	4	8	$6^{1\frac{1}{2}}$	5^{6}	5^{2}	8	8	Guidry M	41.50

OFF AT 5:16 Start Good For All But THAT'S AN OUTRAGE. Won driving. Track fast.

TIME :23^{3}, :46^{3}, 1:11, 1:36^{4}, 1:49^{2} (:23.70, :46.60, 1:11.12, 1:36.91, 1:49.42)

$2 Mutuel Prices:				
	3 – THE CLIFF'S EDGE	13.40	4.40	3.00
	6 – LION HEART		3.00	2.40
	4 – LIMEHOUSE			3.40

$2 EXACTA 3–6 PAID $40.80 $2 TRIFECTA 3–6–4 PAID $160.40
$2 SUPERFECTA 3–6–4–7 PAID $949.60 $2 QUINELLA 3–6 PAID $14.80

Dk. b or br. c, (Apr), by Gulch – Zigember , by Danzig . Trainer Zito Nicholas P. Bred by Stonerside Stable (Ky).

THE CLIFF'S EDGE unhurried early off the inside, moved out to the four path on the backstretch, angled back in to advance in the two path after five furlongs, angled three wide leaving the second turn when rallying and finished willingly to be up in time. LION HEART vied for the early lead three wide, took over before a half, moved in to be off the inside on the second turn, responded willingly in the stretch and held on gamely only to be outfinished. LIMEHOUSE contested the pace from the inside, could not keep pace with LION HEART after a half, stayed on well to midstretch and tired. MUSTANFAR steadied briefly behind the leaders when near the inside early on the first turn, raced forwardly near the rail, split rivals with three furlongs to go, but had no further response. BREAKAWAY outrun for six furlongs, split horses entering the stretch but could not threaten. ACTION THIS DAY reserved early, was no factor. PREACHINATTHEBAR prompted the early pace between rivals, dropped back a bit before a half then faded in the final three furlongs. THAT'S AN OUTRAGE hesitated at the start, was wide early, made a steady run to within striking distance with three furlongs to go but stopped.

Owners– 1, LaPenta Robert V; 2, Smith Derrick and Tabor Michael; 3, Dogwood Stable; 4, Shadwell Stable Hamdan Al Maktoum; 5, Farish William S; 6, Hughes B Wayne; 7, Pegram Michael E; 8, Bull Stick Stables LLC and Mercedes Stables LLC

Trainers– 1, Zito Nicholas P; 2, Biancone Patrick L; 3, Pletcher Todd A; 4, McLaughlin Kiaran P; 5, Howard Neil J; 6, Mandella Richard; 7, Baffert Bob; 8, Puhich Michael

Scratched– Birdstone (20Mar04 ^{8}TP ^{5})

$2 Pick Three (4/13/14–7–3) Paid $328.00 ; Pick Three Pool $76,334 .
$2 Pick Four (2–4/13/14–7–3) Paid $1,546.40 ; Pick Four Pool $113,595 .

NINTH RACE
Oaklawn
APRIL 10, 2004

1⅛ MILES. (1.46^3) 68TH RUNNING OF THE ARKANSAS DERBY. Grade II. Purse $1,000,000 THREE YEAR OLDS. By subscription of $1,000 which shall accompany the nomination, original nominators paying $7,500 to pass the entry box and $7,500 additional to start. Supplementary nominations may be made by the closing time of entries at a fee of $500,000 which qualifies to start. WEIGHTS: Colts and Geldings 122 lbs.; Fillies 117 lbs. Non–winners of a Sweepstakes allowed 4 lbs. In Allowance Stakes starting preference will be given to horses that have accumulated the highest earnings, excluding money won in restricted races. (See reverse side for additional starting limitation infformation). Early Bird closed Saturday, February 14, 2004 with 140 nominees at $300 for both The Rebel and The Arkansas Derby. Oaklawn's Centennial Bonus: Five million to the official winner of all three: 2004 Rebel Stakes, 2004 Arkansas Derby and 2004 Kentucky Derby. Regular nominations closed Saturday, March 20, 2004 with 12 nominees.

Value of Race: $1,000,000 Winner $600,000; second $200,000; third $100,000; fourth $50,000; fifth $30,000; sixth $20,000. Mutuel Pool $1,690,031.00 Exacta Pool $997,907.00 Trifecta Pool $913,928.00

Last Raced	Horse	M/Eqt.	A.	Wt	PP	St	¼	½	¾	Str	Fin	Jockey	Odds $1
20Mar04 ^{10}OP^{1}	Smarty Jones	f	3	122	11	2	$2^{1\frac{1}{2}}$	$2^{1\frac{1}{2}}$	1^{hd}	1^{3}	$1^{1\frac{1}{2}}$	Elliott S	1.00
7Mar04 ^{9}FG^{2}	Borrego	L b	3	118	1	7	4^{hd}	5^{2}	4^{hd}	$2^{\frac{1}{2}}$	$2^{1\frac{1}{2}}$	Espinoza V	3.30
20Mar04 ^{10}OP^{3}	Pro Prado	L	3	122	10	1	8^{1}	$8^{\frac{1}{2}}$	$7^{1\frac{1}{2}}$	$3^{2\frac{1}{2}}$	$3^{3\frac{1}{2}}$	McKee J	17.70
14Mar04 ^{5}SA^{3}	Harvard Avenue	L	3	122	9	6	$6^{\frac{1}{2}}$	6^{3}	$6^{2\frac{1}{2}}$	$5^{1\frac{1}{2}}$	$4^{\frac{3}{4}}$	Court J K	19.10
20Mar04 ^{10}OP^{2}	Purge	L	3	118	5	5	$1^{\frac{1}{2}}$	$1^{\frac{1}{2}}$	2^{2}	4^{2}	$5^{3\frac{1}{4}}$	Velasquez C	5.80
7Feb04 ^{8}TuP^{1}	Mambo Train	L b	3	122	2	3	$3^{\frac{1}{2}}$	4^{hd}	$5^{2\frac{1}{2}}$	7^{5}	6^{1}	Ramsammy E	57.00
7Mar04 ^{9}FG^{7}	Shadowland	L	3	118	3	4	$5^{2\frac{1}{2}}$	3^{hd}	3^{hd}	$6^{\frac{1}{2}}$	$7^{3\frac{1}{2}}$	Day P	8.80
13Mar04 ^{10}DeD^{2}	Every Advantage	L	3	118	4	9	9^{1}	10^{6}	9^{2}	8^{1}	$8^{3\frac{3}{4}}$	Borel C H	86.60
20Mar04 ^{10}OP^{6}	Mr. Jester	L	3	122	7	10	$10^{4\frac{1}{2}}$	9^{1}	8^{1}	9^{15}	$9^{9\frac{1}{2}}$	Chapa R	14.20
20Mar04 ^{8}TP^{2}	Tricky Taboo	L f	3	118	6	11	11	11	11	10^{5}	$10^{10\frac{3}{4}}$	D'Amico A J	28.80
20Mar04 ^{8}TP^{6}	Hasslefree	L b	3	118	8	8	$7^{3\frac{1}{2}}$	$7^{1\frac{1}{2}}$	10^{5}	11	11	Doocy T T	51.10

OFF AT 4:47 Start Good . Won driving. Track muddy.

TIME :22^3, :46^4, 1:11^3, 1:36^4, 1:49^2 (:22.64, :46.95, 1:11.71, 1:36.87, 1:49.41)

$2 Mutuel Prices:				
	11 – SMARTY JONES	4.00	3.00	2.60
	1 – BORREGO		3.20	2.80
	10 – PRO PRADO			4.40

$2 EXACTA 11–1 PAID $15.20 $2 TRIFECTA 11–1–10 PAID $124.00

Ch. c, (Feb), by Elusive Quality – I'll Get Along , by Smile . Trainer Servis John C. Bred by Someday Farm (Pa).

SMARTY JONES away well, pressed the leader under kind handling in first turn, put a head in front in the far turn, cleared at will from off the inside late in the second turn, kept to task through the lane. BORREGO allowed to settle, second flight turning for home, roused right handed when straightened for home, slowly getting to the winner late outside that one. PRO PRADO off the pace, saved ground with a golden trip along the inside, proved best of the others while not at threat to the winner. HARVARD AVENUE moved closer five wide turning for home, lacked the needed late kick. PURGE narrowly set the pace, gave up the lead to the winner in the far turn, staged a steady retreat. MAMBO TRAIN within striking distance, raced in some traffic turning for home, backed up. SHADOWLAND within striking distance, in good position in the second flight on the outside into the far turn, empty. EVERY ADVANTAGE made little impact. MR. JESTER remained back throughout in a dull effort. TRICKY TABOO last away, never close. HASSLEFREE -steadied past the wire the first time, gave way after a half, far back.

Owners– 1, Someday Farm; 2, Ralls & Foster LLC BGreely JKelly & BScott R Ralls & D Foster; 3, Winn Mrs James A; 4, Ron Crockett Inc Ronald D Crockett; 5, Starlight Stables LLC Saylor Paul and Martin John; 6, Everest Stables Inc; 7, Team Valor Stables LLC; 8, New Walter L; 9, Biggs Kaaren J; 10, Oak Haven Farm; 11, Lewis Robert B and Beverly J

Trainers– 1, Servis John C; 2, Greely C Beau; 3, Holthus Robert E; 4, O'Neill Doug; 5, Pletcher Todd A; 6, Polanco Marcelo; 7, Nicks Ralph E; 8, Amoss Thomas; 9, Wren Steve; 10, Frederick Edward; 11, Lukas D Wayne

$2 Pick Three (2–3–11) Paid $359.00 ; Pick Three Pool $1,216,666 .
$2 Pick Three (3–3/6–11) Paid $48.60 ; Pick Three Pool $36,622 .

EIGHTH RACE
Aqueduct
APRIL 17, 2004

1 MILE. (1.32^2) 48TH RUNNING OF THE BED O' ROSES BREEDERS' CUP HANDICAP. Grade III. Purse $150,000 (includes $50,000 BC – Breeders' Cup) A HANDICAP FOR FILLIES AND MARES THREE YEARS OLD AND UPWARD. By subscription of $100 each, which should accompany the nomination; $500 to pass the entry box; $500 to start, with $100,000 added and an additional $50,000 from the Breeders' Cup Fund for Cupnominees only. The NYRA added money and all fees to be divided 60% to the winner, 20% to second, 10% to third, 5% to fourth, 3% to fifth and 2% divided equally among the remaining finishers. Breeders' Cup Fund monies also correspondingly divided, provided a Breeders' Cup nominee has finished in an award position. Any Breeders' Cup Fund monies not awarded will revert back to the Fund. Trophy to the winning owner given by Breeders' Cup Ltd. Closed Saturday, April 3, 2004 with 19 Nominations.

Value of Race: $156,900 Winner $95,040; second $31,680; third $15,840; fourth $7,920; fifth $3,252; sixth $3,168. Mutuel Pool $414,747.00 Exacta Pool $363,869.00 Trifecta Pool $260,878.00

Last Raced	Horse	M/Eqt.	A.	Wt	PP	St	¼	½	¾	Str	Fin	Jockey	Odds $1
14Mar04 ^{8}Aqu^{4}	Passing Shot	L	5	115	1	6	$4^{1\frac{1}{2}}$	4^{1}	4^{hd}	2^{hd}	$1^{2\frac{1}{4}}$	Santos J A	7.30
14Mar04 ^{8}Aqu^{1}	Smok'n Frolic	L b	5	119	6	1	$3^{\frac{1}{2}}$	3^{hd}	$3^{\frac{1}{2}}$	$3^{\frac{1}{2}}$	2^{hd}	Velazquez J R	0.75
4Apr04 ^{10}GP^{1}	Nonsuch Bay	L	5	116	2	5	6	6	6	$5^{\frac{1}{2}}$	3no	Chavez J F	4.90
14Feb04 ^{8}SA^{8}	Victory Encounter	L	4	118	3	3	$1^{\frac{1}{2}}$	$1^{\frac{1}{2}}$	1^{hd}	1^{hd}	4^{1}	Bridgmohan S X	5.10
30Nov03 ^{8}Aqu^{3}	Princess Dixie	L b	5	113	5	4	5^{5}	5^{5}	$5^{2\frac{1}{2}}$	$4^{\frac{1}{2}}$	$5^{5\frac{1}{2}}$	Luzzi M J	21.20
27Mar04 ^{8}Aqu^{2}	Chirimoya	L f	5	111	4	2	$2^{\frac{1}{2}}$	$2^{\frac{1}{2}}$	2^{hd}	6	6	Cotto P L Jr	9.20

OFF AT 4:20 Start Good . Won driving. Track fast.

TIME :23^2, :46^3, 1:10^2, 1:35^2 (:23.46, :46.63, 1:10.57, 1:35.50)

$2 Mutuel Prices:				
	1 – PASSING SHOT	16.60	4.60	3.20
	7 – SMOK'N FROLIC		2.60	2.20
	3 – NONSUCH BAY			2.80

$2 EXACTA 1–7 PAID $39.40 $2 TRIFECTA 1–7–3 PAID $104.50

Dk. b or br. m, (Apr), by A.P. Indy – Aucilla , by Relaunch . Trainer Jerkens H Allen. Bred by J V Shields Jr (Ky).

PASSING SHOT was urged up along the inside early, raced close up for three quarters, found room on the rail turning for home, dug in when roused and drew clear under a drive. SMOK'N FROLIC raced with the pace while three wide, rallied approaching the stretch, dug in between rivals and got the nod for the place. NONSUCH BAY was outrun early, swung wide entering the stretch and finished gamely outside. VICTORY ENCOUNTER set the pace along the inside while in hand and stayed on stubbornly in the stretch. PRINCESS DIXIE was hustled along early, rallied four wide approaching the stretch and lacked a solid finishing kick. CHIRIMOYA contested the pace while between rivals and tired in the stretch.

Owners– 1, Shields Joseph V Jr; 2, Dogwood Stable; 3, Thorn Stable; 4, Mankiewicz Tom; 5, Edwards James F; 6, Rising Graph Stable

Trainers– 1, Jerkens H Allen; 2, Pletcher Todd A; 3, Alexander Frank A; 4, Sadler John W; 5, Bond Harold James; 6, Hushion Michael E

Scratched– Buy the Sport (25Oct03 ^{2}SA ^{5})

EIGHTH RACE
Hawthorne
APRIL 17, 2004

1⅛ MILES. (1.46³) 18TH RUNNING OF THE NATIONAL JOCKEY CLUB HANDICAP. Grade III. Purse $250,000 $250,000 Guaranteed. A HANDICAP FOR THREE-YEAR-OLDS AND UPWARD. By subscription of $100 each, which shall accompany the nomination, $1,250 to pass the entry box, $1,250 additional to start. With $250,000 Guaranteed, of which 60 percent to the winner, 20 percent to second, 11 percent to third, 6 percent to fourth, 3 percent to fifth. Nominations closed Monday, April 5, 2004 with 19.

Value of Race: $250,000 Winner $150,000; second $50,000; third $27,500; fourth $15,000; fifth $7,500. Mutuel Pool $237,192.00 Exacta Pool $107,929.00 Trifecta Pool $91,991.00 Superfecta Pool $27,878.00

Last Raced	Horse	M/Eqt.	A.	Wt	PP	St	¼	½	¾	Str	Fin	Jockey	Odds $1
29Feb04 9FG5	Ten Most Wanted	L b	4	121	4	4	3½	3⁴	3⁷	1⁵	16¾	Flores D R	0.20
18Mar04 9FG3	Colonial Colony	L	6	113	6	6	5½	51½	51½	3⁴	24¼	Lopez J	18.30
3Apr04 2Kee3	New York Hero	L bf	4	113	5	1	2⁴	2⁷	1½	2hd	31¾	Thornton T	4.00
27Dec03 8Haw4	Fighting Indians	L b	5	114	2	5	6	6	6	4½	41¼	Meier R	52.70
27Mar04 8DeD4	Parrott Bay	L b	7	114	1	3	41½	41½	4hd	5²	517¾	Campbell J M	18.40
4Apr04 1Haw1	Flemish Cap	L b	6	116	3	2	1½	1½	2²	6	6	Razo E Jr	7.70

OFF AT 4:27 Start Good. Won handily. Track fast.

TIME :23², :46⁴, 1:11², 1:36³, 1:49² (:23.52, :46.90, 1:11.50, 1:36.76, 1:49.54)

$2 Mutuel Prices:

4 – TEN MOST WANTED	2.40	2.10	2.10
6 – COLONIAL COLONY		3.00	2.10
5 – NEW YORK HERO			2.10

$2 EXACTA 4–6 PAID $12.40 $2 TRIFECTA 4–6–5 PAID $27.60
$2 SUPERFECTA 4–6–5–2 PAID $142.20

Dk. b or br. c, (Feb), by Deputy Commander – Wanted Again , by Criminal Type . Trainer Dollase Wallace. Bred by Jim H Plemmons (Ky).

TEN MOST WANTED was allowed to settle off the rail near the middle of the field, began moving up on his own courage on the second turn, took command entering the stretch and drew well off while under a mild hand ride. COLONIAL COLONY was void off speed while just off the rail, responded when asked for run turning for home and gained the place while no threat to the winner. NEW YORK HERO went up to press the pace of FLEMISH CAP from just outside, took over from that rival on the final turn then was no match for the top two in the drive. FIGHTING INDIANS trailed to the stretch then improved his position in the drive while not a danger. PARROTT BAY saved ground near the middle of the field but was never a factor. FLEMISH CAP set the pace from the inside under pressure but tired on the final turn.

Owners– 1, James Chisholm Michael Jarvis and J Paul Reddam etal; 2, Lakeside Farms LLC; 3, Paraneck Stable; 4, C B Racing Inc and Calkins Linne and Nancy; 5, Hoffman Kenneth E; 6, Papiese Rich

Trainers– 1, Dollase Wallace; 2, Bindner Walter M Jr; 3, Pedersen Jennifer; 4, Bettis Charles L; 5, Hoffman Kenneth E; 6, Gryczewski Jerry L

$2 Pick Three (1–6–4) Paid $28.60 ; Pick Three Pool $7,290 .
$2 Pick Six (6–3–7–1–6–4) 5 Correct Paid $75.20 ; Pick Six Pool $1,606 ; Carryover Pool $5,577.

NINTH RACE
Santa Anita
APRIL 17, 2004

1¼ MILES. (Turf) (1.57²) 56TH RUNNING OF THE SANTA BARBARA HANDICAP. Grade II. Purse $200,000 FOR FILLIES AND MARES FOUR YEARS OLD AND UPWARD. By subscription of $200 each to accompany the nomiation or by supplementary nomination of $4,000 by Sunday, April 11. $2,000 additonal to start, with $200,000 guaranteed, of which $120,000 to first, $40,000 to second, $24,000 to third, $12,000 to fourth and $4,000 to fifth. Weights Tuesday, April 13. High weights preferred. Starters to be named through the entry box by the closing time of entries. A trophy will be presented to the owner of the winner. Closed with 13 nominations.

Value of Race: $200,000 Winner $120,000; second $40,000; third $24,000; fourth $12,000; fifth $4,000. Mutuel Pool $658,653.00 Exacta Pool $202,662.00 Quinella Pool $17,193.00 Trifecta Pool $205,043.00

Last Raced	Horse	M/Eqt.	A.	Wt	PP	¼	½	¾	1	Str	Fin	Jockey	Odds $1
27Mar04 9SA7	Megahertz-GB	LB	5	121	2	5	5	5	4¹	3hd	1¹	Solis A	0.40
28Mar04 2SA4	Noches DeRosa-Chi	LB b	6	116	5	32½	21½	2²	11½	1²	22½	Baze T C	3.70
27Mar04 9SA4	Mandela-Ger	LB	4	111	4	4³	44½	3½	3hd	2hd	3²	Santiago Javier	7.10
28Mar04 7SA1	Uraib-Ire	LB	4	115	1	2¹	3½	4¹	5	5	4½	Leyva J C	11.70
14Mar04 10Tam6	Star Vega-GB	LB b	4	113	3	1½	1¹	1¹	2½	4¹	5	Espinoza V	14.80

OFF AT 4:44 Start Good. Won driving. Course firm.

TIME :24¹, :48, 1:13, 1:37, 2:00³ (:24.30, :48.04, 1:13.17, 1:37.15, 2:00.71)

$2 Mutuel Prices:

2 – MEGAHERTZ-GB	2.80	2.10	2.10
6 – NOCHES DE ROSA-CHI		2.40	2.10
4 – MANDELA-GER			2.10

$1 EXACTA 2–6 PAID $3.10 $2 QUINELLA 2–6 PAID $4.60
$1 TRIFECTA 2–6–4 PAID $5.90

Ch. m, (May), by Pivotal-GB – Heavenly Ray , by Rahy . Trainer Frankel Robert. Bred by Cheveley Park Stud Ltd (GB).

MEGAHERTZ (GB) saved ground off the early pace, inched forward a bit off the rail on the backstretch, continued outside a rival into and on the second turn, tried to go between foes leaving that turn but steadied in tight, swung out into the stretch, rallied to the front under a tap of the whip and good handling past midstretch and proved best. NOCHES DE ROSA (CHI) floated wide on the dirt crossing, stalked off the rail, bid outside a rival and took the lead on the second turn, inched away on that bend, could not match the winner in the final furlong but was clearly second best. MANDELA (GER) chased a bit off the rail then outside a foe, came three deep into the stretch and picked up the show. URAIB (IRE) rank along the inside pressing the early pace, stalked from the rail, was in a bit tight leaving the second turn and lacked the needed response. STAR VEGA (GB) drifted out on the dirt crossing, pulled her way to the front outside a rival, angled in and set the pace inside, dueled into and early on the second turn, came out a bit into the stretch and weakened.

Owners– 1, Bello Michael; 2, Diamond A Racing Corporation; 3, Tanaka Gary A; 4, Charles Ronald L and Clear Valley Stables; 5, Cuchna John R Jim Ford Inc and Pearson Deron

Trainers– 1, Frankel Robert; 2, Mandella Richard; 3, Frankel Robert; 4, Shulman Sanford; 5, Cassidy James

Scratched– Bartok's Blithe (14Feb04 8SA 5)

$2 Daily Double (7–2) Paid $48.40 ; Daily Double Pool $41,875 .
$1 Pick Three (3–7–2/5) Paid $122.50 ; Pick Three Pool $83,833 .

NINTH RACE
Keeneland
APRIL 17, 2004

1 1/16 MILES. (1.40⁴) 23RD RUNNING OF THE COOLMORE LEXINGTON. Grade II. Purse $325,000 FOR THREE YEAR OLDS. By subscription of $250 each, which should accompany the nomination; $3,250 to enter and start with $325,000 guaranteed, of which $201,500 to the owner of the winner, $65,000 to second, $32,500 to third, $16,250 to fourth and $9,750to fifth. Weight: 123 lbs. Non-winners of $60,000 twice at a mile or over allowed, 3 lbs.; $45,000 twice at a mile or over, 5 lbs.; $30,000 twice at a mile or over, 7 lbs. The maximum number of starters for the Coolmore Lexington will be limited to fourteen. In the event that more than fourteen pass the entry box, the fourteen starters will be determined at that time with preference given to graded stakes winners, then those that have accumulated the highest earnings. Starters to be named through the entry box by the usual time of closing. A gold julep cup will be presented to the owner of the winner. Closed Wednesday, April 7, 2004 with 51 nominations.

Value of Race: $325,000 Winner $201,500; second $65,000; third $32,500; fourth $16,250; fifth $9,750. Mutuel Pool $1,164,834.00 Exacta Pool $725,616.00 Trifecta Pool $608,810.00 Superfecta Pool $188,495.00 Quinella Pool $27,102.00

Last Raced	Horse	M/Eqt.	A.	Wt	PP	St	¼	½	¾	Str	Fin	Jockey	Odds $1
3Apr04 8SA4	Quintons Gold Rush	L	3	116	10	5	2hd	21	1hd	12	12¾	Bailey J D	5.70
7Mar04 9FG5	Fire Slam	L	3	116	6	7	51	51½	6½	2½	2nk	Day P	4.50
3Apr04 7Haw2	Song of the Sword	L bf	3	116	2	13	81	6½	4½	3½	32	Arroyo N Jr	4.00
20Mar04 7Aqu2	Pomeroy	b	3	116	4	2	31	3hd	3hd	45	47½	Blanc B	6.90
13Mar04 10GP3	DashboardDrummer	L	3	116	8	4	11½	11	21	51½	5½	Dominguez R A	23.00
20Mar04 7TP4	El Prado Rob	L	3	117	12	11	123	101½	112	72	61¼	Sellers S J	28.80
20Mar04 7Aqu1	Saratoga County	L bf	3	116	14	12	101	9½	72	6½	71	Castellano J J	9.60
13Mar04 7GG6	Totally Platinum	L	3	116	13	14	14	12½	9½	103	83½	Borel C H	71.30
7Apr04 6Kee1	Tiger Heart	L	3	116	1	1	9hd	113	10½	91	9½	Perret C	29.10
20Mar04 7TP3	Gamblin	L b	3	116	3	10	71	7½	82½	118	103¼	Albarado R J	62.60
22Mar04 1GP1	Bride's Best Boy	L	3	116	11	8	4½	41	51½	82½	1114½	Prado E S	13.30
3Apr04 7Haw3	Suave	L b	3	116	5	3	11hd	138	132½	125	129½	Velasquez C	14.00
2Apr04 7Kee6	Race for Glory	L	3	116	9	6	13½	14	14	131½	131½	McKee J	46.60
27Mar04 6SA1	Boomzeeboom	L b	3	116	7	9	6½	8½	12hd	14	14	Bejarano R	5.60

OFF AT 5:17 Start Good . Won driving. Track fast.

TIME :23¹, :47¹, 1:12, 1:37¹, 1:43⁴ (:23.32, :47.29, 1:12.00, 1:37.36, 1:43.82)

$2 Mutuel Prices:

10 – QUINTONS GOLD RUSH	13.40	6.00	4.00
6 – FIRE SLAM		5.60	3.40
2 – SONG OF THE SWORD			3.80

$2 EXACTA 10-6 PAID $83.80 $2 TRIFECTA 10-6-2 PAID $285.40
$2 SUPERFECTA 10-6-2-4 PAID $1,884.80 $2 QUINELLA 6-10 PAID $34.00

Ch. c, (Mar), by Wild Rush – Hollywood Gold , by Mr. Prospector . Trainer Asmussen Steven M. Bred by Toyomi Omiya (Ky).

QUINTONS GOLD RUSH worked his way in soon after the start to press front-running DASHBOARD DRUMMER under light restraint four wide, inched to challenge early on the second turn, took over just prior to going six furlongs, settled into the stretch with a clear lead, then continued under solid right-handed encouragement to maintain his advantage. FIRE SLAM, nicely positioned under light rating while between foes three or four wide, moved a bit wider concluding the second turn, loomed prominently outside the winner through the drive and wasn't good enough. SONG OF THE SWORD bobbled at the start, was caught in close quarters soon after when TIGER HEART came out and GAMBLIN was forced in, settled near the inside, reached easy striking distance midway on the backstretch, saved ground while advancing approaching the stretch, angled three wide in the upper stretch, was inside the top two for the final sixteenth and couldn't muster the needed response. POMEROY leaned in at the start bumping GAMBLIN, forced that one in on SONG OF THE SWORD, raced within easy striking distance three or four wide, remained prominent to the stretch and flattened out. DASHBOARD DRUMMER gained the lead early, maneuvered near the inside, showed the way for nearly six furlongs and weakened gradually. EL PRADO ROB, outrun early, angled near the inside approaching the first turn, remained three wide while edging closer around the far turn, came out five or six wide for the drive but was empty. SARATOGA COUNTY, seven wide early, angled in to race between foes five wide, made a mild move to reach contention just before going six furlongs but failed to continue. TOTALLY PLATINUM lightly bumped the gate at the start, quickly angled in four wide and never was a serious factor. TIGER HEART came out at the start putting SONG OF THE SWORD in tight quarters while bumping him, appeared to be climbing a bit while racing inside into the first turn, moved out four wide on the backstretch and failed to menace. GAMBLIN, bumped at the start by POMEROY and forced in, raced in behind rivals and was through after six furlongs. BRIDE'S BEST BOY edged in to track the pace four or five wide, was asked for his best three furlongs out and couldn't keep pace. SUAVE, ridden away from the gate, was steadied behind horses entering the first turn and never was prominent. RACE FOR GLORY was outrun. BOOMZEEBOOM faded after a half.

Owners– 1, Padua Stables Satish K Sanan and Jay Manoogian; 2, Fulton Stan E; 3, Paraneck Stable; 4, Smith Derrick and Tabor Michael; 5, Double S Stable Preferred Pals Stables and Wachtel Edwin; 6, LaPenta Robert V; 7, Pollard Evelyn M; 8, Chess Phil and Sheva; 9, Buckram Oak Farm; 10, Pabst Henry E; 11, John M Sullivan Jr; 12, Jay Em Ess Stable; 13, Lewis Robert B and Beverly J; 14, John Karubian Alan Landsburg and Larry Postaer

Trainers– 1, Asmussen Steven M; 2, Carroll David; 3, Pedersen Jennifer; 4, Biancone Patrick L; 5, Iwinski Allen; 6, Zito Nicholas P; 7, Weaver George; 8, Baffert Bob; 9, McPeek Kenneth G; 10, O'Callaghan Niall M; 11, Tagg Barclay; 12, McGee Paul J; 13, Lukas D Wayne; 14, Cerin Vladimir

Scratched– New Element (20Mar04 8TP 9)

EIGHTH RACE
Keeneland
APRIL 18, 2004

$1\frac{1}{16}$ MILES. (Turf) (1.40[2]) 16TH RUNNING OF THE JENNY WILEY. Grade III. Purse $100,000 FOR FILLIES AND MARES FOUR YEARS OLD AND UPWARD. By subscription of $100 each, which should accompany the nomination; $1,000 to enter and start with $100,000 added, of which 62% of all monies to the owner of the winner, 20% to second, 10% to third, 5% tofourth and 3% to fifth. Weight 123 lbs. Non-winners of Grade I or II stakes on the turf since September 1 allowed 3 lbs.; $60,000 twice on the turf since August 1, 5 lbs.; $45,000 twice on the turf since July 4, 7 lbs. Starters to be named through theentry box by the usual time of closing. A gold julep cup will be presented to the owner of the winner. Closed Wednesday, April 7, 2004 with 23 nominations. HAGGIN COURSE.

Value of Race: $110,300 Winner $68,386; second $22,060; third $11,030; fourth $5,515; fifth $3,309. Mutuel Pool $498,987.00 Exacta Pool $304,661.00 Trifecta Pool $263,693.00 Superfecta Pool $88,298.00 Quinella Pool $11,050.00

Last Raced	Horse	M/Eqt.	A.	Wt	PP	St	¼	½	¾	Str	Fin	Jockey	Odds $1
28Mar04 2SA1	Intercontinentl-GB	L	4	116	3	7	6hd	5hd	42	2hd	11	Bailey J D	0.80
13Mar04 11GP2	Ocean Drive	L	4	116	5	5	3$1\frac{1}{2}$	3$\frac{1}{2}$	2hd	3$2\frac{1}{2}$	2$1\frac{1}{2}$	Velazquez J R	4.40
14Mar04 10Tam2	Madeira Mist-Ire	L	5	118	8	6	51	6hd	71	41	3nk	Castellano J J	14.40
5Mar04 9GP5	Vanguardia-Arg	L	6	116	4	1	2$1\frac{1}{2}$	2$\frac{1}{2}$	11	1hd	4$2\frac{3}{4}$	Albarado R J	16.30
14Mar04 10Tam1	Coney Kitty-Ire	L	6	116	7	8	8	8	8	5$\frac{1}{2}$	5nk	Santos J A	12.90
15Nov03 9CD8	Film Maker	L b	4	123	2	4	4hd	4hd	51	6$\frac{1}{2}$	6$1\frac{3}{4}$	Prado E S	4.10
13Mar04 11GP3	Vespers	L	6	116	1	2	7$1\frac{1}{2}$	7$1\frac{1}{2}$	61	8	7$1\frac{1}{4}$	Day P	13.50
7Apr04 8Kee4	Virgin Voyage	L b	4	116	6	3	1$1\frac{1}{2}$	1$1\frac{1}{2}$	3hd	7hd	8	Bejarano R	74.10

OFF AT 4:46 Start Good For All But CONEY KITTY (IRE). Won driving. Course firm.
TIME :23[2], :48, 1:12, 1:35[2], 1:41[2] (:23.51, :48.18, 1:12.10, 1:35.43, 1:41.41)

$2 Mutuel Prices:

3 – INTERCONTINENTAL–GB	3.60	2.80	2.60
5 – OCEAN DRIVE		3.40	2.60
8 – MADEIRA MIST–IRE			4.60

$2 EXACTA 3–5 PAID $15.80 $2 TRIFECTA 3–5–8 PAID $103.80
$2 SUPERFECTA 3–5–8–4 PAID $866.80 $2 QUINELLA 3–5 PAID $9.20

B. f, (Mar), by Danehill – Hasili-Ire , by Kahyasi . Trainer Frankel Robert. Bred by Juddmonte Farms (GB).

INTERCONTINENTAL (GB) settled early, was taken out seven or eight wide on the backstretch to race widest, edged in a bit around the far turn, was five wide in the drive and was ridden hard to prevail. OCEAN DRIVE, always well placed while following the leaders under light rating four wide, moved with the winner while inside that one entering the upper stretch, battled on even terms leaving the eighth pole but couldn't sustain the needed momentum. MADEIRA MIST (IRE) drifted out at the start, gained a decent position between foes three or four wide, continued in that position on the course entering the lane and finished determinedly for her position. VANGUARDIA (ARG), in front briefly after the start, was eased back outside of CONEY KITTY (IRE), pressed that one four wide, took over on the far turn, made the pace into the final furlong and weakened. CONEY KITTY (IRE) lunged in the air at the start, settled four wide, was outrun for six furlongs, raced into contention six side on the far turn, was eight wide when straightened for the drive and failed to gain in the final furlong. FILM MAKER, within easy striking distance while racing near the inside between foes to the stretch, eased out five wide and lacked a rally. VESPERS, unhurried early while saving ground in hand, continued near the rail into the stretch, eased out three or four wide, was steadied between rivals leaving the three-sixteenths pole and never menaced thereafter. VIRGIN VOYAGE moved to the front early, edged near the inside, made the pace for nearly six furlongs and tired.

Owners– 1, Juddmonte Farms Inc; 2, Baskin Bonnie and Sy; 3, Skymarc Farm Inc Chryss OReilly; 4, Mack Earle I; 5, J William Betz Steve Humphrey and Arthur Seelbinder; 6, Courtlandt Farms; 7, Janney Stuart S III; 8, Paraneck Stable

Trainers– 1, Frankel Robert; 2, Pletcher Todd A; 3, Clement Christophe; 4, Penna Angel Jr; 5, Toner James J; 6, Motion H Graham; 7, McGaughey III Claude R; 8, Pedersen Jennifer

$2 Pick Three (7–1–3) Paid $87.80 ; Pick Three Pool $46,795 .

SEVENTH RACE
Santa Anita
APRIL 18, 2004

ABOUT $6\frac{1}{2}$ FURLONGS. (Turf) (1.11) 37TH RUNNING OF THE SAN SIMEON HANDICAP. Grade III. Purse $100,000 DOWNHILL TURF FOR FOUR YEARS OLD AND UPWARD. By subscription of $100 each to accompany the nomiation or by supplementary nomination of $2500 by Sunday, April 11. $1000 additonal to start, with $100,000 added. The added money and all fees to be divided 60% to the winner, 20% to second, 12% to third, 6% to fourth and 2% to fifth. Weights Tuesday, April 13. High weights preferred. Starters to be named through the entry box by the closing time of entries. A trophy will be presented to the owner of the winner. Closed with 13 nominations.

Value of Race: $107,300 Winner $64,380; second $21,460; third $12,876; fourth $6,438; fifth $2,146. Mutuel Pool $484,845.00 Exacta Pool $272,410.00 Quinella Pool $31,325.00 Trifecta Pool $270,261.00 Superfecta Pool $98,158.00

Last Raced	Horse	M/Eqt.	A.	Wt	PP	St	¼	½	Str	Fin	Jockey	Odds $1
12Mar04 2SA1	Glick	LB b	8	117	5	3	21	2$1\frac{1}{2}$	1hd	1$\frac{3}{4}$	Solis A	1.00
21Mar04 3SA1	Cayoke-FR	LB b	7	116	6	1	4$1\frac{1}{2}$	4$1\frac{1}{2}$	31	24	Baze T C	3.30
14Mar04 2SA1	Summer Service	LB bf	4	117	4	4	3hd	3hd	4$2\frac{1}{2}$	3$\frac{1}{2}$	Nakatani C S	5.20
21Mar04 3SA4	Grandiser-Aus	LB	6	115	3	2	1$\frac{1}{2}$	1$\frac{1}{2}$	2$1\frac{1}{2}$	4$\frac{1}{2}$	Espinoza V	6.20
12Mar04 2SA2	Van Rouge	LB	5	114	2	6	6	5hd	51	54	Santiago Javier	9.20
20Mar04 1SA4	Island Light-GB	LB	6	116	1	5	5hd	6	6	6	Desormeaux K J	13.80

OFF AT 3:43 Start Good . Won driving. Course firm.
TIME :22, :44, 1:05[3], 1:11[2] (:22.14, :44.15, 1:05.73, 1:11.46)

$2 Mutuel Prices:

7 – GLICK	4.00	2.60	2.20
8 – CAYOKE–FR		3.20	2.60
5 – SUMMER SERVICE			2.80

$1 EXACTA 7–8 PAID $5.00 $2 QUINELLA 7–8 PAID $6.40
$1 TRIFECTA 7–8–5 PAID $15.30 $1 SUPERFECTA 7–8–5–4 PAID $30.40

B. h, (Mar), by Theatrical–Ire – Bejat , by Mr. Prospector . Trainer Mullins Jeff. Bred by Allen E Paulson (Ky).

GLICK prompted the pace outside a rival, took the lead into the stretch, inched away past midstretch and held gamely under some light urging and good handling. CAYOKE (FR) stalked the pace outside a rival, came out into the stretch and continued willingly to the wire. SUMMER SERVICE bobbled at the start, stalked inside down the hill, then went around the early pacesetter late for third. GRANDISER (AUS) sped to the early lead, angled in and dueled inside the winner, fought back into the stretch and to midstretch but weakened in the final furlong and lost third late, then did not return to be unsaddled when bleeding from the nostrils and was vanned off. VAN ROUGE chased outside a rival down the hill, came three deep into the stretch and lacked the needed rally. ISLAND LIGHT (GB) saved ground chasing the pace, came a bit off the rail in the stretch and could not offer the necessary response. Rail on hill at zero.

Owners– 1, Bone Robert D; 2, House Michael; 3, Weatherwatch Farm and Valente Roddy; 4, Vasili Angelo; 5, Moss Mr and Mrs Jerome S; 6, Charles Ronald L and Clear Valley Stables

Trainers– 1, Mullins Jeff; 2, Mullins Jeff; 3, Spawr Bill; 4, McAnally Ronald; 5, Shirreffs John; 6, Shulman Sanford

Scratched– Spinelessjellyfish (13Mar04 3SA 2) , Echo Eddie (06Sep03 3BM 2) , De La Costa (AUS) (24Jan04 61117TRE5)

$2 Daily Double (5–7) Paid $8.40 ; Daily Double Pool $34,388 .
$1 Pick Three (11–5/6–3/6/7/9) Paid $109.60 ; Pick Three Pool $103,155 .

NINTH RACE
Santa Anita
APRIL 18, 2004

ABOUT 1¾ MILES. (Turf) (2.42^4) 65TH RUNNING OF THE SAN JUAN CAPISTRANO INVITATIONAL HANDICAP. Grade II. Purse $250,000 FOR FOUR-YEAR-OLDS AND UPWARD. By invitation, with no nomination or starting fees. The winner to receive $150,000, with $50,000 to second, $30,000 to third, $15,000 to fourth and $5,000 to fifth. Invitations and weights to be published Sunday, April 11Santa Anita reserves the right to assign or reassign weight to any horse prior to time of entry. A trophy will be presented to the owner of the winner.

Value of Race: $250,000 Winner $150,000; second $50,000; third $30,000; fourth $15,000; fifth $5,000. Mutuel Pool $526,695.00 Exacta Pool $260,243.00 Quinella Pool $29,860.00 Trifecta Pool $291,612.00 Superfecta Pool $120,845.00

Last Raced	Horse	M/Eqt.		A.	Wt	PP	½	1	1¼	1½	Str	Fin	Jockey	Odds $1
20Mar04 9SA1	Meteor Storm-GB	LB		5	116	4	3hd	31½	31	31½	12½	11½	Valdivia J Jr	2.80
18Mar04 5SA1	Rhythm Mad-FR	LB		4	115	7	71	71	7hd	81	51	21	Solis A	3.30
20Mar04 9SA4	Runaway Dancer	LB	b	5	115	5	8½	9	81	6hd	4hd	32½	Smith M E	4.00
20Mar04 9SA8	Special Matter	LB	b	6	113	2	41	62½	62½	71½	61½	4hd	Baze T C	14.50
13Mar04 3SA3	Ringaskiddy	LB	b	8	114	9	9	8½	9	9	8½	53	Espinoza V	6.20
20Mar04 9SA6	White Buck	LB	b	4	113	6	61½	4hd	52	51	7hd	6½	Court J K	20.80
3Apr04 3SA6	Gigli-Brz	LB		6	114	8	5½	22½	23½	21	3hd	71½	Santiago Javier	10.50
20Mar04 9SA3	GenedeCampeo-Brz	LB	f	5	113	3	21	52½	4hd	41	9	81	Berrio O A	10.30
18Mar04 5SA5	All the Boys	LB	f	7	114	1	11½	1hd	1hd	1hd	2hd	9	Bisono A	13.00

OFF AT 4:46 Start Good. Won driving. Course firm.

TIME :49^4, 1:13^4, 1:39^1, 2:03^4, 2:28^1, 2:45^4 (:49.85, 1:13.89, 1:39.39, 2:03.92, 2:28.32, 2:45.98)

$2 Mutuel Prices:				
	4 – METEOR STORM–GB	7.60	3.80	2.40
	7 – RHYTHM MAD–FR		5.00	3.20
	5 – RUNAWAY DANCER			2.80

$1 EXACTA 4–7 PAID $14.10 $2 QUINELLA 4–7 PAID $14.40
$1 TRIFECTA 4–7–5 PAID $48.20 $1 SUPERFECTA 4–7–5–2 PAID $333.70

B. h, (Apr), by Bigstone–Ire – Hunt the Sun–GB , by Rainbow Quest . Trainer Dollase Wallace. Bred by Juddmonte Farms (GB).

METEOR STORM (GB) chased outside a rival then a bit off the rail, moved up boldly three deep leaving the second turn and into the stretch to gain the lead, kicked clear and held under urging. RHYTHM MAD (FR) angled in and saved ground off the early pace, went outside a rival leaving the backstretch, split horses leaving the second turn, steadied off heels briefly in midstretch, then rallied between foes and finished well. RUNAWAY DANCER saved ground off the pace, moved up leaving the second turn, split rivals in midstretch and rallied inside. SPECIAL MATTER chased inside then came a bit off the rail into the backstretch, went three deep on the second turn and into the stretch and could not summon the necessary late kick. RINGASKIDDY unhurried outside a rival or off the rail early, also went three deep on the second turn and into the stretch and improved position. WHITE BUCK pulled between horses early then chased outside a rival, continued between foes on the second turn, came out some into the stretch and lacked the needed rally. GIGLI (BRZ) pulled early and was taken back outside on the hill, moved up four wide crossing the dirt, bid outside the leader, prompted the pace outside that one, was between horses into the stretch and weakened. GENE DE CAMPEAO (BRZ) pulled his way along a bit off the rail then between foes into the stretch the first time, stalked inside, lacked room off heels in midstretch but also weakened. ALL THE BOYS took the early lead and went the opening quarter in :24.87, set a pressured pace inside, dropped back when headed into the stretch and had little left. Rail on hill at zero.

Owners– 1, Jarvis Michael Margolis Gary and Smole Ken et al; 2, Four Star Stables LLC; 3, R L Stables; 4, Elder Nancy and McClintock Janice and George et al; 5, Garcia Juan and Scofield Leonard L; 6, Manoogian Jay; 7, T N T Stud; 8, Bandeirantes Stable; 9, Jpf Investments I LLC

Trainers– 1, Dollase Wallace; 2, Headley Bruce; 3, Hendricks Dan L; 4, Becerra Rafael; 5, Garcia Juan; 6, Mitchell Mike; 7, Frankel Robert; 8, Avila A C; 9, Aguirre Paul G

$2 Daily Double (5–4) Paid $13.00 ; Daily Double Pool $50,185 .
$1 Pick Three (3/6/7/9–3/5/6–4) Paid $12.20 ; Pick Three Pool $106,061 .

EIGHTH RACE
Keeneland
APRIL 21, 2004

1½ MILES. (Turf) (2.27²) BEWITCH S. Grade III. Purse $100,000 FOR FILLIES AND MARES FOUR YEARS OLD AND UPWARD. By subscription of $100 each, which should accompany the nomination; $1,000 to enter and start with $100,000 added, of which 62% to the owner of the winner, 20% to second, 10% to third, 5% to fourth and 3%to fifth. Weight: 123 lbs. Non-winners of $60,000 twice over nine furlongs on the turf since October 3 allowed 3 lbs.; $45,000 twice over nine furlongs on the turf since August 1, 5 lbs.; $45,000 over nine furlongs on the turf in 2004, 7 lbs. The maximum number of starters for the Bewitch will be limited to ten. In the event that more than ten fillies or mares pass the entry box, the ten starters will be determined at that time with preference given to graded stakes winners, then highest turf earnings in 2003–2004. Starters to be named through the entry box by the usual time of closing. A gold julep cup will be presented to the owner of the winner. Closed Wednesday, April 14, 2004 with 24 nominations. KEENELAND COURSE. (Rail at 15 feet).

Value of Race: $113,400 Winner $70,308; second $22,680; third $11,340; fourth $5,670; fifth $3,402. Mutuel Pool $420,595.00 Exacta Pool $265,112.00 Trifecta Pool $245,263.00 Superfecta Pool $91,378.00 Quinella Pool $11,919.00

Last Raced	Horse	M/Eqt.	A.	Wt	PP	¼	½	1	1¼	Str	Fin	Jockey	Odds $1
21Mar04 11GP1	Meridiana-Ger	L	4	118	2	4½	3½	41	4½	31	1no	Prado E S	5.00
14Mar04 10Tam3	Alternate	L b	5	116	9	5½	5½	6hd	61½	2hd	21½	Velasquez C	12.30
28Feb04 11GP1	Binya-Ger	L	5	118	5	31	41½	3hd	31	11½	3nk	Velazquez J R	1.30
21Mar04 11GP8	Ocean Silk	L	4	116	7	82	7hd	5hd	5hd	5½	4¾	Day P	5.50
4Apr04 4Kee1	Lady Liberty	L	5	116	4	92½	92	10	10	61	5¾	Albarado R J	52.00
21Mar04 11GP3	Miss Hellie	L	5	116	3	10	10	9½	8hd	71	62	Santos J A	10.40
21Mar04 11GP4	Boana-Ger	L	6	116	6	61½	61½	72	71	81	7nk	Blanc B	19.00
4Apr04 4Kee2	Mexican Moonlight	L	4	116	8	21	21	2½	2hd	4hd	82	McKee J	51.40
31Mar04 7SA3	Juliette-Ire	L	4	116	1	7hd	82	8½	91	98	922	Bailey J D	4.60
24Mar04 9TP1	Tempus Fugit	L	4	116	10	1hd	1½	1½	1hd	10	10	D'Amico A J	61.10

OFF AT 4:46 Start Good . Won driving. Course good.

TIME :25⁴, :50³, 1:15², 1:41¹, 2:06⁴, 2:31 (:25.80, :50.73, 1:15.54, 1:41.28, 2:06.88, 2:31.05)

$2 Mutuel Prices:				
	2 – MERIDIANA-GER	12.00	6.00	3.40
	10 – ALTERNATE		11.60	6.00
	5 – BINYA-GER			2.80

$2 EXACTA 2–10 PAID $143.00 $2 TRIFECTA 2–10–5 PAID $524.00
$2 SUPERFECTA 2–10–5–8 PAID $3,084.00 $2 QUINELLA 2–10 PAID $84.20

Ch. f, (May), by Lomitas-GB – Monbijou , by Dashing Blade . Trainer Clement Christophe. Bred by Gestut Etzean (Ger).

MERIDIANA (GER), rated in a forward position from early on near the inside, lacked room briefly a quarter-mile out, came around a tiring TEMPUS FUGIT, angled back to the rail, then was fully extended to prevail. ALTERNATE edged in early to track the pace three or four wide, was between rivals and lacked room between the five-sixteenths and quarter-mile pole, moved out five wide for the drive and was going well at the end. BINYA (GER) stalked the pace from early on while four wide, gained the lead entering the upper stretch, briefly was clear, then was checked nearing the wire when in a bit tight while weakening. OCEAN SILK, unhurried early, edged up four or five wide upon going a half, raced within easy striking distance five or six wide into the final furlong but couldn't offer the needed late gain. LADY LIBERTY, reserved near the inside from the outset, was unhurried, reached contention as the field tightened nearing the final quarter, moved between foes five wide and was unable to offer a late response. MISS HELLIE, outrun five wide early, moved out six or seven wide on the backstretch, was nine abreast entering the upper stretch and improved position. BOANA (GER) raced within striking distance near the inside to the stretch and came up empty. MEXICAN MOONLIGHT angled in early to press front-running TEMPUS FUGIT, stuck a head in front for a stride between calls when straightened into the stretch and faltered soon after. JULIETTE (IRE) wasn't a factor. TEMPUS FUGIT gained the lead early, maneuvered near the inside, made the pace for 10 furlongs and gave way readily in the drive.

Owners– 1, Kelly Jon and Sarah; 2, Pin Oak Stable LLC; 3, Allen Joseph; 4, Estate of Robert E Sangster Ben Sangster; 5, Janney Stuart S III; 6, Hamilton Emory A; 7, Tanaka Gary A; 8, Pass Taggart Racing; 9, MacDonald Mark; 10, Briland Farm

Trainers– 1, Clement Christophe; 2, Motion H Graham; 3, McLaughlin Kiaran P; 4, Byrne Patrick B; 5, McGaughey III Claude R; 6, McGaughey III Claude R; 7, Attfield Roger L; 8, Murphy Paul H; 9, Frankel Robert; 10, McPeek Kenneth G

Scratched– Spice Island (21Mar04 11GP 6) , Goosey Gander (12Feb04 7GP 9)

$2 Pick Three (3/5/9–5–2) Paid $153.40 ; Pick Three Pool $30,020 .

EIGHTH RACE
Keeneland
APRIL 22, 2004

1⅛ MILES. (1.46³) 74TH RUNNING OF THE BEN ALI. Grade III. Purse $150,000 FOR FOUR YEAR OLDS AND UPWARD. By subscription of $150 each, which should accompany the nomination; $1,500 to enter and start with $150,000 guaranteed, of which $93,000 to the owner of the winner, $30,000 to second, $15,000 to third, $7,500 to fourth and$4,500 to fifth. Weight: 123 lbs. Non–winners of $60,000 twice over a mile since September 1 allowed 3 lbs.; $60,000 over a mile in 2004, 5 lbs.; $45,000 twice over a mile since September 1, 7 lbs. Starters to be named through the entry box by the usual time of closing. A gold julep cup will be presented to the owner of the winner. Closed Wednesday, April 14, 2004 with 24 nominations.

Value of Race: $150,000 Winner $93,000; second $30,000; third $15,000; fourth $7,500; fifth $4,500. Mutuel Pool $357,937.00 Exacta Pool $232,830.00 Trifecta Pool $130,721.00 Superfecta Pool $46,798.00 Quinella Pool $8,193.00

Last Raced	Horse	M/Eqt.	A.	Wt	PP	St	¼	½	¾	Str	Fin	Jockey	Odds $1
18Mar04 9FG4	Midway Road	L	4	116	5	2	1hd	12½	12½	17	111¼	Albarado R J	5.10
3Apr04 8Aqu2	Evening Attire	L b	6	116	1	3	43½	45½	31	34½	2½	Velasquez C	0.50
3Apr04 11OP5	Sir Cherokee	L	4	120	4	5	5	5	5	2hd	312¼	Borel C H	5.40
27Mar04 11GP5	Jersey Giant	L b	5	116	3	4	32	3½	44	5	4½	Bailey J D	11.00
3Apr04 2Kee2	American Style	L	5	117	2	1	23	25	24	41½	5	Sellers S J	6.70

OFF AT 4:45 Start Good . Won driving. Track sloppy.

TIME :23³, :46², 1:10², 1:34⁴, 1:46³ (:23.77, :46.57, 1:10.51, 1:34.89, 1:46.78)

(New Track Record)

$2 Mutuel Prices:				
	7 – MIDWAY ROAD	12.20	3.20	2.10
	2 – EVENING ATTIRE		2.20	2.10
	6 – SIR CHEROKEE			2.10

$2 EXACTA 7–2 PAID $24.00 $2 TRIFECTA 7–2–6 PAID $59.40
$2 SUPERFECTA 7–2–6–4 PAID $141.80 $2 QUINELLA 2–7 PAID $7.60

B. c, (Apr), by Jade Hunter – Fleet Road , by Magesterial . Trainer Howard Neil J. Bred by W S Farish (Ky).

MIDWAY ROAD went up at once to contest the pace outside of AMERICAN STYLE, reached the front just prior to going a quarter, moved clear on the backstretch, drew off with authority entering the upper stretch, then expanded his advantage under hand urging to prevail in track record time. EVENING ATTIRE, close up inside early, was checked behind JERSEY GIANT nearing the first turn, moved out four or five wide on the backstretch, gained second position briefly in the upper stretch, lost it for a stride or two when SIR CHEROKEE advanced to his outside, then dug in gamely to maintain the runner-up spot while no match for the winner. SIR CHEROKEE, reserved early and angled inside, came out leaving the three-eighths pole to commence his rally, was six wide entering the stretch, then flattened out late. JERSEY GIANT tracked the pace four wide for nearly six furlongs and tired. AMERICAN STYLE, in front after the start, dueled inside the winner the opening quarter, eased outside that one on the backstretch, continued forwardly for seven furlongs and gave way.

Owners– 1, Farish William S; 2, Grant Mary and Joseph and Kelly Thomas J; 3, Domino Stud of Lex LLC; 4, Kligman Joel A; 5, Buckram Oak Farm

Trainers– 1, Howard Neil J; 2, Kelly Patrick J; 3, Tomlinson Michael A; 4, Ryerson James T; 5, Zito Nicholas P

Scratched– Congrats (03Apr04 2Kee1) , Sarava (14Feb04 6SA 5)

$2 Pick Three (10–2/3/6/7/8/11/12–7) Paid $155.20 ; Pick Three Pool $35,839 .

NINTH RACE
Keeneland
APRIL 23, 2004

1½ MILES. (Turf) (2.27^{2}) 19TH RUNNING OF THE ELKHORN. Grade III. Purse $150,000 FOR FOUR YEAR OLDS AND UPWARD. By subscription of $150 each, which should accompany the nomination; $1,500 to enter and start with $150,000 guaranteed, of which $93,000 to the owner of the winner, $30,000 to second, $15,000 to third, $7,500 to fourth and$4,500 to fifth. Weight: 123 lbs. Non-winners of $60,000 twice over ten furlongs on the turf since October 3 allowed 3 lbs.; $45,000 twice over nine furlongs on the turf since August 1, 5 lbs.; $60,000 over nine furlongs on the turf in 2004, 7 lbs.Starters to be named through the entry box by the usual time of closing. A gold julep cup will be presented to the owner of the winner. Closed Wednesday, April 14, 2004 with 25 nominations. Keeneland Course. (Rail at 15 feet).

Value of Race: $150,000 Winner $93,000; second $30,000; third $15,000; fourth $7,500; fifth $4,500. Mutuel Pool $482,058.00 Exacta Pool $357,388.00 Trifecta Pool $317,885.00 Superfecta Pool $111,108.00 Quinella Pool $14,231.00

Last Raced	Horse	M/Eqt.	A.	Wt	PP	¼	½	1	1¼	Str	Fin	Jockey	Odds $1
14Mar04 ^{7}GG^{5}	Epicentre	L	5	116	2	5^{hd}	5½	4^{hd}	4^{2}	2^{1}	1$^{4\frac{3}{4}}$	Bailey J D	1.20
11Jan04 ^{8}GP^{7}	Rochester	L	8	116	7	9$^{1\frac{1}{2}}$	7½	7^{3}	5^{hd}	3½	2^{nk}	Velasquez C	15.30
7Apr04 ^{9}Kee^{1}	Art Variety-Brz	L b	6	116	8	10	10	8^{hd}	8$^{3\frac{1}{2}}$	5$^{1\frac{1}{2}}$	3½	Blanc B	6.90
4Oct03 ^{7}Kee^{6}	Kim Loves Bucky	L	7	117	9	3^{hd}	2^{hd}	2^{2}	1^{1}	1^{hd}	4$^{2\frac{1}{2}}$	Sellers S J	6.70
19Mar04 ^{8}GP^{1}	Host	L	4	116	4	6½	4^{hd}	5^{hd}	6½	6½	5$^{1\frac{1}{4}}$	Day P	12.70
3Apr04 ^{8}Kee^{1}	National Pride-GB	L b	4	116	3	4^{2}	3$^{1\frac{1}{2}}$	3^{2}	2^{hd}	4^{3}	6$^{5\frac{1}{4}}$	Velazquez J R	7.90
7Apr04 ^{9}Kee^{3}	Grand-Ire	L f	4	116	6	1½	1$^{1\frac{1}{2}}$	1^{hd}	3^{hd}	7^{3}	7$^{1\frac{1}{2}}$	Albarado R J	14.10
19Jan04 ^{8}SA^{8}	Californian-GB	L	4	116	5	8^{hd}	9½	6^{2}	7$^{1\frac{1}{2}}$	8$^{1\frac{1}{2}}$	8$^{5\frac{1}{4}}$	Lumpkins J	9.60
9Apr04 ^{9}Kee^{7}	Freefourinternet	L	6	116	1	2^{hd}	8^{1}	10	9^{6}	9^{6}	9$^{7\frac{1}{2}}$	Perret C	13.20
29Mar04 ^{4}GP^{3}	Autonomy-Ire	L f	7	116	10	7^{2}	6^{1}	9^{2}	10	10	10	Marquez C H Jr	67.00

OFF AT 5:21 Start Good . Won driving. Course good.

TIME :26^{3}, :51^{4}, 1:17^{2}, 1:42, 2:07^{1}, 2:31^{4} (:26.79, :51.85, 1:17.46, 1:42.18, 2:07.29, 2:31.96)

$2 Mutuel Prices:				
	2 – EPICENTRE	4.40	3.40	2.60
	7 – ROCHESTER		11.20	6.60
	8 – ART VARIETY–BRZ			3.80

$2 EXACTA 2–7 PAID $49.20 $2 TRIFECTA 2–7–8 PAID $307.80
$2 SUPERFECTA 2–7–8–9 PAID $1,139.20 $2 QUINELLA 2–7 PAID $38.20

B. h, (Mar), by Kris S. – Carya , by Northern Dancer . Trainer Frankel Robert. Bred by Juddmonte Farms Inc (Ky).

EPICENTRE, well placed inside from the outset, raced under light rating, eased out between foes leaving the quarter-mile ground, placed GRAND (IRE) in tight, angled outside of front-running KIM LOVES BUCKY, took over leaving the eighth pole and drew off under strong hand urging. ROCHESTER, unhurried early, worked his way inside, saved ground for nearly a mile, came out five or six wide for the drive and was fully extended to earn second position. ART VARIETY (BRZ), outrun to the final turn while four wide, moved out six abreast when straightened for the drive and offered a minor gain. KIM LOVES BUCKY stalked the pace four or five wide, inched to challenge approaching the stretch, took over, held on well until the final furlong and faltered. HOST, lightly rated near the inside between foes, was never far back, came out six wide for the drive but couldn't muster the needed response. NATIONAL PRIDE (GB), well placed near the inside from the outset, angled four wide into the lane and flattened out the last eighth. GRAND (IRE) gained the lead early, edged inside, made the pace until nearing the final quarter, weakened and was checked when in tight next to the winner when that one advanced . CALIFORNIAN (GB), five or six wide most of the way, offered a mild bid nearing the stretch and failed to continue . FREEFOURINTERNET, close up inside early, tired upon going five furlongs. AUTONOMY (IRE) stalked the pace five wide for six furlongs and weakened gradually thereafter.

Owners– 1, Juddmonte Farms Inc; 2, Augustin Stable; 3, Team Victory II; 4, Glenney Kim; 5, C G Zoe Stable Caesar P Kimmel and Philip J Solondz; 6, Ryan Michael J and Dilger Jerry; 7, Team Valor Stables LLC; 8, Noctis LLC Michael Mulhall Neil Papiano and Steve Taub; 9, EquiraceCom LLC; 10, Shining Armor Stable

Trainers– 1, Frankel Robert; 2, Sheppard Jonathan E; 3, McPeek Kenneth G; 4, Glenney John; 5, Kimmel John C; 6, McLaughlin Kiaran P; 7, Nicks Ralph E; 8, Mulhall Kristin; 9, Scott Joan; 10, Oliver Philip J

$2 Pick Three (1/2/4/10–1/2/7–2) Paid $18.60 ; Pick Three Pool $56,272 .
$2 Pick Four (2–1/2/4/10–1/2/7–2) Paid $66.20 ; Pick Four Pool $77,803 .

EIGHTH RACE
Aqueduct
APRIL 24, 2004

1$\frac{1}{16}$ MILES. (Turf) (1.40^{4}) 28TH RUNNING OF THE FORT MARCY HANDICAP. Grade III. Purse $100,000 A HANDICAP FOR THREE YEAR OLDS AND UPWARD. By subscription of $100 each, which should accompany the nomination; $500 to pass the entry box; $500 to start, with $100,000 added. The added money and all fees to be divided 60% to the winner, 20% to second, 10% to third, 5% to fourth, 3% to fifth and 2% divided equally among the remaining finishers. Weights Sunday, April 18. Starters to be named at the closing time of entries. A trophy will be presented to the winning owner. The New York Racing Association reserves the right to transfer this race to the Main Track. In the event that this race is taken off the turf, it may be subject to downgrading upon review by the Graded Stakes Committee. Closed Saturday, April 10, 2004 with 29 Nominations. (If the Stewardsconsider it inadvisable to run this race on the turf course, this race will be run at One Mile on the main track.).

Value of Race: $111,400 Winner $66,840; second $22,280; third $11,140; fourth $5,570; fifth $3,342; sixth $743; seventh $743; eighth $742. Mutuel Pool $535,980.00 Exacta Pool $425,015.00 Trifecta Pool $315,117.00

Last Raced	Horse	M/Eqt.	A.	Wt	PP	St	¼	½	¾	Str	Fin	Jockey	Odds $1
25Mar04 ^{6}GP^{4}	Chilly Rooster	L b	4	113	5	5	4½	4½	3^{hd}	1^{hd}	1½	Uske S	32.25
12Mar04 ^{9}GP^{9}	Union Place	L	5	113	3	3	3^{1}	3½	2^{hd}	2^{3}	2^{1}	Castellano J J	50.50
12Mar04 ^{9}GP^{1}	Slew Valley	L	7	119	2	6	7^{hd}	8	5$^{1\frac{1}{2}}$	3^{hd}	3½	Chavez J F	2.70
20Mar04 ^{6}GP^{5}	Charge	L	4	114	6	2	8	7$^{1\frac{1}{2}}$	6^{hd}	4½	4$^{2\frac{1}{4}}$	Prado E S	7.40
25Mar04 ^{6}GP^{1}	Remind	L	4	115	7	7	5^{1}	6$^{1\frac{1}{2}}$	7^{1}	6^{7}	5$^{2\frac{3}{4}}$	Bailey J D	1.35
7Apr04 ^{8}Aqu^{2}	Rogue Agent	L b	5	112	4	1	1^{1}	1^{1}	1^{1}	5$^{1\frac{1}{2}}$	6$^{5\frac{1}{2}}$	Arroyo N Jr	12.90
9Apr04 ^{7}Kee^{2}	Steadfast and True	L	5	113	8	8	6½	5^{hd}	8	7½	7$^{4\frac{1}{2}}$	Velazquez J R	6.60
20Mar04 ^{9}SA^{7}	Toccet	L b	4	113	1	4	2^{hd}	2½	4½	8	8	Luzzi M J	8.80

OFF AT 4:23 Start Good . Won driving. Course firm.

TIME :23^{3}, :48^{1}, 1:12^{4}, 1:36^{2}, 1:42^{2} (:23.60, :48.34, 1:12.82, 1:36.59, 1:42.47)

$2 Mutuel Prices:				
	5 – CHILLY ROOSTER	66.50	25.80	11.80
	3 – UNION PLACE		43.20	18.80
	2 – SLEW VALLEY			4.30

$2 EXACTA 5–3 PAID $1,109.00 $2 TRIFECTA 5–3–2 PAID $4,774.00

Dk. b or br. g, (May), by Arch – Chilly Chick , by Raise a Native . Trainer Jerkens H Allen. Bred by Hobeau Farm Ltd (Fla).

CHILLY ROOSTER raced close up along the inside while in hand, advanced inside on the second turn, split rivals entering the stretch, dug in gamely on the rail and prevailed after a long drive. UNION PLACE raced close up while three wide, rallied three wide on the second turn and finished gamely outside. SLEW VALLEY was rated along early, put in a four wide run on the second turn and finished well outside. CHARGE was outrun early, advanced inside on the second turn and finished gamely along the inside. REMIND raced between rivals while in hand and had no response when roused. ROGUE AGENT set the pace along the inside and tired in the stretch. STEADFAST AND TRUE raced wide throughout and tired in the stretch. TOCCET chased the pace from the outside and tired after three quarters.

Owners– 1, Hobeau Farm; 2, Sorokolit Sr William A; 3, Rich Meadow Farm; 4, Whitney Wheelock; 5, Claiborne Farm; 6, Fein Scott My Goose Stables Oringer Jay; 7, Al Maktoum Sheik Maktoum b; 8, Borislow Daniel M

Trainers– 1, Jerkens H Allen; 2, Schulhofer Randy; 3, Sciacca Gary; 4, McGaughey III Claude R; 5, Mott William I; 6, Brice Michael; 7, McLaughlin Kiaran P; 8, Scanlan John F

Scratched– Bowman's Band (13Mar04 ^{13}GP ^{3}) , Black Silk (GB) (02Apr04 ^{8}Aqu^{1})

THIRD RACE
Bay Meadows
APRIL 24, 2004

1 MILE. (Turf) (1.34^{3}) 55TH RUNNING OF THE SAN FRANCISCO BREEDERS' CUP MILE HANDICAP. Grade II. Purse $150,000 (includes $50,000 BC – Breeders' Cup) FOR THREE-YEAR-OLDS AND UPWARD. By supscription of $100 each to accompany the nomination or by supplementary nomination of $2,000 by Noon, Sunday, April 18, 2004. $500 to pass the entry box and $500 additional to start with $100,000 Guaranteed and an additional $50,000 from Breeders' Cup Fund for Breeders' Cup eligibles only. The host association's Guaranteed monies to be divided 55% to the winner, 20% to second, 15% to third, 7.5% to fourth and 2.5% to fifth. Breeders' Cup Fund monies also correspondingly divided providing a Breeders' Cup nominee has finished in an awarded position. Any Breeders' Cup Fund monies not awarded will revert back to the Fund. A trophy will be presented to the owner of the winner by Breeders' Cup Ltd. Closed Thursday, April 15, 2004 with 18 nominations.

Value of Race: $148,750 Winner $82,500; second $30,000; third $22,500; fourth $11,250; fifth $2,500. Mutuel Pool $231,280.00 Exacta Pool $110,078.00 Quinella Pool $13,586.00 Trifecta Pool $156,418.00

Last Raced	Horse	M/Eqt.	A.	Wt	PP	St	¼	½	¾	Str	Fin	Jockey	Odds $1
6Mar04 9SA2	Singletary	LB	4	119	7	4	3½	41½	2hd	1hd	1¾	Valdivia J Jr	0.70
19Mar04 7SA1	Captain Squire	LB	5	116	1	2	11½	11	11	23	22	Rollins C J	2.40
27Mar04 7GG4	Gold Ruckus	LB bf	6	116	3	3	7	7	7	52½	31¼	Baze R A	10.50
26Oct03 7BM2	Ninebanks	LB b	6	118	5	5	6hd	5hd	5hd	3hd	4½	Warren R J Jr	7.70
14Feb04 6SA8	Sanderman-Chi	LB b	4	117	4	6	5½	6½	6½	41	52	Carr D	23.60
3Apr04 7SA2	Laidlow	LB	4	112	6	7	41	3hd	4hd	7	63	Schvaneveldt C P	32.50
20Mar04 8GG1	Motel Staff	LB b	7	110	2	1	21	21	32	6hd	7	Duran F	20.10

OFF AT 2:08 Start Good . Won driving. Course firm.

TIME :23^{1}, :47, 1:10^{4}, 1:22^{4}, 1:35 (:23.35, :47.16, 1:10.88, 1:22.89, 1:35.16)

$2 Mutuel Prices:				
	7 – SINGLETARY	3.40	2.20	2.10
	1 – CAPTAIN SQUIRE		2.60	2.40
	3 – GOLD RUCKUS			2.80

$1 EXACTA 7–1 PAID $4.10 $2 QUINELLA 1–7 PAID $3.80
$1 TRIFECTA 7–1–3 PAID $13.70

B. g, (Mar), by Sultry Song – Joiski's Star , by Star de Naskra . Trainer Chatlos Donald Jr. Bred by Disler Farms Ltd (Ky).

SINGLETARY was used some early to establish a good position into the first turn, stalked the pace to the second turn, eased off the rail and split rivals into the stretch, took command leaving the furlong pole and held under steady urging. CAPTAIN SQUIRE was rated on the front end to the half, responded to urging to the stretch, resisted the winner briefly in mid stretch then gamely held the place. GOLD RUCKUS had no speed, was between horses and shuffled back at the half, was forced to circle rivals five wide to the stretch then had a mild late bid. NINEBANKS was unhurried three wide to the backstretch, settled to the second turn, was asked for speed two deep to the stretch but could not muster the needed response. SANDERMAN (CHI) was allowed to settle to the half, saved ground to the stretch but finished evenly in the drive. LAIDLOW tracked the leaders three wide to the half, tried to rally but was fanned four wide to the stretch and flattened out late. MOTEL STAFF pressed the pace to the second turn then weakened in the stretch.

Owners– 1, Little Red Feather Racing; 2, Bone Robert D and Diener Jeffrey S; 3, Franks Farms; 4, Abruzzo Peter; 5, Al Kabeer Sultan and Zarour Marcel; 6, Dorfman Steve; 7, G C C I

Trainers– 1, Chatlos Donald Jr; 2, Mullins Jeff; 3, Hollendorfer Jerry; 4, Hollendorfer Jerry; 5, De Seroux Laura; 6, Chew Matthew; 7, Delima Clifford

---

$2 Daily Double (3–7) Paid $7.80 ; Daily Double Pool $13,510 .
$1 Pick Three (1/4–3–7) Paid $6.80 ; Pick Three Pool $36,050 .

NINTH RACE
Churchill
APRIL 24, 2004

1 MILE. (1.33^{2}) 80TH RUNNING OF THE DERBY TRIAL. Grade III. Purse $100,000 FOR THREE-YEAR-OLDS. By subscription of $100 each on or before April 10, 2004 or by Supplementary Nomination of $5,000 at time of entry. $500 to pass the entry box; $500 additional to start, with $100,000 added of which 62% to the owner of the winner, 20%to second, 10% to third, 5% to fourth and 3% to fifth. Weight 122 lbs. Non-winners of $50,000 allowed 2 lbs.; three races other than maiden or claiming, 4 lbs.; two races other than maiden or claiming, 6 lbs.; a race other than maiden or claiming, 8 lbbs. Starters to be named through the entry box at the usual time of closing. Trophy to winning owner. Nominations closed Saturday, April 10, 2004 with 53 nominations.

Value of Race: $110,800 Winner $68,696; second $22,160; third $11,080; fourth $5,540; fifth $3,324. Mutuel Pool $484,337.00 Exacta Pool $285,365.00 Trifecta Pool $141,206.00 Superfecta Pool $43,241.00

Last Raced	Horse	M/Eqt.	A.	Wt	PP	St	¼	½	¾	Str	Fin	Jockey	Odds $1
9Apr04 6Kee1	Sir Shackleton	L	3	116	2	3	3½	2½	21½	11	11¾	Bejarano R	1.20
27Mar04 3SA1	Courageous Act	L	3	116	5	4	5	5	3hd	21	28½	Velasquez C	3.60
4Apr04 8Kee1	Bwana Charlie	L	3	122	3	2	1hd	3hd	1hd	35½	35¼	Sellers S J	1.40
8Apr04 4Kee1	Honolua Storm	L	3	114	4	5	41	4hd	5	5	43	Albarado R J	22.60
4Apr04 8Kee2	Quick Action	L	3	116	1	1	2hd	1½	43½	4½	5	McKee J	11.10

OFF AT 4:46 Start Good . Won driving. Track fast.

TIME :22^{4}, :46^{1}, 1:11^{3}, 1:24^{1}, 1:37^{3} (:22.86, :46.33, 1:11.67, 1:24.35, 1:37.61)

$2 Mutuel Prices:				
	2 – SIR SHACKLETON	4.40	3.20	2.10
	5 – COURAGEOUS ACT		3.80	2.10
	3 – BWANA CHARLIE			2.10

$2 EXACTA 2–5 PAID $15.20 $2 TRIFECTA 2–5–3 PAID $33.40
$2 SUPERFECTA 2–5–3–4 PAID $66.80

Ch. c, (Mar), by Miswaki – Naskra Colors , by Star de Naskra . Trainer Zito Nicholas P. Bred by Tracy Farmer (Ky).

SIR SHACKLETON attended the pace at once while near the inside between rivals, inched to a slight advantage entering the turn, was headed about the three-furlong pole from the outside by BWANA CHARLIE, regained the top position entering the upper stretch while two wide, then was ridden hard the remainder and kept to his task to slightly increase his margin in a game effort. COURAGEOUS ACT drifted out a bit at the break, quickly recovered, followed the leaders within easy striking distance five wide on the backstretch, made a menacing run outside the winner into the upper stretch and wasn't a match for SIR SHACKLETON late while clearly superior to the rest. BWANA CHARLIE forced the pace at once while three abreast, put a head in front just before going a quarter, surrendered to QUICK ACTION from the inside, regained the advantage three furlongs out, lost it to the winner leaving the turn and tired. HONOLUA STORM moved inside upon going a quarter, swung out four wide into the stretch but was empty. QUICK ACTION vied for the lead along the inside, gained a slight edge before going a half but tired approaching the stretch.

Owners– 1, Farmer Tracy; 2, Lewis Robert B and Beverly J; 3, Heiligbrodt Racing Stable; 4, Attfield Roger L and Werner William; 5, Overbrook Farm

Trainers– 1, Zito Nicholas P; 2, Baffert Bob; 3, Asmussen Steven M; 4, Attfield Roger L; 5, Lukas D Wayne

Scratched– Rock Hard Ten

$2 Pick Three (7–4–2/6) Paid $103.40 ; Pick Three Pool $19,376 .

EIGHTH RACE
Hawthorne
APRIL 24, 2004

1⅛ MILES. (1.46^3) 39TH RUNNING OF THE SIXTY SAILS HANDICAP. Grade III. Purse $250,000 $250,000 Guaranteed. A HANDICAP FOR FILLIES AND MARES, THREE-YEARS-OLD AND UPWARD. By subscription of $100 each, which shall accompany the nomination, $1,250 to pass the entry box, $1,250 additional to start. With $250,000 Guaranteed, of which 60 percen tto the winner, 20 percent to second, 1 percent to third, 6 percent to fourth, 3 percent to fifth. Nominations closed Monday, April 12, 2004 with 17.

Value of Race: $250,000 Winner $150,000; second $50,000; third $27,500; fourth $15,000; fifth $7,500. Mutuel Pool $147,734.00 Exacta Pool $99,952.00 Trifecta Pool $87,268.00 Superfecta Pool $25,507.00

Last Raced	Horse	M/Eqt.	A.	Wt	PP	St	¼	½	¾	Str	Fin	Jockey	Odds $1
25Mar04 8FG2	Allspice	L b	4	115	6	3	21½	21½	21½	2½	1hd	Emigh C A	21.40
14Mar04 8SA3	Bare Necessities	L	5	122	2	1	4½	41	42½	33	21¼	Douglas R R	0.30
5Apr04 8Haw1	Mavoreen	L bf	4	114	3	2	11	11	11	1hd	32¼	Campbell J M	48.30
10Apr04 4Haw1	Julie's Prize	L b	4	115	5	4	3hd	31	3hd	48	413	Sterling L J Jr	3.10
4Apr04 10OP3	Sue's Good News	L f	4	113	4	5	51	6	5hd	51	51	Doocy T T	9.20
20Dec03 8Aqu3	Retroactive	L	4	113	1	6	6	5hd	6	6	6	Thornton T	18.80

OFF AT 4:27 Start Good For All But SUE'S GOOD NEWS. Won driving. Track fast.

TIME :24^1, :49, 1:13^2, 1:38, 1:50^3 (:24.32, :49.00, 1:13.57, 1:38.09, 1:50.66)

$2 Mutuel Prices:

7 – ALLSPICE	44.80	7.20	2.40
2 – BARE NECESSITIES		2.60	2.10
3 – MAVOREEN			2.80

$2 EXACTA 7–2 PAID $99.20 $2 TRIFECTA 7–2–3 PAID $955.40
$2 SUPERFECTA 7–2–3–5 PAID $2,118.60

B. f, (Mar), by Coronado's Quest – Music House , by Sadler's Wells . Trainer Geier Greg. Bred by Jim Tafel LLC (Ky).

ALLSPICE prompted the pace from just off the rail, continued to push the issue to the stretch, challenged near the furlong marker, took over late and held on stubbornly. BARE NECESSITIES saved ground near the middle of the field, lacked room turning for home, angled out for room and rallied but could not get past the winner. MAVOREEN quickly made the lead from the inside, set all of the pace then held on gamely when confronted in the stretch. JULIE'S PRIZE raced close up just outside but lacked a rally. SUE'S GOOD NEWS hopped at the start to get away poorly and was always outrun. RETROACTIVE was also outrun.

Owners– 1, Tafel James B; 2, Iron County Farms Inc; 3, Ten Broeck Farm Inc; 4, Richard Otto Stables Inc; 5, Cresran LLC; 6, Humphrey G Watts Jr

Trainers– 1, Geier Greg; 2, Dollase Wallace; 3, Forster Grant T; 4, Mitchell Anthony; 5, Hobby Steve; 6, Arnold George R II

Scratched– La Reason (04Apr04 10OP 1)

$2 Pick Three (5–3–7) Paid $1,584.20 ; Pick Three Pool $6,337 .
$2 Pick Six (2/6–1–1–5–3–7) 3 Correct Paid $165.60 ; Pick Six Pool $884 ; Carryover Pool $1,983.

EIGHTH RACE
Lone Star
APRIL 24, 2004

1 MILE. (1.34^2) 8TH RUNNING OF THE TEXAS MILE. Grade III. Purse $300,000 (PLUS UP TO $11,250 Open ATB) FOR THREE YEARS OLD AND UPWARD. No nomination fee. $2,250 to pass the entry box and an additional $2,250 to start with $300,000 guaranteed of which $165,000 to the owner of the winner, $55,000 to second , $30,250 to third, $16,500 to fourth and $8,250 too fifth and $5,000 for placing sixth through tenth. If less than 10 horses start, the purse money not distributed will revert to the winning owner. Weights: Three Year Olds, 114lbs. Older, 123 lbs. Non-winners of $90,000 at a mile or over in 2004 allowed 3 lbs.; $60,000 since November 1, 2003, 5 lbs.; $30,000 in 2004, 7 lbs.; $30,000 in 2003 –2004, 10 lbs. Maiden and claiming races not considered in weight allowances. Starters to be named through the entry box by theusual time of closing. High weights preferred (on the scale). Total earnings in 2003 –2004 will be used in determining the order of preference of horses assigned equal weights. The field will be limited to twelve starters. Horses not drawing a starting position in the gate willl receive a refund of the entry fee. A suitable award will be presented to the winning owner. Nominations closed Wednesday, April 14, 2004 with 43 nominations.

Value of Race: $300,000 Winner $175,000; second $55,000; third $30,250; fourth $16,500; fifth $8,250; sixth $5,000; seventh $5,000; eighth $5,000. Mutuel Pool $303,720.00 Exacta Pool $174,491.00 Quinella Pool $12,077.00 Trifecta Pool $159,084.00 Superfecta Pool $53,280.00

Last Raced	Horse	M/Eqt.	A.	Wt	PP	St	¼	½	¾	Str	Fin	Jockey	Odds $1
3Apr04 10SA5	Kela	L b	6	119	7	4	22½	23	26	12½	15¼	Nuesch D	5.40
2Apr04 8GP2	Supah Blitz	L b	4	116	4	8	61	61½	3½	33½	21½	Castro E	4.20
4Mar04 9FG1	Yessirgeneralsir	L	4	114	6	3	12	12	12	23	3nk	Figueroa O	14.20
27Mar04 7GG1	Snorter	L b	4	118	5	7	7½	72½	6½	43½	45¼	Flores D R	2.30
27Mar04 7GG3	Taste of Paradise	L	5	116	2	5	3½	3½	41½	54	53¼	Lovato A J	8.70
27Mar04 8DeD8	Winning Fans	L	4	113	8	2	41½	4½	5hd	6½	62	Jacinto J	52.10
14Mar04 9FG2	Mountain General	L b	6	119	3	1	5hd	5½	74	73	71¼	Martin E M Jr	6.50
14Mar04 9OP3	Pie N Burger	L b	6	118	1	6	8	8	8	8	8	Theriot H J II	2.80

OFF AT 5:14 Start Good . Won driving. Track sloppy.

TIME :23^1, :46^1, 1:10, 1:22^3, 1:35^3 (:23.32, :46.28, 1:10.15, 1:22.68, 1:35.64)

$2 Mutuel Prices:

7 – KELA	12.80	6.20	4.40
4 – SUPAH BLITZ		5.60	3.60
6 – YESSIRGENERALSIR			5.40

$2 EXACTA 7–4 PAID $69.40 $2 QUINELLA 4–7 PAID $43.20
$2 TRIFECTA 7–4–6 PAID $777.20 $2 SUPERFECTA 7–4–6–5 PAID $3,330.00

B. h, (Mar), by Numerous – Bolshoi Comedy , by Sovereign Dancer . Trainer Mitchell Mike. Bred by Cypress Farms 1991 (Ky).

KELA tracked the pace while three wide, was asked near the five-sixteenths marker, engaged the leader leaving the far turn, took the lead in upper stretch, and drew away under strong left hand urging. SUPAH BLITZ was unhurried towards the rear of the field, rallied between rivals midway through the far turn, came out for the stretch drive, and finished willingly to be second best. YESSIRGENERALSIR set the clear pace through solid fractions, remained clear through the far turn, lost the lead in upper stretch, and tired in the final furlong. SNORTER raced four wide on the first turn, was reserved near the back of the field, came between rivals leaving the far turn, and lacked the needed rally. TASTE OF PARADISE was jostled in the hind quarters near the seven furlong marker, settled on the inside, saved ground throughout, and failed to rally. WINNING FANS went four wide on the first turn, raced near the middle of the pack, went four wide on the second turn, and came up empty. MOUNTAIN GENERAL settled off the pace, was roused while saving ground on the far turn, and failed to respond. PIE N BURGER was checked sharply near the seven furlong marker, dropped to the rear of the field, and trailed.

Owners– 1, Manoogian Jay; 2, Bee Bee Stables Inc and Tortora Jacqueline; 3, Jackson James D; 4, Gary and Mary West Stables Inc; 5, Bloom David B; 6, Cuadra Valedor Inc; 7, Asmussen Keith I; 8, Kagele Brothers Inc

Trainers– 1, Mitchell Mike; 2, Tortora Emanuel; 3, Keen Dallas E; 4, Frankel Robert; 5, Stidham Michael; 6, Martinez Eleuterio Jr; 7, Asmussen Steven M; 8, Norman Cole

---

$2 Pick Three (8–10–7) Paid $1,017.40 ; Pick Three Pool $6,783 .

SEVENTH RACE
Hollywood
APRIL 25, 2004

1 MILE. (Turf) (1.323) 43RD RUNNING OF THE WILSHIRE HANDICAP. Grade III. Purse $100,000 FOR FILLIES AND MARES THREE YEARS OLD AND UPWARD. By subscription of $100 each on or before Wednesday, April 14. $1,000 additional to start, with $100,000 added. The added money and all fees to be divided 60% to the winner, 20% to second, 12% to third, 6%to fourth and 2% to fifth. A trophy will be presented to the winning owner. Nominations Closed Wednesday, April 14th, 2004 with 19.

Value of Race: $110,900 Winner $66,540; second $22,180; third $13,308; fourth $6,654; fifth $2,218. Mutuel Pool $512,130.00 Exacta Pool $260,398.00 Quinella Pool $29,503.00 Trifecta Pool $297,530.00 Superfecta Pool $124,684.00

Last Raced	Horse	M/Eqt.	A.	Wt	PP	St	¼	½	¾	Str	Fin	Jockey	Odds $1
29Dec03 5SA3	Spring Star-FR	LB	5	117	9	5	21½	22	21½	1½	12½	Solis A	6.60
11Mar04 3SA1	Quero Quero	LB	4	115	4	4	6½	81	9	61	2no	Espinoza V	11.40
28Mar04 2SA2	Dublino	LB	5	120	1	6	5hd	6½	6½	4hd	31	Valdivia J Jr	2.40
25Oct03 6SA12	Dimitrova	LB	4	122	5	3	42	31	31½	31½	4½	Desormeaux K J	1.80
27Mar04 9SA1	Katdogawn-GB	LB	4	118	7	8	9	7hd	5½	5½	51	Smith M E	4.90
17May03 3Hol1	Makeup Artist	LB	4	119	3	9	8½	9	8hd	83	6½	Valenzuela P A	13.20
4Apr04 8SA8	Fudge Fatale	LB	4	114	8	1	11½	11½	11	22½	71½	Ruis M	54.50
27Mar04 9SA2	Fun House	LB	5	117	2	2	3hd	4hd	4hd	7hd	84½	Santiago Javier	13.40
31Mar04 7SA2	Esmay-Aus	LB	5	116	6	7	71½	51	71½	9	9	Flores D R	87.20

OFF AT 4:27 Start Good. Won driving. Course firm.

TIME :232, :464, 1:102, 1:22, 1:332 (:23.48, :46.95, 1:10.49, 1:22.04, 1:33.41)

$2 Mutuel Prices:				
	9 – SPRING STAR–FR	15.20	8.00	4.80
	4 – QUERO QUERO		9.60	4.60
	1 – DUBLINO			3.00

$1 EXACTA 9–4 PAID $72.90 $2 QUINELLA 4–9 PAID $87.80
$1 TRIFECTA 9–4–1 PAID $333.50 $1 SUPERFECTA 9–4–1–5 PAID $1,118.20

B. m, (May), by Danehill – L'Irlandaise, by Irish River–Fr. Trainer Mandella Richard. Bred by Wertheimer Et Frere (Fr).

SPRING STAR (FR) reluctant to load, pulled her way along and angled in outside a rival early, stalked off the rail, bid outside the pacesetter into the stretch and gained a short lead, then drew clear under some urging and good handling. QUERO QUERO chased between horses or outside a rival, swung four wide into the stretch, came in a bit in deep stretch but closed gamely for the place. DUBLINO saved ground stalking the pace, went between horses on the second turn, drifted out some past midstretch, then split foes late and just missed second. DIMITROVA stalked the pace outside a rival then a bit off the rail on the second turn, came out some in the stretch, was between foes in deep stretch and lacked the needed late kick. KATDOGAWN (GB) chased outside or off the rail, launched a bid four wide on the second turn and into the stretch, steadied when crowded in deep stretch and could not offer the necessary response. MAKEUP ARTIST hesitated in a bit of a slow start, saved ground off the pace, came out into the stretch and lacked the needed rally. FUDGE FATALE sped to the early lead and angled in, set the pace inside, battled inside the winner into the stretch and to midstretch, then weakened. FUN HOUSE saved ground stalking the pace to the stretch and also weakened. ESMAY (AUS) was in a good position stalking the pace three deep then between foes on the second turn, dropped back into the stretch and had little left.

Owners– 1, Wertheimer and Frere; 2, Old Friends Inc; 3, Geringer Robert Klein Michael and Naify Marsha et al; 4, Higgins Joseph; 5, Cuchna John R Jim Ford Inc and Pearson Deron; 6, Krikorian George; 7, Greely John J III; 8, Winchell Thoroughbreds LLC; 9, Burns Mike and Kolbe Al

Trainers– 1, Mandella Richard; 2, Lobo Paulo H; 3, De Seroux Laura; 4, Drysdale Neil; 5, Cassidy James; 6, Shirreffs John; 7, Greely C Beau; 8, McAnally Ronald; 9, Carno Louis R

$2 Daily Double (8–9) Paid $153.80 ; Daily Double Pool $33,276 .
$1 Pick Three (6–8–9) Paid $600.10 ; Pick Three Pool $93,230 .

NINTH RACE
Churchill
APRIL 29, 2004

7½ FURLONGS. (1.28) 49TH RUNNING OF THE LA TROIENNE. Grade III. Purse $100,000 FOR FILLIES, THREE YEARS OLD. By subscription of $100 each on or before April 10, 2004 or by Supplementary Nomination of $5,000 at time of entry. $500 to pass the entry box; $500 additional to start, with $100,000 added of which 62% of all monies to theowner of the winner, 20% to second, 10% to third, 5% to fourth and 3% fifth. Weight 122 lbs. Non–winners of $50,000 allowed 2 lbs.; three races other than maiden or claiming, 4 lbs.; two races other than maiden or claming, 6 lbs.; a race other than maiden or claiming, 8 lbs. Starters to be named through the entry box at the usual time of closing. Trophy to winning owner. Closed Saturday, April 10, 2004 with 52 nominations.

Value of Race: $112,200 Winner $69,564; second $22,440; third $11,220; fourth $5,610; fifth $3,366. Mutuel Pool $436,586.00 Exacta Pool $272,905.00 Trifecta Pool $204,087.00 Superfecta Pool $56,431.00

Last Raced	Horse	M/Eqt.	A.	Wt	PP	St	¼	½	Str	Fin	Jockey	Odds $1
21Mar04 8SA1	Friendly Michelle	L b	3	118	3	6	1hd	1hd	36½	1½	Solis A	2.40
14Mar04 9Tam1	Ender's Sister	L	3	122	4	3	21½	21½	2½	2hd	Day P	4.20
20Mar04 9Aqu1	Bohemian Lady	L	3	122	6	5	31	31½	1hd	35¾	Prado E S	1.00
17Apr04 4Kee1	Pick of the Pack	L b	3	118	1	1	7	52	41	42¼	Bejarano R	47.00
16Apr04 8PrM1	Saltwater Runner	L f	3	120	2	2	61½	7	53	57¾	McKee J	6.50
8Apr04 8Kee4	Ktestormedthebird	L b	3	116	5	7	42	45	68	614¾	Albarado R J	20.70
20Mar04 9TP6	Fond	L	3	118	7	4	53½	62	7	7	Perret C	45.50

OFF AT 5:00 Start Good. Won driving. Track fast.

TIME :213, :44, 1:084, 1:281 (:21.77, :44.09, 1:08.86, 1:28.26)

$2 Mutuel Prices:				
	3 – FRIENDLY MICHELLE	6.80	3.80	2.60
	4 – ENDER'S SISTER		4.20	2.60
	6 – BOHEMIAN LADY			2.20

$2 EXACTA 3–4 PAID $30.60 $2 TRIFECTA 3–4–6 PAID $65.20
$2 SUPERFECTA 3–4–6–1 PAID $425.20

Ch. f, (May), by Artax – Valiant Jewel, by Buckley Boy. Trainer Baffert Bob. Bred by Ronald Fein (Ky).

FRIENDLY MICHELLE went up to contest the pace from near the inside early, gained a slight edge, was headed approaching the final quarter from the outside by ENDER'S SISTER, dropped back into third position nearing the final furlong, then, after the rider switched the whip to his left hand a sixteenth out, dug in gamely while continuing inside to prevail. ENDER'S SISTER, briefly in front after the start, allowed the winner the lead soon after, pressed FRIENDLY MICHELLE three or four wide, inched to the front approaching the stretch, then wasn't good enough. BOHEMIAN LADY, always well placed while tracking the top two four or five wide, moved boldly to reach the front at the eighth pole, then failed to sustain the needed momentum. PICK OF THE PACK, outrun inside to the turn, swung out six or seven wide entering the upper stretch but lacked a late response. SALTWATER RUNNER raced near the inside throughout and failed to rally. KATESTORMEDTHEBIRD bobbled sharply at the start, settled in behind the leaders, moved out five wide for the stretch run and was empty. FOND tired on the turn.

Owners– 1, Friendly Ed; 2, Green Lantern Stables LLC Richard Mason; 3, Padua Stables; 4, Durst Murray; 5, Lakin Lewis G; 6, Rafter L Stables; 7, Dogwood Stable

Trainers– 1, Baffert Bob; 2, Arnold George R II; 3, Pletcher Todd A; 4, Flint Bernard S; 5, Holthus Robert E; 6, Lukas D Wayne; 7, Weaver George

---

$2 Pick Three (6–2–3) Paid $93.00 ; Pick Three Pool $47,286 .

SEVENTH RACE
Churchill
APRIL 30, 2004

5 FURLONGS. (Turf) (.55^{2}) 10TH RUNNING OF THE AEGON TURF SPRINT. Grade III. Purse $100,000 FOR THREE-YEAR-OLDS AND UPWARD. By subscription of $100 each on or before April 10, 2004. $500 to pass entry box, $500 additional to start. Three year olds 115 lbs.; Older 122 lbs. Non-winners of $50,000 on the turf in 2003–2004 allowed 2 lbs.; a sweepstakes on the turf in 2003–2004, 4 lbs; $30,000 on the turf since July 4, 6 lbs.; three races other than maiden, claiming or starter on the turf, 8 lbs. (If this race is taken off of the turf it will be downgraded one grade level for this running only in accordance with American Graded Stakes Committee policy).

Value of Race: $114,700 Winner $71,114; second $22,940; third $11,470; fourth $5,735; fifth $3,441. Mutuel Pool $1,194,349.00 Exacta Pool $916,720.00 Trifecta Pool $649,307.00 Superfecta Pool $194,477.00

Last Raced	Horse	M/Eqt.	A.	Wt	PP	St	$\frac{3}{16}$	$\frac{3}{8}$	Str	Fin	Jockey	Odds $1
4Apr04 ^{2}SA^{2}	Lydgate	L	4	114	11	8	7^{hd}	$7^{\frac{1}{2}}$	4^{1}	1^{1}	Day P	7.70
12Mar04 ^{2}SA^{7}	Mighty Beau	L	5	117	2	2	2^{1}	$1^{\frac{1}{2}}$	$1^{1\frac{1}{2}}$	$2^{\frac{1}{2}}$	Sellers S J	3.30
10Apr04 ^{7}Kee^{3}	Banned in Boston	L	4	114	3	5	6^{2}	$5^{\frac{1}{2}}$	5^{2}	$3^{1\frac{3}{4}}$	Blanc B	4.20
10Apr04 ^{7}Kee^{4}	Cat Singer	L	4	114	7	7	$8^{2\frac{1}{2}}$	8^{1}	$6^{\frac{1}{2}}$	$4^{\frac{1}{2}}$	Albarado R J	9.40
11Apr04 ^{9}GP^{2}	Take AchanceOnMe	L bf	6	114	8	11	10^{2}	10^{4}	9^{1}	5^{nk}	Santana J Z	6.50
9Apr04 ^{4}Kee^{2}	Seventh Inning	L	4	114	10	6	$5^{\frac{1}{2}}$	$3^{\frac{1}{2}}$	3^{1}	$6^{\frac{1}{2}}$	Borel C H	9.70
10Apr04 ^{7}Kee^{8}	Fiscally Speaking	L f	5	122	9	10	$9^{1\frac{1}{2}}$	9^{2}	8^{hd}	$7^{\frac{1}{2}}$	Santos J A	17.00
10Apr04 ^{7}Kee^{5}	Day Trader	L b	5	114	4	3	$3^{\frac{1}{2}}$	$2^{\frac{1}{2}}$	2^{hd}	8^{hd}	Prado E S	9.80
29Nov03 ^{9}CD^{4}	Testify	L	7	122	6	9	11	11	11	9^{1}	McKee J	12.90
10Apr04 ^{7}Kee^{2}	Chosen Chief	L b	5	114	1	4	4^{hd}	$6^{\frac{1}{2}}$	$7^{1\frac{1}{2}}$	$10^{11\frac{1}{4}}$	Butler D P	6.10
27Mar04 ^{8}FG^{7}	Bayou Buster	L	5	114	5	1	$1^{\frac{1}{2}}$	$4^{\frac{1}{2}}$	10^{2}	11	Perret C	42.30

OFF AT 3:05 Start Good . Won driving. Course good.

TIME $:21^{4}$, $:44^{3}$, $:56^{2}$ (:21.84, :44.60, :56.56)

$2 Mutuel Prices:				
	11 – LYDGATE	17.40	7.40	4.60
	2 – MIGHTY BEAU		5.00	3.20
	3 – BANNED IN BOSTON			3.60

$2 EXACTA 11–2 PAID $76.20 $2 TRIFECTA 11–2–3 PAID $438.60
$2 SUPERFECTA 11–2–3–7 PAID $2,282.80

B. c, (Feb), by Pulpit – Mariuka , by Danzig . Trainer Harty Eoin. Bred by Kennelot Stables Limited (Ky).

LYDGATE worked her way in four wide concluding the backstretch, angled six abreast when straightened for the drive, then closed under solid right-handed encouragement to prevail. MIGHTY BEAU went up outside front-running BAYOU BUSTER early, took over on the turn, opened a clear advantage in the upper stretch but couldn't handle the winner late. BANNED IN BOSTON, within striking distance while racing in behind the leaders to the stretch, eased out between foes six wide for the drive and was slowly gaining. CAT SINGER came out at the start bumping TAKE ACHANCE ON ME, followed the leaders in a striking position five or six wide into the final furlong and lacked a serious late account. TAKE ACHANCE ON ME, bumped at the start by CAT SINGER and forced out on FISCALLY SPEAKING, raced four or five wide, came to the extreme outside to be 10 abreast for the drive and offered a mild gain. SEVENTH INNING followed the leaders in a striking position four or five wide into the final furlong and flattened out. FISCALLY SPEAKING broke awkwardly and sluggishly, was bumped and checked afterwards, raced eight wide early, edged in around the turn, came out again to be eight or nine wide for the stretch run and improved position while unable to menace. DAY TRADER came out and brushed the side of the gate, followed the leaders four or five wide, loomed between foes for the last eighth but came up empty. TESTIFY, outrun from the beginning and three or four wide, eased out nine wide for the drive but failed to rally. CHOSEN CHIEF raced in contention near the inside, was steadied behind rivals nearing the lane, angled out three or four wide and weakened. BAYOU BUSTER sprinted clear early, lost the advantage midway on the turn to MIGHTY BEAU from the outside and faded thereafter.

Owners– 1, Darley Stable; 2, M C Stable Michael P Cloonan and Anthony Carolan; 3, Hubbard R D; 4, Sugar Jr Joe and Daniels Eugene; 5, Wilbur Dale and Joan Parker Everett; 6, Tom Boy Stable; 7, Whitham Janis R; 8, Overbrook Farm; 9, Robert S Mitchell Trust; 10, Lynch Emmy; 11, Cohn Alice and Levy Robert P

Trainers– 1, Harty Eoin; 2, Asmussen Steven M; 3, Hennig John K; 4, Gabriel Toni; 5, Aguirre Anthony; 6, Amoss Thomas; 7, Nafzger Carl A; 8, Lukas D Wayne; 9, Morse Randy L; 10, Porter Ron; 11, Cohn Alice G

$2 Pick Three (8–2–11) Paid $691.80 ; Pick Three Pool $147,369 .

EIGHTH RACE
Churchill
APRIL 30, 2004

1$\frac{1}{16}$ MILES. (1.41^{3}) 19TH RUNNING OF THE LOUISVIILLE BREEDERS' CUP HANDICAP. Grade II. Purse $300,000 (includes $100,000 BC – Breeders' Cup) A HANDICAP FOR FILLIES AND MARES THREE YEARS OLD AND UPWARD. By subscription of $300 each on or before April 10, 2004 or by Supplementary Nomination of $15,000 each by the closing of entries on April, 23, 2004. $1,500 to pass the entry box; $1,500 additional to start, with $200,000 added and an additional $100,000 from the Breeders' Cup Fund for Cup Nominees only. The host association's added monies to be divided 62% to the owner of the winner, 20% to second, 10% to third, 5% to fourth and 3% to fifth. Breeders' Cup Fund monies also correspondingly divided providing a Breeders' Cup nominee has finished in an awarded position. Any Breeders' Cup Fund monies not awarded will revert back to the Fund. Weights to be announced April 24. Trophy to winning ownergiven by Breeders' Cup Ltd. Closed April 10, 2004 with 25 nominations.

Value of Race: $327,000 Winner $202,740; second $65,400; third $32,700; fourth $16,350; fifth $9,810. Mutuel Pool $1,297,663.00 Exacta Pool $809,695.00 Trifecta Pool $544,790.00 Superfecta Pool $152,977.00

Last Raced	Horse	M/Eqt.	A.	Wt	PP	St	¼	½	¾	Str	Fin	Jockey	Odds $1
14Mar04 ^{6}GP^{3}	Lead Story	L	5	116	3	5	6	6	$4^{1\frac{1}{2}}$	$1^{1\frac{1}{2}}$	$1^{\frac{3}{4}}$	Borel C H	10.00
7Apr04 ^{8}Kee^{3}	Yell	L	4	114	1	3	4^{3}	3^{hd}	$3^{\frac{1}{2}}$	3^{1}	2^{3}	Day P	5.20
16Apr04 ^{9}Kee^{2}	Cat Fighter	L b	4	116	4	1	1^{1}	$1^{1\frac{1}{2}}$	$1^{\frac{1}{2}}$	2^{1}	$3^{3\frac{1}{4}}$	Solis A	6.80
14Mar04 ^{6}GP^{1}	Sightseek	L	5	122	2	4	3^{hd}	2^{hd}	2^{1}	4^{hd}	$4^{2\frac{1}{4}}$	Bailey J D	0.40
4Apr04 ^{10}OP^{1}	La Reason	L f	4	111	5	2	5^{3}	$5^{2\frac{1}{2}}$	5^{4}	5^{15}	$5^{25\frac{3}{4}}$	Shepherd J	30.30
28Nov03 ^{9}Aqu^{3}	Pocus Hocus	L b	6	115	6	6	$2^{\frac{1}{2}}$	$4^{2\frac{1}{2}}$	6	6	6	Santos J A	12.30

OFF AT 3:54 Start Good . Won driving. Track sloppy.

TIME :24^{1}, :47^{4}, 1:12^{3}, 1:37^{4}, 1:44^{1} (:24.38, :47.89, 1:12.77, 1:37.96, 1:44.37)

$2 Mutuel Prices:				
	3 – LEAD STORY	22.00	8.20	6.20
	1 – YELL		7.20	5.40
	4 – CAT FIGHTER			5.20

$2 EXACTA 3–1 PAID $80.20 $2 TRIFECTA 3–1–4 PAID $285.20
$2 SUPERFECTA 3–1–4–2 PAID $342.60

Ch. m, (Apr), by Editor's Note – Gwenjinsky , by Seattle Dancer . Trainer Nafzger Carl A. Bred by Cabotaba Partnership (Ky).

LEAD STORY, reserved along the inside soon after the start, remained inside while advancing on the far turn, eased out between rivals four wide at the quarter-mile ground, wrested command, opened a clear advantage and held sway under stout left-handed encouragement. YELL, in and along the inside from early on, angled outside the winner for the drive and was slowly gaining late. CAT FIGHTER gained the lead early, raced near the inside, made the pace until entering the stretch and weakened. SIGHTSEEK, forwardly placed between foes early, continued between rivals to stick her head in front for a stride entering the upper stretch but faltered soon after. LA REASON, four or five wide, moved to the two path on the backstretch, came out again to follow the winner five or six wide into the lane but flattened out. POCUS HOCUS broke sluggishly and awkwardly, tracked the pace four wide for a half, weakened thereafter and wasn't persevered with in the drive when hopelessly beaten.

Owners– 1, Miles A Stevens Jr; 2, Claiborne Farm and Dilschneider Adele B; 3, Never Tell Farm Audry and Richard Haisfield and John G Sikura; 4, Juddmonte Farms Inc; 5, K and K Racing Stable LLC; 6, Moore Susan and John

Trainers– 1, Nafzger Carl A; 2, McGaughey III Claude R; 3, Baffert Bob; 4, Frankel Robert; 5, Vance David R; 6, Jerkens James A

Scratched– My Ro (13Mar04 ^{11}GP ^{7})

$2 Pick Three (2–11–3) Paid $1,187.80 ; Pick Three Pool $161,317 .

NINTH RACE
Churchill
APRIL 30, 2004

1$\frac{1}{16}$ MILES. (Turf) (1.40^{4}) 13TH RUNNING OF THE CROWN ROYAL AMERICAN TURF. Grade III. Purse $100,000 FOR THREE–YEAR–OLDS. By subscription of $100 each on or before April 10, 2004 or by Supplementary Nomination of $5,000 at time of entry. $500 to pass the entry box; $500 additional to start. Weight 123 lbs. Non–winners of a sweepstakes on the turf allowed2 lbs.; three races other than maiden or claiming, 4 lbs.; two races other than maiden or claiming, 6 lbs.; a race other than maiden or claiming, 8 lbs. If the race is moved to the main track after the time of closing, a horse may scratch for any reasonat any time up to 15 minutes prior to post time for the race preceding this race or thereafter with a valid physical reason and approved by stewards. Entry fee shall be refunded for scratches made in compliance with the above conditions. (If this race istaken off the turf it will be downgraded one grade level for this running only in accordance with American Graded Stakes Committee policy). Closed April 10, 2004 with 48 nominations.

Value of Race: $113,800 Winner $70,556; second $22,760; third $11,380; fourth $5,690; fifth $3,414. Mutuel Pool $1,511,713.00 Exacta Pool $1,030,605.00 Trifecta Pool $823,769.00 Superfecta Pool $253,888.00

Last Raced	Horse	M/Eqt.	A.	Wt	PP	St	¼	½	¾	Str	Fin	Jockey	Odds $1
21Feb04 ^{11}GP^{1}	Kitten's Joy	L	3	123	4	9	9	$8^{2\frac{1}{2}}$	$4^{\frac{1}{2}}$	$1^{\frac{1}{2}}$	$1^{2\frac{1}{2}}$	Bailey J D	1.10
15Apr04 ^{8}Kee^{1}	Prince Arch	L b	3	123	3	7	7^{hd}	5^{hd}	6^{2}	4^{hd}	$2^{\frac{1}{2}}$	Blanc B	3.60
3Apr04 ^{6}Kee^{1}	Capo	L b	3	117	2	1	1^{hd}	$1^{\frac{1}{2}}$	$1^{1\frac{1}{2}}$	$2^{2\frac{1}{2}}$	$3^{2\frac{1}{4}}$	Prado E S	12.80
15Apr04 ^{8}Kee^{2}	Brass Hat	L b	3	117	9	4	$3^{\frac{1}{2}}$	$3^{\frac{1}{2}}$	3^{1}	3^{hd}	4^{1}	Lumpkins J	13.50
17Apr04 ^{9}Kee^{6}	El Prado Rob	L	3	117	5	2	4^{1}	4^{hd}	5^{2}	$5^{\frac{1}{2}}$	$5^{1\frac{3}{4}}$	Sellers S J	15.40
10Apr04 ^{5}OP^{3}	Level Playingfield	L b	3	119	1	5	$8^{\frac{1}{2}}$	$7^{\frac{1}{2}}$	8^{4}	$7^{2\frac{1}{2}}$	$6^{\frac{1}{2}}$	McKee J	37.80
2Apr04 ^{9}Kee^{4}	Grand Heritage	L b	3	123	6	3	2^{1}	$2^{\frac{1}{2}}$	2^{hd}	6^{3}	7^{4}	Day P	5.20
3Apr04 ^{4}Kee^{1}	Knox	L b	3	117	8	6	$6^{\frac{1}{2}}$	$6^{\frac{1}{2}}$	$7^{2\frac{1}{2}}$	8^{3}	$8^{\frac{3}{4}}$	Santos J A	9.00
10Apr04 ^{11}OP^{3}	Archie B	L b	3	115	7	8	5^{hd}	9	9	9	9	Albarado R J	46.40

OFF AT 4:47 Start Good . Won driving. Course good.

TIME :24^{3}, :49^{2}, 1:13^{1}, 1:37, 1:43^{1} (:24.70, :49.43, 1:13.37, 1:37.12, 1:43.31)

$2 Mutuel Prices:				
	4 – KITTEN'S JOY	4.20	2.80	2.60
	3 – PRINCE ARCH		3.40	2.80
	2 – CAPO			4.80

$2 EXACTA 4–3 PAID $13.40 $2 TRIFECTA 4–3–2 PAID $92.60
$2 SUPERFECTA 4–3–2–9 PAID $555.00

Ch. c, (May), by El Prado–Ire – Kitten's First , by Lear Fan . Trainer Romans Dale. Bred by Kenneth L Ramsey & Sarah K Ramsey (Ky).

KITTEN'S JOY ducked in at the start and bumped the side of the gate, was checked and bumped soon after by PRINCE ARCH, eased back last, swung out six wide while under rating on the backstretch, continued in that position on the course while advancing into the stretch and drove clear under hand urging. PRINCE ARCH broke out on the winner at the start, settled near the inside, raced closer than usual early, inched up two or three wide on the far turn, angled five wide when straightened for the drive and finished willingly for second position. CAPO gained a slight edge inside, raced under light rating while dueling with GRAND HERITAGE, shook off that one nearing the lane, held on well until about the final furlong and weakened. BRASS HAT went up soon after the break to track the leaders four or five wide, remained prominent into the upper stretch but flattened out late. EL PRADO ROB, bumped just after the start by the winner when that one was forced out, settled within easy striking distance while in behind the leaders, remained prominent in behind pacesetting CAPO into the final furlong but was empty thereafter. LEVEL PLAYINGFIELD, rated along three or four wide for six furlongs, angled seven wide into the lane but failed to rally. GRAND HERITAGE went up early to contest the pace outside of CAPO, battled close up to the final quarter and faltered. KNOX, bumped at the start by ARCHIE B, tired after five furlongs. ARCHIE B came out at the start bumping KNOX at the start and tired on the far turn.

Owners– 1, Ramsey Kenneth L and Sarah K; 2, Cottrell Raymond H Sr; 3, Eaglestone Farm; 4, Bradley Fred F; 5, LaPenta Robert V; 6, Fly Racing LLC; 7, Firestone Diane and B R; 8, Runnymede Farm and Hancock III Arthur B; 9, Spence James C

Trainers– 1, Romans Dale; 2, McPeek Kenneth G; 3, Nafzger Carl A; 4, Bradley William; 5, Zito Nicholas P; 6, Holthus Robert E; 7, Mott William I; 8, McPeek Kenneth G; 9, Nicks Morris G

$2 Pick Three (11–3–4) Paid $782.80 ; Pick Three Pool $130,015 .

TENTH RACE
Churchill
APRIL 30, 2004

1⅛ MILES. (1.47^{1}) 130TH RUNNING OF THE KENTUCKY OAKS. Grade I. Purse $500,000 FILLIES THREE YEARS OLD. By subscription of $100 each on or before February 14, 2004, or by SUPPLEMENTARY NOMINATION OF $2,500 AT TIME OF ENTRY. $2,500 to pass entry box; $2,500 additional to start. Weight 121 lbs. The maximum number of starters for the Kentucky Oaks will be limited to 14. If more than 14 entries pass the entry box, preference will be given to those horses that have accumulated the highest earnings in the Graded Stakes races, including all monies actually paid for performance in such Graded Stakes Races. For purposes of this preference the graded status of each race shall be the graded status assigned to the race by the International Cataloguing Standards Committee in Part I of the International Cataloguing Standards as published by The Jockey Club Information Systems, Incorporated each year. Should additional starters be needed to bring the field to 14 the remaining starters shall be determined at the Closing with preference given to those horses that have accumulated and actually been paid the highest earnings in Non–Restricted Sweepstakes.

Value of Race: $572,000 Winner $354,640; second $114,400; third $57,200; fourth $28,600; fifth $17,160. Mutuel Pool $3,213,237.00 Exacta Pool $1,943,055.00 Trifecta Pool $1,597,617.00 Superfecta Pool $528,870.00

Last Raced	Horse	M/Eqt.	A.	Wt	PP	St	¼	½	¾	Str	Fin	Jockey	Odds $1
3Apr04 ^{9}Kee^{2}	Ashado	L	3	121	1	3	3^{hd}	$2^{\frac{1}{2}}$	2^{2}	$2^{2\frac{1}{2}}$	$1^{1\frac{1}{4}}$	Velazquez J R	2.30
9Apr04 ^{10}OP^{2}	Island Sand	L b	3	121	3	10	$10^{1\frac{1}{2}}$	7^{hd}	5^{hd}	3^{3}	$2^{1\frac{3}{4}}$	Thompson T J	16.80
3Apr04 ^{9}Kee^{1}	Madcap Escapade	L	3	121	5	2	1^{3}	$1^{4\frac{1}{2}}$	1^{4}	1^{hd}	$3^{1\frac{1}{4}}$	Bailey J D	3.40
8Apr04 ^{8}Kee^{1}	Victory U. S. A.	L	3	121	7	1	$2^{\frac{1}{2}}$	$3^{\frac{1}{2}}$	6^{2}	$4^{1\frac{1}{2}}$	$4^{1\frac{1}{2}}$	Day P	10.50
13Mar04 ^{8}SA^{4}	Hollywood Story	L b	3	121	2	9	$7^{\frac{1}{2}}$	8^{3}	7^{3}	5^{3}	$5^{3\frac{3}{4}}$	Espinoza V	25.30
13Mar04 ^{8}SA^{3}	A. P. Adventure	L	3	121	8	11	11	11	9^{2}	6^{hd}	$6^{\frac{1}{2}}$	Smith M E	6.30
9Apr04 ^{10}OP^{3}	Stellar Jayne	L b	3	121	11	7	$9^{\frac{1}{2}}$	9^{hd}	8^{2}	$7^{\frac{1}{2}}$	$7^{1\frac{1}{2}}$	Albarado R J	40.80
9Apr04 ^{10}OP^{1}	House of Fortune	L	3	121	4	4	6^{2}	$5^{\frac{1}{2}}$	3^{hd}	8^{3}	8^{hd}	Sellers S J	8.30
3Apr04 ^{9}Kee^{3}	Last Song	L	3	121	9	6	$8^{\frac{1}{2}}$	10^{3}	10^{1}	9^{2}	$9^{15\frac{3}{4}}$	Prado E S	11.10
13Mar04 ^{8}SA^{1}	Silent Sighs	L b	3	121	6	5	$4^{1\frac{1}{2}}$	$4^{2\frac{1}{2}}$	4^{hd}	10^{8}	$10^{4\frac{1}{4}}$	Flores D R	7.90
20Mar04 ^{9}TP^{1}	Class Above	L b	3	121	10	8	5^{hd}	$6^{2\frac{1}{2}}$	11	11	11	Nakatani C S	35.80

OFF AT 5:45 Start Good . Won driving. Track muddy.

TIME :23^{1}, :46, 1:09^{4}, 1:36^{3}, 1:50^{4} (:23.29, :46.00, 1:09.99, 1:36.73, 1:50.81)

$2 Mutuel Prices:				
	1 – ASHADO	6.60	4.20	3.00
	3 – ISLAND SAND		12.00	5.80
	6 – MADCAP ESCAPADE			3.60

$2 EXACTA 1–3 PAID $126.60 $2 TRIFECTA 1–3–6 PAID $492.80
$2 SUPERFECTA 1–3–6–8 PAID $3,824.80

Dk. b or br. f, (Feb), by Saint Ballado – Goulash , by Mari's Book . Trainer Pletcher Todd A. Bred by Aaron U Jones & Marie D Jones (Ky).

ASHADO, under light restraint from early on, raced in behind front-running MADCAP ESCAPADE around the first turn, eased outside of her entering the backstretch to be three wide while patiently handled, was put to a drive approaching the five-sixteenths pole, drifted in for a stride at the furlong pole when strapped right-handed, then, after the rider changed the stick to his left hand, was roused five times to edge clear late. ISLAND SAND, edgy in the gate prior to the start, leaned in after hopping at the break and bumped twice with HOLLYWOOD STORY, was checked lightly and maneuvered in behind horses, saved ground while rallying on the backstretch, split foes four wide approaching the stretch, loomed prominently five wide into the final furlong and was second best. MADCAP ESCAPADE gained the lead soon after the start, angled near the inside, drew well clear while accomplishing rapid early fractions, showed the way into the upper stretch and weakened. VICTORY U. S. A., away in good order, raced within easy striking distance while between rivals four wide, was with the winner while outside that one leaving the backstretch, but was empty when asked in the drive. HOLLYWOOD STORY, bumped twice after the start by ISLAND SAND and checked, raced near the inside into the backstretch, came out four or five wide, raced within striking distance to the stretch but lacked a closing account. A. P. ADVENTURE, outrun early and angled in three wide, moved out six abreast on the backstretch, worked her way to the rail on the far turn, angled three or four wide for the drive but failed to gain in the final furlong. STELLAR JAYNE edged in four wide on the first turn, came out two paths on the backstretch and failed to reach serious contention. HOUSE OF FORTUNE, never far back after moving near the inside, made a mild run midway on the far turn but faltered soon after. LAST SONG wasn't a factor. SILENT SIGHS followed the leaders in a striking position for six furlongs and weakened soon after. CLASS ABOVE bobbled lightly at the start and faded upon going a half.

Owners– 1, Starlight Stables Jack Wolf Paul Saylor and Johns Martin; 2, B A Man Inc; 3, Lunsford Bruce; 4, Van Meter Thomas F II; 5, Krikorian George; 6, Lewis Robert B and Beverly J; 7, Spendthrift Farm LLC Kidder Cole and Strong; 8, Arnold Zetcher LLC; 9, Buckram Oak Farm; 10, Wygod Mr and Mrs Martin J; 11, Padua Stables

Trainers– 1, Pletcher Todd A; 2, Jones J Larry; 3, Brothers Frank L; 4, Baffert Bob; 5, Shirreffs John; 6, Dollase Wallace; 7, Lukas D Wayne; 8, McAnally Ronald; 9, Nafzger Carl A; 10, Canani Julio C; 11, Baffert Bob

Scratched– Halfbridled (08Apr04 ^{8}Kee^{2})

$2 Pick Three (11–3–1/4) Paid $266.00 ; Pick Three Pool $275,114 .
$2 Pick Four (11–3–4–1/4) Paid $3,120.80 ; Pick Four Pool $333,278 .
$2 Pick Six (8–2–11–3–4–1/4) 6 Correct Paid $39,953.40 .
$2 Pick Six (8–2–11–3–4–1/4) 5 Correct Paid $416.00 ; Pick Six Pool $65,767 .
$2 Daily Double (4–1) Paid $14.20 ; Daily Double Pool $953,605 .

EIGHTH RACE
Aqueduct
MAY 1, 2004

1 MILE. (1.32^{2}) 129TH RUNNING OF THE WITHERS. Grade III. Purse $150,000 FOR THREE YEAR OLDS. By subscription of $150 each, which should accompany the nomination; $750 to pass the entry box; $750 to start. The purse to be divided 60% to the winner, 20% to second, 10% to third, 5% to fourth, 3% to fifth and 2% divided equally among the remaining finishers. 123 lbs. Non–winners of $60,000 in 2004 other than restricted stake allowed 3 lbs.; $45,000; or three races other than maiden or claiming, 5 lbs.; $30,000; or two races other than maiden or claiming, 7 lbs. A trophy will bepresented to the winning owner. Closed Saturday, April 17, 2004 with 27 Nominations.

Value of Race: $147,000 Winner $90,000; second $30,000; third $15,000; fourth $7,500; fifth $4,500. Mutuel Pool $774,086.00 Exacta Pool $580,572.00 Trifecta Pool $289,705.00

Last Raced	Horse	M/Eqt.	A.	Wt	PP	St	¼	½	¾	Str	Fin	Jockey	Odds $1
31Mar04 ^{8}GP^{2}	Medallist		3	116	3	3	$2^{2\frac{1}{2}}$	$1^{\frac{1}{2}}$	1^{hd}	$1^{1\frac{1}{2}}$	$1^{3\frac{1}{4}}$	Chavez J F	8.50
10Apr04 ^{7}Aqu^{1}	Forest Danger	L	3	123	5	1	1^{hd}	$2^{3\frac{1}{2}}$	$2^{3\frac{1}{2}}$	2^{1}	2^{1}	Coa E M	0.45
10Apr04 ^{5}OP^{1}	TwoDownAutomtic	L b	3	120	1	5	3^{hd}	$3^{\frac{1}{2}}$	4^{10}	$3^{3\frac{1}{2}}$	$3^{5\frac{1}{4}}$	Castellano J J	5.40
17Apr04 ^{9}Kee^{7}	Saratoga County	L bf	3	123	2	4	5	$4^{4\frac{1}{2}}$	3^{hd}	4^{20}	$4^{25\frac{1}{4}}$	Luzzi M J	5.30
24Mar04 ^{5}Aqu^{1}	One Tough Dude	L f	3	116	4	2	4^{hd}	5	5	5	5	Gryder A T	14.60

OFF AT 4:32 Start Good . Won driving. Track fast.

TIME :22^{2}, :44, 1:07^{4}, 1:34^{2} (:22.50, :44.06, 1:07.90, 1:34.49)

$2 Mutuel Prices:				
	4 – **MEDALLIST**	19.00	4.80	2.10
	1A– **FOREST DANGER**		2.40	2.10
	2 – **TWO DOWN AUTOMATIC**			2.10

$2 EXACTA 4–1 PAID $34.40 $2 TRIFECTA 4–1–2 PAID $114.00

Dk. b or br. c, (Feb), by Touch Gold – Santaria , by Star de Naskra . Trainer Jerkens H Allen. Bred by Robert N Clay & The Albert G Clay &1990 Revocable Trust (Ky).

MEDALLIST was sent up inside, contested a demanding pace along the rail, drew clear in upper stretch, drifted out despite right handed whipping and remained clear while continuing to drift out. FOREST DANGER contested the pace from the outside, angled in behind the winner in the stretch and stayed on gamely to the wire. TWO DOWN AUTOMATIC was urged along inside, chased the pace along the rail and lacked a rally. SARATOGA COUNTY chased the pace from the outside and tired in the stretch. ONE TOUGH DUDE dropped back early, raced inside and tired.

Owners– 1, Clay Robert N; 2, Jones Aaron U and Marie D; 3, Dapple Stable LLC; 4, Pollard Evelyn M; 5, Walsh Elizabeth

Trainers– 1, Jerkens H Allen; 2, Pletcher Todd A; 3, Asmussen Steven M; 4, Weaver George; 5, Hushion Michael E

Scratched– Shaniko (10Apr04 ^{5}Aqu^{1}) , Redskin Warrior (20Mar04 ^{7}Aqu^{5})

$2 Pick Three (4–7–4) Paid $368.00 ; Pick Three Pool $90,066 .

NINTH RACE
Aqueduct
MAY 1, 2004

$1\frac{1}{16}$ MILES. (Turf) (1.40^{4}) 27TH RUNNING OF THE BEAUGAY HANDICAP. Grade III. Purse $100,000 A HANDICAP FOR FILLIES AND MARES THREE YEARS OLD AND UPWARD. By subscription of $100 each, which should accompany the nomination; $500 to pass the entry box: $500 to start, with $100,000 added. The added money and all fees to be divided 60% to the winner,20% to second, 10% to third, 5% to fourth, 3% to fifth and 2% divided equally among the remaining finishers. Starters to be named at the closing time of entries. A trophy will be presented to the winning owner. The New York Racing Association reserves the right to transfer this race to the Main Track. In the event that this race is taken off the turf, it may be subject to downgrading upon review by the Graded Stakes Committee.Closed Saturday, April 17, 2004 with 30 Nominations. (If the Stewards considerit inadvisable to run this race on the turf course, this race will be run at One Mile on the main track.).

Value of Race: $110,000 Winner $66,000; second $22,000; third $11,000; fourth $5,500; fifth $3,300; sixth $1,100; seventh $1,100. Mutuel Pool $538,955.00 Exacta Pool $424,561.00 Trifecta Pool $304,824.00

Last Raced	Horse	M/Eqt.	A.	Wt	PP	St	¼	½	¾	Str	Fin	Jockey	Odds $1
4Apr04 ^{8}SA^{2}	Dedication-FR	L	5	118	2	4	3^{1}	3^{1}	3^{2}	$1^{\frac{1}{2}}$	$1^{\frac{1}{2}}$	Castellano J J	0.80
15Nov03 ^{9}CD^{2}	Aud	L	4	117	4	2	$4^{1\frac{1}{2}}$	4^{2}	$4^{\frac{1}{2}}$	2^{hd}	$2^{\frac{1}{2}}$	Peck B D	4.10
14Mar04 ^{10}Tam^{12}	Caught in the Rain	L	5	114	5	5	1^{1}	1^{2}	1^{hd}	$3^{\frac{1}{2}}$	3^{hd}	Chavez J F	11.70
13Mar04 ^{11}GP^{4}	Delta Princess	L	5	114	6	6	$6^{\frac{1}{2}}$	6^{2}	$5^{\frac{1}{2}}$	5^{hd}	$4^{1\frac{1}{4}}$	Luzzi M J	5.70
14Mar04 ^{10}Tam^{11}	Brandala	L	6	114	3	1	7	7	7	$6^{2\frac{1}{2}}$	$5^{\frac{3}{4}}$	Espinoza J L	44.50
8Nov03 ^{9}Aqu^{2}	Lojo	L	5	114	7	3	2^{1}	$2^{\frac{1}{2}}$	2^{1}	$4^{1\frac{1}{2}}$	$6^{1\frac{1}{4}}$	Bridgmohan S X	6.20
14Mar04 ^{11}GP^{1}	Bijou	L	5	113	1	7	$5^{\frac{1}{2}}$	5^{hd}	$6^{\frac{1}{2}}$	7	7	Gryder A T	30.75

OFF AT 5:00 Start Good . Won driving. Course good.

TIME :25^{3}, :51^{2}, 1:16^{3}, 1:40^{1}, 1:46^{1} (:25.75, :51.42, 1:16.66, 1:40.38, 1:46.38)

$2 Mutuel Prices:				
	2 – **DEDICATION–FR**	3.60	2.60	2.20
	4 – **AUD**		3.50	2.60
	5 – **CAUGHT IN THE RAIN**			3.30

$2 EXACTA 2–4 PAID $13.20 $2 TRIFECTA 2–4–5 PAID $69.00

Gr/ro. m, (Feb), by Highest Honor–Fr – Dissertation , by Sillery . Trainer Clement Christophe. Bred by Alec Head & Ghislaine Head (Fr).

DEDICATION (FR) raced close up outside while in hand, rallied three wide on the second turn, drifted in under right handed pressure in the stretch and prevailed under a drive. AUD was rated along inside, saved ground and finished gamely on the rail. CAUGHT IN THE RAIN quickly showed in front, set the pace while in hand and stayed on stubbornly to the wire. DELTA PRINCESS was outrun early, rallied nearing the stretch and finished well while between rivals in the drive. BRANDALA was outrun early, came wide into the stretch and lacked a rally. LOJO raced with the pace from the outside and tired in the final furlong. BIJOU was rated along inside, saved ground and lacked a rally.

Owners– 1, Head Ghislaine; 2, Willmott Stables Inc; 3, Heiligbrodt Stable New Walter L; 4, Khaled Saud b; 5, Sorin Stables; 6, Durocher Jr Lawrence and Hampshire Farm; 7, Zwerling Gary L

Trainers– 1, Clement Christophe; 2, Reinstedler Anthony; 3, Preciado Guadalupe; 4, Mott William I; 5, Walsh Thomas M; 6, Hills Timothy A; 7, Hauswald Philip M

FIFTH RACE
Churchill
MAY 1, 2004

7 FURLONGS. (1.20^{2}) 70TH RUNNING OF THE CHURCHILL DOWNS HANDICAP. Grade II. Purse $200,000 A HANDICAP FOR FOUR-YEAR-OLDS AND UPWARD. By subscription of $200 each on or before April 10, 2004 or by Supplementary Nomination of $10,000 by the closing of entries Friday, April 23, 2004. $1,000 to pass the entry box; $1,000 additional to start, with $200,000 added of which 62% of all monies to the owner of the winner, 20% to second, 10% to third, 5% to fourth and 3% to fifth. Starters to be named through the entry box at the usual time of closing. Trophy to winning owner. Closed Saturday, April 10, 2004 with 34 nominations.

Value of Race: $221,800 Winner $137,516; second $44,360; third $22,180; fourth $11,090; fifth $6,654. Mutuel Pool $1,797,241.00 Exacta Pool $1,359,245.00 Trifecta Pool $1,058,171.00 Superfecta Pool $254,426.00

Last Raced	Horse	M/Eqt.	A.	Wt	PP	St	¼	½	Str	Fin	Jockey	Odds $1
27Mar04 ^{11}GP^{1}	Speightstown	L	6	115	1	3	1^{1}	1^{1}	$1^{2\frac{1}{2}}$	$1^{3\frac{1}{2}}$	Velazquez J R	5.40
28Mar04 ^{8}SA^{1}	McCann's Mojave	L	4	117	4	1	2^{hd}	2^{hd}	$2^{1\frac{1}{2}}$	2^{2}	Valdivia J Jr	6.60
7Mar04 ^{8}SA^{2}	Publication	L b	5	116	7	2	$6^{2\frac{1}{2}}$	6^{3}	4^{1}	3^{2}	Desormeaux K J	4.00
31Jan04 ^{8}SA^{4}	Congaree	L	6	123	5	4	$5^{3\frac{1}{2}}$	$4^{\frac{1}{2}}$	3^{hd}	$4^{2\frac{1}{4}}$	Bailey J D	0.90
17Apr04 ^{8}Haw^{3}	New York Hero	L b	4	112	3	5	4^{1}	$5^{3\frac{1}{2}}$	5^{1}	$5^{2\frac{1}{2}}$	Arroyo N Jr	27.90
10Apr04 ^{5}Kee^{6}	Saint Waki	L	4	114	6	6	7	7	7	6^{2}	Borel C H	34.60
10Apr04 ^{5}Kee^{2}	Private Horde	L bf	5	117	2	7	$3^{\frac{1}{2}}$	3^{hd}	$6^{1\frac{1}{2}}$	7	Lumpkins J	7.00

OFF AT 1:22 Start Good . Won driving. Track good.

TIME :22^{2}, :45^{1}, 1:08^{4}, 1:21^{1} (:22.48, :45.27, 1:08.87, 1:21.38)

$2 Mutuel Prices:				
	1 – SPEIGHTSTOWN	12.80	5.60	3.60
	5 – MCCANN'S MOJAVE		6.60	4.20
	8 – PUBLICATION			3.40

$2 EXACTA 1–5 PAID $67.60 $2 TRIFECTA 1–5–8 PAID $190.20
$2 SUPERFECTA 1–5–8–6 PAID $416.20

Ch. h, (Feb), by Gone West – Silken Cat , by Storm Cat . Trainer Pletcher Todd A. Bred by Aaron U Jones & Marie Jones (Ky).

SPEIGHTSTOWN broke out a bit, sped to the early lead, set the pace toward the inside, inched away in the stretch and won clear under some urging. MCCANN'S MOJAVE stalked the pace three deep on the backstretch and into the turn, was between foes midway on the bend, continued off the rail into the stretch and was second best. PUBLICATION dropped back off the rail early then angled in, came out leaving the turn and a bit wide into the stretch and picked up the show. CONGAREE chased off the rail on the backstretch, advanced three deep on the turn to loom a threat, lacked the needed response, then drifted inward in deep stretch and weakened. NEW YORK HERO stalked the winner between horses on the backstretch and into the turn, continued outside a rival leaving the turn and also weakened. SAINT WAKI dropped back without early speed, angled in early and saved ground but was outrun. PRIVATE HORDE squeezed back at the start, pulled his way up inside to stalk the pace on the backstretch and turn but had little left for the stretch.

Owners– 1, Melnyk Eugene and Laura; 2, Alix Nikke Hunt and Mike Willman; 3, Mercedes Stables LLC E W Moody and Marie M Villa; 4, Stonerside Stable LLC; 5, Paraneck Stable; 6, Carey Thomas M; 7, Tucker Billy R

Trainers– 1, Pletcher Todd A; 2, Dorfman Leonard; 3, Cerin Vladimir; 4, Baffert Bob; 5, Pedersen Jennifer; 6, Vestal Peter M; 7, Cain Joe

Scratched– Key Deputy (06Mar04 ^{6}GP ^{1})

$2 Pick Three (7–9–1) Paid $801.20 ; Pick Three Pool $181,516 .

SEVENTH RACE
Churchill
MAY 1, 2004

1 MILE. (Turf) (1.33 3) 15TH RUNNING OF THE ARGENT MORTGAGE. Grade III. Purse $100,000 FOR FILLIES AND MARES, THREE YEARS OLD AND UPWARD. By subscription of $100 each on or before April 10, 2004 or by Supplementary Nomination of $5,000 at time of entry. $500 to pass the entry box; $500 additional to start. Three-year-olds 115 lbs.; Older 123 lbs. Non-winners of $50,000 on the turf in 2004 allowed 2 lbs.; a sweepstakes on the turf in 2003–2004, 4 lbs.; $30,000 twice on the turf since July 4, 2003, 6 lbs.; $18,000 twice on the turf in 2003–2004, 8 lbs. If the race is moved to the main track after the time of closing, a horse may be scratched for any reason at any time up to 15 minutes prior to post time for the race preceding this race or thereafter with a valid physical reason and approved by the stewards. The entry fee shall be refunded forscratches made in compliance with the above conditions. (If this race is taken off the turf it will be downgraded one grade level for this running only in accordance with American Graded Stakes Committee policy). Closed April 10, 2004 with 33 nominations.

Value of Race: $113,300 Winner $70,246; second $22,660; third $11,330; fourth $5,665; fifth $3,399. Mutuel Pool $2,194,096.00 Exacta Pool $1,551,310.00 Trifecta Pool $1,242,988.00 Superfecta Pool $336,438.00

Last Raced	Horse	M/Eqt.	A.	Wt	PP	St	¼	½	¾	Str	Fin	Jockey	Odds $1
10Apr04 10Kee7	Shaconage	L	4	121	2	7	8 2½	6½	6hd	4 5	1no	Blanc B	19.30
4Apr04 8SA1	Etoile Montante	L	4	123	3	3	5½	5 1	3½	1½	2 2	Bailey J D	0.70
21Mar04 9FG1	Chance Dance	L	4	117	7	1	4 1	4hd	2½	3 1	3½	Albarado R J	17.60
11Oct03 8Kee9	Sand Springs	L	4	121	6	5	1 1½	1 3	1 1	2hd	4 2¾	Guidry M	4.10
17Apr04 5Kee5	Flager-Arg	L	5	117	4	10	10	9hd	8 2	5½	5 3¼	McKee J	9.70
14Feb04 9OP4	Reason to Talk	L f	5	121	9	9	9½	10	10	8 2	6hd	Shepherd J	32.60
8Apr04 9Kee1	Honorable Cat	L	5	115	1	4	3hd	2hd	5hd	7 1½	7 1¾	Perret C	31.60
28Mar04 2SA3	Abbey Bridge	L b	6	121	8	8	6hd	7 1	7 1½	6hd	8 6½	Day P	7.30
31Mar04 9OP2	Blu Spur	L	5	115	5	2	2½	3 1½	4 1	9 2	9nk	Borel C H	37.00
18Apr04 7Kee2	Darby's Charm	L b	5	115	10	6	7 1½	8 2½	9 2	10	10	Bejarano R	33.00

OFF AT 3:04 Start Good . Won driving. Course good.

TIME :23 3, :47 1, 1:11 4, 1:23 4, 1:36 (:23.78, :47.28, 1:11.82, 1:23.82, 1:36.10)

$2 Mutuel Prices:			
2 – SHACONAGE	40.60	11.00	7.00
3 – ETOILE MONTANTE		3.20	2.40
7 – CHANCE DANCE			5.00

$2 EXACTA 2–3 PAID $98.60 $2 TRIFECTA 2–3–7 PAID $1,146.00
$2 SUPERFECTA 2–3–7–6 PAID $3,449.40

Gr/ro. f, (Jun), by El Prado-Ire – Carita Tostada-Chi , by Gallantsky . Trainer Shirota Mitch. Bred by Andrena Van Doren (Ky).

SHACONAGE reserved along the inside, moved to contention along the hedge after a half, continued to save ground rallying into the stretch and finished with good determination to be up in the final stride. ETOILE MONTANTE forwardly placed in the two path, angled to the rail approaching the second turn, moved up inside the leader nearing the stretch to challenge, came off the inside for the drive, shook off SAND SPRINGS inside the final furlong to open a clear lead with a sixteenth to go but missed. CHANCE DANCE never far back three wide, advanced four wide into the second turn, challenged from the outside entering the stretch, held on well to inside the final furlong and weakened. SAND SPRINGS sprinted clear, set the pace in the two path, responded willingly when challenged after six furlongs, held on well to inside the final furlong and weakened. FLAGER (ARG) unhurried for a half while outrun, commenced her rally three wide after five furlongs, came out five wide leaving the second turn, improved her position through midstretch but lodged only a mild late bid. REASON TO TALK outrun for six furlongs, angled outside for the drive and rallied belatedly. HONORABLE CAT close up along the inside, moved off the inside after a half, stayed on well on the second turn, bumped with BLUE SPUR approaching the stretch when CHANCE DANCE rallied past then tired in the drive. ABBEY BRIDGE within striking distance three wide, made a mild middle move but gave way in the drive. BLU SPUR closest to the pace in the two path, bumped with HONORABLE CAT near the five-sixteenths pole when in close quarters then faded. DARBY'S CHARM four wide on the first turn, was no threat.

Owners– 1, Van Doren Andrena; 2, Juddmonte Farms Inc; 3, Bernacki Robert Burek Tom and Scherer Merrill R; 4, Willmott Stables Inc; 5, Stony Oak Farm LLC; 6, K and K Racing Stable LLC; 7, McKee Stables Inc; 8, Robertson Sanford R; 9, Cella Charles J; 10, McCarty George S

Trainers– 1, Shirota Mitch; 2, Frankel Robert; 3, Scherer Merrill R; 4, Reinstedler Anthony; 5, Barnett Bobby C; 6, Vance David R; 7, Simon Charles; 8, Walsh Kathy; 9, Vestal Peter M; 10, McCarty George S

$2 Pick Three (1–1/3/7–2) Paid $608.40 ; Pick Three Pool $306,508 .

EIGHTH RACE
Churchill
MAY 1, 2004

7 FURLONGS. (1.20 2) 18TH RUNNING OF THE HUMANA DISTAFF HANDICAP. Grade I. Purse $250,000 A HANDICAP FOR FILLIES AND MARES, FOUR YEARS OLD AND UPWARD. By subscription of $250 each on or before April 10, 2004 or by Supplementary Nomination of $12,500 by the closing of entries on April 23, 2004. $1,250 to pass the entry box; $1,250 additional tostart, with $250,000 added of which 62% of all monies to the owner of the winner, 20% to second, 10% to third, 5% to fourth, 3% to fifth. Starters to be named through the entry box at the usual time of closing. All supplementary nominations are requiredto pay entry and starting fees if they participate. Trophy to winning owner given by Humana. Closed April 10, 2004 with 20 nominations.

Value of Race: $272,813 Winner $174,375; second $56,250; third $28,125; fourth $14,063. Mutuel Pool $1,815,754.00 Exacta Pool $1,102,886.00 Trifecta Pool $401,108.00 Superfecta Pool $149,752.00

Last Raced	Horse	M/Eqt.	A.	Wt	PP	St	¼	½	Str	Fin	Jockey	Odds $1
16Apr04 9Kee1	Mayo On the Side	L bf	5	114	3	3	4	3 2	1hd	1hd	Day P	5.50
3Apr04 9OP1	Azeri	L	6	125	2	4	2 1	2 1½	2 2½	2 7¼	Smith M E	0.70
27Mar04 8Aqu1	Randaroo	L	4	121	1	2	1 1	1 1½	3 1½	3nk	Velazquez J R	1.50
20Mar04 3GP6	Keiai Sakura	L b	4	110	4	1	3hd	4	4	4	McKee J	16.00

OFF AT 3:57 Start Good . Won driving. Track fast.

TIME :22 2, :45, 1:09 3, 1:22 3 (:22.49, :45.04, 1:09.65, 1:22.78)

$2 Mutuel Prices:			
5 – MAYO ON THE SIDE	13.00	3.20	—
3 – AZERI		2.40	—
2 – RANDAROO		—	—

$2 EXACTA 5–3 PAID $27.60 $2 TRIFECTA 5–3–2 PAID $30.20
$2 SUPERFECTA 5–3–2–7 PAID $48.20

B. m, (Feb), by French Deputy – Slewveau , by Slew o' Gold . Trainer Nafzger Carl A. Bred by Robert Lothenbach (Ky).

MAYO ON THE SIDE stalked the pace off the rail, bid three deep leaving the turn and into the stretch, gained a short lead nearing midstretch, then gamely prevailed under urging following a stiff drive. AZERI a bit slow to begin, went up inside to stalk the pace, came off the rail leaving the backstretch, bid between foes leaving the turn and put a head in front into the stretch, fought back inside the winner through the final furlong and continued gamely to the wire. RANDAROO lugged out a bit while speeding to the early lead, set the pace just off the inside, dueled inside rivals leaving the turn and into the stretch, came off the rail in midstretch and just held third. KEIAI SAKURA stalked outside a rival then off the rail, angled in leaving the turn, came out in the stretch and was edged for the show.

Owners– 1, Lothenbach Stables Inc; 2, Allen E Paulson Living Trust; 3, Allen Joseph; 4, Kameda Morihiro

Trainers– 1, Nafzger Carl A; 2, Lukas D Wayne; 3, McLaughlin Kiaran P; 4, Gothard Akiko

Scratched– Cat Fighter (30Apr04 8CD 3) , Bear Fan (17Mar04 5SA 1) , Halory Leigh (07Mar04 11GP 9)

$2 Pick Three (1/3/7–2–5) Paid $996.60 ; Pick Three Pool $344,507 .

NINTH RACE
Churchill
MAY 1, 2004

1⅛ MILES. (Turf) (1.46^{1}) 18TH RUNNING OF THE WOODFORD RESERVE TURF CLASSIC. Grade I. Purse $400,000 FOR THREE-YEAR-OLDS AND UPWARD. By subscription of $100 each on or before February 14, 2004 or by SUPPLEMENTARY NOMINATION OF $20,000 AT TIME OF ENTRY. $2,000 to pass the entry box; $2,000 additional to start. Three-year-olds 115 lbs. Older 123 lbs. Non-winners of $200,000 at a mile or over since August 1 allowed 2 lbs.; $100,000 at a mile or over since June 30, 4 lbs.; $50,000 twice at a mile or over in 2003-2004, 6 lbs.; $50,000 at a mile or over in 2004, 8 lbs. If the race is moved to the main track after the time of closing, a horse may be scratched for any reason at any time up to 15 minutes prior to post time for the race preceding this race or thereafter with a valid physical reason and approved by the stewards. (If this race is taken off the turfit will be downgraded one grade level for this running only in accordance with the American Graded Stakes Committee Policy). Closed February 14, 2004 with 99 nominations.

Value of Race: $453,900 Winner $281,418; second $90,780; third $45,390; fourth $22,695; fifth $13,617. Mutuel Pool $2,905,217.00 Exacta Pool $1,952,366.00 Trifecta Pool $1,584,638.00 Superfecta Pool $406,009.00

Last Raced	Horse	M/Eqt.	A.	Wt	PP	St	¼	½	¾	Str	Fin	Jockey	Odds $1
9Apr04 ^{9}Kee^{5}	Stroll	L	4	121	10	7	2^{1}	2^{1}	1^{hd}	$1^{\frac{1}{2}}$	$1^{2\frac{1}{2}}$	Bailey J D	4.80
6Mar04 ^{9}SA^{1}	Sweet Return-GB	L	4	123	6	4	1^{2}	1^{1}	$2^{1\frac{1}{2}}$	$2^{2\frac{1}{2}}$	2no	Day P	4.40
21Mar04 ^{8}FG^{1}	Mystery Giver	L	6	123	7	5	$5^{\frac{1}{2}}$	8^{1}	7^{1}	$4^{\frac{1}{2}}$	$3^{\frac{3}{4}}$	Albarado R J	9.70
21Mar04 ^{8}FG^{4}	Burning Sun	L	5	116	2	1	3^{hd}	$3^{\frac{1}{2}}$	3^{hd}	3^{1}	4^{3}	Solis A	8.40
9Apr04 ^{9}Kee^{4}	Honor in War	L	5	121	5	2	$8^{\frac{1}{2}}$	$9^{\frac{1}{2}}$	$6^{\frac{1}{2}}$	5^{3}	$5^{1\frac{1}{2}}$	Flores D R	7.00
22Feb04 ^{11}GP^{3}	Kicken Kris	L	4	123	9	9	$7^{\frac{1}{2}}$	5^{1}	$4^{2\frac{1}{2}}$	$6^{\frac{1}{2}}$	$6^{1\frac{1}{4}}$	Velazquez J R	6.10
15Apr04 ^{4}Kee^{1}	Everything to Gain	L	5	115	4	3	$9^{\frac{1}{2}}$	10^{4}	9^{8}	$7^{\frac{1}{2}}$	7no	Guidry M	28.20
22Apr04 ^{8}Kee^{3}	Sir Cherokee	L	4	119	8	11	11	11	10^{12}	$9^{1\frac{1}{2}}$	$8^{5\frac{1}{4}}$	Borel C H	14.80
9Apr04 ^{7}Kee^{1}	Stage Call-Ire	L b	5	116	11	8	$4^{1\frac{1}{2}}$	$4^{\frac{1}{2}}$	5^{2}	8^{2}	$9^{2\frac{1}{2}}$	Nakatani C S	27.20
9Apr04 ^{9}Kee^{1}	Perfect Soul-Ire	L b	6	123	1	6	6^{1}	6^{1}	8^{hd}	10	10	Prado E S	4.50
10Apr04 ^{7}Hou^{2}	Skate Away	L	5	116	3	10	10^{3}	7^{hd}	11	—	—	Desormeaux K J	16.00

OFF AT 4:53 Start Good . Won driving. Course yielding.

TIME :25^{1}, :51, 1:15^{2}, 1:39^{3}, 1:53 (:25.36, :51.04, 1:15.54, 1:39.72, 1:53.00)

$2 Mutuel Prices:				
	10 – STROLL	11.60	6.00	4.60
	6 – SWEET RETURN-GB		5.60	3.60
	7 – MYSTERY GIVER			5.20

$2 EXACTA 10-6 PAID $50.40 $2 TRIFECTA 10-6-7 PAID $430.00
$2 SUPERFECTA 10-6-7-2 PAID $4,599.40

Dk. b or br. c, (Apr), by Pulpit – Maid for Walking-GB , by Prince Sabo . Trainer Mott William I. Bred by Claiborne Farm (Ky).

STROLL closest to the pace while reserved, challenged from the three path with three furlongs to go, shook off SWEET RETURN inside the final furlong and drew clear under steady urging. SWEET RETURN (GB) sprinted clear, set a slow pace while off the hedge, responded willingly when challenged on the second turn, held on well to inside the final furlong, could not stay with the winner late and outfinished MYSTERY GIVER for the place. MYSTERY GIVER drifted out at the start tightening up outer rivals, was straightened to be forwardly placed between rivals, steadied once in the first turn when in tight, advanced three wide after six furlongs, split rivals in upper stretch, angled out with a furlong to go and rallied willingly. BURNING SUN forwardly placed off the inside, angled out four wide late on the second turn for clear room but lacked a late bid. HONOR IN WAR reserved off the inside, steadied entering the first turn when in tight, made a mild middle move off the hedge then lacked a closing bid. KICKEN KRIS bumped at the start, was in tight soon after when the winner came in a bit and MYSTERY GIVER drifted out, recovered to race within striking distance four wide but tired. EVERYTHING TO GAIN outrun early, raced in the four path on the second turn and was no threat. SIR CHEROKEE bumped at the start and then steadied when MYSTERY GIVER drifted out, was outrun for six furlongs and rallied belatedly. STAGE CALL (IRE) forwardly placed four wide, faded in the final three furlongs. PERFECT SOUL (IRE) pulled a bit early along the inside when within striking distance, faded after a half. SKATE AWAY outrun, lost his rider after six furlongs. SKATE AWAY was vanned off.

Owners– 1, Claiborne Farm; 2, Red Oak Stable; 3, Team Block; 4, Juddmonte Farms Inc; 5, 3rd Turn Stables LLC; 6, Brushwood Stable; 7, Ramsey Kenneth L and Sarah K; 8, Domino Stud of Lex LLC; 9, WinStar Farm LLC Gaines-Gentry and Nip Richard; 10, Fipke Charles E; 11, Robinson J Mack

Trainers– 1, Mott William I; 2, McAnally Ronald; 3, Block Chris M; 4, Frankel Robert; 5, McGee Paul J; 6, Matz Michael R; 7, Romans Dale; 8, Tomlinson Michael A; 9, Walden W Elliott; 10, Attfield Roger L; 11, Trosclair Jeff

$2 Pick Three (2-5-10) Paid $3,226.80 ; Pick Three Pool $252,972 .

TENTH RACE
Churchill
MAY 1, 2004

1¼ MILES. (1.59^{2}) 130TH RUNNING OF THE KENTUCKY DERBY. Grade I. Purse $1,000,000 (plus $5,000,000 Racing Series Bonus) FOR THREE-YEAR-OLDS. $15,000 to pass the entry box and $15,000 additional to start. Supplemental nominations may be made upon payment of $150,000 and in accordance with the rules set forth. All fees, including supplemental nominations, in excess of $500,000 in the aggregate shall be paid to the winner. Churchill Downs Incorporated shall guarantee a minimum gross purse of $1,000,000. The winner shall receive $700,000, second place shall receive $170,000, third place shall receive $85,000 and fourth place shall receive $45,000. Starters shall be named through the entry box on April 28, 2004. The maximum number of starters shall be limited to 20. Colts and Geldings shall each carry a weight of one hundred twenty-six (126) pounds; Fillies shall each carry onehundred twenty-one (121) pounds. Supplemental Nominees will be allowed to enter but will not have preference over any Original Nominee and will not be allowed to start in the Race if the maximum number of starters has otherwise been reached by Original Nominees prior to or at the Closing. Closed with 448 nominations.

Value of Race: $6,184,800 Winner $5,884,800; second $170,000; third $85,000; fourth $45,000. Mutuel Pool $42,409,001.00 Exacta Pool $19,599,574.00 Trifecta Pool $20,500,979.00 Superfecta Pool $5,261,943.00

Last Raced	Horse	M/Eqt.	A.	Wt	PP	¼	½	¾	1	Str	Fin	Jockey	Odds $1
10Apr04 ^{9}OP^{1}	Smarty Jones	L f	3	126	13	$4^{\frac{1}{2}}$	$4^{1\frac{1}{2}}$	2^{hd}	2^{4}	1^{hd}	$1^{2\frac{3}{4}}$	Elliott S	4.10
10Apr04 ^{9}Kee^{2}	Lion Heart		3	126	3	$1^{1\frac{1}{2}}$	1^{2}	$1^{1\frac{1}{2}}$	1^{hd}	$2^{3\frac{1}{2}}$	$2^{3\frac{1}{4}}$	Smith M E	5.40
3Apr04 ^{8}SA^{2}	Imperialism	L b	3	126	8	$15^{\frac{1}{2}}$	17^{3}	13^{hd}	$10^{\frac{1}{2}}$	$6^{\frac{1}{2}}$	3^{2}	Desormeaux K J	10.90
10Apr04 ^{9}Kee^{3}	Limehouse	L	3	126	1	7^{hd}	8^{hd}	$6^{\frac{1}{2}}$	$6^{\frac{1}{2}}$	3^{2}	$4^{4\frac{1}{2}}$	Santos J A	41.70
10Apr04 ^{9}Kee^{1}	The Cliff's Edge	L	3	126	9	$16^{\frac{1}{2}}$	15^{hd}	17^{2}	8^{2}	5^{1}	$5^{1\frac{1}{4}}$	Sellers S J	8.20
10Apr04 ^{9}Kee^{6}	Action This Day	L	3	126	4	18	18	18	14^{2}	12^{hd}	6^{1}	Flores D R	43.40
13Mar04 ^{9}GP^{4}	Read the Footnotes	L	3	126	12	$5^{\frac{1}{2}}$	6^{hd}	$4^{\frac{1}{2}}$	3^{1}	4^{hd}	$7^{\frac{1}{2}}$	Albarado R J	22.50
20Mar04 ^{8}TP^{5}	Birdstone	L	3	126	11	14^{2}	$11^{\frac{1}{2}}$	10^{hd}	$9^{\frac{1}{2}}$	$9^{\frac{1}{2}}$	$8^{\frac{1}{2}}$	Prado E S	21.20
10Apr04 ^{8}Aqu^{1}	Tapit	L f	3	126	16	17^{3}	16^{hd}	$12^{\frac{1}{2}}$	7^{hd}	$10^{1\frac{1}{2}}$	$9^{\frac{1}{2}}$	Dominguez R A	6.40
10Apr04 ^{9}OP^{2}	Borrego	L b	3	126	10	9^{hd}	7^{2}	$9^{\frac{1}{2}}$	4^{hd}	7^{hd}	$10^{1\frac{1}{4}}$	Espinoza V	14.20
17Apr04 ^{9}Kee^{3}	Song of the Sword	L b	3	126	2	$11^{\frac{1}{2}}$	$13^{\frac{1}{2}}$	$7^{\frac{1}{2}}$	$12^{1\frac{1}{2}}$	$11^{1\frac{1}{2}}$	11^{1}	Arroyo N Jr	55.90
10Apr04 ^{8}Aqu^{2}	Master David	L	3	126	7	8^{hd}	9^{hd}	14^{hd}	$11^{1\frac{1}{2}}$	13^{3}	$12^{1\frac{1}{2}}$	Solis A	10.60
10Apr04 ^{9}OP^{3}	Pro Prado	L	3	126	17	10^{2}	$10^{1\frac{1}{2}}$	8^{hd}	5^{hd}	8^{hd}	$13^{5\frac{1}{4}}$	McKee J	53.50
3Apr04 ^{8}SA^{1}	Castledale-Ire	L	3	126	14	13^{hd}	12^{hd}	15^{hd}	17^{20}	14^{3}	$14^{11\frac{1}{2}}$	Valdivia J Jr	21.90
13Mar04 ^{9}GP^{1}	Friends Lake	L	3	126	5	12^{hd}	14^{1}	$16^{1\frac{1}{2}}$	16^{hd}	$15^{\frac{1}{2}}$	$15^{\frac{1}{2}}$	Migliore R	18.50
14Apr04 ^{7}Kee^{1}	Minister Eric	L	3	126	6	$6^{1\frac{1}{2}}$	5^{hd}	$3^{\frac{1}{2}}$	$13^{\frac{1}{2}}$	17^{20}	$16^{3\frac{1}{2}}$	Day P	22.50
3Apr04 ^{7}Haw^{1}	Pollard's Vision	L	3	126	15	3^{hd}	$2^{\frac{1}{2}}$	5^{1}	$15^{1\frac{1}{2}}$	16^{hd}	17	Velazquez J R	24.00
17Apr04 ^{9}Kee^{1}	Quintons Gold Rush	L	3	126	18	2^{hd}	3^{hd}	11^{hd}	18	18	—	Nakatani C S	51.20

OFF AT 6:12 Start Good . Won driving. Track sloppy.

TIME :22^{4}, :46^{3}, 1:11^{4}, 1:37^{1}, 2:04 (:22.99, :46.73, 1:11.80, 1:37.35, 2:04.06)

$2 Mutuel Prices:

15 – SMARTY JONES	10.20	6.20	4.80
3 – LION HEART		8.20	5.80
10 – IMPERIALISM			6.20

$2 EXACTA 15 3 PAID $65.20 $2 TRIFECTA 15-3-10 PAID $987.60
$2 SUPERFECTA 15-3-10-1 PAID $41,380.20

Ch. c, (Feb), by Elusive Quality – I'll Get Along , by Smile . Trainer Servis John C. Bred by Someday Farm (Pa).

SMARTY JONES, bumped between horses approaching the first turn, settled in good position along the backstretch, raced just behind the pacesetter leaving the far turn, closed the gap from outside midway on the turn, made a run to challenge at the top of the stretch, surged to the front with a furlong remaining then edged away under steady right and left hand encouragement. LION HEART rushed up to gain the early advantage, raced uncontested on the lead along the backstretch, set a rapid pace along the rail for a mile, dug in when challenged leaving the quarter pole, battled heads apart into midstretch but couldn't stay with the winner through the final sixteenth. IMPERIALISM bumped and steadied in traffic at the seven-eighths pole, raced far back for six furlongs, saved ground into the far turn, began to work his way out for room on the turn, swung six wide at the top of the stretch then closed late while drifting in through the stretch to gain a share. LIMEHOUSE was shuffled back a bit along the inside on the first turn, raced in the middle of the pack for six furlongs, saved ground while launching his bid approaching the quarter pole, made a run to reach contention in midstretch but couldn't sustain his bid. THE CLIFF'S EDGE broke a bit slowly, was outrun while strung out five wide going into the first turn, moved to the outside of TAPIT midway down the backstretch, continued wide while moving into contention on the second turn then failed to threaten while improving his position in the middle of the track. ACTION THIS DAY was unhurried in the early going while racing well off the pace, steadied along the inside midway on the turn, swung out in upper stretch then passed mostly tiring horses. READ THE FOOTNOTES steadied in traffic between horses on the first turn, raced three wide while gaining ground along the backstretch, launched his bid between horses on the far turn, made a run to reach contention midway on the turn but couldn't sustain his rally. BIRDSTONE was pinched back a bit at the start then steadied in traffic in the early stages, worked his way forward between horses at the half mile pole, raced within striking distance on the turn then lacked a strong closing response. TAPIT broke a bit slowly, steadied in traffic at the seven-eighths pole, was caught five wide leaving the first turn, continued well off the rail along the backstretch, angled in a bit while gaining slightly at the top of the stretch then lacked a further response. BORREGO was reserved for a half, steadied in traffic between horses at the half mile pole, made a move to reach contention leaving the turn then faded in the stretch. SONG OF THE SWORD checked along the inside on the first turn and failed to seriously threaten thereafter. MASTER DAVID bumped while between horses on the first turn, raced well back for six furlongs, steadied in traffic at the half mile pole and was never close thereafter while six wide at the top of the stretch. PRO PRADO was caught four wide on the first turn, chased the leaders from outside along the backstretch, edged a bit closer midway on the turn then flattened out. CASTLEDALE (IRE) swerved out in the early stages, raced in tight approaching the far turn then failed to mount a serious rally thereafter. FRIENDS LAKE steadied between horses while in tight on the first turn and never reached contention. MINISTER ERIC steadied along the rail leaving the first turn, moved up along the inside through the backstretch, dropped back on the turn and gave way in the stretch. POLLARD'S VISION bumped at the start, stalked the leaders while four wide for six furlongs then gave way. QUINTONS GOLD RUSH up close early, took up between horses at the half mile pole then gave way and was eased late. Due to the scratches of WIMBLEDON and ST. AVERIL, the two inside stalls in the main gate were not utilized.

Owners– 1, Someday Farm; 2, Smith Derrick and Tabor Michael; 3, Taub Steve; 4, Dogwood Stable; 5, LaPenta Robert V; 6, Hughes B Wayne; 7, Klaravich Stables Inc; 8, Marylou Whitney Stables; 9, Winchell Thoroughbreds LLC; 10, Jon and Sara Kelly R Ralls D Foster B Scott and C B Greely; 11, Paraneck Stable; 12, Georgica Stable Mack Stephen and Star Crown Stable; 13, Winn Mrs James A; 14, Frank Lyons and Greg Knee; 15, Broman Sr Mary and Chester; 16, Diamond A Racing Corporation; 17, Edgewood Farm; 18, Padua Stables and Manoogian Jay

Trainers– 1, Servis John C; 2, Biancone Patrick L; 3, Mulhall Kristin; 4, Pletcher Todd A; 5, Zito Nicholas P; 6, Mandella Richard; 7, Violette Richard A Jr; 8, Zito Nicholas P; 9, Dickinson Michael W; 10, Greely C Beau; 11, Pedersen Jennifer; 12, Frankel Robert; 13, Holthus Robert E; 14, Mullins Jeff; 15, Kimmel John C; 16, Mandella Richard; 17, Pletcher Todd A; 18, Asmussen Steven M

Scratched– Wimbledon , St Averil

$2 Pick Three (5-10-5/9/15) Paid $1,470.80 ; Pick Three Pool $987,799 .
$2 Pick Four (2-5-10-5/9/15) Paid $38,594.20 ; Pick Four Pool $2,130,894 .
$2 Pick Six (1-1/3/7-2-5-10-5/9/15) 5 Correct Paid $6,878.00 ; Pick Six Pool $441,558 ; Carryover Pool $268,246.
$2 Daily Double (10-15) Paid $103.60 ; Daily Double Pool $615,859 .
$2 Daily Double (OAKS/DERBY (1-15)) Paid $60.20 ; Daily Double Pool $2,038,878 .

SIXTH RACE
Hollywood
MAY 1, 2004

$1\frac{1}{16}$ MILES. (Turf) (1.38^2) 64TH RUNNING OF THE INGLEWOOD HANDICAP. Grade III. Purse $100,000 FOR THREE YEAR OLDS AND UPWARD. By subscription of $100 each on or before Wednesday, April 21 or by supplementary nomination of $2,000 each by noon Saturday, April 24. $1,000 additional to start, with $100,000 added. The added money and all fees to be divided 60% to the winner, 20% to second, 12% to third, 6% to fourth and 2% to fifth. Weights Sunday, April 25. Starters to be named through the entry box by closing time of entries. A trophy will be presented to the winning owner. Closed with 19 nominations.

Value of Race: $110,900 Winner $66,540; second $22,180; third $13,308; fourth $6,654; fifth $2,218. Mutuel Pool $641,827.00 Exacta Pool $338,984.00 Quinella Pool $31,526.00 Trifecta Pool $343,212.00 Superfecta Pool $104,843.00

Last Raced	Horse	M/Eqt.	A.	Wt	PP	St	¼	½	¾	Str	Fin	Jockey	Odds $1
20Mar04 ^{1}SA^1	Leroidesnimux-Brz	LB	4	114	4	3	1^{hd}	1^{hd}	1^{hd}	1^1	1^2	Court J K	5.80
6Mar04 ^{9}SA^5	Designed for Luck	LB b	7	118	6	1	3^1	$3^{1\frac{1}{2}}$	$3^{1\frac{1}{2}}$	$3^{1\frac{1}{2}}$	2^2	Valenzuela P A	2.40
11Feb04 ^{7}SA^6	Devious Boy-GB	LB	4	115	5	2	2^1	2^1	2^1	$2^{\frac{1}{2}}$	3^{nk}	Sorenson D	21.80
6Mar04 ^{9}SA^{10}	Irish Warrior	LB	6	117	8	8	$6^{1\frac{1}{2}}$	$6^{1\frac{1}{2}}$	6^{hd}	5^1	4^{nk}	Douglas R R	2.60
21Mar04 ^{3}SA^2	Just Wonder-GB	LB	4	118	9	9	9	9	9	$7^{1\frac{1}{2}}$	5^1	Baze R A	5.20
14Mar04 ^{7}GG^1	Tronare-Chi	LB b	6	117	2	5	$4^{1\frac{1}{2}}$	4^{hd}	4^{hd}	4^{hd}	$6^{\frac{1}{2}}$	Steiner J J	a- 4.10
3Apr04 ^{3}SA^3	Seinne-Chi	LB	7	115	7	6	8^{hd}	8^{hd}	7^2	9	7^1	John K	16.90
3Apr04 ^{3}SA^2	Statement	LB	6	115	1	4	5^{hd}	5^{hd}	5^{hd}	6^1	8^1	Santiago Javier	a- 4.10
6Mar04 ^{9}SA^{12}	Golden Dragon-GB	LB bf	6	112	3	7	7^{hd}	7^{hd}	8^{hd}	$8^{\frac{1}{2}}$	9	Bisono A	37.90

a-Coupled: Tronare-Chi and Statement.

OFF AT 4:40 Start Good. Won driving. Course firm.

TIME :23^3, :46^4, 1:09^3, 1:32^3, 1:38^2 (:23.71, :46.90, 1:09.75, 1:32.76, 1:38.45)

(New Course Record)

$2 Mutuel Prices:				
	3 – LEROIDESANIMAUX-BRZ	13.60	6.40	5.20
	5 – DESIGNED FOR LUCK		4.20	3.60
	4 – DEVIOUS BOY-GB			12.20

$1 EXACTA 3–5 PAID $30.00 $2 QUINELLA 3–5 PAID $28.80
$1 TRIFECTA 3–5–4 PAID $376.30 $1 SUPERFECTA 3–5–4–7 PAID $1,578.90

Ch. c, (Sep), by Candy Stripes – Dissemble-GB , by Ahonoora-GB . Trainer Frankel Robert. Bred by Haras Bage Do Sul (Brz).

LEROIDESANIMAUX (BRZ) pulled his way up inside to set or force the fractions, remained along the rail, edged away entering the stretch and padded cushion late under strong handling. DESIGNED FOR LUCK tucked in behind the dueling leaders and appeared perfectly placed a bit off the rail, angled off slightly late on the final bend, raced three wide into the lane and chased the winner home. DEVIOUS BOY (GB) contested the pace outside the winner into the final turn, could not match that foe in upper stretch but gamely held for the show. IRISH WARRIOR reserved outside foe early, chased three deep into and around the second turn, remained on same path into the stretch and almost gained third. JUST WONDER (GB) settled off the fence, reserved while three deep in the final trio, continued on same path around the final turn and into and stretch and improved placing from the outside. TRONARE (CHI) prominent early from along the, continued on a rail-hugging trip and weakened in the drive. SEINNE (CHI) chased from between foes, remained on two wide path leaving the final turn and failed to produce any late punch. STATEMENT eased back into the first turn and taken off the fence, stalked from between foes and on two wide path to the stretch and never menaced. GOLDEN DRAGON (GB) unhurried while securing the inside, had a ground-saving trip into the stretch and never reached contention.

Owners– 1, T N T Stud; 2, Wilson David W and Holly F; 3, Vreeland James R; 4, Coleman John Dasaro George Thompson James et al; 5, Naify Sugarman and Vistas LLC et al; 6, Noctis LLC Papiano Neil and Taub Steve; 7, Hunt Nelson B; 8, Bienstock Winner Stables Mandabach Paul and Papiano Neil; 9, Cobra Farm Inc

Trainers– 1, Frankel Robert; 2, Cerin Vladimir; 3, Walsh Kathy; 4, Dollase Wallace; 5, De Seroux Laura; 6, Mulhall Kristin; 7, McAnally Ronald; 8, Mulhall Kristin; 9, Puype Mike

---

$2 Daily Double (3–3) Paid $41.80 ; Daily Double Pool $41,113 .
$1 Pick Three (1–3–3) Paid $117.40 ; Pick Three Pool $100,475 .

EIGHTH RACE
Hollywood
MAY 2, 2004

7 FURLONGS. (1.19 4) 42ND RUNNING OF THE RAILBIRD. Grade III. Purse $100,000 FOR FILLIES THREE YEARS OLD. By subscription of $100 each on or before Wednesday, April 21, or by supplementary nomination of $2,000 each by closing time of entries. $1,000 additional to start, with $100,000 added.The added money and all fees to be divided 60% to the winner, 20% to second,12% to third,6% to fourth and 2% to fifth. Weight 123 lbs. Non-winners of $90,000 allowed 3 lbs., a race of $60,000 since December 25, 5 lbs., two races other than claiming or starter 8 lbs., such a race 10 lbs. Starters to be named through the entry box by the closing time of entries. A trophy will be presented to the winning owner. Closed with 16 nominations.

Value of Race: $109,600 Winner $65,760; second $21,920; third $13,152; fourth $6,576; fifth $2,192. Mutuel Pool $442,185.00 Exacta Pool $220,917.00 Quinella Pool $21,171.00 Trifecta Pool $243,248.00 Superfecta Pool $129,635.00

Last Raced	Horse	M/Eqt.	A.	Wt	PP	St	¼	½	Str	Fin	Jockey	Odds $1
9Apr04 10OP4	Elusive Diva	LB b	3	118	4	5	4½	3hd	2½	1nk	Valenzuela P A	4.90
11Apr04 6SA2	M. A. Fox	LB	3	116	8	1	8	74	53½	2nk	Desormeaux K J	10.00
27Mar04 8Sun1	Speedy Falcon	LB	3	123	6	3	2½	21	1hd	3no	Espinoza V	4.30
29Feb04 8SA2	Aspen Gal	LB	3	118	7	2	3½	41½	3hd	45	Solis A	1.30
4Apr04 3SA1	Healthy Addiction	LB b	3	118	3	6	51	51	62	54	Smith M E	4.40
21Mar04 8SA5	Mazella	LB b	3	118	5	4	61	6hd	71½	6½	Court J K	59.00
18Apr04 3BM1	Allswellthatnswell	LB	3	118	1	8	1hd	1½	4hd	7hd	Flores D R	11.30
7Apr04 7SA3	A Precious Memory	LB	3	117	2	7	7hd	8	8	8	Nakatani C S	37.20

OFF AT 4:54 Start Good . Won driving. Track fast.
TIME :21 3, :44, 1:08 2, 1:21 1 (:21.74, :44.16, 1:08.55, 1:21.36)

$2 Mutuel Prices:				
	4 – ELUSIVE DIVA	11.80	5.40	3.60
	10 – M. A. FOX		7.60	3.80
	8 – SPEEDY FALCON			4.20

$1 EXACTA 4–10 PAID $51.50 $2 QUINELLA 4–10 PAID $60.60
$1 TRIFECTA 4–10–8 PAID $287.60 $1 SUPERFECTA 4–10–8–9 PAID $907.60

B. f, (Mar), by Elusive Quality – Taj Aire , by Taj Alriyadh Trainer Glatt Mark. Bred by John William Konecny & Doris Konecny (Ky).

ELUSIVE DIVA stalked the leaders from the inside, awaited room approaching the stretch, split rivals in upper stretch, forged to front from inside passing sixteenth marker, inched away and desperately held under string handling. M. A. FOX reserved while extremely wide leaving the chute, angled to the rail entering the turn, was steered back out leaving that bend and closed furiously from far outside to narrowly miss while four deep at the wire. SPEEDY FALCON pulled her way up to force the pace outside rival into and around the turn, drifted out slightly into the stretch and battled bravely through the drive from between foes. ASPEN GAL advanced the boldly loomed three deep on the turn, continued prominently from outside entering the stretch and fought gamely through the drive. HEALTHY ADDICTION reserved from the inside, chased three wide on the turn, was forced out further entering the lane and lacked the needed late response. MAZELLA was taken off the early leaders, chased off the rail and outside the runner-up around the turn, and weakened. ALLSWELLTHATNSWELL rushed up from the inside to engage leaders, gained slim advantage, continued along the fence, resisted but weakened in the final sixteenth. A PRECIOUS MEMORY lagged back from the inside, remained along the fence, brushed the rail passing the eighth marker and was outrun.

Owners– 1, Branch Allen Konecny John W and Doris et al; 2, Hughes B Wayne; 3, Coleman G Chris; 4, Gann Edmund A; 5, Ziebarth Pamela C; 6, Becker Barry and Judith; 7, Johnston E W and Judy; 8, Barber Chaiken Trust Green Lantern et al

Trainers– 1, Glatt Mark; 2, Stute Warren; 3, Dominguez Henry; 4, Frankel Robert; 5, Sadler John W; 6, Robbins Jay M; 7, Warren Donald; 8, Sahadi Jenine

Scratched– Church Editor (27Mar04 2TuP1) , Highest Honoree (07Apr04 7SA 1)

$2 Daily Double (1–4) Paid $50.80 ; Daily Double Pool $39,447 .
$1 Pick Three (10–1–4) Paid $170.20 ; Pick Three Pool $63,767 .

EIGHTH RACE
Belmont
MAY 5, 2004

1 MILE. (1.32 1) 80TH RUNNING OF THE WESTCHESTER HANDICAP. Grade III. Purse $100,000 (Up To $19,000 NYSBFOA) A HANDICAP FOR THREE YEAR OLDS AND UPWARD. By subscription of $100 each, which should accompany the nomination; $500 to pass the entry box; $500 to start, with $100,000 added. The added money and all fees to be divided 60% to the winner, 20% to second, 10% to third, 5% to fourth, 3% to fifth and 2% divided equally among remaining finishers. A trophy will be presented to the winning owner. Closed Saturday, April 24, 2004 with 25 Nominations.

Value of Race: $109,500 Winner $65,700; second $21,900; third $10,950; fourth $5,475; fifth $3,285; sixth $1,095; seventh $1,095. Mutuel Pool $474,807.00 Exacta Pool $370,073.00 Trifecta Pool $313,492.00

Last Raced	Horse	M/Eqt.	A.	Wt	PP	St	¼	½	¾	Str	Fin	Jockey	Odds $1
10Apr04 9Aqu4	Gygistar	L	5	115	7	1	4hd	4hd	1½	13	14¼	Bravo J	4.00
18Mar04 8Aqu4	Saarland	L bf	5	114	2	6	7	6hd	4½	21½	22¾	Bailey J D	2.85
2Apr04 8Aqu1	Black Silk-GB	L f	8	113	6	3	3½	31	5hd	41	3nk	Arroyo N Jr	9.90
27Mar04 7GG5	Jets Fan	L f	4	113	5	2	5½	5½	6½	62½	4½	Castellano J J	21.10
10Apr04 5Kee1	Lion Tamer	L	4	119	4	4	61½	7	7	5hd	5½	Velazquez J R	1.50
7Feb04 9SA5	Formal Attire	L b	4	113	3	7	2hd	2½	2hd	3hd	66	Prado E S	7.40
24Apr04 8Aqu8	Toccet	L b	4	114	1	5	1½	1½	3½	7	7	Luzzi M J	17.00

OFF AT 4:41 Start Good . Won driving. Track fast.
TIME :24 1, :47 2, 1:11 3, 1:35 4 (:24.26, :47.54, 1:11.64, 1:35.89)

$2 Mutuel Prices:				
	7 – GYGISTAR	10.00	5.30	3.60
	2 – SAARLAND		5.00	3.40
	6 – BLACK SILK–GB			5.00

$2 EXACTA 7–2 PAID $40.60 $2 TRIFECTA 7–2–6 PAID $240.50

Ch. g, (Apr), by Prospector's Music – Starr County , by Ogygian . Trainer Hennig Mark. Bred by Edward P Evans (Ky).

GYGISTAR raced close up outside while in hand, cruised up four wide approaching the stretch, responded when roused, drew clear and remained well clear under a vigorous hand ride. SAARLAND was outrun early, rallied five wide on the turn and finished well outside. BLACK SILK (GB) raced close up while between rivals three wide and lacked a rally. JETS FAN was rated along inside, raced on the rail, was blocked in traffic along the inside in upper stretch, angled out, was bumped and lacked a rally. LION TAMER was rated along early, raced three wide and had no response when roused. FORMAL ATTIRE broke awkwardly, moved up quickly along the inside, argued the pace and tired in the final furlong. TOCCET quickly showed in front, set the pace while between rivals and was bumped while tiring in upper stretch.

Owners– 1, Evans Edward P; 2, Phipps Cynthia; 3, Fustok Salah M; 4, Schwartz Barry K Double S Stable Wachtel Stable; 5, Tabor Michael B; 6, Flying Zee Stable; 7, Borislow Daniel M

Trainers– 1, Hennig Mark; 2, McGaughey III Claude R; 3, LaFavers Laurie; 4, Hushion Michael E; 5, Pletcher Todd A; 6, Serpe Philip M; 7, Scanlan John F

SEVENTH RACE
Belmont
MAY 8, 2004

6 FURLONGS. (1.07^{3}) 29TH RUNNING OF THE BOLD RULER HANDICAP. Grade III. Purse $100,000 A HANDICAP FOR THREE YEAR OLDS AND UPWARD. By subscription of $100 each, which should accompany the nomination; $500 to pass the entry box; $500 to start, with $100,000 added. The added money and all fees to be divided 60% to the winner, 20% to second, 10% to third, 5% to fourth, 3% to fifth and 2% divided equally among remaining finishers. A trophy will be presented to the winning owner. Closed Saturday, April 24, 2004 with 17 Nominations.

Value of Race: $107,700 Winner $64,620; second $21,540; third $10,770; fourth $5,385; fifth $3,231; sixth $2,154. Mutuel Pool $630,538.00 Exacta Pool $564,251.00 Trifecta Pool $363,585.00

Last Raced	Horse	M/Eqt.	A.	Wt	PP	St	¼	½	Str	Fin	Jockey	Odds $1
11Apr04 ^{9}GP^{4}	Canadian Frontier	L f	5	111	3	3	2^{hd}	1^{hd}	11½	13¾	Castellano J J	20.50
6Mar04 ^{6}GP^{1}	Key Deputy	L	4	114	4	2	1½	2^{hd}	3½	2no	Bailey J D	3.45
23Apr04 ^{8}Aqu^{1}	First Blush	b	4	113	5	4	3½	4½	5^{hd}	3^{nk}	Luzzi M J	4.80
10Apr04 ^{9}Aqu^{9}	Secret Run	L b	4	113	6	5	4½	3½	2½	4^{nk}	Arroyo N Jr	6.90
2Apr04 ^{8}Aqu^{6}	Aggadan	L f	5	113	2	1	5^{hd}	6	41½	52½	Prado E S	9.70
8Apr04 ^{10}OP^{1}	Shake You Down	L bf	6	121	1	6	6	5^{hd}	6	6	Dominguez R A	0.95

OFF AT 4:14 Start Good For All But SHAKE YOU DOWN. Won driving. Track fast.

TIME :22^{2}, :44^{4}, :56^{2}, 1:08^{4} (:22.51, :44.92, :56.52, 1:08.97)

$2 Mutuel Prices:				
	3 – CANADIAN FRONTIER	43.00	15.40	9.70
	4 – KEY DEPUTY		5.10	4.50
	5 – FIRST BLUSH			4.30

$2 EXACTA 3–4 PAID $209.50 $2 TRIFECTA 3–4–5 PAID $841.00

B. h, (Feb), by Gone West – Borodislew , by Seattle Slew . Trainer Hough Stanley M. Bred by Marshall Naify Revocable Trust (Ky).

CANADIAN FRONTIER flashed good speed along the inside, contested the pace, showed in front turning for home, dug in resolutely when roused, drew clear then widened under a drive. KEY DEPUTY contested the pace while between rivals, dug in in the stretch and came again gamely to get the place prize. FIRST BLUSH contested the pace while three wide, dropped back in upper stretch then came again gamely outside. SECRET RUN argued the pace while four wide and weakened in the final furlong. AGGADAN was bumped at the start, was hustled up inside, chased the pace and lacked a rally. SHAKE YOU DOWN stumbled badly at the start, was bumped then was taken up, raced wide and had no rally. Following a general Stewards' inquiry the result was declared official.

Owners– 1, Robsham Mrs E P; 2, Live Oak Plantation; 3, Cowan Marjorie and Irving M; 4, Chapman Laz K Wexler Avers and Stiegal Michael; 5, Goldfarb S J Carney C L Fleisig J Rosenfeld N and Hochman J; 6, Cole Jr Robert L

Trainers– 1, Hough Stanley M; 2, Mott William I; 3, Jerkens H Allen; 4, Laboccetta Frank Jr; 5, Dutrow Richard E Jr; 6, Lake Scott A

$2 Daily Double (2–3) Paid $352.00 ; Daily Double Pool $153,317 .
$2 Pick Three (3–2–3) Paid $2,880.00 ; Pick Three Pool $115,211 .

EIGHTH RACE
Belmont
MAY 8, 2004

7 FURLONGS. (1.20) 9TH RUNNING OF THE NASSAU COUNTY BREEDERS' CUP. Grade II. Purse $200,000 (includes $50,000 BC – Breeders' Cup) (Up To $28,500 NYSBFOA) FOR FILLIES THREE YEARS OLDS. By subscription of $150 each, which should accompany the nomination; $750 to pass the entry box; $750 to start. The NYRA purse to be divided 60% to the winner, 20% to second, 10% to third, 5% to fourth, 3% to fifth and 2% divided equally among remaining finishers. Breeders' Cup fund monies also correspondingly divided provided a Breeders' Cup nominee has finished in an award position. Any Breeders' Cup fund monies not awarded will revert back to the fund. In the event this race overfills, starters will be determined with preference given to Breeders' Cup nominees only of equal racing quality or weight assignment. 122 lbs. Non–winners of $60,000 other than restricted stake since October 1 allowed 2 lbs.; $45,000 other than restricted stake, 4 lbs.; $30,000 or three races other than maiden or claiming, 6 lbs. Trophy to the winning owner presented by Breeders' Cup Ltd. Closed Saturday, April 24, 2004 with 27 Nominations.

Value of Race: $195,000 Winner $120,000; second $40,000; third $15,000; fourth $10,000; fifth $6,000; sixth $4,000. Mutuel Pool $624,431.00 Exacta Pool $446,993.00 Trifecta Pool $349,257.00

Last Raced	Horse	M/Eqt.	A.	Wt	PP	St	¼	½	Str	Fin	Jockey	Odds $1
9Apr04 ^{8}Aqu^{2}	Bending Strings	L	3	116	1	1	4^{hd}	3^{1}	12½	14¾	Bailey J D	2.85
4Apr04 ^{6}SA^{1}	Grey Traffic	L	3	116	4	3	2½	21½	21½	2^{4}	Prado E S	1.75
9Apr04 ^{8}Aqu^{8}	A Lulu Ofa Menifee	L b	3	116	3	6	6	4^{hd}	42½	32¾	Bravo J	21.50
21Apr04 ^{3}Aqu^{1}	Delta Sensation	L	3	116	6	5	5^{hd}	6	5^{12}	4no	Chavez J F	6.30
8Apr04 ^{5}Kee^{1}	Cherry Bomb	L	3	118	5	2	1^{hd}	1^{hd}	3^{hd}	5^{18}	Velazquez J R	2.00
17Apr04 ^{4}Kee^{2}	Whirlwind Charlott	L b	3	116	2	4	3½	51½	6	6	Migliore R	32.50

OFF AT 4:46 Start Good . Won driving. Track fast.

TIME :22^{2}, :45^{1}, 1:10, 1:22^{3} (:22.55, :45.39, 1:10.09, 1:22.70)

$2 Mutuel Prices:				
	3 – BENDING STRINGS	7.70	3.90	3.20
	6 – GREY TRAFFIC		3.60	3.30
	5 – A LULU OFA MENIFEE			6.70

$2 EXACTA 3–6 PAID $26.40 $2 TRIFECTA 3–6–5 PAID $182.50

Dk. b or br. f, (May), by American Chance – Straight South , by Hail the Pirates . Trainer McLaughlin Kiaran P. Bred by John D Gunther (Ky).

BENDING STRINGS raced in hand early on, angled out and rallied three wide approaching the stretch, responded when roused and drew away under constant handling. GREY TRAFFIC contested the pace along the inside, could not handle the winner but continued on gamely to be second best. A LULU OFA MENIFEE raced in hand while between rivals early, put in a four wide run nearing the stretch and tired in the final furlong. DELTA SENSATION was hustled along early and had no response when roused. CHERRY BOMB contested the pace from the outside and tired in the stretch. WHIRLWIND CHARLOTT bobbled at the start, chased the pace while three wide and tired after a half mile.

Owners– 1, Gunther John D; 2, Amerman John W Amerman Jerry; 3, Lael Stables; 4, Cay John E III; 5, Peachtree Stable; 6, Classic Star Stable LLC

Trainers– 1, McLaughlin Kiaran P; 2, Frankel Robert; 3, Tagg Barclay; 4, Alexander Frank A; 5, Pletcher Todd A; 6, Dowd John F

Scratched– Frenchglen (21Apr04 ^{5}Kee^{1}) , Slewville (10Apr04 ^{8}Haw^{1}) , Forestier (13Mar04 ^{7}Aqu^{1})

THIRD RACE
Bay Meadows
MAY 8, 2004

ABOUT 1⅛ MILES. (Turf) (1.45¹) 31ST RUNNING OF THE YERBA BUENA BREEDERS' CUP HANDICAP. Grade III. Purse $125,000 (includes$50,000 BC - Breeders' Cup) FOR FILLIES AND MARES THREE YEARS OLD AND UPWARD. By supscription of $75 each to accompany the nomination or by supplementary nomination of $1,500 by Noon, Sunday, May 2, 2004. 4375 to pass the entry box and $375 additional to start with $75,000 Guaranteed and an additional $50,000 from breeders' Cup Fund for Breeders' Cup eligibles only. The host association's Guaranteed monies to be divided 55% to the winner, 20% to second, 15% to third, 7.5% to fourth and 2.5% to fifth. Breeders' Cup Fund monies alsocorrespondingly divided providing a Breeders' Cup nominee has finished in an awarded position. Any Breeders' Cup Fund monies not awarded will revert back to the Fund. A trophy will be presented to the owner of the winner by Breeders' Cup Ltd. Closed Thurrsday, April 29, 2004 with 13 nominations. (Rail at 12 feet).

Value of Race: $113,750 Winner $68,750; second $25,000; third $11,250; fourth $5,625; fifth $3,125. Mutuel Pool $185,275.00 Exacta Pool $121,832.00 Quinella Pool $10,614.00 Trifecta Pool $138,624.00

Last Raced	Horse	M/Eqt.	A.	Wt	PP	St	¼	½	¾	Str	Fin	Jockey	Odds $1
10Apr04 7BM3	A B Noodle	LB	5	116	1	2	1hd	1 1½	11	1 3½	13	Castro J M	7.10
10Apr04 7BM2	Marwood	LB	4	116	2	3	32	33	34	2 3½	22	Warren R J Jr	5.80
10Apr04 7BM4	Hooked On Niners	LB f	5	116	3	5	5hd	41	41	4 2½	32	Baze R A	3.10
27Mar04 9SA3	Arabic Song-Ire	LB	5	117	6	6	6	6	54	512	4 1½	Blanc B	0.90
10Apr04 7BM1	Hippogator	LB b	4	116	4	1	24	22	23	3hd	519	Gonzalez R M	6.80
21Apr04 7BM2	Sister Mary Hugh	LB	5	113	5	4	41	5hd	6	6	6	Perez M A	23.00

OFF AT 2:10 Start Good. Won driving. Course firm.

TIME :23⁴, :47⁴, 1:12¹, 1:36, 1:46³ (:23.85, :47.92, 1:12.37, 1:36.05, 1:46.66)

$2 Mutuel Prices:

1 – A B NOODLE	16.20	8.20	6.80
2 – MARWOOD		7.00	6.20
3 – HOOKED ON NINERS			3.60

$1 EXACTA 1–2 PAID $41.40 $2 QUINELLA 1–2 PAID $37.40
$1 TRIFECTA 1–2–3 PAID $137.60

Dk. b or br. m, (May), by Alphabet Soup – Rasant, by Assert-Ire. Trainer Jenda Charles J. Bred by Adena Springs (Ky).

A B NOODLE had good speed, dictated the terms to the second bend, responded and edged away to mid stretch then held under steady encouragement. MARWOOD chased the pace to the half while racing inside, remained inside and slipped past HIPPOGATOR on the second turn then could not impact the winner while second best. HOOKED ON NINERS was outrun to the half, bid two wide on the second turn then had a mild late rally. ARABIC SONG (IRE) had no speed, saved ground throughout but did not threaten. HIPPOGATOR contested the pace to the backstretch, was outrun by the winner to the second turn then gave way after six furlongs. SISTER MARY HUGH had no speed, tired on the second turn and was not persevered with late.

Owners– 1, Amity and Bench; 2, Franks Farms; 3, Langbein Trust Morey Jr Robinson and Sandall; 4, Speelman Anthony; 5, Blanchard Bob Maser Tom and Todaro George; 6, Candell Andrew and Linda

Trainers– 1, Jenda Charles J; 2, Hollendorfer Jerry; 3, Morey William J Jr; 4, Drysdale Neil; 5, Hollendorfer Jerry; 6, Miller Quentin B

$2 Daily Double (5–1) Paid $55.40 ; Daily Double Pool $12,595 .
$1 Pick Three (2–5–1) Paid $245.30 ; Pick Three Pool $30,739 .

SIXTH RACE
Hollywood
MAY 8, 2004

6 FURLONGS. (1.07²) 52ND RUNNING OF THE LOS ANGELES TIMES HANDICAP. Grade III. Purse $150,000 FOR THREE YEAR OLDS AND UPWARD. By subscription of $150 each on or before April 28, 2004, or by supplementary nomination of $3,000 each by 3:00 pm Saturday, May 1,2004. $2,000 additional to start, with $90,000 to the winner, $30,000 to second, $18,000 tothird, $9,000 to fourth and $3,000 to fifth. Weights Sunday, May 2. Starters to be named through the entry box by closing time of entries. A trophy will be presented to the winning owner. Closed with 21 nominations.

Value of Race: $150,000 Winner $90,000; second $30,000; third $18,000; fourth $9,000; fifth $3,000. Mutuel Pool $600,634.00 Exacta Pool $374,901.00 Quinella Pool $27,592.00 Trifecta Pool $332,203.00 Superfecta Pool $110,707.00

Last Raced	Horse	M/Eqt.	A.	Wt	PP	St	¼	½	Str	Fin	Jockey	Odds $1
7Mar04 8SA3	Pohave	LB	6	114	1	7	3hd	2hd	1hd	11	Court J K	4.30
10Apr04 5Kee3	Marino Marini	LB	4	119	8	1	4 1½	3 2½	2½	2 3½	Baze T C	2.50
18Apr04 7SA3	Summer Service	LB bf	4	117	6	3	11	1½	34	3hd	Nakatani C S	8.80
24Jan04 8GP4	Hasty Kris	LB b	7	117	3	8	7 1½	5½	5hd	4½	John K	27.00
18Apr04 7SA2	Cayoke-FR	LB b	7	118	5	5	81	72	6 3½	54	Solis A	5.10
10May03 6Hol1	Hombre Rapido	LB b	7	119	2	4	2 1½	43	41	6 1½	Valdivia J Jr	5.00
21Mar04 2GG1	T S Eliot	LB	4	111	7	2	6 3½	9	7hd	7½	Santiago Javier	15.00
16Feb04 7SA3	Kewen	LB	4	113	9	9	9	8hd	9	82	Espinoza V	16.00
23Apr04 3Hol4	Seattle Shamus	LB	5	118	4	6	5hd	6hd	8hd	9	Valenzuela P A	7.10

OFF AT 3:57 Start Good. Won driving. Track fast.

TIME :21, :43¹, :55, 1:08 (:21.00, :43.23, :55.15, 1:08.12)

$2 Mutuel Prices:

1 – POHAVE	10.60	5.00	3.60
10 – MARINO MARINI		4.00	3.20
7 – SUMMER SERVICE			4.60

$1 EXACTA 1–10 PAID $15.50 $2 QUINELLA 1–10 PAID $20.00
$1 TRIFECTA 1–10–7 PAID $91.60 $1 SUPERFECTA 1–10–7–3 PAID $1,472.70

Gr/ro. g, (Apr), by Holy Bull – Trail Robbery, by Alydar. Trainer O'Neill Doug. Bred by H E Pabst & T J Pabst (Ky).

POHAVE stalked the pace inside on the backstretch, went between foes into the turn, bid between horses leaving the bend, gained a short lead nearing midstretch and gamely inched away under urging. MARINO MARINI broke out a bit, tracked the pace outside on the backstretch, bid three deep on the turn and into the stretch, battled outside the winner past midstretch but could not quite match that one late. SUMMER SERVICE sped to the early lead off the rail, dueled outside a rival then inched away and angled in a half mile out, fought back inside on the turn in the stretch, weakened late and just held third. HASTY KRIS chased a bit off the rail then along the inside, came out into the stretch, split rivals in midstretch and just missed the show. CAYOKE (FR) bobbled at the start, settled off the rail, came three deep into the stretch and also was edged for third. HOMBRE RAPIDO sent along inside to press the early pace, came a bit off the rail and stalked into and on the turn and weakened. T S ELIOT had speed between horses then stalked on the backstretch, dropped back outside a half mile out, angled in leaving the turn and lacked the needed response. KEWEN fell back off the rail soon after the start, settled off the pace, came a bit wide into the stretch and did not rally. SEATTLE SHAMUS stalked between foes then off the rail, dropped back on the turn and weakened.

Owners– 1, Kagele Brothers Inc Leatherman Ty and Leib Mark A; 2, Rancho San Miguel; 3, Weatherwatch Farm and Valente Roddy; 4, C R K Stable; 5, House Michael; 6, Granja Vista Del Rio Stable; 7, Darley Stable; 8, Grossman Jack and Oliver Hal; 9, Finney Albert and Taylor Mickey and Karen LLC

Trainers– 1, O'Neill Doug; 2, O'Neill Doug; 3, Spawr Bill; 4, Sadler John W; 5, Mullins Jeff; 6, Sadler John W; 7, Harty Eoin; 8, Mandella Gary; 9, French Neil

Scratched– Revello (04Mar04 6SA 1), Our Bobby V. (15Apr04 6SA 2)

$2 Daily Double (5–1) Paid $66.60 ; Daily Double Pool $32,585 .
$1 Pick Three (5–5–1) Paid $249.90 ; Pick Three Pool $115,563 .

NINTH RACE
Hollywood
MAY 8, 2004

1$\frac{1}{16}$ MILES. (1.40) 25TH RUNNING OF THE MERVYN LEROY HANDICAP. Grade II. Purse $150,000 FOR THREE-YEAR-OLDS AND UPWARD. By subscription of $150 each on or before Wednesday, April 28 or by supplementary nomination of $3,000 each by 3:00 pm Saturday, May 1. $1,500 additional to start, with $90,000 to the winner, $30,000 to second, $18,000 to third, $9,000 to fourth and $3,000 to fifth. Weights Sunday, May 2. Starters to be named through the entry box by closing time of entries. A trophy will be presented to the winning owner. Closed with 12 nominations.

Value of Race: $150,000 Winner $90,000; second $30,000; third $18,000; fourth $9,000; fifth $3,000. Mutuel Pool $382,524.00 Exacta Pool $244,890.00 Quinella Pool $23,017.00 Trifecta Pool $251,049.00 Superfecta Pool $111,288.00

Last Raced	Horse	M/Eqt.	A.	Wt	PP	St	¼	½	¾	Str	Fin	Jockey	Odds $1
3Apr04 ^{10}SA^{3}	Even the Score	LB b	6	116	4	6	$6^{2\frac{1}{2}}$	4^{1}	4^{2}	2^{1}	1^{2}	Flores D R	5.00
3Apr04 ^{10}SA^{4}	Ender's Shadow	LB bf	4	113	6	1	1^{hd}	1^{hd}	1^{1}	$1^{\frac{1}{2}}$	2^{3}	Ruis M	15.20
3Apr04 ^{10}SA^{2}	Total Impact-Chi	LB b	6	116	8	4	4^{2}	$3^{1\frac{1}{2}}$	3^{1}	3^{1}	3^{1}	Smith M E	4.90
6Mar04 ^{10}SA^{4}	Olmodavor	LB b	5	121	3	8	7^{hd}	$7^{\frac{1}{2}}$	6^{4}	$5^{2\frac{1}{2}}$	$4^{\frac{1}{2}}$	Solis A	2.00
6Mar04 ^{9}SA^{6}	Buckland Manor	LB	4	117	7	3	$3^{\frac{1}{2}}$	$2^{\frac{1}{2}}$	2^{hd}	4^{hd}	5^{4}	Nakatani C S	2.90
13Mar04 ^{6}SA^{3}	Gift of the Eagle	LB b	6	118	1	5	5^{hd}	5^{hd}	$5^{\frac{1}{2}}$	$6^{3\frac{1}{2}}$	6^{4}	Valenzuela P A	14.30
14Feb04 ^{6}SA^{7}	The Eden-Arg	LB	4	113	2	2	2^{1}	$6^{2\frac{1}{2}}$	$7^{2\frac{1}{2}}$	7^{8}	7^{20}	Santiago Javier	21.70
3Apr04 ^{10}SA^{6}	Star Cross-Arg	LB b	7	113	5	7	8	8	8	8	8	Espinoza V	8.90

OFF AT 5:25 Start Good . Won driving. Track fast.

TIME $:23^{1}$, $:45^{4}$, $1:09^{2}$, $1:34^{2}$, $1:40^{4}$ (:23.36, :45.86, 1:09.49, 1:34.52, 1:40.81)

$2 Mutuel Prices:				
	4 – EVEN THE SCORE	12.00	6.00	5.00
	6 – ENDER'S SHADOW		15.20	7.60
	8 – TOTAL IMPACT–CHI			4.20

$1 EXACTA 4–6 PAID $81.00 $2 QUINELLA 4–6 PAID $109.80
$1 TRIFECTA 4–6–8 PAID $430.50 $1 SUPERFECTA 4–6–8–3 PAID $3,087.40

Gr/ro. h, (Apr), by Unbridled's Song – Ashtabula , by Rahy . Trainer Cerin Vladimir. Bred by Aspiration Stable (Ky).

EVEN THE SCORE stalked the pace a bit off the rail early, moved up three deep midway on the backstretch, continued just off the inside on the second turn, awaited room leaving that bend, came out into the stretch, threw his head when just behind the pacesetter nearing midstretch, collared that one under left handed urging past the eighth pole and pulled clear. ENDER'S SHADOW had speed off the rail and set a pressured pace, angled in leaving the backstretch, inched away on the second turn, fought back inside in the stretch, could not match the winner late but was clearly second best. TOTAL IMPACT (CHI) five wide into the first turn, stalked outside, bid three deep on the backstretch, continued outside on the second turn and into the stretch and held third. OLMODAVOR off a bit slowly, pulled inside then came off the rail on the first turn, chased outside a rival, advanced outside on the second turn, came four wide into the stretch and lacked the needed rally. BUCKLAND MANOR four wide into the first turn, stalked outside then bid between foes, continued off the rail on the second turn and weakened. GIFT OF THE EAGLE pulled inside and steadied hard into the first turn, chased outside a rival then between foes midway on the backstretch and did not rally. THE EDEN (ARG) had speed between foes then angled in and stalked inside, dropped back on the backstretch, came out into the stretch and weakened. STAR CROSS (ARG) settled off the rail, dropped back leaving the backstretch, gave way and was eased in the stretch.

Owners– 1, Parra Rosendo G; 2, Green Lantern Stables LLC; 3, Al Kabeer Sultan Mohammed Saud and Bridport S A; 4, Wertheimer and Frere; 5, McCaffery Trudy and Toffan John A; 6, Bell Lance and Krikorian George; 7, Conese Hirsch Nestor Et Al; 8, E A Ranches

Trainers– 1, Cerin Vladimir; 2, Sahadi Jenine; 3, De Seroux Laura; 4, Mandella Richard; 5, Gonzalez J Paco; 6, Shirreffs John; 7, Mullins Jeff; 8, Vienna Darrell

---

$2 Daily Double (11–4) Paid $55.00 ; Daily Double Pool $37,246 .
$1 Pick Three (3–2/11–4) Paid $89.40 ; Pick Three Pool $74,981 .

EIGHTH RACE
Belmont
MAY 9, 2004

6 FURLONGS. (1.07^{3}) 21ST RUNNING OF THE GENUINE RISK HANDICAP. Grade II. Purse $150,000 A HANDICAP FOR FILLIES AND MARES THREE YEARS OLD AND UPWARD. By subscription of $150 each, which should accompany the nomination; $750 to pass the entry box; $750 to start. The purse to be divided 60% to the winner, 20% to second, 10% to third, 5% to fourth, 3% to fifth and 2% divided equally among remaining finishers. A trophy will be presented to the winning owner. Closed Saturday, April 24, 2004 with 14 Nominations.

Value of Race: $147,000 Winner $90,000; second $30,000; third $15,000; fourth $7,500; fifth $4,500. Mutuel Pool $361,755.00 Exacta Pool $302,539.00 Trifecta Pool $152,117.00

Last Raced	Horse	M/Eqt.	A.	Wt	PP	St	¼	½	Str	Fin	Jockey	Odds $1
17Mar04 ^{5}SA^{1}	Bear Fan	L f	5	117	1	3	3^{1}	$1^{\frac{1}{2}}$	1^{5}	1^{5}	Velazquez J R	1.45
7Apr04 ^{8}Kee^{2}	Harmony Lodge	L	6	120	3	2	$2^{\frac{1}{2}}$	2^{hd}	2^{3}	2^{3}	Migliore R	1.25
21Apr04 ^{8}Aqu^{1}	Kitty Knight	L	4	114	4	4	$4^{1\frac{1}{2}}$	$4^{\frac{1}{2}}$	$3^{\frac{1}{2}}$	$3^{2\frac{1}{4}}$	Arroyo N Jr	7.00
8Apr04 ^{8}Aqu^{1}	Our Royal Dancer		4	113	5	5	5	5	5	4^{3}	Luzzi M J	13.30
17Apr04 ^{7}Kee^{10}	Mooji Moo	L	5	115	2	1	$1^{\frac{1}{2}}$	$3^{3\frac{1}{2}}$	4^{1}	5	Aguilar M	7.10

OFF AT 4:45 Start Good . Won driving. Track fast.

TIME $:22^{2}$, $:44^{4}$, $:56^{2}$, $1:08^{4}$ (:22.59, :44.99, :56.47, 1:08.85)

$2 Mutuel Prices:				
	1 – BEAR FAN	4.90	2.50	2.20
	3 – HARMONY LODGE		2.30	2.10
	4 – KITTY KNIGHT			2.40

$2 EXACTA 1–3 PAID $10.80 $2 TRIFECTA 1–3–4 PAID $29.40

B. m, (Mar), by Pine Bluff – Shezalong , by Shimatoree . Trainer Ward Wesley A. Bred by Wesley Ward (Cal).

BEAR FAN raced with the pace along the inside, drew away when asked and remained well clear under a vigorous hand ride. HARMONY LODGE contested the pace while three wide, was no match for the winner but was clearly best of the others. KITTY KNIGHT was bumped at the start, raced four wide and had her rider lose his whip over three eighths from home. OUR ROYAL DANCER was bumped at the start, dropped back inside early, came wide into the stretch and had no rally. MOOJI MOO contested the pace while between rivals and tired in the stretch.

Owners– 1, Wesley Ward Fan Peter; 2, Melnyk Eugene and Laura; 3, Bohemia Stable; 4, Fink Morton; 5, Deckert Sr Robert Deckert Jr Robert

Trainers– 1, Ward Wesley A; 2, Pletcher Todd A; 3, Jerkens H Allen; 4, Levine Bruce N; 5, Hills Timothy A

EIGHTH RACE
Hollywood
MAY 9, 2004

1⅛ MILES. (1.45[1]) 63RD RUNNING OF THE VANITY HANDICAP. Grade I. Purse $250,000 FOR FILLIES AND MARES THREE YEARS OLD AND UPWARD. By subscription of $250 each on or before Wednesday, April 28 or by supplementary nomination of $5,000 each by 3:00 pm Saturday, May 1. $1,000 to pass the entry box and an additional $1,500 to start, with$150,000 to the winner, $50,000 to second, $30,000 to third, $15,000 to fourth and $5,000 to fifth. Weights Sunday, May 2. Starters to be named through the entry box by closing time of entries. Trophies will be presented to the winning owner and trainer.Closed with 8 nominations.

Value of Race: $245,000 Winner $150,000; second $50,000; third $30,000; fourth $15,000. Mutuel Pool $281,292.00 Exacta Pool $149,361.00 Quinella Pool $15,320.00 Trifecta Pool $94,135.00

Last Raced	Horse	M/Eqt.	A.	Wt	PP	St	¼	½	¾	Str	Fin	Jockey	Odds $1
17Apr04 [8]Aqu[4]	Victory Encounter	LB	4	116	4	4	4	4	4	3[1½]	1[2½]	Solis A	7.30
14Mar04 [8]SA[1]	Adoration	LB	5	122	1	1	1[1]	1[hd]	1[½]	1[1]	2[1]	Smith M E	0.80
3Apr04 [9]OP[2]	Star Parade-Arg	LB	5	117	3	2	2[1½]	2[3½]	2[3]	2[1½]	3[5]	Espinoza V	1.60
4Apr04 [7]SA[1]	Hope Rises	LB	4	116	2	3	3[6]	3[7]	3[7]	4	4	Flores D R	6.50

OFF AT 4:55 Start Good . Won driving. Track fast.

TIME :23[2], :46[1], 1:09[3], 1:35[2], 1:48[1] (:23.51, :46.26, 1:09.76, 1:35.44, 1:48.28)

$2 Mutuel Prices:

5 – VICTORY ENCOUNTER	16.60	3.20	—
1 – ADORATION		2.20	—
4 – STAR PARADE–ARG		—	—

$1 EXACTA 5–1 PAID $21.20 $2 QUINELLA 1–5 PAID $13.20
$1 TRIFECTA 5–1–4 PAID $29.90

B. f, (Mar), by Victory Speech – Marvelous Moment , by Raise a Native . Trainer Sadler John W. Bred by Helen Smith (Ky).

VICTORY ENCOUNTER unhurried off the rail early, angled in and lagged back, moved up some on the second turn, then rallied along the rail under urging to collar ADORATION late and pulled clear. ADORATION sped to the early lead, set a pressured pace a bit off the rail, came out some into the stretch, inched away under urging but could not hold off the winner. STAR PARADE (ARG) stalked the early pace off the rail, bid outside the runner-up and pressed that rival's pace, was floated out a bit into the stretch and weakened some. HOPE RISES bobbled slightly at the start, stalked inside, came out leaving the second turn and into the stretch, angled inward in upper stretch, then drifted out late and weakened.

Owners– 1, Mankiewicz Tom; 2, Amerman Racing Stables LLC; 3, Tanaka Gary A; 4, Jay Em Ess Stable

Trainers– 1, Sadler John W; 2, Hofmans David; 3, Vienna Darrell; 4, Ellis Ronald W

Scratched– Coconut Girl (02May04 [8]BM [3]) , Beaucette (22Apr04 [1]Hol[1])

$2 Daily Double (4–5) Paid $95.80 ; Daily Double Pool $26,391 .
$1 Pick Three (5–4–5) Paid $299.30 ; Pick Three Pool $70,495 .

EIGHTH RACE
Pimlico
MAY 14, 2004

1 1/16 MILES. (1.40[4]) 13TH RUNNING OF THE PIMLICO BREEDERS' CUP DISTAFF HANDICAP. Grade III. Purse $150,000 (includes$50,000 BC – Breeders' Cup) FOR FILLIES AND MARES, THREE-YEARS-OLD AND UPWARD. By subscription of $100 each which should accompany the nomination, $500 to pass the entry box, $500 additional to start, with $100,000 Guaranteed, and an additional $50,000 from the Breeders' Cup Fundfor Cup nominees only. The Host Association's added monies to be divided, 60% of all monies to the winner, 20% to second, 11% to third, 6% to fourth and 3% to fifth. Breeders' Cup Fund monies also correspondingly divided provided a Breeders' Cup Nomineehas finished in an awarded position. Any Breeders' Cup Fund money not awarded will revert back to the fund. Supplemental nominations of $1000 each will be accepted by Friday, May 7, 2004 with all other fees due as noted. Weights Saturday, May 8, 2004. Preference given to Breeders' Cup nominees only of equal racing quality or highest weight assignment (respective of sex and weight for age). Starters to be named through the entry box by the usual time of closing. Trophy to the winning owner given by the Breeders' Cup Ltd. Closed Sunday, May 2, 2004 with 24 Nominations.

Value of Race: $150,000 Winner $90,000; second $30,000; third $16,500; fourth $9,000; fifth $4,500. Mutuel Pool $424,491.00 Exacta Pool $316,043.00 Superfecta Pool $59,178.00 Trifecta Pool $216,908.00

Last Raced	Horse	M/Eqt.	A.	Wt	PP	St	¼	½	¾	Str	Fin	Jockey	Odds $1
30Apr04 [3]Aqu[1]	Friel's for Real	L f	4	115	3	1	6[3½]	6[4]	4[1]	1[½]	1[2¼]	Castellano A Jr	11.40
16Apr04 [9]Kee[4]	Saintly Action	L	5	114	1	8	5[hd]	5[hd]	5[1½]	6[5]	2[2]	Bailey J D	3.50
17Apr04 [8]Aqu[3]	Nonsuch Bay	L	5	116	2	4	7[2]	7[½]	7[½]	5[hd]	3[hd]	Velasquez C	3.10
9Apr04 [8]Pim[1]	Shiny Sheet	L b	6	116	8	6	3[hd]	4[2]	2[hd]	4[½]	4[no]	Rose J	18.60
18Apr04 [7]Kee[1]	Fircroft	L	4	113	7	7	4[2]	3[1]	3[½]	2[hd]	5[3½]	Day P	4.30
27Mar04 [10]TP[1]	Angela's Love	L	4	115	6	2	1[1½]	1[½]	1[hd]	3[hd]	6[1½]	Guidry M	1.80
4Apr04 [10]GP[8]	Redoubled Miss	L bf	5	115	4	3	8	8	8	7[4]	7[12¾]	Dominguez R A	23.80
9Apr04 [8]Pim[3]	Gazillion	L f	5	114	5	5	2[½]	2[hd]	6[1]	8	8	Hamilton S D	16.20

OFF AT 4:12 Start Good . Won driving. Track fast.

TIME :24[3], :48[3], 1:12[4], 1:38[2], 1:45 (:24.65, :40.63, 1:12.98, 1:38.57, 1:45.03)

$2 Mutuel Prices:

3 – FRIEL'S FOR REAL	24.80	9.20	4.80
1 – SAINTLY ACTION		5.60	4.00
2 – NONSUCH BAY			2.80

$2 EXACTA 3–1 PAID $104.80 $1 SUPERFECTA 3–1–2–10 PAID $1,830.80
$2 TRIFECTA 3–1–2 PAID $350.40

Dk. b or br. f, (Apr), by Sword Dance-Ire – Beaties for Real , by Unreal Zeal . Trainer Allard Edward T. Bred by Gilbert G Campbell (Fla).

FRIEL'S FOR REAL settled four wide while not far back, moved closer leaving the far turn, lodged a bid nearing the quarter pole, took a short lead in upper stretch, edged clear leaving the furlong marker and held sway under strong handling. SAINTLY ACTION , saved ground the first turn, angled out three wide down the backstretch, moved closer leaving the three eighths pole, angled out five wide from behind rivals for the drive, closed steadily between horses and was game for the place. NONSUCH BAY , unhurried early while two wide, gained ground nearing the quarter pole, swung out six wide for the drive and finished willingly. SHINY SHEET was astutely angled to the rail around the first turn, prompted the pace under rating, lodged a rail bid leaving the three eighths pole, dueled into the stretch then gave way grudgingly in the final sixteenth. FIRCROFT , four wide the first turn, continued four wide down the backstretch attending the pace, lodged a three wide bid leaving the far turn, dueled into the stretch then faded in the final seventy yards. ANGELA'S LOVE cleared early, set a moderate pace off the rail, was joined after six furlongs, dueled to mid stretch then surrendered. REDOUBLED MISS lacked speed along the inside, angled out four wide for the drive and failed to menace. GAZILLION bobbled a bit leaving the gate, pressed the pace three wide between rivals and faltered leaving the three furlong pole.

Owners– 1, Campbell Gilbert G; 2, Live Oak Plantation; 3, Thorn Stable; 4, Rathbun Mrs Henry T; 5, Humphrey G Watts Jr; 6, Poston Bill and Vicki; 7, Centaur Farms Inc; 8, Kessler Lucy C

Trainers– 1, Allard Edward T; 2, Mott William I; 3, Alexander Frank A; 4, Hadry Charles J; 5, Arnold George R II; 6, Romans Dale; 7, Capuano Gary; 8, Smith Hamilton A

Scratched– Roar Emotion (16Apr04 [9]Kee[3]) , Smok'n Frolic (17Apr04 [8]Aqu[2])

$2 Pick Three (1–12–3) Paid $1,342.60 ; Pick Three Pool $43,397 .

NINTH RACE
Pimlico
MAY 14, 2004

6 FURLONGS. (1.09) 19TH RUNNING OF THE ADENA STALLIONS' MISS PREAKNESS. Grade III. Purse $100,000 FOR FILLIES, THREE-YEARS-OLD. By free subscription. $500 to pass the entry box, $500 additional to start, with $100,000 Guaranteed, of which 60% to the winner, 20% to second, 11% to third, 6% to fourth and 3% to fifth. Weight 122 lbs. Non-winners of arace of $50,000, allowed, 3 lbs.; a race of $30,000, 5 lbs.; a race of $20,000, 7 lbs. (Maiden and Claiming races not considered in estimating allowances). Trophy to the owner of the winner. Adena Springs will offer to the first three finishers, a breeding season to one of the following: Red Bullet, Macho Uno, Milwaukee Brew. Closed Sunday, May 2, 2004 with 38 Nominations.

Value of Race: $100,000 Winner $60,000; second $20,000; third $11,000; fourth $6,000; fifth $3,000. Mutuel Pool $482,555.00 Exacta Pool $369,963.00 Superfecta Pool $66,461.00 Trifecta Pool $263,112.00

Last Raced	Horse	M/Eqt.	A.	Wt	PP	St	¼	½	Str	Fin	Jockey	Odds $1
12Dec03 $^{8}Aqu^{3}$	Forest Music	L	3	115	4	6	4^{2}	5^{3}	1^{hd}	1^{hd}	Dominguez R A	8.90
9Apr04 $^{10}OP^{7}$	Stephan's Angel	L f	3	119	1	9	10^{3}	10^{3}	5^{2}	$2^{4\frac{1}{4}}$	Elliott S	6.50
16Apr04 $^{8}GP^{1}$	Fall Fashion	L b	3	119	8	3	3^{hd}	3^{hd}	3^{2}	3^{1}	Prado E S	32.80
13Mar04 $^{7}Aqu^{1}$	Forestier	L	3	117	7	4	5^{1}	4^{1}	2^{hd}	4^{1}	Lopez C C	3.60
27Apr04 $^{9}CD^{4}$	Preach It	L	3	115	5	2	1^{hd}	2^{1}	4^{hd}	$5^{1\frac{1}{2}}$	Day P	29.20
9Apr04 $^{5}Aqu^{1}$	Areek	L	3	117	2	7	$6^{2\frac{1}{2}}$	6^{2}	6^{1}	6^{hd}	Bailey J D	1.70
9Apr04 $^{8}Aqu^{4}$	Baldomera	L b	3	119	10	8	11	11	9	$7^{5\frac{1}{4}}$	Vega H	38.60
2May04 $^{6}Pim^{1}$	A Case of Class	L f	3	115	3	1	2^{1}	1^{hd}	7^{5}	$8^{2\frac{3}{4}}$	Chavez S N	75.30
16Apr04 $^{10}Kee^{1}$	Ruthless Babe	L	3	115	11	10	8^{2}	8^{1}	8^{1}	9	Smith M E	39.80
24Apr04 $^{9}Pim^{1}$	Perilous Night	L	3	115	6	11	9^{2}	$9^{1\frac{1}{2}}$	—	—	Santana J Z	22.50
14Feb04 $^{9}Aqu^{1}$	AmongMySouvenirs	L f	3	119	9	5	$7^{\frac{1}{2}}$	$7^{1\frac{1}{2}}$	—	—	Pino M G	3.20

OFF AT 4:42 Start Good . Won driving. Track fast.

TIME :23, :45^{4}, :58, 1:10^{4} (:23.00, :45.80, :58.16, 1:10.97)

$2 Mutuel Prices:

4 – FOREST MUSIC	19.80	11.20	10.20
1 – STEPHAN'S ANGEL		8.40	6.60
8 – FALL FASHION			15.20

$2 EXACTA 4–1 PAID $133.20 $1 SUPERFECTA 4–1–8–7 PAID $9,869.40

$2 TRIFECTA 4–1–8 PAID $2,325.60

Gr/ro. f, (Apr), by Unbridled's Song – Defer West , by Gone West . Trainer Shuman Mark. Bred by Twin Hopes Farm Inc (Ky).

FOREST MUSIC , bumped leaving the starting gate, stalked the pace, swung wide in upper stretch, opened a clear lead near the sixteenth pole, drifted out late and lasted. STEPHAN'S ANGEL lacked speed, swung six wide at the head of the stretch and closed gamely. FALL FASHION , three wide on the turn, chased pace, was brushed by FORESTIER in midstretch then weakened. FORESTIER , wide around the turn, drifted in near the eighth pole and and gave way. PREACH IT , two wide, disputed the pace and gave way. AREEK , swung wide in upper stretch, failed to rally. BALDOMERA , outrun, raced eight wide in the stretch. A CASE OF CLASS dueled along the rail and gave way. RUTHLESS BABE , outrun, raced seven wide in the stretch. PERILOUS NIGHT , outrun, unseated her rider when clipping heels with AMONG MY SOUVENIRS approaching the eighth pole. AMONG MY SOUVENIRS , outrun, broke down approaching the eighth pole. There was a stewards' inquiry concerning the run through the stretch.

Owners– 1, Gill Michael J; 2, Fox Hill Farms Inc; 3, Courtlandt Farms; 4, Kline Alan S; 5, Live Oak Plantation; 6, Shadwell Stable; 7, Hidden Lane Farms Inc; 8, Gamber Robert E; 9, Andrew Farm; 10, Fitzhugh LLC; 11, Marathon Farms Inc

Trainers– 1, Shuman Mark; 2, Servis John C; 3, Motion H Graham; 4, Pletcher Todd A; 5, Zito Nicholas P; 6, Hennig Mark; 7, Preciado Guadalupe; 8, Gamber Robert E; 9, Biancone Patrick L; 10, Small Richard W; 11, Dutrow Anthony W

$2 Pick Three (12–3–4) Paid $2,718.60 ; Pick Three Pool $49,432 .

TENTH RACE
Pimlico
MAY 14, 2004

1⅛ MILES. (1.47^{1}) 80TH RUNNING OF THE BLACK-EYED SUSAN. Grade II. Purse $200,000 FOR FILLIES, THREE-YEARS-OLD. By free subscription. $1000 to pass the entry box, $1000 additional to start, with $200,000 Guaranteed, of which 60% to the winner, 20% to second, 11% to third, 6% to fourth and 3% to fifth. Weight 122 lbs. Non-winners of$75,000 at one mile or over, allowed, 3 lbs.; $50,000 at one mile or over, 5 lbs.; $30,000 at one mile or over 7 lbs. (Maiden and Claiming races not considered in estimating allowances). Trophy to the owner of the winner. Closed Sunday, May 2, 2004 with 32 Nominations.

Value of Race: $200,000 Winner $120,000; second $40,000; third $22,000; fourth $12,000; fifth $6,000. Mutuel Pool $624,381.00 Exacta Pool $461,842.00 Superfecta Pool $124,344.00 Trifecta Pool $118,542.00

Last Raced	Horse	M/Eqt.	A.	Wt	PP	St	¼	½	¾	Str	Fin	Jockey	Odds $1
24Apr04 $^{3}Hol^{1}$	Yearly Report	L	3	122	5	4	3^{hd}	$3^{\frac{1}{2}}$	$2^{\frac{1}{2}}$	2^{2}	$1^{1\frac{1}{2}}$	Bailey J D	0.50
17Apr04 $^{9}Pim^{2}$	Pawyne Princess	L b	3	115	1	3	$5^{\frac{1}{2}}$	$5^{3\frac{1}{2}}$	$5^{3\frac{1}{2}}$	4^{4}	2^{nk}	Dominguez R A	3.20
16Apr04 $^{8}Aqu^{3}$	Rare Gift	L	3	115	4	5	2^{1}	1^{hd}	$1^{\frac{1}{2}}$	1^{hd}	$3^{1\frac{1}{2}}$	Prado E S	8.30
20Mar04 $^{9}TP^{3}$	Native Annie	L	3	122	6	6	4^{hd}	$4^{\frac{1}{2}}$	$3^{\frac{1}{2}}$	3^{hd}	$4^{6\frac{1}{4}}$	Espinoza V	40.50
14Mar04 $^{9}Tam^{2}$	Menifeeque	L b	3	115	7	1	6^{3}	6^{1}	7	$5^{1\frac{1}{2}}$	$5^{2\frac{1}{2}}$	Velasquez C	24.30
10Apr04 $^{8}Kee^{1}$	Song Track	L	3	117	3	7	7	7	6^{1}	6^{3}	$6^{10\frac{3}{4}}$	Albarado R J	5.10
27Mar04 $^{8}Sun^{4}$	America America		3	122	2	2	$1^{\frac{1}{2}}$	2^{hd}	$4^{\frac{1}{2}}$	7	7	Umana J L	62.30

OFF AT 5:16 Start Good . Won driving. Track fast.

TIME :25^{1}, :49^{3}, 1:13^{4}, 1:39^{2}, 1:52^{3} (:25.21, :49.71, 1:13.97, 1:39.49, 1:52.65)

$2 Mutuel Prices:

6 – YEARLY REPORT	3.00	2.20	2.10
2 – PAWYNE PRINCESS		2.60	2.10
5 – RARE GIFT			2.10

$2 EXACTA 6–2 PAID $8.00 $1 SUPERFECTA 6–2–5–7 PAID $69.60

$2 TRIFECTA 6–2–5 PAID $24.60

B. f, (Jan), by General Meeting – Fiscal Year , by Half a Year . Trainer Baffert Bob. Bred by Mr & Mrs John C Mabee (Cal).

YEARLY REPORT raced three to four wide prompting the pace under rating, drew on near even terms between rivals entering the lane, dueled outside of RARE GIFT past the eighth pole, drifted in a bit then edged clear under strong left handed encouragement. PAWYNE PRINCESS rated close up behind rivals, angled out for room leaving the eighth pole then finished gamely to just get the place. RARE GIFT disputed slow fractions while two and three wide between rivals, dueled inside of YEARLY REPORT past the furlong marker and stayed on well. NATIVE ANNIE lost ground four to five wide while racing in close attendance, lodged a bid leaving the far turn, forced the issue past the three sixteenths pole, drifted a bit and weakened late. MENIFEEQUE , a bit fractious in the gate, settled off the rail, came four wide for the drive and lacked a response. SONG TRACK , unhurried early while saving some ground, raced between rivals into the stretch and failed to threaten. AMERICA AMERICA went to a brief early lead, disputed the pace inside of rivals for nearly six furlongs then faltered.

Owners– 1, Golden Eagle Farm; 2, Gill Michael J; 3, Bolton George Dipietro David and Honour Roger; 4, Stonerside Stable LLC; 5, Live Oak Plantation; 6, Farish William S and Phipps Ogden Mills; 7, Cameron Express Inc

Trainers– 1, Baffert Bob; 2, Robb John J; 3, Kimmel John C; 4, Stidham Michael; 5, Mott William I; 6, Howard Neil J; 7, Mourier Franck

Scratched– Pilfer (10Apr04 $^{7}OP^{2}$)

$2 Pick Three (3–4–1/6) Paid $359.40 ; Pick Three Pool $79,879 .

ELEVENTH RACE
Pimlico
MAY 14, 2004

$1\frac{3}{16}$ MILES. (1.52^2) 38TH RUNNING OF THE PIMLICO SPECIAL HANDICAP. Grade I. Purse $500,000 FOR FOUR-YEAR-OLDS AND UPWARD. By subscription of $500 each which should accompany the nomination. All horses shall pay $5,000 to pass the entry box and $5,000 additional to start. $500,000 Guaranteed, of which 60% to the winner, 20% to second, 11% to third, 6% to fourth, and 3% to fifth. Trophies will be presented to the winning owner, trainer and jockey. Closed Sunday, May 2, 2004 with 13 Nominations.

Value of Race: $500,000 Winner $300,000; second $100,000; third $55,000; fourth $30,000; fifth $15,000. Mutuel Pool $915,668.00 Exacta Pool $571,206.00 Superfecta Pool $107,542.00 Trifecta Pool $377,934.00

Last Raced	Horse	M/Eqt.	A.	Wt	PP	St	¼	½	¾	Str	Fin	Jockey	Odds $1
6Mar04 ^{10}SA^1	Southern Image	L	4	120	4	1	$2^{2\frac{1}{2}}$	$2^{2\frac{1}{2}}$	2^2	$1^{\frac{1}{2}}$	$1^{1\frac{1}{4}}$	Espinoza V	1.90
22Apr04 ^{8}Kee^1	Midway Road	L	4	116	1	4	$1^{\frac{1}{2}}$	1^1	$1^{\frac{1}{2}}$	$2^{3\frac{1}{2}}$	$2^{2\frac{1}{2}}$	Albarado R J	3.30
13Mar04 ^{13}GP^3	Bowman's Band	L	6	114	5	2	$3^{\frac{1}{2}}$	3^1	3^2	3^5	$3^{4\frac{3}{4}}$	Dominguez R A	20.60
22Apr04 ^{8}Kee^2	Evening Attire	L b	6	115	3	6	5^{hd}	6	6	5^7	$4^{2\frac{3}{4}}$	Prado E S	5.70
3Apr04 ^{10}SA^1	Dynever	L	4	117	6	5	6	5^{hd}	4^2	$4^{1\frac{1}{2}}$	$5^{8\frac{3}{4}}$	Nakatani C S	1.70
3Apr04 ^{11}OP^2	Ole Faunty	L	5	114	2	3	4^2	$4^{\frac{1}{2}}$	$5^{\frac{1}{2}}$	6	6	Day P	9.70

OFF AT 5:47 Start Good . Won driving. Track fast.

TIME :24^2, :47^2, 1:11^4, 1:36^1, 1:55^4 (:24.42, :47.53, 1:11.88, 1:36.25, 1:55.89)

$2 Mutuel Prices:

4 – SOUTHERN IMAGE	5.80	3.20	3.00
1 – MIDWAY ROAD		4.20	3.60
6 – BOWMAN'S BAND			6.40

$2 EXACTA 4–1 PAID $34.00 $1 SUPERFECTA 4–1–6–3 PAID $336.90
$2 TRIFECTA 4–1–6 PAID $250.80

Dk. b or br. c, (Apr), by Halo's Image – Pleasant Dixie , by Dixieland Band . Trainer Machowsky Michael. Bred by Arthur I Appleton (Fla).

SOUTHERN IMAGE , snugly rated outside MIDWAY ROAD, bid for the lead entering the stretch, dueled through the lane and drove clear. MIDWAY ROAD set the pace along the rail, dueled with the winner through the stretch, switched leads twice in the drive and weakened. BOWMAN'S BAND stalked the pace, raced three wide entering the far turn, attempted to drift in in midstretch and failed to rally in an even effort. EVENING ATTIRE lacked speed, raced in the two path and passed tired ones. DYNEVER , three wide the first turn, raced four wide entering the far turn and was outrun. OLE FAUNTY raced along the rail and dropped back.

Owners– 1, Blahut Stables LLC Kagele Brothers Tepper Allen et al; 2, Farish William S; 3, Schwartz Martin S; 4, Grant Mary and Joseph and Kelly Thomas J; 5, Peter Karches & Catherine Wills; 6, Van Meter II Thomas and Hendrickson Doug

Trainers– 1, Machowsky Michael; 2, Howard Neil J; 3, Jerkens H Allen; 4, Kelly Patrick J; 5, Clement Christophe; 6, Walden W Elliott

Scratched– Funny Cide (03Apr04 ^{8}Aqu^1)

$2 Daily Double (6–4) Paid $7.40 ; Daily Double Pool $141,152 .

EIGHTH RACE
Hollywood
MAY 15, 2004

1 MILE. (Turf) (1.32^3) 36TH RUNNING OF THE SENORITA. Grade III. Purse $100,000 FOR FILLIES THREE-YEARS-OLD. By subscription of $100 each on or before Wednesday, May 5, or by supplementary nomination of $2,000 each by closing time of entries. $1,000 additional to start, with $100,000 added. The added money and all fees to be divided60% to the winner, 20% to second, 12% to third, 6% to fourth and 2% to fifth. Weight 123 lbs. Non-winners of $100,000 at a mile or over allowed 2 lbs.; such a race of $50,000 allowed 4 lbs.; non-winners of two races other than claiming or starter at a mile or over allowed 6 lbs.; such a race allowed 8 lbs. Starters to be named through the entry box by closing time of entries. A trophy will be presented to the winning owner. Closed with 19 nominations.

Value of Race: $108,900 Winner $65,340; second $21,780; third $13,068; fourth $6,534; fifth $2,178. Mutuel Pool $473,845.00 Exacta Pool $248,254.00 Quinella Pool $21,886.00 Trifecta Pool $256,285.00 Superfecta Pool $100,991.00

Last Raced	Horse	M/Eqt.	A.	Wt	PP	St	¼	½	¾	Str	Fin	Jockey	Odds $1
16Nov03 Rom^1	Miss Vegas-Ire	LB	3	115	3	4	1^2	$1^{2\frac{1}{2}}$	$1^{3\frac{1}{2}}$	1^1	1^{hd}	Solis A	2.40
11Apr04 ^{8}SA^1	Ticker Tape-GB	LB	3	121	7	7	6^{hd}	6^{hd}	5^2	2^{hd}	2^3	Nakatani C S	1.30
11Apr04 ^{8}SA^2	Amorama-FR	LB b	3	116	1	6	5^2	5^1	3^{hd}	4^5	3no	Flores D R	5.10
11Apr04 ^{8}SA^3	Winendynme	LB	3	115	4	1	3^{hd}	$4^{\frac{1}{2}}$	$4^{1\frac{1}{2}}$	$3^{\frac{1}{2}}$	4^5	Valdivia J Jr	16.60
9Apr04 ^{8}SA^1	Freakin Streakin	LB	3	118	5	2	7	7	6^{hd}	$5^{1\frac{1}{2}}$	5^2	Valenzuela P A	9.90
23Apr04 ^{8}Hol^1	Taygete	LB	3	119	6	3	$4^{\frac{1}{2}}$	3^{hd}	7	6^{hd}	$6^{4\frac{1}{2}}$	Santiago Javier	10.80
24Apr04 ^{3}TuP^1	Sauceonside	LB	3	115	2	5	$2^{2\frac{1}{2}}$	$2^{1\frac{1}{2}}$	$2^{\frac{1}{2}}$	7	7	Baze T C	14.70

OFF AT 5:56 Start Good . Won driving. Course firm.

TIME :23^3, :46^3, 1:10, 1:22^2, 1:34^1 (:23.60, :46.62, 1:10.14, 1:22.43, 1:34.25)

$2 Mutuel Prices:

4 – MISS VEGAS–IRE	6.80	3.60	2.80
8 – TICKER TAPE–GB		2.60	2.20
2 – AMORAMA–FR			2.60

$1 EXACTA 4–8 PAID $8.70 $2 QUINELLA 4–8 PAID $6.40
$1 TRIFECTA 4–8–2 PAID $28.30 $1 SUPERFECTA 4–8–2–5 PAID $114.10

B. f, (Feb), by Efisio – Dwingeloo–Ire , by Dancing Dissident . Trainer Frankel Robert. Bred by J C Condon (Ire).

MISS VEGAS (IRE) sped between horses to the early lead, angled in and set the pace inside, responded along the rail when challenged in the stretch and held on gamely under urging. TICKER TAPE (GB) off a bit slowly, angled in and saved ground chasing the pace, came out leaving the second turn and three deep into the stretch, bid alongside the winner past midstretch but could not get by. AMORAMA (FR) stalked the pace along the inside, was boxed in a bit along the fence in midstretch, could not match the top pair but edged a rival for third. WINENDYNME pulled her way between foes to stalk the pace, went three deep leaving the second turn, continued outside a rival into the stretch and was edged for the show. FREAKIN STREAKIN allowed to settle outside the winner, continued a bit off the rail on the second turn, came out into the stretch and lacked the needed rally. TAYGETE was in a good position stalking the pace three deep, came out a bit into the stretch and weakened. SAUCEONSIDE close up tracking the winner a bit off the rail, was between foes leaving the second turn, dropped back into the stretch and also weakened, then was vanned off after being unsaddled.

Owners– 1, Gann Edmund A; 2, Jim Ford Inc Pearson Daron and Sweesy Jack; 3, Naify and Woodside Farms LLC; 4, Sahadi Fred N; 5, Mercedes Stables LLC; 6, Flaxman Holdings Ltd; 7, Triple AAA Ranch

Trainers– 1, Frankel Robert; 2, Cassidy James; 3, Canani Julio C; 4, Sahadi Jenine; 5, Cerin Vladimir; 6, Frankel Robert; 7, Owens R Kory

Scratched– Fortunately (GB) (06May04 ^{2}Hol^4)

$2 Daily Double (4–4) Paid $22.80 ; Daily Double Pool $42,163 .
$1 Pick Three (13–4–4) Paid $271.50 ; Pick Three Pool $78,918 .

EIGHTH RACE
Belmont
MAY 15, 2004

1 MILE. (1.32[1]) 29TH RUNNING OF THE SHUVEE HANDICAP. Grade II. Purse $200,000 (UP TO $34,000 NYSBFOA) A HANDICAP FOR FILLIES AND MARES THREE YEARS OLD AND UPWARD. By subscription of $200 each, which should accompany the nomination; $1,000 to pass the entry box; $1,000 to start. The purse to be divided 60% to the winner, 20% to second, 10% to third, 5% to fourth, 3% to fifth and 2% divided equally among remaining finishers. A trophy will be presented to the winning owner. Closed Saturday, May 1, 2004 with 17 Nominations.

Value of Race: $200,000 Winner $120,000; second $40,000; third $20,000; fourth $10,000; fifth $6,000; sixth $4,000. Mutuel Pool $743,476.00 Exacta Pool $595,419.00 Trifecta Pool $387,902.00

Last Raced	Horse	M/Eqt.	A.	Wt	PP	St	¼	½	¾	Str	Fin	Jockey	Odds $1
27Mar04 8Aqu3	Storm Flag Flying	L	4	116	2	6	4hd	3hd	4 1½	36	1½	Velazquez J R	1.00
17Apr04 8Aqu1	Passing Shot	L	5	117	4	3	3 1½	41	1hd	1hd	2no	Santos J A	5.50
16Apr04 9Kee3	Roar Emotion	L	4	117	6	1	2½	2½	2½	2 1½	3 8¾	Luzzi M J	3.10
8Apr04 7Kee1	Final Round	L	4	114	5	4	53	5 4½	5 2½	52	4 2½	Castellano J J	5.50
21Apr04 8Aqu2	Elegant Mercedes	L f	4	114	1	5	6	6	6	6	5½	Gryder A T	23.20
14Apr04 3Kee3	Cherokee Lite	L	4	113	3	2	1½	1½	3½	4½	6	Arroyo N Jr	11.80

OFF AT 4:49 Start Good. Won driving. Track fast.

TIME :23[4], :46[3], 1:11[1], 1:36 (:23.96, :46.76, 1:11.28, 1:36.10)

$2 Mutuel Prices:

2 – STORM FLAG FLYING	4.00	3.00	2.40
4 – PASSING SHOT		4.20	2.80
6 – ROAR EMOTION			2.60

$2 EXACTA 2–4 PAID $16.80 $2 TRIFECTA 2–4–6 PAID $27.80

Dk. b or br. f, (Apr), by Storm Cat – My Flag, by Easy Goer. Trainer McGaughey III Claude R. Bred by Phipps Stable (Ky).

STORM FLAG FLYING was urged up outside on the backstretch, raced with the pace while three wide, lugged in a bit from a right hand whip in upper stretch, dug in resolutely and finished strongly under left hand whipping and was along late from the outside. PASSING SHOT raced close up inside, rallied on the rail nearing the stretch and fought it out gamely to the wire. ROAR EMOTION argued the pace from the outside and dug in gamely in the stretch. FINAL ROUND raced close up outside, chased the pace while four wide and tired in the stretch. ELEGANT MERCEDES was outrun early and had no response when roused. CHEROKEE LITE quickly showed in front, set the pace along the inside and tired after three quarters.

Owners– 1, Phipps Ogden Mills et al; 2, Shields Joseph V Jr; 3, Allen Joseph; 4, Humphrey G Watts Jr; 5, Sullivan Lane Stable Williams Trevor and Scuderi Vincent; 6, Double C Stable

Trainers– 1, McGaughey III Claude R; 2, Jerkens H Allen; 3, McLaughlin Kiaran P; 4, Arnold George R II; 5, Dutrow Richard E Jr; 6, Zito Nicholas P

FIFTH RACE
Pimlico
MAY 15, 2004

1 1/16 MILES. (Turf) (1.40[1]) 53RD RUNNING OF THE GALLORETTE HANDICAP. Grade III. Purse $100,000 FOR FILLIES AND MARES, THREE-YEARS-OLD AND UPWARD. By subscription of $100. $450 to pass the entry box, $450 additional to start, with $100,000 Guaranteed, of which 60% to the winner, 20% to second, 11% to third, 6% to fourth and 3% to fifth. Supplemental nominations of $1000 each will be accepted by Saturday, May 8, 2004 with all other fees due as noted. Weights Sunday, May 9, 2004. Preference to starters high weights on the scale. Horses may be placed on the also eligible list. Starters to be namedthrough the entry box by the usual time of closing. Trophy to the owner of the winner. (If deemed inadvisable by management to run this race on the Turf course, it will be run on tha main track at One Mile and One Sixteenth).

Value of Race: $100,000 Winner $60,000; second $20,000; third $11,000; fourth $6,000; fifth $3,000. Mutuel Pool $649,148.00 Exacta Pool $601,057.00 Superfecta Pool $140,229.00 Trifecta Pool $464,911.00

Last Raced	Horse	M/Eqt.	A.	Wt	PP	St	¼	½	¾	Str	Fin	Jockey	Odds $1
18Apr04 8Kee2	Ocean Drive	L	4	117	3	5	31	3 1½	2 1½	13	1½	Bailey J D	1.10
18Apr04 8Kee6	Film Maker	L b	4	120	7	4	7 1½	6½	7½	5½	2 3½	Prado E S	2.20
29Apr04 7Aqu1	With Patience	L f	5	112	6	3	4hd	52	51	3½	31	Day P	13.20
1May04 9Aqu3	Caught in the Rain	L	5	114	2	7	8	8	8	7 5½	4hd	Migliore R	10.50
4Apr04 9Tam1	Skip to Savannah	L b	6	114	4	6	51	4hd	4½	4½	5nk	Dominguez R A	11.10
28Feb04 9FG3	Lady Linda	L b	6	115	1	8	61	7 1½	6 1½	61	6 3½	Fogelsonger R	6.20
11Mar04 6FG1	Lavender Baby	L b	5	114	8	1	1 1½	1½	11	2½	74	Karamanos H A	19.80
5May04 7Del4	Bluffie Slew	L b	4	111	5	2	2½	2hd	3½	8	8	Chavez S N	59.10

OFF AT 12:47 Start Good. Won driving. Course firm.

TIME :24[1], :48[1], 1:11[3], 1:34[4], 1:40[4] (:24.38, :48.31, 1:11.70, 1:34.99, 1:40.85)

$2 Mutuel Prices:

3 – OCEAN DRIVE	4.20	2.40	2.20
9 – FILM MAKER		2.80	2.60
6 – WITH PATIENCE			3.40

$2 EXACTA 3–9 PAID $10.40 $1 SUPERFECTA 3–9–6–2 PAID $116.20
$2 TRIFECTA 3–9–6 PAID $59.00

Dk. b or br. f, (Feb), by Belong to Me – Clever But Costly, by Clever Trick. Trainer Pletcher Todd A. Bred by James D Conway & Thomas C Mueller (Ky).

OCEAN DRIVE stalked the pace, advanced two wide entering the stretch, took command in upper stretch and lasted under brisk urging. FILM MAKER, unhurried early, swung wide in upper stretch and closed gamely. WITH PATIENCE, three wide the first turn, raced two wide between horses on the far turn, eased out for the drive and rallied mildly. CAUGHT IN THE RAIN, unhurried, swung wide in upper stretch and passed tired ones. SKIP TO SAVANNAH stalked the pace inside horses and weakened. LADY LINDA raced along the rail and was blocked in midstretch. LAVENDER BABY set the pace near the rail, ducked out in midstretch and dropped back. BLUFFIE SLEW raced wide entering the stretch and faltered.

Owners– 1, Baskin Bonnie and Sy; 2, Courtlandt Farms; 3, Hendriks Elizabeth M; 4, Heiligbrodt Stable & Walter L New; 5, Super Thoroughbreds I LLC; 6, Domino Stud of Lex LLC; 7, Gill Michael J; 8, Owens Warren

Trainers– 1, Pletcher Todd A; 2, Motion H Graham; 3, Hendriks Elizabeth M; 4, Preciado Guadalupe; 5, Campitelli Francis P; 6, Eppler Mary E; 7, Vazquez Gamaliel; 8, Magee Walter B

Scratched– Lady of the Future (14Dec03 5Crc5), True Sensation (07Dec03 9Lrl4)

$2 Pick Three (4–6–3/7/8) Paid $222.40 ; Pick Three Pool $56,044.
$2 Daily Double (6–3) Paid $23.40 ; Daily Double Pool $52,615.

EIGHTH RACE
Pimlico
MAY 15, 2004

1⅛ MILES. (1.47[1]) 18TH RUNNING OF THE WILLIAM DONALD SCHAEFER HANDICAP. Grade III. Purse $100,000 A HANDICAP FOR THREE-YEAR-OLDS AND UPWARD. By free subscription. $500 to pass the entry box, $500 to start, with $100,000 Guaranteed, of which 60% to the winner, 20% to second, 11% to third, 6% to fourth and 3% to fifth. Supplemental nominations of $1000each will be accepted by Saturday, May 8, 2004 with all other fees due as noted. Trophy to the owner of the winner. Closed Sunday, May 2, 2004 with 32 Nominations.

Value of Race: $100,000 Winner $60,000; second $20,000; third $11,000; fourth $6,000; fifth $3,000. Mutuel Pool $963,126.00 Exacta Pool $749,527.00 Superfecta Pool $147,010.00 Trifecta Pool $549,879.00

Last Raced	Horse	M/Eqt.	A.	Wt	PP	St	¼	½	¾	Str	Fin	Jockey	Odds $1
3Apr04 9GP6	Seattle Fitz-Arg	L	5	116	4	2	3 2½	3 2½	2 ½	1 1½	1 1½	Migliore R	1.50
17Apr04 8Pim1	The Lady's Groom	L bf	4	115	8	4	1 ½	1 hd	1 ½	2 5½	2 5¼	Karamanos H A	2.00
28Apr04 8Aqu3	Roaring Fever	L b	4	114	3	1	4 1½	4 ½	4 2	3 ½	3 1	Bailey J D	3.80
2Apr04 8Aqu4	Deeliteful Guy	L f	5	114	1	5	6 1½	6 hd	5 hd	4 1½	4 1¼	Castellano A Jr	17.70
29Apr04 4Hol7	White Buck	L b	4	114	2	8	8	7 1	7 6	5 5	5 7	Dominguez R A	21.00
17Apr04 8Pim4	Jorgie Stover	L	6	112	7	3	2 1	2 1	3 3	6 2	6 1	Kreidel K J	19.80
17Apr04 8Pim5	Your Bluffing	L b	4	114	6	6	5 3	5 3	6 hd	7 5½	7 10½	Prado E S	8.00
17Apr04 6Pim1	Off the Glass	L bf	5	114	5	7	7 hd	8	8	8	8	Santana J Z	22.10

OFF AT 2:53 Start Good . Won driving. Track fast.

TIME :23[4], :47[4], 1:12, 1:36[3], 1:49[2] (:23.88, :47.81, 1:12.08, 1:36.77, 1:49.43)

$2 Mutuel Prices:				
	5 – SEATTLE FITZ-ARG	5.00	3.00	2.40
	10 – THE LADY'S GROOM		3.00	2.40
	3 – ROARING FEVER			2.80

$2 EXACTA 5–10 PAID $13.80 $1 SUPERFECTA 5–10–3–2 PAID $86.00
$2 TRIFECTA 5–10–3 PAID $39.60

Dk. b or br. h, (Oct), by Fitzcarraldo-Arg – Hug a Slew , by Seattle Slew . Trainer McLaughlin Kiaran P. Bred by Firmamento (Arg).

SEATTLE FITZ (ARG) was rated back from between rivals around the first turn, eased out and stalked the pace three wide, moved up under confident handling leaving the far turn, drew even nearing the lane, dueled briefly, went clear a furlong out and held sway under pressure. THE LADY'S GROOM , hustled to the front, set a pressured pace along the inside, was pushed along around the far turn, altered course to the outside leaving the eighth pole and continued gamely. ROARING FEVER settled two wide, was hustled along around the final turn but lacked a finishing response. DEELITEFUL GUY , unhurried early, made a mild four wide run in mid stretch then flattened out. WHITE BUCK , unhurried early, saved ground into the stretch but lacked a response. JORGIE STOVER , three wide early, pressed the pace two wide to the three eighths pole then gave way. YOUR BLUFFING saved ground and weakened. OFF THE GLASS put in a dull effort.

Owners– 1, West Point Stable; 2, Murphy John D Sr; 3, Evans Edward P; 4, C D and G Stable; 5, Gill Michael J; 6, P and J Stable; 7, R D M Racing Stable; 8, The Nonsequitur Stable LLC

Trainers– 1, McLaughlin Kiaran P; 2, Gorham Michael E; 3, Hennig Mark; 4, Klesaris Robert P; 5, Shuman Mark; 6, Alecci John V; 7, Trombetta Michael J; 8, Albert Linda L

Scratched– One Eyed Joker (01May04 9Pim8) , Cherokee's Boy (03May04 7Del5) , Ole Faunty (14May04 11Pim6)

$2 Pick Three (2–8–4/5/8) Paid $162.00 ; Pick Three Pool $56,699 .
$2 Daily Double (8–5) Paid $21.00 ; Daily Double Pool $56,877 .

TENTH RACE
Pimlico
MAY 15, 2004

1⅛ MILES. (Turf) (1.46^{1}) 103TH RUNNING OF THE ARGENT DIXIE. Grade II. Purse $200,000 FOR THREE-YEAR-OLDS AND UPWARD. By subscription of $100. $950 to pass the entry box, $950 additional to start, with $200,000 Guaranteed, of which 60% to the winner, 20% to second, 11% to third, 6% to fourth and 3% to fifth. Supplemental nominations of $2000 each will be accepted by the usual time of entry with all other fees due as noted. Weights: Three-Year-olds, 116 lbs.; Older 124 lbs.; Non-winners of $100,000 at one mile or over in 2004, allowed 3 lbs.; $60,000 at one mile or over in 2004, allowed, 5 lbs. (Maiden and claiming races not considered in estimating allowances). Preference to starters with highest earnings in 2003–04. Horses may be placed on the also eligible list. Starters to be named through the entry box by the usual time of closing. Trophy to the owner of the winner. (If deemed inadvisable by management to run this race on the Turf course, it will be run on the main track at One Mile and One Eighth). Supplemental nominee: My Lord.

Value of Race: $200,000 Winner $120,000; second $40,000; third $22,000; fourth $12,000; fifth $6,000. Mutuel Pool $1,376,983.00 Exacta Pool $1,029,023.00 Superfecta Pool $197,885.00 Trifecta Pool $792,779.00

Last Raced	Horse	M/Eqt.	A.	Wt	PP	St	¼	½	¾	Str	Fin	Jockey	Odds $1
1May04 ^{9}Pim^{1}	Mr O'Brien-Ire	L	5	119	8	8	7^{1}	$7^{1\frac{1}{2}}$	5^{hd}	$2^{\frac{1}{2}}$	1^{2}	Dominguez R A	11.40
9Apr04 ^{9}Kee^{6}	MillnnumDrgon-GB	L	5	121	6	4	3^{2}	$3^{\frac{1}{2}}$	$3^{\frac{1}{2}}$	4^{2}	2^{hd}	Migliore R	7.00
10Apr04 ^{7}Hou^{1}	Warleigh	L	6	124	1	2	$6^{2\frac{1}{2}}$	$5^{\frac{1}{2}}$	$6^{2\frac{1}{2}}$	5^{3}	3^{nk}	Sellers S J	8.90
20Mar04 ^{6}GP^{3}	Megantic	L	6	119	7	11	11	11	11	8^{2}	4^{nk}	Bravo J	32.50
29Apr04 ^{6}CD^{1}	Senor Swinger	L	4	119	2	6	8^{1}	$9^{\frac{1}{2}}$	9^{1}	$7^{1\frac{1}{2}}$	5^{1}	Day P	4.80
12Mar04 ^{9}FG^{2}	Wudantunoit	L b	6	119	3	1	1^{hd}	$1^{\frac{1}{2}}$	$1^{1\frac{1}{2}}$	1^{1}	$6^{\frac{1}{2}}$	Karamanos H A	a- 36.10
18Apr04 ^{6}Kee^{1}	Wando	L	4	119	11	7	2^{2}	2^{2}	2^{hd}	3^{hd}	7^{1}	Husbands P	3.60
21Mar04 ^{8}FG^{8}	Silver Tree	L	4	119	5	3	$4^{\frac{1}{2}}$	4^{2}	4^{1}	6^{hd}	$8^{\frac{3}{4}}$	Bailey J D	5.00
10Apr04 ^{7}Hou^{8}	Better Talk Now	L bf	5	119	10	10	10^{hd}	10^{1}	$10^{\frac{1}{2}}$	10^{1}	9^{3}	Prado E S	10.70
21Mar04 ^{8}FG^{2}	Herculated	L	4	119	9	9	$9^{2\frac{1}{2}}$	8^{hd}	$8^{\frac{1}{2}}$	9^{hd}	$10^{1\frac{1}{4}}$	Lovato F Jr	3.50
27Mar04 ^{8}FG^{1}	My Lord	L b	5	119	4	5	5^{hd}	6^{1}	7^{1}	11	11	Castellano A Jr	a- 36.10

a–Coupled: Wudantunoit and My Lord.

OFF AT 4:26 Start Good. Won driving. Course firm.

TIME :23^{4}, :46^{4}, 1:10, 1:33^{4}, 1:46^{1} (:23.89, :46.80, 1:10.03, 1:33.93, 1:46.34)

(New Course Record)

$2 Mutuel Prices:

7 – MR O'BRIEN–IRE	24.80	12.60	7.40
5 – MILLENNIUM DRAGON–GB		8.20	5.80
2 – WARLEIGH			6.00

$2 EXACTA 7–5 PAID $201.80 $1 SUPERFECTA 7–5–2–6 PAID $6,678.60
$2 TRIFECTA 7–5–2 PAID $1,334.60

Ch. g, (Apr), by Mukaddamah – Laurel Delight–GB, by Presidium–GB. Trainer Graham Robin L. Bred by Jack Ronan & Des Vere Hunt Farm Co (Ire).

MR O'BRIEN (IRE) settled off the rail, steadily advanced four wide nearing the lane, surged to command nearing the sixteenth marker, kicked clear racing on his left lead then held sway under a drive. MILLENNIUM DRAGON (GB), forwardly placed along the inside, was put to urging nearing the quarter pole, was brushed and forced in by WANDO when attempting to get out for room in upper stretch, continued to lack room to the sixteenth marker then finished sharply once clear. WARLEIGH saved ground while never far back, moved closer nearing the lane, angled out leaving the three sixteenths marker and closed willingly. MEGANTIC hopped at the break then was angled in to settle along the rail, continued inside into the stretch, altered course to the outside in mid stretch then finished gamely. SENOR SWINGER saved ground while unhurried early, angled out in upper stretch then closed belatedly between rivals. WUDANTUNOIT broke alertly, set the pace along the inside, was collared leaving the furlong marker then weakened a bit. WANDO, sent up outside to prompt the pace, was put to urging leaving the three furlong marker, remained a presence to the eighth pole then faded. SILVER TREE, three wide most of the trip, stalked the pace to the head of the lane then gave way gradually. BETTER TALK NOW, unhurried early, came four wide for the drive and failed to respond. HERCULATED lost ground four wide, was urged along into the far turn and came up empty. MY LORD, rated between rivals early, dropped back after six and a half furlongs.

Owners– 1, Skeedattle II; 2, Darley Stable; 3, Parra Rosendo G; 4, Runnin Horse Farm Inc; 5, Lewis Robert B and Beverly J; 6, Gill Michael J; 7, Schickedanz Gustav; 8, Vegso Racing Stable; 9, Bushwood Stables; 10, Oak Crest Farm; 11, Gill Michael J

Trainers– 1, Graham Robin L; 2, McLaughlin Kiaran P; 3, Asmussen Steven M; 4, Pointer Norman R; 5, Baffert Bob; 6, Vazquez Gamaliel; 7, Keogh Michael; 8, Mott William I; 9, Motion H Graham; 10, Stidham Michael; 11, Vazquez Gamaliel

Scratched– White Buck (29Apr04 ^{4}Hol^{7})

$2 Pick Three (4/5/8–9–7) Paid $357.60 ; Pick Three Pool $134,441 .
$2 Daily Double (9–7) Paid $149.20 ; Daily Double Pool $79,284 .

ELEVENTH RACE
Pimlico
MAY 15, 2004

6 FURLONGS. (1.09) 18TH RUNNING OF THE MARYLAND BREEDERS' CUP HANDICAP. Grade III. Purse $200,000 (includes $100,000 BC - Breeders' Cup) FOR THREE-YEAR-OLDS AND UPWARD. By subscription of $100 each, which should accompany the nomination, $700 to pass the entry box, $700 additional to start, with $100,000 Guaranteed and an additional $100,000 from the Breeders' Cup Fund for Cup nominees only. The Host Association's guaranteed monies to be divided, 60% of all monies to the owner of the winner, 20% to second, 11% to third, 6% to fourth and 3% to fifth. Supplemental nominations of $1000 each will be accepted by Saturday, May 8, 2004 with all other fees due as noted. Weights Sunday, May 9, 2004. Breeders' Cup Fund monies, also correspondingly divided providing a Breeders' Cup Nominee has finished in an awarded position. Any Breeders' Cup fund monies not awarded will revert back to the fund. This race will not be divided. Preference to Breeders' Cup nominees only of equal racing quality or weight assignment (respective of sex and weight for age). Starters to be named through the entry box by the usual time of closing. Trophy to the winning owner given by Breeders' Cup Ltd. Supplemental nominee: Iron Halo.

Value of Race: $186,000 Winner $120,000; second $40,000; third $11,000; fourth $12,000; fifth $3,000. Mutuel Pool $1,399,970.00 Exacta Pool $1,082,559.00 Superfecta Pool $202,281.00 Trifecta Pool $838,535.00

Last Raced	Horse	M/Eqt.	A.	Wt	PP	St	¼	½	Str	Fin	Jockey	Odds $1
13Mar04 ^{8}Aqu^{2}	Gators N Bears	L bf	4	117	3	4	3½	4½	1½	11¼	Lopez C C	2.50
15Nov03 ^{10}Lrl^{10}	HighwayProspector	L b	7	114	4	8	9	9	6½	21¼	Dominguez R A	a- 15.30
10Apr04 ^{8}Pim^{1}	Sassy Hound	L b	7	115	7	6	85½	6½	41	3½	Castellano A Jr	12.60
28Mar04 ^{8}Aqu^{2}	Gracious Humor	L	4	114	5	5	4½	3½	2hd	42	Prado E S	6.30
15Apr04 ^{6}SA^{1}	Iron Halo-Arg	L	5	112	2	9	6½	84	5½	5nk	Espinoza V	5.50
18Apr04 ^{8}Pim^{1}	Fine Stormy	L f	5	117	6	1	22	21	31½	6nk	Desormeaux K J	14.70
1May04 ^{7}Del^{5}	Mt. Carson	L	4	114	1	7	7hd	7hd	73	73¾	Bailey J D	7.60
10Apr04 ^{7}Kee^{1}	Soaring Free	L	5	121	8	2	5½	5½	8½	82½	Sellers S J	2.00
7Apr04 ^{8}CT^{3}	Native Heir	L b	6	113	9	3	12	1hd	9	9	Fogelsonger R	a- 15.30

a-Coupled: Highway Prospector and Native Heir.

OFF AT 5:11 Start Good . Won driving. Track fast.

TIME :22^{3}, :45^{4}, :58^{1}, 1:10^{4} (:22.77, :45.99, :58.39, 1:10.84)

$2 Mutuel Prices:				
	4 – GATORS N BEARS	7.00	4.00	3.00
	1 – HIGHWAY PROSPECTOR(a-entry)		11.60	5.80
	7 – SASSY HOUND			5.20

$2 EXACTA 4–1 PAID $71.00 $1 SUPERFECTA 4–1–7–5 PAID $1,262.10
$2 TRIFECTA 4–1–7 PAID $444.80

B. c, (Feb), by Stormy Atlantic – I'll Be Along , by Notebook . Trainer Nechamkin Leo S II. Bred by Robert W Camac (NJ).

GATORS N BEARS raced along the rail stalking the pace, eased out two wide on the turn, brushed with NATIVE HEIR near the three sixteenths pole, accelerated to take command in midstretch and drove clear. HIGHWAY PROSPECTOR lacked speed, swung to the seven path entering the stretch and rallied under a hand ride. SASSY HOUND , five wide around the turn, failed to sustain his bid. GRACIOUS HUMOR chased the pace, raced three wide around the turn, bid for the lead in upper and gave way the final furlong. IRON HALO (ARG) lacked speed, was checked in tight quarters entering the turn, raced between horses and failed to rally. FINE STORMY prompted the pace two wide, gained a short lead in upper stretch, dueled to midstretch then gave way. MT. CARSON lacked speed, raced in the three path between horses entering the stretch and failed to rally. SOARING FREE , wide around the turn, gave way after a half mile. NATIVE HEIR , sent to the front, set the pace along the rail, brushed with the winner in upper stretch and faltered.

Owners– 1, Nechamkin Leo S II; 2, Gill Michael J; 3, Roth Toby; 4, Manorwood Stables S Goldfarb & I Davis; 5, S M Mitchell Ranch LLC; 6, Moss Maggi; 7, Reynolds David P; 8, Sam-Son Farms; 9, Gill Michael J

Trainers– 1, Nechamkin Leo S II; 2, Shuman Mark; 3, Feliciano Ben M Jr; 4, Dutrow Richard E Jr; 5, Kruljac J Eric; 6, Pino Michael V; 7, Jenkins Rodney; 8, Frostad Mark; 9, Shuman Mark

Scratched– Crossing Point (01May04 ^{9}Mnr^{2})

$2 Daily Double (7–4) Paid $102.00 ; Daily Double Pool $65,489 .

TWELFTH RACE
Pimlico
MAY 15, 2004

$1\frac{3}{16}$ MILES. (1.52^{2}) 129TH RUNNING OF THE PREAKNESS. Grade I. Purse $1,000,000 FOR THREE-YEAR-OLDS. $10,000 to pass the entry box, starters to pay $10,000 additional. Supplemental nominations may be made in accordance with the rules, upon payment of $100,000, 65% of the purse to the winner, 20% to second, 10% to third, and 5% to fourth. Weight 126 pounds for colts and geldings, 121 lbs., for fillies. A replica of the Woodlawn Vase will be presented to the winning owner to remain his or her personal property.

Value of Race: $1,000,000 Winner $650,000; second $200,000; third $100,000; fourth $50,000. Mutuel Pool $21,823,303.00 Exacta Pool $12,034,370.00 Superfecta Pool $5,713,723.00 Trifecta Pool $15,096,739.00

Last Raced	Horse	M/Eqt.	A.	Wt	PP	St	¼	½	¾	Str	Fin	Jockey	Odds $1
1May04 ^{10}CD^{1}	Smarty Jones	L f	3	126	6	1	$2^{\frac{1}{2}}$	2^{2}	$2^{2\frac{1}{2}}$	1^{5}	$1^{11\frac{1}{2}}$	Elliott S	0.70
3Apr04 ^{8}SA^{3}	Rock Hard Ten	L	3	126	9	4	$7^{\frac{1}{2}}$	7^{hd}	6^{1}	2^{hd}	2^{2}	Stevens G L	6.90
10Apr04 ^{8}Aqu^{3}	Eddington	L b	3	126	8	8	6^{1}	6^{2}	$8^{3\frac{1}{2}}$	7^{5}	3^{hd}	Bailey J D	13.20
1May04 ^{10}CD^{2}	Lion Heart		3	126	1	2	$1^{1\frac{1}{2}}$	$1^{2\frac{1}{2}}$	1^{1}	$3^{4\frac{1}{2}}$	4^{hd}	Smith M E	4.90
1May04 ^{10}CD^{3}	Imperialism	L b	3	126	7	3	3^{1}	4^{hd}	$5^{\frac{1}{2}}$	4^{2}	5^{1}	Desormeaux K J	6.60
24Apr04 ^{9}CD^{1}	Sir Shackleton	L	3	126	5	7	$5^{\frac{1}{2}}$	$5^{\frac{1}{2}}$	4^{hd}	5^{hd}	$6^{\frac{3}{4}}$	Bejarano R	37.50
1May04 ^{10}CD^{10}	Borrego	L b	3	126	2	5	$8^{2\frac{1}{2}}$	8^{4}	7^{hd}	$6^{\frac{1}{2}}$	$7^{5\frac{1}{2}}$	Espinoza V	12.80
10Apr04 ^{8}Aqu^{7}	Little Matth Man	L	3	126	3	10	10	10	10	$8^{2\frac{1}{2}}$	8^{2}	Migliore R	45.00
1May04 ^{10}CD^{11}	Song of the Sword	L b	3	126	4	6	4^{hd}	3^{hd}	$3^{\frac{1}{2}}$	9^{2}	$9^{3\frac{1}{2}}$	Chavez J F	51.00
17Apr04 ^{9}Pim^{1}	Water Cannon	L b	3	126	10	9	$9^{3\frac{1}{2}}$	$9^{\frac{1}{2}}$	$9^{\frac{1}{2}}$	10	10	Fogelsonger R	39.50

OFF AT 6:25 Start Good For All But LITTLE MATTH MAN. Won driving. Track fast.

TIME :23^{3}, :47^{1}, 1:11^{2}, 1:36^{2}, 1:55^{2} (:23.65, :47.32, 1:11.53, 1:36.44, 1:55.59)

$2 Mutuel Prices:				
	7 – SMARTY JONES	3.40	3.00	2.60
	10 – ROCK HARD TEN		5.00	4.00
	9 – EDDINGTON			5.20

$2 EXACTA 7–10 PAID $24.60 $1 SUPERFECTA 7–10–9–1 PAID $230.70
$2 TRIFECTA 7–10–9 PAID $177.20

Ch. c, (Feb), by Elusive Quality – I'll Get Along, by Smile. Trainer Servis John C. Bred by Someday Farm (Pa).

SMARTY JONES, away alertly, was taken in hand going past the wire the first time, tracked the leader while racing well off the rail into the backstretch, continued in hand to the far turn, launched his rally leaving the three eighths pole, angled to the inside of LION HEART mid way on the turn, drew on nearly even terms with that one approaching the quarter pole, took charge at the top of the stretch, quickly opened a commanding lead in mid stretch, extended his advantage when struck twice right handed leaving the furlong marker then drew off with authority under a vigorous hand ride. ROCK HARD TEN, fractious behind the gate delaying the start for several minutes, was strung out six wide around the first turn, raced in mid pack while continuing wide down the backstretch, made a sharp move from outside to reach contention leaving the three furlong marker, angled to the inside mid way on the turn, followed the winner into the stretch but was no match for that one while clearly besting the others. EDDINGTON, unhurried for a half while racing well off the rail, gradually gained five wide nearing the far turn, moved inside IMPERIALISM at the three eighths pole, circled five wide advancing into the stretch, altered course between rivals at the three sixteenths pole but failed to threaten while improving his position. LION HEART was guided well off the rail while sprinting clear soon after the start, set a moderate pace while four wide down the backstretch, continued on the front while remaining well out from the rail around the far turn, relinquished the lead to the winner entering the lane then tired from his early efforts. IMPERIALISM returned to the paddock prior to the post parade for a repair of his left front shoe, raced five wide around the first turn, continued wide in mid pack for six furlongs then lacked a late response when called upon. SIR SHACKLETON, between rivals the first turn, chased the pace in the two to three path down the backstretch, angled to the inside while racing within striking distance to the top of the stretch then steadily tired thereafter. BORREGO broke outward then steadied on heels soon after the start, saved ground to the quarter pole, angled out at the top of the stretch, raced between rivals past the eighth pole and came up empty. LITTLE MATTH MAN was bumped and pinched back at the start, trailed for a good part of the way then failed to mount a serious rally. SONG OF THE SWORD broke inward and bobbled at the start, raced close up for a half, made a run inside the winner to threaten nearing the far turn then gave way. WATER CANNON failed to threaten.

Owners– 1, Someday Farm; 2, Mercedes Stables LLC and Paulson; 3, Willmott Stables Inc; 4, Smith Derrick and Tabor Michael; 5, Taub Steve; 6, Farmer Tracy; 7, J & S Kelly R Ralls D Foster B Scott & B Greely; 8, Papandrea Vincent; 9, Paraneck Stable; 10, The Nonsequitur Stable LLC

Trainers– 1, Servis John C; 2, Orman Jason; 3, Hennig Mark; 4, Biancone Patrick L; 5, Mulhall Kristin; 6, Zito Nicholas P; 7, Greely C Beau; 8, Ciresa Martin E; 9, Pedersen Jennifer; 10, Albert Linda L

Scratched– The Cliff's Edge

$2 Pick Three (7–4–4/7) Paid $143.20 ; Pick Three Pool $373,852 .
$2 Pick Four (9–7–4–4/7) Paid $1,506.40 ; Pick Four Pool $1,248,189 .
$2 Daily Double (4–7) Paid $15.40 ; Daily Double Pool $370,222 .
$2 Daily Double ((SPECIAL/PREAKNESS) 4–7) Paid $10.40 ; Daily Double Pool $475,094 .

EIGHTH RACE
Belmont
MAY 22, 2004

1⅛ MILES. (1.452) 51ST RUNNING OF THE PETER PAN. Grade II. Purse $200,000 (UP TO $34,000 NYSBFOA) FOR THREE YEAR OLDS. By subscription of $200 each, which should accompany the nomination; $1,000 to pass the entry box; $1,000 to start. The purse to be divided 60% to the winner, 20% to second, 10% to third, 5% to fourth, 3% to fifth and 2% divided equally among remaining finishers. 123 lbs. Non–winners of $100,000 at a mile or over in 2004 allowed 2 lbs.; $50,000 other than restricted at a mile or over, or $35,000 twice at a mile or over 4 lbs.; $50,000, or three races other thanmaiden or claiming, 6 lbs.; two races other than maiden or claiming, 8 lbs. A trophy will be presented to the winning owner. Closed Saturday, May 8, 2004 with 31 Nominations.

Value of Race: $200,000 Winner $120,000; second $40,000; third $20,000; fourth $10,000; fifth $6,000; sixth $800; seventh $800; eighth $800; ninth $800; tenth $800. Mutuel Pool $1,204,911.00 Exacta Pool $841,853.00 Trifecta Pool $723,249.00

Last Raced	Horse	M/Eqt.	A.	Wt	PP	St	¼	½	¾	Str	Fin	Jockey	Odds $1
10Apr04 9OP5	Purge	L	3	115	10	2	3½	3½	2hd	16	16¾	Velazquez J R	2.40
10Apr04 8Aqu4	Swingforthefences	L	3	115	6	8	91	8½	7½	2hd	21¼	Bridgmohan S X	6.50
1May04 10CD12	Master David	L f	3	115	4	10	10	10	9hd	5½	32¼	Solis A	1.70
5May04 6Bel1	Pies Prospect	L	3	115	2	7	4½	4½	42½	3hd	4nk	Castellano J J	9.90
1May04 4Aqu4	Intimidator	L f	3	115	9	3	2½	2½	1hd	42	51½	Prado E S	70.50
3Apr04 11GP4	Zakocity	L b	3	115	3	6	5hd	5hd	6½	67	63¼	Santos J A	44.75
1May04 10CD15	Friends Lake	L	3	123	5	5	8hd	92	10	7½	77¾	Migliore R	6.70
10Apr04 8Aqu10	Sinister G	L b	3	123	1	9	11½	1½	3hd	82	84¾	Toscano P R	39.00
10Apr04 8Aqu9	Consecrate	L b	3	115	8	4	71½	6hd	5hd	912	915	Bailey J D	18.00
24Apr04 7Aqu1	Wild Wadi	L	3	115	7	1	6hd	72	8hd	10	10	Luzzi M J	27.75

OFF AT 4:46 Start Good. Won driving. Track fast.

TIME :231, :46, 1:10, 1:35, 1:474 (:23.25, :46.05, 1:10.11, 1:35.01, 1:47.98)

$2 Mutuel Prices:

10 – PURGE	6.80	4.60	2.70
6 – SWINGFORTHEFENCES		7.10	3.30
4 – MASTER DAVID			2.50

$2 EXACTA 10–6 PAID $38.20 $2 TRIFECTA 10–6–4 PAID $104.00

B. c, (Apr), by Pulpit – Copelan's Bid Gal, by Copelan. Trainer Pletcher Todd A. Bred by Glory Days Breeding Inc (Ky).

PURGE raced with the pace from the outside while in hand, advanced four wide on the turn, responded when set down turning for home, drew away when roused and was kept to the task to the wire. SWINGFORTHEFENCES was outrun early along the inside, angled out on the turn, rallied four wide approaching the stretch and finished gamely outside to be second best. MASTER DAVID was outrun early, advanced outside on the turn and finished well. PIES PROSPECT raced close up inside early, joined the leaders from the inside on the turn, could not stay with the winner entering the stretch and tired on the rail in the final furlong. INTIMIDATOR was bumped at the start, argued the pace while between rivals three wide and tired in the stretch. ZAKOCITY raced between rivals early, put in a run along the inside on the turn and had nothing left for the stretch drive. FRIENDS LAKE was outrun early, raced four wide throughout and had no response when roused. SINISTER G was hustled up inside, contested the pace for three quarters and tired. CONSECRATE was bumped at the start, was steadied then raced four wide and tired in the stretch. WILD WADI raced between rivals and tired.

Owners– 1, Starlight Stables Saylor Paul H Johns Martin; 2, Klaravich Stables Inc; 3, Georgica Stable Mack Stephen Star Crown Stable; 4, LaPenta Robert V; 5, Evans Robert S; 6, Pompa Paul P Jr; 7, Broman Sr Mary and Chester; 8, Toscano III John T Corrado Kim Carlat Yamile Toscano Robert; 9, McIngvale James; 10, Kelly Jon and Sarah

Trainers– 1, Pletcher Todd A; 2, Violette Richard A Jr; 3, Frankel Robert; 4, Zito Nicholas P; 5, Schulhofer Randy; 6, Reynolds Patrick L; 7, Kimmel John C; 8, Toscano John T Jr; 9, Baffert Bob; 10, Young Steven W

EIGHTH RACE
Hollywood
MAY 22, 2004

1 MILE. (Turf) (1.323) 64TH RUNNING OF THE WILL ROGERS. Grade III. Purse $100,000 FOR THREE YEAR OLDS. By subscription of $100 each on or before Wednesday, May 12, or by supplementary nomination of $2,000 each by closing time of entries. $1,000 additional to start, with $100,000 added. The added money and all fees to be divided 60% tothe winner, 20% to second, 12% to third, 6% to fourth and 2% to fifth. Weights: 123 lbs. Non–winners of $100,000 at a mile or over allowed 2 lbs.; such a race of $50,000, 4 lbs.; non–winners of two races other than claiming or starter at a mile or over,6lbs.; such a race, 8 lbs. Starters to be named through the entry box by the closing time of entries. A trophy will be presented to the winning owner. (Rail at 10 feet). Closed with 14 nominations.

Value of Race: $109,400 Winner $65,640; second $21,880; third $13,128; fourth $6,564; fifth $2,188. Mutuel Pool $471,823.00 Exacta Pool $253,513.00 Quinella Pool $23,042.00 Trifecta Pool $246,993.00 Superfecta Pool $108,382.00

Last Raced	Horse	M/Eqt.	A.	Wt	PP	St	¼	½	¾	Str	Fin	Jockey	Odds $1
28Apr04 2Hol1	Laura's Lucky Boy	LB	3	119	7	3	51½	5½	1hd	14	14	Valenzuela P A	2.60
10Apr04 8SA1	Toasted	LB	3	121	2	7	71	7½	51	21½	21	Almeida G F	2.00
16Apr04 9SA1	Street Theatre	LB b	3	117	8	8	8	8	72	41	33½	Flores D R	4.90
5May04 6Hol2	Tricky Flash Flood	LB b	3	115	6	6	6½	61	4½	31½	41	Vergara O	61.10
10Apr04 9OP6	Mambo Train	LB b	3	121	5	1	3hd	3hd	61	62	52½	Desormeaux K J	6.40
30Apr04 8Hol1	Running Free	LB	3	117	1	2	1½	1hd	2hd	5hd	64	Martinez F F	54.50
17Apr04 9Kee14	Boomzeeboom	LB b	3	117	3	5	22½	23½	31	72	72	Nakatani C S	5.50
27Mar04 3SA3	Stalking Tiger	LB f	3	115	4	4	42½	41½	8	8	8	Espinoza V	10.00

OFF AT 4:57 Start Good. Won driving. Course firm.

TIME :223, :452, 1:092, 1:212, 1:332 (:22.79, :45.49, 1:09.57, 1:21.52, 1:33.45)

$2 Mutuel Prices:

7 – LAURA'S LUCKY BOY	7.20	3.00	2.40
2 – TOASTED		3.00	2.20
8 – STREET THEATRE			2.80

$1 EXACTA 7–2 PAID $8.40 $2 QUINELLA 2–7 PAID $7.60

$1 TRIFECTA 7–2–8 PAID $37.60 $1 SUPERFECTA 7–2–8–6 PAID $311.40

B. c, (Jan), by Theatrical–Ire – Corridora Slew–Arg, by Corridor Key. Trainer Orman Jason. Bred by Madeleine A Paulson (Ky).

LAURA'S LUCKY BOY chased outside a rival, moved up three deep into and on the second turn to take the lead, kicked clear and angled in entering the stretch and proved best under urging. TOASTED squeezed a bit at the start, settled inside then between horses on the backstretch, went three deep on the second turn and four wide into the stretch and gained the place. STREET THEATRE off a bit slowly, settled off the rail then three deep on the backstretch, also came four wide into the stretch, then angled in and picked up the show. TRICKY FLASH FLOOD angled in and chased inside, moved up into and on the second turn, got through into the stretch, then came out and lacked the needed rally. MAMBO TRAIN three deep early, stalked outside a rival, went between horses into and on the second turn, was boxed in midway on that bend, angled in entering the stretch and weakened. RUNNING FREE sped to the early lead, dueled inside, fought back on the second turn but weakened in the stretch. BOOMZEEBOOM vied for command outside a rival then between horses leaving the second turn, came three deep into the stretch, drifted out in the lane and also weakened. STALKING TIGER chased inside, was in a bit tight between while beginning to weaken leaving the backstretch, came out into the stretch and had little left.

Owners– 1, Mercedes Stables LLC; 2, Port Sidney L and Trust 720270; 3, Darley Stable; 4, Sides Clay R; 5, Everest Stables Inc; 6, Southern Nevada Racing Stables Inc; 7, Karubian John Landsburg Alan and Postaer Larry; 8, Davis John Milch David and Rocchio Al

Trainers– 1, Orman Jason; 2, De Seroux Laura; 3, Harty Eoin; 4, Sides Robert C; 5, Polanco Marcelo; 6, Cassidy James; 7, Cerin Vladimir; 8, Aguirre Paul G

$2 Daily Double (8–7) Paid $14.20 ; Daily Double Pool $42,535 .

$1 Pick Three (1/3–5/8–7) Paid $29.60 ; Pick Three Pool $85,106 .

NINTH RACE
Arlington
MAY 29, 2004

1 MILE. (1.32^{1}) 52ND RUNNING OF THE HANSHIN CUP HANDICAP. Grade III. Purse $100,000 FOR THREE-YEAR-OLDS AND UPWARD. By subscription of $75 each, which should accompany the nomination. A Supplementary Nomination of $4,000 may be made on Saturday, May 22, 2004, which includes entry and starting fees. Original Nominees to pay $750 to pass the entry box and an additional $750 to start, with $100,000 Guaranteed, of which $60,000 to the winner; $20,000 to second; $11,000 to third; $6,000 to fourth and $3,000 to fifth. WEIGHTS: Sunday, May 23, 2004. This event will be limited to fourteen (14) starters. Preference will be Highweights (on the scale). *Total Earnings in 2004 will be used to determine the order of preference of horses assigned equal weight (on the scale). Failure to draw into this race at time of entry cancels all fees with the exception of the nominating fee(s). Starters to be named through the entry box by usual time of closing. Two (2) horses having common ties through ownership cannot start to the exclusion of a single ownership interest. Trophy to the owner of the winner. Closed Wednesday, May 19, 2004 with 19 nominations.

Value of Race: $100,000 Winner $60,000; second $20,000; third $11,000; fourth $6,000; fifth $3,000. Mutuel Pool $251,487.00 Exacta Pool $141,982.00 Trifecta Pool $120,646.00 Superfecta Pool $34,558.00

Last Raced	Horse	M/Eqt.	A.	Wt	PP	St	¼	½	¾	Str	Fin	Jockey	Odds $1
7Apr04 ^{9}OP^{2}	Crafty Shaw	L	6	119	5	3	$2^{1\frac{1}{2}}$	$2^{1\frac{1}{2}}$	$1^{\frac{1}{2}}$	1^{1}	$1^{1\frac{1}{4}}$	Perret C	1.80
2May04 ^{6}Haw^{7}	Apt to Be	L b	7	119	7	2	$3^{\frac{1}{2}}$	3^{hd}	$3^{1\frac{1}{2}}$	$2^{2\frac{1}{2}}$	$2^{2\frac{1}{2}}$	Marquez C H Jr	4.20
30Apr04 ^{6}CD^{3}	Kodema	L f	5	116	4	4	$5^{1\frac{1}{2}}$	$5^{1\frac{1}{2}}$	$5^{1\frac{1}{2}}$	3^{hd}	$3^{1\frac{3}{4}}$	Martinez J R Jr	5.30
1May04 ^{8}PrM^{2}	Coach Jimi Lee	L	4	117	2	5	4^{hd}	$4^{\frac{1}{2}}$	$4^{\frac{1}{2}}$	4^{hd}	$4^{1\frac{1}{4}}$	Douglas R R	2.30
4Apr04 ^{11}Tam^{6}	Attack the Books	L f	5	115	6	1	6^{1}	7	$6^{2\frac{1}{2}}$	6^{6}	$5^{4\frac{1}{2}}$	Laviolette B S	19.20
8May04 ^{6}PrM^{1}	Wiggins	L	4	118	1	6	1^{hd}	$1^{\frac{1}{2}}$	2^{hd}	5^{1}	6^{6}	Razo E Jr	7.10
16May04 ^{8}AP^{10}	Fighting Indians	L b	5	113	3	7	7	6^{hd}	7	7	7	Sibille R	39.70

OFF AT 5:10 Start Good . Won driving. Track fast.

TIME :23^{4}, :47^{1}, 1:11^{1}, 1:23, 1:35^{1} (:23.95, :47.22, 1:11.27, 1:23.16, 1:35.36)

$2 Mutuel Prices:

5 – CRAFTY SHAW	5.60	3.60	2.80
7 – APT TO BE		5.00	4.00
4 – KODEMA			3.80

$2 EXACTA 5–7 PAID $22.40 $2 TRIFECTA 5–7–4 PAID $93.00
$2 SUPERFECTA 5–7–4–2 PAID $226.20

Ch. h, (Apr), by Crafty Prospector – Her She Shawklit , by Air Forbes Won . Trainer Vestal Peter M. Bred by Lance K Robinson (Ky).

CRAFTY SHAW pressed the pace just outside, took over on the turn and held sway in the run to the wire. APT TO BE raced close up three wide, rallied in the stretch then could not get past the winner in the drive. KODEMA raced between horses near the middle of the field, rallied closer in the stretch then lacked a winning bid. COACH JIMI LEE raced near the middle of the field and lacked a rally. ATTACK THE BOOKS lacked speed and passed a pair of beaten rivals. WIGGINS set the pace from the inside while pressed and tired. FIGHTING INDIANS was always outrun.

Owners– 1, Cella Charles J; 2, Duchossois Richard L; 3, Farfellow Farms Ltd; 4, Battaglia Lee and Divito James P; 5, Michael W and Judy Crowe; 6, Pacella William Rizza Joseph and Schwed Ronald; 7, Linne and Nancy Calkins and C B Racing Inc Charles L and Janelle Bettis

Trainers– 1, Vestal Peter M; 2, Block Chris M; 3, Carroll David; 4, DiVito James P; 5, Hinsley David H; 6, Granitz Anthony J; 7, Bettis Charles L

$1 Pick Three (4–1–5) Paid $459.80 ; Pick Three Pool $11,649 .

EIGHTH RACE
Belmont
MAY 29, 2004

1⅜ MILES. (Inner Turf) (2.10^{1}) 46TH RUNNING OF THE SHEEPHEAD BAY HANDICAP. Grade II. Purse $150,000 A HANDICAP FOR FILLIES AND MARES THREE YEARS OLD AND UPWARD. By subscription of $150 each, which should accompany the nomination; $750 to pass the entry box; $750 to start. The purse to be divided 60% to the winner, 20% to second, 10% to third, 5% to fourth, 3% to fifth and 2% divided equally among remaining finishers. A trophy will be presented to the winning owner. The New York Racing Association reserves the right to transfer this race to the Main Track. In the event that this race is taken off the turf, it may be subject to downgrading upon review by the Graded Stakes Committee. Closed Saturday, May 15, 2004 with22 Nominations. (Rail at 18 feet).

Value of Race: $150,000 Winner $90,000; second $30,000; third $15,000; fourth $7,500; fifth $4,500; sixth $1,500; seventh $1,500. Mutuel Pool $811,405.00 Exacta Pool $594,151.00 Trifecta Pool $471,333.00

Last Raced	Horse	M/Eqt.	A.	Wt	PP	¼	½	¾	1	Str	Fin	Jockey	Odds $1
24Apr04 ^{1}Hol^{1}	Moscow Burning	L	4	114	6	1^{1}	1^{1}	1^{1}	$1^{1\frac{1}{2}}$	1^{3}	1^{1}	Smith M E	4.20
29Apr04 ^{6}CD^{2}	Spice Island	L b	5	119	2	4^{1}	$4^{\frac{1}{2}}$	4^{1}	$3^{\frac{1}{2}}$	$2^{\frac{1}{2}}$	2^{4}	Bailey J D	1.90
21Apr04 ^{8}Kee^{1}	Meridiana-Ger	L	4	119	7	$2^{\frac{1}{2}}$	$2^{\frac{1}{2}}$	$2^{\frac{1}{2}}$	$2^{\frac{1}{2}}$	$3^{\frac{1}{2}}$	$3^{\frac{1}{2}}$	Prado E S	2.90
21Apr04 ^{8}Kee^{6}	[D]Miss Hellie	L	5	115	4	7	7	7	7	$6^{\frac{1}{2}}$	$4^{1\frac{1}{2}}$	Santos J A	16.30
23Apr04 ^{4}Kee^{1}	Andover Lady	L	4	115	5	$6^{2\frac{1}{2}}$	$6^{2\frac{1}{2}}$	$6^{2\frac{1}{2}}$	$5^{\frac{1}{2}}$	$5^{\frac{1}{2}}$	5^{hd}	Migliore R	18.00
21Apr04 ^{8}Kee^{2}	Alternate	L b	5	116	3	$3^{1\frac{1}{2}}$	$3^{\frac{1}{2}}$	3^{hd}	4^{1}	$4^{2\frac{1}{2}}$	6^{4}	Velasquez C	4.80
21Mar04 ^{11}GP^{2}	Savedbythelight	L b	4	115	1	$5^{\frac{1}{2}}$	$5^{1\frac{1}{2}}$	5^{hd}	6^{2}	7	7	Velazquez J R	5.30

[D] – Miss Hellie disqualified and placed 4th

OFF AT 4:45 Start Good . Won driving. Course yielding.

TIME :25^{1}, :51^{2}, 1:17^{3}, 1:42^{2}, 2:06^{2}, 2:18^{1} (:25.34, :51.57, 1:17.60, 1:42.48, 2:06.42, 2:18.24)

$2 Mutuel Prices:

7 – MOSCOW BURNING	10.40	4.50	2.60
3 – SPICE ISLAND		3.50	2.50
8 – MERIDIANA-GER			2.50

$2 EXACTA 7–3 PAID $39.00 $2 TRIFECTA 7–3–8 PAID $110.50

B. f, (Mar), by Moscow Ballet – Burning Desire , by Mr. Leader . Trainer Cassidy James. Bred by Harris Farms Inc & Ken Maddy Trust (Cal).

MOSCOW BURNING soon opened a clear lead, made the pace while well in hand, spurted away when roused and remained clear under a drive. SPICE ISLAND raced close up while three wide in hand and finished gamely outside. MERIDIANA (GER) attended the pace from the outside while in hand and came up empty when asked. ALTERNATE raced inside while in hand, saved ground and had no response when roused. ANDOVER LADY was outrun early, raced outside and had no response when roused. MISS HELLIE was outrun early, came wide into the stretch and had no rally. SAVEDBYTHELIGHT was rated along inside and tired.

Owners– 1, Mariani Jeffrey Nentwig Michael Van Kempen Dallas; 2, Denlea Park Ltd; 3, Kelly Jon and Sarah; 4, Hamilton Emory A; 5, Farmer Tracy; 6, Pin Oak Stable LLC; 7, Mack Earle I

Trainers– 1, Cassidy James; 2, Pregman John S Jr; 3, Clement Christophe; 4, McGaughey III Claude R; 5, Kimmel John C; 6, Motion H Graham; 7, Violette Richard A Jr

Scratched– Primetimevalentine (12May04 ^{8}Bel^{3})

NINTH RACE
Churchill
MAY 29, 2004

1 1/16 MILES. (Turf) (1.40^{4}) 28TH RUNNING OF THE EARLY TIMES MINT JULEP HANDICAP. Grade III. Purse $150,000 FOR FILLIES AND MARES, FOUR YEARS OLD AND UPWARD. By subscription of $150 each on or before May 15, 2004 or by Supplementary Nomination of $7,500 each by the closing of entries May 21, 2004. $750 to pass the entry box; $750 additional to start. Weights tobe announced May 22. If the race is moved to the main track after the time of closing, a horse may be scratched for any reason at any time up to 15 minutes prior to post time for the race preceding this race or thereafter with a valid physical reason andapproved by the stewards. The entry fee shall be refunded for scratches made in compliance with the above conditions. (If this race is taken off the turf it will be downgraded one grade level for this running only in accordance with American Graded Stakes Committee policy). Closed May 15, 2004 with 32 nominations.

Value of Race: $168,300 Winner $104,346; second $33,660; third $16,830; fourth $8,415; fifth $5,049. Mutuel Pool $493,910.00 Exacta Pool $321,630.00 Trifecta Pool $261,574.00 Superfecta Pool $84,394.00

Last Raced	Horse	M/Eqt.	A.	Wt	PP	St	¼	½	¾	Str	Fin	Jockey	Odds $1
1May04 ^{5}Crc^{1}	Stay Forever	L b	7	116	3	7	6^{hd}	9	8^{2}	4^{2}	$1\frac{1}{2}$	Castro E	5.00
1May04 ^{7}CD^{4}	Sand Springs	L	4	120	8	2	2^{2}	2^{1}	$2^{1\frac{1}{2}}$	1^{1}	2^{nk}	Guidry M	3.40
17Jan04 Tre^{8}	Eternal Melody-NZ	L	4	115	5	9	8^{hd}	6^{1}	5^{1}	3^{3}	$3^{2\frac{1}{4}}$	Day P	3.30
6May04 ^{9}CD^{1}	Two Dot Slew	L	7	114	2	1	1^{1}	$1^{1\frac{1}{2}}$	$1^{1\frac{1}{2}}$	$2^{1\frac{1}{2}}$	$4\frac{3}{4}$	Bejarano R	10.90
1May04 ^{7}CD^{1}	Shaconage	L	4	117	7	5	$5\frac{1}{2}$	$8\frac{1}{2}$	$6\frac{1}{2}$	6^{2}	5^{hd}	Blanc B	7.90
17Apr04 ^{5}Kee^{1}	River Flower	L b	6	113	1	3	$3^{1\frac{1}{2}}$	4^{hd}	4^{hd}	$5\frac{1}{2}$	$6^{2\frac{3}{4}}$	Doser M E	21.70
1May04 ^{9}Aqu^{2}	Aud	L	4	117	9	8	9	7^{hd}	$7\frac{1}{2}$	7^{2}	7^{3}	Peck B D	2.50
6May04 ^{9}CD^{2}	Daisyago	L	5	113	4	4	7^{1}	$5^{1\frac{1}{2}}$	$3^{1\frac{1}{2}}$	8^{18}	8	McKee J	41.50
25Apr04 ^{9}CD^{1}	Kitty's Legend	L bf	4	114	6	6	$4^{1\frac{1}{2}}$	3^{hd}	9	9	—	Albarado R J	41.60

OFF AT 5:33 Start Good . Won driving. Course firm.

TIME :24^{1}, :48^{3}, 1:12^{4}, 1:36^{3}, 1:42^{3} (:24.36, :48.74, 1:12.80, 1:36.72, 1:42.66)

$2 Mutuel Prices:

3 – STAY FOREVER	12.00	5.60	4.20
8 – SAND SPRINGS		4.40	3.40
5 – ETERNAL MELODY-NZ			4.40

$2 EXACTA 3–8 PAID $69.40 $2 TRIFECTA 3–8–5 PAID $297.80
$2 SUPERFECTA 3–8–5–2 PAID $1,798.80

Ch. m, (Apr), by Stack – Forever Lady , by Forever Sparkle . Trainer Wolfson Martin D. Bred by Santa Cruz Ranch Inc (Fla).

STAY FOREVER settled in behind horses early, fell back last entering the far turn, came out seven or eight wide entering the stretch and closed determinedly under strong handling to prevail. SAND SPRINGS went up early to press front-running TWO DOT SLEW, raced four or five wide as the leader remained well off the hedge for five furlongs, took over in the upper stretch, then failed to contain the winner's surge. ETERNAL MELODY (NZ), a bit sluggish to start, was unhurried while edging inside, advanced between rivals four wide on the far turn, angled back to the rail in the upper stretch and was going well at the end. TWO DOT SLEW gained the lead early, raced three or four wide under careful handling, made the pace until the upper stretch and weakened. SHACONAGE, well placed early, was allowed to fall back on the backstretch, maneuvered inside, remained near the hedge entering the stretch and lacked a serious late response. RIVER FLOWER raced in contention inside into the upper stretch and faltered. AUD, four or five wide most of the trip, never menaced. DAISYAGO stalked the pace five wide to the stretch and flattened out. KITTY'S LEGEND, a bit edgy in the gate prior to the start, gave way after a half and was distanced in the stretch when not persevered with.

Owners– 1, Santa Cruz Ranch Inc Juan Rizo; 2, Willmott Stables Inc; 3, Bello Michael; 4, Chastain Rick; 5, Van Doren Andrena; 6, Stronach Stable; 7, Willmott Stables Inc; 8, Glenney John and Kim; 9, Millard R Seldin Revocable Trust

Trainers– 1, Wolfson Martin D; 2, Reinstedler Anthony; 3, Frankel Robert; 4, Gibson Dewayne C; 5, Shirota Mitch; 6, Sowle Scott; 7, Reinstedler Anthony; 8, Glenney John; 9, Thomas Gary S

$2 Pick Three (5–4–3) Paid $102.80 ; Pick Three Pool $34,777 .

NINTH RACE
Philadelphia
MAY 29, 2004

6 FURLONGS. (1.07^{4}) 4TH RUNNING OF THE DONALD LEVINE MEMORIAL HANDICAP. Grade III. Purse $100,000 FOR THREE YEAR OLDS AND UPWARD. By subscription of $100 each which should accompany the nomination, $300 to pass the entry box, $300 additional to start, with $100,000 guaranteed. The winner to receive $60,000 with $20,000 to second, $11,000 to third, $6,000 to fourth and $3,000 to fifth. Weights, Saturday, May 22, 2004 Starters to be named through the entry box by the usual time of closing, on Tuesday, May 25, 2004. Trophy will be presented to the winning owner, trainer and jockey. Nominations closed Saturday, May 15, 2004 with 28.

Value of Race: $100,000 Winner $60,000; second $20,000; third $11,000; fourth $6,000; fifth $3,000. Mutuel Pool $63,961.00 Exacta Pool $52,222.00 Trifecta Pool $32,127.00

Last Raced	Horse	M/Eqt.	A.	Wt	PP	St	¼	½	Str	Fin	Jockey	Odds $1
10Apr04 ^{9}Aqu^{7}	Peeping Tom	L b	7	116	2	6	6^{1}	6^{1}	6^{hd}	$1\frac{1}{2}$	Smith A E	4.30
15May04 ^{11}Pim^{2}	HighwayProspector	L b	7	117	4	7	7	7	7	2^{nk}	Potts C L	2.00
11May04 ^{9}Pha^{4}	Richierichierich	L f	5	113	5	4	5^{5}	4^{hd}	$1\frac{1}{2}$	$3^{1\frac{1}{2}}$	Molina V H	11.40
13May04 ^{6}Bel^{1}	Spooky Mulder	L	6	114	6	3	3^{hd}	3^{hd}	4^{1}	$4\frac{3}{4}$	Flores J L	4.20
1May04 ^{9}Mnr^{2}	Crossing Point	L f	7	116	7	1	$2^{1\frac{1}{2}}$	1^{hd}	2^{1}	$5^{4\frac{1}{4}}$	Fogelsonger R	9.40
8May04 ^{7}Bel^{4}	Secret Run	L bf	4	114	1	5	4^{2}	5^{3}	5^{hd}	$6^{1\frac{3}{4}}$	Arroyo N Jr	4.80
23Apr04 ^{8}Aqu^{2}	Kazoo	L bf	6	114	3	2	1^{hd}	2^{1}	3^{hd}	7	Vega H	5.40

OFF AT 3:53 Start Good . Won driving. Track fast.

TIME :22, :45^{1}, :57^{4}, 1:11 (:22.12, :45.36, :57.87, 1:11.05)

$2 Mutuel Prices:

3 – PEEPING TOM	10.60	3.80	3.20
1A– HIGHWAY PROSPECTOR		3.60	2.60
6 – RICHIERICHIERICH			3.20

$2 EXACTA 3–1 PAID $38.20 $2 TRIFECTA 3–1–6 PAID $369.20

B. g, (Mar), by Eagle Eyed – Artful Pleasure , by Nasty and Bold . Trainer Reynolds Patrick L. Bred by Finney & Taylor (Ky).

PEEPING TOM raced far back early, angled wide rallying into the stretch and just got up. HIGHWAY PROSPECTOR trailed early, circled the field on the turn while rallying, took a bad step at the head of the stretch, another bad step near the sixteenth pole and was outfinished. RICHIERICHIERICH was outrun early, was steered wide rallying on the turn, lugged in with a clear lead and yielded late. SPOOKY MULDER raced just off the leaders in the three path and continued gamely. CROSSING POINT dueled in the two path to the stretch and yielded in the final furlong. SECRET RUN inside and just off the leaders, angled out, came up empty. KAZOO dueled inside to the stretch and tired in the final furlong.

Owners– 1, Flatbird Stable; 2, Gill Michael J; 3, Walsh Richard; 4, Home Team Stables and Golden Bruce; 5, Clark Nancy and Heyman Fred; 6, Chapman Laz K; 7, Cunningham Marty

Trainers– 1, Reynolds Patrick L; 2, Shuman Mark; 3, Swentkowski Kimberly B; 4, Lake Scott A; 5, Feliciano Ben M Jr; 6, Laboccetta Frank Jr; 7, Hushion Michael E

Scratched– Out of Fashion (10Apr04 ^{8}Pim^{2}) , True Passion (11May04 ^{9}Pha^{1})

$2 Daily Double (5–3) Paid $12.80 ; Daily Double Pool $9,044 .
$2 Pick Three (6–5–3) Paid $85.60 ; Pick Three Pool $3,761 .

EIGHTH RACE

Hollywood

MAY 29, 2004

7 FURLONGS. (1.19^{4}) 11TH RUNNING OF THE LAZARO BARRERA MEMORIAL. Grade II. Purse $150,000 FOR THREE YEAR OLDS. By subscription of $150 each on or before Wednesday, May 12 or by supplementary nomination of $3,000 each by closing time of entries. $1,500 additional to start, with $90,000 to the winner,$30,000 to second, $18,000 to third, $9,000 to fourth and $3,000 to fifth. Weight 123 lbs. Non–winners of $60,000 allowed 3 lbs.; A race of $40,000 since December 25 allowed 5 lbs.; Non–winners of two races other than maiden, claiming or starter allowed 8 lbs.; Of such a race 10 lbs. Starters to benamed through the entry box by closing time of entries. A trophy will be presented to the winning owner. Closed with 19 nominations.

Value of Race: $150,000 Winner $90,000; second $30,000; third $18,000; fourth $9,000; fifth $3,000. Mutuel Pool $460,126.00 Exacta Pool $269,983.00 Quinella Pool $22,976.00 Trifecta Pool $289,093.00 Superfecta Pool $112,961.00

Last Raced	Horse	M/Eqt.	A.	Wt	PP	St	¼	½	Str	Fin	Jockey	Odds $1
13Dec03 ^{9}Crc^{2}	Twice as Bad	LB	3	116	6	3	3^{1}	$3^{1\frac{1}{2}}$	1^{2}	1^{3}	Solis A	2.10
21Apr04 ^{7}Hol^{2}	Wimplestiltskin	LB b	3	116	4	4	1^{hd}	2^{hd}	$2^{1\frac{1}{2}}$	$2^{2\frac{1}{2}}$	Valdivia J Jr	6.30
24Apr04 ^{9}Hol^{2}	Don'tsellmeshort	LB	3	123	2	6	$4^{\frac{1}{2}}$	4^{2}	$3^{2\frac{1}{2}}$	3^{3}	Flores D R	2.30
1May04 ^{7}Hol^{1}	Cape Flyaway	LB b	3	113	7	1	6^{hd}	6^{hd}	$4^{1\frac{1}{2}}$	$4^{2\frac{1}{2}}$	Santiago Javier	6.80
20Mar04 ^{8}OP^{1}	Number Juan	LB b	3	115	3	8	8	8	5^{3}	$5^{3\frac{1}{2}}$	Court J K	17.50
3Apr04 ^{7}Haw^{5}	Skipaslew	LB b	3	120	5	5	7^{hd}	7^{hd}	$6^{1\frac{1}{2}}$	6^{7}	Ruis M	16.10
8May04 ^{10}Hol^{1}	Courtnall	LB b	3	116	8	2	5^{1}	5^{hd}	8	$7^{2\frac{1}{2}}$	Desormeaux K J	21.80
1May04 ^{3}Hol^{2}	Evolution	LB b	3	114	1	7	2^{hd}	$1^{\frac{1}{2}}$	$7^{\frac{1}{2}}$	8	Espinoza V	5.90

OFF AT 4:57 Start Good . Won ridden out. Track fast.

TIME :21^{4}, :44, 1:08^{4}, 1:21^{2} (:21.90, :44.12, 1:08.82, 1:21.57)

$2 Mutuel Prices:				
	7 – TWICE AS BAD	6.20	4.20	2.80
	4 – WIMPLESTILTSKIN		6.00	3.00
	2 – DON'TSELLMESHORT			2.60

$1 EXACTA 7–4 PAID $16.90 $2 QUINELLA 4–7 PAID $29.20
$1 TRIFECTA 7–4–2 PAID $51.30 $1 SUPERFECTA 7–4–2–9 PAID $200.40

Gr/ro. c, (Feb), by Stormy Atlantic – Two Bad Girls , by Diablo . Trainer Cerin Vladimir. Bred by Linda S Rosenblatt (Fla).

TWICE AS BAD between horses early, forced the pace three deep, gained the advantage nearing midway on the turn, kicked clear and angled in entering the stretch and proved best under a brisk hand ride. WIMPLESTILTSKIN sent between horses to duel for the lead, fought back a bit off the rail inside the winner leaving the turn, angled in, came out in the stretch and held second. DON'TSELLMESHORT bumped at the start, had speed between horses then stalked a bit off the rail, came out on the turn and into the stretch and bested the others. CAPE FLYAWAY fractious in the gate, chased outside, went four wide leaving the backstretch and into the turn, continued three deep into the stretch and lacked the needed rally. NUMBER JUAN chased a bit off the rail then inside into and on the turn, split horses into the stretch and could not summon the necessary late response. SKIPASLEW settled between horses chasing the pace, came out four wide into the stretch and did not rally. COURTNALL broke through the gate before the start, had speed outside then stalked four wide, dropped back on the turn, drifted five wide into the stretch, gave way and was not persevered with late. EVOLUTION had good early speed and dueled inside, dropped back past midway on the turn, also gave way and was not urged late.

Owners– 1, Mercedes Stables LLC; 2, Everest Stables Inc; 3, Peacock Cecil N; 4, Gilbert Allan; 5, Pegram Michael E; 6, The Merv Griffin Ranch Co; 7, Reddam J Paul; 8, CRK Stable and Alsdorf Gregg

Trainers– 1, Cerin Vladimir; 2, Polanco Marcelo; 3, Hendricks Dan L; 4, Baffert Bob; 5, Puhich Michael; 6, O'Neill Doug; 7, Dollase Craig; 8, Sadler John W

Scratched– Hosco (28Mar04 ^{8}Sun^{10}) , Siphonizer (24Apr04 ^{7}CD ^{1})

$2 Daily Double (1–7) Paid $36.20 ; Daily Double Pool $27,865 .
$1 Pick Three (10–1–6/7/8) Paid $84.20 ; Pick Three Pool $70,389 .

TENTH RACE
Monmouth
MAY 29, 2004

1 MILE. (Turf) (1.33^{1}) 31ST RUNNING OF THE RED BANK HANDICAP. Grade III. Purse $100,000 FOR THREE-YEAR-OLDS AND UPWARD. By subscription of $100 each, which should accompany the nomination, and $1,500 to pass the entry box. The winning owner to receive $60,000, $20,000 to second, $11,000 to third, $6,000 to fourth and $3,000 to fifth. The owner of the winner to receive a trophy. Closed Monday, May 17, 2004 with 48 nominations.

Value of Race: $100,000 Winner $60,000; second $20,000; third $11,000; fourth $6,000; fifth $3,000. Mutuel Pool $230,613.00 Exacta Pool $178,590.00 Trifecta Pool $108,119.00 Superfecta Pool $19,805.00

Last Raced	Horse	M/Eqt.	A.	Wt	PP	St	¼	½	¾	Str	Fin	Jockey	Odds $1
9Apr04 ^{9}Kee^{2}	Burning Roma	L	6	120	3	5	2^{1}	$2^{\frac{1}{2}}$	$2^{1\frac{1}{2}}$	1^{hd}	1^{hd}	Castanon J L	1.80
24Apr04 ^{8}Aqu^{5}	Remind	L	4	117	10	10	$9^{1\frac{1}{2}}$	$8^{1\frac{1}{2}}$	6^{hd}	5^{1}	$2^{2\frac{3}{4}}$	Bravo J	7.20
18Oct03 ^{8}Del^{4}	American Freedom	L b	6	115	9	7	5^{1}	5^{2}	$5^{1\frac{1}{2}}$	3^{1}	$3^{1\frac{3}{4}}$	Velez J A Jr	47.10
15May04 ^{10}Pim^{6}	Wudantunoit	L b	6	116	8	2	1^{2}	1^{3}	1^{1}	$2^{1\frac{1}{2}}$	4no	Lopez C C	a- 8.20
24Jan04 ^{10}GP^{6}	Stormy Roman	L	5	115	4	8	8^{hd}	9^{1}	7^{1}	$6^{1\frac{1}{2}}$	$5^{\frac{1}{2}}$	Coa E M	10.70
2May04 ^{5}Hol^{1}	Sardaukar-GB	L	8	115	11	11	11	$10^{\frac{1}{2}}$	$9^{1\frac{1}{2}}$	8^{hd}	$6^{1\frac{1}{4}}$	Elliott S	a- 8.20
9May04 ^{7}Bel^{4}	Chilly Rooster	L b	4	116	7	9	10^{hd}	11	11	11	$7^{\frac{1}{2}}$	Uske S	15.10
7Jun03 ^{5}Bel^{1}	Navesink	L	6	115	1	1	$4^{1\frac{1}{2}}$	4^{2}	4^{hd}	4^{hd}	8^{nk}	Pimentel J	3.80
1May04 ^{9}Pim^{2}	Spruce Run	L b	6	115	6	4	7^{1}	6^{1}	$8^{\frac{1}{2}}$	7^{hd}	$9^{\frac{1}{2}}$	Ferrer J C	15.50
9May04 ^{7}Bel^{3}	Pisces	L b	7	115	2	6	$6^{1\frac{1}{2}}$	7^{hd}	10^{1}	10^{hd}	10^{1}	Decarlo C P	9.10
1May04 ^{9}Pim^{3}	Tam's Terms	L	6	116	5	3	3^{hd}	3^{1}	3^{hd}	$9^{1\frac{1}{2}}$	11	Karamanos H A	9.30

a-Coupled: Wudantunoit and Sardaukar-GB.

OFF AT 5:24 Start Good. Won driving. Course good.
TIME :23^{2}, :46^{2}, 1:10^{2}, 1:34^{3} (:23.48, :46.52, 1:10.43, 1:34.73)

(New Course Record)

$2 Mutuel Prices:

5 – BURNING ROMA	5.60	4.00	3.20
12 – REMIND		6.80	5.00
11 – AMERICAN FREEDOM			7.20

$2 EXACTA 5–12 PAID $41.80 $2 TRIFECTA 5–12–11 PAID $849.00
$1 SUPERFECTA 5–12–11–1 PAID $2,121.90

B. h, (Mar), by Rubiano – While Rome Burns, by Overskate. Trainer Giglio Heather A. Bred by William S Farish Jr (Ky).

BURNING ROMA rated off the pace inside, moved closer through the final turn, started a solid drive entering the stretch and just lasted. REMIND rated off the pace in mid track, saved some ground on the final turn, eased out for the stretch run, closed steadily and just missed. AMERICAN FREEDOM rated off the pace in mid track, closed ground to late stretch then flattened out. WUDANTUNOIT advanced to the lead early rating the pace inside, dueled from the top of the stretch but weakened through the final furlong. STORMY ROMAN, unhurried early, bid outside on the final turn and finished evenly. SARDAUKAR (GB), unhurried, bid in the three path on the final turn, closed mildly and finished evenly. CHILLY ROOSTER raced unhurriedly inside, angled out leaving the quarter pole and finished evenly outside. NAVESINK was kept off the pace inside, gave chase through the final turn then weakened in the stretch. SPRUCE RUN raced unhurriedly toward mid track and offered no rally. PISCES was through early. TAM'S TERMS was kept off the pace toward the outside and gave way entering the stretch.

Owners– 1, Queen Harold L; 2, Claiborne Farm; 3, Freedom Acres Inc; 4, Gill Michael J; 5, Croley Thomas L; 6, Gill Michael J; 7, Hobeau Farm; 8, Jayeff B Stables; 9, Golden Dome Stable; 10, Gary Shapiro; 11, Bender Sondra D

Trainers– 1, Giglio Heather A; 2, Mott William I; 3, Woodington Jamie; 4, Vazquez Gamaliel; 5, Hills Timothy A; 6, Shuman Mark; 7, Jerkens H Allen; 8, Goldberg Alan E; 9, Rice Linda; 10, Weaver George; 11, Murray Lawrence E

Scratched– Ricardo A (24Apr04 ^{10}GP ^{4}), Cool N Collective (15Nov03 ^{8}Hoo^{2})

$2 Pick Four (7–2–5–5) Paid $1,405.60 ; Pick Four Pool $26,461 .

EIGHTH RACE
Belmont
MAY 30, 2004

7 FURLONGS. (Turf) (1.19^{4}) 21ST RUNNING OF THE JAIPUR HANDICAP. Grade III. Purse $100,000 WIDENER TURF. (UP TO $19,000 NYSBFOA) A HANDICAP FOR THREE YEAR OLDS AND UPWARD. By subscription of $100 each, which should accompany the nomination; $500 to pass the entry box; $500 to start, with $100,000 added. The added money and all fees to be divided 60% to the winner, 20% to second, 10% to third, 5% to fourth, 3% to fifth and 2% divided equally among remaining finishers. A trophy will be presented to the winning owner. The New York Racing Association reserves the right to transfer this race to the Main Track. In the event that this race is taken off the turf, it may be subject to downgrading upon review by the Graded Stakes Committee. Closed Saturday, May 15, 2004 with 42 Nominations. (If the Stewards consider it inadvisable to run this race on the turf course, this race will be run at Seven Furlongs on the main track.). (Rail at 18 feet).

Value of Race: $112,200 Winner $67,320; second $22,440; third $11,220; fourth $5,610; fifth $3,366; sixth $748; seventh $748; eighth $748. Mutuel Pool $566,136.00 Exacta Pool $461,412.00 Trifecta Pool $354,569.00

Last Raced	Horse	M/Eqt.	A.	Wt	PP	St	¼	½	Str	Fin	Jockey	Odds $1
20May04 ^{8}Bel^{2}	Multiple Choice	L b	6	113	1	8	$4^{2\frac{1}{2}}$	$4^{\frac{1}{2}}$	$4^{1\frac{1}{2}}$	$1^{\frac{1}{2}}$	Castellano J J	14.50
1May04 ^{9}Aqu^{1}	Dedication-FR	L	5	114	7	2	5^{hd}	6^{hd}	2^{hd}	$2^{1\frac{1}{2}}$	Prado E S	2.65
23Apr04 ^{3}Hol^{2}	Geronimo-Chi	L b	5	118	8	1	$7^{4\frac{1}{2}}$	8	6^{hd}	3^{hd}	Santos J A	4.40
30Apr04 ^{7}CD^{3}	Banned in Boston	L	4	116	4	4	3^{hd}	$3^{1\frac{1}{2}}$	$1^{\frac{1}{2}}$	$4^{\frac{1}{2}}$	Migliore R	5.40
18Oct03 ^{8}Haw^{5}	Lismore Knight	L	4	118	6	6	8	7^{hd}	7^{7}	5^{1}	Velazquez J R	6.90
15Apr04 ^{4}Kee^{2}	He's Crafty	L	5	116	3	5	2^{2}	$2^{\frac{1}{2}}$	3^{hd}	6^{1}	Bailey J D	3.65
25Oct03 ^{5}SA^{11}	Great Notion	L f	4	115	2	7	1^{hd}	1^{hd}	5^{hd}	$7^{5\frac{3}{4}}$	Bejarano R	6.50
24Apr04 ^{3}Aqu^{5}	Unswept	L b	4	112	5	3	6^{hd}	$5^{\frac{1}{2}}$	8	8	Arroyo N Jr	67.25

OFF AT 4:50 Start Good. Won driving. Course good.
TIME :22^{2}, :45^{3}, 1:09^{2}, 1:22^{1} (:22.57, :45.62, 1:09.54, 1:22.32)

$2 Mutuel Prices:

1 – MULTIPLE CHOICE	31.00	13.40	6.80
7 – DEDICATION-FR		4.50	3.00
8 – GERONIMO-CHI			4.10

$2 EXACTA 1–7 PAID $150.00 $2 TRIFECTA 1–7–8 PAID $646.00

B. g, (Feb), by Mt. Livermore – Lady of Choice, by Storm Bird. Trainer Jerkens James A. Bred by Peter E Blum (Ky).

MULTIPLE CHOICE raced close up inside while in hand, came wide into the stretch, responded when roused, dug in gamely outside and prevailed after a hard drive. DEDICATION (FR) was bumped at the start, was bumped repeatedly on the backstretch, came wide into the stretch and dug in gamely to the wire. GERONIMO (CHI) was bumped at the start, was bumped repeatedly on the backstretch, was steadied when in tight quarters between rivals on the turn and finished gamely. BANNED IN BOSTON raced close up outside, rallied three wide on the turn, earned a short lead in the stretch and faded in the final furlong. LISMORE KNIGHT was bumped at the start, dropped back early, put in a four wide run approaching the stretch and had little left for the drive. HE'S CRAFTY contested the pace from the outside and tired in the final furlong. GREAT NOTION contested the pace along the inside and tired in the stretch. UNSWEPT raced three wide, was steadied entering the stretch and tired.

Owners– 1, Blum Peter E; 2, Head Ghislaine; 3, Buster Jr William C Machowsky Dana; 4, Hubbard R D; 5, Pletcher Jacob J Simon Barry W; 6, Live Oak Plantation; 7, Silverton Hill LLC; 8, Andrew Farm and Cassidy David

Trainers– 1, Jerkens James A; 2, Clement Christophe; 3, Machowsky Michael; 4, Hennig John K; 5, Pletcher Todd A; 6, Mott William I; 7, Miller Darrin; 8, Contessa Gary C

Scratched– Savoy Special (27Nov03 ^{8}Aqu^{3})

NINTH RACE
Belmont
MAY 31, 2004

1 MILE. (1.32^{1}) 111TH RUNNING OF THE METROPOLITAN HANDICAP. Grade I. Purse $750,000 (Up to $62,500 NYSBFOA) A HANDICAP FOR THREE YEAR OLDS AND UPWARD. By subscription of $750 each, which should accompany the nomination, $3,500 to pass the entry box; $4,000 to start. The purse to be divided 60% to the winner, 20% to second, 10% to third,5% to fourth, 3% to fifth and 2% divided equally among remaining finishers. Trophies will be presented to the winning owner, trainer and jockey. Closed Saturday, May 15, 2004 with 24 Nominations.

Value of Race: $750,000 Winner $450,000; second $150,000; third $75,000; fourth $37,500; fifth $22,500; sixth $3,750; seventh $3,750; eighth $3,750; ninth $3,750. Mutuel Pool $1,361,124.00 Exacta Pool $854,090.00 Trifecta Pool $690,977.00 Superfecta Pool $189,710.00

Last Raced	Horse	M/Eqt.	A.	Wt	PP	St	¼	½	¾	Str	Fin	Jockey	Odds $1
10Apr04 ^{9}Aqu^{1}	Pico Central-Brz	L	5	119	8	3	2^{2}	2^{hd}	$2^{\frac{1}{2}}$	1^{hd}	$1^{\frac{3}{4}}$	Solis A	3.45
14May04 ^{11}Pim^{3}	Bowman's Band	L	6	114	1	8	5^{hd}	7^{6}	$7^{2\frac{1}{2}}$	4^{hd}	$2^{2\frac{1}{4}}$	Chavez J F	18.20
10Apr04 ^{9}Aqu^{2}	Strong Hope	L	4	119	6	2	$1^{\frac{1}{2}}$	$1^{\frac{1}{2}}$	1^{hd}	2^{2}	$3^{1\frac{1}{2}}$	Velazquez J R	1.95
5May04 ^{8}Bel^{1}	Gygistar	L	5	115	5	5	6^{hd}	4^{hd}	$3^{\frac{1}{2}}$	3^{hd}	$4^{\frac{3}{4}}$	Bravo J	13.30
3Apr04 ^{8}Aqu^{1}	Funny Cide	L	4	118	9	1	$4^{1\frac{1}{2}}$	$5^{\frac{1}{2}}$	4^{hd}	$5^{\frac{1}{2}}$	$5^{\frac{1}{2}}$	Santos J A	4.20
5May04 ^{8}Bel^{2}	Saarland	L b	5	114	4	9	9	9	$8^{4\frac{1}{2}}$	$8^{4\frac{1}{2}}$	6^{1}	Bailey J D	15.00
10Apr04 ^{9}Aqu^{3}	Eye of the Tiger	L	4	114	2	7	$7^{4\frac{1}{2}}$	6^{hd}	6^{hd}	$7^{\frac{1}{2}}$	7^{hd}	Prado E S	14.30
1May04 ^{8}CD^{2}	Azeri	L	6	117	3	6	3^{hd}	3^{1}	5^{hd}	6^{2}	$8^{4\frac{3}{4}}$	Day P	5.80
1May04 ^{8}WO^{1}	Mobil	L f	4	115	7	4	8^{5}	8^{1}	9	9	9	Kabel T K	53.75

OFF AT 5:19 Start Good . Won driving. Track fast.

TIME :23^{2}, :46, 1:10, 1:35^{2} (:23.46, :46.00, 1:10.04, 1:35.47)

$2 Mutuel Prices:				
	8 – **PICO CENTRAL–BRZ**	8.90	5.60	3.40
	1 – **BOWMAN'S BAND**		13.20	6.50
	6 – **STRONG HOPE**			2.80

$2 EXACTA 8–1 PAID $134.50 $2 TRIFECTA 8–1–6 PAID $474.50
$2 SUPERFECTA 8–1–6–5 PAID $2,817.00

Dk. b or br. h, (Oct), by Spend a Buck – Sheila Purple , by Purple Mountain . Trainer Lobo Paulo H. Bred by Haras Fronteira PAP (Brz).

PICO CENTRAL (BRZ) bobbled at the start, raced with the pace from the outside while in hand, responded when roused in upper stretch, drew clear inside the eighth pole then dug in gamely and held off BOWMAN'S BAND under strong handling. BOWMAN'S BAND was urged along inside, was in tight quarters on the rail on the turn, angled out in upper stretch and finished fast from the outside. STRONG HOPE quickly showed in front, set the pace under pressure from the winner, could not stay with that rival leaving the eighth pole and weakened in deep stretch. GYGISTAR was unhurried outside early, put in a four wide run on the turn and faded in the final furlong. FUNNY CIDE raced close up while between rivals three wide and had no response when roused. SAARLAND was outrun early, advanced four wide on the turn, came widest into the stretch and was no real threat with a mild rally outside. EYE OF THE TIGER raced in hand while between rivals early, angled out and rallied four wide approaching the stretch and had nothing left for the drive. AZERI raced close up inside while in hand and came up empty when called on. MOBIL was outrun early, raced inside and had no response when roused.

Owners– 1, Tanaka Gary A; 2, Schwartz Martin S; 3, Melnyk Eugene and Laura; 4, Evans Edward P; 5, Sackatoga Stable; 6, Phipps Cynthia; 7, Gunther John D; 8, Allen E Paulson Living Trust; 9, Schickedanz Gustav

Trainers– 1, Lobo Paulo H; 2, Jerkens H Allen; 3, Pletcher Todd A; 4, Hennig Mark; 5, Tagg Barclay; 6, McGaughey III Claude R; 7, McLaughlin Kiaran P; 8, Lukas D Wayne; 9, Keogh Michael

---

TENTH RACE
Calder
MAY 31, 2004

$1\frac{1}{16}$ MILES. (1.42^{2}) 30TH RUNNING OF THE MEMORIAL DAY HANDICAP. Grade III. Purse $100,000 FOR THREE YEAR OLDS AND UPWARD. By subscription of $100 each which shall accompany the nomination, $1,000 to pass the entry box and an additional $1,000 to start – with $100,000 guaranteed. The owner of the winner to receive $60,000, $20,000 to second, $11,000 to third, $6,000 to fourth and $3,000 to fifth. A trophy will be presented to the winning Owner. Closed Saturday, May 22, 2004 with (15) nominations.

Value of Race: $100,000 Winner $60,000; second $20,000; third $11,000; fourth $6,000; fifth $3,000. Mutuel Pool $163,193.00 Exacta Pool $150,333.00 Trifecta Pool $133,947.00 Superfecta Pool $58,566.00

Last Raced	Horse	M/Eqt.	A.	Wt	PP	St	¼	½	¾	Str	Fin	Jockey	Odds $1
26Apr04 ^{8}Crc^{1}	Twilight Road	L	7	111	1	1	$5^{\frac{1}{2}}$	5^{hd}	$5^{3\frac{1}{2}}$	1^{hd}	$1^{5\frac{1}{4}}$	Teator P A	7.60
8May04 ^{8}Crc^{6}	Hear No Evil	L bf	4	115	11	7	$1^{2\frac{1}{2}}$	1^{2}	1^{4}	$2^{2\frac{1}{2}}$	2^{1}	Toscano P R	13.00
11May04 ^{3}Crc^{3}	Gold Dollar	L b	5	112	8	9	12	11^{hd}	$10^{2\frac{1}{2}}$	6^{hd}	$3^{\frac{1}{2}}$	Lopez J E	59.40
8May04 ^{8}Crc^{7}	Super Frolic	L f	4	115	2	3	$9^{\frac{1}{2}}$	$9^{2\frac{1}{2}}$	$8^{1\frac{1}{2}}$	$5^{1\frac{1}{2}}$	4^{2}	Garcia J A	4.90
9May04 ^{9}Crc^{1}	Romolo's Fritzi	L	6	113	3	2	3^{1}	3^{hd}	$4^{\frac{1}{2}}$	3^{1}	5^{nk}	Nunez E O	7.20
26Apr04 ^{6}Crc^{4}	Whos Crying Now	L bf	4	115	6	4	$4^{\frac{1}{2}}$	$4^{1\frac{1}{2}}$	3^{hd}	4^{hd}	$6^{3\frac{3}{4}}$	Cruz M R	40.10
24Apr04 ^{8}LS^{2}	Supah Blitz	L b	4	116	7	12	10^{1}	8^{hd}	$9^{\frac{1}{2}}$	7^{3}	$7^{5\frac{3}{4}}$	Castro E	1.30
15May04 ^{8}Crc^{2}	Patriotic Flame	L b	4	114	9	10	6^{hd}	6^{hd}	7^{hd}	$8^{2\frac{1}{2}}$	$8^{4\frac{3}{4}}$	Toribio A R	19.40
1May04 ^{8}EvD^{1}	Kiss a Native	L f	7	115	5	5	$8^{1\frac{1}{2}}$	$10^{1\frac{1}{2}}$	$11^{2\frac{1}{2}}$	10^{1}	$9^{1\frac{3}{4}}$	Wright M L	34.00
27Apr04 ^{8}Crc^{1}	Predawn Raid	L b	5	116	12	11	2^{3}	2^{4}	$2^{1\frac{1}{2}}$	9^{3}	$10^{1\frac{3}{4}}$	Boulanger G	7.80
15May04 ^{8}Crc^{3}	Dancing Guy	L bf	9	115	4	6	11^{2}	12	12	12	11^{3}	Aguilar M	13.90
27Apr04 ^{8}Crc^{3}	Verkade	L b	4	110	10	8	$7^{1\frac{1}{2}}$	$7^{1\frac{1}{2}}$	6^{hd}	11^{2}	12	Penalba C	52.40

OFF AT 5:02 Start Good . Won driving. Track fast.

TIME :23^{2}, :47, 1:11^{4}, 1:38^{3}, 1:45^{3} (:23.40, :47.17, 1:11.97, 1:38.77, 1:45.79)

$2 Mutuel Prices:				
	1 – **TWILIGHT ROAD**	17.20	9.20	8.60
	11 – **HEAR NO EVIL**		15.40	9.00
	8 – **GOLD DOLLAR**			20.00

$2 EXACTA 1–11 PAID $345.40 $2 TRIFECTA 1–11–8 PAID $10,864.40
$2 SUPERFECTA 1–11–8–2 PAID $28,502.00

Ch. g, (Apr), by Cahill Road – Glory's Light , by Halo . Trainer Fawkes David. Bred by Mira Ball (Ky).

TWILIGHT ROAD reserved while saving ground, angled four wide midway of the far turn, rallied to catch HEAR NO EVIL at the eighth pole and drew away under pressure. HEAR NO EVIL quickly moved to the fore, made the pace off the rail into the stretch, then was no match for the winner while holding the place. GOLD DOLLAR outrun early, came between horses on the far turn, angled out and closed to gain the show. SUPER FROLIC unhurried after being steadied entering the first turn, saved ground into the stretch, eased out and improved his position in the drive without threatening. ROMOLO'S FRITZI tracked the pace along the rail into the stretch and gave way. WHOS CRYING NOW well placed racing off the rail, tired in the drive. SUPAH BLITZ allowed to settle, bumped with DANCING GUY entering the first turn and lacked a rally. PATRIOTIC FLAME rated in striking position off the pace, faltered leaving the far turn. KISS A NATIVE was not a factor. PREDAWN RAID chased the pacesetter three wide to nearing the stretch and faded. DANCING GUY bumped with SUPAH BLITZ and steadied racing into the first turn, then was outrun. VERKADE raced three wide and stopped.

Owners– 1, Donamire Farm; 2, Jacks or Better Farm Inc; 3, Pazos Julio; 4, Stride Rite Racing Stable Inc; 5, Naranjo Carlos; 6, Lewis James R Jr; 7, Bee Bee Stables Inc and Tortora Jacqueline; 8, Kinsman Stable; 9, Castille Carrol; 10, Mount Joy Stables Inc; 11, Green Newcomb; 12, H B Stables and Ziadie Sonia

Trainers– 1, Fawkes David; 2, Hatchett James; 3, Azpurua Manuel J; 4, Wolfson Milton W; 5, Canet Julian; 6, Tortora Emanuel; 7, Tortora Emanuel; 8, Ziadie Kirk; 9, Castille Carrol; 10, Stutts Bennie F Jr; 11, Green Newcomb; 12, Ziadie Ralph

---

$2 Pick Three (2–2–1) Paid $335.60 ; Pick Three Pool $11,924 .

THIRD RACE
Bay Meadows
MAY 31, 2004

$1\frac{1}{16}$ MILES. (1.38^{2}) 37TH RUNNING OF THE SEABISCUT BREEDERS' CUP HANDICAP. Grade III. Purse $100,000 (includes $25,000 BC – Breeders' Cup) FOR THREE-YEAR-OLDS AND UPWARD. By subscription of $75 each to accompany the nomination or by supplementary nomination of $1,500 by Noon, Sunday, May 23, 2004. $375 to pass the entry box and $375 additional to start with $75,000 Guaranteed and an additional $25,000 from Breeders' Cup Fund for Breeders' Cup eligibles only. The host association's Guaranteed monies to be divided 55% to the winner, 20% to second, 15% to third, 7.5% to fourth and 2.5% to fifth. Breeders' Cup Fund monies also correspondinglydivided providing a Breeders' Cup nominee has finished in an awarded position. Any Breeders' Cup Fund monies not awarded will revert back to the Fund. A trophy will be presented to the owner of the winner by Breeders' Cup Ltd. Closed Thursday, May 20, 22004 with 17 nominations.

Value of Race: $86,250 Winner $41,250; second $20,000; third $15,000; fourth $7,500; fifth $2,500. Mutuel Pool $155,978.00 Exacta Pool $117,698.00 Quinella Pool $11,142.00

Last Raced	Horse	M/Eqt.	A.	Wt	PP	St	¼	½	¾	Str	Fin	Jockey	Odds $1
22Apr04 ^{3}BM^{1}	Yougottawanna	LB bf	5	116	4	1	1^{1}	1^{1}	1^{1}	1^{2}	$1^{\frac{3}{4}}$	Baze R A	1.30
24Apr04 ^{3}BM^{3}	Gold Ruckus	LB bf	6	115	1	2	$3^{\frac{1}{2}}$	3^{hd}	3^{hd}	2^{hd}	2^{3}	Schvaneveldt C P	8.80
24Apr04 ^{8}LS^{4}	Snorter	LB b	4	118	3	3	$4^{3\frac{1}{2}}$	4^{6}	4^{4}	4^{2}	$3^{\frac{1}{2}}$	Carr D	1.80
4Oct03 ^{5}SA^{6}	Reba's Gold	LB b	7	117	5	4	$2^{1\frac{1}{2}}$	2^{1}	$2^{1\frac{1}{2}}$	3^{2}	4^{nk}	Rollins C J	2.90
3Apr04 ^{10}SA^{7}	Calkins Road	LB f	5	116	2	5	5	5	5	5	5	Warren R J Jr	17.90

OFF AT 2:11 Start Good . Won driving. Track fast.

TIME $:23^{1}$, :46, $1:09^{2}$, $1:33^{3}$, 1:40 (:23.25, :46.03, 1:09.49, 1:33.67, 1:40.08)

$2 Mutuel Prices:

4 – YOUGOTTAWANNA	4.60	3.20	2.20
1 – GOLD RUCKUS		5.20	3.00
3 – SNORTER			2.60

$1 EXACTA 4–1 PAID $10.10 $2 QUINELLA 1–4 PAID $14.00

Ch. g, (Feb), by Candi's Gold – Chapel's Sister , by Midway Circle . Trainer Hollendorfer Jerry. Bred by Halo Farms (Cal).

YOUGOTTAWANNA set the pace in hand to the second turn, responded to urging to mid stretch while racing in the two path then held off his stable mate under steady pressure. GOLD RUCKUS tracked the winner's pace from the rail to the second turn, remained inside and rallied to the stretch, shifted out in upper stretch then finished willingly late. SNORTER was allowed to settle to the half, tried to rally but was fanned four wide to the stretch and flattened out in mid stretch. REBA'S GOLD prompted the pace three wide to the second turn, bid three wide to the stretch, could not impact the winner and weakened late. CALKINS ROAD lagged to the half, took closer order from the rail to the stretch then could not sustain that run.

Owners– 1, Peter Redekop B C Ltd; 2, Franks Farms; 3, Gary and Mary West Stables Inc; 4, Creston Farms; 5, Shapiro Mr and Mrs Thomas A

Trainers– 1, Hollendorfer Jerry; 2, Hollendorfer Jerry; 3, Frankel Robert; 4, Hendricks Dan L; 5, Shirreffs John

$2 Daily Double (1–4) Paid $44.80 ; Daily Double Pool $7,793 .
$1 Pick Three (4–1–4) Paid $82.70 ; Pick Three Pool $30,653 .

NINTH RACE
Churchill
MAY 31, 2004

$1\frac{3}{8}$ MILES. (Turf) (2.13) 67TH RUNNING OF THE LOUISVILLE HANDICAP. Grade III. Purse $100,000 FOR THREE-YEAR-OLDS AND UPWARD. By subscription of $100 each on or before May 15, 2004 or by Supplementary Nomination of $5,000 each by the closing of entries Friday, May 21, 2004. $500 to pass the entry box; $500 additional to start. Weights to be announced Saturday, May 22, 2004. If the race is moved to the main track after the time of closing, a horse may be scratched for any reason at any time up to fifteen (15) minutes prior to post time for the race preceding this race or thereafter with a validphysical reason and approved by the stewards. The entry fee shall be refunded for scratches made in compliance with the above conditions. (If this race is taken off the turf it will be downgraded one grade level for this running only in accordance withAmerican Graded StakesCommittee policy). Closed Saturday, May 15, 2004 with 34 nominations.

Value of Race: $112,400 Winner $69,688; second $22,480; third $11,240; fourth $4,496; fourth $4,496. Mutuel Pool $416,842.00 Exacta Pool $252,586.00 Trifecta Pool $237,370.00 Superfecta Pool $83,666.00

Last Raced	Horse	M/Eqt.	A.	Wt	PP	¼	½	¾	1	Str	Fin	Jockey	Odds $1
8May04 ^{8}CD^{1}	Silverfoot	L	4	114	3	5^{1}	6^{2}	$6^{1\frac{1}{2}}$	5^{hd}	$2^{1\frac{1}{2}}$	1no	Albarado R J	4.20
23Apr04 ^{9}Kee^{2}	Rochester	L	8	116	2	7^{3}	7^{4}	$7^{3\frac{1}{2}}$	7^{3}	$1^{1\frac{1}{2}}$	$2^{1\frac{1}{4}}$	Velasquez C	5.40
8May04 ^{7}Hol^{4}	Ballingarry-Ire	L	5	120	5	8^{4}	8^{4}	8^{4}	$8^{7\frac{1}{2}}$	4^{2}	$3^{1\frac{1}{2}}$	Guidry M	1.10
23Apr04 ^{9}Kee^{3}	DH Art Variety-Brz	L b	6	115	6	6^{3}	5^{2}	4^{2}	4^{hd}	5^{hd}	4	Blanc B	7.00
23Apr04 ^{9}Kee^{4}	DH Kim Loves Bucky	L	7	117	8	$3^{\frac{1}{2}}$	$4^{\frac{1}{2}}$	3^{hd}	3^{2}	3^{2}	$4^{7\frac{1}{2}}$	Bejarano R	5.00
26May04 ^{8}CD^{2}	Feel the Wind	L b	5	110	7	$1^{\frac{1}{2}}$	1^{3}	1^{2}	2^{1}	7^{1}	$6^{1\frac{1}{2}}$	McKee J	25.90
13May04 ^{9}CD^{7}	Gottabeachboy	L b	4	108	9	4^{3}	3^{hd}	$5^{\frac{1}{2}}$	$6^{\frac{1}{2}}$	8^{4}	$7^{\frac{1}{2}}$	Hernandez B J Jr	115.10
9May04 ^{3}CD^{3}	Dia Alegre-Chi	L	5	112	1	2^{2}	2^{2}	$2^{1\frac{1}{2}}$	1^{hd}	6^{3}	$8^{\frac{3}{4}}$	Melancon L	43.00
24Apr04 ^{8}CD^{7}	Spruce Hero	L	4	114	4	9	9	9	9	9	9	Borel C H	30.30

DH–Dead Heat.

OFF AT 5:34 Start Good For All But GOTTABEACHBOY. Won driving. Course yielding.

TIME $:25^{1}$, :50, $1:15^{1}$, 1:40, 2:05, $2:17^{3}$ (:25.90, :50.03, 1:15.36, 1:40.19, 2:05.05, 2:17.63)

$2 Mutuel Prices:

3 – SILVERFOOT	10.40	5.00	3.00
2 – ROCHESTER		6.00	3.20
5 – BALLINGARRY-IRE			2.40

$2 EXACTA 3–2 PAID $48.40 $2 TRIFECTA 3–2–5 PAID $127.60
$2 SUPERFECTA 3–2–5–8 PAID $280.80 $2 SUPERFECTA 3–2–5–6 PAID $201.20

Gr/ro. g, (May), by With Approval – Northern Silver , by Silver Ghost . Trainer Stewart Dallas. Bred by Stephanie S Clark (Ky).

SILVERFOOT, unhurried early while racing in behind horses three or four wide, edged closer between foes on the far turn, advanced through close quarters a quarter-mile out, bumped with ROCHESTER immediately to his inside as those two both were in tight, as a result came out into FEEL THE WIND, then wore down ROCHESTER in the closing strides. ROCHESTER, never far back, raced under light rating four wide, moved with the winner while inside that one, was in extremely close quarters, bumped with SILVERFOOT, gained a clear advantage at the furlong grounds and failed to last. BALLINGARRY (IRE), outrun early, raced three wide while advancing on the far turn, worked his way out seven wide at the eighth pole and was gaining late. ART VARIETY (BRZ), within easy striking distance while racing near the inside, angled out four wide for the drive and couldn't offer the needed response while dead heating for fourth with KIM LOVES BUCKY. The latter tracked the pace from early on while four wide, was carried out a bit entering the stretch by FEEL THE WIND, continued close up into the final furlong and flattened out to finish evenly with ART VARIETY (BRZ). FEEL THE WIND gained the lead early, edged in to show the way three wide, moved clear on the backstretch, drifted out, carrying KIM LOVES BUCKY out in the process at the quarter-mile pole, was soundly bumped shortly after by SILVERFOOT when straightened, then gradually weakened. GOTTABEACHBOY broke in the air, bobbled when landing, raced in contention to the stretch while five or six wide and weakened. DIA ALEGRE (CHI), nicely placed along the inside from early on, inched to challenge upon going six furlongs, continued close up to the stretch and faltered. SPRUCE HERO was outrun. A FOUL CLAIM LODGED BY THE RIDER OF FEEL THE WIND AGAINST SILVERFOOT FOR ALLEGED INTERFERENCE AT THE QUARTER-MILE GROUND WAS DISALLOWED.

Owners– 1, Chrysalis Stables LLC; 2, Augustin Stable; 3, Port Trust Naify Marsha and San Gabriel Investments; 4, Team Victory II Shirley Cunningham William Gallion and Rick Pitino; 5, Glenney Kim; 6, WinStar Farm LLC; 7, Hackworth Robert S Jr; 8, Panic Stable LLC; 9, Lakeside Farms LLC

Trainers– 1, Stewart Dallas; 2, Sheppard Jonathan E; 3, De Seroux Laura; 4, McPeek Kenneth G; 5, Glenney John; 6, Walden W Elliott; 7, Hackworth Robert S; 8, Amoss Thomas; 9, Bindner Walter M Jr

$2 Pick Three (4–7–3) Paid $364.20 ; Pick Three Pool $34,848 .

SECOND RACE
Hollywood
MAY 31, 2004

1⅛ MILES. (Turf Chute) 38TH RUNNING OF THE GAMELY BREEDERS' CUP HANDICAP. Grade I. Purse $350,000 (includes $100,000 BC – Breeders' Cup) CHUTE START. FOR FILLIES AND MARES THREE YEARS OLD AND UPWARD. By subscription of $500 each on or before Friday, February 27, 2004 which should accompany the nomination. To remain eligible the following payment must be made; $1,500 on or before Friday, April 23, 2004. Late nominations for horses not previously nominated or not remaining eligible, may be made on or before Wednesday, May 26, 2004 by payment of $7,000, which should accompany the nomination, of which $5,000 is refundable if the nominee is entered and does not draw into the body of the race or if the nominee is not entered and a veterinarian certificate is produced indicating the horse is unfit to run. All nominees to pay $2,500 to enter and an additional $3,000 to start. Weights Sunday, May 23. Late nominee weights: Thursday, May 27. Nominations Close Friday, February 27, 2004. Closed with 33 original nominations and 16 sustained.

Value of Race: $324,250 Winner $187,500; second $62,500; third $49,500; fourth $24,750. Mutuel Pool $266,187.00 Exacta Pool $186,016.00 Quinella Pool $13,765.00

Last Raced	Horse	M/Eqt.	A.	Wt	PP	St	¼	½	¾	Str	Fin	Jockey	Odds $1
17Apr04 ^{9}SA^{2}	Noches DeRosa-Chi	LB b	6	115	1	2	1^{hd}	2^{3}	2^{2}	$2^{\frac{1}{2}}$	1^{1}	Smith M E	3.30
17Apr04 ^{9}SA^{1}	Megahertz-GB	LB	5	122	3	1	4	4	4	4	2^{hd}	Espinoza V	0.60
25Apr04 ^{7}Hol^{2}	Quero Quero	LB	4	115	4	3	2^{2}	1^{hd}	1^{1}	1^{hd}	3^{2}	Santiago Javier	7.50
25Apr04 ^{7}Hol^{4}	Dimitrova	LB f	4	122	2	4	3^{8}	3^{10}	3^{12}	$3^{4\frac{1}{2}}$	4	Desormeaux K J	3.10

OFF AT 1:53 Start Good. Won driving. Course firm.

TIME :25^{2}, :49^{2}, 1:12, 1:36, 1:48^{1} (:25.40, :49.57, 1:12.08, 1:36.14, 1:48.34)

$2 Mutuel Prices:

	Win	Place	Show
1 – NOCHES DE ROSA–CHI	8.60	2.80	—
3 – MEGAHERTZ–GB		2.20	—
4 – QUERO QUERO		—	—

$1 EXACTA 1–3 PAID $7.20 $2 QUINELLA 1–3 PAID $4.20

Dk. b or br. m, (Aug), by Stagecraft–GB – Night Girl, by Noble Fighter. Trainer Mandella Richard. Bred by Haras Don Alberto (Chi).

NOCHES DE ROSA (CHI) took the early lead and set the pace toward the inside, dueled inside QUERO QUERO on the backstretch, had that one slip away into the second turn, came out on that turn and re-bid between horses into the stretch, regained the advantage a sixteenth out and gamely prevailed under urging. MEGAHERTZ (GB) lagged well back while saving ground, began to advance inside on the second turn, cut the corner into the stretch and closed with a rush along the rail. QUERO QUERO stalked the early pace off the rail, bid outside the winner on the backstretch and took a short lead, dueled for command, inched away and angled in entering the second turn, came a bit off the fence in upper stretch, fought back through the lane and was outfinished between foes late. DIMITROVA stalked the pace along the inside, went outside the winner on the second turn, bid three deep into the stretch, drifted out some in midstretch and weakened.

Owners– 1, Diamond A Racing Corporation; 2, Bello Michael; 3, Old Friends Inc; 4, Higgins Joseph

Trainers– 1, Mandella Richard; 2, Frankel Robert; 3, Lobo Paulo H; 4, Drysdale Neil

$2 Daily Double (3–1) Paid $55.60 ; Daily Double Pool $103,422 .

SEVENTH RACE
Hollywood
MAY 31, 2004

1 MILE. (Turf) (1.32^{3}) 61ST RUNNING OF THE SHOEMAKER BREEDERS' CUP MILE. Grade I. Purse $350,000 (includes $100,000 BC – Breeders' Cup) FOR THREE-YEAR-OLDS AND UPWARD. By subscription of $500 each on or before Friday, February 27, 2004 which should accompany the nomination. To remain eligible the following payment must be made; $1,500 on or before Friday, April 23, 2004. Late nominations, for horses not previously nominated or not remaining eligible, may be made on or before Wednesday, May 26, 2004 by payment of $7,000, which should accompany the nomination, of which $5,000 is refundable if the nominee is entered and does not draw intothe body of the race or if the nominee is not entered and a veterinarian certificate is produced indicating the horse is unfit to run. All nominees to pay $2,500 to enter and an additional $3,000 to start. Three-year-olds 113 lbs. Older 124 lbs. Nominations Close Friday, February 27, 2004. Closed with 40 original nominations, 17 sustained, and 4 supplemental: Glick, Leroidesanimaux, Momentum and Dell Place.

Value of Race: $456,000 Winner $282,000; second $94,000; third $44,400; fourth $28,200; fifth $7,400. Mutuel Pool $584,584.00 Exacta Pool $333,671.00 Quinella Pool $29,469.00 Trifecta Pool $357,326.00 Superfecta Pool $134,269.00

Last Raced	Horse	M/Eqt.	A.	Wt	PP	St	¼	½	¾	Str	Fin	Jockey	Odds $1
1May04 ^{6}Hol^{2}	Designed for Luck	LB b	7	124	8	3	2^{1}	2^{1}	2^{1}	1^{1}	$1^{1\frac{1}{2}}$	Valenzuela P A	5.90
24Apr04 ^{3}BM^{1}	Singletary	LB	4	124	1	1	4^{1}	3^{hd}	3^{hd}	$4^{1\frac{1}{2}}$	2^{hd}	Valdivia J Jr	4.00
27Mar04 ^{7}NAS^{6}	Tsigane-FR	LB b	5	124	2	6	$6^{1\frac{1}{2}}$	$6^{1\frac{1}{2}}$	$5^{\frac{1}{2}}$	5^{hd}	3^{1}	Flores D R	10.20
13May04 ^{7}Hol^{1}	King of Happiness	LB	5	124	5	8	7^{2}	$7^{2\frac{1}{2}}$	8	7^{4}	4^{hd}	Desormeaux K J	4.30
1May04 ^{9}CD^{2}	Sweet Return-GB	LB	4	124	4	4	3^{hd}	$4^{1\frac{1}{2}}$	$4^{1\frac{1}{2}}$	3^{hd}	$5^{1\frac{1}{2}}$	Espinoza V	1.90
21Apr04 ^{5}Hol^{1}	Dell Place	LB b	5	124	7	7	8	8	$7^{\frac{1}{2}}$	6^{1}	6^{hd}	Santiago Javier	20.30
18Apr04 ^{7}SA^{1}	Glick	LB b	8	124	3	2	1^{1}	1^{2}	1^{1}	2^{hd}	7^{9}	John K	9.70
6Oct02 ^{7}SA^{2}	Momentum	LB	6	124	6	5	$5^{\frac{1}{2}}$	5^{hd}	$6^{1\frac{1}{2}}$	8	8	Nakatani C S	11.00

OFF AT 4:38 Start Good. Won driving. Course firm.

TIME :23^{2}, :46, 1:09, 1:20^{4}, 1:32^{4} (:23.44, :46.13, 1:09.17, 1:20.93, 1:32.81)

$2 Mutuel Prices:

	Win	Place	Show
9 – DESIGNED FOR LUCK	13.80	6.20	4.60
1 – SINGLETARY		5.40	4.00
2 – TSIGANE–FR			8.00

$1 EXACTA 9–1 PAID $27.00 $2 QUINELLA 1–9 PAID $27.00
$1 TRIFECTA 9–1–2 PAID $273.30 $1 SUPERFECTA 9–1–2–5 PAID $1,210.20

Ch. g, (Apr), by Rahy – Fantastic Look, by Green Dancer. Trainer Cerin Vladimir. Bred by Mr & Mrs John C Mabee (Ky).

DESIGNED FOR LUCK stalked the pace off the rail, bid outside GLICK into the stretch, gained the lead in upper stretch, inched away in midstretch and won clear under left handed urging. SINGLETARY stalked the pace inside, came out for room into the stretch, was between horses in midstretch, could not catch the winner and just held second. TSIGANE (FR) chased a bit off the rail, came out leaving the second turn and three deep into the stretch and finished well. KING OF HAPPINESS off a bit slowly and slightly in the air, settled off the rail, went outside a rival on the second turn, also came out three deep into the stretch and could not quite offer the necessary late response. SWEET RETURN (GB) stalked the pace outside a rival, came three wide into the stretch with a bid but was outfinished. DELL PLACE unhurried off the inside early, angled to the rail leaving the second turn, came out in the stretch and lacked the needed rally. GLICK washy at the gate, sped to the early lead, set the pace inside, fought back into the stretch, then weakened. MOMENTUM three wide on the first turn, chased outside, came four wide into the stretch and had little left.

Owners– 1, Wilson David W and Holly F; 2, Little Red Feather Racing; 3, Prestonwood Farm LLC; 4, Al Maktoum Sheik Maktoum b; 5, Red Oak Stable; 6, Manoogian Jay; 7, Bone Robert D; 8, Reddam J Paul

Trainers– 1, Cerin Vladimir; 2, Chatlos Donald Jr; 3, Canani Julio C; 4, Drysdale Neil; 5, McAnally Ronald; 6, Mitchell Mike; 7, Mullins Jeff; 8, Dollase Craig

Scratched– Leroidesanimaux (BRZ) (01May04 ^{6}Hol^{1})

$2 Daily Double (4–9) Paid $33.20 ; Daily Double Pool $39,128 .
$1 Pick Three (7–1/4/6/10–9) Paid $104.00 ; Pick Three Pool $137,739 .

EIGHTH RACE
Lone Star
MAY 31, 2004

1 MILE. (Turf) (1.33^{2}) 6TH RUNNING OF THE WINSTAR DISTAFF HANDICAP. Grade III. Purse $200,000 (PLUS UP TO $11,250 Open ATB) FOR FILLIES AND MARES, THREE YEARS OLD AND UPWARD. No nomination fee. $1,500 to pass the entry box and an additional $1,500 to start with $200,000 guaranteed of which $120,000 to the owner of the winner, $40,000 to second,$22,000 to third, $12,000 to fourth and $6,000 to fifth. Weights: Sunday, May 23, 2004. Starters to be named through the entry box by the usual time of closing. High weights preferred. The field will be limited to twelve starters. Horses not drawinga starting position in thegate will receive a refund of the entry fee. A suitable award will be presented to the winning owner. Nominations closed Wednesday, May 19, 2004 with 50 nominations. (If Deemed inadvisable by management to run this race over the Turf course, it will be run on the main track at One Mile.).

Value of Race: $200,000 Winner $120,000; second $40,000; third $22,000; fourth $12,000; fifth $6,000. Mutuel Pool $257,967.00 Exacta Pool $156,013.00 Quinella Pool $10,958.00 Trifecta Pool $153,176.00 Superfecta Pool $56,165.00

Last Raced	Horse	M/Eqt.	A.	Wt	PP	St	¼	½	¾	Str	Fin	Jockey	Odds $1
4Apr04 ^{11}Sun^{1}	Academic Angel	L	5	117	7	7	10^{2}	$10^{\frac{1}{2}}$	$8^{1\frac{1}{2}}$	3^{1}	$1^{\frac{3}{4}}$	Sellers S J	11.10
17Apr04 ^{9}LS^{1}	Janeian-NZ	L	6	119	11	5	$4^{1\frac{1}{2}}$	4^{1}	3^{2}	$1^{1\frac{1}{2}}$	2^{nk}	Martin E M Jr	3.10
25Apr04 ^{7}Hol^{5}	Katdogawn-GB	L	4	120	2	12	$9^{\frac{1}{2}}$	$8^{\frac{1}{2}}$	$7^{\frac{1}{2}}$	$5^{\frac{1}{2}}$	$3^{\frac{1}{2}}$	Perrodin E J	1.90
15May04 ^{10}LaD^{4}	Cherylville Slew	L	5	116	1	10	12	11^{hd}	9^{hd}	6^{hd}	$4^{1\frac{3}{4}}$	Berry M C	60.50
17Apr04 ^{9}LS^{2}	Cat's Cat	L b	4	115	9	6	2^{2}	2^{2}	$2^{\frac{1}{2}}$	$2^{\frac{1}{2}}$	$5^{1\frac{1}{2}}$	Gondron T D	68.30
24Apr04 ^{1}Hol^{2}	Super High	L f	5	116	12	1	3^{2}	$3^{\frac{1}{2}}$	5^{1}	7^{1}	6^{hd}	Nuesch D	10.00
15May04 ^{10}LaD^{1}	Due to Win Again	L b	6	118	6	4	$6^{1\frac{1}{2}}$	$5^{\frac{1}{2}}$	4^{hd}	4^{hd}	7^{nk}	LeBlanc K P	18.00
17Apr04 ^{9}LS^{3}	Bedanken	L f	5	119	8	8	$8^{\frac{1}{2}}$	7^{hd}	$6^{\frac{1}{2}}$	8^{hd}	8no	Pettinger D R	2.70
15Apr04 ^{9}LS^{1}	Breach of Promise	L	5	117	5	11	$11^{\frac{1}{2}}$	12	11^{2}	$9^{\frac{1}{2}}$	9^{1}	Beasley J A	47.10
15May04 ^{10}LaD^{2}	Titia	L	6	115	4	2	$7^{\frac{1}{2}}$	$9^{1\frac{1}{2}}$	10^{hd}	10^{hd}	$10^{1\frac{1}{4}}$	Chapa R	45.70
21Apr04 ^{8}Kee^{8}	Mexican Moonlight	L	4	114	10	9	5^{hd}	6^{1}	12	12	$11^{2\frac{3}{4}}$	Martinez W	55.00
25Apr04 ^{7}Hol^{7}	Fudge Fatale	L	4	116	3	3	$1^{\frac{1}{2}}$	1^{2}	1^{hd}	$11^{1\frac{1}{2}}$	12	Baze T C	14.90

OFF AT 5:14 Start Good . Won driving. Course firm.

TIME :22^{4}, :46^{2}, 1:10^{2}, 1:23, 1:35^{4} (:22.98, :46.50, 1:10.43, 1:23.10, 1:35.98)

$2 Mutuel Prices:				
	7 – ACADEMIC ANGEL	**24.20**	**10.60**	**4.40**
	11 – JANEIAN-NZ		**4.80**	**3.20**
	2 – KATDOGAWN-GB			**2.80**

$2 EXACTA 7–11 PAID $92.40 $2 QUINELLA 7–11 PAID $37.60
$2 TRIFECTA 7–11–2 PAID $340.80 $2 SUPERFECTA 7–11–2–1 PAID $9,360.80

B. m, (Feb), by Royal Academy – Magic Lass , by Damascus . Trainer Asmussen Steven M. Bred by Cashmark Farms Inc (Ky).

ACADEMIC ANGEL settled near the back of the field, advanced while three wide on the second turn, rallied in upper stretch, and closed strongly under right hand urging. JANEIAN (NZ) crossed over passing the wire the first time, was well placed just off the pace, raced four wide and brushed with SUPER HIGH leaving the backstretch, ranged up while three wide on the far turn, took the lead in upper stretch, inched away inside the furlong marker, but failed to fend off the winner. KATDOGAWN (GB) was urged along a bit while saving ground, continued to save ground through the far turn, split rivals passing the furlong marker,and finished willingly while lacking the needed kick. CHERYLVILLE SLEW lagged near the back of the field, saved ground into the stretch, shifted out near the furlong marker, and also finished willingly. CAT'S CAT crossed over shortly after the start, tracked the solo leader through the backstretch, engaged that rival on the far turn, led briefly entering the stretch, but was quickly headed and weakened. SUPER HIGH crossed over passing the wire the first time, angled to the rail entering the first turn, was forwardly placed down the backstretch, brushed with JANEIAN(NZ) entering the far turn, was roused near the quarter-pole, but failed to respond and gave way. DUE TO WIN AGAIN was bumped at the start, raced off the pace, moved closer while saving ground on the turn, but lacked the needed response. BEDANKEN raced three wide on the first turn, settled near the middle of the field, was roused while three wide on the far turn, came four wide into the stretch, and failed to rally. BREACH OF PROMISE broke outward and bumped a rival, was unhurried near the back of the field, raced three wide on the second turn, swung five wide into the stretch, and failed to threaten. TITIA settled near the middle of the field, raced between rivals on the backstretch, dropped back a bit entering the far turn, and failed to menace. MEXICAN MOONLIGHT went three wide on the first turn, raced in the front half of the field, went four wide on the second turn, and faded. FUDGE FATALE set the clear pace, lost the lead leaving the second turn, and stopped.

Owners– 1, Asmussen Cash; 2, England Greg L; 3, John R Cuchna Jim Ford Inc & Deron Pearson; 4, Trout C R; 5, Frankel Jerry; 6, Harris Farms Inc; 7, Scarberry Howard and Penny; 8, Pin Oak Stable LLC; 9, Arnold Douglas S; 10, Seelig Stanley B; 11, Pass Taggart Racing; 12, Greely John J III

Trainers– 1, Asmussen Steven M; 2, Calhoun William Bret; 3, Cassidy James; 4, Trout C R; 5, Stidham Michael; 6, Gaines Carla; 7, Scarberry Howard; 8, Von Hemel Donnie K; 9, Stidham Michael; 10, Mouton Patrick; 11, Murphy Paul H; 12, Greely C Beau

$2 Pick Three (2–4–7) Paid $106.20 ; Pick Three Pool $14,606 .

NINTH RACE
Lone Star
MAY 31, 2004

$1\frac{1}{16}$ MILES. (1.40^{2}) 8TH RUNNING OF THE LONE STAR PARK HANDICAP. Grade III. Purse $300,000 (PLUS UP TO $11,250 Open ATB) FOR THREE YEAR OLDS AND UPWARD. No nomination fee. $2,250 to pass the entry box and an additional $2,250 to start with $300,000 guaranteed of which $180,000 to the owner of the winner, $60,000 to second $33,000 to third, $18,000 to fourth and $9,000 to fifth. Weights; Sunday, May 23, 2004. Starters to be named through the entry box by the usual time of closing. High weights preferred. The field will be limited to fourteen starters. Horses not drawing a starting poristion in the gate will receive a refund of the entry fee. A suitable award will be presented to the winning owner. Nominations closed Wednesday, May 19, 2004 with 36 nominations.

Value of Race: $300,000 Winner $180,000; second $60,000; third $33,000; fourth $18,000; fifth $9,000. Mutuel Pool $220,875.00 Exacta Pool $119,021.00 Quinella Pool $7,990.00 Trifecta Pool $120,441.00

Last Raced	Horse	M/Eqt.	A.	Wt	PP	St	¼	½	¾	Str	Fin	Jockey	Odds $1
24Apr04 $^{8}LS^{3}$	Yessirgeneralsir	L	4	114	6	1	$1^{1\frac{1}{2}}$	$1^{1\frac{1}{2}}$	1^{5}	1^{6}	$1^{2\frac{1}{4}}$	Figueroa O	11.60
24Apr04 $^{9}Fon^{1}$	Sonic West	L bf	5	117	2	3	5^{hd}	$5^{3\frac{1}{2}}$	4^{hd}	3^{hd}	2^{1}	Martinez W	5.40
30Apr04 $^{6}CD^{7}$	Spanish Empire	L	4	117	1	2	4^{1}	4^{1}	5^{10}	4^{4}	3^{nk}	Sellers S J	4.60
24Apr04 $^{8}LS^{1}$	Kela	L b	6	121	3	4	$2^{\frac{1}{2}}$	$2^{\frac{1}{2}}$	$2^{1\frac{1}{2}}$	$2^{\frac{1}{2}}$	4^{nk}	Nuesch D	1.20
9May04 $^{7}LS^{2}$	Maysville Slew	L f	8	116	4	6	6	6	6	5^{3}	$5^{14\frac{1}{4}}$	Berry M C	32.90
5May04 $^{5}Hol^{2}$	Saint Buddy	L b	4	115	5	5	3^{2}	3^{5}	3^{1}	6	6	Baze T C	2.00

OFF AT 5:42 Start Good . Won driving. Track fast.

TIME :22^{4}, :45^{3}, 1:08^{2}, 1:34, 1:41^{1} (:22.85, :45.67, 1:08.54, 1:34.07, 1:41.29)

$2 Mutuel Prices:				
	6 – YESSIRGENERALSIR	25.20	9.40	4.20
	2 – SONIC WEST		6.00	3.40
	1 – SPANISH EMPIRE			3.20

$2 EXACTA 6–2 PAID $109.20 $2 QUINELLA 2–6 PAID $52.80
$2 TRIFECTA 6–2–1 PAID $497.60

B. g, (Jan), by Patton – Honeydoon , by My Favorite Moment . Trainer Keen Dallas E. Bred by Jim D Jackson (Tex).

YESSIRGENERALSIR set the clear pace while off the rail, drew off on the second turn, and maintained a safe advantage while kept to task. SONIC WEST was unhurried while off the rail, roused on the second turn, moved to the rail near the quarter-pole, brushed with KELA near the furlong marker, and finished willingly for second. SPANISH EMPIRE was hustled from the start, angled out to be three wide midway through the first turn, settled well off the pace, raced three wide on the second turn, and lacked the needed rally. KELA raced three wide on the first turn, came four wide onto the backstretch, tracked the pace set by the winner, dropped back while under a ride on the far turn, brushed with SONIC WEST near the furlong marker, and gave way. MAYSVILLE SLEW lagged well behind the field, saved ground into the stretch, angled out near the furlong marker, angled further out passing the sixteenth pole, and failed to reach serious contention. SAINT BUDDY raced four wide on the first turn, came five wide onto the backstretch, was forwardly placed on the outside, faltered on the far turn, and retreated then was not urged late.

Owners– 1, Jackson James D; 2, Stone Spire LLC; 3, Jubilee Stable Martin L Cherry & Twin Creeks Farm; 4, Manoogian Jay; 5, Trout C R; 6, Fulton Stan E

Trainers– 1, Keen Dallas E; 2, Van Berg Thomas L; 3, Asmussen Steven M; 4, Mitchell Mike; 5, Trout C R; 6, Becerra Rafael

$2 Pick Three (4–7–6) Paid $534.40 ; Pick Three Pool $13,895 .
$2 Daily Double (7–6) Paid $850.40 ; Daily Double Pool $16,150 .

TENTH RACE
Monmouth
MAY 31, 2004

$1\frac{1}{16}$ MILES. (Turf) (1.40^{1}) 60TH RUNNING OF THE JERSEY DERBY. Grade III. Purse $100,000 FOR THREE YEAR OLDS. By subscription of $100 each, which should accompany the nomination and $1,500 to pass the entry box. The winning owner to receive $60,000, $20,000 to second, $11,000 to third, $6,000 to fourth and $3,000 to fifth. Weight: 122 lbs. Non–winners of $60,000 at a mile or over on the turf allowed, 3 lbs.; $45,000 at a mile or over or $60,000, 5 lbs.; A sweepstakes anytime, 7 lbs.; $20,000 at a mile or over, 10 lbs. (Maiden, Claiming and Starter races not considered.) The owner of the winner to receive a trophy. Closed Monday, May 17, 2004 with 36 nominations.

Value of Race: $100,000 Winner $60,000; second $20,000; third $11,000; fourth $6,000; fifth $3,000. Mutuel Pool $171,500.00 Exacta Pool $120,757.00 Trifecta Pool $73,285.00 Superfecta Pool $18,411.00

Last Raced	Horse	M/Eqt.	A.	Wt	PP	St	¼	½	¾	Str	Fin	Jockey	Odds $1
24Apr04 $^{9}Aqu^{1}$	Icy Atlantic	L	3	115	7	3	$4^{1\frac{1}{2}}$	$4^{\frac{1}{2}}$	4^{hd}	1^{hd}	$1^{1\frac{1}{4}}$	Lopez C C	2.70
2Apr04 $^{9}Kee^{5}$	Commendation	L	3	122	5	4	6^{12}	6^{14}	6^{14}	$5^{\frac{1}{2}}$	$2^{\frac{3}{4}}$	Coa E M	2.80
30Apr04 $^{9}CD^{7}$	Grand Heritage	L	3	117	2	5	5^{1}	5^{1}	$5^{1\frac{1}{2}}$	4^{1}	$3^{\frac{3}{4}}$	Pimentel J	3.80
15May04 $^{7}Pim^{2}$	Lipan	L	3	115	4	1	$2^{\frac{1}{2}}$	2^{hd}	2^{hd}	3^{2}	4no	Elliott S	6.70
6May04 $^{7}Bel^{1}$	Nooligan	L b	3	115	6	2	1^{3}	$1^{4\frac{1}{2}}$	1^{1}	$2^{\frac{1}{2}}$	$5^{4\frac{3}{4}}$	Decarlo C P	17.10
13May04 $^{7}Bel^{4}$	Shining Hawk	L b	3	117	1	6	3^{hd}	$3^{1\frac{1}{2}}$	3^{1}	6^{10}	$6^{8\frac{1}{2}}$	Ferrer J C	7.70
3Apr04 $^{4}Kee^{4}$	Master William	L b	3	122	3	7	7	7	7	7	7	Velez J A Jr	4.70

OFF AT 5:11 Start Good For All But MASTER WILLIAM. Won driving. Course good.

TIME :24^{4}, :48^{4}, 1:13^{3}, 1:38, 1:44^{2} (:24.94, :48.83, 1:13.64, 1:38.12, 1:44.51)

$2 Mutuel Prices:				
	1A – ICY ATLANTIC	7.40	3.40	2.20
	6 – COMMENDATION		3.80	2.60
	3 – GRAND HERITAGE			2.80

$2 EXACTA 1–6 PAID $30.80 $2 TRIFECTA 1–6–3 PAID $90.20
$1 SUPERFECTA 1–6–3–5 PAID $276.10

B. c, (Mar), by Stormy Atlantic – Frosty Promise , by Frosty the Snowman . Trainer Pletcher Todd A. Bred by Arthur I Appleton (Fla).

ICY ATLANTIC rated in good position about the four path, was strung five wide entering the stretch, dug in dueling clear leaving the furlong pole then held well with steady handling. COMMENDATION, unhurriedly toward mid track, was eased out to make his bid entering the stretch then advanced steadily taking place in the final seventy yards and finishing well. GRAND HERITAGE rated back inside, lacked room through the upper stretch, eased out approaching the furlong pole and finished well to show. LIPAN rated off the pace and off the rail, started his drive in the three path of the final turn, dueled between horses through the upper stretch then yielded the final sixteenth. NOOLIGAN advanced to a clear lead toward the rail into the opening turn, dueled through the upper stretch then relented the final sixteenth. SHINING HAWK was kept off the pace and off the rail, came four wide through the final turn and weakened in the stretch. MASTER WILLIAM dwelt then never factored.

Owners– 1, Appleton Arthur I; 2, Courtlandt Farms; 3, Diane and Bertram R Firestone; 4, Gill Michael J; 5, EquiraceCom LLC; 6, Ieah Stables; 7, Ramsey Kenneth L and Sarah K

Trainers– 1, Pletcher Todd A; 2, Motion H Graham; 3, Mott William I; 4, Vazquez Gamaliel; 5, Maker Michael J; 6, Dutrow Richard E Jr; 7, Dickinson Michael W

Scratched– Forest Grove (03Apr04 $^{11}GP^{7}$) , Carrots Only (27Mar04 $^{9}GP^{1}$)

$2 Pick Four (6–7–1–1/7) Paid $3,864.20 ; Pick Four Pool $18,185 .

NINTH RACE
Belmont
JUNE 4, 2004

5 FURLONGS. (.55^3) 104TH RUNNING OF THE FLASH. Grade III. Purse $100,000 (Up To $19,000 NYSBFOA) FOR TWO YEAR OLDS. By subscription of $100 each, which should accompany the nomination; $500 to pass the entry box; $500 to start, with $100,000 added. The added money and all fees to be divided 60% to the winner, 20% to second, 10% to third, 5% to fourth, 3% to fifth and 2% divided equally among remaining finishers. 119 lbs. Non-winners of $40,000 allowed 2 lbs.; a race other than maiden or claiming, 4 lbs. A trophy will be presented to the winning owner. Closed Saturday, May 22,2004 with 13 nominations.

Value of Race: $104,300 Winner $63,780; second $21,260; third $10,693; fourth $5,378; fifth $3,189. Mutuel Pool $460,345.00 Exacta Pool $373,290.00 Trifecta Pool $178,617.00

Last Raced	Horse	M/Eqt.	A.	Wt	PP	St	3/16	3/8	Str	Fin	Jockey	Odds $1
29Apr04 3CD1	Primal Storm	L	2	116	4	2	1 1½	1½	1 6	1 7	Sellers S J	0.80
6May04 3Bel1	Winning Expression	L	2	115	3	3	2 hd	2½	2 2	2 3¾	Prado E S	5.40
22Apr04 3Aqu1	Gold Joy	L b	2	115	5	5	5	5	5	3 4	Luzzi M J	21.40
22Apr04 2Kee1	Departing Now		2	115	1	4	4 7	3½	3 3½	4 nk	Day P	3.15
21May04 3Bel1	Dubleo	L	2	115	2	1	3½	4 8	4 3½	5	Velazquez J R	4.40

OFF AT 5:10 Start Good. Won handily. Track fast.
TIME :22, :44^4, :57^2 (:22.00, :44.94, :57.49)

$2 Mutuel Prices:

4 – PRIMAL STORM	3.60	2.60	2.10
3 – WINNING EXPRESSION		3.70	2.70
5 – GOLD JOY			2.90

$2 EXACTA 4–3 PAID $11.00 $2 TRIFECTA 4–3–5 PAID $81.00

B. c, (May), by Storm Boot – Primistal, by Stalwart. Trainer Asmussen Steven M. Bred by Everest Stables Inc (Ky).

PRIMAL STORM came in on the backstretch, drew clear on the turn, set the pace, drew away when roused and remained well clear under wraps. WINNING EXPRESSION was bumped on the backstretch, was checked when put in tight quarters nearing the turn, rallied three wide and continued on gamely. GOLD JOY was outrun early, raced inside and was going well too late. DEPARTING NOW was bumped on the backstretch, was in tight quarters on the rail nearing the turn, chased the pace along the inside and tired. DUBLEO was bumped on the backstretch, was steadied when out in tight quarters nearing the turn, chased the pace while between rivals and tired. Following a Stewards' inquiry concerning the run into the turn the result was declared official.

Owners– 1, Asmussen Keith I Winchell Ronald Cassels James Scherr Connie; 2, Flying Zee Stable; 3, Taylor Kenneth Salzman Timothy E; 4, Dogwood Stable; 5, Scatuorchio James T Pletcher Jake and Wetterman Pete

Trainers– 1, Asmussen Steven M; 2, Serpe Philip M; 3, Salzman Timothy; 4, Maker Rebecca; 5, Pletcher Todd A

TENTH RACE
Belmont
JUNE 4, 2004

1 MILE. (1.32^1) 74TH RUNNING OF THE ACORN. Grade I. Purse $250,000 (Up To $37500 NYSBFOA) FOR FILLIES THREE YEARS OLD. By subscription of $250 each, which should accompany the nomination; $1,250 to pass the entry box; $1,250 to start. The purse to be divided 60% to the winner, 20% to second, 10% to third, 5% to fourth, 3% to fifth and 2% divided equally among remaining finishers. 121 lbs. Trophies will be presented to the winning owner, trainer and jockey. Closed Saturday, May 22, 2004 with 21 Nominations.

Value of Race: $250,000 Winner $150,000; second $50,000; third $25,000; fourth $12,500; fifth $7,500; sixth $1,667; seventh $1,667; eighth $1,666. Mutuel Pool $779,300.00 Exacta Pool $573,226.00 Trifecta Pool $454,923.00 Superfecta Pool $160,566.00

Last Raced	Horse	M/Eqt.	A.	Wt	PP	St	1/4	1/2	3/4	Str	Fin	Jockey	Odds $1
30Apr04 10CD2	Island Sand	L b	3	121	4	6	7 hd	7 hd	5½	2½	1 1¾	Thompson T J	4.00
9Apr04 8Aqu1	Society Selection		3	121	2	7	8	8	7 hd	5 hd	2 no	Chavez J F	2.15
29Apr04 9CD1	Friendly Michelle	L b	3	121	8	3	2 hd	2½	2 2	1 hd	3¾	Solis A	7.10
8May04 8Bel1	Bending Strings	L	3	121	3	5	5 2	5½	3½	3½	4 2½	Day P	13.00
9May04 3Bel1	Magical Illusion	L b	3	121	1	8	3½	4½	4 1½	4½	5¾	Santos J A	21.70
30Apr04 10CD4	Victory U. S. A.	L	3	121	6	4	6 2½	6 2	8	7 8	6 5	Bailey J D	3.15
29Apr04 9CD3	Bohemian Lady	L	3	121	5	2	1½	1½	1 hd	6 2½	7 6½	Prado E S	12.90
3Apr04 9Kee4	La Reina	L b	3	121	7	1	4 hd	3½	6½	8	8	Velazquez J R	8.90

OFF AT 5:42 Start Good. Won driving. Track fast.
TIME :23^2, :45^4, 1:09^4, 1:34^4 (:23.52, :45.95, 1:09.95, 1:34.89)

$2 Mutuel Prices:

5 – ISLAND SAND	10.00	3.60	2.90
2 – SOCIETY SELECTION		3.50	2.60
10 – FRIENDLY MICHELLE			4.30

$2 EXACTA 5–2 PAID $31.20 $2 TRIFECTA 5–2–10 PAID $209.00
$2 SUPERFECTA 5–2–10–3 PAID $987.00

Dk. b or br. f, (Feb), by Tabasco Cat – Sue's Last Dance, by Forty Niner. Trainer Jones J Larry. Bred by Richard D Maynard (Ky).

ISLAND SAND was outrun early outside, advanced between rivals nearing the stretch, came wide for the drive, responded when roused and drew clear late under a drive. SOCIETY SELECTION was outrun along the inside early, angled out entering the stretch, finished gamely from the outside and was up on the line to earn the place award. FRIENDLY MICHELLE contested the pace from the outside and dug in gamely along the inside in the stretch. BENDING STRINGS raced close up early while between rivals, came wide into the stretch and stayed on gamely to the wire. MAGICAL ILLUSION chased the pace along the inside and weakened in the final furlong. VICTORY U. S. A. was outrun early, raced three wide and had no response when roused. BOHEMIAN LADY contested the pace along the inside and tired after three quarters. LA REINA chased the pace while three wide and tired in the stretch.

Owners– 1, Osborne James L; 2, Cowan Marjorie and Irving M; 3, Friendly Ed; 4, Gunther John D; 5, Clifton William L Jr; 6, Van Meter II Thomas F; 7, Padua Stables; 8, Hamilton Emory A

Trainers– 1, Jones J Larry; 2, Jerkens H Allen; 3, Baffert Bob; 4, McLaughlin Kiaran P; 5, Bond Harold James; 6, Baffert Bob; 7, Pletcher Todd A; 8, McGaughey III Claude R

Scratched– Pawyne Princess (14May04 10Pim2), Grey Traffic (08May04 8Bel2)

$2 Daily Double (4–5) Paid $20.20; Daily Double Pool $369,183.
$2 Pick Three (1–4–5) Paid $54.50; Pick Three Pool $205,952.
$2 Pick Four (4–1–4–5) Paid $545.00; Pick Four Pool $350,311.
$2 Pick Six (1–3–4–1–4–5) 6 Correct Paid $10,836.00; Pick Six Pool $237,670.
$2 Pick Six (1–3–4–1–4–5) 5 Correct Paid $113.50.

Belmont Park Attendance: 12,268 Mutuel Pool: $1,700,811.00 ITW Mutuel Pool: $3,465,488.00 ISW Mutuel Pool: $8,982,822.00

SIXTH RACE
Belmont
JUNE 5, 2004

6½ FURLONGS. (1.142) 54TH RUNNING OF THE VAGRANCY HANDICAP. Grade II. Purse $150,000 (Up To $28,500 NYSBFOA) A HANDICAP FOR FILLIES AND MARES THREE YEARS OLD AND UPWARD. By subscription of $150 each, which should accompany the nomination; $750 to pass the entry box; $750 to start. The purse to be divided 60% to the winner, 20% to second,10% to third, 5% to fourth, 3% to fifth and 2% divided equally among remaining finishers. A trophy will be presented to the winning owner. Closed Saturday, May 22, 2004 with 22 Nominations.

Value of Race: $150,000 Winner $90,000; second $30,000; third $15,000; fourth $7,500; fifth $4,500; sixth $750; seventh $750; eighth $750; ninth $750. Mutuel Pool $1,521,699.00 Exacta Pool $1,303,091.00 Trifecta Pool $1,065,114.00

Last Raced	Horse	M/Eqt.	A.	Wt	PP	St	¼	½	Str	Fin	Jockey	Odds $1
9May04 8Bel1	Bear Fan	L f	5	121	4	5	12½	11½	110	19	Velazquez J R	0.75
17Apr04 8Aqu2	Smok'n Frolic	L b	5	117	3	8	87	76	3hd	21¼	Prado E S	6.30
2May04 8Hol4	Aspen Gal	L	3	109	7	6	4½	2hd	22½	32	Chavez J F	10.40
16Apr04 9Kee7	Zawzooth	L	5	116	2	9	9	9	6hd	4nk	Solis A	21.00
9May04 8Bel3	Kitty Knight	L	4	114	1	3	3½	4hd	4½	5no	Velasquez C	15.60
17Apr04 8Aqu6	Chirimoya	L f	5	112	9	1	6½	62	53	65¾	Luzzi M J	38.75
19May04 9CD2	Molto Vita	L	4	115	6	7	73½	83	9	7½	Santos J A	25.75
23Apr04 6Kee1	Kuanyan	L	4	111	5	4	2½	3½	81½	8hd	Day P	17.20
28Nov03 9Aqu2	Beauty Halo-Arg	L	5	114	8	2	5½	51	7hd	9	Bailey J D	5.40

OFF AT 3:12 Start Good . Won ridden out. Track fast.
TIME :214, :443, 1:08, 1:142 (:21.93, :44.68, 1:08.15, 1:14.46)

(New Track Record)

$2 Mutuel Prices:

4 – BEAR FAN	3.50	2.70	2.50
3 – SMOK'N FROLIC		4.30	3.40
7 – ASPEN GAL			4.50

$2 EXACTA 4–3 PAID $13.80 $2 TRIFECTA 4–3–7 PAID $73.50

B. m, (Mar), by Pine Bluff – Shezalong , by Shimatoree . Trainer Ward Wesley A. Bred by Wesley Ward (Cal).

BEAR FAN took charge soon after the start, set the pace along the inside, drew away when asked for run and was ridden out to the wire in track record time. SMOK'N FROLIC was outrun early, came wide nearing the stretch and rallied outside to earn the place prize. ASPEN GAL chased the pace while three wide and tired in the final furlong. ZAWZOOTH was outrun early, came wide into the stretch and had no rally. KITTY KNIGHT chased the pace along the inside and tired in the stretch. CHIRIMOYA raced close up along the inside and tired. MOLTO VITA raced inside and had no response when roused. KUANYAN chased the pace while between rivals and tired after a half mile. BEAUTY HALO (ARG) raced four wide and tired.

Owners– 1, Fan Peter and Ward Wesley; 2, Dogwood Stable; 3, Gann Edmund A; 4, Starlight Stable LLC; 5, Bohemia Stable; 6, Rising Graph Stable; 7, Gunther John D; 8, Live Oak Plantation; 9, WinStar Farm LLC

Trainers– 1, Ward Wesley A; 2, Pletcher Todd A; 3, Frankel Robert; 4, Pletcher Todd A; 5, Jerkens H Allen; 6, Hushion Michael E; 7, Stewart Dallas; 8, Kimmel John C; 9, Walden W Elliott

$2 Pick Three (6–2–4) Paid $1,661.00 ; Pick Three Pool $228,119 .

SEVENTH RACE
Belmont
JUNE 5, 2004

6 FURLONGS. (1.073) 26TH RUNNING OF THE TRUE NORTH BREEDERS' CUP HANDICAP. Grade II. Purse $200,000 (includes $100,000 BC – Breeders' Cup) (Up To $19,000 NYSBFOA) A HANDICAP FOR THREE YEAR OLDS AND UPWARD. By subscription of $100 each, which should accompany the nomination; $500 to pass the entry box; $500 to start. The NYRA purse to be divided 60% to the winner, 20% to second, 10% to third,5% to fourth, 3% to fifth and 2% divided equally among remaining finishers. Breeders' Cup fund monies correspondingly divided. Any Breeders' Cup fund monies not awarded will revert back to the fund. Trophy to the winning owner will be given by Breeders'Cup Ltd. Closed Saturday, May 22, 2004 with 19 Nominations.

Value of Race: $210,830 Winner $126,840; second $42,280; third $21,140; fourth $10,000; fifth $6,342; sixth $1,057; seventh $1,057; eighth $1,057; ninth $1,057. Mutuel Pool $1,802,640.00 Exacta Pool $1,560,038.00 Trifecta Pool $1,241,526.00

Last Raced	Horse	M/Eqt.	A.	Wt	PP	St	¼	½	Str	Fin	Jockey	Odds $1
1May04 5CD1	Speightstown	L	6	119	3	1	2hd	1½	11½	11½	Velazquez J R	1.80
15May04 9Mnr1	Cat Genius	L	4	116	4	3	12½	22½	22½	21¾	Migliore R	7.80
8May04 6Hol1	Pohave	L	6	117	8	4	4½	32	32½	3nk	Court J K	2.65
3May04 7Del2	Sing Me Back Home	L b	6	114	6	8	72½	6½	4hd	42	Dominguez R A	20.70
8May04 7Bel1	Canadian Frontier	L f	5	115	5	7	62½	4hd	53	53	Castellano J J	5.70
8May04 7Bel3	First Blush	b	4	113	1	2	81½	83	6hd	63½	Luzzi M J	17.10
21Apr04 7Kee6	Maybry's Boy	L	5	111	9	9	9	9	812	71¼	Day P	48.25
21May04 8Bel1	Buzzy's Gold	L b	4	114	2	5	51½	51½	72½	830	Velasquez C	34.25
8May04 7Bel2	Key Deputy	L	4	114	7	6	3hd	7hd	9	9	Bailey J D	6.70

OFF AT 3:53 Start Good . Won driving. Track fast.
TIME :212, :433, :551, 1:08 (:21.58, :43.72, :55.35, 1:08.04)

$2 Mutuel Prices:

3 – SPEIGHTSTOWN	5.60	3.70	2.60
4 – CAT GENIUS		6.60	3.60
9 – POHAVE			2.90

$2 EXACTA 3–4 PAID $34.00 $2 TRIFECTA 3–4–9 PAID $75.50

Ch. h, (Feb), by Gone West – Silken Cat , by Storm Cat . Trainer Pletcher Todd A. Bred by Aaron U Jones & Marie Jones (Ky).

SPEIGHTSTOWN broke running, raced with the pace along the inside, came to the outside approaching the stretch, took over from CAT GENIUS in upper stretch, drew clear when roused and remained clear while being kept to the task to the wire. CAT GENIUS flashed good speed from the outside, drew clear into the turn, set the pace and dug in gamely along the inside in the stretch. POHAVE raced close up while three wide and finished well outside. SING ME BACK HOME was hustled along early, raced inside and finished well inside. CANADIAN FRONTIER was hustled outside, raced three wide and lacked a rally. FIRST BLUSH raced inside and had no response when roused. MAYBRY'S BOY had no rally. BUZZY'S GOLD chased the pace along the inside and tired in the stretch. KEY DEPUTY chased the pace while four wide, tired badly and was eased in the stretch.

Owners– 1, Melnyk Eugene and Laura; 2, Parker John R; 3, Leib Mark A Leatherman Ty Kagele Jerry Kagele Tom; 4, Wachtel Stable and Double S Stable; 5, Robsham Mrs E P; 6, Cowan Marjorie and Irving M; 7, RC Hill Stable; 8, Schwartz Martin S; 9, Live Oak Plantation

Trainers– 1, Pletcher Todd A; 2, Amoss Thomas; 3, O'Neill Doug; 4, Iwinski Allen; 5, Hough Stanley M; 6, Jerkens H Allen; 7, Weaver George; 8, Jerkens H Allen; 9, Mott William I

Scratched– Gracious Humor (15May04 11Pim4)

$2 Pick Three (2–4–3) Paid $165.00 ; Pick Three Pool $309,654 .
$2 Daily Double (4–3) Paid $8.30 ; Daily Double Pool $229,360 .

EIGHTH RACE
Belmont
JUNE 5, 2004

1 MILE. (Turf) (1.313) 11TH RUNNING OF THE JUST A GAME BREEDERS' CUP HANDICAP. Grade II. Purse $250,000 (includes $100,000 BC – Breeders' Cup) WIDENER TURF (Up To $28,500 NYSBFOA) A HANDICAP FOR FILLIES AND MARES THREE YEARS OLD AND UPWARD. By subscription of $150 each, which should accompany the nomination; $750 to pass the entry box; $750 to start. The NYRA Purse to be divided 60% to the winner, 20% to second, 10% to third, 5% to fourth, 3% to fifth and 2% divided equally among remaining finishers. Breeders' Cup fund monies also correspondingly divided. Any Breeders' Cup monies not awarded will revert back to the fund. Breeders' Cup Limited shall present a trophy to the winning owner. The New York Racing Association reserves the right to transfer this race to the Main Track. In the event that this race is taken off the turf, it may be subject to downgrading upon review by the Graded Stakes Committee. Closed Saturday, May 22, 2004 with 30 Nominations. (If the Stewards consider it inadvisable to run this race on the turf course, this race will be run at One Mile on the main track.).

Value of Race: $226,333 Winner $150,000; second $30,000; third $25,000; fourth $12,500; fifth $4,500; sixth $1,667; seventh $1,000; eighth $1,666. Mutuel Pool $1,834,235.00 Exacta Pool $1,395,818.00 Trifecta Pool $1,096,266.00

Last Raced	Horse	M/Eqt.	A.	Wt	PP	St	¼	½	¾	Str	Fin	Jockey	Odds $1
18Apr04 8Kee1	Intercontinentl-GB	L	4	118	1	8	7½	7½	5½	2hd	11¼	Bailey J D	a- 0.70
18Apr04 8Kee4	Vanguardia-Arg	L	6	113	6	1	2hd	1hd	1½	11½	2½	Velazquez J R	24.50
1May04 7CD2	Etoile Montante	L	4	121	3	5	4½	3hd	4½	41½	3¾	Solis A	a- 0.70
22Nov03 9CD1	Riskaverse	L	5	118	7	2	1½	21	21½	3½	41	Day P	4.90
30May04 8Bel2	Dedication-FR	L	5	117	4	3	8	8	6hd	5½	5nk	Castellano J J	6.00
5Oct03 6Kee4	Wonder Again	L	5	116	5	6	5hd	6½	71½	76	62	Prado E S	10.30
18Apr04 8Kee5	Coney Kitty-Ire	L f	6	115	2	7	6½	5½	3hd	6½	73½	Santos J A	28.75
9May04 9CD1	Fast Cookie	L b	4	114	8	4	3½	4hd	8	8	8	Velasquez C	7.50

a–Coupled: Intercontinental–GB and Etoile Montante.

OFF AT 4:32 Start Good. Won driving. Course firm.

TIME :233, :464, 1:101, 1:331 (:23.66, :46.90, 1:10.32, 1:33.33)

$2 Mutuel Prices:

1 – INTERCONTINENTL–GB(a–entry).....	3.40	2.60	2.60
6 – VANGUARDIA–ARG..................		10.60	6.20
1A– ETOILE MONTANTE(a–entry).........	3.40	2.60	2.60

$2 EXACTA 1–6 PAID $55.50 $2 TRIFECTA 1–6–7 PAID $197.00

B. f, (Mar), by Danehill – Hasili–Ire , by Kahyasi . Trainer Frankel Robert. Bred by Juddmonte Farms (GB).

INTERCONTINENTAL (GB) raced inside early while under wraps, was steadied along the hedge into the turn, split rivals in upper stretch, ran to the front when shaken up and drew clear in the final sixteenth. VANGUARDIA (ARG) contested the pace along the inside, drew clear when roused and stayed on gamely inside. ETOILE MONTANTE raced close up inside early, raced when roused and finished gamely. RISKAVERSE contested the pace from the outside and weakened in the final furlong. DEDICATION (FR) was outrun early early, came five wide approaching the stretch and offered a mild rally outside. WONDER AGAIN was unhurried early, raced wide and lacked a rally. CONEY KITTY (IRE) was rated along early, raced between rivals and had no response when roused. FAST COOKIE chased the pace while four wide and tired in the stretch.

Owners– 1, Juddmonte Farms Inc; 2, Mack Earle I; 3, Juddmonte Farms Inc; 4, Fox Ridge Farm Inc; 5, Head Ghislaine; 6, Phillips Joan G John W Phillips; 7, Steve R Humphrey Seelbinder G Arthur William J Betz; 8, Stonerside Stable LLC

Trainers– 1, Frankel Robert; 2, Penna Angel Jr; 3, Frankel Robert; 4, Kelly Patrick J; 5, Clement Christophe; 6, Toner James J; 7, Toner James J; 8, Mott William I

Scratched– Caught in the Rain (15May04 5Pim4)

$2 Pick Three (4–3–1) Paid $12.00 ; Pick Three Pool $278,043 .

NINTH RACE
Belmont
JUNE 5, 2004

7 FURLONGS. (1.20) 20TH RUNNING OF THE RIVA RIDGE BREEDERS' CUP. Grade II. Purse $200,000 (includes $50,000 BC – Breeders' Cup) (Up To $28,500 NYSBFOA) FOR THREE YEAR OLDS. By subscription of $150 each, which should accompany the nomination; $750 to pass the entry box; $750 to start. The NYRA purse to be divided 60% to the winner, 20% to second, 10% to third, 5% to fourth, 3% to fifth and 2% divided equally among remaining finishers. Breeders' Cup monies also correspondingly divided. Any Breeders' Cup fund monies not awarded will revert back to the fund. 123 lbs. Non–winners of $60,000 other than restricted in 2004 or $45,000 twice in 2004 allowed 2 lbs.; $50,000 other than restricted, 4 lbs.; $35,000, or three races other than maiden or claiming, 6 lbs.; two races other than maiden or claiming, 8 lbs. Trophy to winning owner presented by Breeders' Cup Ltd. Closed Saturday, May 22, 2004 with 26 nominations.

Value of Race: $200,000 Winner $120,000; second $40,000; third $20,000; fourth $10,000; fifth $6,000; sixth $2,000; seventh $2,000. Mutuel Pool $1,762,729.00 Exacta Pool $1,409,423.00 Trifecta Pool $1,081,103.00

Last Raced	Horse	M/Eqt.	A.	Wt	PP	St	¼	½	Str	Fin	Jockey	Odds $1
8May04 9CD1	Fire Slam	L	3	123	2	6	52	52½	22	1hd	Day P	2.80
15May04 6Pim4	Teton Forest	L b	3	115	4	3	2½	2½	1hd	23¼	Bailey J D	4.10
15May04 6Pim1	Abbondanza	L f	3	123	6	2	4½	4½	33½	31¾	Dominguez R A	6.00
1May04 8Aqu4	Saratoga County	L bf	3	123	1	7	7	7	52½	47¼	Castellano J J	17.40
29May04 8Mth1	Smokume	L	3	119	3	5	1hd	1hd	4hd	5nk	Uske S	15.60
10Apr04 8Aqu6	Value Plus	L	3	115	5	4	3½	3½	61½	61	Velazquez J R	1.35
12May04 9CD1	Stolen Time	L	3	121	7	1	62½	63½	7	7	Velasquez C	26.75

OFF AT 5:12 Start Good. Won driving. Track fast.

TIME :222, :45, 1:084, 1:204 (:22.40, :45.08, 1:08.83, 1:20.94)

$2 Mutuel Prices:

3 – FIRE SLAM.........................	7.60	3.70	2.90
6 – TETON FOREST......................		4.00	3.30
7 – ABBONDANZA........................			3.50

$2 EXACTA 3–6 PAID $33.80 $2 TRIFECTA 3–6–7 PAID $123.50

B. c, (Jan), by Grand Slam – Miss Firefly , by Salt Lake . Trainer Carroll David. Bred by Julie Jones Mogge (Ky).

FIRE SLAM was urged along early, raced close up inside, found room on the rail in upper stretch, dug in gamely and prevailed after a hard drive. TETON FOREST contested the pace while between rivals and fought it out gamely to the wire. ABBONDANZA raced close up early while between rivals, came wide into the stretch and finished well outside. SARATOGA COUNTY was outrun early, came wide into the stretch and offered a mild rally outside. SMOKUME contested the pace along the inside and drifted out while tiring in the stretch. VALUE PLUS chased the pace while three wide and was carried out while tiring in the stretch. STOLEN TIME was hustled along outside and had no response when roused.

Owners– 1, Fulton Stan E; 2, Hughes B Wayne; 3, Aldie Germania Farms Inc; 4, Pollard Evelyn M; 5, Hobeau Farm; 6, Jones Aaron U and Marie D; 7, Smith Robert K

Trainers– 1, Carroll David; 2, Baffert Bob; 3, Tullock Timothy Jr; 4, Weaver George; 5, Jerkens H Allen; 6, Pletcher Todd A; 7, Mott William I

Scratched– Forest Danger (01May04 8Aqu2) , Indian War Dance (14May04 8Bel1)

$2 Daily Double (1–3) Paid $13.60 ; Daily Double Pool $177,007 .
$2 Pick Three (3–1–3) Paid $64.50 ; Pick Three Pool $279,995 .

TENTH RACE

Belmont

JUNE 5, 2004

1¼ MILES. (Inner Turf) (1.57^{3}) 103RD RUNNING OF THE MANHATTAN HANDICAP. Grade I. Purse $400,000 INNER TURF (Up To $48,000 NYSBFOA) A HANDICAP FOR THREE YEAR OLDS AND UPWARD. By subscription of $400 each, which should accompany the nomination; $2,000 to pass the entry box; $2,000 to start. The purse to be divided 60% to the winner, 20% to second, 10% to third, 5% to fourth, 3% to fifth and 2% divided equally among remaining finishers. Trophies will be presented to the winning owner, trainer and jockey. The New York Racing Association reserves the right to transfer this race to the Main Track. In theevent that this race is taken off the turf, it may be subject to downgrading upon review by the Graded Stakes Committee. Closed Saturday May,22 2004 with 23 nominations.

Value of Race: $400,000 Winner $240,000; second $80,000; third $40,000; fourth $20,000; fifth $12,000; sixth $2,000; seventh $2,000; eighth $2,000; ninth $2,000. Mutuel Pool $2,210,955.00 Exacta Pool $1,615,501.00 Trifecta Pool $1,344,462.00

Last Raced	Horse	M/Eqt.	A.	Wt	PP	¼	½	¾	1	Str	Fin	Jockey	Odds $1
18Apr04 ^{9}SA^{1}	Meteor Storm-GB	L	5	117	5	8½	8^{1}	8½	7½	5½	1^{1¼}	Valdivia J Jr	6.00
15May04 ^{10}Pim^{2}	MillnnumDrgon-GB	L	5	116	6	7^{hd}	7½	7^{hd}	6^{2}	3^{hd}	2no	Migliore R	12.40
15May04 ^{10}Pim^{1}	Mr O'Brien-Ire	L	5	116	3	3^{hd}	4½	3^{hd}	5^{hd}	6^{hd}	3¾	Dominguez R A	4.90
1May04 ^{11}STC^{7}	King's Drama-Ire	L	4	115	1	1½	1^{hd}	1^{hd}	2½	1½	4¾	Chavez J F	45.00
20Mar04 ^{6}GP^{2}	Request for Parole	L	5	115	7	9	9	9	8^{2}	7½	5½	Santos J A	13.10
1May04 ^{9}CD^{1}	Stroll	L	4	121	4	4^{hd}	3^{hd}	4^{hd}	3^{hd}	4^{hd}	6¾	Bailey J D	1.55
10Apr04 ^{7}Hou^{4}	Quest Star	L b	5	115	2	2^{1½}	2^{1½}	2^{1½}	1^{hd}	2^{hd}	7^{1½}	Day P	20.00
23Apr04 ^{9}Kee^{1}	Epicentre	L	5	118	8	5^{1½}	5½	5½	4^{hd}	8^{4½}	8¾	Prado E S	11.10
1May04 ^{9}CD^{6}	Kicken Kris	L	4	118	9	6^{hd}	6^{hd}	6½	9	9	9	Velazquez J R	4.90

OFF AT 5:52 Start Good . Won driving. Course firm.

TIME :23^{4}, :48^{2}, 1:12^{1}, 1:35^{4}, 1:59^{1} (:23.98, :48.48, 1:12.30, 1:35.83, 1:59.34)

$2 Mutuel Prices:

5 – METEOR STORM–GB	14.00	7.20	4.60
6 – MILLENNIUM DRAGON–GB		11.20	6.50
3 – MR O'BRIEN–IRE			4.80

$2 EXACTA 5–6 PAID $147.50 $2 TRIFECTA 5–6–3 PAID $736.00

B. h, (Apr), by Bigstone–Ire – Hunt the Sun–GB , by Rainbow Quest . Trainer Dollase Wallace. Bred by Juddmonte Farms (GB).

METEOR STORM (GB) was rated along inside, saved ground on both turns, swung wide into the stretch, responded when roused, finished strongly outside and was clear under the line. MILLENNIUM DRAGON (GB) raced in hand while between rivals early, rallied four wide approaching the stretch and finished gamely. MR O'BRIEN (IRE) raced close up early while between rivals, angled out in upper stretch and finished gamely outside. KING'S DRAMA (IRE) contested the pace along the inside and stayed on gamely on the rail. REQUEST FOR PAROLE was taken back early, raced outside, angled nearing the stretch and finished well while in traffic in the drive. STROLL raced with the pace while three wide on both turns and tired in the final furlong. QUEST STAR contested the pace from the outside and tired in the stretch. EPICENTRE raced close up inside while in hand, saved ground and came up empty when asked. KICKEN KRIS raced wide throughout and tired.

Owners– 1, The Horizon Stable; 2, Darley Stable; 3, Skeedattle Stable; 4, Tanaka Gary A; 5, Knighton Jeri and Sam; 6, Claiborne Farm; 7, Mansell Stables LLC; 8, Juddmonte Farms Inc; 9, Brushwood Stable

Trainers– 1, Dollase Wallace; 2, McLaughlin Kiaran P; 3, Graham Robin L; 4, Collet Robert; 5, Hough Stanley M; 6, Mott William I; 7, Walden W Elliott; 8, Frankel Robert; 9, Matz Michael R

Scratched– Better Talk Now (15May04 ^{10}Pim^{9})

ELEVENTH RACE
Belmont
JUNE 5, 2004

1½ MILES. (2.24) 136TH RUNNING OF THE BELMONT. Grade I. Purse $1,000,000 (Up To $70,000 NYSBFOA) FOR THREE YEAR OLDS. By subscription of $600 each, to accompany the nomination, if made on or before January 17, 2004, or $6,000, if made on or before March 27, 2004, $10,000 to pass the entry box and $10,000 additional to start. The purse to be divided 60% to the winner, 20% to second, 11% to third, 6% to fourth and 3% to fifth. Colts and Geldings, 126 lbs.; Fillies, 121 lbs. The winning owner will be presented with the August Belmont Memorial Cup to be retained for one year as well as a trophy for permanent possession and trophies to the winning trainer and jockey.

Value of Race: $1,000,000 Winner $600,000; second $200,000; third $110,000; fourth $60,000; fifth $30,000. Mutuel Pool $23,355,741.00 Exacta Pool $13,047,212.00 Trifecta Pool $17,922,977.00 Superfecta Pool $6,470,512.00

Last Raced	Horse	M/Eqt.	A.	Wt	PP	¼	½	1	1¼	Str	Fin	Jockey	Odds $1
1May04 ^{10}CD^{8}	Birdstone	L	3	126	4	$7^{1\frac{1}{2}}$	$5^{\frac{1}{2}}$	4^{6}	$2^{1\frac{1}{2}}$	2^{6}	1^{1}	Prado E S	36.00
15May04 ^{12}Pim^{1}	Smarty Jones	L f	3	126	9	$3^{\frac{1}{2}}$	$3^{\frac{1}{2}}$	$1^{\frac{1}{2}}$	$1^{3\frac{1}{2}}$	$1^{1\frac{1}{2}}$	2^{8}	Elliott S	0.35
15May04 ^{9}Pim^{1}	Royal Assault	L	3	126	6	6^{hd}	$6^{1\frac{1}{2}}$	6^{1}	5^{2}	5^{10}	3^{3}	Day P	27.75
15May04 ^{12}Pim^{3}	Eddington	L b	3	126	8	5^{hd}	$4^{1\frac{1}{2}}$	$3^{3\frac{1}{2}}$	4^{8}	4^{6}	4no	Bailey J D	14.20
15May04 ^{12}Pim^{2}	Rock Hard Ten	L	3	126	5	$2^{\frac{1}{2}}$	2^{1}	2^{1}	3^{2}	$3^{2\frac{1}{2}}$	5^{14}	Solis A	6.70
15May04 ^{9}Pim^{4}	Tap Dancer	L f	3	126	7	9	9	8^{10}	$7^{\frac{1}{2}}$	6^{hd}	$6^{4\frac{1}{4}}$	Castellano J J	40.50
22May04 ^{8}Bel^{3}	Master David	L f	3	126	1	8^{1}	8^{hd}	7^{hd}	6^{hd}	7^{8}	7^{1}	Santos J A	24.50
1May04 ^{10}Haw^{1}	Caiman	L	3	126	3	4^{hd}	7^{hd}	9	9	9	$8^{6\frac{1}{4}}$	Dominguez R A	49.75
22May04 ^{8}Bel^{1}	Purge	L	3	126	2	$1^{\frac{1}{2}}$	1^{hd}	5^{6}	8^{6}	8^{2}	9	Velazquez J R	9.60

OFF AT 6:48 Start Good. Won driving. Track fast.

TIME :24^{1}, :48^{3}, 1:11^{3}, 1:35^{2}, 2:00^{2}, 2:27^{2} (:24.33, :48.65, 1:11.76, 1:35.44, 2:00.52, 2:27.50)

$2 Mutuel Prices:				
	4 – BIRDSTONE	74.00	14.00	8.60
	9 – SMARTY JONES		3.30	2.60
	6 – ROYAL ASSAULT			6.10

$2 EXACTA 4–9 PAID $139.00 $2 TRIFECTA 4–9–6 PAID $1,589.00
$2 SUPERFECTA 4–9–6–8 PAID $11,679.00

B. c, (May), by Grindstone – Dear Birdie , by Storm Bird . Trainer Zito Nicholas P. Bred by Marylou Whitney Stables (Ky).

BIRDSTONE was unhurried while between horses on the first turn, swung out entering the backstretch, settled in the middle of the pack while racing five wide along the backstretch, took up chase after SMARTY JONES from outside on the far turn, moved around EDDINGTON while gaining ground midway on the turn, circled five wide while launching his bid at the top of the stretch, drifted out in upper stretch, straightened his course when struck right handed nearing the furlong marker, closed steadily under steady right hand encouragement a sixteenth out then wore down SMARTY JONES in the final seventy yards. SMARTY JONES moved up from outside to contest the early pace, pressed the pace while four wide entering the backstretch, surged to the front just after going a half mile, battled heads apart while continuing wide to the far turn, shook off ROCK HARD TEN to get clear leaving the three-eighths pole, extended his lead approaching the quarter pole, drifted out when struck left handed with the whip in upper stretch and again nearing the eighth pole, maintained a clear lead inside the furlong marker, fought gamely into deep stretch then yielded grudgingly while weakening in the late stages. ROYAL ASSAULT checked in tight while being bothered by ROCK HARD TEN at the start, raced well back through the opening half mile, moved up a bit between horses along the backstretch, launched a mild rally three wide on the turn then failed to threaten while improving his position in the stretch. EDDINGTON was hustled up from outside in the early stages, stalked the pace while five wide along the backstretch, raced just outside SMARTY JONES leaving the far turn, dropped back a bit leaving the three-eighths pole then steadily tired thereafter. ROCK HARD TEN fractious behind the gate at the start, broke outward causing crowding leaving the gate, moved up between horses on the first turn, pressed the pace inside SMARTY JONES along the backstretch, made a run along the inside to threaten on the far turn, forced the issue to the turn then tired from his early efforts. TAP DANCER never reached contention while five wide throughout. MASTER DAVID steadied along the inside on the first turn, lagged behind between horses entering the backstretch then failed to mount a serious rally while four wide throughout. CAIMAN showed brief speed along the inside, saved ground along the backstretch and faded before going a mile. PURGE rushed up while rank in the early stages, set the pace along the rail for nearly a half, dropped back on the far turn and steadily tired thereafter.

Owners– 1, Marylou Whitney Stables; 2, Someday Farm; 3, Farmer Tracy; 4, Willmott Stables Inc; 5, Mercedes Stables Paulson Madeleine A; 6, Campbell Gilbert G; 7, Georgica Stable Mack Stephen and Star Crown Stable; 8, Achar Victor; 9, Starlight Stables LLC Saylor Paul and Martin Johns

Trainers– 1, Zito Nicholas P; 2, Servis John C; 3, Zito Nicholas P; 4, Hennig Mark; 5, Orman Jason; 6, Allard Edward T; 7, Frankel Robert; 8, Medina Angel M; 9, Pletcher Todd A

$2 Daily Double (5–4) Paid $526.00 ; Daily Double Pool $446,089 .
$2 Daily Double (5–4 (ACORN/BELMONT)) Paid $466.00 ; Daily Double Pool $441,507 .
$2 Pick Three (3–5–4) Paid $2,910.00 ; Pick Three Pool $454,107 .
$2 Pick Four (1–3–5–4) Paid $7,309.00 ; Pick Four Pool $1,739,609 .
$2 Pick Six (4–3–1–3–5–4) 6 Correct Paid $47,421.00 ; Pick Six Pool $1,487,744 .
$2 Pick Six (4–3–1–3–5–4) 5 Correct Paid $146.00 .

EIGHTH RACE
Churchill
JUNE 5, 2004

5½ FURLONGS. (1.02²) 17TH RUNNING OF THE KENTUCKY BREEDERS' CUP. Grade III. Purse $125,000 (includes $50,000 BC - Breeders' Cup) FOR TWO-YEAR-OLDS. By subscription of $125 each on or before May 22, 2004 or by Supplementary Nomination of $6,250 at time of entry. $625 to pass the entry box; $625 additional to start, with $75,000 added and an additional $50,000 from the Breeders' CupFund for Cup nominees only. The host association's added monies to be divided 62% to the owner of the winner, 20% to second, 10% to third, 5% to fourth and 3% to fifth. Breeders' Cup Fund monies also correspondingly divided providing a Breeders' Cup nominee has finished in an awarded position. Any Breeders' Cup Fund monies not awarded will revert back to the Fund. Colts and geldings 121 lbs.; Fillies 118 lbs. Non-winners of a sweepstakes allowed 2 lbs.; a race other than maiden or claiming 4 lbs.; arace other than claiming 6 lbs. Starters to be named through the entry box at the usual time of closing. All supplementary nominations will be required to pay entry and starting fees if they participate. Trophy to winning owner given by Breeders' CupLtd. Closed Saturday, May 22, 2004 with 15 nominations and 1 supplementary nomination: Consolidator.

Value of Race: $132,088 Winner $86,025; second $27,750; third $13,875; fourth $4,438. Mutuel Pool $413,092.00 Exacta Pool $209,025.00 Trifecta Pool $75,861.00 Superfecta Pool $32,065.00

Last Raced	Horse	M/Eqt.	A.	Wt	PP	St	¼	⅜	Str	Fin	Jockey	Odds $1
1May04 6CD1	Lunarpal	L	2	121	4	1	1hd	1½	12	1nk	Sellers S J	0.10
29Apr04 3CD5	Consolidator		2	115	3	2	31	2½	22½	2¾	Bejarano R	7.10
22May04 1CD1	Smoke Warning	L	2	117	2	4	4	3hd	33	38	Guidry M	6.10
6May04 2CD1	Cat Tourn	L	2	115	1	3	2½	4	4	4	Hernandez B J Jr	17.40

OFF AT 4:39 Start Good. Won driving. Track fast.
TIME :22¹, :46¹, :57², 1:04 (:22.22, :46.25, :57.52, 1:04.07)

$2 Mutuel Prices:				
	5 – LUNARPAL	2.20	2.10	—
	4 – CONSOLIDATOR		2.10	—
	2 – SMOKE WARNING			—

$2 EXACTA 5–4 PAID $7.40 $2 TRIFECTA 5–4–2 PAID $9.00
$2 SUPERFECTA 5–4–2–1 PAID $11.20

B. c, (Apr), by Successful Appeal – Quiet Eclipse, by Quiet American. Trainer Asmussen Steven M. Bred by L William Heiligbrodt (Fla).

LUNARPAL hopped while breaking to the outside, quickly was straightened and sent up to force the pace, gained a slim lead, edged clear on the turn, came out a bit in the upper stretch, then leaned in while lasting under pressure and placed CONSOLIDATOR in a bit tight at the end. CONSOLIDATOR drifted in at the start bumping the side of the gate, tracked the pace four wide, moved inside the winner in the upper stretch and was gaining late despite being in close quarters at the finish. SMOKE WARNING bobbled at the start and leaned in bumping CAT TOURN, raced four or five wide and and was slowly gaining in the late stages. CAT TOURN, bumped at the start by SMOKE WARNING, contested the pace inside and tired.

Owners– 1, Heiligbrodt Racing Stable; 2, Lewis Robert B and Beverly J; 3, Jones Frank L Jr; 4, Marshall Jon A
Trainers– 1, Asmussen Steven M; 2, Lukas D Wayne; 3, Romans Dale; 4, Werner Ronny
Scratched– Maximus C (15May04 1CD 1)

$2 Pick Three (8–2–5) Paid $165.60 ; Pick Three Pool $48,671 .

TENTH RACE
Churchill
JUNE 5, 2004

1 1/16 MILES. (1.41³) 30TH RUNNING OF THE DOGWOOD BREEDERS' CUP. Grade III. Purse $150,000 (includes $50,000 BC - Breeders' Cup) FOR FILLIES, THREE YEARS OLD. By subscription of $150 each on or before May 15, 2004 or by Supplementary Nomination of $7,500 at time of entry. $750 to pass the entry box; $750 additional to start with $100,000 added and an additional $50,000 from the Breeders' Cup Fund for Cup Nominees only. The host association's monies to be divided 62% to the owner of the winner, 20% to second, 10% to third, 5% to fourth and 3% to fifth. Breeders' Cup Fund monies also correspondingly divided providing a Breeders'Cup nominee has finished in an awarded position. Any Breeders' Cup Fund monies not awarded will revert back to the Fund. Weight 122 lbs. Non-winners of $50,000 twice at a mile or over allowed 2 lbs.; $50,000 at a mile or over, 4 lbs.; three races at a mile or over other than maiden or claiming, 6 lbs.; two races at a mile or over other than maiden or claiming, 8 lbs. Starters to be named through the entry box at the usual time of closing. Trophy to winning owner given by Breeders' Cup Ltd. Closed SSaturday, May 15, 2004 with 21 nominations.

Value of Race: $161,400 Winner $100,068; second $32,280; third $16,140; fourth $8,070; fifth $4,842. Mutuel Pool $394,848.00 Exacta Pool $249,192.00 Trifecta Pool $142,394.00 Superfecta Pool $46,075.00

Last Raced	Horse	M/Eqt.	A.	Wt	PP	St	¼	½	¾	Str	Fin	Jockey	Odds $1
30Apr04 10CD7	Stellar Jayne	L b	3	120	5	2	2½	2½	22	11½	13¼	Albarado R J	2.40
30Apr04 5CD3	Dynaville	L	3	114	3	4	3½	42	31	33	21¾	Perret C	5.80
29Apr04 9CD2	Ender's Sister	L	3	122	2	1	12	11	1hd	2½	3½	Borel C H	0.80
30Apr04 5CD1	Galloping Gal	L	3	122	1	5	4½	31½	43	43	43½	Blanc B	6.20
14May04 10Pim6	Song Track	L f	3	114	4	3	5	5	5	5	5	Guidry M	11.00

OFF AT 5:44 Start Good. Won driving. Track fast.
TIME :24³, :48³, 1:12⁴, 1:36⁴, 1:43 (:24.69, :48.61, 1:12.86, 1:36.94, 1:43.14)

$2 Mutuel Prices:				
	6 – STELLAR JAYNE	6.80	3.60	2.10
	3 – DYNAVILLE		5.40	2.20
	2 – ENDER'S SISTER			2.10

$2 EXACTA 6–3 PAID $35.80 $2 TRIFECTA 6–3–2 PAID $62.60
$2 SUPERFECTA 6–3–2–1 PAID $150.00

Gr/ro. f, (Feb), by Wild Rush – To the Hunt, by Relaunch. Trainer Lukas D Wayne. Bred by Wind Hill Farm (Ky).

STELLAR JAYNE went up early to press front-running ENDER'S SISTER, raced under light restraint while three wide, inched to challenge just after going six furlongs, took over, moved clear, was sharply roused left-handed at the eighth pole and widened a bit at the end under hand urging. DYNAVILLE, lightly bumped at the start by SONG TRACK, was never far back, moved out four or five wide concluding the backstretch, loomed a threat into the final furlong but couldn't offer a late response as second best. ENDER'S SISTER gained the lead at the start, raced two or three wide while in hand, went along through modest early fractions, made the pace for six furlongs and weakened. GALLOPING GAL, never far back while racing near the inside swung out five wide into the upper stretch but failed to fire. SONG TRACK leaned in at the break lightly bumping DYNAVILLE, settled near the inside and failed to menace.

Owners– 1, Spendthrift Farm LLC Kidder Cole and Strong; 2, Fox Nathan and Kaster Richard; 3, Green Lantern Stables LLC; 4, Carl William A; 5, Farish William S and Phipps Ogden Mills
Trainers– 1, Lukas D Wayne; 2, Romans Dale; 3, Arnold George R II; 4, McPeek Kenneth G; 5, Howard Neil J
Scratched– Family Business (31May04 8CD 3)

$2 Pick Three (5–1–6) Paid $35.60 ; Pick Three Pool $26,193 .

FIRST RACE
Hollywood
JUNE 5, 2004

6 FURLONGS. (1.07^2) 8TH RUNNING OF THE DESERT STORMER HANDICAP. Grade III. Purse $100,000 FOR FILLIES AND MARES THREE YEARS OLD AND UPWARD. By subscription of $100 each on or before Wednesday, May 26 or by supplementary nomination of $2,000 each by 3:00 pm Saturday, May 29. $1,000 additional to start, with $100,000 Added. The added money andall fees to be divided 60% to the winner, 20% to second, 12% to third, 6% to fourth and 2% to fifth. Weights Sunday, May 30. Starters to be named through the entry box by closing time of entries. A trophy will be presented to the winning owner. Closedwith 10 nominations. (Clear. 80.)

Value of Race: $106,000 Winner $63,600; second $21,200; third $12,720; fourth $6,360; fifth $2,120. Mutuel Pool $357,125.00 Exacta Pool $200,664.00 Quinella Pool $16,753.00

Last Raced	Horse	M/Eqt.	A.	Wt	PP	St	¼	½	Str	Fin	Jockey	Odds $1
12May04 ^{7}Hol^2	Coconut Girl	LB f	5	115	2	1	2^{hd}	2^1	1^2	$1^{1\frac{1}{4}}$	Espinoza V	5.50
7Apr04 ^{8}Kee^1	Ema Bovary-Chi	LB	5	123	1	4	4^1	$4^{4\frac{1}{2}}$	2^1	$2^{5\frac{1}{2}}$	Gonzalez R M	0.40
2May04 ^{8}BM^2	Stormica	LB	4	115	4	5	$3^{\frac{1}{2}}$	3^{hd}	4^6	3^2	Smith M E	9.60
23Aug03 ^{8}Dmr^7	Jetinto Houston	LB	5	115	3	2	$1^{\frac{1}{2}}$	$1^{\frac{1}{2}}$	3^1	$4^{4\frac{1}{2}}$	Baze T C	9.30
9May04 ^{8}Hol^4	Hope Rises	LB	4	116	5	3	5	5	5	5	Flores D R	5.80

OFF AT 12:51 Start Good. Won driving. Track fast.
TIME :22^2, :44^4, :56^3, 1:08^4 (:22.44, :44.94, :56.60, 1:08.91)

$2 Mutuel Prices:				
	2 – **COCONUT GIRL**	13.00	3.20	2.10
	1 – **EMA BOVARY-CHI**		2.20	2.10
	4 – **STORMICA**			2.10

$1 EXACTA 2–1 PAID $10.70 $2 QUINELLA 1–2 PAID $5.80

Dk. b or br. m, (Jan), by Cryptoclearance – Sarabi, by Lost Code. Trainer Aguirre Paul G. Bred by Leslie R Grimm & Flint S Schulhofer (Ky).

COCONUT GIRL went up to prompt the pace between horses on the backstretch and most of the turn, battled outside a rival leaving the bend, took a short lead into the stretch, kicked clear inside and held under left handed urging. EMA BOVARY (CHI) stalked the pace inside, was in close off heels and shuffled back a bit into the turn, came out for room into the stretch and finished willingly but could not catch the winner. STORMICA broke in a bit, was between horses early then pressed the pace three deep, came out some into the stretch and bested the others. JETINTO HOUSTON sped to the early lead a bit off the rail, set a pressured pace inside and weakened in the stretch. HOPE RISES four wide early, chased off the rail and lacked a response in the stretch, then tied up while being led back to the barn but was walked off.

Owners– 1, Jpf Investments I LLC; 2, Beal Jr & Ramsey-Brog; 3, Wertheimer and Frere; 4, Team Valor Stables LLC and Barber Gary; 5, Jay Em Ess Stable

Trainers– 1, Aguirre Paul G; 2, Ross Larry; 3, Mandella Gary; 4, Sadler John W; 5, Ellis Ronald W

EIGHTH RACE
Hollywood
JUNE 5, 2004

1⅛ MILES. (Turf Chute) 53RD RUNNING OF THE HONEYMOON BREEDERS' CUP HANDICAP. Grade II. Purse $175,000 (includes $50,000 BC – Breeders' Cup) CHUTE START. FOR FILLIES THREE-YEARS-OLD. By subscription of $175 each on or before Wednesday, May 26 or by supplemental nomination of $3,500 each by 3:00 pm Saturday, May 29. $1,500 additional to start, with $125,000 added and an additional $50,000 fromthe Breeders' Cup Fund for Cup nominees only. The host association's added money and all fees to be divided 60% to the winner, 20% to second, 12% to third, 6% to fourth and 2% to fifth.Breeders' Cup monies also correspondingly divided providing a Breeders' Cup nominee has finished in an awarded position. Any Breeders' Cup monies not awarded will revert to the fund. Weights Sunday, May 30. Starters to be named through the entry box by closing time of entries. Preference will be given in the following order: Highweights will be preferred under the following conditions–Breeders' Cup Nominees will be preferred over Non-Breeders Cup nominees assigned equal weights on the scale. Total earnings in 2004 will be used in determining the preference of horses withequal nomination status and equal weight assigned on the scale. All fees for entrants that fail to draw into this race will be cancelled. A trophy will be presented to the winning owner. Closed with 11 nominations.

Value of Race: $184,925 Winner $113,355; second $37,785; third $22,671; fourth $8,335; fifth $2,779. Mutuel Pool $582,160.00 Exacta Pool $314,214.00 Quinella Pool $26,938.00 Trifecta Pool $342,537.00 Superfecta Pool $145,780.00

Last Raced	Horse	M/Eqt.	A.	Wt	PP	St	¼	½	¾	Str	Fin	Jockey	Odds $1
19May04 ^{5}Hol^2	Lovely Rafaela	LB	3	114	4	1	2^1	2^3	2^1	1^{hd}	1no	Espinoza V	16.20
14May04 ^{5}Hol^1	WesternHemispher	LB b	3	114	3	2	$1^{1\frac{1}{2}}$	$1^{4\frac{1}{2}}$	$1^{\frac{1}{2}}$	$2^{1\frac{1}{2}}$	$2^{1\frac{1}{2}}$	Santiago Javier	3.20
6May04 ^{2}Hol^2	Sagitta Ra	LB	3	116	2	3	$4^{\frac{1}{2}}$	$4^{\frac{1}{2}}$	5^1	$4^{1\frac{1}{2}}$	3^{nk}	Nakatani C S	7.00
15May04 ^{8}Hol^2	Ticker Tape-GB	LB	3	121	8	8	$7^{\frac{1}{2}}$	$5^{\frac{1}{2}}$	4^{hd}	3^{hd}	$4^{\frac{1}{2}}$	Desormeaux K J	1.10
15May04 ^{8}Hol^3	Amorama-FR	LB b	3	116	7	7	$5^{\frac{1}{2}}$	6^1	6^1	$6^{1\frac{1}{2}}$	$5^{2\frac{1}{2}}$	Flores D R	5.10
5May04 ^{3}Hol^1	Rather Have Rubies	LB b	3	114	6	5	3^1	$3^{\frac{1}{2}}$	3^{hd}	5^1	6no	John K	26.40
6May04 ^{2}Hol^3	Shake Off	LB	3	114	5	6	8	8	8	8	7^{nk}	Baze T C	18.70
23Apr04 ^{8}Hol^2	Vencedora Amiga	LB	3	114	1	4	6^1	$7^{\frac{1}{2}}$	7^{hd}	$7^{\frac{1}{2}}$	8	Smith M E	18.90

OFF AT 5:20 Start Good. Won driving. Course firm.
TIME :25^3, :50^1, 1:15, 1:38^1, 1:49^4 (:25.77, :50.39, 1:15.09, 1:38.39, 1:49.96)

$2 Mutuel Prices:				
	4 – **LOVELY RAFAELA**	34.40	12.80	7.80
	3 – **WESTERN HEMISPHERE**		5.20	3.80
	2 – **SAGITTA RA**			5.20

$1 EXACTA 4–3 PAID $77.70 $2 QUINELLA 3–4 PAID $66.20
$1 TRIFECTA 4–3–2 PAID $529.60 $1 SUPERFECTA 4–3–2–8 PAID $2,028.60

Dk. b or br. f, (Apr), by A.P. Indy – Campagnarde-Arg, by Oak Dancer-GB. Trainer Lobo Paulo H. Bred by Diamond A Racing Corporation (Ky).

LOVELY RAFAELA stalked the pace off the rail, bid outside the runner-up into the second turn, bid again into the stretch, put a head in front in midstretch, battled through a stiff drive alongside that rival and got up again at the wire under urging. WESTERN HEMISPHERE took the early lead and set the pace inside, opened up on the backstretch, responded when challenged into the second turn, inched away briefly, came out a bit into the stretch, then angled in and fought back along the rail, regained a short advantage past midstretch but was edged on the line. SAGITTA RA saved ground stalking the pace, came a bit off the rail in the stretch and continued willingly to edge a rival for third. TICKER TAPE (GB) angled in some in the chute, chased outside, went three deep into and on the second turn and into the stretch and was edged for the show. AMORAMA (FR) chased outside a rival then between foes on the backstretch, continued off the rail on the second turn, came out some in the stretch and put in a late bid at a minor award. RATHER HAVE RUBIES stalked the pace outside a rival then between foes on the second turn, was a bit crowded in midstretch and lacked the needed response in the stretch. SHAKE OFF settled between horses then outside a rival, came three deep into the stretch and did not rally. VENCEDORA AMIGA saved ground chasing the pace, continued inside throughout and could not offer the necessary response in the lane.

Owners– 1, T N T Stud; 2, Golden Eagle Farm; 3, Frankel Robert J; 4, Jim Ford Inc Pearson Daron and Sweesy Jack; 5, Naify and Woodside Farms LLC; 6, Everest Stables Inc; 7, Hughes B Wayne; 8, Old Friends Inc and Winner Silk Inc

Trainers– 1, Lobo Paulo H; 2, Baffert Bob; 3, Frankel Robert; 4, Cassidy James; 5, Canani Julio C; 6, Polanco Marcelo; 7, Baffert Bob; 8, Lobo Paulo H

$2 Daily Double (1–4) Paid $90.00 ; Daily Double Pool $32,369 .
$1 Pick Three (1–1/2/5/9–4) Paid $516.60 ; Pick Three Pool $104,222 .

EIGHTH RACE
Belmont
JUNE 6, 2004

1⅛ MILES. (Inner Turf) (1.45^{3}) 30TH RUNNING OF THE HILL PRINCE. Grade III. Purse $100,000 (UP TO $19,000 NYSBFOA) 3-YEAR OLDS. By subscription of $100 each, which should accompany the nomination; $500 to pass the entry box; $500 to start, with $100,000 added. The added money and all fees to be divided 60% to the winner, 20%to second, 10% to third, 5% to fourth, 3% to fifth and 2% divided equally among remaining finishers. 122 lbs. Non-winners of $35,000 twice on the turf allowed 2 lbs.; $45,000 at a mile or over; or $35,000 at a mile or over in 2004, 4 lbs.; $30,000, or two races at a mile orover, 6 lbs.; two races, 8 lbs. (Maiden, Claiming and Restricted races not considered in allowances.) A trophy will be presented to the winning owner. The New York Racing Association reserves the right to transfer this race to the Main Track. In the event that this race is taken off the turf, it may be subject to downgrading upon review by the Graded Stakes Committee. Closed Saturday, May 22, 2004 with 40 Nominations.

Value of Race: $110,000 Winner $66,000; second $22,000; third $11,000; fourth $5,500; fifth $3,300; sixth $2,200. Mutuel Pool $522,572.00 Exacta Pool $424,570.00 Trifecta Pool $327,189.00

Last Raced	Horse	M/Eqt.	A.	Wt	PP	St	¼	½	¾	Str	Fin	Jockey	Odds $1
15May04 ^{7}Pim^{1}	Artie Schiller	L	3	120	6	4	$2\frac{1}{2}$	$1\frac{1}{2}$	$1\frac{1}{2}$	$1^{2\frac{1}{2}}$	$1^{1\frac{3}{4}}$	Migliore R	0.95
15May04 ^{7}Pim^{3}	Timo	L b	3	122	4	2	$3\frac{1}{2}$	$3\frac{1}{2}$	$2\frac{1}{2}$	$2^{1\frac{1}{2}}$	$2^{2\frac{1}{4}}$	Velazquez J R	2.65
15May04 ^{7}Pim^{7}	Big Booster	L b	3	114	5	5	$4\frac{1}{2}$	$5\frac{1}{2}$	3^{hd}	$3\frac{1}{2}$	$3\frac{3}{4}$	Castellano J J	19.40
18Apr04 ^{9}Kee^{1}	Good Reward	L	3	118	2	3	6	6	6	6	$4\frac{3}{4}$	Santos J A	6.20
13May04 ^{7}Bel^{1}	War Trace	L	3	114	1	6	5^{hd}	4^{1}	$5\frac{1}{2}$	4^{hd}	$5^{1\frac{1}{4}}$	Bailey J D	6.00
22May04 ^{7}Bel^{6}	Kennel Up		3	114	3	1	$1^{1\frac{1}{2}}$	$2\frac{1}{2}$	$4\frac{1}{2}$	$5\frac{1}{2}$	6	Chavez J F	16.70

OFF AT 4:45 Start Good . Won driving. Course firm.

TIME :26, :51^{2}, 1:16, 1:38^{4}, 1:50 (:26.18, :51.42, 1:16.05, 1:38.96, 1:50.06)

$2 Mutuel Prices:				
	6 – ARTIE SCHILLER	3.90	2.40	2.10
	4 – TIMO		2.60	2.30
	5 – BIG BOOSTER			3.40

$2 EXACTA 6–4 PAID $9.20 $2 TRIFECTA 6–4–5 PAID $48.00

B. c, (Apr), by El Prado-Ire – Hidden Light , by Majestic Light . Trainer Jerkens James A. Bred by Haras Du Mezeray SA (Ky).

ARTIE SCHILLER came away well and raced near the front while well in hand, soon gained control of the pace, sprinted clear when asked for run and was kept busy to the wire. TIMO raced close up outside, advanced outside on the second turn, responded when roused and stayed on gamely while chasing the winner home. BIG BOOSTER was rated along while three wide on both turns and finished well outside. GOOD REWARD was rated along inside, angled out on the second turn, rallied four wide into the stretch and was going well late outside. WAR TRACE broke awkwardly, was rated along between rivals and lacked a rally. KENNEL UP raced with the pace along the inside while in hand, saved ground and had no response when roused.

Owners– 1, Timber Bay Farm and Walsh Mrs Thomas J; 2, C K Woods Stable; 3, Broman Sr Mary and Chester; 4, Phipps Ogden Mills et al; 5, Phillips Joan G John W Phillips; 6, Shields Joseph V Jr

Trainers– 1, Jerkens James A; 2, Badgett William Jr; 3, Kimmel John C; 4, McGaughey III Claude R; 5, Toner James J; 6, Jerkens H Allen

Scratched– West Virginia (25Apr04 ^{8}Aqu^{1}) , Master David (05Jun04 ^{11}Bel^{7}) , Forest Grove (03Apr04 ^{11}GP ^{7}) , Ecclesiastic (12May04 ^{7}Bel^{1})

EIGHTH RACE
Hollywood
JUNE 6, 2004

1$\frac{1}{16}$ MILES. (1.40) 31ST RUNNING OF THE HAWTHORNE HANDICAP. Grade III. Purse $100,000 FOR FILLES AND MARES THREE-YEARS-OLD AND UPWARD. By subscription of $100 each on or before Wednesday, May 26 or by supplementary nomination of $2,000 each by 3:00 pm Saturday, May 29. $1,000 additional to start, with $100,000 added. The added money and all fees to be divided 60% to the winner, 20% to second, 12% to third, 6% to fourth and 2% to fifth. Weights Sunday, May 30. Starters to be named through the entry box by closing time of entries. A trophy will be presented to the winning owner. Closed with16 nominations.

Value of Race: $108,600 Winner $65,160; second $21,720; third $13,032; fourth $6,516; fifth $2,172. Mutuel Pool $402,054.00 Exacta Pool $224,112.00 Quinella Pool $22,912.00 Trifecta Pool $254,835.00 Superfecta Pool $111,412.00

Last Raced	Horse	M/Eqt.	A.	Wt	PP	St	¼	½	¾	Str	Fin	Jockey	Odds $1
24Apr04 ^{4}Hol^{2}	SummerWindDncer	LB b	4	116	2	4	$6^{2\frac{1}{2}}$	4^{2}	2^{hd}	$2^{4\frac{1}{2}}$	1^{1}	Espinoza V	2.20
30Apr04 ^{2}Hol^{1}	Pesci	LB b	4	115	5	3	$1^{1\frac{1}{2}}$	$1^{1\frac{1}{2}}$	1^{2}	$1\frac{1}{2}$	2^{10}	Smith M E	0.90
7Feb04 ^{8}SI^{3}	Miss Loren-Arg	LB	6	116	6	2	3^{hd}	$6^{3\frac{1}{2}}$	6^{hd}	6^{3}	$3\frac{1}{2}$	Desormeaux K J	15.50
12May04 ^{7}Hol^{5}	Sparkling Ava	LB bf	5	112	1	5	$2^{1\frac{1}{2}}$	$2^{1\frac{1}{2}}$	$3^{2\frac{1}{2}}$	3^{hd}	4no	Garcia M S	33.20
6May04 ^{7}Hol^{4}	Honeypenny	LB b	5	116	7	6	$5\frac{1}{2}$	5^{hd}	$4^{3\frac{1}{2}}$	$4^{3\frac{1}{2}}$	5^{1}	Flores D R	19.20
13May04 ^{5}Hol^{1}	Lady Thatcher-Chi	LB	5	115	3	1	7	7	7	5^{hd}	6^{11}	Valdivia J Jr	29.50
25Apr04 ^{7}Hol^{6}	Makeup Artist	LB	4	115	4	7	4^{1}	$3\frac{1}{2}$	$5^{2\frac{1}{2}}$	7	7	Santiago Javier	4.40

OFF AT 4:56 Start Good . Won driving. Track fast.

TIME :23^{2}, :46^{1}, 1:10, 1:34^{4}, 1:41^{2} (:23.48, :46.31, 1:10.14, 1:34.91, 1:41.56)

$2 Mutuel Prices:				
	2 – SUMMER WIND DANCER	6.40	2.80	2.20
	6 – PESCI		2.60	2.20
	7 – MISS LOREN-ARG			3.20

$1 EXACTA 2–6 PAID $5.30 $2 QUINELLA 2–6 PAID $4.00
$1 TRIFECTA 2–6–7 PAID $29.30 $1 SUPERFECTA 2–6–7–1 PAID $129.90

Gr/ro. f, (Mar), by Siberian Summer – Native Wind Dancer , by Incinderator . Trainer Mullins Jeff. Bred by Richard Wira Yvette Wira Linda Vetter && Deborah Penny (Cal).

SUMMER WIND DANCER between foes early, angled in and chased inside, moved up into the second turn, came out into the stretch, bid outside the runner-up, took the lead past midstretch and inched away under urging. PESCI sped to the early lead, angled in on the first turn, set the pace inside, fought back inside the winner in midstretch, could not match that one late but was clearly best of the rest. MISS LOREN (ARG) chased outside then off the rail, came three deep into the stretch and gained the show late outside. SPARKLING AVA stalked the pace inside, came off the rail on the backstretch, continued outside the winner into and on the second turn, went three deep into the stretch and lost the show between foes late. HONEYPENNY four wide into the first turn, chased outside, angled in on the second turn, then was edged for third toward the rail. LADY THATCHER (CHI) bumped into the first turn, angled in on that bend and saved ground off the pace, came out into the stretch and did not rally. MAKEUP ARTIST bumped when three deep between foes into the first turn, moved up between horses on the backstretch, stalked outside the winner, dropped back and angled in on the second turn and gave way.

Owners– 1, Vetter Linda and Wira Richard and Yvette; 2, Giardino Pesci & Ward; 3, Llers Corporation; 4, Schwartz Barry K; 5, Straeter Terry; 6, Sivage W D and Ella; 7, Krikorian George

Trainers– 1, Mullins Jeff; 2, Ward Wesley A; 3, Seglin Luis E; 4, Inda Eduardo; 5, Canani Julio C; 6, Saavedra Anthony K; 7, Shirreffs John

Scratched– Stormica (05Jun04 ^{1}Hol^{3})

$2 Daily Double (1–2) Paid $37.00 ; Daily Double Pool $42,928 .
$1 Pick Three (2–1–2) Paid $110.70 ; Pick Three Pool $74,396 .

SEVENTH RACE
Belmont
JUNE 12, 2004

1⅛ MILES. (1.45^2) 116TH RUNNING OF THE BROOKLYN HANDICAP. Grade II. Purse $250,000 (Up To $37,500 NYSBFOA) A HANDICAP FOR THREE YEAR OLDS AND UPWARD. By subscription of $250 each, which should accompany the nomination; $1,250 to pass the entry box; $1,250 to start. The purse to be divided 60% to the winner, 20% to second, 10% to third,5% to fourth, 3% to fifth and 2% divided equally among remaining finishers. A trophy will be presented to the winning owner. Closed Saturday, May 29, 2004 with 25 Nominations.

Value of Race: $250,000 Winner $150,000; second $50,000; third $25,000; fourth $12,500; fifth $7,500; sixth $5,000. Mutuel Pool $716,348.00 Exacta Pool $475,030.00 Trifecta Pool $306,399.00

Last Raced	Horse	M/Eqt.	A.	Wt	PP	St	¼	½	¾	Str	Fin	Jockey	Odds $1
15May04 8Pim1	Seattle Fitz-Arg	L	5	116	1	3	2½	1hd	1½	1½	1½	Migliore R	3.00
14May04 11Pim5	Dynever	L	4	117	4	4	6	5½	4½	22½	22¾	Nakatani C S	1.60
3Apr04 9GP2	Newfoundland	L b	4	115	2	6	4½	24½	25½	37	35¾	Velazquez J R	3.25
13May04 8Bel1	Angelic Aura	L b	4	111	6	1	1hd	43	57	510	41¼	Bridgmohan S X	10.30
30Apr04 6CD1	Congrats	L	4	115	3	5	3hd	3hd	3hd	41½	514¾	Castellano J J	4.80
2May04 8Aqu1	Gander	L	8	114	5	2	54½	6	6	6	6	Gryder A T	25.50

OFF AT 4:20 Start Good . Won driving. Track fast.

TIME :23^2, :45^1, 1:08^2, 1:33^2, 1:46^1 (:23.41, :45.34, 1:08.56, 1:33.40, 1:46.30)

$2 Mutuel Prices:				
	1 – SEATTLE FITZ-ARG	8.00	3.60	2.40
	4 – DYNEVER		3.00	2.20
	2 – NEWFOUNDLAND			2.40

$2 EXACTA 1–4 PAID $20.40 $2 TRIFECTA 1–4–2 PAID $41.60

Dk. b or br. h, (Oct), by Fitzcarraldo–Arg – Hug a Slew , by Seattle Slew . Trainer McLaughlin Kiaran P. Bred by Firmamento (Arg).

SEATTLE FITZ (ARG) contested the pace from the outside, drew clear between calls entering the stretch, dug in gamely on the rail and held off DYNEVER after a long drive. DYNEVER was outrun early, rallied inside on the turn, came wide into the stretch and finished gamely outside. NEWFOUNDLAND contested the pace along the inside and tired in the stretch. ANGELIC AURA showed speed while three wide and faded after the opening half mile. CONGRATS raced close up inside, chased the pace for three quarters and tired. GANDER was hustled along outside, had no response when roused and tired.

Owners– 1, West Point Stable; 2, Karches Peter F Wills Catherine R; 3, Sumaya Us Stables; 4, Goldfarb Sanford J; 5, Dilschneider Adele B Claiborne Farm; 6, Gatsas Thoroughbreds LLC

Trainers– 1, McLaughlin Kiaran P; 2, Clement Christophe; 3, Pletcher Todd A; 4, Klesaris Steve; 5, McGaughey III Claude R; 6, Terranova John P II

Scratched– Country Be Gold (25May04 8Del2)

$2 Pick Three (12–1–1) Paid $350.00 ; Pick Three Pool $108,606 .
$2 Daily Double (1–1) Paid $41.20 ; Daily Double Pool $145,729 .

FIFTH RACE
Churchill
JUNE 12, 2004

1⅛ MILES. (Turf) (1.46^1) 27TH RUNNING OF THE JEFFERSON CUP. Grade III. Purse $200,000 FOR THREE-YEAR-OLDS. By subscription of $200 each on or before May 29, 2004 or by supplementary nomination of $10,000 at time of entry. $1,000 to pass the entry box; $1,000 additional to star. Weight 122 lbs. Non-winners of $50,000 twice on the turf allowed 2 lbs.; a sweepstakes on the turf, 4 lbs.; two races at a mile or over other than maiden or claiming, 6 lbs.; a race other than claiming on the turf, 8 lbs. If the race is moved to the main track after the time of closing, a horse may be scratched forany reason at any time up to 15 minutes prior to post time for the race preceding this race or thereafter with a valid physical reason and approved by the stewards. (If this race is taken off the turf it will be downgraded one grade level for this running only in accordance with American Graded Stakes Committee policy). Closed May 29, 2004 with 36 nominations.

Value of Race: $226,200 Winner $140,244; second $45,240; third $22,620; fourth $11,310; fifth $6,786. Mutuel Pool $379,475.00 Exacta Pool $289,040.00 Trifecta Pool $248,999.00 Superfecta Pool $90,621.00

Last Raced	Horse	M/Eqt.	A.	Wt	PP	St	¼	½	¾	Str	Fin	Jockey	Odds $1
30Apr04 9CD2	Prince Arch	L b	3	120	3	9	9	7½	85	32½	1hd	Blanc B	5.50
30Apr04 9CD1	Kitten's Joy	L	3	122	8	4	8hd	6½	41½	1hd	24¾	Bailey J D	0.70
16May04 9CD1	Cool Conductor	b	3	116	4	2	12	12	1½	22	31¼	Velasquez C	10.70
5May04 7Hol1	Terroplane-FR	L b	3	118	5	7	4hd	4hd	6hd	41½	41½	Espinoza V	4.40
26May04 4CD3	Mighty Military	L b	3	116	2	6	31	31	5hd	62	5no	McKee J	10.90
30Apr04 9CD3	Capo	L b	3	116	7	8	7hd	81	71½	51½	68½	Day P	17.30
23May04 9Crc1	More Bourb	L	3	118	9	5	51½	5½	3hd	73	72	Douglas R R	29.40
22May04 10CD1	Radiant Cat	L	3	116	1	3	6hd	9	9	9	83½	Guidry M	54.10
26May04 4CD4	Bogangles	L f	3	116	6	1	2hd	2½	2½	83	9	Albarado R J	58.90

OFF AT 3:13 Start Good . Won driving. Course yielding.

TIME :24, :49, 1:13^4, 1:38^1, 1:50^3 (:24.14, :49.18, 1:13.98, 1:38.36, 1:50.61)

$2 Mutuel Prices:				
	4 – PRINCE ARCH	13.00	3.40	2.80
	9 – KITTEN'S JOY		2.40	2.20
	5 – COOL CONDUCTOR			3.60

$2 EXACTA 4–9 PAID $28.20 $2 TRIFECTA 4–9–5 PAID $136.80
$2 SUPERFECTA 4–9–5–6 PAID $430.40

B. c, (May), by Arch – Princess Kris–GB , by Kris–GB . Trainer McPeek Kenneth G. Bred by Pine Lake Bloodstock LLC (Ky).

PRINCE ARCH broke out bumping COOL CONDUCTOR at the start, settled inside, saved ground when rallying into the stretch, worked his way out five wide in the final sixteenth and closed relentlessly under pressure to be along in time. KITTEN'S JOY, unhurried early, edged up four or five wide on the backstretch, commenced his bid three furlongs out, took over nearing the final furlong, opened a clear lead, then failed to contain the winner's surge. COOL CONDUCTOR, bumped by the winner at the start, moved to the fore near the inside soon after, made the pace until the final furlong and faltered. TERROPLANE (FR), never far back while racing between foes, eased outside rivals to be seven wide at the quarter-mile ground, remained prominent into the final furlong but was empty late. MIGHTY MILITARY, forwardly placed inside early, was shuffled back a bit on the far turn, came out five or six wide for the drive and failed to respond. CAPO, unhurried early, raced five or six wide, was between horses while continuing off the inside into the final furlong and flattened out. MORE BOURB followed the leaders in a striking position five wide to the stretch and tired. RADIANT CAT, inside early, moved out six or seven wide on the backstretch, continued wide and never menaced. BOGANGLES chased front-running COOL CONDUCTOR from between horses four wide for six furlongs and tired.

Owners– 1, Cottrell Raymond H Sr; 2, Ramsey Kenneth L and Sarah K; 3, Garner David E; 4, David Bienstock Neil Papiano and Charles Winner; 5, Walts David Stable LLC; 6, Eaglestone Farm; 7, Oxbow Racing LLC; 8, McKee Stables Inc; 9, Mahler Ken

Trainers– 1, McPeek Kenneth G; 2, Romans Dale; 3, Mott William I; 4, Drysdale Neil; 5, Holthus Robert E; 6, Nafzger Carl A; 7, Preston Stephanie; 8, Romans Dale; 9, Kenneally Eddie

Scratched– Lods (21May04 8AP 2)

$2 Pick Three (3–6–4) Paid $649.80 ; Pick Three Pool $57,359 .

SIXTH RACE
Churchill
JUNE 12, 2004

$1\frac{1}{16}$ MILES. (1.41^{3}) 3RD RUNNING OF THE NORTHERN DANCER. Grade III. Purse $200,000 FOR THREE-YEAR-OLDS. By subscription of $200 each on or before May 29, 2004 or by supplementary nomination of $10,000 at time of entry. $1,000 to pass the entry box; $1,000 additional to start, with $200,000 added of which 62% of all monies to the ownerof the winner, 20% to second, 10% to third, 5% to fourth and 3% to fifth. Weight 122 lbs. Non-winners of $50,000 twice at a mile or over allowed 2 lbs.; $50,000 at a mile or over, 4 lbs.; three races at a mile or over other than maiden or claiming, 6lbs.; two races at a mile or over other than maiden or claiming, 8 lbs. Starters to be named through the entry box at the usual time of closing. All supplementary nominations will be required to pay entry and starting fees if they participate. Trophy to winning owner. Closed Saturday, May 29, 2004 with 42 nominations.

Value of Race: $232,400 Winner $144,088; second $46,480; third $23,240; fourth $11,620; fifth $6,972. Mutuel Pool $474,020.00 Exacta Pool $376,519.00 Trifecta Pool $282,712.00 Superfecta Pool $85,269.00

Last Raced	Horse	M/Eqt.	A.	Wt	PP	St	¼	½	¾	Str	Fin	Jockey	Odds $1
17Apr04 ^{9}Kee^{12}	Suave	L b	3	114	4	1	2^{1}	2^{hd}	$2\frac{1}{2}$	$2^{1\frac{1}{2}}$	1^{3}	Bejarano R	11.60
8May04 ^{7}CD^{1}	J Town	L	3	114	10	4	$1^{1\frac{1}{2}}$	$1^{2\frac{1}{2}}$	$1\frac{1}{2}$	1^{1}	2^{3}	Day P	2.90
12May04 ^{7}Bel^{1}	Ecclesiastic	L	3	114	6	5	$5\frac{1}{2}$	$6\frac{1}{2}$	4^{hd}	$4\frac{1}{2}$	$3\frac{3}{4}$	Bailey J D	10.60
22May04 ^{8}CD^{2}	TwoDownAutomtic	L b	3	114	9	3	$3^{1\frac{1}{2}}$	3^{2}	3^{3}	3^{3}	$4\frac{1}{2}$	Albarado R J	2.40
27May04 ^{5}CD^{1}	Chippewa Trail	L	3	114	7	12	10^{4}	8^{1}	7^{hd}	5^{4}	5^{nk}	Peck B D	91.30
27Mar04 NAS^{5}	Ascertain-Ire	L	3	116	11	11	12	12	12	$9\frac{1}{2}$	6^{4}	Guidry M	41.10
12May04 ^{9}CD^{4}	Gran Prospect	L f	3	114	2	10	11^{1}	$11^{5\frac{1}{2}}$	11^{5}	10^{1}	7no	Perret C	13.70
20May04 ^{8}CD^{2}	Texas Deputy	L f	3	114	1	2	$7\frac{1}{2}$	$9\frac{1}{2}$	10^{1}	$7\frac{1}{2}$	8^{1}	Melancon L	46.10
14May04 ^{8}Bel^{1}	Indian War Dance	L b	3	114	12	8	6^{1}	5^{2}	6^{1}	6^{1}	$9^{1\frac{3}{4}}$	McKee J	16.10
8May04 ^{7}CD^{2}	Grande's Grandslam	L	3	114	5	9	$9\frac{1}{2}$	10^{4}	9^{1}	8^{hd}	10^{3}	Blanc B	17.20
14May04 ^{7}Bel^{2}	Shaniko	L b	3	114	3	7	8^{2}	7^{1}	8^{1}	12	$11^{2\frac{1}{2}}$	Espinoza V	5.60
22May04 ^{8}CD^{1}	Courageous Act	L	3	114	8	6	$4\frac{1}{2}$	4^{hd}	5^{hd}	11^{1}	12	Velasquez C	9.30

OFF AT 3:45 Start Good . Won driving. Track sloppy.

TIME :23^{3}, :47^{2}, 1:12, 1:37^{4}, 1:44^{2} (:23.77, :47.46, 1:12.12, 1:37.82, 1:44.50)

$2 Mutuel Prices:				
	4 – SUAVE	**25.20**	**11.80**	**7.60**
	10 – J TOWN		**5.40**	**4.20**
	6 – ECCLESIASTIC			**7.40**

$2 EXACTA 4–10 PAID $126.20 $2 TRIFECTA 4–10–6 PAID $1,214.80
$2 SUPERFECTA 4–10–6–9 PAID $3,212.40

B. c, (May), by A.P. Indy – Urbane , by Citidancer . Trainer McGee Paul J. Bred by Jan Siegel Mace Siegel & &Samantha Siegel (Ky).

SUAVE tracked front-running J TOWN from early on while three or four wide, was asked for more leaving the three furlong marker, took over nearing the final sixteenth and drove clear. J TOWN gained the lead early, edged near the inside while opening a clear advantage, made the pace into the final furlong but wasn't a match for the winner late. ECCLESIASTIC, well placed near the inside to the stretch, eased out four or five wide for the drive but lacked a late response. TWO DOWN AUTOMATIC stalked the pace four or five wide, moved with the winner while outside that one into the stretch but weakened. CHIPPEWA TRAIL hoped while breaking slowly, moved inside, made a mild run near the inside into the upper stretch but couldn't sustain the needed momentum. ASCERTAIN (IRE), outrun early, angled in a bit, circled horses 10 wide into the upper stretch and offered a minor gain. GRAN PROSPECT, outrun to the stretch, came out six or seven wide and improved position. TEXAS DEPUTY raced near the inside and failed to rally. INDIAN WAR DANCE raced forwardly for six furlongs and tired. GRANDE'S GRANDSLAM wasn't a factor. SHANIKO failed to menace. COURAGEOUS ACT faded after six furlongs.

Owners– 1, Jay Em Ess Stable; 2, Golden Orb Farm; 3, Allen Joseph; 4, Dapple Stable LLC; 5, Briland Farm; 6, Paul J Dixon Gene Voss and Mrs S K Johnston Jr; 7, Carey Thomas M; 8, Stonerside Stable LLC; 9, Goldfarb Sanford et al; 10, Fulton Stan E; 11, Jones Aaron U and Marie D; 12, Lewis Robert B and Beverly J

Trainers– 1, McGee Paul J; 2, McPeek Kenneth G; 3, McLaughlin Kiaran P; 4, Asmussen Steven M; 5, Reinstedler Anthony; 6, O'Callaghan Niall M; 7, Vestal Peter M; 8, Flint Bernard S; 9, Dutrow Richard E Jr; 10, Carroll David; 11, Pletcher Todd A; 12, Baffert Bob

$2 Pick Three (6–4–4) Paid $1,891.20 ; Pick Three Pool $52,536 .

SEVENTH RACE
Churchill
JUNE 12, 2004

1⅛ MILES. (Turf) (1.46^{1}) 35TH RUNNING OF THE REGRET. Grade III. Purse $200,000 FOR FILLIES, THREE YEARS OLD. By subscription of $200 each on or before May 29, 2004 or by supplementary nomination of $10,000 at time of entry. $1,000 to pass the entry box; $1,000 additional to start, with $200,000 added of which 62% of all monies tothe owner of the winner, 20% to second, 10% to third, 5% to fourth and 3% to fifth. Weight 122 lbs. Non–winners of $50,000 twice on the turf allowed 2 lbs.; a sweepstakes on the turf, 4 lbs.; two races at a mile or over other than maiden or claiming, 6lbs.; a race other than claiming on the turf, 8 lbs. If the race is moved to the main track after the time of closing, a horse may be scratched for any reason at any time up to fifteen (15) minutes prior to post time for the race preceding this race orthereafter with a valid physical reason and approved by the stewards. The entry fee if applicable, will be refunded for scratches made in compliance with the above conditions. Starters to be named through the entry box at the usual time of closing.Trophy to winning owner. (If this race is taken off the turf it will be downgraded one grade level for this running only in accordance with American Graded Stakes Committee policy). Closed Saturday, May 29, 2004 with 34 nominations.

Value of Race: $221,800 Winner $137,516; second $44,360; third $22,180; fourth $11,090; fifth $6,654. Mutuel Pool $466,777.00 Exacta Pool $323,664.00 Trifecta Pool $254,444.00 Superfecta Pool $71,639.00

Last Raced	Horse	M/Eqt.	A.	Wt	PP	St	¼	½	¾	Str	Fin	Jockey	Odds $1
22May04 ^{4}CD^{2}	Sister Star	L	3	116	4	5	2^{1}	2^{hd}	$2^{\frac{1}{2}}$	1^{hd}	$1^{3\frac{3}{4}}$	Blanc B	8.00
8May04 ^{9}Pim^{1}	Western Ransom	L	3	120	1	2	3^{hd}	$3^{1\frac{1}{2}}$	4^{hd}	$3^{2\frac{1}{2}}$	2^{hd}	Day P	2.50
22May04 ^{4}CD^{1}	Jinny's Gold	L	3	118	3	1	$1^{1\frac{1}{2}}$	$1^{1\frac{1}{2}}$	1^{1}	2^{2}	$3^{1\frac{1}{4}}$	Guidry M	3.10
22May04 ^{4}CD^{3}	Shadow Cast	L b	3	118	5	4	4^{1}	$4^{\frac{1}{2}}$	3^{1}	4^{hd}	$4^{1\frac{1}{4}}$	Albarado R J	9.20
24Apr04 ^{6}CD^{2}	Pretty Jane	L b	3	116	2	3	$5^{\frac{1}{2}}$	$6^{2\frac{1}{2}}$	7	6^{1}	5^{2}	Velasquez C	28.50
30Apr04 ^{5}CD^{2}	Gingham and Lace	L	3	116	7	7	$6^{1\frac{1}{2}}$	5^{hd}	5^{2}	$5^{1\frac{1}{2}}$	$6^{\frac{1}{2}}$	Bailey J D	2.60
19May04 ^{7}CD^{3}	Baxter Hall	L	3	116	6	6	7	7	6^{hd}	7	7	Peck B D	5.40

OFF AT 4:15 Start Good . Won driving. Course yielding.

TIME :24, :49^{3}, 1:14^{2}, 1:39, 1:51^{2} (:24.19, :49.70, 1:14.46, 1:39.06, 1:51.40)

$2 Mutuel Prices:				
	4 – SISTER STAR	18.00	7.00	4.20
	1 – WESTERN RANSOM		3.40	2.80
	3 – JINNY'S GOLD			3.40

$2 EXACTA 4–1 PAID $61.00 $2 TRIFECTA 4–1–3 PAID $325.20
$2 SUPERFECTA 4–1–3–5 PAID $1,706.60

Dk. b or br. f, (Jan), by Langfuhr – Little Irish Nut , by Irish Tower . Trainer McPeek Kenneth G. Bred by John C Marker (Ky).

SISTER STAR tracked front-running JINNY'S GOLD from early on under light rating four wide, was put to a drive leaving the three-eighths pole, came out farther on the course entering the upper stretch when the leader floated out, reached the front just before the eighth pole, edged nearer the inside soon after and drove clear. WESTERN RANSOM, well placed inside from the start, saved ground to the stretch, angled out five wide into the stretch and closed determinedly to wear down JINNY'S GOLD for the place. JINNY'S GOLD gained the lead early, raced in the three path, floated out five or six wide entering the stretch and weakened the last eighth. SHADOW CAST followed the leaders within easy striking distance five wide into the stretch and failed to offer a closing account. PRETTY JANE settled near the inside, lost a bit of position on the far turn, angled out six or seven wide entering the lane and lacked a closing bid. GINGHAM AND LACE, between foes early, was in placed in a striking position five wide from the backstretch on and came up empty. BAXTER HALL failed to menace.

Owners– 1, Marker John C and Julie; 2, Chandler Dr John A; 3, Richard S Kaster and Frederick C Wieting; 4, Farish William S Jr; 5, Redmond Garrett; 6, Lazy Lane Farms Inc; 7, Willmott Stables Inc

Trainers– 1, McPeek Kenneth G; 2, Dickinson Michael W; 3, Romans Dale; 4, Howard Neil J; 5, Caramori Eduardo; 6, Brothers Frank L; 7, Reinstedler Anthony

Scratched– Avaricity (29May04 ^{8}CD ^{4})

$2 Pick Three (4–4–4) Paid $942.80 ; Pick Three Pool $72,027 .
$2 Consolation Pick 3 (4–4–6) Paid $143.20 .

EIGHTH RACE
Churchill
JUNE 12, 2004

1⅛ MILES. (1.47^{1}) 30TH RUNNING OF THE FLEUR DE LIS HANDICAP. Grade II. Purse $400,000 FOR FILLIES AND MARES, THREE YEARS OLD AND UPWARD. By subscription of $400 each on or before May 29, 2004 or by supplementary nomination of $20,000 each by the closing of entries Friday, June 4, 2004. $2,000 to pass the entry box; $2,000 additional to start, with $400,000 added of which 62% of all monies to the owner of the winner, 20% to second, 10% to third, 5% to fourth and 3% to fifth. Weights to be announced Saturday, June 5, 2004. Starters to be named through the entry box at the usual time ofclosing. Trophy to winning owner. Closed Saturday, May 29, 2004 with 23 nominations.

Value of Race: $439,200 Winner $272,304; second $87,840; third $43,920; fourth $21,960; fifth $13,176. Mutuel Pool $495,580.00 Exacta Pool $316,030.00 Trifecta Pool $225,742.00 Superfecta Pool $68,389.00

Last Raced	Horse	M/Eqt.	A.	Wt	PP	St	¼	½	¾	Str	Fin	Jockey	Odds $1
9May04 ^{8}Hol^{2}	Adoration	L	5	122	1	3	$2^{1\frac{1}{2}}$	$2^{\frac{1}{2}}$	2^{1}	$1^{2\frac{1}{2}}$	$1^{1\frac{1}{4}}$	Espinoza V	2.50
24Apr04 ^{8}Haw^{2}	Bare Necessities	L	5	120	5	5	5^{hd}	$5^{1\frac{1}{2}}$	$5^{2\frac{1}{2}}$	$2^{\frac{1}{2}}$	$2^{3\frac{3}{4}}$	Douglas R R	2.40
30Apr04 ^{8}CD^{5}	La Reason	L f	4	110	6	6	6	6	6	4^{hd}	3^{2}	McKee J	50.20
14May04 ^{8}Pim^{6}	Angela's Love	L	4	114	4	2	3^{hd}	$4^{2\frac{1}{2}}$	3^{hd}	$3^{1\frac{1}{2}}$	4^{3}	Guidry M	11.00
30Apr04 ^{8}CD^{2}	Yell	L	4	115	2	1	4^{5}	$3^{\frac{1}{2}}$	4^{1}	6	$5^{5\frac{3}{4}}$	Day P	2.10
15May04 ^{8}Bel^{3}	Roar Emotion	L	4	115	3	4	1^{1}	1^{1}	$1^{\frac{1}{2}}$	$5^{\frac{1}{2}}$	6	Bailey J D	4.00

OFF AT 4:44 Start Good . Won driving. Track sloppy.

TIME :23^{1}, :47^{3}, 1:12^{4}, 1:38^{4}, 1:52 (:23.34, :47.78, 1:12.85, 1:38.93, 1:52.15)

$2 Mutuel Prices:				
	1 – ADORATION	7.00	3.60	3.00
	8 – BARE NECESSITIES		3.40	2.80
	9 – LA REASON			4.60

$2 EXACTA 1–8 PAID $19.40 $2 TRIFECTA 1–8–9 PAID $269.60
$2 SUPERFECTA 1–8–9–4 PAID $1,096.80

B. m, (Apr), by Honor Grades – Sewing Lady , by Key to the Mint . Trainer Hofmans David. Bred by Lucy G Bassett (Ky).

ADORATION eased off the inside on the first turn, tracked front-running ROAR EMOTION three wide under light rating, inched to challenge midway on the far turn, reached the front entering the upper stretch, took over, opened a clear lead, then was under stout right-handed encouragement the remainder to hold sway. BARE NECESSITIES, unhurried early, raced three or four wide, briefly awaited room leaving the three-sixteenths pole, angled outside the winner to made a bid between foes five wide and was second best. LA REASON, reserved early and angled inside, saved ground into the stretch, came out four wide, angled inside the winner in the late going and offered a minor gain. ANGELA'S LOVE stalked the pace within easy striking distance four or five wide into the stretch and came up empty. YELL, close up at once, was eased back from between foes approaching the first turn, raced in behind front-running ROAR EMOTION, raced in a challenging position to the stretch, eased out three wide but was empty. ROAR EMOTION bobbled lightly at the start, moved to the fore soon after, raced near the inside, managed a narrow advantage to the stretch and faded.

Owners– 1, Amerman Racing Stables LLC; 2, Iron County Farms Inc; 3, K and K Racing Stable LLC; 4, Poston Bill and Vicki; 5, Claiborne Farm and Dilschneider Adele B; 6, Allen Joseph

Trainers– 1, Hofmans David; 2, Kirby Frank J; 3, Vance David R; 4, Romans Dale; 5, McGaughey III Claude R; 6, McLaughlin Kiaran P

Scratched– Miss Fortunate (05May04 ^{9}CD ^{1}) , Mayo On the Side (01May04 ^{8}CD ^{1}) , Cat Fighter (30Apr04 ^{8}CD ^{3})

$2 Pick Three (4–4–1) Paid $1,335.40 ; Pick Three Pool $49,733 .
$2 Consolation Pick 3 (4–6–1) Paid $87.60 .

NINTH RACE
Churchill
JUNE 12, 2004

1⅛ MILES. (1.47¹) 23RD RUNNING OF THE STEPHEN FOSTER HANDICAP. Grade I. Purse $750,000 FOR THREE-YEAR-OLDS AND UPWARD. By subscription of $750 each on or before May 29, 2004 or by supplementary nomination of $37,500 each by the closing of entries Friday, June 4, 2004. $3,750 to pass the entry box; $3,750 additional to start, with $750,000added of which 62% of all monies to the owner of the winner, 20% to second, 10% to third, 5% to fourth and 3% to fifth. Weights to be announced Saturday, June 5, 2004. Starters to be named through the entry box at the usual time of closing. Trophy to winning owner. Closed Saturday, May 29, 2004 with 21 nominations.

Value of Race: $810,750 Winner $502,665; second $162,150; third $81,075; fourth $40,538; fifth $24,322. Mutuel Pool $893,725.00 Exacta Pool $471,839.00 Trifecta Pool $349,654.00 Superfecta Pool $125,155.00

Last Raced	Horse	M/Eqt.	A.	Wt	PP	St	¼	½	¾	Str	Fin	Jockey	Odds $1
23May04 9CD5	Colonial Colony	L f	6	111	6	3	6	6	2hd	2 1½	1no	Bejarano R	62.60
14May04 11Pim1	Southern Image	L f	4	122	3	6	3 1½	2hd	4 2	1hd	2 5	Espinoza V	1.50
30Apr04 6CD2	Perfect Drift	L	5	119	1	4	5 4½	5 2½	5hd	3½	3 3¾	Day P	4.20
3Apr04 11OP1	Peace Rules	L	4	121	2	2	1 1½	1 1½	1 1½	4 7	4 7½	Bailey J D	2.80
20May04 8CD1	Best Minister	L	4	113	5	1	4½	4hd	6	6	5nk	Blanc B	29.30
14May04 11Pim2	Midway Road	L	4	116	4	5	2hd	3 1½	3hd	5 1½	6	Albarado R J	2.20

OFF AT 5:15 Start Good. Won driving. Track sloppy.

TIME :23⁴, :47³, 1:12², 1:37², 1:50² (:23.89, :47.77, 1:12.40, 1:37.44, 1:50.40)

$2 Mutuel Prices:			
6 – COLONIAL COLONY	127.20	22.00	5.40
3 – SOUTHERN IMAGE		3.40	2.60
1 – PERFECT DRIFT			3.40

$2 EXACTA 6–3 PAID $348.20 $2 TRIFECTA 6–3–1 PAID $1,264.20
$2 SUPERFECTA 6–3–1–2 PAID $2,938.40

Dk. b or br. h, (Apr), by Pleasant Colony – Jen's Fashion, by Northern Fashion. Trainer Bindner Walter M Jr. Bred by Chris Nolan (Ky).

COLONIAL COLONY, reserved early and angled in to race two or three wide, moved out five or six wide entering the backstretch, was put to a drive leaving the half-mile ground while continuing well off the inside, engaged SOUTHERN IMAGE a furlong out, headed that one about the sixteenth pole, lost the advantage back to SOUTNERN IMAGE when bumped by that one soon after, then came again under vigorous hand urging to prevail in the last lunge. SOUTHERN IMAGE, well placed inside from early on, was a bit rank during the much of the backstretch when lacking room and pocketed inside of MIDWAY ROAD and behind front-running PEACE RULES, eased outside latter at the five-sixteenth when an opening appeared, reached the front in the upper stretch while four or five wide, was headed about the sixteenth-pole from the outside by COLONIAL COLONY, recaptured the advantage soon after when roused left-handed, bumped with COLONIAL COLONY, then was outfinished. PERFECT DRIFT, lightly rated within easy striking distance near the inside from early on, eased out five wide approaching the stretch, made a bold run outside the top two into the final furlong but flattened out when the test came. PEACE RULES moved to the fore near the inside early, opened a clear advantage, made the pace into the upper stretch and weakened. BEST MINISTER, lightly rated early while tracking the leaders four or five wide, was with the winner while inside that one leaving the backstretch but couldn't keep pace. MIDWAY ROAD hopped at the start, moved up soon after to press pacesetting PEACE RULES three or four wide, continued forwardly until nearing the stretch and faded.

Owners– 1, Lakeside Farms LLC; 2, Blahut Stables LLC Kagele Brothers Tepper Allen et al; 3, Stonecrest Farm; 4, Gann Edmund A; 5, Phillips Racing Partnership; 6, Farish William S

Trainers– 1, Bindner Walter M Jr; 2, Machowsky Michael; 3, Johnson Murray W; 4, Frankel Robert; 5, McPeek Kenneth G; 6, Howard Neil J

$2 Pick Three (4–1–6) Paid $5,518.00; Pick Three Pool $74,938.
$2 Pick Four (4–4–1–6) Paid $120,119.60; Pick Four Pool $296,592.
$2 Pick Six (6–4–4–4–1–6) 4 Correct Paid $614.60; Pick Six Pool $48,561; Carryover Pool $70,884.

THIRD RACE
Hollywood
JUNE 12, 2004

$1\frac{1}{4}$ MILES. (Turf) (1.57^{3}) 36TH RUNNING OF THE CHARLES WHITTINGHAM MEMORIAL HANDICAP. Grade I. Purse $350,000 FOR THREE YEAR OLDS AND UPWARD. By subscription of $350 each on or before Thursday, June 3 or by supplementary nomination of $7,000 each by 3:00 pm Saturday, June 5. $1,750 additional to pass the entry box and $1,750 additional to start, with $210,000 tothe winner, $70,000 to second, $42,000 to third, $21,000 to fourth and $7,000 to fifth. Weights Sunday, June 6. Starters to be named through the entry box by closing time of entries. Trophies will be presented to the winning owner and trainer. Closed with 21 nominations.

Value of Race: $350,000 Winner $210,000; second $70,000; third $42,000; fourth $21,000; fifth $7,000. Mutuel Pool $633,836.00 Exacta Pool $373,929.00 Quinella Pool $30,356.00 Trifecta Pool $337,066.00 Superfecta Pool $115,224.00

Last Raced	Horse	M/Eqt.	A.	Wt	PP	¼	½	¾	1	Str	Fin	Jockey	Odds $1
14Dec03 ^{9}ST^{14}	Sabiango-Ger	LB	6	116	3	1^{1}	$1^{1\frac{1}{2}}$	$1^{2\frac{1}{2}}$	1^{3}	$1^{1\frac{1}{2}}$	$1^{\frac{3}{4}}$	Baze T C	13.40
5May04 ^{5}Hol^{1}	Bayamo-Ire	LB	5	116	4	8^{hd}	8^{1}	7^{hd}	4^{1}	2^{1}	2no	Flores D R	5.40
1May04 ^{6}Hol^{5}	Just Wonder-GB	LB	4	116	5	$10^{1\frac{1}{2}}$	10^{1}	9^{1}	$6^{1\frac{1}{2}}$	3^{hd}	$3^{2\frac{1}{2}}$	Smith M E	11.70
2May04 ^{10}LCH^{7}	Vangelis	L	5	117	11	7^{1}	$7^{\frac{1}{2}}$	8^{1}	9^{2}	$8^{1\frac{1}{2}}$	4^{nk}	Santiago Javier	7.70
8May04 ^{7}Hol^{2}	Continental Red	LB	8	116	10	2^{hd}	$2^{\frac{1}{2}}$	2^{1}	2^{1}	$4^{\frac{1}{2}}$	5no	Court J K	12.10
16Feb04 ^{9}SA^{2}	Continuously	LB	5	116	9	11	11	11	8^{1}	7^{2}	$6^{\frac{1}{2}}$	Solis A	3.60
30May04 ^{1}Hol^{2}	Musical Chimes	LB	4	116	1	$4^{\frac{1}{2}}$	$4^{\frac{1}{2}}$	$3^{\frac{1}{2}}$	3^{hd}	$5^{1\frac{1}{2}}$	$7^{\frac{1}{2}}$	Desormeaux K J	4.10
1May04 ^{6}Hol^{7}	Seinne-Chi	LB	7	113	7	3^{1}	3^{1}	4^{hd}	5^{1}	$6^{\frac{1}{2}}$	8^{1}	Ruis M	38.20
8May04 ^{7}Hol^{3}	Gassan Royal	LB	4	113	6	$9^{1\frac{1}{2}}$	$9^{\frac{1}{2}}$	10^{hd}	10^{hd}	9^{3}	9^{5}	Bisono A	10.70
13May04 ^{7}Hol^{4}	Hawkeye-Ire	LB	6	112	8	5^{1}	5^{1}	5^{1}	11	10	10	Almeida G F	52.00
1May04 ^{6}Hol^{4}	Irish Warrior	LB	6	115	2	6^{hd}	6^{1}	6^{1}	7^{hd}	—	—	Valdivia J Jr	5.60

OFF AT 2:33 Start Good . Won driving. Course firm.

TIME :25^{4}, :50^{3}, 1:15, 1:38^{1}, 2:01^{2} (:25.91, :50.68, 1:15.12, 1:38.39, 2:01.52)

$2 Mutuel Prices:

3 – SABIANGO–GER	28.80	14.60	12.00
4 – BAYAMO–IRE		9.20	6.60
5 – JUST WONDER–GB			8.80

$1 EXACTA 3–4 PAID $117.40 $2 QUINELLA 3–4 PAID $130.80
$1 TRIFECTA 3–4–5 PAID $1,310.50 $1 SUPERFECTA 3–4–5–11 PAID $22,848.90

Ch. h, (Apr), by Acatenango-Ger – Spirit of Eagles , by Beau's Eagle . Trainer Baffert Bob. Bred by Stiftung Gestut Fahrhof (Ger).

SABIANGO (GER) took the early lead, set a slow pace along the inside, opened up some on the backstretch, continued clear into the stretch and held on gamely under urging. BAYAMO (IRE) off a bit slowly and brushed with JUST WONDER, chased inside, split horses into the second turn, moved up on that bend, continued just off the inside into the stretch, could not quite catch the winner but narrowly held second. JUST WONDER (GB) settled inside, moved up outside a rival on the second turn, bid inside in the stretch, had the rider lose the whip late and just missed the place. VANGELIS settled three deep then outside a rival, came out into the stretch and found his best stride late. CONTINENTAL RED stalked outside a rival then off the rail, was between horses on the second turn and into the stretch and weakened. CONTINUOUSLY unhurried and angled in early, settled off the rail on the backstretch, moved up inside on the second turn, came out into the stretch and could not offer the necessary late kick. MUSICAL CHIMES stalked inside then came out when in tight off heels into the first turn, stalked between horses on the backstretch, went three deep on the second turn, came out some into the stretch and weakened. SEINNE (CHI) angled in entering the first turn,.stalked inside, dropped back some leaving the second turn and also weakened. GASSAN ROYAL allowed to settle outside a rival, continued off the rail on the second turn, came out into the stretch and did not rally. HAWKEYE (IRE) forced out into the first turn, stalked three deep on the backstretch, fell back on the second turn and had little left. IRISH WARRIOR stalked inside then a bit off the rail, was between horses leaving the backstretch, then was pulled up into the stretch and was vanned off.

Owners– 1, Monty Roberts; 2, Prestonwood Farm LLC; 3, Naify Sugarman and Vistas LLC et al; 4, Bloodstock Management Services Inc; 5, Fitzpatrick Sharon M; 6, Khaled Saud b; 7, Al Maktoum Sheik Maktoum b; 8, Hunt Nelson B; 9, Hatake Shigehiro and Nishimura Semji; 10, Tanaka Gary A; 11, Coleman John Dasaro George Thompson James et al

Trainers– 1, Baffert Bob; 2, Canani Julio C; 3, De Seroux Laura; 4, Dupre Alain D; 5, Jory Ian P D; 6, Frankel Robert; 7, Drysdale Neil; 8, McAnally Ronald; 9, Frankel Robert; 10, Burke Donald J II; 11, Dollase Wallace

$2 Daily Double (8–3) Paid $177.20 ; Daily Double Pool $36,320 .
$1 Pick Three (10–8–3) Paid $1,642.40 ; Pick Three Pool $115,954 .

FOURTH RACE Hollywood JUNE 12, 2004

1 1/16 MILES. (1.40) 59TH RUNNING OF THE HOLLYWOOD BREEDERS' CUP OAKS. Grade II. Purse $175,000 (includes $50,000 BC – Breeders' Cup) FOR FILLIES THREE-YEARS-OLD. Closed with 13 nominations.

Value of Race: $182,875 Winner $109,725; second $36,575; third $21,945; fourth $10,972; fifth $3,658. Mutuel Pool $451,938.00 Exacta Pool $245,385.00 Quinella Pool $21,794.00 Trifecta Pool $194,202.00

Last Raced	Horse	M/Eqt.	A.	Wt	PP	St	1/4	1/2	3/4	Str	Fin	Jockey	Odds $1
30Apr04 10CD8	House of Fortune	LB	3	119	3	2	1^1	1^½	1^½	1^1½	1^3	Solis A	1.20
2May04 8Hol1	Elusive Diva	LB b	3	115	5	3	2^½	2^1	2^1½	2^1½	2^3	Baze T C	9.70
30Apr04 10CD5	Hollywood Story	LB b	3	119	4	4	5	4^hd	5	3^3	3^8	Smith M E	1.70
2May04 8Hol2	M. A. Fox	LB	3	116	2	1	4^1	5	4^hd	4^hd	4^3½	Desormeaux K J	4.90
30Apr04 10CD11	Class Above	LB b	3	119	1	5	3^1½	3^½	3^½	5	5	Flores D R	7.80

OFF AT 3:05 Start Good. Won ridden out. Track fast.

TIME :23, :46, 1:10, 1:35, 1:41² (:23.12, :46.13, 1:10.17, 1:35.03, 1:41.55)

$2 Mutuel Prices:				
	3 – HOUSE OF FORTUNE	4.40	2.80	2.10
	5 – ELUSIVE DIVA		7.00	2.80
	4 – HOLLYWOOD STORY			2.40

$1 EXACTA 3–5 PAID $14.00 $2 QUINELLA 3–5 PAID $24.40
$1 TRIFECTA 3–5–4 PAID $31.70

Dk. b or br. f, (Mar), by Free House – So Fortunate , by Garthorn . Trainer McAnally Ronald. Bred by John Treasure (Cal).

HOUSE OF FORTUNE took the early lead and set the pace inside, responded when headed leaving the second turn and into the stretch, regained the advantage in upper stretch and pulled clear under a steady hand ride while being shown the whip right handed. ELUSIVE DIVA pulled her way along four wide then three deep early on the first turn, stalked outside a rival then bid outside the winner on the backstretch and second turn, put a head in front leaving that turn, then could not match strides in the stretch but was second best. HOLLYWOOD STORY stalked outside, went three deep on the backstretch and second turn and into the stretch, drifted in late and bested the others. M. A. FOX stalked off the rail then between horses, came out into the stretch and weakened. CLASS ABOVE off a bit slowly, pulled a bit along the inside stalking the pace, dropped back into the stretch and also weakened.

Owners– 1, Zetcher Arnold; 2, Branch Branch Konecny Et Al; 3, Krikorian George; 4, Hughes B Wayne; 5, Padua Stables

Trainers– 1, McAnally Ronald; 2, Glatt Mark; 3, Shirreffs John; 4, Stute Warren; 5, Baffert Bob

Scratched– Boasting (22May04 6Bel1)

$2 Daily Double (3–3) Paid $60.40 ; Daily Double Pool $31,653 .
$1 Pick Three (8–3–3/6) Paid $176.30 ; Pick Three Pool $100,067 .

NINTH RACE Hollywood JUNE 12, 2004

1⅛ MILES. (1.45¹) 51ST RUNNING OF THE CALIFORNIAN. Grade II. Purse $250,000 FOR THREE YEAR OLDS AND UPWARD. Closed with 19 nominations.

Value of Race: $250,000 Winner $150,000; second $50,000; third $30,000; fourth $15,000; fifth $5,000. Mutuel Pool $394,888.00 Exacta Pool $231,318.00 Quinella Pool $17,941.00 Trifecta Pool $247,533.00 Superfecta Pool $125,723.00

Last Raced	Horse	M/Eqt.	A.	Wt	PP	St	1/4	1/2	3/4	Str	Fin	Jockey	Odds $1
8May04 9Hol1	Even the Score	LB b	6	118	8	4	6^2½	6^4	4^hd	1^1	1^3½	Flores D R	0.90
8May04 9Hol3	Total Impact-Chi	LB b	6	116	7	3	4^1	3^½	2^1	2^hd	2^2	Smith M E	5.60
13Mar04 6SA9	Nose The Trade-GB	LB	6	116	2	5	3^hd	4^1	3^hd	4^hd	3^nk	Solis A	5.30
8May04 9Hol6	Gift of the Eagle	LB b	6	116	5	6	5^2	5^½	5^½	5^3	4^1	Court J K	20.80
8May04 9Hol2	Ender's Shadow	LB bf	4	116	3	1	1^½	1^1	1^½	3^1½	5^3	Ruis M	8.40
8May04 9Hol5	Buckland Manor	LB	4	116	6	2	2^½	2^hd	6^6	6^1½	6^½	Santiago Javier	5.90
28May04 5Hol5	Mud Shark	LB b	4	116	4	8	7^10	7^8	7^3½	7^1	7^1	Pedroza M A	32.20
8May04 7Hol5	GenedeCampeo-Brz	LB f	5	116	1	7	8	8	8	8	8	Berrio O A	37.10

OFF AT 5:42 Start Good. Won driving. Track fast.

TIME :23², :46³, 1:10¹, 1:35, 1:47³ (:23.56, :46.66, 1:10.30, 1:35.05, 1:47.64)

$2 Mutuel Prices:				
	9 – EVEN THE SCORE	3.80	2.80	2.20
	8 – TOTAL IMPACT-CHI		4.20	2.60
	2 – NOSE THE TRADE-GB			3.00

$1 EXACTA 9–8 PAID $7.30 $2 QUINELLA 8–9 PAID $10.40
$1 TRIFECTA 9–8–2 PAID $29.60 $1 SUPERFECTA 9–8–2–5 PAID $177.70

Gr/ro. h, (Apr), by Unbridled's Song – Ashtabula , by Rahy . Trainer Cerin Vladimir. Bred by Aspiration Stable (Ky).

EVEN THE SCORE chased outside, moved up four wide on the second turn and three deep into the stretch, gained the lead in upper stretch, inched away in midstretch and won clear under some urging. TOTAL IMPACT (CHI) stalked the pace outside on the first turn and backstretch, bid three deep into the second turn, battled between horses into the stretch, could not match the winner but was clearly second best. NOSE THE TRADE (GB) stalked the leaders along the inside, was bumped into the second turn, came out into the stretch and edged a rival for third. GIFT OF THE EAGLE chased outside a rival then between horses on the second turn, came three deep into the stretch and just missed the show. ENDER'S SHADOW had good early speed outside a rival, angled in leaving the first turn, inched away on the backstretch, dueled inside on the second turn and into the stretch and weakened late. BUCKLAND MANOR forced the pace outside a rival then stalked between foes, was bumped into the second turn and weakened. MUD SHARK off a bit slowly, settled inside chasing the pace and did not rally. GENE DE CAMPEAO (BRZ) bobbled at the start, lagged back inside, came out into the stretch and was not a threat.

Owners– 1, Parra Rosendo G; 2, Al Kabeer Sultan Mohammed Saud and Bridport S A; 3, Tanaka Gary A; 4, Bell Lance and Krikorian George; 5, Green Lantern Stables LLC; 6, McCaffery Trudy and Toffan John A; 7, Jacobs and Pegram; 8, Bandeirantes Stable

Trainers– 1, Cerin Vladimir; 2, De Seroux Laura; 3, Frankel Robert; 4, Shirreffs John; 5, Sahadi Jenine; 6, Gonzalez J Paco; 7, Baffert Bob; 8, Avila A C

Scratched– Fonz's (28May04 5Hol2)

$2 Daily Double (3–9) Paid $24.80 ; Daily Double Pool $33,002 .
$1 Pick Three (5–3–6/9) Paid $32.60 ; Pick Three Pool $76,119 .

FOURTEENTH RACE
Thistledown
JUNE 12, 2004

1⅛ MILES. (1.47^{2}) 70TH RUNNING OF THE OHIO DERBY. Grade II. Purse $350,000 (plus $5,000 OTF – Ohio Thoroughbred Fund) FOR THREE-YEAR-OLDS. By subscription of $350 by Wednesday May 26,2004, Supplementary nominations accepted to the Ohio Derby of $10,000 due Tuesday June 8,2004, $2,500 to enter and $1,000 additional to start with $350,000 Guaranteed, of which 60% to the winner; 20% to second; 10% to third; 5% to fourth; 3% to fifth; and 2% to sixth. Weight: 124 lbs. Non-Winners of $100,000 twice at a mile or over in 2004 allowed 3 lbs; of $100,000 at a mile or over in 2004; 6 lbs; of $100,000 at any distance 9 lbs; of $50,000 at any distance 12 lbs. (MCOS not considered in weight allowances) The Ohio Derby will be limited to fourteen (14) starters, in the event more than fourteen (14) entries pass the entry box by 10:30 A.M.Eastern Standard Time, Wednesday June 9, 2004, preference will be given to those horses having accumulated the highest lifetime earnings at the time of closing entries. Lifetime earnings will be determined according to statistics provided by Equibase. A Trophy to the winning Owner, Trainer & Jockey.

Value of Race: $350,000 Winner $210,000; second $70,000; third $35,000; fourth $17,500; fifth $10,500; sixth $7,000. Mutuel Pool $259,434.00 Exacta Pool $172,438.00 Superfecta Pool $62,725.00 Trifecta Pool $166,862.00

Last Raced	Horse	M/Eqt.	A.	Wt	PP	St	¼	½	¾	Str	Fin	Jockey	Odds $1
19May04 ^{4}CD^{2}	Brass Hat	L b	3	115	5	7	9	9	$8\frac{1}{2}$	$1\frac{1}{2}$	1^{3}	Martinez W	21.40
1May04 ^{10}CD^{17}	Pollard's Vision	L	3	121	1	3	3^{hd}	$4\frac{1}{2}$	$3\frac{1}{2}$	2^{2}	2^{5}	Coa E M	2.30
17Apr04 ^{7}BM^{1}	Trieste's Honor	L b	3	115	8	8	4^{1}	3^{1}	1^{hd}	$3^{1\frac{1}{2}}$	3^{3}	Baze R A	5.80
15May04 ^{9}Pim^{2}	DashboardDrummer	L	3	115	6	6	8^{hd}	8^{1}	5^{hd}	$4^{1\frac{1}{2}}$	$4\frac{3}{4}$	Dominguez R A	6.60
22May04 ^{8}Hol^{5}	Mambo Train	L b	3	115	4	5	$7^{1\frac{1}{2}}$	7^{1}	$7\frac{1}{2}$	6^{2}	$5^{5\frac{1}{2}}$	John K	24.50
1May04 ^{10}CD^{4}	Limehouse	L	3	121	3	2	$5\frac{1}{2}$	$5\frac{1}{2}$	4^{1}	5^{1}	$6^{2\frac{1}{2}}$	Santos J A	1.00
15May04 ^{9}Mnr^{5}	Avid Skier	L b	3	115	2	1	$1\frac{1}{2}$	$2\frac{1}{2}$	2^{1}	$7\frac{1}{2}$	7no	Spieth S	103.30
13May04 ^{7}Tdn^{1}	Jandemar	L f	3	114	7	4	2^{1}	1^{hd}	6^{hd}	8^{2}	8^{1}	Rosendo I J	88.80
5Jun04 ^{8}Pim^{3}	Water Cannon	L b	3	115	9	9	6^{1}	$6^{2\frac{1}{2}}$	9	9	9	Villa-Gomez H	17.30

OFF AT 5:49 Start Good. Won ridden out. Track fast.

TIME :23^{2}, :47^{1}, 1:11^{2}, 1:37, 1:49^{2} (:23.40, :47.20, 1:11.48, 1:37.00, 1:49.50)

$2 Mutuel Prices:				
	5 – BRASS HAT	**44.80**	**15.40**	**11.40**
	1 – POLLARD'S VISION		**5.00**	**3.80**
	8 – TRIESTE'S HONOR			**5.00**

$2 EXACTA 5-1 PAID $178.00 $2 SUPERFECTA 5-1-8-6 PAID $4,629.60
$2 TRIFECTA 5-1-8 PAID $1,124.40

B. g, (May), by Prized – Brassy , by Dixie Brass . Trainer Bradley William. Bred by Fred F Bradley (Ky).

BRASS HAT unhurried while trailing into the second turn, responded readily when asked, angled four wide while rallying to make the lead entering the stretch then drew off the final eighth while being ridden out. POLLARD'S VISION settled just off the leaders for six furlongs, rallied three wide to make the lead near the quarter pole, was quickly headed by the winner, altered course outside that one at the eighth pole then finished second best. TRIESTE'S HONOR also with the pace, assumed command going into the second turn, led until the quarter pole then gradually weakened. DASHBOARD DRUMMER settled well back for a half, offered a mild bid on the second turn then leveled off. MAMBO TRAIN failed to menace. LIMEHOUSE well placed just off the leaders along the inside, also bid on the second turn then came up empty. AVID SKIER broke alertly to set a pressured pace around the first turn, had speed into the second turn then flattened out. JANDEMAR pressed the pace off the rail around the first turn, assumed command before a half then stopped after six furlongs. WATER CANNON was through after a half.

Owners– 1, Bradley Fred F; 2, Edgewood Farm; 3, Cobra Farm and Castletop Stable; 4, Double S Stable Preferred Pals Stables and Edwin Wachtel; 5, Everest Stables Inc; 6, Dogwood Stable; 7, France Wilbur K; 8, Miller Jack A; 9, The Nonsequitur Stable LLC

Trainers– 1, Bradley William; 2, Pletcher Todd A; 3, Matz Michael R; 4, Iwinski Allen; 5, Polanco Marcelo; 6, Pletcher Todd A; 7, Bennett Gerald S; 8, Cartwright Michael; 9, Albert Linda L

$2 Pick Three (10-2-5) Paid $710.60 ; Pick Three Pool $3,210 .

EIGHTH RACE
Belmont
JUNE 13, 2004

1⅛ MILES. (Inner Turf) (1.45^3) 10TH RUNNING OF THE SANDS POINT. Grade III. Purse $100,000 (Up tp $19,000 NYSBFOA) FOR FILLIES THREE YEARS OLD. By subscription of $100 each, which should accompany the nomination; $500 to pass the entry box; $500 to start, with $100,000 added. The added money and all fees to be divided 60% to the winner, 20% tosecond, 10% to third, 5% to fourth, 3% to fifth and 2% divided equally among remaining finishers. 122 lbs. Non-winners of $45,000 at a mile or over in 2004 allowed 3 lbs.; $35,000 at a mile or over on the turf, 5 lbs.; two races a mile or over, 7 lbs. (Maiden, Claiming and Restricted races not considered in allowances). A trophy will be presented to the winning owner. The New York Racing Association reserves the right to tranfser this race ot the Main Track. In the event that this race is taken off the turf, it may be subject to downgrading upon review by the Graded Stakes Committee. Closed Saturday, May 29, 2004 with 38 Nominations.

Value of Race: $114,800 Winner $68,880; second $22,960; third $11,480; fourth $5,740; fifth $3,444; sixth $460; seventh $460; eighth $460; ninth $460; tenth $456. Mutuel Pool $672,450.00 Exacta Pool $510,178.00 Trifecta Pool $446,499.00

Last Raced	Horse	M/Eqt.	A.	Wt	PP	St	¼	½	¾	Str	Fin	Jockey	Odds $1
11Apr04 8SA10	Mambo Slew		3	122	3	4	7hd	7hd	8½	4½	1nk	Prado E S	5.00
14Apr04 8Kee1	Lucifer's Stone	L b	3	122	4	2	82	6hd	4½	1½	21¾	Santos J A	2.25
30May04 9Mth4	Vous	L b	3	119	9	3	61½	81½	7hd	5hd	3nk	Fernandez V	16.30
27May04 8Bel1	Delta Sensation	L	3	119	6	8	9½	10	9½	6hd	4no	Chavez J F	5.90
9May04 5Bel4	Fortunate Damsel	L b	3	115	10	9	4hd	51½	61	3hd	5½	Bridgmohan S X	37.50
21Mar04 8GP1	Minge Cove	L	3	119	2	7	5½	4hd	5hd	71½	6¾	Decarlo C P	7.10
16May04 7Bel2	Serendipitous	L b	3	115	5	10	10	9½	10	8½	7½	Luzzi M J	23.10
9May04 5Bel1	Please Take Me Out	L	3	119	8	1	31	31½	3hd	2½	84	Gryder A T	a- 9.50
27May04 8Bel2	Savage Beauty	L	3	115	1	5	1hd	21½	1hd	915	924¼	Migliore R	3.85
26May04 8Bel5	Cherry's Hunter	L	3	115	7	6	2½	1½	21	10	10	Jara F	a- 9.50

a–Coupled: Please Take Me Out and Cherry's Hunter.

OFF AT 4:48 Start Good. Won driving. Course firm.

TIME :24, :47^1, 1:11, 1:35^1, 1:47^1 (:24.06, :47.30, 1:11.00, 1:35.29, 1:47.24)

$2 Mutuel Prices:				
	5 – MAMBO SLEW	12.00	6.10	4.80
	6 – LUCIFER'S STONE		3.80	2.90
	10 – VOUS			7.20

$2 EXACTA 5–6 PAID $44.60 $2 TRIFECTA 5–6–10 PAID $413.00

Dk. b or br. f, (Apr), by Kingmambo – Slew Boyera, by Seattle Slew. Trainer Biancone Patrick L. Bred by FJFM LLC (Ky).

MAMBO SLEW was taken back after the start, was rated along inside, advanced in traffic nearing the stretch, split rivals in upper stretch, found room on the rail, dug in resolutely along the inside and prevailed under a drive. LUCIFER'S STONE was rated along outside, put in a four wide run on the second turn, gained a short lead nearing the eighth pole and dug in gamely to the wire. VOUS stumbled at the start, raced in hand early, rallied four wide approaching the stretch and finished gamely outside. DELTA SENSATION was bumped after the start, was outrun early, rallied five wide approaching the stretch and finished gamely. FORTUNATE DAMSEL broke awkwardly, raced close up early, came wide into the stretch and stayed on gamely to the finish. MINGE COVE raced close up early along the inside and lacked a rally while between rivals in the stretch. SERENDIPITOUS broke slowly, was steadied after the start, dropped back early, raced inside and had no rally. PLEASE TAKE ME OUT stumbled after the start, was steadied, raced with the pace while three wide, put in a three wide run on the second turn and tired in the stretch. SAVAGE BEAUTY leapt in the air at the start, contested the pace along the inside and tired in the stretch. CHERRY'S HUNTER was bumped after the start, was steadied then contested the pace from the outside and tired nearing the stretch.

Owners– 1, Manganaro Frank; 2, Team Solaris Stable; 3, Tee N Jay Stable; 4, Cay John E III; 5, Spruce Pond Stable; 6, Double S Stable Wachtel Stable Friedman Leonard M Iwinski Allen; 7, Clifton William L Jr; 8, Perez Robert; 9, Schwartz Martin S; 10, Perez Robert

Trainers– 1, Biancone Patrick L; 2, Rice Linda; 3, Hills Timothy A; 4, Alexander Frank A; 5, Johnson Philip G; 6, Iwinski Allen; 7, Bond Harold James; 8, Callejas Alfredo; 9, Jerkens H Allen; 10, Callejas Alfredo

Scratched– Miss Coronado (25Apr04 9CD 4), Gracefully (IRE) (11Apr04 8SA 4)

EIGHTH RACE
Arlington
JUNE 19, 2004

7 FURLONGS. (1.20^2) 16TH RUNNING OF THE CHICAGO BREEDERS' CUP HANDICAP. Grade III. Purse $175,000 (includes $75,000 BC – Breeders' Cup) FOR FILLIES AND MARES, THREE–YEARS–OLD AND UPWARD.

Value of Race: $175,000 Winner $105,000; second $35,000; third $19,250; fourth $10,500; fifth $5,250. Mutuel Pool $351,811.00 Exacta Pool $78,279.00 Trifecta Pool $44,432.00

Last Raced	Horse	M/Eqt.	A.	Wt	PP	St	¼	½	Str	Fin	Jockey	Odds $1
22May04 9CD4	My Trusty Cat	L bf	4	116	1	4	5	5	3hd	11¾	Douglas R R	4.50
1Jun04 9Mnr1	Our Josephina	L	4	112	3	3	1hd	1½	21½	21½	Murphy C K	14.90
15May04 8AP1	Smoke Chaser	L	5	116	2	5	3½	2hd	1hd	34	Perez E E	5.40
1May04 8CD1	Mayo On the Side	L bf	5	118	4	2	21	31½	41	41½	Razo E Jr	0.30
26May04 8AP1	Rich City Girl	L	4	114	5	1	41½	4½	5	5	Lopez J	17.50

OFF AT 4:38 Start Good. Won driving. Track fast.

TIME :22^4, :45^4, 1:11, 1:23^2 (:22.93, :45.96, 1:11.12, 1:23.54)

$2 Mutuel Prices:				
	1 – MY TRUSTY CAT	11.00	6.00	22.80
	3 – OUR JOSEPHINA		12.20	34.60
	2 – SMOKE CHASER			24.60

$2 EXACTA 1–3 PAID $118.20 $2 TRIFECTA 1–3–2 PAID $308.40

B. f, (Apr), by Tale of the Cat – Entrusted, by Private Account. Trainer Vance David R. Bred by Vintage Racing (Ky).

MY TRUSTY CAT lacked speed off the rail while not far back, split foes while rallying in the stretch, struck the front nearing the sixteenth pole and drew off late. OUR JOSEPHINA set the pace while pressured between horses, battled gamely in deep stretch then could not hold off the winner while best of the others. SMOKE CHASER raced close up also the rail, slipped through on the inside on the turn, put a head in front in the stretch but could not sustain her bid. MAYO ON THE SIDE pressed the pace while three wide, did not respond when asked for her best in the stretch and weakened thereafter. RICH CITY GIRL lacked speed while not far back but was never a serious factor.

Owners– 1, Pollard Carl F; 2, Brunacini George; 3, Goldish Marc D and Savoy Stable; 4, Lothenbach Stables Inc; 5, Tanis Allen

Trainers– 1, Vance David R; 2, Fojan Emilie; 3, Bennett Dale; 4, Nafzger Carl A; 5, Janks Christine K

$1 Pick Three (3–7–1) Paid $122.60 ; Pick Three Pool $8,668 .

NINTH RACE
Belmont
JUNE 19, 2004

1⅛ MILES. (1.39^{2}) 36TH RUNNING OF THE OGDEN PHIPPS HANDICAP. Grade I. Purse $300,000 (UP TO $41,000 NYSBFOA) A HANDICAP FOR FILLIES AND MARES THREE YEARS OLD AND UPWARD. By subscription of $300 each, which should accompany the nomination; $1,500 to pass the entry box; $1,500 to start. The purse to be divided 60% to the winner, 20% to second, 10% to third, 5% to fourth, 3% to fifth and 2% divided equally among remaining finishers. Trophies will be presented to the winning owner, trainer and jockey. Closed Saturday, June 5, 2004 with 14 Nominations.

Value of Race: $285,000 Winner $180,000; second $60,000; third $30,000; fourth $15,000. Mutuel Pool $588,839.00 Exacta Pool $366,681.00

Last Raced	Horse	M/Eqt.	A.	Wt	PP	St	¼	½	¾	Str	Fin	Jockey	Odds $1
30Apr04 ^{8}CD^{4}	Sightseek	L	5	120	3	1	2$^{\frac{1}{2}}$	2$^{\frac{1}{2}}$	1$^{\frac{1}{2}}$	1^{6}	1$^{3\frac{1}{4}}$	Bailey J D	2.35
15May04 ^{8}Bel^{1}	Storm Flag Flying	L	4	117	4	2	3$^{\frac{1}{2}}$	3^{1}	3$^{1\frac{1}{2}}$	2$^{2\frac{1}{2}}$	2$^{6\frac{1}{2}}$	Velazquez J R	3.00
15May04 ^{8}Bel^{2}	Passing Shot	L	5	116	2	3	4	4	4	3$^{1\frac{1}{2}}$	3^{2}	Migliore R	11.70
31May04 ^{9}Bel^{8}	Azeri	L	6	123	1	4	1$^{\frac{1}{2}}$	1^{hd}	2^{hd}	4	4	Day P	0.80

OFF AT 5:15 Start Good . Won ridden out. Track fast.

TIME :23^{1}, :45^{3}, 1:10, 1:34^{3}, 1:41^{2} (:23.32, :45.73, 1:10.18, 1:34.65, 1:41.46)

$2 Mutuel Prices:				
	3 – SIGHTSEEK	6.70	4.40	—
	4 – STORM FLAG FLYING		4.10	—
	2 – PASSING SHOT		—	—

$2 EXACTA 3–4 PAID $18.60

Ch. m, (Feb), by Distant View – Viviana , by Nureyev . Trainer Frankel Robert. Bred by Juddmonte Farms Inc (Ky).

SIGHTSEEK came away fast, argued the pace while between rivals, drew away when shaken up, was well clear into deep stretch and was taken in hand in the final yards. STORM FLAG FLYING raced with the pace while three wide and finished gamely outside while no real threat to the winner. PASSING SHOT raced close up along the inside and had no response when roused. AZERI was hustled up inside, set the pace and tired after the opening three quarters.

Owners– 1, Juddmonte Farms Inc; 2, Phipps Ogden Mills et al; 3, Shields Joseph V Jr; 4, Allen E Paulson Living Trust

Trainers– 1, Frankel Robert; 2, McGaughey III Claude R; 3, Jerkens H Allen; 4, Lukas D Wayne

---

EIGHTH RACE
Bay Meadows
JUNE 19, 2004

6 FURLONGS. (1.07^{1}) 19TH RUNNING OF THE BAY MEADOWS BREEDERS' CUP SPRINT HANDICAP. Grade III. Purse $125,000 (includes $50,000 BC – Breeders' Cup) FOR THREE-YEAR-OLDS AND UPWARD. By subscripton of $75 each to accompany the nomination or by supplementary nomination of $1,500 by Noon, Sunday, June 13, 2004. $375 to pass the entry box and $375 additional to start with $75,000 Guaranteed and an additional $50,000 from Breeders' Cup Fund for Breeders' Cup eligibles only. The host association's Guaranteed monies to be divided 55% to the winner, 20% to second, 15% to third, 7.5% to fourth and 2.5% to fifth. Breeders' Cup Fund monies also correspondingly divided providing a Breeders' Cup nominee has finished in an awarded position. Any Breeders' Cup Fund monies not awarded will revert back to the Fund. A trophy will be presented to the owner of the winner by Breeders' Cup Ltd. Closed Thursday, June 10, 2004with 16 nominations.

Value of Race: $80,000 Winner $41,250; second $15,000; third $11,250; fourth $9,375; fifth $3,125. Mutuel Pool $255,164.00 Exacta Pool $138,564.00 Quinella Pool $13,641.00 Trifecta Pool $150,565.00 Superfecta Pool $58,970.00

Last Raced	Horse	M/Eqt.	A.	Wt	PP	St	¼	½	Str	Fin	Jockey	Odds $1
3Jun04 ^{7}BM^{1}	Court's in Session	LB bf	5	115	6	5	5^{1}	3$^{1\frac{1}{2}}$	1$^{\frac{1}{2}}$	1$^{2\frac{1}{4}}$	Gonzalez R M	7.90
22May04 ^{8}BM^{3}	Debonair Joe	LB	5	117	4	8	8^{hd}	7^{3}	5^{2}	2^{nk}	Lopez D G	8.90
8May04 ^{6}Hol^{6}	Hombre Rapido	LB b	7	118	3	2	1$^{\frac{1}{2}}$	1^{hd}	2^{2}	3^{nk}	Baze R A	2.90
24Apr04 ^{6}Hol^{6}	Green Team	LB	5	119	5	9	6$^{2\frac{1}{2}}$	6^{2}	4^{1}	4^{4}	Alvarado F T	2.20
22May04 ^{8}BM^{5}	El Dorado Shooter	LB	7	116	9	1	2^{1}	2^{3}	3$^{1\frac{1}{2}}$	5^{2}	Carr D	12.70
31May04 ^{9}Hol^{6}	Smile n Wildcat	LB	5	115	1	4	3^{2}	4^{2}	6$^{3\frac{1}{2}}$	6^{3}	Schvaneveldt C P	4.50
22Apr04 ^{3}BM^{4}	Sirpa	LB b	6	115	7	6	9	9	8^{hd}	7$^{\frac{3}{4}}$	Perez M A	a- 16.50
31May04 ^{9}Hol^{8}	Cappuchino	LB bf	5	116	2	7	7^{1}	8^{hd}	9	8^{4}	Rollins C J	a- 16.50
13Mar04 ^{9}TuP^{5}	Giovannetti	LB	5	117	8	3	4^{2}	5^{hd}	7^{1}	9	Sorenson D	7.30

a–Coupled: Sirpa and Cappuchino.

OFF AT 4:42 Start Good . Won driving. Track fast.

TIME :21^{4}, :44, :56^{1}, 1:08^{4} (:21.91, :44.19, :56.24, 1:08.91)

$2 Mutuel Prices:				
	7 – COURT'S IN SESSION	17.80	8.20	4.00
	5 – DEBONAIR JOE		9.00	4.40
	4 – HOMBRE RAPIDO			3.20

$1 EXACTA 7–5 PAID $62.00 $2 QUINELLA 5–7 PAID $74.80

$1 TRIFECTA 7–5–4 PAID $371.50 $1 SUPERFECTA 7–5–4–6 PAID $836.00

Dk. b or br. g, (Mar), by Petersburg – Crafty Court , by Crafty Native . Trainer Koriner Brian. Bred by Mr & Mrs Guy C Roberts (Wash).

COURT'S IN SESSION was permitted to settle early but was always within striking distance, commenced his bid from the inside on the turn, rallied quickly to gain command inside HOMBRE RAPIDO nearing the furlong pole then drew clear driving. DEBONAIR JOE lagged early, came through inside on the turn and finished willingly but too late. HOMBRE RAPIDO was in front shortly after the start to set all of the pace to the upper stretch then slackened. GREEN TEAM steadied in the earliest stages and fell behind, raced unhurried to the turn, came two wide to the stretch and closed ground steadily. EL DORADO SHOOTER prompted the pace two wide into the lane and slackened. SMILE N WILDCAT tracked the dueling leaders from the inside to the turn, angled three wide near the quarter pole but had no response. SIRPA was never a factor. CAPPUCHINO failed to reach serious contention. GIOVANNETTI stalked the leaders early between horses but stopped suddenly leaving the three eighths.

Owners– 1, Wind River Stables; 2, Ristad-Lidgett Lynne; 3, Granja Vista Del Rio Stable; 4, Ferro Family Trust and Bonde Jeff; 5, DeLima Barbara; 6, David J Lanzman Racing Stable Inc; 7, Marta Racing Ventures and Todaro George; 8, Hollendorfer Litt and Todaro; 9, Schiappa Bernard C

Trainers– 1, Koriner Brian; 2, Ledezma Sergio; 3, Sadler John W; 4, Bonde Jeff; 5, Delima Clifford; 6, O'Neill Doug; 7, Hollendorfer Jerry; 8, Hollendorfer Jerry; 9, Monteleone Frank J

Scratched– R. Baggio (22May04 ^{8}BM ^{2})

$2 Daily Double (6–7) Paid $66.00 ; Daily Double Pool $11,727 .

$1 Pick Three (12–6–7) Paid $51.80 ; Pick Three Pool $18,031 .

NINTH RACE
Churchill
JUNE 19, 2004

6 FURLONGS. (1.07^{3}) 16TH RUNNING OF THE ARISTIDES BREEDERS' CUP HANDICAP. Grade III. Purse $150,000 (includes $50,000 BC – Breeders' Cup) FOR THREE-YEAR-OLDS AND UPWARD. By subscription of $150 each on or before June 5, 2004 or by supplementary nomination of $7,500 each by the closing of entries Friday June 11, 2004. $750 to pass the entry box; $750 additional to start, with $100,000 added and an additional $50,000 from the Breeders' Cup Fund for Cup nominees only. The host association's added monies to be divided 62% of all monies to the owner of the winner, 20% to second, 10% to third, 5% to fourth and 3% to fifth. Breeders' Cup Fundmonies also correspondingly divided providing a Breeders' Cup nominee has finished in an awarded position. Any Breeders' Cup Fund monies not awarded will revert back to the Fund. Weights to be announced Saturday, June 12, 2004. Starters to be named thhrough the entry box at the usual time of closing. Trophy to winning owner given by Breeders' Cup Ltd. Closed Saturday, June 5, 2004 with 21 nominations.

Value of Race: $162,150 Winner $100,533; second $32,430; third $16,215; fourth $8,108; fifth $4,864. Mutuel Pool $387,240.00 Exacta Pool $216,979.00 Trifecta Pool $146,521.00 Superfecta Pool $40,013.00

Last Raced	Horse	M/Eqt.	A.	Wt	PP	St	¼	½	Str	Fin	Jockey	Odds $1
26May04 ^{2}CD^{1}	Champali	L	4	116	5	2	4^{3}	3^{hd}	1^{1}	$1^{3\frac{1}{4}}$	Bejarano R	4.10
8May04 ^{9}LS^{1}	Beau's Town	L b	6	121	3	3	1^{hd}	$1^{\frac{1}{2}}$	2^{hd}	2^{nk}	Borel C H	2.50
19May04 ^{8}CD^{1}	Battle Won	L	4	114	1	6	$5^{2\frac{1}{2}}$	5^{2}	5^{4}	$3^{1\frac{1}{4}}$	McKee J	6.80
20May04 ^{9}CD^{2}	Mountain General	L b	6	115	6	1	6	6	4^{hd}	$4^{3\frac{3}{4}}$.	Velasquez C	3.60
20May04 ^{9}CD^{1}	Cloud Walker	L f	4	115	2	5	2^{hd}	2^{1}	$3^{3\frac{1}{2}}$	$5^{9\frac{1}{2}}$	Albarado R J	2.90
30May04 ^{8}Bel^{7}	Great Notion	L bf	4	114	4	4	3^{3}	4^{3}	6	6	Guidry M	7.30

OFF AT 5:35 Start Good . Won driving. Track fast.
TIME :21, :44, :56^{1}, 1:09 (:21.13, :44.19, :56.37, 1:09.04)

$2 Mutuel Prices:

5 – **CHAMPALI**	10.20	4.60	3.20
3 – **BEAU'S TOWN**		3.80	2.80
1 – **BATTLE WON**			4.20

$2 EXACTA 5–3 PAID $39.20 $2 TRIFECTA 5–3–1 PAID $150.80
$2 SUPERFECTA 5–3–1–6 PAID $440.80

B. c, (Feb), by Glitterman – Radioactivity , by Dixieland Band . Trainer Foley Gregory D. Bred by McKee Stables Inc (Ky).

CHAMPALI, reluctant to load into the gate, bobbled slightly when breaking, bumped lightly with GREAT NOTION when that one came out, settled five wide, commend a sweeping rally five wide at the five-sixteenths pole, took over in the upper stretch and drove clear under energetic handling. BEAU'S TOWN broke to the inside bumping with CLOUD WALKER, gained a slight edge while dueling outside that one, was briefly clear between calls on the turn, then couldn't handle CHAMPALI in the drive while fully extended. BATTLE WON bore in at the break, was steadied, settled near the inside, eased out three or four wide in the final furlong and offered a mild gain. MOUNTAIN GENERAL broke in front, settled three wide, came out five or six wide for the drive but lacked a late response. CLOUD WALKER, bumped at the start by BEAU'S TOWN and forced in, went up soon after to duel for the lead, held on stubbornly into the upper stretch and faltered. GREAT NOTION bobbled at the start, came out bumping the winner, went up and forced the pace for a half and faded.

Owners– 1, Lloyd Madison Farms IV LLC; 2, Hulkewicz David J; 3, Manoogian Jay; 4, Asmussen Keith I; 5, Farmer Tracy; 6, Silverton Hill LLC

Trainers– 1, Foley Gregory D; 2, Norman Cole; 3, Simon Charles; 4, Asmussen Steven M; 5, Amoss Thomas; 6, Miller Darrin

$2 Pick Three (3–5–5) Paid $236.20 ; Pick Three Pool $35,751 .

SEVENTH RACE
Hollywood
JUNE 19, 2004

1$\frac{1}{16}$ MILES. (1.40) 26TH RUNNING OF THE AFFIRMED HANDICAP. Grade III. Purse $100,000 FOR THREE YEAR OLDS. By subscription of $100 each on or before Wednesday, June 9 or by supplementary nomination of $2,000 each by 3:00 pm Saturday, June 12. $1,000 additional to start, with $100,000 added. The added money and all fees to be divided 60% tothe winner, 20% to second, 12% to third,6% to fourth and 2% to fifth. Weights Sunday, June 13. Starters to be named through the entry box by closing time of entries. A trophy will be presented to the winning owner. Closed with 12 nominations.

Value of Race: $110,200 Winner $66,120; second $22,040; third $13,224; fourth $6,612; fifth $2,204. Mutuel Pool $467,430.00 Exacta Pool $241,052.00 Quinella Pool $20,341.00 Trifecta Pool $252,529.00 Superfecta Pool $103,733.00

Last Raced	Horse	M/Eqt.	A.	Wt	PP	St	¼	½	¾	Str	Fin	Jockey	Odds $1
22May04 ^{8}Hol^{7}	Boomzeeboom	LB b	3	115	7	4	$1^{1\frac{1}{2}}$	$1^{1\frac{1}{2}}$	$1^{\frac{1}{2}}$	$2^{2\frac{1}{2}}$	$1^{\frac{1}{2}}$	Espinoza V	12.60
29May04 ^{8}Hol^{1}	Twice as Bad	LB	3	121	1	1	$3^{\frac{1}{2}}$	3^{hd}	$2^{1\frac{1}{2}}$	1^{hd}	$2^{1\frac{1}{4}}$	Nakatani C S	2.50
29May04 ^{8}Hol^{2}	Wimplestiltskin	LB b	3	116	6	2	2^{1}	2^{1}	$3^{\frac{1}{2}}$	$3^{\frac{1}{2}}$	3^{2}	Valdivia J Jr	16.10
24Apr04 ^{9}Hol^{1}	Cheiron	LB	3	120	4	8	8^{hd}	9	5^{1}	4^{3}	4^{6}	Solis A	1.30
15May04 ^{3}Hol^{3}	Hippocrates	LB	3	115	2	6	6^{2}	5^{hd}	6^{1}	$5^{\frac{1}{2}}$	5^{hd}	Smith M E	14.60
15May04 ^{4}Hol^{1}	Vencer	LB b	3	113	8	5	4^{hd}	4^{1}	4^{hd}	$6^{\frac{1}{2}}$	6^{2}	Baze T C	4.40
6Jun04 ^{7}Hol^{4}	Lindero	LB b	3	115	3	3	$5^{1\frac{1}{2}}$	6^{1}	$8^{2\frac{1}{2}}$	7^{1}	7^{4}	Pedroza M A	43.40
24Apr04 ^{9}Hol^{6}	O. K. Mikie	LB b	3	115	9	9	9	$8^{\frac{1}{2}}$	7^{hd}	8^{5}	8^{11}	Santiago Javier	24.80
20Feb04 ^{6}SA^{5}	Coldntight	LB	3	116	5	7	7^{2}	7^{hd}	9	9	9	Flores D R	34.50

OFF AT 4:26 Start Good . Won driving. Track fast.
TIME :23^{3}, :47, 1:11^{1}, 1:35^{3}, 1:42 (:23.62, :47.01, 1:11.31, 1:35.62, 1:42.11)

$2 Mutuel Prices:

8 – **BOOMZEEBOOM**	27.20	12.20	8.00
2 – **TWICE AS BAD**		4.60	4.20
7 – **WIMPLESTILTSKIN**			8.60

$1 EXACTA 8–2 PAID $42.10 $2 QUINELLA 2–8 PAID $37.80
$1 TRIFECTA 8–2–7 PAID $377.90 $1 SUPERFECTA 8–2–7–5 PAID $1,469.30

B. c, (Feb), by Explosive Red – Zee Lady , by Unreal Zeal . Trainer Cerin Vladimir. Bred by Adena Springs (Fla).

BOOMZEEBOOM had good early speed three deep then angled in, set the pace inside, fought back on the second turn, was headed in midstretch but came back on under left handed urging to prove best. TWICE AS BAD stalked inside, bid outside the winner on the second turn, put a head in front in midstretch but was outgamed. WIMPLESTILTSKIN stalked outside a rival or off the rail, was three deep leaving the second turn, could not match the top pair but held third. CHEIRON settled toward the inside then between foes, moved up between rivals on the second turn, angled in some leaving that bend and lacked the needed rally. HIPPOCRATES chased a bit off the inside, angled in on the second turn and did not rally. VENCER was in a good position stalking the pace three deep but weakened in the stretch. LINDERO sent between horses then pulled under a hold into the first turn, stalked outside a rival, went up four wide leaving the backstretch and into the second turn, angled in off the rail leaving that turn and weakened. O. K. MIKIE off a bit slowly, settled out from the inside, went up five wide leaving the backstretch and into the second turn, continued outside and failed to sustain the bid. COLDNTIGHT allowed to settle inside chasing the pace, dropped back into and on the second turn and gave way.

Owners– 1, Karubian John Landsburg Alan and Postaer Larry; 2, Mercedes Stables LLC; 3, Everest Stables Inc; 4, Noctis LLC Papiano Neil and Taub Steve; 5, Robertson Sanford R; 6, Fulton Stan E; 7, Cubanacan Stables; 8, Lo Charles; 9, Pegram Michael E

Trainers– 1, Cerin Vladimir; 2, Cerin Vladimir; 3, Polanco Marcelo; 4, Mulhall Kristin; 5, Walsh Kathy; 6, Becerra Rafael; 7, Garcia Juan; 8, McArthur Jerry; 9, Baffert Bob

Scratched– Capitano (15May04 ^{3}Hol^{1})

$2 Daily Double (10–8) Paid $62.40 ; Daily Double Pool $37,326 .
$1 Pick Three (2–10–8) Paid $198.20 ; Pick Three Pool $108,949 .

TENTH RACE
Suffolk
JUNE 19, 2004

1⅛ MILES. (1.47^{1}) 65TH RUNNING OF THE MASSACHUSETTS HANDICAP. Grade II. Purse $500,000 A HANDICAP FOR THREE-YEAR-OLDS AND UPWARD. By subscription of $100 each by Saturday June 5. $2,000 to pass the entry box and $3,000 to start. If this race is not divided it will be limited to 14 starters. NOMINATIONS CLOSED Saturday, June 5, 2004 with THIRTY FIVE (35).

Value of Race: $500,000 Winner $300,000; second $100,000; third $50,000; fourth $25,000; fifth $15,000; sixth $10,000. Mutuel Pool $605,471.00 Perfecta Pool $364,792.00 Trifecta Pool $322,804.00 Superfecta Pool $95,677.00

Last Raced	Horse	M/Eqt.	A.	Wt	PP	St	¼	½	¾	Str	Fin	Jockey	Odds $1
14May04 ^{7}Bel^{1}	Offlee Wild	LB	4	111	1	2	3^{1}	4^{1}	3^{1}	1^{hd}	1^{hd}	Prado E S	3.20
31May04 ^{9}Bel^{5}	Funny Cide	LB	4	117	7	4	2^{hd}	$2^{1\frac{1}{2}}$	$2^{1\frac{1}{2}}$	3^{2}	2^{hd}	Santos J A	2.10
15May04 ^{8}Pim^{2}	The Lady's Groom	LB bf	4	116	2	1	1^{1}	$1^{\frac{1}{2}}$	1^{hd}	2^{hd}	$3^{1\frac{1}{2}}$	Karamanos H A	5.50
31May04 ^{9}Bel^{4}	Gygistar	LB	5	113	4	6	6^{1}	7^{hd}	4^{hd}	4^{5}	$4^{4\frac{3}{4}}$	Bravo J	5.80
14May04 ^{11}Pim^{4}	Evening Attire	LB b	6	114	8	8	$7^{1\frac{1}{2}}$	8^{3}	8^{3}	5^{3}	5^{8}	Bridgmohan S X	4.10
30Apr04 ^{6}CD^{4}	Sarava	LB	5	112	5	5	$5^{\frac{1}{2}}$	5^{hd}	7^{2}	$6^{1\frac{1}{2}}$	6^{4}	Castellano J J	9.70
28May04 ^{8}Bel^{1}	Rogue Agent	LB b	5	111	9	7	4^{hd}	3^{hd}	$6^{1\frac{1}{2}}$	$7^{1\frac{1}{2}}$	$7^{2\frac{1}{4}}$	Chavez J F	13.50
9Jun04 ^{8}Suf^{2}	Basil's Rhythm	LB f	6	114	3	9	9	9	9	9	8^{2}	Bush W V	94.70
22May04 ^{8}Suf^{1}	On the Game	LB bf	6	112	6	3	$8^{2\frac{1}{2}}$	$6^{\frac{1}{2}}$	5^{hd}	8^{1}	9	Rojas R I	63.90

OFF AT 5:32 Start Good. Won driving. Track fast.

TIME :24, :48^{3}, 1:12^{2}, 1:36^{3}, 1:49 (:24.02, :48.63, 1:12.45, 1:36.76, 1:49.14)

$2 Mutuel Prices:			
1 – OFFLEE WILD	8.40	3.80	3.20
7 – FUNNY CIDE		3.40	2.60
2 – THE LADY'S GROOM			3.40

$2 PERFECTA 1–7 PAID $38.40 $2 TRIFECTA 1–7–2 PAID $195.40
$2 SUPERFECTA 1–7–2–4 PAID $761.20

Dk. b or br. c, (Apr), by Wild Again – Alvear, by Seattle Slew. Trainer Dutrow Richard E Jr. Bred by Dorothy A Matz (Ky).

OFFLEE WILD stalked the early leaders from the two path, moved out to be three wide midway along the far turn, battled outside those rivals through the final furlong and prevailed under strong urging. FUNNY CIDE prompted the pace two wide, battled heads apart and between rivals through the lane and gamely just missed. THE LADY'S GROOM assumed the early lead, was rated along while on the rail, continued determinedly through the final furlong but was outfinished late. GYGISTAR stalked from the inside, was bottled up on the rail while inside rivals heading into far the turn, swung out four wide into upper stretch but could not continue with a late bid. EVENING ATTIRE, raced in contention from the outside, was five wide leaving the far turn then finished evenly through the stretch run. SARAVA bobbled slightly at the break but was never far back racing three wide but had no late impact. ROGUE AGENT raced up close four wide early, was three wide into the final turn while in striking position but soon tired. BASIL'S RHYTHM was off slow, saved all ground but was never involved. ON THE GAME raced in contention three-four wide early, made a bid four wide into the far turn then soon tired.

Owners– 1, Azalea Stables LLC; 2, Sackatoga Stable; 3, Murphy John D Sr; 4, Evans Edward P; 5, Grant Mary and Joseph and Kelly Thomas J; 6, New Phoenix Stable & Mrs Susan Roy; 7, Scott & Eric Fein; 8, Kavazis Stella Stathas William and Maniatis Judy; 9, G Lack Farms

Trainers– 1, Dutrow Richard E Jr; 2, Tagg Barclay; 3, Gorham Michael E; 4, Hennig Mark; 5, Kelly Patrick J; 6, Baffert Bob; 7, Brice Michael; 8, Maniatis Arthur F; 9, Bazeos Peter

$2 Pick Four (1–4–2–1) Paid $5,995.00 ; Pick Four Pool $20,254 .

NINTH RACE
Belmont
JUNE 26, 2004

1⅛ MILES. (1.45^{2}) 48TH RUNNING OF THE MOTHER GOOSE. Grade I. Purse $300,000 (UP TO $41,000 NYSBFOA) FOR FILLIES THREE YEARS OLD. By subscription of $300 each, which should accompany the nomination; $1,500 to pass the entry box; $1,500 to start. The purse to be divided 60% to the winner, 20% to second, 10% to third, 5% to fourth,3% to fifth and 2% divided equally among remaining finishers. 121 lbs. Trophies will be presented to the winning owner, trainer and jockey. A special permanent trophy will be presented to the owner of the winner if the filly wins all legs of the Triple Tiara (The Mother Goose, The Coaching Club American Oaks and The Alabama). Closed Saturday, June 12, 2004 with 11 Nominations.

Value of Race: $300,000 Winner $180,000; second $60,000; third $30,000; fourth $15,000; fifth $9,000; sixth $6,000. Mutuel Pool $758,195.00 Exacta Pool $485,251.00 Trifecta Pool $370,160.00

Last Raced	Horse	M/Eqt.	A.	Wt	PP	St	¼	½	¾	Str	Fin	Jockey	Odds $1
5Jun04 ^{10}CD^{1}	Stellar Jayne	L b	3	121	2	6	$3^{\frac{1}{2}}$	1^{hd}	$2^{1\frac{1}{2}}$	$1^{\frac{1}{2}}$	$1^{2\frac{1}{2}}$	Albarado R J	29.75
30Apr04 ^{10}CD^{1}	Ashado	L	3	121	4	1	1^{hd}	2^{2}	1^{hd}	$2^{3\frac{1}{2}}$	$2^{1\frac{3}{4}}$	Velazquez J R	0.90
4Jun04 ^{10}Bel^{1}	Island Sand	L b	3	121	3	2	5^{hd}	6	5^{hd}	$3^{4\frac{1}{2}}$	3^{5}	Thompson T J	2.90
25Apr04 ^{9}CD^{4}	Miss Coronado	L	3	121	5	3	4^{1}	4^{hd}	4^{hd}	4^{hd}	$4^{1\frac{1}{2}}$	Santos J A	24.75
6May04 ^{8}Bel^{1}	Daydreaming	L	3	121	1	5	6	5^{1}	6	$5^{3\frac{1}{2}}$	5^{4}	Bailey J D	7.60
4Jun04 ^{10}Bel^{2}	Society Selection		3	121	6	4	$2^{\frac{1}{2}}$	3^{hd}	3^{hd}	6	6	Prado E S	3.80

OFF AT 5:15 Start Good. Won driving. Track fast.

TIME :23^{4}, :47, 1:10^{4}, 1:35^{2}, 1:48 (:23.83, :47.00, 1:10.97, 1:35.44, 1:48.13)

$2 Mutuel Prices:			
2 – STELLAR JAYNE	61.50	12.60	4.00
4 – ASHADO		2.90	2.20
3 – ISLAND SAND			2.60

$2 EXACTA 2–4 PAID $146.50 $2 TRIFECTA 2–4–3 PAID $386.50

Gr/ro. f, (Feb), by Wild Rush – To the Hunt, by Relaunch. Trainer Lukas D Wayne. Bred by Wind Hill Farm (Ky).

STELLAR JAYNE came away in good order, sparred for the lead along the inside, dug in resolutely on the rail in the stretch drew clear in the final yards. ASHADO argued the pace from the outside, could not stay with the winner in the final furlong and continued on to hold on to the place award. ISLAND SAND was unhurried early on, split rivals on the turn, put in a three wide move approaching the stretch and had little left for the drive. MISS CORONADO raced close up outside early, chased the pace while four wide and tired nearing the stretch. DAYDREAMING raced close up inside and had no response when roused. SOCIETY SELECTION raced with the pace while three wide and was finished after the opening three quarters.

Owners– 1, Spendthrift Farm Cole Nancy M Kidder Charles Strong Nick; 2, Starlight Stables Saylor Paul H Martin Johns; 3, Osborne James L; 4, Stonerside Stable LLC; 5, Phipps Ogden M; 6, Cowan Marjorie and Irving M

Trainers– 1, Lukas D Wayne; 2, Pletcher Todd A; 3, Jones J Larry; 4, Frankel Robert; 5, McGaughey III Claude R; 6, Jerkens H Allen

NINTH RACE
Churchill
JUNE 26, 2004

1⅛ MILES. (Turf) (1.46¹) 23RD RUNNING OF THE LOCUST GROVE HANDICAP. Grade III. Purse $150,000 FOR FILLIES AND MARES, THREE YEARS OLD AND UPWARD. By subscription of $150 each on or before June 12, 2004 or by supplementary nomination of $7,500 each by the close of entries Friday, June 18, 2004. $750 to pass the entry box; $750 additional to start,with $150,000 added of which 62% to the owner of the winner, 20% to second, 10% to third, 5% to fourth and 3% to fifth. Weights to be announced Saturday, June 19, 2004. If the race is moved to the main track after the time of closing, a horse may bescratched for any reason at any time up to fifteen minutes prior to post time for the race preceding this race or thereafter with a valid physical reason and approved by the stewards. The entry fee shall be refunded for scratches made in compliance withthe above conditions. Starters to be named through the entry box at the usual time of closing. Trophy to winning owner. (If this race is taken off the turf it will be downgraded one grade level for this running only in accordance with American GradedStakes Committee policy). Closed Saturday, June 12, 2004 with 40 nominations.

Value of Race: $165,750 Winner $102,765; second $33,150; third $16,575; fourth $8,288; fifth $4,972. Mutuel Pool $356,630.00 Exacta Pool $242,947.00 Trifecta Pool $205,188.00 Superfecta Pool $68,736.00

Last Raced	Horse	M/Eqt.	A.	Wt	PP	St	¼	½	¾	Str	Fin	Jockey	Odds $1
29May04 9CD5	Shaconage	L	4	116	5	4	53	53½	41½	2hd	11¼	Blanc B	7.20
22May04 9CD5	Halory Leigh	L	4	111	3	6	6	6	6	52	2no	McKee J	29.10
29May04 9CD2	Sand Springs	L	4	119	4	2	11½	12½	11	11	31¾	Guidry M	2.60
29May04 9CD4	Two Dot Slew	L	7	113	6	3	21½	2½	21	3hd	41¼	Bejarano R	14.00
5Jun04 8Bel4	Riskaverse	L	5	118	2	1	3hd	31	3½	42½	58½	Day P	0.60
19May04 7CD1	Modena Bay-NZ	L	6	114	1	5	4½	41½	51½	6	6	Velasquez C	8.10

OFF AT 5:33 Start Good . Won driving. Course firm.

TIME :23⁴, :47, 1:10³, 1:34³, 1:46³ (:23.97, :47.07, 1:10.66, 1:34.73, 1:46.75)

$2 Mutuel Prices:

6 – SHACONAGE	16.40	7.80	4.80
3 – HALORY LEIGH		22.20	8.80
5 – SAND SPRINGS			3.80

$2 EXACTA 6–3 PAID $304.60 $2 TRIFECTA 6–3–5 PAID $1,195.60
$2 SUPERFECTA 6–3–5–7 PAID $9,279.20

Gr/ro. f, (Jun), by El Prado–Ire – Carita Tostada–Chi , by Gallantsky . Trainer Shirota Mitch. Bred by Andrena Van Doren (Ky).

SHACONAGE, in hand early while following the leaders four wide, advanced steadily entering the stretch, took over a sixteenth out and drove clear. HALORY LEIGH, reserved early and three wide, moved four wide entering the lane, lugged in at the eighth pole, quickly was straightened, angled six wide soon after and was fully extended for the place. SAND SPRINGS gained the lead early, went along in the three path under careful handling, showed the way into deep stretch and weakened. TWO DOT SLEW went up early to press front-running SAND SPRINGS four wide, loomed boldly between foes in the final furlong but came up empty. RISKAVERSE, between horses under light rating to the end of the backstretch, edged near the hedge, loomed a solid threat inside through the drive but flattened out. MODENA BAY (NZ) raced in contention near the inside for six furlongs, was angled widest into the upper stretch while tiring and continued to fade.

Owners– 1, Van Doren Andrena; 2, Crawford Jerry Gannon Matt and Grask Charlie; 3, Willmott Stables Inc; 4, Chastain Rick; 5, Fox Ridge Farm Inc; 6, Silverton Hill LLC

Trainers– 1, Shirota Mitch; 2, Romans Dale; 3, Reinstedler Anthony; 4, Gibson Dewayne C; 5, Kelly Patrick J; 6, Miller Darrin

Scratched– Ocean Silk (25Jun04 9CD 1)

$2 Pick Three (7–3–6) Paid $312.60 ; Pick Three Pool $33,787 .

EIGHTH RACE
Delaware
JUNE 26, 2004

1⅛ MILES. (Turf) (1.47²) 40TH RUNNING OF THE KENT BREEDERS' CUP. Grade III. Purse $250,000 (plus $100,000 Starters Bonus) FOR THREE YEAR OLDS. By subscription of $250 each, which shall accompany the nomination;; $1,000 to enter and $1,000 to start. Supplemental nominations of $3,000 will be accepted at time of entry and shall include all fees. $250,000 Guaranteed *(includes $100,000 from Breeders' Cup fund for cup nominees only). The host association's money to be divided 60% to the winner, 20% to second, 11% to third, 6% to fourth and 3% to fifth. Any Breeders' Cup fund monies not awarded reverts back to the fund. Weight; 122 lbs. Non-winners of $120,000 at a mile or over in 2004 allowed 3 lbs.; $90,000 at a mile or over in 2004, 5 lbs.; $45,000 at a mile or over in 2004, 7 lbs. (Maiden and Claiming races not considered in estimating allowances.) The winner to receive a trophy from Breeders' Cup Limited. Closed Saturday, June 12th, 2004 with 31 nominations. (If deemed inadvisable by management not to run this race over the turf course, it will be run on the main track at One Mile and One Eighth). (Rail at 15 feet).

Value of Race: $250,900 Winner $150,000; second $50,000; third $27,500; fourth $15,000; fifth $7,500; sixth $300; seventh $300; eighth $300. Mutuel Pool $173,055.00 Exacta Pool $124,284.00 Trifecta Pool $86,518.00 Superfecta Pool $18,512.00

Last Raced	Horse	M/Eqt.	A.	Wt	PP	St	¼	½	¾	Str	Fin	Jockey	Odds $1
6Jun04 8Bel2	Timo	L b	3	117	4	6	51½	5½	61½	4½	1no	Migliore R	2.90
31May04 10Mth1	Icy Atlantic	L	3	117	5	3	1½	11	1½	11	21¼	Lopez C C	4.50
31May04 10Mth2	Commendation	L	3	115	8	5	71½	72	8	5½	3nk	Dominguez R A	4.80
11Jun04 4Cnl2	King's Coronation	L b	3	115	6	2	21	21½	21½	21	41¾	Pindell M D	29.10
22May04 7Crc1	Wire Bound	L b	3	115	2	1	41½	41½	42	3½	5hd	Toscano P R	4.70
5Jun04 11Bel7	Master David	L	3	117	1	8	61½	62	5hd	7hd	6hd	Bridgmohan S X	1.90
6Jun04 8Bel3	Big Booster	L b	3	115	3	7	8	8	7½	61½	71	Pino M G	27.60
29May04 5Pim1	Expletive		3	115	7	4	3½	3½	3½	8	8	Monterrey R	44.90

OFF AT 3:56 Start Good . Won driving. Course soft.

TIME :26², :52², 1:18², 1:43⁴, 1:55³ (:26.48, :52.46, 1:18.47, 1:43.89, 1:55.75)

$2 Mutuel Prices:

4 – TIMO	7.80	4.20	3.20
5 – ICY ATLANTIC		5.80	4.40
9 – COMMENDATION			3.60

$2 EXACTA 4–5 PAID $29.60 $2 TRIFECTA 4–5–9 PAID $95.00
$1 SUPERFECTA 4–5–9–7 PAID $661.10

Gr/ro. c, (Mar), by El Prado–Ire – Elocat's Burglar , by Criminal Type . Trainer Badgett William Jr. Bred by CK Woods Stables Inc (Ky).

TIMO was never far back, was boxed through the second turn angled off the rail leaving the the furlong grounds and ran down the leader in the final strides. ICY ATLANTIC broke sharp, set a slow pace under good handling, gained a clear lead entering the final furlong then just failed to last. COMMENDATION fanned six wide out of the final turn then was slowly gaining late outside. KING'S CORONATION raced close up from the outset, bid outside the leader after six furlongs, continued to be a threat to mid stretch then weakened late. WIRE BOUND was well placed inside but was outkicked late. MASTER DAVID made a mild middle move outside then came up empty. BIG BOOSTER failed to menace. EXPLETIVE stopped after six furlongs. The portable inner rail was set at zero feet.

Owners– 1, C K Woods Stable; 2, Appleton Arthur I; 3, Courtlandt Farms; 4, Cartagena Julio R; 5, Silver Diamond Thoroughbreds Inc; 6, Georgica Stable Stephen Mack and Star Crown Stable; 7, Broman Sr Mary and Chester; 8, Erdenheim Farm

Trainers– 1, Badgett William Jr; 2, Pletcher Todd A; 3, Motion H Graham; 4, Cartagena Julio R; 5, Criollo Manuel; 6, Frankel Robert; 7, Kimmel John C; 8, Matz Michael R

Scratched– Second Performance (04Jun04 4Bel1)

$2 Daily Double (1–4) Paid $34.60 ; Daily Double Pool $9,388 .
$2 Pick Three (4–1–4) Paid $72.20 ; Pick Three Pool $4,145 .
$2 Pick Four (2/3/4/5/6/11/13–4–1–4) Paid $230.20 ; Pick Four Pool $5,067 .

THIRD RACE
Hollywood
JUNE 26, 2004

1⅛ MILES. (Turf Chute) 58TH RUNNING OF THE CINEMA BREEDERS' CUP HANDICAP. Grade III. Purse $150,000 (includes $50,000 BC – Breeders' Cup) FOR THREE YEAR OLDS. By subscription of $150 each on or before Wednesday, June 16 or by supplementary nomination of $3,000 each by 3:00 pm Saturday, June 19. $1,500 additional to start, with $100,000 added and an additional $50,000 from the Breeders' CupFund for Cup nominees only. The host assosiations added money and all fees to be divided 60% to the winner, 20% to second, 12% to third, 6% to fourth and 2% to fifth. Breeders' Cup monies also correspondingly divided provided a Breeders' Cup nominee hasfinished in an awarded position. Any Breeders' Cup monies not awarded will revert to the fund. Weights Sunday, June 20. Starters to be named through the entry box by closing time of entries. Preference will be given in the following order: Highweights willlbe prefered under the following conditions–Breeders' Cup nominees will be preferred over Non–Breeders' Cup nominees assigned equal weights on the scale. Total earnings in 2004 will be used in determining the preference of horses with equal nomination status and equal weight assigned on the scale. All fees for entrants that fail to draw into this race will be canceled. Closed with 13 nominations.CHUTE START.

Value of Race: $153,450 Winner $97,470; second $32,490; third $13,494; fourth $6,747; fifth $3,249. Mutuel Pool $401,695.00 Exacta Pool $239,275.00 Quinella Pool $21,766.00 Trifecta Pool $246,478.00

Last Raced	Horse	M/Eqt.	A.	Wt	PP	St	¼	½	¾	Str	Fin	Jockey	Odds $1
29Dec03 ^{1}SA^{1}	Greek Sun	LB	3	120	3	5	2^{hd}	3^{4}	$3^{2\frac{1}{2}}$	$2^{2\frac{1}{2}}$	1^{2}	Solis A	2.50
22May04 ^{8}Hol^{1}	Laura's Lucky Boy	LB	3	122	7	2	1^{1}	$2^{3\frac{1}{2}}$	1^{hd}	$1^{2\frac{1}{2}}$	$2^{3\frac{1}{2}}$	Smith M E	0.60
30May04 ^{2}Rom^{8}	Whilly-Ire	B	3	117	2	1	$4^{2\frac{1}{2}}$	4^{1}	4^{hd}	5^{1}	3no	Baze T C	13.20
3Apr04 ^{7}Haw^{6}	Kilgowan	LB b	3	116	4	4	7	7	$6^{1\frac{1}{2}}$	3^{hd}	4^{3}	Santiago Javier	21.50
6Jun04 ^{7}Hol^{3}	Chubasco Red	LB	3	117	1	6	5^{1}	6^{1}	7	$6^{1\frac{1}{2}}$	5^{3}	Nakatani C S	22.80
31May04 ^{10}LS^{5}	Unrivalled-GB	LB	3	116	5	3	$3^{1\frac{1}{2}}$	1^{hd}	2^{3}	$4^{\frac{1}{2}}$	6^{3}	Desormeaux K J	a- 6.40
16Jan04 WOL^{6}	Blofeld-GB	LB	3	114	6	7	$6^{\frac{1}{2}}$	5^{hd}	$5^{\frac{1}{2}}$	7	7	Espinoza V	a- 6.40

a–Coupled: Unrivalled–GB and Blofeld–GB.

OFF AT 2:24 Start Good. Won driving. Course firm.

TIME $:24^{1}$, $:47^{3}$, $1:11^{2}$, $1:36^{1}$, $1:48^{2}$ (:24.32, :47.60, 1:11.40, 1:36.31, 1:48.40)

$2 Mutuel Prices:				
	4 – GREEK SUN	7.00	2.80	2.20
	6 – LAURA'S LUCKY BOY		2.20	2.10
	3 – WHILLY–IRE			2.80

$1 EXACTA 4–6 PAID $6.90 $2 QUINELLA 4–6 PAID $4.20
$1 TRIFECTA 4–6–3 PAID $36.10

Dk. b or br. c, (Mar), by Danzig – Sunlit Silence , by Trempolino . Trainer Frankel Robert. Bred by E K Gaylord II & Cheyenne Stables LLC (Ky).

GREEK SUN pulled between horses early then stalked inside, came out leaving the second turn and into the stretch and rallied under some urging to prove best. LAURA'S LUCKY BOY had speed three deep then angled in on the lead on the first turn, dueled inside on the backstretch and into the second turn, kicked clear but could not hold off the winner. WHILLY (IRE) saved ground chasing the pace, split horses in midstretch and edged a rival for third. KILGOWAN chased outside, went three deep on the second turn and into the stretch and lost the show late. CHUBASCO RED settled just off the rail, angled in on the second turn, waited a bit then went around a rival in midstretch and lacked the needed rally. UNRIVALLED (GB) three deep early, went up to press the pace outside the runner-up, came under urging on the second turn then had the rider lose the whip nearing the quarter pole and weakened. BLOFELD (GB) off a bit slowly, went four wide into the first turn, chased outside a rival then between foes on the second turn and also weakened.

Owners– 1, Angelos Peter G; 2, Mercedes Stables LLC; 3, Triple B Farms; 4, Ann Marie Farm; 5, Royce S Jaime Racing Stable Inc; 6, Jim Ford Inc Pearson Daron and Sweesy Jack; 7, Jim Ford Inc or Cassidy or Cuchna

Trainers– 1, Frankel Robert; 2, Orman Jason; 3, O'Neill Doug; 4, Arterburn Lonnie; 5, O'Neill Doug; 6, Cassidy James; 7, Cassidy James

$2 Daily Double (8–4) Paid $22.40 ; Daily Double Pool $38,584 .
$1 Pick Three (7–3/8–4) Paid $639.70 ; Pick Three Pool $141,155 .

NINTH RACE
Monmouth
JUNE 26, 2004

6 FURLONGS. (1.07^{4}) 13TH RUNNING OF THE JERSEY SHORE BREEDERS' CUP. Grade III. Purse $100,000 (includes $25,000 BC – Breeders' Cup) FOR THREE–YEAR–OLDS. By subscription of $100 each, which should accompany the nomination, $1,500 to pass the entry box with $100,000 guaranteed, which includes $25,000 from the Breeders' Cup Fund for Cup nominees only. The Host Association's money to bedivided 60% to the winning owner, 20% to second, 11% to third, 6% to fourth and 3% to fifth. Breeders' Cup Fund money also correspondingly divided providing a Breeders' Cup nominee has finished in an awarded position. Any Breeders' Cup money not awardedreverts to the Fund. Weight: 122 lbs. Non–winners of $60,000 in 2004 allowed 3 lbs.; $45,000 in 2004, 5 lbs.; $45,000, 7 lbs.; A sweepstakes or two races other than maiden or claiming, 9 lbs. The owner of the winner to receive a trophy. Closed Saturday, June 12, 2004 with 28 nominations. A $5,000 supplemental nomination, which includes all fees, was made at time of entry, Thursday, June 24, 2004.

Value of Race: $95,000 Winner $60,000; second $15,000; third $11,000; fourth $6,000; fifth $3,000. Mutuel Pool $117,682.00 Exacta Pool $105,010.00

Last Raced	Horse	M/Eqt.	A.	Wt	PP	St	¼	½	Str	Fin	Jockey	Odds $1
17Apr04 ^{9}Kee^{4}	Pomeroy	b	3	113	1	3	1^{hd}	1^{2}	$1^{4\frac{1}{2}}$	1^{4}	Bravo J	0.80
12Jun04 ^{7}Del^{1}	Gotaghostofachnce	b	3	115	4	1	3^{2}	3^{5}	$3^{3\frac{1}{2}}$	2^{4}	Elliott S	3.70
10Jun04 ^{8}Mth^{5}	Midnight Express	L bf	3	113	2	5	5	$4^{1\frac{1}{2}}$	4^{5}	3^{hd}	Baze M C	23.10
5Jun04 ^{9}Bel^{6}	Value Plus	L b	3	113	3	4	$2^{2\frac{1}{2}}$	$2^{1\frac{1}{2}}$	2^{hd}	$4^{6\frac{1}{2}}$	Coa E M	1.60
30May04 ^{6}Mth^{1}	Dandoon	L bf	3	115	5	2	4^{1}	5	5	5	Velez J A Jr	20.30

OFF AT 4:41 Start Good. Won ridden out. Track fast.

TIME $:22^{2}$, $:44^{2}$, $:56^{2}$, 1:09 (:22.43, :44.53, :56.46, 1:09.07)

$2 Mutuel Prices:				
	1 – POMEROY	3.60	2.20	—
	4 – GOTAGHOSTOFACHANCE		2.80	—
	2 – MIDNIGHT EXPRESS		—	—

$2 EXACTA 1–4 PAID $10.00

B. c, (Apr), by Boundary – Questress , by Seeking the Gold . Trainer Biancone Patrick L. Bred by Cherry Valley Farm LLC (Ky).

POMEROY held a narrow early advantage inside of VALUE PLUS, drew clear on the turn and widened into midstretch then was ridden out. GOTAGHOSTOFACHANCE bobbled at the start, lodged a bid outside turning for home and finished steadily while second best. MIDNIGHT EXPRESS saved ground on the turn and was gaining some at the end. VALUE PLUS prompted the early issue, continued to chase into upper stretch and weakened. DANDOON broke a bit awkwardly, stayed outside and had little left nearing the stretch.

Owners– 1, Smith Derrick and Tabor Michael; 2, Torsney Phillip J; 3, Ocean View Stables; 4, Jones Aaron U and Marie D; 5, D J Stable and Neuwirth Frank

Trainers– 1, Biancone Patrick L; 2, Allard Edward T; 3, Thompson Glenn R; 4, Pletcher Todd A; 5, Kelly Timothy J

EIGHTH RACE
Hollywood
JUNE 27, 2004

1¼ MILES. (Turf) (1.57^{3}) 39TH RUNNING OF THE BEVERLY HILLS HANDICAP. Grade II. Purse $200,000 FOR FILLIES AND MARES THREE YEARS OLD AND UPWARD. By subscription of $200 each on or before Wednesday, June 16 or by supplementary nomination of $4,000 each by 3:00 pm Saturday, June 19. $2,000 additional to start, with $120,000 to the winner, $40,000 tosecond, $24,000 to third, $12,000 to fourth and $4,000 to fifth. Weights Sunday, June 20. Starters to be named through the entry box by closing time of entries. A trophy will be presented to the winning owner and trainer. Closed with 15 nominations. (Railat 10 feet).

Value of Race: $200,000 Winner $120,000; second $40,000; third $24,000; fourth $12,000; fifth $4,000. Mutuel Pool $374,827.00 Exacta Pool $173,884.00 Quinella Pool $18,386.00 Trifecta Pool $208,445.00

Last Raced	Horse	M/Eqt.	A.	Wt	PP	¼	½	¾	1	Str	Fin	Jockey	Odds $1
26May04 ^{5}Hol^{1}	Light Jig-GB	LB	4	114	1	5^{1}	3^{hd}	4^{1}	4^{1}	$4^{2\frac{1}{2}}$	1^{1}	Solis A	2.00
29May04 ^{8}Bel^{1}	Moscow Burning	LB	4	117	4	3½	4½	3^{hd}	3^{hd}	1^{1}	$2^{1\frac{1}{2}}$	Desormeaux K J	2.30
31May04 ^{2}Hol^{1}	Noches DeRosa-Chi	LB b	6	118	2	2^{1}	1½	1^{hd}	1^{hd}	2½	3^{1}	Smith M E	2.20
6Jun04 ^{8}Hol^{3}	Miss Loren-Arg	LB	6	114	5	1^{hd}	2^{1}	2^{1}	2^{1}	3½	$4^{2\frac{1}{2}}$	Court J K	19.20
27May04 ^{7}Hol^{1}	Notting Hill-Brz	LB	5	114	3	4^{hd}	$5^{1\frac{1}{2}}$	5½	6	6	5^{nk}	Baze T C	6.90
29May04 ^{5}Hol^{1}	Ardum Relaunch	LB	5	114	6	6	6	6	5½	5^{hd}	6	Espinoza V	14.80

OFF AT 4:53 Start Good. Won driving. Course firm.

TIME :25^{2}, :49^{3}, 1:13^{3}, 1:37^{4}, 2:01^{2} (:25.47, :49.71, 1:13.78, 1:37.83, 2:01.52)

$2 Mutuel Prices:

1 – LIGHT JIG–GB	6.00	3.60	2.40
4 – MOSCOW BURNING		3.40	2.40
2 – NOCHES DE ROSA–CHI			2.20

$1 EXACTA 1–4 PAID $9.00 $2 QUINELLA 1–4 PAID $8.60
$1 TRIFECTA 1–4–2 PAID $18.80

B. f, (Apr), by Danehill – Nashmeel, by Blushing Groom–Fr. Trainer Frankel Robert. Bred by Juddmonte Farms (GB).

LIGHT JIG (GB) saved ground stalking the pace, swung three deep into the stretch and closed gamely under some urging to prove best. MOSCOW BURNING was in a good position stalking the pace three deep then outside on the backstretch, continued three wide on the second turn, bid into the stretch, gained the lead in upper stretch, inched away in midstretch but could not hold off the winner. NOCHES DE ROSA (CHI) dueled inside a rival, fought back on the second turn and in the stretch but settled for the show. MISS LOREN (ARG) wide in the chute, angled in and dueled outside a foe, was between horses into the stretch and weakened in the final furlong. NOTTING HILL (BRZ) was a bit rank between horses stalking the pace, tugged her way along a bit off the rail on the backstretch and lacked the needed rally. ARDUM RELAUNCH wide in the chute, angled in and chased a bit off the rail, went three deep on the second turn and four wide into the stretch and could not summon the necessary response.

Owners– 1, Juddmonte Farms Inc; 2, Nentwig & Van Kempen; 3, Diamond A Racing Corporation; 4, Llers Corporation; 5, Green Lantern Stables LLC and Barber Gary; 6, Greely C Beau and Mudra Bill

Trainers– 1, Frankel Robert; 2, Cassidy James; 3, Mandella Richard; 4, Seglin Luis E; 5, Sahadi Jenine; 6, Greely C Beau

$2 Daily Double (5–1) Paid $14.00 ; Daily Double Pool $32,516 .
$1 Pick Three (5/6/7–5–1) Paid $24.40 ; Pick Three Pool $85,392 .

NINTH RACE
Prairie Mdw
JULY 2, 2004

1$\frac{1}{16}$ MILES. (1.40^{4}) 6TH RUNNING OF THE IOWA OAKS. Grade III. Purse $125,000 FOR THREE–YEAR–OLD FILLIES. Weights: 121 lbs. Non–winners of $50,000 at one mile or over in 2004 allowed 3 lbs.; non–winners of $40,000 in 2004 allowed 6 lbs.; non–winners of $20,000 in 2004 allowed 9 lbs. No nomination fee. $750.00 to pass the entry–boxon Monday, June 28. $1,000.00 additional to start on Friday, July 2 with $125,000 guaranteed of which $75,000 to the owner of the winner, $25,000 to second, $12,500 to third, $6,250 to fourth, $3,750 to fifth, $2,500 to sixth. SUPPLEMENTAL NOMINATIONS ATTIME OF ENTRY WITH A FEE OF $3,500 TO ENTER AND START. Starters to be named through the entry box by the usual time of closing. Failure to draw intothe race cancels all fees. Closed Tuesday, June 15, 2004 with Fifty–five (55) Nominations.

Value of Race: $125,000 Winner $75,000; second $25,000; third $12,500; fourth $6,250; fifth $3,750; sixth $2,500. Mutuel Pool $57,678.00 Exacta Pool $28,489.00 Quinella Pool $3,476.00 Trifecta Pool $25,420.00

Last Raced	Horse	M/Eqt.	A.	Wt	PP	St	¼	½	¾	Str	Fin	Jockey	Odds $1
31May04 ^{8}Pim^{1}	He Loves Me	LB	3	118	5	7	5½	5^{2}	2^{hd}	2^{4}	1¾	Santana J Z	3.10
17Jun04 ^{2}CD^{5}	Prospective Saint	LB	3	115	6	1	1^{1}	$1^{1\frac{1}{2}}$	1^{1}	1½	$2^{6\frac{1}{4}}$	Sellers S J	8.00
6Jun04 ^{8}AP^{3}	Home Court	LB	3	115	3	3	$3^{1\frac{1}{2}}$	2½	3^{1}	3^{2}	$3^{1\frac{1}{4}}$	Day P	1.60
13Jun04 ^{10}CD^{2}	Family Business	LB	3	115	7	5	6½	6^{hd}	8	4^{hd}	4^{nk}	Martinez J R Jr	13.50
12Jun04 ^{7}Mth^{2}	Menifeeque	LB b	3	115	1	8	8	8	6^{hd}	5½	5¾	Bridgmohan S X	4.00
19Jun04 ^{7}Cby^{3}	Platinum Ballet	LB b	3	112	8	6	$7^{1\frac{1}{2}}$	$7^{1\frac{1}{2}}$	7½	6½	$6^{3\frac{1}{4}}$	Corbett G W	22.90
5Jun04 ^{9}PrM^{1}	Josh's Madelyn	LB b	3	115	4	2	4^{5}	4^{3}	4^{1}	7^{5}	$7^{9\frac{1}{4}}$	Doocy T T	6.40
18Jun04 ^{10}PrM^{2}	Take D' Tour	B	3	114	2	4	2½	3^{3}	5½	8	8	Blanc B	51.70

OFF AT 9:44 Start Good. Won driving. Track fast.

TIME :23, :46^{3}, 1:11^{2}, 1:36^{2}, 1:42^{4} (:23.14, :46.67, 1:11.58, 1:36.42, 1:42.80)

$2 Mutuel Prices:

5 – HE LOVES ME	8.20	4.80	3.60
6 – PROSPECTIVE SAINT		7.40	4.80
3 – HOME COURT			3.60

$2 EXACTA 5–6 PAID $77.20 $2 QUINELLA 5–6 PAID $28.80
$2 TRIFECTA 5–6–3 PAID $203.20

B. f, (Mar), by Not For Love – Palliser Bay, by Frosty the Snowman. Trainer Small Richard W. Bred by Buckingham Farm (Md).

HE LOVES ME settled well off the early pace while saving ground on the first turn, angled off the inside early on the backstretch, made a quick four wide move entering the final turn, chased the runner up around the bend, wore that one down through the final furlong under strong handling. PROSPECTIVE SAINT sprinted clear early and set the pace racing well in hand for the first half mile, continued on the lead to midstretch, fought on willingly inside of the winner but could not quite match strides late. HOME COURT chased the pace from the two path to the stretch before weakening. FAMILY BUSINESS raced well off the pace to the stretch before passing a few tired ones. MENIFEEQUE was taken back to trail early, raced five wide on the final turn but failed to produce a rally. PLATINUM BALLET showed little while racing inside. JOSH'S MADELYN raced three wide chasing the pacesetter around the first turn, was four wide on the final turn while remaining a forward factor, tired through the stretch. TAKE D' TOUR raced close up along the rail while pulling a bit early, remained within range to midway on the final turn before faltering through the stretch.

Owners– 1, Buckingham Farm; 2, M-2 Stable LLC; 3, Alnoff Stable; 4, Overbrook Farm; 5, Live Oak Plantation; 6, Sanders Wayne R; 7, Pressley Michael and Neidig Jim; 8, Muller Alice

Trainers– 1, Small Richard W; 2, Byrne Patrick B; 3, McPeek Kenneth G; 4, Stewart Dallas; 5, Mott William I; 6, Von Hemel Donnie K; 7, Jones J Larry; 8, Hickey P Noel

Scratched– Native Annie (19Jun04 ^{8}Del^{5})

$2 Pick Three (5–7–5) Paid $456.40 ; Pick Three Pool $9,070 .

NINTH RACE
Arlington
JULY 3, 2004

$1\frac{1}{16}$ MILES. (Turf) (1.41) 70TH RUNNING OF THE ARLINGTON CLASSIC. Grade II. Purse $200,000 FOR THREE-YEAR-OLDS. By subscription of $300 each horse (Early) Wednesday, April 14, 2004; $500 each horse (Late Nomination) on Wednesday, June 16, 2004. Fee to accompany the nomination. A Supplementary Nomination of $8,000 may be made on Wednesday, June30, 2004, which includes entry and starting fees. Original nominees to pay $1,500 to pass the entry box and $1,500 additional to start, with $200,000 Guaranteed, of which $120,000 to the winner; $40,000 to second; $22,000 to third; $12,000 to fourth and$6,000 to fifth. WEIGHT: 126 lbs. Non-winners of $100,000 twice at one mile or over in 2004, allowed 3 lbs.; $100,000 once or $60,000 twice at one mile or over in 2004, 5 lbs.; $60,000 once at one mile or over in 2004, 7 lbs. (Maiden and Claiming races noot considered.) Trophy to the owner of the winner. Lane 1 Early nomations closed Wed. April 14, 2004 with 174 nomations, late nomations closed Wed, June 16, 2004 with 7 nomations. (If the management considers it inadvisable to run this race on the Turf Course, it will be run on the main track at One Mile and One Eighth).

Value of Race: $200,000 Winner $120,000; second $40,000; third $22,000; fourth $12,000; fifth $6,000. Mutuel Pool $349,194.00 Exacta Pool $234,839.00 Trifecta Pool $212,987.00 Superfecta Pool $68,864.00

Last Raced	Horse	M/Eqt.	A.	Wt	PP	St	¼	½	¾	Str	Fin	Jockey	Odds $1
22May04 ^{8}Hol^{2}	Toasted	L	3	121	1	4	5^{1}	$6^{\frac{1}{2}}$	$6^{1\frac{1}{2}}$	$3^{\frac{1}{2}}$	$1^{3\frac{1}{4}}$	Douglas R R	1.40
22May04 ^{8}Hol^{3}	Street Theatre	L b	3	119	3	6	7^{2}	7^{2}	$7^{\frac{1}{2}}$	6^{1}	2^{nk}	Marquez C H Jr	5.40
12Jun04 ^{5}CD^{3}	Cool Conductor	b	3	119	4	2	$1^{\frac{1}{2}}$	$1^{\frac{1}{2}}$	$1^{\frac{1}{2}}$	$1^{\frac{1}{2}}$	3^{hd}	Velasquez C	2.80
5Jun04 ^{9}AP^{1}	Up Anchor	L	3	119	7	8	6^{hd}	4^{1}	$5^{\frac{1}{2}}$	4^{3}	$4^{3\frac{1}{4}}$	Emigh C A	11.50
20Jun04 ^{7}CD^{1}	Old Deuteronomy	L	3	119	2	1	$2^{2\frac{1}{2}}$	$2^{\frac{1}{2}}$	$2^{\frac{1}{2}}$	2^{hd}	5^{3}	Razo E Jr	5.50
31May04 ^{7}CD^{1}	Count On the Tuna	L	3	119	8	7	4^{1}	$5^{\frac{1}{2}}$	$4^{\frac{1}{2}}$	5^{hd}	$6^{\frac{1}{2}}$	Campbell J M	11.40
20Jun04 ^{4}AP^{7}	Caiman	L	3	119	6	3	8	8	8	7^{5}	$7^{7\frac{3}{4}}$	Sterling L J Jr	32.00
31May04 ^{5}CD^{3}	Exploited Storm	L	3	119	5	5	$3^{1\frac{1}{2}}$	3^{hd}	$3^{\frac{1}{2}}$	8	8	Lovato F Jr	22.60

OFF AT 5:12 Start Good. Won driving. Course soft.

TIME :24^{3}, :51, 1:17^{4}, 1:44^{2}, 1:50^{4} (:24.72, :51.02, 1:17.82, 1:44.44, 1:50.91)

$2 Mutuel Prices:			
1 – TOASTED	4.80	3.20	2.40
3 – STREET THEATRE		5.20	3.20
4 – COOL CONDUCTOR			2.80

$2 EXACTA 1–3 PAID $21.20 $2 TRIFECTA 1–3–4 PAID $61.60
$2 SUPERFECTA 1–3–4–7 PAID $260.80

Dk. b or br. c, (Apr), by Hennessy – Burrows, by Seattle Song. Trainer De Seroux Laura. Bred by James D Haley (Ky).

TOASTED raced just outside near the middle of the field, split horses turning for home, rallied to the lead in deep stretch and drew off under urging. STREET THEATRE was allowed to settle while not far back, came out five wide for the drive, rallied in the stretch and gained the place while no danger to the winner. COOL CONDUCTOR was a bit rank in the early going, set the pace from the rail while pressed, maintained the advantage to deep stretch and weakened a bit late. UP ANCHOR raced inside near the middle of the field, rallied to loom a threat in the stretch then could not find a winning bid. OLD DEUTERONOMY pressed the pace from just outside, remained prominent to the stretch and tired in the final furlong. COUNT ON THE TUNA raced off the rail near the middle of the field and also tired. CAIMAN lacked speed and was always outrun. EXPLOITED STORM raced close up three wide and tired.

Owners– 1, Sidney L Port Trust S Port; 2, Darley Stable J Bell et al; 3, Garner David E; 4, Ralls and Foster LLC; 5, Gene Voss Abbott Properties and Hardeman LLC; 6, Crawford Jerry; 7, Achar Victor; 8, Stony Oak Farm LLC

Trainers– 1, De Seroux Laura; 2, Harty Eoin; 3, Mott William I; 4, McGee Paul J; 5, O'Callaghan Niall M; 6, Romans Dale; 7, Medina Angel M; 8, Barnett Bobby C

$1 Pick Three (2–8–1) Paid $214.50 ; Pick Three Pool $8,580 .

SEVENTH RACE
Belmont
JULY 3, 2004

$1\frac{1}{4}$ MILES. (1.58^{1}) 118TH RUNNING OF THE SUBURBAN HANDICAP. Grade I. Purse $500,000 (Up To $55,000 NYSBFOA) A HANDICAP FOR THREE YEAR OLDS AND UPWARD. By subscription of $500 each, which should accompany the nomination; $2,500 to pass the entry box; $2,500 to start. The purse to be divided 60% to the winner, 20% to second, 10% to third,5% to fourth, 3% to fifth and 2% divided equally among remaining finishers. Closed June 19, 2004 with 21 Nominations. The NTRA National Pick 4 is a wager that includes the 7th race at Belmont as Leg A, the 8th race at Churchill Downs as Leg B, the 10th race at Monmouth as Leg C, and the 6th race at Hollywood as Leg D.

Value of Race: $500,000 Winner $300,000; second $100,000; third $50,000; fourth $25,000; fifth $15,000; sixth $3,334; seventh $3,334; eighth $3,332. Mutuel Pool $1,077,067.00 Exacta Pool $721,416.00 Trifecta Pool $525,445.00 Superfecta Pool $107,572.00

Last Raced	Horse	M/Eqt.	A.	Wt	PP	¼	½	¾	1	Str	Fin	Jockey	Odds $1
12Jun04 ^{9}CD^{4}	Peace Rules	L	4	120	3	$1^{1\frac{1}{2}}$	1^{1}	$1^{\frac{1}{2}}$	1^{hd}	2^{hd}	1^{nk}	Bailey J D	3.20
12Jun04 ^{7}Bel^{3}	Newfoundland	L b	4	114	2	2^{hd}	2^{hd}	3^{7}	3^{2}	$3^{2\frac{1}{2}}$	2no	Velazquez J R	8.40
19Jun04 ^{10}Suf^{2}	Funny Cide	L	4	117	1	3^{5}	3^{8}	2^{hd}	2^{1}	$1^{\frac{1}{2}}$	$3^{\frac{3}{4}}$	Santos J A	4.10
12Jun04 ^{9}CD^{1}	Colonial Colony	L f	6	116	6	7^{hd}	8	6^{hd}	7^{10}	$4^{\frac{1}{2}}$	4no	Bejarano R	21.80
19Jun04 ^{10}Suf^{6}	Sarava	L	5	113	4	$4^{2\frac{1}{2}}$	4^{1}	$5^{3\frac{1}{2}}$	$5^{1\frac{1}{2}}$	6^{hd}	$5^{1\frac{1}{4}}$	Castellano J J	22.60
12Jun04 ^{7}Bel^{2}	Dynever	L	4	116	7	$6^{\frac{1}{2}}$	$7^{\frac{1}{2}}$	$7^{2\frac{1}{2}}$	$6^{\frac{1}{2}}$	7^{12}	$6^{2\frac{1}{2}}$	Nakatani C S	2.35
31May04 ^{9}Bel^{2}	Bowman's Band	L	6	115	8	8	$6^{1\frac{1}{2}}$	4^{hd}	4^{hd}	5^{hd}	$7^{16\frac{3}{4}}$	Chavez J F	3.45
23May04 ^{9}CD^{2}	Devil Time	L	7	113	5	$5^{3\frac{1}{2}}$	5^{hd}	8	8	8	8	Troilo W D	46.25

OFF AT 4:21 Start Good. Won driving. Track fast.

TIME :23^{4}, :46^{1}, 1:09^{1}, 1:33^{4}, 1:59^{2} (:23.85, :46.36, 1:09.33, 1:33.93, 1:59.52)

$2 Mutuel Prices:			
3 – PEACE RULES	8.40	5.40	4.10
2 – NEWFOUNDLAND		8.40	6.00
1 – FUNNY CIDE			4.40

$2 EXACTA 3–2 PAID $64.50 $2 TRIFECTA 3–2–1 PAID $198.50
$2 SUPERFECTA 3–2–1–6 PAID $2,123.00

Ch. c, (Apr), by Jules – Hold to Fashion, by Hold Your Peace. Trainer Frankel Robert. Bred by Newchance Farm (Fla).

PEACE RULES took charge from the outset, set a strong pace while in hand, responded when joined by FUNNY CIDE from the inside and NEWFOUNDLAND from the outside, dug in gamely after losing the lead by the eighth pole, came again while between those two rivals and proved best after a long drive. NEWFOUNDLAND raced with the pace from the outside, advanced three wide on the second turn, loomed boldly approaching the eighth pole and stayed on gamely but could not handle the winner late. FUNNY CIDE raced with the pace along the inside, came through on the rail on the second turn, earned a short lead in the stretch and stayed on gamely on the rail. COLONIAL COLONY was outrun early on, advanced on the second turn, swung wide into the stretch, responded when roused and finished gamely outside. SARAVA was urged along to stay close early, rallied three wide approaching the stretch and dug in gamely to the wire. DYNEVER was outrun early, rallied along the inside on the second turn and finished well. BOWMAN'S BAND was unhurried outside while outrun early, was angled to the inside on the backstretch, put in a run along the rail on the second turn and had little left for the stretch drive. DEVIL TIME dropped back after the opening half mile.

Owners– 1, Gann Edmund A; 2, Sumaya Us Stables; 3, Sackatoga Stable; 4, Nolan Chris; 5, New Phoenix Stable and Roy Mrs Susan; 6, Wills Catherine and Karches Peter; 7, Schwartz Martin S; 8, Anderson Brad

Trainers– 1, Frankel Robert; 2, Pletcher Todd A; 3, Tagg Barclay; 4, Bindner Walter M Jr; 5, Baffert Bob; 6, Clement Christophe; 7, Jerkens H Allen; 8, Carroll David

$2 Pick Three (13–6–3) Paid $705.00 ; Pick Three Pool $113,310 .
$2 Daily Double (6–3) Paid $53.00 ; Daily Double Pool $173,495 .

EIGHTH RACE
Belmont
JULY 3, 2004

6 FURLONGS. (1.07^{3}) 57TH RUNNING OF THE PRIORESS. Grade I. Purse $250,000 (Up To $37,500 NYSBFOA) FOR FILLIES THREE YEARS OLD. By subscription of $250 each, which should accompany the nomination; $1,250 to pass the entry box; $1,250 to start. The purse to be divided 60% to the winner, 20% to second, 10% to third, 5% to fourth,3% to fifth and 2% divided equally among remaining finishers. 121 lbs. Non–winners of $60,000 twice allowed 2 lbs.; $60,000; or $45,000 in 2004, 4 lbs.; $30,000, or two races, 6 lbs. (Maiden, claiming, starter, restricted and restricted stake races not considered in allowances.) Closed Saturday, June 19,2004 with 24 Nominations. Trophies will be presented to the winning owner, trainer and jockey.

Value of Race: $250,000 Winner $150,000; second $50,000; third $25,000; fourth $12,500; fifth $7,500; sixth $1,250; seventh $1,250; eighth $1,250; ninth $1,250. Mutuel Pool $760,442.00 Exacta Pool $563,251.00 Trifecta Pool $459,809.00

Last Raced	Horse	M/Eqt.	A.	Wt	PP	St	¼	½	Str	Fin	Jockey	Odds $1
4Jun04 ^{10}Bel^{3}	Friendly Michelle	L b	3	119	8	6	3½	2½	1^{hd}	12¼	Nakatani C S	1.85
12Jun04 ^{8}Bel^{2}	Feline Story	L	3	121	3	3	41½	4½	3½	2no	Castellano J J	26.75
6Jun04 ^{9}Mth^{1}	Forest Music	L	3	119	2	2	11½	11½	24½	3¾	Bridgmohan S X	5.60
10Jun04 ^{8}Bel^{3}	Why You	f	3	115	4	9	9	9	7^{hd}	4¾	Chavez J F	5.50
12Jun04 ^{8}Bel^{1}	She's a Mugs	L	3	117	7	7	83½	81½	5½	51¾	Bejarano R	26.00
5Jun04 ^{6}Bel^{3}	Aspen Gal	L b	3	117	5	5	5^{hd}	6½	8^{3}	6½	Gryder A T	14.00
4Jun04 ^{10}Bel^{4}	Bending Strings	L	3	119	1	1	6½	5^{hd}	4½	72¼	Bailey J D	3.95
4Jun04 ^{10}Bel^{7}	Bohemian Lady	L	3	119	9	8	72½	7^{1}	9	81¾	Velazquez J R	5.90
30May04 ^{8}Hol^{2}	Very Vegas	L	3	119	6	4	2^{1}	31½	6^{hd}	9	Santos J A	31.75

OFF AT 4:53 Start Good . Won driving. Track fast.

TIME :21^{4}, :44^{2}, :56^{1}, 1:09 (:21.82, :44.43, :56.34, 1:09.09)

$2 Mutuel Prices:

9 – FRIENDLY MICHELLE	5.70	3.40	2.80
5 – FELINE STORY		14.00	8.40
4 – FOREST MUSIC			5.20

$2 EXACTA 9–5 PAID $87.50 $2 TRIFECTA 9–5–4 PAID $435.00

Ch. f, (May), by Artax – Valiant Jewel , by Buckley Boy . Trainer Baffert Bob. Bred by Ronald Fein (Ky).

FRIENDLY MICHELLE raced close up outside while in hand, rallied three wide nearing the stretch, responded when roused, reached the front approaching the eighth pole and drew clear late under a drive. FELINE STORY was urged along early on, came wide into the stretch and finished gamely outside to earn the place award. FOREST MUSIC quickly opened a clear lead, set the pace while in hand and weakened in the final furlong. WHY YOU broke slowly, was outrun early, came wide entering the stretch and was going late. SHE'S A MUGS was outrun early, raced inside, rallied nearing the stretch and finished well. ASPEN GAL was hustled along outside, chased the pace while four wide and weakened in the stretch. BENDING STRINGS raced inside and had no response when roused. BOHEMIAN LADY raced wide throughout and tired. VERY VEGAS chased the pace along the inside and tired after a half mile.

Owners– 1, Friendly Ed; 2, Robsham Mrs E P; 3, Gill Michael J; 4, Bohemia Stable; 5, Lucky Shamrock Stable; 6, Gann Edmund A; 7, Gunther John D; 8, Padua Stables; 9, Nielsen Jeffrey L

Trainers– 1, Baffert Bob; 2, Hough Stanley M; 3, Shuman Mark; 4, Jerkens H Allen; 5, Zito Nicholas P; 6, Frankel Robert; 7, McLaughlin Kiaran P; 8, Pletcher Todd A; 9, Polanco Marcelo

Scratched– Reforest (19Jun04 ^{8}Bel^{1}) , Frenchglen (26May04 ^{8}Bel^{1}) , Rodeo Licious (12Jun04 ^{7}Mth^{5})

EIGHTH RACE
Churchill
JULY 3, 2004

1 MILE. (Turf) (1.33^{3}) 15TH RUNNING OF THE FIRECRACKER BREEDERS' CUP HANDICAP. Grade II. Purse $250,000 (includes $75,000 BC – Breeders' Cup) FOR THREE–YEAR–OLDS AND UPWARD.

Value of Race: $287,750 Winner $178,405; third $28,775; second $57,550; fourth $14,388; fifth $8,632. Mutuel Pool $399,056.00 Exacta Pool $288,911.00 Trifecta Pool $244,800.00 Superfecta Pool $77,752.00

Last Raced	Horse	M/Eqt.	A.	Wt	PP	St	¼	½	¾	Str	Fin	Jockey	Odds $1
23May04 ^{8}Bel^{1}	Quantum Merit	L	5	117	7	1	33½	32½	31½	2^{3}	11½	Sellers S J	5.70
12Jun04 ^{10}CD^{1}	[D]Senor Swinger	L	4	117	3	4	4^{hd}	51½	51½	3½	2^{2}	Day P	2.40
1May04 ^{9}CD^{10}	Perfect Soul-Ire	L b	6	121	4	8	7½	7½	6½	6^{1}	3^{1}	Melancon L	1.90
8May04 ^{8}CD^{3}	Mr. Krisley	L f	6	113	6	6	5^{3}	42½	4^{3}	41½	4^{1}	Perret C	58.70
9Apr04 ^{9}Kee^{3}	Royal Spy	L	6	118	1	3	1^{2}	1^{hd}	1^{hd}	1½	5½	Albarado R J	4.60
3Jun04 ^{8}AP^{1}	On the Course	L	4	112	5	9	9	9	9	9	6½	McKee J	8.50
12Jun04 ^{10}CD^{6}	Everything to Gain	L	5	114	8	5	82½	8^{4}	7½	7^{3}	77½	Guidry M	13.00
4Jun04 ^{9}CD^{8}	Puget Sound	L b	4	112	2	2	22½	2^{4}	2^{2}	5^{hd}	8^{1}	Coa D	51.60
12Jun04 ^{10}CD^{3}	Majestic Thief	L b	5	115	9	7	6½	61½	8^{8}	8^{hd}	9	Castanon J L	41.50

[D] – Senor Swinger disqualified and placed 3rd

OFF AT 4:53 Start Good . Won driving. Course firm.

TIME :22^{4}, :45^{4}, 1:09^{3}, 1:21^{4}, 1:34 (:22.97, :45.94, 1:09.62, 1:21.94, 1:34.15)

$2 Mutuel Prices:

7 – QUANTUM MERIT	13.40	6.00	3.80
4 – PERFECT SOUL–IRE		4.20	2.60
3 – SENOR SWINGER			2.40

$2 EXACTA 7–4 PAID $53.60 $2 TRIFECTA 7–4–3 PAID $141.20
$2 SUPERFECTA 7–4–3–6 PAID $2,624.00

Dk. b or br. g, (May), by Hansel – Just Flirting , by Green Dancer . Trainer Carroll Del W II. Bred by Mr & Mrs Gerald Nielsen (NY).

QUANTUM MERIT, well placed from the outset, was rated along three wide, eased out five wide entering the stretch, took over leaving the eighth pole, was roused with the whip on the right side and continued to the wire under solid hand encouragement. SENOR SWINGER settled near the inside within easy striking distance, raced under light restraint, continued inside into the lane, came out under left-handed urging leaving the eighth pole bothering PERFECT SOUL (IRE), was outside the winner five wide late but couldn't offer the needed response. PERFECT SOUL (IRE), reserved soon after the start and three wide for six furlongs, came out between horses four or five wide when advancing into the stretch, was steadied sharply, taken up briefly leaving the eighth pole and forced out when SENOR SWINGER suddenly came out in front of him, quickly recovered and finished with good courage. MR. KRISLEY, never far back and following the leaders four or five wide, came out farther on the course for the drive but couldn't offer a closing threat. ROYAL SPY gained a clear lead near the inside early, was joined early on the backstretch from the outside by PUGET SOUND, battled with that one to the stretch, shook him off but faltered the last eighth. ON THE COURSE, outrun to the stretch while three wide, remained in that position on the course and improved position while unable to menace. EVERYTHING TO GAIN, unhurried early and four wide, worked his way out eight wide for the drive but was empty. PUGET SOUND chased front-running ROYAL SPY from the outset, went up to vie for the lead outside that one on the backstretch, raced close up to the stretch, weakened and swerved out and in leaving the furlong grounds. MAJESTIC THIEF raced four wide and tired. FOLLOWING A FOUL CLAIM LODGED BY THE RIDER OF PERFECT SOUL (IRE) AND STEWARDS' INQUIRY, SENOR SWINGER WAS DISQUALIFIED FROM SECOND AND PLACED THIRD.

Owners– 1, Very Un Stable Joseph Gioia; 2, Lewis Robert B and Beverly J; 3, Fipke Charles E; 4, Arnold Donna C; 5, Jayaraman Kalarikkal K and Vilasini D; 6, Golden Barry; 7, Ramsey Kenneth L and Sarah K; 8, Overbrook Farm; 9, Freeman Walt Rudd Mason and McClinton Don

Trainers– 1, Carroll Del W II; 2, Baffert Bob; 3, Attfield Roger L; 4, Lopresti Charles; 5, Amoss Thomas; 6, Stidham Michael; 7, Romans Dale; 8, Lukas D Wayne; 9, Bindner Walter M Jr

---

$2 Pick Three (4–5–7) Paid $2,263.20 ; Pick Three Pool $43,309 .

FOURTH RACE
Hollywood
JULY 3, 2004

1 MILE. (Turf) (1.32³) 7TH RUNNING OF THE ROYAL HEROINE. Grade III. Purse $100,000 FOR FILLIES AND MARES THREE-YEAR-OLDS AND UPWARD. By subscription of $100 each on or before Wednesday, June 23 or by supplementary nomination of $2,000 each by closing time of entries. $1,000 additional to start, with $100,000 added, of which 60% to the winner, 20% to second, 12% to third, 6% to fourth and 2% to fifth. Three year olds 114 lbs. Older 123 lbs. Non-winners of $60,000 at a mile or over in 2004 allowed 2 lbs. Such a race in 2003 allowed 4 lbs. Non-winners of two races other than maiden, claiming or starter at a mile over in 2004 allowed 6 lbs. Such a race in 2004 allowed 8 lbs. Starters to be named through the entry box by closing time of entries. A trophy will be presented to the winning owner. Closed with 17 nominations. 1supplementary nomination: Etoile Montante

Value of Race: $109,700 Winner $65,820; second $21,940; third $13,164; fourth $6,582; fifth $2,194. Mutuel Pool $402,135.00 Exacta Pool $218,027.00 Quinella Pool $19,545.00 Trifecta Pool $209,792.00

Last Raced	Horse	M/Eqt.	A.	Wt	PP	St	1/4	1/2	3/4	Str	Fin	Jockey	Odds $1
31May04 8LS2	Janeian-NZ	LB	6	121	4	4	3 2 1/2	3 2	3 2	1 hd	1 2	Desormeaux K J	1.90
31May04 8LS3	Katdogawn-GB	LB	4	123	6	6	6	6	6	4 hd	2 1/2	Smith M E	1.50
6Jun04 8Hol7	Makeup Artist	LB	4	121	1	5	5 1 1/2	4 hd	4 hd	3 1	3 1	Espinoza V	4.40
6Jun04 8Hol4	Sparkling Ava	LB bf	5	115	5	3	2 2 1/2	2 2 1/2	1 hd	2 1 1/2	4 hd	Garcia M S	44.40
25Apr04 7Hol8	Fun House	LB	5	123	2	2	4 1	5 1 1/2	5 1	5 1/2	5 8 1/2	Baze T C	4.90
29May04 3BM5	Hippogator	LB b	4	117	3	1	1 1	1 1	2 1 1/2	6	6	Santiago Javier	12.50

OFF AT 1:33 Start Good . Won driving. Course firm.

TIME :23³, :47¹, 1:11, 1:23, 1:34³ (:23.70, :47.20, 1:11.03, 1:23.09, 1:34.79)

$2 Mutuel Prices:				
	5 – JANEIAN-NZ	5.80	2.60	2.20
	7 – KATDOGAWN-GB		2.40	2.10
	1 – MAKEUP ARTIST			2.40

$1 EXACTA 5–7 PAID $5.90 $2 QUINELLA 5–7 PAID $5.00
$1 TRIFECTA 5–7–1 PAID $19.00

B. m, (Oct), by The Jogger – Taipari–NZ , by McGinty–NZ . Trainer Calhoun William Bret. Bred by G A McMullin I A McMullin & &Mrs A J Nooyen (NZ).

JANEIAN (NZ) angled in and saved ground then stalked a bit off the rail, went outside a rival into the stretch, came out in upper stretch, surged to the front under urging in midstretch and pulled clear. KATDOGAWN (GB) broke slowly, angled in and saved ground off the pace, continued a bit off the rail on the second turn, split rivals in midstretch then angled in again and finished with interest inside. MAKEUP ARTIST came a bit off the inside into the first turn, chased just off the rail then outside a rival on the second turn, went three deep into the stretch and was outfinished. SPARKLING AVA pulled a bit early, stalked off the rail, bid outside the pacesetter on the second turn and took a short lead, inched away into the stretch, could not match the winner, was in a bit tight late and was outfinished for a minor award. FUN HOUSE saved ground chasing the pace, came out in upper stretch, split horses in midstretch and could not summon the necessary late response. HIPPOGATOR sped to the early lead, set the pace inside, dueled along the rail on the second turn and weakened in the stretch.

Owners– 1, England Greg L; 2, Cuchna John R Jim Ford Inc and Pearson Deron; 3, Krikorian George; 4, Schwartz Barry K; 5, Winchell Thoroughbreds LLC; 6, Blanchard or Maser or Todaro

Trainers– 1, Calhoun William Bret; 2, Cassidy James; 3, Shirreffs John; 4, Inda Eduardo; 5, McAnally Ronald; 6, Hollendorfer Jerry

Scratched– Etoile Montante (05Jun04 8Bel3)

$2 Daily Double (4–5) Paid $11.20 ; Daily Double Pool $26,363 .
$1 Pick Three (4–4–5) Paid $182.30 ; Pick Three Pool $73,343 .

SIXTH RACE
Hollywood
JULY 3, 2004

1$\frac{1}{4}$ MILES. (Turf) (1.57^{3}) 3RD RUNNING OF THE AMERICAN OAKS. Grade I. Purse $750,000 FOR NORTHERN HEMISPHERE AND SOUTHERN HEMISPHERE (AUSTRALIAN AND NEW ZEALAND. Foaled after August 1, 2000 and before July 31, 2001) FILLIES THREE-YEARS-OLD. The owner of the winner to receive $450,000, with $150,000 to second, $90,000 to third, $45,000 tofourth and $15,000 to fifth. Weights: Northern Hemisphere: 121 lbs. Sourthern Hemisphere (Australian & New Zealand): 125 lbs. Pre-entry fee requirements – In order to be eligible for entry in the American Oaks, horses accepting invitations must make a pre-entry payment of $5,000 (US). Entry fee requirements – Entries for the American Oaks will promptly close at 10:00am (PST), Wednesday, June 30, 2004. An entry fee of $5,000 (US) will be due at the time of entry. A trophy will be presented to the winning owner and trainer.

Value of Race: $750,000 Winner $450,000; second $150,000; third $90,000; fourth $45,000; fifth $15,000. Mutuel Pool $1,038,674.00 Exacta Pool $640,550.00 Quinella Pool $44,125.00 Trifecta Pool $566,335.00 Superfecta Pool $200,280.00

Last Raced	Horse	M/Eqt.	A.	Wt	PP	1/4	1/2	3/4	1	Str	Fin	Jockey	Odds $1
5Jun04 ^{8}Hol^{4}	Ticker Tape-GB	LB	3	121	7	$5^{1\frac{1}{2}}$	4^{1}	$4^{1\frac{1}{2}}$	$2^{\frac{1}{2}}$	1^{2}	1^{1}	Desormeaux K J	12.00
23May04 ^{11}Tok^{4}	DnceinthMood-Jpn		3	121	6	2^{1}	3^{1}	3^{hd}	3^{hd}	$3^{2\frac{1}{2}}$	2^{2}	Take Y	1.40
12Jun04 ^{4}Hol^{3}	Hollywood Story	LB b	3	121	4	4^{hd}	$5^{\frac{1}{2}}$	5^{hd}	5^{hd}	6^{hd}	$3^{\frac{1}{2}}$	Sorenson D	16.10
5Jun04 ^{8}Hol^{2}	WesternHemispher	LB	3	121	10	1^{1}	$1^{1\frac{1}{2}}$	1^{1}	$1^{1\frac{1}{2}}$	$2^{\frac{1}{2}}$	$4^{\frac{1}{2}}$	Flores D R	11.60
5Jun04 ^{8}Hol^{5}	Amorama-FR	LB b	3	121	5	13	13	13	10^{1}	$8^{\frac{1}{2}}$	$5^{\frac{1}{2}}$	John K	62.70
13Jun04 ^{8}Bel^{1}	Mambo Slew	B	3	121	2	10^{hd}	$10^{\frac{1}{2}}$	11^{1}	8^{hd}	$7^{1\frac{1}{2}}$	6^{1}	Smith M E	6.80
12Jun04 ^{5}Avo^{6}	Boulevrdofdrms-NZ	B b	4	125	3	$11^{\frac{1}{2}}$	11^{1}	9^{1}	$9^{1\frac{1}{2}}$	5^{hd}	$7^{\frac{1}{2}}$	Grylls G	57.30
29May04 ^{9}CD^{3}	Eternal Melody-NZ	LB	4	125	11	12^{2}	$12^{\frac{1}{2}}$	$12^{\frac{1}{2}}$	13	11^{2}	$8^{\frac{1}{2}}$	Solis A	6.10
6Jun04 Gow^{1}	Misty Heights-GB	LB	3	121	1	7^{1}	$9^{1\frac{1}{2}}$	7^{hd}	6^{hd}	9^{1}	9no	Espinoza V	9.60
12Jun04 ^{7}CD^{2}	Western Ransom	LB	3	121	9	3^{1}	2^{hd}	2^{1}	$4^{1\frac{1}{2}}$	4^{2}	$10^{\frac{1}{2}}$	Santiago Javier	20.40
13Jun04 CHY^{10}	Steel Princess-Ire	B	3	121	13	9^{1}	8^{hd}	10^{hd}	11^{1}	10^{hd}	11^{4}	Baze T C	17.10
5Jun04 ^{8}Hol^{1}	Lovely Rafaela	LB	3	121	12	$8^{\frac{1}{2}}$	7^{2}	6^{1}	7^{1}	$12^{1\frac{1}{2}}$	12^{1}	Pedroza M A	22.20
5Jun04 ^{3}EF^{11}	French Lady-NZ	LB	4	125	8	6^{hd}	6^{hd}	8^{1}	12^{hd}	13	13	Court J K	58.00

OFF AT 2:48 Start Good. Won driving. Course firm.

TIME :24^{1}, :49, 1:14, 1:38^{1}, 2:01^{2} (:24.23, :49.18, 1:14.10, 1:38.20, 2:01.54)

$2 Mutuel Prices:			
7 – TICKER TAPE-GB	26.00	6.80	6.00
6 – DANCE IN THE MOOD-JPN		3.60	3.00
4 – HOLLYWOOD STORY			8.00

$1 EXACTA 7–6 PAID $47.70 $2 QUINELLA 6–7 PAID $29.20
$1 TRIFECTA 7–6–4 PAID $498.50 $1 SUPERFECTA 7–6–4–10 PAID $4,672.40

B. f, (Jan), by Royal Applause-GB – Argent Du Bois , by Silver Hawk . Trainer Cassidy James. Bred by Car Colston Hall Stud (GB).

TICKER TAPE (GB) stalked the pace between foes early then outside, moved up three deep on the second turn, took the lead outside the pacesetter into the stretch, kicked clear, drifted in under urging but held gamely. DANCE IN THE MOOD (JPN) pulled her way along early, stalked inside, came out into the stretch, could not catch the winner but was clearly second best. HOLLYWOOD STORY also pulled early, stalked inside then a bit off the rail, awaited room leaving the second turn, came out in upper stretch and finished well for third. WESTERN HEMISPHERE wide in the chute, took the lead and angled in, set the pace inside, dueled inside the winner into the stretch and weakened some but lost third late. AMORAMA (FR) angled in and raced unhurried inside, came out on the second turn and four wide into the stretch and put in a late bid at a minor award. MAMBO SLEW chased between horses or outside a rival, split foes in the stretch and could not summon the needed late kick. BOULEVARDOFDREAMS (NZ) saved ground off the pace, moved up inside into the stretch but also lacked the necessary late response. ETERNAL MELODY (NZ) off a bit slowly, settled outside, came five wide into the stretch and was not a threat. MISTY HEIGHTS (GB) pulled her way into a bit of a tight spot into the first turn, chased inside then a bit off the rail, went between foes into and on the second turn, moved up some leaving that bend but could not sustain the bid. WESTERN RANSOM close up stalking the pace outside the runner-up then between foes leaving the second turn, weakened. STEEL PRINCESS (IRE) allowed to settle outside chasing the pace, was in tight off heels into the stretch and failed to menace. LOVELY RAFAELA angled in and chased outside a rival or between foes, went three deep into the second turn and four wide into the stretch and weakened. FRENCH LADY (NZ) between horses early, stalked outside then three deep, came four wide into the stretch and also weakened.

Owners– 1, Jim Ford Inc Pearson Daron and Sweesy Jack; 2, Shadai Race Horse; 3, Krikorian George; 4, Golden Eagle Farm; 5, Naify and Woodside Farms LLC; 6, Manganaro Frank; 7, Ted Van Beurden; 8, Bello Michael; 9, O'Reilly Lady; 10, Chandler Dr John A; 11, Richard Barnes; 12, T N T Stud; 13, Augustin Stable

Trainers– 1, Cassidy James; 2, Fujisawa Kazuo; 3, Shirreffs John; 4, Baffert Bob; 5, Canani Julio C; 6, Biancone Patrick L; 7, Hillis Wayne; 8, Frankel Robert; 9, Weld Dermot K; 10, Dickinson Michael W; 11, Gibson R; 12, Lobo Paulo H; 13, Drysdale Neil

Scratched– Sagitta Ra (05Jun04 ^{8}Hol^{3})

$2 Daily Double (1–7) Paid $171.80 ; Daily Double Pool $51,019 .
$1 Pick Three (5–1–7) Paid $200.90 ; Pick Three Pool $108,687 .
$1 Pick Four ((NATIONAL PICK 4) 3–7–2–7) Paid $3,939.50 ; Pick Four Pool $992,784 .

NINTH RACE

Hollywood

JULY 3, 2004

7 FURLONGS. (1.19^{4}) 53RD RUNNING OF THE TRIPLE BEND BREEDERS' CUP INVITATIONAL HANDICAP. Grade I. Purse $300,000 (includes $50,000 BC – Breeders' Cup) FOR THREE YEAR OLDS AND UPWARD. No Nominating or Starting Fees. With $250,000 guaranteed, and an additional $50,000 from the Breeders' Cup Fund for Breeders' Cup nominees only. The host association's money to be divided 60% to the winner, 20% to second, 12% to third, 6% to fourth and 2% to fifth. Breeders' Cup monies also correspondingly divided providing a Breeders' Cup nominee has finished in an awarded position. Any Breeders' Cup monies not awarded will revert to the fund. A Trophy will be presented to the winning owner. Breeders' Cup Limited shall also present a trophy to the winning owner.

Value of Race: $300,000 Winner $180,000; second $60,000; third $36,000; fourth $18,000; fifth $6,000. Mutuel Pool $619,566.00 Exacta Pool $385,502.00 Quinella Pool $33,214.00 Trifecta Pool $362,420.00 Superfecta Pool $153,630.00

Last Raced	Horse	M/Eqt.	A.	Wt	PP	St	¼	½	Str	Fin	Jockey	Odds $1
5Jun04 ^{7}Bel^{3}	Pohave	LB	6	116	7	5	$6^{\frac{1}{2}}$	3^{hd}	$3^{2\frac{1}{2}}$	$1^{\frac{3}{4}}$	Espinoza V	2.30
7May04 ^{6}Hol^{7}	Rojo Toro	LB b	4	115	11	2	$2^{\frac{1}{2}}$	2^{1}	$2^{\frac{1}{2}}$	$2^{\frac{1}{2}}$	Steiner J J	52.10
31May04 ^{4}Hol^{1}	Revello	LB b	6	110	12	3	5^{hd}	4^{1}	1^{hd}	3^{1}	Santiago Javier	8.30
31May04 ^{9}LS^{4}	Kela	LB b	6	114	1	12	9^{hd}	$10^{2\frac{1}{2}}$	6^{1}	4^{2}	Smith M E	3.60
8May04 ^{6}Hol^{4}	Hasty Kris	LB b	7	114	2	13	13	11^{1}	$7^{1\frac{1}{2}}$	$5^{\frac{1}{2}}$	Baze T C	15.60
31May04 ^{9}Hol^{1}	Taste of Paradise	LB	5	114	3	9	$7^{2\frac{1}{2}}$	$7^{1\frac{1}{2}}$	4^{1}	6^{2}	Court J K	6.50
15May04 ^{11}Pim^{5}	Iron Halo-Arg	LB	5	110	6	7	4^{1}	6^{hd}	$8^{1\frac{1}{2}}$	$7^{1\frac{1}{2}}$	Garcia M S	22.10
31May04 ^{3}BM^{4}	Reba's Gold	LB b	7	116	13	1	8^{hd}	8^{hd}	9^{hd}	8^{1}	Flores D R	14.70
12Jun04 ^{9}Hol^{3}	Nose The Trade-GB	LB	6	115	10	8	12^{hd}	13	11^{3}	$9^{\frac{1}{2}}$	Solis A	9.20
22May04 ^{8}BM^{2}	R. Baggio	LB b	6	112	8	10	11^{1}	12^{hd}	13	$10^{\frac{1}{2}}$	Ruis M	30.90
19Jun04 ^{8}BM^{2}	Debonair Joe	LB	5	112	4	11	10^{2}	$9^{\frac{1}{2}}$	10^{hd}	11^{5}	Bisono A	36.40
16May04 ^{3}Bel^{3}	Ministers Wild Cat	LB	4	113	5	6	3^{hd}	5^{1}	12^{1}	$12^{2\frac{1}{2}}$	Take Y	14.10
19Jun04 ^{8}BM^{6}	Smile n Wildcat	LB	5	116	9	4	1^{hd}	1^{hd}	5^{hd}	13	Desormeaux K J	38.90

OFF AT 4:20 Start Good . Won driving. Track fast.

TIME :21^{4}, :44, 1:08^{1}, 1:21 (:21.98, :44.01, 1:08.32, 1:21.06)

$2 Mutuel Prices:				
	8 – POHAVE	6.60	3.80	3.20
	12 – ROJO TORO		32.80	12.60
	13 – REVELLO			4.60

$1 EXACTA 8–12 PAID $176.30 $2 QUINELLA 8–12 PAID $182.20

$1 TRIFECTA 8–12–13 PAID $2,010.20 $1 SUPERFECTA 8–12–13–1 PAID $20,309.80

Gr/ro. g, (Apr), by Holy Bull – Trail Robbery , by Alydar . Trainer O'Neill Doug. Bred by H E Pabst & T J Pabst (Ky).

POHAVE stalked between horses on the backstretch and into the turn, continued off the rail, came out in the stretch, bid three deep, gained the lead past midstretch and gamely prevailed under urging. ROJO TORO prompted the pace four wide then three deep on the backstretch and outside a rival into and on the turn, gained the advantage into the stretch, fought back toward the inside in the final furlong and continued willingly to the wire. REVELLO stalked the pace outside, bid three deep into the stretch, put a head in front between foes in midstretch and also went on well to the end. KELA chased inside, came off the rail on the turn, split rivals, came out three deep into the stretch and found his best stride late. HASTY KRIS unhurried a bit off the rail then inside, moved up leaving the turn, came out into the stretch and put in a late bid. TASTE OF PARADISE saved ground stalking the pace, also came out into the stretch and lacked the needed rally. IRON HALO (ARG) had speed between horses then stalked outside a rival, went three deep midway on the turn and again into the stretch and weakened. REBA'S GOLD allowed to settle outside chasing the pace, went four wide on the turn and into the stretch and lacked a further response. NOSE THE TRADE (GB) wide early, settled outside without early speed, angled in some on the turn, came out into the stretch and was not a threat. R. BAGGIO settled between horses then dropped back outside into the turn, came four wide into the stretch and was not a factor. DEBONAIR JOE chased between foes on the backstretch and into the turn, came out into the stretch and did not rally. MINISTERS WILD CAT prompted the early pace inside then stalked along the rail, dropped back on the turn and had nothing left for the stretch. SMILE N WILDCAT had speed off the rail then dueled between horses, battled inside on the turn, fell back into the stretch and gave way.

Owners– 1, Kagele Brothers Inc Leatherman Ty and Leib Mark A; 2, Earnhardt III Patti and Hal J; 3, Sengara Jeffrey; 4, Manoogian Jay; 5, C R K Stable; 6, Bloom David B; 7, S M Mitchell Ranch LLC; 8, Creston Farms; 9, Tanaka Gary A; 10, Lewkowitz Frank and Karen; 11, Ristad-Lidgett Lynne; 12, Cowan Marjorie and Irving M; 13, David J Lanzman Racing Stable Inc

Trainers– 1, O'Neill Doug; 2, Baffert Bob; 3, West Ted H; 4, Mitchell Mike; 5, Sadler John W; 6, Pearson Molly J; 7, Kruljac J Eric; 8, Hendricks Dan L; 9, Frankel Robert; 10, Kruljac J Eric; 11, Ledezma Sergio; 12, Drysdale Neil; 13, O'Neill Doug

Scratched– Lifestyle (05Jun04 ^{1}Bel^{4})

$2 Daily Double (5–8) Paid $8.40 ; Daily Double Pool $44,378 .

$1 Pick Three (2–2/5–3/8) Paid $23.00 ; Pick Three Pool $154,326 .

TENTH RACE
Monmouth
JULY 3, 2004

1⅜ MILES. (Turf) (2.15^{4}) 51ST RUNNING OF THE UNITED NATIONS. Grade I. Purse $750,000 FOR THREE-YEAR-OLDS AND UPWARD. By subcription of $500 each, which should accompany the nomination and $7,500 to pass the entry box. The winning owner to receive $450,000, $150,000 to second, $80,000 to third, $42,500 to fourth, $20,000 to fifth and $7,500 to sixth. Weight: 122 lbs.; Non-Winners of a Grade I Stake in 2004 allowed 2 lbs.; Non-winners of a Grade II Stake in 2004, 4 lbs. The owner of the winner to receive a trophy. Closed Sunday, June 20, 2004 with 27 nominations. If deemed inadvisable by management to run this race over the turf course it will be run on the main track at One Mile and One Quarter .

Value of Race: $750,000 Winner $450,000; second $150,000; third $80,000; fourth $42,500; fifth $20,000; sixth $7,500. Mutuel Pool $617,163.00 Exacta Pool $395,620.00 Trifecta Pool $263,618.00 Superfecta Pool $70,774.00

Last Raced	Horse	M/Eqt.	A.	Wt	PP	¼	½	¾	1	Str	Fin	Jockey	Odds $1
5Jun04 ^{10}Bel^{5}	Request for Parole	L	5	118	2	3^{hd}	3^{hd}	3^{hd}	3^{hd}	$3^{1/2}$	$1^{1/2}$	Prado E S	4.70
5Jun04 ^{10}Bel^{3}	Mr O'Brien-Ire	L	5	120	7	$5^{1/2}$	7^{hd}	6^{hd}	7^{hd}	4^{3}	$2^{3/4}$	Dominguez R A	3.10
16Jun04 ^{8}Bel^{2}	Nothing to Lose	L b	4	118	4	$2^{1/2}$	$2^{1/2}$	2^{1}	2^{1}	1^{1}	3^{1}	Migliore R	11.00
12Jun04 ^{9}Mth^{1}	Megantic	L	6	118	8	$8^{1/2}$	8^{hd}	9^{2}	6^{hd}	5^{hd}	$4^{2 1/4}$	Pimentel J	34.90
12Jun04 ^{10}CD^{2}	Hard Buck-Brz	L	5	122	6	7^{1}	9^{1}	8^{hd}	8^{hd}	7^{5}	5no	Blanc B	6.30
22Feb04 ^{11}GP^{2}	Balto Star	L	6	118	3	$1^{1/2}$	1^{1}	1^{1}	$1^{1/2}$	2^{1}	$6^{3 1/2}$	Velez J A Jr	6.10
5Jun04 ^{10}Bel^{1}	Meteor Storm-GB	L	5	122	11	6^{hd}	5^{hd}	$5^{1/2}$	4^{hd}	$6^{1/2}$	$7^{3/4}$	Valdivia J Jr	2.30
5Jun04 ^{9}Pha^{1}	In Hand	L f	4	118	1	11	11	11	11	$8^{1 1/2}$	$8^{3 1/4}$	Elliott S	63.10
12Jun04 ^{4}Mth^{5}	Catechol	L	7	118	9	10^{4}	$10^{5 1/2}$	10^{3}	$9^{1/2}$	$9^{1 1/2}$	9^{2}	Baze M C	205.60
12Jun04 ^{9}Mth^{4}	Final Prophecy	L b	5	118	10	9^{hd}	6^{1}	$7^{1/2}$	10^{3}	11	10no	King E L Jr	222.20
11Jun04 ^{7}Cnl^{4}	Bowman Mill	L	6	118	5	4^{1}	$4^{1/2}$	$4^{1/2}$	5^{1}	10^{hd}	11	Bravo J	12.00

OFF AT 5:21 Start Good . Won driving. Course firm.

TIME :24^{1}, :48^{3}, 1:14, 1:37^{2}, 2:01^{1}, 2:13^{1} (:24.35, :48.74, 1:14.11, 1:37.45, 2:01.31, 2:13.37)

(New Course Record)

$2 Mutuel Prices:				
	2 – REQUEST FOR PAROLE	11.40	5.00	4.00
	7 – MR O'BRIEN-IRE		4.60	3.60
	4 – NOTHING TO LOSE			7.20

$2 EXACTA 2–7 PAID $49.20 $2 TRIFECTA 2–7–4 PAID $524.40
$1 SUPERFECTA 2–7–4–8 PAID $2,123.20

Dk. b or br. h, (Feb), by Judge T C – Madison's Quest , by Deputy Minister . Trainer Hough Stanley M. Bred by Robert H Roberts & Bea Roberts (Ky).

REQUEST FOR PAROLE rated close off the rail, eased slightly out making his bid entering the stretch, closed with the runner up through the lane and dug in determinedly to prevail. MR O'BRIEN (IRE) rated back toward the inside, rallied off the rail entering the stretch, closed with the winner, was between horses leaving the eighth pole, continued in a game duel but was outfinished. NOTHING TO LOSE rated close in the three path, urged to a short lead approaching the quarter pole, dueled briefly clear toward the eighth pole then grudgingly yielded the final sixteenth. MEGANTIC rated back toward the outside, started his drive six wide entering the stretch, closed steadily and finished well. HARD BUCK (BRZ) rated back inside, gave chase nearing the final turn and finished evenly off the rail. BALTO STAR set the pace from the inside, was pressured entering the final turn, contested the rail through the turn then weakened the final furlong. METEOR STORM (GB) rated just off the pace outside, picked up the chase in mid track on the final turn then weakened a furlong out. IN HAND, unhurried while saving ground, eased out making a mild bid on the final turn and finished evenly. CATECHOL, unhurried and off the rail, made a mild outside bid on the final turn then leveled off. FINAL PROPHECY rated off the pace widest, was steadied from between rivals entering the final turn then weakened from there. BOWMAN MILL was kept close to the pace toward mid track and gave way into the final turn.

Owners– 1, Knighton Jeri and Sam; 2, Skeedattle Stable; 3, Ramsey Kenneth L and Sarah K; 4, Runnin Horse Farm Inc; 5, Team Victory II; 6, Anstu Stables Inc; 7, The Horizon Stable; 8, Shining Armor Stable & Humphrey Jr; 9, Ocean View Stables and Thompson Glenn R; 10, Howes Dale and Jean; 11, Chandler Dr John A

Trainers– 1, Hough Stanley M; 2, Graham Robin L; 3, Frankel Robert; 4, Pointer Norman R; 5, McPeek Kenneth G; 6, Pletcher Todd A; 7, Dollase Wallace; 8, Oliver Philip J; 9, Thompson Glenn R; 10, Cibelli Jane; 11, Dickinson Michael W

Scratched– Better Talk Now (12Jun04 ^{9}Mth^{2})

NINTH RACE
Prairie Mdw
JULY 3, 2004

1⅛ MILES. (1.46^{3}) 8TH RUNNING OF THE PRAIRIE MEADOWS CORNHUSKER BREEDERS' CUP HANDICAP. Grade III. Purse $300,000 (includes $50,000 BC – Breeders' Cup) FOR THREE-YEAR-OLDS AND UPWARD.

Value of Race: $300,000 Winner $180,000; second $60,000; third $30,000; fourth $15,000; fifth $9,000; sixth $6,000. Mutuel Pool $130,966.00 Exacta Pool $45,592.00 Quinella Pool $5,631.00 Trifecta Pool $39,757.00

Last Raced	Horse	M/Eqt.	A.	Wt	PP	St	¼	½	¾	Str	Fin	Jockey	Odds $1
21May04 ^{3}CD^{1}	Roses in May	LB	4	115	1	3	1^{1}	1^{1}	$1^{1/2}$	$1^{1/2}$	$1^{1 1/2}$	Guidry M	2.70
12Jun04 ^{9}CD^{3}	Perfect Drift	LB	5	119	3	6	$4^{1 1/2}$	3^{1}	$2^{1/2}$	$2^{3 1/2}$	2^{4}	Day P	0.80
29May04 ^{9}AP^{1}	Crafty Shaw	L	6	117	6	1	$2^{1/2}$	$2^{1/2}$	3^{1}	3^{2}	$3^{4 3/4}$	Perret C	4.70
31May04 ^{9}LS^{2}	Sonic West	LB bf	5	115	5	2	$5^{1/2}$	5^{1}	4^{1}	4^{4}	$4^{8 3/4}$	Martinez W	17.30
12Jun04 ^{7}Cby^{1}	Native Hawk	LB b	4	114	2	4	3^{hd}	4^{hd}	5^{2}	5^{10}	5^{18}	Nolan P M	55.70
14May04 ^{11}Pim^{6}	Ole Faunty	LB	5	116	4	5	6	6	6	6	6	Albarado R J	5.90

OFF AT 9:44 Start Good . Won driving. Track fast.

TIME :23^{2}, :46^{4}, 1:10^{1}, 1:34^{2}, 1:46^{3} (:23.57, :46.98, 1:10.26, 1:34.43, 1:46.63)

$2 Mutuel Prices:				
	1 – ROSES IN MAY	7.40	3.40	2.20
	3 – PERFECT DRIFT		2.40	2.20
	6 – CRAFTY SHAW			2.20

$2 EXACTA 1–3 PAID $14.80 $2 QUINELLA 1–3 PAID $7.00
$2 TRIFECTA 1–3–6 PAID $48.20

Dk. b or br. c, (Feb), by Devil His Due – Tell a Secret , by Speak John . Trainer Romans Dale. Bred by Margaux Farm LLC (Ky).

ROSES IN MAY went clear early, set the pace from the three path on the first turn, was well rated on the lead to the final turn, was headed on his inside by PERFECT DRIFT approaching the stretch, regained a narrow advantage in upper stretch, switched leads nearing the sixteenth marker and inched clear at the wire under steady pressure. PERFECT DRIFT raced within easy striking range while saving ground in midpack early, came through inside of the winner entering the second turn, got on even terms entering the stretch, dueled through the lane but could not match strides in the final sixteenth while easily besting the rest. CRAFTY SHAW chased the pace racing three wide to the stretch before weakening. SONIC WEST raced three wide on the first turn, was within easy striking range to the final turn before giving way. NATIVE HAWK raced close up from between rivals around the first turn, continued between foes to the final turn, came under a ride early on the bend and tired thereafter. OLE FAUNTY was outrun while racing inside.

Owners– 1, Ramsey Kenneth L and Sarah K; 2, Stonecrest Farm; 3, Cella Charles J; 4, Stone Spire LLC; 5, Rice Brett; 6, Van Meter II Thomas and Hendrickson Doug

Trainers– 1, Romans Dale; 2, Johnson Murray W; 3, Vestal Peter M; 4, Van Berg Thomas L; 5, Cheeks Kitty; 6, Walden W Elliott

---

$2 Pick Three (6–2–1) Paid $126.20 ; Pick Three Pool $9,558 .

SEVENTH RACE
Arlington
JULY 4, 2004

1½ MILES. (Turf) (2.27²) 73RD RUNNING OF THE STARS AND STRIPES BREEDERS' CUP TURF HANDICAP. Grade III. Purse $200,000 (includes $75,000 BC – Breeders' Cup) FOR THREE-YEAR-OLDS AND UPWARD.

Value of Race: $200,000 Winner $120,000; fourth $12,000; second $40,000; third $22,000; fifth $6,000. Mutuel Pool $326,379.00 Exacta Pool $181,018.00 Trifecta Pool $181,356.00 Superfecta Pool $63,559.00

Last Raced	Horse	M/Eqt.	A.	Wt	PP	¼	½	1	1¼	Str	Fin	Jockey	Odds $1
31May04 9CD3	Ballingarry-Ire	L b	5	120	2	5½	5¹	4hd	3hd	1³	1¾	Douglas R R	1.80
31May04 9CD1	[D]Silverfoot	L	4	116	5	7¹	72½	7¹	7hd	4hd	2nk	Albarado R J	2.90
28May04 9Mnr2	Grey Beard	L b	5	117	4	6½	6²	5¹	6¹	2½	32¾	Lovato F Jr	37.90
13Jun04 5AP1	Art Variety-Brz	L b	6	116	8	4½	4½	6¹	5hd	52½	43½	Blanc B	5.00
13May04 9CD1	Balustrade	L b	4	112	7	8	8	8	8	71½	51½	Lopez J	15.80
17Jun04 8AP1	Cloudy's Knight	L	4	112	6	2½	2²	2¹	2hd	6¹	61¼	Perez E E	26.20
5Jun04 10Bel7	Quest Star	L b	5	116	1	1hd	1½	1½	11½	3½	7⁵	Marquez C H Jr	2.60
13Jun04 5AP3	Prodigus-Brz	L	5	116	3	3¹	3½	3¹	41½	8	8	Razo E Jr	28.60

[D] – Silverfoot disqualified and placed 4th

OFF AT 5:40 Start Good. Won driving. Course soft.

TIME :26, :52³, 1:19², 1:45¹, 2:10⁴, 2:36¹ (:26.00, :52.68, 1:19.48, 1:45.21, 2:10.90, 2:36.30)

$2 Mutuel Prices:				
	2 – BALLINGARRY-IRE	5.60	4.00	3.00
	4 – GREY BEARD		21.80	7.80
	9 – ART VARIETY-BRZ			4.20

$2 EXACTA 2–4 PAID $181.20 $2 TRIFECTA 2–4–9 PAID $663.40
$2 SUPERFECTA 2–4–9–5 PAID $2,638.80

B. h, (Apr), by Sadler's Wells – Flamenco Wave , by Desert Wine . Trainer De Seroux Laura. Bred by Orpendale (Ire).

BALLINGARRY (IRE) was allowed to settle inside near the middle of the field, angled out turning for home, rallied to a clear lead in the stretch and held sway while kept to his task. SILVERFOOT was void of early speed, checked when he ran up on horses turning for home, forced his way out bothering ART VARIETY (BRZ) and BALUSTRADE then rallied through the stretch but could not reach the winner. GREY BEARD was void of early speed along the rail began working his way up in upper stretch but could not reach the winner and lost the place late. ART VARIETY (BRZ) raced off the rail near the middle of the field, was bumped and carried out by SILVERFOOT turning for home and failed to respond in the stretch. BALUSTRADE was bumped at the break, lacked speed, was carried out turning for home and improved his position without threatening. CLOUDY'S KNIGHT went up to press the pace from just outside and tired turning for home. QUEST STAR set the pace from the inside while pressed, shook loose on the final turn then had nothing left for the drive and also tired. PRODIGUS (BRZ) raced close up just off the rail and tired. AFTER A CLAIM OF FOUL BY THE RIDER OF ART VARIETY (BRZ), SILVERFOOT WAS DISQUALIFIED FROM SECOND AND PLACED FOURTH FOR INTERFERENCE IN THE STRETCH. (Race run in lane 5, rail at 0.)

Owners– 1, Port Trust Naify Marsha and San Gabriel Investments; 2, Chrysalis Stables LLC; 3, Brunacini George; 4, Midnight Cry Stable S Cunningham & W Gallion & Team Victory II Rick Pitino; 5, Hiram Polk Jr and J David Richardson; 6, Schwartz Jerrold; 7, Mansell Stables LLC; 8, Late Night Stables LLC

Trainers– 1, De Seroux Laura; 2, Stewart Dallas; 3, Fojan Emilie; 4, McPeek Kenneth G; 5, Mott William I; 6, Kirby Frank J; 7, Walden W Elliott; 8, McPeek Kenneth G

Scratched– Major Rhythm (12Jun04 10CD 7)

$1 Pick Three (9/13–4/7–2/8) Paid $19.60 ; Pick Three Pool $7,808 .

NINTH RACE
Belmont
JULY 4, 2004

7 FURLONGS. (1.20) 30TH RUNNING OF THE TOM FOOL HANDICAP. Grade II. Purse $150,000 (UP TO $28,500 NYSBFOA) A HANDICAP FOR THREE YEAR OLDS AND UPWARD. By subscription of $150 each, which should accompany the nomination; $750 to pass the entry box; $750 to start. The purse to be divided 60% to the winner, 20% to second, 10% to third, 5% to fourth, 3% to fifth and 2% divided equally among remaining finishers. A trophy will be presented to the winning owner. Closed Saturday, June 19, 2004 with 18 Nominations.

Value of Race: $142,500 Winner $90,000; second $30,000; third $15,000; fourth $7,500. Mutuel Pool $504,874.00 Exacta Pool $392,462.00

Last Raced	Horse	M/Eqt.	A.	Wt	PP	St	¼	½	Str	Fin	Jockey	Odds $1
27Sep03 7Bel1	Ghostzapper	L b	4	119	3	2	3hd	2hd	14½	14¼	Castellano J J	1.35
18Jun04 3Bel1	Aggadan	L f	5	114	2	1	1hd	4	2½	23½	Prado E S	5.90
30May04 5Mth5	Unforgettable Max	L f	4	114	4	3	2²	3½	3hd	3½	Bailey J D	1.90
5May04 8Bel5	Lion Tamer	L	4	118	1	4	4	1hd	4	4	Velazquez J R	3.00

OFF AT 5:13 Start Good. Won ridden out. Track fast.

TIME :22², :44³, 1:08¹, 1:20² (:22.54, :44.79, 1:08.26, 1:20.42)

$2 Mutuel Prices:				
	4 – GHOSTZAPPER	4.70	3.20	—
	3 – AGGADAN		5.40	—
	5 – UNFORGETTABLE MAX		—	—

$2 EXACTA 4–3 PAID $22.40

B. c, (Apr), by Awesome Again – Baby Zip , by Relaunch . Trainer Frankel Robert. Bred by Adena Springs (Ky).

GHOSTZAPPER raced close up outside, cruised up four wide on the turn, drew clear when shaken up and was ridden out to the wire. AGGADAN argued the pace along the inside, dropped back a bit on the turn, came wide into the stretch and rallied to earn the place award. UNFORGETTABLE MAX argued the pace while in hand and tired in the stretch. LION TAMER argued the pace while between rivals three wide and tired in the stretch.

Owners– 1, Stronach Stable; 2, Goldfarb S J Carney C L Fleisig J Rosenfeld N and Hochman J; 3, Dweck Raymond; 4, Tabor Michael B

Trainers– 1, Frankel Robert; 2, Dutrow Richard E Jr; 3, Levine Bruce N; 4, Pletcher Todd A

Scratched– Eye of the Tiger (31May04 9Bel7)

ELEVENTH RACE
Churchill
JULY 4, 2004

5½ FURLONGS. (1.02²) 104TH RUNNING OF THE DEBUTANTE. Grade III. Purse $100,000 FOR FILLIES, TWO YEARS OLD. By subscription of $100 each on or before June 19, 2004 or by supplementary nomination of $5,000 at time of entry. $500 to pass the entry box; $500 additional to start with $100,000 added of which 62% of all monies to the owner of the winner, 20% to second, 10% to third, 5% to fourth and 3% to fifth. Weight 121 lbs. Non–winners of a sweepstakes allowed 2 lbs.; a race other than maiden or claiming, 4 lbs.; a race other than claiming, 6 lbs. Starters to be named through theentry box at the usual time of closing. All supplementary nominations will be required to pay entry and starting fees if they participate. Trophy to winning owner. Closed Saturday, June 19, 2004 with 18 nominations.

Value of Race: $110,800 Winner $68,696; second $22,160; third $11,080; fourth $5,540; fifth $3,324. Mutuel Pool $343,088.00 Exacta Pool $248,670.00 Trifecta Pool $245,197.00 Superfecta Pool $85,438.00

Last Raced	Horse	M/Eqt.	A.	Wt	PP	St	¼	⅜	Str	Fin	Jockey	Odds $1
1May04 6CD3	Classic Elegance		2	117	6	3	3hd	32	21½	11	Day P	1.80
13Jun04 5CD1	Paragon Queen	L	2	117	3	5	11½	1½	12	23½	Coa D	8.00
23May04 4CD1	Cool Spell	L	2	117	9	9	9	82½	5hd	3nk	Velasquez C	16.10
18Jun04 4CD1	Im a Dixie Girl	L	2	115	4	2	2½	4hd	4hd	4nk	McKee J	51.80
8Apr04 2Kee1	Lisa's Cat	L	2	117	1	4	61	7½	6½	5¾	Melancon L	37.50
18Jun04 9CD1	Sweet Miss El	L	2	119	5	6	42	2½	33	6½	Bejarano R	3.20
6Jun04 5CD1	Runway Model		2	117	8	8	8hd	6½	73½	74¾	Martinez W	8.90
18Jun04 9CD3	Jules Best	L	2	117	2	1	71	9	81½	86¼	Guidry M	22.10
21Apr04 1Kee1	Limitless Lady	L	2	117	7	7	5hd	5½	9	9	Sellers S J	3.10

OFF AT 6:21 Start Good . Won driving. Track fast.

TIME :21³, :45², :57³, 1:04 (:21.78, :45.41, :57.68, 1:04.18)

$2 Mutuel Prices:

6 – CLASSIC ELEGANCE	5.60	4.00	3.20
3 – PARAGON QUEEN		6.80	4.80
9 – COOL SPELL			9.40

$2 EXACTA 6–3 PAID $36.00 $2 TRIFECTA 6–3–9 PAID $271.00
$2 SUPERFECTA 6–3–9–4 PAID $4,325.20

B. f, (Mar), by Carson City – Taegu , by Halo . Trainer Lukas D Wayne. Bred by Brereton C Jones (Ky).

CLASSIC ELEGANCE, never far back and tracking the leaders five or six wide, caught front-running PARAGON QUEEN a sixteenth out and was hard ridden the remainder. PARAGON QUEEN gained a clear advantage near the inside early, shook off a challenge from SWEET MISS EL approaching the stretch, settled into the final furlong with a clear advantage but couldn't handle CLASSIC ELEGANCE in the late stages. COOL SPELL settled in behind horses early, was outrun to the stretch, split rivals three or four wide in the final furlong and offered a mild gain. IM A DIXIE GIRL bobbled at the break, gained a forward position between foes soon after four wide and weakened nearing the stretch. LISA'S CAT raced near the inside most of the way and offered a slight late gain. SWEET MISS EL, well placed in behind front-running PARAGON QUEEN early, moved with the winner four wide while rallying into the stretch but flattened out the last eighth. RUNWAY MODEL, outsprinted early and five or six wide to the stretch, angled wider for the drive but lacked a closing account. JULES BEST settled inside, was outrun to the stretch, swung out six wide for the drive but never menaced. LIMITLESS LADY raced in contention until the final quarter while four wide and tired.

Owners– 1, Lewis Robert B and Beverly J; 2, Lewis Robert B and Beverly J; 3, Burris Mr and Mrs W D; 4, Carl William A; 5, Ramsey Kenneth L and Sarah K; 6, Bakster Farm; 7, Chowhan Naveed; 8, Bowling Carl Velotta Robert Foley Vickie L et al; 9, Heiligbrodt Racing Stable

Trainers– 1, Lukas D Wayne; 2, Lukas D Wayne; 3, Hennig John K; 4, Flint Bernard S; 5, Werner Ronny; 6, Foley Gregory D; 7, Flint Bernard S; 8, Foley Vickie L; 9, Asmussen Steven M

$2 Pick Three (1–4–6) Paid $232.00 ; Pick Three Pool $26,220 .

EIGHTH RACE
Hollywood
JULY 4, 2004

1⅛ MILES. (Turf Chute) 65TH RUNNING OF THE AMERICAN HANDICAP. Grade II. Purse $150,000 FOR THREE–YEAR–OLDS AND UPWARD. By subscription of $150 each on or before Wednesday, June 23 or by supplementary nomination of $3,000 each by noon Friday, June 25. $1,500 additional to start, with $90,000 to the winner, $30,000 to second, $18,000 to third, $9,000 to fourth and $3,000 to fifth. Weights Saturday, June 26. Starters to be named through the entry box by closing time of entries. A trophy will be presented to the winning owner. (Rail at 10 feet). Closed with 18 nominations. CHUTE START.

Value of Race: $150,000 Winner $90,000; second $30,000; third $18,000; fourth $9,000; fifth $3,000. Mutuel Pool $383,224.00 Exacta Pool $230,182.00 Quinella Pool $22,494.00

Last Raced	Horse	M/Eqt.	A.	Wt	PP	St	¼	½	¾	Str	Fin	Jockey	Odds $1
12Jun04 3Hol2	Bayamo-Ire	LB	5	117	4	5	4½	41	41	12½	14½	Flores D R	0.70
25Apr04 8ST12	Sarafan	LB	7	119	2	4	5	5	5	2½	24	Nakatani C S	3.60
6Jun04 5Hol5	Night Patrol	LB b	8	114	5	1	1½	11½	11	33	31½	Espinoza V	13.10
13Jun04 8Hol1	Black Bart	LB	5	116	1	2	31	31½	3½	4hd	44	Solis A	2.70
20Jun04 5Hol1	R McLennen	LB f	6	110	3	3	21	2½	21½	5	5	Bisono A	20.80

OFF AT 5:01 Start Good . Won handily. Course firm.

TIME :23¹, :46¹, 1:09³, 1:34¹, 1:46³ (:23.26, :46.33, 1:09.77, 1:34.21, 1:46.60)

$2 Mutuel Prices:

4 – BAYAMO–IRE	3.40	2.40	2.10
2 – SARAFAN		3.20	2.10
5 – NIGHT PATROL			2.10

$1 EXACTA 4–2 PAID $5.10 $2 QUINELLA 2–4 PAID $6.80

Ch. g, (Mar), by Valanour–Ire – Clare Bridge , by Little Current . Trainer Canani Julio C. Bred by Horse Breeding Company (Ire).

BAYAMO (IRE) stalked the pace outside, moved up three deep leaving the second turn, took command outside the pacesetter into the stretch, kicked clear while being mildly hand ridden then was under a long hold late. SARAFAN chased a bit off the rail then inside, moved up along the fence on the second turn, came out into the stretch and was second best. NIGHT PATROL sped to the early lead outside a rival, angled in on the first turn, set the pace inside, was no match for the top pair in the stretch but held third. BLACK BART pulled a bit inside early then came off the rail in the run to the first turn, stalked outside a rival, dropped back on the second turn, came three deep into the stretch and weakened. R MCLENNEN prompted the early pace inside then stalked a bit off the rail, loomed a threat leaving the second turn but also weakened.

Owners– 1, Prestonwood Farm LLC; 2, Tanaka Gary A; 3, Everest Stables Inc; 4, Metzger Thomas F Sr; 5, Carney Brian M

Trainers– 1, Canani Julio C; 2, Drysdale Neil; 3, Polanco Marcelo; 4, Bainum Troy; 5, Hines N J

$2 Daily Double (4–4) Paid $9.20 ; Daily Double Pool $33,577 .
$1 Pick Three (1–1/3/4–4) Paid $58.10 ; Pick Three Pool $58,011 .

TENTH RACE
Monmouth
JULY 4, 2004

1⅛ MILES. (1.46^{4}) 59TH RUNNING OF THE MOLLY PITCHER BREEDERS' CUP HANDICAP. Grade II. Purse $300,000 (includes $100,000 BC – Breeders' Cup) FOR FILLIES AND MARES, THREE YEARS OLD AND UPWARD. By subcription of $250 each, which should accompany the nomination. $3,500 to pass the entry box with $300,000 Guaranteed, which includes $100,000 from the Breeders' Cup Fund for Cup nominees only. The host association's money to be divided 60% to the winning owner, 20% to second, 11% to third, 6% to fourth and 3% to fifth. Breeders' Cup Fund money correspondingly divided providing a Breeders' Cup nominee has finished in an awarded position. Any Breeders' Cup Fund money not awarded reverts to the fund. The owner of the winner to receive a trophy from Breeders' Cup Limited. Closed Sunday, June 20, 2004 with 17 nominations.

Value of Race: $300,000 Winner $180,000; second $60,000; third $33,000; fourth $18,000; fifth $9,000. Mutuel Pool $146,939.00 Exacta Pool $104,849.00 Trifecta Pool $67,615.00 Superfecta Pool $18,278.00

Last Raced	Horse	M/Eqt.	A.	Wt	PP	St	¼	½	¾	Str	Fin	Jockey	Odds $1
12Jun04 ^{8}CD^{3}	La Reason	L f	4	111	5	2	5^{1}	5^{1}	5^{4}	1^{1}	1^{3}	Lopez C C	22.70
12Jun04 ^{8}CD^{5}	Yell	L	4	114	7	6	4^{1}	$4^{\frac{1}{2}}$	2^{hd}	$3^{\frac{1}{2}}$	2^{nk}	Bravo J	3.00
12Jun04 ^{8}CD^{2}	Bare Necessities	L	5	119	1	7	3^{hd}	$3^{1\frac{1}{2}}$	4^{2}	$5^{5\frac{1}{2}}$	3no	Valdivia J Jr	1.50
13Jun04 ^{9}Mth^{1}	Pocus Hocus	L b	6	116	4	3	$1^{\frac{1}{2}}$	1^{1}	1^{2}	$2^{2\frac{1}{2}}$	4^{2}	Santos J A	4.20
5Jun04 ^{6}Bel^{2}	Smok'n Frolic	L b	5	118	3	1	2^{1}	$2^{1\frac{1}{2}}$	3^{hd}	4^{2}	5^{7}	Coa E M	2.60
18Jun04 ^{8}Mth^{3}	Fircroft	L	4	115	2	5	7	$6^{3\frac{1}{2}}$	6^{3}	$6^{\frac{1}{2}}$	6^{4}	Elliott S	35.40
17Jan04 ^{9}Aqu^{5}	Queen's Triomphe	L	5	115	6	4	6^{hd}	7	7	7	7	Velez J A Jr	31.60

OFF AT 5:17 Start Good For All But BARE NECESSITIES. Won driving. Track fast.
TIME :24^{1}, :47^{4}, 1:11^{2}, 1:36^{4}, 1:51 (:24.28, :47.96, 1:11.44, 1:36.92, 1:51.10)

$2 Mutuel Prices:

5 – LA REASON	47.40	18.00	4.00
7 – YELL		5.00	2.20
1 – BARE NECESSITIES			2.10

$2 EXACTA 5–7 PAID $212.00 $2 TRIFECTA 5–7–1 PAID $569.60
$1 SUPERFECTA 5–7–1–4 PAID $1,713.50

B. f, (Apr), by Labeeb–GB – Reasoning , by Naskra . Trainer Vance David R. Bred by Ron Kirby & Tom Kirby (Ky).

LA REASON rated back inside, advanced along the rail through the final turn, angled outside Pocus Hocus turning for home, dueled clear of that one approaching the furlong pole then held well with steady insistence. YELL rated back toward the outside, advanced to contention nearing the final turn, endured a long stretch drive to get place the final yards and held on. BARE NECESSITIES stumbled at the break, rated off the pace about the three path, was shuffled back midway on the final turn, angled to the outside leaving the quarter pole and recovered well through the stretch, just missing place. POCUS HOCUS set the pace just off the rail, was under solid pressure entering the stretch and gradually gave way the last furlong. SMOK'N FROLIC steadied in tight on the rail leaving the seven eighths pole into the opening turn, stalked the leader off the rail, came slightly out midway on the final turn impeding Bare Necessities, angled back inward entering the stretch then leveled off. FIRCROFT raced unhurriedly off the rail and had no rally. QUEEN'S TRIOMPHE raced unhurriedly toward mid track and offered no rally. A claim of foul lodged against the rider of the second place finisher, by the rider of the third place finisher provided no change.

Owners– 1, K and K Racing Stable LLC; 2, Claiborne Farm & A B Dilschneider; 3, Iron County Farms Inc; 4, Moore Susan and John; 5, Dogwood Stable; 6, Humphrey G Watts Jr; 7, Gregory W and Stephen P Kelly

Trainers– 1, Vance David R; 2, McGaughey III Claude R; 3, Kirby Frank J; 4, Jerkens James A; 5, Pletcher Todd A; 6, Arnold George R II; 7, Bush Thomas M

NINTH RACE
Belmont
JULY 5, 2004

1¼ MILES. (Inner Turf) (1.57^{3}) 61ST RUNNING OF THE NEW YORK HANDICAP. Grade II. Purse $250,000 INNER TURF (Up to $37,500 NYSBFOA) A HANDICAP FOR FILLIES AND MARES THREE YEARS OLD AND UPWARD. By subscription of $250 each, which should accompany the nomination; $1,250 to pass the entry box; $1,250 to start. The purse to be divided 60% to the winner,20% to second, 10% to third, 5% to fourth, 3% to fifth and 2% divided equally among remaining finishers. A trophy will be presented to the winning owner. The New York Racing Association reserves the right to transfer this race to the Main Track. In the event that this race is taken off the turf, it may be subject to downgrading upon review by the Graded Stakes Committee. Closed Saturday, June 19, 2004 with 25 Nominations. (Rail at 9 feet).

Value of Race: $250,000 Winner $150,000; second $50,000; third $25,000; fourth $12,500; fifth $7,500; sixth $2,500; seventh $2,500. Mutuel Pool $555,888.00 Exacta Pool $468,101.00 Trifecta Pool $350,360.00

Last Raced	Horse	M/Eqt.	A.	Wt	PP	¼	½	¾	1	Str	Fin	Jockey	Odds $1
5Jun04 ^{8}Bel^{6}	Wonder Again	L	5	115	3	$3^{1\frac{1}{2}}$	3^{1}	2^{hd}	$2^{1\frac{1}{2}}$	1^{5}	$1^{3\frac{1}{4}}$	Prado E S	3.95
29May04 ^{9}CD^{1}	Stay Forever	L b	7	115	2	5^{1}	5^{2}	$5^{3\frac{1}{2}}$	$3^{\frac{1}{2}}$	2^{hd}	2no	Castro E	8.70
29May04 ^{8}Bel^{2}	Spice Island	L b	5	118	4	$4^{\frac{1}{2}}$	$4^{\frac{1}{2}}$	4^{hd}	$4^{2\frac{1}{2}}$	$3^{1\frac{1}{2}}$	$3^{6\frac{1}{2}}$	Bailey J D	1.35
12May04 ^{8}Bel^{1}	Humaita-Ger	L	4	115	6	$6^{\frac{1}{2}}$	$6^{2\frac{1}{2}}$	6^{3}	$5^{\frac{1}{2}}$	5^{6}	4^{nk}	Migliore R	24.25
21Apr04 ^{8}Kee^{3}	Binya-Ger	L	5	117	1	1^{2}	$1^{1\frac{1}{2}}$	$1^{1\frac{1}{2}}$	1^{hd}	$4^{1\frac{1}{2}}$	$5^{6\frac{1}{4}}$	Velazquez J R	2.90
17Jun04 ^{3}Bel^{2}	Alchemist	L	4	114	5	7	7	7	7	7	6^{hd}	Santos J A	17.80
17Jun04 ^{3}Bel^{1}	Potra Fabulous-Arg	L	5	114	7	2^{hd}	2^{hd}	$3^{2\frac{1}{2}}$	6^{5}	6^{2}	7	Chavez J F	9.80

OFF AT 5:12 Start Good . Won driving. Course soft.
TIME :25, :50, 1:15, 1:40^{2}, 2:05^{3} (:25.05, :50.08, 1:15.10, 1:40.51, 2:05.60)

$2 Mutuel Prices:

4 – WONDER AGAIN	9.90	5.70	3.10
2 – STAY FOREVER		8.60	3.60
5 – SPICE ISLAND			2.40

$2 EXACTA 4–2 PAID $63.50 $2 TRIFECTA 4–2–5 PAID $171.50

B. m, (Feb), by Silver Hawk – Ameriflora , by Danzig . Trainer Toner James J. Bred by Phillips Racing Partnership & John &Phillips (Ky).

WONDER AGAIN raced close up along the inside while in hand, came wide approaching the stretch, responded when roused, drew away and was kept to the task to the wire. STAY FOREVER was rated along inside, angled out for the drive, dug in gamely while being brushed by SPICE ISLAND in the stretch and stayed on to earn the place award. SPICE ISLAND was rated along outside, rallied three wide, came in in the stretch, brushing STAY FOREVER then was outfinished for the place. HUMAITA (GER) was outrun early, raced inside and had no response when roused. BINYA (GER) quickly opened a clear lead, set the pace along the inside and tired in the stretch. ALCHEMIST was outrun early and had no response when roused. POTRA FABULOUS (ARG) raced with the pace from the outside and tired after the opening three quarters. A claim of foul against the second place finisher by the rider of the third place finisher, alleging interference in the stretch, was dismissed.

Owners– 1, Phillips Joan G and John W; 2, Rizo-Patron Jamie; 3, Denlea Park Ltd; 4, Jacobs Andreas; 5, Allen Joseph; 6, Alexander Helen C Groves Helen K and Dorothy A Matz LLC; 7, Tanaka Gary A

Trainers– 1, Toner James J; 2, Wolfson Martin D; 3, Pregman John S Jr; 4, Motion H Graham; 5, McLaughlin Kiaran P; 6, McGaughey III Claude R; 7, Frankel Robert

Scratched– Meridiana (GER) (29May04 ^{8}Bel^{3})

TENTH RACE
Churchill
JULY 5, 2004

6 FURLONGS. (1.07^{3}) 103RD RUNNING OF THE BASHFORD MANOR. Grade III. Purse $150,000 FOR TWO-YEAR-OLDS. By subscription of $150 each on or before June 19, 2004 or by supplementary nomination of $7,500 at time of entry. $750 to pass the entry box; $750 additional to start, with $150,000 added of which 62% of all monies to the owner of the winner, 20% to second, 10% to third, 5% to fourth and 3% to fifth. Colts and Geldings 121 lbs. Fillies 118 lbs. Non-winners of a sweepstakes allowed 2 lbs.; a race other than maiden or claiming, 4 lbs.; a race other than claiming, 6 lbs. Starters to be named through the entry box at the usual time of closing. Trophy to winning owner. Closed Saturday, June 19, 2004 with 18 nominations.

Value of Race: $163,200 Winner $101,184; second $32,640; third $16,320; fourth $8,160; fifth $4,896. Mutuel Pool $421,246.00 Exacta Pool $305,390.00 Trifecta Pool $242,235.00 Superfecta Pool $75,794.00

Last Raced	Horse	M/Eqt.	A.	Wt	PP	St	¼	½	Str	Fin	Jockey	Odds $1
5Jun04 ^{8}CD^{1}	Lunarpal	L	2	121	3	2	1^{hd}	1^{1½}	½	1^{nk}	Sellers S J	1.10
29May04 ^{4}CD^{1}	Storm Surge	L f	2	117	4	1	2^{hd}	2^{1½}	2^{2}	2^{1¼}	Albarado R J	15.50
15May04 ^{1}CD^{1}	Maximus C	L	2	117	2	6	4^{1½}	3^{1½}	3^{2}	3^{1¼}	Perret C	7.60
5Jun04 ^{8}CD^{3}	Smoke Warning	L	2	117	1	7	6^{3½}	5^{½}	4^{2½}	4^{2}	Guidry M	6.80
5Jun04 ^{6}CD^{1}	Copy My Notes	L	2	117	7	5	7	7	5^{2}	5^{6}	McKee J	17.80
12Jun04 ^{1}CD^{1}	Raise Ole Glory		2	117	5	3	3^{1½}	4^{hd}	6^{1½}	6^{3}	Day P	2.00
19Jun04 ^{1}CD^{1}	Proper Carson	L	2	117	6	4	5^{hd}	6^{hd}	7	7	Bejarano R	31.30

OFF AT 5:51 Start Good. Won driving. Track sloppy.

TIME :21^{4}, :45^{2}, :58, 1:11^{2} (:21.80, :45.49, :58.01, 1:11.54)

$2 Mutuel Prices:

3 – LUNARPAL	4.20	3.00	2.80
4 – STORM SURGE		9.40	6.80
2 – MAXIMUS C			4.20

$2 EXACTA 3–4 PAID $46.00 $2 TRIFECTA 3–4–2 PAID $223.20
$2 SUPERFECTA 3–4–2–1 PAID $767.40

B. c, (Apr), by Successful Appeal – Quiet Eclipse, by Quiet American. Trainer Asmussen Steven M. Bred by L William Heiligbrodt (Fla).

LUNARPAL gained a slight edge early, raced in the three path under careful handling, battled with STORM SURGE most of the way and gamely held that one safe under energetic handling. STORM SURGE vied for the lead from early on while between rivals four wide, loomed boldly outside the winner through the drive and wasn't quite good enough. MAXIMUS C, nicely placed in behind the leaders from early on, came out five wide for the drive and offered a mild gain. SMOKE WARNING settled inside, raced near the rail most of the way and managed only a minor gain. COPY MY NOTES, outrun three wide to the stretch, advanced between horses four wide into the stretch but could gain only slightly at the end. RAISE OLE GLORY forced the pace early while four or five wide, continued in contention for a half and weakened thereafter. PROPER CARSON raced five or six wide most of the way and tired upon going a half.

Owners– 1, Heiligbrodt Racing Stable; 2, Overbrook Farm; 3, Romans Dale Pacella William Bonomo George and Schwed Ronald; 4, Jones Frank L Jr; 5, Iron Horse Racing LLC; 6, Van Meter Thomas F II; 7, Winn Mrs James A

Trainers– 1, Asmussen Steven M; 2, Stewart Dallas; 3, Romans Dale; 4, Romans Dale; 5, Holthus Robert E; 6, Lukas D Wayne; 7, Holthus Robert E

$2 Pick Three (1–2–3) Paid $83.20; Pick Three Pool $34,218.

EIGHTH RACE
Hollywood
JULY 5, 2004

6 FURLONGS. (1.07^{2}) 60TH RUNNING OF THE LANDALUCE. Grade III. Purse $100,000 FOR FILLIES TWO-YEARS-OLD. By subscription of $100 each on or before Wednesday, June 23, or by supplementary nomination of $2,000 each by closing time of entries.$1,000 additional to start, with $100,000 added. The added money and all fees to be divided 60% to the winner, 20% to second, 12% to third, 6% to fourth and 2% to fifth. Weight 119 lbs. Non-winners of a sweepstakes allowed 3 lbs. Maidens allowed 5 lbs. Starters to be named through the entry box by the closing time of entries. A trophy will be presented to the winning owner. Close with 15 nominations. 1 supplementary nomination: Crypto's Wild.

Value of Race: $106,800 Winner $64,080; second $21,360; third $12,816; fourth $6,408; fifth $2,136. Mutuel Pool $606,710.00 Exacta Pool $289,466.00 Quinella Pool $21,715.00 Trifecta Pool $323,149.00 Superfecta Pool $180,302.00

Last Raced	Horse	M/Eqt.	A.	Wt	PP	St	¼	½	Str	Fin	Jockey	Odds $1
6Jun04 ^{3}Hol^{1}	Souvenir Gift	LB	2	119	2	6	3^{1½}	3^{4}	3^{10}	1^{1¼}	Smith M E	4.10
16May04 ^{8}Hol^{2}	Bella Banissa	LB	2	117	6	3	2^{1}	1^{½}	1^{½}	2no	Nakatani C S	6.00
29May04 ^{1}Hol^{1}	My Miss Storm Cat	LB	2	116	9	4	5^{2}	2^{2½}	2^{1½}	3^{8}	Flores D R	0.40
	Crypto's Wild	LB	2	114	8	10	11	10^{hd}	5^{hd}	4^{½}	Sorenson D	80.80
6Jun04 ^{3}Hol^{2}	Fortunate Event	LB	2	115	4	9	7^{2}	7^{2}	4^{2}	5^{3½}	Valdivia J Jr	21.50
6Jun04 ^{3}Hol^{3}	Swiss Please	LB	2	116	1	8	9^{2}	9^{1½}	6^{½}	6^{4}	Pedroza M A	86.20
9Jun04 ^{3}Hol^{1}	I Can Yodele	LB f	2	116	7	11	10^{1½}	11	9^{1½}	7^{2}	Espinoza V	65.60
4Jun04 ^{1}Hol^{1}	Weybridge	LB f	2	116	11	2	8^{½}	8^{hd}	10^{8}	8^{½}	Martinez F F	205.70
13Jun04 ^{7}Hol^{3}	Wild Humor	LB	2	114	3	1	4^{hd}	5^{hd}	7^{hd}	9^{2}	Garcia M S	113.50
29May04 ^{12}Crc^{1}	Kash Klip	LB	2	116	10	7	6^{hd}	6^{1½}	8^{2}	10	Desormeaux K J	23.60
13Jun04 ^{8}BM^{4}	Kitty and Boo	LB	2	116	5	5	1^{hd}	4^{1½}	11	—	Baze T C	33.70

OFF AT 5:02 Start Good. Won driving. Track fast.

TIME :21^{4}, :44^{2}, :56^{3}, 1:09^{3} (:21.86, :44.58, :56.61, 1:09.75)

$2 Mutuel Prices:

2 – SOUVENIR GIFT	10.20	4.60	2.10
6 – BELLA BANISSA		8.00	2.10
9 – MY MISS STORM CAT			2.10

$1 EXACTA 2–6 PAID $29.20 $2 QUINELLA 2–6 PAID $28.00
$1 TRIFECTA 2–6–9 PAID $53.70 $1 SUPERFECTA 2–6–9–8 PAID $1,362.00

B. f, (Apr), by Souvenir Copy – Alleged Gift, by Alleged. Trainer Semkin Sam. Bred by Mrs John C Mabee (Ky).

SOUVENIR GIFT saved ground stalking the pace, went around the early leader on the turn, continued inside and rallied along the rail in deep stretch under some urging to prove best. BELLA BANISSA crowded at the start, dueled outside a rival, took command and inched away between calls on the turn, responded when challenged leaving the turn and in the stretch, could not hold off the winner but saved second. MY MISS STORM CAT broke inward and was bumped at the start, had the rider nearly lose an iron, chased outside, moved up three deep then challenged outside the runner-up leaving the turn and in the stretch but could not get by that one. CRYPTO'S WILD squeezed a bit at the start, settled off the rail then angled in leaving the backstretch, came out leaving the turn and four wide into the stretch and improved position but was not a threat. FORTUNATE EVENT forced out at the start, settled between foes then a bit off the rail, split horses into the stretch and lacked a further response. SWISS PLEASE allowed to settle inside, remained along the rail and failed to menace. I CAN YODELE steadied hard at the start, settled off the rail, went four wide leaving the turn, angled in entering the stretch and did not rally. WEYBRIDGE wide early, settled outside, angled in off the rail on the turn, came out into the stretch and also lacked a rally. WILD HUMOR broke out onto foes, settled outside the winner then a bit off the rail, came three deep into the stretch and weakened. KASH KLIP bobbled at the start, chased outside, came four wide into the stretch and also weakened. KITTY AND BOO had good early speed and dueled a bit off the rail, angled in on the turn, dropped back fast, gave way readily and was eased in the stretch.

Owners– 1, Semkin Sam and Unruh Gregory; 2, Legacy Ranch; 3, Friendly Ed; 4, Jarvis & Young; 5, Bienstock Winner Stables Mandabach Paul and Papiano Neil; 6, Harrington Vanderhouwen Vanderhouwen et al; 7, Steinmann Heinz; 8, Harlequin Stable; 9, The Hat Ranch Mullens Kathleen A and Stute Annabelle; 10, Claimboxdotcom and Carrier R; 11, Wood Jason

Trainers– 1, Semkin Sam; 2, Hofmans David; 3, Baffert Bob; 4, Sauque Alex; 5, Mulhall Kristin; 6, Harrington Mike; 7, Harrington Mike; 8, Dee Tony; 9, Stute Melvin F; 10, O'Neill Doug; 11, O'Neill Doug

---

$2 Daily Double (1–2) Paid $101.20; Daily Double Pool $38,371.
$1 Pick Three (3–1–2) Paid $327.00; Pick Three Pool $84,926.

EIGHTH RACE
Belmont
JULY 10, 2004

1 MILE. (Turf) (1.31^3) 20TH RUNNING OF THE POKER HANDICAP. Grade III. Purse $100,000 WIDENER TURF. (UP TO $19,000 NYSBFOA) A HANDICAP FOR THREE YEAR OLDS AND UPWARD. By subscription of $100 each, which should accompany the nomination; $500 to pass the entry box; $500 to start, with $100,000 added. The added money and all fees to be divided 60% to the winner, 20% to second, 10% to third, 5% to fourth, 3% to fifth and 2% divided equally among remaining finishers. A trophy will be presented to the winning owner. The New York Racing Association reserves the right to transfer this race to theMain Track. In the event that this race is taken off the turf, it may be subject to downgrading upon review by the Graded Stakes Committee. Closed Saturday, June 26, 2004 with 36 Nominations. (If the Stewards consider it inadvisable to run this race on the turf course, this race will be runat One Mile on the main track.). (Rail at 18 feet).

Value of Race: $112,600 Winner $67,560; second $22,520; third $11,260; fourth $5,630; fifth $3,378; sixth $563; seventh $563; eighth $563; ninth $563. Mutuel Pool $688,295.00 Exacta Pool $504,267.00 Trifecta Pool $389,085.00

Last Raced	Horse	M/Eqt.	A.	Wt	PP	St	¼	½	¾	Str	Fin	Jockey	Odds $1
20Jun04 5Bel1	Christine's Outlaw	L	4	113	2	2	1½	1½	1½	11	1nk	Bridgmohan S X	13.80
5Jun04 10Bel2	MillnnumDrgon-GB	L	5	120	6	8	5hd	4hd	41½	2½	22½	Luzzi M J	2.15
16Jun04 8Bel1	Silver Tree	L	4	117	5	6	3½	3½	3½	3hd	31	Santos J A	2.70
16Jun04 8Bel4	Megoman	L b	4	113	1	9	8hd	9	61½	5hd	4¾	Fragoso P	21.30
16Jun04 8Bel3	Chilly Rooster	L b	4	114	4	3	41½	5½	5½	61½	5no	Uske S	18.20
29May04 10Mth1	Burning Roma	L	6	120	3	4	2hd	2½	2½	41½	61¾	Castanon J L	3.30
20Jun04 5Bel3	Provincetown	L	4	112	9	1	71	71½	8hd	7½	7hd	Chavez J F	27.50
16Jun04 8Bel5	Pisces	L b	7	113	8	7	9	8½	9	8½	82¼	Samyn J L	39.00
30May04 0Bel1	Multiple Choice	L b	6	115	7	5	6hd	6½	7½	9	9	Castellano J J	7.20

OFF AT 4:46 Start Good . Won driving. Course firm.

TIME :23, :46, 1:09, 1:32^2 (:23.14, :46.00, 1:09.19, 1:32.46)

$2 Mutuel Prices:				
	2 – CHRISTINE'S OUTLAW	29.60	10.60	5.80
	6 – MILLENNIUM DRAGON–GB		3.90	2.70
	5 – SILVER TREE			2.90

$2 EXACTA 2–6 PAID $119.00 $2 TRIFECTA 2–6–5 PAID $415.00

Dk. b or br. c, (Mar), by Wild Again – Marianna's Girl , by Dewan . Trainer Weaver George. Bred by Albert G Clay 1990 Rev Trust & &John W Clay (Ky).

CHRISTINE'S OUTLAW quickly showed in front, set the pace along the inside, drifted out a bit in the stretch, was straightened away, dug in determinedly and held on after a hard drive. MILLENNIUM DRAGON (GB) raced close up inside while in hand, rallied into the stretch, angled out in upper stretch and finished gamely outside. SILVER TREE chased the pace while three wide and weakened in the final furlong. MEGOMAN was outrun early along the inside, came wide for the drive and finished well outside. CHILLY ROOSTER raced close up while in hand three wide and had no response when roused. BURNING ROMA raced with the pace while between rivals and was steadied while tiring in the stretch. PROVINCETOWN was outrun early, raced four wide and had no response when roused. PISCES was outrun early, raced between rivals and had no rally. MULTIPLE CHOICE raced three wide and tired in the stretch. A claim of foul lodged by the rider of MILLENNIUM DRAGON against the winner, alleging interference during the stretch run, was dismissed.

Owners– 1, RC Hill Stable; 2, Darley Stable; 3, Vegso Peter; 4, Falco Joseph N Lansdon B Robbins III; 5, Hobeau Farm; 6, Queen Harold L; 7, Flying Zee Stable; 8, Shapiro Gary L; 9, Blum Peter E

Trainers– 1, Weaver George; 2, McLaughlin Kiaran P; 3, Mott William I; 4, McLaughlin Kiaran P; 5, Jerkens H Allen; 6, Giglio Heather A; 7, Biancone Patrick L; 8, Weaver George; 9, Jerkens James A

EIGHTH RACE
Colonial
JULY 10, 2004

1⅛ MILES. (Turf) (1.47^2) 16TH RUNNING OF THE ALL ALONG BREEDERS' CUP. Grade III. Purse $200,000 (Includes $50,000 BC – Breeders' Cup) OUTER TURF FOR FILLIES AND MARES, THREE–YEARS–OLD AND UPWARD. By subscription of $100 each which should accompany the nomination. $950 to pass the entry box. $950 additional to start with $150,000 Guaranteed,and an additional $50,000 from the Breeders' Cup Fund for Cup nominees only. The Host Association's added monies to be divided, of which 60% to the winner, 20% to second, 11% to third, 6% to fourth, and 3% to fifth. Breeders' Cup Fund monies also correspondingly divided provided a Breeders' Cup Nominee has finished in an awarded position. Any Breeders' Cup Fund money not awarded will revert back to the fund. Weights Three–year–olds 117., Older 124 lbs. Non–winners of two races of $50,000 at one mile or over since April 1 2004, allowed 3 lbs.; of such since then, 5 lbs. (Maiden and claiming races not considered in estimating allowances). Starters to be named through the entry box by the usual time of closing. Nominations closed June 28, 2004, with 32 nominations. Trophy to the winning owner given by the Breeders' Cup Ltd.

Value of Race: $200,000 Winner $120,000; second $40,000; third $22,000; fourth $12,000; fifth $6,000. Mutuel Pool $130,222.00 Exacta Pool $81,626.00 Trifecta Pool $67,522.00

Last Raced	Horse	M/Eqt.	A.	Wt	PP	St	¼	½	¾	Str	Fin	Jockey	Odds $1
15May04 5Pim2	Film Maker	L b	4	119	1	3	42	43	4hd	22½	13	Prado E S	1.20
20Jun04 9Mth2	Noisette	L	4	119	7	2	11½	1hd	1½	1½	21¾	Migliore R	2.80
20Jun04 7Cnl1	Lady Linda	L b	6	119	4	5	62½	65	32	3hd	31	Fogelsonger R	8.60
19Jun04 9Cnl1	With Patience	L f	5	119	3	1	2½	3hd	51	44	41¾	Castillo O O	22.80
19Jun04 7Cnl1	Tanwi Spring	L	6	119	5	6	7	7	7	7	56	Van Hassel C	28.20
20Jun04 8Bel1	Brandala	L	6	121	6	4	51½	51	612	51½	6½	Blanc B	20.00
26Jun04 9CD3	Sand Springs	L	4	119	2	7	3½	21½	2hd	64	7	Guidry M	2.40

OFF AT 4:54 Start Good . Won driving. Course firm.

TIME :25^4, :50^3, 1:14^4, 1:38^1, 1:50 (:25.85, :50.61, 1:14.89, 1:38.28, 1:50.08)

$2 Mutuel Prices:				
	1 – FILM MAKER	4.40	2.40	2.40
	9 – NOISETTE		3.20	2.80
	4 – LADY LINDA			2.80

$2 EXACTA 1–9 PAID $17.80 $2 TRIFECTA 1–9–4 PAID $70.20

Dk. b or br. f, (Mar), by Dynaformer – Miss Du Bois , by Mr. Prospector . Trainer Motion H Graham. Bred by TAC Holdings Inc (Ky).

FILM MAKER saved ground under patient rating, eased out near the three sixteenths pole, closed nicely and drew off. NOISETTE , quickly clear, set the pace along the rail and was no match for the winner. LADY LINDA advanced three wide on the far turn, drifted in near the three sixteenths pole and weakened in the drive. WITH PATIENCE stalked the pace two wide, swung four wide in upper stretch and gave way. TANWI SPRING , very wide, was no factor. BRANDALA , three wide on the turns, dropped back. SAND SPRINGS broke slowly, raced four wide on the first turn, was steadied in close quarters near the three sixteenths pole then stopped.

Owners– 1, Courtlandt Farms; 2, Haras Santa Maria de Araras; 3, Domino Stud of Lex LLC; 4, Hendriks Elizabeth M; 5, Augustin Stable; 6, Sorin Stables; 7, Willmott Stables Inc

Trainers– 1, Motion H Graham; 2, Mott William I; 3, Eppler Mary E; 4, Hendriks Elizabeth M; 5, Sheppard Jonathan E; 6, Walsh Thomas M; 7, Reinstedler Anthony

Scratched– Romancin Dixie (20Jun04 7Cnl2) , High Court (BRZ) (30May04 11Mth1)

$2 Pick Six (6/7–6–7–14–4–1/7/8) 5 Correct Paid $214.60 ; Pick Six Pool $2,752 ; Carryover Pool $1,609.

NINTH RACE
Colonial
JULY 10, 2004

$1\frac{1}{4}$ MILES. (Turf) (1.59^4) 7TH RUNNING OF THE VIRGINIA DERBY. Grade III. Purse $500,000 OUTER TURF FOR THREE YEAR OLDS. Early closing June 1, 2004 at a fee of $150. Late nominations close Monday, June 28, 2004 at a fee of $500. $2425 to pass the entry box. $2425 additional to start with $500,000 Guaranteed, of which 60% to the winner, 20%to second, 11% to third, 6% to fourth, and 3% to fifth. Weight 122 lbs. Non–winners of two races of $75,000 at one mile or over since April 1, 2004 allowed 3 lbs.; of such a race since then, 5 lbs.; of a race of $50,000 at a mile or over in 2004, 7 lbs.(Maiden and claiming races not considered in estimating allowances). Starters to be named through the entry box by the usual time of closing. Nominations Closed June 1, 2004, with 61 nominations. Trophy presented to the winning owner, trainer, and jockey.

Value of Race: $500,000 Winner $300,000; second $100,000; third $55,000; fourth $30,000; fifth $15,000. Mutuel Pool $362,887.00 Exacta Pool $215,528.00 Superfecta Pool $72,900.00 Trifecta Pool $201,932.00

Last Raced	Horse	M/Eqt.	A.	Wt	PP	¼	½	¾	1	Str	Fin	Jockey	Odds $1
12Jun04 ^{5}CD^{2}	Kitten's Joy	L	3	117	2	6^{hd}	$6^{1\frac{1}{2}}$	$4^{\frac{1}{2}}$	$3^{4\frac{1}{2}}$	$1^{\frac{1}{2}}$	$1^{2\frac{3}{4}}$	Prado E S	1.70
6Jun04 ^{8}Bel^{1}	Artie Schiller	L	3	117	7	5^{1}	5^{hd}	5^{hd}	$2^{\frac{1}{2}}$	2^{8}	$2^{4\frac{3}{4}}$	Migliore R	1.10
12Jun04 ^{5}CD^{1}	Prince Arch	L b	3	119	1	7^{hd}	8	8	7^{4}	3^{5}	$3^{12\frac{3}{4}}$	Blanc B	3.50
31May04 ^{10}Mth^{4}	Lipan	L	3	115	4	4^{1}	4^{2}	6^{2}	5^{1}	$6^{4\frac{1}{2}}$	4^{1}	Monterrey R	47.00
17Jun04 ^{2}Pen^{2}	Class Concern	L b	3	115	3	$2^{2\frac{1}{2}}$	$2^{4\frac{1}{2}}$	2^{2}	$4^{2\frac{1}{2}}$	4^{hd}	$5^{\frac{3}{4}}$	Boucher R	86.70
5Jun04 ^{8}Pim^{1}	Jane's Luck	L	3	115	5	$1^{3\frac{1}{2}}$	1^{8}	1^{10}	1^{3}	$5^{\frac{1}{2}}$	$6^{7\frac{3}{4}}$	Castillo O O	13.80
6Jun04 ^{8}Del^{4}	Irish Laddie	L b	3	115	6	$3^{1\frac{1}{2}}$	3^{2}	3^{1}	$6^{1\frac{1}{2}}$	7^{4}	$7^{\frac{1}{2}}$	Karamanos H A	50.40
31May04 ^{10}LS^{1}	No Place Like It	L	3	119	8	8	$7^{\frac{1}{2}}$	7^{hd}	8	8	8	Walker B J Jr	17.00

OFF AT 5:41 Start Good. Won driving. Course firm.

TIME :23^2, :47^1, 1:11^2, 1:36^4, 2:01^1 (:23.57, :47.30, 1:11.50, 1:36.98, 2:01.22)

$2 Mutuel Prices:			
2 – KITTEN'S JOY	5.40	2.60	2.10
8 – ARTIE SCHILLER		2.60	2.10
1 – PRINCE ARCH			2.10

$2 EXACTA 2–8 PAID $10.80 $1 SUPERFECTA 2–8–1–4 PAID $45.10
$2 TRIFECTA 2–8–1 PAID $19.40

Ch. c, (May), by El Prado–Ire – Kitten's First, by Lear Fan. Trainer Romans Dale. Bred by Kenneth L Ramsey & Sarah K Ramsey (Ky).

KITTEN'S JOY was taken to rate early while saving ground, angled out leaving the far turn, advanced four wide to even terms entering the lane, gained a short advantage leaving the three sixteenths marker, drifted out late and edged away under a drive. ARTIE SCHILLER settled well off the rail, quickly gained three wide to take a short lead into the lane, dueled briefly inside of the winner and continued gamely to the wire. PRINCE ARCH encountered some traffic entering the first turn, was taken to rate off the rail down the backstretch, came four wide for the drive and finished with interest though no threat to the top two. LIPAN , three wide early, failed to menace. CLASS CONCERN saved ground chasing the pace and gave way. JANE'S LUCK opened up when a bit difficult to settle, set a brisk pace along the inside for a mile then faltered three sixteenths from the wire. IRISH LADDIE ,checked when in tight between rivals near the three furlong marker, failed to recover. NO PLACE LIKE IT lost ground five wide and dropped back.

Owners– 1, Ramsey Kenneth L and Sarah K; 2, Timber Bay Farm and Mrs Thomas J Walsh; 3, Cottrell Raymond H Sr; 4, Gill Michael J; 5, Star Ten Stable; 6, Dresden Farm; 7, Johnson R Larry; 8, Durant Tom R

Trainers– 1, Romans Dale; 2, Jerkens James A; 3, McPeek Kenneth G; 4, Vazquez Gamaliel; 5, Boucher Lilith; 6, Lawrence James L II; 7, Trombetta Michael J; 8, Bruner Jack A

Scratched– Commendation (26Jun04 ^{8}Del^{3}) , King's Coronation (26Jun04 ^{8}Del^{4})

$2 Pick Three (4–1/7/8–2) Paid $117.40 ; Pick Three Pool $23,586 .

EIGHTH RACE
Calder
JULY 10, 2004

6 FURLONGS. (1.08^4) 6TH RUNNING OF THE AZALEA BREEDERS' CUP. Grade III. Purse $300,000 FOR FILLIES, THREE YEARS OLD. By subscription of $300 each which shall accompany the nomination, $1,500 to pass the entry box and an additional $1,500 to start – with $225,000 Guaranteed, and an additional $75,000 from the Breeders' Cup Fund for Cup nominees only. The host association's monies to be divided $132,000 to the owner of the winner, $45,000 to second, $24,750 to third, $13,500 to fourth, $6,750 to fifth, and $3,000 to sixth. Breeders' Cup Fund monies also correspondingly divided. Weight: 121 lbs. Non–winners of $50,000 twice allowed 3 lbs.; once, 5 lbs.; $35,000, 7 lbs.; $25,000 or two races other than Maiden or Claiming, 9 lbs. Closed Saturday, June 26, 2004 with 20 nominations.

Value of Race: $300,000 Winner $177,000; second $60,000; third $33,000; fourth $18,000; fifth $9,000; sixth $3,000. Mutuel Pool $351,778.00 Exacta Pool $265,640.00 Trifecta Pool $202,700.00 Superfecta Pool $74,446.00

Last Raced	Horse	M/Eqt.	A.	Wt	PP	St	¼	½	Str	Fin	Jockey	Odds $1
20Jun04 ^{8}CD^{1}	Dazzle Me	L	3	115	3	5	1^{1}	$1^{1\frac{1}{2}}$	1^{2}	$1^{6\frac{1}{2}}$	Sellers S J	8.90
19Jun04 ^{8}Bel^{1}	Reforest	L	3	114	7	3	3^{hd}	3^{hd}	3^{4}	$2^{\frac{3}{4}}$	Bailey J D	1.10
12Jun04 ^{10}LaD^{1}	Boston Express	L b	3	114	1	6	$4^{1\frac{1}{2}}$	4^{4}	2^{hd}	3^{3}	Castro E	5.90
26May04 ^{8}Bel^{1}	Frenchglen	L	3	116	5	2	$5^{\frac{1}{2}}$	$5^{2\frac{1}{2}}$	4^{2}	4^{3}	Velazquez J R	3.60
13Dec03 ^{12}Crc^{5}	Chatter Chatter	L	3	121	2	7	7	7	$5^{1\frac{1}{2}}$	5^{13}	Bravo J	18.20
23Jun04 ^{9}CD^{1}	Anna Em	L b	3	118	4	1	$2^{\frac{1}{2}}$	2^{hd}	$6^{2\frac{1}{2}}$	6^{3}	Dominguez R A	8.80
14Jun04 ^{8}Crc^{1}	French Village	L	3	118	6	4	6^{7}	$6^{\frac{1}{2}}$	7	7	Velasquez C	6.20

OFF AT 4:10 Start Good. Won driving. Track fast.

TIME :21^1, :44^1, :57, 1:11^2 (:21.24, :44.39, :57.15, 1:11.40)

$2 Mutuel Prices:			
3 – DAZZLE ME	19.80	6.60	3.80
7 – REFOREST		3.40	2.60
1 – BOSTON EXPRESS			4.40

$2 EXACTA 3–7 PAID $73.40 $2 TRIFECTA 3–7–1 PAID $327.60
$2 SUPERFECTA 3–7–1–5 PAID $823.40

Gr/ro. f, (Mar), by Tactical Cat – Social Girl, by Chief's Crown. Trainer Asmussen Steven M. Bred by Mrs J G Jones Sr & R J Judy (Ky).

DAZZLE ME showed speed off the rail into the stretch, then drew away under pressure. REFOREST chased the pace four wide into the stretch, then was no match for the winner while continuing on with good courage for the place. BOSTON EXPRESS chased the pace along the rail, was steadied briefly to avoid being caught in tight quarters entering the turn, continued to chase the winner in the stretch and gave way. FRENCHGLEN allowed to settle, had no response when asked. CHATTER CHATTER was no factor after being outrun early. ANNA EM chased the pace three wide around the turn and faltered. FRENCH VILLAGE was through early.

Owners– 1, Padua Stables; 2, Gann Edmund A; 3, Brooks Jack G; 4, Jones Aaron U and Marie D; 5, Franks Farms; 6, GWM Farms; 7, Melnyk Eugene and Laura

Trainers– 1, Asmussen Steven M; 2, Frankel Robert; 3, Norman Cole; 4, Pletcher Todd A; 5, Wolfson Martin D; 6, Amoss Thomas; 7, White William P

Scratched– Special Report (12Jun04 ^{9}Crc^{4})

$2 Pick Three (11–10–3) Paid $717.60 ; Pick Three Pool $35,883 .

NINTH RACE
Calder
JULY 10, 2004

6 FURLONGS. (1.084) 30TH RUNNING OF THE CARRY BACK. Grade III. Purse $300,000 FOR THREE YEAR OLDS. By subscription of $300 each which shall accompany the nomination, $1,500 to pass the entry box and an additional $1,500 to start – with $300,000 guaranteed. The owner of the winner to receive $177,000, $60,000 to second, $33,000 to third, $18,000 to fourth, $9,000 to fifth and $3,000 to sixth. Weight: 122 lbs. Non–winners of $50,000 twice allowed 3 lbs.; once, 5 lbs.; $35,000, 7 lbs.; $25,000 or two races other than Maiden or Claiming, 10 lbs. A trophy will be presented to the winning Owner. Closed Saturday, June 26, 2004 with 22 nominations.

Value of Race: $300,000 Winner $177,000; second $60,000; third $33,000; fourth $18,000; fifth $9,000; sixth $3,000. Mutuel Pool $473,336.00 Exacta Pool $339,280.00 Trifecta Pool $253,227.00 Superfecta Pool $94,046.00

Last Raced	Horse	M/Eqt.	A.	Wt	PP	St	¼	½	Str	Fin	Jockey	Odds $1
29May04 3Crc2	Weigelia	L	3	117	4	4	41½	32½	1hd	1½	Toribio A Jr	10.50
15Jun04 8Crc2	Classy Migration	L bf	3	112	7	3	1hd	1½	23	24	Day P	13.00
15May04 6Pim2	Bwana Charlie	L	3	119	10	2	81½	4hd	31	34	Sellers S J	5.00
19Jun04 9Crc3	Caballero Negro	L bf	3	115	1	8	91½	9½	6hd	4no	Castro E	28.80
20Jun04 7Bel1	Ice Wynnd Fire	L b	3	115	6	6	6hd	81	51	53¾	Bailey J D	1.50
13Mar04 9GP8	Sir Oscar	L b	3	122	5	10	11	11	8½	6¾	Garcia J A	18.40
19Jun04 7Hol2	Twice as Bad	L	3	119	2	9	2½	2hd	42	7¾	Court J K	4.70
5Jun04 9Bel3	Abbondanza	L f	3	119	11	11	105	6½	72½	86¼	Dominguez R A	3.70
18Jun04 8Crc3	Misguided Left	L b	3	115	3	5	5½	7½	91	93¾	Toribio A R	114.40
18Jun04 8Crc2	Bourbon N Blues	L bf	3	115	9	1	3hd	5½	103	104¼	Velasquez C	67.50
18Jun04 8Crc4	Sami's Majic	L b	3	115	8	7	7½	103½	11	11	Bravo J	63.20

OFF AT 4:42 Start Good . Won driving. Track fast.

TIME :212, :442, :57, 1:102 (:21.42, :44.46, :57.07, 1:10.50)

$2 Mutuel Prices:				
	4 – WEIGELIA	23.00	11.20	6.60
	7 – CLASSY MIGRATION		13.80	6.00
	11 – BWANA CHARLIE			4.40

$2 EXACTA 4–7 PAID $187.00 $2 TRIFECTA 4–7–11 PAID $1,001.80

$2 SUPERFECTA 4–7–11–1 PAID $11,442.20

B. c, (Feb), by Safely's Mark – Turning North , by Obligato . Trainer Azpurua Manuel J. Bred by Shelley Huber (Fla).

WEIGELIA chased the pace, angled three wide on the turn, rallied to gain a slim lead at the top of the stretch and was fully extended to prevail. CLASSY MIGRATION vied for the lead outside TWICE AS BAD, responded when headed at the top of the stretch and continued on gamely while being edged to the wire. BWANA CHARLIE reserved early, bumped with SAMI'S MAJIC entering the turn, advanced off the rail to reach contention entering the stretch, then flattened out. CABALLERO NEGRO unhurried early, passed tired rivals without threatening. ICE WYNND FIRE allowed to settle, lacked a late response. SIR OSCAR off slowly, failed to menace. TWICE AS BAD broke slowly, moved up quickly to vie for the lead along the inside, then gave way in the drive. ABBONDANZA off slowly, advanced four wide around the turn to reach contention at the quarter pole, then tired. MISGUIDED LEFT well placed early, raced four wide on the turn and faltered. BOURBON N BLUES showed brief speed, raced three wide on the turn and faded. SAMI'S MAJIC was racing three wide when he bumped with BWANA CHARLIE entering the turn and stopped.

Owners– 1, Balsamo Joseph J; 2, Buckram Oak Farm; 3, Heiligbrodt Racing Stable; 4, Veranda Farm Inc; 5, Amerman Racing Stables LLC; 6, International Fair Play Inc; 7, Mercedes Stables LLC; 8, Germania Farms Inc; 9, Sainer Joel W; 10, Jacks or Better Farm Inc; 11, Solomon Linda

Trainers– 1, Azpurua Manuel J; 2, Mikhalides George; 3, Asmussen Steven M; 4, Morales Mario; 5, Frankel Robert; 6, Sacco Richard W; 7, Cerin Vladimir; 8, Tullock Timothy Jr; 9, Braddy J David; 10, Hatchett James; 11, Gatis Christos

Scratched– Forest Danger (01May04 8Aqu2) , Stormin' Lyon (12Jun04 4BM 1)

TENTH RACE
Calder
JULY 10, 2004

6 FURLONGS. (1.084) 6TH RUNNING OF THE SMILE SPRINT HANDICAP. Grade III. Purse $500,000 FOR THREE YEAR OLDS AND UPWARD. By subscription of $500 each which shall accompany the nomination, $2,000 to pass the entry box and an additional $2000 to start – with $500,000 guaranteed. The owner of the winner to receive $294,000, $100,000 to seceond,$55,000 to third, $30,000 to fourth, $15,000 to fifth, and $6,000 to sixth. A trophy will be presented to the winning Owner. Closed Saturday, June 26, 2004 with 25 nominations.

Value of Race: $500,000 Winner $294,000; second $100,000; third $55,000; fourth $30,000; fifth $15,000; sixth $6,000. Mutuel Pool $511,016.00 Exacta Pool $363,530.00 Trifecta Pool $274,703.00 Superfecta Pool $94,465.00

Last Raced	Horse	M/Eqt.	A.	Wt	PP	St	¼	½	Str	Fin	Jockey	Odds $1
19Jun04 9CD1	Champali	L	4	117	1	7	11	1hd	11	1no	Bailey J D	2.60
9Jun04 4CD1	Clock Stopper	L b	4	115	5	9	6hd	6hd	3½	2nk	Day P	1.80
29May04 3Crc1	Built Up	L	6	114	4	6	2½	21½	2hd	3nk	Madrid S O	11.10
19Jun04 9Suf3	My Cousin Matt	L f	5	114	2	8	3½	3hd	43	44¾	Dominguez R A	7.20
31May04 10Crc1	Twilight Road	L	7	114	7	5	85	83½	82	54¾	Teator P A	16.30
19Jun04 9Suf2	Valid Video	L b	4	117	8	4	71½	51	5hd	6½	Bravo J	5.10
13Jun04 9Crc1	Gold Dollar	L b	5	114	9	1	915	920	920	7¾	Toribio A Jr	108.90
13Dec03 11Crc5	Love That Moon	L	5	116	6	2	4hd	7½	61	81¼	Garcia J A	67.90
29May04 11LaD3	Aloha Bold	L	6	114	10	3	51½	4½	7hd	923¾	Velasquez C	12.70
23Apr04 8Aqu4	Super Fuse	L b	4	115	3	10	10	10	10	10	Sellers S J	12.10

OFF AT 5:13 Start Good For All But SUPER FUSE. Won driving. Track fast.

TIME :214, :443, :57, 1:10 (:21.90, :44.79, :57.03, 1:10.14)

$2 Mutuel Prices:				
	1 – CHAMPALI	7.20	3.80	3.20
	5 – CLOCK STOPPER		3.20	2.60
	4 – BUILT UP			4.60

$2 EXACTA 1–5 PAID $20.00 $2 TRIFECTA 1–5–4 PAID $129.40

$2 SUPERFECTA 1–5–4–2 PAID $597.00

B. c, (Feb), by Glitterman – Radioactivity , by Dixieland Band . Trainer Foley Gregory D. Bred by McKee Stables Inc (Ky).

CHAMPALI set the pace under pressure along the inside, came off the rail while edging away a bit in midstretch, then was all out to just last over CLOCK STOPPER. The latter, reserved racing along the rail, rallied to reach CHAMPALI in deep stretch and just missed. BUILT UP prompted the pace outside CHAMPALI, was outmoved by that rival in midstretch, then finished willingly while being edged to the wire. MY COUSIN MATT tracked the pace into the stretch, angled outside the leaders and was gaining slowly at the finish. TWILIGHT ROAD unhurried early, raced three wide on the turn and passed tired rivals. VALID VIDEO reserved in striking position off the pace, raced three wide around the turn and tired. GOLD DOLLAR was never a factor. LOVE THAT MOON showed some early foot and faltered. ALOHA BOLD was outrun. SUPER FUSE was never close after breaking poorly.

Owners– 1, Lloyd Madison Farms IV LLC; 2, Overbrook Farm; 3, Susi Raymond; 4, Englander Richard A; 5, Donamire Farm; 6, Fehsenfeld Mac; 7, Pazos Julio; 8, Bakerman Robert; 9, Cooper Michael E; 10, Alpha One Stable

Trainers– 1, Foley Gregory D; 2, Stewart Dallas; 3, Alonso Enrique; 4, Lake Scott A; 5, Fawkes David; 6, Manning Dennis J; 7, Azpurua Manuel J; 8, Wolfendale Ross B; 9, Hawley Wesley; 10, Asmussen Steven M

Scratched– Hombre Rapido (19Jun04 8BM 3) , Super Frolic (15Jun04 7Crc1) , Alke (27Mar04 4056NAS2)

$2 Pick Three (3–4–1) Paid $1,273.20 ; Pick Three Pool $76,229 .

ELEVENTH RACE
Calder
JULY 10, 2004

6 FURLONGS. (1.08[4]) 20TH RUNNING OF THE PRINCESS ROONEY HANDICAP. Grade II. Purse $500,000 FOR FILLIES AND MARES, THREE YEARS OLD AND UPWARD. By subscription of $500 each which shall accompany the nomination, $2,000 to pass the entry box and an additional $2,000 to start – with $500,000 guaranteed. The owner of the winner to receive $294,000, $100,000 to second, $55,000 to third, $30,000 to fourth, $15,000 to fifth, and $6,000 to sixth. A trophy will be presented to the winning Owner. Closed Saturday, June 26, 2004 with 11 nominations.

Value of Race: $500,000 Winner $294,000; second $100,000; third $55,000; fourth $30,000; fifth $15,000; sixth $6,000. Mutuel Pool $501,064.00 Exacta Pool $318,980.00 Trifecta Pool $226,200.00 Superfecta Pool $87,301.00

Last Raced	Horse	M/Eqt.	A.	Wt	PP	St	¼	½	Str	Fin	Jockey	Odds $1
5Jun04 1Hol2	Ema Bovary-Chi	L	5	119	6	1	4hd	3 2½	3 3½	1 2	Gonzalez R M	3.60
5Jun04 6Bel1	Bear Fan	L f	5	122	5	2	2 1½	2 2½	1hd	2 3¾	Velazquez J R	0.80
22May04 9CD1	Lady Tak	L	4	119	2	5	1hd	1½	2 1	3 2	Sellers S J	2.90
30May04 6Crc1	Mary Murphy	L b	4	110	3	4	6	5hd	6	4 1	Homeister R B Jr	18.10
20Jun04 8Hol1	Puxa Saco	L	4	112	4	3	5hd	6	5 1	5½	Castro E	35.10
9May04 8Bel2	Harmony Lodge	L	6	119	1	6	3 2	4 2	4hd	6	Bailey J D	6.90

OFF AT 5:45 Start Good. Won driving. Track fast.
TIME :21[2], :44, :56[4], 1:10[4] (:21.56, :44.12, :56.91, 1:10.81)

$2 Mutuel Prices:			
6 – EMA BOVARY-CHI	9.20	3.00	2.10
5 – BEAR FAN		2.40	2.10
2 – LADY TAK			2.10

$2 EXACTA 6–5 PAID $19.20 $2 TRIFECTA 6–5–2 PAID $51.80
$2 SUPERFECTA 6–5–2–3 PAID $175.00

B. m, (Oct), by Edgy Diplomat – Coqueta, by Domineau. Trainer Ross Larry. Bred by Haras San Patricio (Chi).

EMA BOVARY (CHI) reserved early, raced three wide on the turn, rallied under pressure to gain the lead at the sixteenth pole and edged away. BEAR FAN vied for the lead outside LADY TAK to inside the eighth pole and continued on with good courage to prove second best while unable to stay with the winner late. LADY TAK vied for the lead along the inside to past the eighth pole and tired. MARY MURPHY reserved early, bumped with PUXA SACO and steadied entering the turn, then failed to menace. PUXA SACO allowed to settle, was no factor after she bumped with MARY MURPHY and steadied entering the turn. HARMONY LODGE chased the pace along the inside into the turn and faltered.

Owners– 1, Richard T Beal Jr & Lana Ramsey-Borg; 2, Fan Peter and Ward Wesley; 3, Heiligbrodt Racing Stable; 4, M375 Thoroughbreds Inc; 5, Rowan Richard; 6, Melnyk Eugene and Laura

Trainers– 1, Ross Larry; 2, Ward Wesley A; 3, Asmussen Steven M; 4, Waunsch Joseph J; 5, Sahadi Jenine; 6, Pletcher Todd A

$2 Pick Three (4–1–6) Paid $454.00 ; Pick Three Pool $97,382 .
$1 Pick Five (10–3–4–1–6) Paid $18,409.00 ; Pick Five Pool $469,505 .

FIFTH RACE
Hollywood
JULY 10, 2004

7 FURLONGS. (1.19[4]) 50TH RUNNING OF THE A GLEAM INVITATIONAL HANDICAP. Grade II. Purse $150,000 FOR FILLIES AND MARES THREE YEARS OLD AND UPWARD. No Nominating or Starting Fees. The owner of the winner to receive $ 90,000, with $30,000 to second, $18,000 to third, $9,000 to fourth and $3,000 to fifth. A trophy will be presented to the winning owner.

Value of Race: $150,000 Winner $90,000; second $30,000; third $18,000; fourth $9,000; fifth $3,000. Mutuel Pool $631,479.00 Exacta Pool $371,064.00 Quinella Pool $30,887.00 Trifecta Pool $365,921.00 Superfecta Pool $118,411.00

Last Raced	Horse	M/Eqt.	A.	Wt	PP	St	¼	½	Str	Fin	Jockey	Odds $1
4Jun04 2Hol1	Dream of Summer	LB b	5	114	9	2	1 1	1 2	1 3½	1 3½	Smith M E	9.30
24Apr04 4Hol3	Tucked Away	LB b	4	116	4	9	9	8hd	5 1½	2nk	Desormeaux K J	14.00
12Jun04 4Hol2	Elusive Diva	LB b	3	112	6	4	4 2	2½	2 1	3 1	Bejarano R	5.10
5Jun04 1Hol1	Coconut Girl	LB f	5	116	1	6	6hd	6hd	4 1	4½	Espinoza V	4.20
5Jun04 1Hol3	Stormica	LB	4	113	7	5	8 1½	9	6 1½	5½	Santiago Javier	20.20
27Dec03 7SA6	Elloluv	LB	4	121	5	3	2hd	4½	3½	6 1½	Nakatani C S	1.90
31May04 7LS7	Pocketfullofpesos	LB b	4	114	8	1	3hd	3 1½	7 3	7 7	Baze T C	16.90
14Mar04 8SA5	Fencelineneighbor	LB b	4	116	2	8	7 3½	7 1½	9	8½	Flores D R	21.90
24Apr04 4Hol1	Royally Chosen	LB	6	116	3	7	5 1	5 1	8hd	9	Solis A	4.60

OFF AT 3:39 Start Good. Won ridden out. Track fast.
TIME :22, :44, 1:08, 1:21 (:22.03, :44.02, 1:08.00, 1:21.16)

$2 Mutuel Prices:			
9 – DREAM OF SUMMER	20.60	10.40	6.60
4 – TUCKED AWAY		12.00	6.20
6 – ELUSIVE DIVA			5.20

$1 EXACTA 9–4 PAID $125.20 $2 QUINELLA 4–9 PAID $151.20
$1 TRIFECTA 9–4–6 PAID $879.50 $1 SUPERFECTA 9–4–6–1 PAID $3,913.40

Gr/ro. m, (Apr), by Siberian Summer – Mary's Dream, by Skywalker. Trainer Garcia Juan. Bred by James Weigel (Cal).

DREAM OF SUMMER sped to the early lead, set the pace off the rail, angled in and kicked clear into the turn and proved best under a brisk hand ride until the final strides. TUCKED AWAY unhurried a bit off the rail then inside, moved up some on the turn, came off the rail and waited off heels into the stretch, angled out nearing midstretch and just got the place. ELUSIVE DIVA stalked between horses on the backstretch and off the rail on the turn and into the stretch, could not catch the winner and lost second late. COCONUT GIRL chased inside then a bit off the rail, went between foes leaving the backstretch and on the turn and was outfinished. STORMICA settled off the rail then outside into the turn, went three deep on the bend, angled in approaching the stretch, lacked room into the lane, came out in upper stretch and could not summon the necessary late kick. ELLOLUV had speed to stalk the winner off the rail, angled in and fell back some into the turn, inched forward into the stretch, continued inside and lacked a further response. POCKETFULLOFPESOS stalked outside then three deep leaving the backstretch and off the rail leaving the turn and weakened. FENCELINENEIGHBOR taken outside in the early going, went four wide into and on the turn and into the stretch and did not rally. ROYALLY CHOSEN went up inside to stalk the pace, waited a bit into the turn, fell back on the bend, steadied while weakening nearing the stretch and had little left.

Owners– 1, Weigel James; 2, Nierenberg Nico; 3, Branch Branch Konecny Et Al; 4, Jpf Investments I LLC; 5, Wertheimer and Frere; 6, Reddam J Paul; 7, G Racing Belmonte Phil Shapiro Barry et al; 8, Amerman Racing Stables LLC; 9, Abruzzo Peter Johnston E W Zehenni Tony V et al

Trainers– 1, Garcia Juan; 2, Gallagher Patrick; 3, Glatt Mark; 4, Aguirre Paul G; 5, Mandella Gary; 6, Dollase Craig; 7, Mitchell Mike; 8, Machowsky Michael; 9, Headley Bruce

$2 Daily Double (3–9) Paid $69.60 ; Daily Double Pool $37,827 .
$1 Pick Three (2–3–9) Paid $303.00 ; Pick Three Pool $95,121 .

SEVENTH RACE
Hollywood
JULY 10, 2004

1⅛ MILES. (1.45^{1}) 31ST RUNNING OF THE SWAPS BREEDERS' CUP. Grade II. Purse $400,000 (includes $100,000 BC – Breeders' Cup) FOR THREE YEAR OLDS. By subscription of $300 each, on or before June 30, 2004, which shall accompany the nomination. A supplementary nomination of $8000 maybe made at the time of entry. All horses to pay $3000 additional to start. Weight 124 lbs. Winnersof $250,000 at a mile or over three times in 2004, 2 lbs. additional. Non–winners of two such races in 2004 allowed 2 lbs. Such a race in 2004, 4 lbs. Such a race of $100,000 in 2003–04 allowed 6lbs. Such a race of $50,000 in 2003–04 allowed 8 lbs. Non–winners of three races other than maiden or claiming allowed 10 lbs.; two such races allowed 12 lbs. Nominations closed June 30, 2004. Closed with 11 nominations.

Value of Race: $409,300 Winner $252,780; second $84,260; third $38,556; fourth $25,278; fifth $8,426. Mutuel Pool $666,344.00 Exacta Pool $350,122.00 Quinella Pool $28,097.00 Trifecta Pool $344,862.00

Last Raced	Horse	M/Eqt.	A.	Wt	PP	St	¼	½	¾	Str	Fin	Jockey	Odds $1
5Jun04 ^{11}Bel^{5}	Rock Hard Ten	LB	3	116	3	4	$2^{1\frac{1}{2}}$	$2^{\frac{1}{2}}$	$2^{2\frac{1}{2}}$	$1^{2\frac{1}{2}}$	$1^{3\frac{3}{4}}$	Nakatani C S	0.60
12Jun04 ^{6}CD^{1}	Suave	LB b	3	120	5	2	4^{1}	4^{2}	4^{2}	$3^{1\frac{1}{2}}$	2^{3}	Bejarano R	4.70
19Jun04 ^{7}Hol^{1}	Boomzeeboom	LB b	3	118	6	3	$1^{2\frac{1}{2}}$	1^{1}	1^{1}	2^{2}	$3^{2\frac{1}{2}}$	Espinoza V	4.40
15May04 ^{3}Hol^{1}	Capitano	LB	3	115	1	5	$3^{\frac{1}{2}}$	3^{1}	3^{hd}	4^{1}	4^{nk}	Solis A	7.50
18Jun04 ^{3}Hol^{1}	Brands Hatch	LB	3	114	4	6	6	6	6	6	$5^{\frac{1}{2}}$	Smith M E	15.40
17Jun04 ^{5}Hol^{4}	Bear in the Woods	LB	3	112	2	1	5^{hd}	5^{1}	$5^{1\frac{1}{2}}$	5^{2}	6	Baze T C	27.70

OFF AT 4:41 Start Good . Won driving. Track fast.
TIME :23^{2}, :47, 1:10^{2}, 1:34^{3}, 1:47^{2} (:23.48, :47.07, 1:10.55, 1:34.62, 1:47.47)

$2 Mutuel Prices:

3 – ROCK HARD TEN	3.20	2.40	2.10
5 – SUAVE		3.40	2.10
6 – BOOMZEEBOOM			2.10

$1 EXACTA 3–5 PAID $4.70 $2 QUINELLA 3–5 PAID $6.80
$1 TRIFECTA 3–5–6 PAID $11.30

Dk. b or br. c, (Apr), by Kris S. – Tersa , by Mr. Prospector . Trainer Orman Jason. Bred by Madeleine A Paulson (Ky).

ROCK HARD TEN stalked the leader off the rail, bid outside that one leaving the second turn, took command into the stretch, drifted out some in the drive but pulled clear under some left handed urging and strong handling. SUAVE bobbled at the start, stalked outside a rival or off the rail, came three deep into the stretch, then drifted inward in the drive but picked up the place. BOOMZEEBOOM broke out a bit, sped to the early lead and angled in, set the pace along the inside under a snug hold, fought back leaving the second turn, could not match the top pair in the stretch but saved third. CAPITANO saved ground stalking the pace and weakened in the stretch. BRANDS HATCH allowed to settle outside a rival then off the rail, came out into the stretch and did not rally. BEAR IN THE WOODS pulled his way between horses then chased inside, split rivals into the stretch, came out in the drive and lacked a further response.

Owners– 1, Mercedes Stables LLC and Paulson Madeline; 2, Jay Em Ess Stable; 3, Karubian John Landsburg Alan and Postaer Larry; 4, Meguerditchian Mr and Mrs; 5, Darley Stable; 6, Reddam J Paul

Trainers– 1, Orman Jason; 2, McGee Paul J; 3, Cerin Vladimir; 4, Bell Thomas R II; 5, Harty Eoin, 6, Dollase Craig

$2 Daily Double (6–3) Paid $14.20 ; Daily Double Pool $42,307 .
$1 Pick Three (9–6–3) Paid $123.20 ; Pick Three Pool $132,181 .

NINTH RACE
Hollywood
JULY 10, 2004

1¼ MILES. (1.58^{2}) 65TH RUNNING OF THE HOLLYWOOD GOLD CUP. Grade I. Purse $750,000 FOR THREE YEAR OLDS AND UPWARD. By subscription of $1,000 each on or before Wednesday, June 30, 2004 which should accompany the nomination. Supplementary nominations may be made at time of entry by payment of $15,000 each. All nominees to pay $3,750 to enter and an additional $3,750 to start. Gross Purse $750,000 of which $450,000 to be paid to the winner, $150,000 to second, $90,000 to third, $45,000 to fourth and $15,000 to fifth. Weight: Older, 124 lbs.; 3–Year–Olds, 112 lbs. Starters to be named through the entry box by closing time of entries. This race will not be divided. If the number of entries exceed fourteen (14) horses, preference will be given to Graded or Group Stakes winners in 2004. Second preference will be given to horses with the highest total earnings from Graded or Group races since June 1, 2003. Total earnings in 2004 will be used in determining the order of preference for horses with equal status. Entry fees will be refunded to all horses which fail to draw into this race. Trophieswill be presented to the winning owner and trainer. Closed with 12 nominations.

Value of Race: $750,000 Winner $450,000; second $150,000; third $90,000; fourth $45,000; fifth $15,000. Mutuel Pool $620,652.00 Exacta Pool $311,971.00 Quinella Pool $25,890.00 Trifecta Pool $373,503.00

Last Raced	Horse	M/Eqt.	A.	Wt	PP	¼	½	¾	1	Str	Fin	Jockey	Odds $1
12Jun04 ^{9}Hol^{2}	Total Impact-Chi	LB b	6	124	2	2^{hd}	3^{1}	3^{hd}	2^{hd}	1^{hd}	$1^{1\frac{1}{4}}$	Smith M E	6.70
8May04 ^{9}Hol^{4}	Olmodavor	LB b	5	124	1	5^{1}	$5^{\frac{1}{2}}$	5^{hd}	$4^{\frac{1}{2}}$	$4^{2\frac{1}{2}}$	$2^{\frac{1}{2}}$	Solis A	3.40
12Jun04 ^{9}Hol^{1}	Even the Score	LB b	6	124	7	4^{hd}	$4^{1\frac{1}{2}}$	4^{1}	$3^{1\frac{1}{2}}$	$3^{1\frac{1}{2}}$	3^{4}	Flores D R	0.70
31May04 ^{9}LS^{1}	Yessirgeneralsir	LB	4	124	4	1^{1}	$1^{2\frac{1}{2}}$	1^{hd}	$1^{1\frac{1}{2}}$	$2^{\frac{1}{2}}$	4^{4}	Figueroa O	8.00
26Jun04 ^{8}Hol^{1}	Royal Moro	LB b	5	124	6	3^{1}	$2^{\frac{1}{2}}$	2^{1}	$5^{2\frac{1}{2}}$	$5^{3\frac{1}{2}}$	5^{2}	Nakatani C S	17.50
12Jun04 ^{9}Hol^{4}	Gift of the Eagle	LB b	6	124	5	7	6^{3}	$6^{2\frac{1}{2}}$	6^{2}	$6^{2\frac{1}{2}}$	$6^{3\frac{1}{2}}$	Santiago Javier	41.20
12Jun04 ^{3}Hol^{5}	Continental Red	LB	8	124	3	6^{hd}	7	7	7	7	7	Espinoza V	13.80

OFF AT 5:42 Start Good . Won driving. Track fast.
TIME :23^{4}, :46^{4}, 1:10^{2}, 1:34^{4}, 2:00^{3} (:23.93, :46.97, 1:10.59, 1:34.91, 2:00.72)

$2 Mutuel Prices:

2 – TOTAL IMPACT–CHI	15.40	6.20	2.80
1 – OLMODAVOR		4.60	2.60
7 – EVEN THE SCORE			2.10

$1 EXACTA 2–1 PAID $28.80 $2 QUINELLA 1–2 PAID $27.20
$1 TRIFECTA 2–1–7 PAID $54.80

Ch. h, (Aug), by Stuka – Pebbles–Chi , by Manos de Piedra . Trainer De Seroux Laura. Bred by Haras Don Alberto (Chi).

TOTAL IMPACT (CHI) between horses early, angled to the inside into the first turn, stalked along the rail, slipped through inside brushing with the pacesetter to take a short lead in midstretch and gamely prevailed under urging. OLMODAVOR in a bit tight inside early and again into the first turn, chased a bit off the rail, came out on the second turn and three deep into the stretch, could not catch the winner but edged EVEN THE SCORE late for second. EVEN THE SCORE four wide early, went three deep into the first turn, stalked three wide or outside a rival, bid outside foes in midstretch but was outfinished. YESSIRGENERALSIR sped to the early lead and angled in, set the pace inside, turned back the bid of ROYAL MORO on the second turn to inch clear again, came a bit off the rail into the stretch, battled between foes and brushed with the winner in midstretch, then weakened late. ROYAL MORO stalked outside the winner then bid outside the pacesetter on the backstretch and dueled for the lead, dropped back on the second turn, angled to the inside in the stretch and also weakened. GIFT OF THE EAGLE bumped into the first turn, chased outside a rival then three deep, angled in off the rail on the second turn and did not rally. CONTINENTAL RED also bumped when between horses into the first turn, chased just off the inside, came out on the second turn and failed to menace.

Owners– 1, Al Kabeer Sultan Mohammed Saud and Bridport S A; 2, Wertheimer and Frere; 3, Parra Rosendo G; 4, Jackson James D; 5, Reddam J Paul; 6, Bell Lance and Krikorian George; 7, Fitzpatrick Sharon M

Trainers– 1, De Seroux Laura; 2, Mandella Richard; 3, Cerin Vladimir; 4, Keen Dallas E; 5, Dollase Craig; 6, Shirreffs John; 7, Jory Ian P D

$2 Daily Double (12–2) Paid $79.60 ; Daily Double Pool $37,815 .
$1 Pick Three (3–12–2) Paid $91.90 ; Pick Three Pool $115,533 .

NINTH RACE
Monmouth
JULY 10, 2004

$1\frac{1}{16}$ MILES. (Turf Chute) (1.40) 34TH RUNNING OF THE EATONTOWN HANDICAP. Grade III. Purse $100,000 FOR FILLIES AND MARES, THREE YEARS OLD AND UPWARD. By subscription of $100 each, which should accompany the nomination and $1,500 to pass the entry box. The winning owner to receive $60,000, $20,000 to second, $11,000 to third, $6,000 to fourth and $3,000to fifth. The owner of the winner to receive a trophy. Closed Saturday, June 26, 2004 with 28 nominations. (Rail at 10 feet).

Value of Race: $100,000 Winner $60,000; second $20,000; third $11,000; fourth $6,000; fifth $3,000. Mutuel Pool $147,041.00 Exacta Pool $95,161.00 Trifecta Pool $60,145.00 Superfecta Pool $13,084.00

Last Raced	Horse	M/Eqt.	A.	Wt	PP	St	¼	½	¾	Str	Fin	Jockey	Odds $1
5Jun04 ^{8}WO^{2}	Ocean Drive	L	4	120	1	3	$2^{1\frac{1}{2}}$	$2^{\frac{1}{2}}$	$2^{1\frac{1}{2}}$	1^{hd}	$1^{2\frac{3}{4}}$	Coa E M	1.20
24Jun04 ^{8}Mth^{4}	Honorable Cat	L	5	114	2	1	1^{2}	1^{2}	$1^{\frac{1}{2}}$	2^{3}	$2^{1\frac{1}{2}}$	King E L Jr	27.30
5Jun04 ^{8}Bel^{8}	Fast Cookie	L	4	118	4	5	$4^{\frac{1}{2}}$	$4^{\frac{1}{2}}$	$4^{1\frac{1}{2}}$	3^{hd}	$3^{1\frac{1}{4}}$	Pimentel J	4.00
30May04 ^{11}Mth^{1}	High Court-Brz	L	4	118	6	4	$5^{1\frac{1}{2}}$	$5^{2\frac{1}{2}}$	$5^{2\frac{1}{2}}$	5^{2}	$4^{1\frac{1}{2}}$	Decarlo C P	1.60
20Jun04 ^{9}Mth^{3}	Lojo	L	5	116	5	2	3^{hd}	3^{1}	3^{hd}	$4^{1\frac{1}{2}}$	$5^{2\frac{3}{4}}$	Clemente A V	9.50
5Jun04 ^{8}Del^{2}	Aztec Pearl	L	5	115	3	6	6	6	6	6	6	Velez J A Jr	16.70

OFF AT 4:51 Start Good . Won driving. Course firm.

TIME :24^{4}, :49^{1}, 1:12^{3}, 1:36, 1:41^{3} (:24.80, :49.30, 1:12.75, 1:36.11, 1:41.79)

(New Course Record)

$2 Mutuel Prices:

1 – OCEAN DRIVE	4.40	2.80	2.10
2 – HONORABLE CAT		10.80	3.00
4 – FAST COOKIE			2.60

$2 EXACTA 1–2 PAID $82.80 $2 TRIFECTA 1–2–4 PAID $279.20
$1 SUPERFECTA 1–2–4–6 PAID $280.30

Dk. b or br. f, (Feb), by Belong to Me – Clever But Costly , by Clever Trick . Trainer Pletcher Todd A. Bred by James D Conway & Thomas C Mueller (Ky).

OCEAN DRIVE settled behind the early leader, moved closer midway on the final turn, reached the front passing the furlong marker then drove clear. HONORABLE CAT drew clear early and rated on the pace, saved ground and responded well in the drive but was no match late while remaining clear for the place. FAST COOKIE close up while saving ground, stayed inside for the drive and lacked the needed late response. HIGH COURT (BRZ) never far back from the outside, lacked a rally. LOJO in good position early, raced outside into the lane and weakened. AZTEC PEARL trailed while not far back and lacked a rally.

Owners– 1, Baskin Bonnie and Sy; 2, McKee Stables Inc; 3, Stonerside Stable LLC; 4, Lael Stables; 5, Durocher Jr Lawrence and Hampshire Farm; 6, Alexander & Groves Revocable Trust

Trainers– 1, Pletcher Todd A; 2, Simon Charles; 3, Mott William I; 4, Matz Michael R; 5, Hills Timothy A; 6, McGaughey III Claude R

EIGHTH RACE
Hollywood
JULY 11, 2004

$1\frac{1}{16}$ MILES. (1.40) 53RD RUNNING OF THE MILADY BREEDERS' CUP HANDICAP. Grade I. Purse $250,000 (includes $50,000 BC – Breeders' Cup) FOR FILLIES AND MARES THREE YEARS OLD AND UPWARD. Closed with 13 nominations.

Value of Race: $228,450 Winner $125,670; second $51,890; third $31,134; fourth $15,567; fifth $4,189. Mutuel Pool $446,850.00 Exacta Pool $211,667.00 Quinella Pool $19,992.00 Trifecta Pool $188,927.00

Last Raced	Horse	M/Eqt.	A.	Wt	PP	St	¼	½	¾	Str	Fin	Jockey	Odds $1
9May04 ^{8}Hol^{3}	Star Parade-Arg	LB	5	116	2	1	1^{1}	1^{1}	2^{1}	$1^{\frac{1}{2}}$	$1^{3\frac{1}{2}}$	Espinoza V	1.90
31May04 ^{2}Hol^{3}	Quero Quero	LB	4	115	3	4	4^{3}	$3^{2\frac{1}{2}}$	1^{hd}	2^{1}	2^{hd}	Santiago Javier	10.20
6Jun04 ^{8}Hol^{2}	Pesci	LB b	4	114	4	2	$2^{1\frac{1}{2}}$	$2^{1\frac{1}{2}}$	$3^{4\frac{1}{2}}$	$3^{2\frac{1}{2}}$	3^{2}	Smith M E	2.50
9May04 ^{8}Hol^{1}	Victory Encounter	LB	4	119	1	3	5	5	5	4^{5}	4^{10}	Solis A	2.30
27Jun04 ^{6}Hol^{1}	Tangle-Ire	LB	4	116	5	5	3^{hd}	4^{5}	4^{3}	5	5	Nakatani C S	4.70

OFF AT 4:54 Start Good . Won driving. Track fast.

TIME :23^{3}, :46^{1}, 1:09^{4}, 1:35, 1:41^{4} (:23.77, :46.29, 1:09.89, 1:35.03, 1:41.83)

$2 Mutuel Prices:

2 – STAR PARADE–ARG	5.80	3.40	2.40
5 – QUERO QUERO		5.20	3.00
6 – PESCI			2.60

$1 EXACTA 2–5 PAID $21.30 $2 QUINELLA 2–5 PAID $24.60
$1 TRIFECTA 2–5–6 PAID $67.50

Dk. b or br. m, (Oct), by Parade Marshal – Clerical Etoile–Arg , by The Watcher . Trainer Vienna Darrell. Bred by Firmamento (Arg).

STAR PARADE (ARG) sped to the early lead, set the pace a bit off the rail, responded when headed outside the runner-up on the second turn, regained the advantage in upper stretch, inched away under urging then pulled clear in the final sixteenth. QUERO QUERO bobbled a bit at the start, pulled her way between horses then stalked a bit off the rail, bid inside on the second turn and put a head in front, battled inside the winner into the stretch and until past midstretch, could not match that one but held second. PESCI stalked the winner off the rail, went three deep on the second turn and into the stretch and was edged for the place. VICTORY ENCOUNTER saved ground off the pace, moved up inside leaving the second turn and into the stretch but lacked the needed late response. TANGLE (IRE) three deep into the first turn, chased off the rail, angled in some on the second turn, came out into the stretch and weakened.

Owners– 1, Tanaka Gary A; 2, Old Friends Inc; 3, Giordano Mark Pesci Joe and Ward Wesley A; 4, Mankiewicz Tom; 5, Reddam J Paul

Trainers– 1, Vienna Darrell; 2, Lobo Paulo H; 3, Ward Wesley A; 4, Sadler John W; 5, Dollase Craig

Scratched– Summer Wind Dancer (06Jun04 ^{8}Hol^{1}) , Lady Thatcher (CHI) (06Jun04 ^{8}Hol^{6})

$2 Daily Double (8–2) Paid $36.00 ; Daily Double Pool $35,171 .
$1 Pick Three (5–8–2/3/4) Paid $88.80 ; Pick Three Pool $76,831 .

EIGHTH RACE
Belmont
JULY 11, 2004

1 1/16 MILES. (1.39^2) 87TH RUNNING OF THE DWYER. Grade II. Purse $150,000 (UP TO $28,500 NYSBFOA) FOR THREE YEAR OLDS. By subscription of $150 each, which should accompany the nomination; $750 to pass the entry box; $750 to start. The purse to be divided 60% to the winner, 20% to second, 10% to third, 5% to fourth, 3% to fifthand 2% divided equally among remaining finishers. 123 lbs. Non-winners of $200,000 at a mile or over in 2004 allowed 2 lbs. $60,000 at a mile or over in 2004 or $40,000 twice in 2004, 4 lbs.; $50,000; or $30,000 twice at a mile or over, 6 lbs. $30,000, orthree races, 8 lbs. (Maiden, claiming, starter, restricted or restricted stake races not considered in allowances.) A trophy will be presented to the winning owner. Closed Saturday, June 26, 2004 with 24 Nominations.

Value of Race: $150,000 Winner $90,000; second $30,000; third $15,000; fourth $7,500; fifth $4,500; sixth $3,000. Mutuel Pool $599,716.00 Exacta Pool $409,003.00 Trifecta Pool $213,789.00

Last Raced	Horse	M/Eqt.	A.	Wt	PP	St	¼	½	¾	Str	Fin	Jockey	Odds $1
1May04 8Aqu1	Medallist		3	121	2	4	1 2	1 6	1 8	1 7	1 3¾	Chavez J F	3.40
1May04 10CD5	The Cliff's Edge	L	3	123	4	3	6	6	5 6	2 ½	2 ½	Sellers S J	a- 0.65
15May04 12Pim6	Sir Shackleton	L	3	121	1	5	2 hd	2 1½	2 ½	3 8	3 14½	Bejarano R	a- 0.65
12Jun04 2Bel1	Golden Look	L	3	115	5	1	5 7	4 ½	3 hd	4 1½	4 1	Prado E S	8.10
15May04 9Pim5	Preachinatthebar	L b	3	121	6	2	4 ½	5 7	4 2	5 6	5 6	Bailey J D	5.20
12Jun04 6CD11	Shaniko	L b	3	115	3	6	3 1½	3 hd	6	6	6	Velazquez J R	13.40

a–Coupled: The Cliff's Edge and Sir Shackleton.

OFF AT 4:47 Start Good. Won driving. Track fast.

TIME :22^4, :44^2, 1:07^4, 1:33^1, 1:40 (:22.83, :44.45, 1:07.96, 1:33.27, 1:40.02)

$2 Mutuel Prices:				
	2 – MEDALLIST	8.80	3.20	2.70
	1A – THE CLIFF'S EDGE(a–entry)		2.20	2.10
	1 – SIR SHACKLETON(a–entry)		2.20	2.10

$2 EXACTA 2–1 PAID $13.40 $2 TRIFECTA 2–1–5 PAID $43.60

Dk. b or br. c, (Feb), by Touch Gold – Santaria, by Star de Naskra. Trainer Jerkens H Allen. Bred by Robert N Clay & The Albert G Clay &1990 Revocable Trust (Ky).

MEDALLIST came away well and sprinted out to a clear lead, set the pace along the inside, ran off to a long lead on the turn, settled into the stretch well in front and remained safely clear while being kept to the task to the wire. THE CLIFF'S EDGE was outrun early, rallied four wide on the turn and finished gamely outside. SIR SHACKLETON chased the pace while between rivals and stayed on well in the stretch. GOLDEN LOOK was unhurried early on, was hustled along on the rail on the turn but had no response and tired in the stretch. PREACHINATTHEBAR raced three wide and had no response when roused. SHANIKO chased the pace from the outside and tired.

Owners– 1, Clay Robert N; 2, LaPenta Robert V; 3, Farmer Tracy; 4, Janney Stuart S III; 5, Pegram Michael E; 6, Jones Aaron U and Marie D

Trainers– 1, Jerkens H Allen; 2, Zito Nicholas P; 3, Zito Nicholas P; 4, McGaughey III Claude R; 5, Baffert Bob; 6, Pletcher Todd A

Scratched– Ecclesiastic (12Jun04 6CD 3)

EIGHTH RACE
Belmont
JULY 17, 2004

1⅜ MILES. (Inner Turf) (2.10^1) 47TH RUNNING OF THE BOWLING GREEN HANDICAP. Grade II. Purse $150,000 INNER TURF A HANDICAP FOR THREE YEAR OLDS AND UPWARD. By subscription of $150 each, which should accompany the nomination; $750 to pass the entry box; $750 to start. The purse to be divided 60% to the winner, 20% to second, 10% to third, 5% to fourth, 3%to fifth and 2% divided equally among remaining finishers. A trophy will be presented to the winning owner. The New York Racing Association reserves the right to transfer this race to the Main Track. In the event that this race is taken off the turf, it may be subject to downgrading upon review by the Graded Stakes Committee. Closed Saturday, July 3, 2004 with 32 Nominations. (Rail at 18 feet).

Value of Race: $150,000 Winner $90,000; second $30,000; third $15,000; fourth $7,500; fifth $4,500; sixth $600; seventh $600; eighth $600; ninth $600; tenth $600. Mutuel Pool $749,243.00 Exacta Pool $571,529.00 Trifecta Pool $453,196.00

Last Raced	Horse	M/Eqt.	A.	Wt	PP	¼	½	¾	1	Str	Fin	Jockey	Odds $1
5Jun04 10Bel9	Kicken Kris	L	4	117	7	4 ½	4 hd	4 hd	5 1½	1 1	1 1½	Prado E S	1.35
12Jun04 9Mth2	Better Talk Now	L bf	5	115	5	7 hd	6 ½	6 ½	6 ½	2 ½	2 2¼	Santos J A	8.10
18Apr04 9SA7	Gigli-Brz	L	6	113	3	2 hd	2 1	2 ½	2 ½	5 4½	3 nk	Chavez J F	8.80
25Jun04 3Bel1	B. A. Way	L b	4	113	2	5 2½	5 1½	5 2½	4 hd	4 hd	4 2	Bridgmohan S X	3.90
4Jun04 7Bel2	L'Oiseau d'Argent	L	5	115	1	1 1½	1 2	1 2½	1 1½	3 hd	5 1¼	Migliore R	7.20
19Jun04 9LS3	A to the Z	L b	4	113	10	9 ½	9 hd	10	7 hd	6 ½	6 ½	Samyn J L	18.90
3Jly04 10Mth8	In Hand	L bf	4	114	6	10	10	9 ½	10	8 hd	7 hd	Gryder A T	36.25
18Jun04 8Bel1	Vanity Affair	L b	4	112	4	6 1½	7 ½	7 ½	8 ½	7 1½	8 ½	Jara F	39.00
5Jun04 9Pha2	Host	L	4	114	9	8 1	8 ½	8 ½	9 3	9 3½	9 5¾	Castillo H Jr	41.00
25Jun04 3Bel2	ThompsonRoug-Ire	L	5	113	8	3 2½	3 5½	3 1½	3 ½	10	10	Luzzi M J	11.00

OFF AT 4:45 Start Good. Won driving. Course firm.

TIME :23^1, :47^2, 1:10^4, 1:35^4, 2:00^1, 2:12 (:23.36, :47.52, 1:10.85, 1:35.95, 2:00.32, 2:12.19)

$2 Mutuel Prices:				
	7 – KICKEN KRIS	4.70	3.00	3.00
	5 – BETTER TALK NOW		5.60	5.60
	3 – GIGLI–BRZ			5.90

$2 EXACTA 7–5 PAID $28.40 $2 TRIFECTA 7–5–3 PAID $189.00

B. c, (Mar), by Kris S. – Kicken Grass, by Jade Hunter. Trainer Matz Michael R. Bred by Valerie Naify (Ky).

KICKEN KRIS raced in hand outside early on, advanced three wide on the second turn, responded when roused, drew clear and was kept to the task to the finish. BETTER TALK NOW was rated along inside, came wide into the stretch and finished gamely outside. GIGLI (BRZ) chased the pace from the outside and stayed on stubbornly in the stretch. B. A. WAY raced close up inside, saved ground and stayed on well while between rivals in the stretch. L'OISEAU D'ARGENT quickly opened a clear lead, set the pace along the inside and weakened in the final furlong. A TO THE Z was outrun early, raced three wide on the second turn and lacked a rally. IN HAND was outrun early, raced inside and had no rally. VANITY AFFAIR was rated along early, raced inside and had no response when roused. HOST raced between rivals early, came wide into the stretch and had no rally. THOMPSON ROUGE (IRE) chased the pace while three wide and tired in the stretch.

Owners– 1, Brushwood Stable; 2, Bushwood Stables; 3, T N T Stud; 4, Perkins Diane; 5, Al Maktoum Sheik Maktoum b; 6, Ray Susan; 7, Humphrey Jr G Watts Klatsky Brian; 8, Double R Stable Weiss Steve; 9, Kimmel Caesar P Solondz Philip J C G Zoe Stable; 10, Almaddah Abdullah S

Trainers– 1, Matz Michael R; 2, Motion H Graham; 3, Frankel Robert; 4, Violette Richard A Jr; 5, McLaughlin Kiaran P; 6, McBride Burl D; 7, Oliver Philip J; 8, Stoklosa Richard; 9, Kimmel John C; 10, Mott William I

Scratched– Royal Affirmed (30Jun04 7Bel1)

EIGHTH RACE
Delaware
JULY 17, 2004

1$\frac{1}{16}$ MILES. (1.41^{2}) 43RD RUNNING OF THE DELAWARE OAKS. Grade II. Purse $500,000 (plus$900 Starters Bonus) FOR FILLIES THREE YEARS OLD. By subscription of $500 each, which shall accompany the nomination, $2,000 to enter and $2,500 to start. Supplemental nominations of $6,000 will be accepted at time of entry which shall include all fees. $500,000 Guaranteedof which $300,000 to the winner, $100,000 to second, $55,000 to third, $30,000 to fourth and $15,000 to fifth. Weight 122 lbs. Non–winners of $120,000 at a mile or over in 2004 allowed 3 lbs., $90,000 at a mile or over in 2004, 5 lbs., $45,000 at a mile or over in 2004, 7 lbs. (Maiden and Claiming races not considered in estimating allowances). Trophy to the winner. Closed Saturday, July 3rd 2004 with 20 nominations.

Value of Race: $500,900 Winner $300,000; second $100,000; third $55,000; fourth $30,000; fifth $15,000; sixth $300; seventh $300; eighth $300. Mutuel Pool $249,838.00 Exacta Pool $174,395.00 Trifecta Pool $137,677.00 Superfecta Pool $45,158.00

Last Raced	Horse	M/Eqt.	A.	Wt	PP	St	¼	½	¾	Str	Fin	Jockey	Odds $1
14May04 ^{10}Pim^{1}	Yearly Report	L	3	122	4	4	2½	2½	1hd	1½	1^{1}	Bailey J D	0.40
5Jun04 ^{10}CD^{3}	Ender's Sister	L	3	119	8	5	5½	6½	4^{1}	2^{2}½	2^{8}	Velasquez C	7.80
16Jun04 ^{7}Del^{1}	A Lulu Ofa Menifee	L b	3	115	5	7	7^{2}½	7^{2}½	7^{2}	4^{1}	3^{2}	Dominguez R A	14.20
19Jun04 ^{8}Del^{1}	Hopelessly Devoted	L	3	119	6	8	8	8	8	5^{1}	4¾	Alvarado R Jr	8.70
29May04 ^{7}Del^{1}	Pilfer	L f	3	117	3	3	6½	5½	5½	6^{2}	5^{5}	Caraballo J C	19.10
19Jun04 ^{8}Del^{3}	Richetta	L	3	115	2	1	1½	1hd	2^{1}	3^{1}	6¾	Rose J	44.00
27May04 ^{3}Bel^{1}	Irish Melody	L	3	115	7	6	3½	3^{1}	3hd	7^{3}	7^{14}½	Velazquez J R	5.30
15Jun04 ^{8}Del^{1}	Becky in Pink	L	3	115	1	2	4½	4hd	6hd	8	8	Arroyo N Jr	45.90

OFF AT 3:55 Start Good . Won driving. Track fast.

TIME :24^{1}, :48^{1}, 1:12^{3}, 1:37^{2}, 1:43^{4} (:24.30, :48.36, 1:12.61, 1:37.54, 1:43.80)

$2 Mutuel Prices:				
	5 – YEARLY REPORT	2.80	2.40	2.10
	9 – ENDER'S SISTER		3.60	2.10
	6 – A LULU OFA MENIFEE			2.10

$2 EXACTA 5–9 PAID $13.60 $2 TRIFECTA 5–9–6 PAID $79.80
$1 SUPERFECTA 5–9–6–7 PAID $137.10

B. f, (Jan), by General Meeting – Fiscal Year , by Half a Year . Trainer Baffert Bob. Bred by Mr & Mrs John C Mabee (Cal).

YEARLY REPORT pressed the pace from the outset, gained a short lead after five furlongs then after gaining a clear lead into the stretch, turned back a bid from ENDER'S SISTER through the furlong grounds and was under brisk handling to prevail. ENDER'S SISTER was hung four and five wide from the outset, ranged up four wide out of the turn to go after the leader, looked a threat a furlong out but hung late while easily second best. A LULU OFA MENIFEE was blocked through the second turn then failed to gain once clear. HOPELESSLY DEVOTED passed tiring rivals. PILFER was well placed for six furlongs then gave way. RICHETTA dueled for six furlongs then came up empty. IRISH MELODY pressed the pace three wide for six furlongs then stopped. BECKY IN PINK stalked the pace inside to the second turn then stopped.

Owners– 1, Golden Eagle Farm; 2, Green Lantern Stables LLC; 3, Lael Stables; 4, Liberty Stable; 5, Fox Hill Farms Inc; 6, Higgins and Bowman; 7, Jones Aaron U and Marie D; 8, Cohen Philip and Marcia and Klesaris Steve

Trainers– 1, Baffert Bob; 2, Arnold George R II; 3, Tagg Barclay; 4, Slivka Sandra L; 5, Servis John C; 6, Graham Robin L; 7, Pletcher Todd A; 8, Klesaris Steve

Scratched– Strategy (01Jul04 ^{8}Bel^{2}) , Bending Strings (03Jul04 ^{8}Bel^{7})

$2 Daily Double (1–5) Paid $13.80 ; Daily Double Pool $20,325 .
$2 Pick Three (2/8/12/13–1–2/5/10) Paid $44.20 ; Pick Three Pool $11,268 .
$2 Pick Four (7–2/8/12/13–1–2/5/10) Paid $166.40 ; Pick Four Pool $13,991 .

THIRD RACE
Hollywood
JULY 17, 2004

6 FURLONGS. (1.07^{2}) 65TH RUNNING OF THE HOLLYWOOD JUVENILE CHAMPIONSHIP. Grade III. Purse $100,000 FOR TWO YEAR OLDS. By subscription of $100 each on or before Thursday, July 8, or by supplementary nomination of $2,000 each by closing time of entries. $1,000 additional to start, with $100,000 added. The added money and all fees to be divided 60% to thewinner, 20% to second, 12% to third, 6% to fourth and 2% to fifth. Weight 120 lbs. Non–winners of a sweepstakes allowed 3 lbs. Maidens allowed 5 lbs. Starters to be named through the entry box by closing time of entries. A trophy will be presented to thewinning owner. Closed with 7 nominations.

Value of Race: $104,272 Winner $63,840; second $21,280; third $12,768; fourth $6,384. Mutuel Pool $321,595.00 Exacta Pool $176,407.00 Quinella Pool $16,001.00

Last Raced	Horse	M/Eqt.	A.	Wt	PP	St	¼	½	Str	Fin	Jockey	Odds $1
20Jun04 ^{3}Hol^{1}	Chandtrue	LB	2	120	4	1	3^{1}½	3^{2}	1½	1½	Espinoza V	0.30
20Jun04 ^{3}Hol^{4}	Actxecutive	LB b	2	117	2	3	1hd	1^{1}	2^{3}	2^{7}	Flores D R	1.90
	Commandant	B b	2	115	3	4	4	4	4	3^{5}½	Court J K	12.50
30Jun04 ^{2}Hol^{1}	Great Power	LB bf	2	117	1	2	2^{1}	2hd	3½	4	Martinez F F	20.00

OFF AT 2:23 Start Good . Won driving. Track fast.

TIME :22, :45^{3}, :58, 1:10^{4} (:22.19, :45.66, :58.03, 1:10.88)

$2 Mutuel Prices:				
	4 – CHANDTRUE	2.60	2.10	—
	2 – ACTXECUTIVE		2.10	—
	3 – COMMANDANT		—	—

$1 EXACTA 4–2 PAID $1.80 $2 QUINELLA 2–4 PAID $2.60

B. c, (Apr), by Yes It's True – Chandelle , by Crafty Prospector . Trainer Hess R B Jr. Bred by W E Waltrip (Fla).

CHANDTRUE took an awkward first step then settled into stride stalking the leaders off the rail, ranged up outside a rival leaving the turn and three deep into the stretch to gain the lead, then held sway under some left handed urging and steady handling late. ACTXECUTIVE had good early speed and dueled outside a rival, inched away leaving the turn, fought back inside the winner through the stretch and continued willingly to the wire. COMMANDANT angled in and was roused early, saved ground off the pace, went around a rival in midstretch and picked up the show. GREAT POWER dueled inside on the backstretch and most of the turn, dropped back leaving the turn and into the stretch and weakened.

Owners– 1, Greene Harold F; 2, McIngvale James; 3, Currin William L and Eisman Alvin; 4, Carney Brian M

Trainers– 1, Hess R B Jr; 2, Baffert Bob; 3, Currin William L; 4, Hines N J

Scratched– Gentleman Count (20Jun04 ^{3}Hol^{2})

$2 Daily Double (7–4) Paid $20.80 ; Daily Double Pool $21,082 .
$1 Pick Three (5–7–4) Paid $136.60 ; Pick Three Pool $108,048 .

NINTH RACE
Monmouth
JULY 17, 2004

1$\frac{1}{16}$ MILES. (1.40^{1}) 70TH RUNNING OF THE LONG BRANCH BREEDERS' CUP. Grade III. Purse $100,000 (includes $25,000 BC – Breeders' Cup) FOR THREE-YEAR-OLDS. By subcription of $100 each, which should accompany the nomination, $1,500 to pass the entry box with $100,000 guaranteed, which includes $25,000 from the Breeders' Cup Fund for Cup nominees only. The host association's money to be divided 60% to the winning owner, 20% to second, 11% to third, 6% to fourth and 3% to fifth. Breeders' Cup Fund money correspondingly divided providing a Breeders' Cup nominee has finished in an awarded position. Any Breeders' Cup Fund money not awarded reverts to the Fund. Weight: 122 lbs. Non-winners of $60,000 at a mile or over in 2004 allowed 2 lbs.; $45,000 at a mile or over in 2004, 4 lbs.; A sweepstakes at a mile or over in 2004, 6 lbs.; A sweepstakes anytime, 8 lbs.; Two races other than maiden orclaiming, 10 lbs. The owner of the winner to receive a trophy presented by Breeders' Cup Limited. Closed Saturday, July 3, 2004 with 35 nominations.

Value of Race: $100,000 Winner $60,000; second $20,000; third $11,000; fourth $6,000; fifth $3,000. Mutuel Pool $235,202.00 Exacta Pool $159,557.00 Trifecta Pool $106,868.00 Superfecta Pool $32,377.00

Last Raced	Horse	M/Eqt.	A.	Wt	PP	St	¼	½	¾	Str	Fin	Jockey	Odds $1
15May04 ^{12}Pim^{4}	Lion Heart		3	116	4	3	3^{2}	$3^{2\frac{1}{2}}$	1^{hd}	2^{5}	1^{hd}	Bravo J	0.30
27Jun04 ^{7}Mth^{1}	My Snookie's Boy	L	3	115	3	2	$2^{\frac{1}{2}}$	2^{hd}	2^{3}	1^{hd}	$2^{5\frac{1}{2}}$	Elliott S	12.00
5Jun04 ^{11}Bel^{3}	Royal Assault	L	3	122	7	7	6^{hd}	$6^{1\frac{1}{2}}$	5^{hd}	3^{2}	$3^{3\frac{1}{2}}$	Lopez C C	3.60
12Jun04 ^{6}CD^{3}	Ecclesiastic	L	3	113	6	5	5^{1}	$5^{\frac{1}{2}}$	6^{2}	4^{1}	$4^{1\frac{1}{4}}$	Decarlo C P	14.10
22Jun04 ^{8}Del^{3}	Zakocity	L	3	114	1	4	$4^{\frac{1}{2}}$	4^{hd}	4^{hd}	$5^{\frac{1}{2}}$	$5^{\frac{3}{4}}$	Coa E M	24.90
22Jun04 ^{8}Del^{4}	Gadace's Khamseh	L	3	114	5	6	7	7	7	6^{3}	6^{16}	Ferrer J C	41.90
27Jun04 ^{7}Mth^{8}	Choose	L bf	3	114	2	1	$1^{\frac{1}{2}}$	$1^{\frac{1}{2}}$	$3^{\frac{1}{2}}$	7	7	Turner T G	39.60

OFF AT 4:51 Start Good . Won driving. Track fast.

TIME :23, :46^{2}, 1:10, 1:36^{2}, 1:43^{2} (:23.18, :46.41, 1:10.17, 1:36.53, 1:43.51)

$2 Mutuel Prices:			
5 – LION HEART	2.60	2.20	2.10
4 – MY SNOOKIE'S BOY		3.80	2.10
8 – ROYAL ASSAULT			2.10

$2 EXACTA 5–4 PAID $14.20 $2 TRIFECTA 5–4–8 PAID $29.60
$1 SUPERFECTA 5–4–8–7 PAID $25.90

Ch. c, (Jan), by Tale of the Cat – Satin Sunrise , by Mr. Leader . Trainer Biancone Patrick L. Bred by Sabine Stable (Ky).

LION HEART content to prompt the early issue outside foes, moved to the front three deep in the vicinity of the three-eighths pole, battled heads apart with MY SNOOKIE'S BOY then narrowly prevailed after a long drive. MY SNOOKIE'S BOY pressed the early issue between foes, raced inside the top one on the final turn and moved to the lead nearing the top of the lane, dug in gamely then just failed to stay. ROYAL ASSAULT saved ground into the backstretch, was asked for run between foes midway on the final turn then lacked the needed late response. ECCLESIASTIC never far back and five wide into the lane, lacked the needed response. ZAKOCITY saved ground early while well placed, was between rivals nearing the end of the backstretch, raced in the four path turning for home and offered little in the drive. GADACE'S KHAMSEH raced six wide into the stretch and lacked a rally. CHOOSE set the early pace, saved ground and had little left nearing the lane.

Owners– 1, Smith Derrick and Tabor Michael; 2, Preferred Pals Stable; 3, Farmer Tracy; 4, Allen Joseph; 5, Pompa Paul P Jr; 6, Chinnici Angelo; 7, Dinan James M

Trainers– 1, Biancone Patrick L; 2, Iwinski Allen; 3, Zito Nicholas P; 4, McLaughlin Kiaran P; 5, Reynolds Patrick L; 6, Aristone Philip T; 7, Forbes John H

Scratched– Cherokee Spook (19Jun04 ^{7}Bel^{2})

$2 Pick Three (5–4–5) Paid $53.00 ; Pick Three Pool $21,192 .

EIGHTH RACE
Belmont
JULY 18, 2004

1$\frac{1}{4}$ MILES. (Inner Turf) (1.57^{3}) 40TH RUNNING OF THE LEXINGTON. Grade III. Purse $100,000 (UP TO $19,000 NYSBFOA) INNER TURF FOR THREE YEAR OLDS. By subscription of $100 each, which should accompany the nomination; $500 to pass the entry box; $500 to start, with $100,000 added. The added money and all fees to be divided 60% to the winner, 20%to second, 10% to third, 5% to fourth, 3% to fifth and 2% divided equally among remaining finishers. 122 lbs. Non-winners of $45,000 over a mile on the turf in 2004 allowed 2 lbs.; $30,000 twice over a mile, 4 lbs.; $30,000 over a mile, or three races 6lbs.; two races at a mile or over, 8 lbs. (Maiden, claiming, starter, restricted races not considered in allowances.) A trophy will be presented to the winning owner. The New York Racing Association reserves the right to transfer this race to the Main Track. In the event this race is taken off the turf it may be subject to a downgrade by the Graded Stakes Committee. Closed Saturday, July 3, 2004 with 26 Nominations.

Value of Race: $111,100second $22,220; Winner $66,660; third $11,110; fourth $5,555; fifth $3,333; sixth $741; seventh $741; eighth $740. Mutuel Pool $539,991.00 Exacta Pool $414,034.00 Trifecta Pool $347,506.00

Last Raced	Horse	M/Eqt.	A.	Wt	PP	¼	½	¾	1	Str	Fin	Jockey	Odds $1
26Jun04 ^{8}Del^{2}	[D]Icy Atlantic	L	3	122	5	$2^{\frac{1}{2}}$	$1^{\frac{1}{2}}$	$2^{1\frac{1}{2}}$	$1^{\frac{1}{2}}$	$1^{1\frac{1}{2}}$	1no	Velazquez J R	1.90
27Jun04 ^{7}Bel^{4}	Mustanfar	L b	3	114	7	6^{3}	$5^{\frac{1}{2}}$	5^{2}	$3^{2\frac{1}{2}}$	$2^{2\frac{1}{2}}$	$2^{2\frac{1}{4}}$	Santos J A	5.70
27Jun04 ^{7}Bel^{1}	SecondPerformnce	L b	3	118	1	$4^{\frac{1}{2}}$	2^{hd}	1^{hd}	2^{hd}	$3^{4\frac{1}{2}}$	$3^{1\frac{3}{4}}$	Migliore R	2.80
26Jun04 ^{8}Del^{7}	Big Booster	L b	3	114	3	$1^{\frac{1}{2}}$	4^{1}	$6^{2\frac{1}{2}}$	$6^{1\frac{1}{2}}$	4^{hd}	4^{2}	Chavez J F	20.30
24Jun04 ^{5}Bel^{1}	Agent Danseur	L b	3	114	4	8	8	8	$7^{\frac{1}{2}}$	$6^{\frac{1}{2}}$	$5^{\frac{1}{2}}$	Luzzi M J	49.00
26Jun04 ^{8}Del^{3}	Commendation	L	3	118	2	5^{hd}	$6^{3\frac{1}{2}}$	4^{hd}	$4^{2\frac{1}{2}}$	$5^{\frac{1}{2}}$	6^{nk}	Prado E S	3.50
30Jun04 ^{6}Bel^{1}	Inducement	b	3	114	6	3^{hd}	$3^{\frac{1}{2}}$	3^{hd}	5^{hd}	7^{3}	$7^{3\frac{1}{2}}$	Castillo H Jr	9.10
16Jun04 ^{5}Bel^{1}	Tomorrows Champ	L	3	114	8	7^{hd}	$7^{\frac{1}{2}}$	$7^{\frac{1}{2}}$	8	8	8	Fragoso P	39.75

[D] – Icy Atlantic disqualified and placed 2nd

OFF AT 4:40 Start Good . Won driving. Course firm.

TIME :24^{4}, :48^{4}, 1:12^{3}, 1:34^{4}, 2:01 (:24.94, :48.81, 1:12.66, 1:34.81, 2:01.15)

$2 Mutuel Prices:			
8 – MUSTANFAR	13.40	6.10	3.50
5 – ICY ATLANTIC		3.70	2.50
1 – SECOND PERFORMANCE			2.80

$2 EXACTA 8–5 PAID $61.50 $2 TRIFECTA 8–5–1 PAID $174.00

Ch. c, (Mar), by Unbridled – Manwah , by Lyphard . Trainer McLaughlin Kiaran P. Bred by Shadwell Farm LLC (Ky).

ICY ATLANTIC argued the pace from the outside, dug in resolutely in the stretch, came out in deep stretch under left handed whipping, brushing with MUSTANFAR, then outfinished that rival after a hard drive. MUSTANFAR was in hand early, rallied three wide approaching the stretch, came inward in the stretch under right handed whipping, brushing with the winner then was outfinished by that rival. SECOND PERFORMANCE argued the pace along the inside and weakened in the stretch. BIG BOOSTER was rated along inside, angled out in the stretch and offered a mild rally outside. AGENT DANSEUR raced inside and had no rally. COMMENDATION had no response when roused. INDUCEMENT chased the pace while three wide and tired. TOMORROWS CHAMP had no response when roused. Following a Stewards' inquiry into the stretch run, ICY ATLANTIC was disqualified from first position and placed second.

Owners– 1, Appleton Arthur I; 2, Shadwell Stable; 3, Bloom William Behrendt John T and Marquis Charles K; 4, Broman Sr Mary and Chester; 5, C D and G Stable; 6, Adam Donald A; 7, Centennial Farms; 8, Zuckerman Donald S and Roberta Mary

Trainers– 1, Pletcher Todd A; 2, McLaughlin Kiaran P; 3, Donk David; 4, Kimmel John C; 5, Klesaris Robert P; 6, Motion H Graham; 7, Mott William I; 8, Pletcher Todd A

Scratched– Victory Circle (11Jun04 ^{8}Bel^{3}) , Eddington (05Jun04 ^{11}Bel^{4})

NINTH RACE
Delaware
JULY 18, 2004

1$\frac{1}{16}$ MILES. (1.41^{2}) 54TH RUNNING OF THE LEONARD RICHARDS. Grade III. Purse $250,000 (plus $600 Starters Bonus) FOR THREE YEAR OLDS. By subscription of $250 each which shall accompany the nomination; $1,000 to enter and $1,250 to start. Supplemental nominations of $3,000 will be accepted at time of entry and shall include all fees. $250,000 Guaranteed, of which$150,000 to the winner, $50,000 to second, $27,500 to third, $15,000 to fourth and $7,500 to fifth. Weight 122 lbs. Non–winners of $90,000 at a mile or over in 2004 allowed 3 lbs.; $60,000 twice at a mile or over in 2004, 5 lbs.; one such race, 7 lbs. (Maiden and claiming races not considered in estimating allowances). Trophy to the winner. Closed Saturday, July 3rd, 2004 with 31 nominations.

Value of Race: $250,600 Winner $150,000; second $50,000; third $27,500; fourth $15,000; fifth $7,500; sixth $300; seventh $300. Mutuel Pool $180,536.00 Exacta Pool $115,036.00 Trifecta Pool $91,406.00 Superfecta Pool $23,073.00

Last Raced	Horse	M/Eqt.	A.	Wt	PP	St	¼	½	¾	Str	Fin	Jockey	Odds $1
12Jun04 ^{14}Tdn^{2}	Pollard's Vision	L	3	122	4	3	$3^{1\frac{1}{2}}$	$3^{1\frac{1}{2}}$	3^{3}	2^{3}	1^{2}	Bailey J D	1.00
26Jun04 ^{9}LaD^{1}	Britt's Jules	L b	3	116	3	1	1^{3}	1^{3}	$1^{1\frac{1}{2}}$	1^{1}	$2^{\frac{1}{2}}$	Smith G S	13.20
22Jun04 ^{8}Del^{1}	Pies Prospect	L	3	115	2	7	$4^{1\frac{1}{2}}$	$4^{\frac{1}{2}}$	2^{hd}	3^{6}	$3^{7\frac{1}{4}}$	Arroyo N Jr	2.30
15Jun04 ^{7}Del^{3}	Joe Six Pack	L b	3	115	6	6	$5^{1\frac{1}{2}}$	5^{2}	$5^{\frac{1}{2}}$	5^{hd}	$4^{1\frac{3}{4}}$	Pino M G	10.70
12Jun04 ^{14}Tdn^{3}	Trieste's Honor	L b	3	115	1	2	$2^{\frac{1}{2}}$	2^{2}	$4^{2\frac{1}{2}}$	$4^{\frac{1}{2}}$	$5^{2\frac{3}{4}}$	Velasquez C	9.10
22Jun04 ^{8}Del^{2}	Gmork	L b	3	115	5	5	7	7	7	$6^{\frac{1}{2}}$	6no	Rose J	49.40
12Jun04 ^{14}Tdn^{4}	DashboardDrummer	L	3	115	7	4	6^{1}	6^{1}	$6^{\frac{1}{2}}$	7	7	Dominguez R A	5.60

OFF AT 4:44 Start Good . Won driving. Track sloppy.

TIME :22^{4}, :46^{2}, 1:11, 1:37^{1}, 1:43^{4} (:22.88, :46.57, 1:11.19, 1:37.31, 1:43.85)

$2 Mutuel Prices:

4 – POLLARD'S VISION	4.00	3.20	2.10
3 – BRITT'S JULES		7.40	2.80
2 – PIES PROSPECT			2.20

$2 EXACTA 4–3 PAID $46.80 $2 TRIFECTA 4–3–2 PAID $109.00
$1 SUPERFECTA 4–3–2–6 PAID $298.30

Dk. b or br. c, (Jan), by Carson City – Etats Unis , by Dixieland Band . Trainer Pletcher Todd A. Bred by Charles A Smith (Ky).

POLLARD'S VISION was allowed settle early, moved up between rivals into the far turn then was hard ridden to run down the leader about 70 yards out and edge clear late. BRITT'S JULES quickly to the front, was well handled setting pace and fought it out gamely to the end. PIES PROSPECT was shuffled back at the start, moved up outside three wide in the second flight into the far turn then lacked the needed stretch response and was easily third. JOE SIX PACK lacked a solid rally. TRIESTE'S HONOR was forwardly placed along the inside to the far turn then weakened. GMORK showed little. DASHBOARD DRUMMER was outrun.

Owners– 1, Edgewood Farm; 2, Southern Equine Stables LLC; 3, LaPenta Robert V; 4, West Gary L and Mary E; 5, Cobra Farm and Castletop Stable; 6, Dixon Phyllis and Paula; 7, Double S Stable Preferred Pals Stables and Wachtel Edwin

Trainers– 1, Pletcher Todd A; 2, Guillot Eric; 3, Zito Nicholas P; 4, Dutrow Anthony W; 5, Matz Michael R; 6, Ritchey Tim F; 7, Iwinski Allen

Scratched– Big City Spender (17Jul04 ^{9}ElP^{2}) , Ecclesiastic (17Jul04 ^{9}Mth^{4})

$2 Daily Double (6–4) Paid $13.80 ; Daily Double Pool $11,611 .
$2 Pick Three (8–6–4/8/9) Paid $81.40 ; Pick Three Pool $6,790 .

TENTH RACE
Delaware
JULY 18, 2004

1¼ MILES. (1.59^{4}) 69TH RUNNING OF THE DELAWARE HANDICAP. Grade II. Purse $750,000 (plus $900 Starters Bonus) FOR FILLIES AND MARES THREE YEARS OLD AND UPWARD. By subscription of $750 each, which shall accompany the nomination, $3,000 to enter and $4,000 to start. $750,000 Guaranteed, of which $450,000 to the winner, $150,000 to second, $82,500 to third, $45,000 to fourth and $22,500 to fifth. A trophy to the winning owner, trainer and jockey. Closed Saturday. July 3rd, 2004 with 19 nominations.

Value of Race: $750,900 Winner $450,000; second $150,000; third $82,500; fourth $45,000; fifth $22,500; sixth $300; seventh $300; eighth $300. Mutuel Pool $293,181.00 Exacta Pool $180,034.00 Trifecta Pool $149,511.00 Superfecta Pool $43,212.00

Last Raced	Horse	M/Eqt.	A.	Wt	PP	¼	½	¾	1	Str	Fin	Jockey	Odds $1
6Jun04 ^{8}Hol^{1}	SummerWindDncer	L b	4	116	8	6^{1}	6^{hd}	5^{hd}	3^{1}	$2^{2\frac{1}{2}}$	$1^{1\frac{1}{4}}$	Espinoza V	1.00
12Jun04 ^{8}CD^{6}	Roar Emotion	L	4	117	5	$1^{1\frac{1}{2}}$	$1^{2\frac{1}{2}}$	$1^{1\frac{1}{2}}$	1^{2}	1^{4}	$2^{5\frac{3}{4}}$	Bailey J D	3.60
19Jun04 ^{7}Del^{1}	Misty Sixes	L	6	116	2	$2^{\frac{1}{2}}$	2^{hd}	$2^{\frac{1}{2}}$	2^{1}	3^{1}	$3^{\frac{3}{4}}$	Pino M G	3.00
17Jun04 ^{2}CD^{4}	Cloakof Vagueness	L	4	112	6	8	7^{3}	6^{4}	4^{hd}	4^{2}	$4^{4\frac{3}{4}}$	Arroyo N Jr	8.40
19Jun04 ^{7}Del^{5}	Shiny Sheet	L b	6	115	1	4^{2}	$3^{1\frac{1}{2}}$	3^{1}	5^{1}	5^{2}	$5^{1\frac{1}{4}}$	Rose J	19.30
19Jun04 ^{7}Del^{2}	Redoubled Miss	L bf	5	115	7	$5^{\frac{1}{2}}$	$4^{\frac{1}{2}}$	4^{hd}	6^{5}	6^{8}	$6^{10\frac{1}{4}}$	Dominguez R A	12.80
19Jun04 ^{7}Del^{4}	Gelli	L f	4	115	4	7^{hd}	8	8	7^{7}	7^{20}	$7^{35\frac{1}{4}}$	Caraballo J C	31.20
27Jun04 ^{6}Hol^{2}	Go On Baby	L f	6	112	3	$3^{\frac{1}{2}}$	5^{2}	7^{2}	8	8	8	Castellano A Jr	30.10

OFF AT 5:17 Start Good . Won driving. Track sloppy.

TIME :23^{1}, :47, 1:11^{3}, 1:36^{4}, 2:03^{3} (:23.27, :47.12, 1:11.63, 1:36.93, 2:03.63)

$2 Mutuel Prices:

9 – SUMMER WIND DANCER	4.00	2.80	2.10
5 – ROAR EMOTION		3.60	2.20
2 – MISTY SIXES			2.20

$2 EXACTA 9–5 PAID $13.60 $2 TRIFECTA 9–5–2 PAID $34.60
$1 SUPERFECTA 9–5–2–6 PAID $47.20

Gr/ro. f, (Mar), by Siberian Summer – Native Wind Dancer , by Incinderator . Trainer Mullins Jeff. Bred by Richard Wira Yvette Wira Linda Vetter && Deborah Penny (Cal).

SUMMER WIND DANCER advanced from the outside into the far turn then was under a long, hard drive to run down the leader in the final 70 yards and edge clear in the final strides. ROAR EMOTION quickly went to the front, was well handled setting the pace and held on gamely to the end. MISTY SIXES was well placed racing in close pursuit of the pacesetter for a mile then faded in the drive. CLOAKOF VAGUENESS was unhurried early, moved into contention into the far turn then needed more in the stretch run. SHINY SHEET was well placed racing close up along the inside then lacked a solid response. REDOUBLED MISS, forwardly placed, was shuffled back between rivals into the far turn. GELLI was never a factor. GO ON BABY showed early speed racing outside rivals and tired then was being eased up in deep stretch.

Owners– 1, Linda Vetter and Richard and Yvette Wira; 2, Allen Joseph; 3, Puglisi Stables; 4, Duncker C Steven; 5, Rathbun Mrs Henry T; 6, Centaur Farms Inc; 7, Gelli Partnership LLC; 8, Shah Stables

Trainers– 1, Mullins Jeff; 2, McLaughlin Kiaran P; 3, Klesaris Steve; 4, Hauswald Philip M; 5, Hadry Charles J; 6, Capuano Gary; 7, Hadry Charles J; 8, O'Neill Doug

Scratched– Firecard (26Jun04 ^{8}Mth^{1}) , Savedbythelight (29May04 ^{8}Bel^{7})

$2 Daily Double (4–9) Paid $6.00 ; Daily Double Pool $11,601 .
$2 Pick Three (6–4/8/9–8/9/10) Paid $56.40 ; Pick Three Pool $11,621 .

EIGHTH RACE
Hollywood
JULY 18, 2004

1½ MILES. (Turf) (2.232) 63RD RUNNING OF THE SUNSET HANDICAP. Grade II. Purse $150,000 FOR THREE YEAR OLDS AND UPWARD. By subscription of $150 each on or before Thursday, July 8 or by supplementary nomination of $3,000 each by 3:00 pm Saturday, July 10. $500 additional to pass the entry box, and $1,000 additional to start, with $90,000 to the winner, $30,000 to second, $18,000 to third, $9,000 to fourth and $3,000 to fifth. Weights Sunday July 11.Starters to be named through the entry box by the closing time of entries. A trophy will be presented to the winning owner. Closed with 15 nominations.

Value of Race: $150,000 Winner $90,000; second $30,000; third $18,000; fourth $9,000; fifth $3,000. Mutuel Pool $422,996.00 Exacta Pool $234,223.00 Quinella Pool $19,761.00 Trifecta Pool $275,038.00

Last Raced	Horse	M/Eqt.	A.	Wt	PP	¼	½	1	1¼	Str	Fin	Jockey	Odds $1
19Jun04 9LS2	Star Over the Bay	LB	6	113	4	12½	13½	11½	12	11½	1no	Baze T C	3.00
12Jun04 3Hol6	Continuously	LB	5	116	6	7	6½	5½	32½	21½	21	Solis A	0.80
27May04 5Hol1	Leprechaun Kid	LB b	5	114	3	33	21½	23	23	34½	39	Santiago Javier	10.00
8May04 7Hol7	Runaway Dancer	LB b	5	115	5	52	4hd	42½	43	43	44	Smith M E	9.00
14Dec02 13SI1	Freddy-Arg	LB	5	116	1	61	7	7	62	53	58	Desormeaux K J	5.80
2Jly04 1Hol2	Gallant-GB	LB	7	113	7	2hd	33	3hd	5hd	64	613	Pedroza M A	32.60
2Jly04 1Hol5	Gulchie-GB	LB	6	116	2	41	52	61½	7	7	7	Flores D R	39.30

OFF AT 4:59 Start Good . Won driving. Course firm.

TIME :242, :474, 1:113, 1:364, 2:011, 2:262 (:24.49, :47.93, 1:11.74, 1:36.95, 2:01.34, 2:26.47)

$2 Mutuel Prices:				
	4 – STAR OVER THE BAY	8.00	3.20	3.00
	6 – CONTINUOUSLY		2.60	2.20
	3 – LEPRECHAUN KID			3.20

$1 EXACTA 4–6 PAID $7.50 $2 QUINELLA 4–6 PAID $6.80
$1 TRIFECTA 4–6–3 PAID $39.10

Gr/ro. g, (Feb), by Cozzene – Lituya Bay , by Empery . Trainer Mitchell Mike. Bred by Four Horsemen's Ranch (Fla).

STAR OVER THE BAY took the early lead and angled in, was well rated in front along the inside, inched away again into the stretch and held on gamely under urging CONTINUOUSLY settled outside a rival then a bit off the rail, moved up inside on the final turn, came out in midstretch, drew alongside the winner in deep stretch but could not get by. LEPRECHAUN KID between horses early, angled in on the first turn, stalked inside then a bit off the rail on the last turn and into the stretch and continued willingly to best the others. RUNAWAY DANCER was in a good position chasing outside a rival then off the rail on the final turn and weakened. FREDDY (ARG) broke a bit slowly, saved ground off the pace, went outside a rival on the third turn and did not rally. GALLANT (GB) three deep into the first turn, angled to the inside in the run to the clubhouse turn, saved ground stalking the pace, dropped back on the final turn and gave way. GULCHIE (GB) saved ground chasing the pace, also fell back into and on the last turn and had nothing left.

Owners– 1, G Racing VanBurger and Vaughn; 2, Khaled Saud b; 3, Friendly Ed; 4, R L Stables; 5, Tanaka Gary A; 6, Fisher Derrick; 7, Visionary Racing and Wiles Robert A

Trainers– 1, Mitchell Mike; 2, Frankel Robert; 3, Machowsky Michael; 4, Hendricks Dan L; 5, Burke Donald J II; 6, Jory Ian P D; 7, Mulhall Kristin

$2 Daily Double (4–4) Paid $624.40 ; Daily Double Pool $34,245 .
$1 Pick Three (1–4–4) Paid $4,661.70 ; Pick Three Pool $105,789 .

FIFTH RACE
Arlington
JULY 24, 2004

1 3/16 MILES. (Turf) (1.531) 90TH RUNNING OF THE AMERICAN DERBY. Grade II. Purse $250,000 FOR THREE-YEAR-OLDS.

Value of Race: $250,000 Winner $150,000; second $50,000; third $27,500; fourth $15,000; fifth $7,500. Mutuel Pool $450,179.00 Exacta Pool $261,159.00 Trifecta Pool $247,433.00 Superfecta Pool $87,366.00

Last Raced	Horse	M/Eqt.	A.	Wt	PP	St	¼	½	¾	Str	Fin	Jockey	Odds $1
17Jun04 ASC4	SimpleExchnge-Ire	L	3	119	2	1	31	31	2½	1hd	1nk	Smullen P J	2.20
3Jly04 9AP3	Cool Conductor	L	3	119	8	6	41½	4½	72½	32	2¾	Velasquez C	3.00
3Jly04 9AP1	Toasted	L	3	123	1	2	6hd	61	4hd	43	31¼	Douglas R R	1.20
8Jly04 7AP1	Gwaihir-Ire	L b	3	119	5	3	11	11	11½	2hd	44¼	Campbell J M	49.30
3Jly04 9AP4	Up Anchor	L	3	119	7	7	8	8	8	62½	5½	Bejarano R	15.20
24Jun04 5Hol1	Samwise	L b	3	119	3	5	7hd	71½	6½	5½	65	John K	13.00
26Jun04 3Hol4	Kilgowan	L b	3	123	6	8	5hd	5½	51½	75	78¾	Marquez C H Jr	22.70
3Jly04 9AP7	Caiman	L	3	119	4	4	2hd	2½	31	8	8	Razo E Jr	07.60

OFF AT 3:06 Start Good . Won driving. Course firm.

TIME :241, :482, 1:124, 1:372, 1:544 (:24.31, :48.47, 1:12.80, 1:37.58, 1:54.93)

$2 Mutuel Prices:				
	2 – SIMPLE EXCHANGE-IRE	6.40	4.80	2.40
	8 – COOL CONDUCTOR		3.80	2.20
	1 – TOASTED			2.10

$2 EXACTA 2–8 PAID $29.40 $2 TRIFECTA 2–8–1 PAID $54.40
$2 SUPERFECTA 2–8–1–5 PAID $412.00

B. c, (May), by Danehill – Summer Trysting , by Alleged . Trainer Weld Dermot K. Bred by Moyglare Stud Farm Ltd (Ire).

SIMPLE EXCHANGE (IRE) settled in close up along the rail, remained well placed to the stretch, came just out to challenge in the lane and prevailed at the end of a hard drive. COOL CONDUCTOR raced three wide near the middle of the field, dropped back a bit on the final turn, rallied in the stretch and just missed. TOASTED saved ground near the middle of the field, worked his way out for the drive, gained ground in the stretch but lacked a winning bid. GWAIHIR (IRE) made the front into the first turn, set the pace from the inside, took a clear lead on the second turn but weakened a bit in the drive. UP ANCHOR was four wide on the first turn, continued four to five wide and rallied mildly in the stretch. SAMWISE was crowded a bit at the start, steadied on the first turn and was never a factor. KILGOWAN raced four to five wide near the middle of the field and tired. CAIMAN was crowded a bit at the start, stalked the pace and tired. (Race run in lane 5, rail at 0.)

Owners– 1, Moyglare Stud Farm Ltd Walter Haefner; 2, Garner David E; 3, Sidney L Port Trust; 4, Kirkwood Al and Saundra S; 5, Ralls and Foster LLC; 6, Spendthrift Farm LLC; 7, Ann Marie Farm Terence ONeil; 8, Achar Victor

Trainers– 1, Weld Dermot K; 2, Mott William I; 3, De Seroux Laura; 4, Forster Grant T; 5, McGee Paul J; 6, Hofmans David; 7, Stidham Michael; 8, Medina Angel M

$1 Pick Three (4/5–5–2) Paid $37.90 ; Pick Three Pool $40,357 .
$1 Pick Four (1–4/5–5–2) Paid $199.00 ; Pick Four Pool $40,050 .

SEVENTH RACE **1¼ MILES. (Turf) (1.58^{3}) 69TH RUNNING OF THE ARLINGTON HANDICAP. Grade III. Purse $250,000 FOR THREE-YEAR-OLDS AND UPWARD.**

Arlington

JULY 24, 2004

Value of Race: $250,000 Winner $150,000; second $50,000; third $27,500; fourth $15,000; fifth $7,500. Mutuel Pool $373,583.00 Exacta Pool $228,373.00 Trifecta Pool $174,981.00 Superfecta Pool $44,406.00

Last Raced	Horse	M/Eqt.	A.	Wt	PP	¼	½	¾	1	Str	Fin	Jockey	Odds $1
3Jly04 ^{8}CD^{3}	Senor Swinger	L	4	118	1	3^{1}	3½	5½	3^{hd}	2½	1^{hd}	Blanc B	1.80
26Jun04 ^{8}AP^{6}	Mystery Giver	L	6	120	3	7	7	7	6^{1}	5^{4}	21½	Marquez C H Jr	4.80
4Jly04 ^{7}AP^{1}	Ballingarry-Ire	L b	5	121	5	4½	51½	4^{hd}	4^{hd}	4½	3no	Douglas R R	1.70
3Jly04 ^{8}CD^{6}	On the Course	L	4	114	2	1½	1½	1^{hd}	1½	1½	41¾	Guidry M	8.30
3Apr04 ^{10}Kee^{7}	Rowans Park	L	4	116	7	2^{1}	2^{1}	2^{hd}	21½	3½	5^{3}	Razo E Jr	12.20
19Jan04 ^{8}SA^{5}	Sharbayan-Ire	L bf	6	117	6	6½	61½	31½	51½	6^{5}	64¾	Bejarano R	8.10
4Jly04 ^{7}AP^{2}	Grey Beard	L b	5	116	4	5^{1}	4½	61½	7	7	7	Lovato F Jr	34.10

OFF AT 4:04 Start Good . Won driving. Course firm.

TIME :25, :49^{4}, 1:15, 1:39^{4}, 2:03^{1} (:25.00, :49.95, 1:15.16, 1:39.92, 2:03.38)

$2 Mutuel Prices:

1 – SENOR SWINGER	5.60	3.20	2.20
3 – MYSTERY GIVER		4.60	2.60
5 – BALLINGARRY-IRE			2.10

$2 EXACTA 1–3 PAID $25.80 $2 TRIFECTA 1–3–5 PAID $50.40
$2 SUPERFECTA 1–3–5–2 PAID $186.40

Gr/ro. c, (Apr), by El Prado-Ire – Smooth Swinger , by Kris S.. Trainer Baffert Bob. Bred by Bob Ackerman (Ky).

SENOR SWINGER steadied at the start, raced close up from the rail, continued forwardly to the stretch, found room to get through inside and rallied for a narrow decision. MYSTERY GIVER was bumped at the start, trailed for six furlongs, came out five wide for the drive, rallied in the stretch, came in in front of rivals in deep stretch and just missed. BALLINGARRY (IRE) was bumped at the start, raced just outside near the middle of the field, checked in the stretch then lacked a winning bid. ON THE COURSE came out at the start causing chain reaction bumping, set the pace from the inside while pressed and weakened in the final furlong. ROWANS PARK pressed the pace just outside and steadied while tiring in the stretch. SHARBAYAN (IRE) was bumped at the start, made a four wide bid on the backstretch and tired. GREY BEARD was bumped at the start, raced near the middle of the field and was through early. THERE WAS A TRAINER'S CLAIM OF FOUL BY THE TRAINER OF MYSTERY GIVER AGAINST SENOR SWINGER ALLEGING INTERFERENCE AT THE START BUT IT WAS NOT ALLOWED. IN ADDITION THE RIDER OF BALLINGARRY (IRE) LODGED A CLAIM OF FOUL AGAINST MYSTERY GIVER ALLEGING INTERFERENCE IN THE STRETCH BUT IT WAS ALSO DISALLOWED. (Race run in lane 5, rail at 0.)

Owners– 1, Lewis Robert B and Beverly J; 2, Team Block; 3, Port Trust Naify Marsha and San Gabriel Investments; 4, Golden Barry; 5, Melnyk Eugene and Laura; 6, Iron County Farms Inc and Miller Trust; 7, Brunacini George

Trainers– 1, Baffert Bob; 2, Block Chris M; 3, De Seroux Laura; 4, Stidham Michael; 5, Reinstedler Anthony; 6, Kirby Frank J; 7, Fojan Emilie

$1 Pick Three (2–8/10–1) Paid $24.80 ; Pick Three Pool $50,550 .

NINTH RACE **1$\frac{3}{16}$ MILES. (Turf) (1.53^{1}) 48TH RUNNING OF THE MODESTY HANDICAP. Grade III. Purse $150,000 FOR FILLIES AND MARES, THREE-YEARS-OLD AND UPWARD.**

Arlington

JULY 24, 2004

Value of Race: $150,000 Winner $90,000; second $30,000; third $16,500; fourth $9,000; fifth $4,500. Mutuel Pool $415,637.00 Exacta Pool $252,360.00 Trifecta Pool $206,472.00 Superfecta Pool $65,887.00

Last Raced	Horse	M/Eqt.	A.	Wt	PP	St	¼	½	¾	Str	Fin	Jockey	Odds $1
5Jly04 ^{8}AP^{1}	Bedanken	L f	5	119	7	6	4^{1}	1^{hd}	21½	12½	1¾	Pettinger D R	1.40
5Jly04 ^{8}AP^{4}	Aud	L	4	116	2	4	7	7	6^{hd}	2^{hd}	2½	Razo E Jr	8.70
26Jun04 ^{9}CD^{1}	Shaconage	L	4	118	6	7	6^{1}	4½	4½	4^{hd}	3^{3}	Blanc B	2.00
5Jly04 ^{8}AP^{3}	Delicatessa	L	5	115	5	3	2½	6^{1}	7	6^{1}	4^{nk}	Campbell J M	75.90
25Jun04 ^{9}CD^{1}	Ocean Silk	L b	4	116	3	2	3½	32½	3^{2}	5^{2}	5^{3}	Douglas R R	5.20
12Jun04 ^{9}AP^{2}	Julie's Prize	L b	4	116	8	5	1½	2½	1^{hd}	3½	6^{7}	Sterling L J Jr	6.80
3Jly04 ^{10}CD^{3}	Blue Sky Baby	L	6	116	1	1	5^{hd}	51½	5^{1}	7	7	Lovato F Jr	37.60
3Jly04 ^{10}CD^{1}	Beret	L f	5	115	4	8		—	—	—	—	Emigh C A	19.40

OFF AT 5:12 Start Good For All But BERET. Won driving. Course firm.

TIME :25^{1}, :50^{3}, 1:15, 1:39^{3}, 1:57 (:25.37, :50.67, 1:15.10, 1:39.61, 1:57.00)

$2 Mutuel Prices:

7 – BEDANKEN	4.80	3.40	2.20
2 – AUD		7.40	3.40
6 – SHACONAGE			2.40

$2 EXACTA 7–2 PAID $40.40 $2 TRIFECTA 7–2–6 PAID $113.40
$2 SUPERFECTA 7–2–6–5 PAID $1,411.80

Gr/ro. m, (Feb), by Geri – Danka , by Strawberry Road-Aus . Trainer Von Hemel Donnie K. Bred by Pin Oak Stud LLC (Ky).

BEDANKEN went up to contest the pace three wide, alternated for command for six furlongs, opened a clear lead in the stretch and held sway under a mild drive. AUD was void of early speed, began working her way forward on the final turn, split foes in the stretch and rallied but could not get to the winner. SHACONAGE raced near the middle of the field, came into the stretch four deep and rallied belatedly for minor awards. DELICATESSA raced close up just outside, dropped back steadily then improved her position in the drive. OCEAN SILK raced close up inside and weakened. JULIE'S PRIZE vied for the lead just outside and tired. BLUE SKY BABY raced inside near the middle of the field and tired. BERET stumbled badly at the start and lost her rider. (Race run in lane 5, rail at 0.).

Owners– 1, Pin Oak Stable LLC; 2, Willmott Stables Inc; 3, Van Doren Andrena; 4, Inman Barr H; 5, Estate of Robert E Sangster; 6, Richard Otto Stables Inc; 7, N J Samford Trust; 8, Vanier Nancy A and Williamson Lyda

Trainers– 1, Von Hemel Donnie K; 2, Reinstedler Anthony; 3, Shirota Mitch; 4, Livesay Charlie; 5, Byrne Patrick B; 6, Mitchell Anthony; 7, Maker Rebecca; 8, Vanier Harvey L

$1 Pick Three (1–7–7) Paid $68.90 ; Pick Three Pool $26,564 .

EIGHTH RACE
Belmont
JULY 24, 2004

1¼ MILES. (1.58^1) 87TH RUNNING OF THE COACHING CLUB AMERICAN OAKS. Grade I. Purse $500,000 (Up To $55,000 NYSBFOA) FOR FILLIES THREE YEARS OLD. By subscription of $500 each, which should accompany the nomination; $2,500 to pass the entry box; $2,500 to start. The purse to be divided 60% to the winner, 20% to second, 10% to third, 5% to fourth,3% to fifth and 2% divided equally among remaining finishers. 121 lbs. Trophies will be presented to the winning owner, trainer and jockey. A special permanent trophy will be presented to the owner of the winner if the filly wins all legs of the Triple Tiara (The Mother Goose, The Coaching Club American Oaks and The Alabama). Closed Saturday, July 10,2004 with 14 Nominations.

Value of Race: $500,000 Winner $300,000; second $100,000; third $50,000; fourth $25,000; fifth $15,000; sixth $10,000. Mutuel Pool $705,116.00 Exacta Pool $514,249.00 Trifecta Pool $413,012.00

Last Raced	Horse	M/Eqt.	A.	Wt	PP	¼	½	¾	1	Str	Fin	Jockey	Odds $1
26Jun04 ^{9}Bel^2	Ashado	L	3	121	4	$2^{1\frac{1}{2}}$	$2^{1\frac{1}{2}}$	$2^{\frac{1}{2}}$	$1^{1\frac{1}{2}}$	1^5	$1^{4\frac{1}{2}}$	Velazquez J R	0.75
26Jun04 ^{9}Bel^1	Stellar Jayne	L b	3	121	1	1^{hd}	$1^{\frac{1}{2}}$	$1^{\frac{1}{2}}$	3^7	$2^{2\frac{1}{2}}$	$2^{7\frac{1}{2}}$	Albarado R J	3.60
1Jly04 ^{8}Bel^1	Magical Illusion	L b	3	121	6	3^{hd}	3^{hd}	$3^{1\frac{1}{2}}$	2^{hd}	$3^{5\frac{1}{2}}$	3^4	Prado E S	3.20
27Jun04 ^{5}Bel^4	Honor Point		3	121	5	5^6	$5^{4\frac{1}{2}}$	5^6	5^{10}	$4^{3\frac{1}{2}}$	4^4	Chavez J F	25.50
19Jun04 ^{8}CD^1	Dynaville	L	3	121	2	$4^{2\frac{1}{2}}$	$4^{2\frac{1}{2}}$	$4^{2\frac{1}{2}}$	4^{hd}	5^{10}	$5^{8\frac{3}{4}}$	Bailey J D	9.70
4Jly04 ^{9}LS^1	America America		3	121	3	6	6	6	6	6	6	Samyn J L	65.75

OFF AT 4:45 Start Good. Won driving. Track muddy.

TIME :24^2, :48^3, 1:12^2, 1:36^3, 2:02^2 (:24.54, :48.64, 1:12.53, 1:36.62, 2:02.43)

$2 Mutuel Prices:			
4 – ASHADO	3.50	2.30	2.10
1 – STELLAR JAYNE		2.90	2.10
6 – MAGICAL ILLUSION			2.10

$2 EXACTA 4–1 PAID $9.60 $2 TRIFECTA 4–1–6 PAID $17.20

Dk. b or br. f, (Feb), by Saint Ballado – Goulash , by Mari's Book . Trainer Pletcher Todd A. Bred by Aaron U Jones & Marie D Jones (Ky).

ASHADO prompted the pace from the outside while in hand, took over when asked on the second turn, drew clear into the stretch, widened when roused and remained well clear while being kept to the task to the wire. STELLAR JAYNE quickly showed in front, set the pace along the inside, could not stay with the winner turning for home but continued on well to be easily best of the others. MAGICAL ILLUSION raced close up outside while in hand, put in a three wide run on the second turn and tired in the stretch. HONOR POINT was urged along on the rail, raced inside and had no response when roused. DYNAVILLE raced close up inside, chased the pace for three quarters and tired. AMERICA AMERICA dropped back along the inside, trailed throughout and was vanned off after the finish.

Owners– 1, Starlight Stables LLC Saylor Paul and Martin Johns; 2, Spendthrift Farm LLC Kidder Chuck Cole Nancy and Strong Nick; 3, Clifton William L Jr; 4, Shields Joseph V Jr; 5, Wafare Farm Kaster Richard S; 6, Mourier Franck

Trainers– 1, Pletcher Todd A; 2, Lukas D Wayne; 3, Bond Harold James; 4, Jerkens H Allen; 5, Romans Dale; 6, Mourier Franck

---

SIXTH RACE
Del Mar
JULY 24, 2004

1⅛ MILES. (Turf) (1.45^4) 47TH RUNNING OF THE JOHN C. MABEE HANDICAP. Grade I. Purse $400,000 FOR FILLIES AND MARES,THREE-YEAR-OLDS AND UPWARD. By subscription of $400 each, which shall accompany the nomination, or by supplementary nomination of $4,000 each by Sunday, July 18, $4,000 additional to start, with $400,000 Guaranteed, of which $240,000to first, $80,000 to second, $48,000 to third, $24,000 to fourth and $8,000 to fifth. Weights Monday, July 19. High weights preferred. A trophy will be presented to the owner of the winner. Nominations closed Thrusday, July 15, 2004 with 13 nominations.

Value of Race: $400,000 Winner $240,000; second $80,000; third $48,000; fourth $24,000; fifth $8,000. Mutuel Pool $804,592.00 Exacta Pool $371,868.00 Quinella Pool $35,770.00 Trifecta Pool $339,669.00

Last Raced	Horse	M/Eqt.	A.	Wt	PP	St	¼	½	¾	Str	Fin	Jockey	Odds $1
12Jun04 ^{3}Hol^7	Musical Chimes	LB	4	116	4	4	4^{hd}	$5^{1\frac{1}{2}}$	3^{hd}	$3^{\frac{1}{2}}$	$1^{1\frac{1}{4}}$	Desormeaux K J	2.10
27Jun04 ^{8}Hol^2	Moscow Burning	LB	4	117	3	1	$3^{1\frac{1}{2}}$	3^1	2^1	$1^{\frac{1}{2}}$	2no	Valdivia J Jr	3.60
27Jun04 ^{8}Hol^5	Notting Hill-Brz	LB	5	113	5	2	1^1	$1^{2\frac{1}{2}}$	$1^{\frac{1}{2}}$	2^1	3^1	Baze T C	21.80
31May04 ^{2}Hol^4	Dimitrova	LB f	4	120	6	3	2^1	$2^{\frac{1}{2}}$	$5^{\frac{1}{2}}$	5^2	$4^{\frac{1}{2}}$	Nakatani C S	8.50
3Jly04 ^{4}Hol^2	Katdogawn-GB	LB	4	116	2	5	5^1	$4^{\frac{1}{2}}$	4^{hd}	4^{hd}	5^{nk}	Smith M E	9.60
27Jun04 ^{8}Hol^1	Light Jig-GB	LB	4	116	1	6	6	6	6	6	6	Flores D R	1.40

OFF AT 4:47 Start Good. Won driving. Course firm.

TIME :23^4, :47^4, 1:12, 1:35^2, 1:47 (:23.87, :47.96, 1:12.12, 1:35.42, 1:47.09)

$2 Mutuel Prices:			
5 – MUSICAL CHIMES	6.20	3.60	3.20
3 – MOSCOW BURNING		4.40	3.60
6 – NOTTING HILL-BRZ			4.60

$1 EXACTA 5–3 PAID $13.10 $2 QUINELLA 3–5 PAID $13.40
$1 TRIFECTA 5–3–6 PAID $149.20

Dk. b or br. f, (Apr), by In Excess-Ire – Note Musicale-GB , by Sadler's Wells . Trainer Drysdale Neil. Bred by Gainsborough Farm LLC (Ky).

MUSICAL CHIMES chased outside a rival, went three deep between foes on the second turn, continued three wide into the stretch, loomed up under confident handling in midstretch, made the lead under brisk handling in deep stretch and inched away. MOSCOW BURNING stalked inside then drifted out on the first turn and tracked the pace off the rail, went between foes into and on the second turn, bid outside the pacesetter and took a short advantage in upper stretch, could not match the winner late but gamely held second. NOTTING HILL (BRZ) pulled a bit early, went to the front off the rail, angled in nearing the first turn, kicked clear on the backstretch, battled inside into and on the second turn, fought back in the stretch and was narrowly edged for the place. DIMITROVA stalked the early pace off the rail, bid three deep leaving the backstretch, continued between horses on the second turn and into the stretch and could not quite summon the necessary late response. KATDOGAWN (GB) saved ground stalking the pace, remained inside to bid in the drive but lacked the needed rally. LIGHT JIG (GB) settled inside then a bit off the rail, went four wide into and on the second turn and three deep into the stretch and also could not offer the necessary late kick.

Owners– 1, Al Maktoum Sheik Maktoum b; 2, Nentwig Michael and Van Kempen Dallas; 3, Green Lantern Stables LLC and Barber Gary; 4, Higgins Joseph; 5, Cuchna John R Jim Ford Inc and Pearson Deron; 6, Juddmonte Farms Inc

Trainers– 1, Drysdale Neil; 2, Cassidy James; 3, Sahadi Jenine; 4, Drysdale Neil; 5, Cassidy James; 6, Frankel Robert

Scratched– Makeup Artist (03Jul04 ^{4}Hol^3)

$2 Daily Double (12–5) Paid $45.20 ; Daily Double Pool $56,271 .
$1 Pick Three (3–12–5) Paid $1,107.40 ; Pick Three Pool $164,750 .

SECOND RACE
Del Mar
JULY 25, 2004

6 FURLONGS. (1.073) 59TH RUNNING OF THE BING CROSBY BREEDERS' CUP HANDICAP. Grade I. Purse $250,000 (includes $50,000 BC – Breeders' Cup) FOR THREE-YEAR-OLDS AND UPWARD. By subscription of $200 each, which shall accompany the nomination, or by supplementary nomination of $2,000 each by Sunday, July 18, $2,000 additional to start, with $200,000 and an additional $50,000 from Breeders' Cup Fund for Cup nominees only. The host association's monies to be divided 60% to the winner; 20% to second; 12% to third; 6% to fourth and 2% to fifth. Breeders' Cup Fund monies also correspondingly divided, provided a Breeders' Cup nominee has finished in an awarded position. Any unearned Breeders' Cup Fund monies will revert to the Fund. Weights Monday, July 19. A trophy will be presented to the owner of the winner. Nominations closed Thursday, July 15, 2004 with 14 nominations.

Value of Race: $244,000 Winner $150,000; second $50,000; third $24,000; fourth $15,000; fifth $5,000. Mutuel Pool $782,065.00 Exacta Pool $463,906.00 Quinella Pool $43,208.00 Trifecta Pool $417,617.00 Superfecta Pool $163,517.00

Last Raced	Horse	M/Eqt.	A.	Wt	PP	St	¼	½	Str	Fin	Jockey	Odds $1
3Jly04 9Hol4	Kela	LB b	6	113	6	10	10	5hd	2½	11¼	Baze T C	8.80
3Jly04 9Hol1	Pohave	LB	6	118	7	4	51½	3hd	1hd	22½	Court J K	2.20
19Jun04 8BM3	Hombre Rapido	LB b	7	115	10	1	11½	11	31½	33	Valdivia J Jr	10.50
3Jly04 9Hol3	Revello	LB b	6	110	1	7	61½	61½	51½	4no	Santiago Javier	8.80
17Jun04 3Hol1	Attack Alert	LB b	3	115	2	8	2hd	41½	41½	52½	Bailey J D	11.70
19Jun04 8BM4	Green Team	LB	5	114	9	5	9hd	7hd	81½	6½	Espinoza V	13.80
19Jun04 8BM1	Court's in Session	LB bf	5	116	8	3	7hd	8½	71	7½	Atkinson P	22.60
31May04 7Hol7	Glick	LB b	8	117	5	2	3½	2hd	6hd	82	Nakatani C S	15.50
17Aug03 8Dmr1	Disturbingthepeace	LB	6	117	4	9	8hd	10	10	92½	Flores D R	16.50
19Jun04 9CD2	Beau's Town	LB b	6	119	3	6	4hd	92	9hd	10	Smith M E	2.60

OFF AT 2:48 Start Good. Won driving. Track fast.

TIME :212, :434, :56, 1:082 (:21.45, :43.96, :56.07, 1:08.51)

$2 Mutuel Prices:			
7 – KELA	19.60	8.40	4.60
8 – POHAVE		3.80	2.80
11 – HOMBRE RAPIDO			6.80

$1 EXACTA 7–8 PAID $35.70 $2 QUINELLA 7–8 PAID $28.20

$1 TRIFECTA 7–8–11 PAID $375.10 $1 SUPERFECTA 7–8–11–2 PAID $2,126.20

B. h, (Mar), by Numerous – Bolshoi Comedy , by Sovereign Dancer . Trainer Mitchell Mike. Bred by Cypress Farms 1991 (Ky).

KELA dropped back off the rail without early speed, moved up boldly four wide on the turn and into the stretch, gained the lead three deep just past the eighth pole and gamely prevailed under some urging and good handling. POHAVE four wide early, stalked three deep, took a short lead between horses nearing midstretch, could not match the winner but was clearly second best. HOMBRE RAPIDO sped to the early lead and angled in, set the pace a bit off the rail, fought back in midstretch and bested the others. REVELLO stalked inside then fell back some a half mile out, came out into the turn and three deep into the stretch and lacked the needed rally. ATTACK ALERT between horses early, stalked along the inside to the stretch and weakened. GREEN TEAM wide early, chased outside, split horses early on the turn, came three deep into the stretch and could not offer the necessary response. COURT'S IN SESSION also wide early, chased outside then between foes, split horses twice on the turn and did not rally. GLICK close up stalking the pace between horses to the stretch, weakened. DISTURBINGTHEPEACE a bit crowded at the start, settled just off the rail, came out in the stretch and failed to menace. BEAU'S TOWN had good early speed to stalk between horses, was shuffled back leaving the backstretch, dropped back and angled in on the turn and weakened.

Owners– 1, Manoogian Jay; 2, Kagele Brothers Inc Leatherman Ty and Leib Mark A; 3, Granja Vista Del Rio Stable; 4, Sengara Jeffrey; 5, McIngvale James; 6, Ferro Family Trust and Bonde Jeff; 7, Wind River Stables; 8, Bone Robert D; 9, Milch David S and Rita and Herrick Racing; 10, Hulkewicz David J

Trainers– 1, Mitchell Mike; 2, O'Neill Doug; 3, Sadler John W; 4, West Ted H; 5, Baffert Bob; 6, Bonde Jeff; 7, Koriner Brian; 8, Mullins Jeff; 9, Vienna Darrell; 10, Norman Cole

Scratched– Rojo Toro (03Jul04 9Hol2)

$2 Daily Double (1–7) Paid $37.60 ; Daily Double Pool $154,232 .

EIGHTH RACE
Del Mar
JULY 25, 2004

1⅛ MILES. (Turf) (1.45^4) 31ST RUNNING OF THE EDDIE READ HANDICAP. Grade I. Purse $400,000 FOR THREE-YEAR-OLDS AND UPWARD. By subscription of $400 each, which shall accompany the nomination, or by supplementary nomination of $4,000 by Sunday, July 18, $4,000 additional to start, with $400,000 Guaranteed, of which $240,000 to first, $80,000 tosecond, $48,000 to third, $24,000 to fourth and $8,000 to fifth. Weights Monday, July 19. High weights preferred. A trophy will be presented to the owner of the winner. Nominations closed Thursday, July 15, 2004 with 14 nominations.

Value of Race: $400,000 Winner $240,000; second $80,000; third $48,000; fourth $24,000; fifth $8,000. Mutuel Pool $787,221.00 Exacta Pool $378,448.00 Quinella Pool $34,133.00 Trifecta Pool $330,301.00 Superfecta Pool $154,200.00

Last Raced	Horse	M/Eqt.	A.	Wt	PP	St	¼	½	¾	Str	Fin	Jockey	Odds $1
25Oct03 ^{4}SA^8	Special Ring	LB b	7	118	9	3	$1^{1\frac{1}{2}}$	$1^{3\frac{1}{2}}$	1^{1}	$1^{1\frac{1}{2}}$	$1^{\frac{3}{4}}$	Espinoza V	a- 0.90
4Jly04 ^{8}Hol^1	Bayamo-Ire	LB	5	119	7	2	4^{1}	$4^{1\frac{1}{2}}$	4^{1}	$2^{\frac{1}{2}}$	$2^{\frac{3}{4}}$	Flores D R	a- 0.90
31May04 ^{7}Hol^5	Sweet Return-GB	LB	4	119	1	5	3^{1}	3^{1}	$3^{\frac{1}{2}}$	$3^{2\frac{1}{2}}$	$3^{\frac{3}{4}}$	Bailey J D	4.60
31May04 ^{7}Hol^4	King of Happiness	LB	5	116	4	6	$6^{1\frac{1}{2}}$	6^{1}	7^{2}	4^{1}	4^{hd}	Desormeaux K J	6.60
23Jun04 ^{7}Hol^3	Green Line-GB	LB	5	112	10	7	$7^{1\frac{1}{2}}$	7^{2}	5^{hd}	5^{2}	5^{1}	Sorenson D	68.00
12Jun04 ^{3}Hol^4	Vangelis	LB	5	116	5	10	10	10	10	$8^{\frac{1}{2}}$	$6^{1\frac{1}{2}}$	Valdivia J Jr	6.80
4Jly04 ^{8}Hol^2	Sarafan	LB	7	117	2	8	8^{1}	$8^{\frac{1}{2}}$	8^{hd}	$7^{1\frac{1}{2}}$	$7^{\frac{1}{2}}$	Nakatani C S	11.00
12Jun04 ^{3}Hol^3	Just Wonder-GB	LB	4	116	3	9	$9^{2\frac{1}{2}}$	$9^{1\frac{1}{2}}$	$9^{1\frac{1}{2}}$	9^{1}	8no	Smith M E	10.70
5Jly04 ^{2}Hol^1	Cayoke-FR	LB b	7	114	6	1	$5^{\frac{1}{2}}$	5^{hd}	6^{1}	6^{hd}	9^{6}	Baze T C	19.10
8May04 ^{8}Crc^1	Mr. Livingston	LB f	7	113	8	4	$2^{1\frac{1}{2}}$	2^{1}	$2^{1\frac{1}{2}}$	10	10	Morales C E	60.60

a-Coupled: Special Ring and Bayamo-Ire.

OFF AT 5:46 Start Good. Won driving. Course firm.

TIME :23^3, :47, 1:11, 1:34^2, 1:45^4 (:23.64, :47.12, 1:11.03, 1:34.59, 1:45.90)

$2 Mutuel Prices:				
	1A– SPECIAL RING(a–entry)	3.80	3.80	2.60
	1 – BAYAMO–IRE(a–entry)	3.80	3.80	2.60
	2 – SWEET RETURN–GB			3.80

$1 EXACTA 1–2 PAID $7.20 $2 QUINELLA 1–2 PAID $8.80

$1 TRIFECTA 1–2–5 PAID $32.30 $1 SUPERFECTA 1–2–5–9 PAID $558.40

B. g, (Mar), by Nureyev – Ring Beaune, by Bering–GB. Trainer Canani Julio C. Bred by Wertheimer & Frere (Ky).

SPECIAL RING sped to the early lead, set the pace off the rail, responded into the second turn, angled in on that turn, came a bit off the rail again in the stretch and held on gamely under urging. BAYAMO (IRE) stalked the winner off the rail or outside a rival, came three deep into the stretch and continued willingly. SWEET RETURN (GB) pulled along the inside and steadied slightly, stalked inside, came off the rail on the second turn, was boxed in a bit off heels in upper stretch, angled in and also went on with interest to the end. KING OF HAPPINESS angled in and saved ground chasing the pace, came out on the second turn and three deep into the stretch and finished well. GREEN LINE (GB) angled in and chased a bit off the rail then inside, waited off heels leaving the second turn, split rivals in midstretch and also found his best stride late. VANGELIS unhurried along the inside for more than a mile, came out into the stretch and again in midstretch and finished with interest too late. SARAFAN saved ground off the pace, came out into the stretch and lacked the needed response. JUST WONDER (GB) allowed to settle outside a rival, came three deep into the stretch and was not a threat. CAYOKE (FR) pulled early and was in a bit tight, chased outside a rival then three deep into and on the second turn and four wide into the stretch and could not offer the necessary rally. MR. LIVINGSTON stalked the winner off the rail then angled in and saved ground, inched forward leaving the backstretch, continued inside on the second turn and weakened in the stretch.

Owners– 1, Prestonwood Farm LLC; 2, Prestonwood Farm LLC; 3, Red Oak Stable; 4, Al Maktoum Sheik Maktoum b; 5, Harlequin Ranches and Conroy Ian; 6, Bloodstock Mgn Services Inc or Cheveley Park StbLtd; 7, Tanaka Gary A; 8, Naify Sugarman and Vistas LLC et al; 9, House Michael; 10, Palmer Teresa and David

Trainers– 1, Canani Julio C; 2, Canani Julio C; 3, McAnally Ronald; 4, Drysdale Neil; 5, Gallagher Patrick; 6, Frankel Robert; 7, Drysdale Neil; 8, De Seroux Laura; 9, Mullins Jeff; 10, Kaplan William A

$2 Daily Double (9–1) Paid $60.40 ; Daily Double Pool $47,751 .
$1 Pick Three (5–9–1) Paid $1,037.40 ; Pick Three Pool $96,784 .

TENTH RACE
Monmouth
JULY 25, 2004

1 MILE. (1.33^4) 57TH RUNNING OF THE SALVATOR MILE HANDICAP. Grade III. Purse $100,000 FOR THREE-YEAR-OLDS AND UPWARD. By subcription of $100 each, which should accompany the nomination and $1,500 to pass the entry box. The winning owner to receive $60,000, $20,000 to second, $11,000 to third, $6,000 to fourth and $3,000 to fifth. The owner of the winner to receive a trophy. Closed Sunday, July 11, 2004 with 22 nominations.

Value of Race: $100,000 Winner $60,000; second $20,000; third $11,000; fourth $6,000; fifth $3,000. Mutuel Pool $138,509.00 Exacta Pool $120,782.00

Last Raced	Horse	M/Eqt.	A.	Wt	PP	St	¼	½	¾	Str	Fin	Jockey	Odds $1
5Jly04 ^{5}Mth^1	Presidentialaffair	L	5	117	1	1	$1^{1\frac{1}{2}}$	1^{3}	$1^{\frac{1}{2}}$	$1^{\frac{1}{2}}$	1^{1}	Elliott S	2.30
4Jly04 ^{9}Bel^3	Unforgettable Max	L f	4	117	5	2	$2^{1\frac{1}{2}}$	$2^{2\frac{1}{2}}$	2^{4}	$2^{3\frac{1}{2}}$	2^{4}	Coa E M	1.60
30Jun04 ^{8}Bel^5	Roaring Fever	L b	4	115	2	3	$4^{\frac{1}{2}}$	5	3^{1}	3^{3}	3^{5}	Velez J A Jr	11.70
3Jly04 ^{9}PrM^3	Crafty Shaw	L	6	118	4	4	$3^{2\frac{1}{2}}$	3^{3}	4^{1}	4^{4}	$4^{16\frac{1}{4}}$	Perret C	1.80
24Jun04 ^{8}Bel^4	Cherry Pickings	L	7	114	3	5	5	4^{hd}	5	5	5	Bravo J	8.40

OFF AT 5:16 Start Good. Won driving. Track fast.

TIME :23^2, :46^1, 1:10, 1:35^1 (:23.58, :46.26, 1:10.03, 1:35.27)

$2 Mutuel Prices:				
	1 – PRESIDENTIALAFFAIR	6.60	3.20	3.00
	6 – UNFORGETTABLE MAX		3.00	2.80
	2 – ROARING FEVER			3.80

$2 EXACTA 1–6 PAID $16.80

B. g, (Apr), by Not For Love – Quite Amazing, by Bear Hunt. Trainer Ciresa Martin E. Bred by Will Run Farm (Pa).

PRESIDENTIALAFFAIR rated a clear pace off the rail, was challenged approaching the quarter pole and persevered responsively with steady encouragement. UNFORGETTABLE MAX rated close about the three path, made his move on the winner approaching the quarter pole, dueled close to midstretch, drifted out losing a bit of momentum under a left hand drive then recovered well to come back toward the wire. ROARING FEVER, unhurried inside, bid into the final turn and finished evenly toward the rail. CRAFTY SHAW kept off the early pace about the five path, picked up the chase into the final turn then weakened through the stretch. CHERRY PICKINGS broke a bit awkwardly, rated back in the four path, gave chase into the final turn, eased to the outside entering the stretch, had nothing left and was not abused.

Owners– 1, V Papandrea & E Ciresa; 2, Dweck Raymond; 3, Evans Edward P; 4, Cella Charles J; 5, Darley Stable

Trainers– 1, Ciresa Martin E; 2, Levine Bruce N; 3, Hennig Mark; 4, Vestal Peter M; 5, McLaughlin Kiaran P

Scratched– Polish Pride (07Jun03 ^{11}Pim^3)

NINTH RACE
Saratoga
JULY 28, 2004

6 FURLONGS. (1.08) 87TH RUNNING OF THE SCHUYLERVILLE. Grade II. Purse $150,000 (Up to $28,500 NYSBFOA) FOR FILLIES TWO YEARS OLD. By subscription of $150 each, which should accompany the nomination; $750 to pass the entry box; $750 to start. The purse to be divided 60% to the winner, 20% to second, 10% to third, 5% to fourth, 3% tofifth and 2% divided equally among remaining finishers. 122 lbs. Non–winners of $40,000 allowed 2 lbs.; a race other than maiden or claiming, 4 lbs.; a race other than claiming, 6 lbs. A Trophy will be presented to the winning owner. Closed Saturday, July 17, 2004 with 28 Nominations.

Value of Race: $150,000 Winner $90,000; second $30,000; third $15,000; fourth $7,500; fifth $4,500; sixth $600; seventh $600; eighth $600; ninth $600; tenth $600. Mutuel Pool $638,387.00 Exacta Pool $535,464.00 Trifecta Pool $422,874.00

Last Raced	Horse	M/Eqt.	A.	Wt	PP	St	¼	½	Str	Fin	Jockey	Odds $1
4Jly04 ^{11}CD^{1}	Classic Elegance		2	122	1	7	7^{2}	$6^{\frac{1}{2}}$	5^{3}	1^{1}	Day P	2.90
24Jun04 ^{6}CD^{1}	Angel Trumpet	L	2	118	7	3	1^{hd}	$1^{1\frac{1}{2}}$	$1^{3\frac{1}{2}}$	$2^{1\frac{3}{4}}$	Albarado R J	18.10
4Jun04 ^{2}Mth^{1}	Wild Chick	L	2	118	9	4	5^{1}	2^{hd}	$4^{1\frac{1}{2}}$	3no	Velazquez J R	6.70
10Jly04 ^{3}Bel^{1}	Darn That Girl	L	2	118	10	1	$3^{\frac{1}{2}}$	$3^{\frac{1}{2}}$	2^{hd}	$4^{2\frac{3}{4}}$	Bridgmohan S X	3.70
27Jun04 ^{8}Bel^{1}	Broadway Gold	L b	2	122	6	8	6^{2}	$4^{\frac{1}{2}}$	$3^{\frac{1}{2}}$	$5^{4\frac{1}{4}}$	Bailey J D	2.35
14Jly04 ^{9}Mth^{1}	Dressed for Succes		2	118	8	2	$4^{\frac{1}{2}}$	$7^{\frac{1}{2}}$	$6^{\frac{1}{2}}$	$6^{\frac{3}{4}}$	Bravo J	13.20
11Jly04 ^{8}Cnl^{1}	Partners Due	L	2	118	5	5	$2^{1\frac{1}{2}}$	5^{1}	7^{1}	$7^{\frac{1}{2}}$	Chavez J F	14.60
4Jly04 ^{12}CD^{1}	Lady Dynasty	L	2	118	2	10	$8^{2\frac{1}{2}}$	8^{3}	8^{1}	$8^{\frac{3}{4}}$	Migliore R	50.00
4Jly04 ^{8}WO^{3}	Coconut Popsicle	L	2	118	4	6	9^{hd}	$9^{4\frac{1}{2}}$	9^{6}	$9^{8\frac{1}{2}}$	Fragoso P	55.00
23Jun04 ^{2}Bel^{1}	Pelham Bay		2	118	3	9	10	10	10	10	Prado E S	18.50

OFF AT 5:19 Start Good . Won driving. Track muddy.

TIME :21^{4}, :45^{2}, :58^{2}, 1:12^{2} (:21.80, :45.49, :58.41, 1:12.48)

$2 Mutuel Prices:

1 – CLASSIC ELEGANCE	7.80	4.60	3.80
7 – ANGEL TRUMPET		14.60	10.00
9 – WILD CHICK			5.50

$2 EXACTA 1–7 PAID $100.50 $2 TRIFECTA 1–7–9 PAID $576.00

B. f, (Mar), by Carson City – Taegu , by Halo . Trainer Lukas D Wayne. Bred by Brereton C Jones (Ky).

CLASSIC ELEGANCE was hustled from the gate but dropped back along the inside on the turn, angled out in upper stretch, responded when roused, finished determinedly and was along in time outside. ANGEL TRUMPET was hustled to the front, set the pace, drew clear into the stretch, widened when roused and was caught nearing the finish. WILD CHICK was hustled outside, put in a four wide run on the turn and had little left for the stretch drive. DARN THAT GIRL was hustled along outside, chased the pace while three wide and weakened in the final furlong. BROADWAY GOLD was outrun early, put in a run along the inside on the turn and had nothing left for the drive. DRESSED FOR SUCCES chased the pace from the outside and tired after a half mile. PARTNERS DUE chased the pace along the inside and tired in the stretch. LADY DYNASTY was outrun early, came wide into the stretch and had no rally. COCONUT POPSICLE had no response when roused. PELHAM BAY raced inside and tired.

Owners– 1, Lewis Robert B and Beverly J; 2, Copeland Dreabon; 3, New Farm; 4, Silver Earl I and Eiserman Michael; 5, Robsham Mrs E P; 6, Giacopelli Richard J; 7, Ghost Stable; 8, Kaster Richard S Nancy R Kaster; 9, Singer Craig B; 10, Pollard Evelyn M

Trainers– 1, Lukas D Wayne; 2, Levine Bruce N; 3, Perkins Ben W Jr; 4, Violette Richard A Jr; 5, Hough Stanley M; 6, Biancone Patrick L; 7, Trombetta Michael J; 8, Romans Dale; 9, Tesher Howard M; 10, Kelly Patrick J

Scratched– Smokin Sylvia (23Jun04 ^{4}Bel^{1})

EIGHTH RACE
Saratoga
JULY 29, 2004

6 FURLONGS. (1.08) 91ST RUNNING OF THE SANFORD. Grade II. Purse $150,000 (Up To $28,500 NYSBFOA) FOR TWO YEAR OLDS. By subscription of $150 each, which should accompany the nomination; $750 to pass the entry box; $750 to start. The purse to be divided 60% to the winner, 20% to second, 10% to third, 5% to fourth, 3% to fifth and 2% divided equally among remaining finishers. 122 lbs. Non–winners of $40,000 allowed 2 lbs.; a race other than maiden or claiming, 4 lbs.; a race other than claiming, 6 lbs. A Trophy will be presented to the winning owner. Closed Saturday, July 17, 2004 with 26 nominations.

Value of Race: $150,000 Winner $90,000; second $30,000; third $15,000; fourth $7,500; fifth $4,500; sixth $500; seventh $500; eighth $500; ninth $500; tenth $500; eleventh $500. Mutuel Pool $633,191.00 Exacta Pool $502,890.00 Trifecta Pool $371,215.00

Last Raced	Horse	M/Eqt.	A.	Wt	PP	St	¼	½	Str	Fin	Jockey	Odds $1
12Jly04 ^{7}Del^{1}	Afleet Alex	L	2	120	8	5	$6^{1\frac{1}{2}}$	$1^{\frac{1}{2}}$	$1^{1\frac{1}{2}}$	$1^{5\frac{1}{4}}$	Rose J	3.00
26Jun04 ^{8}WO^{1}	Flamenco	L	2	122	3	8	4^{hd}	$6^{\frac{1}{2}}$	$3^{\frac{1}{2}}$	2^{nk}	Bailey J D	5.80
3Jly04 ^{11}CD^{1}	Consolidator	L	2	118	9	6	3^{hd}	4^{hd}	5^{hd}	$3^{\frac{3}{4}}$	Day P	3.20
26Jun04 ^{3}Bel^{2}	Winning Expression	L	2	118	11	1	2^{1}	$2^{\frac{1}{2}}$	2^{hd}	4^{3}	Prado E S	30.75
1Jly04 ^{8}PrM^{1}	Departing Now	L	2	120	1	3	$5^{1\frac{1}{2}}$	$5^{\frac{1}{2}}$	$4^{\frac{1}{2}}$	$5^{\frac{3}{4}}$	Lovato F Jr	22.90
5Jly04 ^{10}CD^{1}	Lunarpal	L	2	122	2	2	1^{hd}	3^{1}	$6^{2\frac{1}{2}}$	6^{nk}	Sellers S J	5.30
19Jun04 ^{3}Mth^{1}	Smokescreen	L	2	118	4	11	9^{6}	7^{hd}	7^{hd}	7^{1}	Velazquez J R	5.80
25Jun04 ^{4}Bel^{1}	Calypso Band	L	2	118	5	4	$7^{\frac{1}{2}}$	8^{hd}	8^{1}	$8^{1\frac{3}{4}}$	Fragoso P	20.40
5Jly04 ^{10}CD^{3}	Maximus C	L	2	118	10	7	8^{hd}	$9^{3\frac{1}{2}}$	$9^{2\frac{1}{2}}$	$9^{1\frac{1}{2}}$	Albarado R J	13.70
26Jun04 ^{3}Bel^{1}	Gold Joy	L b	2	122	6	9	$10^{\frac{1}{2}}$	$10^{1\frac{1}{2}}$	$10^{\frac{1}{2}}$	$10^{1\frac{1}{4}}$	Velasquez C	46.00
19Jun04 ^{8}Crc^{1}	Fire Path	bf	2	118	7	10	11	11	11	11	Castellano J J	51.75

OFF AT 4:48 Start Good . Won driving. Track fast.

TIME :22^{1}, :45^{2}, :57^{1}, 1:09^{1} (:22.29, :45.58, :57.26, 1:09.32)

$2 Mutuel Prices:

8 – AFLEET ALEX	8.00	4.90	3.60
3 – FLAMENCO		7.50	5.00
9 – CONSOLIDATOR			2.90

$2 EXACTA 8–3 PAID $47.20 $2 TRIFECTA 8–3–9 PAID $169.50

B. c, (May), by Northern Afleet – Maggy Hawk , by Hawkster . Trainer Ritchey Tim F. Bred by John Martin Silvertand (Fla).

AFLEET ALEX was unhurried while racing well off the rail along the backstretch, rapidly gained while circling five wide on the turn, charged to the front in upper stretch then drew off with authority under steady right hand encouragement. FLAMENCO raced up close early between horses, dropped back a bit on the turn then battled back through the stretch to gain the place. CONSOLIDATOR stalked the leaders while four wide for a half and closed late from outside to gain a share. WINNING EXPRESSION pressed the pace in the two path to the far turn, gained a slim lead on the turn then weakened from his early efforts. DEPARTING NOW raced just off the pace while saving ground, made a run along the rail to threaten in upper stretch and lacked a strong closing bid. LUNARPAL set or forced the pace along the rail to the top of the stretch and tired. SMOKESCREEN was outrun for a half after breaking awkwardly and failed to menace thereafter. CALYPSO BAND failed to mount a serious rally while between rivals. MAXIMUS C was outrun early, rallied mildly while five wide on the turn and lacked a strong closing bid. GOLD JOY bumped at the start, was never a factor. FIRE PATH broke inward bumping with GOLD JOY at the start and was never close thereafter.

Owners– 1, Cash is King Stable; 2, Peachtree Stable; 3, Lewis Robert B and Beverly J; 4, Flying Zee Stable; 5, Dogwood Stable; 6, Heiligbrodt Racing Stable; 7, New Farm; 8, Evans Edward P; 9, Pacella William Romans Dale L Bonomo George Schwed Ronald T; 10, Taylor Kenneth and Salzman Sr John E; 11, Buckram Oak Farm

Trainers– 1, Ritchey Tim F; 2, Pletcher Todd A; 3, Lukas D Wayne; 4, Serpe Philip M; 5, Maker Rebecca; 6, Asmussen Steven M; 7, Perkins Ben W Jr; 8, Hennig Mark; 9, Romans Dale; 10, Salzman Timothy; 11, Mikhalides George

EIGHTH RACE
Saratoga
JULY 30, 2004

1⅛ MILES. (Inner Turf) (1.461) 46TH RUNNING OF THE BERNARD BARUCH HANDICAP. Grade II. Purse $150,000 INNER TURF (Up To $28,500 NYSBFOA) A HANDICAP FOR THREE YEAR OLDS AND UPWARD. By subscription of $150 each, which should accompany the nomination; $750 to pass the entry box, $750 to start. The purse to be divided 60% to the winner, 20% to second, 10% tothird, 5% to fourth, 3% to fifth and 2% divided equally among remaining finishers. A Trophy will be presented to the winning owner. The New York Racing Association reserves the right to transfer this race to the Main Track. In the event that this race istaken off the turf, it may be subject to downgrading upon review by the Graded Stakes Committee. Closed Saturday, July 17, 2004 with 37 Nominations. (Rail at 9 feet).

Value of Race: $150,000 Winner $90,000; second $30,000; third $15,000; fourth $7,500; fifth $4,500; sixth $1,500; seventh $1,500. Mutuel Pool $582,238.00 Exacta Pool $489,178.00 Trifecta Pool $359,197.00

Last Raced	Horse	M/Eqt.	A.	Wt	PP	St	¼	½	¾	Str	Fin	Jockey	Odds $1
10Jly04 ^{8}Bel^{3}	Silver Tree	L	4	116	5	6	$6^{3\frac{1}{2}}$	6^{7}	3^{2}	1^{hd}	1^{nk}	Bailey J D	2.75
3Jly04 ^{10}Mth^{3}	Nothing to Lose	L b	4	117	6	5	3^{1}	$3^{\frac{1}{2}}$	2^{hd}	2^{hd}	$2^{\frac{1}{2}}$	Velazquez J R	1.05
9Jly04 ^{6}Bel^{3}	Irish Colonial	L	5	113	2	2	$5^{\frac{1}{2}}$	5^{hd}	4^{1}	4^{hd}	3^{nk}	Samyn J L	13.10
4Jun04 ^{7}Bel^{1}	Union Place	L	5	113	7	4	1^{1}	$1^{1\frac{1}{2}}$	$1^{\frac{1}{2}}$	$3^{1\frac{1}{2}}$	$4^{1\frac{3}{4}}$	Castellano J J	9.80
4Jly04 ^{7}AP^{7}	Quest Star	L b	5	114	1	1	4^{hd}	$4^{\frac{1}{2}}$	$5^{3\frac{1}{2}}$	5^{3}	5^{hd}	Day P	5.30
27Jun04 ^{3}Bel^{4}	Quiet Ruler	L	6	114	3	7	7	7	7	6^{6}	$6^{5\frac{1}{4}}$	Albarado R J	25.00
20Jun04 ^{5}Bel^{2}	Mr. Light-Arg	L	5	115	4	3	2^{hd}	2^{hd}	6^{3}	7	7	Migliore R	17.50

OFF AT 4:47 Start Good . Won driving. Course yielding.

TIME :24^{4}, :49^{1}, 1:13^{1}, 1:37^{1}, 1:49^{3} (:24.84, :49.26, 1:13.21, 1:37.28, 1:49.66)

$2 Mutuel Prices:				
	6 – SILVER TREE	7.50	3.10	2.60
	7 – NOTHING TO LOSE		2.60	2.20
	3 – IRISH COLONIAL			3.40

$2 EXACTA 6–7 PAID $12.80 $2 TRIFECTA 6–7–3 PAID $89.50

Ch. c, (Feb), by Hennessy – Blue Begum , by With Approval . Trainer Mott William I. Bred by Vegso Racing Stable (Fla).

SILVER TREE was rated in good position just off the early pace, moved up a bit leaving the backstretch, ranged up three wide to challenge leaving the turn, battled gamely from outside into deep stretch and prevailed after a long drive. NOTHING TO LOSE moved up three wide on the first turn, forced the pace from outside for five furlongs, engaged UNION PLACE for the lead on the turn, fought heads apart between horses through the lane but couldn't hold the winner safe. IRISH COLONIAL was unhurried early, raced in the middle of the pack for six furlongs, circled four wide to launch his bid on the turn then rallied belatedly in the middle of the track. UNION PLACE angled in after gaining the early advantage, set the pace along the rail into midstretch then yielded grudgingly. QUEST STAR checked slightly on the first turn, was rated just off the pace along the rail, made a run along the inside to reach contention in upper stretch then lacked a strong closing bid. QUIET RULER trailed to the turn then rallied mildly from outside. MR. LIGHT (ARG) hit the rail causing the rider to briefly lose his irons on the first turn, raced up close between horses, was in traffic on the far turn then steadily tired thereafter. There was a Stewards' inquiry focusing on the incident on the first turn before the result was declared official.

Owners– 1, Vegso Peter; 2, Ramsey Kenneth L and Sarah K; 3, Blue Sky Farm and Martin Fred; 4, Sorokolit William A Sr; 5, Mansell Stables LLC; 6, Sarf Leslie and Old Brookside Farm; 7, Mack Earle I

Trainers– 1, Mott William I; 2, Frankel Robert; 3, Schulhofer Randy; 4, Schulhofer Randy; 5, Walden W Elliott; 6, Mueller Russell; 7, Penna Angel Jr

Scratched– Evening Attire , Gygistar

EIGHTH RACE
Arlington
JULY 31, 2004

1$\frac{3}{16}$ MILES. (1.55) 72ND RUNNING OF THE WASHINGTON PARK HANDICAP. Grade II. Purse $350,000 FOR THREE-YEAR-OLDS AND UPWARD. By subscription of $250 each, which should accompany the nomination. A Supplementary Nomination of $12,000 may be made on Saturday, July 24, 2004, which includes entry and starting fees. Original nominees to pay $2,500 to pass the entry box and an additional $2,500 to start, with $350,000 Guaranteed, of which $210,000 to the winner; $70,000 to second; $38,500 to third; $21,000 to fourth and $10,500 to fifth. WEIGHTS: Sunday, July 25, 2004. This event will be limited to fourteen (14) starters. Preference will be Highweights (on the scale). *Total Earnings in 2004 will be used to determine the order of preference of horses assigned equal weight (on the scale). Failure to draw into this race at time of entry cancels all fees with the exception of the nominating fee(s). Starters to be named through the entry box by usual time of closing. Two (2) horses having common ties through ownership cannot start to the exclusion of a single ownership interest. Trophy to the owner of the winner. Closed July 21, 2004 with 14 nominations.

Value of Race: $350,000 Winner $210,000; second $70,000; third $38,500; fourth $21,000; fifth $10,500. Mutuel Pool $214,749.00 Exacta Pool $122,575.00 Trifecta Pool $49,272.00 Superfecta Pool $18,051.00

Last Raced	Horse	M/Eqt.	A.	Wt	PP	St	¼	½	¾	Str	Fin	Jockey	Odds $1
16Jly04 ^{5}Bel^{1}	Eye of the Tiger	L	4	116	5	4	3^{1}	3^{hd}	$3^{\frac{1}{2}}$	1^{hd}	1^{hd}	Razo E Jr	6.80
10Jly04 ^{9}Hol^{2}	Olmodavor	L b	5	121	4	5	5	5	5	$4^{1\frac{1}{2}}$	$2^{1\frac{1}{2}}$	McKee J	2.10
12Jun04 ^{7}Bel^{5}	Congrats	L	4	116	1	1	$1^{\frac{1}{2}}$	$1^{\frac{1}{2}}$	$1^{\frac{1}{2}}$	$2^{\frac{1}{2}}$	3^{nk}	Douglas R R	3.80
3Jly04 ^{7}Bel^{4}	Colonial Colony	L f	6	118	3	3	$4^{\frac{1}{2}}$	4^{2}	4^{1}	5	4^{hd}	Bejarano R	1.60
17Jly04 ^{7}Del^{2}	The Lady's Groom	L b	4	118	2	2	2^{1}	2^{1}	$2^{1\frac{1}{2}}$	3^{hd}	5	Arroyo N Jr	4.80

OFF AT 4:35 Start Good . Won driving. Track fast.

TIME :24^{1}, :48^{2}, 1:12^{4}, 1:36^{3}, 1:56^{4} (:24.29, :48.54, 1:12.92, 1:36.68, 1:56.87)

$2 Mutuel Prices:				
	5 – EYE OF THE TIGER	15.60	5.40	3.40
	4 – OLMODAVOR		3.40	2.80
	1 – CONGRATS			3.20

$2 EXACTA 5–4 PAID $60.20 $2 TRIFECTA 5–4–1 PAID $228.80
$2 SUPERFECTA 5–4–1–3 PAID $282.00

B. c, (Apr), by American Chance – Dial a Trick , by Phone Trick . Trainer McLaughlin Kiaran P. Bred by John D Gunther (Ky).

EYE OF THE TIGER was five wide on the first turn, raced close up four wide, rallied to get a head in front near the furlong marker then resisted stubbornly in the run to the wire. OLMODAVOR raced four wide around the first turn, continued outside while trailing through not far back, was brushed by EYE OF THE TIGER nearing the quarter pole, came four wide into the stretch and rallied but just missed while drifting out. CONGRATS went up from the inside to make a short early lead while kept off the rail, set a pressured pace, could not resist the winner and lost the place late. COLONIAL COLONY was void of early speed while not far back, saved ground to the stretch then had no response when asked for his best. THE LADY'S GROOM went up to press the pace from off the rail, continued forwardly to the stretch then weakened a bit in the drive. THERE WAS A CLAIM OF FOUL BY THE RIDER OF OLMODAVOR AGAINST EYE OF THE TIGER ALLEGING INTERFERENCE NEARING THE QUARTER POLE BUT IT WAS NOT ALLOWED.

Owners– 1, Gunther John D; 2, Wertheimer and Frere; 3, Adele B Dilschneider and Claiborne Farm Mrs A B Hancock; 4, Lakeside Farms LLC; 5, Murphy John D Sr

Trainers– 1, McLaughlin Kiaran P; 2, Mandella Richard; 3, McGaughey III Claude R; 4, Bindner Walter M Jr; 5, Gorham Michael E

$1 Pick Three (5/8/13–6/11–6) Paid $37.40 ; Pick Three Pool $23,211 .

FOURTH RACE
Del Mar
JULY 31, 2004

1 MILE. (Turf) (1.32^{1}) 36TH RUNNING OF THE SAN CLEMENTE HANDICAP. Grade II. Purse $150,000 FOR FILLIES, THREE-YEAR-OLDS. By subscription of $150 each, which shall accompany the nomination, or by supplementary nomination of $1,500 each by Sunday, July 25, $500 to pass the entry box and $1,000 additional to start, with $150,000 Guaranteed, of which $90,000 to first, $30,000 to second, $18,000 to third, $9,000 to fourth and $3,000 to fifth. Weights Monday, July 26. High weights preferred. A trophy will be presented to the owner of the winner. Closed Thursday, July 22, 2004 with 10 nominations.(Rail at 7 feet).

Value of Race: $150,000 Winner $90,000; second $30,000; third $18,000; fourth $9,000; fifth $3,000. Mutuel Pool $876,087.00 Exacta Pool $460,004.00 Quinella Pool $42,776.00

Last Raced	Horse	M/Eqt.	A.	Wt	PP	St	¼	½	¾	Str	Fin	Jockey	Odds $1
13Jun04 4Crc1	Sweet Win	LB	3	114	5	3	$3^{1/2}$	3^{2}	3^{3}	$2^{1 1/2}$	1^{hd}	Espinoza V	8.30
3Jly04 8Hol1	Miss Vegas-Ire	LB	3	121	2	1	1^{1}	1^{2}	1^{2}	1^{1}	2no	Flores D R	0.40
4Jun04 10Bel6	Victory U. S. A.	LB	3	119	1	2	$4^{3 1/2}$	4^{hd}	4^{3}	3^{hd}	$3^{4 1/2}$	Nakatani C S	4.40
15Jly04 7Hol3	Bonaire-GB	LB	3	117	3	4	$2^{2 1/2}$	2^{8}	$2^{2 1/2}$	$4^{2 1/2}$	4^{2}	Desormeaux K J	4.90
9Jly04 7Hol5	Shadow of Mine	LB b	3	113	4	5	5	5	5	5	5	Baze T C	25.70

OFF AT 3:35 Start Good . Won driving. Course firm.

TIME :23^{2}, :46^{2}, 1:10, 1:22^{1}, 1:34 (:23.54, :46.50, 1:10.12, 1:22.29, 1:34.11)

$2 Mutuel Prices:				
	5 – SWEET WIN	18.60	3.40	2.10
	2 – MISS VEGAS–IRE		2.20	2.10
	1 – VICTORY U. S. A.			2.10

$1 EXACTA 5–2 PAID $17.80 $2 QUINELLA 2–5 PAID $8.40

Ch. f, (Feb), by King of Kings–Ire – Win for Juno , by St. Jovite . Trainer Mullins Jeff. Bred by Sez Who Thoroughbreds & Bonnie Heath &Farm (Ky).

SWEET WIN settled outside a rival then a bit off the rail, came three deep into the stretch, altered path inside in midstretch and finished gamely along the rail under left handed urging to narrowly prevail. MISS VEGAS (IRE) took the early lead and angled in on the first turn, set the pace inside under a long hold, came off the rail into the stretch, drifted out in midstretch and held on gamely until the final strides while between horses late. VICTORY U. S. A. saved ground chasing the pace, dropped back on the backstretch, came out in upper stretch and closed willingly three deep on the wire. BONAIRE (GB) stalked a bit off the rail then inside, came out into the stretch, angled to the inside in upper stretch and weakened. SHADOW OF MINE allowed to settle a bit off the rail, angled in on the backstretch, came out into the stretch and lacked the needed rally.

Owners– 1, Fogelson Gayle; 2, Gann Edmund A; 3, Van Meter Thomas F II; 4, Lael Stables; 5, Nichols Thomas L

Trainers– 1, Mullins Jeff; 2, Frankel Robert; 3, Baffert Bob; 4, Drysdale Neil; 5, Greely C Beau

---

$2 Daily Double (1–5) Paid $273.60 ; Daily Double Pool $49,353 .
$1 Pick Three (2–1–5) Paid $637.20 ; Pick Three Pool $120,510 .

SEVENTH RACE
Saratoga
JULY 31, 2004

1⅛ MILES. (Turf) (1.45^{2}) 5TH RUNNING OF THE DIANA HANDICAP. Grade I. Purse $500,000 MELLON TURF. (UP TO 55,000 NYSBFOA) FOR FILLIES AND MARES THREE YEARS OLD AND UPWARD. By subscription of $500 each, which should accompany the nomination; $2,500 to pass the entry box, $2,500 to start. The purse to be divided 60% to the owner of the winner, 20% to second, 10% to third, 5% to fourth, 3% to fifth and 2% divided equally among remaining finishers. Three year olds, 118 lbs.; Older, 123 lbs. Non–winners of a Grade 1 twice on the turf in 2003–04 or a Grade 2 twice on the turf in 2004 allowed 3 lbs.; a Grade 1 in 2003–04 or a Grade 2 in 2004, 5 lbs. Trophies will be presented to the winning owner, trainer and jockey. The New York Racing Association reserves the right to transfer this race to the Main Track. In the event that this race is taken off the turf, it may be subject to downgrading upon review by the Graded Stakes Committee. Closed Saturday, July 17, 2004 with 21 Nominations. (If the Stewards consider it inadvisable to run this race on the turf course, this race will be run at One Mile and One Eighth on the main track.).

Value of Race: $500,000 Winner $300,000; second $100,000; third $50,000; fourth $25,000; fifth $15,000; sixth $5,000; seventh $5,000. Mutuel Pool $1,101,962.00 Exacta Pool $823,986.00 Trifecta Pool $613,969.00

Last Raced	Horse	M/Eqt.	A.	Wt	PP	St	¼	½	¾	Str	Fin	Jockey	Odds $1
5Jly04 9Bel1	Wonder Again	L	5	120	4	2	$3^{1/2}$	3^{1}	$4^{1/2}$	1^{5}	$1^{5 3/4}$	Prado E S	3.10
26Jun04 9CD5	Riskaverse	L	5	118	7	4	4^{3}	$4^{1/2}$	$3^{1/2}$	4^{2}	$2^{2 1/4}$	Day P	9.40
10Jly04 9Mth1	Ocean Drive	L	4	118	2	1	2^{2}	$2^{1 1/2}$	$2^{1/2}$	2^{hd}	$3^{2 1/4}$	Velazquez J R	8.00
10Jly04 8Cnl7	Sand Springs	L	4	118	1	3	$1^{3 1/2}$	1^{6}	$1^{1 1/2}$	$3^{1/2}$	$4^{1 1/4}$	Samyn J L	17.00
5Jun04 8Bel1	Intercontinentl-GB	L	4	120	3	7	7	$5^{1/2}$	$5^{4 1/2}$	$5^{5 1/2}$	$5^{1 1/4}$	Bailey J D	0.80
5Jly04 9Bel3	Spice Island	L b	5	118	5	5	5^{hd}	6^{hd}	7	7	$6^{1 3/4}$	Migliore R	13.00
26Jun04 9CD2	Halory Leigh	L	4	118	6	6	$6^{1 1/2}$	7	$6^{1 1/2}$	$6^{1/2}$	7	Albarado R J	26.25

OFF AT 4:14 Start Good . Won driving. Course yielding.

TIME :23^{3}, :47^{3}, 1:11^{3}, 1:36^{3}, 1:48^{4} (:23.75, :47.61, 1:11.71, 1:36.63, 1:48.99)

$2 Mutuel Prices:				
	4 – WONDER AGAIN	8.20	4.50	3.50
	7 – RISKAVERSE		7.60	5.60
	2 – OCEAN DRIVE			4.60

$2 EXACTA 4–7 PAID $57.50 $2 TRIFECTA 4–7–2 PAID $248.50

B. m, (Feb), by Silver Hawk – Ameriflora , by Danzig . Trainer Toner James J. Bred by Phillips Racing Partnership & John &Phillips (Ky).

WONDER AGAIN settled in good position in the early stages, raced just off while pace while saving ground along the backstretch, waited patiently while continuing to save ground on the turn, slipped through along the inside to take charge in upper stretch then drew off under a vigorous hand ride. RISKAVERSE raced in the middle of the pack for five furlongs, launched a rally three wide on the run, closed the gap in upper stretch and finished willingly to clearly best the others. OCEAN DRIVE was rated just behind the early leader, steadily gained in the two path on the turn, made a run to challenge approaching the stretch but couldn't sustain her bid. SAND SPRINGS sprinted clear in the early stages, extended her lead along the backstretch, set the pace for seven furlongs, drifted off the rail while battling heads apart at the top of the stretch and weakened from her early efforts. INTERCONTINENTAL (GB) was taken well back in the early stages, trailed for nearly a half, gained some ground while four wide nearing the far turn then lacked the needed response when called upon. SPICE ISLAND failed to mount a serious rally while saving ground throughout. HALORY LEIGH was outrun for six furlongs, swung three wide on the turn and lacked a strong closing response.

Owners– 1, Phillips Joan G and John W; 2, Fox Ridge Farm Inc; 3, Baskin Bonnie Baskin Sy; 4, Willmott Stables Inc; 5, Juddmonte Farms Inc; 6, Denlea Park Ltd; 7, Crawford Jerry Gannon Matt Grask Charlie

Trainers– 1, Toner James J; 2, Kelly Patrick J; 3, Pletcher Todd A; 4, Reinstedler Anthony; 5, Frankel Robert; 6, Pregman John S Jr; 7, Romans Dale

Scratched– Buy the Sport (21Jul04 7Bel7) , Nevermore (23May04 7Bel1) , Alchemist (05Jul04 9Bel6)

$2 Daily Double (3–4) Paid $25.80 ; Daily Double Pool $187,007 .
$2 Pick Three (7–3–4) Paid $751.00 ; Pick Three Pool $145,697 .

EIGHTH RACE
Saratoga
JULY 31, 2004

7 FURLONGS. (1.20^{2}) 78TH RUNNING OF THE TEST. Grade I. Purse $250,000 (UP TO 37,500 NYSBFOA) FOR FILLIES THREE YEARS OLD. By subscription of $250 each, which should accompany the nomination; $1,250 to pass the entry box, $1,250 to start. The purse to be divided 60% to the winner, 20% to second, 10% to third, 5% to fourth, 3% to fifth and 2% divided equally among remaining finishers. 122 lbs. Non-winners of a Grade 1 in 2004 allowed 2 lbs.; a Grade 1 in 2003 or Grade 2 in 2004, 4 lbs.; $50,000; or three races, 6 lbs. (Maiden, claiming or restricted allowance races not considered). Trophies will be presented to the winning owner, trainer and jockey. Closed Saturday, July 17, 2004 with 26 Nominations.

Value of Race: $250,000 Winner $150,000; second $50,000; third $25,000; fourth $12,500; fifth $7,500; sixth $715; seventh $715; eighth $715; ninth $715; tenth $715; eleventh $715; twelfth $710. Mutuel Pool $1,128,269.00 Exacta Pool $900,112.00 Trifecta Pool $610,960.00

Last Raced	Horse	M/Eqt.	A.	Wt	PP	St	¼	½	Str	Fin	Jockey	Odds $1
26Jun04 ^{9}Bel^{6}	Society Selection	L	3	120	7	11	10^{hd}	6^{5}	2^{6}	1^{6¼}	Prado E S	3.35
3Jly04 ^{8}Bel^{7}	Bending Strings	L	3	120	6	5	12	9½	3½	2^{3¾}	Day P	13.00
3Jly04 ^{8}Bel^{3}	Forest Music	L f	3	118	12	1	1½	1^{3½}	1^{hd}	3^{4¼}	Bridgmohan S X	12.10
3Jly04 ^{8}Bel^{1}	Friendly Michelle	L b	3	122	10	4	9^{3}	4^{hd}	6½	4^{2¼}	Bailey J D	2.40
2Jly04 ^{9}PrM^{2}	Prospective Saint	L	3	116	9	2	4½	2^{1½}	5½	5^{hd}	Albarado R J	26.50
10Jly04 ^{5}Hol^{3}	Elusive Diva	L b	3	118	8	6	7½	5^{1½}	7^{hd}	6^{nk}	Chavez J F	9.40
10Jly04 ^{8}Crc^{1}	Dazzle Me	L	3	118	5	7	3½	3½	4½	7^{nk}	Sellers S J	5.40
3Jly04 ^{8}Bel^{5}	She's a Mugs	L	3	116	4	12	11^{hd}	8^{hd}	9^{3½}	8^{5}	Velasquez C	44.50
10Jly04 ^{8}Crc^{2}	Reforest	L	3	116	1	10	6½	11^{8}	10^{2}	9^{nk}	Migliore R	19.70
12Jly04 ^{8}Del^{1}	Humor Me Molly	L	3	118	11	3	8^{hd}	7^{hd}	11^{15}	10¾	Velazquez J R	19.40
3Jly04 ^{8}Bel^{2}	Feline Story	L	3	118	3	8	5^{hd}	10½	8½	11^{26¼}	Castellano J J	13.30
12Jun04 ^{7}Mth^{5}	Rodeo Licious	L f	3	118	2	9	2½	12	12	12	Gryder A T	53.50

OFF AT 4:46 Start Good . Won driving. Track muddy.

TIME :21^{2}, :44, 1:10^{1}, 1:23^{3} (:21.51, :44.19, 1:10.22, 1:23.69)

$2 Mutuel Prices:

7 – SOCIETY SELECTION	8.70	5.50	3.90
6 – BENDING STRINGS		11.00	7.60
12 – FOREST MUSIC			9.30

$2 EXACTA 7–6 PAID $106.50 $2 TRIFECTA 7–6–12 PAID $1,307.00

B. f, (Apr), by Coronado's Quest – Love That Jazz , by Dixieland Band . Trainer Jerkens H Allen. Bred by Marjorie Cowan & Irving Cowan (Ky).

SOCIETY SELECTION checked slightly while breaking outward at the start, raced far back through the opening quarter, rapidly closed the gap while rallying five wide on the turn, charged past FOREST MUSIC to take command in upper stretch then drew away under steady left hand encouragement. BENDING STRINGS trailed along the backstretch, was outrun while racing wide for a half, circled six wide while gaining at the top of the stretch then closed late in the middle of the track to best the others. FOREST MUSIC sprinted clear soon after the start, extended her lead midway on the turn, set the pace along the inside into upper stretch and weakened from her early efforts. FRIENDLY MICHELLE ducked out along the backstretch, raced well back while five wide to the turn then failed to threaten while improving her position. PROSPECTIVE SAINT settled just off the early pace, took up chase after the leader in the two path on the turn then faded in the stretch. ELUSIVE DIVA raced in the middle of the pack between horses and lacked the needed response when called upon. DAZZLE ME raced up close along the rail for five furlongs and steadily tired thereafter. SHE'S A MUGS bumped at the start, raced five wide to the turn, checked while bumping with BENDING STRINGS at the top of the stretch and lacked a further response. REFOREST steadied behind a tiring rival on the far turn and failed to mount a serious rally thereafter. HUMOR ME MOLLY was never a factor while four wide. FELINE STORY bumped at the start, checked between horses on the far turn, never reached contention. RODEO LICIOUS pressed the early pace along the rail then took up in tight while giving way on the far turn.

Owners– 1, Cowan Marjorie and Irving M; 2, Gunther John D; 3, Gill Michael J; 4, Friendly Ed; 5, Stuart John D; 6, Branch Allen Konecny John William Konecny Doris Branch Susan; 7, Padua Stables; 8, Lucky Shamrock Stable; 9, Gann Edmund A; 10, Stefanski Stan; 11, Robsham Mrs E P; 12, Our Blue Streaks Stable

Trainers– 1, Jerkens H Allen; 2, McLaughlin Kiaran P; 3, Shuman Mark; 4, Baffert Bob; 5, Byrne Patrick B; 6, Glatt Mark; 7, Asmussen Steven M; 8, Zito Nicholas P; 9, Frankel Robert; 10, Iwinski Allen; 11, Hough Stanley M; 12, Levine Bruce N

$2 Pick Three (3–4–7) Paid $101.00 ; Pick Three Pool $189,195 .

NINTH RACE
Saratoga
AUGUST 1, 2004

1⅛ MILES. (1.47) 51ST RUNNING OF THE GO FOR WAND HANDICAP. Grade I. Purse $250,000 (UP TO 37,500 NYSBFOA) A HANDICAP FOR FILLIES AND MARES THREE YEARS OLD AND UPWARD. By subscription of $250 each, which should accompany the nomination; $1,250 to pass the entry box, $1,250 to start. The purse to be divided 60% to the winner, 20% to second, 10% to third, 5% to fourth, 3% to fifth and 2% divided equally among remaining finishers. Trophies will be presented to the winning owner, trainer and jockey. Closed Saturday, July 17, 2004 with 15 Nominations.

Value of Race: $245,000 Winner $150,000; second $50,000; third $25,000; fourth $12,500; fifth $7,500. Mutuel Pool $776,999.00 Exacta Pool $524,323.00 Trifecta Pool $354,421.00

Last Raced	Horse	M/Eqt.	A.	Wt	PP	St	¼	½	¾	Str	Fin	Jockey	Odds $1
19Jun04 ^{9}Bel^{4}	Azeri	L	6	120	5	4	1^{1½}	1½	1½	1^{hd}	1^{1¾}	Day P	2.95
19Jun04 ^{9}Bel^{1}	Sightseek	L	5	122	4	1	2^{hd}	2½	2^{1½}	2^{3½}	2^{2}	Bailey J D	0.75
19Jun04 ^{9}Bel^{2}	Storm Flag Flying	L	4	117	1	2	3^{1½}	3^{1½}	4^{2½}	3^{3½}	3^{7}	Velazquez J R	3.05
10Jly04 ^{9}ElP^{2}	Mayo On the Side	L bf	5	115	2	5	4^{hd}	5	5	4^{2½}	4^{21¼}	Albarado R J	15.70
4Jly04 ^{10}Mth^{1}	La Reason	L f	4	113	3	3	5	4½	3^{hd}	5	5	Prado E S	21.00

OFF AT 5:21 Start Good . Won driving. Track fast.

TIME :24^{1}, :47^{3}, 1:10^{4}, 1:35, 1:47^{4} (:24.33, :47.75, 1:10.90, 1:35.12, 1:47.86)

$2 Mutuel Prices:

6 – AZERI	7.90	3.10	2.10
5 – SIGHTSEEK		2.40	2.10
1 – STORM FLAG FLYING			2.10

$2 EXACTA 6–5 PAID $15.00 $2 TRIFECTA 6–5–1 PAID $24.00

Ch. m, (May), by Jade Hunter – Zodiac Miss-Aus , by Ahonoora-GB . Trainer Lukas D Wayne. Bred by Allen E Paulson (Ky).

AZERI sprinted clear soon after the start, moved well off the rail leaving the first turn, set the pace in hand while in the five path along the backstretch, was rated on the front while continuing wide through the turn, dug in when challenged in upper stretch, repulsed a bid from SIGHTSEEK leaving the furlong marker then edged away under steady left hand encouragement. SIGHTSEEK settled just off the early pace, moved to the outside of AZERI while stalking along the backstretch, launched a bid while in the six path leaving the far turn, made a run to threaten at the top of the stretch, drew on nearly even terms with the winner in upper stretch but couldn't stay with that one through the final eighth. STORM FLAG FLYING checked slightly along the inside on the first turn, raced in good position while three wide for six furlongs, took up chase after the leaders along the inside on the turn, drifted out while rallying mildly in upper stretch then lacked a strong closing bid. MAYO ON THE SIDE checked slightly after breaking slowly, was unhurried for seven furlongs while three wide then lacked the needed response when called upon. LA REASON settled in good position while saving ground, lodged a mild rally along the inside on the turn then flattened out.

Owners– 1, Allen E Paulson Living Trust; 2, Juddmonte Farms Inc; 3, Phipps Ogden Mills et al; 4, Lothenbach Robert J; 5, Kirby Tommy Kirby Ronald

Trainers– 1, Lukas D Wayne; 2, Frankel Robert; 3, McGaughey III Claude R; 4, Nafzger Carl A; 5, Vance David R

Scratched– Board Elligible (20Jun04 ^{6}Bel^{7})

EIGHTH RACE
Del Mar
AUGUST 1, 2004

$1\frac{1}{16}$ MILES. (1.40) 63RD RUNNING OF THE SAN DIEGO HANDICAP. Grade II. Purse $250,000 FOR THREE-YEAR-OLDS AND UPWARD. By subscription of $250 each, which shall accompany the nomination, or by supplementary nomination of $2,500 each by Sunday, July 25, $2,500 additional to start, with $250,000 Guaranteed, of which $150,000 to first, $50,000to second, $30,000 to third, $15,000 to fourth and $5,000 to fifth. Weights Monday, July 26. A trophy will be presented to the owner of the winner. Nominations closed Thursday, July 22, 2004 with 11 nominations.

Value of Race: $250,000 Winner $150,000; second $50,000; third $30,000; fourth $15,000; fifth $5,000. Mutuel Pool $593,903.00 Exacta Pool $296,254.00 Quinella Pool $26,819.00 Trifecta Pool $309,120.00 Superfecta Pool $151,138.00

Last Raced	Horse	M/Eqt.	A.	Wt	PP	St	¼	½	¾	Str	Fin	Jockey	Odds $1
28May04 ^{5}Hol^{1}	Choctaw Nation	LB b	4	114	1	4	6^{2}	6^{2}	6^{3}	2^{hd}	$1^{\frac{3}{4}}$	Espinoza V	6.30
27Mar04 ^{8}NAS^{1}	Pleasantly Perfect	LB b	6	124	6	5	4^{1}	1^{hd}	2^{hd}	$1^{1\frac{1}{2}}$	2^{5}	Smith M E	0.60
27Mar04 ^{9}NAS^{6}	During	LB b	4	118	2	1	$1^{\frac{1}{2}}$	2^{hd}	1^{hd}	3^{2}	$3^{1\frac{1}{2}}$	Nakatani C S	4.30
3Jly04 ^{9}Hol^{8}	Reba's Gold	LB b	7	116	7	3	$5^{4\frac{1}{2}}$	5^{6}	$5^{2\frac{1}{2}}$	$6^{3\frac{1}{2}}$	$4^{\frac{1}{2}}$	Flores D R	17.90
4Jly04 ^{8}Hol^{3}	Night Patrol	LB b	8	112	4	7	2^{1}	$4^{1\frac{1}{2}}$	$4^{\frac{1}{2}}$	5^{hd}	$5^{\frac{1}{2}}$	Baze T C	20.50
3Jly04 ^{9}Hol^{6}	Taste of Paradise	LB	5	115	3	2	$3^{\frac{1}{2}}$	$3^{1\frac{1}{2}}$	3^{2}	4^{1}	$6^{4\frac{1}{2}}$	Court J K	6.50
2Jly04 ^{2}Crc^{5}	Decorador-Arg	LB bf	5	113	5	6	7	7	7	7	7	Almeida G F	35.50

OFF AT 5:41 Start Good For All But NIGHT PATROL. Won driving. Track fast.

TIME :24, :47^{2}, 1:11^{1}, 1:36, 1:42^{1} (:24.07, :47.50, 1:11.25, 1:36.12, 1:42.32)

$2 Mutuel Prices:			
1 – CHOCTAW NATION	14.60	3.40	2.10
7 – PLEASANTLY PERFECT		2.20	2.10
2 – DURING			2.10

$1 EXACTA 1-7 PAID $13.80 $2 QUINELLA 1-7 PAID $9.20
$1 TRIFECTA 1-7-2 PAID $33.90 $1 SUPERFECTA 1-7-2-8 PAID $148.10

B. g, (Mar), by Louis Quatorze – Melisma , by Well Decorated . Trainer Mullins Jeff. Bred by Loch Lea Farm Inc (Ky).

CHOCTAW NATION unhurried inside then a bit off the rail, moved up outside on the second turn and four wide into the stretch, rallied under steady left handed urging to gain the lead in deep stretch and gamely prevailed. PLEASANTLY PERFECT stalked off the rail then steadied in tight on the first turn, pulled his way up three deep between foes on the backstretch, and briefly put his head in front, dueled between rivals into and on the second turn, regained the advantage a quarter mile out, inched clear in the stretch, fought back toward the inside in deep stretch and continued willingly to the wire. DURING sped to the early lead a bit off the rail, dueled between horses on the first turn then just off the inside on the backstretch, found the fence and fought back on the second turn, then could not match the top pair in the final furlong but held third. REBA'S GOLD four wide into the first turn, stalked outside then off the rail, was outside a rival into the stretch, came out and lacked the needed rally. NIGHT PATROL stumbled to his nose at the start, went up inside to press the pace on the first turn, stalked along the rail on the backstretch and second turn, came out in midstretch and could not summon the necessary response. TASTE OF PARADISE stalked outside then moved up four wide on the backstretch, dueled three deep into and on the second turn and weakened in the stretch. DECORADOR (ARG) unhurried off the rail then along the inside, came out into the stretch and was outrun.

Owners– 1, Bone Robert D; 2, Diamond A Racing Corporation; 3, McIngvale James; 4, Creston Farms; 5, Everest Stables Inc; 6, Bloom David B; 7, Giussepe Iadisernia

Trainers– 1, Mullins Jeff; 2, Mandella Richard; 3, Baffert Bob; 4, Hendricks Dan L; 5, Polanco Marcelo; 6, Pearson Molly J; 7, Reviriego Juan

Scratched– Nose The Trade (GB) (03Jul04 ^{9}Hol^{9})

$2 Daily Double (7–1) Paid $121.20 ; Daily Double Pool $42,733 .
$1 Pick Three (2–7–1) Paid $3,246.40 ; Pick Three Pool $90,042 .

EIGHTH RACE
Saratoga
AUGUST 2, 2004

1 1/16 MILES. (Turf) (1.384) 9TH RUNNING OF THE LAKE GEORGE. Grade III. Purse $100,000 MELLON TURF. (UP TO $19,000 NYSBFOA) FOR FILLIES THREE YEARS OLD. By subscription of $100 each, which should accompany the nomination; $500 to pass the entry box; $500 to start, with $100,000 added. The added money and all fees to be divided 60% to the winner, 20% to second, 10% to third, 5% to fourth, 3% to fifth and 2% divided equally among remaining finishers. 122 lbs. Non-winners of a graded sweepstake on the turf in 2004 allowed 3 lbs.; $45,000 on the turf, 5 lbs.; two races, 7 lbs. (maiden, claiming, or restricted allowance races not considered). A trophy will be presented to the winning owner. The New York Racing Association reserves the right to transfer this race to the main track. In the event that this race is taken off the turf, it may be subject to downgrading upon review by the Graded Stakes Committee. Closed Saturday, July 17, 2004 with 39 Nominations. (If the Stewards consider it inadvisable to run this race on the turf course, this race will be run at One Mile and One Eighth on the main track.).

Value of Race: $113,900 Winner $68,340; second $22,780; third $11,390; fourth $5,695; fifth $3,417; sixth $456; seventh $456; eighth $456; ninth $456; tenth $454. Mutuel Pool $557,621.00 Exacta Pool $468,834.00 Trifecta Pool $340,841.00

Last Raced	Horse	M/Eqt.	A.	Wt	PP	St	¼	½	¾	Str	Fin	Jockey	Odds $1
2Jly04 8Bel2	Seducer's Song	L	3	115	5	4	8½	71½	41½	1hd	11½	Bailey J D	6.70
21Sep03 Cur1	Venturi-GB	L	3	119	4	8	6½	51½	51½	52	2no	Prado E S	3.15
2Jly04 8Bel1	Fortunate Damsel	L b	3	117	1	1	3½	3hd	3hd	4½	3nk	Castellano J J	13.30
10Jly04 7Cnl1	Art Fan	L	3	119	8	2	2½	21½	1½	2½	41¾	Fogelsonger R	16.50
13Jun04 8Bel2	Lucifer's Stone	L b	3	122	10	10	7½	83½	6hd	6½	5½	Day P	3.35
4Jly04 4Bel1	La Reina	L	3	117	2	3	1½	1hd	21½	3½	6hd	Velazquez J R	7.80
14Jly04 3Bel1	Delta Sensation	L	3	117	7	7	4½	6½	72½	72½	72½	Chavez J F	6.10
10Jly04 7Cnl2	Galloping Gal	L	3	119	3	6	9hd	10	10	95½	81	Blanc B	8.40
5Jly04 10Mth2	Really American	L	3	115	9	9	10	94½	91½	8½	93½	Samyn J L	60.25
13Jun04 8Bel9	Savage Beauty	L	3	115	6	5	5½	4hd	82½	10	10	Migliore R	14.40

OFF AT 4:47 Start Good . Won driving. Course good.

TIME :25, :49, 1:121, 1:354, 1:42 (:25.00, :49.09, 1:12.34, 1:35.88, 1:42.01)

$2 Mutuel Prices:				
	5 – SEDUCER'S SONG	15.40	7.80	5.50
	4 – VENTURI–GB		4.80	3.90
	1 – FORTUNATE DAMSEL			8.80

$2 EXACTA 5–4 PAID $90.50 $2 TRIFECTA 5–4–1 PAID $1,016.00

Gr/ro. f, (Apr), by Unbridled's Song – Seducer , by Housebuster . Trainer Clement Christophe. Bred by Peter Karches (Ky).

SEDUCER'S SONG was steadied between rivals when in tight quarters entering the first turn, was rated along inside, advanced inside on the second turn, split rivals approaching the stretch, came wide, responded when roused and drew clear late. VENTURI (GB) was steadied along inside on the first turn, saved ground, swung wide entering the stretch and finished gamely outside to get the place award. FORTUNATE DAMSEL raced close up inside, advanced on the second turn, responded when roused and finished gamely while between rivals in the stretch. ART FAN lunged in the air at the start, contested the pace from the outside and stayed on stubbornly in the stretch. LUCIFER'S STONE was rated along while three wide early, angled in on the backstretch, put in a run along the inside on the second turn, came wide into the stretch and had little left for the drive. LA REINA contested the pace along the inside and tired in the final furlong. DELTA SENSATION was rated along outside, raced three wide on both turns and had no response when roused. GALLOPING GAL dropped back early despite being hustled along and had no response when put to the whip. REALLY AMERICAN was outrun early, raced wide on the first turn, was inside on the second turn and had no rally. SAVAGE BEAUTY was rank under restraint early on, raced between rivals for a half mile and was wide thereafter.

Owners– 1, Karches Peter F; 2, Gann Edmund A; 3, Spruce Pond Stable; 4, Backer William M; 5, Team Solaris Stable; 6, Hamilton Emory A; 7, Cay John E III; 8, Carl William A; 9, Dudley William H and Gaviria Eduardo; 10, Schwartz Martin S

Trainers– 1, Clement Christophe; 2, Frankel Robert; 3, Johnson Philip G; 4, Smith Hamilton A; 5, Rice Linda; 6, McGaughey III Claude R; 7, Alexander Frank A; 8, McPeek Kenneth G; 9, Weaver George; 10, Jerkens H Allen

Scratched– Capeside Lady (05Jul04 10Mth1)

EIGHTH RACE
Saratoga
AUGUST 6, 2004

6 FURLONGS. (1.08) 10TH RUNNING OF THE HONORABLE MISS HANDICAP. Grade II. Purse $150,000 (Up To $28,500 NYSBFOA) A HANDICAP FOR FILLIES AND MARES THREE YEARS OLD AND UPWARD. By subscription of $150 each which should accompany the nomination; $750 to pass the entry box; $750 to start. The purse to be divided 60% to the winner, 20% to second, 10% to third, 5% to fourth, 3% to fifth and 2% divided equally among remaining finishers. A trophy will be presented to the winning owner. Closed Saturday, July 24, 2004 with 17 Nominations.

Value of Race: $150,000 Winner $90,000; second $30,000; third $15,000; fourth $7,500; fifth $4,500; sixth $1,000; seventh $1,000; eighth $1,000. Mutuel Pool $684,648.00 Exacta Pool $529,690.00 Trifecta Pool $375,615.00

Last Raced	Horse	M/Eqt.	A.	Wt	PP	St	¼	½	Str	Fin	Jockey	Odds $1
10Jly04 9ElP5	My Trusty Cat	L bf	4	115	5	8	8	7½	4hd	1no	Day P	14.10
26Jun04 9Pha1	Ebony Breeze	L	4	115	1	6	5hd	4hd	23	22¾	Bailey J D	2.95
4Jly04 10Mth5	Smok'n Frolic	L b	5	116	6	1	4hd	6hd	5½	3½	Prado E S	6.10
16Jly04 8Bel1	Cologny	L b	4	114	4	2	1hd	1½	1hd	41	Alvarado R Jr	9.00
4Jly04 6PrM1	Summer Mis	L b	5	115	2	5	2½	3hd	31	51¼	Sterling L J Jr	8.40
4Jly04 10Mth2	Yell	L	4	115	7	3	7½	8	8	64½	Velazquez J R	4.10
4Jly04 6PrM2	Savorthetime	L	5	115	3	7	3½	51½	7hd	72½	Sellers S J	2.70
5Jly04 7Bel1	Belong to Sea	L bf	4	113	8	4	61½	2hd	6hd	8	Castellano J J	24.50

OFF AT 4:47 Start Good . Won driving. Track fast.

TIME :223, :451, :572, 1:101 (:22.63, :45.31, :57.49, 1:10.37)

$2 Mutuel Prices:				
	6 – MY TRUSTY CAT	30.20	10.40	5.90
	1 – EBONY BREEZE		4.80	3.10
	7 – SMOK'N FROLIC			4.40

$2 EXACTA 6–1 PAID $123.50 $2 TRIFECTA 6–1–7 PAID $686.00

B. f, (Apr), by Tale of the Cat – Entrusted , by Private Account . Trainer Vance David R. Bred by Vintage Racing (Ky).

MY TRUSTY CAT was outrun early, advanced inside on the turn, angled out in upper stretch, split rivals, finished resolutely and was up on the line. EBONY BREEZE raced close up early, rallied inside nearing the stretch, split rivals, drew clear inside the eighth pole and dug in gamely but was caught in the last stride. SMOK'N FROLIC chased the pace while four wide and finished well outside. COLOGNY stumbled at the start, was hustled up inside, set the pace and tired in the final furlong. SUMMER MIS stumbled after the start, was hustled up outside, contested the pace and tired in the stretch. YELL was outrun early, came wide for the drive and had no response when roused. SAVORTHETIME contested the pace while three wide and tired in the stretch. BELONG TO SEA raced close up outside, put in a five wide run on the turn and had nothing left for the stretch drive.

Owners– 1, Pollard Carl F; 2, Kinsman Stable; 3, Dogwood Stable; 4, Gewirtz Evan; 5, Richard Otto; 6, Claiborne Farm and Dilschneider Adele B; 7, Robertson Philip Robertson Brenda; 8, Amling Jeffery S Duncker C Steven Quartucci Alan and Hudson River Farms

Trainers– 1, Vance David R; 2, Mott William I; 3, Pletcher Todd A; 4, Lake Scott A; 5, Mitchell Anthony; 6, McGaughey III Claude R; 7, Asmussen Steven M; 8, Lewis Lisa L

Scratched– Travelator (16Jul04 8Bel2)

EIGHTH RACE
Del Mar
AUGUST 7, 2004

6½ FURLONGS. (1.13^{3}) 36TH RUNNING OF THE SORRENTO. Grade III. Purse $150,000 FOR FILLIES, TWO-YEAR-OLDS. (FOALS OF 2002.) By subscription of $150 each, which shall accompany the nomination, or by supplementary nomination of $1,500 each by closing time of entries, $1,500 additional to start, with $150,000 Guaranteed, of which $90,000 to first, $30,000 to second, $18,000 to third, $9,000 to fourth and $3,000 to fifth. Weight 122 lbs. Non-winners of $50,000 allowed 2 lbs.; of $25,000 other than maiden or claiming, 4 lbs,; of a race other than claiming, 6 lbs. A trophy will be presented to the owner of the winner. Closed with 13 nominations.

Value of Race: $150,000 Winner $90,000; second $30,000; third $18,000; fourth $9,000; fifth $3,000. Mutuel Pool $625,798.00 Exacta Pool $313,290.00 Quinella Pool $37,174.00 Trifecta Pool $325,683.00 Superfecta Pool $140,338.00

Last Raced	Horse	M/Eqt.	A.	Wt	PP	St	¼	½	Str	Fin	Jockey	Odds $1
5Jly04 ^{5}Hol^{1}	Inspiring	LB b	2	118	7	2	1^{hd}	$1^{\frac{1}{2}}$	1^{1}	$1^{2\frac{1}{2}}$	Flores D R	0.90
5Jly04 ^{8}Hol^{1}	Souvenir Gift	LB	2	122	4	6	$2^{\frac{1}{2}}$	$2^{2\frac{1}{2}}$	$2^{2\frac{1}{2}}$	$2^{2\frac{1}{2}}$	Smith M E	1.50
11Jly04 ^{10}Crc^{1}	Hello Lucky	LB	2	118	5	5	3^{2}	$3^{1\frac{1}{2}}$	$4^{1\frac{1}{2}}$	$3^{\frac{1}{2}}$	Court J K	32.10
5Jly04 ^{8}Hol^{4}	Crypto's Wild	LB	2	116	1	8	8	6^{hd}	5^{hd}	4^{1}	Sorenson D	40.30
11Jly04 ^{2}Hol^{1}	Wise Investor	LB	2	118	2	7	$7^{\frac{1}{2}}$	$7^{\frac{1}{2}}$	$6^{3\frac{1}{2}}$	5^{3}	Valdivia J Jr	26.80
3Jly04 ^{11}Pln^{1}	Timeintown	LB	2	118	3	4	$5^{\frac{1}{2}}$	$5^{2\frac{1}{2}}$	3^{hd}	6^{3}	Baze T C	14.80
25Jly04 ^{5}Dmr^{1}	Starleena	LB	2	118	8	3	6^{5}	4^{1}	7^{8}	7^{17}	Ruis M	21.90
20Jun04 ^{1}Hol^{1}	Excusabull	LB	2	118	6	1	$4^{\frac{1}{2}}$	8	8	8	Nakatani C S	12.10

OFF AT 5:37 Start Good . Won driving. Track fast.

TIME :21^{3}, :44^{4}, 1:11, 1:18^{1} (:21.79, :44.93, 1:11.17, 1:18.29)

$2 Mutuel Prices:

7 – INSPIRING	3.80	2.40	2.40
4 – SOUVENIR GIFT		2.40	2.40
5 – HELLO LUCKY			4.80

$1 EXACTA 7–4 PAID $3.50 $2 QUINELLA 4–7 PAID $3.40
$1 TRIFECTA 7–4–5 PAID $24.30 $1 SUPERFECTA 7–4–5–1 PAID $156.30

Ch. f, (Mar), by Golden Missile – Arches of Gold , by Strike Gold . Trainer Baffert Bob. Bred by Timothy Thornton Meg Buckley & Mike &Buckley (Ky).

INSPIRING dueled four wide then outside the runner-up, inched away leaving the turn, continued a bit off the rail in the stretch and proved best under urging. SOUVENIR GIFT went up between horses to duel for the lead, continued off the rail on the backstretch, angled to the fence and fought back on the turn, came out into the stretch and went willingly to the wire. HELLO LUCKY had speed between the top pair then stalked a bit off the rail, came out into the stretch and edged a rival for third. CRYPTO'S WILD taken off the rail early, settled outside a rival chasing the pace, split horses in deep stretch and was edged for the show. WISE INVESTOR unhurried inside on the backstretch and turn, continued inside and lacked the needed response. TIMEINTOWN chased a bit off the rail on the backstretch and turn, came out in the stretch and moved up some, then weakened in the final furlong. STARLEENA settled off the rail then moved up outside leaving the backstretch and on the turn, went three deep into the stretch and weakened. EXCUSABULL had speed between horses early then stalked outside, dropped back on the turn, came wide into the stretch and gave way.

Owners– 1, Lewis Robert B and Beverly J; 2, Semkin Sam and Unruh Gregory; 3, C R Cono LLC; 4, Jarvis Patsy and Young Candace; 5, Williamson Warren B; 6, Royce S Jaime Racing Stable Inc; 7, Hughes B Wayne; 8, Earnhardt III Patti and Hal J

Trainers– 1, Baffert Bob; 2, Semkin Sam; 3, Paasch Christopher S; 4, Sauque Alex; 5, Gaines Carla; 6, O'Neill Doug; 7, Stute Melvin F; 8, Baffert Bob

---

$2 Daily Double (10–7) Paid $70.60 ; Daily Double Pool $37,785 .
$1 Pick Three (1–10–7) Paid $83.00 ; Pick Three Pool $154,157 .

TENTH RACE
Ellis Park
AUGUST 7, 2004

1⅛ MILES. (1.47^{3}) 23RD RUNNING OF THE GARDENIA HANDICAP. Grade III. Purse $200,000 FOR FILLIES AND MARES THREE-YEARS-OLD AND UPWARD. By subscription of $200 each to accompany the nomination, $1,000 to pass the entry box and $1,000 additional to start. $200,000 Guaranteed. The Association's money to be divided: $120,000 to the winner, $40,000 to second, $22,000 to third, $12,000 to fourth and $6,000 to fifth. Starters to be named through the entry box by the usual time of closing. A trophy will be presented to the winning owner. Nominations closed Saturday, July 24, 2004 with 16 nominations.

Value of Race: $200,000 Winner $120,000; second $40,000; third $22,000; fourth $12,000; fifth $6,000. Mutuel Pool $171,298.00 Exacta Pool $131,678.00 Trifecta Pool $98,087.00 Superfecta Pool $30,823.00

Last Raced	Horse	M/Eqt.	A.	Wt	PP	St	¼	½	¾	Str	Fin	Jockey	Odds $1
12Jun04 ^{8}CD^{4}	Angela's Love	L	4	115	1	4	$3^{1\frac{1}{2}}$	2^{hd}	$2^{\frac{1}{2}}$	1^{3}	$1^{4\frac{3}{4}}$	Guidry M	4.50
10Jly04 ^{9}ElP^{1}	Miss Fortunate	L	4	116	5	3	$4^{1\frac{1}{2}}$	$5^{\frac{1}{2}}$	5^{3}	$4^{4\frac{1}{2}}$	$2^{\frac{1}{2}}$	Peck B D	3.80
4Jly04 ^{10}Mth^{3}	Bare Necessities	L	5	119	6	5	5^{hd}	4^{hd}	$3^{\frac{1}{2}}$	2^{hd}	3no	Douglas R R	0.90
3Jly04 ^{8}PrM^{1}	Wildwood Royal	L bf	4	117	2	1	1^{2}	$1^{\frac{1}{2}}$	$1^{1\frac{1}{2}}$	$3^{\frac{1}{2}}$	$4^{5\frac{3}{4}}$	Sukie D G	4.00
17Jun04 ^{2}CD^{1}	New Dreams-Brz	L b	5	114	4	6	6	6	6	5^{hd}	$5^{4\frac{1}{2}}$	Blanc B	9.30
15Jun04 ^{9}Mnr^{5}	Salzurita-Arg	L f	6	115	3	2	2^{1}	3^{2}	$4^{1\frac{1}{2}}$	6	6	Martinez W	47.40

OFF AT 5:34 Start Good . Won driving. Track fast.

TIME :23^{3}, :47^{2}, 1:11^{3}, 1:36^{3}, 1:49^{2} (:23.68, :47.54, 1:11.67, 1:36.61, 1:49.54)

$2 Mutuel Prices:

1 – ANGELA'S LOVE	11.00	5.00	3.00
5 – MISS FORTUNATE		4.60	2.60
6 – BARE NECESSITIES			2.10

$2 EXACTA 1–5 PAID $36.60 $2 TRIFECTA 1–5–6 PAID $72.00
$2 SUPERFECTA 1–5–6–2 PAID $258.40

Dk. b or br. f, (Apr), by Not For Love – Goldgorian's Alden , by John Alden . Trainer Romans Dale. Bred by Dr George E Harmening Kimberly &Harmening & William Campbell (Md).

ANGELA'S LOVE, lightly rated along the inside from early on, advanced inside nearing the final quarter, took over when straightened for the drive, came out a bit farther on the track and widened when kept to her task. MISS FORTUNATE followed the leaders from early on while four or five wide, angled in leaving the second turn, was in behind the winner three or four wide for the drive and couldn't threaten ANGELA'S LOVE while outgaming BARE NECESSITIES for the place. BARE NECESSITIES, never far back and five wide early, moved between horses leaving the backstretch to edge closer, maneuvered five wide while rallying with the winner, loomed a threat into the final furlong but flattened out. WILDWOOD ROYAL sprinted to the fore at once, was three wide on the first turn, moved five wide on the backstretch while showing the way, edged in a bit on the far turn, held the advantage to the stretch and tired. NEW DREAMS (BRZ), sluggish early, angled inside, saved ground and failed to menace while remaining inside for the drive. SALZURITA (ARG) chased front-running WILDWOOD ROYAL five wide and tired on the far turn.

Owners– 1, Poston Bill and Vicki; 2, Lyon Stables; 3, Iron County Farms Inc; 4, Stiritz William; 5, Estrela Energia Stable; 6, Korkames David

Trainers– 1, Romans Dale; 2, Mott William I; 3, Kirby Frank J; 4, Zook Jimmy; 5, McPeek Kenneth G; 6, Van Berg Thomas L

$1 Pick Three (9–5–1) Paid $149.80 ; Pick Three Pool $9,801 .

EIGHTH RACE
Mountaineer
AUGUST 7, 2004

1⅛ MILES. (1.46¹) 35TH RUNNING OF THE WEST VIRGINIA DERBY. Grade III. Purse $600,000 FOR THREE YEAR OLDS. No Nomination Fee. $750.00 to pass the entry box. $2,000.00 additional to start. Money to be divided: $360,000 to Winner; $120,000 to Second; $60,000 to Third; $30,000 to Fourth; $15,000 to Fifth; $9,000 to Sixth and $3,000 for Seventh and Eighth. WEIGHTS 122 LBS. Winners of Two Grade I races at One Mile or Over in 2004... 3 lbs. Additional; Non-winners of a Grade I race at One Mile or Over in 2004... allowed 3 lbs.; Non-winners of a Grade II race at One Mile or Over in 2004... 5 lbs.; Non-winners of a Grade III race at One Mile or Over in 2004...7 lbs.; Non-winners of $150,000 at One Mile or Over in 2004... 9 lbs.; Non-winners of a Sweepstakes at One Mile or Over in 2004... 11 lbs. TROPHY TO THE WINNING OWNER, TRAINER AND JOCKEY. CLOSED SATURDAY, JULY 24, 2004 WITH 55 NOMINATIONS.

Value of Race: $600,000 Winner $363,000; second $120,000; third $60,000; fourth $30,000; fifth $15,000; sixth $9,000; seventh $3,000. Mutuel Pool $217,326.00 Perfecta Pool $149,707.00 Trifecta Pool $144,530.00

Last Raced	Horse	M/Eqt.	A.	Wt	PP	St	¼	½	¾	Str	Fin	Jockey	Odds $1
11Jly04 8Bel3	Sir Shackleton	LB	3	117	5	4	5^{hd}	6^{6}	5^{1}	2^{2}	1^{3}	Bejarano R	1.20
18Jly04 9Del1	Pollard's Vision	LB	3	119	2	3	4^{2}	4^{1}	3^{hd}	3^{2}	$2^{\frac{1}{2}}$	Coa E M	1.30
18Jly04 9Del2	Britt's Jules	LB b	3	115	4	1	$1^{1\frac{1}{2}}$	1^{1}	$1^{2\frac{1}{2}}$	$1^{1\frac{1}{2}}$	3^{5}	Lanerie C J	8.00
17Jly04 9AP5	Avid Skier	LB b	3	113	1	2	$2^{\frac{1}{2}}$	2^{1}	2^{3}	4^{4}	4no	Lester R N	42.70
17Jly04 9AP2	Fantasticat	LB	3	114	7	7	7	7	7	5^{15}	5^{25}	Borel C H	12.60
19Jun04 9Crc1	Mister Fotis	LB b	3	113	3	6	3^{1}	$3^{\frac{1}{2}}$	6^{3}	$6^{\frac{1}{2}}$	6	Castro E	26.90
17Jly04 9Mth4	Ecclesiastic	LB b	3	111	6	5	6^{4}	$5^{\frac{1}{2}}$	$4^{1\frac{1}{2}}$	7	—	Castillo H Jr	9.30

OFF AT 5:27 Start Good. Won driving. Track fast.

TIME :23¹, :47, 1:10³, 1:35⁴, 1:49 (:23.28, :47.14, 1:10.68, 1:35.83, 1:49.16)

$2 Mutuel Prices:				
	7 – SIR SHACKLETON	4.40	2.40	2.20
	3 – POLLARD'S VISION		2.60	2.20
	6 – BRITT'S JULES			2.40

$2 PERFECTA 7–3 PAID $7.60 $2 TRIFECTA 7–3–6 PAID $25.80

Ch. c, (Mar), by Miswaki – Naskra Colors, by Star de Naskra. Trainer Zito Nicholas P. Bred by Tracy Farmer (Ky).

SIR SHACKLETON taken in hand and tucked inside at the break, sat patient off a moderate pace to the 1/2 mile pole, roused to contention advancing through the final turn, continued to respond getting to a weary BRITT'S JULE outside the 1/16 pole, was full of run in the closing stages drawing away to the wire. POLLARD'S VISION was well placed laying close up 4 wide into the backstretch, stalked with even action to the 3/8 pole, asked into final turn putting in an extended bid near mid track in upper stretch, gave a willing response salvaging place in the final yards. BRITT'S JULES broke alertly to go clear under little pressure, allowed to measure on moderate splits to the 1/2 mile pole, edged away into final turn, taken off the inside entering the stretch, became leg weary inside the 1/16 pole, had little left at the end. AVID SKIER came away well to lay close up, stalked BRITT'S JULES on modest opening fractions, remained a threat on the final turn, began to weaken in upper stretch, wore down gradually under a drive. FANTASTICAT off slowly, trailed well back to the 1/2 mile pole, kept along the inside into stretch, was no late factor. MISTER FOTIS prompted close up from the break, chased for a 1/2 mile, wavered leaving the backstretch, had nothing left for drive and was put away. ECCLESIASTIC dropped back at the break, raced evenly to the 1/2 mile pole, still in contention on far turn, wilted at the head of stretch, was eased to the wire.

Owners– 1, Farmer Tracy; 2, Edgewood Farm; 3, Southern Equine Stables LLC; 4, France Wilbur K; 5, R Bar S Thoroughbreds LLP; 6, Alago Inc; 7, Allen Joseph

Trainers– 1, Zito Nicholas P; 2, Pletcher Todd A; 3, Guillot Eric; 4, Bennett Gerald S; 5, Barnett Bobby C; 6, Wolfson Martin D; 7, McLaughlin Kiaran P

Scratched– Rockem Sockem (17Jul04 7GLD1), Line of Scrimmage (27Jul04 2Mnr2)

$2 Pick Three (1–6–7) Paid $203.60 ; Pick Three Pool $15,745 .

EIGHTH RACE
Saratoga
AUGUST 7, 2004

6 FURLONGS. (1.08) 12TH RUNNING OF THE AMSTERDAM. Grade II. Purse $150,000 (Up to $28,500 NYSBFOA) FOR THREE YEAR OLDS. By subscription of $150 each, which should accompany the nomination; $750 to pass the entry box; $750 to start. The purse to be divided 60% to the winner, 20% to second, 10% to third, 5% to fourth, 3% to fifthand 2% divided equally among remaining finishers. 123 lbs. Non-winners of a Graded Sweepstake in 2004 allowed 2 lbs.; $45,000 since October 1, 4 lbs.; three races, 6 lbs.; two races, 8 lbs. (maiden, claiming, and restricted allowance races not considered).A trophy will be presented to the winning owner. Closed Saturday, July 24, 2004 with 17 Nominations.

Value of Race: $150,000 Winner $90,000; second $30,000; third $15,000; fourth $7,500; fifth $4,500; sixth $1,500; seventh $1,500. Mutuel Pool $1,029,412.00 Exacta Pool $827,344.00 Trifecta Pool $545,033.00

Last Raced	Horse	M/Eqt.	A.	Wt	PP	St	¼	½	Str	Fin	Jockey	Odds $1
10Jly04 9Crc3	Bwana Charlie	L	3	123	4	7	7	$6^{\frac{1}{2}}$	$2^{1\frac{1}{2}}$	$1^{\frac{3}{4}}$	Sellers S J	3.70
26Jun04 9Mth1	Pomeroy	b	3	123	7	3	$4^{\frac{1}{2}}$	$2^{\frac{1}{2}}$	$1^{1\frac{1}{2}}$	2^{2}	Prado E S	1.70
10Jly04 9Crc1	Weigelia	L	3	123	2	4	5^{3}	4^{1}	$4^{\frac{1}{2}}$	$3^{\frac{1}{2}}$	Toribio A Jr	7.20
9Jly04 8Bel1	Smokume	L	3	121	5	1	6^{3}	5^{hd}	3^{hd}	$4^{7\frac{3}{4}}$	Uske S	4.90
10Jly04 9Crc2	Classy Migration	L b	3	115	1	5	1^{hd}	3^{hd}	6^{3}	$5^{\frac{1}{2}}$	Day P	8.90
25Jly04 9Mth1	Quick Action	L	3	121	6	2	$2^{2\frac{1}{2}}$	1^{hd}	5^{hd}	$6^{\frac{3}{4}}$	Albarado R J	35.00
23Jun04 8Bel1	Mass Media	L b	3	117	3	6	3^{hd}	7	7	7	Bailey J D	5.10

OFF AT 5:10 Start Good. Won driving. Track fast.

TIME :21⁴, :44³, :56⁴, 1:09² (:21.98, :44.69, :56.82, 1:09.40)

$2 Mutuel Prices:				
	4 – BWANA CHARLIE	9.40	4.00	2.80
	7 – POMEROY		3.30	2.60
	2 – WEIGELIA			3.30

$2 EXACTA 4–7 PAID $28.80 $2 TRIFECTA 4–7–2 PAID $145.00

B. c, (Mar), by Indian Charlie – Shahalo, by Halo. Trainer Asmussen Steven M. Bred by E & D Enterprises (Ky).

BWANA CHARLIE trailed along the backstretch after breaking slowly, closed a lengthy gap while saving ground to the turn, angled five wide for clear sailing at the top of the stretch, drew along side POMEROY to challenge inside the furlong marker then edged clear under brisk urging. POMEROY stalked the pace from outside along the backstretch, launched a rally four wide on the turn, accelerated to the front in upper stretch, opened a clear advantage in midstretch, dug in when challenged leaving the furlong marker then yielded to the winner in the final seventy yards. WEIGELIA stumbled at the start, rushed up along the inside, raced just off the pace along the rail leaving the far turn, angled out midway on the turn, split horses at the top of the stretch then finished willingly between rivals to gain a share. SMOKUME was outrun along the backstretch, gradually gained while five wide on the turn, swung six wide to reach contention while just outside the winner at the top of the stretch then flattened out. CLASSY MIGRATION dueled through rapid fractions along the rail for a half and tired from his early efforts. QUICK ACTION battled heads apart from outside to the turn and steadily tired thereafter. MASS MEDIA chased the leaders slightly off the rail to the turn, checked behind WEIGELIA nearing the quarter pole then gave way.

Owners– 1, Heiligbrodt Racing Stable; 2, Smith Derrick and Tabor Michael; 3, Balsamo Joseph J; 4, Hobeau Farm; 5, Buckram Oak Farm; 6, Overbrook Farm; 7, West Gary L and Mary E

Trainers– 1, Asmussen Steven M; 2, Biancone Patrick L; 3, Azpurua Manuel J; 4, Jerkens H Allen; 5, Mikhalides George; 6, Lukas D Wayne; 7, Frankel Robert

$2 Pick Three (11–7–4) Paid $166.00 ; Pick Three Pool $168,447 .

NINTH RACE
Saratoga
AUGUST 7, 2004

1⅛ MILES. (1.47) 77TH RUNNING OF THE WHITNEY HANDICAP. Grade I. Purse $750,000 (Up to $62,500 NYSBFOA) A HANDICAP FOR THREE YEAR OLDS AND UPWARD. By subscription of $750 each,which should accompany the nomination; $3,500 to pass the entry box, $4,000 to start. The purse to be divided 60% to the winner, 20% to second, 10% to third, 5% to fourth, 3% to fifth and 2% divided equally among remaining finishers. Trophies will be presented to the winning owner, trainer and jockey. Closed Saturday, July 24, 2004 with 20 Nominations.

Value of Race: $750,000 Winner $450,000; second $150,000; third $75,000; fourth $37,500; fifth $22,500; sixth $3,750; seventh $3,750; eighth $3,750; ninth $3,750. Mutuel Pool $1,486,816.00 Exacta Pool $1,039,235.00 Trifecta Pool $752,490.00 Superfecta Pool $188,214.00

Last Raced	Horse	M/Eqt.	A.	Wt	PP	St	¼	½	¾	Str	Fin	Jockey	Odds $1
3Jly04 ^{9}PrM^{1}	Roses in May	L	4	114	2	3	2½	2½	2^{1½}	1^{hd}	1no	Prado E S	7.40
3Jly04 ^{9}PrM^{2}	Perfect Drift	L	5	117	1	1	8^{1}	8^{hd}	5½	2^{2½}	2^{2¼}	Day P	3.30
3Jly04 ^{7}Bel^{7}	Bowman's Band	L	6	114	4	9	9	9	7^{2}	3^{hd}	3no	Chavez J F	7.20
3Jly04 ^{7}Bel^{5}	Sarava	L	5	113	5	4	6^{hd}	7^{1}	8½	7^{5½}	4^{3½}	Castellano J J	14.50
19Jun04 ^{10}Suf^{4}	Gygistar	L	5	113	6	5	5^{hd}	5^{hd}	6½	4^{hd}	5^{2½}	Bravo J	16.50
3Jly04 ^{7}Bel^{1}	Peace Rules	L	4	121	8	6	3^{2½}	3^{1½}	3^{1½}	6^{hd}	6^{1½}	Bailey J D	3.05
3Jly04 ^{7}Bel^{2}	Newfoundland	L b	4	114	9	8	7^{2½}	6^{hd}	9	8^{2½}	7^{4¼}	Velazquez J R	5.60
10Jly04 ^{9}Hol^{4}	Yessirgeneralsir	L	4	113	3	2	1½	1½	1^{2½}	5^{1}	8^{1}	Figueroa O	49.00
12Jun04 ^{7}Bel^{1}	Seattle Fitz-Arg	L	5	117	7	7	4^{1½}	4½	4^{hd}	9	9	Migliore R	5.50

OFF AT 5:44 Start Good . Won driving. Track fast.

TIME :22^{3}, :45^{1}, 1:08^{4}, 1:34^{4}, 1:48^{2} (:22.64, :45.25, 1:08.92, 1:34.89, 1:48.54)

$2 Mutuel Prices:				
	2 – ROSES IN MAY	16.80	7.90	5.40
	1 – PERFECT DRIFT		5.00	3.30
	4 – BOWMAN'S BAND			5.10

$2 EXACTA 2–1 PAID $78.00 $2 TRIFECTA 2–1–4 PAID $525.00
$2 SUPERFECTA 2–1–4–5 PAID $5,228.00

Dk. b or br. c, (Feb), by Devil His Due – Tell a Secret , by Speak John . Trainer Romans Dale. Bred by Margaux Farm LLC (Ky).

ROSES IN MAY moved up rapidly to contest the early pace, pressed the pace between horses through rapid fractions along the backstretch, settled just outside the leader on the far turn, closed the gap nearing the quarter pole, surged to the front in upper stretch, dug in when challenged in midstretch, battled heads apart into deep stretch and prevailed under strong left hand encouragement. PERFECT DRIFT was unhurried though the opening half mile, steadily worked his way forward along the inside on the turn, angled three wide to reach contention at the top of the stretch, drew on nearly even terms with the winner in midstretch, but couldn't overtake that one through the final eighth. BOWMAN'S BAND was outrun for five furlongs, launched a rally along the inside leaving the backstretch, angled out while gaining on the far turn, checked between horses midway on the turn, angled four wide into the stretch then closed late between horses to gain a share. SARAVA was unhurried for six furlongs, saved ground to the turn, swung five wide entering the stretch then improved his position with a mild late rally. GYGISTAR raced in the middle of the pack while saving ground, rallied mildly along the rail leaving the turn, drifted to the three path in upper stretch then lacked a strong closing response. PEACE RULES chased a rapid pace while four wide along the backstretch, remained a factor to the turn then steadily tired thereafter. NEWFOUNDLAND failed to mount a serious rally while five wide throughout. YESSIRGENERALSIR rushed up to gain the early advantage, set a rapid pace along the rail to the top of the stretch and gave way. SEATTLE FITZ (ARG) broke a bit slowly, moved up four wide on the first turn, chased the leaders while continuing wide along the backstretch, dropped back leaving the turn and faded in the stretch.

Owners– 1, Ramsey Kenneth L and Sarah K; 2, Reed William A Reed Mary; 3, Schwartz Martin S; 4, New Phoenix Stable and Roy Mrs Susan; 5, Evans Edward P; 6, Gann Edmund A; 7, Sumaya Us Stables; 8, Jackson James D; 9, West Point Stable

Trainers– 1, Romans Dale; 2, Johnson Murray W; 3, Jerkens H Allen; 4, Baffert Bob; 5, Hennig Mark; 6, Frankel Robert; 7, Pletcher Todd A; 8, Keen Dallas E; 9, McLaughlin Kiaran P

EIGHTH RACE
Del Mar
AUGUST 8, 2004

1$\frac{1}{16}$ MILES. (1.40) 34TH RUNNING OF THE CLEMENT L HIRSCH HANDICAP. Grade II. Purse $300,000 FOR FILLIES AND MARES, THREE-YEAR-OLDS AND UPWARD. By subscription of $300 each, which shall accompany the nomination, or by supplementary nomination of $3,000 each by Sunday, August 1, $3,000 additional to start, with $300,000 Guaranteed, of which $180,000 to first, $60,000 to second, $36,000 to third, $18,000 to fourth and $6,000 to fifth. Weights Monday, August 2. A trophy will be presented to the owner of the winner. Closed with 13 nominations.

Value of Race: $300,000 Winner $180,000; second $60,000; third $36,000; fourth $18,000; fifth $6,000. Mutuel Pool $556,218.00 Exacta Pool $262,353.00 Quinella Pool $27,247.00 Trifecta Pool $272,784.00 Superfecta Pool $129,938.00

Last Raced	Horse	M/Eqt.	A.	Wt	PP	St	¼	½	¾	Str	Fin	Jockey	Odds $1
27Jun04 ^{8}Hol^{4}	Miss Loren-Arg	LB f	6	114	5	5	5^{hd}	5^{hd}	5^{3}	2^{hd}	1^{3¼}	Court J K	34.00
12Jun04 ^{4}Hol^{1}	House of Fortune	LB	3	113	7	4	3^{1}	3^{hd}	3^{1}	1^{hd}	2^{1}	Baze T C	2.80
10Jly04 ^{5}Hol^{9}	Royally Chosen	LB	6	116	3	1	1^{1}	1^{1}	1½	3½	3^{1}	Flores D R	27.70
11Jly04 ^{8}Hol^{1}	Star Parade-Arg	LB	5	119	6	2	2^{1}	2^{1½}	2^{1½}	4^{3}	4½	Espinoza V	1.80
10Jly04 ^{5}Hol^{2}	Tucked Away	LB b	4	116	1	7	8	7^{hd}	8	6^{4}	5^{2½}	Desormeaux K J	11.60
10Jly04 ^{5}Hol^{6}	Elloluv	LB	4	117	8	3	6^{10}	4^{1½}	4^{hd}	5½	6^{9½}	Valdivia J Jr	5.50
11Jly04 ^{8}Hol^{4}	Victory Encounter	LB	4	118	2	6	7^{hd}	8	7^{hd}	7^{2}	7½	Smith M E	3.60
13Jun04 ^{10}CD^{1}	Indy Groove	LB	4	115	4	8	4½	6^{8}	6^{2}	8	8	Guidry M	13.80

OFF AT 5:46 Start Good . Won driving. Track fast.

TIME :22^{2}, :46, 1:10^{3}, 1:36^{2}, 1:42^{4} (:22.59, :46.09, 1:10.76, 1:36.43, 1:42.93)

$2 Mutuel Prices:				
	5 – MISS LOREN–ARG	70.00	25.80	9.00
	7 – HOUSE OF FORTUNE		5.00	4.00
	3 – ROYALLY CHOSEN			10.20

$1 EXACTA 5–7 PAID $168.60 $2 QUINELLA 5–7 PAID $126.60
$1 TRIFECTA 5–7–3 PAID $2,671.20 $1 SUPERFECTA 5–7–3–6 PAID $5,424.50

Dk. b or br. m, (Aug), by Numerous – Luminare–Arg , by Forlitano–Arg . Trainer Seglin Luis E. Bred by Firmamento (Arg).

MISS LOREN (ARG) chased outside a rival, swung out into the stretch and in upper stretch, bid four wide, gained the lead under left handed urging past the eighth pole and pulled clear. HOUSE OF FORTUNE between horses early, stalked outside or off the rail, bid three deep into the stretch, put a head in front nearing midstretch, could not match the winner but held second. ROYALLY CHOSEN sped to the early lead, set the pace inside, fought back on the second turn and inside rivals but a bit off the rail in the stretch and saved the show. STAR PARADE (ARG) between horses early, stalked off the rail, bid outside ROYALLY CHOSEN on the second turn and between horses into and through the stretch and was outfinished. TUCKED AWAY allowed to settle outside a rival, angled to the inside for the stretch and lacked the needed rally. ELLOLUV four wide into the first turn, chased outside, came three deep into the stretch and weakened. VICTORY ENCOUNTER saved ground well off the pace, moved up some inside on the second turn, steadied off heels nearing the quarter pole, came out into the stretch and did not rally. INDY GROOVE off a bit slowly, saved ground chasing the pace, dropped back on the second turn and weakened.

Owners– 1, Llers Corporation; 2, Zetcher Arnold; 3, Abruzzo Peter Johnston E W Zehenni Tony V et al; 4, Tanaka Gary A; 5, Nierenberg Nico; 6, Reddam J Paul; 7, Mankiewicz Tom; 8, Glen Hill Farm

Trainers– 1, Seglin Luis E; 2, McAnally Ronald; 3, Headley Bruce; 4, Vienna Darrell; 5, Gallagher Patrick; 6, Dollase Craig; 7, Sadler John W; 8, Proctor Thomas F

$2 Daily Double (8–5) Paid $1,329.60 ; Daily Double Pool $44,424 .
$1 Pick Three (8–8–5) Paid $4,964.20 ; Pick Three Pool $100,136 .

NINTH RACE
Monmouth
AUGUST 8, 2004

1⅛ MILES. (Turf) (1.46) 35TH RUNNING OF THE MATCHMAKER. Grade III. Purse $100,000 FOR FILLIES AND MARES, THREE YEARS OLD AND UPWARD. By subscription of $100 each, which should accompany the nomination and $1,500 to pass the entry box. Three-Year-Olds: 118 lbs.; Older: 122 lbs. Non-winners of $60,000 twice at a mile or over since November 1 allowed 2 lbs.; $45,000 twice at a mile or over in 2004, 4 lbs.; $30,000 at a mile or over in 2004, 6 lbs. Maiden, claiming and starter races not considered. The owner of the winner to receive a trophy. Closed Sunday, July 25, 2004 with 35 nominations.

Value of Race: $100,000 Winner $60,000; second $20,000; third $11,000; fourth $6,000; fifth $3,000. Mutuel Pool $384,673.00 Exacta Pool $309,313.00 Trifecta Pool $232,382.00

Last Raced	Horse	M/Eqt.	A.	Wt	PP	St	¼	½	¾	Str	Fin	Jockey	Odds $1
21Jly04 7Bel1	WhereWLftOff-GB	L	4	118	7	6	72½	71	81½	3hd	11	Nakatani C S	2.50
3Jly04 6Bel3	Mrs. M	L f	5	118	8	2	11½	11½	11	13	21¾	Lopez C C	12.00
20Jun04 9Mth4	Spin Control	L	4	116	3	5	62	62	6hd	43	31	Bravo J	5.80
3Jly04 4Hol1	Janeian-NZ	L	6	118	4	1	3½	3hd	3hd	2½	41¾	Martin E M Jr	1.70
24Jun04 8Mth1	Bitterroot River	L	4	116	1	9	9	9	9	6hd	5hd	Turner T G	26.90
20Jun04 9Mth6	Constant Touch	L	4	118	2	8	82	82	7½	7hd	6nk	Elliott S	17.80
7Jly04 8Mth1	Jacqui's Promise	L	4	116	5	3	41	51	5½	51	74½	Pimentel J	16.70
17Jly04 9Del1	Alternate	L b	5	118	6	4	5hd	4½	4½	8hd	81	Coa E M	4.70
7Jly04 8Mth8	Cocktailsandreams	L	7	116	9	7	21	2½	2½	9	9	Velez J A Jr	61.60

OFF AT 4:05 Start Good. Won driving. Course firm.

TIME :23, :48¹, 1:12², 1:36³, 1:48⁴ (:23.18, :48.26, 1:12.44, 1:36.68, 1:48.80)

$2 Mutuel Prices:				
	7 – WHERE WE LEFT OFF-GB	7.00	4.40	3.40
	8 – MRS. M		10.60	6.00
	3 – SPIN CONTROL			4.40

$2 EXACTA 7–8 PAID $81.80 $2 TRIFECTA 7–8–3 PAID $423.40

Ch. f, (Feb), by Dr Devious-Ire – Rekindled Affair-Ire, by Rainbow Quest. Trainer Clement Christophe. Bred by Moyglare Stud Farm Ltd (GB).

WHERE WE LEFT OFF (GB) unhurried early while not far back, raced along the inside into the lane, eased out some late and closed strongly. MRS. M set the early pace, responded when asked and widened into midstretch then continued on gamely while unable to contain the top one late. SPIN CONTROL saved ground to the lane, moved out some and finished willingly while not good enough. JANEIAN (NZ) close up while saving ground, advanced some into upper stretch and lacked the needed late response. BITTERROOT RIVER broke slowly, raced in the three path turning for home, was behind rivals briefly, moved inside and gained some. CONSTANT TOUCH raced five wide into the lane and lacked a solid rally. JACQUI'S PROMISE well placed early, raced just off the inside and weakened in the drive. ALTERNATE in good position early, raced four wide into the lane and tired. COCKTAILSANDREAMS stalked early from the outside, remained a factor until nearing the lane and tired.

Owners– 1, Moyglare Stud Farm Ltd; 2, Acclaimed Racing Stable; 3, Evans Robert S; 4, England Greg L; 5, Hunter Barbara; 6, Humphrey G Watts Jr; 7, Double H Stable; 8, Pin Oak Stable LLC; 9, Generazio Patricia A

Trainers– 1, Clement Christophe; 2, Ciardullo Richard Jr; 3, Motion H Graham; 4, Calhoun William Bret; 5, Skiffington Thomas J; 6, Oliver Victoria; 7, Goldberg Alan E; 8, Motion H Graham; 9, Laudati Kim

---

ELEVENTH RACE
Monmouth
AUGUST 8, 2004

1 1/16 MILES. (Turf Chute) (1.39²) 57TH RUNNING OF THE OCEANPORT HANDICAP. Grade III. Purse $100,000 FOR THREE-YEAR-OLDS AND UPWARD. By subcription of $100 each, which should accompany the nomination and $1,500 to pass the entry box. The winning owner to receive $60,000, $20,000 to second, $11,000 to third, $6,000 to fourth and $3,000 to fifth. The ownerof the winner to receive a trophy. Closed Sunday, July 25, 2004 with 35 nominations.

Value of Race: $100,000 Winner $60,000; second $20,000; third $11,000; fourth $6,000; fifth $3,000. Mutuel Pool $446,179.00 Exacta Pool $330,964.00 Trifecta Pool $256,067.00

Last Raced	Horse	M/Eqt.	A.	Wt	PP	St	¼	½	¾	Str	Fin	Jockey	Odds $1
17Jly04 5Mth1	Gulch Approval	L	4	117	2	1	31	31	3hd	2hd	1no	Day P	3.60
27Jun04 8Mth1	Kathir	L	7	116	4	2	51	5hd	5hd	51	2no	Lopez C C	2.40
17Jly04 8Mth2	Stormy Roman	L	5	115	3	7	6hd	71	71½	6hd	3½	Clemente A V	10.30
17Jly04 5Mth2	Royal Affirmed	L	6	114	6	5	2hd	2½	2½	31½	4nk	Pezua J M	24.40
10Jly04 8Bel6	Burning Roma	L	6	120	10	4	4hd	4½	41½	4hd	5½	Coa E M	3.20
12Jun04 9Mth3	Del Mar Show	L	7	117	7	9	10	9½	8hd	8½	6hd	Nakatani C S	3.80
17Jly04 5Mth3	Stormy Ray	L b	5	115	1	6	7hd	8hd	9hd	72	72¼	King E L Jr	30.90
14Jly04 8Mth1	Max's Buddy	L	5	113	5	3	11	1½	11	1hd	8nk	Ferrer J C	47.50
26Jun04 9Cnl1	Mt. Carson	L f	4	115	8	10	9hd	10	10	91½	92¼	Bravo J	22.90
17Jly04 8Mth3	First Lieutenant	L bf	7	115	9	8	81	6½	6hd	10	10	Elliott S	26.20

OFF AT 5:12 Start Good. Won driving. Course firm.

TIME :23⁴, :48¹, 1:12¹, 1:36¹, 1:42¹ (:23.98, :48.32, 1:12.25, 1:36.38, 1:42.31)

$2 Mutuel Prices:				
	2 – GULCH APPROVAL	9.20	4.00	3.40
	4 – KATHIR		3.60	3.00
	3 – STORMY ROMAN			5.20

$2 EXACTA 2–4 PAID $26.00 $2 TRIFECTA 2–4–3 PAID $211.20

Dk. b or br. g, (Jan), by Gulch – Classic Approval, by With Approval. Trainer Zito Nicholas P. Bred by Milton Hendry & WS Farish (Ky).

GULCH APPROVAL close up early while saving ground, stayed inside and advanced into midstretch, reached the front leaving the furlong grounds then prevailed by a narrow margin. KATHIR well placed while along the inside, eased out some in upper stretch, brushed with a foe and moved into a narrow opening between rivals late and closed gamely. STORMY ROMAN never far back and between foes on the final turn, finished gamely outside. ROYAL AFFIRMED prompted the early issue, lodged a bid into the lane and finished willingly. BURNING ROMA close up early from the outside, was brushed while holding his position leaving the furlong grounds while directly outside of KATHIR and lacked the needed late response. DEL MAR SHOW raced four wide turning for home and lacked a solid rally. STORMY RAY saved ground throughout and was gaining some late. MAX'S BUDDY set the pace and weakened in the drive. MT. CARSON broke slowly and lacked a rally. FIRST LIEUTENANT never far back and in the three path turning for home, lacked a bid.

Owners– 1, Marylou Whitney Stables; 2, Melnyk Eugene and Laura; 3, Croley Thomas L; 4, Falcone Robert and Lee John J; 5, Queen Harold L; 6, Allen E Paulson Living Trust; 7, Mamone Raymond; 8, Dweck Raymond; 9, Reynolds David P; 10, Humphrey G Watts Jr

Trainers– 1, Zito Nicholas P; 2, Pletcher Todd A; 3, Hills Timothy A; 4, Ramos Faustino F; 5, Giglio Heather A; 6, Mott William I; 7, Durso Robert J; 8, Levine Bruce N; 9, Jenkins Rodney; 10, Oliver Philip J

$2 Pick Three (7–11–2) Paid $119.80 ; Pick Three Pool $39,698 .

THIRTEENTH RACE
Monmouth
AUGUST 8, 2004

1⅛ MILES. (1.46⁴) 37TH RUNNING OF THE HASKELL INVITATIONAL HANDICAP. Grade I. Purse $1,000,000 FOR THREE-YEAR-OLDS. By invitation only, with no nomination, entry or starting fees. The winning owner to receive $600,000, $200,000 to second, $100,000 to third, $60,000 to fourth, $30,000 to fifth and $10,000 to sixth. The owner and trainer of the winner to receive a trophy.

Value of Race: $1,000,000 Winner $600,000; second $200,000; third $100,000; fourth $60,000; fifth $30,000; sixth $10,000. Mutuel Pool $1,160,071.00 Exacta Pool $733,886.00 Superfecta Pool $199,130.00 Trifecta Pool $604,150.00

Last Raced	Horse	M/Eqt.	A.	Wt	PP	St	¼	½	¾	Str	Fin	Jockey	Odds $1
17Jly04 9Mth1	Lion Heart		3	121	4	1	1½	11½	12	12	11	Bravo J	1.90
17Jly04 9Mth2	My Snookie's Boy	L	3	116	1	4	3hd	3hd	2hd	22	22¼	Elliott S	20.80
18Jly04 9Del3	Pies Prospect	L	3	116	2	2	61	71	5½	32	33¼	Lopez C C	16.80
17Jly04 9Mth3	Royal Assault	L	3	117	3	6	41	51	6hd	42½	45	Day P	9.20
2Jly04 7PrM1	Swingforthefences	L	3	117	8	8	8	8	72	62½	54	Bridgmohan S X	8.40
10Jly04 7Hol1	Rock Hard Ten	L	3	120	5	5	2hd	2½	3hd	51	62	Nakatani C S	0.90
2Jly04 7Mth1	Tap Day	L b	3	116	7	7	72	6hd	8	74	714½	Velez J A Jr	31.00
19Jun04 7Hol3	Wimplestiltskin	L b	3	116	6	3	5hd	4hd	41½	8	8	Coa E M	41.70

OFF AT 6:26 Start Good. Won driving. Track fast.

TIME :23, :46⁴, 1:10², 1:35³, 1:48⁴ (:23.18, :46.81, 1:10.42, 1:35.78, 1:48.95)

$2 Mutuel Prices:			
4 – LION HEART	5.80	4.40	3.80
1 – MY SNOOKIE'S BOY		12.80	7.60
2 – PIES PROSPECT			10.40

$2 EXACTA 4–1 PAID $81.40 $1 SUPERFECTA 4–1–2–3 PAID $1,298.60
$2 TRIFECTA 4–1–2 PAID $509.80

Ch. c, (Jan), by Tale of the Cat – Satin Sunrise, by Mr. Leader. Trainer Biancone Patrick L. Bred by Sabine Stable (Ky).

LION HEART broke alertly and posted the early fractions, showed the way to the lane and held a clear advantage in midstretch then responded well and maintained a safe margin to the wire. MY SNOOKIE'S BOY close up early while along the inside, lodged a bid on the final turn, eased out some and finished gamely. PIES PROSPECT never far back, saved ground and advanced some turning for home then lacked the needed late response. ROYAL ASSAULT close up early, raced between rivals into the far turn, moved briefly with PIES PROSPECT, was near the inside into the lane and lacked the needed late bid. SWINGFORTHEFENCES trailed early while not far back, advanced some four deep into the far turn then offered little in the drive. ROCK HARD TEN prompted the early issue, raced between rivals into the far turn, was asked then raced outside into the lane and tired then was not urged late. TAP DAY between rivals leaving the backstretch, was steadied nearing the three-eighths pole, dropped back and tired. WIMPLESTILTSKIN moved up from the outside on the backstretch, loomed a threat into the far turn, remained a factor until nearing the lane and gave way.

Owners– 1, Smith Derrick and Tabor Michael; 2, Preferred Pals Stable; 3, LaPenta Robert V; 4, Farmer Tracy; 5, Klaravich Stables Inc; 6, Mercedes Stables LLC & M Paulson; 7, Evans Edward P; 8, Everest Stables Inc

Trainers– 1, Biancone Patrick L; 2, Iwinski Allen; 3, Zito Nicholas P; 4, Zito Nicholas P; 5, Violette Richard A Jr; 6, Orman Jason; 7, Hennig Mark; 8, Polanco Marcelo

Scratched– Pollard's Vision (07Aug04 8Mnr2)

NINTH RACE
Saratoga
AUGUST 8, 2004

1⅛ MILES. (1.47) 41ST RUNNING OF THE JIM DANDY. Grade II. Purse $500,000 (Up to $55,000 NYSBFOA) FOR THREE YEAR OLDS. By subscription of $500 each, which should accompany the nomination; $2,500 to pass the entry box, $2,500 to start. The purse to be divided 60% to the winner, 20% to second, 10% to third, 5% to fourth, 3% to fifth and 2% divided equally among remaining finishers. 123 lbs. Non-winners of a Grade 1 in 2004 allowed 2 lbs.; a Grade 2 over a mile in 2004, 4 lbs.; a Graded Sweepstake at a mile or over, 6 lbs.; $40,000 at a mile or over or three races, 8 lbs. (Maiden,claiming and restricted allowance races not considered). A trophy will be presented to the winning owner. Closed Saturday, July 24, 2004 with 25 nominations.

Value of Race: $500,000 Winner $300,000; second $100,000; fourth $25,000; third $50,000; fifth $15,000; sixth $10,000. Mutuel Pool $1,110,422.00 Exacta Pool $705,154.00 Trifecta Pool $487,687.00

Last Raced	Horse	M/Eqt.	A.	Wt	PP	St	¼	½	¾	Str	Fin	Jockey	Odds $1
5Jun04 11Bel9	Purge	L	3	121	6	2	2hd	2½	26	17	14½	Velazquez J R	2.80
11Jly04 8Bel2	The Cliff's Edge	L	3	123	3	6	6	6	6	2hd	2½	Sellers S J	1.70
5Jun04 11Bel4	[D]Eddington	L b	3	115	5	4	56	56	53½	33½	37¼	Migliore R	7.00
18Jly04 9FE2	Niigon	L f	3	117	4	3	46	45	31½	520	43¾	Landry R C	24.75
11Jly04 8Bel1	Medallist		3	121	1	5	12	13½	1½	4hd	525½	Chavez J F	2.00
2Jly04 7PrM2	Courageous Act	L	3	117	2	1	33	33	4hd	6	6	Prado E S	21.20

[D] – Eddington disqualified and placed 4th

OFF AT 5:25 Start Good. Won driving. Track fast.

TIME :23, :45³, 1:09³, 1:34³, 1:47² (:23.09, :45.73, 1:09.64, 1:34.66, 1:47.56)

$2 Mutuel Prices:			
7 – PURGE	7.60	3.60	2.80
3 – THE CLIFF'S EDGE		2.70	2.30
4 – NIIGON			3.40

$2 EXACTA 7–3 PAID $22.60 $2 TRIFECTA 7–3–4 PAID $151.50

B. c, (Apr), by Pulpit – Copelan's Bid Gal, by Copelan. Trainer Pletcher Todd A. Bred by Glory Days Breeding Inc (Ky).

PURGE settled in good position behind the early leader, swung out to the three path entering the backstretch, was rated just behind MEDALLIST to the far turn, charged past that one to take command midway on the turn, extended his advantage opening a comfortable lead in upper stretch then drew away under a vigorous hand ride. THE CLIFF'S EDGE stumbled slightly at the start, raced far back while trailing for six furlongs, launched a rally on the far turn, closed a lengthy gap to reach contention on the turn, swung to the outside of EDDINGTON at the top of the stretch, then closed steadily in the middle of the track but couldn't threaten the winner. EDDINGTON was outrun for a half mile, gradually worked his way forward from outside on the turn, circled four wide into the stretch, drifted in to soundly bump NIIGON in upper stretch then continued on willingly to gain a share. NIIGON was reserved for five furlongs while saving ground, angled three wide on the turn, lodged a mild bid in upper stretch, was bumped off stride at the three-sixteenths pole then weakened in the final eighth. MEDALLIST sprinted clear early, set a rapid pace along the rail for six furlongs, relinquished the lead on the turn then gave way. COURAGEOUS ACT chased the pacesetter along the rail for five furlongs and steadily tired thereafter. Following a stewards inquiry into the stretch run along with a claim of foul by the rider of NIIGON, EDDINGTON was disqualified from third and placed fourth for interference.

Owners– 1, Starlight Stables LLC Saylor Paul and Martin Johns; 2, LaPenta Robert V; 3, Willmott Stables Inc; 4, Chiefswood Stables; 5, Clay Robert N; 6, Lewis Robert B and Beverly J

Trainers– 1, Pletcher Todd A; 2, Zito Nicholas P; 3, Hennig Mark; 4, Coatrieux Eric; 5, Jerkens H Allen; 6, Baffert Bob

Scratched– Swingforthefences (02Jul04 7PrM1)

EIGHTH RACE
Saratoga
AUGUST 9, 2004

1⅛ MILES. (Inner Turf) (1.46^{1}) 19TH RUNNING OF THE NATIONAL MUSEUM OF RACING HALL OF FAME HANDICAP. Grade II. Purse $150,000 (UP TO $28,500 NYSBFOA) INNER TURF FOR THREE YEAR OLDS. By subscription of $150 each, which should accompany the nomination; $750 to pass the entry box, $750 to start. The purse to be divided 60% to the winner, 20% to second, 10% to third, 5% to fourth, 3% to fifth and 2% divided equally among remaining finishers. 122 lbs.; Non-winners of a Graded Sweepstake on the turf in 2004 allowed 3 lbs.; $45,000 on the turf, 5 lbs., two races, 7 lbs. (Maiden, claiming, or restricted allowance races not considered).A trophy will be presented to the winning owner. The New York Racing Association reserves the right to transfer this race to the Main Track. In the event that this race is taken off the turf, it may be subject to downgrading upon review by the Graded Stakes Committee. Closed Saturday, July 24, 2004 with 38 nominations. (Rail at 9 feet).

Value of Race: $150,000 Winner $90,000; second $30,000; third $15,000; fourth $7,500; fifth $4,500; sixth $1,000; seventh $1,000; eighth $1,000. Mutuel Pool $574,389.00 Exacta Pool $469,420.00 Trifecta Pool $375,400.00

Last Raced	Horse	M/Eqt.	A.	Wt	PP	St	¼	½	¾	Str	Fin	Jockey	Odds $1
10Jly04 9Cnl2	Artie Schiller	L	3	122	7	5	3hd	3hd	4hd	1½	1¼	Migliore R	1.00
18Jly04 8Bel1	Mustanfar	L b	3	122	6	8	8	8	7½	5½	2no	Day P	11.10
27Jun04 7Bel2	Good Reward	L b	3	115	2	3	52½	4½	3½	4hd	31½	Prado E S	10.40
18Jly04 8Bel3	SecondPerformnce	L b	3	115	8	7	4hd	55½	53½	2½	43¾	Albarado R J	13.50
18Jly04 8Bel2	Icy Atlantic	L	3	122	3	2	21	1½	1½	3½	51½	Velazquez J R	4.30
11Jly04 8Bel5	Preachinatthebar	L b	3	115	5	6	7½	72½	8	8	6hd	Fragoso P	27.50
11Jly04 7Bel4	Broadway View	L b	3	115	1	1	6½	6hd	6hd	7½	7hd	Sellers S J	31.50
3Jly04 9AP2	Street Theatre	L b	3	115	4	4	1½	21	2½	61	8	Bailey J D	4.40

OFF AT 4:47 Start Good. Won driving. Course firm.

TIME :23^{1}, :47^{1}, 1:10^{3}, 1:35^{3}, 1:47^{3} (:23.34, :47.26, 1:10.72, 1:35.72, 1:47.71)

$2 Mutuel Prices:				
	8 – ARTIE SCHILLER	4.00	2.90	2.60
	7 – MUSTANFAR		6.80	4.90
	3 – GOOD REWARD			5.30

$2 EXACTA 8–7 PAID $27.00 $2 TRIFECTA 8–7–3 PAID $137.00

B. c, (Apr), by El Prado Ire – Hidden Light, by Majestic Light. Trainer Jerkens James A. Bred by Haras Du Mezeray SA (Ky).

ARTIE SCHILLER raced along between rivals while well in hand, was confidently handled around the second turn, came wide into the stretch, responded when asked, quickly drew clear and widened while being kept busy to the finish. MUSTANFAR hit the gate at the start, was outrun early, rallied four wide on the second turn, dug in gamely outside and got the nod for the place award. GOOD REWARD, close up inside while well in hand, was steadied in upper stretch, altered course to the outside and dug in gamely to the finish, just missing for the place prize. SECOND PERFORMANCE raced close up while three wide, rallied three wide on the second turn, earned a short lead between calls in upper stretch then weakened in the final furlong. ICY ATLANTIC showed good speed along the inside, contested the pace into the stretch and tired on the rail in the final furlong. PREACHINATTHEBAR was outrun while between rivals early, came wide into the stretch and had no response when roused. BROADWAY VIEW bobbled at the start, dropped back early, raced inside and tired.. STREET THEATRE contested the pace from the outside, clipped heels in upper stretch, stumbled and dropped back. Following a Stewards' inquiry into the stretch run the result was declared official.

Owners– 1, Timber Bay Farm and Walsh Mrs Thomas J; 2, Shadwell Stable; 3, Phipps Ogden Mills et al; 4, Bloom William Behrendt John T and Marquis Charles K; 5, Appleton Arthur I; 6, Pegram Michael E; 7, Live Oak Plantation; 8, Darley Stable

Trainers– 1, Jerkens James A; 2, McLaughlin Kiaran P; 3, McGaughey III Claude R; 4, Donk David; 5, Pletcher Todd A; 6, Baffert Bob; 7, Zito Nicholas P; 8, Harty Eoin

Scratched– Kennel Up (31Jul04 6Sar5), Dealer Choice (FR) (27Jun04 7Bel3)

EIGHTH RACE
Arlington
AUGUST 14, 2004

1$\frac{3}{16}$ MILES. (Turf) (1.53^{1}) 15TH RUNNING OF THE BEVERLY D. Grade I. Purse $750,000 FOR FILLIES AND MARES, THREE-YEARS-OLD AND UPWARD. By subscription of $300 if made on or before Wednesday, May 12, 2004, with fee to accompany the nomination. Late nomination of $1,500 (each horse) on Wednesday, July 21, 2004. Nominees of May 12 and July21 to pay $5,000 to pass the entry box and $5,000 to start. $750,000 Guaranteed, of which $450,000 to the winner; $150,000 to second; $75,000 to third; $37,500 to fourth; $22,500 to fifth and $15,000 to sixth. WEIGHT-FOR-AGE: NORTHERN HEMISPHERE: Three-Year-Old Fillies, 117 lbs.; Older, 123 lbs.; SOUTHERN HEMISPHERE: Three-Year-Old Fillies, 111 lbs.; Four-Year-Old Fillies, 118 lbs.; Older, 123 lbs. Failure to draw into this race at time of entry cancels all fees with the exception of the nominating fee(s). Starters to be named through the entry box on Wednesday, August 11, 2004. Two (2) horses having common ties through ownership cannot start to the exclusion of a single ownership interest. Trophy to the winning owner. Closed Wednesday, July 21, 2004 with 81 nominations. (If the management considers it inadvisable to run this race on the Turf Course, it will be run on the main track at One Mile and Three Sixteenths).

Value of Race: $750,000 Winner $450,000; second $150,000; third $75,000; fourth $37,500; fifth $22,500; sixth $15,000. Mutuel Pool $1,121,007.00 Exacta Pool $744,170.00 Trifecta Pool $542,962.00 Superfecta Pool $163,267.00

Last Raced	Horse	M/Eqt.	A.	Wt	PP	St	¼	½	¾	Str	Fin	Jockey	Odds $1
16Jun04 ASC^{6}	Crimson Palace-Saf	L f	5	123	9	7	3½	3^{hd}	4½	3^{1}	1½	Dettori L	9.90
31Jly04 ^{7}Sar^{2}	Riskaverse	L	5	123	1	1	4^{hd}	4½	5^{hd}	$4^{1½}$	2^{hd}	Day P	8.40
4Jun04 EPS^{4}	Necklace-GB	L	3	117	5	6	$8^{1½}$	6½	7½	6½	3^{nk}	Spencer J P	25.40
24Jly04 ^{6}Dmr^{1}	Musical Chimes	L	4	123	4	3	1½	2^{1}	2^{1}	2^{hd}	4¾	Desormeaux K J	2.10
24Jly04 ^{9}AP^{1}	Bedanken	L f	5	123	8	8	9^{hd}	9½	3½	5½	5^{nk}	Pettinger D R	8.10
17Jun04 LCH^{1}	Aubonne-Ger		4	123	2	2	2^{1}	1½	1^{1}	1½	6½	Prado E S	7.10
24Jly04 ^{9}AP^{2}	Aud	L	4	123	7	9	10^{1}	$10^{1½}$	9^{hd}	$7^{1½}$	7^{1}	Razo E Jr	38.20
24Jly04 ^{9}AP^{3}	Shaconage	L	4	123	6	5	7^{hd}	8^{2}	8^{1}	10½	8^{1}	Blanc B	17.30
29May04 ^{3}Bel^{1}	Commercante-FR	L	4	123	10	10	6^{hd}	7½	$10^{1½}$	9^{hd}	9^{hd}	Bailey J D	3.30
11Jly04 ^{8}Hol^{2}	Quero Quero	L	4	123	11	11	11	11	11	8½	10½	Espinoza V	23.80
27Jun04 ^{8}Hol^{3}	Noches DeRosa-Chi	L b	6	123	3	4	5^{1}	5^{1}	6½	11	11	Smith M E	13.50

OFF AT 3:38 Start Good . Won driving. Course firm.

TIME :24^{4}, :49^{4}, 1:15^{2}, 1:39^{3}, 1:56^{2} (:24.83, :49.89, 1:15.48, 1:39.76, 1:56.58)

$2 Mutuel Prices:				
	9 – CRIMSON PALACE-SAF	21.80	11.00	9.00
	1 – RISKAVERSE		8.00	7.00
	5 – NECKLACE-GB			11.80

$2 EXACTA 9–1 PAID $216.40 $2 TRIFECTA 9–1–5 PAID $4,286.40
$2 SUPERFECTA 9–1–5–4 PAID $11,661.80

Dk. b or br. m, (Sep), by Elliodor-Fr – Perfect Guest , by Northern Guest . Trainer bin Suroor Saeed. Bred by Adv A P Joubert (Saf).

CRIMSON PALACE (SAF) moved up from outside on the first turn, stalked the pace while four wide along the backstretch, raced just outside the leaders to the top of the stretch, made a run to challenge inside the furlong marker then edged clear in the final twenty yards. RISKAVERSE settled in good position along the inside, saved ground while in good position along the backstretch, launched a rally along the inside on the turn, angled out in mid stretch, split rivals while rallying in deep stretch and finished well to gain the place. NECKLACE (GB) was rated in the middle of the pack for six furlongs, raced in traffic along the inside leaving the turn, angled out in upper stretch then rallied belatedly to gain a share. MUSICAL CHIMES set or forced the pace while three wide to the top of the stretch, battled heads apart into deep stretch then weakened in the final seventy yards. BEDANKEN was reserved for six furlongs while well off the lodged a strong move while five wide to reach contention the turn then flattened out in the stretch. AUBONNE (GER) moved up along the rail to gain a slim early advantage, set the pace under pressure into upper stretch, battled into mid stretch and yielded late. AUD raced well back to the far turn, closed a lengthy gap to reach contention in upper stretch but couldn't sustain her bid. SHACONAGE failed to mount a serious rally. COMMERCANTE (FR) raced in the middle of the pack while four wide, was caught in traffic between horses on the turn then steadied in tight while tiring in the stretch. QUERO QUERO never reached contention. NOCHES DE ROSA (CHI) raced up close between horses while three wide to the turn and gave way. (Race run in lane 5, rail at 0.)

Owners– 1, Godolphin Racing Inc; 2, Fox Ridge Farm Inc; 3, Tabor Michael and Magnier Mrs John; 4, Gainsborough Farm Phillip Scott Director; 5, Pin Oak Stable LLC; 6, Ingeborg Von Shubert and Gary A Tanaka; 7, Willmott Stables Inc; 8, Van Doren Andrena; 9, Alain Falourd Hubert Guy and Robert Trussell Jr; 10, Old Friends Inc Julio Gerin Camargo; 11, Diamond A Racing Corporation Gerald Ford

Trainers– 1, bin Suroor Saeed; 2, Kelly Patrick J; 3, O'Brien Aidan P; 4, Drysdale Neil; 5, Von Hemel Donnie K; 6, Libaud Eric; 7, Reinstedler Anthony; 8, Shirota Mitch; 9, Frankel Robert; 10, Lobo Paulo H; 11, Mandella Richard

$1 Pick Three (4–7–9) Paid $304.50 ; Pick Three Pool $68,622 .

NINTH RACE **$1\frac{1}{4}$ MILES. (Turf) (1.58^{3}) 22ND RUNNING OF THE ARLINGTON MILLION. Grade I. Purse $1,000,000 FOR THREE–YEAR–OLDS AND UPWARD.**

Arlington

AUGUST 14, 2004

Value of Race: $1,000,000fourth $50,000; Winner $600,000; second $200,000; third $100,000; fifth $30,000; sixth $20,000. Mutuel Pool $1,876,200.00 Exacta Pool $1,140,384.00 Trifecta Pool $926,290.00 Superfecta Pool $297,924.00

Last Raced	Horse	M/Eqt.	A.	Wt	PP	¼	½	¾	1	Str	Fin	Jockey	Odds $1
1Aug04 Mch^{2}	[D]Powerscourt-GB	L b	4	126	10	10^{2}	$10^{1\frac{1}{2}}$	$10^{\frac{1}{2}}$	10^{hd}	$1^{\frac{1}{2}}$	$1^{1\frac{1}{2}}$	Spencer J P	4.60
17Jly04 ^{8}Bel^{1}	Kicken Kris	L	4	126	4	5^{1}	$6^{\frac{1}{2}}$	$7^{\frac{1}{2}}$	$4^{\frac{1}{2}}$	$3^{1\frac{1}{2}}$	2^{1}	Desormeaux K J	9.70
17Jly04 NBY^{4}	Magistretti	L b	4	126	12	$9^{2\frac{1}{2}}$	$9^{1\frac{1}{2}}$	$9^{\frac{1}{2}}$	$9^{1\frac{1}{2}}$	4^{1}	$3^{\frac{1}{2}}$	Prado E S	24.00
1Aug04 ^{9}Kol^{2}	Epalo-Ger		5	126	7	$3^{\frac{1}{2}}$	3^{1}	$3^{1\frac{1}{2}}$	$3^{1\frac{1}{2}}$	$2^{\frac{1}{2}}$	$4^{1\frac{1}{2}}$	Starke A	4.10
25Jly04 ^{8}Dmr^{6}	Vangelis	L b	5	126	9	$11^{\frac{1}{2}}$	$11^{1\frac{1}{2}}$	$11^{1\frac{1}{2}}$	$11^{1\frac{1}{2}}$	$5^{\frac{1}{2}}$	$5^{\frac{3}{4}}$	Valdivia J Jr	11.20
3Jly04 ^{10}Mth^{2}	Mr O'Brien-Ire	L	5	126	1	6^{hd}	5^{hd}	6^{hd}	$6^{\frac{1}{2}}$	$6^{\frac{1}{2}}$	$6^{\frac{1}{2}}$	Day P	4.70
24Jly04 ^{7}AP^{1}	Senor Swinger	L	4	126	8	$8^{\frac{1}{2}}$	$8^{\frac{1}{2}}$	$8^{\frac{1}{2}}$	8^{hd}	7^{1}	$7^{\frac{3}{4}}$	Blanc B	21.70
25Jly04 ^{8}Dmr^{3}	Sweet Return-GB	L	4	126	3	$4^{\frac{1}{2}}$	4^{1}	4^{1}	7^{hd}	8^{2}	$8^{1\frac{3}{4}}$	Bailey J D	5.30
25Jly04 ^{8}WO^{2}	Mobil	L f	4	126	13	$7^{1\frac{1}{2}}$	7^{1}	5^{1}	$5^{\frac{1}{2}}$	9^{2}	$9^{\frac{1}{2}}$	Jones J	40.20
24Jly04 ^{7}AP^{2}	Mystery Giver	L	6	126	6	12^{2}	13	12^{1}	12^{7}	10^{4}	$10^{2\frac{3}{4}}$	Douglas R R	20.90
12Jun04 ^{3}Hol^{1}	Sabiango-Ger	L	6	126	5	$2^{\frac{1}{2}}$	$2^{1\frac{1}{2}}$	$2^{\frac{1}{2}}$	1^{hd}	11^{4}	11^{2}	Espinoza V	15.00
17Jly04 NBY^{2}	Vespone-Ire	L b	4	126	2	1^{1}	$1^{1\frac{1}{2}}$	1^{1}	$2^{\frac{1}{2}}$	12^{4}	12^{7}	Dettori L	9.50
26Jly04 ^{7}Dmr^{1}	Hatif-Brz	L	5	126	11	13	$12^{\frac{1}{2}}$	13	13	13	13	Smith M E	56.80

[D] – Powerscourt-GB disqualified and placed 4th

OFF AT 4:38 Start Good . Won driving. Course firm.

TIME :23^{3}, :47^{2}, 1:12, 1:36^{3}, 2:00 (:23.75, :47.49, 1:12.04, 1:36.60, 2:00.08)

$2 Mutuel Prices:				
	4 – KICKEN KRIS	21.40	11.20	6.60
	12 – MAGISTRETTI		25.00	11.60
	7 – EPALO-GER			4.00

$2 EXACTA 4–12 PAID $678.80 $2 TRIFECTA 4–12–7 PAID $7,390.60
$2 SUPERFECTA 4–12–7–10 PAID $31,920.40

B. c, (Mar), by Kris S. – Kicken Grass , by Jade Hunter . Trainer Matz Michael R. Bred by Valerie Naify (Ky).

POWERSCOURT (GB) raced far back for seven furlongs after being pinched back at the start, launched a rally from outside on the far turn, circled six wide while rapidly gaining at the top of the stretch, charged to the front nearing the furlong marker, drifted in under right hand whipping a sixteenth out then edged clear in the final seventy yards. Following a stewards inquiry into the stretch run, POWERSCOURT was disqualified from first and placed fourth for interference in deep stretch. KICKEN KRIS was shuffled back a bit in the early stages, raced in the middle of the pack along the backstretch, closed the gap between horses on the turn, rallied four wide to reach contention in upper stretch, made a run to threaten inside the furlong marker then checked in tight quarters while bumping the rail in the late stages. MAGISTRETTI raced well back early, worked his way forward from outside on the turn, advanced five wide into the stretch then rallied belatedly to gain a share. EPALO (GER) settled in good position along the backstretch, edged closer on the turn, rallied between horses entering the stretch, surged to the front in upper stretch, battled between horses in deep stretch then checked and altered course while being bumped in deep stretch. VANGELIS checked and was pinched back at the start, worked his way forward from outside on the turn, circled six wide entering the stretch then closed late in the middle of the track. MR O'BRIEN (IRE) tucked in along the rail in the early stages, steadied in traffic along the backstretch, gained a bit while saving ground on the turn then lacked a strong closing response. SENOR SWINGER was unhurried for seven furlongs after being pinched back at the start, made a run along the inside to reach contention at the top of the stretch and flattened out. SWEET RETURN (GB) steadied along the inside nearing the first turn, moved out on the first turn, stalked the leaders while four wide for a mile, dropped back on the turn and steadily tired thereafter. MOBIL raced in the middle of the pack while well off the rail to the far turn and faded at the top of the stretch. MYSTERY GIVER never reached contention. SABIANGO (GER) pressed the pace from outside along the backstretch, gained a slim lead on the turn then gave way in the stretch. VESPONE (IRE) set the pace under pressure to the turn and tired from his early efforts. HATIF (BRZ) checked at the start and was never close thereafter. (Race run in lane 5, rail at 0.)

Owners– 1, Magnier Mrs John; 2, Brushwood Stable; 3, Tabor Michael B; 4, Tanaka Gary A; 5, Bloodstock Management Services Inc and Cheveley Park Stud Ltd; 6, Skeedattle II Robert White and Louis Rehak; 7, Lewis Robert B and Beverly J; 8, Red Oak Stable; 9, Schickedanz Gustav; 10, Team Block; 11, Roberts Monty; 12, Godolphin Racing Inc; 13, Belmont Stable D Franceschi & Old Friends Inc J G Camargo

Trainers– 1, O'Brien Aidan P; 2, Matz Michael R; 3, Callaghan Neville A; 4, Schutz Andreas; 5, Frankel Robert; 6, Graham Robin L; 7, Baffert Bob; 8, McAnally Ronald; 9, Keogh Michael; 10, Block Chris M; 11, Baffert Bob; 12, bin Suroor Saeed; 13, Lobo Paulo H

$1 Pick Three (7–9–4) Paid $620.10 ; Pick Three Pool $79,385 .
$1 Pick Four (NTRA–P4–2–9–3–4) Paid $2,705.00 ; Pick Four Pool $1,208,442 .
$2 Daily Double (9–4) Paid $326.80 ; Daily Double Pool $120,884 .

ELEVENTH RACE
Arlington
AUGUST 14, 2004

1¼ MILES. (Turf) (1.58^{3}) 28TH RUNNING OF THE SECRETARIAT. Grade I. Purse $400,000 FOR THREE-YEAR-OLDS. By subscription of $300 each horse (Early) Wednesday, April 14, 2004; $800 each horse (Late Nomination) on Wednesday, July 28, 2004. Fee to accompany the nomination. Original Nominees to pay $3,000 to pass the entry box and $3,000 additional to start, with $400,000 Guaranteed, of which $240,000 to the winner; $80,000 to second; $40,000 to third; $20,000 to fourth; $12,000 to fifth and $8,000 to sixth. WEIGHT: 126 lbs. Non-winners of $100,000 twice at one mile or over in 2004, allowed3 lbs.; $100,000 once or $60,000 twice at one mile or over in 2004, 5 lbs.; $60,000 once at one mile or over in 2004, 7 lbs. (Maiden and Claiming races not considered.) Failure to draw into this race at time of entry cancels all fees with the exceptionof the nominating fee(s). Starters to be named through the entry box on Wednesday, August 11, 2004. Two (2) horses having common ties through ownership cannot start to the exclusion of a single ownership interest. Trophy to the winning owner. Closed Wednesday, July 28, 2004 with 177 nominations. (If the management considers it inadvisable to run this race on the Turf Course, it will be run on the main track at One Mile and One Quarter).

Value of Race: $400,000 Winner $240,000; second $80,000; third $40,000; fourth $20,000; fifth $12,000; sixth $8,000. Mutuel Pool $748,557.00 Exacta Pool $409,810.00 Trifecta Pool $326,416.00 Superfecta Pool $106,601.00

Last Raced	Horse	M/Eqt.	A.	Wt	PP	¼	½	¾	1	Str	Fin	Jockey	Odds $1
10Jly04 ^{9}Cnl^{1}	Kitten's Joy	L	3	123	1	$6^{2\frac{1}{2}}$	$6^{1\frac{1}{2}}$	6^{4}	$5^{1\frac{1}{2}}$	$1^{\frac{1}{2}}$	$1^{3\frac{1}{4}}$	Bailey J D	0.90
26Jun04 ^{3}Hol^{1}	Greek Sun	L	3	121	3	5^{4}	5^{3}	$5^{2\frac{1}{2}}$	6^{4}	4^{1}	$2^{1\frac{1}{4}}$	Prado E S	2.90
27Jun04 Cur^{7}	Moscow Ballet-Ire	L	3	119	6	$3^{1\frac{1}{2}}$	$3^{1\frac{1}{2}}$	$4^{1\frac{1}{2}}$	$4^{1\frac{1}{2}}$	2^{hd}	3^{1}	Spencer J P	7.40
24Jly04 ^{5}AP^{1}	SimpleExchnge-Ire	L	3	123	7	$4^{1\frac{1}{2}}$	$4^{\frac{1}{2}}$	3^{hd}	2^{hd}	$3^{\frac{1}{2}}$	4^{3}	Smullen P J	7.90
24Jly04 ^{5}AP^{2}	Cool Conductor	L	3	119	5	1^{1}	1^{5}	1^{5}	1^{1}	5^{3}	$5^{1\frac{1}{4}}$	Day P	9.20
14Jly04 ML^{3}	Hazyview-GB	L	3	119	2	2^{1}	2^{1}	2^{1}	3^{hd}	6^{4}	$6^{5\frac{3}{4}}$	Dettori L	9.00
24Jly04 ^{5}AP^{5}	Up Anchor	L	3	119	4	7	7	7	7	7	7	Douglas R R	52.80

OFF AT6:00 Start Good . Won driving. Course firm.

TIME :23^{1}, :46^{3}, 1:11, 1:35^{1}, 1:59^{3} (:23.26, :46.70, 1:11.13, 1:35.38, 1:59.65)

$2 Mutuel Prices:				
	1 – KITTEN'S JOY	3.80	2.20	2.10
	3 – GREEK SUN		3.00	2.60
	6 – MOSCOW BALLET–IRE			2.80

$2 EXACTA 1–3 PAID $10.00 $2 TRIFECTA 1–3–6 PAID $55.60
$2 SUPERFECTA 1–3–6–7 PAID $171.40

Ch. c, (May), by El Prado–Ire – Kitten's First , by Lear Fan . Trainer Romans Dale. Bred by Kenneth L Ramsey & Sarah K Ramsey (Ky).

KITTEN'S JOY was taken in hand soon after the start, settled well back while saving ground along the backstretch, angled out to make his moved on the far turn, rapidly closed the gap while angling four wide midway on the turn, charged to the front in upper stretch then drew off with authority under a vigorous hand ride. GREEK SUN was rated just off the early pace while four wide, angled to the inside along the backstretch, was shuffled back while saving ground behind a wall of horses on the turn, waited patiently for room while boxed in behind the leaders at the top of the stretch, steadied and altered course to the outside in upper stretch then finished well in the middle of the track to best the others. MOSCOW BALLET (IRE) raced just off the pace while three wide along the backstretch, made a run between horses to threaten midway on the turn then lacked a strong closing bid. SIMPLE EXCHANGE (IRE) raced in the middle of the pack for seven furlongs, rallied along the inside to reach contention on the turn, lodged a mile bid to challenge nearing the quarter pole then faded in the stretch. COOL CONDUCTOR opened a wide gap in the early stages, set a rapid pace along the inside to the turn then faltered from his early efforts. HAZYVIEW (GB) raced up close along the inside to the turn and gave way. UP ANCHOR taken in hand leaving he gate, never reached contention. (Race run in lane 5, rail at 0.)

Owners– 1, Ramsey Kenneth L and Sarah K; 2, Angelos Peter G; 3, Tabor Michael and Magnier Mrs John; 4, Moyglare Stud Farm Ltd; 5, Garner David E; 6, Thomas Mohan; 7, Ralls and Foster LLC

Trainers– 1, Romans Dale; 2, Frankel Robert; 3, O'Brien Aidan P; 4, Weld Dermot K; 5, Mott William I; 6, Callaghan Neville A; 7, McGee Paul J

$1 Pick Three (FESTIVAL P3 9–4–1) Paid $324.00 ; Pick Three Pool $225,541 .

SEVENTH RACE
Saratoga
AUGUST 14, 2004

6 FURLONGS. (1.08) 20TH RUNNING OF THE ALFRED G. VANDERBILT HANDICAP. Grade II. Purse $200,000 (Up To $34,000 NYSBFOA) A HANDICAP FOR THREE YEAR OLDS AND UPWARD. By subscription of $200 each, which should accompany the nomination; $1,000 to pass the entry box, $1,000 to start. The purse to be divided 60% to the winner, 20% to second, 10% to third,5% to fourth, 3% to fifth and 2% divided equally among remaining finishers. A trophy will be presented to the winning owner. Closed Saturday, July 31, 2004 with 22 Nominations. The National Pick 4 is a wager that includes the 7th race at Saratoga as Leg A,the 8th race at Arlington Park as Leg B, the 8th race at Saratoga as Leg C, and the 9th race at Arlington Park as Leg D.

Value of Race: $200,000 Winner $120,000; second $40,000; third $20,000; fourth $10,000; fifth $6,000; sixth $4,000. Mutuel Pool $1,038,383.00 Exacta Pool $814,218.00 Trifecta Pool $496,199.00

Last Raced	Horse	M/Eqt.	A.	Wt	PP	St	¼	½	Str	Fin	Jockey	Odds $1
5Jun04 ^{7}Bel^{1}	Speightstown	L	6	120	2	5	1^{hd}	2^{hd}	$1^{2\frac{1}{2}}$	$1^{1\frac{1}{2}}$	Velazquez J R	0.90
10Jly04 ^{10}Crc^{2}	Clock Stopper	L b	4	115	1	6	$4^{\frac{1}{2}}$	4^{3}	$4^{3\frac{1}{2}}$	$2^{1\frac{1}{2}}$	Albarado R J	2.80
19Jun04 ^{9}Suf^{1}	Gators N Bears	L bf	4	118	5	2	3^{6}	$3^{2\frac{1}{2}}$	$3^{\frac{1}{2}}$	3^{2}	Lopez C C	5.30
22Jly04 ^{3}Bel^{1}	Mike's Classic	L bf	5	113	3	1	$2^{1\frac{1}{2}}$	1^{hd}	$2^{\frac{1}{2}}$	$4^{2\frac{3}{4}}$	Ganpath R	11.00
31Jly04 ^{9}Crc^{1}	Gold Dollar	L b	5	112	6	3	6	6	6	$5^{1\frac{1}{2}}$	Velasquez C	35.50
10Jly04 ^{10}Crc^{4}	My Cousin Matt	L f	5	114	4	4	$5^{5\frac{1}{2}}$	$5^{4\frac{1}{2}}$	$5^{1\frac{1}{2}}$	6	Dominguez R A	8.30

OFF AT4:21 Start Good . Won driving. Track fast.

TIME :22, :44^{2}, :55^{4}, 1:08 (:22.05, :44.40, :55.95, 1:08.04)

$2 Mutuel Prices:				
	2 – SPEIGHTSTOWN	3.80	2.60	2.10
	1 – CLOCK STOPPER		3.20	2.30
	5 – GATORS N BEARS			2.40

$2 EXACTA 2–1 PAID $9.60 $2 TRIFECTA 2–1–5 PAID $20.00

Ch. h, (Feb), by Gone West – Silken Cat , by Storm Cat . Trainer Pletcher Todd A. Bred by Aaron U Jones & Marie Jones (Ky).

SPEIGHTSTOWN flashed good speed along the inside, contested the pace along the rail, drew clear when asked entering the stretch, opened up when roused and remained clear while being kept busy to the wire. CLOCK STOPPER was outrun early, swung wide approaching the stretch, responded when roused and finished gamely outside but could not get to the winner. GATORS N BEARS raced close up early while in hand, rallied three wide nearing the stretch, could not handle the winner and faded in the final furlong. MIKE'S CLASSIC contested the pace from the outside and tired in the final furlong. GOLD DOLLAR was outrun early, came wide into the stretch and had no rally. MY COUSIN MATT was outrun early, raced inside and had no response when roused.

Owners– 1, Melnyk Eugene and Laura; 2, Overbrook Farm; 3, Nechamkin Leo S II; 4, Middletown Stables; 5, Pazos Julio; 6, Englander Richard A

Trainers– 1, Pletcher Todd A; 2, Stewart Dallas; 3, Nechamkin Leo S II; 4, Jerkens H Allen; 5, Azpurua Manuel J; 6, Lake Scott A

$2 Daily Double (9–2) Paid $70.50 ; Daily Double Pool $158,428 .
$2 Pick Three (2–9–2) Paid $662.00 ; Pick Three Pool $145,400 .

EIGHTH RACE
Saratoga
AUGUST 14, 2004

1½ MILES. (Inner Turf) (2.23^{1}) 30TH RUNNING OF THE SWORD DANCER INVITATIONAL HANDICAP. Grade I. Purse $500,000 INNER TURF (Up To $55,000 NYSBFOA) FOR THREE YEAR OLDS AND UPWARD. By invitation only with no subscription, entry or starting fees. The purse to be divided 60% to the owner of the winner, 20% to second, 10% to third, 5% to fourth, 3% to fifth and 2% divided equally among remaining finishers. Three Year Olds, 115 lbs.; Older, 123 lbs. Non–winners of a Grade 1 on the turf in 2004 allowed 3 lbs.; a Grade 1 on the turf in 2003 or a Grade 2 twice on the turf in 2003–04, 5 lbs; a Grade 2 on the turf in 2003–04,7 lbs. Selection of field of fourteen (14) invitees, Saturday July 31. Acceptance to participate in the Sword Dancer Invitational by Saturday, August 7. Alternate list Monday, August 9. Trophies will be presented to the winning owner, trainer and jockey.The New York Racing Association reserves the right to transfer this race to the Main Track. In the event that this race it taken off the turf, it may be subject to downgrading upon review by the Graded Stakes Committee. Closed Saturday, July 31, 2004 with 16 nominations.

Value of Race: $500,000 Winner $300,000; second $100,000; third $50,000; fourth $25,000; fifth $15,000; sixth $10,000. Mutuel Pool $967,398.00 Exacta Pool $753,742.00 Trifecta Pool $452,055.00

Last Raced	Horse	M/Eqt.	A.	Wt	PP	¼	½	1	1¼	Str	Fin	Jockey	Odds $1
17Jly04 ^{8}Bel^{2}	Better Talk Now	L bf	5	118	3	6	6	6	4^{hd}	3^{hd}	$1^{1\frac{1}{2}}$	Dominguez R A	7.90
3Jly04 ^{10}Mth^{1}	Request for Parole	L	5	123	4	3^{3}	$3^{\frac{1}{2}}$	3^{hd}	2^{2}	2^{1}	$2^{\frac{3}{4}}$	Castellano J J	2.20
3Jly04 ^{10}Mth^{6}	Balto Star	L	6	120	1	$1^{\frac{1}{2}}$	$1^{1\frac{1}{2}}$	$1^{\frac{1}{2}}$	$1^{\frac{1}{2}}$	$1^{\frac{1}{2}}$	3^{1}	Velazquez J R	1.55
31May04 ^{9}CD^{2}	Rochester	L	8	116	5	5^{1}	5^{1}	5^{hd}	3^{1}	4^{2}	$4^{2\frac{1}{4}}$	Velasquez C	10.70
4Jly04 ^{7}AP^{4}	Silverfoot	L	4	116	2	$4^{2\frac{1}{2}}$	$4^{\frac{1}{2}}$	4^{hd}	6	$5^{1\frac{1}{2}}$	$5^{4\frac{1}{4}}$	Albarado R J	3.75
17Jly04 ^{8}Bel^{4}	B. A. Way	L b	4	116	6	2^{1}	$2^{2\frac{1}{2}}$	$2^{\frac{1}{2}}$	$5^{1\frac{1}{2}}$	6	6	Bridgmohan S X	15.80

OFF AT 5:00 Start Good . Won driving. Course yielding.

TIME :24^{2}, :49^{4}, 1:15, 1:40^{1}, 2:04^{3}, 2:28^{2} (:24.48, :49.87, 1:15.08, 1:40.23, 2:04.62, 2:28.49)

$2 Mutuel Prices:				
	3 – BETTER TALK NOW	17.80	6.40	3.60
	4 – REQUEST FOR PAROLE		3.30	2.50
	1 – BALTO STAR			2.60

$2 EXACTA 3–4 PAID $53.50 $2 TRIFECTA 3–4–1 PAID $105.50

B. g, (Feb), by Talkin Man – Bendita , by Baldski . Trainer Motion H Graham. Bred by Wimborne Farm Inc (Ky).

BETTER TALK NOW was rated along inside, saved ground while well in hand, angled out and advanced nearing the stretch, responded when roused, finished gamely outside and was clear under the wire. REQUEST FOR PAROLE raced close up outside while in hand, raced three wide much of the trip, rallied three wide on the final turn, reached the front inside the eighth pole and dug in gamely but could not resist the winner. BALTO STAR quickly showed in front, set the pace along the inside while in hand, led into the final furlong and weakened inside late. ROCHESTER was outrun early, raced outside, advanced three wide on the last turn and lacked a rally. SILVERFOOT was taken in hand early, saved ground throughout and had no response when roused. B. A. WAY prompted the pace from the outside and tired in the stretch.

Owners– 1, Bushwood Stables; 2, Knighton Jeri and Sam; 3, Anstu Stables Inc; 4, Augustin Stable; 5, Clark Stephanie S; 6, Perkins Diane

Trainers– 1, Motion H Graham; 2, Hough Stanley M; 3, Pletcher Todd A; 4, Sheppard Jonathan E; 5, Stewart Dallas; 6, Violette Richard A Jr

---

EIGHTH RACE
Del Mar
AUGUST 14, 2004

1$\frac{1}{16}$ MILES. (Turf) (1.39^{4}) 64TH RUNNING OF THE LA JOLLA HANDICAP. Grade II. Purse $150,000 FOR THREE–YEAR OLDS. By subscription of $150 each, which shall accompany the nomination, or by supplementary nomination of $1,500 each by Sunday, August 8, $500 to pass the entry box and $1,000 additional to start, with $150,000 Guaranteed, of which $90,000 to first, $30,000 to second, $18,000 to third, $9,000 to fourth and $3,000 to fifth. Weights Monday, August 9. High weights preferred. A trophy will be presented to the owner of the winner. Closed Thursday, August 5, 2004 with 18 nominations.

Value of Race: $150,000 Winner $90,000; second $30,000; third $18,000; fourth $9,000; fifth $3,000. Mutuel Pool $623,997.00 Exacta Pool $279,616.00 Quinella Pool $29,618.00 Trifecta Pool $309,013.00

Last Raced	Horse	M/Eqt.	A.	Wt	PP	St	¼	½	¾	Str	Fin	Jockey	Odds $1
21Jly04 ^{8}Dmr^{1}	Blackdoun-FR	LB b	3	120	5	7	6^{hd}	6^{hd}	6^{hd}	$4^{\frac{1}{2}}$	$1^{\frac{3}{4}}$	Nakatani C S	0.90
21Jly04 ^{6}Dmr^{2}	Semi Lost	LB	3	116	7	3	7	7	7	$1^{\frac{1}{2}}$	$2^{\frac{3}{4}}$	Baze T C	3.30
21Jly04 ^{6}Dmr^{4}	Bedmar-GB	LB b	3	113	3	6	4^{1}	$4^{\frac{1}{2}}$	$4^{1\frac{1}{2}}$	2^{1}	$3^{\frac{1}{2}}$	Santiago Javier	41.60
21Jun04 CHY^{4}	Sujimoto	LB	3	116	6	4	5^{2}	$5^{1\frac{1}{2}}$	$5^{\frac{1}{2}}$	6^{5}	$4^{\frac{3}{4}}$	Flores D R	6.00
26Jun04 ^{3}Hol^{2}	Laura's Lucky Boy	LB	3	120	2	1	$3^{\frac{1}{2}}$	3^{1}	3^{hd}	5^{hd}	5^{3}	Court J K	3.40
21Jly04 ^{8}Dmr^{5}	Austin Barber	LB	3	115	1	2	$1^{3\frac{1}{2}}$	$1^{2\frac{1}{2}}$	1^{1}	$3^{\frac{1}{2}}$	6^{7}	Puglisi I	42.40
26Jun04 ^{3}Hol^{6}	Unrivalled-GB	LB	3	115	4	5	2^{1}	2^{1}	$2^{\frac{1}{2}}$	7	7	John K	36.70

OFF AT 5:39 Start Good . Won driving. Course firm.

TIME :23^{4}, :47^{3}, 1:11^{2}, 1:35^{1}, 1:41 (:23.92, :47.62, 1:11.45, 1:35.29, 1:41.03)

$2 Mutuel Prices:				
	5 – BLACKDOUN–FR	3.80	2.60	2.40
	7 – SEMI LOST		3.20	3.00
	3 – BEDMAR–GB			4.80

$1 EXACTA 5–7 PAID $5.90 $2 QUINELLA 5–7 PAID $7.60
$1 TRIFECTA 5–7–3 PAID $47.80

Gr/ro. c, (Apr), by Verglas–Ire – Rade , by Kaldoun–Fr . Trainer Canani Julio C. Bred by Sabine Charpentier & &Anne–Charlotte Charpentier (Fr).

BLACKDOUN (FR) angled in and settled inside chasing the pace, waited behind foes leaving the second turn, came out in upper stretch, steadied off heels nearing midstretch, then split horses under brisk hand urging in deep stretch to gain the lead and proved best. SEMI LOST wide in the chute, angled in and chased outside the winner, went three deep leaving the second turn and four wide into the stretch, took a short lead while lugging inward, could not match the winner late but held second. BEDMAR (GB) saved ground stalking the pace, came out into the stretch, went between foes with a bid nearing midstretch, drifted back to the rail and held third. SUJIMOTO angled in and chased outside a rival then off the rail leaving the backstretch, continued outside on the second turn and three deep into the stretch and was edged for third. LAURA'S LUCKY BOY stalked outside a rival, went three deep into and on the second turn and into the stretch, steadied slightly when the runner-up went past in upper stretch and lacked the needed response. AUSTIN BARBER sped to the early lead, set the pace along the inside but weakened in the stretch. UNRIVALLED (GB) pulled his way between foes then stalked a bit off the rail, was between horses leaving the second turn and also weakened.

Owners– 1, Naify and Woodside Farms LLC; 2, Bone Robert D and Desperado Stables; 3, Brown Ann H; 4, Amerman Racing Stables LLC; 5, Mercedes Stables LLC; 6, Dunford Jeri Montgomery Greg Sharpe Scott et al; 7, Jim Ford Inc Pearson Daron and Sweesy Jack

Trainers– 1, Canani Julio C; 2, Mullins Jeff; 3, Greely C Beau; 4, Frankel Robert; 5, Orman Jason; 6, Halpern Edward; 7, Cassidy James

---

$2 Daily Double (6–5) Paid $10.00 ; Daily Double Pool $39,813 .
$1 Pick Three (7–6–5) Paid $31.00 ; Pick Three Pool $117,490 .

SECOND RACE
Del Mar
AUGUST 15, 2004

6½ FURLONGS. (1.13^{3}) 34TH RUNNING OF THE BEST PAL. Grade II. Purse $150,000 FOR TWO-YEAR-OLDS. By subscription of $150 each, which shall accompany the nomination, or by supplementary nomination of $1,500 each by closing time of entries, $1,500 additional to start, with $150,000 Guaranteed, of which $90,000 to first, $30,000 to second, $18,000 to third, $9,000 to fourth and $3,000 to fifth. Weight 122 lbs.; Non-winners of $50,000 allowed 2 lbs.; of a race of $25,000 other than maiden or claiming, 4 lbs.; of a race other than claiming, 6 lbs. A trophy will be presented to the owner of the winner. Closed Thursday, August 5, 2004 with 10 nominations.

Value of Race: $147,000 Winner $90,000; second $30,000; third $18,000; fourth $9,000. Mutuel Pool $507,276.00 Exacta Pool $325,013.00 Quinella Pool $38,095.00

Last Raced	Horse	M/Eqt.	A.	Wt	PP	St	¼	½	Str	Fin	Jockey	Odds $1
19Jun04 ^{6}Hol^{1}	Roman Ruler	LB	2	118	2	5	4^{4}	4^{5}	1^{2}	1^{7}	Nakatani C S	0.50
17Jly04 ^{3}Hol^{2}	Actxecutive	LB	2	118	1	2	$2^{\frac{1}{2}}$	1^{hd}	2^{5}	2^{10}	Flores D R	4.90
21Jly04 ^{5}Dmr^{4}	Slewsbag	LB	2	116	4	4	5	5	4	$3^{1\frac{1}{2}}$	Valdivia J Jr	26.70
15Jly04 ^{4}Hol^{1}	Things Happen	LB b	2	118	5	1	1^{1}	$2^{1\frac{1}{2}}$	3^{2}	4	Pedroza M A	3.20
24Jly04 ^{2}Dmr^{1}	Wetherly	B	2	118	3	3	3^{7}	3^{4}	—	—	Desormeaux K J	11.20

OFF AT 2:44 Start Good . Won ridden out. Track fast.

TIME :21^{4}, :44^{4}, 1:09^{3}, 1:15^{4} (:21.82, :44.93, 1:09.68, 1:15.93)

$2 Mutuel Prices:

2 – **ROMAN RULER**....................	3.00	2.20	2.10
1 – **ACTXECUTIVE**....................		3.00	2.10
4 – **SLEWSBAG**........................			2.10

$1 EXACTA 2–1 PAID $4.20 $2 QUINELLA 1–2 PAID $32.20

Dk. b or br. c, (Mar), by Fusaichi Pegasus – Silvery Swan , by Silver Deputy . Trainer Baffert Bob. Bred by Needham/ Betz Thoroughbreds Liberation&Farm & Ashford Stud (Ky).

ROMAN RULER broke a bit slowly and was squeezed back, drifted out and settled off the pace, angled in some leaving the backstretch, steadied at the fallen horse midway on the turn, came out leaving the bend, swept to the front in upper stretch and drew off under a moderate hand ride. ACTXECUTIVE broke outward, stalked the early leader inside, bid along the rail and dueled for the lead, inched away leaving the turn, was no match for the winner in the stretch but clearly second best. SLEWSBAG off a bit slowly, settled out from the inside, angled in on the turn then swerved outward around the fallen foe, came out into the stretch, then drifted back to the rail but got the show. THINGS HAPPEN had good early speed three deep, inched away and angled in some, dueled outside the runner-up on the turn, began to weaken approaching the stretch and gave way. WETHERLY broke inward, raced between horses early, chased off the rail on the backstretch and into the turn and broke down midway on the turn.

Owners– 1, Fog City Stable; 2, McIngvale James; 3, Spencer Gary D; 4, Harris Farms Inc and Antonsen Per; 5, Currin William L and Eisman Alvin

Trainers– 1, Baffert Bob; 2, Baffert Bob; 3, Polanco Marcelo; 4, Jones Martin F; 5, Currin William L

$2 Daily Double (1–2) Paid $32.20 ; Daily Double Pool $131,111 .

EIGHTH RACE
Del Mar
AUGUST 15, 2004

7 FURLONGS. (1.20) 19TH RUNNING OF THE PAT O'BRIEN BREEDERS' CUP HANDICAP. Grade II. Purse $200,000 (includes $50,000 BC – Breeders' Cup) FOR THREE-YEAR-OLDS AND UPWARD. By subscription of $150 each, which shall accompany the nomination, or by supplementary nomination of $1,500 each by Sunday, August 8, $1,500 additional to start, with $150,000 and an additional $50,000 from the Breeders' Cup Fund for Cup nominees only. The host association's monies to be divided 60% to the winner, 20% to second, 12% to third, 6% to fourth and 2% to fifth. Breeders' Cup monies also correspondingly divided, provided a Breeders' Cup nominee has finished inan awarded position. Any Breeders' Cup Fund monies not awarded will revert to the Fund. Weights Monday, August 9. High weights preferred. The starters will be determined at entry time with preference given to Breeders' Cup nominees only of equal racinng quality or weight assignment (respective of sex and weight for age). A trophy will be presented to the winning owner by Breeders' Cup Ltd. Cosed Thursday, August 5, 2004 with 12 nominations.

Value of Race: $194,000 Winner $120,000; second $40,000; third $18,000; fourth $12,000; fifth $4,000. Mutuel Pool $598,895.00 Exacta Pool $291,457.00 Quinella Pool $28,477.00 Trifecta Pool $202,066.00 Superfecta Pool $90,472.00

Last Raced	Horse	M/Eqt.	A.	Wt	PP	St	¼	½	Str	Fin	Jockey	Odds $1
25Jly04 ^{2}Dmr^{1}	Kela	LB b	6	116	4	5	5	5	1^{2}	$1^{4\frac{1}{2}}$	Baze T C	2.60
27Mar04 ^{9}NAS^{6}	Domestic Dispute	LB	4	116	2	3	4^{4}	$3^{1\frac{1}{2}}$	$3^{\frac{1}{2}}$	$2^{1\frac{1}{4}}$	Desormeaux K J	13.10
31May04 ^{9}Bel^{1}	Pico Central-Brz	LB	5	122	3	1	1^{hd}	1^{hd}	2^{2}	3^{4}	Flores D R	0.40
30Jly04 ^{2}Dmr^{2}	Hasty Kris	LB b	7	114	1	4	3^{hd}	4^{hd}	5	$4^{2\frac{1}{2}}$	Espinoza V	12.30
1Aug04 ^{8}Dmr^{6}	Taste of Paradise	LB b	5	114	5	2	$2^{1\frac{1}{2}}$	2^{3}	4^{2}	5	Court J K	16.00

OFF AT 5:47 Start Good . Won driving. Track fast.

TIME :21^{4}, :43^{4}, 1:08^{1}, 1:21 (:21.98, :43.92, 1:08.37, 1:21.17)

$2 Mutuel Prices:

6 – **KELA**.............................	7.20	4.20	2.10
2 – **DOMESTIC DISPUTE**...............		8.60	2.10
3 – **PICO CENTRAL–BRZ**...............			2.10

$1 EXACTA 6–2 PAID $29.30 $2 QUINELLA 2–6 PAID $31.20

$1 TRIFECTA 6–2–3 PAID $37.70 $1 SUPERFECTA 6–2–3–1 PAID $133.30

B. h, (Mar), by Numerous – Bolshoi Comedy , by Sovereign Dancer . Trainer Mitchell Mike. Bred by Cypress Farms 1991 (Ky).

KELA unhurried off the rail on the backstretch, moved up outside on the turn, swept to the front three deep into the stretch and pulled clear under some urging. DOMESTIC DISPUTE stalked outside a rival then off the rail leaving the turn, came out into the stretch and gained the place. PICO CENTRAL (BRZ) had good early speed and dueled inside a rival but a bit off the rail, angled in and fought back on the turn, and weakened in the stretch but held third. HASTY KRIS saved ground stalking the pace, came out into the stretch and weakened. TASTE OF PARADISE angled in and dueled outside PICO CENTRAL, put a head in front on the turn, was between horses into the stretch and also weakened.

Owners– 1, Manoogian Jay; 2, Bienstock Mandabach & Winner; 3, Tanaka Gary A; 4, C R K Stable; 5, Bloom David B

Trainers– 1, Mitchell Mike; 2, Gallagher Patrick; 3, Lobo Paulo H; 4, Sadler John W; 5, Pearson Molly J

Scratched– Disturbingthepeace (25Jul04 ^{2}Dmr^{9}) , Amerindio (ARG) (10Jul04 ^{3}Hol^{2}) , Marino Marini (08May04 ^{6}Hol^{2})

$2 Daily Double (10–6) Paid $57.00 ; Daily Double Pool $33,228 .
$1 Pick Three (8–10–6) Paid $125.40 ; Pick Three Pool $89,868 .

TENTH RACE
Monmouth
AUGUST 15, 2004

$1\frac{1}{16}$ MILES. (1.40^{1}) 80TH RUNNING OF THE MONMOUTH BRREEDERS' CUP OAKS. Grade II. Purse $200,000 (includes $100,000 BC – Breeders' Cup) FOR FILLIES, THREE YEARS OLD. By subscription of $200 each, which should accompany the nomination and $3,000 to pass the entry box with $200,000 guaranteed which includes $100,000 from the Breeders' Cup Fund for Cup nominees only. The host association's money to be divided 60% to the owner of the winner, 20% to second, 11% to third, 6% to fourth and 3% to fifth. Breeders' Cup money also correspondingly divided providing a Breeders' Cup nominee has finished in an awarded position. Any Breeders' Cup money not awarded will revert to the Fund. Weight: 121 lbs. Non-winners of a Graded Stake at a mile or over in 2004 allowed 3 lbs.; $60,000 in 2004, 6 lbs. Breeders' Cup Limited will present a trophy to the winning owner. Closed Sunday, August 1, 2004 with 18 nominations.

Value of Race: $200,000 Winner $120,000; second $40,000; third $22,000; fourth $12,000; fifth $6,000. Mutuel Pool $197,979.00 Exacta Pool $161,462.00 Trifecta Pool $89,596.00 Superfecta Pool $26,352.00

Last Raced	Horse	M/Eqt.	A.	Wt	PP	St	¼	½	¾	Str	Fin	Jockey	Odds $1
5Jly04 ^{10}Mth^{1}	Capeside Lady	L	3	115	2	1	$1^{1\frac{1}{2}}$	$1^{\frac{1}{2}}$	1^{1}	1^{5}	$1^{6\frac{1}{2}}$	Decarlo C P	1.70
17Jly04 ^{8}Del^{4}	Hopelessly Devoted	L	3	118	1	2	6	6	5^{1}	3^{hd}	$2^{3\frac{1}{4}}$	Guidry M	9.90
29Jly04 ^{7}Mth^{1}	Habiboo	L	3	115	5	3	3^{hd}	3^{hd}	$3^{1\frac{1}{2}}$	4^{5}	3no	Soto J A Jr	16.40
17Jly04 ^{8}Del^{2}	Ender's Sister	L	3	118	6	5	5^{3}	$4^{\frac{1}{2}}$	$2^{\frac{1}{2}}$	$2^{\frac{1}{2}}$	$4^{8\frac{1}{2}}$	Velasquez C	1.00
29Jly04 ^{6}Mth^{1}	Rings and Things	L	3	115	4	6	4^{hd}	5^{3}	6	5^{hd}	$5^{3\frac{3}{4}}$	Bravo J	6.80
17Jly04 ^{8}Del^{5}	Pilfer	L bf	3	118	3	4	$2^{\frac{1}{2}}$	$2^{\frac{1}{2}}$	$4^{\frac{1}{2}}$	6	6	Elliott S	11.20

OFF AT 5:15 Start Good . Won driving. Track muddy.

TIME :23^{4}, :47^{3}, 1:11^{2}, 1:35^{4}, 1:42 (:23.80, :47.60, 1:11.51, 1:35.90, 1:42.18)

$2 Mutuel Prices:

2 – CAPESIDE LADY	5.40	3.40	2.80
1 – HOPELESSLY DEVOTED		7.20	4.80
5 – HABIBOO			3.80

$2 EXACTA 2–1 PAID $32.80 $2 TRIFECTA 2–1–5 PAID $314.00
$1 SUPERFECTA 2–1–5–6 PAID $270.70

B. f, (Apr), by Cape Town – Gray Lady Type , by Zen . Trainer Pletcher Todd A. Bred by Thomas/Lakin (NY).

CAPESIDE LADY rated the pace inside, was urged clear entering the stretch then widened with a mostly hand ride. HOPELESSLY DEVOTED, unhurriedly, started her drive outside into the final turn, reached place an eighth out and proved best of the rest. HABIBOO rated just off the pace about the four path, made her bid entering the stretch, drifted slightly in and leveled off. ENDER'S SISTER made light contact with Rings And Things entering the opening turn, was kept just off the pace in the three path, began her push into the final turn then weakened from the furlong pole. RINGS AND THINGS broke awkwardly, made light contact with Ender's Sister into the opening turn, rated just off the pace toward the inside, angled out into the final turn then weakened outside. PILFER rated close just off the rail, picked up the chase into the final turn the faded through the turn.

Owners– 1, So Madcapt Stable; 2, Liberty Stable; 3, Hardacre Farm LLC; 4, Green Lantern Stables LLC; 5, Andrew Farm and Tabor Michael; 6, Fox Hill Farms Inc

Trainers– 1, Pletcher Todd A; 2, Slivka Sandra L; 3, Tarrant Amy; 4, Arnold George R II; 5, Biancone Patrick L; 6, Servis John C

Scratched– Hopelessly Devoted (17Jul04 ^{8}Del^{4}) , Capeside Lady (05Jul04 ^{10}Mth^{1}) , Pilfer (17Jul04 ^{8}Del^{5}) , Rings and Things (29Jul04 ^{6}Mth^{1}) , Habiboo (29Jul04 ^{7}Mth^{1}) , Ender's Sister (17Jul04 ^{8}Del^{2})

EIGHTH RACE
Saratoga
AUGUST 20, 2004

7 FURLONGS. (1.20^{2}) 113TH RUNNING OF THE SPINAWAY. Grade II. Purse $250,000 (Up To $37,500) FOR FILLIES TWO YEARS OLD. By subscription of $250 each, which should accompany the nomination; $1,250 to pass the entry box, $1,250 to start. The purse to be divided 60% to the winner, 20% to second, 10% to third, 5% to fourth, 3% to fifth and 2% divided equally among remaining finishers. 121 lbs. A trophy will be presented to the winning owner. Closed Saturday, August 7, 2004 with 24 Nominations.

Value of Race: $250,000 Winner $150,000; second $50,000; third $25,000; fourth $12,500; fifth $7,500; sixth $2,500; seventh $2,500. Mutuel Pool $738,787.00 Exacta Pool $583,292.00 Trifecta Pool $403,089.00

Last Raced	Horse	M/Eqt.	A.	Wt	PP	St	¼	½	Str	Fin	Jockey	Odds $1
1Aug04 ^{4}Sar^{1}	Sense of Style		2	121	4	4	3^{hd}	$3^{1\frac{1}{2}}$	$1^{\frac{1}{2}}$	$1^{6\frac{3}{4}}$	Prado E S	0.95
15Jly04 ^{6}Mth^{1}	Miss Matched	L	2	121	3	6	4^{hd}	$2^{\frac{1}{2}}$	2^{hd}	$2^{\frac{3}{4}}$	Albarado R J	7.40
29Jly04 ^{4}Sar^{1}	Play With Fire	L	2	121	6	2	7	7	6^{1}	$3^{\frac{1}{2}}$	Fragoso P	17.60
28Jly04 ^{9}Sar^{5}	Broadway Gold	L b	2	121	7	3	$5^{\frac{1}{2}}$	4^{3}	4^{1}	$4^{\frac{3}{4}}$	Bailey J D	4.90
23Jly04 ^{9}Crc^{1}	Punch Appeal	L	2	121	2	7	$6^{2\frac{1}{2}}$	$6^{2\frac{1}{2}}$	$5^{2\frac{1}{2}}$	5^{1}	Velasquez C	21.00
29Jly04 ^{5}Mth^{1}	Portsea	L	2	121	5	1	$1^{\frac{1}{2}}$	$1^{\frac{1}{2}}$	$3^{3\frac{1}{2}}$	$6^{7\frac{3}{4}}$	Velazquez J R	18.20
28Jly04 ^{9}Sar^{1}	Classic Elegance		2	121	1	5	$2^{\frac{1}{2}}$	5^{hd}	7	7	Day P	3.60

OFF AT 4:47 Start Good . Won driving. Track fast.

TIME :22^{3}, :45^{3}, 1:10^{3}, 1:23^{1} (:22.73, :45.70, 1:10.68, 1:23.83)

$2 Mutuel Prices:

4 – SENSE OF STYLE	3.90	2.90	2.40
3 – MISS MATCHED		4.90	4.50
6 – PLAY WITH FIRE			5.30

$2 EXACTA 4–3 PAID $20.60 $2 TRIFECTA 4–3–6 PAID $152.00

B. f, (Mar), by Thunder Gulch – Save Me the Waltz-Ire , by Kings Lake . Trainer Biancone Patrick L. Bred by Twelve Oaks Stud (Ky).

SENSE OF STYLE came away well, raced close up outside while in hand, moved to the leaders approaching the stretch, responded when roused, quickly drew away and was under a vigorous hand ride to the wire. MISS MATCHED stumbled at the start, was bumped after the start, was urged up along the inside, argued the pace into the stretch, was no match for the winner and dug on the rail to hold the place. PLAY WITH FIRE bobbled at the start, was outrun early, came wide approaching the stretch and finished well outside. BROADWAY GOLD raced four wide while in hand and had no response when roused. PUNCH APPEAL was bumped at the start, was outrun early and had no rally. PORTSEA quickly showed in front, set the pace while between rivals and tired in the final furlong. CLASSIC ELEGANCE was bumped at the start, showed speed along the inside, was shuffled back entering the turn and tired.

Owners– 1, Smith Derrick and Tabor Michael; 2, Oxley John C; 3, Zwerling Gary L; 4, Robsham Mrs E P; 5, Heiligbrodt Stable Masterson Robert E Burning Day Farm Waldron Dianne K; 6, Vinery Stables; 7, Lewis Robert B and Beverly J

Trainers– 1, Biancone Patrick L; 2, Ward John T Jr; 3, Hennig Mark; 4, Hough Stanley M; 5, Asmussen Steven M; 6, Pletcher Todd A; 7, Lukas D Wayne

---

NINTH RACE
Arlington
AUGUST 21, 2004

1⅛ MILES. (1.46[1]) 25TH RUNNING OF THE ARLINGTON BREEDERS' CUP OAKS. Grade III. Purse $150,000 (includes $50,000 BC – Breeders' Cup) FOR FILLIES, THREE-YEARS-OLD. By subscription of $100 each, which should accompany the nomination. Original nominees to pay $750 to pass the entry box and an additional $750 to start, with $100,000 Guaranteed by Arlington Park and an additional $50,000 from the Breeders' Cup Fund for Cup eligibles only. The $100,000 Guaranteed by Arlington Park to be divided $60,000 to the winner; $20,000 to second; $11,000 to third; $6,000 to fourth and $3,000 to fifth. Breeders' Cup Fund monies also correspondingly divided providing a Breeders' Cup nominee has finished in an awarded position. Any Breeders' Cup Fund monies not awarded will revert back to the fund. WEIGHT: 122 lbs. Non-winners of $50,000 once at one mile or over in 2004, allowed 2 lbs.; $40,000 once or$25,000 twice at one mile or over in 2004, 4 lbs.; a sweepstakes at one mile or over in 2003–2004 or $20,000 twice at one mile or over in 2004, 6 lbs. (Maiden and Claiming races not considered.) Starters to be named through the entry box by usual time offclosing. Two (2) horses having common ties through ownership cannot start to the exclusion of a single ownership interest. Trophy to the owner of the winner given by Breeders' Cup Ltd. Nominations closed Wednesday August 11, with 22.

Value of Race: $150,000 Winner $60,000; Winner $60,000; third $16,500; fourth $9,000; fifth $4,500. Mutuel Pool $227,307.00 Exacta Pool $138,152.00 Trifecta Pool $121,278.00 Superfecta Pool $47,336.00

Last Raced	Horse	M/Eqt.	A.	Wt	PP	St	¼	½	¾	Str	Fin	Jockey	Odds $1
15Jly04 8AP2	DH Lovely Afternoon	L	3	116	2	5	$2^{\frac{1}{2}}$	2^{hd}	2^{hd}	3^{2}	1	Graham J	17.30
30Jly04 8AP2	DH Catboat	L b	3	118	3	10	$6^{\frac{1}{2}}$	6^{1}	$5^{\frac{1}{2}}$	$1^{1\frac{1}{2}}$	$1^{1\frac{3}{4}}$	Martin E M Jr	4.50
8Aug04 8AP1	My Time Now	L bf	3	116	4	6	$5^{\frac{1}{2}}$	5^{hd}	6^{1}	$4^{\frac{1}{2}}$	3^{1}	Meier R	15.50
30Jly04 8AP1	Fly Away Angel	L bf	3	118	1	4	$1^{1\frac{1}{2}}$	$1^{1\frac{1}{2}}$	1^{1}	2^{hd}	4^{3}	Lumpkins J	2.40
28Jly04 5AP2	Platinum Ballet	L b	3	116	9	7	8^{1}	9^{3}	8^{2}	$7^{1\frac{1}{2}}$	5^{1}	Emigh C A	11.30
30Jly04 8AP3	Miss Moses	L	3	116	5	1	$3^{\frac{1}{2}}$	$3^{\frac{1}{2}}$	3^{hd}	6^{hd}	6no	Marquez C H Jr	3.60
30Jly04 8AP7	Touch of Victory	L	3	116	8	8	$9^{2\frac{1}{2}}$	8^{hd}	$7^{\frac{1}{2}}$	5^{2}	$7^{4\frac{1}{2}}$	Douglas R R	11.60
17Jly04 3EIP3	Teenage Temper	L f	3	116	6	3	7^{1}	$7^{1\frac{1}{2}}$	9^{7}	8^{3}	$8^{2\frac{1}{4}}$	Blanc B	4.50
30Jly04 7AP1	Flashy	L f	3	116	7	2	$4^{1\frac{1}{2}}$	$4^{1\frac{1}{2}}$	$4^{\frac{1}{2}}$	9^{7}	$9^{11\frac{1}{2}}$	Razo E Jr	23.20
11Aug04 8AP2	Chancey Light	L b	3	117	10	9	10	10	10	10	10	Lovato F Jr	49.00

DH-Dead Heat.

OFF AT 4:56 Start Good . Won driving. Track fast.

TIME :24[2], :48[2], 1:13, 1:38, 1:51 (:24.53, :48.42, 1:13.07, 1:38.15, 1:51.06)

$2 Mutuel Prices:

2 – DH LOVELY AFTERNOON	16.00	15.20	8.60
3 – DH CATBOAT	6.20	7.20	5.80
4 – MY TIME NOW			10.60

$2 EXACTA 2-3 PAID $101.60 $2 EXACTA 3-2 PAID $76.20
$2 TRIFECTA 2-3-4 PAID $783.80 $2 TRIFECTA 3-2-4 PAID $659.20
$2 SUPERFECTA 2-3-4-1 PAID $1,543.20 $2 SUPERFECTA 3-2-4-1 PAID $1,244.40

Lovely Afternoon —Dk. b or br. f, (Apr), by Afternoon Deelites – Lovely Later , by Green Dancer . Trainer Mitchell Anthony. Bred by Two Sisters Farm (Pa).

Catboat —Dk. b or br. f, (Mar), by Tale of the Cat – Northern Fleet , by Afleet . Trainer Flint Bernard S. Bred by Stonerside Stable (Ky).

LOVELY AFTERNOON raced close up while three wide, remained in good position to the stretch, rallied in the final furlong and was along to finish on even terms with CATBOAT. CATBOAT broke slowly, quickly recovered to race inside near the middle of the field, moved up on the rail, slipped through on the rail and dead heated for the win. MY TIME NOW raced just outside near the middle of the field, responded in the stretch and did not miss by much. FLY AWAY ANGEL set the pace from just outside and weakened. PLATINUM BALLET was void of speed and improved her position. MISS MOSES raced close up four wide and weakened. TOUCH OF VICTORY made a mild bid in the stretch and faltered. TEENAGE TEMPER was always outrun. FLASHY raced close up five wide and tired. CHANCEY LIGHT trailed throughout.

Owners– 1, Richard Otto Stables Inc; 2, Stonerside Stable LLC; 3, Phillips Racing Partnership; 4, Schaeffer Bernard G; 5, Sanders Wayne R; 6, Mount Brilliant Stable LLC; 7, Cranston Mel; 8, Stanley Mark H; 9, Tafel James B; 10, J D Farms and Dellheim Peggy

Trainers– 1, Mitchell Anthony; 2, Flint Bernard S; 3, Nafzger Carl A; 4, Connelly William R; 5, Von Hemel Donnie K; 6, Stidham Michael; 7, Hobby Steve; 8, Fortner David; 9, Nafzger Carl A; 10, Weipert Brian

$1 Pick Three (6-2-2/3) Paid $554.40 ; Pick Three Pool $15,524 .

NINTH RACE
Saratoga
AUGUST 21, 2004

7 FURLONGS. (1.20[2]) 100TH RUNNING OF THE HOPEFUL. Grade I. Purse $250,000 FOR TWO YEAR OLDS. By subscription of $250 each, which should accompany the nomination; $1,250 to pass the entry box, $1,250 to start. The purse to be divided 60% to the winner, 20% to second, 10% to third, 5% to fourth, 3% to fifth and 2% divided equallyamong remaining finishers. 122 lbs. Trophies will be presented to the winning owner, trainer and jockey. Closed Saturday, August 7, 2004 with 22 Nominations.

Value of Race: $250,000 Winner $150,000; second $50,000; third $25,000; fourth $12,500; fifth $7,500; sixth $2,500; seventh $2,500. Mutuel Pool $959,530.00 Exacta Pool $725,971.00 Trifecta Pool $537,316.00

Last Raced	Horse	M/Eqt.	A.	Wt	PP	St	¼	½	Str	Fin	Jockey	Odds $1
29Jly04 8Sar1	Afleet Alex	L	2	122	6	3	5^{hd}	$4^{\frac{1}{2}}$	3^{6}	1^{nk}	Rose J	0.70
25Jly04 6Crc1	Devils Disciple	L bf	2	122	1	7	2^{hd}	1^{hd}	$1^{\frac{1}{2}}$	$2^{1\frac{3}{4}}$	Velasquez C	2.95
29Jly04 8Sar2	Flamenco	L	2	122	3	4	$3^{2\frac{1}{2}}$	2^{hd}	$2^{1\frac{1}{2}}$	3^{11}	Bailey J D	8.00
29Jly04 8Sar3	Consolidator	L b	2	122	7	2	$6^{\frac{1}{2}}$	6^{6}	4^{1}	$4^{4\frac{1}{4}}$	Day P	8.60
4Aug04 7Sar1	Storm Surge	L f	2	122	5	1	4^{hd}	$5^{1\frac{1}{2}}$	$5^{3\frac{1}{2}}$	5^{12}	Albarado R J	13.70
4Aug04 7Sar2	Wild Nature-GB	L f	2	122	4	6	7	7	7	$6^{\frac{3}{4}}$	Migliore R	45.50
29Jly04 8Sar4	Winning Expression	L	2	122	2	5	$1^{\frac{1}{2}}$	3^{2}	$6^{1\frac{1}{2}}$	7	Prado E S	33.50

OFF AT 5:19 Start Good . Won driving. Track sloppy.

TIME :22, :44[3], 1:09[4], 1:23[2] (:22.00, :44.79, 1:09.90, 1:23.58)

$2 Mutuel Prices:

6 – AFLEET ALEX	3.40	2.40	2.10
1 – DEVILS DISCIPLE		3.20	2.10
3 – FLAMENCO			2.10

$2 EXACTA 6-1 PAID $8.20 $2 TRIFECTA 6-1-3 PAID $21.40

B. c, (May), by Northern Afleet – Maggy Hawk , by Hawkster . Trainer Ritchey Tim F. Bred by John Martin Silvertand (Fla).

AFLEET ALEX bumped with CONSOLIDATOR in the early stages, angled to the inside along the backstretch, moved up a bit while saving ground to the far turn, swung to the outside for clear sailing on the turn, launched a rally four wide entering the stretch, closed the gap a bit in upper stretch, drifted out considerably under left hand whipping in midstretch, straightened away under right hand urging a sixteenth out then finished with a flourish to wear down DEVILS DISCIPLE in the final strides. DEVILS DISCIPLE bobbled at the start, rushed up along the rail, surged to the front on the far turn, battled heads apart along the rail into upper stretch, fought gamely into deep stretch and yielded grudgingly. FLAMENCO pressed the pace three wide along the backstretch, drew along side DEVILS DISCIPLE to challenge on the turn, dueled outside that into midstretch and weakened in the final seventy yards. CONSOLIDATOR hit the gate then bumped with the winner at the start, raced well back to the turn, advanced four wide into the stretch and failed to threaten while improving his position. STORM SURGE raced between horses while just off the early pace, swung five wide on the turn then lacked a strong closing bid. WILD NATURE (GB) never reached contention. WINNING EXPRESSION dueled between horses for a half and tired from his early efforts.

Owners– 1, Cash is King LLC; 2, Somers John; 3, Peachtree Stable; 4, Lewis Robert B and Beverly J; 5, Overbrook Farm; 6, Buckram Oak Farm; 7, Flying Zee Stable

Trainers– 1, Ritchey Tim F; 2, Waunsch Joseph J; 3, Pletcher Todd A; 4, Lukas D Wayne; 5, Stewart Dallas; 6, Mikhalides George; 7, Serpe Philip M

TENTH RACE
Saratoga
AUGUST 21, 2004

1¼ MILES. (2.00) 124TH RUNNING OF THE ALABAMA. Grade I. Purse $750,000 (UP TO $62,500 NYSBFOA) FOR FILLIES THREE YEARS OLD. By subscription of $750 each, which should accompany the nomination; $3,500 to pass the entry box, $4,000 to start. The purse to be divided 60% to the winner, 20% to second, 10% to third, 5% to fourth,3% to fifth and 2% divided equally among remaining finishers. 121 lbs. Trophies will be presented to the winning owner, trainer and jockey. A special permanent trophy will be presented to the owner of the filly that wins The Alabama, The Mother Goose andThe Coaching Club American Oaks. Closed Saturday, August 7, 2004 with 15 Nominations.

Value of Race: $750,000 Winner $450,000; second $150,000; third $75,000; fourth $37,500; fifth $22,500; sixth $5,000; seventh $5,000; eighth $5,000. Mutuel Pool $1,035,978.00 Exacta Pool $803,927.00 Trifecta Pool $622,739.00 Superfecta Pool $274,358.00

Last Raced	Horse	M/Eqt.	A.	Wt	PP	¼	½	¾	1	Str	Fin	Jockey	Odds $1
31Jly04 8Sar1	Society Selection	L	3	121	7	8	7hd	62½	51½	31	12½	Velasquez C	5.70
24Jly04 8Bel2	Stellar Jayne	L b	3	121	4	4hd	4hd	4hd	22½	1hd	2½	Albarado R J	10.20
24Jly04 8Bel1	Ashado	L	3	121	5	2hd	32½	31½	1hd	21	35¼	Velazquez J R	0.60
17Jly04 8Del1	Yearly Report	L	3	121	1	3½	2½	2hd	4hd	4½	46	Bailey J D	4.70
15Jly04 8Bel1	Fleet Indian	L	3	121	3	6½	6½	5hd	61½	6½	52	Prado E S	21.00
24Jly04 9Mth1	Susan's Angel	L	3	121	2	1½	1hd	1hd	3½	54½	6nk	Day P	21.30
17Jly04 8Del3	A Lulu Ofa Menifee	L b	3	121	6	7hd	8	76	7	7	7	Dominguez R A	55.00
30Jly04 8AP5	Last Song	L b	3	121	8	5hd	5hd	8	—	—	—	Migliore R	36.00

OFF AT 5:50 Start Good . Won driving. Track sloppy.

TIME :233, :471, 1:112, 1:362, 2:023 (:23.65, :47.23, 1:11.42, 1:36.43, 2:02.70)

$2 Mutuel Prices:			
8 – SOCIETY SELECTION	13.40	6.30	2.70
4 – STELLAR JAYNE		8.70	2.80
6 – ASHADO			2.10

$2 EXACTA 8–4 PAID $98.00 $2 TRIFECTA 8–4–6 PAID $183.50
$2 SUPERFECTA 8–4–6–1 PAID $372.50

B. f, (Apr), by Coronado's Quest – Love That Jazz , by Dixieland Band . Trainer Jerkens H Allen. Bred by Marjorie Cowan & Irving Cowan (Ky).

SOCIETY SELECTION raced in hand outside early on, was shaken up after entering the second turn, advanced four wide approaching the stretch, came in a bit in upper stretch, was straightened away, responded to steady pressure and drew clear in the final yards. STELLAR JAYNE raced close up while four wide and in hand, was urged after the leaders nearing the second turn, rallied four wide, earned a short lead coming to the eighth pole and dug in gamely but had no answer for the winner late. ASHADO argued the pace while three wide, rallied three wide on the second turn, dug in stubbornly in the stretch but weakened in the final sixteenth. YEARLY REPORT showed good speed from the start, contested the pace while between rivals and tired in the final furlong. FLEET INDIAN raced close up inside while in hand, angled out entering the stretch and had no response when roused. SUSAN'S ANGEL was hustled up inside, contested the pace along the rail and tired in upper stretch. A LULU OFA MENIFEE was outrun early, raced inside and had no response when roused. LAST SONG raced close up early while five wide, tired after the opening half mile and was eased after the first three quarters.

Owners– 1, Cowan Irving M Cowan Marjorie; 2, Spendthrift Farm LLC Kidder Chuck Cole Nancy and Strong Nick; 3, Starlight Stable Saylor Paul H Martin Johns; 4, Golden Eagle Farm; 5, Fulton Stan E; 6, S Angel Stable Jackson James H Jackson Thomas W ONeil Conn; 7, Lael Stables; 8, Masri Kassem H

Trainers– 1, Jerkens H Allen; 2, Lukas D Wayne; 3, Pletcher Todd A; 4, Baffert Bob; 5, Toner James J; 6, Lukas D Wayne; 7, Tagg Barclay; 8, Nafzger Carl A

Scratched– Honor Point (24Jul04 8Bel4)

$2 Daily Double (6–8) Paid $29.20 ; Daily Double Pool $408,814 .
$2 Pick Three (8–6–8) Paid $48.60 ; Pick Three Pool $233,173 .
$2 Pick Four (3–8–6–8) Paid $94.00 ; Pick Four Pool $691,373 .
$2 Pick Six (8–2–3–8–6–8) 6 Correct Paid $443.00 ; Pick Six Pool $200,837 .
$2 Pick Six (8–2–3–8–6–8) 5 Correct Paid $8.60 .

Saratoga Attendance: 24,650 Mutuel Pool: $4,162,737.00 ITW Mutuel Pool: $4,538,100.00 ISW Mutuel Pool: $10,931,768.00

NINTH RACE
Monmouth
AUGUST 21, 2004

1⅛ MILES. (1.464) 69TH RUNNING OF THE PHILLIP H. ISELIN BREEDERS' CUP HANDICAP. Grade III. Purse $200,000 (includes $100,000 BC – Breeders' Cup) FOR THREE-YEAR-OLDS AND UPWARD. By subscription of $200 each, which should accompany the nomination and $2,500 to pass the entry box with $200,000 Guaranteed which includes $100,000 from the Breeders' Cup Fund for Cup nominees only. The host association's money to be divided 60% to winning owner, 20% to second, 11% to third, 6% to fourth and 3% to fifth. Breeders' Cup Fund money also correspondingly divided providing a Breeders' Cup nominee has finished in an awarded position. Any Breeders' Cup moneynot awarded will revert to the Fund. The owner of the winner to receive a trophy from Breeders' Cup Limited. Closed Saturday, August 7, 2004 with 19 nominations.

Value of Race: $194,000 Winner $120,000; second $40,000; third $22,000; fourth $12,000. Mutuel Pool $139,987.00 Exacta Pool $146,563.00

Last Raced	Horse	M/Eqt.	A.	Wt	PP	St	¼	½	¾	Str	Fin	Jockey	Odds $1
4Jly04 9Bel1	Ghostzapper	L b	4	120	3	2	2½	21½	25	12	110¾	Castellano J J	0.40
25Jly04 10Mth1	Presidentialaffair	L	5	117	2	1	11½	11½	1½	220	221¼	Elliott S	1.70
29Jly04 8Mth2	Zoffinger	L bf	4	115	1	4	4	4	4	4	3no	Velez J A Jr	23.70
17Jly04 5Mth8	Private Lap	L	5	114	4	3	312	318	318	35	4	Bravo J	7.30

OFF AT 4:44 Start Good . Won ridden out. Track sloppy.

TIME :224, :454, 1:093, 1:351, 1:473 (:22.84, :45.92, 1:09.77, 1:35.20, 1:47.66)

$2 Mutuel Prices:			
5 – GHOSTZAPPER	2.80	2.10	—
2 – PRESIDENTIALAFFAIR		2.10	—
1 – ZOFFINGER		—	—

$2 EXACTA 5–2 PAID $3.80

B. c, (Apr), by Awesome Again – Baby Zip , by Relaunch . Trainer Frankel Robert. Bred by Adena Springs (Ky).

GHOSTZAPPER allowed to track the early leader, moved closer from the outside on the final turn, took command nearing the lane and drew clear then widened while being ridden out to the final yards. PRESIDENTIALAFFAIR set the early pace, raced off the rail turning for home and was no match through the final furlong while second best. ZOFFINGER was far back to the lane then gained some late while earning the show award at the wire. PRIVATE LAP moved inside early, saved ground while close up to the far turn then weakened.

Owners– 1, Stronach Stables; 2, Ciresa Edward and Papapandrea Vincent; 3, Drazin Dennis A; 4, Puglisi Stables

Trainers– 1, Frankel Robert; 2, Ciresa Martin E; 3, Forbes John H; 4, Klesaris Steve

Scratched– Country Be Gold (09Aug04 8Del1) , Colita (28Jul04 8Sar2) , Sherpa Guide (25Jul04 8Bel2)

THIRD RACE
Del Mar
AUGUST 21, 2004

1⅛ MILES. (Turf) (1.45^{4}) 48TH RUNNING OF THE DEL MAR OAKS. Grade I. Purse $300,000 FOR FILLIES, THREE-YEAR-OLDS. By subscription of $300 each, which shall accompany the nomination, or by supplementary nomination of $3,000 each by closing time of entries, with $1,000 to pass the entry box and $2,000 additional to start, with $300,000 guaranteed, of which $180,000 to first, $60,000 to second, $36,000 to third, $18,000 to fourth and $6,000 to fifth. Weight 122 lbs. First preference will be given to graded or group stakes winners. Second preference will be given to fillies which have finished second or third in graded or group stakes. Total non-claiming purse earnings will determine the order of preference for fillies of equal status. Entry fees will be refunded to all fillies which fail to draw into this race. The field will be drawn by the closing time of entries, Thursday, August 19. A trophy will be presented to the owner of the winner. Closed with 16 nominations.

Value of Race: $300,000 Winner $180,000; second $60,000; third $36,000; fourth $18,000; fifth $6,000. Mutuel Pool $864,536.00 Exacta Pool $429,536.00 Quinella Pool $44,190.00 Trifecta Pool $400,963.00

Last Raced	Horse	M/Eqt.	A.	Wt	PP	St	¼	½	¾	Str	Fin	Jockey	Odds $1
3Jly04 ^{6}Hol^{5}	Amorama-FR	LB b	3	122	6	5	7	7	7	6^{5}	1no	Flores D R	19.30
3Jly04 ^{6}Hol^{1}	Ticker Tape-GB	LB	3	122	2	4	4^{1}	3^{½}	3^{1½}	1^{½}	2^{1}	Desormeaux K J	2.20
31Jly04 ^{4}Dmr^{1}	Sweet Win	LB	3	122	4	1	3^{hd}	4^{2½}	4^{1}	3^{½}	3^{½}	Espinoza V	4.60
2Aug04 ^{8}Sar^{1}	Seducer's Song	LB	3	122	5	3	2^{1}	2^{1½}	1^{hd}	2^{1}	4^{1}	Smith M E	3.00
29Jly04 ^{4}Dmr^{2}	Sagitta Ra	LB	3	122	3	7	6^{1}	5^{½}	5^{½}	4^{½}	5^{3½}	Nakatani C S	4.90
24Jly04 ^{8}Dmr^{1}	WesternHemispher	LB	3	122	1	2	1^{½}	1^{1}	2^{1}	5^{1}	6^{3}	Baze T C	3.60
9Jly04 CHE^{1}	Red Top-Ire	LB	3	122	7	6	5^{½}	6^{1}	6^{1}	7	7	Valdivia J Jr	43.90

OFF AT 3:16 Start Good. Won driving. Course firm.

TIME :23, :46^{2}, 1:10^{1}, 1:34^{2}, 1:46^{1} (:23.15, :46.57, 1:10.34, 1:34.53, 1:46.26)

$2 Mutuel Prices:				
	6 – **AMORAMA-FR**	40.60	13.20	5.40
	2 – **TICKER TAPE-GB**		4.00	2.60
	4 – **SWEET WIN**			3.40

$1 EXACTA 6–2 PAID $61.40 $2 QUINELLA 2–6 PAID $42.60
$1 TRIFECTA 6–2–4 PAID $300.30

Dk. b or br. f, (Feb), by Sri Pekan – Tanzania-Ire, by Alzao. Trainer Canani Julio C. Bred by Jean Etienne Dubois (Fr).

AMORAMA (FR) settled outside a rival then inside, came out leaving the second turn, swung out in upper stretch and closed gamely under left handed urging to get up at the wire. TICKER TAPE (GB) stalked the pace inside then a bit off the rail, came three deep into the stretch, rallied to the front nearing midstretch and held on well but was caught on the line. SWEET WIN broke out a bit, pulled her way between horses then stalked outside a rival, swung four wide into the stretch and finished with interest while in a bit tight late, then returned cut on the right fore. SEDUCER'S SONG pulled three deep leaving the chute, pressed the pace outside WESTERN HEMISPHERE, briefly put a head in front into the second turn, led again into the stretch, fought back in midstretch but was outfinished. SAGITTA RA settled inside, came out into the stretch and could not summon the necessary late response. WESTERN HEMISPHERE pulled her way to the front and set a pressured pace inside, regained the advantage on the second turn but weakened in the stretch. RED TOP (IRE) pulled early, went wide leaving the chute, chased outside a rival, angled in leaving the second turn and also weakened.

Owners– 1, Naify and Woodside Farms LLC; 2, Jim Ford Inc Pearson Daron and Sweesy Jack; 3, Fogelson Gayle; 4, Karches Peter F; 5, Frankel Robert J; 6, Golden Eagle Farm; 7, Pabst Henry E

Trainers– 1, Canani Julio C; 2, Cassidy James; 3, Mullins Jeff; 4, Clement Christophe; 5, Frankel Robert; 6, Baffert Bob; 7, Gallagher Patrick

---

$2 Daily Double (4–6) Paid $158.40 ; Daily Double Pool $42,739 .
$1 Pick Three (3/8–4–6) Paid $170.50 ; Pick Three Pool $158,207 .

EIGHTH RACE
Del Mar
AUGUST 21, 2004

6½ FURLONGS. (1.13^{3}) 33RD RUNNING OF THE RANCHO BERNARDO HANDICAP. Grade III. Purse $150,000 FOR FILLIES AND MARES, THREE-YEAR-OLDS AND UPWARD. By subscription of $150 each, which shall accompany the nomination, or by supplementary nomination of $1,500 each by Sunday, August 15, $1,500 additional to start, with $150,000 Guaranteed, of which $90,000 to first, $30,000 to second, $18,000 to third, $9,000 to fourth and $3,000 to fifth. Weights Monday, August 16. High weights preferred. A trophy will be presented to the owner of the winner. Nominations closed Thursday, August 12, 2004 with 9 nominations.

Value of Race: $150,000 Winner $90,000; second $30,000; third $18,000; fourth $9,000; fifth $3,000. Mutuel Pool $542,316.00 Exacta Pool $296,748.00 Quinella Pool $30,087.00 Trifecta Pool $329,782.00

Last Raced	Horse	M/Eqt.	A.	Wt	PP	St	¼	½	Str	Fin	Jockey	Odds $1
10Jly04 ^{5}Hol^{1}	Dream of Summer	LB b	5	118	6	1	2^{½}	1^{hd}	1^{½}	1^{nk}	Smith M E	1.00
14Jly04 ^{7}Hol^{1}	Barbara Orr	LB	4	113	4	3	1^{hd}	2^{2}	2^{1½}	2^{3½}	Baze T C	5.30
23Jly04 ^{6}Dmr^{1}	Cyber Slew	LB b	4	117	3	6	7	6^{1}	4^{1½}	3^{hd}	Nakatani C S	4.10
10Jly04 ^{5}Hol^{4}	Coconut Girl	LB f	5	116	2	5	4^{1}	3^{1½}	3^{3½}	4^{6}	Espinoza V	3.00
2May04 ^{8}BM^{6}	Bold Roberta	LB b	6	116	7	2	6^{2½}	4^{1½}	5^{3}	5^{6}	Nuesch D	29.40
30Jly04 ^{7}Dmr^{1}	Icantgoforthat	LB b	5	117	1	7	3^{½}	5^{2}	6^{7}	6^{8}	Steiner J J	27.60
6May04 HCH^{2}	All Glory	LB	5	115	5	4	5^{hd}	7	7	7	John K	26.80

OFF AT 5:46 Start Good. Won driving. Track fast.

TIME :21^{4}, :44^{1}, 1:09, 1:15^{4} (:21.93, :44.29, 1:09.17, 1:15.85)

$2 Mutuel Prices:				
	6 – **DREAM OF SUMMER**	4.00	2.80	2.20
	4 – **BARBARA ORR**		4.40	3.40
	3 – **CYBER SLEW**			2.80

$1 EXACTA 6–4 PAID $8.90 $2 QUINELLA 4–6 PAID $10.60
$1 TRIFECTA 6–4–3 PAID $29.60

Gr/ro. m, (Apr), by Siberian Summer – Mary's Dream, by Skywalker. Trainer Garcia Juan. Bred by James Weigel (Cal).

DREAM OF SUMMER had good early speed and dueled outside the runner-up throughout, put a head in front on the turn, came out a bit into the stretch but held on gamely following a long drive. BARBARA ORR sped to the early lead, dueled between horses early then inside the winner but a bit off the rail, angled to the fence on the turn, fought back through the stretch and continued gamely to the wire. CYBER SLEW dropped back early and settled a bit off the rail, moved up toward the inside on the turn, came out three deep into the stretch and just got the show. COCONUT GIRL stalked a bit off the rail then between horses into the turn, continued just off the rail, angled inward in deep stretch and lost third late. BOLD ROBERTA four wide early, chased outside then three deep into the turn, continued off the rail and lacked a response in the stretch. ICANTGOFORTHAT bobbled at the start, went up inside to press the early pace then stalked along the rail, dropped back on the turn and weakened. ALL GLORY chased three deep between horses, dropped back off the rail on the turn and gave way.

Owners– 1, Weigel James; 2, Mercedes Stables LLC; 3, Rancho Ballena LLC; 4, Jpf Investments I LLC; 5, S L U Inc; 6, Broberg Andy and Knapp Palmer; 7, Allende Jaime M

Trainers– 1, Garcia Juan; 2, Orman Jason; 3, O'Neill Doug; 4, Aguirre Paul G; 5, Warren Donald; 6, Knapp Steve; 7, Polanco Marcelo

---

$2 Daily Double (5–6) Paid $13.00 ; Daily Double Pool $159,980 .
$1 Pick Three (4/5/8–5–6) Paid $15.70 ; Pick Three Pool $81,480 .

EIGHTH RACE
Del Mar
AUGUST 22, 2004

1¼ MILES. (1.59) 14TH RUNNING OF THE PACIFIC CLASSIC. Grade I. Purse $1,000,000 FOR THREE-YEAR-OLDS AND UPWARD. By subscription of $200 each to accompany the nomination. For horses not nominated, supplementary nominations of $10,000 each will close at the time of entry Wednesday, August 18. All horses shall pay $10,000 additional tostart, with $1,000,000 Guaranteed, with $600,000 to the winner, $200,000 to second, $120,000 to third, $60,000 to fourth and $20,000 to fifth. Three-year-olds, 117 lbs.; older, 124 lbs. This race will not be divided. Trophies will be presented to the winning owner, trainer and jockey. Closed Thursday, August 12, 2004 with 15 nominations.

Value of Race: $1,000,000 Winner $600,000; second $200,000; third $120,000; fourth $60,000; fifth $20,000. Mutuel Pool $1,305,294.00 Exacta Pool $570,827.00 Quinella Pool $55,440.00 Trifecta Pool $553,496.00 Superfecta Pool $231,557.00

Last Raced	Horse	M/Eqt.	A.	Wt	PP	¼	½	¾	1	Str	Fin	Jockey	Odds $1
1Aug04 ^{8}Dmr^{2}	Pleasantly Perfect	LB b	6	124	5	6^{5}	$6^{3\frac{1}{2}}$	6^{6}	4^{2}	1½	1^{1}	Bailey J D	1.00
7Aug04 ^{9}Sar^{2}	Perfect Drift	L	5	124	4	5^{1}	$5^{2\frac{1}{2}}$	5^{hd}	$5^{1\frac{1}{2}}$	$3^{1\frac{1}{2}}$	2¾	Day P	4.40
10Jly04 ^{9}Hol^{1}	Total Impact-Chi	LB b	6	124	6	4½	4^{hd}	$3^{1\frac{1}{2}}$	1^{1}	$2^{1\frac{1}{2}}$	$3^{4\frac{3}{4}}$	Smith M E	6.20
1Aug04 ^{8}Dmr^{1}	Choctaw Nation	LB b	4	124	3	8	8	8	8	6^{hd}	4^{1}	Espinoza V	4.40
1Aug04 ^{8}Dmr^{3}	During	LB b	4	124	8	3^{1}	3½	2^{hd}	2^{hd}	4^{hd}	5^{1}	Nakatani C S	13.40
31Jly04 ^{8}AP^{4}	Colonial Colony	LB f	6	124	2	7^{hd}	$7^{1\frac{1}{2}}$	7^{1}	6^{1}	7^{4}	6^{1}	Bejarano R	14.40
25Jly04 ^{3}Dmr^{2}	El Elogiado-Arg	LB	4	124	1	1^{hd}	1½	1^{hd}	3½	5^{2}	7^{8}	Desormeaux K J	33.40
1Aug04 ^{8}Dmr^{5}	Night Patrol	LB b	8	124	7	2^{1}	$2^{1\frac{1}{2}}$	$4^{1\frac{1}{2}}$	7½	8	8	Baze T C	53.00

OFF AT 4:50 Start Good . Won driving. Track fast.

TIME $:23^{2}$, $:46^{4}$, $1:10^{4}$, $1:35^{2}$, 2:01 (:23.45, :46.82, 1:10.90, 1:35.48, 2:01.17)

$2 Mutuel Prices:

5 – PLEASANTLY PERFECT	4.00	2.60	2.20
4 – PERFECT DRIFT		4.00	3.20
6 – TOTAL IMPACT–CHI			3.20

$1 EXACTA 5–4 PAID $6.40 $2 QUINELLA 4–5 PAID $8.20
$1 TRIFECTA 5–4–6 PAID $23.60 $1 SUPERFECTA 5–4–6–3 PAID $51.40

B. h, (Apr), by Pleasant Colony – Regal State , by Affirmed . Trainer Mandella Richard. Bred by Clovelly Farms (Ky).

PLEASANTLY PERFECT a half step slow to begin, pulled between horses early, chased off the rail, moved up outside on the second turn, bid four wide into the stretch, bumped with TOTAL IMPACT into the lane, gained the lead nearing midstretch, inched away in deep stretch and held gamely under urging. PERFECT DRIFT chased a bit off the inside, went outside a rival on the second turn, came out into the stretch and closed willingly. TOTAL IMPACT (CHI) pulled early, was a bit wide into the first turn, launched a bid four wide on the backstretch, gained the lead three deep on the second turn, inched away leaving that bend, bumped with the winner into the stretch, fought back inside in midstretch, then could not match the winner, was caught for second late but bested the rest. CHOCTAW NATION unhurried outside a rival then off the rail, inched forward outside on the second turn, came five wide into the stretch and improved position. DURING stalked the early pace outside then off the rail, went up three deep between rivals on the backstretch, dueled between foes on the second turn and weakened. COLONIAL COLONY unhurried a bit off the rail early, came out into the stretch and did not rally. EL ELOGIADO (ARG) went up inside to duel for the lead, fought back into the second turn, dropped back some leaving that turn and weakened. NIGHT PATROL had speed between horses then dueled outside a rival, fell back toward the inside nearing the second turn, came out into the stretch and gave way.

Owners– 1, Diamond A Racing Corporation; 2, Stonecrest Farm; 3, Al Kabeer Sultan Mohammed Saud and Bridport S A; 4, Bone Robert D; 5, McIngvale James; 6, Nolan Chris; 7, Craig Sidney H and Jenny; 8, Everest Stables Inc

Trainers– 1, Mandella Richard; 2, Johnson Murray W; 3, De Seroux Laura; 4, Mullins Jeff; 5, Baffert Bob; 6, Bindner Walter M Jr; 7, McAnally Ronald; 8, Polanco Marcelo

---

$2 Daily Double (9–5) Paid $13.60 ; Daily Double Pool $65,617 .
$1 Pick Three (8–9–5) Paid $58.20 ; Pick Three Pool $192,031 .

NINTH RACE
Saratoga
AUGUST 22, 2004

1¼ MILES. (2.00) 87TH RUNNING OF THE SARATOGA BREEDERS' CUP HANDICAP. Grade II. Purse $250,000 (includes $100,000 BC – Breeders' Cup) (UP TO $28,500 NYSBFOA) A HANDICAP FOR THREE YEAR OLDS AND UPWARD. By subscription of $150 each, which should accompany the nomination; $750 to pass the entry box; $750 to start. The NYRA purse to be divided 60% to the winner, 20% to second, 10% to third,5% to fourth, 3% to fifth and 2% divided equally among remaining finishers. The Breeders' Cup fund monies also correspondingly divided. Any Breeders' Cup monies not awarded will revert back to the fund. Breeders' Cup trophy will be presented to the winning owner. Closed Saturday, August 7,2004 with 22 Nominations.

Value of Race: $250,000 Winner $150,000; second $50,000; third $25,000; fourth $12,500; fifth $7,500; sixth $2,500; seventh $2,500. Mutuel Pool $1,063,400.00 Exacta Pool $789,511.00 Trifecta Pool $620,630.00

Last Raced	Horse	M/Eqt.	A.	Wt	PP	¼	½	¾	1	Str	Fin	Jockey	Odds $1
19Jun04 ^{10}Suf^{5}	Evening Attire	L b	6	115	7	$5^{2\frac{1}{2}}$	$5^{1\frac{1}{2}}$	6^{1}	5½	1½	1^{5}	Velasquez C	7.50
3Jly04 ^{7}Bel^{3}	Funny Cide	L	4	118	5	$3^{1\frac{1}{2}}$	$3^{1\frac{1}{2}}$	4^{hd}	2½	2^{hd}	$2^{3\frac{3}{4}}$	Prado E S	1.00
7Aug04 ^{9}Sar^{3}	Bowman's Band	L	6	116	4	6½	6^{hd}	3^{hd}	1½	$3^{4\frac{1}{2}}$	$3^{1\frac{1}{4}}$	Chavez J F	3.95
10Jly04 ^{9}AP^{1}	Alumni Hall	L b	5	115	6	7	7	7	4^{hd}	4^{2}	$4^{4\frac{1}{2}}$	Albarado R J	6.80
7Aug04 ^{9}Sar^{4}	Sarava	L	5	115	3	4^{hd}	4½	5½	6^{5}	5^{2}	5½	Castellano J J	6.30
31Jly04 ^{8}AP^{3}	Congrats	L	4	114	2	2^{hd}	$2^{1\frac{1}{2}}$	2^{1}	3½	6^{6}	$6^{20\frac{1}{2}}$	Velazquez J R	16.80
31Jly04 ^{8}AP^{5}	The Lady's Groom	L bf	4	116	1	1½	1^{hd}	1½	7	7	7	Migliore R	29.00

OFF AT 5:23 Start Good . Won driving. Track fast.

TIME :23, $:46^{2}$, $1:10^{4}$, 1:36, $2:00^{4}$ (:23.15, :46.40, 1:10.90, 1:36.02, 2:00.83)

$2 Mutuel Prices:

8 – EVENING ATTIRE	17.00	5.20	3.30
6 – FUNNY CIDE		3.00	2.30
5 – BOWMAN'S BAND			3.10

$2 EXACTA 8–6 PAID $35.40 $2 TRIFECTA 8–6–5 PAID $99.50

Gr/ro. g, (Feb), by Black Tie Affair-Ire – Concolour , by Our Native . Trainer Kelly Patrick J. Bred by Thomas J Kelly & Joseph M Grant (Ky).

EVENING ATTIRE was taken in hand and patiently handled while outside early on, advanced outside on the second turn, rallied four wide approaching the stretch, responded when roused, reached the front nearing the eighth pole and drew away late under a drive. FUNNY CIDE raced with the pace while three wide in hand, responded when asked for run on the second turn, could not stay with the winner in the final furlong while clearly best of the others. BOWMAN'S BAND was rated along inside, advanced inside on the backstretch, slipped through on the rail on the second turn, led into the stretch and tired in the final furlong. ALUMNI HALL was taken back after the start, advanced outside on the backstretch, put in a five wide run on the second turn and tired in the drive. SARAVA raced in hand while between rivals and had no response when roused. CONGRATS pressed the pace while between rivals and tired after the opening three quarters. THE LADY'S GROOM quickly showed in front, set the pace for a half mile and tired.

Owners– 1, Grant Mary and Joseph and Kelly Thomas J; 2, Sackatoga Stable; 3, Schwartz Martin S; 4, Farish William S Elkins Jr James A and Webber Jr W Temple; 5, New Phoenix Stable and Roy Mrs Susan; 6, Claiborne Farm and Dilschneider Adele B; 7, Murphy John D Sr

Trainers– 1, Kelly Patrick J; 2, Tagg Barclay; 3, Jerkens H Allen; 4, Howard Neil J; 5, Baffert Bob; 6, McGaughey III Claude R; 7, Gorham Michael E

Scratched– Presidentialaffair (21Aug04 ^{9}Mth^{2})

SEVENTH RACE
Emerald
AUGUST 22, 2004

1 MILE. (1.33) 69TH RUNNING OF THE LONGACRES MILE HANDICAP. Grade III. Purse $250,000 FOR THREE-YEAR-OLDS AND UPWARD. By subscription of $250 each, which shall accompany the nomination, $1,250 to enter, $1,250 additional to start with $137,500 guaranteed to the owner of the winner, $50,000 to second, $37,500 to third, $18,750 to fourthand $6,250 to fifth. High weights preferred. Field size will be limited to 12 starters with no also eligibles. Starters to be named through the entry box by closing time of entries. Nominations closed Sunday, August 8, 2004 with 32.

Value of Race: $250,000 Winner $137,500; second $50,000; third $37,500; fourth $18,750; fifth $6,250. Mutuel Pool $234,955.00 Exacta Pool $86,883.00 Trifecta Pool $84,489.00 Head2Head Pool $1,598.00 Superfecta Pool $28,146.00

Last Raced		Horse	M/Eqt.	A.	Wt	PP	St	¼	½	¾	Str	Fin	Jockey	Odds $1
11Jly04 ^{11}Pln^{1}		Adreamisborn	LB b	5	116	7	12	11^{4}	10^{hd}	7^{hd}	1^{2}	1^{1}	Baze R A	4.40
25Jly04 ^{8}EmD^{3}		Demon Warlock	LB	4	114	5	4	6^{hd}	$7^{1\frac{1}{2}}$	6^{hd}	2^{2}	$2^{5\frac{3}{4}}$	Chaves N J	10.10
25Jly04 ^{8}EmD^{2}		Mr. Makah	LB b	4	112	12	10	12	12	12	$7^{2\frac{1}{2}}$	$3^{\frac{3}{4}}$	Saito S T	30.80
2Aug04 ^{7}Dmr^{1}		American Fury	LB	4	114	10	11	10^{2}	$9^{1\frac{1}{2}}$	$8^{\frac{1}{2}}$	5^{hd}	4^{nk}	Vergara O	a- 11.70
2Aug04 ^{1}Hst^{1}		Metatron	LB f	5	114	2	2	$1^{2\frac{1}{2}}$	$1^{1\frac{1}{2}}$	1^{1}	3^{2}	$5^{1\frac{1}{2}}$	Hoverson C	31.10
1Jly04 ^{9}Hst^{1}		Royal Place	LB f	4	118	11	7	7^{hd}	5^{1}	4^{1}	6^{hd}	$6^{1\frac{1}{2}}$	Valdivia J Jr	6.20
5Aug04 ^{7}Dmr^{2}		Verkade	LB b	4	113	8	6	$5^{1\frac{1}{2}}$	$3^{1\frac{1}{2}}$	2^{hd}	4^{1}	$7^{1\frac{1}{2}}$	Gann S L	6.50
25Jly04 ^{8}EmD^{1}		Poker Brad	LB	6	117	9	8	9^{1}	8^{hd}	9^{1}	8^{3}	$8^{4\frac{1}{4}}$	Frazier R L	3.40
25Jly04 ^{8}EmD^{7}		Gratitude Attack	LB bf	4	115	1	9	$8^{2\frac{1}{2}}$	11^{8}	$11^{\frac{1}{2}}$	9^{hd}	9^{hd}	Wilson D H	5.60
8Aug04 ^{9}EmD^{2}		Best On Tap	LB bf	4	110	4	1	$4^{1\frac{1}{2}}$	$6^{\frac{1}{2}}$	10^{2}	$11^{1\frac{1}{2}}$	$10^{3\frac{3}{4}}$	Russell B R	a- 11.70
2Aug04 ^{8}NP^{1}	DH	Deputy Country	LB	6	115	3	5	2^{hd}	4^{hd}	$5^{\frac{1}{2}}$	12	11	Hamel R	39.50
8Aug04 ^{9}EmD^{1}	DH	Salt Grinder	LB bf	5	116	6	3	3^{1}	2^{hd}	3^{2}	10^{hd}	11	Mitchell G V	8.20

DH–Dead Heat.

a–Coupled: American Fury and Best On Tap.

OFF AT 4:23 Start Good . Won driving. Track sloppy.

TIME :22^{1}, :44^{3}, 1:09^{1}, 1:22, 1:34^{4} (:22.20, :44.60, 1:09.20, 1:22.00, 1:34.80)

$2 Mutuel Prices:				
	7 – ADREAMISBORN	**10.80**	**6.20**	**5.20**
	5 – DEMON WARLOCK		**8.60**	**6.20**
	11 – MR. MAKAH			**9.80**

$1 EXACTA 7–5 PAID $55.50 $1 TRIFECTA 7–5–11 PAID $494.80
$2 HEAD2HEAD 6VS.8(WINNER8) PAID $4.60
$1 SUPERFECTA 7–5–11–1 PAID $5,481.40

Dk. b or br. g, (Feb), by Kris S. – Erica's Dream , by Two's a Plenty . Trainer Hollendorfer Jerry. Bred by John Franks & Jonabell Farm (Ky).

ADREAMISBORN was off a step slow then allowed to settle well off the leaders, began to advance nearing the three-eighths pole, drifted in while rallying into the lane, opened a clear lead in mid-stretch and held DEMON WARLOCK at bay to the wire. DEMON WARLOCK raced just off the leaders from the inside, responded when set down for the drive, moved to within striking distance of the winner in deep stretch but could not reach that rival late. MR. MAKAH was void of early speed, moved far outside approaching the stretch and finished with good energy. AMERICAN FURY lacked early foot, moved into contention into the lane from between rivals, was bumped and lost an iron with three-sixteenths to run and stayed on to improve his position late. METATRON went to the front at once, opened a clear lead before going a quarter, saved ground while setting the pace and gave way in the drive. ROYAL PLACE raced wide into both turns, was bumped nearing the sixteenth pole and finished willingly. VERKADE chased the leaders from the outside early, offered a bid nearing the quarter and failed to sustain his rally. POKER BRAD showed no early speed, raced wide into the stretch and failed to threaten. GRATITUDE ATTACK saved ground throughout to no avail. BEST ON TAP broke sharply to show brief speed and weakened. DEPUTY COUNTRY chased the leaders from the outside for three-quarters and weakened. SALT GRINDER chased the leaders from the outside, drifted out to bump rival while tiring into the lane and gave way. The rider of AMERICAN FURY called an objection against the winner concerning the bumped incident nearing the three-sixteenths pole and after reviewing the films the Stewards concluded that SALT GRINDER had drifted out and bumped AMERICAN FURY and therefore held ADREAMISBORN blameless in the incident.

Owners– 1, Franks Farms; 2, Floyd Tim and Allen and Nist Mike; 3, Friendship Stable and McDonald Frank; 4, Ingalls James L; 5, Coyote Creek Racing Stable; 6, Sangara K K; 7, R D Bone Ralph Hawkins & Dan Robinson; 8, Quadrun Farm LLC; 9, Two of Spades; 10, Ingalls James L; 11, Heppner Arnold; 12, Homestretch Farms Inc

Trainers– 1, Hollendorfer Jerry; 2, Gillihan Terry; 3, Jenne Bonnie; 4, Robbins Carlton T; 5, Snow Mel; 6, Becerra Rafael; 7, Mullins Jeff; 8, McCanna Tim; 9, Forster Grant T; 10, Driever Douglas; 11, Smith Ron K; 12, Penney Jim

---

$1 Pick Three (6–3–7) Paid $591.70 ; Pick Three Pool $8,356 .

EIGHTH RACE
Saratoga
AUGUST 23, 2004

1⅛ MILES. (Turf) (1.45^{2}) 22ND RUNNING OF THE LAKE PLACID HANDICAP. Grade II. Purse $150,000 MELLON TURF. (UP TO $28,500 NYSBFOA) FOR FILLIES THREE YEARS OLD. By subscription of $150 each, which should accompany the nomination; $750 to pass the entry box; $750 to start. The purse to be divided 60% to the winner, 20% to second, 10% to third, 5% tofourth, 3% to fifth and 2% divided equally among remaining finishers. 122 lbs. Non-winners of a graded sweepstake twice on the turf in 2004 allowed 2 lbs.; such a race in 2004, 4 lbs.; $40,000; or three races, 6 lbs.; two races, 8 lbs. (Maiden, claimingand restricted allowance races not considered). A trophy will be presented to the winning owner. The New York Racing Association reserves the right to transfer this race to the Main Track. In the event that this race is taken off the turf, it may be subject to downgrading upon review by theGraded Stakes Committee. Closed Saturday, August 7, 2004 with 36 Nominations. (If the Stewards consider it inadvisable to run this race on the turf course, this race will be run at One Mile and One Eighth on the main track.). (Rail at 12 feet).

Value of Race: $150,000 Winner $90,000; second $30,000; third $15,000; fourth $7,500; fifth $4,500; sixth $1,500; seventh $1,500. Mutuel Pool $513,363.00 Exacta Pool $406,774.00 Trifecta Pool $342,106.00

Last Raced	Horse	M/Eqt.	A.	Wt	PP	St	¼	½	¾	Str	Fin	Jockey	Odds $1
23Jly04 8Bel1	Spotlight-GB	L	3	116	5	3	3 2½	2 1	2 3½	1 ½	1 3½	Bailey J D	1.55
3Jly04 6Hol6	Mambo Slew		3	120	2	5	6 1	6 2½	6 2	3 2½	2 ¾	Prado E S	1.80
2Aug04 8Sar3	Fortunate Damsel	L b	3	116	7	6	1 2	1 1	1 ½	2 2½	3 3	Castellano J J	5.60
2Aug04 8Sar7	Delta Sensation	L	3	118	6	7	7	7	7	5 2½	4 nk	Sellers S J	6.60
10Jly04 7Cnl3	Vous	L b	3	118	3	4	2 hd	3 ½	3 ½	4 hd	5 4	Velasquez C	11.20
6Aug04 3Sar7	Minge Cove	L	3	118	1	1	5 1	5 ½	5 ½	6 7	6 4	Velazquez J R	25.50
23Jly04 8Bel5	Indy Charmer	L b	3	114	4	2	4 ½	4 ½	4 1	7	7	Albarado R J	45.25

OFF AT 4:47 Start Good. Won driving. Course good.

TIME :24^{3}, :50, 1:14^{1}, 1:38^{1}, 1:50^{2} (:24.75, :50.08, 1:14.34, 1:38.33, 1:50.54)

$2 Mutuel Prices:

7 – SPOTLIGHT–GB	5.10	2.90	2.10
2 – MAMBO SLEW		3.00	2.30
9 – FORTUNATE DAMSEL			2.50

$2 EXACTA 7–2 PAID $12.60 $2 TRIFECTA 7–2–9 PAID $36.60

Ch. f, (Apr), by Dr Fong – Dust Dancer–GB, by Suave Dancer. Trainer Clement Christophe. Bred by Hesmonds Stud Ltd (GB).

SPOTLIGHT (GB) came away well and raced close up outside while in hand, advanced outside when ready, responded when asked, drew clear leaving the eighth pole and was kept to the task to the finish. MAMBO SLEW was unhurried while outrun early, rallied inside approaching the stretch, angled out in upper stretch and finished gamely to get the place award. FORTUNATE DAMSEL quickly opened a clear lead, set the pace along the inside while in hand, could not stay with the winner in the final furlong and was outfinished for the place. DELTA SENSATION was outrun early, raced inside and had no response when roused. VOUS raced close up inside while well in hand, saved ground and came up empty when asked. MINGE COVE was rated along inside, advanced inside on the second turn, came wide for the drive and tired. INDY CHARMER was outrun early, raced three wide and tired in the stretch.

Owners– 1, Green Hills Farm; 2, Manganaro Frank; 3, Spruce Pond Stable; 4, Cay John E III; 5, Tee N Jay Stable; 6, Double S Stable Wachtel Stable Friedman Leonard M and Iwinski Allen; 7, Robsham Mrs E P

Trainers– 1, Clement Christophe; 2, Biancone Patrick L; 3, Cedano Heriberto; 4, Alexander Frank A; 5, Hills Timothy A; 6, Iwinski Allen; 7, Hough Stanley M

Scratched– Lucifer's Stone (02Aug04 8Sar5), Ohbeegeewhyen (02Jul04 8Bel4), Shadow Cast (04Aug04 5Sar3), Bending Strings (31Jul04 8Sar2)

NINTH RACE
Saratoga
AUGUST 27, 2004

1¼ MILES. (2.00) 57TH RUNNING OF THE PERSONAL ENSIGN HANDICAP. Grade I. Purse $400,000 A HANDICAP FOR FILLIES AND MARES THREE YEARS OLD AND UPWARD. By subscription of $400 each, which should accompany the nomination; $2,000 to pass the entry box and $2,000 to start. The purse to be divided 60% to the winner, 20% to second, 10% to third, 5%to fourth, 3% to fifth and 2% divided equally among remaining finishers.Trophies will be presented to the winning owner, trainer and jockey. Closed Saturday, August 14,2004 with 12 Nominations.

Value of Race: $392,000 Winner $240,000; second $80,000; third $40,000; fourth $20,000; fifth $12,000. Mutuel Pool $680,050.00 Exacta Pool $467,919.00 Trifecta Pool $272,368.00

Last Raced	Horse	M/Eqt.	A.	Wt	PP	¼	½	¾	1	Str	Fin	Jockey	Odds $1
1Aug04 9Sar3	Storm Flag Flying	L	4	116	1	3 2½	3 3½	3 2½	3 1½	1 hd	1 1¼	Velazquez J R	2.15
1Aug04 9Sar1	Azeri	L	6	122	2	2 3½	2 6	2 7	1 1½	2 2½	2 ½	Day P	0.60
1Aug04 7Sar2	Nevermore	L	4	114	3	4 6	4 4½	4 1½	4 3	3 3	3 4½	Prado E S	18.30
12Aug04 8Sar1	Board Elligible	L b	4	112	5	5	5	5	5	4 7	4 16	Fragoso P	17.10
18Jly04 10Del2	Roar Emotion	L	4	115	4	1 1½	1 1½	1 hd	2 hd	5	5	Bailey J D	7.10

OFF AT 5:18 Start Good. Won driving. Track fast.

TIME :23, :46^{1}, 1:09^{3}, 1:35^{4}, 2:03^{3} (:23.15, :46.26, 1:09.78, 1:35.94, 2:03.63)

$2 Mutuel Prices:

1 – STORM FLAG FLYING	6.30	2.50	2.10
2 – AZERI		2.30	2.10
3 – NEVERMORE			2.10

$2 EXACTA 1–2 PAID $11.00 $2 TRIFECTA 1–2–3 PAID $50.50

Dk. b or br. f, (Apr), by Storm Cat – My Flag, by Easy Goer. Trainer McGaughey III Claude R. Bred by Phipps Stable (Ky).

STORM FLAG FLYING was unhurried while racing away from the rail early on, was patiently handled on the backstretch, advanced three wide approaching the stretch, responded when roused, collared AZERI coming to the eighth pole, dug in resolutely and was clear under the wire. AZERI raced in hand along the inside early, was eased to the outside after allowing ROAR EMOTION to set the pace, advanced outside on the backstretch, took over from that rival entering the second turn, drew clear, responded when joined by the winner in upper stretch, could not stay with that one in the final sixteenth and dug in determinedly on the rail to earn the place award. NEVERMORE was unhurried while outrun early, advanced inside on the second turn, came wide into the stretch, responded to steady pressure and finished gamely outside. BOARD ELLIGIBLE was outrun early along the inside, angled out entering the stretch and lacked a rally. ROAR EMOTION showed good speed while in hand, soon had a clear lead, set the pace along the inside, could not keep up with AZERI after entering the second turn and tired in the stretch.

Owners– 1, Phipps Ogden Mills et al; 2, Allen E Paulson Living Trust; 3, Clifton William L Jr; 4, Rudina Stable; 5, Allen Joseph

Trainers– 1, McGaughey III Claude R; 2, Lukas D Wayne; 3, Bond Harold James; 4, Ferraro James W; 5, McLaughlin Kiaran P

EIGHTH RACE
Del Mar
AUGUST 28, 2004

7 FURLONGS. (1.20) 54TH RUNNING OF THE DEL MAR DEBUTANTE. Grade I. Purse $250,000 FOR FILLIES, TWO-YEAR-OLDS (FOALS OF 2002). By subscription of $250 each, on or before June 4, 2004, the fee to accompany the nomination. For horses not nominated, supplementary nominations of $10,000 each will close at the time of entry, Thursday, August 26, 2004. All horses shall pay $500 to pass the entry box and $2,000 additional to start, with $250,000 Guaranteed, of which $150,000 to first, $50,000 to second, $30,000 to third, $15,000 to fourth and $5,000 to fifth. Weight 122 lbs.; Non-winners of $50,000 twice allowed 2 lbs.; of such a race, 4 lbs.; of $25,000 other than maiden or claiming, 6 lbs.; of a race other than claiming, 8 lbs. Starters to be named through the entry box Thursday, August 26, by the closing time of entries. Total non-claiming purse earnings will determine the order of preference for fillies of equal status. A trophy will be presented to the owner of the winner. Closed with 129 nominations. 1 supplementary nomination: Hello Lucky.

Value of Race: $250,000 Winner $150,000; second $50,000; third $30,000; fourth $15,000; fifth $2,500; fifth $2,500. Mutuel Pool $631,405.00 Exacta Pool $321,201.00 Quinella Pool $29,859.00 Trifecta Pool $301,298.00 Superfecta Pool $126,393.00

Last Raced	Horse	M/Eqt.	A.	Wt	PP	St	¼	½	Str	Fin	Jockey	Odds $1
31Jly04 ^{1}Dmr^{2}	Sweet Catomine	LB b	2	114	7	9	9	7^{2}	3^{hd}	$1^{3/4}$	Espinoza V	a- 1.60
7Aug04 ^{8}Dmr^{2}	Souvenir Gift	LB	2	120	6	4	$5^{1/2}$	5^{4}	$2^{2\frac{1}{2}}$	$2^{1\frac{1}{2}}$	Baze T C	3.10
7Aug04 ^{8}Dmr^{3}	Hello Lucky	LB	2	116	2	5	$1^{1/2}$	$1^{1/2}$	$1^{1/2}$	$3^{2\frac{1}{2}}$	Smith M E	12.30
2Aug04 ^{1}Dmr^{1}	Ninadivina	LB	2	117	1	7	6^{2}	6^{hd}	$4^{1\frac{1}{2}}$	4^{5}	Atkinson P	43.20
31Jly04 ^{1}Dmr^{5}	DH Girly Girl	LB	2	115	3	8	7^{hd}	8^{4}	8^{12}	5	Valdivia J Jr	14.20
31Jly04 ^{1}Dmr^{1}	DH She's Salty	LB	2	116	9	2	$4^{2\frac{1}{2}}$	$4^{3\frac{1}{2}}$	$6^{1/2}$	5^{2}	Court J K	5.60
23Jly04 ^{7}Dmr^{3}	Proposed	LB b	2	116	5	3	3^{hd}	3^{hd}	5^{hd}	7^{6}	Flores D R	a- 1.60
15Aug04 ^{4}Dmr^{1}	No Bull Baby	LB b	2	116	4	1	2^{hd}	2^{hd}	7^{1}	8^{9}	Nakatani C S	3.30
19May04 ^{4}Hol^{4}	Princess Godiva	LB b	2	114	8	6	$8^{1/2}$	9	9	9	Garcia M S	46.80

DH-Dead Heat.
a-Coupled: Sweet Catomine and Proposed.

OFF AT 5:38 Start Good. Won driving. Track fast.
TIME :22, :44^{2}, 1:10^{2}, 1:24 (:22.07, :44.51, 1:10.40, 1:24.18)

$2 Mutuel Prices:				
	1A- SWEET CATOMINE(a-entry)	5.20	2.60	2.40
	6 - SOUVENIR GIFT		3.00	2.60
	3 - HELLO LUCKY			4.20

$1 EXACTA 1-6 PAID $8.10 $2 QUINELLA 1-6 PAID $8.80
$1 TRIFECTA 1-6-3 PAID $44.20 $1 SUPERFECTA 1-6-3-2 PAID $407.50

B. f, (Feb), by Storm Cat - Sweet Life , by Kris S.. Trainer Canani Julio C. Bred by Mr & Mrs Martin J Wygod (Ky).

SWEET CATOMINE hopped slightly at the break, reserved while well off the rail, advanced four and then five wide around the turn and into the stretch, came in slightly through drive, responded from steady right hand encouragement and reeled in leader in deep stretch. SOUVENIR GIFT settled off the rail, launched rally while four wide leaving the backstretch, continued further out entering the stretch, collared rival passing sixteenth marker, edged away but could stave off the winner late. HELLO LUCKY was sent up inside leaving the chute, set a pressured pace from just off the rail, headed passing the sixteenth marker and gave ground grudgingly late in a game effort. NINADIVINA settled along the fence, continued on a rail-hugging trip into the stretch and finished very willingly from the inside. GIRLY GIRL reserved a bit off the rail, saved ground into the stretch and finished on even terms for a minor award. SHE'S SALTY prompted the early issue from the outside, caught four wide into and around the bend, remained wide into the stretch and lacked the needed late punch while finishing on even terms with foe. PROPOSED prompted the early pace from between rivals, then three deep into the turn, continued on same path and weakened. NO BULL BABY forced the pace while outside foe and then between rivals leaving the backstretch, remained two wide, lost contact and gave way. PRINCESS GODIVA was bit fractious in the gate, chased while outside foe leaving the chute, dropped back leaving the backstretch and weakened.

Owners- 1, Wygod Mr and Mrs Martin J; 2, Semkin Sam and Unruh Gregory; 3, Cono Charles; 4, Niederrad Stables; 5, Norman Greg; 6, Guiol or Suarez Racing Inc; 7, Wygod Mr and Mrs Martin J; 8, Earnhardt III Patti and Hal J; 9, Merrell Scott P

Trainers- 1, Canani Julio C; 2, Semkin Sam; 3, Paasch Christopher S; 4, Meairs John M; 5, Gonzalez Salvador G; 6, O'Neill Doug; 7, Canani Julio C; 8, Baffert Bob; 9, Ward Wesley A

$2 Daily Double (1-1) Paid $10.60 ; Daily Double Pool $47,041 .
$1 Pick Three (1-1-1) Paid $261.00 ; Pick Three Pool $136,591 .

ELEVENTH RACE
Monmouth
AUGUST 28, 2004

6 FURLONGS. (1.07^{4}) 70TH RUNNING OF THE SAPLING. Grade III. Purse $100,000 FOR TWO-YEAR-OLDS. By Subscription of $100 each, which should accompany the nomination and $1,500 to pass the entry box. The winning owner to receive $60,000, $20,000 to second, $11,000 to third, $6,000 to fourth and $3,000 to fifth. Weight: 120 lbs. Maidens allowed 5 lbs. The owner of the winner to receive a trophy. Closed Saturday, August 14, 2004 with 23 nominations.

Value of Race: $100,000 Winner $60,000; second $20,000; third $11,000; fourth $6,000; fifth $3,000. Mutuel Pool $205,027.00 Exacta Pool $137,028.00 Superfecta Pool $22,703.00 Trifecta Pool $91,942.00

Last Raced	Horse	M/Eqt.	A.	Wt	PP	St	¼	½	Str	Fin	Jockey	Odds $1
1Aug04 ^{5}Pim^{1}	Evil Minister	L f	2	120	5	6	8	5^{2}	3^{4}	$1^{3/4}$	Pimentel J	24.50
31Jly04 ^{5}Mth^{1}	Park Avenue Ball	L	2	120	4	5	6^{2}	$4^{1\frac{1}{2}}$	1^{hd}	$2^{2\frac{3}{4}}$	Beckner D V	2.10
4Aug04 ^{3}Sar^{1}	Upscaled	L	2	120	1	8	1^{hd}	1^{hd}	$2^{1/2}$	3^{6}	Santos J A	3.50
4Aug04 ^{7}Sar^{4}	Vicarage	L	2	120	6	3	$3^{1/2}$	3^{hd}	4^{hd}	$4^{4\frac{3}{4}}$	Coa E M	7.70
15Aug04 ^{11}Mth^{1}	Punch the Odds	L	2	120	3	4	$2^{1/2}$	2^{2}	5^{6}	$5^{6\frac{1}{4}}$	Lopez C C	15.20
26Jun04 ^{3}Bel^{3}	Primal Storm	L	2	120	8	1	$5^{2\frac{1}{2}}$	7	6^{hd}	6^{2}	Elliott S	2.00
26Jun04 ^{3}Bel^{4}	June the Tiger	L	2	120	7	2	4^{hd}	6^{hd}	7	7	Decarlo C P	17.70
17Jly04 ^{1}Mth^{1}	Pop the Question	L	2	120	2	7	7^{1}	—	—	—	Molina V H	14.00

OFF AT 5:36 Start Good. Won driving. Track fast.
TIME :21^{3}, :44^{3}, :58, 1:11^{1} (:21.63, :44.70, :58.01, 1:11.21)

$2 Mutuel Prices:				
	5 - EVIL MINISTER	51.00	14.00	4.80
	4 - PARK AVENUE BALL		3.80	2.80
	1 - UPSCALED			3.00

$2 EXACTA 5-4 PAID $132.20 $1 SUPERFECTA 5-4-1-6 PAID $1,216.20
$2 TRIFECTA 5-4-1 PAID $545.00

Ch. c, (Feb), by Deputy Minister - Evil's Pic , by Piccolino . Trainer Juvonen Erik. Bred by ClassicStar LLC (Ky).

EVIL MINISTER raced just off the inside on the turn, eased out nearing the furlong marker and finished gamely to prevail. PARK AVENUE BALL saved ground on the turn, eased out some for the drive, reached the front passing the furlong marker, responded well but could not contain the top one. UPSCALED broke a bit slowly, advanced along the inside and vied for the early lead, drew clear between calls entering the lane then weakened in the drive. VICARAGE between foes down the backstretch, raced four wide turning for home and tired. PUNCH THE ODDS between foes early, pressed the pace until nearing the lane and weakened. PRIMAL STORM broke alertly, battled early, raced five deep into the turn and weakened. JUNE THE TIGER chased early between foes, raced four deep into the turn and tired. POP THE QUESTION was steadied slightly dropping back from between foes on the backstretch, was eased then walked off.

Owners- 1, Namcook Stables LLC; 2, Char-Mari Stable; 3, Lewis Robert B and Beverly J; 4, Dogwood Stable; 5, Malouf Richard; 6, Asmussen Winchell Cassels & Scherr; 7, Peachtree Stable; 8, Team Derby Dreams Stable

Trainers- 1, Juvonen Erik; 2, Ryerson James T; 3, Pletcher Todd A; 4, Pletcher Todd A; 5, Broome Edwin T; 6, Asmussen Steven M; 7, Pletcher Todd A; 8, Dowd John F

NINTH RACE
Saratoga
AUGUST 28, 2004

$1\frac{1}{16}$ MILES. (Turf) (1.38^{4}) 20TH RUNNING OF THE FOURSTARDAVE HANDICAP. Grade II. Purse $200,000 MELLON TURF. (UP TO $34,000 NYSBFOA) A HANDICAP FOR THREE YEAR OLDS AND UPWARD. By subscription of $200 each, which should accompany the nomination; $1,000 to pass the entry box and $1,000 to start. The purse to be divided 60% to the winner, 20% to second, 10% to third, 5% to fourth, 3% to fifth and 2% divided equally among remaining finishers. A trophy will be presented to the winning owner. The New York Racing Association reserves the right to transfer this race to the Main Track. In the event that this race is taken off the turf, it may be subject to downgrading upon review by the Graded Stakes Committee. Closed Saturday, August 14, 2004 with 43 Nominations. (If the Stewards consider it inadvisable to run this race on the turf course, this race will be run at One Mile and One Eighth on the main track.).

Value of Race: $200,000 Winner $120,000; second $40,000; third $20,000; fourth $10,000; fifth $6,000; sixth $800; seventh $800; eighth $800; ninth $800; tenth $800. Mutuel Pool $1,302,313.00 Exacta Pool $1,067,964.00 Trifecta Pool $768,050.00

Last Raced	Horse	M/Eqt.	A.	Wt	PP	St	¼	½	¾	Str	Fin	Jockey	Odds $1
30Jly04 ^{8}Sar^{2}	Nothing to Lose	L b	4	117	2	4	7^{hd}	$6^{\frac{1}{2}}$	5^{hd}	$3^{\frac{1}{2}}$	$1^{\frac{1}{2}}$	Velazquez J R	1.90
30Jly04 ^{8}Sar^{1}	Silver Tree	L	4	117	7	8	9^{7}	9^{8}	$6^{1\frac{1}{2}}$	2^{hd}	2^{1}	Bailey J D	3.20
1Jly04 ^{2}WO^{1}	Royal Regalia	L b	6	114	4	2	$1^{1\frac{1}{2}}$	1^{hd}	1^{hd}	1^{hd}	$3^{1\frac{3}{4}}$	Chavez J F	16.10
8Aug04 ^{5}Mth^{1}	Hotstufanthensome	L	4	113	9	7	8^{2}	8^{2}	8^{5}	5^{hd}	4no	Bravo J	19.60
30Jly04 ^{8}Sar^{4}	Union Place	L	5	113	1	1	$4^{\frac{1}{2}}$	5^{1}	7^{2}	$6^{\frac{1}{2}}$	5^{1}	Castellano J J	21.50
5Jly04 ^{2}CD^{1}	Ay Caramba-Brz	L	4	115	6	6	10	10	10	8^{2}	$6^{\frac{1}{2}}$	Velasquez C	7.10
8Aug04 ^{11}Mth^{1}	Gulch Approval	L	4	117	3	5	3^{hd}	$3^{\frac{1}{2}}$	$4^{1\frac{1}{2}}$	4^{2}	$7^{4\frac{3}{4}}$	Day P	11.00
5Aug04 ^{7}Sar^{1}	L'Oiseau d'Argent	L	5	115	10	9	$2^{\frac{1}{2}}$	$2^{2\frac{1}{2}}$	$2^{1\frac{1}{2}}$	9^{3}	8^{2}	Migliore R	11.50
10Jly04 ^{8}Bel^{1}	Christine's Outlaw	L	4	115	5	3	$5^{1\frac{1}{2}}$	$4^{1\frac{1}{2}}$	3^{hd}	10	$9^{4\frac{1}{4}}$	Prado E S	7.80
3Jly04 ^{8}CD^{5}	Royal Spy	L	6	117	8	10	6^{hd}	7^{hd}	9^{2}	7^{hd}	10	Albarado R J	30.50

OFF AT 5:14 Start Good For All But ROYAL SPY. Won driving. Course firm.

TIME :23^{3}, :46^{2}, 1:09^{1}, 1:33^{2}, 1:39^{2} (:23.70, :46.47, 1:09.30, 1:33.42, 1:39.50)

$2 Mutuel Prices:				
	2 – NOTHING TO LOSE....................	5.80	3.10	2.60
	7 – SILVER TREE......................		3.80	3.00
	4 – ROYAL REGALIA....................			6.30

$2 EXACTA 2–7 PAID $16.80 $2 TRIFECTA 2–7–4 PAID $203.50

B. c, (Jan), by Sky Classic – Cherlindrea , by Clever Trick . Trainer Frankel Robert. Bred by Kenneth L Ramsey & Sarah K Ramsey (Ky).

NOTHING TO LOSE was reserved for five furlongs, closed the gap along the inside on the turn, swung out entering the stretch, split rivals in upper stretch, altered course back to the inside in midstretch then finished well along the hedge to get up in the final seventy yards. SILVER TREE was outrun for a half, worked his way forward leaving the backstretch, closed the gap while four wide on the turn, made a run to challenge in midstretch, battled into deep stretch and yielded grudgingly. ROYAL REGALIA rushed up to gain a clear early advantage, set the pace under pressure along the backstretch, maintained a slim lead through the turn, battled into deep stretch and weakened late. HOTSTUFANTHENSOME raced far back for six furlongs, rallied four wide to reach contention on the turn then finished willingly while in traffic through the stretch. UNION PLACE raced just off the early pace, moved up along the backstretch, dropped back while three wide on the turn, steadied in traffic after being bumped in upper stretch then closed mildly in the middle of the track. AY CARAMBA (BRZ) was outrun to the turn, saved ground advancing into the stretch then rallied belatedly in traffic through the stretch. GULCH APPROVAL bobbled at the start, steadied along the rail on the first turn, raced in close contention while saving ground to the turn, lodged a brief bid along the rail in upper stretch and flattened out. L'OISEAU D'ARGENT pressed the pace from outside to the turn and steadily tired thereafter. CHRISTINE'S OUTLAW raced just off the early pace while three wide, made a run between horses to reach contention on the turn then gave way in the stretch. ROYAL SPY stumbled badly at the start, was finished after going six furlongs.

Owners– 1, Ramsey Kenneth L and Sarah K; 2, Vegso Peter; 3, Stronach Stables; 4, Steinger Lesley; 5, Sorokolit William A Sr; 6, Bozzano Patricia; 7, Marylou Whitney Stables; 8, Al Maktoum Sheik Maktoum b; 9, RC Hill Stable; 10, Jayaraman Kalarikkal K Jayaraman Vilasini D

Trainers– 1, Frankel Robert; 2, Mott William I; 3, Nixon Justin; 4, Pointer Norman R; 5, Schulhofer Randy; 6, Caramori Eduardo; 7, Zito Nicholas P; 8, McLaughlin Kiaran P; 9, Weaver George; 10, Asmussen Steven M

$2 Pick Three (9–3–2) Paid $61.00 ; Pick Three Pool $196,436 .

TENTH RACE
Saratoga
AUGUST 28, 2004

7 FURLONGS. (1.20²) 20TH RUNNING OF THE KING'S BISHOP. Grade I. Purse $250,000 (UP TO $37,500 NYSBFOA) FOR THREE YEAR OLDS. By subscription of $250 each, which should accompany the nomination; $1,250 to pass the entry box, $1,250 to start. The purse to be divided 60% to the winner, 20% to second, 10% to third, 5% to fourth, 3% to fifth and 2% divided equally among remaining finishers. 123 lbs. Non-winners of a Grade 1 or Grade 2 since March 1 allowed 2 lbs.; a Graded Sweepstakes, 4 lbs.; $50,000, or three races, 6 lbs. (Maiden, claiming or restricted allowance races not considered). Trophies will be presented to the winning owner, trainer and jockey. Closed Saturday, August 14, 2004 with 15 Nominations.

Value of Race: $250,000 Winner $150,000; second $50,000; third $25,000; fourth $12,500; fifth $7,500; sixth $1,667; seventh $1,667; eighth $1,666. Mutuel Pool $1,371,321.00 Exacta Pool $1,018,667.00 Trifecta Pool $753,813.00

Last Raced	Horse	M/Eqt.	A.	Wt	PP	St	¼	½	Str	Fin	Jockey	Odds $1
7Aug04 8Sar2	Pomeroy		3	121	3	4	4²	4²	1hd	1½	Prado E S	4.70
7Aug04 8Sar3	Weigelia	L	3	121	5	2	3½	3½	2³	2¹	Velazquez J R	7.70
10Jly04 9Crc5	Ice Wynnd Fire	L	3	117	6	6	8	7¹	3½	3¼	Bailey J D	13.60
7Aug04 8Sar1	Bwana Charlie	L	3	123	2	8	5hd	6½	4⁶	4⁴	Sellers S J	8.30
31Jly04 9Sar4	Saratoga County	L b	3	121	7	1	6hd	8	6½	5½	Castellano J J	36.75
24Jly04 4EIP1	Fire Slam	L	3	123	8	3	7²	5½	5hd	6½	Day P	2.45
8Aug04 9Sar5	Medallist	L	3	123	1	7	1hd	1½	7¹	7½	Chavez J F	1.75
28Mar04 8Sun10	Hosco	L b	3	121	4	5	2½	2hd	8	8	Velasquez C	37.00

OFF AT 5:50 Start Good For All But FIRE SLAM. Won driving. Track fast.

TIME :22, :44³, 1:08², 1:20⁴ (:22.18, :44.61, 1:08.51, 1:20.99)

$2 Mutuel Prices:				
	3 – POMEROY	11.40	6.30	4.80
	5 – WEIGELIA		8.30	6.10
	6 – ICE WYNND FIRE			6.80

$2 EXACTA 3–5 PAID $64.50 $2 TRIFECTA 3–5–6 PAID $604.00

B. c, (Apr), by Boundary – Questress , by Seeking the Gold . Trainer Biancone Patrick L. Bred by Cherry Valley Farm LLC (Ky).

POMEROY broke awkwardly, settled in good position along the backstretch, closed the gap while launching his bid on the turn, charged through along the rail to challenge in upper stretch, surged to the front in midstretch then turned back WEIGELIA under steady right hand encouragement. WEIGELIA stalked the pace while three wide along the backstretch, made a run from outside to challenge on the turn, was carried out at the top of the stretch, surged to the front leaving the quarter pole, battled into deep stretch and yielded grudgingly. ICE WYNND FIRE trailed along the backstretch, moved out on the far turn, rallied three wide on the turn, went to the inside of MEDALLIST at the top of the stretch then finished willingly to gain a share. BWANA CHARLIE bumped at the start, steadied sharply along the rail on the far turn, dropped back midway on the turn and failed to threaten thereafter. SARATOGA COUNTY failed to mount a serious rally while between horses. FIRE SLAM stumbled badly at the start, raced wide along the backstretch, dropped back between horses on the turn and failed to threaten thereafter. MEDALLIST bumped after breaking a bit slowly, rushed up along the rail, dueled heads apart to the turn, steadied sharply while drifting out at the quarter pole then gave way in the stretch. HOSCO battled three wide to the turn, was carried out at the quarter pole then faltered badly in the stretch.

Owners– 1, Smith Derrick and Tabor Michael; 2, Balsamo Joseph J; 3, Amerman Racing Stables LLC; 4, Heiligbrodt Racing Stable; 5, Pollard Evelyn M; 6, Fulton Stan E; 7, Clay Robert N; 8, Rodriguez Lorraine and Rod

Trainers– 1, Biancone Patrick L; 2, Azpurua Manuel J; 3, Frankel Robert; 4, Asmussen Steven M; 5, Weaver George; 6, Carroll David; 7, Jerkens H Allen; 8, O'Neill Doug

$2 Daily Double (2–3) Paid $43.40 ; Daily Double Pool $183,034 .

ELEVENTH RACE
Saratoga
AUGUST 28, 2004

1¼ MILES. (2.00) 135TH RUNNING OF THE TRAVERS. Grade I. Purse $1,000,000 (UP TO $70,000 NYSBFOA) FOR THREE YEAR OLDS. By subscription of $1,000 each, which should accompany the nomination; $5,000 to pass the entry box, $5,000 to start. The purse to be divided 60% to the winner, 20% to second, 10% to third, 5% to fourth, 3% tofifth and 2% divided equally among remaining finishers. 126 lbs. Trophies will be presented to the winning owner, trainer and jockey. Closed Saturday, August 14, 2004 with 12 Nominations.

Value of Race: $1,000,000 Winner $600,000; second $200,000; third $100,000; fourth $50,000; fifth $30,000; sixth $10,000; seventh $10,000. Mutuel Pool $2,167,135.00 Exacta Pool $1,280,324.00 Trifecta Pool $1,003,804.00

Last Raced	Horse	M/Eqt.	A.	Wt	PP	¼	½	¾	1	Str	Fin	Jockey	Odds $1
5Jun04 11Bel1	Birdstone	L	3	126	5	6 4½	5 ½	4 2½	2 1½	1 1½	1 2½	Prado E S	4.80
8Aug04 9Sar2	The Cliff's Edge	L	3	126	6	7	7	5 4½	3 ½	2 hd	2 3½	Sellers S J	3.15
8Aug04 9Sar4	Eddington	L b	3	126	1	3 1½	3 2½	3 hd	4 hd	4 6	3 nk	Migliore R	9.70
8Aug04 9Sar1	Purge	L	3	126	3	2 ½	2 1	2 1	1 hd	3 2½	4 5	Velazquez J R	4.00
7Aug04 8Mnr1	Sir Shackleton	L	3	126	4	4 hd	6 ½	6 ½	6 ½	5 5	5 5½	Bejarano R	7.20
10Jly04 7Hol2	Suave	L b	3	126	7	5 ½	4 ½	7	7	6 1½	6 5¼	Day P	14.20
8Aug04 13Mth1	Lion Heart		3	126	2	1 1½	1 1½	1 hd	5 3½	7	7	Bravo J	2.60

OFF AT 6:22 Start Good . Won driving. Track fast.

TIME :24^2, :49, 1:12^4, 1:37, 2:02^2 (:24.48, :49.15, 1:12.82, 1:37.15, 2:02.45)

$2 Mutuel Prices:				
	5 – BIRDSTONE	11.60	5.70	4.00
	6 – THE CLIFF'S EDGE		3.90	3.00
	1 – EDDINGTON			4.30

$2 EXACTA 5–6 PAID $46.40 $2 TRIFECTA 5–6–1 PAID $277.50

B. c, (May), by Grindstone – Dear Birdie , by Storm Bird . Trainer Zito Nicholas P. Bred by Marylou Whitney Stables (Ky).

BIRDSTONE was unhurried in the early stages, angled to the rail approaching the first turn, saved ground entering the backstretch, gradually closed the gap midway down the backstretch, angled out nearing the far turn, moved up three wide to challenge at the quarter pole, took charge in upper stretch, shook off LION HEART to get clear in midstretch then turned back THE CLIFF'S EDGE under steady left hand encouragement. THE CLIFF'S EDGE was outrun in the early stages, trailed for nearly a half, rapidly gained while four wide nearing the far turn, closed the gap from outside leaving the quarter pole, made a run to threaten in midstretch but was no match for the winner. EDDINGTON was taken in hand in the early stages, was rated just behind the leaders along the backstretch, moved out briefly on the turn, angled back to the rail in upper stretch then lacked a strong closing response. PURGE moved up from outside in the early stages, stalked the pace from outside along the backstretch, took up chase after LION HEART midway on the turn, surged to the front nearing the quarter pole, battled into upper stretch and weakened in the final eighth. SIR SHACKLETON was rated along the inside in the early stages, moved between horses along the backstretch, dropped back on the far turn and steadily tired thereafter. SUAVE raced in the middle of the pack while four wide along the backstretch, trailed on the far turn and was never close thereafter. LION HEART rushed up to gain the early advantage, set a moderate pace along the inside to the turn, relinquished the lead nearing the top of the stretch then gave way.

Owners– 1, Marylou Whitney Stables; 2, LaPenta Robert V; 3, Willmott Stables Inc; 4, Starlight Stable Saylor Paul H Martin Johns; 5, Farmer Tracy; 6, Jay Em Ess Stable; 7, Smith Derrick and Tabor Michael

Trainers– 1, Zito Nicholas P; 2, Zito Nicholas P; 3, Hennig Mark; 4, Pletcher Todd A; 5, Zito Nicholas P; 6, McGee Paul J; 7, Biancone Patrick L

$2 Pick Three (2–3–5) Paid $314.00 ; Pick Three Pool $325,624 .
$2 Pick Four (3–2–3–5) Paid $1,314.00 ; Pick Four Pool $1,479,908 .
$2 Pick Six (9–3–2–3–5–ALL) 6 Correct Paid $1,991.00 ; Pick Six Pool $263,567 .
$2 Pick Six (9–3–2–3–5–ALL) 5 Correct Paid $16.00 .
$2 Daily Double (3–5) Paid $93.00 ; Daily Double Pool $232,322 .
$2 Consolation Pick 3 (3–5–ALL (RACES 10–12)) Paid $90.50 ; Consolation Pick 3 Pool $267,405 .
$2 Consolation Daily Double (5–ALL (RACES 11& 12)) Paid $12.60 ; Consolation Daily Double Pool $421,247 .

Saratoga Attendance: 48,894 Mutuel Pool: $7,391,420.00 ITW Mutuel Pool: $7,027,672.00 ISW Mutuel Pool: $18,653,928.00

NINTH RACE
Saratoga
AUGUST 29, 2004

7 FURLONGS. (1.20^2) 16TH RUNNING OF THE BALLERINA HANDICAP. Grade I. Purse $250,000 (Up To $37,500 NYSBFOA) A HANDICAP FOR FILLIES AND MARES THREE YEARS OLD AND UPWARD. By subscription of $250 each, which should accompany the nomination; $1,250 to pass the entry box, $1,250 to start. The purse to be divided 60% to the winner, 20% to second, 10% to third, 5% tofourth, 3% to fifth and 2% divided equally among remaining finishers. Trophies will be presented to the winning owner, trainer and jockey. Closed Saturday, August 14, 2004 with 17 Nominations.

Value of Race: $250,000 Winner $150,000; second $50,000; third $25,000; fourth $12,500; fifth $7,500; sixth $2,500; seventh $2,500. Mutuel Pool $650,470.00 Exacta Pool $540,417.00 Trifecta Pool $433,326.00

Last Raced	Horse	M/Eqt.	A.	Wt	PP	St	¼	½	Str	Fin	Jockey	Odds $1
10Jly04 11Crc3	Lady Tak	L	4	119	3	5	1 1½	1 2½	1 2½	1 hd	Bailey J D	0.85
6Aug04 8Sar1	My Trusty Cat	L bf	4	116	6	4	4 ½	4 3½	4 6	2 hd	Velazquez J R	5.10
10Jly04 11Crc6	Harmony Lodge		6	119	4	3	2 2½	2 3½	2 1½	3 1	Migliore R	6.00
14Aug04 9EIP1	Molto Vita	L	4	114	5	1	3 1	3 hd	3 hd	4 5¼	Chavez J F	29.75
6Aug04 8Sar3	Smok'n Frolic	L b	5	115	7	2	5 ½	5 2½	5 3½	5 5	Prado E S	9.40
18Jly04 9Mth1	Final Round	L	4	113	2	6	7	6 hd	7	6 1¼	Castellano J J	29.75
23Jly04 9EIP2	My Boston Gal	L	4	117	1	7	6 hd	7	6 hd	7	Albarado R J	5.20

OFF AT 5:20 Start Good . Won driving. Track good.

TIME :22^1, :44^2, 1:07^4, 1:21 (:22.35, :44.49, 1:07.90, 1:21.09)

$2 Mutuel Prices:				
	3 – LADY TAK	3.70	2.70	2.20
	7 – MY TRUSTY CAT		4.00	2.80
	4 – HARMONY LODGE			2.90

$2 EXACTA 3–7 PAID $15.40 $2 TRIFECTA 3–7–4 PAID $42.80

Ch. f, (Apr), by Mutakddim – Star of My Eye , by Lucky North . Trainer Asmussen Steven M. Bred by John Franks (Fla).

LADY TAK was hustled up along the inside, soon opened a clear lead, set the pace, responded when roused, dug in resolutely on the rail and prevailed while coming out a step at the wire. MY TRUSTY CAT raced close up inside, came wide into the stretch, was bumped, angled back to the inside, rallied between rivals in deep stretch and dug in gamely despite being inadvertently punched in the nose nearing the wire. HARMONY LODGE raced close up early, came wide into the stretch and finished gamely outside. MOLTO VITA was hustled along outside, was bumped in upper stretch and finished gamely outside. SMOK'N FROLIC was urged along outside, raced wide throughout and tired in the stretch. FINAL ROUND raced between rivals early, dropped back on the turn and had no response when roused. MY BOSTON GAL was outrun early, raced inside and had no response when roused. Following a Stewards' inquiry into the stretch run, as well as a claim of foul against the second place finisher by the rider of the third place finisher, the result was declared official.

Owners– 1, Heiligbrodt Racing Stable; 2, Pollard Carl F; 3, Melnyk Eugene and Laura; 4, Gunther John D; 5, Dogwood Stable; 6, Humphrey G Watts Jr; 7, Porter J Chester Bloch Randy L Milner Phil

Trainers– 1, Asmussen Steven M; 2, Vance David R; 3, Pletcher Todd A; 4, Stewart Dallas; 5, Pletcher Todd A; 6, Arnold George R II; 7, Nafzger Carl A

Scratched– Ebony Breeze (06Aug04 8Sar2)

EIGHTH RACE
Del Mar
AUGUST 29, 2004

1⅜ MILES. (Turf) (2.12) 65TH RUNNING OF THE DEL MAR HANDICAP. Grade II. Purse $250,000 FOR THREE-YEAR-OLDS AND UPWARD. By subscription of $250 each, which shall accompany the nomination, or by supplementary nomination of $2,500 by Sunday, August 22, $2,500 additional to start, with $250,000 Guaranteed, of which $150,000 to first, $50,000 to second, $30,000 to third, $15,000 to fourth and $5,000 to fifth. Weights Monday, August 23. High weights preferred. STARTERS TO BE NAMED THROUGH THE ENTRY BOX THURSDAY, AUGUST 26, BY THE CLOSING TIME OF ENTRIES. A trophy will be presented to the owner of the winner. Closed Thursday, August 19 with 13 nominations. (Rail at 14 feet).

Value of Race: $250,000 Winner $150,000; second $50,000; third $30,000; fourth $15,000; fifth $5,000. Mutuel Pool $632,978.00 Exacta Pool $313,720.00 Quinella Pool $32,335.00 Trifecta Pool $315,102.00 Superfecta Pool $138,500.00

Last Raced	Horse	M/Eqt.	A.	Wt	PP	¼	½	¾	1	Str	Fin	Jockey	Odds $1
18Jly04 ^{8}Hol^{1}	Star Over the Bay	LB	6	116	1	$1^{3\frac{1}{2}}$	$1^{3\frac{1}{2}}$	$1^{2\frac{1}{2}}$	1^{1}	$1^{1\frac{1}{2}}$	1^{nk}	Baze T C	a- 2.60
4Aug04 ^{7}Dmr^{1}	Sarafan	LB	7	121	6	$3^{1\frac{1}{2}}$	3^{1}	$3^{\frac{1}{2}}$	5^{2}	$2^{\frac{1}{2}}$	2^{2}	Nakatani C S	3.10
24Jly04 ^{6}Dmr^{2}	Moscow Burning	LB	4	114	5	2^{2}	2^{4}	$2^{4\frac{1}{2}}$	2^{1}	$3^{1\frac{1}{2}}$	3^{hd}	Valdivia J Jr	7.80
24Jly04 ^{6}Dmr^{4}	Dimitrova	LB f	4	114	9	$4^{1\frac{1}{2}}$	4^{2}	5^{1}	$7^{1\frac{1}{2}}$	$6^{1\frac{1}{2}}$	4^{nk}	Espinoza V	10.20
4Aug04 ^{7}Dmr^{2}	GenedeCampeo-Brz	LB	5	113	4	5^{hd}	$5^{\frac{1}{2}}$	6^{1}	$3^{\frac{1}{2}}$	4^{hd}	5no	Berrio O A	32.80
14Aug04 ^{10}Dmr^{1}	Murano	LB b	5	112	8	9	9	9	9	$8^{1\frac{1}{2}}$	6^{1}	Santiago Javier	a- 2.60
18Jly04 ^{8}Hol^{2}	Continuously	LB	5	117	3	8^{2}	$8^{2\frac{1}{2}}$	$7^{2\frac{1}{2}}$	6^{hd}	7^{hd}	$7^{\frac{1}{2}}$	Desormeaux K J	2.10
4Aug04 ^{7}Dmr^{3}	Outta Here	LB	4	113	2	$7^{\frac{1}{2}}$	7^{hd}	8^{2}	$8^{1\frac{1}{2}}$	9	8^{hd}	Court J K	18.80
28Jly04 ^{3}Dmr^{1}	Mananan McLir	LB	5	116	7	6^{1}	6^{1}	4^{hd}	4^{1}	5^{hd}	9	Flores D R	13.20

a–Coupled: Star Over the Bay and Murano.

OFF AT 5:43 Start Good . Won driving. Course firm.

TIME :24, :47^{3}, 1:12^{1}, 1:36^{4}, 2:00^{3}, 2:12^{3} (:24.14, :47.71, 1:12.26, 1:36.95, 2:00.76, 2:12.71)

$2 Mutuel Prices:				
	1 – STAR OVER THE BAY(a–entry).......	7.20	3.60	3.20
	6 – SARAFAN..........................		4.00	3.00
	5 – MOSCOW BURNING...................			4.40

$1 EXACTA 1–6 PAID $14.00 $2 QUINELLA 1–6 PAID $13.60
$1 TRIFECTA 1–6–5 PAID $76.80 $1 SUPERFECTA 1–6–5–8 PAID $442.90

Gr/ro. g, (Feb), by Cozzene – Lituya Bay , by Empery . Trainer Mitchell Mike. Bred by Four Horsemen's Ranch (Fla).

STAR OVER THE BAY took the early lead and set the pace inside, responded when rivals loomed on the final turn, came a bit off the rail and held on gamely under urging. SARAFAN stalked the pace inside, split horses into the stretch, bid outside the winner past midstretch and continued willingly but could not get by. MOSCOW BURNING stalked the winner a bit off the rail, inched forward leaving the backstretch, loomed boldly on the final turn and just held third. DIMITROVA chased a bit off the rail then inside, came out into the stretch, split rivals in midstretch and was edged for the show. GENE DE CAMPEAO (BRZ) between horses early, chased inside, moved up leaving the backstretch, was in a bit tight nearing midstretch and could not summon the necessary late response. MURANO unhurried and angled in to save ground off the pace, came out leaving the final turn and into the stretch, angled back in past midstretch and found his best stride late. CONTINUOUSLY settled outside a rival off the early pace, came out leaving the last turn and three deep into the stretch and lacked the needed rally. OUTTA HERE steadied in tight on the first turn, saved ground chasing the pace, came out on the final turn and four wide into the stretch and could not offer the needed rally. MANANAN MCLIR settled outside a rival stalking the pace, continued three deep on the backstretch and final turn and into the stretch and weakened. A claim of foul by the rider of GENE DE CAMPEAO against MOSCOW BURNING for alleged interference in the stretch was not allowed by the stewards, who ruled the videotape failed to substantiate the claim.

Owners– 1, G Racing VanBurger and Vaughn; 2, Tanaka Gary A; 3, Mariani Jeffrey J Nentwig Michael and Van Kempen Dallas; 4, Higgins Joseph; 5, Bandeirantes Stable; 6, Coleman James G Racing and Van Burger Carl; 7, Khaled Saud b; 8, Currin William L and Eisman Alvin; 9, Horizon Stable Jarvis and Margolis et al

Trainers– 1, Mitchell Mike; 2, Drysdale Neil; 3, Cassidy James; 4, Drysdale Neil; 5, Avila A C; 6, Mitchell Mike; 7, Frankel Robert; 8, Currin William L; 9, Dollase Wallace

$2 Daily Double (9–1) Paid $281.80 ; Daily Double Pool $36,610 .
$1 Pick Three (10–9–1) Paid $1,109.90 ; Pick Three Pool $82,563 .

EIGHTH RACE
Saratoga
AUGUST 30, 2004

1 1/16 MILES. (Inner Turf) (1.39 4) 16TH RUNNING OF THE BALLSTON SPA BREEDERS' CUP HANDICAP. Grade III. Purse $200,000 (includes $100,000 BC – Breeders' Cup) INNER TURF. (UP TO $19,000 NYSBFOA) A HANDICAP FOR FILLIES AND MARES THREE YEARS OLD AND UPWARD. By subscription of $500 each, which should accompany the nomination; $500 to pass the entry box; $500 to start, with $100,000 added and an additional $100,000 from the Breeders' Cup Fund for Cup nominees only. The NYRA added monies will be divided 60% to the winner, 20% to second, 10% to third, 5% to fourth, 3% to fifth and 2% divided equally among remaining finishers. Any Breeders' Cup fund monies not awarded will revert back to the Fund. A Breeders' Cup trophy will be presented to the owner of the winner. The New York Racing Association reserves the right to transfer this race to the Main Track. In the event that this race is taken off the turf, it may besubject to downgrading upon review by the Graded Stakes Committee. Closed Saturday, August 14, 2004 with 35 Nominations. (Rail at 9 feet).

Value of Race: $201,000 Winner $128,400; second $42,800; third $11,400; fourth $10,700; fifth $3,420; sixth $856; seventh $856; eighth $856; ninth $856; tenth $856. Mutuel Pool $544,565.00 Exacta Pool $428,585.00 Trifecta Pool $340,071.00

Last Raced	Horse	M/Eqt.	A.	Wt	PP	St	¼	½	¾	Str	Fin	Jockey	Odds $1
31Jly04 7Sar3	Ocean Drive	L	4	119	4	4	2½	2½	2½	1½	1 1¼	Velazquez J R	2.10
11Aug04 6Sar1	Personal Legend	L b	4	115	1	2	4hd	41	4½	33	2 1¾	Bailey J D	3.05
11Aug04 8Sar5	High Court-Brz	L	4	114	5	5	7hd	6½	5 1½	4½	3 1¾	Albarado R J	8.20
3Jly04 6Bel1	Delta Princess	L	5	114	6	7	8 1½	8hd	8½	7½	4¾	Castillo H Jr	5.20
17Jly04 4WO1	Mona Rose		4	114	8	8	6½	5½	61	6hd	5¾	Chavez J F	12.90
31Jly04 7Sar4	Sand Springs	L	4	117	2	1	13	18	16	2 1½	6nk	Guidry M	10.70
31Jly04 7Sar7	Halory Leigh	L	4	113	3	3	5½	7hd	9 1½	5½	7nk	Blanc B	43.50
15Aug04 8Sar3	Mariakel	L	4	112	10	10	10	10	10	9hd	8 5½	Fragoso P	39.50
1May04 5Crc9	Derrianne	L	4	115	9	9	9 3½	93	7hd	81	9 3½	Prado E S	9.50
8Aug04 9Mth2	Mrs. M	L f	5	114	7	6	3hd	3½	31	10	10	Santos J A	29.75

OFF AT 4:47 Start Good . Won driving. Course yielding.
TIME :24, :49, 1:12, 1:37, 1:43 4 (:24.02, :49.00, 1:12.05, 1.37.06, 1:43.82)

$2 Mutuel Prices:

4 – OCEAN DRIVE	6.20	3.60	2.70
1 – PERSONAL LEGEND		3.90	3.00
5 – HIGH COURT–BRZ			5.40

$2 EXACTA 4–1 PAID $19.80 $2 TRIFECTA 4–1–5 PAID $114.50

Dk. b or br. f, (Feb), by Belong to Me – Clever But Costly , by Clever Trick . Trainer Pletcher Todd A. Bred by James D Conway & Thomas C Mueller (Ky).

OCEAN DRIVE raced in hand along the inside early, saved ground, advanced inside nearing the stretch, angled out, responded when roused, drew clear and remained clear under a drive. PERSONAL LEGEND was rated along inside, saved ground, responded when roused and finished gamely but could not get to the winner. HIGH COURT (BRZ) was rated along early, came wide into the stretch and finished well outside. DELTA PRINCESS was rated along early, raced between rivals, came wide for the drive and lacked a rally. MONA ROSE was outrun early, raced wide on both turns and had no rally. SAND SPRINGS quickly opened a clear lead, set the pace, ran off to a long lead on the backstretch and tired in the drive. HALORY LEIGH raced in hand early while between rivals and had no response when roused. MARIAKEL was outrun early, came wide into the stretch and had no rally. DERRIANNE raced wide and tired. MRS. M chased the pace from the outside and tired.

Owners– 1, Baskin Bonnie and Sy; 2, Gann Edmund A; 3, Lael Stables; 4, Khaled Saud b; 5, OBrien Frank OBrien Paul; 6, Willmott Stables Inc; 7, Crawford Jerry Gannon Matt and Grask Charlie; 8, Crown Stable; 9, Waterville Lake Stable; 10, Acclaimed Raysing Stable

Trainers– 1, Pletcher Todd A; 2, Frankel Robert; 3, Matz Michael R; 4, Mott William I; 5, Barnett Robert E; 6, Reinstedler Anthony; 7, Romans Dale; 8, Martin Carlos F; 9, Clement Christophe; 10, Ciardullo Richard Jr

Scratched– Film Maker (10Jul04 8Cnl1) , Misty Sixes (08Aug04 8Mth2) , Bounding Charm (13Aug04 8Sar1)

EIGHTH RACE
Saratoga
SEPTEMBER 4, 2004

7 FURLONGS. (1.20 2) 25TH RUNNING OF THE FOREGO HANDICAP. Grade I. Purse $250,000 (Up To $37,500 NYSBFOA) A HANDICAP FOR THREE YEAR OLDS AND UPWARD. By subscription of $250 each, which should accompany the nomination; $1,250 to pass the entry box, $1,250 to start. The purse to be divided 60% to the winner, 20% to second, 10% to third,5% to fourth, 3% to fifth and 2% divided equally among remaining finishers. Trophies will be presented to the winning owner, trainer and jockey. Closed Saturday, August 21, 2004 with 27 Nominations.

Value of Race: $250,000 Winner $150,000; second $50,000; third $25,000; fourth $12,500; fifth $7,500; sixth $1,250; seventh $1,250; eighth $1,250; ninth $1,250. Mutuel Pool $1,187,514.00 Exacta Pool $903,909.00 Trifecta Pool $701,527.00

Last Raced	Horse	M/Eqt.	A.	Wt	PP	St	¼	½	Str	Fin	Jockey	Odds $1
25Aug04 7Sar1	Midas Eyes	L	4	117	3	5	3 5½	38	1½	1 1¾	Prado E S	3.60
14Aug04 7Sar2	Clock Stopper	L b	4	114	2	9	87	86	5½	2 1¼	Day P	2.60
7Aug04 9Sar5	Gygistar	L	5	114	6	4	4 1½	4 1½	4½	3no	Fragoso P	9.80
31May04 9Bel3	Strong Hope	L	4	118	7	3	2 1½	1hd	2 5½	42	Velazquez J R	1.85
25Jly04 10Mth2	Unforgettable Max	L f	4	115	1	7	6½	6½	65	5 2½	Migliore R	22.90
14Aug04 7Sar5	Gold Dollar	L b	5	113	8	1	9	9	8hd	6 3½	Bridgmohan S X	104.00
15Nov03 10Lrl1	A Huevo	L f	8	116	5	8	7 1½	5½	7 2½	7½	Dominguez R A	6.10
7Aug04 9Sar8	Yessirgeneralsir	L	4	114	4	6	1 1½	2½	3hd	8½	Albarado R J	39.00
7Aug04 6Mnr1	Eavesdropper	L	4	114	9	2	5hd	72	9	9	Velasquez C	90.00

OFF AT 4:45 Start Good . Won driving. Track fast.
TIME :22 1, :44 4, 1:09, 1:22 1 (:22.37, :44.91, 1:09.18, 1:22.22)

$2 Mutuel Prices:

1 – MIDAS EYES	9.20	4.30	3.00
4 – CLOCK STOPPER		3.40	2.70
7 – GYGISTAR			4.80

$2 EXACTA 1–4 PAID $32.00 $2 TRIFECTA 1–4–7 PAID $168.50

B. c, (Apr), by Touch Gold – Bayou Plans , by Bayou Hebert . Trainer Frankel Robert. Bred by Jacks or Better Farm Inc (Fla).

MIDAS EYES raced close up early while in hand, advanced three wide on the turn, responded when roused in upper stretch, drew clear then dug in gamely and held CLOCK STOPPER safe under a drive. CLOCK STOPPER was outrun early, came wide into the stretch and finished gamely outside but could not get to the winner. GYGISTAR bobbled after the start, raced in hand along the inside early, came wide for the drive and finished gamely outside. STRONG HOPE raced with the pace from the outside, gained a short lead on the turn then tired along the inside in the final furlong. UNFORGETTABLE MAX was hustled along early, raced inside and offered a mild rally on the rail. GOLD DOLLAR was outrun early, came wide into the stretch and lacked a rally. A HUEVO was outrun early, raced between rivals and had no response when roused. YESSIRGENERALSIR quickly opened a clear lead, set the pace along the inside and tired in the stretch. EAVESDROPPER raced three wide and tired.

Owners– 1, Gann Edmund A; 2, Overbrook Farm; 3, Evans Edward P; 4, Melnyk Eugene and Laura; 5, Dweck Raymond; 6, Pazos Julio; 7, Hopkins Mark S; 8, Jackson James D; 9, De Renzo Dean and Hartley Randall

Trainers– 1, Frankel Robert; 2, Stewart Dallas; 3, Hennig Mark; 4, Pletcher Todd A; 5, Levine Bruce N; 6, Azpurua Manuel J; 7, Dickinson Michael W; 8, Keen Dallas E; 9, McLaughlin Kiaran P

Scratched– Watchem Smokey (28Mar04 8SA 4) , Toccet (05May04 8Bel7)

$2 Pick Three (7–10–1) Paid $87.50 ; Pick Three Pool $163,018 .

SEVENTH RACE
Del Mar
SEPTEMBER 4, 2004

1⅛ MILES. (Turf) (1.39⁴) 51ST RUNNING OF THE PALOMAR BREEDERS' CUP HANDICAP. Grade II. Purse $200,000 (includes $50,000 BC – Breeders' Cup) FOR FILLIES AND MARES, THREE-YEAR-OLDS AND UPWARD. By subscription of $150 each, which shall accompany the nomination, or by supplementary nomination of $1,500 each by Sunday, August 29, $500 to pass the entry box and $1,000 additional to start, with $150,000 and an additional $50,000 from the Breeders' Cup fund for Cup nominees only. The host association's monies to be divided 60% to the winner, 20% to second, 12% to third, 6% to fourth and 2% to fifth. Breeders' Cup monies also correspondingly divided,provided a Breeders' Cup nominee has finished in an awarded position. Any Breeders' Cup fund monies not awarded will revert to the fund. Weights Monday, August 30. The field will be limited to 10 starters. High weights preferred. If more than 10 entries ppass the entry box, the starters will be determined at the time of entry with preference given to Breeders' Cup nominees of equal racing quality or weight assignment (respective of age). Starters to be named through the entry box, Thursday, September 2 bythe closing time of entries. A trophy will be presented to the owner of the winner. Closed with 12 nominations.

Value of Race: $180,000 Winner $120,000; second $30,000; third $18,000; fourth $9,000; fifth $3,000. Mutuel Pool $530,719.00 Exacta Pool $266,828.00 Quinella Pool $27,681.00 Trifecta Pool $268,147.00

Last Raced	Horse	M/Eqt.	A.	Wt	PP	St	¼	½	¾	Str	Fin	Jockey	Odds $1
11Aug04 7Dmr4	Etoile Montante	LB	4	120	2	2	$2^{1½}$	$2^{1½}$	$2^{1½}$	$1^{½}$	$1^{¾}$	Valdivia J Jr	1.90
24Jly04 6Dmr5	Katdogawn-GB	LB	4	117	4	5	6^{1}	$6^{½}$	3^{hd}	3^{hd}	$2^{½}$	Desormeaux K J	3.00
11Jly04 8Hol5	Tangle-Ire	LB	4	117	1	6	4^{hd}	4^{hd}	5^{1}	4^{1}	3^{1}	Nakatani C S	5.50
24Jly04 6Dmr3	Notting Hill-Brz	LB f	5	116	5	1	1^{1}	$1^{1½}$	$1^{1½}$	$2^{1½}$	$4^{½}$	Flores D R	4.80
11Aug04 7Dmr1	VozDeColegiala-Chi	LB	5	114	3	3	5^{1}	5^{1}	7	5^{2}	5^{2}	Court J K	13.80
11Aug04 7Dmr2	Makeup Artist	LB	4	115	6	7	7	7	$6^{½}$	6^{hd}	6^{1}	Smith M E	11.00
3Jly04 4Hol5	Fun House	LB	5	116	7	4	$3^{½}$	3^{1}	4^{hd}	7	7	Stevens G L	7.50

OFF AT 5:14 Start Good . Won driving. Course firm.

TIME :23⁴, :48¹, 1:11⁴, 1:34³, 1:40² (:23.90, :48.28, 1:11.82, 1:34.79, 1:40.59)

$2 Mutuel Prices:			
1 – ETOILE MONTANTE	5.80	3.20	2.60
4 – KATDOGAWN-GB		3.40	3.00
2 – TANGLE-IRE			3.60

$1 EXACTA 1–4 PAID $10.80 $2 QUINELLA 1–4 PAID $11.40
$1 TRIFECTA 1–4–2 PAID $40.70

Ch. f, (Feb), by Miswaki – Willstar , by Nureyev . Trainer Frankel Robert. Bred by Juddmonte Farms Inc (Ky).

ETOILE MONTANTE pulled a bit along the inside pressing the early pace then stalked approaching the first turn, came a bit off the rail into the backstretch, tracked the leader down the backstretch and on the second turn, bid outside that one into the stretch, gained a short lead, inched clear under urging and held on gamely. KATDOGAWN (GB) saved ground chasing the pace, moved up inside leaving the backstretch, came out in upper stretch and closed gamely. TANGLE (IRE) stalked inside then a bit off the rail, was between foes leaving the backstretch and on the second turn, also came out in upper stretch and finished willingly. NOTTING HILL (BRZ) had good early speed outside the winner, inched away and angled in on the first turn, set the pace inside, fought back into the stretch and past midstretch but was outfinished. VOZ DE COLEGIALA (CHI) chased between foes then outside a rival, continued a bit off the rail into and on the second turn, angled in for the stretch, came off the rail in deep stretch and could not quite summon the necessary response. MAKEUP ARTIST settled inside then a bit off the rail, came out four wide on the second turn and into the stretch and lacked the needed rally. FUN HOUSE stalked the pace outside, went three deep into and on the second turn and into the stretch, drifted in some in the drive and weakened.

Owners– 1, Juddmonte Farms Inc; 2, Cuchna John R Jim Ford Inc and Pearson Deron; 3, Reddam J Paul; 4, Green Lantern Stables LLC and Barber Gary; 5, Hunt Nelson B; 6, Krikorian George; 7, Winchell Thoroughbreds LLC

Trainers– 1, Frankel Robert; 2, Cassidy James; 3, Dollase Craig; 4, Sahadi Jenine; 5, McAnally Ronald; 6, Shirreffs John; 7, McAnally Ronald

Scratched– Intercontinental (GB) (31Jul04 7Sar5)

$2 Daily Double (8–1) Paid $7.20 ; Daily Double Pool $35,935 .
$1 Pick Three (12–2/8–1) Paid $53.30 ; Pick Three Pool $115,436 .

NINTH RACE
Arlington
SEPTEMBER 4, 2004

1⅛ MILES. (1.46¹) 68TH RUNNING OF THE ARLINGTON MATRON HANDICAP. Grade III. Purse $150,000 FOR FILLIES AND MARES, THREE-YEARS-OLD AND UPWARD. By subscription of $100 each, which should accompany the nomination. A Supplementary Nomination of $6,000 may be made on Saturday, August 28, 2004, which includes entry and starting fees. Original nominees to pay $1,000 to pass the entry box and an additional $1,000 to start, with $150,000 Guaranteed, of which $90,000 to the winner; $30,000 to second; $16,500 to third; $9,000 to fourth and $4,500 to fifth. WEIGHTS: Sunday, August 29, 2004. This event will be limited to fourteen (14) starters. Preference will be Highweights (on the scale). Total Earnings in 2004 will be used to determine the order of preference of horses assigned equal weight (on the scale). Failure to draw into this race at time of entrycancels all fees with the exception of the nominating fee(s). Starters to be named through the entry box by usual time of closing. Two (2) horses having common ties through ownership cannot start to the exclusion of a single ownership interest. Trophy to the owner of the winner. Closed Wednesday, August 25, 2004 with 20 nominations.

Value of Race: $150,000 Winner $90,000; second $30,000; third $16,500; fourth $9,000; fifth $4,500. Mutuel Pool $276,105.00 Exacta Pool $167,510.00 Trifecta Pool $161,592.00 Superfecta Pool $59,987.00

Last Raced	Horse	M/Eqt.	A.	Wt	PP	St	¼	½	¾	Str	Fin	Jockey	Odds $1
12Jun04 8CD1	Adoration	L	5	123	4	4	1^{1}	$1^{½}$	$1^{½}$	$1^{1½}$	1^{2}	Espinoza V	1.10
13Aug04 8AP1	Tamweel	L	4	116	5	2	2^{hd}	3^{1}	$2^{½}$	2^{4}	$2^{2¾}$	Douglas R R	1.70
8Aug04 8Dmr8	Indy Groove	L	4	116	6	1	5^{2}	5^{2}	4^{1}	3^{2}	$3^{2¾}$	Fires E	22.20
13Aug04 8AP3	Julie's Prize	L bf	4	116	2	7	$6^{1½}$	7	7	4^{hd}	$4^{1¼}$	Razo E Jr	12.20
7Aug04 10ElP3	Bare Necessities	L	5	118	3	5	7	6^{1}	6^{1}	5^{3}	5^{7}	Marquez C H Jr	4.70
13Aug04 8AP4	Allspice	L b	4	116	7	3	$4^{½}$	$2^{½}$	$3^{1½}$	6^{1}	6^{4}	Emigh C A	28.90
13Aug04 8AP6	Hennie's Song	L	4	114	1	6	$3^{½}$	$4^{1½}$	5^{hd}	7	7	Graham J	24.90

OFF AT 4:57 Start Good . Won ridden out. Track fast.

TIME :24³, :48³, 1:12³, 1:37, 1:49³ (:24.71, :48.66, 1:12.72, 1:37.00, 1:49.75)

$2 Mutuel Prices:			
4 – ADORATION	4.20	2.40	2.10
5 – TAMWEEL		2.60	2.20
6 – INDY GROOVE			3.20

$2 EXACTA 4–5 PAID $9.20 $2 TRIFECTA 4–5–6 PAID $68.60
$2 SUPERFECTA 4–5–6–2 PAID $212.60

B. m, (Apr), by Honor Grades – Sewing Lady , by Key to the Mint . Trainer Hofmans David. Bred by Lucy G Bassett (Ky).

ADORATION broke in good order, quickly established the lead from the inside, was shown the whip to draw off in upper stretch then finished under a brisk hand ride. TAMWEEL went up to press the pace from just outside, remained lapped on the winner to the stretch then could not stay with that one in the final furlong and settled for the place. INDY GROOVE was taken back after breaking alertly, raced four to five wide, near the middle of the field, launched a bid in upper stretch then could not rally late. JULIE'S PRIZE lacked speed three to four wide then rallied mildly in the stretch but could not sustain her bid. BARE NECESSITIES lacked speed four to five wide and was never prominent. ALLSPICE raced close up three to four wide and tired. HENNIE'S SONG raced close up inside and steadily lost ground.

Owners– 1, Amerman Racing Stables LLC; 2, Turf Express Inc and Darrell and Evelyn Yates Ltd; 3, Glen Hill Farm; 4, Richard Otto Stables Inc; 5, Iron County Farms Inc; 6, Tafel James B; 7, Godolphin Racing Inc

Trainers– 1, Hofmans David; 2, Catalano Wayne M; 3, Proctor Thomas F; 4, Mitchell Anthony; 5, Kirby Frank J; 6, Geier Greg; 7, bin Suroor Saeed

Scratched– Miss Fortunate (07Aug04 10ElP2) , La Reason (01Aug04 9Sar5)

$1 Pick Three (3–5–4/8/9) Paid $81.70 ; Pick Three Pool $15,254 .

SEVENTH RACE
Saratoga
SEPTEMBER 5, 2004

1⅜ MILES. (Inner Turf) (2.12) 9TH RUNNING OF THE GLENS FALLS HANDICAP. 1ST DIVISION Grade III. Purse $100,000 INNER TURF A HANDICAP FOR FILLIES AND MARES THREE YEARS OLD AND UPWARD. By subscription of $100 each, which should accompany the nomination; $500 to pass the entry box, $500 to start, with $100,000 added. The added money and all fees to be divided 60% to the winner, 20% to second, 10% to third, 5% to fourth, 3% to fifth and 2% divided equally among remaining finishers. A trophy will be presented to the winning owner. The New York Racing Association reserves the right to transfer this race to the Main Track. In the event that this race is taken off the turf, it may be subject to downgrading upon review by the Graded Stakes Committee. Closed Saturday, August 21, 2004 with 27 Nominations.

Value of Race: $110,400 Winner $66,240; second $22,080; third $11,040; fourth $5,520; fifth $3,312; sixth $552; seventh $552; eighth $552; ninth $552. Mutuel Pool $619,702.00 Exacta Pool $596,107.00 Trifecta Pool $443,669.00

Last Raced	Horse	M/Eqt.	A.	Wt	PP	¼	½	¾	1	Str	Fin	Jockey	Odds $1
5Jly04 9Bel4	Humaita-Ger	L	4	114	9	4½	41½	41	41½	3hd	1½	Velasquez C	5.70
8Aug04 9Mth1	WhereWLftOff-GB	L	4	116	4	31	3hd	3hd	3½	2½	21¼	Prado E S	0.90
13Aug04 8Sar2	Savedbythelight	L b	4	115	3	1½	1½	1½	1½	1hd	32	Migliore R	7.40
17Jly04 9Del7	Lady Liberty	L	5	114	8	9	9	9	9	5½	4hd	Santos J A	41.75
8Aug04 9Mth8	Alternate	L b	5	116	6	2½	21½	21	2½	44½	51¾	Dominguez R A	4.90
25Aug04 7Mth2	Strategy-GB	b	4	112	1	51½	5hd	7½	6½	62½	63	Farina T	14.40
19Aug04 7Sar3	Ocean Silk	L b	4	112	5	7hd	82	6hd	7hd	73	72	Samyn J L	12.80
8Jly04 8Bel6	Shining Jewel	L	4	112	7	6½	6hd	5hd	5hd	8hd	81½	Fragoso P	38.75
27Aug04 8Sar6	Gal O Gal	L	4	114	2	82½	71	82	82	9	9	Albarado R J	51.00

OFF AT 4:13 Start Good . Won driving. Course firm.

TIME :24^{3}, :50^{1}, 1:16, 1:40^{1}, 2:03^{2}, 2:15^{1} (:24.76, :50.36, 1:16.16, 1:40.25, 2:03.57, 2:15.25)

$2 Mutuel Prices:

9 – HUMAITA–GER	13.40	4.20	3.20
4 – WHERE WE LEFT OFF–GB		2.70	2.30
3 – SAVEDBYTHELIGHT			3.70

$2 EXACTA 9–4 PAID $33.00 $2 TRIFECTA 9–4–3 PAID $147.00

Ch. f, (Feb), by Surumu–Ger – Happy Gini , by Ginistrelli . Trainer Motion H Graham. Bred by Stiftung Gestut Fahrhof (Ger).

HUMAITA (GER) raced close up outside while in hand, responded when roused in upper stretch, dug in gamely outside and prevailed under a drive. WHERE WE LEFT OFF (GB) raced close up inside while well in hand, saved ground throughout, got through on the rail in the stretch and dug in gamely to the wire. SAVEDBYTHELIGHT quickly showed in front, set the pace along the inside and weakened in the final furlong. LADY LIBERTY was outrun early, raced inside, rallied nearing the stretch and finished gamely. ALTERNATE prompted the pace from the outside while in hand and tired in the final furlong. STRATEGY (GB) was rated along inside, saved ground and lacked a rally. OCEAN SILK was unhurried while outrun early, raced inside, came wide into the stretch and had no rally. SHINING JEWEL was rated along early, raced between rivals, was three wide on the final turn and tired in the stretch. GAL O GAL was outrun early, raced four wide on the final turn and tired in the stretch.

Owners– 1, Jacobs Andreas; 2, Moyglare Stud Farm Ltd; 3, Mack Earle I; 4, Janney Stuart S III; 5, Pin Oak Stable LLC; 6, Fab Oak Stable; 7, Sangster Ben; 8, Dicresce Gary P; 9, Hugel Max

Trainers– 1, Motion H Graham; 2, Clement Christophe; 3, Violette Richard A Jr; 4, McGaughey III Claude R; 5, Motion H Graham; 6, Biancone Patrick L; 7, Byrne Patrick B; 8, Bond Harold James; 9, Blengs Vincent L

$2 Daily Double (1–9) Paid $49.60 ; Daily Double Pool $132,680 .
$2 Pick Three (4–1–9) Paid $749.00 ; Pick Three Pool $128,354 .

TENTH RACE
Saratoga
SEPTEMBER 5, 2004

1⅜ MILES. (Inner Turf) (2.12) 9TH RUNNING OF THE GLENS FALLS HANDICAP. 2ND DIVISION Grade III. Purse $100,000 INNER TURF A HANDICAP FOR FILLIES AND MARES THREE YEARS OLD AND UPWARD. By subscription of $100 each, which should accompany the nomination; $500 to pass the entry box, $500 to start, with $100,000 added. The added money and all fees to be divided 60% to the winner, 20% to second, 10% to third, 5% to fourth, 3% to fifth and 2% divided equally among remaining finishers. A trophy will be presented to the winning owner. The New York Racing Association reserves the right to transfer this race to the Main Track. In the event that this race is taken off the turf, it may be subject to downgrading upon review by the Graded Stakes Committee. Closed Saturday, August 21, 2004 with 27 Nominations.

Value of Race: $109,300 Winner $65,580; second $21,860; third $10,930; fourth $5,465; fifth $3,279; sixth $729; seventh $729; eighth $728. Mutuel Pool $552,500.00 Exacta Pool $434,039.00 Trifecta Pool $343,351.00

Last Raced	Horse	M/Eqt.	A.	Wt	PP	¼	½	¾	1	Str	Fin	Jockey	Odds $1
11Aug04 4Sar1	Arvada-GB	L	4	112	4	11½	1½	11½	1½	12½	1½	Velazquez J R	3.25
31Jly04 7Sar6	Spice Island	L b	5	118	7	2hd	31	3½	4½	21½	2no	Prado E S	2.20
10Jly04 8Cnl1	Film Maker	L b	4	121	5	5hd	52	6½	52½	3hd	32¼	Dominguez R A	2.80
14Aug04 8AP7	Aud	L	4	115	6	62½	6hd	5hd	6hd	4½	43	Day P	7.20
7Aug04 5Mnr1	Lady of the Future	L	6	116	3	73	73	71	72	6hd	51	Vega H	11.80
11Aug04 8Sar4	Nannycam	L	4	112	8	3½	2½	2½	3½	72½	61	Chavez J F	25.50
17Jly04 9Del3	Primetimevalentine	L b	5	113	1	42	4hd	41½	2½	52	7hd	Castellano J J	11.00
17Jly04 9Del4	Miss Hellie	L	5	114	2	8	8	8	8	8	8	Santos J A	26.00

OFF AT 5:48 Start Good . Won driving. Course firm.

TIME :25^{3}, :50, 1:15, 1:39, 2:02^{1}, 2:14 (:25.64, :50.16, 1:15.08, 1:39.04, 2:02.39, 2:14.12)

$2 Mutuel Prices:

4 – ARVADA–GB	8.50	4.80	3.00
7 – SPICE ISLAND		3.60	2.70
5 – FILM MAKER			2.50

$2 EXACTA 4–7 PAID $36.80 $2 TRIFECTA 4–7–5 PAID $79.50

B. f, (Mar), by Hernando–Fr – Lalindi–Ire , by Cadeaux Genereux–GB . Trainer Frankel Robert. Bred by Myriad Communications and &New England Stud (GB).

ARVADA (GB) quickly showed in front, set the pace along the inside while in hand, drew clear when roused in upper stretch then dug in gamely and held on after a long drive. SPICE ISLAND was rated along inside, saved ground, angled out in the stretch and finished gamely to earn the place award. FILM MAKER was rated along outside, advanced three wide on the final turn and finished gamely outside. AUD raced inside while in hand, saved ground, responded when roused in upper stretch and finished well inside. LADY OF THE FUTURE was outrun early, put in a three wide run on the final turn and had nothing left for the stretch drive. NANNYCAM attended the pace from the outside and tired in the stretch. PRIMETIMEVALENTINE raced close up inside, put in a three wide run on the final turn and tired in the stretch. MISS HELLIE was outrun early, raced inside and had no response when roused.

Owners– 1, Gordon Giles Pritchard; 2, Denlea Park Ltd; 3, Adam Donald A; 4, Willmott Stables Inc; 5, Pearson Max H; 6, Oxley John C; 7, Low Robert and Lawana; 8, Hamilton Emory A

Trainers– 1, Frankel Robert; 2, Clement Christophe; 3, Motion H Graham; 4, Reinstedler Anthony; 5, Greene Thomas M; 6, Ward John T Jr; 7, Peitz Daniel C; 8, McGaughey III Claude R

EIGHTH RACE
Del Mar
SEPTEMBER 5, 2004

1 MILE. (1.33[1]) 18TH RUNNING OF THE DEL MAR BREEDERS' CUP HANDICAP. Grade II. Purse $250,000 (includes $100,000 BC – Breeders' Cup) FOR THREE-YEAR-OLDS AND UPWARD. By subscription of $150 each, which shall accompany the nomination, or by supplementary nomination of $1,500 each by Sunday, August 29, $1,500 additional to start, with $150,000 and an additional $100,000 from the Breeders' Cup Fund for Cup nominees only. The host association's monies to be divided 60% to the winner, 20% to second, 12% to third, 6% to fourth and 2% to fifth. Breeders' Cup monies also correspondingly divided, provided a Breeders' Cup nominee has finished inan awarded position. Any Breeders' Cup Fund monies not awarded will revert to the Fund. Weights Monday, August 30. The field will be limited to 12 starters. High weights preferred. If more than 12 entries pass the entry box, the starters will be determmined at that time with preference given to Breeders' Cup nominees only of equal racing quality or weight assignment (respective of sex and weight for age). STARTERS TO BE NAMED THROUGH THE ENTRY BOX THURSDAY, SEPTEMBER 2, BY THE CLOSING TIME OF ENTRIES. A trophy will be presented to the winning owner by Breeders' Cup Ltd. Closed with 13 nominations.

Value of Race: $250,000 Winner $150,000; second $50,000; third $30,000; fourth $15,000; fifth $5,000. Mutuel Pool $498,978.00 Exacta Pool $250,945.00 Quinella Pool $30,996.00 Trifecta Pool $219,732.00

Last Raced	Horse	M/Eqt.	A.	Wt	PP	St	¼	½	¾	Str	Fin	Jockey	Odds $1
9Aug04 8Del2	Supah Blitz	LB	4	116	2	1	3¹	4²	3¹½	1¹½	1no	Espinoza V	4.20
15Aug04 8Dmr2	Domestic Dispute	LB	4	117	6	3	2¹	3¹	4¹	3½	2⁴	Desormeaux K J	2.50
22Aug04 8Dmr5	During	LB b	4	117	5	2	1hd	2hd	1hd	2¹	3¹	Nakatani C S	2.10
5Aug04 7Dmr1	Touch the Wire	LB b	4	115	3	5	5⁶	5hd	5½	4hd	4²	Court J K	9.80
31May04 3BM3	Snorter	LB b	4	116	4	4	4¹½	1½	2hd	5²½	5⁵½	Baze T C	6.10
30Jly04 2Dmr4	Rushin' to Altar	LB f	5	116	1	6	6	6	6	6	6	Stevens G L	5.30

OFF AT 5:47 Start Good. Won driving. Track fast.

TIME :22², :46, 1:10, 1:22², 1:35 (:22.45, :46.07, 1:10.18, 1:22.53, 1:35.14)

$2 Mutuel Prices:				
	3 – SUPAH BLITZ	10.40	5.40	3.00
	7 – DOMESTIC DISPUTE		4.00	2.60
	6 – DURING			2.60

$1 EXACTA 3–7 PAID $17.60 $2 QUINELLA 3–7 PAID $20.00
$1 TRIFECTA 3–7–6 PAID $43.30

Dk. b or br. c, (Feb), by Mecke – Boots 'n Jackie, by Major Moran. Trainer O'Neill Doug. Bred by Bee Bee Stables Inc & Equitor Inc (Fla).

SUPAH BLITZ chased inside then a bit off the rail, came out on the second turn, bid three deep leaving that turn, gained the lead, inched clear and held on gamely under urging. DOMESTIC DISPUTE three deep early, angled in and dueled outside a rival then briefly between foes on the backstretch, fell back a bit off the rail into the second turn, came out leaving that turn and into the stretch and re-rallied in the lane to just miss. DURING had speed between foes then dueled inside, fought back to a short lead leaving the second turn and weakened in the final furlong but held third. TOUCH THE WIRE chased between foes then a bit off the rail, came out on the second turn and four wide into the stretch and lacked the needed rally. SNORTER stalked outside then bid three deep on the backstretch to gain the lead, battled outside DURING on the second turn and between foes leaving that bend and weakened. RUSHIN' TO ALTAR broke awkwardly and a bit slowly, settled a bit off the rail then outside a rival on the backstretch, came out on the second turn and five wide into the stretch and did not rally.

Owners– 1, Kagele Bros & Leib; 2, Bienstock David Mandabach Paul and Winner Charles; 3, McIngvale James; 4, Creel Allan Lanni J Terrance and Schiappa Bernard C; 5, Gary and Mary West Stables Inc; 6, Vogel Arthur

Trainers– 1, O'Neill Doug; 2, Gallagher Patrick; 3, Baffert Bob; 4, Dollase Craig; 5, Frankel Robert; 6, McAnally Ronald

Scratched– Night Patrol (22Aug04 8Dmr8)

$2 Daily Double (7–3) Paid $39.60 ; Daily Double Pool $36,030 .
$1 Pick Three (8–2/3/7–3) Paid $483.20 ; Pick Three Pool $113,930 .

TENTH RACE
Saratoga
SEPTEMBER 6, 2004

1$\frac{3}{16}$ MILES. (Turf) (1.51[3]) 97TH RUNNING OF THE SARANAC HANDICAP. Grade III. Purse $100,000 MELLON TURF (Up To $19,000 NYSBFOA) FOR THREE YEAR OLDS. By subscription of $100 each, which should accompany the nomination; $500 to pass the entry box; $500 to start, with $100,000 added. The added money and all fees to be divided 60% to the winner, 20% to second, 10% to third, 5% to fourth, 3% to fifth and 2% divided equally among remaining finishers. 123 lbs. Non-winners of $60,000 twice on the turf in 2004 allowed 2 lbs.; such a race in 2004, 4 lbs.; $45,000; or three races, 6 lbs.; two races, 8 lbs. (Maiden, claiming and restricted allowance races not considered). A trophy will be presented to the winning owner. The New York Racing Association reserves the right to transfer this race to the Main Track. In the event that this race is taken off the turf, it may be subject to downgrading upon review by the Graded Stakes Committee. Closed Saturday, August 21, 2004 with 22 Nominations. (If the Stewards consider it inadvisable to run this race on the turf course, this race will be run at One Mile and OneEighth on the main track.).

Value of Race: $108,200 Winner $64,920; second $21,640; third $10,820; fourth $5,410; fifth $3,246; sixth $2,164. Mutuel Pool $614,518.00 Exacta Pool $466,765.00 Trifecta Pool $318,609.00

Last Raced	Horse	M/Eqt.	A.	Wt	PP	St	¼	½	¾	Str	Fin	Jockey	Odds $1
10Jly04 9Cnl3	Prince Arch	L b	3	123	1	2	6	6	6	4hd	1hd	Castellano J J	2.05
9Aug04 8Sar2	Mustanfar	L b	3	121	6	6	3¹½	3hd	3½	1½	2²¼	Velasquez C	2.45
7Aug04 4Sar1	Catch the Glory	L b	3	115	4	5	1¹	1³	1½	2¹	3¹½	Chavez J F	12.40
9Aug04 8Sar3	Good Reward	L b	3	115	2	1	5½	5¹½	5½	5½	4²	Santos J A	4.10
8Aug04 7Mth3	Grand Heritage	L	3	117	3	4	4¹½	4½	4hd	6	5¹	Sellers S J	11.80
8Aug04 8Sar1	Dynamite Flyer	L	3	117	5	3	2½	2¹½	2½	3hd	6	Migliore R	3.85

OFF AT 5:48 Start Good. Won driving. Course firm.

TIME :24¹, :48², 1:12³, 1:36², 1:53⁴ (:24.20, :48.49, 1:12.70, 1:36.58, 1:53.89)

$2 Mutuel Prices:				
	1 – PRINCE ARCH	6.10	2.90	2.60
	6 – MUSTANFAR		3.10	2.80
	4 – CATCH THE GLORY			4.20

$2 EXACTA 1–6 PAID $13.60 $2 TRIFECTA 1–6–4 PAID $96.50

B. c, (May), by Arch – Princess Kris-GB, by Kris-GB. Trainer McPeek Kenneth G. Bred by Pine Lake Bloodstock LLC (Ky).

PRINCE ARCH was unhurried while outrun early, rallied four wide approaching the stretch, bumped with GOOD REWARD in upper stretch, dug in resolutely outside and was up in time. MUSTANFAR raced close up outside while in hand, rallied three wide on the second turn, reached the front nearing the eighth pole, drew clear in deep stretch and dug in gamely but could not hold off the winner. CATCH THE GLORY hit the gate at the start, quickly showed in front, set the pace along the inside while in hand, was bumped in upper stretch and tired in the final furlong. GOOD REWARD was rated along while between rivals, came wide into the stretch, bumped with the winner in upper stretch and lacked a rally. GRAND HERITAGE was rated along early, raced inside and had no response when roused. DYNAMITE FLYER raced close up outside, chased the pace, was bumped in upper stretch and tired.

Owners– 1, Cottrell Raymond H Sr; 2, Shadwell Stable; 3, Sovereign Stable and Gatsas Stables; 4, Phipps Ogden Mills et al; 5, Firestone Mr and Mrs B; 6, Augustin Stable

Trainers– 1, McPeek Kenneth G; 2, McLaughlin Kiaran P; 3, Terranova John P II; 4, McGaughey III Claude R; 5, Mott William I; 6, Hendriks Sanna N

EIGHTH RACE
Del Mar
SEPTEMBER 6, 2004

1$\frac{1}{8}$ MILES. (Turf) (1.45^{4}) 60TH RUNNING OF THE DEL MAR DERBY. Grade II. Purse $400,000 FOR THREE-YEAR-OLDS. By subscription of $400 each, which shall accompany the nomination, or by supplementary nomination of $4,000 each by closing time of entries, $1,000 to pass the entry box and $3,000 additional to start, with $400,000 Guaranteed, of which $240,000 to first, $80,000 to second, $48,000 to third, $24,000 to fourth and $8,000 to fifth. Weight 122 lbs. First preference will be given to the winner(s) of the Oceanside Stakes. Second preference will be given to graded or group stakes winners.Third preference will be given to horses which have finished second or third in graded or group stakes. Total non-claiming purse earnings will determine the order of preference for horses of equal status. Entry fees will be refunded to all horses which fail to draw into this race. The field will be drawn by the closing time of entries, Saturday, September 4. A trophy will be presented to the owner of the winner. Closed with 18 nominations.

Value of Race: $400,000 Winner $240,000; second $80,000; third $48,000; fourth $24,000; fifth $8,000. Mutuel Pool $648,385.00 Exacta Pool $339,570.00 Quinella Pool $33,199.00 Trifecta Pool $349,145.00 Superfecta Pool $164,084.00

Last Raced	Horse	M/Eqt.	A.	Wt	PP	St	1/4	1/2	3/4	Str	Fin	Jockey	Odds $1
14Aug04 ^{8}Dmr^{1}	Blackdoun-FR	LB b	3	122	10	8	10	10	10	$5\frac{1}{2}$	1^{nk}	Nakatani C S	0.90
24Jly04 ^{5}AP^{3}	Toasted	LB	3	122	3	4	3^{hd}	3^{hd}	3^{hd}	3^{1}	2no	Douglas R R	6.50
14Aug04 ^{8}Dmr^{5}	Laura's Lucky Boy	LB	3	122	2	3	$2^{1\frac{1}{2}}$	$2^{2\frac{1}{2}}$	2^{2}	$1^{1\frac{1}{2}}$	$3^{\frac{1}{2}}$	Stevens G L	6.70
21Jly04 ^{8}Dmr^{2}	Terroplane-FR	LB b	3	122	6	6	6^{2}	5^{hd}	$6^{1\frac{1}{2}}$	6^{1}	4^{1}	Desormeaux K J	12.10
20Jun04 TOU^{1}	Fast andFurious-FR	LB	3	122	9	9	9^{1}	$9^{1\frac{1}{2}}$	9^{hd}	$8^{1\frac{1}{2}}$	5no	Espinoza V	7.70
14Aug04 ^{8}Dmr^{2}	Semi Lost	LB	3	122	7	2	4^{1}	4^{2}	$4^{1\frac{1}{2}}$	2^{hd}	6^{1}	Baze T C	10.40
15Jly04 EPS^{6}	Place Cowboy-Ire	B	3	122	1	10	8^{1}	8^{3}	8^{1}	7^{2}	7^{3}	Valdivia J Jr	75.40
14Aug04 ^{8}Dmr^{3}	Bedmar-GB	LB b	3	122	4	7	$7^{\frac{1}{2}}$	7^{hd}	7^{hd}	9^{6}	8^{2}	Smith M E	61.50
21Jly04 ^{8}Dmr^{3}	Lucky Pulpit	LB bf	3	122	5	1	$1^{1\frac{1}{2}}$	$1^{2\frac{1}{2}}$	$1^{\frac{1}{2}}$	4^{hd}	$9^{15\frac{1}{2}}$	Puglisi I	24.80
14Aug04 ^{8}Dmr^{4}	Sujimoto	LB	3	122	8	5	5^{hd}	6^{2}	5^{hd}	10	10	Flores D R	12.80

OFF AT 5:36 Start Good . Won driving. Course firm.

TIME :24, :47^{3}, 1:11^{4}, 1:35, 1:48^{3} (:24.04, .47.73, 1:11.43, 1:35.06, 1:46.75)

$2 Mutuel Prices:				
	10 – BLACKDOUN-FR	3.80	2.80	2.20
	3 – TOASTED		4.80	3.80
	2 – LAURA'S LUCKY BOY			3.80

$1 EXACTA 10–3 PAID $11.60 $2 QUINELLA 3–10 PAID $16.20
$1 TRIFECTA 10–3–2 PAID $50.50 $1 SUPERFECTA 10–3–2–6 PAID $233.20

Gr/ro. c, (Apr), by Verglas-Ire – Rade , by Kaldoun-Fr . Trainer Canani Julio C. Bred by Sabine Charpentier & &Anne-Charlotte Charpentier (Fr).

BLACKDOUN (FR) unhurried and angled in early, settled a bit off the rail, was in a bit tight off heels on the second turn, rallied between horses in the stretch, gained a short lead under left handed urging in deep stretch and held gamely. TOASTED saved ground stalking the pace, came out into the stretch, also rallied between foes in the drive and continued willingly between horses late. LAURA'S LUCKY BOY stalked the pace inside then a bit off the rail, bid outside the pacesetter leaving the backstretch and on the second turn, took a short lead into the stretch, inched clear, then fought back inside the top pair to the wire. TERROPLANE (FR) pulled between horses then chased a bit off the rail, came out on the second turn and four wide into the stretch and found his best stride late. FAST AND FURIOUS (FR) angled in and settled just off the inside, steadied off heels midway on the second turn, came out in midstretch and also put in a late bid outside. SEMI LOST stalked outside a rival, bid three deep into the stretch, steadied late when the top pair went past and was outfinished. PLACE COWBOY (IRE) saved ground off the pace, came out a bit in the stretch and lacked the needed rally. BEDMAR (GB) pulled between foes and steadied in tight leaving the chute, chased outside a rival, came three deep into the stretch and could not summon the necessary late kick. LUCKY PULPIT pulled his way to the early lead, drifted out a bit leaving the chute then angled in and set the pace inside, dueled along the rail into and on the second turn and weakened in the stretch. SUJIMOTO pulled a bit early, stalked outside then three deep into the second turn, dropped back on that turn and gave way. A claim of foul by the rider of SEMI LOST against the winner was not allowed by the stewards, who ruled the latter was not the cause of that one's trouble.

Owners– 1, Naify and Woodside Farms LLC; 2, Port Sidney L and Trust 720270; 3, Mercedes Stables LLC; 4, Bienstock David Papiano Neil and Winner Charles; 5, Zetcher Arnold; 6, Bone Robert D and Desperado Stables; 7, Gould Family Trust; 8, Brown Ann H; 9, Williams Mr and Mrs Larry D; 10, Amerman Racing Stables LLC

Trainers– 1, Canani Julio C; 2, De Seroux Laura; 3, Orman Jason; 4, Drysdale Neil; 5, McAnally Ronald; 6, Mullins Jeff; 7, Cassidy James; 8, Greely C Beau; 9, Sise Clifford Jr; 10, Frankel Robert

---

$2 Daily Double (9–10) Paid $15.00 ; Daily Double Pool $50,993 .
$1 Pick Three (9–9–10) Paid $40.90 ; Pick Three Pool $149,704 .

THIRTEENTH RACE
River Downs
SEPTEMBER 6, 2004

$1\frac{1}{16}$ MILES. (1.41^{4}) 28TH RUNNING OF THE MILLER GENUINE DRAFT CRADLE. Grade III. Purse $200,000 (plus $5,000 OTF – Ohio Thoroughbred Fund) FOR TWO YEAR OLDS. Weight.....120 lbs. $25 Early Bird nominations closed December 31, 2003. $100 Last Chance Reservations closed on May 7, 2004. Fees due to remain eligible: $200 due by June 25, 2004; $400 by July 31, 2004. $1,500 to enter by the usual time of closing. The first three finishers in the Cradle Prep may supplement with a fee of $3,000 at the time of entry. A supplemental entry may be made upon payment of $12,000 at the time of entry. The purse to be distributed: 60% to the winner; 20% to second; 10% to third; 5% to fourth; 3% to fifth; 2% to sixth. A trophy will be presented to the winning owner. No owner may start (2) two or more horses to the exclusion of a single entry. Should the race have more entries than management feels can be accomodated, River Downs reserves the right to limit the field to (12) twelve starters with preference given to those with the highest total earnings. Entry fees for excluded horses to be returned.

Value of Race: $200,000 Winner $120,000; second $40,000; third $20,000; fourth $10,000; fifth $6,000; sixth $4,000. Mutuel Pool $130,621.00 Exacta Pool $67,529.00 Superfecta Pool $20,038.00 Trifecta Pool $58,626.00

Last Raced	Horse	M/Eqt.	A.	Wt	PP	St	¼	½	¾	Str	Fin	Jockey	Odds $1
3Aug04 ^{4}Del^{1}	Bellamy Road	L f	2	120	2	2	$1\frac{1}{2}$	1^{1}	$1^{1\frac{1}{2}}$	1^{6}	$1^{2\frac{3}{4}}$	Castellano A Jr	2.20
5Jly04 ^{3}CD^{1}	Diamond Isle	L	2	120	5	3	4^{1}	4^{hd}	2^{hd}	2^{1}	2^{nk}	Blanc B	2.40
14Aug04 ^{2}Sar^{1}	Scipion	b	2	120	1	4	2^{1}	2^{hd}	$3\frac{1}{2}$	$3^{3\frac{1}{2}}$	$3^{6\frac{3}{4}}$	Prado E S	1.00
14Aug04 ^{11}RD^{2}	Flyrock	L b	2	120	8	5	7^{5}	7^{15}	7^{25}	4^{hd}	4no	Johnston J A	39.60
1Aug04 ^{8}AP^{5}	Copy My Notes	L	2	120	3	6	6^{2}	$6^{2\frac{1}{2}}$	6^{hd}	5^{3}	5^{6}	McKee J	20.10
14Aug04 ^{11}RD^{3}	Quick Blend	L	2	120	4	7	5^{1}	5^{5}	5^{5}	7	$6^{1\frac{1}{2}}$	Owens A	62.20
14Aug04 ^{11}RD^{1}	Cat Tourn	L	2	120	7	1	3^{hd}	3^{hd}	4^{hd}	6^{hd}	7	Coa D	19.10
	Capwikann	L	2	120	6	8	8	8	8	—	—	Solomon N G	120.70

OFF AT 5:17 Start Good For All But CAPWIKANN. Won ridden out. Track fast.

TIME :25^{1}, :49^{2}, 1:12^{2}, 1:38, 1:45 (:25.20, :49.40, 1:12.40, 1:38.00, 1:45.00)

$2 Mutuel Prices:			
2 – BELLAMY ROAD	6.40	3.60	2.10
5 – DIAMOND ISLE		3.60	2.10
1 – SCIPION			2.10

$2 EXACTA 2–5 PAID $14.60 $2 SUPERFECTA 2–5–1–8 PAID $228.20
$2 TRIFECTA 2–5–1 PAID $32.60

Dk. b or br. c, (Apr), by Concerto – Hurry Home Hillary , by Deputed Testamony . Trainer Dickinson Michael W. Bred by Dianne D Cotter (Fla).

BELLAMY ROAD set all of the pace while racing in the three and four path, was able to set a slow pace, drew off in upper stretch, was shown the whip in mid stretch, was ridden out to the wire. DIAMOND ISLE was well placed while between horses early, rallied on the far turn, could not get to the winner but gamely held the place. SCIPION pressed the pace and dueled for the lead from the inside early, was angled out in the stretch, ran evenly late and had no closing response. FLYROCK was unhurried early, improved position in the stretch on the outside but was no threat to the top three. COPY MY NOTES was well placed on the inside early, ran evenly throughout and had no rally. QUICK BLEND was pinched back at the start, was in a good stalking position on the outside in mid pack, had no rally. CAT TOURN pressed the pace with good early speed, faltered in the stretch and faded. CAPWIKANN hit the gate, clipped heels soon after the start, gave way and was eased.

Owners– 1, Kinsman Stable; 2, Buckram Oak Farm; 3, Kraft-Payson Virginia; 4, Silverton Hill LLC; 5, Iron Horse Racing LLC; 6, Hays Billy; 7, Panic Stable LLC; 8, Cole Mrs Carlton

Trainers– 1, Dickinson Michael W; 2, McPeek Kenneth G; 3, Biancone Patrick L; 4, Miller Darrin; 5, Holthus Robert E; 6, Woodard Joe; 7, Amoss Thomas; 8, Ortiz Jeff

---

$2 Pick Three (2–3/7–2) Paid $218.00 ; Pick Three Pool $6,258 .

TENTH RACE
Philadelphia
SEPTEMBER 6, 2004

1⅛ MILES. 26TH RUNNING OF THE PENNSYLVANIA DERBY. Grade II. Purse $750,000 FOR THREE YEAR OLDS. By subscription of $750 each which should accompany the nomination, $1,000 to pass the entry box, $1,000 additional to start. Weight 122 lbs. Non-winners of a graded race at a mile or over in 2004 allowed 3 lbs.; of a $60,000 at a mile or over in 2004, 5 lbs.; of three races at a mile or over other than maiden or claiming in 2004, 8 lbs. This race will not be divided. A field of 14 horses will be drawn with the preference given to Graded/Group stakes winners in order (I–II–III), stakes winners, then highest career earnings. Nominations closed Monday, August 23, 2004.

Value of Race: $750,000 Winner $418,500; second $139,500; third $76,725; fourth $41,850; fifth $20,925; sixth $7,500; seventh $7,500; eighth $7,500; ninth $7,500; tenth $7,500; eleventh $7,500; twelfth $7,500. Mutuel Pool $596,090.00 Exacta Pool $416,955.00 Trifecta Pool $321,089.00 Superfecta Pool $82,987.00

Last Raced	Horse	M/Eqt.	A.	Wt	PP	St	¼	½	¾	Str	Fin	Jockey	Odds $1
12Aug04 ^{7}Sar^{1}	Love of Money	L	3	116	4	2	$1^{\frac{1}{2}}$	1^{1}	1^{1}	1^{4}	$1^{8\frac{1}{2}}$	Albarado R J	12.70
7Aug04 ^{8}Mnr^{2}	Pollard's Vision	L	3	122	8	1	$2^{1\frac{1}{2}}$	2^{1}	2^{1}	2^{3}	2^{1}	Velazquez J R	3.90
8Aug04 ^{13}Mth^{5}	Swingforthefences	L f	3	119	5	5	$10^{\frac{1}{2}}$	10^{1}	9^{hd}	$4^{2\frac{1}{2}}$	$3^{3\frac{1}{4}}$	Bridgmohan S X	20.00
8Aug04 ^{9}Sar^{3}	Niigon	L f	3	119	9	6	3^{hd}	4^{hd}	$3^{\frac{1}{2}}$	$3^{\frac{1}{2}}$	$4^{1\frac{1}{4}}$	Landry R C	28.40
8Aug04 ^{13}Mth^{3}	Pies Prospect	L	3	114	3	4	8^{hd}	$8^{\frac{1}{2}}$	8^{hd}	$5^{\frac{1}{2}}$	$5^{\frac{1}{2}}$	Lopez C C	10.90
14Aug04 ^{8}Pha^{1}	Separato	L	3	119	10	12	12	12	12	7^{hd}	6^{nk}	Rose J	12.10
15May04 ^{12}Pim^{9}	Song of the Sword	L bf	3	115	2	11	11^{6}	11^{5}	11^{5}	$8^{\frac{1}{2}}$	$7^{2\frac{1}{4}}$	Black A S	23.60
8Aug04 ^{13}Mth^{4}	Royal Assault	L b	3	119	6	8	9^{2}	9^{2}	5^{hd}	6^{hd}	$8^{\frac{1}{2}}$	Day P	11.50
1May04 ^{10}CD^{9}	Tapit	L f	3	122	12	10	$4^{\frac{1}{2}}$	3^{hd}	4^{2}	9^{5}	$9^{3\frac{3}{4}}$	Dominguez R A	3.30
8Aug04 ^{13}Mth^{2}	My Snookie's Boy	L	3	114	1	3	$5^{\frac{1}{2}}$	5^{1}	10^{hd}	11^{1}	10^{3}	Elliott S	3.80
8Aug04 ^{13}Mth^{8}	Wimplestiltskin	L b	3	114	11	9	$7^{\frac{1}{2}}$	7^{hd}	$7^{\frac{1}{2}}$	10^{1}	11^{4}	Rivera H G	83.20
26Jun04 ^{8}Del^{6}	Master David	L b	3	114	7	7	6^{hd}	6^{2}	6^{hd}	12	12	Coa E M	7.40

OFF AT 5:10 Start Good . Won ridden out. Track fast.

TIME :23^{3}, :47^{3}, 1:11^{1}, 1:35^{3}, 1:48^{2} (:23.63, :47.62, 1:11.26, 1:35.61, 1:48.42)

$2 Mutuel Prices:				
	4 – LOVE OF MONEY	27.40	12.40	9.00
	8 – POLLARD'S VISION		6.00	4.00
	5 – SWINGFORTHEFENCES			9.20

$2 EXACTA 4–8 PAID $120.00 $2 TRIFECTA 4–8–5 PAID $2,598.40
$2 SUPERFECTA 4–8–5–9 PAID $16,597.40

Dk. b or br. c, (Apr), by Not For Love – Mescalina , by Smarten . Trainer Dutrow Richard E Jr. Bred by Dr & Mrs Thomas Bowman Mr & Mrs &Thomas Sutton & Milton P Higgins III (Md).

LOVE OF MONEY took the lead soon after the start, set pace inside under rating, tried to bear out entering the stretch, was quickly straightened away, he was roused once right handed in mid stretch and then was hand ridden out to the wire. POLLARD'S VISION raced off the rail while always in closest pursuit, was no match through the stretch. SWINGFORTHEFENCES was outrun early, raced outside and passed tiring foes while no real threat. NIIGON was between foes and just off the pace, was left with the rail on the final turn and dropped back. PIES PROSPECT failed to menace. SEPARATO was outrun early and then only passed tiring foes. SONG OF THE SWORD failed to menace. ROYAL ASSAULT was steadied into the first turn and then failed to menace. TAPIT bobbled leaving the gate, recovered quickly and was sent up to be well placed racing wide and then dropped back suddenly. MY SNOOKIE'S BOY saved ground just off the early pace and was finished after after half. WIMPLESTILTSKIN steadied in tight soon after start, raced outside and tired. MASTER DAVID was also in tight early, raced outside, tired.

Owners– 1, Jay Em Ess Stable; 2, Edgewood Farm; 3, Klaravich Stables Inc; 4, Chiefswood Stable; 5, LaPenta Robert V; 6, CJZ Racing Stable; 7, Paraneck Stable; 8, Farmer Tracy; 9, Winchell Thoroughbreds LLC; 10, Preferred Pals Stable; 11, Everest Stables Inc; 12, Georgica Stable and Star Crown Stable

Trainers– 1, Dutrow Richard E Jr; 2, Pletcher Todd A; 3, Violette Richard A Jr; 4, Coatrieux Eric; 5, Zito Nicholas P; 6, Ritchey Tim F; 7, Pedersen Jennifer; 8, Zito Nicholas P; 9, Dickinson Michael W; 10, Iwinski Allen; 11, Coletti Edward J Jr; 12, Frankel Robert

$2 Pick Three (1–3/8–4) Paid $134.60 ; Pick Three Pool $19,671 .

EIGHTH RACE
Del Mar
SEPTEMBER 8, 2004

7 FURLONGS. (1.20) 57TH RUNNING OF THE DEL MAR FUTURITY. Grade II. Purse $250,000 FOR TWO-YEAR-OLDS (FOALS OF 2002). By subscription of $250 each if made on or before June 4, 2004, the fee to accompany the nomination. For horses not nominated, supplementary nominations of $10,000 each will close at the time of entry, Sunday, September5. All horses shall pay $500 to pass the entry box and $2,000 additional to start, with $250,000 Guaranteed, of which $150,000 to first, $50,000 to second, $30,000 to third, $15,000 to fourth and $5,000 to fifth. Weights: colts and geldings, 122 lbs.; fillies, 119 lbs. Non-winners of $50,000 twice allowed 2 lbs.; of such a race, 4 lbs. of $25,000 other than maiden or claiming, 6 lbs.; of a race other than claiming, 8 lbs. Starters to be named through the entry box Sunday, September 5, by the closing timeof entries. High weights preferred. Total non-claiming purse earnings will determine the order of preference for horses of equal status. A trophy will be presented to the owner of the winner. Closed with 193 nominations.

Value of Race: $245,000 Winner $150,000; second $50,000; third $30,000; fourth $15,000. Mutuel Pool $617,282.00 Exacta Pool $204,430.00 Quinella Pool $19,679.00 Trifecta Pool $105,460.00

Last Raced	Horse	M/Eqt.	A.	Wt	PP	St	¼	½	Str	Fin	Jockey	Odds $1
31Jly04 ^{3}Dmr^{1}	Declan's Moon	LB	2	116	1	3	2^{1}	$2^{1\frac{1}{2}}$	$2^{3\frac{1}{2}}$	1^{nk}	Espinoza V	6.20
15Aug04 ^{2}Dmr^{1}	Roman Ruler	LB	2	120	2	4	3^{hd}	$3^{1\frac{1}{2}}$	$1^{\frac{1}{2}}$	$2^{9\frac{1}{2}}$	Nakatani C S	0.10
21Aug04 ^{6}Dmr^{1}	Swiss Lad	LB	2	116	3	1	4	4	4	3^{4}	Baze T C	7.80
28Aug04 ^{2}Dmr^{1}	Gentleman Count	LB b	2	116	4	2	$1^{3\frac{1}{2}}$	1^{4}	$3^{1\frac{1}{2}}$	4	John K	18.20

OFF AT 5:41 Start Good . Won driving. Track fast.

TIME :22^{1}, :44^{3}, 1:08^{4}, 1:21^{1} (:22.25, :44.73, 1:08.87, 1:21.29)

$2 Mutuel Prices:				
	3 – DECLAN'S MOON	14.40	2.10	—
	4 – ROMAN RULER		2.10	—
	5 – SWISS LAD		—	—

$1 EXACTA 3–4 PAID $11.00 $2 QUINELLA 3–4 PAID $3.80
$1 TRIFECTA 3–4–5 PAID $15.30

Dk. b or br. g, (Feb), by Malibu Moon – Vee Vee Star , by Norquestor . Trainer Ellis Ronald W. Bred by Brice Ridgely (Md).

DECLAN'S MOON drifted out some early, chased off the rail, bid between horses into the stretch, fought back along the rail in the final furlong, put a head in front in deep stretch, brushed with the runner-up late but gamely prevailed under urging. ROMAN RULER off a bit slowly, steadied briefly in a bit tight behind the winner early, also chased off the inside, bid three deep leaving the turn and into the stretch, took a short lead in upper stretch, also fought back and continued willingly to the wire while brushing the winner late. SWISS LAD chased outside, went four wide into the turn, angled in on the turn and lacked a further response. GENTLEMAN COUNT sped to the early lead, angled in and set the pace inside, dueled along the rail leaving the turn and into the stretch and weakened.

Owners– 1, Jay Em Ess Stable; 2, Fog City Stable; 3, Waranch Ronald C; 4, Carney Brian M

Trainers– 1, Ellis Ronald W; 2, Baffert Bob; 3, Mullins Jeff; 4, Hines N J

Scratched– Notarized (21Aug04 ^{6}Dmr^{2}) , Allright (21Aug04 ^{6}Dmr^{7}) , Chandtrue (17Jul04 ^{3}Hol^{1})

$2 Daily Double (2–3) Paid $229.20 ; Daily Double Pool $33,976 .
$1 Pick Three (3–2–3) Paid $1,211.70 ; Pick Three Pool $103,880 .

EIGHTH RACE
Belmont
SEPTEMBER 11, 2004

1⅛ MILES. (1.45^2) 109TH RUNNING OF THE GAZELLE HANDICAP. Grade I. Purse $250,000 (UP TO $37,500 NYSBFOA) FOR FILLIES THREE YEARS OLD. By subscription of $250 each, which should accompany the nomination; $1,250 to pass the entry box and $1,250 to start. The purse to be divided 60% to the winner, 20% to second, 10% to third, 5% to fourth, 3% to fifth and 2% divided equally among remaining finishers. 122 lbs. Non-winners of a Grade 1 at a mile or over in 2004 allowed 3 lbs.; a Grade 1or a Grade 2 at a mile or over, 5 lbs. a Graded Sweepstakes; or $45,000 at a mile or over in 2004, 7 lbs. Trophies will be presented to the winning owner, trainer and jockey. Closed Saturday, August 28, 2004 with 21 Nominations.

Value of Race: $250,000 Winner $150,000; second $50,000; third $25,000; fourth $12,500; fifth $7,500; sixth $5,000. Mutuel Pool $623,040.00 Exacta Pool $517,073.00 Trifecta Pool $373,574.00

Last Raced	Horse	M/Eqt.	A.	Wt	PP	St	¼	½	¾	Str	Fin	Jockey	Odds $1
21Aug04 10Sar2	Stellar Jayne	L b	3	122	2	5	11½	1½	1hd	22½	11	Albarado R J	0.50
4Aug04 5Sar1	Daydreaming	L	3	115	1	6	3hd	2hd	21	1hd	21¾	Velazquez J R	5.20
31Jly04 8Pim1	He Loves Me	L	3	117	4	3	6	6	3½	3½	3no	Santana J Z	7.40
25Aug04 3Sar1	Shadow Cast	L	3	119	3	4	5½	51½	6	4½	41¼	Migliore R	22.90
14Aug04 7WO3	My Lordship	L	3	117	6	2	41½	4½	5½	57	56¾	Velasquez C	11.70
31Jly04 8Sar2	Bending Strings	L	3	117	5	1	2½	3½	4hd	6	6	Day P	7.70

OFF AT 4:43 Start Good. Won driving. Track fast.

TIME :24, :48, 1:12^2, 1:36^2, 1:48^1 (:24.11, :48.11, 1:12.56, 1:36.53, 1:48.25)

$2 Mutuel Prices:

2 – STELLAR JAYNE	3.00	2.30	2.10
1 – DAYDREAMING		3.50	2.10
6 – HE LOVES ME			2.10

$2 EXACTA 2–1 PAID $10.20 $2 TRIFECTA 2–1–6 PAID $26.80

Gr/ro. f, (Feb), by Wild Rush – To the Hunt, by Relaunch. Trainer Lukas D Wayne. Bred by Wind Hill Farm (Ky).

STELLAR JAYNE quickly showed in front, set the pace along the inside, dug in determinedly when headed turning for home, came again on the rail and was clear under the wire. DAYDREAMING raced close up along the inside, angled out and moved up to join the lead from the outside approaching the stretch, earned a short lead and dug in gamely but could not stay with the winner late. HE LOVES ME was rated along outside, put in a four wide run on the turn and finished gamely outside. SHADOW CAST raced in hand early along the inside, rallied inside nearing the stretch and finished gamely on the rail. MY LORDSHIP raced close up while three wide and had no response when roused. BENDING STRINGS raced with the pace from the outside and tired after the opening three quarters.

Owners– 1, Spendthrift Farm LLC Kidder Chuck Cole Nancy and Strong Nick; 2, Phipps Ogden M; 3, Buckingham Farm; 4, Farish William S Jr; 5, Live Oak Plantation; 6, Gunther John D

Trainers– 1, Lukas D Wayne; 2, McGaughey III Claude R; 3, Small Richard W; 4, Howard Neil J; 5, Mott William I; 6, McLaughlin Kiaran P

Scratched– Capeside Lady (15Aug04 10Mth1), Mambo Bell (15Aug04 4Sar1), Magical Illusion (24Jul04 8Bel3)

$2 Pick Three (4–6–2) Paid $62.50; Pick Three Pool $106,205.

NINTH RACE
Belmont
SEPTEMBER 11, 2004

1⅜ MILES. (Turf) (2.11) 46TH RUNNING OF THE MAN O' WAR. Grade I. Purse $500,000 WIDENER TURF (UP TO $55,000 NYSBFOA) FOR THREE YEAR OLDS AND UPWARD. By subscription of $500 each, which should accompany the nomination; $2,500 to pass the entry box and $2,500 to start. The purse to be divided 60% to the winner, 20% to second, 10% to third, 5% to fourth, 3% to fifth and 2% divided equally among remaining finishers. Weight for age. Three year olds, 121 lbs.; older, 126 lbs. The New York Racing Association to add the Man o'War Bowl to be won three times, not necessarily consecutively, bythe same owner before becoming his or her property. The owner of the winner will also receive a trophy for permanent possession and trophies will be presented to the winning trainer and jockey. The New York Racing Association reserves the right to transfer this race to the Main Track. In the event that this race is taken off the turf, it may be subject to downgrading upon review by the Graded Stakes Committee. Closed Saturday, August 28, 2004 with 24 Nominations. (If the Stewards consider it inadvisable to run this race on the turf course, this race will be run at One Mile and One Eighth on the main track.).

Value of Race: $500,000 Winner $300,000; second $100,000; third $50,000; fourth $25,000; fifth $15,000; sixth $3,334; seventh $3,334; eighth $3,332. Mutuel Pool $825,529.00 Exacta Pool $600,767.00 Trifecta Pool $464,167.00

Last Raced	Horse	M/Eqt.	A.	Wt	PP	¼	½	¾	1	Str	Fin	Jockey	Odds $1
14Aug04 9AP2	Magistretti	L b	4	126	3	71½	73½	72½	8	4hd	11¼	Prado E S	3.15
14Aug04 9AP3	Epalo-Ger		5	126	6	11½	1½	1½	11	13½	22	Starke A	a- 2.40
1Sep04 7Sar1	King's Drama-Ire	L	4	126	7	2½	2½	2½	21½	22	3¾	Chavez J F	a- 2.40
14Aug04 8Sar1	Better Talk Now	L bf	5	126	1	8	8	8	7hd	3hd	4½	Dominguez R A	6.10
14Aug04 8Sar2	Request for Parole	L	5	126	4	4½	4½	4½	4hd	5½	52½	Castellano J J	6.40
24Jly04 7AP3	Ballingarry-Ire	L b	5	126	2	61	6½	5hd	51½	64½	62¼	Douglas R R	15.90
14Aug04 8Sar3	Balto Star	L	6	126	8	3hd	31½	3½	3hd	71	7¾	Velazquez J R	9.70
14Aug04 11AP2	Greek Sun	L	3	121	5	5½	51½	61½	6½	8	8	Velasquez C	3.85

a–Coupled: Epalo–Ger and King's Drama–Ire.

OFF AT 5:15 Start Good. Won driving. Course yielding.

TIME :24^2, :50, 1:14^2, 1:38, 2:02, 2:14^3 (:24.53, :50.05, 1:14.43, 1:38.17, 2:02.14, 2:14.65)

$2 Mutuel Prices:

4 – MAGISTRETTI	8.30	3.90	3.00
1 – EPALO–GER(a–entry)		3.30	3.40
1A– KING'S DRAMA–IRE(a–entry)		3.30	3.40

$2 EXACTA 4–1 PAID $20.20 $2 TRIFECTA 4–1–2 PAID $85.50

B. c, (Mar), by Diesis–GB – Ms. Strike Zone, by Deputy Minister. Trainer Biancone Patrick L. Bred by Tri–County Farms LLC (Ky).

MAGISTRETTI was taken back after the start, was rated along, raced inside on the second turn, swung to the outside turning for home, responded when asked for run, finished with a rush from the outside and was clear under the wire. EPALO (GER) quickly showed in front, set the pace along the inside, drew away when roused in upper stretch, took a clear lead into deep stretch and stayed on gamely but could not withstand the winner late. KING'S DRAMA (IRE) raced with the pace from the outside while in hand and stayed on well in the stretch. BETTER TALK NOW was outrun early, moved into contention with a four wide run on the second turn and had little left for the stretch drive. REQUEST FOR PAROLE was rated along early, advanced between rivals on the second turn and lacked a rally. BALLINGARRY (IRE) was rated along inside, saved ground and had no response when roused. BALTO STAR raced with the pace from the outside, was three wide on both turns and tired in the stretch. GREEK SUN raced in hand while three wide and tired in the stretch.

Owners– 1, Tabor Michael B; 2, Tanaka Gary A; 3, Tanaka Gary A; 4, Bushwood Stables; 5, Knighton Jeri and Sam; 6, Port Sidney L Naify Marsha De Seroux Laura De Seroux Emmanuel; 7, Anstu Stables Inc; 8, Angelos Peter G

Trainers– 1, Biancone Patrick L; 2, Schutz Andreas; 3, Frankel Robert; 4, Motion H Graham; 5, Hough Stanley M; 6, De Seroux Laura; 7, Pletcher Todd A; 8, Frankel Robert

TENTH RACE
Belmont
SEPTEMBER 11, 2004

1⅛ MILES. (1.45²) 51ST RUNNING OF THE WOODWARD. Grade I. Purse $500,000 (UP TO $55,000 NYSBFOA) FOR THREE YEAR OLDS AND UPWARD. By subscription of $500 each, which should accompany the nomination; $2,500 to pass the entry box and $2,500 to start. The purse to be divided 60% to the winner, 20% to second, 10% to third, 5% to fourth, 3% to fifth and 2% divided equally among remaining finishers. Weight for age. Three year olds, 122 lbs.; older, 126 lbs. The estate of Mrs. William Woodward, Sr. to add the Woodward Challenge Cup, to be won three times, not necessarily consecutively, by the same owner before becoming his or her property. The owner of the winner will also receive a trophy for permanent possession and trophies will be presented to the winning trainer and jockey. Closed Saturday, August 28, 2004 with 18 Nominations.

Value of Race: $500,000 Winner $300,000; second $100,000; third $50,000; fourth $25,000; fifth $15,000; sixth $5,000; seventh $5,000. Mutuel Pool $862,072.00 Exacta Pool $633,521.00 Trifecta Pool $608,466.00

Last Raced	Horse	M/Eqt.	A.	Wt	PP	St	¼	½	¾	Str	Fin	Jockey	Odds $1
21Aug04 9Mth1	Ghostzapper	L b	4	126	3	4	3½	2½	25½	26	1nk	Castellano J J	0.40
3Apr04 11OP3	Saint Liam	L	4	126	1	7	2hd	1½	1hd	1hd	29¼	Prado E S	11.70
22Aug04 9Sar3	Bowman's Band	L	6	126	6	3	62½	4hd	3½	38	37¼	Dominguez R A	9.10
18Aug04 3Sar1	Seek Gold	L	4	126	5	1	7	7	7	4½	41½	Velasquez C	41.00
7Aug04 9Sar7	Newfoundland	L b	4	126	4	5	5½	5½	51	57	57½	Velazquez J R	6.10
21Aug04 7Sar1	Midway Road	L	4	126	2	6	42½	67	6½	62½	610¼	Albarado R J	8.90
21Aug04 9Mth2	Presidentialaffair	L	5	126	7	2	1hd	31½	43½	7	7	Fragoso P	37.50

OFF AT 5:48 Start Good. Won driving. Track fast.

TIME :23³, :45³, 1:08³, 1:33¹, 1:46¹ (:23.66, :45.70, 1:08.75, 1:33.35, 1:46.38)

$2 Mutuel Prices:

	Win	Place	Show
4 – GHOSTZAPPER	2.80	2.40	2.10
2 – SAINT LIAM		5.60	2.20
7 – BOWMAN'S BAND			2.10

$2 EXACTA 4–2 PAID $14.20 $2 TRIFECTA 4–2–7 PAID $59.00

B. c, (Apr), by Awesome Again – Baby Zip, by Relaunch. Trainer Frankel Robert. Bred by Adena Springs (Ky).

GHOSTZAPPER argued the pace while between rivals, was carried out into the stretch, bumped with SAINT LIAM in the drive and bested that rival after a prolonged battle. SAINT LIAM contested the pace along the inside, drifted out entering the stretch, bumped with the winner in the drive and dug in gamely to the wire. BOWMAN'S BAND was bumped at the start, raced in hand outside, angled in into the turn, put in a run along the rail nearing the stretch and had nothing left for the drive. SEEK GOLD was crowded at the start, was hustled along to keep up early, raced inside on the turn, came wide into the stretch and had no response when roused. NEWFOUNDLAND was hustled along outside, raced wide and tired in the stretch. MIDWAY ROAD raced close up inside early, had no response when roused and tired. PRESIDENTIALAFFAIR, bumped at the start, contested the pace while three wide and tired after a half mile.

Owners– 1, Stronach Stables; 2, Warren Jr Mr and Mrs William K; 3, Schwartz Martin S; 4, LaPenta Robert V; 5, Sumaya Us Stables; 6, Farish William S; 7, Ciresa Edward and Papapandrea Vincent

Trainers– 1, Frankel Robert; 2, Dutrow Richard E Jr; 3, Jerkens H Allen; 4, Zito Nicholas P; 5, Pletcher Todd A; 6, Howard Neil J; 7, Ciresa Martin E

Scratched– Colita (28Jul04 8Sar2)

$2 Daily Double (4–4) Paid $12.60; Daily Double Pool $321,337.
$2 Pick Three (2–4–4) Paid $20.60; Pick Three Pool $256,513.
$2 Pick Four (6–2–4–4) Paid $95.50; Pick Four Pool $592,763.
$2 Pick Six (5–4–6–2–4–4) 6 Correct Paid $1,401.00; Pick Six Pool $302,944.
$2 Pick Six (5–4–6–2–4–4) 5 Correct Paid $23.80.

Belmont Park Attendance: 10,251 Mutuel Pool: $1,758,743.00 ITW Mutuel Pool: $3,493,302.00 ISW Mutuel Pool: $10,105,218.00

EIGHTH RACE
Delaware
SEPTEMBER 11, 2004

6 FURLONGS. (1.08¹) 21ST RUNNING OF THE ENDINE HANDICAP. Grade III. Purse $200,000 (plus $300 Starters Bonus) FOR FILLIES AND MARES THREE YEARS OLD AND UPWARD. By subscription of $200 each which shall accompany the nomination; $900 to enter and $900 to start. $200,000 Guaranteed of which $120,000 to the winner, $40,000 to second, $22,000 to third, $12,000 to fourth and $6,000 to fifth. Trophy to the winner. Closed Saturday, August 28th, 2004 with 20 nominations.

Value of Race: $200,300 Winner $120,000; second $40,000; third $22,000; fourth $12,000; fifth $6,000; sixth $300. Mutuel Pool $91,154.00 Exacta Pool $75,508.00 Trifecta Pool $45,631.00

Last Raced	Horse	M/Eqt.	A.	Wt	PP	St	¼	½	Str	Fin	Jockey	Odds $1
6Aug04 8Sar2	Ebony Breeze	L	4	119	6	6	6	6	3½	13	Castillo H Jr	0.80
8Aug04 12Mth4	Umpateedle	L b	5	117	3	3	42	3½	22½	22¾	Castellano A Jr	a- 9.80
18Jly04 5Del2	Bronze Abe	L f	5	119	4	5	53	4½	42½	3½	Pino M G	4.10
23Aug04 8Del1	Electrical Carlita	L b	4	116	5	1	12½	12½	12	41¾	Potts C L	6.00
8Aug04 12Mth1	Travelator	L	4	118	2	4	3½	52	51½	56½	Gryder A T	3.20
13Aug04 5Sar1	Read Me My Rights	L	5	114	1	2	21½	2hd	6	6	Rose J	a- 9.80

a–Coupled: Umpateedle and Read Me My Rights.

OFF AT 3:55 Start Good. Won driving. Track fast.

TIME :21³, :44², :57¹, 1:09³ (:21.64, :44.53, :57.29, 1:09.73)

$2 Mutuel Prices:

	Win	Place	Show
6 – EBONY BREEZE	3.60	2.60	2.10
1A – UMPATEEDLE(a–entry)		4.60	2.10
3 – BRONZE ABE			2.10

$2 EXACTA 6–1 PAID $19.80 $2 TRIFECTA 6–1–3 PAID $49.80

B. f, (Jan), by Belong to Me – Valid Carnauba, by Valid Appeal. Trainer Mott William I. Bred by Kinsman Farm (Ky).

EBONY BREEZE was void of early speed, fanned five wide out of the turn then ran past the leaders leaving the furlong grounds to be along in time. UMPATEEDLE made a three wide middle move to contention after three furlongs, loomed a threat outside ELECTRICAL CARLITA leaving the furlong marker but was no match for the winner late while second best. BRONZE ABE lodged a mild belated rally. ELECTRICAL CARLITA broke sharp to gain the early lead, set a fast pace past mid stretch then gave way in the final furlong. TRAVELATOR was through early. READ ME MY RIGHTS stopped after a half.

Owners– 1, Kinsman Stable; 2, Gill Michael J; 3, Bayard Samuel F; 4, Gumpster Stable LLC; 5, Our Sugar Bear Stable; 6, Gill Michael J

Trainers– 1, Mott William I; 2, Shuman Mark; 3, Delp Grover G; 4, Lake Scott A; 5, Hough Stanley M; 6, Shuman Mark

Scratched– Chirimoya (08Aug04 12Mth8)

$2 Pick Three (3–6–5/6) Paid $93.40; Pick Three Pool $6,041.
$2 Pick Four (1/2/4/5/10/12–3–6–5/6) Paid $195.80; Pick Four Pool $5,352.
$2 Daily Double (6–6) Paid $8.00; Daily Double Pool $11,646.

SEVENTH RACE
Calder
SEPTEMBER 11, 2004

1 MILE. (Turf) (1.33^3) 18TH RUNNING OF THE MIAMI MILE BREEDERS' CUP HANDICAP. Grade III. Purse $150,000 (includes $75,000 BC – Breeders' Cup) FOR THREE YEAR OLDS AND UPWARD. By subscription of $150 each which shall accompany the nomination, $1,000 to pass the entry box and an additional $1,000 to start – with $75,000 Guaranteed and an additional $75,000 from the Breeders' Cup for Cup nominees only. The host association's monies to be divided $45,000 to the owner of the winner, $15,000 to second, $8,350 to third, $4,500 to fourth and $2,250 to fifth. Breeders' Cup monies also correspondingly divided providing a Breeders' Cup Nominee has finished in an awarded position. Any Breeders' Cup Fund monies not awarded will revert back to the fund. This race will not be divided. Preference will be given in the following order: High Weights will be preferred under the following conditions – Breeders CupNominees will be preferred over non–Breeders' Cup Nominees assigned equal weights. Trophy to winning Owner provided by Breeders' Cup Limited. This race will be limited to 12 Starters, with Also Eligibles. (High Weights Preferred) 2 Supplemental Nominations of $3,000 to enter and start. Closed Saturday, August 21, 2004 with 18 nominations. (If deemed inadvisable to run this race over the Turf course, it will be run on the main track at One Mile).

Value of Race: $150,000 Winner $90,000; second $30,000; third $16,500; fourth $9,000; fifth $4,500. Mutuel Pool $117,844.00 Exacta Pool $97,974.00 Trifecta Pool $63,159.00 Superfecta Pool $25,367.00

Last Raced	Horse	M/Eqt.	A.	Wt	PP	St	¼	½	¾	Str	Fin	Jockey	Odds $1
10Jly04 10Crc5	Twilight Road	L	7	114	2	2	3½	3hd	3½	2hd	1½	Teator P A	5.30
4Sep04 8Sar6	Gold Dollar	L b	5	114	9	9	8½	8hd	71½	41½	2¾	Lopez J E	12.20
15Aug04 5Crc2	Paradise Dancer	L f	4	115	8	7	2½	21	21	3½	3hd	Aguilar M	9.70
26Jun04 8Del5	Wire Bound	L b	3	116	3	4	5½	51	5½	52	41¾	Toscano P R	3.30
4Jly04 6Crc7	Hear No Evil	L bf	4	114	1	1	12	11½	12	11½	52¼	Garcia J A	8.20
15Aug04 5Crc1	Class of Seventy	L b	5	116	6	8	9	9	88	61	62	Cruz M R	7.00
15Aug04 5Crc7	Tour of the Cat	L f	6	115	5	5	73½	71	6½	71½	76¼	Boulanger G	11.50
15Aug04 5Crc3	Unbridels King	L b	4	118	7	6	61½	4hd	4½	8	8	Castro E	3.00
31Jly04 9Crc6	Built Up	L	6	115	4	3	4hd	61½	9	—	—	Madrid S O	8.40

OFF AT 2:38 Start Good . Won driving. Course yielding.
TIME :24, :48^4, 1:13^1, 1:39^2 (:24.06, :48.85, 1:13.28, 1:39.56)

$2 Mutuel Prices:				
	3 – TWILIGHT ROAD	12.60	7.20	5.60
	12 – GOLD DOLLAR		11.20	7.20
	11 – PARADISE DANCER			9.20

$2 EXACTA 3–12 PAID $206.80 $2 TRIFECTA 3–12–11 PAID $2,144.40
$2 SUPERFECTA 3–12–11–5 PAID $6,172.60

Ch. g, (Apr), by Cahill Road – Glory's Light , by Halo . Trainer Fawkes David. Bred by Mira Ball (Ky).

TWILIGHT ROAD tracked the pace along the hedge, eased outside HEAR NO EVIL in the stretch, rallied to catch that rival just inside the sixteenth pole and was fully extended to prevail. GOLD DOLLAR unhurried early, rallied along the hedge through the stretch to be up for the place. PARADISE DANCER stalked the pace, made a run outside TWILIGHT ROAD to reach near even terms for command at the sixteenth pole but was outfinished. WIRE BOUND rated off the pace, angled to the outside in the stretch and closed with a belated rally. HEAR NO EVIL set the pace along the hedge to inside the sixteenth pole and gave way. CLASS OF SEVENTY outrun early, lacked a rally. TOUR OF THE CAT allowed to settle, raced four wide on the far turn and tired. UNBRIDELS KING tracked the leaders three wide around the far turn and faltered. BUILT UP was done early and eased in the stretch run.

Owners– 1, Donamire Farm; 2, Pazos Julio; 3, Sessa Ralph C; 4, Silver Diamond Thoroughbreds Inc; 5, Jacks or Better Farm Inc; 6, Rey Wan Racing; 7, Double G Stable; 8, Oxenberg Bea and Montanari Marion; 9, Susi Raymond

Trainers– 1, Fawkes David; 2, Azpurua Manuel J; 3, Musgrave Shawn; 4, Criollo Manuel; 5, Hatchett James; 6, Ritvo Timothy; 7, Wayar Manuel J; 8, Plesa Edward Jr; 9, Alonso Enrique

Scratched– French Charmer (14Feb04 8Tam7) , Romolo's Fritzi (15Aug04 5Crc4) , Stay Forever (05Jul04 9Bel2) , Super Frolic (15Aug04 5Crc11)

$2 Pick Three (2–4–3) Paid $59.00 ; Pick Three Pool $11,671 .

NINTH RACE
Belmont
SEPTEMBER 12, 2004

1⅛ MILES. (Inner Turf) (1.45^3) 10TH RUNNING OF THE GARDEN CITY BREEDERS' CUP HANDICAP. Grade I. Purse $300,000 (includes $100,000 BC – Breeders' Cup) (Up To $34,000 NYSBFOA) INNER TURF FOR FILLIES THREE YEAR OLDS. By subscription of $200 each, which should accompany the nomination; $1,000 to pass the entry box; $1,000 additional to start. The NYRA purse to be divided 60% to the winner, 20% to second, 10% to third, 5% to fourth, 3% to fifth and 2% divided equally among remaining finishers. Breeders' Cup Fund monies also correspondingly divided. Any Breeders' Cup fund monies not awarded will revert back to the fund. 122 lbs. Non–winners of a Grade 1 on the turf allowed 2 lbs.;a Grade 2 on the turf, 4 lbs.; a Graded Sweepstakes, 6 lbs. A trophy to winning owner given by Breeders' Cup Ltd. The New York Racing Association will present trophies to the winning trainer and jockey. The New York Racing Association reserves the right to transfer this race to the Main Track. In the event that this race is taken off the turf, it may be subject to downgrading upon review by the Graded Stakes Committee. Closed Saturday, August 28, 2004 with 32 Nominations.

Value of Race: $264,000 Winner $180,000; second $40,000; third $20,000; fourth $10,000; fifth $9,000; sixth $2,000; seventh $3,000. Mutuel Pool $542,485.00 Exacta Pool $369,156.00 Trifecta Pool $295,549.00

Last Raced	Horse	M/Eqt.	A.	Wt	PP	St	¼	½	¾	Str	Fin	Jockey	Odds $1
2Aug04 8Sar5	Lucifer's Stone	L b	3	118	2	1	31½	5½	4hd	3hd	11¼	Santos J A	9.20
24Aug04 DEA5	Barancella-FR	L	3	116	3	6	6hd	6hd	5hd	41	2¾	Chavez J F	25.00
15Aug04 Leo1	Noahs Ark-Ire	L	3	116	6	3	22½	2½	1hd	1hd	3nk	Castellano J J	6.90
14Aug04 8AP3	Necklace-GB	L	3	122	1	7	7	7	7	58	4¾	Spencer J P	1.80
23Aug04 8Sar2	Mambo Slew		3	118	5	2	4hd	4½	3½	21	59	Prado E S	a- 4.30
13Jun04 CHY11	Torrestrella-Ire	L	3	122	4	4	51	3hd	6½	63	65¼	Nakatani C S	1.75
25Aug04 4Sar2	Saratoga Sugar		3	116	7	5	11½	11	2½	7	7	Farina T	a- 4.30

a–Coupled: Mambo Slew and Saratoga Sugar.

OFF AT 5:14 Start Good . Won driving. Course good.
TIME :25, :49^3, 1:13^4, 1:37^2, 1:48^4 (:25.14, :49.70, 1:13.94, 1:37.48, 1:48.88)

$2 Mutuel Prices:				
	4 – LUCIFER'S STONE	20.40	7.50	5.50
	5 – BARANCELLA–FR		19.00	8.90
	8 – NOAHS ARK–IRE			4.90

$2 EXACTA 4–5 PAID $259.50 $2 TRIFECTA 4–5–8 PAID $1,296.00

B. f, (Mar), by Horse Chestnut–Saf – Ladue , by Demons Begone . Trainer Rice Linda. Bred by Mega Stable (Ky).

LUCIFER'S STONE was rated along early, raced between rivals, responded when set down in upper stretch, found room between rivals and scampered clear late. BARANCELLA (FR) was taken in hand after the start, was rated along outside, rallied four wide on the second turn and finished gamely outside. NOAHS ARK (IRE) raced close up early while in hand, advanced outside on the second turn and dug in gamely on the rail in the stretch. NECKLACE (GB) broke slowly, was rated inside, swung wide into the stretch and lacked a solid finishing kick. MAMBO SLEW raced in hand while outside early on, put in a three wide run on the second turn and faded in the final furlong. TORRESTRELLA (IRE) was rank under restraint along the inside, was steadied repeatedly, raced inside and tired. SARATOGA SUGAR was hustled to the front, set the pace along the inside and tired in the stretch.

Owners– 1, Team Solaris Stable; 2, Tanaka Gary A; 3, OFlynn Denis Sheehy Denis Cashman Liam; 4, Tabor Michael B Magnier Mrs John; 5, Manganaro Frank; 6, Karches Peter and Rankowitz Michael; 7, Manganaro Frank

Trainers– 1, Rice Linda; 2, Head Freddie; 3, Weld Dermot K; 4, O'Brien Aidan P; 5, Biancone Patrick L; 6, Clement Christophe; 7, Biancone Patrick L

Scratched– Spotlight (GB) (23Aug04 8Sar1) , Venturi (GB) (02Aug04 8Sar2)

NINTH RACE
Monmouth
SEPTEMBER 12, 2004

1$\frac{1}{16}$ MILES. (Turf Chute) (1.39^{2}) 28TH RUNNING OF THE BOILING SPRINGS. Grade III. Purse $150,000 FOR FILLIES, THREE YEARS OLD. By subscription of $100 each, which should accompany the nomination and $1,500 to pass the entry box. Weight: 121 lbs. Non–winners of $60,000 twice at a mile or over in 2004 allowed 2 lbs.; $45,000 at a mile or over in 2004,4 lbs. The winning owner to receive a trophy. Closed Sunday, August 29, 2004 with 38 nominations.

Value of Race: $150,000 Winner $90,000; second $30,000; third $16,500; fourth $9,000; fifth $4,500. Mutuel Pool $115,433.00 Exacta Pool $102,310.00 Trifecta Pool $73,647.00 Superfecta Pool $21,483.00

Last Raced	Horse	M/Eqt.	A.	Wt	PP	St	¼	½	¾	Str	Fin	Jockey	Odds $1
21Aug04 ^{3}Dmr^{4}	Seducer's Song	L	3	119	8	3	5^{hd}	$6^{1\frac{1}{2}}$	3^{hd}	$2^{\frac{1}{2}}$	$1^{\frac{1}{2}}$	Bravo J	1.00
22Aug04 ^{8}Sar^{1}	Go Robin	L	3	117	7	8	7^{1}	7^{hd}	7^{hd}	5^{1}	$2^{\frac{1}{2}}$	Velez J A Jr	9.90
7Aug04 ^{6}Sar^{1}	River Belle-GB	L	3	117	4	6	$6^{1\frac{1}{2}}$	5^{hd}	1^{hd}	1^{hd}	3^{1}	Coa E M	2.40
23Aug04 ^{8}Sar^{5}	Vous	L b	3	117	6	1	$4^{1\frac{1}{2}}$	4^{hd}	5^{hd}	$6^{\frac{1}{2}}$	4^{1}	Clemente A V	17.40
2Aug04 ^{8}Sar^{4}	Art Fan	L f	3	119	5	5	2^{hd}	2^{hd}	$2^{1\frac{1}{2}}$	3^{hd}	5^{hd}	Pimentel J	6.70
23Aug04 ^{8}Sar^{4}	Delta Sensation	L	3	117	3	9	9	8^{1}	8^{3}	7^{5}	6^{hd}	Castillo H Jr	11.00
15Aug04 ^{10}Mth^{3}	Habiboo	L	3	117	2	4	3^{hd}	1^{hd}	4^{hd}	4^{hd}	$7^{7\frac{3}{4}}$	Soto J A Jr	39.00
8Aug04 ^{6}Crc^{1}	Format	L	3	117	1	7	8^{1}	9	9	8^{5}	$8^{8\frac{1}{2}}$	Ferrer J C	35.20
21Aug04 ^{7}Del^{1}	Present Danger	L f	3	117	9	2	1^{hd}	3^{1}	6^{1}	9	9	Elliott S	57.10

OFF AT 4:55 Start Good . Won driving. Course good.

TIME :24^{4}, :50, 1:14^{1}, 1:39^{1}, 1:45^{3} (:24.94, :50.06, 1:14.31, 1:39.39, 1:45.66)

$2 Mutuel Prices:

10 – SEDUCER'S SONG	4.00	3.00	2.10
8 – GO ROBIN		6.00	2.60
4 – RIVER BELLE–GB			2.20

$2 EXACTA 10–8 PAID $33.00 $2 TRIFECTA 10–8–4 PAID $89.80
$1 SUPERFECTA 10–8–4–7 PAID $350.20

Gr/ro. f, (Apr), by Unbridled's Song – Seducer , by Housebuster . Trainer Clement Christophe. Bred by Peter Karches (Ky).

SEDUCER'S SONG rated kindly in the second flight between rivals, came three wide into the lane, responded when roused and closed well for the win. GO ROBIN rated off the pace inside, angled out, rallied four wide and finished gamely outside. RIVER BELLE (GB) raced close up on the inside, came through on the rail entering the far turn and finished gamely inside. VOUS stalked four wide and failed to sustain a bid. ART FAN vied between rivals and tired. DELTA SENSATION lacked a sufficient rally. HABIBOO set the pace on the inside and tired. FORMAT did not factor. PRESENT DANGER showed speed racing four wide into the clubhouse turn, raced three wide on the backside and gave way.

Owners– 1, Karches Peter F; 2, Casby Camelia Hennig Mark and Radar Robby; 3, Team Valor Helligbrodt & D R Masson; 4, Tee-N-Jay Farm; 5, Backer William M; 6, Cay John E III; 7, Hardacre Farm LLC; 8, Silly Goose Racing Stable; 9, Humphrey G Watts Jr

Trainers– 1, Clement Christophe; 2, Hennig Mark; 3, Pletcher Todd A; 4, Hills Timothy A; 5, Smith Hamilton A; 6, Alexander Frank A; 7, Tarrant Amy; 8, Breen Kelly J; 9, Oliver Victoria

Scratched– Lucifer's Stone (02Aug04 ^{8}Sar^{5}) , Sabellina (18Aug04 ^{8}Sar^{1})

NINTH RACE
Arlington
SEPTEMBER 18, 2004

1⅛ MILES. (Turf) (1.47^{2}) 41ST RUNNING OF THE PUCKER UP. Grade III. Purse $200,000 FOR FILLIES, THREE–YEARS–OLD.

Value of Race: $200,000 Winner $120,000; second $40,000; third $22,000; fourth $12,000; fifth $6,000. Mutuel Pool $332,433.00 Exacta Pool $235,611.00 Trifecta Pool $214,180.00 Superfecta Pool $90,107.00

Last Raced	Horse	M/Eqt.	A.	Wt	PP	St	¼	½	¾	Str	Fin	Jockey	Odds $1
21Aug04 ^{3}Dmr^{2}	Ticker Tape-GB	L	3	122	8	6	$8^{1\frac{1}{2}}$	$8^{1\frac{1}{2}}$	$4^{\frac{1}{2}}$	3^{1}	$1^{2\frac{3}{4}}$	Desormeaux K J	1.20
23Aug04 ^{8}Sar^{1}	Spotlight-GB	L	3	122	10	9	9^{3}	9^{2}	$6^{\frac{1}{2}}$	5^{1}	2^{hd}	Douglas R R	1.30
22Aug04 ^{8}AP^{1}	Sister Swank	L	3	116	2	3	$2^{\frac{1}{2}}$	3^{1}	$3^{\frac{1}{2}}$	2^{hd}	$3^{\frac{1}{2}}$	Lovato F Jr	25.90
28Aug04 ^{8}AP^{1}	Humorous Miss	L b	3	118	5	8	5^{hd}	6^{hd}	$7^{1\frac{1}{2}}$	$4^{\frac{1}{2}}$	$4^{1\frac{1}{2}}$	Graham J	9.40
28Aug04 ^{8}AP^{5}	Bonanza Jellybean	L	3	116	1	1	$1^{1\frac{1}{2}}$	1^{1}	1^{1}	1^{2}	5^{nk}	Fires E	39.20
21Aug04 ^{8}Mth^{3}	Skip Poker	L b	3	116	11	11	11	10^{hd}	11	8^{3}	$6^{1\frac{1}{2}}$	Marquez C H Jr	32.00
11Aug04 ^{8}AP^{1}	Erhu	L	3	116	3	2	$4^{\frac{1}{2}}$	4^{hd}	5^{1}	6^{1}	$7^{1\frac{3}{4}}$	Molina T	36.80
3Sep04 ^{10}AP^{2}	Dancing Liebling	L	3	116	7	10	$10^{\frac{1}{2}}$	11	9^{hd}	$7^{\frac{1}{2}}$	8^{4}	Sterling L J Jr	68.80
25Aug04 ^{8}AP^{1}	Ms. Lydonia	L	3	116	9	7	7^{2}	$7^{1\frac{1}{2}}$	10^{hd}	10^{5}	$9^{3\frac{1}{2}}$	Emigh C A	47.10
28Aug04 ^{8}AP^{2}	Code of Ethics	L	3	116	4	4	$3^{\frac{1}{2}}$	2^{1}	$2^{\frac{1}{2}}$	9^{1}	$10^{\frac{1}{2}}$	Razo E Jr	30.90
22Aug04 ^{8}ElP^{1}	Unbridled Echo	L b	3	116	6	5	$6^{\frac{1}{2}}$	$5^{1\frac{1}{2}}$	8^{1}	11	11	Campbell J M	17.80

OFF AT 4:58 Start Good . Won ridden out. Course firm.

TIME :23^{2}, :47^{4}, 1:12^{1}, 1:36^{4}, 1:48^{3} (:23.52, :47.82, 1:12.22, 1:36.80, 1:48.63)

$2 Mutuel Prices:

10 – TICKER TAPE–GB	4.40	2.40	2.40
12 – SPOTLIGHT–GB		2.60	2.80
2 – SISTER SWANK			5.40

$2 EXACTA 10–12 PAID $8.60 $2 TRIFECTA 10–12–2 PAID $77.00
$2 SUPERFECTA 10–12–2–6 PAID $209.20

B. f, (Jan), by Royal Applause–GB – Argent Du Bois , by Silver Hawk . Trainer Cassidy James. Bred by Car Colston Hall Stud (GB).

TICKER TAPE (GB) lacked speed three wide, began moving up on the final turn took the lead in deep stretch and drew off under moderate urging. SPOTLIGHT (GB) was void of early speed while racing four to five wide, rallied in the stretch and gained the place while no danger to the top one. SISTER SWANK raced close up inside, maintained a rail position to the stretch then lacked a winning response when asked for her best. HUMOROUS MISS raced just outside near the middle of the field and improved her position in the drive. BONANZA JELLYBEAN made the lead from the inside, set all of the pace from the rail and had a clear margin in the stretch but weakened late. SKIP POKER lacked speed, came seven wide into the stretch and lacked a serious bid. ERHU raced close up just outside and tired. DANCING LIEBLING was void of speed and was always outrun. MS. LYDONIA was five wide on the first turn and was never a factor. CODE OF ETHICS raced close up just outside and tired. UNBRIDLED ECHO was four wide on the first turn and gave way after a half. (Race run in lane 5, rail at 0.).

Owners– 1, Jim Ford Inc Daron Pearson and Jack Sweesy; 2, Green Hills Farm Leo Liaskos; 3, Heiligbrodt Racing Stable; 4, Russell L Reineman Stable Inc; 5, Gray Carolyn L; 6, Team Victory; 7, Select Stable One LLC; 8, Parra Rosendo G; 9, Lydon William and Carson Springs Farm; 10, Jeremiah Stable and Nelson Joi; 11, Stoneway Farm LLC

Trainers– 1, Cassidy James; 2, Clement Christophe; 3, Asmussen Steven M; 4, Springer Frank R; 5, Barnett Bobby C; 6, McPeek Kenneth G; 7, Daly Patrick J; 8, Asmussen Steven M; 9, Janks Christine K; 10, Granitz Anthony J; 11, Montano Angel

Scratched– Key to the Cat (15Aug04 ^{9}ElP^{3}) , Lenatareese (31Jul04 ^{9}ElP^{1})

$1 Pick Three (5–2–4/9/10) Paid $339.10 ; Pick Three Pool $20,346 .

SEVENTH RACE
Belmont
SEPTEMBER 18, 2004

6 FURLONGS. (1.07^{3}) 10TH RUNNING OF THE FLORAL PARK HANDICAP. Grade III. Purse $100,000 (UP TO $19,000 NYSBFOA) A HANDICAP FOR FILLIES AND MARES THREE YEARS OLD AND UPWARD. By subscription of $100 each, which should accompany the nomination; $500 to pass the entry box; $500 to start, with $100,000 added. The added money and all fees to be divided 60% to the winner, 20% to second, 10% to third, 5% to fourth, 3% to fifth and 2% divided equally among remaining finishers. A trophy will be presented to the winning owner. Closed Saturday, September 4, 2004 with 14 Nominations.

Value of Race: $104,400 Winner $63,840; second $21,280; third $10,704; fourth $5,384; fifth $3,192. Mutuel Pool $348,745.00 Exacta Pool $264,797.00 Trifecta Pool $117,438.00

Last Raced	Horse	M/Eqt.	A.	Wt	PP	St	¼	½	Str	Fin	Jockey	Odds $1
28Aug04 ^{8}Sar^{3}	Feline Story	L	3	114	5	5	$4^{3\frac{1}{2}}$	3^{hd}	3^{1}	1^{nk}	Prado E S	1.35
26Aug04 ^{8}Sar^{3}	Cologny	L b	4	115	1	1	$1^{1\frac{1}{2}}$	1^{2}	1^{2}	$2^{2\frac{1}{2}}$	Gryder A T	3.25
11Sep04 ^{8}Del^{5}	Travelator	L	4	116	4	3	3^{3}	2^{3}	$2^{1\frac{1}{2}}$	$3^{\frac{1}{2}}$	Velasquez C	3.15
8Aug04 ^{12}Mth^{3}	Hidden Ransom	L b	4	112	3	4	5	5	4^{6}	4^{13}	Fragoso P	6.80
3Apr04 ^{5}Aqu^{1}	Sensibly Chic	L bf	4	115	2	2	2^{hd}	4^{1}	5	5	Migliore R	6.00

OFF AT 4:08 Start Good . Won driving. Track sloppy.

TIME :22, :44^{4}, :57^{1}, 1:10^{3} (:22.07, :44.93, :57.24, 1:10.69)

$2 Mutuel Prices:			
5 – FELINE STORY	4.70	2.90	2.20
1 – COLOGNY		3.30	2.20
4 – TRAVELATOR			2.30

$2 EXACTA 5–1 PAID $16.40 $2 TRIFECTA 5–1–4 PAID $26.80

B. f, (Apr), by Tale of the Cat – Shappy , by Really Secret . Trainer Hough Stanley M. Bred by Eclipse Thoroughbreds Inc (Ky).

FELINE STORY was outrun early, was hustled along while three wide, finished determinedly outside and was along in the final yards. COLOGNY quickly opened a clear lead, set the pace while in hand, took a clear advantage into deep stretch and dug in gamely but was caught in the final strides. TRAVELATOR chased the pace while three wide and had no response when roused. HIDDEN RANSOM was outrun early, came wide into the stretch and finished well outside. SENSIBLY CHIC broke awkwardly, chased the pace for a half mile and tired.

Owners– 1, Robsham Mrs E P; 2, Gewirtz Evan; 3, Our Sugar Bear Stable; 4, Evans Edward P; 5, Nervitt Lois S

Trainers– 1, Hough Stanley M; 2, Lake Scott A; 3, Hough Stanley M; 4, Hennig Mark; 5, Tullock Timothy Jr

$2 Daily Double (5–5) Paid $12.20 ; Daily Double Pool $92,952 .
$2 Pick Three (5–5–5) Paid $46.60 ; Pick Three Pool $87,861 .

EIGHTH RACE
Belmont
SEPTEMBER 18, 2004

1⅛ MILES. (Inner Turf) (1.45^{3}) 19TH RUNNING OF THE BELMONT BREEDERS' CUP HANDICAP. Grade II. Purse $200,000 (includes $100,000 BC – Breeders' Cup) (UP TO $19,000 NYSBFOA) INNER TURF A HANDICAP FOR THREE YEAR OLDS AND UPWARD. By subscription of $100 each, which should accompany the nomination; $500 to pass the entry box; $500 additional to start, with $100,000 added and an additional $100,000 from the Breeders' Cup Fund for Cup nominees only. The NYRA added money and all fees to be divided 60% to the winner, 20% to second, 10% to third, 5% to fourth, 3% to fifth and 2% divided equally among remaining finishers. Breeders' Cup Fund monies also correspondingly divided. Trophy to winning owner given by Breeders' Cup Ltd. The New York Racing Association reserves the right to transfer this race to the Main Track. In the event that this race is taken off the turf, it may be subject to downgrading upon review by the Graded Stakes Committee. Closed Saturday, September 4, 2004 with 28 Nominations.

Value of Race: $197,800 Winner $124,680; second $41,716; third $20,936; fourth $10,468. Mutuel Pool $282,139.00 Exacta Pool $235,142.00

Last Raced	Horse	M/Eqt.	A.	Wt	PP	St	¼	½	¾	Str	Fin	Jockey	Odds $1
14Aug04 ^{9}AP^{7}	Senor Swinger	L	4	117	3	1	$3^{4\frac{1}{2}}$	$3^{1\frac{1}{2}}$	$3^{3\frac{1}{2}}$	1^{1}	1^{4}	Prado E S	2.40
5Jun04 ^{10}Bel^{6}	Stroll	L	4	120	1	3	2^{3}	2^{5}	$2^{2\frac{1}{2}}$	$2^{1\frac{1}{2}}$	$2^{3\frac{1}{2}}$	Velasquez C	0.60
14Aug04 ^{8}Sar^{6}	B. A. Way	L b	4	113	2	4	4	4	4	4	$3^{\frac{3}{4}}$	Bridgmohan S X	10.30
28Aug04 ^{9}Sar^{7}	Gulch Approval	L	4	115	4	2	1^{1}	$1^{\frac{1}{2}}$	1^{hd}	3^{3}	4	Nakatani C S	5.00

OFF AT 4:40 Start Good . Won ridden out. Course soft.

TIME :25^{2}, :50, 1:15^{1}, 1:40^{1}, 1:52^{3} (:25.50, :50.15, 1:15.30, 1:40.32, 1:52.72)

$2 Mutuel Prices:			
3 – SENOR SWINGER	6.80	2.50	—
1 – STROLL		2.20	—
2 – B. A. WAY		—	—

$2 EXACTA 3–1 PAID $10.00

Gr/ro. c, (Apr), by El Prado-Ire – Smooth Swinger , by Kris S. . Trainer Baffert Bob. Bred by Bob Ackerman (Ky).

SENOR SWINGER raced in hand early on, advanced on the second turn, rallied three wide approaching the stretch, blew past the leaders at the eighth pole and drew away under a vigorous hand ride. STROLL came out at the start, bumping B. A. WAY, then raced with the pace from the outside, earned the lead between calls in upper stretch but could not stay with the winner in the final furlong while clearly best of the others. B. A. WAY was bumped at the start, was outrun along the inside early, saved ground, angled out in the stretch and lacked a rally. GULCH APPROVAL was urged to the front, set the pace along the inside and tired in the stretch.

Owners– 1, Lewis Robert B and Beverly J; 2, Claiborne Farm; 3, Perkins Diane; 4, Marylou Whitney Stables

Trainers– 1, Baffert Bob; 2, Mott William I; 3, Violette Richard A Jr; 4, Zito Nicholas P

Scratched– Hotstufanthensome (28Aug04 ^{9}Sar^{4}) , Gygistar (04Sep04 ^{8}Sar^{3}) , Colita (28Jul04 ^{8}Sar^{2})

$2 Pick Three (5–5–3) Paid $45.40 ; Pick Three Pool $68,246 .
$2 Consolation Pick 3 (5–5–4) Paid $13.40 .

NINTH RACE
Belmont
SEPTEMBER 18, 2004

1 MILE. (1.32^{1}) 135TH RUNNING OF THE JEROME HANDICAP. Grade II. Purse $150,000 (UP TO $28,500 NYSBFOA) A HANDICAP FOR THREE YEAR OLDS. By subscription of $150 each, which should accompany the nomination; $750 to pass the entry box and $750 to start. The purse to be divided 60% to the winner, 20% to second, 10% to third, 5% to fourth, 3% to fifth and 2% divided equally among remaining finishers. A trophy will be presented to the winning owner. Closed Saturday, September 4, 2004 with 28 Nominations.

Value of Race: $150,000 Winner $90,000; second $30,000; third $15,000; fourth $7,500; fifth $4,500; sixth $1,500; seventh $1,500. Mutuel Pool $403,118.00 Exacta Pool $328,106.00 Trifecta Pool $258,103.00

Last Raced	Horse	M/Eqt.	A.	Wt	PP	St	¼	½	¾	Str	Fin	Jockey	Odds $1
5Jun04 ^{9}Bel^{2}	Teton Forest	L b	3	116	6	1	1^{1}	$1^{1\frac{1}{2}}$	1^{5}	1^{7}	1^{6}	Bridgmohan S X	2.30
28Aug04 ^{10}Sar^{3}	Ice Wynnd Fire	L	3	116	7	3	3^{hd}	3^{hd}	$3^{1\frac{1}{2}}$	2^{hd}	$2^{\frac{3}{4}}$	Prado E S	1.35
28Aug04 ^{5}Sar^{5}	Mahzouz	L f	3	112	5	4	6^{5}	6^{6}	5^{2}	4^{5}	$3^{2\frac{3}{4}}$	Fragoso P	23.90
28Aug04 ^{10}Sar^{5}	Saratoga County	L bf	3	115	3	5	$2^{\frac{1}{2}}$	2^{hd}	$2^{\frac{1}{2}}$	3^{hd}	$4^{1\frac{1}{2}}$	Velasquez C	11.50
25Aug04 ^{8}Sar^{1}	West Virginia	L	3	116	2	7	7	7	$6^{\frac{1}{2}}$	6^{8}	$5^{2\frac{3}{4}}$	Nakatani C S	4.40
28Aug04 ^{5}Sar^{3}	Coded Warning	L b	3	113	1	6	5^{6}	5^{5}	$4^{1\frac{1}{2}}$	5^{hd}	6^{15}	Castellano J J	8.50
14Aug04 ^{9}Mth^{8}	Sir Oscar	L bf	3	113	4	2	$4^{2\frac{1}{2}}$	$4^{2\frac{1}{2}}$	7	7	7	Chavez J F	36.00

OFF AT 5:12 Start Good. Won driving. Track sloppy.

TIME :23^{3}, :46^{3}, 1:10^{3}, 1:35^{3} (:23.68, :46.66, 1:10.73, 1:35.74)

$2 Mutuel Prices:

6 – **TETON FOREST**	6.60	3.10	2.70
7 – **ICE WYNND FIRE**		2.70	2.40
5 – **MAHZOUZ**			4.60

$2 EXACTA 6–7 PAID $12.40 $2 TRIFECTA 6–7–5 PAID $100.50

Dk. b or br. c, (Mar), by Forestry – Tomorrow's Child, by Al Nasr-Fr. Trainer Baffert Bob. Bred by Donald S & R Mary Zuckerman as &Tenants by the Entireties (Ky).

TETON FOREST flashed good speed from the start, soon opened a clear lead, set the pace while in hand, drew away when roused in upper stretch and remained well clear under a drive. ICE WYNND FIRE raced close up outside, chased the pace while three wide and rallied outside to earn the place award. MAHZOUZ was outrun early early, put in a run along the inside on the turn and was outfinished for the place. SARATOGA COUNTY was bumped at the start, was hustled up inside, chased the pace into the stretch and tired in the final furlong. WEST VIRGINIA was bumped at the start, dropped back early, raced wide throughout and had no rally. CODED WARNING was bumped at the start, raced close up while well in hand, was wide on the turn and tired in the stretch. SIR OSCAR chased the pace while between rivals and tired.

Owners– 1, Hughes B Wayne; 2, Amerman Racing Stables LLC; 3, Buckram Oak Farm; 4, Pollard Evelyn M; 5, Zuckerman Donald S and Roberta Mary; 6, Juddmonte Farms Inc; 7, Novo Oscar

Trainers– 1, Baffert Bob; 2, Frankel Robert; 3, LaFavers Laurie; 4, Weaver George; 5, Pletcher Todd A; 6, Frankel Robert; 7, Sacco Gregory D

TENTH RACE
Turfway Park
SEPTEMBER 18, 2004

1$\frac{1}{16}$ MILES. (1.40^{3}) 11TH RUNNING OF THE KENTUCKY CUP JUVENILE. Grade III. Purse $100,000 FOR TWO-YEAR-OLDS. By subscription of $100, $500 to enter and $500 additional to start. Supplementary nominations may be made at the time of entry Thursday, September 16, 2004 by payment of $5,000 each (includes all fees). $100,000 Guaranteed. Monies tobe divided 62% to the owner of the winner, 20% to second, 10% to third, 5% to fourth and 3% to fifth. Weight: 120 lbs. Non-winners of a Graded Stake allowed 2 lbs.; of a non-graded stake, 4 lbs.; of two races other than claiming, 6 lbs. Starters and riders must be named through the entry box by the usual time of closing. This race will be limited to twelve (12) starters. Preference to start will be given in the following order: Graded/Group Stakes Winners (in order I-II-III). Stakes winners, then highesttotal earnings. Failure to draw into the race cancels all fees. Closed Wednesday, September 8, 2004 with 31 Nominations.

Value of Race: $100,000 Winner $62,000; second $20,000; third $10,000; fourth $5,000; fifth $3,000. Mutuel Pool $210,695.00 Exacta Pool $150,342.00 Trifecta Pool $127,881.00 Superfecta Pool $36,453.00

Last Raced	Horse	M/Eqt.	A.	Wt	PP	St	¼	½	¾	Str	Fin	Jockey	Odds $1
7Aug04 ^{7}ElP^{1}	Greater Good	L	2	114	1	6	6	6	6	2^{4}	$1^{2\frac{3}{4}}$	McKee J	6.00
18Aug04 ^{1}ElP^{1}	Magna Graduate	L	2	114	4	2	$1^{\frac{1}{2}}$	$1^{\frac{1}{2}}$	$1^{1\frac{1}{2}}$	$1^{\frac{1}{2}}$	$2^{6\frac{3}{4}}$	Martinez W	11.20
22Aug04 ^{9}ElP^{3}	Norainonthisparty		2	114	3	5	5^{4}	5^{4}	$5^{\frac{1}{2}}$	5^{5}	3^{nk}	Johnson P A	34.20
5Sep04 ^{8}Mth^{2}	United	L b	2	114	2	3	$3^{1\frac{1}{2}}$	4^{12}	3^{1}	3^{1}	$4^{6\frac{1}{2}}$	Velazquez J R	3.80
21Aug04 ^{5}Sar^{1}	Storied Cat	L	2	114	6	1	2^{1}	$2^{\frac{1}{2}}$	$2^{\frac{1}{2}}$	4^{hd}	$5^{4\frac{1}{4}}$	Day P	0.60
4Sep04 ^{11}ElP^{1}	Sequoia Grove	L	2	114	5	4	4^{12}	$3^{\frac{1}{2}}$	4^{5}	6	6	Albarado R J	6.40

OFF AT 5:10 Start Good. Won driving. Track fast.

TIME :22^{4}, :46, 1:10^{4}, 1:38, 1:44^{4} (:22.88, :46.18, 1:10.96, 1:38.14, 1:44.96)

$2 Mutuel Prices:

2 – **GREATER GOOD**	14.00	6.80	5.80
5 – **MAGNA GRADUATE**		9.80	5.80
4 – **NORAINONTHISPARTY**			7.00

$2 EXACTA 2–5 PAID $106.00 $2 TRIFECTA 2–5–4 PAID $602.60
$2 SUPERFECTA 2–5–4–3 PAID $4,372.20

B. c, (Apr), by Intidab – Gather The Clan-Ire, by General Assembly. Trainer Holthus Robert E. Bred by A Lakin & Sons Inc (Ky).

GREATER GOOD far back early along the inside, made a run three wide on the second turn, angled out in upper stretch and closed fast to win going away. MAGNA GRADUATE set the early pace off the inside, moved to the rail and opened a clear lead on the second turn, drifted out a bit near the furlong marker when the winner was moving to challenge, could not stay with that one late but was clearly second best. NORAINONTHISPARTY outrun early in the two path, made a solid middle move, angled out for clear room in upper stretch but had no late bid. UNITED close up along the inside, stayed on well to the stretch and tired. STORIED CAT pressed the pace three wide, moved in a bit after a half, held well to the stretch and gave way in the drive. SEQUOIA GROVE forwardly placed four wide, stayed in that path on the second turn and faded.

Owners– 1, Lakin Lewis G; 2, Travis Burr J; 3, Lawrence Leslie; 4, Dogwood Stable; 5, Atkins Clinton C and Susan A; 6, Spence James C

Trainers– 1, Holthus Robert E; 2, Simms Garry W; 3, Stidham Susan; 4, Weaver George; 5, Lukas D Wayne; 6, Nicks Ralph E
Scratched– Oro Bravo (11Sep04 ^{3}TP ^{2})

$2 Pick Three (12–5–2) Paid $3,336.00 ; Pick Three Pool $19,254.
$2 Pick Four (4–12–5–2) Paid $18,429.80 ; Pick Four Pool $23,627.
$1 Daily Double (5–2) Paid $40.40 ; Daily Double Pool $8,395.

ELEVENTH RACE
Turfway Park
SEPTEMBER 18, 2004

1⅛ MILES. (1.463) 11TH RUNNING OF THE KENTUCKY CUP CLASSIC HANDICAP. Grade II. Purse $350,000 (includes $150,000 KTDF - KY TB Devt Fund) FOR THREE-YEAR-OLDS AND UPWARD. By subscription of $200, $1,750 to enter and $1,750 additional to start. Supplementary nominations may be made by the closing of entries Saturday, September 11, 2004 by payment of $20,000 each (includes all fees). $200,000 Guaranteed plus $150,000 KTDF for KTDF eligibles only. Monies to be divided: 62% to the owner of the winner; 20% to second; 10% to third; 5% to fourth and 3% to fifth. Any KTDF money not awarded will revert back to the fund. Weights to be announced Sunday, September 12, 2004. Starters and riders must be named through the entry box by the usual time of closing. This race will be limited to twelve (12) starters. Preference to start will be given to those horses having been assigned the highest weight (scale considered). Total 2004 earnings will be used in determining order of preference for horses assigned equal weights (scale considered). Failure to draw into the race cancels all fees. Closed Wednesday, September 8, 2004 with 18 nominations.

Value of Race: $350,000 Winner $221,500; second $70,000; third $35,000; fourth $17,500; fifth $6,000. Mutuel Pool $435,376.00 Exacta Pool $178,935.00 Trifecta Pool $140,283.00 Superfecta Pool $46,789.00

Last Raced	Horse	M/Eqt.	A.	Wt	PP	St	¼	½	¾	Str	Fin	Jockey	Odds $1
7Aug04 9Sar1	Roses in May	L	4	118	5	2	1hd	1hd	24	12½	14	Velazquez J R	0.30
14Aug04 8EvD1	Pie N Burger	L b	6	117	4	1	24	25	1hd	22	2¾	Theriot H J II	11.30
28Aug04 9ElP5	Sonic West	L f	5	113	6	5	55	41½	52½	55	3nk	Day P	8.30
11Sep04 7Del3	Country Be Gold	L	7	114	3	6	6	6	42	41½	4hd	Bejarano R	51.20
22Aug04 7EmD1	Adreamisborn	L b	5	114	2	4	3hd	31½	32	3½	55½	Baze R A	4.20
14Aug04 3Sar3	Stratostar	L	4	111	1	3	41½	55	6	6	6	McKee J	29.20

OFF AT 5:42 Start Good. Won driving. Track fast.

TIME :234, :472, 1:113, 1:362, 1:49 (:23.89, :47.41, 1:11.66, 1:36.41, 1:49.13)

$2 Mutuel Prices:			
5 – ROSES IN MAY	2.60	2.10	2.10
4 – PIE N BURGER		3.20	2.10
6 – SONIC WEST			2.10

$2 EXACTA 5–4 PAID $11.20 $2 TRIFECTA 5–4–6 PAID $44.00
$2 SUPERFECTA 5–4–6–3 PAID $129.00

Dk. b or br. c, (Feb), by Devil His Due – Tell a Secret , by Speak John . Trainer Romans Dale. Bred by Margaux Farm LLC (Ky).

ROSES IN MAY rated on the pace outside PIE N BURGER, drew clear when ready entering the stretch, drifted to the inside approaching the furlong marker when shown the whip on the right side then increased his lead under steady handling. ROSES IN MAY went an additional furlong getting the mile and a quarter in 2:02 3/5. PIE N BURGER vied for the lead inside the winner, could not stay with that one leaving the second turn, angled out when displaced in upper stretch and held on for the place. SONIC WEST reserved early four wide, stayed out in that path around the second turn when dropping back a bit then lodged a mild bid on the outside. COUNTRY BE GOLD outrun for a half along the inside, made a run on the rail into the stretch, angled out for the drive but hung. ADREAMISBORN behind the leaders off the rail, moved out to the four path on the backstretch, came in just a bit with three furlongs to go, stayed on well to midstretch and had no late bid. STRATOSTAR within striking distance off the inside, moved out four wide with three furlongs to go and tired.

Owners– 1, Ramsey Kenneth L and Sarah K; 2, Kagele Brothers Inc Tom Kagele; 3, Stone Spire LLC; 4, S A Partnership; 5, Franks John; 6, Allen E Paulson Living Trust

Trainers– 1, Romans Dale; 2, Norman Cole; 3, Van Berg Thomas L; 4, Nobles Reynaldo H; 5, Hollendorfer Jerry; 6, Lukas D Wayne

$2 Pick Three (5–2–5) Paid $88.00 ; Pick Three Pool $36,918 .
$1 Daily Double (2–5) Paid $14.00 ; Daily Double Pool $9,512 .

TWELFTH RACE
Turfway Park
SEPTEMBER 18, 2004

1$\frac{1}{16}$ MILES. (1.403) 19TH RUNNING OF THE TURFWAY BREEDERS' CUP. Grade III. Purse $175,000 (includes $75,000 BC - Breeders' Cup) FOR FILLIES AND MARES THREE-YEARS-OLD AND UPWARD.

Value of Race: $175,000 Winner $108,500; second $35,000; third $17,500; fourth $8,750; fifth $5,250. Mutuel Pool $261,205.00 Exacta Pool $174,100.00 Trifecta Pool $151,126.00 Superfecta Pool $43,034.00

Last Raced	Horse	M/Eqt.	A.	Wt	PP	St	¼	½	¾	Str	Fin	Jockey	Odds $1
21Aug04 10Sar6	Susan's Angel	L	3	116	5	2	2½	2½	22	1½	1¾	Bejarano R	6.20
1Aug04 9Sar4	Mayo On the Side	L bf	5	120	2	6	6	6	4½	32	21½	Albarado R J	2.50
7Aug04 10ElP1	Angela's Love	L	4	122	3	3	11	1½	1hd	21	32	Guidry M	1.80
7Aug04 10ElP2	Miss Fortunate	L	4	120	1	1	4hd	54	5hd	56	4¾	Sellers S J	4.20
1Aug04 9Sar5	La Reason	L f	4	122	4	5	53½	4hd	6	4½	511¾	Day P	5.20
22Aug04 9EmD3	Hippogator	L b	4	120	6	4	34	34	31½	6	6	Baze R A	13.20

OFF AT 6:15 Start Good. Won driving. Track fast.

TIME :232, :464, 1:113, 1:371, 1:441 (:23.45, :46.99, 1:11.61, 1:37.38, 1:44.21)

$2 Mutuel Prices:			
6 – SUSAN'S ANGEL	14.40	5.80	2.80
2 – MAYO ON THE SIDE		4.20	2.40
3 – ANGELA'S LOVE			2.40

$2 EXACTA 6–2 PAID $62.00 $2 TRIFECTA 6–2–3 PAID $127.40
$2 SUPERFECTA 6–2–3–1 PAID $325.80

Dk. b or br. f, (Mar), by Cape Town – Copeaway , by Copelan . Trainer Lukas D Wayne. Bred by Captain W Jakeman & Mrs K C Jakeman (Ky).

SUSAN'S ANGEL closest to the pace in the two path, challenged in earnest midway down the backstretch, gained a short lead in upper stretch then edged off and held sway late under pressure. MAYO ON THE SIDE in tight after the start, dropped well back while three wide, made a solid gain four wide on the second turn, reached a forward position with a furlong to go but lodged only a mild late bid. ANGELA'S LOVE set the pace near the rail, stayed on with the winner to deep stretch and held on gamely. MISS FORTUNATE drifted out after the start, was straightened and reserved along the inside then went evenly the final three furlongs. LA REASON well placed early, maintained good position for five furlongs, split rivals approaching the stretch but had nothing left late. HIPPOGATOR prompted the pace three wide, held on well to the stretch and faded.

Owners– 1, S Angel Stable Kris Jakeman et al; 2, Lothenbach Stables Inc; 3, Poston Bill and Vicki; 4, Lyon Stables; 5, K and K Racing Stable LLC; 6, Blanchard Bob Maser Tom and Todaro George

Trainers– 1, Lukas D Wayne; 2, Nafzger Carl A; 3, Romans Dale; 4, Mott William I; 5, Vance David R; 6, Hollendorfer Jerry

Scratched– Our Josephina (07Aug04 2Mnr3)

$2 Pick Three (2–5–6) Paid $287.20 ; Pick Three Pool $22,353 .
$1 Daily Double (5–6) Paid $12.10 ; Daily Double Pool $10,832 .
$2 Consolation Pick 3 (2–5–4) Paid $29.00 .
$2 Consolation Daily Double (5–4) Paid $2.40 .

THIRTEENTH RACE
Turfway Park
SEPTEMBER 18, 2004

6 FURLONGS. (1.08^{1}) 11TH RUNNING OF THE KENTUCKY CUP SPRINT. Grade III. Purse $100,000 FOR THREE-YEAR-OLDS. By subscription of $100, $500 to enter and $500 additional to start. Supplementary nominations may be made at the time of entry Thursday, September 16, 2004 by payment of $5,000 each (includes all fees). $100,000 Guaranteed. Monies to be divided 62% to the owner of the winner, 20% to second, 10% to third, 5% to fourth and 3% to fifth. Weight: 122 lbs. Non-winners of a $50,000 since April 3 allowed 3 lbs.; non-winners of $30,000 twice in 2004, 6 lbs. Starters and riders must be named through the entry box by the usual time of closing. This race will be limited to twelve (12) starters. Preference to start will be given in the following order: Graded/Group Stakes Winners (in order I–II–III). Stakes winners, then highest total earnings in 2004. Failure to draw into the race cancels all fees. Closed Wednesday, September 8, 2004 with 22 Nominations.

Value of Race: $100,000 Winner $62,000; second $20,000; third $10,000; fourth $5,000; fifth $3,000. Mutuel Pool $224,185.00 Exacta Pool $153,584.00 Trifecta Pool $85,625.00 Superfecta Pool $29,516.00

Last Raced	Horse	M/Eqt.	A.	Wt	PP	St	¼	½	Str	Fin	Jockey	Odds $1
29Aug04 4EIP2	Level Playingfield	L b	3	116	2	5	5	5	3^{hd}	1$^{2\frac{1}{2}}$	McKee J	10.40
8May04 9CD2	Cuvee	L	3	116	4	2	1^{hd}	1^{hd}	2$^{3\frac{1}{2}}$	2$^{1\frac{1}{4}}$	Sellers S J	1.30
12Aug04 7Sar4	Swift Attraction	L b	3	116	1	4	2^{1}	3^{3}	4^{2}	3$^{\frac{1}{2}}$	Day P	4.00
28Aug04 5Sar2	Heckle	L	3	116	5	1	3^{3}	2$^{1\frac{1}{2}}$	1^{hd}	4$^{2\frac{3}{4}}$	Velazquez J R	1.70
7Aug04 6EIP5	Silver Minister	L	3	119	3	3	4^{10}	4^{3}	5	5	Bejarano R	6.40

OFF AT 6:43 Start Good. Won driving. Track fast.
TIME :21^{2}, :44^{1}, :56^{3}, 1:09^{3} (:21.52, :44.27, :56.72, 1:09.76)

$2 Mutuel Prices:

2 – LEVEL PLAYINGFIELD	22.80	5.40	3.40
4 – CUVEE		3.20	2.80
1 – SWIFT ATTRACTION			3.00

$2 EXACTA 2–4 PAID $73.60 $2 TRIFECTA 2–4–1 PAID $242.00
$2 SUPERFECTA 2–4–1–6 PAID $428.00

Dk. b or br. c, (Apr), by Level Sands – Chao Praya, by Gold Legend. Trainer Holthus Robert E. Bred by Briland Farm & Mrs Stacy L Mitchell (Ky).

LEVEL PLAYINGFIELD bumped with SWIFT ATTRACTION after the start, was outrun for three furlongs, advanced three wide thereafter and closed well to be clear. CUVEE with the pace out in the strip, raced three wide into the turn, moved in a bit, responded willingly when joined by HECKLE with three furlongs to go, drifted out to bump that one in midstretch then held on for the place. SWIFT ATTRACTION bumped with the winner after the start, recovered quickly, vied for the lead along the inside, could not keep pace with the leaders on the turn, angled out in upper stretch and went evenly to be up for the show. HECKLE close up outside, was four wide into the turn, challenged CUVEE with three furlongs to go, stayed on well to midstretch, was bumped with a furlong to go and tired late. SILVER MINISTER drifted in at the start, raced behind the leaders off the rail and tired.

Owners– 1, Fly Racing LLC; 2, Winchell Thoroughbreds LLC and Spendthrift Farm; 3, Overbrook Farm; 4, Dogwood Stable; 5, Lloyd Madison Farms LLC

Trainers– 1, Holthus Robert E; 2, Asmussen Steven M; 3, Lukas D Wayne; 4, Pletcher Todd A; 5, Foley Gregory D

Scratched– Quick Action (25Aug04 7Sar6)

$2 Pick Three (5–6–2) Paid $253.80; Pick Three Pool $36,998.
$2 Pick Four (2–5–6–2) Paid $3,538.40; Pick Four Pool $56,702.
$1 Daily Double (6–2) Paid $110.60; Daily Double Pool $16,744.
$2 Consolation Pick 3 (5–4–2) Paid $29.00.

SIXTH RACE
Arlington
SEPTEMBER 19, 2004

1 MILE. (1.32^{1}) 70TH RUNNING OF THE ARLINGTON-WASHINGTON FUTURITY. Grade III. Purse $200,000 (includes $50,000 BC – Breeders' Cup) FOR TWO-YEAR-OLDS.

Value of Race: $200,000 Winner $120,000; second $31,000; second $31,000; fourth $12,000; fifth $6,000. Mutuel Pool $197,413.00 Exacta Pool $124,911.00 Trifecta Pool $105,035.00 Superfecta Pool $35,382.00

Last Raced	Horse	M/Eqt.	A.	Wt	PP	St	¼	½	¾	Str	Fin	Jockey	Odds $1
29Aug04 5AP1	Three Hour Nap	L	2	119	6	2	4$^{1\frac{1}{2}}$	4^{1}	4^{1}	3$^{1\frac{1}{2}}$	1^{nk}	Razo E Jr	3.10
22Aug04 9EIP1	[DH] Elusive Chris	L f	2	122	1	4	2^{hd}	2$^{1\frac{1}{2}}$	2$^{\frac{1}{2}}$	2^{1}	2	McKee J	5.40
22Aug04 9EIP8	[DH] Straight Line		2	119	2	5	5$^{\frac{1}{2}}$	5$^{2\frac{1}{2}}$	5^{hd}	4^{5}	2^{8}	Marquez C H Jr	12.70
29Aug04 8AP1	Rocky River	L	2	119	4	1	1$^{\frac{1}{2}}$	1$^{\frac{1}{2}}$	1$^{2\frac{1}{2}}$	1^{hd}	4^{4}	Emigh C A	0.60
29Aug04 8AP2	Santana Strings		2	117	3	6	6	6	6	5^{1}	5^{hd}	Cosme E	19.90
29Aug04 5AP3	Exceptional Ride	L b	2	117	5	3	3^{hd}	3$^{1\frac{1}{2}}$	3^{hd}	6	6	Albarado R J	9.30

[DH]–Dead Heat.

OFF AT 3:26 Start Good. Won driving. Track fast.
TIME :22^{4}, :45^{1}, 1:10^{3}, 1:24^{1}, 1:38^{2} (:22.99, :45.34, 1:10.78, 1:24.39, 1:38.56)

$2 Mutuel Prices:

6 – THREE HOUR NAP	8.20	4.00	3.20
1 – [DH]ELUSIVE CHRIS		3.60	3.80
2 – [DH]STRAIGHT LINE		4.80	5.60

$2 EXACTA 6–1 PAID $19.60 $2 EXACTA 6–2 PAID $41.20
$2 TRIFECTA 6–1–2 PAID $114.80 $2 TRIFECTA 6–2–1 PAID $182.00
$2 SUPERFECTA 6–1–2–4 PAID $285.60 $2 SUPERFECTA 6–2–1–4 PAID $420.60

B. c, (Mar), by Afternoon Deelites – Pilgrim's Treasure, by Pilgrim. Trainer Robertson Hugh H. Bred by Frank A Penn Jr & D Flannigan (Ky).

THREE HOUR NAP raced four wide near the middle of the field, rallied in the stretch and prevailed after being bumped late. ELUSIVE CHRIS pressed the pace from the inside and held on gamely to finish on even terms for the place. STRAIGHT LINE lacked speed, came four wide into the stretch and rallied in the drive but missed. ROCKY RIVER was rank in the early going, set the pace from just outside and weakened. SANTANA STRINGS was always outrun. EXCEPTIONAL RIDE raced close up three wide and weakened.

Owners– 1, Homewrecker Racing LLC and Robertson Hugh; 2, Hines James T Jr; 3, Nancy A Vanier and Cartwright Thoroughbreds LLC II B Cartwright et al; 4, Thunderhead Farms; 5, Shamrock Hill Farm; 6, Kahn Eliah and Lisa

Trainers– 1, Robertson Hugh H; 2, Holthus Robert E; 3, Vanier Harvey L; 4, Von Hemel Don; 5, Tomillo Thomas F; 6, McPeek Kenneth G

$1 Pick Three (9–10–6) Paid $397.10; Pick Three Pool $22,243.
$2 Daily Double (10–6) Paid $51.00; Daily Double Pool $19,908.

NINTH RACE
Arlington
SEPTEMBER 19, 2004

1 MILE. (1.32[1]) 70TH RUNNING OF THE ARLINGTON-WASHINGTON LASSIE. Grade III. Purse $100,000 FOR FILLIES, TWO-YEARS-OLD. By subscription of $75 each, which should accompany the nomination. A Supplementary Nomination of $4,000 may be made on Thursday, September 16, 2004, which includes entry and starting fees. Original nominees to pay $750 to pass the entry box and an additional $750 to start, with $100,000 Guaranteed, of which $60,000 to the winner; $20,000 to second; $11,000 to third; $6,000 to fourth and $3,000 to fifth. WEIGHT: 121 lbs. Non-winners of $50,000 once, allowed 3 lbs.; $35,000 once or a race other than Maiden or Claiming, 5 lbs. This event will be limited to fourteen (14) starters. Preference will be to winners of Graded/Group Stakes (in order of I-II-III), next preference, Highest Lifetime Earnings. Failure to draw into this raceat time of entry cancels all fees with the exception of the nominating fee(s). Starters to be named through the entry box by usual time of closing. Two (2) horses having common ties through ownership cannot start to the exclusion of a single ownership intterest. Trophy to the owner of the winner. Closed Wednesday, September 8, 2004 with 22 nominations.

Value of Race: $100,000 Winner $60,000; second $20,000; third $11,000; fourth $6,000; fifth $3,000. Mutuel Pool $249,464.00 Exacta Pool $153,890.00 Trifecta Pool $155,032.00 Superfecta Pool $55,869.00

Last Raced	Horse	M/Eqt.	A.	Wt	PP	St	¼	½	¾	Str	Fin	Jockey	Odds $1
12Aug04 ^{6}AP^{1}	Culinary	L	2	116	2	8	6^{1}	$4\frac{1}{2}$	$3\frac{1}{2}$	2^{2}	1^{2}	Marquez C H Jr	7.00
4Sep04 ^{10}RD^{2}	Runway Model		2	118	3	6	7^{2}	$5^{1\frac{1}{2}}$	5^{2}	$3\frac{1}{2}$	$2^{3\frac{1}{2}}$	Albarado R J	2.20
21Aug04 ^{9}EIP^{1}	Kota	L	2	118	7	3	4^{hd}	6^{2}	$6\frac{1}{2}$	$5^{1\frac{1}{2}}$	3^{2}	McKee J	2.70
29Aug04 ^{5}AP^{2}	Mary Alex	L f	2	116	5	2	1^{1}	1^{1}	$1^{1\frac{1}{2}}$	$1\frac{1}{2}$	$4\frac{3}{4}$	Douglas R R	2.40
4Sep04 ^{6}PrM^{1}	My Three Sisters	L	2	118	4	7	8	$7\frac{1}{2}$	7^{4}	6^{3}	5^{2}	Campbell J M	28.80
29Aug04 ^{9}AP^{1}	Bubble N Squeak	L	2	116	1	4	3^{hd}	$3^{1\frac{1}{2}}$	$4\frac{1}{2}$	4^{1}	$6\frac{3}{4}$	Emigh C A	25.80
21Aug04 ^{9}EIP^{3}	Patience Pays	L b	2	116	6	1	2^{2}	2^{1}	2^{1}	7^{4}	$7^{3\frac{1}{2}}$	Razo E Jr	8.60
28Aug04 ^{1}PrM^{1}	Queansco		2	118	8	5	$5\frac{1}{2}$	8	8	8	8	Doocy T T	24.40

OFF AT 4:56 Start Good. Won driving. Track fast.

TIME :23^{3}, :47, 1:12, 1:24^{3}, 1:36^{4} (:23.74, :47.01, 1:12.02, 1:24.61, 1:36.98)

$2 Mutuel Prices:

2 – CULINARY	16.00	7.80	4.00
3 – RUNWAY MODEL		4.20	3.00
7 – KOTA			3.00

$2 EXACTA 2–3 PAID $89.00 $2 TRIFECTA 2–3–7 PAID $299.60
$2 SUPERFECTA 2–3–7–5 PAID $625.00

Gr/ro. f, (May), by El Amante – Volunteer-Arg, by Ski Champ. Trainer Stidham Michael. Bred by Diana Snowden & Guy B Snowden (Ky).

CULINARY raced three wide near the middle of the field, rallied in the stretch and drew off late. RUNWAY MODEL raced close up just outside and rallied for the place while no danger to the winner. KOTA lacked speed, came five wide into the stretch and gained belatedly. MARY ALEX set the pace inside and weakened. MY THREE SISTERS lacked speed and improved her position. BUBBLE N SQUEAK raced close up inside and tired. PATIENCE PAYS stalked the pace just outside and tired. QUEANSCO was through early.

Owners– 1, Jack H Smith III Thoroughbreds; 2, Chowhan Naveed; 3, OFER Stables LLC; 4, Lieblong Alex and Joanne; 5, William Gessman and Ed Casady; 6, Carl William A; 7, Minnic Stan and Hundley C Bruce; 8, Hammersmith Dennis L

Trainers– 1, Stidham Michael; 2, Flint Bernard S; 3, Holthus Robert E; 4, Hobby Steve; 5, Von Hemel Kelly; 6, McPeek Kenneth G; 7, Amoss Thomas; 8, Von Hemel Don

Scratched– Lady Dynasty (22Aug04 ^{9}Mth^{5})

$1 Pick Three (10–2/4/13–2) Paid $365.00 ; Pick Three Pool $15,576 .

SEVENTH RACE
Belmont
SEPTEMBER 19, 2004

1 MILE. (1.32[1]) 115TH RUNNING OF THE FUTURITY. Grade II. Purse $300,000 (Up To $41,000 NYSBFOA) FOR TWO YEAR OLDS. By subscription of $300 each, which should accompany the nomination; $1,500 to pass the entry box and $1,500 to start. The purse to be divided 60% to the winner, 20% to second, 10% to third, 5% to fourth, 3% to fifth and 2% divided equally among remaining finishers. 120 lbs. A trophy will be presented to the winning owner. Closed Saturday, September 4, 2004 with 23 Nominations.

Value of Race: $300,000 Winner $180,000; second $60,000; third $30,000; fourth $15,000; fifth $9,000; sixth $6,000. Mutuel Pool $401,506.00 Exacta Pool $305,087.00 Trifecta Pool $208,942.00

Last Raced	Horse	M/Eqt.	A.	Wt	PP	St	¼	½	¾	Str	Fin	Jockey	Odds $1
28Aug04 ^{11}Mth^{2}	Park Avenue Ball	L	2	120	3	3	6	$5\frac{1}{2}$	3^{hd}	$1^{2\frac{1}{2}}$	1^{3}	Castellano J J	10.80
16Aug04 ^{2}Sar^{1}	Wallstreet Scandal	L	2	120	1	4	1^{hd}	$4\frac{1}{2}$	5^{2}	4^{2}	$2^{1\frac{1}{2}}$	Bridgmohan S X	3.55
28Aug04 ^{11}Mth^{1}	Evil Minister	L f	2	120	2	5	$4\frac{1}{2}$	6	6	5^{hd}	3^{2}	Pimentel J	10.20
28Aug04 ^{11}Mth^{3}	Upscaled	L	2	120	6	2	3^{hd}	1^{hd}	1^{hd}	2^{hd}	$4^{1\frac{1}{4}}$	Velazquez J R	4.30
7Aug04 ^{6}Dmr^{1}	Fusaichi Rock Star	L b	2	120	4	6	$5\frac{1}{2}$	$2\frac{1}{2}$	$2\frac{1}{2}$	3^{hd}	5^{2}	Desormeaux K J	1.15
15Aug04 ^{5}Sar^{1}	Comacina	b	2	117	5	1	2^{hd}	$3^{1\frac{1}{2}}$	$4\frac{1}{2}$	6	6	Prado E S	7.00

OFF AT 4:14 Start Good. Won driving. Track fast.

TIME :24, :46^{4}, 1:12^{1}, 1:38^{4} (:24.02, :46.88, 1:12.31, 1:38.84)

$2 Mutuel Prices:

3 – PARK AVENUE BALL	23.60	9.30	5.20
1 – WALLSTREET SCANDAL		4.60	3.50
2 – EVIL MINISTER			5.10

$2 EXACTA 3–1 PAID $77.50 $2 TRIFECTA 3–1–2 PAID $250.50

Ch. c, (May), by Citidancer – Road to the Ball, by Cahill Road. Trainer Ryerson James T. Bred by C J Hesse Inc (NJ).

PARK AVENUE BALL was taken in hand early, angled out and advanced four wide on the turn, reached the front in upper stretch, drew clear when roused and remained well clear while being kept to the task to the finish. WALLSTREET SCANDAL raced with the pace along the inside, was eased back nearing the turn, angled out and came wide approaching the stretch and finished gamely outside. EVIL MINISTER raced with the pace while between rivals, dropped back nearing the turn, came wide into the stretch and offered a mild rally outside. UPSCALED contested the pace while between rivals and tired in the final furlong. FUSAICHI ROCK STAR broke sluggishly, was a bit rank outside early on, put in a three wide run on the turn and tired in the stretch. COMACINA stumbled at the start, contested the pace along the inside and tired in the stretch.

Owners– 1, Char-Mari Stable; 2, Klaravich Stables Inc; 3, Namcook Stables LLC; 4, Lewis Robert B and Beverly J; 5, Sekiguchi Fusao; 6, Flying Zee Stable

Trainers– 1, Ryerson James T; 2, Violette Richard A Jr; 3, Juvonen Erik; 4, Pletcher Todd A; 5, Baffert Bob; 6, Biancone Patrick L

$2 Daily Double (1–3) Paid $182.00 ; Daily Double Pool $97,672 .
$2 Pick Three (7–1–3) Paid $334.50 ; Pick Three Pool $62,452 .

EIGHTH RACE
Belmont
SEPTEMBER 19, 2004

1 MILE. (1.32^{1}) 98TH RUNNING OF THE MATRON. Grade I. Purse $300,000 (Up To $41,000 NYSBFOA) FOR FILLIES TWO YEARS OLD. By subscription of $300 each, which should accompany the nomination; $1,500 to pass the entry box and $1,500 to start. The purse to be divided 60% to the winner, 20% to second, 10% to third, 5% to fourth, 3% to fifth and 2%divided equally among remaining finishers. 119 lbs. Trophies will be presented to the winning owner, trainer and jockey. Closed Saturday, September 4, 2004 with 19 Nominations.

Value of Race: $300,000 Winner $180,000; second $60,000; third $30,000; fourth $15,000; fifth $9,000; sixth $6,000. Mutuel Pool $458,097.00 Exacta Pool $364,312.00 Trifecta Pool $231,740.00

Last Raced	Horse	M/Eqt.	A.	Wt	PP	St	¼	½	¾	Str	Fin	Jockey	Odds $1
20Aug04 8Sar1	Sense of Style		2	119	4	6	6	6	1½	1½	1^{1}	Prado E S	0.35
2Aug04 3Sar1	Balletto-UAE	L	2	119	2	4	4½	3^{hd}	5^{5}	$3^{2\frac{1}{2}}$	2¾	Gryder A T	7.90
20Aug04 8Sar3	Play With Fire	L	2	119	3	2	3^{hd}	4½	4½	2^{1}	$3^{7\frac{1}{4}}$	Fragoso P	16.90
28Jly04 9Sar4	Darn That Girl	L	2	119	6	3	$5^{2\frac{1}{2}}$	5½	6	6	$4^{2\frac{3}{4}}$	Bridgmohan S X	9.70
22Aug04 4Sar1	Graceful Nancy	L	2	119	1	5	1½	1½	3^{hd}	5½	5no	Castellano J J	12.10
29Aug04 4Sar1	Summer Raven	L	2	119	5	1	2½	2½	$2^{1\frac{1}{2}}$	4^{1}	6	Velazquez J R	9.60

OFF AT 4:45 Start Good . Won driving. Track fast.

TIME :24^{2}, :48, 1:12, 1:37^{3} (:24.46, :48.03, 1:12.12, 1:37.67)

$2 Mutuel Prices:

4 – SENSE OF STYLE	2.70	2.20	2.10
2 – BALLETTO-UAE		3.80	2.10
3 – PLAY WITH FIRE			2.10

$2 EXACTA 4–2 PAID $11.80 $2 TRIFECTA 4–2–3 PAID $43.00

B. f, (Mar), by Thunder Gulch – Save Me the Waltz-Ire , by Kings Lake . Trainer Biancone Patrick L. Bred by Twelve Oaks Stud (Ky).

SENSE OF STYLE was unprepared for the start, was away slowly and unhurried outside early, advanced quickly while four wide on the turn, took over entering the stretch, turned back a bid from PLAY WITH FIRE nearing the eighth pole then held BALLETTO safe under a drive. BALLETTO (UAE) raced close up early inside, came wide into the stretch, angled back to the inside in deep stretch and finished gamely. PLAY WITH FIRE raced close up while between rivals, rallied wide nearing the stretch, took a run at the winner approaching the eighth pole, could not get by that rival and weakened in the final yards. DARN THAT GIRL raced close up outside, was three wide on the turn and had no response when roused. GRACEFUL NANCY was hustled up inside, contested the pace into the stretch and tired. SUMMER RAVEN contested the pace from the outside and tired in the stretch.

Owners– 1, Smith Derrick and Tabor Michael; 2, Darley Stable; 3, Zwerling Gary L; 4, Silver Earl I and Eiserman Michael; 5, LaPenta Robert V; 6, Edgewood Farm

Trainers– 1, Biancone Patrick L; 2, Albertrani Thomas; 3, Hennig Mark; 4, Violette Richard A Jr; 5, Zito Nicholas P; 6, Pletcher Todd A

NINTH RACE
Belmont
SEPTEMBER 19, 2004

1$\frac{1}{16}$ MILES. (1.39^{2}) 29TH RUNNING OF THE RUFFIAN HANDICAP. Grade I. Purse $300,000 (Up to $41,000 NYSBFOA) A HANDICAP FOR FILLIES AND MARES THREE YEARS OLD AND UPWARD. By subscription of $300 each, which should accompany the nomination; $1,500 to pass the entry box and $1,500 to start. The purse to be divided 60% to the winner, 20% to second, 10% to third, 5%to fourth, 3% to fifth and 2% divided equally among remaining finishers. Trophies will be presented to the winning owner, trainer and jockey. Closed Saturday, September 4, 2004 with 16 Nominations.

Value of Race: $294,000 Winner $180,000; second $60,000; third $30,000; fourth $15,000; fifth $9,000. Mutuel Pool $410,448.00 Exacta Pool $298,799.00 Trifecta Pool $179,210.00

Last Raced	Horse	M/Eqt.	A.	Wt	PP	St	¼	½	¾	Str	Fin	Jockey	Odds $1
1Aug04 9Sar2	Sightseek	L	5	122	3	3	3½	$3^{1\frac{1}{2}}$	1½	1^{8}	$1^{11\frac{1}{4}}$	Velazquez J R	0.25
4Jly04 10Mth4	Pocus Hocus	L b	6	114	1	4	1½	1^{hd}	$3^{3\frac{1}{2}}$	2^{hd}	$2^{2\frac{1}{2}}$	Santos J A	12.10
8Aug04 8Dmr1	Miss Loren-Arg	L f	6	117	4	2	5	5	5	$4^{5\frac{1}{2}}$	3½	Court J K	4.60
12Jun04 4Hol5	Class Above	L b	3	108	5	1	2^{hd}	2½	$2^{1\frac{1}{2}}$	$3^{3\frac{1}{2}}$	$4^{7\frac{1}{4}}$	Jara F	24.00
13Aug04 8Sar1	Bounding Charm	L	4	114	2	5	4^{3}	4^{3}	4^{hd}	5	5	Prado E S	11.80

OFF AT 5:40 Start Good . Won ridden out. Track fast.

TIME :23^{3}, :46^{1}, 1:10^{3}, 1:35, 1:41^{2} (:23.62, :46.32, 1:10.68, 1:35.00, 1:41.51)

$2 Mutuel Prices:

3 – SIGHTSEEK	2.50	2.10	—
1 – POCUS HOCUS		2.10	—
4 – MISS LOREN-ARG		—	—

$2 EXACTA 3–1 PAID $10.00 $2 TRIFECTA 3–1–4 PAID $25.40

Ch. m, (Feb), by Distant View – Viviana , by Nureyev . Trainer Frankel Robert. Bred by Juddmonte Farms Inc (Ky).

SIGHTSEEK came away in good order, raced with the pace while well in hand, advanced three wide on the turn, took over after a slap on the shoulder, quickly drew away and widened while under a hand ride through the stretch. POCUS HOCUS argued the pace along the inside, was no match for the winner and stayed on on the rail to earn the place award. MISS LOREN (ARG) was outrun early, was shaken up on the turn, came four wide approaching the stretch and had no rally. CLASS ABOVE ducked out at the start, argued the pace from the outside and tired in the stretch. BOUNDING CHARM stumbled at the start, chased the pace while three wide and tired after three quarters.

Owners– 1, Juddmonte Farms Inc; 2, Moore Susan and John; 3, Bago Maria A Bago Juan Carlos Goldberg Gabriel; 4, Padua Stables; 5, Trade Winds Farm

Trainers– 1, Frankel Robert; 2, Jerkens James A; 3, Seglin Luis E; 4, McLaughlin Kiaran P; 5, Mott William I

$2 Pick Three (3–4–3) Paid $37.00 ; Pick Three Pool $109,156 .
$2 Pick Four (1–3–4–3) Paid $304.00 ; Pick Four Pool $215,378 .
$2 Pick Four (3–4–11–3 (NTRA NATIONAL)) Paid $178.50 ; Pick Four Pool $493,939 .

NINTH RACE
Belmont
SEPTEMBER 25, 2004

1 MILE. (Turf) (1.31^{3}) 17TH RUNNING OF THE NOBLE DAMSEL HANDICAP. Grade III. Purse $150,000 WIDENER TURF. (UP TO $28,500 NYSBFOA) A HANDICAP FOR FILLIES AND MARES THREE YEARS OLD AND UPWARD. By subscription of $150 each, which should accompany the nomination; $750 to pass the entry box; $750 to start. The purse to be divided 60% to the winner, 20% to second, 10% to third, 5% to fourth, 3% to fifth and 2% divided equally among remaining finishers. A trophy will be presented to the winning owner. The New York Racing Association reserves the right to transfer this race to the Main Track. In the event that this race is taken off the turf, it may be subject to downgrading upon review by the Graded Stakes Committee. Closed Saturday, September 11, 2004 with 36 Nominations. (If the Stewards consider it inadvisable to run this race on the turf course, this race will be run at One Mile on the main track.). (Rail at 9 feet).

Value of Race: $150,000 Winner $90,000; second $30,000; third $15,000; fourth $7,500; fifth $4,500; sixth $750; seventh $750; eighth $750; ninth $750. Mutuel Pool $560,559.00 Exacta Pool $378,300.00 Trifecta Pool $330,961.00

Last Raced	Horse	M/Eqt.	A.	Wt	PP	St	¼	½	¾	Str	Fin	Jockey	Odds $1
30Aug04 ^{8}Sar^{1}	Ocean Drive	L	4	120	9	2	5^{hd}	3½	1^{hd}	1^{hd}	1¼	Velazquez J R	*2.75
30Aug04 ^{8}Sar^{3}	High Court-Brz	L	4	115	7	5	9	7^{1½}	5½	4^{hd}	2¾	Migliore R	21.70
28Aug04 ^{10}WO^{1}	Hour of Justice	L	4	116	4	3	1^{hd}	2½	3½	2^{3}	3^{2}	Kabel T K	2.75
19Aug04 ^{7}Sar^{1}	Changing World	L	4	113	6	4	3^{hd}	6½	6½	5^{hd}	4^{nk}	Castellano J J	15.10
27Aug04 ^{8}Sar^{2}	Finery	L	4	114	8	1	2½	1^{hd}	4^{2}	6^{2½}	5½	Gryder A T	38.25
6Aug04 ^{8}Sar^{6}	Yell	L	4	112	5	7	8½	9	8½	7^{1}	6^{2}	Velasquez C	9.80
30Aug04 ^{8}Sar^{2}	Personal Legend	L b	4	115	1	6	7^{hd}	8½	9	9	7^{1¼}	Chavez J F	5.30
5Jun04 ^{8}Bel^{5}	Dedication-FR	L	5	117	3	9	6^{1½}	5½	2^{hd}	3^{hd}	8^{1¼}	Prado E S	3.65
28Aug04 ^{10}Mth^{1}	Coney Kitty-Ire	L f	6	115	2	8	4^{hd}	4^{hd}	7^{1½}	8^{hd}	9	Santos J A	26.00

***–Actual Betting Favorite.**

OFF AT 5:12 Start Good . Won driving. Course firm.

TIME :24^{1}, :47^{3}, 1:11^{2}, 1:34^{3} (:24.23, :47.70, 1:11.40, 1:34.71)

$2 Mutuel Prices:				
	9 – OCEAN DRIVE	7.50	4.80	2.60
	7 – HIGH COURT–BRZ		17.60	6.10
	4 – HOUR OF JUSTICE			2.80

$2 EXACTA 9–7 PAID $117.00 $2 TRIFECTA 9–7–4 PAID $573.00

Dk. b or br. f, (Feb), by Belong to Me – Clever But Costly , by Clever Trick . Trainer Pletcher Todd A. Bred by James D Conway & Thomas C Mueller (Ky).

OCEAN DRIVE raced close up outside while in hand, advanced four wide on the turn, responded when roused and drew clear late. HIGH COURT (BRZ) was outrun early, rallied three wide on the turn and finished gamely outside. HOUR OF JUSTICE contested the pace along the inside and dug in stubbornly along the inside in the stretch. CHANGING WORLD raced close up early while between rivals and lacked a rally. FINERY contested the pace from the outside and tired in the stretch. YELL raced in hand outside early, clipped heels and stumbled badly entering the turn, came wide into the stretch and finished well outside. PERSONAL LEGEND was outrun early along the inside, angled out in upper stretch and lacked a rally. DEDICATION (FR) raced close up while in hand, put in a three wide run on the turn and tired in the stretch. CONEY KITTY (IRE) raced close up along the inside, chased the pace and tired in the stretch.

Owners– 1, Baskin Bonnie and Sy; 2, Lael Stables; 3, Stronach Stables; 4, Rogers Samuel H Jr; 5, Richards Althea D; 6, Claiborne Farm and Dilschneider Adele B; 7, Gann Edmund A; 8, Head Ghislaine; 9, Betz William J Humphrey Steve and Seelbinder Arthur

Trainers– 1, Pletcher Todd A; 2, Matz Michael R; 3, Keogh Michael; 4, Tagg Barclay; 5, Turner William H Jr; 6, McGaughey III Claude R; 7, Frankel Robert; 8, Clement Christophe; 9, Toner James J

FOURTEENTH RACE
Ky Downs
SEPTEMBER 25, 2004

1½ MILES. (Turf) (2.27^{3}) 7TH RUNNING OF THE KENTUCKY TURF CUP HANDICAP. Grade III. Purse $200,000 FOR THREE YEAR OLDS AND UPWARD. By subscription of $200, $1,000 to enter and an additional $1,000 to start. $200,000 Guaranteed of which all monies to be divided $124,000 to the owner of the winner, $40,000 to second, $20,000 to third, $10,000 to fourth and $6,000 to fifth. Weights to be announced Sunday, September 19, 2004. Starters and riders must be named through the entry box by the usual time of closing. Nominations closed Wednesday, September 15, 2004 with 18 nominations. (Rail at 27 feet).

Value of Race: $200,000 Winner $124,000; second $40,000; third $20,000; fourth $10,000; fifth $6,000. Mutuel Pool $174,803.00 Exacta Pool $100,951.00 Superfecta Pool $29,801.00 Trifecta Pool $83,643.00

Last Raced	Horse	M/Eqt.	A.	Wt	PP	¼	½	1	1¼	Str	Fin	Jockey	Odds $1
14Aug04 ^{9}AP^{11}	Sabiango-Ger	L	6	119	4	1^{3}	1^{3½}	1^{1}	1^{1}	1^{2}	1^{3}	Blanc B	1.30
14Aug04 ^{8}Sar^{4}	Rochester	L	8	117	5	3½	3^{1}	2^{hd}	3^{hd}	2^{hd}	2½	Day P	2.20
4Sep04 ^{7}AP^{6}	Gottabeachboy	L bf	4	115	2	4^{1½}	5^{hd}	6	5	4^{1}	3^{nk}	Graham J	57.30
6Sep04 ^{10}EIP^{8}	Gorylla-Brz	L	7	114	1	2^{1½}	2^{1½}	4^{1½}	4^{1}	3^{hd}	4^{6¼}	Bejarano R	4.00
6Sep04 ^{10}Cby^{1}	Dontbothrknocking	L b	6	114	6	6	4½	3^{1}	2^{1½}	5	5	Guidry M	14.80
4Sep04 ^{7}AP^{2}	Sharbayan-Ire	L bf	6	115	3	5^{hd}	6	5½	—	—	—	Albarado R J	3.80

OFF AT 5:02 Start Good . Won driving. Course firm.

TIME :53^{4}, 1:22^{3}, 1:44^{3}, 2:10^{2}, 2:33^{3} (:53.99, 1:22.77, 1:44.63, 2:10.44, 2:33.70)

$2 Mutuel Prices:				
	5 – SABIANGO–GER	4.60	3.20	2.60
	6 – ROCHESTER		2.60	2.20
	2 – GOTTABEACHBOY			4.80

$2 EXACTA 5–6 PAID $9.20 $2 SUPERFECTA 5–6–2–1 PAID $294.20
$2 TRIFECTA 5–6–2 PAID $97.60

Ch. h, (Apr), by Acatenango-Ger – Spirit of Eagles , by Beau's Eagle . Trainer Yakteen Tim. Bred by Stiftung Gestut Fahrhof (Ger).

SABIANGO (GER) gained a clear lead early while allowed to establish modest fractions, went along under careful handling, briefly surrendered the advantage to GORYLLA (BRZ) soon after going six furlongs, regained the top position when called upon, reopened a clear lead and prevailed under hand urging. ROCHESTER, always well placed while four or five wide, loomed a solid threat from between horses in the final furlong but couldn't offer the needed response. GOTTABEACHBOY settled in behind horses early, was never far back, swung out six wide for the drive and offered a mild gain. GORYLLA (BRZ), close up inside from the outset, moved boldly to take over just after going six furlongs, lost the advantage back to the winner entering the far turn, remained close up into the final furlong and came up empty. DONTBOTHERKNOCKING followed the leaders four or five wide, was just off the winner entering the stretch and flattened out when the test came. SHARBAYAN (IRE), within easy striking distance while racing in behind the leaders three or four wide, appeared to take a bad step approaching the final quarter, bore out entering the stretch and was pulled up soon after appearing lame in his right front. ALL RACES AT KENTUCKY DOWNS ARE HAND TIMED BY THE ASSOCIATION.

Owners– 1, Roberts Monty; 2, Augustin Stable; 3, Hackworth Robert S Jr; 4, Stud Colorado; 5, Jedlicki Frank F; 6, Iron County Farms Inc and Miller Trust

Trainers– 1, Yakteen Tim; 2, Sheppard Jonathan E; 3, Hackworth Robert S; 4, McPeek Kenneth G; 5, Rhone Bernell B; 6, Kirby Frank J

Scratched– Art Variety (BRZ) (04Sep04 ^{7}AP ^{5}) , Quest Star (01Sep04 ^{7}Sar^{4})

$2 Pick Three (3–6–5) Paid $166.40 ; Pick Three Pool $16,439 .

TENTH RACE
La. Downs
SEPTEMBER 25, 2004

1⅛ MILES. (1.48) 25TH RUNNING OF THE SUPER DERBY. Grade II. Purse $500,000 FOR THREE YEAR OLDS. Weights: Colts and Geldings –124 lbs.; Fillies – 121 lbs. $500,000 Guaranteed of which $300,000 to the winner, $100,000 to second, $50,000 to the third, $25,000 to fourth, $15,000 to fifth, and $10,000 to sixth. Starters to be namedthrough the entry box on Wednesday, September 22.

Value of Race: $500,000 Winner $300,000; second $100,000; third $50,000; fourth $25,000; fifth $15,000; sixth $10,000. Mutuel Pool $598,986.00 Exacta Pool $389,652.00 Quinella Pool $26,868.00 Trifecta Pool $355,470.00 Superfecta Pool $120,738.00

Last Raced	Horse	M/Eqt.	A.	Wt	PP	St	¼	½	¾	Str	Fin	Jockey	Odds $1
28Aug04 ^{10}LaD^{2}	Fantasticat	L b	3	124	5	6	$7^{3\frac{1}{2}}$	7^{2}	$6^{1\frac{1}{2}}$	1^{hd}	$1^{\frac{1}{2}}$	Melancon G	14.70
3Sep04 ^{6}Dmr^{2}	Borrego	L	3	124	6	3	$3^{1\frac{1}{2}}$	$3^{\frac{1}{2}}$	$3^{1\frac{1}{2}}$	$3^{3\frac{1}{2}}$	$2^{1\frac{1}{4}}$	Baze T C	2.40
28Aug04 ^{10}LaD^{3}	Britt's Jules	L	3	124	2	2	2^{4}	$2^{5\frac{1}{2}}$	$1^{1\frac{1}{2}}$	2^{hd}	3^{4}	Smith G S	6.90
15May04 ^{12}Pim^{5}	Imperialism	L b	3	124	7	9	$8^{1\frac{1}{2}}$	9	7^{hd}	$5^{\frac{1}{2}}$	4no	Desormeaux K J	2.00
7Aug04 ^{6}Crc^{1}	Caballero Negro	L f	3	124	9	4	$5^{2\frac{1}{2}}$	5^{hd}	4^{hd}	4^{hd}	$5^{1\frac{1}{4}}$	Lanerie C J	14.30
17Jly04 ^{9}AP^{1}	Cryptograph	L	3	124	1	8	9	8^{hd}	8^{hd}	$6^{2\frac{1}{2}}$	$6^{5\frac{3}{4}}$	Pettinger D R	4.30
28Aug04 ^{10}LaD^{4}	Xirius	L	3	124	4	5	$4^{\frac{1}{2}}$	4^{2}	5^{1}	8^{15}	7^{nk}	Jara F	22.30
28Aug04 ^{10}LaD^{6}	Mr. Jester	L	3	124	8	7	6^{hd}	$6^{2\frac{1}{2}}$	9	7^{1}	$8^{17\frac{1}{4}}$	Meche L J	29.10
28Aug04 ^{10}LaD^{1}	South Africa	L b	3	124	3	1	1^{hd}	$1^{\frac{1}{2}}$	2^{5}	9	9	Jacinto J	12.70

OFF AT 5:09 Start Good. Won driving. Track muddy.

TIME :23, :47^{1}, 1:12, 1:38, 1:51^{2} (:23.06, :47.39, 1:12.02, 1:38.01, 1:51.40)

$2 Mutuel Prices:			
5 – FANTASTICAT	31.40	12.20	7.40
6 – BORREGO		4.40	4.00
2 – BRITT'S JULES			5.40

$2 EXACTA 5–6 PAID $121.60 $2 QUINELLA 5–6 PAID $44.60
$2 TRIFECTA 5–6–2 PAID $985.40 $2 SUPERFECTA 5–6–2–7 PAID $3,696.00

D. o, (Mar), by Storm Cat – Lotta Dancing, by Alydar. Trainer Barnett Bobby C. Bred by Pacelco SA & Chelston Ireland Ltd (Ky).

FANTASTICAT unhurried early, advanced quickly toward the fore in the two path late in the second turn, angled out just a bit to engage the leader entering the stretch, eventually put that foe away inside the furlong grounds, enough left to hold the runner up safe in the waning strides. BORREGO allowed the speed to go early, began to move closer on the outside midway on the second turn, reached a striking position entering the stretch, slowly gaining on the winner in the late going. BRITT'S JULES set or forced the pace along the inside, shook off the other speed turning for home, gave ground grudgingly to the top two. IMPERIALISM off a bit slow, raced back and to the inside, moved out and around a tiring foe along the rail late in the second turn, roused soon after, lacked the necessary response after moving back to the inside and finished evenly. CABALLERO NEGRO settled off the pace and the inside, asked for some run three wide into the stretch, lacked a response. CRYPTOGRAPH void of early foot, came five wide into the stretch, also failed to produce a late kick. XIRIUS raced in the second flight inside, weakened. MR. JESTER four wide into the stretch when well off the pace, no rally. SOUTH AFRICA dueled off the inside, gave way suddenly with a quarter to run, stopped in the drive.

Owners– 1, R Bar S Thoroughbreds LLP; 2, Kelly Jon Scott Brad Ralls and Foster LLC et al; 3, Southern Equine Stable LLC; 4, Taub Steve; 5, Veranda Farm Inc Alfonso Andrade; 6, Pin Oak Stable LLC; 7, Carbonel Celestino; 8, Biggs Kaaren J; 9, Gary and Mary West Stables Inc

Trainers– 1, Barnett Bobby C; 2, Greely C Beau; 3, Guillot Eric; 4, Mulhall Kristin; 5, Morales Mario; 6, Von Hemel Donnie K; 7, Keen Dallas E; 8, Wren Steve; 9, Norman Cole

$2 Pick Three (7–1–5) Paid $4,966.20; Pick Three Pool $26,487.

NINTH RACE
Pimlico
SEPTEMBER 25, 2004

1$\frac{1}{16}$ MILES. (Turf) (1.40^{1}) 23RD RUNNING OF THE MARTHA WASHINGTON BREEDERS' CUP. Grade III. Purse $150,000 (includes $50,000 BC – Breeders' Cup) FOR FILLIES, THREE–YEARS–OLD. (Rail at 15 feet).

Value of Race: $148,500 Winner $90,000; second $30,000; third $16,500; fourth $9,000; fifth $3,000. Mutuel Pool $67,187.00 Exacta Pool $60,527.00 Superfecta Pool $10,723.00 Trifecta Pool $43,791.00

Last Raced	Horse	M/Eqt.	A.	Wt	PP	St	¼	½	¾	Str	Fin	Jockey	Odds $1
3Jly04 ^{6}Hol^{10}	Western Ransom	L	3	122	6	5	8^{2}	8^{2}	8^{2}	$4^{\frac{1}{2}}$	1^{hd}	Fogelsonger R	2.10
4Aug04 ^{6}Sar^{1}	Plenty	L	3	115	3	12	12	$1^{1\frac{1}{2}}$	$1^{3\frac{1}{2}}$	1^{4}	2^{nk}	Castellano A Jr	2.40
15Sep04 ^{8}Del^{1}	With Affection	L b	3	115	5	2	4^{hd}	$5^{2\frac{1}{2}}$	3^{1}	$2^{\frac{1}{2}}$	$3^{3\frac{3}{4}}$	Monterrey R	29.80
12Sep04 ^{8}Pim^{1}	Academic Queen	L b	3	115	2	10	$7^{\frac{1}{2}}$	7^{1}	$7^{2\frac{1}{2}}$	$3^{\frac{1}{2}}$	$4^{1\frac{1}{4}}$	Hamilton S D	16.40
3Aug04 DEA^{8}	Bay Tree-Ire	L	3	115	12	9	12	12	11^{2}	9^{3}	5^{nk}	Dunkelberger T L	11.60
29Jun04 ^{6}Cnl^{1}	Humoristic	L b	3	115	7	1	5^{2}	$4^{\frac{1}{2}}$	$6^{\frac{1}{2}}$	$7^{1\frac{1}{2}}$	6no	Garcia Luis	46.00
12Sep04 ^{9}Mth^{5}	Art Fan	L	3	122	8	4	$6^{1\frac{1}{2}}$	$6^{2\frac{1}{2}}$	5^{hd}	6^{2}	7^{nk}	Potts C L	6.20
26Jly04 ^{8}Del^{1}	Saree-GB	L	3	115	4	3	2^{hd}	$2^{\frac{1}{2}}$	2^{1}	5^{hd}	$8^{1\frac{3}{4}}$	Arroyo N Jr	13.90
3Sep04 ^{7}Mth^{1}	Diavla	L b	3	115	11	8	10^{2}	10^{2}	9^{2}	8^{3}	$9^{6\frac{1}{4}}$	Camacho E	76.40
6Sep04 ^{9}Pha^{6}	Perilous Night	L	3	115	1	11	$11^{\frac{1}{2}}$	11^{hd}	12	$11^{1\frac{1}{2}}$	$10^{\frac{1}{2}}$	Santana J Z	6.90
11Sep04 ^{8}Pim^{3}	Richetta	L	3	122	10	6	$3^{1\frac{1}{2}}$	3^{2}	4^{hd}	10^{2}	$11^{2\frac{1}{4}}$	Goodwin N	14.20
15Aug04 ^{7}Del^{1}	Pour It On	L	3	115	9	7	9^{hd}	$9^{\frac{1}{2}}$	10^{1}	12	12	Karamanos H A	64.70

OFF AT 4:57 Start Good. Won driving. Course firm.

TIME :23^{3}, :47^{2}, 1:11^{2}, 1:36^{4}, 1:43^{1} (:23.67, :47.56, 1:11.55, 1:36.85, 1:43.26)

$2 Mutuel Prices:			
8 – WESTERN RANSOM	6.20	3.40	2.60
3 – PLENTY		3.20	3.00
6 – WITH AFFECTION			6.80

$2 EXACTA 8–3 PAID $17.80 $1 SUPERFECTA 8–3–6–2 PAID $995.20
$2 TRIFECTA 8–3–6 PAID $216.00

Dk. b or br. f, (Feb), by Red Ransom – Western Wind, by Gone West. Trainer Dickinson Michael W. Bred by Dr John A Chandler (Ky).

WESTERN RANSOM lacked speed, raced six wide turning for home, closed and was along in time. PLENTY broke a step slowly, set the pace along the rail, was asked to open up on the far turn and tired in the drive. WITH AFFECTION saved ground, eased out for the drive and finished willingly between the top pair. ACADEMIC QUEEN worked between horses on the far turn, raced in the three path in upper stretch and failed to sustain her bid. BAY TREE (IRE) broke slowly, raced very wide and passed tired ones. HUMORISTIC raced well off the rail and weakened. ART FAN raced wide entering the stretch and came up empty. SAREE (GB) chased the pace two wide and gave way. DIAVLA, no factor, raced along the rail in the stretch. PERILOUS NIGHT was checked in tight quarters along the rail entering the first turn. RICHETTA, fanned very wide entering the stretch, gave way. POUR IT ON was outrun.

Owners– 1, Chandler Dr John A; 2, Claiborne Farm; 3, Bailey Morris; 4, Wirth Eric J; 5, Prince Faisal Salman; 6, Peralta-Ramos Jaqueline; 7, Backer William M; 8, Mack Earle I; 9, Devil Eleven Stable and Perri Tom; 10, Fitzhugh LLC; 11, Higgins and Bowman; 12, Hickory Plains

Trainers– 1, Dickinson Michael W; 2, Young Steven W; 3, Gaudet Edmond D; 4, Cartwright Ronald; 5, Motion H Graham; 6, Smith Hamilton A; 7, Smith Hamilton A; 8, McLaughlin Kiaran P; 9, Dowd John F; 10, Small Richard W; 11, Graham Robin L; 12, Smith Hamilton A

Scratched– Leopard Hunt (01Sep04 ^{8}Del^{1}), From Away (06Sep04 ^{7}Del^{1}), Many Many Bows (13Sep04 ^{7}Del^{2})

NINTH RACE Belmont SEPTEMBER 26, 2004

1⅛ MILES. (Inner Turf) (1.45^{2}) 55TH RUNNING OF THE JAMAICA HANDICAP. Grade II. Purse $200,000 (Up To $34,000 NYSBFOA) INNER TURF A HANDICAP FOR THREE YEAR OLDS. By subscription of $200 each, which should accompany the nomination; $1,000 to pass the entry box and $1,000 to start. The purse to be divided 60% to the winner, 20% to second, 10% to third, 5% to fourth, 3% to fifth and 2% divided equally among remaining finishers. A trophy will be presented to the winning owner. The New York Racing Association reserves the right to transfer this race to the Main Track. In the event that this race is taken off the turf, it may be subject to downgrading upon review by the Graded Stakes Committee. Closed Saturday, September 11, 2004 with 26 Nominations. (Rail at 9 feet).

Value of Race: $200,000 Winner $120,000; second $40,000; third $20,000; fourth $10,000; fifth $6,000; sixth $4,000. Mutuel Pool $580,586.00 Exacta Pool $270,499.00 Trifecta Pool $227,606.00

Last Raced	Horse	M/Eqt.	A.	Wt	PP	St	¼	½	¾	Str	Fin	Jockey	Odds $1
9Aug04 8Sar1	Artie Schiller	L	3	123	2	2	$2\frac{1}{2}$	$2\frac{1}{2}$	$2\frac{1}{2}$	$1^{4\frac{1}{2}}$	$1^{5\frac{1}{4}}$	Migliore R	0.30
2Sep04 8Sar1	Rousing Victory	L b	3	113	3	1	5^{2}	5^{hd}	5^{6}	4^{hd}	$2^{1\frac{1}{4}}$	Velasquez C	30.75
9Aug04 8Sar5	Icy Atlantic	L	3	120	4	4	$1^{1\frac{1}{2}}$	$1^{1\frac{1}{2}}$	$1\frac{1}{2}$	2^{2}	3^{hd}	Velazquez J R	7.10
27Jun04 7Bel3	Dealer Choice-FR	L	3	117	6	6	3^{hd}	3^{hd}	$3\frac{1}{2}$	3^{hd}	4^{1}	Castellano J J	5.60
28Aug04 6Sar2	Kennel Up		3	114	1	3	$4^{1\frac{1}{2}}$	4^{3}	$4\frac{1}{2}$	5^{10}	$5^{7\frac{3}{4}}$	Santos J A	13.70
1Aug04 5Sar1	Reggie for Three	L b	3	114	5	5	6	6	6	6	6	Prado E S	19.60

OFF AT 5:12 Start Good. Won driving. Course firm.

TIME :24^{3}, :48, 1:11^{3}, 1:34, 1:45^{2} (:24.60, :48.15, 1:11.71, 1:34.09, 1:45.50)

(New Course Record)

$2 Mutuel Prices:

2 – ARTIE SCHILLER	2.60	2.30	2.10
3 – ROUSING VICTORY		8.40	2.10
4 – ICY ATLANTIC			2.10

$2 EXACTA 2–3 PAID $26.00 $2 TRIFECTA 2–3–4 PAID $82.50

B. c, (Apr), by El Prado-Ire – Hidden Light, by Majestic Light. Trainer Jerkens James A. Bred by Haras Du Mezeray SA (Ky).

ARTIE SCHILLER came away in good order, raced with the pace from the outside while well in hand, advanced outside on the second turn, took over with a rush when asked, drew away and was under a vigorous hand ride to finish in course record time. ROUSING VICTORY raced in hand along the inside, saved ground, split rivals leaving the eighth pole and finished gamely. ICY ATLANTIC quickly showed in front, set the pace along the inside, proved no match for the winner turning for home and weakened inside in the final furlong. DEALER CHOICE (FR) raced close up outside while in hand, was three wide on both turns and had no response when roused. KENNEL UP was rated along early, raced inside and had no response when roused. REGGIE FOR THREE dropped back early, raced inside and had no rally.

Owners– 1, Timber Bay Farm and Walsh Mrs Thomas J; 2, Hilly Fields Stable and Moran Thomas; 3, Appleton Arthur I; 4, Amerman Racing Stables LLC; 5, Shields Joseph V Jr; 6, Martin Edmund W Jr

Trainers– 1, Jerkens James A; 2, Serpe Philip M; 3, Pletcher Todd A; 4, Frankel Robert; 5, Jerkens H Allen; 6, Bond Harold James

---

SEVENTH RACE Santa Anita SEPTEMBER 29, 2004

ABOUT 6½ FURLONGS. (Turf) (1.11) 36TH RUNNING OF THE SENATOR KEN MADDY HANDICAP. Grade III. Purse $100,000 DOWNHILL TURF FOR FILLIES AND MARES, THREE YEARS OLD AND UPWARD. By subscription of $100 each if made on or before Thursday, September 23 or by supplementary nomination of $2,000 by 10 AM Satuday, September 25. All horses to pay $1,000 to start with $100,000 guaranteed of which $60,000 to the winner, $20,000 to second, $12,000 to third, $6,000 to fourth and $2,000 to fifth. Weights: Saturday, September 25. Starters to be named through the entry box by the closing time of entries. A trophy will be presented to the owner of the winner. Closed Thursday, September 23 with 16 nominations.

Value of Race: $100,000 Winner $60,000; second $20,000; third $12,000; fourth $6,000; fifth $2,000. Mutuel Pool $329,023.00 Exacta Pool $184,543.00 Quinella Pool $16,351.00 Trifecta Pool $169,583.00 Superfecta Pool $71,856.00

Last Raced	Horse	M/Eqt.	A.	Wt	PP	St	¼	½	Str	Fin	Jockey	Odds $1
26Aug04 7Dmr1	Belleski	LB	5	118	2	4	$2^{2\frac{1}{2}}$	$2^{2\frac{1}{2}}$	1^{hd}	$1\frac{1}{2}$	Nakatani C S	1.60
31Jly04 7Sar5	Intercontinentl-GB	LB	4	120	9	2	6^{1}	3^{hd}	$2^{1\frac{1}{2}}$	2^{2}	Flores D R	1.80
27Dec03 7SA5	Acago	LB	4	116	1	9	9	7^{hd}	$7^{1\frac{1}{2}}$	3no	Espinoza V	a- 2.20
30Aug04 7Dmr1	Navaja-NZ	LB b	4	115	3	8	7^{hd}	$8^{1\frac{1}{2}}$	5^{hd}	4^{2}	Douglas R R	47.50
26Aug04 7Dmr3	Fencelineneighbor	LB b	4	116	7	3	4^{1}	6^{1}	6^{hd}	$5\frac{1}{2}$	Valdivia J Jr	19.40
22Jan04 8Ohi8	Festival-Jpn	LB b	5	114	4	5	5^{hd}	9	9	6no	Sorenson D	73.20
8Sep04 1Dmr1	Lady Sabrina	LB	4	114	8	1	$1^{1\frac{1}{2}}$	$1^{1\frac{1}{2}}$	3^{2}	7^{1}	Smith M E	12.30
10Jly04 5Hol5	Stormica	LB	4	114	5	6	3^{hd}	$4^{1\frac{1}{2}}$	4^{hd}	8^{2}	Court J K	a- 2.20
4Apr04 8SA4	Polygreen-FR	LB	5	116	6	7	8^{3}	5^{hd}	8^{hd}	9	Stevens G L	a- 2.20

a–Coupled: Acago and Stormica and Polygreen–Fr.

OFF AT 4:11 Start Good. Won driving. Course firm.

TIME :22^{2}, :44^{2}, 1:06^{4}, 1:12^{4} (:22.54, :44.46, 1:06.99, 1:12.86)

$2 Mutuel Prices:

2 – BELLESKI	5.20	2.40	2.10
8 – INTERCONTINENTAL–GB		2.60	2.20
1 – ACAGO(a–entry)			2.20

$1 EXACTA 2–8 PAID $6.70 $2 QUINELLA 2–8 PAID $6.40

$1 TRIFECTA 2–8–1 PAID $13.80 $1 SUPERFECTA 2–8–1–3 PAID $51.10

B. m, (Feb), by Polish Numbers – Rangoon Belle, by Alysheba. Trainer Sadler John W. Bred by David Garvin David Camball Garvin Gabriel Duignan & Willard Raymer (Ky).

BELLESKI cut the corner at the right hand curve then angled in and stalked inside, came out leaving the hill, bid three deep into the stretch and outside the runner-up through the final furlong and gamely prevailed under a tap of the whip and good handling. INTERCONTINENTAL (GB) stalked outside then alongside a rival on the hill, cut to the inside crossing the dirt, bid along the rail and continued gamely to the wire. ACAGO off a bit slowly, settled just off the inside, swung four wide into the stretch and rallied late for third. NAVAJA (NZ) chased a bit off the rail then angled in on the hill, bid inside in the stretch and was edged for the show. FENCELINENEIGHBOR pulled her way between horses then chased a bit off the rail, came out some into the stretch and lacked the necessary late kick. FESTIVAL (JPN) also pulled early, angled in and saved ground stalking the pace, dropped back leaving the hill, came out into the stretch and was outfinished. LADY SABRINA sped to the early lead, set the pace a bit off the rail, was between foes into the stretch and weakened. STORMICA chased between horses then inside on the hill and also weakened. POLYGREEN (FR) allowed to settle three deep early, moved up outside leaving the hill but weakened in the stretch. Rail on hill at zero.

Owners– 1, Moss Mr and Mrs Jerome S; 2, Juddmonte Farms Inc; 3, Wertheimer and Frere; 4, Cooperstone Martin Doll Ford et al; 5, Amerman Racing Stables LLC; 6, Grand Farm; 7, Roncelli Family Trust or Barron or Bassett; 8, Wertheimer and Frere; 9, Wertheimer and Frere

Trainers– 1, Sadler John W; 2, Frankel Robert; 3, Mandella Richard; 4, Stein Roger M; 5, Machowsky Michael; 6, Gallagher Patrick; 7, Knapp Steve; 8, Mandella Gary; 9, Mandella Richard

Scratched– Bonaire (GB) (22Aug04 4Dmr3)

$2 Daily Double (6–2) Paid $13.00 ; Daily Double Pool $26,654 .

$1 Pick Three (12–6–2/6) Paid $29.20 ; Pick Three Pool $67,694 .

NINTH RACE
Hoosier Park
OCTOBER 1, 2004

$1\frac{1}{16}$ MILES. (1.41) 10TH RUNNING OF THE INDIANA BREEDERS' CUP OAKS. Grade III. Purse $400,000 (includes $50,000 BC – Breeders' Cup) FOR FILLIES, THREE YEARS OLD.

Value of Race: $406,300 Winner $243,780; second $81,260; third $44,693; fourth $24,378; fifth $12,189. Mutuel Pool $73,327.00 Exacta Pool $45,225.00 Trifecta Pool $52,783.00 Superfecta Pool $16,827.00

Last Raced	Horse	M/Eqt.	A.	Wt	PP	St	¼	½	¾	Str	Fin	Jockey	Odds $1
11Sep04 ^{8}Bel^{2}	Daydreaming	LB	3	118	6	3	4^{1}	$4\frac{1}{2}$	4^{3}	$2\frac{1}{2}$	$1^{1\frac{1}{2}}$	Velazquez J R	2.60
15Aug04 ^{10}Mth^{1}	Capeside Lady	LB	3	121	3	1	1^{hd}	1^{1}	$1\frac{1}{2}$	1^{hd}	2^{hd}	Decarlo C P	2.20
11Sep04 ^{8}Bel^{1}	Stellar Jayne	LB b	3	121	5	5	$3^{1\frac{1}{2}}$	$3^{1\frac{1}{2}}$	3^{2}	3^{4}	$3^{5\frac{1}{2}}$	Albarado R J	1.00
27Aug04 ^{9}Crc^{1}	Adobe Gold	LB	3	116	1	2	$5\frac{1}{2}$	$5^{1\frac{1}{2}}$	5^{7}	5^{12}	$4^{3\frac{1}{4}}$	Castro E	9.80
8Sep04 ^{8}AP^{1}	Storm's Darling	LB	3	116	7	4	$2^{1\frac{1}{2}}$	$2\frac{1}{2}$	2^{hd}	$4\frac{1}{2}$	5^{13}	Zimmerman R	22.00
17Sep04 ^{8}GLD^{2}	Lunes Grito	LB	3	117	4	6	6^{1}	6^{1}	6^{4}	6^{10}	$6^{27\frac{3}{4}}$	Delgado J H	122.70
4Sep04 ^{8}EIP^{2}	Slewpy's Storm	LB f	3	114	2	7	7	7	7	7	7	Byrne J	85.70

OFF AT 9:46 Start Good . Won driving. Track fast.

TIME :23^{2}, :48, 1:12, 1:37, 1:43^{3} (:23.52, :48.03, 1:12.18, 1:37.05, 1:43.65)

$2 Mutuel Prices:			
7 – DAYDREAMING	7.20	5.20	2.10
4 – CAPESIDE LADY		4.20	2.10
6 – STELLAR JAYNE			2.10

$2 EXACTA 7–4 PAID $28.80 $2 TRIFECTA 7–4–6 PAID $44.20
$2 SUPERFECTA 7–4–6–1 PAID $92.00

B. f, (Mar), by A.P. Indy – Get Lucky , by Mr. Prospector . Trainer McGaughey III Claude R. Bred by Ogden Mills Phipps (Ky).

DAYDREAMING settled outside off the early pace, made a strong move to contention through the far turn nearing the stretch to challenge, came in a bit through midstretch, continued on willingly and moved clear under steady handling. CAPESIDE LADY was on the pace inside STORM'S DARLING to edge clear heading up the backstretch, was again challenged by that one through the far turn, dug in through the lane and came out a bit midstretch as the winner loomed then could not match strides in the late going. STELLAR JAYNE stalked the pace from three wide while never far back, moved to challenge three abreast nearing the stretch, was caught in a little tight through midstretch from between the top pair and altered course outward then could not produce the needed late surge. ADOBE GOLD settled along the inside and lacked a final closing response. STORM'S DARLING pressed the pace outside CAPESIDE LADY to upper stretch and had little left for the final furlong. LUNES GRITO saved ground in the reach of the pace to the far turn and tired. SLEWPY'S STORM broke in a tangle and trailed throughout to give way in the late going. The stewards conducted an inquiry into the stretch run concerning the top three finishers but found no action to be necessary.

Owners– 1, Phipps Ogden M; 2, So Madcapt Stable Michael Cascio; 3, Spendthrift Farm LLCBKline C Kidder N Cole and N Strong; 4, Villareal Leo Jr; 5, Vogel Arthur; 6, Gilmore Gene and Phyllis; 7, Oak Haven Farm

Trainers– 1, McGaughey III Claude R; 2, Pletcher Todd A; 3, Lukas D Wayne; 4, Wolfson Martin D; 5, Barnett Bobby C; 6, Bennett Gerald S; 7, Frederick Edward

Scratched– Family Business (25Aug04 ^{5}Sar^{2}) , Lenatareese (31Jul04 ^{9}EIP^{1})

$2 Pick Three (4–10–7) Paid $29.80 ; Pick Three Pool $5,357 .

SEVENTH RACE
Meadowlands
OCTOBER 1, 2004

1⅛ MILES. (1.45^{2}) 23RD RUNNING OF THE PEGASUS HANDICAP. Grade III. Purse $300,000 FOR THREE–YEAR–OLDS. By subscription of $200 each, which should accompany the nomination, $1,500 to pass the entry box and an additional $1,500 to start. Weight: 122 lbs. Non–winners of $45,000 twice at a mile or over in 2004 allowed 2 lbs.; $60,000 at a mile or over in 2004, 4 lbs. The winning owner and trainer to receive a trophy. Closed Sunday, September 19, 2004 with 24 nominations.

Value of Race: $300,000 Winner $180,000; second $60,000; third $33,000; fourth $18,000; fifth $9,000. Mutuel Pool $193,920.00 Exacta Pool $138,645.00 Trifecta Pool $93,904.00 Superfecta Pool $22,678.00

Last Raced	Horse	M/Eqt.	A.	Wt	PP	St	¼	½	¾	Str	Fin	Jockey	Odds $1
6Sep04 ^{10}Pha^{5}	Pies Prospect	L	3	118	8	5	4^{hd}	3^{hd}	$3\frac{1}{2}$	1^{hd}	1^{nk}	Prado E S	4.90
28Aug04 ^{11}Sar^{3}	Eddington	L b	3	118	4	8	8	8	5^{hd}	2^{1}	$2^{3\frac{1}{2}}$	Migliore R	1.10
30Aug04 ^{7}Sar^{1}	Zakocity	L b	3	118	1	1	3^{1}	$4\frac{1}{2}$	1^{hd}	$3^{2\frac{1}{2}}$	3^{hd}	Castellano J J	6.20
30Aug04 ^{3}Sar^{1}	Navesink River	L	3	118	3	2	7^{1}	7^{hd}	4^{hd}	4^{hd}	4^{nk}	Dominguez R A	5.40
19Sep04 ^{6}Bel^{4}	Golden Look	L	3	118	5	7	$5^{1\frac{1}{2}}$	$5\frac{1}{2}$	6^{1}	5^{3}	5^{6}	Bravo J	20.00
6Sep04 ^{10}Pha^{3}	Swingforthefences	L	3	120	7	6	6^{hd}	6^{1}	7^{5}	6^{2}	6^{4}	Bridgmohan S X	5.90
5Sep04 ^{3}Sar^{2}	Tales of Glory	L	3	118	6	4	1^{1}	1^{hd}	$2\frac{1}{2}$	7^{15}	$7^{18\frac{3}{4}}$	Coa E M	17.50
1Sep04 ^{5}Mth^{1}	Rat Like Cunning	L b	3	118	2	3	$2\frac{1}{2}$	$2\frac{1}{2}$	8	8	8	Elliott S	30.30

OFF AT 9:56 Start Good . Won driving. Track fast.

TIME :23^{2}, :46^{4}, 1:10^{3}, 1:35^{3}, 1:48^{2} (:23.46, :46.84, 1:10.63, 1:35.63, 1:48.57)

$2 Mutuel Prices:			
10 – PIES PROSPECT	11.80	4.60	3.80
6 – EDDINGTON		3.00	3.00
1 – ZAKOCITY			4.40

$2 EXACTA 10–6 PAID $32.40 $2 TRIFECTA 10–6–1 PAID $144.20
$1 SUPERFECTA 10–6–1–4 PAID $296.30

Ch. c, (Apr), by Crafty Prospector – Hot Pillow , by Bates Motel . Trainer Zito Nicholas P. Bred by Gordon Wootton & Mary Lou Wootton (Ky).

PIES PROSPECT stalked three wide, bid between rivals on the far turn, was bumped in upper stretch then dug in gamely and prevailed. EDDINGTON settled into stride well off the pace, moved boldly four wide to challenge midway on the far turn, bumped PIES PROSPECT at the three sixteenths marker and was outfinished in the final furlong. ZAKOCITY was steadied midway on the clubhouse turn, raced close up inside, moved through on the rail to take over entering the far turn and weakened in the stretch. NAVESINK RIVER saved ground and lacked a rally. GOLDEN LOOK raced close up between rivals and failed to respond when asked. SWINGFORTHEFENCES raced off the pace never factored. TALES OF GLORY set the pace racing just off the rail and faded. RAT LIKE CUNNING pressed the pace and gave way.

Owners– 1, LaPenta Robert V; 2, Willmott Stables Inc; 3, Pompa Paul P Jr; 4, Char-Mari Stable; 5, Janney Stuart S III; 6, Klaravich Stables Inc; 7, Carliwood Farms and Herrell John; 8, Pretty Boys Stable 3

Trainers– 1, Zito Nicholas P; 2, Hennig Mark; 3, Reynolds Patrick L; 4, Pletcher Todd A; 5, McGaughey III Claude R; 6, Violette Richard A Jr; 7, Pletcher Todd A; 8, Bottazzi Patrick L

Scratched– Grancentral Pkwy. (15Sep04 ^{3}Bel^{3}) , Pollard's Vision (06Sep04 ^{57}Mth^{2})

$2 Pick Three (8–7–10) Paid $189.80 ; Pick Three Pool $12,781 .

SEVENTH RACE
Belmont
OCTOBER 2, 2004

1¼ MILES. (Inner Turf) (1.57^3) 27TH RUNNING OF THE FLOWER BOWL INVITATIONAL. Grade I. Purse $750,000 (UP TO $62,500 NYSBFOA) INNER TURF FOR FILLIES AND MARES THREE YEARS OLD AND UPWARD. By invitation only with no subscription fees. The purse to be divided 60% to the winner, 20% to second, 10% to third, 5% to fourth, 3% to fifth and 2% divided equally among remaining finishers. Three year olds, 119 lbs.; older, 123 lbs. Non-winners of a Grade 1 since April 1, 2004 allowed 3 lbs.; a Grade 1 since October 1, 2003, or a Grade 2 since April 1, 2004, 5 lbs. The New York Racing Association will select a field of (14) invitees by Saturday, September 18. A list of alternates will be published on Sunday, September 26.Trophies will be presented to the winning owner, trainer and jockey. The New York Racing Association reserves the right to transfer this race to the Main Track. In the event that this race is taken off the turf, it may be subject to downgrading upon review by the Graded Stakes Committee.

Value of Race: $750,000 Winner $450,000; second $150,000; third $75,000; fourth $37,500; fifth $22,500; sixth $5,000; seventh $5,000; eighth $5,000. Mutuel Pool $738,854.00 Exacta Pool $562,392.00 Trifecta Pool $395,753.00 Superfecta Pool $86,718.00

Last Raced	Horse	M/Eqt.	A.	Wt	PP	¼	½	¾	1	Str	Fin	Jockey	Odds $1
14Aug04 8AP2	Riskaverse	L	5	118	8	51	5½	5hd	5hd	4hd	1¾	Velasquez C	8.70
14Aug04 8AP9	Commercante-FR	L	4	118	5	4½	4½	4½	41½	2½	2hd	Velazquez J R	3.40
29Aug04 8Dmr3	Moscow Burning	L	4	120	3	11½	1½	11	11	1½	3nk	Valdivia J Jr	6.40
5Sep04 10Sar3	Film Maker	L b	4	120	2	8	8	7hd	710	724	4hd	Dominguez R A	12.30
14Aug04 8AP6	Aubonne-Ger		4	118	6	71½	6½	61½	61	61½	5½	Santos J A	15.60
31Jly04 7Sar1	Wonder Again	L	5	123	4	2hd	2½	2hd	2½	5hd	6nk	Prado E S	0.95
5Sep04 7Sar1	Humaita-Ger	L	4	118	1	3½	3hd	3hd	3hd	3½	735¼	Stevens G L	26.00
23Sep04 7Bel7	Indy Five Hundred	L	4	118	7	6hd	72½	8	8	8	8	Fragoso P	34.25

OFF AT 4:09 Start Good. Won driving. Course yielding.

TIME :25^2, :52^2, 1:17^4, 1:41^2, 2:04^3 (:25.45, :52.55, 1:17.85, 1:41.55, 2:04.65)

$2 Mutuel Prices:

9 – RISKAVERSE	19.40	7.10	4.60
6 – COMMERCANTE-FR		4.70	3.90
4 – MOSCOW BURNING			4.60

$2 EXACTA 9–6 PAID $73.50 $2 TRIFECTA 9–6–4 PAID $381.00
$2 SUPERFECTA 9–6–4–3 PAID $2,282.00

Dk. b or br. m, (Apr), by Dynaformer – The Bink, by Seeking the Gold. Trainer Kelly Patrick J. Bred by Fox Ridge Farm Inc (Ky).

RISKAVERSE came away well and was angled over to the inside after the start, raced between rivals while well in hand, came wide into the stretch, responded when set down, finished resolutely outside and was up late after a furious finish. COMMERCANTE (FR) raced close up outside while in hand, advanced three wide on the second turn and dug in gamely while between rivals in the stretch. MOSCOW BURNING was sent to the front from the start, set the pace along the inside while well in hand, drew clear entering the stretch and dug in gamely to the finish. FILM MAKER was outrun early, swung wide entering the stretch, responded when roused and finished gamely outside. AUBONNE (GER) was rated along inside, saved ground, angled out for the drive and finished gamely while in traffic in the stretch. WONDER AGAIN raced with the pace from the outside, advanced outside approaching the stretch and had no response when roused. HUMAITA (GER) raced close up inside, saved ground into the stretch and weakened on the rail late. INDY FIVE HUNDRED raced wide and tired.

Owners– 1, Fox Ridge Farm Inc; 2, Falourd Alain Guy Hubert and Trussell Robert; 3, Van Kempen Dallas Nentwig Michael; 4, Adam Donald A; 5, Tanaka Gary A; 6, Phillips Joan G and John W; 7, Jacobs Andreas; 8, Georgica Stable

Trainers– 1, Kelly Patrick J; 2, Frankel Robert; 3, Cassidy James; 4, Motion H Graham; 5, Libaud Eric; 6, Toner James J; 7, Motion H Graham; 8, Barbara Robert

Scratched– Super Brand (SAF) (11Aug04 8Sar3)

$2 Pick Three (9–5–9) Paid $460.00; Pick Three Pool $117,239.
$2 Daily Double (5–9) Paid $125.50; Daily Double Pool $133,708.

EIGHTH RACE
Belmont
OCTOBER 2, 2004

6 FURLONGS. (1.07^3) 65TH RUNNING OF THE VOSBURGH. Grade I. Purse $500,000 (UP TO $55,000 NYSBFOA) FOR THREE YEAR OLDS AND UPWARD. By subscription of $500 each, which should accompany the nomination; $2,500 to pass the entry box and $2,500 to start. The purse to be divided 60% to the winner, 20% to second, 10% to third, 5% to fourth, 3% to fifth and 2% divided equally among remaining finishers. Three year olds, 122 lbs.; older, 124 lbs. Trophies will be presented to the winning owner, trainer and jockey. Closed Saturday, September 18, 2004 with 19 Nominations. The National Pick 4 is a wager that includes the 8th race at Belmont as Leg A, the 9th race at Belmont as Leg B, the 4th race at Santa Anita as Leg C, and the 10th race at Belmont as Leg D.

Value of Race: $490,000 Winner $300,000; second $100,000; third $50,000; fourth $25,000; fifth $15,000. Mutuel Pool $786,915.00 Exacta Pool $514,775.00 Trifecta Pool $260,393.00

Last Raced	Horse	M/Eqt.	A.	Wt	PP	St	¼	½	Str	Fin	Jockey	Odds $1
15Aug04 8Dmr3	Pico Central-Brz	L	5	124	5	4	2½	1hd	1½	14	Espinoza V	2.20
3Sep04 8Sar8	Voodoo	L b	6	124	4	5	41½	42	42½	2½	Chavez J F	23.40
14Aug04 7Sar1	Speightstown	L	6	124	2	2	1½	2hd	2hd	3hd	Velazquez J R	0.80
27Mar04 11NAS4	Cajun Beat	L b	4	124	1	3	3hd	3hd	31½	43	Velasquez C	6.40
15Sep04 8Bel1	Watchem Smokey	L	4	124	3	1	5	5	5	5	Prado E S	6.50

OFF AT 4:41 Start Good. Won driving. Track fast.

TIME :22^3, :45^3, :57^1, 1:09^3 (:22.61, :45.62, :57.28, 1:09.74)

$2 Mutuel Prices:

6 – PICO CENTRAL-BRZ	6.40	5.00	2.10
4 – VOODOO		13.20	2.10
2 – SPEIGHTSTOWN			2.10

$2 EXACTA 6–4 PAID $97.50 $2 TRIFECTA 6–4–2 PAID $148.50

Dk. b or br. h, (Oct), by Spend a Buck – Sheila Purple, by Purple Mountain. Trainer Lobo Paulo H. Bred by Haras Fronteira PAP (Brz).

PICO CENTRAL (BRZ) raced with the pace while three wide between rivals, responded when roused in upper stretch and drew away late. VOODOO raced with the pace while four wide and finished gamely outside to earn the place award. SPEIGHTSTOWN bobbled at the start, argued the pace while between rivals and weakened in the final furlong. CAJUN BEAT raced with the pace along the inside and weakened on the rail in deep stretch. WATCHEM SMOKEY was outrun early, angled out in upper stretch and lacked a rally.

Owners– 1, Tanaka Gary A; 2, Moore Susan and John; 3, Melnyk Eugene and Laura; 4, Padua Stables Iracane Joseph A Iracane John; 5, Gann Edmund A

Trainers– 1, Lobo Paulo H; 2, Jerkens James A; 3, Pletcher Todd A; 4, Frankel Robert; 5, Frankel Robert

Scratched– Eavesdropper (04Sep04 8Sar9)

$2 Pick Three (5–9–6) Paid $574.00; Pick Three Pool $95,741.

NINTH RACE
Belmont
OCTOBER 2, 2004

1½ MILES. (Turf) (2.24^1) 28TH RUNNING OF THE JOE HIRSCH TURF CLASSIC INVITATIONAL. Grade I. Purse $750,000 WIDENER TURF. (UP TO $62,500 NYSBFOA) FOR THREE YEAR OLDS AND UPWARD. By invitation only with no subscription fees. The purse to be divided 60% to the winner, 20% to second, 10% to third, 5% to fourth, 3% to fifth and 2% divided equally among remaining finishers. Weight for age. Three year olds, 121 lbs.; older, 126 lbs. Fillies and Mares allowed 3 lbs. The New York Racing Association will select a field of (14) invitees by Saturday, September 18. A list of alternates will be published on Sunday, September 26. Trophies will be presented to the winning owner, trainer and jockey. The New York Racing Association reserves the right to transfer this race to the Main Track. In the event that this race is taken off the turf, it may be subject to downgrading upon review by the Graded Stakes Committee. (If the Stewards consider it in advisable to run this race on the turf course, this race will be run at One Mile and One Eighth on the main track.).

Value of Race: $750,000 Winner $450,000; second $150,000; third $75,000; fourth $37,500; fifth $22,500; sixth $7,500; seventh $7,500. Mutuel Pool $853,436.00 Exacta Pool $566,231.00 Trifecta Pool $433,443.00

Last Raced	Horse	M/Eqt.	A.	Wt	PP	¼	½	1	1¼	Str	Fin	Jockey	Odds $1
14Aug04 11AP1	Kitten's Joy	L	3	121	5	51½	4hd	41½	21½	1hd	12½	Velazquez J R	2.40
11Sep04 9Bel1	Magistretti	L b	4	126	4	31½	2½	21½	11½	22½	2¾	Prado E S	1.70
11Sep04 DON3	Tycoon-GB	L	3	121	6	61½	61½	62	3hd	33½	33	Spencer J P	9.20
11Sep04 9Bel5	Request for Parole	L	5	126	2	4hd	51½	5hd	620	4hd	42¼	Velasquez C	14.50
12Sep04 9LCH4	Polish Summer-GB		7	126	7	7	7	7	5hd	5hd	51½	Stevens G L	8.40
14Aug04 9AP1	Kicken Kris	L f	4	126	1	2hd	3½	3hd	42	624	632¼	Castellano J J	4.00
11Sep04 Ist2	Maktub-Ity	L	5	126	3	1½	11½	1hd	7	7	7	Chavez J F	23.40

OFF AT 5:14 Start Good. Won driving. Course yielding.

TIME :25, :50^4, 1:17^1, 1:42^3, 2:07^1, 2:29^4 (:25.19, :50.90, 1:17.25, 1:42.65, 2:07.31, 2:29.97)

$2 Mutuel Prices:				
	5 – KITTEN'S JOY	6.80	3.30	2.80
	4 – MAGISTRETTI		2.90	2.50
	6 – TYCOON-GB			4.00

$2 EXACTA 5–4 PAID $17.20 $2 TRIFECTA 5–4–6 PAID $106.00

Ch. c, (May), by El Prado–Ire – Kitten's First, by Lear Fan. Trainer Romans Dale. Bred by Kenneth L Ramsey & Sarah K Ramsey (Ky).

KITTEN'S JOY raced in hand early on, advanced outside on the second turn, responded readily when set down, ran by MAGISTRETTI leaving the eighth pole and drew clear. MAGISTRETTI raced close up outside while well in hand, ran to the front with a quick move entering the second turn, drew clear but proved no match for the winner while staying on gamely to hold the place. TYCOON (GB) came away sluggishly, was outrun early, advanced outside on the second turn, came three wide into the stretch and finished well outside. REQUEST FOR PAROLE was rated along inside, saved ground and lacked a rally. POLISH SUMMER (GB) was outrun early, moved up three wide approaching the stretch and had no response when roused. KICKEN KRIS raced close up along the inside and tired in the stretch. MAKTUB (ITY) quickly showed in front, set the pace along the inside and was finished after the opening mile.

Owners– 1, Ramsey Kenneth L and Sarah K; 2, Tabor Michael B; 3, Magnier Mrs John; 4, Knighton Jeri and Sam; 5, Juddmonte Farms Inc; 6, Brushwood Stable; 7, Tanaka Gary A

Trainers– 1, Romans Dale; 2, Biancone Patrick L; 3, O'Brien Aidan P; 4, Hough Stanley M; 5, Fabre Andre; 6, Matz Michael R; 7, Jarvis Michael A

TENTH RACE
Belmont
OCTOBER 2, 2004

1¼ MILES. (1.58^1) 86TH RUNNING OF THE JOCKEY CLUB GOLD CUP. Grade I. Purse $1,000,000 (UP TO $70,000 NYSBFOA) FOR THREE YEAR OLDS AND UPWARD. By subscription of $1,000 each, which should accompany the nomination; $5,000 to pass the entry box and $5,000 to start. The purse to be divided 60% to the winner, 20% to second, 10% to third, 5% tofourth, 3% to fifth and2% divided equally among remaining finishers. Weight for age. Three year olds, 122 lbs., older, 126 lbs.The New York Racing Association will present a Gold Cup to the winning owner and trophies to the winning trainer and jockey. Closed Saturday, September 18, 2004 with 26 Nominations.

Value of Race: $1,000,000 Winner $600,000; second $200,000; third $100,000; fourth $50,000; fifth $30,000; sixth $10,000; seventh $10,000. Mutuel Pool $1,010,306.00 Exacta Pool $554,918.00 Trifecta Pool $460,479.00

Last Raced	Horse	M/Eqt.	A.	Wt	PP	¼	½	¾	1	Str	Fin	Jockey	Odds $1
22Aug04 9Sar2	Funny Cide	L	4	126	7	2½	2hd	33½	3hd	2hd	1¾	Santos J A	2.80
11Sep04 10Bel5	Newfoundland	L bf	4	126	6	3½	3½	2hd	1½	1½	21	Prado E S	20.30
28Aug04 11Sar2	The Cliff's Edge	L	3	122	1	7	7	7	42½	33½	33¾	Stevens G L	3.50
22Aug04 9Sar1	Evening Attire	L b	6	126	4	6½	5hd	5hd	5½	4hd	44½	Velasquez C	3.50
11Sep04 10Bel3	Bowman's Band	L	6	126	5	5hd	62	6hd	6½	63½	55	Dominguez R A	14.90
6Sep04 10Pha1	Love of Money	L	3	122	2	1½	1½	1hd	21½	51½	61	Albarado R J	*2.80
5Sep04 8Dmr2	Domestic Dispute	L	4	126	3	41½	4½	4hd	7	7	7	Velazquez J R	10.30

***–Actual Betting Favorite.**

OFF AT 5:45 Start Good. Won driving. Track fast.

TIME :24, :47^3, 1:11^3, 1:36^2, 2:02^2 (:24.01, :47.65, 1:11.62, 1:36.44, 2:02.44)

$2 Mutuel Prices:				
	7 – FUNNY CIDE	7.60	4.80	2.50
	6 – NEWFOUNDLAND		11.60	5.50
	1 – THE CLIFF'S EDGE			2.90

$2 EXACTA 7–6 PAID $97.00 $2 TRIFECTA 7–6–1 PAID $356.00

Ch. g, (Apr), by Distorted Humor – Belle's Good Cide, by Slewacide. Trainer Tagg Barclay. Bred by Win Star Farm LLC (NY).

FUNNY CIDE raced with the pace from the outside while in hand, dropped back a bit on the second turn, came again when put to the task, dug in determinedly while between rivals in the stretch and wore down NEWFOUNDLAND after a hard drive. NEWFOUNDLAND raced close up outside while well in hand, advanced outside leaving the backstretch, showed in front on the second turn and dug in gamely while drifting out in the stretch. THE CLIFF'S EDGE was rated along inside, put in a four wide run on the second turn and weakened outside in the final furlong. EVENING ATTIRE was outrun early, raced between rivals and offered a mild rally along the inside. BOWMAN'S BAND was outrun early, raced three wide on both turns and had no response when roused. LOVE OF MONEY was sent up along the inside, contested the pace for the opening mile and tired in the stretch. DOMESTIC DISPUTE raced close up along the inside and tired after three quarters.

Owners– 1, Sackatoga Stable; 2, Sumaya Us Stables; 3, LaPenta Robert V; 4, Grant Mary and Joseph and Kelly Thomas J; 5, Schwartz Martin S; 6, Jay Em Ess Stable; 7, Winner Charles Bienstock David Mandabach Paul

Trainers– 1, Tagg Barclay; 2, Pletcher Todd A; 3, Zito Nicholas P; 4, Kelly Patrick J; 5, Jerkens H Allen; 6, Dutrow Richard E Jr; 7, Gallagher Patrick

---

$2 Pick Three (6–5–7) Paid $120.50 ; Pick Three Pool $174,231 .
$2 Pick Four (9–6–5–7) 3 Correct Paid $1,394.00 ; Pick Four Pool $534,654 .
$2 Pick Four (6–5–1–7 (NTRA NATIONAL)) 3 Correct Paid $359.50 ; Pick Four Pool $718,822 .

SEVENTH RACE
Bay Meadows
OCTOBER 2, 2004

ABOUT 1⅛ MILES. (Turf) (1.45^{1}) 29TH RUNNING OF THE BAY MEADOWS BREEDERS' CUP HANDICAP. Grade III. Purse $150,000 (includes $50,000 BC – Breeders' Cup) FOR THREE-YEAR-OLDS AND UPWARD. By subscription of $100 each to accompany the nomination or by supplementary nominations of $2,000 by Noon, Sunday, September 21, 2003. $500 to pass the entry box and $500 additional to start and an additional $50,000 from Breeders' Cup Fund for Breeders' Cup eligibles only. This race will not be divided. Starters to be named through the entry box by the closing time of entries. The starters will be determined at that time with preference given to Breeders' Cup nominees only of equal racing quality or weight assignment (respective of sex and weight for age). Preference to Non-Breeders' Cup nominees follow the same stipulation. Closed Thursday, September 23, 2004 with 14 nominations.

Value of Race: $112,500 Winner $55,000; second $20,000; third $22,500; fourth $11,250; fifth $3,750. Mutuel Pool $255,210.00 Exacta Pool $152,397.00 Quinella Pool $12,410.00 Trifecta Pool $159,299.00

Last Raced	Horse	M/Eqt.	A.	Wt	PP	St	¼	½	¾	Str	Fin	Jockey	Odds $1
8Sep04 ^{6}Dmr^{4}	NeedwoodBlde-GB	LB b	6	116	6	7	6^{2}	$6^{3\frac{1}{2}}$	$6^{2\frac{1}{2}}$	$4^{\frac{1}{2}}$	1^{1}	Carr D	11.10
8Sep04 ^{6}Dmr^{6}	Seinne-Chi	LB	7	116	4	5	7	7	7	$6^{\frac{1}{2}}$	2^{2}	Alvarado F T	6.00
26May04 ^{7}Hol^{2}	Balestrini-Ire	LB	4	117	2	3	4^{1}	3^{hd}	3^{1}	$3^{\frac{1}{2}}$	$3^{1\frac{1}{4}}$	Almeida G F	5.40
6Sep04 ^{8}BM^{2}	Ninebanks	LB b	6	117	5	6	3^{1}	4^{1}	$5^{\frac{1}{2}}$	7	4^{2}	Warren R J Jr	2.10
22Aug04 ^{8}Dmr^{8}	Night Patrol	LB b	8	114	7	1	1^{1}	$1^{\frac{1}{2}}$	$1^{\frac{1}{2}}$	1^{hd}	5^{1}	Duran F	6.10
29Aug04 ^{8}Dmr^{9}	Mananan McLir	LB	5	116	3	4	$5^{1\frac{1}{2}}$	$5^{\frac{1}{2}}$	$4^{\frac{1}{2}}$	$5^{\frac{1}{2}}$	6^{nk}	Baze R A	4.00
29Aug04 ^{8}Dmr^{6}	Murano	LB b	5	114	1	2	2^{1}	$2^{1\frac{1}{2}}$	2^{2}	$2^{\frac{1}{2}}$	7	Lumpkins J	5.60

OFF AT 4:17 Start Good. Won driving. Course firm.

TIME :23, :47^{2}, 1:11^{2}, 1:36^{3}, 1:46^{2} (:23.05, :47.41, 1:11.42, 1:36.67, 1:46.55)

$2 Mutuel Prices:

6 – NEEDWOOD BLADE-GB	24.20	11.60	7.20
4 – SEINNE-CHI		7.60	5.40
2 – BALESTRINI-IRE			5.40

$1 EXACTA 6–4 PAID $54.80 $2 QUINELLA 4–6 PAID $44.40
$1 TRIFECTA 6–4–2 PAID $432.70

Ch. h, (Mar), by Pivotal-GB – Finlaggan-GB , by Be My Chief . Trainer Gallagher Patrick. Bred by Mr & Mrs C R Philipson (GB).

NEEDWOOD BLADE (GB) raced unhurried and gained the rail on the first turn, remained inside on the second turn to quickly rally to contention, was blocked behind the leaders on the rail at the furlong pole, steadied briefly then found a narrow path between those rivals, responded quickly and outraced SEINNE to the line. SEINNE (CHI) trailed to the second turn, quickly circled horses five wide on the second turn, offered a bold rally in the lane, got to terms in the deep stretch but was outfinished by the winner. BALESTRINI (IRE) took back between horses into the first turn then stalked the leaders two wide, was fanned three wide into the lane, was in tight at the furlong pole but lacked a closing response. NINEBANKS was permitted to settle early but was always within striking distance, raced three wide and slipped back into the stretch, came on late but was not a serious threat. NIGHT PATROL was quickly in front and gained the rail into the first turn, set all of the pace to the furlong pole and slackened. MANANAN MCLIR settled early from off the rail, offered his best bid four wide into the stretch, challenged in the upper stretch but slackened in the lane. MURANO prompted the pace two wide into the stretch and slackened.

Owners– 1, Harlequin Ranches & Richard Duggan; 2, Hunt Nelson B; 3, Carl Holt; 4, Hollendorfer & Jamgotchian; 5, Everest Stables Inc; 6, Horizon Stable Jarvis and Margolis et al; 7, James Coleman G Racing & Carl Van Burger

Trainers– 1, Gallagher Patrick; 2, McAnally Ronald; 3, Drysdale Neil; 4, Hollendorfer Jerry; 5, Polanco Marcelo; 6, Dollase Wallace; 7, Mitchell Mike

$2 Daily Double (6–6) Paid $90.80 ; Daily Double Pool $10,144 .
$1 Pick Three (5–6–6) Paid $1,564.70 ; Pick Three Pool $18,727 .

SEVENTH RACE
Hawthorne
OCTOBER 2, 2004

1¼ MILES. (1.58^{4}) 68TH RUNNING OF THE HAWTHRONE GOLD CUP HANDICAP. Grade II. Purse $750,000 FOR THREE-YEAR-OLDS AND UPWARD. By subscription of $100 each, which shall accompany the nomination. $1,500 to pass the entry box and $1,500 additional to start. With $750,000 Guaranteed, of which $450,000 to the winner, $150,000 to second, $82,500 to third, $45,000 to fourth and $22,500 to fifth. Nominations closed Wednesday, September 22, 2004 with 21.

Value of Race: $750,000 Winner $450,000; second $150,000; third $82,500; fourth $45,000; fifth $22,500. Mutuel Pool $416,266.00 Exacta Pool $164,260.00 Trifecta Pool $161,637.00 Superfecta Pool $58,433.00

Last Raced	Horse	M/Eqt.	A.	Wt	PP	¼	½	¾	1	Str	Fin	Jockey	Odds $1
6Sep04 ^{3}Mnr^{1}	Freefourinternet	L	6	112	6	7	7	7	$6^{\frac{1}{2}}$	1^{hd}	$1^{1\frac{3}{4}}$	Kuntzweiler G	27.00
22Aug04 ^{8}Dmr^{2}	Perfect Drift	L	5	121	4	$3^{1\frac{1}{2}}$	$3^{3\frac{1}{2}}$	3^{7}	2^{2}	2^{hd}	$2^{2\frac{1}{4}}$	Day P	0.50
18Sep04 ^{11}TP^{3}	Sonic West	L bf	5	115	7	5^{1}	5^{4}	$4^{\frac{1}{2}}$	3^{2}	4^{2}	$3^{2\frac{1}{4}}$	Razo E Jr	14.00
1Sep04 ^{7}Sar^{4}	Quest Star	L b	5	113	1	$2^{\frac{1}{2}}$	$1^{\frac{1}{2}}$	$1^{\frac{1}{2}}$	1^{hd}	3^{1}	$4^{\frac{3}{4}}$	Melancon L	24.50
11Sep04 ^{8}AP^{5}	Caiman	L	3	110	3	6^{8}	6^{12}	6^{10}	5^{hd}	5^{4}	5^{4}	Cosme E	57.50
6Sep04 ^{3}Sar^{5}	Kissin Saint	L b	4	115	5	$4^{3\frac{1}{2}}$	4^{5}	5^{4}	7	6^{7}	6^{13}	Emigh C A	21.80
6Sep04 ^{3}Sar^{1}	Powerful Touch	L	4	114	2	1^{hd}	2^{hd}	2^{hd}	4^{2}	7	7	Marquez C H Jr	1.70

OFF AT 4:05 Start Good. Won driving. Track fast.

TIME :23^{2}, :47^{1}, 1:11^{1}, 1:36^{4}, 2:03^{1} (:23.40, :47.32, 1:11.24, 1:36.93, 2:03.34)

$2 Mutuel Prices:

6 – FREEFOURINTERNET	56.00	7.00	2.10
4 – PERFECT DRIFT		2.20	2.10
7 – SONIC WEST			2.10

$2 EXACTA 6–4 PAID $120.20 $2 TRIFECTA 6–4–7 PAID $534.00
$2 SUPERFECTA 6–4–7–1 PAID $3,371.00

B. h, (Apr), by Tabasco Cat – Dixie Chimes , by Dixieland Band . Trainer Maker Michael J. Bred by Edward P Evans (Ky).

FREEFOURINTERNET was void of early speed, closed a gap on the final turn, came out six wide for the drive, responded through the stretch and won going away. PERFECT DRIFT raced close up three wide, challenged for the lead nearing the eighth pole then could not resist the winner in the final furlong. SONIC WEST raced three wide near the middle of the field then gained belatedly in the stretch for minor awards. QUEST STAR set the pace from the inside under pressure and weakened. CAIMAN lacked speed and was not a factor. KISSIN SAINT raced four wide near the middle of the field and tired. POWERFUL TOUCH pressed the pace from just outside and tired.

Owners– 1, EquiraseCom LLC Ron Peltz; 2, Stonecrest Farm; 3, Stone Spire LLC; 4, Mansell Stables LLC; 5, Achar Victor; 6, Karches Peter and Rankowitz Michael; 7, Stronach Stables Elfriede Belinda & Andrew Stronach

Trainers– 1, Maker Michael J; 2, Johnson Murray W; 3, Van Berg Thomas L; 4, Walden W Elliott; 5, Medina Angel M; 6, Lewis Lisa L; 7, Frankel Robert

$1 Pick Three (2–3–6) Paid $9,125.20 ; Pick Three Pool $12,167 .

NINTH RACE
Hoosier Park
OCTOBER 2, 2004

1 1/16 MILES. (1.41) 10TH RUNNING OF THE INDIANA DERBY. Grade II. Purse $500,000 FOR THREE YEAR OLDS. By subscription of $100 each which shall accompany the nomination, $400 to pass the entry box and $500 additional to start. With $500,000 added, of which 60% to the winner, 20% to second, 11% to third, 6% to fourth and 3% to fifth. Weight: 124 lbs. Fillies: 121 lbs. Non-winners of $50,000 at one mile or over in 2004, 3 lbs.; of $30,000 at any distance in 2004, 5 lbs.; three races other than maiden or claiming, 7 lbs.; two such races, 9 lbs. Starters to be named through the entry box by the usual time of closing (72 Hour Closing). Trophy to the winning owner. High weights preferred. NOTE: This stake will be limited to twelve starters. If more than twelve horses pass the entry box, preference will be (1) High weights; (2) Highest Lifetime Earnings. Two horses having common ties through ownership cannot start to the exclusion of a single interest. Entry fee only will be refunded if failure to draw into the race.

Value of Race: $511,300 Winner $306,780; second $102,260; third $56,243; fourth $30,678; fifth $15,339. Mutuel Pool $141,982.00 Exacta Pool $88,592.00 Trifecta Pool $82,839.00 Superfecta Pool $26,124.00

Last Raced	Horse	M/Eqt.	A.	Wt	PP	St	¼	½	¾	Str	Fin	Jockey	Odds $1
12Jun04 14Tdn1	Brass Hat	LB b	3	124	8	9	9	9	5½	1hd	11¾	Martinez W	10.00
28Aug04 11Sar6	Suave	LB b	3	124	7	8	83	2hd	1½	2½	2¾	Peck B D	9.50
27Aug04 5Sar2	Hasslefree	LB b	3	115	3	6	21½	41	21½	31	3½	McKee J	29.50
28Aug04 11Sar5	Sir Shackleton	LB	3	124	2	4	6hd	82½	41	4½	41	Bejarano R	2.20
3Sep04 6Dmr1	Perfect Moon	LB	3	121	4	2	51½	71½	63	67	5hd	Court J K	5.90
6Sep04 10Pha2	Pollard's Vision	LB	3	124	1	3	3hd	6½	3hd	53	618	Velazquez J R	2.10
28Aug04 6AP4	Avid Skier	LB b	3	119	6	1	1hd	3hd	81½	710	712¼	Delgado J H	51.20
10Sep04 1PrM1	Edgerrin	LB b	3	119	9	7	4hd	5½	9	8½	88½	Pompell T L	43.30
1May04 10CD18	Quintons Gold Rush	LB	3	124	5	5	72	1hd	7hd	9	9	Sellers S J	4.20

OFF AT 9:49 Start Good. Won driving. Track fast.

TIME :224, :47, 1:12, 1:371, 1:44 (:22.80, :47.19, 1:12.11, 1:37.39, 1:44.04)

$2 Mutuel Prices:				
	8 – BRASS HAT	22.00	8.00	5.60
	7 – SUAVE		9.80	7.20
	3 – HASSLEFREE			11.20

$2 EXACTA 8–7 PAID $109.00 $2 TRIFECTA 8–7–3 PAID $3,024.40
$2 SUPERFECTA 8–7–3–2 PAID $10,253.60

B. g, (May), by Prized – Brassy, by Dixie Brass. Trainer Bradley William. Bred by Fred F Bradley (Ky).

BRASS HAT settled well off the pace while unhurried and racing out from the rail, angled out to rally five wide through the far turn, continued on strongly to reach the front through midstretch and moved clear under steady handling. SUAVE moved up quickly to bid midway up the backstretch while five wide, continued on between rivals through the far turn, resisted then could not handle the winner late. HASSLEFREE was on the pace inside AVID SKIER, continued gamely and dug in through midstretch but could not contain the top pair in the final furlong. SIR SHACKLETON was along the inside while never far back, angled four wide through the far turn to bid into the stretch, lugged in upper stretch then came back out and could not get by the top ones. PERFECT MOON saved ground in good striking position, swung six wide into the lane for room as the field bunched and made a mild late run. POLLARD'S VISION was along the inside, was forced in as SIR SHACKLETON lugged in upper stretch and weakened in the late going. AVID SKIER was on the pace outside HASSLEFREE to late in the far turn and gave way through the lane. EDGERRIN was close up to the pace racing three to four wide between rivals and tired. QUINTONS GOLD RUSH was climbing on the first turn and ran up heels nearing the backstretch to be steadied, quickly moved to contention from five deep heading up the backstretch then gave way into the stretch.

Owners– 1, Bradley Fred F; 2, Jay Em Ess Stable; 3, Lewis Robert B and Beverly J; 4, Farmer Tracy; 5, Royce S Jaime Racing Stable Inc Royce S Jaime; 6, Edgewood Farm; 7, France Wilbur K; 8, Likens Herbert and Darlene; 9, Padua Stables Satish Sanan and Jay Manoogian

Trainers– 1, Bradley William; 2, McGee Paul J; 3, Lukas D Wayne; 4, Zito Nicholas P; 5, O'Neill Doug; 6, Pletcher Todd A; 7, Bennett Gerald S; 8, Roberts Stanley W; 9, Asmussen Steven M

$2 Pick Three (6–7–8) Paid $334.00 ; Pick Three Pool $6,598 .

NINTH RACE
Philadelphia
OCTOBER 2, 2004

1 1/16 MILES. 35TH RUNNING OF THE COTILLION HANDICAP. Grade II. Purse $250,000 FOR FILLIES THREE YEARS OLD. By subscription of $250 each which should accompany the nomination, $600 to pass the entry box, $800 additional to start, with $250,000 guaranteed. The winner to receive $150,000 with $50,000 to second, $27,500 to third, $15,000 to fourth and $7,500 to fifth. Weights: Saturday, September 25, 2004. Starters to be named through the entry box by the usual time of closing, on Tuesday, September 28, 2004. (Highweights preferred). Trophy will be presented to the winning owner, trainer and jockey. Nominations closed Saturday, September 18, 2004 with 22.

Value of Race: $250,000 Winner $150,000; second $50,000; third $27,500; fourth $15,000; fifth $7,500. Mutuel Pool $72,836.00 Exacta Pool $45,436.00 Trifecta Pool $35,915.00

Last Raced	Horse	M/Eqt.	A.	Wt	PP	St	¼	½	¾	Str	Fin	Jockey	Odds $1
21Aug04 10Sar3	Ashado	L	3	124	5	2	2hd	2½	21	1½	12¾	Coa E M	0.20
15Aug04 10Mth4	Ender's Sister	L	3	117	2	1	11½	11	1½	23	23½	Velez J A Jr	9.80
11Sep04 8Bel5	My Lordship	L	3	115	1	3	32	32	3½	3½	31¼	Castillo H Jr	12.00
11Sep04 8Bel3	He Loves Me	L	3	117	7	4	41	4½	42	43	43	Santana J Z	5.70
21Aug04 9AP1	Catboat	L b	3	116	4	7	7	7	6hd	5hd	5nk	Murphy C K	25.00
15Aug04 10Mth6	Pilfer	L bf	3	115	3	6	5hd	5½	5hd	63	64½	Arguello F A Jr	40.50
1Sep04 8Sar1	Fait Accompli	L f	3	115	6	5	63	63	7	7	7	Vega H	40.60

OFF AT 4:01 Start Good. Won ridden out. Track fast.

TIME :234, :473, 1:111, 1:352, 1:413 (:23.99, :47.68, 1:11.37, 1:35.43, 1:41.68)

$2 Mutuel Prices:				
	7 – ASHADO	2.40	2.20	2.10
	2 – ENDER'S SISTER		3.60	2.10
	1 – MY LORDSHIP			2.10

$2 EXACTA 7–2 PAID $10.60 $2 TRIFECTA 7–2–1 PAID $36.40

Dk. b or br. f, (Feb), by Saint Ballado – Goulash, by Mari's Book. Trainer Pletcher Todd A. Bred by Aaron U Jones & Marie D Jones (Ky).

ASHADO stalked the early pace while three wide, made a bid past the quarter pole when ready, was carried out slightly leaving the second turn, then drew clear past the furlong marker and widened late while being ridden out. ENDER'S SISTER set the early pace while being well handled, drifted out slightly at the top of the stretch, proved to be no match for the winner late while clearly second best. MY LORDSHIP was well placed on the inside but faded while besting the rest. HE LOVES ME was rated early, came four wide into the stretch, but had no rally. CATBOAT was settled back early, came wide for the drive but had no rally. PILFER failed to menace. FAIT ACCOMPLI was not a factor.

Owners– 1, Starlight Stables LLC; 2, Richard Masson; 3, Live Oak Plantation; 4, Buckingham Farm; 5, Stonerside Stable LLC; 6, Fox Hill Farms Inc; 7, Berkshire Stud

Trainers– 1, Pletcher Todd A; 2, Arnold George R II; 3, Mott William I; 4, Small Richard W; 5, Flint Bernard S; 6, Servis John C; 7, Bush Thomas M

Scratched– Hopelessly Devoted (06Sep04 9Pha5), Schedule (GB) (06Sep04 9Pha4)

$2 Daily Double (2–7) Paid $8.40 ; Daily Double Pool $9,652 .
$2 Pick Three (1–2–7) Paid $157.00 ; Pick Three Pool $5,625 .

NINTH RACE
Pimlico
OCTOBER 2, 2004

6 FURLONGS. (1.09) 17TH RUNNINGS OF THE SAFELY KEPT BREEDERS' CUP Grade III. Purse $150,000 (includes $50,000 BC - Breeders' Cup) FOR FILLIES, THREE-YEARS-OLD. By subscription of $100 each which should accompnay the nomination. $500 to pass the entry box. $500 additional to start with $100,000 Guaranteed, and an additional $50,000 from the Breeders' Cup fund for Cup nominees only.The Host Association's guaranteed monies to be divided 60% of all monies to the winner, 20% to second, 11% to third, 6% to fourth, and 3% to fifth. Supplemental nominations of $1500 each will be accepted by the usual time of entry with all other fees dueas noted. Breeders' Cup fund monies, also correspondingly divided providing a Breeders' Cup nominee has finished in an awarded position. Any Breeders' Cup fund monies not awarded will revert back to the fund. Weight 122 lbs. Non-winners of $50,000 twice,allowed 3 lbs.; once, 5 lbs.; $25,000 once, 7 lbs. (Maiden and Claiming races not considered in estimating allowances). Preference to Breeders' Cup nominees only of equal racing quality or starters with the highest career earnings. Horses may be placedon the also-eligible list. Starters to be named through the entry box by the usual time of closing. Trophy to the winning owner given by the Breeders' Cup Ltd. Closed, September 23, 2004 with 19 Nominations.

Value of Race: $143,000 Winner $90,000; second $30,000; third $11,000; fourth $9,000; fifth $3,000. Mutuel Pool $83,381.00 Exacta Pool $69,356.00 Superfecta Pool $9,734.00 Trifecta Pool $46,593.00

Last Raced	Horse	M/Eqt.	A.	Wt	PP	St	¼	½	Str	Fin	Jockey	Odds $1
11Sep04 ^{8}Bel^{6}	Bending Strings	L	3	119	6	5	6	$5^{1\frac{1}{2}}$	3^{1}	$1^{2\frac{1}{4}}$	Karamanos H A	3.90
28Aug04 ^{8}Sar^{1}	Smokey Glacken	L	3	119	1	3	1^{hd}	$1^{\frac{1}{2}}$	1^{hd}	$2^{\frac{1}{2}}$	Bravo J	1.00
22Aug04 ^{8}Mth^{1}	Then She Laughs	L f	3	117	4	1	3^{1}	2^{1}	$2^{1\frac{1}{2}}$	$3^{1\frac{1}{2}}$	Elliott S	7.10
3Sep04 ^{5}AP^{2}	Liz On Polk Street	L	3	115	5	4	$5^{2\frac{1}{2}}$	6	$5^{2\frac{1}{2}}$	$4^{2\frac{1}{2}}$	Laviolette B S	24.90
3Sep04 ^{5}AP^{1}	Gilded Gold	L	3	117	2	2	4^{1}	$4^{\frac{1}{2}}$	$4^{1\frac{1}{2}}$	$5^{5\frac{3}{4}}$	Fogelsonger R	2.30
6Sep04 ^{11}Mth^{1}	Ambition Unbridled	L	3	117	3	6	$2^{\frac{1}{2}}$	3^{2}	6	6	Castellano A Jr	12.80

OFF AT 4:59 Start Good . Won driving. Track fast.

TIME :22^{2}, :45^{1}, :57^{2}, 1:10 (:22.55, :45.21, :57.54, 1:10.11)

$2 Mutuel Prices:				
	7 – BENDING STRINGS	9.80	3.60	2.80
	1 – SMOKEY GLACKEN		2.40	2.20
	5 – THEN SHE LAUGHS			3.00

$2 EXACTA 7-1 PAID $27.40 $1 SUPERFECTA 7-1-5-6 PAID $185.30
$2 TRIFECTA 7-1-5 PAID $105.20

Dk. b or br. f, (May), by American Chance - Straight South , by Hail the Pirates . Trainer McLaughlin Kiaran P. Bred by John D Gunther (Ky).

BENDING STRINGS lacked speed, began her move leaving the turn, swung to the four path in midstretch, closed nicely and drew off. SMOKEY GLACKEN set a pressured pace along the rail, drifted out a bit in midstretch and weakened late. THEN SHE LAUGHS chased the pace three wide and weakened. LIZ ON POLK STREET , unhurried early, circled the turn, raced in the six path in midstretch and failed to menace. GILDED GOLD circled the turn, was fanned five wide in midstretch and gave way. AMBITION UNBRIDLED pressed the pace two wide and dropped back.

Owners– 1, Gunther John D; 2, Moore Susan and John; 3, Papandrea Vincent; 4, Calabrese Frank C; 5, Bobby Flay Robert E Masterson & Barry L Weisbord; 6, Gill Michael J

Trainers– 1, McLaughlin Kiaran P; 2, Jerkens James A; 3, Ciresa Martin E; 4, Sinclair Jodie L; 5, Amoss Thomas; 6, Shuman Mark

Scratched– Brilliant Peaks (18Sep04 ^{8}Pim^{1})

NINTH RACE
Turfway Park
OCTOBER 2, 2004

1 MILE. (1.34) 55TH RUNNING OF THE TURFWAY PARK FALL CHAMPIONSHIP. Grade III. Purse $100,000 FOR THREE-YEAR-OLDS AND UPWARD. By subscription of $100, $500 to enter and $500 additional to start. Supplementary nominations may be made at the time of entry Thursday, September 30, 2004 by payment of $5,000 each (includes all fees). Monies to be divided 62% to the owner of the winner, 20% to second, 10% to third, 5% to fourth and 3% to fifth. Weights:Three-year-olds 119 lbs.; older 122 lbs. Non-winners of a Graded Stake at a mile or over since May 15 allowed 3 lbs.; non-winners of a non-graded stake at a mile or over in 2004, 5 lbs.; 30,000 twice at a mile or over in 2003-2004, 7 lbs. Starters and riders must be named through the entry box by the usual time of closing. This race will be limited to twelve (12) starters. Preference to start will be given in the following order: Graded/Group Stakes Winners (in order I-II-III). Stakes winners, then highest total earnings in 2004. Failure to draw into the race cancels all fees. Closed Wednesday, September 22, 2004 with 27 Nominations.

Value of Race: $100,000 Winner $62,000; second $20,000; third $10,000; fourth $5,000; fifth $3,000. Mutuel Pool $126,168.00 Exacta Pool $74,092.00 Trifecta Pool $63,203.00 Superfecta Pool $21,919.00

Last Raced	Horse	M/Eqt.	A.	Wt	PP	St	¼	½	¾	Str	Fin	Jockey	Odds $1
11Jly04 ^{11}Pln^{4}	Cappuchino	L bf	5	115	4	1	$1^{\frac{1}{2}}$	$1^{1\frac{1}{2}}$	$1^{2\frac{1}{2}}$	1^{4}	1^{4}	Sarvis D A	31.90
25Jly04 ^{10}Mth^{4}	Crafty Shaw	L	6	122	3	5	4^{4}	4^{3}	3^{hd}	$3^{1\frac{1}{2}}$	2^{nk}	Perret C	2.60
28Aug04 ^{9}ElP^{1}	Added Edge	L	4	119	6	3	2^{1}	$2^{\frac{1}{2}}$	$2^{\frac{1}{2}}$	$2^{\frac{1}{2}}$	3^{1}	Guidry M	3.20
28Aug04 ^{9}ElP^{6}	Ask the Lord	L	7	119	2	4	5^{hd}	$5^{\frac{1}{2}}$	$5^{\frac{1}{2}}$	$4^{\frac{1}{2}}$	4^{hd}	Bejarano R	7.40
28Aug04 ^{9}ElP^{8}	Eagle Time	L f	7	115	1	6	$6^{1\frac{1}{2}}$	6^{hd}	6^{1}	5^{hd}	5^{hd}	Melancon P	95.00
22Aug04 ^{9}Sar^{4}	Alumni Hall	L b	5	119	5	7	7	7	7	$6^{2\frac{1}{2}}$	$6^{9\frac{3}{4}}$	Martinez W	2.00
31May04 ^{9}LS^{3}	Spanish Empire	L	4	119	7	2	3^{2}	$3^{\frac{1}{2}}$	4^{3}	7	7	Sellers S J	3.70

OFF AT 4:58 Start Good . Won driving. Track fast.

TIME :22^{4}, :46^{1}, 1:11, 1:24, 1:37 (:22.87, :46.38, 1:11.18, 1:24.02, 1:37.19)

$2 Mutuel Prices:				
	4 – CAPPUCHINO	65.80	25.20	8.40
	3 – CRAFTY SHAW		5.00	3.00
	8 – ADDED EDGE			3.00

$2 EXACTA 4-3 PAID $235.80 $2 TRIFECTA 4-3-8 PAID $1,095.40
$2 SUPERFECTA 4-3-8-2 PAID $2,279.40

B. h, (Mar), by Capote - Tara Roma , by Lyphard . Trainer Hollendorfer Jerry. Bred by Emory A Hamilton (Ky).

CAPPUCHINO set the early pace while out in the three path, opened a clear lead once on the backstretch, moved in a bit for the second turn, increased his lead into the stretch and was not menaced while under steady urging. CRAFTY SHAW within striking distance off the rail, moved to the inside on the second turn and outfinished ADED EDGE for the place. ADDED EDGE pressed the early pace ofu8r wide, moved in to the three path on the second turn but weakened in the drive. ASK THE LORD reserved along the inside, saved ground to the stretch and lacked a late bid on the inside. EAGLE TIME outsprinted early off the inside, had nothing left late. ALUMNI HALL outrun early three wide, moved out to the four path on the second turn and lacked a closing bid. SPANISH EMPIRE pressed the early pace five wide, held on well for six furlongs and faded.

Owners– 1, Hollendorfer Jerry Litt Howard and Todaro George; 2, Cella Charles J; 3, Team Valor Stables and Wilson Robert J; 4, L T B Inc and Williams R A; 5, Kempthorne Loy; 6, Farish William S Elkins Jr James A and Webber Jr W Temple; 7, Jubilee Stable Cherry Martin L and Twin Creeks Farm

Trainers– 1, Hollendorfer Jerry; 2, Vestal Peter M; 3, Romans Dale; 4, Flint Bernard S; 5, Jordan Rick; 6, Howard Neil J; 7, Asmussen Steven M

Scratched– Intelligent Male (21Aug04 ^{7}AP ^{1}) , Ministers Wild Cat (05Aug04 ^{7}Dmr^{5})

$2 Pick Three (7-1-4) Paid $834.20 ; Pick Three Pool $8,556 .

FOURTH RACE
Santa Anita
OCTOBER 2, 2004

1¼ MILES. (Turf) (1.57^{2}) 28TH RUNNING OF THE YELLOW RIBBON. Grade I. Purse $500,000 FOR FILLIES AND MARES, THREE YEARS OLD AND UPWARD. By subscription of $500 each if made on or before Thursday, September 2, 2004 or by supplementary nomination of $10,000 at time of entry. All horses shall pay $5,000 to start with $500,000 guaranteed,of which $300,000 to the winner, $100,000 to second, $60,000 to third, $30,000 to fourth and $10,000 to fifth. Three–Year–Olds: 118 lbs. Older: 123 lbs. Starters to be named through the entry box by the closing time of entries. This race will not bedivided. If the number exceeds fourteen (14), preference will be determined in the following order: First preference will be given to graded or group winners in 2004. Second preference will be given to those horses with the highest total earnings in 20004. Entry and supplementary fees will be refunded to all horses which fail to draw into this race. A trophy will be presented to the winning owner. Closed with 38 nominations.

Value of Race: $500,000 Winner $300,000; second $100,000; third $60,000; fourth $30,000; fifth $10,000. Mutuel Pool $660,540.00 Exacta Pool $353,266.00 Quinella Pool $31,533.00 Trifecta Pool $355,261.00 Superfecta Pool $137,628.00

Last Raced	Horse	M/Eqt.	A.	Wt	PP	¼	½	¾	1	Str	Fin	Jockey	Odds $1
24Jly04 ^{6}Dmr^{6}	Light Jig-GB	LB	4	123	1	8^{hd}	8^{1}	$7^{\frac{1}{2}}$	$5^{1\frac{1}{2}}$	$3^{\frac{1}{2}}$	1^{4}	Douglas R R	1.30
4Sep04 ^{7}Dmr^{3}	Tangle-Ire	LB	4	123	2	7^{hd}	$5^{\frac{1}{2}}$	5^{hd}	7^{1}	6^{hd}	2^{1}	Nakatani C S	9.50
4Sep04 ^{7}Dmr^{2}	Katdogawn-GB	LB	4	123	3	4^{1}	$3^{1\frac{1}{2}}$	3^{hd}	3^{1}	2^{hd}	3^{hd}	Desormeaux K J	5.00
2Sep04 ^{6}Dmr^{1}	Good Student-Arg	LB	4	123	8	2^{1}	$2^{\frac{1}{2}}$	2^{1}	$2^{\frac{1}{2}}$	$4^{1\frac{1}{2}}$	$4^{\frac{1}{2}}$	Smith M E	13.30
21Aug04 ^{3}Dmr^{1}	Amorama-FR	LB b	3	118	9	9^{6}	9^{7}	9^{8}	$8^{1\frac{1}{2}}$	$9^{2\frac{1}{2}}$	5^{hd}	Flores D R	3.50
20Dec03 ^{9}Hol^{5}	Hoh Buzzard-Ire	LB b	4	123	10	3^{hd}	$4^{\frac{1}{2}}$	$4^{2\frac{1}{2}}$	4^{hd}	$5^{\frac{1}{2}}$	$6^{\frac{1}{2}}$	Blanc B	30.20
14Aug04 ^{8}AP^{11}	Noches DeRosa-Chi	LB b	6	123	5	5^{hd}	6^{hd}	8^{2}	9^{3}	7^{2}	$7^{\frac{1}{2}}$	Baze T C	7.60
4Sep04 ^{7}Dmr^{5}	VozDeColegiala-Chi	LB	5	123	6	6^{1}	7^{1}	6^{hd}	6^{hd}	8^{hd}	$8^{\frac{1}{2}}$	Bisono A	66.40
4Sep04 ^{7}Dmr^{4}	Notting Hill-Brz	LB f	5	123	4	1^{1}	1^{1}	$1^{3\frac{1}{2}}$	1^{2}	1^{hd}	$9^{\frac{1}{2}}$	Gomez G K	32.10
23Aug04 ^{7}Dmr^{2}	Cozie Advantage	LB b	5	123	7	10	10	10	10	10	10	Pedroza M A	49.20

OFF AT 2:28 Start Good. Won driving. Course firm.

TIME :23^{1}, :46^{2}, 1:10, 1:34^{2}, 1:59^{1} (:23.29, :46.41, 1:10.09, 1:34.49, 1:59.28)

$2 Mutuel Prices:				
	1 – **LIGHT JIG–GB**	**4.60**	**3.20**	**2.60**
	2 – **TANGLE–IRE**		**7.40**	**5.00**
	3 – **KATDOGAWN–GB**			**3.60**

$1 EXACTA 1–2 PAID $17.30 $2 QUINELLA 1–2 PAID $22.40
$1 TRIFECTA 1–2–3 PAID $47.30 $1 SUPERFECTA 1–2–3–8 PAID $394.10

B. f, (Apr), by Danehill – Nashmeel, by Blushing Groom–Fr. Trainer Frankel Robert. Bred by Juddmonte Farms (GB).

LIGHT JIG (GB) saved ground off the pace, moved up inside leaving the backstretch, continued between foes and behind rivals leaving the turn, swung three deep for room into the stretch, surged to the front four wide under urging just past the eighth pole and pulled clear. TANGLE (IRE) chased inside, split horses into the second turn, continued a bit off the rail, waited a bit off heels three deep into the stretch, then rallied between foes in the drive and gained the place. KATDOGAWN (GB) close up stalking the pace inside, bid between horses in midstretch and was outfinished but held third. GOOD STUDENT (ARG) pulled a bit early, stalked outside a rival or off the rail, bid three deep between foes in the stretch and also was outfinished. AMORAMA (FR) unhurried off the rail early, moved up outside leaving the second turn, came three deep into the stretch and put in a late bid. HOH BUZZARD (IRE) close up stalking the pace three deep, was forced four wide into the stretch and lacked the needed response. NOCHES DE ROSA (CHI) pulled early, chased between horses, steadied in tight into the second turn, continued just off the inside and lacked the needed rally. VOZ DE COLEGIALA (CHI) stalked between foes then outside, went three deep on the second turn, was a bit crowded off heels four wide into the stretch and could not offer the necessary response. NOTTING HILL (BRZ) sped to the early lead, set the pace inside, fought back in upper and midstretch but weakened. COZIE ADVANTAGE angled in and saved ground off the pace, came out into the stretch and again in midstretch and was not a threat.

Owners– 1, Juddmonte Farms Inc; 2, Reddam J Paul; 3, Cuchna John R Jim Ford Inc and Pearson Deron; 4, Zetcher Arnold; 5, Naify and Woodside Farms LLC; 6, Tanaka Gary A; 7, Diamond A Racing Corporation; 8, Hunt Nelson B; 9, Green Lantern Stables LLC and Barber Gary; 10, Red Oak Stable

Trainers– 1, Frankel Robert; 2, Dollase Craig; 3, Cassidy James; 4, McAnally Ronald; 5, Canani Julio C; 6, Cecil B D A; 7, Mandella Richard; 8, McAnally Ronald; 9, Sahadi Jenine; 10, McAnally Ronald

---

$2 Daily Double (7–1) Paid $22.40 ; Daily Double Pool $34,405 .
$1 Pick Three (5–7–1) Paid $710.10 ; Pick Three Pool $67,145 .

EIGHTH RACE Santa Anita OCTOBER 2, 2004

1⅛ MILES. (1.45⁴) 23RD RUNNING OF THE GOODWOOD BREEDERS' CUP HANDICAP. Grade II. Purse $500,000 (includes $100,000 BC - Breeders' Cup) FOR THREE-YEAR-OLDS AND UPWARD. By subscription of $500 each if made on or before Thursday, September 2, 2004 or by supplementary nomination of $10,000 by 10 AM Sunday, September 26.. All horses shall pay $5,000 additional to start, with $400,000 guaranteed and an additional $100,000 from Breeders' Cup Fund for Cup nominees only. The host association's money to be divided 60% to the winner, 20% to second, 12% to third, 6% to fourth and 2% to fifth. Breeders' Cup Fund monies also correspondingly divided provided a Breeders' Cup nominee has finished in an awarded position. Any Breeders' Cup Fund monies not awarded will revert to the Fund. Weights: Sunday, September 26. The starters will be determined at entry time with preference given to Breeders' Cup nominees only of equal racing quality or weight assignment (respective of sex and weight for age). Starters to be named through the entry box by the closing time of entries. A trophy will be presented to the owner of the winner. Closed with 30 nominations.

Value of Race: $480,000 Winner $300,000; second $80,000; third $60,000; fourth $30,000; fifth $10,000. Mutuel Pool $386,090.00 Exacta Pool $183,363.00 Quinella Pool $16,330.00 Trifecta Pool $160,974.00

Last Raced	Horse	M/Eqt.	A.	Wt	PP	St	¼	½	¾	Str	Fin	Jockey	Odds $1
27Mar04 NAS1	LundysLiability-Brz	LB	4	118	2	3	1hd	2 1½	1½	2 1	1hd	Flores D R	2.30
22Aug04 8Dmr3	Total Impact-Chi	LB b	6	119	5	2	2 1½	1hd	2 1	1hd	2 2	Smith M E	1.10
5Sep04 8Dmr1	Supah Blitz	LB	4	117	3	1	4 1½	4 7	3½	3 4	3 6	Nakatani C S	2.30
25Aug04 3Dmr1	Truly a Judge	LB	6	115	4	5	3hd	3hd	4 7	4 2½	4no	Douglas R R	14.30
23Apr04 9Kee8	Californian-GB	LB	4	114	1	4	5	5	5	5	5	Pedroza M A	19.50

OFF AT 4:35 Start Good. Won driving. Track fast.

TIME :24¹, :48, 1:11², 1:35³, 1:48¹ (:24.28, :48.10, 1:11.42, 1:35.63, 1:48.39)

$2 Mutuel Prices:

2 - LUNDY'S LIABILITY-BRZ	6.60	2.60	2.20
5 - TOTAL IMPACT-CHI		2.20	2.10
3 - SUPAH BLITZ			2.20

$1 EXACTA 2-5 PAID $7.30 $2 QUINELLA 2-5 PAID $7.00
$1 TRIFECTA 2-5-3 PAID $13.50

B. c, (Sep), by Candy Stripes - Emerald Counter , by Geiger Counter . Trainer Frankel Robert. Bred by Stud Tnt (Brz).

LUNDY'S LIABILITY (BRZ) dueled inside, fought back a bit off the rail on the second turn and into the stretch, drifted in a bit in midstretch and gamely prevailed under urging. TOTAL IMPACT (CHI) alternated in front outside the winner to the stretch, fought back to a short lead in midstretch, continued lapped on that rival through a stiff drive and was outgamed. SUPAH BLITZ stalked the pace off the rail then angled in leaving the backstretch, tried to get through inside the top pair in midstretch but steadied and altered course outside and bested the others. TRULY A JUDGE broke slowly, stalked the dueling pair outside SUPAH BLITZ then off the rail on the second turn and weakened. CALIFORNIAN (GB) unhurried early, dropped back along the inside on the backstretch, continued on the rail and lacked a response in the stretch. A claim of foul by the rider of SUPAH BLITZ against the winner for alleged interference in midstretch was not allowed by the stewards, who ruled the incident did not alter the original order of finish.

Owners- 1, Slack & Stud TNT; 2, Al Kabeer Sultan Mohammed Saud and Bridport S A; 3, Black Saddle Stable or Kagele Bros Inc or Leib; 4, Aidekman Alan Ailshie Gaylord and Harris Tom; 5, Noctis LLC Papiano Neil and Taub Steve

Trainers- 1, Frankel Robert; 2, De Seroux Laura; 3, O'Neill Doug; 4, Bernstein David; 5, Mulhall Kristin

Scratched- During (05Sep04 8Dmr3)

$2 Daily Double (8-2) Paid $25.80 ; Daily Double Pool $24,231 .
$1 Pick Three (9-8-2) Paid $136.10 ; Pick Three Pool $88,921 .

NINTH RACE Santa Anita OCTOBER 2, 2004

1 1/16 MILES. (1.39) 36TH RUNNING OF THE OAK LEAF. Grade II. Purse $200,000 FOR FILLIES, TWO YEARS OLD. By subscription of $200 each if made on or before Thursday, September 2, 2004 or by supplementary nomination of $4,000 at time of entry. All horses shall pay $2,000 to start, with $200,000 guaranteed of which $120,000 to thewinner, $40,000 to second, $24,000 to third, $12,000 to fourth and $4,000 to fifth. Weight: 119 lbs. Starters to be named through the entry box by the closing time of entries. Those horses with the highest earnings at time of entry will be preferred. A trophy will be presented to the owner of the winner. Closed with 31 nominations.

Value of Race: $200,000 Winner $120,000; second $40,000; third $24,000; fourth $12,000; fifth $4,000. Mutuel Pool $422,945.00 Exacta Pool $266,354.00 Quinella Pool $26,495.00 Trifecta Pool $278,221.00 Superfecta Pool $126,034.00

Last Raced	Horse	M/Eqt.	A.	Wt	PP	St	¼	½	¾	Str	Fin	Jockey	Odds $1
28Aug04 8Dmr1	Sweet Catomine	LB b	2	119	9	9	7 1	6 3	5 3	1 2½	1 4	Nakatani C S	2.00
6Sep04 4Dmr1	Splendid Blended	LB	2	119	3	5	4 1	3 2	3hd	2 2	2 2½	Desormeaux K J	1.40
1Sep04 7Dmr2	Memorette	B	2	119	7	7	9	9	7 5	5 1½	3 4	Baze T C	10.70
5Sep04 6Dmr1	Culture Clash	LB b	2	119	4	6	5hd	4 1	4 1	3hd	4 6	John K	16.40
28Aug04 8Dmr3	Hello Lucky	LB	2	119	1	1	2½	2½	2 1	6 3	5 3	Smith M E	11.00
28Aug04 8Dmr4	Ninadivina	LB f	2	119	6	4	3hd	5 2½	6 1	7 5	6 1½	Atkinson P	44.40
28Aug04 8Dmr8	No Bull Baby	LB b	2	119	5	3	1hd	1hd	1hd	4hd	7 9	Douglas R R	15.30
12Sep04 8WO1	Fearless Flyer-Ire	LB	2	119	8	8	8hd	8hd	9	8hd	8 2	Flores D R	7.90
16Sep04 10Fpx4	Seeking the Heat	LB b	2	119	2	2	6 1	7 1	8hd	9	9	Pedroza M A	40.60

OFF AT 5:07 Start Good. Won driving. Track fast.

TIME :23, :46⁴, 1:11¹, 1:36², 1:42⁴ (:23.10, :46.86, 1:11.36, 1:36.40, 1:42.98)

$2 Mutuel Prices:

9 - SWEET CATOMINE	6.00	2.80	2.40
3 - SPLENDID BLENDED		2.80	2.40
7 - MEMORETTE			3.20

$1 EXACTA 9-3 PAID $8.30 $2 QUINELLA 3-9 PAID $5.80
$1 TRIFECTA 9-3-7 PAID $38.70 $1 SUPERFECTA 9-3-7-4 PAID $187.90

B. f, (Feb), by Storm Cat - Sweet Life , by Kris S.. Trainer Canani Julio C. Bred by Mr & Mrs Martin J Wygod (Ky).

SWEET CATOMINE three deep into the first turn, chased outside, moved up on the second turn, surged to the front four wide leaving that turn and drew clear under a strong hand ride. SPLENDID BLENDED was rank early and drifted wide into the first turn, moved up four wide leaving that turn, bid three deep and dueled for the lead, angled in a bit into the stretch, was no match for the winner but second best. MEMORETTE settled outside a rival then three deep leaving the backstretch, angled in on the second turn, came out into the stretch and picked up the show. CULTURE CLASH forced wide into the first turn, angled in off the rail to chase the pace, moved up inside on the second turn, steadied off heels midway on that bend, came out a bit into the stretch and lacked a further response. HELLO LUCKY rank inside and steadied early, came out on the first turn, bid between foes and dueled for the lead, dropped back nearing the stretch and weakened. NINADIVINA stalked off the rail then inside into the second turn and weakened. NO BULL BABY had speed outside a rival then angled in on the first turn, dueled inside and also weakened in the stretch. FEARLESS FLYER (IRE) angled in early and saved ground to no avail. SEEKING THE HEAT chased inside then a bit off the rail, was between foes leaving the backstretch and outside a rival on the second turn and gave way.

Owners- 1, Wygod Mr and Mrs Martin J; 2, Vegso Peter; 3, Currin Betty J; 4, Everest Stables Inc; 5, Cono Charles; 6, Niederrad Stables; 7, Earnhardt III Patti and Hal J; 8, Reddam J Paul; 9, Pegram Michael E

Trainers- 1, Canani Julio C; 2, Drysdale Neil; 3, Currin William L; 4, Polanco Marcelo; 5, Paasch Christopher S; 6, Meairs John M; 7, Baffert Bob; 8, Cecil B D A; 9, Baffert Bob

---

$2 Daily Double (2-9) Paid $24.20 ; Daily Double Pool $35,860 .
$1 Pick Three (8-2-9) Paid $44.90 ; Pick Three Pool $79,124 .

FIFTH RACE
Santa Anita
OCTOBER 3, 2004

1¼ MILES. (Turf) (1.57²) 36TH RUNNING OF THE CLEMENT L. HIRSCH MEMORIAL TURF CHAMPIONSHIP. Grade I. Purse $250,000 FOR THREE-YEAR-OLDS AND UPWARD. By subscription of $250 each if made on or before Thursday, September 2, 2004 or by supplementary nomination of $5,000 at time of entry. All horses shall pay $2,500 to start, with $250,000 guaranteed of which $150,000 tothe winner, $50,000 to second, $30,000 to third, $15,000 to fourth and $5,000 to fifth. Three-Year-Olds: 119 lbs. Older: 124 lbs. Starters to be named through the entry box by the closing time of entries. This race will not be divided. If the numberof entries exceeds fourteen (14), preference will be determined in the following order: First preference will be given to greded or group stakes winners in 2004 Second preference will be given to those horses with highest total earnings in 2004. Entryand supplementary fees will be refunded to all horses which fail to draw into this race. A trophy will be presented to the winning owner. Closed with 30 nominations.

Value of Race: $250,000 Winner $150,000; second $50,000; third $30,000; fourth $15,000; fifth $5,000. Mutuel Pool $450,690.00 Exacta Pool $222,787.00 Quinella Pool $22,822.00 Trifecta Pool $241,764.00

Last Raced	Horse	M/Eqt.	A.	Wt	PP	¼	½	¾	1	Str	Fin	Jockey	Odds $1
29Aug04 8Dmr1	Star Over the Bay	LB	6	124	5	1 2½	1 8	1 8	1 2½	1 2	1 ¾	Baze T C	4.90
29Aug04 8Dmr2	Sarafan	LB f	7	124	4	5 2	5 2	5 2½	4 1½	3 1½	2 ¾	Nakatani C S	7.60
14Aug04 9AP5	Vangelis	LB b	5	124	7	6 2	6 2	6 1½	5 1	4 1½	3 ¾	Valdivia J Jr	2.70
8Sep04 6Dmr9	The Tin Man	LB	6	124	1	2 1	2 ½	2 ½	2 1½	2 hd	4 4½	Smith M E	6.30
11Sep04 9Bel6	Ballingarry-Ire	LB b	5	124	3	4 2	3 1	3 1	3 hd	5 1½	5 1½	Douglas R R	27.30
20Mar04 9SA5	Puerto Banus	LB b	5	124	2	7	7	7	6	6	6	Espinoza V	21.80
25Jly04 8Dmr2	Bayamo-Ire	LB	5	124	6	3 hd	4 3	4 4	—	—	—	Flores D R	1.40

OFF AT 2:40 Start Good . Won driving. Course firm.

TIME :24¹, :47, 1:11, 1:35, 1:58³ (:24.27, :47.02, 1:11.08, 1:35.19, 1:58.70)

$2 Mutuel Prices:				
	5 – STAR OVER THE BAY	11.80	5.80	4.40
	4 – SARAFAN		7.40	4.60
	7 – VANGELIS			3.80

$1 EXACTA 5–4 PAID $31.60 $2 QUINELLA 4–5 PAID $28.60
$1 TRIFECTA 5–4–7 PAID $142.00

Gr/ro. g, (Feb), by Cozzene – Lituya Bay , by Empery . Trainer Mitchell Mike. Bred by Four Horsemen's Ranch (Fla).

STAR OVER THE BAY sped to the early lead and angled in, opened a commanding advantage along the inside through the stretch the first time, continued clear on the backstretch and second turn and into the stretch and held on gamely under some urging and strong handling. SARAFAN in a bit tight between foes crossing the dirt early, took back and angled in, saved ground, moved up outside a rival on the second turn and into the stretch and closed willingly. VANGELIS angled in and saved ground off the pace, came out into the second turn and three deep into the stretch and also rallied gamely. THE TIN MAN stalked the pace a bit off the rail then outside a rival, moved up inside on the second turn, came a bit off the fence in the stretch and lacked the needed late kick. BALLINGARRY (IRE) steadied in a bit tight between foes crossing the dirt, angled in and saved ground chasing the pace and did not rally. PUERTO BANUS allowed to settle inside, came off the rail on the backstretch, went outside a rival into the second turn and four wide into the stretch and was not a threat. BAYAMO (IRE) was in a good position chasing the winner outside a rival, then pulled up lame into the second turn and was vanned off.

Owners– 1, G Racing VanBurger Carl F and Vaughn Howard; 2, Tanaka Gary A; 3, Bloodstock Management Services Inc and Cheveley Park Stud Ltd; 4, Todd Aury and Ralph E; 5, Port Trust Naify Marsha and San Gabriel Investments; 6, Noctis LLC Papiano Neil and Taub Steve; 7, Prestonwood Farm LLC

Trainers– 1, Mitchell Mike; 2, Drysdale Neil; 3, Frankel Robert; 4, Mandella Richard; 5, De Seroux Laura; 6, Mulhall Kristin; 7, Canani Julio C

$2 Daily Double (5–5) Paid $395.60 ; Daily Double Pool $20,953 .
$1 Pick Three (10–5–5) Paid $550.30 ; Pick Three Pool $79,092 .

SIXTH RACE
Santa Anita
OCTOBER 3, 2004

$1\frac{1}{16}$ MILES. (1.39) 12TH RUNNING OF THE LADY'S SECRET BREEDERS' CUP HANDICAP. Grade II. Purse $250,000 (includes $75,000 BC – Breeders' Cup) FOR FILLIES AND MARES, THREE YEARS OLD AND UPWARD. By subscription of $250 each if made on or before Thursday, September 2, 2004 or by supplementary nomination of $5,000 by 10 AM Tuesday, September 28. All horses shall pay $2,500 to start, with $175,000 guaranteed and an additional $75,000 from the Breeders' Cup Fund for Cup nominees only. The host association's money to be divided 60% to the winner, 20% to second, 12% to third, 6% to fourth and 2% to fifth. Breeders' Cup Fund monies also correspondingly divided provided a Breeders' Cup nominee has finished in an awarded position. Any Breeders' Cup Fund monies not awarded will revert back to the Fund. Weights: Tuesday, September 28. The starters will be determined at entry time with preference given to Breeders' Cup nominees only of equal racing quality or weight assignment (respective of sex and weight for age.) Starters to be named through the entry box by the closing time of entries. A trophy will be presented to the owner of the winner. Closed with 21 nominations.

Value of Race: $235,000 Winner $150,000; second $35,000; third $30,000; fourth $15,000; fifth $5,000. Mutuel Pool $418,503.00 Exacta Pool $212,403.00 Quinella Pool $18,928.00 Trifecta Pool $231,344.00

Last Raced	Horse	M/Eqt.	A.	Wt	PP	St	¼	½	¾	Str	Fin	Jockey	Odds $1
6Jun04 ^{11}Tok^{16}	Island Fashion	LB b	4	120	2	1	$4^{1\frac{1}{2}}$	4^{1}	$3^{1\frac{1}{2}}$	1^{hd}	$1^{\frac{1}{2}}$	John K	a- 2.70
19Sep04 ^{9}Bel^{3}	Miss Loren-Arg	LB f	6	116	6	5	5^{hd}	7	7	$4^{\frac{1}{2}}$	2^{hd}	Court J K	7.50
2Sep04 ^{7}Dmr^{1}	Elloluv	LB b	4	118	4	4	$2^{\frac{1}{2}}$	$2^{\frac{1}{2}}$	2^{hd}	2^{3}	$3^{3\frac{1}{2}}$	Nakatani C S	3.10
18Jly04 ^{10}Del^{1}	SummerWindDncer	LB b	4	118	1	6	7	6^{hd}	4^{hd}	$3^{\frac{1}{2}}$	4^{3}	Espinoza V	1.20
10Aug03 ^{8}Dmr^{4}	Sister Girl Blues	LB	5	109	3	3	3^{1}	3^{hd}	5^{2}	5^{2}	5^{6}	Martinez F F	a- 2.70
3Apr04 ^{9}OP^{5}	Keys to the Heart	LB	5	115	5	7	$6^{1\frac{1}{2}}$	5^{hd}	$6^{\frac{1}{2}}$	6^{hd}	6^{3}	Gomez G K	38.80
21Aug04 ^{8}Dmr^{2}	Barbara Orr	LB	4	112	7	2	$1^{1\frac{1}{2}}$	1^{1}	$1^{\frac{1}{2}}$	7	7	Baze T C	9.90

a–Coupled: Island Fashion and Sister Girl Blues.

OFF AT 3:13 Start Good . Won driving. Track fast.

TIME :24, :48^{1}, 1:11^{4}, 1:36^{3}, 1:43^{2} (:24.04, :48.31, 1:11.90, 1:36.66, 1:43.43)

$2 Mutuel Prices:			
1 – ISLAND FASHION(a–entry)	**7.40**	**4.20**	**2.80**
6 – MISS LOREN-ARG		**6.80**	**3.80**
4 – ELLOLUV			**2.80**

$1 EXACTA 1–6 PAID $22.20 $2 QUINELLA 1–6 PAID $27.60
$1 TRIFECTA 1–6–4 PAID $80.80

Gr/ro. f, (Mar), by Petionville – Danzigs Fashion , by A Native Danzig . Trainer Polanco Marcelo. Bred by Everest Stables Inc (Ky).

ISLAND FASHION came off the inside into the first turn, chased outside on the backstretch, bid three deep on the second turn and outside ELLOLUV into the stretch, gained a short lead in upper stretch and held on gamely under urging while between foes late. MISS LOREN (ARG) chased outside a rival or between horses, continued outside a foe on the second turn and three deep into the stretch and closed willingly to just miss. ELLOLUV stalked outside a rival, bid between horses on the second turn, took a short lead past midway on that turn, fought back along the rail through a long drive and continued gamely to the end. SUMMER WIND DANCER settled inside, was roused into the first turn, came off the rail, chased outside, went four wide into the stretch, then drifted in and lacked the needed rally. SISTER GIRL BLUES saved ground stalking the pace, came out leaving the second turn and into the stretch and weakened. KEYS TO THE HEART off a bit slowly, angled in on the first turn and saved ground off the pace, came a bit off the rail on the second turn and did not rally. BARBARA ORR sped to the early lead outside foes, angled in on the first turn, set the pace inside, dueled briefly along the rail on the second turn, then dropped back and had little left for the stretch.

Owners– 1, Everest Stables Inc; 2, Llers Corporation; 3, Reddam J Paul; 4, Vetter Linda and Wira Richard and Yvette; 5, Everest Stables Inc; 6, Nichols Thomas L; 7, Mercedes Stables LLC

Trainers– 1, Polanco Marcelo; 2, Seglin Luis E; 3, Dollase Craig; 4, Mullins Jeff; 5, Polanco Marcelo; 6, Greely C Beau; 7, Orman Jason

Scratched– Royally Chosen (08Aug04 ^{8}Dmr^{3})

$2 Daily Double (5–1) Paid $50.00 ; Daily Double Pool $31,301 .
$1 Pick Three (5–5–1) Paid $573.90 ; Pick Three Pool $78,877 .

SEVENTH RACE
Santa Anita
OCTOBER 3, 2004

$1\frac{1}{16}$ MILES. (1.39) 35TH RUNNING OF THE NORFOLK. Grade II. Purse $200,000 FOR TWO-YEAR-OLDS. By subscription of $200 each if made on or before Thursday, September 2, 2004 or by supplementary nomination of $4,000 at time of entry. All horses to pay $2000 to start, with $200,000 guaranteed of which $120,000 to the winner, $40,000 to second, $24,000 to third, $12,000 to fourth and $4,000 to fifth. Weight: 120 lbs. Starters to be named through the entry box by the closing time of entries. Those horses with the highest earnings at time of entry will be preferred. A trophy willbe presented to the owner of the winner. Closed with 24 nominations.

Value of Race: $196,000 Winner $120,000; second $40,000; third $24,000; fourth $12,000. Mutuel Pool $1,037,161.00 Exacta Pool $271,841.00 Quinella Pool $17,238.00

Last Raced	Horse	M/Eqt.	A.	Wt	PP	St	¼	½	¾	Str	Fin	Jockey	Odds $1
8Sep04 ^{8}Dmr^{2}	Roman Ruler	LB b	2	120	4	4	$2^{1\frac{1}{2}}$	$2^{2\frac{1}{2}}$	$2^{3\frac{1}{2}}$	1^{4}	$1^{4\frac{1}{2}}$	Nakatani C S	0.05
18Sep04 ^{8}BM^{3}	Boston Glory	LB	2	120	2	3	4	4	4	$2^{2\frac{1}{2}}$	2^{13}	Baze T C	15.10
25Aug04 ^{4}Dmr^{1}	Littlebitofzip	LB b	2	120	3	2	1^{1}	1^{1}	1^{hd}	3^{2}	3^{2}	Flores D R	7.70
14Sep04 ^{9}Fpx^{1}	Forever Foxy	LB b	2	120	1	1	$3^{3\frac{1}{2}}$	3^{8}	3^{2}	4	4	Sorenson D	10.30

OFF AT 3:45 Start Good . Won driving. Track fast.

TIME :23, :46, 1:10^{3}, 1:37, 1:44^{1} (:23.02, :46.05, 1:10.66, 1:37.13, 1:44.27)

$2 Mutuel Prices:			
5 – ROMAN RULER	**2.10**	**2.10**	—
3 – BOSTON GLORY		**2.10**	—
4 – LITTLEBITOFZIP		—	—

$1 EXACTA 5–3 PAID $3.50 $2 QUINELLA 3–5 PAID $6.60

Dk. b or br. c, (Mar), by Fusaichi Pegasus – Silvery Swan , by Silver Deputy . Trainer Baffert Bob. Bred by Needham/ Betz Thoroughbreds Liberation Farm & Ashford Stud (Ky).

ROMAN RULER pulled his way along a bit wide into the first turn, stalked off the rail under a snug hold, ranged up outside LITTLEBITOFZIP to gain the lead past midway on the second turn, kicked clear nearing the quarter pole and proved best under a couple cracks of the whip and a strong hand ride while drifting in some. BOSTON GLORY trailed a bit off the rail, went outside a rival leaving the second turn, came out into the stretch and was second best. LITTLEBITOFZIP sped to the lead outside a rival early, angled in and set the pace inside and weakened once headed on the second turn. FOREVER FOXY rank along the inside early, saved ground chasing the pace and gave way.

Owners– 1, Fog City Stable; 2, Eagle Oak Ranch LLC; 3, Peacock Cecil N; 4, Hoffman Lathrop G

Trainers– 1, Baffert Bob; 2, Harty Eoin; 3, Hendricks Dan L; 4, Fanning Jerry

Scratched– Compulsive (14Aug04 ^{2}Dmr^{1})

$2 Daily Double (1–5) Paid $10.00 ; Daily Double Pool $34,336 .
$1 Pick Three (5–1–2/5) Paid $26.40 ; Pick Three Pool $96,435 .

SEVENTH RACE
Keeneland
OCTOBER 8, 2004

6 FURLONGS. (1.07³) 152ND RUNNING OF THE PHOENIX BREEDERS' CUP. Grade III. Purse $250,000 (includes $100,000 BC – Breeders' Cup) FOR THREE YEAR OLDS AND UPWARD. By subscription of $250 each, which should accompany the nomination; $750 to enter and an additional $750 to start, with $150,000 guaranteed, and an additional $100,000 from Breeders' Cup for Cup eligibles only. Keeneland Association added monies and all fees to be divided 62% to the owner of the winner, 20% to second, 10% to third, 5% to fourth and 3% to fifth. Breeders' Cup fund monies also correspondingly divided providing a Breeders' Cup nominee has finished in an awarded position. Any Breeders' Cup monies not awarded will revert back to the fund. Weight: Three-year-olds, 122 lbs.; Older, 124 lbs. Non-winners of a Grade I or II in 2004 allowed 2 lbs.; Grade III or $60,000 twice in 2004, 4 lbs; $45,000 twice in 2004, 6 lbs. Starters to be named through the entry box by usual time of closing. A gold julep cup and a Breeders' Cup trophy will be presented to the owner of the winner. Closed Wednesday, September 29, 2004 with 19 nominations.

Value of Race: $271,250 Winner $168,175; second $54,250; third $27,125; fourth $10,850; fourth $10,850. Mutuel Pool $440,655.00 Exacta Pool $317,708.00 Trifecta Pool $233,970.00 Superfecta Pool $68,135.00 Quinella Pool $13,754.00

Last Raced		Horse	M/Eqt.	A.	Wt	PP	St	¼	½	Str	Fin	Jockey	Odds $1
28Aug04 6AP3		Champali	L	4	122	7	2	4 2½	4½	3 1	1¾	Bejarano R	4.00
28Aug04 6AP1		Gold Storm	L b	4	118	1	5	2 1½	1 1	1½	2nk	Taylor L	4.70
4Sep04 8Sar2		Clock Stopper	L b	4	118	10	9	9 2½	7hd	4 1	3nk	Day P	1.90
28Aug04 6AP2	DH	Super Fuse	L b	4	118	3	11	11	10½	6 3	4	McKee J	9.60
6Sep04 9Mth1	DH	Wildcat Heir	L f	4	118	4	10	3hd	3 1½	2½	4 1½	Albarado R J	8.10
28Aug04 6AP5		Coach Jimi Lee	L	4	118	9	1	6hd	8½	5 1	6 3¼	Perret C	25.60
25Sep04 13TP1		Private Horde	L bf	5	118	5	8	8hd	9 2	8 1	7 1¼	Guidry M	31.40
15Sep04 8AP2		Arbitrate	L b	4	118	8	7	10 1½	11	9 1½	8nk	Dominguez R A	38.90
8Aug04 10Mth1		Canadian Frontier	L f	5	122	6	6	5hd	5hd	11	9 6	Castellano J J	8.80
27Mar04 11GP9		Deer Lake	L	5	118	11	3	7 1½	6hd	7hd	10 2	Prado E S	65.50
28Aug04 10Sar8		Hosco	L bf	3	120	2	4	1hd	2½	10hd	11	Nakatani C S	13.70

DH–Dead Heat.

OFF AT 4:16 Start Good. Won driving. Track fast.
TIME :21, :43⁴, :56, 1:08³ (:21.19, :43.95, :56.09, 1:08.72)

$2 Mutuel Prices:

7 – CHAMPALI	10.00	5.20	3.20
1 – GOLD STORM		6.00	3.60
10 – CLOCK STOPPER			2.40

$2 EXACTA 7–1 PAID $57.20 $2 TRIFECTA 7–1–10 PAID $137.60
$2 SUPERFECTA 7–1–10–3 PAID $434.40 $2 SUPERFECTA 7–1–10–4 PAID $424.40
$2 QUINELLA 1–7 PAID $30.80

B. c, (Feb), by Glitterman – Radioactivity , by Dixieland Band . Trainer Foley Gregory D. Bred by McKee Stables Inc (Ky).

CHAMPALI, well placed from the beginning while following the dueling leaders four or five wide, reached the front leaving the sixteenth pole while continuing five wide and was hard ridden the remainder. GOLD STORM, hustled along the inside early to contest the pace, gained the advantage on the turn, made the pace into deep stretch and couldn't contain CHAMPALI'S surge. CLOCK STOPPER, outsprinted early and six wide, edged in on the turn, advanced from between rivals into the stretch, briefly lacked room at the furlong grounds, worked his way out seven wide in the late going but couldn't muster the needed response. SUPER FUSE, outrun for a half, rallied from between horses five wide into the lane, angled to the rail at the sixteenth pole and offered a minor gain to dead heat with WILDCAT HEIR for fourth position. WILDCAT HEIR, forwardly placed between foes three or four wide into the stretch, loomed boldly for the last eighth but came up empty while finishing evenly with SUPER FUSE for fourth. COACH JIMI LEE, between foes four or five wide, wide, flattened out when the test came. PRIVATE HORDE, outsprinted early, raced near the inside, eased out five wide leaving the eighth pole but lacked a rally. ARBITRATE failed to menace. CANADIAN FRONTIER, in a striking position to the stretch while three or four wide, weakened thereafter. DEER LAKE followed the leaders five or six wide to the stretch and tired. HOSCO, sent to the fore early while three or four wide, lost the edge to GOLD STORM on the turn, continued forwardly for a half and tired.

Owners– 1, Lloyd Madison Farms IV LLC; 2, McKinney Keith and Sweesy Jack; 3, Overbrook Farm; 4, Alpha One Stable; 5, New Farm; 6, Battaglia Lee and Divito James P; 7, Tucker Billy R; 8, Lewis Robert B and Beverly J; 9, Robsham Mrs E P; 10, Fugitte Steve; 11, Rodriguez Lorraine and Rod

Trainers– 1, Foley Gregory D; 2, Cascio C W Bubba; 3, Stewart Dallas; 4, Asmussen Steven M; 5, Perkins Ben W Jr; 6, DiVito James P; 7, Cain Joe; 8, Lukas D Wayne; 9, Hough Stanley M; 10, Simon Charles; 11, O'Neill Doug

---

$2 Pick Three (6–5–7) Paid $130.60 ; Pick Three Pool $47,413 .
$2 Pick Four (1–6–5–7) Paid $1,751.60 ; Pick Four Pool $30,603 .

NINTH RACE
Keeneland
OCTOBER 8, 2004

1 1/16 MILES. (1.404) 53RD RUNNING OF THE DARLEY ALCIBIADES. Grade II. Purse $400,000 FOR FILLIES, TWO YEARS OLD. By subscription of $200 each, which should accompany the nomination. $2,000 to enter and an additional $2,000 to start, with $400,000 guaranteed, of which $248,000 to the owner of the winner, $80,000 to second, $40,000 to third, $20,000 to fourth and $12,000 to fifth. Weight: 118 lbs. Starters to be named through the entry box by usual time of closing. A gold julep cup will be presented to the owner of the winner. The owner of the winner will receive a complimentary 2005 nomination to Quiet American. The breeder of the winner will receive a complimentary 2005 nomination to Street Cry. The first four finishers in the Darley Alcibiades are automatically made eligible for the Ashland Stakes of 2005 as to nomination fees. ClosedWednesday, September 29, 2004 with 24 nominations.

Value of Race: $400,000 Winner $248,000; second $80,000; third $40,000; fourth $20,000; fifth $12,000. Mutuel Pool $343,121.00 Exacta Pool $217,835.00 Trifecta Pool $169,479.00 Superfecta Pool $66,589.00 Quinella Pool $7,447.00

Last Raced	Horse	M/Eqt.	A.	Wt	PP	St	¼	½	¾	Str	Fin	Jockey	Odds $1
19Sep04 9AP2	Runway Model	L	2	118	8	9	8½	61½	6hd	63½	1hd	Bejarano R	17.20
12Sep04 1Crc1	Sharp Lisa	L f	2	118	7	8	5½	5hd	5hd	3hd	2no	Nakatani C S	11.70
18Sep04 3Bel1	In the Gold	L	2	118	1	3	42	3hd	2½	11	3½	Castellano J J	11.20
25Sep04 7Del1	Dance Away Capote	L	2	118	10	10	10	95½	73	2hd	41½	Dominguez R A	27.80
19Sep04 8Bel1	Sense of Style		2	118	5	5	3½	42	3hd	51	53¾	Prado E S	0.60
20Aug04 8Sar2	Miss Matched	L	2	118	2	2	11½	1½	1½	41	62	Albarado R J	4.70
18Sep04 9TP1	Punch Appeal	L	2	118	3	1	21½	2½	41	76	77½	McKee J	17.10
17Sep04 7AP1	Sweet Talker	L f	2	118	4	4	62	71	8½	83	86¼	Santos J A	46.10
4Sep04 10RD3	Gallant Secret	L	2	118	6	6	7½	82	912	9	9	Houghton T D	52.10
20Aug04 8Sar7	Classic Elegance		2	118	9	7	91	10	10	—	—	Day P	12.80

OFF AT 5:15 Start Good . Won driving. Track fast.

TIME :223, :464, 1:113, 1:372, 1:441 (:22.76, :46.99, 1:11.78, 1:37.52, 1:44.31)

$2 Mutuel Prices:

8 – RUNWAY MODEL	36.40	17.40	19.20
7 – SHARP LISA		11.20	16.80
1 – IN THE GOLD			15.60

$2 EXACTA 8–7 PAID $226.00 $2 TRIFECTA 8–7–1 PAID $6,863.80
$2 SUPERFECTA 8–7–1–10 PAID $26,968.40 $2 QUINELLA 7–8 PAID $317.40

Dk. b or br. f, (Mar), by Petionville – Ticket to Houston , by Houston . Trainer Flint Bernard S. Bred by Everest Stables Inc (Ky).

RUNWAY MODEL, unhurried early, moved inside, edged up along the rail on the far turn, swung out five wide into the stretch, then closed determinedly under strong handling to capture a close decision. SHARP LISA, never far back, raced between rivals four wide around the far turn and into the stretch, angled to rail about the sixteenth pole and was going well only to be outfinished. IN THE GOLD eased off the inside early, followed the leaders four or five wide, inched to challenge front-running MISS MATCHED approaching the stretch, took over, then couldn't sustain the needed momentum. DANCE AWAY CAPOTE broke to the outside, quickly was angled to the inside, saved ground to the end of the backstretch, eased out five wide when put to a drive, loomed prominently just inside the winner for the drive but couldn't offer the needed response. SENSE OF STYLE, well placed in behind rivals under light rating early, lacked room approaching the stretch, continued in contention and lacked a response when clear. MISS MATCHED gained the lead early, raced two or three wide, made the pace until nearing the stretch and faltered. PUNCH APPEAL tracked front-running MISS MATCHED three or four wide and weakened upon going six furlongs. SWEET TALKER weakened upon going a half. GALLANT SECRET bore out on the first turn, continued six wide and tired. CLASSIC ELEGANCE faded early and was pulled up nearing the final furlong.

Owners– 1, Chowhan Naveed; 2, J Paul Reddam and Suarez Racing Inc Pablo Suarez; 3, Live Oak Plantation; 4, Pandora Farms LLC Lyn Merritt; 5, Derrick Smith and Michael B Tabor; 6, Oxley John C; 7, Heiligbrodt Stable and Burning Day Farm; 8, Kahn Eliah and Lisa; 9, Elkhorn Oaks Inc Martha D and James F Fortney; 10, Lewis Robert B and Beverly J

Trainers– 1, Flint Bernard S; 2, O'Neill Doug; 3, Zito Nicholas P; 4, Motion H Graham; 5, Biancone Patrick L; 6, Ward John T Jr; 7, Asmussen Steven M; 8, McPeek Kenneth G; 9, Jackson James R; 10, Lukas D Wayne

Scratched– Shebelongstoyou (05Sep04 4Mth1)

$2 Pick Three (7–6–8) Paid $2,686.60 ; Pick Three Pool $48,556 .

SEVENTH RACE
Meadowlands
OCTOBER 8, 2004

1⅛ MILES. (1.452) 27TH RUNNING OF THE MEADOWLANDS BREEDERS' CUP. Grade II. Purse $500,000 (includes $100,000 BC – Breeders' Cup) FOR THREE–YEAR–OLDS AND UPWARD. By subscription of $300 each, which should accompany the nomination, $2,000 to pass the entry box and an additional $2,000 to start. Purse $400,000 guaranteed with $100,000 from the Breeders' Cup Fund for Cup nominees only. The host association's money to be divided 60% to the owner of the winner, 20% to second, 10% to third, 6% to fourth, 3% to fifth and 1% to sixth. Breeders' Cup Fund money also correspondingly divided provided a Breeders' Cup nominee has finished in anawarded position. Any Breeders' Cup Fund money not awarded reverts to the Fund. Three–Year–Olds: 120 lbs.; Older: 123 lbs.; Non–winners of $100,000 at a mile or over since October 15, 2003 allowed 2 lbs.; $75,000 at a mile or over in 2004, 4 lbs. The winnning owner, trainer and jockey to recieve a trophy. Closed Saturday, September 25, 2004 with 22 nominations.

Value of Race: $500,000 Winner $300,000; second $100,000; third $50,000; fourth $30,000; fifth $15,000; sixth $5,000. Mutuel Pool $205,268.00 Exacta Pool $149,757.00 Trifecta Pool $102,878.00 Superfecta Pool $28,463.00

Last Raced	Horse	M/Eqt.	A.	Wt	PP	St	¼	½	¾	Str	Fin	Jockey	Odds $1
11Sep04 9Bel7	Balto Star	L	6	123	6	5	31½	21	21	11½	1½	Velazquez J R	6.00
3Jly04 7Bel6	Dynever	L	4	119	2	6	6hd	75	61½	31	21½	Nakatani C S	1.10
4Sep04 8Sar3	Gygistar	L	5	119	7	4	4½	41½	31	2½	33¾	Bravo J	4.40
4Sep04 8Sar5	Unforgettable Max	L f	4	119	3	3	1½	11½	1hd	42½	4no	Black A S	8.70
18Sep04 9Pim1	Lusty Latin	L b	5	121	4	2	51	5hd	72	5½	5no	Fogelsonger R	12.90
6Sep04 3Sar2	Toccet	L b	4	119	1	1	2½	3hd	5hd	61	63½	Chavez J F	7.80
11Sep04 10Bel4	Seek Gold	L	4	119	8	8	8	8	8	8	72	Velasquez C	18.10
11Sep04 3Mth1	Lion Tamer	L	4	119	5	7	72½	61½	4½	7hd	8	Coa E M	11.90

OFF AT 9:59 Start Good . Won driving. Track fast.

TIME :232, :464, 1:11, 1:354, 1:483 (:23.48, :46.97, 1:11.15, 1:35.97, 1:48.68)

$2 Mutuel Prices:

6 – BALTO STAR	14.00	5.40	3.80
2 – DYNEVER		2.60	2.40
7 – GYGISTAR			3.20

$2 EXACTA 6–2 PAID $37.00 $2 TRIFECTA 6–2–7 PAID $121.00
$1 SUPERFECTA 6–2–7–3 PAID $298.60

Dk. b or br. g, (Mar), by Glitterman – Miss Livi , by Devil's Bag . Trainer Pletcher Todd A. Bred by Anstu Stables Inc (Ky).

BALTO STAR tracked the leader racing just off the rail, moved up outside of UNFORGETTABLE MAX to take over entering the far turn, kicked clear in upper stretch and held well under urging. DYNEVER saved ground racing off the pace, advanced between rivals on the turn, angled out at the top of the lane and closed gamely outside. GYGISTAR raced three wide into the clubhouse turn, stalked the leaders, bid three wide on the far turn and was outfinished. UNFORGETTABLE MAX set the pace and weakened in the stretch. LUSTY LATIN saved ground off the pace, came four wide into the lane and lacked a rally. TOCCET raced close up on the inside and failed to sustain a rally when asked. SEEK GOLD was outrun early, came five wide into the lane and had no rally. LION TAMER rated outside a rival, moved three wide into contention on the second turn and lacked a response after that.

Owners– 1, Anstu Stables Inc; 2, Wills Catherine and Karches Peter; 3, Evans Edward P; 4, Dweck Raymond; 5, Gill Michael J; 6, Borislow Daniel M; 7, LaPenta Robert V; 8, Tabor Michael B

Trainers– 1, Pletcher Todd A; 2, Clement Christophe; 3, Hennig Mark; 4, Preciado Guadalupe; 5, Shuman Mark; 6, Frankel Robert; 7, Zito Nicholas P; 8, Pletcher Todd A

$2 Pick Three (7–8–6) Paid $276.40 ; Pick Three Pool $14,561 .

SIXTH RACE
Belmont
OCTOBER 9, 2004

$1\frac{1}{16}$ MILES. (1.39^{2}) 57TH RUNNING OF THE FRIZETTE. Grade I. Purse $500,000 (UP TO $55,000 NYSBFOA) FOR FILLIES TWO YEARS OLD. By subscription of $500 each, which should accompany the nomination; $2,500 to pass the entry box and $2,500 to start. The purse to be divided 60% to the winner, 20% to second, 10% to third, 5% to fourth, 3% to fifth and 2% divided equally among remaining finishers. 120 lbs. Trophies will be presented to the winning owner, trainer and jockey. Closed Saturday, September 25, 2004 with 16 Nominations.

Value of Race: $500,000 Winner $300,000; second $100,000; third $50,000; fourth $25,000; fifth $15,000; sixth $3,334; seventh $3,334; eighth $3,332. Mutuel Pool $557,902.00 Exacta Pool $433,076.00 Trifecta Pool $316,858.00 Superfecta Pool $60,772.00

Last Raced	Horse	M/Eqt.	A.	Wt	PP	St	¼	½	¾	Str	Fin	Jockey	Odds $1
19Sep04 ^{8}Bel^{2}	Balletto-UAE	L	2	120	1	8	7^{6}	7^{5}	$5\frac{1}{2}$	2^{hd}	$1\frac{3}{4}$	Nakatani C S	1.35
30Aug04 ^{5}Sar^{1}	Ready's Gal	L	2	120	8	3	$5\frac{1}{2}$	5^{hd}	$4\frac{1}{2}$	3^{5}	$2\frac{3}{4}$	Velazquez J R	2.65
12Sep04 ^{8}Mth^{1}	Sis City	L	2	120	2	6	$1\frac{1}{2}$	$1\frac{1}{2}$	1^{1}	$1^{1\frac{1}{2}}$	$3^{2\frac{1}{4}}$	Coa E M	10.10
19Sep04 ^{8}Bel^{3}	Play With Fire	L	2	120	5	5	8	8	7^{5}	$4\frac{1}{2}$	4^{4}	Fragoso P	4.30
5Sep04 ^{4}Mth^{1}	Shebelongstoyou	L	2	120	3	7	4^{hd}	$4\frac{1}{2}$	6^{1}	$6\frac{1}{2}$	5^{1}	Bravo J	72.75
19Sep04 ^{8}Bel^{4}	Darn That Girl	L	2	120	6	1	$2\frac{1}{2}$	3^{hd}	3^{hd}	7^{10}	$6\frac{1}{2}$	Velasquez C	19.30
3Sep04 ^{4}Sar^{1}	J P Jewel	L	2	120	4	2	$3\frac{1}{2}$	2^{1}	2^{hd}	5^{hd}	7^{17}	Castellano J J	10.10
19Sep04 ^{7}Bel^{6}	Comacina	bf	2	120	7	4	6^{hd}	$6\frac{1}{2}$	8	8	8	Farina T	26.75

OFF AT 3:50 Start Good . Won driving. Track fast.

TIME :23, :46^{1}, 1:10^{3}, 1:36^{2}, 1:43^{2} (:23.13, :46.28, 1:10.77, 1:36.59, 1:43.52)

$2 Mutuel Prices:				
	1 – BALLETTO–UAE	4.70	2.70	2.30
	8 – READY'S GAL		3.30	3.10
	2 – SIS CITY			3.70

$2 EXACTA 1–8 PAID $14.00 $2 TRIFECTA 1–8–2 PAID $51.50
$2 SUPERFECTA 1–8–2–5 PAID $84.50

Ch. f, (Mar), by Timber Country – Destiny Dance , by Nijinsky II . Trainer Albertrani Thomas. Bred by Darley (UAE).

BALLETTO (UAE) raced in hand along the inside early, advanced inside on the turn, dug in resolutely along the inside when roused and prevailed after a long drive. READY'S GAL was unhurried early on, rallied four wide approaching the stretch and finished gamely outside. SIS CITY was hustled to the front, set the pace along the inside, drifted out in upper stretch and dug in gamely despite racing a bit erratically in the final furlong. PLAY WITH FIRE was outrun early, came wide nearing the stretch and finished well outside. SHEBELONGSTOYOU raced close up inside, chased the pace and tired in the stretch. DARN THAT GIRL chased the pace while three wide and tired after the opening three quarters. J P JEWEL pressed the pace while between rivals and tired. COMACINA hit the gate at the start, raced three wide and tired.

Owners– 1, Darley Stable; 2, Scatuorchio James T; 3, Goldfarb Sanford J Torre Joe Dubb Michael Davis Ira; 4, Zwerling Gary L; 5, Narlinger Dennis; 6, Silver Earl I and Eiserman Michael; 7, Ol Memorial Stable; 8, Flying Zee Stable

Trainers– 1, Albertrani Thomas; 2, Pletcher Todd A; 3, Dutrow Richard E Jr; 4, Hennig Mark; 5, Breen Kelly J; 6, Violette Richard A Jr; 7, Zito Nicholas P; 8, Biancone Patrick L

$2 Pick Three (3–8–1) Paid $43.80 ; Pick Three Pool $95,266 .

SEVENTH RACE
Belmont
OCTOBER 9, 2004

$1\frac{1}{16}$ MILES. (1.39^{2}) 133RD RUNNING OF THE CHAMPAGNE. Grade I. Purse $500,000 (UP TO $55,000 NYSBFOA) FOR TWO YEAR OLDS. By subscription of $500 each, which should accompany the nomination; $2,500 to pass the entry box and $2,500 to start. The purse to be divided 60% to the winner, 20% to second, 10% to third, 5% to fourth, 3% to fifth and 2% divided equally among remaining finishers. 122 lbs. The New York Racing Association to add The Champagne Challenge Cup, to be won three times, not necessarily consecutively, by the same owner before becoming his or her property. The owner of the winner will also receive a trophy for permanent possession and trophies will be presented to the winning trainer and jockey. The winning horse will receive a free nomination to the 2005 Triple Crown. Closed Saturday, September 25, 2004 with 17 Nominations.

Value of Race: $500,000 Winner $300,000; second $100,000; third $50,000; fourth $25,000; fifth $15,000; sixth $3,334; seventh $3,334; eighth $3,332. Mutuel Pool $626,873.00 Exacta Pool $501,266.00 Trifecta Pool $382,383.00 Superfecta Pool $86,107.00

Last Raced	Horse	M/Eqt.	A.	Wt	PP	St	¼	½	¾	Str	Fin	Jockey	Odds $1
1Sep04 ^{5}Sar^{1}	Proud Accolade	L	2	122	8	1	4^{hd}	$4\frac{1}{2}$	$3\frac{1}{2}$	$1\frac{1}{2}$	$1\frac{1}{2}$	Velazquez J R	2.40
21Aug04 ^{9}Sar^{1}	Afleet Alex	L	2	122	6	3	$6^{2\frac{1}{2}}$	$5\frac{1}{2}$	4^{hd}	3^{5}	$2^{1\frac{1}{4}}$	Rose J	1.25
17Sep04 ^{6}Bel^{1}	Sun King	L	2	122	7	2	$2\frac{1}{2}$	$3\frac{1}{2}$	2^{hd}	2^{1}	$3^{11\frac{3}{4}}$	Castellano J J	3.90
28Aug04 ^{3}Sar^{1}	Silver Train	L f	2	122	5	4	$1\frac{1}{2}$	1^{hd}	1^{hd}	$4^{1\frac{1}{2}}$	$4^{1\frac{3}{4}}$	Smith M E	14.20
19Sep04 ^{7}Bel^{1}	Park Avenue Ball	L	2	122	2	6	$7\frac{1}{2}$	8	8	$7\frac{1}{2}$	5^{1}	Bravo J	12.50
11Sep04 ^{6}Bel^{3}	One Fein Dad	L	2	122	4	8	8	7^{1}	$6\frac{1}{2}$	5^{2}	$6^{1\frac{1}{4}}$	Migliore R	67.50
19Sep04 ^{7}Bel^{2}	Wallstreet Scandal	L	2	122	1	5	5^{hd}	$6^{1\frac{1}{2}}$	$7^{2\frac{1}{2}}$	$6\frac{1}{2}$	7^{4}	Bridgmohan S X	17.80
4Sep04 ^{4}Sar^{1}	All Trumps	L	2	122	3	7	$3\frac{1}{2}$	2^{hd}	$5^{1\frac{1}{2}}$	8	8	Velasquez C	47.25

OFF AT 4:28 Start Good . Won driving. Track fast.

TIME :23^{3}, :47^{1}, 1:11^{2}, 1:36, 1:42^{1} (:23.71, :47.20, 1:11.49, 1:36.09, 1:42.30)

$2 Mutuel Prices:				
	8 – PROUD ACCOLADE	6.80	3.10	2.40
	6 – AFLEET ALEX		2.80	2.30
	7 – SUN KING			2.60

$2 EXACTA 8–6 PAID $13.40 $2 TRIFECTA 8–6–7 PAID $38.00
$2 SUPERFECTA 8–6–7–5 PAID $130.50

Dk. b or br. c, (Apr), by Yes It's True – Proud Ciel , by Septieme Ciel . Trainer Pletcher Todd A. Bred by Marion G Montanari (Fla).

PROUD ACCOLADE came away well and was confidently handled while racing close up outside, advanced in hand while four wide on the turn, responded when asked for run turning for home, drew clear under steady pressure inside the eighth pole then dug in resolutely and held off AFLEET ALEX under a drive. AFLEET ALEX raced in hand while between rivals early, swung to the outside entering the stretch, responded when roused and finished gamely but could not get to the winner. SUN KING was hustled along outside, contested the pace while three wide, dug in when confronted by the winner entering the stretch but weakened along the inside in the final furlong. SILVER TRAIN bobbled after the start, was hustled to the front, set the pace while between rivals and tired in the stretch. PARK AVENUE BALL was outrun early along the inside, was put to the whip midway on the turn, came wide into the stretch and had no rally. ONE FEIN DAD ducked in at the start, bumping ALL TRUMPS, was hustled along outside, raced four wide and tired in the stretch. WALLSTREET SCANDAL raced close up early, was hard ridden to keep up after a half mile and tired. ALL TRUMPS was bumped at the start, raced close up inside for a half mile and tired.

Owners– 1, Padua Stables; 2, Cash is King LLC; 3, Farmer Tracy; 4, Buckram Oak Farm; 5, Char-Mari Stable; 6, One Fein Stable; 7, Klaravich Stables Inc; 8, Lazy F Ranch

Trainers– 1, Pletcher Todd A; 2, Ritchey Tim F; 3, Zito Nicholas P; 4, Mikhalides George; 5, Ryerson James T; 6, Brice Michael; 7, Violette Richard A Jr; 8, Penna Angel Jr

$2 Daily Double (1–8) Paid $21.60 ; Daily Double Pool $124,712 .
$2 Pick Three (8–1–8) Paid $43.40 ; Pick Three Pool $95,814 .

EIGHTH RACE
Belmont
OCTOBER 9, 2004

1 MILE. (Turf) (1.31^{3}) 24TH RUNNING OF THE KELSO BREEDERS' CUP HANDICAP. Grade II. Purse $350,000 (includes $100,000 BC – Breeders' Cup) WIDENER TURF (UP TO $37,500 NYSBFOA) A HANDICAP FOR THREE YEAR OLDS AND UPWARD. By subscription of $250 each, which should accompany the nomination; $1,250 to pass the entry box and $1,250 to start. The NYRA purse to be divided 60% to the winner, 20% to second, 10% to third, 5% to fourth, 3% to fifth and 2% divided equally among remaining finishers. Breeders' Cup monies also correspondingly divided. Any Breeders' Cup fund monies not awarded will revert back to the fund.Trophy to the winning owner given by Breeders' Cup Ltd. The New York Racing Association reserves the right to transfer this race to the Main Track. In the event that this race is taken off the turf, it may be subject to downgrading upon review by the Graded Stakes Committee. Closed Saturday, September 25, 2004 with 30 Nominations. (If the Stewards consider it inadvisable to run this race on the turf course, this race will be run at One Mile on the main track.).

Value of Race: $270,000 Winner $150,000; second $50,000; third $35,000; fourth $17,500; fifth $10,500; sixth $2,334; seventh $2,334; eighth $2,332. Mutuel Pool $593,212.00 Exacta Pool $426,010.00 Trifecta Pool $320,231.00

Last Raced	Horse	M/Eqt.	A.	Wt	PP	St	¼	½	¾	Str	Fin	Jockey	Odds $1
18Sep04 ^{9}Pim^{5}	Mr O'Brien-Ire	L	5	119	1	7	4^{hd}	4½	4^{hd}	2^{hd}	1$1\frac{1}{2}$	Coa E M	4.90
19Sep04 ^{9}WO^{9}	MillnnumDrgon-GB	L	5	119	3	6	6½	6^{1}	$7^{3\frac{1}{2}}$	$5^{1\frac{1}{2}}$	2no	Migliore R	6.80
18Sep04 ^{8}Bel^{4}	Gulch Approval	L	4	114	7	1	$3^{1\frac{1}{2}}$	3½	2^{hd}	1^{hd}	3½	Castellano J J	32.25
18Sep04 ^{8}Bel^{2}	Stroll	L	4	119	4	5	2½	$2^{1\frac{1}{2}}$	1^{hd}	3½	4no	Velasquez C	2.40
20Aug04 ^{7}Dmr^{3}	King of Happiness	L	5	117	8	2	5^{2}	$5^{3\frac{1}{2}}$	5½	4½	5no	Espinoza V	2.60
3Sep04 ^{8}Sar^{1}	Willard Straight	L	4	114	6	8	8	8	8	7^{hd}	6^{2}	Velazquez J R	5.90
21Mar04 ^{8}FG^{5}	Proud Man	L b	6	115	5	3	7^{7}	7^{6}	6½	6^{1}	$7^{3\frac{1}{2}}$	Nakatani C S	12.30
19Sep04 ^{9}WO^{10}	Christine's Outlaw	L	4	114	2	4	1½	1½	$3^{1\frac{1}{2}}$	8	8	Bridgmohan S X	18.40

OFF AT 4:58 Start Good . Won driving. Course firm.

TIME :23^{2}, :46, 1:09^{1}, 1:32^{3} (:23.45, :46.11, 1:09.25, 1:32.69)

$2 Mutuel Prices:

1 – MR O'BRIEN–IRE	11.80	5.70	4.70
3 – MILLENNIUM DRAGON–GB		7.10	4.60
7 – GULCH APPROVAL			12.60

$2 EXACTA 1–3 PAID $63.50 $2 TRIFECTA 1–3–7 PAID $1,106.00

Ch. g, (Apr), by Mukaddamah – Laurel Delight–GB , by Presidium–GB . Trainer Graham Robin L. Bred by Jack Ronan & Des Vere Hunt Farm Co (Ire).

MR O'BRIEN (IRE) raced close up along the inside while in hand, came wide entering the stretch, responded when roused and drew clear under a drive. MILLENNIUM DRAGON (GB) raced inside while in hand, found room in the stretch and finished gamely. GULCH APPROVAL bobbled at the start, contested the pace while three wide and dug in gamely in the stretch. STROLL pressed the pace from the outside and weakened in the stretch. KING OF HAPPINESS raced close up while in hand and lacked a rally. WILLARD STRAIGHT was outrun early, advanced inside on the turn, altered course to the outside in the stretch and finished well. PROUD MAN was outrun early, put in a four wide run on the turn and tired in the stretch. CHRISTINE'S OUTLAW quickly showed in front, set the pace along the inside and tired after three quarters.

Owners– 1, Skeedattle Stable; 2, Darley Stable; 3, Marylou Whitney Stables; 4, Claiborne Farm; 5, Al Maktoum Sheik Maktoum b; 6, Goichman Lawrence; 7, Kaufman Robert Double R Stable Weiss Stephen; 8, RC Hill Stable

Trainers– 1, Graham Robin L; 2, McLaughlin Kiaran P; 3, Zito Nicholas P; 4, Mott William I; 5, Drysdale Neil; 6, Pletcher Todd A; 7, Clement Christophe; 8, Weaver George

---

$2 Pick Three (1–8–1) Paid $87.00 ; Pick Three Pool $114,562 .

NINTH RACE
Belmont
OCTOBER 9, 2004

1⅛ MILES. (1.45^{2}) 66TH RUNNING OF THE BELDAME. Grade I. Purse $750,000 (UP TO $62,500 NYSBFOA) FOR FILLIES AND MARES THREE YEARS OLD AND UPWARD. By subscription of $750 each, which should accompany the nomination; $3,500 to pass the entry box and $4,000 to start. The purse to be divided 60% to the winner, 20% to second, 10%to third, 5% to fourth, 3% to fifth and 2% divided equally among remaining finishers. Weight for age. Three–year–olds. 120 lbs.; older, 123 lbs. Mrs. John E. Cowdin has donated a perpetual cup to be held by the owner of the winner for one year. Trophies will be presented to the winning owner, trainer and jockey. Closed Saturday, September 25, 2004 with 15 Nominations.

Value of Race: $735,000 Winner $450,000; second $150,000; third $75,000; fourth $37,500; fifth $22,500. Mutuel Pool $942,251.00 Exacta Pool $359,169.00 Trifecta Pool $258,640.00

Last Raced	Horse	M/Eqt.	A.	Wt	PP	St	¼	½	¾	Str	Fin	Jockey	Odds $1
19Sep04 ^{9}Bel^{1}	Sightseek	L	5	123	1	3	1^{hd}	1^{1}	1½	1^{6}	$1^{2\frac{3}{4}}$	Castellano J J	0.30
21Aug04 ^{10}Sar^{1}	Society Selection	L	3	120	4	1	$3^{1\frac{1}{2}}$	$3^{1\frac{1}{2}}$	3^{hd}	2½	$2^{1\frac{1}{4}}$	Velasquez C	4.70
27Aug04 ^{9}Sar^{1}	Storm Flag Flying	L	4	123	5	2	2^{1}	2^{1}	2^{hd}	$4^{5\frac{1}{2}}$	3¾	Velazquez J R	4.40
27Aug04 ^{9}Sar^{4}	Board Elligible	L bf	4	123	3	4	5	5	4^{hd}	3^{hd}	$4^{6\frac{1}{4}}$	Fragoso P	51.25
27Aug04 ^{9}Sar^{3}	Nevermore	L	4	123	2	5	4^{2}	4^{hd}	5	5	5	Espinoza V	28.50

OFF AT 5:30 Start Good . Won handily. Track fast.

TIME :24^{4}, :48^{2}, 1:12^{4}, 1:36^{4}, 1:49^{3} (:24.82, :48.40, 1:12.86, 1:36.95, 1:49.60)

$2 Mutuel Prices:

1 – SIGHTSEEK	2.60	2.10	2.10
5 – SOCIETY SELECTION		2.50	2.10
6 – STORM FLAG FLYING			2.10

$2 EXACTA 1–5 PAID $6.40 $2 TRIFECTA 1–5–6 PAID $8.00

Ch. m, (Feb), by Distant View – Viviana , by Nureyev . Trainer Frankel Robert. Bred by Juddmonte Farms Inc (Ky).

SIGHTSEEK took charge soon after the start, dictated the pace while well in hand, burst away from the field entering the stretch and was wrapped up in the final furlong, a handy winner. SOCIETY SELECTION raced close up early while between rivals and finished gamely to earn the place award. STORM FLAG FLYING pressed the pace from the outside, raced three wide on the turn and stayed on stubbornly in the stretch. BOARD ELLIGIBLE was unhurried early on, raced inside, put in a run on the rail entering the stretch and tired in the final furlong. NEVERMORE raced in hand early, moved up while four wide on the turn and tired in the stretch.

Owners– 1, Juddmonte Farms Inc; 2, Cowan Marjorie and Irving M; 3, Phipps Ogden Mills et al; 4, Rudina Stable; 5, Clifton William L Jr

Trainers– 1, Frankel Robert; 2, Jerkens H Allen; 3, McGaughey III Claude R; 4, Ferraro James W; 5, Bond Harold James

Scratched– Personal Legend (25Sep04 ^{9}Bel^{7})

EIGHTH RACE
Hawthorne
OCTOBER 9, 2004

1 MILE. (Turf) (1.33^{2}) 22ND RUNNING OF THE ROBERT F. CAREY MEMORIAL HANDICAP. Grade III. Purse $150,000 FOR THREE-YEAR-OLDS AND UPWARD. By subscription of $100 each which shall accompany the nomination. $1,000 to pass the entry box, $1,000 additional to start. With $150,000 Guaranteed, of which $90,000 to the winner, $30,000 to second, $16,500 to third, $9,000 to fourth and $4,500 to fifth. Nominations closed Wednesday, September 29, 2004 with 20. (Rail at 10 feet).

Value of Race: $150,000 Winner $90,000; second $30,000; third $16,500; fourth $9,000; fifth $4,500. Mutuel Pool $135,219.00 Exacta Pool $92,362.00 Trifecta Pool $77,938.00 Superfecta Pool $23,370.00

Last Raced	Horse	M/Eqt.	A.	Wt	PP	St	¼	½	¾	Str	Fin	Jockey	Odds $1
10Sep04 8AP3	Scooter Roach	L	5	115	4	2	61	61	5hd	3½	1nk	Campbell J M	18.60
18Sep04 6AP2	Gin and Sin	L	4	116	7	3	11	1½	1½	11	2½	Sterling L J Jr	9.10
18Sep04 6AP1	Cloudy's Knight	L	4	116	2	9	9	7hd	7½	43	31	Emigh C A	8.30
6Sep04 10EIP1	G P Fleet	L	4	114	3	4	81	9	9	8½	41¾	Mojica R Jr	8.50
6Sep04 8RP1	Major Rhythm	L b	5	117	6	5	51	51	61½	7hd	5hd	Fires E	5.20
4Sep04 7AP3	False Promises	L	4	116	5	8	7½	81	81½	6hd	6hd	Razo E Jr	5.70
1Sep04 7AP3	Holy Conflict	L	7	112	1	1	4½	3hd	21½	2hd	71¼	Montalvo C	47.60
7Aug04 8AP1	Herculated	L	4	119	8	7	3½	41	3hd	5hd	8nk	Marquez C H Jr	1.30
25Sep04 9KD1	Missme	L b	5	114	9	6	2hd	21	41½	9	9	Butler D P	10.30

OFF AT 4:28 Start Good. Won driving. Course firm.

TIME :23^{4}, :47^{2}, 1:11, 1:22^{4}, 1:34^{2} (:23.92, :47.50, 1:11.09, 1:22.80, 1:34.51)

$2 Mutuel Prices:			
4 – SCOOTER ROACH	39.20	17.80	8.00
7 – GIN AND SIN		9.60	5.40
2 – CLOUDY'S KNIGHT			7.80

$2 EXACTA 4–7 PAID $343.00 $2 TRIFECTA 4–7–2 PAID $2,087.60
$2 SUPERFECTA 4–7–2–3 PAID $5,704.40

B. g, (Mar), by Mi Cielo – Heroic Dreams, by Mr. Leader. Trainer Kassen David C. Bred by Mr & Mrs Terrel Gore (Ill).

SCOOTER ROACH saved ground near the middle of the field, angled out for the drive, rallied through the lane and was along in the final strides. GIN AND SIN set the pace from the rail while pressed and just failed to hold off the winner. CLOUDY'S KNIGHT steadied at the start, lacked speed inside, checked off of heels in the stretch angled out in deep stretch and rallied belatedly when clear. G P FLEET lacked speed, angled out for the drive and gained belatedly. MAJOR RHYTHM failed to reach a contending position. FALSE PROMISES lacked speed and was never a factor. HOLY CONFLICT raced close up inside and tired. HERCULATED raced close up just outside and tired. MISSME was five wide on the first turn, pressed the pace and gave way.

Owners– 1, Butterfly Stable Larry Slavin Lois Temkin & David Flanzbaum; 2, Silverton Hill LLC; 3, Schwartz Jerrold; 4, Richard Elaine & Bertram Klein; 5, Messino James M; 6, Maraclch David; 7, J S Cubcd Stable John F John A & James Shemroske; 8, Oakcrest Farm LLC Theresa Hodge & Jack Hodge Jr; 9, Whippoorwill Farm Inc

Trainers– 1, Kassen David C; 2, Miller Darrin; 3, Kirby Frank J; 4, Flint Steve; 5, Beam Edward; 6, Granitz Anthony J; 7, Geier Greg; 8, Stidham Michael; 9, Whiting Lynn S

$2 Pick Three (2–1–4) Paid $5,704.40 ; Pick Three Pool $3,800 .
$2 Pick Six (4–5–2–2–1–4) 3 Correct Paid $14.00 ; Pick Six Pool $525 ; Carryover Pool $3,101.

FIFTH RACE
Keeneland
OCTOBER 9, 2004

1½ MILES. (Turf) (2.27^{2}) 10TH RUNNING OF THE SYCAMORE BREEDERS' CUP. Grade III. Purse $150,000 (includes $50,000 BC – Breeders' Cup) HAGGIN COURSE. FOR THREE YEAR OLDS AND UPWARD. By subscription of $150 each, which should accompany the nomination; $500 to enter and an additional $500 to start with $100,000 added and an additional $50,000 from the Breeders' Cup for Cup eligibles only.Keeneland Association added monies and all fees to be divided 62% to the owner of the winner, 20% to second, 10% to third, 5% to fourth and 3% to fifth. Breeders' Cup fund monies also correspondingly divided providing a Breeders' Cup nominee has finishedin an awarded position. Any Breeders' Cup monies not awarded will revert back to the fund. Weight: Three year olds, 121 lbs.; Older, 125 lbs. Non-winners of a Grade I or II over ten furlongs on the turf in 2004 allowed 3 lbs.; a Grade III or Listed race over nine furlongs in 2003–2004, 5lbs. Starters to be named through the entry box by the usual time of closing. A gold julep cup and a Breeders' Cup trophy will be presented to the owner of the winner. Closed Wednesday, September 29, 2004 with 22 nominations.

Value of Race: $152,300 Winner $100,626; second $22,460; third $16,230; fourth $8,115; fifth $4,869. Mutuel Pool $425,515.00 Exacta Pool $297,760.00 Trifecta Pool $229,670.00 Superfecta Pool $62,870.00 Quinella Pool $13,028.00

Last Raced	Horse	M/Eqt.	A.	Wt	PP	¼	½	1	1¼	Str	Fin	Jockey	Odds $1
6Sep04 10Sar2	Mustanfar	L b	3	118	2	83	82½	82½	7½	4hd	13	Santos J A	2.90
27Aug04 10Sar1	Deputy Strike	L	6	120	5	52½	3½	31	2½	1hd	21	Guidry M	9.60
25Sep04 14KD2	Rochester	L	8	122	1	6hd	6hd	5½	5hd	52	31¼	Day P	3.70
4Sep04 7AP1	On the Course	L	4	120	7	2hd	2½	2hd	1hd	31½	4¾	Albarado R J	7.40
14Dec03 10ST11	Denon	L	6	122	8	31½	4½	4hd	4hd	2hd	52	Prado E S	1.50
25Sep04 14KD3	Gottabeachboy	L b	4	120	4	72	71½	7hd	61	62	63	Graham J	75.80
18Sep04 11TP6	Stratostar	L b	4	120	6	9	9	9	9	9	7hd	Bejarano R	34.00
25Sep04 14KD4	Gorylla-Brz	L	7	122	3	4hd	51	61½	81	7hd	8hd	Stevens G L	16.30
4Sep04 7AP8	Grey Beard	L b	5	120	9	11½	11	1hd	31	8hd	9	Blanc B	66.20

OFF AT 3:13 Start Good. Won driving. Course firm.

TIME :26, :51^{2}, 1:16^{1}, 1:41^{3}, 2:07, 2:30^{4} (:26.03, :51.54, 1:16.24, 1:41.74, 2:07.07, 2:30.88)

$2 Mutuel Prices:			
2 – MUSTANFAR	7.80	4.60	3.20
5 – DEPUTY STRIKE		8.80	5.00
1 – ROCHESTER			3.20

$2 EXACTA 2–5 PAID $53.20 $2 TRIFECTA 2–5–1 PAID $203.60
$2 SUPERFECTA 2–5–1–7 PAID $841.60 $2 QUINELLA 2–5 PAID $31.40

Ch. c, (Mar), by Unbridled – Manwah, by Lyphard. Trainer McLaughlin Kiaran P. Bred by Shadwell Farm LLC (Ky).

MUSTANFAR, rated near the inside from early on, came out leaving the five-sixteenths pole, advanced seven wide into the stretch and drove clear under energetic handling. DEPUTY STRIKE tracked the pace from early on while in hand four wide, inched to challenge approaching the stretch, gained a slight edge, then wasn't a match for the winner late. ROCHESTER, never far back, went along under light restraint while between foes three or four wide, came out wider for the drive but lacked a serious late response. ON THE COURSE went up early to press front-running GREY BEARD three or four wide, reached the front approaching the final quarter, then weakened in the final furlong. DENON moved inside early, made a bold run from the rail to gain even terms for the lead leaving the furlong grounds and failed to sustain the needed momentum. GOTTABEACHBOY, six wide much of the way while within striking distance, failed to rally. STRATOSTAR settled in behind horses early and never menaced. GORYLLA (BRZ), four wide, weakened gradually after going nine furlongs. GREY BEARD gained the lead, moved inside, managed the lead through modest fractions, battled close up to the stretch and tired.

Owners– 1, Shadwell Farm LLC; 2, Ramsey Kenneth L and Sarah K; 3, Augustin Stable; 4, Golden Barry; 5, Sekiguchi Fusao; 6, Hackworth Robert S Jr; 7, Allen E Paulson Living Trust; 8, Stud Colorado; 9, Brunacini George

Trainers– 1, McLaughlin Kiaran P; 2, Romans Dale; 3, Sheppard Jonathan E; 4, Stidham Michael; 5, Frankel Robert; 6, Hackworth Robert S; 7, Lukas D Wayne; 8, McPeek Kenneth G; 9, Fojan Emilie

---

$2 Pick Three (1–2–2) Paid $243.80 ; Pick Three Pool $52,740 .
$2 Pick Four (1–1–2–2) Paid $1,428.80 ; Pick Four Pool $45,619 .

SEVENTH RACE
Keeneland
OCTOBER 9, 2004

1 1/16 MILES. (1.40⁴) 91ST RUNNING OF THE LANE'S END BREEDERS' FUTURITY. Grade I. Purse $500,000 FOR TWO YEAR OLDS. By subscription of $300 each, which should accompany the nomination; $2,500 to enter and an additional $2,500 to start with $500,000 guaranteed, of which $310,000 to the owner of the winner, $100,000 to second, $50,000 to third, $25,000 to fourth and $15,000 to fifth. Weight; Fillies, 118 lbs.; Colts and Geldings, 121 lbs. Starters to be named through the entry box by usual time of closing. A gold julep cup will be presented to the owner of the winner. A silver julep cup will be presented to the winning trainer and jockey. The first four finishers in the Lane's End Breeders' Futurity are automatically made eligible for the Toyota Blue Grass Stakes of 2005 as to nomination fees. Closed Wednesday, September 29, 2004 with 29 nominations.

Value of Race: $500,000 Winner $310,000; second $100,000; third $50,000; fourth $25,000; fifth $15,000. Mutuel Pool $624,239.00 Exacta Pool $393,505.00 Trifecta Pool $291,786.00 Superfecta Pool $76,388.00 Quinella Pool $15,953.00

Last Raced	Horse	M/Eqt.	A.	Wt	PP	St	¼	½	¾	Str	Fin	Jockey	Odds $1
21Aug04 9Sar4	Consolidator	L	2	121	6	1	2 1½	2hd	2½	1 2½	1 2	Bejarano R	5.90
17Sep04 6Bel2	Patriot Act	L	2	121	9	3	7 2	8½	5 1½	2 1	2 3¼	Albarado R J	3.30
6Sep04 13RD2	Diamond Isle	L	2	121	3	6	5hd	5 2	6 1½	5 2	3½	Day P	5.70
19Sep04 6AP2	Straight Line		2	121	7	7	3hd	3½	3 2	3 2	4 5½	Blanc B	28.60
19Sep04 7Bel3	Evil Minister	L f	2	121	5	8	9½	7hd	8 2	6hd	5½	Stevens G L	18.60
19Sep04 6AP1	Three Hour Nap	L	2	121	8	9	10	9 2½	7hd	8 4	6nk	Guidry M	11.10
6Sep04 13RD1	Bellamy Road	L f	2	121	2	4	1½	1 1½	1½	4hd	7no	Dominguez R A	2.10
6Sep04 13RD3	Scipion	b	2	121	10	2	4 4½	4 4½	4 1	7hd	8 5	Prado E S	7.20
11Sep04 4Bel1	Father Weist	L	2	121	1	5	6½	6½	9 1½	9 4	9 9¼	Martinez W	23.90
28Aug04 11Mth8	Pop the Question	L	2	121	4	10	8½	10	10	10	10	Perret C	51.10

OFF AT 4:13 Start Good . Won driving. Track fast.

TIME :23, :47, 1:12, 1:37¹, 1:43³ (:23.19, :47.14, 1:12.04, 1:37.34, 1:43.67)

$2 Mutuel Prices:				
	7 – CONSOLIDATOR	13.80	6.20	4.60
	10 – PATRIOT ACT		4.60	3.20
	4 – DIAMOND ISLE			4.20

$2 EXACTA 7–10 PAID $70.00 $2 TRIFECTA 7–10–4 PAID $359.60
$2 SUPERFECTA 7–10–4–8 PAID $6,187.40 $2 QUINELLA 7–10 PAID $37.80

Ch. c, (May), by Storm Cat – Good Example–Fr , by Crystal Glitters . Trainer Lukas D Wayne. Bred by Pacelco SA (Ky).

CONSOLIDATOR went up at once to press front-running BELLAMY ROAD three or four wide, was eased back slightly early on the backstretch, went along under careful handling, was asked for a bit more entering the far turn, took over approaching the five-sixteenths pole, settled into the stretch with a clear advantage and continued under energetic handling. PATRIOT ACT, unhurried for a half, followed the leaders five wide, made a solid run to be just off the winner while outside that one entering the stretch and couldn't offer the needed response as second best. DIAMOND ISLE, never far back, raced under light restraint three wide, lost a bit of position on the far turn while continuing near the inside, swung out five or six wide when straightened for the drive and bested the others while unable to challenge the top two. STRAIGHT LINE worked his way inside early while gaining a forward position, raced along the rail on the far turn, moved with CONSOLIDATOR while inside that one approaching the stretch and flattened out in the drive. EVIL MINISTER, reserved three wide early, was outrun for six furlongs while inside, eased out three or four wide for the stretch run and improved position while not a threat. THREE HOUR NAP hopped at the start, was outrun until the stretch and unable to menace while improving position slightly. BELLAMY ROAD was sent to the fore inside at once, made the pace for six furlongs and gradually weakened thereafter. SCIPION maneuvered in early to follow the leaders four or five wide and also weakened after three-quarters. FATHER WEIST drifted out slightly on the first turn, continued in contention between horses four or five wide to the end of the backstretch and lacked a further account. POP THE QUESTION hopped slightly at the start while breaking sluggishly and never menaced.

Owners– 1, Lewis Robert B and Beverly J; 2, Farish William S; 3, Buckram Oak Farm; 4, Vanier Nancy A and Cartwright Thoroughbreds LLC; 5, Namcook Stables LLC Terrance Murray; 6, Homewrecker Racing LLC Ron and Ricki Rashinski and Hugh H Robertson; 7, Kinsman Stable; 8, Kraft-Payson Virginia; 9, Double C Stable; 10, Team Derby Dreams Stable John F Goldthorp and Robert Hurley

Trainers– 1, Lukas D Wayne; 2, Howard Neil J; 3, McPeek Kenneth G; 4, Vanier Harvey L; 5, Juvonen Erik; 6, Robertson Hugh H; 7, Dickinson Michael W; 8, Biancone Patrick L; 9, Zito Nicholas P; 10, Dowd John F

Scratched– Magna Graduate (18Sep04 10TP 2) , Copy My Notes (06Sep04 13RD 5)

$2 Pick Three (2–11–7) Paid $3,246.40 ; Pick Three Pool $64,537 .
$2 Pick Four (2–2–11–7) Paid $21,382.00 ; Pick Four Pool $51,523 .

EIGHTH RACE
Keeneland
OCTOBER 9, 2004

1 MILE. (Turf) (1.33²) 19TH RUNNING OF THE SHADWELL TURF MILE. Grade I. Purse $600,000 HAGGIN COURSE. FOR THREE YEAR OLDS AND UPWARD. By subscription of $400 each, which should accompany the nomination; $3,000 to enter and an additional $3,000 to start with $600,000 guaranteed, of which $372,000 to the owner of the winner, $120,000 to second, $60,000 to third, $30,000 to fourth and $18,000 to fifth. Weight: Three year olds, 123 lbs.; Older, 126 lbs. Starters to be named through the entry box by the usual time of closing. A gold julep cup will be presented to the owner of the winner. A silver julep cup will be presented to the winning trainer and jockey. Closed Wednesday, September 29, 2004 with 21 nominations.

Value of Race: $600,000 Winner $372,000; second $120,000; third $60,000; fourth $30,000; fifth $18,000. Mutuel Pool $614,674.00 Exacta Pool $371,144.00 Trifecta Pool $285,983.00 Superfecta Pool $71,810.00 Quinella Pool $16,713.00

Last Raced	Horse	M/Eqt.	A.	Wt	PP	St	¼	½	¾	Str	Fin	Jockey	Odds $1
28Aug04 9Sar1	Nothing to Lose	L b	4	126	9	9	7 1½	7 1½	3hd	1 1½	1 4½	Albarado R J	4.60
18Sep04 6AP3	Honor in War	L	5	126	5	8	9	9	9	2hd	2¾	Borel C H	10.30
28Aug04 9Sar2	Silver Tree	L	4	126	4	3	4 2½	5hd	6 1	5hd	3 1¼	Day P	4.30
28Aug04 9Sar6	Ay Caramba-Brz	L	4	126	1	4	8 1	8 1½	7hd	6½	4no	Santos J A	10.10
18Sep04 LCH2	Puppeteer-GB	L	4	126	6	7	6 2½	6 3	8½	7 1½	5 1	Blanc B	17.40
14Aug04 9AP8	Sweet Return-GB	L	4	126	8	5	2hd	2hd	2½	3hd	6 4	Stevens G L	4.60
19Sep04 9WO2	Perfect Soul-Ire	L b	6	126	7	6	5hd	4½	4½	8 1½	7½	Prado E S	2.20
26Sep04 9LaD1	Warleigh	L	6	126	3	1	1 1½	1 1½	1 1	4 1½	8hd	Melancon L	16.70
19Sep04 9WO4	Surging River	L	4	126	2	2	3 2	3 1	5hd	9	9	Bejarano R	18.10

OFF AT 4:45 Start Good . Won driving. Course firm.

TIME :23², :47¹, 1:11⁴, 1:23³, 1:35² (:23.56, :47.20, 1:11.94, 1:23.68, 1:35.55)

$2 Mutuel Prices:				
	9 – NOTHING TO LOSE	11.20	6.40	4.20
	5 – HONOR IN WAR		9.20	6.40
	4 – SILVER TREE			4.00

$2 EXACTA 9–5 PAID $152.80 $2 TRIFECTA 9–5–4 PAID $710.40
$2 SUPERFECTA 9–5–4–1 PAID $9,694.20 $2 QUINELLA 5–9 PAID $92.00

B. c, (Jan), by Sky Classic – Cherlindrea , by Clever Trick . Trainer Frankel Robert. Bred by Kenneth L Ramsey & Sarah K Ramsey (Ky).

NOTHING TO LOSE, lightly rated early and four or five wide most of the way, moved to the fore entering the upper stretch and was going away at the end when kept to his task. HONOR IN WAR, reserved after the start and angled inside, moved five wide on the backstretch, came out farther on the course for the stretch run and was up for the place. SILVER TREE, well positioned between horses from early on, remained within easy striking distance while continuing between foes into deep stretch and failed to respond. AY CARAMBA (BRZ) settled inside early, swung out seven or eight wide entering the stretch and lacked a serious response. PUPPETEER (GB), rated near the inside from early on, eased out four wide for the stretch run and couldn't challenge while slightly improving position. SWEET RETURN (GB), well placed from the start while tracking front-running WARLEIGH in hand three or four wide, remained close up into the stretch and failed to continue. PERFECT SOUL (IRE) followed the leaders in a striking position four or five wide to the stretch and weakened. WARLEIGH gained the lead early while dueling outside of SURGING RIVER, opened a clear advantage on the first turn, made the pace into the stretch and faltered. SURGING RIVER, close up inside from the outset, continued prominently for about six furlongs and weakened.

Owners– 1, Ramsey Kenneth L and Sarah K; 2, 3rd Turn Stables LLC Will Wolford et al; 3, Vegso Peter; 4, Patricia Bozano; 5, House Michael; 6, Red Oak Stable; 7, Fipke Charles E; 8, Parra Rosendo G; 9, Sam-Son Farms

Trainers– 1, Frankel Robert; 2, McGee Paul J; 3, Mott William I; 4, Caramori Eduardo; 5, Dupre Alain D; 6, McAnally Ronald; 7, Attfield Roger L; 8, Asmussen Steven M; 9, Frostad Mark

$2 Pick Three (11–7–9) Paid $6,532.80 ; Pick Three Pool $59,032 .

NINTH RACE
Santa Anita
OCTOBER 9, 2004

1 MILE. (Turf) (1.31[4]) 19TH RUNNING OF THE OAK TREE BREEDERS' CUP MILE. Grade II. Purse $250,000 (includes $50,000 BC - Breeders' Cup) FOR THREE-YEAR-OLDS AND UPWARD. Closed Thursday, September 2 with 32 nominations. 2 supplementary nominations: Buckland Manor and Royal Price(Ger).

Value of Race: $246,000 Winner $150,000; second $50,000; third $30,000; fourth $12,000; fifth $4,000. Mutuel Pool $465,772.00 Exacta Pool $238,713.00 Quinella Pool $23,933.00 Trifecta Pool $240,969.00

Last Raced	Horse	M/Eqt.	A.	Wt	PP	St	¼	½	¾	Str	Fin	Jockey	Odds $1
14Aug04 8AP4	Musical Chimes	LB	4	118	3	3	3hd	4hd	3½	3hd	1no	Desormeaux K J	4.00
12Jun04 9Hol6	Buckland Manor	LB	4	119	2	1	2½	2½	2½	21	2no	Douglas R R	5.90
31May04 7Hol2	Singletary	LB	4	119	5	4	5½	51	51	53	3½	Flores D R	1.50
25Aug04 3Dmr2	Gondolieri-Chi	LB b	5	119	1	2	11½	11	11	1hd	4½	Baze T C	9.90
8Sep04 6Dmr3	Tsigane-FR	LB b	5	119	6	6	6	6	4hd	4½	55½	Valdivia J Jr	2.70
27Aug04 7Dmr1	Royal Price-Ger	LB	4	119	4	5	41	31	6	6	6	Court J K	9.10

OFF AT 4:42 Start Good. Won driving. Course firm.

TIME :23, :46[4], 1:09[3], 1:21[1], 1:33[1] (:23.00, :46.99, 1:09.60, 1:21.38, 1:33.29)

$2 Mutuel Prices:

3 – MUSICAL CHIMES	10.00	5.40	2.60
2 – BUCKLAND MANOR		7.60	3.40
6 – SINGLETARY			2.40

$1 EXACTA 3-2 PAID $30.70 $2 QUINELLA 2-3 PAID $35.60
$1 TRIFECTA 3-2-6 PAID $93.00

Dk. b or br. f, (Apr), by In Excess-Ire - Note Musicale-GB , by Sadler's Wells . Trainer Drysdale Neil. Bred by Gainsborough Farm LLC (Ky).

MUSICAL CHIMES saved ground stalking the pace, came out leaving the second turn and three deep into the stretch and rallied gamely between foes under urging to get up late. BUCKLAND MANOR pulled a bit early, stalked the pace just off the rail, bid outside a rival in the stretch, put a head in front between horses in deep stretch but was caught late. SINGLETARY was in a good position stalking the pace three deep then outside a rival on the backstretch, continued three wide on the second turn and four wide into the stretch and closed gamely. GONDOLIERI (CHI) bobbled slightly at the start, sped to the early lead, set the pace inside, fought back gamely through a hard drive and continued willingly to the wire. TSIGANE (FR) angled in and saved ground chasing the pace, moved up inside into the stretch, was blocked off heels from midstretch to deep stretch and could not recover. ROYAL PRICE (GER) well placed stalking the pace between foes then outside a rival on the backstretch, continued between horses on the second turn and weakened.

Owners– 1, Al Maktoum Sheik Maktoum b; 2, McCaffery Trudy and Toffan John A; 3, Little Red Feather Racing; 4, Hunt Nelson B; 5, Prestonwood Farm LLC; 6, Bello Michael

Trainers– 1, Drysdale Neil; 2, Gonzalez J Paco; 3, Chatlos Donald Jr; 4, McAnally Ronald; 5, Canani Julio C; 6, Frankel Robert

Scratched– Needwood Blade (GB) (02Oct04 7BM 1)

$2 Daily Double (7-3) Paid $108.40 ; Daily Double Pool $30,234 .
$1 Pick Three (10-7-3) Paid $597.00 ; Pick Three Pool $76,020 .

NINTH RACE
Belmont
OCTOBER 10, 2004

6½ FURLONGS. (1.14[2]) 11TH RUNNING OF THE GALLANT BLOOM HANDICAP. Grade II. Purse $150,000 (Up to $28,500 NYSBFOA) A HANDICAP FOR FILLIES AND MARES THREE YEARS OLD AND UPWARD. By subscription of $150 each, which should accompany the nomination; $750 to pass the entry box and $750 to start. The purse to be divided 60% to the winner, 20% to second, 10% to third, 5% to fourth, 3% to fifth and 2% divided equally among remaining finishers. A trophy will be presented to the winning owner. Closed Saturday, September 25, 2004 with 18 Nominations.

Value of Race: $150,000 Winner $90,000; second $30,000; third $15,000; fourth $7,500; fifth $4,500; sixth $1,500; seventh $1,500. Mutuel Pool $273,466.00 Exacta Pool $236,405.00 Trifecta Pool $210,343.00

Last Raced	Horse	M/Eqt.	A.	Wt	PP	St	¼	½	Str	Fin	Jockey	Odds $1
29Aug04 9Sar1	Lady Tak	L	4	122	7	1	2½	21½	1½	12	Velazquez J R	0.80
29Aug04 9Sar4	Molto Vita	L	4	115	6	2	1½	1hd	26	24¼	Castellano J J	8.90
23Jun04 5Bel1	Zawzooth	L	5	115	2	3	3½	3hd	3hd	3hd	Santos J A	15.20
11Sep04 8Del1	Ebony Breeze	L	4	118	1	6	6½	7	52½	43½	Velasquez C	2.20
22Aug04 8Mth2	Forty Moves	L	3	112	5	4	4hd	41	4½	51½	Bravo J	37.25
19Sep04 9Bel4	Class Above	L b	3	115	3	7	7	62	65	67¼	Migliore R	19.30
31Jly04 8Sar3	Forest Music	L f	3	114	4	5	51½	5hd	7	7	Gryder A T	12.50

OFF AT 5:12 Start Good. Won ridden out. Track fast.

TIME :23[1], :46[4], 1:09[4], 1:16 (:23.37, :46.84, 1:09.81, 1:16.04)

$2 Mutuel Prices:

7 – LADY TAK	3.60	2.70	2.30
6 – MOLTO VITA		6.40	5.40
2 – ZAWZOOTH			5.00

$2 EXACTA 7-6 PAID $16.40 $2 TRIFECTA 7-6-2 PAID $96.50

Ch. f, (Apr), by Mutakddim - Star of My Eye , by Lucky North . Trainer Asmussen Steven M. Bred by John Franks (Fla).

LADY TAK came away fast and prompted the pace from the outside while well in hand, cruised up to engage MOLTO VITA approaching the stretch, showed in front of that rival when asked for run, drew clear inside the eighth pole and was ridden out to the wire. MOLTO VITA broke running, quickly showed in front, set the pace under pressure from the winner, proved no match for that one in the stretch but dug in gamely to be clearly best of the others. ZAWZOOTH was bumped at the start, raced close up inside, chased the pace and lacked a rally. EBONY BREEZE stumbled at the start, was outrun early, raced inside on the turn, angled out in upper stretch and had no rally. FORTY MOVES raced in hand outside early, put in a three wide run on the turn and faded in the stretch. CLASS ABOVE was bumped at the start, was pinched back after the start, put in a four wide run on the turn and tired in the stretch. FOREST MUSIC raced close up while between rivals and tired in the stretch.

Owners– 1, Heiligbrodt Racing Stable; 2, Gunther John D; 3, Starlight Stable LLC; 4, Kinsman Stable; 5, Evans Edward P; 6, Padua Stables; 7, Gill Michael J

Trainers– 1, Asmussen Steven M; 2, Stewart Dallas; 3, Pletcher Todd A; 4, Mott William I; 5, Hennig Mark; 6, McLaughlin Kiaran P; 7, Shuman Mark

SIXTH RACE
Keeneland
OCTOBER 10, 2004

$1\frac{1}{16}$ MILES. (Turf) (1.53^{4}) 7TH RUNNING OF THE WINSTAR GALAXY. Grade II. Purse $500,000 Haggin Course. FOR FILLIES AND MARES, THREE YEARS OLD AND UPWARD. By subscription of $300 each, which should accompany the nomination; $2,500 to enter and an additional $2,500 to start, with $500,000 guaranteed, of which $310,000 to the owner of the winner, $100,000 to second, $50,000 to third, $25,000 to fourth and $15,000 to fifth. Weight: Three-year-old fillies, 122 lbs.; Older fillies and mares, 125 lbs. Non-winners of a Grade or Group I on the turf in 2004 allowed 2 lbs.; a Grade or Group II over a mile on the turf in 2004, 4 lbs.; a Grade or Group III over a mile on the turf in 2004 or $60,000 twice over a mile on the turf in 2003-2004, 6 lbs. Starters to be named through the entry box by the usual time of closing. A gold julep cup will be presented to the ownerof the winner. Closed Wednesday, September 29, 2004 with 28 nominations.

Value of Race: $500,000 Winner $310,000; second $100,000; third $50,000; fourth $25,000; fifth $15,000. Mutuel Pool $343,275.00 Exacta Pool $218,853.00 Trifecta Pool $167,354.00 Superfecta Pool $46,722.00 Quinella Pool $11,747.00

Last Raced	Horse	M/Eqt.	A.	Wt	PP	St	¼	½	¾	Str	Fin	Jockey	Odds $1
5Jly04 ^{9}Bel^{2}	Stay Forever	L b	7	121	5	8	9	9	8^{hd}	$5^{1\frac{1}{2}}$	$1^{\frac{1}{2}}$	Castro E	8.00
11Aug04 ^{8}Sar^{3}	Super Brand-Saf	L	5	119	2	7	$4^{1\frac{1}{2}}$	5^{1}	$5^{3\frac{1}{2}}$	4^{1}	$2^{1\frac{1}{2}}$	Day P	10.10
14Aug04 ^{8}AP^{8}	Shaconage	L	4	121	4	4	1^{1}	1^{1}	$1^{\frac{1}{2}}$	2^{hd}	3no	Bejarano R	7.20
29Aug04 ^{8}Dmr^{4}	Dimitrova	L	4	121	9	1	2^{hd}	2^{hd}	$4^{\frac{1}{2}}$	1^{hd}	4^{1}	Douglas R R	2.80
23Sep04 ^{7}Bel^{1}	Alchemist	L	4	119	8	2	5^{hd}	$7^{1\frac{1}{2}}$	7^{2}	7^{1}	$5^{\frac{1}{2}}$	Stevens G L	18.70
15Aug04 SAB^{1}	Jacira-FR		5	119	6	9	$6^{\frac{1}{2}}$	$3^{\frac{1}{2}}$	2^{1}	3^{hd}	6^{hd}	Albarado R J	18.90
5Sep04 ^{10}Sar^{2}	Spice Island	L b	5	121	1	6	3^{hd}	$4^{\frac{1}{2}}$	3^{hd}	$6^{\frac{1}{2}}$	7^{nk}	Prado E S	*2.80
14Aug04 ^{8}AP^{5}	Bedanken	L f	5	121	7	3	8^{hd}	8^{hd}	9	8^{3}	8^{8}	Pettinger D R	3.40
5Sep04 ^{7}Sar^{4}	Lady Liberty	L	5	119	3	5	$7^{\frac{1}{2}}$	$6^{2\frac{1}{2}}$	$6^{\frac{1}{2}}$	9	9	Blanc B	54.40

***-Actual Betting Favorite.**

OFF AT 3:45 Start Good . Won driving. Course firm.

TIME :25^{1}, :50, 1:14^{2}, 1:39^{1}, 1:57 (:25.20, :50.08, 1:14.55, 1:39.33, 1:57.08)

$2 Mutuel Prices:

5 – STAY FOREVER	18.00	9.20	7.00
2 – SUPER BRAND–SAF		9.80	6.60
4 – SHACONAGE			6.40

$2 EXACTA 5–2 PAID $216.00 $2 TRIFECTA 5–2–4 PAID $1,978.80
$2 SUPERFECTA 5–2–4–9 PAID $7,568.80 $2 QUINELLA 2–5 PAID $142.00

Ch. m, (Apr), by Stack – Forever Lady , by Forever Sparkle . Trainer Wolfson Martin D. Bred by Santa Cruz Ranch Inc (Fla).

STAY FOREVER, unhurried early and five wide, advanced steadily from that position on the course around the far turn, came out seven or eight wide when straightened for the drive and was ridden hard to prevail. SUPER BRAND (SAF), never far back, raced under light restraint while tracking the leaders four or five wide, continued in that position on the course entering the stretch, was just inside that winner, gained even terms in the late going but wasn't quite good enough. SHACONAGE moved to the front early, raced two or three wide, drifted out for a stride nearing the final furlong bumping with JACIRA (FR), then grudgingly weakened. DIMITROVA pressed front-running SHACONAGE from early on while three or four wide, slipped down along the inside on the far turn, made a bold run from the rail to reach the front briefly at the eighth pole, then failed to sustain the needed momentum. ALCHEMIST, within striking distance always and four or five wide to the stretch, angled a bit wider for the drive and offered a minor gain in the late going. JACIRA (FR), sluggish early, worked her way forward four wide on the first turn, went up to press front-running SHACONAGE, gained even terms while between horses outside that rival nearing the final furlong, was bumped for a stride by SHACONAGE when she came out, then came up empty. SPICE ISLAND, well placed inside early, eased out five wide leaving the second turn and was empty in the drive. BEDANKEN moved near the inside early, swung out seven wide entering the stretch and lacked a response. LADY LIBERTY raced in contention near the inside until midway on the far turn and tired.

Owners– 1, Santa Cruz Ranch Inc; 2, Team Valor Stables LLC Barry Irwin et al; 3, Van Doren Andrena; 4, Higgins Joseph; 5, Alexander Helen C Groves Helen K and Dorothy A Matz LLC; 6, Cuadra Madronos Felix Sanz-Blanco and Eduardo Sanz-Moraga; 7, Denlea Park Ltd; 8, Pin Oak Stable LLC; 9, Janney Stuart S III

Trainers– 1, Wolfson Martin D; 2, McLaughlin Kiaran P; 3, Shirota Mitch; 4, Drysdale Neil; 5, McGaughey III Claude R; 6, Delcher-Sanchez Mauricio; 7, Clement Christophe; 8, Von Hemel Donnie K; 9, McGaughey III Claude R

$2 Daily Double (6–5) Paid $84.40 ; Daily Double Pool $12,219 .
$2 Pick Three (6–6–5) Paid $343.20 : Pick Three Pool $47,368 .

EIGHTH RACE
Keeneland
OCTOBER 10, 2004

1⅛ MILES. (1.46^{3}) 49TH RUNNING OF THE OVERBROOK SPINSTER. Grade I. Purse $500,000 FOR FILLIES AND MARES, THREE YEARS OLD AND UPWARD. By subscription of $300 each, which should accompany the nomination; $2,500 to enter and an additional $2,500 to start, with $500,000 guaranteed, of which $310,000 to the owner of the winner, $100,000 tosecond, $50,000 to third, $25,000 to fourth and $15,000 to fifth. Weight: Three year olds, 120 lbs.; Older, 123 lbs. Starters to be named through the entry box by the usual time of closing. A gold julep cup will be presented to the owner of the winner.A silver julep cup will be presented to the winning trainer and jockey. Closed Wednesday, September 29, 2004 with 19 nominations.

Value of Race: $500,000 Winner $310,000; second $100,000; third $50,000; fourth $25,000; fifth $15,000. Mutuel Pool $354,977.00 Exacta Pool $209,329.00 Trifecta Pool $180,059.00 Superfecta Pool $56,831.00 Quinella Pool $8,149.00

Last Raced	Horse	M/Eqt.	A.	Wt	PP	St	¼	½	¾	Str	Fin	Jockey	Odds $1
27Aug04 ^{9}Sar^{2}	Azeri	L	6	123	1	3	$2^{1\frac{1}{2}}$	2^{1}	$2^{1\frac{1}{2}}$	1^{hd}	1^{3}	Day P	0.40
4Sep04 ^{9}AP^{2}	Tamweel	L	4	123	3	2	$1^{1\frac{1}{2}}$	$1^{1\frac{1}{2}}$	1^{hd}	$2^{1\frac{1}{2}}$	$2^{\frac{1}{2}}$	Douglas R R	10.10
18Sep04 ^{12}TP^{2}	Mayo On the Side	L bf	5	123	5	4	6^{2}	4^{hd}	6^{1}	3^{2}	$3^{3\frac{3}{4}}$	Albarado R J	10.80
5Sep04 ^{4}WO^{1}	One for Rose	L	5	123	2	5	$4^{\frac{1}{2}}$	5^{hd}	5^{hd}	4^{hd}	4no	Ramsammy E	7.70
18Sep04 ^{12}TP^{5}	La Reason	L f	4	123	6	7	7	7	7	$5^{2\frac{1}{2}}$	$5^{5\frac{1}{4}}$	Bejarano R	46.20
18Sep04 ^{12}TP^{3}	Angela's Love	L	4	123	4	1	$3^{\frac{1}{2}}$	3^{hd}	4^{hd}	6^{1}	$6^{4\frac{1}{2}}$	Guidry M	40.70
8Aug04 ^{8}Dmr^{2}	House of Fortune	L	3	120	7	6	5^{hd}	$6^{1\frac{1}{2}}$	3^{hd}	7	7	Stevens G L	4.20

OFF AT 4:45 Start Good . Won driving. Track fast.

TIME :23^{1}, :46^{4}, 1:11^{3}, 1:37, 1:49^{3} (:23.35, :46.99, 1:11.71, 1:37.00, 1:49.74)

$2 Mutuel Prices:

1 – AZERI	2.80	2.20	2.10
3 – TAMWEEL		4.60	2.10
5 – MAYO ON THE SIDE			2.10

$2 EXACTA 1–3 PAID $14.60 $2 TRIFECTA 1–3–5 PAID $59.40
$2 SUPERFECTA 1–3–5–2 PAID $190.60 $2 QUINELLA 1–3 PAID $11.60

Ch. m, (May), by Jade Hunter – Zodiac Miss-Aus , by Ahonoora-GB . Trainer Lukas D Wayne. Bred by Allen E Paulson (Ky).

AZERI, close up inside early, edged out a bit to stalk front-running TAMWEEL three or four wide, inched to challenge nearing the stretch, put a head in front about the three-sixteenths pole, battled TAMHEEL into submission leaving the furlong grounds and moved well clear under mild hand urging. TAMHEEL gained the lead early, edged clear, raced two or three wide, lost the advantage to AZERI about the three-sixteenths pole, then held on stubbornly the remainder to save the place. MAYO ON THE SIDE maneuvered inside early, saved ground while edging up approaching the stretch, eased out four wide for the drive, remained prominent outside the top two in the final furlong and failed to respond. ONE FOR ROSE, well placed between horses three or four wide, came out a bit farther on the track for the drive, remained a threat into the final furlong and failed to fire. LA REASON moved inside early while under restraint, eased out to make a six wide run leaving the five-sixteenths pole but failed to gain in the final furlong. ANGELA'S LOVE went up early to track the pace four wide, held on well for six furlongs and tired. HOUSE OF FORTUNE, five wide from early on, raced in contention until approaching the final quarter and weakened thereafter.

Owners– 1, Allen E Paulson Living Trust; 2, Turf Express Inc and Darrell and Evelyn Yates Ltd; 3, Lothenbach Stables Inc; 4, Tucci Stables Lou Tucci; 5, K and K Racing Stable LLC Tom and Ronald L Kirby; 6, Poston Bill and Vicki; 7, Arnold Zetcher LLC

Trainers– 1, Lukas D Wayne; 2, Catalano Wayne M; 3, Nafzger Carl A; 4, Attard Sid C; 5, Vance David R; 6, Romans Dale; 7, McAnally Ronald

---

$2 Pick Three (5–8–1) Paid $81.80 ; Pick Three Pool $35,984 .

EIGHTH RACE
Santa Anita
OCTOBER 10, 2004

6 FURLONGS. (1.07^{1}) 20TH RUNNING OF THE ANCIENT TITLE BREEDERS' CUP HANDICAP. Grade I. Purse $250,000 (includes $50,000 BC - Breeders' Cup) FOR THREE-YEAR-OLDS AND UPWARD. By subscription of $250 each if made on or before Thursday, September 2, 2004 or by supplementary nomination of $5,000 by 10 AM Tuesday, October 5. All horses shall pay $2,500 to start, with $200,000 added and an additional $50,000 from Breeders' Cup Fund for Cup nominees only. The host association's money to be divided 60% to the winner, 20% to second, 12% to third, 6% to fourth and 2% to fifth. Breeders' Cup Fund monies also correspondingly divided provided a Breeders' Cup nominee has finished in an awarded position. Any Breeders' Cup Fund monies not awarded will revert to the Fund. Weights: Tuesday, October 5. The starters will be determined at entry time with preference given to Breeders' Cup nominees only of equal racing quality or weight assignment (respective of sex and weight for age). Starters to be named through the entry box by the closing time of entries. A troply will be presented to the owner of the winner. Closed Thursday, September 2 with 21 nominations. 2 supplementary nominations: During and Omega Code.

Value of Race: $213,000 Winner $120,000; second $50,000; third $24,000; fourth $15,000; fifth $4,000. Mutuel Pool $432,227.00 Exacta Pool $249,455.00 Quinella Pool $20,623.00 Trifecta Pool $251,070.00 Superfecta Pool $102,269.00

Last Raced	Horse	M/Eqt.	A.	Wt	PP	St	¼	½	Str	Fin	Jockey	Odds $1
10Sep04 ^{11}Fpx^{2}	Pt's Grey Eagle	LB b	3	109	7	2	7^{1}	6½	4½	1½	Bisono A	29.80
25Jly04 ^{2}Dmr^{2}	Pohave	LB	6	118	2	8	3½	2^{1}	1½	2^{2}	Court J K	1.30
25Jly04 ^{2}Dmr^{3}	Hombre Rapido	LB b	7	114	8	1	1^{1}	1^{1}	2½	3^{hd}	Baze T C	5.00
6Sep04 ^{6}Dmr^{4}	Kamsack	LB f	5	116	4	5	4½	4^{hd}	3^{hd}	4½	Desormeaux K J	14.90
6Sep04 ^{6}Dmr^{2}	Bluesthestandard	LB	7	118	5	4	5½	5½	5^{2}	5½	Smith M E	2.90
5Sep04 ^{8}Dmr^{3}	During	LB b	4	116	3	6	6½	7^{2}	7^{3}	6^{5}	Santiago Javier	9.20
30Jly04 ^{2}Dmr^{3}	Rojo Toro	LB b	4	114	1	7	2^{hd}	3^{hd}	6½	7^{4}	Esplnoza V	8.00
28Aug04 ^{7}Sar^{7}	Omega Code	LB	4	114	6	3	8	8	8	8	Pedroza M A	34.50

OFF AT 4:09 Start Good . Won driving. Track fast.

TIME :21, :43^{3}, :55^{4}, 1:08^{4} (:21.04, :43.79, :55.91, 1:08.84)

$2 Mutuel Prices:				
	7 – PT'S GREY EAGLE	61.60	15.40	4.60
	2 – POHAVE		3.20	2.40
	8 – HOMBRE RAPIDO			3.00

$1 EXACTA 7–2 PAID $81.80 $2 QUINELLA 2–7 PAID $57.40
$1 TRIFECTA 7–2–8 PAID $500.30 $1 SUPERFECTA 7–2–8–4 PAID $3,687.20

Gr/ro. g, (Feb), by Pleasant Tap – Hemet Eagle , by Swing Till Dawn . Trainer Dollase Craig. Bred by Farrell W Jones (Ky).

PT'S GREY EAGLE settled outside, went four wide on the turn and five wide into the stretch, then rallied under some left handed urging to get up late. POHAVE a bit slow to begin, stalked between horses on the backstretch and outside a rival on the turn, took a short lead outside HOMBRE RAPIDO into the stretch, inched away past midstretch but could not hold off the winner. HOMBRE RAPIDO sped to the early lead, set the pace off the rail, angled to the inside on the turn, dueled inside the runner-up into the stretch and until midstretch, then just held third. KAMSACK bumped lightly at the start, stalked outside then between foes on the backstretch, went three deep on the turn and into the stretch and just missed the show. BLUESTHESTANDARD broke in a bit and was bumped lightly, stalked outside on the backstretch and four wide on the turn and into the stretch and lacked the needed response. DURING chased between horses then a bit off the rail and weakened in the stretch. ROJO TORO went up inside to track the leader, dropped back into the stretch and also weakened. OMEGA CODE allowed to settle a bit off the rail, angled in on the backstretch, came out into the stretch and was outrun.

Owners– 1, Reddam J Paul; 2, Darley Stable; 3, Granja Vista Del Rio Stable; 4, Rodriguez Lorraine and Rod; 5, Sengara Jeffrey; 6, McIngvale James; 7, Earnhardt III Patti and Hal J; 8, Trussell Robert

Trainers– 1, Dollase Craig; 2, O'Neill Doug; 3, Sadler John W; 4, O'Neill Doug; 5, West Ted H; 6, Hines N J; 7, Baffert Bob; 8, Ward Wesley A

$2 Daily Double (6–7) Paid $574.60 ; Daily Double Pool $35,140 .
$1 Pick Three (7–6–7) Paid $2,036.30 ; Pick Three Pool $64,181 .

NINTH RACE
Belmont
OCTOBER 11, 2004

1⅛ MILES. (Inner Turf) (1.45^{2}) 12TH RUNNING OF THE PEBBLES. Grade III. Purse $100,000 INNER TURF FOR FILLIES THREE YEARS OLD. By subscription of $100 each, which should accompany the nomination; $500 to pass the entry box; $500 to start, with $100,000 added. The added money and all fees to be divided 60% to the winner, 20% to second, 10% to third, 5% to fourth, 3% to fifth and 2% divided equally among remaining finishers. 123 lbs. Non-winners of a Grade 1 or Grade 2 on the turf in 2004 allowed 2 lbs.; a Graded Sweepstake, 4 lbs.; a Sweepstake on the turf; or two races on the turf, 6 lbs.;a race on the turf, 8 lbs. (Maiden, claiming and restricted allowance races not considered). A trophy will be presented to the winning owner. The New York Racing Association reserves the right to transfer this race to the Main Track. In the event that thiis race is taken off the turf, it may be subject to downgrading upon review by the Graded Stakes Committee. Closed Saturday, September 25, 2004 with 38 Nominations. (Rail at 18 feet).

Value of Race: $112,300 Winner $67,380; second $22,460; third $11,230; fourth $5,615; fifth $3,369; sixth $749; seventh $749; eighth $748. Mutuel Pool $299,394.00 Exacta Pool $262,079.00 Trifecta Pool $216,210.00

Last Raced	Horse	M/Eqt.	A.	Wt	PP	St	¼	½	¾	Str	Fin	Jockey	Odds $1
23Aug04 ^{8}Sar^{3}	Fortunate Damsel	L	3	119	7	2	1½	1½	1½	1^{2}	1^{hd}	Castellano J J	6.50
2Aug04 ^{8}Sar^{2}	Venturi-GB	L	3	121	3	4	5½	6½	6^{2}	4½	2^{1}	Velazquez J R	0.80
12Sep04 ^{9}Mth^{6}	Delta Sensation	L	3	119	5	1	2½	2½	3½	2½	3no	Velasquez C	17.10
12Sep04 ^{9}Mth^{2}	Go Robin	L	3	117	4	6	6^{hd}	7^{hd}	7½	5^{hd}	4^{nk}	Bravo J	8.60
5Sep04 ^{5}Sar^{1}	Right This Way	L	3	117	2	3	3½	3^{hd}	5^{hd}	7^{3}	5¼	Espinoza J L	35.50
12Sep04 ^{8}Bel^{11}	Sabellina	L	3	119	1	7	8	5^{hd}	2½	3^{hd}	6^{nk}	Chavez J F	10.50
30Aug04 ^{6}Sar^{1}	Serendipitous	L b	3	117	6	5	4½	4½	4½	6^{hd}	7^{2}	Prado E S	10.30
31Jly04 ^{9}ElP^{1}	Lenatareese	L	3	119	8	8	7^{2}	8	8	8	8	Blanc B	7.30

OFF AT 5:12 Start Good . Won driving. Course firm.

TIME :25^{3}, :50^{2}, 1:13^{4}, 1:36^{4}, 1:48^{4} (:25.72, :50.51, 1:13.85, 1:36.97, 1:48.80)

$2 Mutuel Prices:				
	8 – FORTUNATE DAMSEL	15.00	4.40	3.70
	3 – VENTURI–GB		2.80	2.60
	5 – DELTA SENSATION			5.80

$2 EXACTA 8–3 PAID $33.40 $2 TRIFECTA 8–3–5 PAID $208.00

Dk. b or br. f, (Mar), by Runaway Groom – Consider It Done , by Green Dancer . Trainer Cedano Heriberto. Bred by Edward J Messina (NY).

FORTUNATE DAMSEL quickly showed in front, soon opened a clear lead, set the pace along the inside while well in hand, responded when roused in upper stretch, took a clear lead into deep stretch then dug in gamely and held on under a drive. VENTURI (GB) was a bit rank along the inside early on, was rated along rallied inside into the stretch, split rivals and finished gamely. DELTA SENSATION raced close up in hand, rallied along the inside turning for home and dug in gamely to the wire. GO ROBIN was rated along inside, angled out on the second turn, rallied three wide approaching the stretch and finished gamely outside. RIGHT THIS WAY raced close up inside while in hand, was shuffled back inside on the second turn, angled out in the stretch and finished well. SABELLINA was outrun early, put in a quick move from the outside nearing the second turn and tired in the stretch. SERENDIPITOUS was rated along outside, raced three wide on both turns and lacked a rally. LENATAREESE leapt in the air at the start, was outrun early, came wide into the stretch and had no rally.

Owners– 1, Spruce Pond Stable; 2, Gann Edmund A; 3, Cay John E III; 4, Casby Camelia Hennig Mark and Radar Robby; 5, Pesch Alan; 6, Lieberman Jay A and Scharfman Mark; 7, Clifton William L Jr; 8, Anderson Brad

Trainers– 1, Cedano Heriberto; 2, Frankel Robert; 3, Alexander Frank A; 4, Hennig Mark; 5, Tagg Barclay; 6, Aquilino Joseph; 7, Bond Harold James; 8, Carroll David

Scratched– Tigi (22Sep04 ^{7}Bel^{4})

NINTH RACE
Keeneland
OCTOBER 15, 2004

7 FURLONGS. (1.20^{1}) 6TH RUNNING OF THE RAVEN RUN. Grade II. Purse $200,000 FOR FILLIES, THREE YEARS OLD. By subscription of $200 each, which should accompany the nomination; $1,000 to enter and an additional $1,000 to start, with $200,000 added, of which 62% of all monies to the owner of the winner, 20% to second, 10% to third,5% to fourth and 3% to fifth. Weight: 123 lbs. Non-winners of a Grade I or II race allowed 3 lbs.; $60,000 twice in 2004 allowed 5 lbs.; three races other than maiden or claiming allowed 7 lbs. Starters to be named through the entry box by the usual timeof closing. A gold julep cup will be presented to the owner of the winner. Closed Wednesday, October 6, 2004 with 21 nominations.

Value of Race: $224,200 Winner $139,004; second $44,840; third $22,420; fourth $11,210; fifth $6,726. Mutuel Pool $358,955.00 Exacta Pool $226,049.00 Trifecta Pool $189,114.00 Superfecta Pool $67,922.00 Quinella Pool $8,242.00

Last Raced	Horse	M/Eqt.	A.	Wt	PP	St	¼	½	Str	Fin	Jockey	Odds $1
5Sep04 ^{10}ElP^{1}	Josh's Madelyn	L b	3	118	5	10	10	10	$2^{1\frac{1}{2}}$	$1^{1\frac{1}{4}}$	Shepherd J	5.60
5Sep04 ^{8}Sar^{1}	Vision of Beauty	L	3	116	2	4	$1^{\frac{1}{2}}$	$1^{\frac{1}{2}}$	1^{2}	$2^{9\frac{1}{2}}$	Chavez J F	3.30
18Sep04 ^{7}Bel^{1}	Feline Story	L	3	118	9	2	$6^{2\frac{1}{2}}$	6^{1}	3^{hd}	$3^{\frac{1}{2}}$	Albarado R J	5.80
24Sep04 ^{8}Bel^{1}	Dance Tune	L	3	116	8	9	$7^{\frac{1}{2}}$	7^{2}	6^{1}	4no	Bejarano R	15.30
12Sep04 ^{9}Mth^{8}	Format	L	3	118	4	7	9^{4}	9^{hd}	$7^{4\frac{1}{2}}$	5^{hd}	McKee J	29.30
1Oct04 ^{9}Hoo^{5}	Storm's Darling	L f	3	116	7	1	$2^{\frac{1}{2}}$	2^{2}	$4^{1\frac{1}{2}}$	6^{2}	Borel C H	47.40
18Sep04 ^{6}PrM^{1}	Miss Moses	L	3	116	6	8	8^{hd}	8^{2}	5^{1}	7^{7}	Guidry M	39.30
11Sep04 ^{7}Bel^{1}	Salty Romance	f	3	116	3	5	4^{hd}	$3^{\frac{1}{2}}$	8^{2}	$8^{5\frac{3}{4}}$	Prado E S	6.40
31Jly04 ^{8}Sar^{4}	Friendly Michelle	L b	3	123	10	3	5^{2}	5^{hd}	10	9^{nk}	Day P	1.80
14Aug04 ^{3}AP^{3}	Silver Crown	L	3	118	1	6	$3^{\frac{1}{2}}$	4^{hd}	9^{hd}	10	Graham J	22.60

OFF AT 5:16 Start Good. Won driving. Track muddy.

TIME :21^{3}, :44^{1}, 1:09^{4}, 1:22^{4} (:21.73, :44.38, 1:09.94, 1:22.86)

$2 Mutuel Prices:

5 – JOSH'S MADELYN	13.20	6.20	4.60
2 – VISION OF BEAUTY		4.60	3.60
9 – FELINE STORY			3.80

$2 EXACTA 5–2 PAID $57.20 $2 TRIFECTA 5–2–9 PAID $281.40
$2 SUPERFECTA 5–2–9–8 PAID $3,056.40 $2 QUINELLA 2–5 PAID $27.00

B. f, (Mar), by Quiet American – Intend to Win, by Housebuster. Trainer Jones J Larry. Bred by Mt Brilliant Farm LLC (Ky).

JOSH'S MADELYN bobbled while drifting out slightly at the start, moved out five or six wide on the backstretch, trailed for a half, came out eight wide at the quarter-mile ground, caught front-running VISION OF BEAUTY in the final sixteenth and edged clear late under urging. VISION OF BEAUTY gained the lead early while two or three wide, managed a clear advantage into the final furlong and wasn't a match for the winner late. FELINE STORY drifted in at the start, settled four wide, came out six wide for the drive, loomed a threat for last eighth and came up empty. DANCE TUNE, shuffled back at the start when FELINE STORY drifted in, raced between rivals on the turn, came out seven wide for the drive and improved position while unable to menace. FORMAT, outrun to the stretch while near the inside, eased out a bit for the drive and passed tired foes. STORM'S DARLING went up early to press front-running VISION OF BEAUTY four wide, held on well for five furlongs and weakened. MISS MOSES, outrun and near the inside to the stretch, eased out a bit for the drive, reached contention at the furlong grounds and failed to continue. SALTY ROMANCE stalked the pace four wide until the final quarter and tired. FRIENDLY MICHELLE tracked the leaders five wide for a half and gradually weakened. SILVER CROWN raced forwardly near the inside for a half and weakened thereafter.

Owners– 1, Pressley Michael and Neidig Jim; 2, Oxley Debby M; 3, Robsham Mrs E P; 4, Overbrook Farm; 5, Miller Brian; 6, Vogel Arthur; 7, Mount Brilliant Stable LLC; 8, Flying Zee Stable; 9, Friendly Ed; 10, Russell L Reineman Stable Inc Jennifer L McCutcheon

Trainers– 1, Jones J Larry; 2, Ward John T Jr; 3, Hough Stanley M; 4, Lukas D Wayne; 5, Breen Kelly J; 6, Barnett Bobby C; 7, Stidham Michael; 8, Biancone Patrick L; 9, Baffert Bob; 10, Springer Frank R

$2 Pick Three (1–5–5) Paid $1,263.80 ; Pick Three Pool $23,603 .

EIGHTH RACE
Meadowlands
OCTOBER 15, 2004

$1\frac{1}{16}$ MILES. (Turf) (1.39^{2}) 27TH RUNNING OF THE CLIFF HANGER HANDICAP. Grade III. Purse $200,000 FOR THREE–YEAR–OLDS AND UPWARD. By subscription of $200 each, which should accompany the nomination and $1,500 to pass the entry box. The owner of the winner to receive 60% of the purse, 20% to second, 11% to third, 6% to fourth and 3% to fifth. The winning owner to receive a trophy. Closed Saturday, October 2, 2004 with 38 nominations. (Rail at 10 feet).

Value of Race: $200,000 Winner $120,000; second $40,000; third $22,000; fourth $12,000; fifth $6,000. Mutuel Pool $126,090.00 Exacta Pool $98,451.00 Trifecta Pool $72,308.00 Superfecta Pool $19,082.00

Last Raced	Horse	M/Eqt.	A.	Wt	PP	St	¼	½	¾	Str	Fin	Jockey	Odds $1
1Oct04 ^{4}Med^{5}	Dr. Kashnikow	L	7	116	5	8	8	8	8	$6^{\frac{1}{2}}$	$1^{\frac{1}{2}}$	Migliore R	15.90
1Oct04 ^{4}Med^{1}	Tam's Terms	L	6	116	6	6	$5^{\frac{1}{2}}$	5^{1}	6^{1}	4^{hd}	$2^{\frac{3}{4}}$	Dominguez R A	2.90
3Apr04 ^{8}Aqu^{3}	Host-Chi	L	4	117	1	1	$6^{\frac{1}{2}}$	$6^{\frac{1}{2}}$	7^{hd}	$7^{2\frac{1}{2}}$	3no	Velazquez J R	1.80
23Sep04 ^{8}Mth^{1}	Hotstufanthensome	L	4	115	3	7	7^{1}	$7^{1\frac{1}{2}}$	$5^{\frac{1}{2}}$	5^{hd}	4^{nk}	Bravo J	2.90
5Sep04 ^{10}Mth^{7}	Spruce Run	L b	6	116	7	4	$1^{1\frac{1}{2}}$	$1^{1\frac{1}{2}}$	1^{1}	$1^{\frac{1}{2}}$	$5^{\frac{1}{2}}$	Coa E M	33.80
1Oct04 ^{4}Med^{3}	American Freedom	L b	6	115	2	2	4^{1}	4^{1}	$4^{\frac{1}{2}}$	2^{hd}	6^{hd}	Velez J A Jr	26.50
1Oct04 ^{4}Med^{2}	Stormy Roman	L	5	116	8	5	$3^{\frac{1}{2}}$	$3^{\frac{1}{2}}$	$3^{\frac{1}{2}}$	3^{hd}	$7^{5\frac{3}{4}}$	Clemente A V	5.50
25Sep04 ^{6}Bel^{1}	Royal Affirmed	L	6	115	4	3	$2^{\frac{1}{2}}$	$2^{\frac{1}{2}}$	2^{hd}	8	8	Elliott S	14.00

OFF AT 10:21 Start Good. Won driving. Course good.

TIME :23^{1}, :48, 1:12^{1}, 1:36^{2}, 1:42^{2} (:23.33, :48.05, 1:12.22, 1:36.48, 1:42.41)

$2 Mutuel Prices:

7 – DR. KASHNIKOW	33.80	9.40	5.20
8 – TAM'S TERMS		4.40	3.00
1 – HOST–CHI			3.00

$2 EXACTA 7–8 PAID $125.60 $2 TRIFECTA 7–8–1 PAID $573.80
$1 SUPERFECTA 7–8–1–3 PAID $954.10

Gr/ro. g, (Apr), by El Gran Senor – One More Breeze, by Mythical Ruler. Trainer Fisher John R S. Bred by Stan Dodson (Ont–C).

DR. KASHNIKOW steadied at the start, raced unhurriedly off the rail, advanced angling widest on the final turn, started a long drive entering the stretch, drifted slightly in after taking the lead in late stretch and edged ahead the closing yards. TAM'S TERMS rated off the pace toward the outside, rallied splitting horses in midstretch, took a short but brief lead in late stretch then outfinished in the final yards. HOST (CHI) rated back off the rail, was steadied in tight into the final turn, boxed in on the final turn, lacked room angling to the outside through the stretch and finished well when clear. HOTSTUFANTHENSOME, unhurriedly while never far from the front, advanced outside on the final turn, dueled between horses through the stretch then steadied late. SPRUCE RUN rated a clear lead just off the rail, was pressured approaching the quarter pole, drifted slightly outward toward the eighth pole, dueled between rivals from there but was outfinished from the seventy yard pole. AMERICAN FREEDOM rated off the pace inside, was boxed in on the rail on the final turn, made his bid entering the stretch, looked a factor an eighth away then lost momentum in the final yards. STORMY ROMAN rated in good position about the three path, dueled between horses through the stretch but weakened late. ROYAL AFFIRMED rated close in the three path but weakened entering the stretch. A claim of foul lodged against the winning rider by the rider of the fourth place finisher, was dismissed

Owners– 1, Erdenheim Farm; 2, Bender Sondra D; 3, Melnyk Eugene and Laura; 4, Runnin Horse Farm Inc; 5, Golden Dome Stable; 6, Freedom Acres Inc; 7, Croley Thomas L; 8, Falcone Robert and Lee John J

Trainers– 1, Fisher John R S; 2, Murray Lawrence E; 3, Pletcher Todd A; 4, Pointer Norman R; 5, Rice Linda; 6, Woodington Jamie; 7, Hills Timothy A; 8, Ramos Faustino F

Scratched– Stormy Ray (23Sep04 ^{8}Mth^{2}), One Nice Cat (11Sep04 ^{3}Mth^{2}), Mr. Light (ARG) (25Sep04 ^{4}Bel^{3})

NINTH RACE
Belmont
OCTOBER 16, 2004

1½ MILES. (Turf) (2.241) 111TH RUNNING OF THE LAWRENCE REALIZATION. Grade III. Purse $100,000 WIDENER TURF. (UP TO $19,000 NYSBFOA) FOR THREE YEAR OLDS. By subscription of $100 each, which should accompany the nomination; $500 to pass the entry box and $500 to start, with $100,000 added. The added money and all fees to be divided 60% to the winner, 20% to second, 10% to third, 5% to fourth, 3% to fifth and 2% divided equally among remaining finishers. 123 lbs. Non-winners of a $50,000 twice over a mile on the turf in 2004 allowed 2 lbs.; such a race in 2004, 4 lbs.; a Sweepstake on the turf; or three races at a mile or over, 6 lbs.; two races at a mile or over, 8 lbs. (Maiden, claiming and restricted allowance races not considered). Trophies will be presented to the winning owner, trainer and jockey. The New York Racing Association reserves the right to transfer this race to the Main Track. In the event that this race is taken off the turf, it may be subject to downgrading upon review by the Graded Stakes Committee. Closed Saturday, October 2, 2004 with 26 Nominations. (If the Stewards consider it in advisable to run this race on the turf course, this race will be run at One Mile and One Eighth on the main track.). (Rail at 18 feet).

Value of Race: $110,100 Winner $66,060; second $22,020; third $11,010; fourth $5,505; fifth $3,303; sixth $1,101; seventh $1,101. Mutuel Pool $456,104.00 Exacta Pool $344,621.00 Trifecta Pool $297,621.00

Last Raced	Horse	M/Eqt.	A.	Wt	PP	¼	½	1	1¼	Str	Fin	Jockey	Odds $1
8Oct04 6Med3	Gunning For	L	3	119	7	7	7	64½	1½	11½	1½	Bravo J	16.00
26Sep04 9Bel2	Rousing Victory	L b	3	115	3	56	51½	3hd	2hd	22½	23½	Velasquez C	1.45
3Oct04 7Bel4	SecondPerformnce	L b	3	119	4	1hd	1hd	1hd	31	35	34¾	Velazquez J R	3.85
26Sep04 10Bel1	Dark Equation	L	3	115	5	21	23	21½	41½	45	42¾	Coa E M	9.30
4Sep04 9Sar6	Victory Circle	L b	3	115	2	63	65½	7	6hd	62	52¾	Jara F	36.25
4Sep04 9Sar2	Generous One	L bf	3	115	1	3hd	3hd	4½	53½	5½	62½	Gryder A T	6.40
6Sep04 10Pha8	Royal Assault	L	3	115	6	4½	42½	51	7	7	7	Castellano J J	3.25

OFF AT 5:12 Start Good. Won driving. Course yielding.

TIME :232, :472, 1:121, 1:372, 2:032, 2:294 (:23.59, :47.51, 1:12.28, 1:37.59, 2:03.59, 2:29.91)

$2 Mutuel Prices:				
	8 – GUNNING FOR	34.00	9.40	4.80
	3 – ROUSING VICTORY		3.10	2.60
	5 – SECOND PERFORMANCE			3.30

$2 EXACTA 8–3 PAID $114.50 $2 TRIFECTA 8–3–5 PAID $390.50

B. g, (Apr), by Dove Hunt – Hopalina , by Trempolino . Trainer Walsh Timothy. Bred by Denise Walsh & Tom Walsh (Fla).

GUNNING FOR was unhurried while outrun early, rallied four wide on the second turn, drew clear in the stretch then dug in resolutely and held off ROUSING VICTORY under a drive. ROUSING VICTORY raced in hand outside early, rallied three wide nearing the stretch and stayed on gamely inside. SECOND PERFORMANCE contested the pace along the inside and weakened in the stretch. DARK EQUATION contested the pace from the outside and tired in the drive. VICTORY CIRCLE was outrun early, raced inside and had no response when roused. GENEROUS ONE raced close up inside, chased the pace and tired in the stretch. ROYAL ASSAULT was hustled along outside, was hard ridden while three wide and tired.

Owners– 1, Walsh Mrs Thomas J; 2, Hilly Fields Stable and Moran Thomas; 3, Bloom William Behrendt John T and Marquis Charles K; 4, Live Oak Plantation; 5, Flying Zee Stable; 6, Nicholson Patricia E and Ronald; 7, Farmer Tracy

Trainers– 1, Walsh Timothy; 2, Serpe Philip M; 3, Donk David; 4, Clement Christophe; 5, Serpe Philip M; 6, Toner James J; 7, Zito Nicholas P

Scratched– Defrocked (11Oct04 5Del6) , Zakocity (01Oct04 7Med3) , Navesink River (01Oct04 7Med4)

EIGHTH RACE
Hawthorne
OCTOBER 16, 2004

1⅛ MILES. (Turf) (1.443) 40TH RUNNING OF THE HAWTHORNE DERBY. Grade III. Purse $250,000 FOR THREE–YEAR–OLDS. By subscription of $100 each which shall accompany the nomination. $1,250 to pass the entry box and $1,250 additional to start. With $250,000 Guaranteed, of which $150,000 to the winner, $50,000 to second, $27,500 to third, $15,000 to fourth and $7,500 to fifth. Weight, 122 lbs. Non–winners of $100,000 at a mile or over in 2004, allowed 3 lbs.; Of $55,000 at a mile or over in 2004, 5 lbs.; Of $55,000 at a mile or over anytime, 7 lbs.; Of $25,000 or $15,000 twice at a mile or over in 2004, 9 lbs.; Of $20,000 at a mile or over at any time, 11 lbs. (Maiden and Claiming races not considered). Nominations closed Wednesday, October 6, 2004 with 26.

Value of Race: $250,000 Winner $150,000; second $50,000; third $27,500; fourth $15,000; fifth $7,500. Mutuel Pool $214,987.00 Exacta Pool $135,035.00 Trifecta Pool $127,025.00 Superfecta Pool $44,117.00

Last Raced	Horse	M/Eqt.	A.	Wt	PP	St	¼	½	¾	Str	Fin	Jockey	Odds $1
10Oct04 4Kee4	Cool Conductor	L	3	115	5	5	61½	61	6hd	21½	1nk	Santos J A	1.50
25Sep04 6Bel2	Bankruptcy Court	L	3	115	3	1	32½	31½	3hd	12	22¼	Bridgmohan S X	4.60
25Sep04 10Haw8	Crown Prince	L	3	113	2	10	10	10	10	4½	3¾	Sterling L J Jr	45.60
6Sep04 8Del4	Cockleshell	L f	3	115	6	6	41	4½	42	32	43	Dominguez R A	2.60
11Sep04 8AP3	Gwaihir-Ire	L b	3	117	8	4	2½	21½	21½	6½	5no	Campbell J M	10.70
25Sep04 10Haw7	Lord Carmen	L f	3	116	1	7	7hd	81	8hd	5½	6nk	Emigh C A	10.60
25Sep04 10Haw1	Hunting Hillbilly	L	3	115	10	9	82	7½	71	73	71¾	Perez E E	9.50
17Sep04 9AP1	Cowboy Code	L bf	3	116	4	8	91½	92½	9½	8hd	81¼	Fires E	31.20
1Oct04 9Haw9	Western Ridge	L b	3	113	9	2	11½	12½	1½	94	95¼	Morris L K	91.30
18Sep04 4KD1	Double Shotgun	L	3	115	7	3	5hd	51½	5hd	10	10	Marquez C H Jr	35.50

OFF AT 4:29 Start Good. Won driving. Course firm.

TIME :232, :472, 1:112, 1:352, 1:474 (:23.56, :47.40, 1:11.43, 1:35.54, 1:47.89)

$2 Mutuel Prices:				
	5 – COOL CONDUCTOR	5.00	3.00	2.60
	3 – BANKRUPTCY COURT		4.20	3.20
	2 – CROWN PRINCE			9.40

$2 EXACTA 5–3 PAID $20.20 $2 TRIFECTA 5–3–2 PAID $280.60
$2 SUPERFECTA 5–3–2–6 PAID $1,654.20

B. c, (Jan), by Stravinsky – Verinha-Brz , by Baronius-Brz . Trainer Mott William I. Bred by Rio Claro Tbs Inc R D Hubbard & C Sczesny (Ky).

COOL CONDUCTOR saved ground near the middle of the field, came just out for the drive and rallied to be up in the final strides. BANKRUPTCY COURT raced close up inside, slipped through on the rail on the final turn and took a clear lead in the stretch but could not hold off the winner. CROWN PRINCE lacked speed inside, got through on the rail turning for home and gained belatedly for a share. COCKLESHELL raced close up four wide but lacked a winning bid. GWAIHIR (IRE) raced close up just outside and weakened. LORD CARMEN lacked speed inside and showed little. HUNTING HILLBILLY raced near the middle of the field and gave way in the drive. COWBOY CODE was always outrun. WESTERN RIDGE set the pace from the inside on a clear lead and tired. DOUBLE SHOTGUN raced close up but gave way in the drive.

Owners– 1, Garner David E; 2, Klaravich Stables Inc Seth Klarman & Jess Ravich; 3, Jayaraman Kalarikkal K and Vilasini D; 4, Chandler Dr John A; 5, Kirkwood Al and Saundra S; 6, Calabrese Frank C; 7, Rich Ege & Team Block David Patricia & Ryan Block; 8, Thunderhead Farms; 9, Richards Gerald and Francione Thomas; 10, Silverton Hill LLC

Trainers– 1, Mott William I; 2, Violette Richard A Jr; 3, Hobby Steve; 4, Dickinson Michael W; 5, Forster Grant T; 6, Catalano Wayne M; 7, Block Chris M; 8, Von Hemel Don; 9, Arnett Jon G; 10, Miller Darrin

---

$2 Pick Three (2–4–5) Paid $1,043.40 ; Pick Three Pool $11,826 .
$2 Pick Six (4–3–2/7–2–4–5) 5 Correct Paid $129.60 ; Pick Six Pool $692 ; Carryover Pool $6,498.

EIGHTH RACE
Keeneland
OCTOBER 16, 2004

1⅛ MILES. (Turf) (1.45^{4}) 21ST RUNNING OF THE QUEEN ELIZABETH II CHALLENGE CUP. Grade I. Purse $500,000 HAGGIN COURSE. FOR FILLIES, THREE YEARS OLD. By invitation with no nomination or starting fee. The owner of the winner to receive $310,000, with $100,000 to second, $50,000 to third, $25,000 to fourth and $15,000 to fifth. Weight: 121 lbs. The field willbe drawn by the usual time of closing. A gold julep cup will be presented to the owner of the winner. A silver julep cup will be presented to the winning trainer and jockey.

Value of Race: $500,000 Winner $310,000; second $100,000; third $50,000; fourth $25,000; fifth $15,000. Mutuel Pool $639,802.00 Exacta Pool $356,329.00 Trifecta Pool $261,267.00 Superfecta Pool $64,276.00 Quinella Pool $15,963.00

Last Raced	Horse	M/Eqt.	A.	Wt	PP	St	¼	½	¾	Str	Fin	Jockey	Odds $1
18Sep04 ^{9}AP^{1}	Ticker Tape-GB	L	3	121	5	1	$6^{1\frac{1}{2}}$	$6^{1\frac{1}{2}}$	$6^{\frac{1}{2}}$	$1^{\frac{1}{2}}$	$1^{\frac{1}{2}}$	Desormeaux K J	1.70
12Sep04 ^{9}Bel^{2}	Barancella-FR	L	3	121	3	7	5^{hd}	$5^{\frac{1}{2}}$	5^{1}	$3^{1\frac{1}{2}}$	$2^{\frac{1}{2}}$	Prado E S	2.30
12Sep04 ^{9}Mth^{3}	River Belle-GB	L	3	121	2	5	$1^{\frac{1}{2}}$	1^{2}	1^{2}	$2^{1\frac{1}{2}}$	3^{1}	Bejarano R	13.60
11Sep04 Leo^{3}	Phantom Wind		3	121	6	3	4^{1}	$4^{\frac{1}{2}}$	$4^{\frac{1}{2}}$	4^{hd}	$4^{4\frac{1}{2}}$	Bailey J D	3.90
12Sep04 ^{9}Bel^{5}	Mambo Slew		3	121	1	6	$3^{\frac{1}{2}}$	$3^{1\frac{1}{2}}$	2^{1}	5^{5}	$5^{4\frac{1}{2}}$	Farina T	11.00
18Sep04 ^{9}AP^{4}	Humorous Miss	L b	3	121	7	2	7	7	7	$6^{\frac{1}{2}}$	6^{3}	Graham J	37.60
26Jun04 ^{9}Bel^{3}	Island Sand	L b	3	121	4	4	2^{1}	2^{hd}	3^{1}	7	7	Day P	6.00

OFF AT 4:45 Start Good . Won driving. Course good.

TIME :25, :49^{3}, 1:14^{2}, 1:38^{4}, 1:51^{1} (:25.06, :49.64, 1:14.43, 1:38.83, 1:51.35)

$2 Mutuel Prices:

5 – TICKER TAPE–GB	5.40	2.80	2.40
3 – BARANCELLA–FR		3.00	2.80
2 – RIVER BELLE–GB			3.20

$2 EXACTA 5–3 PAID $14.40 $2 TRIFECTA 5–3–2 PAID $114.20
$2 SUPERFECTA 5–3–2–6 PAID $319.40 $2 QUINELLA 3–5 PAID $7.00

B. f, (Jan), by Royal Applause–GB – Argent Du Bois , by Silver Hawk . Trainer Cassidy James. Bred by Car Colston Hall Stud (GB).

TICKER TAPE (GB), lightly rated early while three or four wide, advanced four abreast entering the upper stretch, took over approaching the final furlong, expanded her advantage slightly, then held sway under strong handling. BARANCELLA (FR) settled inside early, moved two or three wide on the second turn, angled outside the winner in the final furlong to be four or five wide and finished well for the place. RIVER BELLE (GB) moved to the fore early, raced two or three wide while accomplishing a modest pace, edged clear on the backstretch, expanded her advantage between calls approaching the final quarter, then couldn't last. PHANTOM WIND, within easy striking distance while following the leaders four wide into the final furlong, lacked a final response. MAMBO SLEW, well placed inside from the start, inched up a bit leaving the backstretch, eased out to continue prominently from between foes three or four wide into the stretch and came up empty. HUMOROUS MISS, outrun early and three wide, eased out five abreast on the backstretch, continued in that position on the course much of the remainder and failed to rally. ISLAND SAND bobbled at the start, was a bit rank during the run to the first turn while prompting a modest pace outside of front-running RIVER BELLE (GB), settled on the backstretch, continued in a striking position for seven furlongs and weakened thereafter.

Owners– 1, Jim Ford Inc Jim Ford Daron Pearson and Jack Sweesy; 2, Tanaka Gary A; 3, Team Valor Stables Heiligbrodt Racing Stable and Green Lantern StablesLLC; 4, Juddmonte Farms Inc; 5, Manganaro Frank; 6, Russell L Reineman Stable Inc Jennifer L McCutcheon; 7, B A Man Inc

Trainers– 1, Cassidy James; 2, Frankel Robert; 3, Pletcher Todd A; 4, Gosden John H M; 5, Biancone Patrick L; 6, Springer Frank R; 7, Jones J Larry

$2 Pick Three (4–7–5) Paid $31.80 ; Pick Three Pool $73,945 .

EIGHTH RACE
Belmont
OCTOBER 17, 2004

6½ FURLONGS. (1.14^{2}) 56TH RUNNING OF THE ASTARITA. Grade III. Purse $100,000 (UP TO $19,000 NYSBFOA) FOR FILLIES TWO YEARS OLD. By subscription of $100 each, which should accompany the nomination; $500 to pass the entry box; $500 to start, with $100,000 added. The added money and all fees to be divided 60% to the winner, 20% to second, 10% to third, 5% to fourth, 3% to fifth and 2% divided equally among remaining finishers. 120 lbs. Non–winners of $50,000 other than restricted allowed 3 lbs. A trophy will be presented to the winning owner. Closed Saturday, October 2, 2004 with 20Nominations.

Value of Race: $108,000 Winner $64,800; second $21,600; third $10,800; fourth $5,400; fifth $3,240; sixth $2,160. Mutuel Pool $291,703.00 Exacta Pool $223,207.00 Trifecta Pool $162,224.00

Last Raced	Horse	M/Eqt.	A.	Wt	PP	St	¼	½	Str	Fin	Jockey	Odds $1
10Sep04 ^{7}Mth^{1}	Toll Taker	L	2	117	2	1	4^{1}	$3^{\frac{1}{2}}$	$1^{\frac{1}{2}}$	$1^{3\frac{1}{4}}$	Coa E M	6.70
18Sep04 ^{9}TP^{5}	Im a Dixie Girl	L	2	120	3	4	1^{hd}	$2^{\frac{1}{2}}$	$2^{\frac{1}{2}}$	$2^{1\frac{1}{2}}$	Migliore R	1.70
19Sep04 ^{8}Bel^{6}	Summer Raven	L	2	117	4	5	$3^{\frac{1}{2}}$	$1^{\frac{1}{2}}$	3^{7}	$3^{11\frac{1}{2}}$	Castellano J J	2.15
2Oct04 ^{8}FL^{1}	Roving Angel		2	117	5	3	5^{hd}	5^{3}	4^{12}	$4^{12\frac{3}{4}}$	Velasquez C	6.00
4Sep04 ^{10}Mth^{1}	Queens Plaza	L f	2	120	1	2	$2^{\frac{1}{2}}$	$4^{\frac{1}{2}}$	$5^{1\frac{1}{2}}$	$5^{\frac{3}{4}}$	Bailey J D	6.30
26Sep04 ^{3}Bel^{1}	Five Star Fund	L	2	117	6	6	6	6	6	6	Bridgmohan S X	12.60

OFF AT 4:40 Start Good . Won driving. Track fast.

TIME :22^{4}, :47, 1:11^{3}, 1:18 (:22.96, :47.02, 1:11.71, 1:18.16)

$2 Mutuel Prices:

2 – TOLL TAKER	15.40	5.50	3.00
3 – IM A DIXIE GIRL		3.40	2.60
4 – SUMMER RAVEN			2.40

$2 EXACTA 2–3 PAID $49.60 $2 TRIFECTA 2–3–4 PAID $166.00

B. f, (Apr), by Bernstein – Tappanzee , by Bet Big . Trainer Hills Timothy A. Bred by Lothenbach Stables Inc (Ill).

TOLL TAKER raced in hand along the inside early, angled out and advanced four wide approaching the stretch, responded when roused in upper stretch and drew clear under a drive. IM A DIXIE GIRL contested the pace from the outside, dug in gamely in the stretch and came again along the inside late. SUMMER RAVEN raced close up early, rallied three wide on the turn, led into the stretch and faltered in the final furlong. ROVING ANGEL was outrun early, raced inside and had no response when roused. QUEENS PLAZA contested the pace along the inside and tired after a half mile. FIVE STAR FUND was outrun early, came wide into the stretch and tired.

Owners– 1, Patrick Welsh; 2, Carl William A; 3, Edgewood Farm; 4, McClelland Rachel McClelland Keith; 5, Candy Stables; 6, Klaravich Stables Inc

Trainers– 1, Hills Timothy A; 2, Levine Bruce N; 3, Pletcher Todd A; 4, Pion Robert A; 5, Bush Thomas M; 6, Violette Richard A Jr

EIGHTH RACE Keeneland OCTOBER 17, 2004

6 FURLONGS. (1.073) 24TH RUNNING OF THE THOROUGHBRED CLUB OF AMERICA. Grade III. Purse $125,000 FOR FILLIES AND MARES, THREE YEARS OLD AND UPWARD. By subscription of $125 each, which should accompany the nomination; $625 to enter and an additional $625 to start, with $125,000 guaranteed, of which the owner of the winner to receive $77,500, with $25,000 to second, $12,500 to third, $6,250 to fourth and $3,750 to fifth. Weight: Three year old fillies, 122 lbs., Older, 124 lbs. Non–winners of a graded stakes in 2004 allowed 2 lbs.; a sweepstakes in 2004, 4 lbs.; $30,000 twice in 2004, 6 lbs. Starters to be named through the entry box by the usual time of closing. A gold julep cup and a Thoroughbred Club of America trophy will be presented to the owner of the winner. Closed Wednesday, October 6, 2004 with 16 nominations.

Value of Race: $125,000 Winner $77,500; second $25,000; third $12,500; fourth $6,250; fifth $3,750. Mutuel Pool $270,514.00 Exacta Pool $174,351.00 Trifecta Pool $120,899.00 Superfecta Pool $35,291.00 Quinella Pool $6,551.00

Last Raced	Horse	M/Eqt.	A.	Wt	PP	St	¼	½	Str	Fin	Jockey	Odds $1
10Oct04 9Bel2	Molto Vita	L	4	122	6	1	11½	11½	11½	1¾	Bejarano R	2.60
29Aug04 9Sar2	My Trusty Cat	L bf	4	124	2	5	53	52½	33	2nk	Day P	1.10
29Aug04 9Sar7	My Boston Gal	L f	4	118	4	4	41½	31½	21	31¾	Borel C H	4.70
6Sep04 8AP1	Souris	L b	4	122	1	6	6	6	4hd	46½	Albarado R J	9.00
7Aug04 2Mnr3	Our Josephina	L	4	122	5	2	3½	2hd	52	52	McKee J	28.60
6Sep04 8AP3	Summer Mis	L b	5	122	3	3	2½	41	6	6	Sterling L J Jr	5.50

OFF AT 4:45 Start Good . Won driving. Track fast.

TIME :22, :453, :573, 1:094 (:22.09, :45.75, :57.65, 1:09.92)

$2 Mutuel Prices:			
6 – MOLTO VITA	7.20	3.00	2.60
2 – MY TRUSTY CAT		2.40	2.40
4 – MY BOSTON GAL			2.80

$2 EXACTA 6–2 PAID $15.00 $2 TRIFECTA 6–2–4 PAID $55.00

$2 SUPERFECTA 6–2–4–1 PAID $123.20 $2 QUINELLA 2–6 PAID $7.00

B. f, (Mar), by Carson City – Princess Polonia , by Danzig . Trainer Stewart Dallas. Bred by TAC Holding Inc (Ky).

MOLTO VITA broke in front, raced in the three path, opened a clear advantage just prior to going a quarter, made the balance of the pace and held sway under strong handling. MY TRUSTY CAT, never far back and positioned in behind the leaders two or three wide, swung out six wide for the drive and was slowly gaining at the end . MY BOSTON GAL tracked the winner four wide from early on, was just off MOTO VITA for the final furlong and couldn't muster the needed response. SOURIS, outrun inside for a half, maneuvered out four wide for the drive and offered a slight gain. OUR JOSEPHINA, bobbled lightly at the start, was checked at the five furlong marker, continued close up four wide into the stretch and tired. SUMMER MIS, close up inside the winner early, continued forwardly for a half, weakened and was angled out four wide for the drive to no avail.

Owners– 1, Gunther John D; 2, Pollard Carl F; 3, Porter J Chester Bloch Randy and Milner Phil; 4, Hunt Nelson B; 5, Brunacini George; 6, Richard Otto Stables Inc

Trainers– 1, Stewart Dallas; 2, Vance David R; 3, Nafzger Carl A; 4, Asmussen Steven M; 5, Fojan Emilie; 6, Mitchell Anthony

$2 Pick Three (3–5–6) Paid $251.00 ; Pick Three Pool $31,919 .

EIGHTH RACE Santa Anita OCTOBER 17, 2004

1⅛ MILES. (Turf) (1.434) 35TH RUNNING OF THE OAK TREE DERBY. Grade II. Purse $150,000 FOR THREE–YEAR–OLDS. By subscription of $150 if made on or before Thursday, September 9, 2004. Closed with 30. All horses shall pay $1,500 to start with $150,000 guaranteed of which $90,000 to first, $30,000 to second, $18,000 to third, $9,000 to fourthand $3,000 to fifth. 122 lbs. Non–winners of $100,000 twice at one mile or over in 2004 allowed 2 lbs.; $100,000 at one mile or over in 2004, 4 lbs. A trophy will be presented to the owner of the winner. Closed with 27 nominations. (Rail at 15 feet).

Value of Race: $150,000 Winner $90,000; second $30,000; third $18,000; fourth $9,000; fifth $3,000. Mutuel Pool $506,696.00 Exacta Pool $291,048.00 Quinella Pool $26,235.00 Trifecta Pool $317,625.00 Superfecta Pool $146,177.00

Last Raced	Horse	M/Eqt.	A.	Wt	PP	St	¼	½	¾	Str	Fin	Jockey	Odds $1
11Sep04 9Bel8	Greek Sun	LB	3	118	8	9	71	84	71	71	1¾	Prado E S	1.40
6Sep04 8Dmr3	Laura's Lucky Boy	LB	3	118	6	3	2½	2½	21	1½	21	Stevens G L	4.30
19Sep04 3BM4	Hendrix	LB b	3	118	3	1	5hd	4hd	41	31½	3no	Flores D R	56.10
25Sep04 10LaD4	Imperialism	LB b	3	120	2	7	9	9	9	8hd	41	Espinoza V	7.20
25Sep04 11Fpx1	Semi Lost	LB	3	118	7	4	4hd	5½	51	4hd	5no	Pedroza M A	8.20
6Sep04 8Dmr4	Terroplane-FR	LB b	3	118	9	6	31	31	3hd	51	6nk	Desormeaux K J	6.80
5Sep04 1Dmr1	On the Acorn-GB	LB	3	118	1	8	82	7hd	82½	9	7no	Sorenson D	43.40
26Jun04 3Hol3	Whilly-Ire	LB	3	118	4	2	1hd	1½	1hd	2hd	8hd	Martinez F F	29.40
25Sep04 10LaD2	Borrego	LB	3	118	5	5	61½	61½	6½	6hd	9	Baze T C	5.40

OFF AT 4:09 Start Good . Won driving. Course good.

TIME :234, :482, 1:122, 1:362, 1:48 (:23.88, :40.53, 1:12.55, 1:36.55, 1:48.08)

$2 Mutuel Prices:			
9 – GREEK SUN	4.80	3.20	2.80
7 – LAURA'S LUCKY BOY		4.20	3.80
3 – HENDRIX			8.20

$1 EXACTA 9–7 PAID $9.60 $2 QUINELLA 7–9 PAID $12.00

$1 TRIFECTA 9–7–3 PAID $236.10 $1 SUPERFECTA 9–7–3–2 PAID $1,413.10

Dk. b or br. c, (Mar), by Danzig – Sunlit Silence , by Trempolino . Trainer Frankel Robert. Bred by E K Gaylord II & Cheyenne Stables LLC (Ky).

GREEK SUN off a bit slowly, settled outside a rival, moved up outside leaving the second turn and five wide into the stretch and closed gamely under some left handed urging to get up late. LAURA'S LUCKY BOY forced the pace between horses, took a short lead three deep into the stretch and held on gamely but was caught late. HENDRIX bumped into the first turn, raced close up stalking the pace inside, bid along the rail in the stretch and continued willingly to just hold third. IMPERIALISM unhurried outside a rival then along the inside, came out on the second turn and five wide into the stretch and finished well. SEMI LOST between foes early, was bumped into the first turn, stalked three deep, came four wide into the stretch and was outfinished. TERROPLANE (FR) prompted the pace three deep, fell back a bit into the stretch and lacked the needed response. ON THE ACORN (GB) saved ground off the pace, came out into the stretch and could not summon the necessary late kick. WHILLY (IRE) sped to the early lead and angled in, was briefly clear leaving the first turn, set a pressured pace inside, came out into the stretch, fought back between horses in midstretch and weakened some late. BORREGO pulled early, chased between foes and was bumped between rivals into the first turn, continued a bit off the rail leaving the backstretch and on the second turn, lacked room off heels in deep stretch, angled in and lacked the needed response.

Owners– 1, Angelos Peter G; 2, Mercedes Stables LLC; 3, Reddam J Paul; 4, Taub Steve; 5, Bone Robert D and Desperado Stables; 6, Bienstock David Papiano Neil and Winner Charles; 7, Cassidy James M Jim Ford Inc and Pearson Deron; 8, Triple B Farms; 9, Kelly Jon Scott Brad Ralls and Foster LLC et al

Trainers– 1, Frankel Robert; 2, Orman Jason; 3, Dollase Craig; 4, Mulhall Kristin; 5, Mullins Jeff; 6, Drysdale Neil; 7, Cassidy James; 8, O'Neill Doug; 9, Greely C Beau

Scratched– We All Love Aleyna (25Sep04 11Fpx7)

$2 Daily Double (2–9) Paid $30.40 ; Daily Double Pool $35,020 .

$1 Pick Three (2/5/8/10/11–2–6/9) Paid $36.60 ; Pick Three Pool $78,403 .

EIGHTH RACE
Meadowlands
OCTOBER 22, 2004

$1\frac{1}{16}$ MILES. (Turf) (1.39^2) 28TH RUNNING OF THE VIOLET HANDICAP. Grade III. Purse $200,000 FOR FILLIES AND MARES, THREE YEARS OLD AND UPWARD. By subscription of $200 each, which should accompany the nomination and $1,500 to pass the entry box. The purse to be divided 60% to the owner of the winner, 20% to second, 11% to third, 6% to fourth and 3% to fifth. The winning owner to receive a trophy. Closed Friday, October 8, 2004 with 20 nominations.

Value of Race: $200,000 Winner $120,000; second $40,000; third $22,000; fourth $12,000; fifth $6,000. Mutuel Pool $113,018.00 Exacta Pool $96,295.00 Trifecta Pool $77,404.00 Superfecta Pool $19,841.00

Last Raced	Horse	M/Eqt.	A.	Wt	PP	St	¼	½	¾	Str	Fin	Jockey	Odds $1
25Sep04 ^{9}Bel^{4}	Changing World	L	4	113	6	1	$1^{1\frac{1}{2}}$	$1^{3\frac{1}{2}}$	1^{4}	1^{3}	$1^{1\frac{1}{4}}$	Fragoso P	13.40
25Sep04 ^{9}Bel^{2}	High Court-Brz	L	4	117	7	6	7	7	$5^{1\frac{1}{2}}$	4^{1}	2^{hd}	Migliore R	5.10
25Sep04 ^{9}Bel^{1}	Ocean Drive	L	4	121	4	3	2^{1}	$2^{2\frac{1}{2}}$	2^{2}	2^{2}	$3^{2\frac{1}{2}}$	Velazquez J R	0.50
5Sep04 ^{7}Sar^{2}	WhereWLftOff-GB	L	4	118	1	5	4^{hd}	3^{hd}	3^{1}	$3^{1\frac{1}{2}}$	4^{1}	Bravo J	6.30
9Oct04 ^{9}Pha^{1}	Caught in the Rain	L	5	116	2	4	5^{1}	$5^{\frac{1}{2}}$	4^{1}	$5^{\frac{1}{2}}$	5^{1}	Molina V H	15.50
12Sep04 ^{8}Bel^{3}	Fast Cookie	L	4	118	3	7	6^{2}	$6^{1\frac{1}{2}}$	7	6^{4}	$6^{10\frac{1}{4}}$	Velasquez C	10.00
5Oct04 ^{6}Med^{1}	Smart N Classy	L	4	115	5	2	3^{hd}	4^{1}	6^{hd}	7	7	Velez J A Jr	44.70

OFF AT 10:17 Start Good . Won driving. Course good.

TIME :24^{3}, :48^{2}, 1:11^{3}, 1:35^{1}, 1:41^{2} (:24.63, :48.40, 1:11.65, 1:35.34, 1:41.53)

$2 Mutuel Prices:			
6 – CHANGING WORLD	28.80	11.40	2.20
7 – HIGH COURT–BRZ		6.60	2.10
4 – OCEAN DRIVE			2.10

$2 EXACTA 6–7 PAID $188.00 $2 TRIFECTA 6–7–4 PAID $457.00
$1 SUPERFECTA 6–7–4–1 PAID $766.50

B. f, (Jan), by Spinning World – Reach the Top , by Cozzene . Trainer Tagg Barclay. Bred by Mr & Mrs S H Rogers Jr (Fla).

CHANGING WORLD firmly rated a clear lead inside, felt steady pressure the final furlong and held on well. HIGH COURT (BRZ), unhurried inside, bid saving ground on the final turn, built momentum through the final furlong, was up the final yards for place and finished well. OCEAN DRIVE kept off the pace and off the rail, gave chase into the final turn, closed well to late stretch, couldn't threaten the winner and was outfinished for place the closing yards. WHERE WE LEFT OFF (GB) rated off the pace inside, gave chase through the final turn then finished evenly. CAUGHT IN THE RAIN steadied into the opening turn, again entering the backstretch then showed no significant response on the final turn. FAST COOKIE was shuffled back early and never a threat. SMART N CLASSY was through after half.

Owners– 1, Rogers Samuel H Jr; 2, Lael Stables; 3, Baskin Bonnie and Sy; 4, Moyglare Stud Farm Ltd; 5, Heiligbrodt Racing & W L New; 6, Stonerside Stable LLC; 7, Roseland Farm Stable

Trainers– 1, Tagg Barclay; 2, Matz Michael R; 3, Pletcher Todd A; 4, Clement Christophe; 5, Preciado Guadalupe; 6, Mott William I; 7, Tammaro John J III

TENTH RACE
Calder
OCTOBER 23, 2004

1⅛ MILES. (Turf) (1.44^{4}) 33RD RUNNING OF THE CALDER DERBY. Grade III. Purse $200,000 FOR THREE YEARS OLD. By subscription of $200 each which shall accompany the nomination, $2,000 to pass the entry box and an additional $2,000 to start – with $200,000 guaranteed. The owner of the winner to receive $120,000, $40,000 to second, $22,000 to third, $12,000 to fourth and $6,000 to fifth. Weight: 121 lbs. Non–winners of a sweepstakes of $75,000 at a mile or over allowed 3 lbs.; non–winners of a sweepstakes of $50,000 at a mile or over, 5 lbs.; non–winners of two races other than Maiden or Claiming at a mile or over, 7 lbs.; non–winners of a race other than Maiden or Claiming at a mile or over, 9 lbs. Graded placed horses at equal weights preferred. A trophy will be presented to the winning Owner. This race will be limited to 12 Starters, with Also Eligibles. (High Weights Preferred) Closed Saturday, October 9, 2004 with 26 nominations. (If deemed inadvisable to run this race over the Turf course, it will be run on the main track at One Mile and One Eighth).

Value of Race: $200,000 Winner $120,000; second $40,000; third $22,000; fourth $12,000; fifth $6,000. Mutuel Pool $196,160.00 Exacta Pool $210,338.00 Trifecta Pool $171,522.00 Superfecta Pool $61,780.00

Last Raced	Horse	M/Eqt.		A.	Wt	PP	St	¼	½	¾	Str	Fin	Jockey	Odds $1
1Oct04 ^{7}Med^{2}	Eddington	L	b	3	114	3	8	11^{2}	9^{hd}	7^{1}	4^{1}	1^{hd}	Coa E M	2.70
1Oct04 ^{9}Crc^{1}	Bob'sProudMoment	L		3	116	1	2	$1^{\frac{1}{2}}$	1^{1}	1^{hd}	1^{2}	2^{1}	Madrid S O	42.10
9Jly04 ^{3}Crc^{1}	[D]Capias	L		3	116	2	3	5^{hd}	$8^{1\frac{1}{2}}$	$8^{\frac{1}{2}}$	$6^{1\frac{1}{2}}$	$3^{2\frac{1}{2}}$	Velasquez C	6.10
25Sep04 ^{10}LaD^{5}	Caballero Negro	L	f	3	114	9	1	$3^{\frac{1}{2}}$	4^{hd}	$4^{1\frac{1}{2}}$	3^{hd}	4^{1}	Peltroche E	19.90
25Sep04 ^{4}Crc^{1}	Wire Bound	L	b	3	116	4	7	$8^{\frac{1}{2}}$	7^{hd}	$5^{\frac{1}{2}}$	5^{hd}	5^{nk}	Cruz M R	2.30
25Sep04 ^{4}Crc^{4}	Silversandsoftime	L	b	3	116	6	12	12	12	12	8^{3}	$6^{\frac{3}{4}}$	Boulanger G	58.60
26Sep04 ^{9}Bel^{3}	Icy Atlantic	L		3	118	5	5	4^{1}	$3^{\frac{1}{2}}$	$3^{\frac{1}{2}}$	$2^{\frac{1}{2}}$	$7^{4\frac{1}{4}}$	Bailey J D	*2.30
25Sep04 ^{4}Crc^{6}	Soverign Honor	L	b	3	116	11	4	2^{1}	2^{1}	2^{1}	7^{1}	$8^{\frac{3}{4}}$	Aguilar M	61.50
4Oct04 ^{5}Crc^{2}	Uncivil	L	b	3	116	7	9	9^{1}	10^{1}	10^{hd}	$9^{3\frac{1}{2}}$	9^{2}	Castro E	84.00
9Oct04 ^{10}Crc^{5}	Halo Goodbye	L	b	3	114	10	10	$10^{\frac{1}{2}}$	11^{1}	$11^{\frac{1}{2}}$	10^{hd}	$10^{4\frac{3}{4}}$	Nelson L C	95.20
25Sep04 ^{4}Crc^{3}	Frolic for Joy	L	b	3	114	12	11	$7^{\frac{1}{2}}$	5^{hd}	$6^{\frac{1}{2}}$	11^{1}	$11^{2\frac{1}{2}}$	Bravo J	42.10
25Sep04 ^{4}Crc^{2}	Cervelo	L		3	116	8	6	6^{hd}	6^{hd}	$9^{1\frac{1}{2}}$	12	12	Garcia J A	13.20

[D] – Capias disqualified and placed 12th
***–Actual Betting Favorite.**

OFF AT 4:01 Start Good . Won driving. Course good.

TIME :24^{2}, :49, 1:14^{1}, 1:38^{4}, 1:51^{1} (:24.57, :49.09, 1:14.34, 1:38.91, 1:51.25)

$2 Mutuel Prices:			
3 – EDDINGTON	7.40	4.40	3.20
1 – BOB'S PROUD MOMENT		24.80	10.20
9 – CABALLERO NEGRO			9.40

$2 EXACTA 3–1 PAID $166.60 $2 TRIFECTA 3–1–9 PAID $1,788.60
$2 SUPERFECTA 3–1–9–4 PAID $6,013.20

Ch. c, (Mar), by Unbridled – Fashion Star , by Chief's Crown . Trainer Hennig Mark. Bred by Carl Rosen Associates (Ky).

EDDINGTON reserved after being steadied in close quarters in the early going, saved ground while moving up on the far turn, worked his way through traffic in early stretch, eased outside the leader inside the eighth pole and rallied to be just up at the wire. BOB'S PROUD MOMENT set the pace along the hedge, drew clear in midstretch, then just failed to last. CAPIAS rated off the pace, angled out for the stretch run, then drifted in impeding several rivals just inside the sixteenth pole while rallying to be up for the show. CABALLERO NEGRO well placed racing along the hedge, was bumped hard by WIRE BOUND inside the sixteenth pole and weakened. WIRE BOUND allowed to settle, raced three wide on the far turn, then was moving into contention when checked inside CAPIAS just past the sixteenth pole and gave way. SILVERSANDSOFTIME outrun early, angled to the outside in the stretch and passed tired rivals. ICY ATLANTIC chased the pace three wide into the stretch, then bumped with CABALLERO NEGRO when forced in inside the sixteenth pole, steadied and tired. SOVERIGN HONOR prompted the pace outside BOB'S PROUD MOMENT into the far turn and faltered. UNCIVIL failed to menace. HALO GOODBYE was not a factor. FROLIC FOR JOY raced in striking position three wide into the far turn and faded. CERVELO was through after a half mile. Following a stewards inquiry and a claim of foul by the rider of WIRE BOUND, CAPIAS was disqualified and placed twelfth for interference to several rivals just inside the sixteenth pole.

Owners– 1, Willmott Stables Inc; 2, Dubois Robert M; 3, Etarip Stables Ltd; 4, Veranda Farm Inc; 5, Silver Diamond Thoroughbreds Inc; 6, Lundock Rodney G; 7, Appleton Arthur I; 8, Chin James; 9, Mount Joy Stables Inc; 10, Collazo Henry and Beda Ron; 11, Stride Rite Racing Stable Inc; 12, Denes Paul R

Trainers– 1, Hennig Mark; 2, Potter Douglas; 3, White William P; 4, Morales Mario; 5, Criollo Manuel; 6, Tortora Emanuel; 7, Pletcher Todd A; 8, Pinchin Jose; 9, Stutts Bennie F Jr; 10, Collazo Henry; 11, Wolfson Milton W; 12, Hatchett James

Scratched– Cool Conductor (16Oct04 ^{8}Haw^{1}) , Dashboard Drummer (02Oct04 ^{7}Med^{2}) , Nightmare Affair (09Sep04 ^{8}Crc^{2})

$2 Pick Three (10–1–3) Paid $1,355.80 ; Pick Three Pool $21,408 .

THIRTEENTH RACE

Calder

OCTOBER 23, 2004

1 1/16 MILES. (1.42^{2}) 13TH RUNNING OF THE SPEND A BUCK HANDICAP. Grade III. Purse $100,000 FOR THREE YEARS OLD AND UPWARD. By subscription of $100 each which shall accompany the nomination, $1,000 to pass the entry box and an additional $1,000 to start – with $100,000 guaranteed. The owner of the winner to receive $60,000, $20,000 to second, $11,000 to third, $6,000 to fourth and $3,000 to fifth. A trophy will be presented to the winning Owner. Closed Saturday, October 9, 2004 with 15 nominations.

Value of Race: $100,000 Winner $60,000; second $20,000; third $11,000; fourth $6,000; fifth $3,000. Mutuel Pool $193,273.00 Exacta Pool $146,784.00 Trifecta Pool $107,996.00 Superfecta Pool $32,445.00

Last Raced	Horse	M/Eqt.	A.	Wt	PP	St	¼	½	¾	Str	Fin	Jockey	Odds $1
26Sep04 ^{8}Crc^{2}	Built Up	L	6	115	1	1	5½	5^{1½}	3^{1½}	1^{2½}	1^{hd}	Coa E M	2.60
26Sep04 ^{8}Crc^{3}	Super Frolic	L f	4	117	2	4	7^{1}	6½	4½	2^{1½}	2^{4¼}	Bravo J	2.80
9Oct04 ^{7}Crc^{10}	Gold Dollar	L b	5	115	6	7	9^{1½}	10^{1}	6^{hd}	4^{2}	3^{3½}	Lopez J E	13.30
9Oct04 ^{7}Crc^{2}	Twilight Road	L	7	117	7	6	8^{1½}	8½	5^{1}	6½	4^{1½}	Teator P A	2.20
26Sep04 ^{8}Crc^{7}	Hear No Evil	L bf	4	114	11	5	2^{hd}	2^{hd}	2^{hd}	3^{hd}	5^{1}	Velasquez C	11.10
3Oct04 ^{9}Crc^{2}	Black Mambo	L f	5	113	5	8	10^{1}	9^{hd}	7^{hd}	5^{1}	6^{1¾}	Ferrer J C	17.00
3Oct04 ^{9}Crc^{9}	Puck	L b	5	114	9	9	3^{1}	3½	1^{1}	7^{1}	7^{1¾}	Aguilar M	27.20
2Oct04 ^{3}Crc^{1}	Dependable Herbie	L b	4	112	8	10	11	11	9^{1½}	8^{6}	8^{8¾}	Castro E	16.10
20Jun04 ^{9}Mon^{1}	Big Luck-Per	L f	6	117	3	2	1^{1½}	1^{hd}	11	10^{8}	9^{5½}	Talaverano R	32.30
26Sep04 ^{8}Crc^{6}	Dancing Guy	L bf	9	114	4	3	6^{1}	7½	8^{1½}	9^{hd}	10	Cruz M R	42.90
15Jun04 ^{7}Crc^{6}	Predawn Raid	L b	5	115	10	11	4^{hd}	4^{1}	10^{1}	11	—	Velez J A Jr	31.80

OFF AT 5:24 Start Good For All But PREDAWN RAID. Won driving. Track fast.

TIME :23^{4}, :48, 1:13, 1:38^{4}, 1:45^{4} (:23.82, :48.16, 1:13.04, 1:38.98, 1:45.86)

$2 Mutuel Prices:

1 – BUILT UP	7.20	4.00	4.20
2 – SUPER FROLIC		3.80	3.80
6 – GOLD DOLLAR			6.60

$2 EXACTA 1–2 PAID $23.60 $2 TRIFECTA 1–2–6 PAID $140.40
$2 SUPERFECTA 1–2–6–7 PAID $358.80

B. g, (Apr), by Homebuilder – Toned Up, by Herat. Trainer Alonso Enrique. Bred by John Franks (Fla).

BUILT UP rated off the pace, rallied three wide to take over leaving the far turn and opened a clear lead, then was all out to last over SUPER FROLIC. The latter, reserved early, angled outside the leaders for the stretch run and rallied to just miss. GOLD DOLLAR unhurried while saving ground, steadied in behind BIG LUCK on the far turn, angled out in the stretch and closed to gain the show. TWILIGHT ROAD reserved early, advanced into contention on the far turn, then couldn't keep pace with the top ones in the drive. HEAR NO EVIL chased the pace into the stretch and gave way. BLACK MAMBO outrun early, passed tired rivals. PUCK chased the pace, moved to take over on the far turn, then tired in the drive. DEPENDABLE HERBIE was not a factor. BIG LUCK (PER) set the pace along the inside into the far turn and faltered. DANCING GUY allowed to settle, bore out leaving the backstretch and around the far turn, then faded. PREDAWN RAID hesitated at the start, moved up to chase the leaders three wide to the far turn, stopped and was eased in the stretch run.

Owners– 1, Susi Raymond; 2, Stride Rite Racing Stable Inc; 3, Pazos Julio; 4, Donamire Farm; 5, Jacks or Better Farm Inc; 6, Murphy William F; 7, Oxbow Racing LLC; 8, Sullivan Joseph J; 9, Salas Jorge M; 10, Green Newcomb; 11, Mount Joy Stables Inc

Trainers– 1, Alonso Enrique; 2, Wolfson Milton W; 3, Azpurua Manuel J; 4, Fawkes David; 5, Hatchett James; 6, Gomez Frank; 7, White William P; 8, Wolfson Martin D; 9, Rosas-Canessa Walter; 10, Green Newcomb; 11, Stutts Bennie F Jr

$2 Pick Three (7–8–1) Paid $137.60 ; Pick Three Pool $31,431 .
$1 Pick Four (3–7–8–1) Paid $344.20 ; Pick Four Pool $96,040 .

NINTH RACE
Keeneland
OCTOBER 23, 2004

$1\frac{1}{16}$ MILES. (Turf) (1.40^{1}) 14TH RUNNING OF THE VALLEY VIEW. Grade III. Purse $100,000 HAGGIN COURSE. FOR FILLIES, THREE YEARS OLD. By subscription of $100 each which should accompany the nomination; $500 to enter and an additional $500 to start, with $100,000 added, of which 62% of all monies to the owner of the winner, 20% to second, 10%to third, 5% to fourth and 3% to fifth. Weight: 123 lbs. Non-winners of a graded or group stakes on the turf allowed 4 lbs.; a sweepstakes, 7 lbs. The maximum number of starters for the Valley View will be limited to twelve. In the event that more than twelve fillies pass the entry box, the twelve starters will be determined at that time with preference by condition eligibility, beginning with graded or group stakes winners. Starters to be named through the entry box by the usual time of closing. A gold julep cup will be presented to the owner of the winner. Closed Wednesday, October 13, 2004 with 43 nominations.

Value of Race: $116,300 Winner $72,106; second $23,260; third $11,630; fourth $5,815; fifth $3,489. Mutuel Pool $401,681.00 Exacta Pool $280,471.00 Trifecta Pool $222,333.00 Superfecta Pool $79,472.00 Quinella Pool $10,005.00

Last Raced	Horse	M/Eqt.	A.	Wt	PP	St	¼	½	¾	Str	Fin	Jockey	Odds $1
18Sep04 ^{9}AP^{3}	Sister Swank	L	3	116	7	5	5^{hd}	3^{1}	2^{1}	2^{hd}	$1^{1\frac{1}{4}}$	Day P	3.30
4Sep04 ^{8}WO^{3}	Jinny's Gold	L	3	116	3	3	$2^{1\frac{1}{2}}$	1^{hd}	$1^{1\frac{1}{2}}$	$1^{2\frac{1}{2}}$	$2^{1\frac{1}{2}}$	Borel C H	6.90
11Sep04 ^{8}Bel^{4}	Shadow Cast	L	3	119	12	10	9^{2}	$5^{\frac{1}{2}}$	3^{hd}	3^{3}	$3^{4\frac{1}{2}}$	Albarado R J	4.60
25Sep04 ^{6}LaD^{5}	Topango	L f	3	119	9	8	$7^{\frac{1}{2}}$	$4^{\frac{1}{2}}$	4^{2}	$4^{1\frac{1}{2}}$	$4^{1\frac{1}{2}}$	Martinez J R Jr	30.00
2Oct04 ^{9}Pha^{5}	Catboat	L b	3	119	6	9	8^{hd}	$8^{1\frac{1}{2}}$	7^{1}	$5^{\frac{1}{2}}$	$5^{\frac{1}{2}}$	Bejarano R	7.10
18Sep04 ^{8}KD^{5}	Rich Find	L	3	119	5	1	$3^{\frac{1}{2}}$	7^{2}	6^{hd}	6^{3}	6^{1}	Perret C	28.90
25Sep04 ^{9}Pim^{5}	Bay Tree-Ire	L	3	119	11	12	11^{5}	11^{3}	$11^{4\frac{1}{2}}$	$8^{\frac{1}{2}}$	7^{nk}	Guidry M	7.00
11Oct04 ^{9}Bel^{8}	Lenatareese	L	3	119	2	7	$10^{2\frac{1}{2}}$	$10^{\frac{1}{2}}$	10^{hd}	7^{1}	$8^{8\frac{1}{4}}$	Melancon L	3.10
18Sep04 ^{6}PrM^{4}	This One for Abbey	L	3	119	8	4	$4^{1\frac{1}{2}}$	2^{hd}	$5^{\frac{1}{2}}$	9^{2}	$9^{\frac{1}{2}}$	McKee J	66.50
21Sep04 ^{6}KD^{1}	Pretty Jane	L	3	116	4	6	6^{hd}	9^{hd}	9^{1}	10^{2}	$10^{2\frac{3}{4}}$	Castanon J L	38.00
31Jly04 ^{10}RD^{1}	Barnsy		3	119	10	11	12	12	12	11^{hd}	11^{2}	Martinez W	48.40
18Sep04 ^{8}KD^{1}	Beau Watch	L b	3	119	1	2	1^{1}	6^{hd}	8^{2}	12	12	Blanc B	20.10

OFF AT 5:16 Start Good . Won driving. Course yielding.

TIME :23^{2}, :48^{3}, 1:14^{1}, 1:40^{1}, 1:46^{3} (:23.53, :48.72, 1:14.32, 1:40.22, 1:46.75)

$2 Mutuel Prices:

7 – SISTER SWANK	**8.60**	**6.00**	**4.20**
3 – JINNY'S GOLD		**7.20**	**4.80**
12 – SHADOW CAST			**4.00**

$2 EXACTA 7–3 PAID $56.60 $2 TRIFECTA 7–3–12 PAID $263.60
$2 SUPERFECTA 7–3–12–9 PAID $7,573.20 $2 QUINELLA 3–7 PAID $29.20

Ch. f, (Mar), by Skip Away – Max Donnell , by Critique . Trainer Asmussen Steven M. Bred by Kenirey Stud Farm (Ky).

SISTER SWANK, in hand from early on, followed the leaders four or five wide, came out farther on the course when advancing into the stretch, was sharply roused in the upper stretch and edged clear late. JINNY'S GOLD forced the pace from early on while four or five wide, took over and continued five wide, moved wider when managing a clear advantage into the stretch and couldn't handle the winner late. SHADOW CAST leaned in at the start exchanging bumps with BAY TREE (IRE), was unhurried, worked her way inward, edged up between rivals on the far turn, was with the winner while inside that one approaching the stretch, loomed a threat into the final furlong but couldn't muster the needed response. TOPANGO, in a striking position throughout while following the leaders five or six wide, failed to fire. CATBOAT bobbled at the start and leaned in bumping RICH FIND, was unhurried, edged to contention between foes approaching the stretch but lacked a further account when straightened for the drive. RICH FIND, bumped at the start, was well placed between foes four wide to the stretch and came up empty. BAY TREE (IRE) came out at the break exchanging bumps with CHADOW CAST, was outrun to the lane and unable to menace while improving position. LENATAREESE, outrun into the backstretch, moved up four wide on the far turn but never reached serous contention. THIS ONE FOR ABBEY, rated between horses four or five wide for six furlongs, weakened thereafter. PRETTY JANE tired early. BARNSY was outrun. BEAU WATCH gained the lead inside early but began to fade early on the backstretch.

Owners– 1, Heiligbrodt Racing Stable; 2, Kaster Richard S and Wieting Frederick C; 3, Farish William S Jr; 4, HSB Racing John G Locke et al; 5, Stonerside Stable LLC; 6, Shadowfax Stable; 7, Salman Prince Faisal; 8, Anderson Brad; 9, DeBruycker Lloyd; 10, Redmond Garrett; 11, Destiny Farm LLC; 12, Reed Kay and Wright Timothy

Trainers– 1, Asmussen Steven M; 2, Fox Jamie; 3, Howard Neil J; 4, Locke John G; 5, Flint Bernard S; 6, Foley Gregory D; 7, Motion H Graham; 8, Carroll David; 9, Tracy Ray E Jr; 10, Caramori Eduardo; 11, Hamm Timothy; 12, Reed Eric R

Scratched– Cape Town Lass (17Sep04 ^{6}AP ^{1}) , Lady Offense (13Oct04 ^{6}Kee^{8})

$2 Pick Three (1–8–7) Paid $559.00 ; Pick Three Pool $27,285 .

NINTH RACE
Santa Anita
OCTOBER 23, 2004

1½ MILES. (Turf) (2.22^{4}) 36TH RUNNING OF THE CARLETON F. BURKE HANDICAP. Grade III. Purse $100,000 FOR THREE-YEAR-OLDS AND UPWARD. By subscription of $100 each if made on or before Thursday, October 14, 2004 or by supplementary nomination of $2,000 by 10 AM Tuesday, October 19. All horses shall pay $1,000 to start with $100,000 guaranteed of which $60,000 to the winner, $20,000 to second, $12,000 to third, $6,000 to fourth and $2,000 to fifth. Weights: Tuesday, October 19. Starters to be named through the entry box by the closing time of entries. A trophy will be presented to the owner of the winner. (Rail at 8 feet). Closed with 18 nominations.

Value of Race: $100,000 Winner $60,000; second $20,000; third $12,000; fourth $6,000; fifth $2,000. Mutuel Pool $427,555.00 Exacta Pool $239,207.00 Quinella Pool $24,082.00 Trifecta Pool $265,508.00 Superfecta Pool $120,472.00

Last Raced	Horse	M/Eqt.	A.	Wt	PP	¼	½	1	1¼	Str	Fin	Jockey	Odds $1
11Oct04 ^{4}SA^{2}	Habaneros	LB bf	5	116	2	1^{1}	$1^{1\frac{1}{2}}$	$1^{\frac{1}{2}}$	$1^{1\frac{1}{2}}$	1^{2}	$1^{\frac{3}{4}}$	Flores D R	14.10
4Aug04 ^{7}Dmr^{4}	Pellegrino-Brz	LB	5	116	5	$6^{\frac{1}{2}}$	$6^{\frac{1}{2}}$	7^{2}	7^{1}	$4^{1\frac{1}{2}}$	2^{nk}	Stevens G L	14.10
3Sep04 ^{4}Dmr^{1}	Gallant-GB	LB	7	113	3	5^{2}	$3^{\frac{1}{2}}$	$4^{1\frac{1}{2}}$	$2^{\frac{1}{2}}$	2^{hd}	3no	Pedroza M A	29.30
3Oct04 ^{5}SA^{6}	Puerto Banus	LB b	5	115	8	$7^{1\frac{1}{2}}$	$7^{1\frac{1}{2}}$	6^{hd}	5^{1}	$3^{\frac{1}{2}}$	4^{1}	Espinoza V	2.60
14Aug04 ^{9}AP^{13}	Hatif-Brz	LB	5	112	4	$2^{\frac{1}{2}}$	$2^{1\frac{1}{2}}$	2^{hd}	3^{1}	$5^{\frac{1}{2}}$	5^{1}	Baze T C	7.80
8Sep04 ^{6}Dmr^{8}	Special Matter	LB b	6	116	7	4^{hd}	$5^{1\frac{1}{2}}$	$5^{1\frac{1}{2}}$	4^{hd}	6^{hd}	6^{nk}	Desormeaux K J	9.00
29Aug04 ^{8}Dmr^{7}	Continuously	LB	5	117	6	8	8	8	8	$7^{1\frac{1}{2}}$	7^{2}	Nakatani C S	1.30
4Aug04 ^{7}Dmr^{6}	Leprechaun Kid	LB b	5	114	1	3^{1}	4^{1}	3^{1}	6^{hd}	8	8	Smith M E	7.60

OFF AT 4:38 Start Good . Won driving. Course firm.

TIME :25^{1}, :49^{1}, 1:13^{4}, 1:38^{3}, 2:02^{3}, 2:26^{4} (:25.26, :49.30, 1:13.83, 1:38.62, 2:02.65, 2:26.91)

$2 Mutuel Prices:				
	2 – HABANEROS	30.20	13.20	8.20
	5 – PELLEGRINO–BRZ		11.40	7.80
	3 – GALLANT–GB			11.20

$1 EXACTA 2–5 PAID $176.60 $2 QUINELLA 2–5 PAID $161.80
$1 TRIFECTA 2–5–3 PAID $2,064.70 $1 SUPERFECTA 2–5–3–8 PAID $8,687.10

Ch. g, (Feb), by Tabasco Cat – Innocently Astray , by Gone West . Trainer Bell Thomas R II. Bred by Louie Roussel III (Ky).

HABANEROS went between horses to the early lead, set the pace inside, shook off rivals leaving the backstretch, came a bit off the rail in the stretch and held on gamely under urging. PELLEGRINO (BRZ) angled in and saved ground off the pace, moved up inside leaving the second turn, slipped through along the rail in the stretch and finished willingly. GALLANT (GB) stalked the pace inside, was in tight into the second turn, came out into the stretch, was between foes in midstretch and just held third. PUERTO BANUS chased outside a rival, went three deep on the second turn and five wide into the stretch and just missed the show. HATIF (BRZ) stalked the pace off the rail, bid between horses on the backstretch then outside the winner, tracked that one outside a rival on the second turn, came three deep into the stretch and lacked the needed late response. SPECIAL MATTER chased off the rail then angled in past the wire the first time, came out into the second turn and four wide into the stretch and could not offer the necessary late kick. CONTINUOUSLY unhurried along the inside to the second turn, came outside foes on that turn and five wide into the stretch and lacked the needed rally. LEPRECHAUN KID pulled inside then outside a rival, bid three deep on the backstretch, steadied while dropping back between horses leaving the second turn and weakened. Rail on hill at zero.

Owners– 1, Bell John C Lessee; 2, Tanaka Gary A; 3, Fisher Derrick; 4, Noctis LLC Papiano Neil and Taub Steve; 5, Belmont Stable and Old Friends Inc; 6, Elder Nancy and McClintock Janice and George et al; 7, Khaled Saud b; 8, Friendly Ed

Trainers– 1, Bell Thomas R II; 2, Burke Donald J II; 3, Jory Ian P D; 4, Mulhall Kristin; 5, Lobo Paulo H; 6, Becerra Rafael; 7, Frankel Robert; 8, Machowsky Michael

$2 Daily Double (8–2) Paid $122.60 ; Daily Double Pool $35,817 .
$1 Pick Three (4–8–2) Paid $381.10 ; Pick Three Pool $71,600 .

EIGHTH RACE
Aqueduct
OCTOBER 27, 2004

1⅛ MILES. (1.47) 60TH RUNNING OF THE DISCOVERY HANDICAP. Grade III. Purse $100,000 (Up To $19,000 NYSBFOA) A HANDICAP FOR THREE YEAR OLDS. By subscription of $100 each, which should accompany the nomination; $500 to pass the entry box; $500 to start, with $100,000 added. The added money and all fees to be divided 60% to the winner, 20%to second, 10% to third, 5% to fourth, 3% to fifth and 2% divided equally among remaining finishers. Weights Thursday, October 21. The owner of the winner to receive the Walter J. Salmon Challenge Trophy presented by the family of late Walter J. Salmon tobe retained for one year. A trophy will be presented to the winning owner for permanent possession. Closed Saturday, October 16, 2004 with 21 Nominations.

Value of Race: $110,100 Winner $66,060; second $22,020; third $11,010; fourth $5,505; fifth $3,303; sixth $734; seventh $734; eighth $734. Mutuel Pool $312,254.00 Exacta Pool $256,905.00 Trifecta Pool $189,328.00

Last Raced	Horse	M/Eqt.	A.	Wt	PP	St	¼	½	¾	Str	Fin	Jockey	Odds $1
10Oct04 ^{7}Med^{3}	Zakocity	L b	3	116	7	5	$1^{\frac{1}{2}}$	$1^{\frac{1}{2}}$	1^{1}	$1^{4\frac{1}{2}}$	$1^{3\frac{1}{2}}$	Castellano J J	6.50
11Oct04 ^{8}Bel^{1}	Stolen Time	L	3	116	5	4	$2^{\frac{1}{2}}$	$2^{\frac{1}{2}}$	$2^{\frac{1}{2}}$	$2^{\frac{1}{2}}$	$2^{\frac{3}{4}}$	Santos J A	4.60
11Oct04 ^{8}Bel^{3}	Mahzouz	L f	3	115	4	1	4^{hd}	7^{2}	4^{hd}	$4^{1\frac{1}{2}}$	$3^{\frac{1}{2}}$	Fragoso P	21.90
10Oct04 ^{7}Med^{4}	Navesink River	L	3	115	8	8	$5^{1\frac{1}{2}}$	$3^{\frac{1}{2}}$	$5^{\frac{1}{2}}$	$5^{1\frac{1}{2}}$	4no	Velazquez J R	3.45
2Oct04 ^{4}Bel^{1}	Go Now	L b	3	114	3	3	6^{2}	5^{hd}	3^{hd}	3^{hd}	5^{1}	Chavez J F	9.70
6Sep04 ^{10}Pha^{10}	My Snookie's Boy	L	3	119	2	2	$3^{\frac{1}{2}}$	4^{hd}	$6^{2\frac{1}{2}}$	6^{7}	$6^{6\frac{1}{4}}$	Bravo J	2.05
26Sep04 ^{9}Bel^{6}	Reggie for Three	L b	3	114	6	6	$7^{\frac{1}{2}}$	6^{hd}	7^{3}	$7^{1\frac{1}{2}}$	$7^{4\frac{3}{4}}$	Arroyo N Jr	29.75
9Oct04 ^{4}Bel^{5}	Coded Warning	L	3	114	1	7	8	8	8	8	8	Velasquez C	6.50

OFF AT 3:46 Start Good . Won driving. Track fast.

TIME :24^{2}, :48^{4}, 1:13^{1}, 1:37^{1}, 1:49^{3} (:24.42, :48.99, 1:13.27, 1:37.22, 1:49.78)

$2 Mutuel Prices:				
	7 – ZAKOCITY	15.00	6.20	4.50
	5 – STOLEN TIME		5.30	4.80
	4 – MAHZOUZ			5.30

$2 EXACTA 7–5 PAID $79.50 $2 TRIFECTA 7–5–4 PAID $704.00

B. c, (May), by Precocity – Zakcat , by Vilzak . Trainer Reynolds Patrick L. Bred by John Franks (Fla).

ZAKOCITY quickly showed in front, set the pace along the inside, drew clear when roused in upper stretch and remained clear under a steady drive. STOLEN TIME prompted the pace from the outside and stayed on gamely to hold the place prize. MAHZOUZ raced close up early along the inside and finished well on the rail. NAVESINK RIVER raced in hand outside early, was three wide on both turns and lacked a rally. GO NOW was outrun early, put in a four wide run on the second turn and faded in the stretch. MY SNOOKIE'S BOY was rated along while between rivals, came wide into the stretch and had no rally. REGGIE FOR THREE raced wide and tired in the stretch. CODED WARNING was outrun early, raced inside and tired.

Owners– 1, Pompa Paul P Jr; 2, Smith Robert K; 3, Buckram Oak Farm; 4, Char-Mari Stable; 5, LaPenta Robert V; 6, Preferred Pals Stable; 7, Martin Edmund W Jr; 8, Juddmonte Farms Inc

Trainers– 1, Reynolds Patrick L; 2, Mott William I; 3, LaFavers Laurie; 4, Pletcher Todd A; 5, Zito Nicholas P; 6, Iwinski Allen; 7, Bond Harold James; 8, Frankel Robert

SEVENTH RACE
Lone Star
OCTOBER 29, 2004

1$\frac{1}{16}$ MILES. (1.40^{2}) 8TH RUNNING OF THE LONE STAR DERBY. Grade III. Purse $250,000 (PLUS UP TO $11,250 Open ATB) FOR THREE YEAR OLDS. No nomination fee. $2,000 to pass the entry box and an additional $2,000 to start with $250,000 guaranteed of which $150,000 to the owner of the winner, $50,000 to second, $27,500 to third, $15,000 to fourth and $7,500 to fifth. Weight: Colts and Geldings, 122 lbs. Fillies, 119 lbs. Starters to be named through the entry box by the usual time of closing. In allowance stakes starting preference will be given to horses that have accumulated the highest earnings at time of entry. The field will be limited to fourteen starters. Horses not drawing a starting position in the gate will receive a refund of the entry fee. A suitable award will be presented to the winning owner, trainer, and jockey. Nominations closed Wednesday, October 20, 2004 with 34 nominations.

Value of Race: $250,000 Winner $150,000; second $50,000; third $27,500; fourth $15,000; fifth $7,500. Mutuel Pool $537,953.00 Exacta Pool $333,455.00 Quinella Pool $18,691.00 Trifecta Pool $283,432.00 Superfecta Pool $99,989.00

Last Raced	Horse	M/Eqt.	A.	Wt	PP	St	¼	½	¾	Str	Fin	Jockey	Odds $1
2Oct04 ^{9}Hoo^{6}	Pollard's Vision	L	3	122	3	4	6^{½}	8^{2}	6^{hd}	3^{2}	1^{½}	Velazquez J R	3.20
25Sep04 ^{10}LaD^{6}	Cryptograph	L b	3	122	2	11	10^{1½}	10^{1}	9^{1½}	4^{1½}	2^{½}	Pettinger D R	9.90
26Sep04 ^{8}Hst^{1}	Flamethrowintexan	L f	3	122	4	2	1^{1½}	1^{½}	1^{1}	1^{hd}	3^{3¼}	Frazier R L	15.20
25Sep04 ^{11}Fpx^{4}	Skipaslew	L b	3	122	1	7	3^{2}	4^{1½}	4^{½}	6^{2}	4^{hd}	Dettori L	31.80
25Sep04 ^{10}LaD^{3}	Britt's Jules	L	3	122	6	1	4^{1}	5^{½}	2^{hd}	2^{½}	5^{1¼}	Flores D R	9.20
5Sep04 ^{2}AP^{1}	With Distinction	L b	3	122	10	3	2^{hd}	2^{hd}	3^{1}	5^{hd}	6^{1¾}	Bejarano R	9.00
1Oct04 ^{7}Med^{1}	Pies Prospect	L	3	122	9	5	5^{hd}	7^{hd}	8^{hd}	8^{2½}	7^{¾}	Prado E S	3.90
6Sep04 ^{9}EmD^{1}	My Creed	L b	3	122	11	8	8^{½}	6^{½}	5^{hd}	7^{hd}	8^{6¼}	Perez M A	33.10
2Oct04 ^{9}Hoo^{1}	Brass Hat	L b	3	122	5	10	11^{hd}	11^{hd}	10^{1}	9^{2}	9^{2}	Martinez W	2.00
9Oct04 ^{3}LS^{1}	Willionaire	L	3	122	7	9	12	12	12	10^{3½}	10^{4¾}	Lambert C T	179.80
2Oct04 ^{9}LS^{1}	Charming Socialite	L b	3	122	12	12	7^{hd}	3^{hd}	7^{hd}	11^{2}	11^{6½}	Taylor L	106.10
18Sep04 ^{4}WO^{2}	Cut and Shoot	L	3	122	8	6	9^{hd}	9^{hd}	11^{½}	12	12	Santos J A	38.80

OFF AT 4:54 Start Good . Won driving. Track fast.

TIME :22^{4}, :46^{2}, 1:10^{2}, 1:35^{3}, 1:42 (:22.97, :46.40, 1:10.50, 1:35.66, 1:42.10)

$2 Mutuel Prices:				
	4 – POLLARD'S VISION..................	8.40	4.80	4.20
	2 – CRYPTOGRAPH......................		8.80	7.00
	5 – FLAMETHROWINTEXAN............			9.40

$2 EXACTA 4–2 PAID $67.20 $2 QUINELLA 2–4 PAID $39.20

$2 TRIFECTA 4–2–5 PAID $1,029.40 $2 SUPERFECTA 4–2–5–1 PAID $14,998.20

Dk. b or br. c, (Jan), by Carson City – Etats Unis , by Dixieland Band . Trainer Pletcher Todd A. Bred by Charles A Smith (Ky).

POLLARD'S VISION settled while off the rail, was roused while between rivals on the far turn, rallied three wide passing the quarter-pole and closed strongly to get up late. CRYPTOGRAPH was kicked by an unruly rival in the gate, saved ground near the back of the field, came off the rail leaving the backstretch, raced four wide on the far turn, rallied five wide into the stretch and closed fast but was too late. FLAMETHROWINTEXAN set the pace while off the rail, dropped to the rail with three furlongs to run, responded gamely when challenged in upper stretch, battled determinedly into the final sixteenth and gave way very grudgingly. SKIPASLEW raced up close on the inside, was asked to go inside the leader near the half-mile marker, dropped back a bit while saving ground on the far turn and lacked the needed response. BRITT'S JULES raced three wide on the first turn, was well placed just off the pace, ranged up while three wide on the far turn, engaged FLAMETHROWINTEXAN in upper stretch, vied into the final furlong and gave way. WITH DISTINCTION tracked the pace while off the rail, was urged along on the backstretch, vied through the far turn and tired. PIES PROSPECT was caught four wide on the first turn, settled near the middle of the field, raced three wide on the second turn and failed to rally. MY CREED was caught five wide on the first turn, settled on the outside, roused while five wide on the far turn, dropped to four wide near the quarter-pole and had nothing left. BRASS HAT was in tight entering the first turn, raced unhurried near the back of the field, lacked room leaving the backstretch, saved ground on the far turn and failed to threaten. WILLIONAIRE raced three wide on the first turn, lagged near the back of the field, was roused on the far turn and failed to respond. CHARMING SOCIALITE was off a tad slow, advanced while six wide on the first turn, raced up close on the outside, came up empty while four wide on the far turn and stopped. CUT AND SHOOT raced three wide on the first turn, settled towards the rear of the field, went five wide on the second turn and showed little.

Owners– 1, Edgewood Farm; 2, Pin Oak Stable LLC; 3, Grasshopper Stable; 4, The Merv Griffin Ranch Co; 5, Southern Equine Stable LLC; 6, Lewis Robert B and Beverly J; 7, LaPenta Robert V; 8, Seven Star Racing Stable and Hess Sr R B; 9, Bradley Fred F; 10, Clifton William L Jr; 11, Sutton Paul A and Pettit William; 12, Stonerside Stable LLC

Trainers– 1, Pletcher Todd A; 2, Von Hemel Donnie K; 3, Penney Jim; 4, O'Neill Doug; 5, Guillot Eric; 6, Lukas D Wayne; 7, Zito Nicholas P; 8, Hess R B; 9, Bradley William; 10, Leach William F; 11, Pettit William A; 12, Casse Mark

Scratched– Tricky Taboo (13Aug04 ^{9}ElP^{7})

$2 Pick Three (5–4/6/10/12–4) Paid $482.40 ; Pick Three Pool $22,842 .

$2 Pick Four (3–5–4/6/10/12–4) Paid $2,392.00 ; Pick Four Pool $27,111 .

FOURTH RACE
Aqueduct
OCTOBER 30, 2004

7 FURLONGS. (1.20) 27TH RUNNING OF THE FIRST FLIGHT HANDICAP. Grade II. Purse $150,000 (Up To $28,500 NYSBFOA) A HANDICAP FOR FILLIES AND MARES THREE YEARS OLD AND UPWARD. By subscription of $150 each, which should accompany the nomination; $750 to pass the entry box; $750 to start. The purse to be divided 60% to the winner, 20% to second,10% to third, 5% to fourth, 3% to fifth and 2% divided equally among remaining finishers . A trophy will be presented to the winning owner. Closed Saturday, October 16, 2004 with 14 nominations.

Value of Race: $150,000 Winner $90,000; second $30,000; third $15,000; fourth $7,500; fifth $4,500; sixth $3,000. Mutuel Pool $352,531.00 Exacta Pool $340,810.00 Quinella Pool $22,730.00 Trifecta Pool $206,351.00

Last Raced	Horse	M/Eqt.	A.	Wt	PP	St	¼	½	Str	Fin	Jockey	Odds $1
20ct04 9Pim1	Bending Strings	L	3	116	5	3	51½	42½	1½	15¾	Bridgmohan S X	2.00
20ct04 9Pim2	Smokey Glacken	L	3	115	1	6	35½	2hd	25	22¾	Bravo J	2.35
19Jun04 9Bel3	Passing Shot	L	5	118	4	4	6	6	5hd	34	Gryder A T	3.30
18Sep04 7Bel5	Sensibly Chic	L bf	4	113	2	2	1hd	1hd	31½	41	Espinoza J L	23.60
150ct04 6Med1	Schedule-GB	L bf	3	114	6	1	2hd	32½	4hd	52¾	Elliott S	5.30
80ct04 8Bel4	Hidden Ransom	L b	4	112	3	5	4hd	53½	6	6	Fragoso P	8.30

OFF AT 12:25 Start Good . Won driving. Track fast.

TIME :22^{2}, :44^{3}, 1:09^{1}, 1:22 (:22.43, :44.65, 1:09.33, 1:22.13)

$2 Mutuel Prices:			
5 – BENDING STRINGS	6.00	3.10	2.30
1 – SMOKEY GLACKEN		3.50	2.50
4 – PASSING SHOT			2.60

$2 EXACTA 5–1 PAID $18.00 $2 QUINELLA 1–5 PAID $9.90
$2 TRIFECTA 5–1–4 PAID $49.80

Dk. b or br. f, (May), by American Chance – Straight South , by Hail the Pirates . Trainer McLaughlin Kiaran P. Bred by John D Gunther (Ky).

BENDING STRINGS was outrun early, rallied four wide approaching the stretch, responded when roused and drew away late. SMOKEY GLACKEN ducked in at the start, contested the pace along the inside and continued on to get the place award. PASSING SHOT was outrun early, raced inside and offered a mild rally along the inside. SENSIBLY CHIC contested the pace while between rivals and tired in the stretch. SCHEDULE (GB) contested the pace while three wide and tired in the stretch. HIDDEN RANSOM was outrun early, raced inside and had no response when roused.

Owners– 1, Gunther John D; 2, Moore Susan and John; 3, Shields Joseph V Jr; 4, Nervitt Lois S; 5, Jayeff B Stables; 6, Evans Edward P

Trainers– 1, McLaughlin Kiaran P; 2, Jerkens James A; 3, Jerkens H Allen; 4, Tullock Timothy Jr; 5, Goldberg Alan E; 6, Hennig Mark

$2 Pick Three (5–3–5) Paid $77.00 ; Pick Three Pool $57,177 .

FIFTH RACE
Aqueduct
OCTOBER 30, 2004

1⅛ MILES. (Turf) (1.47) 45TH RUNNING OF THE KNICKERBOCKER HANDICAP. Grade II. Purse $150,000 (Up To $28,500 NYSBFOA) A HANDICAP FOR THREE YEAR OLDS AND UPWARD. By subscription of $150 each, which should accompany the nomination; $750 to pass the entry box; $750 to start. The purse to be divided 60% to the winner, 20% to second, 10% to third, 5% to fourth, 3% to fifth and 2% divided equally among remaining finishers. A trophy will be presented to the winning owner. The New York Racing Association reserves the right to transfer this race to the Main Track. In the event that this race is taken offthe turf, it may be subject to downgrading upon review by the Graded Stakes Committee. Closed Saturday, October 16, 2004 with 41 Nominations. (If the Stewards consider it inadvisable to run this race on the turf course, this race will be run at One Mile and One Furlong on the main track.). (Rail at 18 feet).

Value of Race: $150,000 Winner $90,000; second $30,000; third $15,000; fourth $7,500; fifth $4,500; sixth $750; seventh $750; eighth $750; ninth $750. Mutuel Pool $480,537.00 Exacta Pool $431,961.00 Trifecta Pool $271,410.00 Superfecta Pool $65,580.00

Last Raced	Horse	M/Eqt.	A.	Wt	PP	St	¼	½	¾	Str	Fin	Jockey	Odds $1
150ct04 8Med3	Host-Chi	L	4	115	6	3	7hd	7hd	81½	6½	11½	Decarlo C P	4.00
20ct04 10Bel4	Evening Attire	L b	6	114	3	4	31	2hd	21½	1hd	2hd	Espinoza J L	3.40
30ct04 7Bel2	Sailaway	L f	4	113	9	7	81½	82½	72	4hd	3½	Bridgmohan S X	16.40
60ct04 8Bel1	L'Oiseau d'Argent	L	5	115	5	2	12	13½	11½	22½	42	Gryder A T	4.20
25Sep04 4Bel3	Mr. Light-Arg	L	5	113	8	8	4hd	62½	4½	5hd	5no	Bravo J	16.30
150ct04 8Med1	Dr. Kashnikow	L	7	116	4	1	9	9	9	9	6no	Samyn J L	10.40
22Jly04 10VHY6	Caesarion-Ire	L	5	114	1	5	2hd	32	3½	3½	7hd	Chavez J F	17.90
150ct04 8Med4	Hotstufanthensome	L	4	114	2	6	5hd	5hd	5hd	71	81¼	Pimentel J	8.10
20ct04 7BM3	Balestrini-Ire	L	4	116	7	9	61½	4hd	61	8hd	9	Almeida G F	4.40

OFF AT 12:56 Start Good . Won driving. Course firm.

TIME :24^{3}, :49^{2}, 1:13^{4}, 1:38, 1:49^{4} (:24.75, :49.45, 1:13.84, 1:38.11, 1:49.95)

$2 Mutuel Prices:			
6 – HOST–CHI	10.00	4.60	3.80
3 – EVENING ATTIRE		4.80	3.80
9 – SAILAWAY			5.70

$2 EXACTA 6–3 PAID $63.50 $2 TRIFECTA 6–3–9 PAID $537.00
$2 SUPERFECTA 6–3–9–5 PAID $3,643.00

Ch. c, (Aug), by Hussonet – Colonna Traiana–Chi , by Roy . Trainer Pletcher Todd A. Bred by Haras De Pirque (Chi).

HOST (CHI) was outrun early, came wide for the drive, responded when set down, finished fast outside and was clear under the wire. EVENING ATTIRE raced close up early, rallied outside on the second turn, earned a short lead in the stretch and stayed on to hold the place. SAILAWAY was outrun early, rallied three wide on the second turn and finished well outside. L'OISEAU D'ARGENT quickly opened a clear lead, set the pace along the inside and weakened in the final furlong. MR. LIGHT (ARG) raced in hand early, put in a three wide run on the second turn and had nothing left for the stretch drive. DR. KASHNIKOW was outrun early, came wide into the stretch and had no rally. CAESARION (IRE) chased the pace along the inside and had no response when roused. HOTSTUFANTHENSOME raced inside and had no rally. BALESTRINI (IRE) raced three wide and tired in the stretch.

Owners– 1, Melnyk Eugene and Laura; 2, Grant Mary and Joseph and Kelly Thomas J; 3, Phipps Ogden M; 4, Al Maktoum Sheikh Maktoum b; 5, Mack Earle I; 6, Erdenheim Farm; 7, Tanaka Gary A; 8, Steinger Lesley; 9, Holt Carl

Trainers– 1, Pletcher Todd A; 2, Kelly Patrick J; 3, McGaughey III Claude R; 4, McLaughlin Kiaran P; 5, Penna Angel Jr; 6, Fisher John R S; 7, De Roualle Jean; 8, Pointer Norman R; 9, Drysdale Neil

Scratched– Denon (09Oct04 5Kee5)

$2 Daily Double (5–6) Paid $31.80 ; Daily Double Pool $121,451 .
$2 Pick Three (3–5–6) Paid $42.80 ; Pick Three Pool $111,614 .
$2 Pick Four (5–3–5–6) Paid $458.00 ; Pick Four Pool $118,225 .

Aqueduct Attendance: 6,112 Mutuel Pool: $398,985.00 ITW Mutuel Pool: $1,471,560.00 ISW Mutuel Pool: $3,096,042.00

FIFTH RACE
Keeneland
OCTOBER 30, 2004

1⅛ MILES. (1.46³) 46TH RUNNING OF THE FAYETTE. Grade III. Purse $150,000 FOR THREE YEAR OLDS AND UPWARD. By subscription of $150 each, which should accompany the nomination; $750 to enter and an additional $750 to start, with $150,000 added, of which 62% of all monies to the owner of the winner, 20% to second, 10% to third, 5% to fourth and 3% to fifth. Weight: Three year olds, 122 lbs.; Older, 125 lbs. Non-winners of a Grade I stakes over a mile in 2004 allowed 2 lbs.; a Grade II stakes over a mile in 2004 allowed 4 lbs.; a Grade III stakes at a mile or over in 2004 or $60,000 twice at a mile or over in 2003–2004, 6 lbs. Starters to be named through the entry box by the usual time of closing. A gold julep cup will be presented to the owner of the winner. Closed Wednesday, October 20, 2004 with 20 nominations.

Value of Race: $161,250 Winner $99,975; second $32,250; third $16,125; fourth $8,063; fifth $4,837. Mutuel Pool $435,923.00 Exacta Pool $322,815.00 Quinella Pool $12,831.00 Trifecta Pool $189,971.00

Last Raced	Horse	M/Eqt.	A.	Wt	PP	St	¼	½	¾	Str	Fin	Jockey	Odds $1
11Sep04 ¹⁰Bel⁶	Midway Road	L	4	121	1	1	$1^{1\frac{1}{2}}$	$1^{\frac{1}{2}}$	$1^{\frac{1}{2}}$	1^{hd}	1no	Borel C H	1.50
2Oct04 ⁸SA²	Total Impact-Chi	L b	6	125	3	2	$2^{2\frac{1}{2}}$	$2^{3\frac{1}{2}}$	$2^{3\frac{1}{2}}$	$2^{3\frac{1}{2}}$	2^{6}	Perret C	1.30
2Oct04 ⁹TP⁶	Alumni Hall	L b	5	119	5	5	5	3^{hd}	$3^{2\frac{1}{2}}$	$3^{2\frac{1}{2}}$	$3^{6\frac{3}{4}}$	Melancon L	7.20
2Oct04 ⁷Haw³	Sonic West	L bf	5	121	2	4	$3^{\frac{1}{2}}$	5	5	$4^{2\frac{1}{2}}$	$4^{8\frac{3}{4}}$	Martinez W	12.80
23Sep04 ⁸Bel⁴	Quest	L	5	119	4	3	$4^{1\frac{1}{2}}$	$4^{\frac{1}{2}}$	4^{1}	5	5	Hernandez B J Jr	4.60

OFF AT 2:11 Start Good. Won driving. Track fast.

TIME :23³, :47¹, 1:11², 1:36⁴, 1:50¹ (:23.70, :47.35, 1:11.53, 1:36.99, 1:50.39)

$2 Mutuel Prices:			
1 – MIDWAY ROAD	5.00	2.80	2.20
3 – TOTAL IMPACT-CHI		2.40	2.20
6 – ALUMNI HALL			2.40

$2 EXACTA 1–3 PAID $10.40 $2 QUINELLA 1–3 PAID $5.00
$2 TRIFECTA 1–3–6 PAID $36.00

B. c, (Apr), by Jade Hunter – Fleet Road, by Magesterial. Trainer Howard Neil J. Bred by W S Farish (Ky).

MIDWAY ROAD gained the lead inside early, edged clear for nearly a half while rated along under careful handling, was engaged by TOTAL IMPACT (CHI) from the outside nearing the five-sixteenths pole, was repeatedly bumped by that one from the three-sixteenths pole to the wire and proved gamely best under strong handling. TOTAL IMPACT (CHI) tracked front-running MIDWAY ROAD from early on while four wide, moved earnestly to challenge approaching the stretch, leaned in through the drive bumping the winner repeatedly thereafter and missed. ALUMNI HALL, unhurried early and four wide, inched to within striking distance on the far turn, moved five wide into the stretch, loomed a threat for the last eighth and came up empty. SONIC WEST settled near the inside early, swung out five or six wide entering the stretch and failed to menace. QUEST hopped at the start, raced in contention four wide until midway on the far turn and tired.

Owners– 1, Farish William S; 2, Mohammed Saud Al Kabeer and Bridport S A Lillian Solari; 3, Farish William S Elkins Jr James A and Webber Jr W Temple; 4, Stone Spire LLC; 5, Hancock III Arthur B and Healy Gerald F

Trainers– 1, Howard Neil J; 2, De Seroux Laura; 3, Howard Neil J; 4, Van Berg Thomas L; 5, Zito Nicholas P

Scratched– Grey Beard (09Oct04 ⁵Kee⁹)

$2 Pick Three (4–5–1) Paid $864.00 ; Pick Three Pool $54,284 .
$2 Daily Double (5–1) Paid $56.00 ; Daily Double Pool $38,519 .

Keeneland Attendance: Unavailable Mutuel Pool: $506,449.00 ITW Mutuel Pool: $241,707.00 ISW Mutuel Pool: $3,187,946.00

SECOND RACE
Lone Star
OCTOBER 30, 2004

1⅛ MILES. (1.48¹) 21ST RUNNING OF THE BREEDERS' CUP DISTAFF PRESENTED BY NEXTEL Grade I. Purse $2,000,000 FOR FILLIES AND MARES, THREE-YEAR-OLDS AND UPWARD. Northern Hemisphere three-year-olds, 119 lbs.; Older, 123 lbs.; Southern Hemisphere three-year-olds, 114 lbs.; Older, 123 lbs. $20,000 to pre-enter, $40,000 to enter, with guaranteed $2 million purse including nominator awards (plus Net Supplementary Fees, if any), of which 52% of all monies to the owner of the winner, 20% to second, 11% to third, 5.7% to fourth and 3% to fifth; plus stallion nominator awards of 2.6% of all monies to the winner, 1% to second and 0.55% to third and foal nominator awards of 2.6% of all monies to the winner, 1% to second and 0.55% to third. Closed with 12 pre-entries.

Value of Race: $1,834,000 Winner $1,040,000; second $400,000; third $220,000; fourth $114,000; fifth $60,000. Mutuel Pool $3,097,057.00 Exacta Pool $2,292,119.00 Trifecta Pool $1,842,795.00 Superfecta Pool $527,612.00 Head2Head Pool $52,041.00

Last Raced	Horse	M/Eqt.	A.	Wt	PP	St	¼	½	¾	Str	Fin	Jockey	Odds $1
2Oct04 9Pha1	Ashado	L	3	119	1	1	3½	5½	4hd	1½	11¼	Velazquez J R	2.00
9Oct04 9Bel3	Storm Flag Flying	L	4	123	7	10	101½	11	8½	52½	2nk	Bailey J D	4.60
1Oct04 9Hoo3	Stellar Jayne	L b	3	119	11	11	11	10½	6hd	4½	31½	Albarado R J	10.30
10Oct04 8Kee2	Tamweel	L	4	123	3	2	11	1½	1½	21	41¾	Douglas R R	9.00
3Oct04 6SA1	Island Fashion	L b	4	123	10	9	81	4½	2hd	3hd	53¾	John K	6.60
28Sep04 9Mnr1	Indy Groove	L	4	123	8	5	41	31	31	62	61	Guidry M	48.80
3Oct04 6SA3	Elloluv	L b	4	123	2	3	5½	71	71	72	7nk	Nakatani C S	21.20
2Oct04 NEW3	Nebraska Tornado		4	123	5	6	2hd	2hd	51	8½	8nk	Prado E S	7.30
9Oct04 9Bel2	Society Selection	L	3	119	4	8	6hd	6hd	91½	92½	9½	Velasquez C	5.10
3Jly04 6Hol3	Hollywood Story	L b	3	119	6	4	7hd	9hd	11	11	101¾	Baze T C	32.40
4Sep04 9AP5	Bare Necessities	L	5	123	9	7	9hd	8½	102	102	11	Valdivia J Jr	57.10

OFF AT 12:21 Start Good. Won driving. Track good.

TIME :22^{1}, :46^{3}, 1:10^{2}, 1:35^{2}, 1:48^{1} (:22.03, :46.70, 1:10.50, 1:35.48, 1:48.26)

(New Track Record)

$2 Mutuel Prices:				
	1 – ASHADO	6.00	3.60	2.80
	7 – STORM FLAG FLYING		7.00	4.00
	11 – STELLAR JAYNE			4.80

$2 EXACTA 1-7 PAID $34.80 $2 TRIFECTA 1-7-11 PAID $178.00
$2 SUPERFECTA 1-7-11-3 PAID $1,191.80
$2 HEAD2HEAD 1VS7-WINNER1 PAID $3.20

Dk. b or br. f, (Feb), by Saint Ballado – Goulash, by Mari's Book. Trainer Pletcher Todd A. Bred by Aaron U Jones & Marie D Jones (Ky).

ASHADO settled in good position along the inside, was well placed just behind the leaders along the backstretch, waited patiently while saving ground through the turn, checked briefly while awaiting room nearing the quarter pole, split rivals to get clear entering the stretch, surged to the front nearing the furlong marker then edged clear under strong right hand encouragement. STORM FLAG FLYING checked slightly when SOCIETY SELECTION angled in on the first turn, was unhurried while saving ground along the backstretch, worked her way forward along the rail midway on the turn, launched a bid along the inside entering the stretch, angled between horses while gaining in midstretch then finished well between horses while drifting out a bit to edge STELLAR JAYNE for the place. STELLAR JAYNE raced far back for a half after breaking a bit slowly, launched a rally while five wide leaving the three-eighths pole, closed the gap while continuing wide at the top of the stretch, made a run to reach contention in midstretch then flattened out a bit in the late stages. TAMWEEL, bobbled at the start, rushed up along the rail to gain a clear early advantage, set the pace along the inside rail while being pressured along the backstretch, dug in when challenged on the turn, battled heads apart inside the winner into midstretch then weakened from her early efforts. ISLAND FASHION was strung out four wide on the first turn, continued wide while closing the gap along the backstretch, circled four wide to reach contention on the turn, made a run from outside to threaten at the quarter pole, remained a factor into midstretch then weakened in the final eighth. INDY GROOVE raced in traffic on the first turn, moved up between horses before going a half, pressed the pace between horses to the turn, steadied in traffic nearing the quarter pole then gradually tired thereafter. ELLOLUV eased back along the inside in the early stages, moved out along the backstretch, lodged a mild rally while five wide on the turn then lacked a further response. NEBRASKA TORNADO pressed the pace between horses along the backstretch, raced up close to the turn and tired. SOCIETY SELECTION checked slightly and angled to the rail nearing the first turn, angled between horses along the backstretch, raced in the middle of the pack for seven furlongs and steadily tired thereafter. HOLLYWOOD STORY was in tight on the first turn, moved up a bit before going a half then faded on the far turn. BARE NECESSITIES raced in traffic on the first turn, steadied between horses nearing the far turn and was never close thereafter.

Owners– 1, Starlight Stables LLC Saylor Paul and Martin Johns; 2, Phipps Ogden M; 3, Spendthrift Farm LLC Kidder Chuck Cole Nancy and Strong Nick; 4, Turf Express Inc and Yates Darrell and Evelyn; 5, Everest Stables Inc; 6, Glen Hill Farm; 7, Reddam J Paul; 8, Juddmonte Farms Inc; 9, Cowan Marjorie and Irving M; 10, Krikorian George; 11, Iron County Farms Inc

Trainers– 1, Pletcher Todd A; 2, McGaughey III Claude R; 3, Lukas D Wayne; 4, Catalano Wayne M; 5, Polanco Marcelo; 6, Proctor Thomas F; 7, Dollase Craig; 8, Fabre Andre; 9, Jerkens H Allen; 10, Shirreffs John; 11, Kirby Frank J

$2 Daily Double (4-1) Paid $297.60 ; Daily Double Pool $392,550 .

THIRD RACE

Lone Star

OCTOBER 30, 2004

1 1/16 MILES. (1.40²) 21ST RUNNING OF THE BREEDERS' CUP JUVENILE FILLIES Grade I. Purse $1,000,000 FOR FILLIES, TWO YEARS OLD. Weight, 119 lbs. $10,000 to pre–enter, $20,000 to enter, with guaranteed $1 million purse including nominator awards (plus Net Supplementary Fees, if any), of which 52% of all monies to the owner of the winner, 20% to second,11% to third, 5.7% to fourth and 3% to fifth; plus stallion nominator awards of 2.6% of all monies to the winner, 1% to second and 0.55% to third and foal nominator awards of 2.6% of all monies to the winner, 1% to second and 0.55% to third. Closed with 16 pre–entries.

Value of Race: $917,000 Winner $520,000; second $200,000; third $110,000; fourth $57,000; fifth $30,000. Mutuel Pool $3,452,881.00 Exacta Pool $2,684,520.00 Trifecta Pool $2,159,267.00 Superfecta Pool $684,872.00 Head2Head Pool $58,939.00

Last Raced	Horse	M/Eqt.	A.	Wt	PP	St	¼	½	¾	Str	Fin	Jockey	Odds $1
2Oct04 9SA1	Sweet Catomine	L b	2	119	9	7	7 1½	7½	7½	2½	1 3¾	Nakatani C S	2.30
9Oct04 6Bel1	Balletto-UAE	L	2	119	1	5	3 1½	3 1	2½	3½	2 1¼	Bailey J D	4.10
8Oct04 9Kee1	Runway Model	L	2	119	3	1	5 hd	6 1	6½	4 2½	3¾	Bejarano R	10.00
9Oct04 6Bel3	Sis City	L	2	119	6	3	2 2	2 1½	1½	1 hd	4 nk	Velazquez J R	20.20
8Oct04 9Kee4	Dance Away Capote	L	2	119	5	9	9½	9½	9½	5½	5 1¼	Dominguez R A	15.70
8Oct04 9Kee2	Sharp Lisa	L f	2	119	11	6	6½	5½	5 hd	6 1	6 2¼	Dettori L	12.10
19Sep04 9AP1	Culinary	L	2	119	4	2	4 1	4 hd	3 hd	7 1½	7 hd	Marquez C H Jr	7.30
9Oct04 6Bel4	Play With Fire	L	2	119	12	8	10 1	12	12	9½	8 3	Day P	28.80
8Oct04 9Kee5	Sense of Style	L	2	119	8	11	8½	8 1	8 hd	8 1½	9 1	Prado E S	3.50
2Oct04 9SA4	Culture Clash	L b	2	119	10	10	11½	10½	10 2	10 2	10 5¼	John K	61.60
25Sep04 ASC4	Mona Lisa-GB	L	2	119	7	12	12	11 1	11 hd	12	11 2¼	Spencer J P	18.50
3Oct04 9WO1	Higher World	L	2	119	2	4	1½	1 hd	4 hd	11 2½	12	Husbands P	60.80

OFF AT 12:56 Start Good . Won driving. Track fast.

TIME :22⁴, :46², 1:10³, 1:35², 1:41³ (:22.99, :46.44, 1:10.69, 1:35.47, 1:41.65)

$2 Mutuel Prices:				
	10 – SWEET CATOMINE	6.60	4.00	3.00
	1 – BALLETTO–UAE		4.80	3.40
	4 – RUNWAY MODEL			5.00

$2 EXACTA 10–1 PAID $29.00 $2 TRIFECTA 10–1–4 PAID $174.20
$2 SUPERFECTA 10–1–4–7 PAID $1,561.20
$2 HEAD2HEAD 5VS12VS13–WINNER12 PAID $5.60

B. f, (Feb), by Storm Cat – Sweet Life , by Kris S.. Trainer Canani Julio C. Bred by Mr & Mrs Martin J Wygod (Ky).

SWEET CATOMINE raced in traffic between horses while four wide on the first turn, was unhurried along the backstretch, launched a rally between horses leaving the far turn, steadied sharply while lacking room midway on the turn, swung between horses for clear sailing at the top of the stretch, made a strong run to challenge while drifting in a bit nearing the furlong marker, took control approaching the sixteenth pole then drew away with authority through the final seventy yards. BALLETTO settled in good position in the early stages, raced just behind the leaders while saving ground along the backstretch, angled three wide on the far turn, ranged up from outside to challenge on the turn, battled between horses into upper stretch, was in a bit tight while dueling for the lead in midstretch then continued on well to best the others. RUNWAY MODEL settled in the middle of the pack for six furlongs, moved around rivals while rallying on the far turn, lacked room while saving ground at the top of the stretch, steadied in traffic between horses and the eighth pole and again a sixteenth out and failed to threaten thereafter. SIS CITY was carried wide on the first turn, pressed the pace from outside for five furlongs, surged to the front on the far turn, continued on the lead into upper stretch, battled heads apart into midstretch then weakened under pressure in the final eighth. DANCE AWAY CAPOTE, broke a bit slowly was bounced away between horses while in tight on the first turn, raced well back for six furlongs, closed the gap midway on the turn, steadied while blocked in traffic at the five-sixteenths pole, made a run to reach contention in upper stretch then lacked a strong closing response. SHARP LISA was strung out four wide on the first turn, continued wide while in the middle of the pack to the far turn, lodged a mild bid while being forced six wide at the quarter pole then flattened out. CULINARY settled just off the early pace, moved into contention while four wide leaving the backstretch, raced just off the pace while being carried five wide on the turn then faded in the stretch. PLAY WITH FIRE failed to mount a serious rally while four wide. SENSE OF STYLE broke in the air at the start while coming away awkwardly, was bumped along the inside on the first turn, raced well back for six furlongs, was behind a wall of horses on the turn then lacked the needed response when called upon. CULTURE CLASH broke outward and steadied at the start and was never close thereafter. MONA LISA broke in the air at the start and never reached contention. HIGHER WORLD drifted out while taking the lead on the first turn, dueled along the inside for five furlongs and gave way.

Owners– 1, Wygod Mr and Mrs Martin J; 2, Darley Stable; 3, Chowhan Naveed; 4, Goldfarb&Torre&Dubb&Davis; 5, Pandora Farms LLC; 6, Reddam J Paul Suarez Racing Inc and Schlesinger Mark; 7, Jack H Smith III Thoroughbreds; 8, Zwerling Gary L; 9, Smith Derrick and Tabor Michael; 10, Everest Stables Inc; 11, Tabor Michael and Magnier Mrs John; 12, Simeone Sal and Colleen

Trainers– 1, Canani Julio C; 2, Albertrani Thomas; 3, Flint Bernard S; 4, Dutrow Richard E Jr; 5, Motion H Graham; 6, O'Neill Doug; 7, Stidham Michael; 8, Hennig Mark; 9, Biancone Patrick L; 10, Polanco Marcelo; 11, O'Brien Aidan P; 12, Casse Mark

Scratched– In the Gold (08Oct04 9Kee3)

$2 Pick Three (4–1–3/10) Paid $1,629.40 ; Pick Three Pool $334,583 .
$2 Daily Double (1–10) Paid $19.60 ; Daily Double Pool $346,470 .

FOURTH RACE
Lone Star
OCTOBER 30, 2004

1 MILE. (Turf) (1.33^{2}) 21ST RUNNING OF THE NETJETS BREEDERS' CUP MILE Grade I. Purse $1,500,000 FOR THREE-YEAR-OLDS AND UPWARD. Northern Hemisphere Three-Year-Olds, 122 lbs.; Older, 126 lbs. Southern Hemisphere Three-Year-Olds, 119 lbs.; Older, 126 lbs. All Fillies and Mares allowed 3 lbs. $15,000 to pre-enter, $30,000 to enter, with guaranteed $1.5 million purse including nominator awards (plus Net Supplementary Fees, if any), of which 52% of all monies to the owner of the winner, 20% to second, 11% to third, 5.7% to fourth and 3% to fifth; plus stallion nominator awards of 2.6% of all monies to the winner, 1% to second and 0.55% to third and foal nominator awards of 2.6% of all monies to the winner, 1% to second and 0.55% to third. Closed with 19 pre-entries. Supplemental nominees: Blackdoun and Mr O'Brien.

Value of Race: $1,540,560 Winner $873,600; second $336,000; third $184,800; fourth $95,760; fifth $50,400. Mutuel Pool $4,143,442.00 Exacta Pool $3,250,944.00 Trifecta Pool $2,526,857.00 Superfecta Pool $787,513.00 Head2Head Pool $62,822.00

Last Raced	Horse	M/Eqt.	A.	Wt	PP	St	¼	½	¾	Str	Fin	Jockey	Odds $1
9Oct04 ^{9}SA^{3}	Singletary	L	4	126	10	7	5^{1}	5½	4^{hd}	1^{1}	1½	Flores D R	16.50
25Sep04 ASC^{9}	Antonius Pius	L	3	122	7	10	$12^{1\frac{1}{2}}$	12^{1}	10^{hd}	4^{1}	$2^{1\frac{1}{2}}$	Spencer J P	31.40
15Aug04 ^{4}DEA^{2}	Six Perfections-FR	L	4	123	11	11	8^{1}	8½	7^{1}	7^{hd}	3^{nk}	Bailey J D	5.90
19Sep04 ^{9}WO^{1}	Soaring Free	L	5	126	4	3	$1^{1\frac{1}{2}}$	1^{1}	1½	2^{1}	4¾	Kabel T K	10.90
9Oct04 ^{8}Kee^{3}	Silver Tree	L	4	126	2	2	7^{1}	7½	8½	5^{hd}	5^{nk}	Prado E S	21.90
9Oct04 ^{9}SA^{1}	Musical Chimes	L	4	123	9	9	10^{hd}	9½	11^{hd}	8^{hd}	6^{nk}	Desormeaux K J	22.90
6Sep04 ^{8}Dmr^{1}	Blackdoun-FR	L b	3	122	13	14	14	14	$13^{1\frac{1}{2}}$	11^{hd}	7^{nk}	Nakatani C S	10.60
25Sep04 ASC^{8}	Diamond Green-FR		3	122	8	13	13^{1}	13^{hd}	14	$10^{1\frac{1}{2}}$	8^{1}	Dettori L	19.70
9Oct04 ^{8}Bel^{1}	Mr O'Brien-Ire	L	5	126	14	8	6^{hd}	6^{1}	5½	6½	9no	Coa E M	20.70
5Sep04 LCH^{5}	Whipper	L	3	122	1	5	$4^{1\frac{1}{2}}$	4½	2^{hd}	3^{hd}	10no	Soumillon C	7.10
9Oct04 ^{8}Kee^{1}	Nothing to Lose	L b	4	126	12	12	11^{hd}	10½	9^{hd}	12^{1}	11½	Velazquez J R	4.30
26Sep04 ^{9}Bel^{1}	Artie Schiller	L	3	122	6	6	9½	11½	12½	$9^{1\frac{1}{2}}$	$12^{3\frac{3}{4}}$	Migliore R	3.80
25Jly04 ^{8}Dmr^{1}	Special Ring	L b	7	126	3	1	3^{hd}	2^{hd}	3^{hd}	13^{3}	$13^{3\frac{1}{2}}$	Espinoza V	8.60
2Oct04 ^{10}Bel^{7}	Domestic Dispute	L	4	126	5	4	2^{hd}	3^{1}	6^{hd}	14	14	John K	53.80

OFF AT 1:37 Start Good . Won driving. Course yielding.

TIME :24, :48^{3}, 1:12^{3}, 1:24^{3}, 1:36^{4} (:24.03, :48.65, 1:12.71, 1:24.77, 1:36.90)

$2 Mutuel Prices:

10 – SINGLETARY	35.00	15.60	9.80
7 – ANTONIUS PIUS		37.60	13.60
11 – SIX PERFECTIONS–FR			5.00

$2 EXACTA 10–7 PAID $1,495.60 $2 TRIFECTA 10–7–11 PAID $12,435.20
$2 SUPERFECTA 10–7–11–4 PAID $107,388.00
$2 HEAD2HEAD 11VS12–WINNER11 PAID $3.80

B. c, (May), by Sultry Song – Joiski's Star , by Star de Naskra . Trainer Chatlos Donald Jr. Bred by Disler Farms Ltd (Ky).

SINGLETARY was rated in good position between horses for five furlongs, waited patiently for room while gaining on the turn, split horses while angling out at the top of the stretch, took charge at the three-sixteenths pole, opened a clear advantage in midstretch then held off ANTONIUS PIUS under steady right hand urging. ANTONIUS PIUS steadied in tight on the first turn, raced well back for seven furlongs, steadied sharply while in traffic on the turn, moved between horses to get clear in upper stretch, lugged in while gaining in midstretch, closed strongly from outside nearing the sixteenth pole then checked behind the winner while lugging in again in the late stages. SIX PERFECTIONS (FR) was unhurried for a half, launched a bid between horses on the far turn, steadied in traffic midway on the turn, swung wide entering the stretch then rallied belatedly to gain a share. SOARING FREE sprinted clear in the early stages, raced uncontested on the lead for a half, continued on the front while saving ground to the turn, relinquished the lead to the winner in upper stretch then weakened from his early efforts. SILVER TREE was reserved for a half while saving ground, rallied along the rail midway on the turn, was blocked along the inside nearing the quarter pole, lodged a mild bid to reach contention in upper stretch then flattened out. MUSICAL CHIMES raced well back for a half, steadied while trapped between horses on the turn and in upper stretch then lacked a strong closing bid. BLACKDOUN (FR) was outrun for five furlongs, steadied sharply in traffic on the turn, swung seven wide entering the stretch then failed to threaten thereafter. DIAMOND GREEN (FR) raced far back for a half after breaking slowly, steadied along the rail behind a wall of horses on the turn then failed to threaten while improving his position. MR O'BRIEN (IRE) raced in the middle of the pack while four wide along the backstretch, lodged a mild rally five wide on the turn then faded in the stretch. WHIPPER raced in close contention along the inside for a half, made a run to challenge on the turn, remained a factor into upper stretch then tired in the final eighth. NOTHING TO LOSE failed to mount a serious rally while wide throughout. ARTIE SCHILLER steadied along the inside on the first turn, tucked in along the rail on the backstretch, saved ground to the turn, awaited room nearing the quarter pole, rallied briefly along the rail in upper stretch then flattened out. SPECIAL RING bobbled at the start, raced up close between horses for five furlongs, made a mild bid on the turn, steadied sharply in upper stretch and steadily tired thereafter. DOMESTIC DISPUTE showed speed for five furlongs and tired.

Owners– 1, Little Red Feather Racing; 2, Tabor Michael and Magnier Mrs John; 3, Flaxman Holdings Ltd; 4, Sam-Son Farms; 5, Vegso Peter; 6, Al Maktoum Sheikh Maktoum b; 7, Naify Marsha and Woodside Farms LLC; 8, Lagardere Family; 9, Skeedattle II; 10, Strauss Richard C; 11, Ramsey Kenneth L and Sarah K; 12, Timber Bay Farm and Walsh Mrs Thomas J; 13, Prestonwood Racing LLC; 14, Bienstock&Mandabach&Winner

Trainers– 1, Chatlos Donald Jr; 2, O'Brien Aidan P; 3, Bary Pascal F; 4, Frostad Mark; 5, Mott William I; 6, Drysdale Neil; 7, Canani Julio C; 8, Fabre Andre; 9, Graham Robin L; 10, Collet Robert; 11, Frankel Robert; 12, Jerkens James A; 13, Canani Julio C; 14, Gallagher Patrick

$2 Pick Three (1–3/10–10) Paid $474.00 ; Pick Three Pool $795,946 .

FIFTH RACE

Lone Star

OCTOBER 30, 2004

6 FURLONGS. (1.07^{4}) 21ST RUNNING OF THE BREEDERS' CUP SPRINT Grade I. Purse $1,000,000 FOR THREE-YEAR-OLDS AND UPWARD. Northern Hemisphere Three-Year-Olds, 123 lbs.; Older, 126 lbs.; Southern Hemisphere Three-Year-Olds, 121 lbs.; Older, 126 lbs. All Fillies and Mares allowed 3 lbs. $10,000 to pre-enter, $20,000 to enter, with guaranteed $1 million purse including nominator awards (plus Net Supplementary Fees, if any), of which 52% of all monies to the owner of the winner, 20% to second, 11% to third, 5.7% to fourth and 3% to fifth; plus stallion nominator awards of 2.6% of all monies to the winner, 1% to second and 0.55% to third and foal nominator awards of 2.6% of all monies to the winner, 1% to second and 0.55% to third. Closed with 15 pre-entries. Supplemental nomination: Pt's Grey Eagle.

Value of Race: $972,020 Winner $551,200; second $212,000; third $116,600; fourth $60,420; fifth $31,800. Mutuel Pool $4,140,082.00 Exacta Pool $3,231,926.00 Trifecta Pool $2,623,198.00 Superfecta Pool $847,305.00 Head2Head Pool $60,145.00

Last Raced	Horse	M/Eqt.	A.	Wt	PP	St	¼	½	Str	Fin	Jockey	Odds $1
20Oct04 ^{8}Bel^{3}	Speightstown	L	6	126	2	8	4^{1}	3^{1}	1^{1}½	1^{1}¼	Velazquez J R	3.70
15Aug04 ^{8}Dmr^{1}	Kela	L b	6	126	5	10	10^{1}½	10^{1}	7½	2¾	Bailey J D	4.00
30Sep04 ^{7}SA^{5}	My Cousin Matt	L f	5	126	12	2	9^{1}½	9½	4^{1}	3½	Dominguez R A	60.70
20Oct04 ^{9}LS^{2}	Bwana Charlie	L	3	123	1	11	11^{3}½	11^{3}	8^{hd}	4¾	Migliore R	35.30
20Oct04 ^{8}Bel^{4}	Cajun Beat	L b	4	126	11	3	6^{1}½	5^{1}	5^{1}	5^{hd}	Velasquez C	14.80
8Oct04 ^{7}Kee^{3}	Clock Stopper	L b	4	126	7	13	13	13	11^{hd}	6^{hd}	Day P	7.70
8Oct04 ^{7}Kee^{1}	Champali	L	4	126	3	9	7^{hd}	8½	6½	7^{nk}	Bejarano R	7.30
10Oct04 ^{8}SA^{1}	Pt's Grey Eagle	L b	3	123	8	12	12^{2}	12^{2}	10^{1}½	8^{nk}	Nakatani C S	23.70
8Oct04 ^{7}Kee^{2}	Gold Storm	L b	4	126	9	7	3^{1}	2^{hd}	2½	9^{1}½	Taylor L	18.70
4Sep04 ^{8}Sar^{1}	Midas Eyes	L	4	126	13	1	8^{1}	7½	9^{2}	10^{3}½	Prado E S	3.60
20Oct04 ^{8}Pha^{1}	Abbondanza	L f	3	123	6	6	1½	1^{1}	3^{hd}	11^{1}¼	Coa E M	25.70
6Sep04 ^{6}Dmr^{1}	Our New Recruit	L	5	126	4	5	5^{hd}	6^{hd}	12^{hd}	12^{8}½	Baze T C	8.90
18Sep04 ^{13}TP^{2}	Cuvee	L	3	123	10	4	2^{hd}	4^{1}	13	13	Albarado R J	39.20

OFF AT 2:13 Start Good. Won driving. Track fast.

TIME :21^{1}, :43^{2}, :55^{2}, 1:08 (:21.23, :43.47, :55.56, 1:08.11)

$2 Mutuel Prices:				
	2 – SPEIGHTSTOWN	9.40	5.20	4.00
	5 – KELA		5.00	4.00
	12 – MY COUSIN MATT			15.00

$2 EXACTA 2–5 PAID $41.60 $2 TRIFECTA 2–5–12 PAID $2,684.20
$2 SUPERFECTA 2–5–12–1 PAID $42,365.20
$2 HEAD2HEAD 7VS11–WINNER11 PAID $4.20

Ch. h, (Feb), by Gone West – Silken Cat, by Storm Cat. Trainer Pletcher Todd A. Bred by Aaron U Jones & Marie Jones (Ky).

SPEIGHTSTOWN was well placed on the inside, saved ground on the turn, slipped through to make a bid at the top of the stretch, edged clear into the final furlong and held well under strong right hand urging. KELA was outrun early, raced three to four wide on the turn, swung seven wide leaving the turn, drifted inward in upper stretch and finished well while unable to reach the winner. MY COUSIN MATT settled towards the rear of the field, angled in late on the backstretch, saved ground on the turn, shifted out near the furlong marker and finished willingly. BWANA CHARLIE lacked early speed, shifted five wide near the quarter-pole, swung eight wide into the stretch and improved position. CAJUN BEAT was ridden along on the outside, vied three to four wide on the turn, lacked room near the sixteenth-pole and failed to rally. CLOCK STOPPER was completely void of speed, saved ground on the turn, angled out in upper stretch then again near the sixteenth-pole and failed to menace while finishing with some interest. CHAMPALI shifted outside near the five-furlong marker, was ridden along while three wide on the turn, bumped repeatedly with OUR NEW RECRUIT near the three-sixteenths marker and came up empty. PT'S GREY EAGLE dropped well back in the field, saved ground on the turn, angled out in upper stretch, lacked room late and never reached serious contention. GOLD STORM was bumped at the start, chased the pace on the outside, vied three wide on the turn, made a bid near the quarter-pole, drifted in while briefly in the lead passing the three-sixteenths marker and tired. MIDAS EYES was urged along on the outside, raced four wide on the turn, floated six wide leaving the turn, was forced inward in upper stretch and had nothing left. ABBONDANZA set the pace through quick fractions, was in tight while losing the lead near the three-sixteenths marker and faded. OUR NEW RECRUIT steadied repeatedly on the backstretch, raced off the rail on the turn, bumped repeatedly with CHAMPALI and steadied near the three-sixteenths marker then stopped in a rough trip. CUVEE broke inward and bumped a rival, chased the pace on the outside, vied three wide on the turn, was jostled in upper stretch and stopped.

Owners– 1, Melnyk Eugene and Laura; 2, Manoogian Jay; 3, Englander Richard A; 4, Heiligbrodt Racing Stable; 5, Padua St & Iracane J & J; 6, Overbrook Farm; 7, Lloyd Madison Farms IV LLC; 8, Reddam J Paul; 9, McKinney Keith and Sweesy Jack; 10, Gann Edmund A; 11, Germania Farms Inc; 12, C R K Stable; 13, Winchell Tbreds&Spendthrift Farm

Trainers– 1, Pletcher Todd A; 2, Mitchell Mike; 3, Mullins Jeff; 4, Asmussen Steven M; 5, Frankel Robert; 6, Stewart Dallas; 7, Foley Gregory D; 8, Dollase Craig; 9, Cascio C W Bubba; 10, Frankel Robert; 11, Tullock Timothy Jr; 12, Sadler John W; 13, Asmussen Steven M

$2 Pick Three (3/10–10–2) Paid $761.00; Pick Three Pool $762,652.
$2 Pick Four (1–3/10–10–2) Paid $3,130.20; Pick Four Pool $1,032,983.

SIXTH RACE
Lone Star
OCTOBER 30, 2004

1⅜ MILES. (Turf) (2.13^2) 6TH RUNNING OF THE V05 BREEDERS' CUP FILLY & MARE TURF. Grade I. Purse $1,000,000 FOR FILLIES AND MARES, THREE-YEAR-OLDS AND UPWARD. Northern Hemisphere Three-Year-Olds, 118 lbs.; Older, 123 lbs. Southern Hemisphere Three-Year-Olds, 113 lbs. Older, 122 lbs. $10,000 to pre-enter, $20,000 to enter, with guaranteed $1 million purse including nominator awards (plus Net Supplementary Fees, if any), of which 52% of all monies to the owner of the winner, 20% to second, 11% to third, 5.7% to fourth and 3% to fifth; plus stallion nominator awards of 2.6% of all monies to the winner, 1% to second and 0.55% to third and foal nominator awards of 2.6% of all monies to the winner, 1% to second and 0.55% to third. Closed with 14 pre-entries. Supplemental nominees: Aubonne, Katdogawn, Megahertz, Moscow Burning, Ouija Board and Super Brand.

Value of Race: $1,292,970 Winner $733,200; second $282,000; third $155,100; fourth $80,370; fifth $42,300. Mutuel Pool $4,014,411.00 Exacta Pool $3,085,646.00 Trifecta Pool $2,530,006.00 Superfecta Pool $879,527.00 Head2Head Pool $75,922.00

Last Raced	Horse	M/Eqt.	A.	Wt	PP	¼	½	¾	1	Str	Fin	Jockey	Odds $1
3Oct04 LCH3	Ouija Board-GB	L	3	118	5	6½	5½	4hd	41	2½	11½	Fallon K	0.90
2Oct04 7Bel4	Film Maker	L b	4	123	3	2½	2½	2½	21½	31½	2nk	Velazquez J R	16.50
2Oct04 7Bel6	Wonder Again	L	5	123	12	11½	112	112½	101	4½	32¾	Prado E S	10.70
2Oct04 7Bel3	Moscow Burning	L	4	123	4	12	14	11½	11½	1hd	41¼	Valdivia J Jr	18.80
3Oct04 6LCH4	Yesterday-Ire	L b	4	123	11	81	81	71½	6hd	53	51	Spencer J P	9.00
10Oct04 6Kee3	Shaconage	L	4	123	6	12	12	12	12	7hd	6¾	Bejarano R	62.40
2Oct04 4SA1	Light Jig-GB	L	4	123	7	101½	101	8½	111	82½	7½	Douglas R R	6.40
2Oct04 7Bel1	Riskaverse	L	5	123	9	4½	4hd	5½	5hd	61½	81	Velasquez C	13.70
10Oct04 6Kee2	Super Brand-SAf	L	5	123	1	7½	7hd	9½	9hd	9hd	95½	Day P	32.60
2Oct04 4SA3	Katdogawn-GB	L	4	123	2	9½	9½	101½	8hd	102½	101	Desormeaux K J	55.40
31May04 2Hol2	Megahertz-GB	L	5	123	10	5hd	6½	61	71½	11hd	11nk	Nakatani C S	10.10
2Oct04 7Bel5	Aubonne-Ger		4	123	8	31	31	31½	3hd	12	12	Bailey J D	16.80

OFF AT 2:48 Start Good . Won driving. Course yielding.

TIME :26^2, :52^2, 1:18^2, 1:42^1, 2:06^1, 2:18^1 (:26.42, :52.47, 1:18.50, 1:42.36, 2:06.34, 2:18.25)

$2 Mutuel Prices:

5 – OUIJA BOARD-GB	3.80	3.00	2.80
3 – FILM MAKER		9.00	6.60
12 – WONDER AGAIN			6.60

$2 EXACTA 5-3 PAID $43.40 $2 TRIFECTA 5-3-12 PAID $364.00
$2 SUPERFECTA 5-3-12-4 PAID $3,257.40
$2 HEAD2HEAD 3VS10VS11-WINNER3 PAID $5.60

B. f, (Mar), by Cape Cross-Ire - Selection Board-GB , by Welsh Pageant-Fr . Trainer Dunlop Edward. Bred by Stanley Estate and Stud Co (GB).

OUIJA BOARD (GB) taken in hand soon after the start, was rated in good position for a mile, launched a rally three wide leaving the turn, rapidly closed the gap in upper stretch, accelerated to the front inside the furlong marker then drew clear under steady right hand encouragement. FILM MAKER settled just behind the early leader, raced just off the pace for a mile, edged closer on the turn, made a run to threaten at the quarter pole, battled into upper stretch, but couldn't stay with the winner while holding well for the place. WONDER AGAIN was outrun for six furlongs, gradually worked her way forward along the inside midway on the turn, saved ground into the stretch, angled out in upper stretch then rallied belatedly to gain a share. MOSCOW BURNING sprinted well clear in the early stages, set a moderate pace along the inside to the top of the stretch, fought gamely into midstretch then weakened from her early efforts. YESTERDAY (IRE) dwelt at the start breaking well behind the field, rushed up between horses shortly thereafter, was in the middle of the pack for seven furlongs, rallied inside the winner to threaten nearing the quarter pole but couldn't sustain her bid. SHACONAGE raced far back to the turn and failed to threaten while improving her position. LIGHT JIG (GB) failed to mount a serious rally. RISKAVERSE steadied while rank in the early stages, raced in the middle of the pack along the backstretch, lodged a brief bid while three wide on the turn then faded in the stretch. SUPER BRAND (SAF) was unhurried for a half, angled out along the backstretch, swung seven wide leaving the turn then lacked a strong closing response. KATDOGAWN (GB) checked between horses in the early stages, was outrun for a mile, circled six wide entering the stretch then lacked a further response. MEGAHERTZ (GB) raced within striking distance while five wide for most of the way and faded in the stretch. AUBONNE (GER), up close while three wide for a mile, dropped back on the turn and steadily tired thereafter.

Owners– 1, Lord Derby; 2, Courtlandt Farms; 3, Phillips Racing Partnership; 4, Van Kempen Dallas Nentwig Mike and Mariani Jeff; 5, Magnier Mrs John and Henry Mrs Richard; 6, Van Doren Andrena; 7, Juddmonte Farms Inc; 8, Fox Ridge Farm Inc; 9, Team Valor Stables LLC; 10, Cuchna John R Jim Ford Inc and Pearson Deron; 11, Bello Michael; 12, Tanaka Gary A

Trainers– 1, Dunlop Edward; 2, Motion H Graham; 3, Toner James J; 4, Cassidy James; 5, O'Brien Aidan P; 6, Shirota Mitch; 7, Frankel Robert; 8, Kelly Patrick J; 9, McLaughlin Kiaran P; 10, Cassidy James; 11, Frankel Robert; 12, Libaud Eric

$2 Pick Three (10-2-5) Paid $505.80 ; Pick Three Pool $791,548 .

SEVENTH RACE
Lone Star
OCTOBER 30, 2004

$1\frac{1}{16}$ MILES. (1.40^{2}) 21ST RUNNING OF THE BESSEMER TRUST BREEDERS' CUP JUVENILE. Grade I. Purse $1,500,000 FOR COLTS AND GELDINGS, TWO YEARS OLD. Weight: 122 lbs.; $15,000 to pre-enter, $30,000 to enter, with guaranteed $1.5 million purse including nominator awards (plus Net Supplementary Fees, if any) of which 52% of all monies to the owner of the winner, 20% to second, 11% to third, 5.7% to fourth and 3% to fifth; plus stallion nominator awards of 2.6% of all monies to the winner, 1% to second and 0.55% to third and foal nominator awards of 2.6% of all monies to the winner, 1% to second and 0.55% to third.Closed with 8 pre-entries.

Value of Race: $1,375,500 Winner $780,000; second $300,000; third $165,000; fourth $85,500; fifth $45,000. Mutuel Pool $3,893,107.00 Exacta Pool $2,669,146.00 Trifecta Pool $2,125,441.00 Superfecta Pool $691,187.00 Head2Head Pool $81,464.00

Last Raced	Horse	M/Eqt.	A.	Wt	PP	St	¼	½	¾	Str	Fin	Jockey	Odds $1
25Sep04 ASC^{3}	Wilko	L	2	122	8	5	3^{1}	3^{hd}	$4^{2\frac{1}{2}}$	4^{2}	$1^{\frac{3}{4}}$	Dettori L	28.30
9Oct04 ^{7}Bel^{2}	Afleet Alex	L	2	122	3	7	8	$6^{1\frac{1}{2}}$	$3^{\frac{1}{2}}$	1^{hd}	2^{nk}	Rose J	3.00
9Oct04 ^{7}Bel^{3}	Sun King	L	2	122	1	2	$5^{1\frac{1}{2}}$	$4^{\frac{1}{2}}$	1^{hd}	$2^{\frac{1}{2}}$	$3^{1\frac{1}{4}}$	Prado E S	6.90
9Oct04 ^{7}Kee^{1}	Consolidator	L	2	122	4	1	$2^{\frac{1}{2}}$	2^{1}	2^{hd}	$3^{\frac{1}{2}}$	$4^{1\frac{1}{2}}$	Bejarano R	7.50
3Oct04 ^{7}SA^{1}	Roman Ruler	L	2	122	2	3	7^{1}	7^{hd}	$5^{\frac{1}{2}}$	5^{2}	$5^{1\frac{1}{4}}$	Nakatani C S	2.00
9Oct04 ^{7}Bel^{1}	Proud Accolade	L	2	122	6	6	4^{hd}	5^{hd}	6^{hd}	6^{5}	$6^{9\frac{3}{4}}$	Velazquez J R	2.60
3Oct04 ^{3}SA^{5}	Twice Unbridled	b	2	122	7	4	$1^{1\frac{1}{2}}$	1^{1}	$7^{\frac{1}{2}}$	7^{1}	$7^{1\frac{1}{4}}$	Espinoza V	33.20
25Sep04 ASC^{2}	Scandinavia	L	2	122	5	8	6^{hd}	8	8	8	8	Spencer J P	14.50

OFF AT 3:24 Start Good . Won driving. Track fast.

TIME :23^{2}, :47^{2}, 1:11^{1}, 1:35^{3}, 1:42 (:23.54, :47.49, 1:11.25, 1:35.77, 1:42.09)

$2 Mutuel Prices:				
	8 – WILKO	58.60	18.20	6.80
	3 – AFLEET ALEX		5.00	3.60
	1 – SUN KING			5.60

$2 EXACTA 8–3 PAID $254.00 $2 TRIFECTA 8–3–1 PAID $1,424.60
$2 SUPERFECTA 8–3–1–4 PAID $7,150.20
$2 HEAD2HEAD 1VS4–WINNER1 PAID $3.20

Ch. c, (Jan), by Awesome Again – Native Roots–Ire , by Indian Ridge–Ire . Trainer Noseda Jeremy. Bred by Ro Parra (Ky).

WILKO settled on the outside while three wide, made a four wide bid leaving the backstretch, moved to three wide midway through the turn, dropped back passing the quarter-pole, rallied again outside the furlong marker, surged to the lead near the sixteenth-pole and inched clear under steady left hand encouragement. AFLEET ALEX bobbled at the start then bumped with CONSOLIDATOR and ROMAN RULER, shifted four wide early on the initial turn, settled on the outside, engaged the leaders while five wide leaving the backstretch, dropped to four wide midway through the turn, took the lead passing the quarter-pole, led gamely into the final furlong, was collared near the sixteenth-pole then outfinished. SUN KING was rated while eager to run on the inside, settled a bit on the backstretch, moved through to contest the lead leaving the backstretch, dueled through the turn, bumped with CONSOLIDATOR in upper stretch, battled gamely into the final sixteenth and weakened slightly. CONSOLIDATOR was bumped at the start, tracked the pace on the outside, made a bid between rivals entering the far turn, dueled into the stretch, bumped with SUN KING inside the three-sixteenths marker, fought determinedly into the final sixteenth and gave way grudgingly. ROMAN RULER bumped with AFLEET ALEX after the start, steadied off heels approaching the first turn, continued just off heels into the backstretch, was hard held near the back of the field, saved ground on the far turn, angled out sharply near the furlong marker and came up empty. PROUD ACCOLADE leaned out at the start, settled between rivals, came under a ride leaving the backstretch, moved around TWICE UNBRIDLED midway through the turn and failed to respond. TWICE UNBRIDLED set the pace under moderate pressure, steadied while being passed with three furlongs to run and stopped. SCANDINAVIA hesitated at the start, raced three wide on the first turn, was reserved near the back of the field, roused while three wide on the far turn, moved to four wide near the quarter-pole and had nothing left.

Owners– 1, Reddam J Paul and Roy Susan; 2, Cash is King LLC; 3, Farmer Tracy; 4, Lewis Robert B and Beverly J; 5, Fog City Stable; 6, Padua Stables; 7, McBride Renn Labrum Lyle and Jensen Daniel M; 8, Tabor Michael and Magnier Mrs John

Trainers– 1, Noseda Jeremy; 2, Ritchey Tim F; 3, Zito Nicholas P; 4, Lukas D Wayne; 5, Baffert Bob; 6, Pletcher Todd A; 7, Jensen Daniel M; 8, O'Brien Aidan P

$2 Pick Three (2–5–8) Paid $1,114.40 ; Pick Three Pool $850,832 .

EIGHTH RACE
Lone Star
OCTOBER 30, 2004

$1\frac{1}{2}$ MILES. (Turf) (2.28^{1}) 21ST RUNNING OF THE JOHN DEERE BREEDERS' CUP TURF. Grade I. Purse $2,000,000 FOR THREE-YEAR-OLDS AND UPWARD. Northern Hemisphere Three-Year-Olds, 121 lbs.; Older, 126 lbs.; Southern Hemisphere Three-Year-Olds, 116 lbs.; Older, 125 lbs. All Fillies and Mares allowed 3 lbs. $20,000 to pre-enter, $40,000 to enter, with guaranteed $2million purse including nominator awards (plus Net Supplementary fees, if any) of which 52% of all monies to the owner of the winner, 20% to second, 11% to third, 5.7% to fourth and 3% to fifth; plus stallion nominator awards of 2.6% of all monies to thewinner, 1% to second and 0.55% to third and foal nominator awards of 2.6% of all monies to the winner, 1% to second and 0.55% to third. Closed with 11 pre-entries.

Value of Race: $1,834,000 Winner $1,040,000; second $400,000; third $220,000; fourth $114,000; fifth $60,000. Mutuel Pool $3,942,242.00 Exacta Pool $2,676,912.00 Trifecta Pool $2,357,798.00 Superfecta Pool $903,935.00 Head2Head Pool $56,680.00

Last Raced	Horse	M/Eqt.	A.	Wt	PP	¼	½	1	1¼	Str	Fin	Jockey	Odds $1
11Sep04 ^{9}Bel^{4}	Better Talk Now	L bf	5	126	5	8	7^{hd}	$6^{2\frac{1}{2}}$	$4^{\frac{1}{2}}$	$2^{1\frac{1}{2}}$	$1^{1\frac{3}{4}}$	Dominguez R A	27.90
2Oct04 ^{9}Bel^{1}	Kitten's Joy	L	3	121	4	$3^{\frac{1}{2}}$	3^{2}	3^{1}	3^{1}	3^{2}	2^{1}	Velazquez J R	0.70
11Sep04 ^{9}Leo^{3}	Powerscourt-GB	L b	4	126	1	6^{2}	$6^{1\frac{1}{2}}$	$2^{\frac{1}{2}}$	1^{2}	1^{hd}	$3^{2\frac{1}{4}}$	Spencer J P	2.90
2Oct04 ^{9}Bel^{2}	Magistretti	L b	4	126	6	5^{2}	$4^{1\frac{1}{2}}$	5^{2}	2^{hd}	$4^{2\frac{1}{2}}$	$4^{2\frac{3}{4}}$	Prado E S	6.10
9Oct04 ^{5}Kee^{1}	Mustanfar	L b	3	121	8	7^{hd}	8	8	7^{1}	5^{2}	5^{nk}	Santos J A	23.40
2Oct04 ^{9}Bel^{4}	Request for Parole	L	5	126	2	4^{hd}	5^{hd}	7^{hd}	8	$6^{\frac{1}{2}}$	6^{4}	Day P	22.20
2Oct04 ^{8}WO^{7}	Strut the Stage	L b	6	126	3	2^{2}	2^{2}	$4^{\frac{1}{2}}$	$6^{\frac{1}{2}}$	$7^{\frac{1}{2}}$	$7^{3\frac{3}{4}}$	Nakatani C S	27.40
3Oct04 ^{5}SA^{1}	Star Over the Bay	L	6	126	7	$1^{3\frac{1}{2}}$	1^{5}	1^{2}	$5^{2\frac{1}{2}}$	8	8	Baze T C	8.10

OFF AT 3:59 Start Good. Won driving. Course yielding.

TIME :24^{4}, :49, 1:13^{4}, 1:40, 2:04, 2:29^{3} (:24.90, :49.16, 1:13.96, 1:40.14, 2:04.15, 2:29.70)

$2 Mutuel Prices:

5 – BETTER TALK NOW	57.80	12.40	5.20
4 – KITTEN'S JOY		2.80	2.20
1 – POWERSCOURT-GB			3.00

$2 EXACTA 5–4 PAID $134.80 $2 TRIFECTA 5–4–1 PAID $492.00
$2 SUPERFECTA 5–4–1–6 PAID $1,483.40
$2 HEAD2HEAD 1VS4–WINNER4 PAID $2.80

B. g, (Feb), by Talkin Man – Bendita , by Baldski . Trainer Motion H Graham. Bred by Wimborne Farm Inc (Ky).

BETTER TALK NOW was unhurried for a mile, angled out on the far turn, rapidly closed the gap on the turn, circled five wide rallying into the stretch, charged to the front while drifting in slightly in midstretch then drew away under steady left hand urging. KITTEN'S JOY was well placed slightly off the rail along the backstretch, launched a rally in the two path on the turn, made a run along the inside to threaten in upper stretch but was no match for the winner while outfinishing POWERSCOURT for the place. POWERSCOURT (GB) was unhurried early after breaking poorly, made a strong middle move while four wide along the backstretch, opened a clear advantage on the far turn, maintained a slim lead into upper stretch, brushed with the winner while drifting out in midstretch then weakened under pressure in the final eighth. MAGISTRETTI was taken in hand for six furlongs, eased back slightly on the far turn, rallied three wide to reach contention on the turn, moved up between horses in upper stretch, steadied in traffic nearing the furlong marker then weakened late. MUSTANFAR was outrun for a mile and failed to threaten while improving his position. REQUEST FOR PAROLE raced up close while saving ground for a mile and steadily tired thereafter. STRUT THE STAGE chased the pacesetter along the rail to the far turn and faltered. STAR OVER THE BAY was used up setting the early pace. Following a stewards inquiry into the stretch run there was no change in the order of finish.

Owners– 1, Bushwood Racing Partners; 2, Ramsey Kenneth L and Sarah K; 3, Magnier Mrs John; 4, Tabor Michael B; 5, Shadwell Stable; 6, Knighton Jeri and Sam; 7, Sam-Son Farms; 8, G Racing VanBurger Carl F and Vaughn Landon

Trainers– 1, Motion H Graham; 2, Romans Dale; 3, O'Brien Aidan P; 4, Biancone Patrick L; 5, McLaughlin Kiaran P; 6, Hough Stanley M; 7, Frostad Mark; 8, Mitchell Mike

$2 Pick Three (5–8–5) Paid $4,007.40 ; Pick Three Pool $550,358 .

NINTH RACE
Lone Star
OCTOBER 30, 2004

1¼ MILES. (1.59) 21ST RUNNING OF THE BREEDERS' CUP CLASSIC POWERED BY DODGE. Grade I. Purse $4,000,000 FOR THREE-YEAR-OLDS AND UPWARD. Northern Hemisphere Three-Year-Olds, 121 lbs.; Older, 126 lbs.; Southern Hemisphere Three-Year-Olds, 116 lbs.; Older, 126 lbs. All Fillies and Mares allowed 3 lbs. $40,000 to pre-enter, $80,000 to enter, with guaranteed $4million purse including nominator awards (plus Net Supplementary Fees, if any) of which 52% of all monies to the owner of the winner, 20% to second, 11% to third, 5.7% to fourth and 3% to fifth; plus stallion nominator awards of 2.6% of all monies to thewinner, 1% to second and 0.55% to third and foal nominator awards of 2.6% of all monies to the winner, 1% to second and 0.55% to third. Closed with 13 pre-entries.

Value of Race: $3,668,000 Winner $2,080,000; second $800,000; third $440,000; fourth $228,000; fifth $120,000. Mutuel Pool $8,498,771.00 Exacta Pool $4,955,254.00 Trifecta Pool $4,726,585.00 Superfecta Pool $1,856,002.00 Head2Head Pool $85,255.00

Last Raced	Horse	M/Eqt.	A.	Wt	PP	¼	½	¾	1	Str	Fin	Jockey	Odds $1
11Sep04 ^{10}Bel^{1}	Ghostzapper	L b	4	126	1	1^{hd}	$1^{1/2}$	$1^{1/2}$	1^{1}	1^{2}	1^{3}	Castellano J J	*2.50
18Sep04 ^{11}TP^{1}	Roses in May	L	4	126	6	$2^{1/2}$	$2^{1/2}$	2^{1}	2^{1}	2^{3}	2^{4}	Velazquez J R	8.70
22Aug04 ^{8}Dmr^{1}	Pleasantly Perfect	L b	6	126	12	$9^{1/2}$	$10^{1/2}$	$10^{1/2}$	$5^{1/2}$	3^{hd}	$3^{3/4}$	Bailey J D	2.50
2Oct04 ^{7}Haw^{2}	Perfect Drift	L	5	126	4	$6^{1/2}$	6^{hd}	8^{hd}	6^{hd}	$4^{1/2}$	4^{2}	Desormeaux K J	13.80
10Oct04 ^{8}Kee^{1}	Azeri	L	6	123	3	3^{1}	$3^{1/2}$	$4^{1/2}$	7^{1}	5^{2}	5^{2}	Day P	15.20
20Sep04 ^{10}Mor^{1}	Personal Rush	b	3	121	8	$5^{1/2}$	5^{1}	$5^{1/2}$	$8^{1/2}$	7^{hd}	$6^{3/4}$	Dettori L	25.10
28Aug04 ^{11}Sar^{1}	Birdstone	L	3	121	7	10^{1}	$9^{1 1/2}$	9^{2}	9^{1}	$9^{1/2}$	7^{nk}	Prado E S	6.50
8Oct04 ^{7}Med^{2}	Dynever	L	4	126	13	7^{1}	$8^{1/2}$	7^{1}	$3^{1/2}$	$6^{1/2}$	$8^{3/4}$	Nakatani C S	15.30
25Sep04 ^{10}LaD^{1}	Fantasticat	L b	3	121	5	12^{12}	12^{20}	12^{25}	12^{15}	$11^{2 1/2}$	$9^{3/4}$	Melancon G	59.90
2Oct04 ^{10}Bel^{1}	Funny Cide	L	4	126	9	$8^{1/2}$	$7^{1/2}$	$6^{1/2}$	$4^{1/2}$	8^{1}	10^{nk}	Santos J A	7.70
2Oct04 ^{10}Bel^{5}	Bowman's Band	L	6	126	11	$11^{2 1/2}$	11^{4}	11^{3}	10^{1}	10^{hd}	11^{3}	Velasquez C	61.70
2Oct04 ^{10}Bel^{2}	Newfoundland	L b	4	126	10	$4^{1/2}$	$4^{1/2}$	$3^{1/2}$	$11^{2 1/2}$	12^{10}	12^{6}	Coa E M	38.80
2Oct04 ^{7}Haw^{1}	Freefourinternet	L	6	126	2	13	13	13	13	13	13	Kuntzweiler G	54.30

***-Actual Betting Favorite.**

OFF AT 4:42 Start Good. Won driving. Track fast.

TIME :23^{2}, :47, 1:11^{1}, 1:35^{1}, 1:59 (:23.42, :47.00, 1:11.32, 1:35.38, 1:59.02)

(New Track Record)

$2 Mutuel Prices:				
	1 – GHOSTZAPPER	7.00	4.00	3.60
	6 – ROSES IN MAY		8.20	5.20
	12 – PLEASANTLY PERFECT			3.00

$2 EXACTA 1-6 PAID $46.60 $2 TRIFECTA 1-6-12 PAID $164.00
$2 SUPERFECTA 1-6-12-4 PAID $1,297.80
$2 HEAD2HEAD 7VS9-WINNER7 PAID $3.60

B. c, (Apr), by Awesome Again – Baby Zip , by Relaunch . Trainer Frankel Robert. Bred by Adena Springs (Ky).

GHOSTZAPPER rushed up along the inside to gain a slim early advantage, set the pace under pressure from ROSES IN MAY along the backstretch, opened a clear lead approaching the quarter pole, shook loose in upper stretch then drew away under intermittent right hand encouragement. ROSES IN MAY moved up from outside to contest the early pace, pressed the pace outside the winner for a mile, couldn't stay with that one in upper stretch but continued on well to clearly best the others. PLEASANTLY PERFECT raced well back for six furlongs after breaking a bit slowly, circled six wide while gaining a bit leaving the turn, was brushed a bit at the top of the stretch then rallied mildly to gain a share. PERFECT DRIFT was taken in hand along the rail on the first turn, settled in midpack for six furlongs, was shuffled back along the inside on the far turn, swung out on the turn, brushed with PLEASANTLY PERFECT while angling five wide entering the stretch then failed to threaten while improving his position. AZERI broke a bit slowly, rushed up along the rail, raced in good position just behind the top two while saving ground to the top of the stretch then weakened in the final eighth. PERSONAL RUSH rushed up after breaking slowly, raced within striking distance between horses along the backstretch, remained a factor to the turn and gradually tired thereafter. BIRDSTONE in traffic early, raced well back for seven furlongs, advanced four wide nearing the quarter pole and passed mostly tiring rivals. DYNEVER raced in the middle of the pack while five wide for six furlongs, lodged a brief bid on the turn and flattened out. FANTASTICAT never reached contention while saving ground. FUNNY CIDE was taken in hand while in traffic nearing the first turn, moved up five wide along the backstretch, lodged a mild bid between horses on the turn then gave way. BOWMAN'S BAND checked early along the rail then never reached contention. NEWFOUNDLAND raced up close while four wide for seven furlongs and gave way. FREEFOURINTERNET never reached contention.

Owners– 1, Stronach Stables; 2, Ramsey Kenneth L and Sarah K; 3, Diamond A Racing Corporation; 4, Stonecrest Farm; 5, Allen E Paulson Living Trust; 6, Fukami Tomiro; 7, Marylou Whitney Stables; 8, Wills Catherine and Karches Peter; 9, R Bar S Thoroughbreds LLP; 10, Sackatoga Stable; 11, Schwartz Martin S; 12, Sumaya Us Stables; 13, EquiraceCom LLC

Trainers– 1, Frankel Robert; 2, Romans Dale; 3, Mandella Richard; 4, Johnson Murray W; 5, Lukas D Wayne; 6, Yamauchi Kenji; 7, Zito Nicholas P; 8, Clement Christophe; 9, Barnett Bobby C; 10, Tagg Barclay; 11, Jerkens H Allen; 12, Pletcher Todd A; 13, Maker Michael J

$2 Pick Three (8-5-1) Paid $9,884.20 ; Pick Three Pool $1,034,563 .
$2 Pick Four (5-8-5-1) Paid $46,791.20 ; Pick Four Pool $1,466,130 .
$2 Pick Six (10-2-5-8-5-1) 5 Correct Paid $56,149.60 ; Pick Six Pool $4,566,837 .
$2 Daily Double (5-1) Paid $390.40 ; Daily Double Pool $999,821 .

SIXTH RACE
Santa Anita
OCTOBER 30, 2004

ABOUT 6½ FURLONGS. (Turf) (1.11) 31ST RUNNING OF THE MORVICH HANDICAP. Grade III. Purse $100,000 DOWNHILL TURF FOR THREE-YEAR-OLDS AND UPWARD. By subscription of $100 each if made on or before Thursday, October 21, 2004 or by supplementary nomination of $2,000 by 10 AM Tuesday, October 26.. All horses shall pay $1,000 to start, with $100,000 guaranteed of which $60,000 to the winner, $20,000 to second, $12,000 to third, $6,000 to fourth, and $2,000 to fifth. Weights: Tuesday, October 26. Starters to be named through the entry box by the closing time of entries. A trophy will be presented to the owner of the winner. Closed with 15 nominations.

Value of Race: $100,000 Winner $60,000; second $20,000; third $12,000; fourth $6,000; fifth $2,000. Mutuel Pool $480,166.00 Exacta Pool $216,354.00 Quinella Pool $19,424.00 Trifecta Pool $251,333.00

Last Raced	Horse	M/Eqt.	A.	Wt	PP	St	¼	½	Str	Fin	Jockey	Odds $1
1May04 6Hol1	Leroidesnimux-Brz	LB	4	117	4	1	4^{2}	$3^{1\frac{1}{2}}$	$3^{2\frac{1}{2}}$	$1^{1\frac{1}{4}}$	Court J K	3.00
30Sep04 7SA1	De Valmont-Aus	LB b	7	115	1	3	$1^{1\frac{1}{2}}$	1^{2}	1^{1}	2no	Smith M E	2.10
8Sep04 6Dmr2	Cayoke-FR	LB b	7	116	6	2	2^{1}	$2^{1\frac{1}{2}}$	$2^{1\frac{1}{2}}$	$3^{1\frac{1}{2}}$	Stevens G L	1.70
30Sep04 7SA2	Geronimo-Chi	LB b	5	118	3	5	5^{1}	$5^{1\frac{1}{2}}$	4^{4}	4^{10}	Gomez G K	4.30
28Feb04 8RAN6	Irgunette-Aus	LB	5	114	5	4	3^{1}	4^{hd}	$5^{1\frac{1}{2}}$	5^{2}	Fusilier C	24.60
19Sep04 CRA9	Vasywait-FR	B	5	115	2	6	6	6	6	6	Figueroa O	37.20

OFF AT 5:10 Start Good . Won driving. Course firm.

TIME :21[2], :43[1], 1:05[4], 1:11[3] (:21.45, :43.31, 1:05.88, 1:11.76)

$2 Mutuel Prices:				
	4 – LEROIDESANIMAUX-BRZ	8.00	4.00	2.60
	1 – DE VALMONT-AUS		3.20	2.40
	6 – CAYOKE-FR			2.40

$1 EXACTA 4–1 PAID $13.70 $2 QUINELLA 1–4 PAID $11.80
$1 TRIFECTA 4–1–6 PAID $29.60

Ch. c, (Sep), by Candy Stripes – Dissemble-GB , by Ahonoora-GB . Trainer Frankel Robert. Bred by Haras Bage Do Sul (Brz).

LEROIDESANIMAUX (BRZ) stalked inside on the hill, came out crossing the dirt, bid three deep under urging in the stretch, lugged in a bit but gained the lead in deep stretch and inched clear. DE VALMONT (AUS) sped to the early lead in the middle of the course, angled in after the right hand curve, set the pace inside, fought back along the rail in the stretch, could not quite match the winner late but held second. CAYOKE (FR) bobbled at the start, stalked off the rail then angled in, came out nearing the stretch, bid between foes past midstretch and continued willingly to the wire. GERONIMO (CHI) between horses early, stalked a bit off the rail then inside, came out into the stretch and lacked the needed rally. IRGUNETTE (AUS) was in a good position stalking the pace outside a rival, came three deep into the stretch and weakened. VASYWAIT (FR) unhurried a bit off the inside down the hill, came out into the stretch and lacked a further response. Rail on hill at zero.

Owners– 1, T N T Stud; 2, O'Connor David; 3, House Michael; 4, Buster Jr William C Hays Rusty Surfside Equine et al; 5, Epic Racing; 6, Mrs Andree Gay

Trainers– 1, Frankel Robert; 2, Cardenas Ruben; 3, Mullins Jeff; 4, Machowsky Michael; 5, Hines N J; 6, Powell Leonard

Scratched– Coded Message (26Sep04 9Fpx1)

$2 Daily Double (4 4) Paid $32.00 ; Daily Double Pool $29,480 .
$1 Pick Three (2–4–4) Paid $234.50 ; Pick Three Pool $50,274 .

SEVENTH RACE
Aqueduct
OCTOBER 31, 2004

7 FURLONGS. (1.20) 52ND RUNNING OF THE SPORT PAGE HANDICAP. Grade III. Purse $100,000 (UP TO $19,000 NYSBFOA) A HANDICAP FOR THREE YEAR OLDS AND UPWARD. By subscription of $100 each, which should accompany the nomination; $500 to pass the entry box; $500 to start, with $100,000 added. The added money and all fees to be divided 60% to the winner, 20% to second, 10% to third, 5% to fourth, 3% to fifth and 2% divided equally among remaining finishers. A trophy will be presented to the winning owner. Closed Saturday, October 16, 2004 with 22 Nominations.

Value of Race: $111,200 Winner $66,720; second $22,240; third $11,120; fourth $5,560; fifth $3,336; sixth $556; seventh $556; eighth $556; ninth $556. Mutuel Pool $451,629.00 Exacta Pool $395,693.00 Trifecta Pool $301,187.00

Last Raced	Horse	M/Eqt.	A.	Wt	PP	St	¼	½	Str	Fin	Jockey	Odds $1
12Sep04 7Bel1	Mass Media	L b	3	113	7	2	2^{hd}	$2^{1\frac{1}{2}}$	$1^{3\frac{1}{2}}$	$1^{3\frac{1}{2}}$	Castellano J J	8.30
8Oct04 7Med8	Lion Tamer	L	4	118	8	5	8^{3}	5^{hd}	$4^{2\frac{1}{2}}$	2^{2}	Velazquez J R	4.40
8Oct04 7Med3	Gygistar	L	5	120	9	1	$4^{\frac{1}{2}}$	3^{2}	3^{hd}	3no	Bravo J	2.20
2Oct04 8Bel2	Voodoo	L b	6	117	5	4	1^{hd}	$1^{1\frac{1}{2}}$	$2^{1\frac{1}{2}}$	$4^{3\frac{1}{2}}$	Chavez J F	3.20
23Sep04 8Bel2	Personal Touch	L b	4	113	3	7	6^{hd}	$6^{1\frac{1}{2}}$	$5^{3\frac{1}{2}}$	5^{4}	Fragoso P	11.50
8Oct04 7Kee4	Super Fuse	L b	4	117	2	9	7^{1}	8^{6}	6^{6}	$6^{2\frac{1}{4}}$	Velasquez C	4.40
4Sep04 8Sar9	Eavesdropper	L	4	114	1	8	9	9	8^{1}	$7^{2\frac{3}{4}}$	Castillo H Jr	74.25
6Sep04 9Tim3	Conservation	L b	4	114	6	3	5^{6}	$7^{1\frac{1}{2}}$	$7^{1\frac{1}{2}}$	$8^{7\frac{1}{4}}$	Prado E S	37.75
2Apr04 8Kee9	Tomahawk	L	4	115	4	6	3^{2}	$4^{2\frac{1}{2}}$	9	9	Santos J A	42.50

OFF AT 3:16 Start Good . Won driving. Track fast.

TIME :22[1], :44[3], 1:08[2], 1:21 (:22.32, :44.60, 1:08.49, 1:21.10)

$2 Mutuel Prices:				
	7 – MASS MEDIA	18.60	9.00	5.40
	8 – LION TAMER		7.20	4.00
	9 – GYGISTAR			2.80

$2 EXACTA 7–8 PAID $127.50 $2 TRIFECTA 7–8–9 PAID $352.00

Dk. b or br. c, (Mar), by Touch Gold – Sultry Allure , by Forty Niner . Trainer Frankel Robert. Bred by Live Oak Stud (Ky).

MASS MEDIA was bumped at the start, raced with the pace while three wide, responded when roused, drew clear and was kept to a drive to the wire. LION TAMER was bumped at the start, was outrun early, rallied three wide nearing the stretch and finished gamely outside. GYGISTAR raced close up early, was three wide on the turn and had no response when roused. VOODOO set the pace while between rivals, drew clear on the turn and tired in the final furlong. PERSONAL TOUCH was outrun early, raced inside and had no rally. SUPER FUSE was outrun early along the inside, angled out in the stretch and had no response when roused. EAVESDROPPER was outrun early, came wide into the stretch and had no rally. CONSERVATION raced close up early and tired after a half mile. TOMAHAWK contested the pace along the inside and tired.

Owners– 1, West Gary L and Mary E; 2, Tabor Michael B; 3, Evans Edward P; 4, Moore Susan and John; 5, Amendola Robert J; 6, Alpha One Stable; 7, De Renzo Dean and Hartley Randall; 8, McCarthy James; 9, Firestone D Morgan

Trainers– 1, Frankel Robert; 2, Pletcher Todd A; 3, Hennig Mark; 4, Jerkens James A; 5, Iwinski Allen; 6, Asmussen Steven M; 7, McLaughlin Kiaran P; 8, Tagg Barclay; 9, Pletcher Todd A

$2 Daily Double (8–7) Paid $118.50 ; Daily Double Pool $106,817 .
$2 Pick Three (7–8–7) Paid $1,874.00 ; Pick Three Pool $67,470 .

EIGHTH RACE
Aqueduct
OCTOBER 31, 2004

1$\frac{1}{16}$ MILES. (Turf) (1.40^{4}) 27TH RUNNING OF THE ATHENIA. Grade III. Purse $100,000 (UP TO $19,000 NYSBFOA) A HANDICAP FOR FILLIES AND MARES THREE YEARS OLD AND UPWARD. By subscription of $100 each, which should accompany the nomination; $500 to pass the entry box; $500 to start, with $100,000 added. The added money and all fees to be divided 60% to the winner, 20% to second, 10% to third, 5% to fourth, 3% to fifth and 2% divided equally among remaining finishers. A trophy will be presented to the winning owner. The New York Racing Association reserves the right to transfer this race to the Main Track. In the event that this race is taken off the turf, it may be subject to downgrading by the Graded Stakes Committee. Closed Saturday, October 16, 2004 with 42 Nominations. (If the Stewards consider it inadvisable to run this race on the turf course, this race will be run at One Mile on the main track.).

Value of Race: $115,700 Winner $69,420; second $23,140; third $11,570; fourth $5,785; fifth $3,471; sixth $386; seventh $386; eighth $386; ninth $386; tenth $386; eleventh $384. Mutuel Pool $434,897.00 Exacta Pool $357,818.00 Trifecta Pool $282,332.00

Last Raced	Horse	M/Eqt.	A.	Wt	PP	St	¼	½	¾	Str	Fin	Jockey	Odds $1
17Oct04 6Bel1	Finery	L	4	113	3	3	4½	5½	5½	3hd	1½	Fragoso P	6.60
11Oct04 8Del1	Madeira Mist-Ire	L	5	118	11	7	21½	11½	1½	1hd	2nk	Santos J A	8.40
1Oct04 6Med4	With Patience	L f	5	114	1	1	1hd	2½	2½	21½	3½	Castellano J J	8.80
11Aug04 8Sar2	Snowdrops-GB	L	4	116	8	8	7hd	6½	6½	4hd	4½	Prado E S	1.60
1Oct04 6Med1	Delta Princess	L	5	115	7	6	6½	8½	8½	61½	52¼	Castillo H Jr	4.20
11Oct04 8Del2	Mystery Itself	L	4	114	5	2	3½	3½	3½	52½	6¾	Espinoza J L	41.75
1Oct04 6Med3	Coney Kitty-Ire	L f	6	114	4	5	9hd	9½	9½	71	71¾	Coa E M	14.10
19Sep04 4Bel1	French Hideaway	L f	5	112	9	4	81½	10hd	101½	81½	8hd	Garcia Alan	63.50
23Oct04 9Pim2	Lady of the Future	L	6	115	2	11	11	11	11	96	95½	Bridgmohan S X	45.75
1Oct04 6Med2	SomethingVentured	L b	5	114	6	10	103	7½	7½	106	106¼	Velazquez J R	8.70
10Oct04 8Bel4	Andover Lady	L	4	113	10	9	51½	4hd	4hd	11	11	Bravo J	35.00

OFF AT 3:45 Start Good. Won driving. Course firm.

TIME :25^{2}, :50^{1}, 1:14^{3}, 1:38, 1:43^{3} (:25.44, :50.29, 1:14.64, 1:38.01, 1:43.73)

$2 Mutuel Prices:			
3 – FINERY	15.20	8.30	6.00
12 – MADEIRA MIST–IRE		8.90	5.10
1 – WITH PATIENCE			5.80

$2 EXACTA 3–12 PAID $133.50 $2 TRIFECTA 3–12–1 PAID $970.00

B. f, (Feb), by Lear Fan – Duds, by Ack Ack. Trainer Turner William H Jr. Bred by Althea Richards (Va).

FINERY raced close up inside while in hand, saved ground throughout, angled out in the stretch, responded quickly once clear and was up in time. MADEIRA MIST (IRE) argued the pace from the outside, drew clear on the backstretch then dug in gamely along the inside in the stretch. WITH PATIENCE raced with the pace along the inside, was eased back on the backstretch, moved up outside on the second turn and dug in gamely to the wire. SNOWDROPS (GB) was rated along inside, came wide into the stretch and finished gamely. DELTA PRINCESS was rated along inside, angled out in upper stretch and finished gamely outside. MYSTERY ITSELF raced close up early while in hand, put in a three wide run on the second turn and faded in the final furlong. CONEY KITTY (IRE) was rated along early, raced inside and had no rally. FRENCH HIDEAWAY was outrun early, raced inside and had no response when roused. LADY OF THE FUTURE was outrun early, raced wide and lacked a rally. SOMETHING VENTURED raced wide throughout, rallied four wide into the second turn, was forced to check nearing the stretch and tired. ANDOVER LADY raced close up while three wide, stumbled on the second turn and tired.

Owners– 1, Richards Althea D; 2, Skymarc Farm Inc; 3, Merryman Elizabeth M; 4, Spink G Howard; 5, Khaled Saud b; 6, Lael Stables; 7, Betz William J Humphrey Steve and Seelbinder Arthur; 8, Anstu Stables Inc; 9, Pearson Max H; 10, McLane John and Wiemer Irwin; 11, Farmer Tracy

Trainers– 1, Turner William H Jr; 2, Clement Christophe; 3, Merryman Elizabeth M; 4, Clement Christophe; 5, Mott William I; 6, Matz Michael R; 7, Toner James J; 8, Moloney James J; 9, Greene Thomas M; 10, Pletcher Todd A; 11, Kimmel John C

Scratched– Vespers (08Oct04 8Bel3), Cloakof Vagueness (30Sep04 3Bel2)

NINTH RACE
Churchill
OCTOBER 31, 2004

7½ FURLONGS. (1.28) 12TH RUNNING OF THE ACK ACK HANDICAP. Grade III. Purse $150,000 FOR THREE–YEAR–OLDS AND UPWARD. By subscription of $150 each on or before October 16, 2004 or by supplementary nomination of $7,500 each by 12:00 noon (EST) Friday, October 22, 2004. $750 to pass the entry box; $750 additional to start, with $150,000 added of which 62% of all monies to the owner of the winner, 20% to second, 10% to third, 5% to fourth and 3% to fifth. Weights to be announced Saturday, October 23. Starters to be named through the entry box by the usual time of closing. All supplementary nominations will be required to pay entry and starting fees if they participate. Trophy to winning owner. Closed Saturday, October 16,2004 with 37 nominations.

Value of Race: $165,300 Winner $102,486; second $33,060; third $16,530; fourth $8,265; fifth $4,959. Mutuel Pool $200,117.00 Exacta Pool $147,596.00 Trifecta Pool $119,726.00 Superfecta Pool $31,128.00

Last Raced	Horse	M/Eqt.	A.	Wt	PP	St	¼	½	Str	Fin	Jockey	Odds $1
5Jun04 9Mnr3	Sir Cherokee	L	4	114	2	6	6	6	11½	15¼	Borel C H	6.40
28Aug04 10Sar6	Fire Slam	L	3	117	4	4	3hd	52½	43	2nk	Day P	0.60
14Oct04 7Kee1	Slate Run	L	4	106	3	3	2hd	31	2hd	3nk	Martinez W	12.10
8Oct04 7Kee7	Private Horde	L bf	5	115	1	5	41	21½	31½	47½	Bejarano R	6.00
13Oct04 5Kee1	Sterling Gold	L bf	5	115	6	2	53½	4½	52½	53	Castanon J L	11.00
2Oct04 9TP1	Cappuchino	L bf	5	118	5	1	1½	1hd	6	6	Albarado R J	5.00

OFF AT 4:40 Start Good. Won driving. Track fast.

TIME :22^{4}, :45^{2}, 1:10^{1}, 1:29^{2} (:22.82, :45.49, 1:10.39, 1:29.48)

$2 Mutuel Prices:			
2 – SIR CHEROKEE	14.80	3.80	3.60
5 – FIRE SLAM		2.60	2.20
4 – SLATE RUN			3.40

$2 EXACTA 2–5 PAID $32.00 $2 TRIFECTA 2–5–4 PAID $278.20
$1 SUPERFECTA 2–5–4–1 PAID $525.20

B. c, (Feb), by Cherokee Run – La Cucina–Ire, by Last Tycoon–Ire. Trainer Tomlinson Michael A. Bred by Domino Stud of Lexington LLC (Ky).

SIR CHEROKEE, reserved early and five wide, was unhurried for a half, edged closer nearing the stretch while remaining off the inside, wrested command in the upper stretch and drew off under urging. FIRE SLAM raced forwardly from the outset, was eased back four wide leaving the backstretch, came out six wide when straightened into the stretch and was fully extended for the place. SLATE RUN, close up three or four wide from the outset, continued four wide, was with the winner while inside that one entering the upper stretch but couldn't keep pace. PRIVATE HORDE, forwardly placed between foes early four wide, reached the front between calls on the turn, held on well until the stretch and weakened. STERLING GOLD, five or six wide to the end of the backstretch while within easy striking distance, continued four wide around the bend and tired in the drive. CAPPUCHINO sprinted clear soon after the start, maneuvered in to race two or three wide, made the pace for a half and gradually weakened.

Owners– 1, Domino Stud of Lex LLC; 2, Fulton Stan E; 3, Kingsbury Alan; 4, Tucker Billy R; 5, Hays Billy; 6, Hollendorfer Jerry Litt Howard and Todaro George

Trainers– 1, Tomlinson Michael A; 2, Carroll David; 3, Aubrey J Kevin; 4, Cain Joe; 5, Woodard Joe; 6, Hollendorfer Jerry

Scratched– Battle Won (22Oct04 9Kee1)

$2 Pick Three (8–8–2) Paid $4,641.20 ; Pick Three Pool $22,920 .

EIGHTH RACE
Santa Anita
OCTOBER 31, 2004

1⅛ MILES. (Turf) (1.43^{4}) 35TH RUNNING OF THE LAS PALMAS HANDICAP. Grade II. Purse $150,000 FOR FILLIES AND MARES, THREE YEARS OLD AND UPWARD. By subscription of $150 if made on or before Thursday, October 21 or by supplementary nomination of $3,000 by 10 AM Tuesday, October 26. All horses shall pay $1,500 to start with $150,000 guaranteed ofwhich $90,000 to the winner, $30,000 to second, $18,000 to third, $9,000 to fourth and $3,000 to fifth. Weights: Tu[illegible]day, October 26. Starters to be named throught the entry box by the usual time of entries. a tropiy will b[illegible] presented to the owner ofthe winner. Closed with 19 nominations.

Value of Race: $150,000 Winner $90,000; second $30,000; third $18,000; fourth $9,000; fifth $3,000. Mutuel Pool $406,117.00 Exacta Pool $211,524.00 Quinella Pool $21,118.00 Trifecta Pool $235,801.00 Superfecta Pool $100,751.00

Last Raced	Horse	M/Eqt.	A.	Wt	PP	St	¼	½	¾	Str	Fin	Jockey	Odds $1
21Jly04 ^{4}Dmr^{1}	Theater R. N.	LB	4	114	3	7	5½	5^{hd}	5½	3½	1½	Douglas R R	5.90
2Sep04 ^{6}Dmr^{2}	Lots of Hope-Brz	LB	4	117	5	2	3^{hd}	3^{1}	3^{1}	2^{1½}	2½	Nakatani C S	4.40
2Oct04 ^{4}SA^{4}	Good Student-Arg	LB	4	114	4	1	2^{2½}	1½	1^{3}	1^{1½}	3^{1}	Smith M E	2.10
3Oct04 ^{6}SA^{2}	Miss Loren-Arg	LB f	6	116	7	4	4^{2}	4^{2½}	4^{1½}	4^{1}	4^{1}	Court J K	2.40
25Sep04 ^{3}BM^{1}	Uraib-Ire	LB	4	115	1	5	7	7	7	7	5^{1½}	Baze T C	8.30
21Oct04 ^{7}SA^{5}	Navaja-NZ	LB b	4	114	6	6	6^{1½}	6^{3}	6^{2½}	6^{1½}	6^{4}	Gomez G K	21.80
29Sep04 ^{7}SA^{5}	Fencelineneighbor	LB b	4	115	2	3	1^{1}	2^{4}	2^{3}	5^{hd}	7	Valdivia J Jr	8.50

OFF AT 4:16 Start Good . Won driving. Course firm.

TIME :24, :48^{3}, 1:12^{3}, 1:36^{1}, 1:47^{4} (:24.16, :48.69, 1:12.70, 1:36.38, 1:47.81)

$2 Mutuel Prices:				
	3 – THEATER R. N.	13.80	7.60	4.40
	5 – LOTS OF HOPE–BRZ		6.00	3.20
	4 – GOOD STUDENT–ARG			2.80

$1 EXACTA 3–5 PAID $25.80 $2 QUINELLA 3–5 PAID $22.20
$1 TRIFECTA 3–5–4 PAID $100.00 $1 SUPERFECTA 3–5–4–8 PAID $275.50

Ch. f, (Mar), by Theatrical–Ire – Yokama , by Irish River–Fr . Trainer Frankel Robert. Bred by Allen E Paulson (Ky).

THEATER R. N. broke a bit slowly, saved ground off the pace, came out in upper stretch and rallied gamely under urging to get up three deep on the line. LOTS OF HOPE (BRZ) angled in and chased inside, moved up along the rail on the second turn, came out into the stretch, bid outside GOOD STUDENT past midstretch, put a head in front in deep stretch and was caught between foes late. GOOD STUDENT (ARG) stalked off the rail then bid outside a rival on the backstretch, kicked clear and angled in, opened up into the second turn, fought back through the final furlong and continued willingly to the wire. MISS LOREN (ARG) was in a good position stalking the pace outside a rival then off the rail to the stretch and had a mild bid in the drive. URAIB (IRE) saved ground off the pace, came out into the stretch and lacked the needed rally. NAVAJA (NZ) chased outside then alongside a foe, came three deep into the stretch and could not summon the needed late kick. FENCELINENEIGHBOR pulled her way to the early lead, drifted out a bit into the first turn then angled in, stalked a bit off the rail on the backstretch, lugged out into and out of the second turn and weakened.

Owners– 1, Pegasus Thoroughbred Training Center LLC; 2, T N T Stud; 3, Zetcher Arnold; 4, Llers Corporation; 5, Charles Ronald L and Clear Valley Stables; 6, Cooperstone Martin Doll Ford et al; 7, Amerman Racing Stables LLC

Trainers– 1, Frankel Robert; 2, Frankel Robert; 3, McAnally Ronald; 4, Seglin Luis E; 5, Shulman Sanford; 6, Stein Roger M; 7, Machowsky Michael

Scratched– Hoh Buzzard (IRE) (02Oct04 ^{4}SA ^{6})

$2 Daily Double (7–3) Paid $75.80 ; Daily Double Pool $27,532 .
$1 Pick Three (1–7–3) Paid $328.50 ; Pick Three Pool $59,236 .

SIXTH RACE
Aqueduct
NOVEMBER 2, 2004

1 MILE. (1.32^{2}) 29TH RUNNING OF THE TEMPTED. Grade III. Purse $100,000 (Up To $19,000 NYSBFOA) FOR FILLIES TWO YEARS OLD. By subscription of $100 each, which should accompany the nomination; $500 to pass the entry box; $500 to start, with $100,000 added. The added money and all fees to be divided 60% to the winner, 20% to second, 10% to third, 5% to fourth, 3% to fifth and 2% divided equally among remaining finishers. 121 lbs. Non–winners of $50,000 allowed 2 lbs.; two races, 4 lbs.; a race, 6 lbs. (Maiden and claiming races not considered). A trophy will be presented to the winning owner. ClosedSaturday, October 16, 2004 with 16 Nominations.

Value of Race: $104,600 Winner $63,960; second $21,320; third $10,726; fourth $5,396; fifth $3,198. Mutuel Pool $187,085.00 Exacta Pool $195,950.00 Trifecta Pool $90,371.00

Last Raced	Horse	M/Eqt.	A.	Wt	PP	St	¼	½	¾	Str	Fin	Jockey	Odds $1
17Oct04 ^{8}Bel^{3}	Summer Raven	L f	2	115	4	1	1½	1½	1½	1^{2½}	1^{2}	Elliott S	6.60
29Oct04 ^{4}Aqu^{3}	K. D.'s Shady Lady	L	2	115	2	2	3½	4^{2½}	3^{2}	3^{3½}	2^{2¼}	Prado E S	6.30
8Oct04 ^{4}Bel^{1}	Salute	L	2	115	5	4	2^{1½}	2^{1½}	2^{1½}	2^{hd}	3^{5}	Velazquez J R	0.55
3Oct04 ^{5}Bel^{1}	Winsome		2	115	1	5	4^{hd}	3^{hd}	4^{7}	4^{10}	4^{16}	Chavez J F	3.80
29Sep04 ^{6}Bel^{4}	Hide and Chic	L	2	115	3	3	5	5	5	5	5	Castellano J J	15.50

OFF AT 2:48 Start Good . Won driving. Track fast.

TIME :23^{1}, :46^{1}, 1:10^{1}, 1:36 (:23.37, :46.30, 1:10.28, 1:36.09)

$2 Mutuel Prices:				
	4 – SUMMER RAVEN	15.20	6.40	2.60
	2 – K. D.'S SHADY LADY		6.90	2.60
	5 – SALUTE			2.10

$2 EXACTA 4–2 PAID $87.00 $2 TRIFECTA 4–2–5 PAID $147.00

B. f, (Feb), by Summer Squall – Rahy Rose , by Rahy . Trainer Pletcher Todd A. Bred by Mt Brilliant Farm LLC (Ky).

SUMMER RAVEN was hustled to the front, set the pace along the inside, responded when roused in upper stretch, drew clear and remained clear under a steady drive. K. D.'S SHADY LADY raced close up early, rallied three wide approaching the stretch and finished gamely outside. SALUTE pressed the pace from the outside and weakened in the stretch. WINSOME raced in hand along the inside and had no response when roused. HIDE AND CHIC was hustled along inside and tired.

Owners– 1, Edgewood Farm; 2, Goldfarb Sanford J Dubb Michael Gargano Carmen Joscelyn Robert; 3, Phipps Ogden Mills et al; 4, Clay Robert Nand Cowan Irving M and Marjorie; 5, Live Oak Plantation

Trainers– 1, Pletcher Todd A; 2, Dutrow Richard E Jr; 3, McGaughey III Claude R; 4, Jerkens H Allen; 5, Mott William I

$2 Pick Three (11–5–4) Paid $106.00 ; Pick Three Pool $42,459 .

EIGHTH RACE
Aqueduct
NOVEMBER 2, 2004

1 MILE. (1.32²) 29TH RUNNING OF THE NASHUA. Grade III. Purse $100,000 (Up To $19,000 NYSBFOA) FOR TWO YEAR OLDS. By subscription of $100 each, which should accompany the nomination; $500 to pass the entry box; $500 to start, with $100,000 added. The added money and all fees to be divided 60% to the winner, 20% to second, 10% to third, 5% to fourth, 3% to fifth and 2% divided equally among remaining finishers. 122 lbs. Non-winners of $50,000 allowed 2 lbs.; two races, 4 lbs.; a race 6 lbs. (Maiden and claiming races not considered). A trophy will be presented to the winning owner. Closed Saturday, October 16, 2004 with 30 Nominations.

Value of Race: $109,500 Winner $65,700; second $21,900; third $10,950; fourth $5,475; fifth $3,285; sixth $2,190. Mutuel Pool $275,735.00 Exacta Pool $265,736.00 Trifecta Pool $166,183.00

Last Raced	Horse	M/Eqt.	A.	Wt	PP	St	¼	½	¾	Str	Fin	Jockey	Odds $1
12Oct04 9Pha1	Rockport Harbor	L	2	118	3	5	1hd	1 1½	1½	1 5½	1 6¼	Elliott S	0.90
2Oct04 3Bel1	Defer		2	116	6	3	3½	3½	2 2	2 1	2hd	Castellano J J	3.50
17Oct04 7Bel2	Better Than Bonds	L b	2	116	2	4	5hd	5hd	4hd	3hd	3 2¼	Velasquez C	3.50
15Oct04 7Med3	Doctor Voodoo	L b	2	120	4	1	4hd	6	3½	4 2½	4 4¼	Coa E M	10.40
11Sep04 6Bel1	Reverberate	L	2	116	1	6	6	4½	5 7	5 8	5 11	Prado E S	12.20
15Oct04 7Med1	Favalora	L f	2	118	5	2	2½	2hd	6	6	6	Vega H	25.75

OFF AT 3:44 Start Good. Won handily. Track fast.
TIME :22⁴, :45², 1:10, 1:36³ (:22.88, :45.50, 1:10.18, 1:36.67)

$2 Mutuel Prices:				
	3 – ROCKPORT HARBOR	3.80	2.50	2.30
	7 – DEFER		3.40	2.80
	2 – BETTER THAN BONDS			2.60

$2 EXACTA 3–7 PAID $14.00 $2 TRIFECTA 3–7–2 PAID $29.40

Gr/ro. c, (Apr), by Unbridled's Song – Regal Miss Copelan , by Copelan . Trainer Servis John C. Bred by Heiligbrodt Racing Stable & Taylor Made Farm Inc (Ky).

ROCKPORT HARBOR quickly showed in front, soon opened a clear lead, drew away on his own courage and was in hand through the final furlong. DEFER raced close up outside, put in a three wide run on the turn, could not get by the winner and continued on to hold the place. BETTER THAN BONDS was rated along early, raced three wide on the turn and finished well outside. DOCTOR VOODOO was bumped at the start, was rated along between rivals, put in a four wide run on the turn and tired in the final furlong. REVERBERATE broke awkwardly, chased the pace along the inside and tired in the stretch. FAVALORA was bumped at the start, raced with the pace while between rivals and tired after a half mile.

Owners– 1, Fox Hill Farms Inc; 2, Phipps Ogden M; 3, Abbo Robert D; 4, Kligman Joel A; 5, Centennial Farms; 6, Campbell Gilbert G

Trainers– 1, Servis John C; 2, McGaughey III Claude R; 3, Reinacher Robert Jr; 4, Ryerson James T; 5, Russo Sal; 6, Allard Edward T

Scratched– All Trumps (09Oct04 7Bel8)

EIGHTH RACE
Aqueduct
NOVEMBER 6, 2004

1½ MILES. (Turf) (2.27) 48TH RUNNING OF THE LONG ISLAND HANDICAP. Grade II. Purse $150,000 (UP TO $28,500 NYSBFOA) A HANDICAP FOR FILLIES AND MARES THREE YEARS OLD AND UPWARD. By subscription of $150 each, which should accompany the nomination; $750 to pass the entry box; $750 to start. The purse to be divided 60% to the winner, 20% to second,10% to third, 5% to fourth, 3% to fifth and 2% divided equally among remaining finishers. A trophy will be presented to the winning owner. The New York Racing Association reserves the right to transfer this race to the Main Track. In the event that thisrace is taken off the turf, it may be subject to downgrading by the Graded Stakes Committee. Closed Saturday, October 23, 2004 with 26 Nominations. (If the Stewards consider it inadvisable to run this race on the turf course, this race will be run at OneMile and One Quarter onthe main track.).

Value of Race: $150,000 Winner $90,000; second $30,000; third $15,000; fourth $7,500; fifth $4,500; sixth $1,500; seventh $1,500. Mutuel Pool $401,945.00 Exacta Pool $314,930.00 Trifecta Pool $224,461.00

Last Raced	Horse	M/Eqt.	A.	Wt	PP	¼	½	1	1¼	Str	Fin	Jockey	Odds $1
1Oct04 CHY1	Eleusis		3	115	3	3 1	3½	3 1½	3½	2 2½	1 2¼	Santos J A	a- 1.65
24Oct04 8Kee3	Literacy	L	4	114	1	5½	6½	5hd	4 1½	3½	2½	Prado E S	16.70
5Sep04 10Sar1	Arvada-GB	L	4	117	6	2 2½	2 1	2½	2 1½	1½	3 1¾	Velazquez J R	1.35
5Sep04 7Sar3	Savedbythelight	L b	4	117	4	7	7	7	5½	4 1	4 4½	Bailey J D	4.70
10Oct04 1Mil1	Noble Stella-Ger		3	114	7	4½	4½	6hd	7	7	5 3	Velasquez C	a- 1.65
24Oct04 4Bel1	Belles Lettres	L b	5	113	2	1½	1½	1½	1hd	5 2	6hd	Espinoza J L	21.90
18Oct04 TOU1	Briviesca-GB	L	3	111	5	6½	5hd	4½	6 5	6 1½	7	Chavez J F	9.40

a-Coupled: Eleusis and Noble Stella-Ger.

OFF AT 3:37 Start Good. Won driving. Course good.
TIME :24, :50¹, 1:16, 1:40⁴, 2:05³, 2:31² (:24.10, :50.35, 1:16.03, 1:40.91, 2:05.68, 2:31.51)

$2 Mutuel Prices:				
	1 – ELEUSIS(a–entry)	5.30	3.00	2.10
	2 – LITERACY		9.00	3.20
	7 – ARVADA–GB			2.20

$2 EXACTA 1–2 PAID $54.00 $2 TRIFECTA 1–2–7 PAID $118.00

B. f, (Mar), by Diesis–GB – Balancing Act , by Spectacular Bid . Trainer Rouget Jean–Claude. Bred by Nancy S Dillman (Ky).

ELEUSIS was rated along, saved ground throughout, angled out in the stretch, responded when roused and drew clear. LITERACY was rated along inside, saved ground, came wide into the stretch and finished gamely outside. ARVADA (GB) prompted the pace from the outside and weakened along the inside in the final furlong. SAVEDBYTHELIGHT was outrun early, rallied on the final turn and stayed on well to the wire. NOBLE STELLA (GER) was rated along between rivals and lacked a rally. BELLES LETTRES set the pace along the inside and tired in the stretch. BRIVIESCA (GB) raced three wide and tired.

Owners– 1, Tanaka Gary A; 2, Goodman Gerald and Pregman Jr John S; 3, Gordon Giles Pritchard; 4, Mack Earle I; 5, Tanaka Gary A; 6, Robbins William G; 7, Darpat SL Stables

Trainers– 1, Rouget Jean-Claude; 2, Pregman John S Jr; 3, Frankel Robert; 4, Violette Richard A Jr; 5, Attfield Roger L; 6, Carroll Del W II; 7, Laffon-Parias Carlos

Scratched– Primetimevalentine (10Oct04 8Bel2) , Bounding Charm (19Sep04 9Bel5)

$2 Pick Three (5–2–1) Paid $176.50 ; Pick Three Pool $76,962 .

NINTH RACE
Aqueduct
NOVEMBER 6, 2004

1⅛ MILES. (1.47) 18TH RUNNING OF THE TURNBACK THE ALARM HANDICAP. Grade III. Purse $100,000 (UP TO $19,000 NYSBFOA) A HANDICAP FOR FILLIES AND MARES THREE YEARS OLD AND UPWARD. By subscription of $100 each, which should accompany the nomination; $500 to pass the entry box; $500 to start, with $100,000 added. The added money and all fees to be divided 60% to the winner, 20% to second, 10% to third, 5% to fourth, 3% to fifth and 2% divided equally among remaining finishers. A trophy will be presented to the winning owner. Closed Saturday, October 23, 2004 with 17 Nominations.

Value of Race: $110,700 Winner $66,420; second $22,140; third $11,070; fourth $5,535; fifth $3,321; sixth $554; seventh $554; eighth $554; ninth $552. Mutuel Pool $441,225.00 Exacta Pool $380,594.00 Trifecta Pool $268,376.00

Last Raced	Horse	M/Eqt.	A.	Wt	PP	St	¼	½	¾	Str	Fin	Jockey	Odds $1
25Sep04 ^{9}Bel^{7}	Personal Legend	L b	4	115	1	7	6^{1}	$5^{\frac{1}{2}}$	$6^{\frac{1}{2}}$	$2^{\frac{1}{2}}$	$1^{\frac{1}{2}}$	Bailey J D	3.95
27Aug04 ^{9}Sar^{5}	Roar Emotion	L	4	117	7	6	$3^{\frac{1}{2}}$	3^{hd}	$3^{\frac{1}{2}}$	$1^{\frac{1}{2}}$	$2^{4\frac{3}{4}}$	Velazquez J R	7.10
22Oct04 ^{8}Med^{6}	Fast Cookie	L	4	114	4	5	4^{1}	4^{1}	2^{hd}	$3^{\frac{1}{2}}$	3^{2}	Velasquez C	11.50
1Oct04 ^{9}Hoo^{2}	Capeside Lady	L	3	117	2	3	$1^{\frac{1}{2}}$	$1^{\frac{1}{2}}$	1^{hd}	$4^{4\frac{1}{2}}$	$4^{1\frac{1}{4}}$	Decarlo C P	2.60
30Sep04 ^{3}Bel^{2}	Cloakof Vagueness	L	4	114	9	9	$8^{2\frac{1}{2}}$	7^{hd}	$8^{1\frac{1}{2}}$	5^{1}	$5^{1\frac{3}{4}}$	Prado E S	10.30
27Sep04 ^{8}Del^{2}	Misty Sixes	L	6	116	3	2	$2^{\frac{1}{2}}$	$2^{\frac{1}{2}}$	$4^{\frac{1}{2}}$	$8^{1\frac{1}{2}}$	6no	Arroyo N Jr	23.40
11Oct04 ^{9}Bel^{1}	Fortunate Damsel	L	3	112	8	1	$5^{\frac{1}{2}}$	6^{hd}	7^{hd}	$7^{\frac{1}{2}}$	7^{1}	Castellano J J	27.50
9Oct04 ^{9}Bel^{5}	Nevermore	L	4	115	6	8	9	9	9	9	$8^{\frac{3}{4}}$	Fragoso P	4.70
19Sep04 ^{9}Bel^{2}	Pocus Hocus	L b	6	116	5	4	$7^{\frac{1}{2}}$	$8^{1\frac{1}{2}}$	5^{hd}	6^{hd}	9	Santos J A	5.90

OFF AT 4:05 Start Good . Won driving. Track fast.

TIME :24^{1}, :48^{4}, 1:13, 1:38^{1}, 1:51^{1} (:24.36, :48.88, 1:13.14, 1:38.33, 1:51.27)

$2 Mutuel Prices:				
	1 – PERSONAL LEGEND	9.90	5.90	3.90
	7 – ROAR EMOTION		9.00	5.00
	4 – FAST COOKIE			6.80

$2 EXACTA 1–7 PAID $64.00 $2 TRIFECTA 1 7 4 PAID $440.50

Ch. f, (Jan), by Awesome Again – Highland Legend , by Storm Bird . Trainer Frankel Robert. Bred by G Watts Humphrey Jr & Louise I Humphrey (Ky).

PERSONAL LEGEND was rated along inside, came wide into the stretch, dug in gamely when roused and prevailed after a long drive. ROAR EMOTION raced with the pace while three wide on the first turn, rallied four wide on the second turn and dug in gamely to the finish. FAST COOKIE raced close up early along the inside and lacked a rally. CAPESIDE LADY quickly showed in front, set the pace along the inside and tired in the final furlong. CLOAKOF VAGUENESS was outrun early, advanced inside on the backstretch and weakened in the stretch. MISTY SIXES pressed the pace while three wide and tired after three quarters. FORTUNATE DAMSEL stumbled at the start, raced three wide and tired in the stretch. NEVERMORE was outrun early, came wide into the stretch and had no rally. POCUS HOCUS was rated outside, put in a five wide run on the second turn and tired in the stretch.

Owners– 1, Gann Edmund A; 2, Allen Joseph; 3, Stonerside Stable LLC; 4, So Madcapt Stable; 5, Duncker C Steven; 6, Puglisi Stables; 7, Spruce Pond Stable; 8, Clifton William L Jr; 9, Moore Susan and John

Trainers– 1, Frankel Robert; 2, McLaughlin Kiaran P; 3, Mott William I; 4, Pletcher Todd A; 5, Hauswald Philip M; 6, Klesaris Steve; 7, Cedano Heriberto; 8, Bond Harold James; 9, Jerkens James A

EIGHTH RACE
Bay Meadows
NOVEMBER 6, 2004

ABOUT 1⅛ MILES. (Turf) (1.45^{1}) 29TH RUNNING OF THE BAY MEADOWS DERBY. Grade III. Purse $100,000 FOR THREE–YEAR–OLDS. By subscription of $100 each to accompany the nomination or by supplementary nomination of $2,000 by Noon, Sunday, October 31, 2004. $500 to pass the entry box and $500 additional to start with $100,000 Guaranteed of which $55,000 to the winner, $20,000 to second, $15,000 to third, $7,500 to fourth and $2,500 to fifth. A trophy will be presented to the owner of the winner. High weights preferred. Closed Thursday, October 28, 2004 with 14 nominations.

Value of Race: $100,000 Winner $55,000; second $20,000; third $15,000; fourth $7,500; fifth $2,500. Mutuel Pool $241,652.00 Exacta Pool $134,362.00 Quinella Pool $12,037.00 Trifecta Pool $165,035.00 Superfecta Pool $78,365.00

Last Raced	Horse	M/Eqt.	A.	Wt	PP	St	¼	½	¾	Str	Fin	Jockey	Odds $1
20Oct04 ^{4}BM^{2}	Congressionalhonor	LB b	3	115	8	1	$5^{2\frac{1}{2}}$	5^{2}	$6^{1\frac{1}{2}}$	6^{6}	$1^{2\frac{1}{4}}$	Baze R A	9.20
20Oct04 ^{4}BM^{1}	Talaris	LB b	3	116	7	2	1^{hd}	1^{2}	$1^{\frac{1}{2}}$	1^{1}	2no	Carr D	20.80
17Oct04 ^{8}SA^{3}	[D]Hendrix	LB b	3	117	2	4	$4^{\frac{1}{2}}$	4^{3}	4^{4}	4^{hd}	3no	Gomez G K	1.30
17Oct04 ^{8}SA^{7}	On the Acorn-GB	LB	3	116	1	7	$7^{\frac{1}{2}}$	6^{2}	5^{hd}	5^{1}	$4^{1\frac{1}{2}}$	Lopez A D	3.60
10Oct04 ^{7}Hst^{2}	Rules of War	LB b	3	116	5	6	6^{1}	8	8	8	$5^{\frac{1}{2}}$	Alvarado F T	49.80
3Oct04 ^{3}BM^{1}	New Course	LB b	3	110	6	8	8	7^{2}	7^{4}	7^{1}	6^{nk}	Duran F	59.10
16Oct04 ^{8}BM^{1}	Kingdom Come-Ire	LB	3	116	4	5	$3^{\frac{1}{2}}$	3^{1}	3^{2}	$3^{\frac{1}{2}}$	7^{1}	Gonzalez R M	2.50
10Oct04 ^{7}SA^{4}	Big Squeeze	LB bf	3	116	3	3	2^{1}	2^{1}	$2^{\frac{1}{2}}$	2^{hd}	8	John K	11.30

[D] – Hendrix disqualified and placed 8th

OFF AT 4:21 Start Good . Won driving. Course yielding.

TIME :23^{1}, :47^{1}, 1:11^{4}, 1:38, 1:48^{4} (:23.38, :47.20, 1:11.91, 1:38.07, 1:48.92)

$2 Mutuel Prices:				
	8 – CONGRESSIONALHONOR	20.40	8.60	4.40
	7 – TALARIS		19.80	11.20
	1 – ON THE ACORN–GB			4.20

$1 EXACTA 8–7 PAID $85.70 $2 QUINELLA 7–8 PAID $74.20
$1 TRIFECTA 8–7–1 PAID $452.90 $1 SUPERFECTA 8–7–1–5 PAID $4,781.40

Gr/ro. c, (Apr), by Forestry – Quiet Dance , by Quiet American . Trainer Hollendorfer Jerry. Bred by Edward P Evans (Ky).

CONGRESSIONALHONOR was permitted to settle early while three wide to the backstretch, remained unhurried to the second turn, quickly circled rivals four wide into the stretch, took command leaving the furlong pole and drew driving. TALARIS set a pressured pace from the rail throughout, responded in the stretch but could not stall the winner. HENDRIX tracked the leaders from the inside early, remained directly behind the leaders on the second turn under stout restraint and blocked, forced his way through tight quarters leaving the furlong pole, bumped repeatedly BIG SQUEEZE, forcing that rival into KINGDOM COME, finally got through the opening then closed willingly. ON THE ACORN (GB) was not asked for speed early from the rail, moved closer on the second turn from the inside, was put in tight quarters trying to get through inside HENDRIX at the furlong pole and remained blocked to the finish. RULES OF WAR lagged early, raced two wide throughout and closed late. NEW COURSE was void of early speed, raced three wide to the stretch and closed a gap late. KINGDOM COME (IRE) stalked the pace two wide early, eased out three wide on the second turn while challenging for command, was bumped repeatedly in the stretch by BIG SQUEEZE and faltered. BIG SQUEEZE pressed the pace from the inside, moved two wide to challenge on the second turn then was bumped off stride repeatedly leaving the furlong pole by HENDRIX. Following a stewards inquiry, HENDRIX was disqualified from third and placed last.

Owners– 1, Rancho San Miguel Anderson Norma Hollendorfer Jerry et al; 2, Jeffin Racing LLC; 3, Reddam J Paul; 4, Cassidy or Jim Ford Inc or Pearson; 5, Gilker Rob; 6, Alberts Lon and Connors James M; 7, Strauss Richard and Williford Ward; 8, Everest Stables Inc

Trainers– 1, Hollendorfer Jerry; 2, Gallagher Patrick; 3, Dollase Craig; 4, Cassidy James; 5, McLean Bill; 6, Peery Chuck; 7, Gallagher Patrick; 8, Polanco Marcelo

---

$2 Daily Double (2–8) Paid $109.80 ; Daily Double Pool $12,196 .
$1 Pick Three (8–2–8) Paid $151.30 ; Pick Three Pool $21,184 .

TENTH RACE
Churchill
NOVEMBER 6, 2004

1 MILE. (1.33^{2}) 23RD RUNNING OF THE IROQUOIS. Grade III. Purse $100,000 FOR TWO YEAR OLDS. By subscription of $100 each on or before October 23, 2004 or by supplementary nomination of $5,000 each at time of entry. $500 to pass the entry box; $500 additional to start, with $100,000 added of which 62% of all monies to the owner of the winner, 20% to second, 10% to third, 5% to fourth and 3% to fifth. Weight 122 lbs. Non–winners of a sweepstakes allowed 2 lbs.; two races other than claiming, 4 lbs.; a race other than claiming 6 lbs. Starters to be named through the entry box by the usual time of closing. Trophy to winning owner. Closed Saturday, October 23, 2004 with 26 nominations.

Value of Race: $109,600 Winner $67,952; second $21,920; third $10,960; fourth $5,480; fifth $3,288. Mutuel Pool $403,047.00 Exacta Pool $280,895.00 Trifecta Pool $219,219.00 Superfecta Pool $63,763.00

Last Raced	Horse	M/Eqt.	A.	Wt	PP	St	¼	½	¾	Str	Fin	Jockey	Odds $1
9Oct04 ^{7}Kee^{4}	Straight Line		2	122	2	1	$4^{1\frac{1}{2}}$	2^{hd}	1^{hd}	1^{2}	1^{5}	Blanc B	2.20
22Aug04 ^{9}ElP^{4}	Social Probation	L	2	120	1	7	6^{4}	$3^{\frac{1}{2}}$	4^{hd}	2^{hd}	2^{2}	Borel C H	5.10
18Sep04 ^{10}TP^{1}	Greater Good	L	2	122	5	6	7	7	6	$4^{2\frac{1}{2}}$	$3^{1\frac{3}{4}}$	McKee J	2.30
15Oct04 ^{10}Kee^{1}	Chief Commander	L	2	118	6	4	3^{1}	$5^{1\frac{1}{2}}$	2^{2}	3^{3}	$4^{6\frac{1}{4}}$	Bejarano R	7.40
15Oct04 ^{6}Kee^{1}	Highgrove	L	2	118	7	5	2^{hd}	$4^{1\frac{1}{2}}$	$3^{\frac{1}{2}}$	$5^{3\frac{1}{2}}$	5^{6}	Day P	3.20
21Oct04 ^{3}Kee^{1}	Can't Trick Jake	L b	2	118	3	3	1^{hd}	1^{1}	5^{5}	6	6	Hernandez B J Jr	20.70
14Oct04 ^{6}Kee^{7}	Norainonthisparty		2	116	4	2	$5^{\frac{1}{2}}$	6^{4}	—	—	—	Krigger K	44.90

OFF AT 5:01 Start Good. Won driving. Track fast.

TIME :22^{3}, :45^{3}, 1:10^{4}, 1:23^{3}, 1:36^{3} (:22.63, :45.65, 1:10.96, 1:23.68, 1:36.62)

$2 Mutuel Prices:			
2 – STRAIGHT LINE	6.40	3.80	3.00
1 – SOCIAL PROBATION		5.40	3.40
5 – GREATER GOOD			2.40

$2 EXACTA 2–1 PAID $26.40 $2 TRIFECTA 2–1–5 PAID $53.40
$1 SUPERFECTA 2–1–5–6 PAID $210.80

Dk. b or br. c, (May), by Boundary – Zanti, by Strawberry Road–Aus. Trainer Vanier Harvey L. Bred by R Alex Rankin & Louis Wright (Ky).

STRAIGHT LINE eased out three or four wide on the backstretch to track the pace in hand, inched to challenge front-running CAN'T TRICK JAKE on the turn, reached the front approaching the stretch, repelled a challenge from CHIEF COMMANDER entering the lane, then moved clear under energetic hand urging. SOCIAL PROBATION, unhurried early but never far back, edged up along the inside leaving the backstretch, moved between foes into the lane, angled four or five wide and was second best. GREATER GOOD, bumped at the start by CHIEF COMMANDER, was outrun four or five wide to the turn, was put to a drive three furlongs out, was forced to steady nearing the quarter-mile ground to avoid NORAINONTHISPARTY when that one fell, hurdled the fallen rider, bobbled, came to the outside, swerved a bit in the final furlong and improved position. CHIEF COMMANDER leaned in at the start bumping GREATER GOOD, was never far back while three ore four wide, moved after the winner nearing the lane, gained about even terms for the drive but flattened out. HIGHGROVE went up early to vie for the lead four or five wide, remained a factor when bumped by NORAINONTHISPARTY in tight at the quarter-mile ground, then weakened in the drive. CAN'T TRICK JAKE gained a slim lead early while three or four wide, lost the edge to the winner approaching the stretch and tired. NORAINONTHISPARTY, never far back while racing under light restraint three or four wide, was attempting to advance in tight quarters between SOCIAL PROBATION and HIGHGROVE approaching the quarter-mile ground when he appeared to lose his action and fell.

Owners– 1, Vanier Nancy A and Cartwright Thoroughbreds LLC; 2, Old School Stable; 3, Lakin Lewis G; 4, Farmer Tracy; 5, Farmer Tracy; 6, Robert S Mitchell Trust; 7, Lawrence Leslie

Trainers– 1, Vanier Harvey L; 2, Nafzger Carl A; 3, Holthus Robert E; 4, Zito Nicholas P; 5, Zito Nicholas P; 6, Morse Randy L; 7, Stidham Susan

$2 Pick Three (8–4–2) Paid $100.80 ; Pick Three Pool $37,533.

TENTH RACE
Churchill
NOVEMBER 7, 2004

1 MILE. (1.33^{2}) 19TH RUNNING OF THE CHURCHILL DOWNS DISTAFF HANDICAP. Grade II. Purse $200,000 FOR FILLIES AND MARES, THREE-YEAR-OLDS AND UPWARD. By subscription of $200 each on or before October 23, 2004 or by supplementary nomination of $10,000 each by the close of entries on Friday, October 29, 2004. $1,000 to pass the entry box; $1,000 additional to start, with $200,000 added of which 62% of all monies to the owner of the winner, 20% to second, 10% to third, 5% to fourth and 3% to fifth. Weights to be announced Saturday, October 30. Starters to be named through the entry box by the usual time of closing. Trophy to winning owner. Closed Saturday, October 23, 2004 with 32 nominations.

Value of Race: $230,400 Winner $142,848; second $46,080; third $23,040; fourth $11,520; fifth $6,912. Mutuel Pool $432,306.00 Exacta Pool $298,637.00 Trifecta Pool $252,587.00 Superfecta Pool $90,792.00

Last Raced	Horse	M/Eqt.	A.	Wt	PP	St	¼	½	¾	Str	Fin	Jockey	Odds $1
10Oct04 ^{5}Kee^{1}	Halory Leigh	L	4	115	11	8	10½	9$1\frac{1}{2}$	7^{3}	2^{hd}	1^{5}	Perret C	14.60
10Oct04 ^{9}Bel^{1}	Lady Tak	L	4	123	3	2	2^{1}	1½	1½	1^{2}	2¾	Velazquez J R	1.30
18Sep04 ^{12}TP^{1}	Susan's Angel	L	3	115	1	11	5$1\frac{1}{2}$	4½	2^{1}	3$1\frac{1}{2}$	3¾	Bejarano R	18.30
17Oct04 ^{8}Kee^{3}	My Boston Gal	L f	4	116	2	12	7^{hd}	3^{hd}	4^{hd}	4$2\frac{1}{2}$	4^{hd}	Borel C H	14.30
16Oct04 ^{8}Kee^{7}	Island Sand	L b	3	119	12	6	6^{hd}	7^{1}	6$1\frac{1}{2}$	5^{2}	5$1\frac{1}{2}$	Shepherd J	6.00
10Oct04 ^{8}Kee^{3}	Mayo On the Side	L bf	5	118	10	7	9^{hd}	10½	8^{hd}	6^{1}	6^{3}	Albarado R J	4.80
17Oct04 ^{8}Kee^{2}	My Trusty Cat	L bf	4	118	6	4	4^{hd}	6½	5^{hd}	7^{2}	7$1\frac{1}{2}$	Day P	4.40
10Oct04 ^{5}Kee^{3}	There Runs Hattie	L b	5	113	8	9	12	12	11$1\frac{1}{2}$	8^{1}	8no	Martinez W	121.10
10Oct04 ^{9}Wds^{1}	Wildwood Royal	L bf	4	115	5	3	3½	5½	9^{1}	10½	9$2\frac{1}{2}$	Guidry M	28.60
18Sep04 ^{12}TP^{4}	Miss Fortunate	L	4	115	7	5	8$2\frac{1}{2}$	8^{hd}	10^{1}	11½	10$1\frac{3}{4}$	Peck B D	51.10
10Oct04 ^{8}Kee^{5}	La Reason	L f	4	114	9	10	11^{2}	11^{3}	12	9½	11$1\frac{1}{2}$	Melancon L	79.10
16Oct04 ^{9}Kee^{1}	Revolutionary Act	L	4	111	4	1	1½	2$1\frac{1}{2}$	3^{hd}	12	12	Blanc B	61.10

OFF AT 5:07 Start Good. Won driving. Track fast.

TIME :22^{3}, :45^{3}, 1:10^{2}, 1:22^{3}, 1:35 (:22.64, :45.60, 1:10.40, 1:22.70, 1:35.05)

$2 Mutuel Prices:			
11 – HALORY LEIGH	31.20	8.80	7.00
3 – LADY TAK		3.20	3.00
1 – SUSAN'S ANGEL			8.40

$2 EXACTA 11-3 PAID $115.80 $2 TRIFECTA 11-3-1 PAID $1,192.80
$1 SUPERFECTA 11-3-1-2 PAID $5,657.00

Ch. f, (Feb), by Halory Hunter – Graceful Leigh, by Clever Trick. Trainer Romans Dale. Bred by Al Profitt & Larry Demeritte (Ky).

HALORY LEIGH, unhurried early, moved closer on the turn while between foes four wide, angled five or six wide for the drive, took over a sixteenth out and drew off under strong handling. LADY TAK contested the pace from early on while near the inside, took over before going a half, opened a clear advantage in the upper stretch but wasn't a match for the winner late. SUSAN'S ANGEL eased off the inside early to gain a striking position four wide, loomed a solid threat into the final furlong but came up empty. MY BOSTON GAL, well placed near the inside throughout, failed to rally. ISLAND SAND, hung seven or eight wide during the early going, edged in five wide on the turn, came out again to be six or seven wide for the drive and lacked a closing bid. MAYO ON THE SIDE, unhurried early, raced in behind horses, edged up between foes four or five wide on the turn, angled six wide for the drive but failed to fire. MY TRUSTY CAT, bumped at the start, was never far back, raced between foes five wide around the turn and was empty in the drive. THERE RUNS HATTIE, bumped at the start by LA REASON, was outrun five wide to the stretch, came a bit wider for the drive and improved position. WILDWOOD ROYAL, bumped at the start by REVOLUTIONARY ACT and forced out, raced in contention for five furlongs and weakened thereafter. MISS FORTUNATE, bumped at the start by MY TRUSTY CAT, tired leaving the backstretch. LA REASON leaned in at the break bumping THERE RUNS HATTIE, angled inside soon after and never was prominent. REVOLUTIONARY ACT came out at the start bumping WILDWOOD ROYAL, forced that one out, went up to gain a slight edge while dueling with LADY TAK, lost the edge to that one before going a half, continued forwardly for six furlongs and faded.

Owners– 1, Crawford Jerry Gannon Matt and Grask Charlie; 2, Heiligbrodt Racing Stable; 3, S Angel Stable; 4, Porter J Chester Bloch Randy and Milner Phil; 5, B A Man Inc; 6, Lothenbach Stables Inc; 7, Pollard Carl F; 8, Markwell Steve and Froedge Samuel; 9, Stiritz William; 10, Lyon Stables; 11, K and K Racing Stable LLC; 12, Casby Camelia J

Trainers– 1, Romans Dale; 2, Asmussen Steven M; 3, Lukas D Wayne; 4, Nafzger Carl A; 5, Jones J Larry; 6, Nafzger Carl A; 7, Vance David R; 8, Huffman William G; 9, Zook Jimmy; 10, Mott William I; 11, Vance David R; 12, Huffman Pat

$2 Pick Three (5-7-11) Paid $1,922.00; Pick Three Pool $37,968.

EIGHTH RACE
Aqueduct
NOVEMBER 13, 2004

1⅛ MILES. (1.47) 54TH RUNNING OF THE STUYVESANT HANDICAP. Grade III. Purse $100,000 (UP TO $19,000 NYSBFOA) A HANDICAP FOR THREE YEAR OLDS AND UPWARD. By subscription of $100 each, which should accompany the nomination; $500 to pass the entry box; $500 to start, with $100,000 added. The added money and all fees to be divided 60% to the winner, 20% to second, 10% to third, 5% to fourth, 3% to fifth and 2% divided equally among remaining finishers. A trophy will be presented to the winning owner. Closed Saturday, October 30, 2004 with 24 Nominations.

Value of Race: $109,900 Winner $65,940; second $21,980; third $10,990; fourth $5,495; fifth $3,297; sixth $1,099; seventh $1,099. Mutuel Pool $568,474.00 Exacta Pool $421,640.00 Trifecta Pool $328,347.00

Last Raced	Horse	M/Eqt.	A.	Wt	PP	St	¼	½	¾	Str	Fin	Jockey	Odds $1
29Sep04 8Bel1	Classic Endeavor	L f	6	114	1	5	11½	1½	12½	13½	11½	Prado E S	3.30
14Oct04 8Bel1	Colita	L bf	4	115	4	3	3½	4hd	5hd	21½	24¼	Bejarano R	2.95
14Oct04 8Bel4	Snake Mountain	L	6	115	7	6	6hd	61	63	31½	3½	Santos J A	7.30
2Oct04 7Del5	Country Be Gold	L	7	114	3	7	7	7	7	5½	42½	Fragoso P	11.80
28Oct04 8Aqu2	Trapped Again	L bf	4	114	2	1	2½	2½	4½	6hd	52¼	Bridgmohan S X	17.20
2Oct04 7Haw7	Powerful Touch	L	4	116	5	4	5hd	5½	31	4hd	63¾	Chavez J F	1.50
23Oct04 10Bel4	Everydayissaturday	L b	3	112	6	2	41	3hd	2hd	7	7	Arroyo N Jr	31.50

OFF AT 3:45 Start Good. Won handily. Track good.

TIME :24^{1}, :48^{3}, 1:12^{4}, 1:37^{1}, 1:49^{3} (:24.26, :48.74, 1:12.86, 1:37.37, 1:49.70)

$2 Mutuel Prices:

1 – CLASSIC ENDEAVOR	8.60	3.80	4.50
4 – COLITA		3.80	3.50
8 – SNAKE MOUNTAIN			5.80

$2 EXACTA 1–4 PAID $28.80 $2 TRIFECTA 1–4–8 PAID $126.00

Dk. b or br. h, (Mar), by Silver Buck – Bold Juana, by John Alden. Trainer Dutrow Richard E Jr. Bred by Diane H Flowers (Fla).

CLASSIC ENDEAVOR soon opened a clear lead, made the pace while well in hand, drew away when ready and cruised home a handy winner. COLITA raced close up along the inside, dropped back into the second turn, rallied three wide approaching the stretch and finished gamely outside. SNAKE MOUNTAIN was rated along early, raced four wide on the second turn and had no response when roused. COUNTRY BE GOLD was outrun early, came wide for the drive and had no rally. TRAPPED AGAIN raced with the pace from the outside and tired after the opening three quarters. POWERFUL TOUCH was rated along outside, raced wide throughout and tired. EVERYDAYISSATURDAY raced close up outside, chased the pace and tired.

Owners– 1, Sullivan Lane Stable Scuderi Vincent and L Hollow Farm; 2, Team Valor Stables LLC; 3, Shelley Jack and Buzas Paul J; 4, Seinfeld Barry and Dodson Elizabeth K; 5, Steeplechase Farm; 6, Stronach Stables; 7, Schwartz Barry K

Trainers– 1, Dutrow Richard E Jr; 2, Pletcher Todd A; 3, Jerkens James A; 4, Nobles Reynaldo H; 5, Gorham Michael E; 6, Frankel Robert; 7, Hushion Michael E

Scratched– Kissin Saint (28Oct04 8Aqu1)

NINTH RACE
Churchill
NOVEMBER 13, 2004

1$\frac{1}{16}$ MILES. (Turf) (1.40^{4}) 14TH RUNNING OF THE MRS. REVERE. Grade II. Purse $150,000 FOR FILLIES, THREE YEARS OLD. By subscription of $150 each on or before October 30, 2004 or by supplementary nomination of $7,500 each at time of entry. $750 to pass the entry box; $750 additional to start. Weights 122 lbs. Grade/Group 1 stakes winners on the turf to carry 2 lbs. additional. Non–winners of $50,000 twice at a mile or over on the turf allowed 2 lbs.; a sweepstakes on the turf, 4 lbs.; $50,000 at a mile or over, 6 lbs.; three races other than maiden or claiming, 8 lbs. (If this race is taken off the turf it will be downgraded one grade level for this running only in accordance with American Graded Stakes Committee policy). Closed October 30, 2004 with 36 nominations.

Value of Race: $171,150 Winner $106,113; second $34,230; third $17,115; fourth $8,558; fifth $5,134. Mutuel Pool $444,860.00 Exacta Pool $239,039.00 Trifecta Pool $311,378.00 Superfecta Pool $130,646.00

Last Raced	Horse	M/Eqt.	A.	Wt	PP	St	¼	½	¾	Str	Fin	Jockey	Odds $1
16Oct04 8Kee3	River Belle-GB	L	3	120	2	8	4½	4hd	4½	21	1no	Fallon K	1.60
23Oct04 9Kee8	Lenatareese	L	3	120	5	7	92	82½	62	51	2no	Melancon L	9.50
24Oct04 9Kee5	Cape Town Lass	L	3	114	9	10	10	10	7hd	32	3½	Sarvis D A	47.90
23Oct04 9Kee1	Sister Swank	L	3	120	10	9	82	5½	52	4½	41¼	Day P	3.00
23Oct04 9Kee2	Jinny's Gold	L	3	116	7	2	51	3½	1½	11½	55	Martin E M Jr	8.30
9Oct04 8WO1	Black Rock Road	L b	3	120	1	5	1hd	1½	21	66	66¼	Blanc B	3.30
23Oct04 9Kee4	Topango	L	3	120	8	6	7hd	7hd	82½	7½	7nk	Krigger K	57.00
20Oct04 6Suf4	Casa Nekia	L f	3	114	6	1	2hd	62	93½	91	81¾	Hernandez B J Jr	130.90
24Oct04 9Kee10	Sahmkindwonderful	L	3	120	4	3	6hd	9hd	10	10	91¼	Coa D	54.20
23Oct04 9Pim1	With Affection	L bf	3	120	3	4	3½	2½	3hd	82	10	Monterrey R	11.60

OFF AT 4:40 Start Good. Won driving. Course good.

TIME :23^{3}, :48^{1}, 1:13^{2}, 1:38^{1}, 1:44^{2} (:23.71, :48.30, 1:13.48, 1:38.30, 1:44.59)

$2 Mutuel Prices:

2 – RIVER BELLE–GB	5.20	3.60	3.00
5 – LENATAREESE		7.60	5.40
9 – CAPE TOWN LASS			9.80

$2 EXACTA 2–5 PAID $49.00 $2 TRIFECTA 2–5–9 PAID $923.80
$1 SUPERFECTA 2–5–9–10 PAID $2,351.60

Ch. f, (Mar), by Lahib – Dixie Favor, by Dixieland Band. Trainer Pletcher Todd A. Bred by Mrs S Camacho (GB).

RIVER BELLE (GB), lightly rated near the inside early, was never far back, angled four wide entering the stretch, was between horses in the late going and proved gamely best under strong handling. LENATAREESE, unhurried early while in behind horses four or five wide, came out seven wide for the drive, loomed boldly through deep stretch and missed. CAPE TOWN LASS, outrun for a half while near the inside, continued near the inside around the far turn, came out between four wide entering the stretch, angled to the hedge in deep stretch, bumped with a tiring BLACK ROCK ROAD, reached the front briefly, then was outfinished. SISTER SWANK, rated between foes early and four wide, advanced five wide into the stretch, was prominent in deep stretch but gained only slightly. JINNY'S GOLD, never far back while following the leaders four or five wide, took over on the far turn, managed a clear advantage into the final furlong and faltered. BLACK ROCK ROAD contested the pace inside from early on, held on well until the final quarter, weakened in the drive and was bumped in deep stretch by CAPE TOWN LASS. TOPANGO, near the inside, failed to rally. CASA NEKIA forced the pace around the first turn while three abreast and couldn't keep pace after going a half. SAHMKINDAWONDERFUL tired midway on the backstretch. WITH AFFECTION, close up between foes early while attending the pace, continued in a striking position for six furlongs and weakened thereafter.

Owners– 1, Team Valor Stables Heiligbrodt Racing Stable and Green Lantern StablesLLC; 2, Anderson Brad; 3, Ralls and Foster LLC Raleigh Ralls and Dennis Foster and Richard Banas; 4, Heiligbrodt Racing Stable; 5, Kaster Richard S and Wieting Frederick C; 6, Melnyk Eugene and Laura; 7, H S B Racing; 8, Gray Dennis; 9, Dare To Dream Stable LLC; 10, Bailey Morris

Trainers– 1, Pletcher Todd A; 2, Carroll David; 3, McGee Paul J; 4, Asmussen Steven M; 5, Fox Jamie; 6, Bell David R; 7, Locke John G; 8, Gray Dennis; 9, Maker Rebecca; 10, Gaudet Edmond D

Scratched– Family Business (23Oct04 3Kee2)

$2 Pick Three (10–4–2) Paid $440.80; Pick Three Pool $35,660.

EIGHTH RACE
Aqueduct
NOVEMBER 20, 2004

1⅜ MILES. (Turf) (2.14^{1}) 45TH RUNNING OF THE RED SMITH HANDICAP. Grade II. Purse $150,000 A HANDICAP FOR THREE YEAR OLDS AND UPWARD. By subscription of $150 each, which should accompany the nomination; $750 to pass the entry box; $750 to start. The purse to be divided 60% to the winner, 20% to second, 10% to third, 5% to fourth, 3% to fifth and 2% divided equally among remaining finishers. A trophy will be presented to the winning owner. The New York Racing Association reserves the right to transfer this race to the Main Track. In the event that this race is taken off the turf, it may be subject to downgrading upon review by the Graded Stakes Committee. Closed Saturday, November 6, 2004 with 28 Nominations. (If the Stewards consider it inadvisable to run this race on the turf course, this race will be run at One Mile and One Quarter on the main track.). (Rail at 9 feet).

Value of Race: $150,000 Winner $90,000; second $30,000; third $15,000; fourth $7,500; fifth $4,500; sixth $600; seventh $600; eighth $600; ninth $600; tenth $600. Mutuel Pool $686,327.00 Exacta Pool $575,380.00 Trifecta Pool $452,078.00

Last Raced	Horse	M/Eqt.	A.	Wt	PP	¼	½	¾	1	Str	Fin	Jockey	Odds $1
29Oct04 ^{9}Med^{2}	Dreadnaught	L	4	115	4	5^{1}	$5^{\frac12}$	$5^{\frac12}$	4^{hd}	1^{hd}	1no	Samyn J L	5.60
23Oct04 ^{7}Bel^{2}	Certifiably Crazy	L b	4	112	3	$1^{\frac12}$	1^{1}	$1^{\frac12}$	$1^{\frac12}$	2^{3}	2^{3}	Fragoso P	8.30
13Oct04 LBS^{1}	Alost-FR	L	4	116	8	9^{1}	9^{hd}	$9^{\frac12}$	$9^{\frac12}$	$8^{1\frac12}$	3^{nk}	Gryder A T	22.60
23Oct04 ^{7}Bel^{1}	Irish Colonial	L	5	115	7	$3^{\frac12}$	3^{1}	$3^{\frac12}$	3^{1}	$7^{\frac12}$	4^{nk}	Bridgmohan S X	5.70
27Oct04 ^{8}Aqu^{4}	Navesink River	L	3	109	6	2^{1}	$2^{\frac12}$	$2^{\frac12}$	2^{hd}	3^{hd}	5^{hd}	Chavez J F	22.10
15Oct04 ^{8}Kee^{2}	Dr. Brendler	L f	6	120	10	8^{3}	8^{2}	7^{1}	$8^{1\frac12}$	$5^{\frac12}$	6^{hd}	Santos J A	3.00
16Oct04 ^{9}Bel^{3}	SecondPerformnce	L b	3	112	5	$6^{\frac12}$	6^{hd}	6^{1}	7^{hd}	6^{1}	7^{1}	Arroyo N Jr	24.50
30Oct04 ^{5}Aqu^{2}	Evening Attire	L b	6	116	1	10	10	10	10	9^{8}	8^{hd}	Espinoza J L	2.60
5Nov04 ^{7}CD^{5}	Rochester	L	8	116	2	$4^{\frac12}$	4^{hd}	4^{hd}	$5^{\frac12}$	4^{hd}	$9^{7\frac34}$	Velasquez C	10.00
23Oct04 ^{7}Bel^{11}	Quiet Ruler	L	6	114	9	$7^{\frac12}$	7^{hd}	8^{hd}	6^{hd}	10	10	Pimentel J	55.00

OFF AT 3:49 Start Good . Won driving. Course good.

TIME :26, :51^{4}, 1:17^{4}, 1:43^{1}, 2:07^{1}, 2:18^{4} (:26.10, :51.95, 1:17.80, 1:43.35, 2:07.22, 2:18.87)

$2 Mutuel Prices:				
	4 – DREADNAUGHT....................	13.20	6.70	4.40
	3 – CERTIFIABLY CRAZY...............		9.60	7.10
	8 – ALOST-FR..........................			10.80

$2 EXACTA 4–3 PAID $84.50 $2 TRIFECTA 4–3–8 PAID $1,474.00

B. g, (Feb), by Lac Ouimet – Wings of Dreams , by Sovereign Dancer . Trainer Voss Thomas H. Bred by David S Pennington (Ky).

DREADNAUGHT was rank in the gate, was rated along outside, rallied four wide on the final turn, dug in determinedly in the stretch and prevailed after a long drive. CERTIFIABLY CRAZY quickly showed in front, made the pace along the inside and dug in gamely to the wire, just missing. ALOST (FR) was outrun early, came wide into the stretch and finished well outside. IRISH COLONIAL raced close up outside, was three wide on each turn and stayed on stubbornly to the finish. NAVESINK RIVER prompted the pace from the outside and weakened in the final furlong. DR. BRENDLER was outrun early, came wide for the drive and lacked a rally. SECOND PERFORMANCE was rated along early, saved ground and lacked a rally while between rivals in the stretch. EVENING ATTIRE was outrun early, came wide approaching the stretch and had no rally. ROCHESTER was rated inside, saved ground and tired in the stretch. QUIET RULER raced wide and tired.

Owners– 1, Trillium Stable; 2, Double S Stable Avanzino Kenneth and Wachtel Stable; 3, Bayel Dominique; 4, Blue Sky Farm and Martin Fred; 5, Char-Mari Stable; 6, OToole Francis J; 7, Bloom William Behrendt John T and Marquis Charles K; 8, Grant Mary and Joseph and Kelly Thomas J; 9, Augustin Stable; 10, Sarf Leslie and Old Brookside Farm

Trainers– 1, Voss Thomas H; 2, Destefano John M Jr; 3, Spanu Antonio; 4, Schulhofer Randy; 5, Pletcher Todd A; 6, Motion H Graham; 7, Donk David; 8, Kelly Patrick J; 9, Sheppard Jonathan E; 10, Mueller Russell

Scratched– Sailaway (30Oct04 ^{5}Aqu^{3}) , Zakocity (27Oct04 ^{8}Aqu^{1}) , Kissin Saint (28Oct04 ^{8}Aqu^{1})

NINTH RACE
Churchill
NOVEMBER 20, 2004

1⅛ MILES. (Turf) (1.46^{1}) 31ST RUNNING OF THE CARDINAL HANDICAP. Grade III. Purse $150,000 FOR FILLIES AND MARES, THREE–YEARS–OLD AND UPWARD.

Value of Race: $173,550 Winner $107,601; second $34,710; third $17,355; fourth $8,678; fifth $5,206. Mutuel Pool $509,169.00 Exacta Pool $358,783.00 Trifecta Pool $295,563.00 Superfecta Pool $123,571.00

Last Raced	Horse	M/Eqt.	A.	Wt	PP	St	¼	½	¾	Str	Fin	Jockey	Odds $1
24Oct04 ^{8}Kee^{2}	Aud	L	4	115	5	11	11	11	8^{1}	3^{2}	1^{nk}	Blanc B	3.50
5Nov04 ^{4}CD^{3}	May Gator	L b	5	117	4	1	$2^{\frac12}$	$2^{2\frac12}$	2^{3}	$2^{2\frac12}$	2^{hd}	Martinez J R Jr	51.70
10Oct04 ^{8}Kee^{6}	Angela's Love	L	4	114	11	2	$1^{1\frac12}$	1^{1}	$1^{1\frac12}$	1^{2}	$3^{4\frac14}$	Fox T L	38.10
8Oct04 ^{8}Bel^{1}	Noisette	L	4	114	10	7	5^{hd}	$5^{\frac12}$	$5^{1\frac12}$	7^{2}	4^{nk}	Melancon L	15.30
24Oct04 ^{6}WO^{3}	Classic Stamp	L	4	119	1	3	$6^{\frac12}$	$3^{\frac12}$	$3^{\frac12}$	$4^{1\frac12}$	$5^{2\frac14}$	Day P	1.70
31Oct04 ^{8}Aqu^{1}	Finery	L	4	115	6	10	9^{hd}	$9^{\frac12}$	10^{2}	10^{8}	6no	McKee J	5.00
2Oct04 ^{8}Haw^{1}	Beret	L f	5	117	2	4	10^{6}	$10^{2\frac12}$	$7^{\frac12}$	$6^{\frac12}$	7^{hd}	Sarvis D A	19.50
30Oct04 ^{6}LS^{6}	Shaconage	L	4	118	3	9	7^{hd}	6^{hd}	$4^{1\frac12}$	5^{hd}	8^{nk}	Johnson J M	5.90
23Oct04 ^{9}Bel^{1}	On the Bus	L	4	116	9	8	$8^{1\frac12}$	$8^{\frac12}$	$9^{1\frac12}$	$9^{\frac12}$	$9^{3\frac34}$	Martin E M Jr	8.60
29Oct04 ^{4}Kee^{2}	Chance Dance	L	4	116	7	5	4^{hd}	7^{2}	$6^{\frac12}$	8^{3}	$10^{12\frac14}$	Hernandez B J Jr	33.80
13Oct04 ^{8}Kee^{1}	Nannycam	L	4	113	8	6	3^{1}	$4^{\frac12}$	11	11	11	Troilo W D	71.80

OFF AT 4:39 Start Good . Won driving. Course yielding.

TIME :24^{3}, :49^{2}, 1:14, 1:40^{1}, 1:53^{4} (:24.71, :49.49, 1:14.01, 1:40.24, 1:53.94)

$2 Mutuel Prices:				
	6 – AUD....................................	9.00	4.20	3.60
	5 – MAY GATOR........................		36.00	19.00
	12 – ANGELA'S LOVE..................			16.40

$2 EXACTA 6–5 PAID $287.60 $2 TRIFECTA 6–5–12 PAID $6,939.20
$1 SUPERFECTA 6–5–12–11 PAID $100,092.50

Dk. b or br. f, (Feb), by Wild Again – Gail's Brush , by Broad Brush . Trainer Reinstedler Anthony. Bred by Willmott Stable (Ky).

AUD, outrun from the beginning, settled inside, remained inside when advancing on the far turn, eased around BERET nearing the stretch, maneuvered back inside, came out between foes four wide in the final furlong and was hard ridden to be along in time. MAY GATOR stalked front-running ANGELA'S LOVE from early on, raced five or six wide most of the way, loomed boldly outside the winner through the drive and was outfinished when drifting out at the wire. ANGELA'S LOVE gained the advantage early, worked her way nicely to the inside during the opening quarter, managed a clear lead into the final furlong and couldn't last in a strong try. NOISETTE, never far back, followed the leaders five or six wide into the stretch but couldn't produce a closing bid. CLASSIC STAMP, well placed inside to the stretch, angled four wide for the drive, then lacked a late response. FINERY, five wide early, moved seven or eight wide on the backstretch, then remained off the inside while improving position. BERET settled inside, was unhurried, inched to contention on the far turn, came out four or five wide for the drive but failed to fire. SHACONAGE, never far back, edged up between foes four wide around the far turn, remained a threat into the final furlong and flattened out. ON THE BUS, never far back, edged up between foes four wide on the far turn, remained a threat until straightened into the stretch and weakened. CHANCE DANCE, forwardly placed five wide early, moved out seven or eight wide on the backstretch, remained in contention for seven furlongs and weakened. NANNYCAM tracked the pace to the far turn while four or five wide and faded.

Owners– 1, Willmott Stables Inc; 2, Klein Richard Bertram and Elaine; 3, Poston Bill and Vicki; 4, Haras Santa Maria de Araras; 5, Sorokolit William A Sr; 6, Richards Althea D; 7, Vanier Nancy A and Williamson Lyda; 8, Van Doren Andrena; 9, Ramsey Kenneth L and Sarah K; 10, Bernacki Robert Hall Robert and Scherer Merrill R; 11, Oxley John C

Trainers– 1, Reinstedler Anthony; 2, Flint Steve; 3, Romans Dale; 4, Mott William I; 5, Hopmans C C Jr; 6, Turner William H Jr; 7, Vanier Harvey L; 8, Shirota Mitch; 9, Romans Dale; 10, Scherer Merrill R; 11, Ward John T Jr

Scratched– Beautiful Bets (22Oct04 ^{7}Haw^{4}) , Ocean Silk (02Nov04 ^{9}CD ^{3})

$2 Pick Three (3–9–6) Paid $138.20 ; Pick Three Pool $38,064 .

EIGHTH RACE
Hollywood
NOVEMBER 20, 2004

7 FURLONGS. (1.19^{4}) 23RD RUNNING OF THE HOLLYWOOD PREVUE. Grade III. Purse $100,000 FOR TWO-YEAR-OLDS. By subscription of $100 each, on or before Wednesday, November 10, or by supplementary nomination of $2,000 each by closing time of entries. $1,000 additional to start, with $60,000 to the winner, $20,000 to second, $12,000 to third, $6,000 to fourth and $2,000 to fifth. 122 lbs. Non-winners of $60,000 or $45,000 twice allowed 3 lbs. ; $45,000 or two races other than maiden or claiming, 5 lbs. ; of a sweepstakes of any value, 7 lbs. ; of a race other than maiden or claiming , 9 lbs. Starters to be named through the entry box by closing time of entries. Total earnings in 2004 will be used in determining the order of presence of horses assigned equal weights. All fees for entrants that fail to draw into this race will be cancelled. A trophy will be presented to the owner of the winner. No fees to any horse originally nominated to the 2004 Hollywood Futurity. (Does not include supplementary nomination). Closed with 12 nominations.

Value of Race: $100,000 Winner $60,000; second $20,000; third $12,000; fourth $6,000; fifth $2,000. Mutuel Pool $437,843.00 Exacta Pool $258,284.00 Quinella Pool $23,383.00 Trifecta Pool $296,263.00 Superfecta Pool $145,539.00

Last Raced	Horse	M/Eqt.	A.	Wt	PP	St	¼	½	Str	Fin	Jockey	Odds $1
8Sep04 ^{8}Dmr^{1}	Declan's Moon	LB	2	122	5	5	$3\frac{1}{2}$	3^{3}	$1\frac{1}{2}$	1^{2}	Espinoza V	0.40
6Nov04 ^{9}Hol^{1}	Bushwacker	LB b	2	114	8	3	$1^{1\frac{1}{2}}$	1^{1}	2^{2}	2^{hd}	Douglas R R	16.70
11Oct04 ^{5}SA^{1}	Seize the Day	LB	2	117	6	2	$2\frac{1}{2}$	2^{hd}	3^{2}	3^{2}	Nakatani C S	3.30
25Jly04 ASC^{1}	Southern Africa	LB	2	115	1	8	7^{hd}	$6^{1\frac{1}{2}}$	4^{1}	$4^{3\frac{1}{2}}$	Baze T C	22.40
23Oct04 ^{2}SA^{1}	Megabyte	LB b	2	114	7	1	4^{1}	$4^{1\frac{1}{2}}$	5^{hd}	$5^{1\frac{1}{2}}$	Smith M E	12.50
14Oct04 ^{6}BM^{1}	Beat the Chalk	LB b	2	122	3	4	$5^{1\frac{1}{2}}$	5^{hd}	$6^{4\frac{1}{2}}$	6^{2}	Pedroza M A	18.10
30Oct04 ^{7}LS^{7}	Twice Unbridled	B	2	113	2	7	6^{hd}	7^{2}	$7\frac{1}{2}$	7^{3}	Martinez F F	49.00
16Oct04 ^{8}TuP^{1}	Power Wave	LB	2	119	4	6	8	8	8	8	Hernandez M G	27.90

OFF AT 4:10 Start Good . Won ridden out. Track fast.

TIME :21^{4}, :44^{1}, 1:08^{2}, 1:21^{3} (:21.96, :44.22, 1:08.54, 1:21.74)

$2 Mutuel Prices:

5 – DECLAN'S MOON	2.80	2.20	2.10
8 – BUSHWACKER		6.20	2.60
6 – SEIZE THE DAY			2.20

$1 EXACTA 5–8 PAID $16.60 $2 QUINELLA 5–8 PAID $29.80
$1 TRIFECTA 5–8–6 PAID $43.50 $1 SUPERFECTA 5–8–6–1 PAID $252.00

Dk. b or br. g, (Feb), by Malibu Moon – Vee Vee Star , by Norquestor . Trainer Ellis Ronald W. Bred by Brice Ridgely (Md).

DECLAN'S MOON stalked between foes then outside a rival, bid three deep into the stretch, gained the lead in upper stretch and pulled clear under a steady hand ride until the final strides. BUSHWACKER broke out a bit, sped to the lead outside rivals then set the pace a bit off the rail, found the fence into the stretch, fought back inside the winner but could not match that one late and just held second. SEIZE THE DAY had speed off the rail then stalked the pace just off the inside, angled to the rail for the turn, came out in upper stretch and just missed the place. SOUTHERN AFRICA off a bit slowly, saved ground off the pace, went outside a rival on the turn, split horses into the stretch and lacked the needed late kick. MEGABYTE stalked outside on the backstretch and turn, came three deep into the stretch and weakened. BEAT THE CHALK angled in and saved ground chasing the pace and lacked a response in the stretch. TWICE UNBRIDLED chased outside a rival then a bit off the rail on the turn and failed to menace. POWER WAVE allowed to settle off the pace three deep, angled to the inside on the turn and was outrun.

Owners– 1, Jay Em Ess Stable; 2, Currin William L and Eisman Alvin; 3, American Equistock Racing & Shepard; 4, Kirkwood Al and Saundra S; 5, Mercedes Stables LLC; 6, House Michael; 7, McBride Labrum & Jensen; 8, Bryant Monty Howard Neil and Marrone Gary

Trainers– 1, Ellis Ronald W; 2, Currin William L; 3, Mulhall Kristin; 4, Puhich Michael; 5, Cerin Vladimir; 6, Mullins Jeff; 7, Jensen Daniel M; 8, Lenzini Michael

$2 Daily Double (10–5) Paid $19.20 ; Daily Double Pool $32,293 .
$1 Pick Three (10–10–5) Paid $57.60 ; Pick Three Pool $81,593 .

FIFTH RACE
Pimlico
NOVEMBER 20, 2004

$1\frac{1}{16}$ MILES. (1.40^{4}) 81ST RUNNING OF THE LAUREL FUTURITY. Grade III. Purse $100,000 FOR TWO-YEAR-OLDS. By free subscription, $500 to pass the entry box, $500 additional to start, with $100,000 Guaranteed, of which 60% to the winner, 20% to second, 11% to third, 6% to fourth and 3% to fifth. Weight 122 lbs. Fillies allowed 3 lbs., Maiden allowed, 5 lbs. Trophy to the owner of the winner. Closed Wednesday, November 10, 2004 with 23 Nominations.

Value of Race: $100,000 Winner $60,000; second $20,000; third $11,000; fourth $6,000; fifth $3,000. Mutuel Pool $103,816.00 Exacta Pool $78,678.00 Trifecta Pool $30,509.00

Last Raced	Horse	M/Eqt.	A.	Wt	PP	St	¼	½	¾	Str	Fin	Jockey	Odds $1
2Nov04 ^{8}Aqu^{2}	Defer	L	2	122	1	4	3^{5}	3^{3}	3^{3}	$1\frac{1}{2}$	1^{2}	Bailey J D	0.70
14Oct04 ^{7}Med^{1}	Funk	L	2	122	2	2	$2^{1\frac{1}{2}}$	2^{2}	2^{2}	$2^{1\frac{1}{2}}$	$2^{3\frac{3}{4}}$	Velazquez J R	1.20
10Nov04 ^{7}Pim^{3}	Woody's Apache	L b	2	122	5	3	5	$4^{1\frac{1}{2}}$	4^{4}	4^{7}	3^{hd}	Dominguez R A	a- 7.90
30Oct04 ^{3}Med^{2}	Elusive Thunder	L b	2	122	4	1	$1^{1\frac{1}{2}}$	$1\frac{1}{2}$	1^{hd}	3^{3}	$4^{7\frac{1}{2}}$	Elliott S	10.40
19Sep04 ^{6}Pim^{1}	Malibu Moonshine		2	122	3	5	4^{1}	5	5	5	5	Monterrey R	a- 7.90

a–Coupled: Woody's Apache and Malibu Moonshine.

OFF AT 2:10 Start Good For All But MALIBU MOONSHINE. Won driving. Track fast.

TIME :24^{3}, :49^{1}, 1:13^{3}, 1:38^{4}, 1:45^{2} (:24.77, :49.23, 1:13.71, 1:38.95, 1:45.48)

$2 Mutuel Prices:

2 – DEFER	3.40	2.20	—
3 – FUNK		2.40	—
1A– WOODY'S APACHE(a–entry)		—	—

$2 EXACTA 2–3 PAID $5.80 $2 TRIFECTA 2–3–1 PAID $8.20

B. c, (May), by Danzig – Hidden Reserve , by Mr. Prospector . Trainer McGaughey III Claude R. Bred by Ogden Mills Phipps (Ky).

DEFER stalked the pace, eased outside when set down in upper stretch, secured command in midstretch then drew off under brisk urging. FUNK prompted the pace outside ELUSIVE THUNDER, gained a short lead in upper stretch, lugged in near the eighth pole and gave way. WOODY'S APACHE raced well off the rail in the stretch and was no factor. ELUSIVE THUNDER set the pace along the rail and gave way. MALIBU MOONSHINE hesitated at the break and trailed.

Owners– 1, Phipps Ogden M; 2, Starlight Stables Paul H Saylor & Barbara Kurtin; 3, Marriott Woodrow; 4, Winged Foot Stables; 5, Marriott Woodrow

Trainers– 1, McGaughey III Claude R; 2, Pletcher Todd A; 3, Leatherbury King T; 4, Ryan Derek S; 5, Leatherbury King T

Scratched– Killenaule (30Oct04 ^{3}Med^{1}) , Monster Chaser (30Oct04 ^{8}Pim^{1})

$2 Pick Three (8–2–2/4/5) Paid $436.80 ; Pick Three Pool $7,649 .

NINTH RACE
Pimlico
NOVEMBER 20, 2004

1⅛ MILES. (1.47¹) 30TH RUNNING OF THE ANNE ARUNDEL. Grade III. Purse $100,000 FOR FILLIES, THREE-YEARS-OLD. By free subscription. $500 to pass the entry box, $500 additional to start, with $100,000 Guaranteed, of which 60% to the winner, 20% to second, 11% to third, 6% to fourth and 3% to fifth. Supplemental nominations of $1000 each will be accepted by the usual time of entry with all other fees due as noted. Weight 122 lbs. Non-winners of a race of $50,000 at one mile or over allowed, 3 lbs.; $30,000 twice at one mile or over, 5 lbs.; once 7 lbs. (Maiden and Claiming racesnot considered in estimating allowances). Trophy to the owner of the winner. Closed Wednesday, November 10, 2004 with 29 Nominations.

Value of Race: $100,000 Winner $60,000; second $20,000; third $11,000; fourth $6,000; fifth $3,000. Mutuel Pool $190,827.00 Exacta Pool $145,968.00 Superfecta Pool $26,563.00 Trifecta Pool $100,580.00

Last Raced	Horse	M/Eqt.	A.	Wt	PP	St	¼	½	¾	Str	Fin	Jockey	Odds $1
13Oct04 7Kee1	Essence	L	3	115	1	3	11	1½	1½	11	1nk	Velazquez J R	3.20
24Oct04 8Bel4	Rare Gift	L	3	115	4	6	3½	4½	3hd	22½	22½	Prado E S	4.90
23Oct04 3Kee2	Family Business	L	3	115	5	8	93	7hd	83	6½	3½	Bailey J D	7.00
2Oct04 9Pha4	He Loves Me	L	3	122	8	10	103	104½	94	4½	4no	Hamilton S D	1.60
9Oct04 3Pim1	Silmaril	L f	3	122	7	4	61	62	41	3½	5¾	Castellano A Jr	5.60
25Sep04 9Pim12	Pour It On	L	3	122	2	9	71	81	6hd	78	61½	Dominguez R A	24.70
1Nov04 7Del1	Summer Rainbow	L	3	115	3	1	2½	21	21½	5hd	76¾	Fogelsonger R	40.30
9Oct04 8Del1	Jazz Legend	L f	3	115	10	2	4½	3hd	51	83	84¼	Castillo O O	49.10
25Oct04 9Del2	Blind Canyon	L b	3	115	11	7	5½	5hd	7½	96	92¼	Elliott S	48.90
9Oct04 10Pim6	NagemNagemNgem	L f	3	115	6	11	11	11	11	101	104¼	Delgado A	72.10
9Oct04 8WO9	Touchnow	L b	3	122	9	5	8hd	92	104	11	11	Bejarano R	19.10

OFF AT 4:03 Start Good . Won driving. Track fast.
TIME :23³, :47⁴, 1:11⁴, 1:36², 1:49¹ (:23.74, :47.96, 1:11.83, 1:36.59, 1:49.37)

$2 Mutuel Prices:				
	1 – ESSENCE	8.40	5.00	3.40
	4 – RARE GIFT		5.80	3.60
	5 – FAMILY BUSINESS			4.00

$2 EXACTA 1–4 PAID $50.80 $1 SUPERFECTA 1–4–5–9 PAID $493.00
$2 TRIFECTA 1–4–5 PAID $203.40

B. f, (Apr), by Gulch – Patelin's Legacy , by Cherokee Colony . Trainer Pletcher Todd A. Bred by Mrs C Oliver Iselin III (Va).

ESSENCE set the pace along the rail, opened a clear lead in upper stretch and dug in tenaciously to prevail. RARE GIFT saved ground stalking the pace, eased out two wide in upper stretch and closed gamely. FAMILY BUSINESS , unhurried early, raced in the two path, swung five wide in upper stretch and rallied. HE LOVES ME lacked speed, raced inside horses on the far turn, swung to the six path at the head of the stretch and offered a slight rally. SILMARIL stalked the pace between horses, swung four wide entering the stretch and came up empty. POUR IT ON raced along the rail and failed to rally. SUMMER RAINBOW pressed the pace outside the winner and gave way. JAZZ LEGEND , three wide both turns, gave way. BLIND CANYON , four wide on the turns, fell back. NAGEM NAGEM NAGEM was outrun. TOUCHNOW dropped back.

Owners– 1, Padua Stables; 2, Bolton George Dipietro David and Honour Roger; 3, Overbrook Farm; 4, Buckingham Farm; 5, Quick Stephen E and Feifarek Christopher J; 6, Hickory Plains; 7, Dogwood Stable; 8, Farish Sarah S; 9, Knew Stable; 10, Aiken Jerome; 11, Farr George

Trainers– 1, Pletcher Todd A; 2, Kimmel John C; 3, Stewart Dallas; 4, Small Richard W; 5, Grove Christopher W; 6, Smith Hamilton A; 7, Motion H Graham; 8, Zwiesler Michael; 9, Dunn John J; 10, Aguirre Anthony; 11, Baker Reade

Scratched– Pawyne Princess (29Oct04 3Med1)

TENTH RACE
Pimlico
NOVEMBER 20, 2004

6 FURLONGS. (1.09) 15TH RUNNING OF THE FRANK J. DE FRANCIS MEMORIAL DASH. Grade I. Purse $300,000 FOR THREE-YEAR-OLDS AND UPWARD. By free subscription. $3000 to pass the entry box. $3000 additional to start with $300,000 Guaranteed of which 60% to the winner, 20% to second, 11% to third, 6% to fourth and 3% to fifth. Weights: Three-Year-Olds, 122 lbs., Older, 126 lbs. Non-winners of $100,000 twice in 2004 allowed 3 lbs.; Once, 5 lbs.; $60,000 Twice in 2004, 7 lbs. Trophy to the owner of the winner. Closed Wednesday, November 10, 2004 with 25 Nominations.

Value of Race: $300,000 Winner $180,000; second $60,000; third $33,000; fourth $18,000; fifth $9,000. Mutuel Pool $464,221.00 Exacta Pool $330,543.00 Superfecta Pool $82,961.00 Trifecta Pool $249,417.00

Last Raced	Horse	M/Eqt.	A.	Wt	PP	St	¼	½	Str	Fin	Jockey	Odds $1
8Oct04 7Kee4	Wildcat Heir	L f	4	119	8	1	31	31	12	1nk	Elliott S	16.00
30Oct04 5LS10	Midas Eyes	L	4	123	1	4	5hd	51½	41½	21½	Prado E S	1.30
30Oct04 5LS6	Clock Stopper	L b	4	119	7	10	10	10	7hd	3¾	Bailey J D	4.60
14Aug04 7Sar3	Gators N Bears	L bf	4	126	4	7	4hd	61	61½	42	Castellano J J	8.90
24Oct04 7Del1	Philadelphia Jim	L	4	119	3	6	2½	1hd	3½	51	Beasley J A	84.70
9Oct04 7CT1	A Huevo	L f	8	123	2	9	96	7½	83	61¼	Dominguez R A	6.70
30Oct04 5LS11	Abbondanza	L f	3	117	9	2	6½	4½	21	71½	Castellano A Jr	12.70
30Oct04 5LS7	Champali	L	4	126	6	8	71½	83	91½	81	Bejarano R	5.70
23Sep04 8Pim2	True Direction	L b	5	119	10	3	82½	91½	10	91½	Velazquez J R	39.70
8May04 7Bel6	Shake You Down	L bf	6	123	5	5	1hd	21	5hd	10	Luzzi M J	12.50

OFF AT 4:34 Start Good . Won driving. Track fast.
TIME :22³, :45², :57¹, 1:09² (:22.77, :45.42, :57.28, 1:09.45)

$2 Mutuel Prices:				
	8 – WILDCAT HEIR	34.00	10.00	5.80
	1 – MIDAS EYES		3.60	2.80
	7 – CLOCK STOPPER			2.80

$2 EXACTA 8–1 PAID $138.40 $1 SUPERFECTA 8–1–7–4 PAID $1,162.20
$2 TRIFECTA 8–1–7 PAID $551.00

B. c, (Feb), by Forest Wildcat – Penniless Heiress , by Pentelicus . Trainer Perkins Ben W Jr. Bred by New Farm (Ky).

WILDCAT HEIR , away alertly, tracked a contested pace while three wide, moved to even terms between rivals in upper stretch, shook clear a furlong out, drifted in then back out and was fully extended to hold off MIDAS EYES. MIDAS EYES , forwardly placed along the rail, angled out nearing the lane, swung out wider in mid stretch, closed sharply and was getting to the winner. CLOCK STOPPER broke slowly, trailed for a half mile, swung out seven wide leaving the furlong marker and finished with good energy. GATORS N BEARS , between rivals early, chased the pace off the rail on the turn, made a mild run in the six path leaving the eighth pole then flattened out. PHILADELPHIA JIM dueled inside of SHAKE YOU DOWN through brisk fractions, remained a solid presence to the three sixteenths marker then faded. A HUEVO , taken to rate, saved ground into the lane, angled out but lacked a solid response. ABBONDANZA , taken to rate off the rail, ranged up four wide nearing the quarter pole, drew on near even terms in upper stretch, battled briefly then gave way. CHAMPALI , three to four wide, failed to respond. TRUE DIRECTION , four wide past the three furlong marker, came up empty. SHAKE YOU DOWN was sent up between rivals, dueled two wide and tired nearing mid stretch.

Owners– 1, New Farm; 2, Gann Edmund A; 3, Overbrook Farm; 4, Nechamkin Leo S II; 5, Gill Michael J; 6, Hopkins Mark S; 7, Germania Farms Inc; 8, Lloyd Madison Farms IV LLC; 9, Binn Moreton; 10, Cole Robert L Jr

Trainers– 1, Perkins Ben W Jr; 2, Frankel Robert; 3, Stewart Dallas; 4, Nechamkin Leo S II; 5, Shuman Mark; 6, Dickinson Michael W; 7, Tullock Timothy Jr; 8, Foley Gregory D; 9, Pletcher Todd A; 10, Lake Scott A

Scratched– Lion Tamer (31Oct04 7Aqu2)

$2 Pick Three (6–1–8) Paid $1,970.80 ; Pick Three Pool $33,181 .
$2 Pick Four (6–6–1–8) Paid $46,531.00 ; Pick Four Pool $54,106 .
$2 Daily Double (1–8) Paid $196.40 ; Daily Double Pool $47,398 .

Pimlico Attendance: Unavailable Mutuel Pool: $.00

EIGHTH RACE
Aqueduct
NOVEMBER 21, 2004

6 FURLONGS. (1.07^{2}) 10TH RUNNING OF THE VALLEY STREAM. Grade III. Purse $100,000 (UP TO $19,000 NYSBFOA) FOR FILLIES TWO YEARS OLD. By subscription of $100 each, which should accompany the nomination; $500 to pass the entry box; $500 to start, with $100,000 added. The added money and all fees to be divided 60% to the winner, 20% to second, 10% to third, 5% to fourth, 3% to fifth and 2% divided equally among remaining finishers. 122 lbs. Non-winners of $40,000 allowed 2 lbs.; two races other than maiden or claiming, 4 lbs.; a race other than maiden or claiming 6 lbs. A trophy will bepresented to the winning owner. Closed Saturday, November 6, 2004 with 15 Nominations.

Value of Race: $101,500 Winner $63,900; second $21,430; third $10,780; fourth $5,390. Mutuel Pool $384,814.00 Exacta Pool $268,222.00 Trifecta Pool $141,409.00

Last Raced	Horse	M/Eqt.	A.	Wt	PP	St	¼	½	Str	Fin	Jockey	Odds $1
23Oct04 ^{5}Bel^{6}	Megascape	L	2	122	1	3	1^{1}	$1^{1\frac{1}{2}}$	$1^{3\frac{1}{2}}$	$1^{2\frac{1}{4}}$	Velazquez J R	4.80
4Nov04 ^{7}Aqu^{1}	Alfonsina	L	2	118	4	4	$4^{\frac{1}{2}}$	3^{1}	$3^{3\frac{1}{2}}$	$2^{\frac{3}{4}}$	Velasquez C	0.70
23Oct04 ^{8}Med^{1}	More Moonlight	L	2	118	5	1	3^{2}	$2^{\frac{1}{2}}$	2^{hd}	$3^{5\frac{3}{4}}$	Elliott S	3.35
2Nov04 ^{6}Aqu^{4}	Winsome		2	116	2	5	5	4	4	4	Santos J A	6.30
23Oct04 ^{8}Med^{3}	Galactic Cat	L	2	118	3	2	2^{hd}	—	—	—	Gryder A T	20.80

OFF AT 3:44 Start Good. Won driving. Track good.

TIME :22, :45^{1}, :57^{1}, 1:10^{1} (:22.16, :45.39, :57.37, 1:10.38)

$2 Mutuel Prices:				
	1 – MEGASCAPE	11.60	3.40	2.10
	4 – ALFONSINA		2.50	2.10
	5 – MORE MOONLIGHT			2.10

$2 EXACTA 1–4 PAID $30.80 $2 TRIFECTA 1–4–5 PAID $57.50

Dk. b or br. f, (Apr), by Cape Canaveral – Bigger Half, by Megaturn. Trainer Asmussen Steven M. Bred by Sez Who Thoroughbreds (NY).

MEGASCAPE quickly showed in front, soon opened a clear lead, set the pace along the inside, widened when roused and was kept to a drive to the wire. ALFONSINA stumbled at the start, was bumped after the start, raced three wide and rallied to earn the place prize. MORE MOONLIGHT chased the pace from the outside and was outfinished for the place. WINSOME raced inside and had no response when roused. GALACTIC CAT was bumped after the start, showed speed while between rivals and was pulled up after the opening quarter mile.

Owners– 1, Beck Robert L; 2, Mandara Michael A; 3, Vinery Stables; 4, Clay Robert Nand Cowan Irving M and Marjorie; 5, Dare To Dream Stable

Trainers– 1, Asmussen Steven M; 2, Zito Nicholas P; 3, Asmussen Steven M; 4, Jerkens H Allen; 5, Maker Rebecca

---

NINTH RACE
Churchill
NOVEMBER 21, 2004

1⅛ MILES. (Turf) (1.46^{1}) 27TH RUNNING OF THE RIVER CITY HANDICAP. Grade III. Purse $150,000 FOR THREE–YEARS–OLD AND UPWARD.

Value of Race: $174,300 Winner $108,066; second $34,860; third $17,430; fourth $8,715; fifth $5,229. Mutuel Pool $369,656.00 Exacta Pool $284,425.00 Trifecta Pool $240,642.00 Superfecta Pool $82,977.00

Last Raced	Horse	M/Eqt.	A.	Wt	PP	St	¼	½	¾	Str	Fin	Jockey	Odds $1
3Nov04 ^{9}CD^{1}	G P Fleet	L	4	115	2	2	5^{hd}	4^{1}	4^{2}	2^{2}	$1^{\frac{1}{2}}$	Martinez J R Jr	12.30
5Nov04 ^{7}CD^{4}	Cloudy's Knight	L	4	115	11	6	2^{hd}	$3^{1\frac{1}{2}}$	$3^{1\frac{1}{2}}$	1^{hd}	$2^{5\frac{1}{4}}$	Emigh C A	16.10
5Nov04 ^{9}CD^{2}	Ay Caramba-Brz	L b	4	115	5	5	7^{4}	7^{hd}	$5^{\frac{1}{2}}$	3^{1}	3no	Cruz M R	4.70
9Oct04 ^{5}Kee^{2}	Deputy Strike	L	6	116	12	12	12	$10^{1\frac{1}{2}}$	9^{3}	7^{3}	$4^{\frac{1}{2}}$	Martin E M Jr	15.60
5Nov04 ^{7}CD^{7}	Honor in War	L	5	118	6	8	8^{1}	8^{1}	7^{1}	$5^{2\frac{1}{2}}$	5^{1}	Day P	3.60
15Oct04 ^{8}Med^{2}	Tam's Terms	L	6	116	9	10	$9^{\frac{1}{2}}$	9^{2}	8^{2}	$6^{1\frac{1}{2}}$	6^{2}	Marquez C H Jr	8.50
9Oct04 ^{8}Kee^{8}	Warleigh	L	6	116	1	3	$3^{1\frac{1}{2}}$	$2^{1\frac{1}{2}}$	$2^{1\frac{1}{2}}$	$4^{1\frac{1}{2}}$	$7^{5\frac{1}{2}}$	McKee J	2.70
23Oct04 ^{7}Kee^{5}	False Promises	L	4	114	8	7	4^{hd}	5^{2}	6^{1}	$8^{\frac{1}{2}}$	$8^{6\frac{3}{4}}$	Perez E E	83.40
7Nov04 ^{4}WO^{4}	Dumaani Star	L	6	114	7	11	$11^{\frac{1}{2}}$	12	12	$10^{1\frac{1}{2}}$	$9^{\frac{3}{4}}$	Troilo W D	132.30
5Nov04 ^{7}CD^{1}	Quest Star	L b	5	116	10	1	1^{hd}	1^{hd}	1^{hd}	9^{8}	$10^{6\frac{3}{4}}$	Melancon L	9.70
24Oct04 ^{3}WO^{7}	French Lieutenant	L	4	113	3	4	6^{hd}	$6^{1\frac{1}{2}}$	10^{2}	12	$11^{1\frac{1}{4}}$	Sarvis D A	50.90
30Oct04 ^{5}Aqu^{6}	Dr. Kashnikow	L	7	117	4	9	10^{1}	$11^{\frac{1}{2}}$	$11^{2\frac{1}{2}}$	11^{1}	12	Blanc B	8.30

OFF AT 4:39 Start Good. Won driving. Course yielding.

TIME :24, :48^{1}, 1:13, 1:38^{4}, 1:51^{1} (:24.01, :48.27, 1:13.07, 1:38.83, 1:51.26)

$2 Mutuel Prices:				
	2 – G P FLEET	26.60	12.80	8.00
	12 – CLOUDY'S KNIGHT		16.20	9.60
	5 – AY CARAMBA-BRZ			4.60

$2 EXACTA 2–12 PAID $424.20 $2 TRIFECTA 2–12–5 PAID $2,745.20
$1 SUPERFECTA 2–12–5–13 PAID $9,601.60

Ch. g, (May), by Northern Afleet – Come On Bid, by Spectacular Bid. Trainer Flint Steve. Bred by George Parrish (Fla).

G P FLEET, well placed inside from early on, eased out and split rivals approaching the final furlong and proved gamely best under brisk left-handed urging. CLOUDY'S KNIGHT maneuvered in early to force the pace four wide, stuck his head in front at the furlong grounds, then was outfinished in a long drive. AY CARAMBA (BRZ), reserved in behind horses early, was never far back, made a bold run five wide into the final furlong, loomed a solid threat but lacked a late account. DEPUTY STRIKE, outrun for six furlongs, swung out 10 wide entering the stretch and offered a minor gain while not a serious threat. HONOR IN WAR settled near the inside early, inched closer on the far turn, came out six wide to make a run nearing the final eighth but lacked a serious response. TAM'S TERMS, unhurried early, edged up between calls approaching the stretch while four wide, came out seven abreast for the drive and was empty the last eighth. WARLEIGH eased off the inside early to force the pace between foes, battled close up to the stretch and weakened. FALSE PROMISES followed the leaders in a striking position four or five wide and weakened after seven furlongs. DUMAANI STAR never was prominent. QUEST STAR bobbled at the break, moved to the front soon after, worked his way inside, made the pace until the final quarter, gave way, then was gathered up in deep stretch and taken to the outside after bobbling leaving the sixteenth pole. FRENCH LIEUTENANT tired after five furlongs. DR. KASHNIKOW, five wide much of the way, was outrun.

Owners– 1, Klein Richard Bertram and Elaine; 2, Schwartz Jerrold; 3, Bozano Patricia; 4, Ramsey Kenneth L and Sarah K; 5, 3rd Turn Stables LLC; 6, Bender Sondra D; 7, Parra Rosendo G; 8, Maracich David; 9, Castle Peak Farm Ltd Joann Walker Ng; 10, Mansell Stables LLC; 11, Glennwood Farm Inc John D Gunther; 12, Erdenheim Farm

Trainers– 1, Flint Steve; 2, Kirby Frank J; 3, Caramori Eduardo; 4, Romans Dale; 5, McGee Paul J; 6, Murray Lawrence E; 7, Asmussen Steven M; 8, Granitz Anthony J; 9, Simon Charles; 10, Walden W Elliott; 11, Day-Phillips Catherine; 12, Fisher John R S

Scratched– Prince Prado (05Nov04 ^{7}CD ^{3})

$2 Pick Three (9–7–2) Paid $6,526.80; Pick Three Pool $28,203.

EIGHTH RACE
Remington
NOVEMBER 21, 2004

1⅛ MILES. (1.48) 16TH RUNNING OF THE OKLAHOMA DERBY. Grade III. Purse $150,000 (plus $1,300 OBP – Oklahoma Bred Pgm) FOR THREE–YEAR–OLDS. No nomination fee. $750 to pass the entry box. Starters to pay $750 additional with $150,000 added. The added money and all fees to be divided 60% to the winner, 20% to second, 11% to third, 6% to fourth and 3% to fifth. Weights: Colts and Geldings, 124 lbs.; Fillies, 119 lbs. Non–winners of $100,000 twice at a mile or over in 2004 allowed 3 lbs.; $100,000 once at a mile or over in 2004, 6 lbs.; $50,000 at a mile or over in 2004, 9 lbs.; $50,000 at any distance in 2003–2004, 12 lbs.Trophy to the winning Owner, Trainer and Jockey.

Value of Race: $167,250 Winner $100,350; second $33,450; third $18,398; fourth $10,035; fifth $5,017. Mutuel Pool $60,111.00 Exacta Pool $38,611.00 Quinella Pool $2,425.00 Trifecta Pool $40,352.00 Superfecta Pool $12,426.00

Last Raced	Horse	M/Eqt.	A.	Wt	PP	St	¼	½	¾	Str	Fin	Jockey	Odds $1
24Oct04 9Wds1	Wally's Choice	LB	3	115	2	10	11	11	$9^{\frac{1}{2}}$	3^{2}	1^{1}	Quinonez L S	33.90
27Oct04 4Kee1	Golden Glen	LB	3	112	3	9	10^{5}	7^{hd}	4^{hd}	2^{hd}	$2^{1\frac{1}{2}}$	Hernandez B J Jr	8.00
29Oct04 7LS2	Cryptograph	LB b	3	118	11	8	9^{4}	$8^{1\frac{1}{2}}$	$6^{\frac{1}{2}}$	$1^{\frac{1}{2}}$	$3^{6\frac{1}{2}}$	Pettinger D R	1.70
27Oct04 8Kee3	Slew Slayer	LB	3	116	4	5	$7^{\frac{1}{2}}$	6^{hd}	8^{3}	4^{3}	$4^{7\frac{1}{4}}$	Fires E	22.90
1Nov04 7RP6	Foreign Justice	LB	3	112	5	4	$5^{\frac{1}{2}}$	5^{3}	5^{hd}	$5^{1\frac{1}{2}}$	5^{7}	Matz N	78.00
29Oct04 7LS5	Britt's Jules	LB b	3	116	1	3	$3^{\frac{1}{2}}$	$3^{1\frac{1}{2}}$	$1^{\frac{1}{2}}$	$6^{1\frac{1}{2}}$	6^{nk}	Lanerie C J	3.40
24Oct04 9Wds2	Roarofvictory	LB b	3	112	7	11	8^{hd}	10^{5}	10^{2}	8^{5}	$7^{2\frac{3}{4}}$	Noll C S	57.50
2Nov04 8CD1	Quintons Gold Rush	LB	3	121	8	2	2^{2}	$2^{1\frac{1}{2}}$	$2^{\frac{1}{2}}$	7^{2}	$8^{6\frac{3}{4}}$	Berry M C	2.60
21Oct04 7Kee6	Gamblin	LB b	3	116	6	1	$1^{\frac{1}{2}}$	$1^{\frac{1}{2}}$	7^{hd}	9^{8}	9^{4}	Lopez J	26.70
1Nov04 5RP1	Commander Buck	LB	3	116	10	7	$6^{\frac{1}{2}}$	$9^{\frac{1}{2}}$	11	10	10	Williams R D	57.80
24Oct04 5LaD2	Mr. Jester	LB b	3	116	9	6	4^{2}	$4^{1\frac{1}{2}}$	$3^{\frac{1}{2}}$	—	—	Melancon G	9.40

OFF AT 4:33 Start Good. Won driving. Track muddy.

TIME :22^{2}, :45^{4}, 1:10^{4}, 1:37^{2}, 1:50^{1} (:22.43, :45.87, 1:10.90, 1:37.48, 1:50.26)

$2 Mutuel Prices:				
	2 – WALLY'S CHOICE	69.80	28.40	9.40
	3 – GOLDEN GLEN		9.20	4.60
	12 – CRYPTOGRAPH			3.20

$2 EXACTA 2–3 PAID $604.00 $2 QUINELLA 2–3 PAID $319.00
$2 TRIFECTA 2–3–12 PAID $2,555.00 $1 SUPERFECTA 2–3–12–4 PAID $9,437.60

B. g, (Feb), by Quick Cut – L'Etoile Jolie , by Commemorate . Trainer Biehler Michael. Bred by Curtis A Sampson (Minn).

WALLY'S CHOICE outrun early, tracked the pace up the backstretch while inside, reached a striking position entering the second turn, altered course outside, responded when asked to find his best stride in time. GOLDEN GLEN unhurried early while inside, crept closer up the backstretch, reached a forward position entering the second turn, responded to pressure while inside upper stretch but could not keep pace. CRYPTOGRAPH stalked the early pace from the outside, crept closer entering the second turn, gained a short advantage at the eighth pole but flattened out late. SLEW SLAYER well placed from between foes, tracked the pace up the backstretch, advanced entering the second turn, responded when asked but was too late. FOREIGN JUSTICE went evenly. BRITT'S JULES chased the pace from the inside, inched closer up the backstretch, gained the advantage entering the second turn but faltered in the drive. ROAROFVICTORY could only pass tried ones. QUINTONS GOLD RUSH dueled from the outside and tired. GAMBLIN dueled from the inside and tired. COMMANDER BUCK had a steady fade. MR. JESTER up close outside, stopped after going three quarters and was eased both stretch and finish.

Owners– 1, McNeil Joyce and Wally and Sampson Curtis; 2, Stony Oak Farm LLC; 3, Pin Oak Stable LLC; 4, Messino James M; 5, Salisbury Duane; 6, Southern Equine Stable LLC; 7, Orion Stables; 8, Padua Stables & Jay Manoogian; 9, Pabst Henry E; 10, Prentice Bryant H III; 11, Biggs Kaaren J

Trainers– 1, Biehler Michael; 2, Barnett Bobby C; 3, Von Hemel Donnie K; 4, Beam Edward; 5, Salisbury Joyce; 6, Guillot Eric; 7, McCoy James B; 8, Asmussen Steven M; 9, O'Callaghan Niall M; 10, Ingram Steve; 11, Wren Steve

Scratched– Shrewd Deputy (12Jul04 9EIP5)

TENTH RACE
Churchill
NOVEMBER 25, 2004

1⅛ MILES. (1.47^{1}) 89TH RUNNING OF THE FALLS CITY HANDICAP. Grade II. Purse $300,000 FOR FILLIES AND MARES, THREE–YEARS–OLD AND UPWARD. By subscription of $300 each on or before November 13, 2004. $1,500 to pass the entry box; $1,500 additional to start, with $300,000 added of which 62% of all monies to the owner of the winner, 20% to second, 10% to third, 5% to fourth and 3% to fifth. Weights to be announced Saturday, November 20, 2004. Starters to be named through the entry box by the usual time of closing. Trophy to winning owner. Closed Saturday, November 13, 2004 with 14 nominations.

Value of Race: $325,200 Winner $201,624; second $65,040; third $32,520; fourth $16,260; fifth $9,756. Mutuel Pool $218,150.00 Exacta Pool $140,628.00 Trifecta Pool $121,288.00 Superfecta Pool $40,010.00

Last Raced	Horse	M/Eqt.	A.	Wt	PP	St	¼	½	¾	Str	Fin	Jockey	Odds $1
7Nov04 10CD1	Halory Leigh	L	4	116	3	3	$5^{\frac{1}{2}}$	4^{hd}	$3^{1\frac{1}{2}}$	1^{hd}	$1^{2\frac{3}{4}}$	Martin E M Jr	1.20
7Nov04 10CD3	Susan's Angel	L	3	114	4	2	$2^{1\frac{1}{2}}$	2^{1}	1^{hd}	$2^{2\frac{1}{2}}$	$2^{3\frac{1}{4}}$	Day P	4.60
7Nov04 10CD10	Miss Fortunate	L	4	113	2	6	4^{1}	$3^{\frac{1}{2}}$	$4^{\frac{1}{2}}$	3^{hd}	$3^{2\frac{1}{4}}$	Melancon L	20.50
30Oct04 2LS6	Indy Groove	L	4	114	1	5	1^{1}	1^{1}	$2^{\frac{1}{2}}$	$4^{2\frac{1}{2}}$	4^{3}	Blanc B	3.20
25Oct04 8Del1	Flower Forest	L b	4	116	5	7	6^{2}	6^{hd}	$6^{3\frac{1}{2}}$	$6^{2\frac{1}{2}}$	5^{hd}	Razo E Jr	13.80
7Nov04 10CD6	Mayo On the Side	L bf	5	116	6	4	3^{hd}	$5^{\frac{1}{2}}$	$5^{1\frac{1}{2}}$	$5^{1\frac{1}{2}}$	$6^{1\frac{1}{2}}$	McKee J	4.10
31Oct04 5CD3	Red Cell	L f	4	111	7	1	7	7	7	7	7	Hernandez B J Jr	48.20

OFF AT 3:53 Start Good. Won driving. Track good.

TIME :24^{1}, :48^{3}, 1:13^{1}, 1:38^{4}, 1:51^{4} (:24.20, :48.70, 1:13.28, 1:38.80, 1:51.81)

$2 Mutuel Prices:				
	3 – HALORY LEIGH	4.40	3.00	2.40
	4 – SUSAN'S ANGEL		3.60	3.00
	2 – MISS FORTUNATE			5.20

$2 EXACTA 3–4 PAID $16.40 $2 TRIFECTA 3–4–2 PAID $124.20
$1 SUPERFECTA 3–4–2–1 PAID $171.40

Ch. f, (Feb), by Halory Hunter – Graceful Leigh , by Clever Trick . Trainer Romans Dale. Bred by Al Profitt & Larry Demeritte (Ky).

HALORY LEIGH, well placed from the outset while lightly rated between foes, raced four wide on the backstretch, came a bit wider to take over leaving the three-sixteenths pole, then was under strong left-handed whipping to draw clear. SUSAN'S ANGEL bobbled lightly just after the break, went up soon after to press front-running INDY GROOVE three or four wide, gained a slight edge just before going six furlongs, was headed by the winner entering the upper stretch and continued on as second best. MISS FORTUNATE, checked in behind horses during the opening furlong and angled to the inside, was never far back, maneuvered out four or five wide entering the lane, loomed a solid threat for the last eighth but couldn't produce the needed response. INDY GROOVE gained the advantage near the inside early, made the pace for nearly six furlongs, lost the edge to SUSAN'S ANGEL and gradually weakened. FLOWER FOREST, four or five wide throughout, failed to rally. MAYO ON THE SIDE, close up outside the leaders early while four or five wide, continued within striking distance to the stretch while remaining off the inside and flattened out. RED CELL broke in front, was five or six wide into the first turn, settled in behind the leaders on the backstretch and never menaced.

Owners– 1, Crawford Jerry Gannon Matt and Grask Charlie; 2, S Angel Stable; 3, Lyon Stables; 4, Glen Hill Farm; 5, Melnyk Eugene and Laura; 6, Lothenbach Stables Inc; 7, McEwan Fred and Wilhemina M

Trainers– 1, Romans Dale; 2, Lukas D Wayne; 3, Mott William I; 4, Proctor Thomas F; 5, Reinstedler Anthony; 6, Nafzger Carl A; 7, Vance David R

$2 Pick Three (10–1–3) Paid $67.00 ; Pick Three Pool $28,958 .

NINTH RACE
Aqueduct
NOVEMBER 26, 2004

1 MILE. (1.32^{2}) 65TH RUNNING OF THE TOP FLIGHT HANDICAP. Grade II. Purse $150,000 (UP TO $28,500 NYSBFOA) A HANDICAP FOR FILLIES AND MARES THREE YEARS OLD AND UPWARD. By subscription of $150 each, which should accompany the nomination; $750 to pass the entry box; $750 to start. The purse to be divided 60% to the winner, 20% to second,10% to third, 5% to fourth, 3% to fifth and 2% divided equally among remaining finishers. A trophy will be presented to the winning owner. Closed Saturday, November 13, 2004 with 19 nominations.

Value of Race: $150,000 Winner $90,000; second $30,000; third $15,000; fourth $7,500; fifth $4,500; sixth $3,000. Mutuel Pool $450,179.00 Exacta Pool $367,465.00 Trifecta Pool $277,940.00

Last Raced	Horse	M/Eqt.	A.	Wt	PP	St	¼	½	¾	Str	Fin	Jockey	Odds $1
1Oct04 ^{9}Hoo^{1}	Daydreaming	L	3	117	6	2	$4^{\frac{1}{2}}$	4^{hd}	4^{1}	$2^{1\frac{1}{2}}$	1no	Bailey J D	1.05
30Oct04 ^{4}Aqu^{1}	Bending Strings	L	3	118	2	4	$5^{\frac{1}{2}}$	$5^{\frac{1}{2}}$	5^{1}	3^{hd}	$2^{2\frac{1}{4}}$	Bridgmohan S X	3.25
6Nov04 ^{9}Aqu^{2}	Roar Emotion	L	4	116	3	3	$3^{1\frac{1}{2}}$	$3^{1\frac{1}{2}}$	2^{hd}	1^{hd}	$3^{2\frac{1}{4}}$	Velazquez J R	3.50
29Oct04 ^{8}Aqu^{1}	Pop Princess	L b	4	112	1	6	2^{1}	1^{hd}	1^{hd}	$4^{\frac{1}{2}}$	4^{2}	Bejarano R	5.60
4Nov04 ^{9}CD^{1}	Tempus Fugit	L	4	114	5	1	1^{hd}	$2^{1\frac{1}{2}}$	$3^{\frac{1}{2}}$	5^{7}	$5^{4\frac{1}{2}}$	Elliott S	20.70
22Oct04 ^{8}Med^{5}	Caught in the Rain	L f	5	114	4	5	6	6	6	6	6	Velasquez C	31.00

OFF AT 3:48 Start Good . Won driving. Track fast.

TIME :23^{4}, :46^{4}, 1:11, 1:35^{1} (:23.87, :46.88, 1:11.04, 1:35.29)

$2 Mutuel Prices:

7 – DAYDREAMING	4.10	2.60	2.20
2 – BENDING STRINGS		3.10	2.40
3 – ROAR EMOTION			2.50

$2 EXACTA 7–2 PAID $11.60 $2 TRIFECTA 7–2–3 PAID $25.40

B. f, (Mar), by A.P. Indy – Get Lucky , by Mr. Prospector . Trainer McGaughey III Claude R. Bred by Ogden Mills Phipps (Ky).

DAYDREAMING raced close up outside, rallied four wide approaching the stretch, dug in resolutely when roused and prevailed after a rousing finish. BENDING STRINGS raced in hand along the inside early, came wide for the drive, drifted out in the stretch and finished gamely outside, just missing. ROAR EMOTION raced with the pace while in hand, rallied three wide on the turn, reached the front approaching the eighth pole and weakened in the final furlong. POP PRINCESS argued the pace along the inside and tired on the rail in the stretch. TEMPUS FUGIT contested the pace from the outside and tired in the stretch. CAUGHT IN THE RAIN was bothered at the start, was outrun early and had no response when roused.

Owners– 1, Phipps Ogden M; 2, Gunther John D; 3, Allen Joseph; 4, Stronach Stables; 5, Briland Farm; 6, Heiligbrodt Racing Stable and New Walter L

Trainers– 1, McGaughey III Claude R; 2, McLaughlin Kiaran P; 3, McLaughlin Kiaran P; 4, Frankel Robert; 5, Levine Bruce N; 6, Preciado Guadalupe

Scratched– Distinctive Kitten (23Oct04 ^{6}Bel^{3})

ELEVENTH RACE
Churchill
NOVEMBER 26, 2004

1⅛ MILES. (1.47^{1}) 130TH RUNNING OF THE CLARK HANDICAP. Grade II. Purse $500,000 FOR THREE-YEAR-OLDS AND UPWARD. By subscription of $500 each on or before November 13, 2004. $2,500 to pass the entry box; $2,500 additional to start, with $500,000 added of which 62% of all monies to the owner of the winner, 20% to second, 10% to third, 5% to fourth and 3% to fifth. Weights to be announced Saturday, November 20. Starters to be named through the entry box by the usual time of closing. Trophy to winning owner. Closed, Saturday November 13, 2004 with 21 nominations.

Value of Race: $558,000 Winner $345,960; second $111,600; third $55,800; fourth $27,900; fifth $16,740. Mutuel Pool $733,307.00 Exacta Pool $474,275.00 Trifecta Pool $400,865.00 Superfecta Pool $155,233.00

Last Raced	Horse	M/Eqt.	A.	Wt	PP	St	¼	½	¾	Str	Fin	Jockey	Odds $1
11Sep04 ^{10}Bel^{2}	Saint Liam	L b	4	117	2	6	$2^{\frac{1}{2}}$	$2^{1\frac{1}{2}}$	$2^{2\frac{1}{2}}$	$1^{1\frac{1}{2}}$	$1^{1\frac{1}{4}}$	Prado E S	1.20
30Oct04 ^{1}LS^{2}	Seek Gold	L	4	111	3	9	9	9	9	$5^{2\frac{1}{2}}$	2no	Melancon L	42.20
30Oct04 ^{9}LS^{4}	Perfect Drift	L	5	118	8	3	3^{hd}	3^{hd}	$3^{\frac{1}{2}}$	$2^{1\frac{1}{2}}$	$3^{1\frac{1}{4}}$	Desormeaux K J	3.00
2Oct04 ^{9}Hoo^{2}	Suave	L b	3	113	6	1	4^{1}	$5^{2\frac{1}{2}}$	$4^{\frac{1}{2}}$	4^{hd}	$4^{1\frac{1}{4}}$	Sarvis D A	39.40
14Oct04 ^{8}Kee^{2}	Eurosilver	L	3	113	7	2	6^{hd}	$7^{\frac{1}{2}}$	$8^{3\frac{1}{2}}$	6^{1}	$5^{1\frac{1}{4}}$	Castellano J J	8.80
2Oct04 ^{8}SA^{1}	LundysLiability-Brz	L	4	120	4	5	$1^{\frac{1}{2}}$	$1^{1\frac{1}{2}}$	1^{hd}	$3^{2\frac{1}{2}}$	$6^{1\frac{1}{2}}$	Flores D R	4.10
29Oct04 ^{7}LS^{7}	Pies Prospect	L	3	112	9	4	5^{hd}	$8^{4\frac{1}{2}}$	6^{hd}	8^{4}	$7^{\frac{1}{2}}$	McKee J	46.60
22Aug04 ^{8}Dmr^{6}	Colonial Colony	L	6	116	1	8	8^{4}	6^{hd}	7^{hd}	7^{1}	$8^{13\frac{1}{4}}$	Day P	19.20
31Oct04 ^{9}CD^{1}	Sir Cherokee	L	4	116	5	7	7^{2}	$4^{\frac{1}{2}}$	$5^{2\frac{1}{2}}$	9	9	Blanc B	10.20

OFF AT 4:31 Start Good . Won driving. Track fast.

TIME :24, :48, 1:12, 1:37^{2}, 1:50^{4} (:24.03, :48.03, 1:12.13, 1:37.44, 1:50.81)

$2 Mutuel Prices:

2 – SAINT LIAM	4.40	3.40	2.60
3 – SEEK GOLD		25.60	7.60
9 – PERFECT DRIFT			2.60

$2 EXACTA 2–3 PAID $100.60 $2 TRIFECTA 2–3–9 PAID $365.80
$1 SUPERFECTA 2–3–9–6 PAID $1,654.40

B. c, (Apr), by Saint Ballado – Quiet Dance , by Quiet American . Trainer Dutrow Richard E Jr. Bred by Edward P Evans (Ky).

SAINT LIAM bumped soundly with SEEK GOLD at the start, was rated in behind front-running LUNDY'S IIABILITY (BRZ), eased out to press that one four wide on the backstretch, reached the front at the quarter-mile ground, drifted out for a stride while edging clear at the furlong grounds and was kept to his task. SEEK GOLD broke in badly at the start and exchanged bumps with the winner, was bumped soon after by LUNDY'S LIABILITY (BRZ) and had to steady sharply, quickly settled, was outrun to the far turn while three wide, split foes nicely in the upper stretch and was going well at the end in a good effort despite an eventful trip. PERFECT DRIFT stalked the pace under light rating from early on, loomed menacingly outside the winner five wide for the drive, was carried out for a stride at the eighth pole, then came up empty. SUAVE, well placed within easy striking distance between horses four wide around the far turn, angled six wide for the drive, was a prominent factor for the last eighth but failed to muster a further account. EUROSILVER, four or five wide, was between horses approaching the stretch, continued five wide and gained only slightly at the end. LUNDY'S LIABILITY (BRZ) drifted in at the start bumping SEEK GOLD, continued inside to gain the lead, was clear on the backstretch, managed a narrow advantage until the final quarter, lost the lead to the winner and weakened along the inside. PIES PROSPECT followed the pace five or six wide and couldn't keep pace after six furlongs while coming wider into the lane. COLONIAL COLONY settled inside early, moved between foes on the far turn, angled five wide into the stretch but never menaced. SIR CHEROKEE, closer than usual early, was checked in behind horses approaching the first turn, saved ground while remaining a threat for seven furlongs and weakened gradually thereafter.

Owners– 1, Warren Jr Mr and Mrs William K; 2, LaPenta Robert V; 3, Stonecrest Farm; 4, Jay Em Ess Stable; 5, Buckram Oak Farm; 6, Stud TNT Gonzalo Torrealba and Mrs M Slack; 7, LaPenta Robert V; 8, Lakeside Farms LLC; 9, Domino Stud of Lex LLC

Trainers– 1, Dutrow Richard E Jr; 2, Zito Nicholas P; 3, Johnson Murray W; 4, McGee Paul J; 5, Nafzger Carl A; 6, Frankel Robert; 7, Zito Nicholas P; 8, Stewart Dallas; 9, Tomlinson Michael A

Scratched– Fantasticat (30Oct04 ^{9}LS ^{9})

$2 Pick Three (12–3–2) Paid $283.20 ; Pick Three Pool $36,545 .

THIRD RACE
Hollywood
NOVEMBER 26, 2004

1 MILE. (Turf) (1.32^3) 14TH RUNNING OF THE MIESQUE(1ST DIVISION). Grade III. Purse $75,000 FOR FILLIES TWO-YEARS-OLD. By subscription of $100 each on or before Wednesday, November 17, or by supplementary nomination of $2,000 each by closing time of entries. All nominees to pay $500 to enter and an additional $1,000 to start. Gross purse $75,000 of which $45,000 to be paid to the winner, $15,000 to second, $9,000 to third, $4,500 to fourth and $1,500 to fifth. 121 lbs. Non-winners of $60,000 at one mile or over allowed 3 lbs. ; non winners of two races other than claiming at one mile or over, 5 lbs. ; a race other than claimimg, 7 lbs. Hollywood Park reserves the right not to divide this race. Should this race not be divided and the number of entries exceed the starting gate capacity , first preference will be given to graded or group stakes winners. Second preference will be given to those horses with the highest total earnings. Entry fees will be refunded to all horses which fail to draw into this race. A trophy will be presented to the winning owner. Closed Wednesday, November 17 with 21 nominations.

Value of Race: $75,000 Winner $45,000; second $15,000; third $9,000; fourth $4,500; fifth $1,500. Mutuel Pool $277,882.00 Exacta Pool $185,185.00 Quinella Pool $16,101.00 Trifecta Pool $182,481.00 Superfecta Pool $68,922.00

Last Raced	Horse	M/Eqt.	A.	Wt	PP	St	¼	½	¾	Str	Fin	Jockey	Odds $1
4Sep04 CRA3	Louvain-Ire	LB	2	115	1	7	8	7	5^{1}	3^{hd}	1^{2}	Dominguez R A	2.00
21Aug04 DEA2	RoylCopenhgen-FR	B	2	114	5	8	7^{2}	4^{hd}	3^{hd}	2^{hd}	2^{nk}	Douglas R R	1.60
24Jly04 Leo4	La Maitresse-Ire	LB f	2	114	3	4	$3^{1/2}$	3^{1}	4^{2}	$4^{1\frac12}$	$3^{2\frac12}$	Court J K	11.70
16Oct04 10SA4	Lunar Flight	LB	2	114	8	1	2^{1}	$2^{1\frac12}$	$2^{1\frac12}$	1^{1}	4^{4}	Martinez F F	30.90
16Oct04 10SA7	Kachina Dream	LB b	2	116	2	5	5^{1}	5^{1}	7	7	$5^{1/2}$	Figueroa O	72.60
16Oct04 10SA1	Lady Truffles	LB	2	121	7	2	1^{1}	1^{hd}	1^{hd}	$5^{2\frac12}$	6^{2}	Pedroza M A	7.30
10Nov04 5Hol2	Crystal House	LB	2	114	6	6	$6^{1/2}$	6^{1}	$6^{1/2}$	6^{hd}	7	Espinoza V	8.40
30Oct04 3LS10	Culture Clash	LB b	2	115	4	3	4^{2}	—	—	—	—	Gomez G K	6.70

OFF AT 1:35 Start Good . Won driving. Course firm.

TIME :24^1, :48^4, 1:13, 1:25^1, 1:37 (:24.32, :48.87, 1:13.15, 1:25.27, 1:37.19)

$2 Mutuel Prices:

1 – LOUVAIN-IRE	6.00	3.20	3.00
5 – ROYAL COPENHAGEN-FR		3.20	2.80
3 – LA MAITRESSE-IRE			4.20

$1 EXACTA 1–5 PAID $7.20 $2 QUINELLA 1–5 PAID $6.40
$1 TRIFECTA 1–5–3 PAID $34.70 $1 SUPERFECTA 1–5–3–8 PAID $251.90

B. f, (Feb), by Sinndar-Ire – Flanders-Ire , by Common Grounds . Trainer Frankel Robert. Bred by Twelve Oaks Stud Establishment (Ire).

LOUVAIN (IRE) a bit slow to begin, saved ground off the pace, moved up a bit off the rail on the second turn, swung three deep into the stretch, gained the lead four across the course past midstretch and pulled clear under a couple cracks of the whip and good handling. ROYAL COPENHAGEN (FR) also off a bit slowly, settled just off the rail then angled in, advanced inside leaving the backstretch and on the second turn, came out into the stretch, bid between horses in the drive, could not match the winner but gamely edged a rival for second. LA MAITRESSE (IRE) pulled her way along early and steadied off heels into the first turn, stalked just off the rail then outside the runner-up on the second turn, came out into the stretch, also bid between foes in the drive and was edged for the place. LUNAR FLIGHT three deep into the first turn, stalked off the rail then bid outside a foe and dueled for the lead, gained the advantage into the stretch, inched away but weakened late. KACHINA DREAM chased inside then outside a rival, dropped back three deep on the second turn then passed tiring rivals in the stretch. LADY TRUFFLES sped to the early lead and angled in, set the pace inside, dueled along the rail on the backstretch and second turn and weakened in the stretch. CRYSTAL HOUSE three deep into the first turn, settled outside a rival then off the rail on the second turn and did not rally. CULTURE CLASH steadied off heels into the first turn, stalked outside a rival, was pulled up lame on the backstretch and vanned off.

Owners– 1, Gann Edmund A; 2, Duchossois Richard L; 3, Williamson Gross Dineo Et Al; 4, Beaumont Maurie; 5, Edmunds Frank and Jeff; 6, Janavar Thoroughbreds LLC; 7, Vreeland James R; 8, Everest Stables Inc

Trainers– 1, Frankel Robert; 2, De Seroux Laura; 3, Gaines Carla; 4, Jory Ian P D; 5, Stute Melvin F; 6, Sadler John W; 7, Walsh Kathy; 8, Polanco Marcelo

$2 Daily Double (1–1) Paid $71.40 ; Daily Double Pool $19,108 .
$1 Pick Three (2–1–1) Paid $335.20 ; Pick Three Pool $95,092 .

SIXTH RACE
Hollywood
NOVEMBER 26, 2004

1 MILE. (Turf) (1.32^3) 14TH RUNNING OF THE MIESQUE(2ND DIVISION). Grade III. Purse $75,000 FOR FILLIES TWO-YEARS-OLD. By subscription of $100 each on or before Wednesday, November 17, or by supplementary nomination of $2,000 each by closing time of entries. All nominees to pay $500 to enter and an additional $1,000 to start. Gross purse $75,000 of which $45,000 to be paid to the winner, $15,000 to second, $9,000 to third, $4,500 to fourth and $1,500 to fifth. 121 lbs. Non-winners of $60,000 at one mile or over allowed 3 lbs. ; non winners of two races other than claiming at one mile or over, 5 lbs. ; a race other than claimimg, 7 lbs. Hollywood Park reserves the right not to divide this race. Should this race not be divided and the number of entries exceed the starting gate capacity , first preference will be given to graded or group stakes winners. Second preference will be given to those horses with the highest total earnings. Entry fees will be refunded to all horses which fail to draw into this race. A trophy will be presented to the winning owner. Closed Wednesday, November 17 with 21nominations

Value of Race: $75,000 Winner $45,000; second $15,000; third $9,000; fourth $4,500; fifth $1,500. Mutuel Pool $438,347.00 Exacta Pool $284,631.00 Quinella Pool $24,473.00 Trifecta Pool $301,972.00 Superfecta Pool $129,046.00

Last Raced	Horse	M/Eqt.	A.	Wt	PP	St	¼	½	¾	Str	Fin	Jockey	Odds $1
28Oct04 8Kee1	Paddy's Daisy	LB	2	121	6	6	$6^{1/2}$	$6^{1\frac12}$	$5^{1/2}$	2^{2}	1^{nk}	Nakatani C S	1.70
27Oct04 3SA1	Conveyor's Angel	LB	2	118	4	3	$5^{1\frac12}$	$5^{2\frac12}$	$4^{1\frac12}$	1^{1}	2^{5}	Stevens G L	3.50
10Nov04 6Hol1	Kenza	LB	2	116	7	1	8	8	8	$6^{1\frac12}$	$3^{1/2}$	Espinoza V	10.20
10Jly04 Mil2	Mac Rhapsody-GB	LB	2	115	5	7	$7^{1\frac12}$	$7^{1\frac12}$	$7^{1\frac12}$	3^{1}	$4^{3\frac12}$	Gomez G K	19.40
2Oct04 NEW7	Lady Le Quesne-Ire	B	2	114	2	8	3^{2}	$3^{2\frac12}$	$3^{1/2}$	5^{hd}	5^{3}	Farina T	40.90
27Oct04 3SA3	Wise Investor	LB	2	115	3	4	4^{2}	4^{hd}	6^{1}	7^{hd}	6^{1}	Valdivia J Jr	7.70
13Oct04 LBS1	Witten	f	2	116	8	2	$1^{1/2}$	1^{hd}	1^{hd}	4^{hd}	$7^{5\frac12}$	Baze T C	2.30
20Oct04 1SA1	She Sings	LB b	2	116	1	5	$2^{2\frac12}$	2^{2}	2^{1}	8	8	Almeida G F	35.90

OFF AT 3:09 Start Good . Won driving. Course firm.

TIME :23^1, :47^3, 1:12, 1:24^2, 1:36^4 (:23.33, :47.66, 1:12.15, 1:24.50, 1:36.92)

$2 Mutuel Prices:

6 – PADDY'S DAISY	5.40	3.00	2.60
4 – CONVEYOR'S ANGEL		3.60	2.80
7 – KENZA			3.80

$1 EXACTA 6–4 PAID $9.10 $2 QUINELLA 4–6 PAID $10.40
$1 TRIFECTA 6–4–7 PAID $51.30 $1 SUPERFECTA 6–4–7–5 PAID $316.90

Ch. f, (Apr), by King of Kings-Ire – Mrs. Paddy , by Woodman . Trainer Pletcher Todd A. Bred by Stonehaven Farm (Ky).

PADDY'S DAISY four wide into the first turn, chased outside a rival, moved up on the second turn, came four wide into the stretch, bid outside the runner-up past midstretch and gamely but narrowly prevailed late under urging. CONVEYOR'S ANGEL bumped at the start, went three deep into the first turn, stalked outside a rival then off the rail, advanced outside a foe on the second turn, gained the advantage three wide into the stretch, inched away, fought back inside the winner and continued willingly to the wire. KENZA five wide into the first turn, settled off the rail, circled four wide into the stretch and just got the show. MAC RHAPSODY (GB) pulled early, angled in and saved ground off the pace, came out on the second turn and four wide into the stretch with a move forward and was edged late for third. LADY LE QUESNE (IRE) stalked the pace inside, waited off heels leaving the second turn, came out into the stretch and lacked the needed late kick. WISE INVESTOR bumped at the start, chased between foes then a bit off the rail, continued inside into and on the second turn, came out leaving that bend and three deep into the stretch and weakened. WITTEN pulled her way along and angled in early, dueled outside a rival then between horses into the stretch and weakened. SHE SINGS had good early speed and dueled inside to the stretch and also weakened.

Owners– 1, Stonehaven Farm; 2, Cono Charles; 3, Moss Mr and Mrs Jerome S; 4, Gould Family Trust; 5, A and R Stables LLC and Class Racing Stable; 6, Williamson Warren B; 7, Scheumann Theiline P; 8, Everest Stables Inc

Trainers– 1, Pletcher Todd A; 2, Paasch Christopher S; 3, Shirreffs John; 4, Cassidy James; 5, Hofmans David; 6, Gaines Carla; 7, Rouget Jean-Claude; 8, Polanco Marcelo

$2 Daily Double (4–6) Paid $55.40 ; Daily Double Pool $30,472 .
$1 Pick Three (1–4–6) Paid $146.40 ; Pick Three Pool $70,896 .

EIGHTH RACE
Hollywood
NOVEMBER 26, 2004

5½ FURLONGS. (Turf) (1.00^{2}) 20TH RUNNING OF THE HOLLYWOOD TURF EXPRESS HANDICAP. Grade III. Purse $150,000 FOR THREE-YEAR-OLDS AND UPWARD. By subscription of $150 each on or before Wednesday, November 17 or by supplementary nomination of $3,000 each by 3:00 pm Friday, November 19. All nominees to pay $1,000 to enter and an additional $1,000 to start. Gross purse $150,000 of which $90,000 to be paid to the winner, $30,000 to second, $18,000 to third, $9,000 to fourth and $3,000 to fifth. Weights Saturday, November 20. Starters to be named through the entry box by closing time of entries. Hollywood Park reserves the right not to divide this race. Should this race not be divided and the number of entries exceed twelve (12), highweights on the weight scale will be preferred. Total earnings in 2004 will used in determining the order of preference of horses assigned equal weights on the scale. Entry fees will be refunded to all horses which fail to draw into this race. A trophy will be presented to the winning owner. Closed Wednesday, November 17 with 21 nominations.

Value of Race: $150,000 Winner $90,000; second $30,000; third $18,000; fourth $9,000; fifth $3,000. Mutuel Pool $462,824.00 Exacta Pool $292,315.00 Quinella Pool $25,008.00 Trifecta Pool $296,429.00 Superfecta Pool $125,098.00

Last Raced	Horse	M/Eqt.	A.	Wt	PP	St	¼	⅜	Str	Fin	Jockey	Odds $1
30Oct04 ^{5}LS^{5}	Cajun Beat	LB b	4	122	3	7	7^{hd}	$7^{1\frac{1}{2}}$	5^{1}	1^{3}	Dominguez R A	2.20
30Oct04 ^{6}SA^{4}	Geronimo-Chi	LB b	5	117	6	9	9	9	$7^{2\frac{1}{2}}$	2^{nk}	Nakatani C S	3.20
22Oct04 ^{9}Kee^{7}	Mighty Beau	LB f	5	117	2	6	3^{hd}	$4^{1\frac{1}{2}}$	$3^{\frac{1}{2}}$	$3^{\frac{1}{2}}$	Gomez G K	22.50
13Nov04 ^{8}Hol^{1}	Golden Arrow	LB	5	115	1	8	8^{2}	6^{hd}	4^{hd}	4^{1}	Douglas R R	13.30
30Oct04 ^{6}SA^{2}	De Valmont-Aus	LB b	7	115	8	2	$1^{\frac{1}{2}}$	$1^{2\frac{1}{2}}$	1^{3}	$5^{1\frac{1}{2}}$	Espinoza V	2.90
14Nov04 ^{7}CD^{1}	WorldwindRomance	LB	6	118	9	1	6^{2}	$8^{\frac{1}{2}}$	$8^{\frac{1}{2}}$	6^{hd}	Fogelsonger R	6.30
10Oct04 ^{8}SA^{3}	Hombre Rapido	LB b	7	117	4	4	2^{2}	$3^{1\frac{1}{2}}$	2^{hd}	$7^{3\frac{1}{2}}$	Baze T C	11.50
16Oct04 ^{6}SA^{5}	Only the Best	LB bf	4	113	5	5	$5^{\frac{1}{2}}$	5^{1}	9	8^{1}	Bisono A	47.30
26Sep04 ^{9}Fpx^{1}	Coded Message	LB f	6	113	7	3	$4^{1\frac{1}{2}}$	2^{hd}	$6^{\frac{1}{2}}$	9	Court J K	27.30

OFF AT 4:09 Start Good. Won driving. Course firm.

TIME :21^{1}, :43^{3}, :56, 1:02 (:21.25, :43.60, :56.15, 1:02.08)

$2 Mutuel Prices:				
	3 – CAJUN BEAT	6.40	3.80	3.20
	6 – GERONIMO-CHI		3.80	2.80
	2 – MIGHTY BEAU			6.60

$1 EXACTA 3–6 PAID $11.90 $2 QUINELLA 3–6 PAID $12.60
$1 TRIFECTA 3–6–2 PAID $118.40 $1 SUPERFECTA 3–6–2–1 PAID $560.60

Dk. b or br. g, (Mar), by Grand Slam – Beckys Shirt, by Cure the Blues. Trainer Frankel Robert. Bred by John T L Jones Jr & H Smoot Fahlgren (Ky).

CAJUN BEAT settled outside a rival, came out in upper stretch and rallied gamely under some left handed urging to gain the lead in deep stretch and won clear. GERONIMO (CHI) steadied when squeezed after the start, trailed off the rail, angled in on the turn, came out in the stretch and finished well to get the place late. MIGHTY BEAU stalked inside then a bit off the rail on the turn, came out in the stretch and was edged for second between foes late. GOLDEN ARROW allowed to settle inside, moved up along the rail on the turn, came out in the stretch, split horses in midstretch and again nearing the wire and just missed a minor award. DE VALMONT (AUS) angled in and dueled outside a rival, kicked clear and angled in on the turn, remained clear past midstretch but weakened late. WORLDWIND ROMANCE chased outside, went three deep on the turn and into the stretch and could not summon the necessary late response. HOMBRE RAPIDO had speed between foes then angled in and dueled inside a rival, stalked along the rail on the turn and weakened. ONLY THE BEST chased between horses then off the rail, went outside a rival on the turn and three deep into the stretch and also weakened. CODED MESSAGE stalked between horses then outside a rival into and on the turn, was between horses nearing midstretch and had little left in the final furlong.

Owners– 1, Padua Stable Ircan & Ircan; 2, Buster Jr William C Hays Rusty Surfside Equine et al; 3, Cloonan Mike and Carolan Anthony; 4, Pabst Henry E; 5, O'Connor David; 6, Gill Michael J; 7, Granja Vista Del Rio Stable; 8, Puglisi Stables; 9, STD Racing Stable

Trainers– 1, Frankel Robert; 2, Machowsky Michael; 3, Mullins Jeff; 4, Drysdale Neil; 5, Cardenas Ruben; 6, Shuman Mark; 7, Sadler John W; 8, Mullins Jeff; 9, Aguirre Paul G

$2 Daily Double (4–3) Paid $172.00 ; Daily Double Pool $32,993 .
$1 Pick Three (6–4–3) Paid $294.90 ; Pick Three Pool $119,741 .

SEVENTH RACE
Aqueduct
NOVEMBER 27, 2004

1⅛ MILES. (1.47) 83RD RUNNING OF THE DEMOISELLE. Grade II. Purse $200,000 FOR FILLIES TWO YEARS OLD. By subscription of $200 each, which should accompany the nomination; $1,000 to pass the entry box; $1,000 to start. The purse to be divided 60% to the winner, 20% to second, 10% to third, 5% to fourth, 3% to fifth and 2% divided equally among remaining finishers. 121 lbs. Non-winners of $100,000 at a mile or over other than restricted allowed 2 lbs.; $35,000 at a mile or over, 4 lbs.; two races other than maiden or claiming, 6 lbs. A trophy will be presented to the winning owner. Closed Saturday, November 13, 2004 with 14 Nominations.

Value of Race: $200,000 Winner $120,000; second $40,000; third $20,000; fourth $10,000; fifth $6,000; sixth $2,000; seventh $2,000. Mutuel Pool $772,266.00 Exacta Pool $421,647.00 Trifecta Pool $303,773.00

Last Raced	Horse	M/Eqt.	A.	Wt	PP	St	¼	½	¾	Str	Fin	Jockey	Odds $1
30Oct04 ^{3}LS^{4}	Sis City	L	2	119	4	2	1^{1}	$1^{\frac{1}{2}}$	$1^{\frac{1}{2}}$	$1^{3\frac{1}{2}}$	$1^{3\frac{3}{4}}$	Velazquez J R	a- 0.40
2Nov04 ^{6}Aqu^{3}	Salute	L b	2	115	2	5	$2^{\frac{1}{2}}$	$2^{1\frac{1}{2}}$	2^{1}	$2^{1\frac{1}{2}}$	2no	Bailey J D	2.90
2Nov04 ^{2}CD^{1}	Winning Season	L	2	115	5	4	$3^{\frac{1}{2}}$	$3^{\frac{1}{2}}$	$3^{\frac{1}{2}}$	3^{5}	3^{5}	Bejarano R	16.00
11Nov04 ^{3}Aqu^{3}	Secrets Galore	L b	2	115	1	1	4^{hd}	5^{5}	$5^{4\frac{1}{2}}$	$5^{5\frac{1}{2}}$	$4^{\frac{1}{2}}$	Elliott S	34.25
2Nov04 ^{6}Aqu^{2}	K. D.'s Shady Lady	L	2	115	3	3	$5^{1\frac{1}{2}}$	$4^{\frac{1}{2}}$	$4^{3\frac{1}{2}}$	4^{1}	$5^{8\frac{1}{2}}$	Velasquez C	a- 0.40
30Oct04 NEW^{3}	Natalie Jane-Ire		2	115	6	7	7	7	7	6^{6}	$6^{6\frac{3}{4}}$	Castellano J J	9.90
11Nov04 ^{6}Aqu^{2}	Money Helps	L	2	115	7	6	6^{3}	6^{6}	$6^{\frac{1}{2}}$	7	7	Santos J A	42.00

a–Coupled: Sis City and K. D.'s Shady Lady.

OFF AT 2:47 Start Good. Won driving. Track fast.

TIME :24^{2}, :48^{1}, 1:12^{2}, 1:37^{1}, 1:50^{1} (:24.55, :48.30, 1:12.49, 1:37.20, 1:50.39)

$2 Mutuel Prices:				
	1A – SIS CITY (a–entry)	2.80	2.10	2.10
	3 – SALUTE		2.20	2.10
	4 – WINNING SEASON			2.10

$2 EXACTA 1–3 PAID $4.50 $2 TRIFECTA 1–3–4 PAID $16.00

B. f, (Mar), by Slew City Slew – Smart Sis, by Beau Genius. Trainer Dutrow Richard E Jr. Bred by Heiligbrodt Racing Stable (Ky).

SIS CITY was hustled to the front, set the pace along the inside, drew clear when roused and remained safely clear under a drive. SALUTE prompted the pace from the outside, could not stay with the winner in the stretch and continued on to hold the place. WINNING SEASON raced with the pace while three wide and offered a mild rally outside. SECRETS GALORE raced close up along the inside early, came wide into the stretch and had no rally. K. D.'S SHADY LADY raced in hand along the inside and had no response when roused. NATALIE JANE (IRE) broke awkwardly, was outrun early, raced inside and had no rally. MONEY HELPS raced three wide on the first turn and tired.

Owners– 1, Goldfarb Sanford J Torre Joe Dubb Michael Davis Ira; 2, Phipps Ogden Mills et al; 3, Overbrook Farm; 4, Heiligbrodt Racing Stable; 5, Goldfarb Sanford Dubb Michael Gargano Carmen and Joscelyn Robert; 6, Woodcote Stud; 7, Gunther John D

Trainers– 1, Dutrow Richard E Jr; 2, McGaughey III Claude R; 3, Lukas D Wayne; 4, Preciado Guadalupe; 5, Dutrow Richard E Jr; 6, Butler Gerard A; 7, McLaughlin Kiaran P

$2 Daily Double (5–1) Paid $11.40 ; Daily Double Pool $117,157 .
$2 Pick Three (10–5–1) Paid $33.40 ; Pick Three Pool $91,399 .

EIGHTH RACE
Aqueduct
NOVEMBER 27, 2004

1⅛ MILES. (1.47) 91ST RUNNING OF THE REMSEN. Grade II. Purse $200,000 FOR TWO YEAR OLDS. By subscription of $200 each, which should accompany the nomination; $1,000 to pass the entry box; $1,000 to start. The purse to be divided 60% to the winner, 20% to second, 10% to third, 5% to fourth, 3% to fifth and 2% divided equally among remaining finishers. 122 lbs. Non–winners of $100,000 at a mile or over other than restricted allowed 2 lbs.; $35,000 at a mile or over, 4 lbs.; two races other than maiden or claiming, 6 lbs. A trophy will be presented to the winning owner. Closed Saturday, November 13, 2004 with 20 Nominations.

Value of Race: $200,000 Winner $120,000; second $40,000; third $20,000; fourth $10,000; fifth $6,000; sixth $4,000. Mutuel Pool $609,872.00 Exacta Pool $509,581.00 Trifecta Pool $366,259.00

Last Raced	Horse	M/Eqt.	A.	Wt	PP	St	¼	½	¾	Str	Fin	Jockey	Odds $1
2Nov04 ^{8}Aqu^{1}	Rockport Harbor	L	2	120	2	1	1^{1}	$1^{1\frac{1}{2}}$	1^{hd}	1^{hd}	1^{nk}	Elliott S	1.30
23Oct04 ^{4}Bel^{1}	Galloping Grocer	L	2	120	6	2	$2^{\frac{1}{2}}$	2^{1}	$2^{1\frac{1}{2}}$	2^{8}	$2^{8\frac{1}{4}}$	Velazquez J R	1.20
30Oct04 ^{3}Med^{1}	Killenaule	L f	2	120	4	4	$4^{4\frac{1}{2}}$	$4^{5\frac{1}{2}}$	3^{2}	$3^{3\frac{1}{2}}$	$3^{3\frac{1}{2}}$	Bailey J D	9.30
10Nov04 ^{3}Aqu^{1}	Stormy Jim	L	2	116	3	5	5^{5}	5^{3}	$5^{3\frac{1}{2}}$	$4^{1\frac{1}{2}}$	$4^{\frac{3}{4}}$	Castellano J J	37.00
22Oct04 ^{8}Kee^{2}	Father Weist	L	2	116	5	3	6	6	6	$5^{\frac{1}{2}}$	$5^{2\frac{3}{4}}$	Bejarano R	5.80
2Nov04 ^{4}Aqu^{1}	Pavo	L	2	116	1	6	$3^{1\frac{1}{2}}$	3^{hd}	$4^{\frac{1}{2}}$	6	6	Garcia Alan	50.00

OFF AT 3:15 Start Good . Won driving. Track fast.

TIME :23^{4}, :47^{1}, 1:11, 1:35^{2}, 1:48^{4} (:23.80, :47.20, 1:11.04, 1:35.58, 1:48.88)

$2 Mutuel Prices:			
2 – ROCKPORT HARBOR	4.60	2.50	2.10
6 – GALLOPING GROCER		2.40	2.10
4 – KILLENAULE			2.20

$2 EXACTA 2–6 PAID $8.80 $2 TRIFECTA 2–6–4 PAID $22.80

Gr/ro. c, (Apr), by Unbridled's Song – Regal Miss Copelan , by Copelan . Trainer Servis John C. Bred by Heiligbrodt Racing Stable & Taylor Made Farm Inc (Ky).

ROCKPORT HARBOR broke running, quickly showed in front, set the pace along inside, responded when joined by GALLOPING GROCER on the second turn, dug in resolutely on the rail in the stretch and held off that rival after a long drive. GALLOPING GROCER raced with the pace from the outside while in hand, moved up to engage the winner entering the second turn and fought it out gamely to the finish. KILLENAULE raced close up early, put in a three wide run on the second turn and tired in the stretch. STORMY JIM raced in hand early, rallied three wide on the second turn and had nothing left for the stretch drive. FATHER WEIST was outrun early, raced inside and had no response when roused. PAVO chased the pace along the inside and tired after the opening three quarters.

Owners– 1, Fox Hill Farms Inc; 2, Rosenthal Robert D and Waldbaum Bernice; 3, Tabor Michael B; 4, Carrion Jaime S; 5, Double C Stable; 6, Paraneck Stable

Trainers– 1, Servis John C; 2, Schettino Dominick A; 3, Pletcher Todd A; 4, Plesa Edward Jr; 5, Zito Nicholas P; 6, Pedersen Jennifer

$2 Pick Three (5–1–2) Paid $24.60 ; Pick Three Pool $94,933 .

NINTH RACE
Aqueduct
NOVEMBER 27, 2004

1 MILE. (1.32^{2}) 16TH RUNNING OF THE CIGAR MILE HANDICAP. Grade I. Purse $350,000 A HANDICAP FOR THREE YEAR OLDS AND UPWARD. By subscription of $350 each, which should accompany the nomination; $1,500 to pass the entry box; $2,000 to start. The purse to be divided 60% to the winner, 20% to second, 10% to third, 5 to fourth, 3% to fifth and 2% divided equally among remaining finishers. Trophies will be presented to the winning owner, trainer and jockey. Closed Saturday, November 13, 2004 with 24 Nominations.

Value of Race: $350,000 Winner $210,000; second $70,000; third $35,000; fourth $17,500; fifth $10,500; sixth $2,334; seventh $2,334; eighth $2,332. Mutuel Pool $733,817.00 Exacta Pool $582,733.00 Trifecta Pool $498,562.00

Last Raced	Horse	M/Eqt.	A.	Wt	PP	St	¼	½	¾	Str	Fin	Jockey	Odds $1
31Oct04 ^{7}Aqu^{2}	Lion Tamer	L f	4	115	5	6	8	8	2^{hd}	1^{hd}	$1^{1\frac{1}{4}}$	Santos J A	12.00
16Oct04 ^{8}Bel^{2}	Badge of Silver	L	4	115	6	3	3^{hd}	$3^{\frac{1}{2}}$	$3^{2\frac{1}{2}}$	$3^{3\frac{1}{2}}$	2no	Bailey J D	3.45
2Oct04 ^{8}Bel^{1}	Pico Central-Brz	L	5	123	1	5	1^{hd}	$1^{\frac{1}{2}}$	1^{hd}	$2^{2\frac{1}{2}}$	$3^{4\frac{3}{4}}$	Espinoza V	0.95
6Nov04 ^{8}Del^{1}	Unforgettable Max	L f	4	114	2	7	4^{3}	$4^{2\frac{1}{2}}$	$4^{1\frac{1}{2}}$	4^{1}	$4^{\frac{1}{2}}$	Velasquez C	13.10
21Oct04 ^{7}Bel^{1}	Potrisunrise-Arg	L b	7	114	3	8	7^{3}	7^{hd}	$6^{1\frac{1}{2}}$	$5^{3\frac{1}{2}}$	5^{5}	Luzzi M J	40.00
28Aug04 ^{11}Sar^{4}	Purge	L	3	116	4	4	2^{hd}	2^{hd}	5^{hd}	6^{hd}	$6^{1\frac{3}{4}}$	Velazquez J R	3.95
30Oct04 ^{1}LS^{3}	During	L	4	116	8	2	$5^{\frac{1}{2}}$	6^{hd}	0	7^{5}	7^{7}	Bejarano R	35.50
31Oct04 ^{7}Aqu^{4}	Voodoo	L b	6	114	7	1	6^{hd}	5^{hd}	7^{hd}	8	8	Chavez J F	28.75

OFF AT 3:49 Start Good . Won driving. Track fast.

TIME :22^{2}, :44^{1}, 1:08^{1}, 1:33^{2} (:22.47, :44.29, 1:08.23, 1:33.46)

$2 Mutuel Prices:			
5 – LION TAMER	26.00	9.40	3.70
6 – BADGE OF SILVER		5.80	3.10
1 – PICO CENTRAL–BRZ			2.20

$2 EXACTA 5–6 PAID $110.50 $2 TRIFECTA 5–6–1 PAID $358.50

Ch. c, (Feb), by Will's Way – Tippecanoe Creek , by Olympio . Trainer Pletcher Todd A. Bred by Paul Smith (Ky).

LION TAMER was unhurried while outrun early, advanced quickly with a four wide sweep on the turn, reached the front nearing the eighth pole, dug in gamely when roused and drew clear late. BADGE OF SILVER chased the pace while three wide, dropped back in upper stretch then dug in gamely and came again to get the place award. PICO CENTRAL (BRZ) was hustled up inside, set the pace and weakened along the inside in the final furlong. UNFORGETTABLE MAX raced with the pace while between rivals, was eased back on the backstretch, rallied inside nearing the stretch, angled out for the drive and lacked a rally. POTRISUNRISE (ARG) was a bit rank early on, was steadied while between rivals in the chute, put in a run along the inside on the turn and had little left for the stretch drive. PURGE contested the pace while between rivals and tired in the stretch. DURING was outrun early, raced between rivals and had no response when roused. VOODOO was outrun early, raced four wide and tired.

Owners– 1, Tabor Michael B; 2, Ramsey Kenneth L and Sarah K; 3, Tanaka Gary A; 4, Dweck Raymond; 5, Valente Roddy J; 6, Starlight Stables LLC Saylor Paul and Martin Johns; 7, McIngvale James; 8, Moore Susan and John

Trainers– 1, Pletcher Todd A; 2, Frankel Robert; 3, Lobo Paulo H; 4, Preciado Guadalupe; 5, Levine Bruce N; 6, Pletcher Todd A; 7, Hines N J; 8, Jerkens James A

Scratched– Kela (30Oct04 ^{5}LS ^{2})

NINTH RACE
Churchill
NOVEMBER 27, 2004

$1\frac{1}{16}$ MILES. (1.41^{3}) 61ST RUNNING OF THE GOLDEN ROD. Grade II. Purse $200,000 FOR FILLIES, TWO YEARS OLD. By subscription of $200 each on or before November 13, 2004. $1,000 to pass the entry box; $1,000 additional to start, with $200,000 added of which 62% of all monies to the owner of the winner, 20% to second, 10% to third, 5% to fourth and 3% to fifth. Weight 122 lbs. Non-winners of a sweepstakes at a mile or over allowed 2 lbs; two races other than maiden or claiming 4 lbs; a race other than maiden or claiming 6 lbs. Trophy to winning owner. The Golden Rod Stakes winner will automatically be nominated to the 2005 Kentucky Oaks, as far as nomination fee. Closed Saturday, November 13, 2004 with 17 nominations.

Value of Race: $215,400 Winner $133,548; second $43,080; third $21,540; fourth $10,770; fifth $6,462. Mutuel Pool $328,800.00 Exacta Pool $218,948.00 Trifecta Pool $160,792.00 Superfecta Pool $44,910.00

Last Raced	Horse	M/Eqt.	A.	Wt	PP	St	¼	½	¾	Str	Fin	Jockey	Odds $1
30Oct04 ^{3}LS^{3}	Runway Model	L	2	122	1	4	$4^{\frac{1}{2}}$	4^{5}	1^{hd}	$1^{1\frac{1}{2}}$	1^{3}	Martin E M Jr	1.10
6Nov04 ^{8}CD^{3}	Kota	L	2	118	5	2	$5^{1\frac{1}{2}}$	6	6	3^{2}	$2^{1\frac{3}{4}}$	McKee J	8.10
8Oct04 ^{3}Kee^{1}	Summerly	L	2	116	6	3	$1^{2\frac{1}{2}}$	$1^{\frac{1}{2}}$	$2^{\frac{1}{2}}$	2^{2}	3^{4}	Hernandez B J Jr	11.70
7Nov04 ^{1}CD^{1}	Mille Lacs	L	2	116	3	6	6	5^{1}	$5^{1\frac{1}{2}}$	5^{4}	4^{nk}	Melancon L	12.90
8Oct04 ^{9}Kee^{3}	In the Gold	L	2	116	2	5	$3^{2\frac{1}{2}}$	3^{hd}	4^{2}	$4^{1\frac{1}{2}}$	5^{15}	Day P	1.20
6Nov04 ^{8}CD^{4}	Quiet Optimism	L	2	118	4	1	2^{1}	$2^{1\frac{1}{2}}$	3^{2}	6	6	Castro E	34.30

OFF AT 3:30 Start Good . Won driving. Track fast.

TIME :24, :47^{2}, 1:13, 1:39, 1:45^{4} (:24.00, :47.58, 1:13.05, 1:39.15, 1:45.97)

$2 Mutuel Prices:			
1 – RUNWAY MODEL	4.20	2.80	2.80
5 – KOTA		4.60	3.80
6 – SUMMERLY			5.20

$2 EXACTA 1–5 PAID $29.60 $2 TRIFECTA 1–5–6 PAID $146.60
$1 SUPERFECTA 1–5–6–3 PAID $240.90

Dk. b or br. f, (Mar), by Petionville – Ticket to Houston , by Houston . Trainer Flint Bernard S. Bred by Everest Stables Inc (Ky).

RUNWAY MODEL settled near the inside early, was never far back, eased out three or four wide on the backstretch to edge closer, headed front-running SUMMERLY just before going three-quarters, lost the lead back to that one soon after, recaptured it when straightened into the lane, then was ridden hard in the drive to kick clear. KOTA, outrun early, moved inside, remained near the rail into the lane, maneuvered out five wide at the eighth pole and was second best. SUMMERLY bobbled at the start, gained the lead, moved inside, was a bit rank early, settled on the backstretch, was headed briefly from the outside just prior to going six furlongs by RUNAWAY MODEL, regained a slight edge soon after, the weakened in the drive. MILLE LACS, sluggish to start and three or four wide, swung out six wide for the drive but lacked a rally. IN THE GOLD, well placed near the inside early, raced within easy striking distance, came out five wide for the drive and was empty. QUIET OPTIMISM went up early to press front-running SUMMERLY four wide, gained even terms for the lead just before going six furlongs but tired soon after.

Owners– 1, Chowhan Naveed; 2, OFER Stables LLC; 3, Winchell Thoroughbreds LLC; 4, Smith Bentley L; 5, Live Oak Plantation; 6, Bowling Carl Foley Vickie L et al

Trainers– 1, Flint Bernard S; 2, Holthus Robert E; 3, Asmussen Steven M; 4, Nafzger Carl A; 5, Zito Nicholas P; 6, Foley Vickie L

$2 Pick Three (4–11–1) Paid $240.00 ; Pick Three Pool $50,696 .

ELEVENTH RACE
Churchill
NOVEMBER 27, 2004

$1\frac{1}{16}$ MILES. (1.41^{3}) 78TH RUNNING OF THE KENTUCKY JOCKEY CLUB. Grade II. Purse $200,000 FOR TWO YEAR OLDS. By subscription of $200 each on or before November 13, 2004. $1,000 to pass the entry box; $1,000 additional to start, with $200,000 added of which 62% of all monies to the owner of the winner; 20% to second; 10% to third; 5% to fourth and 3% to fifth. Weight 122 lbs. Non-winners of a sweepstakes at a mile or over allowed 2 lbs.; two races other than maiden or claiming 4 lbs.; a race other than maiden or claiming 6 lbs. Starters to be named through the entry box by the usual time of closing. Trophy to winning owner. The Kentucky Jockey Club Stakes winner will automatically be nominated to the 2005 Visa Triple Crown, as far as nomination fee. Closed Saturday, November 13, 2004 with 26 nominations.

Value of Race: $223,200 Winner $138,384; second $44,640; third $22,320; fourth $11,160; fifth $6,696. Mutuel Pool $450,990.00 Exacta Pool $314,148.00 Trifecta Pool $259,366.00 Superfecta Pool $86,210.00

Last Raced	Horse	M/Eqt.	A.	Wt	PP	St	¼	½	¾	Str	Fin	Jockey	Odds $1
6Nov04 ^{10}CD^{3}	Greater Good	L	2	122	4	2	7^{hd}	$8^{2\frac{1}{2}}$	7^{2}	3^{hd}	$1^{1\frac{3}{4}}$	McKee J	4.40
31Oct04 ^{4}CD^{1}	Rush Bay	L	2	116	2	6	5^{hd}	6^{2}	$6^{2\frac{1}{2}}$	$4^{\frac{1}{2}}$	$2^{\frac{1}{2}}$	Razo E Jr	5.50
29Oct04 ^{9}Kee^{5}	Wild Desert	L b	2	118	3	9	9	9	8^{5}	6^{3}	3^{nk}	Blanc B	33.00
23Oct04 ^{12}Crc^{1}	B. B. Best	L	2	122	6	5	3^{4}	1^{hd}	1^{1}	$1^{1\frac{1}{2}}$	$4^{2\frac{1}{4}}$	Castro E	6.00
22Oct04 ^{8}Kee^{1}	Magna Graduate	L	2	118	8	4	4^{2}	$4^{1\frac{1}{2}}$	2^{hd}	2^{hd}	5^{5}	Day P	4.80
30Oct04 ^{11}LS^{1}	Storm Surge	L f	2	120	5	1	$2^{\frac{1}{2}}$	$2^{\frac{1}{2}}$	$3^{\frac{1}{2}}$	$5^{2\frac{1}{2}}$	$6^{2\frac{1}{4}}$	Hernandez B J Jr	2.80
13Nov04 ^{8}CD^{2}	Drum Major	L	2	116	7	8	8^{5}	7^{2}	5^{2}	7^{1}	$7^{2\frac{1}{2}}$	Johnson J M	14.10
6Nov04 ^{10}CD^{2}	Social Probation	L	2	118	9	7	$6^{1\frac{1}{2}}$	5^{hd}	4^{hd}	8^{15}	8	Melancon L	5.90
6Nov04 ^{10}CD^{5}	Highgrove	L	2	116	1	3	1^{hd}	3^{4}	9	9	—	Martin E M Jr	21.00

OFF AT 4:34 Start Good . Won driving. Track fast.

TIME :23^{2}, :47, 1:12^{4}, 1:38^{3}, 1:45 (:23.56, :47.11, 1:12.87, 1:38.74, 1:45.14)

$2 Mutuel Prices:			
4 – GREATER GOOD	10.80	5.40	3.80
2 – RUSH BAY		6.40	4.20
3 – WILD DESERT			8.40

$2 EXACTA 4–2 PAID $75.80 $2 TRIFECTA 4–2–3 PAID $1,045.20
$1 SUPERFECTA 4–2–3–6 PAID $5,371.50

B. c, (Apr), by Intidab – Gather The Clan–Ire , by General Assembly . Trainer Holthus Robert E. Bred by A Lakin & Sons Inc (Ky).

GREATER GOOD, reserved near the inside soon after the start, was patiently handled, came out four wide midway on the far turn, was alertly angled back to the inside entering the lane, came through fairly close quarters along the rail at the furlong grounds and drove clear late under energetic handling. RUSH BAY settled near the inside early, followed the leaders three wide on the backstretch, awaited room briefly at the five-sixteenths, was four wide when straightened for the drive, loomed outside the winner late but wasn't a match. WILD DESERT, reserved near the inside early, moved with the winner while outside that one five wide on the far turn, came out eight abreast when straightened for the drive and finished willingly. B. B. BEST came out bumping DRUM MAJOR at the start, went up soon after to force the pace three abreast, gained the advantage just before going a half, raced three or four wide while opening a clear margin in the upper stretch, then weakened late. MAGNA GRADUATE gained a forward position in behind the leaders entering the first turn, followed them four wide on the backstretch, leaned in at the five-sixteenths pole and bumped for a stride with STORM SURGE, loomed boldly while coming a bit wider for the drive and flattened out late. STORM SURGE went up early to vie for the lead between foes, battled close up for six furlongs, was bumped for a stride by MAGNA GRADUATE approaching the stretch and weakened. DRUM MAJOR, bumped at the break by B. B. BEST, raced five or six wide, was a factor for six furlongs and weakened thereafter. SOCIAL PROBATION, a bit awkward at the start, raced within easy striking distance five wide to the final quarter and faltered. HIGHGROVE gained a slim lead inside early, battled close up on for a half, gave way on the far turn and was distanced in the stretch when not persevered with.

Owners– 1, Lakin Lewis G; 2, Phoebe Ann Mueller Trust; 3, Sarah-Lyn Stables LLC and Gessler Jr Carl; 4, Bea Oxenberg and Laurie Plesa; 5, Alexander Elisabeth H; 6, Overbrook Farm; 7, Dogwood Stable; 8, Old School Stable; 9, Farmer Tracy

Trainers– 1, Holthus Robert E; 2, Amoss Thomas; 3, McPeek Kenneth G; 4, Plesa Edward Jr; 5, Byrne Patrick B; 6, Stewart Dallas; 7, Weaver George; 8, Nafzger Carl A; 9, Zito Nicholas P

$2 Pick Three (1–12–4) Paid $210.80 ; Pick Three Pool $42,568 .
$2 Consolation Pick 3 (1–10–4) Paid $24.60 .

SEVENTH RACE
Hollywood
NOVEMBER 27, 2004

1$\frac{1}{16}$ MILES. (Turf) (1.38^{2}) 28TH RUNNING OF THE CITATION HANDICAP Grade I. Purse $400,000 FOR THREE-YEAR-OLD AND UPWARD. Gross purse $400,000 of which $240,000 to be paid to the winner, $80,000 to second, $48,000 to third, $24,000 to fourth and $8,000 to fifth. Weights Sunday, November 21. Starters to be named through the entry box by closingtime of entries. Closed with 45 early nominations Aug 13, 3 late nominations Oct 6, and 4 supplements: Three Valleys, A to the Z, Buckland Manor, and Mingun on Nov 17.

Value of Race: $400,000 Winner $240,000; second $80,000; third $48,000; fourth $24,000; fifth $8,000. Mutuel Pool $626,486.00 Exacta Pool $385,209.00 Quinella Pool $30,844.00 Trifecta Pool $355,942.00 Superfecta Pool $120,819.00

Last Raced	Horse	M/Eqt.	A.	Wt	PP	St	¼	½	¾	Str	Fin	Jockey	Odds $1
30Oct04 ^{6}SA^{1}	Leroidesnimux-Brz	LB	4	117	2	1	3^{1}	5^{1}	3^{hd}	1^{1}	$1^{\frac{1}{2}}$	Court J K	3.10
16Oct04 ^{9}SA^{1}	A to the Z	LB b	4	115	1	8	$9^{2\frac{1}{2}}$	$9^{1\frac{1}{2}}$	7^{hd}	$4^{1\frac{1}{2}}$	2^{1}	Gomez G K	41.10
1May04 NEW^{11}	Three Valleys	LB	3	115	8	9	10	10	10	5^{1}	$3^{\frac{1}{2}}$	Dominguez R A	7.80
16Oct04 NEW^{8}	Mingun	LB	4	116	7	10	4^{1}	$3^{\frac{1}{2}}$	$4^{\frac{1}{2}}$	2^{hd}	4^{1}	Desormeaux K J	12.90
9Oct04 ^{9}SA^{2}	Buckland Manor	LB	4	116	5	2	$1^{\frac{1}{2}}$	1^{1}	1^{1}	3^{hd}	5^{1}	Douglas R R	12.50
30Oct04 ^{4}LS^{11}	Nothing to Lose	LB b	4	120	3	7	7^{hd}	$7^{\frac{1}{2}}$	$8^{1\frac{1}{2}}$	$7^{1\frac{1}{2}}$	6^{hd}	Prado E S	2.50
9Oct04 ^{9}SA^{5}	Tsigane-FR	LB b	5	116	4	5	5^{hd}	$6^{\frac{1}{2}}$	6^{1}	$6^{\frac{1}{2}}$	7^{2}	Pedroza M A	8.40
6Nov04 ^{7}Hol^{1}	Fairly Ransom	LB	4	116	9	6	8^{1}	8^{1}	9^{hd}	8^{4}	$8^{9\frac{1}{2}}$	Flores D R	12.00
9Oct04 ^{9}SA^{4}	Gondolieri-Chi	LB b	5	116	6	3	2^{1}	2^{hd}	2^{hd}	10	9^{hd}	Stevens G L	28.20
30Oct04 ^{4}LS^{13}	Special Ring	LB b	7	120	10	4	$6^{1\frac{1}{2}}$	4^{hd}	$5^{1\frac{1}{2}}$	9^{1}	10	Nakatani C S	5.20

OFF AT 3:39 Start Good. Won driving. Course firm.

TIME :23^{3}, :48, 1:11^{2}, 1:35^{2}, 1:41^{1} (:23.71, :48.18, 1:11.48, 1:35.44, 1:41.36)

$2 Mutuel Prices:			
2 – LEROIDESANIMAUX-BRZ	8.20	5.80	4.80
1 – A TO THE Z		25.80	13.00
8 – THREE VALLEYS			7.40

$1 EXACTA 2–1 PAID $94.80 $2 QUINELLA 1–2 PAID $112.40
$1 TRIFECTA 2–1–8 PAID $1,081.70 $1 SUPERFECTA 2–1–8–7 PAID $8,712.10

Ch. c, (Sep), by Candy Stripes – Dissemble-GB , by Ahonoora-GB . Trainer Frankel Robert. Bred by Haras Bage Do Sul (Brz).

LEROIDESANIMAUX (BRZ) pulled a bit early, stalked inside, bid between foes leaving the second turn, took a short lead into the stretch, inched away nearing midstretch and held on gamely under left handed urging. A TO THE Z settled inside, moved up on the second turn, waited momentarily then split horses in midstretch, rallied inside the winner and continued gamely but could not get by. THREE VALLEYS broke slowly, raced unhurried inside, got through with a forward move into the stretch then altered course outside for room in midstretch and just got third. MINGUN also broke slowly, pulled his way between horses to stalk the pace, went four wide leaving the second turn and three deep into the stretch to loom a threat and was edged for third late. BUCKLAND MANOR sped to the early lead, angled in on the first turn, set the pace inside, dueled along the rail leaving the second turn and into the stretch and weakened in the final furlong. NOTHING TO LOSE was in a good position stalking the pace between horses, came out leaving the second turn and four wide into the stretch and lacked the needed rally. TSIGANE (FR) chased inside then a bit off the rail, was between horses leaving the second turn, came out in the stretch and weakened. FAIRLY RANSOM pulled early, chased three deep, waited a bit off heels while four wide into the stretch and could not summon the necessary late kick. GONDOLIERI (CHI) pulled while pressing the early pace outside a rival, stalked outside the winner on the backstretch and second turn, was in a bit tight between horses into the stretch and weakened. SPECIAL RING stalked the pace three deep, came out five wide leaving the second turn and into the stretch and gave way.

Owners– 1, T N T Stud; 2, Capestro Andrew and Paula S; 3, Juddmonte Farms Inc; 4, Flaxman Holdings Ltd; 5, McCaffery Trudy and Toffan John A; 6, Ramsey Kenneth L and Sarah K; 7, Prestonwood Farm LLC; 8, Zetcher Arnold; 9, Hunt Nelson B; 10, Prestonwood Farm LLC

Trainers– 1, Frankel Robert; 2, Capestro Paula S; 3, Frankel Robert; 4, O'Brien Aidan P; 5, Gonzalez J Paco; 6, Frankel Robert; 7, Canani Julio C; 8, McAnally Ronald; 9, McAnally Ronald; 10, Canani Julio C

Scratched– Mananan McLir (06Nov04 ^{7}Hol^{3})

$2 Daily Double (1–2) Paid $15.40 ; Daily Double Pool $45,449 .
$1 Pick Three (9–1/7–2) Paid $102.60 ; Pick Three Pool $104,478 .

NINTH RACE
Hollywood
NOVEMBER 27, 2004

1 MILE. (Turf) (1.32^{3}) 23RD RUNNING OF THE GENEROUS. Grade III. Purse $100,000 FOR TWO-YEAR-OLDS. By subscription of $100 each on or before Wednesday, November 17, or by supplementary nomination of $2,000 each by closing time of entries. All nominees to pay $500 to enter and an additional $1,000 to start. Gross purse $100,000 of which $60,000 to be paid to the winner, $20,000 to second, $12,000 to third, $6,000 to fourth and $2,000 to fifth. 121 lbs. Non-winners of $60,000 at one mile or over allowed 3 lbs.; non winners of two races other than claiming at one mile or over, 5 lbs. ;a race other than claiming, 7 lbs. Hollywood Park reserves the right not to divide this race. Should this race not be divided and the number of entries exceed the starting gate capacity, first preference will be given to graded or group stakes winners. Seecond preference will be given to those horses with the highest total earnings. Entry fees will be refunded to all horses which fail to draw into this race. A trophy will be presented to the winning owner. Closed Wednesday, November 17 with 19 nominations.

Value of Race: $100,000 Winner $60,000; second $20,000; third $12,000; fourth $6,000; fifth $2,000. Mutuel Pool $480,027.00 Exacta Pool $288,238.00 Quinella Pool $22,650.00 Trifecta Pool $260,389.00 Superfecta Pool $101,715.00

Last Raced	Horse	M/Eqt.	A.	Wt	PP	St	¼	½	¾	Str	Fin	Jockey	Odds $1
29Oct04 ^{9}Kee^{2}	Dubleo	LB	2	121	9	1	$2^{1\frac{1}{2}}$	$2^{3\frac{1}{2}}$	2^{2}	2^{3}	$1^{\frac{3}{4}}$	Nakatani C S	1.40
29Oct04 ^{3}SA^{3}	Littlebitofzip	LB	2	116	4	3	$1^{1\frac{1}{2}}$	1^{4}	1^{4}	$1^{1\frac{1}{2}}$	2no	Bisono A	41.40
4Nov04 NAN^{1}	Sunny Sky-FR	LB b	2	116	10	9	9^{1}	$10^{1\frac{1}{2}}$	$5^{1\frac{1}{2}}$	$3^{\frac{1}{2}}$	3^{3}	Douglas R R	8.00
15Oct04 ^{3}SA^{1}	Chattahoochee War	LB b	2	115	6	11	$10^{\frac{1}{2}}$	11^{5}	8^{hd}	8^{3}	$4^{\frac{1}{2}}$	Dominguez R A	4.30
13Nov04 LIN^{1}	Forzeen-GB	B	2	115	1	4	$3^{1\frac{1}{2}}$	3^{hd}	3^{hd}	$4^{1\frac{1}{2}}$	5^{hd}	Valdivia J Jr	53.30
4Nov04 ^{6}Hol^{1}	Petrus	LB	2	116	7	8	5^{1}	$5^{2\frac{1}{2}}$	$4^{1\frac{1}{2}}$	5^{2}	$6^{1\frac{1}{2}}$	Baze T C	13.00
29Oct04 ^{3}SA^{1}	Veiled Speed	LB	2	116	11	6	8^{1}	8^{1}	10^{2}	6^{1}	$7^{\frac{1}{2}}$	Flores D R	13.80
29Oct04 ^{3}SA^{4}	Generalist	LB	2	114	2	5	$4^{\frac{1}{2}}$	4^{hd}	7^{1}	7^{hd}	8^{2}	Court J K	28.60
17Oct04 ^{2}Bel^{1}	Vitruvian	LB	2	116	5	2	$6^{\frac{1}{2}}$	6^{hd}	$6^{2\frac{1}{2}}$	$9^{\frac{1}{2}}$	9^{2}	Prado E S	4.30
29Oct04 ^{3}SA^{2}	Lucky Bid	LB	2	116	12	7	$11^{2\frac{1}{2}}$	9^{hd}	$9^{1\frac{1}{2}}$	10^{1}	$10^{\frac{1}{2}}$	Stevens G L	19.80
7Nov04 ^{3}Pha^{1}	Quiet Money	LB b	2	116	3	10	$7^{\frac{1}{2}}$	$7^{\frac{1}{2}}$	11^{2}	$11^{1\frac{1}{2}}$	11^{hd}	Farina T	48.60
23Jly04 Fah^{1}	Doctor Kananga-Ire	LB b	2	114	8	12	12	12	12	12	12	Martinez F F	90.50

OFF AT 4:44 Start Good . Won driving. Course firm.

TIME :23^{4}, :47^{2}, 1:12, 1:24^{1}, 1:37^{1} (:23.96, :47.56, 1:12.00, 1:24.32, 1:37.21)

$2 Mutuel Prices:

10 – DUBLEO	4.80	3.40	3.00
5 – LITTLEBITOFZIP		18.00	9.40
11 – SUNNY SKY–FR			5.80

$1 EXACTA 10–5 PAID $51.50 $2 QUINELLA 5–10 PAID $76.60
$1 TRIFECTA 10–5–11 PAID $495.30 $1 SUPERFECTA 10–5–11–7 PAID $4,482.20

Dk. b or br. c, (Mar), by Southern Halo – Secret Red , by Secretariat . Trainer Pletcher Todd A. Bred by Anzac LLC (Ky).

DUBLEO pulled early and angled in, stalked inside, came out in the stretch and wore down the runner-up under some urging. LITTLEBITOFZIP sped to the early lead, angled in and set the pace on a clear lead inside, remained clear past midstretch but was worn down late. SUNNY SKY (FR) three deep into the first turn, chased outside a rival, moved up quickly four wide on the second turn and into the stretch and just missed the place. CHATTAHOOCHEE WAR angled in and settled inside then a bit off the rail, came out on the second turn, was four wide into the stretch and improved position. FORZEEN (GB) was in a good position chasing inside to the stretch and lacked the needed response. PETRUS chased outside a rival to the stretch and also lacked the needed rally. VEILED SPEED four wide into the first turn, chased three deep, split foes on the second turn and did not rally. GENERALIST stalked between horses then inside and weakened. VITRUVIAN chased between foes or outside a rival and also weakened. LUCKY BID four wide into the first turn, chased outside, went three deep between foes on the second turn and was not a threat. QUIET MONEY saved ground in midpack, dropped back into and on the second turn and had little left for the stretch. DOCTOR KANANGA (IRE) off slowly then steadied when squeezed, saved ground off the pace, came out into the stretch and was outrun.

Owners– 1, Scataurchio Pletcher & Wetterman; 2, Peacock Cecil N; 3, Naify Marsha and Woodside Farms LLC; 4, Amerman Racing Stables LLC; 5, Cassidy James M; 6, Relatively Stable Browne Sean and Dundon Desmond; 7, Cono Charles; 8, Malmuth Marvin and Sonya and McCay Nathan; 9, Flaxman Holdings Ltd; 10, Whetstone Ilona; 11, Everest Stables Inc; 12, Howard Roberts Farm

Trainers– 1, Pletcher Todd A; 2, Hendricks Dan L; 3, Zilber Maurice; 4, Frankel Robert; 5, Cassidy James; 6, Drysdale Neil; 7, Paasch Christopher S; 8, Garcia Juan; 9, Frankel Robert; 10, McAnally Ronald; 11, Polanco Marcelo; 12, Knapp Steve

Scratched– Moth Ball (GB) (09Oct04 46502YOR1)

$2 Daily Double (8–10) Paid $58.60 ; Daily Double Pool $35,235 .
$1 Pick Three (2–8–4/10) Paid $139.70 ; Pick Three Pool $94,414 .
$2 Consolation Daily Double (8–4) Paid $18.20 .

NINTH RACE
Aqueduct
NOVEMBER 28, 2004

6 FURLONGS. (1.07^{2}) THE 91ST RUNNING OF FALL HIGHWEIGHT HANDICAP. Purse $100,000 (UP TO $19,000 NYSBFOA) A HANDICAP FOR THREE YEAR OLDS AND UPWARD. By subscription of $100 each, which should accompany the nomination; $500 to pass the entry box; $500 to start, with $100,000 added. The added money and all fees to be divided 60% to the winner, 20% to second, 10% to third, 5% to fourth, 3% to fifth and 2% divided among remaining finishers. A trophy will be presented to the winning owner. Closed Saturday, November 13, 2004 with 26 Nominations.

Value of Race: $111,600 Winner $66,960; second $22,320; third $11,160; fourth $5,580; fifth $3,348; sixth $558; seventh $558; eighth $558; ninth $558. Mutuel Pool $376,293.00 Exacta Pool $333,703.00 Trifecta Pool $271,784.00

Last Raced	Horse	M/Eqt.	A.	Wt	PP	St	¼	½	Str	Fin	Jockey	Odds $1
14Oct04 ^{3}Bel^{1}	Thunder Touch	L f	3	126	3	4	5^{hd}	4^{hd}	2^{hd}	$1^{1\frac{1}{4}}$	Bejarano R	6.90
23Oct04 ^{8}Bel^{3}	Papua	L bf	5	128	7	8	7^{hd}	6^{2}	$3^{1\frac{1}{2}}$	$2^{\frac{1}{2}}$	Castellano J J	6.30
31Oct04 ^{7}Aqu^{7}	Eavesdropper	L	4	127	5	7	9	8^{2}	$6^{\frac{1}{2}}$	3^{nk}	Gryder A T	33.25
23Oct04 ^{8}Bel^{5}	Uncle Camie	L f	4	128	1	5	1^{1}	$1^{1\frac{1}{2}}$	1^{3}	$4^{3\frac{1}{2}}$	Luzzi M J	24.00
28Aug04 ^{10}Sar^{7}	Medallist	L	3	134	9	9	6^{3}	3^{hd}	$4^{\frac{1}{2}}$	5^{2}	Santos J A	2.00
30Oct04 ^{3}Aqu^{1}	Primary Suspect	L	3	126	8	1	8^{hd}	7^{1}	$7^{\frac{1}{2}}$	6^{3}	Fragoso P	3.00
23Oct04 ^{8}Bel^{1}	Friendly Island	L f	3	130	6	3	3^{hd}	$2^{2\frac{1}{2}}$	$5^{\frac{1}{2}}$	7^{nk}	Elliott S	4.70
8Oct04 ^{4}Med^{9}	Don Six	L	4	128	2	6	$2^{\frac{1}{2}}$	5^{1}	8^{12}	$8^{20\frac{1}{4}}$	Bridgmohan S X	17.10
24Oct04 ^{7}Del^{3}	Max's Buddy	L f	5	127	4	2	$4^{3\frac{1}{2}}$	9	9	9	Velasquez C	49.00

OFF AT 3:48 Start Good . Won driving. Track sloppy.

TIME :21^{2}, :44^{1}, :56^{4}, 1:09^{4} (:21.45, :44.36, :56.81, 1:09.83)

$2 Mutuel Prices:

3 – THUNDER TOUCH	15.80	7.90	5.10
7 – PAPUA		6.80	5.20
5 – EAVESDROPPER			11.80

$2 EXACTA 3–7 PAID $94.50 $2 TRIFECTA 3–7–5 PAID $1,202.00

Ch. c, (Jan), by Gulch – Highland Vixen , by Highland Ruckus . Trainer McLaughlin Kiaran P. Bred by Adena Springs (Ky).

THUNDER TOUCH was hustled along inside early, angled out and rallied three wide approaching the stretch, dug in gamely when roused and was clear under the wire. PAPUA was outrun early, rallied inside on the turn, came wide into traffic in upper stretch, altered course to the inside, was steadied while attempting to split rivals in deep stretch, altered course again and finished gamely. EAVESDROPPER was outrun early, swung wide entering the stretch and finished gamely outside. UNCLE CAMIE was hustled to the front, set the pace along the inside, took a clear lead into deep stretch and weakened inside late. MEDALLIST broke awkwardly, was outrun early, put in a four wide run on the turn and tired in the stretch. PRIMARY SUSPECT was outrun early, raced three wide and lacked a rally. FRIENDLY ISLAND raced close up outside, put in a three wide run on the turn and tired in the final furlong. DON SIX raced with the pace along the inside while in hand and tired after a half mile. MAX'S BUDDY chased the pace along the inside and tired. After a Stewards' inquiry focusing on the stretch run, as well as a claim of foul lodged by the rider of PAPUA against the winner alleging interference inside the furlong grounds, the result was declared official.

Owners– 1, Stronach Stables; 2, Schwartz Barry K; 3, De Renzo Dean and Hartley Randall; 4, Telesca Carmine and Guerrera John and Marilyn; 5, Clay Robert N; 6, Lewis Lee; 7, Anstu Stables Inc; 8, Generazio Patricia A; 9, Dweck Raymond

Trainers– 1, McLaughlin Kiaran P; 2, Hushion Michael E; 3, McLaughlin Kiaran P; 4, Hushion Michael E; 5, Jerkens H Allen; 6, Hennig Mark; 7, Pletcher Todd A; 8, Generazio Frank Jr; 9, Preciado Guadalupe

SEVENTH RACE
Hollywood
NOVEMBER 28, 2004

1 MILE. (Turf) (1.32^3) 24TH RUNNING OF THE MATRIARCH. Grade I. Purse $500,000 FOR FILLIES AND MARES THREE-YEAR-OLD AND UPWARD. Gross purse $500,000 of which $300,000 to be paid to the winner, $100,000 to second, $60,000 to third, $30,000 to fourth and $10,000 to fifth. Three year olds 120 lbs. Older 123 lbs. Starters to be namedthrough the entry box by closing time of entries. Closed with 62 early nominations Aug 13 and 6 late nominations Oct 6.

Value of Race: $500,000 Winner $300,000; second $100,000; third $60,000; fourth $30,000; fifth $10,000. Mutuel Pool $572,865.00 Exacta Pool $320,036.00 Quinella Pool $30,442.00 Trifecta Pool $311,510.00 Superfecta Pool $121,358.00

Last Raced	Horse	M/Eqt.	A.	Wt	PP	St	¼	½	¾	Str	Fin	Jockey	Odds $1
29Sep04 ^{7}SA^2	Intercontinentl-GB	LB	4	123	4	6	$6^{\frac12}$	6^1	$4^{\frac12}$	$3^{1\frac12}$	1^2	Bailey J D	4.60
4Sep04 ^{7}Dmr^1	Etoile Montante	LB	4	123	9	4	1^1	1^{hd}	1^{hd}	1^{hd}	2no	Prado E S	12.00
16Oct04 ^{8}Kee^1	Ticker Tape-GB	LB	3	120	6	7	$8^{\frac12}$	8^1	$6^{1\frac12}$	$4^{2\frac12}$	$3^{1\frac12}$	Espinoza V	6.90
30Oct04 ^{2}LS^5	Island Fashion	LB b	4	123	8	3	$7^{1\frac12}$	7^{hd}	9	$7^{\frac12}$	4no	Baze T C	7.10
2Oct04 ^{4}SA^6	Hoh Buzzard-Ire	LB b	4	123	1	2	2^{hd}	2^{hd}	2^1	$2^{\frac12}$	5^1	Flores D R	27.60
30Oct04 ^{4}LS^6	Musical Chimes	LB	4	123	7	8	9	9	$7^{1\frac12}$	5^1	$6^{4\frac12}$	Desormeaux K J	1.80
22Oct04 ^{8}Med^3	Ocean Drive	LB	4	123	5	1	$4^{1\frac12}$	4^1	8^1	9	$7^{\frac12}$	Velazquez J R	9.90
9Oct04 LCH^2	Denebola	LB	3	120	3	9	5^{hd}	5^{hd}	5^1	6^{hd}	8^9	Stevens G L	5.10
3Nov04 ^{6}Hol^2	Quero Quero	LB	4	123	2	5	3^{hd}	3^{hd}	3^1	8^2	9	Nakatani C S	25.10

OFF AT 3:52 Start Good . Won driving. Course firm.

TIME :24, :47^3, 1:11^2, 1:23^3, 1:35^4 (:24.00, :47.77, 1:11.41, 1:23.61, 1:35.87)

$2 Mutuel Prices:				
	4 – INTERCONTINENTAL–GB	11.20	6.20	4.80
	9 – ETOILE MONTANTE		12.40	9.00
	6 – TICKER TAPE–GB			5.40

$1 EXACTA 4–9 PAID $44.10 $2 QUINELLA 4–9 PAID $40.80
$1 TRIFECTA 4–9–6 PAID $276.30 $1 SUPERFECTA 4–9–6–8 PAID $2,468.20

B. f, (Mar), by Danehill – Hasili–Ire , by Kahyasi . Trainer Frankel Robert. Bred by Juddmonte Farms (GB).

INTERCONTINENTAL (GB) pulled her way between horses chasing the pace, continued outside a rival leaving the backstretch and on the second turn, came out in the stretch, bid three deep, gained the lead past midstretch and won clear under urging. ETOILE MONTANTE sped to the early lead, angled in on the first turn, dueled inside a rival on the backstretch and second turn, fought back in the stretch but could not match the winner and just held second. TICKER TAPE (GB) angled in on the first turn and settled a bit off the rail, came outside rivals leaving the second turn and four wide into the stretch and finished well. ISLAND FASHION chased three deep, was in tight between horses into the second turn, steadied in traffic midway on that turn, came out nearing the stretch and finished with interest too late. HOH BUZZARD (IRE) came off the rail leaving the first turn, bid outside the runner-up then between foes, battled outside that one again on the second turn and between horses in midstretch and weakened late. MUSICAL CHIMES chased outside then off the rail, moved up four wide into and on the second turn and into the stretch but lacked the needed response. OCEAN DRIVE chased three deep, bid four wide on the backstretch, dropped back and angled in on the second turn and weakened. DENEBOLA pulled a bit early, stalked the pace inside to the stretch and weakened. QUERO QUERO stalked between foes early, bid three deep between horses on the backstretch, fell back some on the second turn and gave way in the stretch.

Owners– 1, Juddmonte Farms Inc; 2, Juddmonte Farms Inc; 3, Jim Ford Inc Pearson Deron and Sweesy Jack; 4, Everest Stables Inc; 5, Tanaka Gary A; 6, Al Maktoum Sheikh Maktoum b; 7, Baskin Bonnie and Sy; 8, Flaxman Holdings Ltd; 9, Old Friends Inc

Trainers– 1, Frankel Robert; 2, Frankel Robert; 3, Cassidy James; 4, Polanco Marcelo; 5, Cecil B D A; 6, Drysdale Neil; 7, Pletcher Todd A; 8, Bary Pascal F; 9, Lobo Paulo H

$2 Daily Double (6–4) Paid $97.00 ; Daily Double Pool $40,084 .
$1 Pick Three (6–6–4) Paid $226.40 ; Pick Three Pool $129,631 .

NINTH RACE
Hollywood
NOVEMBER 28, 2004

$1\frac{1}{4}$ MILES. (Turf) (1.57^3) 64TH RUNNING OF THE HOLLYWOOD DERBY. Grade I. Purse $500,000 FOR THREE-YEAR-OLDS. Gross purse $500,000 of which $300,000 to be paid to the winner, $100,000 to second, $60,000 to third, $30,000 to fourth and $10,000 to fifth. Weight 122 lbs. Starters to be named through the entry box by closing time of entries. Closed with 69 early nominations Aug 13, 5 late nominations Oct 6, and 3 supplements: Good Reward, Hendrix, Joursanvault on Nov 17.

Value of Race: $500,000 Winner $300,000; second $100,000; third $60,000; fourth $30,000; fifth $10,000. Mutuel Pool $583,335.00 Exacta Pool $330,165.00 Quinella Pool $28,882.00 Trifecta Pool $344,108.00 Superfecta Pool $180,293.00

Last Raced	Horse	M/Eqt.	A.	Wt	PP	¼	½	¾	1	Str	Fin	Jockey	Odds $1
10Oct04 ^{4}Kee^1	Good Reward	LB b	3	122	5	6^{hd}	8^1	8^1	7^{hd}	4^{hd}	$1\frac{1}{2}$	Bailey J D	16.10
6Sep04 ^{8}Dmr^5	Fast andFurious-FR	LB	3	122	11	$12\frac{1}{2}$	13	12^1	$10^{1\frac{1}{2}}$	5^{hd}	2^1	Espinoza V	4.40
17Oct04 ^{8}SA^4	Imperialism	LB b	3	122	13	10^{hd}	$11^{1\frac{1}{2}}$	11^1	9^{hd}	$6\frac{1}{2}$	3^2	Desormeaux K J	7.10
6Nov04 ^{5}Hol^1	Whilly-Ire	LB	3	122	4	$4\frac{1}{2}$	$3\frac{1}{2}$	4^{hd}	$6^{1\frac{1}{2}}$	7^2	4^{hd}	Martinez F F	41.30
17Oct04 ^{8}SA^2	Laura's Lucky Boy	LB	3	122	12	2^{hd}	2^1	1^{hd}	1^1	1^1	$5^{2\frac{1}{2}}$	Stevens G L	7.30
6Nov04 ^{8}BM^8	Hendrix	LB b	3	122	1	7^{hd}	7^{hd}	7^{hd}	$8\frac{1}{2}$	$9\frac{1}{2}$	$6\frac{1}{2}$	Flores D R	23.60
26Jun04 ^{8}Del^1	Timo	LB b	3	122	6	3^{hd}	4^1	$3\frac{1}{2}$	2^1	2^{hd}	$7\frac{1}{2}$	Velazquez J R	8.60
19Sep04 CRA^5	Joursanvault-FR	LB	3	122	10	$11^{1\frac{1}{2}}$	10^{hd}	9^1	12^1	8^{hd}	8no	Valdivia J Jr	40.80
30Oct04 ^{4}LS^7	Blackdoun-FR	LB b	3	122	3	13	12^{hd}	13	11^1	$10^{1\frac{1}{2}}$	9no	Nakatani C S	1.80
24Oct04 Bad^5	Fight Club-Ger	LB	3	122	9	$9\frac{1}{2}$	6^{hd}	$6\frac{1}{2}$	4^{hd}	3^{hd}	10^4	Baze T C	12.30
6Nov04 ^{8}BM^3	On the Acorn-GB	LB	3	122	8	8^1	$9\frac{1}{2}$	10^1	13	12^2	11^1	Gomez G K	80.70
6Nov04 ^{8}BM^7	Big Squeeze	LB bf	3	122	2	1^2	$1\frac{1}{2}$	$2\frac{1}{2}$	5^{hd}	11^1	12^4	Court J K	117.30
17Oct04 ^{8}SA^6	Terroplane-FR	LB b	3	122	7	$5^{1\frac{1}{2}}$	$5\frac{1}{2}$	5^{hd}	$3\frac{1}{2}$	13	13	Douglas R R	15.80

OFF AT 4:55 Start Good . Won driving. Course firm.

TIME $:22^3$, $:47^1$, $1:12^1$, 1:37, $2:01^2$ (:22.75, :47.20, 1:12.30, 1:37.19, 2:01.53)

$2 Mutuel Prices:				
	5 – GOOD REWARD	34.20	13.60	10.20
	11 – FAST AND FURIOUS-FR		5.60	4.80
	13 – IMPERIALISM			5.80

$1 EXACTA 5–11 PAID $88.70 $2 QUINELLA 5–11 PAID $75.60

$1 TRIFECTA 5–11–13 PAID $1,151.60 $1 SUPERFECTA 5–11–13–4 PAID $14,300.80

B. c, (Mar), by Storm Cat – Heavenly Prize , by Seeking the Gold . Trainer McGaughey III Claude R. Bred by Phipps Stable (Ky).

GOOD REWARD chased between horses, came out four wide into the stretch, rallied between rivals while being bumped past the eighth pole and proved best under urging. FAST AND FURIOUS (FR) angled in outside a rival after the chute, advanced four then five wide on the second turn and six wide into the stretch, drifted in a bit and bumped with the winner in the stretch but closed gamely. IMPERIALISM in tight early, chased between foes then a bit off the rail, came out in traffic four wide on the second turn and five wide into the stretch, also was bumped in the lane but finished well. WHILLY (IRE) stalked inside, went between horses leaving the backstretch, steadied twice in traffic on the second turn, was in tight off heels in midstretch and was outfinished. LAURA'S LUCKY BOY four wide leaving the chute, angled in and dueled outside a rival, took the lead on the backstretch, inched away on the second turn, held on well until past midstretch and weakened late. HENDRIX chased inside, came out for room and waited off heels into the stretch, came out a bit again in the drive and lacked the needed response. TIMO stalked between horses then outside a rival, continued off the rail on the second turn and weakened in the final furlong. JOURSANVAULT (FR) pulled his way between horses and steadied on the first turn, went up between foes leaving the backstretch, steadied in tight early on the second turn, came out into the stretch and could not summon the needed late kick. BLACKDOUN (FR) saved ground off the pace, awaited room into the stretch and in midstretch, split foes late and was not a threat. FIGHT CLUB (GER) fanned wide into the first turn, chased outside, moved up five wide on the second turn and four wide into the stretch and weakened. ON THE ACORN (GB) steadied into the first turn, chased outside, dropped back on the second turn, came four wide into the stretch and did not rally. BIG SQUEEZE sped to the early lead inside, dueled inside a rival on the first turn and backstretch, stalked along the rail on the second turn and weakened. TERROPLANE (FR) chased between horses, went four wide on the second turn and three deep into the stretch and also weakened. The stewards conducted an inquiry into the bumping among the top three finisher but made no change when they ruled the contact incidental.

Owners– 1, Phipps Ogden M; 2, Zetcher Arnold; 3, Taub Steve; 4, Triple B Farms; 5, Mercedes Stables LLC; 6, Reddam J Paul; 7, C K Wood Stable; 8, Kenis Charles; 9, Naify Marsha and Woodside Farms LLC; 10, Tanaka Gary A; 11, Cassidy James M Jim Ford Inc and Pearson Deron; 12, Everest Stables Inc; 13, Bienstock David Papiano Neil and Winner Charles

Trainers– 1, McGaughey III Claude R; 2, McAnally Ronald; 3, Mulhall Kristin; 4, O'Neill Doug; 5, Orman Jason; 6, Dollase Craig; 7, Badgett William Jr; 8, Sahadi Jenine; 9, Canani Julio C; 10, Schutz Andreas; 11, Cassidy James; 12, Polanco Marcelo; 13, Drysdale Neil

---

$2 Daily Double (6–5) Paid $100.20 ; Daily Double Pool $42,386 .
$1 Pick Three (4–4/6–5) Paid $262.00 ; Pick Three Pool $113,644 .

EIGHTH RACE
Aqueduct
DECEMBER 4, 2004

$1\frac{1}{8}$ MILES. (1.54^{2}) 99TH RUNNING OF THE QUEENS COUNTY HANDICAP. Grade III. Purse $100,000 (Up To $19,000 NYSBFOA) INNER DIRT A HANDICAP FOR THREE YEAR OLDS AND UPWARD. By subscription of $100 each, which should accompany the nomination; $500 to pass the entry box; $500 to start with $100,000 added. The added money and all fees to be divided 60% to the winner, 20% to second, 10% to third, 5% to fourth, 3% to fifth and 2% divided equally among remaining finishers. A trophy will be presented to the winning owner. Closed Saturday, November 20, 2004 with 26 Nominations.

Value of Race: $112,100 Winner $67,260; second $22,420; third $11,210; fourth $5,605; fifth $3,363; sixth $561; seventh $561; eighth $561; ninth $559. Mutuel Pool $646,754.00 Exacta Pool $522,348.00 Trifecta Pool $417,275.00

Last Raced	Horse	M/Eqt.	A.	Wt	PP	St	¼	½	¾	Str	Fin	Jockey	Odds $1
13Nov04 ^{8}Aqu^{1}	Classic Endeavor	L f	6	117	1	5	$1^{\frac{1}{2}}$	$1^{1\frac{1}{2}}$	1^{1}	1^{3}	$1^{\frac{3}{4}}$	Gryder A T	2.75
20Nov04 ^{8}Aqu^{8}	Evening Attire	L b	6	123	5	9	7^{1}	$7^{1\frac{1}{2}}$	$7^{2\frac{1}{2}}$	2^{hd}	$2^{\frac{1}{2}}$	Espinoza J L	2.35
13Nov04 ^{8}Aqu^{2}	Colita	L bf	4	115	2	3	4^{hd}	$4^{\frac{1}{2}}$	4^{hd}	$4^{2\frac{1}{2}}$	3no	Bejarano R	2.85
28Oct04 ^{8}Aqu^{1}	Kissin Saint	L bf	4	114	8	7	8^{10}	8^{5}	8^{4}	5^{hd}	$4^{\frac{1}{2}}$	Bridgmohan S X	25.00
27Oct04 ^{8}Aqu^{1}	Zakocity	L b	3	115	9	4	3^{3}	$3^{1\frac{1}{2}}$	$3^{\frac{1}{2}}$	3^{hd}	5^{3}	Castellano J J	8.30
6Nov04 ^{8}Del^{2}	Hydrogen	L	5	114	7	6	$6^{\frac{1}{2}}$	5^{hd}	5^{hd}	6^{1}	6^{4}	Luzzi M J	11.50
13Nov04 ^{8}Aqu^{4}	Country Be Gold	L	7	113	4	8	9	9	9	$8^{\frac{1}{2}}$	$7^{4\frac{1}{4}}$	Garcia Alan	37.00
29Oct04 ^{8}Med^{1}	Roaring Fever	L b	4	115	6	1	$5^{2\frac{1}{2}}$	6^{2}	$6^{\frac{1}{2}}$	9	$8^{\frac{3}{4}}$	Fragoso P	24.00
9Nov04 ^{8}Med^{1}	Admiralty Arch	L	4	115	3	2	$2^{\frac{1}{2}}$	$2^{\frac{1}{2}}$	2^{hd}	$7^{\frac{1}{2}}$	9	Elliott S	17.30

OFF AT 3:45 Start Good . Won driving. Track fast.

TIME :23^{1}, :47^{4}, 1:12^{2}, 1:38, 1:57 (:23.20, :47.90, 1:12.56, 1:38.01, 1:57.13)

$2 Mutuel Prices:

1 – CLASSIC ENDEAVOR	7.50	3.90	2.80
5 – EVENING ATTIRE		3.70	2.60
2 – COLITA			2.70

$2 EXACTA 1–5 PAID $30.80 $2 TRIFECTA 1–5–2 PAID $66.00

Dk. b or br. h, (Mar), by Silver Buck - Gold Juana , by John Alden Trainer Dutrow Richard E Jr. Bred by Diane H Flowers (Fla).

CLASSIC ENDEAVOR rated the pace inside, remained under a firm hold through the final turn, was pressured into the stretch and held on well with steady encouragement. EVENING ATTIRE was off slowly, rated back toward mid track, started his drive into the final turn, closed through the stretch and finished well. COLITA rated off the pace inside, made his bid entering the stretch, dueled on the rail but was outfinished for place. KISSIN SAINT rated off the pace about the four path, lost some momentum in the upper stretch, angled out making his bid and finished well. ZAKOCITY rated just off the early pace about the four path, began his push into the final turn then leveled off at the eighth pole. HYDROGEN rated back in the four path and finished evenly. COUNTRY BE GOLD never factored. ROARING FEVER rated off the pace toward mid track then tired inside. ADMIRALTY ARCH rated close just off the rail, drew near on the final turn toward the quarter pole then faded through the stretch.

Owners– 1, Sullivan Lane Stable and Scuderi Vincent S; 2, Grant Mary and Joseph and Kelly Thomas J; 3, Team Valor Stables LLC; 4, Karches Peter and Rankowitz Michael; 5, Pompa Paul P Jr; 6, Mack Earle I; 7, Seinfeld Barry and Dodson Elizabeth K; 8, Evans Edward P; 9, Moss Maggi

Trainers– 1, Dutrow Richard E Jr; 2, Kelly Patrick J; 3, Pletcher Todd A; 4, Lewis Lisa L; 5, Reynolds Patrick L; 6, Levine Bruce N; 7, Kappes Steven W; 8, Hennig Mark; 9, Contessa Gary C

Scratched– Private Lap (06Nov04 ^{8}Del^{6})

EIGHTH RACE
Calder
DECEMBER 4, 2004

$1\frac{1}{8}$ MILES. (Turf) (1.44^{4}) 22ND RUNNING OF THE MY CHARMER HANDICAP. Grade III. Purse $100,000 FOR FILLIES AND MARES, THREE YEARS OLD AND UPWARD. By subscription of $100 each which shall accompany the nomination, $1,000 to pass the entry box and an additional $1,000 to start – with $100,000 guaranteed. The owner of the winner to receive $60,000, $20,000 to second, $11,000 to third, $6,000 to fourth and $3,000 to fifth. A trophy will be presented to the winning Owner. This race will be limited to 12 Starters, with Also Eligibles. (High Weights Preferred) Closed Saturday, November 20, 2004 with 33nominations. (If deemed inadvisable to run this race over the Turf course, it will be run on the main track at One Mile and One Eighth).

Value of Race: $100,000 Winner $60,000; second $20,000; third $11,000; fourth $6,000; fifth $3,000. Mutuel Pool $396,968.00 Exacta Pool $314,086.00 Trifecta Pool $206,566.00 Superfecta Pool $66,633.00

Last Raced	Horse	M/Eqt.	A.	Wt	PP	St	¼	½	¾	Str	Fin	Jockey	Odds $1
31Oct04 ^{8}Aqu^{10}	SomethingVentured	L b	5	115	12	12	$4^{1\frac{1}{2}}$	$3^{1\frac{1}{2}}$	$3^{2\frac{1}{2}}$	$2^{1\frac{1}{2}}$	1^{1}	Velazquez J R	6.10
31Oct04 ^{8}Aqu^{4}	Snowdrops-GB	L	4	115	10	6	$6^{1\frac{1}{2}}$	5^{1}	5^{hd}	$3^{\frac{1}{2}}$	$2^{\frac{1}{2}}$	Blanc B	3.20
22Oct04 ^{8}Med^{1}	Changing World	L	4	117	3	5	1^{5}	1^{9}	1^{8}	1^{4}	$3^{3\frac{1}{4}}$	Boulanger G	1.70
31Oct04 ^{8}Aqu^{6}	Mystery Itself	L	4	112	9	11	$9^{1\frac{1}{2}}$	$9^{\frac{1}{2}}$	$7^{\frac{1}{2}}$	6^{1}	4^{nk}	Castro E	22.30
11Nov04 ^{4}CD^{1}	Hail Hillary	L	4	114	6	3	$5^{\frac{1}{2}}$	4^{hd}	4^{hd}	$5^{1\frac{1}{2}}$	$5^{2\frac{1}{4}}$	Razo E Jr	10.80
10Oct04 ^{6}Kee^{5}	Alchemist	L	4	116	11	10	8^{1}	7^{1}	6^{2}	$7^{1\frac{1}{2}}$	6^{nk}	Coa E M	9.10
11Nov04 ^{8}Aqu^{1}	Right This Way	L	3	115	2	4	$7^{1\frac{1}{2}}$	8^{1}	8^{1}	$8^{\frac{1}{2}}$	7^{nk}	Aguilar M	16.00
6Nov04 ^{5}Crc^{1}	Formal Miss	L b	4	117	1	8	12	12	12	10^{2}	8^{nk}	Cruz M R	8.70
6Nov04 ^{8}Crc^{2}	Love Sting	L	4	114	8	2	$2^{2\frac{1}{2}}$	2^{7}	2^{10}	$4^{1\frac{1}{2}}$	9^{nk}	Bain G W	78.10
25Sep04 ^{12}KD^{3}	Omeya-Chi	L	4	115	4	7	11^{3}	11^{6}	$11^{\frac{1}{2}}$	$9^{\frac{1}{2}}$	$10^{1\frac{1}{4}}$	Chavez J F	25.20
17Nov04 ^{8}Aqu^{1}	Broadway Lady	L b	4	114	5	9	10^{1}	10^{1}	9^{1}	$11^{\frac{1}{2}}$	$11^{\frac{1}{2}}$	Castillo H Jr	52.00
14Nov04 ^{5}CD^{1}	Anegada		3	113	7	1	3^{hd}	6^{hd}	$10^{1\frac{1}{2}}$	12	12	Decarlo C P	37.80

OFF AT 3:33 Start Good . Won driving. Course firm.

TIME :24, :47, 1:09^{4}, 1:34^{1}, 1:46^{3} (:24.08, :47.16, 1:09.94, 1:34.38, 1:46.79)

$2 Mutuel Prices:

12 – SOMETHING VENTURED	14.20	6.40	3.80
10 – SNOWDROPS–GB		4.00	2.80
3 – CHANGING WORLD			2.40

$2 EXACTA 12–10 PAID $60.80 $2 TRIFECTA 12–10–3 PAID $197.60

$2 SUPERFECTA 12–10–3–9 PAID $2,161.80

Dk. b or br. m, (Mar), by Cobra King - Intend , by Seattle Slew . Trainer Pletcher Todd A. Bred by Tomaeato Farm (Ky).

SOMETHING VENTURED rated off the pace, eased outside the leader for the stretch run and rallied to be up late. SNOWDROPS (GB) allowed to settle, angled out for the stretch run and rallied to be up for the place. CHANGING WORLD sprinted to a long lead along the hedge, made the pace to deep stretch and gave way. MYSTERY ITSELF unhurried early, raced three wide on the far turn and found her best stride late. HAIL HILLARY reserved off the pace, didn't do enough late. ALCHEMIST raced three wide on the far turn and failed to menace. RIGHT THIS WAY was not a factor. FORMAL MISS failed to threaten after being outrun early. LOVE STING chased the pacesetter into the stretch and tired. OMEYA (CHI) was outrun. BROADWAY LADY showed little. ANEGADA saved ground and faltered.

Owners– 1, Wiemer Irvin and McLane John; 2, Spink G Howard; 3, Rogers Samuel H Jr; 4, Lael Stables; 5, Butterfly Stable; 6, Alexander Helen C; 7, Pesch Alan; 8, Elite Racing Fornaro N et al; 9, Emerald Pastures Corp Inc; 10, Augustin Stable; 11, Punk Jr William J and Dileo Philip; 12, Kiowa Stable

Trainers– 1, Pletcher Todd A; 2, Clement Christophe; 3, Tagg Barclay; 4, Matz Michael R; 5, Kassen David C; 6, McGaughey III Claude R; 7, Tagg Barclay; 8, Maxwell Paul M; 9, Stewart Cecil; 10, Sheppard Jonathan E; 11, O'Brien Keith; 12, Reinstedler Anthony

Scratched– Cloudy Gray (19Nov04 ^{1}Crc^{1}) , Redoubled Miss (13Nov04 ^{7}Crc^{4}) , Pampered Princess (23Oct04 ^{6}Crc^{5})

$2 Pick Three (10–3–12) Paid $1,065.00 ; Pick Three Pool $28,728 .

ELEVENTH RACE
Calder
DECEMBER 4, 2004

1⅛ MILES. (Turf) (1.44^{4}) 28TH RUNNING OF THE TROPICAL TURF HANDICAP. Grade III. Purse $100,000 FOR THREE YEAR OLDS AND UPWARD. By subscription of $100 each which shall accompany the nomination, $1,000 to pass the entry box and an additional $1,000 to start – with $100,000 guaranteed. The owner of the winner to receive $60,000, $20,000 to second, $11,000 to third, $6,000 to fourth and $3,000 to fifth. A trophy will be presented to the winning Owner. This race will be limited to 12 Starters, with Also Eligibles. (High Weights Preferred) Supplemental Nominations at time of entry with a fee of $3,000to enter and start. Closed Saturday, November 20, 2004 with 32 nominations. (If deemed inadvisable to run this race over the Turf course, it will be run on the main track at One Mile and One Eighth).

Value of Race: $100,000 Winner $60,000; second $20,000; third $11,000; fourth $6,000; fifth $3,000. Mutuel Pool $444,125.00 Exacta Pool $332,503.00 Trifecta Pool $285,405.00 Superfecta Pool $117,212.00

Last Raced	Horse	M/Eqt.	A.	Wt	PP	St	¼	½	¾	Str	Fin	Jockey	Odds $1
30Oct04 ^{5}Aqu^{1}	Host-Chi	L	4	118	7	6	6^{2}	6^{2}	6^{1}	3^{hd}	1^{nk}	Velazquez J R	*1.70
30Oct04 ^{4}LS^{5}	Silver Tree	L	4	118	3	2	5^{2}	$4^{1\frac{1}{2}}$	2^{1}	$2^{1\frac{1}{2}}$	$2^{\frac{1}{2}}$	Coa E M	1.70
4Oct04 ^{5}Crc^{1}	Demeteor	L	5	114	2	4	1^{hd}	2^{1}	$3^{\frac{1}{2}}$	4^{2}	3^{1}	Chavez J F	48.80
6Oct04 ^{8}Bel^{2}	Mogador	L	4	115	10	7	7^{1}	$7^{\frac{1}{2}}$	7^{hd}	$5^{\frac{1}{2}}$	$4^{\frac{3}{4}}$	Blanc B	5.30
15Oct04 ^{8}Kee^{1}	In Hand	L bf	4	115	1	8	$9^{1\frac{1}{2}}$	10^{2}	11^{7}	$7^{1\frac{1}{2}}$	5no	Boulanger G	22.60
13Nov04 ^{10}Crc^{7}	Keep Cool	L f	4	115	5	1	$2^{1\frac{1}{2}}$	1^{1}	$1^{1\frac{1}{2}}$	$1^{1\frac{1}{2}}$	$6^{1\frac{1}{2}}$	Rivera J A II	23.20
18Nov04 ^{8}Aqu^{1}	Private Scandal	L b	4	115	9	10	$8^{\frac{1}{2}}$	8^{1}	9^{1}	8^{1}	7no	Toribio A R	26.70
28Oct04 ^{3}Crc^{6}	Sea Pleasure	L b	4	115	8	9	$11^{3\frac{1}{2}}$	$9^{\frac{1}{2}}$	$8^{\frac{1}{2}}$	6^{1}	$8^{1\frac{1}{2}}$	Toribio A Jr	112.50
13Nov04 ^{10}Crc^{3}	Bob'sProudMoment	L	3	115	4	11	10^{hd}	11^{6}	10^{1}	10^{2}	$9^{3\frac{1}{4}}$	Cruz M R	13.60
13Nov04 ^{9}Crc^{1}	Final Prophecy	L b	5	115	6	5	$3^{\frac{1}{2}}$	3^{hd}	4^{1}	11^{7}	$10^{\frac{1}{2}}$	Olivero C A	24.20
6Oct04 ^{8}Bel^{4}	Colonial Bay	L b	5	113	12	3	$4^{\frac{1}{2}}$	5^{2}	$5^{\frac{1}{2}}$	$9^{\frac{1}{2}}$	$11^{7\frac{3}{4}}$	Castillo H Jr	15.60
9Oct04 ^{7}Crc^{4}	Pah	L b	5	114	11	12	12	12	12	12	12	Castro E	61.20

***-Actual Betting Favorite.**

OFF AT 4:53 Start Good. Won driving. Course firm.

TIME :23^{1}, :47, 1:10, 1:33^{4}, 1:45^{3} (:23.30, :47.18, 1:10.09, 1:33.81, 1:45.74)

$2 Mutuel Prices:			
7 – HOST–CHI	5.40	2.80	2.80
3 – SILVER TREE		2.80	2.60
2 – DEMETEOR			11.20

$2 EXACTA 7–3 PAID $13.00 $2 TRIFECTA 7–3–2 PAID $288.80
$2 SUPERFECTA 7–3–2–10 PAID $2,139.00

Ch. c, (Aug), by Hussonet – Colonna Traiana–Chi, by Roy. Trainer Pletcher Todd A. Bred by Haras De Pirque (Chi).

HOST (CHI) drifted slightly out entering the opening turn, rated just off the pace toward the outside, made his bid entering the stretch, endured a long drive, dueled the final yards and inched up nearing the wire. SILVER TREE rated just off the early pace about the three path, started his drive entering the stretch, had a short lead a sixteenth out, picked up the winner from there and was outfinished through the the closing yards. DEMETEOR rated close to the pace inside, felt solid steady pressure from the quarter pole and finished well. MOGADOR rated back about the four path, was in tight through the final turn, bid entering the stretch and finished well. IN HAND, unhurried inside, angled out to start his drive into the final turn and finished evenly outside. KEEP COOL rated the pace two deep on the backstretch, moved clear through the final turn, was under a solid drive entering the stretch but weakened toward the sixteenth pole. PRIVATE SCANDAL, unhurried toward mid track, made a mild bid into the final turn and finished evenly outside. SEA PLEASURE saved ground, steadied lacking room approaching the quarter pole and finished evenly. BOB'S PROUD MOMENT steadied at the start and was never a factor. FINAL PROPHECY drifted out into the opening turn, rated off the pace about the five path then weakened the final quarter. COLONIAL BAY was carried slightly out into the opening turn and through after half. PAH never factored.

Owners– 1, Melnyk Eugene and Laura; 2, Vegso Peter; 3, Hoffman Kenneth E; 4, Brushwood Stable; 5, Shining Armor Stable and Humphrey Jr G Watts; 6, Skys The Limit Racing LLC; 7, Pompa Paul P Jr; 8, A O Lewis; 9, Dubois Robert M; 10, Howes Dale and Jean; 11, Dogwood Stable; 12, Falls Racing Stable

Trainers– 1, Pletcher Todd A; 2, Mott William I; 3, Hoffman Kenneth E; 4, Clement Christophe; 5, Oliver Philip J; 6, Falzone Victor; 7, Sciacca Gary; 8, Tortora Emanuel; 9, Potter Douglas; 10, Brownlee David R; 11, Motion H Graham; 12, Wolfson Martin D

Scratched– Twilight Road (23Oct04 ^{13}Crc^{4}), Sir Walter Rahy (26Oct04 ^{8}Med^{1}), Gold Dollar (25Nov04 ^{3}Crc^{3}), Dependable Herbie (13Nov04 ^{10}Crc^{4})

$2 Pick Three (1–3–7) Paid $912.60 ; Pick Three Pool $52,239 .
$1 Pick Four (12–1–3–7) Paid $4,557.50 ; Pick Four Pool $269,857 .

SEVENTH RACE
Hollywood
DECEMBER 4, 2004

1½ MILES. (Turf) (2.23^{2}) 24TH RUNNING OF THE HOLLYWOOD TURF CUP. Grade I. Purse $250,000 FOR THREE-YEAR-OLDS AND UPWARD. By subscription of $250 each, on or before November 24, or by supplementary nomination of $5,000 each by closing time of entries. $1,250 to pass the entry box and $1,250 additional to start, with $150,000 to the winner, $50,000 to second, $30,000 to third, $15,000 to fourth and $5,000 to fifth. Three-year-olds 122 lbs. Older 126 lbs. Starters to be named through the entry box by the closing time of entries. This race will not be divided. If the number of entries exceed fourteen(14), first preference will be given to graded or group stakes winners in 2004. Second preference will be given to horses placed (second or third) in a graded or grouped stakes in 2004. Total earnings in 2004 will be used in determining the order of preference of horses with equal status. All fees for entrants that fail to draw into this race will be cancelled. Trophies will be presented to the winning owner and trainer. Closed with 13 nominations.

Value of Race: $250,000 Winner $150,000; second $50,000; third $30,000; fourth $15,000; fifth $5,000. Mutuel Pool $612,971.00 Exacta Pool $344,366.00 Quinella Pool $28,547.00 Trifecta Pool $365,677.00 Superfecta Pool $134,416.00

Last Raced	Horse	M/Eqt.	A.	Wt	PP	¼	½	1	1¼	Str	Fin	Jockey	Odds $1
23Oct04 ^{9}SA^{2}	Pellegrino-Brz	LB	5	126	7	$7^{1\frac{1}{2}}$	7^{hd}	7^{hd}	$6^{2\frac{1}{2}}$	$4^{\frac{1}{2}}$	1^{hd}	Stevens G L	10.20
30Oct04 ^{6}LS^{11}	Megahertz-GB	LB	5	123	8	8^{hd}	9	9	5^{1}	2^{hd}	2^{hd}	Douglas R R	4.90
16May04 CJD^{16}	License To Run-Brz	LB	4	126	4	$3^{1\frac{1}{2}}$	4^{1}	5^{hd}	7^{hd}	6^{3}	$3^{\frac{1}{2}}$	Gomez G K	10.50
30Oct04 ^{6}LS^{4}	Moscow Burning	LB	4	123	5	2^{hd}	$3^{1\frac{1}{2}}$	4^{1}	$3^{\frac{1}{2}}$	$5^{1\frac{1}{2}}$	4^{2}	Valdivia J Jr	11.90
24Nov04 ^{7}Hol^{2}	Balestrini-Ire	LB b	4	126	1	1^{1}	$1^{\frac{1}{2}}$	$1^{\frac{1}{2}}$	1^{hd}	3^{hd}	5no	Smith M E	27.40
30Oct04 ^{8}LS^{1}	Better Talk Now	LB bf	5	126	3	6^{hd}	5^{hd}	3^{1}	$2^{1\frac{1}{2}}$	1^{hd}	6^{8}	Dominguez R A	1.10
23Oct04 ^{9}SA^{5}	Hatif-Brz	LB	5	126	9	$5^{1\frac{1}{2}}$	6^{2}	6^{1}	9	8^{2}	$7^{\frac{1}{2}}$	Baze T C	47.00
23Oct04 ^{9}SA^{1}	Habaneros	LB bf	5	126	6	9	8^{1}	$8^{1\frac{1}{2}}$	$8^{1\frac{1}{2}}$	$7^{2\frac{1}{2}}$	8^{6}	Flores D R	8.20
23Oct04 ^{9}SA^{4}	Puerto Banus	LB b	5	126	2	4^{1}	2^{1}	2^{hd}	4^{hd}	9	9	Desormeaux K J	5.90

OFF AT 3:37 Start Good. Won driving. Course firm.

TIME :25^{3}, :50^{2}, 1:15^{3}, 1:39^{4}, 2:04, 2:29^{3} (:25.72, :50.50, 1:15.61, 1:39.97, 2:04.18, 2:29.73)

$2 Mutuel Prices:			
7 – PELLEGRINO-BRZ	22.40	10.00	6.20
8 – MEGAHERTZ-GB		7.20	6.00
4 – LICENSE TO RUN-BRZ			9.80

$1 EXACTA 7-8 PAID $74.70 $2 QUINELLA 7-8 PAID $64.60
$1 TRIFECTA 7-8-4 PAID $843.10 $1 SUPERFECTA 7-8-4-5 PAID $6,271.60

Dk. b or br. h, (Aug), by Nugget Point-Ire – Vale Mas, by Good Bloke-Arg. Trainer Burke Donald J II. Bred by Haras Equilia (Brz).

PELLEGRINO (BRZ) chased outside a rival then along the inside leaving the backstretch, was in tight into the final turn and again leaving that turn, continued inside, bid along the rail under urging in midstretch and gamely prevailed. MEGAHERTZ (GB) settled outside a rival then a bit off the rail, split horses into the last turn, came three deep into the stretch, gained a short lead past midstretch and continued gamely between foes late. LICENSE TO RUN (BRZ) stalked inside then just off the rail on the backstretch, dropped back between horses approaching the final turn, swung out on that bend and three deep into the stretch and closed willingly. MOSCOW BURNING stalked outside a rival then inside, came out into the stretch, steadied in tight approaching midstretch but continued willingly between foes late. BALESTRINI (IRE) took the early lead, set the pace inside, dueled along the rail on the backstretch and final turn, fought back between horses in midstretch but weakened. BETTER TALK NOW pulled inside then outside a rival, tugged his way up three deep to prompt the pace on the backstretch and last turn, took a short lead into the stretch, battled between horses and drifted out a bit in midstretch and also weakened in the final furlong. HATIF (BRZ) chased outside then three deep on the backstretch, dropped back off the rail on the final turn and lacked a further response. HABANEROS off a step slowly, saved ground off the pace and did not rally. PUERTO BANUS steadied in tight on the first turn, came off the rail leaving that bend, bid outside a rival in the stretch the first time, battled between horses on the second turn and backstretch and into the final turn, dropped back approaching the stretch, gave way and was eased in the drive. A claim of foul by the rider of MOSCOW BURNING against MEGAHERTZ for alleged interference in the stretch was not allowed by the stewards, who ruled the trouble to the former was caused by BETTER TALK NOW.

Owners– 1, Tanaka Gary A; 2, Bello Michael; 3, T N T Stud; 4, Mariani Jeffrey J Nentwig Michael and Van Kempen Dallas; 5, Carl Holt; 6, Bushwood Racing Partners; 7, Belmont Stable and Old Friends Inc; 8, Bell John C Lessee; 9, Noctis LLC Papiano Neil and Taub Steve

Trainers– 1, Burke Donald J II; 2, Frankel Robert; 3, Frankel Robert; 4, Cassidy James; 5, Drysdale Neil; 6, Motion H Graham; 7, Lobo Paulo H; 8, Bell Thomas R II; 9, Mulhall Kristin

$2 Daily Double (8–7) Paid $115.20; Daily Double Pool $31,909.
$1 Pick Three (4–8–7) Paid $940.80; Pick Three Pool $91,333.

SIXTH RACE
Hollywood
DECEMBER 5, 2004

6 FURLONGS. (1.07^{2}) 24TH RUNNING OF THE VERNON O. UNDERWOOD. Grade III. Purse $100,000 FOR THREE-YEAR-OLDS AND UPWARD. By subscription of $100 each, on or before November 24. Or by supplementary nomination of $2,000 each by the closing time of entries. $1,000 additional to start, with $60,000 to the winner, $20,000 to second, $12,000 to third, $6,000 to fourth and $2,000 to fifth. Three-year-olds 122 lbs. Older 124 lbs. Winners of two races of $60,000 in 2004, 2 lbs additional. Non-winners of two races of $45,000 since April 20 allowed 2 lbs. ; of three races of $25,000 or a race of $45,000 in 2004, 4 lbs. ; of $35,000 twice in 2004, 6 lbs. ; of $35,000 or two races of $20,000 in 2004, 8 lbs. (Claiming races not considered). A trophy will be presented to the owner of the winner. Closed with 14 nominations. Supplemental nomination: KELA.

Value of Race: $100,000 Winner $60,000; second $20,000; third $12,000; fourth $6,000; fifth $2,000. Mutuel Pool $404,058.00 Exacta Pool $217,249.00 Quinella Pool $19,425.00 Trifecta Pool $224,541.00 Superfecta Pool $88,105.00

Last Raced	Horse	M/Eqt.	A.	Wt	PP	St	¼	½	Str	Fin	Jockey	Odds $1
15Aug04 ^{8}Dmr^{5}	Taste of Paradise	LB	5	122	3	4	3^{hd}	$3^{1\frac{1}{2}}$	4^{3}	1no	Valdivia J Jr	26.40
5Nov04 ^{8}Aqu^{2}	Watchem Smokey	LB	4	116	5	5	5^{1}	5^{2}	$3^{\frac{1}{2}}$	2^{2}	Douglas R R	4.70
7Nov04 ^{6}Hol^{2}	My Master-Arg	LB b	5	116	2	2	1^{hd}	1^{hd}	1^{hd}	3^{3}	Court J K	11.30
30Oct04 ^{5}LS^{2}	Kela	LB b	6	126	7	3	7	7	$5^{\frac{1}{2}}$	$4^{\frac{1}{2}}$	Nakatani C S	1.50
30Oct04 ^{5}LS^{12}	Our New Recruit	LB	5	122	4	1	2^{6}	2^{3}	2^{1}	$5^{3\frac{1}{2}}$	Baze T C	2.50
1Nov04 ^{4}TuP^{1}	Newark	LB	4	118	6	6	4^{1}	4^{hd}	6^{hd}	6^{2}	Espinoza V	21.10
30Oct04 ^{5}LS^{3}	My Cousin Matt	LB f	5	116	1	7	6^{hd}	6^{hd}	7	7	Dominguez R A	4.80

OFF AT 3:05 Start Good For All But MY COUSIN MATT. Won driving. Track wet fast.

TIME :21^{3}, :44, :55^{4}, 1:08 (:21.64, :44.07, :55.92, 1:08.04)

$2 Mutuel Prices:			
3 – TASTE OF PARADISE	54.80	20.40	8.40
5 – WATCHEM SMOKEY		6.80	5.20
2 – MY MASTER-ARG			7.00

$1 EXACTA 3–5 PAID $128.70 $2 QUINELLA 3–5 PAID $101.20
$1 TRIFECTA 3–5–2 PAID $1,000.50 $1 SUPERFECTA 3–5–2–8 PAID $3,031.60

Dk. b or br. h, (Apr), by Conquistador Cielo – Tastetheteardrops , by What Luck . Trainer Mandella Gary. Bred by Abrahams Snukal & Bloom (Ky).

TASTE OF PARADISE chased off the rail then between foes leaving the backstretch, angled in midway on the turn, swung out into the stretch and rallied under urging to get up at the wire. WATCHEM SMOKEY also chased off the rail early, angled in on the backstretch, steadied briefly behind the winner midway on the turn, rallied along the fence in the lane to gain a short lead in deep stretch but was caught on the line. MY MASTER (ARG) had good early speed and dueled inside a rival but a bit off the rail, fought back into the stretch, could not match the top pair late but held third. KELA chased outside then between foes leaving the backstretch, continued alongside a rival on the turn, swung out into the stretch and lacked the needed rally. OUR NEW RECRUIT dueled outside a rival, fought back alongside that one to midstretch, then weakened. NEWARK steadied when squeezed at the start, went up four wide on the backstretch to chase the pace, continued outside on the turn and three deep into the stretch and also weakened. MY COUSIN MATT tried to rear at the start and broke in the air and slowly, settled inside, came a bit off the rail on the turn, angled back in nearing the stretch and did not rally.

Owners– 1, Bloom David B; 2, Gann Edmund A; 3, Sengara Jeffrey; 4, Manoogian Jay; 5, C R K Stable; 6, Bob or Shenen Dietrich or Patsy Leavitt; 7, Englander Richard A

Trainers– 1, Mandella Gary; 2, Frankel Robert; 3, West Ted H; 4, Mitchell Mike; 5, Sadler John W; 6, Bennett Keith; 7, Mullins Jeff

Scratched– Star Cross (ARG) (08May04 ^{9}Hol^{8})

$2 Daily Double (6–3) Paid $314.80 ; Daily Double Pool $30,763 .
$1 Pick Three (2/5–6–3) Paid $1,122.50 ; Pick Three Pool $75,006 .

SEVENTH RACE
Hollywood
DECEMBER 11, 2004

1⅛ MILES. (1.45^{1}) 26TH RUNNING OF THE NATIVE DIVER HANDICAP. Grade III. Purse $100,000 FOR THREE-YEAR-OLDS AND UPWARD. By subscription of $100 each, on or before December 1, or by supplementary nomination of $2,000 each by 3:00 pm Saturday, December 4. $1,000 additional to start, with $60,000 to the winner, $20,000 to second, $12,000 to third, $6,000 to fourth and $2,000 to fifth. Weights Sunday, December 5. Starters to be named through the entry box by closing time of entries. Hollywood Park reserves the right not to divide this race. Should this race not be divided and the number of entries exceed the starting gate capacity, high weights on the scale will be preferred. Total earnings in 2004 will be used in determining the order of preference of horses assigned equal weight on the scale. All fees for entrants that fail to draw into this race will be cancelled. A trophy will be presented to the owner of the winner. Closed with 23 nominations.

Value of Race: $100,000 Winner $60,000; second $20,000; third $12,000; fourth $6,000; fifth $2,000. Mutuel Pool $562,957.00 Exacta Pool $352,551.00 Quinella Pool $28,020.00 Trifecta Pool $362,256.00 Superfecta Pool $161,309.00

Last Raced	Horse	M/Eqt.	A.	Wt	PP	St	¼	½	¾	Str	Fin	Jockey	Odds $1
18Nov04 ^{5}Hol^{1}	Truly a Judge	LB	6	115	8	3	1^{1}	1^{1}	1^{1}	$1^{2\frac{1}{2}}$	1^{2}	Pedroza M A	6.40
30Oct04 ^{9}LS^{8}	Dynever	LB	4	119	6	7	7^{hd}	8	7^{2}	$3^{2\frac{1}{2}}$	2^{7}	Nakatani C S	1.10
16Oct04 ^{8}SA^{4}	Calkins Road	LB f	5	116	2	2	$6^{2\frac{1}{2}}$	6^{1}	6^{hd}	$5^{1\frac{1}{2}}$	3^{2}	Flores D R	31.00
16Oct04 ^{8}SA^{5}	Tizbud	LB	5	115	3	6	$4^{\frac{1}{2}}$	3^{hd}	$4^{1\frac{1}{2}}$	7^{1}	4^{hd}	Gomez G K	10.80
13Nov04 ^{10}Crc^{1}	Supah Blitz	LB	4	118	1	4	3^{1}	4^{1}	3^{1}	$4^{\frac{1}{2}}$	$5^{2\frac{1}{2}}$	Espinoza V	3.20
22Aug04 ^{9}Sar^{6}	Congrats	LB	4	115	5	5	5^{hd}	5^{1}	5^{hd}	8	6^{3}	Baze T C	5.90
3Nov04 ^{7}Hol^{1}	Mud Shark	LB b	4	115	7	8	8	$7^{\frac{1}{2}}$	8	6^{hd}	7^{11}	Douglas R R	23.10
6Nov04 ^{8}TuP^{1}	Black Bart	LB	5	114	4	1	2^{hd}	$2^{\frac{1}{2}}$	2^{1}	2^{hd}	8	Gann S L	19.10

OFF AT 3:45 Start Good . Won driving. Track fast.

TIME :23^{3}, :47^{2}, 1:11^{1}, 1:34^{4}, 1:47 (:23.67, :47.50, 1:11.32, 1:34.90, 1:47.06)

$2 Mutuel Prices:			
10 – TRULY A JUDGE	14.80	5.40	4.20
7 – DYNEVER		2.80	2.60
2 – CALKINS ROAD			9.00

$1 EXACTA 10–7 PAID $20.00 $2 QUINELLA 7–10 PAID $15.40
$1 TRIFECTA 10–7–2 PAID $229.10 $1 SUPERFECTA 10–7–2–3 PAID $1,304.50

Dk. b or br. g, (May), by Judge T C – Truly Needy , by Yukon . Trainer Bernstein David. Bred by Robert H Roberts & Bea Roberts (Ky).

TRULY A JUDGE had speed three deep then angled in on the lead, set the pace along the inside, inched away on the second turn, kicked clear in the stretch and held on gamely under urging. DYNEVER angled in and saved ground off the pace, moved up inside on the second turn, came out into the stretch and finished with interest but could not catch the winner. CALKINS ROAD chased inside then between horses into and on the second turn, found the rail again nearing the stretch and picked up the show. TIZBUD stalked between horses then outside a rival leaving the backstretch, came three deep into the stretch, steadied and was forced out a sixteenth from the wire and lacked the needed response. SUPAH BLITZ saved ground stalking the pace, was between foes leaving the second turn, steadied and was forced out past midstretch and weakened. CONGRATS chased three deep, was briefly four wide on the second turn, came three wide into the stretch, also steadied and was forced out in deep stretch and did not rally. MUD SHARK allowed to settle outside a rival, came out into the stretch, also steadied when crowded in deep stretch and was not a threat. BLACK BART stalked the winner outside a rival then off the rail on the second turn, took a bad step in midstretch, drifted out while being pulled up in the final furlong, was unsaddled a pole from the wire and vanned off.

Owners– 1, Aidekman Alan Ailshie Gaylord and Harris Tom; 2, Wills Catherine and Karches Peter; 3, Shapiro Mr and Mrs Thomas A; 4, Cees Stable LLC; 5, Black Saddle Stable Kagele Brothers Inc and Leib Mark; 6, Claiborne Farm & Dilschneider; 7, Jacobs and Pegram; 8, Metzger Thomas F Sr

Trainers– 1, Bernstein David; 2, Clement Christophe; 3, Shirreffs John; 4, Sadler John W; 5, O'Neill Doug; 6, Mandella Richard; 7, Baffert Bob; 8, Bainum Troy

Scratched– Formal Attire (05Sep04 ^{3}Sar^{3}) , Valid Again (18Nov04 ^{5}Hol^{9}) , Sigfreto (13Nov04 ^{9}Crc^{6})

$2 Daily Double (6–10) Paid $90.00 ; Daily Double Pool $31,496 .
$1 Pick Three (11/12–6–10) Paid $105.70 ; Pick Three Pool $107,728 .

EIGHTH RACE
Hollywood
DECEMBER 12, 2004

$1\frac{1}{16}$ MILES. (1.40) 23RD RUNNING OF THE BAYAKOA HANDICAP. Grade II. Purse $150,000 FOR FILLIES AND MARES THREE -YEAR-OLDS AND UPWARD. By subscription of $150 each, on or before December 1, or by supplementary nomination of $3,000 each by 3:00 pm Saturday, December 4. $1,500 additional to start, with $90,000 to the winner, $30,000 to second, $18,000 to third, $9,000 to fourth and $3,000 to fifth. Weights Sunday, December 5. Starters to be named through the entry box by closing time of entries. Hollywood Park reserves the right not to divide this race. Should this race not be divided and the number of entries exceed the starting gate capacity, high weights on the scale will be preferred. Total earnings in 2004 will be used in determining the order of preference of horses assigned equal weight on the scale. All fees for entrants that fail to draw into this race will be cancelled. A trophy will be presented to the owner of the winner. Closed Wednesday, December 1 with 15 nominations.

Value of Race: $150,000 Winner $90,000; second $30,000; third $18,000; fourth $9,000; fifth $3,000. Mutuel Pool $397,498.00 Exacta Pool $194,842.00 Quinella Pool $17,711.00 Trifecta Pool $214,460.00 Superfecta Pool $97,621.00

Last Raced	Horse	M/Eqt.	A.	Wt	PP	St	¼	½	¾	Str	Fin	Jockey	Odds $1
30Oct04 2LS10	Hollywood Story	LB b	3	115	7	6	5^{3}	$5^{1\frac{1}{2}}$	4^{hd}	3^{1}	1^{1}	Espinoza V	5.10
14Nov04 8Hol1	Royally Chosen	LB	6	116	4	2	$2^{1\frac{1}{2}}$	$2^{1\frac{1}{2}}$	2^{1}	$1^{\frac{1}{2}}$	2^{2}	Flores D R	4.50
30Apr04 10CD6	A. P. Adventure	LB	3	117	1	5	$4^{\frac{1}{2}}$	4^{1}	$5^{2\frac{1}{2}}$	4^{hd}	$3^{\frac{1}{2}}$	Smith M E	1.70
31Oct04 8SA4	Miss Loren-Arg	LB f	6	116	6	1	3^{hd}	3^{hd}	3^{1}	5^{2}	4^{2}	Valdivia J Jr	3.60
21Nov04 6Hol2	Keys to the Heart	LB	5	115	2	4	6^{2}	6^{3}	$6^{1\frac{1}{2}}$	$6^{2\frac{1}{2}}$	$5^{2\frac{1}{2}}$	Gomez G K	23.30
20Nov04 9Pim1	Essence	LB	3	117	3	3	$1^{1\frac{1}{2}}$	1^{1}	1^{1}	2^{hd}	$6^{2\frac{1}{2}}$	Nakatani C S	4.10
14May04 5GLD2	Born to Dance	LB bf	5	115	5	7	7	7	7	7	7	Douglas R R	31.90

OFF AT 1:06 Start Good For All But BORN TO DANCE. Won driving. Track fast.
TIME :23^{3}, :47, 1:11, 1:34^{4}, 1:41 (:23.67, :47.09, 1:11.08, 1:34.94, 1:41.11)

$2 Mutuel Prices:				
	8 – HOLLYWOOD STORY	12.20	5.60	3.00
	5 – ROYALLY CHOSEN		5.80	3.40
	1 – A. P. ADVENTURE			2.60

$1 EXACTA 8–5 PAID $39.10 $2 QUINELLA 5–8 PAID $36.00
$1 TRIFECTA 8–5–1 PAID $140.00 $1 SUPERFECTA 8–5–1–7 PAID $380.10

Dk. b or br. f, (Mar), by Wild Rush – Wife for Life , by Dynaformer . Trainer Shirreffs John. Bred by Vinery (Ky).

HOLLYWOOD STORY chased three deep on the first turn, continued outside, ranged up four wide into the stretch, bid outside and took the lead past midstretch and proved best under good handling. ROYALLY CHOSEN stalked off the rail, took command outside the pacesetter into the stretch, battled between foes in midstretch, fought back inside the winner but could not match that one late. A. P. ADVENTURE saved ground stalking the pace, came out into the stretch, split rivals in midstretch and edged a foe inside for third. MISS LOREN (ARG) chased between horses then outside a rival, came three deep into the stretch and just missed the show. KEYS TO THE HEART chased a bit off the rail then inside, came out into the stretch and lacked the needed rally. ESSENCE sped to the early lead, set the pace inside, dueled inside the runner-up into the stretch and to midstretch, then weakened. BORN TO DANCE had her head turned and broke slowly, settled off the rail, angled in some leaving the backstretch and was outrun.

Owners– 1, Krikorian George; 2, Abruzzo Peter Johnston E W Zehenni Tony V et al; 3, Lewis Robert B and Beverly J; 4, Llers Corporation; 5, Nichols Thomas L; 6, Padua Stables; 7, Parra Rosendo G

Trainers– 1, Shirreffs John; 2, Headley Bruce; 3, Dollase Wallace; 4, Seglin Luis E; 5, Greely C Beau; 6, Pletcher Todd A; 7, Cerin Vladimir

Scratched– Coconut Girl (02Sep04 7Dmr4)

$2 Daily Double (2–8) Paid $73.80 ; Daily Double Pool $38,871 .
$1 Pick Three (7–2–8) Paid $181.00 ; Pick Three Pool $59,121 .

EIGHTH RACE
Aqueduct
DECEMBER 18, 2004

$1\frac{1}{4}$ MILES. (2.01^{2}) 134TH RUNNING OF THE LADIES HANDICAP. Grade III. Purse $100,000 INNER DIRT (Up To $19,000 NYSBFOA) A HANDICAP FOR FILLIES AND MARES THREE YEARS OLD AND UPWARD. By subscription of $100 each, which should accompany the nomination; $500 to pass the entry box; $500 to start, with $100,000 added. The added money and all fees to be divided 60% to the winner, 20% to second, 10% to third, 5% to fourth, 3% to fifth and 2% divided equally among remaining finishers. A trophy will be presented to the winning owner. Closed Saturday, December 4, 2004 with 14 Nominations.

Value of Race: $109,400 Winner $65,640; second $21,880; third $10,940; fourth $5,470; fifth $3,282; sixth $730; seventh $730; eighth $728. Mutuel Pool $510,773.00 Exacta Pool $443,217.00 Trifecta Pool $347,674.00

Last Raced	Horse	M/Eqt.	A.	Wt	PP	¼	½	¾	1	Str	Fin	Jockey	Odds $1
20Nov04 9Pim2	Rare Gift	L	3	115	3	1^{hd}	$1^{\frac{1}{2}}$	1^{1}	1^{1}	1^{4}	1^{6}	Migliore R	4.20
28Nov04 8Aqu1	Board Elligible	L bf	4	117	2	4^{hd}	4^{1}	4^{hd}	5^{3}	3^{1}	2^{nk}	Fragoso P	4.40
25Nov04 10CD3	Miss Fortunate	L	4	117	6	3^{2}	3^{hd}	3^{hd}	$3^{\frac{1}{2}}$	2^{hd}	3^{3}	Bridgmohan S X	6.60
6Nov04 9Aqu8	Nevermore	L f	4	116	1	6^{1}	7^{hd}	6^{hd}	$6^{2\frac{1}{2}}$	5^{hd}	4^{1}	Bejarano R	4.30
26Nov04 9Aqu3	Roar Emotion	L	4	119	5	2^{1}	2^{2}	$2^{1\frac{1}{2}}$	2^{1}	4^{3}	$5^{1\frac{1}{2}}$	Luzzi M J	1.70
13Nov04 7Aqu1	Points West	L	4	114	4	5^{2}	$5^{\frac{1}{2}}$	5^{2}	4^{hd}	6^{1}	$6^{\frac{3}{4}}$	Carrero V	37.25
28Nov04 8Aqu4	French Hideaway	L f	5	112	8	8	8	8	8	$7^{\frac{1}{2}}$	$7^{2\frac{1}{4}}$	Jara F	65.75
10Nov04 LIN1	Rendezvous Point		3	113	7	7^{hd}	6^{1}	$7^{\frac{1}{2}}$	7^{1}	8	8	Arroyo N Jr	14.40

OFF AT 3:47 Start Good . Won driving. Track fast.
TIME :25, :49^{4}, 1:14^{4}, 1:39^{3}, 2:05^{2} (:25.05, :49.91, 1:14.83, 1:39.71, 2:05.51)

$2 Mutuel Prices:				
	3 – RARE GIFT	10.40	5.50	4.50
	2 – BOARD ELLIGIBLE		5.00	4.00
	6 – MISS FORTUNATE			4.40

$2 EXACTA 3–2 PAID $42.60 $2 TRIFECTA 3–2–6 PAID $189.50

Gr/ro. f, (Apr), by Unbridled's Song – Rare Blend , by Bates Motel . Trainer Kimmel John C. Bred by Joseph Allen (Ky).

RARE GIFT set the pace inside and drew off under urging. BOARD ELLIGIBLE saved ground and rallied up the rail for second. MISS FORTUNATE stalked outside, bid three wide into the lane and was outfinished for the place. NEVERMORE raced off the pace on the inside and lacked a rally. ROAR EMOTION was content to sit second outside of RARE GIFT and came up empty in the stretch. POINTS WEST had a wide trip and tired. FRENCH HIDEAWAY was outrun. RENDEZVOUS POINT was outrun.

Owners– 1, Bolton George Dipietro David and Honour Roger; 2, Rudina Stable; 3, Lyon Stables; 4, Scarborough Robert; 5, Allen Joseph; 6, Peace John H; 7, Anstu Stables Inc; 8, Augustin Stable

Trainers– 1, Kimmel John C; 2, Ferraro James W; 3, Mott William I; 4, Bond Harold James; 5, McLaughlin Kiaran P; 6, Weaver George; 7, Moloney James J; 8, Gosden John H M

NINTH RACE
Calder
DECEMBER 18, 2004

$1\frac{1}{2}$ MILES. (Turf) (2.24) 30TH RUNNING OF THE LA PREVOYANTE HANDICAP. Grade II. Purse $200,000 FOR FILLIES AND MARES, THREE YEARS OLD AND UPWARD. By subscription of $200 each which shall accompany the nomination, $2,000 to pass the entry box and an additional $2,000 to start – with 200,000 guaranteed. The owner of the winner to receive $120,000, $40,000 to second, $22,000 to third, $12,000 to fourth and $6,000 to fifth. A trophy will be presented to the winning Owner, Trainer and Jockey. This race will be limited to 12 Starters, with Also Eligibles. (High Weights Preferred) Closed Saturday, December 4, 2004 with 25 nominations. (If deemed inadvisable to run this race over the Turf course, it will be run on the main track at One Mile and One Half).

Value of Race: $200,000 Winner $120,000; second $40,000; third $22,000; fourth $12,000; fifth $6,000. Mutuel Pool $317,795.00 Exacta Pool $241,766.00 Trifecta Pool $161,352.00 Superfecta Pool $52,328.00

Last Raced	Horse	M/Eqt.	A.	Wt	PP	¼	½	1	1¼	Str	Fin	Jockey	Odds $1
6Nov04 ^{8}Aqu^{3}	Arvada-GB	L	4	117	9	$2\frac{1}{2}$	$2\frac{1}{2}$	1^{1}	$1^{1\frac{1}{2}}$	$1^{1\frac{1}{2}}$	1^{hd}	Prado E S	3.00
24Oct04 ^{8}Kee^{1}	Humaita-Ger	L	4	119	8	$5\frac{1}{2}$	$5^{1\frac{1}{2}}$	6^{1}	$4^{2\frac{1}{2}}$	$2^{1\frac{1}{2}}$	$2^{1\frac{1}{2}}$	Velasquez C	2.50
20Nov04 ^{4}Crc^{1}	Honey Ryder	L b	3	113	10	11	11	11	10^{2}	$6^{1\frac{1}{2}}$	$3\frac{3}{4}$	Cruz M R	34.00
2Nov04 ^{9}CD^{3}	Ocean Silk	L b	4	115	6	10^{hd}	10^{3}	8^{1}	8^{1}	7^{hd}	4^{nk}	Boulanger G	43.70
6Nov04 ^{5}Crc^{6}	Iowa's Image	L	5	113	11	9^{2}	9^{1}	9^{hd}	$7\frac{1}{2}$	4^{hd}	$5^{1\frac{1}{2}}$	Samyn J L	54.90
13Nov04 ^{9}CD^{2}	Lenatareese	L	3	113	3	$1\frac{1}{2}$	$1\frac{1}{2}$	$4\frac{1}{2}$	3^{hd}	3^{2}	6^{nk}	Dominguez R A	6.40
22Oct04 ^{6}Kee^{3}	My Dear Lady-Arg	L	4	114	5	$6\frac{1}{2}$	8^{hd}	$10^{2\frac{1}{2}}$	$9\frac{1}{2}$	8^{3}	7^{1}	Chavez J F	7.60
6Nov04 ^{8}Aqu^{4}	Savedbythelight	L b	4	115	1	$3\frac{1}{2}$	3^{hd}	2^{hd}	2^{hd}	5^{1}	8^{5}	Valdivia J Jr	11.60
4Dec04 ^{8}Crc^{1}	SomethingVentured	L b	5	115	2	$7^{1\frac{1}{2}}$	6^{hd}	5^{hd}	$6\frac{1}{2}$	10^{3}	$9^{1\frac{1}{4}}$	Bailey J D	3.70
6Nov04 ^{8}Aqu^{2}	Literacy	L	4	114	4	8^{hd}	$7^{1\frac{1}{2}}$	$7^{1\frac{1}{2}}$	5^{hd}	$9\frac{1}{2}$	$10^{1\frac{1}{4}}$	Bravo J	14.20
2Oct04 ^{4}SA^{10}	Cozie Advantage	L b	5	113	7	4^{1}	4^{hd}	3^{1}	11	11	11	Ferrer J C	64.00

OFF AT 4:00 Start Good. Won driving. Course firm.

TIME :24^{4}, :50^{3}, 1:14^{4}, 1:39^{1}, 2:03^{1}, 2:27 (:24.93, :50.67, 1:14.84, 1:39.27, 2:03.30, 2:27.19)

$2 Mutuel Prices:

10 – ARVADA-GB	8.00	3.80	3.40
9 – HUMAITA-GER		3.60	3.00
11 – HONEY RYDER			9.40

$2 EXACTA 10–9 PAID $26.20 $2 TRIFECTA 10–9–11 PAID $439.40
$2 SUPERFECTA 10–9–11–7 PAID $6,945.20

B. f, (Mar), by Hernando-Fr – Lalindi-Ire , by Cadeaux Genereux-GB . Trainer Frankel Robert. Bred by Myriad Communications and New England Stud (GB).

ARVADA (GB) battled along the outside for the opening furlong, gave a bit of ground nearing the first turn, ran again to set the pace midway, maintained her advantage into the stretch and was able to last under serious pressure. HUMAITA (GER) placed close up early on, retreated slightly towards one mile, kept to task with a sustained drive but was unable to run down the winner and just missed. HONEY RYDER trailed the field most of the way, advanced late with a stiff drive through the lane and finished strong. OCEAN SILK raced unhurried early on, maintained position towards the rear most of the way, offered a late bid into the stretch and was gaining at the end. IOWA'S IMAGE raced without speed from the outset, ran on evenly to to the stretch and rallied late. LENATAREESE battled in the opening furlong while between foes, gave way after a half mile and had nothing late. MY DEAR LADY (ARG) placed towards the outside from early on, made a move towards the rail nearing the first turn, bothered foes during path, raced along the rail but failed to respond. SAVEDBYTHELIGHT battled from the inside for the opening furlong, pressed the pace for a mile then tired. SOMETHING VENTURED checked badly nearing the first turn when MY DEAR LADY(ARG) moved toward the rail, circled that one to race outside, was four wide around the second turn then faded. LITERACY forwardly placed from the outset, was steadied a bit when MY DEAR LADY(ARG) moved toward the rail, was then taken back, saved ground for the remainder but was unable to rally. COZIE ADVANTAGE raced just off the pace around the first two turns while three wide and tired.

Owners– 1, Gordon Giles Pritchard; 2, Jacobs Andreas; 3, Glencrest Farm LLC; 4, Swettenham Stud; 5, Ersoff Racing Stable Inc; 6, Anderson Brad; 7, Oxley John C; 8, Mack Earle I; 9, Wiemer Irvin and McLane John; 10, John S Pregman Jr & Gerald Goodman; 11, Red Oak Stable

Trainers– 1, Frankel Robert; 2, Motion H Graham; 3, Pletcher Todd A; 4, Byrne Patrick B; 5, Ersoff Stanley M; 6, Carroll David; 7, Ward John T Jr; 8, Violette Richard A Jr; 9, Pletcher Todd A; 10, Pregman John S Jr; 11, Sacco Richard W

Scratched– Derrianne (06Nov04 ^{8}Crc^{3}) , Krasnaya (20Nov04 ^{4}Crc^{4})

$2 Pick Three (1–2–10) Paid $152.60 ; Pick Three Pool $24,206 .

ELEVENTH RACE
Calder
DECEMBER 18, 2004

$1\frac{1}{2}$ MILES. (Turf) (2.24) 33RD RUNNING OF THE W L MCKNIGHT HANDICAP. Grade II. Purse $200,000 FOR THREE YEAR OLDS AND UPWARD. By subscription of $200 each which shall accompany the nomination, $2,000 to pass the entry box and an additional $2,000 to start – with 200,000 guaranteed. The owner of the winner to receive $120,000, $40,000 to second, $22,000 to third, $12,000 to fourth and $6,000 to fifth. A trophy will be presented to the winning Owner, Trainer and Jockey. Closed Saturday, December 4, 2004 with 20 nominations. (If deemed inadvisable to run this race over the Turf course, it will berun on the main track at One Mile and One Half).

Value of Race: $200,000 Winner $120,000; second $40,000; third $22,000; fourth $12,000; fifth $6,000. Mutuel Pool $436,913.00 Exacta Pool $318,359.00 Trifecta Pool $227,270.00 Superfecta Pool $70,374.00

Last Raced	Horse	M/Eqt.	A.	Wt	PP	¼	½	1	1¼	Str	Fin	Jockey	Odds $1
20Nov04 ^{8}Aqu^{1}	Dreadnaught	L	4	116	4	$7^{1\frac{1}{2}}$	7^{1}	$7^{\frac{1}{2}}$	6^{hd}	4^{hd}	1^{nk}	Samyn J L	3.10
4Dec04 ^{11}Crc^{3}	Demeteor	L	5	112	8	$2^{\frac{1}{2}}$	$2^{\frac{1}{2}}$	2^{1}	2^{1}	1^{hd}	$2^{\frac{1}{2}}$	Chavez J F	12.50
13Nov04 ^{9}Haw^{5}	Scooter Roach	L	5	115	3	3^{1}	3^{1}	3^{hd}	3^{hd}	$5^{1\frac{1}{2}}$	$3^{\frac{1}{2}}$	Bravo J	35.00
4Dec04 ^{11}Crc^{11}	Colonial Bay	L b	5	112	1	8^{1}	8^{1}	8^{hd}	$9^{\frac{1}{2}}$	7^{hd}	$4^{\frac{1}{2}}$	Dominguez R A	23.20
9Oct04 ^{8}Kee^{5}	Puppeteer-GB	L	4	115	11	$9^{\frac{1}{2}}$	$9^{\frac{1}{2}}$	$10^{\frac{1}{2}}$	8^{hd}	$8^{\frac{1}{2}}$	5^{nk}	Valdivia J Jr	4.80
20Nov04 ^{8}Aqu^{4}	Irish Colonial	L	5	114	9	6^{2}	6^{2}	5^{hd}	4^{hd}	3^{hd}	6^{nk}	Prado E S	4.10
20Nov04 ^{8}Aqu^{2}	Certifiably Crazy	L b	4	114	2	1^{1}	$1^{1\frac{1}{2}}$	$1^{\frac{1}{2}}$	$1^{\frac{1}{2}}$	2^{2}	7^{1}	Velasquez C	5.20
29Oct04 ^{9}Med^{1}	Macaw-Ire	L bf	5	115	5	$10^{\frac{1}{2}}$	$10^{1\frac{1}{2}}$	9^{1}	7^{1}	$9^{1\frac{1}{2}}$	8^{nk}	Castro E	9.90
4Dec04 ^{11}Crc^{5}	In Hand	L bf	4	115	7	12	12	11^{hd}	11^{4}	11^{12}	$9^{\frac{3}{4}}$	Boulanger G	10.70
20Nov04 ^{8}Aqu^{6}	Dr. Brendler	L	6	116	6	$11^{1\frac{1}{2}}$	11^{1}	12	10^{1}	10^{hd}	$10^{1\frac{1}{2}}$	Santos J A	7.60
27Oct04 ^{9}Aqu^{1}	Latino-Per		5	113	10	4^{hd}	$5^{\frac{1}{2}}$	$4^{1\frac{1}{2}}$	5^{1}	6^{hd}	$11^{20\frac{3}{4}}$	Cruz M R	71.80
11Dec04 ^{11}Crc^{7}	Rays a Ruler	L bf	7	113	12	5^{hd}	4^{hd}	6^{hd}	12	12	12	Pezua J M	158.70

OFF AT 4:54 Start Good . Won driving. Course firm.

TIME :24, :49^{1}, 1:13^{4}, 1:39^{1}, 2:03, 2:26^{3} (:24.12, :49.37, 1:13.85, 1:39.39, 2:03.17, 2:26.60)

$2 Mutuel Prices:				
	4 – DREADNAUGHT	**8.20**	**4.60**	**3.80**
	8 – DEMETEOR		**13.40**	**8.40**
	3 – SCOOTER ROACH			**11.40**

$2 EXACTA 4–8 PAID $140.80 $2 TRIFECTA 4–8–3 PAID $2,494.80
$2 SUPERFECTA 4–8–3–All PAID $7,903.40

B. g, (Feb), by Lac Ouimet – Wings of Dreams , by Sovereign Dancer . Trainer Voss Thomas H. Bred by David S Pennington (Ky).

DREADNAUGHT raced a bit wide while placed near mid pack, was three wide around the second turn, came out four wide for the stretch drive and responded well when asked. DEMETEOR was out quickly to challenge for the early lead, went stride for stride with pace to the stretch, put away that one to take a short lead near the eight pole, then dug in to finish gamely when challenged by winner but couldn't last. SCOOTER ROACH placed on the rail while just behind leaders to the stretch, gave up ground through the lane, but managed to rally to regain show. COLONIAL BAY positioned along the rail, came out from behind horses for the stretch drive, found room between foes and responded well when asked and finished strong. PUPPETEER (GB) raced from well off the pace for a mile, moved up with a drive between horses then moved out five wide entering the lane. IRISH COLONIAL settled in good position to rate from the outset, reached striking position in the upper stretch then flattened out. CERTIFIABLY CRAZY showed early speed to take the advantage, was pressed while stride for stride with DEMETEOR most of the way then tired in the upper stretch. MACAW (IRE) hesitated a bit at the start, made a middle move to improve his position with half mile to go but was no real threat. IN HAND was outrun early and passed only tiring rivals. DR. BRENDLER lacked speed in the early going and was unable to menace. LATINO (PER) sat between horses around the first turn, closed to reach a good position around the third turn and failed to respond. RAYS A RULER raced three wide around the first turn, fanned four wide around the second turn, made a mild bid midway and faded quickly thereafter.

Owners– 1, Trillium Stable; 2, Hoffman Kenneth E; 3, Butterfly Stable; 4, Dogwood Stable; 5, House Michael; 6, Martin F and Nolan H; 7, Double S Stable K Avanzino & E Wachtel; 8, Melillo George and Sandra; 9, Shining Armor Stable and Humphrey Jr G Watts; 10, O'Toole Francis J; 11, Santa Cruz Ranch Inc; 12, Fernandez Jose N

Trainers– 1, Voss Thomas H; 2, Hoffman Kenneth E; 3, Kassen David C; 4, Motion H Graham; 5, Mullins Jeff; 6, Schulhofer Randy; 7, Destefano John M Jr; 8, Penna Angel Jr; 9, Oliver Philip J; 10, Motion H Graham; 11, Pompay Terri; 12, Fernandez Jose N

TWELFTH RACE
Calder
DECEMBER 18, 2004

1⅛ MILES. (1.50) 21ST RUNNING OF THE FRED W HOOPER HANDICAP. Grade III. Purse $100,000 FOR THREE YEAR OLDS AND UPWARD. By subscription of $100 each which shall accompany the nomination, $1,000 to pass the entry box and an additional $1,000 to start – with $100,000 guaranteed. The owner of the winner to receive $60,000, $20,000 to second, $11,000 to third, $6,000 to fourth and $3,000 to fifth. A trophy will be presented to the winning Owner. Supplemental Nomination for $3,000 to enter and start. Closed Saturday, December 4, 2004 with 14 nominations. Pies Prospect supplemental nominated.

Value of Race: $100,000 Winner $60,000; second $20,000; third $11,000; fourth $6,000; fifth $3,000. Mutuel Pool $270,739.00 Exacta Pool $205,789.00 Trifecta Pool $155,565.00 Superfecta Pool $58,322.00

Last Raced	Horse	M/Eqt.	A.	Wt	PP	St	¼	½	¾	Str	Fin	Jockey	Odds $1
26Nov04 ^{11}CD^{7}	Pies Prospect	L	3	114	3	2	3^{hd}	$4^{1\frac{1}{2}}$	3^{2}	1^{1}	$1^{8\frac{1}{2}}$	Prado E S	3.20
23Oct04 ^{13}Crc^{4}	Twilight Road	L	7	115	7	7	$6^{1\frac{1}{2}}$	$6^{2\frac{1}{2}}$	$5^{\frac{1}{2}}$	$3^{2\frac{1}{2}}$	2^{1}	Teator P A	9.70
13Nov04 ^{10}Crc^{2}	Hear No Evil	L bf	4	112	6	3	1^{1}	$1^{\frac{1}{2}}$	1^{1}	2^{3}	$3^{3\frac{1}{4}}$	Castro E	12.50
28Nov04 ^{9}Crc^{5}	The Judge Sez Who	L	5	114	4	6	11	11	8^{1}	$6^{\frac{1}{2}}$	$4^{1\frac{1}{4}}$	Santos J A	23.00
19Nov04 ^{9}Crc^{1}	Uncivil	L b	3	111	11	9	7^{hd}	7^{2}	7^{1}	7^{2}	$5^{\frac{3}{4}}$	Chavez J F	12.90
11Dec04 ^{8}Crc^{11}	Caiman	L	3	112	10	10	10^{3}	10^{hd}	11	8^{hd}	$6^{\frac{1}{2}}$	Nunez E O	137.90
25Nov04 ^{3}Crc^{3}	Gold Dollar	L b	5	113	5	5	9^{hd}	9^{hd}	10^{hd}	9^{hd}	7^{nk}	Lopez J E	24.80
28Nov04 ^{9}Crc^{1}	Super Frolic	L f	4	117	8	8	5^{hd}	5^{1}	$6^{3\frac{1}{2}}$	4^{hd}	8^{3}	Bravo J	4.00
28Nov04 ^{9}Crc^{2}	Dustys Birthday	L b	5	112	1	4	8^{2}	$8^{2\frac{1}{2}}$	$9^{2\frac{1}{2}}$	10^{5}	$9^{2\frac{1}{2}}$	Penalba C	68.60
4Dec04 ^{11}Crc^{9}	Bob'sProudMoment	L	3	113	2	1	$2^{1\frac{1}{2}}$	2^{3}	$2^{2\frac{1}{2}}$	5^{1}	10^{12}	Cruz M R	5.70
20Nov04 ^{10}Pim^{6}	A Huevo	L f	8	117	9	11	$4^{1\frac{1}{2}}$	3^{hd}	4^{2}	11	11	Dominguez R A	2.30

OFF AT 5:19 Start Good . Won driving. Track fast.

TIME :23^{3}, :47^{4}, 1:11^{2}, 1:37^{3}, 1:50^{3} (:23.79, :47.88, 1:11.55, 1:37.72, 1:50.74)

$2 Mutuel Prices:				
	4 – PIES PROSPECT	8.40	4.60	4.20
	8 – TWILIGHT ROAD		9.00	7.40
	7 – HEAR NO EVIL			6.00

$2 EXACTA 4–8 PAID $76.80 $2 TRIFECTA 4–8–7 PAID $772.40
$2 SUPERFECTA 4–8–7–5 PAID $9,461.00

Ch. c, (Apr), by Crafty Prospector – Hot Pillow , by Bates Motel . Trainer Zito Nicholas P. Bred by Gordon Wootton & Mary Lou Wootton (Ky).

PIES PROSPECT sat off the pace prior to reaching mid turn, came on strong to take the advantage in the stretch, dueled with HEAR NO EVIL in the upper stretch and drew off. TWILIGHT ROAD settled to race in mid pack to the stretch, moved in towards the rail around the turn, came out four wide entering the stretch was up for place after a strong bid through the lane. HEAR NO EVIL sprinted out to take a clear lead from early on, was pressured by BOB'S PROUND MOMENT for six furlongs, put that one away around the turn to take a brief lead, dueled with winner in the upper stretch but was used up and faded. THE JUDGE SEZ WHO trailed the field in the opening half, and improved after a strong rally. UNCIVIL was forced five wide around the first turn, came in to save ground and finished evenly. CAIMAN along unhurried most way, fanned three wide out of the far turn and improved position. GOLD DOLLAR placed towards the rear early, drifted three wide around the second turn then had no bid in the lane. SUPER FROLIC between foe in the early stages, dropped back after racing in good position from the opening half mile and had no rally. DUSTYS BIRTHDAY not a factor. BOB'S PROUD MOMENT pressed the pace from just outside HEAR NO EVIL to the second turn, gave ground readily and was outmatched. A HUEVO settled two wide behind the first flight, maintained position for seven furlongs and stopped.

Owners– 1, LaPenta Robert V; 2, Donamire Farm; 3, Jacks or Better Farm Inc; 4, Sez Who Racing; 5, Mount Joy Stables Inc; 6, Achar Victor; 7, Pazos Julio; 8, Stride Rite Racing Stable Inc; 9, Curry Diane and Gentry Lloyd; 10, Dubois Robert M; 11, Hopkins Mark S

Trainers– 1, Zito Nicholas P; 2, Fawkes David; 3, Pilotti Larry; 4, Wolfson Milton W; 5, Stutts Bennie F Jr; 6, Medina Angel M; 7, Azpurua Manuel J; 8, Wolfson Milton W; 9, Nazareth John A; 10, Potter Douglas; 11, Dickinson Michael W

Scratched– Scooter Roach (13Nov04 ^{9}Haw^{5})

$2 Daily Double (4–4) Paid $41.00 ; Daily Double Pool $87,782 .
$2 Pick Three (8–4–4) Paid $422.00 ; Pick Three Pool $52,200 .
$1 Pick Four (10–8–4–4) Paid $1,079.10 ; Pick Four Pool $311,750 .

Calder Race Course Attendance: 8,456 Mutuel Pool: $1,097,605.00 ITW Mutuel Pool: $510,362.00 ISW Mutuel Pool: $6,561,862.00

EIGHTH RACE
Hollywood
DECEMBER 18, 2004

1$\frac{1}{16}$ MILES. (1.40) 24TH RUNNING OF THE HOLLYWOOD FUTURITY. Grade I. Purse $449,500 FOR TWO YEAR OLDS (FOALS OF 2002).Supplementary nominations may be made at time of entry by a payment of $10,000 each which qualifies to enter and an additional $10,000 to start. Closed with 244 original and 167 sustained nominations. 3 supplementary nominations: Southern Africa, Proud Accolade and General Jumbo.

Value of Race: $446,500 Winner $267,900; second $89,300; third $53,580; fourth $26,790; fifth $8,930. Mutuel Pool $680,546.00 Exacta Pool $340,108.00 Quinella Pool $28,399.00 Trifecta Pool $366,846.00 Superfecta Pool $165,638.00

Last Raced	Horse	M/Eqt.	A.	Wt	PP	St	¼	½	¾	Str	Fin	Jockey	Odds $1
20Nov04 ^{8}Hol^{1}	Declan's Moon	LB	2	121	3	1	2^{hd}	2^{hd}	1^{hd}	1^{1}	1^{1}	Espinoza V	1.20
14Nov04 ^{4}Hol^{3}	Giacomo	LB	2	121	4	7	$6^{\frac{1}{2}}$	6^{1}	4^{hd}	3^{2}	2no	Smith M E	15.90
30Oct04 ^{7}LS^{1}	Wilko	LB	2	121	1	4	3^{hd}	$4^{2\frac{1}{2}}$	$2^{\frac{1}{2}}$	2^{1}	3^{2}	Nakatani C S	2.80
20Nov04 ^{8}Hol^{4}	Southern Africa	LB	2	121	2	2	$5^{1\frac{1}{2}}$	$5^{1\frac{1}{2}}$	5^{1}	$4^{2\frac{1}{2}}$	4^{10}	Baze T C	23.80
30Oct04 ^{7}LS^{6}	Proud Accolade	LB b	2	121	5	5	$4^{2\frac{1}{2}}$	3^{1}	$3^{1\frac{1}{2}}$	5^{3}	5^{2}	Velazquez J R	2.20
27Nov04 ^{9}Hol^{10}	Lucky Bid	LB	2	121	7	6	7	7	7	6	6	Desormeaux K J	43.90
20Nov04 ^{8}Hol^{2}	Bushwacker	LB b	2	121	6	3	1^{1}	$1^{\frac{1}{2}}$	6^{2}	—	—	Douglas R R	17.90

OFF AT 4:06 Start Good . Won driving. Track fast.

TIME :23^{2}, :46, 1:10, 1:35, 1:41^{3} (:23.46, :46.13, 1:10.15, 1:35.07, 1:41.63)

$2 Mutuel Prices:				
	3 – DECLAN'S MOON	4.40	3.00	2.40
	4 – GIACOMO		7.60	3.60
	1 – WILKO			2.80

$1 EXACTA 3–4 PAID $19.80 $2 QUINELLA 3–4 PAID $29.00
$1 TRIFECTA 3–4–1 PAID $72.20 $1 SUPERFECTA 3–4–1–2 PAID $336.80

Dk. b or br. g, (Feb), by Malibu Moon – Vee Vee Star , by Norquestor . Trainer Ellis Ronald W. Bred by Brice Ridgely (Md).

DECLAN'S MOON pulled a bit between horses early, stalked into the backstretch, bid inside and dueled a bit off the rail on the backstretch and into the second turn, continued between foes midway on that turn, battled outside WILKO nearing the stretch, inched away and held on gamely under urging then was under steady handling late. GIACOMO off a bit slowly, settled outside a rival, moved up on the second turn, came out in the stretch and closed willingly. WILKO had speed inside then stalked along the rail, bid from the inside on the second turn, came out nearing midstretch and just lost the place. SOUTHERN AFRICA saved ground stalking the pace, waited a bit off heels past midway on the second turn, came out leaving that turn and into the stretch and could not offer the necessary late kick. PROUD ACCOLADE stalked outside then three deep, bid three wide on the backstretch and second turn, dropped back leaving that turn, angled in entering the stretch and weakened. LUCKY BID angled in on the first turn and saved ground off the pace, came out into the stretch and did not rally. BUSHWACKER pulled his way along four wide into the first turn, took the lead three deep then inched away leaving the first turn as the saddle slipped, dueled outside on the backstretch, dropped back and drifted out on the second turn, gave way and was eased in the stretch.

Owners– 1, Jay Em Ess Stable; 2, Moss Mr and Mrs Jerome S; 3, Reddam & Roy; 4, Kirkwood Al and Saundra S; 5, Padua Stables; 6, Whetstone Ilona; 7, Currin William L and Eisman Alvin

Trainers– 1, Ellis Ronald W; 2, Shirreffs John; 3, Dollase Craig; 4, Puhich Michael; 5, Pletcher Todd A; 6, McAnally Ronald; 7, Currin William L

Scratched– General Jumbo (GB) (13Nov04 ^{6}70031LIN^{1})

$2 Daily Double (10–3) Paid $9.00 ; Daily Double Pool $38,772 .
$1 Pick Three (8–3/5/6/8/10–3/7) Paid $16.30 ; Pick Three Pool $118,276 .

EIGHTH RACE
Aqueduct
DECEMBER 19, 2004

6 FURLONGS. (1.07^{4}) 46TH RUNNING OF THE GRAVESEND HANDICAP. Grade III. Purse $100,000 (UP TO $19,000 NYSBFOA) INNER DIRT A HANDICAP FOR THREE YEAR OLDS AND UPWARD. By subscription of $100 each, which should accompany the nomination; $500 to pass the entry box; $500 to start, with $100,000 added. The added money and all fees to be divided 60% to the winner, 20% to second, 10% to third, 5% to fourth, 3% to fifth and 2% divided equally among remaining finishers. A trophy will be presented to the winning owner. Closed Saturday, December 4, 2004 with 24 Nominations.

Value of Race: $109,400 Winner $65,640; second $21,880; third $10,940; fourth $5,470; fifth $3,282; sixth $2,188. Mutuel Pool $346,740.00 Exacta Pool $288,641.00 Trifecta Pool $230,297.00

Last Raced	Horse	M/Eqt.	A.	Wt	PP	St	¼	½	Str	Fin	Jockey	Odds $1
28Nov04 ^{9}Aqu^{8}	Don Six	L f	4	114	3	1	1^{2}	$1^{1\frac{1}{2}}$	$1^{1\frac{1}{2}}$	$1^{1\frac{1}{4}}$	Luzzi M J	5.00
5Nov04 ^{8}Aqu^{1}	Mr. Whitestone	L b	4	114	1	6	$5^{\frac{1}{2}}$	5^{8}	2^{hd}	$2^{\frac{1}{2}}$	Pimentel J	3.60
28Nov04 ^{9}Aqu^{2}	Papua	L b	5	114	2	5	3^{2}	$3^{2\frac{1}{2}}$	4^{4}	3^{2}	Bridgmohan S X	7.40
20Nov04 ^{10}Pim^{4}	Gators N Bears	L bf	4	121	5	2	2^{hd}	$2^{\frac{1}{2}}$	3^{hd}	4^{4}	Castellano J J	0.80
27Nov04 ^{4}Aqu^{1}	Black Silk-GB	L f	8	114	4	4	4^{hd}	4^{hd}	5^{8}	5^{7}	Fragoso P	15.90
28Nov04 ^{9}Aqu^{3}	Eavesdropper	L	4	115	6	3	6	6	6	6	Gryder A T	19.40

OFF AT 3:44 Start Good . Won driving. Track fast.

TIME $:22^{4}$, $:45^{1}$, :57, $1:08^{4}$ (:22.84, :45.35, :57.01, 1:08.97)

$2 Mutuel Prices:				
	3 – DON SIX	12.00	6.90	4.60
	1 – MR. WHITESTONE		4.40	3.40
	2 – PAPUA			3.90

$2 EXACTA 3–1 PAID $44.80 $2 TRIFECTA 3–1–2 PAID $164.50

Dk. b or br. c, (May), by Wild Escapade – Concorde's Beauty , by Concorde Bound . Trainer Lake Scott A. Bred by Patricia Generazio (Fla).

DON SIX sped clear early, set the pace on the inside, responded when roused and held on well under urging. MR. WHITESTONE saved ground, angled out at the top of the lane and closed gamely outside. PAPUA chased the pace on the rail and finished gamely inside. GATORS N BEARS stalked outside, bid three wide and came up empty. BLACK SILK (GB) raced off the rail and tired. EAVESDROPPER was outrun.

Owners– 1, Generazio Patricia A; 2, Steel Your Face Stables; 3, Schwartz Barry K; 4, Nechamkin Leo S II; 5, Fustok Salah M; 6, De Renzo Dean and Hartley Randall

Trainers– 1, Lake Scott A; 2, Dutrow Richard E Jr; 3, Hushion Michael E; 4, Nechamkin Leo S II; 5, LaFavers Laurie; 6, McLaughlin Kiaran P

Scratched– Ameri Brilliance (08Dec04 ^{7}Pim^{2}) , Uncle Camie (28Nov04 ^{9}Aqu^{4})

EIGHTH RACE
Hollywood
DECEMBER 19, 2004

$1\frac{1}{16}$ MILES. (1.40) 24TH RUNNING OF THE HOLLYWOOD STARLET. Grade I. Purse $380,000 FOR FILLIES TWO YEARS OLD (FOALS OF 2002). Supplementary nominations may be made at time of entry by a payment of $10,000 each which qualifies to enter and an additional $10,000 to start. Closed with 152 original nominations, 114 sustained nominations and four supplemental: CHARMING COLLEEN, SHARP LISA, MEMORETTE, and SPLENDID BLENDED.

Value of Race: $389,000 Winner $233,400; second $77,800; third $46,680; fourth $23,340; fifth $7,780. Mutuel Pool $463,554.00 Exacta Pool $247,210.00 Quinella Pool $24,839.00 Trifecta Pool $314,925.00

Last Raced	Horse	M/Eqt.	A.	Wt	PP	St	¼	½	¾	Str	Fin	Jockey	Odds $1
14Nov04 ^{2}Hol^{1}	Splendid Blended	LB	2	120	7	3	2^{1}	2^{2}	2^{1}	$1^{1\frac{1}{2}}$	1^{2}	Desormeaux K J	1.30
30Oct04 ^{3}LS^{6}	Sharp Lisa	LB	2	120	3	1	4^{1}	4^{1}	3^{1}	$3^{\frac{1}{2}}$	2^{2}	Nakatani C S	1.60
21Nov04 ^{8}Hol^{4}	Northern Mischief	LB	2	120	1	4	$3^{\frac{1}{2}}$	3^{hd}	$4^{1\frac{1}{2}}$	$4^{4\frac{1}{2}}$	3^{3}	Stevens G L	10.10
21Nov04 ^{8}Hol^{1}	No Bull Baby	LB b	2	120	6	2	$1^{\frac{1}{2}}$	1^{hd}	1^{hd}	2^{hd}	4^{4}	Douglas R R	8.70
19Sep04 ^{9}EmD^{2}	Charming Colleen	LB b	2	120	2	5	5^{hd}	6^{hd}	$5^{1\frac{1}{2}}$	5^{2}	5^{nk}	Gomez G K	17.20
26Nov04 ^{6}Hol^{3}	Kenza	LB	2	120	4	7	7	5^{hd}	$6^{1\frac{1}{2}}$	$6^{\frac{1}{2}}$	$6^{1\frac{1}{2}}$	Smith M E	20.20
2Oct04 ^{9}SA^{3}	Memorette	LB b	2	120	5	6	6^{hd}	7	7	7	7	Baze T C	11.00

OFF AT 4:06 Start Good . Won driving. Track fast.

TIME $:23^{3}$, $:46^{4}$, 1:11, $1:35^{2}$, $1:41^{4}$ (:23.62, :46.84, 1:11.00, 1:35.48, 1:41.82)

$2 Mutuel Prices:				
	7 – SPLENDID BLENDED	4.60	2.60	2.40
	3 – SHARP LISA		2.60	2.40
	1 – NORTHERN MISCHIEF			3.40

$1 EXACTA 7–3 PAID $5.50 $2 QUINELLA 3–7 PAID $5.20
$1 TRIFECTA 7–3–1 PAID $23.20

Ch. f, (May), by Unbridled's Song – Valid Blend , by Valid Appeal . Trainer Drysdale Neil. Bred by Peter Vegso Racing Stable (Fla).

SPLENDID BLENDED pulled her way along three deep into the first turn, dueled outside a rival, gained the advantage into the stretch and drove clear under urging. SHARP LISA bobbled at the start, stalked outside a rival, came out into the stretch and gained the place. NORTHERN MISCHIEF close up tracking the dueling leaders inside, came out in upper stretch, split rivals in midstretch and bested the others. NO BULL BABY had good early speed and angled in on the first turn, dueled inside the winner, fought back on the second turn and into the stretch but weakened in the final furlong. CHARMING COLLEEN chased inside then a bit off the rail on the second turn, came out into the stretch and lacked the needed rally. KENZA a bit awkwardly into stride, pulled her way between foes chasing the pace, continued off the rail on the second turn and three deep into the stretch and had little left. MEMORETTE chased three deep then off the inside on the second turn, angled in some leaving that turn and lacked a further response.

Owners– 1, Vegso Peter; 2, Reddam Suarez Racing Inc & Schlesinger; 3, Lakin Lewis A; 4, Earnhardt III Patti and Hal J; 5, McIngvale James; 6, Moss Mr and Mrs Jerome S; 7, Currin Betty J

Trainers– 1, Drysdale Neil; 2, O'Neill Doug; 3, McAnally Ronald; 4, Baffert Bob; 5, Hines N J; 6, Shirreffs John; 7, Currin William L

$2 Daily Double (9–7) Paid $14.40 ; Daily Double Pool $38,824 .
$1 Pick Three (5–4/6/9–7) Paid $22.70 ; Pick Three Pool $67,888 .

SEVENTH RACE
Hollywood
DECEMBER 20, 2004

1$\frac{1}{16}$ MILES. (1.40) 23RD RUNNING OF THE DAHLIA HANDICAP. Grade III. Purse $150,000 FOR FILLIES AND MARES THREE-YEARS-OLD AND UPWARD. By subscription of $150 each, on or before December 8, or by supplementary nomination of $3,000 each by 3:00 pm Saturday, December 11. $1,500 additional to start, with $90,000 to the winner, $30,000 tosecond, $18,000 to third, $9,000 to fourth and $3,000 to fifth. Weights Sunday, December 12. Starters to be named through the entry box by closing time of entries. Hollywood Park reserves the right not to divide this race. Should this race not be divided and the number of entries exceed the starting gate capacity, high weights on the scale will be preferred. Total earnings in 2004 will be used in determining the order of preference of horses assigned equal weight on the scale. All fees for entrants that fail to draw into this race will be cancelled. A trophy will be presented to the owner of the winner. Closed with 27 nominations.(ORIGINALLY SCHEDULED FOR TURF).

Value of Race: $150,000 Winner $90,000; second $30,000; third $18,000; fourth $9,000; fifth $3,000. Mutuel Pool $174,944.00 Exacta Pool $98,456.00 Quinella Pool $8,172.00 Trifecta Pool $77,003.00 Superfecta Pool $40,559.00

Last Raced	Horse	M/Eqt.	A.	Wt	PP	St	¼	½	¾	Str	Fin	Jockey	Odds $1
29Sep04 ^{7}SA^{6}	Festival-Jpn	LB b	5	111	3	3	5	4^{1}	$2^{1\frac{1}{2}}$	2^{6}	1^{6}	Sorenson D	5.70
19Nov04 ^{6}Hol^{3}	Irgunette-Aus	LB	5	113	1	1	1^{2}	1^{7}	1^{7}	$1^{\frac{1}{2}}$	2^{9}	Bisono A	3.30
7Nov04 ^{8}Hol^{4}	Belle Ange-FR	LB	3	114	2	5	2^{1}	$2^{\frac{1}{2}}$	$3^{1\frac{1}{2}}$	$3^{2\frac{1}{2}}$	3^{3}	Farina T	4.10
9Oct04 ^{7}BM^{1}	Midwife	LB	3	115	4	2	$3^{2\frac{1}{2}}$	$3^{2\frac{1}{2}}$	4^{8}	4^{8}	4^{13}	Douglas R R	1.20
17Nov04 ^{7}Hol^{1}	Navaja-NZ	LB b	4	114	5	4	4^{hd}	5	5	5	5	Pedroza M A	5.10

OFF AT 3:36 Start Good . Won driving. Track fast.

TIME :23^{1}, :45^{3}, 1:09^{3}, 1:35^{3}, 1:42 (:23.32, :45.61, 1:09.74, 1:35.61, 1:42.11)

$2 Mutuel Prices:				
	7 – FESTIVAL-JPN	13.40	5.80	5.40
	3 – IRGUNETTE-AUS		5.60	4.40
	5 – BELLE ANGE-FR			4.00

$1 EXACTA 7–3 PAID $25.70 $2 QUINELLA 3–7 PAID $34.40
$1 TRIFECTA 7–3–5 PAID $73.60 $1 SUPERFECTA 7–3–5–9 PAID $181.70

B. m, (Apr), by Assatis – North Cape , by Crowned Prince . Trainer Gallagher Patrick. Bred by Grand Stud (Jpn).

FESTIVAL (JPN) settled a bit off the rail, angled in on the backstretch, slipped through inside on the second turn, came out leaving that turn, bid outside the runner-up in midstretch, gained the lead past the eighth pole and pulled clear under left handed urging. IRGUNETTE (AUS) quickly sprinted clear, set the pace under a long hold inside, opened up on the backstretch, could not match the winner in the final furlong but was clearly second best. BELLE ANGE (FR) broke a bit slowly, chased just off the inside, was between horses into the second turn, angled in on that turn and saved the show. MIDWIFE chased outside a rival then three deep into the second turn, angled in some and weakened. NAVAJA (NZ) allowed to settle outside, dropped back off the rail into the second turn and gave way.

Owners– 1, Grand Farm; 2, Epic Racing; 3, Guedj Fanny; 4, Doyle Jr & Josephson; 5, Cooperstone Martin Doll Ford et al

Trainers– 1, Gallagher Patrick; 2, Hines N J; 3, Powell Leonard; 4, Josephson J B; 5, Stein Roger M

Scratched– Janeian (NZ) (31Oct04 ^{9}LS ^{4}) , Katdogawn (GB) (30Oct04 ^{6}LS ^{10}) , Penny's Fortune (07Nov04 ^{8}Hol^{1}) , Hoh Buzzard (IRE) (28Nov04 ^{7}Hol^{5}) , Belleski (03Nov04 ^{6}Hol^{1})

$2 Daily Double (7–7) Paid $31.20 ; Daily Double Pool $15,501 .
$1 Pick Three (1–1/7–7) Paid $118.60 ; Pick Three Pool $51,301 .

EIGHTH RACE
Santa Anita
DECEMBER 26, 2004

7 FURLONGS. (1.20) 53RD RUNNING OF THE MALIBU. Grade I. Purse $250,000 FOR THREE-YEAR-OLDS. (Foals of 2001). By subscription of $250 each to accompany the nomination or by supplementary nomination of $5,000 by time of entry. $1000 to pass the entry box and $1,500 additional to start, with $250,000 guaranteed, of which $150,000 to first, $50,000 to second, $30,000 to third, $15,000 to fourth and $5,000 to fifth. 123 lbs. Non-winners of $200,000 twice in 2004 allowed 2 lbs.; $200,000 once in 2004, 4 lbs.; of $100,000 in 2004 or $60,000 since September 25, 6 lbs.; of $60,000 in 2004 or $30,000 since September 25, 8 lbs. (Claiming races not considered). Starters to be named through the entry box by the closing time of entries. A trophy will be presented to the owner of the winner. Closed with 31 nominations.

Value of Race: $250,000 Winner $150,000; second $50,000; third $30,000; fourth $15,000; fifth $5,000. Mutuel Pool $835,018.00 Exacta Pool $459,563.00 Quinella Pool $43,728.00 Trifecta Pool $460,842.00 Superfecta Pool $187,715.00

Last Raced	Horse	M/Eqt.	A.	Wt	PP	St	¼	½	Str	Fin	Jockey	Odds $1
8Aug04 ^{13}Mth^{6}	Rock Hard Ten	LB	3	121	9	9	10	10	5^{hd}	$1^{\frac{1}{2}}$	Stevens G L	2.40
13Nov04 ^{7}Hol^{2}	Lava Man	LB	3	115	7	1	$4^{\frac{1}{2}}$	3^{hd}	$3^{\frac{1}{2}}$	2no	Court J K	8.90
17Nov04 ^{6}Hol^{2}	Harvard Avenue	LB	3	115	2	7	7^{hd}	7^{hd}	$6^{2\frac{1}{2}}$	3no	Gomez G K	21.80
6Nov04 ^{5}Hol^{2}	Perfect Moon	LB	3	115	6	4	2^{hd}	$2^{\frac{1}{2}}$	1^{hd}	$4^{1\frac{1}{2}}$	Smith M E	34.60
31Oct04 ^{7}Aqu^{1}	Mass Media	LB b	3	119	1	8	6^{hd}	$4^{\frac{1}{2}}$	$4^{1\frac{1}{2}}$	5^{3}	Castellano J J	1.20
17Nov04 ^{6}Hol^{1}	Stone Rain	LB	3	115	3	3	$1^{\frac{1}{2}}$	1^{1}	2^{1}	6^{3}	Pedroza M A	16.80
17Nov04 ^{6}Hol^{3}	Minister Eric	LB b	3	115	10	2	8^{1}	9^{2}	$7^{\frac{1}{2}}$	7^{13}	Douglas R R	8.20
10Oct04 Cur^{2}	Grand Reward	LB b	3	116	5	10	$9^{3\frac{1}{2}}$	8^{hd}	9^{3}	8^{1}	Flores D R	29.90
21Nov04 ^{8}RP^{8}	Quintons Gold Rush	LB	3	121	8	5	3^{hd}	6^{hd}	10	9	Espinoza V	16.50
25Nov04 ^{9}CD^{7}	Jeffries Bay	LB	3	117	4	6	5^{1}	5^{2}	8^{3}	—	Valdivia J Jr	54.30

OFF AT 4:04 Start Good . Won driving. Track fast.

TIME :22^{1}, :44^{1}, 1:08^{1}, 1:21^{4} (:22.20, :44.35, 1:08.31, 1:21.89)

$2 Mutuel Prices:				
	11 – ROCK HARD TEN	6.80	4.00	3.60
	9 – LAVA MAN		5.80	4.20
	3 – HARVARD AVENUE			7.20

$1 EXACTA 11–9 PAID $22.70 $2 QUINELLA 9–11 PAID $25.40
$1 TRIFECTA 11–9–3 PAID $214.60 $1 SUPERFECTA 11–9–3–7 PAID $2,156.70

Dk. b or br. c, (Apr), by Kris S. – Tersa , by Mr. Prospector . Trainer Mandella Richard. Bred by Madeleine A Paulson (Ky).

ROCK HARD TEN settled off the rail, angled in some for the turn, came out in the stretch and rallied between horses under urging to get up late. LAVA MAN forced the early pace between foes then stalked outside, bid between horses past midstretch, put a head in front late but could not hold off the winner. HARVARD AVENUE stalked outside a rival then along the inside, steadied off heels in midstretch, came out and surged between foes nearing the wire. PERFECT MOON dueled between foes early, stalked off the rail into and on the turn, gained a short lead outside the pacesetter in upper stretch and fought back gamely to the wire. MASS MEDIA stalked inside, came out into the stretch, angled back in passing the eighth pole, awaited room briefly then got through along the rail past midstretch and was outfinished. STONE RAIN had good early speed and dueled inside, inched away into the turn, came a bit off the rail in the stretch and weakened late. MINISTER ERIC stalked outside on the backstretch, split rivals on the turn, came three deep into the stretch and lacked the needed rally. GRAND REWARD off a bit slowly, settled off the rail then outside a rival on the turn, drifted inward in the stretch and had little left. QUINTONS GOLD RUSH forced the pace five wide then stalked outside, dropped back into and on the turn and gave way. JEFFRIES BAY prompted the pace between horses then stalked between foes, dropped back in the stretch, was eased past midstretch but walked off.

Owners– 1, Mercedes Stables LLC and Paulson Madeleine; 2, STD Racing Stable and Wood Jason; 3, Ron Crockett Inc; 4, Royce S Jaime Racing Stable Inc; 5, Gary and Mary West Stables Inc; 6, McAtee Ronald and Melodie; 7, Diamond A Racing Corporation; 8, Lewis Magnier S and Tabor; 9, Padua Stables and Manoogian Jay; 10, Rancho San Miguel Hollendorfer Litt et al

Trainers– 1, Mandella Richard; 2, O'Neill Doug; 3, O'Neill Doug; 4, O'Neill Doug; 5, Frankel Robert; 6, Sadler John W; 7, Mandella Richard; 8, Lukas D Wayne; 9, Mitchell Mike; 10, Hollendorfer Jerry

Scratched– Love of Money (02Oct04 ^{10}Bel^{6}) , Spellbinder (22Oct04 ^{3}SA ^{3})

$2 Daily Double (9–11) Paid $39.80 ; Daily Double Pool $57,245 .
$1 Pick Three (10–9–11) Paid $107.00 ; Pick Three Pool $97,690 .

EIGHTH RACE
Santa Anita
DECEMBER 27, 2004

7 FURLONGS. (1.20) 32ND RUNNING OF THE LA BREA. Grade I. Purse $250,000 FOR FILLIES, THREE YEARS OLD. (Foals of 2001). By subscription of $250 each to accompany the nomination or by supplementary nomination of $5,000 by time of entry. $2,500 additional to start, with $250,000 guaranteed, of which $150,000 to first, $50,000 to second, $30,000 to third, $15,000 to fourth and $5,000 to fifth. 123 lbs. Non-winners of $100,000 twice in 2004 allowed 2 lbs.; $100,000 once in 2004, 4 lbs.; of $60,000 in 2004 or $35,000 since September 25, 6 lbs.; of $30,000 anytime, 8 lbs. (Maidenand claiming races not considered). Starters to be named through the entry box by the closing time of entries. A trophy will be presented to the owner of the winner. Closed Thursday December 16 with 21 nominations.

Value of Race: $250,000 Winner $150,000; second $50,000; third $30,000; fourth $15,000; fifth $5,000. Mutuel Pool $394,498.00 Exacta Pool $229,233.00 Quinella Pool $21,059.00 Trifecta Pool $235,682.00 Superfecta Pool $120,046.00

Last Raced	Horse	M/Eqt.	A.	Wt	PP	St	1/4	1/2	Str	Fin	Jockey	Odds $1
3Dec04 7Hol1	Alphabet Kisses	LB b	3	117	9	1	1 1	2 1½	2 1	1 1	Smith M E	20.10
26Nov04 9Aqu2	Bending Strings	LB	3	121	7	5	7 1½	4 hd	3 2½	2 2	Espinoza V	1.60
31Jly04 8Sar6	Elusive Diva	LB	3	119	3	4	2½	1 hd	1 hd	3 2	Desormeaux K J	5.30
25Nov04 10CD2	Susan's Angel	LB	3	121	6	3	6 hd	7½	4 hd	4½	Baze T C	8.80
2Oct04 4SA5	Amorama-FR	LB b	3	121	8	7	9 3	9 3½	8 2½	5½	Flores D R	18.90
11Oct04 8SA1	Mea Domina	LB	3	119	5	9	5 hd	6 1	6 1	6 no	Stevens G L	3.10
21Nov04 5Hol1	Costume Designer	LB	3	115	1	6	4 hd	5 hd	5 1½	7 2	Court J K	42.10
8Dec04 7Hol3	Nyramba-GB	LB	3	117	4	8	8 2½	8 4½	7 hd	8 2	Douglas R R	19.60
21Nov04 6Hol1	Sweet Lips	LB	3	117	2	10	10	10	9 1	9 5	Gomez G K	8.60
15Oct04 9Kee8	Salty Romance	B	3	117	10	2	3 1½	3 1	10	10	Farina T	24.40

OFF AT 4:09 Start Good. Won driving. Track fast.
TIME :22 1, :44 2, 1:08 3, 1:21 1 (:22.28, :44.58, 1:08.60, 1:21.38)

$2 Mutuel Prices:				
	12 – ALPHABET KISSES	42.20	12.80	6.20
	9 – BENDING STRINGS		3.60	2.80
	3 – ELUSIVE DIVA			4.20

$1 EXACTA 12–9 PAID $97.90 $2 QUINELLA 9–12 PAID $54.40
$1 TRIFECTA 12–9–3 PAID $516.40 $1 SUPERFECTA 12–9–3–7 PAID $3,174.00

Gr/ro. f, (Feb), by Alphabet Soup – Kiss for Six , by Saratoga Six . Trainer Jones Martin F. Bred by Harris Farms Inc (Cal).

ALPHABET KISSES had good early speed well off the rail then angled in and dueled outside a rival, let that one slip away leaving the turn, re-bid outside in the stretch, regained the lead past the eighth pole and held on gamely under urging. BENDING STRINGS stalked four wide on the backstretch, moved up outside foes on the turn, came three deep into the stretch and finished willingly but could not catch the winner. ELUSIVE DIVA stalked the early pace inside, bid along the rail on the backstretch and dueled for the lead, inched clear leaving the turn, fought back inside in midstretch, could not match the top pair but held third. SUSAN'S ANGEL tracked the pace between horses on the backstretch and outside on the turn, came four wide into the stretch and lacked the needed rally. AMORAMA (FR) unhurried off the rail early, angled in a bit off the fence leaving the backstretch, found the inside in midstretch and could not summon the necessary response. MEA DOMINA bobbled at the start, chased between horses to the stretch and did not rally. COSTUME DESIGNER was in a good position stalking the pace inside, came a bit off the rail in the stretch and weakened. NYRAMBA (GB) off a bit awkwardly, settled inside, awaited room off heels midway on the turn, came out four wide into the stretch and lacked a rally. SWEET LIPS saved ground off the pace and was outrun. SALTY ROMANCE close up stalking the pace outside or off the rail, weakened in the stretch.

Owners– 1, Harris Farms Inc; 2, Gunther John D; 3, Branch Branch Konecny et al; 4, Finney Creek Stable; 5, Naify Marsha and Woodside Farms LLC; 6, Whitham Janis R; 7, Krikorian George; 8, Von Boetticher Dietrich; 9, Gary and Mary West Stables Inc; 10, Flying Zee Stable

Trainers– 1, Jones Martin F; 2, McLaughlin Kiaran P; 3, Glatt Mark; 4, Lukas D Wayne; 5, Canani Julio C; 6, McAnally Ronald; 7, Shirreffs John; 8, Drysdale Neil; 9, Frankel Robert; 10, Biancone Patrick L

Scratched– Tizakitty (11Nov04 5Hol1) , Iflookscouldkill (09Dec04 7Hol2) , Yearly Report (29Oct04 10LS 1)

$2 Daily Double (7–12) Paid $284.40 ; Daily Double Pool $27,977 .
$1 Pick Three (8–7–12) Paid $367.90 ; Pick Three Pool $64,952 .

TENTH RACE
Calder
DECEMBER 31, 2004

7 FURLONGS. (1.21[4]) 22ND RUNNING OF THE CHAPOSA SPRINGS HANDICAP. Grade III. Purse $100,000 FOR FILLIES AND MARES, THREE YEARS OLD AND UPWARD. By subscription of $100 each which shall accompany the nomination, $1,000 to pass the entry box and an additional $1,000 to start – with $100,000 guaranteed. The owner of the winner to receive $60,000, $20,000 to second, $11,000 to third, $6,000 to fourth and $3,000 to fifth. A trophy will be presented to the winning Owner. Closed Monday, December 20, 2004 with (13) nominations.

Value of Race: $100,000 Winner $60,000; second $20,000; third $11,000; fourth $6,000; fifth $3,000. Mutuel Pool $177,738.00 Exacta Pool $139,848.00 Trifecta Pool $96,601.00 Superfecta Pool $40,093.00

Last Raced	Horse	M/Eqt.	A.	Wt	PP	St	¼	½	Str	Fin	Jockey	Odds $1
19Dec04 10Crc1	Expect an Angel	L	4	110	2	6	7	6[4]	3hd	1[3]	Lopez J E	39.40
13Dec04 10Crc1	Alix M	L f	4	120	3	3	1hd	2½	½	2½	Velasquez C	2.70
15Oct04 8Bel1	Habiboo	L	3	112	7	1	6[1]	4½	2[1]	3¾	Castro E	a- 10.10
26Nov04 9Aqu4	Pop Princess	L b	4	114	6	2	3[1]	3½	4[2]	4[1]	Prado E S	3.10
30Oct04 9Med5	Ebony Breeze	L	4	116	4	7	4hd	5½	5[1]	5[5]	Bailey J D	1.20
4Dec04 10TP1	Revolutionary Act		4	115	1	4	2½	1hd	6[12]	6[23]	Coa E M	5.30
22Oct04 8Bel2	Lawful Nice	L	3	115	5	5	5hd	7	7	7	Aguilar M	a- 10.10

a–Coupled: Habiboo and Lawful Nice.

OFF AT 4:25 Start Good. Won driving. Track sloppy.
TIME :22[2], :45[4], 1:10[4], 1:23[3] (:22.57, :45.81, 1:10.83, 1:23.66)

$2 Mutuel Prices:				
	3 – EXPECT AN ANGEL	80.80	22.20	7.20
	4 – ALIX M		4.80	3.80
	1A– HABIBOO(a–entry)			3.60

$2 EXACTA 3–4 PAID $242.60 $2 TRIFECTA 3–4–1 PAID $1,052.40
$2 SUPERFECTA 3–4–1–6 PAID $4,502.60

B. f, (Apr), by Valid Expectations – Leah's Angel, by Caller I. D.. Trainer Hale Robert A. Bred by David Robbins (Fla).

EXPECT AN ANGEL reserved early, angled four wide on the turn, rallied to catch ALIX M at the sixteenth pole and drew clear. ALIX M vied for the lead off the rail and continued on with good courage to hold the place while unable to stay with winner late. HABIBOO reserved early, made a run along the inside to loom a threat in midstretch, then gave way. POP PRINCESS chased the pace three wide into the stretch, then faltered. EBONY BREEZE off a step slowly, tracked the pace along the rail into the stretch and tired. REVOLUTIONARY ACT vied for the lead along the inside to nearing the stretch and faded. LAWFUL NICE was through early.

Owners– 1, Hale Kay; 2, Seven Oaks Farm; 3, Hardacre Farm LLC; 4, Stronach Stables; 5, Kinsman Stable; 6, Casby Camelia J; 7, Hardacre Farm LLC

Trainers– 1, Hale Robert A; 2, Spatz Ronald B; 3, Tarrant Amy; 4, Frankel Robert; 5, Mott William I; 6, Huffman Pat; 7, Tarrant Amy

$2 Pick Three (1–7–3) Paid $1,361.00 ; Pick Three Pool $10,745 .

SEVENTH RACE
Santa Anita
DECEMBER 31, 2004

6½ FURLONGS. (1.13[3]) 38TH RUNNING OF THE MONROVIA HANDICAP. Purse $100,000 FOR FILLIES AND MARES THREE YEARS OLD AND UPWARD. By subscription of $100 each to accompany the nomination or by supplementary nomination of $2,000 by 10 AM Monday, December 27.. $250 to pass the entry box and $750 additional to start with $100,000 added. The added monies and all fees to be divided 60% to the winner, 20% to second, 12% to third, 6% to fourth and 2% to fifth. Weights Monday, December 27. High weights preferred. Starters to be named through the entry box by the closing time of entries. A trophy will be presented to the owner of the winner. Closed with 28 nominations.(ORIGINALLY SCHEDULED FOR TURF).

Value of Race: $113,550 Winner $68,130; second $22,710; third $13,626; fourth $6,813; fifth $2,271. Mutuel Pool $358,058.00 Exacta Pool $219,794.00 Quinella Pool $16,783.00 Trifecta Pool $210,361.00 Superfecta Pool $78,842.00

Last Raced	Horse	M/Eqt.	A.	Wt	PP	St	¼	½	Str	Fin	Jockey	Odds $1
11Nov04 5Hol3	Resplendency	LB b	3	112	2	6	3½	1[1]	1[1]	1[1]	Fusilier C	5.30
19Nov04 6Hol4	Puxa Saco	LB	4	115	8	2	8½	8½	3hd	2[3]	Smith M E	10.00
19Nov04 6Hol2	Market Garden	LB bf	4	115	3	4	4[1]½	5[1]	2[1]½	3[4]	Douglas R R	b- 1.40
8Dec04 7Hol1	Cyber Slew	LB b	4	115	1	8	6hd	7hd	7½	4½	Martinez F F	7.80
11Nov04 5Hol7	Delizia	LB	4	115	9	1	2hd	2hd	4[1]½	5[1]½	Valdivia J Jr	10.70
24Oct04 8SA6	Chapeau	LB	5	113	4	7	9	9	5hd	6[1]½	Bisono A	b- 1.40
3Dec04 7Hol4	Woodlass	LB	4	116	5	3	5hd	4½	6[1]	7[2]	Desormeaux K J	14.20
2Sep04 7Dmr4	Coconut Girl	LB f	5	115	7	9	7[1]½	3hd	8[3]	8[9]	Espinoza V	4.70
12Nov04 2Hol1	Spring Festival	LB	3	116	6	5	1hd	6[1]½	9	9	Flores D R	10.10

b–Coupled: Market Garden and Chapeau.

OFF AT 3:37 Start Good. Won driving. Track sloppy.
TIME :21[2], :44[1], 1:08[4], 1:15[1] (:21.59, :44.32, 1:08.84, 1:15.34)

$2 Mutuel Prices:				
	7 – RESPLENDENCY	12.60	8.40	4.60
	14 – PUXA SACO		9.60	4.80
	2 – MARKET GARDEN(b–entry)			2.60

$1 EXACTA 7–14 PAID $65.10 $2 QUINELLA 7–14 PAID $57.40
$1 TRIFECTA 7–14–2 PAID $183.70 $1 SUPERFECTA 7–14–2–5 PAID $772.00

B. f, (Jan), by Tale of the Cat – Doppio Espresso, by Java Gold. Trainer Baffert Bob. Bred by Highclere Inc (Ky).

RESPLENDENCY dueled inside on the backstretch, inched away on the turn and held on gamely under urging. PUXA SACO angled in and settled outside a rival, came out leaving the turn and four wide into the stretch and finished well. MARKET GARDEN stalked just off the inside then along the rail on the turn, came a bit off the fence in the stretch and bested the rest. CYBER SLEW came off the rail on the backstretch, chased off the fence on the turn, came three deep into the stretch and lacked the needed rally. DELIZIA dueled four wide then three deep on the backstretch, stalked between foes on the turn and weakened in the stretch. CHAPEAU allowed to settle a bit off the rail, angled to the inside leaving the backstretch, remained along the fence in the stretch and could not summon the necessary response. WOODLASS chased between rivals, split foes three deep on the turn and weakened in the stretch. COCONUT GIRL chased outside then three deep on the backstretch, advanced four wide on the turn and three wide into the stretch and also weakened. SPRING FESTIVAL dueled between horses on the backstretch, dropped back on the turn and gave way.

Owners– 1, Lewis Robert B and Beverly J; 2, Rowan Richard; 3, Craig Sidney H and Jenny; 4, Rancho Ballena LLC; 5, Moss Mr and Mrs Jerome S; 6, Craig Sidney H and Jenny; 7, Walsh Kathy; 8, Jpf Investments I LLC; 9, Wygod Mr and Mrs Martin J

Trainers– 1, Baffert Bob; 2, Sahadi Jenine; 3, Spawr Bill; 4, O'Neill Doug; 5, Shirreffs John; 6, McAnally Ronald; 7, Walsh Kathy; 8, Aguirre Paul G; 9, Canani Julio C

Scratched– Belleski (03Nov04 6Hol1) , Solar Echo (24Aug03 9Dmr2) , Shezsospiritual (27Nov04 8TuP3) , Mazella (09Dec04 7Hol3) , Valentine Dancer (24Apr04 1Hol6) , Any for Love (ARG) (24Oct04 8SA 1) , Very Vegas (27Nov04 8TuP1)

$2 Daily Double (7–7) Paid $41.00 ; Daily Double Pool $18,083 .
$1 Pick Three (5–2/3/7–7) Paid $46.40 ; Pick Three Pool $69,727 .

CANADIAN GRADED STAKES

EIGHTH RACE
Woodbine
MAY 1, 2004

7 FURLONGS. (1.20³) VIGIL H. Grade III. Purse $150,000 For FOUR YEAR OLDS AND UPWARD. By subscription of $150 each which shall accompany the nomination and an additional $1,500 when making entry; with $150,000 added, plus all fees to be divided: 60% to the winner, 20% to second, 11% to third, 6% to fourth and3% to fifth. Weights Saturday, April 24, 2004. Final entries to be made through the entry box no later than 11:30 AM on Thursday, April 29, 2004. Plus up to $12,420 Ontario Sire/Canadian Bred Breeder Awards. Closed with 22 nominations, Wednesday, April 14, 2004.

Value of Race: $160,800 Winner $96,480; second $32,160; third $17,688; fourth $9,648; fifth $4,824. Mutuel Pool $89,920.00 Exactor Pool $85,032.00

Last Raced	Horse	M/Eqt.	A.	Wt	PP	St	¼	½	Str	Fin	Jockey	Odds $1
8Nov03 8WO2	Mobil	L f	4	120	3	2	3½	31½	23½	11¾	Kabel T K	1.75
17Apr04 9WO1	Chris's Bad Boy	L f	7	122	4	3	1½	11	12½	24	Jones J	0.50
29Nov03 9WO6	Awesome Action	L	4	115	2	1	5	4hd	43	32¾	Landry R C	17.40
17Apr04 9WO7	Anglian Prince	L b	5	115	1	5	21	21½	3hd	41½	McAleney J S	13.85
29Nov03 4WO2	Merlin's Moon	L b	6	114	5	4	4hd	5	5	5	Montpellier C	15.40

OFF AT 4:17 Start Good. Won driving. Track fast.
TIME :22⁴, :45, 1:09, 1:21⁴ (:22.86, :45.02, 1:09.17, 1:21.81)

$2 Mutuel Prices:

3 – MOBIL	5.50	2.60	—
4 – CHRIS'S BAD BOY		2.10	—
2 – AWESOME ACTION		—	—

$2 EXACTOR 3–4 PAID $8.50

B. c, (Jan), by Langfuhr – Kinetigal, by Naskra. Trainer Keogh Michael. Bred by Gustav Schickedanz (Ont–C).

MOBIL stalked the pace, closed late on the turn, had aim on the leader in the stretch, responded to encouragement and swept by CHRIS'S BAD BOY in the late stages.. CHRIS'S BAD BOY stalked the pace, closed three-wide late turn, had aim on the leader in the stretch, responded to encouragement and swept by CHRIS'S BAD BOY in th elate stages. AWESOME ACTION showed speed from the outset, turned back ANGLIAN PRINCE entering the turn and widened at the top of the stretch but failed to contain the winner late. ANGLIAN PRINCE forced issue then tried to match strides with the leader late backstretch, failed, and gave way along the rail. MERLIN'S MOON was close up early but dropped back and trailed without showing a late response.

Owners– 1, Schickedanz Gustav; 2, Alpine Stable; 3, Joseph C and N Meehan D and Leslie S; 4, Prime Acres Inc; 5, Ten Goal Racing Stable

Trainers– 1, Keogh Michael; 2, Armata Vito; 3, Leslie Sue; 4, Hardy James M; 5, Day-Phillips Catherine

$1 Pick Three (6–5/8–3) Paid $131.30 ; Pick Three Pool $6,574 .

EIGHTH RACE
Woodbine
MAY 16, 2004

6½ FURLONGS. (1.14³) 30TH RUNNING OF THE HENDRIE HANDICAP. Grade III. Purse $150,000 (plus $50,000 Other Sources) FOR FILLIES AND MARES, FOUR YEAR OLDS AND UPWARD. By subscription of $150 each which shall accompany the nomination and an additional $1,500 when making entry; with $150,000 added and an additional $50,000 for Canadian Breds, plus all fees to be divided:60% to the winner, 20% to second, 11% to third, 6% to fourth and 3% to fifth. Weights Saturday, May 8, 2004. Final entries to be made through the entry box no later than 11:30 a.m. on Friday, May 14, 2004. Plus $50,000 for Canadian Breds from the Thoroughbred Improvement Program and the Canadian Thoroughbred Horse Society. Plus up to $12,420 Ontario Sire/Canadian Bred Breeder Awards. Closed Wednesday, April 28, 2004 with 15 nominations.

Value of Race: $174,250 Winner $96,750; second $42,250; third $17,738; fourth $12,675; fifth $4,837. Mutuel Pool $91,186.00 Exactor Pool $63,473.00

Last Raced	Horse	M/Eqt.	A.	Wt	PP	St	¼	½	Str	Fin	Jockey	Odds $1
18Apr04 9WO2	Winter Garden	L	4	122	5	1	32	32	12½	13	Clark D	1.80
19Nov03 7WO6	Spanish Decree	L f	5	115	1	4	4hd	42½	41½	2nk	Landry R C	27.35
26Mar04 9DeD1	Handpainted	L	4	119	4	2	2½	1hd	2hd	32	Husbands P	0.80
19Nov03 7WO1	Brass in Pocket	L	5	122	2	5	1hd	2hd	32½	4nk	Kabel T K	3.95
16Nov03 9WO1	Rich Assertion	L b	5	118	3	3	5	5	5	5	Jones J	13.80

OFF AT 4:37 Start Good. Won driving. Track fast.
TIME :22², :45¹, 1:09⁴, 1:16³ (:22.48, :45.33, 1:09.99, 1:16.76)

$2 Mutuel Prices:

6 – WINTER GARDEN	5.60	3.80	2.30
1 – SPANISH DECREE		18.10	3.60
5 – HANDPAINTED			2.10

$2 EXACTOR 6–1 PAID $115.60

B. f, (Mar), by Roy – Hillsburgh Rumors, by Bold Ruckus. Trainer Tiller Robert P. Bred by Anomaly Investments LP (Ky).

WINTER GARDEN stalked the duel three-wide, edged closer then bid midturn, dueled to the top of the stretch and sprinted clear then held sway under light handling. SPANISH DECREE stalked from the rail, angled out late turn then rallied three-wide. HANDPAINTED dueled outside BRASS IN POCKET, wore down that rival midstretch but was no match for the winner from the top of the stretch home. BRASS IN POCKET dueled from the rail and tired midstretch. RICH ASSERTION stalked from the second path, moved to the rail early turn to save ground but lacked the necessary closing response.

Owners– 1, DiGiulio Frank D Jr; 2, Huarte Frank; 3, Sikura John and Glen; 4, DiGiulio Frank D Jr; 5, Alpine Stable

Trainers– 1, Tiller Robert P; 2, Huarte Frank; 3, Carroll Josie; 4, Tiller Robert P; 5, Armata Vito

Scratched– Mille Feville (18Apr04 9WO 3)

$1 Pick Three (5–8–6) Paid $22.60 ; Pick Three Pool $6,331 .

EIGHTH RACE
Woodbine
MAY 22, 2004

$1\frac{1}{16}$ MILES. (1.40[4]) 49TH RUNNING OF THE MARINE. Grade III. Purse $150,000 FOR THREE-YEAR-OLDS. By subscription of $150 each which shall accompany the nomination and an additional $1,500 when making entry; with $150,000 added, plus all fees to be divided: 60% to the winner, 20% to second, 11% to third, 6% to fourth and 3% to fifth. Weight 124 lbs. Non-winners of a sweepstakes of $75,000 three times at a mile or over allowed 3 lbs. Of a sweepstakes of $75,000 twice at a mile or over, 5 lbs.; Of a sweepstakes of $75,000 once at a mile or over, 7 lbs; Of a sweepstakes of $75,000 atany distance, 9 lbs. (No Canadian Bred Allowance). Final entries to be made through the entry box no later than 11:30 a.m. on Thursday, May 20, 2004. Plus up to $12,420 Ontario Sire/Canadian Bred Breeder Awards. Closed Wednesday, May 5, 2004 with 34 nominations.

Value of Race: $164,100 Winner $98,460; second $32,820; third $18,051; fourth $9,846; fifth $4,923. Mutuel Pool $115,603.00 Exactor Pool $37,884.00 Triactor Pool $38,868.00

Last Raced	Horse	M/Eqt.	A.	Wt	PP	St	¼	½	¾	Str	Fin	Jockey	Odds $1
10Apr04 ^{7}Aqu^{6}	Judiths Wild Rush	L b	3	119	3	3	1^{2}	$1^{1\frac{1}{2}}$	1^{2}	1^{2}	1^{1}	Luciani D	1.60
1May04 ^{4}WO^{3}	Organ Grinder	L	3	117	4	2	$3^{3\frac{1}{2}}$	3^{3}	3^{6}	$2^{1\frac{1}{2}}$	$2^{2\frac{1}{4}}$	Husbands S P	12.45
24Apr04 ^{9}CD^{4}	Honolua Storm	L	3	117	1	1	2^{1}	$2^{1\frac{1}{2}}$	$2^{1\frac{1}{2}}$	3^{6}	$3^{9\frac{1}{2}}$	Jones J	8.55
8May04 ^{4}WO^{1}	Burst of Fire	L	3	116	2	4	5^{1}	5^{hd}	$4^{1\frac{1}{2}}$	$4^{1\frac{1}{2}}$	$4^{2\frac{1}{4}}$	Kabel T K	5.65
2May04 ^{10}WO^{4}	Smoocher	L b	3	119	6	6	6	6	$5^{2\frac{1}{2}}$	$5^{2\frac{1}{2}}$	5	McAleney J S	3.60
8May04 ^{8}WO^{3}	Nyuk Nyuk Nyuk	L	3	117	5	5	4^{hd}	4^{hd}	6	6	—	Clark D	2.55

OFF AT 4:38 Start Good. Won driving. Track fast.

TIME :23[1], :47, 1:11[4], 1:38[3], 1:45[4] (:23.32, :47.11, 1:11.80, 1:38.75, 1:45.96)

$2 Mutuel Prices:

3 – JUDITHS WILD RUSH	5.20	3.30	3.00
4 – ORGAN GRINDER		9.00	4.20
1 – HONOLUA STORM			4.70

$2 EXACTOR 3–4 PAID $52.40 $2 TRIACTOR 3–4–1 PAID $259.70

Gr/ro. c, (Mar), by Wild Rush – Tie Talk, by Black Tie Affair-Ire. Trainer Fairlie Scott H. Bred by Sez Who Thoroughbreds (Ky).

JUDITHS WILD RUSH gained command entering the first turn, set a reserved pace then was roused at the 1/4 pole and kept under pressure through the stretch. ORGAN GRINDER stalked the pace from the second path, was sent after the leader on the final turn, responded to steady encouragement in the stretch and gained to deep stretch then hung. HONOLUA STORM stalked the pacesetter from the rail, was all out at the top of the stretch but could not close the gap. BURST OF FIRE raced evenly between rivals, was asked to close on the far turn but failed to respond and finished evenly. SMOOCHER was always well off the pace, raced three-wide on the first turn and came four-wide out of the final turn but lacked a closing response. NYUK NYUK NYUK saved ground while just out of striking range, tired on the far turn and was eased in the stretch.

Owners– 1, Tenenbaum Racing Stables; 2, S and B Stable; 3, Attfield Roger L and Werner William; 4, Sam-Son Farms; 5, Franks Farms; 6, Di Giulio Frank D Jr

Trainers– 1, Fairlie Scott H; 2, Attard Sid C; 3, Attfield Roger L; 4, Frostad Mark; 5, Bell David R; 6, Tiller Robert P

$1 Pick Three (5–3–3) Paid $21.80; Pick Three Pool $8,338.

EIGHTH RACE
Woodbine
MAY 23, 2004

$1\frac{1}{16}$ MILES. (1.40[4]) 51ST RUNNING OF THE SELENE. Grade II. Purse $250,000 FOR THREE YEAR OLD FILLIES. By subscription of $250 each which shall accompany the nomination and an additional $2,500 when making entry; with $250,000 added, plus all fees to be divided: 60% to the winner, 20% to second, 11% to third, 6% to fourth and 3%to fifth. Weight 123 lbs. Non-winners of a sweepstakes of $75,000 twice at a mile or over allowed 3 lbs.; Of a sweepstakes of $75,000 once at a mile or over, 5 lbs.; Of a sweepstakes of $75,000 at any distance, 7 lbs. (No Canadian Bred Allowance.) Finalentries to be made through the entry box no later than 11:30 a.m. on Friday, May 21, 2004. Includes $25,000 from the Thoroughbred Improvement Program and the Canadian Thoroughbred Horse Society. Plus up to $15,180 Ontario Sire/Canadian Bred Breeder Awards. Closed Wednesday, May 5, 2004 with 30 nominations.

Value of Race: $275,000 Winner $165,000; second $55,000; third $30,250; fourth $16,500; fifth $8,250. Mutuel Pool $93,068.00 Exactor Pool $43,675.00 Triactor Pool $53,076.00

Last Raced	Horse	M/Eqt.	A.	Wt	PP	St	¼	½	¾	Str	Fin	Jockey	Odds $1
9May04 ^{8}WO^{1}	Eye of the Sphynx	L	3	118	6	3	2^{1}	2^{1}	$2^{1\frac{1}{2}}$	2^{5}	1^{nk}	Kabel T K	0.25
9May04 ^{8}WO^{2}	Silver Bird	L b	3	118	2	2	3^{hd}	4^{1}	$3^{\frac{1}{2}}$	1^{hd}	$2^{6\frac{3}{4}}$	McAleney J S	4.45
14May04 ^{6}WO^{1}	Sweet Problem	L	3	116	3	5	5^{6}	5^{6}	5^{8}	$3^{1\frac{1}{2}}$	3^{1}	Clark D	15.05
25Apr04 ^{5}WO^{1}	Pandora's Secret	f	3	116	5	4	4^{2}	3^{1}	4^{hd}	$4^{\frac{1}{2}}$	$4^{7\frac{1}{4}}$	Luciani D	31.70
25Apr04 ^{9}WO^{1}	Ontheqt	L b	3	118	4	1	$1^{1\frac{1}{2}}$	1^{1}	1^{hd}	5^{10}	$5^{7\frac{3}{4}}$	Pimentel R M	10.40
17Apr04 ^{10}Kee^{2}	Charming Proposal	L b	3	116	1	6	6	6	6	6	6	Landry R C	13.95

OFF AT 4:37 Start Good. Won driving. Track sloppy.

TIME :22[4], :47[4], 1:13[3], 1:41, 1:48[1] (:22.97, :47.82, 1:13.73, 1:41.13, 1:48.28)

$2 Mutuel Prices:

7 – EYE OF THE SPHYNX	2.50	2.20	2.10
3 – SILVER BIRD		3.00	2.70
4 – SWEET PROBLEM			4.60

$2 EXACTOR 7–3 PAID $5.40 $2 TRIACTOR 7–3–4 PAID $23.00

B. f, (Apr), by Smart Strike – Queen of Egypt, by Vice Regent. Trainer Frostad Mark. Bred by Sam–Son Farm (Ont–C).

EYE OF THE SPHYNX forced the pace from outside the leader, bid in earnest midturn, wore down ONTHEQT but was engaged at the top of the stretch,dueled inside SILVER BIRD, appeared beaten midstretch but dug in and outfinished her in the late stages. SILVER BIRD stalked from the inside, angled out and bid three-wide at the top of the stretch, dueled to the finish and missed. SWEET PROBLEM raced evenly off the rail to the far turn, closed up three-wide approaching the stretch then hung in the final furlong. PANDORA'S SECRET stalked pace from the outside, was roused between horses late turn but lacked a closing response. ONTHEQT led quickly, set a pressured pace from off the rail on the first turn and backstretch, moved to the rail on the final turn, was engaged midturn and tired at the 1/4 pole. CHARMING PROPOSAL trailed throughout and lacked a rally.

Owners– 1, Sam-Son Farms; 2, McAlpine James; 3, Sangara K K; 4, Chynawhite Investments; 5, Maine J and Baker R; 6, Chiefswood Stable

Trainers– 1, Frostad Mark; 2, Baker Reade; 3, Richards Lorne; 4, Paquette Chantal L; 5, Baker Reade; 6, Coatrieux Eric

Scratched– My Vintage Port (09May04 ^{8}WO ^{3})

$1 Pick Three (8–3–1/7) Paid $9.30; Pick Three Pool $7,240.

EIGHTH RACE
Woodbine
MAY 24, 2004

1$\frac{1}{16}$ MILES. (1.40^{4}) 49TH RUNNING OF THE ECLIPSE HANDICAP. Grade III. Purse $150,000 FOR FOUR YEAR OLDS AND UPWARD. By subscription of $150 each which shall accompany the nomination and an additional $1,500 when making entry; with $150,000 added, plus all fees to be divided: 60% to the winner, 20% to second, 11% to third, 6% to fourth and3% to fifth. Weights Saturday, May 15, 2004. Final entries to be made through the entry box no later than 11:30 a.m. on Saturday, May 22, 2004. Closed Wednesday, May 5, 2004 with 19 nominations.

Value of Race: $163,350 Winner $98,010; second $32,670; third $17,969; fourth $9,801; fifth $4,900. Mutuel Pool $137,057.00 Exactor Pool $74,800.00 Triactor Pool $50,955.00

Last Raced	Horse	M/Eqt.	A.	Wt	PP	St	¼	½	¾	Str	Fin	Jockey	Odds $1
2May04 ^{9}WO^{1}	Mark One	L	5	115	1	3	3^{hd}	3^{1}	3^{2}	2^{4}	$1^{2\frac{1}{2}}$	Landry R C	3.60
2May04 ^{9}WO^{2}	Open Concert	L b	5	113	2	1	$1^{1\frac{1}{2}}$	$1^{1\frac{1}{2}}$	$1^{1\frac{1}{2}}$	1^{1}	$2^{4\frac{1}{2}}$	Ramsammy E	1.75
1May04 ^{9}WO^{1}	Rock Again	L	4	115	3	4	4^{5}	4^{6}	4^{5}	4^{5}	$3^{\frac{3}{4}}$	McAleney J S	3.85
27Nov03 ^{7}WO^{1}	One for Rose	L	5	116	4	2	$2^{1\frac{1}{2}}$	2^{1}	$2^{1\frac{1}{2}}$	$3^{1\frac{1}{2}}$	$4^{1\frac{3}{4}}$	Kabel T K	1.55
16Apr04 ^{7}Kee^{4}	Indy Lead	L b	6	109	5	5	5	5	5	5	5	Brimo J	26.20

OFF AT 4:28 Start Good. Won driving. Track sloppy.

TIME :24, :47^{4}, 1:12^{1}, 1:39^{2}, 1:46^{3} (:24.04, :47.91, 1:12.30, 1:39.47, 1:46.70)

$2 Mutuel Prices:				
	2 – MARK ONE	9.20	3.50	3.00
	3 – OPEN CONCERT		3.20	2.30
	4 – ROCK AGAIN			3.50

$2 EXACTOR 2–3 PAID $22.30 $2 TRIACTOR 2–3–4 PAID $57.50

Gr/ro. g, (Apr), by Alphabet Soup – My Marchesa, by Stately Don. Trainer Vella Daniel J. Bred by Adena Springs (Ky).

MARK ONE stalked from the inside, closed late on the backstretch and maintained striking distance through the turn, responded to encouragement in the stretch and got by the leader with a sixteenth to run and drove clear. OPEN CONCERT set a reserved pace, quickened on the far turn then failed to contain the winner in the final sixteenth while best of the others. ROCK AGAIN raced evenly on the third path then was all out in the stretch but could not stay close. ONE FOR ROSE stalked the pace, was roused on the far turn but failed to respond and flattened out. INDY LEAD trailed along the fourth path.

Owners– 1, Stronach Stable; 2, Kelynack Racing Stable Inc; 3, Stronach Stable; 4, Tucci Stables; 5, Fipke Charles E

Trainers– 1, Vella Daniel J; 2, Katryan Abraham R; 3, Vella Daniel J; 4, Attard Sid C; 5, Attfield Roger L

Scratched– No Comprende (07Apr04 ^{9}OP ^{3}), Hydrogen (30Nov03 ^{9}WO ^{1})

$1 Pick Three (7–3–2) Paid $199.75; Pick Three Pool $6,882.

EIGHTH RACE
Woodbine
MAY 30, 2004

1$\frac{1}{16}$ MILES. (Turf) (1.39^{1}) 70TH RUNNING OF THE CONNAUGHT CUP. Grade III. Purse $150,000 FOR FOUR YEAR OLDS AND UPWARD. By subscription of $150 each which shall accompany the nomination and an additional $1,500 when making entry; with $150,000 added plus all fees to be divided: 60% to the winner, 20% to second, 11% to third, 6% to fourth and3% to fifth. Weight 124 lbs. Non-winners of a sweepstakes of $75,000 three times at a mile or over in 2003–2004 allowed 3 lbs.; Of a sweepstakes of $75,000 twice at a mile or over in 2003–2004, 5 lbs.; Of a sweepstakes of $75,000 once at a mile or over in2003–2004, 7 lbs. Final entries to be made through the entry box no later than 11:30 a.m. on Friday, May 28, 2004. Plus up to $12,420 Breeder Awards. Closed Wednesday, May 12, 2004 with 26 nominations. (Rail at 10 feet).

Value of Race: $164,400 Winner $98,640; second $32,880; third $18,084; fourth $9,864; fifth $4,932. Mutuel Pool $122,189.00 Exactor Pool $58,604.00 Triactor Pool $68,715.00

Last Raced	Horse	M/Eqt.	A.	Wt	PP	St	¼	½	¾	Str	Fin	Jockey	Odds $1
24Apr04 ^{8}Aqu^{3}	Slew Valley	L	7	117	5	3	4^{1}	3^{hd}	2^{hd}	1^{hd}	1no	McAleney J S	1.95
15May04 ^{9}WO^{3}	Le Cinquieme Essai	L	5	117	3	5	2^{1}	$2^{\frac{1}{2}}$	$3^{2\frac{1}{2}}$	$2^{\frac{1}{2}}$	$2^{\frac{3}{4}}$	Bahen S R	8.10
15May04 ^{9}WO^{1}	Shoal Water	L	4	117	1	4	$1^{\frac{1}{2}}$	$1^{\frac{1}{2}}$	1^{hd}	3^{1}	$3^{1\frac{1}{2}}$	Kabel T K	0.85
15May04 ^{9}WO^{2}	Prince Alphie	L bf	4	117	2	6	3^{hd}	$4^{2\frac{1}{2}}$	$4^{1\frac{1}{2}}$	4^{hd}	4^{nk}	Husbands P	8.25
15May04 ^{9}WO^{4}	Mr. Sulu	L	6	117	4	2	6	6	5^{hd}	5^{2}	$5^{1\frac{3}{4}}$	Landry R C	19.70
23Apr04 ^{10}Kee^{4}	Puffer	L	5	117	6	1	5^{1}	$5^{\frac{1}{2}}$	6	6	6	Callaghan S	13.35

OFF AT 4:39 Start Good. Won driving. Course firm.

TIME :24, :47, 1:10^{1}, 1:33^{4}, 1:40^{1} (:24.02, :47.19, 1:10.37, 1:33.97, 1:40.24)

$2 Mutuel Prices:				
	6 – SLEW VALLEY	5.90	4.10	2.70
	4 – LE CINQUIEME ESSAI		5.60	2.70
	2 – SHOAL WATER			2.10

$2 EXACTOR 6–4 PAID $34.70 $2 TRIACTOR 6–4–2 PAID $63.40

B. h, (May), by Valley Crossing – Slewway, by Slewpy. Trainer Baker Reade. Bred by W James Hindman (Md).

SLEW VALLEY stalked the pacesetter three-wide, challenged midway through the turn, vied four-wide into the stretch then outfinished LE CINQUIEME ESSAI in a stretch-long duel to the finish. LE CINQUIEME ESSAI stalked up close on the second path while well in hand, bid between horses late turn then dueled inside SLEW VALLEY to the end and just missed. SHOAL WATER led quickly and set a reserved pace from the rail, was engaged on the turn, dueled into the stretch then gave way very grudgingly in the final furlong. PRINCE ALPHIE was always close on the rail, attempted to lodge a bid at the top of the stretch, was all out but could not get up then tired in the late stages. MR. SULU closed late on the turn and tried to get up to the leaders, could not sustain the bid and flattened out in the stretch. PUFFER raced three-wide on the turn and was always in striking range but hung in the stretch.

Owners– 1, Rich Meadow Farm; 2, William Scott; 3, Sam-Son Farms; 4, Schettine William C; 5, McMurray A L and Carroll Josie; 6, Sam-Son Farms

Trainers– 1, Baker Reade; 2, Nielsen Paul; 3, Frostad Mark; 4, Carroll Josie; 5, Carroll Josie; 6, Frostad Mark

Scratched– Tusayan (15May04 ^{9}WO ^{5})

$1 Pick Three (5–7–6) Paid $265.45; Pick Three Pool $8,061.

EIGHTH RACE
Woodbine
JUNE 5, 2004

1$\frac{1}{16}$ MILES. (Turf) (1.39^{1}) 49TH RUNNING OF THE NASSAU. Grade III. Purse $250,000 (plus $50,000 Other Sources) FOR FILLIES AND MARES, THREE-YEAR-OLDS AND UPWARD. By subscription of $250 each which shall accompany the nomination and an additional $2,500 when making entry; with $250,000 added plus all fees to be divided: 60% to the winner, 20% to second, 11% to third, 6% to fourth and 3% to fifth. Weight: Three year olds 117 lbs.; Older 124 lbs. Non-winners of a sweepstakes of $75,000 three times at a mile or over in 2003-2004 allowed 3 lbs.; Of a sweepstakes of $75,000 twice at a mile or over in 2003-2004, 5 lbs.;Of a sweepstakes of $75,000 once at a mile or over in 2003-2004, 7 lbs.; Of $51,840 at a mile or over in 2003-2004, 9 lbs.(No Canadian Bred Allowance) (Maiden or claiming races not considered.) Final entries to be made through the entry box no later than11:30 a.m. on Thursday, June 3, 2004. Plus $50,000 for Canadian Breds from the Thoroughbred Improvement Program and Canadian Thoroughbred Horse Society. Closed Wednesday, May 19, 2004 with 29 nominations. Plus up to $12,420 Ontario Sire/Canadian Bred Breeder Awards. (Rail at 30 feet).

Value of Race: $310,750 Winner $193,350; second $54,450; third $35,448; fourth $19,335; fifth $8,167. Mutuel Pool $115,894.00 Exactor Pool $52,284.00 Triactor Pool $57,707.00

Last Raced	Horse	M/Eqt.	A.	Wt	PP	St	¼	½	¾	Str	Fin	Jockey	Odds $1
16May04 ^{6}WO^{1}	Inish Glora	L	6	121	5	1	$1^{\frac{1}{2}}$	$1^{1\frac{1}{2}}$	$1^{1\frac{1}{2}}$	$1^{1\frac{1}{2}}$	$1^{\frac{3}{4}}$	Kabel T K	3.50
15May04 ^{5}Pim^{1}	Ocean Drive	L	4	117	6	2	3^{1}	2^{hd}	$2^{\frac{1}{2}}$	$2^{2\frac{1}{2}}$	$2^{2\frac{1}{2}}$	Douglas R R	0.65
16May04 ^{6}WO^{2}	Classic Stamp	L	4	119	3	5	4^{1}	4^{2}	4^{2}	$3^{1\frac{1}{2}}$	$3^{\frac{3}{4}}$	Husbands P	7.05
16May04 ^{6}WO^{5}	First Quarter	L	5	115	2	4	6	5^{hd}	$5^{1\frac{1}{2}}$	$4^{\frac{1}{2}}$	4^{nk}	Montpellier C	44.95
17Apr04 ^{7}Kee^{1}	Dyna Da Wyna	L f	4	117	1	3	$2^{\frac{1}{2}}$	$3^{1\frac{1}{2}}$	3^{1}	$5^{3\frac{1}{2}}$	5^{4}	Landry R C	4.20
21Apr04 ^{8}Kee^{7}	Boana-Ger	L	6	115	4	6	5^{hd}	6	6	6	6	Ramsammy E	19.70

OFF AT 4:40 Start Good . Won driving. Course firm.

TIME :25, :48^{4}, 1:12, 1:34^{1}, 1:40^{1} (:25.08, :48.99, 1:12.01, 1:34.36, 1:40.38)

$2 Mutuel Prices:			
5 – INISH GLORA	9.00	3.20	2.60
6 – OCEAN DRIVE		2.60	2.20
3 – CLASSIC STAMP			2.80

$2 EXACTOR 5–6 PAID $20.90 $2 TRIACTOR 5–6–3 PAID $64.20

B. m, (May), by Regal Classic – Star Guest, by Assert-Ire . Trainer Benson MacDonald. Bred by C G Scott DVM (Ont-C).

INISH GLORA had command from an alert break, set a pressured pace but still in hand, quickened entering the turn and drew clear then held OCEAN DRIVE safe through the stretch under left-handed encouragement. OCEAN DRIVE stalked from the third path, kept the leader in her sights on the turn, was set down at the head of the stretch and finished determinedly but showed only a mild late gain. CLASSIC STAMP stalked from the second path, moved three-wide for the run through the turn, closed approaching the top of the stretch then hung in the final furlong. FIRST QUARTER saved ground, gained a bit in the final furlong but did not menace. DYNA DA WYNA moved up inside and abreast of the leader early on the backstretch, took back slightly and forced the issue from INISH GLORA's inside flank, continued to stay close on the turn then lacked the necessary closing response. BOANA (GER) trailed the field from the third path then lacked a rally.

Owners– 1, Costigan Robert J; 2, Sy & Bonnie Baskin; 3, Sorokolit William A Sr; 4, Come By Chance Stable; 5, WinStar Farm LLC; 6, Tanaka Gary A

Trainers– 1, Benson MacDonald; 2, Pletcher Todd A; 3, Hopmans C C Jr; 4, Day James E; 5, Walden W Elliott; 6, Attfield Roger L

$1 Pick Three (1–4–5) Paid $22.25 ; Pick Three Pool $7,889 .

EIGHTH RACE
Woodbine
JUNE 13, 2004

1⅛ MILES. (1.48) 49TH RUNNING OF THE LABATT WOODBINE OAKS. Purse $500,000 FOR THREE-YEAR-OLD FILLIES, FOALED IN CANADA. By subscription of $50 each to accompany the nomination by February 1, 2003 (296 nominations). To continue eligibility, the following payments must be made: second subscription of $100 by February 1st, 2004 (154 remained eligible). Third subscription of $250 by May 1st, 2004 (63 remained eligible). Plus 3 supplements at $5000 each and an additional $5,000 when making final entry The added money and all fees to be divided: 60% to the winner, 20% to second, 11%to third, 6% to fourth and 3% to fifth. Weight 121 lbs. Final entries to be made through the entry box no later than 11:30 a.m. on Friday, June 11, 2004. Plus up to $17,940 Ontario Sire/Canadian Bred Breeder Awards. $275,000 of this purse has been providedthrough the Canadian Thoroughbred Horse Society and the Thoroughbred Improvement Program.

Value of Race: $500,000 Winner $300,000; second $100,000; third $55,000; fourth $30,000; fifth $15,000. Mutuel Pool $149,905.00 Exactor Pool $95,240.00

Last Raced	Horse	M/Eqt.	A.	Wt	PP	St	¼	½	¾	Str	Fin	Jockey	Odds $1
23May04 ^{8}WO^{1}	Eye of the Sphynx	L	3	121	2	1	$1^{\frac{1}{2}}$	2^{hd}	$2^{\frac{1}{2}}$	1^{3}	$1^{4\frac{1}{4}}$	Kabel T K	0.80
22May04 ^{6}WO^{5}	Touchnow	L b	3	121	4	4	5	5	5	2^{5}	2^{9}	Husbands P	29.35
29May04 ^{8}WO^{2}	My Vintage Port	L	3	121	3	5	4^{hd}	4^{hd}	4^{hd}	4^{5}	$3^{1\frac{1}{4}}$	Jones J	6.95
22May04 ^{6}WO^{1}	Hong Kong Dancer	L	3	121	5	2	2^{hd}	3^{1}	$3^{\frac{1}{2}}$	3^{1}	4^{16}	Pimentel R M	2.60
23May04 ^{8}WO^{2}	Silver Bird	L b	3	121	1	3	$3^{\frac{1}{2}}$	1^{1}	$1^{\frac{1}{2}}$	5	5	McAleney J S	3.60

OFF AT 4:42 Start Good . Won driving. Track fast.

TIME :23^{3}, :48^{1}, 1:13^{3}, 1:39^{4}, 1:53 (:23.72, :48.21, 1:13.72, 1:39.97, 1:53.11)

$2 Mutuel Prices:			
2 – EYE OF THE SPHYNX	3.60	3.10	2.20
4 – TOUCHNOW		13.90	5.00
3 – MY VINTAGE PORT			4.10

$2 EXACTOR 2–4 PAID $45.00

B. f, (Apr), by Smart Strike – Queen of Egypt , by Vice Regent . Trainer Frostad Mark. Bred by Sam-Son Farm (Ont-C).

EYE OF THE SPHYNX showed early foot then settled and stalked the pacesetter in hand through the backstretch, swept to the lead early on the far turn, responded smartly when roused at the top of the stretch and drew off. TOUCHNOW stalked from the second path, closed up between rivals late on the final turn and was all out in the stretch to be second best. MY VINTAGE PORT stalked the leader from the rail, was roused late on the turn and launched an all-out rally but could not close the gap. HONG KONG DANCER forced the pace on the first turn then stalked to the far turn, chased after the leader while three-wide but flattened out in the stretch. SILVER BIRD raced forwardly from the outset, shook clear leaving the clubhouse turn, set a reserved pace to the far turn but yielded quickly when challenged and faded.

Owners– 1, Sam-Son Farms; 2, Farr George; 3, Parsley Ken and Pettifer Rick; 4, Ho Peter; 5, McAlpine James

Trainers– 1, Frostad Mark; 2, Baker Reade; 3, Parsley Ken B; 4, Baker Reade; 5, Baker Reade

$1 Pick Three (1–4–2) Paid $55.30 ; Pick Three Pool $10,135 .

EIGHTH RACE
Woodbine
JUNE 19, 2004

1⅛ MILES. (Turf) (1.45^{1}) 97TH RUNNING OF THE KING EDWARD BREEDERS' CUP HANDICAP. Grade II. Purse $300,000 (includes $100,000 BC – Breeders' Cup) FOR THREE-YEAR-OLDS AND UPWARD. By subscription of $300 each which shall accompany the nomination and an additional $3000 when making entry; with $200,000 added and an additional $100,000 from the Breeders' Cup Fund for Cup nominees only. The host associations added monies and all fees to be divided: 60% to the winner, 20% to second, 11% to third, 6% to fourth and 3% to fifth. Breeders' Cup Fund monies also correspondingly divided provided a Breeders' Cup nominee has finished in an awarded position. Any Breeders' Cup Fund monies not awarded will revert back to the fund. Weights Saturday, June 12, 2004. This race will not be divided, the starters will be determined at the time of entry with preference given to Breeders' Cup nominees only of equal racing quality or weight assignment (respective of sex and weight for age). Final entries to be made through the entry box no later than 11:30 a.m. on Thursday, June 17, 2004. Plus up to $15,180 Ontario Sire/Canadian Bred Breeder Awards. Closed Wednesday, June 2,2004 with 31 nominations. (Rail at 20 feet).

Value of Race: $324,300 Winner $194,580; second $64,860; third $35,673; fourth $19,458; fifth $9,729. Mutuel Pool $92,260.00 Exactor Pool $69,978.00

Last Raced	Horse	M/Eqt.	A.	Wt	PP	St	¼	½	¾	Str	Fin	Jockey	Odds $1
30May04 ^{8}WO^{1}	Slew Valley	L	7	117	3	3	$3^{\frac{1}{2}}$	$3^{\frac{1}{2}}$	3^{hd}	$3^{1\frac{1}{2}}$	1^{nk}	McAleney J S	4.30
30May04 ^{8}WO^{3}	Shoal Water	L	4	116	1	1	$2^{1\frac{1}{2}}$	$2^{1\frac{1}{2}}$	$2^{1\frac{1}{2}}$	2^{hd}	$2^{2\frac{1}{2}}$	Kabel T K	4.80
28May04 ^{9}WO^{1}	Surging River	L	4	112	5	4	$4^{\frac{1}{2}}$	5	5	4^{2}	3^{hd}	McKnight J	11.70
15May04 ^{10}Pim^{7}	Wando	L	4	118	2	2	1^{1}	1^{hd}	1^{hd}	1^{hd}	$4^{2\frac{1}{2}}$	Husbands P	0.75
29May04 ^{10}Mth^{2}	Remind	L	4	114	4	5	5	$4^{\frac{1}{2}}$	$4^{\frac{1}{2}}$	5	5	Ramsammy E	3.95

OFF AT 4:38 Start Good . Won driving. Course yielding.

TIME $:23^{2}$, $:46^{2}$, 1:10, $1:35^{1}$, $1:48^{2}$ (:23.52, :46.45, 1:10.16, 1:35.31, 1:48.42)

$2 Mutuel Prices:

3 – SLEW VALLEY	10.60	5.80	3.90
1 – SHOAL WATER		5.50	4.80
5 – SURGING RIVER			7.00

$2 EXACTOR 3–1 PAID $48.10

B. h, (May), by Valley Crossing – Slewway, by Slewpy. Trainer Baker Reade. Bred by W James Hindman (Md).

SLEW VALLEY stalked the pace from the second path, came three-wide into the stretch, responded gamely when asked and wore down the leader in deep stretch. SHOAL WATER forced the issue from the rail, dueled in earnest through the stretch, battled to a short lead inside the furlong marker but failed to contain the winner. SURGING RIVER was always in range while on the third path, finished determinedly to no avail. WANDO set the pace under pressure, dueled into the stretch then gave way grudgingly in the final furlong. REMIND always in range along the inside, lacked a response in the final furlong.

Owners– 1, Rich Meadow Farm and Burkhard Alan; 2, Sam-Son Farms; 3, Sam-Son Farms; 4, Schickedanz Gustav; 5, Claiborne Farm

Trainers– 1, Baker Reade; 2, Frostad Mark; 3, Frostad Mark; 4, Keogh Michael; 5, Mott William I

$1 Pick Three (1–9–3) Paid $226.25 ; Pick Three Pool $8,212 .

FOURTH RACE
Woodbine
JUNE 27, 2004

6 FURLONGS. (Turf) (1.07^{3}) 47TH RUNNING OF THE SCOTTS HIGHLANDER HANDICAP. Grade III. Purse $200,000 FOR THREE-YEAR-OLDS AND UPWARD. By subscription of $200 each which shall accompany the nomination and an additional $2,000 when making entry; with $200,000 added, plus all fees to be divided: 60% to the winner, 20% to second, 11% to third, 6% to fourth and 3% to fifth. Weights, Saturday, June 19, 2004. Final entries to be made through the entry box no later than 11:30 a.m. on Friday, June 25, 2004. Plus up to $12,420 Ontario Sire/Canadian Bred Breeder Awards. Closed Wednesday, June 9, 2004 with 25 nominations.

Value of Race: $219,000 Winner $131,400; second $43,800; third $24,090; fourth $13,140; fifth $6,570. Mutuel Pool $159,217.00 Exactor Pool $95,525.00 Triactor Pool $118,862.00

Last Raced	Horse	M/Eqt.	A.	Wt	PP	St	¼	½	Str	Fin	Jockey	Odds $1
6Jun04 ^{3}WO^{1}	Soaring Free	L	5	123	1	1	1^{1}	1^{1}	1^{2}	$1^{2\frac{1}{4}}$	Kabel T K	0.45
24May04 ^{8}WO^{2}	Open Concert	L b	5	115	6	5	$5^{1\frac{1}{2}}$	$3^{1\frac{1}{2}}$	3^{1}	$2^{\frac{3}{4}}$	Ramsammy E	7.20
31May04 ^{9}Pha^{5}	Take AchanceOnMe	L bf	6	116	5	2	2^{1}	$2^{1\frac{1}{2}}$	$2^{1\frac{1}{2}}$	3no	Delgado A	14.00
6Jun04 ^{3}WO^{3}	Waltzin' Storm	L	6	117	4	3	$3^{\frac{1}{2}}$	$4^{\frac{1}{2}}$	$4^{\frac{1}{2}}$	4^{nk}	Husbands P	7.90
6Jun04 ^{3}WO^{6}	Tusayan	L	4	110	2	6	$6^{1\frac{1}{2}}$	7	$5^{1\frac{1}{2}}$	5^{2}	Pimentel R M	35.20
6Jun04 ^{3}WO^{2}	My Lucky Strike	L f	5	116	7	7	7	6^{hd}	$6^{1\frac{1}{2}}$	$6^{1\frac{1}{4}}$	Elliott S	5.25
12Jun04 ^{8}FE^{3}	Frank's Selection	L b	8	115	3	4	4^{1}	5^{hd}	7	7	Poznansky N E	29.65

OFF AT 1:59 Start Good . Won driving. Course firm.

TIME $:22^{3}$, $:45^{3}$, $:56^{4}$, $1:08^{3}$ (:22.73, :45.62, :56.82, 1:08.72)

$2 Mutuel Prices:

1 – SOARING FREE	2.90	2.40	2.10
6 – OPEN CONCERT		4.30	3.50
5 – TAKE ACHANCE ON ME			4.70

$2 EXACTOR 1–6 PAID $11.10 $2 TRIACTOR 1–6–5 PAID $66.80

Dk. b or br. g, (Jan), by Smart Strike – Dancing With Wings, by Danzig. Trainer Frostad Mark. Bred by Sam-Son Farm (Ont-C).

SOARING FREE broke alertly and sprinted to the early lead, set a reserved pace from the hedge, turned back TAKE ACHANCE ON ME upper stretch and held sway under a drive. OPEN CONCERT rated just off the pace while three-wide, came four-wide into the stretch and launched an all-out rally and gained the place. TAKE ACHANCE ON ME pressed the pace in hand along the second path, loomed up late turn and flanked the leader but could not match strides and gave way. WALTZIN' STORM stalked the pace then was all out late between rivals. TUSAYAN was well back on the rail, gained late turn then evened out in the stretch. MY LUCKY STRIKE was well off the pace, closed four-wide late turn then flattened out. FRANK'S SELECTION raced midpack along the rail, closed up late turn then flattened out in the stretch.

Owners– 1, Sam-Son Farms; 2, Kelynack Racing Stable Inc; 3, Ben Dover Stable; 4, Melnyk Eugene and Laura; 5, Silvera Laurie and Kilambi Sriniva; 6, Billy Wine and Joe Ferraro; 7, Elliott-Griem Lynda

Trainers– 1, Frostad Mark; 2, Katryan Abraham R; 3, Aguirre Anthony; 4, Casse Mark; 5, Silvera Laurie; 6, Cirillo John; 7, Griem Robert J

$1 Pick Three (8–5–1) Paid $196.50 ; Pick Three Pool $11,927 .

NINTH RACE
Woodbine
JUNE 27, 2004

$1\frac{1}{4}$ MILES. (2.01) 145TH RUNNING OF THE QUEEN'S PLATE. Purse $1,000,000 FOR THREE-YEAR-OLDS, FOALED IN CANADA. Weight; Colts and Geldings 126 lbs. Fillies, 121 lbs. By subscription of $150 each to accompany the nomination by February 1st, 2003 (417 nominations); second subscription of $500 by February 1st, 2004 (186 remainedeligible plus 4 supplements at $7,500 each); third subscription of $1,000 by May 15th, 2004 (68 remained eligible, plus 4 supplements at $15,000 each); and an additional $10,000 when making final entry no later than June 25, 2004. Horses not originally nominated may be made eligible by payment of a late nomination fee of $7,500 on or before February 1st, 2004 or of $15,000 on or before May 15th, 2004. All monies received from the original nomination (February 1st, 2003) and the February 1st, 2004, payments will be divided equally between the gross purses of the Queen's Plate, Prince of Wales and Breeders' Stakes. $300,000 of this purse has been provided through the Thoroughbred Improvement Program and Canadian Thoroughbred Horse Society.

Value of Race: $1,000,000 Winner $600,000; second $200,000; third $110,000; fourth $60,000; fifth $30,000. Mutuel Pool $658,208.00 Exactor Pool $250,771.00 Triactor Pool $350,036.00 Superfecta Pool $99,355.00

Last Raced	Horse	M/Eqt.	A.	Wt	PP	1/4	1/2	3/4	1	Str	Fin	Jockey	Odds $1
6Jun04 ^{8}WO^{2}	Niigon	L f	3	126	13	$2^{\frac{1}{2}}$	2^{1}	1^{hd}	$1^{1\frac{1}{2}}$	1^{2}	$1^{\frac{3}{4}}$	Landry R C	5.90
6Jun04 ^{8}WO^{1}	A Bit O'Gold	L	3	126	10	7^{1}	5^{hd}	$4^{2\frac{1}{2}}$	2^{4}	2^{8}	$2^{7\frac{3}{4}}$	Jones J	1.35
5Jun04 ^{5}WO^{1}	Will He Crow	L	3	126	3	$12^{\frac{1}{2}}$	12^{hd}	12^{hd}	9^{5}	$4^{1\frac{1}{2}}$	3^{1}	Bahen S R	30.45
12Jun04 ^{2}WO^{1}	Just in Case Jimmy	L	3	126	12	11^{6}	9^{hd}	6^{hd}	4^{1}	$3^{\frac{1}{2}}$	4^{hd}	Dos Ramos R A	23.55
13Jun04 ^{11}WO^{6}	His Smoothness	L	3	126	11	8^{hd}	$11^{4\frac{1}{2}}$	9^{3}	7^{1}	5^{6}	5^{6}	McKnight J	45.80
6Jun04 ^{8}WO^{4}	Strike Em Hard	L	3	126	5	9^{hd}	7^{hd}	$7^{\frac{1}{2}}$	8^{2}	7^{2}	6^{1}	Ramsammy E	46.90
29May04 ^{7}WO^{1}	Alleged Ruler	L	3	126	6	$10^{1\frac{1}{2}}$	$10^{\frac{1}{2}}$	8^{1}	5^{hd}	6^{hd}	$7^{2\frac{1}{2}}$	Callaghan S	15.10
5Jun04 ^{9}WO^{1}	Silver Ticket	L	3	126	9	1^{1}	1^{1}	2^{2}	$3^{2\frac{1}{2}}$	8^{4}	$8^{2\frac{1}{2}}$	Kabel T K	5.65
13Jun04 ^{7}WO^{2}	Copper Trail	L	3	126	2	13	13	13	10^{5}	9^{hd}	$9^{3\frac{1}{4}}$	Somsanith N	10.20
21May04 ^{7}WO^{1}	Kent Ridge	L b	3	126	8	6^{hd}	$8^{\frac{1}{2}}$	3^{hd}	6^{1}	10^{15}	$10^{22\frac{3}{4}}$	Husbands P	23.45
21May04 ^{7}WO^{2}	Archer Fleet	L b	3	126	4	4^{hd}	3^{hd}	$10^{1\frac{1}{2}}$	12^{3}	12^{1}	11no	Husbands S P	33.25
4Jun04 ^{7}WO^{1}	Night Sky	L	3	126	7	5^{hd}	6^{2}	5^{hd}	11^{5}	$11^{\frac{1}{2}}$	12no	McAleney J S	11.60
6Jun04 ^{10}WO^{1}	Long Pond	L b	3	126	1	3^{hd}	$4^{\frac{1}{2}}$	11^{hd}	13	13	13	Elliott S	12.45

OFF AT 5:06 Start Good . Won driving. Track fast.

TIME :23^{1}, :47^{4}, 1:12^{4}, 1:37^{4}, 2:04^{3} (:23.31, :47.83, 1:12.94, 1:37.87, 2:04.72)

$2 Mutuel Prices:				
	13 – NIIGON	**13.80**	**5.10**	**4.10**
	10 – A BIT O'GOLD		**3.10**	**2.90**
	3 – WILL HE CROW			**9.60**

$2 EXACTOR 13–10 PAID $33.80 $2 TRIACTOR 13–10–3 PAID $742.40
$1 SUPERFECTA 13–10–3–12 PAID $5,343.70

Dk. b or br. c, (Mar), by Unbridled – Savethelastdance , by Nureyev . Trainer Coatrieux Eric. Bred by Chiefswood Stables Limited (Ont–C).

NIIGON stalked the pacesetter just to the outside, moved up outside him late backstretch and moved clear quickly early turn, had command to the stretch then held A BIT O'GOLD safe under steady pressure. A BIT O'GOLD rated early in striking range, moved sharply after the leader late backstretch then was determined and gaining gradually to the end. WILL HE CROW was unhurried to the final turn, closed four-wide but never reached contention. JUST IN CASE JIMMY raced evenly while four-wide, advanced outside horses but lacked a late response. HIS SMOOTHNESS was well off the early pace, came four-wide through the turn then hung in the stretch. STRIKE EM HARD raced evenly on the second path, was roused on the far turn but lacked the necessary response. ALLEGED RULER raced midpack along the rail, was hustled through the far turn but flattened out in the stretch. SILVER TICKET set a pressured pace in hand, was no match for the winner at the far turn and tired. COPPER TRAIL trailed early and passed tiring horses. KENT RIDGE stalked the pace, was hustled on the far turn then tired at the top of the stretch. ARCHER FLEET was close early then faded between foes on the backstretch. NIGHT SKY close early while three-deep, tired on the far turn. LONG POND saved ground but was through early and faded on the backstretch.

Owners– 1, Chiefswood Stable; 2, The Two Bit Racing Stable; 3, Regan Lawrence D; 4, Attfield Roger L and Werner William; 5, Come By Chance Stable; 6, Dominion Bloodstock Ball Derek Galbraith Hugh and Peacock G; 7, Chiefswood Stable; 8, Sam-Son Farms; 9, Stolar Stables; 10, Melnyk Eugene and Laura and Bristow Bill and Iris; 11, Armata John and Mazarese Giuseppe; 12, Stronach Stable; 13, Melnyk Eugene and Laura

Trainers– 1, Coatrieux Eric; 2, Day-Phillips Catherine; 3, Regan Timothy; 4, Attfield Roger L; 5, Day James E; 6, Cotey David; 7, Coatrieux Eric; 8, Frostad Mark; 9, Day James E; 10, Casse Mark; 11, Armata Vito; 12, Vella Daniel J; 13, Casse Mark

$1 Pick Three (4–5–13) Paid $3,106.80 ; Pick Three Pool $12,464 .
$1 Pick Six (1–7–6–4–5–13) 5 Correct Paid $2,728.05 ; Pick Six Pool $25,915 .

EIGHTH RACE
Woodbine
JULY 1, 2004

1¼ MILES. (2.01) 52ND RUNNING OF THE DOMINION DAY HANDICAP. Grade III. Purse $200,000 FOR THREE-YEAR-OLDS AND UPWARD. By subscription of $200 each which shall accompany the nomination and an additional $2,000 when making entry; with $200,000 added, plus all fees to be divided: 60% to the winner, 20% to second, 11% to third, 6% to fourth and 3% to fifth. Weights, Thursday, June 24, 2004. Final entries to be made through the entry box at the closing time then in effect for overnight events. Plus up to $12,420 Ontario Sire/Canadian Bred Breeder Awards. Closed Wednesday, June 16, 2004 with 16nominations.

Value of Race: $217,200 Winner $130,320; second $43,440; third $23,892; fourth $13,032; fifth $6,516. Mutuel Pool $127,428.00 Exactor Pool $70,226.00 Triactor Pool $87,726.00

Last Raced	Horse	M/Eqt.	A.	Wt	PP	¼	½	¾	1	Str	Fin	Jockey	Odds $1
31May04 ^{9}Bel^{9}	Mobil	L f	4	122	4	$4^{1\frac{1}{2}}$	$4^{2\frac{1}{2}}$	3^{hd}	$1^{\frac{1}{2}}$	1^{7}	$1^{12\frac{3}{4}}$	Kabel T K	0.60
24May04 ^{8}WO^{1}	Mark One	L	5	118	5	5^{hd}	6^{7}	5^{hd}	$5^{\frac{1}{2}}$	$3^{1\frac{1}{2}}$	2^{nk}	Landry R C	2.85
3Apr04 ^{9}GP^{4}	The Judge Sez Who	L	5	119	6	7	7	7	4^{2}	2^{1}	$3^{3\frac{1}{4}}$	Husbands P	5.15
30May04 ^{1}WO^{1}	Parrott Bay	L bf	7	113	2	3^{1}	3^{hd}	$4^{1\frac{1}{2}}$	7	$5^{\frac{1}{2}}$	$4^{1\frac{1}{2}}$	Ramsammy E	33.80
30Nov03 ^{9}WO^{1}	Hydrogen	L	5	115	7	6^{5}	5^{hd}	$6^{2\frac{1}{2}}$	6^{2}	6^{4}	$5^{1\frac{1}{4}}$	McAleney J S	11.75
13Jun04 ^{2}WO^{1}	Tackling Stress	L	4	115	3	2^{1}	2^{1}	2^{1}	$2^{2\frac{1}{2}}$	4^{2}	6^{9}	Montpellier C	29.90
12Jun04 ^{5}WO^{7}	Slim Dusty	L f	5	113	1	$1^{1\frac{1}{2}}$	$1^{4\frac{1}{2}}$	$1^{\frac{1}{2}}$	$3^{\frac{1}{2}}$	7	7	Singh S	31.60

OFF AT 4:30 Start Good. Won ridden out. Track fast.

TIME :23^{3}, :47, 1:12, 1:37^{2}, 2:03^{1} (:23.61, :47.02, 1:12.08, 1:37.55, 2:03.34)

$2 Mutuel Prices:				
	4 – MOBIL	3.20	2.10	2.10
	5 – MARK ONE		2.60	2.20
	6 – THE JUDGE SEZ WHO			2.70

$2 EXACTOR 4–5 PAID $7.40 $2 TRIACTOR 4–5–6 PAID $14.30

B. c, (Jan), by Langfuhr – Kinetigal, by Naskra. Trainer Keogh Michael. Bred by Gustav Schickedanz (Ont–C).

MOBIL stalked the pace, closed three-wide and bid outside two others midturn, edged clear late turn and drew off in the stretch under light handling. MARK ONE was unhurried to the far turn then closed between horses and was all out in the stretch. THE JUDGE SEZ WHO was devoid of speed, trailed to the far turn then closed four-wide, was roused at the top of the stretch and was all out in the stretch. PARROTT BAY stalked from the rail, fell back on the far turn then angled out at the top of the stretch and failed to menace. HYDROGEN was well back, closed mildly three-deep late turn then hung in the stretch. TACKLING STRESS broke alertly, settled, stalked the pace then bid between foes on the far turn, was no match for MOBIL and tired at the head of the stretch. SLIM DUSTY led early, set the pace to midway of the final turn, yielded when challenged and was through.

Owners– 1, Schickedanz Gustav; 2, Stronach Stable; 3, Sez Who Racing; 4, Kelynack Racing Stable Inc; 5, Mack Earle I; 6, Dominion Bloodstock Ball Derek and Galbraith Hugh; 7, Kelynack Racing Stable Inc

Trainers– 1, Keogh Michael; 2, Vella Daniel J; 3, Casse Mark; 4, Katryan Abraham R; 5, Casse Mark; 6, Cotey David; 7, Katryan Abraham R

$1 Pick Three (2–1/3–4) Paid $11.25 ; Pick Three Pool $6,865 .

NINTH RACE
Hastings
JULY 1, 2004

1⅛ MILES. (1.46^{4}) LIEUTENANT GOVERNORS' H. Grade III. Purse $100,000 (plus $12,500 THRIF – British Columbia Bred) A Handicap for Three Year Olds and Upward. $200 to nominate. $1,000 to enter and $1,000 to pass scratch time. With $100,000 guaranteed, of which 60% goes to the winner, 20% to second, 11% to third, 6% to fourth, and 3% to fifth.

Value of Race: $103,598 Winner $60,000; second $22,116; third $12,164; fourth $6,000; fifth $3,318. Mutuel Pool $64,056.00 Triactor Pool $35,660.00 Exactor Pool $24,181.00

Last Raced	Horse	M/Eqt.	A.	Wt	PP	St	¼	½	¾	Str	Fin	Jockey	Odds $1
19May04 ^{7}Hol^{4}	Royal Place	L	4	119	5	1	2^{1}	2^{1}	$2^{\frac{1}{2}}$	$2^{2\frac{1}{2}}$	1^{nk}	Olguin G L	5.45
23May04 ^{7}Hst^{1}	Lord Nelson	L f	7	123	6	8	3^{hd}	3^{hd}	$3^{1\frac{1}{2}}$	1^{hd}	$2^{4\frac{1}{4}}$	Fuentes F P	2.10
12Jun04 ^{8}Hst^{1}	Roscoe Pito	L	4	119	1	2	1^{1}	$1^{\frac{1}{2}}$	$1^{\frac{1}{2}}$	$3^{2\frac{1}{2}}$	3^{hd}	Hoverson C	6.20
20Jun04 ^{9}EmD^{4}	Ezra	L	5	117	7	7	6^{2}	6^{3}	6^{4}	4^{1}	$4^{1\frac{1}{4}}$	Valdez F S	45.55
20Jun04 ^{3}Hst^{1}	Steady Smiler	L	4	116	8	6	7	7	7	6^{3}	$5^{\frac{1}{2}}$	May R H	75.25
12Jun04 ^{8}Hst^{4}	Illusive Force	L	4	114	2	5	4^{2}	4^{1}	$4^{\frac{1}{2}}$	5^{hd}	6^{3}	Wilson D H	18.20
31May04 ^{3}BM^{1}	Yougottawanna	L bf	5	122	4	4	5^{5}	5^{3}	5^{4}	7	7	Alvarado P V	1.10
20Jun04 ^{10}Hst^{2}	Mister Mane Man	L	4	113	3	3		—	—	—	—	Wright N	49.90

OFF AT 4:56 Start Good. Won driving. Track fast.

TIME :22^{4}, :46^{3}, 1:11^{1}, 1:35^{3}, 1:49 (:22.80, :46.63, 1:11.22, 1:35.66, 1:49.08)

$2 Mutuel Prices:				
	5 – ROYAL PLACE	12.90	7.30	4.50
	6 – LORD NELSON		3.00	2.50
	1 – ROSCOE PITO			4.00

$2 TRIACTOR 5–6–1 PAID $172.50 $2 EXACTOR 5–6 PAID $53.10

B. c, (Feb), by Out of Place – British Bauble, by Kris S.. Trainer Becerra Rafael. Bred by Meadowbrook Farms Inc (Fla).

ROYAL PLACE broke sharply, pressed the pace from the outside, rallied, gained the rail when the pace setter gave way, gained the lead late in the stretch driving under left handed pressure. LORD NELSON hustled along to be close up, rallied from three wide on the backstretch, gained the lead from three wide on the final turn, was outfinished in the late stages. ROSCOE PITO broke sharply, assumed command form the inside, set a brisk pace, gave way on the final turn. EZRA slow early, put in a mild late rally from three wide down the stretch and was outrun. STEADY SMILER trailed for the first three quarters, put in a late gain from four wide down the stretch. ILLUSIVE FORCE away alertly and close up on the inside, chased the leaders, was through after three quarters. YOUGOTTAWANNA away alertly, steadied early when MISTER MANE MAN lost his rider, stalked the leaders, gave way after three quarters. MISTER MANE MAN broke sharply, ran up on and clipped the heels of ROYAL PLACE before the quarter, stumbled and lost his jockey. Following the race there was a stewards enquiry into the incident away from the gate. After review no action was taken the result was left to stand.

Owners– 1, Sangara K K; 2, Bennett Mr and Mrs R J; 3, Snow John Wildcard Stable Punjab Foods Mutti Raj and Gomes Gus; 4, Rakis Michael and Hughes David J; 5, Maybin Rob; 6, Canyon Farms; 7, Peter Redekop B C Ltd; 8, Hart Kim N

Trainers– 1, Becerra Rafael; 2, Condilenios Dino; 3, Snow John; 4, Giesbrecht Brian; 5, Maybin Robert; 6, VanOverschot Robert; 7, Hollendorfer Jerry; 8, Heads Barbara

$2 Pick Three (6–5–5) Paid $69.30 ; Pick Three Pool $3,923 .
$2 Pick Four (8–6–5–5) Paid $224.20 ; Pick Four Pool $7,455 .

FOURTH RACE
Woodbine
JULY 17, 2004

1⅛ MILES. (Turf) (1.45^{1}) 9TH RUNNING OF THE DANCE SMARTLY HANDICAP. Grade III. Purse $150,000 (plus $50,000 Other Sources) FOR FILLIES AND MARES, THREE-YEAR-OLDS AND UPWARD. By subscription of $150 each to accompany the nomination and an additional $1,500 when making entry; with $150,000 added and an additional $50,000 for Canadian Breds plus all fees to be divided: 60% to the winner, 20% to second, 11% to third, 6% to fourth and 3% to fifth. Weights Saturday, July 10, 2004. Final entries to be made through the entry box no later than 11:30 a.m. on Thursday, July 15, 2004. Closed Wednesday, June 30, 2004 with 23 nominations.Plus $50,000 for Canadian Breds from the Thoroughbred Improvement Program and Canadian Thoroughbred Horse Society. Plus up to $12,420 Ontario Sire/Canadian Bred Breeder Awards. (Rail at 20 feet).

Value of Race: $209,450 Winner $133,844; second $42,490; third $23,369; fourth $9,747. Mutuel Pool $53,901.00 Exactor Pool $52,133.00

Last Raced	Horse	M/Eqt.	A.	Wt	PP	St	¼	½	¾	Str	Fin	Jockey	Odds $1
26Jun04 ^{5}WO^{1}	Mona Rose		4	112	3	3	3^{hd}	4	4	2^{hd}	1^{1}	Da Silva E R	5.60
5Jun04 ^{8}WO^{1}	Inish Glora	L	6	122	2	2	2^{1}	1^{hd}	1^{hd}	1^{2}	$2^{1\frac{1}{2}}$	Kabel T K	0.60
26Jun04 ^{2}WO^{1}	Classic Stamp	L	4	116	1	4	4	2^{hd}	2^{hd}	3^{5}	$3^{11\frac{1}{4}}$	Husbands P	2.05
14Mar04 ^{10}Tam^{4}	Strait From Texas	L	5	117	4	1	1^{1}	$3^{2\frac{1}{2}}$	$3^{2\frac{1}{2}}$	4	4	Dos Ramos R A	8.35

OFF AT 2:23 Start Good . Won driving. Course yielding.

TIME $:24^{4}$, :48, $1:11^{2}$, $1:35^{2}$, 1:48 (:24.94, :48.17, 1:11.40, 1:35.44, 1:48.18)

$2 Mutuel Prices:			
5 – MONA ROSE	13.20	—	—
3 – INISH GLORA		—	—
1 – CLASSIC STAMP		—	—

$2 EXACTOR 5–3 PAID $28.40

B. f, (Feb), by Gold Legend – Royal Charmer , by Lomond . Trainer Barnett Robert E. Bred by Paul O''Brien & Frank O''Brien (Ont-C).

MONA ROSE stalked the pace from the rail, remained unhurried to the stretch, angled out and rallied three-wide and got by the leader in the late stages. INISH GLORA pressed the pacesetter early, moved to the fore on the backstretch, dueled inside two others, shook clear approaching the furlong marker then failed to contain the winner. CLASSIC STAMP moved off the rail and up between horses on the backstretch, dueled to the stretch, was no match for INISH GLORA approaching the eighth pole and evened out. STRAIT FROM TEXAS broke alertly and had a clear early lead, was joined on the backstretch, dueled three-wide through the turn and into the stretch then tired.

Owners– 1, O'Brien P and F; 2, Costigan Robert J; 3, Sorokolit William A Sr; 4, Michael James A

Trainers– 1, Barnett Robert E; 2, Benson MacDonald; 3, Hopmans C C Jr; 4, Buttigieg Paul M

Scratched– One for Rose (20Jun04 ^{3}WO ^{1}) , Raylene (12Jun04 ^{8}Stp^{1})

$1 Pick Three (5–4–5) Paid $250.00 ; Pick Three Pool $8,456 .

EIGHTH RACE
Woodbine
JULY 17, 2004

1⅛ MILES. (Turf) (1.45^{1}) 105TH RUNNING OF THE TORONTO CUP HANDICAP. Grade III. Purse $150,000 FOR THREE-YEAR-OLDS. By subscription of $150 each to accompany the nomination and an additional $1,500 when making entry; with $150,000 added, plus all fees to be divided: 60% to the winner, 20% to second, 11% to third, 6% to fourth and 3% to fifth. Weights, Saturday, July 10, 2004. Final entries to be made through the entry box no later than 11:30 a.m. on Thursday, July 15, 2004. Closed Wednesday, June 30, 2004 with 24 nominations. Plus up to $12,420 Ontario Sire/Canadian Bred Breeder Awards. (Rail at 20 feet).

Value of Race: $168,600 Winner $101,160; second $33,720; third $18,546; fourth $10,116; fifth $5,058. Mutuel Pool $130,712.00 Exactor Pool $54,237.00 Triactor Pool $73,582.00

Last Raced	Horse	M/Eqt.	A.	Wt	PP	St	¼	½	¾	Str	Fin	Jockey	Odds $1
27Jun04 ^{9}WO^{8}	Silver Ticket	L	3	117	3	4	$4^{1\frac{1}{2}}$	$4^{1\frac{1}{2}}$	3^{hd}	1^{hd}	$1^{1\frac{3}{4}}$	Kabel T K	1.65
27Jun04 ^{6}WO^{3}	Bachelor Blues	L	3	118	4	3	$1^{2\frac{1}{2}}$	$1^{3\frac{1}{2}}$	1^{3}	2^{3}	$2^{2\frac{1}{4}}$	Ramsammy E	12.10
27Jun04 ^{6}WO^{2}	Burst of Fire	L b	3	116	2	8	3^{hd}	3^{hd}	4^{2}	4^{4}	3^{2}	Callaghan S	20.95
27Jun04 ^{1}WO^{1}	Honolua Storm	L	3	118	7	5	2^{2}	$2^{1\frac{1}{2}}$	2^{1}	3^{hd}	$4^{1\frac{1}{4}}$	Jones J	7.30
27Jun04 ^{11}WO^{1}	Gangster	L b	3	115	10	6	10	$7^{\frac{1}{2}}$	$7^{2\frac{1}{2}}$	7^{2}	5^{1}	McAleney J S	10.50
25Jun04 ^{4}WO^{5}	Northtobaghdad	L	3	110	1	10	6^{hd}	$5^{\frac{1}{2}}$	6^{1}	$6^{\frac{1}{2}}$	$6^{\frac{1}{2}}$	Brimo J	55.05
23Jun04 ^{8}Mth^{1}	Dynalympic	L f	3	116	6	7	5^{hd}	6^{2}	$5^{1\frac{1}{2}}$	$5^{1\frac{1}{2}}$	$7^{\frac{1}{2}}$	Husbands P	1.70
18Jun04 ^{5}WO^{6}	Kintu	L b	3	111	5	9	9^{hd}	10	8^{2}	$9^{2\frac{1}{2}}$	8^{nk}	Da Silva E R	48.80
27Jun04 ^{6}WO^{5}	Lone Arrow	L	3	114	9	1	$8^{\frac{1}{2}}$	9^{1}	$9^{1\frac{1}{2}}$	$8^{\frac{1}{2}}$	$9^{1\frac{1}{2}}$	Dos Ramos R A	37.05
27Jun04 ^{9}WO^{7}	Alleged Ruler	L	3	115	8	2	7^{2}	8^{hd}	10	10	10	Landry R C	13.50

OFF AT 4:27 Start Good . Won driving. Course good.

TIME $:23^{2}$, $:46^{1}$, $1:10^{2}$, $1:34^{4}$, $1:47^{1}$ (:23.54, :46.25, 1:10.49, 1:34.87, 1:47.35)

$2 Mutuel Prices:			
3 – SILVER TICKET	5.30	3.50	2.80
4 – BACHELOR BLUES		8.70	4.70
2 – BURST OF FIRE			7.40

$2 EXACTOR 3–4 PAID $47.90 $2 TRIACTOR 3–4–2 PAID $295.00

B. g, (Mar), by Silver Deputy – Go First Class , by Easy Goer . Trainer Frostad Mark. Bred by Sam-Son Farm (Ont-C).

SILVER TICKET stalked from the third path, responded to rousing upper stretch, collared BACHELOR BLUES a furlong out and drove clear. BACHELOR BLUES led quickly, set a reserved pace to upper stretch, quickened, but failed to stave off the winner with a furlong to run. BURST OF FIRE stalked the leader from the rail, began to close late turn then was all out in the stretch. HONOLUA STORM stalked from the second path, closed late turn then flattened out in the late stages. GANGSTER well back early, closed late on the turn and continued on with a mild rally but failed reach contention. NORTHTOBAGHDAD raced midpack between horses then lacked a late response. DYNALYMPIC rated early, came three-wide through the turn, was set down at the top of the stretch but flattened out. KINTU was well back early, saved ground then lacked a closing response. LONE ARROW raced far off the early pace, came through the turn along the fourth path then lacked a rally. ALLEGED RULER raced along the second path and was through early.

Owners– 1, Sam-Son Farms; 2, Schettine William C; 3, Sam-Son Farms; 4, Attfield Roger L and Werner William; 5, Goldmart Farms; 6, Silvera Laurie; 7, John R Kelley Jr and Carol Griseto; 8, Oxbridge Farm; 9, Attfield Roger L and Werner William; 10, Chiefswood Stable

Trainers– 1, Frostad Mark; 2, Carroll Josie; 3, Frostad Mark; 4, Attfield Roger L; 5, Attard Sid C; 6, Silvera Laurie; 7, Dickinson Michael W; 8, Burke Ronald G; 9, Attfield Roger L; 10, Coatrieux Eric

$1 Pick Three (2–2–3) Paid $60.00 ; Pick Three Pool $9,326 .

EIGHTH RACE
Woodbine
JULY 25, 2004

1⅜ MILES. (Turf) (2.12^{1}) 2ND RUNNING OF THE CHINESE CULTURAL CENTRE. Grade II. Purse $300,000 FOR THREE-YEAR-OLDS AND UPWARD. By subscription of $300 each which shall accompany the nomination and an additional $3,000 when making entry; with $300,000 added, plus all fees to be divided: 60% to the winner, 20% to second, 11% to third, 6% to fourth and 3% to fifth. Weights: Three-Year-Olds, 118 lbs. Older, 124 lbs. Winners of $750,000 at a mile or over since October 1, 2003, additional 2 lbs.; Non-winners of $100,000 three times at a mile or over in 2003–2004, 3 lbs.; Of $100,000 twice at a mile or over in 2003–2004, 5 lbs.; Of $100,000 once at a mile or over in 2003–2004, 7 lbs.; Of $75,000 at a mile or over in 2003–2004, 9 lbs. (No Canadian Bred Allowance.) Final entries to be made through the entry box no later than 10:30 a.m. on Friday, July 23, 2004. Plus up to $15,180 Ontario Sire/Canadian Bred Breeder Awards. Closed Wednesday, July 7, 2004 with 31 nominations.

Value of Race: $333,300 Winner $199,980; second $66,660; third $36,663; fourth $19,998; fifth $9,999. Mutuel Pool $189,354.00 Exactor Pool $91,291.00 Triactor Pool $110,926.00

Last Raced	Horse	M/Eqt.	A.	Wt	PP	¼	½	¾	1	Str	Fin	Jockey	Odds $1
19Jun04 ^{8}WO^{2}	Shoal Water	L	4	116	5	2^{1}	2^{1}	2^{1}	2^{1}	1^{1}	1^{nk}	Kabel T K	5.35
1Jly04 ^{8}WO^{1}	Mobil	L	4	121	1	1^{1}	$1^{1\frac{1}{2}}$	1^{1}	$1^{\frac{1}{2}}$	$2^{3\frac{1}{2}}$	$2^{2\frac{1}{4}}$	Jones J	6.55
28Sep03 ^{8}WO^{4}	Strut the Stage	L bf	6	121	2	4^{hd}	6^{hd}	7^{1}	$7^{\frac{1}{2}}$	$4^{1\frac{1}{2}}$	$3^{\frac{3}{4}}$	Callaghan S	6.50
1Jly04 ^{2}WO^{3}	Control Tower	L b	5	115	4	$3^{2\frac{1}{2}}$	3^{1}	$3^{\frac{1}{2}}$	$3^{1\frac{1}{2}}$	3^{hd}	4^{2}	Ramsammy E	24.70
3Jly04 ^{8}CD^{2}	Perfect Soul-Ire	L b	6	124	3	5^{hd}	5^{1}	6^{hd}	5^{hd}	5^{1}	$5^{3\frac{1}{4}}$	Landry R C	1.60
19Jun04 ^{8}WO^{1}	Slew Valley	L	7	119	8	$6^{2\frac{1}{2}}$	4^{hd}	$4^{\frac{1}{2}}$	4^{hd}	6^{2}	$6^{\frac{1}{2}}$	McAleney J S	3.65
3Jly04 ^{10}Mth^{11}	Bowman Mill	L	6	119	7	$7^{3\frac{1}{2}}$	$7^{1\frac{1}{2}}$	5^{hd}	$6^{1\frac{1}{2}}$	$7^{2\frac{1}{2}}$	$7^{\frac{1}{2}}$	Husbands P	12.65
27Dec03 ^{11}Crc^{7}	Cetewayo	L b	10	115	6	8	8	8	8	8	8	Blanc B	12.25

OFF AT 4:41 Start Good . Won driving. Course firm.

TIME :24, :48^{2}, 1:12^{3}, 1:36^{4}, 2:00^{1}, 2:12^{1} (:24.19, :48.56, 1:12.72, 1:36.82, 2:00.31, 2:12.37)

(New Course Record)

$2 Mutuel Prices:				
	5 – SHOAL WATER	12.70	5.70	5.40
	1 – MOBIL		7.90	5.90
	2 – STRUT THE STAGE			5.50

$2 EXACTOR 5–1 PAID $89.00 $2 TRIACTOR 5–1–2 PAID $515.40

B. g, (Feb), by Smart Strike – Puffin Island , by Pleasant Colony . Trainer Frostad Mark. Bred by Sam–Son Farm (Ont–C).

SHOAL WATER stalked the pace from the second path, edged up outside MOBIL midway through the far turn, engaged that one in earnest at the top of the stretch, took a short lead then held him safe under steady pressure. MOBIL set a reserved pace from the rail, was engaged at the top of the stretch, was well-headed with a furlong to run but finished very gamely. STRUT THE STAGE in hand early along the rail, angled out at the top of the stretch and rallied willingly. CONTROL TOWER stalked from the rail and was always in striking range then launched an all-out drive in the stretch but hung. PERFECT SOUL (IRE) raced midpack and was four-wide early, gained slightly three-deep on the far turn but hung in the stretch. SLEW VALLEY ..stalked the pace from the fourth path then evened out In the stretch. BOWMAN MILL was well back early and under strong restraint, raced along the second path and lacked a response when asked. CETEWAYO moved to the rail shortly after leaving the gate, saved ground to the backstretch then moved four-wide and trailed to the finish.

Owners– 1, Sam-Son Farms; 2, Schickedanz Gustav; 3, Sam-Son Farms; 4, Pin Oak Stable LLC; 5, Fipke Charles E; 6, Rich Meadow Farm and Burkhard Alan; 7, Chandler Dr John A; 8, Chandler Dr John A

Trainers– 1, Frostad Mark; 2, Keogh Michael; 3, Frostad Mark; 4, Pierce Malcolm; 5, Attfield Roger L; 6, Baker Reade; 7, Dickinson Michael W; 8, Dickinson Michael W

$1 Pick Three (4–7–5) Paid $599.80 ; Pick Three Pool $8,147 .

NINTH RACE
Fort Erie
JULY 18, 2004

1$\frac{3}{16}$ MILES. (1.53^{1}) 69TH RUNNING OF THE PRINCE OF WALES. Purse $500,000 For Three–Year–Old Canadian–Breds. By subscription of $150 each to accompany the nomination by February 1st, 2003 [417 Nominations]; second subscription of $500 by February 1st, 2004[186 remained eligible, 4 supplements]; third subscription of $1,000 by July 1st, 2004; and an additional $5,000 when making final entry at the closing time then in effect for overnight events. Horses not originally nominated may be made eligible by payment of a late nomination fee of $7,500 on or before February 1st, 2004, or $15,000 on or before May 15th, 2004. The added money and all fees to be divided as set forth by the Association. Closed with 17 nominations. All monies received from the original nomination, February 1st, 2003 and the February 1st, 2004 payments will be divided equally between the gross purses of the Queens' Plate, Prince of Wales and Breeders' Stakes. Weight: Colts and Geldings 126 lbs.;Fillies 122 lbs. $197,000 of this purse has been provided through the Thoroughbred Improvement Program/Canadian Thoroughbred Horse Society. Plus up to $17,940 Breeder Awards for the 1st, 2nd, and 3rd. place finishers.

Value of Race: $500,000 Winner $300,000; second $100,000; third $50,000; fourth $25,000; fifth $15,000; sixth $5,000; seventh $5,000. Mutuel Pool $174,868.00 Exactor Pool $63,735.00 Triactor Pool $82,646.00 Superfecta Pool $14,910.00

Last Raced	Horse	M/Eqt.	A.	Wt	PP	St	¼	½	¾	Str	Fin	Jockey	Odds $1
27Jun04 ^{9}WO^{2}	A Bit O'Gold	L	3	126	4	4	$3^{\frac{1}{2}}$	3^{hd}	2^{hd}	2^{10}	1^{hd}	Jones J	1.15
27Jun04 ^{9}WO^{1}	Niigon	L f	3	126	3	3	1^{hd}	1^{hd}	$1^{2\frac{1}{2}}$	1^{1}	$2^{15\frac{1}{4}}$	Landry R C	1.25
27Jun04 ^{9}WO^{5}	His Smoothness	L f	3	126	5	5	5^{hd}	$5^{2\frac{1}{2}}$	4^{hd}	$3^{1\frac{1}{2}}$	$3^{1\frac{3}{4}}$	McKnight J	20.70
27Jun04 ^{9}WO^{4}	Just in Case Jimmy	L b	3	126	1	6	4^{1}	$4^{2\frac{1}{2}}$	5^{hd}	5^{1}	4^{nk}	Dos Ramos R A	11.90
27Jun04 ^{9}WO^{9}	Copper Trail	L	3	126	6	7	7	7	7	4^{hd}	$5^{2\frac{3}{4}}$	Somsanith N	18.45
13Jun04 ^{7}WO^{5}	Picadilly Bay	L	3	126	7	1	6^{hd}	6^{hd}	6^{3}	6^{8}	$6^{9\frac{1}{4}}$	Montpellier C	11.35
1Jly04 ^{3}WO^{1}	One to Celebrate	L b	3	126	2	2	2^{2}	$2^{1\frac{1}{2}}$	3^{2}	7	7	Pimentel R M	19.10

OFF AT 5:08 Start Good . Won driving. Track sloppy.

TIME :23^{2}, :47^{3}, 1:12^{2}, 1:37^{3}, 1:57^{3} (:23.52, :47.79, 1:12.49, 1:37.75, 1:57.69)

$2 Mutuel Prices:				
	4 – A BIT O'GOLD	4.30	2.20	2.20
	3 – NIIGON		2.50	2.10
	5 – HIS SMOOTHNESS			4.60

$2 EXACTOR 4–3 PAID $5.80 $2 TRIACTOR 4–3–5 PAID $39.40
$1 SUPERFECTA 4–3–5–1 PAID $52.10

Ch. g, (Mar), by Gold Fever – Annasan , by Corporate Report . Trainer Day–Phillips Catherine. Bred by Beclawat Stable (Ont–C).

A BIT O'GOLD never far back, stalked the leaders from off the rail into the clubhouse turn, kept contact then tracked the leader through the turn, began to close in the stretch drive, got alongside the leader inside the final sixteenth and edged a nose in front at the wire. NIIGON had early speed to vie for the lead outside of rival, held a slim edge after going a half, cleared into the far turn, opened a gap, held it into the final furlong then was full out in a 4-path drive but outnosed in the final yards. HIS SMOOTHNESS off the early pace, was in striking distance into the far turn, could not match the leaders in the final half but came on to best the rest with a 3-path stretch run. JUST IN CASE JIMMY on the inside early, stalked the leaders into the far turn, then lost ground and finished inside through the stretch. COPPER TRAIL trailed while inside rival in the early going, continued to tag along at the back of the pack, made a run to catch the show spot but needed more. PICADILLY BAY was off the pace throughout and not a threat. ONE TO CELEBRATE on the inside and pressing the pace, kept at it for five then backed off and faded.

Owners– 1, The Two Bit Racing Stable; 2, Chiefswood Stable; 3, Come By Chance Stable; 4, Attfield Roger L and Werner William; 5, Stolar Stables; 6, Wellwood Gary and Titchner L; 7, Curraghmore Farm and Formal Racing Stable

Trainers– 1, Day-Phillips Catherine; 2, Coatrieux Eric; 3, Day James E; 4, Attfield Roger L; 5, Day James E; 6, Ross John A; 7, Baker Reade

$1 Pick Three (1–2–4) Paid $7.95 ; Pick Three Pool $3,641 .

EIGHTH RACE
Woodbine
AUGUST 2, 2004

6 FURLONGS. (Turf) (1.07³) 16TH RUNNING OF THE ROYAL NORTH HANDICAP. Grade III. Purse $150,000 (plus $50,000 Other Sources) FOR FILLIES AND MARES, THREE-YEAR-OLDS AND UPWARD. By subscription of $150 each which shall accompany the nomination and an additional $1,500 when making entry; with $150,000 added and an additional $50,000 for Canadian Breds, plus all fees to be divided:60% to the winner, 20% to second, 11% to third, 6% to fourth and 3% to fifth. Weights, Saturday, July 24, 2004. Final entries to be made through the entry box no later than 11:30 a.m. on Saturday, July 31, 2004. $50,000 for Canadian Breds from the Thoroughbred Improvement Program and Canadian Thoroughbred Horse Society. Plus up to $11,040 Ontario Sire/Canadian Bred Breeder Awards. Closed Wednesday, July 14, 2004 with 27 nominations. (Rail at 10 feet).

Value of Race: $170,550 Winner $100,530; second $33,510; third $18,431; fourth $13,053; fifth $5,026. Mutuel Pool $142,380.00 Exactor Pool $64,658.00 Triactor Pool $88,519.00

Last Raced	Horse	M/Eqt.	A.	Wt	PP	St	¼	½	Str	Fin	Jockey	Odds $1
11Jly04 4WO1	Hour of Justice	L	4	118	4	1	2hd	2hd	13½	13½	Kabel T K	0.80
10Jly04 8Cnl4	With Patience	L f	5	118	5	9	7½	72	31½	21¾	Jones J	8.30
3Jly04 9Pha6	Boozin' Susan	L	5	120	8	7	61	5hd	2hd	31¼	Ramsammy E	3.50
10Jly04 9WO1	Velvet Snow	L	3	110	2	3	5hd	4½	5½	41¾	Fraser C	11.85
7Jly04 4WO1	Pucker	L	4	114	3	5	4hd	6hd	61½	5½	Baird J	42.35
3Jun04 3WO3	Swift of Flight	L	4	109	7	2	31½	1hd	4½	61¼	Pimentel R M	43.25
3Jly04 9Cnl3	Glowing Breeze	L f	4	114	9	8	9	9	83	7½	Decarlo C P	15.85
3Jly04 8WO2	Sweet Problem	L	3	114	6	6	8hd	8½	7hd	84	McAleney J S	6.70
11Jly04 4WO8	Leading Role	L f	6	115	1	4	1hd	32	9	9	Landry R C	53.80

OFF AT 4:26 Start Good For All But WITH PATIENCE, SWEET PROBLEM. Won driving. Course firm.

TIME :22³, :45², :56², 1:07⁴ (:22.67, :45.47, :56.40, 1:07.83)

$2 Mutuel Prices:

4 – HOUR OF JUSTICE	3.60	2.60	2.40
5 – WITH PATIENCE		6.40	3.70
8 – BOOZIN' SUSAN			3.00

$2 EXACTOR 4–5 PAID $19.20 $2 TRIACTOR 4–5–8 PAID $54.10

B. f, (Apr), by Lit de Justice – Dark Hours, by Dynaformer. Trainer Keogh Michael. Bred by Adena Springs (Ky).

HOUR OF JUSTICE dueled between horses, shook clear at the top of the stretch then held sway under a light drive. WITH PATIENCE broke outward, rated early, moved out between horses near the 1/4 pole and was all out through the stretch. BOOZIN' SUSAN stalked three-wide, closed at the top of the stretch then flattened out late. VELVET SNOW raced midpack in hand, closed to the top of the stretch but lacked the necessary stretch response. PUCKER stalked between horses, was in range at the top of the stretch but hung. SWIFT OF FLIGHT dueled three-wide, held a slight lead at the top of the stretch then tired in the late stages. GLOWING BREEZE well back early, raced four-wide on the turn then lacked a rally. SWEET PROBLEM bobbled leaving the gate, remained well back early, raced three-deep and lacked a closing response. LEADING ROLE dueled from the rail then tired at the top of the stretch.

Owners– 1, Stronach Stables; 2, Hendriks Elizabeth M; 3, Weber Larry; 4, Di Giulio Frank D Jr; 5, Spring Farm; 6, Sam-Son Farms; 7, Bushwood Stables; 8, Sangara K K; 9, Colne Farm Casselman Gail and Mitchell J

Trainers– 1, Keogh Michael; 2, Hendriks Elizabeth M; 3, Dickinson Michael W; 4, Tiller Robert P; 5, Ranford Kathryn; 6, Frostad Mark; 7, Motion H Graham; 8, Richards Lorne; 9, Casselman Gail

$1 Pick Three (2–5–4) Paid $218.95; Pick Three Pool $10,082.

NINTH RACE
Woodbine
AUGUST 8, 2004

1½ MILES. (Turf) (2.25³) 114TH RUNNING OF THE BREEDERS'. Purse $500,000 FOR THREE-YEAR-OLDS, FOALED IN CANADA. Weight; Colts and Geldings 126 lbs. Fillies, 121 lbs. By subscription of $150 each to accompany the nomination by February 1st, 2003 (417 nominations); second subscription of $500 by February 1st, 2004 (186 remainedeligible, plus 4 supplements at $7,500 each); third subscription of $1,000 by May 15th, 2004 (68 remained eligible, plus 4 supplements at $15,000 each); and an additional $5,000 due at time of final entry. Final entries to be made through the entry box nolater than 10:30 a.m. on Friday, August 6, 2004. Total purse to be divided: 60% to the winner, 20% to second, 11% to third, 6% to fourth and 3% to fifth. All monies received from the original nomination (February 1st, 2003) and the February 1st, 2004 payments will be divided equally between the gross purses of the Queen's Plate, Prince of Wales and Breeders' Stakes. Plus up to $17,940 Ontario Sire/Canadian Bred Breeder Awards.

Value of Race: $500,000 Winner $300,000; second $100,000; third $55,000; fourth $30,000; fifth $15,000. Mutuel Pool $230,891.00 Exactor Pool $92,710.00 Triactor Pool $153,716.00

Last Raced	Horse	M/Eqt.	A.	Wt	PP	¼	½	1	1¼	Str	Fin	Jockey	Odds $1
18Jly04 9FE1	A Bit O'Gold	L	3	126	4	2hd	2½	2hd	21½	11½	11¾	Jones J	2.45
17Jly04 8WO3	Burst of Fire	L b	3	126	3	12	14½	11½	11½	22½	21¼	Callaghan S	18.45
17Jly04 8WO1	Silver Ticket	L	3	126	6	5hd	41	4½	31	32½	31¼	Kabel T K	1.55
30Jun04 9AP1	Lord Carmen	L f	3	126	10	9hd	91½	6½	4½	41½	4¾	Ramsammy E	7.75
11Jly04 7WO3	Rainbows for Luck	L	3	126	9	11	10hd	10hd	6½	51	52	McAleney J S	6.35
17Jly04 8WO9	Lone Arrow	L	3	126	11	10hd	72	81	72	63½	63¾	Dos Ramos R A	47.85
24Jly04 3WO3	Hunt the Rainbow		3	126	1	8hd	8hd	91	81½	84	7½	Da Silva E R	38.65
25Jly04 4WO2	Strike Em Hard	L b	3	126	2	4½	51	5hd	52	7½	83½	Montpellier C	28.40
18Jly04 9FE3	His Smoothness	L f	3	126	5	31½	3½	3hd	11	101	9nk	McKnight J	22.95
24Jly04 3WO1	Cavans Lane	L f	3	126	7	62	6hd	7hd	92	9½	10¾	Husbands P	10.35
27Jun04 6WO4	Witness This	L	3	126	8	7hd	11	11	10hd	11	11	Luciani D	60.10

OFF AT 5:17 Start Good. Won driving. Course firm.

TIME :24³, :48⁴, 1:14, 1:38³, 2:03, 2:27 (:24.61, :48.95, 1:14.16, 1:38.79, 2:03.15, 2:27.15)

$2 Mutuel Prices:

4 – A BIT O'GOLD	6.90	4.50	2.70
3 – BURST OF FIRE		14.30	5.20
6 – SILVER TICKET			2.30

$2 EXACTOR 4–3 PAID $81.20 $2 TRIACTOR 4–3–6 PAID $170.60

Ch. g, (Mar), by Gold Fever – Annasan, by Corporate Report. Trainer Day–Phillips Catherine. Bred by Beclawat Stable (Ont–C).

A BIT O'GOLD stalked the pace, bid outside BURST OF FIRE at the 3/16th pole, drew clear quickly then held sway under pressure. BURST OF FIRE set a reserved pace from the outset, was engaged upper stretch but could not match strides with the winner but stayed gamely for the place. SILVER TICKET stalked three-wide then launched an all-out rally in the stretch. LORD CARMEN closed between horses on the far turn, angled out sharply at the top of the stretch then finished gamely to no avail. RAINBOWS FOR LUCK, unhurried early, circled four-wide on the far turn, came widest into the stretch and hung. LONE ARROW traced midpack, circled five-wide late turn but evened out in the stretch. HUNT THE RAINBOW, always far back, saved ground but never reached contention. STRIKE EM HARD stalked from the rail, was roused at the top of the stretch then flattened out. HIS SMOOTHNESS stalked the pace to the far turn then faded quickly between horses. CAVANS LANE raced midpack while three-deep and lacked a rally. WITNESS THIS, always far back, lacked a closing response.

Owners– 1, The Two Bit Racing Stable; 2, Sam-Son Farms; 3, Sam-Son Farms; 4, Calabrese Frank C; 5, Sam-Son Farms; 6, Attfield Roger L and Werner William; 7, Sam-Son Farms; 8, Dominion Bloodstock Ball Derek Galbraith Hugh and Peacock G; 9, Come By Chance Stable; 10, Melnyk Eugene and Laura and Bristow Iris; 11, Gaillardia Racing LLC

Trainers– 1, Day-Phillips Catherine; 2, Frostad Mark; 3, Frostad Mark; 4, Carroll Josie; 5, Frostad Mark; 6, Attfield Roger L; 7, Frostad Mark; 8, Cotey David; 9, Day James E; 10, Bell David R; 11, Casse Mark

$1 Pick Three (10–7–4) Paid $246.80; Pick Three Pool $7,478.

EIGHTH RACE
Woodbine
AUGUST 21, 2004

7 FURLONGS. (1.20^{3}) 49TH RUNNING OF THE DUCHESS. Grade III. Purse $150,000 (plus $50,000 Other Sources) FOR THREE-YEAR-OLD FILLIES. By subscription of $150 each which shall accompany the nomination and an additional $1,500 when making entry; with $150,000 added and an additional $50,000 for Canadian Breds, plus all fees to be divided: 60% to the winner, 20%to second, 11% to third, 6% to fourth and 3% to fifth. Weight, 123 lbs. Winners of a sweepstakes of $75,000 three times in 2004 additional 2 lbs.; Non-winners of a sweepstakes of $75,000 twice in 2004 allowed 3 lbs.; Of a sweepstakes of $75,000 once in 2004, 5 lbs.; Of a sweepstakes of $75,000 in 2003, 7 lbs.; Of $47,100, 9 lbs. (No Canadian Bred Allowance.) Final entries to be made through the entry box no later than 11:30 a.m. on Thursday, August 19, 2004. Plus up to $12,420 Ontario Sire/Canadian BredBreeder Awards. Plus $50,000 for Canadian Breds from the Thoroughbred Improvement Program and the Canadian Thoroughbred Horse Society. Closed Wednesday, August 4, 2004 with 21 nominations.

Value of Race: $206,150 Winner $126,390; second $42,130; third $23,172; fourth $9,639; fifth $4,819. Mutuel Pool $98,590.00 Exactor Pool $66,575.00

Last Raced	Horse	M/Eqt.	A.	Wt	PP	St	¼	½	Str	Fin	Jockey	Odds $1
28Jly04 ^{3}WO^{1}	Blonde Executive	L f	3	123	2	2	$1^{\frac{1}{2}}$	$1^{\frac{1}{2}}$	$1^{1\frac{1}{2}}$	1^{nk}	Dos Ramos R A	2.40
6Aug04 ^{4}WO^{2}	Silver Bird	L b	3	118	5	3	4^{3}	$4^{3\frac{1}{2}}$	2^{hd}	2^{4}	McAleney J S	1.75
7Aug04 ^{7}WO^{2}	Search the Church	L	3	114	4	1	$3^{2\frac{1}{2}}$	$3^{1\frac{1}{2}}$	$3^{4\frac{1}{2}}$	$3^{2\frac{3}{4}}$	Ramsammy E	12.25
1Aug04 ^{9}Mth^{7}	Cherish Destiny	L b	3	116	1	5	5	5	5	$4^{1\frac{3}{4}}$	Kabel T K	7.90
10Jly04 ^{8}Crc^{3}	Boston Express	L b	3	117	3	4	$2^{1\frac{1}{2}}$	$2^{2\frac{1}{2}}$	$4^{2\frac{1}{2}}$	5	Husbands P	1.70

OFF AT 4:24 Start Good For All But CHERISH DESTINY. Won driving. Track fast.

TIME :22, :44^{2}, 1:09^{4}, 1:23^{1} (:22.18, :44.49, 1:09.82, 1:23.26)

$2 Mutuel Prices:

2 – BLONDE EXECUTIVE	6.80	2.90	2.70
5 – SILVER BIRD		2.60	2.10
4 – SEARCH THE CHURCH			3.20

$2 EXACTOR 2–5 PAID $14.20

Ch. f, (Feb), by Bold Executive – Dream Smartly , by Smarten . Trainer Loney Radlie A. Bred by Bruno Brothers Farm (Ont-C).

BLONDE EXECUTIVE sprinted up quickly to take a short lead, was under pressure from BOSTON EXPRESS through the backstretch and quickened on the turn, turned back a challenge from SEARCH THE CHURCH at the top of the stretch then held SILVER BIRD safe under left-handed encouragement through the final sixteenth. SILVER BIRD unhurried early and well off the rail, closed on the third path late turn, came four-wide into the stretch, launched her rally and finished determinedly but could not get by the winner. SEARCH THE CHURCH stalked the pace from the rail, was hustled from the 1/4 pole and bid inside BLONDE EXECUTIVE at the top of the stretch but was no match for that one and flattened out. CHERISH DESTINY broke slightly outward and was steadied, remained unhurried while saving ground, angled out at the head of the stretch but had too little too late. BOSTON EXPRESS pressed the pace on the backstretch and early turn, chased after the leader but tired at the top of the stretch.

Owners– 1, Bruno Brothers Farms; 2, McAlpine James; 3, Jim Dandy Stable; 4, David J Lanzman Racing Inc; 5, Brooks Jack G

Trainers– 1, Loney Radlie A; 2, Baker Reade; 3, Attard Sid C; 4, O'Neill Doug; 5, Jerkens James A

$1 Pick Three (2–4–2) Paid $61.25 ; Pick Three Pool $9,854 .

NINTH RACE
Northlands
AUGUST 28, 2004

1⅜ MILES. (2.15^{4}) 75TH RUNNING OF THE CANADIAN DERBY. Grade III. Purse $250,000 FOR THREE YEAR OLDS. By subscription of $500.00 each and a further payment of $2,500.00 to pass the entry box and an additional $2,000.00 to pass scratch time. Guaranteed with $157,500 to the winner, $50,000 to second, $25,000 to third, $12,500 to fourth, and $5,000 to fifth. Preference conditions apply. Weights: Fillies...121lbs. Colts & Geldings...126lbs. Field limited to 12 starters.

Value of Race: $250,000 Winner $157,500; second $50,000; third $18,750; third $18,750; fifth $5,000. Mutuel Pool $129,026.00 Triactor Pool $58,406.00 Exacta Pool $37,148.00 Superfecta Pool $25,929.00

Last Raced	Horse	M/Eqt.	A.	Wt	PP	¼	½	¾	1	Str	Fin	Jockey	Odds $1
25Jly04 ^{4}WO^{1}	Organ Grinder	L	3	126	3	6^{1}	$5^{1\frac{1}{2}}$	$3^{1\frac{1}{2}}$	2^{hd}	2^{hd}	1^{hd}	McAleney J S	0.85
24Jly04 ^{9}NP^{1}	Controlled Meeting	L bf	3	126	10	3^{1}	1^{hd}	2^{hd}	1^{hd}	1^{1}	$2^{3\frac{1}{4}}$	Hamel R	34.05
14Aug04 ^{7}NP^{1}	[DH] Bonspiel		3	126	2	10^{4}	10^{2}	8^{hd}	7^{1}	$4^{\frac{1}{2}}$	3	Iammarino M P	29.70
14Aug04 ^{10}Hst^{2}	[DH] Cariboo Prospector	L b	3	126	7	$7^{1\frac{1}{2}}$	$7^{1\frac{1}{2}}$	$4^{\frac{1}{2}}$	4^{1}	3^{2}	3^{1}	Walcott R	19.70
13Aug04 ^{1}Dmr^{5}	Plenty of Heat	L b	3	126	9	9^{1}	$8^{\frac{1}{2}}$	9^{1}	5^{hd}	5^{3}	$5^{\frac{3}{4}}$	Puglisi I	16.65
7Aug04 ^{8}NP^{1}	Kat Kool	L	3	126	11	8^{hd}	$9^{1\frac{1}{2}}$	10^{2}	8^{hd}	6^{1}	6^{1}	Welch Q K	8.70
14Aug04 ^{10}Hst^{3}	Joyride	L	3	126	5	11	11	11	10^{6}	$7^{2\frac{1}{2}}$	$7^{6\frac{1}{2}}$	Loseth C	25.75
2Aug04 ^{8}AsD^{1}	Royalty Boy	b	3	126	6	2^{hd}	6^{hd}	6^{1}	6^{hd}	8^{hd}	$8^{4\frac{1}{2}}$	Simard R E	5.45
2Aug04 ^{2}Hst^{1}	Lord Samarai	L b	3	126	8	$5^{\frac{1}{2}}$	2^{2}	1^{hd}	$3^{\frac{1}{2}}$	$9^{2\frac{1}{2}}$	9^{2}	Wilson D H	9.45
22Aug04 ^{3}Hst^{1}	Proud Son	L	3	126	4	4^{hd}	3^{hd}	$5^{\frac{1}{2}}$	$9^{1\frac{1}{2}}$	10^{20}	$10^{24\frac{1}{4}}$	Shirley S H	34.10
14Aug04 ^{8}NP^{1}	Overact	L	3	121	1	1^{hd}	4^{hd}	7^{hd}	11	11	11	Skelly R V	13.80

[DH]–Dead Heat.

OFF AT 4:48 Start Good . Won driving. Track fast.

TIME :23^{4}, :48^{2}, 1:15, 1:42^{1}, 2:08^{3}, 2:22^{3} (:23.80, :48.40, 1:15.00, 1:42.20, 2:08.60, 2:22.60)

$2 Mutuel Prices:

3 – ORGAN GRINDER	3.70	3.30	3.00
10 – CONTROLLED MEETING		19.90	11.90
2 – [DH] BONSPIEL			4.70
7 – [DH] CARIBOO PROSPECTOR			4.80

$2 TRIACTOR 3–10–2 PAID $844.30 $2 TRIACTOR 3–10–7 PAID $646.00
$2 EXACTA 3–10 PAID $137.40 $2 SUPERFECTA 3–10–2–All PAID $649.50
$2 SUPERFECTA 3–10–7–All PAID $304.85

Gr/ro. c, (Mar), by Grindstone – Caveanella , by Caveat . Trainer Attard Sid C. Bred by Nancy B Stone (Ky).

ORGAN GRINDER rail, bid 3 wide 3/8 pole, rallied stretch, all out, prevailed late. CONTROLLED MEETING wide early, vied for lead, gamely, led late, gamely, outfinished. BONSPIEL rail, evenly, steady gain, rallied stretch, altered course. CARIBOO PROSPECTOR wide early, gaining, bid 1/4 pole, vied, weakened stretch. PLENTY OF HEAT evenly, 3 wide, gaining backstretch, evenly stretch. KAT KOOL 5 wide early, dropped back, gaining backstretch, mild bid. JOYRIDE slow early, rallied 3/8 pole, gaining, evenly stretch. ROYALTY BOY vied for lead early, between horses, dropped back. LORD SAMARAI 4 wide early, bid 3rd turn, vied, weakened 3/8 pole, gave way. PROUD SON close up early, outside, weakened backstretch, dropped back. OVERACT rail, close up, dropped back backstretch, eased.

Owners– 1, S and B Stable; 2, Wiest Rick; 3, McFadyen Jim; 4, George Gilbert Raymond Hanson Glyn Kelly and Karen Chan; 5, Elick John W; 6, Derby Stable Red Ron Farms and Tosh David; 7, Bennett Mr and Mrs R J; 8, Antingham Derrick Propp Donald and Gromoff Brian; 9, Canyon Farms; 10, Hart Kim N; 11, Exclusive Stable and Hanson Raymond

Trainers– 1, Attard Sid C; 2, Diodoro Robertino; 3, Saunders Dale L; 4, Forster David; 5, Simon Stuart; 6, Smith Ron K; 7, Heads Barbara; 8, Phelan Bruce; 9, VanOverschot Robert; 10, Lemasurier Paul; 11, Forster David

$1 Pick Three (1–4–3) Paid $493.95 ; Pick Three Pool $5,237 .

EIGHTH RACE
Woodbine
AUGUST 28, 2004

7 FURLONGS. (Turf) (1.19^1) 10TH RUNNING OF THE PLAY THE KING HANDICAP. Grade III. Purse $150,000 FOR THREE-YEAR-OLDS AND UPWARD. By subscription of $150 each which shall accompany the nomination and an additional $1,500 when making entry; with $150,000 added, plus all fees to be divided: 60% to the winner, 20% to second, 11% to third, 6% to fourth and 3% to fifth. Weights, Saturday, August 21, 2004. Closed Wednesday, August 11, 2004 with 36 nominations. Final entries to be made through the entry box no later than 11:30 a.m. on Thursday, August 26, 2004. Plus up to $12,420 Ontario Sire/Canadian BredBreeder Awards. (Rail at 10 feet).

Value of Race: $173,400 Winner $104,040; second $34,680; third $19,074; fourth $10,404; fifth $5,202. Mutuel Pool $179,378.00 Exactor Pool $100,083.00 Triactor Pool $130,118.00

Last Raced	Horse	M/Eqt.	A.	Wt	PP	St	¼	½	Str	Fin	Jockey	Odds $1
24Jly04 ^{8}WO^{1}	Soaring Free	L	5	126	8	2	3^1	3^{hd}	1^1	$1\frac{3}{4}$	Kabel T K	0.60
7Aug04 ^{2}WO^{2}	Frank's Selection	L b	8	115	7	3	9^{hd}	10^1	4^{hd}	2^2	Montpellier C	40.25
28Jly04 ^{7}WO^{1}	Dancin Joey	L	4	116	2	7	11^6	7^{hd}	$2^{2\frac{1}{2}}$	$3\frac{3}{4}$	McKnight J	40.70
24Jly04 ^{8}WO^{2}	Super Case	L	4	114	6	4	4^{hd}	5^{hd}	3^1	$4\frac{1}{2}$	Landry R C	12.50
29Jly04 ^{2}WO^{1}	Prince Alphie	L bf	4	115	3	11	7^{hd}	$4^{1\frac{1}{2}}$	$9^{2\frac{1}{2}}$	$5\frac{3}{4}$	Luciani D	32.40
7Aug04 ^{2}WO^{4}	My Lucky Strike	L f	5	115	10	9	12	12	$10\frac{1}{2}$	6^{nk}	Clark D	22.50
7Aug04 ^{2}WO^{1}	Chris's Bad Boy	L f	7	119	5	12	$10^{1\frac{1}{2}}$	$11^{2\frac{1}{2}}$	6^{hd}	7no	Jones J	10.55
31Jly04 ^{3}WO^{2}	Dalavin	L b	3	117	9	8	$6\frac{1}{2}$	8^{hd}	7^{hd}	$8^{1\frac{1}{4}}$	Husbands P	7.65
7Aug04 ^{2}WO^{3}	Very Professional	L bf	6	116	12	1	$8\frac{1}{2}$	$6\frac{1}{2}$	8^2	$9^{1\frac{3}{4}}$	Callaghan S	44.70
7Aug04 ^{2}WO^{6}	Lucky Tom	L	4	111	11	5	5^{hd}	9^{hd}	$11^{3\frac{1}{2}}$	$10^{1\frac{1}{4}}$	Sutherland C	60.45
17Jly04 ^{8}WO^{2}	Bachelor Blues	L	3	113	1	6	1^{hd}	$1\frac{1}{2}$	$5\frac{1}{2}$	$11^{2\frac{1}{4}}$	Ramsammy E	24.50
24Jly04 ^{4}EIP^{3}	Cat Genius	L f	4	121	4	10	2^{hd}	2^1	12	12	Blanc B	7.50

OFF AT 4:22 Start Good For All But SOARING FREE. Won driving. Course good.

TIME :22^2, :45^1, 1:08^4, 1:20^4 (:22.59, :45.33, 1:08.97, 1:20.97)

$2 Mutuel Prices:

8 – SOARING FREE	3.20	2.60	2.20
7 – FRANK'S SELECTION		15.80	12.10
2 – DANCIN JOEY			10.90

$2 EXACTOR 8–7 PAID $80.50 $2 TRIACTOR 8–7–2 PAID $1,307.00

Dk. b or br. g, (Jan), by Smart Strike – Dancing With Wings , by Danzig . Trainer Frostad Mark. Bred by Sam-Son Farm (Ont-C).

SOARING FREE broke outward and bumped with DALAVIN then stumbled, recovered quickly and stalked the pace three-wide, took command sharply upper stretch and drew clear then held sway under a drive. FRANK'S SELECTION back between foes early, was checked in traffic early turn then moved to the rail, closed leaving the turn, lacked a path midstretch then found racing room and finished full of run. DANCIN JOEY was unhurried early on the rail, moved five-wide and closed leaving the turn, took a strong run at the leader upper stretch but could not get up and flattened out. SUPER CASE stalked the pace from between horses, was always in range but hung in the stretch. PRINCE ALPHIE stalked from the rail, lacked a path midstretch and failed to menace. MY LUCKY STRIKE trailed from the fourth path, came widest into the stretch and finished gamely in vain. CHRIS'S BAD BOY raced well back early, closed five-wide into the stretch but never reached contention. DALAVIN bumped with SOARING FREE at the start, was under severe restraint and steadied repeatedly on the turn in traffic then flattened out in the stretch. VERY PROFESSIONAL raced midpack four-wide and flattened out in the late stages. LUCKY TOM was in touch early, raced four-wide on the turn but lacked a rally. BACHELOR BLUES raced forwardly, dueled into the turn, held a short lead at the top of the stretch and gave way when headed. CAT GENIUS raced forwardly, dueled into the turn, forced the issue but tired at the top of the stretch.

Owners– 1, Sam-Son Farms; 2, Elliott-Griem Lynda; 3, Cappuccitti G Terra Racing Stable and Mattine Tony; 4, Stronach Stables; 5, Schettine William C; 6, Wine Billy and Ferraro Joe; 7, Alpine Stable Ltd; 8, Cappuccitti Audre and Gordon; 9, D'Amato Carlo; 10, Stronach Stables; 11, Schettine William C; 12, Parker John R

Trainers– 1, Frostad Mark; 2, Griem Robert J; 3, Mattine Tony; 4, Vella Daniel J; 5, Carroll Josie; 6, Cirillo John; 7, Armata Vito; 8, Cappuccitti Audre; 9, Wilcox Warren; 10, Keogh Michael; 11, Carroll Josie; 12, McPeek Kenneth G

$1 Pick Three (1–7–8) Paid $307.20 ; Pick Three Pool $8,585 .

EIGHTH RACE
Woodbine
SEPTEMBER 6, 2004

1½ MILES. (Turf) (2.25^3) 52ND RUNNING OF THE NIAGARA BREEDERS' CUP HANDICAP. Grade II. Purse $300,000 (includes $100,000 Other Sources) FOR THREE-YEAR-OLDS AND UPWARD. By subscription of $300 each which shall accompany the nomination and an additional $3,000 when making entry; with $200,000 added and an additional $100,000 from the Breeders' Cup Fund for Cup nominees only. The host associations added monies and all fees to be divided: 60% to the winner, 20% to second, 11% to third, 6% to fourth and 3% to fifth. Breeders' Cup Fund monies also correspondingly divided provided a Breeders' Cup nominee has finished in an awarded position. AnyBreeders' Cup Fund monies not awarded will revert back to the Fund. Weights Saturday, August 28, 2004. This field will be limited to seventeen starters. If more than seventeen entries pass the entry box, the starters will be determined at that time with preference given to Breeders' Cup nominees only of equal racing quality or weight assignment (respective of sex and weight for age). Final entries to be made through the entry box no later than 11:30 a.m. on Saturday, September 4, 2004. Plus up to $15,180Ontario Sire/Canadian Bred Breeder Awards. Closed Wednesday August 18, 2004 with 20 nominations. (Rail at 20 feet).

Value of Race: $324,000 Winner $194,400; second $64,800; third $35,640; fourth $19,440; fifth $9,720. Mutuel Pool $99,437.00 Exactor Pool $42,241.00 Triactor Pool $46,993.00

Last Raced	Horse	M/Eqt.	A.	Wt	PP	¼	½	1	1¼	Str	Fin	Jockey	Odds $1
25Jly04 ^{8}WO^{3}	Strut the Stage	L bf	6	121	3	6	6	5^1	$1^{2\frac{1}{2}}$	1^4	1^4	Kabel T K	0.25
18Jly04 ^{3}WO^{1}	Colorful Judgement	L	4	115	1	$4\frac{1}{2}$	4^{hd}	6	3^2	2^2	$2^{3\frac{3}{4}}$	Callaghan S	7.15
7Aug04 ^{8}WO^{2}	Mark One	L	5	115	4	5^2	$5^{2\frac{1}{2}}$	2^{hd}	2^{hd}	$3^{2\frac{1}{2}}$	$3^{1\frac{1}{4}}$	McAleney J S	7.30
7Aug04 ^{8}WO^{3}	Hydrogen	L	5	113	5	$3^{1\frac{1}{2}}$	3^2	4^{hd}	5^7	5^{15}	4^{nk}	McKnight J	22.50
25Jly04 ^{8}WO^{4}	Control Tower	L b	5	112	2	1^{hd}	2^1	3^2	$4^{1\frac{1}{2}}$	$4\frac{1}{2}$	5^{25}	Ramsammy E	7.90
18Jly04 ^{4}FE^{3}	Longship	L f	4	109	6	2^1	$1\frac{1}{2}$	1^{hd}	6	6	6	Pimentel R M	28.05

OFF AT 4:27 Start Good . Won ridden out. Course firm.

TIME :25, :49^1, 1:13^2, 1:37^3, 2:01^4, 2:25^4 (:25.11, :49.23, 1:13.56, 1:37.66, 2:01.94, 2:25.87)

$2 Mutuel Prices:

3 – STRUT THE STAGE	2.50	2.10	2.10
1 – COLORFUL JUDGEMENT		4.20	2.70
4 – MARK ONE			2.30

$2 EXACTOR 3–1 PAID $9.80 $2 TRIACTOR 3–1–4 PAID $25.60

Ch. h, (Mar), by Theatrical-Ire – Ruby Ransom , by Red Ransom . Trainer Frostad Mark. Bred by Jamm Ltd (Ky).

STRUT THE STAGE was unhurried early, closed up on the far turn, moved quickly between foes late turn and took command at the top of the stretch, drew away when asked then held sway under a hand ride. COLORFUL JUDGEMENT was unhurried along the rail while always in range, followed STRUT THE STAGE into the stretch,chased after him and finished gamely to be best of the rest. MARK ONE stalked three-wide to the far turn then bid sharply outside rivals, dueled to the top of the stretch and yielded. HYDROGEN stalked from the fourth path, was always in striking range but lacked the needed rally. CONTROL TOWER forced the issue from the rail, bid in earnest on the far turn, dueled to the top of the stretch and gave way. LONGSHIP held a narrow lead while setting the pace from off the rail, was engaged on the far turn, dueled to the top of the stretch and tired.

Owners– 1, Sam-Son Farms; 2, Sam-Son Farms; 3, Stronach Stables; 4, Mack Earle I; 5, Pin Oak Stable LLC; 6, Sam-Son Farms

Trainers– 1, Frostad Mark; 2, Frostad Mark; 3, Vella Daniel J; 4, Casse Mark; 5, Pierce Malcolm; 6, Frostad Mark

$1 Pick Three (6–4–3) Paid $22.40 ; Pick Three Pool $7,469 .

EIGHTH RACE
Woodbine
SEPTEMBER 11, 2004

7 FURLONGS. (1.20³) 37TH RUNNING OF THE SEAWAY. Grade III. Purse $125,000 (plus $50,000 Other Sources) FOR FILLIES AND MARES, THREE-YEAR-OLDS AND UPWARD. By subscription of $125 each which shall accompany the nomination and an additional $1,250 when making entry; with $125,000 added and an additional $50,000 for Canadian Breds, plus all fees to be divided: 60% to the winner, 20% to second, 11% to third, 6% to fourth and 3% to fifth. Three-year-olds, 121 lbs.; Older, 124 lbs. Winners of a sweepstakes of $75,000 four times in 2004, additional 2 lbs.; Non-winners of a sweepstakes of $75,000 three times in 2004 allowed 3 lbs.; Of a sweepstakes of $75,000 twice in 2004, 5 lbs.; Of a sweepstakes of $75,000 once in 2004, 7 lbs.; Of $47,100 in 2004, 9 lbs. (Maiden or claiming races not considered.) (No Canadian Bred Allowances.) Final entries to be made through the entry box no later than 11:30 a.m. on Thursday, September 9, 2004. Plus $50,000 for Canadian Breds from the Thoroughbred Improvement Program and Canadian Thoroughbred Horse Society. Plus up to $12,420 Ontario Sire/Canadian Bred Breeder Awards. Closed Wednesday, August 25, 2004 with 22 nominations.

Value of Race: $178,000 Winner $111,900; second $37,300; third $15,015; fourth $8,190; fifth $5,595. Mutuel Pool $117,984.00 Exactor Pool $62,292.00 Triactor Pool $72,369.00

Last Raced	Horse	M/Eqt.	A.	Wt	PP	St	¼	½	Str	Fin	Jockey	Odds $1
29Aug04 7WO1	Brass in Pocket	L	5	119	7	2	11½	11	12½	12¼	Kabel T K	3.25
22Aug04 7WO1	Winter Garden	L	4	119	4	7	7	7	4hd	22¼	Clark D	1.60
22Aug04 7WO2	El Prado Essence	L bf	7	117	3	3	5½	4hd	53	31	Husbands P	4.75
7Aug04 7WO1	La Trillium	L	4	115	2	5	2½	31	31	4nk	Callaghan S	2.80
22Aug04 7WO3	Spanish Decree	L f	5	116	1	4	4½	2hd	21½	52	Landry R C	24.95
20Jun04 8WO7	Alpha Heat	L	5	115	5	6	64	62	6hd	63	McAleney J S	13.35
13Aug04 3WO4	Mille Feville	L	5	118	6	1	3½	51½	7	7	Jones J	21.85

OFF AT 4:37 Start Good For All But WINTER GARDEN. Won ridden out. Track fast.

TIME :22², :45¹, 1:09², 1:22¹ (:22.51, :45.32, 1:09.46, 1:22.26)

$2 Mutuel Prices:				
	7 – BRASS IN POCKET	8.50	4.00	2.60
	4 – WINTER GARDEN		3.20	2.30
	3 – EL PRADO ESSENCE			2.80

$2 EXACTOR 7–4 PAID $20.10 $2 TRIACTOR 7–4–3 PAID $62.00

B. m, (Mar), by Domasca Dan – Luck In My Pocket , by Lucky North . Trainer Tiller Robert P. Bred by Frank Digiulio & Frank DiGiulio Jr (Ont-C).

BRASS IN POCKET led quickly, moved to the rail and set a reserved pace then held sway under a hand ride. WINTER GARDEN broke in the air then remained unhurried, launched her rally four-wide from midturn, drifted out at the top of the stretch then finished willingly, but late. EL PRADO ESSENCE was always in range, raced along the second path and finished gamely to no avail. LA TRILLIUM stalked the pace, closed along the third path from midturn then flattened out in the stretch. SPANISH DECREE closed along the rail late backstretch, stalked through the turn, was roused at the top of the stretch but flattened out in the final furlong. ALPHA HEAT was hustled along the rail through the turn then lacked a rally. MILLE FEVILLE stalked the pace three wide then tired at the top of the stretch.

Owners– 1, Di Giulio Frank D Jr; 2, Di Giulio Frank D Jr; 3, Cappuccitti Audre and Gordon; 4, Jasmine Stables; 5, Huarte Frank; 6, Stronach Stables; 7, Haras Santa Maria de Araras

Trainers– 1, Tiller Robert P; 2, Tiller Robert P; 3, Cappuccitti Audre; 4, Nielsen Paul; 5, Huarte Frank; 6, Vella Daniel J; 7, Attfield Roger L

$1 Pick Three (6–2–7) Paid $28.00 ; Pick Three Pool $8,014 .

EIGHTH RACE
Woodbine
SEPTEMBER 12, 2004

1 MILE. (Turf) (1.31⁴) 40TH RUNNING OF THE NATALMA. Grade III. Purse $150,000 (plus $50,000 Other Sources) FOR TWO-YEAR-OLD FILLIES. By subscription of $150 each which shall accompany the nomination and an additional $1,500 when making entry; with $150,000 added and an additional $50,000 for Canadian Breds, plus all fees to be divided: 60% to the winner, 20% to second, 11% to third, 6% to fourth and 3% to fifth. Weight 119 lbs. winners of a sweepstakes of $75,000 twice, additional 2 lbs.; Non-winners of a sweepstakes of $75,000 once allowed 3 lbs.; Of a race other than maiden or claiming, 5 lbs. (No Canadian Bred Allowance.) Final entries to be made through the entry box no later than 11:30 a.m. on Friday, September 10, 2004. Plus $50,000 for Canadian Breds from the Thoroughbred Improvement Program and Canadian Thoroughbred Horse Society. Plus up to $12,420 Ontario Sire/Canadian Bred Breeder Awards. Closed Wednesday, August 25, 2004 with 42 nominations. (Rail at 30 feet).

Value of Race: $177,300 Winner $106,380; second $35,460; third $19,503; fourth $10,638; fifth $5,319. Mutuel Pool $125,483.00 Exactor Pool $57,589.00 Triactor Pool $86,798.00

Last Raced	Horse	M/Eqt.	A.	Wt	PP	St	¼	½	¾	Str	Fin	Jockey	Odds $1
24Jly04 Leo7	Fearless Flyer-Ire	L	2	114	6	10	101	101½	92½	31	11½	Ramsammy E	6.85
20Aug04 6WO1	Sweet Solairo	L	2	114	1	4	11	11½	11	11½	2¾	Somsanith N	30.20
20Aug04 2WO1	Little Hussy	L	2	117	11	3	3½	2hd	2½	2½	3nk	Husbands P	1.50
8Aug04 4Sar1	Paddy's Daisy	L	2	119	7	9	81	7½	6½	52	4½	Decarlo C P	6.05
22Aug04 8WO2	Extra Bases	L	2	118	5	7	6hd	61	51	42	5¾	Jones J	29.50
9Jly04 4Bel1	Accretion	L	2	116	9	1	4hd	5½	7hd	61	6nk	Kabel T K	3.10
20Aug04 6WO3	Miss Adelaide	L b	2	116	2	11	11	11	11	71½	72½	Luciani D	24.85
15Aug04 3WO1	Feistee Deer	L	2	115	4	5	92½	91	8hd	81½	83	McAleney J S	21.80
28Jly04 9Sar9	Coconut Popsicle	L	2	115	3	8	5hd	8½	10½	103	9nk	Callaghan S	37.35
15Aug04 3WO2	Elle Runaway	L b	2	114	8	6	7½	4hd	31½	91	104½	Dos Ramos R A	10.75
29Aug04 2WO1	Canadian Gem	L	2	117	10	2	2½	31	41	11	11	Landry R C	24.90

OFF AT 4:22 Start Good . Won driving. Course firm.

TIME :23, :46¹, 1:10¹, 1:34⁴ (:23.04, :46.20, 1:10.34, 1:34.99)

$2 Mutuel Prices:				
	7 – FEARLESS FLYER–IRE	15.70	11.40	5.80
	1 – SWEET SOLAIRO		28.40	11.40
	13 – LITTLE HUSSY			2.90

$2 EXACTOR 7–1 PAID $415.30 $2 TRIACTOR 7–1–13 PAID $1,972.40

Dk. b or br. f, (Feb), by Brave Act-GB – Canary Bird-Ire , by Catrail . Trainer Stack Tommy. Bred by Mr Yakup Demir Tokdemir (Ire).

FEARLESS FLYER (IRE) unhurried early, came three-wide through the turn, swung wide at the top of the stretch and rallied willingly. SWEET SOLAIRO led quickly, set a reserved pace, had command to deep stretch then failed to stave off the winner. LITTLE HUSSY pressed the pace three-wide, closed leaving the turn and finished determinedly. PADDY'S DAISY closed steadily three-wide and was still gaining late. EXTRA BASES in touch two deep, was blocked at the sixteenth pole then evened out. ACCRETION was taken under a strong hold early, moved to the rail on the backstretch and stalked the pace then lacked the necessary closing response. MISS ADELAIDE trailed along the second path and rallied mildly outside the field. FEISTEE DEER bumped with COCONUT POPSICLE at the start, raced evenly along the second path. COCONUT POPSICLE, bumped at the start, was in touch early but faded steadily along the rail. ELLE RUNAWAY closed four-wide late turn, was in striking position at the top of the stretch then tired. CANADIAN GEM pressed the pace along the rail then tired at the top of the stretch.

Owners– 1, Reddam J Paul; 2, Shultz Richard L; 3, Oxley John C; 4, Stonehaven Farm; 5, Wilson R J and Hunsicker G; 6, Klaravich Stables Inc; 7, Shaw Richard F and Jo Ellen; 8, McAlpine James; 9, Singer Craig B; 10, Live Oak Plantation; 11, Fipke Charles E

Trainers– 1, Stack Tommy; 2, Silvera Laurie; 3, Casse Mark; 4, Pletcher Todd A; 5, Casse Mark; 6, Violette Richard A Jr; 7, Bell David R; 8, Baker Reade; 9, Tesher Howard M; 10, Pierce Malcolm; 11, Attfield Roger L

Scratched– Hassayampa (20Aug04 2WO 3) , Higher World (14Aug04 6WO 1) , Shout to the North (22Aug04 8WO 5)

$1 Pick Three (1–7–7) Paid $3,271.50 ; Pick Three Pool $8,885 .

NINTH RACE
Woodbine
SEPTEMBER 19, 2004

1 MILE. (Turf) (1.31⁴) 8TH RUNNING OF THE ATTO MILE. Grade I. Purse $1,000,000 FOR THREE-YEAR-OLDS AND UPWARD. By subscription of $750 each which shall accompany the nomination and an additional $10,000 when making entry. The added money and all fees to be divided: 60% to the winner, 20% to second, 11% to third, 6% to fourth and 3%to fifth. Three-year-olds, 119 lbs.; Older 124 lbs. Non-winners of a Gr. 1 Race in 2004 allowed 3 lbs.; Of a Gr. II Race in 2004 or a Gr. I Race in 2003 allowed 5 lbs.; Of a Gr. III Race in 2004 or a Gr. II race in 2003 allowed 7 lbs. (Note: Grades as recognized by the International Cataloguing Standards Committee.) (No Canadian-Bred Allowance.) (Maiden or claiming not considered.) Final entries to be made through the entry box no later than 10:30 a.m. on Friday, September 17, 2004. (A supplemental nomination fee of $50,000 which includes the entry fee may be made no later than the time of final entry. Plus up to $17,940 Ontario Sire/Canadian Bred Breeder Awards.

Value of Race: $1,000,000 Winner $600,000; second $200,000; third $110,000; fourth $60,000; fifth $30,000. Mutuel Pool $660,357.00 Exactor Pool $364,317.00 Triactor Pool $354,387.00 Superfecta Pool $103,641.00

Last Raced	Horse	M/Eqt.	A.	Wt	PP	St	¼	½	¾	Str	Fin	Jockey	Odds $1
28Aug04 8WO1	Soaring Free	L	5	119	11	1	1½	21½	1½	11	1¾	Kabel T K	2.15
25Jly04 8WO5	Perfect Soul-Ire	L b	6	121	8	8	11	105	61½	3½	2hd	Nakatani C S	3.55
28Aug04 9Sar3	Royal Regalia	L	6	118	9	3	21½	1hd	21½	22½	31¼	Jones J	7.30
3Sep04 8Sar7	Surging River	L	4	117	3	6	7hd	6½	4hd	42	42¾	Landry R C	25.60
5Sep04 2WO1	Mobil	L	4	119	7	5	51½	51	5½	51½	5¾	Husbands P	9.70
8Aug04 11Mth2	Kathir	L	7	117	10	2	6hd	82	8½	7hd	6nk	Callaghan S	21.65
25Jly04 8WO6	Slew Valley	L	7	121	5	10	94½	7½	7½	61	7nk	McAleney J S	20.55
28Aug04 7WO8	Dumaani Star	L f	6	117	1	11	81	92½	106	81½	81¼	Husbands S P	132.85
10Jly04 8Bel2	MillnnumDrgon-GB	L	5	119	6	4	3hd	3½	3hd	94	92¾	Migliore R	4.10
28Aug04 9Sar9	Christine's Outlaw	L	4	119	4	7	4½	4hd	9hd	102	10¾	Dominguez R A	8.80
28Aug04 8WO6	My Lucky Strike	L bf	5	117	2	9	10hd	11	11	11	11	Clark D	44.80

OFF AT 5:10 Start Good For All But DUMAANI STAR. Won driving. Course firm.
TIME :23², :46, 1:09, 1:32³ (:23.48, :46.01, 1:09.19, 1:32.72)

$2 Mutuel Prices:

11 – SOARING FREE	6.30	3.20	2.70
8 – PERFECT SOUL–IRE		4.20	3.30
9 – ROYAL REGALIA			4.50

$2 EXACTOR 11–8 PAID $27.20 $2 TRIACTOR 11–8–9 PAID $149.90
$1 SUPERFECTA 11–8–9–3 PAID $990.65

Dk. b or br. g, (Jan), by Smart Strike – Dancing With Wings , by Danzig . Trainer Frostad Mark. Bred by Sam–Son Farm (Ont–C).

SOARING FREE broke alertly, raced forwardly under pressure from ROYAL REGALIA, traded the lead with that one off and on but took command in earnest leaving the turn then held under steady pressure. PERFECT SOUL (IRE) unhurried on the second path until late turn, swung wide at the top of the stretch and rallied willingly. ROYAL REGALIA forced the issue from the rail on the backstretch, led briefly on the turn, was headed entering the stretch but raced very gamely through the stretch and just missed the place. SURGING RIVER raced midpack, closed between rivals leaving the turn, was all out in the stretch and evened out late. MOBIL stalked the pace, raced four-wide in the turn and maintained striking range but evened out in the stretch. KATHIR raced midpack, closed three-deep late turn, rallied mildly in the stretch and failed to menace. SLEW VALLEY was well off the early pace, came five-wide through the turn then hung in the stretch. DUMAANI STAR off a step slowly, saved ground, was behind traffic at the head of the stretch and never reached contention. MILLENNIUM DRAGON (GB) stalked the pace three-deep to the top of the stretch then tired. CHRISTINE'S OUTLAW stalked the pace from the rail, gave way late turn and tired in the stretch. MY LUCKY STRIKE trailed throughout.

Owners– 1, Sam-Son Farms; 2, Fipke Charles E; 3, Stronach Stables; 4, Sam-Son Farms; 5, Schickedanz Gustav; 6, Melnyk Eugene and Laura; 7, Rich Meadow Farm and Burkhard Alan; 8, Castle Peak Farm Ltd; 9, Darley Stable; 10, RC Hill Stable; 11, Wine Billy and Ferraro Joe

Trainers– 1, Frostad Mark; 2, Attfield Roger L; 3, Nixon Justin; 4, Frostad Mark; 5, Keogh Michael; 6, Pletcher Todd A; 7, Baker Reade; 8, Yu Danny; 9, McLaughlin Kiaran P; 10, Weaver George; 11, Cirillo John

$1 Pick Three (6–8–11) Paid $64.45 ; Pick Three Pool $18,477 .
$1 Pick Six (1/7–3/8/9–2–6–8–11) 6 Correct Paid $6,356.00 ; Pick Six Pool $14,377 .
$1 Pick Six (1/7–3/8/9–2–6–8–11) 5 Correct Paid $151.30 .
$1 Win Four (2–6–8–11) Paid $1,032.50 ; Win Four Pool $52,470 .

SIXTH RACE
Woodbine
SEPTEMBER 19, 2004

ABOUT 1⅛ MILES. (Turf) (1.42[4]) 50TH RUNNING OF THE CANADIAN HANDICAP. Grade II. Purse $250,000 (plus $50,000 Other Sources) FOR FILLIES AND MARES, THREE-YEAR-OLDS AND UPWARD. By subscription of $250 each which shall accompany the nomination and an additional $2,500 when making entry; with $250,000 added and an additional $50,000 for Canadian Breds, plus all fees to be divided: 60% to the winner, 20% to second, 11% to third, 6% to fourth and 3% to fifth. Weights, Saturday, September 11, 2004. Final entries to be made through the entry box no later than 11:30 a.m. on Friday, September 17, 2004. Plus $50,000 for Canadian Breds from the Thoroughbred Improvement Program and Canadian Thoroughbred Horse Society. Plus up to $15,180 Ontario Sire/Canadian Bred Breeder Awards. Closed Wednesday, September 1, 2004 with 32 nominations.

Value of Race: $327,500 Winner $198,300; second $66,100; third $36,355; fourth $16,830; fifth $9,915. Mutuel Pool $201,596.00 Exactor Pool $101,352.00 Triactor Pool $120,460.00 Superfecta Pool $30,075.00

Last Raced	Horse	M/Eqt.	A.	Wt	PP	St	¼	½	¾	Str	Fin	Jockey	Odds $1
28Aug04 [10]WO[2]	Classic Stamp	L	4	117	2	9	9	8[½]	7[hd]	3[2½]	1[1]	Husbands P	10.95
14Aug04 [4]WO[1]	Inish Glora	L f	6	121	1	5	2[½]	2[½]	2[2½]	1[1]	2[1¾]	Kabel T K	1.85
28Aug04 [10]WO[4]	Heyahohowdy	L bf	5	114	9	1	1[1½]	1[1]	1[½]	2[hd]	3[½]	Sabourin R B	35.50
27Aug04 [8]Sar[1]	Madeira Mist-Ire	L	5	119	5	3	4[½]	5[1½]	3[hd]	4[3]	4[2¼]	Nakatani C S	3.15
30Aug04 [8]Sar[5]	Mona Rose		4	114	6	6	7[1]	7[hd]	6[hd]	5[hd]	5[1]	Da Silva E R	8.65
10Jly04 [8]Cnl[2]	Noisette	L	4	116	7	7	8[½]	6[hd]	5[hd]	6[hd]	6[2¼]	Castillo H Jr	10.45
5Jly04 [9]Bel[5]	Binya-Ger	L	5	118	8	2	3[½]	4[½]	4[1½]	7[3]	7[nk]	Migliore R	3.65
29Aug04 [7]WO[2]	Raylene	L b	4	115	3	4	5[hd]	9	9	8[1]	8[3]	McAleney J S	32.30
8Aug04 [9]Mth[3]	Spin Control	L	4	115	4	8	6[hd]	3[hd]	8[3]	9	9	Dominguez R A	12.45

OFF AT 3:27 Start Good . Won driving. Course firm.

TIME :23[2], :46, 1:43[2] (:23.46, :46.01, 1:43.59)

$2 Mutuel Prices:

2 – CLASSIC STAMP	23.90	8.30	5.00
1 – INISH GLORA		3.60	2.90
9 – HEYAHOHOWDY			6.70

$2 EXACTOR 2–1 PAID $68.00 $2 TRIACTOR 2–1–9 PAID $986.90
$1 SUPERFECTA 2–1–9–5 PAID $3,515.95

Dk. b or br. f, (Apr), by Regal Classic – Native Rights , by Our Native . Trainer Hopmans C C Jr. Bred by William Sorokolit (Ont-C).

CLASSIC STAMP, unhurried early, closed between horses leaving the turn, angled out midstretch and launched a strong rally and got up with a sixteenth to run. INISH GLORA stalked close up, bid outside HEYAHOHOWDY late turn, shook clear at the eighth pole but failed to contain the winner. HEYAHOHOWDY led quickly, set a reserved pace, was under pressure from INISH GLORA late turn, was engaged by that one at the top of the stretch and yielded. MADEIRA MIST (IRE), always in touch between horses, closed late turn then evened out. MONA ROSE, well back early, raced three-deep on the turn, then hung in the stretch. NOISETTE, well back early, raced four-wide on the turn, was set down approaching the top of the stretch but hung. BINYA (GER) stalked three-wide, chased into the stretch then flattened out. RAYLENE dropped back along the rail late backstretch and lacked a rally. SPIN CONTROL stalked from the rail but gave way late turn.

Owners– 1, Sorokolit William A Sr; 2, Costigan Robert J; 3, Kelynack Racing Stable Inc; 4, Skymarc Farm Inc; 5, O'Brien P and F; 6, Haras Santa Maria de Araras; 7, Allen Joseph; 8, Calmar Stables and Ranch; 9, Evans Robert S

Trainers– 1, Hopmans C C Jr; 2, Benson MacDonald; 3, Katryan Abraham R; 4, Clement Christophe; 5, Barnett Robert E; 6, Mott William I; 7, McLaughlin Kiaran P; 8, Baker Reade; 9, Motion H Graham

$1 Pick Three (1–8–2) Paid $141.70 ; Pick Three Pool $8,940 .

THIRD RACE
Woodbine
SEPTEMBER 19, 2004

1 MILE. (Turf) (1.31[4]) 52ND RUNNING OF THE SUMMER. Grade II. Purse $250,000 FOR TWO-YEAR-OLDS. By subscription of $250 each which shall accompany the nomination and an additional $2,500 when making entry; with $250,000 added, plus all fees to be divided: 60% to the winner, 20% to second, 11% to third, 6% to fourth and 3% to fifth. Weights 122 lbs. Fillies allowed 3 lbs. (No Canadian Bred Allowance.) Final entries to be made through the entry box no later than 11:30 a.m. on Friday, September 17, 2004. Plus up to $11,040 Ontario Sire/Canadian Bred Breeder Awards. Closed Wednesday,September 1, 2004 with 31 nominations.

Value of Race: $277,750 Winner $166,650; second $55,550; third $30,553; fourth $16,665; fifth $8,332. Mutuel Pool $154,371.00 Exactor Pool $81,259.00 Triactor Pool $89,800.00

Last Raced	Horse	M/Eqt.	A.	Wt	PP	St	¼	½	¾	Str	Fin	Jockey	Odds $1
5Sep04 [8]Mth[1]	Dubleo	L	2	122	2	4	2[4]	1[2½]	1[2]	1[2½]	1[2¼]	Nakatani C S	2.25
22Aug04 [5]WO[3]	Dance With Ravens	L b	2	122	4	1	3[1]	3[hd]	2[1½]	2[2½]	2[1]	Kabel T K	2.55
4Sep04 [5]WO[1]	Go to the Sun	L	2	122	5	2	5[2½]	5[1½]	5[hd]	3[½]	3[¾]	Callaghan S	11.90
21Aug04 [3]WO[1]	Strike a Bargain	L b	2	122	1	7	4[½]	4[2]	6[3]	4[2½]	4[4¼]	Ramsammy E	10.50
22Aug04 [5]WO[1]	Stag Nation	L	2	122	7	8	8	6[½]	4[hd]	5[1½]	5[no]	Landry R C	14.20
5Sep04 [8]Mth[5]	Copyco	L	2	122	8	5	6[½]	7[hd]	7[1]	7[2]	6[1¼]	Migliore R	3.90
27Aug04 [6]Mth[1]	Elusive Thunder	L	2	122	6	6	7[½]	8	8	8	7[2]	Dominguez R A	7.45
28Aug04 [3]WO[1]	Tommy's Topper	L b	2	122	3	3	1[hd]	2[½]	3[½]	6[1]	8	Husbands P	13.50

OFF AT 1:55 Start Good For All But TOMMY'S TOPPER, ELUSIVE THUNDER, STAG NATION. Won driving. Course firm.

TIME :22[2], :45[1], 1:10, 1:34[3] (:22.55, :45.27, 1:10.00, 1:34.69)

$2 Mutuel Prices:

2 – DUBLEO	6.50	3.60	3.20
4 – DANCE WITH RAVENS		3.10	2.80
5 – GO TO THE SUN			4.90

$2 EXACTOR 2–4 PAID $23.30 $2 TRIACTOR 2–4–5 PAID $143.40

Dk. b or br. c, (Mar), by Southern Halo – Secret Red , by Secretariat . Trainer Pletcher Todd A. Bred by Anzac LLC (Ky).

DUBLEO paired up with TOMMEY'S TOPPER early, drew clear entering the turn, set a reserved pace then held sway under steady pressure through the stretch. DANCE WITH RAVENS was unhurried early, closed three-wide on the turn then was all out in the stretch to no avail. GO TO THE SUN was well back early on the inside, closed between horses on the turn then evened out in the stretch. STRIKE A BARGAIN was unhurried along the hedge, closed on the turn, was in tight upper stretch then evened out. STAG NATION broke in the air and raced well off the pace, advanced three-wide on the turn then finished evenly. COPYCO was well off the early pace, raced three-wide then lacked a closing response. ELUSIVE THUNDER broke outward, raced well back and was never a serious factor. TOMMY'S TOPPER broke in the air but sprinted to the lead, was joined early by DUBLEO, remained outside that one to the turn, stalked from between rivals to the stretch and tired. AN OBJECTION BY THE RIDER ON STRIKE A BARGAIN AGAINST GO TO THE SUN FOR INTERFERENCE UPPERSTRETCH WAS DISALLOWED.

Owners– 1, J T Scatuorchio P Wetterman and JJ Pletcher; 2, Sam-Son Farms; 3, Sam-Son Farms; 4, Pin Oak Stable LLC; 5, Class Action Stable; 6, Wertheimer; 7, Winged Foot Stable; 8, Tommy Town Thoroughbreds LLC

Trainers– 1, Pletcher Todd A; 2, Frostad Mark; 3, Frostad Mark; 4, Bell David R; 5, Vella Daniel J; 6, Pletcher Todd A; 7, Ryan Derek S; 8, Casse Mark

$1 Pick Three (1–1–2) Paid $304.60 ; Pick Three Pool $12,269 .

EIGHTH RACE
Hastings
SEPTEMBER 25, 2004

1⅛ MILES. (1.464) 42ND RUNNING OF THE BRITISH COLUMBIA BREEDERS' CUP OAKS. Grade III. Purse $125,000 (plus $16,000 THRIF – British Columbia Bred) A Scale Weight Stakes for Three Year Old Fillies. By subscription of $200 to accompany the nomination due on Wednesday, September 15, 2004. $1,250 to enter and $1,250 to pass scratch time. With $125,000 added and an additional $25,000 from the Breeders'Cup Fund for Cup nominees only. All Hastings Entertainment Inc. purse money to be divided 60% to the winner, 20% to second, 11% to third, 6% to fourth, and 3% to fifth. Breeders' Cup Fund monies correspondingly divided providing a Breeders' Cup nominee has finished in an awarded position. Any Breeders' Cup Fund monies not awarded will revert back to the Fund. Preference will be based on lifetime earnings as recorded by The Daily Racing Form at time of entry. In a case where horses have identical earnings,preference will be given to the Breeders' Cup eligible horse. Scale Weight: 121 lbs.

Value of Race: $174,087 Winner $105,660; second $33,470; third $19,371; fourth $10,566; fifth $5,020. Mutuel Pool $40,167.00 Triactor Pool $36,141.00 Exactor Pool $27,270.00

Last Raced	Horse	M/Eqt.	A.	Wt	PP	St	¼	½	¾	Str	Fin	Jockey	Odds $1
5Sep04 4Hst4	Summer Symphony	L	3	121	4	7	7½	71½	71	31½	1½	Hoverson C	a- 0.40
5Sep04 4Hst1	Socorro County	L	3	121	2	6	61½	62	5hd	2hd	22¾	Skelly R V	a- 0.40
5Sep04 4Hst7	See Me Through	L f	3	121	7	1	11	11	12	11½	31¼	Alvarado P V	9.40
28Aug04 9NP11	Overact	L	3	121	9	2	21	2hd	2½	42½	42¼	Barton J	a- 0.40
29Aug04 4Hst1	Skyhyla	L b	3	121	1	8	85	86	83	51½	51½	Stephen A	9.40
29Aug04 3Hst1	Galica	L b	3	121	6	9	9	9	9	61	62¾	Loseth C	30.70
25Aug04 1Dmr1	Palace Rose	L b	3	121	8	5	41½	31½	3½	81½	7¾	Wilson D H	3.20
19Sep04 8Hst1	Bullseye Bess	L b	3	121	5	3	3½	42½	42	7½	81½	Fuentes F P	26.90
5Sep04 4Hst2	Gold Accent	L	3	121	3	4	51½	5hd	61	9	9	Ramirez Roberto	a- 0.40

a–Coupled: Summer Symphony and Socorro County and Overact and Gold Accent.

OFF AT 4:21 Start Good . Won driving. Track fast.

TIME :231, :472, 1:121, 1:374, 1:51 (:23.26, :47.58, 1:12.21, 1:37.91, 1:51.08)

$2 Mutuel Prices:			
1X– SUMMER SYMPHONY(a–entry).......	2.80	—	—
1 – SOCORRO COUNTY(a–entry)..........	2.80	—	—
5 – SEE ME THROUGH....................		—	—

$2 TRIACTOR 1–5–2 PAID $44.30 $2 EXACTOR 1–5 PAID $15.60

Ch. f, (Apr), by Summer Squall – Second Symphony , by Mining . Trainer Forster David. Bred by Janis R Whitham (Ky).

SUMMER SYMPHONY never far back, stalked the leaders, rallied from between horses on the final turn, gained the lead at mid stretch and won driving. SOCORRO COUNTY never far back and gaining, rallied from four wide around the final turn, closed well and was second best. SEE ME THROUGH broke sharply, assumed command from between horses, set a moderate pace, gave way in the stretch. OVERACT broke sharply, chased the pace setter from the inside, weakened after three quarters and gave way. SKYHYLA slow early, rallied from three wide down the stretch and was outrun. GALICA trailed for the first three quarters, put in a mild bid from five wide in the stretch, was also outrun. PALACE ROSE away alertly and well placed, made a middle move from three wide, was through after three quarters. BULLSEYE BESS broke sharply, close up, chased the leaders, was through after three quarters. GOLD ACCENT away alertly, in the middle of the pack, stalked the pace, dropped back after three quarters.

Owners– 1, Whitham Janis R; 2, Forster Stable and Kelly Glyn; 3, Jawl Michael; 4, Exclusive Stable and Hanson Raymond; 5, Bellevue Oaks; 6, Bennett Mr and Mrs R J; 7, Carter Michael Snow John and Crown Stables; 8, MacDougall Lorne and Susan; 9, Hanson Ray Gilbert George Chan Dr K and Kelly Glyn

Trainers– 1, Forster David; 2, Forster David; 3, Krasner Cindy; 4, Forster David; 5, Cloutier Jacobson Toni; 6, Heads Barbara; 7, Snow John; 8, Brown Jim R; 9, Forster David

---

EIGHTH RACE
Hastings
SEPTEMBER 26, 2004

1⅛ MILES. (1.464) 59TH RUNNING OF THE BRITISH COLUMBIA DERBY. Grade III. Purse $250,000 (plus $32,000 THRIF – British Columbia Bred) A Scale Weight Stakes for Three Year Olds. $250 to nominate. $2,500 to enter and $2,500 to pass scratch time. With $250,000 added, of which 60% goes to the winner, 20% to second, 11% to third, 6% to fourth, and 3% to fifth. Weights: Colts & Geldings 126lbs., Fillies 121 lbs. Preference will be based on lifetime earnings as recorded by The Daily Racing Form at time of entry. Field will be limited to 12 starters.

Value of Race: $325,500 Winner $191,400; second $70,300; third $35,090; fourth $19,140; fifth $9,570. Mutuel Pool $111,339.00 Triactor Pool $72,838.00 Exactor Pool $47,526.00

Last Raced	Horse	M/Eqt.	A.	Wt	PP	St	¼	½	¾	Str	Fin	Jockey	Odds $1
6Sep04 9EmD2	Flamethrowintexan	L f	3	126	5	3	21	21½	21	15	18½	Frazier R L	3.00
28Aug04 9NP9	Lord Samarai	L b	3	126	11	11	11	11	11	5½	22¼	Wilson D H	18.90
28Aug04 7WO3	Strike Em Hard	L b	3	126	10	6	71	71½	61	31	3nk	Montpellier C	17.00
28Aug04 9NP3	Cariboo Prospector	L b	3	126	6	10	102	106	8hd	61½	41	Barton J	20.55
10Sep04 11Fpx5	Don'tsellmeshort	L	3	126	9	1	11	11½	11½	2½	51½	Fuentes F P	14.10
6Sep04 9Hst3	Victory Light	L bf	3	126	1	2	61½	61	5hd	41½	63	Welch Q K	15.85
28Aug04 9Mth1	Gotaghostofachnce	b	3	126	7	7	4hd	52	3½	71	7¾	Alvarado P V	2.00
6Sep04 9Hst2	Future Flash	L b	3	126	4	8	91½	9½	91½	83	86¼	Skelly R V	34.20
29Aug04 5Dmr1	Quiet Cash	L b	3	126	8	4	51	4hd	4hd	92	93¼	Hoverson C	20.85
28Aug04 9NP5	Plenty of Heat	L b	3	126	3	9	82	82	102½	102½	102½	Hamel R	34.30
22Aug04 6Sar2	Garret's Gulch	L b	3	126	2	5	31	3hd	72	11	11	Olguin G L	6.55
6Sep04 9Hst1	Rules of War	L b	3	126	12	12		—	—	—	—	Ramirez Roberto	9.25

OFF AT 4:27 Start Good For All But. Won driving. Track fast.

TIME :221, :453, 1:102, 1:36, 1:492 (:22.30, :45.70, 1:10.52, 1:36.09, 1:49.58)

$2 Mutuel Prices:			
5 – FLAMETHROWINTEXAN............	8.00	4.10	4.30
11 – LORD SAMARAI......................		15.50	11.30
10 – STRIKE EM HARD....................			8.20

$2 TRIACTOR 5–11–10 PAID $1,689.00 $2 EXACTOR 5–11 PAID $164.30

Ch. g, (Feb), by Way West–Fr – Willalady , by Citidancer . Trainer Cooper Kay. Bred by Moloney & Thompson (Fla).

FLAMETHROWINTEXAN broke sharply, chased the pace setter from off the rail, rallied and gained the lead nearing the quarter pole, drew off driving. LORD SAMARAI slow early, rallied from six wide down the stretch, finished well as second best but was no match for the winner. STRIKE EM HARD in the middle of the pack and off the rail, rallied from four wide on the backstretch, finished well. CARIBOO PROSPECTOR slow early, gaining, rallied from three wide on the final turn and six wide in the stretch, gained a minor share. DON'TSELLMESHORT broke sharply, assumed command from the outside, set a rapid pace from off the rail, gave way leaving the backstretch. VICTORY LIGHT broke sharply, close up, chased from the inside, weakened in the stretch. GOTAGHOSTOFACHANCE away alertly and well placed, stalked the pace, weakened after three quarters. FUTURE FLASH unhurried early, showed little and was never a threat. QUIET CASH away alertly and well placed, rallied from three wide on the backstretch, weakened in the stretch. PLENTY OF HEAT unhurried early, stalked the pace, gave way after a half. GARRET'S GULCH away alertly, chased the leaders, was through after a half. RULES OF WAR stumbled at the start and lost his rider. Following the race there was a stewards enquiry into the start of the race. After review it was deemed that all horses received a fair start and no action was taken.

Owners– 1, Grasshopper Stable Inc; 2, Canyon Farms; 3, Dominion Bloodstock D Ball H Galbraith and G Peacock; 4, Gilbert George Hanson Raymond Kelly Glyn and Chan Karen; 5, Peacock Cecil N; 6, Double Down Stable; 7, McLeod Ross and Ming Charles; 8, Snow Daryl and Spevakow Robert and Jason; 9, Cheema Bahadur; 10, Elick John W; 11, Sangara K K; 12, Lucky 8 Racing Stables

Trainers– 1, Cooper Kay; 2, VanOverschot Robert; 3, Cotey David; 4, Forster David; 5, Giesbrecht Lance; 6, Longstaff Tom; 7, Bryant Steve; 8, Snow Daryl; 9, Jordan Terry; 10, Simon Stuart; 11, Barroby Harold J; 12, Gilker Robert

Scratched– Joyride (28Aug04 9NP 7)

EIGHTH RACE
Woodbine
OCTOBER 2, 2004

1⅜ MILES. (Turf) (2.12[1]) 10TH RUNNING OF THE SKY CLASSIC HANDICAP. Grade II. Purse $250,000 FOR THREE-YEAR-OLDS AND UPWARD. By subscription of $250 each which shall accompany the nomination and an additional $2,500 when making entry; with $250,000 added, plus all fees to be divided: 60% to the winner, 20% to second, 11% to third, 6% to fourth and 3% to fifth. Weights, Saturday, September 25, 2004. Final entries to be made through the entry box no later than 11:30 a. m. on Thursday, September 30, 2004. Plus up to $11,040 Ontario Sire/ Canadian Breeder Awards. Closed Wednesday, September 15, 2004with 21 nominations. (Rail at 20 feet).

Value of Race: $275,250 Winner $165,150; second $55,050; third $30,278; fourth $16,515; fifth $8,257. Mutuel Pool $175,994.00 Exactor Pool $95,993.00 Triactor Pool $127,937.00

Last Raced	Horse	M/Eqt.	A.	Wt	PP	¼	½	¾	1	Str	Fin	Jockey	Odds $1
6Sep04 8WO2	Colorful Judgement	L	4	114	2	4hd	31	3hd	51½	32½	1nk	Callaghan S	5.80
5Sep04 2WO2	Lenny the Lender	L bf	8	110	1	3hd	52½	2hd	21	1hd	21	Sutherland C	9.05
6Sep04 8WO6	Longship	L f	4	107	5	12	11½	11	1hd	21	3nk	Pimentel R M	51.15
6Sep04 9WO1	Rainbows for Luck	L	3	108	3	2½	2hd	41	3½	41	4hd	Singh S	20.55
5Sep04 2WO3	Jambalar	L b	4	109	6	7	7	7	7	6½	51½	Fraser C	37.10
4Sep04 9WO1	French Lieutenant	L	4	116	4	61½	61½	61	63	5hd	6nk	Husbands S P	8.95
6Sep04 8WO1	Strut the Stage	L bf	6	123	7	53	4hd	52	4hd	7	7	Kabel T K	0.30

OFF AT 4:23 Start Good . Won driving. Course firm.

TIME :25[4], :51, 1:15[2], 1:40, 2:03[3], 2:16 (:25.85, :51.19, 1:15.50, 1:40.19, 2:03.77, 2:16.19)

$2 Mutuel Prices:

2 – COLORFUL JUDGEMENT	13.60	7.50	9.70
1 – LENNY THE LENDER		11.70	18.40
5 – LONGSHIP			55.10

$2 EXACTOR 2–1 PAID $118.60 $2 TRIACTOR 2–1–5 PAID $1,338.30

Ch. g, (Feb), by Diesis-GB – Colorful Vices , by Regal Classic . Trainer Frostad Mark. Bred by Sam-Son Farm (Ont-C).

COLORFUL JUDGEMENT stalked the pace from the second path, moved to the rail for the stretch run, closed gamely inside LENNY THE LENDER and got up with a strong effort in the late stages. LENNY THE LENDER stalked from the rail, moved up to force the issue early turn, bid in earnest approaching the top of the stretch, dueled inside LONGSHIP, wore that one down inside the final sixteenth then failed to contain the winner late. LONGSHIP led quickly, set a reserved pace, was under pressure from LENNY THE LENDER on the far turn, entertained a challenge from that one approaching the top of the stretch, dueled to the late stages and weakened. RAINBOWS FOR LUCK stalked close up on the third path then was all out in the stretch. JAMBALAR was unhurried early, moved to the rail for the run through the far turn, was in range at the top of the stretch but lacked the necessary closing response. FRENCH LIEUTENANT rated early, maintained striking distance on the second path then evened out in the stretch. STRUT THE STAGE stalked the pace from the outside, came four-wide through the far turn then flattened out.

Owners– 1, Sam-Son Farms; 2, Jukosky Richard H; 3, Sam-Son Farms; 4, Sam-Son Farms; 5, Shaw Richard F and Jo Ellen; 6, Glenwood Farm; 7, Sam-Son Farms

Trainers– 1, Frostad Mark; 2, Jukosky Richard H; 3, Frostad Mark; 4, Frostad Mark; 5, Bell David R; 6, Day-Phillips Catherine; 7, Frostad Mark

Scratched– Last Answer (10Sep04 9WO 2)

$1 Pick Three (6–2–2) Paid $121.90 ; Pick Three Pool $12,827 .

NINTH RACE
Woodbine
OCTOBER 3, 2004

1 1/16 MILES. (1.40[4]) 39TH RUNNING OF THE MAZARINE BREEDERS' CUP. Grade II. Purse $250,000 (plus $75,000 BC – Breeders' Cup) FOR TWO-YEAR-OLD FILLIES. By subscription of $250 each which shall accompany the nomination and an additional $2,500 when making entry; with $175,000 added, and an additional $75,000 from the Breeders' Cup Fund for Cup nominees only. The host association's added monies and all fees to be divided: 60% to the winner, 20% to second, 11% to third, 6% to fourth and 3% to fifth. Breeders' Cup Fund monies correspondingly divided provided a Breeders' Cup nominee has finished in an awarded position. Any Breeders'Cup Fund monies not awarded will revert back to the fund. Weight 120 lbs. Winners of a sweepstakes of $75,000 at a mile or over, or a sweepstakes of $75,000 three times at any distance, additional 2 lbs.; Non-winners of a sweepstakes of $75,000 twice at any distance allowed 3 lbs.; Of a sweepstakes of $75,000 once, 5 lbs.; Of a race other than claiming, 7 lbs. (No Canadian Bred Allowance.) Closed Wednesday, September 15 with 25 nominations. Plus up to $15,180 Ontario Sire/Canadian Bred Breeder Awards. Includes $25,000 from the Thoroughbred Improvement Program and Canadian Thoroughbred Horse Society.

Value of Race: $278,750 Winner $167,250; second $55,750; third $30,663; fourth $16,725; fifth $8,362. Mutuel Pool $125,339.00 Exactor Pool $62,739.00 Triactor Pool $91,735.00

Last Raced	Horse	M/Eqt.	A.	Wt	PP	St	¼	½	¾	Str	Fin	Jockey	Odds $1
14Aug04 6WO1	Higher World	L	2	117	6	5	11	11½	11	1½	1nk	Husbands P	1.50
28Aug04 4WO1	Didycheatmndhowe	L	2	115	9	8	51	4½	32½	23	27½	Clark D	8.20
17Sep04 7WO1	Dancehall Deelites	L	2	116	4	3	2½	22	21	33½	32½	Kabel T K	2.30
12Sep04 8WO11	Canadian Gem	I	2	116	2	4	4½	52½	4½	43	43	Landry R C	22.75
17Sep04 7WO6	Rude Behavior	L f	2	113	5	7	73	6hd	7½	62	5nk	Baird J	67.10
12Sep04 8WO5	Extra Bases	L	2	115	1	1	8½	8½	6½	51½	63¼	Luciani D	3.90
22Sep04 2WO1	Good as Gold	L	2	115	8	9	9	9	8½	71½	72½	McAleney J S	39.10
10Sep04 8WO4	Ring City	L	2	115	3	2	6½	73	9	9	83¼	Ramsammy E	18.90
23Sep04 4WO1	Hassayampa	L f	2	118	7	6	31	3½	52½	8½	9	Jones J	14.00

OFF AT 5:09 Start Good . Won driving. Track fast.

TIME :24[2], :49[2], 1:14[2], 1:41, 1:47[4] (:24.47, :49.42, 1:14.59, 1:41.05, 1:47.99)

$2 Mutuel Prices:

6 – HIGHER WORLD	5.00	4.00	2.80
9 – DIDYCHEATAMANDHOWE		6.90	3.70
4 – DANCEHALL DEELITES			3.00

$2 EXACTOR 6–9 PAID $34.70 $2 TRIACTOR 6–9–4 PAID $103.60

Gr/ro. f, (Jan), by Peaks and Valleys – Sarah's World , by Holy Bull . Trainer Casse Mark. Bred by Thomas J Vanderhyde (Ky).

HIGHER WORLD set a reserved pace, drifted out late turn then held DIDYCHEATAMANDHOWE safe under steady pressure. DIDYCHEATAMANDHOWE in range from the outset, closed three-wide on the far turn, launched an all-out bid at the top of the stretch, finished determinedly but was not getting by the winner. DANCEHALL DEELITES stalked the pace in hand, bid at the top of the stretch, curt inside the leader but flattened out when unable to match strides. CANADIAN GEM saved ground, was roused midturn then hung in the stretch. RUDE BEHAVIOR raced well off the pace, came three-wide through the far turn, was roused but lacked a strong response. EXTRA BASES was well back early, saved ground and lacked a rally. GOOD AS GOLD trailed on the third path and was never a threat. RING CITY faded two deep on the far turn and lacked a rally. HASSAYAMPA stalked the pace, closed leaving the backstretch, was roused late turn but lacked a response.

Owners– 1, Sea Soft Stable; 2, Miller Martin; 3, Robert Harvey; 4, Fipke Charles E; 5, Fernung Brent; 6, Wilson R J and Hunsicker G; 7, Lickrish Elizabeth and Gordon; 8, Windways Farm and Quinn Stable; 9, Behind The Mask Stables

Trainers– 1, Casse Mark; 2, McPherson Alex; 3, Attard Sid C; 4, Attfield Roger L; 5, Silvera Arthur; 6, Casse Mark; 7, Buck Beverly; 8, Pierce Malcolm; 9, McPherson Alex

$1 Pick Three (1–1–6) Paid $60.80 ; Pick Three Pool $9,535 .

EIGHTH RACE
Woodbine
OCTOBER 11, 2004

$1\frac{1}{16}$ MILES. (1.40^{4}) 96TH RUNNING OF THE GREY BREEDERS' CUP. Grade II. Purse $175,000 (plus $75,000 BC – Breeders' Cup) FOR TWO-YEAR-OLDS. By subscription of $250 each which shall accompany the nomination and an additional $2,500 when making entry; with $175,000 added and an additional $75,000 from the Breeders' Cup Fund for Cup nominees only. The host association's addedmonies and all the fees to be divided: 60% to the winner, 20% to second, 11% to third, 6% to fourth and 3% to fifth. Breeders' Cup Fund monies also correspondingly divided provided a Breeders' Cup nominee has finished in an awarded position. Any Breeders' Cup monies not awarded will revert back to the Fund. Weight 122 lbs. Non-winners of a sweepstakes of $75,000 once at a mile or over or a sweepstakes of $75,000 three times at any distance allowed 3 lbs.; Of a sweepstakes of $75,000 twice, 5 lbs.; Of a sweepstakes of $75,000 once, 7 lbs.; Of a race other than maiden or claiming, 9 lbs. (No Canadian Bred Allowance.) This field will be limited to 14 entries. If more than fourteen entries pass the entry box, the starters will be determined at that time withpreference given to the Breeders' Cup nominees only of equal racing quality or weight assignment (respective to sex and weight for age).

Value of Race: $261,750 Winner $162,000; second $54,000; third $21,450; fourth $16,200; fifth $8,100. Mutuel Pool $96,024.00 Exactor Pool $54,955.00 Triactor Pool $68,860.00

Last Raced	Horse	M/Eqt.	A.	Wt	PP	St	¼	½	¾	Str	Fin	Jockey	Odds $1
19Sep04 ^{3}WO^{2}	Dance With Ravens	L b	2	116	1	1	$2^{1\frac{1}{2}}$	$3^{\frac{1}{2}}$	$3^{2\frac{1}{2}}$	1^{hd}	$1^{\frac{1}{2}}$	Kabel T K	1.40
14Aug04 ^{3}WO^{1}	Accountforthegold	L	2	114	4	5	$1^{\frac{1}{2}}$	1^{1}	1^{1}	2^{3}	$2^{1\frac{1}{4}}$	Ramsammy E	11.40
19Sep04 ^{7}WO^{2}	Criminal Mind	L f	2	113	6	3	5^{1}	4^{1}	$4^{1\frac{1}{2}}$	4^{4}	$3^{1\frac{1}{2}}$	Montpellier C	6.00
25Sep04 ^{6}WO^{1}	What's Up Dude	L bf	2	117	2	2	$3^{\frac{1}{2}}$	2^{hd}	$2^{\frac{1}{2}}$	$3^{1\frac{1}{2}}$	$4^{\frac{3}{4}}$	Husbands P	1.10
19Sep04 ^{7}WO^{3}	Lucky Cielo	L b	2	113	5	4	6	6	$5^{\frac{1}{2}}$	$5^{3\frac{1}{2}}$	5^{4}	Baird J	28.10
26Sep04 ^{3}WO^{2}	En El Fuego	L b	2	116	3	6	4^{1}	5^{hd}	6	6	6	Luciani D	14.85

OFF AT 4:27 Start Good . Won driving. Track fast.

TIME :23^{3}, :48^{2}, 1:13^{4}, 1:40^{2}, 1:47^{3} (:23.77, :48.51, 1:13.83, 1:40.54, 1:47.79)

$2 Mutuel Prices:

1 – DANCE WITH RAVENS	4.80	3.40	3.10
4 – ACCOUNTFORTHEGOLD		7.80	4.80
6 – CRIMINAL MIND			4.80

$2 EXACTOR 1–4 PAID $50.50 $2 TRIACTOR 1–4–6 PAID $156.20

B. c, (Apr), by A.P. Indy – Dance Smartly , by Danzig . Trainer Frostad Mark. Bred by Sam–Son Farm (Ont–C).

DANCE WITH RAVENS broke alertly and raced forwardly into the clubhouse turn, settled when headed by ACCOUNTFORTHEGOLD, stalked that one from the rail while WHAT'S UP DUDE sat just outside him, was set down late turn when DANCE WITH RAVENS came off the rail, challenged at the top of the stretch, dueled to the late stages and outfinished him with a strong late effort. ACCOUNTFORTHEGOLD gained a short lead on the clubhouse turn, moved clear to set a reserved pace on the backstretch, drifted out late turn, turned back WHAT'S UP DUDE but was engaged to the inside by DANCE WITH RAVENS, battled through the stretch but yielded in the late stages. CRIMINAL MIND was always in touch just off the rail, responded when roused on the far turn and finished determinedly. WHAT'S UP DUDE stalked the pace from the second path, went after the leader midway through the far turn, was forced out at the top of the stretch and gave way. LUCKY CIELO was always in touch while saving ground then was all out in the stretch. EN EL FUEGO was under strong rating while off the rail then lacked a late response.

Owners– 1, Sam-Son Farms; 2, Sez Who Racing; 3, Moldofsky Jeff and Ortofsky Norm; 4, Kuehne Racing; 5, Wellwood G Titchner L and Ross JA; 6, Wilson Robert J and HorseN Around Racing Stable

Trainers– 1, Frostad Mark; 2, Casse Mark; 3, Silvera Arthur; 4, Mareina Michael; 5, Ross John A; 6, Casse Mark

---

$1 Pick Three (6–10–1) Paid $38.15 ; Pick Three Pool $10,935 .

EIGHTH RACE
Hastings
OCTOBER 16, 2004

$1\frac{1}{8}$ MILES. (1.46^{4}) 34TH RUNNING OF THE BALLERINA BREEDERS' CUP. Grade III. Purse $125,000 (plus $16,000 THRIF – British Columbia Bred) A Scale Weight Stakes for Three Year Olds and Upward Fillies and Mares. By subscription of $200 to accompany the nomination due on Wednesday, October 6, 2004. $1,250 to enter and $1,250 to pass scratch time. With $125,000 added and an additional $25,000from the Breeders' Cup Fund for Cup nominees only. All Hastings Entertainment Inc. purse money to be divided 60% to the winner, 20% to second, 11% to third, 6% to fourth, and 3% to fifth. Breeders' Cup Fund monies correspondingly divided providing a Breeders' Cup nominee has finished in an awarded position. Any Breeders' Cup Fund monies not awarded will revert back to the Fund. Preference will be based on lifetime earnings as recorded by The Daily Racing Form at time of entry. In a case where horses have identical earnings, preference will be given to the Breeders' Cup eligible horse. Scale Weights: 3 year olds 121 lbs,Older 124 lbs.

Value of Race: $180,637 Winner $108,540; second $36,180; third $19,899; fourth $10,854; fifth $5,164. Mutuel Pool $62,693.00 Triactor Pool $51,439.00 Exactor Pool $30,966.00 Superfecta Pool $18,857.00

Last Raced	Horse	M/Eqt.	A.	Wt	PP	St	¼	½	¾	Str	Fin	Jockey	Odds $1
25Sep04 ^{8}Hst^{3}	See Me Through	L f	3	121	4	1	1^{1}	1^{hd}	1^{1}	$1^{3\frac{1}{2}}$	$1^{3\frac{1}{2}}$	Alvarado P V	8.45
25Sep04 ^{8}Hst^{1}	Summer Symphony	L	3	121	6	6	7^{1}	7^{hd}	6^{1}	2^{1}	$2^{2\frac{3}{4}}$	Hoverson C	a- 2.05
26Sep04 ^{6}Hst^{7}	You and Nelly	L	4	124	10	10	10^{10}	$8^{1\frac{1}{2}}$	$9^{1\frac{1}{2}}$	$7^{2\frac{1}{2}}$	$3^{\frac{1}{2}}$	Fuentes F P	15.10
26Sep04 ^{6}Hst^{2}	Stormented	L bf	5	124	7	2	2^{2}	$3^{1\frac{1}{2}}$	3^{1}	$3^{2\frac{1}{2}}$	$4^{\frac{3}{4}}$	Espitia J	8.20
25Sep04 ^{8}Hst^{2}	Socorro County	L	3	121	11	9	9^{8}	9^{hd}	8^{1}	4^{1}	5^{1}	Skelly R V	a- 2.05
26Sep04 ^{6}Hst^{1}	La Belle Fleur	L b	4	124	2	4	5^{hd}	4^{hd}	7^{hd}	$6^{\frac{1}{2}}$	6^{3}	Hamel R	15.40
26Sep04 ^{6}Hst^{4}	Defrere's Image	L	5	124	1	11	11	11	11	9^{2}	$7^{\frac{3}{4}}$	May R H	46.95
25Sep04 ^{8}Hst^{7}	Palace Rose	L bf	3	121	5	3	3^{1}	2^{1}	2^{2}	5^{hd}	$8^{\frac{1}{2}}$	Wilson D H	15.55
19Sep04 ^{3}EmD^{5}	Brave Miss	L b	4	124	9	8	8^{hd}	10^{12}	10^{8}	8^{hd}	9^{3}	Trimble P	62.10
19Sep04 ^{3}EmD^{1}	Aunt Sophie	L b	6	124	8	5	$4^{\frac{1}{2}}$	$6^{1\frac{1}{2}}$	$5^{\frac{1}{2}}$	10^{6}	$10^{14\frac{1}{2}}$	Gonzalez R M	1.45
26Sep04 ^{6}Hst^{5}	Ice Girl	L	4	124	3	7	$6^{1\frac{1}{2}}$	5^{hd}	$4^{\frac{1}{2}}$	11	11	Barton J	46.50

a–Coupled: Summer Symphony and Socorro County.

OFF AT 4:17 Start Good For All But DEFRERE'S IMAGE. Won driving. Track good.

TIME :23^{1}, :47^{4}, 1:12^{3}, 1:38, 1:51^{2} (:23.28, :47.87, 1:12.69, 1:38.13, 1:51.42)

$2 Mutuel Prices:

5 – SEE ME THROUGH	18.90	8.30	5.50
1 – SUMMER SYMPHONY(a–entry)		3.20	2.50
10 – YOU AND NELLY			7.10

$2 TRIACTOR 5–1–10 PAID $623.60 $2 EXACTOR 5–1 PAID $65.60
$2 SUPERFECTA 5–1–10–7 PAID $2,924.80

Ch. f, (Jan), by Sky Classic – Youcan'taffordher , by Carson City . Trainer Krasner Cindy. Bred by Upson Downs Farm & Alistin Farms (Ky).

SEE ME THROUGH broke sharply, assumed command, being well rated, led throughout, drew clear on the final turn and won driving. SUMMER SYMPHONY away alertly and unhurried on the inside, angled out to rally from four wide on the final turn, finished well as second best. YOU AND NELLY unhurried early, rallied from four wide around the final turn and down the stretch, was next best. STORMENTED broke sharply, chased the winner from off the rail, weakened in the stretch. SOCORRO COUNTY unhurried early and three wide, five wide on the backstretch, put in a bid from four wide and weakened. LA BELLE FLEUR away alertly and well placed on the inside, was through after a half. DEFRERE'S IMAGE broke slowly, trailed far back, made a late rally but was not a threat. PALACE ROSE broke sharply, pressed the pace from off the rail, gave way after three quarters. BRAVE MISS unhurried early, showed little and was not a factor. AUNT SOPHIE away alertly, stalked the pace from a three wide trip, four wide on the backstretch, gave way after three quarters. ICE GIRL in the middle of the pack, gaining on the two path, was through after three quarter.

Owners– 1, Jawl Michael; 2, Whitham Janis R; 3, Poladian Carlo; 4, Budget Stable; 5, Forster Stable and Kelly Glyn; 6, Braithwaite E M and Gorasht I M; 7, McLellan Roy E; 8, Michael Carter John Snow & Crown Stables; 9, Nordahl Leif S; 10, Barth Dr Charles and Barbara; 11, Nebssor Racing Stable

Trainers– 1, Krasner Cindy; 2, Forster David; 3, Armstrong Janet; 4, Armstrong Janet; 5, Forster David; 6, Barroby Frank E; 7, Barroby Harold J; 8, Snow John; 9, Heads Barbara; 10, Barth Charles J; 11, Richardson Donald P

EIGHTH RACE
Woodbine
OCTOBER 16, 2004

1⅛ MILES. (1.48) 94TH RUNNING OF THE DURHAM CUP HANDICAP. Grade III. Purse $150,000 FOR THREE-YEAR-OLDS AND UPWARD. By subscription of $150 each to accompany the nomination and an additional $1,500 when making entry; with $150,000 added, plus all fees to be divided: 60% to the winner, 20% to second, 11% to third, 6% to fourth and 3% to fifth. Weights, Saturday, October 9, 2004. Closed Wednesday, September 29, 2004 with 13 nominations. Final entries to be made through the entry box no later than 11:30 a.m. on Thursday October 14, 2004. Plus up to $12,420 Breeder Awards.

Value of Race: $159,450 Winner $95,670; second $31,890; third $17,540; fourth $9,567; fifth $4,783. Mutuel Pool $82,037.00 Exactor Pool $73,135.00 Triactor Pool $37,783.00

Last Raced	Horse	M/Eqt.	A.	Wt	PP	St	¼	½	¾	Str	Fin	Jockey	Odds $1
26Sep04 ^{2}WO^{1}	Norfolk Knight	L	5	116	2	4	$1^{\frac{1}{2}}$	1^{1}	$1^{1\frac{1}{2}}$	$1^{1\frac{1}{2}}$	1^{nk}	Scharfstein J	5.95
19Sep04 ^{9}WO^{5}	Mobil	L f	4	126	4	5	5	$4^{\frac{1}{2}}$	3^{5}	2^{5}	$2^{11\frac{3}{4}}$	Kabel T K	0.45
23Sep04 ^{2}WO^{1}	Sky Diamond	L b	4	117	5	2	$4^{\frac{1}{2}}$	$3^{\frac{1}{2}}$	2^{hd}	3^{8}	$3^{7\frac{3}{4}}$	Husbands P	2.50
23Sep04 ^{2}WO^{5}	Dance Engagement	L	4	111	1	3	3^{2}	5	5	4^{4}	$4^{14\frac{3}{4}}$	Sutherland C	25.40
19Sep04 ^{10}WO^{3}	Adjalah	L b	5	109	3	1	2^{hd}	$2^{1\frac{1}{2}}$	4^{hd}	5	5	Fraser C	16.75

OFF AT 4:26 Start Good . Won driving. Track fast.

TIME :23^{3}, :47^{1}, 1:11^{2}, 1:37^{2}, 1:51^{2} (:23.74, :47.29, 1:11.44, 1:37.48, 1:51.56)

$2 Mutuel Prices:

2 – NORFOLK KNIGHT	13.90	4.00	—
4 – MOBIL		2.20	—
5 – SKY DIAMOND		—	—

$2 EXACTOR 2–4 PAID $31.30 $2 TRIACTOR 2–4–5 PAID $46.40

Dk. b or br. g, (Apr), by Tejabo – Artic Bleu , by Nain Bleu-Fr . Trainer Dittfach Hugo. Bred by Margaret Squires (Ont-C).

NORFOLK KNIGHT showed speed from the outset, was under pressure through the first turn then shook clear early backstretch, set the pace, was asked twice upper stretch and once midstretch then held MOBIL safe under a hand ride. MOBIL settled early and stalked the pace, was set down midturn, launched an all-out drive in the stretch, gained to a certain point but was not getting by the leader. SKY DIAMOND stalked the pacesetter from off the rail, chased on the far turn then flattened out in the stretch. DANCE ENGAGEMENT showed brief early foot then settled on the first turn, remained in touch to the far turn then faded. ADJALAH showed brief speed, forced the pace to the backstretch then dropped back, stalked to the far turn and faded.

Owners– 1, Squires Margaret; 2, Schickedanz Gustav; 3, Patten Roger W; 4, Hillsbrook Farms; 5, Beclawat Stable

Trainers– 1, Dittfach Hugo; 2, Keogh Michael; 3, Attard Sid C; 4, Pierce Malcolm; 5, Attard Steve

$1 Pick Three (4–10–2) Paid $694.65 ; Pick Three Pool $10,854 .

EIGHTH RACE
Hastings
OCTOBER 17, 2004

1⅜ MILES. PREMIER'S H. Grade III. Purse $100,000 (plus $13,000 THRIF – British Columbia Bred) A Handicap for Three Year Olds and Upward. $200 to nominate. $1,000 to enter and $1,000 to pass scratch time. With $100,000 added, of which 60% goes to the winner, 20% to second, 11% to third, 6% to fourth, and 3% to fifth. Preference will be based on lifetime earnings as recorded by The Daily Racing Form at time of entry.

Value of Race: $128,590 Winner $75,360; second $27,720; third $13,816; fourth $7,536; fifth $4,158. Mutuel Pool $61,848.00 Triactor Pool $45,625.00 Exactor Pool $31,374.00 Superfecta Pool $20,428.00

Last Raced	Horse	M/Eqt.	A.	Wt	PP	¼	½	¾	1	Str	Fin	Jockey	Odds $1
25Sep04 ^{6}Hst^{5}	Blowin in the Wind	L	5	114	7	8^{4}	7^{hd}	$5^{\frac{1}{2}}$	3^{hd}	2^{2}	1^{nk}	Skelly R V	b- 4.80
25Sep04 ^{6}Hst^{3}	Illusive Force	L	4	119	2	3^{2}	3^{3}	2^{hd}	2^{1}	1^{1}	$2^{2\frac{1}{2}}$	Wilson D H	a- 2.85
26Sep04 ^{11}Fpx^{4}	Royal Place	L	4	121	6	5^{1}	4^{hd}	$4^{\frac{1}{2}}$	5^{1}	$4^{\frac{1}{2}}$	3^{hd}	Alvarado P V	2.90
19Sep04 ^{10}EmD^{5}	Mr. Makah	L b	4	117	1	$7^{1\frac{1}{2}}$	$6^{1\frac{1}{2}}$	7^{1}	8^{5}	$3^{1\frac{1}{2}}$	$4^{\frac{3}{4}}$	Barton J	8.05
25Sep04 ^{6}Hst^{4}	Steady Smiler	L	4	117	5	9^{3}	9^{6}	9^{2}	$6^{\frac{1}{2}}$	$5^{1\frac{1}{2}}$	5^{5}	Stephen A	21.70
3Oct04 ^{9}AsD^{2}	Indy Lead	L b	6	117	4	10	10	10	7^{hd}	6^{4}	$6^{4\frac{1}{2}}$	Loseth C	14.75
26Sep04 ^{8}Hst^{4}	Cariboo Prospector	L	3	113	10	$4^{\frac{1}{2}}$	$5^{\frac{1}{2}}$	8^{hd}	$9^{1\frac{1}{2}}$	7^{2}	$7^{3\frac{1}{4}}$	Espitia J	b- 4.80
25Sep04 ^{9}NP^{1}	Beau Brass	L	4	119	8	6^{1}	8^{3}	6^{1}	$4^{\frac{1}{2}}$	8^{3}	$8^{7\frac{1}{4}}$	Simard R E	13.05
25Sep04 ^{6}Hst^{1}	Metatron	L	5	119	9	$1^{1\frac{1}{2}}$	1^{1}	$1^{1\frac{1}{2}}$	1^{1}	9^{12}	$9^{23\frac{1}{2}}$	Hoverson C	3.60
26Sep04 ^{8}Hst^{2}	Lord Samarai	L b	3	116	3	2^{3}	2^{6}	$3^{1\frac{1}{2}}$	10	10	10	Hamel R	a- 2.85

a–Coupled: Illusive Force and Lord Samarai.

b–Coupled: Blowin in the Wind and Cariboo Prospector.

OFF AT 4:21 Start Good . Won driving. Track sloppy.

TIME :23^{3}, :46^{4}, 1:13^{4}, 1:41, 2:06^{4}, 2:19^{3} (:23.65, :46.96, 1:13.98, 1:41.13, 2:06.86, 2:19.64)

$2 Mutuel Prices:

2 – BLOWIN IN THE WIND(b–entry)	11.60	4.80	3.50
1 – ILLUSIVE FORCE(a–entry)		4.80	3.00
6 – ROYAL PLACE			2.70

$2 TRIACTOR 2–1–6 PAID $119.00 $2 EXACTOR 2–1 PAID $33.20

$2 SUPERFECTA 2–1–6–3 PAID $493.60

Gr/ro. g, (Mar), by Dumaani – Stray , by Wander Kind . Trainer Forster David. Bred by David V Forster (Ky).

BLOWIN IN THE WIND never far back, gaining from between horses on the backstretch, checked on the final turn, rallied on the inside into the stretch, gained the lead at mid stretch and prevailed driving. ILLUSIVE FORCE broke sharply, well placed on the inside, rallied from off the rail, gained the lead on the final turn, was outfinished in the stretch run. ROYAL PLACE away alertly and well placed on the inside, stalked the leaders, rallied from three wide and finished well. MR. MAKAH away alertly and allowed to settle off the rail, rallied from four wide on the final turn and down the stretch, also finished well. STEADY SMILER slow early, gaining on the outside, rallied from five wide into the stretch, he too finished well. INDY LEAD trailed for the first three quarters, put in a mild rally and was outrun. CARIBOO PROSPECTOR away alertly, stalked the pace from a three wide trip, was through after three quarters. BEAU BRASS unhurried early on a four wide trip, failed to menace. METATRON broke sharply, assumed command from the outside, set the pace from off the rail, gave way on the final turn. LORD SAMARAI broke sharply, chased the pace setter from the outside, was through after three quarters.

Owners– 1, Forster Stable; 2, Canyon Farms; 3, Sangara K K; 4, Frank McDonald & Bonnie Jenne; 5, Maybin Rob; 6, Fipke Charles E; 7, Gilbert George Hanson Raymond Kelly Glyn and Chan Karen; 8, White Tom; 9, Coyote Creek Racing Stable; 10, Canyon Farms

Trainers– 1, Forster David; 2, VanOverschot Robert; 3, Barroby Harold J; 4, Penney Jim; 5, Maybin Robert; 6, Anderson Carl N; 7, Forster David; 8, Hedge Rick; 9, Snow Mel; 10, VanOverschot Robert

Scratched– Shacane (25Sep04 ^{6}Hst^{2})

NINTH RACE
Woodbine
OCTOBER 24, 2004

1½ MILES. (Turf) (2.25^{3}) 67TH RUNNING OF THE PATTISON CANADIAN INTERNATIONAL. Grade I. Purse $1,500,000 FOR THREE-YEAR-OLDS AND UPWARD. By subscription of $1,000 each which shall accompany the nomination and an additional $15,000 when making final entry. The added money and all fees to be divided: 60% to the winner, 20% to second, 11% to third, 6% to fourth and 3% to fifth. Three-Year-Olds, 119 lbs. (54 kg); Older, 126 lbs. (57 kg). (European Scale.) Fillies and Mares 3 lbs. (1.4 kg) allowance. (No Canadian Bred Allowance.) Final entries to be made through the entry box no later than 10:30 a.m. on Friday,October 22, 2004. Supplementary nominations may be made no later than the time of final entry by payment of a non-refundable fee of $60,000 which shall include the entry fee. A trophy will be presented to the winning owner. Closed Wednesday, October 6, 2004 with 47 nominations. Plus up to $17,940 Ontario Sire/Canadian Bred Breeder Awards.

Value of Race: $1,500,000 Winner $900,000; second $300,000; third $165,000; fourth $90,000; fifth $45,000. Mutuel Pool $471,025.00 Exactor Pool $216,558.00 Triactor Pool $254,694.00 Superfecta Pool $89,278.00

Last Raced	Horse	M/Eqt.	A.	Wt	PP	¼	½	1	1¼	Str	Fin	Jockey	Odds $1
17Aug04 ^{8}YOR^{1}	Sulamani-Ire	L	5	126	3	9^{1}	$8^{1/2}$	$7^{1/2}$	$6^{1/2}$	$2^{2 1/2}$	$1^{1 1/2}$	Dettori L	0.85
5Sep04 Bad^{4}	Simonas-Ire		5	126	9	$8^{1/2}$	$9^{1 1/2}$	$8^{1/2}$	1^{hd}	$1^{1/2}$	2^{2}	Fallon K	21.35
18Sep04 ^{9}Cur^{2}	Brian Boru-GB	L	4	126	5	10	10	9^{hd}	10	4^{hd}	$3^{3/4}$	Spencer J P	4.90
5Sep04 Bad^{7}	Mubtaker		7	126	1	$7^{1 1/2}$	6^{1}	$6^{1/2}$	$5^{1 1/2}$	$3^{1/2}$	$4^{4 1/4}$	Hills R	5.50
11Sep04 ^{9}Bel^{3}	King's Drama-Ire	L	4	126	2	3^{hd}	3^{hd}	$3^{1/2}$	4^{hd}	5^{4}	$5^{3 3/4}$	Velazquez J R	11.00
18Sep04 ^{8}Bel^{1}	Senor Swinger	L	4	126	6	$5^{1/2}$	7^{hd}	10	9^{hd}	6^{7}	$6^{7 1/4}$	Prado E S	9.20
15Sep04 ^{1}WO^{1}	Burst of Fire	L b	3	119	8	$1^{1 1/2}$	1^{1}	$2^{2 1/2}$	$3^{1/2}$	$7^{2 1/2}$	$7^{2 1/2}$	Callaghan S	35.45
2Oct04 ^{8}WO^{1}	Colorful Judgement	L	4	126	7	4^{hd}	$4^{1/2}$	$4^{1/2}$	8^{1}	8^{hd}	8^{1}	Kabel T K	31.55
25Sep04 ^{14}KD^{1}	Sabiango-Ger	L	6	126	10	$2^{1/2}$	$2^{1 1/2}$	1^{hd}	2^{hd}	9^{1}	9^{1}	Blanc B	22.25
2Oct04 ^{8}WO^{2}	Lenny the Lender	L bf	8	126	4	6^{hd}	$5^{1 1/2}$	5^{1}	7^{hd}	10	10	Sutherland C	37.80

OFF AT 5:09 Start Good . Won driving. Course good.

TIME :24^{2}, :49^{4}, 1:14^{1}, 1:38^{4}, 2:04^{4}, 2:28^{3} (:24.58, :49.86, 1:14.27, 1:38.95, 2:04.91, 2:28.64)

$2 Mutuel Prices:			
3 – **SULAMANI-IRE**	3.70	2.70	2.30
10 – **SIMONAS-IRE**		11.00	5.70
5 – **BRIAN BORU-GB**			3.60

$2 EXACTOR 3-10 PAID $59.60 $2 TRIACTOR 3-10-5 PAID $214.80
$1 SUPERFECTA 3-10-5-1 PAID $359.00

B. h, (Apr), by Hernando-Fr – Soul Dream , by Alleged . Trainer bin Suroor Saeed. Bred by The Niarchos Family (Ire).

SULAMANI (IRE) settled early, raced in striking range three-deep, swung out upper stretch to launch his rally, collared SIMONAS a sixteenth out and drove clear. SIMONAS (IRE) was unhurried early, closed five-wide on the turn, gained command from KING'S drama upper stretch then failed to stave off the winner in the final sixteenth. BRIAN BORU (GB) well off the pace, came three-wide through the far turn then rallied gamely in the stretch and was full out at the finish. MUBTAKER raced midpack three-deep, was contentious at the head of the stretch but hung. KING'S DRAMA (IRE) stalked the pace from the inside, took command briefly at the top of the stretch, gave way to SIMONAS then flattened out. SENOR SWINGER well off the early pace, came five-wide late turn then flattened out in the stretch. BURST OF FIRE led early, set a reserved pace, was headed by SABIANGO late on the backstretch, rebid inside him early turn, dueled to the stretch and tired. COLORFUL JUDGEMENT was always in touch while racing two-deep but lacked a rally. SABIANGO (GER) stalked the pace, took command late backstretch, was engaged early turn, dueled to the head of the stretch and tired. LENNY THE LENDER steadied in traffic entering the first turn, was well positioned along the inside to the top of the stretch, lacked a rally.

Owners– 1, Godolphin Racing Inc; 2, Turf Syndikat 2001; 3, Magnier Mrs John; 4, Shadwell Stable; 5, Tanaka Gary A; 6, Lewis Robert B and Beverly J; 7, Sam-Son Farms; 8, Sam-Son Farms; 9, Roberts Monty; 10, Jukosky Richard H

Trainers– 1, bin Suroor Saeed; 2, Wohler Andreas; 3, O'Brien Aidan P; 4, Tregoning Marcus P; 5, Frankel Robert; 6, Baffert Bob; 7, Frostad Mark; 8, Frostad Mark; 9, Yakteen Tim; 10, Jukosky Richard H

Scratched– Ecomium (IRE) (02Oct04 ^{596659}CUR^{2})

$1 Pick Three (1-9-3) Paid $127.15 ; Pick Three Pool $16,734 .
$1 Pick Six (3/7-2-6-1-6/9-3/8) 6 Correct Paid $10,799.30 ; Pick Six Pool $24,457 .
$1 Pick Six (3/7-2-6-1-6/9-3/8) 5 Correct Paid $116.65 .
$1 Win Four (6-1-6/9-3/8) Paid $506.00 ; Win Four Pool $70,778 .

SIXTH RACE
Woodbine
OCTOBER 24, 2004

1¼ MILES. (Turf) (2.01) 49TH RUNNING OF THE E. P. TAYLOR. Grade I. Purse $750,000 FOR FILLIES AND MARES, THREE-YEAR-OLDS AND UPWARD. By subscription of $750 each which shall accompany the nomination and an additional $7,500 when making entry; the added money and all fees to be divided: 60% to the winner, 20% to second, 11% to third, 6% to fourth and 3% to fifth. Three-Year-Olds 118 lbs. (53.5 kg); Older, 123 lbs. (55.5 kg) (European Scale). (No Canadian Bred Allowance). Final entries to be made through the entry box no later than 10:30 a.m. on Friday, October 22, 2004. Supplementary nominations may be made no later than the time of final entry by payment of a non-refundable fee of $30,000 which shall include the entry fee. $50,000 of this purse has been provided through the Thoroughbred Improvement Program and Canadian Thoroughbred Horse Society. Plus up to $17,940 Ontario Sire/Canadian Bred Breeder Awards. Closed Wednesday, October 6, 2004 with 38 nominations.

Value of Race: $750,000 Winner $450,000; second $150,000; third $82,500; fourth $45,000; fifth $22,500. Mutuel Pool $279,022.00 Exactor Pool $150,057.00 Triactor Pool $158,090.00 Superfecta Pool $44,639.00

Last Raced	Horse	M/Eqt.	A.	Wt	PP	¼	½	¾	1	Str	Fin	Jockey	Odds $1
20Oct04 7Bel2	Commercante-FR	L	4	123	5	6 1½	6½	6 2	3 hd	2 hd	1½	Velazquez J R	2.55
18Aug04 YOR4	Punctilious-GB	L f	3	118	8	5 2½	5 1½	5 1½	5 hd	1 hd	2 nk	Dettori L	1.10
19Sep04 6WO1	Classic Stamp	L	4	123	1	8	8	8	7 2½	4 1½	3 2¼	Husbands P	10.45
20Oct04 LCH1	Samando-FR	L	4	123	2	3 1	4½	4 hd	6 hd	5 2	4 no	Blanc B	8.55
10Oct04 4WO1	Mona Rose	L	4	123	3	4 hd	3 hd	2 hd	2 1½	3 1½	5 1	Da Silva E R	29.60
20Oct04 LCH4	Asti-Ire		3	118	6	7 2½	7 4½	7 2	8	7 1½	6 2¼	Migliore R	14.65
5Sep04 LCH1	Ometsz-Ire	L	3	118	4	1 1	1 hd	1½	1 hd	6 hd	7½	Prado E S	5.95
10Oct04 4WO2	Heyahohowdy	L bf	5	123	7	2 hd	2½	3 1	4½	8	8	Sabourin R B	58.45

OFF AT 3:28 Start Good. Won driving. Course good.

TIME :26, :50 4, 1:15 2, 1:40, 2:04 (:26.03, :50.87, 1:15.54, 1:40.05, 2:04.02)

$2 Mutuel Prices:				
	6 – COMMERCANTE-FR	7.10	3.00	2.60
	10 – PUNCTILIOUS-GB		2.50	2.20
	2 – CLASSIC STAMP			3.30

$2 EXACTOR 6–10 PAID $16.40 $2 TRIACTOR 6–10–2 PAID $82.30
$1 SUPERFECTA 6–10–2–3 PAID $134.00

B. f, (Jan), by Marchand de Sable – Deception , by Tropular . Trainer Frankel Robert. Bred by Har De Bernesq & SC Ecurie Ouaki Fabien (Fr).

COMMERCANTE (FR) was unhurried early, closed outside rivals leaving the final turn, responded smartly, gained command inside the sixteenth pole and held well. PUNCTILIOUS (GB) stalked pace, launched her bid four-wide at the top of the stretch, had command a furlong out, came in through the stretch then was outfinished in the final sixteenth. CLASSIC STAMP saved ground while unhurried, angled out upper stretch and rallied gamely. SAMANDO (FR) stalked the pace two deep, launched her bid upper stretch but was squeezed and bumped with HEYAHOHOWDY then rallied gamely. MONA ROSE forced the issue from the rail, bid upper stretch, was checked hard a sixteenth out and was through. ASTI (IRE) was always well back and lacked a strong closing response. OMETSZ (IRE) was prominent from the outset, was under pressure on the backstretch and far turn, entertained challengers upper stretch, dueled briefly and tired. HEYAHOHOWDY forced the issue three-wide, launched her bid at the top of the stretch but appeared to be tiring, bumped with SAMANDO and was through. A CLAIM OF FOUL BY THE RIDERS ON SAMANDO AND HEYAHOHOWDY AGAINST PUNCTILIOUS FOR INTERFERENCE UPPER STRETCH WAS DISALLOWED. A CLAIM OF FOUL BY THE RIDER OF MONA ROSE AGAINST PUNCTILIOUS FOR INTERFERENCE AT THE SIXTEENTH POLE WAS ALSO DISALLOWED.

Owners– 1, Alain Falourd Hubert Guy and Robert Trussell; 2, Godolphin Racing Inc; 3, Sorokolit William A Sr; 4, Mr Hans Wirth; 5, O'Brien P and F; 6, Allen Joseph; 7, Ecurie Fabien Ouaki; 8, Kelynack Racing Stable Inc

Trainers– 1, Frankel Robert; 2, bin Suroor Saeed; 3, Hopmans C C Jr; 4, Doumen Francois; 5, Barnett Robert E; 6, Lellouche Elie; 7, Collet Rodolphe; 8, Katryan Abraham R

Scratched– Dimitrova (10Oct04 6KEE4), Inish Glora (19Sep04 6WO 2)

THIRD RACE
Woodbine
OCTOBER 24, 2004

6 FURLONGS. (Turf) (1.07^{3}) 32ND RUNNING OF THE NEARCTIC HANDICAP. Grade II. Purse $250,000 FOR THREE-YEAR-OLDS AND UPWARD. By subscription of $250 each which shall accompany the nomination and an additional $2,500 when making entry; with $250,000 added plus all fees to be divided: 60% to the winner, 20% to second, 11% to third, 6% to fourth and 3% to fifth. Weights, Saturday, October 16, 2004. Final entries to be made through the entry box no later than 11:30 a.m. on Friday, October 22, 2004. Plus up to $15,180 Ontario Sire/Canadian Bred Breeder Awards. Closed Wednesday, October 6, 2004 with 31 nominations. (Rail at 40 feet).

Value of Race: $282,750 Winner $169,650; second $56,550; third $31,103; fourth $16,965; fifth $8,482. Mutuel Pool $173,433.00 Exactor Pool $101,156.00 Triactor Pool $116,403.00

Last Raced	Horse	M/Eqt.	A.	Wt	PP	St	¼	½	Str	Fin	Jockey	Odds $1
1Oct04 ^{9}WO^{1}	I Thee Wed	L b	4	114	4	6	7^{2}	$7^{\frac{1}{2}}$	$4^{1\frac{1}{2}}$	1^{nk}	McAleney J S	26.70
28Aug04 ^{8}WO^{7}	Chris's Bad Boy	L f	7	118	9	3	$2^{1\frac{1}{2}}$	$1^{2\frac{1}{2}}$	$1^{2\frac{1}{2}}$	2^{nk}	Jones J	6.45
25Sep04 ^{9}Bel^{3}	Hour of Justice	L	4	116	7	5	4^{1}	$2^{\frac{1}{2}}$	2^{1}	3^{hd}	Kabel T K	1.25
1Oct04 ^{10}WO^{1}	Dalavin	L b	3	117	5	8	5^{hd}	$4^{\frac{1}{2}}$	$3^{\frac{1}{2}}$	$4^{1\frac{1}{4}}$	Husbands P	15.20
8Aug04 ^{5}DEA^{17}	Crystal Castle		6	118	6	10	9^{1}	$8^{\frac{1}{2}}$	$5^{\frac{1}{2}}$	$5^{\frac{1}{2}}$	Fallon K	4.15
11Oct04 ^{7}WO^{3}	Frank's Selection	L b	8	115	1	1	6^{3}	$6^{\frac{1}{2}}$	6^{hd}	$6^{\frac{3}{4}}$	Montpellier C	11.40
2Oct04 ^{8}WO^{6}	French Lieutenant	L	4	116	10	9	$8^{\frac{1}{2}}$	10	8^{4}	7^{hd}	Husbands S P	36.90
16Sep04 ^{6}WO^{2}	Parasail	L b	4	113	3	2	$3^{\frac{1}{2}}$	$5^{1\frac{1}{2}}$	7^{2}	$8^{3\frac{1}{4}}$	Landry R C	10.95
24Sep04 ^{8}Mth^{2}	Blakelock	L	4	115	2	7	10	9^{2}	9^{4}	$9^{5\frac{1}{4}}$	Coa E M	8.40
1Oct04 ^{10}WO^{2}	As Expected	L b	5	114	8	4	1^{hd}	3^{hd}	10	10	Dos Ramos R A	20.80

OFF AT 1:55 Start Good For All But CRYSTAL CASTLE. Won driving. Course good.

TIME :22^{3}, :44^{4}, :56^{2}, 1:09^{1} (:22.63, :44.98, :56.59, 1:09.36)

$2 Mutuel Prices:			
4 – I THEE WED	55.40	21.70	6.80
9 – CHRIS'S BAD BOY		6.90	4.00
7 – HOUR OF JUSTICE			2.50

$2 EXACTOR 4–9 PAID $386.30 $2 TRIACTOR 4–9–7 PAID $1,565.50

Ch. g, (Feb), by Affirmed – With This Ring , by Green Dancer . Trainer Bell David R. Bred by Pin Oak Stud LLC (Ky).

I THEE WED raced midpack three-deep, closed outside rivals in the stretch, finished fastest and just got up. CHRIS'S BAD BOY raced prominently on the outside, dueled briefly then shook clear midturn, had command to the final yards and failed to contain the winner. HOUR OF JUSTICE stalked from the third path, was all out in the stretch and gaining late. DALAVIN always in range, raced three-wide, closed leaving the turn and gained steadily through the stretch. CRYSTAL CASTLE off a step slowly, attained striking range three-wide ate turn then finished gamely in vain. FRANK'S SELECTION raced midpack along the inside then hung in the stretch. FRENCH LIEUTENANT raced off the pace on the fourth path, was gaining mildly in the stretch but needed more to menace. PARASAIL raced forwardly on the backstretch, took back from the duel at the turn, stalked on the rail then flattened out in the stretch. BLAKELOCK always well back, raced between foes on the second path and was never in contention. AS EXPECTED prominent from the outset, bid in earnest between horses entering the turn, dueled to midturn and could no longer stay with the leader, chased briefly and tired.

Owners– 1, Pin Oak Stable LLC; 2, Alpine Stable Ltd; 3, Stronach Stables; 4, Cappuccitti Audre and Gordon; 5, Herrick Racing LLC; 6, Elliott-Griem Lynda; 7, Glenwood Farm; 8, Sam-Son Farms; 9, Stillmeadow Farm Inc; 10, Bruno Brothers Farms

Trainers– 1, Bell David R; 2, Armata Vito; 3, Keogh Michael; 4, Cappuccitti Audre; 5, Vienna Darrell; 6, Griem Robert J; 7, Day-Phillips Catherine; 8, Frostad Mark; 9, Weaver George; 10, Loney Radlie A

$1 Pick Three (7–9–4) Paid $1,894.65 ; Pick Three Pool $16,049 .

SIXTH RACE
Woodbine
NOVEMBER 13, 2004

1¼ MILES. (2.01) 111TH RUNNING OF THE MAPLE LEAF. Grade III. Purse $175,000 (plus $50,000 Other Sources) FOR FILLIES AND MARES, THREE-YEAR-OLDS AND UPWARD. By subscription of $175 each which shall accompany the nomination and an additional $1,750 when making entry; with $175,000 added and an additional $50,000 for Canadian Breds, plus all fees to be divided: 60% to the winner, 20% to second, 11% to third, 6% to fourth and 3% to fifth. Three-Year-Olds 119 lbs., Older 124 lbs. Winners of a sweepstakes of $75,000 three times at a mile or over in 2004, additional 2 lbs.; Non-winners of a sweepstakes of $75,000 twice at a mile or over in 2004 allowed 3 lbs.; Of a sweepstakes of $75,000 once at a mile or over in 2004, 5 lbs.; Of $51,840 at a mile or over in 2004, 7 lbs. (Maiden or claiming races not considered.) (No Canadian Bred Allowance.) Final entries to be made through the entry box no later than 11:30 a.m. on Thursday, November 11, 2004. Plus $50,000 for Canadian Breds from the Thoroughbred Improvement Program and Canadian Thoroughbred Horse Society. Plus up to $11,040 Breeder Awards. Closed Wednesday, October 27, 2004 with 12 nominations.

Value of Race: $218,850 Winner $141,510; second $37,170; third $20,444; fourth $14,151; fifth $5,575. Mutuel Pool $86,338.00 Exactor Pool $76,553.00

Last Raced	Horse	M/Eqt.	A.	Wt	PP	¼	½	¾	1	Str	Fin	Jockey	Odds $1
24Oct04 ^{5}WO^{2}	One for Rose	L	5	126	4	$1^{\frac{1}{2}}$	$1^{1\frac{1}{2}}$	$1^{\frac{1}{2}}$	1^{3}	1^{6}	$1^{6\frac{1}{2}}$	Ramsammy E	0.50
24Oct04 ^{5}WO^{3}	Clouds of Gold	L	5	118	3	$2^{\frac{1}{2}}$	2^{1}	$2^{3\frac{1}{2}}$	2^{2}	$2^{\frac{1}{2}}$	$2^{\frac{1}{2}}$	Jones J	3.20
24Oct04 ^{5}WO^{1}	Raylene	L b	4	117	1	3^{1}	$3^{\frac{1}{2}}$	$3^{2\frac{1}{2}}$	3^{6}	3^{7}	$3^{7\frac{3}{4}}$	McAleney J S	3.65
10Oct04 ^{4}WO^{7}	Appleby Gardens	L	4	117	2	5	4^{1}	5	$4^{1\frac{1}{2}}$	$4^{1\frac{1}{2}}$	$4^{\frac{1}{2}}$	Husbands P	11.95
16Oct04 ^{7}WO^{6}	Six Jiggles	L	4	118	5	4^{1}	5	4^{hd}	5	5	5	Husbands S P	37.80

OFF AT 3:28 Start Good For All But APPLEBY GARDENS. Won driving. Track fast.

TIME :24^{4}, :49^{4}, 1:14^{2}, 1:39^{1}, 2:04^{4} (:24.87, :49.97, 1:14.56, 1:39.22, 2:04.87)

$2 Mutuel Prices:			
4 – ONE FOR ROSE	3.00	2.30	—
3 – CLOUDS OF GOLD		3.40	—
1 – RAYLENE		—	—

$2 EXACTOR 4–3 PAID $9.90

Dk. b or br. m, (May), by Tejano Run – Saucyladygaylord , by Lord Gaylord . Trainer Attard Sid C. Bred by Hill 'N' Dale Farms (Ont-C).

ONE FOR ROSE led quickly, set a reserved pace, was put under pressure by CLOUDS OF GOLD from midbackstretch, quickened on the turn then held sway under a strong ride. CLOUDS OF GOLD stalked from off the rail, moved up outside ONE FOR ROSE after three-quarters of a mile, forced the issue into the turn, chased after that one but could not stay close and was all out to save the place. RAYLENE stalked from the rail, chased hard from midway of the far turn and finished best of the others. APPLEBY GARDENS off a step slowly, gained contention quickly but altered course to the outside when up on heels on the first turn, forcing SIX JIGGLES out a bit, remained off the pace, saved ground, but lacked a closing response. SIX JIGGLES forced out slightly on the first turn, raced in range to the far turn then evened out.

Owners– 1, Tucci Stables; 2, The Valiant Stable and Parsley K; 3, Calmar Stables and Ranch; 4, Melnyk Eugene and Laura; 5, Box Arrow Farm

Trainers– 1, Attard Sid C; 2, Parsley Ken B; 3, Baker Reade; 4, Bell David R; 5, Colbourne Gordon C

EIGHTH RACE
Woodbine
NOVEMBER 20, 2004

$1\frac{1}{16}$ MILES. (1.40[4]) 3RD RUNNING OF THE WOODBINE SLOTS CUP HANDICAP. Grade III. Purse $150,000 FOR THREE-YEAR-OLDS AND UPWARD. By subscription of $150 each which shall accompany the nomination and an additional $1,500 when making entry; with $150,000 added plus all fees to be divided: 60% to the winner, 20% to second, 11% to third, 6% to fourth and 3% to fifth. Weights, Saturday, November 13, 2004. Final entries to be made through the entry box no later than 11:30 a.m. on Thursday, November 18, 2004. Plus up to $12,420 Ontario Sire/Canadian Bred Breeder Awards. Closed Wednesday, November 3, 2004 with 13 nominations.

Value of Race: $157,950 Winner $99,508; second $31,590; third $17,375; fourth $9,477. Mutuel Pool $69,849.00 Exactor Pool $59,252.00

Last Raced	Horse	M/Eqt.	A.	Wt	PP	St	¼	½	¾	Str	Fin	Jockey	Odds $1
30Oct04 9WO7	Mark One	L	5	119	3	2	3$3\frac{1}{2}$	3$5$	3$4$	3$3\frac{1}{2}$	1hd	Landry R C	6.25
10Oct04 8WO1	A Bit O'Gold	L	3	120	2	4	2$\frac{1}{2}$	2$1$	2$1\frac{1}{2}$	1hd	2$2\frac{1}{2}$	Jones J	1.85
31Oct04 4WO1	Norfolk Knight	L	5	120	1	1	1$2\frac{1}{2}$	1$5$	1$1\frac{1}{2}$	2$2$	3$2\frac{1}{4}$	Scharfstein J	0.50
31Oct04 4WO2	Open Lock	L	3	116	4	3	4	4	4	4	4	Kabel T K	13.75

OFF AT 4:27 Start Good. Won driving. Track muddy.

TIME :23[4], :47[3], 1:12[1], 1:38[1], 1:45 (:23.92, :47.62, 1:12.27, 1:38.27, 1:45.00)

$2 Mutuel Prices:				
	3 – MARK ONE	14.50	4.30	—
	2 – A BIT O'GOLD		3.50	—
	1 – NORFOLK KNIGHT		—	—

$2 EXACTOR 3–2 PAID $34.90

Gr/ro. g, (Apr), by Alphabet Soup – My Marchesa, by Stately Don. Trainer Vella Daniel J. Bred by Adena Springs (Ky).

MARK ONE stalked the pace in hand, closed three-wide on the far turn, was determined in the stretch and jut got by A BIT O' GOLD in the final strides. A BIT O'GOLD got off just a touch slowly but stalked the leader from the rail, went after the leader on the far turn, challenged at the top of the stretch, had NORFOLK KNIGHT'S MEASURE inside the eighth pole then failed to stave off the winner in the final strides. NORFOLK KNIGHT led quickly, drew off a long lead on the backstretch, set a reserved pace, was engaged at the top of the stretch and yielded inside the eighth pole. OPEN LOCK settled quickly, saved ground but lacked a rally.

Owners– 1, Stronach Stables; 2, The Two Bit Racing Stable; 3, Squires Margaret; 4, James Perron Racing Stable

Trainers– 1, Vella Daniel J; 2, Day-Phillips Catherine; 3, Dittfach Hugo; 4, Creath Heather

$1 Pick Three (6–2–3) Paid $47.50 ; Pick Three Pool $10,421 .

EIGHTH RACE
Woodbine
NOVEMBER 28, 2004

7 FURLONGS. (1.20[3]) 10TH RUNNING OF THE BESSARABIAN HANDICAP. Grade III. Purse $150,000 (plus $50,000 Other Sources) FOR FILLIES AND MARES, THREE-YEAR-OLDS AND UPWARD. By subscription of $150 each which shall accompany the nomination and an additional $1,500 when making entry; with $150,000 added and an additional $50,000 for Canadian Breds, plus all fees to be divided: 60% to the winner, 20% to second, 11% to third, 6% to fourth and 3% to fifth. Weights, Saturday, November 20, 2004. Final entries to be made through the entry box no later than 11:30 a.m. on Friday, November 26, 2004. Plus $50,000 from the Thoroughbred Improvement Program and Canadian Thoroughbred Horse Society for Canadian Breds. Plus up to $12,420 Ontario Sire/Canadian Bred Breeder Awards. Closed Wednesday, November 10, 2004 with 15 nominations.

Value of Race: $164,250 Winner $97,650; second $32,550; third $17,903; fourth $9,765; fifth $6,382. Mutuel Pool $92,985.00 Exactor Pool $51,020.00 Triactor Pool $60,302.00

Last Raced	Horse	M/Eqt.	A.	Wt	PP	St	¼	½	Str	Fin	Jockey	Odds $1
6Nov04 8WO4	Miss Grindstone	L	5	113	4	3	1hd	1$\frac{1}{2}$	1$1$	1$3$	Sabourin R B	4.05
6Nov04 8WO2	El Prado Essence	L b	7	118	5	1	2$1\frac{1}{2}$	2$2$	2$2\frac{1}{2}$	2$1\frac{3}{4}$	Husbands P	0.85
24Oct04 5WO4	Surprised Humor	L	3	117	1	6	5$1$	4$1\frac{1}{2}$	4$2$	3hd	Kabel T K	6.05
19Nov04 2WO1	Sweet Problem	L	3	115	2	5	4hd	5$2$	3$2$	4$2\frac{3}{4}$	McAleney J S	6.25
31Oct04 7WO10	Spanish Decree	L f	5	113	3	4	3$1\frac{1}{2}$	3$1$	6	5$1$	Ramsammy E	14.50
10Nov04 2WO1	Colonial Surprise	L b	4	117	6	2	6	6	5$1$	6	Olguin G L	6.75

OFF AT 4:32 Start Good. Won driving. Track sloppy.

TIME :22[2], :45, 1:09[3], 1:23[1] (:22.52, :45.04, 1:09.64, 1:23.21)

$2 Mutuel Prices:				
	5 – MISS GRINDSTONE	10.10	3.20	2.70
	6 – EL PRADO ESSENCE		2.40	2.10
	1 – SURPRISED HUMOR			3.50

$2 EXACTOR 5–6 PAID $22.70 $2 TRIACTOR 5–6–1 PAID $94.70

Dk. b or br. m, (Jan), by Grindstone – Dancing in Seattle, by Seattle Song. Trainer Passero Frank A Jr. Bred by Dancing in Seattle LLC (Ky).

MISS GRINDSTONE moved up quickly to duel, edged clear midway of the backstretch, had command to midturn and engaged by EL PRADO ESSENCE, dueled inside that one to upper stretch and shook clear approaching the furlong marker then widened under a drive. EL PRADO ESSENCE broke alertly, was joined in a duel, settled just off the pace midway of the backstretch, rebid outside MISS GRINDSTONE midturn, dueled to the stretch and yielded. SURPRISED HUMOR closed along the rail on the backstretch to stalk the pace, chased on the turn, came three-wide into the stretch then hung. SWEET PROBLEM always in range, was set down midturn, closed along the rail then flattened out in the late stages. SPANISH DECREE stalked from the rail, chased along the second path through the turn then lacked a closing response. COLONIAL SURPRISE trailed throughout, came four-wide through the turn and lacked a rally.

Owners– 1, Robbins William G; 2, Cappuccitti Audre and Gordon; 3, Norseman Racing Stable; 4, Sangara K K; 5, Huarte Frank; 6, DeToro Nickolas

Trainers– 1, Passero Frank A Jr; 2, Cappuccitti Audre; 3, Attard Sid C; 4, Richards Lorne; 5, Huarte Frank; 6, DeToro Nicholas

Scratched– Ginger Gold (06Nov04 5WO 2)

$1 Pick Three (6–5–5) Paid $334.90 ; Pick Three Pool $7,810 .

A B Noodle

Own: Amity and Bench

Dk. b or b. m. 6 (May)
Sire: Alphabet Soup (Cozzene) $20,000
Dam: Rasant (Assert*Ire)
Br: Adena Springs (Ky)
Tr: Jenda Charles J(0 0 0 0 .00) 2004:(268 36 .13)

Life	22	7	4	4	$303,110	94
2004	8	3	1	3	$161,550	94
2003	6	0	1	0	$16,200	84
	0	0	0	0	$0	-

D.Fst	8	1	3	1	$60,075	92
Wet(357)	1	1	0	0	$22,000	89
Turf(316)	13	5	1	3	$221,035	94
Dst(0)	0	0	0	0	$0	-

25Sep04-3BM fm 1 1/16 Ⓣ :233 :47 1:103 1:421 3↑Ⓕ HillsboroH55k 94 6 11 1/2 11 1/2 12 11 1/2 3 3/4 Gonzalez R M LB118 4.00 94-12 Uraib117no *Cat Alert*117 3/4 A B Noodle1183 Gave way late inside 7
4Sep04-8BM fm 1 Ⓣ :223 :462 1:101 1:351 3↑Ⓕ AutmnLvesH55k 84 6 12 11 1/2 11 1/2 2 1/2 44 1/4 Gonzalez R M LB119 2.00 93-03 Marwood1193 Cat Alert117no Sea Jewel1161 1/4 Pace off rail, wknd 7
29May04-3BM fst 1 :222 :46 1:101 1:344 3↑Ⓕ SntaClaraH58k 92 3 1 1/2 1 1/2 11 2hd 24 Castro J M LB119 2.30 92-04 Gonetorule1164 A B Noodle1192 Bartok's Blithe1183 Set pace, held 2d 6
8May04-3BM fm *1 1/8 Ⓣ :474 1:121 1:36 1:463 3↑Ⓕ YrbBnBCH-G3 94 1 1hd 11 1/2 11 13 1/2 13 Castro J M LB116 7.10 94-12 A BNoodle1163 *Marwood*1162 HookedOnNiners1162 Dictated pace, driving 6
10Apr04-7BM fm 1 1/16 Ⓣ :23 :47 1:113 1:412 3↑Ⓕ MsAmericaH83k 85 9 31 22 22 22 1/2 31 3/4 Castro J M LB117 4.80 97-07 Hippogator115 3/4 Marwood1161 *A B Noodle*117nk Chasd winnr thruout 10
11Mar04-3GG fst 1 :233 :472 1:112 1:362 4↑Ⓕ Alw 37538n$y 83 1 11 1 1/2 11 11 1/2 11 1/4 Castro J M LB118 1.50 87-20 ABNoodle1181 1/4 HookedOnNiners1162 *Hippogator*1165 Pace off rail, drvng 4
31Jan04-3GG sf 1 1/16 Ⓣ :232 :481 1:124 1:46 +4↑Ⓕ BrwnBssH-G3 82 4 33 33 2hd 12 1/2 32 1/4 Gonzalez R M LB116 5.90 78-20 RedRioj1171 HookedOnNiners1171 1/4 *ABNoodle*1161 Stalked,led,overtaken 11
3Jan04-7GG wf 1 1/16 :224 :46 1:10 1:42 4↑Ⓕ Alw 40000n$my 89 5 11 1/2 11 1/2 11 1/2 12 1/2 11 1/2 Gonzalez R M LB116 5.10 93-17 ABNoodle1161 1/2 HookedOnNiners1184 FriscoBell1162 Pace off rail, drvng 7

A Bit O'Gold

Own: The Two Bit Racing Stable

Ch. g. 4 (Mar) ONTSEP02 $38,642
Sire: Gold Fever (Forty Niner) $5,000
Dam: Annasan (Corporate Report)
Br: Beclawat Stable (Ont-C)
Tr: Day Phillips Catherine(0 0 0 0 .00) 2004:(88 15 .17)

Life	11	7	3	0	$1,290,819	100
2004	7	4	3	0	$1,060,790	100
2003	4	3	0	0	$230,029	85
	0	0	0	0	$0	-

D.Fst	7	5	1	0	$625,959	96
Wet(333)	3	1	2	0	$364,860	100
Turf(269)	1	1	0	0	$300,000	93
Dst(0)	0	0	0	0	$0	-

20Nov04-8WO my 1 1/16 :234 :473 1:121 1:45 3↑ WoSltCpH-G3 97 2 22 1/2 25 21 1/2 1hd 2hd Jones J L120 1.85 86-27 Mark One119hd A Bit O'Gold1202 1/2 Norfolk Knight1202 1/4 Just failed to hold 4
10Oct04-8WO fst 1 1/8 :491 1:142 1:40 1:53 OntarDby160k 84 3 31 1/2 31 1/2 31 1/2 12 11 1/4 Jones J L124 *.70 83-29 A Bit O'Gold1241 1/4 OrganGrinder1211 AllegedRuler1174 1/4 Bid 3w,clear,held 5
8Aug04-9WO fm 1 1/2 Ⓣ :484 1:14 2:03 2:27 Ⓡ Breeders500k 93 4 24 1/2 21 1/2 21 1/2 11 1/2 11 3/4 Jones J L126 2.45 95 - *ABitO'Gold*1261 3/4 *BurstofFire*1261 1/4 SilverTicket1261 1/4 Bid stretch,clear,held 11
18Jly04-9FE sly 1 3/16 :473 1:122 1:373 1:573 Ⓡ PrncOWales500k 100 4 32 31 1/2 22 1/2 21 1hd Jones J L126 *1.15 91-27 *A Bit O'Gold*126hd Niigon12615 1/4 His Smoothness1261 3/4 Stalk, bid, just up 7
27Jun04-9WO fst 1 1/4 :474 1:124 1:374 2:043 Ⓡ QueensPlt1000k 96 10 52 1/2 42 1/4 21 1/2 22 2 3/4 Jones J L126 *1.35 81-17 Niigon1262 3/4 *A Bit O'Gold*1267 3/4 Will He Crow1261 Determinedly,gaining 13
6Jun04-8WO fst 1 1/8 :483 1:14 1:39 1:513 Ⓡ PlateTrial166k 96 7 54 1/4 53 51 3/4 13 13 1/4 Jones J L126 *1.80 90-20 A Bit O'Gold1263 1/4 *Niigon*1261 3/4 Little Bentley12610 3/4 Off step slow,drvg 8
8May04-8WO sly 7f :231 :461 1:103 1:231 Ⓡ Queenston166k 95 1 7 51 3/4 2hd 2 1/2 22 1/2 Jones J L119 5.65 88-17 TwistdWit1212 1/2 *ABitOGold*1192 1/4 NyukNyukNyuk1195 1/2 Off step slow,rebid 7

Note: Ages on all past performances are as of 2005

A. P. Adventure
Own: Lewis Robert B. and Beverly J

B. f. 4 (Jan) FTFFEB03 $425,000
Sire: A.P. Indy (Seattle Slew) $300,000
Dam: Nataliano (Fappiano)
Br: Lazy E Ranch Inc. (Ky)
Tr: Dollase Wallace A(0 0 0 0 .00) 2004:(111 21 .19)

Life	6	3	0	2	$295,080	98	D.Fst	5 3 0 2	$295,080 98
2004	5	2	0	2	$268,080	98	Wet(439)	1 0 0 0	$0 87
2003	1	1	0	0	$27,000	86	Turf(304)	0 0 0 0	$0 –
	0	0	0	0	$0	–	Dst(0)	0 0 0 0	$0 –

12Dec04–8Hol fst 1 1/16 :233 :47 1:11 1:41 3↑ⒻBayakoaH-G2 92 1 43 42½ 53 41½ 33 Smith M E LB117 *1.70 93–09 HollywoodStory1151 RoyllyChosen1162 APAdvntur117½ Split foes,rail bid 7

30Apr04–10CD my 1⅛ :46 1:094 1:363 1:504 ⒻKyOaks-G1 87 8 1110 1117 913 610 69½ Smith M E L121 6.30 73–17 Ashado1211¼ *IslandSand*1211¾ MadcapEscpde1211¼ 6w much of way,no bid 11

13Mar04–8SA fst 1 1/16 :224 :462 1:104 1:424 ⒻSAOaks-G1 91 5 43½ 32½ 52¼ 44 33 Solis A LB117 3.30 88–08 Silent Sighs1171½ Halfbridled1171½ A. P. Adventure117½ Shuffled bit 1/4 7

15Feb04–8SA fst 1 :223 :46 1:102 1:362 ⒻLsVrgnes-G1 98 1 66 54 44 42 1½ Solis A LB118 *1.10 89–18 APAdvntur118½ HollywoodStory1202½ *FrindlyMichl*1161 Split foes,rallied 8

4Jan04–6SA fst 1 1/16 :231 :464 1:111 1:441 ⒻSntYsabl-G3 94 3 66 43 33 34 13½ Solis A LB115 *.90 84–16 *APAdvntur*1153½ SltyRomnc120½ WildwoodFlowr115½ Off bit slw,late rally 6

Academic Angel
Own: Asmussen Cash

B. m. 6 (Feb)
Sire: Royal Academy (Nijinsky II) $17,500
Dam: Magic Lass (Damascus)
Br: Cashmark Farms, Inc. (Ky)
Tr: Asmussen Steven M(0 0 0 0 .00) 2004:(2293 555 .24)

Life	24	9	4	3	$427,065	95	D.Fst	5 4 0 0	$130,145 92
2004	7	3	0	2	$210,520	95	Wet(340)	5 1 2 2	$43,740 89
2003	9	4	2	0	$136,730	94	Turf(350)	14 4 2 1	$253,180 95
	0	0	0	0	$0	–	Dst(0)	0 0 0 0	$0 –

27Nov04–9FG my 1 ⊗:243 :49 1:143 1:40 3↑ⒻOC 80k/c-N 82 4 21½ 21 2hd 21½ 33¾ Meche D J L121 *1.60 79–28 Flager1191¼ MissMoses1182½ AcdemicAngel1214¾ Stalked, bid,held show 6

31Oct04–9LS gd 1 1/16 Ⓣ:242 :494 1:14 1:45 3↑ⒻBluebonnet100k 82 3 42 52½ 62¼ 73¾ 74¾ Chapa R L123 2.90 74–28 My Misty Princess119no Queena Corrina119¾ Bonnie J.1192 Checked 1/8 8

25Sep04–12KD fm 1 Ⓣ:252 :464 1:122 1:364 3↑ⒻKyCpLdsTrf100k 62 9 86¾ 67 66½ 810 916¾ Sellers S J L122 *1.70 79–15 Sand Springs1153¼ *Wildwood Royal*1162 Omeya115¾ Tired 9

31May04–8LS fm 1 Ⓣ:224 :462 1:102 1:354 3↑ⒻWnStDstH-G3 95 7 109 109 84¾ 32 1¾ Sellers S J L117 11.10 91–13 Academic Angel117¾ *Janeian*119nk Katdogawn120½ 3w 2nd turn,closd fast 12

4Apr04–11Sun fst 1 :23 :461 1:11 1:364 3↑ⒻHHensonH105k 90 9 31 3½ 1½ 14 12¼ Tohill K S L123 *.60 93–07 *Academic Angel*1232¼ Sideways1192¼ Blue Guru119¾ 4wd 1st turn, driving 9

22Feb04–11Sun fst 1 :23 :462 1:11 1:352 4↑ⒻAlw 31900N2Y 92 5 13 11 1½ 13½ 16¾ Tohill K S L118 *.80 100–12 *Academic Angel*1186¾ Runawayfun1161¼ Sideways1227 2path, ridden out 6

30Jan04–9FG sly 1 ⊗:242 :482 1:14 1:404 4↑ⒻOC 80k/c-N 66 5 43 42 1hd 21 37½ Albarado R J L120 *.50 71–20 DuetoWinAgin1201 Decnci1186½ *AcdmicAngl*1206 3-w bid,edge, weakened 5

Adoration

Own: Ameriman Racing Stables LLC

B. m. 6 (Apr)
Sire: Honor Grades (Danzig) $15,000
Dam: Sewing Lady (Key to the Mint)
Br: Lucy G. Bassett (Ky)
Tr: Hofmans David E(0 0 0 0 .00) 2004:(102 16 .16)

Life	20	8	3	1	$2,051,160	107
2004	5	3	1	0	$607,304	107
2003	5	2	1	1	$1,160,750	101
	0	0	0	0	$0	–
D.Fst	15	6	2	1	$1,697,030	107
Wet(356)	1	1	0	0	$272,304	94
Turf(273)	4	1	1	0	$81,826	93
Dst(0)	0	0	0	0	$0	–

Date-Race	Cond	Dist	Fractions	Race	Fig	PP	St	1C	2C	Str	Fin	Jockey	Med/Wt	Odds		Top Finishers	Comment	Fld
4Sep04-9AP	fst	1⅛	:48 3 1:12 3 1:37 1:49 3	3↑Ⓕ ArlMtrnH-G3	97	4	1 1	1½	1½	1 1½	1 2	Espinoza V	L123	*1.10	95-14	Adoration123 2 Tamweel116 2¾ *Indy Groove*116 2¾	Inside, ridden out	7
12Jun04-8CD	sly	1⅛	:47 3 1:12 4 1:38 4 1:52	3↑Ⓕ FlrDLisH-G2	94	1	2 1	2 1	2½	1 2½	1 1¼	Espinoza V	L122	2.50	77-17	*Adoration*122 1¼ Bare Necessities120 3¾ *La Reason*110 2	3-4w,steady drive	6
9May04-8Hol	fst	1⅛	:46 1 1:09 3 1:35 2 1:48 1	3↑Ⓕ VanityH-G1	89	1	1 1	1 hd	1½	1 1	2 2½	Smith M E	LB122	*.80	95-02	VictoryEncounter116 2½ *Adoration*122 1 *StarParade*117 5	Bit off rail,held 2nd	4
14Mar04-8SA	fst	1⅛	:46 3 1:11 1:35 4 1:48 4	4↑Ⓕ SMrgrtaH-G1	107	5	2 1	2 2	2 1	1 1	1 2	Smith M E	LB118	2.30e	90-09	Adoration118 2 Star Parade115 hd BareNecessities118 2	Stalked,led,gamely	5
16Feb04-8SA	fst	1 1/16	:22 2 :46 1:10 2 1:43 4	4↑Ⓕ SntMriaH-G1	92	5	2 1	2 1½	2 1½	2 1½	4 4	Smith M E	LB120	2.30	82-18	StarParade114 hd BreNecessities118 2 LTour115 2	Stalked pace, weakened	6

Adreamisborn

Own: Franks Farms

Dk. b or b. g. 6 (Feb)
Sire: Kris S. (Roberto) $150,000
Dam: Erica's Dream (Two's a Plenty)
Br: John Franks & Jonabell Farm (Ky)
Tr: Hollendorfer Jerry(0 0 0 0 .00) 2004:(1300 308 .24)

Life	18	5	6	2	$286,680	99
2004	10	5	2	2	$257,740	99
2003	7	M	4	0	$28,940	86
	0	0	0	0	$0	–
D.Fst	3	1	1	0	$48,585	97
Wet(381)	2	2	0	0	$152,295	99
Turf(338)	13	2	5	2	$85,800	97
Dst(0)	0	0	0	0	$0	–

Date-Race	Cond	Dist	Fractions	Race	Fig	PP	St	1C	2C	Str	Fin	Jockey	Med/Wt	Odds		Top Finishers	Comment	Fld
26Nov04-8GG	fst	1 1/16	:22 3 :46 2 1:10 4 1:42	3↑ FortyNinrH82k	97	4	8 8	8 7¼	7 5½	2 2½	2 nk	Baze R A	LB119 b	*.90e	93-20	Yougottawanna118 nk Adremisborn119 3½ MyCreed114 1	Circled 4w, rallied	9
18Sep04-11TP	fst	1⅛	:47 2 1:11 3 1:36 2 1:49	3↑ KyCpClH-G2	97	2	3 4	3 5	3 4	3 4½	5 5	Baze R A	L114 b	4.20	86-11	Roses in May118 4 Pie N Burger117¾ Sonic West113 nk	3 path 2nd turn	6
22Aug04-7EmD	sly	1	:22 1 :44 3 1:09 1 1:34 4	3↑ LgaMileH-G3	99	7	11 12	10 7¾	7 4¾	1 2	1 1	Baze R A	LB116 b	4.40	91-21	Adreamisborn116 1 *DemonWarlock*114 5¾ MrMkh112¾	Off slow,drifted,clear	12
11Jly04-11Pln	fst	1 1/16	:22 2 :45 2 1:09 1:40	3↑ AlamedanH50k	97	5	7 10	6 12	5 5¼	3 1	1 1	Baze R A	LB117 b	*.60e	101-10	*Adrmisborn*117 1 SurprisHlo116 1¼ GoldRuckus118 1½	Willingly 2d trn,drvng	8
20Jun04-7BM	fm	1 1/16 Ⓣ	:23 1 :46 4 1:11 1 1:42 3	3↑ FosterCtyH65k	97	8	7 9	6 10	5 6	4 3½	2 1¼	Baze R A	LB116 b	2.50	92-16	Ninebanks118 1¼ *Adreamisborn*116 no HandymnBill115 2½	2w 2nd turn, rallied	8
30May04-8BM	fm	1 Ⓣ	:24 4 :49 1 1:12 4 1:37	3↑ OC 80k/N3x-N	89	2	6 7½	7 7¾	7 7¼	7 5¼	3 hd	Warren R J Jr	LB120 b	*1.80	88-12	Vallarta118 no Boss Ego118 no Adreamisborn120 1¼	Split foes, jst missed	7
1May04-3BM	fm	1 1/16 Ⓣ	:22 4 :46 1:10 2 1:41 3	3↑ OC 50k/N2x-N	95	6	8 10	8 13	7 7	3 3	1 3	Warren R J Jr	LB118 b	8.00	98-10	Adreamisborn118 3 *True Dancer*120½ Sanger118 2	Bid 2w,exploded,clear	8
17Apr04-5BM	fm	7½f Ⓣ	:23 1 :47 1:11 2 1:29 3	4↑ Alw 33840N1x	85	3	9	7 6¾	5 2¾	3 2½	1¾	Baze R A	LB119 b	3.00	106 -	*Adreamisborn*119¾ *Foxlair*119 no High Alert119 2½	Saved ground, late bid	10
27Mar04-5GG	fm	1 1/16 Ⓣ	:23 1 :47 1 1:11 1 1:42 1	+4↑ Alw 33840N1x	81	8	5 5½	5 4¾	4 3½	3 4	3 2½	Radke K	LB119 b	*2.90	96-10	*True Dancer*119 2½ Foxlair119 hd *Adreamisborn*119 2½	3w trip gaining	11
26Feb04-3GG	sly	1	:22 3 :45 3 1:09 4 1:34 3	4↑ Md Sp Wt 27k	86	2	3 2½	3 2½	3 2½	1 1	1 3	Radke K	LB120 b	6.50	96-04	Adrmisborn120 3 *AmricnLbrty*119 6½ DolphnBnd116 6	Shifted 3w 1/4p, handy	6

Afleet Alex

Own: Cash is King LLC

B. c. 3 (May) EASMAY04 $75,000
Sire: Northern Afleet (Afleet) $5,000
Dam: Maggy Hawk (Hawkster)
Br: John Martin Silvertand (Fla)
Tr: Ritchey Timothy F(0 0 0 0 .00) 2004:(414 86 .21)

Life	6	4	2	0	$680,800	102	**D.Fst**	4 2 2 0	$509,800 102
2004	6	4	2	0	$680,800	102	**Wet(276)**	2 2 0 0	$171,000 90
2003	0	M	0	0	$0	–	**Turf(357)**	0 0 0 0	$0 –
	0	0	0	0	$0	–	**Dst(0)**	0 0 0 0	$0 –

30Oct04–7LS	fst	$1\frac{1}{16}$	:23²	:47²	1:11¹	1:42	BCJuvnle-G1	**97**	3	$8^{5\frac{3}{4}}$	$6^{2\frac{3}{4}}$	3^{nk}	1^{hd}	$2^{\frac{3}{4}}$	Rose J	L122	3.00	91– 02	Wilko$122^{\frac{3}{4}}$ Afleet Alex122^{nk} Sun King$122^{1\frac{1}{4}}$	4-5w trns,led,outfnshd	8
9Oct04–7Bel	fst	$1\frac{1}{16}$	:23³	:47¹	1:11²	1:42¹	Champagn-G1	**99**	6	$6^{1\frac{3}{4}}$	$5^{1\frac{1}{4}}$	$4^{\frac{3}{4}}$	$3^{1\frac{1}{2}}$	$2^{\frac{1}{2}}$	Rose J	L122	*1.25	88– 20	Proud Accolade$122^{\frac{1}{2}}$ AfleetAlex$122^{1\frac{1}{4}}$ SunKing$122^{1\frac{3}{4}}$	Game finish outside	8
21Aug04–9Sar	sly	7f	:22	:44³	1:09⁴	1:23²	Hopeful-G1	**90**	6	3	$5^{3\frac{1}{4}}$	$4^{2\frac{1}{4}}$	3^{2}	1^{nk}	Rose J	L122	*.70	87– 13	Afleet Alex122^{nk} Devils Disciple$122^{1\frac{3}{4}}$ *Flamenco*122^{11}	Ducked out stretch	7
29Jly04–8Sar	fst	6f	:22¹	:45²	:57¹	1:09¹	Sanford-G2	**102**	8	5	$6^{2\frac{3}{4}}$	$1^{\frac{1}{2}}$	$1^{1\frac{1}{2}}$	$1^{5\frac{1}{4}}$	Rose J	L120	*3.00	96– 11	*AfleetAlex*$120^{5\frac{1}{4}}$ Flamenco122^{nk} Consolidtor$118^{\frac{3}{4}}$	Drew away when roused	11
12Jly04–7Del	sly	$5\frac{1}{2}$f	:21⁴	:45⁴	:57³	1:03⁴	Alw 35000N1x	**89**	2	4	3^{1}	2^{hd}	$1^{3\frac{1}{2}}$	1^{12}	Rose J	L118	*.20	98– 13	*Afleet Alex*118^{12} *Monster Chaser*115^{1} Chazmandu$118^{6\frac{1}{4}}$	Bid turn, handily	5
26Jun04–3Del	fst	$5\frac{1}{2}$f	:22¹	:45³	:57³	1:03⁴	Md Sp Wt 33k	**83**	3	4	$3^{\frac{1}{2}}$	2^{hd}	$1^{3\frac{1}{2}}$	$1^{11\frac{1}{4}}$	Rose J	118	1.70	98– 12	*AfleetAlex*$118^{11\frac{1}{4}}$ BTrick$118^{6\frac{3}{4}}$ PrecisionPerfect$118^{8\frac{1}{2}}$	Bid, drew off handily	6

Alke

Own: Kenneth D English & Alan Braun

Dk. b or b. h. 5 (May)
Sire: Grand Slam (Gone West) $85,000
Dam: Pasampsi (Crow*Fr)
Br: White Fox Farm (Ky)
Tr: Todd Pletcher(0 0 0 0 .00) 2004:(0 0 .00)

Life	10	5	4	0	$619,385	110	**D.Fst**	9 5 3 0	$604,385 110
2004	3	2	1	0	$482,800	110	**Wet(375)**	1 0 1 0	$15,000 88
2003	4	2	1	0	$77,600	102	**Turf(287)**	0 0 0 0	$0 –
	0	0	0	0	$0	–	**Dst(0)**	0 0 0 0	$0 –

27Mar04 Nad Al Sheba (UAE) ft *6f Str 1:10¹ 3↑ Dubai Golden Shaheer-G1 Stk 2000000 — 2^{2} Velazquez J R 126 - *Our New Recruit*126^{2} Alke$126^{1\frac{1}{2}}$ Conroy$126^{\frac{1}{2}}$ 12
Timeform rating: 118 — Close up in 5th,strong bid over 1f out,outfinished

7Feb04–11GP	fst	$6\frac{1}{2}$f	:23	:46	1:09³	1:15⁴	3↑ DpMnstrH-G3	**108**	5	3	$2^{\frac{1}{2}}$	2^{hd}	1^{hd}	$1^{2\frac{1}{2}}$	Velazquez J R	L112	4.40	96– 11	Alke$112^{2\frac{1}{2}}$ Cajun Beat$123^{1\frac{1}{4}}$ Coach Jimi Lee$115^{2\frac{1}{4}}$	Vied, edged away late	7
8Jan04–8GP	fst	6f	:21³	:45¹	:56³	1:08¹	4↑ OC 75k/N3x-N	**110**	5	5	3^{2}	$3^{\frac{1}{2}}$	2^{hd}	$1^{\frac{1}{2}}$	Velazquez J R	L120	*1.00	101– 11	*Alke*$120^{\frac{1}{2}}$ *I'm the Tiger*$120^{7\frac{1}{4}}$ *First Blush*$118^{7\frac{1}{4}}$	3 wide, fully extended	7

Allspice
Own: Tafel James B

B. m. 5 (Mar)
Sire: Coronado's Quest (Forty Niner) $50,000
Dam: Music House (Sadler's Wells)
Br: Jim Tafel, LLC (Ky)
Tr: Geier Greg(0 0 0 0 .00) 2004:(184 21 .11)

Life	15	4	3	1	$317,496	99
2004	8	2	2	0	$191,394	99
2003	4	0	1	1	$49,302	88
	0	0	0	0	$0	-

D.Fst	13	4	2	1	$311,096	99
Wet(353)	1	0	1	0	$6,400	85
Turf(294)	1	0	0	0	$0	58
Dst(0)	0	0	0	0	$0	-

4Sep04-9AP fst 1⅛ :48³ 1:12³ 1:37 1:49³ 3↑Ⓕ ArlMtrnH-G3 **71** 7 4¹½ 2½ 3¹ 6¹⁰ 6¹⁵¾ Emigh C A L116 b 28.90 79-14 Adoration123² Tamweel116²¾ *Indy Groove*116²¾ 3-4 wide, tired 7
13Aug04-8AP fst 1⅛ :49 1:13¹ 1:38 1:50⁴ 3↑Ⓕ MariahStrm52k **79** 4 3² 3¹½ 3¹½ 5⁶½ 4¹³½ Emigh C A L123 b 3.70 75-30 Tamweel121⁵ *Casual Attitude*119² Julie's Prize123⁶½ 4 wide, weakened 6
3Jly04-8PrM fst 1 1/16 :23² :46³ 1:10² 1:41³ 3↑Ⓕ IaDistafBC122k **80** 5 5³ 5³ 4³ 4⁹ 4¹⁰¾ Emigh C A LB123 b 5.40 85-12 Wildwood Royal120² Chance Dance120⁴¼ Cat Fighter123⁴½ 3-4 wide trip 5
12Jun04-5AP fst 1⅛ :49³ 1:14⁴ 1:39⁴ 1:52¹ 3↑Ⓕ OC 62k/N3x-N **85** 3 2² 2² 2½ 1² 1²¾ Emigh C A L122 b *.40 82-14 Allspice122²¾ *Quest for Truth*120¾ True Ruby120hd Fractious post parade 6
24Apr04-8Haw fst 1⅛ :49 1:13² 1:38 1:50³ 3↑Ⓕ SixtySIH-G3 **99** 6 2¹ 2¹ 2¹ 2hd 1hd Emigh C A L115 b 21.40 104-25 *Allspice*115hd Bare Necessities122¹¼ Mavoreen114²¼ Game effort, driving 6
25Mar04-8FG fst 1 :24² :47³ 1:12¹ 1:37³ 4↑Ⓕ OC 40k/N2x-N **88** 1 3¹½ 2¹ 2¹ 2²½ 2² Lovato F Jr L117 b *1.30 93-15 Mamboalot117² *Allspice*117⁵ Mini Brush117⁴¾ Best of rest 6
13Mar04-9FG fst 6f 1:09⁴ 4↑Ⓕ MKrantzMmH75k **72** 8 2 8⁷¼ 8¹¹ 7¹⁰ 7⁹¼ Lovato F Jr L117 b 9.30 82-14 Put Me In118¹½ *Savorthetime*116hd *Tina Bull*117²½ Trailed, no factor 8
12Feb04-9FG gd 5½f ⊗ :22⁴ :46¹ :58³ 1:05¹ 4↑Ⓕ OC 40k/N2x-N **85** 4 5 4²½ 4¹¾ 4² 2½ Albarado R J L118 b 4.80 90-18 *Comalagold*118½ Allspice118nk Cabo Sunrise118no Split foes, late 6

Alphabet Kisses
Own: Harris Farms Inc

Gr/ro. f. 4 (Feb)
Sire: Alphabet Soup (Cozzene) $20,000
Dam: Kiss for Six (Saratoga Six)
Br: Harris Farms Inc. (Cal)
Tr: Jones Martin F(0 0 0 0 .00) 2004:(176 30 .17)

Life	9	5	2	1	$326,910	101
2004	9	5	2	1	$326,910	101
2003	0	M	0	0	$0	-
	0	0	0	0	$0	-

D.Fst	7	4	2	1	$287,910	101
Wet(384)	0	0	0	0	$0	-
Turf(290)	2	1	0	0	$39,000	85
Dst(0)	0	0	0	0	$0	-

27Dec04-8SA fst 7f :22¹ :44² 1:08³ 1:21¹ Ⓕ LaBrea-G1 **101** 9 1 1¹ 2hd 2hd 1¹ Smith M E LB117 b 20.10 99-07 AlphbtKisss117¹ BndingStrings121² ElusivDv119² Re-bid,led,held gamely 10
3Dec04-7Hol fst 1 1/16 :23³ :46⁴ 1:10³ 1:42 3↑Ⓕ OC 62k/N2x-N **84** 3 1¹½ 1¹½ 2½ 1½ 1¹ Stevens G L LB116 b 2.10 91-10 *AlphabetKisses*116¹ Trlow116nk MoonlightCruise118½ Btwn 2nd turn,game 6
16Oct04-7SA fm *6½f Ⓣ :21 :43 1:06¹ 1:12³ 3↑ⒻⓈ CalCupDisH150k **79** 5 5 4nk 6⁴½ 9⁶¼ 9⁶ Stevens G L LB116 6.10 88-06 OurMngo116no WestrnHmisphr119½ MrktGrdn119¹ 6wd into lane,wkened 12
4Sep04-3Dmr fst 1 :21³ :44⁴ 1:10² 1:37⁴ ⒻⓇ TorryPines81k **82** 1 1¹ 1½ 1¹ 1hd 3² Ruis M LB120 3.40 83-10 *MuirBech*118² Resplendency118hd AlphbetKisss120⁷ Bit off rail,bumpd 1/1 6
24Jly04-8Dmr fst 7f :22¹ :45¹ 1:10 1:22³ ⒻⓈ FleetTreat100k **86** 5 3 2hd 1hd 1¹ 2² Ruis M LB122 3.20 87-12 WstrnHmisphr120² AlphbtKisss122³½ MrisRos118½ Dueled,clear,2nd best 9
10Jun04-5Hol fm 1 1/16 Ⓣ :23 :47⁴ 1:12² 1:42³ Ⓕ OC 80k/N1x-N **85** 7 1¹½ 1½ 1hd 1½ 1¾ Ruis M⁵ LB113 *2.60 83-20 AlphbtKisss113¾ *OldChinsCopy*118¹ FivNickls120no Inside, held on gamely 7
16May04-3Hol fst 6f :21³ :44 :56¹ 1:09³ 3↑ⒻⓈ Alw 47000N1x **94** 1 5 3¹ 2²½ 2²½ 1¹½ Ruis M⁵ LB113 *1.60 89-13 *AlphbetKisses*113¹½ PreciousBg116¹ *MrisRos*116³ Came out,wore down foe 8
24Apr04-2Hol fst 6½f :21³ :44² 1:09³ 1:16¹ 3↑ⒻⓈ MagaliFms60k **80** 7 4 4¹¼ 2hd 1³½ 1⁶½ Ruis M LB117 2.40 92-06 *AlphbtKisss*117⁶½ PowrfulSstr117nk DncngEvnt117⁴ 3wd bid turn,drew off 9
28Mar04-1SA fst 6f :21¹ :44³ :56⁴ 1:09³ ⒻⓈ Md Sp Wt 44k **72** 3 5 3¹½ 3³ 2⁴ 2⁸ Ruis M⁵ LB115 3.60 82-12 BuffyMyLov120⁸ *AlphbtKisss*115⁴ FourtnRoss120⁴ Angld out,3w into lane 6

Amorama (Fr)

Own: Naify Marsha and Woodside Farms LLC

Dk. b or b. f. 4 (Feb)
Sire: Sri Pekan (Red Ransom) $10,000
Dam: Tanzania*Ire (Alzao)
Br: Jean Etienne Dubois (Fr)
Tr: Canani Julio C(0 0 0 0 .00) 2004:(186 42 .23)

Life	14	3	1	3	$291,729	99	D.Fst	1	0	0	0	$5,000	89
2004	8	1	1	2	$257,683	99	Wet(279*)	0	0	0	0	$0	-
2003	6	2	0	1	$34,046	75	Turf(379)	13	3	1	3	$286,729	99
	0	0	0	0	$0	-	Dst(0)	0	0	0	0	$0	-

Date/Track	Cond	Dist	Fractions	Race	Fig	Running line	Jockey	Med/Wt	Odds	Pace	Top finishers	Comment	Field
27Dec04-8SA	fst	7f	:221 :442 1:083 1:211	ⓕLaBrea-G1	89	8 7 97¼ 98¾ 86¼ 55½	Flores D R	LB121 b	18.90	93-07	AlphbetKisses1171 BndingStrings1212 ElusivDiv1192	Angled in, no threat	10
20ct04-4SA	fm	1¼	Ⓣ:462 1:10 1:342 1:591	3↑ⓕYlwRibbn-G1	91	9 96 99¾ 86¼ 95 55½	Flores D R	LB118 b	3.50	87-09	Light Jig1234 Tangle1231 Katdogawn123hd	3wd into str,late bid	10
21Aug04-3Dmr	fm	1⅛	Ⓣ:462 1:101 1:342 1:461	ⓕDmrOaks-G1	99	6 74 77 75 63½ 1no	Flores D R	LB122 b	19.30	98-02	Amorama122no *Ticker Tape*1221 Sweet Win122½	Swung out,up at wire	7
3Jly04-6Hol	fm	1¼	Ⓣ:49 1:14 1:381 2:012	ⓕAmrcnOks-G1	91	5 139¾ 138½ 106½ 88¾ 54	John K	LB121 b	62.70	81-13	TickrTp1211 DncinthMood1212 HollywoodStory121½	Swung 4w, belatedly	13
5Jun04-8Hol	fm	1⅛	Ⓣ:501 1:15 1:381 1:494	+ⓕHnymnBCH-G2	88	7 54 69 62¾ 64¼ 52¼	Flores D R	LB116 b	5.10	80-14	LovelyRfel114no WesternHemispher1141½ SgittR116nk	Chased,missed 3rd	8
15May04-8Hol	fm	1	Ⓣ:233 :463 1:10 1:341	ⓕSenorita-G3	87	1 55 54½ 34 41½ 33	Flores D R	LB116 b	5.10	90-09	*Miss Vegas*115hd Ticker Tape1213 Amorama116no	Boxed bit 1/8,rail	7
11Apr04-8SA	fm	1	Ⓣ:222 :453 1:101 1:342	ⓕProvidncia113k	83	1012 1012 1210 85¼ 22½	Baze T C	LB114 b	7.70	87-10	TickerTape1182½ Amorama1141 Winendynme1151	Swung 5wd lane,late 2d	12
18Mar04-7SA	fm	1	Ⓣ:24 :482 1:123 1:361	ⓕChinaDoll75k	80	10104¾ 87¼ 106 95¾ 32¼	Stevens G L	LB116	6.10	79-13	*Ticker Tape*117¾ Mambo Slew1221½ Amorama116no	Rail rally, split foes	10

Angela's Love

Own: Poston Bill and Vicki

Dk. b or b. m. 5 (Apr)
Sire: Not For Love (Mr. Prospector) $25,000
Dam: Goldgorian's Alden (John Alden)
Br: Dr. George E. Harmening, Kimberly Harmening & William (Md)
Tr: Romans Dale L(0 0 0 0 .00) 2004:(580 109 .19)

Life	14	6	0	2	$291,135	100	D.Fst	11	5	0	1	$227,020	100
2004	9	3	0	2	$224,795	100	Wet(420)	2	1	0	0	$46,760	83
2003	5	3	0	0	$66,340	93	Turf(273)	1	0	0	1	$17,355	98
	0	0	0	0	$0	-	Dst(0)	0	0	0	0	$0	-

Date/Track	Cond	Dist	Fractions	Race	Fig	Running line	Jockey	Med/Wt	Odds	Pace	Top finishers	Comment	Field
20Nov04-9CD	yl	1⅛	Ⓣ:492 1:14 1:401 1:534	3↑ⓕCardinlH-G3	98	11 11½ 11 11½ 12 3nk	Fox T L	L114	38.10	64-34	Aud115nk May Gator117hd Angela's Love1144¼	Moved inside,outgamed	11
10Oct04-8Kee	fst	1⅛	:464 1:113 1:37 1:493	3↑ⓕSpinster-G1	87	4 33 32½ 41¾ 66¼ 612½	Guidry M	L123	40.70	80-12	Azeri1233 Tamweel123½ Mayo On the Side1233¾	Tracked 4w,weakened	7
18Sep04-12TP	fst	1 1/16	:232 :464 1:113 1:441	3↑ⓕTPBC-G3	85	3 11 1½ 1hd 2½ 32¼	Guidry M	L122	*1.80	89-11	SusansAngel116¾ MayoOntheSide1201½ AngelsLove1222	Near rail, gamely	6
7Aug04-10EIP	fst	1⅛	:472 1:113 1:363 1:492	3↑ⓕGrdeniaH-G3	98	1 33 2½ 21½ 13 14¾	Guidry M	L115	4.50	101 -	AngelsLove1154¾ MissFortunt116½ BrNcssitis119no	2-3w trip,steady drive	6
12Jun04-8CD	sly	1⅛	:473 1:124 1:384 1:52	3↑ⓕFirDLisH-G2	83	4 32½ 42 31½ 33 47	Guidry M	L114	11.00	70-17	*Adoration*1221¼ Bare Necessities1203¾ *La Reason*1102	Well placed,empty	6
14May04-8Pim	fst	1 1/16	:243 :483 1:124 1:45	3↑ⓕPmBCDsfH-G3	81	6 11½ 1½ 1hd 3½ 68	Guidry M	L115	*1.80	74-17	FrilsforRl1152¼ SintlyAction1142 NonsuchBy116hd	Pace 2w,dueled,wkned	8
27Mar04-10TP	fst	1 1/16	:234 :464 1:103 1:404	4↑ⓕFairwayFun43k	100	7 11 11 1½ 15 18¼	Guidry M	L116	*1.80	108-14	AnglsLov1168¼ ScondrySchool1144½ JrmrRin1141¼	Inside,steady handling	7
22Feb04-9GP	fst	1 1/16	:23 :47 1:12 1:444	4↑ⓕOC 75k/N3x-N	89	1 11½ 12 11½ 12½ 13½	Perret C	L117	3.60	35-22	*Angela's Love*1173½ Serenity's Smile1176¼ Sniffles1199½	Inside, drew clear	7
11Jan04-9GP	fst	6f	:22 :452 :573 1:102	4↑ⓕOC 75k/N3x-N	81	1 10 84¼ 96 66½ 64¾	Perret C	L119	2.70	85-12	Kitty Knight1171¼ Honeymooner117¾ Final Round1171¾	Failed to menace	12

Artie Schiller

Own: Timber Bay Farm and Walsh Mrs. Thomas

B. c. 4 (Apr) KEESEP02 $67,000
Sire: El Prado*Ire (Sadler's Wells) $100,000
Dam: Hidden Light (Majestic Light)
Br: Haras Du Mezeray S.A. (Ky)
Tr: Jerkens James A(0 0 0 0 .00) 2004:(207 43 .21)

Life	13	7	2	1	$555,853	105	D.Fst	2 0 0 1	$17,170	83
2004	8	5	1	0	$467,578	105	Wet(322)	1 0 0 0	$3,978	75
2003	5	2	1	1	$88,275	87	Turf(309)	10 7 2 0	$534,705	105
	0	0	0	0	$0	–	Dst(0)	0 0 0 0	$0	–

Date/Race	Cond	Dist	Fractions	Race	Fig	PP	Calls	Jockey	Wt	Odds	Pace	Company Line	Comment	Fld
30Oct04–4LS	yl	1	Ⓣ:24 :483 1:1231:364	3↑BCMile-G1	**97**	6	96¼ 116 123¼ 94 125¼	Migliore R	L122	*3.80	81–07	Singletry126½ AntoniusPius1221½ SixPerfctions123nk	Steadied both turns	14
26Sep04–9Bel	fm	1⅛	🅃:48 1:113 1:34 1:452	JamaicaH-G2	**105**	2	21½ 21½ 2½ 14½ 15¼	Migliore R	L123	*.30	103–04	ArtiSchillr1235¼ RousingVictory1131¼ IcyAtlntic120hd	Vigorous hand ride	6
9Aug04–8Sar	fm	1⅛	🅃:4711:103 1:3531:473	HalOFmeH-G2	**103**	7	31½ 31½ 41½ 11½ 14¼	Migliore R	L122	*1.00	99–09	*ArtieSchiller*1224¼ Mustnfr122no GoodRewrd1151½	Drew away when asked	8
10Jly04–9Cnl	fm	1¼	Ⓣ:4711:112 1:3642:011	VaDby-G3	**103**	7	516 513 23 2½ 22¾	Migliore R	L117	*1.10	96–16	*KittensJoy*1172¾ *ArtieSchillr*1174¾ *PrincArch*11912¾	4-3wd,led upper,gamely	8
6Jun04–8Bel	fm	1⅛	🅃:5121:16 1:3841:50	HillPrnc-G3	**97**	6	21½ 1½ 1½ 12½ 11¾	Migliore R	L120	*.95	80–20	Artie Schiller1201¾ *Timo*1222¼ Big Booster114¾	Sprinted away stretch	6
15May04–7Pim	fm	1 1/16	Ⓣ:242 :481 1:1211:414	Woodlawn100k	**89**	7	62¼ 64 64¾ 2hd 13¾	Migliore R	L115	2.70	93 –	*Artie Schiller*1153¾ Lipan115nk Timo122hd	Steadied 3/8,driving	13
1May04–6Aqu	gd	1	Ⓣ:231 :481 1:1221:361	3↑Alw 46000N2x	**96**	3	22 21½ 32½ 21½ 1½	Luzzi M J	L115	3.25	96–10	*ArtieSchillr*115½ CIticMmoris1222½ GovrnorBrown1225	Game finish on rail	7
18Jan04–10GP	sly	1 1/16	⊗:241 :484 1:13 1:454	DaveFeldmn66k	**75**	5	74¼ 74½ 41½ 44½ 44¾	Migliore R	L118	*2.00	75–25	Tap Day118hd Zakocity1202¾ Commendation1222	5 wide move, tired	8

Arvada (GB)

Own: Gordon Giles, Pritchard

B. f. 5 (Mar)
Sire: Hernando*Fr (Niniski) $23,022
Dam: Lalindi*Ire (Cadeaux Genereux*GB)
Br: Myriad Communications and New England Stud (GB)
Tr: Frankel Robert J(0 0 0 0 .00) 2004:(491 135 .27)

Life	18	4	2	4	$309,651	103	D.Fst	0 0 0 0	$0	–
2004	7	3	2	1	$251,700	103	Wet(280*)	0 0 0 0	$0	–
2003	6	0	0	1	$30,883	–	Turf(289)	18 4 2 4	$309,651	103
	0	0	0	0	$0	–	Dst(0)	0 0 0 0	$0	–

Date/Race	Cond	Dist	Fractions	Race	Fig	PP	Calls	Jockey	Wt	Odds	Pace	Company Line	Comment	Fld
18Dec04–9Crc	fm	1½	Ⓣ:5031:144 2:0312:27	3↑ⒻLaPvyteH-G2	**97**	9	2½ 11 11½ 11½ 1hd	Prado E S	L117	3.00	89–10	Arvada117hd Humaita1191½ Honey Ryder113¾	Pace,clear,just lasted	11
6Nov04–8Aqu	gd	1½	Ⓣ:5011:16 2:0532:312	3↑ⒻLngIlndH-G2	**94**	6	2½ 2½ 2hd 1½ 32¾	Velazquez J R	L117	*1.35	86–11	Eleusis1152¼ Literacy114½ *Arvada*1171¾	Prompt pace, weakened	7
5Sep04–10Sar	fm	1⅜	🅃:50 1:15 1:39 2:14	3↑ⒻGlenFlsH-G3	**103**	4	1½ 11½ 1½ 12½ 1½	Velazquez J R	L112	3.25	99–06	Arvada112½ Spice Island118no Film Maker1212¼	Pace, dug in, held on	8
Run in divisions														
11Aug04–4Sar	fm	1⅜	🅃:4841:142 1:3842:142	3↑ⒻAlw 48000N1x	**89**	4	2hd 2½ 1hd 16 13¼	Bailey J D	L121	*1.35	97–03	*Arvada*1213¼ Chic Joy121nk Belles Lettres1211½	Took over when asked	9
9Jun04–8Bel	fm	1¼	🅃:51 1:162 1:4022:031	3↑ⒻAlw 46000N1x	**86**	1	41½ 41 32 31 2hd	Bailey J D	L121	*.65	78–20	Indy Charmer115hd *Arvada*1212¾ Shadow Play124hd	Angled in, outfinished	8
22Apr04–7Hol	fm	1¼	Ⓣ:4911:132 1:3642:011	4↑ⒻOC 50k/N1x-N	**84**	1	32½ 2½ 2½ 1hd 2no	Espinoza V	LB122	*.80	86–14	JordynMacoma120no Arvada1221 HrborBlues1223	Pulled,btwn lane,game	5
28Mar04–7SA	fm	1⅛	Ⓣ:4621:103 1:35 1:47	4↑ⒻOC 40k/N1x-N	**83**	2	68 67½ 64¼ 54 42½	Espinoza V	LB118	3.80	91–10	Uraib1182 *Night Games*118½ Harbor Blues118no	2-3w to lane,willingly	9

Ashado
Own: Starlight Stables LLC Saylor, Paul an

Dk. b or b. f. 4 (Feb) KEESEP02 $170,000
Sire: Saint Ballado (Halo) $125,000
Dam: Goulash (Mari's Book)
Br: Aaron U. Jones & Marie D. Jones (Ky)
Tr: Pletcher Todd A(0 0 0 0 .00) 2004:(948 240 .25)

Life	14	9	3	2	$2,870,440	106	D.Fst	8 4 3 1		$985,000	103
2004	8	5	2	1	$2,259,640	106	Wet(364)	6 5 0 1		$1,885,440	106
2003	6	4	1	1	$610,800	95	Turf(306)	0 0 0 0		$0	–
	0	0	0	0	$0	–	Dst(0)	0 0 0 0		$0	–

30Oct04-2LS gd 1⅛ :46³ 1:10² 1:35² 1:48¹ 3↑ⒻBCDistaf-G1 **102** 1 3¹ 5² 41½ 1½ 11¼ Velazquez J R L119 *2.00 108–02 Ashado1191¼ StormFlagFlying123nk StellrJyne1191½ Blocked 1/4,steadied 11
2Oct04-9Pha fst 1 1/16 :23⁴ :47³ 1:11¹ 1:41³ ⒻCotillnH-G2 **103** 5 21½ 2¹ 2½ 1½ 12¾ Coa E M L124 *.20 107–13 *Ashado*1242¾ Ender'sSister1173½ MyLordship1151¼ When ready,drew clear 7
21Aug04-10Sar sly 1¼ :47¹ 1:11² 1:36² 2:02³ ⒻAlabama-G1 **103** 5 3½ 3nk 1hd 2hd 3³ Velazquez J R L121 *.60 91–18 SocietySelection1212½ *StellarJyne*121½ *Ashdo*1215¼ Vied 3 wide, weakened 8
24Jly04-8Bel my 1¼ :48³ 1:12² 1:36³ 2:02² ⒻCCAOaks-G1 **106** 4 2½ 2½ 11½ 1⁵ 14½ Velazquez J R L121 *.75 85–22 Ashado1214½ StellarJayne1217½ *MagicIllusion*121⁴ Drew clear when asked 6
25Jun04-9Bel fst 1⅛ :47 1:10⁴ 1:35² 1:48 ⒻMthrGoos-G1 **96** 4 1hd 2hd 1hd 2½ 22½ Velazquez J R L121 *.90 88–11 Stellar Jayne1212½ *Ashado*1211¾ Island Sand121⁵ Stayed on for place 6
30Apr04-10CD my 1⅛ :46 1:09⁴ 1:36³ 1:50⁴ ⒻKyOaks-G1 **102** 1 33½ 24½ 2⁴ 2hd 11¼ Velazquez J R L121 *2.30 83–17 Ashado1211¼ *IslandSand*1211¾ MadcapEscapde1211¼ Moved 4w,stiff drive 11
3Apr04-9Kee fst 1 1/16 :24 :47² 1:11² 1:44² ⒻAshland-G1 **97** 1 3¹ 3² 3² 22½ 2½ Velasquez C L123 1.70 89–14 Madcap Escapade118½ *Ashado*123⁴ Last Song120³ Ck 1st turn,4w bid 4
5Mar04-9FG fst 1 1/16 :23⁴ :47³ 1:12¹ 1:43 ⒻFGOaks-G2 **94** 1 3² 32½ 31½ 12½ 13¾ Velasquez C L121 *1.10 95–10 Ashado1213¾ *Victory U. S. A.*121¹¼ Shadow Cast121½ 3-w bid, clear,driving 6

Aud
Own: Willmott Stables Inc

Dk. b or b. m. 5 (Feb)
Sire: Wild Again (Icecapade) $50,000
Dam: Gail's Brush (Broad Brush)
Br: Willmott Stable (Ky)
Tr: Reinstedler Anthony L(0 0 0 0 .00) 2004:(201 31 .15)

Life	20	6	5	0	$485,623	101	D.Fst	2 1 0 0		$26,030	83
2004	9	2	3	0	$257,578	101	Wet(399)	1 0 0 0		$340	36
2003	11	4	2	0	$228,045	97	Turf(316)	17 5 5 0		$459,253	101
	0	0	0	0	$0	–	Dst(0)	0 0 0 0		$0	–

20Nov04-9CD yl 1⅛ Ⓣ:49² 1:14 1:40¹ 1:53⁴ 3↑ⒻCardinlH-G3 **99** 5 11¹¹ 11¹⁰ 8⁹ 34½ 1nk Blanc B L115 3.50 64–34 Aud115nk May Gator117hd Angela's Love1144¼ Angle 4w late,drvg 11
24Oct04-8Kee sf 1½ Ⓣ:51 1:17 2:08³ 2:33¹ 3↑ⒻDowager150k **101** 5 67½ 42½ 3¹ 2hd 2no Day P L120 2.00 79–21 Humaita122no *Aud*120⁸ Literacy1201¼ 5w,long drive,outgamed 7
3Oct04-8LS fm 1⅛ Ⓣ:47³ 1:11⁴ 1:36² 1:48² 3↑ⒻYellowRsBC92k **88** 8 8¹¹ 89½ 86¾ 5⁴ 21¼ Borel C H L119 2.10 100–08 Ⓓ*My Misty Princess*1191¼ Aud119hd Janeian123½ 4w into lane,clsd well 8
Placed first through disqualification
5Sep04-10Sar fm 1⅜ 🅃:50 1:15 1:39 2:14 3↑ⒻGlenFlsH-G3 **98** 6 6⁴ 5⁴ 64½ 4⁴ 42¾ Day P L115 7.20 96–06 Arvada112½ Spice Island118no Film Maker1212¼ Good finish inside 8
Run in divisions
14Aug04-8AP fm 1 3/16 Ⓣ:49⁴ 1:15² 1:39³ 1:56² 3↑ⒻBeverlyD-G1 **97** 7 10⁵ 106½ 9⁵ 7⁴ 72¼ Razo E Jr L123 33.20 90 – Crimson Palace123½ *Riskaverse*123hd Necklace117nk Bid, flattened out 11
24Jly04-9AP fm 1 3/16 Ⓣ:50³ 1:15 1:39³ 1:57 3↑ⒻModestyH-G3 **94** 2 73½ 7⁶ 6⁵ 22½ 2¾ Razo E Jr L116 8.70 88–05 Bedanken119¾ Aud116½ Shaconage118³ Split horses, missed 8
5Jly04-8AP yl *1⅛ Ⓣ:50 1:17 1:55³ 3↑ⒻPsblyPrfct41k **81** 5 6⁵ 6⁵ 63½ 4³ 46¼ Peck B D L121 *1.40 57–35 *Bedanken*1232¾ Cat's Cat119½ Delicatessa119³ Flattened out 6
29May04-9CD fm 1 1/16 Ⓣ:24¹ :48³ 1:12⁴ 1:42³ 4↑ⒻMntJulpH-G3 **81** 9 97¾ 75¼ 7⁶ 7¹⁰ 76½ Peck B D L117 *2.50 84–13 StayForever116= SndSprings120nk EternlMelody1152¼ Never menaced,5w 9
1May04-9Aqu gd 1 1/16 Ⓣ:25³ :51² 1:16³ 1:46¹ 3↑ⒻBeaugayH-G3 **96** 4 4³ 43½ 4³ 2½ 2½ Peck B D L117 4.10 75–10 Dedication118½ Aud117½ Caught in the Rain114hd Game finish on rail 7

Austin's Mom

Own: Friedman Len, Nilsen, Jan and Keifetz

B. f. 5 (Feb)
Sire: Sefapiano (Fappiano) $3,500
Dam: Precious Brenda (Habitonia)
Br: Sefa's Farm (Ky)
Tr: Iwinski Allen(0 0 0 0 .00) 2004:(506 98 .19)

Life	20	6	5	2	$246,170	100	D.Fst	16	5	4	2	$228,075	100
2004	2	2	0	0	$114,720	100	Wet(390)	3	1	1	0	$17,915	75
2003	10	4	1	0	$105,190	85	Turf(253)	1	0	0	0	$180	40
	0	0	0	0	$0	-	Dst(0)	0	0	0	0	$0	-

16Feb04- 8Aqu fst 1⅛ ⊡ :491 1:142 1:402 1:523 3↑ⒻRareTreatH81k 87 5 53½ 56½ 55½ 12 11¾ Fragoso P L118 *.85 79- 20 AustinsMom1181¾ UKTrick1115¼ BiogiosBeauty1122½ Found room on rail 7
17Jan04- 9Aqu fst 1 1/16 ⊡ :231 :474 1:123 1:44 3↑ⒻAfectnyH-G3 100 6 510 68¾ 76¼ 32½ 15½ Fragoso P L112 11.50 91- 13 *Austin's Mom*1125½ GoldenDamsel1141 ConsortMusic114¾ Going away late 8

Azeri

Own: Allen E. Paulson Living Trust

Ch. m. 7 (May)
Sire: Jade Hunter (Mr. Prospector) $10,000
Dam: Zodiac Miss*Aus (Ahonoora*GB)
Br: Allen E. Paulson (Ky)
Tr: Lukas D. W(0 0 0 0 .00) 2004:(577 67 .12)

Life	24	17	4	0	$4,079,820	112	D.Fst	23	16	4	0	$3,039,820	112
2004	8	3	2	0	$1,035,000	112	Wet(329)	1	1	0	0	$1,040,000	111
2003	5	4	1	0	$817,080	109	Turf(272)	0	0	0	0	$0	-
	0	0	0	0	$0	-	Dst(0)	0	0	0	0	$0	-

30Oct04- 9LS fst 1¼ :47 1:111 1:351 1:59 3↑BCClasic-G1 109 3 31 42 73½ 55½ 59¾ Day P L123 15.20 - - Ghostzpper1263 RosesinMy1264 PlesntlyPerfect126¾ Broke slow, rail trip 13
10Oct04- 8Kee fst 1⅛ :464 1:113 1:37 1:493 3↑ⒻSpinster-G1 108 1 21½ 21½ 2hd 1hd 13 Day P L123 *.40 93- 12 Azeri1233 Tamweel123½ Mayo On the Side1233¾ 3-4w,mild hand urging 7
27Aug04- 9Sar fst 1¼ :461 1:093 1:354 2:033 3↑ⒻPrsnlEnH-G1 97 2 21½ 2hd 11½ 2hd 21¼ Day P L122 *.60 88- 11 StormFlagFlying1161¼ *Azeri*122½ Nevermore1144½ Stalked fast pace game 5
1Aug04- 9Sar fst 1⅛ :473 1:104 1:35 1:474 3↑ⒻGoFWandH-G1 106 5 11½ 1½ 1½ 1hd 11¾ Day P L120 2.95 96- 14 Azeri1201¾ *Sightseek*1222 *Storm Flag Flying*1177 Pace, resolute, clear 5
19Jun04- 9Bel fst 1 1/16 :231 :453 1:10 1:412 3↑ⒻOPhippsH-G1 78 1 1½ 1hd 2½ 410 411¾ Day P L123 *.80 81- 20 Sightseek1203¼ Storm Flag Flying1176½ Passing Shot1162 Set pace, tired 4
31May04- 9Bel fst 1 :232 :46 1:10 1:352 3↑MtropltH-G1 103 3 32½ 3½ 51¼ 62¾ 86¾ Day P L117 5.80 77- 34 PicoCntrl119¾ BowmnsBnd1142¼ StrongHop1191½ Close up inside, empty 9
1May04- 8CD fst 7f :222 :45 1:093 1:223 4↑ⒻHmnaDstH-G1 99 2 4 21 21½ 2hd 2hd Smith M E L125 *.70 89- 06 Mayo On the Side114hd Azeri1257¼ Randaroo121nk Bid btwn,game rail 4
3Apr04- 9OP fst 1 1/16 :231 :463 1:104 1:411 4↑ⒻAplBlsmH-G1 112 1 11 1½ 11½ 12½ 11½ Smith M E L123 2.00 104- 09 Azeri1231½ ⒹWild Spirit1191¾ Star Parade1147¼ Pace off rail, driving 6

Balletto (UAE)

Own: Darley Stable

Ch. f. 3 (Mar)
Sire: Timber Country (Woodman) $15,000
Dam: Destiny Dance (Nijinsky II)
Br: Darley (UAE)
Tr: Albertrani Thomas(0 0 0 0 .00) 2004:(65 11 .17)

Life	5	3	2	0	$614,000	95	D.Fst	5	3	2	0	$614,000	95
2004	5	3	2	0	$614,000	95	Wet(238)	0	0	0	0	$0	-
2003	0	M	0	0	$0	-	Turf(304*)	0	0	0	0	$0	-
	0	0	0	0	$0	-	Dst(0)	0	0	0	0	$0	-

30Oct04- 3LS fst 1 1/16 :224 :462 1:103 1:413 ⒻBCJuvFil-G1 95 1 32½ 31½ 2½ 3½ 23¾ Bailey J D L119 4.10 90- 02 SweetCatomine1193¾ Blletto1191¼ *RunwyModel*119¾ In tight 1/8,no match 12
9Oct04- 6Bel fst 1 1/16 :23 :461 1:103 1:432 ⒻFrizette-G1 89 1 72¼ 72¾ 51¾ 21½ 1¾ Nakatani C S L120 *1.35 83- 20 Balletto120¾ Ready's Gal120¾ Sis City1202¼ Dug in gamely inside 8
19Sep04- 8Bel fst 1 :242 :48 1:12 1:373 ⒻMatron-G1 89 2 41 31 52½ 31½ 21 Gryder A T L119 7.90 72- 25 Sense of Style1191 *Balletto*119¾ Play With Fire1197¼ Game finish inside 6
2Aug04- 3Sar fst 6½f :213 :444 1:111 1:181 ⒻAlw 46060N1x 74 3 5 41½ 42¾ 31½ 1¾ Velazquez J R L120 3.00 84- 16 Balletto120¾ ParagonQueen1203¾ *BrassyBoots*1183¼ Bothered start, inside 5
18Jly04- 4Bel fst 5½f :221 :454 :59 1:053 ⒻMd Sp Wt 43k 69 4 8 79 78¾ 33½ 12¼ Prado E S 118 16.50 85- 21 *Balletto*1182¼ Winsome118½ Amoureux1181¾ Came wide, along late 9

Ballingarry (Ire)
Own: Port Trust Naify, Marsha and San Gabr
B. h. 6 (Apr)
Sire: Sadler's Wells (Northern Dancer)
Dam: Flamenco Wave (Desert Wine)
Br: Orpendale (Ire)
Tr: De Seroux Laura(0 0 0 0 .00) 2004:(98 8 .08)

Life	23	6	1	6	$1,741,049	111	D.Fst	0 0 0 0	$0	–
2004	7	1	0	2	$197,074	99	Wet(281)	0 0 0 0	$0	–
2003	5	1	0	1	$194,700	100	Turf(292)	23 6 1 6	$1,741,049	111
	0	0	0	0	$0	–	Dst(0)	0 0 0 0	$0	–

30Oct04–5SA fm 1¼ Ⓣ:47 1:11 1:35 1:58³ 3↑CLHirsch-G1 **93** 3 38½ 38½ 34 55 56¾ Douglas R R LB124 b 27.30 89– 09 Star Over the Eay124¾ Sarafan124¾ Vangelis124¾ Steadied bit early 7
11Sep04–9Bel yl 1⅜ Ⓣ:50 1:14² 1:38 2:14³ 3↑ManOWar-G1 **98** 2 64½ 52 52¾ 66¼ 67 Douglas R R L126 b 15.90 83– 10 Magistretti126 ¼ Epalo126² King's Drama126¾ Inside, no response 8
24Jly04–7AP fm 1¼ Ⓣ:49⁴1:15 1:39⁴2:03¹ 3↑ArlngtnH-G3 **99** 5 52½ 41¾ 42 41½ 31½ Douglas R R L121 b *1.70 93– 05 SenorSwinger118hd MysteryGiver120 1½ Ballingarry121no Checked stretch 7
4Jly04–7AP sf 1½ Ⓣ:52³1:19² 2:10⁴2:36¹ 3↑StrStBCH-G3 **99** 2 53½ 42½ 31½ 13 11¾ Douglas R R L120 b *1.80 56– 44 Ballingarry120 1¾ DSilverfoot116nk Grey Beard117 2¾ Angled out, driving 8
31May04–9CD yl 1⅜ Ⓣ:50 1:15¹ 1:40 2:17³ 3↑LsvillH-G3 **97** 5 813 811 86¾ 45 31¼ Guidry M L120 *1.10 81– 18 Silverfoot114nc Rochester116 1¼ *Ballingarry*120 1½ 7w 1/8p,mild gain 9
8May04–7Hol fm 1½ Ⓣ:49¹1:14⁴ 2:02⁴2:26³ 3↑JMurryMemH350k **95** 6 56½ 53½ 54 42½ 43¾ Smith M E LB119 3.30 89– 11 RhythmMad116nk ContinentlRed117½ GssnRoyl113³ Btwn 3rd turn,no bid 7
3Apr04–3SA fm 1⅛ Ⓣ:48³1:12³ 1:36¹1:47⁴ 4↑ArcadiaH-G2 **95** 6 76 77½ 76¼ 64½ 43¾ Valdivia J Jr LB118 7.80 86– 13 Diplomatic Bag116¾ Statement114² Seinne115¹ Chased,split foes late 7

Balto Star
Own: Anstu Stables Inc
Dk. b or b. g. 7 (Mar)
Sire: Glitterman (Dewan) $15,000
Dam: Miss Livi (Devil's Bag)
Br: Anstu Stables, Inc. (Ky)
Tr: Pletcher Todd A(0 0 0 0 .00) 2004:(948 240 .25)

Life	38	12	7	3	$2,363,780	113	D.Fst	17 6 4 1	$993,126	113
2004	5	1	1	1	$410,834	107	Wet(386)	4 1 1 0	$322,520	109
2003	13	4	2	1	$907,500	111	Turf(326)	17 5 2 2	$1,048,134	110
	0	0	0	0	$0	–	Dst(0)	0 0 0 0	$0	–

8Oct04–7Med fst 1⅛ :46⁴1:11 1:35⁴1:48³ 3↑MedBC-G2 **107** 6 31 21½ 2hd 11½ 1½ Velazquez J R L123 6.00 89– 15 Balto Star123½ Dynever119 1½ Gygistar119¾ Bid 2w, kicked clear 8
11Sep04–9Bel yl 1⅜ Ⓣ:50 1:14² 1:38 2:14³ 3↑ManOWar-G1 **94** 8 31 31 32½ 710 79¼ Velazquez J R L126 9.70 81– 10 Magistretti126 1¼ Epalo126² King's Drama126¾ 3 wide both turns 8
14Aug04–8Sar yl 1½ 🅃:49⁴1:15 2:04³2:28² 3↑SwrdDncr-G1 **102** 1 11½ 1½ 1½ 1½ 32¼ Velazquez J R L120 *1.55 76– 22 BetterTlkNow118 1½ RequestforProl123¾ BltoStr120¹ Set pace, weakened 6
3Jly04–10Mth fm 1⅜ Ⓣ:48³1:14 1:37²2:13¹ 3↑UnitdNtn-G1 **100** 3 11 11 1½ 21 64½ Velez J A Jr L118 6.10 92– 09 RequstforProl118½ MrOBrin120¾ NothingtoLos118¹ Pace,pressured,tired 11
22Feb04–11GP fm 1⅜ Ⓣ:48⁴ 1:36¹2:11² 3↑GPBCH-G1 **104** 7 11 11½ 12 11½ 2hd Velazquez J R L122 *2.30 101– 10 Hard Buck117hc Balto Star122½ Kicken Kris118¹ On hedge, just failed 8

Bayamo (Ire)
Own: Prestonwood Farm LLC
Ch. g. 6 (Mar)
Sire: Valanour*Ire (Lomond)
Dam: Clare Bridge (Little Current)
Br: Horse Breeding Company (Ire)
Tr: Canani Julio C(0 0 0 0 .00) 2004:(186 42 .23)

Life	11	4	2	2	$321,428	109	D.Fst	0 0 0 0	$0	–
2004	5	2	2	0	$272,400	109	Wet(255)	0 0 0 0	$0	–
2003	2	1	0	1	$36,720	94	Turf(271*)	11 4 2 2	$321,428	109
	0	0	0	0	$0	–	Dst(0)	0 0 0 0	$0	–

30Oct04–5SA fm 1¼ Ⓣ:47 1:11 1:35 1:58³ 3↑CLHirsch-G1 – 6 49½ 49½ - - - Flores D R LB124 *1.40 - 09 Star Over the Bay124¾ Sarafan124¾ Vangelis124¾ Pulled up lame,vanned 7
25Jly04–8Dmr fm 1⅛ Ⓣ:47 1:11 1:34²1:45⁴ 3↑EdReadH-G1 **108** 7 44 45½ 43 21½ 2¾ Flores D R LB119 *.90e 99– 03 Special Ring119¾ Bayamo119¾ Sweet Return119¾ Stalked pace,willingly 10
4Jly04–8Hol fm 1⅛ Ⓣ:46¹1:09³ 1:34¹1:46³+3↑AmericnH-G2 **109** 4 42½ 43½ 43 12½ 14½ Flores D R LB117 *.70 98– 07 Bayamo117 4½ Sarafan119⁴ Night Patrol114 1½ 3wd move,led,handily 5
12Jun04–3Hol fm 1¼ Ⓣ:50³1:15 1:38¹2:01² 3↑CWhtghmH-G1 **105** 4 86 76 44 21½ 2¾ Flores D R LB116 5.40 84– 12 Sabiango116¾ *Bayamo*116no Just Wonder116 2½ Off bit slow,held 2nd 11
5May04–5Hol fm 1¹⁄₁₆ Ⓣ:24 :48 1:11 1:40³ 4↑Alw 54000N2X **97** 4 52 52¼ 31 2½ 11¼ Flores D R LB118 3.50 93– 09 Bayamo118 1¼ Saint Buddy120nc *Grafton*122³ 4wd,3wd,rallied 7

Bear Fan
Own: Fan Peter and Ward, Wesley

B. m. 6 (Mar)
Sire: Pine Bluff (Danzig) $10,000
Dam: Shezalong (Shimatoree)
Br: Wesley Ward (Cal)
Tr: Ward Wesley A(0 0 0 0 .00) 2004:(447 75 .17)

Life	13 8 3 1	$688,150	112	D.Fst	12 7 3 1	$621,970	112
2004	6 4 1 1	$496,180	112	Wet(367)	0 0 0 0	$0	-
2003	4 1 2 0	$67,170	102	Turf(280)	1 1 0 0	$66,180	92
	0 0 0 0	$0	-	Dst(0)	0 0 0 0	$0	-

10Jly04-11Crc fst 6f :212 :44 :5641:104 3↑Ⓕ PrcsRnyH-G2 102 5 2 2hd 2½ 1hd 22 Velazquez J R L122f *.80 93-09 Ema Bovary1192 Bear Fan1223¾ *Lady Tak*1192 Vied, outfinished 6
5Jun04-6Bel fst 6½f :214 :443 1:08 1:142 3↑Ⓕ VagrncyH-G2 112 4 5 12½ 11½ 110 19 Velazquez J R L121f *.75 101-07 Bear Fan1219 Smok'n Frolic1171¼ Aspen Gal1092 In charge from start 9
9May04-8Bel fst 6f :222 :444 :5621:084 3↑Ⓕ GnunRskH-G2 107 1 3 31 1½ 15 15 Velazquez J R L117f 1.45 95-11 *Bear Fan*1175 Harmony Lodge1203 Kitty Knight1142¼ Vigorous hand ride 5
17Mar04-5SA fm *6½f Ⓣ :212 :432 1:0611:123 4↑ⒻⓈ IrshOBrien110k 92 3 7 21 21½ 1hd 11 Smith M E LB121 2.50 94-06 *Bear Fan*1211 Super High121¾ Bold Roberta116no Bid,led, came in bit 9
14Feb04-9Lrl fst 7f :232 :462 1:1031:232 3↑Ⓕ BFrtcheH-G2 94 6 5 5¾ 2hd 13 11 Fogelsonger R L116f *1.10 93-13 *Bear Fan*1161 Gazillion1161½ *Bronze Abe*1171¼ Prompted 4wd, driving 9
24Jan04-4SA fst 6f :213 :441 :5611:091 4↑ⒻⓇ SMF&MSprnt300k 89 3 10 61¾ 63½ 63¾ 31½ •Bailey J D LB120 *1.50 90-09 MoojiMoo120¾ BoldRoberta120¾ DH ChnningWy120 Off slow,pulld,box 1/8 10

Bedanken
Own: Pin Oak Stable LLC

Gr/ro. m. 6 (Feb)
Sire: Geri (Theatrical*Ire) $9,000
Dam: Danka (Strawberry Road*Aus)
Br: Pin Oak Stud, LLC (Ky)
Tr: Von Hemel Donnie K(0 0 0 0 .00) 2004:(479 91 .19)

Life	19 11 1 3	$539,629	105	D.Fst	6 4 1 1	$102,590	96
2004	8 3 0 1	$222,555	98	Wet(336)	0 0 0 0	$0	-
2003	1 1 0 0	$36,000	98	Turf(284)	13 7 0 2	$437,039	105
	0 0 0 0	$0	-	Dst(0)	0 0 0 0	$0	-

5Nov04-4CD gd 1 1/16 Ⓣ :241 :484 1:1321:45 3↑Ⓕ Alw 68300c 82 5 56½ 52¼ 3½ 43 54¼ Pettinger D R L117f *.80 75-20 Mymich119no Fun House112¾ May Gator1193 4-5w,empty late 7
10Oct04-6Kee fm 1 3/16 Ⓣ :50 1:142 1:3911:57 3↑Ⓕ WnStGlxy-G2 87 7 83¾ 87 98¼ 84¼ 84 Pettinger D R L121f 3.40 82-12 Stay Forever121½ Super Brand1191½ Shaconage121no No threat 9
14Aug04-8AP fm 1 3/16 Ⓣ :4941:152 1:3931:562 3↑Ⓕ BeverlyD-G1 98 8 94¾ 96 32 53 51½ Pettinger D R L123f 8.10 90 - Crimson Palace123½ *Riskaverse*123hd Necklace117nk 5wd 1/4, no rally 11
24Jly04-9AP fm 1 3/16 Ⓣ :5031:15 1:3931:57 3↑Ⓕ ModestyH-G3 96 7 41½ 1hd 2hd 12½ 1¾ Pettinger D R L119f *1.40 89-05 Bedanken119¾ Aud116½ Shaconage1183 3 wide, mild drive 8
5Jly04-8AP yl *1⅛ Ⓣ :50 1:17 1:553 3↑Ⓕ PsblyPrfct41k 95 3 43 43 42½ 32 12¾ Pettinger D R L123f 1.90 63-35 *Bedanken*1232¾ Cat's Cat119½ Delicatessa1193 Driving 6
31May04-8LS fm 1 Ⓣ :224 :462 1:1021:354 3↑Ⓕ WnStDstH-G3 84 8 88 77 63¾ 84¾ 85 Pettinger D R L119f 2.70 86-13 Academic Angel117¾ *Janeian*119nk Katdogawn120½ 3wide turns,4wide 1/4 12
17Apr04-9LS fm 7½f Ⓣ :232 :462 1:10 1:281 3↑Ⓕ IrvingDstf75k 87 2 5 54½ 63¾ 56½ 34½ Pettinger D R L123f *.40 99 - Janeian1184 Cat's Cat118½ Bedanken1231 Jostled with foe early 8
28Feb04-9FG fm *1⅛ Ⓣ :5011:15 1:4011:523 4↑Ⓕ BayuBCH-G3 95 3 44½ 46 43½ 11½ 11¾ Pettinger D R L121f *1.50 81-19 Bedanken1211¾ *DuetoWinAgain*118no LadyLind1151¼ Mild encouragement 10

Bellamy Road
Own: Kinsman Stable

Dk. b or b. c. 3 (Apr) OBSAPR04 $87,000
Sire: Concerto (Chief's Crown) $5,000
Dam: Hurry Home Hillary (Deputed Testamony)
Br: Dianne D. Cotter (Fla)
Tr: Dickinson Michael W(0 0 0 0 .00) 2004:(190 39 .21)

Life	3 2 0 0	$140,400	82	D.Fst	3 2 0 0	$140,400	82
2004	3 2 0 0	$140,400	82	Wet(422)	0 0 0 0	$0	-
2003	0 M 0 0	$0	-	Turf(237)	0 0 0 0	$0	-
	0 0 0 0	$0	-	Dst(0)	0 0 0 0	$0	-

9Oct04-7Kee fst 1 1/16 :23 :47 1:12 1:433 BrdrsFut-G1 72 2 1½ 11½ 1½ 45½ 712 Dominguez R A L121f *2.10 82-13 Consolidator1212 Patriot Act1213¼ DiamondIsle121½ Weakened after 3/4s 10
6Sep04-13RD fst 1 1/16 :251 :492 1:1221:45 MGDCrdle-G3 82 2 1½ 11 11½ 16 12¾ Castellano A Jr L120f 2.20 97-11 Bellamy Road1202¾ Diamond Isle120nk Scipion1206¾ Off rail, ridden out 8
3Aug04-4Del fst 6f :221 :46 :5821:104 Md Sp Wt 35k 81 2 6 42½ 2hd 11½ 17½ Castellano A Jr L119f 5.00 87-16 *Bellamy Road*1197½ B Trick1191½ Straw Hat1195½ Drew away easily 10

Belleski

Own: Moss Mr. and Mrs. Jerome S

B. m. 6 (Feb)
Sire: Polish Numbers (Danzig) $20,000
Dam: Rangoon Belle (Alysheba)
Br: David Garvin, David Camball Garvin, Gabriel Duignan & (Ky)
Tr: Sadler John W(0 0 0 0 .00) 2004:(396 65 .16)

Life	15	8	2	1	$374,586	99	D.Fst	3	0	1	0	$12,960	76
2004	4	3	0	0	$136,567	99	Wet(349)	0	0	0	0	$0	–
2003	7	4	1	1	$195,059	99	Turf(333)	12	8	1	1	$361,626	99
	0	0	0	0	$0	–	Dst(0)	0	0	0	0	$0	–

3Nov04–6Hol fm 1 Ⓣ :244 :482 1:114 1:361 3↑Ⓕ Alw 51600N$MY **98** 8 52¼ 52¼ 43 1½ 12¼ Nakatani C S **LB**121 *1.90 83– 17 Belleski1212¼ Cuero Quero123no Betty's Wish123no Waited 1/4,bid btwn 9
29Sep04–7SA fm *6½f Ⓣ :222 :442 1:064 1:124 3↑Ⓕ SKMaddyH-G3 **99** 2 4 21½ 21½ 1hd 1½ Nakatani C S **LB**118 *1.60 93– 07 *Belleski*118½ *Intercontinental*1202 Acago116no 3wd into lane,gamely 9
26Aug04–7Dmr fm 1 Ⓣ :223 :461 1:092 1:332 3↑Ⓕ OC 100k/c -N **97** 4 43 43 42½ 32 12¼ Nakatani C S **LB**119 *1.10 94– 07 *Belleski*1192¼ *MarketGrden*119½ Fencelineneighbor1192 Lugged in str,clear 7
30Jly04–7Dmr fm 5f Ⓣ :22 :45 :554 3↑Ⓕ DaisycutrH96k **88** 4 3 73¾ 74¼ 53¼ 41¼ Espinoza V **LB**121 *1.00 95– 04 Icntgoforitht117¾ MrketGrden116no LdyGenerl112½ Stdied 4-1/2& into str 8

Bending Strings

Own: Gunther John D

Dk. b or b. f. 4 (May)
Sire: American Chance (Cure the Blues) $7,500
Dam: Straight South (Hail the Pirates)
Br: John D. Gunther (Ky)
Tr: McLaughlin Kiaran P(0 0 0 0 .00) 2004:(462 84 .18)

Life	16	5	6	0	$534,300	99	D.Fst	13	3	5	0	$450,750	99
2004	13	3	5	0	$495,150	99	Wet(294)	3	2	1	0	$83,550	92
2003	3	2	1	0	$39,150	92	Turf(275)	0	0	0	0	$0	–
	0	0	0	0	$0	–	Dst(0)	0	0	0	0	$0	–

27Dec04–8SA fst 7f :221 :442 1:083 1:211 Ⓕ LaBrea-G1 **99** 7 5 73¼ 42½ 31 21 Espinoza V **LB**121 *1.60 98– 07 AlphbetKisses1171 BendingStrings1212 ElusiveDiv1192 4wd,3wd,willingly 10
26Nov04–9Aqu fst 1 :234 :464 1:11 1:351 3↑Ⓕ TopFlgtH-G2 **98** 2 53 53¼ 51¾ 31½ 2no Bridgmohan S X L118 3.25 89– 17 Dydrmng117no BndngStrngs1182¼ RorEmotn1162¼ Drifted stretch, game 6
30Oct04–4Aqu fst 7f :222 :443 1:091 1:22 3↑Ⓕ FrstFltH-G2 **98** 5 3 55¾ 42¾ 1½ 15¾ Bridgmohan S X L116 *2.00 95– 08 BndingStrings1165¾ SmokyGlckn1152¾ PssngShot1184 4 wide move, clear 6
2Oct04–9Pim fst 6f :222 :451 :572 1:10 Ⓕ SflyKtBC-G3 **95** 6 5 65 54 31½ 12¼ Karamanos H A L119 3.90 95– 12 *BndngStrngs*1192¼ SmkGlckn119½ ThnShLghs1171½ Swung 4wd 1/8,driving 6
11Sep04–8Bel fst 1⅛ :48 1:122 1:362 1:481 Ⓕ Gazelle-G1 **79** 5 21½ 3½ 41½ 610 610¾ Day P L117 7.70 79– 15 StellarJayne1221 *Daydreming*1151¾ HeLovesMe117no Speed outside, tired 6
31Jly04–8Sar my 7f :212 :44 1:101 1:233 Ⓕ Test-G1 **83** 6 5 126½ 912 36 26¼ Day P L120 13.00 80– 11 *SoctySlcton*1206¼ BndngStrngs1203¾ ForstMsc1184¼ 5 wide, bump 1/4 pole 12
3Jly04–8Bel fst 6f :214 :442 :561 1:09 Ⓕ Frioress-G1 **82** 1 1 64½ 54 45 76 Bailey J D L119 3.95 88– 08 FriendlyMichel 1192¼ FlinStory121no ForstMusic119¾ Inside, no response 9
4Jun04–10Bel fst 1 :232 :454 1:094 1:344 Ⓕ Acorn-G1 **96** 3 51¼ 52 32 3½ 42½ Day P L121 13.00 84– 17 IslndSnd1211¾ SocitySlcton121no *FrndlyMchl*1213¾ Between rivals, gamely 8
8May04–8Bel fst 7f :222 :451 1:10 1:223 Ⓕ NasauCBC-G2 **94** 1 1 41 31½ 12½ 14¾ Bailey J D L116 2.85 87– 18 BendingStrings1164¾ GryTrffic1164 ALuluOfMnif1162¾ 3 wide move, clear 6
9Apr04–8Aqu fst 1 :224 :453 1:104 1:354 Ⓕ Comely-G3 **84** 6 2hd 2½ 11½ 2½ 23 Luzzi M J L116 10.40 83– 15 SocitySlction1223 *BndingStrngs*1162¾ *Dydrmng*1168½ Pressed pace, gamely 8
Previously trained by Hollendorfer Jerry
6Mar04–9FG fst 1$\frac{1}{16}$:234 :473 1:121 1:43 Ⓕ FGOaks-G2 **81** 4 43 53½ 43 67 67½ Martin E M Jr L121 27.30 87– 10 Ashado1213¾ *Victory U. S. A.*1211¼ ShadowCast121½ 4w bckstrtch & 2nd trn 6
8Feb04–8GG fst 1 :231 :464 1:111 1:372 GldnStMile83k **81** 1 42½ 32 1hd 1½ 2½ Baze R A **LB**117 b *1.90 81– 27 O. K. Mikie116½ Bending Strings1173 Point Dume115¾ Rank early, bid 3w 8
19Jan04–5SA fst 7f :22 :441 1:082 1:21 Ⓕ SntaYnez-G2 **81** 8 1 32 51¾ 54¾ 411½ Espinoza V **LB**114 16.50 88– 07 *YearlyReport*1141 *HouseofFortune*1214½ *PapatoKinzie*1153 4 wide, weakened 8

Better Talk Now
Own: Bushwood Racing Partners

B. g. 6 (Feb)
Sire: Talkin Man (With Approval) $1,568
Dam: Bendita (Baldski)
Br: Wimborne Farm, Inc. (Ky)
Tr: Motion H. G(0 0 0 0 .00) 2004:(424 81 .19)

Life	25	8	5	2	$1,744,437	111	D.Fst	4	0	2	0	$16,360	90
2004	8	2	2	0	$1,407,000	111	Wet(290)	0	0	0	0	$0	-
2003	7	3	1	2	$240,152	101	Turf(307)	21	8	3	2	$1,728,077	111
	0	0	0	0	$0	-	Dst(0)	0	0	0	0	$0	-

4Dec04–7Hol fm 1½ Ⓣ :502 1:153 2:04 2:293 3↑HolTrfCp-G1 **96** 3 54 3½ 2hd 1hd 62¾ Dominguez R A LB126 fb *1.10 75–22 Pellegrino126hd Meghertz123hd LicensToRun126½ Pulled,3wd bid,wkened 9
30Oct04–8LS yl 1½ Ⓣ :49 1:134 2:04 2:293 3↑BCTurf-G1 **111** 5 712 66 43 2hd 11¾ Dominguez R A L126 fb 27.90 123–07 BettrTlkNow1261¾ KittnsJoy1211 Powrscourt1262¼ Five wide move, clear 8
11Sep04–9Bel yl 1⅜ Ⓣ :50 1:142 1:38 2:143 3↑ManOWar-G1 **104** 1 88½ 86 74¾ 35½ 44 Dominguez R A L126 fb 6.10 86–10 Magistretti1261¼ Epalo1262 King's Drama126¾ 4 wide run second turn 8
14Aug04–8Sar yl 1½ Ⓣ :494 1:15 2:043 2:282 3↑SwrdDncr-G1 **106** 3 66 61¼ 43½ 31½ 11½ Dominguez R A L118 fb 7.90 78–22 BetterTlkNow1181½ RequestforProl123¾ BltoStr1201 Saved ground, clear 6
17Jly04–8Bel fm 1⅜ Ⓣ :472 1:104 1:354 2:12 3↑BwlnGrnH-G2 **103** 5 610 67 64 21 21½ Santos J A L115 fb 8.10 91–10 *Kicken Kris*1171½ *Better Talk Now*1152¼ Gigli113nk Game finish outside 10
12Jun04–9Mth fm 1⅛ Ⓣ :49 1:13 1:36 1:48 3↑Battlfield60k **99** 1 52½ 52½ 51¾ 1hd 21½ Elliott S L115 fb 3.00 88–13 Megantic1151½ BetterTalkNow1151 DelMrShow1171¼ 4-deep bid,good try 6
15May04–10Pim fm 1⅛ Ⓣ :464 1:10 1:334 1:461 3↑Dixie-G2 **93** 1010 11 108½ 108¼ 1010 95¾ Prado E S L119 fb 10.70 105 – MrOBrien1192 MillenniumDrgon121hd Wrleigh124nk 4wd upper, no factor 11
10Apr04–7Hou yl 1⅛ Ⓣ 1:53 3↑JBConlyBCH222k **88** 11 94½ 96 96¼ 87¼ 86¼ Douglas R R L119 fb 5.70 80–17 Warleigh116½ Skate Away1171 Gentlemen J J109¾ Failed to menace 11

Binya (Ger)
Own: Allen Joseph

Ch. m. 6 (Mar)
Sire: Royal Solo*Ire (Sadler's Wells)
Dam: Beaconaire (Vaguely Noble)
Br: Gestut Hof Iserneichen (Ger)
Tr: McLaughlin Kiaran P(0 0 0 0 .00) 2004:(462 84 .18)

Life	14	5	2	3	$176,855	98	D.Fst	0	0	0	0	$0	-
2004	5	2	0	1	$101,640	98	Wet(238*)	0	0	0	0	$0	-
2002	8	3	2	2	$75,215	-	Turf(321)	14	5	2	3	$176,855	98
	0	0	0	0	$0	-	Dst(0)	0	0	0	0	$0	-

19Sep04–6WO fm *1⅛ Ⓣ :46 1:432 3↑ⒻCanadinH-G2 **78** 8 32 41½ 43 76¾ 78¾ Migliore R L118 3.65 92–03 Classic Stamp1171 Inish Glora1211¾ Heyahohowdy114½ 3wd,flattened out 9
5Jly04–9Bel sf 1¼ 🅃 :50 1:15 1:402 2:053 3↑ⒻNewYorkH-G2 **85** 1 11½ 11½ 1hd 46½ 510 Velazquez J R L117 2.90 56–34 *Wonder Again*1153¼ *Stay Forever*115no Spice Island1186½ Set pace, tired 7
21Apr04–8Kee gd 1½ Ⓣ :503 1:152 2:064 2:31 4↑ⒻBewitch-G3 **94** 5 42 31 3nk 11½ 31½ Velazquez J R L118 *1.30 88–13 Meridiana118no Alternate1161½ Binya118nk Weaken late,ck wire 10
28Feb04–11GP fm 1⅜ Ⓣ :51 1:172 1:423 2:193 3↑ⒻVeryOneH-G3 **98** 8 21½ 21 21½ 12½ 12½ Velazquez J R L114 *2.10 60–34 Binya1142½ Ocean Silk115½ Boana114¾ Stalked, drew clear 12
16Jan04–8GP fm *1⅛ Ⓣ :471 1:11 1:364 1:49 4↑ⒻAlw 38000N3x **97** 6 31½ 21 21 11½ 13¼ Velazquez J R L117 3.60 97–04 *Binya*1173¼ Russian Sweetiepie117½ Lady Liberty117½ Stalked, drew clear 9

Birdstone
Own: Marylou Whitney Stables

B. c. 4 (May)
Sire: Grindstone (Unbridled) $10,000
Dam: Dear Birdie (Storm Bird)
Br: Marylou Whitney Stables (Ky)
Tr: Zito Nicholas P(0 0 0 0 .00) 2004:(452 86 .19)

Life	9	5	0	0	$1,575,600	108	D.Fst 7 4 0 0 $1,548,600 108
2004	6	3	0	0	$1,236,600	108	Wet(361) 2 1 0 0 $27,000 99
2003	3	2	0	0	$339,000	99	Turf(177) 0 0 0 0 $0 –
	0	0	0	0	$0	–	Dst(0) 0 0 0 0 $0 –

30Oct04–9LS fst 1¼ :47 1:111 1:351 1:59 3↑BCClasic-G1 **105** 7 94 94½ 95 99¼ 712½ Prado E S L121 6.50 - - Ghostzpper1263 RosesinMy1264 PlesntlyPerfect126¾ Traffic early, no bid 13
28Aug04–11Sar fst 1¼ :49 1:124 1:37 2:022 Travers-G1 **108** 5 55½ 41¼ 2hd 11½ 12½ Prado E S L126 4.80 95– 05 Birdstone1262½ The Cliff's Edge1263½ Eddington126nk Quick 3 wide move 7
5Jun04–11Bel fst 1½ :483 1:113 2:002 2:272 Belmont-G1 **101** 4 53 45 23½ 21½ 11 Prado E S L126 36.00 95– 10 *Birdstone*1261 Smarty Jones1268 Royal Assault1263 4 wide, determined 9
1May04–10CD sly 1¼ :463 1:114 1:371 2:04 KyDerby-G1 **85** 11118 105¼ 98 97½ 815¼ Prado E S L126 21.20 64– 21 *Smarty Jones*1262¾ Lion Heart1263¼ Imperialism1262 Stdied,shuffled early 18
20Mar04–8TP fst 1⅛ :471 1:112 1:371 1:503 LanesEnd-G2 **76** 1 53 62¾ 51¾ 58½ 510¾ Bailey J D L121 *.60 72– 17 Sinister G1211½ Tricky Taboo121¾ Little Matth Man1211 Steadied twice 11
14Feb04–1GP fst 170 :241 :484 1:124 1:422 Alw 36000N2x **93** 6 42 31 3nk 1½ 13 Bailey J D L118 *.20 85– 14 Birdstone1183 Capejinsky118½ Caiman1182½ 3 wide, ridden out 6

Blackdoun (Fr)
Own: Naify Marsha and Woodside Farms LLC

Gr/ro. c. 4 (Apr)
Sire: Verglas*Ire (Highest Honor*Fr) $10,238
Dam: Rade (Kaldoun*Fr)
Br: Mme Sabine Charpentier & Mlle Anne Charlotte Charpent (Fr)
Tr: Canani Julio C(0 0 0 0 .00) 2004:(186 42 .23)

Life	16	6	4	2	$477,765	102	D.Fst 0 0 0 0 $0 –
2004	9	4	2	1	$440,864	102	Wet(280*) 0 0 0 0 $0 –
2003	7	2	2	1	$36,901	–	Turf(261*) 16 6 4 2 $477,765 102
	0	0	0	0	$0	–	Dst(0) 0 0 0 0 $0 –

28Nov04–9Hol fm 1¼ Ⓣ:471 1:121 1:37 2:012 HolDerby-G1 **91** 3 126¾137 116½ 104½ 97¼ Nakatani C S LB122 b *1.80 78– 17 Good Reward122½ FastandFurious1221 Imperialism1222 Waited 1/8,no bid 13
30Oct04–4LS yl 1 Ⓣ:24 :483 1:123 1:364 3↑BCMile-G1 **101** 13149½147¾ 133¾ 117 73½ Nakatani C S L122 b 10.60 82– 07 Singltry126½ ArtoniusPius1221½ SixPrfctons123nk Stead block turn, wide 14
6Sep04–8Dmr fm 1⅛ Ⓣ:473 1:112 1:35 1:463 DmrDerby-G2 **102** 101083¾1013 107 52¾ 1nk Nakatani C S LB122 b *.90 96– 10 Blackdoun122ns Toasted122no LaursLuckyBoy122½ Tight 5/16,rallied btw 10
14Aug04–8Dmr fm 1 1/16 Ⓣ:234 :473 1:112 1:41 LaJollaH-G2 **95** 5 68 66½ 63½ 42 1¾ Nakatani C S LB120 b *.90 94– 07 *Blackdoun*120¾ Semi Lost116¾ Bedmar113½ Waited 1/4,stdied 1/8 7
21Jly04–8Dmr fm 1 Ⓣ:221 :452 1:10 1:332 ⓇOceanside85k **102** 3 79 77¾ 42½ 1½ 12½ Nakatani C S LB118 b 2.00 94– 09 *Blackdoun*1182½ Terroplane1202 Lucky Pulpit1183½ Off slw,4w bid,rid out 8
Run in divisions Previously trained by Jean-Luc Pelletan
25Apr04 Longchamp (Fr) gs *1 Ⓣ RH 1:382 Prix de Fontainebleau-G3 Stk 82100 33 Spanu F 128 10.00 *American Post*1281 ⒹAntonius Pius1282 *Blackdoun*128¾ 4
Timeform rating: 108 *Trckd in 3rd,stayed on.Diamond Green placed 3rd*
Placed second through disqualification
31Mar04 Saint-Cloud (Fr) gd *1 Ⓣ LH 1:43 Prix Omnium II (Listed) Stk 55300 34½ Eyquem J-B 128 15.00 *American Post*1284 Joursanvault128½ Blackdoun128½ 5
Timeform rating: 101? *Trailed,bid 1-1/2f out,drifted left,lost 2nd late*
14Feb04 Cagnes-sur-Mer (Fr) gs *7½f Ⓣ LH 1:342 Prix de la Californie (Listed) Stk 57300 1hd Spanu F 123 4.80 Blackdoun123hd Ancerwert1232 Kensington123hd 7
Timeform rating: 93 *Rated in 4th,dueled 120y out,prevailed*
7Feb04 Cagnes-sur-Mer (Fr) gd *7½f Ⓣ LH 1:332 Prix de la Baie des Anges Alw 25600 2no Spanu F 128 6.70 Sixela123no *Blackdoun*1283 Nasaria1173 11
Timeform rating: 93 *Rated at rear,bid 2f out,dueled 1f out,just missed*

Blonde Executive

Own: Bruno Brothers Farms

Ch. f. 4 (Feb)
Sire: Bold Executive (Bold Ruckus) $10,000
Dam: Dream Smartly (Smarten)
Br: Bruno Brothers Farm (Ont-C)
Tr: Loney A. R(0 0 0 0 .00) 2004:(36 8 .22)

Life	13	8	1	1	$610,591	95	D.Fst	7	5	0	0	$376,996 95
2004	6	5	0	0	$414,263	95	Wet(346)	4	1	1	1	$75,345 93
2003	7	3	1	1	$196,328	83	Turf(276)	2	2	0	0	$158,250 85
	0	0	0	0	$0	-	Dst(0)	0	0	0	0	$0 -

26Sep04-8WO fm 1 Ⓣ :232 :461 1:092 1:343 ⒻⓈLaPrevynte132k 85 6 1½ 1hd 2hd 1hd 1nk Dos Ramos R A L118 *.70 90-12 BlondeExecutiv118nk *Finncingvilbl*1162¾ GlditorQun114¾ Bmp'd,prevailed 7
21Aug04-8WO fst 7f :22 :442 1:094 1:231 ⒻDuchess-G3 88 2 2 1½ 1½ 11½ 1nk Dos Ramos R A L123 f 2.40 91-17 *BlondeExecutive*123nk SilvrBird1184 SrchthChurch1142¾ Held gamely,drvg 5
28Jly04-3WO yl 7f Ⓣ :224 :461 1:103 1:223 ⒻⓈPassinMood131k 85 1 1 11 11 11 12¼ Dos Ramos R A L124 f 2.15 89-11 *BlondeExecutiv*1242¼ FlshyAnn1152¼ LovlyLol115hd Turned back rivals str 7
30Jun04-7WO fst 6f :214 :441 :561 1:09 3↑ⒻⓈBallade127k 68 5 1 2½ 2hd 34 47 Dos Ramos R A L117 f *.55 88-13 *Brass in Pocket*1261¾ Regal'nBold1174¾ BoldestofAll117½ Dueled turn,tired 5
29May04-8WO fst 7f :222 :444 1:092 1:224 ⒻⓈLadyAngela133k 95 1 1 11½ 11½ 16 16¼ Dos Ramos R A L118 *.65 93-14 BlondeExecutive1186¼ MyVintgePort1232¾ AshlsBll114½ Kept to business 8
2May04-3WO sly 5f :213 :451 :58 3↑ⒻOC 80k/N3x-N 93 4 1 2hd 1hd 1hd 11¾ Dos Ramos R A L117 7.10 89-15 *BlondExcutiv*1171¾ MistyExpctton120hd ExpctdSong1202 Vied,drove clear 6

Blowin in the Wind

Own: Forster Stable

Gr/ro. g. 6 (Mar)
Sire: Dumaani (Danzig) $3,000
Dam: Stray (Wander Kind)
Br: David V. Forster (Ky)
Tr: Forster David(0 0 0 0 .00) 2004:(116 20 .17)

Life	27	5	8	5	$267,749	91	D.Fst	22	4	5	5	$159,569 90
2004	9	3	2	0	$121,410	90	Wet(292)	5	1	3	0	$108,180 91
2003	9	1	3	2	$53,019	91	Turf(281)	0	0	0	0	$0 -
	0	0	0	0	$0	-	Dst(0)	0	0	0	0	$0 -

17Oct04-8Hst sly 1⅜ :464 1:134 1:41 2:193 3↑PremierH-G3 90 7 712 53½ 32 21 1nk Skelly R V L114 4.80e 86-14 BlowinintheWind114nk IllusiveForce1192½ RoyalPlce121hd Inside, driving 10
25Sep04-6Hst fst 1⅛ :452 1:094 1:353 1:491 3↑WChurchilH41k 85 5 79½ 713 711 66 56¼ Skelly R V L115 3.80 93-08 Metatron117hd Shacane1163¾ Illusive Force120½ Outrun 8
6Sep04-8Hst fst 1⅛ :454 1:104 1:36 1:494 3↑SWRandlPlH43k 89 2 67¼ 510 56¼ 43½ 2hd Skelly R V L115 15.05 96-03 LordNelson122hd BlowinintheWind1151 *Metatron*118¾ Closed, just missed 7
2Aug04-1Hst fst 1 1/16 :224 :461 1:102 1:422 3↑Alw 27500NC 89 1 22½ 23 22½ 23 24½ Skelly R V L115 5.65 100-05 Metatron1154½ Blowin in the Wind1151½ Road Afleet1153¾ Second best 6
18Jly04-7Hst fst 1 1/16 :234 :474 1:114 1:431 3↑Alw 25748N$Y 89 7 21 21 21 21½ 21¼ Skelly R V L115 9.90 100-07 Ⓓ*Metatron*1151¼ Blowin in the Wind1151¾ *Illusive Force*1151¾ Second best 7
Awarded first purse money Previously trained by Forster Grant T
4Jly04-9EmD fst 1 1/16 :232 :47 1:11 1:412 3↑IndepDayH40k 76 6 78½ 86¼ 77 79½ 79½ Cedeno A LB118 9.50 84-21 Briartic Gold115½ Metatron116no Mr. Makah1143 Failed to respond 8
Previously trained by Forster David
12Jun04-8Hst fst 1 1/16 :234 :47 1:112 1:434 3↑JLongdenH49k 82 8 3nk 31 31½ 44 55¾ Wright N L115 13.90 92-10 RoscoePito1172¾ Dncewithvixn117no CommodorCrig1182½ Chased, 3 wide 10
23May04-7Hst fst 6½f :212 :442 1:091 1:16 3↑HKJockClbH44k 78 7 8 87¼ 98¼ 96¾ 98¼ Hoverson C L117 13.10 90-13 LordNelson1232¾ CommodoreCraig1181½ Dancewithvixen117no No threat 10
2May04-7Hst fst 6½f :221 :461 1:103 1:17 3↑OC 50k/N2x-N 89 1 3 77 73¾ 41¾ 1nk Skelly R V L119 3.50 93-16 BlowinintheWind119nk *BoldTexs*116nk Ninlvnturbo116hd 3 wide, up in time 8

Bluesthestandard
Own: Sengara Jeffrey

B. g. 8 (Apr)
Sire: American Standard (In Reality) $2,500
Dam: Bob's Blue (Bob's Dusty)
Br: Terry Brown (Ga)
Tr: West Ted H(0 0 0 0 .00) 2004:(142 30 .21)

Life	33	15	8	4	$939,818	114	D.Fst	32	15	7	4	$929,818	114
2004	6	1	2	1	$132,633	114	Wet(313)	1	0	1	0	$10,000	104
2003	10	4	2	2	$631,975	114	Turf(208)	0	0	0	0	$0	–
	0	0	0	0	$0	–	Dst(0)	0	0	0	0	$0	–

11Dec04–8GG wf 6f :21^{3} :43^{3} :55^{1}1:07^{3} 3↑OaklandH58k **104** 7 1 2$1\frac{1}{2}$ 2$1\frac{1}{2}$ 2$2\frac{1}{2}$ 2$3\frac{1}{4}$ Court J K LB120 *1.40 96– 11 GreenTem119$3\frac{1}{2}$ Bluesthestndrd120^{2} Onebdshrk116$\frac{1}{2}$ Stlkd outside, no bid 7
10Oct04–8SA fst 6f :21 :43^{3} :55^{4}1:08^{4} 3↑AnTtlBCH-G1 **85** 5 4 5^{2} 5$2\frac{1}{4}$ 5$2\frac{1}{2}$ 5^{7} Smith M E LB118 2.90 87– 12 Pt's Grey Eagle109$\frac{1}{2}$ Pohave118^{2} Hombre Rapido114^{hd} 4 wide turn,no bid 8
6Sep04–6Dmr fst 6f :21^{3} :44 :55^{4}1:08^{1} 3↑ⓇPirtsBntyH76k **101** 4 4 4$1\frac{3}{4}$ 1^{hd} 2$\frac{1}{2}$ 2^{2} Smith M E LB122 2.40 96– 06 OurNewRecruit121^{2} Bluesthestndrd122^{2} *Nwrk*114$2\frac{1}{2}$ Led btwn 1/4,2nd best 8
28Mar04–8SA fst 6½f :21^{4} :44^{1} 1:08^{4}1:15^{3} 4↑PtrGrBCH-G2 **96** 1 2 3^{nk} 3^{1} 3$2\frac{1}{2}$ 3$3\frac{1}{2}$ Smith M E LB118 *.80 90– 12 McCnnsMjv118$1\frac{3}{4}$ UnfrlthFlg114$1\frac{3}{4}$ Blsthstndrd118 Angld out, evenly late 5
7Mar04–8SA fst 7f :22^{1} :44 1:08^{2}1:21 4↑SnCrlosH-G2 **98** 1 7 6$3\frac{1}{2}$ 6$2\frac{1}{2}$ 5$3\frac{1}{4}$ 7$6\frac{3}{4}$ Smith M E LB119 *1.60 93– 11 *Pico Central*116^{2} Publication116^{2} *Pohave*112^{1} Came out turn,no bid 10
1Feb04–7SA fst 6f :21 :43^{2} :55^{2}1:08 4↑PlsVrdsH-G2 **114** 7 1 4$1\frac{1}{4}$ 2$\frac{1}{2}$ 2^{hd} 1^{1} Smith M E LB117 *1.80 98– 12 Bluesthestndrd117^{1} MrinoMrini115^{4} *OurNwRcruit*114$\frac{1}{2}$ 3wd bid,led,gamely 7

Bohemian Lady
Own: Padua Stables

B. f. 4 (Feb) FTKJUL02 $150,000
Sire: Carson City (Mr. Prospector) $35,000
Dam: Weekend in Indy (A.P. Indy)
Br: WinStar Farm, LLC (Ky)
Tr: Pletcher Todd A(0 0 0 0 .00) 2004:(948 240 .25)

Life	7	3	1	1	$146,282	97	D.Fst	6	2	1	1	$80,822	97
2004	6	2	1	1	$121,682	97	Wet(445)	1	1	0	0	$65,460	89
2003	1	1	0	0	$24,600	84	Turf(262)	0	0	0	0	$0	–
	0	0	0	0	$0	–	Dst(0)	0	0	0	0	$0	–

3Jly04–8Bel fst 6f :21^{4} :44^{2} :56^{1}1:09 ⒻPrioress-G1 **76** 9 8 7^{5} 7$4\frac{1}{2}$ 9$9\frac{1}{4}$ 8$8\frac{1}{4}$ Velazquez J R L119 5.90 86– 08 FrindlyMichll119$2\frac{1}{4}$ FlnStory121^{no} ForstMusc119$\frac{3}{4}$ Wide throughout, tired 9
4Jun04–10Bel fst 1 :23^{2} :45^{4} 1:09^{4}1:34^{4} ⒻAcorn-G1 **81** 5 1$\frac{1}{2}$ 1$\frac{1}{2}$ 1^{hd} 6$1\frac{3}{4}$ 7$10\frac{3}{4}$ Prado E S L121 12.90 76– 17 IslndSnd121$1\frac{3}{4}$ SocietySelection121^{no} *FriendlyMichll*121$\frac{3}{4}$ Vied inside, tired 8
29Apr04–9CD fst 7½f :21^{3} :44 1:08^{4}1:28^{1} ⒻLaTroien-G3 **97** 6 5 3$1\frac{1}{2}$ 3$1\frac{1}{2}$ 1^{hd} 3$\frac{1}{2}$ Prado E S L122 *1.00 98– 08 FrindlyMichll118$\frac{1}{2}$ EndrsSistr122^{hd} BohminLdy122$5\frac{3}{4}$ Tracked,led,weaken 7
20Mar04–9Aqu gd 7f :22 :44^{3} 1:09^{4}1:23^{1} ⒻCicada-G3 **89** 3 2 2^{1} 2$\frac{1}{2}$ 1$5\frac{1}{2}$ 1$6\frac{1}{2}$ Prado E S L116 1.55 89– 17 BohemianLdy116$6\frac{1}{2}$ WhoopiCt116$4\frac{3}{4}$ Bldomer122^{nk} When asked, kept busy 6
14Feb04–9Aqu fst 6f ⊡ :23^{2} :47 :59^{1}1:11^{3} ⒻDrlyPrcius81k **79** 3 6 2$\frac{1}{2}$ 1^{hd} 1$\frac{1}{2}$ 2$1\frac{1}{2}$ Migliore R L118 *.85 79– 22 AmongMySovnrs118$1\frac{1}{2}$ *BohmnLdy*118$3\frac{1}{4}$ Bldomr122$\frac{1}{2}$ Awkward start, game 6
23Jan04–8Aqu fst 6f ⊡ :22^{4} :46^{3} :59^{2}1:12^{1} ⒻAlw 43000N1x **84** 3 3 2$\frac{1}{2}$ 1$\frac{1}{2}$ 1$1\frac{1}{2}$ 1^{2} Castellano J J L122 *.45 78– 26 BohemianLady122^{2} *PacificIslnd*114$6\frac{1}{4}$ ForMyWife119$2\frac{1}{4}$ Vied outside, clear 6

Boomzeeboom

Own: Karubian John, Landsburg, Alan and Po

B. c. 4 (Feb) ADSSPR03 $30,000
Sire: Explosive Red (Explodent) $500
Dam: Zee Lady (Unreal Zeal)
Br: Adena Springs (Fla)
Tr: Cerin Vladimir(0 0 0 0 .00) 2004:(339 59 .17)

Life	10	3	3	1	$190,096	106	D.Fst	9	3	3	1	$190,096 106
2004	6	3	0	1	$162,276	106	Wet(314)	0	0	0	0	$0 –
2003	4	M	3	0	$27,820	93	Turf(274)	1	0	0	0	$0 65
	0	0	0	0	$0	–	Dst(0)	0	0	0	0	$0 –

Date/Race	Trk	Dist	Fractions	Race	Fig	PP	St	1C	2C	Str	Fin	Jockey	Wt	Odds	Pace	Top Finishers	Comment	Fld
10Jly04-7Hol	fst	1⅛	:47 1:102 1:343 1:472	SwapsBC-G2	98	6	12½	11	11	22½	36¾	Espinoza V	LB118 b	4.40	95 -	Rock HardTen1163¾ Suave1203 Boomzeeboom1182½	Speed,inside,held 3rd	6
19Jun04-7Hol	fst	1 1/16	:233 :47 1:111 1:42	AffirmdH-G3	102	7	11½	11½	1½	2hd	1½	Espinoza V	LB115 b	12.60	91- 17	Boomzboom115½ TwicsBd1211¼ Wmplstltskn1162	Angled in,headed,game	9
22May04-8Hol	fm	1	Ⓣ :223 :452 1:092 1:332	WilRogrs-G3	65	3	2½	2hd	3nk	710	716	Nakatani C S	LB117 b	5.50	81- 05	Laura'sLuckyBoy1194 *Toasted*1211 StreetTheatre1173½	Dueled, weakened	8
17Apr04-9Kee	fst	1 1/16	:231 :471 1:12 1:434	Lexingtn-G2	19	7	64	85½	1211	1433	1448	Bejarano R	L116 b	5.60	45- 11	QuintonsGoldRush1162¾ *FirSlm*116nk SongofthSword1162	Faded after 1/2	14
27Mar04-6SA	fst	1 1/16	:233 :464 1:111 1:414	Alw 52000N1x	102	7	1½	11	11	11	1½	Nakatani C S	LB118 b	1.70	96- 11	Boomzeeboom118½ *MinisterEric*1188 DremPlce1184	Repulsed rival in lane	8
6Mar04-11SA	fst	6f	:213 :442 :561 1:083	Md Sp Wt 44k	106	1	3	1½	13½	15	18½	Nakatani C S	LB120 b	*1.60	95- 14	*Boomzboom*1208½ HrocMomnt1201½ EstrnPnt1201	Speed,clear,ridden out	12

Boston Common

Own: Minichiello Fashion Stable

B. g. 6 (Apr)
Sire: Boston Harbor (Capote) $23,576
Dam: Especially (Mr. Prospector)
Br: Overbrook Farm (Ky)
Tr: Duncan Leonard M(0 0 0 0 .00) 2004:(102 12 .12)

Life	33	12	8	4	$609,317	107	D.Fst	23	8	7	3	$445,667 107
2004	6	3	1	0	$141,960	105	Wet(379)	5	2	1	1	$103,250 106
2003	8	4	1	0	$105,930	102	Turf(291)	5	2	0	0	$60,400 100
	0	0	0	0	$0	–	Dst(0)	0	0	0	0	$0 –

Date/Race	Trk	Dist	Fractions	Race	Fig	PP	St	1C	2C	Str	Fin	Jockey	Wt	Odds	Pace	Top Finishers	Comment	Fld
27Jun04-4Hol	fm	5½f	Ⓣ :213 :441 :554 1:013	4↑ Clm c-(62.5-55)	–	2	4	31½	33½	-	-	Santiago Javier	LB122	*1.10	- 03	F J's Pace1221½ Full Moon Madness118½ Los Solano1183	Broke down turn	6
Claimed from Englander Richard A. for $62,500, Mullins Jeff Trainer 2004(as of 6/27): (257 74 55 19 0.29)																		
29May04-3Hol	fm	5½f	Ⓣ :212 :432 :552 1:011	3↑ OC 80k/N2x	100	6	1	43½	45	31½	11	Santiago Javier	LB121	3.70	99- 01	BostonCommon1211 FllMoonMdnss1191½ *FJsPc*119no	Inside rally,gamely	8
7May04-5Hol	fm	5½f	Ⓣ :211 :434 :552 1:012	3↑ OC 80k/N2x	98	2	4	31	62¼	2hd	1nk	Santiago Javier	LB121	3.70	98- 02	*BostonCommon*121nk *StgePlyer*1211 VlleysPssion121nk	Rail bid,drifted out	9
21Feb04-7TuP	fst	6f	:213 :432 :551 1:072	4↑ CoyoteH40k	86	3	4	31	32½	24	26¾	Barton J	L123	*.30	97- 05	Taiaslew1196¾ *BostonCommon*123no Plmerton119½	Pressd 2-3wd,lugged in	7
1Feb04-7SA	fst	6f	:21 :432 :552 1:08	4↑ PlsVrdsH-G2	99	4	3	51¼	64	44	45½	Stevens G L	LB117	4.80	92- 12	Blusthstndrd1171 MrinoMrin1154 *OurNwRcrut*114½	Came out str,missd 3rd	7
1Jan04-8SA	fst	5½f	:211 :434 :554 1:021	4↑ ElCnejoH-G3	105	4	1	41½	33	21	1nk	Stevens G L	LB117	4.80	101- 10	BostonCommn117nk *SmmrSrvc*1121½ KngRbyn1192½	3wd bid,lugged in str	6

Brass Hat
Own: Bradley Fred F

B. g. 4 (May)
Sire: Prized (Kris S.) $5,000
Dam: Brassy (Dixie Brass)
Br: Fred F. Bradley (Ky)
Tr: Bradley William(0 0 0 0 .00) 2004:(229 24 .10)

Life	9	3	4	0	$624,430	106	D.Fst 7 3 3 0 $596,520 106
2004	9	3	4	0	$624,430	106	Wet(357) 0 0 0 0 $0 –
2003	0	M	0	0	$0	–	Turf(317) 2 0 1 0 $27,910 84
	0	0	0	0	$0	–	Dst(0) 0 0 0 0 $0 –

29Oct04-7LS	fst	1 1/16	:224 :462 1:102 1:42	LnStrDby-G3	77	5	117 1/2	116 1/2	104 1/2	98 3/4	914 1/4	Martinez W	L122 b	*2.00	78-17	PollrdsVson122 1/2 Cryptgrph122 1/2 Flmthrwntxn122 3 1/4	Vanned off after race	12
2Oct04-9Hoo	fst	1 1/16	:224 :47 1:12 1:44	IndnaDby-G2	106	8	98 1/2	96 1/4	53	1hd	11 3/4	Martinez W	LB124 b	10.00	91-21	Brass Hat124 1 3/4 Suave124 3/4 Hasslefree115 1/2	5wd rally, strongly	9
12Jun04-14Tdn	fst	1 1/8	:471 1:112 1:37 1:492	OhioDrby-G2	103	5	95 3/4	97	83 1/4	1 1/2	13	Martinez W	L115 b	21.40	96-06	*BrassHat*115 3 *PollrdsVision*121 5 TriestesHonor115 3	Going away,ridden out	9
19May04-4CD	fst	1 1/8	:474 1:121 1:374 1:503	3↑ Alw 48595N1x	90	5	31 1/2	2hd	1hd	2hd	22 1/2	McKee J	L114 b	4.30	81-16	*Alumni Hall*117 2 1/2 *Brass Hat*114 3 1/2 *Fantasticat*114 1 1/4	Tracked,led,no match	7
30Apr04-9CD	gd	1 1/16 Ⓣ	:243 :492 1:131 1:431	AmerTurf-G3	81	9	31	31	31 1/2	33	45 1/4	Lumpkins J	L117 b	13.50	83-11	Kitten's Joy123 2 1/2 *Prince Arch*123 1/2 Capo117 2 1/4	Tracked,flatten out	9
15Apr04-8Kee	fm	1 1/8 Ⓣ	:462 1:11 1:363 1:483	Forerunner111k	84	3	79 1/4	811	47 1/2	53	25 3/4	Lumpkins J	L116 b	8.00	88-05	Prince Arch116 5 3/4 Brass Hat116 2 Big Booster117no	Ck start,bmp,2ndbest	8
20Mar04-7TP	fst	1 1/16	:224 :462 1:111 1:441	Rushaway100k	89	8	43 1/2	31	1 1/2	11	13 3/4	Lumpkins J	L114 b	38.80	91-17	Brass Hat114 3 3/4 Tales of Glory114 1 1/4 Gamblin114 3	4 wide 1st turn	10
27Feb04-8TP	fst	1	:23 :471 1:124 1:381	Md Sp Wt 29k	75	2	54 1/2	56	31 1/2	21 1/2	21 3/4	Panas D A	L121 b	3.70	81-25	Heroic Deed121 1 3/4 *Brass Hat*121 5 1/4 Uppercut121 6 3/4	3w run, 2nd best	10
29Jan04-9TP	fst	6f	:221 :453 :582 1:113	Md 15000(15-10)	55	10	11	76 1/2		57 3/4	23 1/2	Panas D A	L122 b	32.10	83-09	Sleet Rod122 3 1/2 Brass Hat122 2 1/4 *Swerve*122 1 1/4	Snow, closed well	12

Brass in Pocket
Own: Di Giulio F D Jr

B. m. 6 (Mar)
Sire: Domasca Dan (Same Direction) $1,500
Dam: Luck In My Pocket (Lucky North)
Br: Frank Digiulio & Frank DiGiulio Jr. (Ont-C)
Tr: Tiller Robert P(0 0 0 0 .00) 2004:(282 69 .24)

Life	24	14	3	2	$1,146,023	98	D.Fst 18 10 3 0 $867,518 98
2004	9	4	2	0	$371,038	98	Wet(305) 6 4 0 2 $278,505 93
2003	7	5	0	1	$475,830	92	Turf(305) 0 0 0 0 $0 –
	0	0	0	0	$0	–	Dst(0) 0 0 0 0 $0 –

1Dec04-7WO	gd	1 1/16	:241 :48 1:121 1:46	3↑ⒻⓇClssyNSmrt129k	84	3	12	11 1/2	12	14	13	Kabel T K	L119	*.75	81-25	BrssinPocket119 3 BySwetiBb114hd RomnRomnc116 5	Set pace,ridden out	6
6Nov04-8WO	fst	6f	:221 :443 :57 1:101	3↑ⒻOntFashnH137k	79	8	4	2 1/2	56	67 1/2	55 3/4	Kabel T K	L123	2.95	83-16	WintrGrdn122 1 3/4 ElPrdoEssnc118 3/4 BigChqu113 1 1/4	Stalked 3wd,evened out	8
24Oct04-5WO	fst	1 1/8	:482 1:124 1:384 1:522	3↑ⒻAlw 83700NC	85	4	1hd	1hd	1 1/2	2 1/2	53 1/2	Kabel T K	L117	3.40	82-23	Raylene117 1/2 *One forRose*123 1 1/4 CloudsofGold118 1 1/4	Vied,weakened 1/8 pole	9
3Oct04-4WO	fst	1 1/16	:233 :473 1:124 1:463	3↑ⒻAlw 83700N$MY	86	2	11	11	11 1/2	21	22 3/4	Kabel T K	L120	*.35	75-28	KssdbyPrnc120 2 3/4 BrssnPockt120 4 1/4 SMchMr116 5 1/2	Yielded top str,gamely	6
11Sep04-8WO	fst	7f	:222 :451 1:092 1:221	3↑ⒻSeaway-G3	98	7	2	11 1/2	11	12 1/2	12 1/4	Kabel T K	L119	3.25	96-13	Brass in Pocket119 2 1/4 *WinterGarden*119 2 1/4 ElPradoEssence117 1	Ridden out	7
29Aug04-7WO	sly	1 1/16	:231 :462 1:104 1:452	3↑ⒻAlw 83700N$MY	93	4	12	11	11	13 1/2	13 1/2	Kabel T K	L122	*1.50	84-22	*Brass in Pocket*122 3 1/2 Raylene120 1 1/2 Royal Dalliance116 3/4	Ridden out	6
30Jun04-7WO	fst	6f	:214 :441 :561 1:09	3↑ⒻⓈBallade127k	86	1	5	1 1/2	1hd	11	11 3/4	Kabel T K	L126	2.00	95-13	*BrssinPocket*126 1 3/4 ReglnBold117 4 3/4 BoldstofAll117 1/2	Dueled turn,clear,held	5
30May04-2WO	fst	1 1/16	:231 :473 1:121 1:44	3↑ⒻAlw 86400NC	84	2	11	1 1/2	2hd	25	28 1/2	Clark D	L118	1.75	82-15	WinnngChnc113 8 1/2 *BrssnPockt*118 3 1/2 CloudsofGold118 1/2	Set pace,no match	5
16May04-8WO	fst	6 1/2f	:222 :451 1:094 1:163	4↑ⒻGCHndriH-G3	87	2	5	1hd	2hd	32 1/2	45 1/4	Kabel T K	L122	3.95	90-14	*WinterGrden*122 3 SpnishDecree115nk Hndpinted119 2	Vied rail,tired midstr	5

Built Up
Own: Susi Raymond

B. g. 7 (Apr)
Sire: Homebuilder (Mr. Prospector) $2,000
Dam: Toned Up (Herat)
Br: John Franks (Fla)
Tr: Alonso Enrique(0 0 0 0 .00) 2004:(215 30 .14)

Life	48	14	7	8	$758,518	110	D.Fst	36	13	4	7	$669,249	110
2004	13	3	2	2	$217,195	110	Wet(296)	4	0	2	1	$37,749	96
2003	9	3	0	1	$169,539	103	Turf(218)	8	1	1	0	$51,520	89
	0	0	0	0	$0	-	Dst(0)	0	0	0	0	$0	-

18Dec04-10Crc fst 7f :221 :45 1:093 1:223 3↑KenyNoeJrH100k 74 2 5 2hd 74¼ 810 818 Aguilar M L116 19.40 85- 11 Medallist1144½ Paradise Dancer113¾ Hasty Kris1151¾ Battled, gave way 10
13Nov04-11Crc fst 6f :214 :444 :571 1:101 3↑[S]JDudlySprH150k 89 5 4 52 52½ 64½ 67¾ Coa E M L118 3.70 90- 10 Weigelia1161 Onebadshark1163 Love That Moon1162 3 wide, faltered 10
23Oct04-13Crc fst 1 1/16 :234 :48 1:13 1:454 3↑SpdABckH-G3 102 1 52¾ 51¾ 31 12½ 1hd Coa E M L115 2.60 83- 26 Built Up115hd *Super Frolic*1174¼ Gold Dollar1153½ 3 wide, lasted 11
26Sep04-8Crc sly 1 1/16 :232 :473 1:13 1:461 3↑Sumter40k 96 4 43 42½ 42 22 22½ Aguilar M L115 6.30 78- 26 Tour of the Cat1152½ *Built Up*1156¼ Super Frolic119¾ Angled out, 2nd best 9
11Sep04-7Crc yl 1 Ⓣ:24 :484 1:131 1:392 3↑MiaMIBCH-G3 - 4 43 63¾ 914 - - Madrid S O L115 8.40 - 32 TwilightRoad114½ GoldDollar114¾ ParadiseDancer115hd Done early, eased 9
31Jly04-9Crc fst 6½f :22 :452 1:113 1:182 3↑GroomstckH75k 82 5 5 3nk 1hd 1½ 64¼ Madrid S O L118 *.70 83- 19 GoldDollar1151½ FormalCharde114nk MyLstChnce1121 Slim lead, faltered 9
10Jly04-10Crc fst 6f :214 :443 :57 1:10 3↑SmlSprtH-G3 110 4 6 21 2hd 21 3nk Madrid S O L114 11.10 99- 09 Champali117no Clock Stopper115nk Built Up114nk Finished willingly 10
29May04-3Crc fst 6f :222 :453 :574 1:11 3↑PoncheH75k 108 5 1 31 3nk 1½ 14¼ Madrid S O L116 5.70 94- 13 Built Up1164¼ *Weigelia*1142 Bernard's Candy114½ 3 wide, drew away 5
26Apr04-6Crc fst 7f :23 :46 1:11 1:241 3↑ThtsOurBck40k 89 6 2 21 2½ 33 25 Madrid S O L119 9.60 90- 17 Sea of Tranquility1155 *Built Up*119¾ Scrubs1224¼ Chased, no match 8
Run in divisions
14Apr04-8GP fst 6f :23 :462 :584 1:113 4↑OC 80k/N$Y-N 82 6 1 31 2hd 2½ 1nk Madrid S O L118 4.50 84- 17 Built Up118nk *Twilight Road*1181¼ Royal Lad1111 Long drive, prevailed 6
4Apr04-10Tam fst 6f :221 :451 :573 1:103 4↑Sprint81k 79 7 3 43½ 32½ 34 37 Castanon J L L116 3.20 90- 16 Scrubs1166½ Rock County116½ *Built Up*116½ Mild rally outside 7
10Mar04-8GP fst 6f :223 :451 :564 1:083 4↑OC 125k/N$Y-N 70 5 6 21½ 32½ 48 516¾ Coa E M L116 24.80 82- 18 StrongHop1169¾ DvidsExpcttion116½ Vinmistr1204¾ Steadied st, faltered 8
24Jan04-10Tam fst 7f :222 :444 1:10 1:233 4↑Super50k 47 3 7 75 87¼ 1413 1419¼ Nunez E O L116 6.80 76- 14 Above the Wind1221½ *Scrubs*1163½ Attack the Books116½ Stopped 14

Burning Roma
Own: Queen Harold L

B. h. 7 (Mar)
Sire: Rubiano (Fappiano) $10,000
Dam: While Rome Burns (Overskate)
Br: William S. Farish, Jr. (Ky)
Tr: Giglio Heather A(0 0 0 0 .00) 2004:(64 5 .08)

Life	36	13	5	7	$1,500,200	114	D.Fst	27	9	3	6	$1,140,537	108
2004	8	2	1	2	$176,163	104	Wet(323)	1	1	0	0	$120,000	114
2003	5	1	2	0	$118,500	107	Turf(278)	8	3	2	1	$239,663	104
	0	0	0	0	$0	-	Dst(0)	0	0	0	0	$0	-

5Sep04-10Mth fm 1 Ⓣ:241 :474 1:114 1:364 3↑BobHarding60k 96 6 32 31½ 2½ 1½ 31½ Coa E M L119 3.60 86- 17 StormyRoman115¾ GreenLine115¾ BurningRom1191 Led,brushed,yielded 8
8Aug04-11Mth fm 1 1/16 Ⓣ:234 :481 1:121 1:421+3↑OcenprtH-G3 94 10 42 42 41½ 41¾ 5¾ Coa E M L120 3.20 87- 12 GulchApproval117no Kathir116no *StormyRomn*115½ No solid late response 10
10Jly04-8Bel fm 1 Ⓣ:23 :46 1:09 1:322 3↑PokerH-G3 98 3 2½ 2½ 2½ 41½ 64½ Castanon J L L120 3.30 93- 05 ChristnsOutlw113nk MllnnumDrgon1202½ *SlvrTr*1171 Steadied while tiring 9
29May04-10Mth gd 1 Ⓣ:232 :462 1:102 1:343 3↑RedBankH-G3 102 3 22 23 21 1hd 1hd Castanon J L L120 *1.80 99- 01 BurningRom120hd Remind1172¾ AmricnFrdom1151¾ Solid drive,just lastd 11
9Apr04-9Kee fm 1 Ⓣ:23 :451 1:09 1:332 4↑MakrsMrk-G2 104 3 33½ 33½ 2½ 21½ 2½ Castanon J L L116 18.90 104 - Perfect Soul116½ *Burning Roma*116hd RoyalSpy1161 Bump,carried out late 10
6Mar04-10Tam fst 1 1/16 :234 :47 1:111 1:442 4↑BudChalngr75k 96 10 64½ 53¼ 52¼ 2½ 3¾ Castanon J L L122 *2.50 95- 04 *AttckthBooks*116hd NtivHwk116¾ BurningRom1221¾ Loomed boldly, hung 10
14Feb04-8Tam fm 1 1/16 Ⓣ:223 :46 1:101 1:413 3↑TampaBayBC100k 99 2 72½ 41¾ 42 11½ 1nk Castanon J L L123 3.40 95- 05 Burning Roma123nk *Remind*1232½ Native Hawk1171½ Bid,clear,lasted 12
24Jan04-10Tam fst 7f :222 :444 1:10 1:233 4↑Super50k 72 5 6 42½ 33 35 67¼ Castanon J L L116 *1.30 88- 14 AbovetheWind1221½ *Scrubs*1163½ AttckthBooks116½ Stalked pace, empty 14

Bwana Charlie
Own: Heiligbrodt Racing Stable

B. c. 4 (Mar) TEXMAR03 $240,000
Sire: Indian Charlie (In Excess*Ire) $15,000
Dam: Shahalo (Halo)
Br: E & D Enterprises (Ky)
Tr: Asmussen Steven M(0 0 0 0 .00) 2004:(2293 555 .24)

Life	15	4	4	5	$381,350	106	D.Fst	13 4 3 4 $368,420 106
2004	10	4	2	2	$349,690	106	Wet(385)	2 0 1 1 $12,930 82
2003	5	M	2	3	$31,660	82	Turf(303)	0 0 0 0 $0 –
	0	0	0	0	$0	–	Dst(0)	0 0 0 0 $0 –

30Oct04–5LS fst 6f :211 :432 :552 1:08 3↑BCSprint-G1 105 1 11 118¼ 116¾ 85 42½ Migliore R L123 35.30 97–04 Speightstown126 1¼ Kela126¾ My Cousin Matt126½ 5w 1/4,8w into stretch 13
2Oct04–9LS fst 6f :213 :44 :563 1:093 AlyshebaBC67k 92 5 5 45 36½ 23 2¾ Meche D J L123 *.60 91–13 ChrmingSocilite118¾ BwnChrlie1232½ *Dniltown*1202 4wide turn,closed well 6
28Aug04–10Sar fst 7f :22 :443 1:082 1:204 KngsBshp-G1 93 2 8 54 65½ 43½ 46¾ Sellers S J L123 8.30 93–04 Pomeroy1211½ Weigelia1211 Ice Wynnd Fire1174¼ Bumped start, steadied 8
7Aug04–8Sar fst 6f :214 :443 :564 1:092 Amstrdam-G2 106 4 7 79¼ 61¾ 21½ 1¾ Sellers S J L123 3.70 95–13 Bwana Charlie123¾ *Pomeroy*1232 Weigelia123½ Off slowly, gamely 7
10Jly04–9Crc fst 6f :212 :442 :57 1:102 CarryBck-G3 97 10 2 83¼ 43 33 34½ Sellers S J L119 5.00 92–09 Weigelia117½ ClassyMigration1124 *BwanChrlie*1194 Bumped entering turn 11
15May04–6Pim fst 6f :223 :451 :573 1:103 HrshJacobs100k 102 6 4 66¾ 66½ 42½ 2hd Sellers S J L122 5.70 92–11 Abbondanza115hd BwanaCharlie122¾ PennPcific117nk 4-5wd trip, gamely 9
24Apr04–9CD fst 1 :224 :461 1:113 1:373 DerbyTrl-G3 74 3 1hd 31 1hd 32 310¼ Sellers S J L122 1.40 72–22 SirShcklton1161¾ *CourgousAct*116 8½ BwnChrli1225¼ Vied 3abreast,weaken 5
4Apr04–8Kee fst 7f :213 :44 1:10 1:243 Lafayett-G3 91 3 2 2½ 2hd 11½ 13¼ Sellers S J L117 2.30 84–18 BwanChrlie1173¼ QuickAction1167 TlesofGlory1163 Drifted bit, 1/8p,drvg 6
6Mar04–7FG fst 1 :24 :474 1:111 1:364 OC 50k/n1x-N 93 2 31½ 3nk 11 14 111¾ Sellers S J L117 *.90 99–10 *Bwana Charlie*117 11¾ *AppleKrisp*117no Blackmailer1171¼ Surged, ridden out 9
8Feb04–7FG fst 6f :221 :46 :581 1:104 Md Sp Wt 28k 87 7 6 62¾ 42 2hd 1½ Sellers S J L120 *.80 86–20 *BwanChrlie*120½ Dncemker1153½ WllStreetAfleet1204¼ Confident handling 9

Cajun Beat
Own: Padua Stables and Iracane John and Jo

Dk. b or b. g. 5 (Mar)
Sire: Grand Slam (Gone West) $85,000
Dam: Beckys Shirt (Cure the Blues)
Br: John T. L. Jones Jr. & H. Smoot Fahlgren (Ky)
Tr: Frankel Robert J(0 0 0 0 .00) 2004:(491 135 .27)

Life	17	7	3	0	$1,159,100	120	D.Fst	14 6 2 0 $1,056,300 120
2004	6	2	1	0	$326,800	107	Wet(394)	1 0 0 0 $0 49
2003	9	4	2	0	$820,000	120	Turf(296)	2 1 1 0 $102,800 107
	0	0	0	0	$0	–	Dst(0)	0 0 0 0 $0 –

26Nov04–8Hol fm 5½f Ⓣ :211 :433 :56 1:02 3↑HolTrExH-G3 107 3 7 76½ 76¾ 53¾ 13 Dominguez R A LB122 b *2.20 95–09 Cajun Beat1223 Geronimo117nk Mighty Beau117½ Came out str,rallied 9
30Oct04–5LS fst 6f :211 :432 :552 1:08 3↑BCSprint-G1 103 11 3 62¾ 53 53 53¼ Velasquez C L126 b 14.80 97–04 Speightstown1261¼ Kela126¾ My Cousin Matt126½ 3-4wide turn,no rally 13
2Oct04–8Bel fst 6f :223 :453 :571 1:093 3↑Vosburgh-G1 102 1 3 31 3nk 3½ 44½ Velasquez C L124 b 6.40 86–22 Pico Central1244 Voodoo124½ *Speightstown*124hd Speed inside, weakened 5
Previously trained by Steve Margolis
27Mar04 Nad Al Sheba (UAE) ft *6f Str 1:101 3↑Dubai Golden Shaheen-G1 Stk 2000000 44 Bailey J D 126 b – *Our New Recruit*1262 Alke1261½ Conroy126½ 12
Timeform rating: 114 *Close up in 4th,2nd over 1f out,faded late*
7Feb04–11GP fst 6½f :23 :46 1:093 1:154 3↑DpMnstrH-G3 102 4 1 1½ 1hd 2hd 22½ Velasquez C L123 b *.90 93–11 Alke1122½ Cajun Beat1231¼ Coach Jimi Lee1152¼ Vied inside, held 2nd 7
3Jan04–10GP fst 6f :221 :444 :563 1:09 3↑MrProspH-G3 105 6 2 1hd 1hd 11½ 11½ Velasquez C L121 b *.80 97–10 Cajun Beat1211½ Gygistar118¾ Deer Lake1153 Clear, good response 6

Canadian Frontier
Own: Robsham Mrs. E P

B. h. 6 (Feb)
Sire: Gone West (Mr. Prospector) $150,000
Dam: Borodislew (Seattle Slew)
Br: Marshall Naify Revocable Trust (Ky)
Tr: Hough Stanley M(0 0 0 0 .00) 2004:(259 53 .20)

Life	13	6	1	1	$253,239	107	D.Fst	11	6	1	1	$248,859	107
2004	8	5	0	0	$214,962	107	Wet(390)	0	0	0	0	$0	–
2003	3	1	1	1	$36,897	96	Turf(298)	2	0	0	0	$4,380	93
	0	0	0	0	$0	–	Dst(0)	0	0	0	0	$0	–

8Oct04-7Kee fst 6f :21 :434 :56 1:083 3↑PhoenxBC-G3 93 6 6 54¼ 53½ 119¾ 97½ Castellano J J L122 f 8.80 90-08 Champali122¾ Gold Storm118nk Clock Stopper118nk Weakened in drive 11

8Aug04-10Mth fst 6f :214 :443 :563 1:09 3↑TeddyDrone100k 104 7 3 32 21 21 11 Coa E M L122 f 2.50 95-11 CndinFrontier1221 *WildctHeir*1172 HrsZlous115¾ Lost ground,came back 7

3Jly04-9Mth fst 6f :22 :444 :563 1:084 3↑Longfellow65k 107 5 2 22½ 12 12 1½ Prado E S L119 f *.60 96-15 *CndnFrontr*119½ HghwyPrspctr1155½ Rchrchrch115nk Off rail into lane,drv 5

5Jun04-7Bel fst 6f :212 :433 :551 1:08 3↑TrNthBCH-G2 100 5 7 64¾ 45 56½ 55½ Castellano J J L115 f 5.70 93-07 *Speightstown*1191½ Cat Genius1161¾ *Pohave*117nk 3 wide trip, no rally 9

8May04-7Bel fst 6f :222 :444 :562 1:084 3↑BoldRlrH-G3 107 3 3 2½ 1hd 11½ 13¾ Castellano J J L111 f 20.50 95-18 CanadinFrontier1113¾ KeyDeputy114no FirstBlush113nk Resolutely inside 6

11Apr04-9GP fm 5f Ⓣ :223 :444 :56 3↑YankeeAffr50k 93 5 3 41¾ 43 41¾ 41¾ Boulanger G L118 4.50 93-05 TrLovsScrt120nk TkAchncOnM1201 GhstlyNmbrs124½ Hedge, no late gain 7

17Mar04-7GP fst 7f :221 :45 1:103 1:234 4↑Alw 36000N2x 89 2 3 1½ 11 11 11 Prado E S L122 f *.90 83-20 Canadian Frontier1221 Y. V.Five118¾ AnyWayAtAll118¾ Inside, prevailed 6

7Feb04-12GP fst 6f :222 :453 :573 1:101 4↑Alw 34000N1x 95 2 6 1½ 1hd 11½ 12½ Prado E S L118 f *1.40 91-11 *CndinFrontier*1182½ *Rufustherodrunner*1131½ MeggGee1113¾ Inside, handily 12

Capeside Lady
Own: So Madcapt Stable

B. f. 4 (Apr) EASMAY03 $65,000
Sire: Cape Town (Seeking the Gold) $20,000
Dam: Gray Lady Type (Zen)
Br: Thomas/Lakin (NY)
Tr: Pletcher Todd A(0 0 0 0 .00) 2004:(948 240 .25)

Life	11	5	1	2	$416,160	106	D.Fst	5	1	1	2	$128,820	105
2004	7	2	1	2	$266,220	106	Wet(398)	5	4	0	0	$281,340	106
2003	4	3	0	0	$149,940	86	Turf(306)	1	0	0	0	$6,000	83
	0	0	0	0	$0	–	Dst(0)	0	0	0	0	$0	–

27Nov04-8Crc fm 7½f Ⓣ :23 :453 1:094 1:28 ⒻFAGenter100k 83 8 5 63 64 34½ 43¾ Decarlo C P L121 *1.80 93-03 RObsssion1211¼ OurExploit1162½ MrndChvon118hd 4 wd, no late response 12

6Nov04-9Aqu fst 1⅛ :484 1:13 1:381 1:511 3↑ⒻTnbkAlmH-G3 85 2 1½ 1½ 1hd 41½ 47¼ Decarlo C P L117 *2.60 76-24 Personal Legend115½ Roar Emotion1174¾ Fast Cookie1142 Set pace, tired 9

10Oct04-9Hoo fst 1 1/16 :232 :48 1:12 1:433 ⒻInBCOaks-G3 105 3 1hd 11 1½ 1hd 21½ Decarlo C P LB121 2.20 91-27 *Daydreaming*1181½ CapesideLady121hd StellrJyne1215½ Pace inside, dug in 7

15Aug04-10Mth my 1 1/16 :234 :473 1:112 1:42 ⒻMthBCOks-G2 106 2 11½ 1½ 11 15 16½ Decarlo C P L115 1.70 95-14 CpesidLdy1156½ HoplsslyDvotd1183¼ Hbiboo115no Clear,mostly hand ride 6

5Jly04-10Mth sly 1 1/16 ⊗ :231 :462 1:104 1:421 ⒻLitlSilver60k 103 6 2½ 1hd 11½ 16 113½ Decarlo C P L114 *1.50 94-11 *CpsdLdy*11413½ RllyAmrcn1182¾ LgndryJrny1148½ Drew off,steady hndlng 6

12Jun04-8Bel fst 6f :221 :452 :572 1:103 ⒻFunistrada60k 79 4 6 2½ 21 32½ 34¼ Velazquez J R L119 3.30 82-12 ShesaMugs117hd FelineStory1224¼ *CpesideLdy*1191¾ Bumped backstretch 6

16May04-8Bel fst 7f :22 :452 1:10 1:23 ⒻⓈBouwerie113k 83 1 11 21½ 2½ 2½ 32¼ Velazquez J R L120 *1.60 83-14 RodeoLicious1201 *Mistda*1201¼ CpesideLdy1205¼ Tried winner, weakened 11

Cappuchino

Own: Hollendorfer Jerry, Litt, Howard and

B. h. 6 (Mar)
Sire: Capote (Seattle Slew) $30,000
Dam: Tara Roma (Lyphard)
Br: Emory A. Hamilton (Ky)
Tr: Hollendorfer Jerry(0 0 0 0 .00) 2004:(1300 308 .24)

Life	32	8	2	5	$509,220	105
2004	7	1	0	0	$71,460	97
2003	10	2	0	3	$201,712	105
	0	0	0	0	$0	-

D.Fst	21	5	1	5	$314,216	105
Wet(384)	6	2	1	0	$164,004	99
Turf(290)	5	1	0	0	$31,000	92
Dst(0)	0	0	0	0	$0	-

31Oct04–9CD fst 7½f :22⁴ :45² 1:10¹ 1:29² 3↑AckAckH-G3 74 5 1 1½ 1hd 68½ 616¼ Albarado R J L118 fb 5.00 77–14 Sir Cherokee114⁵¼ Fire Slam117nk Slate Run106nk Clear early,3w,tired 6
2Oct04–9TP fst 1 :22⁴ :46¹ 1:11 1:37 3↑TPFallCh-G3 97 4 1½ 11½ 12½ 14 14 Sarvis D A L115 fb 31.90 89–19 Cappuchino115⁴ Crafty Shaw122nk *Added Edge*119¹ 3 path early, driving 7
11Jly04–11Pln fst 1 1/16 :22² :45² 1:09 1:40 3↑AlamedanH50k 90 8 12 12 1hd 2hd 43¾ Warren R J Jr LB116 fb 7.40 97–10 *Adreamisborn*117¹ SurpriseHalo116¹¼ GoldRuckus118¹½ Hustled, tired late 8
19Jun04–8BM fst 6f :21⁴ :44 :56¹ 1:08⁴ 3↑BMBCSprH-G3 72 2 7 7⁹ 8¹¹ 9¹¹ 812½ Rollins C J LB116 fb 16.50e 82–11 Court's in Session115²¼ Debonair Joe117nk Hombre Rapido118nk Outrun 9
31May04–9Hol fst 7½f :22 :44 1:08² 1:28 3↑AckAckH81k 73 5 1 1hd 2hd 66¾ 815¾ Valenzuela P A LB118 fb 15.80 79–08 Taste of Parad se116¾ Buddy Gil122³½ *Black Bart*116¹½ Dueled, weakened 8
7Feb04–7GG yl 1 1/16 Ⓣ :23⁴ :48² 1:13 1:45¹+4↑TnforanH84k 79 2 31 32½ 32½ 97 1010¼ Warren R J Jr LB116 fb 9.50 74–23 Wixoe Express114² Aly Bubba116² Gold Ruckus116¹½ Stlkd 2-3w, empty 10
1Jan04–8GG wf 1 :23² :46³ 1:10 1:34² 4↑LafayetteH81k 90 1 11½ 1½ 1hd 22 44¾ Warren R J Jr LB119 fb *2.10 92–03 GoldRuckus116¹ TrulyJudge116³ BringHomeThgold116¾ Gave way inside 6

Castledale (Ire)

Own: Lyons Frank and Knee, Greg

B. c. 4 (Apr)
Sire: Peintre Celebre (Nureyev) $37,632
Dam: Louju (Silver Hawk)
Br: Gigginstown House Stud (Ire)
Tr: Mullins Jeff(0 0 0 0 .00) 2004:(538 140 .26)

Life	11	3	4	1	$559,623	103
2004	3	1	0	0	$450,000	103
2003	8	2	4	1	$109,623	91
	0	0	0	0	$0	-

D.Fst	2	1	0	0	$450,000	103
Wet(289)	1	0	0	0	$0	70
Turf(355)	8	2	4	1	$109,623	91
Dst(0)	0	0	0	0	$0	-

1May04–10CD sly 1¼ :46³ 1:11⁴ 1:37¹ 2:04 KyDerby-G1 70 14 1412¾ 156 1716 1414 1425¼ Valdivia J Jr L126 21.90 54–21 *Smarty Jones*126²¾ Lion Heart126³¼ Imperialism126² Wide,in tight 1/2 18
3Apr04–8SA fst 1⅛ :46⁴ 1:11 1:36² 1:49¹ SADerby-G1 103 4 64½ 64¾ 52¾ 31 1hd Valdivia J Jr LB122 30.00 88–09 Castledale122hd DRockHrdTen122² Imperilism122¹ Lost whip 1/8,drftd in 7
6Mar04–7SA fst 1 :22³ :45³ 1:10 1:36 SnRafael-G2 89 5 72¾ 74¼ 53½ 53½ 68¼ Flores D R LB118 11.00 83–11 Imperialism118nk Lion Heart121⁴½ Consecrate115¹ 4wd,angled in,no bid 10

Cat Fighter

Own: Never Tell Farm and Sikura John G

Dk. b or b. m. 5 (Mar)
Sire: Storm Cat (Storm Bird) $500,000
Dam: Strategic Maneuver (Cryptoclearance)
Br: Brushwood Stable (Ky)
Tr: Baffert Bob(0 0 0 0 .00) 2004:(562 105 .19)

Life	10	3	3	3	$277,860	96
2004	5	1	1	3	$206,060	96
2003	4	2	2	0	$68,800	88
	0	0	0	0	$0	-

D.Fst	9	3	3	2	$245,160	96
Wet(407)	1	0	0	1	$32,700	93
Turf(316)	0	0	0	0	$0	-
Dst(0)	0	0	0	0	$0	-

3Jly04–8PrM fst 1 1/16 :23² :46³ 1:10² 1:41³ 3↑ⒻIaDistafBC122k 88 3 2½ 2½ 21 33 36¼ Day P LB123 b *.60 90–12 WildwoodRoyal120² ChnceDnce120⁴¼ CtFighter123⁴½ Pressed, weakened 5
30Apr04–8CD sly 1 1/16 :24¹ :47⁴ 1:12³ 1:44¹ 3↑ⒻLouvlBCH-G2 93 4 11 11½ 1½ 21½ 33¾ Solis A L116 b 6.80 83–17 Lead Story116½ Yell114³ Cat Fighter116³¼ Pace,weakened 6
16Apr04–9Kee fst 1 1/16 :23¹ :47³ 1:12² 1:43⁴ 4↑ⒻDbldogdare114k 96 1 2hd 2hd 1hd 1hd 21¾ Velasquez C L116 b 3.50 91–16 *MayoOntheSide*116¹¾ CtFighter116²¼ RorEmotion116½ Dueled,outfinished 8
14Feb04–8SA fst 1⅛ :46³ 1:11 1:36⁴ 1:50² ⒻLaCanada-G2 91 3 1½ 1hd 1½ 21 1hd Solis A LB115 b 3.40e 82–15 CtFighter115hd Fencelineneignbor116nk Tngl116² Inside,came back,game 8
18Jan04–7SA fst 1 1/16 :22³ :46 1:10² 1:42² ⒻElEncino-G2 87 5 33 33 2hd 2½ 31¾ Fogelsonger R LB115 b 13.90 91–13 VctoryEncountr117¹¼ PrsonlLgnd115½ *CtFghtr*115½ 3wd bid,led,outkicked 7

Catboat

Own: Stonerside Stable LLC

Dk. b or b. f. 4 (Mar)
Sire: Tale of the Cat (Storm Cat) $65,000
Dam: Northern Fleet (Afleet)
Br: Stonerside Stable (Ky)
Tr: Flint Bernard S(0 0 0 0 .00) 2004:(575 124 .22)

Life	15	6	3	2	$185,988	90	D.Fst	9	3	2	1	$112,123 90
2004	12	6	3	1	$184,598	90	Wet(395)	4	2	1	1	$54,020 77
2003	3	M	0	1	$1,390	50	Turf(275)	2	1	0	0	$19,845 73
	0	0	0	0	$0	–	Dst(0)	0	0	0	0	$0 –

Date/Track	Cond	Dist	Fractions	Race	Fig	PP	St	1C	2C	Str	Fin	Jockey	Med/Wt	Odds	Pace	Top Finishers	Comment	Fld
26Nov04-9Mnr	gd	1^{70}	:23^2 :47^1 1:13 1:45^1	3↑ Ⓕ Alw 47800NC	77	6	4^2	21	2½	1^{hd}	1½	Murphy C K	LB112 b	*.90	70– 38	Catboat112½ Ashwood C C115½ Kissinleaf118¼	Bid-3W1/4,edged clear	6
23Oct04-9Kee	yl	1 1/16 Ⓣ	:23^2 :48^3 1:14^1 1:46^3	Ⓕ VllyView-G3	71	6	85¼	84¼	75¼	57	58¾	Bejarano R	L119 b	7.10	62– 29	Sister Swank116¼ Jinny's Gold116½ *Shadow Cast*1194½	Bobble,bmp start	12
2Oct04-9Pha	fst	1 1/16	:23^4 :47^3 1:11^1 1:41^3	Ⓕ CotillnH-G2	84	4	77¾	77½	64	57	510½	Murphy C K	L116 b	25.00	96– 13	*Ashado*1242¾ Ender's Sister1173½ My Lordship1151¼	Came wide, no rally	7
21Aug04-9AP	fst	1⅛	:48^2 1:13 1:38 1:51	Ⓕ ArlBCOks-G3	90	3	64½	63¾	51¾	11½	11¾	♦Martin E M Jr	L118 b	4.50	88– 16	DH LovlyAftrnoon116 DH Ctbot1181¾ MyTmNw116^1	Broke slowly, driving	10
30Jly04-8AP	fst	1	:22^4 :45^3 1:10^3 1:36^4	Ⓕ SweetChant54k	90	5	32½	35½	21	2^{hd}	2½	Martin E M Jr	L118 b	23.80	83– 24	Fly Away Angel115½ *Catboat*1181½ Miss Moses115^1	Off rail, outfinished	10
5Jly04-4Mnr	gd	1 ⊗	:24^1 :47^4 1:13 1:40	3↑ Ⓕ Alw 36500N4L	76	7	2½	2^{hd}	13	14	14½	Murphy C K	LB109 b	*.80	73– 32	Catboat1094½ *Deed to the Gate*1152¼ Bolaro115^5	Shook clear, held firm	8
5Jun04-4Mnr	fm	7f Ⓣ	:23^1 :46^1 1:11^3 1:24^1	3↑ Ⓕ Alw 28200N3L	73	6	9	78¼	21	1½	12¾	Murphy C K	LB111 b	*1.80	86– 13	*Catboat*1112¾ Loving Feeling115½ Excuse1151½	Patient, surged clear	10
30Apr04-7Mnr	fst	1	:24 :48 1:13^2 1:40^2	Ⓕ Alw 25000N1X	73	3	32½	1^{hd}	1½	13	14	Murphy C K	LB118 b	*.70	71– 37	*Ctbot*118^4 WestwrdMiss113^3 SunshinSummr1121¾	Rail bid,drew off,easy	6
5Apr04-6Mnr	fst	1	:23^4 :47^4 1:14^2 1:42^2	Ⓕ Md Sp Wt 21k	68	6	31½	1^{hd}	14	110	111½	Murphy C K	LB117 b	*.30	61– 36	*Catboat*11711½ Wildaboutaunty1177¼ No No Cielo1172½	Much the best	7
24Mar04-7TP	fst	6½f	:23 :46 1:10^4 1:17^1	Ⓕ Md 40000(50–40)	68	3	5	53¼	41¼	32½	2¾	Bejarano R	L118 b	*1.80	93– 07	*Wild Bertie*118¾ *Catboat*1183¼ Weatherwise122^5	Inside to stretch	9
18Feb04-4TP	fst	5½f	:22^2 :46 :58^1 1:04^3	Ⓕ Md Sp Wt 26k	49	5	3	55½	55½	35	38¼	Prescott R	L122 b	4.20	87– 09	*Thisgirldontlaugh*122^7 We Can Do1221¼ Catboat1223¼	Stumbled after start	9
6Feb04-3TP	my	5½f	:23^4 :48^3 1:01^2 1:08	Ⓕ Md 50000(50–40)	56	4	4	31½	3½	1^{hd}	2½	Prescott R	L122 b	*1.50	77– 27	Regal Case122½ Catboat1223½ *Prison of Love*1224¼	Outfinished	7

Champali

Own: Lloyd Madison Farms IV LLC

B. h. 5 (Feb)
Sire: Glitterman (Dewan) $15,000
Dam: Radioactivity (Dixieland Band)
Br: McKee Stables, Inc. (Ky)
Tr: Foley Gregory D(0 0 0 0 .00) 2004:(283 66 .23)

Life	22	11	2	4	$1,073,794	113	D.Fst	16	7	1	4	$890,774 113
2004	8	4	1	1	$634,398	113	Wet(399)	5	4	1	0	$179,790 101
2003	10	4	1	3	$313,522	104	Turf(338)	1	0	0	0	$3,230 96
	0	0	0	0	$0	–	Dst(0)	0	0	0	0	$0 –

Date/Track	Cond	Dist	Fractions	Race	Fig	PP	St	1C	2C	Str	Fin	Jockey	Med/Wt	Odds	Pace	Top Finishers	Comment	Fld
20Nov04-10Pim	fst	6f	:22^3 :45^2 :57^1 1:09^2	3↑ DeFrncsM-G1	88	6	8	72¼	85½	99¾	88¼	Bejarano R	L126	5.70	90– 13	Wildcat Heir119^{nk} MidasEyes1231½ ClockStopper119¾	3-4wd, no response	10
30Oct04-5LS	fst	6f	:21^1 :43^2 :55^2 1:08	3↑ BCSprint-G1	103	3	9	74¼	84¾	64	73½	Bejarano R	L126	7.30	97– 04	Speightstown1261¼ Kela126¾ My Cousin Matt126½	3w turn,bumped 3/16	13
8Oct04-7Kee	fst	6f	:21 :43^4 :56 1:08^3	3↑ PhoenxBC-G3	113	7	2	41¾	43	31	1¾	Bejarano R	L122	4.00	98– 08	Champali122¾ GoldStorm118^{nk} ClockStopper118^{nk}	Tracked,4w,stiff drive	11
28Aug04-6AP	fst	6f	:22^3 :45^2 :57 1:08^3	3↑ ArSprntBCH147k	95	4	4	3½	1½	32½	36	Douglas R R	L120	*.60	95– 11	Gold Storm115¾ Super Fuse1185¼ *Champali*120^1	Between foes, weakened	5
10Jly04-10Crc	fst	6f	:21^4 :44^3 :57 1:10	3↑ SmlSprtH-G3	111	1	7	11	1^{hd}	11	1no	Bailey J D	L117	2.60	99– 09	Champali117^{no} Clock Stopper115^{nk} Built Up114^{nk}	Pressured, just lasted	10
19Jun04-9CD	fst	6f	:21 :44 :56^1 1:09	3↑ AristdsH-G3	105	5	2	43¼	31½	11	13¼	Bejarano R	L116	4.10	96– 11	*Champali*1163¼ Beau's Town121^{nk} BattleWon1141¼	Bobble,bmp strt,5w,drv	6
26May04-2CD	my	6½f	:23^2 :46^1 1:10 1:16^1	3↑ Alw 66800N$Y	101	4	1	11½	11½	11½	11¼	Day P	L117	*.40	90– 17	*Champali*1171¼ *Premier Performer*123^2 Saint Waki119^{nk}	3path,hand urging	5
1May04-4CD	my	6f	:21^1 :43^4 :56 1:09^2	3↑ Alw 66800N$Y	97	5	2	2½	3^{nk}	21	22	Day P	L117	3.30	92– 14	SmilenWildcat123^2 *Champli*1171½ StrengthndHonor123½	Dueled, held well	8

Chandtrue

Own: Greene Harold F

B. c. 3 (Apr) KEESEP03 $130,000
Sire: Yes It's True (Is It True) $10,000
Dam: Chandelle (Crafty Prospector)
Br: W. E. Waltrip (Fla)
Tr: Hess R B Jr(0 0 0 0 .00) 2004:(183 31 .17)

Life	4	4	0	0	$182,970	82	D.Fst	4 4 0 0	$182,970 82
2004	4	4	0	0	$182,970	82	Wet(363)	0 0 0 0	$0 –
2003	0	M	0	0	$0	–	Turf(256*)	0 0 0 0	$0 –
	0	0	0	0	$0	–	Dst(0)	0 0 0 0	$0 –

17Jly04–3Hol fst 6f :22 :453 :58 1:104 HolJuvCh-G3 80 4 1 31 31 1½ 1½ Espinoza V LB120 *.30 83–15 Chandtrue120½ Actxecutive1177 Commandant1155½ 3wd into lane,gamely 4
20Jun04–3Hol fst 5½f :212 :444 :572 1:04 Haggin80k 80 2 5 42 31½ 2hd 17 Nakatani C S LB119 1.50 88–11 *Chandtrue*1197 *Gentleman Count*116½ Fallfree1143½ 3wd bid,ridden out 6
23May04–8Hol fst 5f :214 :46 :581 ®WProctrMem79k 79 7 5 4nk 3nk 1½ 14 Nakatani C S LB119 *.40 93–11 *Chandtrue*1194 OnceThief1142 GentlemnCount1184 Bobbled bit strt,5-4wd 8
29Apr04–8Hol fst 4½f :22 :443 :504 Md Sp Wt 43k 82 7 1 1½ 12 14½ Nakatani C S LB119 *1.30 102–06 *Chndtrue*1194½ IllPreyforYou119hd *DilgntProspct*1191½ Speed, rail, cleared 9

Changing World

Own: Rogers S H Jr

B. m. 5 (Jan)
Sire: Spinning World (Nureyev) $21,952
Dam: Reach the Top (Cozzene)
Br: Mr. & Mrs. S. H. Rogers Jr. (Fla)
Tr: Tagg Barclay(0 0 0 0 .00) 2004:(235 32 .14)

Life	13	5	0	4	$292,189	100	D.Fst	3 0 0 1	$3,500 51
2004	4	2	0	1	$168,500	100	Wet(330)	1 1 0 0	$20,400 60
2003	6	3	0	2	$120,189	94	Turf(391)	9 4 0 3	$268,289 100
	0	0	0	0	$0	–	Dst(0)	0 0 0 0	$0 –

4Dec04–8Crc fm 1⅛ Ⓣ:47 1:094 1:341 1:463 3↑ⒻMyChrmrH-G3 95 3 15 19 18 14 31½ Boulanger G L117 *1.70 94–03 SomthngVntre1151 Snwdrps115½ ChngngWrld1173¼ Hedge, gave way late 12
22Oct04–8Med gd 1 1/16 Ⓣ:243 :482 1:113 1:412 3↑ⒻVioletH-G3 100 6 11½ 13½ 14 13 11¼ Fragoso P L113 13.40 91–12 ChngingWorld1131¼ HighCourt117hd OcnDriv1212½ Steady drive,held well 7
25Sep04–9Bel fm 1 Ⓣ:241 :473 1:112 1:343 3↑ⒻNblDmslH-G3 95 6 3½ 61¾ 63¼ 53¼ 44 Castellano J J L113 15.10 83–16 OcenDrive1201¼ HighCourt115¾ HourofJustice1162 Between foes, no rally 9
19Aug04–7Sar yl 1 1/16 Ⓣ:24 :482 1:132 1:45 4↑ⒻOC 75k/N3x-N 93 4 21½ 2hd 12½ 12½ 1nk Castellano J J L118 *2.00 70–30 ChngingWorld118nk Alchemist1182¼ OcenSilk120¾ Determined, prevailed 6

Chilly Rooster

Own: Hobeau Farm

Dk. b or b. g. 5 (May)
Sire: Arch (Kris S.) $10,000
Dam: Chilly Chick (Raise a Native)
Br: Hobeau Farm Ltd. (Fla)
Tr: Jerkens H. A(0 0 0 0 .00) 2004:(374 72 .19)

Life	22	4	4	6	$232,959	99	D.Fst	10 3 3 3	$119,200 95
2004	9	1	0	1	$86,218	99	Wet(398)	4 0 1 2	$29,441 96
2003	13	3	4	5	$146,741	95	Turf(307)	8 1 0 1	$84,318 99
	0	0	0	0	$0	–	Dst(0)	0 0 0 0	$0 –

10Jly04–8Bel fm 1 Ⓣ:23 :46 1:09 1:322 3↑PokerH-G3 98 4 41 51½ 53 63¼ 54½ Uske S L114 b 18.20 93–05 ChristinsOutlw113nk MillnniumDrgon1202½ *SlvrTr*1171 3 wide, no response 9
16Jun04–8Bel fm 1 Ⓣ:231 :46 1:091 1:323 4↑OC 100k/c-N 99 3 1hd 1½ 1hd 2hd 32 Uske S7 L116 b 9.40 95–03 SilverTree1231 NothingtoLos1231 ChillyRoostr1161½ Set pace, weakened 6
29May04–10Mth gd 1 Ⓣ:232 :462 1:102 1:343 3↑RedBankH-G3 88 7 109¾ 1112 118¼ 117 76½ Uske S L116 b 15.10 93–01 BurningRom120hd Remind1172¾ AmericnFrdom1151¾ Even finish outside 11
9May04–7Bel fm 1 Ⓣ:234 :47 1:094 1:332 4↑OC 100k/c-N 98 5 42½ 42 41¾ 33 42¾ Uske S7 L116 b 6.70 90–07 *Quantum Merit*1152¼ *Union Place*117nk Pisces119nk Saved ground, no rally 6
24Apr04–8Aqu fm 1 1/16 Ⓣ:233 :481 1:124 1:422 3↑FtMarcyH-G3 99 5 42 42 31 1hd 1½ Uske S L113 b 32.25 95–09 Chilly Rooster113½ Union Place1131 *Slew Valley*119½ Inside move, gamely 8
25Mar04–6GP fm *1 1/16 Ⓣ:242 :502 1:144 1:443 4↑Alw 38000N3x 88 1 54 63½ 53½ 53¼ 43¾ Cruz M R L118 b 8.90 77–19 Remind1181 *Fast Decision*1181¼ Thefull Circle1181½ Clipped heels bkstr 7
4Mar04–6GP fm *1 1/16 Ⓣ:231 :474 1:113 1:431 4↑Alw 38000N3x 90 9 3nk 32 41¼ 3½ 41½ Uske S7 L111 b 12.60 86–16 L'Oiseau d'Argent120hd *Stage Call*118¾ *Restage*120¾ Bid, weakened late 10
23Jan04–8GP fm *1 1/16 Ⓣ:234 :493 1:14 1:44 4↑Alw 38000N3x 88 4 21½ 21½ 21 32 42 Uske S7 115 8.60 82–16 Spotted Owl118hd Motives1181¼ Thefull Circle118¾ No late response 8
18Jan04–9GP wf 1 1/16 :24 :48 1:122 1:434 4↑OC 75k/N3x-N 96 4 32 42 41¼ 44 43½ Uske S7 115 8.20 86–19 *Ground Storm*1181¼ Flying Free118nk Aeneas1182 Couldn't keep pace 8

Choctaw Nation

Own: Bone Robert D

B. g. 5 (Mar)
Sire: Louis Quatorze (Sovereign Dancer) $6,000
Dam: Melisma (Well Decorated)
Br: Loch Lea Farm Inc. (Ky)
Tr: Mullins Jeff(0 0 0 0 .00) 2004:(538 140 .26)

Life	6	5	0	0	$301,800	103	D.Fst 6 5 0 0 $301,800 103
2004	6	5	0	0	$301,800	103	Wet(356) 0 0 0 0 $0 –
2003	0	M	0	0	$0	–	Turf(218) 0 0 0 0 $0 –
	0	0	0	0	$0	–	Dst(0) 0 0 0 0 $0 –

22Aug04–8Dmr fst 1¼ :464 1:104 1:352 2:01 3↑PacifcCl-G1 **102** 3 810 810 86½ 65½ 46½ Espinoza V LB124 b 4.40 83– 10 PlesntlyPerfect1241 PerfectDrift124¾ TotlImpct1244¾ 5 wide into stretch 8
1Aug04–8Dmr fst 1 1/16 :24 :472 1:111 1:421 3↑SnDiegoH-G2 **103** 1 67½ 69¼ 65¼ 21½ 1¾ Espinoza V LB114 b 6.30 97– 10 ChoctawNtion114¾ *PlesntlyPerfect*1245 During1181½ 4wd into lane,gamely 7
28May04–5Hol fst 1⅛ :48 1:111 1:354 1:482 3↑OC 62k/N2x-N **97** 4 77 67½ 46 1hd 1¾ Espinoza V LB123 b *.60 97– 06 *ChoctawNtion*123¾ Fonzs1191½ FortySuertudo1192 Rail move,led 2wd,held 7
18Apr04–8SA fst 1 1/16 :224 :462 1:103 1:421 4↑OC 50k/N1x-N **102** 4 711 711 710 43¾ 11¼ Espinoza V LB118 b *.70 94– 06 *ChoctwNtion*1181¼ ChestersChoic1183 ThisNTht1183 4wd into lane,rallied 7
28Mar04–3SA fst 1 1/16 :232 :463 1:104 1:421 4↑Alw 40000s **101** 8 87 810 77 41¾ 14½ Espinoza V LB120 b *1.30 94– 11 *ChoctwNton*1204½ Whnthwndblws122¾ MrkfCrg1201 4wd rally,inhaled foes 8
29Feb04–1SA fst 6½f :214 :444 1:102 1:17 4↑Md c-(40-35) **89** 3 7 814 817 58 12¼ Solis A LB122 b *2.70 87– 17 *ChoctwNtion*1222¼ Downtim122¾ OutofthBluSlw1222 Off bit slow,late rush 8
Claimed from Griffith, Joella, Headley, Bruce and Sobel, Norman for $40,000, Headley Bruce Trainer 2003: (138 29 17 26 0.21)

Christine's Outlaw

Own: R.C. Hill Stable

Dk. b or b. h. 5 (Mar)
Sire: Wild Again (Icecapade) $50,000
Dam: Marianna's Girl (Dewan)
Br: Albert G. Clay 1990 Rev. Trust & John W. Clay (Ky)
Tr: Weaver George(0 0 0 0 .00) 2004:(401 46 .11)

Life	19	5	3	1	$351,359	108	D.Fst 11 3 2 1 $193,867 102
2004	9	3	1	0	$145,199	108	Wet(391) 2 0 0 0 $45,000 96
2003	10	2	2	1	$206,160	99	Turf(317) 6 2 1 0 $112,492 108
	0	0	0	0	$0	–	Dst(0) 0 0 0 0 $0 –

9Oct04–8Bel fm 1 Ⓣ:232 :46 1:091 1:323 3↑KelsoBCH-G2 **91** 2 1½ 1½ 3nk 83¾ 87¾ Bridgmohan S X L114 18.40 89– 03 MrOBrien1191½ MillenniumDrgon119no GulchApprovl114½ Set pace, tired 8
19Sep04–9WO fm 1 Ⓣ:232 :46 1:09 1:323 3↑AttoMile-G1 **81** 4 42 42 95¼ 1014 1010 Dominguez R A L119 8.80 90– 03 Soaring Free119¾ Perfect Soul121hd *Royal Regalia*1181¼ Stalked rail,tired 11
28Aug04–9Sar fm 1 1/16 Ⓣ:233 :462 1:091 1:392 3↑4strdavH-G2 **82** 5 52½ 43 31½ 108½ 911½ Prado E S L115 7.80 86– 01 *NothingtoLose*117½ SilverTree1171 RoylRegli1141¾ Bump stretch, steadied 10
10Jly04–8Bel fm 1 Ⓣ:23 :46 1:09 1:322 3↑PokerH-G3 **108** 2 1½ 1½ 1½ 11 1nk Bridgmohan S X L113 13.80 98– 05 ChrstnsOutlw113nk MllnnumDrgon1202½ *SlvrTr*1171 Set pace, game inside 9
20Jun04–5Bel gd 1 1/16 Ⓣ:242 :481 1:121 1:413 3↑Alw 50000N3x **96** 4 3½ 21 2hd 11 11¾ Bailey J D L121 f *2.20 89– 11 *ChristinesOutlw*1211¾ MrLight121hd Provincetown1211 Pressed pace, clear 7
5Jun04–4Bel fm 7f Ⓣ:233 :46 1:091 1:212 4↑Alw 59000N3x **94** 5 4 2hd 2hd 1hd 2nk Solis A L116 f 5.20 93– 07 *GulchApprovl*116nk *ChrstnsOtlw*116½ *PrsonlToch*116nk Between rivals, game 10
10Apr04–5Kee fst 7f :223 :451 1:093 1:23 3↑CmwlthBC-G2 **93** 6 4 42 31½ 53½ 55½ Albarado R J L118 6.70 86– 15 Lion Tamer122¾ Private Horde120½ MarinoMarini1182¼ 5w lane,weakened 6
13Mar04–13GP fst 1 1/16 :24 :481 1:12 1:431 3↑SkipAwyH-G3 **88** 2 1½ 1½ 1hd 31 59½ Prado E S L113 f 4.90 83– 15 Newfoundlnd116½ SuphBlitz1142¼ BowmnsBnd1174¼ Pressured, gave way 10
9Feb04–8GP fst 7f :221 :442 1:083 1:212 4↑Alw 36000N2x **102** 6 4 1hd 11 13 16 Bailey J D L118 f 3.40 95– 12 Christine'sOutlaw1186 *SeekGold*1181¾ *PersonalTouch*1182¾ Inside, drew off 12

Classic Elegance

Own: Lewis Robert B. and Beverly J

B. f. 3 (Mar) KEESEP03 $650,000
Sire: Carson City (Mr. Prospector) $35,000
Dam: Taegu (Halo)
Br: Brereton C. Jones (Ky)
Tr: Lukas D. W(0 0 0 0 .00) 2004:(577 67 .12)

Life	6 3 0 1	$204,006	79	D.Fst	5 2 0 1	$114,006	79
2004	6 3 0 1	$204,006	79	Wet(406)	1 1 0 0	$90,000	79
2003	0 M 0 0	$0	–	Turf(248)	0 0 0 0	$0	–
	0 0 0 0	$0	–	Dst(0)	0 0 0 0	$0	–

```
8Oct04-9Kee fst 1 1/16 :223 :464 1:113 1:441 (F)Alcibiad-G2 – 9 99 1013 1017 - - Day P 118 12.80 - 17 Runway Model118hd Sharp Lisa118no In the Gold118 1/2 Pulled up 10
20Aug04-8Sar fst 7f :223 :453 1:103 1:234 (F)Spinaway-G2 50 1 5 2 1/2 5 5 1/2 7 8 1/2 7 17 1/2 Day P 121 3.50 67- 13 SenseofStyle121 6 3/4 MissMatched121 3/4 PlyWithFire121 1/2 Shuffled back turn 7
28Jly04-9Sar my 6f :214 :452 :582 1:122 (F)SchylrvI-G2 79 1 7 7 5 1/2 6 3 1/2 5 5 1/2 11 Day P 122 2.90 80- 15 ClssicElgnc1221 AnglTrumpt118 1 3/4 WildChick118no Along in time outside 10
4Jly04-11CD fst 5 1/2f :213 :452 :573 1:04 (F)Debutant-G3 79 6 3 32 31 22 11 Day P 117 *1.80 92- 11 ClassicElegnce1171 PrgonQueen117 3 1/2 CoolSpell117nk Rallied 5-6w,driving 9
1May04-6CD fst 5f :213 :45 :574 Juvenile115k 63 1 1 11 2 1/2 32 3 7 1/4 Bailey J D 115 1.50 89- 06 Lunarpal1185 GallantSecret115 2 1/4 ClassicElegnce115 2 3/4 Inside,tired final 1/8 5
16Apr04-5Kee fst 4 1/2f :223 :451 :511 (F)Md Sp Wt 50k – 4 1 1 1/2 12 1/2 17 1/4 Bailey J D 118 *1.10 99- 11 ClassicElegance118 7 1/4 AdriadsCape1186 Sefree118 9 1/4 Drew off,hand urging 6
```

Classic Endeavor

Own: Sullivan Lane Stable and Scuderi Vinc

Dk. b or b. h. 7 (Mar)
Sire: Silver Buck (Buckpasser) $7,500
Dam: Bold Juana (John Alden)
Br: Diane H. Flowers (Fla)
Tr: Dutrow R E Jr(0 0 0 0 .00) 2004:(603 166 .28)

Life	56 16 9 3	$715,153	109	D.Fst	37 11 6 3	$482,322	109
2004	15 5 2 0	$248,798	104	Wet(347)	18 5 3 0	$232,831	104
2003	11 5 2 0	$241,595	109	Turf(207)	1 0 0 0	$0	36
	0 0 0 0	$0	–	Dst(0)	0 0 0 0	$0	–

```
4Dec04-8Aqu fst 1 3/16 [•] :474 1:122 1:38 1:57 3↑QeensCoH-G3 104 1 1 1/2 11 1/2 11 13 1 3/4 Gryder A T L117 f 2.75 94- 18 ClassicEndeavor117 3/4 EveningAttire123 1/2 Colit115no Pace,steady handling 9
13Nov04-8Aqu gd 1 1/8 :483 1:124 1:371 1:493 3↑StuyvntH-G3 104 1 11 1/2 1 1/2 12 1/2 13 1/2 11 1/2 Prado E S L114 f 3.30 91- 14 ClassicEndeavor1141 1/2 Colita1154 1/4 SnkeMountin115 1/2 Cruised home in hand 7
29Sep04-8Bel fst 1 1/16 :23 :46 1:11 1:424 4↑OC 85k/n3x 99 4 2 1/2 1 1/2 11 1/2 12 1/2 11 1/2 Prado E S L118 *1.80 86- 30 ClsscEndvor118 1/2 AdmrltyArch1234 CountryJdg120 1/2 Drifted out badly late 5
1Aug04-3Sar fst 1 1/8 :464 1:111 1:364 1:51 3↑Clm c-(50-40) 85 1 12 1/2 12 1/2 1 1/2 13 11 1/4 Bridgmohan S X L124 f *1.30e 80- 14 ClssicEndevor1241 1/4 LegendryWeve122nk TrilPrep1222 Set pace, drew clear 7
  Claimed from Lake Scott A. for $50,000, Lake Scott A Trainer 2004(as of 8/1): ( 993 218 176 154 0.22 )
18Jly04-6Bel fst 1 :24 :471 1:113 1:363 4↑Clm 45000(50-40) 96 3 43 42 1/2 2hd 2hd 12 Luzzi M J L118 f 5.90 78- 21 Classic Endeavor1182 Ginzano121 3/4 Lott1205 3 wide move, clear 5
20Jun04-9Bel fst 1 :233 :462 1:112 1:37 4↑Clm c-(35-25) 74 2 2hd 6 2 3/4 9 9 3/4 710 612 Castellano J J L120 f 4.20 64- 27 Lott120 7 1/2 Albert E.115 1/2 Left Hook1201 Brief speed, tired 9
  Claimed from Schwartz, Herbert T. and Carol A. for $35,000, Schwartz Scott M Trainer 2004(as of 6/20): ( 98 7 15 19 0.07 )
9Jun04-2Bel fst 1 1/16 :232 :462 1:111 1:423 4↑Clm 35000(35-25) 88 7 1 1/2 1 1/2 1hd 2hd 4 1 1/4 Chavez J F L120 f 4.50 86- 21 YnkeeDoodleBoy120nk BeuTi1171 RunwyRussy120no Set pace, weakened 8
13May04-6Bel fst 1 :234 :462 1:091 1:35 4↑Clm 65000(75-65) 80 3 21 5 1 1/4 65 512 512 Cotto P L Jr5 L111 f 21.20 74- 14 SpookyMldr122 2 1/2 Jstfcton118 1 1/4 ThDptyIsHom1202 Between rivals, tired 6
15Apr04-7Aqu gd 1 :242 :484 1:141 1:384 4↑Clm 75000(75-65) 83 3 11 1/2 1 1/2 2 1/2 4 3/4 4 6 3/4 Lopez C C L120 f 14.80 64- 41 BigSidsPrty1201 Justifiction120nk TheDeputyIsHom120 5 1/2 Set pace, tired 7
2Apr04-8Aqu gd 1 :23 :46 1:103 1:353 4↑OC 85k/c-N 75 4 6 3 1/4 5 2 1/4 7 5 1/4 610 5 15 1/4 Jara F5 L118 f 14.00 72- 29 Black Silk1163 Multiple Choice118nk Peeping Tom118 1 3/4 Inside trip, tired 7
6Mar04-8Aqu sly 1 1/8 [•] :474 1:121 1:38 1:504 3↑StymieH81k 91 4 13 1/2 12 1/2 11 1/2 3 4 1/2 4 8 1/4 Lopez C C L115 f 5.80 80- 16 Ground Storm1151 1/4 Big Sid's Party1134 Nothing Flat1123 Set pace, tired 6
20Feb04-6Aqu fst 1 1/16 [•] :242 :484 1:13 1:432 4↑OC 75k/c-N 92 5 2 1/2 21 2 1/2 2 1/2 43 Lopez C C L120 f 7.80 91- 16 Loving120nk Lord Ofthe Thunder117 2 1/4 Abreeze120 1/2 Speed outside, tired 5
1Feb04-8Aqu fst 170 [•] :23 :461 1:11 1:411 4↑Alw 54000c 93 8 710 612 5 7 1/2 3 1 1/2 23 Lopez C C L122 f 9.30 89- 17 LordOfthThnd1143 ClsscEndvor1221 NwYorkHro112no Game finish inside 8
17Jan04-4Aqu fst 1 1/16 [•] :224 :46 1:101 1:42 3↑AcuH-G3 56 2 6 9 1/2 7 7 1/2 815 820 831 Lopez C C L114 f 10.00 70- 13 Seattle Fitz114no Evening Attire122 1 1/4 Rogue Agent112 8 3/4 Tired 8
2Jan04-8Aqu fst 170 [•] :233 :473 1:12 1:42 4↑OC 75k/c-N 93 1 3 1/2 5 1 1/4 3 2 1/2 2 2 1/2 2 1 1/2 Lopez C C L120 f 11.70 86- 26 Abreez1221 1/2 ClssicEndvor1201 LordOfthThundr116 3/4 Game finish outside 9
```

Classic Stamp
Own: Sorokolit W A Sr

Dk. b or b. m. 5 (Apr)
Sire: Regal Classic (Vice Regent) $10,000
Dam: Native Rights (Our Native)
Br: William Sorokolit (Ont-C)
Tr: Hopmans C C Jr(0 0 0 0 .00) 2004:(146 10 .07)

Life	16	5	4	5	$653,097	99	D.Fst	6	1	2	2	$85,314	85
2004	8	2	2	3	$425,043	99	Wet(332)	0	0	0	0	$0	–
2003	8	3	2	2	$228,054	89	Turf(272)	10	4	2	3	$567,783	99
	0	0	0	0	$0	–	Dst(0)	0	0	0	0	$0	–

20Nov04-9CD yl 1⅛ Ⓣ :492 1:14 1:401 1:534 3↑ⒻCardinlH-G3 **88** 1 6¾ 3½ 3½ 4½ 5¾ Day P L119 *1.70 59-34 Aud115nk May Gator117hd Angela's Love1144¼ 4w bid,empty late 11
24Oct04-6WO gd 1¼ Ⓣ :504 1:152 1:40 2:04 3↑ⒻEPTaylor-G1 **99** 1 8¾ 8¼ 7½ 4¾ 3¾ Husbands P L123 10.45 86-13 Commercante123½ Punctilious118nk ClassicStmp1232¼ Angled out,rallied 8
19Sep04-6WO fm *1⅛ Ⓣ :46 1:432 3↑ⒻCanadinH-G2 **97** 2 9¾ 8¾ 7¾ 31 11 Husbands P L117 10.95 101-03 Classic Stamp1171 Inish Glora1211¾ Heyahohowdy114½ Angled out,drvg 9
28Aug04-10WO gd 1 1/16 Ⓣ :24 :464 1:10 1:40 3↑ⒻAlw 83700NC **95** 5 6¾ 5¼ 4½ 33 2¼ Husbands P L118 3.35 96-02 Hour of Justice1162¼ *Classic Stamp*1182¼ First Quarter116¾ 3wd,all out 8
17Jly04-4WO yl 1⅛ Ⓣ :48 1:112 1:352 1:48 3↑ⒻDncSmrtH-G3 **90** 1 42 2hd 2hd 32 3½ Husbands P L116 2.05 85-12 Mona Rose1121 *InishGlora*1221½ ClassicStamp11611¼ Vied btwn,weakened 4
26Jun04-2WO fm 1 Ⓣ :233 :462 1:102 1:343 3↑OC 80k/N3X-N **94** 2 6¼ 6½ 34 2hd 1¼ Husbands P L117 *1.60 90-09 ClassicStamp1172¼ SirBlitz1201¼ P.J.'sPaulieBoy1202½ Rallied,drove clear 7
5Jun04-8WO fm 1 1/16 Ⓣ :25 :484 1:12 1:401 3↑ⒻNassau-G3 **91** 3 42 43 43 34 3¼ Husbands P L119 7.05 94-02 Inish Glora121¾ *Ocean Drive*1172¼ *Classic Stamp*119¾ Hung 3-wide 6
16May04-6WO fm 1 Ⓣ :231 :463 1:102 1:333 3↑ⒻAlw 86400NC **91** 7 7½ 7½ 5¼ 3½ 2nk Husbands P L118 5.60 95-05 *Inish Glora*120nk Classic Stamp118¾ *Msbaileyscream*1186¼ Dug in late 7

Coconut Girl
Own: Jpf Investments I LLC

Dk. b or b. m. 6 (Jan)
Sire: Cryptoclearance (Fappiano) $12,500
Dam: Sarabi (Lost Code)
Br: Leslie R. Grimm & Flint S. Schulhofer (Ky)
Tr: Aguirre Paul G(0 0 0 0 .00) 2004:(159 29 .18)

Life	20	5	3	4	$277,166	104	D.Fst	12	3	3	3	$209,370	104
2004	9	2	1	2	$154,686	104	Wet(335)	2	0	0	1	$12,876	94
2003	6	1	2	1	$62,640	100	Turf(241)	6	2	0	0	$54,920	87
	0	0	0	0	$0	–	Dst(0)	0	0	0	0	$0	–

31Dec04-7SA sly 6½f ⊗ :212 :441 1:084 1:151 3↑ⒻMnroviaH113k – 7 9 7½ 31 8¾ 813½ Espinoza V LB115 f 4.70 82-12 Resplendency1121 PuxaSco1153 MrketGrden1154 4wd move turn,wkened 9
2Sep04-7Dmr fst 1 :221 :46 1:10 1:353 3↑ⒻⓇPiedraFndH76k **88** 2 67 53 4½ 4½ 4½ Court J K LB117 f 4.40 90-07 Elloluv1222½ LetrdeCmbio1152½ SintlyPrsusion114½ Off bit slow,squeezed 7
21Aug04-8Dmr fst 6½f :214 :441 1:09 1:154 3↑ⒻRchBrdoH-G3 **91** 2 5 41 32 32 4¾ Espinoza V LB116 f 3.00 92-08 *DreamofSummer*118nk BarbarOrr1133½ CyberSlew117hd Bit off rail,lost 3rd 7
10Jly04-5Hol fst 7f :22 :44 1:08 1:21 3↑ⒻAGleamH-G2 **96** 1 6 6¼ 6½ 45 4¾ Espinoza V LB116 f 4.20 92-10 *DremofSummr*1143½ TuckdAwy116nk ElusivDiv1121 Btwn turn,outfinished 9
5Jun04-1Hol fst 6f :222 :444 :563 1:084 3↑ⒻDstStmrH-G3 **104** 2 1 2½ 2½ 12 1¼ Espinoza V LB115 f 5.50 93-13 Coconut Girl1151¼ *Ema Bovary*1235½ Stormica1152 Btwn,led into str,game 5
12May04-7Hol fst 6f :212 :442 :561 1:091 4↑ⒻAlw 63720c **92** 7 2 43 2½ 1½ 2½ Espinoza V LB120 f 2.50 90-11 Pocktfllofpsos118½ *CocontGrl*120¾ DmondTr1181½ 3w,drifted in,outgamed 7
2May04-8BM fst 6f :222 :451 :57 1:092 3↑ⒻWoodsideH56k **91** 6 5 5¼ 4½ 3½ 3¼ Puglisi I LB117 f 2.00 91-12 Christmas Time1181¼ Stormica116no Coconut Girl117no Bid 3w, even late 7
31Mar04-4SA fst 6f :221 :45 :563 1:09 4↑ⒻAlw 61366c **100** 1 4 2hd 1hd 11 11 Espinoza V LB116 f *1.30 93-10 CoconutGirl1161 DeviousImpct1162 DimondTir1161 Inside,good handling 6
22Feb04-8SA wf 6f :211 :434 :553 1:08 4↑ⒻLsFlresH-G3 **94** 1 4 31 2½ 32 3¼ Espinoza V LB113 f 10.70 94-07 *EmBovry*1213¼ Buffythecntrfold1171 *CoconutGirl*1135 Rail trip,best of rest 6

Colonial Colony
Own: Nolan Chris

Dk. b or b. h. 7 (Apr)
Sire: Pleasant Colony (His Majesty)
Dam: Jen's Fashion (Northern Fashion)
Br: Chris Nolan (Ky)
Tr: Stewart Dallas(0 0 0 0 .00) 2004:(295 49 .17)

Life	34	4	7	6	$865,205	110	D.Fst	17	1	4	4	$246,915	109
2004	9	1	1	1	$607,625	110	Wet(358)	3	1	0	0	$534,015	110
2003	10	1	3	0	$164,665	109	Turf(282)	14	2	3	2	$84,275	94
	0	0	0	0	$0	-	Dst(0)	0	0	0	0	$0	-

31Dec04- 9FG fst 1 1/16 :242 :48 1:12 1:432 3↑LouisianaH60k – 5 46 46 44½ 45 47 Melancon L L122 3.70 86- 16 Gigawatt1142¼ Alumni Hall117¾ Kodema1161 Unhrried,even position 7
26Nov04-11CD fst 1⅛ :48 1:12 1:372 1:504 3↑ClarkH-G2 **99** 1 84¼ 66 76¼ 79 87 Day P L116 19.20 76- 25 Saint Liam1171¼ Seek Gold111no Perfect Drift1181¼ 5w into lane,no bid 9
Previously trained by Bindner Walter M Jr
22Aug04- 8Dmr fst 1¼ :464 1:104 1:352 2:01 3↑PacifcCl-G1 **99** 2 78½ 79¼ 65 75¾ 68½ Bejarano R LB124 f 14.40 81- 10 PleasantlyPerfect1241 PerfectDrift124¾ TotalImpct1244¾ Off rail,no rally 8
31Jly04- 8AP fst 1 3/16 :482 1:124 1:363 1:564 3↑WashPkH-G2 **99** 3 42½ 41½ 42½ 52¼ 41¾ Bejarano R L118 f *1.60 89- 18 Eye of the Tiger116hd Olmodavor1211½ Congrats116nk Inside, no rally 5
3Jly04- 7Bel fst 1¼ :461 1:091 1:334 1:592 3↑SuburbnH-G1 **109** 6 812 611 75¼ 43 41 Bejarano R L116 f 21.80 99 - PeaceRules120nk Newfoundlnd114no FunnyCide117¾ Game finish outside 8
12Jun04- 9CD sly 1⅛ :473 1:122 1:372 1:502 3↑SFosterH-G1 **110** 6 68 65¾ 21½ 2hd 1no Bejarano R L111 f 62.60 85- 17 ColonlColony111no SthrnImg1225 PrfctDrft1193¾ Bumped late,6w,gamely 6
23May04- 9CD fm 1⅛ Ⓣ :474 1:113 1:36 1:482 3↑Alw 65200c **90** 4 2hd 33½ 33 42½ 53¼ Velasquez C L117 7.80 88- 06 EverythingtoGin123nk DevilTim1171 GrtBloom1212 Between,forced,tired 6
17Apr04- 8Haw fst 1⅛ :464 1:112 1:363 1:492 3↑NtlJClbH-G3 **99** 6 57½ 513 59½ 35 26¾ Lopez J L113 18.30 103- 07 TnMostWntd1216¾ ColonlClny1134¼ NwYrkHr1131¾ No match for winner 6
18Mar04- 9FG fst 140 :233 :464 1:112 1:383 4↑OC 62k/N3x-N **93** 6 55½ 66¾ 57½ 43½ 32¾ Melancon G L117 4.40 98- 07 Mr. Archibald1182¼ Dance to Destiny112½ Colonial Colony117¾ Mild close 6

Colorful Judgement
Own: Sam-Son Farms

Ch. g. 5 (Feb)
Sire: Diesis*GB (Sharpen Up*GB) $30,000
Dam: Colorful Vices (Regal Classic)
Br: Sam-Son Farm (Ont-C)
Tr: Frostad Mark R(0 0 0 0 .00) 2004:(269 49 .18)

Life	12	4	1	4	$462,178	97	D.Fst	0	0	0	0	$0	-
2004	5	2	1	0	$277,602	97	Wet(253)	0	0	0	0	$0	-
2003	6	2	0	4	$184,576	94	Turf(325)	12	4	1	4	$462,178	97
	0	0	0	0	$0	-	Dst(0)	0	0	0	0	$0	-

24Oct04- 9WO gd 1½ Ⓣ :494 1:141 2:044 2:283 3↑CanIntnl-G1 **75** 7 42½ 43 83 817 822 Kabel T K L126 31.55 65- 13 Sulamani1261½ Simonas1262 Brian Boru126¾ 2-deep,lacked rally 10
2Oct04- 8WO fm 1⅜ Ⓣ :51 1:152 1:40 2:16 3↑SkyClscH-G2 **94** 2 31½ 31 51¾ 31 1nk Callaghan S L114 5.80 85- 14 ColorfulJudgmnt114nk LnnythLndr1101 Longship107nk Strong late effort 7
6Sep04- 8WO fm 1½ Ⓣ :491 1:132 2:014 2:254 3↑NiagrBCH-G2 **97** 1 43½ 63¼ 32½ 24 24 Callaghan S L115 7.15 97- 06 StruttheStage1214 *ColorfulJudgement*1153¾ MrkOne1151¼ Rail trip,gamely 6
18Jly04- 3WO gd 1⅜ Ⓣ :453 1:103 1:372 2:16 3↑Alw 72200N2x **90** 3 320 220 210 1½ 11¾ Callaghan S L120 *1.95 85- 17 ColorfulJudgement1201¾ LstAnswer1201¾ *KingofSim*120¾ Rail trip,driving 6
12Jun04- 3WO fm 1⅛ Ⓣ :452 1:093 1:341 1:463 3↑Alw 72200N2x **82** 5 62¾ 63½ 6½ 3½ 44¼ Callaghan S L120 *2.35 91- 06 PJsPuliBoy120nk WolfHowl1202¼ *HighSpdTrvl*1201¾ 4wd,gamely,hung late 10

Commercante (Fr)
Own: Falourd Alain, Guy, Hubert and Trusse

B. f. 5 (Jan)
Sire: Marchand de Sable (Theatrical*Ire)
Dam: Deception (Tropular)
Br: Har. De Bernesq & S.C. Ecurie Ouaki Fabien (Fr)
Tr: Frankel Robert J(0 0 0 0 .00) 2004:(491 135 .27)

Life	13	4	3	1	$709,791	107	D.Fst	0	0	0	0	$0	–
2004	4	2	1	0	$630,000	107	Wet(311)	0	0	0	0	$0	–
2003	7	1	1	1	$63,420	–	Turf(248)	13	4	3	1	$709,791	107
	0	0	0	0	$0	–	Dst(0)	0	0	0	0	$0	–

24Oct04-6WO	gd	1¼	Ⓣ:504	1:152	1:40	2:04	3↑ⒻEPTaylor-G1	100	5	6²¾	6³¼	3¹½	2hd	1½	Velazquez J R	L123	2.55	87– 13	Commercante123½ Punctilious118nk ClssicStmp123²¼	Led 1/6th pole,drvg	8
2Oct04-7Bel	yl	1¼	🅃:522	1:174	1:412	2:043	3↑ⒻFlwrBlIv-G1	101	5	4¹	4¹¼	4¹½	2½	2¾	Velazquez J R	L118	3.40	70– 25	Riskvrs118¾ *Commrcnt*118hd MoscowBurning120nk	Gamely between rivals	8
14Aug04-8AP	fm	1³⁄₁₆	Ⓣ:494	1:152	1:393	1:562	3↑ⒻBeverlyD-G1	92	10	6³	7³½	10⁵¼	9⁶	9⁴¼	Bailey J D	L123	3.30	88 -	Crimson Palace123½ *Riskaverse*123hd Necklace117nk	Traffic turn, steadied	11
29May04-3Bel	yl	1¹⁄₁₆	Ⓣ:234	:482	1:133	1:443	3↑ⒻAlw 50000N3x	107	3	6¹²	6⁸¾	2²½	1⁶	1¹¹¼	Bailey J D	L121 f	*.45	74– 30	Commercnte121¹¹¼ LdyLibby118²½ Letthefrdomror113³¼	A handy winner	6

Coney Kitty (Ire)
Own: Betz William J., Humphrey, Steve and

Ch. m. 7 (Apr)
Sire: Lycius (Mr. Prospector) $6,000
Dam: Auntie Maureen*Ire (Roi Danzig)
Br: Tony Doyle (Ire)
Tr: Toner James J(0 0 0 0 .00) 2004:(112 19 .17)

Life	34	7	3	5	$345,468	97	D.Fst	2	0	0	1	$3,400	76
2004	9	2	1	2	$136,145	93	Wet(267)	0	0	0	0	$0	–
2003	8	1	0	2	$65,540	95	Turf(310)	32	7	3	4	$342,068	97
	0	0	0	0	$0	–	Dst(0)	0	0	0	0	$0	–

31Oct04-8Aqu	fm	1¹⁄₁₆	Ⓣ:252	:501	1:143	1:433	3↑ⒻAtheniaH-G3	86	4	9⁶½	9⁴½	9³½	7⁵¾	7⁴¾	Coa E M	L114 f	14.10	84– 13	Finery113½ Madeira Mist118nk With Patience114½	Inside trip, no rally	11
10Oct04-6Med	gd	1¹⁄₁₆	Ⓣ:233	:492	1:14	1:443	3↑ⒻNavjoPrcss60k	92	5	5²¼	4¹	3¹½	6¹½	3¹¾	Coa E M	L122 f	4.30	73– 28	DltPrincss119¾ SomthingVnturd115¹ ConyKtty122no	Outside bid,duel 3rd	6
25Sep04-9Bel	fm	1	Ⓣ:241	:473	1:112	1:343	3↑ⒻNblDmslH-G3	84	2	4¾	4¹	7³¾	8⁷	9⁹¼	Santos J A	L115 f	26.00	78– 16	Ocean Drive120¹¼ High Court115¾ HourofJustice116²	Chased inside, tired	9
28Aug04-10Mth	fm	1¹⁄₁₆	Ⓣ:234	:473	1:114	1:431	+3↑ⒻOmnibus60k	93	2	8⁶½	8⁵¾	7³¾	2½	1¹¼	Coa E M	L117 f	*1.10	83– 18	ConeyKitty117¹¼ *WithPtinc*115¹ ConstntTouch116¹½	Blocked into far turn	11
5Jun04-8Bel	fm	1	Ⓣ:233	:464	1:101	1:331	3↑ⒻJsAGmBCH-G2	90	2	6¹¾	5¹¼	3²	6⁴	7⁵¾	Santos J A	L115 f	28.75	88– 06	Intercontinental118¹¼ Vanguardia113½ Etoile Montante121¾	No response	8
18Apr04-8Kee	fm	1¹⁄₁₆	Ⓣ:232	:48	1:12	1:412	4↑ⒻJenyWily-G3	87	7	8⁷¼	8⁴¼	8⁶¼	5³¾	5⁵½	Santos J A	L116	12.90	91– 05	*Intercontinental*116¹ *OceanDrive*116¹½ *MdeirMist*118nk	Lunge in air start,8w	8
14Mar04-10Tam	fm	*1⅛	Ⓣ:49	1:124	1:37	1:484	4↑ⒻHlsborgh-G3	92	3	7³½	6⁵	6⁴½	4¹½	1nk	Santos J A	L116 f	2.90	95– 09	Coney Kitty116nk Madeira Mist122nk Alternate116³½	Split h,came out late	12
10Feb04-8Tam	fm	1¹⁄₁₆	Ⓣ:244	:503	1:154	1:444	4↑ⒻEndeavour100k	88	11	7³½	6⁴	7²¾	9²¾	3¹	Samyn J L	L116 f	6.20	78– 20	MdirMist116¾ SomthingVnturd116nk *ConyKitty*116¾	Boxed,gaining 7 wide	12
3Jan04-11GP	fm	1¹⁄₁₆	Ⓣ:234	:481	1:12	1:411	3↑ⒻHonyFoxH-G3	89	7	4¹¾	4³½	3²	3¹	2½	Velasquez C	L115 f	5.90	90– 07	DelmonicoCt116½ ConeyKitty115nk *MdeirMist*117nk	Game try,outfinished	10

Congressionalhonor
Own: Anderson Hollendorfer, Litt, et al

Gr/ro. c. 4 (Apr) KEESEP02 $67,000
Sire: Forestry (Storm Cat) $75,000
Dam: Quiet Dance (Quiet American)
Br: Edward P. Evans (Ky)
Tr: Hollendorfer Jerry(0 0 0 0 .00) 2004:(1300 308 .24)

Life	10	2	2	3	$99,638	89	D.Fst	3	1	0	1	$21,538	79
2004	10	2	2	3	$99,638	89	Wet(461)	2	0	1	0	$6,000	80
2003	0	M	0	0	$0	-	Turf(311)	5	1	1	2	$72,100	89
	0	0	0	0	$0	-	Dst(0)	0	0	0	0	$0	-

19Dec04-7GG gd 1 Ⓣ:24 :49 1:133 1:381 3↑OC 50k/n2x-N 81 6 44 52½ 32 52½ 62½ Baze R A LB118 b *1.40 85-11 Holdthehelm117no Gambler's Mark1191 DSloatBlvd1171 Stlkd 3w, no rally 8
28Nov04-7GG yl 1$\frac{1}{16}$ Ⓣ:23 :473 1:123 1:441+3↑OC 50k/n2x-N 83 3 65½ 65¼ 52½ 42 31¾ Baze R A LB117 b *.60e 87-09 AngloSxon1171 KingSimpt119¾ Congrssonlhonor117½ Split foes,outfnshd 9
6Nov04-8BM yl *1⅛ Ⓣ:471 1:114 1:38 1:484 BMDerby-G3 89 8 52 57 67 62¾ 12¼ Baze R A LB115 b 9.20 83-24 Congressionalhonor1152¼ Talaris116no DHendrix117no Circled 4w, drvng 8
20Oct04-4BM wf 1$\frac{1}{16}$ ⊗:222 :461 1:11 1:424 OC 40k/n1x-N 80 5 53 54½ 3½ 11 2nk Baze R A LB118 b 2.80 93-10 Talaris118nk Congressionlhonor1185 EpicPower118½ Strong run 3w, caught 6
29Sep04-7BM fm 1$\frac{1}{16}$ Ⓣ:232 :483 1:122 1:442 OC 40k/n1x-N 79 5 32½ 42¼ 31½ 2½ 2no Baze R A LB118 b *1.10 84-16 EpicPower118no Congressionlhonor118¾ RreRqust1188 Bid 3w, outdueled 6
5Sep04-8BM fm 1$\frac{1}{16}$ Ⓣ:231 :471 1:111 1:43 OC 40k/n1x-N 79 5 31½ 31½ 32½ 34 34 Lopez D G LB118 b 25.10 87-08 StrtThtr118hd RmblinBob1184 Congrssionlhonor1186 Bmpd 4w 1/4p, even 8
14Jly04-5Sol fst 1 :24 :471 1:113 1:374 3↑Md Sp Wt 29k 79 6 2hd 2hd 1½ 11 1½ Schvaneveldt C P LB117 b *2.00 87-17 Congrssionlhonor117½ DrbyRidr1222½ DputyGold1175 Dueled,held off foe 6
11Jun04-4BM fst 1 :221 :453 1:101 1:36 3↑Md Sp Wt 33k 66 8 2½ 21 22 33 45¼ Warren R J Jr LB116 b 6.00 85-15 ApolloKing116½ WantedMn116nk CopperMist1164½ Pressed,3w, gave way 8
23May04-2BM fst 6f :221 :443 :563 1:092 3↑Md Sp Wt 27k 65 7 5 65 57½ 59 38½ Warren R J Jr LB117 b 2.00e 83-14 Jeffries Bay1171½ Sloat Blvd1174 Congressionalhonor117¾ 3w, no threat 7
14Jan04-5GG wf 5½f :214 :451 :571 1:034 Md Sp Wt 35k 39 4 4 32 64¼ 79¾ 711¾ Radke K LB118 2.10 79-09 Stacy's Ridge118nk Copper Mist1181 Trevanian1181½ Svd grnd to no avail 7

Consolidator
Own: Lewis Robert B. and Beverly J

Ch. c. 3 (May) KEESEP03 $1,250,000
Sire: Storm Cat (Storm Bird) $500,000
Dam: Good Example*Fr (Crystal Glitters)
Br: Pacelco S.A. (Ky)
Tr: Lukas D. W(0 0 0 0 .00) 2004:(577 67 .12)

Life	7	2	1	1	$480,260	94	D.Fst	6	2	1	1	$467,760	94
2004	7	2	1	1	$480,260	94	Wet(371)	1	0	0	0	$12,500	62
2003	0	M	0	0	$0	-	Turf(328)	0	0	0	0	$0	-
	0	0	0	0	$0	-	Dst(0)	0	0	0	0	$0	-

30Oct04-7LS fst 1$\frac{1}{16}$:232 :472 1:111 1:42 BCJuvnle-G1 94 4 21½ 21 2hd 3½ 42¼ Bejarano R L122 7.50 90-02 Wilko122¾ Afleet Alex122nk Sun King1221¼ Bumped 3/16,gave way 8
9Oct04-7Kee fst 1$\frac{1}{16}$:23 :47 1:12 1:433 BrdrsFut-G1 93 6 2½ 21½ 2½ 12½ 12 Bejarano R L121 5.90 94-13 Consolidator1212 Patriot Act1213¼ Diamond Isle121½ 4w,strong handling 10
21Aug04-9Sar sly 7f :22 :443 1:094 1:232 Hopeful-G1 62 7 2 63¼ 64¼ 48 413 Day P L122 b 8.60 74-13 AfleetAlex122nk DevilsDisciple1221¾ Flmenco12211 Hit gate start, bumped 7
29Jly04-8Sar fst 6f :221 :452 :571 1:091 Sanford-G2 88 9 6 31 42 52½ 35½ Day P L118 3.20 90-11 Afleet Alex1205¼ Flamenco122nk Consolidator118¾ Good finish outside 11
3Jly04-11CD fst 6f :221 :463 :58 1:10 Md Sp Wt 45k 87 7 1 1½ 1hd 12½ 13 McKee J 119 *.60 91-08 Consolidator1193 Belarion1198¼ Mansmind1193½ Dueled,hand urging 10
5Jun04-8CD fst 5½f :221 :461 :572 1:04 KyBC-G3 83 3 2 3½ 21½ 22 2nk Bejarano R 115 7.10 92-12 Lunarpal121nk Consolidator1151¾ SmokeWrning1178 Bmp gate,in tight late 4
29Apr04-3CD fst 4½f :222 :45 :511 Md Sp Wt 44k 46 7 6 2½ 57 510 Velasquez C 118 *1.90 89-08 PrimalStorm1186 SmokeWrning1181¾ IronstoneRod1181 Bore in bmp start 7

Cool Conductor
Own: Garner David E

B. c. 4 (Jan) KEESEP02 $100,000
Sire: Stravinsky (Nureyev) $25,000
Dam: Verinha*Brz (Baronius*Brz)
Br: Rio Claro Tbs. Inc., R D Hubbard & C Sczesny (Ky)
Tr: Mott William I(0 0 0 0 .00) 2004:(680 116 .17)

Life	13	3	1	4	$341,846	99	D.Fst	1	0	0	0	$0	36
2004	9	2	1	3	$298,295	99	Wet(275)	0	0	0	0	$0	-
2003	4	1	0	1	$43,551	86	Turf(310)	12	3	1	4	$341,846	99
	0	0	0	0	$0	-	Dst(0)	0	0	0	0	$0	-

```
14Nov04-9CD fm 1 1/16 Ⓣ :232 :483 1:141 1:443 CmmnwlthTf171k 78 2 810 87½ 73½ 105 96¾ Santos J A L120 *1.10 74-21 Broadway View114no America Alive1161¼ Capo114½ Ck 3/16s, no bid 10
16Oct04-8Haw fm 1⅛ Ⓣ :472 1:112 1:352 1:474 HawDerby-G3 92 5 65½ 67½ 64¼ 22 1nk Santos J A L115 *1.50 101-07 CoolCondctor115nk BnkrptcyCort1152¼ CrwnPrnc113¾ Inside trip, driving 10
10Oct04-4Kee fm 1 Ⓣ :233 :472 1:12 1:362 StormCat110k 95 3 23 12 1½ 1hd 41½ Day P L117 *1.50 88-12 Good Reward117¾ Fort Prado120nk Silver Ticket123½ Bmp gate,weakened 8
14Aug04-11AP fm 1¼ Ⓣ :463 1:11 1:351 1:593 Secretar-G1 98 5 15 15 11 52 58½ Day P L119 9.20 104 - Kitten's Joy1233¼ Greek Sun1211¼ Moscow Ballet1191 Rank early, tired 7
24Jly04-5AP fm 1 3/16 Ⓣ :482 1:124 1:372 1:544 AmercnDb-G2 99 8 42 42½ 75 3nk 2nk Velasquez C L119 3.00 100-05 SimpleExchnge119nk CoolConductor119¾ Tosted1231¼ 3 wide, just missed 8
3Jly04-9AP sf 1 1/16 Ⓣ :243 :51 1:174 1:504 ArlClsc-G2 87 4 1½ 1½ 1½ 1½ 33½ Velasquez C 119 b 2.80 51-45 Toasted1213¼ Street Theatre119nk Cool Conductor119hd Rank early, bled 8
12Jun04-5CD yl 1⅛ Ⓣ :49 1:134 1:381 1:503 JfrsnCup-G3 90 4 12 12 1½ 2hd 34¾ Velasquez C 116 b 10.70 75-25 PrinceArch120hd KittensJoy1224¾ CoolConductor1161¼ Bmp start,faltered 9
16May04-9CD yl 1 1/16 Ⓣ :244 :494 1:144 1:441 Alw 48595N1x 87 2 3½ 32 21½ 12½ 15½ Velasquez C 116 b *.80 83-15 CoolConductor1165½ PryerBell116½ BlldoBrez1161½ Drew off,hand urging 9
18Apr04-9Kee fm 1⅛ Ⓣ :47 1:12 1:37 1:49 Alw 53515N1x 85 3 88½ 710 74¾ 42½ 31½ Bailey J D 120 b 2.50 90-05 GoodRewrd118nk HroicDd1181¼ CoolConductor1202½ Angle in late,gaining 12
```

Court's in Session
Own: Wind River Stables

Dk. b or b. g. 6 (Mar)
Sire: Petersburg (Danzig) $2,000
Dam: Crafty Court (Crafty Native)
Br: Mr. & Mrs. Guy C. Roberts (Wash)
Tr: Koriner Brian J(0 0 0 0 .00) 2004:(288 57 .20)

Life	32	8	6	7	$238,945	105	D.Fst	16	6	1	4	$159,105	105
2004	11	5	0	1	$134,485	105	Wet(360)	2	1	0	1	$17,140	80
2003	6	0	3	2	$30,420	88	Turf(260)	14	1	5	2	$62,700	91
	0	0	0	0	$0	-	Dst(0)	0	0	0	0	$0	-

```
31Oct04-8BM yl 1 1/16 Ⓣ :234 :481 1:124 1:441 3↑PacificaH69k 79 5 97½ 97¾ 85½ 79 77½ Alvarado F T LB116 fb 21.30 77-21 Ninebanks119¾ D True Dancer116nk Motel Staff1171 Clipped heels 1/4p 9
  Placed 6th through disqualification
15Sep04-10Fpx fst 6½f :21 :441 1:093 1:162 3↑GovernrCpH59k 94 5 5 54¾ 44 33 1hd Jauregui L H LB119 fb 11.80 95-10 CourtsinSsson119hd MyMstr1162½ ExcssSummr1213½ 3w into str,rallied,up 8
18Aug04-7Dmr fm 5f Ⓣ :212 :434 :55 3↑GreenFlshH76k 74 2 5 52¾ 67 66½ 69¼ Flores D R LB116 fb 11.20 91 - Geronimo119hd Glick1216 Gray Jag109no Bit off rail,no rally 6
25Jly04-2Dmr fst 6f :212 :434 :56 1:082 3↑BCrsbBCH-G1 86 8 3 75¼ 84½ 75¼ 79¾ Atkinson P LB116 fb 22.60 87-09 Kela1131¼ Pohave1182½ Hombre Rapido1153 Split foes turn,no bid 10
19Jun04-8BM fst 6f :214 :44 :561 1:084 3↑BMBCSprH-G3 105 6 5 55½ 33 1½ 12¼ Gonzalez R M LB115 fb 7.90 95-11 CourtsinSession1152¼ DebonirJoe117nk HombrRpido118nk Bid rail, drvng 9
3Jun04-7BM fst 6f :22 :441 :563 1:09 3↑OC 50k/N2x-N 92 5 1 41¾ 41¾ 52 11¼ Gonzalez R M LB119 b 4.20 94-12 CourtsinSession1191¼ AttackForce1191½ Operatic1172½ Waited 1/4p, drvng 6
9May04-8BM fm 1 1/16 Ⓣ :233 :474 1:121 1:433 4↑Clm c-(32-30) 91 8 63½ 65 63¼ 52 1nk Gonzalez R M LB117 b 10.00 88-18 CourtsnSsson117nk TruckWrror117¾ Trmontm117hd Circled 4w, brshd late 9
  Claimed from Ward Dennis for $32,000, Ward Wesley A Trainer 2004(as of 5/9): (137 19 24 18 0.14) Previously trained by Ward Dennis
10Apr04-9PM fst 1 :232 :472 1:121 1:384 3↑PMMileH40k 87 4 43½ 46 44½ 33½ 33½ Mitchell G V LB120 fb 3.30 85-24 LethalGrnde1221 PokerBrd1232½ CourtsinSession120no 3 wide, up for show 7
  Previously trained by Ward Wesley A
7Mar04-7GG fst 6f :213 :44 :562 1:09 4↑Alw 35742N1x 89 6 6 64½ 66 53 11 Gonzalez R M LB119 fb 13.30 92-15 CourtsinSession1191 AtBoyLuther1192 BlzingRod119no 4w trn, steady bid 10
5Feb04-6GG yl 1 1/16 Ⓣ :241 :482 1:123 1:453+4↑Clm 40000(40-35) 79 7 43½ 35½ 46½ 46½ 57¾ Gonzalez R M LB117 fb 14.00 74-18 MotelStaff1175 LoveThatMan1172 LittleGhzi117no Prompted pace, wknd 9
24Jan04-7GG sf 1 1/16 Ⓣ :241 :492 1:132 1:452+4↑Alw 34732N1x 79 1 65 54 42 34½ 44¾ Gonzalez R M LB120 fb 4.10 78-21 Juniper Kris1192¼ Prairie Predator1201½ Foxlair1191 Rail trip, evenly 10
```

Crafty Shaw
Own: Cella Charles J

Ch. h. 7 (Apr)
Sire: Crafty Prospector (Mr. Prospector) $10,000
Dam: Her She Shawklit (Air Forbes Won)
Br: Lance K. Robinson (Ky)
Tr: Vestal Peter M(0 0 0 0 .00) 2004:(93 9 .10)

Life	42	15	7	7	$1,040,440	113	D.Fst 29 10 6 5 $804,075 113
2004	8	2	3	2	$190,000	111	Wet(388) 11 5 1 2 $234,835 104
2003	14	4	3	2	$351,185	105	Turf(239) 2 0 0 0 $1,530 93
	0	0	0	0	$0	–	Dst(0) 0 0 0 0 $0 –

20Oct04–9TP fst 1 :224 :461 1:11 1:37 3↑TPFallCh-G3 **90** 3 43½ 42½ 33 34½ 24 Perret C L122 2.60 85–19 Cappuchino1154 Crafty Shaw122nk *Added Edge*1191 Inside 2nd turn 7
25Jly04–10Mth fst 1 :232 :461 1:10 1:351 3↑SalvtrMH-G3 **91** 4 33 35½ 45½ 47 410 Perret C L118 1.80 91–19 Presidntilffir117¹ UnforgttblMx1174 RoringFvr1155 5p,chased,weakened 5
3Jly04–9PrM fst 1⅛ :464 1:101 1:342 1:463 3↑CrnhsBCH-G3 **104** 6 21 21 31 34 35½ Perret C L117 4.70 99–12 *Roses in May*1151½ Perfect Drift1194 Crafty Shaw1174¾ 3 wide, weakened 6
29May04–9AP fst 1 :234 :471 1:111 1:351 3↑HanshinH-G3 **111** 5 2hd 2½ 1½ 11 11¼ Perret C L119 *1.80 92–17 Crafty Shaw1191¼ Apt to Be1192½ Kodema1161¾ Driving 7
7Apr04–9OP fst 1 1/16 :23 :462 1:103 1:422 4↑5thSeasn-G3 **99** 1 11 1½ 1hd 3½ 21 Doocy T T L122 1.80 97–10 SpnishEmpire1131 *CrftyShw*122nk NoComprend1222 Came back for place 8
14Mar04–9OP fst 1 1/16 :234 :472 1:114 1:432 4↑RazrbckH-G3 **99** 3 2½ 2hd 1hd 31 22¾ Perret C L117 3.40 90–23 Sonic West1132¾ Crafty Shaw117hd Pie N Burger1192 Game for place 7
21Feb04–9OP fst 1 1/16 :241 :48 1:13 1:433 4↑EssexH-G3 **92** 3 32 32½ 31 34 35¼ Perret C L118 2.40 87–16 PrivteEmblem1131¼ PieNBurger1184 CrftyShw118hd Broke thru prestart 8
1Feb04–9OP fst 1 :242 :483 1:133 1:38 4↑Alw 40000NC **94** 5 11½ 11½ 1hd 2hd 1no Perret C L118 *.60 94–13 Crafty Shaw118no Docent118¾ Missme1183¾ Soft pace, fought back 5

Crimson Palace (SAf)
Own: Godolphin Racing Inc

Dk. b or b. m. 6 (Sep)
Sire: Elliodor*Fr (Lyphard)
Dam: Perfect Guest (Northern Guest)
Br: Adv A P Joubert (SAf)
Tr: bin Suroor Saeed(0 0 0 0 .00) 2004:(9 2 .22)

Life	11	7	0	0	$663,278	102	D.Fst 0 0 0 0 $0 –
2004	5	3	0	0	$637,731	102	Wet(327) 0 0 0 0 $0 –
2003	1	0	0	0	$1,175	–	Turf(432) 11 7 0 0 $663,278 102
	0	0	0	0	$0	–	Dst(0) 0 0 0 0 $0 –

14Aug04–8AP fm 1 3/16 Ⓣ :494 1:152 1:393 1:562 3↑ⒻBeverlyD-G1 **102** 9 31½ 31½ 42½ 3½ 1½ Dettori L L123 f 9.90 92 – Crimson Palace123½ *Riskaverse*123hd Necklace117nk 3 wide, rallied, drvg 11
16Jun04 Ascot (GB) gf 1 Ⓣ Str 1:401 4↑ ⒻWindsor Forest Stakes-G2 Stk 255000 69½ Dettori L 121 *1.20 Favourable Terms1242 Monturani1213½ Soldera1211 10
Timeform rating: 90 *Tracked leaders,weakened over 1f out*
12May04 York (GB) gs 1 5/16 Ⓣ LH 2:153 4↑ ⒻMiddleton Stakes (1 1/4m,88y)-G3 Stk 88600 1¾ Dettori L 121 *1.50 Crimson Palace121¾ Beneventa12411 Summitville1216 6
Timeform rating: 110+ *Rated in 5th,rallied to lead over 1f out,driving*
27Mar04 Nad Al Sheba (UAE) gf *1⅛ Ⓣ LH 1:491 3↑ Dubai Duty Free-G1 Stk 2000000 4¾ Dettori L 121 - DH Right Approach126 DH Paolini126nk Nayyir126½ 11
Timeform rating: 112 *3rd on rail,fnshd well but held by first three*
Previously trained by Mike de Kock
29Jan04 Nad Al Sheba (UAE) gf *1⅛ Ⓣ LH 1:472 3↑ Alhaarth Stakes Alw 50000 14¾ Marwing W 121 - Crimson Palace1214¾ Gateman126½ Hero's Journey126½ 7
Timeform rating: 112+ *Rated in 5th,in tight 1-1/2f out,led 1f out,going away*

Culinary

Own: Jack H. Smith III Thoroughbreds

Gr/ro. f. 3 (May) EASMAY04 $25,000
Sire: El Amante (Wild Again) $1,500
Dam: Volunteer*Arg (Ski Champ)
Br: Diana Snowden & Guy B. Snowden (Ky)
Tr: Stidham Michael(0 0 0 0 .00) 2004:(369 81 .22)

Life	3	2	0	0	$78,000	87	D.Fst	3	2	0	0	$78,000	87
2004	3	2	0	0	$78,000	87	Wet(287)	0	0	0	0	$0	–
2003	0	M	0	0	$0	–	Turf(263*)	0	0	0	0	$0	–
	0	0	0	0	$0	–	Dst(0)	0	0	0	0	$0	–

30Oct04–3LS fst 1 1/16 :22^4 :46^2 1:10^3 1:41^3 ⒻBCJuvFil-G1 **85** 4 4^4 4^{2½} 3^1 7^5 7^{9½} Marquez C H Jr L119 7.30 84–02 SweetCtomine119^{3¾} Blletto119^{1¼} *RunwyMod*119^{¾} 3-4wide turns,gave way 12
19Sep04–9AP fst 1 :23^3 :47 1:12 1:36^4 ⒻArlWaLas-G3 **87** 2 6^{3¾} 4^{3½} 3^{2½} 2^{½} 1^2 Marquez C H Jr L116 7.00 84–20 Culinary116^2 *Runway Model*118^{3½} Kota118^2 3 wide, driving 8
12Aug04–6AP fst 1 :23 :46^3 1:13^4 1:41^2 ⒻMd Sp Wt 30k **60** 4 5^5 4^4 4^{1½} 1^4 1^{11} Marquez C H Jr L118 3.70 61–32 *Culinary*118^{11} Rosegate118^{1¼} Coastal Flag118^{1½} 4 wide, handily 7

Dance With Ravens

Own: Sam-Son Farms

B. c. 3 (Apr)
Sire: A.P. Indy (Seattle Slew) $300,000
Dam: Dance Smartly (Danzig)
Br: Sam-Son Farm (Ont-C)
Tr: Frostad Mark R(0 0 0 0 .00) 2004:(269 49 .18)

Life	3	1	1	1	$223,820	77	D.Fst	1	1	0	0	$162,000	72
2004	3	1	1	1	$223,820	77	Wet(456)	0	0	0	0	$0	–
2003	0	M	0	0	$0	–	Turf(367)	2	0	1	1	$61,820	77
	0	0	0	0	$0	–	Dst(0)	0	0	0	0	$0	–

11Oct04–8WO fst 1 1/16 :23^3 :48^2 1:13^4 1:47^3 GreyBC-G2 **72** 1 2^{½} 3^1 3^{1½} 1^{hd} 1^{½} Kabel T K L116 b 1.40 73–25 DncWthRvns116^{½} Accontforthgld114^{1¼} *CrmnlMnd*113^{1½} Strong late effort 6
19Sep04–3WO fm 1 Ⓣ :22^2 :45^1 1:10 1:34^3 Summer-G2 **77** 4 3^4 3^3 2^2 2^{2½} 2^{2¼} Kabel T K L122 b 2.55 88–03 Dubleo122^{2¼} *Dance With Ravens*122^1 Go to the Sun122^{¾} 3wd,all out 8
22Aug04–5WO fm 7f Ⓣ :22^3 :45^4 1:10^3 1:23^2 Md Sp Wt 57k **64** 6 1 3^2 5^{2¾} 4^{1½} 3^{1½} Kabel T K L116 2.15 83–05 StgNtion116^{no} PurplePssge120^{1½} DnceWithRvns116^{¾} Blocked str,gamely 11

Daydreaming

Own: Phipps Ogden M

B. f. 4 (Mar)
Sire: A.P. Indy (Seattle Slew) $300,000
Dam: Get Lucky (Mr. Prospector)
Br: Ogden Mills Phipps (Ky)
Tr: McGaughey III Claude R(0 0 0 0 .00) 2004:(254 48 .19)

Life	11	6	1	2	$562,180	108	D.Fst	11	6	1	2	$562,180	108
2004	8	5	1	1	$483,180	108	Wet(438)	0	0	0	0	$0	–
2003	3	1	0	1	$79,000	88	Turf(314)	0	0	0	0	$0	–
	0	0	0	0	$0	–	Dst(0)	0	0	0	0	$0	–

26Nov04–9Aqu fst 1 :23^4 :46^4 1:11 1:35^1 3↑ⒻTopFlgtH-G2 **98** 6 4^{2½} 4^3 4^{¾} 2^{hd} 1no Bailey J D L117 *1.05 89–17 Dydrmng117^{no} BndngStrngs118^{2¼} RorEmotn116^{2¼} 4 wide move, resolute 6
10Oct04–9Hoo fst 1 1/16 :23^2 :48 1:12 1:43^3 ⒻInBCOaks-G3 **108** 6 4^3 4^3 4^{2½} 2^{hd} 1^{1½} Velazquez J R LB118 2.60 93–27 *Daydreaming*118^{1½} CpesideLdy121^{hd} StellrJyne121^{5½} 4wd bid 1/4, drove clr 7
11Sep04–8Bel fst 1⅛ :48 1:12^2 1:36^2 1:48^1 ⒻGazelle-G1 **95** 1 3^2 2^{½} 2^{hd} 1^{hd} 2^1 Velazquez J R L115 5.20 89–15 StellarJyne122^1 *Dydreming*115^{1¾} HeLovesMe117^{no} Dug in gamely outside 6
4Aug04–5Sar fst 1⅛ :49^2 1:13^3 1:38 1:51 3↑ⒻOC 75k/N3x -N **94** 5 5^{1¼} 3^{½} 3^{½} 1^{hd} 1^{½} Bailey J D L116 *.95 80–11 Daydreming116^{½} ClokofVgueness121^{5¼} *ShdowCst*115^{6¼} Bumped first turn 6
26Jun04–9Bel fst 1⅛ :47 1:10^4 1:35^2 1:48 ⒻMthrGoos-G1 **82** 1 6^{2¼} 5^{2¼} 6^2 5^{8½} 5^{10¾} Bailey J D L121 7.60 80–11 Stellar Jayne121^{2½} *Ashado*121^{1¾} Island Sand121^5 Inside, no response 6
6May04–8Bel fst 1 1/16 :23^2 :47^1 1:12^1 1:42^3 3↑ⒻAlw 48000N2x **97** 4 3^{2½} 5^{1¼} 2^{hd} 1^8 1^9 Castellano J J L116 *1.55 87–22 Daydreaming116^9 Marylebone114^{½} Gold Player124^{4½} Quick 3 wide move 6
9Apr04–8Aqu fst 1 :22^4 :45^3 1:10^4 1:35^4 ⒻComely-G3 **79** 2 5^{2½} 6^{2¼} 5^{2½} 3^{6½} 3^{5¾} Castellano J J L116 6.50 80–15 SocitySlction122^3 *BndingStrings*116^{2¾} *Dydrming*116^{8½} Good finish outside 8
1Mar04–8GP fst 170 :22^4 :46^4 1:12^3 1:43^4 ⒻAlw 34000N1x **73** 10 7^{6¼} 7^{7½} 6^{3½} 3^2 1^1 Bailey J D L117 1.70 78–21 Dydrming117^1 ⒹSoulofthCt117^{¾} *ChrryBomb*117^{nk} Bmp st, bothered early 11

Dazzle Me
Own: Padua Stables

Gr/ro. f. 4 (Mar) FTSAUG02 $170,000
Sire: Tactical Cat (Storm Cat) $10,000
Dam: Social Girl (Chief's Crown)
Br: Mrs. J. G. Jones Sr. & R. J. Judy (Ky)
Tr: Asmussen Steven M(0 0 0 0 .00) 2004:(2293 555 .24)

Life	6	4	0	0	$266,276	98	D.Fst	4	4	0	0	$259,946	98
2004	6	4	0	0	$266,276	98	Wet(355)	1	0	0	0	$715	60
2003	0	M	0	0	$0	–	Turf(255)	1	0	0	0	$5,615	74
	0	0	0	0	$0	–	Dst(0)	0	0	0	0	$0	–

31Jly04–8Sar my 7f :212 :44 1:101 1:233 ⒻTest-G1 **60** 5 7 31 35 46½ 716¾ Sellers S J L118 5.40 69–11 *SoctySlcton*120¼ BndngStrngs120¾ ForstMusc118¼ Chased inside, tired 12
10Jly04–8Crc fst 6f :211 :441 :57 1:112 ⒻAzaleaBC-G3 **98** 3 5 11 11½ 12 16½ Sellers S J L115 8.90 92–09 Dazzle Me1156½ Reforest114¾ Boston Express1143 Off rail, drew away 7
20Jun04–8CD fst 6½f :221 :452 1:101 1:17 3↑ⒻAlw 51700N3L **91** 3 2 2½ 2hd 12 13 Sellers S J L117 *.90 86–14 *Dazzle Me*1173 Shari's Gold Sole119no *Audrey Hep*1171¾ Forced,4w,driving 7
15May04–9CD yl 5f Ⓣ:22 :443 :571 ⒻOpenMind112k **74** 1 2 22 54¾ 25 48¼ Douglas R R L118 3.30 83–09 Anna Em1146½ Movant118¾ Victoire Bataille1141 Lost position turn 9
4Apr04–7Kee fst 6½f :213 :444 1:104 1:174 ⒻAlw 54000N2L **92** 1 5 1½ 1½ 11½ 13 Sellers S J L118 1.90 87–18 DazzleMe1183 SmileMaker120¼ GoldMargarita118½ Dueled,driving,clear 10
7Feb04–5FG fst 6f :222 :462 :581 1:104 ⒻMd Sp Wt 28k **89** 3 3 11 11 11½ 11½ Sellers S J L120 1.60 86–15 *DzzleM*120½ *FmilyBusinss*1202 *SmokyDiplomcy*120½ Intermittent pressure 9

Declan's Moon
Own: Jay Em Ess Stable

Dk. b or b. g. 3 (Feb) EASSEP03 $125,000
Sire: Malibu Moon (A.P. Indy) $17,500
Dam: Vee Vee Star (Norquestor)
Br: Brice Ridgely (Md)
Tr: Ellis Ronald W(0 0 0 0 .00) 2004:(121 24 .20)

Life	4	4	0	0	$507,300	107	D.Fst	4	4	0	0	$507,300	107
2004	4	4	0	0	$507,300	107	Wet(349)	0	0	0	0	$0	–
2003	0	M	0	0	$0	–	Turf(303)	0	0	0	0	$0	–
	0	0	0	0	$0	–	Dst(0)	0	0	0	0	$0	–

18Dec04–8Hol fst 1 1/16 :232 :46 1:10 1:413 HolFut-G1 **96** 3 21 2½ 1hd 11 11 Espinoza V LB121 *1.20 93–11 Declan's Moon1211 Giacomo121no Wilko1212 Bid,led,held gamely 7
20Nov04–8Hol fst 7f :214 :441 1:082 1:213 HolPrevu-G3 **98** 5 5 32 31 1½ 12 Espinoza V LB122 *.40 94–11 *Declan's Moon*1222 Bushwacker114hd Seize theDay1172 3wd bid,ridden out 8
8Sep04–8Dmr fst 7f :221 :443 1:084 1:211 DmrFut-G2 **107** 1 3 23½ 24 2½ 1nk Espinoza V LB116 6.20 96–11 *DeclansMoon*116nk *RomanRuler*1209½ *SwissLad*1164 Bid btwn,brushed,game 4
31Jly04–3Dmr fst 5½f :22 :451 :572 1:033 Md Sp Wt 49k **87** 1 2 1hd 1hd 11 15 Flores D R LB118 14.70 97–09 *Declan's Moon*1185 Currency Trader1182 Cashmula118½ Inside, ridden out 7

Dedication (Fr)

Own: Head Ghislaine

Gr/ro. m. 6 (Feb)
Sire: Highest Honor*Fr (Kenmare*Fr) $47,484
Dam: Dissertation (Sillery)
Br: Alec Head & Ghislaine Head (Fr)
Tr: Clement Christophe(0 0 0 0 .00) 2004:(344 68 .20)

Life	23	7	6	1	$456,645	102	**D.Fst**	1	0	0	0	$0	75
2004	8	2	2	0	$156,660	100	**Wet(285)**	0	0	0	0	$0	–
2003	5	1	1	1	$128,450	102	**Turf(262)**	22	7	6	1	$456,645	102
	0	0	0	0	$0	–	**Dst(0)**	0	0	0	0	$0	–

6Nov04-5WO	yl	1	Ⓣ	:24	:47^2	1:12^1	1:39^2	3↑ⒻRiverMem112k	–	2	6 1¾	5 7¾	4 9½	11 31	-	Kabel T K	L117	*1.75	- 34	My Pal Lana117 1½ Ginger Gold117^{no} Always Awesome117½	Bled,pulled up	11
25Sep04-9Bel	fm	1	Ⓣ	:24^1	:47^3	1:11^2	1:34^3	3↑ⒻNblDmslH-G3	**86**	3	6 1	5 1¼	2^{hd}	3 3	8 8	Prado E S	L117	3.65	79- 16	Ocean Drive120 1¼ High Court115¾ Hour of Justice116 2	3 wide move, tired	9
5Jun04-8Bel	fm	1	Ⓣ	:23^3	:46^4	1:10^1	1:33^1	3↑ⒻJsAGmBCH-G2	**95**	4	8 2¾	8 2¾	6 3	5 3½	5 3½	Castellano J J	L117	6.00	90- 06	Intercontinental118 1¼ Vngurdi113½ EtoileMontnte121¾	Mild rally outside	8
30May04-8Bel	gd	7f	Ⓣ	:22^2	:45^3	1:09^2	1:22^1	3↑Jaipur-G3	**100**	7	2	5 4¾	6 3	2½	2½	Prado E S	L114	*2.65	88- 11	Multiple Choice113½ Dedication114 1½ *Geronimo*118^{hd}	Bumped repeatedly	8
1May04-9Aqu	gd	1 1/16	Ⓣ	:25^3	:51^2	1:16^3	1:46^1	3↑ⒻBeaugayH-G3	**97**	2	3 2	3 2½	3 1	1½	1½	Castellano J J	L118	*.80	76- 10	Dedication118½ Aud117½ Caught in the Rain114^{hd}	Drifted in stretch	7
4Apr04-8SA	fm	*6½f	Ⓣ	:22	:44^1	1:07^1	1:13^1	4↑ⒻLsCngasH-G3	**92**	6	5	7 3¾	5 3½	4¾	2½	Nakatani C S	LB118	2.70	90- 08	EtoileMontnte121½ *Dediction*118¾ AnyforLov115½	Waitd bit,bid btw,game	9
13Mar04-11GP	fm	1	Ⓣ	:25^1	:49^4	1:13^2	1:37^4	3↑ⒻMrshsRiver67k	**100**	1	3 2½	3 2½	3 2	1 2	1 2	Prado E S	L120	*1.20	77- 13	Dedication120 2 Ocean Drive120 1 Vespers120½	Hedge, stdy far turn	9
8Feb04-11GP	fst	7f		:22^2	:44^4	1:08^4	1:21^2	3↑ⒻShrlJnsH-G3	**75**	1	7	5 3	5 5	5 7	8 14¾	Prado E S	L114	6.20	80- 16	*Randaroo*118 7¼ Harmony Lodge121¾ Halory Leigh114 2½	Faltered	8

Defer

Own: Phipps Ogden M

B. c. 3 (May)
Sire: Danzig (Northern Dancer) $200,000
Dam: Hidden Reserve (Mr. Prospector)
Br: Ogden Mills Phipps (Ky)
Tr: McGaughey III Claude R(0 0 0 0 .00) 2004:(254 48 .19)

Life	3	2	1	0	$108,900	78	**D.Fst**	3	2	1	0	$108,900	78
2004	3	2	1	0	$108,900	78	**Wet(434)**	0	0	0	0	$0	–
2003	0	M	0	0	$0	–	**Turf(390)**	0	0	0	0	$0	–
	0	0	0	0	$0	–	**Dst(0)**	0	0	0	0	$0	–

20Nov04-5Pim	fst	1 1/16	:24^3	:49^1	1:13^3	1:45^2	LrlFut-G3	**78**	1	3 3	3 2½	3 2	1½	1 2	Bailey J D	L122	*.70	80- 15	Defer122 2 Funk122 3¾ Woody's Apache122^{hd}	Stalked pace, driving	5
2Nov04-8Aqu	fst	1	:22^4	:45^2	1:10	1:36^3	Nashua-G3	**72**	6	3½	3 1½	2½	2 5½	2 6¼	Castellano J J	116	3.50	76- 22	*RockportHrbor*118 6¼ *Defer*116^{hd} *BettrThnBonds*116 2¼	3 wide run, held place	6
2Oct04-3Bel	fst	7f	:22^4	:46^1	1:11^2	1:24^4	Md Sp Wt 45k	**75**	3	7	2^{hd}	2^{hd}	1 4½	1 1½	Castellano J J	119	6.70	76- 22	Defer119 1½ Bachelor's Gulch119^{no} *Apprentice*119¾	Vied inside, drew off	12

Delmonico Cat

Own: Wygod Mr. and Mrs. Martin J

Dk. b or b. m. 6 (Feb)
Sire: Storm Cat (Storm Bird) $500,000
Dam: Glass Ceiling (Pirate's Bounty)
Br: Mr. & Mrs. Martin J. Wygod (Ky)
Tr: Mott William I(0 0 0 0 .00) 2004:(680 116 .17)

Life	15	6	5	2	$273,804	90	**D.Fst**	5	1	2	2	$51,580	87
2004	2	1	0	0	$60,000	90	**Wet(419)**	1	0	1	0	$9,690	80
2003	9	3	4	1	$146,764	90	**Turf(362)**	9	5	2	0	$212,534	90
	0	0	0	0	$0	–	**Dst(0)**	0	0	0	0	$0	–

10Feb04-8Tam	fm	1 1/16	Ⓣ	:24^4	:50^3	1:15^4	1:44^4	4↑ⒻEndeavour100k	**81**	6	6 3½	7 5½	12 5½	8 2¼	11 4	Velasquez C	L122	4.80	75- 20	MdeirMist116¾ SomthingVnturd116^{nk} *ConyKitty*116¾	Buried inside, no rly	12
3Jan04-11GP	fm	1 1/16	Ⓣ	:23^4	:48^1	1:12	1:41^1	3↑ⒻHonyFoxH-G3	**90**	6	6 3¼	7 5	7 5	5 2	1½	Bailey J D	L116	4.90	91- 07	DelmonicoCat116½ ConeyKitty115^{nk} *MadeirMist*117^{nk}	Eased out,rallied,up	10

Designed for Luck
Own: Wilson David W. and Holly F

Ch. g. 8 (Apr)
Sire: Rahy (Blushing Groom*Fr) $80,000
Dam: Fantastic Look (Green Dancer)
Br: Mr. & Mrs. John C. Mabee (Ky)
Tr: Cerin Vladimir(0 0 0 0 .00) 2004:(339 59 .17)

Life	25	10	6	2	$915,500	109	D.Fst	2	1	0	0	$14,400	73
2004	4	1	1	0	$311,180	109	Wet(324)	0	0	0	0	$0	–
2003	4	3	0	0	$267,735	107	Turf(356)	24	9	6	2	$901,100	109
	0	0	0	0	$0	–	Dst(0)	0	0	0	0	$0	–

31May04–7Hol fm 1 Ⓣ:232 :46 1:09 1:324 3↑ShoeBCM-G1 **109** 8 21 22 21 11 11½ Valenzuela P A LB124 b 5.90 100–07 Designed forLuck1241½ Singletary124hd Tsigane1241 Stalked,bid,led,clear 8
1May04–6Hol fm 1 1/16 Ⓣ:233 :464 1:093 1:382 3↑InglewdH-G3 **107** 6 31 31 31 31½ 22 Valenzuela P A LB118 b *2.40 102–04 *Lroidsnimux*1142 *DsigndforLuck*1182 DvousBoy115nk Stalked,3wd, 2nd best 9
6Mar04–9SA fm 1 Ⓣ:224 :452 1:094 1:334 4↑FKilroeH-G2 **101** 11 56 57½ 64¾ 1hd 53¼ Baze T C LB118 b 3.10 90–12 Sweet Return119½ *Singletary*1172 Inesperado116½ 4wd bid,led,outkicked 14
11Feb04–7SA fm 1 Ⓣ:231 :464 1:102 1:342 4↑ThunderRdH71k **91** 8 52½ 43 54 74½ 75 Smith M E LB121 *2.10 85–14 Singletary1171 Inesperado118½ Apache Wings116hd 3wd,4wd,no response 8

Diplomatic Bag
Own: Juddmonte Farms Inc

B. h. 5 (Feb)
Sire: Devil's Bag (Halo) $10,000
Dam: Louis d'Or (Mr. Prospector)
Br: Juddmonte Farms Inc (Ky)
Tr: Frankel Robert J(0 0 0 0 .00) 2004:(491 135 .27)

Life	6	4	0	0	$145,019	103	D.Fst	0	0	0	0	$0	–
2004	1	1	0	0	$90,000	103	Wet(367)	0	0	0	0	$0	–
2003	5	3	0	0	$55,019	–	Turf(281)	6	4	0	0	$145,019	103
	0	0	0	0	$0	–	Dst(0)	0	0	0	0	$0	–

3Apr04–3SA fm 1⅛ Ⓣ:483 1:123 1:361 1:474 4↑ArcadiaH-G2 **103** 5 21½ 31½ 32½ 31½ 1¾ Flores D R LB116 4.10 90–13 Diplomatic Bag116¾ Statement1142 Seinne1151 Strong hand ride 7

Domestic Dispute
Own: Bienstock David, Mandabach, Paul and

Ch. h. 5 (Mar)
Sire: Unbridled's Song (Unbridled) $125,000
Dam: Majestical Moment (Magesterial)
Br: Gary Garber (Ky)
Tr: Gallagher Patrick(0 0 0 0 .00) 2004:(220 39 .18)

Life	21	3	4	2	$703,115	108	D.Fst	17	3	4	2	$689,115	108
2004	7	1	2	0	$413,428	108	Wet(360)	2	0	0	0	$5,000	97
2003	8	1	0	1	$155,367	103	Turf(280)	2	0	0	0	$9,000	90
	0	0	0	0	$0	–	Dst(0)	0	0	0	0	$0	–

30Oct04–4LS yl 1 Ⓣ:24 :483 1:123 1:364 3↑BCMile-G1 **81** 5 21½ 31 61¼ 1411 1412½ John K L126 53.80 73–07 Singletary126½ Antonius Pius1221½ Six Perfections123nk Brief speed tired 14
2Oct04–10Bel fst 1¼ :473 1:113 1:362 2:022 3↑JkyClbGC-G1 **88** 3 41 43¾ 75½ 79¼ 716 Velazquez J R L126 10.30 69–13 FunnyCide126¾ NewfoundInd1261 ThCliffsEdg1223¾ Close up inside, tired 7
5Sep04–8Dmr fst 1 :222 :46 1:10 1:35 3↑DmrBCH-G2 **108** 6 2hd 3½ 41¾ 32½ 2no Desormeaux K J LB117 2.50 99–07 Supah Blitz116no Domestic Dispute1174 During1171 3wd into str,re-bid 6
15Aug04–8Dmr fst 7f :214 :434 1:081 1:21 3↑OBrinBCH-G2 **106** 2 3 41¾ 33 34 24½ Desormeaux K J LB116 13.10 92–10 Kela1164½ Domestic Dispute1161¼ *Pico Central*1224 Came out str,best rest 5
27Mar04 Nad Al Sheba (UAE) ft *1¼ LH 2:001 3↑ Dubai World Cup-G1 Stk 6000000 621½ Stevens G L 126 - Pleasantly Perfect126¾ Medaglia d'Oro1265 Victory Moon1267¾ 12
Timeform rating: 95 *Rated in 6th,5th 2-1/2f out,soon weakened*
7Feb04–9SA fst 1⅛ :454 1:101 1:354 1:49 Strub-G2 **107** 7 42 51¾ 62¼ 74¼ 1nk Desormeaux K J LB117 14.30 89–15 DomesticDispute117nk During121¾ BucklandMnor117½ Blocked 1/8,rallied 11
10Jan04–8SA fst 1 1/16 :222 :452 1:091 1:413 SnFndoBC-G2 **99** 6 74¾ 84¾ 85¾ 52¾ 44 Solis A LB116 4.80 93–07 During1201 Toccet1161 Touch the Wire1172 Tight early,waited 3/8 10

Don Six

Own: Generazio Patricia A

Dk. b or b. h. 5 (May)
Sire: Wild Escapade (Wild Again) $2,000
Dam: Concorde's Beauty (Concorde Bound)
Br: Patricia Generazio (Fla)
Tr: Lake Scott A(0 0 0 0 .00) 2004:(1703 379 .22)

Life	23	8	5	3	$412,183	108	D.Fst	18	7	3	3	$336,085 108
2004	11	4	1	2	$218,733	108	Wet(391)	4	1	2	0	$75,498 98
2003	12	4	4	1	$193,450	104	Turf(280)	1	0	0	0	$600 65
	0	0	0	0	$0	–	Dst(0)	0	0	0	0	$0 –

19Dec04–8Aqu fst 6f ⊡ :224 :451 :57 1:084 3↑GravesdH-G3 108 3 1 12 11½ 11½ 11¼ Luzzi M J L114 f 5.00 95–18 Don Six114 1¼ Mr. Whitestone114½ Papua1142 Sped clear, driving 6
Previously trained by Generazio Frank Jr
28Nov04–9Aqu sly 6f :212 :441 :564 1:094 3↑FallHwtH-G3 73 2 6 21 54¼ 86½ 810¾ Bridgmohan S X L128 17.10 78–16 Thunder Touch126 1¼ Papua128½ Eavesdropper127nk Speed in hand, tired 9
8Oct04–4Med fm 5f Ⓣ :211 :434 :56 3↑MyFrnchman60k 65 3 6 63½ 87¾ 911 99 Bridgmohan S X L119 7.50 88–03 Mnofglory115no DH CumbyTexs115 DH Rudirudy1192 Faded saving ground 9
Run in divisions
6Sep04–9Mth fst 6f :213 :441 :563 1:091 3↑Icecapade60k 66 1 6 1hd 2½ 55½ 713¾ Ferrer J C L117 4.60 80–15 WildctHeir1174 SingMBckHom119¾ HrsZlous1151¾ Vied inside,weakened 7
24Jly04–8Del fst 6f :221 :451 :574 1:094 3↑VAMscrliMH97k 105 2 3 21½ 21 31 21¼ Caraballo J C L118 *1.30 91–16 D HghwyProspctr118 1¼ DnSx118¾ SngMBckHm1168½ Bid, outfinished rest 5
Awarded first purse money
3Jly04–8Del fst 6f :22 :45 :571 1:10 3↑MoBay51k 101 1 3 11½ 11½ 11½ 11¾ Caraballo J C L118 *1.20 91–13 Don Six118 1¾ True Direction1185¼ Sassy Hound1185¼ Held safe margin 4
20May04–8Bel fst 6f :213 :442 :563 1:091 4↑OC 100k/c-N 89 2 3 2hd 2hd 21½ 36 Bridgmohan S X L118 *1.75 87–14 My Cousin Matt1182¾ Multiple Choice1183¼ Don Six1182½ Vied inside, tired 5
1May04–7Del fst 6f :212 :434 :563 1:101 3↑OC 50k/N4x-N 103 4 2 1½ 11 1½ 12¼ Caraballo J C L117 *1.50 90–17 Don Six1172¼ Trounce1174¼ Stormin Oedy117¾ Drifted, driving 8
10Apr04–9Aqu fst 7f :213 :432 1:072 1:201 3↑CarterH-G1 92 6 4 1hd 2½ 46½ 610½ Bridgmohan S X L112 37.75 93–04 PicoCentrl117 1¼ StrongHope1192 EyeoftheTiger114¾ Between rivals, tired 9
13Mar04–8Aqu fst 7f :222 :45 1:092 1:22 3↑ToboggnH-G3 105 2 7 12½ 12½ 2hd 32¼ Bridgmohan S X L113 12.80 93–17 Well Fancied1182 Gators N Bears115nk Don Six1131¾ Set pace, weakened 10
24Jan04–8Aqu fst 6f ⊡ :223 :46 :58 1:102 3↑PaumonokH83k 103 1 8 1hd 11½ 12 2hd Bridgmohan S X L113 b 4.40 87–21 Peeping Tom117hd Don Six1132¼ Super Fuse114½ Pace, clear, gamely 9

Dr. Kashnikow

Own: Erdenheim Farm

Gr/ro. g. 8 (Apr)
Sire: El Gran Senor (Northern Dancer)
Dam: One More Breeze (Mythical Ruler)
Br: Stan Dodson (Ont-C)
Tr: Fisher John R(0 0 0 0 .00) 2004:(96 20 .21)

Life	31	8	5	5	$740,571	105	D.Fst	1	0	0	0	$2,880 57
2004	6	1	1	0	$132,080	99	Wet(326)	0	0	0	0	$0 –
2003	7	0	1	2	$37,280	100	Turf(322)	30	8	5	5	$737,691 105
	0	0	0	0	$0	–	Dst(0)	0	0	0	0	$0 –

21Nov04–9CD yl 1⅛ Ⓣ :481 1:13 1:384 1:511 3↑RivrCtyH-G3 38 4 107½ 1112 1114 1121 1230¼ Blanc B L117 8.30 47–26 G P Fleet115½ Cloudy's Knight1155¼ Ay Caramba115no 5w trip,outrun 12
30Oct04–5Aqu fm 1⅛ Ⓣ :492 1:134 1:38 1:494 3↑KnkrbkrH-G2 94 4 96½ 910 98½ 95 64¼ Samyn J L L116 10.40 87–07 Host1151½ Evening Attire114hd Sailaway113½ Came wide, no rally 9
15Oct04–8Med gd 1 1/16 Ⓣ :231 :48 1:121 1:422 3↑ClfHngfH-G3 99 5 85½ 86½ 83¾ 61 1½ Migliore R L116 15.90 86–14 Dr. Kashnikow116½ Tam's Terms116¾ Host117no Steadied start,up late 8
1Oct04–4Med gd 1 1/16 Ⓣ :243 :501 1:143 1:443 3↑Alw 54749c 79 7 85¼ 85½ 84¾ 63¾ 58 Pino M G L116 8.30 67–28 TmsTrms119hd StormyRomn119hd AmrcnFrdm119hd Shuffled back early 8
28Aug04–8Del fm 1 1/16 Ⓣ :243 :481 1:113 1:414 3↑LeadrOBand54k 89 4 611 616 613 48½ 26 Pino M G L115 4.10 91–13 Tam's Terms1166 Dr. Kashnikow115nk Change Course1191 Split h for 2nd 6
29Apr04–6CD fm 1⅛ Ⓣ :482 1:122 1:361 1:481 3↑Alw 64300N1Y – 1 - - - - - Albarado R J L117 6.80 - 07 Senor Swinger117¾ Spice Island1141¼ Startac1171¼ Stumble,lost rider 7

Dreadnaught
Own: Trillium Stable

B. g. 5 (Feb)
Sire: Lac Ouimet (Pleasant Colony) $4,000
Dam: Wings of Dreams (Sovereign Dancer)
Br: David S. Pennington (Ky)
Tr: Voss Thomas H(0 0 0 0 .00) 2004:(151 23 .15)

Life	15	5	4	0	$305,523	101	D.Fst	1	0	0	0	$1,380	26
2004	10	3	4	0	$271,243	101	Wet(383)	0	0	0	0	$0	–
2003	5	2	0	0	$34,280	84	Turf(255)	11	5	2	0	$296,943	101
	0	0	0	0	$0	–	Dst(0)	0	0	0	0	$0	–

18Dec04-11Crc fm 1½ Ⓣ :49¹ 1:13⁴ 2:03 2:26³ 3↑WLMcKntH-G2 **101** 4 75½ 73¼ 62¾ 42¼ 1nk Samyn J L L116 *3.10 91–10 Drednught116nk Demeteor112½ ScooterRoch115½ 4w lane,responded well 12
20Nov04-8Aqu gd 1⅜ Ⓣ :51⁴ 1:17⁴ 1:43¹ 2:18⁴ 3↑RedSmthH-G2 **101** 4 52½ 51½ 41½ 1hd 1no Samyn J L L115 5.60 90–10 *Dreadnaught*115nc Certifiably Crazy112³ Alost116nk Rank gate, 4 wide run 10
29Oct04-9Med fm 1⅜ Ⓣ :47² 1:12¹ 1:37 2:14¹ 3↑JohnHenry60k **94** 3 5⁵ 4¾ 1½ 11 2nk Samyn J L L117 b *2.60 102–04 Macaw115nk *Dreadnaught*117hd Revved Up115no Game finish inside 11
3Oct04-7Bel gd 1⅜ Ⓣ :48² 1:12⁴ 1:37³ 2:15 3↑Alw 50000N2x **96** 4 33½ 31½ 3nk 1hd 11¼ Samyn J L L120 b 9.50 88–18 Dreadnaught120 1¼ Sailaway120 2¾ Rayon120nk 3 wide move, clear 9
16Sep04-8Bel fm 1¼ Ⓣ :49¹ 1:13¹ 1:37 2:01 3↑Alw 50000N2x **93** 2 62½ 64½ 6⁹ 66½ 42¼ Samyn J L L120 b 5.80 87–11 CelticMemories 201½ FortunWritrs124nk PotomcChs118½ Going well late 6
28Aug04-6Sar fm 1 3/16 Ⓣ :47 1:10³ 1:34³ 1:53 3↑Alw 50000N2x **84** 11 12¹⁴ 12¹² 12¹⁴ 10¹² 75¼ Fragoso P L121 b 5.30 95–01 Governor Brown121nk Kennel Up117nk Inducement119 2½ Broke in air 12
8Aug04-8Sar fm 1 3/16 Ⓣ :47 1:11² 1:36² 1:55² 3↑Alw 50000N2x **92** 8 76¾ 8¹⁰ 94¾ 73¼ 2nk Fragoso P L121 b 42.75 88–21 DynmtFlyr117nk Drdnght121nk *GovrnorBrown*121¾ Circled widest, gamely 10
27Jun04-1Cnl gd 1⅞ Hurdles 3:23³ 4↑Md Sp Wt 24k – 1 48½ 38½ 33½ 22½ 23½ Murphy C L147 b *2.00 - - ShadyValley154 3½ Dreadnaught147 3¼ BeuFilou154nk Failed to sustain bid 9
31May04-5Fai yl 2¼ Hurdles 4:16⁴ 4↑Md Sp Wt 15k – 9 2² 4² 41½ 1hd 2no Murphy C L142 5.10 - - ErinGoBrgh154no Drednught142 4½ *NorthrnFntsy*154³ Led late, outfinished 11
8May04-4PW fm 2¼ Hurdles 4:16³ 4↑Md Sp Wt 24k – 6 31½ - - - - - Murphy C L142 - - - NorthrnRn154 1½ ToySoldr139 2½ Cptnofndstry154 5½ Lost jockey 9th fence 10

Dream of Summer
Own: Weigel James

Gr/ro. m. 6 (Apr)
Sire: Siberian Summer (Siberian Express) $6,000
Dam: Mary's Dream (Skywalker)
Br: James Weigel (Cal)
Tr: Garcia Juan J(0 0 0 0 .00) 2004:(263 21 .08)

Life	9	7	1	0	$412,500	107	D.Fst	8	7	1	0	$412,500	107
2004	4	4	0	0	$309,000	107	Wet(328)	0	0	0	0	$0	–
2003	5	3	1	0	$103,500	96	Turf(307)	1	0	0	0	$0	–
	0	0	0	0	$0	–	Dst(0)	0	0	0	0	$0	–

16Oct04-3SA fst 1 1/16 :23¹ :46³ 1:10³ 1:42¹ 3↑ⒻⓈCalCupMatH150k **103** 2 1¹ 11½ 1¹ 2hd 1no Smith M E LB121 b 4.10 94–11 DrmfSmmr121no *YrlyRprt*120⁶ SmmrWndDncr122½ Fought back rail,game 6
21Aug04-8Dmr fst 6½f :21⁴ :44¹ 1:09 1:15⁴ 3↑ⒻRchBrdoH-G3 **100** 6 1 2hd 1hd 1½ 1nk Smith M E LB118 b *1.00 96–08 *Dream of Summer*118nk Barbara Orr113 3½ Cyber Slew117hd Dueled,gamely 7
10Jly04-5Hol fst 7f :22 :44 1:08 1:21 3↑ⒻAGleamH-G2 **107** 9 2 1¹ 1² 13½ 13½ Smith M E LB114 b 9.30 97–10 *DremofSummer*114 3½ TuckdAwy116nk ElusivDiv112¹ Angled in, ridden out 9
4Jun04-2Hol fst 6f :21⁴ :44³ :57 1:10¹ 3↑ⒻOC 62k/N2x-N **86** 3 4 2hd 1¹ 11½ 1⁴ Smith M E LB119 b *.80 86–17 *Dream of Summer*119⁴ StoptheTalking121½ Madrone116½ Clear, ridden out 4

Dubleo

Own: Scatuorchio James T., Pletcher, Jake

Dk. b or b. c. 3 (Mar) FTKJUL03 $90,000
Sire: Southern Halo (Halo) $21,050
Dam: Secret Red (Secretariat)
Br: Anzac LLC (Ky)
Tr: Pletcher Todd A(0 0 0 0 .00) 2004:(948 240 .25)

							D.Fst	3	1	0	1	$33,989	75
Life	9	6	1	1	$360,899	92							
2004	9	6	1	1	$360,899	92	Wet(342)	1	1	0	0	$30,000	55
2003	0	M	0	0	$0	–	Turf(283)	5	4	1	0	$296,910	92
	0	0	0	0	$0	–	Dst(0)	0	0	0	0	$0	–

27Nov04–9Hol fm 1 Ⓣ :234 :472 1:12 1:371 Generous-G3 **92** 9 21½ 24 24 21½ 1¾ Nakatani C S LB121 *1.40 78–17 Dubleo121¾ Littlebitofzip116no Sunny Sky1163 Came out,wore down foe 12
29Oct04–9Kee gd 1 1/16 Ⓣ :232 :474 1:123 1:424 BourbonCo112k **92** 3 11½ 12 11½ 1½ 2nk Decarlo C P L122 *1.70 90–13 Rey de Cafe116nk *Dubleo*1224½ Ready Ruler1224¼ Long drive,outfinished 10
19Sep04–3WO fm 1 Ⓣ :222 :451 1:10 1:343 Summer-G2 **82** 2 2hd 12½ 12 12½ 12¼ Nakatani C S L122 *2.25 90–03 Dubleo1222¼ *Dance With Ravens*1221 Go to the Sun122¾ Held sway,driving 8
5Sep04–8Mth fm 1 Ⓣ :231 :472 1:122 1:383 ContnlMile55k **81** 1 13 14½ 13½ 12½ 1nk Decarlo C P L120 *.40e 79–17 *Dubleo*120nk United1152¼ *Arcturus*117nk Clear pace,held well 10
24Jly04–9Cnl sly 5½f ⊗ :222 :46 :584 1:053 Chenery50k **55** 1 1 1½ 1½ 12½ 1¾ Karamanos H A L117 *.80 85–15 *Dubleo*117¾ Black Tie1172¼ Tip City1171 Pressured 2-3w,driving 5
10Jly04–3Cnl fm 5f 🅃 :222 :454 :573 Alw 26000N1x **78** 4 2 11 11 15½ 18 Prado E S L122 *.60 94–06 *Dubleo*1228 Black Tie1221 It's in the Kiss117nk Off rail,hand pressure 8
4Jun04–9Bel fst 5f :22 :444 :572 Flash-G3 **37** 2 1 31½ 41½ 411 515 Velazquez J R L115 4.40 81–14 PrimlStorm1167 WinningExpression1153¾ *GoldJoy*1154 Bumped, steadied 5
21May04–3Bel fst 5f :224 :454 :583 Md Sp Wt 43k **75** 1 1 11½ 1½ 13 13¼ Velazquez J R L117 *.70 90–15 Dubleo1173¼ WitchWaysWest114¾ GoFernndoGo1142¾ Pace, kept to task 6
9Apr04–3Kee fst 4½f :223 :454 :52 Md Sp Wt 41k – 8 5 2hd 23½ 39½ Bailey J D L118 *1.20 85–09 Goes1189 Palacios Appeal118½ *Dubleo*1187¼ Rushed 5w,faltered 8

During

Own: McIngvale James

Dk. b or b. h. 5 (Feb)
Sire: Cherokee Run (Runaway Groom) $40,000
Dam: Blading Saddle (Blade)
Br: Gulf States Racing Stables II (Ky)
Tr: Hines Nicholas J(0 0 0 0 .00) 2004:(214 24 .11)

							D.Fst	17	5	2	3	$724,284	107
Life	22	6	3	4	$822,364	107							
2004	9	1	1	3	$307,614	107	Wet(369)	5	1	1	1	$98,080	106
2003	13	5	2	1	$514,750	106	Turf(253)	0	0	0	0	$0	–
	0	0	0	0	$0	–	Dst(0)	0	0	0	0	$0	–

27Nov04–9Aqu fst 1 :222 :441 1:081 1:332 3↑CigarMiH-G1 **85** 8 53¼ 63¾ 86 710 713¼ Bejarano R L116 35.50 85–07 Lion Tamer1151¼ Badge of Silver115no Pico Central1234¾ No response 8
30Oct04–1LS gd 1 :232 :463 1:102 1:352 3↑MetrplxMil100k **95** 2 2½ 1hd 1hd 3½ 43½ Nakatani C S L123 b 2.90 92–02 Wishingitws1191¼ 🄳SpnishEmpire123nk SekGold1212 Steadied inside 1/8 11
Placed third through disqualification
10Oct04–8SA fst 6f :21 :433 :554 1:084 3↑AnTtlBCH-G1 **84** 3 6 62½ 74¼ 76 67½ Santiago Javier LB116 b 9.20 86–12 PtsGreyEagle109½ Pohave1182 HombreRapido114hd Bit off rail,weakened 8
Previously trained by Baffert Bob
5Sep04–8Dmr fst 1 :222 :46 1:10 1:35 3↑DmrBCH-G2 **100** 5 1hd 2½ 1hd 21½ 34 Nakatani C S LB117 b *2.10 95–07 Supah Blitz116no Domestic Dispute1174 During1171 Inside,held 3rd 6
22Aug04–8Dmr fst 1¼ :464 1:104 1:352 2:01 3↑PacifcCl-G1 **101** 8 32 2hd 21 43½ 57½ Nakatani C S LB124 b 13.40 82–10 PlesntlyPerfect1241 PrfctDrift124¾ TotlImpct1244¾ 3wd move,weakened 8
1Aug04–8Dmr fst 1 1/16 :24 :472 1:111 1:421 3↑SnDiegoH-G2 **93** 2 1½ 2hd 1hd 31½ 35¾ Nakatani C S LB118 b 4.30 91–10 ChoctawNation114¾ *PlesntlyPerfect*1245 During1181½ Btwn,inside,held 3rd 7
27Mar04 Nad Al Sheba (UAE) ft *1 LH 1:354 3↑Godolphin Mile-G2 Stk 1000000 611¾ JBailey J D 126 b – Firebreak1264½ Tropical Star1262¾ Excessivepleasure1262¼ 9
Timeform rating: 98 *Led to over 3f out,weakened 2-1/2f out.Inamorato 5th*
7Feb04–9SA fst 1⅛ :454 1:101 1:354 1:49 Strub-G2 **107** 11 52 4¾ 41¼ 52¼ 2nk Flores D R LB121 b 5.50 89–15 Domestic Dispute117nk During121¾ Buckland Manor117½ 4wd,bid,led 1/16 11
10Jan04–8SA fst 1 1/16 :222 :452 1:091 1:413 SnFndoBC-G2 **106** 3 2½ 2hd 2hd 21 11 Flores D R LB120 b *4.00 97–07 During1201 Toccet1161 Touch the Wire1172 Came back btwn,game 10

Dynever
Own: Wills Catherine and Karches, Peter

Dk. b or b. h. 5 (Mar)
Sire: Dynaformer (Roberto) $75,000
Dam: Flamboyance (Zilzal)
Br: Catherine Wills (Ky)
Tr: Clement Christophe(0 0 0 0 .00) 2004:(344 68 .20)

Life	16	4	6	1	$1,408,714	116	
2004	7	1	3	0	$254,694	113	
2003	9	3	3	1	$1,154,020	116	
	0	0	0	0	$0	–	
D.Fst	14	4	6	1	$1,348,714	116	
Wet(322)	2	0	0	0	$60,000	98	
Turf(333)	0	0	0	0	$0	–	
Dst(0)	0	0	0	0	$0	–	

11Dec04–7Hol fst 1⅛ :47² 1:11¹ 1:34⁴ 1:47 3↑NtvDivrH-G3 **108** 6 75¼ 85 74¾ 32½ 22 Nakatani C S LB119 *1.10 102– 08 Truly a Judge115² Dynever119⁷ Calkins Road116² Came out lane,2nd best 8
30Oct04–9LS fst 1¼ :47 1:11¹ 1:35¹ 1:59 3↑BCClasic-G1 **105** 13 83½ 73½ 32 67½ 812¾ Nakatani C S L126 15.30 – – Ghostzapper126³ RosesinMay126⁴ PleasntlyPerfect126¾ 5 wide, flattened 13
8Oct04–7Med fst 1⅛ :46⁴ 1:11 1:35⁴ 1:48³ 3↑MedBC-G2 **106** 2 64 75¾ 62¾ 32 2½ Nakatani C S L119 *1.10 88– 15 Balto Star123½ Dynever1191½ Gygistar119³¾ Angled out, gamely 8
3Jly04–7Bel fst 1¼ :46¹ 1:09¹ 1:33⁴ 1:59² 3↑SuburbnH-G1 **107** 7 711 711 64¾ 73¾ 62¼ Nakatani C S L116 *2.35 98 – Peace Rules120nk Newfoundland114no Funny Cide117¾ Good finish inside 8
12Jun04–7Bel fst 1⅛ :45¹ 1:08² 1:33² 1:46¹ 3↑BroklynH-G2 **112** 4 65¾ 57¾ 46 2½ 2½ Nakatani C S L117 *1.60 99– 03 Seattle Fitz116½ Dynever117²¾ Newfoundland115⁵¾ Game finish outside 6
14May04–11Pim fst 1³⁄₁₆ :47² 1:11⁴ 1:36¹ 1:55⁴ 4↑PimSpclH-G1 **101** 6 65½ 55 44½ 49 511¼ Nakatani C S L117 *1.70 87– 17 SouthernImg1201¼ MidwyRod116²½ BowmnsBnd114⁴¾ Lost ground turns 6
3Apr04–10SA fst 1⅛ :47¹ 1:11² 1:35⁴ 1:48 4↑SnBrdnoH-G3 **113** 1 44½ 46½ 32½ 1½ 14½ Nakatani C S LB117 *.60 94– 09 Dynever1174½ Total Impact116² *Even the Score*116² 3wd bid,ridden out 7

Ebony Breeze
Own: Kinsman Stable

B. m. 5 (Jan)
Sire: Belong to Me (Danzig) $25,000
Dam: Valid Carnauba (Valid Appeal)
Br: Kinsman Farm (Ky)
Tr: Mott William I(0 0 0 0 .00) 2004:(680 116 .17)

Life	22	7	6	4	$659,157	102	
2004	9	2	3	1	$255,360	101	
2003	8	4	1	2	$365,887	102	
	0	0	0	0	$0	–	
D.Fst	15	7	5	2	$619,832	102	
Wet(382)	3	0	1	1	$21,350	93	
Turf(290)	4	0	0	1	$17,975	86	
Dst(0)	0	0	0	0	$0	–	

31Dec04–10Crc sly 7f :22² :45⁴ 1:10⁴ 1:23³ 3↑Ⓕ ChSprngH-G3 **77** 4 7 41½ 52½ 53½ 59¼ Bailey J D L116 *1.20 89– 09 Expect an Angel110³ Alix M1201½ Habiboo112³¾ Step slow st, tired 7
30Oct04–9Med gd 5f Ⓣ :21⁴ :45 :57¹ 3↑Ⓕ WitchesBrw60k **82** 4 6 104½ 106 85½ 52¾ Castillo H Jr L122 *2.10 88– 09 KissMeKti116no TightSpin119²½ AmbitionUnbridld115nk Mild rally 5 wide 12
10Oct04–9Bel fst 6½f :23¹ :46⁴ 1:09⁴ 1:16 3↑Ⓕ GlntBlmH-G2 **88** 1 6 63 74¾ 57 46¼ Velasquez C L118 2.20 87– 16 Lady Tak122² *Molto Vita*1154¼ Zawzooth115hd Stumbled start, inside 7
11Sep04–8Del fst 6f :21³ :44² :57¹ 1:09³ 3↑Ⓕ EndineH-G3 **101** 6 6 69½ 65½ 34½ 13 Castillo H Jr L119 *.80 93– 16 Ebony Breeze119³ Umpateedle117²¾ Bronze Abe119½ Ran past leaders 5w 6
6Aug04–8Sar fst 6f :22³ :45¹ :57² 1:10¹ 3↑Ⓕ HnrblMsH-G2 **96** 1 6 51¼ 4¾ 2hd 2no Bailey J D L115 2.95 91– 10 MyTrustyCat115no *EbonyBreeze*115²¾ SmoknFrolic116½ Clear late, caught 8
26Jun04–9Pha fst 6f :22¹ :45² :57³ 1:10³ 3↑Ⓕ MyJuliet100k **100** 1 5 33 32½ 22 11 Castillo H Jr L114 *.60 89– 21 Ebony Breeze114¹ She Is Raging1176½ Balmy114³ Off slow, clear 5
22May04–9CD fst 6f :21² :44 :55⁴ 1:08⁴ 3↑Ⓕ WinColorsH108k **99** 5 3 41½ 33 33½ 32 Velasquez C L116 4.20 95– 11 Lady Tak122¾ *Put Me In*1171¼ *Ebony Breeze*116¹ 6w bid,slight gain 7
14Apr04–3Kee gd 6½f :22¹ :45 1:09⁴ 1:16³ 4↑Ⓕ Alw 67000N$Y **93** 3 3 42½ 43 32 22¼ Velasquez C L120 *.80 91– 14 TinaBull120²¼ EbonyBreeze120¹ CherokeeLite1201²¼ Came out bmp start 5
20Mar04–6TP fst 6f :22¹ :46 :58 1:10¹ 4↑Ⓕ Queen50k **92** 3 6 52¼ 51¾ 21½ 2no Velasquez C L119 *.60 94– 11 GloriousMiss117no EbonyBreeze119²½ AirMarshll115³ Inside turn, missed 6

Eddington
Own: Willmott Stables Inc

Ch. c. 4 (Mar) KEEJUL02 $450,000
Sire: Unbridled (Fappiano) $200,000
Dam: Fashion Star (Chief's Crown)
Br: Carl Rosen Associates (Ky)
Tr: Hennig Mark A(0 0 0 0 .00) 2004:(516 72 .14)

Life	12	3	3	4	$614,560	101	D.Fst 10 2 3 3 $474,560 101
2004	11	3	2	4	$605,360	101	Wet(410) 1 0 0 1 $20,000 90
2003	1	M	1	0	$9,200	75	Turf(286) 1 1 0 0 $120,000 97
	0	0	0	0	$0	-	Dst(0) 0 0 0 0 $0 -

23Oct04-10Crc gd 1⅛ Ⓣ :49 1:141 1:384 1:511 CrcDerby-G3 **97** 3 11 5¾ 9 4½ 74 4 2½ 1hd Coa E M L114 b 2.70 73- 28 Eddington114hd BobsProudMoment1161 ⒹCapis1162½ Stdy early, just up 12
10Oct04-7Med fst 1⅛ :464 1:103 1:353 1:482 Pegasus-G3 **101** 4 8 5¼ 8 2¾ 5 1¼ 2hd 2nk Migliore R L118 b *1.10 90- 11 Pies Prospect118nk *Eddington*1183½ *Zakocity*118hd 4 wide move, outfinish 8
28Aug04-11Sar fst 1¼ :49 1:124 1:37 2:022 Travers-G1 **99** 1 3 2½ 31 42 44 36 Migliore R L126 b 9.70 89- 05 Birdstone1262½ TheCliff'sEdge1263½ Eddington126nk Chased inside, tired 7
8Aug04-9Sar fst 1⅛ :453 1:093 1:343 1:472 JimDandy-G2 **101** 5 511 512 58 37 35 Migliore R L115 b 7.00 93- 02 Purge1214½ The Cliff's Edge123½ ⒹEddington1157¼ Lugged in, bumped 6
Disqualified and placed 4th
5Jun04-11Bel fst 1½ :483 1:113 2:002 2:272 Belmont-G1 **86** 8 4 1½ 3 1½ 47 410 412 Bailey J D L126 b 14.20 83- 10 *Birdstone*1261 Smarty Jones1268 Royal Assault1263 Chased 5 wide, tired 9
15May04-12Pim fst 1 3/16 :471 1:112 1:362 1:552 Preaknes-G1 **97** 8 6 3½ 6 5¼ 8 5¾ 712 3 13½ Bailey J D L126 b 13.20 86- 13 SmrtyJons12611½ RockHrdTn1262 Eddington126hd 4-5wd,altered crse 1/8 10
10Apr04-8Aqu fst 1⅛ :47 1:112 1:37 1:493 WoodMem-G1 **97** 8 52 42 3nk 2hd 3½ Bailey J D L123 b 3.20 90- 12 Tapit123½ Master David123no Eddington1231½ 3 wide move, gamely 11
20Mar04-7Aqu gd 1 :214 :433 1:08 1:352 Gotham-G3 **90** 2 7 5¼ 7 4½ 53 4 3½ 33 Prado E S L116 b *1.35 85- 14 Saratoga County1162¼ Pomeroy116¾ Eddington1165¼ Bumped after start 8
28Feb04-1GP fst 1 1/16 :234 :474 1:114 1:43 Alw 34000n1x **101** 5 21 21 2hd 11 1 5½ Bailey J D L122 b *.30 94- 14 Eddington1225½ *Tiger Heart*1186¾ Capias1225½ Greenly, drew off 6
7Feb04-6GP fst 1 1/16 :233 :473 1:112 1:423 Md Sp Wt 32k **97** 6 21 2½ 2hd 1½ 1 4¾ Bailey J D L122 b *1.20 96- 09 *Eddington*1224¾ *Forty Five*1225¼ Shots122½ Drew away, driving 12
8Jan04-6GP fst 1 1/16 :241 :491 1:14 1:444 Md Sp Wt 32k **77** 10 4 3½ 5 3¼ 42 3 3½ 2 6¾ Bailey J D L122 *2.10 78- 18 Shaniko1226¾ *Eddington*1222½ Radiant Cat1221½ 3 wide, 2nd best 11

Eleusis
Own: Tanaka Gary A

B. f. 4 (Mar) KEESEP02 $67,000
Sire: Diesis*GB (Sharpen Up*GB) $30,000
Dam: Balancing Act (Spectacular Bid)
Br: Nancy S. Dillman (Ky)
Tr: Rouget Jean-Claude(0 0 0 0 .00) 2004:(2 1 .50)

Life	7	6	1	0	$165,801	99	D.Fst 0 0 0 0 $0 -
2004	7	6	1	0	$165,801	99	Wet(246) 0 0 0 0 $0 -
2003	0	M	0	0	$0	-	Turf(336) 7 6 1 0 $165,801 99
	0	0	0	0	$0	-	Dst(0) 0 0 0 0 $0 -

6Nov04-8Aqu gd 1½ Ⓣ :501 1:16 2:053 2:312 3↑ⒻLngIIndH-G2 **99** 3 3 1½ 31 3 1½ 2½ 1 2¼ Santos J A 115 1.65e 89- 11 Eleusis1152¼ Literacy114½ *Arvada*1171¾ Saved ground, clear 7
10Oct04 Chantilly (Fr) gd *1½ Ⓣ RH 2:294 ⒻPrix Joubert (Listed) Stk 55800 1 1½ Mendizabal I 123 *2.20 *Eleusis*1231½ Pink Palace1231½ Berroscoberro1232 13
Timeform rating: 104 *Rated in mid-pack,wide rally to lead 150y out*
10Aug04 Deauville (Fr) sf *1 9/16 Ⓣ RH 2:514 Prix de Pont-Audemer Alw 38000 12 Mendizabal I 121 4.30 *Eleusis*1212 Tamreen1251 Nation State125nk 8
Timeform rating: 91 *Unhurried in 6th,rallied to lead 1f out*
1Jly04 La Teste de Buch (Fr) gs *1⅜ Ⓣ RH 2:141 ⒻPrix Pierre Versein Alw 25500 1no Mendizabal I 121 *1.50 *Eleusis*121no Time Flies1211 Baffling1231 7
Rated in 5th,dueled 1f out,gamely prevailed
31May04 Tarbes (Fr) gs *1 5/16 Ⓣ RH ⒻPrix Soledad de Moratalla Alw 15800 1½ Langlois A 123 *.70 *Eleusis*123½ Staraway1282½ Revolera1281½ 7
Led thruout,repelled late challenge.Time not taken
9May04 Lyon-Parilly (Fr) sf *1⅜ Ⓣ LH Prix Elisee & Hubert Munet Alw 16600 2nk Lemaire C-P 123 - Aaltham123nk *Eleusis*1231½ *Petite Nany*1232 10
Mid-pack,led over 1f out,headed late.Time not taken
12Apr04 Tarbes (Fr) sf *1 7/16 Ⓣ RH Prix de Maubourguet Maiden (FT) 9700 1 3½ Lemaire C-P 124 5.40 Eleusis1243½ Kazimierski1284 Marbeuf1282 13
Tracked in 3rd,led 1f out,drew clear.Time not taken

Elusive Diva
Own: Branch Branch, Konecny, et al

B. f. 4 (Mar)
Sire: Elusive Quality (Gone West) $100,000
Dam: Taj Aire (Taj Alriyadh)
Br: John William Konecny & Doris Konecny (Ky)
Tr: Glatt Mark(0 0 0 0 .00) 2004:(200 19 .10)

Life	9	3	1	2	$221,470	99	D.Fst	8 3 1 2	$220,755 99
2004	9	3	1	2	$221,470	99	Wet(350)	1 0 0 0	$715 60
2003	0	M	0	0	$0	–	Turf(217)	0 0 0 0	$0 –
	0	0	0	0	$0	–	Dst(0)	0 0 0 0	$0 –

27Dec04–8SA fst 7f :221 :442 1:083 1:211 ⓕLaBrea-G1 **94** 3 4 21 1hd 1hd 33 Desormeaux K J LB119 5.30 96–07 AlphbetKisss117[1] BndingStrings121[2] ElusivDiv119[2] Rail,clear 1/4,held 3d 10
31Jly04–8Sar my 7f :212 :44 1:101 1:233 ⓕTest-G1 **60** 8 6 72½ 55½ 78 616½ Chavez J F L118 b 9.40 69–11 *SoctySlcton*120[6½] BndngStrngs120[3¾] FrstMsc118[4¼] Between foes, no rally 12
10Jly04–5Hol fst 7f :22 :44 1:08 1:21 3↑ⓕAGleamH-G2 **99** 6 4 41¼ 22 23½ 33¾ Bejarano R LB112 b 5.10 93–10 *DremofSummer*114[3½] TuckdAwy116[nk] ElusivDiv112[1] Stalked pace,lost 2nd 9
12Jun04–4Hol fst 1 1/16 :23 :46 1:10 1:412 ⓕHolBCOak-G2 **99** 5 21 2½ 2½ 21½ 23 Baze T C LB115 b 9.70 91–08 HousofFortun119[3] ElsvDv115[3] HollywoodStory119[8] Pulled,led 1/4,2d best 5
2May04–8Hol fst 7f :213 :44 1:082 1:211 ⓕRailbird-G3 **88** 4 5 41 31½ 2hd 1nk Valenzuela P A LB118 b 4.90 96–07 ElusiveDiva118[nk] M.A.Fox116[nk] SpeedyFalcon123[no] Spilt,led,gamely held 8
9Apr04–10OP fst 1 1/16 :231 :463 1:11 1:423 ⓕFantasy-G2 **85** 3 3½ 31½ 31½ 67 48 Valdivia J Jr L117 29.90 89–11 HouseofFortune121[1¾] IslndSnd121[4] StellrJyne121[2¼] Traffic early, empty 11
10Mar04–2SA fst 1 :233 :472 1:114 1:373 ⓕOC 80k/n1x-N **84** 3 21 21 21 11½ 11 Stevens G L LB118 *1.30 83–22 ElusiveDiv118[1] RenissnceLdy113[1½] Remembrnces118[3] Pulled,bid,led,held 5
14Feb04–2SA fst 6f :213 :444 :571 1:10 ⓕMd Sp Wt 44k **88** 2 7 42 41¼ 21 1¾ Stevens G L LB120 4.40 88–13 *Elusive Diva*120[¾] *HealthyAddiction*120[5] Tizakitty120[1] Waited 1/4,bid,gamely 9
24Jan04–1SA fst 5½f :213 :444 :571 1:04 ⓕMd Sp Wt 47k **67** 5 2 2hd 3nk 2hd 43½ Stevens G L LB120 *1.00 88–09 DawnsAngel120[½] AllAglow120[½] AnandaParadis120[½] Dueled btwn,lost 3rd 6

Ema Bovary (Chi)
Own: Beal Jr., Richard T. and Ramsey–Brog,

B. m. 6 (Oct)
Sire: Edgy Diplomat (Deputy Minister)
Dam: Coqueta (Domineau)
Br: Haras San Patricio (Chi)
Tr: Ross Larry D(0 0 0 0 .00) 2004:(75 9 .12)

Life	19	13	3	0	$721,642	107	D.Fst	8 6 1 0	$554,990 107
2004	5	4	1	0	$521,780	107	Wet(468)	11 7 2 0	$166,652 105
2003	7	6	0	0	$184,340	103	Turf(288*)	0 0 0 0	$0 –
	0	0	0	0	$0	–	Dst(0)	0 0 0 0	$0 –

10Jly04–11Crc fst 6f :212 :44 :564 1:104 3↑ⓕPrcsRnyH-G2 **107** 6 1 43½ 33 31 12 Gonzalez R M L119 3.60 95–09 Ema Bovary119[2] Bear Fan122[3¾] *Lady Tak*119[2] 3 wd, edged away late 6
5Jun04–1Hol fst 6f :222 :444 :563 1:084 3↑ⓕDstStmrH-G3 **101** 1 4 41 41½ 22 21¼ Gonzalez R M LB123 *.40 92–13 Coconut Girl115[1¼] *Ema Bovary*123[5½] Stormica115[2] Bit tight,shuffled 3/8 5
7Apr04–8Kee fst 7f :22 :441 1:093 1:232 4↑ⓕMadison175k **101** 5 3 43 44½ 1½ 12¼ Gonzalez R M L120 3.10 90–14 Ema Bovary120[2¼] Harmony Lodge123[¾] Yell116[2½] Drift in 1/16p,driving 6
22Feb04–8SA wf 6f :211 :434 :553 1:08 4↑ⓕLsFlresH-G3 **105** 2 3 52¼ 41 11½ 13¼ Gonzalez R M LB121 1.40 98–07 *EmBovry*121[3¼] Buffythecntrfold117[1] *CoconutGirl*113[5] Bit tight 1/2,4wd bid 6
24Jan04–8GG wf 6f :22 :442 :562 1:082 4↑ⓕCrindaH62k **96** 3 6 73¼ 64 31 12 Gonzalez R M LB123 *.40 95–14 *Ema Bovary*123[2] Christmas Time116[1] *Pheiffer*115[2½] Chckd,rank, handily 7

Epicentre
Own: Juddmonte Farms Inc

B. h. 6 (Mar)
Sire: Kris S. (Roberto) $150,000
Dam: Carya (Northern Dancer)
Br: Juddmonte Farms, Inc. (Ky)
Tr: Frankel Robert J(0 0 0 0 .00) 2004:(491 135 .27)

Life	16	5	3	3	$251,382	102	**D.Fst**	0	0	0	0	$0	–
2004	4	2	0	0	$134,125	100	**Wet(365)**	0	0	0	0	$0	–
2003	5	1	1	2	$82,565	102	**Turf(407)**	16	5	3	3	$251,382	102
	0	0	0	0	$0	–	**Dst(0)**	0	0	0	0	$0	–

5Jun04-10Bel fm 1¼ [T] :48² 1:12¹ 1:35⁴ 1:59¹ 3↑ManhttnH-G1 **99** 8 5²¼ 5¹¾ 4¾ 8² 8⁵½ Prado E S L118 11.10 92-05 MtorStorm117¹¼ MillnnumDrgon116^no MrOBrn116¾ Saved ground, empty 9
23Apr04-9Kee gd 1½ Ⓣ :51⁴ 1:17² 2:07¹ 2:31⁴ 4↑Elkhorn-G3 **99** 2 5³¼ 4⁴ 4¹¼ 2^hd 1⁴¾ Bailey J D L116 *1.20 86-14 Epicentre116⁴¾ Rochester116^nk Art Variety116½ Drew off,hand urging 10
14Mar04-7GG fm 1⅛ Ⓣ :47³ 1:11³ 1:36 1:48² 3↑GGBCH-G3 **94** 3 6⁶ 6⁸¼ 6⁴¼ 4⁴ 5³¼ Baze R A LB121 1.90 102-10 Tronare115¹ Soud118² Aly Bubba116^no 4w 2nd turn, mild gain 9
20Feb04-7SA gd 1⅛ Ⓣ :46³ 1:11³ 1:36³ 1:48⁴ 4↑OC 100k/N3x-N **100** 1 5⁴½ 5⁵½ 5²¾ 3^nk 1^hd Desormeaux K J LB119 *.80 85-15 Epicentre119^hd Gent119³ Royal Gem119½ Off bit slow,3wd bid 9

Essence
Own: Padua Stables

B. f. 4 (Apr) FTSAUG02 $120,000
Sire: Gulch (Mr. Prospector) $50,000
Dam: Patelin's Legacy (Cherokee Colony)
Br: Mrs. C. Oliver Iselin III (Va)
Tr: Pletcher Todd A(0 0 0 0 .00) 2004:(948 240 .25)

Life	9	3	1	1	$132,272	94	**D.Fst**	8	2	1	1	$105,860	94
2004	9	3	1	1	$132,272	94	**Wet(357)**	1	1	0	0	$26,412	83
2003	0	M	0	0	$0	–	**Turf(280)**	0	0	0	0	$0	–
	0	0	0	0	$0	–	**Dst(0)**	0	0	0	0	$0	–

12Dec04-8Hol fst 1$\frac{1}{16}$:23³ :47 1:11 1:41 3↑ⒻBayakoaH-G2 **83** 3 1¹½ 1¹ 1¹ 2½ 6⁸ Nakatani C S LB117 4.10 88-09 HollywoodStory115¹ RoyllyChsn116² APAdvntr117½ Speed,inside,wkened 7
20Nov04-9Pim fst 1⅛ :47⁴ 1:11⁴ 1:36² 1:49¹ ⒻAArundel-G3 **94** 1 1¹ 1½ 1½ 1¹ 1^nk Velazquez J R L115 3.20 98-15 Essence115^nk *Rare Gift*115²½ Family Business115½ Rail, pace, driving 11
13Oct04-7Kee my 1⅛ :47⁴ 1:13⁴ 1:39⁴ 1:53 3↑ⒻAlw 45890N1x **83** 1 3¹½ 2½ 1^hd 1³ 1⁸¼ Albarado R J L120 *1.00 76-24 *Essence*120⁸¼ Struttin'119² Dyna's Dynamo116¹¼ Drew off,4w,driving 9
22Sep04-7Bel fst 1$\frac{1}{16}$:23³ :46² 1:10⁴ 1:43⁴ 3↑ⒻAlw 48000N1x **79** 4 2¹½ 2½ 2¹ 3¹ 3³¼ Velazquez J R L117 *.50 78-21 PlesntHome117¹¾ AftertheTone117¹½ *Essnc*117¹½ With pace, no response 8
1Aug04-8Sar fst 1⅛ :47⁴ 1:11⁴ 1:37 1:50² 3↑ⒻAlw 48000N1x **89** 2 2½ 2½ 2½ 2^hd 2no Velazquez J R L116 *1.70 83-14 *Paiota Falls*119no Essence116¹½ Strategy116⁴¾ Fought it out gamely 8
Previously trained by Baffert Bob
18Jun04-7Hol fst 1$\frac{1}{16}$:22⁴ :46 1:10² 1:42³ 3↑ⒻAlw 59000N1x **85** 2 3¹½ 3² 2½ 1¹ 2¾ Nakatani C S LB117 *1.20 87-10 Thunder's Echo114¾ [D]Essence117⁵ Dolly Wells119¹ Came in 1/4,caught 5
Disqualified and placed 5th
13May04-2Hol fst 1$\frac{1}{16}$:23³ :47² 1:12¹ 1:43³ 3↑ⒻMd Sp Wt 47k **78** 3 2¹ 2½ 2½ 1½ 1¹¼ Nakatani C S LB117 *1.20 83-19 Essence117¹¼ *WhyKnottMeToo*123⁴ TinasLove117³ Btwn foes,inched clear 7
25Apr04-3Hol fst 6f :21⁴ :44¹ :56¹ 1:08⁴ 3↑ⒻMd Sp Wt 43k **80** 5 2 3¹½ 4²½ 4⁵ 4⁶ Santiago Javier LB117 b 6.40 87-08 HlekISunrise119¹½ TwoTrilSioux117^hd KlhriCt123⁴½ 3wd into lane,wkened 6
11Apr04-6SA fst 6½f :22¹ :45 1:09³ 1:16² ⒻMd Sp Wt 44k **64** 2 8 3¹½ 3³ 5⁵½ 5⁷ Santiago Javier LB120 b 5.40 83-13 *Tizakitty*120no MAFox120² MysteryMountain120²½ Came out turn,wkened 9

Etoile Montante
Own: Juddmonte Farms Inc

Ch. m. 5 (Feb)
Sire: Miswaki (Mr. Prospector) $30,000
Dam: Willstar (Nureyev)
Br: Juddmonte Farms, Inc. (Ky)
Tr: Frankel Robert J(0 0 0 0 .00) 2004:(491 135 .27)

Life	16	7	4	2	$659,277	99	**D.Fst**	0	0	0	0	$0	–
2004	6	2	2	1	$340,149	99	**Wet(355)**	0	0	0	0	$0	–
2003	7	3	1	1	$240,719	87	**Turf(300)**	16	7	4	2	$659,277	99
	0	0	0	0	$0	–	**Dst(0)**	0	0	0	0	$0	–

Date/Race	Trk	Dist	Surf	Fractions	Race	Fig	PP	St	1C	2C	Str	Fin	Jockey	Med/Wt	Odds	Sp-Var	Top finishers	Comment	Fld
28Nov04–7Hol	fm	1	Ⓣ	:24 :47^3 1:11^2 1:35^4	3↑Ⓕ Matriarc-G1	**97**	9	11	1^{hd}	1^{hd}	1^{hd}	2^2	Prado E S	**LB**123	12.00	83– 17	Intercontinntl123^2 EtoilMontnt123^{no} TickrTp120$1\frac{1}{2}$	Speed,inside,held 2nd	9
4Sep04–7Dmr	fm	$1\frac{1}{16}$	Ⓣ	:23^4 :48^1 1:11^4 1:40^2	3↑Ⓕ PalmrBCH-G2	**98**	2	2^1	2$1\frac{1}{2}$	2$1\frac{1}{2}$	1$\frac{1}{2}$	1$\frac{3}{4}$	Valdivia J Jr	**LB**120	*1.90	97– 09	Etoile Montante120$\frac{3}{4}$ Katdogawn117$\frac{1}{2}$ Tangle117^1	Bid,led,clear,held	7
11Aug04–7Dmr	fm	$1\frac{1}{16}$	Ⓣ	:23^4 :47^3 1:11^3 1:41	3↑ⒻⓇ OsunitasH82k	**91**	5	3^3	4^4	3^1	5$2\frac{3}{4}$	4^1	Nakatani C S	**LB**123	*.60	93– 06	VozDeColegiala113$\frac{1}{2}$ MkeupArtist116$\frac{1}{2}$ Shlini114^{no}	Stdied,blocked 1/4-1/8	8
5Jun04–8Bel	fm	1	Ⓣ	:23^3 :46^4 1:10^1 1:33^1	3↑Ⓕ JsAGmBCH-G2	**99**	3	4^1	3^1	4^2	4^2	3$1\frac{3}{4}$	Solis A	**L**121	*.70e	92– 06	Intercontinentl118$1\frac{1}{4}$ Vngurdi113$\frac{1}{2}$ EtoileMontnte121$\frac{3}{4}$	Game finish inside	8
1May04–7CD	gd	1	Ⓣ	:23^3 :47^1 1:11^4 1:36	3↑Ⓕ ArgntMor-G3	**95**	3	5^3	5$4\frac{3}{4}$	3$1\frac{1}{2}$	1$\frac{1}{2}$	2no	Bailey J D	**L**123	*.70	89– 11	Shaconage121^{no} EtoileMontante123^2 *ChnceDnce*117$\frac{1}{2}$	Inside move, missed	10
4Apr04–8SA	fm	*$6\frac{1}{2}$f	Ⓣ	:22 :44^1 1:07^1 1:13^1	4↑Ⓕ LsCngasH-G3	**93**	1	7	2^1	4^2	1^{hd}	1$\frac{1}{2}$	Santiago Javier	**LB**121	*1.20	91– 08	EtoileMontnte121$\frac{1}{2}$ *Dediction*118$\frac{3}{4}$ AnyforLove115$\frac{1}{2}$	Rail bid,led,held game	9

Even the Score
Own: Parra Rosendo G

Gr/ro. h. 7 (Apr)
Sire: Unbridled's Song (Unbridled) $125,000
Dam: Ashtabula (Rahy)
Br: Aspiration Stable (Ky)
Tr: Cerin Vladimir(0 0 0 0 .00) 2004:(339 59 .17)

Life	29	9	1	9	$751,629	109	**D.Fst**	12	5	0	4	$463,061	109
2004	4	2	0	2	$343,272	109	**Wet(362)**	1	1	0	0	$34,800	102
2003	8	3	0	0	$116,408	103	**Turf(308)**	16	3	1	5	$253,768	99
	0	0	0	0	$0	–	**Dst(0)**	0	0	0	0	$0	–

Date/Race	Trk	Dist	Fractions	Race	Fig	PP	St	1C	2C	Str	Fin	Jockey	Med/Wt	Odds	Sp-Var	Top finishers	Comment	Fld
10Jly04–9Hol	fst	$1\frac{1}{4}$	:46^4 1:10^2 1:34^4 2:00^3	3↑ HolGldCp-G1	**106**	7	4^4	4$1\frac{1}{4}$	3$1\frac{1}{2}$	3$\frac{1}{2}$	3$1\frac{3}{4}$	Flores D R	**LB**124 b	*.70	97 -	TotalImpct124$1\frac{1}{2}$ Olmodvor124$\frac{1}{2}$ EventheScore124^4	Bid 3wd 1/8,outkicked	7
12Jun04–9Hol	fst	$1\frac{1}{8}$	:46^3 1:10^1 1:35 1:47^3	3↑ Calfrnin-G2	**109**	8	6^4	6^3	4$1\frac{1}{2}$	1^1	1$3\frac{1}{2}$	Flores D R	**LB**118 b	*.90	101– 08	EventheScor118$3\frac{1}{2}$ *TotlImpct*116^2 NosThTrd116^{nk}	4wd move,led 3wd,clear	8
8May04–9Hol	fst	$1\frac{1}{16}$	:23^1 :45^4 1:09^2 1:40^4	3↑ MrvnLRyH-G2	**103**	4	6$3\frac{3}{4}$	4^2	4^2	2$\frac{1}{2}$	1^2	Flores D R	**LB**116 b	5.00	97– 04	*EventheScore*116^2 EndersShadow113^3 TotlImpct116^1	Waited 1/4,bid,clear	8
3Apr04–10SA	fst	$1\frac{1}{8}$	:47^1 1:11^2 1:35^4 1:48	4↑ SnBrdnoH-G3	**102**	3	5$4\frac{1}{2}$	5^7	5^4	4^2	3$6\frac{1}{2}$	Flores D R	**LB**116 b	14.80	87– 09	Dynever117$4\frac{1}{2}$ Total Impact116^2 *Even the Score*116^2	In bit tight 3-1/2	7

Evening Attire
Own: Grant Mary and Joseph and Kelly, Thom

Gr/ro. g. 7 (Feb)
Sire: Black Tie Affair*Ire (Miswaki) $7,500
Dam: Concolour (Our Native)
Br: Thomas J. Kelly & Joseph M. Grant (Ky)
Tr: Kelly Patrick J(0 0 0 0 .00) 2004:(238 21 .09)

Life	39	11	12	3	$2,373,010	114	**D.Fst**	27	7	7	3	$1,286,810 114
2004	11	1	6	0	$420,040	114	**Wet(369)**	9	4	4	0	$1,055,600 114
2003	9	2	2	2	$430,160	110	**Turf(278)**	3	0	1	0	$30,600 100
	0	0	0	0	$0	–	**Dst(0)**	0	0	0	0	$0 –

4Dec04–8Aqu fst 1 3/16 ⊡ :47⁴ 1:12² 1:38 1:57 3↑QeensCoH-G3 **103** 5 7⁷ 7⁶ 72¼ 2³ 2¾ Espinoza J L L123 b *2.35 93– 18 ClassicEndevor117¾ EveningAttire123½ Colit115no Closed and finish well 9
20Nov04–8Aqu gd 1⅜ Ⓣ :51⁴ 1:17⁴ 1:43¹ 2:18⁴ 3↑RedSmthH-G2 **92** 1 105½ 104¾ 104½ 96¾ 84¾ Espinoza J L L116 b *2.60 85– 10 *Dreadnaught*115no Certifiably Crazy112³ Alost116nk Came wide, no rally 10
30Oct04–5Aqu fm 1⅛ Ⓣ :49² 1:13⁴ 1:38 1:49⁴ 3↑KnkrbkrH-G2 **100** 3 3² 23½ 21½ 1hd 21½ Espinoza J L L114 b *3.40 89– 07 *Host*1151½ Evening Attire114hd Sailaway113½ Held place 9
2Oct04–10Bel fst 1¼ :47³ 1:11³ 1:36² 2:02² 3↑JkyClbGC-G1 **104** 4 51½ 53¾ 54½ 44 45½ Velasquez C L126 b 3.50 79– 13 Funny Cide126¾ Newfoundland126¹ TheCliff'sEdge1223¾ Mild rally inside 7
22Aug04–9Sar fst 1¼ :46² 1:10⁴ 1:36 2:00⁴ 3↑SarBCH-G2 **114** 7 53½ 62¼ 51½ 1½ 1⁵ Velasquez C L115 b 7.50 103– 11 EveningAttir115⁵ *FunnyCid*1183¾ BowmnsBnd1161¼ 4 wide run, drew away 7
19Jun04–10Suf fst 1⅛ :48³ 1:12² 1:36³ 1:49 3↑MassH-G2 **99** 8 73¾ 83¾ 86¼ 57¼ 56½ Bridgmohan S X LB114 b 4.10 92– 10 OffleWild113hd FunnyCid117hd ThLdysGroom1161½ 4-5wd trip,even finish 9
14May04–11Pim fst 1 3/16 :47² 1:11⁴ 1:36¹ 1:55⁴ 4↑PimSpclH-G1 **105** 3 55½ 6⁵ 6⁷ 5¹⁰ 48½ Prado E S L115 b 5.70 89– 17 SouthrnImg1201¼ MidwyRod1162½ BowmnsBnd1144¾ Passed tiring rivals 6
22Apr04–8Kee sly 1⅛ :46² 1:10² 1:34⁴ 1:46³ 4↑BenAli-G3 **104** 1 4⁵ 4⁸ 36½ 3⁷ 211¼ Velasquez C L116 b *.50 97 – MidwyRod11611¼ EveningAttire116½ SirCheroke1201¼ Ck 1st turn,all out 5
3Apr04–8Aqu my 1⅛ :48 1:12 1:36⁴ 1:49² 3↑ExlsrBCH-G3 **108** 2 54½ 51¾ 51¾ 2² 2½ Bridgmohan S X L119 b 1.45 91– 08 Funny Cide120½ Evening Attire119⁸ Host114nk Game finish outside 5
14Feb04–8Lrl fst 1⅛ :48¹ 1:12¹ 1:36⁴ 1:49 4↑JCampbellH150k **104** 2 5⁵ 4² 3² 4³ 32¾ Bridgmohan S X L122 b *.40 94– 20 OleFunty1141¼ ⓓRogueAgnt1131½ EvningAttir1221½ Shut off,roughed str 8
Placed second through disqualification
17Jan04–4Aqu fst 1 1/16 ⊡ :22⁴ :46 1:10¹ 1:42 3↑AquH-G3 **111** 4 8¹¹ 5⁷ 45½ 32½ 2no Bridgmohan S X L122 b *.90 101– 13 SettleFitz114no EveningAttire1221¼ RogueAgnt1128¾ Game finish outside 8

Evil Minister
Own: Namcook Stables LLC

Ch. c. 3 (Feb) FTFFEB04 $200,000
Sire: Deputy Minister (Vice Regent) $100,000
Dam: Evil's Pic (Piccolino)
Br: ClassicStar, LLC (Ky)
Tr: Juvonen Erik R(0 0 0 0 .00) 2004:(120 20 .17)

Life	5	2	0	1	$120,530	78	**D.Fst**	4	1	0	1	$106,850 78
2004	5	2	0	1	$120,530	78	**Wet(354)**	1	1	0	0	$13,680 67
2003	0	M	0	0	$0	–	**Turf(286)**	0	0	0	0	$0 –
	0	0	0	0	$0	–	**Dst(0)**	0	0	0	0	$0 –

9Oct04–7Kee fst 1 1/16 :23 :47 1:12 1:43³ BrdrsFut-G1 **73** 5 99¾ 7⁹ 8⁷ 67½ 511¼ Stevens G L L121 f 18.60 83– 13 Consolidator121² Patriot Act1213¼ Diamond Isle121½ Improved position 10
19Sep04–7Bel fst 1 :24 :46⁴ 1:12¹ 1:38⁴ Futurity-G2 **72** 2 4nk 6³ 63¼ 54¾ 34½ Pimentel J L120 f 10.20 62– 25 PrkAvenueBll120³ WllstretScndl1201½ EvilMinistr120² Mild rally outside 6
28Aug04–11Mth fst 6f :21³ :44³ :58 1:11¹ Sapling-G3 **78** 5 6 86¾ 53¾ 3½ 1¾ Pimentel J L120 f 24.50 84– 18 EvilMinister120¾ *ParkAvenueBal*l1202¾ Upscled120⁶ Eased out,game score 8
1Aug04–5Pim gd 6f :24 :47³ :59⁴ 1:11⁴ Md Sp Wt 24k **67** 3 1 3¹ 3⁴ 41¼ 12¾ Rodriguez E D L122 f *2.10 86– 15 *EvlMnstr*1222¾ WhtsUpLnl1221¾ BnkOnthChmp122¾ 6wd 1/8,drifted in,drv 7
19Jun04–3Mth fst 5f :22⁴ :46³ :58⁴ Md Sp Wt 37k **50** 6 7 51¾ 62¼ 4³ 4⁹ Pimentel J 118 f 6.10 79– 18 Smokescreen1181½ AllnsKt1183¼ *DoctorVoodoo*1184¼ Broke bit slow,green 8

Expect an Angel
Own: Hale Kay

B. f. 5 (Apr)
Sire: Valid Expectations (Valid Appeal) $17,500
Dam: Leah's Angel (Caller I. D.)
Br: David Robbins (Fla)
Tr: Hale Robert A(0 0 0 0 .00) 2004:(208 37 .18)

Life	13	7	2	0	$150,960	97	D.Fst	11 6 2 0	$90,600 82
2004	8	4	0	0	$106,230	97	Wet(365)	1 1 0 0	$60,000 97
2003	4	2	2	0	$33,730	82	Turf(264)	1 0 0 0	$360 49
	0	0	0	0	$0	–	Dst(0)	0 0 0 0	$0 –

31Dec04-10Crc sly 7f :222 :454 1:104 1:233 3↑ⒻChSprngH-G3 **97** 2 6 72¾ 63 31½ 13 Lopez J E L110 39.40 98-09 Expect an Angel1103 Alix M1201½ Habiboo1123¾ 4 wide, drew clear 7
19Dec04-10Crc fst 7f :231 :464 1:121 1:25 3↑ⒻOC 16k/N1x **82** 8 1 62¾ 62¼ 11 12½ Toribio A Jr L119 2.70 91-14 *ExpectnAngel*1192½ StrletNote1164¼ Showmesomlov1162¼ 4w, drifted late 9
5Nov04-9Crc fst 7f :224 :47 1:124 1:261 3↑ⒻOC 25k/N2x-N – 7 2 54¾ 51¾ 43 – Toribio A Jr L119 3.70 – 17 AwesomePowers119nk CrftyDiv1225¾ DinnerSwts1221¾ Clipped heels, fell 8
11Sep04-6Crc fst 6f :214 :46 :592 1:13 3↑ⒻClm 10000(10-9) **71** 4 7 98¾ 83¾ 31 1nk Toribio A Jr L117 1.70 84-17 Expect an Angel117nk Friendly Mickey1153¾ Seminole Gal117½ Handily 9
3May04-8Crc fst 6½f :223 :464 1:112 1:174 3↑ⒻAlw 25000N2x **64** 8 3 99½ 83¾ 66 610 Toribio A Jr L118 *2.40 80-16 MysterieuseEtcile1184 AmericnMiss1171¼ *JulsforAJ*1151 4 wide, no factor 9
21Apr04-6GP fst 6f :22 :45 :571 1:103 4↑ⒻOC 50k/N2x **79** 3 3 57 45½ 33 4¾ Toribio A Jr L119 3.50 88-11 Is ThatYou121nk Austin'sBelle117½ HowAboutIt117hd Angled out, gaining 6
25Mar04-8GP fm *5f Ⓣ:213 :453 :57 4↑ⒻAlw 36000N2x **49** 4 6 88 88 79¾ 710¾ Toribio A Jr L121 6.90 83-06 ElusiveHoney1171¾ Candybedndy117nk WinnerTkesAll1171 Saved ground 8
20Feb04-8GP fst 6f :214 :45 :58 1:11 4↑ⒻAlw 34000N1x **76** 2 7 79¾ 68 44 1½ Toribio A Jr 117 3.80 87-14 Expect anAngel117½ IndyGroove117¾ *Kuanyan*117nk Swung 6 wide, up late 9

Eye of the Sphynx
Own: Sam-Son Farms

B. f. 4 (Apr)
Sire: Smart Strike (Mr. Prospector) $35,000
Dam: Queen of Egypt (Vice Regent)
Br: Sam-Son Farm (Ont-C)
Tr: Frostad Mark R(0 0 0 0 .00) 2004:(269 49 .18)

Life	7	4	2	0	$688,340	91	D.Fst	2 1 1 0	$350,000 89
2004	7	4	2	0	$688,340	91	Wet(427)	3 3 0 0	$288,340 91
2003	0	M	0	0	$0	–	Turf(349)	2 0 1 0	$50,000 84
	0	0	0	0	$0	–	Dst(0)	0 0 0 0	$0 –

4Sep04-8WO fm 1 Ⓣ:221 :441 1:081 1:332 ⒻOntColeenH143k **60** 3 33½ 35½ 64½ 1116 1113½ Kabel T K L121 *1.05 82-02 Emerald Earrings1151 Faswiga111½ Jinny's Gold1181¾ No response 11
1Aug04-8WO gd 1¼ Ⓣ:503 1:154 1:404 2:05 ⒻⓇWondrWhere250k **84** 1 1½ 1hd 2hd 1hd 2½ Kabel T K L121 *.70 81-18 *MyVintgePort*121½ EyeoftheSphynx1212¼ ShrEnchntmnt121½ Outfinished 8
4Jly04-8FE fst 1 1/16 :232 :464 1:11 1:452 ⒻⓇBisonCity250k **82** 2 31 21 2hd 1hd 2nk Kabel T K L121 *.15 84-20 Tochnow121nk EyofthSphynx1211¾ *MyVntgPort*1214¾ Bid, dueled, missed 6
13Jun04-8WO fst 1⅛ :481 1:133 1:394 1:53 ⒻⓇWoOaks500k **89** 2 1½ 21 2½ 13 14¼ Kabel T K L121 *.80 83-16 EyofthSphynx1214¼ *Tochnow*1219 MyVntgPrt1211¼ Swept to lead far turn 5
23May04-8WO sly 1 1/16 :224 :474 1:133 1:481 ⒻSelene-G2 **82** 6 21½ 21 2hd 2hd 1nk Kabel T K L118 *.25 70-30 *EyeoftheSphynx*118nk SilvrBird1186¾ *SwtProblm*1161 Dueled,beaten,dug in 6
9May04-8WO my 7f :23 :461 1:103 1:231 ⒻⓇFury163k **91** 5 3 11 1hd 11 13¼ Kabel T K L117 1.50 91-07 *EyofthSphynx*1173¼ SilvrBird1186½ MyVintgPort123hd Drove clear 1/8 pole 7
22Apr04-6Kee sly 7f :221 :461 1:114 1:241 ⒻMd Sp Wt 44k **81** 8 1 2½ 2½ 21 13 Blanc B L119 2.30 86-12 *Eye of the Sphynx*1193 Go Robin1197¾ *Present Danger*1194 4w,driving 8

Eye of the Tiger

Own: Gunther John D

B. h. 5 (Apr)
Sire: American Chance (Cure the Blues) $7,500
Dam: Dial a Trick (Phone Trick)
Br: John D. Gunther (Ky)
Tr: McLaughlin Kiaran P(0 0 0 0 .00) 2004:(462 84 .18)

Life	18	5	2	4	$532,779	110	D.Fst	16 5 1 4	$518,079 110
2004	8	2	1	1	$296,450	110	Wet(355)	1 0 1 0	$12,000 95
2003	8	2	1	2	$214,689	107	Turf(254)	1 0 0 0	$2,700 81
	0	0	0	0	$0	–	Dst(0)	0 0 0 0	$0 –

31Jly04–8AP fst 1 3/16 :482 1:124 1:363 1:564 3↑WashPkH-G2 **102** 5 31½ 31½ 32 1hd 1hd Razo E Jr L116 6.80 91–18 Eye oftheTiger116hd Olmodavor1211½ Congrats116nk 4-5 wide, stubbornly 5
16Jly04–5Bel fst 1 :233 :47 1:111 1:353 4↑OC 75k/N3X-N **110** 4 27 23 1½ 1½ 13¼ Bailey J D L118 *.55 83–27 *Eye of the Tiger*1183¼ CountryJudge1239¼ Limero1181¼ When roused, clear 5
31May04–9Bel fst 1 :232 :46 1:10 1:352 3↑MtropltH-G1 **103** 2 74¼ 62¼ 61¼ 74¾ 76¾ Prado E S L114 14.30 77–34 PicoCentral119¾ BowmansBnd1142¼ StrongHope1191½ 4 wide move, tired 9
10Apr04–9Aqu fst 7f :213 :432 1:072 1:201 3↑CarterH-G1 **109** 2 9 79¾ 711 56¾ 33¼ Luzzi M J L114 26.50 101–04 *Pico Central*1171¼ Strong Hope1192 EyeoftheTiger114¾ Game finish inside 9
Previously trained by Hollendorfer Jerry
7Mar04–8SA fst 7f :221 :44 1:082 1:21 4↑SnCrlosH-G2 **100** 8 10 911 98¼ 95½ 56 Stevens G L LB116 12.90 94–11 *Pico Central*1162 Publication1162 *Pohave*1121 3wd into lane,no bid 10
22Feb04–5SA wf 1 :224 :451 1:084 1:35 4↑OC 100k/N3X-N **95** 2 31½ 33½ 22 21 2¾ Espinoza V LB117 *.90 95–04 Calkins Road119¾ Eye of theTiger117¾ RojoToro1172½ Willingly late btwn 4
7Feb04–9SA fst 1⅛ :454 1:101 1:354 1:49 Strub-G2 **103** 9 62½ 3½ 31 21½ 62½ Espinoza V LB117 12.30 86–15 DomesticDisput117nk During121¾ BuckIndMnor117½ 3wd btwn,outkicked 11
15Jan04–4GG sf 1 Ⓣ :242 :49 1:134 1:384 4↑OC 80k/N3X-N **81** 8 44 43 42 45 46 Warren R J Jr LB116 *1.00 79–16 Savage117½ Studio Time1182 Hannibal Lad1173½ Stlkd 3-4w,no response 8

Fantasticat

Own: R Bar S Thoroughbreds LLP

B. c. 4 (Mar)
Sire: Storm Cat (Storm Bird) $500,000
Dam: Lotta Dancing (Alydar)
Br: Pacelco S.A. & Chelston Ireland, Ltd. (Ky)
Tr: Barnett Bobby C(0 0 0 0 .00) 2004:(407 48 .12)

Life	18	3	4	5	$425,384	104	D.Fst	13 2 4 2	$118,180 104
2004	14	3	4	2	$418,400	104	Wet(430)	2 1 0 1	$301,760 103
2003	4	M	0	3	$6,984	69	Turf(349)	3 0 0 2	$5,444 76
	0	0	0	0	$0	–	Dst(0)	0 0 0 0	$0 –

31Dec04–9FG fst 1 1/16 :242 :48 1:12 1:432 3↑LouisianaH60k – 4 710 711 58½ 58 67½ Melancon G L116 b 5.30 85–16 Gigawatt1142¼ Alumni Hall1173¾ Kodema1161 Trailed, no threat 7
4Dec04–9FG fst 1 1/16 :24 :474 1:124 1:452 3↑TenaciousH60k **96** 3 612 612 58 55½ 53¾ Hernandez B J Jr L117 b 4.00 79–25 Midway Road123no Pie N Burger120¾ Kodema116½ No real threat 6
30Oct04–9LS fst 1¼ :47 1:111 1:351 1:59 3↑BCClasic-G1 **104** 5 1210 1210 129½ 119¾ 913½ Melancon G L121 b 59.90 - - Ghostzpper1263 RosesinMy1264 PlesntlyPerfct126¾ Saved grd, no threat 13
25Sep04–10LaD my 1⅛ :471 1:12 1:38 1:512 SuperDby-G2 **103** 5 78¾ 711 69 1hd 1½ Melancon G L124 b 14.70 84–19 Fantasticat124½ Borrego1241¼ Britt's Jules1244 Inside advance, held 9
28Aug04–10LaD fst 1 1/16 :233 :474 1:12 1:434 Prelude60k **94** 3 76½ 66½ 46 43¼ 2nk Melancon G L122 b 7.80 100–12 South Africa122nk *Fantasticat*122nk Britt's Jules1224 Settled, late run rail 10
7Aug04–8Mnr fst 1⅛ :47 1:103 1:354 1:49 WVDerby-G3 **91** 7 79 710 711 59½ 58½ Borel C H LB114 12.60 77–12 SirShckleton1173 PollrdsVision119½ BrittsJuls1155 Well back, inside trip 7
17Jly04–9AP fst 1⅛ :461 1:11 1:38 1:512 RoundTable100k **92** 6 817 817 811 1hd 21 Douglas R R L116 7.90 85–20 Cryptograph1201 Fantastict1165 ChippewTril1161¼ Split foes-outfinished 9
2Jly04–10CD fst 1 1/16 :233 :471 1:12 1:432 3↑Alw 50720N2X **83** 4 811 811 87 56½ 46½ Borel C H L117 b 9.30 84–15 Real Trooper1114 *Danish Dancer*1171¾ One Nice Cat117¾ Inside,minor gain 9
6Jun04–10CD fst 1 1/16 :242 :483 1:133 1:444 Alw 49100N1X **81** 1 74 53 63¾ 32 11½ Borel C H L116 b 3.10 84–17 Fntstict1161½ VictoryLight116hd RogueScholr1222½ Bmp start,inside,drvg 9
19May04–4CD fst 1⅛ :474 1:121 1:374 1:503 3↑Alw 48595N1X **84** 4 21 31½ 51½ 42 36 Borel C H L114 b 19.20 78–16 *Alumni Hall*1172½ *Brass Hat*1143½ *Fantasticat*1141¼ 4w bid,no threat late 7
25Mar04–9FG fm *1 Ⓣ :234 :474 1:121 1:373 OC 50k/N1X-N **76** 2 76¾ 67 75¼ 55½ 34¼ Borel C H L119 b 3.30 88–13 Alpha Capo119no St Regs1174¼ Fantasticat1191½ No final kick 8
Previously trained by Desormeaux J Keith
28Feb04–8FG fst 1 1/16 :234 :484 1:134 1:461 Md Sp Wt 28k **78** 3 811 88 87¼ 63½ 11 Borel C H L119 b 6.30 79–17 Fantasticat1191 *Swaggering*119¾ Wheaty1191 Sandwiched break 8
1Feb04–5FG fst 1 :24 :474 1:13 1:39 Md Sp Wt 28k **70** 1 44 41½ 32½ 46 29¼ Lanerie C J L119 b 5.10 79–17 GrandesGrndslm1199¼ *Fntstict*119nk KisstheGroom119½ Up for second rail 7
12Jan04–7FG fst 1 1/16 :232 :471 1:134 1:48 Md Sp Wt 28k **71** 4 32 33½ 31½ 53½ 2½ Lovato F Jr L119 b 4.10 69–22 Chivalric119½ Fantasticat119½ Wheaty1194¼ Game close 10

Fearless Flyer (Ire)
Own: Reddam J. P

Dk. b or b. f. 3 (Feb)
Sire: Brave Act*GB (Persian Bold*Ire) $9,000
Dam: Canary Bird*Ire (Catrail)
Br: Yakup Demir Tokdemir (Ire)
Tr: Cecil Ben D(0 0 0 0 .00) 2004:(53 4 .08)

Life	6	2	0	2	$119,775	82	D.Fst	1	0	0	0	$0	39
2004	6	2	0	2	$119,775	82	Wet(260)	0	0	0	0	$0	–
2003	0	M	0	0	$0	–	Turf(292)	5	2	0	2	$119,775	82
	0	0	0	0	$0	–	Dst(0)	0	0	0	0	$0	–

20ct04–9SA fst 1 1/16 :23 :464 1:111 1:424 ⒻOakLeaf-G2 **39** 8 83¾ 810 911 814 830 Flores D R LB119 7.90 61–08 *SweetCtomine*1194 *SplendidBlndd*1192½ Mmortt1194 Saved ground, no rally 9
Previously trained by Stack Tommy
12Sep04–8WO fm 1 Ⓣ:23 :461 1:101 1:344 ⒻNatalma-G3 **82** 6 106¼ 106¼ 95¾ 32 11½ Ramsammy E L114 6.85 89–09 FearlessFlyer1141½ SweetSoliro114¾ LittleHussy117nk Swung wide,rallied 11
24Jly04 Leopardstwn (Ire) gf 7f Ⓣ LH 1:29 Tyros Stakes (Listed) Stk 60500 75¼ Lordan W M 123 12.00 Elusive Double1261 Lock And Key123hd Amsterdam126no 7
Timeform rating: 84 *Rated in 5th,3rd over 2f out,soon weakened*
1Jly04 Bellewstown (Ire) gd 1 Ⓣ LH 1:394 Tattersalls Auction Mdn(Rstrctd) Maiden 13400 113 Lordan W M 117 3.30 Fearless Flyer11713 *Arcelie*1073 Brandon Mountain1192 12
Timeform rating: 96 *Tracked in 3rd,led 3f out,soon clear*
11Jun04 Navan (Ire) gd 6f Ⓣ Str 1:101 EBF Median Auction Maiden Maiden 22200 34 Lordan W M 123 5.00 Spring of Pearls1231½ Shamoan1252½ *Fearless Flyer*1237 10
Timeform rating: 71 *Tracked in 3rd,lacked rally*
27May04 Fairyhouse (Ire) fm 6f Ⓣ RH 1:12 EBF Auction Race (Restricted) Alw 23200 34½ Lordan W M 117 7.00 Nepro1231 Value Plus1203½ Fearless Flyer1173 10
Timeform rating: 61 *Tracked in 4th,stayed on*

Feline Story
Own: Robsham Mrs. E P

B. f. 4 (Apr) OBSMAR03 $140,000
Sire: Tale of the Cat (Storm Cat) $65,000
Dam: Shappy (Really Secret)
Br: Eclipse Thoroughbreds Inc. (Ky)
Tr: Hough Stanley M(0 0 0 0 .00) 2004:(259 53 .20)

Life	15	5	5	2	$426,765	93	D.Fst	7	2	3	1	$203,790	92
2004	9	2	4	2	$224,985	93	Wet(346)	8	3	2	1	$222,975	93
2003	6	3	1	0	$201,780	87	Turf(282)	0	0	0	0	$0	–
	0	0	0	0	$0	–	Dst(0)	0	0	0	0	$0	–

13Nov04–10Med fst 6f :214 :441 :563 1:094 ⒻSetonHallU60k **86** 3 5 44½ 46 25½ 21½ Bridgmohan S X L121 2.80 89–13 ForestMusic1181½ FelineStory1217¼ Itsytesthing115¾ Shuffled back start 7
15Oct04–9Kee my 7f :213 :441 1:094 1:224 ⒻRavenRun-G2 **75** 9 2 63½ 63¼ 33½ 310¾ Albarado R J L118 5.80 82–11 JoshsMdelyn1181¼ VisionofButy1169½ FlinStory118½ Drift in start,6w lane 10
18Sep04–7Bel sly 6f :22 :444 :571 1:103 3↑ⒻFlrlPrkH-G3 **93** 5 5 44½ 35 33½ 1nk Prado E S L114 *1.35 86–23 Feline Story114nk Cologny1152½ Travelator116½ 3 wide, along late 5
28Aug04–8Sar fst 6f :213 :444 :564 1:093 ⒻVctoryRide76k **83** 2 7 53 32 22 33¾ Castellano J J L120 *2.60 90–04 Smokey Glacken1203¾ *GrandPrayer*116no *FelineStory*1204 Off slowly, inside 7
31Jly04–8Sar my 7f :212 :44 1:101 1:233 ⒻTest-G1 **46** 3 8 52 1012 88¼ 1123 Castellano J J L118 13.30 63–11 *SoctySlcton*120 6/1 BndngStrngs1203¾ FrstMsc1184¼ Steadied 1/2 mile pole 12
3Jly04–8Bel fst 6f :214 :442 :561 1:09 ⒻPrioress-G1 **92** 3 3 43 43½ 34½ 22¼ Castellano J J L121 26.75 92–08 FriendlyMichll1192¼ FlinStory121no ForstMusic119¾ Game finish outside 9
12Jun04–8Bel fst 6f :221 :452 :572 1:103 ⒻFunistrada60k **90** 1 5 1½ 11 12 2hd Castellano J J L122 *1.35 86–12 ShesMugs117hd FelineStory1224¼ *CpesideLdy*1191¾ Bobbled start, gamely 6
19May04–6Bel sly 6½f :221 :452 1:102 1:171 3↑ⒻOC 100k/c-N **93** 4 1 2hd 2hd 1hd 2no Castellano J J L118 *.75 87–18 BeutifulAmeric121no FelinStory1187 LitrryLight120nk Vied inside, missed 5
24Apr04–8Del fst 6f :221 :46 :584 1:12 ⒻLegalLight75k **79** 2 2 41½ 1hd 11½ 12 Dominguez R A L119 *.50 81–19 Feline Story1192 *She's a Mugs*1151¾ WildBerry117hd Rated rail,bid3w,clear 7

Festival (Jpn)

Own: Grand Farm

B. m. 6 (Apr)
Sire: Assatis (Topsider) $2,186
Dam: North Cape (Crowned Prince)
Br: Grand Stud (Jpn)
Tr: Gallagher Patrick(0 0 0 0 .00) 2004:(220 39 .18)

Life	20	5	0	0	$607,550	90	D.Fst	14	5	0	0	$607,550 90
2004	3	1	0	0	$90,000	90	Wet(227)	4	0	0	0	$0 -
2003	10	0	0	0	$0	-	Turf(254*)	2	0	0	0	$0 87
	0	0	0	0	$0	-	Dst(0)	0	0	0	0	$0 -

20Dec04–7Hol fst 1 1/16 ⊗ :231 :453 1:093 1:42 3↑ ⒻDahliaH-G3 **90** 3 5 5½ 4 10 2 7 2½ 1 6 Sorenson D **LB**111 b 5.70 91– 10 Festival1116 Irgunette1139 Belle Ange1143 Rail move,led 2w,clear 5
29Sep04–7SA fm *6½f Ⓣ :222 :442 1:064 1:124 3↑ ⒻSKMaddyH-G3 **87** 4 5 5 5 9 8¼ 9 5½ 6 5 Sorenson D **LB**114 b 73.20 88– 07 *Belleski*118½ *Intercontinental*1202 Acago116no Pulled,outkicked 9
Previously trained by Shintaro Terade
22Jan04 Ohi (Jpn) ft *6f RH 1:11 4↑ Winter Sprint Alw 160000 8 11 Sakai S 121 - Ebisu Fighter1123 Nice King O1173 Amato Ben Hur1172 11 *Never a factor*

Film Maker

Own: Courtlandt Farms

Dk. b or b. m. 5 (Mar)
Sire: Dynaformer (Roberto) $75,000
Dam: Miss Du Bois (Mr. Prospector)
Br: TAC Holdings, Inc. (Ky)
Tr: Motion H. G(0 0 0 0 .00) 2004:(424 81 .19)

Life	16	5	4	4	$930,290	105	D.Fst	1	0	0	1	$2,640 52
2004	6	1	2	1	$470,430	105	Wet(357)	0	0	0	0	$0 -
2003	9	4	2	2	$457,220	100	Turf(326)	15	5	4	3	$927,650 105
	0	0	0	0	$0	-	Dst(0)	0	0	0	0	$0 -

30Oct04–6LS yl 1⅜ Ⓣ :522 1:182 1:421 2:181 3↑ ⒻBCF&MTrf-G1 **105** 3 2 4 2 1½ 2 1½ 3½ 2 1½ Velazquez J R L123 b 16.50 96– 07 Ouija Board1181½ Film Maker123nk Wonder Again1232¾ Bid turn, 2nd best 12
20ct04–7Bel yl 1¼ 🅃 :522 1:174 1:412 2:043 3↑ ⒻFlwrBlIv-G1 **100** 2 8 5 7 3¼ 7 4¼ 7 3¼ 4 1 Dominguez R A L120 b 12.30 70– 25 Riskverse118¾ *Commercnt*118hd MoscowBurning120nk Swung wide, rallied 8
5Sep04–10Sar fm 1⅜ 🅃 :50 1:15 1:39 2:14 3↑ ⒻGlenFlsH-G3 **102** 5 5 2 6 4 5 2 3 4 3½ Dominguez R A L121 b 2.80 98– 06 Arvada112½ Spice Island118no Film Maker1212¼ Game finish outside 8
Run in divisions
10Jly04–8Cnl fm 1⅛ Ⓣ :503 1:144 1:381 1:50 3↑ ⒻAlAlngBC-G3 **100** 1 4 2½ 4 1¾ 4 2½ 2½ 1 3 Prado E S L119 b *1.20 87– 16 Film Maker1193 Noisette1191¾ Lady Linda1191 Saved ground, driving 7
15May04–5Pim fm 1 1/16 Ⓣ :241 :481 1:113 1:404 3↑ ⒻGalrettH-G3 **98** 7 7 5 6 4¼ 7 6 5 4½ 2½ Prado E S L120 b 2.20 97 - Ocean Drive117½ *Film Maker*1203½ *With Patience*1121 Wide, closed gamely 8
18Apr04–8Kee fm 1 1/16 Ⓣ :232 :48 1:12 1:412 4↑ ⒻJenyWily-G3 **86** 2 4 4½ 4 2½ 5 3¼ 6 4¼ 6 5¾ Prado E S L123 b 4.10 91– 05 *Intercontinental*1161 *OceanDrive*1161½ *MadeiraMist*118nk 5w lane,empty late 8

Finery
Own: Richards Althea D

B. m. 5 (Feb)
Sire: Lear Fan (Roberto) $15,000
Dam: Duds (Ack Ack)
Br: Althea Richards (Va)
Tr: Turner W H Jr(0 0 0 0 .00) 2004:(143 8 .06)

Life	11	4	4	0	$200,320	96	**D.Fst**	2	0	2	0	$19,600	86
2004	7	2	2	0	$127,920	96	**Wet(300)**	2	2	0	0	$52,800	88
2003	4	2	2	0	$72,400	88	**Turf(333)**	7	2	2	0	$127,920	96
	0	0	0	0	$0	–	**Dst(0)**	0	0	0	0	$0	–

20Nov04-9CD yl 1⅛ Ⓣ :492 1:14 1:401 1:534 3↑ⒻCardinlH-G3 **83** 6 9 5¼ 9 7½ 10 11 10 14 6 7 McKee J L115 5.00 57-34 Aud115nk May Gator117hd Angela's Love1144¼ 7-8w much of way 11
31Oct04-8Aqu fm 1 1/16 Ⓣ :252 :501 1:143 1:433 3↑ⒻAtheniaH-G3 **96** 3 4 2 5 2½ 5 1½ 3 1½ 1½ Fragoso P L113 6.60 89-13 Finery113½ Madeira Mist118nk With Patience114½ Quick surge, in time 11
17Oct04-6Bel yl 1 1/16 🅃 :251 :494 1:144 1:44 3↑ⒻAlw 50000N2x **94** 3 3 2 3 1½ 2hd 1 2 1 1¼ Bailey J D L120 2.30 83-21 *Finery*120 1¼ Shoot120 1¾ *Honey Ryder*117 3½ 3 wide move, clear 6
25Sep04-9Bel fm 1 Ⓣ :241 :473 1:112 1:343 3↑ⒻNblDmslH-G3 **95** 8 2hd 1hd 4¾ 6 3½ 5 4¼ Gryder A T L114 38.25 83-16 Ocean Drive120 1¼ High Court115¾ Hour of Justice116 2 Vied outside, tired 9
27Aug04-8Sar fm 1 🅃 :241 :48 1:121 1:353 4↑ⒻAlw 60000c **92** 3 2 1½ 2½ 1hd 2hd 2nk Bailey J D L116 2.95 93-05 Madeira Mist120nk Finery116 2 Bijou116nk Lost whip 3/16, gamely 9
23Jly04-8Bel sf 1⅛ 🅃 :493 1:144 1:403 1:531 3↑ⒻAlw 48000N2x **87** 1 2 1½ 4 3 5 3½ 2 3½ 2 2 Chavez J F L121 5.70 62-40 *Spotlight*115 2 Finery121 3 Pattiano121 3¼ Game finish inside 7
4Jly04-4Bel fm 1 Ⓣ :233 :464 1:103 1:34 3↑ⒻAlw 47040N2x **85** 3 2½ 3 1 4 2 4 2½ 4 3¼ Chavez J F L121 8.30 87-15 La Reina115½ Shoot121 2¼ Erase121½ Stayed on well inside 5

Fire Slam
Own: Fulton Stan E

B. c. 4 (Jan) FTKJUL02 $230,000
Sire: Grand Slam (Gone West) $85,000
Dam: Miss Firefly (Salt Lake)
Br: Julie Jones Mogge (Ky)
Tr: Carroll David M(0 0 0 0 .00) 2004:(157 33 .21)

Life	12	6	3	0	$686,811	109	**D.Fst**	11	5	3	0	$658,606	109
2004	9	4	2	0	$427,381	109	**Wet(407)**	1	1	0	0	$28,205	86
2003	3	2	1	0	$259,430	90	**Turf(291)**	0	0	0	0	$0	–
	0	0	0	0	$0	–	**Dst(0)**	0	0	0	0	$0	–

27Nov04-10CD fst 6½f :224 :454 1:10 1:162 3↑DstrtHumrH71k **97** 3 7 8 2½ 7 5¼ 6 2¾ 6 4 Day P L118 *1.70 85-15 StrngthndHnr11[illegible]nk CchJmL121 2½ LvlPlyngfld114½ Bmp start,no rally,8w 10
31Oct04-9CD fst 7½f :224 :452 1:101 1:292 3↑AckAckH-G3 **96** 4 4 3½ 5 3 4 3 2 5¼ Day P L117 *.60 88-14 Sir Cherokee114 5¼ Fire Slam117nk Slate Run106nk Eased back turn,6w bid 6
28Aug04-10Sar fst 7f :22 :443 1:082 1:204 KngsBshp-G1 **83** 8 3 7 4¼ 5 5 5 9½ 6 11¼ Day P L123 2.45 89-04 Pomeroy121 1½ Weigelia121 1 Ice Wynnd Fire117 4¼ Stumbled badly start 8
24Jly04-4EIP fst 6½f :224 :453 1:094 1:164 3↑DBernhardt97k **99** 1 3 3 3 2 3½ 2hd 1hd Day P L117 .90 95-12 Fire Slam117hd Unbridled America117 5¼ Cat Genius123 8¼ 4w,hand urging 4
5Jun04-9Bel fst 7f :222 :45 1:084 1:204 RvaRdgBC-G2 **109** 2 6 5 1½ 5 1½ 2hd 1hd Day P L123 2.80 96-07 *Fire Slam*123hd *Teton Forest*115 3¼ Abbondanza123 1¾ Found room on rail 7
8May04-9CD fst 6f :203 :433 :561 1:093 MattWinn103k **96** 4 1 4 6 4 2¾ 1 1 1 5¼ Day P L120 *1.10 93-12 *Fire Slam*120 5¼ Cuvee120 2¼ Hasslefree116nk 5w,late hand urging 4
17Apr04-9Kee fst 1 1/16 :231 :471 1:12 1:434 Lexingtn-G2 **97** 6 5 3 5 3 6 3¼ 2 2 2 2¾ Day P L116 4.50 90-11 QuintonsGoldRush116 2¾ *FirSlm*116nk SongofthSword116 2 5w bid,2ndbest 14
7Mar04-9FG fst 1 1/16 :222 :451 1:103 1:423 LaDerby-G2 **86** 10 2½ 2 1 2hd 3 2½ 5 8¼ Sellers S J L122 3.20 89-07 Wimbledon122 2¼ Borrego122hd *Pollard's Vision*122¾ Headed, faltered 11
24Jan04-9FG fst 1 :243 :484 1:134 1:382 Lecomte-G3 **92** 3 2 1 2½ 2hd 1 1½ 1 2 Sellers S J L119 1.70 91-15 FireSlm119 2 ShdowInd118 1½ TwoDownAutomtic117 2½ Clear, kept to task 7

Flamethrowintexan
Own: Grasshopper Stable

Ch. g. 4 (Feb) OBSOCT01 $11,000
Sire: Way West*Fr (Gone West) $2,000
Dam: Willalady (Citidancer)
Br: Moloney & Thompson (Fla)
Tr: Penney Jim(0 0 0 0 .00) 2004:(210 47 .22)

Life	13	8	2	1	$382,588	100	D.Fst	13	8	2	1	$382,588	100
2004	11	7	1	1	$368,813	100	Wet(338)	0	0	0	0	$0	–
2003	2	1	1	0	$13,775	75	Turf(235)	0	0	0	0	$0	–
	0	0	0	0	$0	–	Dst(0)	0	0	0	0	$0	–

29Oct04–7LS fst 1 1/16 :224 :462 1:102 1:42 LnStrDby-G3 **100** 4 11 1/2 1 1/2 11 1hd 31 Frazier R L L122 f 15.20 91–17 PollrdsVson122 1/2 Cryptogrph122 1/2 Flmthrwntxn122 3/4 Gamely, grudgingly 12
Previously trained by Cooper Kay
26Sep04–8Hst fst 1 1/8 :453 1:102 1:36 1:492 BCDerby-G3 **92** 5 21 21 1/2 21 1/2 15 18 1/2 Frazier R L L126 f 3.00 98–05 Flmethrowintexn126 8 1/2 LordSmri126 2 1/4 StrikeEmHrd126nk Much the best 12
Previously trained by Penney Jim
6Sep04–9EmD fst 1 1/8 :46 1:10 1:35 1:472 EmDBCDerby96k **92** 3 11 1 1/2 1hd 11 22 3/4 Frazier R L LB122 *1.50 87–16 MyCred122 2 3/4 *Flmthrowintxn*122nk RndomMmo1224 Long drive 4 w, missed 7
15Aug04–6EmD fst 1 1/16 :224 :46 1:102 1:421 OC 32k/n2x-N **89** 1 1 1/2 11 1hd 11 1/2 12 1/2 Frazier R L LB121 *.50 90–14 Flamethrowintexan121 2 1/2 MilitrySinger121 4 1/2 Skyrider121 1 3/4 Off rail, clear 6
31Jly04–9EmD fst 1 1/16 :23 :464 1:11 1:424 SetlSlwBCH64k **89** 1 12 11 1/2 1 1/2 12 11 Frazier R L LB118 *1.50 87–13 *Flmthrowintxn*1181 PurAmricn116 1 1/2 SoccrDn1201 Hopped start,held sway 9
24Jun04–3Hol fst 6 1/2f :221 :444 1:092 1:154 Clm c-(62.5-55) **86** 2 3 11 1 1/2 11 1/2 12 Smith M E LB120 *.70 94–07 *Flmthrowntxn*1202 RodoShoppr118 1 1/2 RocknthShp1224 Speed,dueled,clear 5
Claimed from Wafer, Jr. Thomas J. for $62,500, Spawr Bill Trainer 2004(as of 6/24): (143 33 27 21 0.23)
27May04–4Hol fst 6 1/2f :212 :433 1:084 1:152 Clm 50000(50-45) **87** 5 3 1 1/2 13 1/2 12 1/2 11 Smith M E LB120 *1.20 96–10 *Flmethrowintexn*1201 HourOutlw1185 OrchidThif1186 Angled in,clear,held 5
29Apr04–3Hol fst 6 1/2f :212 :433 1:082 1:152 Clm c-(40-35) **85** 4 1 11 1hd 1hd 1no Martinez F F LB120 *1.80 96–06 *Flmthrowintxn*120no MmoryMn118 6 1/2 HvnsCt118 3 3/4 Dueled, game, won bob 6
Claimed from Mertus, Ron, Smith, Earl and Wong for $40,000, O'Neill Doug Trainer 2004(as of 4/29): (288 47 47 35 0.16)
10Apr04–3SA fst 6 1/2f :212 :442 1:09 1:15 OC 80k/n1x **73** 1 4 1 1/2 1hd 42 1/2 513 3/4 Baze T C LB118 13.60 83–12 Teton Forest118 3/4 M. P. Cat1207 Tenace1181 Inside duel,weakened 6
11Mar04–2SA fst 7f :222 :451 1:104 1:243 Alw 40000s **76** 4 2 1 1/2 1 1/2 12 12 Baze T C LB120 9.90 82–20 Flmthrowntxn1202 Nmnynmnynmny120 1/2 CgrsDn122 1 1/2 Off rail, drew clear 7
16Jan04–5SA fst 6f :211 :44 :561 1:092 Alw 40000s **71** 1 4 1hd 1 1/2 22 56 Baze T C LB120 6.30 85–15 TundrPonch118 3/4 *Aryotlkntom*120hd RhnoChsr118hd Inside duel,weakened 8

Forest Danger
Own: Jones Aaron U. and Marie D

B. c. 4 (Feb) FTFFEB03 $900,000
Sire: Forestry (Storm Cat) $75,000
Dam: Starry Ice (Ice Age)
Br: Barbara Jean Dutton & Jerry Dutton (Ky)
Tr: Pletcher Todd A(0 0 0 0 .00) 2004:(948 240 .25)

Life	4	3	1	0	$159,600	110	D.Fst	4	3	1	0	$159,600	110
2004	4	3	1	0	$159,600	110	Wet(462)	0	0	0	0	$0	–
2003	0	M	0	0	$0	–	Turf(285)	0	0	0	0	$0	–
	0	0	0	0	$0	–	Dst(0)	0	0	0	0	$0	–

1May04–8Aqu fst 1 :222 :44 1:074 1:342 Withers-G3 **104** 5 1hd 2 1/2 2hd 21 1/2 23 1/4 Coa E M L123 *.45 90–19 *Mdllist*116 3 1/4 ForstDngr1231 TwoDownAutomtc120 5 1/4 Vied outside, gamely 5
10Apr04–7Aqu fst 7f :221 :441 1:081 1:203 BayShore-G3 **110** 2 5 1hd 1 1/2 16 17 1/2 Velazquez J R L116 *1.10 102–04 ForstDngr116 7 1/2 *Abbondnz*116 3 1/2 *IndinWrDnc*116 2 1/2 Drew away when roused 8
13Mar04–2GP fst 7f :22 :441 1:093 1:232 Alw 34000n1x **89** 5 3 1hd 1hd 12 1/2 12 1/2 Velazquez J R L122 *1.00 85–13 *Forest Danger*122 2 1/2 Classic Wine1182 Medallist122hd Vied inside, driving 7
14Feb04–12GP fst 6f :22 :45 :572 1:10 Md Sp Wt 32k **91** 6 10 64 1/4 41 1/2 21 1/2 11 1/2 Velazquez J R L122 *.90 92–07 *ForestDnger*122 1 1/2 *SirShcklton*122 4 1/2 *GoldGunnr*122 3/4 Bounced around st, 4wd 11

Forest Music
Own: Gill Michael J

Gr/ro. f. 4 (Apr) FTFFEB03 $325,000
Sire: Unbridled's Song (Unbridled) $125,000
Dam: Defer West (Gone West)
Br: Twin Hopes Farm, Inc. (Ky)
Tr: Shuman Mark(0 0 0 0 .00) 2004:(987 159 .16)

Life	11	4	0	4	$212,266	105	D.Fst	8 3 0 2	$146,176	105
2004	7	3	0	3	$188,590	100	Wet(377)	3 1 0 2	$66,090	91
2003	4	1	0	1	$23,676	105	Turf(286)	0 0 0 0	$0	–
	0	0	0	0	$0	–	Dst(0)	0 0 0 0	$0	–

```
11Dec04-8Aqu my 6f  ⊡:213 :442 :57 1:103 3↑ⒻGrIndORssH80k  87 1 3 11½ 11 12 3nk Elliott S     L118   2.70 86-14 Trveltor116hd SensiblyChic114nk ForestMusic118½ Fast pace, game effort 6
13Nov04-10Med fst 6f  :214 :441 :563 1:094 ⒻSetonHallU60k  90 7 3 11½ 11½ 15½ 11½ Gryder A T   L118   3.50 91-13 ForestMusic1181½ FelinStory1217¼ Itsytsthing115¾ Urged away,held well 7
10Oct04-9Bel fst 6½f  :231 :464 1:094 1:16 3↑ⒻGlntBlmH-G2  59 4 5 51½ 52¾ 714 718½ Gryder A T   L114f 12.50 74-16 Lady Tak1222 Mo to Vita1154¼ Zawzooth115hd Between rivals, tired 7
31Jly04-8Sar my 7f  :212 :44 1:101 1:233 ⒻTest-G1  74 12 1 1½ 13½ 1hd 310 Bridgmohan S X  L118f 12.10 76-11 SoctySlcton1206¼ BndngStrngs1233¾ FrstMsc1184¼ Faltered final furlong 12
3Jly04-8Bel fst 6f  :214 :442 :561 1:09 ⒻPrioress-G1  92 2 2 11½ 11½ 2hd 32¼ Bridgmohan S X  L119   5.60 92-08 FriendlyMichell1192¼ FlinStory121no ForstMusic119¾ Set pace, weakened 9
6Jun04-9Mth sly 5f  ⊗:214 :442 :564 ⒻCrankItUp55k  91 7 1 11 11½ 11½ 11½ Elliott S  L119  *.70e 98-14 Forest Music1191½ Schedule1171¼ Forty Moves1175½ Pace outside,driving 7
14May04-9Pim fst 6f  :23 :454 :58 1:104 ⒻMsPreakn-G3  100 4 6 41¼ 52¼ 1hd 1hd Dominguez R A  L115   8.90 91-16 ForestMusic115hd StephansAngel1194¼ FallFshion1191 Bumped start,wide 11
```

Fortunate Damsel
Own: Spruce Pond Stable

Dk. b or b. f. 4 (Mar)
Sire: Runaway Groom (Blushing Groom*Fr) $12,500
Dam: Consider It Done (Green Dancer)
Br: Edward J. Messina (NY)
Tr: Cedano Heriberto(0 0 0 0 .00) 2004:(47 2 .04)

Life	15	4	2	3	$200,202	95	D.Fst	7 1 1 1	$28,008	80
2004	12	4	2	2	$192,312	95	Wet(354)	1 0 1 0	$8,800	71
2003	3	M	0	1	$7,890	61	Turf(284)	7 3 0 2	$163,394	95
	0	0	0	0	$0	–	Dst(0)	0 0 0 0	$0	–

```
6Nov04-9Aqu fst 1⅛  :484 1:13 1:381 1:511 3↑ⒻTnbkAlmH-G3  80 8 52½ 62½ 71¾ 77 710¼ Castellano J J  L112  27.50 73-24 PersonlLgnd115½ RorEmotion1174¾ FstCooki1142 Stumbled start, 3 wide 9
11Oct04-9Bel fm 1⅛ Ⓣ:502 1:134 1:364 1:484 ⒻPebbles-G3  94 7 11½ 1½ 1½ 12 1hd Castellano J J  L119  6.50 86-15 FortunateDmsel119hd Venturi1211 DeltSenstion119no Pace, clear, gamely 8
23Aug04-8Sar gd 1⅛ Ⓣ:50 1:141 1:381 1:502 ⒻLakPlcdH-G2  91 7 12 11 1½ 2½ 34¼ Castellano J J  L116b 5.60 74-31 Spotlight1163½ MamboSlew120¾ FortunateDamsel1163 Set pace, weakened 7
  Previously trained by Johnson Philip G
2Aug04-8Sar gd 1 1/16 Ⓣ:25 :49 1:121 1:42 ⒻLkGeorge-G3  95 1 31 31½ 32 41 31½ Castellano J J  L117b 13.30 83-15 SeducersSong1151½ Venturi119no FortunteDmsl117nk Inside trip, gamely 10
2Jly04-8Bel fm 1 Ⓣ:223 :453 1:091 1:331 ⒻⓇFieldy62k  94 2 64½ 55 43 3½ 1½ Castellano J J  L119b 4.60 94-09 FortunteDmsl119½ SducrsSong119½ JinnysGold1227½ Inside move, in time 7
13Jun04-8Bel fm 1⅛ Ⓣ:471 1:11 1:351 1:471 ⒻSandsPnt-G3  88 10 41½ 53½ 61¾ 31 52¼ Bridgmohan S X  L115b 37.50 92-06 MamboSlew122nk Lucifer'sStone122 1¾ Vous119nk Awkward start, gamely 10
9May04-5Bel fm 1 1/16 Ⓣ:25 :491 1:13 1:422 3↑ⒻAlw 48000n2x  86 9 21 2½ 51½ 43½ 42½ Bridgmohan S X  L117b 12.70 88-13 Please TakeMeOut114¾ Coherent124hd Erase1211¾ Stayed on well stretch 9
25Apr04-6Aqu fm 1 Ⓣ:24 :491 1:134 1:38 ⒻAlw 44000n2L  80 3 31½ 41 31½ 1½ 14¾ Fragoso P  L117b 5.10 87-13 FortuntDmsl1174¾ TnTrsurs119½ MissPrkPlc1121 When roused, hand ride 10
18Mar04-5Aqu my 1  :232 :463 1:111 1:382 ⒻAlw 44000n1x  71 6 43 44 42 42 2¾ Perez E R5  L112b 12.80 72-25 GrndPryer117¾ FortunteDmsel1123½ SpecilTctics119½ Game finish outside 6
5Mar04-2Aqu fst 1 ⊡:234 :482 1:14 1:40 ⒻMd 50000(50-40)  55 5 21½ 52½ 51¼ 32½ 11¾ Perez E R5  L116b 2.65 81-17 FortntDmsl1161¾ VldAcqston1122 Commndr1191¼ Stumbled start, steady 7
19Feb04-3Aqu fst 1 ⊡:233 :483 1:142 1:39 ⒻMd 50000(60-50)  55 4 32½ 31½ 22½ 26 26½ Perez E R5  L114  3.25 79-21 BnkAudit1216½ FortuntDmsl1144 VlidAcquiston1148¼ Close up, second best 8
7Jan04-6Aqu fst 6f ⊡:23 :471 :594 1:132 ⒻMd Sp Wt 41k  48 4 8 87¼ 1010 815 811¼ Castillo H Jr  L120  11.20 61-24 SpclTctcs120nk MythclTm1204 ForgottnPrms1201¾ Between foes, no rally 10
```

Freefourinternet
Own: Equirace.Com LLC

B. h. 7 (Apr)
Sire: Tabasco Cat (Storm Cat) $17,490
Dam: Dixie Chimes (Dixieland Band)
Br: Edward P. Evans (Ky)
Tr: Maker Michael J(0 0 0 0 .00) 2004:(200 31 .16)

Life	34	8	3	6	$1,050,275	105	D.Fst	5	2	0	0	$475,893	104
2004	9	2	1	0	$527,693	104	Wet(364)	2	0	1	1	$32,708	99
2003	11	2	1	5	$418,598	105	Turf(318)	27	6	2	5	$541,674	105
	0	0	0	0	$0	-	Dst(0)	0	0	0	0	$0	-

13Nov04- 3Hoo fst 1 :232 :464 1:1121:354 3↑SchaeferMl103k 99 3 613 615 68 56½ 54¾ McKee J LB124 2.30 93- 17 Added Edge121no CoachJimiLee1192 PerfectCut1172½ 4wd, no threat late 6
30Oct04- 9LS fst 1¼ :47 1:111 1:3511:59 3↑BCClasic-G1 88 2 13301335 1324 1322 1323½ Kuntzweiler G L126 54.30 - - Ghostzapper1263 Roses in May1264 Pleasantly Perfect126¾ Never close 13
20Oct04- 7Haw fst 1¼ :4711:111 1:3642:031 3↑HawGldCp-G2 104 6 725 722 66¼ 1hd 11¾ Kuntzweiler G L112 27.00 90- 19 Freefourinternt1121¾ PrfctDrift1212¼ SonicWst1152¼ 4 wide 1/4, late rally 7
6Sep04- 3Mnr fm 1 Ⓣ:231 :463 1:0931:34 3↑LaborDayH75k 91 6 813 813 87 55 1hd Kuntzweiler G LB114 3.70 97- 04 *Freefourinternet*114hd LReinsTrms116¾ StrlingGold1121½ 7w,furious finish 8
Previously trained by Scott Joan
23Apr04- 9Kee gd 1½ Ⓣ:5141:172 2:0712:314 4↑Elkhorn-G3 61 1 85¼1011 98¾ 911 921¼ Perret C L116 13.20 65- 14 Epicentre1164¾ Rochester116nk Art Variety116½ Tired early 10
9Apr04- 9Kee fm 1 Ⓣ:23 :451 1:09 1:332 4↑MakrsMrk-G2 91 1 10241024 1017 1012 76¼ Perret C L116 26.30 99 - Perfect Soul116½ *Burning Roma*116hd Royal Spy1161 Improved position 10
7Feb04- 7TuP fm 1 1/16 Ⓣ:232 :46 1:10 1:404 3↑TuPBCH150k 88 8 915 818 813 58½ 56¼ Lovato F Jr L122 4.60 96 - Irish Warrior123hd *Black Bart*1135 Rock N Rosh1161 4wide 1/4, mild gain 9
17Jan04- 7Hou gd 1⅛ :4821:131 1:3841:513 4↑MaxmGldCpH100k 95 3 85½ 86¾ 43 1½ 2¾ Albarado R J L119 2.90 86- 17 SirCherokee118¾ Frfourintrnt1192½ DustySpik1164½ Rallied, 4w, led, hung 8
3Jan04- 9FG fm *1 1/16 Ⓣ:251 :503 1:1531:45 4↑CERBradlyH60k 91 9 811 812 88¾ 55½ 45¼ Albarado R J L122 1.90 83- 14 Skate Away116nk Warleigh1173 Great Bloom1172 Angled out, hung 9

Friel's for Real
Own: Campbell Gilbert G

Dk. b or b. m. 5 (Apr)
Sire: Sword Dance*Ire (Nijinsky II) $5,000
Dam: Beaties for Real (Unreal Zeal)
Br: Gilbert G. Campbell (Fla)
Tr: Allard Edward T(0 0 0 0 .00) 2004:(348 86 .25)

Life	15	8	3	2	$260,080	106	D.Fst	14	8	3	1	$262,560	106
2004	6	5	1	0	$204,450	106	Wet(320)	2	1	0	1	$16,900	65
2003	5	1	0	2	$22,770	81	Turf(285)	0	0	0	0	$0	-
	0	0	0	0	$0	-	Dst(0)	0	0	0	0	$0	-

14May04- 8Pim fst 1 1/16 :243 :483 1:1241:45 3↑ⒻPmBCDsfH-G3 95 3 64¼ 63¾ 4¾ 1½ 12¼ Castellano A Jr L115 f 11.40 82- 17 FrilsforRl1152¼ SintlyAction1142 NonsuchBy116hd Settled,4wd trip,drvng 8
30Apr04- 3Aqu fst 1⅛ :4921:134 1:3921:523 4↑ⒻOC 75k/c -N 84 1 21 21 1hd 14½ 15 Castellano J J L118 f *1.30 76- 26 *FrilsforRl*1185 ArtstJohnn1181 DvotonUnbrdld11611 When asked, drew off 4
20Mar04- 8Lrl fst 1⅛ :4821:123 1:3731:50 4↑ⒻGalaLil57k 106 2 52¼ 55¼ 55 12½ 16 Castellano A Jr L115 f 3.70 92- 21 *Friel's for Real*1156 Undercover1223¼ City Fire1221¼ Wide, driving 6
21Feb04- 8Lrl fst 1⅛ :5021:151 1:40 1:524 4↑ⒻMdRcngMedH75k 87 2 2hd 42 31½ 23½ 21½ Wilson R L115 f 2.10 76- 33 Undercover1151½ *FrielsforReal*1151¾ Databse118½ Rated bk,angld,4wd mve 5
8Feb04- 8Lrl fst 1 1/16 :242 :482 1:1321:45 4↑ⒻOC 50k/N$Y -N 83 2 21½ 22 2½ 15 14½ Wilson R L119 f *.90 87- 21 Friel's for Real1194½ Lady Linda1172 Kiss aMiss1174¾ 2w,bid 5/16,drove clr 6
8Jan04- 7Lrl fst 1 1/16 :243 :484 1:1331:463 4↑ⒻOC 32k/N3x -N 88 2 57½ 45 32 11½ 12½ Wilson R L119 f 5.00 79- 43 *FrielsforRel*1192½ SwetDynmit1192 *WorldlyPlsur*1174 In close start,driving 8

Friendly Michelle
Own: Friendly Ed

Ch. f. 4 (May) FTKJUL02 $77,000
Sire: Artax (Marquetry) $10,000
Dam: Valiant Jewel (Buckley Boy)
Br: Ronald Fein (Ky)
Tr: Baffert Bob(0 0 0 0 .00) 2004:(562 105 .19)

Life	10	5	0	2	$399,294	98	D.Fst	8	5	0	2	$386,794	98
2004	7	3	0	2	$335,754	98	Wet(300)	2	0	0	0	$12,500	65
2003	3	2	0	0	$63,540	83	Turf(226)	0	0	0	0	$0	–
	0	0	0	0	$0	–	Dst(0)	0	0	0	0	$0	–

Date/Race	Cond	Dist	Fractions	Race	Speed	PP	St	1C	2C	Str	Fin	Jockey	Wt	Odds	Pace	Finishers	Comment	Field
15Oct04–9Kee	my	7f	:213 :441 1:0941:224	ⒻRavenRun-G2	41	10	3	51½	53	1013	926¼	Day P	L123 b	*1.80	67– 11	JoshsMdelyn118¼ VisionofBeuty1169½ FlinStory118½	Tracked,4-5w,tired	10
31Jly04–8Sar	my	7f	:212 :44 1:1011:233	ⒻTest-G1	65	10	4	93¼	45½	67½	414¼	Bailey J D	L122 b	*2.40	72– 11	*SctySlctn*1206¼ BndngStrngs120¾ FrstMsc1184¼	Ducked out backstretch	12
3Jly04–8Bel	fst	6f	:214 :442 :5611:09	ⒻPrioress-G1	98	8	6	32½	21½	1hd	12¼	Nakatani C S	L119 b	*1.85	94– 08	FriendlyMichll1192¼ FlinStory121no ForstMusic119¾	3 wide move, driving	9
4Jun04-10Bel	fst	1	:232 :454 1:0941:344	ⒻAcorn-G1	98	8	2½	2½	2hd	1hd	31¾	Solis A	L121 b	7.10	85– 17	IslndSnd1211¾ ScitySlction121no *FrindlyMichll*121¾	Vied outside, gamely	8
29Apr04–9CD	fst	7½f	:213 :44 1:0841:281	ⒻLaTroien-G3	98	3	6	1hd	1hd	3½	1½	Solis A	L118 b	2.40	99– 08	FriendlyMichll118½ EndrsSistr122hd BohminLdy1225¾	Inside,gamely,drvg	7
21Mar04–8SA	fst	6½f	:214 :443 1:1011:171	ⒻSantaPaula82k	76	2	2	42	43	41	11¼	Baze T C	LB116 b	*.70	86– 12	*FriendlyMichelle*1161¼ LyinGoddess1161 VryVgs118½	4wd, wore down foes	5
15Feb04–8SA	fst	1	:223 :46 1:1021:362	ⒻLsVrgnes-G1	92	2	1½	1hd	1½	11½	33	Baze T C	LB116 b	20.40	86– 18	APAdvntr118½ HollywoodStory1202½ *FrndlyMchll*1161	Inside duel,held 3rd	8

Friends Lake
Own: Broman Sr., Mary and Chester

Ch. c. 4 (Apr)
Sire: A.P. Indy (Seattle Slew) $300,000
Dam: Antespend (Spend a Buck)
Br: Chester Broman & Mary R. Broman (NY)
Tr: Kimmel John C(0 0 0 0 .00) 2004:(281 34 .12)

Life	7	3	0	1	$696,400	99	D.Fst	5	2	0	1	$636,400	92
2004	4	1	0	1	$611,800	92	Wet(412)	2	1	0	0	$60,000	99
2003	3	2	0	0	$84,600	99	Turf(312)	0	0	0	0	$0	–
	0	0	0	0	$0	–	Dst(0)	0	0	0	0	$0	–

Date/Race	Cond	Dist	Fractions	Race	Speed	PP	St	1C	2C	Str	Fin	Jockey	Wt	Odds	Pace	Finishers	Comment	Field
22May04–8Bel	fst	1⅛	:46 1:10 1:35 1:474	PeterPan-G2	83	5	84¾	94¾	104	715	715¼	Migliore R	L123	6.70	77– 24	Purge1156¾ *Swirgforthefences*1151¼ MasterDvid1152¼	4 wide, no response	10
1May04-10CD	sly	1¼	:4631:114 1:3712:04	KyDerby-G1	54	5	149	166¼	1615	1517	1536¾	Migliore R	L126	13.50	42– 21	*Smarty Jones*1262¾ Lion Heart1263¼ Imperialism1262	Steadied 1st turn	18
13Mar04–9GP	fst	1⅛	:47 1:112 1:3731:511	FlaDerby-G1	92	2	44½	68½	64	33	1¾	Migliore R	L122	37.40	83– 15	Friends Lake122¾ Value Plus122¾ *The Cliff's Edge*1222½	4 wide rally, up late	10
17Jan04-10GP	fst	1 1/16	:24 :481 1:1221:43	HolyBull-G3	89	4	51¾	62½	53	48	312¾	Migliore R	L122	3.20	81– 24	SecondofJune1222¾ SilverWgon12010 *FriendsLke*122½	Couldn't keep pace	9

Fun House
Own: Winchell Thoroughbreds LLC

B. m. 6 (Feb)
Sire: Prized (Kris S.) $5,000
Dam: Bistra (Classic Go Go)
Br: Verne H. Winchell (Ky)
Tr: Asmussen Steven M(0 0 0 0 .00) 2004:(2293 555 .24)

Life	29	5	11	6	$432,922	97	D.Fst	6 1 2 1	$66,556 91
2004	10	1	4	2	$175,476	97	Wet(334)	0 0 0 0	$0 –
2003	8	2	3	2	$123,340	96	Turf(310)	23 4 9 5	$366,366 97
	0	0	0	0	$0	–	Dst(0)	0 0 0 0	$0 –

23Dec04–9FG fst 1 1/16 ⊗ :252 :504 1:1541:471 3↑Ⓕ FurlSailH60k 89 7 21 11 1hd 12 2½ Hernandez B J Jr L119 4.80 73–28 Chance Dance119½ Fun House1196 Kitty's Legend116hd No match late 7
4Dec04–8Hou fm 1 1/16 Ⓣ :242 :493 1:1511:474 3↑Ⓕ Katy40k 87 7 51¾ 41½ 41½ 2½ 3½ Hernandez B J Jr L118 *1.20 77–27 Key to the Cat115nk Lady Mallory123nk FunHouse1183 Stalk, inside, hung 11
5Nov04–4CD gd 1 1/16 Ⓣ :241 :484 1:1321:45 3↑Ⓕ Alw 68300c 91 6 21 1hd 4¾ 21½ 2no Hernandez B J Jr5 L112 4.40 79–20 Mymich119no Fun House112¾ May Gator1193 Rail,led,outfinished 7
Previously trained by McAnally Ronald
4Sep04–7Dmr fm 1 1/16 Ⓣ :234 :481 1:1141:402 3↑Ⓕ PalmrBCH-G2 85 7 32½ 33 43 75¼ 75¾ Stevens G L LB116 7.50 91–09 Etoile Montante120¾ Katdogawn117½ Tangle1171 3wd 2nd turn,wkened 7
3Jly04–4Hol fm 1 Ⓣ :233 :471 1:11 1:343 3↑Ⓕ RlHroine-G3 87 2 46 55½ 53¾ 52¾ 53½ Baze T C LB123 4.90 87–13 Janeian1212 Katdogawn123½ Makeup Artist1211 Saved ground to lane 6
25Apr04–7Hol fm 1 Ⓣ :232 :464 1:1021:332 3↑Ⓕ WilshirH-G3 83 2 33 44½ 44 76 87 Santiago Javier LB117 13.40 90–05 Spring Star1172½ QueroQuero115no Dublino1201 Saved ground, weakened 9
27Mar04–9SA fm 1⅛ Ⓣ :4741:12 1:3521:471 4↑Ⓕ SntaAnaH-G2 94 5 33 32 32 21½ 32½ Valdivia J Jr LB118 8.00 90–11 Ⓓ *Megahertz*1201 Katdogawn1171½ Fun House1181½ Bid btwn, willingly 7
Placed second through disqualification
21Feb04–8SA gd 1 Ⓣ :232 :473 1:12 1:36 4↑Ⓕ BnaVstaH-G2 97 5 44½ 43½ 32½ 21½ 12¾ Stevens G L LB116 11.00 82–18 Fun House1162¾ *Katdogawn*117½ Fudge Fatale116½ Rallied,led 1/16,clear 7
28Jan04–7SA fm 1 Ⓣ :23 :461 1:0941:342 4↑Ⓕ TuzlaH76k 91 8 65 54 77½ 76¼ 32¼ Smith M E LB117 6.50 88–14 Fudge Fatale1161¼ Polygreen1171 *Fun House*117hd 4wd into str,late 3rd 9
9Jan04–7SA fm 1 Ⓣ :241 :483 1:1241:361 4↑Ⓕ Alw 70000c 88 4 21 21 2½ 1hd 2½ Smith M E LB116 *1.40 80–18 Abbey Bridge116½ FunHouse1163½ LacrystalClassic116hd Bid,led,willingly 5

Funny Cide
Own: Sackatoga Stable

Ch. g. 5 (Apr)
Sire: Distorted Humor (Forty Niner) $60,000
Dam: Belle's Good Cide (Slewacide)
Br: Win Star Farm, LLC (NY)
Tr: Tagg Barclay(0 0 0 0 .00) 2004:(235 32 .14)

Life	21	8	4	5	$3,174,485	114	D.Fst	17 6 3 4	$2,144,485 112
2004	10	3	2	3	$1,075,100	112	Wet(424)	4 2 1 1	$1,030,000 114
2003	8	2	2	2	$1,963,200	114	Turf(303)	0 0 0 0	$0 –
	0	0	0	0	$0	–	Dst(0)	0 0 0 0	$0 –

30Oct04–9LS fst 1¼ :47 1:111 1:3511:59 3↑ BCClasic-G1 102 9 73 63 42½ 88¼ 1014¼ Santos J A L126 7.70 – – Ghostzapper1263 RosesinMy1264 PlesntlyPerfect126¾ Traffic early, tired 13
2Oct04–10Bel fst 1¼ :4731:113 1:3622:022 3↑ JkyClbGC-G1 112 7 2½ 3nk 32 2½ 1¾ Santos J A L126 *2.80 85–13 FunnyCid126¾ Nwfoundlnd1261 ThCliffsEdg1223¾ Gamely between rivals 7
22Aug04–9Sar fst 1¼ :4621:104 1:36 2:004 3↑ SarBCH-G2 107 5 31½ 41½ 2½ 2½ 25 Prado E S L118 *1.00 98–11 EveningAttire1155 *FunnyCide*1183¾ BowmnsBnd1161¼ 3 wide trip, 2nd best 7
3Jly04–7Bel fst 1¼ :4611:091 1:3341:592 3↑ SuburbnH-G1 111 1 31 2½ 2hd 1½ 3nk Santos J A L117 4.10 100 – PeceRules120nk Newfoundlnd114no FunnyCide117¾ Speed on rail, gamely 8
19Jun04–10Suf fst 1⅛ :4831:122 1:3631:49 3↑ MassH-G2 110 7 21 2½ 2hd 3nk 2hd Santos J A LB117 *2.10 98–10 OfflWild113hd FunnyCid117hd ThLdysGroom1161½ 2wd thru-out,game fin 9
31May04–9Bel fst 1 :232 :46 1:10 1:352 3↑ MtropltH-G1 106 9 42½ 51¾ 41 52¼ 55¼ Santos J A L118 4.20 79–34 PicoCentrl119¾ BowmnsBnd1142¼ StrongHope1191½ Between foes, 3 wide 9
3Apr04–8Aqu my 1⅛ :48 1:12 1:3641:492 3↑ ExlsrBCH-G3 109 3 21½ 2½ 2hd 12 1½ Santos J A L120 *1.30 92–08 Funny Cide120½ Evening Attire1198 Host114nk Dug in gamely inside 5
29Feb04–9FG fst 1⅛ :47 1:102 1:3521:483 4↑ NwOrlnsH-G2 108 2 32½ 33 32 43¼ 32¾ Santos J A L118 5.40 98–05 *Peace Rules*119hd Saint Liam1142¾ *Funny Cide*1181¼ Bumped, game for 3rd 8
7Feb04–10GP fst 1⅛ :4711:11 1:3531:473 3↑ DonnH-G1 103 5 33 31 31½ 34 38½ Santos J A L119 3.00 92–09 Medaglia d'Oro1224¾ Seattle Fitz113¾ Funny Cide1194 3 wide, tired 8
10Jan04–10GP fst 7f :223 :453 1:1011:224 4↑ OC 100k/N$Y-N 102 2 3 4nk 11½ 13 15 Santos J A L118 *.40 88–20 FunnyCide1185 AmericnStyle1167½ WckyforLov1223 Drew off, ridden out 5

G P Fleet

Own: Klein Richard, Bertram and Elaine

Ch. g. 5 (May)
Sire: Northern Afleet (Afleet) $5,000
Dam: Come On Bid (Spectacular Bid)
Br: George Parrish (Fla)
Tr: Flint Steven B(0 0 0 0 .00) 2004:(157 30 .19)

Life	22	7	7	2	$357,504	105	D.Fst 5 2 2 0 $67,694 101
2004	11	4	3	1	$247,786	105	Wet(304) 1 0 1 0 $9,000 92
2003	11	3	4	1	$109,718	99	Turf(379) 16 5 4 2 $280,810 105
	0	0	0	0	$0	–	Dst(0) 0 0 0 0 $0 –

23Dec04–7FG fst 1 1/16 ⊗ :244 :493 1:15 1:46 3↑OC 80k/N$Y-N 98 3 31 3nk 3nk 11 12 3/4 Martinez J R Jr L123 *.50 80–28 G P Fleet123 3/4 Candid Glen1191 Classic Par1191 1/2 Increased margin 7

21Nov04–9CD yl 1 1/8 Ⓣ :481 1:13 1:384 1:511 3↑RivrCtyH-G3 105 2 51 3/4 43 43 2hd 1 1/2 Martinez J R Jr L115 12.30 77–26 *G P Fleet*115 1/2 Cloudy's Knight115 5/4 Ay Caramba115no Split foes,4w,drvg 12

3Nov04–9CD fst 1 1/16 ⊗ :243 :49 1:133 1:443 3↑OC 100k/c-N 101 1 33 1 1/2 1hd 12 1/2 17 1/2 Bejarano R L123 *.70 85–22 *G P Fleet*1237 1/2 Justlikedawg1233 1/2 Woodmoon1192 1/2 Inside trip,driving 4

9Oct04–8Haw fm 1 Ⓣ :234 :472 1:11 1:342 3↑CareyMmH-G3 90 3 84 1/2 95 3/4 97 1/4 85 41 3/4 Mojica R Jr L114 8.50 97–04 ScootrRoch115nk GinndSin116 1/2 CloudysKnight1161 Angled out, belatedly 9

6Sep04–10EIP fm 1 1/16 Ⓣ :24 :463 1:092 1:391 3↑TriStateH75k 97 1 810 610 69 1/2 44 1nk Bejarano R L114 *2.40 100–06 G P Fleet114nk Flying Jazz112 3/4 Gretchen's Star117 3/4 Driving,rail,in time 9

24Jly04–9EIP gd 1 1/16 Ⓣ :234 :471 1:121 1:432 3↑Hcp 40000 99 7 89 3/4 811 84 3/4 42 1/4 2nk Day P L115 *2.30 79–28 Gretchen's Star116nk *G P Fleet*115 1/2 Missme1172 1/2 Angle 6w,closing 8

5Jly04–2CD fm 1 1/16 Ⓣ :233 :471 1:122 1:432 3↑OC 62k/N$Y-N 87 2 510 510 41 1/2 2hd 22 1/2 Albarado R J L117 2.90 84–16 AyCaramb1172 1/2 GPFleet1171 1/4 MoonshineHll1172 1/2 4-5w bid,no match late 6

31May04–5CD fst 1 1/16 ⊗ :241 :48 1:13 1:451 3↑OC 62k/N$Y-N 82 3 46 46 41 3/4 32 1/2 23/4 Albarado R J L117 *1.00 81–18 Justlikedawg123/4 G P Fleet117 1/2 Exploited Storm11211 1/2 5w bid,2ndbest 4

23Apr04–10Kee gd 1 Ⓣ :234 :48 1:123 1:363 4↑Alw 60320N3x 85 8 62 3/4 52 1/2 53 43 1/2 36 Lumpkins J L120 18.60 83–14 ManAmongMen1161 1/4 MoonshireHll1184 3/4 GPFleet120 1/2 5w bid,empty late 10

8Feb04–10GP fst 1 1/16 :232 :473 1:12 1:432 4↑OC 75k/N3x-N 73 5 74 1/4 63 1/2 74 79 1/2 711 Day P L118 4.70 81–15 ThLdysGroom118nk *BdBmBdBoom*1181 PrncBnjmn1181 3/4 3 wide, no factor 8

23Jan04–8GP fm *1 1/16 Ⓣ :234 :493 1:14 1:44 4↑Alw 38000N3x 81 2 54 1/2 53 1/2 53 76 65 1/4 Velazquez J R L120 3.80 79–16 Spotted Owl118hd Motives1181 1/4 Thefull Circle118 3/4 4 wide, lacked a rally 8

Gators N Bears

Own: Nechamkin L S II

B. h. 5 (Feb)
Sire: Stormy Atlantic (Storm Cat) $15,000
Dam: I'll Be Along (Notebook)
Br: Robert W. Camac (NJ)
Tr: Nechamkin L S II(0 0 0 0 .00) 2004:(56 12 .21)

Life	25	10	5	6	$659,750	110	D.Fst 21 9 4 6 $624,930 110
2004	8	3	1	2	$357,910	110	Wet(386) 4 1 1 0 $34,820 92
2003	13	5	3	4	$257,270	108	Turf(294) 0 0 0 0 $0 –
	0	0	0	0	$0	–	Dst(0) 0 0 0 0 $0 –

19Dec04–8Aqu fst 6f ⊡ :224 :451 :57 1:084 3↑GravesdH-G3 98 5 2 22 21 1/2 31 1/2 43 3/4 Castellano J J L121 fb *.80 91–18 Don Six1141 1/4 M. Whitestone1141 1/2 Papua1142 Stalked, bid, empty 6

20Nov04–10Pim fst 6f :223 :452 :571 1:092 3↑DeFrncsM-G1 103 4 7 41 1/2 64 65 42 1/2 Castellano J J L126 fb 8.90 95–13 WildctHeir119nk MidsEys1231 1/2 ClockStoppr119 3/4 Chased,outfinshed 6wd 10

14Aug04–7Sar fst 6f :22 :442 :554 1:08 3↑AGVndbtH-G2 109 5 2 31 1/2 3nk 33 33 Lopez C C L118 fb 5.30 99–12 Speightstown1201 1/2 ClockStoppr1151 1/2 GtorsNBrs1182 3 wide move, faded 6

19Jun04–9Suf fst 6f :214 :442 :563 1:091 3↑JBMoslyBCH198k 110 3 2 21 1 1/2 13 14 1/2 Lopez C C LB118 fb 2.20 102–06 GtorsNBers1184 1/2 VlidVido1182 1/4 MyCousinMtt1153 2wd trn,kept alert str 8

15May04–11Pim fst 6f :223 :454 :581 1:104 3↑MdBCH-G3 105 3 4 34 41 1/2 1 1/2 11 1/4 Lopez C C L117 fb 2.50 91–11 *GtorsNBrs*1171 1/4 HghwyProspctor1141 1/4 SssyHnd115 1/2 Brushed 3/16,driving 9

13Mar04–8Aqu fst 7f :222 :45 1:092 1:22 3↑ToboggnH-G3 106 8 2 33 33 3 1/2 22 Lopez C C L115 fb 11.80 93–17 Well Fancied1132 *Gators N Bears*115nk Don Six1131 3/4 Game finish outside 10

16Feb04–9Lrl fst 7f :223 :452 1:10 1:222 3↑GenGrgeH-G2 105 4 4 31 1/2 31 1/2 42 1/2 31 3/4 Wilson R L116 fb 9.30 96–17 *WellFncied*1151 JnforgttblMx114 3/4 GtorsNBrs116hd Close up ins,held well 9

24Jan04–8Lrl fst 6f :221 :451 :573 1:10 4↑Hoover52k 106 3 4 2 1/2 12 13 1 1/2 Wilson R L117 fb *.70 92–23 GtorsNBrs117 1/2 MyGoodTrck1152 3/4 *SssyHound*1151 1/4 Pressed 3-2w,clr,game 10

Ghostzapper
Own: Stronach Stables

B. h. 5 (Apr)
Sire: Awesome Again (Deputy Minister) $125,000
Dam: Baby Zip (Relaunch)
Br: Adena Springs (Ky)
Tr: Frankel Robert J(0 0 0 0 .00) 2004:(491 135 .27)

Life	10	8	0	1	$2,996,120	128	D.Fst	8 6 0 1	$2,849,120	124
2004	4	4	0	0	$2,590,000	128	Wet(419)	2 2 0 0	$147,000	128
2003	4	3	0	1	$378,400	116	Turf(282)	0 0 0 0	$0	-
	0	0	0	0	$0	-	Dst(0)	0 0 0 0	$0	-

30Oct04–9LS fst 1¼ :47 1:111 1:351 1:59 3↑BCClasic-G1 **124** 1 1½ 1½ 11 12 13 Castellano J J L126 b *2.50 - - Ghostzapper1263 Roses inMay1264 PleasantlyPerfect126¾ Drew clear late 13
11Sep04–10Bel fst 1⅛ :453 1:083 1:331 1:461 3↑Woodward-G1 **114** 3 3nk 2½ 2hd 2hd 1nk Castellano J J L126 b *.40 100– 15 *Ghostzapper*126nk *SaintLiam*1269¼ BowmansBnd1267¼ Carried out, bumped 7
21Aug04–9Mth sly 1⅛ :454 1:093 1:351 1:473 3↑IselnBCH-G3 **128** 3 21½ 21½ 2½ 12 110¾ Castellano J J L120 b *.40 103– 16 *Ghostzpper*12010¾ Prsidntilffir11721¼ Zoffingr115no Drew out,hand ridden 4
4Jly04–9Bel fst 7f :222 :443 1:081 1:202 3↑TomFoolH-G2 **120** 3 2 32 2hd 14½ 14¼ Castellano J J L119 b *1.35 98– 13 *Ghostzpper*1194¼ Aggdn1143½ UnforgettbleMx114½ 4 wide move, hand ride 4

Glick
Own: Bone Robert D

Dk. b or b. h. 9 (Mar)
Sire: Theatrical*Ire (Nureyev) $50,000
Dam: Bejat (Mr. Prospector)
Br: Allen E. Paulson (Ky)
Tr: Mullins Jeff(0 0 0 0 .00) 2004:(538 140 .26)

Life	40	14	7	3	$594,791	110	D.Fst	2 0 0 0	$1,380	85
2004	8	3	2	0	$160,960	110	Wet(367)	0 0 0 0	$0	-
2003	13	4	2	0	$111,330	97	Turf(371)	38 14 7 3	$593,411	110
	0	0	0	0	$0	-	Dst(0)	0 0 0 0	$0	-

8Sep04–6Dmr fm 1 Ⓣ:231 :473 1:112 1:341 3↑LiveDreamH76k **74** 6 86¾ 85½ 95¾ 1010 1013 Stevens G L LB117 b 7.10 77– 11 Statement117hd Cayoke117nk Tsigane1191 Weakened, vanned off 10
18Aug04–7Dmr fm 5f Ⓣ:212 :434 :55 3↑GreenFlshH76k **104** 1 4 3nk 1½ 11 2hd Espinoza V LB121 b *1.50 100 - Geronimo119hd Glick1216 Gray Jag109no Bit off rail str,edged 6
25Jly04–2Dmr fst 6f :212 :434 :56 1:082 3↑BCrsbBCH-G1 **85** 5 2 31½ 21 65 810¼ Nakatani C S LB117 b 15.50 87– 09 *Kela*1131¼ Pohave1182½ Hombre Rapido1153 Stalked btwn,weakened 10
31May04–7Hol fm 1 Ⓣ:232 :46 1:09 1:324 3↑ShoeBCM-G1 **100** 3 11 12 11 21 74¼ John K LB124 b 9.70 96– 07 DesignedforLuck1241½ Singletary124hd Tsigne1241 Washy,inside,wkened 8
18Apr04–7SA fm *6½f Ⓣ:22 :44 1:053 1:112 4↑SnSmeonH-G3 **110** 5 3 2½ 2½ 1hd 1¾ Solis A LB117 b *1.00 100– 06 Glick117¾ Cayoke1164 Summer Service117½ Led,inched clear,held 6
12Mar04–2SA fm *6½f Ⓣ:21 :431 1:051 1:111 4↑OC 100k/N3x **110** 7 3 44 33½ 1hd 12 Stevens G L LB118 b *1.10 101– 04 *Glick*1182 Van Rouge1182 Vronsky120hd 3wd bid,stdy handling 7
15Feb04–7SA fm *6½f Ⓣ:222 :443 1:063 1:122 4↑DaytonaH71k **103** 1 5 43 53 41¼ 2½ Stevens G L LB116 b 3.10 94– 05 Tsigane116½ *Glick*116no *Cayoke*1151 3wd into lane,willing 6
19Jan04–4SA fm *6½f Ⓣ:212 :431 1:051 1:111 4↑OC 62k/N2x **103** 4 6 63¾ 64 31 12½ Stevens G L LB119 b 3.10 101– 02 Glick1192½ Special Rate1182 *F J's Pace*119no 4wd into str,handily 7

Golden Sonata
Own: Spence James C

Dk. b or b. m. 6 (Feb)
Sire: Mr. Prospector (Raise a Native)
Dam: Elissa Beethoven*GB (Royal Academy)
Br: James C. Spence (Ky)
Tr: Nicks Morris G(0 0 0 0 .00) 2004:(186 43 .23)

Life	19	6	4	0	$288,811	92	D.Fst	13	4	3	0	$246,745	92
2004	4	2	0	0	$166,000	92	Wet(384)	2	2	0	0	$40,460	91
2003	10	2	3	0	$88,575	92	Turf(316)	4	0	1	0	$1,606	79
	0	0	0	0	$0	–	Dst(0)	0	0	0	0	$0	–

3Apr04–9OP fst 1 1/16 :231 :463 1:104 1:411 4↑Ⓕ ApIBlsmH-G1 **84** 6 613 615 612 615 615½ Marquez C H Jr L114 34.20 88–09 Azeri1231½ Ⓓ Wild Spirit1191¾ Star Parade1147¼ Fell back, trailed 6
13Mar04–10OP fst 1 1/16 :23 :464 1:12 1:441 3↑Ⓕ OakIwnBC-G3 **92** 8 1017 1020 1010 63½ 11¾ Marquez C H Jr L117 29.30 89–15 GoldenSont117¾ KeystotheHr1173/4 *MyoOnthSid*113½ Full of run midtrack 10
Previously trained by Richards Corale A
21Feb04–9FG fst 1 1/16 :241 :481 1:124 1:432 4↑Ⓕ ChouCroutH100k **86** 3 64½ 77¾ 66 79 68¼ Melancon G L118 10.60 85–15 SpctclrLs1171½ TropclBlossom1171 *PrncssPln*1142 Saved ground, no avail 7
4Jan04–9FG fst 1 1/16 :234 :474 1:124 1:451 4↑Ⓕ TrlyBoundH60k **88** 1110 1110 1011 1011 42½ 1½ Melancon G L116 7.10 84–12 GoldnSont116½ SpiritdMidn117hd Whilthronshot1162 Game finish, in time 11

Good Reward
Own: Phipps Ogden M

B. c. 4 (Mar)
Sire: Storm Cat (Storm Bird) $500,000
Dam: Heavenly Prize (Seeking the Gold)
Br: Phipps Stable (Ky)
Tr: McGaughey III Claude R(0 0 0 0 .00) 2004:(254 48 .19)

Life	12	4	1	2	$477,353	104	D.Fst	4	1	0	0	$33,000	75
2004	8	3	1	2	$444,353	104	Wet(431)	0	0	0	0	$0	–
2003	4	1	0	0	$33,000	75	Turf(333)	8	3	1	2	$444,353	104
	0	0	0	0	$0	–	Dst(0)	0	0	0	0	$0	–

28Nov04–9Hol fm 1¼ Ⓣ :471 1:121 1:37 2:012 HolDerby-G1 **104** 5 83¾ 82 74¼ 41¼ 1½ Bailey J D LB122 b *6.10 85–17 GoodReward122½ FastndFurious1221 Imperilism1222 Bumped lane,rallied 13
10Oct04–4Kee fm 1 Ⓣ :233 :472 1:12 1:362 StormCat110k **98** 6 77½ 75 54 43 1¾ Prado E S L117 b 2.70 90–12 *Good Reward*117¾ Fort Prado120nk Silver Ticket123½ Rallied 6-7w,driving 8
6Sep04–10Sar fm 1 3/16 Ⓣ :482 1:123 1:362 1:534 SaranacH-G3 **89** 2 54½ 55 51½ 51¾ 43¾ Santos J A L115 b 4.10 92–09 PrinceArch123hd *Mustnfr*1212¼ CtchtheGlory1151½ Bumped upper stretch 6
9Aug04–8Sar fm 1⅛ 🅃 :471 1:103 1:353 1:473 HalOFmeH-G2 **94** 2 51¾ 41½ 31 42½ 34¼ Prado E S L115 b 10.40 95–09 *ArtieSchiller*1221¼ Mustanfr122no GoodRewrd1151½ Steady, altered course 8
27Jun04–7Bel gd 1⅛ 🅃 :491 1:124 1:364 1:483 🅁MDiarmida61k **86** 6 65¾ 67 64¾ 43 22¼ Santos J A L118 5.40 85–13 SecondPrformnc1162¼ GoodRwrd118¾ DlrChoic116¾ Game finish outside 8
5Jun04–8Bel fm 1⅛ 🅃 :512 1:16 1:384 1:50 HillPrnc-G3 **87** 2 63 63 62 65 44¾ Santos J A L118 6.20 75–20 Artie Schiller1201¾ *Timo*1222¼ Big Booster114¾ Going well late 6
18Apr04–9Kee fm 1⅛ Ⓣ :47 1:12 1:37 1:49 Alw 53515N1x **88** 2 99½ 912 96¾ 32 1nk Santos J A L118 5.30 92–05 GoodRewrd118nk HeroicDd1181¼ *CoolConductor*1202½ 7w 1/4p,drvg,in time 12
27Mar04–9GP fm *1 Ⓣ :251 :513 1:161 1:401 Alw 34000N1x **77** 9 96¼ 83¼ 84¼ 74¼ 3½ Santos J A L118 *2.00 71–22 Carrots Only118½ Fairforforest118hd *Good Reward*118nk Belated rally 10

Gradepoint
Own: Mount Brilliant Stable LLC and Farish

Dk. b or b. c. 4 (May) OBSFEB03 $77,000
Sire: A.P. Indy (Seattle Slew) $300,000
Dam: Class Kris (Kris S.)
Br: W. S. Farish & H. Greg Goodman (Ky)
Tr: Howard Neil J(0 0 0 0 .00) 2004:(173 37 .21)

Life	5	3	0	1	$144,285	96	D.Fst	5	3	0	1	$144,285	96
2004	3	2	0	0	$108,000	96	Wet(438)	0	0	0	0	$0	-
2003	2	1	0	1	$36,285	73	Turf(346)	0	0	0	0	$0	-
	0	0	0	0	$0	-	Dst(0)	0	0	0	0	$0	-

7Mar04-9FG fst 1 1/16 :222 :451 1:103 1:423 LaDerby-G2 **82** 9 913 913 87 77½ 810¾ Albarado R J L122 *2.30e 86-07 Wimbledon1222¼ Borrego122hd *Pollard's Vision*122¾ No real threat 11
15Feb04-9FG fst 1 1/16 :242 :481 1:132 1:451 RisenStr-G3 **96** 1 66 610 69 42½ 1½ Albarado R J L116 1.90 84-21 Grdepoint116½ MrJester1221 Nightliftbigblu1181¼ Rallied,strong handlng 6
2Jan04-7FG fst 1 1/16 :232 :463 1:121 1:454 Alw 30000N1x **87** 10 810 712 77½ 2hd 1½ Albarado R J L121 2.80 81-18 *Gradepoint*121½ Maisie's Son1163 *Colonel Day*1173¼ Circled, driving 11

Greater Good
Own: Lakin Lewis G

B. c. 3 (Apr)
Sire: Intidab (Phone Trick) $3,500
Dam: Gather The Clan*Ire (General Assembly)
Br: A. Lakin & Sons, Inc. (Ky)
Tr: Holthus Robert E(0 0 0 0 .00) 2004:(364 72 .20)

Life	5	3	0	1	$226,275	91	D.Fst	5	3	0	1	$226,275	91
2004	5	3	0	1	$226,275	91	Wet(346*)	0	0	0	0	$0	-
2003	0	M	0	0	$0	-	Turf(216*)	0	0	0	0	$0	-
	0	0	0	0	$0	-	Dst(0)	0	0	0	0	$0	-

27Nov04-11CD fst 1 1/16 :232 :47 1:124 1:45 KyJC-G2 **91** 4 78¼ 810 76¼ 31½ 11¾ McKee J L122 4.40 83-25 Greater Good1221¾ Rush Bay116½ Wild Desert118nk Near inside,driving 9
6Nov04-10CD fst 1 :223 :453 1:104 1:363 Iroquois-G3 **85** 5 77¼ 78½ 67¾ 45 37 McKee J L122 2.30 80-20 StrightLine1225 SocilProbtion1202 *GretrGood*1221¾ Steady,angle out 1/4p 7
18Sep04-10TP fst 1 1/16 :224 :46 1:104 1:444 KyCupJuv-G3 **81** 1 619 617 68½ 2½ 12¾ McKee J L114 6.00 88-11 GrtrGood1142¾ *MgnGrdt*1146¾ Nornnthsprty114nk Closed fast,going away 6
7Aug04-7EIP fst 7f :223 :463 1:114 1:241 Md Sp Wt 22k **73** 5 2 32 41½ 3½ 11½ McKee J L120 3.00 91-12 *GreaterGood*1201½ MelissasComet1205¾ EdMircle1201 Rated early,drvg,5w 9
24Jly04-5EIP fst 6f :231 :464 :592 1:121 Md Sp Wt 25k **58** 10 6 76½ 812 710 56¼ McKee J L119 3.60 79-12 ClertoClose119nk ClytonsPrty1193¼ BridgetsWildCt1192¼ Evenly,no rally 10

Greek Sun
Own: Angelos Peter G

Dk. b or b. c. 4 (Mar) FTFFEB03 $425,000
Sire: Danzig (Northern Dancer) $200,000
Dam: Sunlit Silence (Trempolino)
Br: E. K. Gaylord II & Cheyenne Stables LLC (Ky)
Tr: Frankel Robert J(0 0 0 0 .00) 2004:(491 135 .27)

Life	6	4	1	0	$342,652	107	D.Fst	0	0	0	0	$0	-
2004	4	2	1	0	$270,802	107	Wet(384)	0	0	0	0	$0	-
2003	2	2	0	0	$71,850	88	Turf(399)	6	4	1	0	$342,652	107
	0	0	0	0	$0	-	Dst(0)	0	0	0	0	$0	-

17Oct04-8SA gd 1⅛ Ⓣ :482 1:122 1:362 1:48 OakTrDby-G2 **105** 8 73¼ 84¼ 73¾ 73¼ 1¾ Prado E S LB118 *1.40 89-11 Greek Sun118¾ Laura's LuckyBoy1181 Hendrix118no Off bit slow,5wd lane 9
11Sep04-9Bel yl 1⅜ Ⓣ :50 1:142 1:38 2:143 3↑ ManOWar-G1 **93** 5 53 62 64¼ 811 810 Velasquez C L121 3.85 80-10 Magistretti1261¼ Epalo1262 King's Drama126¾ 3 wide trip, tired 8
14Aug04-11AP fm 1¼ Ⓣ :463 1:11 1:351 1:593 Secretar-G1 **107** 3 58 57½ 64¼ 41 23¼ Prado E S L121 2.90 110 - *Kitten's Joy*1233¼ Greek Sun1211¼ Moscow Ballet1191 Stead, boxed in turn 7
26Jun04-3Hol fm 1⅛ Ⓣ :473 1:112 1:361 1:482 + CinmaBCH-G3 **96** 3 21 33½ 33 22½ 12 Solis A LB120 2.50 89-14 Greek Sun1202 Laura's LuckyBoy1223½ Whilly117no Pulled,stalked,rallied 7

Gulch Approval

Own: Marylou Whitney Stables

Dk. b or b. g. 5 (Jan)
Sire: Gulch (Mr. Prospector) $50,000
Dam: Classic Approval (With Approval)
Br: Milton Hendry & W.S. Farish (Ky)
Tr: Zito Nicholas P(0 0 0 0 .00) 2004:(452 86 .19)

Life 25 6 3 5 $317,820 105 | D.Fst 17 2 3 4 $106,092 93
2004 11 3 1 1 $192,698 105 | Wet(359) 2 1 0 0 $34,090 92
2003 12 3 2 3 $117,472 93 | Turf(302) 6 3 0 1 $177,638 105
0 0 0 0 $0 – | Dst(0) 0 0 0 0 $0 –

9Oct04–8Bel fm 1 Ⓣ:232 :46 1:091 1:323 3↑KelsoBCH-G2 105 7 31 32 2hd 1hd 31½ Castellano J J L114 32.25 95–03 MrOBrn1191½ MllnnmDrgon119no GlchApprovl114½ Bobbled start, gamely 8
18Sep04–8Bel sf 1⅛ 🅃:50 1:151 1:401 1:523 3↑BelBCH-G2 90 4 11 1½ 1hd 32½ 48¼ Nakatani C S L115 5.00 59–33 Senor Swinger1174 Stroll1203½ B. A. Way113¾ Set pace, tired 4
28Aug04–9Sar fm 1 1/16 Ⓣ:233 :462 1:091 1:392 3↑4strdavH-G2 96 3 32 32½ 41¾ 4¾ 74¾ Day P L117 11.00 93–01 Nothing to Lose117½ Silver Tree1171 Royal Regalia1141¾ Close up, no rally 10
8Aug04–11Mth fm 1 1/16 Ⓣ:234 :481 1:121 1:421+3↑OcenprtH-G3 96 2 31 31 31½ 2hd 1no Day P L117 3.60 88–12 GulchApproval117no Kathir116no StormyRomn115½ Along inside,prevailed 10
17Jly04–5Mth sf 1 1/16 Ⓣ:224 :463 1:103 1:431+3↑Elkwood60k 97 7 41¼ 42¼ 32 3½ 1¾ Lopez C C L117 4.40 83–18 GlchApprovl117¾ RoylAffrmd115no StormyRy117½ Saved ground, driving 9
Run in divisions
5Jun04–4Bel fm 7f Ⓣ:233 :46 1:091 1:212 4↑Alw 59000N3x 95 6 3 1hd 1hd 3nk 1nk Day P L116 19.00 93–07 GulchApprovl116nk ChrstnsOtlw116½ PrsonlToch116nk Vied 3 wide, resolute 10
16Apr04–7Kee fst 1 1/16 :234 :472 1:114 1:434 4↑Alw 60880N3x 86 1 11 11 1hd 21 27½ Sellers S J L117 5.70 85–16 PerfectRide1167½ GulchApproval1172¼ DncetoDestiny112¾ Pace,no match 6
2Apr04–8Kee fst 6½f :214 :444 1:093 1:161 4↑Alw 59200N3x 71 6 1 32 32 1011 1017½ Bailey J D L120 b 19.70 77–13 Strength and Honor1183 Pud1153¼ Saintly Look1161¾ Tired after 1/2 11
28Feb04–9GP fst 1 1/16 :234 :474 1:12 1:44 4↑OC 75k/N3x-N 78 3 1½ 1hd 2hd 43¼ 67 Alvarado R Jr L118 22.30 82–14 BadaBamBadBoom1181½ Jckpot1181 Justifiction1181¼ Vied outside, tired 8
8Feb04–10GP fst 1 1/16 :232 :473 1:12 1:432 4↑OC 75k/N3x-N 87 3 11 11 1hd 31½ 43 Prado E S L118 8.30 89–15 ThLdysGroom118nk BdBmBdBom1181 PrncBnjmn1181¾ Inside, weakened 8
18Jan04–6GP fst 1 1/16 :23 :464 1:112 1:43 4↑OC 75k/N3x-N 81 3 1hd 2hd 42½ 77¾ 615¼ Velasquez C L120 7.90 79–19 SaintLiam1224 TheLadysGroom1182¾ GranCesre1222½ Vied inside, faltered 8

Gunning For

Own: Walsh Mrs. Thomas J

B. g. 4 (Apr)
Sire: Dove Hunt (Danzig) $3,500
Dam: Hopalina (Trempolino)
Br: Denise Walsh & Tom Walsh (Fla)
Tr: Walsh Timothy J(0 0 0 0 .00) 2004:(56 9 .16)

Life 13 5 1 2 $146,495 95 | D.Fst 3 1 1 0 $8,490 49
2004 11 4 0 2 $138,135 95 | Wet(317) 1 0 0 0 $675 50
2003 2 1 1 0 $8,360 39 | Turf(357) 9 4 0 2 $137,330 95
0 0 0 0 $0 – | Dst(0) 0 0 0 0 $0 –

16Oct04–9Bel yl 1½ Ⓣ:472 1:121 2:032 2:294 LawrReal-G3 95 7 712 63¼ 1½ 11½ 1½ Bravo J L119 16.00 72–28 GnnngFor119½ RosngVctry1153½ ScndPrfrmnc1194¾ 4 wide move, gamely 7
8Oct04–6Med fm 1 1/16 Ⓣ:233 :483 1:12 1:421 Paterson60k 89 8 811 85¾ 85½ 66¾ 32¼ Alvarado R Jr L119 6.30 85–15 ForestGrove1191½ Commndtion115¾ GunningFor119½ Off slow,outside bid 8
Run in divisions
6Sep04–8Del fm 1⅛ Ⓣ:482 1:131 1:38 1:494 Stanton55k 88 6 78½ 78 73½ 5¾ 11¼ Alvarado R Jr L117 35.10 88–15 GunningFor1171¼ Commendation119hd Minnmn1192½ Ran past leaders 6w 7
13Aug04–6Mth gd 1 1/16 Ⓣ:233 :48 1:122 1:451 Clm 32000(32-28) 82 5 77½ 77½ 64½ 3½ 1nk Bravo J L116 4.20 73–27 GunningFor116nk MatzohToga116½ TwicetheCat116¾ Split rivals,determind 9
20Jly04–5Cnl fm 1 🅃:254 :50 1:134 1:383 3↑Clm 25000(25-20) 74 1 88 86¾ 85¾ 44½ 31½ Calucag C M L114 15.60 84–17 Grapeshot115¾ Shure119¾ Gunning For114½ 6wd 1/4, rallied 8
27Mar04–10Tam fm 1 Ⓣ:24 :474 1:131 1:38 Alw 16000N1x 72 3 69 68¾ 51¼ 11½ 14¾ Faine C L118 9.30 87–16 GunningFor1184¾ BettrQulity118no PrintrsSon1181¼ Looped 4w, drew off 10
18Mar04–8Tam gd 1 1/16 Ⓣ:243 :504 1:16 1:461 Alw 16000N1x 59 7 88 87½ 86¾ 43 44¾ Faine C L118 22.00 67–25 Indigo Flyer1221¼ Halo for Mary1223 Riddle122½ Passed tiring rivals 8
5Mar04–9Tam fm 1 Ⓣ:23 :472 1:113 1:363 Alw 15500N1x 63 2 810 86¼ 64¼ 43 54¼ Bush W V L118 15.30 90–09 Choice Union1182½ Lycius Two118hd Riddle1221½ Failed to sustain bid 9
24Feb04–8Tam sly 1 1/16 ⊗:234 :484 1:143 1:482 Alw 15500N1x 50 2 2½ 21 31 63½ 410½ Zimmerman R L118 22.60 65–28 SingleFile1182¾ DiamondaDay122¾ ChoiceUnion1187 Bid 2nd turn,flattnd o 10
10Feb04–9Tam fst 6f :214 :45 :574 1:11 Alw 13000N2L 49 7 9 126¾ 1010 87½ 811¾ Zimmerman R L118 b 20.90 83–14 SmileNCrson118nk LittleRedRocket1186 AnnouncofGold122no No factor 12
4Jan04–6Tam fm 1 1/16 Ⓣ:241 :49 1:144 1:464 Alw 15500N1x 46 6 41¼ 45 62½ 66½ 78¾ Castillo O O 118 21.50 60–30 Platinum Priced1181 Jamian1182 Texmckay1182½ Well placed, faded 8

Gygistar
Own: Evans Edward P

Ch. g. 6 (Apr)
Sire: Prospector's Music (Mr. Prospector) $2,000
Dam: Starr County (Ogygian)
Br: Edward P. Evans (Ky)
Tr: Hennig Mark A(0 0 0 0 .00) 2004:(516 72 .14)

Life	23	8	2	4	$842,605	113	D.Fst	22 7 2 4 $722,605 110
2004	12	1	1	3	$295,320	110	Wet(374)	1 1 0 0 $120,000 113
2003	4	1	0	1	$94,100	109	Turf(233)	0 0 0 0 $0 –
	0	0	0	0	$0	–	Dst(0)	0 0 0 0 $0 –

20Nov04–8Pim fst 1 1/16 :233 :473 1:113 1:431 3↑ChasHHadry100k 93 1 22 2½ 2hd 2hd 54 Bailey J D L124 *.70 87–15 IrishColony117 1½ BowmnsBnd124¾ LstIntntion119¾ Pressed 2wd,led,fade 8
31Oct04–7Aqu fst 7f :221 :443 1:082 1:21 3↑SportPgH-G3 103 9 1 42¼ 33 35 35½ Bravo J L120 *2.20 94–13 Mass Media113 3½ *Lion Tamer*118 2 Gygistar120no 3 wide, no response 9
8Oct04–7Med fst 1⅛ :464 1:11 1:354 1:483 3↑MedBC-G2 104 7 42½ 42½ 31 21½ 32 Bravo J L119 4.40 87–15 Balto Star123½ Dynever119 1½ Gygistar119 3¾ 3 wide, outfinished 8
4Sep04–8Sar fst 7f :221 :444 1:09 1:221 3↑ForegoH-G1 106 6 4 48½ 48½ 46 33 Fragoso P L114 9.80 90–19 Midas Eyes117 1¾ Clock Stopper114 1¼ Gygistar114no Bobbled after start 9
7Aug04–9Sar fst 1⅛ :451 1:084 1:344 1:482 3↑WhitneyH-G1 104 6 55 53 66 42¾ 55¾ Bravo J L113 16.50 87–14 *RossinMy*114no PrfctDrift117 2¼ BowmnsBnd114no Inside move, weakened 9
19Jun04–10Suf fst 1⅛ :483 1:122 1:363 1:49 3↑MassH-G2 107 4 62¾ 73¾ 42½ 42¼ 41¾ Bravo J LB113 5.80 96–10 OffIWild113hd FunnyCd117hd ThLdysGroom116 1½ Box in,swung4w top str 9
31May04–9Bel fst 1 :232 :46 1:10 1:352 3↑MtropltH-G1 108 5 64¼ 41½ 3½ 32 44½ Bravo J L115 13.30 79–34 PicoCentral119¾ BowmnsBnd114 2¼ StrongHope119 1½ 4 wide move, faded 9
5May04–8Bel fst 1 :241 :472 1:113 1:354 3↑WschstrH-G3 110 7 41 42 1½ 13 14¼ Bravo J L115 4.00 82–25 Gygistar115 4¼ Saarland114 2¾ *Black Silk*113nk Vigorous hand ride 7
10Apr04–9Aqu fst 7f :213 :432 1:072 1:201 3↑CarterH-G1 107 4 6 69½ 610 36 44 Fragoso P L115 12.30 100–04 *PicoCentral*117 1¼ StrongHope119 2 EyeoftheTiger114¾ Good finish outside 9
6Mar04–11GP fst 7f :22 :441 1:083 1:212 3↑RcSclBCH-G2 102 6 2 64½ 63½ 52¼ 41¼ Bailey J D L117 2.80 94–08 *LionTmer*116¾ CochJimiLee115½ WckyforLove114hd 3 wide, gaining slowly 7
7Feb04–11GP fst 6½f :23 :46 1:093 1:154 3↑DpMnstrH-G3 94 1 6 52¼ 41¾ 44 46 Bailey J D L118 3.50 90–11 Alke112 2½ Cajun Beat123 1¼ Coach Jimi Lee115 2¼ Steadied bkstr, tired 7
3Jan04–10GP fst 6f :221 :444 :563 1:09 3↑MrProspH-G3 101 4 3 2hd 41¼ 43½ 21½ Bailey J D L118 2.30 95–10 Cajun Beat121 1½ Gygistar118¾ Deer Lake115 3 Angled out,finish well 6

Habaneros
Own: Bell John C. Lessee

Ch. g. 6 (Feb)
Sire: Tabasco Cat (Storm Cat) $17,490
Dam: Innocently Astray (Gone West)
Br: Louie Roussel III (Ky)
Tr: Bell T R II(0 0 0 0 .00) 2004:(72 7 .10)

Life	12	4	2	2	$174,400	99	D.Fst	5 2 0 1 $62,400 92
2004	5	3	1	0	$122,800	99	Wet(363)	0 0 0 0 $0 –
2003	2	1	0	0	$30,000	80	Turf(314)	7 2 2 1 $112,000 99
	0	0	0	0	$0	–	Dst(0)	0 0 0 0 $0 –

4Dec04–7Hol fm 1½ Ⓣ :502 1:153 2:04 2:293 3↑HolTrfCp-G1 81 6 86½ 83¾ 85¾ 75¼ 811¼ Flores D R LB126 fb 8.20 67–22 Pellegrino126hd Megahertz123hd License To Run126½ Off step slow,inside 9
23Oct04–9SA fm 1½ Ⓣ :491 1:134 2:023 2:264 3↑CFBurkeH-G3 99 2 11½ 1½ 11½ 12 1¾ Flores D R LB116 fb 14.10 87–13 Habaneros116¾ *Pellegrino*116nk Gallant113no Bit off rail lane,game 8
11Oct04–4SA fm 1⅛ Ⓣ :463 1:10 1:341 1:463 3↑Alw 32000s 93 9 89½ 86¼ 85¾ 33 2¾ Flores D R LB120 fb 5.50 95–05 Sigfreto117¾ *Habaneros*120 1½ Me My Mine120½ 4wd into lane,rallied 9
29Aug04–7Dmr fst 1 1/16 :224 :464 1:111 1:432 3↑Alw 63236n1x 92 9 99 88¾ 64¼ 3nk 1hd Steiner J J LB123 fb 24.50 91–12 Hbneros123hd Lindero116 1½ MusiqueToujours123 3½ 4wd into lane,gamely 12
24Jly04–4Dmr fst 1 1/16 :23 :463 1:111 1:441 3↑Clm 25000(25-22.5) 83 3 77½ 76¾ 54½ 2½ 1nk Steiner J J LB119 fb 26.40 87–13 *Habaneros*119nk With Iris119 1 Desert Boom112 1½ 4wd into lane,gamely 7

Halory Leigh
Own: Crawford Jerry, Gannon, Matt and Gras

Ch. f. 5 (Feb)
Sire: Halory Hunter (Jade Hunter) $2,500
Dam: Graceful Leigh (Clever Trick)
Br: Al Profitt & Larry Demeritte (Ky)
Tr: Romans Dale L(0 0 0 0 .00) 2004:(580 109 .19)

Life	21	7	3	2	$612,872	107	D.Fst	15 6 1 2	$361,442 107
2004	10	3	1	1	$434,634	107	Wet(355)	2 1 1 0	$212,424 99
2003	11	4	2	1	$178,238	100	Turf(192)	4 0 1 0	$39,006 95
	0	0	0	0	$0	–	Dst(0)	0 0 0 0	$0 –

25Nov04-10CD gd 1⅛ :483 1:131 1:384 1:514 3↑ⒻFallCtyH-G2 **99** 3 5³½ 4²½ 3½ 1hd 1²¾ Martin E M Jr L116 *1.20 78– 24 HaloryLeigh116²¾ SusansAngel114³¼ MissFortunte113²¼ 4w,driving,clear 7
7Nov04-10CD fst 1 :223 :453 1:102 1:35 3↑ⒻCDDstafH-G2 **107** 11 11 10⁶½ 9⁴¾ 7³¼ 2² 1⁵ Perret C L115 14.60 95– 13 *Halory Leigh*115⁵ Lady Tak123¾ Susan's Angel115¾ 5-6w,drew off,drvg 12
10Oct04-5Kee fst 7f :222 :452 1:101 1:222 3↑ⒻAlw 59000N$Y **103** 6 9 9⁹¼ 7⁶½ 1½ 1⁴ Perret C L123 4.50 95– 12 *HloryLeigh*123⁴ GoldnMrlin123⁴¼ ThrRunsHtti121¹¾ Angle 5w lane,driving 9
25Sep04-12KD fm 1 Ⓣ:252 :464 1:122 1:364 3↑ⒻKyCpLdsTrf100k **83** 6 7⁶¾ 7⁸½ 9⁷¾ 7⁹½ 7⁷¼ Albarado R J L115 4.80 89– 15 Sand Springs115³¼ *Wildwood Royal*116² Omeya115¾ Not a factor 9
30Aug04-8Sar yl 1 1/16 Ⓣ:24 :47 1:111 1:434 3↑ⒻBlSpaBCH-G3 **87** 3 5³¾ 7¹¹ 9¹¹ 5⁵½ 7⁶½ Blanc B L113 43.50 78– 15 *OcenDrive*119¹¼ PersonlLegnd115¹¾ HighCourt114¹¾ Between rivals, tired 10
31Jly04-7Sar yl 1⅛ Ⓣ:473 1:113 1:363 1:484 3↑ⒻDianaH-G1 **78** 6 6⁹ 7⁹½ 6⁷½ 6¹³ 7¹⁴½ Albarado R J L118 26.25 71– 14 WonderAgin120⁵¾ Riskverse118²¼ *OcenDriv*118²¼ Came wide, no response 7
26Jun04-9CD fm 1⅛ Ⓣ:47 1:103 1:343 1:463 3↑ⒻLcstGrvH-G3 **95** 3 6⁶½ 6⁹ 6⁵½ 5³¾ 2¹¼ McKee J L111 29.10 99– 07 Shaconage116¹¼ HloryLeigh111no SndSprings119¹¾ Lug in 1/8p,all out,6w 6
22May04-9CD fst 6f :212 :44 :554 1:084 3↑ⒻWinColorsH108k **89** 4 7 6⁴¾ 7¹⁰ 6¹⁰ 5⁵¾ Day P L113 11.70 91– 11 Lady Tak122¾ *Fut Me In*117¹¼ *Ebony Breeze*116¹ Slow start,5w late 7
7Mar04-11GP fst 6½f :214 :441 1:084 1:152 3↑ⒻHrrcnBrtiH100k **72** 7 8 8⁶½ 8⁷ 8¹⁰ 9⁹½ Perret C L114 4.40 88– 08 House Party117nk Mooji Moo115³½ Zawzooth113hd Steadied turn 10
8Feb04-11GP fst 7f :222 :444 1:084 1:212 3↑ⒻShrlJnsH-G3 **90** 6 5 7⁶ 7⁶¼ 4⁶½ 3⁸ Perret C L114 13.20 87– 16 *Randaroo*118⁷¼ Harmony Lodge121¾ Halory Leigh114²½ 3 wide, gained 3rd 8

Hard Buck (Brz)
Own: Team Victory

Dk. b or b. h. 6 (Nov)
Sire: Spend a Buck (Buckaroo)
Dam: Social Secret (Secreto)
Br: Haras Old Friends (Brz)
Tr: McPeek Kenneth G(0 0 0 0 .00) 2004:(413 74 .18)

Life	19	9	5	0	$1,073,674	104	D.Fst	1 0 0 0	$0 –
2004	6	1	3	0	$840,526	104	Wet(304)	1 0 0 0	$6,000 76
2003	5	3	1	0	$208,238	104	Turf(283)	17 9 5 0	$1,067,674 104
	0	0	0	0	$0	–	Dst(0)	0 0 0 0	$0 –

24Jly04 Ascot (GB) gf 1½ Ⓣ RH 2:33 3↑ King George VI & Queen Eliz S-G1 Stk 1374000 2³ Stevens G L 133 33.00 Doyen133³ Hard Buck133hd *Sulamani*133¹¾ 11
Timeform rating: 127 *Rank in 2nd,brief lead 2f out,saved 2nd.Warrsan9th*
3Jly04-10Mth fm 1⅜ Ⓣ:483 1:14 1:372 2:131 3↑UnitdNtn-G1 **100** 6 9³½ 8³¾ 8³ 7⁶ 5⁴½ Blanc B L122 6.30 92– 09 RequestforProle118½ MrOBrin120¾ NothingtoLos118¹ Even finish off rail 11
12Jun04-10CD yl 1 1/16 Ⓣ:244 :502 1:153 1:454 3↑OpningVrsH110k **95** 2 3¹½ 3¹½ 4¹ 4¹¾ 2¹¼ Blanc B L123 *1.10 74– 25 Senor Swinger117¹¼ Hard Buck123¹¼ Majestic Thief115² Lack room 1/2p 7
27Mar04 Nad Al Sheba (UAE) gf *1½ Ⓣ LH 2:31 4↑ The Palm Dubai Sheema Classic-G1 Stk 2000000 2½ Velazquez J R 123 – Polish Summer123½ Hard Buck123¾ *Scott's View*123¾ 13
Timeform rating: 119 *Trckd ldr,led 1f to 100y out,gamely.Fair Mix 6th*
22Feb04-11GP fm 1⅜ Ⓣ:484 1:361 2:112 3↑GPBCH-G1 **104** 6 4³ 4³½ 4³½ 4¹¾ 1hd Prado E S L117 11.50 101– 10 Hard Buck117hd Balto Star122½ Kicken Kris118¹ 3 wide, just up 8
31Jan04-8GP sly 1 1/16 ⊗:233 :471 1:114 1:444 3↑CanTurfH-G3 **76** 2 1hd 2½ 3²½ 4⁶½ 4¹⁴ Prado E S L119 3.70 71– 29 *NwfoundInd*115nk MillnniumDrgon118⁸½ EvrythingtoGin113⁵¼ Inside, tired 6

Harmony Lodge
Own: Melnyk Eugene and Laura

Ch. m. 7 (Mar)
Sire: Hennessy (Storm Cat) $35,000
Dam: Win Crafty Lady (Crafty Prospector)
Br: Sabine Stables (Ky)
Tr: Pletcher Todd A(0 0 0 0 .00) 2004:(948 240 .25)

Life	24	10	4	5	$851,120	107	D.Fst	19	8	4	4	$762,020	107
2004	6	1	3	1	$176,000	106	Wet(378)	4	2	0	1	$88,600	105
2003	8	5	1	2	$516,300	107	Turf(281)	1	0	0	0	$500	63
	0	0	0	0	$0	–	Dst(0)	0	0	0	0	$0	–

29Aug04–9Sar gd 7f :221 :442 1:0741:21 3↑ⒻBalrinaH-G1 **102** 4 3 21½ 22½ 22½ 3nk Migliore R 119 6.00 99–05 *LadyTak*119hd MyTrustyCat116hd HrmonyLodge1191 Game finish outside 7
10Jly04–11Crc fst 6f :212 :44 :5641:104 3↑ⒻPrcsRnyH-G2 **83** 1 6 31½ 45½ 44½ 69¼ Bailey J D L119 6.90 86–09 Ema Bovary1192 Bear Fan1223¾ *Lady Tak*1192 Inside, faltered 6
9May04–8Bel fst 6f :222 :444 :5621:084 3↑ⒻGnunRskH-G2 **94** 3 2 2½ 2½ 25 25 Migliore R L120 *1.25 90–11 *Bear Fan*1175 Harmony Lodge1203 Kitty Knight1142¼ 3 wide, second best 5
7Apr04–8Kee fst 7f :22 :441 1:0931:232 4↑ⒻMadison175k **96** 2 1 1hd 2½ 2½ 22¼ Migliore R L123 2.20 88–14 Ema Bovary1202¼ Harmony Lodge123¾ Yell1162½ Ck 1/16p,gamely 6
8Feb04–11GP fst 7f :222 :444 1:0841:212 3↑ⒻShrlJnsH-G3 **92** 8 1 2hd 2½ 22½ 27¼ Migliore R L121 *1.20 88–16 *Randaroo*1187¼ Harmony Lodge121¾ Halory Leigh1142½ 3 wide, no match 8
11Jan04–10GP fst 6f :214 :444 :57 1:093 3↑Ⓕ1stLadyH-G3 **106** 3 5 31½ 3½ 13½ 11¾ Migliore R L119 *1.60 94–12 HrmonyLodge1191¾ HousePrty118½ MyoOntheSid1152 3 wide, drew clear 9

He Loves Me
Own: Buckingham Farm

B. f. 4 (Mar)
Sire: Not For Love (Mr. Prospector) $25,000
Dam: Palliser Bay (Frosty the Snowman)
Br: Buckingham Farm (Md)
Tr: Small Richard W(0 0 0 0 .00) 2004:(181 39 .22)

Life	14	7	1	2	$343,250	95	D.Fst	10	5	1	2	$301,250	95
2004	10	5	0	1	$295,000	95	Wet(425)	2	1	0	0	$24,000	74
2003	4	2	1	1	$48,250	82	Turf(316)	2	1	0	0	$18,000	74
	0	0	0	0	$0	–	Dst(0)	0	0	0	0	$0	–

20Nov04–9Pim fst 1⅛ :4741:114 1:3621:491 ⒻAArundel-G3 **89** 8 108 107¼ 97¾ 44 43¼ Hamilton S D L122 *1.60 95–15 Essence115nk *Rare Gift*1152½ Family Business115½ Swung 6wd 1/4 11
2Oct04–9Pha fst 1 1/16 :234 :473 1:1111:413 ⒻCotillnH-G2 **90** 7 43½ 43½ 42 44 47½ Santana J Z L117 5.70 99–13 *Ashado*1242¾ Ender's Sister1173½ My Lordship1151¼ Came 4 wide, no rally 7
11Sep04–8Bel fst 1⅛ :48 1:122 1:3621:481 ⒻGazelle-G1 **92** 4 64 63 31 32½ 32¾ Santana J Z L117 7.40 87–15 Stellar Jayne1221 *Daydreaming*1151¾ He Loves Me117no 4 wide run, gamely 6
31Jly04–8Pim fst 1⅛ :49 1:13 1:38 1:51 ⒻⓈTwixt100k **93** 8 65 53½ 3½ 13 11¾ Santana J Z L122 *.40 89–26 He Loves Me1221¾ *Richetta*1221 *Pour It On*1223 5-3w,bid in hand,drvng 9
2Jly04–9PrM fst 1 1/16 :23 :463 1:1121:424 ⒻIowaOaks-G3 **95** 5 58 58 21 2½ 1¾ Santana J Z LB118 3.10 90–19 *HeLovesMe*118¾ ProspectivSint1156¼ HomCourt1151¼ Quick move, driving 8
31May04–8Pim fst 1 1/16 ⊗ :24 :482 1:1231:44 ⒻⓈPearlNcklc75k **93** 4 55½ 52¼ 21 1½ 11½ Santana J Z L119 *.40 87–24 *HeLovesMe*1191½ HiFiveRvn1151¼ PourItOn12210¼ When ready 4w,driving 8
8May04–9Pim fm 1 1/16 Ⓣ :23 :472 1:12 1:431 ⒻHilltop50k **74** 3 1113 98 98¾ 710 66¾ Santana J Z L122 5.10 79–14 WesternRansom115¾ ArtFan1153¾ StrofAnziyn1151½ No factor, very wide 11
24Apr04–8Pim fst 1 1/16 :25 :491 1:1321:443 ⒻⓈCaesrsWish72k **82** 3 21½ 21 2hd 1hd 1¾ Santana J Z L122 2.20 84–24 He Loves Me122¾ Plata115¾ Dance Fee1152¼ Prompted 2w,duel,drvng 4
6Mar04–8Lrl gd 1 1/16 :243 :482 1:13 1:471 ⒻWideContry40k **74** 4 66½ 67 45½ 23½ 1¾ Santana J Z L115 4.30 76–24 *He Loves Me*115¾ Via Sacra115nk *PawynePrincess*1153½ 3-4wd turns, driving 8
25Jan04–9FG gd 1 :231 :463 1:1211:384 ⒻTiffnyLass100k **73** 1111111111 106¾ 86 68 Melancon L L114 20.30 81–11 Lotta Kim116¾ Josie G.1185¼ Love Power116½ Improved position 13

Higher World
Own: Simeone Sal and Colleen

Gr/ro. f. 3 (Jan) KEESEP03 $22,000
Sire: Peaks and Valleys (Mt. Livermore) $10,000
Dam: Sarah's World (Holy Bull)
Br: Thomas J Vanderhyde (Ky)
Tr: Casse Mark E(0 0 0 0 .00) 2004:(323 48 .15)

Life	4	2	1	0	$213,210	79	D.Fst	4	2	1	0	$213,210	79
2004	4	2	1	0	$213,210	79	Wet(362)	0	0	0	0	$0	–
2003	0	M	0	0	$0	–	Turf(207)	0	0	0	0	$0	–
	0	0	0	0	$0	–	Dst(0)	0	0	0	0	$0	–

30Oct04–3LS fst $1\frac{1}{16}$:22^4 :46^2 1:10^3 1:41^3 ⒻBCJuvFil-G1 **65** 2 $1\frac{1}{2}$ 1^{hd} 4^1 11^{10} 12^{21} Husbands P L119 60.80 73–02 SweetCatomine119$3\frac{3}{4}$ Balletto119$1\frac{1}{4}$ *RunwyModel*119$\frac{3}{4}$ Drifted out 1st turn 12
30ct04–9WO fst $1\frac{1}{16}$:24^2 :49^2 1:14^2 1:47^4 ⒻMazarnBC-G2 **79** 6 1^1 $1^{1\frac{1}{2}}$ 1^1 $1^{\frac{1}{2}}$ 1^{nk} Husbands P L117 *1.50 72–28 HighrWorld117^{nk} Didychtmndhow115$7\frac{1}{2}$ DnchllDlits116$2\frac{1}{2}$ Drifted out,held 9
14Aug04–6WO fst 7f :23 :46^2 1:11^4 1:24^4 ⒻMd Sp Wt 57k **66** 4 5 1^{hd} 1^1 1^5 $18\frac{3}{4}$ Husbands P L120 *1.05 83–14 *Higher World*120$8\frac{3}{4}$ Silver Impulse110$1\frac{1}{2}$ Vincita116$\frac{3}{4}$ Widened,easily 8
18Jly04–6WO fst 6f :22^3 :46^3 :59^2 1:12 ⒻMd Sp Wt 58k **67** 5 4 3^1 $2^{1\frac{1}{2}}$ $2^{\frac{1}{2}}$ 2^1 Husbands P L120 2.25 79–17 HghButtonShos120^1 *HghrWorld*120$5\frac{3}{4}$ SlvrImpls110^1 Bid top stretch,failed 6

Hollywood Story
Own: Krikorian George

Dk. b or b. f. 4 (Mar) FTKJUL02 $130,000
Sire: Wild Rush (Wild Again) $10,000
Dam: Wife for Life (Dynaformer)
Br: Vinery (Ky)
Tr: Shirreffs John A(0 0 0 0 .00) 2004:(182 23 .13)

Life	12	2	3	3	$643,605	97	D.Fst	9	2	3	2	$536,445	97
2004	7	1	1	2	$287,105	97	Wet(367)	2	0	0	0	$17,160	93
2003	5	1	2	1	$356,500	95	Turf(255)	1	0	0	1	$90,000	93
	0	0	0	0	$0	–	Dst(0)	0	0	0	0	$0	–

12Dec04–8Hol fst $1\frac{1}{16}$:23^3 :47 1:11 1:41 3↑ⒻBayakoaH-G2 **97** 7 $5^{3\frac{1}{2}}$ $5^{3\frac{1}{2}}$ 4^3 $3^{\frac{1}{2}}$ 1^1 Espinoza V LB115 b 5.10 96–09 HollywoodStory115^1 RoyllyChsn116^2 APAdvntr117$\frac{1}{2}$ 4wd into lane,gamely 7
30Oct04–2LS gd $1\frac{1}{8}$:46^3 1:10^2 1:35^2 1:48^1 3↑ⒻBCDistaf-G1 **85** 6 $7^{3\frac{1}{4}}$ $9^{4\frac{1}{4}}$ $11^{7\frac{3}{4}}$ 11^{13} $10^{10\frac{1}{2}}$ Baze T C L119 b 32.40 97–02 Ashado119$1\frac{1}{4}$ StormFlagFlying123^{nk} StellrJyne119$1\frac{1}{2}$ Tight 7/8,4w 1st turn 11
3Jly04–6Hol fm 1¼ Ⓣ :49 1:14 1:38^1 2:01^2 ⒻAmrcnOks-G1 **93** 4 $5^{3\frac{1}{2}}$ $5^{3\frac{1}{2}}$ $5^{3\frac{1}{2}}$ 6^7 3^3 Sorenson D LB121 b 16.10 82–13 TickerTpe121^1 DnceinthMood121^2 HollywoodStory121$\frac{1}{2}$ Pulled,waited 1/4 13
12Jun04–4Hol fst $1\frac{1}{16}$:23 :46 1:10 1:41^2 ⒻHolBCOak-G2 **93** 4 5^4 4^2 $5^{2\frac{1}{2}}$ 3^3 3^6 Smith M E LB119 b 1.70 88–08 HousofFortune119^3 ElusivDiv115^3 HollywoodStory119^8 3wd,drifted in late 5
30Apr04–10CD my $1\frac{1}{8}$:46 1:09^4 1:36^3 1:50^4 ⒻKyOaks-G1 **93** 2 $7^{7\frac{1}{4}}$ 8^{11} $7^{8\frac{1}{4}}$ 5^7 $5^{5\frac{3}{4}}$ Espinoza V L121 b 25.30 77–17 Ashado121$1\frac{1}{4}$ *Island Sand*121$1\frac{3}{4}$ MadcapEscapade121$1\frac{1}{4}$ Bmp start,ck,5w bid 11
13Mar04–8SA fst $1\frac{1}{16}$:22^4 :46^2 1:10^4 1:42^4 ⒻSAOaks-G1 **90** 4 5^4 $5^{3\frac{1}{2}}$ $3^{1\frac{1}{2}}$ 3^3 $4^{3\frac{1}{2}}$ Espinoza V LB117 b 7.50 87–08 SilentSighs117$1\frac{1}{2}$ Hlfbridled117$1\frac{1}{2}$ APAdvntur117$\frac{1}{2}$ 3wd 2nd turn,edged 3rd 7
15Feb04–8SA fst 1 :22^3 :46 1:10^2 1:36^2 ⒻLsVrgnes-G1 **97** 5 $4^{4\frac{1}{2}}$ $4^{3\frac{1}{2}}$ 5^4 $3^{1\frac{1}{2}}$ $2^{\frac{1}{2}}$ Espinoza V LB120 b 2.30 88–18 APAdvntur118$\frac{1}{2}$ HollywoodStory120$2\frac{1}{2}$ *FrindlyMichll*116^1 3wd bid,willingly 8

Hosco
Own: Rodriguez Lorraine and Rod

Dk. b or b. c. 4 (Mar) WASAUG02 $30,000
Sire: Honour and Glory (Relaunch) $15,000
Dam: Cucina Cucina (Carson City)
Br: Northwest Farms (Ky)
Tr: O'Neill Doug(0 0 0 0 .00) 2004:(938 170 .18)

Life	9	3	1	0	$148,186	100	**D.Fst**	9	3	1	0	$148,186	100
2004	7	1	1	0	$101,386	98	**Wet(381)**	0	0	0	0	$0	–
2003	2	2	0	0	$46,800	100	**Turf(254)**	0	0	0	0	$0	–
	0	0	0	0	$0	–	**Dst(0)**	0	0	0	0	$0	–

7Nov04–6Hol fst 6½f :214 :442 1:083 1:143 3↑OC 100k/n3x -N **82** 6 1 11 2hd 2hd 55¾ Pedroza M A **LB**119 b 7.90 94– 06 Saint Afleet117hd My Master1211 Hasty Kris119no Speed,dueled,wkened 7

8Oct04–7Kee fst 6f :21 :434 :56 1:083 3↑PhoenxBC-G3 **72** 2 4 1hd 21 109½ 1115½ Nakatani C S L120 fb 13.70 82– 08 Champali122¾ Gold Storm118nk Clock Stopper118nk Vied for 1/2, tired 11

28Aug04–10Sar fst 7f :22 :443 1:082 1:204 KngsBshp-G1 **61** 4 5 2hd 2½ 813 821¼ Velasquez C L121 b 37.00 79– 04 Pomeroy1211½ Weigelia1211 Ice Wynnd Fire1174¼ Carried out 1/4 pole 8

28Mar04–8Sun fst 1 1/16 :224 :46 1:093 1:431 WinStarDby500k **68** 9 12 1½ 2hd 108¼ 1014¼ Gonzalez R M L122 b 7.50 80– 11 HiTeckMan122½ Consecrate1221½ RockyGulch122½ Rail, snug hold, empty 10

6Mar04–7SA fst 1 :223 :453 1:10 1:36 SnRafael-G2 **91** 6 1½ 2hd 2½ 21½ 56¾ Baze T C **LB**118 b 20.90 84– 11 Imperialism118nk Lion Heart1214½ Consecrate1151 Dueled, weakened 10

7Feb04–3SA fst 7f :222 :443 1:091 1:221 SnVicnte-G2 **98** 6 1 1½ 11 11 21¼ Baze T C **LB**120 b *1.10 93– 11 *Imperialism*1161¼ Hosco120hd Consecrate1161 Angled in,held 2nd 6

11Jan04–7SA fst 6f :21 :434 :56 1:091 SMiguel-G3 **94** 1 3 11 1½ 11½ 11 Baze T C **LB**118 b 4.00 92– 08 Hosco1181 Roi Charmant1173 Gethsemani116hd Bit off rail,held game 7

Host (Chi)
Own: Melnyk Eugene and Laura

Ch. c. 5 (Aug)
Sire: Hussonet (Mr. Prospector) $19,367
Dam: Colonna Traiana*Chi (Roy)
Br: Haras De Pirque (Chi)
Tr: Pletcher Todd A(0 0 0 0 .00) 2004:(948 240 .25)

Life	12	7	2	3	$255,119	103	**D.Fst**	0	0	0	0	$0	–
2004	6	2	2	2	$204,480	103	**Wet(364*)**	2	1	0	1	$36,945	95
2003	6	5	0	1	$50,639	–	**Turf(327)**	10	6	2	2	$218,174	103
	0	0	0	0	$0	–	**Dst(0)**	0	0	0	0	$0	–

4Dec04–11Crc fm 1⅛ Ⓣ :47 1:10 1:334 1:453 3↑TropTrfH-G3 **103** 7 64½ 65½ 64½ 33 1nk Velazquez J R L118 *1.70 101– 03 Host118nk Silver Tree118½ Demeteor1141 Drftd 1st trn,long drv 12

30Oct04–5Aqu fm 1⅛ Ⓣ :492 1:134 1:38 1:494 3↑KnkrbkrH-G2 **103** 6 74¾ 78¼ 87 63¼ 11½ Decarlo C P L115 4.00 91– 07 *Host*1151½ Evening Attire114hd Sailaway113½ Fast finish outside 9

15Oct04–8Med gd 1 1/16 Ⓣ :231 :48 1:121 1:422 3↑ClfHngfH-G3 **96** 1 64 64½ 73½ 71½ 31¼ Velazquez J R L117 *1.80 85– 14 Dr. Kashnikow116½ Tam's Terms116¾ *Host*117no Boxed turn,fin well 8

3Apr04–8Aqu my 1⅛ :48 1:12 1:364 1:492 3↑ExlsrBCH-G3 **95** 5 11½ 1½ 1hd 34½ 38½ Luzzi M J L114 4.70 83– 08 Funny Cide120½ Evening Attire1198 Host114nk Set pace, tired 5

23Feb04–8GP fm *1⅛ Ⓣ :482 1:122 1:383 1:504 4↑Alw 46000c **92** 5 3nk 2hd 1hd 1hd 22 Velazquez J R L118 *.60 86– 19 Full Flow1162 Host118nk First Lieutenant116hd Rail, dueled, held 2nd 8

5Feb04–8GP fm *1 Ⓣ :243 :494 1:153 1:404 4↑Alw 46000c **103** 4 41¾ 21 1½ 1hd 21 Velazquez J R L120 1.90 68– 42 DelMarShow1161 Host1204¼ WithAnticipation1164½ Outfinished, 2nd best 7

Hour of Justice
Own: Stronach Stables

B. m. 5 (Apr)
Sire: Lit de Justice (El Gran Senor) $6,000
Dam: Dark Hours (Dynaformer)
Br: Adena Springs (Ky)
Tr: Keogh Michael(0 0 0 0 .00) 2004:(103 14 .14)

Life	11	7	2	2	$484,608	100	D.Fst 4 3 1 0 $144,780 94
2004	5	3	0	2	$243,953	100	Wet(340) 0 0 0 0 $0 –
2003	4	2	2	0	$166,195	89	Turf(343) 7 4 1 2 $339,828 100
	0	0	0	0	$0	–	Dst(0) 0 0 0 0 $0 –

24Oct04–3WO gd 6f Ⓣ :223 :444 :562 1:091 3↑NearctcH-G2 100 7 5 42 2 2½ 2 2½ 3½ Kabel T K L116 *1.25 91–08 ITheeWd114nk *ChrissBdBoy*118nk HourofJustic116hd Stalked,gaining late 10
25Sep04–9Bel fm 1 Ⓣ :241 :473 1:112 1:343 3↑ⒻNblDmslH-G3 100 4 1hd 2hd 3nk 2hd 32 Kabel T K L116 2.75 85–16 OcenDrive120 1¼ HighCourt115¾ HourofJustice1162 Dug in stubbornly rail 9
28Aug04–10WO gd 1 1/16 Ⓣ :24 :464 1:10 1:40 3↑ⒻAlw 83700NC 100 7 31 3 2½ 2 2½ 13 1 2¼ Kabel T K L116 *1.65 98–02 Hour of Justice116 2¼ *Classic Stamp*118 2¼ FirstQuarter116¾ Stalked,driving 8
2Aug04–8WO fm 6f Ⓣ :223 :452 :562 1:074 3↑ⒻRylNrthH-G3 99 4 1 2hd 2hd 1 3½ 1 3½ Kabel T K L118 *.80 99–01 *HourofJustic*118 3½ WithPtinc118 1¾ BoozinSusn120 1¼ Dueled btwn,driving 9
11Jly04–4WO fm 6f Ⓣ :222 :452 :57 1:084 3↑ⒻAlw 78500NC 95 3 1 2½ 1½ 11 1¾ Kabel T K L116 *1.75 94–09 *HourofJustice*116¾ Heyahohowdy111 3¼ MilleFeville116¾ Clear 1/8 pole,held 8

House of Fortune
Own: Arnold Zetcher LLC

Dk. b or b. f. 4 (Mar) BARMAR03 $125,000
Sire: Free House (Smokester) $15,000
Dam: So Fortunate (Garthorn)
Br: John Treasure (Cal)
Tr: McAnally Ronald L(0 0 0 0 .00) 2004:(249 26 .10)

Life	12	6	2	1	$560,819	104	D.Fst 11 6 2 1 $560,819 104
2004	7	3	2	0	$364,875	104	Wet(316) 1 0 0 0 $0 83
2003	5	3	0	1	$195,944	91	Turf(285) 0 0 0 0 $0 –
	0	0	0	0	$0	–	Dst(0) 0 0 0 0 $0 –

10Oct04–8Kee fst 1⅛ :464 1:113 1:37 1:493 3↑ⒻSpinster-G1 80 7 54 6 2¾ 3 1½ 7 7¼ 717 Stevens G L L120 4.20 76–12 Azeri1233 Tamweel123½ Mayo On the Side123 3¾ 5w trip,tired 7
8Aug04–8Dmr fst 1 1/16 :222 :46 1:103 1:424 3↑ⒻCLHrschH-G2 96 7 32 3 2½ 32 1hd 2 3¼ Baze T C LB113 2.80 91–06 MissLoren114 3¼ HousofFortun1131 RoyllyChosn1161 3wd bid,led,held 2nd 8
12Jun04–4Hol fst 1 1/16 :23 :46 1:10 1:412 ⒻHolBCOak-G2 104 3 11 1½ 1½ 1 1½ 13 Solis A LB119 *1.20 94–08 HosofFortn1193 ElsvDv1153 HollywoodStory1198 Rail,headed,ridden out 5
30Apr04–10CD my 1⅛ :46 1:094 1:363 1:504 ⒻKyOaks-G1 83 4 6 5¼ 58 36 810 8 11½ Sellers S J L121 8.30 71–17 Ashado121 1¼ *IslandSand*121 1¾ MadcapEscapade121 1¼ Inside far turn,tired 11
9Apr04–10OP fst 1 1/16 :231 :463 1:11 1:423 ⒻFantasy-G2 99 1 5 2½ 42 43 1½ 1 1¾ Solis A L121 *.70 97–11 HousofFortun121 1¾ IslndSnd1214 StllrJyn121 2¼ Asked when ready,drvng 11
6Mar04–3GG fst 1 1/16 :231 :464 1:11 1:413 ⒻCalOaks77k 99 3 21 2½ 13 110 117 Warren R J Jr LB121 *.20 95–13 *HouseofFortune*12117 *ChurchEditor*1162 SecretCorsg116 2½ Drew off at will 4
19Jan04–5SA fst 7f :22 :441 1:082 1:21 ⒻSntaYnez-G2 98 7 2 21 4 1½ 32 24 Solis A LB121 4.30 96–07 *YerlyReport*1144 *HouseofFortune*121 4½ *PptoKinzi*1153 Stalked 3wd,2nd best 8

Humaita (Ger)

Own: Jacobs Andreas

Ch. f. 5 (Feb)
Sire: Surumu*Ger (Literat)
Dam: Happy Gini (Ginistrelli)
Br: Stiftung Gestut Fahrhof (Ger)
Tr: Motion H. G(0 0 0 0 .00) 2004:(424 81 .19)

Life	13	5	3	1	$300,210	101	D.Fst	0	0	0	0	$0	–
2004	9	4	2	0	$281,440	101	Wet(303*)	0	0	0	0	$0	–
2003	4	1	1	1	$18,770	–	Turf(356)	13	5	3	1	$300,210	101
	0	0	0	0	$0	–	Dst(0)	0	0	0	0	$0	–

Date/Race	Cond	Dist	Fractions	Race	Fig	PP	St	1C	2C	Str	Fin	Jockey	Wt	Odds	Speed	Top Finishers	Comment	Fld
18Dec04–9Crc	fm	1½	Ⓣ :503 1:144 2:031 2:27	3↑ⒻLaPvyteH-G2	**97**	8	51¼	62¾	41¾	21½	2hd	Velasquez C	L119	*2.50	89– 10	Arvada117hd Humaita1191½ Honey Ryder113¾	Sustainbid,just missed	11
24Oct04–8Kee	sf	1½	Ⓣ :51 1:17 2:083 2:331	3↑ⒻDowager150k	**101**	2	57	54	41½	1hd	1no	Albarado R J	L122	*1.60	79– 21	Humaita122no *Aud*1208 Literacy1201¼	5-6w,gamely,driving	7
2Oct04–7Bel	yl	1¼	🅃 :522 1:174 1:412 2:043	3↑ⒻFlwrBlIv-G1	**98**	1	31	31	31½	31	72	Stevens G L	L118	26.00	69– 25	Riskvers118¾ *Commrcnt*118hd MoscowBurning120nk	Weakened on rail late	8
5Sep04–7Sar	fm	1⅜	🅃 :501 1:16 1:401 2:151	3↑ⒻGlenFlsH-G3	**94**	9	42	41½	41½	3½	1½	Velasquez C	L114	5.70	93– 06	Humit114½ WhereWeLftOff1161¼ Svdbythlight1152	Game outside, prevail	9
Run in divisions																		
5Jly04–9Bel	sf	1¼	🅃 :50 1:15 1:402 2:053	3↑ⒻNewYorkH-G2	**85**	6	65	67¾	54½	58	49¾	Migliore R	L115	24.25	56– 34	*Wonder Again*1153¼ *StayForever*115no SpiceIsland1186½	Inside, no response	7
12May04–8Bel	gd	1¼	🅃 :511 1:161 1:402 2:042	4↑ⒻⓇSabin60k	**96**	5	21	21	2hd	1½	1½	Santos J A	L116	14.30	72– 28	Humaita116½ Noisette123½ Primetimevlentine1161½	With pace, resolutely	7
20Mar04–4GP	fm	1⅜	Ⓣ :493 1:154 1:403 2:16	4↑ⒻAlw 34000N1x	**83**	4	56½	53¾	43	21	1nk	Santos J A	L117	*.90	78– 14	*Humaita*117nk *Bitterroot River*1171 Candy Verse117½	3 wide, driving	9
29Feb04–11GP	fm	*1⅛	Ⓣ :52 1:162 1:411 1:532	4↑ⒻAlw 34000N1x	**82**	1	52½	43	33	33	22	Velasquez C	L117	2.10	73– 25	Coherent1172 *Humaita*1173 *Krasnaya*1172¼	Off slowly, 2nd best	10
7Feb04–5GP	yl	*1½	Ⓣ :52 1:182 2:141 2:412	4↑ⒻAlw 34000N1x	**79**	4	1016	1010	86¼	52¼	42¼	Velasquez C	L117	3.00	33– 65	TwoShrkyBtty117½ BttrrootRvr1171¼ Morlun117½	Bumped, steadied early	10

I Thee Wed

Own: Pin Oak Stable LLC

Ch. g. 5 (Feb)
Sire: Affirmed (Exclusive Native) $30,000
Dam: With This Ring (Green Dancer)
Br: Pin Oak Stud, LLC (Ky)
Tr: Bell David R(0 0 0 0 .00) 2004:(217 36 .17)

Life	15	5	3	4	$405,752	101	D.Fst	5	2	0	2	$101,187	96
2004	8	4	0	2	$314,337	101	Wet(290)	1	1	0	0	$36,960	94
2003	7	1	3	2	$91,415	88	Turf(336)	9	2	3	2	$267,605	101
	0	0	0	0	$0	–	Dst(0)	0	0	0	0	$0	–

Date/Race	Cond	Dist	Fractions	Race	Fig	PP	St	1C	2C	Str	Fin	Jockey	Wt	Odds	Speed	Top Finishers	Comment	Fld
24Oct04–3WO	gd	6f	Ⓣ :223 :444 :562 1:091	3↑NearctcH-G2	**101**	4	6	76¼	75½	44	1nk	McAleney J S	L114 b	26.70	92– 08	ITheeWed114nk *Chris'sBadBoy*118nk HourofJustice116hd	3w,rallied,just up	10
10Oct04–9WO	fm	7f	Ⓣ :214 :443 1:082 1:204	3↑OC 80k/N3x-N	**98**	9	8	96½	54½	2hd	1nk	McAleney J S	L120 b	8.50	98– 02	*I Thee Wed*120nk Sky Hunter1161½ Dumaani Star1201½	5wd,prevailed,drvg	11
4Sep04–9WO	fm	1	Ⓣ :224 :444 1:082 1:324	3↑OC 80k/N3x-N	**87**	10	64½	85¼	53¼	22½	63¼	McAleney J S	L118 b	5.00	96– 02	FrnchLiutnnt120¾ AsExpctd118¾ PJsPuliBoy118nk	Came in,flattened out	10
2Aug04–6WO	fst	6f	:222 :452 :573 1:101	3↑OC 80k/N3x-N	**89**	5	3	2½	3nk	31	32¼	McAleney J S	L120 b	*1.50	87– 20	Dillinger1152 Choreography120nk I Thee Wed1202½	Forced issue 4-wide	7
11Jly04–8WO	fst	6½f	:214 :441 1:09 1:153	3↑BldVenturH141k	**96**	8	2	63¼	64½	54¼	32½	McAleney J S	L115 b	9.15	97– 11	*I'm the Tiger*1161½ Twisted Wit1161 I Thee Wed1151¼	Determinedly 3-wide	10
12Jun04–5WO	fm	1	Ⓣ :223 :451 1:091 1:332	3↑OC 80k/N3x-N	**89**	4	3nk	21	32	11	41¼	McAleney J S	L120 b	*2.05	95– 06	AwesomeAction120nk SophisPrinc1201 SirBlitz120no	Checked rail,bid led	11
14May04–9WO	fst	7f	:22 :441 1:084 1:222	3↑Alw 65600N2x	**93**	6	4	42½	44½	1hd	12½	McAleney J S	L122 b	*2.90	95– 10	ITheeWed1222½ *TheKingNRob*117nk TobeSuave119¾	Closed 4-wide,driving	9
25Apr04–8WO	my	7f	:224 :461 1:11 1:233	3↑Alw 61600N1x	**94**	10	1	32½	2hd	13½	15¼	McAleney J S	L120 b	*2.55	89– 15	*IThWd*1205¼ TrcysTonkToy1202½ SltyLngfuhn117nk	Swept to lead,rdn out	10

Icy Atlantic

Own: Appleton Arthur I

B. c. 4 (Mar) OBSMAR03 $80,000
Sire: Stormy Atlantic (Storm Cat) $15,000
Dam: Frosty Promise (Frosty the Snowman)
Br: Arthur I. Appleton (Fla)
Tr: Pletcher Todd A(0 0 0 0 .00) 2004:(948 240 .25)

Life	11	3	3	1	$219,420	94	D.Fst	4 1 1 0	$36,300 71
2004	9	3	3	1	$216,720	94	Wet(367)	0 0 0 0	$0 –
2003	2	M	0	0	$2,700	65	Turf(324)	7 2 2 1	$183,120 94
	0	0	0	0	$0	–	Dst(0)	0 0 0 0	$0 –

23Oct04-10Crc gd 1⅛ Ⓣ :49 1:141 1:384 1:511 CrcDerby-G3 85 5 42 32 31 22 75½ Bailey J D L118 *2.30 67-28 Eddngton114hd BobsProudMomnt1161 [D]Cps1162½ Bumped, steadied late 12
Placed 6th through disqualification
26Sep04-9Bel fm 1⅛ [T] :48 1:113 1:34 1:452 JamaicaH-G2 91 4 11½ 11½ 1½ 24½ 36½ Velazquez J R L120 7.10 96-04 ArtiSchillr1235¼ RousingVictory1131¼ IcyAtlntc120hd Set pace, weakened 6
9Aug04-8Sar fm 1⅛ [T] :471 1:103 1:353 1:473 HalOFmeH-G2 82 3 2½ 1½ 1½ 32 59½ Velazquez J R L122 4.30 89-09 *ArtieSchiller*1224¼ Mustanfr122no GoodRewrd1151½ Vied inside, weakened 8
18Jly04-8Bel fm 1¼ [T] :484 1:123 1:344 2:01 Lexingtn-G3 94 5 1½ 2hd 1½ 11½ 1no Velazquez J R L122 *1.90 89-11 [D]IcyAtlntic122no Mustnfr1142¼ ScondPrformnc1181¾ Came out, brushed 8
Disqualified and placed second
26Jun04-8Del sf 1⅛ Ⓣ :522 1:182 1:434 1:553 KentBC-G3 90 5 1½ 11 1½ 11 2no Lopez C C L117 4.50 59-38 Timo117no Icy Atlantic1171¼ Commendation115nk Slow pace,just caught 8
31May04-10Mth gd 1 1/16 Ⓣ :244 :484 1:133 1:442 JrsyDrby-G3 93 7 43½ 46 42 1hd 11¼ Lopez C C L115 *2.70 77-18 IcyAtlntic1151¼ Commendtion122¾ GrndHeritge117¾ 5wd bid,clr,held well 7
24Apr04-9Aqu fm 1⅛ Ⓣ :501 1:144 1:391 1:502 3↑ Alw 44000N1x 92 1 83¼ 82¾ 73 2hd 13¾ Velazquez J R L115 10.60 88-09 *IcyAtlntic*1153¾ RunthLight1151 MorningWtch122no Swung wide, drew off 10
14Feb04-7Aqu fst 170 [•] :234 :48 1:141 1:443 Md Sp Wt 42k 71 3 711 78 31 13½ 11¾ Smith A E L121 *2.50 75-19 *IcyAtlntic*1211¾ GrhmCrcker1162¼ GibbonsTerrce121nk 4 wide move, clear 8
17Jan04-6Aqu fst 170 [•] :234 :482 1:134 1:44 Md Sp Wt 42k 68 1 85¾ 74¼ 64½ 3½ 2½ Smith A E L120 11.00 77-13 Hornshope120½ *Icy Atlantic*1201¾ GrahamCracker120¾ Good finish outside 10

Imperialism

Own: Taub Steve

Gr/ro. c. 4 (Apr)
Sire: Langfuhr (Danzig) $30,000
Dam: Bodhavista (Pass the Tab)
Br: Farnsworth Farms (Ky)
Tr: Mulhall Kristin(0 0 0 0 .00) 2004:(154 23 .15)

Life	20	5	4	3	$616,605	104	D.Fst	9 3 2 1	$384,605 104
2004	9	2	1	2	$542,000	104	Wet(333)	6 2 0 1	$135,500 98
2003	11	3	3	1	$74,605	90	Turf(237)	5 0 2 1	$96,500 101
	0	0	0	0	$0	–	Dst(0)	0 0 0 0	$0 –

28Nov04-9Hol fm 1¼ Ⓣ :471 1:121 1:37 2:012 HolDerby-G1 101 13 115¼ 115 94¾ 61½ 31½ Desormeaux K J LB122 b 7.10 83-17 GoodRewrd122½ FstndFurious1221 Imperilism1222 Tight early & 2nd turn 13
17Oct04-8SA gd 1⅛ Ⓣ :482 1:122 1:362 1:48 OakTrDby-G2 101 2 96¼ 98¼ 97¼ 84¼ 41¾ Espinoza V LB120 b 7.20 87-11 Greek Sun118¾ Laura's Lucky Boy1181 Hendrix118no 5wd into lane,rallied 9
25Sep04-10LaD my 1⅛ :471 1:12 1:38 1:512 SuperDby-G2 94 7 812 913 710 53¾ 45¾ Desormeaux K J L124 b *2.00 78-19 Fantasticat124½ Borrego1241¼ Britt's Jules1244 Roused 1/4,evenly late 9
15May04-12Pim fst 1 3/16 :471 1:112 1:362 1:552 Preaknes-G1 97 7 32 44½ 54 49½ 513¾ Desormeaux K J L126 b 6.60 86-13 SmrtyJons12611½ RockHrdTn1262 Eddington126hd Fixed shoe,5-4wd trip 10
1May04-10CD sly 1¼ :463 1:114 1:371 2:04 KyDerby-G1 98 8 1710 136 108½ 66¾ 36 Desormeaux K J L126 b 10.90 73-21 *Smarty Jones*1262¾ Lion Heart1263¼ Imperialism1262 Stdied 7/8,6wd lane 18
3Apr04-8SA fst 1⅛ :464 1:11 1:362 1:491 SADerby-G1 100 1 76 77¾ 74¾ 41¼ 32 Espinoza V LB122 b 4.70 86-09 Castledale122hd [D]RockHrdTen1222 Imperilism1221 Rail bid,steadied 1/16 7
Placed second through disqualification
6Mar04-7SA fst 1 :223 :453 1:10 1:36 SnRafael-G2 104 3 107½ 109¾ 75½ 43 1nk Espinoza V LB118 b 7.40 91-11 Imperialism118nk Lion Heart1214½ Consecrate1151 5wd into lane,rallied 10
7Feb04-3SA fst 7f :222 :443 1:091 1:221 SnVicnte-G2 101 1 6 610 67½ 42½ 11¼ Espinoza V LB116 b 14.10 94-11 *Imperialism*1161¼ Hosco120hd Consecrate1161 4wd rally,lugged in 6
Previously trained by Salinas Angel
1Jan04-9Crc fm 1⅛ Ⓣ :471 1:112 1:351 1:464 + TrpPkDby-G3 78 8 118 97 72¾ 53¼ 55¾ Velazquez J R L115 b 4.90 89-08 *KittensJoy*1194½ BrodwyViw112nk SovrignHonor117hd Even finish outside 11

Inish Glora

Own: Costigan Robert J

B. m. 7 (May)
Sire: Regal Classic (Vice Regent) $10,000
Dam: Star Guest (Assert*Ire)
Br: C. G. Scott DVM (Ont-C)
Tr: Benson Macdonald(0 0 0 0 .00) 2004:(93 13 .14)

Life	32	9	9	4	$977,618	98		D.Fst	17	3	6	2	$147,517	88
2004	5	3	2	0	$433,730	98		Wet(327)	0	0	0	0	$0	-
2003	6	3	1	1	$359,667	98		Turf(276)	15	6	3	2	$830,101	98
	0	0	0	0	$0	-		Dst(0)	0	0	0	0	$0	-

19Sep04-6WO fm *1⅛ (T) :46 1:43² 3↑(F)CanadinH-G2 **95** 1 21½ 21 2½ 11 21 Kabel T K L121 f *1.85 100-03 Classic Stamp117¹ Inish Glora1211¾ Heyahohowdy114½ Failed to hold late 9
14Aug04-4WO fm 1 1/16 (T) :23² :46² 1:11¹ 1:41⁴ 3↑(F)[S]Victoriana133k **94** 1 35½ 34½ 31½ 12½ 12½ Kabel T K L119 f *.70 89-10 InishGlora1192½ Heyahohowdy1171¼ Roshron1151¼ Closed 3wd,clear,held 8
17Jly04-4WO yl 1⅛ (T) :48 1:11² 1:35² 1:48 3↑(F)DncSmrtH-G3 **94** 2 21 1hd 1hd 12 21 Kabel T K L122 *.60 87-12 MonaRose112¹ *InishGlora1221½* ClassicStamp11611¼ Vied rail,clear,missed 4
5Jun04-8WO fm 1 1/16 (T) :25 :48⁴ 1:12 1:40¹ 3↑(F)Nassau-G3 **98** 5 1½ 11½ 11½ 11½ 1¾ Kabel T K L121 3.50 97-02 Inish Glora121¾ *Ocean Drive1172½ Classic Stamp119¾* Set pace,held,driving 6
16May04-6WO fm 1 (T) :23¹ :46³ 1:10² 1:33³ 3↑(F)Alw 86400NC **92** 4 21 2½ 1hd 1hd 1nk Kabel T K L120 *.45 95-05 *InishGlora120nk* ClassicStamp118¾ *Msbileyscrem1186¼* Stalked,dueled,drvg 7

Inspiring

Own: Lewis Robert B. and Beverly J

Ch. f. 3 (Mar) KEESEP03 $450,000
Sire: Golden Missile (A.P. Indy) $25,000
Dam: Arches of Gold (Strike Gold)
Br: Timothy Thornton, Meg Buckley & Mike Buckley (Ky)
Tr: Baffert Bob(0 0 0 0 .00) 2004:(562 105 .19)

Life	2	2	0	0	$115,800	91		D.Fst	2	2	0	0	$115,800	91
2004	2	2	0	0	$115,800	91		Wet(402*)	0	0	0	0	$0	-
2003	0	M	0	0	$0	-		Turf(275*)	0	0	0	0	$0	-
	0	0	0	0	$0	-		Dst(0)	0	0	0	0	$0	-

7Aug04-8Dmr fst 6½f :21³ :44⁴ 1:11 1:18¹ (F)Sorrento-G3 **78** 7 2 1hd 1½ 11 12½ Flores D R LB118 b *.90 84-13 Inspiring1182½ Souvenir Gift1222½ Hello Lucky118½ 4wd early,vied,clear 8
5Jly04-5Hol fst 5f :21⁴ :44³ :57 (F)Md Sp Wt 45k **91** 3 4 31 2½ 11 14 Flores D R LB119 b *.30 99-09 *Inspiring119⁴ She's Salty119⁵* Crafty Vixen119² Bid,led,ridden out 10

Intercontinental (GB)

Own: Juddmonte Farms Inc

B. f. 5 (Mar)
Sire: Danehill (Danzig)
Dam: Hasili*Ire (Kahyasi)
Br: Juddmonte Farms (GB)
Tr: Frankel Robert J(0 0 0 0 .00) 2004:(491 135 .27)

Life	15	8	2	3	$781,263	103		D.Fst	0	0	0	0	$0	-
2004	6	4	1	0	$592,386	103		Wet(371)	0	0	0	0	$0	-
2003	6	2	1	2	$127,098	-		Turf(399)	15	8	2	3	$781,263	103
	0	0	0	0	$0	-		Dst(0)	0	0	0	0	$0	-

28Nov04-7Hol fm 1 (T) :24 :47³ 1:11² 1:35⁴ 3↑(F)Matriarc-G1 **101** 4 62¾ 61½ 42 3½ 12 Bailey J D LB123 4.60 85-17 Intercontinentl123² EtoileMontnt123no TickrTp1201½ Pulled btwn,rallied 9
29Sep04-7SA fm *6½f (T) :22² :44² 1:06⁴ 1:12⁴ 3↑(F)SKMaddyH-G3 **98** 9 2 65¼ 34 2hd 2½ Flores D R LB120 1.80 92-07 *Belleski118½ Intercontinental120²* Acago116no Rail bid lane,willing 9
31Jly04-7Sar yl 1⅛ (T) :47³ 1:11³ 1:36³ 1:48⁴ 3↑(F)DianaH-G1 **85** 3 710 59 53 57½ 511½ Bailey J D L120 *.80 74-14 Wonder Again1205¾ Riskaverse1182¼ *Ocean Drive1182¼* No response 7
5Jun04-8Bel fm 1 (T) :23³ :46⁴ 1:10¹ 1:33¹ 3↑(F)JsAGmBCH-G2 **103** 1 72¼ 72¼ 52½ 21½ 11¼ Bailey J D L118 *.70e 94-06 Intercontinentl1181¼ Vngurdi113½ EtoileMontnt121¾ Steadied inside turn 8
18Apr04-8Kee fm 1 1/16 (T) :23² :48 1:12 1:41² 4↑(F)JenyWily-G3 **99** 3 65½ 52½ 41¼ 2hd 11 Bailey J D L116 *.80 97-05 *Intercontinental116¹ Ocean Drive1161½ Madeira Mist118nk* 8w early,5w turn 8
28Mar04-2SA fm 1 (T) :23¹ :47³ 1:11² 1:34³ 4↑(F)Alw 65000N$MY **93** 2 43 32 21½ 21 11½ Espinoza V LB116 *.80 89-10 *Intercontinentl1161½* Dublino116hd AbbeyBridg1172½ Hesitated str,got foe 5

Island Fashion
Own: Everest Stables Inc

Gr/ro. m. 5 (Mar)
Sire: Petionville (Seeking the Gold) $15,000
Dam: Danzigs Fashion (A Native Danzig)
Br: Everest Stables Inc. (Ky)
Tr: Polanco Marcelo(0 0 0 0 .00) 2004:(245 26 .11)

Life	17	6	2	0	$1,727,970	111	D.Fst	13	6	2	0	$1,607,970	111
2004	7	2	1	0	$615,000	111	Wet(311)	1	0	0	0	$60,000	94
2003	10	4	1	0	$1,112,970	111	Turf(186)	3	0	0	0	$60,000	101
	0	0	0	0	$0	-	Dst(0)	0	0	0	0	$0	-

28Nov04- 7Hol fm 1 Ⓣ :24 :473 1:112 1:354 3↑ⒻMatriarc-G1 **93** 8 7¾ 7½ 9½ 7¾ 4½ Baze T C LB123 b 7.10 81- 17 Intercontinentl1232 EtoilMontnt123no TickrTp120½ Tight 3/8,stdied 5/16 9
30Oct04- 2LS gd 1⅛ :463 1:102 1:352 1:481 3↑ⒻBCDistaf-G1 **94** 10 8¾ 4½ 2½ 3½ 5¾ John K L123 b 6.60 103- 02 Ashado119¼ StormFlagFlying123nk StellarJyne119½ Wide trip, gave way 11
3Oct04- 6SA fst 1 1/16 :24 :481 1:114 1:432 3↑ⒻLdyScBCH-G2 **96** 2 43 4½ 3½ 1hd 1½ John K LB120 b 2.70e 88- 17 Island Fashion120½ Miss Loren116hd Elloluv118½ 3wd bid,led,held game 7
6Jun04 Tokyo (Jpn) gd *1 Ⓣ RH 1:323 3↑ Yasuda Kinen-G1 Stk 1615000 1610¼ Puglisi I 123 b 14.50 Tsurumaru Boy128nk *Telegnosis*128 1¼ Balance of Game128nk 18
Rated in 7th,wknd 2f out.Lohengrin5th,WinRadius14th
3Apr04- 9OP fst 1 1/16 :231 :463 1:104 1:411 4↑ⒻAplBlsmH-G1 **93** 5 3½ 3½ 32 48 410½ Desormeaux K J L118 b 1.80 93- 09 Azeri123 1½ ⓔWild Spirit119¾ Star Parade1147¼ Bothered 1/4pl, no bid 6
6Mar04-10SA fst 1¼ :461 1:101 1:351 2:013 4↑SAH-G1 **111** 4 5¾ 5¾ 42 2½ 2¼ Desormeaux K J LB115 b 6.70 90- 11 *SouthernImge*118 1¼ IslndFshion115 2¼ SintBuddy1114 4wd bid 1/4,willingly 8
25Jan04- 8SA fst 7f :214 :44 1:082 1:211 4↑ⒻSntMncaH-G1 **104** 4 5 4¼ 32 21 1¾ Desormeaux K J LB120 b 1.50 99- 08 IslndFshon120¾ Buffythcntrfold114½ GotKoko119 3½ 3wd into lane,gamely 6

Island Sand
Own: B. A. Man Inc

Dk. b or b. f. 4 (Feb) KEESEP02 $82,000
Sire: Tabasco Cat (Storm Cat) $17,490
Dam: Sue's Last Dance (Forty Niner)
Br: Richard D. Maynard (Ky)
Tr: Jones J. L(0 0 0 0 .00) 2004:(189 35 .19)

Life	11	4	3	1	$438,917	101	D.Fst	8	3	2	1	$310,267	101
2004	7	2	2	1	$391,937	101	Wet(362)	2	1	1	0	$128,650	100
2003	4	2	1	0	$46,980	81	Turf(292)	1	0	0	0	$0	65
	0	0	0	0	$0	-	Dst(0)	0	0	0	0	$0	-

7Nov04-10CD fst 1 :223 :453 1:102 1:35 3↑ⒻCDDstafH-G2 **95** 12 6½ 7½ 6¾ 56 5½ Shepherd J L119 b 6.00 88- 13 *Halory Leigh*1 55 Lady Tak123¾ Susan's Angel115¾ 6w bid,empty late 12
16Oct04- 8Kee gd 1⅛ Ⓣ :493 1:142 1:384 1:511 ⒻQEIICup-G1 **65** 4 2½ 22 33 79 714 Day P L121 b 6.00 67- 20 Ticker Tape121½ Barancella121½ *River Belle*1211 Bobble start,rank,tire 7
26Jun04- 9Bel fst 1⅛ :47 1:104 1:352 1:48 ⒻMthrGoos-G1 **93** 3 52 6¼ 5¾ 34 3¼ Thompson T J L121 b 2.90 87- 11 Stellar Jayne121½ *Ashado*121¾ Island Sand1215 3 wide move, faded 6
4Jun04-10Bel fst 1 :232 :454 1:094 1:344 ⒻAcorn-G1 **101** 4 7¾ 7½ 54 2hd 1¾ Thompson T J L121 b 4.00 87- 17 IslndSnd121¾ SocitySlction121no *FrndlyMchl*121¾ Came wide, drew clear 8
30Apr04-10CD my 1⅛ :46 1:094 1:363 1:504 ⒻKyOaks-G1 **100** 3 10¾ 711 5¼ 3½ 2¼ Thompson T J L121 b 16.80 82- 17 Ashado121 1¼ *Island Sand*121 1¾ MadcapEscapade121 1¼ Edgy,hop start,bmp 11
9Apr04-10OP fst 1 1/16 :231 :463 1:11 1:423 ⒻFantasy-G2 **96** 11 2hd 2hd 1hd 2½ 2¾ Thompson T J L121 b 8.40 95- 11 HouseofFortune121¾ IslndSnd1214 StellrJyn121¼ Lively pace, solid 2nd 11
Previously trained by Dutrow Anthony W
25Jan04- 8Aqu fst 170 ⊡ :231 :472 1:133 1:43 ⒻBusanda84k **86** 8 4½ 5½ 6¼ 3½ 1½ Fragoso P L118 b 2.20 83- 24 IslndSnd118 1½ TmptingNot118¼ *FitAccompli*118¾ Altered course stretch 10

Jackpot

Own: Phipps Cynthia

Ch. h. 7 (Mar)
Sire: Seeking the Gold (Mr. Prospector) $125,000
Dam: Frolic (Cox's Ridge)
Br: Cynthia Phipps (Ky)
Tr: McGaughey III Claude R(0 0 0 0 .00) 2004:(254 48 .19)

Life	16	4	4	1	$288,915	107	**D.Fst**	10	3	3	1	$248,335 107
2004	3	1	1	0	$189,120	107	**Wet(379)**	1	0	0	0	$1,380 83
2003	5	1	1	0	$39,200	102	**Turf(235)**	5	1	1	0	$39,200 102
	0	0	0	0	$0	-	**Dst(0)**	0	0	0	0	$0 -

3Apr04- 9GP fst 1¼ :472 1:112 1:362 2:024 3↑GPH-G2 **107** 2 44½ 44 32½ 22½ 12 Bravo J L113 b 17.10 100- 15 Jackpot1132 Newfoundland1161 *The Lady's Groom*1131¾ 3 wide, up late 6
28Feb04- 9GP fst 1 1/16 :234 :474 1:12 1:44 4↑OC 75k/N3x-N **87** 8 53 42½ 42 33 21½ Douglas R R L118 b 6.70 87- 14 BadaBamBadBoom1181½ *Jckpot*1181 Justifiction1181¼ 3 wide, gaining late 8
7Feb04- 7GP fst 1⅛ ⊗:484 1:13 1:374 1:503 4↑Alw 38000N3x **87** 2 54 42¼ 42½ 42¼ 42 Douglas R R L118 b 3.70 84- 09 LightningStripes118½ ProudPrtnr118½ GrnCsr1201 4 wd, no late response 6

Janeian (NZ)

Own: England Greg L

B. m. 7 (Oct)
Sire: The Jogger (Danzig)
Dam: Taipari*NZ (McGinty*NZ)
Br: G. A. McMullin, I. A. McMullin & Mrs. A. J. Nooyen (NZ)
Tr: Calhoun W. B(0 0 0 0 .00) 2004:(714 148 .21)

Life	35	9	6	6	$368,114	97	**D.Fst**	1	0	0	0	$3,360 70
2004	6	2	2	0	$177,820	97	**Wet(328)**	0	0	0	0	$0 -
2003	13	4	3	3	$183,870	93	**Turf(230)**	34	9	6	6	$364,754 97
	0	0	0	0	$0	-	**Dst(0)**	0	0	0	0	$0 -

31Oct04- 9LS gd 1 1/16 Ⓣ:242 :494 1:14 1:45 3↑ⒻBluebonnet100k **87** 7 63 63½ 42 62¾ 42¾ Martin E M Jr L123 *1.10 76- 28 MyMistyPrincess119no QuenCorrin119¾ BonniJ1192 3wide turns,4wide 1/4 8
3Oct04- 8LS fm 1⅛ Ⓣ:473 1:114 1:362 1:482 3↑ⒻYellowRsBC92k **88** 6 32½ 32 31½ 42½ 31¼ Berry M C L123 *1.30 100- 08 D *My Misty Princess*1191¼ Aud119hd Janeian123½ Boxed in 1/4 to 3/16 8
Placed second through disqualification
8Aug04- 9Mth fm 1⅛ Ⓣ:481 1:122 1:363 1:484 3↑ⒻMatchmkr-G3 **88** 4 32½ 32 31½ 23 43¾ Martin E M Jr L118 *1.70 82- 12 WhereWeLeftOff1181 Mrs.M1181¾ SpinControl1161 Lacked late response 9
3Jly04- 4Hol fm 1 Ⓣ:233 :471 1:11 1:343 3↑ⒻRIHroine-G3 **95** 4 33½ 33½ 31½ 1hd 12 Desormeaux K J LB121 1.90 91- 13 Janeian1212 Katdogawn123½ Makeup Artist1211 Stalked,bid,clear 6
31May04- 8LS fm 1 Ⓣ:224 :462 1:102 1:354 3↑ⒻWnStDstH-G3 **93** 11 44½ 44½ 3½ 11½ 2¾ Martin E M Jr L119 3.10 90- 13 Academic Angel117¾ *Janeian*119nk Katdogawn120½ 3w 2nd turn,caught 12
17Apr04- 9LS fm 7½f Ⓣ:232 :462 1:10 1:281 3↑ⒻIrvingDstf75k **97** 7 7 43½ 3½ 13½ 14 Martin E M Jr L118 3.20 104 - Janeian1184 Cat's Cat118½ Bedanken1231 4w 3/4,stalkd,drw away 8

Josh's Madelyn
Own: Pressley Michael and Neidig, Jim

B. f. 4 (Mar) KEESEP02 $10,000
Sire: Quiet American (Fappiano) $20,000
Dam: Intend to Win (Housebuster)
Br: Mt. Brilliant Farm LLC (Ky)
Tr: Jones J. L(0 0 0 0 .00) 2004:(189 35 .19)

Life	14	6	2	1	$254,202	104	D.Fst 10 5 0 1 $101,898 104
2004	9	6	1	0	$245,172	104	Wet(394) 3 1 2 0 $150,804 98
2003	5	M	1	1	$9,030	66	Turf(263) 1 0 0 0 $1,500 80
	0	0	0	0	$0	–	Dst(0) 0 0 0 0 $0 –

15Oct04–9Kee my 7f :21³ :44¹ 1:09⁴ 1:22⁴ ⒻRavenRun-G2 **98** 5 10 10¹⁰ 108¼ 2² 11¼ Shepherd J L118 b 5.60 93– 11 JoshsMdlyn1181¼ VisionofButy1169½ FlinStory118½ Drft start,8w lane,drv 10
5Sep04–10EIP fst 7f :22 :44⁴ 1:09¹ 1:21¹ 3↑ⒻHcp 38000 **104** 6 2 44¾ 43½ 1⁴ 111½ Shepherd J L112 b 4.30 106– 10 *JoshsMadelyn*11211½ SilentStrem1172 StrikeRte1161¼ 4w,drew off,mild urg 6
31Jly04–9EIP gd 1 1/16 Ⓣ :23 :46 1:10¹ 1:41² ⒻAudubonOak75k **80** 10 89½ 88 84½ 74½ 53½ Shepherd J L121 b 17.50 85– 20 Lenatareese119½ Key to the Cat117¹ Lady Offense1171½ 6 wide 1/4 pole 12
2Jly04–9PrM fst 1 1/16 :23 :46³ 1:11² 1:42⁴ ⒻIowaOaks-G3 **73** 4 4³ 4⁵ 4² 77½ 712½ Doocy T T LB115 b 6.40 77– 19 *He Loves Me*118¾ Prospective Saint1156¼ HomeCourt1151¼ 4 wide 2nd turn 8
5Jun04–9PrM fst 1 :23 :46 1:11 1:36 ⒻPanthers50k **85** 4 2⁶ 2² 1hd 1² 11¾ Thompson T J LB118 b 3.90 100– 13 JoshsMadelyn1181¾ PltinumBllet1182¼ Defuhr1182¼ Stalked pace, driving 7
26Apr04–8PrM fst 6f :23 :47¹ :59⁴ 1:12² 3↑ⒻOC 30k/N2x-N **72** 3 4 3² 2hd 12½ 13¾ Thompson T J LB117 b *.70 79– 28 *Josh's Madelyn*1173¾ Liliana L1204¾ Bonita Rose1172 3wd bid, drove clear 6
2Apr04–5OP fst 6f :22 :45² :57³ 1:10 ⒻAlw 33500N1x **87** 3 2 2hd 1hd 12½ 1⁷ Shepherd J5 L110 b 2.90 90– 15 *Josh's Madelyn*1107 Callone115² Metallic Miss1184¾ Pressed,bid,well clear 6
15Feb04–7OP my 6f :22³ :47 :59⁴ 1:13¹ ⒻAlw 32000N$Y **80** 5 4 5⁴ 4⁴ 3¹ 21¾ Shepherd J5 L117 b 8.60 72– 30 Miss Concerto1181¾ *Josh's Madelyn*1173¼ Brigette's Dream1182 Wide rally 6
23Jan04–4OP fst 6f :22 :45¹ :59 1:12 ⒻMd 50000(50-40) **69** 3 5 63½ 31½ 1½ 11½ Thompson T J L121 b 2.40 80– 18 JoshsMadelyn1211½ PyramidGirl1211¼ *Avaricity*1213¾ 4-w bid, slowly clear 9

Judiths Wild Rush
Own: Tenenbaum Racing Stables

Gr/ro. c. 4 (Mar) OBSAUG02 $7,000
Sire: Wild Rush (Wild Again) $10,000
Dam: Tie Talk (Black Tie Affair*Ire)
Br: Sez Who Thoroughbreds (Ky)
Tr: Fairlie Scott H(0 0 0 0 .00) 2004:(304 48 .16)

Life	12	4	0	2	$264,271	103	D.Fst 9 3 0 1 $218,104 103
2004	8	1	0	2	$122,356	102	Wet(384) 3 1 0 1 $46,167 87
2003	4	3	0	0	$141,915	103	Turf(227) 0 0 0 0 $0 –
	0	0	0	0	$0	–	Dst(0) 0 0 0 0 $0 –

10Dec04–8WO sly 6½f :22 :45¹ 1:10³ 1:17² 3↑OC 62k/N2x **76** 7 4 45½ 6⁶ 68½ 67¾ Luciani D L117 b 7.65 83– 19 Gangster1185 Souvenier Biz118nk Rodeo Fun1211¼ Lacked rally 3w 10
14Nov04–2WO fst 1 1/16 :23² :47 1:11³ 1:46¹ 3↑OC 80k/N3x **79** 6 2hd 2hd 2½ 4⁵ 4⁸ Olguin G L L117 b 3.05 72– 28 MyLuckyStrik1181 SkyDimond1221½ Solihull1095½ Forced pace,gave way 6
31Oct04–4WO gd 1 1/16 :23¹ :46³ 1:10⁴ 1:45³ 3↑Alw 83700NC **81** 2 2hd 2½ 22½ 2⁸ 310¾ Luciani D L116 b 2.85 72– 24 NrflkKnht11510¾ OpnLck118nc JdthsWldRsh1162 Chased to stretch,hung 6
18Sep04–4WO fst 1 1/16 :23³ :47² 1:11³ 1:43⁴ Alw 83700NC **89** 2 1⁵ 1⁷ 1½ 1hd 32¾ Luciani D L120 b 4.50 89– 19 OrgnGrndr122nk CutndShoot1182½ JdthsWldRsh1201¼ Led, weakened ins 7
14Aug04–8Pha fst 170 :22¹ :45² 1:10³ 1:41⁴ PresdntsCp100k **54** 7 1¹ 1² 2½ 67¾ 922¾ Luciani D L122 b 7.30 71– 17 Separato1175 Gadace's Khamseh117½ *Prince Joseph*1192 Used up 10
13Jun04–7WO fst 1⅛ :48 1:13² 1:39¹ 1:51² VictoriaPk140k **70** 9 3¹ 3nk 2hd 5¹⁰ 620¼ Luciani D L123 b 2.15 71– 16 Organ Grinder1176 Copper Trail1192¾ *TobeSuave*1176¼ Bid 3-wide,led,tired 9
22May04–8WO fst 1 1/16 :23¹ :47 1:11⁴ 1:45⁴ Marine-G3 **102** 3 1² 11½ 1² 1² 1¹ Luciani D L119 b *1.60 82– 27 JudithsWildRush1191 *OrgnGrindr*1172¼ *HonoluStorm*1179½ Set pace,driving 6
10Apr04–7Aqu fst 7f :22¹ :44¹ 1:08¹ 1:20³ BayShore-G3 **71** 7 1 62¾ 69½ 7¹⁶ 617½ Luzzi M J L118 b 8.10 84– 04 ForestDnger1157½ *Abbondnz*1163½ *IndinWrDnc*1162½ Close up, no response 8

Katdogawn (GB)
Own: Cuchna John R., Jim Ford, Inc. and Pe

B. f. 5 (Feb)
Sire: Bahhare (Woodman) $6,784
Dam: Trempkate (Trempolino)
Br: Mrs W. H. Gibson Fleming (GB)
Tr: Cassidy James M(0 0 0 0 .00) 2004:(157 18 .11)

Life	24	6	6	4	$594,803	98	D.Fst	0	0	0	0	$0	-
2004	9	1	3	2	$264,158	98	Wet(267*)	0	0	0	0	$0	-
2003	10	4	3	1	$320,580	97	Turf(284)	24	6	6	4	$594,803	98
	0	0	0	0	$0	-	Dst(0)	0	0	0	0	$0	-

30Oct04-6LS yl 1⅜ Ⓣ :522 1:182 1:421 2:181 3↑ⒻBCF&MTrf-G1 **82** 2 97¾ 107½ 85¾ 109¾ 1014½ Desormeaux K J L123 55.40 83-07 Ouija Board1181½ Film Maker123nk Wonder Again1232¾ Check early, wide 12
2Oct04-4SA fm 1¼ Ⓣ :462 1:10 1:342 1:591 3↑ⒻYlwRibbn-G1 **92** 3 31½ 34½ 32½ 2hd 35 Desormeaux K J LB123 5.00 88-09 Light Jig1234 Tangle1231 Katdogawn123hd Bid btwn 1/8,outkicked 10
4Sep04-7Dmr fm 1$\frac{1}{16}$ Ⓣ :234 :481 1:114 1:402 3↑ⒻPalmrBCH-G2 **96** 4 64 65 33 32 2¾ Desormeaux K J LB117 3.00 96-09 Etoile Montante120¾ Katdogawn117½ Tangle1171 Came out str,rallied 7
24Jly04-6Dmr fm 1⅛ Ⓣ :474 1:12 1:352 1:47 3↑ⒻJCMabeeH-G1 **96** 2 53½ 44 41½ 42 52¾ Smith M E LB116 9.60 91-09 MusiclChims1161¼ MoscowBurnng117no NottngHll1131 Inside,no late bid 6
3Jly04-4Hol fm 1 Ⓣ :233 :471 1:11 1:343 3↑ⒻRlHroine-G3 **91** 6 68½ 67 64¾ 42½ 22 Smith M E LB123 *1.50 89-13 Janeian1212 Katdogawn123½ Makeup Artist1211 Off slow,rallied 6
31May04-8LS fm 1 Ⓣ :224 :462 1:102 1:354 3↑ⒻWnStDstH-G3 **93** 2 98½ 87 74¼ 53 31 Perrodin E J L120 *1.90 90-13 Academic Angel117¾ *Janeian*119nk Katdogawn120½ Saved ground,willingly 12
25Apr04-7Hol fm 1 Ⓣ :232 :464 1:102 1:332 3↑ⒻWilshirH-G3 **90** 7 97¾ 76 54 54½ 54 Smith M E LB118 4.90 93-05 Spring Star1172½ Quero Quero115no Dublino1201 4wd move,stdied 1/16 9
27Mar04-9SA fm 1⅛ Ⓣ :474 1:12 1:352 1:471 4↑ⒻSntaAnaH-G2 **98** 2 55 53 53½ 31½ 21 Smith M E LB117 5.30 92-11 Ⓓ*Megahertz*1201 Katdogawn1171½ Fun House1181½ Blockd,angld in, bid 7
Placed first through disqualification
21Feb04-8SA gd 1 Ⓣ :232 :473 1:12 1:36 4↑ⒻBnaVstaH-G2 **91** 2 75¾ 74¾ 54¼ 44 22¾ Smith M E LB117 3.90 79-18 Fun House1162¾ *Katdogawn*117½ Fudge Fatale116½ Off bit slow,late 2nd 7

Kela
Own: Manoogian Jay

B. h. 7 (Mar)
Sire: Numerous (Mr. Prospector) $13,567
Dam: Bolshoi Comedy (Sovereign Dancer)
Br: Cypress Farms 1991 (Ky)
Tr: Mitchell Mike R(0 0 0 0 .00) 2004:(391 97 .25)

Life	25	8	6	0	$1,011,527	116	D.Fst	23	7	6	0	$830,527	116
2004	9	3	1	0	$710,212	116	Wet(343)	2	1	0	0	$181,000	114
2003	6	1	1	0	$81,915	107	Turf(277)	0	0	0	0	$0	-
	0	0	0	0	$0	-	Dst(0)	0	0	0	0	$0	-

5Dec04-6Hol wf 6f :213 :44 :554 1:08 3↑VOUndrwd-G3 **93** 7 3 78¼ 76¾ 54½ 45 Nakatani C S LB126 b *1.50 92-11 TsteofPrdise122no WtchemSmokey1162 MyMstr1163 3wd into lane,no bid 7
30Oct04-5LS fst 6f :211 :432 :552 1:08 3↑BCSprint-G1 **109** 5 10 106¾ 105¾ 74½ 21¼ Bailey J D L126 b 4.00 99-04 Speightstown1261¼ Kela126¾ My Cousin Matt126½ 7w into lane,clsd well 13
15Aug04-8Dmr fst 7f :214 :434 1:081 1:21 3↑OBrinBCH-G2 **116** 4 5 55¾ 54¾ 12 14½ Baze T C LB116 b 2.60 97-10 Kela1164½ Domestic Dispute1161¼ *Pico Central*1224 3wd bid,led,clear 5
25Jly04-2Dmr fst 6f :212 :434 :56 1:082 3↑BCrsbBCH-G1 **112** 6 10 105½ 52¾ 2hd 11¼ Baze T C LB113 b 8.80 97-09 *Kela*1131¼ Pohave1182½ Hombre Rapido1153 4wd move turn,gamely 10
3Jly04-9Hol fst 7f :214 :44 1:081 1:21 3↑TrBndBCH-G1 **98** 1 12 95 105½ 64¼ 42¼ Smith M E LB114 b 3.60 95-12 Pohave116¾ Rojo Toro115½ Revello1101 3wd into lane,late bid 13
31May04-9LS fst 1$\frac{1}{16}$:224 :453 1:082 1:411 3↑LSParkH-G3 **98** 3 21½ 21½ 25 26 43½ Nuesch D L121 b *1.20 92-08 Yessirgnrlsir1142¼ SonicWst1171 SpnishEmpir117nk 3w 1st turn,gave way 6
24Apr04-8LS sly 1 :231 :461 1:10 1:353 3↑TexsMile-G3 **114** 7 22 22 22 12½ 15¼ Nuesch D L119 b 5.40 95-22 Kela1195¼ Supah Blitz1161½ *Yessirgeneralsir*114nk Tracked 3w,drew away 8
3Apr04-10SA fst 1⅛ :471 1:112 1:354 1:48 4↑SnBrdnoH-G3 **98** 7 76¼ 711 76½ 75¾ 59 Baze T C LB114 b 6.20 85-09 Dynever1174½ Total Impact1162 *Even the Score*1162 Widest into lane 7
7Mar04-8SA fst 7f :221 :44 1:082 1:21 4↑SnCrlosH-G2 **102** 6 8 89½ 88 85¼ 45 Nakatani C S LB117 b 27.60 95-11 *Pico Central*1162 Publication1162 *Pohave*1121 Waited 1/8,outkicked 10

Kicken Kris

Own: Brushwood Stable

B. h. 5 (Mar)
Sire: Kris S. (Roberto) $150,000
Dam: Kicker Grass (Jade Hunter)
Br: Valerie Naify (Ky)
Tr: Matz Michael R(0 0 0 0 .00) 2004:(214 32 .15)

Life	19	6	3	3	$1,326,600	106	D.Fst	5	0	0	1	$6,400	67
2004	6	2	0	1	$727,000	106	Wet(380)	0	0	0	0	$0	–
2003	9	4	3	1	$593,540	106	Turf(346)	14	6	3	2	$1,320,200	106
	0	0	0	0	$0	–	Dst(0)	0	0	0	0	$0	–

Date/Race	Cnd	Dist	Surf	Fractions	Race	Spd	PP	St	1C	2C	Str	Fin	Jockey	M/Wt	Odds	Pace	Top Finishers	Comment	Fld
20Oct04–9Bel	yl	1½	Ⓣ	$:50^{4}$ $1:17^{1}$ $2:07^{1}$ $2:29^{4}$	3↑TfClscIv-G1	**96**	1	3^{2}	$3^{1\frac{1}{2}}$	4^{3}	$6^{6\frac{1}{4}}$	6^{10}	Castellano J J	L126 f	4.00	62–22	Kitten's Joy$121^{2\frac{1}{2}}$ Magistretti$126^{\frac{3}{4}}$ Tycoon121^{3}	Close up inside, tired	7
14Aug04–9AP	fm	1¼	Ⓣ	$:47^{2}$ 1:12 $1:36^{3}$ 2:00	3↑ArlMilln-G1	**106**	4	6^{5}	7^{5}	4^{2}	3^{1}	$2^{1\frac{1}{2}}$	Desormeaux K J	L126	9.70	109 –	[D]Powerscourt$126^{1\frac{1}{2}}$ Kicken Kris126^{1} *Magistretti*$126^{\frac{1}{2}}$	Bumped-hit rail	13
Placed first through disqualification																			
17Jly04–8Bel	fm	1⅜	[T]	$:47^{2}$ $1:10^{4}$ $1:35^{4}$ 2:12	3↑BwlnGrnH-G2	**106**	7	$4^{8\frac{1}{2}}$	$4^{4\frac{1}{2}}$	$5^{2\frac{1}{2}}$	1^{1}	$1^{1\frac{1}{2}}$	Prado E S	L117	*1.35	93–10	*Kicken Kris*$117^{1\frac{1}{2}}$ *Better Talk Now*$115^{2\frac{1}{4}}$ Gigli113^{nk}	3 wide move, clear	10
5Jun04–10Bel	fm	1¼	[T]	$:48^{2}$ $1:12^{1}$ $1:35^{4}$ $1:59^{1}$	3↑ManhttnH-G1	**98**	9	$6^{2\frac{3}{4}}$	$6^{2\frac{1}{4}}$	$9^{5\frac{1}{2}}$	$9^{6\frac{1}{2}}$	$9^{6\frac{1}{4}}$	Velazquez J R	L118	4.90	92–05	MtorStorm$117^{1\frac{1}{4}}$ MllnnmDrgon116^{no} MrOBrn$116^{\frac{3}{4}}$	Wide throughout, tired	9
1May04–9CD	yl	1⅛	Ⓣ	:51 $1:15^{2}$ $1:39^{3}$ 1:53	3↑TurfClsc-G1	**90**	9	7^{6}	5^{3}	$4^{1\frac{3}{4}}$	$6^{7\frac{1}{2}}$	$6^{7\frac{3}{4}}$	Velazquez J R	L123	6.10	60–32	Stroll$121^{2\frac{1}{2}}$ Sweet Return123^{no} Mystery Giver$123^{\frac{3}{4}}$	Bumped, in tight	11
22Feb04–11GP	fm	1⅜	Ⓣ	$:48^{4}$ $1:36^{1}$ $2:11^{2}$	3↑GPBCH-G1	**103**	2	$5^{3\frac{1}{2}}$	5^{4}	$5^{4\frac{1}{2}}$	$5^{3\frac{1}{4}}$	$3^{\frac{1}{2}}$	Castellano J J	L118	4.70	100–10	Hard Buck117^{hd} Balto Star$122^{\frac{1}{2}}$ Kicken Kris118^{1}	Lacked room final turn	8

Kilgowan

Own: Ann Marie Farm

Gr/ro. c. 4 (Mar)
Sire: Smoke Glacken (Two Punch) $30,000
Dam: Port Roberto (Dynaformer)
Br: Ann Marie Farm (Ky)
Tr: Stidham Michael(0 0 0 0 .00) 2004:(369 81 .22)

Life	8	3	0	1	$160,122	85	D.Fst	4	1	0	1	$119,825	85
2004	6	2	0	0	$140,522	85	Wet(391)	2	2	0	0	$33,550	73
2003	2	1	0	1	$19,600	75	Turf(270)	2	0	0	0	$6,747	84
	0	0	0	0	$0	–	Dst(0)	0	0	0	0	$0	–

Date/Race	Cnd	Dist	Surf	Fractions	Race	Spd	PP	St	1C	2C	Str	Fin	Jockey	M/Wt	Odds	Pace	Top Finishers	Comment	Fld
24Jly04–5AP	fm	$1\frac{3}{16}$	Ⓣ	$:48^{2}$ $1:12^{4}$ $1:37^{2}$ $1:54^{4}$	AmercnDb-G2	**74**	6	$5^{3\frac{1}{2}}$	5^{3}	5^{3}	$7^{8\frac{1}{4}}$	7^{12}	Marquez C H Jr	L123 b	22.70	88–05	Simple Exchange119^{nk} Cool Conductor$119^{\frac{3}{4}}$ Toasted$123^{1\frac{1}{4}}$	4-5 wide, tired	8
Previously trained by Arterburn Lonnie																			
26Jun04–3Hol	fm	1⅛	Ⓣ	$:47^{3}$ $1:11^{2}$ $1:36^{1}$ $1:48^{2}$	+ CinmaBCH-G3	**84**	4	$7^{6\frac{1}{2}}$	$7^{9\frac{3}{4}}$	$6^{6\frac{1}{4}}$	3^{5}	$4^{5\frac{1}{2}}$	Santiago Javier	LB116 b	21.50	83–14	Greek Sun120^{2} Laura's Lucky Boy$122^{3\frac{1}{2}}$ Whilly117^{no}	3wd 2nd turn,lost 3rd	7
3Apr04–7Haw	fst	1⅛		$:47^{4}$ $1:12^{3}$ $1:37^{4}$ $1:50^{4}$	IlnosDby-G2	**82**	1	$7^{4\frac{1}{4}}$	$7^{5\frac{1}{4}}$	$8^{5\frac{1}{4}}$	6^{10}	$6^{15\frac{1}{4}}$	Rollins C J	L124 b	18.30	88–21	PollardsVision$114^{2\frac{3}{4}}$ SongoftheSword$116^{2\frac{3}{4}}$ Suve$114^{8\frac{1}{2}}$	steadied first turn	11
13Mar04–7GG	fst	$1\frac{1}{16}$		:23 $:46^{4}$ 1:11 $1:43^{4}$	ElCamRlD-G3	**85**	4	$6^{5\frac{1}{4}}$	$7^{4\frac{3}{4}}$	$6^{4\frac{1}{4}}$	$6^{4\frac{1}{2}}$	$1^{\frac{1}{2}}$	Rollins C J	LB116 b	26.90	84–16	Kilgowan$116^{\frac{1}{2}}$ [DH]Cpitno116 [DH]SettleBorders117^{hd}	Bmpd hard 1/8p, drvng	10
8Feb04–8GG	fst	1		$:23^{1}$ $:46^{4}$ $1:11^{1}$ $1:37^{2}$	GldnStMile83k	**74**	7	$7^{5\frac{1}{2}}$	$5^{2\frac{1}{2}}$	4^{3}	4^{5}	$4^{4\frac{1}{4}}$	Rollins C J	LB117 fb	7.80	78–27	O. K. Mikie$116^{\frac{1}{2}}$ Bending Strings117^{3} Point Dume$115^{\frac{3}{4}}$	Drftd wide 2nd turn	8
9Jan04–7GG	sly	1		:22 $:45^{4}$ 1:11 1:37	Alw 35723n1x	**73**	5	6^{7}	4^{3}	$4^{1\frac{1}{4}}$	$2^{\frac{1}{2}}$	1^{nk}	Rollins C J	LB118 fb	*1.90	84–19	Kilgowan118^{nk} Iza Big Star118^{2} Tacky118^{10}	Waited 2d turn,rallied	6

Kitten's Joy
Own: Ramsey Kenneth L. and Sarah K

Ch. c. 4 (May)
Sire: El Prado*Ire (Sadler's Wells) $100,000
Dam: Kitten's First (Lear Fan)
Br: Kenneth L. Ramsey & Sarah K. Ramsey (Ky)
Tr: Romans Dale L(0 0 0 0 .00) 2004:(580 109 .19)

Life	12	8	3	0	$1,705,911	114	D.Fst	2	0	1	0	$10,550	74
2004	8	6	2	0	$1,625,796	114	Wet(346)	0	0	0	0	$0	–
2003	4	2	1	0	$80,115	86	Turf(325)	10	8	2	0	$1,695,361	114
	0	0	0	0	$0	–	Dst(0)	0	0	0	0	$0	–

Date/Race	Trk	Dist	Fractions	Race	Fig	PP	St	1c	2c	Str	Fin	Jockey	Wt	Odds	Spd	Top finishers	Comment	Fld
30Oct04–8LS	yl	1½	Ⓣ:49 1:134 2:04 2:293	3↑BCTurf-G1	108	4	37	32½	32	31½	21¾	Velazquez J R	L121	*.70	121– 07	BettrTlkNow1261¾ KittnsJoy1211 Powrscourt1262¼	Inside move, 2nd best	8
2Oct04–9Bel	yl	1½	Ⓣ:504 1:171 2:071 2:294	3↑TfClscIv-G1	114	5	42½	41¾	21½	1hd	12½	Velazquez J R	L121	2.40	72– 22	Kitten's Joy1212½ Magistretti1263¾ Tycoon1213	Strong when set down	7
14Aug04–11AP	fm	1¼	Ⓣ:463 1:11 1:351 1:593	Secretar-G1	113	1	611	610	52¾	1½	13¼	Bailey J D	L123	*.90	113 -	*KittensJoy*1233¼ GreekSun1211¼ MoscowBallet1191	5w, vigorous hand ride	7
10Jly04–9Cnl	fm	1¼	Ⓣ:471 1:112 1:364 2:011	VaDby-G3	108	2	616	413	33½	1½	12¾	Prado E S	L117	1.70	99– 16	*Kitten'sJoy*1172¾ *ArtieSchiller*1174¾ *PrinceArch*1191 2¾	4wd move,drifted out	8
12Jun04–5CD	yl	1⅛	Ⓣ:49 1:134 1:381 1:503	JfrsnCup-G3	101	8	85	64	41	1hd	2hd	Bailey J D	L122	*.70	80– 25	PrncArch120hd *KttnsJoy*1224¾ CoolCondctor1161¼	5w,bid,clear,outgamed	9
30Apr04–9CD	gd	1 1/16	Ⓣ:243 :492 1:131 1:431	AmerTurf-G3	93	4	93¾	82¾	42½	1½	12½	Bailey J D	L123	*1.10	88– 11	Kitten's Joy1232½ *Prince Arch*1231½ Capo1172¼	Bmp gate,6w,driving	9
21Feb04–11GP	fm	1⅛	Ⓣ:494 1:133 1:371 1:483	PalmBch-G3	91	1	43½	43	52½	3½	11¾	Bailey J D	L122	*.60e	92– 06	*Kitten's Joy*1221¾ Prince Arch118nk Pa Pa Da118¾	Angled out, clear	12
1Jan04–9Crc	fm	1⅛	Ⓣ:471 1:112 1:351 1:464	+ TrpPkDby-G3	91	9	43	64½	41½	1hd	14½	Bailey J D	L119	3.60	95– 08	*KittensJoy*1194½ BrodwyView112nk SoverignHonor117hd	3wd bid,drew off	11

La Reason
Own: K and K Racing Stable LLC

B. m. 5 (Apr)
Sire: Labeeb*GB (Lear Fan) $3,530
Dam: Reasoning (Naskra)
Br: Ron Kirby & Tom Kirby (Ky)
Tr: Vance David R(0 0 0 0 .00) 2004:(260 35 .13)

Life	23	6	2	3	$432,925	96	D.Fst	14	4	2	0	$319,245	96
2004	11	3	0	2	$331,080	96	Wet(311)	7	2	0	3	$112,450	90
2003	12	3	2	1	$101,845	92	Turf(289)	2	0	0	0	$1,230	77
	0	0	0	0	$0	–	Dst(0)	0	0	0	0	$0	–

Date/Race	Trk	Dist	Fractions	Race	Fig	PP	St	1c	2c	Str	Fin	Jockey	Wt	Odds	Spd	Top finishers	Comment	Fld
7Nov04–10CD	fst	1	:223 :453 1:102 1:35	3↑ⒻCDDstafH-G2	75	9	117	116¾	1210	912	1117	Melancon L	L114 f	79.10	78– 13	*Halory Leigh*1155 Lady Tak123¾ Susan's Angel115¾	Lean in bmp start	12
10Oct04–8Kee	fst	1⅛	:464 1:113 1:37 1:493	3↑ⒻSpinster-G1	96	6	76	74¼	73	53¾	57¼	Bejarano R	L123 f	46.20	86– 12	Azeri1233 Tamweel123½ Mayo On the Side1233¾	Angled 6w,no rally	7
18Sep04–12TP	fst	1 1/16	:232 :464 1:113 1:441	3↑ⒻTPBC-G3	80	4	55½	45	64¼	43½	55	Day P	L122 f	5.20	86– 11	SusansAngel116¾ MayoOntheSide1201½ AngelsLove1222	Nothing left late	6
1Aug04–9Sar	fst	1⅛	:473 1:104 1:35 1:474	3↑ⒻGoFWandH-G1	53	3	53¼	42½	32	59½	532	Prado E S	L113 f	21.00	64– 14	Azeri1201¾ *Sightseek*1222 *Storm Flag Flying*1177	Inside run second turn	5
4Jly04–10Mth	fst	1⅛	:474 1:112 1:364 1:51	3↑ⒻMPchrBCH-G2	91	5	52½	54½	54¼	11	13	Lopez C C	L111 f	22.70	86– 19	La Reason1113 Yell114nk Bare Necessities119no	Dueled clear inside	7
12Jun04–8CD	sly	1⅛	:473 1:124 1:384 1:52	3↑ⒻFlrDLisH-G2	86	6	67¾	66	65	44½	35	McKee J	L110 f	50.20	72– 17	*Adoration*1221¼ Bare Necessities1203¾ *La Reason*1102	Mild gain	6
30Apr04–8CD	sly	1 1/16	:241 :474 1:123 1:441	3↑ⒻLouvlBCH-G2	83	5	54½	54½	53½	53½	59¼	Shepherd J	L111 f	30.30	78– 17	Lead Story116¾ Yell1143 Cat Fighter1163¼	6w lane,empty	6
4Apr04–10OP	fst	1 1/16	:232 :471 1:113 1:433	4↑ⒻBayakoa75k	90	2	36½	43¼	43	2½	1¾	Shepherd J	L116 f	9.70	92– 14	LaReason116¾ Pmpered116hd SuesGoodNews1161¾	Angled out, split foes	7
13Mar04–10OP	fst	1 1/16	:23 :464 1:12 1:441	3↑ⒻOaklwnBC-G3	73	10	41½	54½	4nk	86½	811	Johnson J M	L114 f	62.30	78– 15	GoldenSont1171¾ KeystothHrt117¾ *MyoOnthSid*113½	Five wide both turns	10
29Feb04–9OP	sly	1 1/16	:233 :473 1:13 1:452	4↑ⒻOC 60k/N2M-N	84	6	54½	53	52¼	23½	34	Shepherd J5	L117 f	*2.00	79– 17	Small Promises1153½ Due to Win115½ La Reason1173	Outfinished place	6
13Feb04–8OP	gd	1	:25 :493 1:152 1:41	4↑ⒻAlw 35000N$Y	83	1	1hd	32	32	2½	11½	Shepherd J5	L117 f	3.30	79– 22	LRson1171½ ChrylvlISlw1221¾ CurosConndrm1183¼	Got thru rail,exploded	8

Lady Tak

Own: Heiligbrodt Racing Stable

Ch. m. 5 (Apr)
Sire: Mutakddim (Seeking the Gold) $10,000
Dam: Star of My Eye (Lucky North)
Br: John Franks (Fla)
Tr: Asmussen Steven M(0 0 0 0 .00) 2004:(2293 555 .24)

Life	18	10	4	1	$1,155,682	110		
2004	7	4	1	1	$439,412	105		
2003	9	4	3	0	$675,350	110		
	0	0	0	0	$0	-		
D.Fst	16	8	4	1	$985,842	110		
Wet(374)	2	2	0	0	$169,840	102		
Turf(293)	0	0	0	0	$0	-		
Dst(0)	0	0	0	0	$0	-		

Date/Track	Cond	Dist	Fractions	Race	Fig	PP	St	1c	2c	Str	Fin	Jockey	Wt	Odds		Top Finishers	Comment	
7Nov04-10CD	fst	1	:223 :453 1:102 1:35	3↑ⒻCDDstafH-G2	**98**	3	2½	1½	1½	12	25	Velazquez J R	L123	*1.30	90- 13	*Halory Leigh*1155 Lady Tak123¾ Susan's Angel115¾	Dueled,no match	12
10Oct04-9Bel	fst	6½f	:231 :464 1:094 1:16	3↑ⒻGlntBlmH-G2	**103**	7	1	2½	2hd	1½	12	Velazquez J R	L122	*.80	93- 16	Lady Tak1222 *Molto Vita*1154¼ Zawzooth115hd	When asked, ridden out	7
29Aug04-9Sar	gd	7f	:221 :442 1:074 1:21	3↑ⒻBalrinaH-G1	**102**	3	5	11½	12½	12½	1hd	Bailey J D	L119	*.85	99- 05	*Lady Tak*119hd My Trusty Cat116hd Harmony Lodge1191	Resolutely on rail	7
10Jly04-11Crc	fst	6f	:212 :44 :564 1:104	3↑ⒻPrcsRnyH-G2	**92**	2	5	1hd	1½	2hd	35¾	Sellers S J	L119	2.90	89- 09	Ema Bovary1192 Bear Fan1223¾ *Lady Tak*1192	Vied inside, tired	6
22May04-9CD	fst	6f	:212 :44 :554 1:084	3↑ⒻWinColorsH108k	**104**	3	2	2hd	11½	12	1¾	Sellers S J	L122	*.50	97- 11	Lady Tak122¾ *Put Me In*1171¼ *Ebony Breeze*1161	Drft start,4w,driving	7
24Apr04-4CD	fst	6f	:222 :452 :571 1:094	3↑ⒻAlw 54550N1Y	**105**	3	1	11½	13	13½	12	Sellers S J	L117	*.80	92- 16	*Lady Tak*1172 Souris121½ *Golden Marlin*1196¼	3path,hand urging	5
7Apr04-8Kee	fst	7f	:22 :441 1:093 1:232	4↑ⒻMadison175k	**77**	6	2	2hd	1½	42	611	Sellers S J	L117 f	*1.70	79- 14	Ema Bovary1202¼ Harmony Lodge123¾ Yell1162½	Dueled,led,tired	6

Last Song

Own: Three Roses LLC

B. f. 4 (Mar) KEESEP02 $190,000
Sire: Unbridled's Song (Unbridled) $125,000
Dam: Queen of Spirit (Deputy Minister)
Br: Katalpa Farm (Ky)
Tr: Nafzger Carl A(0 0 0 0 .00) 2004:(358 54 .15)

Life	15	4	2	2	$293,183	93		
2004	11	3	1	2	$254,253	93		
2003	4	1	1	0	$38,930	87		
	0	0	0	0	$0	-		
D.Fst	11	2	2	2	$232,760	93		
Wet(379)	4	2	0	0	$60,423	90		
Turf(281)	0	0	0	0	$0	-		
Dst(0)	0	0	0	0	$0	-		

Date/Track	Cond	Dist	Fractions	Race	Fig	PP	St	1c	2c	Str	Fin	Jockey	Wt	Odds		Top Finishers	Comment	
26Nov04-4CD	fst	6½f	:23 :454 1:101 1:164	3↑ⒻDrmSuprmeH71k	**93**	3	4	56½	55½	55¾	44¼	Castellano J J	L114 f	5.10	83- 16	Savorthetime1152½ Hippogator115¾ Souris1201	5w,no late gain	6
24Oct04-3Kee	gd	6f	:214 :45 :572 1:094	3↑ⒻAlw 56000N3X	**83**	1	6	65½	66½	31½	1hd	Borel C H	L116 f	2.20	92- 10	Last Song116hd Flaming Dixie1165 Fashion Girl1161½	Rail late,driving	6
26Sep04-9TP	fst	6½f	:223 :452 1:11 1:18	3↑ⒻAlw 30600N$Y	**65**	2	6	621	612	55	23	Borel C H	L114 f	*1.40	87- 12	Moonlit Romance1163 *Last Song*114nk A Little Gold116no	Inside trip	6
21Aug04-10Sar	sly	1¼	:471 1:112 1:362 2:023	ⒻAlabama-G1	**–**	8	53¼	810	-	-	-	Migliore R	L121 b	36.00	- 18	Society Selection1212½ *Stellar Jayne*121½ *Ashado*1215¼	5 wide, eased	8
30Jly04-8AP	fst	1	:224 :453 1:103 1:364	ⒻSweetChant54k	**83**	2	76	69½	56	53¾	54½	Douglas R R	L121 b	*1.30	79- 24	Fly Away Angel115½ *Catboat*1181½ Miss Moses1151	No factor	10
9Jly04-8AP	fst	1	:241 :472 1:113 1:361	3↑ⒻOC 62k/N3X -N	**78**	4	43	43	52½	44	37	D'Amico A J	L116	*1.00	80- 13	*Tamweel*1235 Balla Twine1192 Last Song116½	Mild rally	7
30Apr04-10CD	my	1⅛	:46 1:094 1:363 1:504	ⒻKyOaks-G1	**83**	9	87¾	1014	1015	913	911½	Prado E S	L121	11.10	71- 17	Ashado1211¼ *Island Sand*1211¾ Madcap Escapade1211¼	Failed to menace	11
3Apr04-9Kee	fst	1 1/16	:24 :472 1:112 1:442	ⒻAshland-G1	**90**	4	43½	45½	44½	47½	34½	Albarado R J	L120	8.50	85- 14	Madcap Escapade118½ *Ashado*1234 Last Song1203	Inside,no late gain	4
6Mar04-8GP	fst	1⅛	:473 1:113 1:37 1:503	ⒻBonnieMs-G2	**92**	5	42½	2½	2½	1hd	12	Prado E S	L118	3.10	86- 21	Last Song1182 *Society Selection*1204¾ Rare Gift1167	Dueled, edged away	5
7Feb04-8GP	fst	1 1/16	:242 :49 1:14 1:443	ⒻDvonaDal-G2	**88**	7	42	2½	2hd	2½	4½	Prado E S	L117 f	2.60	85- 09	MissCorondo117hd EyeDzzler115nk SocitySlction121nk	Bid between, hung	7
19Jan04-8GP	gd	1 1/16	:234 :482 1:132 1:453	ⒻAlw 34000N1X	**90**	5	45	42½	21	12	18¾	Prado E S	L119 f	*1.10	81- 24	Last Song1198¾ Quick Temper1192½ Charity Girl1174	3 wide, handily	7

Laura's Lucky Boy
Own: Mercedes Stables LLC

B. c. 4 (Jan)
Sire: Theatrical*Ire (Nureyev) $50,000
Dam: Corridora Slew*Arg (Corridor Key)
Br: Madeleine A Paulson (Ky)
Tr: Orman Jason R(0 0 0 0 .00) 2004:(53 8 .15)

Life	**9**	**3**	**2**	**1**	**$246,730**	**103**	**D.Fst**	**0**	**0**	**0**	**0**	**$0 –**
2004	**9**	**3**	**2**	**1**	**$246,730**	**103**	**Wet(339)**	**0**	**0**	**0**	**0**	**$0 –**
2003	**0**	**M**	**0**	**0**	**$0**	**–**	**Turf(343)**	**9**	**3**	**2**	**1**	**$246,730 103**
	0	**0**	**0**	**0**	**$0**	**–**	**Dst(0)**	**0**	**0**	**0**	**0**	**$0 –**

28Nov04–9Hol fm 1¼ Ⓣ :471 1:121 1:37 2:012 HolDerby-G1 **98** 12 2½ 1hd 11 11 53½ Stevens G L **LB**122 7.30 81–17 GoodReward122½ FstndFurious1221 Imperilism1222 Dueled,led,outkicked 13
17Oct04–8SA gd 1⅛ Ⓣ :482 1:122 1:362 1:48 OakTrDby-G2 **103** 6 2hd 2½ 2hd 1½ 2¾ Stevens G L **LB**118 4.30 88–11 Greek Sun118¾ Laura's Lucky Boy1181 Hendrix118no Led 3wd into lane 9
6Sep04–8Dmr fm 1⅛ Ⓣ :473 1:112 1:35 1:463 DmrDerby-G2 **101** 2 21½ 22½ 2½ 11½ 3nk Stevens G L **LB**122 6.70 96–10 Blackdoun122nk Toasted122no LaurasLuckyBoy122½ Led into lane,gamely 10
14Aug04–8Dmr fm 1$\frac{1}{16}$ Ⓣ :234 :473 1:112 1:41 LaJollaH-G2 **89** 2 34½ 33½ 31½ 52½ 52¾ Court J K **LB**120 3.40 91–07 *Blackdoun*120¾ Semi Lost116¾ Bedmar113½ Steadied bit near 1/8 7
26Jun04–3Hol fm 1⅛ Ⓣ :473 1:112 1:361 1:482 + CinmaBCH-G3 **92** 7 11 2hd 1hd 12½ 22 Smith M E **LB**122 *.60 87–14 Greek Sun1202 Laura's Lucky Boy1223½ Whilly117no Inside,clear,held 2nd 7
22May04–8Hol fm 1 Ⓣ :223 :452 1:092 1:332 WilRogrs-G3 **100** 7 55½ 55¼ 1hd 14 14 Valenzuela P A **LB**119 2.60 97–05 LaurasLuckyBoy1194 *Toasted*1211 StreetTheatre1173½ 3wd move,led,clear 8
28Apr04–2Hol fm 1$\frac{1}{16}$ Ⓣ :234 :473 1:111 1:401 Alw 50000N1x **88** 1 11 1½ 1hd 2hd 1nk Valenzuela P A **LB**120 *1.00e 95–04 *LaurasLuckyBoy*120nk Richebourg1183½ Bedmar118¾ Fought back rail lane 6
27Mar04–5SA fm 1 Ⓣ :222 :461 1:102 1:34 Md Sp Wt 46k **90** 8 31½ 31½ 21 11½ 12½ Smith M E **LB**120 9.30 92–11 *LaurasLuckyBoy*1202½ MinisterBlir120¾ ArticDrem1201 Bid 1/4, led, cleared 12
28Feb04–6SA gd 1⅛ Ⓣ :471 1:121 1:381 1:504 Md Sp Wt 46k **46** 3 1017 1019 1118 1013 1017 Smith M E **LB**120 6.40 58–25 On the Acorn1202 Artic Dream120½ Wanted Man1201 Off slow,veered in 11

Lead Story
Own: Miles A S Jr

Ch. m. 6 (Apr)
Sire: Editor's Note (Forty Niner) $3,500
Dam: Gwenjinsky (Seattle Dancer)
Br: Cabotaba Partnership (Ky)
Tr: Nafzger Carl A(0 0 0 0 .00) 2004:(358 54 .15)

Life	**32**	**8**	**3**	**6**	**$842,031**	**107**	**D.Fst**	**18**	**4**	**2**	**5**	**$361,928 98**
2004	**3**	**1**	**0**	**2**	**$235,740**	**99**	**Wet(280)**	**7**	**3**	**1**	**0**	**$454,429 107**
2003	**11**	**3**	**1**	**1**	**$449,062**	**107**	**Turf(241)**	**7**	**1**	**0**	**1**	**$25,674 79**
	0	**0**	**0**	**0**	**$0**	**–**	**Dst(0)**	**0**	**0**	**0**	**0**	**$0 –**

30Apr04–8CD sly 1$\frac{1}{16}$:241 :474 1:123 1:441 3↑Ⓕ LouvlBCH-G2 **99** 3 67½ 66¾ 42 11½ 1¾ Borel C H L116 10.00 87–17 Lead Story116¾ Yell1143 Cat Fighter1163¼ Angled 4w lane,driving 6
14Mar04–6GP fst 1⅛ :482 1:114 1:372 1:51 3↑Ⓕ RampartH-G2 **86** 2 45½ 412 414 47½ 39½ Borel C H L117 9.70 74–27 Sightseek1217½ Redoubled Miss1132 *Lead Story*1179 Failed to menace 4
15Feb04–11GP fst 1$\frac{1}{16}$:234 :473 1:114 1:431 3↑Ⓕ SabinH-G3 **89** 9 97¾ 912 97¼ 46 36¼ Borel C H L119 7.40 87–17 RoarEmotion1165½ *NonsuchBy*115¾ LedStory1191¾ Saved grnd, gained 3rd 9

Leroidesanimaux (Brz)

Own: T N T Stud

Ch. c. 5 (Sep)
Sire: Candy Stripes (Blushing Groom*Fr) $6,000
Dam: Dissemble*GB (Ahonoora*GB)
Br: Haras Bage Do Sul (Brz)
Tr: Frankel Robert J(0 0 0 0 .00) 2004:(491 135 .27)

Life	9	6	1	0	$444,337	112	D.Fst	0 0 0 0		$0	–
2004	6	5	0	0	$436,860	112	Wet(311)	1 0 0 0		$0	–
2003	3	1	1	0	$7,477	–	Turf(330)	8 6 1 0		$444,337	112
	0	0	0	0	$0	–	Dst(0)	0 0 0 0		$0	–

27Nov04–7Hol fm 1 1/16 Ⓣ :233 :48 1:112 1:411 3↑ CtationH-G1 112 2 3 1½ 5 1¾ 31 11 1½ Court J K LB117 3.10 90– 17 Leroidesnimux117½ AtotheZ1151 ThreeVlleys115½ Bid btwn,led,held game 10
30Oct04–6SA fm *6½f Ⓣ :212 :431 1:054 1:113 3↑ MorvichH-G3 111 4 1 4 3½ 3 3½ 3 2½ 1 1¼ Court J K LB117 3.00 99– 01 *Leroidesanimaux*117 1¼ DeValmont115no Cayoke116 1½ 3wd bid,lugged in bit 6
1May04–6Hol fm 1 1/16 Ⓣ :233 :464 1:093 1:382 3↑ InglewdH-G3 111 4 1hd 1hd 1hd 11 12 Court J K LB114 5.80 104– 04 *Lroidsnimux*1142 *DsigndforLuck*1182 DvousBoy115nk Duel, rail, edged away 9
20Mar04–1SA fm 1 Ⓣ :223 :453 1:091 1:334 4↑ OC 100k/N3x-N 98 2 3 2½ 3 3½ 2½ 1hd 1¾ Espinoza V LB120 3.00 93– 08 *Leroidesanimaux*120¾ *King ofHappiness*1201 Grafton120½ Bid btwn, led, held 6
31Jan04–5SA fm 1 Ⓣ :213 :443 1:082 1:34 4↑ Alw 54184N1x 98 4 6 8½ 516 4 7½ 3 1½ 1 2½ Desormeaux K J LB117 *2.20 92– 13 *Leroidesanimaux*117 2½ Hsil1211 Pssionforcshin123 2½ 3w bid,lugged in,clear 11
7Jan04–7SA fm *6½f Ⓣ :213 :433 1:061 1:123 4↑ Alw 52000N1x 89 4 6 42 3 2½ 32 4 1¼ Desormeaux K J LB120 4.50 93– 05 *Vronsky*121½ Lydgate120½ Great White Father119nk Pulled,inside,willing 9

Level Playingfield

Own: Fly Racing LLC

Dk. b or b. c. 4 (Apr) OBSAPR03 $15,000
Sire: Level Sands (Storm Cat) $1,500
Dam: Chao Praya (Gold Legend)
Br: Briland Farm & Mrs. Stacy L. Mitchell (Ky)
Tr: Holthus Robert E(0 0 0 0 .00) 2004:(364 72 .20)

Life	16	4	5	4	$216,440	100	D.Fst	6 3 2 1		$147,500	100
2004	13	3	4	3	$166,250	100	Wet(282)	5 1 0 3		$40,740	91
2003	3	1	1	1	$50,190	87	Turf(196)	5 0 3 0		$28,200	93
	0	0	0	0	$0	–	Dst(0)	0 0 0 0		$0	–

27Nov04–10CD fst 6½f :224 :454 1:10 1:162 3↑ DstrtHumrH71k 100 2 10 10 5½ 10 8¾ 7 3¾ 3 2¾ McKee J L114 b 13.80 86– 15 StrngthndHoror118nk CchJmL121 2½ LvlPlyngfld114½ 9w lane,gaining late 10
7Nov04–8CD fst 6f :212 :443 :57 1:094 3↑ Alw 57100N$Y 93 6 8 7 9½ 7 9½ 5 7½ 23 McKee J L119 b 8.80 89– 12 *StrengthndHoror*1173 LevelPlyingfild119 1¼ DrLk1173 Bmp,squeezed start 8
14Oct04–8Kee my *7f :224 :452 1:093 1:25 Perryville112k 91 6 5 3 2½ 3 5½ 34 4 7¾ McKee J L123 b 15.20 93– 11 *Commentator*1177 Eurosilver123½ *Weigelia*123nk Rail stretch,empty 7
18Sep04–13TP fst 6f :212 :441 :563 1:093 KyCpSpnt-G3 97 2 5 514 5 7½ 3 3½ 1 2½ McKee J L116 b 10.40 97– 11 LevelPlyingfield116 2½ Cuv116 1¼ SwiftAttrction116½ 3 wide move, driving 5
29Aug04–4EIP fm 5½f Ⓣ :213 :45 :564 1:024 Hcp 38000 88 3 5 4 4¾ 4 5½ 4 4½ 2 1¼ McKee J L118 b 4.80 87– 14 SgtBert115 1¼ *LvlPlyingfild*118nk JimmyCrckdCorn1203 Bmp start,5w lane 5
7Aug04–6EIP fm 5½f Ⓣ :214 :443 :554 1:014 3↑ Hcp 38000 82 4 3 6 5½ 6 7½ 610 47 McKee J L113 b 4.00 86– 15 ChosenChief117 1½ JusticeforAuston120 5½ Tstify119hd 6w lane,minor gain 6
17Jly04–6AP fm 5f Ⓣ :221 :451 :572 3↑ Hcp 38000 86 2 7 7 6½ 7 7½ 6 5½ 2 1½ Douglas R R L116 b 3.30 92– 06 NicolesDrem117 1½ LevelPlyingfield116hd [DH]SecretRomo117 Second best 10
20Jun04–5CD gd 5f Ⓣ :224 :453 :571 3↑ OC 62k/N$Y-N 93 8 4 4 1½ 32 3nk 2no McKee J L110 b 20.90 91– 09 JstcforAston121no LvlPlyngfld110hd SvnthInnng1171 5w bid,loom,missed 8
30Apr04–9CD gd 1 1/16 Ⓣ :243 :492 1:131 1:431 AmerTurf-G3 75 1 8 3¼ 7 2¼ 8 9½ 7 6¾ 68 McKee J L119 b 37.80 80– 11 Kitten's Joy123 2½ *Prince Arch*123½ Capo117 2¼ 7w lane,no late gain 9
10Apr04–5OP sly 1 :223 :463 1:112 1:371 NrthnSprBC73k 89 3 4 7½ 3 5½ 3 2½ 3 3½ 3 6¾ Martin E M Jr L117 b *0.10 91– 17 TwoDwnAtmtc115 5¾ PrprPrd1191 LvlPlyngfld117 2¼ Getting to runner up 6
29Feb04–7OP sly 6f :211 :451 :582 1:112 OC 60k/N2x-N 84 6 5 69 5 7½ 2 1½ 1 3¼ McKee J L122 b 2.70 83– 22 LevelPlyingfild122 3¼ SouthAfric122 3½ EndofnEr122 1¾ Finished full of run 6
13Feb04–9OP gd 1 1/16 :233 :48 1:14 1:463 OC 75k/N3L-N 82 1 1½ 1hd 1hd 2½ 36 Thompson T J L121 b 6.10 71– 22 Cryptogrph121 ¼ ProprPrdo117 4¾ *LvlPlyingfld*121 10½ Hooked inside,faded 6
23Jan04–10P fst 1 :23 :464 1:12 1:394 Alw 32000N1x 75 7 5 3½ 31 1½ 12 1 1½ McKee J L115 b *1.30 85– 19 LvlPlyngfld115 ¼ Ntntqt119 9¼ PyrmdPrfrmr115 1¾ Stalkd in hand,3-w bid 8

Light Jig (GB)
Own: Juddmonte Farms Inc

B. f. 5 (Apr)
Sire: Danehill (Danzig)
Dam: Nashmeel (Blushing Groom*Fr)
Br: Juddmonte Farms (GB)
Tr: Frankel Robert J(0 0 0 0 .00) 2004:(491 135 .27)

Life	14	5	3	1	$537,819	101	D.Fst	0 0 0 0	$0	-
2004	7	4	1	0	$494,800	101	Wet(432)	0 0 0 0	$0	-
2003	7	1	2	1	$43,019	-	Turf(397)	14 5 3 1	$537,819	101
	0	0	0	0	$0	-	Dst(0)	0 0 0 0	$0	-

30Oct04- 6LS yl 1⅜ Ⓣ :52² 1:18² 1:42¹ 2:18¹ 3↑ⒻBCF&MTrf-G1 **94** 7 10 8¼ 8 6½ 11 7 8 7¼ 7 7½ Douglas R R L123 6.40 90- 07 Ouija Board118 1½ Film Maker123nk Wonder Again123 2¾ No threat 12

20Oct04- 4SA fm 1¼ Ⓣ :46² 1:10 1:34² 1:59¹ 3↑ⒻYlwRibbn-G1 **101** 1 8 5 7 7¼ 5 3½ 3nk 1 4 Douglas R R LB123 *1.30 93- 09 Light Jig123 4 Tangle123 1 Katdogawn123hd 3w into lane,bid,clear 10

24Jly04- 6Dmr fm 1⅛ Ⓣ :47⁴ 1:12 1:35² 1:47 3↑ⒻJCMabeeH-G1 **95** 1 6 4½ 6 6 6 2¼ 6 4 6 3 Flores D R LB116 *1.40 91- 09 MusclChms116 1¼ MoscowBrnng117no NottngHll113 1 4wd 2nd turn,no bid 6

27Jun04- 8Hol fm 1¼ Ⓣ :49³ 1:13³ 1:37⁴ 2:01² 3↑ⒻBevHilsH-G2 **101** 1 3 1½ 4 1¼ 4 1¼ 4 2 1 1 Solis A LB114 *2.00 85- 13 LightJig114 1 MoscowBurning117 1½ NochsDRos118 1 3wd into lane,rallied 6

26May04- 5Hol fm 1¼ Ⓣ :48⁴ 1:12⁴ 1:36⁴ 2:00⁴ 4↑ⒻOC 62k/n2x -N **95** 1 7 3¾ 7 4¾ 5 4 1½ 1 1½ Solis A LB120 *.60 88- 13 *Light Jig*120 1½ Night Games122hd Go On Baby118 6½ 4wd into lane,rallied 9

14Apr04- 7SA fm 1 Ⓣ :23 :46¹ 1:10¹ 1:35 4↑ⒻAlw 56000n2x **90** 5 4 5½ 4 5 4 1¼ 3 1 2no Desormeaux K J LB120 *.50 87- 13 Alozaina118no *Light Jig*120 2 Tamweel118 2 Blocked 1/4-1/8,rail 6

16Feb04- 3SA fm 1 Ⓣ :23⁴ :48 1:11³ 1:34⁴ 4↑ⒻAlw 52000n1x **92** 5 4 2 4 2 3 4½ 3 4½ 1 1 Desormeaux K J LB121 2.70 88- 15 LightJig121 1 PerfectWorld119 1 *LadySabrina*117 4½ Awkward step 1/4,game 7

Limehouse
Own: Dogwood Stable

Ch. c. 4 (Feb) FTSAUG02 $140,000
Sire: Grand Slam (Gone West) $85,000
Dam: Dixieland Blues (Dixieland Band)
Br: Cheryl A. Curtin (Fla)
Tr: Pletcher Todd A(0 0 0 0 .00) 2004:(948 240 .25)

Life	11	5	0	3	$627,435	100	D.Fst	9 5 0 2	$565,935	100
2004	5	2	0	1	$367,000	100	Wet(405)	2 0 0 1	$61,500	95
2003	6	3	0	2	$260,435	92	Turf(310)	0 0 0 0	$0	-
	0	0	0	0	$0	-	Dst(0)	0 0 0 0	$0	-

12Jun04-14Tdn fst 1⅛ :47¹ 1:11² 1:37 1:49² OhioDrby-G2 **75** 3 5 2½ 5 2 4 1½ 5 5½ 6 17¼ Santos J A L121 *1.00 79- 06 *Brass Hat*115 3 *Pollard's Vision*121 5 Trieste's Honor115 3 Bid 2nd turn,empty 9

1May04-10CD sly 1¼ :46³ 1:11⁴ 1:37¹ 2:04 KyDerby-G1 **95** 1 8 6¼ 6 3½ 6 5¼ 3 3½ 4 8 Santos J A L126 41.70 71- 21 *Smarty Jones*126 2¾ Lion Heart126 3¼ Imperialism126 2 Shuffled 7/8,inside 18

10Apr04- 9Kee fst 1⅛ :46³ 1:11 1:36⁴ 1:49² BlueGras-G1 **100** 3 1hd 2 1 2 2½ 3 2½ 3 6½ Santos J A L123 6.30 87- 20 The Cliff's Edge123½ Lion Heart123 6 Limehouse123 3¾ Inside, tired late 8

14Mar04-11Tam fst 1 1/16 :23³ :47³ 1:11⁴ 1:43⁴ TampaDby-G3 **100** 1 2 1½ 4 1½ 5 1½ 3 1½ 1nk Day P L118 *.90 99- 10 Limehouse118nk Mustnfr116 1 Swingforthefencs116 1¾ Angled out, up late 8

14Feb04-10GP fst 7f :21³ :43³ 1:08⁴ 1:22¹ Hutchesn-G2 **99** 1 2 6 3½ 4 2 2 2 1 2¼ Velazquez J R L122 4.20 91- 07 *Limehouse*122 2¼ Deputy Storm118 1¾ *Saratoga County*116 3¾ Drew clear late 10

Lion Heart

Own: Smith Derrick and Tabor, Michael

Ch. c. 4 (Jan) FTFFEB03 $1,400,000
Sire: Tale of the Cat (Storm Cat) $65,000
Dam: Satin Sunrise (Mr. Leader)
Br: Sabine Stable (Ky)
Tr: Biancone Patrick L(0 0 0 0 .00) 2004:(130 29 .22)

Life	10	5	3	0	$1,390,800	110			
2004	7	2	3	0	$1,080,000	110			
2003	3	3	0	0	$310,800	103			
	0	0	0	0	$0	–			

D.Fst	9	5	2	0	$1,220,800	110
Wet(363)	1	0	1	0	$170,000	103
Turf(306)	0	0	0	0	$0	–
Dst(0)	0	0	0	0	$0	–

28Aug04-11Sar fst 1¼ :49 1:12⁴ 1:37 2:02² Travers-G1 **76** 2 11½ 1hd 52¼ 716 722 Bravo J 126 *2.60 73-05 Birdstone1262½ The Cliff's Edge1263½ Eddington126nk Speed inside, tired 7
8Aug04-13Mth fst 1⅛ :46⁴ 1:10² 1:35³ 1:48⁴ HsklInvH-G1 **109** 4 1½ 11½ 12 12 11 Bravo J 121 1.90 97-13 LionHert1211 MySnookiesBoy1162¼ PiesProspect1163¼ Set pace, driving 8
17Jly04-9Mth fst 1$\frac{1}{16}$:23 :46² 1:10 1:43² LBrnchBC-G3 **102** 4 31 3½ 1hd 2hd 1hd Bravo J 116 *.30 88-19 *LionHrt*116hd MySnookisBoy1155½ RoylAssult1223½ Outside bid,prevailed 7
15May04-12Pim fst 1$\frac{3}{16}$:47¹ 1:11² 1:36² 1:55² Preaknes-G1 **97** 1 11½ 12½ 11 35 413½ Smith M E 126 4.90 86-13 SmrtyJons12611½ RockHrdTn1262 Eddington126hd Pace 3-4w,grudgingly 10
1May04-10CD sly 1¼ :46³ 1:11⁴ 1:37¹ 2:04 KyDerby-G1 **103** 3 12 11½ 1hd 2hd 22¾ Smith M E 126 5.40 76-21 *Smarty Jones*1262¾ Lion Heart1263¼ Imperialism1262 Bit off rail,2nd best 18
10Apr04-9Kee fst 1⅛ :46³ 1:11 1:36⁴ 1:49² BlueGras-G1 **110** 5 2hd 11 12½ 11 2½ Smith M E 123 *.90 93-20 The Cliff's Edge123½ LionHeart1236 Limehouse1233¾ 3 wide early, gamely 8
6Mar04-7SA fst 1 :22³ :45³ 1:10 1:36 SnRafael-G2 **104** 7 3½ 1hd 1½ 11½ 2nk Smith M E B121 *1.00 91-11 Imperialism113nk Lion Heart1214½ Consecrate1151 4wd 7/8,clear,caught 10

Lion Tamer

Own: Tabor Michael B

Ch. c. 5 (Feb)
Sire: Will's Way (Easy Goer) $5,000
Dam: Tippecanoe Creek (Olympio)
Br: Paul Smith (Ky)
Tr: Pletcher Todd A(0 0 0 0 .00) 2004:(948 240 .25)

Life	15	8	2	0	$763,380	111
2004	9	5	1	0	$592,380	111
2003	4	2	0	0	$135,400	98
	0	0	0	0	$0	–

D.Fst	14	7	2	0	$736,380	111
Wet(427)	1	1	0	0	$27,000	89
Turf(173)	0	0	0	0	$0	–
Dst(0)	0	0	0	0	$0	–

27Nov04-9Aqu fst 1 :22² :44¹ 1:08¹ 1:33² 3↑CigarMiH-G1 **111** 5 87 84 2hd 1hd 11¼ Santos J A L115 f 12.00 98-07 LionTamer1151¼ BadgeofSilver115no PicoCentrl1234¾ 4 wide sweep, clear 8
31Oct04-7Aqu fst 7f :22¹ :44³ 1:08² 1:21 3↑SportPgH-G3 **107** 8 5 89¾ 57½ 45 23½ Velazquez J R L118 4.40 96-13 Mass Media1133½ *Lion Tamer*1132 Gygistar120no Bumped start, 3 wide 9
8Oct04-7Med fst 1⅛ :46⁴ 1:11 1:35⁴ 1:48³ 3↑MedBC-G2 **88** 5 74 64¼ 42 77 811¼ Coa E M L119 11.90 78-15 Balto Star123½ Dynever1191½ Gygistar1193¾ 3 wide, no response 8
11Sep04-3Mth fst 1$\frac{1}{16}$:24³ :48⁴ 1:13 1:44 3↑FormalGold65k **101** 5 53¾ 53½ 41 1hd 12 Coa E M L115 *.30 85-18 LionTmer1152 OneNiceCt115nk WestonField1153½ 4 wide move,ridden out 6
4Jly04-9Bel fst 7f :22² :44³ 1:08¹ 1:20² 3↑TomFoolH-G2 **102** 1 4 42¼ 1hd 45 48¼ Velazquez J R L118 3.00 90-13 *Ghostzapper*1194¼ Aggdn1143½ UnforgettbleMx114½ 3 wide between rivals 4
5May04-8Bel fst 1 :24¹ :47² 1:11³ 1:35⁴ 3↑WschstrH-G3 **95** 4 61¾ 72¾ 72¼ 55½ 57¾ Velazquez J R L119 *1.50 74-25 Gygistar1154¼ Saarland1142¾ *Black Silk*113nk 3 wide trip, no rally 7
10Apr04-5Kee fst 7f :22³ :45¹ 1:09³ 1:23 3↑CmwlthBC-G2 **105** 4 5 52½ 53½ 3½ 1¾ Smith M E L122 *1.40 92-15 Lion Tamer122¾ Private Horde120½ MarinoMarini1182¼ 5w lane,stiff drive 6
6Mar04-11GP fst 7f :22 :44¹ 1:08³ 1:21² 3↑RcSclBCH-G2 **105** 7 3 42½ 31 3nk 1¾ Velazquez J R L116 *1.60 95-08 *Lion Tamer*116¾ Coach Jimi Lee115½ WackyforLove114hd 3 wide, prevailed 7
28Jan04-8GP fst 7f :22⁴ :46² 1:11² 1:24³ 4↑OC 75k/N3x-N **97** 6 4 3nk 3nk 13 12¼ Velazquez J R L118 *.60 79-22 *LionTamer*1182¼ DvidsExpecttion1184¼ AllAmericnBlue118½ 3 wide, easily 8

Louvain (Ire)
Own: Gann Edmund A

B. f. 3 (Feb)
Sire: Sinndar*Ire (Grand Lodge) $20,350
Dam: Flanders*Ire (Common Grounds)
Br: Twelve Oaks Stud Establishment (Ire)
Tr: Frankel Robert J(0 0 0 0 .00) 2004:(491 135 .27)

Life	6	2	2	2	$87,143	84	D.Fst	0 0 0 0		$0	–
2004	6	2	2	2	$87,143	84	Wet(273)	0 0 0 0		$0	–
2003	0	M	0	0	$0	–	Turf(303*)	6 2 2 2		$87,143	84
	0	0	0	0	$0	–	Dst(0)	0 0 0 0		$0	–

26Nov04–3Hol fm 1 Ⓣ:24 1 :48 4 1:13 1:37 ⒻMiesque-G3 **84** 1 8 8 7 4 3/4 5 3 3/4 3 1 1 2 Dominguez R A LB115 2.00 79–20 Louvain115 2 RoyalCopenhagen114 nk LMitresse114 2 1/2 3wd into lane,rallied 8
Run in divisions Previously trained by Richard Gibson

4Sep04 Craon (Fr) gs *1 Ⓣ RH 1:36 2 Criterium de l'Ouest (Listed) Stk 54200 3 3/4 Jarnet T 124 5.50 Hypnotic128 1/2 River Bride124 nk *Louvain*124 2 11
Timeform rating: 93 *Towards rear,finished well.Ascot Dream 7th*

4Aug04 Vichy (Fr) sf *7f Ⓣ RH 1:29 Pr Jouvenceaux & Jouvencelles(Lstd) Stk 54200 2 1/2 Jarnet T 124 *.90 Ozone Bere125 1/2 Louvain125 2 Ascot Dream125 3/4 7
Timeform rating: 94 *Tracked in 3rd,bid 2f out,held by winner*

16Jly04 Maisons-Laffitte (Fr) gs *7f Ⓣ LH 1:31 Prix Arbele-EBF Alw 28600 1 3 Jarnet T 122 1.90 Louvain122 3 Craft Fair126 1 1/2 Nobelline124 nk 5
Timeform rating: 91 *Rated in last,rallied to lead over 1f out,going away*

27May04 Longchamp (Fr) gs *5f Ⓣ Str :59 Prix du Cherche Midi-EBF Alw 28200 2 1 Jarnet T 120 *.50 Lady Weasley120 1 *Louvain*120 nk Nobelline124 3 6
Timeform rating: 78 *Tracked winner,3rd 1-1/2f out,back up for 2nd*

10May04 Maisons-Laffitte (Fr) hy *4 1/2f Ⓣ Str :56 2 Prix Marigot-EBF Maiden (FT) 21300 3 3 1/2 Jarnet T 124 3.20 Semarang128 2 1/2 Miss Laure124 1 Louvain124 1 1/2 10
Timeform rating: 78 *Dwelt,trailed,finished well along rail*

Love of Money
Own: Jay Em Ess Stable

Dk. b or b. c. 4 (Apr) EASOCT02 $70,000
Sire: Not For Love (Mr. Prospector) $25,000
Dam: Mescalina (Smarten)
Br: Dr. & Mrs. T. Bowman, Mr. & Mrs. T. Sutton & M. Higgin (Md)
Tr: Dutrow R E Jr(0 0 0 0 .00) 2004:(603 166 .28)

Life	5	3	1	0	$491,500	112	D.Fst	4 2 1 0		$463,300	112
2004	5	3	1	0	$491,500	112	Wet(413)	1 1 0 0		$28,200	105
2003	0	M	0	0	$0	–	Turf(315)	0 0 0 0		$0	–
	0	0	0	0	$0	–	Dst(0)	0 0 0 0		$0	–

2Oct04–10Bel fst 1 1/4 :47 3 1:11 3 1:36 2 2:02 2 3↑JkyClbGC-G1 **90** 2 1 1/2 1hd 2 1/2 5 4 1/4 6 15 Albarado R J L122 *2.80 70–13 FunnyCide126 3/4 Newfoundland126 1 TheCliff'sEdge122 3 3/4 Vied inside, tired 7
6Sep04–10Pha fst 1 1/8 :47 3 1:11 1 1:35 3 1:48 2 PaDerby-G2 **112** 4 1 1/2 1 1 1 1 1 4 1 8 1/2 Albarado R J L116 12.70 103–11 LovofMony116 8 1/2 PollrdsVision122 1 Swngforthfncs119 3 1/4 Hand ridden out 12
12Aug04–7Sar sly 7f :22 2 :45 4 1:09 4 1:22 2 3↑Alw 47000N1X **105** 7 1 2hd 1 1/2 1 6 1 6 Velazquez J R L116 2.05 92–08 *LoveofMoney*116 6 TangoTales116 5 *PrimrySuspect*118 1 1/4 Vigorous hand ride 7
9Jly04–5Bel fst 6f :22 2 :45 1 :57 1:09 3↑Alw 44100N2L **88** 3 1 2hd 1 1 2hd 2 2 1/4 Velazquez J R L118 *.45 92–14 ThundrTouch116 2 1/4 *LovofMony*118 10 1/4 ThGrtBzzn111 1 1/4 Vied outside, tired 5
12Jun04–4Bel fst 6f :22 1 :45 :57 1:09 3 3↑Md Sp Wt 43k **96** 2 3 1hd 1hd 1 3 1 6 Velazquez J R L118 3.00 91–12 LoveofMoney118 6 *OldForester*118 no ClertheBss118 1/2 Widened under drive 8

Lovely Afternoon
Own: Richard Otto Stables Inc

Dk. b or b. f. 4 (Apr) KEESEP02 $52,000
Sire: Afternoon Deelites (Private Terms) $4,000
Dam: Lovely Later (Green Dancer)
Br: Two Sisters Farm (Pa)
Tr: Mitchell Anthony(0 0 0 0 .00) 2004:(130 19 .15)

Life	12	4	1	2	$150,076	90		
2004	6	2	1	0	$86,959	90		
2003	6	2	0	2	$63,117	79		
	0	0	0	0	$0	–		
D.Fst	7	2	0	2	$108,801	90		
Wet(364)	1	1	0	0	$18,000	83		
Turf(319)	4	1	1	0	$23,275	80		
Dst(0)	0	0	0	0	$0	–		

21Aug04–9AP fst 1⅛ :48² 1:13 1:38 1:51 ⒻArlBCOks-G3 **90** 2 2½ 2½ 21 3½ 1¾ •Graham J L116 17.30 88–16 DH LovelyAfternoon116 DH Catboat118¾ MyTimeNow116¹ 3 wide, driving 10
15Jly04–8AP fm *1 Ⓣ :24⁴ :49³ 1:15² 1:40 3↑ⒻOC 62k/n3x-N **80** 4 3½ 42 4½ 32 2no Sterling L J Jr L118 18.80 79–22 Mymich119no *Lovely Afternoon*118½ Rich City Girl119hd Just missed 9
20Jun04–8AP gd 1 Ⓣ :24³ :49 1:14¹ 1:38 ⒻDoublDelta42k **78** 9 4½ 32 3½ 4½ 5½ Sterling L J Jr L117 3.70 83–16 Shmkindwor drful116hd ChicDncr116½ *HumorousMiss*115¾ Weakened a bit 10
31May04–5AP sly 1⅛ ⊗ :50¹ 1:14² 1:39³ 1:52³ ⒻOC 62k/n2x-N **83** 4 21 21 2½ 1½ 1¼ Sterling L J Jr L117 5.30 80–23 Lovely Afternoon117¼ Barrel Racer117¾ Dancing Liebling121⁷ Driving 5
26Apr04–9Haw fm 1 Ⓣ :22⁴ :46 1:11³ 1:37⁴ 3↑ⒻAlw 39180n2x **72** 3 6¼ 510 89 7¼ 6¾ Sterling L J Jr L115 3.30 78–21 Lighthouse Lil121½ *Sunset Kisses*121hd Barrel Racer116¾ No factor 10
3Apr04–4Haw fst 6f :21² :45³ :58³ 1:11⁴ ⒻMeafara42k **51** 3 5 59 69 6½ 510½ Sterling L J Jr L115 2.70 66–23 Prevalent113½ Clever Maid115¼ Stoneway115¾ No factor 7

Lovely Rafaela
Own: T N T Stud

Dk. b or b. f. 4 (Apr) KEESEP02 $600,000
Sire: A.P. Indy (Seattle Slew) $300,000
Dam: Campagrarde*Arg (Oak Dancer*GB)
Br: Diamond A Racing Corporation (Ky)
Tr: Lobo Paulo H(0 0 0 0 .00) 2004:(118 22 .19)

Life	9	2	1	0	$162,015	93		
2004	6	1	1	0	$125,535	93		
2003	3	1	0	0	$36,480	73		
	0	0	0	0	$0	–		
D.Fst	3	1	0	0	$36,480	73		
Wet(405)	0	0	0	0	$0	–		
Turf(325)	6	1	1	0	$125,535	93		
Dst(0)	0	0	0	0	$0	–		

7Nov04–8Hol fm 1⅛ Ⓣ :51² 1:16 1:39¹ 1:51² +ⒻASkirball62k **87** 7 5½ 5½ 6½ 5¼ 51 Douglas R R LB120 5.10 73–26 PennysFortune118½ SeekingtheHert116½ SwetWin120no Chased,willingly 7
11Oct04–8SA fm 1 Ⓣ :22⁴ :46⁴ 1:10³ 1:33⁴ ⒻHCRamsrSrH100k **86** 6 6½ 77 6¾ 6½ 6½ John K LB118 15.00 88–05 MeDomin116² *PennysFortune*116½ *CostumDsignr*115no 4 wide into stretch 9
3Jly04–6Hol fm 1¼ Ⓣ :49 1:14 1:38¹ 2:01² ⒻAmrcnOks-G1 **78** 12 7¼ 6¾ 7¾ 1212 1211 Pedroza M A LB121 22.20 74–13 TckrTp121¹ DncnthMood121² HollywoodStory121½ 4wd into lane,wkened 13
5Jun04–8Hol fm 1⅛ Ⓣ :50¹ 1:15 1:38¹ 1:49⁴ +ⒻHnymnBCH-G2 **93** 4 2½ 2½ 2½ 1hd 1no Espinoza V LB114 16.20 82–14 LovelyRfel114no WesternHemisphr114½ SgittR116nk Stalked,bid,up wire 8
19May04–5Hol fm 1$\frac{1}{16}$ Ⓣ :24¹ :49 1:13² 1:43 ⒻOC 80k/n1x-N **82** 2 21 32 4½ 32 2hd Espinoza V LB120 5.40 81–14 DawnsAngel118hd *LovelyRafael*120¹ ChurchEditor122¾ Surged late,missed 9
Previously trained by Mandella Richard
12Mar04–7SA fm *6½f Ⓣ :21¹ :43² 1:06⁴ 1:13¹ ⒻOC 80k/n1x-N **75** 5 5 7¼ 53 3½ 5¾ Solis A LB118 b 8.60 89–04 Cousineau118¾ TheDempseyLook118no HwMhl118¹ 4wd into str,tight1/16 9

Lucifer's Stone
Own: Team Solaris Stable

B. f. 4 (Mar) FTFFEB03 $150,000
Sire: Horse Chestnut*SAf (Fort Wood) $10,000
Dam: Ladue (Demons Begone)
Br: Mega Stable (Ky)
Tr: Rice Linda(0 0 0 0 .00) 2004:(288 38 .13)

Life	10	5	2	1	$405,991	100	D.Fst	0	0	0	0	$0 –
2004	6	4	1	0	$357,147	100	Wet(290)	0	0	0	0	$0 –
2003	4	1	1	1	$48,844	78	Turf(355)	10	5	2	1	$405,991 100
	0	0	0	0	$0	–	Dst(0)	0	0	0	0	$0 –

12Sep04- 9Bel gd 1⅛ Ⓣ :493 1:134 1:372 1:484 ⒻGrdCyBC-G1 **100** 2 34 52 41 31 11¼ Santos J A L118 b 9.20 86- 16 LucifersStone1181¼ Barancell116¾ NohsArk116nk Found room, drew clear 7
2Aug04- 8Sar gd 1 1/16 Ⓣ :25 :49 1:121 1:42 ⒻLkGeorge-G3 **90** 10 73 85¼ 65 63½ 53½ Day P L122 b 3.35 81- 15 SeducrsSong1151½ Vnturi119no FortuntDmsl117nk Inside run second turn 10
13Jun04- 8Bel fm 1⅛ Ⓣ :471 1:11 1:351 1:471 ⒻSandsPnt-G3 **92** 4 83¾ 65 41¼ 1½ 2nk Santos J A L122 b *2.25 94- 06 Mambo Slew122nk Lucifer's Stone1221¾ Vous119nk 4 wide move, gamely 10
14Apr04- 8Kee gd 1 Ⓣ :241 :483 1:13 1:372 ⒻApplachian113k **91** 1 75 84¾ 52¾ 31½ 1hd Santos J A L120 b *2.00 85- 15 LcfrsSton120hd *WstrnRnsom*1164¼ HnyRydr116hd Exch bmp,lost whip,drv 9
28Feb04- 8GP fm 1⅛ Ⓣ :50 1:153 1:404 1:523 ⒻHcmbride-G3 **87** 1 83¾ 94¼ 73¼ 2hd 1½ Santos J A L117 b 3.70 72- 34 *Lucifer's Stone*117½ Dynamia115¾ Honey Ryder1171¼ Hit gate, steadied trn 12
14Jan04- 7GP fm *1 1/16 Ⓣ :232 :49 1:131 1:442 ⒻAlw 34000N1x **82** 8 93 93½ 72¾ 1hd 11 Santos J A L117 b *1.90 82- 23 *LucifersStone*1171 SkipPoker121nk LivWirLucy1171 Ducked in, stdy 1/8 pl 10

Lunarpal
Own: Heiligbrodt Racing Stable

B. c. 3 (Apr)
Sire: Successful Appeal (Valid Appeal) $6,000
Dam: Quiet Eclipse (Quiet American)
Br: L. William Heiligbrodt (Fla)
Tr: Asmussen Steven M(0 0 0 0 .00) 2004:(2293 555 .24)

Life	5	4	0	0	$284,677	85	D.Fst	4	3	0	0	$183,493 85
2004	5	4	0	0	$284,677	85	Wet(365*)	1	1	0	0	$101,184 79
2003	0	M	0	0	$0	–	Turf(259*)	0	0	0	0	$0 –
	0	0	0	0	$0	–	Dst(0)	0	0	0	0	$0 –

29Jly04- 8Sar fst 6f :221 :452 :571 1:091 Sanford-G2 **76** 2 2 1hd 31 62¾ 610 Sellers S J L122 5.30 86- 11 *Afleet Alex*1205¼ Flamenco122nk Consolidator118¾ Vied inside, tired 11
5Jly04-10CD sly 6f :214 :452 :58 1:112 BshfdMnr-G3 **79** 3 2 1hd 11½ 1½ 1nk Sellers S J L121 *1.10 84- 18 Lunarpal121nk *Storm Surge*1171¼ Maximus C1171¼ 3path,gamely,drvg 7
5Jun04- 8CD fst 5½f :221 :461 :572 1:04 KyBC-G3 **84** 4 1 1hd 11½ 12 1nk Sellers S J L121 *.10 92- 12 *Lunarpal*121nk *Consolidator*1151¾ Smoke Warning1178 Hop,broke out start 4
1May04- 6CD fst 5f :213 :45 :574 Juvenile115k **85** 5 2 21 1½ 12 15 Sellers S J L118 *1.30 96- 06 *Lunarpal*1185 GallantSecret1152¼ *ClssicElegnce*1152¾ Bid, drew off, driving 5
18Apr04- 3Kee fst 4½f :221 :452 :513 Md Sp Wt 42k **–** 4 4 2hd 12 17 Sellers S J L118 2.50 97- 14 *Lunarpal*1187 TemporryZone118no HedgeYourBet1187 Drvg,gathered late 7

Lundy's Liability (Brz)

Own: Stud TNT and Slack Mrs. M

B. c. 5 (Sep)
Sire: Candy Stripes (Blushing Groom*Fr) $6,000
Dam: Emerald Counter (Geiger Counter)
Br: Stud Tnt (Brz)
Tr: Frankel Robert J(0 0 0 0 .00) 2004:(491 135 .27)

Life	7	4	1	0	$1,553,930	108	D.Fst	5 2 1 0	$1,542,500 108
2004	5	2	1	0	$1,542,500	108	Wet(332)	0 0 0 0	$0 –
2003	2	2	0	0	$11,430	–	Turf(345)	2 2 0 0	$11,430 –
	0	0	0	0	$0	–	Dst(0)	0 0 0 0	$0 –

26Nov04–11CD fst 1⅛ :48 1:12 1:37^2 1:50^4 3↑ ClarkH-G2 **102** 4 1½ 11½ 1hd 3^3 6^5 Flores D R L120 4.10 78–25 Saint Liam117¹¼ Seek Gold111no Perfect Drift1181¼ Drft in bmp start,tire 9
20Oct04–8SA fst 1⅛ :48 1:11^2 1:35^3 1:48^1 3↑ GdwdBCH-G2 **108** 2 1hd 2hd 1½ 2hd 1hd Flores D R **LB**113 2.30 93–08 LundysLiability118hd TotalImpct119^2 *SuphBlitz*117^6 Drifted in bit,gamely 5
27Mar04 Nad Al Sheba (UAE) ft *1⅛ LH 1:50^4 UAE Derby-G2 Stk 2000000 1¾ Marwing W 130 - *Lundy's Liability*130¾ Petit Paris130¾ Little Jim1303¾ 9
3rd straight, steady headway 400m out, led fnl 150m, driven out
6Mar04 Nad Al Sheba (UAE) ft *1⅓ LH 1:51^2 Al Bastikiya Alw 150000 22¾ Marwing W 132 - Petit Paris1342¾ *Lundy's Liability*1321¾ Little Jim1379½ 6
Timeform rating: 105
Tracked in 3rd,bid 2f out,held by winner
5Feb04 Nad Al Sheba (UAE) ft *1 LH 1:37^3 UAE 2000 Guineas-G3 Alw 250000 43¾ Marwing W 130 - Little Jim1302½ Jack Sullivan121½ *Rosencrans*121¾ 14
Timeform rating: 104
Tracked in 3rd,lacked rally.Petit Paris 5th

Lydgate

Own: Godolphin

B. h. 5 (Feb)
Sire: Pulpit (A.P. Indy) $60,000
Dam: Mariuka (Danzig)
Br: Kennelot Stables Limited (Ky)
Tr: Saeed Bin Suroor(0 0 0 0 .00) 2004:(0 0 .00)

Life	13	2	4	0	$139,769	102	D.Fst	2 0 2 0	$14,200 79
2004	8	1	2	0	$100,069	102	Wet(384)	1 0 0 0	$2,700 73
2003	5	1	2	0	$39,700	92	Turf(345)	10 2 2 0	$122,869 102
	0	0	0	0	$0	–	Dst(0)	0 0 0 0	$0 –

14Oct04 Newmarket (GB) sf 5f Ⓣ 1:00^4 3↑ Thoroughbred Breeders Handicap S. Hcp 37300 83½ Dettori L 133 6.00 Corridor Creeper123½ If Paradise125nk Fruit of Glory119hd 10
Hld up: rdn 1/2-way: r.o ins fnl f: nt trble ldrs
11Sep04 Goodwood (GB) gf 6f Ⓣ Str 1:12^1 3↑ Starlit Stakes (Listed) Stk 53900 43½ Ahern E 133 4.00 Var1261½ Ruby Rocket119½ So Will I1281½ 7
Racd on cuter: hld up: shkn up 2f out: one pce and no imp
15Jun04 Ascot (GB) gf 5f Ⓣ Str 1:00 3↑ King's Stand Stakes-G2 Stk 256000 9^4 Dettori L 128 *6.00 The Tatling128½ Cape of Good Hope128nk *Frizzante*125nk 19
Held up towards rear, ridden over 2f out, never near to challenge
30Apr04–7CD gd 5f Ⓣ :21^4 :44^3 :56^2 3↑ TurfSprt-G3 **102** 11 8 74½ 7^3 42½ 1^1 Day P L114 7.70 95–05 Lydgate114^1 *Mighty Beau*117½ Banned in Boston1141¾ 6w lane,driving 11
4Apr04–2SA fm *6½f Ⓣ :21^2 :44^1 1:06^4 1:12^4 4↑ Alw 49000n1x **97** 2 5 64¾ 5^4 23½ 2½ Nakatani C S **LB**120 *1.00 92–08 The Griff120½ *Lydgate*120^4 Quietly Quick120^2 Came out str,rallied 8
6Mar04–4SA fm *6½f Ⓣ :21^2 :43^4 1:07^1 1:13 4↑ Alw 57820n1x **84** 3 4 2^1 2½ 1^1 41¼ Flores D R **LB**120 *1.10 91–07 Blairs General122hd Quietly Quick120^1 *The Griff*120nk Bid,led,outfinished 10
31Jan04–5SA fm 1 Ⓣ :21^3 :44^3 1:08^2 1:34 4↑ Alw 54184n1x **85** 7 3^5 38½ 2^3 2½ 4^6 Solis A **LB**117 4.50 86–13 *Leroidesanimaux*1172½ Haasil121^1 Pssionforcshin1232½ Chased,bid,wkened 11
7Jan04–7SA fm *6½f Ⓣ :21^3 :43^3 1:06^1 1:12^3 4↑ Alw 52000n1x **91** 1 4 1hd 1^1 1^1 2½ Flores D R **LB**120 *1.50 93–05 *Vronsky*121½ Lydgate120½ Great White Father119nk Inside, game try 9

Madcap Escapade
Own: Lunsford Bruce

B. f. 4 (May) KEESEP02 $160,000
Sire: Hennessy (Storm Cat) $35,000
Dam: Sassy Pants (Saratoga Six)
Br: Needham/ Betz Thoroughbreds & James Blackburn (Ky)
Tr: Brothers Frank L(0 0 0 0 .00) 2004:(83 16 .19)

Life	5	4	0	1	$536,400	108	D.Fst	4	4	0	0	$479,200 108
2004	5	4	0	1	$536,400	108	Wet(373)	1	0	0	1	$57,200 97
2003	0	M	0	0	$0	-	Turf(285)	0	0	0	0	$0 -
	0	0	0	0	$0	-	Dst(0)	0	0	0	0	$0 -

30Apr04-10CD my 1⅛ :46 1:094 1:363 1:504 ⒻKyOaks-G1 **97** 5 13 14½ 14 1hd 33 Bailey J D L121 3.40 80- 17 Ashado1211¼ *IslandSand*1211¾ MadcapEscapade1211¼ Fast pace,weakened 11
3Apr04-9Kee fst 1 1/16 :24 :472 1:112 1:442 ⒻAshland-G1 **98** 2 11 11½ 11½ 12½ 1½ Douglas R R L118 *.70 90- 14 Madcap Escapade118½ *Ashado*1234 Last Song1203 Drift in start,driving 4
13Mar04-4GP fst 7f :214 :443 1:091 1:224 ⒻFrwrdGal-G2 **95** 2 5 11½ 11½ 17 14¾ Bailey J D L121 *.20 88- 13 *MadcapEscapade*1214¾ LaReina1212¼ *Frenchglen*1152¼ Step slow st, handily 5
14Feb04-8GP fst 6f :211 :44 :56 1:084 ⒻOldHat100k **108** 7 4 22 1½ 15 111¾ Douglas R R L115 *.80 98- 07 *MdcpEscpde*11511¾ SwetVision1151¼ *SmokyGlckn*1192 Off rail, kept to task 9
4Jan04-5GP fst 6f :214 :444 :564 1:091 ⒻMd Sp Wt 32k **93** 4 10 11 11 13½ 110 Douglas R R L121 16.30 96- 10 *MdcpEscpd*12110 DnmWldct1215¼ WckdlWs1211¾ Widened,steady coaxing 12

Magistretti
Own: Tabor Michael B

B. h. 5 (Mar)
Sire: Diesis*GB (Sharpen Up*GB) $30,000
Dam: Ms. Strike Zone (Deputy Minister)
Br: Tri-County Farms LLC (Ky)
Tr: Biancone Patrick L(0 0 0 0 .00) 2004:(130 29 .22)

Life	16	4	6	0	$1,264,117	111	D.Fst	0	0	0	0	$0 -
2004	7	1	2	0	$782,981	111	Wet(274)	0	0	0	0	$0 -
2003	5	2	2	0	$458,559	-	Turf(337)	16	4	6	0	$1,264,117 111
	0	0	0	0	$0	-	Dst(0)	0	0	0	0	$0 -

30Oct04-8LS yl 1½ Ⓣ:49 1:134 2:04 2:293 3↑BCTurf-G1 **102** 6 49 54 22 43½ 45 Prado E S L126 b 6.10 118-07 BettrTlkNow1261¾ KittnsJoy1211 Powrscourt1262¼ Steadied 3/16pl, tired 8
2Oct04-9Bel yl 1½ Ⓣ:504 1:171 2:071 2:294 3↑TfClscIv-G1 **109** 4 21½ 2hd 11½ 2hd 22½ Prado E S L126 b *1.70 69- 22 Kitten's Joy1212½ Magistretti126¾ Tycoon1213 Quick move, gamely 7
11Sep04-9Bel yl 1⅜ Ⓣ:50 1:142 1:38 2:143 3↑ManOWar-G1 **111** 3 75 73½ 84¾ 45½ 11¼ Prado E S L126 b 3.15 90- 10 Magistretti1261¼ Epalo1262 King's Drama126¾ Fast finish outside 8
Previously trained by Callaghan Neville A
14Aug04-9AP fm 1¼ Ⓣ:472 1:12 1:363 2:00 3↑ArlMilln-G1 **104** 12 97 96 93¾ 42½ 32½ Prado E S L126 b 24.00 108 - ⒹPowerscourt1261½ Kicken Kris1261 *Magistretti*126½ 4 wide, belatedly 13
Placed second through disqualification
17Jly04 Newbury (GB) gf 1¼ Ⓣ LH 2:04 3↑ Steventon Stakes (Listed) 48¼ Holland D 129 *1.85 Muqbil129¾ Vespone1296 Musanid1291½ 7
Timeform rating: 105 Stk 56100 *Tracked in 3rd,2nd 2f out,weakened 1f out.Kaieteur 5th*
7Jly04 Newmarket (GB) gf 1½ Ⓣ RH 2:324 3↑ Princess of Wales's Stakes-G2 46½ Holland D 128 3.30 Bandari128½ Sulamani1332½ High Accolade1283½ 8
Timeform rating: 113 Stk 185400 *Rated in 6th,mild bid 3f out,weakened over 1f out*
4Jun04 Epsom (GB) gd 1½ Ⓣ LH 2:354 4↑ Coronation Cup-G1 64¼ Murtagh J P 126 7.00 Warrsan1261¾ *Doyen*126no Vallee Enchantee123no 11
Timeform rating: 118 Stk 460000 *Tracked in 4th,outpaced 2f out.Imperial Dancer 9th*

Mambo Slew
Own: Manganaro Frank

Dk. b or b. f. 4 (Apr)
Sire: Kingmambo (Mr. Prospector) $300,000
Dam: Slew Boyera (Seattle Slew)
Br: F.J.F.M., LLC (Ky)
Tr: Biancone Patrick L(0 0 0 0 .00) 2004:(130 29 .22)

Life	11	4	2	0	$272,170	93	D.Fst	1	0	0	0	$1,350	49
2004	8	2	2	0	$183,820	93	Wet(378)	0	0	0	0	$0	–
2003	3	2	0	0	$88,350	81	Turf(323)	10	4	2	0	$270,820	93
	0	0	0	0	$0	–	Dst(0)	0	0	0	0	$0	–

16Oct04-8Kee gd 1⅛ Ⓣ :49³ 1:14² 1:38⁴ 1:51¹ ⒻQEIICup-G1 **82** 1 3¹½ 3² 2² 5³½ 5⁶½ Farina T 121 11.00 74-20 Ticker Tape121½ Barancella121½ *River Belle*121¹ Between lane,empty 7
12Sep04-9Bel gd 1⅛ Ⓣ :49³ 1:13⁴ 1:37² 1:48⁴ ⒻGrdCyBC-G1 **93** 5 4⁵½ 4¹½ 3½ 2ʰᵈ 5³ Prado E S 118 4.30e 83-16 Lucifer's Stone118¹¼ Barancella116¾ Noahs Ark116ⁿᵏ 3 wide move, faded 7
23Aug04-8Sar gd 1⅛ Ⓣ :50 1:14¹ 1:38¹ 1:50² ⒻLakPlcdH-G2 **92** 2 6⁶ 6³½ 6⁶ 3³ 2³½ Prado E S 120 1.80 74-31 Spotlight116³½ MamboSlew120¾ *FortunateDmsel*116³ Inside move, gamely 7
3Jly04-6Hol fm 1¼ Ⓣ :49 1:14 1:38¹ 2:01² ⒻAmrcnOks-G1 **90** 2 10⁷¾ 11⁷ 8⁴¾ 7⁷¼ 6⁴½ Smith M E B121 6.80 80-13 TickerTp121¹ DcinthMood121² HollywoodStory121½ Chased,no late bid 13
13Jun04-8Bel fm 1⅛ Ⓣ :47¹ 1:11 1:35¹ 1:47¹ ⒻSandsPnt-G3 **93** 3 7³¾ 7⁵¼ 8³ 4¹ 1ⁿᵏ Prado E S 122 5.00 94-06 Mambo Slew122ⁿᵏ Lucifer's Stone122¹¾ Vous119ⁿᵏ Got through inside 10
11Apr04-8SA fm 1 Ⓣ :22² :45³ 1:10¹ 1:34² ⒻProvidncia113k **69** 8 11⁹¾ 11¹⁰ 8⁵½ 11⁹¼ 10⁹ Smith M E B120 *2.10 81-10 Ticker Tape118²½ Amorama114¹ Winendynme115¹ Blocked rail lane 12
18Mar04-7SA fm 1 Ⓣ :24 :48² 1:12³ 1:36¹ ⒻChinaDoll75k **83** 7 2½ 2ʰᵈ 2½ 1ʰᵈ 2¾ Smith M E 122 *1.60 80-13 *Ticker Tape*117¾ Mambo Slew122¹½ Amorama116ⁿᵒ Pressed, led, gamely 10
14Jan04-7SA fm 1 Ⓣ :23 :47 1:11 1:34³ ⒻBlueNorthr76k **86** 5 4³½ 4³½ 3² 1¹½ 1³ Smith M E 120 *1.80 89-10 Mambo Slew120³ *Ticker Tape*116² Yingyingying115¹ 3wd bid,led,clear 8

Mark One
Own: Stronach Stables

Gr/ro. g. 6 (Apr)
Sire: Alphabet Soup (Cozzene) $20,000
Dam: My Marchesa (Stately Don)
Br: Adena Springs (Ky)
Tr: Vella Daniel J(0 0 0 0 .00) 2004:(223 37 .17)

Life	29	8	7	4	$726,037	103	D.Fst	16	4	5	2	$340,858	99
2004	10	3	3	1	$378,988	103	Wet(331)	5	3	1	1	$271,575	103
2003	9	3	0	1	$180,972	96	Turf(291)	8	1	1	1	$113,604	96
	0	0	0	0	$0	–	Dst(0)	0	0	0	0	$0	–

20Nov04-8WO my 1¹⁄₁₆ :23⁴ :47³ 1:12¹ 1:45 3↑WoSltCpH-G3 **97** 3 3³ 3⁶ 3³ 3² 1ʰᵈ Landry R C L119 6.25 86-27 MrkOne119ʰᵈ ABitOGold120²½ NorfolkKnight120²¼ Determinedly,just up 4
30Oct04-9WO yl 1¼ Ⓣ :49⁴ 1:15⁴ 1:43 2:09³ 3↑ChfBearhrt108k **77** 2 6³¾ 6¹½ 10¹¼ 7¹⁰ 7⁹¼ Landry R C L120 *1.20 50-41 LstAnswr118½ RnbowsforLck115⁴ ControlTwr118ⁿᵒ Blocked rail late turn 10
26Sep04-2WO fst 1¹⁄₁₆ :24² :48² 1:12³ 1:45¹ 3↑Alw 83700NC **90** 4 3²½ 4⁴½ 4⁴½ 3⁴½ 2⁵½ Landry R C L118 *.75 79-33 *NorfolkKnight*113⁵½ MarkOne118²¼ DreamLuncher116⁴ 3wd,determinedly 5
6Sep04-8WO fm 1½ Ⓣ :49¹ 1:13² 2:01⁴ 2:25⁴ 3↑NiagrBCH-G2 **90** 4 5³½ 2ʰᵈ 2²½ 3⁶ 3⁷¾ McAleney J S L115 7.30 93-06 StruttheStge121⁴ *ColorfulJudgmnt*115³¾ MrkOn115¹¼ Bid 3wd,vied,yielded 6
7Aug04-8WO fst 1¹⁄₁₆ :24¹ :48³ 1:12³ 1:44¹ 3↑SeagramCup136k **93** 1 3³½ 4³ 3²½ 3⁵½ 2⁵ Landry R C L121 *1.45 85-17 *One for Rose*116⁵ Mark One121¾ Hydrogen115ⁿᵏ Stalked rail,all out 7
1Jly04-8WO fst 1¼ :47 1:12 1:37² 2:03¹ 3↑DomDayH-G3 **73** 5 6⁸¼ 5³ 5⁵½ 3⁸ 21²¾ Landry R C L118 2.85 76-11 Mobil122¹²¾ Mark One118ⁿᵏ The Judge Sez Who119³¼ Closed btwn,all out 7
24May04-8WO sly 1¹⁄₁₆ :24 :47⁴ 1:12¹ 1:46³ 4↑EclipseH-G3 **99** 1 3³ 3²½ 3³ 2¹ 1²½ Landry R C L115 3.60 78-26 Mark One115²½ Open Concert113⁴½ RockAgain115¾ Stalked inside,driving 5
2May04-9WO sly 1⁷⁰ :23 :46 1:10² 1:41³ 4↑Alw 86400NC **103** 1 3² 3⁴ 2²½ 2¹½ 1ⁿᵏ Landry R C L116 2.40 101 - *Mark One*116ⁿᵏ Open Concert116⁶ Mortgage Man116² Rallied,just up 6
23Feb04-8GP fm *1⅛ Ⓣ :48² 1:12² 1:38³ 1:50⁴ 4↑Alw 46000c **77** 7 1ʰᵈ 1ʰᵈ 2ʰᵈ 5³½ 7⁸½ Coa E M L120 b 6.20 79-19 Full Flow116² Host118ⁿᵏ First Lieutenant116ʰᵈ Dueled, faltered 8
25Jan04-10GP fm 1⅜ Ⓣ :48³ 1:13² 1:37 2:12² 3↑MDiarmdH-G3 **93** 8 4¾ 4¹½ 4²½ 4⁴ 4⁵½ Coa E M L114 b 20.70 90-07 RqustforProl115¹½ SlwVlly117¾ SrBrnsSword113³¼ Angled out, weakened 12

Mass Media

Own: Gary and Mary West Stables Inc

Dk. b or b. c. 4 (Mar) KEESEP02 $65,000
Sire: Touch Gold (Deputy Minister) $50,000
Dam: Sultry Allure (Forty Niner)
Br: Live Oak Stud (Ky)
Tr: Frankel Robert J(0 0 0 0 .00) 2004:(491 135 .27)

Life	8	5	0	0	$166,550	115	D.Fst	8	5	0	0	$166,550	115
2004	5	3	0	0	$137,750	115	Wet(332)	0	0	0	0	$0	–
2003	3	2	0	0	$28,800	100	Turf(224)	0	0	0	0	$0	–
	0	0	0	0	$0	–	Dst(0)	0	0	0	0	$0	–

Date/Race	Cond	Dist	Fractions	Race	Fig	PP	St	1C	2C	Str	Fin	Jockey	Wt	Odds	Speed	Top Finishers	Comment	Fld
26Dec04-8SA	fst	7f	:221 :441 1:081 1:214	Malibu-G1	**95**	1	8	62¼	41½	41½	52	Castellano J J	LB119 b	*1.20	94-09	RockHardTen121½ LavaMan115no HrvrdAvenue115no	Waited bit,got thru	10
31Oct04-7Aqu	fst	7f	:221 :443 1:082 1:21	3↑SportPgH-G3	**115**	7	2	2hd	21½	13½	13½	Castellano J J	L113 b	8.30	100-13	Mass Media1133½ *Lion Tamer*1182 Gygistar120no	Bumped start, 3 wide	9
12Sep04-7Bel	fst	6f	:214 :442 :562 1:084	FlySoFree59k	**101**	5	4	47	32½	1hd	1hd	Castellano J J	L117 b	12.90	95-14	*MassMedia*117hd Smokume1193¼ AllHailStormy117½	Bumped start, widest	5
7Aug04-8Sar	fst	6f	:214 :443 :564 1:092	Amstrdam-G2	**74**	3	6	32½	72¼	76¾	712¼	Bailey J D	L117 b	5.10	83-13	Bwana Charlie123¾ *Pomeroy*1232 Weigelia123½	Steadied turn, tired	7
23Jun04-8Bel	fst	6f	:22 :443 :564 1:10	3↑Alw 47000n2x	**97**	2	1	2hd	2hd	1hd	1½	Bailey J D	L115 b	*1.40	89-14	Mass Media115½ Forest Grove1151 Introspect118hd	Vied inside, prevailed	7

Mayo On the Side

Own: Lothenbach Stables Inc

B. m. 6 (Feb)
Sire: French Deputy (Deputy Minister) $30,126
Dam: Slewveau (Slew o' Gold)
Br: Robert Lothenbach (Ky)
Tr: Nafzger Carl A(0 0 0 0 .00) 2004:(358 54 .15)

Life	28	7	4	8	$642,366	102	D.Fst	22	6	3	6	$539,446	102
2004	12	2	2	3	$405,241	102	Wet(388)	6	1	1	2	$102,920	96
2003	9	3	1	3	$163,240	101	Turf(308)	0	0	0	0	$0	–
	0	0	0	0	$0	–	Dst(0)	0	0	0	0	$0	–

Date/Race	Cond	Dist	Fractions	Race	Fig	PP	St	1C	2C	Str	Fin	Jockey	Wt	Odds	Speed	Top Finishers	Comment	Fld
25Nov04-10CD	gd	1⅛	:483 1:131 1:384 1:514	3↑ⒻFallCtyH-G2	**81**	6	32½	52½	52½	55¼	611¼	McKee J	L116 fb	4.10	67-24	Halory Leigh1162¾ Susan's Angel1143¼ Miss Fortunate1132¼	5w,weakened	7
7Nov04-10CD	fst	1	:223 :453 1:102 1:35	3↑ⒻCDDstafH-G2	**92**	10	96¼	106¼	86¼	68	68	Albarado R J	L118 fb	4.80	87-13	*Halory Leigh*1155 Lady Tak123¾ Susan's Angel115¾	6w lane,no bid	12
10Oct04-8Kee	fst	1⅛	:464 1:113 1:37 1:493	3↑ⒻSpinster-G1	**102**	5	64	42½	62	31½	33½	Albarado R J	L123 fb	10.80	89-12	Azeri1233 Tamweel123½ Mayo On the Side1233¾	4w lane,no final gain	7
18Sep04-12TP	fst	1 1/16	:232 :464 1:113 1:441	3↑ⒻTPBC-G3	**88**	2	69	69	43½	31½	2¾	Albarado R J	L120 fb	2.50	90-11	Susan's Angel116¾ Mayo OntheSide1201½ Angela'sLove1222	In tight early	6
1Aug04-9Sar	fst	1⅛	:473 1:104 1:35 1:474	3↑ⒻGoFWandH-G1	**88**	2	43	53	54½	47	410¾	Albarado R J	L115 fb	15.70	85-14	Azeri1201¾ *Sightseek*1222 *Storm Flag Flying*1177	3 wide, no response	5
10Jly04-9EIP	fst	1	:24 :472 1:121 1:371	3↑ⒻHBPAH75k	**97**	2	73	64	3nk	11	2½	Borel C H	L120 fb	*1.80	93-13	MissFortunt115½ MyoOnthSd1201 ThrRunsHtt116¾	5w bid,led,outfinished	8
19Jun04-8AP	fst	7f	:224 :454 1:11 1:232	3↑ⒻChcgoBCH-G3	**81**	4	2	2hd	3½	41¾	47¼	Razo E Jr	L118 fb	*.30	85-14	MyTrustyCat1161¾ OurJosephin1121½ SmokeChser1164	3 wide, weakened	5
1May04-8CD	fst	7f	:222 :45 1:093 1:223	4↑ⒻHmnaDstH-G1	**99**	3	3	42	33	1hd	1hd	Day P	L114 fb	5.50	89-06	Mayo On the Side114hd Azeri1257¼ Randaroo121nk	3wd bid,led,gamely	4
16Apr04-9Kee	fst	1 1/16	:231 :473 1:122 1:434	4↑ⒻDbldogdare114k	**99**	4	41½	42	51¼	31½	11¾	Day P	L116 fb	3.40	93-16	*MyoOntheSide*1161¾ CtFightr1162¼ RorEmotion116½	Lack room 5/16s,drvg	8
13Mar04-10OP	fst	1 1/16	:23 :464 1:12 1:441	3↑ⒻOaklwnBC-G3	**88**	2	52½	44	5½	1hd	32½	Doocy T T	L113 fb	3.90	86-15	GoldenSont1171¾ KeystothHrt117¾ *MyoOnthSid*113½	4-w bid 5/16, held 3rd	10
8Feb04-11GP	fst	7f	:222 :444 1:084 1:212	3↑ⒻShrlJnsH-G3	**85**	2	8	86¼	88¾	810	410½	Velez J A Jr	L115 fb	12.80	84-16	*Randaroo*1187¼ Harmony Lodge121¾ Halory Leigh1142½	Passed tired rivals	8
11Jan04-10GP	fst	6f	:214 :444 :57 1:093	3↑Ⓕ1stLadyH-G3	**100**	2	8	911	99¾	76½	32¼	Velez J A Jr	L115 fb	33.20	92-12	HrmonyLodg1191¾ HousPrty118½ MyoOnthSid1152	Swung out, full of run	9

McCann's Mojave

Own: Hunt Alix Nikke and Willman, Mike

B. c. 5 (Feb)
Sire: Memo*Chi (Mocito Guapo) $7,500
Dam: Joni U. Bar (Nordic Prince)
Br: Alix Nikki Hunt & Mike Willman (Cal)
Tr: Dorfman Leonard(0 0 0 0 .00) 2004:(11 2 .18)

Life	7	5	1	0	$280,820	108	**D.Fst**	5	4	0	0	$170,520	104
2004	4	2	1	0	$177,140	108	**Wet(359)**	1	0	1	0	$44,360	108
2003	2	2	0	0	$74,880	100	**Turf(208)**	1	1	0	0	$65,940	105
	0	0	0	0	$0	–	**Dst(0)**	0	0	0	0	$0	–

Date/Race	Trk	Dist	Fractions	Race	Speed	PP	St	1C	2C	Str	Fin	Jockey	Wt	Odds		Top Finishers	Comment	Fld
1May04–5CD	gd	7f	$:22^2$ $:45^1$ $1:08^4$ $1:21^1$	4↑CDH-G2	**108**	4	1	2^1	2^1	$2^{2\frac{1}{2}}$	$2^{3\frac{1}{2}}$	Valdivia J Jr	L117	6.60	92–06	*Spightstown*$115^{3\frac{1}{2}}$ McCnnsMojv117^2 Publiction116^2	Stalked 3wd,2nd best	7
28Mar04–8SA	fst	$6\frac{1}{2}$f	$:21^4$ $:44^1$ $1:08^4$ $1:15^3$	4↑PtrGrBCH-G2	**104**	2	5	2^{hd}	1^{hd}	2^{hd}	$1^{1\frac{3}{4}}$	Valdivia J Jr	LB116	6.90	94–12	McCnnsMjv$116^{1\frac{3}{4}}$ UnfrlthFlg$114^{1\frac{3}{4}}$ Blsthstndrd118	Duel btwn, edged away	5
14Feb04–3SA	fm	*$6\frac{1}{2}$f Ⓣ	$:21^2$ $:43$ $1:06$ $1:12^1$	4↑[S]SensatStrH109k	**105**	5	4	$2^{3\frac{1}{2}}$	2^9	$2^{2\frac{1}{2}}$	$1^{\frac{1}{2}}$	Valdivia J Jr	LB115	10.60	96–07	*McCnnsMojv*$115^{\frac{1}{2}}$ *Lnnyfromlibu*120^1 HmtThought117^1	Bid btwn,led,gamely	8
24Jan04–9SA	fst	$6\frac{1}{2}$f	$:21^4$ $:44^2$ $1:08^1$ $1:14^3$	4↑OC 62k/N2x-N	**92**	2	6	$7^{4\frac{1}{4}}$	$7^{4\frac{3}{4}}$	6^5	$7^{5\frac{1}{2}}$	Stevens G L	LB118	*2.40	93–09	Casas Caballo$118^{2\frac{1}{2}}$ Kewen118^1 Our Bobby V.118^{nk}	Steadied 5-1/2	8

Medaglia d'Oro

Own: Gann Edmund A

Dk. b or b. h. 6 (Apr)
Sire: El Prado*Ire (Sadler's Wells) $100,000
Dam: Cappucino Bay (Bailjumper)
Br: Albert Bell & Joyce Bell (Ky)
Tr: Frankel Robert J(0 0 0 0 .00) 2004:(491 135 .27)

Life	17	8	7	0	$5,754,720	120	**D.Fst**	16	7	7	0	$5,154,720	120
2004	2	1	1	0	$1,500,000	117	**Wet(334)**	1	1	0	0	$600,000	113
2003	5	3	2	0	$1,990,000	119	**Turf(305)**	0	0	0	0	$0	–
	0	0	0	0	$0	–	**Dst(0)**	0	0	0	0	$0	–

Date/Race	Trk	Dist	Fractions	Race	Speed	PP	St	1C	2C	Str	Fin	Jockey	Wt	Odds		Top Finishers	Comment	Fld
27Mar04 Nad Al Sheba (UAE) **Timeform rating: 129**	ft	*$1\frac{1}{4}$	LH $2:00^1$	3↑ Dubai World Cup-G1 Stk 6000000							$2^{\frac{3}{4}}$	Bailey J D	126	-		Pleasantly Perfect$126^{\frac{3}{4}}$ Medaglia d'Oro126^5 Victory Moon$126^{7\frac{3}{4}}$	*Tracked leader,led 2-1/2f out,headed 100y out*	12
7Feb04–10GP	fst	$1\frac{1}{8}$	$:47^1$ $1:11$ $1:35^3$ $1:47^3$	3↑DonnH-G1	**117**	3	2^{hd}	$2^{\frac{1}{2}}$	$2^{\frac{1}{2}}$	1^3	$1^{4\frac{3}{4}}$	Bailey J D	L122	*.60	101–09	Medaglia d'Oro$122^{4\frac{3}{4}}$ Seattle Fitz$113^{3\frac{3}{4}}$ Funny Cide119^4	In tight 1st turn	8

Medallist

Own: Clay Robert N

Dk. b or b. c. 4 (Feb)
Sire: Touch Gold (Deputy Minister) $50,000
Dam: Santaria (Star de Naskra)
Br: Robert N. Clay & The Albert G. Clay 1990 Revocable Tru (Ky)
Tr: Jerkens H. A(0 0 0 0 .00) 2004:(374 72 .19)

Life	10	4	1	1	$291,375	113	D.Fst	9	4	1	1	$288,027 113
2004	10	4	1	1	$291,375	113	Wet(327)	1	0	0	0	$3,348 87
2003	0	M	0	0	$0	–	Turf(224)	0	0	0	0	$0 –
	0	0	0	0	$0	–	Dst(0)	0	0	0	0	$0 –

18Dec04-10Crc fst 7f :221 :45 1:093 1:223 3↑KenyNoeJrH100k 113 8 4 3nk 1hd 13 14½ Santos J A L114 4.60 103–11 Medallist1144½ ParadiseDancer113¾ HastyKris1151¾ 4w early, pace, ran on 10

28Nov04-9Aqu sly 6f :212 :441 :564 1:094 3↑FallHwtH-G3 87 9 9 65¼ 34 44½ 55½ Santos J A L134 *2.00 83–16 ThunderTouch1261¼ Papua128½ Evesdropper127nk Awkward start, 4 wide 9

28Aug04-10Sar fst 7f :22 :443 1:082 1:204 KngsBshp-G1 66 1 7 1hd 1½ 712 718¾ Chavez J F L123 *1.75 81–04 Pomeroy1211½ Weigelia1211 Ice Wynnd Fire1174¼ Drifted out 1/4 pole 8

8Aug04-9Sar fst 1⅛ :453 1:093 1:343 1:472 JimDandy-G2 82 1 12 13½ 1½ 410 516 Chavez J F 121 2.00 82–02 Purge1214½ The Cliff's Edge123½ [D]Eddington1157¼ Set pace, tired 6

11Jly04-8Bel fst 1 1/16 :224 :442 1:074 1:40 Dwyer-G2 112 2 12 16 18 17 13¾ Chavez J F 121 3.40 100–09 Medllist1213¾ TheCliffsEdge123½ *SirShckleton*12114½ Long lead, kept busy 6

1May04-8Aqu fst 1 :222 :44 1:074 1:342 Withers-G3 110 3 2hd 1½ 1hd 11½ 13¼ Chavez J F 116 8.50 93–19 *Medllist*1163¼ ForstDngr1231 TwoDownAutomtic1205¼ Drifted out stretch 5

31Mar04-8GP fst 6f :214 :443 :57 1:102 Alw 34000N1x 83 6 4 4¾ 3nk 32½ 21½ Alvarado R Jr 120 *1.10 88–20 Classy Migration1181½ *Medallist*1201¼ Call Me Moe118nk Floated out turn 7

13Mar04-2GP fst 7f :22 :441 1:093 1:232 Alw 34000N1x 79 7 2 2hd 2hd 22½ 34½ Santos J A 122 1.80 80–13 *Forest Danger*1222½ Classic Wine1182 Medallist122hd Vied, tired 7

8Feb04-8GP fst 7f :224 :454 1:10 1:224 Md Sp Wt 32k 89 5 5 11 11½ 13 13½ Santos J A 122 *1.10 88–16 Medallist1223½ Evening Trial1224¼ Joma122½ Inside, ridden out 10

24Jan04-4GP fst 7f :222 :452 1:102 1:231 Md Sp Wt 32k 72 10 10 2hd 2½ 32 48 Santos J A 122 *2.70 78–11 HarbourGate1226½ *Intimidator*122hd GnnettPek1221½ Off slowly, gave way 12

Megahertz (GB)

Own: Bello Michael

Ch. m. 6 (May)
Sire: Pivotal*GB (Polar Falcon) $71,344
Dam: Heavenly Ray (Rahy)
Br: Cheveley Park Stud Ltd (GB)
Tr: Frankel Robert J(0 0 0 0 .00) 2004:(491 135 .27)

Life	28	10	5	5	$1,481,594	104	D.Fst	0	0	0	0	$0 –
2004	6	2	2	0	$322,500	101	Wet(294)	0	0	0	0	$0 –
2003	7	2	1	3	$534,480	104	Turf(474)	28	10	5	5	$1,481,594 104
	0	0	0	0	$0	–	Dst(0)	0	0	0	0	$0 –

4Dec04-7Hol fm 1½ Ⓣ :502 1:153 2:04 2:293 3↑HolTrfCp-G1 101 8 97¼ 95¼ 52¼ 2hd 2hd Douglas R R LB123 4.90 78–22 Pellegrino126hd Megahertz123hd LicenseToRun126½ 3wd bid,led,btwn late 9

30Oct04-6LS yl 1⅜ Ⓣ :522 1:182 1:421 2:181 3↑ⒻBCF&MTrf-G1 80 10 66 64 74½ 1112 1115½ Nakatani C S L123 10.10 82–07 Ouija Board1181½ Film Maker123nk Wonder Again1232¾ Wide trip tired 12

31May04-2Hol fm 1⅛ Ⓣ :492 1:12 1:36 1:481+3↑ⒻGamlyBCH-G1 94 3 410 413 415 45 21 Espinoza V LB122 *.60 89–07 Noches De Rosa1151 Megahertz122hd Quero Quero1152 Closed fast on rail 4

17Apr04-9SA fm 1¼ Ⓣ :48 1:13 1:37 2:003 4↑ⒻSntBrbrH-G2 100 2 57½ 54½ 42 32 11 Solis A LB121 *.40 86–16 Megahertz1211 *Noches De Rosa*1162½ Mandela1112 Steadied 1/4,3wd rally 5

27Mar04-9SA fm 1⅛ Ⓣ :474 1:12 1:352 1:471 4↑ⒻSntaAnaH-G2 100 4 67 73½ 73¾ 11½ 11 Espinoza V LB120 *.70 93–11 [D]*Megahertz*1201 Katdogawn1171½ Fun House1181½ 5w, swerved in 1/8 7

Disqualified and placed 7th

10Jan04-3SA fm 1⅛ Ⓣ :51 1:143 1:374 1:492 4↑ⒻSnGrgnoH-G2 98 2 42½ 42 41½ 21½ 11 Solis A LB119 *.60 82–18 Meghertz1191 GrdeninthRin1161½ FirthofLorn116hd 3wd into lane,gamely 4

Megascape
Own: Beck Robert L

Dk. b or b. f. 3 (Apr) OBSMAR04 $80,000
Sire: Cape Canaveral (Mr. Prospector) $15,000
Dam: Bigger Half (Megaturn)
Br: Sez Who Thoroughbreds (NY)
Tr: Asmussen Steven M(0 0 0 0 .00) 2004:(2293 555 .24)

Life	5	3	0	1	$161,740	88	
2004	5	3	0	1	$161,740	88	
2003	0	M	0	0	$0	–	
	0	0	0	0	$0	–	
D.Fst	3	2	0	0	$93,140	74	
Wet(356*)	2	1	0	1	$68,600	88	
Turf(232*)	0	0	0	0	$0	–	
Dst(0)	0	0	0	0	$0	–	

21Nov04–8Aqu gd 6f :22 :451 :571 1:101 ⒻVllyStrm-G3 88 1 3 11 1½ 13½ 12¼ Velazquez J R L122 4.80 87–13 Megscpe122 2¼ Alfonsin118¾ MorMoonlight118 5¾ Opened up when roused 5
23Oct04–5Bel fst 1 :224 :46 1:112 1:392 ⒻⓈMaidOTMist100k 43 4 1½ 1½ 1hd 36 617 Velazquez J R L122 *1.10 47–27 PelhamBay118 4½ *KarkorumSplendor*116 1¼ SocilVirtue116 1½ Set pace, tired 9
3Oct04–8Bel fst 7f :22 :451 1:111 1:254 ⒻⓈJoeAGimma113k 74 1 6 1hd 1hd 15½ 13¼ Velazquez J R L117 *2.10 71–22 Megascape117 3¼ SocialVirtue117½ RoyalFudge117 1½ Vied inside, drew off 10
30Aug04–5Sar gd 6½f :213 :442 1:093 1:162 ⒻAlw 47000N1x 63 1 6 2½ 32 41½ 36½ Bailey J D L118 7.60 36–12 ReadysGal120 2 ShouldBeRoyalty120 4½ *Megascpe*118 2¼ Vied inside, no bid 7
2Aug04–4Sar fst 5½f :221 :461 :59 1:054 ⒻⓈMd Sp Wt 41k 64 5 1 2½ 2hd 14½ 15 Sellers S J L118 *.95 87–16 Megscpe118 5 DzzleMeDrlin118½ DylightsEnd118 1¾ Drew clear when asked 10

Meridiana (Ger)
Own: Kelly Jon and Sarah

Ch. f. 5 (May)
Sire: Lomitas*GB (Niniski) $23,022
Dam: Monbijou (Dashing Blade)
Br: Gestut Etzean (Ger)
Tr: Clement Christophe(0 0 0 0 .00) 2004:(344 68 .20)

Life	14	7	0	1	$556,795	97	
2004	5	3	0	1	$231,308	97	
2003	5	2	0	0	$303,478	78	
	0	0	0	0	$0	–	
D.Fst	0	0	0	0	$0	–	
Wet(280*)	0	0	0	0	$0	–	
Turf(347)	14	7	0	1	$556,795	97	
Dst(0)	0	0	0	0	$0	–	

29May04–8Bel yl 1⅜ Ⓣ :512 1:173 1:422 2:181 3↑ⒻShpshdBH-G2 93 7 21 21 21½ 33½ 35 Prado E S L119 2.90 57–38 MoscowBurning114 1 SpiceIsland119 4 Meridin119½ Attended pace, empty 7
21Apr04–8Kee gd 1½ Ⓣ :503 1:152 2:064 2:31 4↑ⒻBewitch-G3 97 2 31½ 41 41¼ 31½ 1no Prado E S L118 5.00 90–13 Meridiana118no Alternate116 1½ Binya118nk Lack room 1/4p,drvg 10
21Mar04–11GP fm 1½ Ⓣ :51 1:151 2:031 2:264 3↑ⒻOrchidH-G2 95 7 11 1hd 11 12 11¼ Prado E S L114 7.40 84–11 *Meridiana*114 1¼ Savedbythelight114½ Miss Hellie114nk On hedge, prevailed 10
5Mar04–9GP fm *1 1/16 Ⓣ :244 :50 1:142 1:443 4↑ⒻOC 100k/N4x -N 91 6 52½ 54½ 62 42 1¾ Prado E S L117 *1.60 81–22 *Meridiana*117¾ Cocktilsndrems117hd Sweettrickydncer117½ 3 wide, up late 9
12Feb04–7GP fm *1 1/16 Ⓣ :243 :50 1:143 1:461 4↑ⒻOC 100k/N4x -N 85 7 43 46 54 74½ 41 Prado E S L117 *2.40 72–26 ShtGnFvrt117nk PrfctEnrg117no Ccktlsndrms117¾ Blocked str, belatedly 9

Meteor Storm (GB)
Own: The Horizon Stable

B. h. 6 (Apr)
Sire: Bigstone*Ire (Last Tycoon*Ire) $4,592
Dam: Hunt the Sun*GB (Rainbow Quest)
Br: Juddmonte Farms (GB)
Tr: Dollase Wallace A(0 0 0 0 .00) 2004:(111 21 .19)

Life	15	6	3	3	$645,884	109	
2004	6	3	0	1	$529,800	109	
2003	4	2	1	1	$80,120	99	
	0	0	0	0	$0	–	
D.Fst	0	0	0	0	$0	–	
Wet(224)	0	0	0	0	$0	–	
Turf(314)	15	6	3	3	$645,884	109	
Dst(0)	0	0	0	0	$0	–	

3Jly04–10Mth fm 1⅜ Ⓣ :483 1:14 1:372 2:131 3↑UnitdNtn-G1 94 11 52 52½ 41½ 65½ 78 Valdivia J Jr L122 *2.30 89–09 RequstforProl118½ MrOBrin120¾ NothingtoLos118 1 Outside,chased,tired 11
5Jun04–10Bel fm 1¼ Ⓣ :482 1:121 1:354 1:591 3↑ManhttnH-G1 109 5 83¼ 83 73 5¾ 11¼ Valdivia J Jr L117 6.00 98–05 MtorStorm117 1¼ MillnnumDrgon116no MrOBrn116¾ Strong finish outside 9
18Apr04–9SA fm *1¾ Ⓣ 1:134 1:391 2:281 2:454 4↑SnJnCpoH-G2 102 4 32½ 33½ 31 12½ 11½ Valdivia J Jr LB116 *2.80 85–17 *MeteorStorm*116 1½ *RhythmMad*115 1 RunawyDncer115 2½ 3wd move,cleared 9
20Mar04–9SA fm 1½ Ⓣ :471 1:12 2:02 2:26 4↑SanLsRyH-G2 102 5 45½ 45 42 2hd 1nk Valdivia J Jr LB115 7.80 91–08 *Meteor Storm*115nk Labirinto114¾ GenedeCampeao114¾ Rail, 3wd, led, held 10
16Feb04–9SA fm 1½ Ⓣ :494 1:15 2:044 2:28 4↑SLsObspH-G2 101 1 11 1hd 1hd 12 4½ Valdivia J Jr LB116 14.50 81–15 PurtoBnus115nk Continuously116hd ContinntlRd117no Inside,game effort 12
8Jan04–2SA fm 1⅛ Ⓣ :46 1:104 1:354 1:48 4↑Alw 65000N3x 91 1 59 45½ 41¾ 1hd 33¼ Stevens G L LB121 *.90 86–13 SpcilMttr119 1¼ *MontSntMch*119 2 MtorStorm121 3½ Bobbld strt,came in1/8 5

Midas Eyes
Own: Gann Edmund A

B. h. 5 (Apr)
Sire: Touch Gold (Deputy Minister) $50,000
Dam: Bayou Plans (Bayou Hebert)
Br: Jacks or Better Farm Inc. (Fla)
Tr: Frankel Robert J(0 0 0 0 .00) 2004:(491 135 .27)

Life	13	5	4	1	$616,528	113	D.Fst	12 5 3 1	$576,528 113
2004	5	2	1	0	$258,600	113	Wet(303)	1 0 1 0	$40,000 111
2003	6	2	2	1	$333,788	111	Turf(202)	0 0 0 0	$0 -
	0	0	0	0	$0	-	Dst(0)	0 0 0 0	$0 -

Date/Race	Cond	Dist	Fractions	Race	Fig	PP/Calls	Fin	Jockey	Wt	Odds	Spd	Top Finishers	Comment	Fld
20Nov04-10Pim	fst	6f	:223 :452 :5711:092	3↑DeFrncsM-G1	108	1 4 51¾ 52½ 43½	2nk	Prado E S	L123	*1.30	98- 13	WildctHeir119nk MidsEyes1231½ ClockStoppr119¾	Rail,swung out,gamely	10
30Oct04-5LS	fst	6f	:211 :432 :5521:08	3↑BCSprint-G1	98	13 1 84¼ 74¼ 95¼	105½	Prado E S	L126	*3.60	95- 04	Speightstown1261¼ Kela126¾ My Cousin Matt126½	4w turn,6w into lane	13
4Sep04-8Sar	fst	7f	:221 :444 1:09 1:221	3↑ForegoH-G1	113	3 5 33 3½ 1½	11¾	Prado E S	L117	3.60	93- 19	Midas Eyes1171¾ Clock Stopper1141¼ Gygistar114no	3 wide move, clear	9
25Aug04-7Sar	fst	6½f	:214 :441 1:0811:144	3↑Alw 51000n3x	111	2 5 2½ 2½ 13½	15¾	Prado E S	L118	*.40	101 -	*MidsEyes*1185¾ MrNncho1183½ DshbordDrummr1142½	Shown whip stretch	6
7Feb04-9SA	fst	1⅛	:4541:101 1:3541:49	Strub-G2	105	10 73½ 72 72¾ 64¼	41½	Solis A	LB119	*2.80	87- 15	Domestic Dispute117nk During121¾ Buckland Manor117½	4wd,5wd,rallied	11

Midway Road
Own: Farish William S

B. h. 5 (Apr)
Sire: Jade Hunter (Mr. Prospector) $10,000
Dam: Fleet Road (Magesterial)
Br: W. S. Farish (Ky)
Tr: Howard Neil J(0 0 0 0 .00) 2004:(173 37 .21)

Life	17	7	2	2	$695,060	123	D.Fst	12 5 1 2	$366,060 116
2004	8	4	1	0	$372,015	123	Wet(342)	4 2 1 0	$329,000 123
2003	5	1	1	2	$270,146	99	Turf(283)	1 0 0 0	$0 80
	0	0	0	0	$0	-	Dst(0)	0 0 0 0	$0 -

Date/Race	Cond	Dist	Fractions	Race	Fig	PP/Calls	Fin	Jockey	Wt	Odds	Spd	Top Finishers	Comment	Fld
4Dec04-9FG	fst	1 1/16	:24 :474 1:1241:452	3↑TenaciousH60k	102	2 11½ 11 1hd 1hd	1no	Albarado R J	L123	*.50	83- 25	Midway Road123no Pie N Burger120¾ Kodema116½	Dueled, prevailed	6
30Oct04-5Kee	fst	1⅛	:4711:112 1:3641:501	3↑Fayette-G3	107	1 11½ 1½ 1½ 1hd	1no	Borel C H	L121	1.50	90- 10	*MidwayRoad*121no TotalImpact1256 AlumniHll1196¾	Repeatedly bmp lane	5
11Sep04-10Bel	fst	1⅛	:4531:083 1:3311:461	3↑Woodward-G1	70	2 4¾ 63 610 621	625¾	Albarado R J	L126	8.90	74- 15	*Ghostzapper*126nk *SaintLiam*1269¼ BowmnsBnd1267¼	Close up inside, tired	7
21Aug04-7Sar	sly	1⅛	:4641:103 1:36 1:492	4↑OC 100k/c-N	106	3 21½ 2½ 22 11½	13¼	Albarado R J	L118	*.70	88- 18	MidwyRod1183¼ Almuhthr118¾ NorthrnRock1182¼	Bothered start, gamely	7
12Jun04-9CD	sly	1⅛	:4731:122 1:3721:502	3↑SFosterH-G1	83	4 21½ 31½ 31½ 59	616½	Albarado R J	L116	2.20	68- 17	ColonilColony111no SouthrnImg1225 PrfctDrift1193¾	Hop start,4w,faded	6
14May04-11Pim	fst	1 3/16	:4721:114 1:3611:554	4↑PimSpclH-G1	116	1 1½ 11 1½ 2½	21¼	Albarado R J	L116	3.30	97- 17	SothrnImg1201¼ MdwyRod1162½ BowmnsBnd1144¾	Rail, pace, weakened	6
22Apr04-8Kee	sly	1⅛	:4621:102 1:3441:463	4↑BenAli-G3	123	5 1hd 12½ 12½ 17	111¼	Albarado R J	L116	5.10	108 -	MidwyRod11611¼ EveningAttir116½ SirChrok12012¼	Drew off,hand urging	5
18Mar04-9FG	fst	140	:233 :464 1:1121:383	4↑OC 62k/n3x-N	92	5 32 32 31 1hd	43½	Albarado R J	L117	*.90	97- 07	MrArchibld1182¼ DnctoDstny112½ ColonlColony117¾	4 wide bid, flattened	6

Millennium Dragon (GB)
Own: Darley Stable

B. h. 6 (Jan)
Sire: Mark of Esteem*Ire (Darshaan*GB) $13,430
Dam: Feather Bride*Ire (Groom Dancer)
Br: Elsdon Farms (GB)
Tr: McLaughlin Kiaran P(0 0 0 0 .00) 2004:(462 84 .18)

Life	27	6	8	2	$492,505	108	D.Fst 0 0 0 0 $0 -
2004	8	1	5	0	$302,520	108	Wet(277*) 2 0 1 1 $25,390 100
2003	8	2	1	2	$112,990	103	Turf(303) 25 6 7 1 $467,115 108
	0	0	0	0	$0	-	Dst(0) 0 0 0 0 $0 -

9Oct04-8Bel fm 1 Ⓣ:232 :46 1:091 1:323 3↑KelsoBCH-G2 **105** 3 64½ 66½ 72¾ 51¼ 21½ Migliore R L119 6.80 95-03 MrOBrn119½ MllnnumDrgon119no GlchApprovl114½ Found room, gamely 8
19Sep04-9WO fm 1 Ⓣ:232 :46 1:09 1:323 3↑AttoMile-G1 **87** 6 32 31½ 32 910 97¼ Migliore R L119 4.10 93-03 SoaringFree119¾ PerfectSoul121hd *RoyalRegalia*118 1¼ Stalked 3deep,tired 11
10Jly04-8Bel fm 1 Ⓣ:23 :46 1:09 1:322 3↑PokerH-G3 **107** 6 52½ 41½ 41½ 21 2nk Luzzi M J L120 *2.15 98-05 ChristinsOutlw113nk MllnnumDrgon120 2½ *SlvrTr*1171 Game finish outside 9
5Jun04-10Bel fm 1¼ 🅃:482 1:121 1:354 1:591 3↑ManhttnH-G1 **107** 6 72¾ 72¾ 61 3½ 21¼ Migliore R L116 12.40 97-05 MtorStorm1171¼ MillnniumDrgon116no MrOBrn116¾ 4 wide move, gamely 9
15May04-10Pim fm 1⅛ Ⓣ:464 1:10 1:334 1:461 3↑Dixie-G2 **102** 6 32 32½ 31½ 41½ 22 Migliore R L121 7.00 109 - MrOBrien1192 MillenniumDragon121hd Wrleigh124nk Rail,boxed 3/16-1/16 11
9Apr04-9Kee fm 1 Ⓣ:23 :451 1:09 1:332 4↑MakrsMrk-G2 **100** 4 65½ 65½ 62½ 66½ 62¼ Migliore R L116 7.50 103 - Perfect Soul116½ *Burning Roma*116hd Royal Spy1161 Between,no late gain 10
31Jan04-8GP sly 1 1/16 ⊗:233 :471 1:114 1:444 3↑CanTurfH-G3 **100** 6 2hd 1½ 1½ 11 2nk Migliore R L118 *2.00 85-29 *NwfondInd*115nk MllnnmDrgn118 8½ EvrythngtGn113 5¼ Drifted out stretch 6
4Jan04-9GP fm 1 Ⓣ:24 :49 1:114 1:342 3↑AppletnH-G3 **108** 7 11 11 1½ 11½ 11¼ Migliore R L116 4.10 94-07 MllnnumDrgon116 1¼ PoltclAttck1184 *ProdMn*116nk Pace,held well driving 12

Miss Coronado
Own: Stonerside Stable LLC

Dk. b or b. f. 4 (May)
Sire: Coronado's Quest (Forty Niner) $50,000
Dam: Miss Caerleona*Fr (Caerleon)
Br: Stonerside Stable (Ky)
Tr: Frankel Robert J(0 0 0 0 .00) 2004:(491 135 .27)

Life	6	2	0	1	$141,965	89	D.Fst 3 1 0 0 $105,000 89
2004	5	2	0	0	$137,045	89	Wet(314) 0 0 0 0 $0 -
2003	1	M	0	1	$4,920	76	Turf(296) 3 1 0 1 $36,965 81
	0	0	0	0	$0	-	Dst(0) 0 0 0 0 $0 -

26Jun04-9Bel fst 1⅛ :47 1:104 1:352 1:48 ⒻMthrGoos-G1 **85** 5 41 42¼ 41¾ 48½ 49¼ Santos J A L121 24.75 82-11 Stellar Jayne121 2½ *Ashado*121 1¾ Island Sand1215 Chased 4 wide, tired 6
25Apr04-9CD yl 1 1/16 Ⓣ:251 :50 1:143 1:451 3↑ⒻAlw 52900N2x **80** 4 31½ 41½ 51¼ 53 41¾ Day P L111 *.80 76-22 KittysLgnd1171 MissGoosbumps117hd ChrylsMyth117¾ Off slow,bobbled 8
9Apr04-10OP fst 1 1/16 :231 :463 1:11 1:423 ⒻFantasy-G2 **80** 5 42 53 55 811 810½ Velasquez C L121 4.50 86-11 HouseofFortune121 1¾ IslandSnd1214 StellrJyne121 2¼ Traffic early, faded 11
7Feb04-8GP fst 1 1/16 :242 :49 1:14 1:443 ⒻDvonaDal-G2 **89** 1 11 1½ 1hd 1½ 1hd Velasquez C L117 8.40 86-09 MissCoronado117hd EyeDzzler115nk SocietySelection121nk On rail, lasted 7
4Jan04-4SA fm 1⅛ Ⓣ:481 1:122 1:373 1:494 ⒻMd Sp Wt 49k **81** 2 54 53¾ 53½ 31½ 12½ Solis A LB120 *1.00 80-20 *Miss Coronado*120 2½ K'ehleyr120 1½ Yingyingying120 2½ 3wd bid,led past 1/8 8

Miss Grindstone
Own: Robbins William G

Dk. b or b. m. 6 (Jan)
Sire: Grindstone (Unbridled) $10,000
Dam: Dancing in Seattle (Seattle Song)
Br: Dancing in Seattle LLC (Ky)
Tr: Passero F A Jr(0 0 0 0 .00) 2004:(9 3 .33)

							D.Fst	19	9	3	4	$380,029	89
Life	26	14	3	4	$608,179	98	D.Fst	19	9	3	4	$380,029	89
2004	8	5	0	2	$271,985	98	Wet(356)	4	4	0	0	$189,210	98
2003	8	4	1	1	$148,176	83	Turf(209)	3	1	0	0	$38,940	80
	0	0	0	0	$0	–	Dst(0)	0	0	0	0	$0	–

28Nov04–8WO sly 7f :222 :45 1:093 1:231 3↑ⒻBessarbH-G3 **98** 4 3 1hd 1½ 11 13 Sabourin R B L113 4.05 91–15 MssGrndston1133 ElPrdEssnc118 1¾ SrprsdHmr117hd Shook clear stretch 6
6Nov04–8WO fst 6f :221 :443 :57 1:101 3↑ⒻOntFashnH137k **84** 3 6 61¾ 68 57 43¾ Sabourin R B L114 8.35 85–16 WinterGrdn122 1¾ ElPrdoEssnc118¾ BigChqu113 1¼ Determinedly between 8
11Oct04–6WO fst 6f :221 :453 :582 1:114 3↑ⒻOC c-77k/N3x **82** 6 7 710 76¾ 53¾ 11 David D J L118 2.55 81–22 MissGrindstone1181 *ColonilSurprise*120¾ RglnBold120 1¾ 3wd,swept by late 9
Claimed from California Stable for $77,500, Lane Robert W Trainer 2004(as of 10/11): (11 2 1 0 0.18)
30Sep04–1WO fst 7f :224 :451 1:103 1:234 3↑ⒻClm c-(50-45) **88** 5 2 2hd 32 11½ 11 Sabourin R B L120 *1.85 88–15 *MissGrindston*1201 RoylDistrcton118 1½ VroomHld118 3¼ Bid 3wd,clear,held 7
Claimed from Cardella John for $50,000, Cardella John Trainer 2004(as of 9/30): (130 18 14 19 0.14)
6Aug04–4WO fst 6f :221 :452 :582 1:113 3↑ⒻOC 75k/N3x **89** 2 3 32½ 55 32 1½ Sabourin R B L116 5.10 82–22 *Miss Grindstone*116½ Silver Bird117 2¼ *Expected Song*122 2¾ Up late inside 6
10Jly04–8FE fst 1 1/16 :233 :472 1:121 1:443 3↑ⒻⓇHHindmarsh75k **82** 3 22 22½ 2hd 33½ 34½ Sabourin R B L116 2.80 83–23 KissdbyPrinc116½ RoylDllinc1164 *MissGrindston*1161 Chased lacked finish 5
24Jun04–3WO fst 6f :22 :45 :572 1:101 3↑ⒻOC 75k/N3x **78** 3 6 54 54½ 55½ 32½ Sabourin R B L116 *1.60 86–19 ExpctdSong1162 HollywoodEndng116½ MssGrndstn1162 Rallied belatedly 6
9May04–7WO sly 5½f :22 :452 :58 1:043 3↑ⒻAlw 65600N2x **84** 4 6 51¾ 53 31½ 1½ Sabourin R B L120 2.45 97–07 MssGrndston120½ *DrssdforActon*120 2¼ RcksnCort119nk Rallied late inside 9

Miss Loren (Arg)
Own: Llers Corporation

Dk. b or b. m. 7 (Aug)
Sire: Numerous (Mr. Prospector) $13,567
Dam: Luminare*Arg (Forlitano*Arg)
Br: Firmamento (Arg)
Tr: Seglin Luis E(0 0 0 0 .00) 2004:(41 2 .05)

Life	43	11	10	7	$419,400	102	D.Fst	22	6	6	3	$320,977	102
2004	9	1	1	3	$290,044	102	Wet(269)	4	2	2	0	$22,533	–
2003	11	3	4	1	$41,597	–	Turf(229)	17	3	2	4	$75,890	95
	0	0	0	0	$0	–	Dst(0)	0	0	0	0	$0	–

12Dec04–8Hol fst 1 1/16 :233 :47 1:11 1:41 3↑ⒻBayakoaH-G2 **91** 6 33 32½ 32 51¾ 43½ Valdivia J Jr LB116 f 3.60 92–09 HollywoodStory1151 RyllyChsn1162 APAdvntr117½ 3wd into str,missed 3d 7
31Oct04–8SA fm 1⅛ Ⓣ :483 1:123 1:361 1:474 3↑ⒻLsPlmasH-G2 **89** 7 43½ 45½ 47 43½ 42 Court J K LB116 f 2.40 88–14 Theater R. N.114½ Lots of Hope117½ Good Student1141 Stalked,mild bid 7
3Oct04–6SA fst 1 1/16 :24 :481 1:114 1:432 3↑ⒻLdyScBCH-G2 **95** 6 54½ 72¾ 74¾ 43½ 2½ Court J K LB116 f 7.50 87–17 Island Fashion120½ Miss Loren116hd Elloluv118 3½ 3wd into lane,rallied 7
19Sep04–9Bel fst 1 1/16 :233 :461 1:103 1:412 3↑ⒻRuffianH-G1 **88** 4 54 55 55½ 411 313¾ Court J K L117 f 4.60 79–25 *Sightseek*122 11¼ Pocus Hocus114 2½ Miss Loren117½ 4 wide into stretch 5
8Aug04–8Dmr fst 1 1/16 :222 :46 1:103 1:424 3↑ⒻCLHrschH-G2 **102** 5 53½ 54 53 2hd 13¼ Court J K LB114 f 34.00 94–06 MissLoren114 3¼ HouseofFortune1131 RoyllyChosn1161 Bid 4wd,led,clear 8
27Jun04–8Hol fm 1¼ Ⓣ :493 1:133 1:374 2:012 3↑ⒻBevHilsH-G2 **95** 5 2½ 2hd 2hd 31½ 43½ Court J K LB114 19.20 81–13 LightJig1141 MoscowBurning117 1½ NochesDeRos1181 Dueled, weakened 6
6Jun04–8Hol fst 1 1/16 :232 :461 1:10 1:412 3↑ⒻHawthrnH-G3 **85** 6 33 65½ 610 68¾ 311 Desormeaux K J LB116 15.50 83–18 *Summer Wind Dancer*1161 Pesci11510 Miss Loren116½ Late for 3rd outside 7
Previously trained by Miguel Angel Garcia
7Feb04 San Isidro (Arg) fm *1⅜ Ⓣ LH 2:142 3↑ Clasico Juan Shaw-G2 ⒻStk 12800 32¼ Gramatica E 133 3.00 FriedaFritz132nk Pulistinh1322 MissLoren133nk *Trckd 3rd,led 2f to 1f out* 8
23Jan04 San Isidro (Arg) fm *1 Ⓣ LH 1:333 3↑ Cls R & E Fernandez Guerrico-G2 ⒻStk 11200 44¾ Gramatica E 132 5.30 Eivissa Jet131¾ *Brunilda*1202 La Virtual1202 *Midpack,lacked rally* 9

Miss Vegas (Ire)
Own: Gann Edmund A

B. f. 4 (Feb)
Sire: Efisio (Formidable) $23,022
Dam: Dwingeloo*Ire (Dancing Dissident)
Br: J. C. Condon (Ire)
Tr: Frankel Robert J(0 0 0 0 .00) 2004:(491 135 .27)

Life	9	7	1	1	$308,762	95	D.Fst	0 0 0 0	$0 –
2004	3	2	1	0	$161,160	95	Wet(338)	0 0 0 0	$0 –
2003	6	5	0	1	$147,602	–	Turf(265)	9 7 1 1	$308,762 95
	0	0	0	0	$0	–	Dst(0)	0 0 0 0	$0 –

31Jly04–4Dmr fm 1 Ⓣ :23^{2} :46^{2} 1:10 1:34 ⒻSnClmntH-G2 **94** 2 1^{1} 1^{2} 1^{2} 1^{1} 2^{hd} Flores D R LB121 *.40 91–07 SweetWin114^{hd} MissVegas121^{no} VictoryUSA119 4½ Drifted out 1/8,gamely 5
3Jly04–8Hol fm 1 Ⓣ :23^{2} :47 1:10^{2} 1:34^{3} ⒻFlawlessly109k **95** 4 1^{1} 1^{1½} 1^{2} 1^{2} 1^{5} Solis A LB121 *.40 91–13 Miss Vegas121^{5} Five Nickels117^{hd} *Shake Off*119^{2} Inside,clear,riddn out 8
15May04–8Hol fm 1 Ⓣ :23^{3} :46^{3} 1:10 1:34^{1} ⒻSenorita-G3 **94** 3 1^{2} 1^{2½} 1^{3½} 1^{1} 1^{hd} Solis A LB115 2.40 93–09 *Miss Vegas*115^{hd} Ticker Tape121^{3} Amorama116^{no} Inside,held on gamely 7

Mobil
Own: Schickedanz Gustav

B. h. 5 (Jan)
Sire: Langfuhr (Danzig) $30,000
Dam: Kinetigal (Naskra)
Br: Gustav Schickedanz (Ont-C)
Tr: Keogh Michael(0 0 0 0 .00) 2004:(103 14 .14)

Life	23	11	5	1	$1,507,924	104	D.Fst	13 6 4 0	$925,033 104
2004	8	3	2	0	$440,213	104	Wet(356)	1 1 0 0	$47,640 79
2003	9	5	2	1	$753,405	98	Turf(270)	9 4 1 1	$535,251 103
	0	0	0	0	$0	–	Dst(0)	0 0 0 0	$0 –

16Oct04–8WO fst 1⅛ :47^{1} 1:11^{2} 1:37^{2} 1:51^{2} 3↑DurhmCpH-G3 **100** 4 5^{3} 4^{3} 3^{1½} 2^{1½} 2^{nk} Kabel T K L126 f *.45 91–24 *Norfolk Knight*116^{nk} Mobil126^{1¾} Sky Diamond117^{7¾} All out drive failed 5
19Sep04–9WO fm 1 Ⓣ :23^{2} :46 1:09 1:32^{3} 3↑AttoMile-G1 **92** 7 5^{2½} 5^{2¼} 5^{2¼} 5^{6} 5^{4¾} Husbands P L119 9.70 95–03 Soaring Free119^{¾} Perfect Soul121^{hd} *Royal Regalia*118^{1¼} 4wd,evened out 11
5Sep04–2WO fm 1⅛ Ⓣ :48 1:12 1:35 1:46^{4} 3↑ⓇHalton128k **97** 4 2^{½} 2^{½} 2^{hd} 1^{4} 1^{3½} Kabel T K L121 *.15 94–09 Mobil121^{3½} Lenny the Lender115^{1½} Jambalar115^{2} Ridden out 4
14Aug04–9AP fm 1¼ Ⓣ :47^{2} 1:12 1:36^{3} 2:00 3↑ArlMilln-G1 **94** 13 7^{5½} 5^{4} 5^{2½} 9^{7½} 9^{8¼} Jones J L126 f 40.20 103 – ⒹPowerscourt126^{1½} Kicken Kris126^{1} *Magistretti*126^{½} 4 wide, tired 13
25Jly04–8WO fm 1⅜ Ⓣ :48^{2} 1:12^{3} 1:36^{4} 2:12^{1} 3↑ChneseCC-G2 **103** 1 1^{1½} 1^{1} 1^{½} 2^{1} 2^{nk} Jones J L121 5.55 104–05 Shoal Water116^{nk} Mobil121^{2¼} *Strut the Stage*121^{¾} Very game stretch 8
1Jly04–8WO fst 1¼ :47 1:12 1:37^{2} 2:03^{1} 3↑DomDayH-G3 **92** 4 4^{5½} 3^{1½} 1^{½} 1^{7} 1^{12¾} Kabel T K L122 f *.60 89–11 Mobil122^{12¾} Mark One118^{nk} The Judge Sez Who119^{3¼} Bid 3wd,drew off 7
31May04–9Bel fst 1 :23^{2} :46 1:10 1:35^{2} 3↑MtropltH-G1 **94** 7 8^{8¾} 8^{8¼} 9^{8½} 9^{9¾} 9^{11½} Kabel T K L115 f 53.75 72–34 PicoCentral119^{½} BowmnsBnd114^{2¼} StrongHope119^{1½} Inside, no response 9
1May04–8WO fst 7f :22^{4} :45 1:09 1:21^{4} 4↑VigilH-G3 **104** 3 2 3^{1½} 3^{2½} 2^{2½} 1^{1¾} Kabel T K L120 f 1.75 98–08 Mobil120^{1¾} Chris's Bad Boy122^{4} Awesome Action115^{2¾} Swept to lead late 5

Molto Vita
Own: Gunther John D

B. m. 5 (Mar)
Sire: Carson City (Mr. Prospector) $35,000
Dam: Princess Polonia (Danzig)
Br: TAC Holding Inc (Ky)
Tr: Stewart Dallas(0 0 0 0 .00) 2004:(295 49 .17)

Life	19	7	3	0	$357,410	105
2004	8	3	2	0	$220,730	105
2003	11	4	1	0	$136,680	94
	0	0	0	0	$0	-

D.Fst	15	7	1	0	$323,610	105
Wet(443)	4	0	2	0	$33,800	99
Turf(300)	0	0	0	0	$0	-
Dst(0)	0	0	0	0	$0	-

17Oct04-8Kee fst 6f :22 :453 :573 1:094 3↑ⒻTCA-G3 **105** 6 1 1½ 1½ 1½ 1¾ Bejarano R L122 2.60 92-12 Molto Vita122¾ My Trusty Cat124nk My Boston Gal118¾ 3w,stiff drive 6
10Oct04-9Bel fst 6½f :231 :464 1:094 1:16 3↑ⒻGlntBlmH-G2 **98** 6 2 1½ 1hd 2½ 22 Castellano J J L115 8.90 91-16 Lady Tak1222 *Molto Vita*1154¼ Zawzooth115hd Set pace, gamely 7
29Aug04-9Sar gd 7f :221 :442 1:074 1:21 3↑ⒻBalrinaH-G1 **99** 5 1 34 36 34 41¼ Chavez J F L114 29.75 98-05 *LadyTk*119hd MyTrustyCt116hd HrmonyLodge1191 Bumped upper stretch 7
14Aug04-9EIP fst 6½f :213 :45 1:102 1:17 3↑ⒻEllisPrkBC103k **98** 1 6 1½ 1½ 1½ 1nk Melancon L L117 14.90 94-18 Molto Vita117nk Tina Bull1192½ Smoke Chaser121½ Off inside, driving 7
23Jly04-9EIP fst 6f :223 :454 :58 1:103 3↑ⒻHcp 40000 **89** 3 1 1hd 2hd 11 1nk Melancon L L117 23.70 93-11 *Molto Vita*117nk My Boston Gal1221¼ *Souris*1182¼ Duel,4w,gamely,drvg 7
2Jly04-4CD fst 6f :213 :452 :572 1:094 3↑ⒻOC 80k/c-N **71** 1 6 32 63 64½ 77½ Borel C H L117 4.40 85-14 [D]VickVllncourt119hd Sours1194½ AdoptdDughtr123hd Stumble start,tired 7
5Jun04-6Bel fst 6½f :214 :443 1:08 1:142 3↑ⒻVagrncyH-G2 **68** 6 7 75 811 917 718¼ Santos J A L115 25.75 83-07 Bear Fan1219 Smok'n Frolic1171¼ Aspen Gal1092 Inside, no response 9
19May04-9CD sly 7f :223 :454 1:104 1:241 3↑ⒻAlw 63000N1Y **90** 2 2 31 3½ 1½ 2½ Borel C H L119 13.50 80-16 Golden Marlin119½ Molto Vita1191 Souris119½ 4w,failed to last 8

Mona Rose
Own: O'Brien P. and F

B. m. 5 (Feb)
Sire: Gold Legend (Seattle Slew) $3,500
Dam: Royal Charmer (Lomond)
Br: Paul O"Brien & Frank O"Brien (Ont-C)
Tr: Barnett Robert E(0 0 0 0 .00) 2004:(117 9 .08)

Life	14	5	2	0	$392,104	96
2004	8	4	0	0	$319,439	96
2003	6	1	2	0	$72,665	80
	0	0	0	0	$0	-

D.Fst	1	0	0	0	$5,184	57
Wet(327)	0	0	0	0	$0	-
Turf(289)	13	5	2	0	$386,920	96
Dst(0)	0	0	0	0	$0	-

6Nov04-5WO yl 1 Ⓣ:24 :472 1:121 1:392 3↑ⒻRiverMem112k **87** 10 10 10 3½ 78 511 43½ 52¼ Da Silva E R L119 2.70 64-34 MyPlLn1171½ GingerGold117no AlwysAwesome117½ Closed 4wd,hung late 11
24Oct04-6WO gd 1¼ Ⓣ:504 1:152 1:40 2:04 3↑ⒻEPTaylor-G1 **95** 3 3½ 2½ 2hd 3nk 53 Da Silva E R L123 29.60 84-13 Commrcnt123½ Punctilious118nk ClssicStmp1232¼ Checked hard 1/16th pl 8
10Oct04-4WO fm 1⅛ Ⓣ:481 1:114 1:353 1:48 3↑Ⓕ[R]BelleGeste104k **93** 4 32 41¾ 42 21½ 12 Da Silva E R L119 *1.95 88-11 Mona Rose1192 Heyahohowdy117nk First Quarter117¾ Swept to lead,drvg 7
19Sep04-6WO fm *1⅛ Ⓣ:46 1:432 3↑ⒻCanadinH-G2 **85** 6 73¼ 73¾ 64¾ 56½ 55½ Da Silva E R 114 8.65 95-03 Classic Stamp1171 Inish Glora1211¾ Heyahohowdy114½ 3deep,hung 9
30Aug04-8Sar yl 1 1/16 [T]:24 :47 1:111 1:434 3↑ⒻBlSpaBCH-G3 **89** 8 64¼ 510 69½ 66 55½ Chavez J F 114 12.90 79-15 *Ocean Drive*1191¼ Personal Legend1151¾ High Court1141¾ Wide both turns 10
17Jly04-4WO yl 1⅛ Ⓣ:48 1:112 1:352 1:48 3↑ⒻDncSmrtH-G3 **96** 3 32 42¾ 42¾ 22 11 Da Silva E R 112 5.60 88-12 Mona Rose1121 *Inish Glora*1221½ Classic Stamp1161¼ Rail to 3wd,rallied 4
26Jun04-5WO fm 1 1/16 Ⓣ:232 :46 1:101 1:411 3↑ⒻAlw 72200N2X **87** 4 93¼ 64¾ 53½ 2hd 1nk Da Silva E R 122 3.80 92-09 *Mona Rose*122nk *Kabul*1204¾ Babeth1202 Rail to 3wd,up late 11
22May04-5WO fm 1 1/16 Ⓣ:232 :461 1:104 1:411 3↑ⒻAlw 67800N1X **85** 9 63 41½ 54 2hd 13½ Da Silva E R 120 9.50 92-08 *Mona Rose*1203½ Faswiga1151¼ Dynamite Cocktail1201¼ Rail bid,drew off 12

Moscow Burning

Own: Mariani Jeffrey J., Nentwig, Michael

B. m. 5 (Mar)
Sire: Moscow Ballet (Nijinsky II) $3,000
Dam: Burning Desire (Mr. Leader)
Br: Harris Farms, Inc. & Ken Maddy Trust (Cal)
Tr: Cassidy James M(0 0 0 0 .00) 2004:(157 18 .11)

Life	20	8	5	2	$807,535	102	D.Fst	3	2	0	0	$13,725 72
2004	11	2	4	2	$627,970	102	Wet(342)	0	0	0	0	$0 –
2003	9	6	1	0	$179,565	93	Turf(288)	17	6	5	2	$793,810 102
	0	0	0	0	$0	–	Dst(0)	0	0	0	0	$0 –

4Dec04-7Hol fm 1½ Ⓣ :50[2] 1:15[3] 2:04 2:29[3] 3↑HolTrfCp-G1 100 5 3[1½] 4[1½] 3[1½] 5[¾] 4[¾] Valdivia J Jr LB123 1.90 77-22 Pellegrino126[hd] Meghertz123[hd] LicensToRun126½ Steadied near 1/8,game 9
30Oct04-6LS yl 1⅜ Ⓣ :52[2] 1:18[2] 1:42[1] 2:18[1] 3↑ⒻBCF&MTrf-G1 100 4 1[4] 1[1½] 1[1½] 1[hd] 4[4½] Valdivia J Jr L123 18.80 93-07 OuijaBord1181½ FilmMker123[nk] WonderAgin123[2¾] Weakened final eighth 12
2Oct04-7Bel yl 1¼ 🅃 :52[2] 1:17[4] 1:41[2] 2:04[3] 3↑ⒻFlwrBlIv-G1 100 3 1[½] 1[1] 1[1] 1[½] 3[¾] Valdivia J Jr L120 6.40 70-25 Riskverse118¾ Commercnt118[hd] MoscowBurning120[nk] Set pace, held well 8
29Aug04-8Dmr fm 1⅜ Ⓣ :47[3] 1:12[1] 1:36[4] 2:12[3] 3↑DelMarH-G2 97 5 2[3½] 2[2½] 2[1] 3[2] 3[2¼] Valdivia J Jr LB114 7.80 95-08 StarOvertheBay116[nk] Sarfn121[2] MoscowBurning114[hd] Bit off rail,held 3rd 9
24Jly04-6Dmr fm 1⅛ Ⓣ :47[4] 1:12 1:35[2] 1:47 3↑ⒻJCMabeeH-G1 99 3 3[2] 3[3] 2[½] 1[½] 2[1¼] Valdivia J Jr LB117 3.60 93-09 MsclChms1161¼ MoscowBrnng117[no] NttngHll113[1] Stalked,led,outkicked 6
27Jun04-8Hol fm 1¼ Ⓣ :49[3] 1:13[3] 1:37[4] 2:01[2] 3↑ⒻBevHilsH-G2 99 4 4[1½] 3[1] 3[1] 1[1] 2[1] Desormeaux K J LB117 2.30 84-13 Light Jig114[1] Moscow Burning1171½ Noches De Rosa118[1] 3wd,led,caught 6
29May04-8Bel yl 1⅜ 🅃 :51[2] 1:17[3] 1:42[2] 2:18[1] 3↑ⒻShpshdBH-G2 102 6 1[1] 1[1] 1[1½] 1[3] 1[1] Smith M E L114 4.20 62-38 MoscowBurning114[1] SpiceIsland119[4] Meridian119½ Soon clear, kept busy 7
24Apr04-1Hol fm 1 1/16 Ⓣ :23[2] :46[3] 1:10 1:39[1] 4↑ⒻⓈFrnsValntn150k 95 6 5[3] 6[4] 6[3½] 2[hd] 1[2½] Desormeaux K J LB122 2.80 100-03 MoscowBurning1222½ SuperHigh122[1] SwetFrippry116[1] 4wd move,bid,clear 7
21Mar04-11GP fm 1½ Ⓣ :51 1:15[1] 2:03[1] 2:26[4] 3↑ⒻOrchidH-G2 91 6 5[3] 5[3] 5[3] 5[3½] 5[2¼] Ramsammy E L115 4.20 82-11 Meridiana1141¼ Savedbythelight114½ Miss Hellie114[nk] Not enough late 10
15Feb04-3SA fm 1 Ⓣ :23[3] :47[3] 1:11[4] 1:35[1] 4↑ⒻⓈProOrConH108k 90 6 3[2½] 3[2] 3[1] 2[1] 2[no] Espinoza V LB118 *.40 86-15 SuprHigh119[no] MoscowBurning1182½ ClzdKid116[2] 3wd into str,outgamed 7
24Jan04-5SA fm 1⅛ Ⓣ :46[3] 1:10[1] 1:34[2] 1:46[1] 4↑ⒻⓇSMF&MTurf500k 94 11 5[2¼] 5[2] 5[2] 5[1¾] 2[¾] Valdivia J Jr LB118 4.10 97-02 VlntinDncr118¾ MoscowBurning118[1] BrtoksBlth118[1] 4wd into lane,rallied 11

Mr O'Brien (Ire)

Own: Skeedattle II

Ch. g. 6 (Apr)
Sire: Mukaddamah (Storm Bird)
Dam: Laurel Delight*GB (Presidium*GB)
Br: Jack Ronan & Des Vere Hunt Farm Co. (Ire)
Tr: Graham Robin L(0 0 0 0 .00) 2004:(130 16 .12)

Life	22	8	4	2	$673,290	108	D.Fst	8	1	3	1	$51,990 98
2004	9	3	1	1	$514,050	108	Wet(311)	1	1	0	0	$25,800 98
2003	7	2	3	1	$73,740	98	Turf(269)	13	6	1	1	$595,500 108
	0	0	0	0	$0	–	Dst(0)	0	0	0	0	$0 –

30Oct04-4LS yl 1 Ⓣ :24 :48[3] 1:12[3] 1:36[4] 3↑BCMile-G1 99 14 6[4¼] 6[3] 5[¾] 6[3¼] 9[4¾] Coa E M L126 20.70 81-07 Singletry126½ AntoniusPius1221½ SixPerfections123[nk] Wide trip, no rally 14
9Oct04-8Bel fm 1 Ⓣ :23[2] :46 1:09[1] 1:32[3] 3↑Kelso3CH-G2 108 1 4[2½] 4[2½] 4[1¾] 2[hd] 1[1½] Coa E M L119 4.90 97-03 MrOBrn1191½ MllnnmDrgon119[no] GlchApprvl114½ Came wide, drew clear 8
18Sep04-9Pim fst 1⅛ ⊗ :47[2] 1:11[4] 1:36[4] 1:49 3↑SchprMmBCH148k 69 5 1[½] 1[hd] 5[2] 5[14] 5[21] Dominguez R A L122 *.40 78-22 LustyLatin1124¾ Foufa'sWarrior1155½ PaythePreacher114[2] Dropped back 5
14Aug04-9AP fm 1¼ Ⓣ :47[2] 1:12 1:36[3] 2:00 3↑ArlMilln-G1 100 1 5[5] 6[5] 6[3] 6[4] 6[5¼] Day P L126 4.70 106 - ⒹPowerscourt1261½ KickenKris126[1] Mgistretti126½ Steadied backstretch 13
3Jly04-10Mth fm 1⅜ Ⓣ :48[3] 1:14 1:37[2] 2:13[1] 3↑UnitdNtn-G1 107 7 7[3¼] 6[3] 7[2¾] 4[2½] 2[½] Dominguez R A L120 3.10 96-09 RequstforProl118½ MrOBrin120¾ NothingtoLos118[1] Btwn 1/8, outfinished 11
5Jun04-10Bel fm 1¼ 🅃 :48[2] 1:12[1] 1:35[4] 1:59[1] 3↑ManhtnH-G1 107 3 4[1¾] 3[1½] 5[¾] 6[1¼] 3[1¼] Dominguez R A L116 4.90 97-05 MeteorStorm1171¼ MillenniumDrgon116[no] MrOBrien116¾ Rallied outside 9
15May04-10Pim fm 1⅛ Ⓣ :46[4] 1:10 1:33[4] 1:46[1] 3↑Dixie-G2 106 8 7[7¼] 7[6½] 5[3] 2[1] 1[2] Dominguez R A L119 11.40 111 - MrOBrien119[2] MillenniumDragon121[hd] Wrleigh124[nk] 4wd move, left lead 11
1May04-9Pim fm 1 Ⓣ :24 :47[3] 1:11[3] 1:35[4] 3↑HenryClark50k 105 2 3[2] 3[1½] 1[2½] 1[8] 1[9] Wilson R L119 8.50 90-11 Mr O'Brien119[9] Spruce Run1192½ Tam's Terms1193¾ Brisk whipping 8
8Jan04-8Lrl fst 6f :22[1] :45[2] :58[2] 1:11[1] 4↑OC75k/N$Y-N 81 4 1 4[5] 4[3] 4[4] 5[6¼] Carabal o J C L117 7.00 80-20 TacticlSide112[1] InsRocket1164½ InnerHrbour117½ Chased,angld in,empty 6

Multiple Choice
Own: Pompa P P Jr

B. g. 7 (Feb)
Sire: Mt. Livermore (Blushing Groom*Fr) $25,000
Dam: Lady of Choice (Storm Bird)
Br: Peter E. Blum (Ky)
Tr: Reynolds Patrick L(0 0 0 0 .00) 2004:(186 25 .13)

Life	42	8	7	6	$584,261	107	D.Fst	34 6 5 6	$424,693 107
2004	14	1	4	1	$123,008	101	Wet(359)	5 1 2 0	$91,440 107
2003	4	0	0	2	$39,121	105	Turf(286)	3 1 0 0	$68,128 101
	0	0	0	0	$0	–	Dst(0)	0 0 0 0	$0 –

12Dec04–7Aqu fst 6f ⊡ :222 :452 :5741:102 3↑OC 65k/N3X 91 3 5 84¼ 65¼ 42¼ 22 Smith A E L119 fb 7.40 85–15 MyPokerPlyer1212 MultipleChoice1191 WildJm118nk Rallied 3w, 2nd best 9
27Nov04–4Aqu fst 6½f :232 :454 1:0931:154 3↑OC 85k/N1Y 86 4 2 42½ 42½ 41¾ 42 Castellano J J L122 fb 7.50 97–08 BlckSilk120no DubiSheikh1181¼ NewYorkHero118¾ 4 wide run, weakened 5
22Oct04–7Bel fst 6f :221 :45 :57 1:10 3↑Clm 75000(75-65) 92 4 6 47½ 46 53 51½ Castellano J J L120 fb 6.50 88–14 Wheaton's Aly120no *First Blush*120½ DubaiSheikh124hd Came wide, gamely 6
28Aug04–4Sar fm 1 Ⓣ :233 :463 1:1031:343 4↑Clm 100000(100-75) 86 4 42½ 43 41 51¼ 65¾ Migliore R L120 fb 9.40 92–04 StageCll1171¼ MiesquesApprovl1202½ FstDecision120½ Steadied first turn 9
13Aug04–7Sar sly 6½f :221 :45 1:09 1:153 4↑Alw 58000c 89 7 1 51½ 52½ 510 59¼ Albarado R J L123 fb 5.70 88–12 PrettyWild1234¼ MountinGnrl120¾ PhildlphiJim1161¼ 4 wide trip, no rally 7
24Jly04–7Bel my 7f ⊗ :223 :452 1:0921:223 4↑Clm c-(100-75) 93 4 3 41¾ 33 32½ 2nk Luzzi M J L123 b 2.25 87–15 Secret Run121nk Multiple Choice1231½ NoParole1212 Game finish outside 6
Claimed from Blum Peter E. for $100,000, Jerkens James A Trainer 2004(as of 7/24): (111 20 17 12 0.18)
10Jly04–8Bel fm 1 Ⓣ :23 :46 1:09 1:322 3↑PokerH-G3 89 7 62¾ 62 75 95¾ 98¾ Castellano J J L115 b 7.20 89–05 ChristinesOutlw113nk MillenniumDrgon1202½ *SilvrTr*1171 3 wide trip, tired 9
30May04–8Bel gd 7f Ⓣ :222 :453 1:0921:221 3↑Jaipur-G3 101 1 8 42¼ 42 4¾ 1½ Castellano J J L113 b 14.50 89–11 MultipleChoice113½ Dediction1141½ *Geronimo*118hd Dug in gamely outside 8
20May04–8Bel fst 6f :213 :442 :5631:091 4↑OC 100k/c-N 98 1 5 47½ 43½ 32 22¾ Castellano J J L118 b 3.15 90–14 MyCousinMtt1182¾ *MultipleChoice*1183¼ *DonSix*1182½ Game finish outside 5
23Apr04–8Aqu fst 6f :224 :453 :5711:093 4↑OC 85k/c-N 97 2 5 42 42¼ 32 31¾ Santos J A L118 b 3.30 88–17 First Blush1161¾ Kazoo118hd Multiple Choice1181¼ Awkward start, inside 5
2Apr04–8Aqu gd 1 :23 :46 1:1031:353 4↑OC 85k/c-N 98 5 3nk 4¾ 2hd 31½ 23 Santos J A L118 b 3.30 84–29 Black Silk1163 Multiple Choice118nk PeepingTom1181¾ 4 wide trip, rallied 7
28Mar04–8Aqu fst 6f :214 :444 :5631:084 4↑OC 85k/c-N 98 2 7 67¾ 52¼ 62¾ 43¼ Jara F5 L113 b 3.85 91–16 SuprFus1181 GrcousHmor116½ SngMBckHom1151¾ Bumped start, rallied 7
6Mar04–11GP fst 7f :22 :441 1:0831:212 3↑RcSclBCH-G2 94 3 7 53 52½ 64¾ 75¼ Chavez J F L113 b 28.00 90–08 *Lion Tamer*116¾ Coach Jimi Lee115½ Wacky for Love114hd Faltered 7
3Jan04–10GP fst 6f :221 :444 :5631:09 3↑MrProspH-G3 80 1 6 63½ 63¼ 67 69¾ Douglas R R L115 b 20.00 87–10 Cajun Beat1211½ Gygistar118¾ Deer Lake1153 No early speed,no bid 6

Musical Chimes
Own: Al Maktoum Sheikh Maktoum b

Dk. b or b. m. 5 (Apr)
Sire: In Excess*Ire (Siberian Express) $25,000
Dam: Note Musicale*GB (Sadler's Wells)
Br: Gainsborough Farm LLC (Ky)
Tr: Drysdale Neil D(0 0 0 0 .00) 2004:(180 37 .21)

Life	18	4	3	1	$954,489	106	D.Fst	0 0 0 0	$0 –
2004	7	2	1	0	$438,300	106	Wet(377)	0 0 0 0	$0 –
2003	8	2	2	1	$513,103	106	Turf(368)	18 4 3 1	$954,489 106
	0	0	0	0	$0	–	Dst(0)	0 0 0 0	$0 –

28Nov04–7Hol fm 1 Ⓣ :24 :473 1:1121:354 3↑ⒻMatriarc-G1 91 7 95¼ 93½ 75 54½ 64½ Desormeaux K J LB123 *1.80 80–17 Intercontinntl1232 EtoilMontnt123no TickrTp1201½ 4wd move,no late bid 9
30Oct04–4LS yl 1 Ⓣ :24 :483 1:1231:364 3↑BCMile-G1 102 9 106¾ 95 113 83¾ 63¼ Desormeaux K J L123 22.90 83–07 Singltry126½ AntoniusPius1221½ SixPrfctons123nk Blockd 2nd turn,stdied 14
9Oct04–9SA fm 1 Ⓣ :23 :464 1:0931:331 3↑OkTrBCMl-G2 106 3 33 42½ 32½ 31 1no Desormeaux K J LB118 4.00 96–11 MusiclChims118no BuckIndMnor119no *Singltry*119½ 3wd bid,rallied btw,up 6
14Aug04–8AP fm 1 3/16 Ⓣ :4941:152 1:3931:562 3↑ⒻBeverlyD-G1 100 4 1½ 2½ 21 2½ 4¾ Desormeaux K J L123 *2.10 91 – Crimson Palace123½ *Riskaverse*123hd Necklace117nk Dueled three wide 11
24Jly04–6Dmr fm 1⅛ Ⓣ :4741:12 1:3521:47 3↑ⒻJCMabeeH-G1 102 4 43½ 54½ 31½ 31½ 11¼ Desormeaux K J LB116 2.10 94–09 MsclChms1161¼ MoscowBrnng117no NttngHll1131 3wd bid,brisk handling 6
12Jun04–3Hol fm 1¼ Ⓣ :5031:15 1:3812:012 3↑CWhtghmH-G1 99 1 43 33½ 34 53 74 Desormeaux K J LB116 4.10 81–12 Sabiango116¾ *Bayamo*116no Just Wonder1162½ Tight 7/8,3wd 2nd turn 11
30May04–1Hol fm 1 Ⓣ :243 :48 1:1111:341 4↑Alw 64120N2X 97 2 55 53½ 53 52½ 2½ Desormeaux K J LB117 *1.20 92–06 *StagePlayer*118½ MusicalChimes117hd *RoylPrice*122nk 3wd into str,willingly 6

Mustanfar
Own: Shadwell Stable

Ch. c. 4 (Mar)
Sire: Unbridled (Fappiano) $200,000
Dam: Manwah (Lyphard)
Br: Shadwell Farm, LLC (Ky)
Tr: McLaughlin Kiaran P(0 0 0 0 .00) 2004:(462 84 .18)

Life	14	4	3	1	$423,696	100	D.Fst	7	2	1	1	$141,680	100
2004	11	3	3	1	$394,716	100	Wet(412)	0	0	0	0	$0	–
2003	3	1	0	0	$28,980	74	Turf(307)	7	2	2	0	$282,016	100
	0	0	0	0	$0	–	Dst(0)	0	0	0	0	$0	–

30Oct04–8LS yl 1½ Ⓣ :49 1:134 2:04 2:293 3↑BCTurf-G1 97 8 812 88½ 76½ 56 57¾ Santos J A L121 b 23.40 115–07 BetterTlkNow126 1¾ KittensJoy1211 Powrscourt1262¼ Improved position 8
9Oct04–5Kee fm 1½ Ⓣ :512 1:161 2:07 2:304 3↑SycamrBC-G3 100 2 85 83½ 72¾ 41¾ 13 Santos J A L118 b 2.90 91–10 Mustanfar1183 Deputy Strike1201 Rochester1221¼ Angle 7w lane,driving 9
6Sep04–10Sar fm 1 3/16 Ⓣ :482 1:123 1:362 1:534 SaranacH-G3 97 6 31½ 34½ 31 1½ 2hd Velasquez C L121 b 2.45 96–09 PrinceArch123hd Mustanfar1212¼ CtchtheGlory1151½ 3 wide move, gamely 6
9Aug04–8Sar fm 1⅛ 🅃 :471 1:103 1:353 1:473 HalOFmeH-G2 94 6 85¼ 810 75¼ 52½ 24¼ Day P L122 b 11.10 95–09 ArtieSchiller1224¼ Mustanfar122no GoodRewrd1151½ Hit gate start, 4 wide 8
18Jly04–8Bel fm 1¼ 🅃 :484 1:123 1:344 2:01 Lexingtn-G3 94 7 52 51¾ 3½ 21½ 2no Santos J A L114 b 5.70 89–11 🄳IcyAtlntic122no Mustnfr1142¼ SecondPrformnc1181¾ Came in, brushed 8
Placed first through disqualification
27Jun04–7Bel gd 1⅛ 🅃 :491 1:124 1:364 1:483 🅁MDiarmida61k 83 1 55½ 56 53¾ 53 43¾ Migliore R L116 b 4.50 83–13 SecondPerformnce1162¼ GoodRewrd118¾ DelerChoic116¾ Svd grd, no bid 8
14May04–7Bel fst 1 1/16 :231 :454 1:101 1:412 3↑Alw 48000n2x 91 4 64½ 46½ 41½ 35 35 Bridgmohan S X L114 b *1.45 88–20 Offlee Wild1214½ Shaniko117½ Mustanfar1147½ Stumbled start, inside 7
10Apr04–9Kee fst 1⅛ :463 1:11 1:364 1:492 BlueGras-G1 94 6 42¼ 43½ 33½ 45 410¼ Migliore R L123 b 10.60 84–20 TheCliff'sEdge123½ LionHeart1236 Limehouse1233¾ Steadied briefly 7/8pl 8
14Mar04–11Tam fst 1 1/16 :233 :473 1:114 1:434 TampaDby-G3 100 3 85 62¾ 41½ 52½ 2nk Judice J C L116 b 7.00 99–10 Limehouse118nk Mustnfr1161 Swingforthefences1161¾ Drew even,missed 8
21Feb04–11GP fm 1⅛ Ⓣ :494 1:133 1:371 1:483 PalmBch-G3 85 6 76½ 74¾ 73½ 63¼ 63 Santos J A L118 b 7.40 89–06 Kitten's Joy1221¼ Prince Arch113nk Pa Pa Da118¾ 5 wide, mild rally 12
24Jan04–3GP fst 1 1/16 :232 :474 1:124 1:441 Alw 34000n1x 86 1 66 64½ 62 43 1hd Velazquez J R L120 b 3.50 88–15 Mustanfar120hd 🄳Suave1201 Swingforthefences1183 Swung out, just up 10

My Trusty Cat
Own: Pollard Carl F

B. m. 5 (Apr)
Sire: Tale of the Cat (Storm Cat) $65,000
Dam: Entrusted (Private Account)
Br: Vintage Racing (Ky)
Tr: Vance David R(0 0 0 0 .00) 2004:(260 35 .13)

Life	24	6	6	2	$633,468	103	D.Fst	19	6	4	2	$560,458	103
2004	10	3	3	0	$311,290	103	Wet(398)	5	0	2	0	$73,010	102
2003	8	1	0	1	$94,153	91	Turf(299)	0	0	0	0	$0	–
	0	0	0	0	$0	–	Dst(0)	0	0	0	0	$0	–

7Nov04–10CD fst 1 :223 :453 1:102 1:35 3↑Ⓕ CDDstafH-G2 86 6 42 63 51¾ 79 711 Day P L118 fb 4.40 84–13 Halory Leigh1155 Lady Tak123¾ Susan's Angel115¾ Bmp start,forced out 12
17Oct04–8Kee fst 6f :22 :453 :573 1:094 3↑Ⓕ TCA-G3 103 2 5 54 54 32½ 2¾ Day P L124 fb *1.10 91–12 MoltoVita122¾ MyTrustyCat124nk MyBostonGl1181¾ 6w lane,gaining late 6
29Aug04–9Sar gd 7f :221 :442 1:074 1:21 3↑Ⓕ BalrinaH-G1 102 6 4 45 46 44 2hd Velazquez J R L116 fb 5.10 99–05 LadyTk119hd MyTrustyCt116hd HrmonyLodge1191 Bumped upper stretch 7
6Aug04–8Sar fst 6f :223 :451 :572 1:101 3↑Ⓕ HnrblMsH-G2 96 5 8 83¼ 72½ 44 1no Day P L115 fb *4.10 91–10 MyTrustyCt115no EbonyBreez1152¾ SmoknFrolic116½ Along in final stride 8
10Jly04–9EIP fst 1 :24 :472 1:121 1:371 3↑Ⓕ HBPAH75k 87 1 42 31½ 61¾ 55½ 56 Martinez W L119 fb 2.90 88–13 MissFortunte115½ MyoOnthSid1201 ThrRunsHtti116¾ Rated inside,empty 8
13Jun04–8AP fst 7f :224 :454 1:11 1:232 3↑Ⓕ ChcgoBCH-G3 97 1 4 53 52½ 31½ 11¾ Douglas R R L116 fb 4.50 92–14 MyTrustyCt1161¾ OurJosephin1121½ SmokeChsr1164 Split horses, driving 5
22May04–9CD fst 6f :212 :44 :554 1:084 3↑Ⓕ WinColorsH108k 96 6 4 74¾ 68 47 43 Shepherd J L115 fb 28.10 94–11 Lady Tak122¾ Fut Me In1171¼ Ebony Breeze1161 5-6w,mild gain 7
1May04–11CD sly 6½f :224 :454 1:11 1:172 3↑Ⓕ Alw 66110n$y 94 4 5 65½ 64 31 2½ Shepherd J5 L114 f 3.50 83–14 MyBostonGal117½ MyTrustyCat1143½ ChrismticAppel109½ 5 wide 1/4 pole 6
13Mar04–10OP fst 1 1/16 :23 :464 1:12 1:441 3↑Ⓕ OaklwnBC-G3 81 3 2hd 2hd 2hd 75 76½ Shepherd J L113 fb 5.20 82–15 GoldnSont1171¾ KystothHrt117¾ MyOnthSd113½ Vied between, weakened 10
19Feb04–9OP fst 6f :213 :444 :573 1:10 4↑Ⓕ Alw 35000n1y 92 1 7 710 66¾ 32½ 12 Shepherd J5 L111 fb 2.20 90–19 MyTrustyCt1112 GilddWings1161½ EmilyRing1167¼ Angld out turn,willing 7

Mystery Giver
Own: Team Block

B. g. 7 (Apr)
Sire: Dynaformer (Roberto) $75,000
Dam: Ioya (Naskra)
Br: David Block & Patricia Block (Ill)
Tr: Block Chris M(0 0 0 0 .00) 2004:(298 51 .17)

Life	33	11	7	2	$1,165,900	105	D.Fst	0	0	0	0	$0	-
2004	6	2	1	1	$470,390	105	Wet(338)	1	0	0	0	$1,560	52
2003	10	2	2	1	$256,260	102	Turf(319)	32	11	7	2	$1,164,340	105
	0	0	0	0	$0	-	Dst(0)	0	0	0	0	$0	-

14Aug04-9AP fm 1¼ Ⓣ:4721:12 1:3632:00 3↑ArlMilln-G1 **93** 6 1312128½ 127 109½ 108¾ Douglas R R L126 20.90 102 - ⒹPowerscourt1261½ Kicken Kris1261 *Magistretti*126½ Never prominent 13

24Jly04-7AP fm 1¼ Ⓣ:4941:15 1:3942:031 3↑ArlngtnH-G3 **102** 3 75½ 73¾ 63¾ 52 2hd Marquez C H Jr L120 4.80 95-05 Senor Swinger118hd Mystery Giver1201½ Ballingarry121no Bumped start 7

26Jun04-8AP gd 1$\frac{1}{16}$ Ⓣ:242 :492 1:14 1:442 3↑ⓈCardinalH84k **79** 3 65½ 52½ 53 62½ 62 Marquez C H Jr L127 *.50 85-14 Runaway Victor112hd Colorful Tour1191 *Home of Stars*115no No rally 7

1May04-9CD yl 1⅛ Ⓣ:51 1:152 1:3931:53 3↑TurfClsc-G1 **101** 7 54½ 85 76¾ 44 32½ Albarado R J L123 9.70 65-32 Stroll1212½ Sweet Return123no Mystery Giver123¾ Steadied 1st turn 11

Previously trained by Scherer Richard R

21Mar04-8FG fm *1⅛ Ⓣ:49 1:122 1:3611:481 4↑MMunzJrH-G2 **105** 10 85¾ 99¾ 95 44½ 1¾ Albarado R J L120 15.00 103-05 MysteryGiver120¾ Herculated116½ SkateAway1171 In time,nw crse record 10

31Jan04-9FG yl *1⅛ Ⓣ:50 1:14 1:3911:513 4↑FGBCH119k **104** 1 75¾ 78 75 31½ 1nk Albarado R J L120 2.50 86-14 *Mystery Giver*120nk Skate Away1182½ Great Bloom1163¾ Up final strides 9

Needwood Blade (GB)
Own: Harlequin Ranches and Duggan Richard

Ch. h. 7 (Mar)
Sire: Pivotal*GB (Polar Falcon) $71,344
Dam: Finlaggan*GB (Be My Chief)
Br: Mr. & Mrs. C. R. Philipson (GB)
Tr: Gallagher Patrick(0 0 0 0 .00) 2004:(220 39 .18)

Life	39	9	3	3	$310,154	104	D.Fst	1	0	0	0	$0	-
2004	7	1	0	0	$68,426	104	Wet(320)	0	0	0	0	$0	-
2003	8	2	0	0	$87,201	95	Turf(430)	38	9	3	3	$310,154	104
	0	0	0	0	$0	-	Dst(0)	0	0	0	0	$0	-

30Oct04-10LS yl 1⅛ Ⓣ:5011:151 1:3931:514 3↑ConGenBfTf100k **94** 9 108¼108 104 85¾ 73¼ Flores D R L121b 3.70 81-07 Royal Regalia1212¼ Kathir123½ Xirius120nk Failed to threaten 12

2Oct04-7BM fm *1⅛ Ⓣ:4721:112 1:3631:462 3↑BMBCH-G3 **104** 6 65½ 63½ 64½ 41 11 Carr D LB116b 11.10 95-16 Needwood Blade1161 Seinne1162 Balestrini1171¼ Blckd 1/8p, drvng 7

8Sep04-6Dmr fm 1 Ⓣ:231 :473 1:1121:341 3↑LiveDreamH76k **100** 1 75¼ 74½ 63 54 41¼ Sorenson D LB114b 19.80 89-11 Statement117hd Cayoke117nk Tsigane1191 Pulled,inside to lane 10

Previously trained by Walsh Kathy

31Jly04-8Dmr fm 1 Ⓣ:224 :463 1:10 1:331 3↑ⓇWickerrH76k **99** 6 53 53¼ 54 52½ 41 Sorenson D LB114f 13.00 94-07 *Statement*116nk Seinne116¾ Golden Arrow114hd Came out str,willingly 7

9Apr04-9Kee fm 1 Ⓣ:23 :451 1:09 1:332 4↑MakrsMrk-G2 **83** 9 99 99 95 910 99¾ Santiago Javier L116 23.30 95 - Perfect Soul116½ *Burning Roma*116hd Royal Spy1161 Outrun 10

6Mar04-9SA fm 1 Ⓣ:224 :452 1:0941:334 4↑FKilroeH-G2 **99** 7 11141116 1311 105½ 84¼ Santiago Javier LB113 27.60 89-12 Sweet Return119½ *Singletary*1172 Inesperado116½ 5wd into lane,no bid 14

15Feb04-7SA fm *6½f Ⓣ:222 :443 1:0631:122 4↑DaytonaH71k **100** 5 6 53½ 42½ 52¾ 41½ Santiago Javier LB115 9.90 93-05 Tsigane116½ *Glick*116no *Cayoke*1151 Off bit slow,3wd,4wd 6

Newfoundland
Own: Sumaya Us Stables

Ch. h. 5 (Feb)
Sire: Storm Cat (Storm Bird) $500,000
Dam: Clear Mandate (Deputy Minister)
Br: G. Watts Humphrey (Ky)
Tr: Pletcher Todd A(0 0 0 0 .00) 2004:(948 240 .25)

Life	22	7	3	2	$677,534	111		D.Fst	14	4	3	2	$569,670	111
2004	9	2	3	1	$523,750	111		Wet(430)	3	2	0	0	$90,954	100
2003	9	4	0	1	$137,234	98		Turf(347)	5	1	0	0	$16,910	73
	0	0	0	0	$0	–		Dst(0)	0	0	0	0	$0	–

30Oct04-9LS fst 1¼ :47 1:111 1:351 1:59 3↑BCClasic-G1 98 10 41½ 31½ 117 1212 1217½ Coa E M L126 b 38.80 - - Ghostzapper1263 RosesinMay1264 PleasantlyPerfect126¾ Wide trip, tired 13
2Oct04-10Bel fst 1¼ :473 1:113 1:362 2:022 3↑JkyClbGC-G1 111 6 3½ 2hd 1½ 1½ 2¾ Prado E S L126 fb 20.30 84-13 FunnyCide126¾ Nwfoundlnd1261 ThCliffsEdg1223¾ Drifted stretch, game 7
11Sep04-10Bel fst 1⅛ :453 1:083 1:331 1:461 3↑Woodward-G1 83 4 53¼ 52½ 59½ 514 518¼ Velazquez J R L126 b 6.10 82-15 *Ghostzapper*126nk *Saint Liam*1269¼ Bowman's Band1267¼ Wide trip, tired 7
7Aug04-9Sar fst 1⅛ :451 1:084 1:344 1:482 3↑WhitneyH-G1 98 9 75¼ 63 99 89½ 79¾ Velazquez J R L114 b 5.60 83-14 *RosesinMy*114no PrfctDrift1172¼ BowmnsBnd114no Wide both turns, tired 9
3Jly04-7Bel fst 1¼ :461 1:091 1:334 1:592 3↑SuburbnH-G1 111 2 21 3½ 31 3½ 2nk Velazquez J R L114 b 8.40 100 - PeceRules120nk Newfoundlnd114no FunnyCide117¾ Speed 3 wide, gamely 8
12Jun04-7Bel fst 1⅛ :451 1:082 1:332 1:461 3↑BrklynH-G2 107 2 4¾ 2hd 2½ 33 33¼ Velazquez J R L115 b 3.25 97-03 Seattle Fitz116½ Dynever1172¾ Newfoundland1155¾ Vied inside, tired 6
3Apr04-9GP fst 1¼ :472 1:112 1:362 2:024 3↑GFH-G2 104 3 22 22½ 21½ 32½ 22 Chavez J F L116 b 1.90 98-15 Jackpot1132 Newfoundland1161 *TheLdysGroom*1131¾ Stalked, outfinished 6
13Mar04-13GP fst 1 1/16 :24 :481 1:12 1:431 3↑SkipAwyH-G3 105 6 42 31½ 3½ 11 1½ Velazquez J R L116 b 6.00 93-15 Newfoundland116½ SupahBlitz1142¼ BowmansBnd1174¼ 3 wide, prevailed 10
31Jan04-8GP sly 1 1/16 ⊗ :233 :471 1:114 1:444 3↑CanTurfH-G3 100 4 52¾ 41½ 2½ 21 1nk Velazquez J R L115 b 2.70 85-29 *Nwfondlnd*115nk MllnnmDrgon1188½ EvrythngtoGn1135¼ Hit gate, just up 6

Niigon
Own: Chiefswood Stable

Dk. b or b. c. 4 (Mar)
Sire: Unbridled (Fappiano) $200,000
Dam: Savethelastdance (Nureyev)
Br: Chiefswood Stables Limited (Ont-C)
Tr: Coatrieux Eric(0 0 0 0 .00) 2004:(71 13 .18)

Life	12	2	3	3	$915,114	100		D.Fst	10	1	2	3	$776,294	97
2004	9	2	2	1	$864,610	100		Wet(409)	2	1	1	0	$138,820	100
2003	3	M	1	2	$50,504	86		Turf(306)	0	0	0	0	$0	–
	0	0	0	0	$0	–		Dst(0)	0	0	0	0	$0	–

6Sep04-10Pha fst 1⅛ :473 1:111 1:353 1:482 PaDerby-G2 91 9 32 42 32 37 412¾ Landry R C L119 f 28.40 90-11 LovofMny1168½ PllrdsVsn1221 Swngfrthfncs1193¼ Dropped back steadily 12
8Aug04-9Sar fst 1⅛ :453 1:093 1:343 1:472 JimDandy-G2 89 4 45 47 36½ 510 412¼ Landry R C L117 f 24.75 86-02 Purge1214½ The Cliff's Edge123½ [D]Eddington1157¼ Bumped stretch 6
Placed third through disqualification
18Jly04-9FE sly 1 3/16 :473 1:122 1:373 1:573 [R]PrncOWales500k 100 3 1hd 1hd 12½ 11 2hd Landry R C L126 f 1.25 91-27 *A Bit O'Gold*126hd Niigon12615¼ His Smoothness1261¾ Caught at wire 7
27Jun04-9WO fst 1¼ :474 1:124 1:374 2:043 [R]QueensPlt1000k 97 13 21 1hd 11½ 12 1¾ Landry R C L126 f 5.90 82-17 Niigon126¾ *A Bit O'Gold*1267¾ Will He Crow1261 Stalked,bid,clear,held 13
6Jun04-8WO fst 1⅛ :483 1:14 1:39 1:513 [R]PlateTrial166k 91 1 32 41½ 31 23 23¼ Landry R C L126 f 7.10 87-20 A Bit O'Gold1233¼ *Niigon*1261¾ Little Bentley12610¾ Steadied,failed bid 8
8May04-9WO sly 1 1/16 :224 :464 1:123 1:45 3↑Md Sp Wt 64k 86 5 63¾ 32 1hd 13½ 16¾ Landry R C L117 f 3.95e 86-18 Niigon1176¾ *Aleged Ruler*1171¼ Frankie's Fire1221¼ Widened,driving 11
17Apr04-6Kee fst 1⅛ :474 1:132 1:393 1:53 Md Sp Wt 44k 40 5 43½ 31½ 53¾ 715 723½ Guidry M L121 fb 9.60 52-11 IndinProspector1216¼ Confirmd1212 Ctsctcn1211½ Tracked,4w,weakened 11
13Mar04-6GP fst 1⅛ :472 1:13 1:39 1:521 Md Sp Wt 32k 61 5 97¼ 76¼ 83¾ 710 615 Migliore R L122 b *3.10 63-15 Go Now1221¼ Mr. Mabee1225½ Summer Book1221 Failed to menace 12
21Feb04-10GP fst 1 1/16 :25 :501 1:144 1:454 Md Sp Wt 32k 67 7 126¾ 115 74¾ 810 712 Landry R C L122 b 4.20 68-23 MorinesVictory122¾ Ctsctcn1224 *ReggieforThree*1223½ Pinch brk, steadied 12

Noches De Rosa (Chi)
Own: Diamond A Racing Corporation

Dk. b or b. m. 7 (Aug)
Sire: Stagecraft*GB (Sadler's Wells)
Dam: Night Girl (Noble Fighter)
Br: Haras Don Alberto (Chi)
Tr: Mandella Richard E(0 0 0 0 .00) 2004:(160 24 .15)

Life	27	7	5	5	$546,073	100		
2004	7	1	1	1	$256,600	98		
2003	5	2	1	1	$192,860	100		
	0	0	0	0	$0	-		
D.Fst	0	0	0	0	$0	-		
Wet(280*)	0	0	0	0	$0	-		
Turf(254)	27	7	5	5	$546,073	100		
Dst(0)	0	0	0	0	$0	-		

25Nov04-6Hol fm 1½ Ⓣ :484 1:141 2:042 2:292 3↑ⒻHermosBchH65k 76 7 5¾ 5¾ 7¾ 5¼ 511½ Baze T C LB121 b 2.50 67-24 Uraib1161½ Nadeszhda1164 Test the Waters1181 3wd,tight 5/16,wkened 8
20Oct04-4SA fm 1¼ Ⓣ :462 1:10 1:342 1:591 3↑ⒻYlwRibbn-G1 90 5 64 87¾ 97¾ 72¾ 76¼ Baze T C LB123 b 7.60 87-09 Light Jig1234 Tangle1231 Katdogawn123hd Steadied 3/8,no bid 10
14Aug04-8AP fm 1 3/16 Ⓣ :494 1:152 1:393 1:562 3↑ⒻBeverlyD-G1 91 3 52 52 63 116¾ 115 Smith M E L123 b 13.50 87 - Crimson Palace123½ *Riskaverse*123hd Necklace117nk Gave way stretch 11
27Jun04-8Hol fm 1¼ Ⓣ :493 1:133 1:374 2:012 3↑ⒻBevHilsH-G2 96 2 1½ 1hd 1hd 21 32½ Smith M E LB118 b 2.20 82-13 Light Jig1141 Moscow Burning1171½ Noches De Rosa1181 Inside, held 3rd 6
31May04-2Hol fm 1⅛ Ⓣ :492 1:12 1:36 1:481+3↑ⒻGamlyBCH-G1 96 1 1hd 2hd 21 2hd 11 Smith M E LB115 b 3.30 90-07 NochesDeRos1151 Meghertz122hd QuroQuro1152 Re-bid btwn foes,game 4
17Apr04-9SA fm 1¼ Ⓣ :48 1:13 1:37 2:003 4↑ⒻSntBrbrH-G2 98 5 21 21 11½ 12 21 Baze T C LB116 b 3.70 85-16 Megahertz1211 *Noches De Rosa*1162½ Mandela1112 Bid,led,clear,2nd best 5
28Mar04-2SA fm 1 Ⓣ :231 :473 1:112 1:343 4↑ⒻAlw 65000N$MY 84 4 32½ 42¼ 53½ 44½ 44 Baze T C LB116 b 4.30 85-10 *Intercontinent*l1161½ Dublino116hd AbbeyBridg1172½ Rail, angld out,evenly 5

Norfolk Knight
Own: Squires Margaret

Dk. b or b. g. 6 (Apr)
Sire: Tejabo (Deputy Minister) $1,500
Dam: Artic Bleu (Nain Bleu*Fr)
Br: Margaret Squires (Ont-C)
Tr: Dittfach Hugo(0 0 0 0 .00) 2004:(43 7 .16)

Life	27	9	3	4	$584,862	100		
2004	13	4	0	4	$338,923	100		
2003	14	5	3	0	$245,939	95		
	0	0	0	0	$0	-		
D.Fst	16	6	1	2	$396,386	100		
Wet(264)	9	3	2	2	$183,766	99		
Turf(191)	2	0	0	0	$4,710	88		
Dst(0)	0	0	0	0	$0	-		

12Dec04-8WO my 1¾ 1:113 1:391 3:032 3↑ValdictryH137k 55 6 1hd 33½ 624 634 644¼ Scharfstein J L120 2.65 25-24 Daddy Cool1179½ Jambalar1162¼ Solihull1116 Dueled,tired 7
20Nov04-8WO my 1 1/16 :234 :473 1:121 1:45 3↑WoSltCpH-G3 93 1 12½ 15 11½ 2hd 32½ Scharfstein J L120 *.50 83-27 Mark One119hd A Bit O'Gold1202½ Norfolk Knight1202¼ Yielded 1/8 pole 4
31Oct04-4WO gd 1 1/16 :231 :463 1:104 1:453 3↑Alw 83700NC 99 1 1hd 1½ 12½ 18 110¾ Scharfstein J5 L115 *1.00 83-24 NorfolkKnght11510¾ OpnLck118no JdthsWldRsh1162 Widened,ridden out 6
16Oct04-8WO fst 1⅛ :471 1:112 1:372 1:512 3↑DurhmCpH-G3 100 2 1½ 11 11½ 11½ 1nk Scharfstein J L116 5.95 91-24 *Norfolk Knight*116nk Mobil12611¾ Sky Diamond1177¾ Set pace,held gamely 5
26Sep04-2WO fst 1 1/16 :242 :482 1:123 1:451 3↑Alw 83700NC 99 5 1hd 11½ 12½ 14½ 15½ Scharfstein J5 L113 3.30 85-33 *Norfolk Knight*1135½ Mark One1182¼ Dream Launcher1164 Ridden out 5
21Aug04-4WO fst 1 1/16 :24 :472 1:12 1:444 3↑ⓇIzvestia104k 83 7 2hd 11½ 1hd 1½ 31 Barton J 120 *2.10 86-19 RefusetoBend114½ IdBGon118½ *NorfolkKnight*120nk Dueled,weakened late 7
7Aug04-8WO fst 1 1/16 :241 :483 1:123 1:441 3↑SeagramCup136k 92 3 12½ 11 2½ 24 46 Barton J 121 15.15 84-17 *One for Rose*1165 Mark One121¾ Hydrogen115nk No match on turn 7
21Jly04-7WO fst 7f :222 :443 1:092 1:23 3↑ⓈOverskate133k 81 8 4 21½ 51¼ 810 86¼ Da Silva E R 122 7.55 86-18 Barath1151 Choreography115¾ Barbeau Ruckus126½ Tired 5-wide top str 8
11Jly04-8WO fst 6½f :214 :441 1:09 1:153 3↑BldVenturH141k 84 4 10 1010 99 910 77½ Scharfstein J 113 15.30 92-11 *I'm the Tiger*1161½ Twisted Wit1161 I TheeWed1151¼ 5wd,passed tired foes 10
12Jun04-8WO fst 1 1/16 :234 :48 1:124 1:442 3↑ⓈStdyGrowth129k 93 4 1½ 12 11½ 12 13¼ Scharfstein J 117 5.25 89-18 Norfolk Knight1173¼ Hot Pepper Hill1173 Barath1192¼ Set reserved pace 6
6Jun04-3WO fm 6f Ⓣ :22 :44 :553 1:08 3↑Alw 78500NC 88 4 8 711 86 46½ 44 Scharfstein J5 111 15.25 94-02 *Soaring Free*1222¾ My LuckyStrike1161 Waltzin'Storm117nk 4-wide,all out 8
15May04-8WO fst 6f :222 :452 :573 1:10 3↑ⓈNwProvdnce134k 94 7 8 84¼ 64 53 32¼ Scharfstein J 115 5.55 88-13 BrbuRuckus121nk Chorogrphy1152 NorfolkKnght1151¼ Rail to 3wd,rallied 8
2May04-8WO sly 5f :214 :451 :581 3↑Alw 78500N$Y 89 5 5 68 58½ 45½ 3¾ Scharfstein J5 115 4.15 87-15 *RreFriends*122½ WildWhiskey120nk NorfolkKnight115½ Checked near wire 6

Nothing to Lose

Own: Ramsey Kenneth L. and Sarah K

B. h. 5 (Jan)
Sire: Sky Classic (Nijinsky II) $12,500
Dam: Cherlindrea (Clever Trick)
Br: Kenneth L. Ramsey & Sarah K. Ramsey (Ky)
Tr: Frankel Robert J(0 0 0 0 .00) 2004:(491 135 .27)

Life	15	6	3	1	$809,210	111
2004	9	2	3	1	$643,200	111
2003	2	2	0	0	$120,000	93
	0	0	0	0	$0	–

D.Fst	1	0	0	0	$2,650	83
Wet(356)	1	0	0	0	$3,160	72
Turf(341)	13	6	3	1	$803,400	111
Dst(0)	0	0	0	0	$0	–

27Nov04– 7Hol fm 1 1/16 Ⓣ :233 :48 1:112 1:411 3↑ CtationH-G1 **103** 3 75 73¼ 84¼ 74¼ 64 Prado E S LB120 b *2.50 86– 17 Leroidesanimaux117½ AtotheZ1151 ThreeValleys115½ 4wd into lane,no bid 10

30Oct04– 4LS yl 1 Ⓣ :24 :483 1:123 1:364 3↑ BCMile-G1 **98** 12 117 105½ 93 127 114¾ Velazquez J R L126 b 4.30 81– 07 Singletry126½ AntoniusPius122 1½ SixPerfections123nk Wide trip, no rally 14

9Oct04– 8Kee fm 1 Ⓣ :232 :471 1:114 1:352 3↑ ShdwlTfM-G1 **111** 9 78¾ 76¼ 31½ 11½ 14½ Albarado R J L126 b 4.60 95– 10 NothingtoLose1264½ HonorinWr126¾ SilverTree1261¼ 5w trip,steady drive 9

28Aug04– 9Sar fm 1 1/16 Ⓣ :233 :462 1:091 1:392 3↑ 4strdavH-G2 **107** 2 74¼ 65½ 53¼ 3nk 1½ Velazquez J R L117 b *1.90 98– 01 *NothingtoLose*117½ SilverTree1171 RoyalRegli1141¾ Got through on hedge 10

30Jly04– 8Sar yl 1⅛ Ⓣ :491 1:131 1:371 1:493 3↑ BBaruchH-G2 **103** 6 31 31½ 2½ 2hd 2nk Velazquez J R L117 b *1.05 89– 11 SilverTree116nk *NothingtoLos*117½ IrishColonil113nk Gamely between foes 7

3Jly04–10Mth fm 1⅜ Ⓣ :483 1:14 1:372 2:131 3↑ UnitdNtn-G1 **106** 4 21 21 2½ 11 31¼ Migliore R L118 b 11.00 96– 09 RequstforProl118½ MrOBrin120¾ NothingtoLos1181 Grudging yielded 1/16 11

16Jun04– 8Bel fm 1 Ⓣ :231 :46 1:091 1:323 4↑ OC 100k/c -N **101** 6 41¾ 32 3½ 3½ 21 Velazquez J R L123 b 1.80 96– 03 SilverTree1231 NothingtoLos1231 ChillyRoostr1161½ Game finish outside 6

21Mar04– 8FG fm *1⅛ Ⓣ :49 1:122 1:361 1:481 4↑ MMunzJrH-G2 **99** 4 31½ 31½ 52¾ 54½ 62¾ Desormeaux K J L118 b 4.30 100– 05 Mystery Giver120¾ Herculated116½ Skate Away1171 No final kick 10

19Jan04– 8SA fm 1¼ Ⓣ :474 1:121 1:353 1:584 4↑ SnMarcos-G2 **99** 5 31½ 21 31 21 2½ Bailey J D LB116 b 4.80 94– 05 *SweetReturn*12½ NothingtoLose1161½ BlueStllr116½ 3wd into lane,willing 9

Ocean Drive

Own: Baskin Bonnie and Sy

Dk. b or b. m. 5 (Feb)
Sire: Belong to Me (Danzig) $25,000
Dam: Clever But Costly (Clever Trick)
Br: James D. Conway & Thomas C. Mueller (Ky)
Tr: Pletcher Todd A(0 0 0 0 .00) 2004:(948 240 .25)

Life	21	9	4	3	$803,986	104
2004	11	4	3	3	$505,900	104
2003	6	2	1	0	$159,356	97
	0	0	0	0	$0	–

D.Fst	0	0	0	0	$0	–
Wet(359)	0	0	0	0	$0	–
Turf(307)	21	9	4	3	$803,986	104
Dst(0)	0	0	0	0	$0	–

28Nov04– 7Hol fm 1 Ⓣ :24 :473 1:112 1:354 3↑ ⒻMatriarc-G1 **81** 5 41½ 4nk 86½ 98¼ 79 Velazquez J R LB123 9.90 76– 17 Intercontinentl1232 EtoileMontnt123no TickrTp1201½ 4wd bid 1/2,wkened 9

22Oct04– 8Med gd 1 1/16 Ⓣ :243 :482 1:113 1:412 3↑ ⒻVioletH-G3 **97** 4 21½ 23½ 24 23 31¼ Velazquez J R L121 *.50 90– 12 ChngingWorld1131¼ HghCourt117hd OcnDrv1212½ Closed,outfinished 2nd 7

25Sep04– 9Bel fm 1 Ⓣ :241 :473 1:112 1:343 3↑ ⒻNblDmslH-G3 **104** 9 5¾ 3½ 1hd 1hd 11¼ Velazquez J R L120 *2.75 87– 16 Ocean Drive1201¼ High Court115¾ Hour of Justice1162 4 wide move, clear 9

30Aug04– 8Sar yl 1 1/16 Ⓣ :24 :47 1:111 1:434 3↑ ⒻBlSpaBCH-G3 **101** 4 23 28 26 1½ 11¼ Velazquez J R L119 *2.10 85– 15 *OcenDrive*1191¼ PersonlLegend1151¾ HighCourt1141¾ Saved ground, clear 10

31Jly04– 7Sar yl 1⅛ Ⓣ :473 1:113 1:363 1:484 3↑ ⒻDianaH-G1 **92** 2 23½ 26 21½ 25 38 Velazquez J R L118 8.00 78– 14 WonderAgain1205¾ Riskverse1182¼ *OcenDrive*1182¼ Inside run second turn 7

10Jly04– 9Mth fm 1 1/16 Ⓣ :244 :491 1:123 1:413+3↑ ⒻEatntwnH-G3 **99** 1 22 22 2½ 1hd 12¾ Coa E M L120 *1.20 91– 08 OceanDrive1202¾ *HonorableCat*1141½ *FastCookie*1181¼ Stalked,kicked clear 6

5Jun04– 8WO fm 1 1/16 Ⓣ :25 :484 1:12 1:401 3↑ ⒻNassau-G3 **96** 6 31 21½ 21½ 21½ 2¾ Douglas R R L117 *.65 96– 02 Inish Glora121¾ *Ocean Drive*1172½ *Classic Stamp*119¾ Stalked 3wd,mild gain 6

15May04– 5Pim fm 1 1/16 Ⓣ :241 :481 1:113 1:404 3↑ ⒻGalrettH-G3 **99** 3 32 3½ 21 13 1½ Bailey J D L117 *1.10 98 - Ocean Drive117½ *Film Maker*1203½ *With Patience*1121 2wd 1/4, driving 8

18Apr04– 8Kee fm 1 1/16 Ⓣ :232 :48 1:12 1:412 4↑ ⒻJenyWily-G3 **97** 5 33 32 21 3nk 21 Velazquez J R L116 4.40 96– 05 *Intercontinental*1161 *Ocean Drive*1161½ *MadeiraMist*118nk 4w bid,outfinished 8

13Mar04–11GP fm 1 Ⓣ :251 :494 1:132 1:374 3↑ ⒻMrshsRiver67k **96** 6 53 54½ 42½ 32½ 22 Velazquez J R L120 4.40 75– 13 Dedication1202 Ocean Drive1201 Vespers120½ Bobbled start, 3 wide 9

6Feb04– 9GP yl *1 Ⓣ :25 :501 1:154 1:412 4↑ ⒻAlw 46000c **94** 5 33 33 2½ 2½ 3½ Velazquez J R L119 3.20 65– 43 Stay Forever115nk Vespers115nk Ocean Drive1191¼ Led late, outfinished 8

Offlee Wild
Own: Azalea Stables LLC

Dk. b or b. h. 5 (Apr)
Sire: Wild Again (Icecapade) $50,000
Dam: Alvear (Seattle Slew)
Br: Dorothy A. Matz (Ky)
Tr: Dutrow R E Jr(0 0 0 0 .00) 2004:(603 166 .28)

Life	14	4	2	2	$523,825	110	D.Fst	14	4	2	2	$523,825	110
2004	4	2	1	0	$335,640	110	Wet(389)	0	0	0	0	$0	–
2003	7	1	0	2	$152,400	99	Turf(298)	0	0	0	0	$0	–
	0	0	0	0	$0	–	Dst(0)	0	0	0	0	$0	–

19Jun04-10Suf fst 1⅛ :483 1:122 1:363 1:49 3↑ MassH-G2 **110** 1 31 42 31½ 1hd 1hd Prado E S LB113 3.20 98– 10 OffleWild113hd FunnyCid117hd ThLdysGroom1161½ 3wd bid 1/4,strong drv 9
14May04- 7Bel fst 1 1/16 :231 :454 1:101 1:412 3↑ Alw 48000N2x **100** 6 54 56½ 2hd 11½ 14½ Castellano J J L121 2.55 93– 20 *Offlee Wild*1214½ Shaniko117½ Mustanfar1147½ 3 wide move, clear 7
Previously trained by Smith Thomas V
13Mar04-13GP fst 1 1/16 :24 :481 1:12 1:431 3↑ SkipAwyH-G3 **85** 8 86¼ 97½ 84¾ 76¼ 811½ Guidry M L114 12.70 81– 15 Newfoundland116½ SupahBlitz1142¼ BowmansBnd1174¼ 3 wide, no factor 10
9Feb04- 5GP fst 1 1/16 :223 :452 1:103 1:434 4↑ Alw 36000N2x **90** 1 511 516 44½ 11 2hd Guidry M L118 *1.40 90– 21 CollateralDamage118hd OffleeWild1185 IndyDncer1181 Drifted str, failed 8

Olmodavor
Own: Wertheimer and Frere

B. h. 6 (Apr)
Sire: A.P. Indy (Seattle Slew) $300,000
Dam: Corrazona (El Gran Senor)
Br: Wertheimer et Frere (Ky)
Tr: Mandella Richard E(0 0 0 0 .00) 2004:(160 24 .15)

Life	15	5	5	1	$706,540	110	D.Fst	14	5	5	1	$703,480	110
2004	6	1	2	1	$367,000	107	Wet(410)	0	0	0	0	$0	–
2003	4	1	2	0	$241,080	110	Turf(335)	1	0	0	0	$3,060	88
	0	0	0	0	$0	–	Dst(0)	0	0	0	0	$0	–

31Jly04- 8AP fst 1 3/16 :482 1:124 1:363 1:564 3↑ WashPkH-G2 **102** 4 53 53½ 53½ 4¾ 2hd McKee J L121 b 2.10 91– 18 Eye of the Tiger116hd Olmodavor1211½ Congrats116nk Brushed 1/4 pole 5
10Jly04- 9Hol fst 1¼ :464 1:102 1:344 2:003 3↑ HolGldCp-G1 **107** 1 55½ 52¼ 43 42 21¼ Solis A LB124 b 3.40 98 – Total Impact1241¼ Olmodavor124½ Even theScore1244 Tight early & 7-1/2 7
8May04- 9Hol fst 1 1/16 :231 :454 1:092 1:404 3↑ MrvnLRyH-G2 **92** 3 76¼ 75¾ 64½ 52½ 46 Solis A LB121 b *2.00 91– 04 *EventheScore*1162 EndersShdow1133 TotlImpct1161 Off bit slow,4wd lane 8
6Mar04-10SA fst 1¼ :461 1:101 1:351 2:013 4↑ SAH-G1 **102** 7 75¼ 76¼ 75¾ 65 47½ Smith M E LB119 4.60 83– 11 *SouthrnImg*1181¼ IslndFshion1152¼ SintBuddy1114 Swung out lane,no bid 8
1Feb04- 8FG fst 1 1/16 :242 :472 1:114 1:452 4↑ WhrlwayH-G3 **107** 9 66 810 56½ 2½ 1¾ Lanerie C J L121 *1.50 83– 17 Olmodavor121¾ Spanish Empire1182¼ Almuhathir114½ 4-w rally, driving 9
3Jan04- 7SA fst 1 1/16 :224 :454 1:093 1:421 4↑ SnPsqalH-G2 **94** 4 64¼ 63 64¾ 34 33½ Solis A LB118 *1.50 90– 13 Star Cross113½ *Nose The Trade*1153 *Olmodavor*1182½ 4wd into lane,along 3d 7

One for Rose
Own: Tucci Stables

Dk. b or b. m. 6 (May)
Sire: Tejano Run (Tejano) $5,000
Dam: Saucyladygaylord (Lord Gaylord)
Br: Hill 'N' Dale Farms (Ont-C)
Tr: Attard Sid C(0 0 0 0 .00) 2004:(315 76 .24)

Life	22	12	4	2	$1,047,243	110	D.Fst	16	10	4	1	$918,365	110
2004	8	4	2	0	$489,832	102	Wet(323)	4	2	0	1	$109,186	93
2003	10	6	2	0	$476,377	110	Turf(252)	2	0	0	0	$19,692	85
	0	0	0	0	$0	-	Dst(0)	0	0	0	0	$0	-

Date/Race	Trk	Dist	Fractions	Race	Fig	PP	St	1C	2C	Str	Fin	Jockey	Wt	Odds	Spd-Var	Top Finishers	Comment	Fld
13Nov04-6WO	fst	1¼	:494 1:142 1:391 2:044	3↑ⒻMaplLeaf-G3	100	4	11½	1½	13	16	16½	Ramsammy E	L126	*.50	81-28	One for Rose1266½ Clouds of Gold118½ Raylene1177¾	Set pace,driving	5
24Oct04-5WO	fst	1⅛	:482 1:124 1:384 1:522	3↑ⒻAlw 83700NC	90	1	41½	42	2½	1½	2½	Ramsammy E	L123	*.70	85-23	Raylene117½ One for Rose1231¼ CloudsofGold1181¼	Bid midtrn,vied,missed	9
10Oct04-8Kee	fst	1⅛	:464 1:113 1:37 1:493	3↑ⒻSpinster-G1	96	2	43½	52¾	51¾	43½	47¼	Ramsammy E	L123	7.70	86-12	Azeri1233 Tamweel123½ Mayo On the Side1233¾	5w lane,empty late	7
5Sep04-4WO	fst	1 1/16	:24 :482 1:122 1:432	3↑ⒻⓇAlgoma125k	100	4	22½	2½	21½	21½	12¼	Ramsammy E	L122	*.50	94-12	OnforRos1222¼ WnnngChnc1169¼ KssdbyPrnc11512	Bothered start,by late	4
7Aug04-8WO	fst	1 1/16	:241 :483 1:123 1:441	3↑SeagramCup136k	102	7	22½	21	1½	14	15	Ramsammy E	L116	2.00	90-17	One for Rose1165 Mark One121¾ Hydrogen115nk	Clear quickly,drvg	7
18Jly04-8WO	fst	1 1/16	:243 :492 1:134 1:451	3↑ⒻBellMahone107k	91	6	31½	33	21½	23	23½	Ramsammy E	L124	*.95	81-26	WinningChnce1193½ OneforRose1241¼ Rylene1212½	Chased 3deep,2nd best	7
20Jun04-3WO	fst	1 1/16	:24 :481 1:113 1:441	3↑ⒻOntMatronH175k	99	3	21½	2hd	1½	11½	11½	Ramsammy E	L123	1.05	90-19	OneforRos1231½ WinningChnc1202½ Hndpintd1171½	Drvg,came out stretch	4
24May04-8WO	sly	1 1/16	:24 :474 1:121 1:463	4↑EclipseH-G3	86	4	21½	21½	21½	35	47¾	Kabel T K	L116	*1.55	70-26	Mark One1152½ Open Concert1134½ Rock Again115¾	Stalked,flattened out	5

Organ Grinder
Own: S and B Stable

Gr/ro. c. 4 (Mar) OBSMAR03 $50,000
Sire: Grindstone (Unbridled) $10,000
Dam: Caveanella (Caveat)
Br: Nancy B. Stone (Ky)
Tr: Attard Sid C(0 0 0 0 .00) 2004:(315 76 .24)

Life	11	5	4	2	$533,473	103	D.Fst	11	5	4	2	$533,473	103
2004	8	4	2	2	$414,813	103	Wet(368)	0	0	0	0	$0	-
2003	3	1	2	0	$118,660	86	Turf(200)	0	0	0	0	$0	-
	0	0	0	0	$0	-	Dst(0)	0	0	0	0	$0	-

Date/Race	Trk	Dist	Fractions	Race	Fig	PP	St	1C	2C	Str	Fin	Jockey	Wt	Odds	Spd-Var	Top Finishers	Comment	Fld
10Oct04-8WO	fst	1⅛	:491 1:142 1:40 1:53	OntarDby160k	82	1	43	42	42	32	21¼	McAleney J S	L121	2.35	82-29	A BitO'Gold1241¼ OrganGrinder1211 AllegedRuler1174¼	4wd,determinedly	5
18Sep04-4WO	fst	1 1/16	:233 :472 1:113 1:434	Alw 83700NC	94	1	36	37½	31½	3½	1nk	McAleney J S	L122	*1.30	92-19	OrgnGrndr122nk CtndShoot1182½ JdthsWldRsh1201¼	Rally 3w, up in time	7
28Aug04-9NP	fst	1⅜	:482 1:15 1:421 2:223	CanDerby-G3	77	3	52¼	3nk	2hd	21	1hd	McAleney J S	L126	*.85	73-21	OrgnGrindr126hd ControlldMting1263¼ DH Bonspi126	Bid 3 wide, prevailed	11
25Jly04-4WO	fst	1 1/16	:233 :47 1:12 1:461	3↑Alw 72200N2x	96	1	43	45½	34½	11½	11¾	Kabel T K	L117	*.55	80-29	OrgnGrinder1171¾ StrikEmHrd115¾ Sttlspctculr12010¾	Rail to 3wd,driving	7
27Jun04-2WO	fst	1 1/16	:241 :483 1:13 1:453	3↑Alw 72200N2x	83	4	51¼	5¾	51¼	42	3¾	Husbands S P	L117	*.30	82-17	IdeBeGone122nk LastAnswer120½ OrgnGrinder1172¾	Stalked,determinedly	8
13Jun04-7WO	fst	1⅛	:48 1:132 1:391 1:512	VictoriaPk140k	103	4	41¼	41¼	41	13½	16	Husbands S P	L117	*1.85	91-16	OrganGrinder1176 CopperTril1192¾ TobeSuve1176¼	Fast move to lead 3 wd	9
22May04-8WO	fst	1 1/16	:231 :47 1:114 1:454	Marine-G3	100	4	33	33	33½	22	21	Husbands S P	L117	12.45	81-27	JudthsWldRush1191 OrgnGrndr1172¼ HonolStorm1179½	Gained steadily str	6
1May04-4WO	fst	6f	:221 :443 :563 1:091	Alw 61600N1x	84	3	3	2½	2½	33	33¾	Husbands S P	L120	3.20	90-08	CutndShoot1183½ ImperilAlydeed117nk OrgnGrindr1205	Forced pace,hung	6

Ouija Board (GB)

Own: Lord Derby

B. f. 4 (Mar)
Sire: Cape Cross*Ire (Green Desert) $67,835
Dam: Selection Board*GB (Welsh Pageant*Fr)
Br: Stanley Estate and Stud Co (GB)
Tr: Dunlop Edward(0 0 0 0 .00) 2004:(1 1 1.00)

Life	8	5	0	3	$1,671,768	108	D.Fst	0 0 0 0		$0	–
2004	5	4	0	1	$1,659,958	108	Wet(280*)	0 0 0 0		$0	–
2003	3	1	0	2	$11,810	–	Turf(263*)	8 5 0 3		$1,671,768	108
	0	0	0	0	$0	–	Dst(0)	0 0 0 0		$0	–

30Oct04–6LS yl 1⅜ Ⓣ :52^2 1:18^2 1:42^1 2:18^1 3↑ ⒻBCF&MTrf-G1 **108** 5 5$5\frac{1}{2}$ 4$3\frac{1}{2}$ 4^3 2^{hd} 1$1\frac{1}{2}$ Fallon K L118 *.90 98– 07 Ouija Board118$1\frac{1}{2}$ Film Maker123^{nk} Wonder Again123$2\frac{3}{4}$ Drew off late 12
30Oct04 Longchamp (Fr) gd *1½ Ⓣ RH 2:25 3↑ Prix de l'Arc de Triomphe-G1 3$1\frac{1}{2}$ Murtagh J P 120 9.00 Bago123½ Cherry Mix123^1 *Ouija Board*120^2 19
Timeform rating: 124+ Stk 1986000 *Rated in 14th,lacked room 2f out,sharp late run into 3rd*
18Jly04 Curragh (Ire) gf 1½ Ⓣ RH 2:28^1 ⒻIrish Oaks-G1 1^1 Fallon K 126 *.57 Ouija Board126^1 Punctilious126$\frac{3}{4}$ Hazarista126^7 7
Timeform rating: 116+ Stk 498000 *Dwelt,rated in 5th,led 1-1/2f out,handily.AllTooBeautiful4th*
4Jun04 Epsom (GB) gd 1½ Ⓣ LH 2:35^2 ⒻEnglish Oaks-G1 1^7 Fallon K 126 3.50 *Ouija Board*126^7 All Too Beautiful126$3\frac{1}{2}$ *Punctilious*126$1\frac{1}{2}$ 7
Timeform rating: 124 Stk 644000 *Dwelt,rated in 6th,led 2f out,surged clear.Necklace4th*
2May04 Newmarket (GB) gd 1¼ Ⓣ Str 2:02^4 ⒻPretty Polly Stakes (Listed) 1^6 Fallon K 120 *2.00 *Ouija Board*120^6 Sahool120½ Rave Reviews120$1\frac{1}{4}$ 9
Timeform rating: 116+ Stk 53300 *Rated in 5th,led over 1f out,ridden clear*

Paddy's Daisy

Own: Stonehaven Farm

Ch. f. 3 (Apr)
Sire: King of Kings*Ire (Sadler's Wells) $5,263
Dam: Mrs. Paddy (Woodman)
Br: Stonehaven Farm (Ky)
Tr: Pletcher Todd A(0 0 0 0 .00) 2004:(948 240 .25)

Life	6	4	0	0	$186,336	87	D.Fst	1 0 0 0		$286	25
2004	6	4	0	0	$186,336	87	Wet(223)	0 0 0 0		$0	–
2003	0	M	0	0	$0	–	Turf(275)	5 4 0 0		$186,050	87
	0	0	0	0	$0	–	Dst(0)	0 0 0 0		$0	–

26Nov04–6Hol fm 1 Ⓣ :23^1 :47^3 1:12 1:36^4 ⒻMiesque-G3 **87** 6 6$8\frac{1}{2}$ 6$7\frac{1}{4}$ 5^3 2^1 1^{nk} Nakatani C S **LB**121 *1.70 80– 20 Paddy'sDaisy121^{nk} Conveyor'sAngel118^5 Kenza116½ 4wd into lane,gamely 8
Run in divisions
28Oct04–8Kee gd 1$\frac{1}{16}$ Ⓣ :22^4 :47^3 1:13^2 1:44^1 ⒻJesamineCo112k **83** 6 6^3 4^1 3½ 2^{hd} 1½ Velazquez J R L120 *.50 83– 17 *Paddy's Daisy*120½ Berbatim116$5\frac{3}{4}$ Jules Best116$4\frac{1}{4}$ 4-5w,stiff drive 10
20Oct04–9Med gd 1^{70} Ⓣ :24 :48^4 1:13^4 1:43^3 ⒻSalemCo55k **80** 5 3^2 3$3\frac{1}{2}$ 2^{hd} 1^{hd} 1$2\frac{1}{4}$ Decarlo C P L115 *.90e 75– 23 *Paddy's Daisy*115$2\frac{1}{4}$ K. D.'s Shady Lady115^1 Elke117^6 3 wide move, drew clr 6
12Sep04–8WO fm 1 Ⓣ :23 :46^1 1:10^1 1:34^4 ⒻNatalma-G3 **76** 7 8$2\frac{3}{4}$ 7$4\frac{1}{4}$ 6^5 5^5 4$2\frac{1}{2}$ Decarlo C P L119 6.05 86– 09 FerlessFlyer114$1\frac{1}{2}$ SwetSoliro114$\frac{3}{4}$ LittlHussy117^{nk} Closed steadily 3-wide 11
8Aug04–4Sar fm 1$\frac{1}{16}$ Ⓣ :23^4 :49 1:14 1:45 ⒻMd Sp Wt 46k **65** 2 3^2 4^1 4$1\frac{1}{2}$ 1$1\frac{1}{2}$ 1^5 Bailey J D L118 *2.25 70– 21 Paddy's Daisy118^5 Nives118^{hd} Clearly Kathy118½ Rank inside, drew away 9
1Jly04–3Bel fst 5½f :22^1 :45^4 :58^3 1:05^2 ⒻMd Sp Wt 43k **25** 7 8 6$7\frac{1}{2}$ 7$6\frac{1}{2}$ 8^{12} 8$13\frac{1}{2}$ Bailey J D L118 *1.25e 72– 11 Extent118^1 Boardwalk Babe118^2 Blitzen118$4\frac{1}{4}$ 3 wide trip, tired 8

Park Avenue Ball
Own: Char-Mari Stable

Ch. c. 3 (May)
Sire: Citidancer (Dixieland Band) $7,500
Dam: Road to the Ball (Cahill Road)
Br: C. J. Hesse, Inc. (NJ)
Tr: Ryerson James T(0 0 0 0 .00) 2004:(192 27 .14)

Life	5	3	1	0	$278,600	80		
2004	5	3	1	0	$278,600	80		
2003	0	M	0	0	$0	-		
	0	0	0	0	$0	-		
D.Fst	5	3	1	0	$278,600	80		
Wet(395)	0	0	0	0	$0	-		
Turf(284)	0	0	0	0	$0	-		
Dst(0)	0	0	0	0	$0	-		

9Oct04-7Bel fst 1 1/16 :233 :471 1:112 1:421 Champagn-G1 **73** 2 7 4¼ 8 4¼ 8 5¼ 7 10 5 15¼ Bravo J L122 12.50 74-20 Proud Accolade122½ Afleet Alex122 1¼ SunKing122 1 1¾ Came wide, no rally 8
19Sep04-7Bel fst 1 :24 :464 1:121 1:384 Futurity-G2 **80** 3 6 1¼ 5 2½ 3½ 1 2½ 1 3 Castellano J J L120 10.80 67-25 PrkAvenueBll1203 WllstretScndl120 1½ EvilMinistr1202 4 wide move, clear 6
28Aug04-11Mth fst 6f :213 :443 :58 1:111 Sapling-G3 **76** 4 5 6 3¾ 4 2¼ 1hd 2¾ Beckner D V L120 2.10 83-18 Evil Minister120¾ *Park Avenue Ball*120 2¾ Upscaled1206 Bid,led,outfinished 8
31Jly04-5Mth fst 5½f :214 :452 :581 1:05 Tyro60k **74** 6 2 4 2½ 4¾ 1 1 1 2½ Beckner D V L118 *.60e 90-15 PrkAvenueBll118 2½ *DoctorVoodoo*116 2½ OnthPorch118¾ 4-wide bid,driving 8
15Jly04-4Mth fst 5f :223 :462 :582 [S]Md Sp Wt 46k **71** 9 4 4nk 2hd 1½ 1 5 Beckner D V L118 6.30 90-13 *PrkAvnBll*1185 *WhosthCowby*118 4¼ DmndClp118nk Dueled,widened driving 12

Passing Shot
Own: Shields J V Jr

Dk. b or b. m. 6 (Apr)
Sire: A.P. Indy (Seattle Slew) $300,000
Dam: Aucilla (Relaunch)
Br: J. V. Shields Jr. (Ky)
Tr: Jerkens H. A(0 0 0 0 .00) 2004:(374 72 .19)

Life	25	6	6	5	$633,857	102		
2004	6	1	1	2	$185,460	102		
2003	10	3	2	2	$362,637	94		
	0	0	0	0	$0	-		
D.Fst	20	6	3	5	$602,880	102		
Wet(447)	4	0	3	0	$30,977	84		
Turf(335)	1	0	0	0	$0	61		
Dst(0)	0	0	0	0	$0	-		

30Oct04-4Aqu fst 7f :222 :443 1:091 1:22 3↑Ⓕ FrstFltH-G2 **79** 4 4 6 7¼ 6 8¾ 5 7 3 8½ Gryder A T L118 3.30 86-08 BendingStrings116 5¾ SmokyGlckn115 2¾ PssingShot1184 Mild rally inside 6
19Jun04-9Bel fst 1 1/16 :231 :453 1:10 1:412 3↑Ⓕ OPhippsH-G1 **82** 2 4 1½ 4 1½ 4 2 3 8½ 3 9¾ Migliore R L116 11.70 83-20 Sightseek120 3¼ StormFlgFlying117 6½ PssingShot1162 Inside, no response 4
15May04-8Bel fst 1 :234 :463 1:111 1:36 3↑Ⓕ ShuveeH-G2 **102** 4 3 1 4 1 1hd 1hd 2½ Santos J A L117 5.50 80-19 StormFlgFlyng116½ PssngShct117no RorEmtn117 8¼ Dug in gamely inside 6
17Apr04-8Aqu fst 1 :232 :463 1:102 1:352 3↑Ⓕ BdORsBCH-G3 **93** 1 4 1½ 4 1 4¾ 2hd 1 2¼ Santos J A L115 7.30 88-16 PssingShot115 2¼ SmoknFrolic119hd NonsuchBy116no Found room on rail 6
14Mar04-8Aqu fst 1⅛ :47 1:111 1:372 1:512 3↑Ⓕ NxtMoveH-G3 **80** 4 4 1¾ 4 2½ 5 5½ 5 9½ 4 6¾ Chavez J F L118 3.10 75-24 Smok'n Frolic119 6½ Stake112no U K Trick110nk Bobbled start, 3 wide 7
15Feb04-11GP fst 1 1/16 :234 :473 1:114 1:431 3↑Ⓕ SabinH-G3 **65** 2 5 2¾ 6 4¼ 5 3¾ 8 14 9 20 Santos J A L117 8.00 73-17 RoarEmotion116 5½ *NonsuchBy*115¾ LedStory119 1¾ Bmpd, steadied 1st trn 9

Peace Rules
Own: Gann Edmund A

Ch. h. 5 (Apr)
Sire: Jules (Forty Niner) $6,000
Dam: Hold to Fashion (Hold Your Peace)
Br: Newchance Farm (Fla)
Tr: Frankel Robert J(0 0 0 0 .00) 2004:(491 135 .27)

Life	19	9	2	2	$3,084,278	113	
2004	6	3	0	0	$1,024,288	113	
2003	7	3	1	1	$1,850,000	109	
	0	0	0	0	$0	-	
D.Fst	11	6	1	2	$2,788,700	113	
Wet(357)	3	0	0	0	$91,888	98	
Turf(225)	5	3	1	0	$203,690	102	
Dst(0)	0	0	0	0	$0	-	

7Aug04- 9Sar fst 1⅛ :451 1:084 1:344 1:482 3↑WhitneyH-G1 **100** 8 31 31 34 63¾ 68¼ Bailey J D L121 *3.05 85- 14 *RosesinMy*114no PerfctDrift1172¼ BowmnsBnd114no Chased outside, tired 9
3Jly04- 7Bel fst 1¼ :461 1:091 1:334 1:592 3↑SuburbnH-G1 **111** 3 11 1½ 1hd 2½ 1nk Bailey J D L120 3.20 100 - PeaceRules120nk Newfoundland114no FunnyCide117¾ Came again gamely 8
12Jun04- 9CD sly 1⅛ :473 1:122 1:372 1:502 3↑SFosterH-G1 **96** 2 11½ 11½ 11½ 42 48¾ Bailey J D L121 2.80 76- 17 ColonilColony111no SouthrnImg1225 PrfctDrft1193¾ Pace,inside,faltered 6
3Apr04- 11OP fst 1⅛ :452 1:093 1:352 1:481 4↑OaklawnH-G2 **112** 3 21 2½ 2hd 11½ 12 Bailey J D L120 *.80 97- 09 Peace Rules1202 Ole Faunty116nk Saint Liam1142¼ Quick duel,stayd clear 6
29Feb04- 9FG fst 1⅛ :47 1:102 1:352 1:483 4↑NwOrlnsH-G2 **113** 5 12 12 11 1hd 1hd Bailey J D L119 3.60 101- 05 *Peace Rules*119hd Saint Liam1142¾ *Funny Cide*1181¼ Headed, fought back 8
24Jan04- 6SA fst 1⅛ :453 1:092 1:342 1:473 4↑[R]SMClassic1000k **93** 6 64½ 54½ 54 46½ 48½ Bailey J D LB120 *1.00 87- 07 *SothrnImg*1203 ExcssSmmr1205 ThJdgSzWho122½ Bobbled bit strt,empty 12

Peeping Tom
Own: Flatbird Stable

B. g. 8 (Mar)
Sire: Eagle Eyed (Danzig) $5,000
Dam: Artful Pleasure (Nasty and Bold)
Br: Finney & Taylor (Ky)
Tr: Reynolds Patrick L(0 0 0 0 .00) 2004:(186 25 .13)

Life	49	14	7	9	$1,398,547	113	
2004	8	2	0	2	$147,531	105	
2003	14	3	4	3	$428,733	108	
	0	0	0	0	$0	-	
D.Fst	41	13	5	6	$1,055,747	113	
Wet(310)	6	1	2	3	$342,800	107	
Turf(294)	2	0	0	0	$0	76	
Dst(0)	0	0	0	0	$0	-	

19Jun04- 9Suf fst 6f :214 :442 :563 1:091 3↑JBMoslyBCH198k **85** 6 8 87¼ 86¼ 67¼ 49¾ Smith A E LB117 b 5.80 92- 06 GtorsNBers1184½ VlidVideo1182¼ MyCousinMtt1153 Outrun 3wd, no rally 8
29May04- 9Pha fst 6f :22 :451 :574 1:11 3↑DLeVinMH-G3 **100** 2 6 68¾ 64¼ 62¾ 1½ Smith A E L116 b 4.30 87- 26 PpngTom116½ HghwyProspctr117nk Rchrchrch1131½ Angled wide, just up 7
10Apr04- 9Aqu fst 7f :213 :432 1:072 1:201 3↑CarterH-G1 **92** 9 1 810 812 810 710½ Smith A E L114 fb 22.60 93- 04 *Pico Central*1171¼ StrongHope1192 EyeoftheTiger114¾ 3 wide trip, no rally 9
2Apr04- 8Aqu gd 1 :23 :46 1:103 1:353 4↑OC 85k/c-N **98** 3 53¼ 3nk 1hd 21 33½ Fragoso P5 L118 fb *2.05 84- 29 BlckSilk1163 MultipleChoice118nk PepingTom1181¾ Rail run, outfinished 7
13Mar04- 8Aqu fst 7f :222 :45 1:092 1:22 3↑ToboggnH-G3 **100** 3 9 108¼ 88¼ 73½ 54¾ Smith A E L117 fb 7.10 90- 17 Well Fancied1182 *Gators NBears*115nk DonSix1131¾ Altered course stretch 10
16Feb04- 9Lrl fst 7f :223 :452 1:10 1:222 3↑GenGrgeH-G2 **105** 1 9 89½ 95½ 54 41¾ Smith A E L117 fb 8.90 96- 17 *WellFncied*1151 UnforgettbleMx114¾ GtorsNBrs116hd Swung 6wd, fin well 9
24Jan04- 8Aqu fst 6f [•] :223 :46 :58 1:102 3↑PaumonokH83k **103** 2 6 84¾ 53¼ 22 1hd Smith A E L117 fb 10.70 87- 21 Peeping Tom117hd Don Six1132¼ Super Fuse114½ 3 wide move, prevailed 9
7Jan04- 8Aqu fst 6f [•] :224 :462 :584 1:113 4↑OC 75k/c-N **89** 1 4 33 42¾ 35½ 34½ Bridgmohan S X L120 fb *1.45 76- 24 Spooky Mulder1163½ *Kazoo*1161 *Peeping Tom*120no Inside trip, no rally 5

Pellegrino (Brz)
Own: Tanaka Gary A

Dk. b or b. h. 6 (Aug)
Sire: Nugget Point*Ire (Nureyev)
Dam: Vale Mas (Good Bloke*Arg)
Br: Haras Equilia (Brz)
Tr: Burke D J II(0 0 0 0 .00) 2004:(21 3 .14)

Life 15 4 4 3 $275,676 101 | D.Fst 1 0 1 0 $4,244 –
2004 9 3 2 2 $260,060 101 | Wet(323*) 0 0 0 0 $0 –
2003 1 0 0 0 $443 – | Turf(322) 14 4 3 3 $271,432 101
0 0 0 0 $0 – | Dst(0) 0 0 0 0 $0 –

4Dec04–7Hol fm 1½ Ⓣ :50²1:15³ 2:04 2:29³ 3↑HolTrfCp-G1 101 7 7⁶ 7³¾ 6³¼ 4nk 1hd Stevens G L LB126 10.20 78– 22 Pellegrino126hd Megahertz123hd LicenseToRun126½ Tight 3/8&1/4,rail bid 9
23Oct04–9SA fm 1½ Ⓣ :49¹1:13⁴ 2:02³2:26⁴ 3↑CFBurkeH-G3 98 5 6⁶ 7⁴¾ 7⁴¼ 4²½ 2¾ Stevens G L LB116 14.10 86– 13 Habaneros116¾ Pellegrino116nk Gallant113no Inside trip,willingly 8
4Aug04–7Dmr fm 1⅜ Ⓣ :48 1:12⁴ 1:36³2:12⁴ 3↑[R]EscondidoH79k 91 4 4³ 4¹¼ 5¹¼ 5⁴ 4⁴ Espinoza V LB116 *.70e 92– 11 Sarafan1211½ Gene de Campeao1161 Outta Here1141½ Chased btwn,no bid 6
2Jly04–1Hol fm 1½ Ⓣ :50 1:14⁴ 2:04¹2:29¹ 4↑OC 80k/n2x-N 98 1 4⁵½ 5⁴½ 4³ 4² 1¹¼ Solis A LB122 *.40e 80– 19 Pellegrino1221¼ Gallant1181 Right Proof118nk Stdied 5/8,shuffled3/8 6
27May04–5Hol fm 1¼ Ⓣ :50 1:14² 1:38 2:01³ 4↑OC 80k/n2x-N 97 4 6³¾ 6²¾ 5¹¾ 4¾ 2½ Solis A LB122 *2.40e 83– 11 Leprechaun Kid118½ Pellegrino122hd Gallant118nk 4wd into lane,willing 8
2May04–3Hol fm 1¼ Ⓣ :46²1:10¹ 1:35²2:00²+4↑Alw 50000n1x 96 1 5⁵ 5⁷ 2¹½ 1hd 1¾ Solis A LB120 4.10 90– 11 Pellegrino120¾ Hawksbill1208½ But of Course1133 Rail,bid,led,edgd away 5
13Mar04–9SA fm 1½ Ⓣ :46²1:10¹ 2:01 2:26¹ 4↑OC 40k/n1x-N 90 1 7¹³ 7⁵¼ 6⁹ 5⁵½ 3¹½ Solis A LB118 7.00 88– 11 Fade to Blue1181 Motto118½ Pellegrino118hd Btwn late for 3rd 9
13Feb04–7SA fm 1¼ Ⓣ :48⁴1:13³ 1:38 2:01² 4↑OC 40k/n1x-N 86 1 4² 4⁴ 4² 2hd 3³ Desormeaux K J LB119 8.40 79– 14 GassanRoyal1172½ BucneroGris117½ Pellegrino1191½ 4wd into lane,lost 2nd 8
3Jan04–8SA gd 1¼ Ⓣ :47⁴1:12³ 1:37⁴2:01¹ 4↑OC 40k/n1x-N 79 7 3² 3¹½ 4³ 7⁶ 6⁷¾ Smith M E LB119 10.80 75– 19 FadetoBlue12¹hd GassanRoyal1176½ BlueBloodBoot117no 3 wide, no late bid 8

Perfect Soul (Ire)
Own: Fipke Charles E

B. h. 7 (Apr)
Sire: Sadler's Wells (Northern Dancer)
Dam: Ball Chairman (Secretariat)
Br: C. Fipke (Ire)
Tr: Attfield Roger L(0 0 0 0 .00) 2004:(292 35 .12)

Life 21 7 5 1 $1,527,764 107 | D.Fst 0 0 0 0 $0 –
2004 6 1 2 0 $391,549 105 | Wet(277) 0 0 0 0 $0 –
2003 8 3 2 1 $856,195 107 | Turf(339) 21 7 5 1 $1,527,764 107
0 0 0 0 $0 – | Dst(0) 0 0 0 0 $0 –

9Oct04–8Kee fm 1 Ⓣ :23² :47¹ 1:11⁴1:35² 3↑SndwlTfM-G1 86 7 5⁶ 4²½ 4¹½ 8⁵¼ 7¹¹½ Prado E S L126 b *2.20 83– 10 Nothing to Lose1264½ Honor in War126¾ Silver Tree1261¼ 4-5w,weakened 9
19Sep04–9WO fm 1 Ⓣ :23² :46 1:09 1:32³ 3↑AttoMile-G1 101 8 11¹⁰10⁸¾ 6²¾ 3³½ 2¾ Nakatani C S L121 b 3.55 99– 03 Soaring Free119¾ Perfect Soul121hd RoyalRegalia1181¼ Swung wide,rallied 11
25Jly04–8WO fm 1⅜ Ⓣ :48²1:12³ 1:36⁴2:12¹ 3↑ChneseCC-G2 94 3 5³½ 6³ 5³ 5⁶ 5⁵¼ Landry R C L124 b *1.60 99– 05 Shoal Water116nk Mobil1212¼ Strut the Stage121¾ Lacked strong rally 8
3Jly04–8CD fm 1 Ⓣ :22⁴ :45⁴ 1:09³1:34 3↑FrckrBCH-G2 99 4 7¹¹ 7¹² 6⁸ 6⁵½ 3³½ Melancon L L121 b *1.90 95– 07 Quantum Merit1171½ [D]Senor Swinger1172 Perfect Soul1211 Stead 1/8 pole 9
Placed second through disqualification
1May04–9CD yl 1⅛ Ⓣ :51 1:15² 1:39³1:53 3↑TurfClsc-G1 70 1 6⁵ 6⁴ 8⁷¾ 10¹² 10¹⁶¾ Prado E S L123 b 4.50 51– 32 Stroll1212½ Sweet Return123no Mystery Giver123¾ Pulled bit early 11
9Apr04–9Kee fm 1 Ⓣ :23 :45¹ 1:09 1:33² 4↑MakrsMrk-G2 105 7 7⁷ 7⁶ 7³ 4⁴½ 1½ Prado E S L116 b 3.40 105 – Perfect Soul116½ Burning Roma116hd Royal Spy1161 Rallied 6w,stiff drive 10

Personal Legend
Own: Gann Edmund A

Ch. m. 5 (Jan)
Sire: Awesome Again (Deputy Minister) $125,000
Dam: Highland Legend (Storm Bird)
Br: G. Watts Humphrey Jr. & Louise I. Humphrey (Ky)
Tr: Frankel Robert J(0 0 0 0 .00) 2004:(491 135 .27)

Life	17	5	5	2	$407,340	98	D.Fst	2	1	1	0	$96,420 97
2004	8	3	2	1	$224,330	98	Wet(379)	2	0	1	0	$4,320 63
2003	9	2	3	1	$183,010	97	Turf(253)	13	4	3	2	$306,600 98
	0	0	0	0	$0	–	Dst(0)	0	0	0	0	$0 –

6Nov04–9Aqu fst 1⅛ :484 1:13 1:381 1:511 3↑ⒻTnbkAlmH-G3 **97** 1 63 52 61¼ 2½ 1½ Bailey J D L115 b 3.95 83– 24 PersonlLegnd115½ RorEmotion1174¾ FstCooki1142 Came wide, prevailed 9
25Sep04–9Bel fm 1 Ⓣ :241 :473 1:112 1:343 3↑ⒻNblDmslH-G3 **89** 1 72½ 83¾ 95¾ 97 76¾ Chavez J F L115 b 5.30 80– 16 Ocean Drive1201¼ High Court115¾ Hour of Justice1162 Inside trip, no rally 9
30Aug04–8Sar yl 1 1/16 🅃 :24 :47 1:111 1:434 3↑ⒻBlSpaBCH-G3 **98** 1 43½ 49 47½ 32 21¼ Bailey J D L115 b 3.05 84– 15 *OcenDrive*1191¼ PersonlLgnd1151¾ HighCourt1141¾ Saved ground, gamely 10
11Aug04–6Sar gd 1 🅃 :243 :49 1:124 1:363 4↑ⒻⓇDeLaRose66k **94** 1 43½ 43 31½ 31½ 1hd Bailey J D L116 b *1.30 88– 13 Personal Legend116hd *Lenti*116nk Vespers120¾ Fast finish, in time 8
Run in divisions
31May04–3Bel fm 1 1/16 🅃 :25 :492 1:124 1:422 3↑ⒻAlw 48000N2X **95** 4 21 2½ 2½ 1½ 12½ Bailey J D L121 b *.60 91– 09 *Personal Legend*1212½ Erase121½ Orkan1211¼ When roused, clear 6
6May04–7Hol fm 1 1/16 Ⓣ :221 :452 1:092 1:401 4↑ⒻAlw 63720N2X **94** 6 612 69½ 65 42½ 3½ Solis A LB118 b *.30 94– 09 IcyAvenue118½ *Chasethegold*118no *PersonlLegend*1181 5wd into lane,rallied 6
21Feb04–8SA gd 1 Ⓣ :232 :473 1:12 1:36 4↑ⒻBnaVstaH-G2 **89** 7 65½ 64½ 75¾ 56½ 43¾ Solis A LB115 b 2.10 78– 18 Fun House1162¾ *Katdogawn*117½ Fudge Fatale116½ Came out 1/8,late bid 7
18Jan04–7SA fst 1 1/16 :223 :46 1:102 1:422 ⒻElEncino-G2 **88** 7 713 710 75¾ 42 21¼ Solis A LB115 b *2.20 92– 13 VictoryEncountr1171¼ PrsonlLgnd115½ *CtFightr*115½ 4wd into lane,willing 7

Pico Central (Brz)
Own: Tanaka Gary A

Dk. b or b. h. 6 (Oct)
Sire: Spend a Buck (Buckaroo)
Dam: Sheila Purple*Brz (Purple Mountain)
Br: Haras Fronteira P.A.P. (Brz)
Tr: Lobo Paulo H(0 0 0 0 .00) 2004:(118 22 .19)

Life	15	9	0	3	$1,183,145	116	D.Fst	7	5	0	2	$1,139,000 116
2004	7	5	0	2	$1,139,000	116	Wet(314)	1	1	0	0	$1,692 –
2003	3	1	0	0	$13,874	–	Turf(269)	7	3	0	1	$42,453 –
	0	0	0	0	$0	–	Dst(0)	0	0	0	0	$0 –

27Nov04–9Aqu fst 1 :222 :441 1:081 1:332 3↑CigarMiH-G1 **108** 1 1hd 1½ 1hd 2hd 31¼ Espinoza V L123 *.95 97– 07 LionTamer1151¼ BdgeofSilver115no PicoCentrl1234¾ Set pace, weakened 8
2Oct04–8Bel fst 6f :223 :453 :571 1:093 3↑Vosburgh-G1 **114** 5 4 2½ 1hd 1½ 14 Espinoza V L124 2.20 91– 22 Pico Central1244 Voodoo124½ *Speightstown*124hd Speed 3 wide, clear 5
15Aug04–8Dmr fst 7f :214 :434 1:081 1:21 3↑OBrinBCH-G2 **103** 3 1 1hd 1hd 22 35¾ Flores D R LB122 *.40 91– 10 Kela1164½ Domestic Dispute1161¼ *Pico Central*1224 Inside duel,held 3rd 5
31May04–9Bel fst 1 :232 :46 1:10 1:352 3↑MtropltH-G1 **116** 8 2½ 2½ 2hd 1hd 1¾ Solis A L119 3.45 84– 34 PicoCentrl119¾ BowmnsBnd1142¼ StrongHop1191½ Bobbled start, gamely 9
10Apr04–9Aqu fst 7f :213 :432 1:072 1:201 3↑CarterH-G1 **116** 3 5 2hd 1½ 2hd 11¼ Solis A L117 4.30 104– 04 *Pico Central*1171¼ Strong Hope1192 EyeoftheTiger114¾ Came again on rail 9
7Mar04–8SA fst 7f :221 :44 1:082 1:21 4↑SnCrlosH-G2 **113** 5 2 1½ 1½ 12½ 12 Flores D R LB116 43.20 100– 11 *Pico Central*1162 Publication1162 *Pohave*1121 Bit off rail,held game 10
25Jan04–7SA fst 6½f :211 :433 1:083 1:151 4↑OC 100k/N3X-N **95** 8 2 1hd 1hd 1½ 2¾ Espinoza V LB119 37.50 95– 08 ⒹRide andShine119¾ *PicoCentral*119½ Arsen119no Dueled,game,edged late 9
Placed first through disqualification

Pies Prospect

Own: LaPenta Robert V

Ch. c. 4 (Apr) KEESEP02 $190,000
Sire: Crafty Prospector (Mr. Prospector) $10,000
Dam: Hot Pillow (Bates Motel)
Br: Gordon Wootton & Mary Lou Wootton (Ky)
Tr: Zito Nicholas P(0 0 0 0 .00) 2004:(452 86 .19)

Life	15	5	1	2	$500,865	110
2004	14	4	1	2	$473,865	110
2003	1	1	0	0	$27,000	80
	0	0	0	0	$0	–

D.Fst	14	5	1	1	$473,365	110
Wet(392)	1	0	0	1	$27,500	101
Turf(227)	0	0	0	0	$0	–
Dst(0)	0	0	0	0	$0	–

Date/Race	Cond	Dist	Fractions	Race	Fig	PP	St	1st	2nd	Str	Fin	Jockey	Wt	Odds	Pace	Top Finishers	Comment	Field
18Dec04-12Crc	fst	1⅛	:474 1:112 1:373 1:503	3↑FHooperH-G3	110	3		32½	43½	33½	11	18½	Prado E S	L114	3.20	99-21	PisProspct1143½ TwilightRod1151 HrNoEvil1123¼	Came on, duel,drew off	11
26Nov04-11CD	fst	1⅛	:48 1:12 1:372 1:504	3↑ClarkH-G2	99	9		52	86¾	66	810	76½	McKee J	L112	46.60	76-25	Saint Liam117¼ Seek Gold111no Perfect Drift1181¼	5-6w trip,weakened	9
29Oct04-7LS	fst	1 1/16	:224 :462 1:102 1:42	LnStrDby-G3	89	9		54½	73¼	83	86¼	77¼	Prado E S	L122	3.90	85-17	PollrdsVson122½ Cryptgrph122½ Flmthrwntxn1223¼	4w 1st turn,3w 2nd trn	12
10ct04-7Med	fst	1⅛	:464 1:103 1:353 1:482	Pegasus-G3	101	8		42½	3½	3½	1hd	1nk	Prado E S	L118	4.90	90-11	Pies Prospect118nk *Eddington*1183½ *Zakocity*118hd	3 wide, bumped 3/16	8
6Sep04-10Pha	fst	1⅛	:473 1:111 1:353 1:482	PaDerby-G2	89	3		83¾	85¼	85¼	510	514	Lopez C C	L114	10.90	89-11	LovofMony118½ PollrdsVson1221 Swngforthfncs1193¼	Failed to menace	12
8Aug04-13Mth	fst	1⅛	:464 1:102 1:353 1:484	HsklInvH-G1	104	2		61¾	73¼	53¾	34	33¼	Lopez C C	L116	16.80	94-13	LionHert1211 MySnookiesBoy1162¼ PiesProspect1163¼	Inside,no late bid	8
18Jly04-9Del	sly	1 1/16	:224 :462 1:11 1:434	LRichrds-G3	101	2		45	46½	21½	34	32½	Arroyo N Jr	L115	2.30	90-15	PollrdsVision1222 BrittsJules116½ PisProspct1157¼	Shuffled start,willing	7
22Jun04-8Del	fst	1 1/16	:233 :471 1:114 1:434	FloorShow55k	98	5		42	32	3nk	11½	15½	Arroyo N Jr	L117	*1.80	93-22	Pies Prospect1175½ Gmork1172½ Zakocity117½	Much the best	8
22May04-8Bel	fst	1⅛	:46 1:10 1:35 1:474	PeterPan-G2	91	2		42½	41½	4nk	36	410¼	Castellano J J	L115	9.90	82-24	Purge1156¾ *Swingforthefences*1151¼ Master David1152¼	Speed inside, tired	10
5May04-6Bel	fst	1 1/16	:23 :454 1:103 1:423	3↑Alw 46000N2L	101	8		41	42½	3nk	12	11¼	Castellano J J	L114	4.20	87-25	Pies Prospect1141¼ *Alumni Hal*1234¼ Bidless1173¾	3 wide, drew clear	8
10Apr04-5Aqu	fst	1	:223 :45 1:094 1:35	3↑Alw 44000N2L	85	5		58	56	31	22½	22¾	Castellano J J	L113	7.60	87-12	Shaniko1162¾ *PiesProspect*1135½ LedingthePrde1161¾	Game finish outside	9
20Mar04-7TP	fst	1 1/16	:224 :462 1:111 1:441	Rushaway100k	55	3		87¼	87¼	77½	514	519½	Bejarano R	L114	*.60	71-17	Brass Hat1143 Tales of Glory1141¼ Gamblin1143	Inside, no factor	10
14Feb04-9GP	fst	1⅛	:471 1:12 1:38 1:503	Alw 34000N1x	81	10		106¼	105¾	73¼	52¼	49¼	Castellano J J	L118	8.70	77-14	Swingforthefences1185¼ Shaniko1223¼ Capias122¾	5 wide bid, tired	11
7Jan04-6GP	fst	7f	:223 :454 1:11 1:24	Alw 34000N1x	75	9	10	95¾	63		75¾	44½	Velazquez J R	L120	2.30	77-21	*FriskySpidr*118 NotoriousRogu1184 ClssicWn122hd	Steadied start, 4 wide	11

Pleasantly Perfect

Own: Diamond A Racing Corporation

B. h. 7 (Apr)
Sire: Pleasant Colony (His Majesty)
Dam: Regal State (Affirmed)
Br: Clovelly Farms (Ky)
Tr: Mandella Richard E(0 0 0 0 .00) 2004:(160 24 .15)

Life	18	9	3	2	$7,789,880	119
2004	5	3	1	1	$4,840,000	113
2003	4	2	0	1	$2,470,000	119
	0	0	0	0	$0	–

D.Fst	16	9	3	2	$7,787,000	119
Wet(371)	0	0	0	0	$0	–
Turf(323)	2	0	0	0	$2,880	76
Dst(0)	0	0	0	0	$0	–

Date/Race	Cond	Dist	Fractions	Race	Fig	PP	1st	2nd	3rd	Str	Fin	Jockey	Wt	Odds	Pace	Top Finishers	Comment	Field
30Oct04-9LS	fst	1¼	:47 1:111 1:351 1:59	3↑BCClasic-G1	113	12	105½	106½	53	35	37	Bailey J D	L126 b	2.50	- -	Ghostzapper1263 RosesinMy1264 PlesntlyPerfect126¾	Broke slow, 6 wide	13
22Aug04-8Dmr	fst	1¼	:464 1:104 1:352 2:01	3↑PacifcCl-G1	112	5	65	63¼	41½	1½	11	Bailey J D	LB124 b	*1.00	90-10	PlesntlyPerfct1241 PrfctDrift124¾ TotlImpct1244¾	4wd bid,bumped,game	8
1Aug04-8Dmr	fst	1 1/16	:24 :472 1:111 1:421	3↑SnDiegoH-G2	102	6	42	1hd	2hd	11½	2¾	Smith M E	LB124 b	*.60	96-10	ChoctwNtion114¾ *PlesntlyPerfect*1245 During1181½	Stdied6-1/2,led,caught	7
27Mar04 Nad Al Sheba (UAE) Timeform rating: 130	ft	*1¼	LH 2:001	3↑Dubai World Cup-G1 Stk 6000000							1¾	Solis A	126 b	-		Pleasantly Perfect126¾ Medaglia d'Oro1265 Victory Moon1267¾	*3rd on rail,bid 2f out,led 100y out.Grand Hombre 4th*	12
31Jan04-8SA	fst	1⅛	:463 1:10 1:343 1:471	4↑SnAntnoH-G2	109	4	41½	41½	2hd	11	14	Solis A	LB121 b	1.90	98-06	*PlesntlyPerfect*1214 StrCross114nk FleetstreetDncr1164	4wd bid,drifted in	4

Pohave
Own: Darley Stable

Gr/ro. g. 7 (Apr)
Sire: Holy Bull (Great Above) $15,000
Dam: Trail Robbery (Alydar)
Br: H. E. Pabst & T. J. Pabst (Ky)
Tr: O'Neill Doug(0 0 0 0 .00) 2004:(938 170 .18)

Life	27	5	9	4	$576,240	112	D.Fst	22 5 7 4	$555,720 112
2004	8	3	3	2	$450,740	112	Wet(394)	1 0 1 0	$9,000 81
2003	12	1	4	0	$64,320	111	Turf(258)	4 0 1 0	$11,520 93
	0	0	0	0	$0	-	Dst(0)	0 0 0 0	$0 -

Date/Race	Cond	Dist	Fractions	Race	Spd	Running line	Jockey	Med/Wt	Odds	Spd-Var	Top three	Comment	Fld
10Oct04-8SA	fst	6f	:21 :43^3 :55^4 1:08^4	3↑AnTtlBCH-G1	103	2 8 3^1 2^1 1^½ 2^½	Court J K	LB118	*1.30	93-12	PtsGreyEagle109^½ Pohave118^2 HombreRpido114^{hd}	Off bit slw,led,caught	8
25Jly04-2Dmr	fst	6f	:21^2 :43^4 :56 1:08^2	3↑BCrsbBCH-G1	109	7 4 5^{2¼} 3^1 1^{hd} 2^{1¼}	Court J K	LB118	*2.20	96-09	*Kela*113^{1¼} Pohave118^{2½} Hombre Rapido115^3	4wd,3wd,led,2nd best	10
3Jly04-9Hol	fst	7f	:21^4 :44 1:08^1 1:21	3↑TrBndBCH-G1	103	7 5 6^{1¾} 3^1 3^½ 1^¾	Espinoza V	LB116	*2.30	97-12	Pohave116^¾ Rojo Toro115^½ Revello110^1	Bid 3wd,gamely	13
5Jun04-7Bel	fst	6f	:21^2 :43^3 :55^1 1:08	3↑TrNthBCH-G2	106	8 4 4^{2¾} 3^3 3^4 3^{3¼}	Court J K	L117	2.65	96-07	*Speightstown*119^{1½} Cat Genius116^{1¾} *Pohave*117^{nk}	Good finish outside	9
8May04-6Hol	fst	6f	:21 :43^1 :55 1:08	3↑LATimesH-G3	105	1 7 3^{2½} 2^½ 1^{hd} 1^1	Court J K	LB114	4.30	97-07	Pohave114^1 MarinoMrini119^{3½} SummerService117^{hd}	Bid btwn,led,gamely	9
7Mar04-8SA	fst	7f	:22^1 :44 1:08^2 1:21	4↑SnCrlosH-G2	104	7 1 5^{2½} 5^{1½} 3^{2½} 3^4	Court J K	LB112	15.20	96-11	*Pico Central*116^2 Publication116^2 *Pohave*112^1	5wd,lost whip into str	10
16Feb04-7SA	fm	*6½f Ⓣ	:21^4 :44 1:06^2 1:12^1	4↑OC 62k/n2x-N	93	3 6 6^{1¾} 4^{1¾} 2^{hd} 2^½	Nakatani C S	LB121	3.40	95-04	Vronsky121^{1½} Pohave121^{nk} Kewen118^{nk}	Bid btwn,outkicked	9
4Jan04-7SA	fst	6f	:21^2 :44 :56 1:08^1	4↑Alw 55120n1x	112	3 6 3^1 1^½ 1^1 1^{3½}	Nakatani C S	LB121	3.10	97-13	Pohave121^{3½} Sun City Bradley122^{3½} Sum Trick122^{nk}	Inside bid,vied,clear	9

Pollard's Vision
Own: Edgewood Farm

Dk. b or b. c. 4 (Jan) KEEAPR03 $70,000
Sire: Carson City (Mr. Prospector) $35,000
Dam: Etats Unis (Dixieland Band)
Br: Charles A. Smith (Ky)
Tr: Pletcher Todd A(0 0 0 0 .00) 2004:(948 240 .25)

Life	17	5	5	3	$1,075,311	107	D.Fst	14 3 5 3	$897,711 107
2004	11	4	4	1	$1,022,020	107	Wet(423)	3 2 0 0	$177,600 105
2003	6	1	1	2	$53,291	84	Turf(257)	0 0 0 0	$0 -
	0	0	0	0	$0	-	Dst(0)	0 0 0 0	$0 -

Date/Race	Cond	Dist	Fractions	Race	Spd	Running line	Jockey	Med/Wt	Odds	Spd-Var	Top three	Comment	Fld
29Oct04-7LS	fst	1$\frac{1}{16}$	:22^4 :46^2 1:10^2 1:42	LnStrDby-G3	102	3 6^{4¾} 8^{3¼} 6^{2¾} 3^½ 1^½	Velazquez J R	L122	3.20	92-17	PollrdsVision122^½ Cryptogrph122^½ Flmethrowintxn122^{3¼}	Closed strongly	12
2Oct04-9Hoo	fst	1$\frac{1}{16}$	:22^4 :47 1:12 1:44	IndnaDby-G2	99	1 3^{1½} 6^{1¾} 3^2 5^2 6^4	Velazquez J R	LB124	*2.10	87-21	Brass Hat124^{1¾} Suave124^¾ Hasslefree115^½	Forced in 3/16, weaken	9
6Sep04-10Pha	fst	1⅛	:47^3 1:11^1 1:35^3 1:48^2	PaDerby-G2	98	8 2^½ 2^1 2^1 2^4 2^{8½}	Velazquez J R	L122	3.90	94-11	LoveofMoney116^{8½} PollrdsVision122^1 Swingforthefences119^{3¼}	No match	12
7Aug04-8Mnr	fst	1⅛	:47 1:10^3 1:35^4 1:49	WVDerby-G3	100	2 4^3 4^{2½} 3^{5½} 3^{3½} 2^3	Coa E M	LB119	1.30	83-12	SirShcklton117^3 PollrdsVision119^½ BrttsJuls115^5	Loomed4w, saved place	7
18Jly04-9Del	sly	1$\frac{1}{16}$	:22^4 :46^2 1:11 1:43^4	LRichrds-G3	105	4 3^{3½} 3^5 3^{1½} 2^1 1^2	Bailey J D	L122	*1.00	93-15	PollrdsVision122^2 BrittsJules116^½ PisProspct115^{7¼}	Hard drive, clear late	7
12Jun04-14Tdn	fst	1⅛	:47^1 1:11^2 1:37 1:49^2	OhioDrby-G2	98	1 3^{1½} 4^{1½} 3^1 2^½ 2^3	Coa E M	L121	2.30	93-06	*BrassHat*115^3 *Pollard'sVision*121^5 TriestesHonor115^3	Led 1/4pole,no match	9
1May04-10CD	sly	1¼	:46^3 1:11^4 1:37^1 2:04	KyDerby-G1	48	15 2^2 5^{2½} 15^{14} 16^{17} 17^{40¾}	Velazquez J R	L126	24.00	38-21	*SmartyJones*126^{2¾} LionHert126^{3¼} Imperilism126^2	Stalked btwn,weakened	18
3Apr04-7Haw	fst	1⅛	:47^4 1:12^3 1:37^4 1:50^4	IlnosDby-G2	107	2 1^{1½} 1^{1½} 1^1 1^2 1^{2¾}	Coa E M	L114	*1.70	103-21	Pollard's Vision114^{2¾} Song of the Sword116^{2¾} Suave114^{8½}	Dug in gamely	11
7Mar04-9FG	fst	1$\frac{1}{16}$	:22^2 :45^1 1:10^3 1:42^3	LaDerby-G2	97	7 4^{4½} 4^5 3^{2½} 1^{1½} 3^{2¼}	Velazquez J R	L122	6.50	95-07	Wimbledon122^{2¼} Borrego122^{hd} *Pollard'sVision*122^¾	3-w bid, weakened late	11
8Feb04-9GP	fst	1$\frac{1}{16}$ ⊗	:23^1 :47^1 1:12 1:42^4	Alw 34000n1x	98	7 2^{1½} 2^1 2^1 1^2 1^{5¾}	Velazquez J R	L118	2.90	95-15	PollrdsVson118^{5¾} MyLckyMrcry118^½ NotorosRog118^{2½}	Strong hand ride	9
7Jan04-8GP	fst	7f	:22^2 :45^3 1:10^2 1:22^4	Alw 34000n1x	83	3 8 3^{nk} 1^{hd} 2^{1½} 2^{7¼}	Velazquez J R	L118	*1.60	81-21	BlushingIndian118^{7¼} *PollardsVision*118^{4¼} Mutchi118^¾	Vied inside, 2nd best	10

Pomeroy
Own: Smith Derrick and Tabor, Michael

B. c. 4 (Apr) FTFFEB03 $300,000
Sire: Boundary (Danzig) $10,000
Dam: Questress (Seeking the Gold)
Br: Cherry Valley Farm LLC (Ky)
Tr: Biancone Patrick L(0 0 0 0 .00) 2004:(130 29 .22)

Life	9	4	3	1	$384,250	108	D.Fst	5	2	1	1	$266,250	108
2004	5	2	2	0	$296,250	108	Wet(404)	4	2	2	0	$118,000	92
2003	4	2	1	1	$88,000	91	Turf(290)	0	0	0	0	$0	–
	0	0	0	0	$0	–	Dst(0)	0	0	0	0	$0	–

28Aug04-10Sar fst 7f :22 :443 1:082 1:204 KngsBshp-G1 **108** 3 4 42 43 1hd 1 1½ Prado E S 121 4.70 100–04 Pomeroy1211½ Weigelia1211 Ice Wynnd Fire1174¼ Awkward start, inside 8
7Aug04-8Sar fst 6f :214 :443 :564 1:092 Amstrdam-G2 **104** 7 3 42¾ 2hd 1 1½ 2¾ Prado E S 123 b *1.70 94–13 Bwana Charlie123¾ *Pomeroy*1232 Weigelia123½ 4 wide move, gamely 7
26Jun04-9Mth fst 6f :222 :442 :562 1:09 JerShrBC-G3 **100** 1 3 1hd 12 14½ 14 Bravo J 113 b *.80 95–09 Pomroy1134 Ctghstfchnc1154 MdnghtExprss113hd Pace inside,ridden out 5
17Apr04-9Kee fst 1 1/16 :231 :471 1:12 1:434 Lexingtn-G2 **93** 4 31½ 32 31 43 45 Blanc B 116 b 6.90 88–11 QntonsGoldRsh1162¾ *FrSlm*116nk SngfthSwrd1162 Drft in bmp strt,empty 14
20Mar04-7Aqu gd 1 :214 :433 1:08 1:352 Gotham-G3 **92** 4 2½ 2½ 1½ 2½ 22¼ Smith M E 116 b 9.20 86–14 SartogCounty1162¼ Pomeroy116¾ Eddington1165¼ Speed outside, gamely 8

Preachinatthebar
Own: Pegram Michael E

Gr/ro. c. 4 (Feb)
Sire: Silver Charm (Silver Buck) $25,000
Dam: Holy Nola (Silver Deputy)
Br: Michael Pegram (Ky)
Tr: Baffert Bob(0 0 0 0 .00) 2004:(562 105 .19)

Life	11	2	0	2	$210,088	101	D.Fst	10	2	0	2	$209,088	101
2004	7	1	0	1	$177,268	101	Wet(363)	0	0	0	0	$0	–
2003	4	1	0	1	$32,820	86	Turf(199)	1	0	0	0	$1,000	79
	0	0	0	0	$0	–	Dst(0)	0	0	0	0	$0	–

9Aug04-8Sar fm 1⅛ Ⓣ :471 1:103 1:353 1:473 HalOFmeH-G2 **79** 5 74¾ 77¾ 85¾ 89½ 611 Fragoso P L115 b 27.50 88–09 *ArtieSchiller*1224¼ Mustnfr122no GoodRwrd1151½ Came wide, no response 8
11Jly04-8Bel fst 1 1/16 :224 :442 1:074 1:40 Dwyer-G2 **76** 6 43½ 58 48½ 517 519¾ Bailey J D L121 b 5.20 80–09 Medallist1213¾ TheCliffsEdge123½ *SirShckleton*12114½ 3 wide, no response 6
15May04-9Pim fst 1 1/16 :242 :482 1:13 1:453 SirBarton100k **83** 8 21½ 21½ 2hd 31 53 Bailey J D L122 b *.90 76–13 RoylAssult1151¾ DshbordDrummr117½ Hmorosly122¾ 4wd early, gave way 8
10Apr04-9Kee fst 1⅛ :463 1:11 1:364 1:492 BlueGras-G1 **61** 7 3nk 32 43½ 715 730½ Santiago Javier L123 b 5.80 63–20 TheCliffsEdge123½ LionHeart1236 Limehouse1233¾ Faded final 3 furlongs 8
14Mar04-5SA fst 1 1/16 :231 :464 1:11 1:424 SnFelipe-G2 **101** 6 32 21½ 1hd 11½ 1no Santiago Javier LB116 b 8.60 91–09 Prechintthebr116no StAveril1224½ HrvrdAvenu1161 Stalked,led,clear,held 9
8Feb04-8SA fst 1⅛ :47 1:11 1:362 1:491 Sham81k **98** 6 55 53¾ 53 31½ 31 Stevens G L LB116 b 7.00 87–13 MasterDavid1161 Borrego120hd *Preachinatthebr*116hd 3wd into lane,willing 7
17Jan04-7SA fst 1 1/16 :223 :453 1:094 1:413 StCtlina-G2 **96** 3 53¾ 83¾ 65¼ 44½ 43½ Flores D R LB116 b 8.20 93–20 St Averil1131½ Lucky Pulpit1152 *Master David*113hd 4wd into str,late bid 9

Presidentialaffair

Own: Ciresa Edward and Papapandrea, Vincen

B. g. 6 (Apr)
Sire: Not For Love (Mr. Prospector) $25,000
Dam: Quite Amazing (Bear Hunt)
Br: Will Run Farm (Pa)
Tr: Ciresa Martin E(0 0 0 0 .00) 2004:(138 19 .14)

Life	21	9	6	1	$495,970	112		
2004	8	3	4	0	$285,040	112		
2003	9	5	1	1	$188,140	106		
	0	0	0	0	$0	–		
D.Fst	16	7	4	1	$378,430	110		
Wet(408)	5	2	2	0	$117,540	112		
Turf(235)	0	0	0	0	$0	–		
Dst(0)	0	0	0	0	$0	–		

9Oct04-11Pim fst 1 3/16 :474 1:112 1:362 1:552 3↑ⓇMdMilClasc190k 105 8 11½ 12½ 12½ 13 11¾ Elliott S L126 *1.40 100– 12 Presidentialaffair1261¾ *Aggadn*1211 *IrishColony*1215¾ Dictated ins, driving 8
11Sep04-10Bel fst 1⅛ :453 1:083 1:331 1:461 3↑Woodward-G1 53 7 1hd 31 46 724 736 Fragoso P L126 37.50 64– 15 *Ghostzapper*126nk *SaintLiam*1269¼ BowmnsBnd1267¼ Bumped start, 3 wide 7
21Aug04-9Mth sly 1⅛ :454 1:093 1:351 1:473 3↑IselnBCH-G3 110 2 11½ 11½ 1½ 22 210¾ Elliott S L117 1.70 92– 16 *Ghostzpper*12010¾ Presidntilffir11721¼ Zoffingr115no Early pace, no match 4
25Jly04-10Mth fst 1 :232 :461 1:10 1:351 3↑SalvtrMH-G3 110 1 11½ 13 1½ 1½ 11 Elliott S L117 2.30 101– 19 Prsidntilffir1171 UnforgttblMx1174 RorngFvr1155 Willing,steady handlng 5
5Jly04-5Mth sly 170 :223 :451 1:091 1:384 3↑SkipAway70k 112 2 12½ 15 14 15 17¾ Elliott S L115 2.20 103– 11 *Prsidntilffir*1157¾ DonldsPrid1152¼ RglSncton1174½ Moderate hand urging 6
20Jun04-3Mth fst 1 1/16 :231 :453 1:10 1:431 3↑Alw 53000c 94 1 12½ 14 14 2hd 23¼ Martinez C L117 *.50 86– 12 GratitudeAttack1173¼ *Presidentilffir*1173 Lyrcist1177½ Well off rail,drifted 5
5Jun04-10Pha sly 7f :223 :451 1:094 1:223 3↑ⓈLymanSpChH54k 94 4 4 2hd 11 12 2nk Martinez C L120 *2.20 96– 18 Docent123nk Presidntilffir1202½ SnorChrismtic1154½ Drifted out, just fail 8
11May04-9Pha fst 6f :213 :44 :564 1:102 4↑Alw 26500N$Y 94 5 3 3½ 3nk 31 22½ Rocco J L116 *1.00 87– 23 TruePassion1142½ Presidentilffir116½ SureYouCn1142¾ Dueled three wide 5

Primal Storm

Own: Asmussen K., Winchell R., Cassels, J.

B. c. 3 (May) KEESEP03 $42,000
Sire: Storm Boot (Storm Cat) $15,000
Dam: Primistal (Stalwart)
Br: Everest Stables Inc. (Ky)
Tr: Asmussen Steven M(0 0 0 0 .00) 2004:(2293 555 .24)

Life	4	2	0	1	$102,798	84		
2004	4	2	0	1	$102,798	84		
2003	0	M	0	0	$0	–		
	0	0	0	0	$0	–		
D.Fst	4	2	0	1	$97,710	84		
Wet(335)	1	0	0	1	$10,588	56		
Turf(295)	0	0	0	0	$0	–		
Dst(0)	0	0	0	0	$0	–		

28Aug04-11Mth fst 6f :213 :443 :58 1:111 Sapling-G3 26 8 1 51¼ 75¾ 610 620½ Elliott S L120 *2.00 63– 18 EvilMinister120¾ *ParkAvenueBall*1202¾ Upscled1206 5-deep into turn,tired 8
26Jun04-3Bel my 5½f :222 :453 :581 1:044 Tremont99k 56 2 1 1½ 1½ 2½ 34½ Sellers S J L119 *.65 84– 14 GoldJoy1151½ WnnngExprsson1153 PrmlStrm1197 Bobbled start, bumped 4
4Jun04-9Bel fst 5f :22 :444 :572 Flash-G3 84 4 2 11½ 1½ 16 17 Sellers S J L116 *.80 96– 14 PrimlStorm1167 WinnngExprsson1153¾ *GoldJoy*1154 Came in backstretch 5
29Apr04-3CD fst 4½f :222 :45 :511 Md Sp Wt 44k 81 5 3 1½ 14½ 16 Sellers S J L118 5.00 99– 08 *PrimlStorm*1186 *SmokeWrning*1181¾ IronstonRod1181 Drew off,much best 7

Prince Arch
Own: Cottrell R H Sr

B. c. 4 (May) KEESEP02 $37,000
Sire: Arch (Kris S.) $10,000
Dam: Princess Kris*GB (Kris*GB)
Br: Pine Lake Bloodstock LLC (Ky)
Tr: McPeek Kenneth G(0 0 0 0 .00) 2004:(413 74 .18)

Life	13	5	4	1	$419,186	101	D.Fst	3 0 1 0	$4,900	54
2004	9	4	3	1	$405,946	101	Wet(377)	1 1 0 0	$8,340	77
2003	4	1	1	0	$13,240	77	Turf(375)	9 4 3 1	$405,946	101
	0	0	0	0	$0	–	Dst(0)	0 0 0 0	$0	–

Date/Race	Trk	Dist	Fractions	Race	Fig	PP	St	1C	2C	Str	Fin	Jockey	Wt	Odds	Pace	Top Finishers	Comment	Fld
6Sep04-10Sar	fm	1$\frac{3}{16}$ Ⓣ	:48^2 1:12^3 1:36^2 1:53^4	SaranacH-G3	**97**	1	6^5	6$^{6\frac12}$	6^2	4$^{1\frac12}$	1^{hd}	Castellano J J	L123 b	*2.05	96– 09	PrinceArch123^{hd} *Mustnfr*1212$\frac14$ CtchtheGlory1151$\frac12$	Bumped upper stretch	6
10Jly04-9Cnl	fm	1¼ Ⓣ	:47^1 1:11^2 1:36^4 2:01^1	VaDby-G3	**94**	1	8^{18}	8^{15}	7^{13}	3$^{8\frac12}$	3$^{7\frac12}$	Blanc B	L119 b	3.50	91– 16	*KittensJoy*117$^{\frac34}$ *ArtieSchiller*1174$\frac34$ *PrinceArch*1191 2$\frac34$	Traffic early,wide run	8
12Jun04-5CD	yl	1⅛ Ⓣ	:49 1:13^4 1:38^1 1:50^3	JfrsnCup-G3	**101**	3	9^5	7$^{4\frac12}$	8$^{4\frac14}$	3^2	1^{hd}	Blanc B	L120 b	5.50	80– 25	PrncArch120^{hd} *KttnsJoy*1224$\frac34$ CoolCondctor1161$\frac14$	Brke out,bmp start,drv	9
30Apr04-9CD	gd	1$\frac{1}{16}$ Ⓣ	:24^3 :49^2 1:13^1 1:43^1	AmerTurf-G3	**87**	3	7$^{3\frac14}$	5$^{1\frac12}$	6^5	4^3	2$^{2\frac12}$	Blanc B	L123 b	3.60	85– 11	Kitten's Joy1232$\frac12$ *Prince Arch*1231$\frac12$ Capo1172$\frac14$	Broke out bmp start	9
15Apr04-8Kee	fm	1⅛ Ⓣ	:46^2 1:11 1:36^3 1:48^3	Forerunner111k	**97**	1	6^9	7^{11}	7^{10}	3^2	1$^{5\frac34}$	Blanc B	L116 b	2.90	94– 05	Prince Arch1165$\frac34$ BrassHat1162 BigBooster117^{no}	Came out bmp start,drv	8
20Mar04-11GP	fm	1⅛ Ⓣ	:49 1:13^1 1:36^3 1:48	Caltech67k	**86**	4	6$^{3\frac14}$	6$^{4\frac14}$	6^4	4$^{2\frac14}$	2$^{2\frac14}$	Blanc B	L116 b	3.50	93– 14	Shakespeare1162$\frac14$ *Prince Arch*1161 Prepster116$\frac12$	Bmpd st, stdy bkstr	11
21Feb04-11GP	fm	1⅛ Ⓣ	:49^4 1:13^3 1:37^1 1:48^3	PalmBch-G3	**87**	3	9^8	8$^{7\frac14}$	9$^{5\frac12}$	9$^{4\frac12}$	2$^{1\frac34}$	Blanc B	L118 b	37.10	90– 06	*Kitten's Joy*1221$\frac34$ Prince Arch118^{nk} Pa Pa Da118$\frac34$	Swung 7w, rallied	12
17Jan04-8GP	fm	1⅛ Ⓣ	:51 1:15^2 1:39^2 1:51	Alw 34000N1x	**84**	2	6^3	6^2	5$^{1\frac34}$	2$^{\frac12}$	1$^{\frac12}$	Blanc B	L118 b	22.70	80– 17	Prince Arch118$\frac12$ Wasabi Cat120$\frac12$ Pa Pa Da118^{no}	Bmpd st, rail, up late	10
1Jan04-11Crc	fm	1$\frac{1}{16}$ Ⓣ	:23^1 :47^3 1:11 1:41^1	Alw 24000N1x	**69**	6	9^7	10^{10}	9^{12}	9^{11}	7$^{6\frac34}$	Blanc B	L117	6.70	86– 08	GnRummyChmp120^1 FlghttoJustc117^1 HntngHllblly117^2	Never factored	11

Private Emblem
Own: Cassels James and Zollars, Bob

Dk. b or b. h. 5 (Mar)
Sire: Our Emblem (Mr. Prospector) $10,000
Dam: Merion Miss (Halo)
Br: Berkshire Stud and Oak Cliff Stable (NY)
Tr: Asmussen Steven M(0 0 0 0 .00) 2004:(2293 555 .24)

Life	24	7	3	5	$783,152	101	D.Fst	17 5 3 2	$660,389	101
2004	4	1	0	0	$80,049	101	Wet(327)	2 1 0 0	$51,000	98
2003	8	1	0	3	$82,863	100	Turf(252)	5 1 0 3	$71,763	93
	0	0	0	0	$0	–	Dst(0)	0 0 0 0	$0	–

Date/Race	Trk	Dist	Fractions	Race	Fig	PP	St	1C	2C	Str	Fin	Jockey	Wt	Odds	Pace	Top Finishers	Comment	Fld
2May04-8Aqu	fst	1⅛	:48^4 1:13 1:38^3 1:52^1	3↑ Ⓢ KngsPointH80k	**78**	1	2^{hd}	1$^{\frac12}$	1$^{\frac12}$	3$^{\frac12}$	4$^{10\frac34}$	Migliore R	L123 f	2.20	67– 25	Gander1221 Levendis1154 Trial Prep1185$\frac34$	Broke down, vanned off	6
3Apr04-11OP	fst	1⅛	:45^2 1:09^3 1:35^2 1:48^1	4↑ OaklawnH-G2	**99**	4	5^{13}	6^{13}	6$^{8\frac12}$	6$^{6\frac12}$	6^8	Doocy T T	L113 f	11.20	89– 09	Peace Rules1202 Ole Faunty116^{nk} Saint Liam1142$\frac14$	Saved ground	6
21Feb04-9OP	fst	1$\frac{1}{16}$	:24^1 :48 1:13 1:43^3	4↑ EssexH-G3	**101**	2	2$^{\frac12}$	2$^{\frac12}$	2^{hd}	1^{hd}	1$^{1\frac14}$	Doocy T T	L113 f	8.70	92– 16	PrivteEmblem1131$\frac14$ PiNBurgr1184 CrftyShw118^{hd}	Outkicked foe to wire	8
17Jan04-7Hou	gd	1⅛	:48^2 1:13^1 1:38^4 1:51^3	4↑ MaxmGldCpH100k	**84**	5	5$^{2\frac12}$	4$^{2\frac14}$	5$^{3\frac12}$	4^5	4$^{7\frac34}$	Beasley J A	L115 f	4.20	79– 17	SirCherokee1183$\frac34$ Frfourintrnt1192$\frac12$ DustySpik1164$\frac12$	2w, failed to respond	8

Proud Accolade

Own: Padua Stables

Dk. b or b. c. 3 (Apr) OBSMAR04 $450,000
Sire: Yes It's True (Is It True) $10,000
Dam: Proud Ciel (Septieme Ciel)
Br: Marion G. Montanari (Fla)
Tr: Pletcher Todd A(0 0 0 0 .00) 2004:(948 240 .25)

Life	5 3 0 0	$364,130	100	D.Fst	5 3 0 0	$364,130	100
2004	5 3 0 0	$364,130	100	Wet(327)	0 0 0 0	$0	–
2003	0 M 0 0	$0	–	Turf(292*)	0 0 0 0	$0	–
	0 0 0 0	$0	–	Dst(0)	0 0 0 0	$0	–

Date/Race	Cond	Dist	Fractions	Race	Fig	PP St 1C 2C Str Fin	Jockey	Wt	Odds	Comment/Winners	Remark	Fld
18Dec04-8Hol	fst	1 1/16	$:23^{2}$:46 1:10 $1:41^{3}$	HolFut-G1	**73**	5 4 1¼ 3½ 3½ 5 6½ 5 13	Velazquez J R	LB121 b	2.20	80- 11 Declan's Moon121 1 Giacomo121no Wilko121 2	Bid 3 wide, weakened	7
30Oct04-7LS	fst	1 1/16	$:23^{2}$ $:47^{2}$ $1:11^{1}$ 1:42	BCJuvnle-G1	**89**	6 4 3 5 2½ 6 3¾ 6 5 6 5	Velazquez J R	L122	2.60	87- 02 Wilko122¾ Afleet Alex122nk Sun King122 1¼	Between,no response	8
9Oct04-7Bel	fst	1 1/16	$:23^{3}$ $:47^{1}$ $1:11^{2}$ $1:42^{1}$	Champagn-G1	**100**	8 4 1½ 4¾ 3nk 1½ 1½	Velazquez J R	L122	2.40	89- 20 Proud Accolade122½ AfleetAlex122 1¼ SunKing122 1¾	4 wide, when roused	8
1Sep04-5Sar	fst	6½f	:22 $:45^{4}$ $1:10^{1}$ $1:16^{3}$	Alw 47000N1x	**88**	6 2 3 1 2½ 1½ 15½	Velazquez J R	L120	*.15	92- 10 *PrdAccld*120 5½ StrmCrkRsng120hd ClypsBnd120½	Drew clear when roused	7
31Jly04-4Sar	fst	6½f	:22 $:45^{2}$ 1:10 $1:16^{2}$	Md Sp Wt 45k	**94**	3 8 1hd 1hd 1 6 17½	Velazquez J R	L118	*1.90e	93- 09 *ProudAccolde*118 7½ MorThnSomwht118 1 *Blrion*118 2¼	Widened under drive	13

Pt's Grey Eagle

Own: Reddam J. P

Gr/ro. g. 4 (Feb) BARMAR03 $80,000
Sire: Pleasant Tap (Pleasant Colony) $10,000
Dam: Hemet Eagle (Swing Till Dawn)
Br: Farrell W. Jones (Ky)
Tr: Dollase Craig(0 0 0 0 .00) 2004:(191 35 .18)

Life	9 3 4 0	$205,540	104	D.Fst	8 3 4 0	$204,600	104
2004	7 2 3 0	$184,340	104	Wet(355)	0 0 0 0	$0	–
2003	2 1 1 0	$21,200	97	Turf(295)	1 0 0 0	$940	82
	0 0 0 0	$0	–	Dst(0)	0 0 0 0	$0	–

Date/Race	Cond	Dist	Fractions	Race	Fig	PP St 1C 2C Str Fin	Jockey	Wt	Odds	Comment/Winners	Remark	Fld
30Oct04-5LS	fst	6f	$:21^{1}$ $:43^{2}$ $:55^{2}$ 1:08	3↑BCSprint-G1	**102**	8 12 12 11 12 9¾ 10 7¼ 8 3¾	Nakatani C S	L123 b	23.70	96- 04 Speightstown126 1¼ Kela126¾ My Cousin Matt126½	No speed, no factor	13
10Oct04-8SA	fst	6f	:21 $:43^{3}$ $:55^{4}$ $1:08^{4}$	3↑AnTtlBCH-G1	**104**	7 2 7 4 6 3¾ 4 2 1½	Bisono A	LB109 b	29.80	94- 12 Pt'sGreyEagle109½ Pohave118 2 HombreRapido114hd	5wd into lane,rallied	8
10Sep04-11Fpx	fst	6½f	$:21^{1}$ $:44^{2}$ $1:09^{3}$ $1:16^{2}$	Foothill58k	**87**	6 2 3 1 2 1 1hd 2 1¼	Pedroza M A	LB122 b	*1.20	94- 09 LstMinutDtil122 1¼ *PtsGryEgl*122 3 TrishsDimond122¾	4wd into str,2nd best	7
22Aug04-2Dmr	fst	6½f	$:21^{4}$ $:44^{2}$ $1:08^{4}$ $1:15^{1}$	3↑Alw 54400N1x	**104**	5 1 2½ 2hd 1½ 1 4½	Flores D R	LB117 b	1.80	99- 09 PtsGryEgl117 4½ GoldnSouvnir119 1½ OutofthBluSlw121 6½	Steady handling	6
7Aug04-7Dmr	fst	6f	$:21^{4}$ $:44^{4}$ $:57^{1}$ 1:10	3↑Alw 56000N1x	**99**	9 1 3 1½ 2 1 1hd 2 1¼	Flores D R	LB117 b	5.60	88- 13 RetireesThree121 1¼ *PtsGryEgl*117 1 LstTiminTown119hd	Bid btwn,held 2nd	10
17Jly04-7Hol	fst	6f	$:21^{4}$ $:44^{3}$:57 $1:09^{4}$	3↑Alw 47400N1x	**89**	6 1 5¾ 5 1¾ 4 1½ 2 1½	Flores D R	LB116 b	4.90	86- 15 *IndinCountry*116 1½ PtsGreyEgle116½ *RetireesThre*119 1½	5 wide, late for 2nd	6
13Jun04-4Hol	fm	5½f	Ⓣ $:21^{2}$ $:43^{3}$ $:55^{3}$ $1:01^{4}$	3↑Alw 49000N1x	**82**	5 7 8 7¼ 9 9¼ 7 8 5 4½	Solis A	LB115 b	4.00	91- 05 *LestWeForget*119 2½ CIticSword123½ Prgmtico123no	3w into str,vanned off	10

Puerto Banus
Own: Noctis LLC Papiano, Neil and Taub, St
Ch. h. 6 (Feb)
Sire: Supremo (Gone West) $2,000
Dam: Drina (Regal and Royal)
Br: The Thoroughbred Corporation (Ky)
Tr: Mulhall Kristin(0 0 0 0 .00) 2004:(154 23 .15)

Life	20	5	3	1	$380,410	102	D.Fst	9 2 2 1 $106,010 100
2004	6	1	0	0	$139,000	102	Wet(298)	0 0 0 0 $0 –
2003	8	3	2	0	$183,560	101	Turf(230)	11 3 1 0 $274,400 102
	0	0	0	0	$0	–	Dst(0)	0 0 0 0 $0 –

4Dec04–7Hol fm 1½ Ⓣ :502 1:153 2:04 2:293 3↑HolTrfCp-G1 70 2 2½ 2½ 42 9¾ 917¼ Desormeaux K J LB126 b 5.90 61–22 Pellegrino126hd Megahertz123hd License To Run126½ Stdied early,eased 9
23Oct04–9SA fm 1½ Ⓣ :491 1:134 2:023 2:264 3↑CFBurkeH-G3 97 8 76½ 64½ 53 32 41 Espinoza V LB115 b 2.60 86–13 Habaneros115¾ *Pellegrino*116nk Gallant113no 5wd into str,missed 3d 8
3Oct04–5SA fm 1¼ Ⓣ :47 1:11 1:35 1:583 3↑CLHirsch-G1 90 2 716 717 66½ 66½ 68¼ Espinoza V LB124 b 21.60 88–09 Star Over the Bay124¾ Sarafan124¾ Vangelis124¾ 4wd into lane,no bid 7
20Mar04–9SA fm 1½ Ⓣ :471 1:12 2:02 2:26 4↑SanLsRyH-G2 99 9 78½ 67½ 53 31½ 51¾ Espinoza V LB116 b *2.80 89–08 *MeteorStorm*115nk Labirinto114¾ GenedeCampeao114¾ 3-4 wide to stretch 10
16Feb04–9SA fm 1½ Ⓣ :494 1:15 2:044 2:28 4↑SLsObspH-G2 102 2 87 85¼ 85½ 63¼ 1nk Espinoza V LB115 b 3.90 81–15 PurtoBnus115nk Contnuosly116hd ContnntlRd117no Rallied btwn,gamely 12
19Jan04–8SA fm 1¼ Ⓣ :474 1:121 1:353 1:584 4↑SnMarcos-G2 95 6 85¾ 74¼ 42½ 42 42½ Espinoza V LB120 b 3.40e 92–05 *SweetReturn*121½ NothingtoLos116 1½ BluStllr116½ 4wd 2nd turn,missed 3d 9

Purge
Own: Starlight Stables LLC Saylor, Paul an
B. c. 4 (Apr) KEESEP02 $180,000
Sire: Pulpit (A.P. Indy) $60,000
Dam: Copelan's Bid Gal (Copelan)
Br: Glory Days Breeding, Inc. (Ky)
Tr: Pletcher Todd A(0 0 0 0 .00) 2004:(948 240 .25)

Life	9	4	1	0	$589,734	109	D.Fst	8 4 1 0 $559,734 109
2004	8	3	1	0	$562,734	109	Wet(370)	1 0 0 0 $30,000 95
2003	1	1	0	0	$27,000	89	Turf(267)	0 0 0 0 $0 –
	0	0	0	0	$0	–	Dst(0)	0 0 0 0 $0 –

27Nov04–9Aqu fst 1 :222 :441 1:081 1:332 3↑CigarMiH-G1 89 4 2hd 2½ 54¼ 610 611½ Velazquez J R L116 3.95 86–07 LionTmer115¼ BdgeofSilver115no PicoCentrl123¾ Between rivals, tired 8
28Aug04–11Sar fst 1¼ :49 1:124 1:37 2:022 Travers-G1 99 3 21½ 2hd 1hd 31½ 46¼ Velazquez J R L126 4.00 89–05 Birdstone126 2½ TheCliffsEdge126 3½ Eddington126nk Speed outside, tired 7
8Aug04–9Sar fst 1⅛ :453 1:093 1:343 1:472 JimDandy-G2 109 6 22 23½ 2½ 17 14½ Velazquez J R L121 2.80 98–02 Purge121 4½ The Cliff's Edge123½ [D]Eddington115 7¼ Shown whip stretch 6
5Jun04–11Bel fst 1½ :483 1:113 2:002 2:272 Belmont-G1 55 2 1hd 511 817 834 937½ Velazquez J R L126 9.60 57–10 *Birdstone*126 1 Smarty Jones126 8 Royal Assault126 3 Vied inside, tired 9
22May04–8Bel fst 1⅛ :46 1:10 1:35 1:474 PeterPan-G2 108 10 32 31 2hd 16 16¾ Velazquez J R L115 2.40 92–24 Purge115 6¾ *Swingforthefences*115 1¼ MstrDvid115 2¼ Speed 4 wide, drew off 10
10Apr04–9OP my 1⅛ :464 1:113 1:364 1:492 ArkDerby-G2 95 5 1½ 1½ 2hd 46 57¼ Velasquez C L118 5.80 84–17 *Smarty Jones*122 1½ Borrego118 1½ Pro Prado122 3½ Gave up lead, faded 11
20Mar04–10OP fst 1 1/16 :232 :473 1:12 1:42 Rebel200k 102 4 11 11 1½ 21 23¼ Velazquez J R L117 b *2.00 97–16 *Smarty Jones*122 3¼ Purge117 3¾ Pro Prado117 3¾ Legit pace, no match 9
22Feb04–3GP fst 6f :221 :45 :561 1:092 Alw 33660N1x 99 1 4 32 3½ 11 13 Velazquez J R L118 b *.70 95–15 Purge118 3 All Hail Stormy122 10½ Grand Score118 1½ 3 wide, drew clear 4

Puzzlement
Own: Shields J V Jr
B. h. 6 (Jan)
Sire: Pine Bluff (Danzig) $10,000
Dam: Taine (Sir Ivor)
Br: J. V. Shields Jr. (Fla)
Tr: Jerkens H. A(0 0 0 0 .00) 2004:(374 72 .19)

Life	22	6	3	5	$717,590	113	D.Fst	15 4 2 5 $587,740 113
2004	2	1	0	0	$90,000	110	Wet(356)	7 2 1 0 $129,850 108
2003	11	2	2	3	$470,450	113	Turf(317)	0 0 0 0 $0 –
	0	0	0	0	$0	–	Dst(0)	0 0 0 0 $0 –

7Feb04–10GP fst 1⅛ :471 1:11 1:353 1:473 3↑DonnH-G1 96 2 714 714 711 511 412½ Chavez J F L115 b 7.80 88–09 Medaglia d'Oro122 4¾ Seattle Fitz113 3¾ FunnyCide119 4 Passed tired rivals 8
3Jan04–9GP fst 1 1/16 :233 :472 1:112 1:421 3↑HalHopeH-G3 110 4 78½ 78½ 65 22½ 1nk Chavez J F L116 b 2.70 98–13 Puzzlement116nk BowmansBnd118 8 Stockholder114 2 Outside bid,up late 7

Quantum Merit
Own: Very Un Stable and Gioia Joseph

Dk. b or b. g. 6 (May)
Sire: Hansel (Woodman) $10,946
Dam: Just Flirting (Green Dancer)
Br: Mr. & Mrs. Gerald Nielsen (NY)
Tr: Carroll D W II(0 0 0 0 .00) 2004:(135 20 .15)

Life	18	8	1	2	$519,525	107	D.Fst	0	0	0	0	$0	–
2004	3	3	0	0	$280,585	107	Wet(328)	0	0	0	0	$0	–
2003	8	3	1	2	$176,180	101	Turf(315)	18	8	1	2	$519,525	107
	0	0	0	0	$0	–	Dst(0)	0	0	0	0	$0	–

3Jly04–8CD fm 1 Ⓣ :22⁴ :45⁴ 1:09³ 1:34 3↑FrckrBCH-G2 **107** 7 3⁴½ 3⁴ 3² 2½ 1¹½ Sellers S J L117 5.70 99–07 QuntumMerit117¹½ D *SenorSwingr*117² PrfctSoul121¹ 5w,late hand urging 9
23May04–8Bel fm 1⅛ Ⓣ :48¹ 1:11⁴ 1:35 1:47 3↑SKingstonH114k **102** 6 1¹½ 1¹ 1²½ 1¹ 1no Migliore R L121 *1.10 95–05 *QuntmMrt*121no Forvrnss116² GoldnCommndr115⁶ Game inside, prevailed 10
9May04–7Bel fm 1 Ⓣ :23⁴ :47 1:09⁴ 1:33² 4↑OC 100k/c -N **104** 2 1¹½ 1½ 1hd 1¹½ 1²¼ Migliore R L115 4.50 93–07 *Quantum Merit*115²¼ *Union Place*117nk Pisces119nk Drew clear when roused 6

Quest Star
Own: Mansell Stables LLC

Dk. b or b. h. 6 (May)
Sire: Broad Brush (Ack Ack) $100,000
Dam: Tinaca (Manila)
Br: John Messara (Ky)
Tr: Walden W. E(0 0 0 0 .00) 2004:(207 33 .16)

Life	34	7	7	4	$798,070	105	D.Fst	7	1	3	1	$103,260	95
2004	10	2	0	0	$238,035	102	Wet(373)	2	0	0	0	$2,800	97
2003	10	3	3	0	$298,380	105	Turf(323)	25	6	4	3	$692,010	105
	0	0	0	0	$0	–	Dst(0)	0	0	0	0	$0	–

21Nov04–9CD yl 1⅛ Ⓣ :48¹ 1:13 1:38⁴ 1:51¹ 3↑RivrCtyH-G3 **56** 10 1hd 1hd 1hd 9¹² 10²²¼ Melancon L L116 b 9.70 55–26 *GPFleet*115½ CloudysKnight115⁵¼ AyCaramb115no Bobble,not persevered 12
5Nov04–7CD gd 1⅛ Ⓣ :49⁴ 1:13³ 1:37⁴ 1:50² 3↑Alw 68300c **100** 5 1¹½ 1² 1²½ 1³ 1¹½ Melancon L L117 b 10.50 81–20 QuestStar117¹½ GretchensStar117½ PrincePrdo123½ Slow early pace,drivg 7
2Oct04–7Haw fst 1¼ :47¹ 1:11¹ 1:36⁴ 2:03¹ 3↑HawGldCp-G2 **95** 1 1½ 1½ 1hd 3nk 4⁶¼ Melancon L L113 b 24.50 84–19 Freefourinternet112¹¾ PerfctDrift121²¼ SonicWst115²¼ Inside, weakened 7
1Sep04–7Sar gd 1³⁄₁₆ Ⓣ :49⁴ 1:14² 1:38² 1:55⁴ 4↑Alw 60000c **88** 4 4¹½ 4¹½ 3¹½ 3⁴ 4⁷¾ Day P L123 b 2.50 78–18 King's Drama117⁵¾ Cottage119¹¾ Third Half117nk Inside, no response 6
30Jly04–8Sar yl 1⅛ Ⓣ :49¹ 1:13¹ 1:37¹ 1:49³ 3↑BBaruchH-G2 **98** 1 4² 4² 5³½ 5¹¾ 5²¾ Day P L114 b 5.30 86–11 SilverTree116nk *NothingtoLos*117½ IrishColonil113nk Saved ground, empty 7
4Jly04–7AP sf 1½ Ⓣ :52³ 1:19² 2:10⁴ 2:36¹ 3↑StrStBCH-G3 **79** 1 1½ 1½ 1¹½ 3³½ 7¹¹ Marquez C H Jr L116 b 2.60 45–44 Ballingarry120¹¾ D Silverfoot116nk Grey Beard117²¾ Tired 8
5Jun04–10Bel fm 1¼ Ⓣ :48² 1:12¹ 1:35⁴ 1:59¹ 3↑ManhttnH-G1 **102** 2 2hd 2hd 1hd 2½ 7⁴ Day P L115 b 20.00 94–05 MetorStorm117¹¼ MillnniumDrgon116no MrOBrin116¾ Vied outside, tired 9
10Apr04–7Hou yl 1⅛ Ⓣ 1:53 3↑JBConlyBCH222k **97** 2 6²¾ 8⁶ 7⁴¼ 6⁴¾ 4²¼ Day P L118 b *1.60 84–17 Warleigh116½ Skate Away117¹ Gentlemen J J109¾ Swung 4w, willingly 11
20Mar04–6GP fm 1½ Ⓣ :50 1:15³ 2:26² 3↑PanAmerH-G2 **101** 3 2¹½ 2hd 1¹ 1³ 1½ Day P L114 b 1.70 86–14 Quest Star114½ Request for Parole115¹¾ Megantic112²½ On hedge, lasted 7
22Feb04–11GP fm 1⅜ Ⓣ :48⁴ 1:36¹ 2:11² 3↑GPBCH-G1 **101** 5 3²½ 3² 3²½ 2¹½ 5¹¾ Day P L115 b 15.40 99–10 Hard Buck117hd Balto Star122½ Kicken Kris118¹ Hedge, no late gain 8

Quintons Gold Rush
Own: Padua Stables and Manoogian Jay

Ch. c. 4 (Mar) OBSMAR03 $60,000
Sire: Wild Rush (Wild Again) $10,000
Dam: Hollywood Gold (Mr. Prospector)
Br: Toyomi Omiya (Ky)
Tr: Mitchell Mike R(0 0 0 0 .00) 2004:(391 97 .25)

Life	10	3	1	0	$329,835	102	D.Fst	7 2 1 0	$295,500	102
2004	9	3	0	0	$322,235	102	Wet(388)	3 1 0 0	$34,335	99
2003	1	M	1	0	$7,600	32	Turf(233)	0 0 0 0	$0	-
	0	0	0	0	$0	-	Dst(0)	0 0 0 0	$0	-

26Dec04-8SA fst 7f :221 :441 1:0811:214 Malibu-G1 **51** 8 5 3½ 64 1012 922 Espinoza V LB121 16.50 74-09 RockHardTen121½ LavaMn115no HrvrdAvenue115no 5wd to turn,gave way 10
Previously trained by Asmussen Steven M
21Nov04-8RP my 1⅛ :4541:104 1:3721:501 OkDerby-G3 **61** 8 2½ 2½ 2½ 78½ 826¼ Berry M C LB121 2.60 69-08 Wally's Choice1151 Golden Glen1121½ Cryptograph1186½ Tired 11
2Nov04-8CD sly 1 :223 :453 1:1031:373 3↑ Alw 53910N2x **99** 5 11 11 11½ 11½ 12¾ Day P L117 *.70 82-27 QuintonsGoldRush1172¾ Intrwovn119¾ EvryAdvntg117¾ 2-3w,hand urging 6
2Oct04-9Hoo fst 1$\frac{1}{16}$:224 :47 1:12 1:44 IndnaDby-G2 **32** 5 73½ 1hd 76½ 922 942¾ Sellers S J LB124 4.20 48-21 Brass Hat1241¾ Suave124¾ Hasslefree115½ Climbing 1st turn,quit 9
1May04-10CD sly 1¼ :4631:114 1:3712:04 KyDerby-G1 **–** 18 32½115¼ 1836 1837 - Nakatani C S L126 51.20 - 21 *Smarty Jones*1262¾ LionHeart1263¼ Imperialism1262 4wd,took up 1/2,eased 18
17Apr04-9Kee fst 1$\frac{1}{16}$:231 :471 1:12 1:434 Lexingtn-G2 **102** 10 21½ 21 1hd 12 12¾ Bailey J D L116 5.70 93-11 QntonsGoldRsh1162¾ *FrSlm*116nk SongofthSword1162 Pressed,4w,driving 14
Previously trained by Mitchell Mike
3Apr04-8SA fst 1⅛ :4641:11 1:3621:491 SADerby-G1 **98** 5 2½ 1hd 2hd 1hd 43 Nakatani C S LB122 7.00 85-09 Castledale122hd [D]Rock Hard Ten1222 Imperialism1221 Dueled, weakened 7
6Mar04-7SA fst 1 :223 :453 1:10 1:36 SnRafael-G2 **93** 9 51¾ 31½ 31½ 32 45¾ Nakatani C S LB116 4.80 85-11 Imperialism118nk Lion Heart1214½ Consecrate1151 4 wide,no late bid 10
18Jan04-6SA fst 1$\frac{1}{16}$:222 :46 1:1011:42 Md Sp Wt 49k **93** 4 2hd 2hd 2hd 11½ 13½ Valenzuela P A LB120 2.80 95-13 QntonsGoldRsh1203½ *Wmbldon*1206½ Onvrycolct1203½ Pulled,dueled,clear 12

Randaroo
Own: Allen Joseph

B. m. 5 (Feb)
Sire: Gold Case (Forty Niner) $7,500
Dam: Validated (Valid Appeal)
Br: Dennis Drazin (Ky)
Tr: McLaughlin Kiaran P(0 0 0 0 .00) 2004:(462 84 .18)

Life	15	8	4	1	$673,045	108	D.Fst	13 7 3 1	$633,045	108
2004	3	2	0	1	$181,365	108	Wet(371)	2 1 1 0	$40,000	94
2003	10	4	4	0	$401,500	102	Turf(284)	0 0 0 0	$0	-
	0	0	0	0	$0	-	Dst(0)	0 0 0 0	$0	-

1May04-8CD fst 7f :222 :45 1:0931:223 4↑ⒻHmnaDstH-G1 **83** 1 2 11 11½ 32½ 37¼ Velazquez J R L121 1.50 82-06 Mayo On the Side114hd Azeri1257¼ Randaroo121nk Speed,held 3rd 4
27Mar04-8Aqu fst 7f :224 :461 1:10 1:223 3↑ⒻDistfBCH-G2 **100** 4 1 1½ 1½ 13 13½ Migliore R L121 *.45 92-17 Randaroo1213½ Chirimoy1102¼ *StormFlgFlying*1181¼ With something left 4
8Feb04-11GP fst 7f :222 :444 1:0841:212 3↑ⒻShrlJnsH-G3 **108** 5 2 1hd 1½ 12½ 17¼ Velazquez J R L118 1.80 95-16 *Randaroo*1187¼ Harmony Lodge121¾ Halory Leigh1142½ Off rail, drew away 8

Rare Gift

Own: Bolton George, Dipietro, David and Ho

Gr/ro. f. 4 (Apr) FTSAUG02 $330,000
Sire: Unbridled's Song (Unbridled) $125,000
Dam: Rare Blend (Bates Motel)
Br: Joseph Allen (Ky)
Tr: Kimmel John C(0 0 0 0 .00) 2004:(281 34 .12)

Life	9	3	1	4	$188,220	94	D.Fst	8	2	1	4	$161,220	94
2004	8	2	1	4	$161,220	94	Wet(365)	1	1	0	0	$27,000	79
2003	1	1	0	0	$27,000	79	Turf(261)	0	0	0	0	$0	-
	0	0	0	0	$0	-	Dst(0)	0	0	0	0	$0	-

18Dec04-8Aqu fst 1¼ ⊡ :494 1:144 1:393 2:052 3↑Ⓕ LadiesH-G3 90 3 1½ 11 11 14 16 Migliore R L115 4.20 88-22 Rare Gift1156 Board Elligible117nk Miss Fortunate1173 Set pace, drew off 8
20Nov04-9Pim fst 1⅛ :474 1:114 1:362 1:491 Ⓕ AArundel-G3 94 4 31½ 41½ 32 21 2nk Prado E S L115 4.90 98-15 Essence115nk *Rare Gift*1152½ Family Business115½ Rail, eased out,closed 11
24Oct04-8Bel fst 1$\frac{1}{16}$:231 :454 1:093 1:422 3↑Ⓕ Alw 49000N2X 75 4 4¾ 43 46½ 414 410 Bravo J L116 10.20 78-17 Magical Illusion1163 La Minuta1191 Pleasant Home1206 Tired after a half 5
14May04-10Pim fst 1⅛ :493 1:134 1:392 1:523 Ⓕ BlkEySsn-G2 84 4 2½ 1hd 1½ 1hd 31¾ Prado E S L115 8.30 79-17 *YerlyReport*1221½ PwynePrincess115nk RreGift1151½ 2-3wd,dueled,gamely 7
16Apr04-8Aqu fst 1⅛ :481 1:124 1:372 1:50 3↑Ⓕ Alw 46000N2X 80 2 56 53½ 32½ 34½ 35¾ Migliore R L117 *.60 83-25 Board Elligible1212½ Chase Gap1223¼ Rare Gift1174 3 wide, no rally 6
6Mar04-8GP fst 1⅛ :473 1:113 1:37 1:503 Ⓕ BonnieMs-G2 81 3 31½ 3½ 31 36 36¾ Day P L116 3.50 79-21 Last Song1182 *Society Selection*1204¾ Rare Gift1167 Off rail, tired 5
7Feb04-3GP fst 1⅛ :482 1:131 1:382 1:504 Ⓕ Alw 34000N1X 78 7 31 31 3½ 1½ 12¾ Prado E S L117 *1.70 85-09 Rare Gift1172¾ Hot Mail1178¼ Special Report117nk 3 wide, drew clear 8
9Jan04-7GP fst 7f :224 :452 1:102 1:231 Ⓕ Alw 34000N1X 74 5 4 2½ 2hd 2hd 34½ Prado E S 117 3.50 81-15 Eye Dazzler1173¾ Dance Fee119¾ *Rare Gift*117½ Vied inside, weakened 9

Read the Footnotes

Own: Klaravich Stables Inc

B. c. 4 (Apr) EASMAY03 $320,000
Sire: Smoke Glacken (Two Punch) $30,000
Dam: Baydon Belle (Al Nasr*Fr)
Br: Lawrence Goichman (NY)
Tr: Violette R A Jr(0 0 0 0 .00) 2004:(249 41 .16)

Life	8	5	0	0	$450,660	113	D.Fst	7	5	0	0	$450,660	113
2004	3	1	0	0	$210,000	113	Wet(378)	1	0	0	0	$0	86
2003	5	4	0	0	$240,660	105	Turf(234)	0	0	0	0	$0	-
	0	0	0	0	$0	-	Dst(0)	0	0	0	0	$0	-

1May04-10CD sly 1¼ :463 1:114 1:371 2:04 KyDerby-G1 86 12 64¼ 42 34 45½ 714¾ Albarado R J L126 22.50 64-21 *SmartyJones*1262¾ LionHeart1263¼ Imperilism1262 Stdied 1st turn,wkened 18
13Mar04-9GP fst 1⅛ :47 1:112 1:373 1:511 FlaDerby-G1 86 3 33 34½ 2hd 2½ 44 Bailey J D L122 *1.00 79-15 Friends Lake122¾ Value Plus122¾ *The Cliff's Edge*1222½ Rail trip, gave way 10
14Feb04-11GP fst 1$\frac{1}{16}$:234 :473 1:111 1:423 FntnOYth-G2 113 8 32½ 31 21 2½ 1nk Bailey J D L122 2.10 96-14 RdthFootnots122nk ScondofJun1207½ SilvrWgon1205½ Long drive, just up 8

Red Rioja (Ire)

Own: Sanderson Dr. Karen

B. m. 6 (Mar)
Sire: King's Theatre*Ire (Sadler's Wells) $9,497
Dam: Foreign Relation*Ire (Distant Relative*Ire)
Br: Dr Karen Monica Sanderson (Ire)
Tr: Cecil Ben D(0 0 0 0 .00) 2004:(53 4 .08)

Life	15	4	1	1	$223,980	98	D.Fst	0	0	0	0	$0	-
2004	1	1	0	0	$55,000	87	Wet(318)	0	0	0	0	$0	-
2003	3	1	1	0	$60,800	98	Turf(288)	15	4	1	1	$223,980	98
	0	0	0	0	$0	-	Dst(0)	0	0	0	0	$0	-

31Jan04-3GG sf 1$\frac{1}{16}$ Ⓣ :232 :481 1:124 1:46 +4↑Ⓕ BrwnBssH-G3 87 7 78½ 78½ 74¼ 42¾ 11 Saint-Martin E LB117 *1.20 80-20 Red Rioja1171 Hooked On Niners1171¼ *A BNoodle*1161 Split 3w, rallied late 11

Request for Parole
Own: Knighton Jeri and Sam

Dk. b or b. h. 6 (Feb)
Sire: Judge T C (Judge Smells) $8,500
Dam: Madison's Quest (Deputy Minister)
Br: Robert H. Roberts & Bea Roberts (Ky)
Tr: Hough Stanley M(0 0 0 0 .00) 2004:(259 53 .20)

Life	34	9	7	3	$1,205,892	108	D.Fst	13	3	2	3	$248,202 102
2004	10	3	2	0	$757,100	108	Wet(349)	5	1	1	0	$111,220 99
2003	12	2	2	1	$103,270	102	Turf(281)	16	5	4	0	$846,470 108
	0	0	0	0	$0	–	Dst(0)	0	0	0	0	$0 –

30Oct04–8LS yl 1½ Ⓣ :49 1:13⁴ 2:04 2:29³ 3↑BCTurf-G1 97 2 5¹⁰ 7⁸½ 8⁷½ 6⁸ 6⁸ Day P L126 22.20 115–07 BetterTlkNow126¹¾ KittnsJoy121¹ Powrscourt126²¼ Saved ground, tired 8
2Oct04–9Bel yl 1½ Ⓣ :50⁴ 1:17¹ 2:07¹ 2:29⁴ 3↑TfClscIv-G1 103 2 5²½ 5³¼ 6⁵¼ 4⁶ 4⁶¼ Velasquez C L126 14.50 66–22 Kitten's Joy121²½ Magistretti126¾ Tycoon121³ Saved ground, no rally 7
11Sep04–9Bel yl 1⅜ Ⓣ :50 1:14² 1:38 2:14³ 3↑ManOWar-G1 103 4 4²½ 4¹½ 4²½ 5⁵¾ 5⁴½ Castellano J J L126 6.40 85–10 Magistretti126¹¼ Epalo126² King's Drama126¾ Between foes, no rally 8
14Aug04–8Sar yl 1½ [T] :49⁴ 1:15 2:04³ 2:28² 3↑SwrdDncr-G1 103 4 3⁴ 3¹ 2½ 2½ 2¹½ Castellano J J L123 2.20 76–22 BetterTlkNow118¹½ RequstfcrProl123¾ BltoStr120¹ 3 wide move, gamely 6
3Jly04–10Mth fm 1⅜ Ⓣ :48³ 1:14 1:37² 2:13¹ 3↑UnitdNtn-G1 108 2 3¹½ 3² 3¹½ 3² 1½ Prado E S L118 4.70 97–09 RqstforProl118½ MrOBrn120¾ NothngtoLos118¹ Eased out,bid,determnd 11
5Jun04–10Bel fm 1¼ [T] :48² 1:12¹ 1:35⁴ 1:59¹ 3↑ManhttnH-G1 104 7 9⁴¼ 9³½ 8³½ 7¹½ 5²¾ Santos J A L115 13.10 95–05 MtorStorm117¹¼ MillnnumDrgon116^no MrOBrn116¾ Traffic inside stretch 9
20Mar04–6GP fm 1½ Ⓣ :50 1:15³ 2:26² 3↑PanAmerH-G2 100 5 4²½ 4² 6²¼ 3⁴ 2½ Santos J A L115 *1.40 85–14 Quest Star114½ Request for Parole115¹¾ Megantic112²½ 3 wide, gaining 7
22Feb04–11GP fm 1⅜ Ⓣ :48⁴ 1:36¹ 2:11² 3↑GPBCH-G1 101 1 6⁴½ 6⁵ 7⁶ 6³¼ 4¹½ Santos J A L116 2.80 99–10 Hard Buck117^hd Balto Star122½ Kicken Kris118¹ Stdy early, mild rally 8
25Jan04–10GP fm 1⅜ Ⓣ :48³ 1:13² 1:37 2:12² 3↑MDiarmdH-G3 103 7 7³¼ 7³¾ 8⁴ 2¹½ 1¹½ Santos J A L115 3.20 96–07 RequstforProl115¹½ SlwVlly117¾ SirBrinsSword113³¼ Steadied final turn 12
11Jan04–8GP fm 1⅛ Ⓣ :49² 1:13⁴ 1:38³ 1:50 4↑Alw 46000c 101 1 7⁵ 8⁶¾ 6⁴ 3¹½ 1no Santos J A L120 4.50 85–20 *RqustforProl*120no *DlMrShow*116²¾ IrishColonil116¹¼ Stdy far turn, just up 10

Riskaverse
Own: Fox Ridge Farm Inc

Dk. b or b. m. 6 (Apr)
Sire: Dynaformer (Roberto) $75,000
Dam: The Bink (Seeking the Gold)
Br: Fox Ridge Farm Inc (Ky)
Tr: Kelly Patrick J(0 0 0 0 .00) 2004:(238 21 .09)

Life	27	8	6	4	$1,717,706	104	D.Fst	2	0	0	2	$59,730 72
2004	6	1	2	0	$717,472	102	Wet(357)	1	1	0	0	$26,400 83
2003	8	2	1	2	$336,324	104	Turf(315)	24	7	6	2	$1,631,576 104
	0	0	0	0	$0	–	Dst(0)	0	0	0	0	$0 –

30Oct04–6LS yl 1⅜ Ⓣ :52² 1:18² 1:42¹ 2:18¹ 3↑ⒻBCF&MTrf-G1 94 9 4⁵½ 5³½ 5⁴ 6⁵½ 8⁸ Velasquez C L123 13.70 90–07 Ouija Board118¹½ Film Maker123^nk Wonder Again123²¾ Stead rank early 12
2Oct04–7Bel yl 1¼ [T] :52² 1:17⁴ 1:41² 2:04³ 3↑ⒻFlwrBlIv-G1 102 8 5¹½ 5¹¾ 5³ 4¹½ 1¾ Velasquez C L118 8.70 71–25 Riskverse118¾ *Commercnt*118^hd MoscowBurning120^nk Resolutely outside 8
14Aug04–8AP fm 1 3/16 Ⓣ :49⁴ 1:15² 1:39³ 1:56² 3↑ⒻBeverlyD-G1 101 1 4² 4¹½ 5³ 4¹½ 2½ Day P L123 8.40 91 – Crimson Palace123½ *Riskaverse*123^hd Necklace117^nk Ins, angled, missed 11
31Jly04–7Sar yl 1⅛ Ⓣ :47³ 1:11³ 1:36³ 1:48⁴ 3↑ⒻDianaH-G1 97 7 4⁶ 4⁸½ 3² 4⁵½ 2⁵¾ Day P L118 9.40 80–14 WonderAgain120⁵¾ Riskaverse118²¼ *OceanDrive*118²¼ Game finish outside 7
26Jun04–9CD fm 1⅛ Ⓣ :47 1:10³ 1:34³ 1:46³ 3↑ⒻLcstGrvH-G3 89 2 3³ 3³ 3² 4¹¼ 5⁴¼ Day P L118 *.60 96–07 Shaconge116¹¼ HloryLeigh111^no SndSprings119¹¾ Near hedge,flatten out 6
5Jun04–8Bel fm 1 Ⓣ :23³ :46⁴ 1:10¹ 1:33¹ 3↑ⒻJsAGmBCH-G2 97 7 1½ 2^hd 2½ 3¹½ 4²½ Day P L118 4.90 91–06 Intrcontinntl118¹¼ Vngurdi113½ EtoilMontnt121¾ Vied outside, weakened 8

River Belle (GB)

Own: Team Valor Stables Heiligbrodt Racing

Ch. f. 4 (Mar)
Sire: Lahib (Riverman) $3,763
Dam: Dixie Favor (Dixieland Band)
Br: Mrs S. Camacho (GB)
Tr: Pletcher Todd A(0 0 0 0 .00) 2004:(948 240 .25)

							D.Fst	0	0	0	0	$0	–
Life	8	4	0	2	$258,831	94	D.Fst	0	0	0	0	$0	–
2004	4	2	0	2	$202,613	94	Wet(320)	0	0	0	0	$0	–
2003	4	2	0	0	$56,218	–	Turf(294)	8	4	0	2	$258,831	94
	0	0	0	0	$0	–	Dst(0)	0	0	0	0	$0	–

13Nov04-9CD gd 1 1/16 Ⓣ :233 :481 1:132 1:442 ⒻMrsRvere-G2 **92** 2 4¾ 41½ 41½ 21½ 1no Fallon K L120 *1.60 82–20 RiverBelle120no Lenatareese120no CpeTownLss114½ 4w,between late,drvg 10

16Oct04-8Kee gd 1⅛ Ⓣ :493 1:142 1:384 1:511 ⒻQEIICup-G1 **94** 2 1½ 12 12 2½ 31 Bejarano R L121 13.60 80–20 Ticker Tape121½ Barancella121½ *River Belle*1211 Clear,couldn't last,3w 7

12Sep04-9Mth gd 1 1/16 Ⓣ :244 :50 1:141 1:453 +ⒻBoilSprn-G3 **91** 4 62 51¼ 1hd 1hd 31 Coa E M L117 2.40 70–32 Seducer's Song119½ Go Robin117½ River Belle1171 Inside trip, gamely 9

7Aug04-6Sar fm 1 Ⓣ :233 :474 1:122 1:362 3↑ⒻAlw 50000N2x **88** 10 98¾ 95½ 63¾ 2hd 11 Velazquez J R L116 2.90 89–11 River Belle1161 Whoopi Cat116½ *Pattiano*1211 Strong finish outside 10

Roar Emotion

Own: Allen Joseph

Dk. b or b. m. 5 (Mar)
Sire: Roar (Forty Niner) $15,000
Dam: Emotional Outburst (Capote)
Br: Brenda Jones (Ky)
Tr: McLaughlin Kiaran P(0 0 0 0 .00) 2004:(462 84 .18)

Life	17	5	4	3	$635,912	102	D.Fst	13	4	2	3	$356,312	102
2004	11	2	2	3	$328,652	102	Wet(382)	4	1	2	0	$279,600	102
2003	3	1	1	0	$150,660	93	Turf(290)	0	0	0	0	$0	–
	0	0	0	0	$0	–	Dst(0)	0	0	0	0	$0	–

18Dec04-8Aqu fst 1¼ ⊡ :494 1:144 1:393 2:052 3↑ⒻLadiesH-G3 **75** 5 2½ 21 21 45 510¼ Luzzi M J L119 *1.70 78–22 RreGift1156 BordElligibl117nk MissFortunt1173 Tracked, came up empty 8

26Nov04-9Aqu fst 1 :234 :464 1:11 1:351 3↑ⒻTopFlgtH-G2 **94** 3 31 31½ 2hd 1hd 32¼ Velazquez J R L116 3.50 87–17 Dydrmng117no BndngStrngs118 2¼ RorEmtn116 2¼ 3 wide move, weakened 6

6Nov04-9Aqu fst 1⅛ :484 1:13 1:381 1:511 3↑ⒻTnbkAlmH-G3 **96** 7 31 31 3nk 1½ 2½ Velazquez J R L117 7.10 82–24 PersonlLgnd115½ RorEmotion1174¾ FstCooki1142 Wide both turns, game 9

27Aug04-9Sar fst 1¼ :461 1:093 1:354 2:033 3↑ⒻPrsnlEnH-G1 **67** 4 11½ 1hd 21½ 512 522¼ Bailey J D L115 7.10 67–11 Storm Flag Flying1161¼ *Azeri*122½ Nevermore1144½ Set pace, tired 5

18Jly04-10Del sly 1¼ :47 1:113 1:364 2:033 3↑ⒻDelH-G2 **102** 5 12½ 11½ 12 14 21¼ Bailey J D L117 3.60 95–15 SummrWindDncr1161¼ RorEmoton1175¾ MstySxs116¾ Gamely to the end 8

12Jun04-8CD sly 1⅛ :473 1:124 1:384 1:52 3↑ⒻFlrDLisH-G2 **69** 3 11 11 1½ 54½ 615¾ Bailey J D L115 4.00 61–17 *Adoration*1221¼ Bare Necessities1203¾ *La Reason*1102 Bobble start,tired 6

15May04-8Bel fst 1 :234 :463 1:111 1:36 3↑ⒻShuveeH-G2 **102** 6 2½ 2½ 2hd 2hd 3½ Luzzi M J L117 3.10 80–19 StormFlgFlyng116½ PssngShot117no RorEmtn1178¼ Vied outside, gamely 6

16Apr04-9Kee fst 1 1/16 :231 :473 1:122 1:434 4↑ⒻDbldogdare114k **92** 6 31 31½ 3nk 2hd 34 Velazquez J R L116 *1.80 89–16 *MayoOntheSide*1161¾ CatFighter1162¼ RorEmotion116½ 4w,loomed,empty 8

14Mar04-6GP fst 1⅛ :482 1:114 1:372 1:51 3↑ⒻRampartH-G2 **71** 1 11½ 11 1hd 26 418½ Velazquez J R L118 1.50 65–27 Sightseek1217½ Redoubled Miss1132 *Lead Story*1179 Inside, nothing left 4

15Feb04-11GP fst 1 1/16 :234 :473 1:114 1:431 3↑ⒻSabinH-G3 **100** 6 21 2hd 2hd 14 15½ Velazquez J R L116 2.20 93–17 Roar Emotion1165½ *Nonsuch Bay*115¾ Lead Story1191¾ Vied, drew off 9

15Jan04-8GP fst 1 1/16 :234 :473 1:122 1:45 4↑ⒻOC 75k/N3x-N **91** 6 11½ 11 11½ 11 11 Velazquez J R L117 *.70 84–24 *Roar Emotion*1171 *Kiss Me Twice*11712¾ Paisley Park1171 Inside, driving 8

Rock Hard Ten
Own: Mercedes Stables LLC and Paulson Made

Dk. b or b. c. 4 (Apr)
Sire: Kris S. (Roberto) $150,000
Dam: Tersa (Mr. Prospector)
Br: Madeleine A. Paulson (Ky)
Tr: Mandella Richard E(0 0 0 0 .00) 2004:(160 24 .15)

Life	8	4	1	1	$790,380	109	D.Fst	8	4	1	1	$790,380	109
2004	8	4	1	1	$790,380	109	Wet(398)	0	0	0	0	$0	–
2003	0	M	0	0	$0	–	Turf(347)	0	0	0	0	$0	–
	0	0	0	0	$0	–	Dst(0)	0	0	0	0	$0	–

26Dec04–8SA fst 7f :221 :441 1:081 1:214 Malibu-G1 **100** 9 9 107 106½ 53 1½ Stevens G L LB121 2.40 96– 09 RockHardTen121½ LavaMan115no HrvrdAvenue115no Rallied btwn,up late 10
Previously trained by Orman Jason
8Aug04–13Mth fst 1⅛ :464 1:102 1:353 1:484 HskIInvH-G1 **83** 5 2½ 21½ 32 58½ 615½ Nakatani C S L120 *.90 81– 13 LionHert1211 MySnookiesBoy1162¼ PisProspct1163¼ Tired,not urged late 8
10Jly04–7Hol fst 1⅛ :47 1:102 1:343 1:472 SwapsBC-G2 **109** 3 22½ 21 21 12½ 13¾ Nakatani C S LB116 *.60 102 - Rock Hard Ten1163¾ Suave1203 Boomzeeboom1182½ Stalked,bid,cleared 6
5Jun04–11Bel fst 1½ :483 1:113 2:002 2:272 Belmont-G1 **86** 5 2hd 2½ 35 37½ 512 Solis A L126 6.70 83– 10 *Birdstone*1261 Smarty Jones1268 Royal Assault1263 Finished after mile 9
15May04–12Pim fst 1 3/16 :471 1:112 1:362 1:552 Preaknes-G1 **100** 9 74½ 77¼ 64½ 25 211½ Stevens G L L126 6.90 88– 13 SmrtyJons12611½ RockHrdTn1262 Eddington126hd 6-5wd to 3/8,angled in 10
3Apr04–8SA fst 1⅛ :464 1:11 1:362 1:491 SADerby-G1 **103** 6 33 32½ 4¾ 2hd 2hd Flores D R LB122 3.00 88– 09 Castledale122hd [D]Rock Hard Ten1222 Imperialism1221 4wd bid,drifted in 7
Disqualified and placed third
3Mar04–2SA fst 1 :224 :454 1:101 1:361 Alw 53872N1x **99** 5 52¼ 41½ 42 21 11¾ Stevens G L LB118 *.60 90– 18 RockHrdTn1181¾ TtonForst118½ JmmysInstnct1185 3 wide bid,ridden out 5
7Feb04–7SA fst 7f :223 :452 1:094 1:221 Md Sp Wt 44k **101** 5 5 32½ 31 21 11¼ Stevens G L LB120 6.40 94– 11 *Rock Hard Ten*1201¼ StormPilot1204 *PointofFlight*1204 Moderate hand ride 8

Rockport Harbor
Own: Fox Hill Farms Inc

Gr/ro. c. 3 (Apr) KEESEP03 $470,000
Sire: Unbridled's Song (Unbridled) $125,000
Dam: Regal Miss Copelan (Copelan)
Br: Heiligbrodt Racing Stable & Taylor Made Farm, Inc. (Ky)
Tr: Servis John C(0 0 0 0 .00) 2004:(284 68 .24)

Life	4	4	0	0	$210,300	102	D.Fst	4	4	0	0	$210,300	102
2004	4	4	0	0	$210,300	102	Wet(383)	0	0	0	0	$0	–
2003	0	M	0	0	$0	–	Turf(255)	0	0	0	0	$0	–
	0	0	0	0	$0	–	Dst(0)	0	0	0	0	$0	–

27Nov04–8Aqu fst 1⅛ :471 1:11 1:352 1:484 Remsen-G2 **102** 2 11 11½ 1hd 1hd 1nk Elliott S L120 1.30 95– 07 RockportHrbor120nk GllopingGrocer1208¼ Killnul1203½ Resolutely on rail 6
2Nov04–8Aqu fst 1 :224 :452 1:10 1:363 Nashua-G3 **84** 3 1hd 11½ 1½ 15½ 16¼ Elliott S L118 *.90 82– 22 *RockportHarbor*1186¼ *Defer*116hd *BetterThanBonds*1162¼ Drew away in hand 6
12Oct04–9Pha fst 6½f :22 :453 1:103 1:17 Alw 21000N1x **85** 1 5 11½ 13 15 17½ Elliott S 115 *.10 90– 18 *RockportHrbor*1157½ ItsTimtoSml1136½ ShnJuls1152¼ Drew off, ridden out 5
12Sep04–1Pha fst 5½f :222 :454 :582 1:05 Md Sp Wt 21k **73** 10 2 11 12 14 18¾ Elliott S 118 *.30 89– 15 *Rockport Harber*1188¾ The Love King118½ *Favalora*1183¾ Drew off, handily 10

Roman Ruler
Own: Fog City Stable

Dk. b or b. c. 3 (Mar) KEESEP03 $500,000
Sire: Fusaichi Pegasus (Mr. Prospector) $100,000
Dam: Silvery Swan (Silver Deputy)
Br: Needham/Betz, Liberation Fm & Ashford Stud (Ky)
Tr: Baffert Bob(0 0 0 0 .00) 2004:(562 105 .19)

Life	5	3	1	0	$330,800	106	**D.Fst** 5 3 1 0 $330,800 106
2004	5	3	1	0	$330,800	106	**Wet(364*)** 0 0 0 0 $0 –
2003	0	M	0	0	$0	–	**Turf(256*)** 0 0 0 0 $0 –
	0	0	0	0	$0	–	**Dst(0)** 0 0 0 0 $0 –

30Oct04–7LS fst 1 1/16 :232 :472 1:111 1:42 BCJuvnle-G1 **91** 2 7¾ 74¼ 53¼ 53 53¾ Nakatani C S L122 *2.00 88– 02 Wilko122¾ Afleet Alex122nk Sun King1221¼ Stdied 7-1/2,hard held 8
3Oct04–7SA fst 1 1/16 :23 :46 1:103 1:441 Norfolk-G2 **87** 4 21 21 2hd 14 14½ Nakatani C S **LB**120 b *.05 84– 17 Roman Ruler1204½ Boston Glory12013 Littlebitofzip1202 Pulled,bid,clear 4
8Sep04–8Dmr fst 7f :221 :443 1:084 1:211 DmrFut-G2 **106** 2 4 34½ 35½ 1½ 2nk Nakatani C S **LB**120 *.10 96– 11 *Declan's Moon*116nk *Roman Ruler*1209½ *Swiss Lad*1164 Off bit slw,stdy early 4
15Aug04–2Dmr fst 6½f :214 :444 1:093 1:154 BestPal-G2 **103** 2 5 48½ 45½ 12 17 Nakatani C S **LB**118 *.50 96– 10 Roman Ruler1187 Actxecutive11810 Slewsbag1161½ Stdied 5/16,ridden out 5
19Jun04–6Hol fst 5f :22 :444 :571 Md Sp Wt 46k **84** 10 6 41 3½ 1½ 14 Nakatani C S **LB**119 *.80 98– 08 *Roman Ruler*1194 Dance Thief119nk Roman Jake119½ 4wd,3wd,ridden out 10

Roses in May
Own: Ramsey Kenneth L. and Sarah K

Dk. b or b. h. 5 (Feb)
Sire: Devil His Due (Devil's Bag) $10,000
Dam: Tell a Secret (Speak John)
Br: Margaux Farm LLC (Ky)
Tr: Romans Dale L(0 0 0 0 .00) 2004:(580 109 .19)

Life	11	7	3	0	$1,795,187	119	**D.Fst** 10 6 3 0 $1,769,497 119
2004	6	5	1	0	$1,723,277	119	**Wet(342)** 1 1 0 0 $25,690 95
2003	5	2	2	0	$71,910	104	**Turf(296)** 0 0 0 0 $0 –
	0	0	0	0	$0	–	**Dst(0)** 0 0 0 0 $0 –

30Oct04–9LS fst 1¼ :47 1:111 1:351 1:59 3↑BCClasic-G1 **119** 6 2½ 2½ 21 22 23 Velazquez J R L126 8.70 – – Ghostzapper1263 RosesinMay1264 PlesntlyPerfect126¾ Held well for 2nd 13
18Sep04–11TP fst 1⅛ :472 1:113 1:362 1:49 3↑KyCpClH-G2 **105** 5 1hd 1hd 2hd 12½ 14 Velazquez J R L118 *.30 91– 11 Roses in May1184 Pie N Burger117¾ Sonic West113nk 2path to str, driving 6
7Aug04–9Sar fst 1⅛ :451 1:084 1:344 1:482 3↑WhitneyH-G1 **114** 2 2½ 2½ 22½ 1hd 1no Prado E S L114 7.40 93– 14 *RosesinMy*114no PerfectDrift1172¼ BowmnsBnd114no Resolutely, got nod 9
3Jly04–9PrM fst 1⅛ :464 1:101 1:342 1:463 3↑CrnhsBCH-G3 **113** 1 11 11 1½ 1½ 11½ Guidry M **LB**115 2.70 105– 12 *Roses in May*1151½ Perfect Drift1194 Crafty Shaw1174¾ Well rated, driving 6
21May04–3CD fst 1 1/16 :231 :462 1:112 1:432 3↑OC 62k/N$Y-N **99** 3 11 11½ 12½ 12 15 Day P L121 *.10 91– 13 *RosesinMay*1215 StrengthWithin121½ TacticalWar121½ Sluggish start,drvg 5
17Apr04–8Kee fst 1 1/16 :231 :471 1:114 1:423 4↑Alw 58000N2X **113** 8 11½ 11½ 11½ 14½ 112 Bailey J D L116 *2.00 99– 11 *RosesinMy*11612 *BestMinister*1161 OneNiceCt1182¾ Hand urging,much best 8

Royal Place
Own: Sangara K. K

B. h. 5 (Feb)
Sire: Out of Place (Cox's Ridge) $7,500
Dam: British Bauble (Kris S.)
Br: Meadowbrook Farms, Inc. (Fla)
Tr: Becerra Rafael(0 0 0 0 .00) 2004:(258 36 .14)

Life	28	6	4	3	$330,266	105	D.Fst	13 4 2 0	$201,340	105
2004	10	2	1	2	$137,696	105	Wet(385)	3 0 0 1	$20,956	86
2003	14	3	2	1	$147,432	99	Turf(297)	12 2 2 2	$107,970	102
	0	0	0	0	$0	–	Dst(0)	0 0 0 0	$0	–

27Dec04–6SA fm 1 Ⓣ :241 :481 1:121 1:352 3↑OC 100k/N$MY 102 6 11½ 12 11½ 1½ 31 Gomez G K LB121 f 22.30 84– 15 BucklandManor119nk Inesperdo119¾ RoylPlce121½ Fought back rail,game 8
26Nov04–8GG fst 1 1/16 :223 :462 1:104 1:42 3↑FortyNinrH82k 62 6 43½ 43½ 64 813 919¾ Carr D LB117 16.30 73– 20 Yougottawn118nk Adremisborn1193½ MyCreed1141 Steadied 3/8p, empty 9
Previously trained by Barroby Harold J
17Oct04–8Hst sly 1⅜ :464 1:134 1:41 2:193 3↑PremierH-G3 86 6 410 43 52½ 44½ 32¾ Alvarado P V L121 2.90 83– 14 BlowininthWind114nk IllusivForc1192½ RoylPlc121hd 3 wide, finished well 10
Previously trained by Becerra Rafael
26Sep04–11Fpx fst *1⅛ :453 1:103 1:361 1:493 3↑HndPomInvH99k 82 1 31 2hd 3nk 68 45¾ Sorenson D LB119 3.70 89– 07 HotelHll115nk NoseTheTrde1204½ KristinesKing1171 3w,chkd 5/16,imprvd 8
22Aug04–7EmD sly 1 :221 :443 1:091 1:344 3↑LgaMileH-G3 81 11 76¾ 53¼ 43 67 69¼ Valdivia J Jr LB118 f 6.20 82– 21 Adremisborn1161 DemonWrlcck1145¾ MrMkh112¾ Wide turns,bumped3/16 12
1Jly04–9Hst fst 1⅛ :463 1:111 1:353 1:49 3↑LtGovrnH-G3 99 5 21 2½ 2½ 2hd 1nk Olguin G L L119 5.45 100– 06 Royal Place119nk Lord Nelson1234¼ Roscoe Pito119hd Rail, driving 8
19May04–7Hol fm 1 1/16 Ⓣ :242 :483 1:114 1:41 4↑Alw 58000N3X 97 7 2½ 1hd 1½ 11 42 Valdivia J Jr LB120 *1.50 89– 14 Sigint118nk Tronare1221½ Wixoe Express120nk Dueled,led,lost 3rd 7
16Apr04–3SA fst 1 :223 :45 1:084 1:343 4↑Alw 63700N$MY 105 1 11 1½ 11 11 2½ Valdivia J Jr LB116 2.10 97– 14 Buddy Gil116½ Royal Place1167 Touch theWire1187 Inside,worn down late 4
6Mar04–10SA fst 1¼ :461 1:101 1:351 2:013 4↑SAH-G1 92 3 2hd 2hd 21½ 55 714 Valdivia J Jr LB114 43.50 77– 11 SouthrnImg1131¼ IslndFshion1152¼ SintBuddy1114 Dueled btwn,gave way 8
31Jan04–6SA fst 1 :222 :454 1:094 1:35 4↑Alw 56000N2X 100 5 31 21 2hd 12½ 13½ Valdivia J Jr LB119 *2.60 96– 06 Royal Place1193½ Hotel Hall119no Infinite Faith119hd Bid,led,drew clear 10

Runway Model
Own: Chowhan Naveed

Dk. b or b. f. 3 (Mar) OBSFEB04 $260,000
Sire: Petionville (Seeking the Gold) $15,000
Dam: Ticket to Houston (Houston)
Br: Everest Stables, Inc. (Ky)
Tr: Flint Bernard S(0 0 0 0 .00) 2004:(575 124 .22)

Life	10	4	2	2	$580,598	93	D.Fst	9 4 2 2	$579,518	93
2004	10	4	2	2	$580,598	93	Wet(313)	1 0 0 0	$1,080	29
2003	0	M	0	0	$0	–	Turf(193)	0 0 0 0	$0	–
	0	0	0	0	$0	–	Dst(0)	0 0 0 0	$0	–

27Nov04–9CD fst 1 1/16 :24 :472 1:13 1:454 ⒻGoldnRod-G2 82 1 46 42 1hd 11½ 13 Martin E M Jr L122 *1.10 79– 25 Runway Model1223 Kota1181¾ Summerly1164 4w,steady drive 6
30Oct04–3LS fst 1 1/16 :224 :462 1:103 1:413 ⒻBCJuvFil-G1 93 3 55 63¼ 61¼ 41 35 Bejarano R L119 10.00 89– 02 SweetCatomine1193¾ Balletto1191¼ RunwyModel119¾ Blocked 1/8 and 1/16 12
8Oct04–9Kee fst 1 1/16 :223 :464 1:113 1:441 ⒻAlcibiad-G2 90 8 88½ 63¼ 62¼ 63¼ 1hd Bejarano R L118 17.20 91– 17 Runway Model118hd Sharp Lisa118no In the Gold118½ Rallied 4-5w,driving 10
19Sep04–9AP fst 1 :233 :47 1:12 1:364 ⒻArlWaLas-G3 83 3 74¾ 54 53½ 32½ 22 Albarado R J 118 *2.20 82– 20 Culinary1162 Runway Model1183½ Kota1182 Just outside, 2nd best 8
4Sep04–10RD fst 6f :221 :45 :58 1:103 ⒻBassinet100k 86 11 7 85¼ 55½ 31 2nk Johnston J A 120 3.30 102– 07 ImDixieGirl120nk RunwyModel1204 GllntScrt1201½ Lunged start, too late 11
15Aug04–10RD fst 6f :221 :453 :582 1:114 ⒻAlw 25000NC 88 9 5 32 1hd 15 19¼ Johnston J A 115 *.70 96– 12 Runway Model1159¼ Swede1175¼ A. P. Sheauxgirl1205¼ Ridden out 9
4Jly04–11CD fst 5½f :213 :452 :573 1:04 ⒻDebutant-G3 61 8 8 86¼ 63½ 77¼ 76¼ Martinez W 117 8.90 86– 11 ClassicElegance1171 PargonQueen1173½ CoolSpell117nk 7-8w lane,no rally 9
6Jun04–5CD fst 5½f :223 :46 :582 1:043 ⒻMd Sp Wt 43k 74 6 2 72½ 41½ 2hd 12½ Martinez W 119 6.00 89– 09 RunwayModel1192½ KristenKristen1191 PrivteGift1195 4-5w,driving,clear 9
16May04–6CD fst 4½f :221 :453 :514 ⒻMd Sp Wt 38k 70 6 4 65½ 55 32½ Martinez W 118 11.60 93– 13 SweetMissE118nk ParagonQueen1182¼ RunwyModel1181½ 5w lane,mild gain 11
30Apr04–1CD sly 4½f :232 :462 :524 ⒻMd Sp Wt 39k 29 6 8 56 68¼ 512¾ Albarado R J 118 6.90 78– 16 Maddalena1185¾ Sutton's Bay118½ Cool Spell1182 Bmp start,checked 8

Sabiango (Ger)
Own: Roberts Monty

Ch. h. 7 (Apr)
Sire: Acatenango*Ger (Surumu*Ger) $15,750
Dam: Spirit of Eagles (Beau's Eagle)
Br: Stiftung Gestut Fahrhof (Ger)
Tr: Yakteen Tim(0 0 0 0 .00) 2004:(28 5 .18)

Life	19	7	1	2	$828,333	106	D.Fst	0 0 0 0	$0	–
2004	4	2	0	0	$334,000	106	Wet(273)	0 0 0 0	$0	–
2003	6	1	0	1	$218,563	103	Turf(359)	19 7 1 2	$828,333	106
	0	0	0	0	$0	–	Dst(0)	0 0 0 0	$0	–

24Oct04–9WO gd 1½ Ⓣ :494 1:141 2:044 2:283 3↑CanIntnl-G1 **74** 10 21 1hd 2hd 917 923 Blanc B L126 22.25 64– 13 Sulamani126 1½ Simonas1262 Brian Boru126¾ Tired top stretch 10
25Sep04–14KD fm 1½ Ⓣ :534 1:223 2:102 2:333 3↑KyCpTrfH-G3 **95** 4 13½ 11 11 12 13 Blanc B L119 *1.30 75– 15 Sabiango1193 Rochester117½ Gottabechboy115nk Rated on pace,hand urg 6
Previously trained by Baffert Bob
14Aug04–9AP fm 1¼ Ⓣ :472 1:12 1:363 2:00 3↑ArlMilln-G1 **88** 5 21½ 21 1hd 1113 1111½ Espinoza V L126 15.00 99 - DPowerscourt126 1½ Kicken Kris1261 *Magistretti*126½ Stalked, tired 13
12Jun04–3Hol fm 1¼ Ⓣ :503 1:15 1:381 2:012 3↑CWhtghmH-G1 **106** 3 11½ 12½ 13 11½ 1¾ Baze T C LB116 13.40 85– 12 Sabiango116¾ *Bayamo*116no Just Wonder1162½ Inside,held gamely 11

Saint Liam
Own: Warren Jr., Mr. and Mrs. William K

B. h. 5 (Apr)
Sire: Saint Ballado (Halo) $125,000
Dam: Quiet Dance (Quiet American)
Br: Edward P. Evans (Ky)
Tr: Dutrow R E Jr(0 0 0 0 .00) 2004:(603 166 .28)

Life	14	5	5	1	$760,035	114	D.Fst	12 5 4 1	$751,335	114
2004	5	2	2	1	$618,760	114	Wet(381)	1 0 1 0	$8,700	96
2003	9	3	3	0	$141,275	100	Turf(270)	1 0 0 0	$0	75
	0	0	0	0	$0	–	Dst(0)	0 0 0 0	$0	–

26Nov04–11CD fst 1⅛ :48 1:12 1:372 1:504 3↑ClarkH-G2 **110** 2 2½ 21½ 2hd 11½ 11¼ Prado E S L117 b *1.20 83– 25 SaintLim1171¼ SeekGold111no PerfectDrift1181¼ Exch bmps start,4w,drv 9
11Sep04–10Bel fst 1⅛ :453 1:083 1:331 1:461 3↑Woodward-G1 **114** 1 2hd 1½ 1hd 1hd 2nk Prado E S L126 11.70 100– 15 *Ghostzapper*126nk *SaintLiam*1269¼ BowmansBnd1267¼ Drifted out, bumped 7
3Apr04–11OP fst 1⅛ :452 1:093 1:352 1:481 4↑OaklawnH-G2 **108** 2 11 1½ 1hd 21½ 32¼ Prado E S L114 1.90 95– 09 Peace Rules1202 Ole Faunty116nk Saint Liam1142¼ Dueled, missed 2nd 6
29Feb04–9FG fst 1⅛ :47 1:102 1:352 1:483 4↑NwOrlnsH-G2 **113** 4 22 22 21 2hd 2hd Prado E S L114 5.60 101– 05 *Peace Rules*119hd Saint Liam1142¾ *Funny Cide*1181¼ Led, out kicked late 8
18Jan04–6GP fst 1 1/16 :23 :464 1:112 1:43 4↑OC 75k/N3x-N **108** 6 52½ 41¼ 21 1hd 14 Prado E S L122 *.90 94– 19 Saint Liam1224 *The Lady'sGroom*1182¾ GranCesare1222½ 4 wide, ridden out 8

Saratoga County
Own: Pollard Evelyn M

B. c. 4 (Mar) OBSFEB03 $100,000
Sire: Valid Expectations (Valid Appeal) $17,500
Dam: Grub's Dancer (Grub)
Br: Round Table LLC (Ky)
Tr: Weaver George(0 0 0 0 .00) 2004:(401 46 .11)

Life 14 3 4 1 $266,590 108 | D.Fst 10 2 3 1 $126,840 108
2004 12 2 3 1 $237,390 108 | Wet(371) 3 1 0 0 $129,950 96
2003 2 1 1 0 $29,200 87 | Turf(238) 1 0 1 0 $9,800 89
0 0 0 0 $0 – | Dst(0) 0 0 0 0 $0 –

27Nov04–7CD fst 7f :22² :44⁴ 1:09² 1:22³ 3↑Alw 46910N2x 108 3 6 3²½ 3½ 1⁴ 1⁵¼ Johnson J M L117 fb 5.10 89–15 Saratoga County117⁵¼ Kenta Kun121¾ Ominous119¹¼ Tracked,4w,driving 12
30Oct04–3Kee fst *7f :22¹ :44⁴ 1:10¹ 1:26³ 3↑Alw 52060N2x 93 5 6 5⁴½ 5³¼ 2¹½ 2⁵¼ Borel C H L116 ft *1.00 88–16 Chachacharlie116⁵¼ *SaratogaCounty*116³½ Kuch119½ Bmp start,5w,2ndbest 7
3Oct04–4Bel fm 7f Ⓣ :23² :45⁴ 1:08⁴ 1:21¹ 3↑Alw 49000N2x 89 2 3 5¹½ 4³ 2⁷ 2¹¼ Velasquez C L117 fb 9.60 93–06 Heckle117¹¼ Saratoga County117¹¾ Ball Four121² Between rivals, gamely 6
18Sep04–9Bel sly 1 :23³ :46³ 1:10³ 1:35³ JeromeH-G2 92 3 21 2¹½ 2⁵ 3⁷ 4⁹½ Velasquez C L115 fb 11.50 73–29 Teton Forest116⁶ Ice WynndFire116¾ Mahzouz112²¾ Bumped start, inside 7
28Aug04–10Sar fst 7f :22 :44³ 1:08² 1:20⁴ KngsBshp-G1 84 7 1 6⁴¼ 8⁷ 6⁹¾ 5¹⁰¾ Castellano J J L121 b 36.75 89–04 Pomeroy121¹½ Weigelia121¹ Ice Wynnd Fire117⁴¼ Between foes, no rally 8
31Jly04–9Sar my 7f :21⁴ :44⁴ 1:09¹ 1:22³ 3↑Alw 49000N2x 80 2 9 5³½ 5³ 4⁸½ 4¹³ Bailey J D L116 fb *1.60 78–11 *Top Shoter*122³½ *Willy o'the Valley*119⁸¼ Wildly117¹¼ Steadied into turn 10
5Jun04–9Bel fst 7f :22² :45 1:08⁴ 1:20⁴ RvaRdgBC-G2 98 1 7 7⁶ 7⁷½ 5⁵¾ 4⁵ Castellano J J L123 fb 17.40 91–07 *Fire Slam*123hd *Teton Forest*115³¼ Abbondanza123¹¾ Mild rally outside 7
1May04–8Aqu fst 1 :22² :44 1:07⁴ 1:34² Withers-G3 92 2 5²¾ 4⁴½ 3³½ 4⁶ 4⁹½ Luzzi M J L123 fb 5.30 83–19 *Mdllst*116³¼ FirstDngr123¹ TwoDownAutomtc120⁵¼ Chased outside, tired 5
17Apr04–9Kee fst 1¹⁄₁₆ :23¹ :47¹ 1:12 1:43⁴ Lexingtn-G2 77 14 10⁶¾ 9⁶ 7³¾ 6⁹½ 7¹⁴¼ Castellano J J L116 fb 9.60 79–11 QuntonsGoldRsh116²¾ *FrSlm*116nk SongofthSword116² Bid far turn,tired 14
20Mar04–7Aqu gd 1 :21⁴ :43³ 1:08 1:35² Gotham-G3 96 5 5¹½ 5¹½ 3² 1½ 1²¼ Castellano J J L116 fb 4.70 88–14 SartogCounty116²¼ Pomeroy116¾ Eddington116⁵¼ Came wide, drew clear 8
14Feb04–10GP fst 7f :21³ :43³ 1:08⁴ 1:22¹ Hutchesn-G2 90 3 10 10¹⁰ 9¹⁰ 6⁷½ 3⁴ Coa E M L116 fb 13.70 87–07 *Limehous*122²½ DputyStorm118¹¾ *SrtogCounty*116¾ Hit gate,checked early 10
10Jan04–8GP fst 6f :22² :45⁴ :58¹ 1:10³ SpectBid-G3 92 5 6 3² 2hd 3¹ 2¹¼ Velazquez J R L116 fb 3.60 88–20 WynnDotComm120¹¼ SrtogConty116¾ GhstMntn120½ Floated out top str 7

Scooter Roach
Own: Butterfly Stable

B. g. 6 (Mar)
Sire: Mi Cielo (Conquistador Cielo) $2,500
Dam: Heroic Dreams (Mr. Leader)
Br: Mr. & Mrs. Terrel Gore (Ill)
Tr: Kassen David C(0 0 0 0 .00) 2004:(140 20 .14)

Life 39 7 6 5 $541,577 100 | D.Fst 21 3 4 4 $194,857 95
2004 12 2 3 3 $213,827 100 | Wet(329) 2 1 0 0 $21,360 78
2003 10 1 2 1 $94,256 92 | Turf(307) 16 3 2 1 $325,360 100
0 0 0 0 $0 – | Dst(0) 0 0 0 0 $0 –

18Dec04–11Crc fm 1½ Ⓣ :49¹ 1:13⁴ 2:03 2:26³ 3↑WLMcKntH-G2 100 3 3² 3¹½ 3¹½ 5²¼ 3¾ Bravo J L115 35.00 90–10 Dreadnaught116nk Demeteor112½ Scooter Roach115½ Gave grnd, rallied 12
13Nov04–9Haw fst 1¹⁄₁₆ :24¹ :48 1:13 1:45¹ 3↑ⓈHiAlexndrH96k 86 2 7⁶¾ 7⁸ 7³¾ 6⁴ 5⁵¼ Campbell J M L121 2.30 74–25 Home of Stars116¹¾ Magic Doe115¹½ Wiggins123¹¾ Improved position 11
9Oct04–8Haw fm 1 Ⓣ :23⁴ :47² 1:11 1:34² 3↑CareyMmH-G3 94 4 6³ 6³½ 5³½ 3¹ 1nk Campbell J M L115 18.60 99–04 ScooterRoch115nk GinndSin116½ CloudysKnight116¹ Angled out, driving 9
10Sep04–8AP fst 1 :24 :47¹ 1:11² 1:36⁴ 3↑OC 62k/N3x 85 7 5²½ 5³½ 5¹¼ 4² 3²½ Campbell J M L118 *1.70 81–24 *Bodgiteer*118¾ *Fiery Diablo*118¹¾ *Scooter Roach*118¹ 4 wide, late bid 7
21Aug04–7AP fst 1⅛ :49 1:12⁴ 1:37² 1:50 3↑OC 62k/N3x 94 7 3⁴ 3² 3² 3² 2³ Campbell J M L119 4.50 90–16 IntelligentMale121³ ScooterRoch119¹¼ BkerRod119⁴ 3 wide, second best 7
29Jly04–7AP fst 1 :23⁴ :46¹ 1:10¹ 1:35¹ 3↑OC 62k/N3x 94 1 6⁶½ 6⁹¾ 6⁸½ 4⁵ 2⁴ Campbell J M L119 5.50 88–16 Sterling Gold119⁴ Scooter Roach119½ Flip123¾ Inside-through traffic 7
10Jly04–9AP fst 1⅛ :47² 1:11⁴ 1:37 1:49² 3↑BlckTiAfrH75k 90 3 6⁷ 6¹⁰ 6⁸½ 4³½ 4⁵½ Campbell J M L115 25.80 90–18 Alumni Hall116²½ *Wiggins*117½ Stratostar114²½ Bit fractious in gate 7
26Jun04–8AP gd 1¹⁄₁₆ Ⓣ :24² :49² 1:14 1:44² 3↑ⓈCardinalH84k 79 6 5³½ 3² 3¹½ 7²¾ 7² Campbell J M L120 7.00 85–14 Runaway Victor112hd Colorful Tour119¹ *Home of Stars*115no Weakened 7
3Jun04–8AP yl *1 Ⓣ :25 :51 1:17³ 1:43³ 3↑OC c-62k/N3x 89 1 1¹ 1¹½ 1¹ 1hd 2¹ Campbell J M L122 2.50 60–45 On the Course122¹ Scooter Roach122¾ Lacer120¹⁰½ Couldn't last 8
Claimed from Win, IV LLC for $62,500, Boyce Michele Trainer 2004(as of 6/3): (72 11 9 10 0.15)
2May04–6Haw fm 1¹⁄₁₆ Ⓣ :23² :47⁴ 1:11³ 1:41 4↑OC 100k/c 87 2 6⁴½ 7⁵ 6³¼ 6³¼ 4¹½ Campbell J M L122 6.20 92–05 Great Bloom120hd Garesche118¹ *Major Rhythm*116½ Belatedly 7
10Apr04–7Haw fst 1¹⁄₁₆ :25¹ :49³ 1:13⁴ 1:46² 3↑ⓈMilwakAveH92k 95 4 5³½ 5³½ 6³¼ 2½ 1½ Campbell J M L116 *3.00 73–33 Scooter Roach116½ *Wiggins*122nk Act of War117²¾ 3 wide, driving 7
15Mar04–4Haw fst 1⁷⁰ :25³ :50 1:14² 1:44 4↑OC 100k/N1Y 85 1 2¹ 5¹¼ 5²¼ 4³½ 3⁵ Campbell J M L116 2.50 73–36 Cat Tracker116²¾ Garesche122²¼ *Scooter Roach*116nk Belatedly 5

Seattle Borders
Own: Gann Edmund A

B. c. 4 (Feb)
Sire: Western Borders (Gone West) $2,500
Dam: Assets On Ice (Seattle Dancer)
Br: CaroLin Stables Inc (Fla)
Tr: Frankel Robert J(0 0 0 0 .00) 2004:(491 135 .27)

Life	10	2	3	1	$151,410	91	D.Fst	4	0	2	0	$43,340	84
2004	5	1	1	1	$116,670	91	Wet(314)	0	0	0	0	$0	-
2003	5	1	2	0	$34,740	76	Turf(274*)	6	2	1	1	$108,070	91
	0	0	0	0	$0	-	Dst(0)	0	0	0	0	$0	-

24Jun04-7Hol fm 5½f Ⓣ :214 :443 :5611:02 3↑Alw 50400N2x 68 5 1 42 55 67¼ 610¾ Solis A LB116 4.90 84-05 *Geronimo*1211½ Tunder Ponche118nk Tikkun1191 3wd to turn,weakened 6
5May04-7Hol fm 1 Ⓣ :231 :461 1:0911:34 Alw 54000N2x 88 3 42½ 41½ 21 21 63¼ Santiago Javier LB118 *2.10 91-09 Terroplane1181 WildBbe118nk KingdomCome122no 3wd move,bid,wkened 7
10Apr04-8SA fm 1 Ⓣ :223 :453 1:0941:34 LaPuente110k 91 7 43½ 46½ 21½ 2hd 31¾ Garcia M S LB116 4.20 90-12 Toasted1151¼ Erewhon116½ Seattle Borders1161 Bid,led,outkicked 9
13Mar04-7GG fst 1 1/16 :23 :464 1:11 1:434 ElCamRID-G3 84 10 33 31 31 31½ 2½ ⬇Desormeaux K J LB117 *1.90 83-16 Kilgowan116½ [DH]Capitano116 [DH]Seattle Borders117hd Stlkd 3w, gamely 10
28Feb04-8SA gd *6½f Ⓣ :221 :444 1:0741:14 Baldwin-G3 90 2 5 4¾ 52¾ 31½ 11 Solis A LB114 5.30 87-13 SettleBorders1141 StlkingTiger117½ JunglPrinc114½ Came out,rallied 3wd 10

Seattle Fitz (Arg)
Own: West Point Stable

Dk. b or b. h. 6 (Oct)
Sire: Fitzcarraldo*Arg (Cipayo*Arg)
Dam: Hug a Slew (Seattle Slew)
Br: Firmamento (Arg)
Tr: McLaughlin Kiaran P(0 0 0 0 .00) 2004:(462 84 .18)

Life	21	6	3	2	$594,371	113	D.Fst	17	6	1	2	$544,231	113
2004	7	3	1	0	$404,810	113	Wet(401)	4	0	2	0	$50,140	102
2003	12	2	2	2	$170,636	111	Turf(317)	0	0	0	0	$0	-
	0	0	0	0	$0	-	Dst(0)	0	0	0	0	$0	-

7Aug04-9Sar fst 1⅛ :4511:084 1:3441:482 3↑WhitneyH-G1 89 7 43½ 42½ 45½ 911 915 Migliore R L117 5.50 78-14 *RosesinMay*114no PerfectDrift1172¼ BowmnsBnd114no 4 wide throughout 9
12Jun04-7Bel fst 1⅛ :4511:082 1:3321:461 3↑BroklynH-G2 113 1 2hd 1hd 1½ 1½ 1½ Migliore R L116 3.00 100-03 Seattle Fitz116½ Dynever1172¾ Newfoundland1155¾ Vied outside, gamely 6
15May04-8Pim fst 1⅛ :4741:12 1:3631:492 3↑WDShferH-G3 111 4 31½ 31 2½ 11½ 11½ Migliore R L116 *1.50 97-13 *SettleFitz*1161½ ThLdysGroom1155¼ RoringFvr1141 Ratd bck 7/8,3w,drivng 8
3Apr04-9GP fst 1¼ :4721:112 1:3622:024 3↑GPH-G2 86 4 33½ 34 43½ 57½ 614½ Gryder A T L115 *.70 85-15 Jackpot1132 Newfoundland1161 *The Lady's Groom*1131¾ Inside, faltered 6
29Feb04-9FG fst 1⅛ :47 1:102 1:3521:483 4↑NwOrlnsH-G2 106 1 44 43½ 43½ 33 44 Velazquez J R L115 *2.60 97-05 *Peace Rules*119hd Saint Liam1142¾ *Funny Cide*1181¼ Inside, lacked kick 8
7Feb04-10GP fst 1⅛ :4711:11 1:3531:473 3↑DonnH-G1 109 7 54¾ 52½ 52½ 23 24¾ Velazquez J R L113 9.80 96-09 MedagliadOro1224¾ SettleFitz1133¾ FunnyCide1194 Angled 4 wd, 2nd best 8
17Jan04-4Aqu fst 1 1/16 [•] :224 :46 1:1011:42 3↑AquH-G3 111 8 21½ 21½ 2½ 1hd 1no Gryder A T L114 2.70 101-13 SettleFitz114no EveningAttir1221¼ RoguAgnt1128¾ Outside move, gamely 8

Second of June
Own: Cesare Barbara

Dk. b or b. c. 4 (Jun) OBSWIN03 $7,500
Sire: Louis Quatorze (Sovereign Dancer) $6,000
Dam: Whow (Spectacular Bid)
Br: Lambholm & E. Felcher (Fla)
Tr: Cesare William J(0 0 0 0 .00) 2004:(202 15 .07)

Life	8	4	3	0	$230,400	113	D.Fst	8	4	3	0	$230,400	113
2004	3	1	2	0	$115,600	113	Wet(351)	0	0	0	0	$0	-
2003	5	3	1	0	$114,800	97	Turf(241)	0	0	0	0	$0	-
	0	0	0	0	$0	-	Dst(0)	0	0	0	0	$0	-

27Dec04-6Crc fst 1 1/16 :244 :492 1:1341:46 3↑OC 62k/N4x-N 100 1 21½ 21 2½ 2hd 2nk Velasquez C L114 f *.70 82-21 SmoothLovr117nk ScondofJn1141 Consrvton1175 Bobbled st,brushed str 5
14Feb04-11GP fst 1 1/16 :234 :473 1:1111:423 FntnOYth-G2 113 7 21½ 2½ 11 1½ 2nk Velasquez C L120 f *1.50 96-14 RedtheFootnots122nk ScondofJun1207½ SilvrWgon1205½ Off rail, gamely 8
17Jan04-10GP fst 1 1/16 :24 :481 1:1221:43 HolyBull-G3 111 5 4¾ 2½ 2hd 11½ 12¾ Velasquez C L122 f 2.80 94-24 SecondofJune1222¾ SilverWagon12010 *FriendsLake*122½ 3 wide, drew clear 9

Seducer's Song
Own: Karches Peter F

Gr/ro. f. 4 (Apr)
Sire: Unbridled's Song (Unbridled) $125,000
Dam: Seducer (Housebuster)
Br: Peter Karches (Ky)
Tr: Clement Christophe(0 0 0 0 .00) 2004:(344 68 .20)

Life	8	4	1	1	$239,760	98	D.Fst	3	1	0	1	$23,360	78
2004	8	4	1	1	$239,760	98	Wet(382)	0	0	0	0	$0	–
2003	0	M	0	0	$0	–	Turf(285)	5	3	1	0	$216,400	98
	0	0	0	0	$0	–	Dst(J)	0	0	0	0	$0	–

12Sep04–9Mth gd 1 1/16 Ⓣ :24[4] :50 1:14[1] 1:45[3] + ⒻBoilSprn-G3 **93** 8 5 1 3/4 6 1 1/2 3 1 1/2 2hd 1 1/2 Bravo J L119 *1.00 71–32 Seducer's Song119 1/2 Go Robin117 1/2 River Belle117[1] Rallied 3 wide 9
21Aug04–3Dmr fm 1 1/8 Ⓣ :46[2] 1:10[1] 1:34[2] 1:46[1] ⒻDmrOaks-G1 **96** 5 2 1/2 21 1hd 2 1/2 4 1 1/2 Smith M E LB122 3.00 96–02 Amorama122no *Ticker Tape*122[1] Sweet Win122 1/2 Led into str,outkicked 7
2Aug04–8Sar gd 1 1/16 Ⓣ :25 :49 1:12[1] 1:42 ⒻLkGeorge-G3 **98** 5 8 3 1/2 7 3 3/4 42 1hd 1 1 1/2 Bailey J D L115 6.70 85–15 SeducersSong115 1 1/2 Venturi119no FortunteDmsl117nk Steadied first turn 10
2Jly04–8Bel fm 1 Ⓣ :22[3] :45[3] 1:09[1] 1:33[1] ⒻⓇFieldy62k **93** 1 3 1 1/2 32 2 1/2 2hd 2 1/2 Santos J A L119 2.35 93–09 FortuntDmsl119 1/2 *SdcrsSong*119 1/2 JnnysGold122 7 1/2 Gamely between rivals 7
4Jun04–8Bel fm 1 Ⓣ :22[3] :45 1:09[1] 1:34[3] 3↑ⒻAlw 46000N1x **88** 2 6 8 3/4 510 37 3 1/2 1 1/2 Santos J A L115 *1.15e 87–14 SducrsSong115 1/2 DH *SvnMoons*124 DH HighSpdAccss117 1 1/2 Clear trip inside 11
4Apr04–7GP fst 1 1/16 :23[3] :47[4] 1:12[1] 1:46[1] ⒻMd Sp Wt 32k **78** 6 3 2 1/2 32 2 1 1/2 2hd 13 Bravo J L121 *1.40 78–23 *SeducersSong*121[3] MrnApprovd121hd *GoldDncr*121[5] Ckd 1st turn, bmpd str 10
7Mar04–9GP fst 6f :21[2] :45 :57[2] 1:10[4] ⒻMd Sp Wt 32k **67** 8 5 56 54 44 3 1 1/4 Santos J A L121 *1.20 87–08 Smile Maker121 1/2 *Wildcard Cat*121 3/4 *Seducer's Song*121[1] Finished willingly 9
15Feb04–4GP fst 6f :22 :45 :57[3] 1:10[2] ⒻMd Sp Wt 32k **44** 9 10 9 4 1/4 76 612 6 14 1/4 Prado E S 121 *2.00 76–11 Areek121 5 1/2 Letussoupriseyou121[7] Joyjoyjoy121no Hit gate, bumped start 10

See Me Through
Own: Jawl Michael

Ch. f. 4 (Jan) KEESEP02 $55,000
Sire: Sky Classic (Nijinsky II) $12,500
Dam: Youcan'taffordher (Carson City)
Br: Upson Downs Farm & Alistin Farms (Ky)
Tr: Peery Chuck(0 0 0 0 .00) 2004:(152 22 .14)

Life	11	2	3	2	$159,164	81	D.Fst	5	0	2	2	$30,694	74
2004	10	2	3	1	$157,041	81	Wet(394)	5	2	1	0	$127,220	81
2003	1	M	0	1	$2,123	53	Turf(300)	1	0	0	0	$1,250	73
	0	0	0	0	$0	–	Dst(0)	0	0	0	0	$0	–

14Nov04–8GG yl 1 1/16 Ⓣ :24[1] :48[2] 1:13[1] 1:45[1] +3↑ⒻStarBallH51k **73** 7 2hd 1hd 2hd 2hd 5 6 3/4 Baze R A LB120 f 6.50 77–16 Frisco Belle118 1/2 Stormica116no Shezsospiritual118no Alternated lead 2w 7
Previously trained by Krasner Cindy
16Oct04–8Hst gd 1 1/8 :47[4] 1:12[3] 1:38 1:51[2] 3↑ⒻBlrinaBC-G3 **81** 4 11 1hd 11 1 3 1/2 1 3 1/2 Alvarado P V L121 f 8.45 88–15 SMThrough121 3 1/2 SummrSymphony121 2 3/4 YoundNlly124 1/2 Led throughout 11
25Sep04–8Hst fst 1 1/8 :47[2] 1:12[1] 1:37[4] 1:51 ⒻBCBCOaks-G3 **74** 7 11 11 12 1 1 1/2 3 3 1/4 Alvarado P V L121 f 9.40 87–08 SmmrSymphony121 1/2 SocorrCnty121 2 3/4 *SMThrgh*121 1 1/4 Set pace, gave way 9
5Sep04–4Hst fst 1 1/16 :23[1] :46[3] 1:11[4] 1:44[3] ⒻOaksPrvwH43k **47** 6 5 3 1/2 3 1/2 2hd 7 9 1/2 7 17 1/2 Loseth C L117 b 4.15 76–09 Socorro County119 5 1/2 Gold Accent115 3 1/2 *Bullseye Bess*115 2 3/4 3 wide trip 8
22Aug04–1Hst gd 1 1/16 :23[4] :47[3] 1:12[1] 1:44[3] 3↑ⒻOC 50k/N2x-N **77** 2 14 1 3 1/2 1 1 1/2 1 1 1/2 22 Loseth C L117 b 5.85 92–14 YoundNelly114[2] SeeMeThrough117[1] FmousSpirit116[4] Set pace, gave way 6
7Aug04–1Hst gd 1 1/16 :24[3] :48[1] 1:13 1:45[4] 3↑ⒻAlw 25000N$Y **60** 3 31 3nk 4 1 3/4 5 3 1/4 4 5 1/2 Wilson D H L115 b 3.15 82–13 SummerSymphony115 2 1/2 GoldAccent115no RiversRch117[3] Pressed 3 wide 5
17Jly04–9Hst fst 6 1/2f :22[1] :45[4] 1:10[3] 1:17[1] ⒻOC 50k/N1x-N **71** 1 3 4 1 1/2 4 2 1/2 32 2 2 1/4 Wilson D H L122 b 3.50 90–14 Literary119 2 1/4 SeeMeThrough122 1 3/4 AvalncheBy120 2 3/4 3 wide, second best 7
30May04–9Hst gd 6 1/2f :21[4] :45[2] 1:11[4] 1:19[1] ⒻOC 50k/N1x-N **62** 4 9 5 6 1/2 45 75 7 2 1/2 Krasner S B L119 b 2.90 79–14 Stole One119hd Bamboo Orient117hd Wild Glory116hd Off slowly 9
15May04–8Hst fst 6 1/2f :22[2] :46 1:11[2] 1:18[2] ⒻOC 50k/N$Y-N **66** 5 6 64 64 64 2 3 1/4 Krasner S B L119 b 3.90 83–14 Wild Glory114 3 1/4 See Me Through119hd Literary119hd Wide bid, placed 10
17Apr04–4Hst gd 6f :23 :47[1] 1:00[2] 1:14[3] ⒻMd Sp Wt 21k **66** 1 2 1hd 1hd 1hd 1 1 1/2 Krasner S B L122 b *.75 83–16 SMThrough122 1 1/2 BsktofDrms117hd DvilsEclps122 1 3/4 Pressured, prevailed 5

Senor Swinger

Own: Lewis Robert B. and Beverly J

Gr/ro. h. 5 (Apr)
Sire: El Prado*Ire (Sadler's Wells) $100,000
Dam: Smooth Swinger (Kris S.)
Br: Bob Ackerman (Ky)
Tr: Baffert Bob(0 0 0 0 .00) 2004:(562 105 .19)

Life	22	8	0	3	$795,068	108	D.Fst	4 2 0 0	$59,640 93
2004	10	4	0	1	$418,178	108	Wet(376)	2 0 0 0	$22,500 96
2003	11	3	0	2	$361,290	103	Turf(339)	16 6 0 3	$712,928 108
	0	0	0	0	$0	–	Dst(0)	0 0 0 0	$0 –

24Oct04-9WO gd 1½ Ⓣ :494 1:141 2:044 2:283 3↑CanIntnl-G1 **93** 6 75½ 106¼ 94 67½ 612¼ Prado E S L126 9.20 75-13 Sulamani126 1½ Simonas126 2 Brian Boru126¾ 5wd,fltnd out 10
18Sep04-8Bel sf 1⅛ 🅃 :50 1:151 1:401 1:523 3↑BelBCH-G2 **108** 3 34 35½ 32½ 11 14 Prado E S L117 2.40 67-33 Senor Swinger117 4 Stroll120 3½ *B. A. Way*113¾ Vigorous hand ride 4
14Aug04-9AP fm 1¼ Ⓣ :472 1:12 1:363 2:00 3↑ArlMilln-G1 **99** 8 86½ 85½ 83¾ 74½ 75¾ Blanc B L126 21.70 105 - ⒹPowerscourt126 1½ Kicken Kris126 1 *Magistretti*126½ Bothered start 13
24Jly04-7AP fm 1¼ Ⓣ :494 1:15 1:394 2:031 3↑ArlngtnH-G3 **102** 1 31½ 51¾ 32 2½ 1hd Blanc B L118 1.80 95-05 SenorSwinger118hd MystryGivr120 1½ Bllingrry121no Steadied start, inside 7
3Jly04-8CD fm 1 Ⓣ :224 :454 1:093 1:34 3↑FrckrBCH-G2 **104** 3 48 59 56½ 33½ 21½ Day P L117 2.40 97-07 QuntumMerit117 1½ Ⓓ*SenorSwinger*117 2 PerfctSoul121 1 Came out 1/8 pole 9
Disqualified and placed third
12Jun04-10CD yl 1 1/16 Ⓣ :244 :502 1:153 1:454 3↑OpningVrsH110k **98** 7 53 53½ 51½ 21½ 11¼ Day P L117 2.10 75-25 Senor Swinger117 1¼ Hard Buck123 1¼ Majestic Thief115 2 4-5w trip,driving 7
15May04-10Pim fm 1⅛ Ⓣ :464 1:10 1:334 1:461 3↑Dixie-G2 **100** 2 88¼ 98 97¼ 76¾ 52½ Day P L119 4.80 108 - MrOBrien119 2 MillenniumDrgon121hd Wrligh124nk Rail,angld,belated btw 11
29Apr04-6CD fm 1⅛ Ⓣ :482 1:122 1:361 1:481 3↑Alw 64300N1Y **101** 7 32½ 43 33 2hd 1¾ Day P L117 *1.00 92-07 Senor Swinger117¾ Spice Island114 1¼ Startac117 1¼ Rated,5w,driving 7
16Feb04-9SA fm 1½ Ⓣ :494 1:15 2:044 2:28 4↑SLsObspH-G2 **95** 3 65½ 74¾ 107 73¾ 113¾ Santiago Javier LB113 b 12.90 77-15 PurtoBnus115nk Continuously116hd ContinntlRd117no Inside,in tight late 12
10Jan04-8SA fst 1 1/16 :222 :452 1:091 1:413 SnFndoBC-G2 **92** 5 64¼ 73¾ 44 63¾ 68 Ramsammy E LB120 b 9.40 89-07 During120 1 Toccet116 1 Touch the Wire117 2 Tight early,waited3/16 10

Sense of Style

Own: Smith Derrick and Tabor, Michael

B. f. 3 (Mar) KEESEP03 $800,000
Sire: Thunder Gulch (Gulch) $40,000
Dam: Save Me the Waltz*Ire (Kings Lake)
Br: Twelve Oaks Stud (Ky)
Tr: Biancone Patrick L(0 0 0 0 .00) 2004:(130 29 .22)

Life	5	3	0	0	$369,000	92	D.Fst	5 3 0 0	$369,000 92
2004	5	3	0	0	$369,000	92	Wet(318)	0 0 0 0	$0 –
2003	0	M	0	0	$0	–	Turf(292)	0 0 0 0	$0 –
	0	0	0	0	$0	–	Dst(0)	0 0 0 0	$0 –

30Oct04-3LS fst 1 1/16 :224 :462 1:103 1:413 ⒻBCJuvFil-G1 **80** 8 87 84¾ 82¼ 86½ 912½ Prado E S L119 3.50 81-02 SweetCtomine119 3¾ Blletto119 1¼ *RunwyModl*119¾ Hoppd strt,4w 2nd turn 12
8Oct04-9Kee fst 1 1/16 :223 :464 1:113 1:441 ⒻAlcibiad-G2 **86** 5 33 41 31 52¼ 52¼ Prado E S 118 *.60 89-17 Runway Model118hd Sharp Lisa118no In the Gold118½ Lack room 1/8p 10
19Sep04-8Bel fst 1 :242 :48 1:12 1:373 ⒻMatron-G1 **91** 4 64 62 1½ 1½ 11 Prado E S 119 *.35 73-25 Sense of Style119 1 *Balletto*119¾ Play With Fire119 7¼ Unprepared for start 6
20Aug04-8Sar fst 7f :223 :453 1:103 1:234 ⒻSpinaway-G2 **88** 4 4 31 31 1½ 16¾ Prado E S 121 *.95 85-13 *SenseofStyle*121 6¾ MissMtchd121¼ PlyWithFir121½ Drew away when asked 7
1Aug04-4Sar fst 6½f :214 :451 1:10 1:162 ⒻMd Sp Wt 45k **92** 9 2 62¼ 34 1hd 12½ Prado E S 118 *1.65 93-12 *SenseofStyle*118 2½ *SummrRvn*118 4½ PpprmintLilly118 1¾ 3 wide move, clear 9

Shaconage

Own: Van Doren Andrena

Gr/ro. f. 5 (Jun)
Sire: El Prado*Ire (Sadler's Wells) $100,000
Dam: Carita Tostada*Chi (Gallantsky)
Br: Andrena Van Doren (Ky)
Tr: Shirota Mitch(0 0 0 0 .00) 2004:(54 6 .11)

Life	20	5	1	4	$391,962	98	D.Fst	1	0	0	0	$2,110	75
2004	11	2	1	3	$256,340	98	Wet(344)	3	0	1	1	$12,220	67
2003	6	2	0	0	$113,822	92	Turf(292)	16	5	0	3	$377,632	98
	0	0	0	0	$0	-	Dst(0)	0	0	0	0	$0	-

20Nov04-9CD yl 1⅛ Ⓣ :49² 1:14 1:40¹ 1:53⁴ 3↑Ⓕ CardinlH-G3 83 3 7³¾ 6⁵ 4⁵ 5⁸ 8⁷¼ Johnson J M L118 5.90 57-34 Aud115nk May Gato117hd Angela's Love1144¼ 4-5w,between,tired 11

30Oct04-6LS yl 1⅜ Ⓣ :52² 1:18² 1:42¹ 2:18¹ 3↑Ⓕ BCF&MTrf-G1 96 6 12¹¹ 12¹¹ 12⁸ 7⁷ 6⁶¾ Bejarano R L123 62.40 91-07 Ouija Board1181½ Film Maker123nk Wonder Again1232¾ No factor 12

10Oct04-6Kee fm 1 3/16 Ⓣ :50 1:14² 1:39¹ 1:57 3↑Ⓕ WnStGlxy-G2 92 4 1¹ 1¹ 1½ 2hd 3² Bejarano R L121 7.20 84-12 Stay Forever121½ Super Brand1191½ Shaconage121no Drift out bmp 1/8p 9

14Aug04-8AP fm 1 3/16 Ⓣ :49⁴ 1:15² 1:39³ 1:56² 3↑Ⓕ BeverlyD-G1 95 6 7³¼ 8⁴ 8⁴ 10⁶¼ 8³¼ Blanc B L123 17.30 89 - Crimson Palace123½ Riskaverse123hd Necklace117nk No factor 11

24Jly04-9AP fm 1 3/16 Ⓣ :50³ 1:15 1:39³ 1:57 3↑Ⓕ ModestyH-G3 93 6 6²½ 4³ 4³½ 4³ 3¹¼ Blanc B L118 2.00 88-05 Bedanken119¾ Aud116½ Shaconage118³ 4 wide 1/4, belatedly 8

26Jun04-9CD fm 1⅛ Ⓣ :47 1:10³ 1:34³ 1:46³ 3↑Ⓕ LcstGrvH-G3 98 5 5³½ 5⁵½ 4²½ 2¹ 1¹¼ Blanc B L116 7.20 100-07 Shaconage1161¼ HaloryLeigh111nc SndSprings1191¾ 4w,driving,clear late 6

29May04-9CD fm 1 1/16 Ⓣ :24¹ :48³ 1:12⁴ 1:42³ 4↑Ⓕ MntJulpH-G3 88 7 5⁶ 8⁵¼ 6⁵½ 6⁸ 5³¾ Blanc B L117 7.90 87-13 StayForever116½ SndSprings120nk EternlMelody1152¼ Near inside,no bid 9

1May04-7CD gd 1 Ⓣ :23³ :47¹ 1:11⁴ 1:36 3↑Ⓕ ArgntMor-G3 95 2 8⁵¼ 6⁵¾ 6³ 4¹½ 1no Blanc B L121 19.30 89-11 Shaconage121no Etoile Montante123² Chance Dance117½ Inside trip 10

10Apr04-10Kee fm 1⅛ Ⓣ :45⁴ 1:10² 1:35 1:47² 4↑Ⓕ Alw 62000N3x 85 9 10¹¹ 10¹⁷ 10⁸½ 10⁸ 7⁴½ Albarado R J L118 7.70 96 - Noisette118¾ Two Dot Slew116² Sun Brightia118hd Belated bid 11

14Mar04-11GP fm *1 1/16 Ⓣ :24 :49⁴ 1:14¹ 1:44⁴ 4↑Ⓕ Alw 38000N3x 83 6 6⁵¼ 6¹¼ 5²¼ 5¹¾ 3²¼ Blanc B L117 b 3.40 78-23 Bijou117½ Alchemist1171¾ Shaconage1171¾ Poor st, stdy early 9

25Feb04-8GP sly 170 ⊗ :22³ :46² 1:12¹ 1:44³ 4↑Ⓕ Alw 38000N3x 67 6 7⁵¾ 7⁸½ 4⁵½ 3⁴ 2⁴ Prado E S L117 b 12.10 70-23 My Ro117⁴ Shaconage117² Askforaraise117¹ 4 wide, gained 2nd 8

Shadow Cast

Own: Farish W S Jr

Ch. f. 4 (Mar)
Sire: Smart Strike (Mr. Prospector) $35,000
Dam: Daily Special (Dayjur)
Br: William S. Farish Jr. (Ky)
Tr: Howard Neil J(0 0 0 0 .00) 2004:(173 37 .21)

Life	14	5	1	5	$297,485	93	D.Fst	8	2	1	3	$115,000	93
2004	12	4	1	4	$267,480	93	Wet(416)	2	2	0	0	$116,705	89
2003	2	1	0	1	$30,005	76	Turf(321)	4	1	0	2	$65,780	86
	0	0	0	0	$0	-	Dst(0)	0	0	0	0	$0	-

18Dec04-9FG fm *1 Ⓣ :23⁴ :48¹ 1:13¹ 1:37⁴ Ⓕ PagoHop60k 86 10 8⁶ 8⁷ 5⁴½ 1½ 1nk Albarado R J L116 9.30 91-10 ShdowCst116nk CodeofEthics116hd SistrSwnk123no Bid 4w, edge, held on 14

23Oct04-9Kee yl 1 1/16 Ⓣ :23² :48³ 1:14¹ 1:46³ Ⓕ VllyView-G3 84 12 9⁵¼ 5¹¾ 3²½ 3²½ 3²¾ Albarado R J L119 4.60 68-29 SistrSwnk1161¼ JinnysGold1161½ ShdowCst1194½ Exch bumps start,empty 12

11Sep04-8Bel fst 1⅛ :48 1:12² 1:36² 1:48¹ Ⓕ Gazelle-G1 92 3 5³½ 5¹½ 6²¼ 4³ 4²¾ Migliore R L119 22.90 87-15 Stellar Jayne122¹ Daydreaming1151¾ He LovesMe117no Game finish on rail 6

25Aug04-3Sar fst 1⅛ :49⁴ 1:13⁴ 1:38 1:50² 3↑Ⓕ OC 75k/N3x-N 93 4 4¹½ 3¹ 3½ 1hd 1¾ Albarado R J L115 5.80 83-19 ShdowCst115¾ ClokofVgueness120⁴ Childrss1202½ 3 wide move, prevailed 6

4Aug04-5Sar fst 1⅛ :49² 1:13³ 1:38 1:51 3↑Ⓕ OC 75k/N3x-N 85 3 3¹ 5¹¾ 4³½ 3⁴½ 3⁵¾ Albarado R J L115 5.40 74-11 Daydreming116½ ClokofVgueness1215¼ ShdowCst1156¼ Bumped first turn 6

12Jun04-7CD yl 1⅛ Ⓣ :49³ 1:14² 1:39 1:51² Ⓕ Regret-G3 82 5 4²½ 4³ 3¹½ 4⁴½ 4⁵ Albarado R J L118 b 9.20 71-25 Sister Star1163¾ Western Ransom120hd Jinny's Gold1181¼ 5w trip,no rally 7

22May04-4CD fm 1 1/16 Ⓣ :24¹ :47⁴ 1:11³ 1:42² Ⓕ Alw 70600NC 76 5 6⁴¾ 6⁶¾ 5⁵½ 3⁵ 3⁷½ Albarado R J L116 b *1.00 84-10 Jinny's Gold1201¾ Sister Star1205¾ Shadow Cast116³ 4-5w,no late gain 6

9Apr04-10OP fst 1 1/16 :23¹ :46³ 1:11 1:42³ Ⓕ Fantasy-G2 85 6 10⁹ 9⁷½ 9⁷¾ 7⁷½ 5⁸ Borel C H L121 b 7.50 89-11 HouseofFortune1211¾ IslndSnd121⁴ StellrJyne1212¼ Tight, rank early,rail 11

6Mar04-9FG fst 1 1/16 :23⁴ :47³ 1:12¹ 1:43 Ⓕ FGOaks-G2 85 2 5⁴ 4³½ 5³½ 5⁵ 3⁵ Albarado R J L121 b 5.70 90-10 Ashado1213¾ Victory U. S. A.1211¼ Shadow Cast121½ Steadied, up for show 6

14Feb04-9FG sly 1 1/16 :24 :48² 1:14¹ 1:46⁴ Ⓕ Slvrbltd-G2 89 4 4³½ 4² 5²¼ 2½ 1¾ Albarado R J L116 b 2.90 76-23 ShdowCst116¾ QuickTemper113⁴ SisterSwnk1173¾ Angled out, prevailed 6

18Jan04-7FG fst 1 1/16 ⊗ :22⁴ :46³ 1:13¹ 1:46² Ⓕ Alw 30000N2L 82 2 4⁶ 4⁴½ 1hd 1² 1²½ Albarado R J L116 b *.60 78-22 Shadow Cast1162½ Twilight Gallop117¹¹ Blondz Away1188½ Driving to wire 7

4Jan04-7FG fst 1 :23³ :47⁴ 1:12⁴ 1:38⁴ Ⓕ Alw 30000N1x 82 5 4³ 5³ 4³ 4²½ 2⁴ Albarado R J L116 *1.20 85-12 All Electric117⁴ Shadow Cast116¾ Perilous Night116⁴ Along for second 7

Shake You Down

Own: Cole R L Jr

Ch. g. 7 (Apr)
Sire: Montbrook (Buckaroo) $20,000
Dam: Mauvin Gway (Rajab)
Br: Ocala Stud Farm (Fla)
Tr: Lake Scott A(0 0 0 0 .00) 2004:(1703 379 .22)

Life	**42**	**17**	**6**	**4**	**$1,277,164**	**121**	**D.Fst**	**34**	**12**	**6**	**4**	**$1,078,984**	**121**
2004	**6**	**3**	**0**	**0**	**$278,604**	**113**	**Wet(363)**	**7**	**5**	**0**	**0**	**$198,180**	**118**
2003	**13**	**7**	**2**	**2**	**$829,160**	**121**	**Turf(260)**	**1**	**0**	**0**	**0**	**$0**	**29**
	0	**0**	**0**	**0**	**$0**	**–**	**Dst(0)**	**0**	**0**	**0**	**0**	**$0**	**–**

Race	Fractions	Class	Spd	Running line	Jockey	Wt/Med	Odds	Spd-Var	Top finishers	Comment	Fld
8Dec04-7Pim fst 5f	:21^4 :44^4 :57^2	3↑OC 75k/N$Y-N	**103**	3 2 4^2 2^2 1$^{1\frac{1}{2}}$ 1^3	Dominguez R A	L119 fb	*1.00	95- 11	ShkeYouDown119^3 AmeriBrillince119$^{3\frac{1}{2}}$ ChoctwRidg119^1	Circled, driving	5
20Nov04-10Pim fst 6f	:22^3 :45^2 :57^1 1:09^2	3↑DeFrncsM-G1	**81**	5 5 1^{hd} 2^{hd} 5^5 10$^{10\frac{3}{4}}$	Luzzi M J	L123 fb	12.50	87- 13	Wildcat Heir119^{nk} Midas Eyes123$^{1\frac{1}{2}}$ Clock Stopper119$^{\frac{3}{4}}$	Dueled 2wd, tired	10
8May04-7Bel fst 6f	:22^2 :44^4 :56^2 1:08^4	3↑BoldRlrH-G3	**89**	1 6 6$^{1\frac{3}{4}}$ 5$^{1\frac{1}{4}}$ 6^4 6$^{6\frac{3}{4}}$	Dominguez R A	L121 fb	*.95	88- 18	CndinFrontier111$^{3\frac{3}{4}}$ KyDputy114^{no} FirstBlush113^{nk}	Stumbled badly start	6
8Apr04-10OP fst 6f	:21^4 :44^3 :56^3 1:09^1	4↑CtFltSpH-G3	**102**	6 5 1^2 1$^{1\frac{1}{2}}$ 1$^{2\frac{1}{2}}$ 1^{hd}	Dominguez R A	L121 fb	*1.40	94- 15	ShkYoDown121^{hd} WhrsthRng115$^{1\frac{1}{4}}$ *AlohBld*114^{nk}	Comfortable pace, held	6
21Mar04-10OP fst 6f	:22 :45 :56^4 1:09^1	4↑HotSprings49k	**85**	4 4 1^{hd} 2^{hd} 3^6 5$^{8\frac{3}{4}}$	Luzzi M J	L122 fb	*.40	85- 19	Skeet119$^{2\frac{1}{4}}$ That Tat118$^{3\frac{1}{2}}$ [DH]Saint Waki119	Off slow,rank,gave way	5
24Jan04-8GP fst 6f	:21^4 :44^1 :56^1 1:09	4↑[R]SunMilSprt300k	**113**	3 2 1^{hd} 1^2 1$^{2\frac{1}{2}}$ 1^3	Luzzi M J	L120 fb	*.60	97- 11	Shake You Down120^3 GreenTeam120^{nk} ValidVideo119$^{1\frac{1}{4}}$	Widened, driving	7

Shoal Water

Own: Sam-Son Farms

B. g. 5 (Feb)
Sire: Smart Strike (Mr. Prospector) $35,000
Dam: Puffin Island (Pleasant Colony)
Br: Sam-Son Farm (Ont-C)
Tr: Frostad Mark R(0 0 0 0 .00) 2004:(269 49 .18)

Life	**15**	**5**	**3**	**3**	**$748,464**	**103**	**D.Fst**	**5**	**2**	**0**	**1**	**$146,770**	**92**
2004	**5**	**2**	**1**	**1**	**$336,414**	**103**	**Wet(448)**	**1**	**0**	**0**	**1**	**$50,000**	**90**
2003	**7**	**2**	**1**	**2**	**$325,690**	**99**	**Turf(345)**	**9**	**3**	**3**	**1**	**$551,694**	**103**
	0	**0**	**0**	**0**	**$0**	**–**	**Dst(0)**	**0**	**0**	**0**	**0**	**$0**	**–**

Race	Fractions	Class	Spd	Running line	Jockey	Wt/Med	Odds	Spd-Var	Top finishers	Comment	Fld
25Jly04-8WO fm 1$\frac{3}{8}$ (T)	:48^2 1:12^3 1:36^4 2:12^1	3↑ChneseCC-G2	**103**	5 2$^{1\frac{1}{2}}$ 2^1 2$^{\frac{1}{2}}$ 1^1 1^{nk}	Kabel T K	L116	5.35	104- 05	Shoal Water116^{nk} Mobil121$^{2\frac{1}{4}}$ *Strut the Stage*121$^{\frac{3}{4}}$	Outfinished rival	8
19Jun04-8WO yl 1$\frac{1}{8}$ (T)	:46^2 1:10 1:35^1 1:48^2	3↑KngEdBCH-G2	**99**	1 2^1 2^{hd} 2^{hd} 2^{hd} 2^{nk}	Kabel T K	L116	4.80	86- 13	SlewValley117^{nk} *ShoalWater*116$^{2\frac{1}{2}}$ *SurgingRiver*112^{hd}	Led briefly late,game	5
30May04-8WO fm 1$\frac{1}{16}$ (T)	:24 :47 1:10^1 1:40^1	4↑ConghtCp-G3	**96**	1 1$^{\frac{1}{2}}$ 1$^{\frac{1}{2}}$ 1^{hd} 3$^{\frac{1}{2}}$ 3$^{\frac{3}{4}}$	Kabel T K	L117	*.85	96- 03	*SlewVlley*117no *LeCinquiemeEssi*117$^{\frac{3}{4}}$ SholWter117$^{1\frac{1}{2}}$	Gave way grudgingly	6
15May04-9WO gd 1 (T)	:23 :46 1:10^2 1:34^2	3↑Alw 86400NC	**97**	9 3^2 3^2 2$^{1\frac{1}{2}}$ 1$^{2\frac{1}{2}}$ 1$^{1\frac{1}{2}}$	Kabel T K	L116	*1.05e	91- 09	SholWter116$^{1\frac{1}{2}}$ PrinceAlphie116^{no} LeCinquiemeEssi116^2	3wd,drove clear	10
18Apr04-6Kee fm 1$\frac{1}{16}$ (T)	:23^3 :47^4 1:11^4 1:41^4	4↑Alw 56200c	**89**	5 1^{hd} 2^{hd} 2$^{\frac{1}{2}}$ 3$^{2\frac{1}{2}}$ 5$^{2\frac{1}{2}}$	Velazquez J R	L118	5.30	92- 05	Wando118$^{\frac{3}{4}}$ Miesque's Approval116^1 Pisces116$^{\frac{1}{2}}$	Bit rank early,weaken	8

Sightseek

Own: Juddmonte Farms Inc

Ch. m. 6 (Feb)
Sire: Distant View (Mr. Prospector) $15,000
Dam: Viviana (Nureyev)
Br: Juddmonte Farms, Inc. (Ky)
Tr: Frankel Robert J(0 0 0 0 .00) 2004:(491 135 .27)

Life	20	12	5	0	$2,445,216	115	D.Fst 17 11 4 0 $2,239,266 115
2004	7	4	1	0	$1,011,350	112	Wet(362) 2 1 0 0 $196,350 110
2003	8	4	3	0	$1,171,888	115	Turf(345) 1 0 1 0 $9,600 85
	0	0	0	0	$0	–	Dst(0) 0 0 0 0 $0 –

Date	Cond	Dist	Fractions	Race	Fig	PP	St	1C	2C	Str	Fin	Jockey	Wt	Odds		Top Finishers	Comment	Fld
9Oct04-9Bel	fst	1⅛	:482 1:124 1:364 1:493	3↑ⒻBeldame-G1	101	1	1hd	11	1½	16	12¾	Castellano J J	L123	*.30	83–20	Sghtsk123 2¾ SoctySlctn120 1¼ StrmFlgFlyng123¾	In command from start	5
19Sep04-9Bel	fst	1 1/16	:233 :461 1:103 1:412	3↑ⒻRuffianH-G1	112	3	3½	3½	1½	18	11 1¼	Velazquez J R	L122	*.25	93–25	*Sightseek*122 11¼ Pocus Hocus114 2½ MissLoren117½	3 wide move, hand ride	5
1Aug04-9Sar	fst	1⅛	:473 1:104 1:35 1:474	3↑ⒻGoFWandH-G1	103	4	2 1½	2½	2½	2hd	21¾	Bailey J D	L122	*.75	94–14	Azeri120 1¾ *Sightseek*122 2 *Storm Flag Flying*117 7	Tried winner 1/4 pole	5
19Jun04-9Bel	fst	1 1/16	:231 :453 1:10 1:412	3↑ⒻOPhippsH-G1	99	3	2½	2hd	1½	16	13¼	Bailey J D	L120	2.35	93–20	Sightseek120 3¼ StormFlagFlying117 6½ PassingShot116 2	Wrapped up late	4
30Apr04-8CD	sly	1 1/16	:241 :474 1:123 1:441	3↑ⒻLouvlBCH-G2	87	2	3 1½	2 1½	2½	4 3½	47	Bailey J D	L122	*.40	80–17	Lead Story116¾ Yell114 3 Cat Fighter116 3¼	Led for stride,tired	6
14Mar04-6GP	fst	1⅛	:482 1:114 1:372 1:51	3↑ⒻRampartH-G2	101	3	2 1½	21	2hd	16	17½	Bailey J D	L121	*.50	84–27	Sightseek121 7½ Recoubled Miss113 2 *Lead Story*117 9	Drew off, easily	4
25Jan04-8SA	fst	7f	:214 :44 1:082 1:211	4↑ⒻSntMncaH-G1	93	2	3	5 4¼	54	4 2½	4 4¾	Bailey J D	LB122	*1.20	94–08	IslndFshion120¾ Bffythcntrfold114 1½ GotKoko119 3½	Stalked pace, no bid	6

Silent Sighs

Own: Wygod Mr. and Mrs. Martin J

Dk. b or b. f. 4 (Mar)
Sire: Benchmark (Alydar) $7,500
Dam: Quiet Romance (Bertrando)
Br: Mr. & Mrs. Martin J. Wygod (Cal)
Tr: Canani Julio C(0 0 0 0 .00) 2004:(186 42 .23)

Life	6	4	1	0	$442,700	107	D.Fst 5 4 1 0 $442,700 107
2004	3	2	0	0	$317,500	96	Wet(400) 1 0 0 0 $0 58
2003	3	2	1	0	$125,200	107	Turf(323) 0 0 0 0 $0 –
	0	0	0	0	$0	–	Dst(0) 0 0 0 0 $0 –

Date	Cond	Dist	Fractions	Race	Fig	PP	St	1C	2C	Str	Fin	Jockey	Wt	Odds		Top Finishers	Comment	Fld
30Apr04-10CD	my	1⅛	:46 1:094 1:363 1:504	ⒻKyOaks-G1	58	6	4 3½	4 5½	46	10 15	10 27¼	Flores D R	L121 b	7.90	56–17	Ashado121 1¼ *IslandSand*121 1¾ MadcapEscapde121 1¼	Weakened after 3/4s	11
13Mar04-8SA	fst	1 1/16	:224 :462 1:104 1:424	ⒻSAOaks-G1	96	3	2 1½	21	2hd	12	1 1½	Flores D R	LB117 b	6.70	91–08	Silent Sighs117 1½ Halfbridled117 1½ A. P. Adventure117½	Bid,cleared,held	7
24Jan04-7GP	fst	6f	:213 :443 :572 1:104	ⒻⓇSunMilOaks250k	90	1	6	32	32	3 2½	1nk	Flores D R	L120 b	*.20	88–11	*Silent Sighs*120nk Wacky Patty120 2 Dixie High120¾	Bmpd st, boxed in str	6

Silver Ticket

Own: Sam-Son Farms

B. g. 4 (Mar)
Sire: Silver Deputy (Deputy Minister) $40,000
Dam: Go First Class (Easy Goer)
Br: Sam-Son Farm (Ont-C)
Tr: Frostad Mark R(0 0 0 0 .00) 2004:(269 49 .18)

Life	9	3	2	2	$319,120	96	D.Fst 3 1 0 0 $40,020 79
2004	6	2	1	2	$229,100	96	Wet(381) 0 0 0 0 $0 –
2003	3	1	1	0	$90,020	79	Turf(272) 6 2 2 2 $279,100 96
	0	0	0	0	$0	–	Dst(0) 0 0 0 0 $0 –

Date	Cond	Dist	Fractions	Race	Fig	PP	St	1C	2C	Str	Fin	Jockey	Wt	Odds		Top Finishers	Comment	Fld
7Nov04-4WO	yl	1	Ⓣ:24 :472 1:121 1:384	3↑Labeeb106k	95	4	3 1½	34	32	2 2½	2 1½	Landry R C	L117	3.30	67–31	LeCinquiemeEssi118 1½ SilvrTickt117hd Tusyn118 2¾	Ducked in 1/8 pl,game	9
10Oct04-4Kee	fm	1	Ⓣ:233 :472 1:12 1:362	StormCat110k	96	8	66	5 3½	43	6 3¾	31	Albarado R J	L123	3.00	89–12	*Good Reward*117¾ Fort Prado120nk Silver Ticket123½	4-5w trip,outfinished	8
8Aug04-9WO	fm	1½	Ⓣ:484 1:14 2:03 2:27	ⓇBreeders500k	88	6	4 5½	4 1¾	33	34	33	Kabel T K	L126	*1.55	92 –	*A Bit O'Gold*126 1¾ *Burst of Fire*126 1¼ Silver Ticket126 1¼	Stalked 3wd,all out	11
17Jly04-8WO	gd	1⅛	Ⓣ:461 1:102 1:344 1:471	TrontoCH-G3	93	3	4 4½	45	34	1hd	1 1¾	Kabel T K	L117	*1.65	92–08	Silver Ticket117 1¾ Bachelor Blues118 2¼ BurstofFire116 2	Bid 1/8 pole,drvg	10
27Jun04-9WO	fst	1¼	:474 1:124 1:374 2:043	ⓇQueensPlt1000k	69	9	11	2hd	3 5½	820	819	Kabel T K	L126	5.65	63–17	Niigon126¾ *A Bit O'Gold*126 7¾ Will He Crow126 1	Set pressured pace	13
5Jun04-9WO	fm	1	Ⓣ:22 :444 1:091 1:33	Alw 67800N1x	90	4	3 1½	31	2hd	12½	14½	Kabel T K	L117	*1.35	98–02	Silver Ticket117 4½ Lone Arrow117 3¾ St Regs120 1¾	Stalked 3wd,driving	8

Silver Tree

Own: Vegso Peter

Ch. c. 5 (Feb)
Sire: Hennessy (Storm Cat) $35,000
Dam: Blue Begum (With Approval)
Br: Vegso Racing Stable (Fla)
Tr: Mott William I(0 0 0 0 .00) 2004:(680 116 .17)

Life	16	6	2	3	$718,720	106	D.Fst	1	0	0	0	$340	52
2004	10	3	2	2	$328,060	106	Wet(354)	0	0	0	0	$0	-
2003	6	3	0	1	$390,660	96	Turf(317)	15	6	2	3	$718,380	106
	0	0	0	0	$0	-	Dst(0)	0	0	0	0	$0	-

4Dec04-11Crc fm 1⅛ Ⓣ :47 1:10 1:33⁴ 1:45³ 3↑ TropTrfH-G3 **102** 3 5 2½ 42 21½ 21½ 2nk Coa E M L118 1.70 101-03 Host118nk Silver Tree118½ Demeteor1141 3p,led 1/16,outfinishd 12
30Oct04-4LS yl 1 Ⓣ :24 :48³ 1:12³ 1:36⁴ 3↑ BCMile-G1 **102** 2 74¼ 74 82½ 53 53 Prado E S L126 21.90 83-07 Singletry126½ AntoniusPius122 1½ SixPerfections123nk Rail trip, flattened 14
9Oct04-8Kee fm 1 Ⓣ :23² :47¹ 1:11⁴ 1:35² 3↑ ShdwlTfM-G1 **99** 4 43½ 53 62¼ 53¼ 35¼ Day P L126 4.30 90-10 NothingtoLose1264½ HonorinWr126¾ SilverTree126 1¼ Between,no late bid 9
28Aug04-9Sar fm 1 1/16 Ⓣ :23³ :46² 1:09¹ 1:39² 3↑ 4strdavH-G2 **106** 7 96½ 98¼ 63¼ 2hd 2½ Bailey J D L117 3.20 97-01 *NothingtoLose*117½ SilverTree1171 RoyalRegalia114 1¾ Game finish outside 10
30Jly04-8Sar yl 1⅛ 🅃 :49¹ 1:13¹ 1:37¹ 1:49³ 3↑ BBaruchH-G2 **104** 5 62¾ 62¾ 3½ 1hd 1nk Bailey J D L116 2.75 89-11 SilverTree116nk *NothingtoLose*117½ IrishColonial113nk 3 wide, determined 7
10Jly04-8Bel fm 1 Ⓣ :23 :46 1:09 1:32² 3↑ PokerH-G3 **102** 5 3½ 31 31 31½ 32¾ Santos J A L117 2.70 95-05 ChrstnsOutlw113nk MllnnmDrgon120 2½ *SlvrTr*1171 Chased 3 wide, weaken 9
16Jun04-8Bel fm 1 Ⓣ :23¹ :46 1:09¹ 1:32³ 4↑ OC 100k/c-N **103** 5 2hd 2½ 2hd 1hd 11 Bailey J D L123 *1.40 97-03 SilverTree1231 NothingtoLose1231 ChillyRoostr116 1½ Pressed pace, clear 6
15May04-10Pim fm 1⅛ Ⓣ :46⁴ 1:10 1:33⁴ 1:46¹ 3↑ Dixie-G2 **95** 5 44 43 42 66½ 85 Bailey J D L119 5.00 106 - MrOBrin1192 MillnniumDrgon121hd Wrligh124nk 3wd most trip,weakened 11
21Mar04-8FG fm *1⅛ Ⓣ :49 1:12² 1:36¹ 1:48¹ 4↑ MMunzJrH-G2 **96** 1 21 1hd 31 22½ 84 Bailey J D L118 *2.30 99-05 Mystery Giver120¾ Herculated116½ Skate Away1171 Faltered mid stretch 10
21Feb04-9GP fm 1 Ⓣ :23¹ :46¹ 1:09² 1:33¹ 4↑ Alw 38000N3x **98** 9 53½ 43½ 21½ 21 12¼ Bailey J D L118 *.70 100-06 Silver Tree1182¼ Tacirring118 1¾ Fast Decision118 1¾ Vigorous hand ride 10

Silverfoot

Own: Clark Stephanie S

Gr/ro. g. 5 (May)
Sire: With Approval (Caro*Ire) $5,000
Dam: Northern Silver (Silver Ghost)
Br: Stephanie S. Clark (Ky)
Tr: Stewart Dallas(0 0 0 0 .00) 2004:(295 49 .17)

Life	10	5	0	1	$189,063	99	D.Fst	2	1	0	0	$13,270	81
2004	9	4	0	1	$177,593	99	Wet(338)	0	0	0	0	$0	-
2003	1	1	0	0	$11,470	76	Turf(320)	8	4	0	1	$175,793	99
	0	0	0	0	$0	-	Dst(0)	0	0	0	0	$0	-

14Aug04-8Sar yl 1½ 🅃 :49⁴ 1:15 2:04³ 2:28² 3↑ SwrdDncr-G1 **96** 2 44½ 41 65 53½ 55½ Albarado R J L116 3.75 72-22 BetterTlkNow118 1½ RequestforProl123¾ BltoStr1201 Inside, no response 6
4Jly04-7AP sf 1½ Ⓣ :52³ 1:19² 2:10⁴ 2:36¹ 3↑ StrStBCH-G3 **96** 5 76½ 74½ 74¼ 44 21¾ Albarado R J L116 2.90 54-44 Ballingarry120 1¾ 🄳Silverfoot116nk Grey Beard1172¾ Forced way out 1/4 8
Disqualified and placed 4th
31May04-9CD yl 1⅜ Ⓣ :50 1:15¹ 1:40 2:17³ 3↑ LsvillH-G3 **99** 3 67½ 66 53¼ 21½ 1no Albarado R J L114 4.20 82-18 Silverfoot114no Rochester116 1¼ *Ballingarry*120 1½ Bump foe 1/4p,drvg 9
8May04-8CD fm 1⅛ Ⓣ :48 1:11⁴ 1:36 1:47⁴ 3↑ OC 62k/N$Y-N **97** 3 66 68 64½ 42 1nk Albarado R J L121 2.20 94-08 *Silverfoot*121nk European121 1½ Mr. Krisley1172½ Lack room 3/16s,drv,6w 7
7Apr04-9Kee fm 1½ Ⓣ :47³ 1:12¹ 2:03² 2:27⁴ 4↑ Alw 53900N3x **93** 5 34 42½ 5¾ 4¾ 41½ Martinez J R Jr L116 4.10 104 - Art Variety116nk *In Hand*118½ Grand116¾ Between,no late gain 10
7Mar04-8FG fm *1 1/16 Ⓣ :23 :48¹ 1:12⁴ 1:43³ 4↑ OC 40k/N2x-N **93** 3 57½ 53¾ 63¾ 42 11½ Martinez J R Jr L119 7.50 95-12 Silverfoot119 1½ Justlikedawg117no *Stone Cat*1171 Split foes, driving 10
9Feb04-9FG fm *1 Ⓣ :25² :49³ 1:15 1:39² 4↑ Alw 30000N1x **89** 6 56½ 55 44½ 33 11¾ Martinez J R Jr L117 *2.80 83-23 *Silverfoot*117 1¾ Gimme an A1181 Neuf de Carreau1173½ Rallied mid track 10
23Jan04-8FG fm *7½f Ⓣ :25³ :49¹ 1:14 1:32¹ 4↑ Alw 30000N1x **73** 6 9 9 10 109¼ 78½ 3¾ Martinez J R Jr L118 2.60 91-06 Duffy118hd Mr. Romeo118¾ *Silverfoot*118hd Late close mid track 10
5Jan04-7FG fst 1 1/16 ⊗ :24¹ :48⁴ 1:14 1:44² 4↑ Alw 30000N1x **81** 9 77 65½ 75¼ 56 48¾ Melancon L L118 4.30 79-22 One Nice Cat1227½ Fehr1181 Reflector120nk Lacked serious rally 9

Simple Exchange (Ire)
Own: Moyglare Stud Farm Ltd

B. c. 4 (May)
Sire: Danehill (Danzig)
Dam: Summer Trysting (Alleged)
Br: Moyglare Stud Farm, Ltd. (Ire)
Tr: Weld D. K(0 0 0 0 .00) 2004:(0 0 .00)

Life	8	3	1	0	$238,270	103	D.Fst	0 0 0 0		$0	–
2004	4	1	0	0	$173,673	103	Wet(362)	0 0 0 0		$0	–
2003	4	2	1	0	$64,597	–	Turf(386)	8 3 1 0		$238,270	103
	0	0	0	0	$0	–	Dst(0)	0 0 0 0		$0	–

20Oct04 Longchamp (Fr) gd *1 3/16 Ⓣ RH 1:581 3↑ Prix Dollar-G2 Stk 130000 66¾ Smullen P J 126 11.00 Touch of Land130nk Gateman1261 Special Kaldoun1261 12
Timeform rating: 111 *Towards rear,some late progress*
14Aug04-11AP fm 1¼ Ⓣ :463 1:11 1:351 1:593 Secretar-G1 **103** 7 47½ 36 21 3½ 45½ Smullen P J L123 7.90 107 - *Kitten's Joy*123¾ Greek Sun1211¼ Moscow Ballet1191 Inside, bid, faltered 7
24Jly04-5AP fm 1 3/16 Ⓣ :482 1:124 1:372 1:544 AmercnDb-G2 **100** 2 31 31½ 21½ 1hd 1nk Smullen P J L119 2.20 100- 05 SimpleExchnge119nk CoolConductor119¾ Tostd1231¼ Rail trip, hard drive 8
17Jun04 Ascot (GB) fm 1¼ Ⓣ RH 2:074 Hampton Court Stakes (Listed) Stk 73400 43 Smullen P J 128 6.00 Moscow Ballet1231¼ *Crocodile Dundee*1231¼ Mutafanen123½ 13
Timeform rating: 110+ *Rated in mid-pack,angled out 2f out,stayed on*

Singletary
Own: Little Red Feather Racing

B. h. 5 (May)
Sire: Sultry Song (Cox's Ridge) $5,000
Dam: Joiski's Star (Star de Naskra)
Br: Disler Farms Ltd (Ky)
Tr: Chatlos D Jr(0 0 0 0 .00) 2004:(76 12 .16)

Life	16	6	5	2	$1,439,732	109	D.Fst	2 0 0 0		$1,120	79
2004	6	3	2	1	$1,192,910	109	Wet(346)	0 0 0 0		$0	–
2003	8	2	2	1	$206,352	99	Turf(273)	14 6 5 2		$1,438,612	109
	0	0	0	0	$0	–	Dst(0)	0 0 0 0		$0	–

30Oct04-4LS yl 1 Ⓣ :24 :483 1:123 1:364 3↑ BCMile-G1 **109** 10 53¼ 52½ 4¾ 11 1½ Flores D R L126 16.50 86- 07 Singltry126½ AntoniusPius1221½ SxPrfctons123nk Swung wide, drew clear 14
9Oct04-9SA fm 1 Ⓣ :23 :464 1:093 1:331 3↑ OkTrBCMl-G2 **106** 5 54 52½ 54 51¾ 3hd Flores D R LB119 *1.50 96- 11 MusiclChimes118no BuckIndMnor119no *Singletry*119½ 4wd into lane,rallied 6
31May04-7Hol fm 1 Ⓣ :232 :46 1:09 1:324 3↑ ShoeBCM-G1 **106** 1 42 33 32 41¼ 21½ Valdivia J Jr LB124 4.00 98- 07 DesignedforLuck1241½ Singletary124hd Tsigne1241 Rail,btwn 1/8,held 2nd 8
24Apr04-3BM fm 1 Ⓣ :231 :47 1:104 1:35 3↑ SnFrnBCH-G2 **99** 7 32½ 42 21 1hd 1¾ Valdivia J Jr LB119 *.70 98- 09 Singletary119¾ CaptainSquire1162 GoldRuckus1161¼ Eased 2w,led,driving 7
6Mar04-9SA fm 1 Ⓣ :224 :452 1:094 1:334 4↑ FKilroeH-G2 **107** 5 67 68 54½ 3nk 2½ Valdivia J Jr LB117 6.90 92- 12 Sweet Return119½ *Singletary*1172 Inesperado116½ 4wd into lane,bid btwn 14
11Feb04-7SA fm 1 Ⓣ :231 :464 1:102 1:342 4↑ ThunderRdH71k **102** 6 62¾ 63¾ 42½ 21 11 Espinoza V LB117 9.30 90- 14 Singletary1171 Inesperado118½ Apache Wings116hd 3wd into lane,rallied 8

Sinister G
Own: Toscano III, John T., Corrado, Kim, C

Dk. b or b. c. 4 (Feb) OBSAPR03 $67,000
Sire: Matty G (Capote) $10,000
Dam: Sinister Punch (Two Punch)
Br: Devonia Stud, Inc. (Fla)
Tr: Toscano J T Jr(0 0 0 0 .00) 2004:(93 6 .06)

Life	11	3	2	1	$384,016	95	D.Fst	10	3	2	1	$383,187	95
2004	8	2	1	0	$342,466	95	Wet(337)	1	0	0	0	$829	18
2003	3	1	1	1	$41,550	74	Turf(136)	0	0	0	0	$0	–
	0	0	0	0	$0	–	Dst(0)	0	0	0	0	$0	–

22Jun04–8Del fst 1 1/16 :233 :471 1:114 1:434 FloorShow55k 78 6 1½ 1hd 1hd 32 611½ Lopez C C L119 3.20 81–22 Pies Prospect1175½ Gmork1172½ Zakocity117½ Dueled, weakened 8
22May04–8Bel fst 1⅛ :46 1:10 1:35 1:474 PeterPan-G2 70 1 11½ 1½ 3nk 816 823 Toscano P R L123 b 39.00 69–24 Purge1156¾ *Swingforthefences*1151¼ Master David1152¼ Vied inside, tired 10
10Apr04–8Aqu fst 1⅛ :47 1:112 1:37 1:493 WoodMem-G1 52 9 1½ 2hd 2hd 1118 1028 Toscano P R L123 17.90 63–12 Tapit123½ Master David123no Eddington1231½ Between rivals, tired 11
20Mar04–8TP fst 1⅛ :471 1:112 1:371 1:503 LanesEnd-G2 93 11 11½ 11 1hd 11 11½ Toscano P R L121 16.40 83–17 SinisterG1211½ TrickyTaboo121¾ LittleMtthMn1211 Repulsed bid, driving 11
5Mar04–8Aqu fst 170 ⊡ :243 :482 1:122 1:411 OC 100k/n3L -N 95 5 1hd 1hd 2no Toscano P R L122 2.95 92–17 SongoftheSword122no *SinisterG*1224¾ DeltGhost11911 Gamely on rail, fog 5
7Feb04–9Aqu my 1 1/16 ⊡ :224 :463 1:12 1:453 Whirlaway82k 18 6 31 3nk 44 722 737¾ Toscano P R 118 3.65 45–19 LittleMtthMn1181½ RiskyTrick1161½ QuickAction11613¼ Vied 3 wide, tired 7
17Jan04–3Aqu fst 1 1/16 ⊡ :224 :463 1:112 1:441 Alw 44000n1x 91 2 2hd 2hd 11½ 17 15¾ Lopez C C 122 *1.60 90–13 Sinister G1225¾ Run the Light112no Parthenon1177 Kept to drive 6
3Jan04–8Aqu fst 170 ⊡ :231 :47 1:113 1:412 CountFleet81k 75 5 2½ 2½ 33 48½ 512¼ Toscano P R 116 13.80 79–21 *Smarty Jones*1165 Risky Trick1166 Mr. Spock116½ Bumped start, tired 7

Sir Cherokee
Own: Domino Stud of Lex LLC

B. h. 5 (Feb)
Sire: Cherokee Run (Runaway Groom) $40,000
Dam: La Cucina*Ire (Last Tycoon*Ire)
Br: Domino Stud of Lexington, LLC (Ky)
Tr: Tomlinson Michael A(0 0 0 0 .00) 2004:(180 27 .15)

Life	19	6	3	2	$628,296	107	D.Fst	11	2	2	1	$459,466	107
2004	8	2	0	2	$199,986	107	Wet(361)	7	4	1	1	$168,830	103
2003	5	3	0	0	$365,535	106	Turf(246)	1	0	0	0	$0	87
	0	0	0	0	$0	–	Dst(0)	0	0	0	0	$0	–

26Nov04–11CD fst 1⅛ :48 1:12 1:372 1:504 3↑ClarkH-G2 77 5 72¼ 43 53½ 914 920¼ Blanc B L116 10.20 63–25 Saint Liam1171¼ Seek Gold111no Perfect Drift1181¼ Ck 1st turn,rail,tired 9
31Oct04–9CD fst 7½f :224 :452 1:101 1:292 3↑AckAckH-G3 107 2 6 65¼ 65½ 11½ 15¼ Borel C H L114 6.40 93–14 Sir Cherokee1145¼ Fire Slam117nk Slate Run106nk 5w trip,drew off,drv 6
5Jun04–9Mnr fst 170 :244 :484 1:122 1:421 3↑SliptnFelH75k 86 4 45½ 49 49 36½ 37¾ Borel C H LB122 *.50 77–25 Ask the Lord1211 *Eagle Time*1166¾ *Sir Cherokee*1221 Ins,never threatened 4
1May04–9CD yl 1⅛ Ⓣ :51 1:152 1:393 1:53 3↑TurfClsc-G1 87 8 1110 1110 1015 910 89 Borel C H L119 14.80 59–32 Stroll1212½ Sweet Return123no Mystery Giver123¾ Bumped, steadied 11
22Apr04–8Kee sly 1⅛ :462 1:102 1:344 1:463 4↑BenAli-G3 103 4 58½ 513 511 27 311¾ Borel C H L120 5.40 96 – MidwyRod11611¼ EveningAttir116½ SirChrok12012¼ Circle 6w lane,empty 5
3Apr04–11OP fst 1⅛ :452 1:093 1:352 1:481 4↑OaklawnH-G2 102 5 614 410 45½ 56 56 Thompson T J L113 7.80 91–09 Peace Rules1202 Ole Faunty116nk Saint Liam1142¼ No late response 6
29Feb04–9FG fst 1⅛ :47 1:102 1:352 1:483 4↑NwOrlnsH-G2 92 6 54 55 811 712 612½ Thompson T J L115 11.70 88–05 *Peace Rules*119hd Saint Liam1142¾ *Funny Cide*1181¼ Steered out, faded 8
17Jan04–7Hou gd 1⅛ :482 1:131 1:384 1:513 4↑MaxmGldCpH100k 96 7 41½ 1hd 1hd 2½ 1¾ Thompson T J L118 *1.40 87–17 SirCherokee118¾ Freefourintrnt1192½ DustySpik1164½ Dueled, 2w, gamely 8

Sir Shackleton

Own: Farmer Tracy

Ch. c. 4 (Mar)
Sire: Miswaki (Mr. Prospector) $30,000
Dam: Naskra Colors (Star de Naskra)
Br: Tracy Farmer (Ky)
Tr: Zito Nicholas P(0 0 0 0 .00) 2004:(452 86 .19)

Life	9	4	1	1	$566,105	105	D.Fst	9 4 1 1 $566,105 105
2004	9	4	1	1	$566,105	105	Wet(354)	0 0 0 0 $0 –
2003	0	M	0	0	$0	–	Turf(266)	0 0 0 0 $0 –
	0	0	0	0	$0	–	Dst(C)	0 0 0 0 $0 –

Date/Track	Cond	Dist	Fractions	Race	Speed	PP	St	1C	2C	Str	Fin	Jockey	Med/Wt	Odds	Pace	Top Finishers	Comment	Fld
2Oct04-9Hoo	fst	$1\frac{1}{16}$	:224 :47 1:12 1:44	IndnaDby-G2	**101**	2	$6^{3\frac{1}{4}}$	$8^{3\frac{3}{4}}$	4^2	$4^{1\frac{1}{2}}$	4^3	Bejarano R	LB124	2.20	88–21	Brass Hat124$1\frac{3}{4}$ Suave124$\frac{3}{4}$ Hasslefree115$\frac{1}{2}$	4wd bid, lug in 3/16	9
28Aug04-11Sar	fst	$1\frac{1}{4}$	:49 1:124 1:37 2:022	Travers-G1	**91**	4	6^6	$6^{8\frac{1}{4}}$	$6^{5\frac{3}{4}}$	5^{10}	$5^{11\frac{1}{4}}$	Bejarano R	L126	7.20	84–05	Birdstone126$2\frac{1}{2}$ The Cliff'sEdge126$3\frac{1}{2}$ Eddington126nk	Inside, no response	7
7Aug04-8Mnr	fst	$1\frac{1}{8}$	:47 1:103 1:354 1:49	WVDerby-G3	**105**	5	5^5	6^4	5^7	$2^{1\frac{1}{2}}$	1^3	Bejarano R	LB117	*1.20	86–12	SirShckleton1173 Pol rdsVision119$\frac{1}{2}$ BrittsJuls1155	Patient, surged up ins	7
11Jly04-8Bel	fst	$1\frac{1}{16}$	:224 :442 1:074 1:40	Dwyer-G2	**104**	1	2^2	2^6	2^8	$3^{7\frac{1}{2}}$	$3^{4\frac{1}{4}}$	Bejarano R	L121	*.65e	96–09	Medllist121$3\frac{3}{4}$ TheCliffsEdg123$\frac{1}{2}$ *SirShcklton*121$4\frac{1}{2}$	Stayed on well stretch	6
15May04-12Pim	fst	$1\frac{3}{16}$	:471 1:112 1:362 1:552	Preaknes-G1	**95**	5	5^3	$5^{4\frac{3}{4}}$	4^4	5^{11}	$6^{14\frac{3}{4}}$	Bejarano R	L126	37.50	85–13	SmrtyJons126$11\frac{1}{2}$ RockHrdTn1262 Eddngton126hd	Chased between,faded	10
24Apr04-9CD	fst	1	:224 :461 1:113 1:373	DerbyTrl-G3	**93**	2	3^{nk}	$2^{\frac{1}{2}}$	2^{hd}	1^1	$1^{1\frac{3}{4}}$	Bejarano R	L116	*1.20	82–22	SirShcklton116$1\frac{3}{4}$ *CorgousAct*116$8\frac{1}{2}$ BwnChrli122$5\frac{1}{4}$	Between,gamely,drvg	5
9Apr04-6Kee	fst	7f	:22 :451 1:102 1:231	Alw 51575n1x	**97**	7	5	5^3	3^3	1^{hd}	$1^{1\frac{1}{4}}$	Bejarano R	L120	*2.10	91–09	*Sir Shackleton*120$1\frac{1}{4}$ MistyAppeal117$13\frac{1}{2}$ Mr.Trieste120hd	4-5w,steady drive	8
13Mar04-3GP	fst	7f	:221 :452 1:104 1:23	Md Sp Wt 32k	**93**	5	3	$3^{\frac{1}{2}}$	1^{hd}	1^2	$1^{1\frac{1}{2}}$	Castellano J J	L122	2.40	87–13	*SrShcklton*122$1\frac{1}{2}$ WllwothVlly122$7\frac{3}{4}$ SlthTroops122$2\frac{1}{2}$	Drifted str, prevailed	11
14Feb04-12GP	fst	6f	:22 :45 :572 1:10	Md Sp Wt 32k	**87**	2	5	3^{nk}	1^{hd}	$1^{1\frac{1}{2}}$	$2^{1\frac{1}{2}}$	Castellano J J	122	15.80	90–07	*Forest Danger*122$1\frac{1}{2}$ *Sir Shackleton*122$4\frac{1}{2}$ *Gold Gunner*122$\frac{3}{4}$	Vied, outfinished	11

Sis City

Own: Goldfarb Sanford, Torre, Joe, Dubb, M

B. f. 3 (Mar)
Sire: Slew City Slew (Seattle Slew) $5,000
Dam: Smart Sis (Beau Genius)
Br: Heiligbrodt Racing Stable (Ky)
Tr: Dutrow R E Jr(0 0 0 0 .00) 2004:(603 166 .28)

Life	7	3	0	2	$282,980	92	D.Fst	7 3 0 2 $282,980 92
2004	7	3	0	2	$282,980	92	Wet(373)	0 0 0 0 $0 –
2003	0	M	0	0	$0	–	Turf(306)	0 0 0 0 $0 –
	0	0	0	0	$0	–	Dst(0)	0 0 0 0 $0 –

Date/Track	Cond	Dist	Fractions	Race	Speed	PP	St	1C	2C	Str	Fin	Jockey	Med/Wt	Odds	Pace	Top Finishers	Comment	Fld
27Nov04-7Aqu	fst	$1\frac{1}{8}$	:481 1:122 1:371 1:501	ⒻDemoisel-G2	**88**	4	1^1	$1^{\frac{1}{2}}$	$1^{\frac{1}{2}}$	$1^{3\frac{1}{2}}$	$1^{3\frac{3}{4}}$	Velazquez J R	L119	*.40e	88–07	Sis City119$3\frac{3}{4}$ Salute115no *Winning Season*1155	Pace, clear, driving	7
30Oct04-3LS	fst	$1\frac{1}{16}$	:224 :462 1:103 1:413	ⒻBCJuvFil-G1	**92**	6	$2^{\frac{1}{2}}$	2^{hd}	$1^{\frac{1}{2}}$	1^{hd}	$4^{5\frac{3}{4}}$	Velazquez J R	L119	20.20	88–02	SweetCatomine119$3\frac{3}{4}$ Balletto119$1\frac{1}{4}$ *RunwayModel*119$\frac{3}{4}$	Carried 4w 1st turn	12
9Oct04-6Bel	fst	$1\frac{1}{16}$	:23 :461 1:103 1:432	ⒻFrizette-G1	**86**	2	$1^{\frac{1}{2}}$	$1^{\frac{1}{2}}$	1^1	$1^{1\frac{1}{2}}$	$3^{1\frac{1}{2}}$	Coa E M	L120	10.10	81–20	Balletto120$\frac{3}{4}$ Ready's Gal120$\frac{3}{4}$ Sis City120$2\frac{1}{4}$	Drifted out stretch	8
12Sep04-8Mth	fst	170	:231 :464 1:12 1:42	ⒻMongoQueen60k	**85**	5	1^1	$1^{\frac{1}{2}}$	1^2	$1^{9\frac{1}{2}}$	1^{16}	Coa E M	L116	*1.50	87–20	Sis City11616 By Grace Alone116$6\frac{1}{4}$ Our Miss Jones116$6\frac{3}{4}$	Drew away,easily	7
5Aug04-2Sar	fst	$5\frac{1}{2}$f	:223 :464 :594 1:063	ⒻMd c-50000	**56**	1	1	1^1	$1^{\frac{1}{2}}$	1^2	1no	Sellers S J	L118	*1.50	83–11	*Sis City*118no My Muchacha1181 *Tizzy Rizzi*118$6\frac{1}{4}$	Pace, game, held on	9
Claimed from Heiligbrodt Racing Stable for $50,000, Asmussen Steven M Trainer 2004(as of 8/5): (1354 342 215 213 0.25)																		
20Jun04-6CD	fst	$5\frac{1}{2}$f	:222 :454 :582 1:05	ⒻMd Sp Wt 39k	**54**	8	3	1^{hd}	2^{hd}	$3^{3\frac{1}{2}}$	5^7	Sellers S J	L119	4.40	80–14	RoyalFudge119$4\frac{1}{4}$ *OurRoyalLdy*119nk PrivteGift119hd	Drift in start,weaken	12
23May04-4CD	fst	5f	:223 :461 :583	ⒻMd Sp Wt 45k	**62**	8	3	$2^{\frac{1}{2}}$	2^{hd}	2^{hd}	3^2	Sellers S J	L118	5.60	90–12	Cool Spell1182 Sutton's Bay118hd Sis City1181	Forced pace,weakened	8

Sister Star

Own: Marker John C. and Julie

Dk. b or b. f. 4 (Jan)
Sire: Langfuhr (Danzig) $30,000
Dam: Little Irish Nut (Irish Tower)
Br: John C. Marker (Ky)
Tr: McPeek Kenneth G(0 0 0 0 .00) 2004:(413 74 .18)

Life	10	3	2	3	$223,665	93	D.Fst	4 1 0 1 $28,184 69
2004	4	2	1	0	$183,710	93	Wet(375)	1 0 0 1 $5,000 -
2003	6	1	1	3	$39,955	69	Turf(254)	5 2 2 1 $190,481 93
	0	0	0	0	$0	-	Dst(0)	0 0 0 0 $0 -

12Jun04- 7CD yl 1⅛ Ⓣ :493 1:142 1:39 1:512 ⒻRegret-G3 **93** 4 21½ 21½ 21 1hd 13¾ Blanc B L116 8.00 76- 25 Sister Star1163¾ Western Ransom120hd Jinny'sGold1181¼ 6w 3/16s,driving 7
22May04- 4CD fm 1 1/16 Ⓣ :241 :474 1:113 1:422 ⒻAlw 70600NC **89** 3 21½ 21½ 21 21½ 21¾ Blanc B L120 2.20 90- 10 Jinny's Gold1201¾ *Sister Star*1205¾ Shadow Cast1163 Chased,4w,2ndbest 6
24Apr04- 6CD fm 1⅛ Ⓣ :472 1:122 1:371 1:491 3↑ⒻAlw 49100N1x **89** 10 34 35 31½ 11½ 12¼ Blanc B L113 9.60 87- 11 Sister Star1132¼ Pretty Jane1152½ *Border Blues*117½ 5w,drove clear late 10
10Apr04- 8Kee fst 1 1/16 :232 :474 1:124 1:454 ⒻAlw 54000N1x **62** 8 74¼ 96¾ 98½ 67½ 515 Blanc B L118 b 22.30 68- 20 Song Track1187½ QuickTemper1202 TangoforTips1202 Improved position 10

Sister Swank

Own: Heiligbrodt Racing Stable

Ch. f. 4 (Mar) KEESEP02 $41,000
Sire: Skip Away (Skip Trial) $15,000
Dam: Max Donnell (Critique)
Br: Kenirey Stud Farm (Ky)
Tr: Asmussen Steven M(0 0 0 0 .00) 2004:(2293 555 .24)

Life	12	4	3	3	$256,479	91	D.Fst	4 1 3 0 $85,715 83
2004	9	2	2	3	$219,679	91	Wet(331)	3 1 0 1 $40,500 81
2003	3	2	1	0	$36,800	78	Turf(281)	5 2 0 2 $130,264 91
	0	0	0	0	$0	-	Dst(0)	0 0 0 0 $0 -

18Dec04- 9FG fm *1 Ⓣ :234 :481 1:131 1:374 ⒻPagoHop60k **85** 8 75½ 66 43½ 31 3nk Meche D J L123 *1.80 91- 10 ShdowCst116nk CodofEthics116hd SistrSwnk123no Split foes,outfinished 14
13Nov04- 9CD gd 1 1/16 Ⓣ :233 :481 1:132 1:442 ⒻMrsRvere-G2 **91** 10 82½ 51½ 52 44½ 4½ Day P L120 3.00 81- 20 River Belle120no Lenatareese120no Cape Town Lass114½ 5w,mild late gain 10
23Oct04- 9Kee yl 1 1/16 Ⓣ :232 :483 1:141 1:463 ⒻVllyView-G3 **90** 7 54½ 3nk 21½ 22½ 11¼ Day P L116 3.30 71- 29 SisterSwank1161¼ JinnysGold1161½ *ShadowCast*1194½ 8w lane,steady drive 12
18Sep04- 9AP fm 1⅛ Ⓣ :474 1:121 1:364 1:483 ⒻPuckerUp-G3 **87** 2 21½ 32 31½ 22 32¾ Lovato F Jr L116 25.90 93- 05 *Ticker Tape*1222¾ Spotlight122hd *Sister Swank*116½ Inside, no winning bid 11
22Aug04- 8AP fm 1 1/16 Ⓣ :241 :483 1:13 1:433 3↑ⒻAlw 35000N2x **82** 5 32 31 41½ 1hd 11¾ Lovato F Jr L117 5.20 91- 09 SisterSwank1171¾ LiftingtheVeil121hd EchoSpring123hd Inside to stretch 10
27Mar04- 8Sun fst 1 :232 :471 1:112 1:362 ⒻSunlandOak260k **80** 3 32½ 21½ 33 26 26 Sellers S J L122 *1.60 89- 16 SpeedyFalcon1226 *SisterSwnk*122¾ Skyldysky1222½ Tracked winner inside 9
14Feb04- 9FG sly 1 1/16 :24 :482 1:141 1:464 ⒻSlvrbltd-G2 **81** 3 32 1½ 1hd 31½ 34¾ Sellers S J L117 5.30 71- 23 ShadowCst116¾ QuickTemper1134 SisterSwnk1173¾ Inside, edge, lasted 3 6
25Jan04- 9FG gd 1 :231 :463 1:121 1:384 ⒻTiffnyLass100k **76** 7 55 64½ 51¾ 43 46½ Sellers S J L117 6.80 82- 11 Lotta Kim116¾ Josie G.1185¼ Love Power116½ Off rail, lacked finsh 13
3Jan04- 8FG fst 6f :222 :461 :582 1:111 ⒻThelma60k **83** 3 2 21 2hd 2hd 2½ Albarado R J L116 1.50 83- 18 Movant117½ Sister Swank1163¼ Turn to Lass1182¾ Exchanged brushes 5

Skipaslew
Own: The Merv Griffin Ranch Co

Ch. c. 4 (Mar) KEESEP02 $18,000
Sire: Skip Away (Skip Trial) $15,000
Dam: Slew Be (Seattle Slew)
Br: Morgan's Ford Farm & Skip Away, LLC (Va)
Tr: O'Neill Doug(0 0 0 0 .00) 2004:(938 170 .18)

Life	14	4	0	2	$203,975	95
2004	7	1	0	0	$92,875	95
2003	7	3	0	2	$111,100	88
	0	0	0	0	$0	-

D.Fst	12	2	0	2	$100,075	95
Wet(376)	2	2	0	0	$103,900	91
Turf(296)	0	0	0	0	$0	-
Dst(0)	0	0	0	0	$0	-

26Nov04-8GG fst 1 1/16 :223 :462 1:104 1:42 3↑ FortyNinrH82k 88 5 33 32 31½ 44 55¼ Gonzalez R M LB115 b 9.10 88-20 Yougottawanna118nk Adreamisbcrn1193½ My Creed1141 Stlkd 3w, wknd 9
29Oct04-7LS fst 1 1/16 :224 :452 1:102 1:42 LnStrDby-G3 95 1 31½ 4¾ 42 64¼ 44¼ Dettori L L122 b 31.80 88-17 PllrdsVsn122½ Cryptgrph122½ Flmthrwntxn1223¼ Saved ground,weakened 12
25Sep04-11Fpx fst *1⅛ :471 1:114 1:363 1:484 PomonaDrby99k 86 5 62¾ 63¼ 51¾ 56 47 Martinez F F LB116 b 15.80 92-15 Semi Lost1204½ *Cozy Guy*1202 Lava Man122½ 2-3w, steadied 5/16 8
29May04-8Hol fst 7f :214 :44 1:084 1:212 LBrreraM-G2 63 5 5 72¾ 74¼ 610 614½ Ruis M LB120 b 16.10 80-09 TwicsBd1163 Wimplstltskn1162½ DontsIlmshort1233 Swung 4wd into lane 8
3Apr04-7Haw fst 1⅛ :474 1:123 1:374 1:504 IlnosDby-G2 83 3 31½ 21½ 41¼ 48 515 Saint-Martin E L118 b 12.10 88-21 Pollard's Vision1142¾ Song oftheSword1162¾ Suave1148½ Saved grd, tired 11
13Mar04-7GG fst 1 1/16 :23 :464 1:11 1:434 ElCamRlD-G3 79 7 53¼ 42 42½ 75 73¼ Saint-Martin E LB120 b 2.10 81-16 Kilgowan116½ DH Capitno116 DH SettleBorders117hd Drftd out, bmpd 1/8p 10
10Jan04-3GG wf 1 1/16 :224 :462 1:101 1:414 GGDerby-G3 91 5 31½ 31½ 31 1½ 12 Saint-Martin E LB120 b *1.00 94-11 Skipaslew1202 *O. K. Mikie*120hd Bensquito1201½ Stalked,bid 3w,driving 5

Slew Valley
Own: Rich Meadow Farm and Burkhard Alan

B. h. 8 (May)
Sire: Valley Crossing (Private Account) $2,500
Dam: Slewway (Slewpy)
Br: W James Hindman (Md)
Tr: Baker Reade(0 0 0 0 .00) 2004:(274 44 .16)

Life	32	7	3	5	$767,040	113
2004	9	3	1	1	$353,360	102
2003	9	0	1	3	$186,880	105
	0	0	0	0	$0	-

D.Fst	5	2	0	0	$56,700	89
Wet(350)	0	0	0	0	$0	-
Turf(279)	27	5	3	5	$710,340	113
Dst(0)	0	0	0	0	$0	-

9Oct04-4Pim fm 1⅛ Ⓣ :493 1:132 1:382 1:504 3↑ [R] MdMillTurf95k 80 4 3½ 31 2½ 34 44¼ Elliott S L126 b *.70 84-12 DrDetroit119no *PrivteScndl*1192½ LReinsTrms1211¾ Stp slw,takn 5wd early 6
19Sep04-9WO fm 1 Ⓣ :232 :46 1:09 1:323 3↑ AttoMile-G1 90 5 95¼ 73¾ 74¼ 67½ 75¾ McAleney J S L121 20.55 94-03 Soaring Free113¾ Perfect Soul121hd *Royal Regalia*1181¼ 5-wide,hung 11
25Jly04-8WO fm 1⅜ Ⓣ :482 1:123 1:364 2:121 3↑ ChneseCC-G2 88 8 43½ 42½ 43 67 68½ McAleney J S L119 3.65 95-05 Shoal Water115nk Mobil1212¼ *Strut the Stage*121¾ 4wd,evened out 8
19Jun04-8WO yl 1⅛ Ⓣ :462 1:10 1:351 1:482 3↑ KngEdBCH-G2 100 3 32½ 31½ 31½ 3nk 1nk McAleney J S L117 4.30 86-13 Slew Valley117nk *Shoal Water*1162½ *Surging River*112hd Stalked,got up late 5
30May04-8WO fm 1 1/16 Ⓣ :24 :47 1:101 1:401 4↑ ConghtCp-G3 98 5 41½ 31 2hd 1hd 1no McAleney J S L117 1.95 97-03 *Slew Valley*117no *Le Cinquieme Essai*117¾ Shoal Water1171½ 3-wide,driving 6
Previously trained by Sciacca Gary
24Apr04-8Aqu fm 1 1/16 Ⓣ :233 :481 1:124 1:422 3↑ FtMarcyH-G3 96 2 74 85½ 51¾ 33 31½ Chavez J F L119 2.70 93-09 ChillyRooster113½ UnionPlace1131 *SlewValley*119½ 4 wide run second turn 8
12Mar04-9GP fm *1⅛ Ⓣ :472 1:11 1:363 1:482 4↑ OC 80k/n4x-N 102 5 59 48 45½ 31½ 11 Chavez J F L118 2.40 100 - Slew Valley1181 He's Crafty1182¾ *EverythingtoGain*1202 Stdy early, up late 10
22Feb04-11GP fm 1⅜ Ⓣ :484 1:361 2:112 3↑ GPBCH-G1 98 8 21 21½ 22 31½ 63¼ Chavez J F L117 21.90 98-10 Hard Buck117nd Balto Star122½ Kicken Kris1181 Stalked, weakened 8
25Jan04-10GP fm 1⅜ Ⓣ :483 1:132 1:37 2:122 3↑ MDiarmdH-G3 100 1 1½ 1½ 11 11½ 21½ Chavez J F L117 7.50 94-07 RqustforProl1151½ SlwVlly117¾ SrBrnsSword1133¼ On hedge, outfinished 12

Smarty Jones
Own: Someday Farm

Ch. c. 4 (Feb)
Sire: Elusive Quality (Gone West) $100,000
Dam: I'll Get Along (Smile)
Br: Someday Farm (Pa)
Tr: Servis John C(0 0 0 0 .00) 2004:(284 68 .24)

Life	9	8	1	0	$7,613,155	118	D.Fst	7 6 1 0 $1,128,355 118
2004	7	6	1	0	$7,563,535	118	Wet(343)	2 2 0 0 $6,484,800 107
2003	2	2	0	0	$49,620	105	Turf(276)	0 0 0 0 $0 –
	0	0	0	0	$0	–	Dst(0)	0 0 0 0 $0 –

Date/Track	Cond	Dist	Fractions	Race								Jockey	Wt	Odds		Top Finishers	Comment	
5Jun04-11Bel	fst	1½	:483 1:113 2:002 2:272	Belmont-G1	100	9	31	1½	13½	11½	21	Elliott S	L126 f	*.35	94- 10	*Birdstone*1261 Smarty Jones1268 Royal Assault1263	Vied, clear, gamely	9
15May04-12Pim	fst	1 3/16	:471 1:112 1:362 1:552	Preaknes-G1	118	6	21½	22½	21	15	111½	Elliott S	L126 f	*.70	100- 13	SmrtyJons12611½ RockHrdTn1262 Eddington126hd	3-4w,angled in,driving	10
1May04-10CD	sly	1¼	:463 1:114 1:371 2:04	KyDerby-G1	107	13	42½	21½	2hd	1hd	12¾	Elliott S	L126 f	*4.10	79- 21	*Smarty Jones*1262¾ Lion Heart1263¼ Imperialism1262	Stalked,bid,clear	18
10Apr04- 9OP	my	1⅛	:464 1:113 1:364 1:492	ArkDerby-G2	107	11	2½	2½	1hd	13	11½	Elliott S	122 f	*1.00	91- 17	*Smarty Jones*1221½ Borrego1181½ Pro Prado1223½	Cleared at will,drivng	11
20Mar04-10OP	fst	1 1/16	:232 :473 1:12 1:42	Rebel200k	108	7	21	21	2½	11	13¼	Elliott S	122 f	3.50	100- 16	*Smarty Jones*1223¼ Purge1173¾ Pro Prado1173¾	Kicked strongly clear	9
28Feb04- 9OP	fst	1	:224 :454 1:111 1:372	Southwest100k	95	6	21½	22½	2hd	12	1¾	Elliott S	122 f	*.50	97- 18	*SmrtyJons*122¾ *TwoDownAtomtc*112½ ProPrd1177¼	Chased,took over,drvng	9
3Jan04- 8Aqu	fst	170	⊡ :231 :47 1:113 1:412	CountFleet81k	97	7	31	31	2hd	1½	15	Elliott S	116 f	*.40	91- 21	*Smarty Jones*1165 Risky Trick1166 Mr. Spock116½	Stumbled start, 3 wide	7

Smok'n Frolic
Own: Dogwood Stable

Gr/ro. m. 6 (Apr)
Sire: Smoke Glacken (Two Punch) $30,000
Dam: Cherokyfrolicflash (Green Dancer)
Br: Cherokee Farms Inc. (Fla)
Tr: Pletcher Todd A(0 0 0 0 .00) 2004:(948 240 .25)

Life	33	9	8	2	$1,534,720	104	D.Fst	27 9 8 1 $1,490,484 100
2004	8	1	3	1	$258,220	93	Wet(374)	4 0 0 1 $37,336 104
2003	11	3	3	1	$776,856	104	Turf(263)	2 0 0 0 $6,900 90
	0	0	0	0	$0	–	Dst(0)	0 0 0 0 $0 –

Date/Track	Cond	Dist	Fractions	Race								Jockey	Wt	Odds		Top Finishers	Comment	
29Aug04- 9Sar	gd	7f	:221 :442 1:074 1:21	3↑Ⓕ BalrinaH-G1	88	7	2	55½	59½	510	56½	Prado E S	L115 b	9.40	93- 05	*LadyTk*119hd MyTrustyCt116hd HrmonyLodge1191	Wide throughout, tired	7
6Aug04- 8Sar	fst	6f	:223 :451 :572 1:101	3↑Ⓕ HnrblMsH-G2	89	6	1	41	62¼	54¼	32¾	Prado E S	L116 b	6.10	88- 10	MyTrustyCt115no *EbonyBreeze*1152¾ SmoknFrolic116½	4 wide, good finish	8
4Jly04-10Mth	fst	1⅛	:474 1:112 1:364 1:51	3↑Ⓕ MPchrBCH-G2	82	3	2½	21	32	44	55¼	Coa E M	L118 b	2.60	81- 19	La Reason1113 Yell114nk Bare Necessities119no	Steadied into 1st turn	7
5Jun04- 6Bel	fst	6½f	:214 :443 1:08 1:142	3↑Ⓕ VagrncyH-G2	90	3	8	88½	75¼	312	29	Prado E S	L117 b	6.30	92- 07	Bear Fan1219 Smok'n Frolic1171¼ Aspen Gal1092	Rallied outside	9
17Apr04- 8Aqu	fst	1	:232 :463 1:102 1:352	3↑Ⓕ BdORsBCH-G3	89	6	31	31	3nk	3nk	22¼	Velazquez J R	L119 b	*.75	86- 16	PassingShot1152¼ SmoknFrolic119hd NonsuchBy116no	Got nod for place	6
14Mar04- 8Aqu	fst	1⅛	:47 1:111 1:372 1:512	3↑Ⓕ NxtMoveH-G3	91	5	51¾	31½	2½	16	16½	Migliore R	L119 b	*.80	82- 24	Smok'n Frolic1196½ Stake112no U K Trick110nk	Stumbled start, wide	7
15Feb04-11GP	fst	1 1/16	:234 :473 1:114 1:431	3↑Ⓕ SabinH-G3	73	1	32½	41¾	64¾	610	715¼	Bailey J D	L117 b	*2.00	78- 17	RorEmotion1165½ *NonsuchBy*115¾ LedStory1191¾	Checked, bmpd 1st turn	9
24Jan04- 9GP	fst	1 1/16	:231 :463 1:111 1:45	4↑Ⓕ Ⓡ SunMilDstf500k	93	10	118¼	910	79½	62¾	2¾	Velazquez J R	L120 b	4.10	83- 15	Secret Request118¾ Smok'n Frolic1201¾ Scapade118¾	In tight st, rallied	12

Snorter

Own: Gary and Mary West Stables Inc

B. h. 5 (Jan)
Sire: Awesome Again (Deputy Minister) $125,000
Dam: Retiro Park (Meadowlake)
Br: John Toffan & Trudy McCaffery (Ky)
Tr: Frankel Robert J(0 0 0 0 .00) 2004:(491 135 .27)

Life	14	4	1	4	$207,930	102	D.Fst	9 4 0 3	$177,170	102
2004	6	2	0	1	$125,100	102	Wet(412)	3 0 1 0	$25,700	101
2003	6	2	1	1	$72,820	93	Turf(233)	2 0 0 1	$5,060	84
	0	0	0	0	$0	–	Dst(0)	0 0 0 0	$0	–

Date/Race	Cond	Dist	Fractions	Race	Fig	PP	St	1C	2C	Str	Fin	Jockey	Wt	Odds		Top Finishers	Comment	Fld
30Oct04-1LS	gd	1	:23^2 :46^3 1:10^2 1:35^2	3↑ MetrplxMil100k	**83**	9	7$3\frac{1}{4}$	73	8$3\frac{1}{4}$	9$8\frac{3}{4}$	7^{10}	Castellano J J	L121 b	5.50	86–02	Wishingitws119$1\frac{1}{4}$ [D]SpnishEmpire123^{nk} SkGold121^2	4-5wide turns,empty	11
5Sep04-8Dmr	fst	1	:22^2 :46 1:10 1:35	3↑ DmrBCH-G2	**95**	4	4^2	1$\frac{1}{2}$	2^{hd}	5^3	5^7	Baze T C	LB116 b	6.10	92–07	SuphBlitz116^{no} DomesticDisput117^4 During117^1	3wd move,led,weakened	6
31May04-3BM	fst	1$\frac{1}{16}$	:23^1 :46 1:09^2 1:40	3↑ SbsctBCH-G3	**96**	3	4^3	4^2	4$2\frac{1}{2}$	4^4	3$3\frac{3}{4}$	Carr D	LB118 b	1.80	103–05	Yougottawanna116$\frac{3}{4}$ Gold Ruckus115^3 Snorter118$\frac{1}{2}$	Fanned 4w, no rally	5
24Apr04-8LS	sly	1	:23^1 :46^1 1:10 1:35^3	3↑ TexsMile-G3	**101**	5	7$7\frac{1}{2}$	7^8	6^{10}	4^9	4^7	Flores D R	L118 b	*2.30	88–22	Kela119$5\frac{1}{4}$ Supah Blitz116$1\frac{1}{2}$ *Yessirgeneralsir*114^{nk}	4w 1st turn,no rally	8
27Mar04-7GG	fst	1	:22^4 :46 1:09^4 1:33^4	3↑ BrklyBCH-G3	**102**	1	3^1	3^2	3$\frac{1}{2}$	3^{nk}	1^1	Baze R A	LB116 b	*2.00	100–09	Snorter116^1 *Yougottawanna*116^{nk} Taste of Paradise116^{hd}	Stlkd rail, drvng	5
4Feb04-6SA	fst	1	:23 :46^2 1:11^1 1:37	4↑ Alw 56000N2x	**99**	5	4$2\frac{1}{4}$	5$2\frac{1}{2}$	5$2\frac{1}{4}$	2$\frac{1}{2}$	1^1	Solis A	LB117 b	4.00	86–19	*Snorter*117^1 Spersive117^5 Traditional119^1	Tight 7/8,bid,gamely	7

Soaring Free

Own: Sam–Son Farms

Dk. b or b. g. 6 (Jan)
Sire: Smart Strike (Mr. Prospector) $35,000
Dam: Dancing With Wings (Danzig)
Br: Sam–Son Farm (Ont–C)
Tr: Frostad Mark R(0 0 0 0 .00) 2004:(269 49 .18)

Life	22	13	3	0	$1,917,544	109	D.Fst	7 3 2 0	$142,520	100
2004	8	6	0	0	$1,113,862	104	Wet(463)	2 1 0 0	$51,062	109
2003	8	5	1	0	$699,200	109	Turf(388)	13 9 1 0	$1,723,962	105
	0	0	0	0	$0	–	Dst(0)	0 0 0 0	$0	–

Date/Race	Cond	Dist	Fractions	Race	Fig	PP	St	1C	2C	Str	Fin	Jockey	Wt	Odds		Top Finishers	Comment	Fld
30Oct04-4LS	yl	1	Ⓣ :24 :48^3 1:12^3 1:36^4	3↑ BCMile-G1	**104**	4	1$1\frac{1}{2}$	1^1	1$\frac{1}{2}$	2^1	4$2\frac{1}{4}$	Kabel T K	L126	10.90	84–07	Singletry126$\frac{1}{2}$ AntoniusPius122$1\frac{1}{2}$ SixPerfctions123^{nk}	Set pace weakened	14
19Sep04-9WO	fm	1	Ⓣ :23^2 :46 1:09 1:32^3	3↑ AttoMile-G1	**103**	11	1$\frac{1}{2}$	2^{hd}	1$\frac{1}{2}$	1^1	1$\frac{3}{4}$	Kabel T K	L119	*2.15	100–03	SoaringFree119$\frac{3}{4}$ PerfectSoul121^{hd} *RoylRegl*118$1\frac{1}{4}$	Prominent throughout	11
28Aug04-8WO	gd	7f	Ⓣ :22^2 :45^1 1:08^4 1:20^4	3↑ PlayKngH-G3	**102**	8	2	3^{nk}	3$1\frac{1}{2}$	1^1	1$\frac{3}{4}$	Kabel T K	L126	*.60	98–09	*SoringFree*126$\frac{3}{4}$ FrnksSelection115^2 DncinJoey116$\frac{3}{4}$	Bmp'd,stumbled,drvg	12
24Jly04-8WO	fm	7f	Ⓣ :23 :45^2 1:08 1:19^1	3↑ [R]OntarioJC107k	**100**	1	2	1^1	1$\frac{1}{2}$	1$1\frac{1}{2}$	1$2\frac{1}{4}$	Kabel T K	L126	*.40	106	– *SoringFree*126$2\frac{1}{4}$ SuprCs118$1\frac{3}{4}$ AwsomAction118$3\frac{1}{4}$	Led throughout,driving	6
27Jun04-4WO	fm	6f	Ⓣ :22^3 :45^3 :56^4 1:08^3	3↑ HilandrH-G3	**98**	1	1	1^1	1^1	1^2	1$2\frac{1}{4}$	Kabel T K	L123	*.45	95–05	*SoringFr*123$2\frac{1}{4}$ DpnConcrt115$\frac{3}{4}$ TkAchncOnM116^{no}	Turned back rival,drvg	7
6Jun04-3WO	fm	6f	Ⓣ :22 :44 :55^3 1:08	3↑ Alw 78500NC	**99**	8	1	1^{hd}	1$\frac{1}{2}$	1$3\frac{1}{2}$	1$2\frac{3}{4}$	Kabel T K	L122	*.40	98–02	*SoringFr*122$2\frac{3}{4}$ MyLuckyStrk116^1 WltznStorm117^{nk}	Dueled 3-wide,driving	8
15May04-11Pim	fst	6f	:22^3 :45^4 :58^1 1:10^4	3↑ MdBCH-G3	**81**	8	2	5^5	5^2	8^7	8$9\frac{1}{4}$	Sellers S J	L121	*2.00	82–11	*GtorsNBers*117$1\frac{1}{4}$ HighwyProspector114$1\frac{1}{4}$ SssyHound115$\frac{1}{2}$	Wide, gave way	9
10Apr04-7Kee	fm	5$\frac{1}{2}$f	Ⓣ :21^2 :44 :55^3 1:01^3	3↑ Shakrtwn-G3	**101**	4	2	2^{hd}	1^{hd}	1^{hd}	1$1\frac{1}{2}$	Sellers S J	L120	*.70	103	– SoringFr120$1\frac{1}{2}$ ChosnChif118$\frac{1}{2}$ BnndinBoston118$\frac{1}{2}$	Bmp start,between,drv	12

Society Selection

Own: Cowan Marjorie and Irving M

B. f. 4 (Apr)
Sire: Coronado's Quest (Forty Niner) $50,000
Dam: Love That Jazz (Dixieland Band)
Br: Marjorie Cowan & Irving Cowan (Ky)
Tr: Jerkens H. A(0 0 0 0 .00) 2004:(374 72 .19)

Life	12	5	3	1	$1,256,700	107	D.Fst	9	3	3	1	$656,700	98
2004	9	3	3	1	$929,700	107	Wet(383)	3	2	0	0	$600,000	107
2003	3	2	0	0	$327,000	95	Turf(287)	0	0	0	0	$0	–
	0	0	0	0	$0	–	Dst(0)	0	0	0	0	$0	–

30Oct04–2LS gd 1⅛ :463 1:102 1:352 1:481 3↑ⒻBCDistaf-G1 **85** 4 63 6 2½ 9 4¼ 99 910 Velasquez C L119 5.10 98–02 Ashado1191¼ Storm Flag Flying123nk Stellar Jayne1191½ Steadied tad 7/8 11

9Oct04–9Bel fst 1⅛ :482 1:124 1:364 1:493 3↑ⒻBeldame-G1 **96** 4 31 32 3½ 26 2 2¾ Velasquez C L120 4.70 80–20 Sghtsk1232¾ SoctySlcton1201¼ StormFlgFlyng123¾ Game finish for place 5

21Aug04–10Sar sly 1¼ :471 1:112 1:362 2:023 ⒻAlabama-G1 **107** 7 7 3¾ 62 5 3¼ 31 1 2½ Velasquez C L121 5.70 94–18 Society Selection1212½ *Stellar Jayne*121½ *Ashado*1215¼ Determined outside 8

31Jly04–8Sar my 7f :212 :44 1:101 1:233 ⒻTest-G1 **96** 7 11 10 6¼ 67 2hd 1 6¼ Prado E S L120 3.35 86–11 *SocitySlcton*1206¼ BndngStrngs1203¾ ForstMusc1184¼ Quick 4 wide sweep 12

26Jun04–9Bel fst 1⅛ :47 1:104 1:352 1:48 ⒻMthrGoos-G1 **75** 6 2hd 32 3 1½ 612 6 14¾ Prado E S 121 3.80 76–11 Stellar Jayne1212½ *Ashado*1211¾ Island Sand1215 Chased 3 wide, tired 6

4Jun04–10Bel fst 1 :232 :454 1:094 1:344 ⒻAcorn-G1 **98** 2 8 5¾ 8 4½ 75 5 1½ 2 1¾ Chavez J F 121 *2.15 85–17 IslndSnd1211¾ SocietySlction121no *FrindlyMichl*121¾ Game finish outside 8

9Apr04–8Aqu fst 1 :224 :453 1:104 1:354 ⒻComely-G3 **90** 5 7 5½ 8 3¾ 2 1½ 1½ 13 Chavez J F 122 *1.65 86–15 SocitySlction1223 *BndingStrings*1162¾ *Dydrmng*1168½ Steadied turn, 5 wide 8

6Mar04–8GP fst 1⅛ :473 1:113 1:37 1:503 ⒻBonnieMs-G2 **89** 4 1 1½ 1½ 1½ 2hd 22 Bailey J D 120 *.50 84–21 Last Song1182 *Society Selection*1204¾ Rare Gift1167 Inside duel, 2nd best 5

7Feb04–8GP fst 1 1/16 :242 :49 1:14 1:443 ⒻDvonaDal-G2 **88** 2 32 42 3½ 31 3nk Bailey J D 121 *.80 86–09 MissCorondo117hd EyDzzlr115nk SocitySlcton121nk 3 wd, not enough late 7

Something Ventured

Own: Wiemer Irvin and McLane, John

Dk. b or b. m. 6 (Mar)
Sire: Cobra King (Farma Way) $5,000
Dam: Intend (Seattle Slew)
Br: Tomaeato Farm (Ky)
Tr: Pletcher Todd A(0 0 0 0 .00) 2004:(948 240 .25)

Life	35	6	9	5	$373,881	101	D.Fst	4	0	0	0	$540	31
2004	11	1	4	0	$114,920	98	Wet(375)	0	0	0	0	$0	–
2003	11	3	3	3	$193,171	101	Turf(309)	31	6	9	5	$373,341	101
	0	0	0	0	$0	–	Dst(0)	0	0	0	0	$0	–

18Dec04–9Crc fm 1½ Ⓣ :503 1:144 2:031 2:27 3↑ⒻLaPvyteH-G2 **78** 2 6 2¾ 5 2½ 6 4¼ 1011 9 10¼ Bailey J D L115 b 3.70 79–10 Arvada117hd Humaita1191½ Honey Ryder113¾ Checked, 4w, faded 11

4Dec04–8Crc fm 1⅛ Ⓣ :47 1:094 1:341 1:463 3↑ⒻMyChrmrH-G3 **98** 12 4 7½ 316 318 24 11 Velazquez J R L115 b 6.10 96–03 SomthingVnturd1151 Snowdrops115½ ChngingWorld1173¼ Rallied, up late 12

31Oct04–8Aqu fm 1 1/16 Ⓣ :252 :501 1:143 1:433 3↑ⒻAtheniaH-G3 **69** 6 10 6¼ 7 3½ 7 2½ 1014 1012 Velazquez J R L114 b 8.70 77–13 Finery113½ Madeira Mist118nk With Patience114½ Checked second turn 11

10Oct04–6Med gd 1 1/16 Ⓣ :233 :492 1:14 1:443 3↑ⒻNavjoPrcss60k **94** 1 32 31 42 3nk 2¾ Prado E S L115 b 2.60 74–28 DltPrncss119¾ SomthngVntrd1151 ConyKtty122no Lacked room near turn 6

12Sep04–8Bel gd 1 Ⓣ :223 :453 1:094 1:343 3↑ⒻⓇVoodooDncr61k **93** 6 7 6¾ 6 5½ 6 3½ 3 1½ 2 1¾ Velazquez J R L122 b 3.75 85–13 WithPtinc1221¾ SomthingVnturd122no FstCook124¾ 4 wide move, gamely 12

11Aug04–6Sar gd 1 🅃 :243 :49 1:124 1:363 4↑ⒻⓇDeLaRose66k **80** 8 5 3½ 54 5 3¾ 8 7½ 8 6¼ Velazquez J R L120 b 2.70 82–13 Personal Legend116hd *Lenti*116nk Vespers120¾ Wide both turns, tired 8

Run in divisions

3Jly04–6Bel fm 1 1/16 Ⓣ :232 :462 1:093 1:383 4↑ⒻAlw 56000c **97** 2 3 3½ 31 3 1½ 2½ 2 4¼ Velazquez J R L118 b 3.00 100–01 DeltPrincess1234¼ SomthingVnturd1184½ MrsM1163¼ 3 wide, second best 7

30May04–11Mth fm 1 Ⓣ :24 :48 1:12 1:36 3↑ⒻFortMth60k **88** 2 4 1½ 4 1½ 10 9¼ 9 4½ 5 3¾ Coa E M L115 b 3.60 88–16 High Court1191½ *Delta Princess*115½ *Mrs. M*115½ Checked 2nd turn 11

14Mar04–10Tam fm *1⅛ Ⓣ :49 1:124 1:37 1:484 4↑ⒻHlsborgh-G3 **79** 5 95 87 107 98 86 Day P L116 b 3.30 89–09 Coney Kitty116nk Madeira Mist122nk Alternate1163½ No factor 12

10Feb04–8Tam fm 1 1/16 Ⓣ :244 :503 1:154 1:444 4↑ⒻEndeavour100k **88** 1 12 6¾ 8 5¾ 6 1¾ 3nk 2¾ Decarlo C P L116 b 4.10 78–20 MdirMist116¾ SomthngVnturd116nk *ConyKtty*116¾ Mid m 4w, bumpd, hung 12

3Jan04–11GP fm 1 1/16 Ⓣ :234 :481 1:12 1:411 3↑ⒻHonyFoxH-G3 **86** 5 8 3¾ 8 5¼ 9 6¾ 8 3¾ 52 Velazquez J R L117 b *2.40 89–07 DelmonicoCt116½ ConeyKitty115nk *MdeirMist*117nk Even finish mid track 10

Sonic West
Own: Stone Spire LLC

B. g. 6 (Feb)
Sire: West by West (Gone West) $5,000
Dam: Contumelious (Northern Baby)
Br: Richard Lake (Ky)
Tr: Van Berg Thomas L(0 0 0 0 .00) 2004:(112 16 .14)

Life	22	7	5	3	$589,453	105
2004	10	2	2	2	$367,813	105
2003	9	4	2	1	$200,970	98
	0	0	0	0	$0	–

D.Fst	20	6	5	3	$529,453	105
Wet(326)	2	1	0	0	$60,000	98
Turf(268)	0	0	0	0	$0	–
Dst(0)	0	0	0	0	$0	–

13Nov04–9Mnr fst 1 :242 :48 1:1321:401 3↑MnrMileH100k 100 2 57¼ 513 59 46½ 24¾ Walker B J Jr LB121 fb *1.30 67– 37 *DiscretHro*1134¾ SonicWst121¾ FrnkiRsWinnr1111¾ Waited, belated bid in 5
30Oct04–5Kee fst 1⅛ :4711:112 1:3641:501 3↑Fayette-G3 86 2 34 54½ 57½ 46 412¾ Martinez W L121 fb 12.80 77– 10 *Midway Road*121no Total Impact1256 Alumni Hall1196¾ 5-6w lane,no threat 5
2Oct04–7Haw fst 1¼ :4711:111 1:3642:031 3↑HawGldCp-G2 98 7 59 47½ 32 41¼ 34 Razo E Jr L115 fb 14.00 86– 19 Freefourinternet1121¾ PerfctDrift1212¼ SonicWst1152¼ 3 wide, belatedly 7
18Sep04–11TP fst 1⅛ :4721:113 1:3621:49 3↑KyCpClH-G2 97 6 55¾ 46½ 58 56½ 34¾ Day P L113 f 8.30 86– 11 Roses in May1184 Pie N Burger117¾ Sonic West113nk 4 wide trip 6
28Aug04–9EIP fst 1 :232 :454 1:1011:351 3↑GovernorsH75k 91 9 97¼ 97¼ 76¾ 44½ 58¼ Martinez W L118 fb *1.80 96– 04 AddedEdge116¾ DiscretHro1127¼ RorofthTigr114nk Bmp start,flatten out 10
3Jly04–9PrM fst 1⅛ :4641:101 1:3421:463 3↑CrnhsBCH-G3 96 5 53 52½ 42 46 410¼ Martinez W LB115 fb 17.30 95– 12 *RosesinMay*1151½ PerfectDrift1194 CrftyShw1174¾ Within range, gave way 6
31May04–9LS fst 1 1/16 :224 :453 1:0821:411 3↑LSParkH-G3 100 2 55 58 47½ 36½ 22¼ Martinez W L117 fb 5.40 94– 08 Yssirgnrlsir1142¼ SonicWst1171 SpnishEmpir117nk Brushed 1/8, willingly 6
24Apr04–9Fon my 1 1/16 :233 :464 1:13 1:464 3↑BslmnGusFn100k 97 1 88 65¾ 63½ 2hd 1¾ Martinez W LB122 fb *.80 84– 15 SonicWst122¾ DustySpik116nk *TonightRinbow*1157 Angled 4wd, gamely up 9
3Apr04–11OP fst 1⅛ :4521:093 1:3521:481 4↑OaklawnH-G2 105 1 412 310 34½ 43 44½ Martinez W L112 b 22.80 92– 09 Peace Rules120¾ Ole Faunty116nk Saint Liam1142¼ Roused, empty 6
14Mar04–9OP fst 1 1/16 :234 :472 1:1141:432 4↑RazrbckH-G3 104 2 43 32½ 3½ 11 12¾ Martinez W L113 b 7.40 93– 23 Sonic West1132¾ Crafty Shaw117hd Pie N Burger1192 Stalked, drove clear 7

Southern Image
Own: Blahut Stables LLC Kagele Brothers, T

Dk. b or b. h. 5 (Apr)
Sire: Halo's Image (Halo) $10,000
Dam: Pleasant Dixie (Dixieland Band)
Br: Arthur I. Appleton (Fla)
Tr: Machowsky Michael(0 0 0 0 .00) 2004:(154 23 .15)

Life	8	6	1	1	$1,843,750	118
2004	4	3	1	0	$1,612,150	118
2003	3	2	0	1	$202,800	108
	0	0	0	0	$0	–

D.Fst	7	6	0	1	$1,681,600	118
Wet(346)	1	0	1	0	$162,150	110
Turf(269)	0	0	0	0	$0	–
Dst(0)	0	0	0	0	$0	–

12Jun04–9CD sly 1⅛ :4731:122 1:3721:502 3↑SFosterH-G1 110 3 31½ 21½ 41¾ 1hd 2no Espinoza V L122 f *1.50 85– 17 ColonilColony111no SouthrnImg1225 PrfctDrift1193¾ Bmp late,outgamed 6
14May04–11Pim fst 1 3/16 :4721:114 1:3611:554 4↑PimSpclH-G1 118 4 2½ 21 2½ 1½ 11¼ Espinoza V L120 1.90 98– 17 SothrnImg1201¼ MdwyRd1162½ BwmnsBnd1144¾ Snugly rated,2wd,drvng 6
6Mar04–10SA fst 1¼ :4611:101 1:3512:013 4↑SAH-G1 113 2 41¼ 3nk 11½ 11½ 11¼ Espinoza V LB118 *1.00 91– 11 *SouthrnImg*1181¼ IslndFshion1152¼ SintBuddy1114 Inside,led,held gamely 8
24Jan04–6SA fst 1⅛ :4531:092 1:3421:473 4↑ⓇSMClassic1000k 107 8 52½ 32 31 1½ 13 Espinoza V LB120 3.10 96– 07 *SouthrnImg*1203 ExcssSummr1205 ThJdgSzWho122½ Pulled,3wd bid,clear 12

Souvenir Gift
Own: Semkin Sam and Unruh, Gregory

B. f. 3 (Apr) BAROCY03 $25,000
Sire: Souvenir Copy (Mr. Prospector) $10,000
Dam: Alleged Gift (Alleged)
Br: Mrs. John C. Mabee (Ky)
Tr: Semkin Sam(0 0 0 0 .00) 2004:(42 5 .12)

Life	5	3	2	0	$211,760	90	D.Fst 5 3 2 0 $211,760 90
2004	5	3	2	0	$211,760	90	Wet(349) 0 0 0 0 $0 –
2003	0	M	0	0	$0	–	Turf(300) 0 0 0 0 $0 –
	0	0	0	0	$0	–	Dst(0) 0 0 0 0 $0 –

28Aug04–8Dmr fst 7f :22 :44² 1:10² 1:24 Ⓕ DmrDeb-G1 **74** 6 4 5³¼ 5⁴¼ 2½ 2¾ Baze T C LB120 3.10 81–13 *SweetCtomin*114¾ SouvnirGift120 1½ HlloLucky116 2½ 5wd rally, led, caught 9
7Aug04–8Dmr fst 6½f :21³ :44⁴ 1:11 1:18¹ Ⓕ Sorrento-G3 **72** 4 6 2hd 2½ 2¹ 2 2½ Smith M E LB122 1.50 81–13 Inspiring118 2½ Souvenir Gift122 2½ Hello Lucky118½ Came out lane,willing 8
5Jly04–8Hol fst 6f :21⁴ :44² :56³ 1:09³ Ⓕ Landaluc-G3 **90** 2 6 3¹ 3³ 3² 1 1¼ Smith M E LB119 4.10 89–09 SouvenirGift119 1¼ BellBniss117no MyMissStormCt116⁸ Rail rally,gamely 11
6Jun04–3Hol fst 5½f :21⁴ :45³ :58 1:04⁴ Ⓕ Cinderella85k **72** 4 3 3¹ 2½ 1 2½ 1 4½ Smith M E LB116 7.00 84–14 *SouvenirGift*116 4½ FortunteEvent112 3½ SwissPls116⁶ 3wd bid,clear,rid out 6
14Apr04–1SA fst 2f :11² :22 Ⓕ Md Sp Wt 40k – 6 2 1 1½ 1 1½ Baze T C LB118 4.80 95–12 *SouvnirGift*118 1½ DownhillChmp118hd SwissLdybug118 1½ Steady handling 9

Spanish Empire
Own: Jubilee Stable Cherry, Martin L. and

Dk. b or b. h. 5 (May)
Sire: Pleasant Colony (His Majesty)
Dam: La Paz (Hold Your Peace)
Br: John R. Gaines Thoroughbreds & Twin Creeks Farm (Ky)
Tr: Asmussen Steven M(0 0 0 0 .00) 2004:(2293 555 .24)

Life	20	5	3	3	$276,714	109	D.Fst 15 4 2 3 $234,314 109
2004	9	2	1	1	$155,000	109	Wet(374) 3 1 0 0 $33,600 100
2003	8	3	2	2	$121,714	99	Turf(274) 2 0 1 0 $8,800 82
	0	0	0	0	$0	–	Dst(0) 0 0 0 0 $0 –

4Dec04–9FG fst 1 1/16 :24 :47⁴ 1:12⁴ 1:45² 3↑ TenaciousH60k – 4 2 1½ 2¹ 6¹⁵ – – Meche L J L119 4.40 – 25 Midway Road123no PieNBurger120¾ Kodema116½ Stopped abruptly,eased 6
30Oct04–1LS gd 1 :23² :46³ 1:10² 1:35² 3↑ MetrplxMil100k **100** 6 3 1½ 3nk 2hd 1½ 2 1¼ Martin E M Jr L123 11.40 95–02 Wishingitws119 1¼ Ⓓ SpnishEmpire123nk SekGold121² Drifted in 1/8,wknd 11
Disqualified and placed 4th
2Oct04–9TP fst 1 :22⁴ :46¹ 1:11 1:37 3↑ TPFallCh-G3 **69** 7 3 1½ 3² 4³ 7⁹ 7 15¼ Sellers S J L119 3.70 74–19 Cappuchino115⁴ Crafty Shaw122nk *Added Edge*119¹ 5 wide early 7
31May04–9LS fst 1 1/16 :22⁴ :45³ 1:08² 1:41¹ 3↑ LSParkH-G3 **98** 1 4⁴ 4⁷ 5 7½ 4 6½ 3 3¼ Sellers S J L117 4.60 93–08 Yessirgenrlsir114 2¼ SonicWst117¹ SpnishEmpir117nk 3w 2nd turn,no rally 6
30Apr04–6CD sly 1 1/16 :24 :48 1:12 1:44¹ 3↑ Alysheba113k **88** 7 5 3¼ 3¹ 2hd 4³ 7⁷ Sellers S J L120 4.70 80–17 Congrats116 1¾ Perfect Drift114¾ Kodema120no Bid 5w,led,faltered 8
7Apr04–9OP fst 1 1/16 :23 :46² 1:10³ 1:42² 4↑ 5thSeasn-G3 **101** 7 3 3½ 3½ 2hd 1½ 1¹ Martin E M Jr L118 *1.80 98–10 SpanishEmpire118¹ *CraftyShw*122nk NoComprende122² Determined drive 8
29Feb04–9FG fst 1⅛ :47 1:10² 1:35² 1:48³ 4↑ NwOrlnsH-G2 **88** 3 6 4¼ 6⁵ 5 6½ 6¹⁰ 7¹⁵ Martin E M Jr L118 21.30 86–05 *Peace Rules*119hd Saint Liam114 2¾ *Funny Cide*118 1¼ Bumped, no real threat 8
1Feb04–8FG fst 1 1/16 :24² :47² 1:11⁴ 1:45² 4↑ WhrlwayH-G3 **106** 2 2½ 2½ 1¹ 1½ 2¾ Martin E M Jr L118 2.40 82–17 Olmodavor121¾ Spanish Empire118 2¼ Almuhathir114½ Out kicked to wire 9
2Jan04–9FG fst 1 1/16 :23⁴ :48 1:12² 1:43² 4↑ LouisianaH60k **109** 7 3 1½ 3½ 1hd 1 1½ 1¹ Martin E M Jr L118 11.80 93–18 Spanish Empire118¹ Tenpins122² Comic Truth118½ Drifted in, held on 7

Special Ring
Own: Prestonwood Farm LLC

B. g. 8 (Mar)
Sire: Nureyev (Northern Dancer) $100,000
Dam: Ring Beaune (Bering*GB)
Br: Wertheimer & Frere (Ky)
Tr: Canani Julio C(0 0 0 0 .00) 2004:(186 42 .23)

Life	**28**	**10**	**4**	**3**	**$915,023**	**111**	**D.Fst**	**0**	**0**	**0**	**0**	**$0**	**–**
2004	**3**	**1**	**0**	**0**	**$240,000**	**110**	**Wet(337)**	**0**	**0**	**0**	**0**	**$0**	**–**
2003	**5**	**1**	**2**	**0**	**$383,000**	**111**	**Turf(325)**	**28**	**10**	**4**	**3**	**$915,023**	**111**
	0	**0**	**0**	**0**	**$0**	**–**	**Dst(0)**	**0**	**0**	**0**	**0**	**$0**	**–**

27Nov04–7Hol fm 1$\frac{1}{16}$ Ⓣ :23^{3} :48 1:11^{2} 1:41^{1} 3↑CtationH-G1 **77** 10 6$3\frac{1}{2}$ 4$1\frac{1}{2}$ 5$1\frac{3}{4}$ 9$9\frac{3}{4}$ 10$15\frac{3}{4}$ Nakatani C S **LB**120 b 5.20 74– 17 Leroidesnimux11$7\frac{1}{2}$ AtotheZ115^{1} ThreeVlleys115$\frac{1}{2}$ 5wd into lane,gave way 10

30Oct04–4LS yl 1 Ⓣ :24 :48^{3} 1:12^{3} 1:36^{4} 3↑BCMile-G1 **89** 3 3$1\frac{1}{2}$ 2^{1} 3$\frac{1}{2}$ 13^{8} 13^{9} Espinoza V L126 b 8.50 77– 07 Singltry126$\frac{1}{2}$ AntcniusPius122$1\frac{1}{2}$ SixPrfctions123^{nk} Bobbled brk, steadied 14

25Jly04–8Dmr fm 1⅛ Ⓣ :47 1:11 1:34^{2} 1:45^{4} 3↑EdReadH-G1 **110** 9 1$1\frac{1}{2}$ 1$3\frac{1}{2}$ 1^{1} 1$1\frac{1}{2}$ 1$\frac{3}{4}$ Espinoza V **LB**118 b *.90e100– 03 Special Ring118$\frac{3}{4}$ Bayamo119$\frac{3}{4}$ Sweet Return119$\frac{3}{4}$ Bit off rail,held game 10

Speightstown
Own: Melnyk Eugene and Laura

Ch. h. 7 (Feb)
Sire: Gone West (Mr. Prospector) $150,000
Dam: Silken Cat (Storm Cat)
Br: Aaron U. Jones & Marie Jones (Ky)
Tr: Pletcher Todd A(0 0 0 0 .00) 2004:(948 240 .25)

Life	**16**	**10**	**2**	**2**	**$1,258,256**	**117**	**D.Fst**	**13**	**8**	**1**	**2**	**$1,064,600**	**117**
2004	**6**	**5**	**0**	**1**	**$1,045,556**	**117**	**Wet(409)**	**3**	**2**	**1**	**0**	**$193,656**	**116**
2003	**2**	**1**	**1**	**0**	**$56,020**	**105**	**Turf(329)**	**0**	**0**	**0**	**0**	**$0**	**–**
	0	**0**	**0**	**0**	**$0**	**–**	**Dst(0)**	**0**	**0**	**0**	**0**	**$0**	**–**

30Oct04–5LS fst 6f :21^{1} :43^{2} :55^{2} 1:08 3↑BCSprint-G1 **112** 2 8 4$1\frac{1}{2}$ 3^{1} 1$1\frac{1}{2}$ 1$1\frac{1}{4}$ Velazquez J R L126 3.70 100– 04 Speightstown126$1\frac{1}{4}$ Kela126$\frac{3}{4}$ My Cousin Matt126$\frac{1}{2}$ Rail trip,edged clear 13

2Oct04–8Bel fst 6f :22^{3} :45^{3} :57^{1} 1:09^{3} 3↑Vosburgh-G1 **102** 2 2 1$\frac{1}{2}$ 2^{hd} 2$\frac{1}{2}$ 3$4\frac{1}{2}$ Velazquez J R L124 *.80 86– 22 Pico Central124^{4} Voodoo124$\frac{1}{2}$ *Speightstown*124^{hd} Bobbled start, between 5

14Aug04–7Sar fst 6f :22 :44^{2} :55^{4} 1:08 3↑AGVndbtH-G2 **117** 2 5 1^{hd} 2^{hd} 1$2\frac{1}{2}$ 1$1\frac{1}{2}$ Velazquez J R L120 *.90 102– 12 Spghtstown120$1\frac{1}{2}$ ClockStopp'115$1\frac{1}{2}$ GtrsNBrs118^{2} Vied inside, kept busy 6

5Jun04–7Bel fst 6f :21^{2} :43^{3} :55^{1} 1:08 3↑TrNthBCH-G2 **115** 3 1 2$2\frac{1}{2}$ 1$\frac{1}{2}$ 1$1\frac{1}{2}$ 1$1\frac{1}{2}$ Velazquez J R L119 *1.80 99– 07 *Speightstown*119$1\frac{1}{2}$ Cat Genius116$1\frac{3}{4}$ *Pohave*117^{nk} When roused, driving 9

1May04–5CD gd 7f :22^{2} :45^{1} 1:08^{4} 1:21^{1} 4↑CDH-G2 **116** 1 3 1^{1} 1^{1} 1$2\frac{1}{2}$ 1$3\frac{1}{2}$ Velazquez J R L115 5.40 96– 06 *Speightstown*115$3\frac{1}{2}$ McCannsMojve117^{2} Publiction116^{2} Speed,inside,clear 7

27Mar04–11GP fst 7f :22^{1} :44^{4} 1:09 1:22 3↑ArtaxH100k **106** 1 1 1^{hd} 1^{hd} 1$3\frac{1}{2}$ 1$4\frac{1}{2}$ Coa E M L116 *3.20 92– 16 *Speightstown*116$4\frac{1}{2}$ *PrttyWild*111no WckyforLov115$3\frac{1}{4}$ Dueled rail, drew off 9

Splendid Blended

Own: Vegso Peter

Ch. f. 3 (May)
Sire: Unbridled's Song (Unbridled) $125,000
Dam: Valid Blend (Valid Appeal)
Br: Peter Vegso Racing Stable (Fla)
Tr: Drysdale Neil D(0 0 0 0 .00) 2004:(180 37 .21)

Life	4	3	1	0	$327,400	92	
2004	4	3	1	0	$327,400	92	
2003	0	M	0	0	$0	–	
	0	0	0	0	$0	–	

D.Fst	4	3	1	0	$327,400	92
Wet(378)	0	0	0	0	$0	–
Turf(283)	0	0	0	0	$0	–
Dst(0)	0	0	0	0	$0	–

19Dec04–8Hol fst 1 1/16 :233 :464 1:11 1:414 ⒻHolStrlt-G1 **92** 7 2½ 2hd 2hd 11½ 12 Desormeaux K J **LB**120 *1.30 92– 10 SplndidBlndd1202 ShrpLis1202 NorthrnMischf1203 Pulled,dueled,cleared 7
14Nov04–2Hol fst 1 1/16 :223 :461 1:104 1:433 ⒻAlw 41974N1x **84** 2 2hd 11½ 12 11 13¼ Desormeaux K J **LB**120 *.10 83– 13 *Splendid Blended*1203¼ Home Ice1187 *Ninadivina*1189 Dueled,clear,handily 6
20Oct04–9SA fst 1 1/16 :23 :464 1:111 1:424 ⒻOakLeaf-G2 **84** 3 4¾ 3½ 31 22½ 24 Desormeaux K J **LB**119 *1.40 87– 08 *SweetCtomine*1194 *SplndidBlndd*1192½ Mmortt1194 Rank,wide 7/8,2nd best 9
6Sep04–4Dmr fst 1 :23 :474 1:123 1:37 ⒻMd Sp Wt 57k **78** 7 1½ 1½ 11 12½ 15 Desormeaux K J **B**118 *1.70 89– 13 SplnddBlndd1185 *SpOnforMom*1184 GrvyCrwn1182 Drifted out,ridden out 9

Spotlight (GB)

Own: Green Hills Farm

Ch. f. 4 (Apr)
Sire: Dr Fong (Kris S.) $16,052
Dam: Dust Dancer*GB (Suave Dancer)
Br: Hesmonds Stud Ltd (GB)
Tr: Clement Christophe(0 0 0 0 .00) 2004:(344 68 .20)

Life	11	4	3	1	$221,793	100	
2004	7	2	2	0	$187,058	100	
2003	4	2	1	1	$34,735	–	
	0	0	0	0	$0	–	

D.Fst	0	0	0	0	$0	–
Wet(338*)	0	0	0	0	$0	–
Turf(326*)	11	4	3	1	$221,793	100
Dst(0)	0	0	0	0	$0	–

23Oct04–7Crc gd 1⅛ Ⓣ:494 1:141 1:39 1:512 ⒻCalderOaks200k **86** 9 76 65¼ 41 41 44 Bailey J D L121 f *.40 68– 28 *HopelesslyDevotd*1212¾ Vous118¾ SkipCommnd116½ Steadied early, 4 wide 12
18Sep04–9AP fm 1⅛ Ⓣ:474 1:121 1:364 1:483 ⒻPuckerUp-G3 **87** 10 97 97¾ 63½ 53½ 22¾ Douglas R R L122 1.30 93– 05 *Ticker Tape*1222¾ Spotlight122hd *Sister Swank*116½ 4-5 wide, second best 11
23Aug04–8Sar gd 1⅛ Ⓣ:50 1:141 1:381 1:502 ⒻLakPlcdH-G2 **100** 5 32 21 2½ 1½ 13½ Bailey J D L116 *1.55 78– 31 Spotlight1163½ Mambo Slew120¾ *FortunateDamsel*1163 When roused, clear 7
23Jly04–8Bel sf 1⅛ Ⓣ:493 1:144 1:403 1:531 3↑ⒻAlw 48000N2x **91** 4 42½ 1½ 12 13½ 12 Bailey J D L115 *1.15 64– 40 *Spotlight*1152 Finery1213 Pattiano1213¼ Took over after a half 7
Previously trained by John Dunlop
19May04 Goodwood (GB) gf 1¼ Ⓣ RH 2:07 ⒻLupe Stakes (Listed) Stk 53400 2nk Kinane M J 123 4.50 Halicardia120nk *Spotlight*1236 Carini1202½ 7
Timeform rating: **106** *Trckd in 4th,led 3f out,clear 1f out,headed near line*
2May04 Newmarket (GB) gd 1 Ⓣ Str 1:363 Ⓕ1000 Guineas Stakes-G1 Stk 573000 1616¾ Ahern E 126 33.00 *Attraction*126½ Sundrop126½ Hathrah1261¼ 16
Timeform rating: **69** *Raced alone in center,angled over 3f out,wknd 2f out*
17Apr04 Newbury (GB) gd 7f Ⓣ Str 1:292 ⒻFred Darling Stakes-G3 Stk 89800 43¼ Murtagh J P 126 3.30 Majestic Desert1261 Nyramba1261 Nataliya1261¼ 8
Timeform rating: **96** *Set slow pace,quickened 2-1/2f out,headed 1f out*

Spring Star (Fr)

Own: Wertheimer and Frere

B. m. 6 (May)
Sire: Danehill (Danzig)
Dam: L'Irlandaise (Irish River*Fr)
Br: Wertheimer Et Frere (Fr)
Tr: Mandella Richard E(0 0 0 0 .00) 2004:(160 24 .15)

Life	12	5	1	4	$320,336	101	
2004	1	1	0	0	$66,540	99	
2003	5	2	0	3	$182,313	101	
	0	0	0	0	$0	–	

D.Fst	0	0	0	0	$0	–
Wet(371)	0	0	0	0	$0	–
Turf(391)	12	5	1	4	$320,336	101
Dst(0)	0	0	0	0	$0	–

25Apr04–7Hol fm 1 Ⓣ:232 :464 1:102 1:332 3↑ⒻWilshirH-G3 **99** 9 21½ 21½ 21 1½ 12½ Solis A **LB**117 6.60 97– 05 Spring Star1172½ Quero Quero115no Dublino1201 Balked gate,gamely 9

St Averil
Own: Fulton Stan E

Dk. b or b. c. 4 (Mar) FTKJUL02 $500,000
Sire: Saint Ballado (Halo) $125,000
Dam: Avie's Fancy (Lord Avie)
Br: Gunsmith Stables (Ky)
Tr: Carroll David M(0 0 0 0 .00) 2004:(157 33 .21)

Life	6	2	2	0	$238,000	102	D.Fst	6	2	2	0	$238,000 102
2004	4	1	1	0	$140,000	102	Wet(382)	0	0	0	0	$0 –
2003	2	1	1	0	$98,000	96	Turf(318)	0	0	0	0	$0 –
	0	0	0	0	$0	–	Dst(0)	0	0	0	0	$0 –

27Nov04–7CD fst 7f :222 :444 1:092 1:223 3↑ Alw 46910N2x **53** 8 8 96 1/4 1110 1217 1225 Melancon L L117 b *2.10 64–15 Saratoga County11751/4 Kenta Kun1213/4 Ominous11911/4 8w lane,outrun 12
Previously trained by Becerra Rafael
3Apr04–8SA fst 1 1/8 :464 1:11 1:362 1:491 SADerby-G1 **86** 7 54 54 3/4 64 1/4 76 1/4 610 1/2 Baze T C LB122 b *2.20 77–09 Castledale122hd Rock Hard Ten1222 Imperialism1221 4wd 7/8,weakened 7
14Mar04–5SA fst 1 1/16 :231 :464 1:11 1:424 SnFelipe-G2 **101** 7 53 1/2 45 32 21 1/2 2no Baze T C LB122 b *1.30 91–09 Preachinatthebar116no StAveril12241/2 HrvrdAvenue1161 4wd,3wd,willingly 9
17Jan04–7SA fst 1 1/16 :223 :453 1:094 1:413 StCtlina-G2 **102** 8 41 3/4 52 31 1/2 31 1/2 11 1/2 Baze T C LB113 b 2.20 97–20 St Averil11311/2 Lucky Pulpit1152 *Master David*113hd 3wd bid,led past 1/8 9

Star Cross (Arg)
Own: E. A. Ranches

Ch. h. 8 (Sep)
Sire: Southern Halo (Halo) $21,050
Dam: Other Star (Logical)
Br: La Quebrada (Arg)
Tr: Vienna Darrell(0 0 0 0 .00) 2004:(162 17 .10)

Life	27	8	2	4	$298,299	102	D.Fst	17	5	1	3	$265,400 102
2004	5	1	1	0	$140,000	102	Wet(345)	4	3	0	1	$21,792 –
2003	4	1	0	1	$101,277	102	Turf(255)	6	0	1	0	$11,107 93
	0	0	0	0	$0	–	Dst(0)	0	0	0	0	$0 –

8May04–9Hol fst 1 1/16 :231 :454 1:092 1:404 3↑ MrvrLRyH-G2 **41** 5 86 1/4 86 1/4 811 816 834 1/2 Espinoza V LB113 b 8.90 62–04 *EventheScore*1162 EndersShdow1133 TotlImpct1161 Wide,gave way,eased 8
3Apr04–10SA fst 1 1/8 :471 1:112 1:354 1:48 4↑ SnBrdnoH-G3 **96** 2 34 35 1/2 43 54 1/2 610 Espinoza V LB114 b 4.70 84–09 Dynever11741/2 Total Impact1162 *Even theScore*1162 Pulled,stalked,wkened 7
6Mar04–10SA fst 1 1/4 :461 1:101 1:351 2:013 4↑ SAH-G1 **83** 5 87 1/4 86 1/4 89 3/4 812 820 Nakatani C S LB116 b 6.90 71–11 *SouthernImage*11811/4 IslandFashion11521/4 SaintBuddy1114 No rally outside 8
31Jan04–8SA fst 1 1/8 :463 1:10 1:343 1:471 4↑ SnAntnoH-G2 **102** 2 21/2 1 1/2 3nk 32 24 Espinoza V LB114 b 10.80 94–06 *PlesntlyPerfect*1214 StrCross114nk FleetstreetDncr1164 Bit tight into lane 4
3Jan04–7SA fst 1 1/16 :224 :454 1:093 1:421 4↑ SnPsqalH-G2 **100** 3 54 53 42 3/4 22 1 1/2 Espinoza V LB113 b 8.70 94–13 Star Cross1131/2 *Nose The Trade*1153 *Olmodavor*11821/2 Bit tight 3/8,rallied 7

Star Over the Bay
Own: G Racing VanBurger, Carl F. and Vaugh

Gr/ro. g. 7 (Feb)
Sire: Cozzene (Caro*Ire) $50,000
Dam: Lituya Bay (Empery)
Br: Four Horsemen's Ranch (Fla)
Tr: Mitchell Mike R(0 0 0 0 .00) 2004:(391 97 .25)

Life	40	9	4	3	$638,353	105	D.Fst	2	0	0	0	$2,400	93
2004	9	5	1	0	$493,960	105	Wet(270)	0	0	0	0	$0	-
2003	7	1	1	0	$32,800	89	Turf(332)	38	9	4	3	$635,953	105
	0	0	0	0	$0	-	Dst(0)	0	0	0	0	$0	-

30Oct04-8LS yl 1½ Ⓣ :49 1:13⁴ 2:04 2:29³ 3↑BCTurf-G1 83 7 1⁵ 1² 5 3½ 8⁹ 8 15¾ Baze T C L126 8.10 107-07 Better Talk Now126 1¾ Kitten's Joy121 1 Powerscourt126 2¼ Used up 8
3Oct04-5SA fm 1¼ Ⓣ :47 1:11 1:35 1:58³ 3↑CLHirsch-G1 105 5 1⁸ 1⁸ 1 2½ 1² 1¾ Baze T C LB124 4.90 96-09 Star Over the Bay124¾ Sarafan124¾ Vangelis124¾ Inside, held on gamely 7
29Aug04-8Dmr fm 1⅜ Ⓣ :47³ 1:12¹ 1:36⁴ 2:12³ 3↑DelMarH-G2 101 1 1 3½ 1 2½ 1¹ 1 1½ 1nk Baze T C LB116 2.60e 97-08 *StrOverthBy*116nk Srfn121 2 MoscowBurning114hd Cleared,held on gamely 9
18Jly04-8Hol fm 1½ Ⓣ :47⁴ 1:11³ 2:01¹ 2:26² 3↑SunsetH-G2 102 4 1 3½ 1 1½ 1² 1 1½ 1no Baze T C LB113 3.00 94-15 *StrOvrthBy*113no Continuously116 1 LprchunKd114 9 Inside,held on gamely 7
19Jun04-9LS fm 1⅛ Ⓣ :47³ 1:11³ 1:36³ 1:49⁴ 3↑DllasTfCpH200k 102 5 2½ 2¹ 2hd 1½ 2nk Court J K L115 2.00 94-14 *MysvilleSlew*115nk *StrOvertheBy*115 1½ AtothZ115 2¼ Trackd 3w,clear,caught 7
16May04-7Hol fm 1 Ⓣ :22⁴ :45⁴ 1:09 1:33 4↑Clm c-(80-70) 102 1 1⁴ 1⁶ 1² 1 3½ 1⁴ Nakatani C S LB118 4.20 99-01 StrOvertheBy118 4 GoldenDrgon120½ SwtStppr120½ Rail,strong hand ride 8
Claimed from Fitzpatrick, Patricia and Stephen for $80,000, Cerin Vladimir Trainer 2004(as of 5/16): (132 23 22 20 0.17)
27Mar04-1SA fst 1 :23 :46¹ 1:10¹ 1:35³ 4↑Alw 35000s 93 4 5 2½ 3 1½ 4 1½ 4 2¾ 4³ Nakatani C S LB120 3.50 90-11 EarlySnow118 2½ *BaldwinCounty*118½ Oberwld118no 3wd to lane,missed 3rd 6
7Mar04-3SA fm 1⅛ Ⓣ :46¹ 1:09² 1:34¹ 1:46³ 4↑Clm 62500(62.5-55) 95 2 2¹ 2hd 1 2½ 1⁴ 1 2½ Baze T C LB118 4.70 96-07 StrOvrthBy118 2½ Adminnistrtor118 2 *LprchunKd*118 3½ Bid,cleared,held rail 5
14Feb04-7SA fm 1 Ⓣ :22⁴ :46³ 1:10⁴ 1:34² 4↑OC 62k/n2x 89 1 3 1½ 4 1½ 4 1½ 5 2½ 4 3½ Ramsammy E LB119 37.60 86-10 KingofHappiness119 1½ *SpecilRte*117 1 DocHolidy112 1 Steadied twice early 9

Star Parade (Arg)
Own: Tanaka Gary A

Dk. b or b. m. 6 (Oct)
Sire: Parade Marshal (Caro*Ire)
Dam: Clerical Etoile*Arg (The Watcher)
Br: Firmamento (Arg)
Tr: Vienna Darrell(0 0 0 0 .00) 2004:(162 17 .10)

Life	18	6	5	2	$659,782	106	D.Fst	14	6	5	1	$656,495	106
2004	6	2	2	1	$483,670	106	Wet(226)	1	0	0	1	$227	-
2003	9	3	3	0	$173,396	106	Turf(217)	3	0	0	0	$3,060	88
	0	0	0	0	$0	-	Dst(0)	0	0	0	0	$0	-

8Aug04-8Dmr fst 1 1/16 :22² :46 1:10³ 1:42⁴ 3↑ⒻCLHrschH-G2 93 6 2¹ 2¹ 2½ 4¾ 4 5¼ Espinoza V LB119 *1.80 89-06 MssLorn114 3¼ HosofFortn113 1 RoyllyChosn116 1 Bid,btwn lane,outkickd 8
11Jly04-8Hol fst 1 1/16 :23³ :46¹ 1:09⁴ 1:41⁴ 3↑ⒻMladyBCH-G1 98 2 1¹ 1¹ 2hd 1½ 1 3½ Espinoza V LB116 *1.90 92-07 Star Parade116 3½ Quero Quero115hd Pesci114 2 Headed,gamely,clear 5
9May04-8Hol fst 1⅛ :46¹ 1:09³ 1:35² 1:48¹ 3↑ⒻVanityH-G1 87 3 2¹ 2hd 2½ 2¹ 3 3½ Espinoza V LB117 1.60 94-02 VictoryEncounter116 2½ *Adoration*122 1 *StarParde*117 5 Bid,vied,outfinished 4
3Apr04-9OP fst 1 1/16 :23¹ :46³ 1:10⁴ 1:41¹ 4↑ⒻAplBlsmH-G1 106 3 2¹ 2½ 2 1½ 3³ 3 3¼ McKee J L114 10.50 101-09 Azeri123 1½ DWild Spirit119 1¾ Star Parade114 7¼ Soundly bumped 1/4 6
Awarded second purse money
14Mar04-8SA fst 1⅛ :46³ 1:11 1:35⁴ 1:48⁴ 4↑ⒻSMrgrtaH-G1 104 2 1¹ 1² 1¹ 2¹ 2² Espinoza V LB115 2.10 88-09 Adoration118 2 Star Parade115hd BareNecessities118 2 Pulled,rail,held 2nd 5
16Feb04-8SA fst 1 1/16 :22² :46 1:10² 1:43⁴ 4↑ⒻSntMriaH-G1 99 6 1¹ 1 1½ 1 1½ 1 1½ 1hd Espinoza V LB114 *1.20 86-18 Star Parade114hd Bare Necessities118 2 La Tour115 2 Pulled,cleared,held 6

Stay Forever
Own: Santa Cruz Ranch Inc

Ch. m. 8 (Apr)
Sire: Stack (Nijinsky II) $4,000
Dam: Forever Lady (Forever Sparkle)
Br: Santa Cruz Ranch Inc. (Fla)
Tr: Wolfson Martin D(0 0 0 0 .00) 2004:(176 39 .22)

Life	17	10	2	1	$910,399	97		
2004	7	4	1	0	$581,946	97		
2003	3	1	0	0	$198,500	97		
	0	0	0	0	$0	–		
D.Fst	0	0	0	0	$0	–		
Wet(225)	0	0	0	0	$0	–		
Turf(253)	17	10	2	1	$910,399	97		
Dst(0)	0	0	0	0	$0	–		

10Oct04–6Kee fm 1 3/16 Ⓣ :50 1:142 1:391 1:57 3↑ⒻWnStGlxy-G2 96 5 94 97¼ 88 51¼ 1½ Castro E L121 b 8.00 86– 12 Stay Forever121½ Super Brand1191½ Shaconage121no 7-8w lane,stiff drive 9
5Jly04–9Bel sf 1¼ Ⓣ :50 1:15 1:402 2:053 3↑ⒻNewYorkH-G2 97 2 53 54¼ 31½ 25 23¼ Castro E L115 b 8.70 63– 34 WonderAgin1153¼ StyForever115no SpiceIslnd1186½ Brushed stretch, game 7
29May04–9CD fm 1 1/16 Ⓣ :241 :483 1:124 1:423 4↑ⒻMntJulpH-G3 96 3 66½ 95¾ 86½ 45½ 1½ Castro E L116 b 5.00 91– 13 StyForever116½ SndSprings120nk EternlMlody1152¼ Circled 8w lane,drvg 9
1May04–5Crc gd 1 1/16 Ⓣ :232 :471 1:104 1:42 3↑ⒻHolWdctBCH145k 94 10 119¾ 1112 76 42 1¾ Castro E L114 b 5.90 89– 18 StayForever114¾ MrsM1131¼ Sweettrickydncer114hd 4 wd, up final strides 11
4Apr04–9Tam fm 1 1/16 Ⓣ :231 :471 1:12 1:42 4↑ⒻTurfDstaff84k 74 1 1113 1117 1112 108 86¼ Santos J A L118 b *1.00 87– 10 ⒹImprovised116¾ SkiptoSavannh116nk FormlMiss116no Failed to threaten 11
28Feb04–11GP fm 1⅜ Ⓣ :51 1:172 1:423 2:193 3↑ⒻVeryOneH-G3 88 1 119¼ 119¾ 108½ 98¼ 85¼ Santos J A L114 b 6.20 55– 34 Binya1142½ Ocean Silk115½ Boana114¾ 4 wide, no factor 12
6Feb04–9GP yl *1 Ⓣ :25 :501 1:154 1:412 4↑ⒻAlw 46000c 95 6 67 65¼ 61¾ 41½ 1nk Santos J A L115 b 7.90 66– 43 Stay Forever115nk Vespers115nk Ocean Drive1191¼ 4 wide, just up 8

Stellar Jayne
Own: Spendthrift Farm LLC Kidder, Chuck, C

Gr/ro. f. 4 (Feb) FTKNOV01 $150,000
Sire: Wild Rush (Wild Again) $10,000
Dam: To the Hunt (Relaunch)
Br: Wind Hill Farm (Ky)
Tr: Lukas D. W(0 0 0 0 .00) 2004:(577 67 .12)

Life	18	6	2	3	$1,111,244	105		
2004	13	3	2	3	$992,169	105		
2003	5	3	0	0	$119,075	78		
	0	0	0	0	$0	–		
D.Fst	13	6	0	2	$641,244	105		
Wet(396)	4	0	2	1	$470,000	103		
Turf(254)	1	0	0	0	$0	67		
Dst(0)	0	0	0	0	$0	–		

30Oct04–2LS gd 1⅛ :463 1:102 1:352 1:481 3↑ⒻBCDistaf-G1 100 11 116 104¼ 62¾ 41½ 31½ Albarado R J L119 b 10.30 106– 02 Ashado1191¼ StormFlgFlying123nk StellrJyne1191½ 4-5w rally,flattnd out 11
10Oct04–9Hoo fst 1 1/16 :232 :48 1:12 1:433 ⒻInBCOaks-G3 105 5 31½ 31½ 3½ 3½ 31½ Albarado R J LB121 b *1.00 91– 27 Daydreaming1181½ CpesideLdy121hd StellrJyne1215½ 3wd bid,alter crs 3/16 7
11Sep04–8Bel fst 1⅛ :48 1:122 1:362 1:481 ⒻGazelle-G1 97 2 11½ 1½ 1hd 2hd 11 Albarado R J L122 b *.50 90– 15 Stellar Jayne1221 Daydreaming1151¾ He LovesMe117no Came again on rail 6
21Aug04–10Sar sly 1¼ :471 1:112 1:362 2:023 ⒻAlabama-G1 103 4 43 41¾ 2hd 1hd 22½ Albarado R J L121 b 10.20 91– 18 Society Selection1212½ Stellar Jayne121½ Ashado1215¼ 4 wide both turns 8
24Jly04–8Bel my 1¼ :483 1:122 1:363 2:022 ⒻCCAOaks-G1 99 1 1½ 1½ 31½ 25 24½ Albarado R J L121 b 3.60 80– 22 Ashado1214½ Stellar Jayne1217½ MagicalIllusion1214 Set pace, second best 6
26Jun04–9Bel fst 1⅛ :47 1:104 1:352 1:48 ⒻMthrGoos-G1 100 2 3½ 1hd 2hd 1½ 12½ Albarado R J L121 b 29.75 91– 11 Stellar Jayne1212½ Ashado1211½ Island Sand1215 Resolutely on rail 6
5Jun04–10CD fst 1 1/16 :243 :483 1:124 1:43 ⒻDgwoodBC-G3 98 5 22 21 2hd 11½ 13¼ Albarado R J L120 b 2.40 93– 16 Stellar Jayne1203¼ Dynaville1141¾ Ender's Sister122½ Tracked,3-4w,driving 5
30Apr04–10CD my 1⅛ :46 1:094 1:363 1:504 ⒻKyOaks-G1 86 11 98¼ 914 811 710 710 Albarado R J L121 b 40.80 73– 17 Ashado1211¼ Island Sand1211¾ Madcap Escapade1211¼ Bid far turn,tired 11
9Apr04–10OP fst 1 1/16 :231 :463 1:11 1:423 ⒻFantasy-G2 89 9 97 107¾ 87¼ 46½ 35¾ McKee J L121 b 10.10 91– 11 HouseofFortune1211¾ IslandSand1214 StellrJyne1212¼ 5-w 1/4, willing 3rd 11
13Mar04–8SA fst 1 1/16 :224 :462 1:104 1:424 ⒻSAOaks-G1 86 7 76½ 75½ 63¼ 54 55½ Santiago Javier LB117 b 34.60 85– 08 SilentSighs1171½ Halfbridled1171½ APAdventure117½ 4wd into lane,no bid 7
15Feb04–8SA fst 1 :223 :46 1:102 1:362 ⒻLsVrgnes-G1 91 8 87½ 87¾ 66½ 65 44 Santiago Javier LB118 b 45.30 85– 18 APAdvntr118½ HollywoodStry1202½ FrndlyMchl1161 Off bit slow,best rest 8
14Jan04–7SA fm 1 Ⓣ :23 :47 1:11 1:343 ⒻBlueNorthr76k 67 7 55½ 55 87½ 75¾ 68½ Stevens G L LB120 6.30 80– 10 MamboSlew1203 TickerTpe1162 Yingyingying1151 Stdied btwn 5/16,wkend 8
4Jan04–6SA fst 1 1/16 :231 :464 1:111 1:441 ⒻSntYsabl-G3 86 4 56 67½ 64¾ 45 44½ Espinoza V LB120 9.00 79– 16 APAdvntr1153½ SltyRomnc120½ WldwoodFlwr115½ 5wd into str,missed 3d 6

Storm Flag Flying

Own: Phipps Ogden M

Dk. b or b. m. 5 (Apr)
Sire: Storm Cat (Storm Bird) $500,000
Dam: My Flag (Easy Goer)
Br: Phipps Stable (Ky)
Tr: McGaughey III Claude R(0 0 0 0 .00) 2004:(254 48 .19)

Life	14	7	3	3	$1,951,828	103	D.Fst	11	5	2	3	$911,828	103
2004	8	3	2	3	$963,248	103	Wet(429)	3	2	1	0	$1,040,000	102
2003	2	0	1	0	$21,580	79	Turf(349)	0	0	0	0	$0	–
	0	0	0	0	$0	–	Dst(0)	0	0	0	0	$0	–

30Oct04–2LS gd 1⅛ :463 1:102 1:352 1:481 3↑ⒻBCDistaf-G1 **100** 7 10 4½ 11 4¾ 8 3¾ 5 2 2 1¼ Bailey J D L123 4.60 107–02 Ashdo119 1¼ StormFlgFlying123nk StellrJyne119 1½ Svd grnd,finished well 11

9Oct04–9Bel fst 1⅛ :482 1:124 1:364 1:493 3↑ⒻBeldame-G1 **94** 5 2hd 2 1 2½ 4 6½ 3 4 Velazquez J R L123 4.40 79–20 Sghtsk123 2¾ SoctySlcton120 1¼ StormFlgFlyng123¾ Stayed on stubbornly 5

27Aug04–9Sar fst 1¼ :461 1:093 1:354 2:033 3↑ⒻPrsnlEnH-G1 **99** 1 3 7½ 3 7 3 1½ 1hd 1 1¼ Velazquez J R L116 2.15 89–11 Storm Flag Flying116 1¼ *Azeri*122½ Nevermore114 4½ 3 wide move, resolute 5

1Aug04–9Sar fst 1⅛ :473 1:104 1:35 1:474 3↑ⒻGoFWandH-G1 **100** 1 3 1½ 3 1 4 2 3 3½ 3 3¾ Velazquez J R L117 3.05 92–14 Azeri120 1¾ *Sightseek*122² *Storm Flag Flying*117⁷ Steadied rail 1st turn 5

19Jun04–9Bel fst 1 1/16 :231 :453 1:10 1:412 3↑ⒻOPhippsH-G1 **93** 4 3 1 3½ 3½ 2 6 2 3¼ Velazquez J R L117 3.00 90–20 Sightsek120 3¼ StormFlgFlying117 6½ PssingShot116² 3 wide bid, no match 4

15May04–8Bel fst 1 :234 :463 1:111 1:36 3↑ⒻShuveeH-G2 **103** 2 4 2½ 3 1 4 1 3 1½ 1½ Velazquez J R L116 *1.00 81–19 StormFlgFlyng116½ PssngShot117no RorEmoton117 8¼ Along late outside 6

27Mar04–8Aqu fst 7f :224 :461 1:10 1:223 3↑ⒻDistfBCH-G2 **87** 2 3 2½ 3 2 3 6½ 3 5¾ Prado E S L118 2.10 86–17 Randaroo121 3½ Chirimoya110 2¼ *StormFlgFlying*118 1¼ Inside, no response 4

26Feb04–8GP fst 170 :224 :462 1:114 1:423 4↑ⒻOC 100k/c-N **92** 7 3 1 2 1½ 2½ 1 1 1 3¾ Velazquez J R L115 *.80 84–28 StormFlgFlying115 3¾ RdoubldMiss119 1¼ KiSkur115 3¼ Drew away, driving 7

Straight Line

Own: Vanier Nancy A. and Cartwright Thorou

Dk. b or b. c. 3 (May) KEESEP03 $15,000
Sire: Boundary (Danzig) $10,000
Dam: Zanti (Strawberry Road*Aus)
Br: R. Alex Rankin & Louis Wright (Ky)
Tr: Vanier Harvey L(0 0 0 0 .00) 2004:(196 29 .15)

Life	6	3	1	0	$166,312	98	D.Fst	6	3	1	0	$166,312	98
2004	6	3	1	0	$166,312	98	Wet(393)	0	0	0	0	$0	–
2003	0	M	0	0	$0	–	Turf(314)	0	0	0	0	$0	–
	0	0	0	0	$0	–	Dst(0)	0	0	0	0	$0	–

6Nov04–10CD fst 1 :223 :453 1:104 1:363 Iroquois-G3 **98** 2 4 1¼ 2 1 1hd 1 2 1 5 Blanc B 122 *2.20 87–20 StraightLine122⁵ SocialProbation120² *GreterGood*122 1¾ Repel bid,driving 7

9Oct04–7Kee fst 1 1/16 :23 :47 1:12 1:433 BrdrsFut-G1 **83** 7 3 2 3 1½ 3 1 3 3½ 4 5¾ Blanc B 121 28.60 88–13 Consolidator121² Patriot Act121 3¼ Diamond Isle121½ Inside,flatten out 10

19Sep04–6AP fst 1 :224 :451 1:103 1:382 ArWBCFut-G3 **80** 2 5 2¼ 5 4½ 5 4 4 2½ 2nk ♦Marquez C H Jr 119 12.70 76–20 ThreHourNp119nk DH ElusivChris122 DH StrightLin119⁸ 4 wide 1/4, missed 6

22Aug04–9EIP fst 7f :214 :444 1:10 1:234 JCEllisJuv98k **47** 8 2 3 1 2 1 5 5½ 8 13¾ Emigh C A 122 2.60 79–14 ElsvChrs116nk Wnsmmnyhny116 5½ Nrnnthsprty116 1¾ Tracked,4w,weaken 9

1Aug04–8AP fst 5½f :223 :454 :58 1:043 HnstPleasr52k **80** 2 1 1 1½ 1 1 1 3 1 1½ Emigh C A 116 7.00 91–13 StrightLin116 1½ Tolivr118 2¾ SmokSmokSmok122³ Green through stretch 6

14Jly04–6AP fst 5f :223 :463 :593 Md 50000(50-40) **66** 2 3 1hd 1½ 1 2½ 1 4 Emigh C A 119 3.10 88–14 *Straight Line*119⁴ Runaround Jonnie119² Stalwart's Heir119⁷ Driving 7

Stroll

Own: Claiborne Farm

Dk. b or b. h. 5 (Apr)
Sire: Pulpit (A.P. Indy) $60,000
Dam: Maid for Walking*GB (Prince Sabo)
Br: Claiborne Farm (Ky)
Tr: Mott William I(0 0 0 0 .00) 2004:(680 116 .17)

Life	16	7	3	1	$795,071	107	D.Fst	3	0	1	0	$14,867	65
2004	5	1	1	0	$348,524	107	Wet(318)	0	0	0	0	$0	-
2003	6	5	1	0	$398,800	105	Turf(273)	13	7	2	1	$780,204	107
	0	0	0	0	$0	-	Dst(0)	0	0	0	0	$0	-

9Oct04–8Bel fm 1 Ⓣ:232 :46 1:091 1:323 3↑KelsoBCH-G2 **103** 4 2½ 2½ 1hd 3nk 42 Velasquez C L119 *2.40 95–03 MrOBrn119 1½ MllnnmDrgn119no GlchApprvl114½ Pressed pace, weakened 8
18Sep04–8Bel sf 1⅛ 🅃:50 1:151 1:401 1:523 3↑BelBCH-G2 **99** 1 21 2½ 2hd 21 24 Velasquez C L120 *.60 63–33 Senor Swinger1`74 Stroll120 3½ *B. A. Way*113¾ Came out start, bumped 4
5Jun04–10Bel fm 1¼ 🅃:482 1:121 1:354 1:591 3↑ManhttnH-G1 **103** 4 3 1½ 4 1¾ 3½ 4¾ 6 3¼ Bailey J D L121 *1.55 95–05 MeteorStorm117 1¼ MillnniumDrgon116no MrOBrin116¾ 3 wide both turns 9
1May04–9CD yl 1⅛ Ⓣ:51 1:152 1:393 1:53 3↑TurfClsc-G1 **107** 10 22 21 1hd 1½ 12½ Bailey J D L121 4.80 68–32 Stroll121 2½ Sweet Return123no Mystery Giver123¾ 3 wide, bid, driving 11
9Apr04–9Kee fm 1 Ⓣ:23 :451 1:09 1:332 4↑MakrsMrk-G2 **100** 6 4 4½ 4 3½ 41 3 2½ 52 Bailey J D L120 *3.10 103 - Perfect Soul116⅓ *Burning Roma*116hd Royal Spy1161 Rail,flattened out 10

Strut the Stage

Own: Sam–Son Farms

Ch. h. 7 (Mar)
Sire: Theatrical*Ire (Nureyev) $50,000
Dam: Ruby Ransom (Red Ransom)
Br: Jamm Ltd. (Ky)
Tr: Frostad Mark R(0 0 0 0 .00) 2004:(269 49 .18)

Life	23	10	2	3	$1,496,986	105	D.Fst	0	0	0	0	$0	-
2004	4	1	0	1	$231,063	104	Wet(332)	0	0	0	0	$0	-
2003	4	2	1	0	$485,085	104	Turf(395)	23	10	2	3	$1,496,986	105
	0	0	0	0	$0	-	Dst(0)	0	0	0	0	$0	-

30Oct04–8LS yl 1½ Ⓣ:49 1:134 2:04 2:293 3↑BCTurf-G1 **89** 3 25 4 3½ 66 7 8½ 712 Nakatani C S L126 b 27.40 111–07 BettrTlkNow126 1¾ KittnsJoy1211 Powrscourt126 2¼ Chased rail, gave way 8
2Oct04–8WO fm 1⅜ Ⓣ:51 1:152 1:40 2:16 3↑SkyClscH-G2 **88** 7 4 2½ 5 2¼ 4 1½ 7 5¼ 7 3¼ Kabel T K L123 fb *.30 82–14 ColorfulJudgmnt114nk LnnythLndr1101 Longship107nk 4wd,flattened out 7
6Sep04–8WO fm 1½ Ⓣ:491 1:132 2:014 2:254 3↑NiagrBCH-G2 **104** 3 66 5 2¼ 1 2½ 14 14 Kabel T K L121 fb *.25 101–06 StruttheStge1214 *ColorfulJudgement*115 3¾ MrkOn115 1¼ Bid btwn,drew off 6
25Jly04–8WO fm 1⅜ Ⓣ:482 1:123 1:364 2:121 3↑ChneseCC-G2 **98** 2 6 4½ 7 3¼ 7 4¾ 4 4½ 3 2½ Callaghan S L121 fb 6.50 101–05 Shoal Water116nk Mobil121 2¼ *Strut the Stage*121¾ Angled out,rallied 8

Suave

Own: Jay Em Ess Stable

B. c. 4 (May)
Sire: A.P. Indy (Seattle Slew) $300,000
Dam: Urbane (Citidancer)
Br: Jan Siegel, Mace Siegel & Samantha Siegel (Ky)
Tr: McGee Paul J(0 0 0 0 .00) 2004:(290 49 .17)

Life	16	3	4	2	$489,683	106	D.Fst	14 2 3 2	$340,195	106
2004	11	2	2	2	$448,328	106	Wet(446)	2 1 1 0	$149,488	103
2003	5	1	2	0	$41,355	79	Turf(307)	0 0 0 0	$0	-
	0	0	0	0	$0	-	Dst(0)	0 0 0 0	$0	-

26Nov04-11CD fst 1⅛ :48 1:12 1:372 1:504 3↑ ClarkH-G2 **106** 6 41 53½ 43 45½ 42½ Sarvis D A L113 b 39.40 80- 25 Saint Liam1171¼ Seek Gold111no Perfect Drift1181¼ 6w late,no response 9
20Oct04-9Hoo fst 1 1/16 :224 :47 1:12 1:44 IndnaDby-G2 **103** 7 85½ 2hd 1½ 2hd 21¾ Peck B D LB124 b 9.50 89- 21 Brass Hat1241¾ Suave124¾ Hasslefree115½ Early bid4-5w,no match 9
28Aug04-11Sar fst 1¼ :49 1:124 1:37 2:022 Travers-G1 **83** 7 45 78¾ 76¼ 615 616¾ Day P L126 b 14.20 78- 05 Birdstone1262½ The Cliff's Edge1263½ Eddington126nk 3 wide trip, tired 7
10Jly04-7Hol fst 1⅛ :47 1:102 1:343 1:472 SwapsBC-G2 **103** 5 44½ 42½ 43½ 34½ 23¾ Bejarano R LB120 b 4.70 98 - RockHardTen1163¾ Suve1203 Boomzeeboom1182½ Bobbled start,2nd best 6
12Jun04-6CD sly 1 1/16 :233 :472 1:12 1:442 NrthDncr-G3 **103** 4 21½ 22½ 2½ 21 13 Bejarano R L114 b 11.60 86- 17 Suave1143 J Town1143 Ecclesiastic114¾ 3-4w,driving,clear 12
17Apr04-9Kee fst 1 1/16 :231 :471 1:12 1:434 Lexingtn-G2 **38** 5 117¾ 1311 1311 1226 1237 Velasquez C L116 b 14.00 56- 11 QuntonsGoldRsh1162¾ *FrSlm*116nk SongofthSword1162 Steadied 1st turn 14
3Apr04-7Haw fst 1⅛ :474 1:123 1:374 1:504 IlnosDby-G2 **98** 4 42 64¼ 51¾ 35 35½ Bejarano R L114 b 4.50 97- 21 Pollard's Vision1142¾ Song of the Sword1162¾ Suave1148½ Four wide trip 11
13Mar04-7GP fst 1⅛ :48 1:124 1:381 1:504 Alw 34000N1x **96** 7 21½ 21 2hd 16 13¾ Douglas R R L118 b 9.00 85- 15 Suave1183¾ Royal Assault1188¾ Intimidator122½ Drew away, driving 10
14Feb04-9GP fst 1⅛ :471 1:12 1:38 1:503 Alw 34000N1x **78** 3 42 42 51¾ 64¼ 511¼ Douglas R R L118 b 9.80 75- 14 Swingforthefences1185¼ Shaniko1223¼ Capias122¾ Faltered 11
24Jan04-3GP fst 1 1/16 :232 :474 1:124 1:441 Alw 34000N1x **86** 8 21 2½ 1½ 11 2hd Velasquez C L120 b 7.20 88- 15 Mustanfar120hd [D]Suve1201 *Swingforthefences*1183 Impeded rival 1/8 pole 10
Disqualified and placed third
3Jan04-6GP fst 1 1/16 :231 :473 1:122 1:45 Alw 34000N1x **71** 7 43 42 73¼ 86½ 66¾ Velasquez C L120 b 5.80 77- 13 Zakocity1181 Battle Hero122nk Nightmare Affair1181¼ Forced out 1/4 12

Sulamani (Ire)

Own: Godolphin Racing Inc

B. h. 6 (Apr)
Sire: Hernando*Fr (Niniski) $23,022
Dam: Soul Dream (Alleged)
Br: The Niarchos Family (Ire)
Tr: bin Suroor Saeed(0 0 0 0 .00) 2004:(9 2 .22)

Life	17	9	3	1	$5,252,368	115	D.Fst	0 0 0 0	$0	-
2004	5	2	1	1	$1,611,523	115	Wet(271*)	0 0 0 0	$0	-
2003	6	3	1	0	$2,603,842	110	Turf(296)	17 9 3 1	$5,252,368	115
	0	0	0	0	$0	-	Dst(0)	0 0 0 0	$0	-

24Oct04-9WO gd 1½ Ⓣ :494 1:141 2:044 2:283 3↑ CanIntnl-G1 **115** 3 85¾ 75 62¼ 2½ 11½ Dettori L L126 *.85 87- 13 Sulamani1261½ Simonas1262 Brian Boru126¾ Took lead 1/16th pole 10
17Aug04 York (GB) gd 1 5/16 Ⓣ LH 2:114 3↑ Juddmonte Intl Stks(1 1/4m,88y)-G1 Stk 840000 1¾ Dettori L 131 3.00 *Sulamani*131¾ Norse Dancer131¾ Bago1235 9
Timeform rating: 126+ *Rated in 6th,long drive to lead 50y out.Cacique4th*
24Jly04 Ascot (GB) gf 1½ Ⓣ RH 2:33 3↑ King George VI & Queen Eliz S-G1 Stk 1374000 33 McEvoy K 133 7.00 Doyen1333 Hard Buck133hd *Sulamani*1331¾ 11
Timeform rating: 127+ *Rated in 8th,bid 1-1/2f out,just missed 2nd.Gamut 4th*
7Jly04 Newmarket (GB) gf 1½ Ⓣ RH 2:324 3↑ Princess of Wales's Stakes-G2 Stk 185400 2½ Dettori L 133 *1.35 Bandari128½ Sulamani1332½ High Accolade1283½ 8
Timeform rating: 128 *Rated at rear,prgrss to lead 1-1/2f out,headed near line*
16Jun04 Ascot (GB) gf 1¼ Ⓣ RH 2:044 4↑ Prince of Wales's Stakes-G1 Stk 639000 44 Dettori L 126 *2.75 Rakti1262 Powerscourt126½ Ikhtyar1261½ 10
Timeform rating: 120 *Rated in 7th,brief bid 2f out,drifted right,up for 4th*

Summer Raven
Own: Edgewood Farm

B. f. 3 (Feb) KEESEP03 $200,000
Sire: Summer Squall (Storm Bird) $50,000
Dam: Rahy Rose (Rahy)
Br: Mt. Brilliant Farm LLC (Ky)
Tr: Pletcher Todd A(0 0 0 0 .00) 2004:(948 240 .25)

Life	7	2	2	1	$168,910	90	D.Fst	6 1 2 1 $141,910 90
2004	7	2	2	1	$168,910	90	Wet(336)	1 1 0 0 $27,000 69
2003	0	M	0	0	$0	-	Turf(318)	0 0 0 0 $0 -
	0	0	0	0	$0	-	Dst(0)	0 0 0 0 $0 -

4Dec04-6DeD fst 1 :23³ :48⁴ 1:14 1:40² ⒻDltaPrncss250k 83 6 41¼ 21 2½ 23 25½ Espinoza V L121 *1.00 79-21 PunchAppl1215½ SummrRvn121⁴ SnipprLou118no No match, clear second 6
2Nov04-6Aqu fst 1 :23¹ :46¹ 1:10¹ 1:36 ⒻTempted-G3 90 4 1½ 1½ 1½ 12½ 12 Elliott S L115 f 6.60 85-22 SummerRaven115² KDsShdyLdy1152¼ Slute115⁵ Drew clear when roused 5
17Oct04-8Bel fst 6½f :22⁴ :47 1:11³ 1:18 ⒻAstarita-G3 68 4 5 3½ 1½ 31 34¾ Castellano J J L117 2.15 78-18 TollTker1173¼ ImDixieGirl1201½ *SummerRven*11711½ 3 wide move, faltered 6
19Sep04-8Bel fst 1 :24² :48 1:12 1:37³ ⒻMatron-G1 69 5 2½ 2½ 2½ 44 611¾ Velazquez J R L119 9.60 61-25 Sense of Style119¹ *Balletto*119¾ Play With Fire1197¼ Vied outside, tired 6
29Aug04-4Sar my 6½f :21² :44¹ 1:10² 1:17³ ⒻMd Sp Wt 45k 69 1 7 1½ 1hd 12 1no Velazquez J R L118 1.65 87-11 SummrRvn118no PpprmintLlly11813½ BobbsthBst118¾ Vied, clear, held on 8
1Aug04-4Sar fst 6½f :21⁴ :45¹ 1:10 1:16² ⒻMd Sp Wt 45k 86 2 7 11½ 11½ 2hd 22½ Velazquez J R L118 1.85 90-12 *SnsofSty*l1182½ *SummrRvn*1184½ PpprmintLilly1181¾ Dug in gamely on rail 9
17Jun04-2Bel fst 5f :22² :45⁴ :58² ⒻMd Sp Wt 43k 56 6 7 51¼ 2hd 46 411¼ Velazquez J R L118 =1.20 80-19 Dream Time118¹ *Darn That Girl*1183½ Comacina1186¾ Sluggish start, 3 wide 7

Summer Symphony
Own: Whitham Janis R

Ch. f. 4 (Apr)
Sire: Summer Squall (Storm Bird) $50,000
Dam: Second Symphony (Mining)
Br: Janis R. Whitham (Ky)
Tr: Forster David(0 0 0 0 .00) 2004:(116 20 .17)

Life	13	3	2	2	$190,464	79	D.Fst	9 2 1 1 $129,661 79
2004	8	3	1	0	$180,729	79	Wet(373)	4 1 1 1 $60,803 75
2003	5	M	1	2	$9,735	63	Turf(274)	0 0 0 0 $0 -
	0	0	0	0	$0	-	Dst(0)	0 0 0 0 $0 -

16Oct04-8Hst gd 1⅛ :47⁴1:12³ 1:38 1:51² 3↑ⒻBlrinaBC-G3 75 6 76 74¼ 65 23½ 23½ Hoverson C L121 2.05e 84-15 SMThrogh121³½ SmmrSymphony1212¾ YondNlly124½ 4 wide, second best 11
25Sep04-8Hst fst 1⅛ :47²1:12¹ 1:37⁴1:51 ⒻBCBCOaks-G3 79 4 77 77¼ 76 31½ 1½ Hoverson C L121 *.40e 90-08 SmmrSymphony121½ SocorroConty1212¾ *SMThrgh*1211¼ Between, driving 9
5Sep04-4Hst fst 1$\frac{1}{16}$:23¹ :46³ 1:11⁴1:44³ ⒻOaksPrvwH43k 57 1 74½ 75¼ 75¼ 47 411¾ Hoverson C L116 *.35e 82-09 SocorroCounty1195½ GoldAccent1153½ *BullseyBss*1152¾ Rallied, weakened 8
Previously trained by Forster Grant T
21Aug04-9EmD wf 1⅛ :45⁴1:10 1:35 1:48⁴ ⒻWashBCOaks100k 68 3 66 66 54 54½ 47¼ Hoverson C LB119 45.20 76-22 Bianconi Baby119¹ Karis Makaw1194½ Sariano1191¾ Off rail, evenly 9
Previously trained by Forster David
7Aug04-1Hst gd 1$\frac{1}{16}$:24³ :48¹ 1:13 1:45⁴ 3↑ⒻAlw 25000N$Y 69 4 53 51¾ 31½ 2hd 12½ Hoverson C L115 6.60 88-13 SummrSymphony1152½ GoldAccnt115no RivrsRch117³ Drew clear, driving 5
18Jly04-4Hst fst 1$\frac{1}{16}$:23³ :46³ 1:11 1:45¹ ⒻNanaimoH42k 63 2 52¾ 44 43½ 55 54½ Hoverson C L114 *1.45e 86-07 SocorroCounty118nk GoldAccent113¹ StoleOn115½ Lacked late response 7
6Jun04-3Hst fst 1$\frac{1}{16}$:23⁴ :48¹ 1:13⁴1:46³ ⒻMd Sp Wt 20k 66 7 68½ 65 52½ 31 1¾ Wright N L122 3.95 84-17 SmmrSymphny122¾ *GldAccnt*1221½ KtlnsStr117no Going away, ridden out 7
8May04-5Hst fst 6½f :22 :45³ 1:11¹1:18 ⒻMd Sp Wt 22k 59 8 6 74½ 65½ 54¼ 57¼ Hoverson C 122 4.15 81-15 Skyhyla117no Double 'd' Special117⁵ *River's Reach*122² Mild bid, outrun 10

Summer Wind Dancer
Own: Vetter Linda and Wira, Richard and Yv

Gr/ro. m. 5 (Mar)
Sire: Siberian Summer (Siberian Express) $6,000
Dam: Native Wind Dancer (Incinderator)
Br: R. Wira, Y. Wira, L. Vetter & D. Penny (Cal)
Tr: Mullins Jeff(0 0 0 0 .00) 2004:(538 140 .26)

Life	18	5	5	4	$898,762	104	D.Fst	14	4	4	4	$421,484	104
2004	7	2	2	1	$598,905	104	Wet(310)	1	1	0	0	$450,000	104
2003	6	0	3	1	$92,692	91	Turf(292)	3	0	1	0	$27,278	88
	0	0	0	0	$0	–	Dst(0)	0	0	0	0	$0	–

16Oct04–3SA fst 1 1/16 :23^{1} :46^{3} 1:10^{3}1:42^{1} 3↑ⒻⓈCalCupMatH150k **92** 6 54½ 53½ 42 43½ 36 Espinoza V LB122 b 2.50 88– 11 DrmfSmmr121^{no} *YrlyRprt*120^{6} SmmrWndDncr122½ Rail bid,edged foe 3rd 6
3Oct04–6SA fst 1 1/16 :24 :48^{1} 1:11^{4}1:43^{2} 3↑ⒻLdyScBCH-G2 **89** 1 76 62¾ 42 33 44 Espinoza V LB118 b *1.20 84– 17 Island Fashion120½ Miss Loren116^{hd} Elloluv118^{3}½ 4wd into str,drift in 7
18Jly04–10Del sly 1¼ :47 1:11^{3} 1:36^{4}2:03^{3} 3↑ⒻDelH-G2 **104** 8 66½ 53 33 24 11¼ Espinoza V L116 b *1.00 96– 15 SmmrWndDncr1161¼ RorEmotn1175¾ MstySxs116¾ Long hard drive, clear 8
6Jun04–8Hol fst 1 1/16 :23^{2} :46^{1} 1:10 1:41^{2} 3↑ⒻHawthrnH-G3 **104** 2 64½ 43½ 22 2½ 11 Espinoza V LB116 b 2.20 94– 18 *Summer Wind Dancer*116^{1} Pesci115^{10} Miss Loren116½ Led past 1/8,game 7
24Apr04–4Hol fst 7f :21^{2} :43^{4} 1:08^{2}1:21^{2} 4↑ⒻⓈBThoughtfl150k **95** 7 6 81^{3} 810 53¾ 2^{hd} Espinoza V LB120 b *1.20 95– 06 RoyllyChosn122^{hd} *SummrWndDncr*120½ TckdAwy122^{2} 3wd into lane,rallied 8
4Apr04–7SA fst 1 1/16 :24 :48^{3} 1:12^{3}1:43^{2} 4↑ⒻⓇSntaLuciaH85k **92** 7 74¾ 74¼ 63¼ 32½ 2^{hd} Espinoza V LB116 b 6.60 88– 19 HopeRises116^{hd} SummerWindDncer116^{5} *Pesci*115^{1} Came out lane,rallied 7
Previously trained by Sahadi Jenine
24Jan04–5SA fm 1⅛ Ⓣ :46^{3}1:10^{1} 1:34^{2}1:46^{1} 4↑ⒻⓇSMF&MTurf500k **88** 10 97¼ 910 96¾ 84¾ 63¾ Nakatani C S LB118 24.20 94– 02 VlntnDncr118¾ MoscowBrnng118^{1} BrtoksBlth118^{1} Saved ground, late bid 11

Supah Blitz
Own: Black Saddle Stable Kagele Brothers,

Dk. b or b. h. 5 (Feb)
Sire: Mecke (Maudlin) $3,500
Dam: Boots 'n Jackie (Major Moran)
Br: Bee Bee Stables, Inc & Equitor, Inc (Fla)
Tr: O'Neill Doug(0 0 0 0 .00) 2004:(938 170 .18)

Life	33	6	12	5	$970,610	110	D.Fst	24	4	10	4	$824,410	108
2004	13	2	5	2	$446,280	108	Wet(325)	5	1	2	0	$115,200	110
2003	10	2	2	2	$278,000	110	Turf(254)	4	1	0	1	$31,000	88
	0	0	0	0	$0	–	Dst(0)	0	0	0	0	$0	–

11Dec04–7Hol fst 1⅛ :47^{2}1:11^{1} 1:34^{4}1:47 3↑NtvDivrH-G3 **92** 1 31 41½ 32 45 511 Espinoza V LB118 3.20 93– 08 Truly a Judge115^{2} Dynever119^{7} Calkins Road116^{2} Stdied 1/16,weakened 8
13Nov04–10Crc fst 1⅛ :49 1:12^{4} 1:38^{3}1:52^{2} 3↑ⓈCGRoseClsH200k **104** 5 54 56 55 21 11 Bailey J D L119 *.40 90– 20 Supah Blitz119^{1} HearNoEvil1121¾ Bob'sProudMoment113¾ 4 wide, up late 7
2Oct04–8SA fst 1⅛ :48 1:11^{2} 1:35^{3}1:48^{1} 3↑GdwdBCH-G2 **105** 3 41¾ 41¾ 31½ 31 32 Nakatani C S LB117 2.30 91– 08 LundysLiability118^{hd} TotlImpct119^{2} *SuphBlitz*117^{6} Steadied,came out 1/8 5
5Sep04–8Dmr fst 1 :22^{2} :46 1:10 1:35 3↑DmrBCH-G2 **108** 2 31 41½ 3^{nk} 11½ 1no Espinoza V LB116 4.20 99– 07 Supah Blitz116^{no} DomesticDispute117^{4} During117^{1} 3wd bid,led,held game 6
Previously trained by Tortora Emanuel
9Aug04–8Del fst 1⅛ :48^{4}1:12^{4} 1:38^{3}1:50^{4} 3↑Alw 44600c **103** 6 53 43½ 32 2½ 2^{nk} Dominguez R A L117 *.80 90– 22 *CountryBGold*117^{nk} *SuphBlitz*1173¾ OfftheGlss119^{4} Got thru,drew even,hng 7
17Jly04–7Del fst 1 1/16 :23^{4} :47 1:11^{3}1:43^{2} 3↑RRMCarpMmH100k **101** 2 55¼ 45½ 32 33 3½ Velasquez C L115 b 6.20 94– 14 AngelicAur114^{nk} ThLdysGroom117^{nk} SuphBlitz115^{1} In tight start, gamely 6
31May04–10Crc fst 1 1/16 :23^{2} :47 1:11^{4}1:45^{3} 3↑MemDayH-G3 **82** 7 10^{11} 89¼ 911 75¼ 712¾ Castro E L116 b *1.30 71– 16 Twilight Road1115¼ Hear No Evil115^{1} *Gold Dollar*112½ Bmpd early, no rally 12
24Apr04–8LS sly 1 :23^{1} :46^{1} 1:10 1:35^{3} 3↑TexsMile-G3 **104** 4 66½ 66½ 38 35½ 25¼ Castro E L116 b 4.20 90– 22 Kela1195¼ Supah Blitz1161½ *Yessirgeneralsir*114^{nk} Willingly, second best 8
2Apr04–8GP fst 1 1/16 :23^{4} :47^{1} 1:11^{3}1:43^{3} 4↑OC 80k/c -N **98** 2 73½ 73¾ 62¾ 32½ 2^{hd} Castro E L120 b *.80 91– 09 SuperFrolic116^{hd} SuphBlitz120^{2} BdBmBdBoom1227¼ Rallied, just missed 7
13Mar04–13GP fst 1 1/16 :24 :48^{1} 1:12 1:43^{1} 3↑SkipAwyH-G3 **104** 4 74¼ 74 73¾ 51¾ 2½ Velasquez C L114 b 14.70 92– 15 Newfoundland116½ SuphBlitz1142¼ BowmnsBnd1174¼ Late bid, outgamed 10
27Feb04–9GP fst 170 :23^{4} :48^{1} 1:13 1:42^{1} 4↑Alw 46000c **96** 6 51¾ 31½ 41½ 1^{hd} 2^{hd} Velasquez C L116 b 2.50 86– 25 WhosCryingNow120^{hd} SuphBlitz1163¼ MBS1223¼ Brushed str, outgamed 7
29Jan04–8GP fm *1 Ⓣ :24^{3} :48^{1} 1:13^{1}1:36 4↑OC 100k/n4x -N **84** 4 911 812 610 56½ 45½ Chavez J F L118 b 7.70 87– 12 *Marco's Word*1222¾ Wild Buddy118^{no} Last Stand1182¾ Passed tired rivals 9
4Jan04–9GP fm 1 Ⓣ :24 :49 1:11^{4}1:34^{2} 3↑AppletnH-G3 **82** 12107¼106¾ 105¼ 12^{10} 12^{12} Velazquez J R L113 b 17.80 82– 07 MillenniumDragon1161¼ PoliticlAttck118^{4} *ProudMn*116^{nk} Never factored 12

Susan's Angel
Own: Finney Creek Stable

Dk. b or b. f. 4 (Mar)
Sire: Cape Town (Seeking the Gold) $20,000
Dam: Copeaway (Copelan)
Br: Captain W. Jakeman & Mrs. K. C. Jakeman (Ky)
Tr: Lukas D. W(0 0 0 0 .00) 2004:(577 67 .12)

Life	14	3	5	2	$350,440	96	D.Fst	8	1	2	2	$175,900 96
2004	12	3	4	2	$338,540	96	Wet(434)	6	2	3	0	$174,540 95
2003	2	M	1	0	$11,900	76	Turf(263)	0	0	0	0	$0 –
	0	0	0	0	$0	–	Dst(0)	0	0	0	0	$0 –

27Dec04–8SA fst 7f :221 :442 1:083 1:211 ⒻLaBrea-G1 **90** 6 3 63¼ 73¾ 43½ 45 Baze T C LB121 8.80 94–07 AlphbetKisses1171 BndingStrings1212 ElusivDiv1192 4wd into lane,no bid 10
25Nov04–10CD gd 1⅛ :483 1:131 1:384 1:514 3↑ⒻFallCtyH-G2 **95** 4 21 21 1hd 2hd 22¾ Day P L114 4.60 75–24 HloryLeigh1162¾ SusnsAngel1143¼ MissFortunt1132¼ Press,led,no match 7
7Nov04–10CD fst 1 :223 :453 1:102 1:35 3↑ⒻCDDstafH-G2 **96** 1 52 42 2½ 32 35¾ Bejarano R L115 18.30 89–13 *Halory Leigh*1155 Lady Tak123¾ Susan's Angel115¾ 4w,loomed,empty 12
18Sep04–12TP fst 1 1/16 :232 :464 1:113 1:441 3↑ⒻTPBC-G3 **89** 5 21 2½ 2hd 1½ 1¾ Bejarano R L116 6.20 91–11 Susan'sAngel116¾ MayoOntheSide1201½ Angela'sLove1222 2 path, driving 6
21Aug04–10Sar sly 1¼ :471 1:112 1:362 2:023 ⒻAlabama-G1 **83** 2 1hd 1hd 32½ 52½ 616¼ Day P L121 21.30 78–18 Society Selection1212½ *Stellar Jayne*121½ *Ashado*1215¼ Vied inside, tired 8
24Jly04–9Mth gd 170 :221 :453 1:10 1:41 ⒻSrenasSong60k **95** 5 43½ 32½ 22 2½ 1hd Coa E M L114 *2.90 92–15 SusnsAngel114hd Schedule1144¼ *TittingerRos*1181 Outside bid,game score 10
9Jun04–9CD fst 1 1/16 :234 :473 1:122 1:443 ⒻAlw 49100n1x **80** 6 31½ 2hd 1½ 2hd 2no Day P L122 *1.00 85–16 Plaid116no *Susan's Angel*1225¼ Quick Temper1168¾ Held on stubbornly 6
26May04–1CD my 1 1/16 :24 :472 1:113 1:442 3↑ⒻMd Sp Wt 44k **92** 3 1½ 11½ 1½ 13 18¼ Day P L116 *.60 86–23 SusnsAngl1168¼ *MoonlghtCrs*1165¾ ScrtConqst1111½ Drew off,hand urging 6
30Apr04–11CD my 1 1/16 :234 :48 1:14 1:461 3↑ⒻMd Sp Wt 45k **81** 1 1hd 11½ 11 11½ 2no Bailey J D L115 *1.50 77–17 TwoMilHill123no *SusnsAngl*1152 MoonlightCruis1158 Came out bmp start 11
9Apr04–5Kee fst *7f :223 :454 1:114 1:283 ⒻMd Sp Wt 49k **65** 6 2 43 41 32½ 34¼ Flores D R L119 2.70 79–09 The K O Touch1192¾ Aurelia1191½ Susan'sAngel1197¾ Ck 3/8s, no late gain 9
20Mar04–9TP wf 1 :223 :461 1:112 1:374 ⒻBourbnttBC150k **79** 1 42½ 52 31½ 34 23¾ Court J K L114 15.50 81–17 Class Above1233¾ Susan's Angel114½ Native Annie1213 Drifted out early 6
31Jan04–2SA fst 7f :222 :45 1:11 1:243 ⒻMd Sp Wt 44k **64** 9 3 42½ 41½ 41½ 45 Stevens G L LB120 2.60 77–09 MmeEspionge1202½ AnAnnikMomnt120½ *Nctrin*1202 4 wide,bid,weakened 11

Sweet Catomine
Own: Wygod Mr. and Mrs. Martin J

B. f. 3 (Feb)
Sire: Storm Cat (Storm Bird) $500,000
Dam: Sweet Life (Kris S.)
Br: Mr. & Mrs. Martin J. Wygod (Ky)
Tr: Canani Julio C(0 0 0 0 .00) 2004:(186 42 .23)

Life	4	3	1	0	$799,800	102	D.Fst	4	3	1	0	$799,800 102
2004	4	3	1	0	$799,800	102	Wet(430)	0	0	0	0	$0 –
2003	0	M	0	0	$0	–	Turf(376)	0	0	0	0	$0 –
	0	0	0	0	$0	–	Dst(0)	0	0	0	0	$0 –

30Oct04–3LS fst 1 1/16 :224 :462 1:103 1:413 ⒻBCJuvFil-G1 **102** 9 75½ 74¼ 71¾ 2hd 13¾ Nakatani C S L119 b *2.30 94–02 SweetCatomine1193¾ Blletto1191¼ *RunwyModel*119¾ Blocked 5/16,checked 12
2Oct04–9SA fst 1 1/16 :23 :464 1:111 1:424 ⒻOakLeaf-G2 **91** 9 72¾ 66 52¼ 12½ 14 Nakatani C S LB119 b 2.00 91–08 *SweetCatomine*1194 *SplendidBlended*1192½ Memorette1194 4wd surge,clear 9
28Aug04–8Dmr fst 7f :22 :442 1:102 1:24 ⒻDmrDeb-G1 **76** 7 9 96¼ 78¼ 33 1¾ Espinoza V LB114 b *1.60e 82–13 *SwtCtomin*114¾ SouvnirGift1201½ HlloLucky1162½ Hopd brk,5w,nailed foe 9
31Jly04–1Dmr fst 5½f :221 :451 :574 1:042 ⒻMd Sp Wt 50k **64** 9 3 42¾ 42½ 33½ 25 Flores D R LB118 b 5.70 88–09 She's Salty1185 *Sweet Catomine*118nk Wild Humor118½ 5wd,3wd,late 2nd 9

Sweet Return (GB)

Own: Red Oak Stable

Ch. c. 5 (Mar)
Sire: Elmaamul (Diesis*GB) $3,837
Dam: Sweet Revival*GB (Claude Monet)
Br: C. S. Tateson (GB)
Tr: McAnally Ronald L(0 0 0 0 .00) 2004:(249 26 .10)

Life	21	5	4	5	$969,211	108	D.Fst	0	0	0	0	$0 -
2004	7	2	1	1	$446,180	108	Wet(229)	0	0	0	0	$0 -
2003	9	2	2	2	$500,360	101	Turf(246)	21	5	4	5	$969,211 108
	0	0	0	0	$0	-	Dst(0)	0	0	0	0	$0 -

Date/Race	Cond	Dist	Fractions	Race	Fig	PP	St	1C	2C	Str	Fin	Jockey	Wt	Odds	Pace	Top Finishers	Comment	Fld
9Oct04-8Kee	fm	1	Ⓣ :232 :471 1:1141:352	3↑ShdwlTfM-G1	94	8	21½	21½	21	31½	67½	Stevens G L	L126	4.60	87- 10	NothingtoLose1264½ HonorinWar126¾ SilverTree1261¼	3-4w,flattened out	9
14Aug04-9AP	fm	1¼	Ⓣ :4721:12 1:3632:00	3↑ArlMilln-G1	97	3	44	43	73½	85½	86½	Bailey J D	L126	5.30	104 -	D Powerscourt1261½ Kicken Kris1261 *Magistretti*126½	Just outside, tired	13
25Jly04-8Dmr	fm	1⅛	Ⓣ :47 1:11 1:3421:454	3↑EdReadH-G1	107	1	33	34½	32½	32	31½	Bailey J D	LB119	4.60	98- 03	Special Ring118¾ Bayamo119¾ Sweet Return119¾	Boxed bit 3/16	10
31May04-7Hol	fm	1	Ⓣ :232 :46 1:09 1:324	3↑ShoeBCM-G1	103	4	32	43	42	31	52¾	Espinoza V	LB124	*1.90	97- 07	DesignedforLuck1241½ Singletry124hd Tsigne1241	3wd into str,outkicked	8
1May04-9CD	yl	1⅛	Ⓣ :51 1:152 1:3931:53	3↑TurfClsc-G1	101	6	12	11	2hd	2½	22½	Day P	L123	*4.40	65- 32	Stroll1212½ Sweet Return123no Mystery Giver123¾	Slow pace, held place	11
6Mar04-9SA	fm	1	Ⓣ :224 :452 1:0941:334	4↑FKilroeH-G2	108	14	79½	711	74¾	2hd	1½	Stevens G L	LB119	9.80	93- 12	Sweet Return119½ *Singletary*1172 Inesperado116½	5wd into lane,gamely	14
19Jan04-8SA	fm	1¼	Ⓣ :4741:121 1:3531:584	4↑SnMarcos-G2	100	9	11	11	11	11	1½	Stevens G L	LB121	6.90	95- 05	*SweetReturn*121½ NothingtoLose1161½ BlueStllr116½	Bit off rail,held game	9

Sweet Win

Own: Fogelson Gayle

Ch. f. 4 (Feb) OBSAPR03 $10,000
Sire: King of Kings*Ire (Sadler's Wells) $5,263
Dam: Win for Juno (St. Jovite)
Br: Sez Who Thoroughbreds & Bonnie Heath Farm (Ky)
Tr: Mullins Jeff(0 0 0 0 .00) 2004:(538 140 .26)

Life	8	3	0	2	$162,980	97	D.Fst	2	1	0	0	$13,760 66
2004	8	3	0	2	$162,980	97	Wet(211)	0	0	0	0	$0 -
2003	0	M	0	0	$0	-	Turf(282)	6	2	0	2	$149,220 97
	0	0	0	0	$0	-	Dst(0)	0	0	0	0	$0 -

Date/Race	Cond	Dist	Fractions	Race	Fig	PP	St	1C	2C	Str	Fin	Jockey	Wt	Odds	Pace	Top Finishers	Comment	Fld
7Nov04-8Hol	fm	1⅛	Ⓣ :5121:16 1:3911:512	+ ⒻASkirball62k	87	6	77	77	76	62¾	31	Espinoza V	LB120	*2.30	73- 26	PennysFortune118½ SeekingthHrt116½ SwtWin120no	Tight,stdied into str	7
11Oct04-8SA	fm	1	Ⓣ :224 :464 1:1031:334	ⒻHCRamsrSrH100k	87	2	54	56	52¾	53	54	Espinoza V	LB119	*1.00	89- 05	MeDomin1162 *PnnysFortun*1161½ *CostumDsignr*115no	Btwn 2nd turn,no bid	9
21Aug04-3Dmr	fm	1⅛	Ⓣ :4621:101 1:3421:461	ⒻDmrOaks-G1	97	4	31½	43	42½	31½	31	Espinoza V	LB122	4.60	97- 02	Amorama122no *Ticker Tape*1221 Sweet Win122½	4wd bid,bit tight late	7
31Jly04-4Dmr	fm	1	Ⓣ :232 :462 1:10 1:34	ⒻSnClmntH-G2	94	5	33½	310	34½	21	1hd	Espinoza V	LB114	8.30	91- 07	Sweet Win114hd MissVegas121no VictoryU.S.A.1194½	Angled in 1/8,gamely	5
Previously trained by Wolfson Milton W																		
13Jun04-4Crc	fm	1 1/16	Ⓣ :221 :48 1:1211:424	3↑ⒻAlw 23000N2L	84	8	814	78	53	13½	16	Toribio A R	117	3.50	85- 15	*SweetWin*1176 MissBradfordCo115½ KingsFncy1192¾	Split rivals, drew off	10
1Jun04-9Crc	fst	1 1/16	:24 :482 1:1421:492	ⒻMd Sp Wt 22k	66	8	76½	59	46	23½	11½	Castro E	121	*1.60	65- 29	*Sweet Win*1211½ *Appealing Pond*1213 Miswaki Lady1213	Saved grnd, up late	8
9May04-10Crc	fm	1 1/16	Ⓣ :23 :481 1:1221:432	3↑ⒻMd Sp Wt 22k	72	9	75½	74¼	64¼	62¾	52¼	Homeister R B Jr	117	6.20	80- 19	*ShoreyVillge*117hd UmNorm1171½ *OldMothrGoos*122½	Lacked late response	10
30Apr04-3Crc	fst	6f	:214 :453 :5841:123	ⒻMd 25000(25-22.5)	56	6	6	74¾	77	53¾	42½	Castro E	121	53.70	83- 11	Actxpresso121½ Tri for the Moon1211½ Montpar121½	Mild response	12

Tapit
Own: Winchell Thoroughbreds LLC

Gr/ro. c. 4 (Feb) KEESEP02 $625,000
Sire: Pulpit (A.P. Indy) $60,000
Dam: Tap Your Heels (Unbridled)
Br: Oldenburg Farms, LLC (Ky)
Tr: Dickinson Michael W(0 0 0 0 .00) 2004:(190 39 .21)

Life	6	3	0	0	$557,300	98	D.Fst	5	3	0	0	$557,300 98
2004	4	1	0	0	$477,500	98	Wet(376)	1	0	0	0	$0 84
2003	2	2	0	0	$79,800	98	Turf(293)	0	0	0	0	$0 –
	0	0	0	0	$0	–	Dst(0)	0	0	0	0	$0 –

6Sep04-10Pha fst 1⅛ :473 1:111 1:353 1:482 PaDerby-G2 **83** 12 42 32 42½ 911 917½ Dominguez R A L122 f *3.30 85– 11 LovofMony1163½ PollrdsVsn1221 Swngfrthfncs1193¼ Bobbled, wide, tired 12
1May04-10CD sly 1¼ :463 1:114 1:371 2:04 KyDerby-G1 **84** 1616 1012 5½ 75¾ 108 915¾ Dominguez R A L126 f 6.40 63– 21 *Smarty Jones*1262¾ Lion Heart1263¼ Imperialism1262 Stdied 7-1/2,no bid 18
10Apr04-8Aqu fst 1⅛ :47 1:112 1:37 1:493 WoodMem-G1 **98** 2 1110 99¼ 74 41¼ 1½ Dominguez R A L123 f 5.30 91– 12 Tapit123½ Master David123no Eddington1231½ Game outside, prevail 11
13Mar04-9GP fst 1⅛ :47 1:112 1:373 1:511 FlaDerby-G1 **83** 4 54½ 45 52 55 65¾ Prado E S L122 f 5.60 77– 15 FriendsLake122¾ ValuePlus122¾ *TheCliffsEdge*1222½ In tight trn, bmpd str 10

Taste of Paradise
Own: Bloom David B

Dk. b or b. h. 6 (Apr)
Sire: Conquistador Cielo (Mr. Prospector) $15,000
Dam: Tastetheteardrops (What Luck)
Br: Abrahams, Snukal & Bloom (Ky)
Tr: Mandella Gary(0 0 0 0 .00) 2004:(121 15 .12)

Life	20	5	2	2	$414,455	106	D.Fst	18	4	2	2	$346,205 105
2004	8	2	0	1	$134,095	106	Wet(369)	2	1	0	0	$68,250 106
2003	7	2	0	0	$222,910	102	Turf(252)	0	0	0	0	$0 –
	0	0	0	0	$0	–	Dst(0)	0	0	0	0	$0 –

5Dec04-6Hol wf 6f :213 :44 :554 1:08 3↑VOUndrwd-G3 **106** 3 4 36 33 41½ 1no Valdivia J Jr LB122 26.40 97– 11 TsteofPrdise122no WtchemSmoky1162 MyMstr1163 Swung out,rallied,up 7
Previously trained by Pearson Molly J
15Aug04-8Dmr fst 7f :214 :434 1:081 1:21 3↑OBrinBCH-G2 **89** 5 2 2hd 2hd 44½ 512¼ Court J K LB114 b 16.00 85– 10 Kela1164½ Domestic Dispute1161¼ *Pico Central*1224 Dueled, weakened 5
1Aug04-8Dmr fst 1 1/16 :24 :472 1:111 1:421 3↑SnDiegoH-G2 **88** 3 31½ 3nk 3nk 43½ 68¼ Court J K LB115 6.50 89– 10 ChoctawNation114¾ *PleasntlyPerfect*1245 During1181½ 4wd,3wd,weakened 7
3Jly04-9Hol fst 7f :214 :44 1:081 1:21 3↑TrBndBCH-G1 **92** 3 9 72¼ 73¼ 43 64¾ Court J K LB114 6.50 92– 12 Pohave116¾ Rojo Toro115½ Revello1101 Saved ground to 1/4 13
31May04-9Hol fst 7½f :22 :44 1:082 1:28 3↑AckAckH81k **105** 4 4 42 51¾ 3nk 1¾ Court J K LB116 5.10 95– 08 Taste of Paradise116¾ Buddy Gil1223½ *Black Bart*1161½ Got thru rail,held 8
Previously trained by Stidham Michael
24Apr04-8LS sly 1 :231 :461 1:10 1:353 3↑TexsMile-G3 **91** 2 34½ 35 48½ 512 512¼ Lovato A J L116 8.70 83– 22 Kela1195¼ Supah Blitz1161½ *Yessirgeneralsir*114nk Saved ground,no rally 8
Previously trained by Robbins Jay M
27Mar04-7GG fst 1 :224 :46 1:094 1:334 3↑BrklyBCH-G3 **100** 5 21 21 2½ 2hd 31¼ Lovato A J LB116 3.40 99– 09 Snorter1161 *Yougottawanna*116nk TsteofPrdise116hd Prssd pace 3w, wknd 5
7Mar04-8SA fst 7f :221 :44 1:082 1:21 4↑SnCrlosH-G2 **92** 9 3 77½ 76½ 64¾ 99¼ Ruis M LB113 62.70 91– 11 *Pico Central*1162 Publication1162 *Pohave*1121 Waited into str,no bid 10

Ten Most Wanted

Own: Chisholm James, Jarvis, Michael and R

Dk. b or b. h. 5 (Feb)
Sire: Deputy Commander (Deputy Minister) $20,000
Dam: Wanted Again (Criminal Type)
Br: Jim H. Plemmons (Ky)
Tr: Dollase Wallace A(0 0 0 0 .00) 2004:(111 21 .19)

Life	13	5	3	1	$1,718,460	112	D.Fst	12	5	2	1	$1,518,460	112
2004	2	1	0	0	$165,000	110	Wet(284)	1	0	1	0	$200,000	109
2003	10	4	2	1	$1,544,860	112	Turf(223)	0	0	0	0	$0	–
	0	0	0	0	$0	–	Dst(0)	0	0	0	0	$0	–

17Apr04–8Haw fst 1⅛ :464 1:112 1:363 1:492 3↑NtlJClbH-G3 **110** 4 34½ 37½ 32½ 15 16¾ Flores D R L121 b *.20 110–07 TnMostWntd1216¾ ColonilColony1134¼ NwYorkHro1131¾ Settled, handily 6
29Feb04–9FG fst 1⅛ :47 1:102 1:352 1:483 4↑NwOrlnsH-G2 **97** 8 76¼ 75½ 66½ 58¼ 59¾ Day P L120 b 2.60 91–05 *Peace Rules*119hd Saint Liam1142¾ *Funny Cide*1181¼ 4-w early, carried out 8

Teton Forest

Own: Hughes B. W

Dk. b or b. c. 4 (Mar)
Sire: Forestry (Storm Cat) $75,000
Dam: Tomorrow's Child (Al Nasr*Fr)
Br: Donald S. & R. Mary Zuckerman, as Tenants by the Entir (Ky)
Tr: Baffert Bob(0 0 0 0 .00) 2004:(562 105 .19)

Life	8	3	2	0	$222,000	110	D.Fst	7	2	2	0	$132,000	109
2004	8	3	2	0	$222,000	110	Wet(431)	1	1	0	0	$90,000	110
2003	0	M	0	0	$0	–	Turf(310)	0	0	0	0	$0	–
	0	0	0	0	$0	–	Dst(0)	0	0	0	0	$0	–

18Sep04–9Bel sly 1 :233 :463 1:103 1:353 JeromeH-G2 **110** 6 11 11½ 15 17 16 Bridgmohan S X L116 b 2.30 83–29 TetonForest1166 IceWynndFir116¾ Mhzouz1122¾ Drew away when roused 7
5Jun04–9Bel fst 7f :222 :45 1:084 1:204 RvaRdgBC-G2 **109** 4 3 2hd 2hd 1hd 2hd Bailey J D L115 b 4.10 96–07 *Fire Slam*123hd *Teton Forest*1153¼ Abbondanza1231¾ Fought it out gamely 7
15May04–6Pim fst 6f :223 :451 :573 1:103 HrshJacobs100k **99** 2 7 45 44½ 52¾ 41 Bailey J D L117 b *1.70 91–11 Abbondanz115hd BwnChrlie122¾ PennPcific117nk Angled 4wd, outkicked 9
10Apr04–3SA fst 6½f :212 :442 1:09 1:15 OC 80k/N1X-N **106** 6 2 42½ 42 31 1¾ Nakatani C S LB118 b *.80 97–12 Teton Forest118¾ M. P. Cat1207 Tenace1181 4wd into lane,gamely 6
28Mar04–8Sun fst 1$\frac{1}{16}$:224 :46 1:093 1:431 WinStarDby500k **82** 6 85¼ 84½ 84 65½ 66¼ Ramsammy E L122 fb 3.90 88–11 Hi Teck Man122½ Consecrate1221½ Rocky Gulch122½ No rally 5wide 10
3Mar04–2SA fst 1 :224 :454 1:101 1:361 Alw 53872N1X **96** 1 32 31½ 31½ 32½ 21¾ Flores D R LB118 b 2.00 88–18 RockHrdTn1181¾ TtonForst118½ JmmysInstnct1185 Came out str,late 2nd 5
7Feb04–3SA fst 7f :222 :443 1:091 1:221 SnVicnte-G2 **94** 3 3 31½ 31 31 53¼ Flores D R LB116 b 1.30 91–11 *Imperialism*1161¼ Hosco120hd Consecrate1161 Waited,boxed rail 1/8 6
3Jan04–4SA fst 7f :222 :451 1:092 1:214 Md Sp Wt 47k **90** 3 4 2½ 1hd 12 11½ Flores D R LB120 b 3.80 96–06 Teton Forest1201½ Storm Pilot1201 *Number Juan*1206 Inside duel,clear 8

The Cliff's Edge
Own: LaPenta Robert V

Dk. b or b. c. 4 (Apr) KEESEP02 $200,000
Sire: Gulch (Mr. Prospector) $50,000
Dam: Zigember (Danzig)
Br: Stoneside Stable (Ky)
Tr: Zito Nicholas P(0 0 0 0 .00) 2004:(452 86 .19)

Life	13	4	5	2	$1,265,258	111
2004	8	1	4	2	$1,010,000	111
2003	5	3	1	0	$255,258	101
	0	0	0	0	$0	-

D.Fst	12	4	5	2	$1,265,258	111
Wet(397)	1	0	0	0	$0	89
Turf(338)	0	0	0	0	$0	-
Dst(0)	0	0	0	0	$0	-

20Oct04-10Bel fst 1¼ :47³ 1:11³ 1:36² 2:02² 3↑JkyClbGC-G1 **109** 1 7³¾ 7⁴ 4² 3½ 3¹¾ Stevens G L L122 3.50 83- 13 FunnyCid126¾ Nwfoundlnd126¹ ThCliffsEdg122³¾ 4 wide move, weakened 7
28Aug04-11Sar fst 1¼ :49 1:12⁴ 1:37 2:02² Travers-G1 **104** 6 7⁶½ 5³¾ 3¹½ 2¹½ 2²½ Sellers S J L126 3.15 92- 05 Birdstone126²½ TheCliff'sEdge126³½ Eddington126nk Game finish outside 7
8Aug04-9Sar fst 1⅛ :45³ 1:09³ 1:34³ 1:47² JimDandy-G2 **101** 3 6¹⁷ 6¹⁸ 6¹¹ 2⁷ 2⁴½ Sellers S J L123 *1.70 93- 02 Purge1214½ The Cliff's Edge123½ [D]Eddington1157¼ Game finish outside 6
11Jly04-8Bel fst 1 1/16 :22⁴ :44² 1:07⁴ 1:40 Dwyer-G2 **105** 4 6¹¹ 6¹⁵ 5¹⁰ 2⁷ 2³¾ Sellers S J L123 *.65e 96- 09 Medllist1213¾ TheCliffsEdge123½ *SirShckleton*12114½ 4 wide move, gamely 6
1May04-10CD sly 1¼ :46³ 1:11⁴ 1:37¹ 2:04 KyDerby-G1 **89** 9 15¹⁰ 17⁷¾ 8⁶ 5⁵¾ 5¹²½ Sellers S J L126 8.20 66- 21 *SmartyJones*1262¾ LionHert1263¼ Imperilism1262 Wide,improved position 18
10Apr04-9Kee fst 1⅛ :46³ 1:11 1:36⁴ 1:49² BlueGras-G1 **111** 2 7¹⁰ 7¹³ 6⁷ 2¹ 1½ Sellers S J L123 5.70 94- 20 TheCliff'sEdge123½ LionHeart1236 Limehouse1233¾ Middle move, in time 8
13Mar04-9GP fst 1⅛ :47 1:11² 1:37³ 1:51¹ FlaDerby-G1 **90** 1 8¹⁰ 8¹³ 7⁵ 4³½ 3¹½ Sellers S J L122 5.20 81- 15 FriendsLake122¾ VluePlus122¾ *TheCliffsEdge*1222½ Fractious, bumped str 10
21Feb04-10Tam fst 1 1/16 :23² :47⁴ 1:12³ 1:44³ SamFDavis100k **88** 11¹¹ 11¹¹ 8⁶¼ 6³ 4¾ 2¹¾ Sellers S J L116 *.50 93- 15 Kaufy Mate1161¾ TheCliff'sEdge1161½ Zakocity1182 Looped 5w,bid,wknd 11

Theater R. N.
Own: Pegasus Thoroughbred Training Center

Ch. m. 5 (Mar)
Sire: Theatrical*Ire (Nureyev) $50,000
Dam: Yokama (Irish River*Fr)
Br: Allen E. Paulson (Ky)
Tr: Frankel Robert J(0 0 0 0 .00) 2004:(491 135 .27)

Life	5	4	0	0	$181,800	93
2004	3	2	0	0	$129,000	93
2003	2	2	0	0	$52,800	85
	0	0	0	0	$0	-

D.Fst	0	0	0	0	$0	-
Wet(333)	0	0	0	0	$0	-
Turf(395)	5	4	0	0	$181,800	93
Dst(0)	0	0	0	0	$0	-

31Oct04-8SA fm 1⅛ Ⓣ :48³ 1:12³ 1:36¹ 1:47⁴ 3↑ⒻLsPlmasH-G2 **93** 3 5⁵½ 5⁸ 5⁸½ 3³ 1½ Douglas R R LB114 5.90 90- 14 TheaterR.N.114½ LotsofHope117½ GoodStudent1141 Off bit slw,up 3w late 7
21Jly04-4Dmr fm 1 1/16 Ⓣ :24³ :48² 1:12² 1:42 3↑ⒻOC 62k/n2x-N **85** 3 8⁵¼ 8⁵¾ 6²¾ 2hd 1¹ Nakatani C S LB119 4.50 89- 09 *Theater R. N.*1191 Uraib119nk Taygete116½ 4wd into lane,rallied 10
8Jan04-7SA fm 1⅛ Ⓣ :48 1:12¹ 1:36³ 1:48⁴ 4↑ⒻOC 80k/n2x-N **83** 9 5¹¼ 5⁴½ 4³ 6²¾ 5³¼ Flores D R LB120 *1.50 82- 13 *Magnificent Val*121¾ Drew Away1191 Esmay1191 3wd into lane,outkickd 9

Three Hour Nap
Own: Homewrecker Racing LLC and Robertson

B. c. 3 (Mar) KEESEP03 $67,000
Sire: Afternoon Deelites (Private Terms) $4,000
Dam: Pilgrim's Treasure (Pilgrim)
Br: Frank A. Penn Jr. & D. Flannigan (Ky)
Tr: Robertson Hugh H(0 0 0 0 .00) 2004:(469 100 .21)

Life	4	3	0	0	$158,400	86
2004	4	3	0	0	$158,400	86
2003	0	M	0	0	$0	-
	0	0	0	0	$0	-

D.Fst	4	3	0	0	$158,400	86
Wet(370)	0	0	0	0	$0	-
Turf(284)	0	0	0	0	$0	-
Dst(0)	0	0	0	0	$0	-

9Oct04-7Kee fst 1 1/16 :23 :47 1:12 1:43³ BrdrsFut-G1 **73** 8 10¹⁰ 9⁹¾ 7⁷ 8⁷¾ 6¹¹¾ Guidry M L121 11.10 82- 13 Consolidator1212 Patriot Act1213¼ Diamond Isle121½ Hop start,no threat 10
19Sep04-6AP fst 1 :22⁴ :45¹ 1:10³ 1:38² A-WBCFut-G3 **80** 6 4¾ 4³½ 4³ 3¹ 1nk Razo E Jr L119 3.10 76- 20 ThreeHourNp119nk [DH]ElusivChris122 [DH]StrightLin1198 Bumped stretch 6
29Aug04-5AP fst 1 :24³ :48 1:12² 1:37 OC 50k/n1x-N **86** 5 2¹½ 2¹½ 2¹ 2¹½ 1²½ Emigh C A L118 2.30 83- 17 *ThreeHourNp*1182½ MryAlex1151¾ ExceptionlRide1208 Stalked, drew clear 6
23Jly04-7AP fst 5½f :23 :47¹ :59² 1:05³ Md Sp Wt 30k **73** 10 6 6³ 6²½ 4nk 1¾ Emigh C A L119 21.90 86- 16 *ThreeHourNp*119¾ SlemSchoolRod1194½ GenrlChrly1192 6 wide 1/4, up late 12

Thunder Touch
Own: Stronach Stables

Ch. c. 4 (Jan) ADSSPR03 $95,000
Sire: Gulch (Mr. Prospector) $50,000
Dam: Highland Vixen (Highland Ruckus)
Br: Adena Springs (Ky)
Tr: McLaughlin Kiaran P(0 0 0 0 .00) 2004:(462 84 .18)

Life	8	4	1	1	$164,750	101	D.Fst	6	2	1	1	$73,190	99
2004	8	4	1	1	$164,750	101	Wet(370)	2	2	0	0	$91,560	101
2003	0	M	0	0	$0	–	Turf(280)	0	0	0	0	$0	–
	0	0	0	0	$0	–	Dst(0)	0	0	0	0	$0	–

28Nov04-9Aqu sly 6f :212 :441 :5641:094 3↑FallHwtH-G3 **101** 3 4 55 44 23 1¼ Bejarano R L126 f 6.90 89-16 Thunder Touch1261¼ Papua128½ Eavesdropper127nk 3 wide move, clear 9
14Oct04-3Bel fst 6½f :223 :452 1:0931:16 3↑Alw 48020N2x **99** 1 2 41½ 41 2½ 1½ Migliore R L118 f *1.40 93-16 *ThunderTouch*118½ LuckyGamble1222¼ *BahmJohn*120¾ Got through on rail 5
19Sep04-6Bel fst 1 :241 :473 1:1131:362 3↑Alw 50000N2x **99** 2 1½ 1½ 1½ 1hd 3hd Gryder A T L118 *1.75 79-25 BrodwyVw116hd *InfntGlory*120no *ThundrToch*118¼ Gamely between rivals 6
16Aug04-7Sar fst 6f :214 :442 :5631:093 3↑Alw 49000N2x **95** 3 4 42½ 47 23½ 21¼ Migliore R L120 *1.55 93-11 AllHIStormy1201¼ ThundrToch12011¼ *BllMrkt*1218¼ Steadied turn, gamely 6
9Jly04-5Bel fst 6f :222 :451 :57 1:09 3↑Alw 44100N2L **94** 4 2 31½ 21 1hd 12¼ Migliore R L116 2.70 94-14 ThndrToch1162¼ *LovofMny*11810¼ ThGrtBzzn1111¼ Wide move, drew clear 5
5Jun04-3Bel fst 7f :222 :451 1:1011:232 3↑Alw 55000N1x **86** 13 2 41 2hd 2hd 23¼ Migliore R L115 12.00e 80-07 *CountryJudg*1213¼ D *ThundrTouch*115nk MxwllTrrc1151¼ Lugged in stretch 14
Disqualified and placed 5th
14Feb04-4GP fst 7f :212 :432 1:09 1:224 Alw 34000N1x **55** 6 7 67¾ 57 58½ 616¼ Bailey J D L122 *1.90 72-07 VeryFormalMD118¾ NightmreAffir1185½ CherokeeSpook1184½ No factor 9
18Jan04-4Aqu my 6f ⊡ :232 :472 :5931:121 Md Sp Wt 41k **82** 1 3 2hd 1hd 14½ 13¾ Gryder A T L120 8.70 78-25 ThunderTouch1203¾ ParkersMill1202¾ JckofClubs1208¾ Vied inside, clear 8

Ticker Tape (GB)
Own: Jim Ford Inc., Pearson, Deron and Swe

B. f. 4 (Jan)
Sire: Royal Applause*GB (Waajib*Ire) $38,370
Dam: Argent Du Bois (Silver Hawk)
Br: Car Colston Hall Stud (GB)
Tr: Cassidy James M(0 0 0 0 .00) 2004:(157 18 .11)

Life	18	7	6	2	$1,267,426	99	D.Fst	0	0	0	0	$0	–
2004	10	5	3	1	$1,159,075	99	Wet(247)	0	0	0	0	$0	–
2003	8	2	3	1	$108,351	78	Turf(354)	18	7	6	2	$1,267,426	99
	0	0	0	0	$0	–	Dst(0)	0	0	0	0	$0	–

28Nov04-7Hol fm 1 Ⓣ:24 :473 1:1121:354 3↑ⒻMatriarc-G1 **96** 6 84¾ 82½ 63½ 42 32 Espinoza V LB120 6.90 83-17 Intercontinentl1232 EtoilMontnt123no TickrTp1201½ 4wd into lane,rallied 9
16Oct04-8Kee gd 1⅛ Ⓣ:4931:142 1:3841:511 ⒻQEIICup-G1 **96** 5 63 64½ 65½ 1½ 1½ Desormeaux K J L121 *1.70 81-20 Ticker Tape121½ Barancella121½ *River Belle*1211 4w,steady drive 7
18Sep04-9AP fm 1⅛ Ⓣ:4741:121 1:3641:483 ⒻPuckerUp-G3 **93** 8 85½ 86¼ 42 32 12¾ Desormeaux K J L122 *1.20 96-05 *Ticker Tape*1222¾ Spotlight122hd *Sister Swank*116½ 3 wide, ridden out 11
21Aug04-3Dmr fm 1⅛ Ⓣ:4621:101 1:3421:461 ⒻDmrOaks-G1 **99** 2 41½ 32½ 31 1½ 2no Desormeaux K J LB122 *2.20 98-02 Amorama122no *Ticker Tape*1221 Sweet Win122½ 3wd into lane,caught 7
3Jly04-6Hol fm 1¼ Ⓣ:49 1:14 1:3812:012 ⒻAmrcnOks-G1 **98** 7 42½ 42 21½ 12 11 Desormeaux K J LB121 12.00 85-13 TickerTpe1211 DncinthMood1212 HollywoodStory121½ 3wd move,led,held 13
5Jun04-8Hol fm 1⅛ Ⓣ:5011:15 1:3811:494 +ⒻHnymnBCH-G2 **89** 8 75½ 58½ 41½ 31½ 41¾ Desormeaux K J LB121 *1.10 80-14 LovelyRfel114no WesternHmisphr1141½ SgittR116nk 3wd 2nd turn,lost 3rd 8
15May04-8Hol fm 1 Ⓣ:233 :463 1:10 1:341 ⒻSenorita-G3 **94** 7 67 65½ 55½ 21 2hd Nakatani C S LB121 *1.30 93-09 *Miss Vegas*115hd Ticker Tape1213 Amorama116no 3wd into str,missed 7
11Apr04-8SA fm 1 Ⓣ:222 :453 1:1011:342 ⒻProvidncia113k **89** 9 75½ 64¾ 3½ 12 12½ Desormeaux K J LB118 4.70 90-10 Ticker Tape1182½ Amorama1141 Winendynme1151 3wd bid,led,clear 12
18Mar04-7SA fm 1 Ⓣ:24 :482 1:1231:361 ⒻChinaDoll75k **85** 9 41½ 31½ 41½ 31½ 1¾ Desormeaux K J LB117 5.00e 81-13 *Ticker Tape*117¾ Mambo Slew1221½ Amorama116no 2-3wd, collared foes 10
14Jan04-7SA fm 1 Ⓣ:23 :47 1:11 1:343 ⒻBlueNorthr76k **79** 6 76½ 76½ 64½ 32 23 Desormeaux K J LB116 2.20 86-10 Mambo Slew1203 *Ticker Tape*1162 Yingyingying1151 Bit tight 6-1/2,4w str 8

Timo

Own: C. K. Woods Stable

Gr/ro. c. 4 (Mar)
Sire: El Prado*Ire (Sadler's Wells) $100,000
Dam: Elocat's Burglar (Criminal Type)
Br: C.K. Woods Stables, Inc (Ky)
Tr: Badgett W Jr(0 0 0 0 .00) 2004:(115 13 .11)

Life	11	5	3	1	$406,823	93	D.Fst	0	0	0	0	$0	–
2004	6	2	1	1	$253,308	93	Wet(318)	0	0	0	0	$0	–
2003	5	3	2	0	$153,515	89	Turf(259)	11	5	3	1	$406,823	93
	0	0	0	0	$0	–	Dst(0)	0	0	0	0	$0	–

28Nov04–9Hol fm 1¼ Ⓣ :47¹ 1:12¹ 1:37 2:01² HolDerby-G1 **92** 6 4² 3½ 2¹ 2¹ 76½ Velazquez J R **LB**122 b 8.60 78–17 GoodRwrd122½ FstndFurious122¹ Imprilism122² Stalked pace, weakened 13
26Jun04–8Del sf 1⅛ Ⓣ :52² 1:18² 1:43⁴ 1:55³ KentBC-G3 **90** 4 53½ 54½ 64½ 42½ 1no Migliore R L117 b 2.90 59–38 Timo117no Icy Atlantic117 1¼ Commendation115nk Split h,up final str 8
6Jun04–8Bel fm 1⅛ 🅃 :51² 1:16 1:38⁴ 1:50 HillPrnc-G3 **93** 4 3² 3¹ 2½ 22½ 21¾ Velazquez J R L122 b 2.65 78–20 Artie Schiller1201¾ *Timo*1222¼ Big Booster114¾ Chased winner stretch 6
15May04–7Pim fm 1 1/16 Ⓣ :24² :48¹ 1:12¹ 1:41⁴ Woodlawn100k **80** 4 52¼ 5³ 54¾ 5⁵ 3⁴ Prado E S L122 b *1.60 89 – *Artie Schiller*1153¾ Lipan115nk Timo122hd Wide turns, rallied 13
2Apr04–9Kee fm 1 Ⓣ :23¹ :47¹ 1:12¹ 1:36² Trnsylvn-G3 **91** 1 3² 31½ 21½ 21½ 1¾ Prado E S L123 b 2.30 90–14 Timo123¾ Mr. J T. L.116nk *America Alive*116nk 4w,bmp 1/8p,drvg 9
1Jan04–9Crc fm 1⅛ Ⓣ :47¹ 1:11² 1:35¹ 1:46⁴ + TrpPkDby-G3 **76** 7 84½ 8⁶ 62¼ 73½ 86½ Coa E M L122 b *1.90 88–08 *KittensJoy*1194½ BroadwayView112nk SoverignHonor117hd Stumbled start 11

Toasted

Own: Port Sidney L. and Trust 720270

Dk. b or b. c. 4 (Apr) KEESEP02 $45,000
Sire: Hennessy (Storm Cat) $35,000
Dam: Burrows (Seattle Song)
Br: James D. Haley (Ky)
Tr: De Seroux Laura(0 0 0 0 .00) 2004:(98 8 .08)

Life	10	4	2	3	$356,171	101	D.Fst	1	0	0	0	$0	82
2004	6	2	2	1	$315,680	101	Wet(338)	0	0	0	0	$0	–
2003	4	2	0	2	$40,491	–	Turf(324)	9	4	2	3	$356,171	101
	0	0	0	0	$0	–	Dst(0)	0	0	0	0	$0	–

6Sep04–8Dmr fm 1⅛ Ⓣ :47³ 1:11² 1:35 1:46³ DmrDerby-G2 **101** 3 3³ 3⁵ 32½ 31½ 2nk Douglas R R **LB**122 6.50 96–10 Blackdoun122nk Toasted122no LaurasLuckyBoy122½ Rallied btwn,gamely 10
24Jly04–5AP fm 1 3/16 Ⓣ :48² 1:12⁴ 1:37² 1:54⁴ AmercnDb-G2 **98** 1 63¾ 63½ 4³ 42¼ 3¹ Douglas R R L123 *1.20 99–05 Simple Exchange119nk Cool Conductor119¾ Toasted1231¼ Inside to lane 8
3Jly04–9AP sf 1 1/16 Ⓣ :24³ :51 1:17⁴ 1:50⁴ ArlClsc-G2 **95** 1 55½ 62½ 62½ 3½ 13¼ Douglas R R L121 *1.40 55–45 Tosted1213¼ StreetThetre119nk CoolConductor119hd Split horses, driving 8
22May04–8Hol fm 1 Ⓣ :22³ :45² 1:09² 1:33² WilRogrs-G3 **91** 2 77½ 76¾ 51¾ 2⁴ 2⁴ Almeida G F **LB**121 *2.00 93–05 LursLuckyBoy119⁴ *Tosted*121¹ StreetThetre1173½ Squeezed strt,4wd lane 8
10Apr04–8SA fm 1 Ⓣ :22³ :45³ 1:09⁴ 1:34 LaPuente110k **95** 6 97¼ 9¹⁰ 86¾ 41¾ 11¼ Almeida G F **LB**115 25.60 92–12 Toasted1151¼ Erewhon116½ Seattle Borders116¹ Waited bit,rallied btw 9
14Mar04–5SA fst 1 1/16 :23¹ :46⁴ 1:11 1:42⁴ SnFelipe-G2 **82** 9 8⁹ 89½ 8⁸ 8⁷ 8¹¹ Stevens G L **LB**116 21.20 80–09 Prechintthebr116no StAveril1224½ HrvrdAvnu116¹ Bit slow,awkward start 9

Toll Taker

Own: Welsh Patrick

B. f. 3 (Apr)
Sire: Bernstein (Storm Cat) $15,000
Dam: Tappanzee (Bet Big)
Br: Lothenbach Stables, Inc. (Ill)
Tr: Hills Timothy A(0 0 0 0 .00) 2004:(585 103 .18)

Life	6	3	0	1	$114,240	79	D.Fst	5	3	0	0	$110,170	79
2004	6	3	0	1	$114,240	79	Wet(379*)	1	0	0	1	$4,070	41
2003	0	M	0	0	$0	–	Turf(293*)	0	0	0	0	$0	–
	0	0	0	0	$0	–	Dst(0)	0	0	0	0	$0	–

13Nov04–6Haw	fst	6f	:22	:462	:59	1:121	ⒻⓈShowtimDeb97k	–	5	11	-	-	-	-	Marquez C H Jr	L121	*.80	- 21	Bluesbdancing1163¼ *MedowBride*116½ CrtsTurn116¾	Stumbled, lost jockey	11
17Oct04–8Bel	fst	6½f	:224	:47	1:113	1:18	ⒻAstarita-G3	**79**	2	1	41	31	1½	13¼	Coa E M	L117	6.70	83– 18	TollTaker1173¼ ImaDixieGirl1201½ *SummerRaven*11711½	4 wide move, clear	6
10Sep04–7Mth	fst	6f	:221	:461	:583	1:11	ⒻAlw 40280N1x	**71**	1	4	52	21	12	110	Coa E M	L118	*1.40	85– 20	*Toll Taker*11810 MurphyStyle1211½ PrincessLana11510¼	Bid 1/4, ridden out	8
12Aug04–4Mth	fst	5½f	:22	:462	:591	1:061	ⒻMd Sp Wt 37k	**50**	9	1	4¾	41	12	15	Coa E M	L118	4.60	84– 14	*TollTkr*1185 *Shblongstoyo*118nk HonorngCrlyn1181¾	6wd bid,drifted,drivng	11
15Jly04–2Mth	gd	5f	:222	:461		:583	ⒻMd Sp Wt 37k	**41**	4	2	1hd	11	22	38	Coa E M	L118 b	6.70	81– 13	JoyousSong1186¾ *SpeedyDeedy*1181¼ *TollTker*118¾	Led,brief duel,weakend	8
17Jun04–5Mth	fst	5f	:214	:453		:591	ⒻMd Sp Wt 37k	**31**	7	4	45½	45¾	56½	67½	Coa E M	118	8.00	78– 15	*Elke*1182 Our Miss Jones118¾ Grecian Lover118no	Chased outside,tired	7

Total Impact (Chi)

Own: Sultan Al Kabeer

Ch. h. 7 (Aug)
Sire: Stuka (Jade Hunter) $1,500
Dam: Pebbles*Chi (Manos de Piedra)
Br: Haras Don Alberto (Chi)
Tr: De Seroux Laura(0 0 0 0 .00) 2004:(0 0 .00)

Life	22	5	8	2	$1,586,778	112	D.Fst	19	3	8	2	$1,562,830	112
2004	11	1	5	2	$988,390	109	Wet(305)	2	2	0	0	$20,288	–
2003	6	2	1	0	$163,400	112	Turf(255)	1	0	0	0	$3,660	95
	0	0	0	0	$0	–	Dst(0)	0	0	0	0	$0	–

28Nov04 Tokyo (Jpn) ft *1 5/16 LH 2:083 3↑ Japan Cup Dirt-G1 Stk 2417000 — 45 Smith M 126 3.40 Time Paradox1262½ Admire Don1261 Gene Crisis1211½ — 16
Timeform rating: 114 — *Tracked in 4th,2nd 4f out,led briefly 2f out,faded*

30Oct04–5Kee	fst	1⅛	:471	1:112	1:364	1:501	3↑Fayette-G3	**107**	3	21½	2½	2½	2hd	2no	Perret C	L125 b	*1.30	90– 10	*Midway Road*121no TotalImpact1256 AlumniHall1196¾	Lean in bmp stretch	5
2Oct04–8SA	fst	1⅛	:48	1:112	1:353	1:481	3↑GdwdBCH-G2	**108**	5	2hd	1hd	2½	1hd	2hd	Smith M E	LB119 b	*1.10	93– 08	LundysLiability118hd TotalImpact1192 *SuphBlitz*1176	Willingly,outgamed	5
22Aug04–8Dmr	fst	1¼	:464	1:104	1:352	2:01	3↑PacifcCl-G1	**109**	6	42½	3nk	11	2½	31¾	Smith M E	LB124 b	6.20	88– 10	PlesntlyPerfct1241 PrfctDrift124¾ TotlImpct1244¾	4wd move,led,held 3rd	8
10Jly04–9Hol	fst	1¼	:464	1:102	1:344	2:003	3↑HolGldCp-G1	**109**	2	33	31	21½	1hd	11¼	Smith M E	LB124 b	6.70	99 -	TotalImpct1241¼ Olmodvor124½ EventheScore1244	Slipped thru rail,game	7
12Jun04–9Hol	fst	1⅛	:463	1:101	1:35	1:473	3↑Calfrnin-G2	**103**	7	41	31	2½	21	23½	Smith M E	LB116 b	5.60	97– 08	EventheScore1183½ *TotlImpct*1162 NosThTrd116nk	3wd bid,btwn,2nd best	8
8May04–9Hol	fst	1 1/16	:231	:454	1:092	1:404	3↑MrvnLRyH-G2	**94**	8	41½	3½	31	31½	35	Smith M E	LB116 b	4.90	92– 04	*EventheScore*1162 Ender'sShadow1133 TotalImpact1161	5wd 7-1/2,3wd bid	8
3Apr04–10SA	fst	1⅛	:471	1:112	1:354	1:48	4↑SnBrdnoH-G3	**106**	5	21½	23	2½	2½	24½	Valdivia J Jr	LB116 b	14.40	89– 09	Dynever1174½ Total Impact1162 *Even the Score*1162	Bid,btwn 1/4,2nd best	7
13Mar04–6SA	fst	1	:224	:454	1:101	1:354	4↑TokyoCityH75k	**95**	4	4¾	2hd	2½	21½	23	Espinoza V	LB118 b	5.10	89– 08	EndrsShdow1143 TotlImpct118no GiftofthEgl1162	Bid btwn,just held 2nd	9
1Feb04–8FG	fst	1 1/16	:242	:472	1:114	1:452	4↑WhrlwayH-G3	**100**	1	32½	32½	43½	75½	54¼	Sellers S J	L118	6.90	79– 17	Olmodavor121¾ SpanishEmpire1182¼ Almuhthir114½	Inside, lacked finish	9
3Jan04–7SA	fst	1 1/16	:224	:454	1:093	1:421	4↑SnPsqalH-G2	**79**	6	31	31	53¼	66¾	512	Smith M E	LB116	2.40	82– 13	Star Cross113½ *Nose The Trade*1153 *Olmodavor*1182½	3wd bid,weakened	7

Tronare (Chi)
Own: Noctis LLC Papiano, Neil and Taub, St

Ch. h. 7 (Jul)
Sire: Stuka (Jade Hunter) $1,500
Dam: Pijama Party (Manos de Piedra)
Br: Haras Don Alberto (Chi)
Tr: Mulhall Kristin(0 0 0 0 .00) 2004:(154 23 .15)

Life	20	3	4	5	$118,921	101		
2004	7	1	2	2	$80,890	101		
2003	2	0	0	0	$4,880	91		
	0	0	0	0	$0	–		
D.Fst	7	1	1	2	$8,341	–		
Wet(305)	1	0	0	0	$0	–		
Turf(255)	12	2	3	3	$110,580	101		
Dst(0)	0	0	0	0	$0	–		

Date/Track	Cond	Dist	Fractions	Race	Speed	PP	St	1C	2C	Str	Fin	Jockey	Med/Wt	Odds	Pace	Top Finishers	Comment	Fld
28Jly04-3Dmr	fm	1$\frac{1}{16}$	Ⓣ :24^4 :48^4 1:12 1:40^4	3↑OC 100k/N3x-N	90	4	1^1	1^{hd}	1^{hd}	3^1	3^2	Valdivia J Jr	LB119 b	2.20	93– 07	Mananan McL r119$\frac{3}{4}$ Bis Repetitas119$1\frac{1}{4}$ Tronare119$\frac{3}{4}$	Inside,held 3rd	5
23Jun04-7Hol	fm	1	Ⓣ :23^4 :46^4 1:10^2 1:35^1	4↑OC 100k/N3x-N	97	2	5^5	5$^{5\frac{1}{2}}$	6$^{4\frac{1}{4}}$	6$^{3\frac{3}{4}}$	5^1	Solis A	LB122 b	*1.70	87– 16	ReelEmIn118^{nk} GoldenArrow118^{no} GreenLine118$\frac{1}{2}$	3wd into str,outkicked	7
19May04-7Hol	fm	1$\frac{1}{16}$	Ⓣ :24^2 :48^3 1:11^4 1:41	4↑Alw 58000N3x	100	5	4^2	3$^{\frac{1}{2}}$	3$^{1\frac{1}{2}}$	2^1	2^{nk}	Solis A	LB122 b	2.60	91– 14	Sigint118^{nk} Tronare122$1\frac{1}{2}$ Wixoe Express120^{nk}	Tight 7/8,led 1/16	7
1May04-6Hol	fm	1$\frac{1}{16}$	Ⓣ :23^3 :46^4 1:09^3 1:38^2	3↑InglewdH-G3	99	2	4^2	4$^{2\frac{1}{2}}$	4$^{2\frac{1}{2}}$	4^3	6$^{5\frac{1}{2}}$	Steiner J J	LB117 b	4.10e	98– 04	*Lroidsnimux*114^2 *DsigndforLuck*118^2 DvousBoy115^{nk}	Inside trip, weakened	9
14Mar04-7GG	fm	1$\frac{1}{8}$	Ⓣ :47^3 1:11^3 1:36 1:48^2	3↑GGBCH-G3	101	4	3^2	3^2	3^1	1^{hd}	1^1	Gonzalez R M	LB115 b	10.70	105– 10	Tronare115^1 Soud118^2 Aly Bubba116^{no}	Bid 3w, dueled, drvng	9
11Feb04-3SA	fm	1$\frac{1}{4}$	Ⓣ :47^1 1:11^2 1:35^1 2:00^1	4↑OC 62k/N2x-N	92	2	2^2	3^2	2$^{2\frac{1}{2}}$	2$^{2\frac{1}{2}}$	3^2	Espinoza V	LB119 b	2.80	86– 14	All the Boys119^{no} Urban King117^2 *Tronare*119^3	Pulled,inside,held 3rd	5
11Jan04-8SA	fm	1	Ⓣ :22^1 :45^2 1:10 1:34^1	4↑OC 80k/N2x-N	88	2	3^2	3$^{2\frac{1}{2}}$	3$^{\frac{1}{2}}$	2^{hd}	2^2	Espinoza V	LB119 b	6.60	89– 11	Academy Spy119^2 Tronare119$1\frac{1}{2}$ Fail Me Not119^1	Bid 3wd,led into lane	10

Truly a Judge
Own: Aidekman Alan, Ailshie, Gaylord and H

Dk. b or b. g. 7 (May)
Sire: Judge T C (Judge Smells) $8,500
Dam: Truly Needy (Yukon)
Br: Robert H. Roberts & Bea Roberts (Ky)
Tr: Bernstein David(0 0 0 0 .00) 2004:(68 10 .15)

Life	41	11	7	8	$595,131	111		
2004	8	3	1	0	$187,218	111		
2003	10	1	3	3	$135,063	105		
	0	0	0	0	$0	–		
D.Fst	37	10	5	7	$512,271	111		
Wet(311)	3	1	2	0	$75,180	103		
Turf(266)	1	0	0	1	$7,680	94		
Dst(0)	0	0	0	0	$0	–		

Date/Track	Cond	Dist	Fractions	Race	Speed	PP	St	1C	2C	Str	Fin	Jockey	Med/Wt	Odds	Pace	Top Finishers	Comment	Fld
11Dec04-7Hol	fst	1$\frac{1}{8}$	:47^2 1:11^1 1:34^4 1:47	3↑NtvDivrH-G3	111	8	1^1	1^1	1^1	1$^{2\frac{1}{2}}$	1^2	Pedroza M A	LB115	6.40	104– 08	Truly a Judge115^2 Dynever119^7 Calkins Road116^2	Speed,inside,held game	8
18Nov04-5Hol	fst	1$\frac{1}{16}$	:23^3 :46^3 1:10^2 1:41^2	3↑OC 80k/c-N	105	9	1^1	1^1	1^2	1$^{2\frac{1}{2}}$	1$^{6\frac{1}{2}}$	Pedroza M A	LB123	8.30	94– 24	*Truly a Judge*123$6\frac{1}{2}$ Verkade123^1 *Special Matter*119^3	Drew off, ridden out	10
2Oct04-8SA	fst	1$\frac{1}{8}$	:48 1:11^2 1:35^3 1:48^1	3↑GdwdBCH-G2	95	4	3$^{1\frac{1}{2}}$	3$^{1\frac{1}{2}}$	4^2	4^5	4^8	Douglas R R	LB115	14.30	85– 08	LundysLiability118^{hd} TotalImpact119^2 *SupahBlitz*117^6	Off slow,weakened	5
25Aug04-3Dmr	fst	1	:22^1 :45^1 1:09^3 1:36	3↑OC 125k/c-N	99	1	2^{hd}	2^{hd}	2^{hd}	2$^{\frac{1}{2}}$	1$^{\frac{1}{2}}$	Nakatani C S	LB117	6.10	94– 06	Truly a Judge117$\frac{1}{2}$ Gondolieri117^6 Waingarth117^2	Inside duel, gamely	5
5Aug04-7Dmr	fst	1	:22 :45 1:09^3 1:36	3↑OC 125k/c-N	83	4	5$^{4\frac{1}{2}}$	4^5	6$^{6\frac{1}{2}}$	6$^{6\frac{1}{4}}$	4^{10}	Baze T C	LB117 b	12.30	84– 06	TouchtheWire119^1 Verkde119^7 NoseTheTrde119^2	Bobbled strt,4w 2-turn	6
13Mar04-6SA	fst	1	:22^4 :45^4 1:10^1 1:35^4	4↑TokyoCityH75k	92	3	6$^{3\frac{1}{4}}$	5$^{2\frac{1}{4}}$	3^2	3$^{2\frac{1}{2}}$	4^5	Smith M E	LB116 b	5.60	87– 08	EndersShdow114^3 TotlImpct118^{no} GiftoftheEgl116^2	Stalked inside,no bid	9
14Feb04-6SA	fst	1$\frac{1}{16}$	:23^3 :47^2 1:11^2 1:43	4↑Alw 65000c	89	2	8$^{5\frac{3}{4}}$	5$^{1\frac{3}{4}}$	4$^{1\frac{1}{4}}$	4^3	4^5	Smith M E	LB117 b	5.40	85– 15	NoseTheTrde120^2 NtionlPrk117^2 GiftoftheEgl120^1	Stumbled start,4wd 1/2	8
1Jan04-8GG	wf	1	:23^2 :46^3 1:10 1:34^2	4↑LafayetteH81k	97	5	2$^{1\frac{1}{2}}$	2$^{\frac{1}{2}}$	2^{hd}	1^2	2^1	Olivares F	LB116 f	2.20	96– 03	GoldRuckus116^1 TrulyJudg116^3 BringHomThgold116$\frac{3}{4}$	Clear lead, tagged	6

Twice as Bad
Own: Mercedes Stables LLC

Gr/ro. c. 4 (Feb) OBSAUG02 $15,000
Sire: Stormy Atlantic (Storm Cat) $15,000
Dam: Two Bad Girls (Diablo)
Br: Linda S. Rosenblatt (Fla)
Tr: Cerin Vladimir(0 0 0 0 .00) 2004:(339 59 .17)

Life	15	3	4	1	$218,320	101	D.Fst 14 3 4 1 $218,090 101
2004	3	1	1	0	$112,040	101	Wet(368) 1 0 0 0 $230 41
2003	12	2	3	1	$106,280	88	Turf(310) 0 0 0 0 $0 –
	0	0	0	0	$0	–	Dst(0) 0 0 0 0 $0 –

10Jly04- 9Crc fst 6f :21^2 :44^2 :57 1:10^2 CarryBck-G3 **75** 2 9 2^{hd} 2½ 4^4 7^{13} Court J K L119 4.70 84- 09 Weigelia117½ Classy Migration112^4 *Bwana Charlie*119^4 Slow st, vied inside 11
19Jun04- 7Hol fst 1$\frac{1}{16}$:23^3 :47 1:11^1 1:42 AffirmdH-G3 **101** 1 3$^{2\frac{1}{2}}$ 3$^{2\frac{1}{2}}$ 2½ 1^{hd} 2½ Nakatani C S LB121 2.50 90- 17 Boomzeeboom115½ TwicesBd1211¼ Wimplstiltskin116^2 Bid,led,outgamed 9
29May04- 8Hol fst 7f :21^4 :44 1:08^4 1:21^2 LBrreraM-G2 **95** 6 3 3^{nk} 3½ 1^2 1^3 Solis A LB116 *2.10 95- 09 TwicsBd116^3 Wimplstltskn1162½ DontsIlmshort123^3 3wd,angled in,rid out 8

Twilight Road
Own: Donamire Farm

Ch. g. 8 (Apr)
Sire: Cahill Road (Fappiano) $4,000
Dam: Glory's Light (Halo)
Br: Mira Ball (Ky)
Tr: Fawkes David(0 0 0 0 .00) 2004:(236 36 .15)

Life	47	11	12	2	$667,557	107	D.Fst 38 10 8 0 $472,472 107
2004	9	3	3	0	$246,500	104	Wet(338) 6 0 3 2 $85,085 107
2003	7	2	0	1	$79,520	101	Turf(313) 3 1 1 0 $110,000 95
	0	0	0	0	$0	–	Dst(0) 0 0 0 0 $0 –

18Dec04-12Crc fst 1⅛ :47^4 1:11^2 1:37^3 1:50^3 3↑ FHooperH-G3 **96** 7 6$^{4\frac{1}{4}}$ 6^6 5$^{7\frac{1}{2}}$ 3^4 2$^{8\frac{1}{2}}$ Teator P A L115 9.70 90- 21 PiesProspect1148½ TwilightRod115^1 HrNoEvil1123¼ Late bid, 4w, up place 11
23Oct04-13Crc fst 1$\frac{1}{16}$:23^4 :48 1:13 1:45^4 3↑ SpdABckH-G3 **89** 7 8$^{5\frac{1}{4}}$ 8$^{4\frac{1}{4}}$ 5^3 6^7 4$^{7\frac{3}{4}}$ Teator P A L117 *2.20 75- 26 Built Up115^{hd} *Super Frolic*1174¼ Gold Dollar1153½ Couldn't keep pace 11
9Oct04- 7Crc fm 1⅛ Ⓣ :50^3 1:14^2 1:38^2 1:50^3 3↑ FlyngPdgnH100k **92** 6 4^2 5$^{3\frac{1}{2}}$ 6^4 3$^{5\frac{1}{2}}$ 2$^{2\frac{3}{4}}$ Teator P A L116 *2.50 73- 24 Keep Cool1162¾ Twilight Road116½ Unbridels King1161½ 3 wide, rallied 11
11Sep04- 7Crc yl 1 Ⓣ :24 :48^4 1:13^1 1:39^2 3↑ MiaMIBCH-G3 **95** 2 3$^{2\frac{1}{2}}$ 3$^{2\frac{1}{2}}$ 3^3 2$^{1\frac{1}{2}}$ 1½ Teator P A L114 5.30 71- 32 TwilightRoad114½ GoldDollar114¾ ParadiseDancer115^{hd} All out, prevailed 9
10Jly04-10Crc fst 6f :21^4 :44^3 :57 1:10 3↑ SmlSprtH-G3 **97** 7 5 8$^{5\frac{1}{4}}$ 8$^{3\frac{3}{4}}$ 8$^{5\frac{3}{4}}$ 5$^{5\frac{1}{4}}$ Teator P A L114 16.30 94- 09 Champali117^{no} Clock Stopper115^{nk} Built Up114^{nk} 3 wide, passed tired 10
31May04-10Crc fst 1$\frac{1}{16}$:23^2 :47 1:11^4 1:45^3 3↑ MemDayH-G3 **104** 1 5^7 5$^{7\frac{1}{2}}$ 5^6 1^{hd} 1$^{5\frac{1}{4}}$ Teator P A L111 7.60 84- 16 Twilight Road1115¼ Hear No Evil115^1 *Gold Dollar*112½ 4 wide, drew away 12
26Apr04- 8Crc fst 7f :22^4 :46 1:11^1 1:24^2 3↑ ThtsOurBck40k **99** 2 8 7^3 7$^{2\frac{1}{4}}$ 2^3 1^1 Teator P A L115 6.10 94- 17 *Twilight Road*115^1 Super Frolic1192¾ Patriotic Flame1152¼ 4 wide, up late 9
Run in divisions
14Apr04- 8GP fst 6f :23 :46^2 :58^4 1:11^3 4↑ OC 80k/N$Y -N **81** 1 5 5^2 4^1 3^1 2^{nk} Bravo J L118 *1.40 84- 17 Built Up118^{nk} *Twilight Road*1181¼ Royal Lad111^1 4 wide, gamely 6
Previously trained by McGee Paul J
10Mar04- 8GP fst 6f :22^3 :45^1 :56^4 1:08^3 4↑ OC 125k/N$Y -N **75** 4 5 8$^{5\frac{1}{4}}$ 6$^{7\frac{1}{4}}$ 6^{11} 4^{15} Douglas R R L116 9.80 84- 18 StrongHope1169¾ DvidsExpcttion116½ Vinmistr1204¾ Drifted out stretch 8

Victory Encounter

Own: Mankiewicz Tom

B. m. 5 (Ma*)
Sire: Victory Speech (Deputy Minister) $10,104
Dam: Marvelous Moment (Raise a Native)
Br: Helen Smith (Ky)
Tr: Sadler John W(0 0 0 0 .00) 2004:(396 65 .16)

Life	14	7	2	1	$430,887	96	D.Fst	13 7 2 0		$424,767	96
2004	7	2	1	0	$274,287	93	Wet(307)	0 0 0 0		$0	–
2003	7	5	1	1	$156,600	96	Turf(194)	1 0 0 1		$6,120	83
	0	0	0	0	$0	–	Dst(0)	0 0 0 0		$0	–

12Sep04-11Fpx fst 1$\frac{1}{16}$:22^{2} :46 1:11^{3} 1:44 3↑ⒻEBJohnston57k **80** 5 55½ 54 42½ 33½ 25½ Pedroza M A **LB**117 *.90 83– 18 Shzsosprtul117$^{5\frac12}$ VctoryEncountr117$^{\frac12}$ LckynLov117^{7} 3wd bid 1/4,late 2nd 5

8Aug04-8Dmr fst 1$\frac{1}{16}$:22^{2} :46 1:10^{3} 1:42^{4} 3↑ⒻCLHrschH-G2 **71** 2 71^{3} 812 78 78¼ 717¾ Smith M E **LB**118 3.60 76– 06 MissLoren114$^{3\frac14}$ HouseofFortune113^{1} RoyllyChosn116^{1} Steadied near 1/4 8

11Jly04-8Hol fst 1$\frac{1}{16}$:23^{3} :46^{1} 1:09^{4} 1:41^{4} 3↑ⒻMladyBCH-G1 **88** 1 55½ 510 58½ 44 45½ Solis A **LB**119 2.30 86– 07 Star Parade116$^{3\frac12}$ Quero Quero115^{hd} Pesci114^{2} Rail trip,no late bid 5

9May04-8Hol fst 1⅛ :46^{1} 1:09^{3} 1:35^{2} 1:48^{1} 3↑ⒻVanityH-G1 **93** 4 48½ 410 410 32½ 12½ Solis A **LB**116 7.30 98– 02 Victory Encounter116$^{2\frac12}$ *Adoration*122^{1} *StarParade*117^{5} Rail rally lane,clear 4

17Apr04-8Aqu fst 1 :23^{2} :46^{3} 1:10^{2} 1:35^{2} 3↑ⒻBdORsBCH-G3 **88** 3 1½ 1½ 1^{hd} 1^{hd} 42½ Bridgmohan S X L118 5.10 86– 16 PssingShot11$^{2\frac14}$ SmoknFrolic119^{hd} NonsuchBy116^{no} Set pace, stubborn 6

14Feb04-8SA fst 1⅛ :46^{3} 1:11 1:36^{4} 1:50^{2} ⒻLaCanada-G2 **45** 1 88¾ 89¾ 810 810 828¼ Smith M E **LB**121 *1.90 54– 15 Cat Fighter115^{hd} Fencelinene ghbor116^{nk} Tangle116^{2} Outrun, eased late 8

18Jan04-7SA fst 1$\frac{1}{16}$:22^{3} :46 1:10^{2} 1:42^{2} ⒻElEncino-G2 **90** 4 69½ 67 53½ 1½ 11¼ Smith M E **LB**117 3.40 93– 13 VictoryEncountr117$^{1\frac14}$ PrsonlLgnd115$^{\frac12}$ *CtFghtr*115$^{\frac12}$ 4wd into lane,gamely 7

Victory U. S. A.

Own: Van Meter T F II

Ch. f. 4 (Feb) FTFFEB03 $525,000
Sire: Victory Gallop (Cryptoclearance) $30,000
Dam: Fordyce (Cox's Ridge)
Br: George Brunacini (Ky)
Tr: Baffert Bob(0 0 0 0 .00) 2004:(562 105 .19)

Life	11	3	2	3	$613,637	95	D.Fst	9 3 2 2		$567,037	94
2004	5	1	1	1	$263,267	95	Wet(325)	1 0 0 0		$28,600	95
2003	6	2	1	2	$350,370	94	Turf(254)	1 0 0 1		$18,000	94
	0	0	0	0	$0	–	Dst(0)	0 0 0 0		$0	–

31Jly04-4Dmr fm 1 Ⓣ :23^{2} :46^{2} 1:10 1:34 ⒻSnClmntH-G2 **94** 1 44 412 47½ 32½ 3^{hd} Nakatani C S **LB**119 4.40 91– 07 Sweet Win114^{hd} Miss Vegas121^{no} VictoryU.S.A.119$^{4\frac12}$ Rail,willing 3wd late 5

4Jun04-10Bel fst 1 :23^{2} :45^{4} 1:09^{4} 1:34^{4} ⒻAcorn-G1 **90** 6 63¼ 62½ 85¼ 74¼ 65¾ Bailey J D L121 3.15 81– 17 IslndSnd121$^{1\frac12}$ SocietySelction121^{no} *FrindlyMichl*121$^{\frac34}$ 3 wide, no response 8

30Apr04-10CD my 1⅛ :46 1:09^{4} 1:36^{3} 1:50^{4} ⒻKyOaks-G1 **95** 7 23 35 66¼ 45½ 44¼ Day P L121 10.50 79– 17 Ashado121$^{1\frac14}$ *Island Sand*121$^{1\frac34}$ Madcap Escapade121$^{1\frac14}$ 4w,between,empty 11

8Apr04-8Kee fst *7f :21^{4} :44^{2} 1:10^{3} 1:27 ⒻBeaumont-G2 **93** 6 3 53¼ 53 11½ 18¼ Bailey J D L118 2.80 91– 09 VctoryUSA113$^{8\frac14}$ Hlfbrdld123$^{1\frac12}$ WldwoodFlwr118$^{1\frac34}$ 4-5w,drew off,driving 8

6Mar04-9FG fst 1$\frac{1}{16}$:23^{4} :47^{3} 1:12^{1} 1:43 ⒻFGOaks-G2 **87** 5 21 21½ 21 22½ 23¾ Lanerie C J L121 3.30 91– 10 Ashado121$^{3\frac34}$ *Vctory U. S. A.*121$^{1\frac14}$ Shadow Cast121$^{\frac12}$ Forward 3w, game 2nd 6

Wally's Choice

Own: McNeil Joyce and Wally and Sampson, C

B. g. 4 (Feb)
Sire: Quick Cut (Storm Cat) $1,500
Dam: L'Etoile Jolie (Commemorate)
Br: Curtis A. Sampson (Minn)
Tr: Biehler Michael E(0 0 0 0 .00) 2004:(191 36 .19)

Life	13	7	0	3	$228,090	104		
2004	8	5	0	1	$199,061	104		
2003	5	2	0	2	$29,029	54		
	0	0	0	0	$0	–		
D.Fst	10	5	0	3	$110,622	86		
Wet(255)	3	2	0	0	$117,468	104		
Turf(317*)	0	0	0	0	$0	–		
Dst(0)	0	0	0	0	$0	–		

Date/Race	Cond	Dist	Fractions	Race	Spd	PP	Calls	Jockey	Med/Wt	Odds	Fig	Top Finishers	Comment	Fld
21Nov04-8RP	my	1⅛	:454 1:104 1:372 1:501	OkDerby-G3	104	2	1115 1115 95¼ 3½ 11	Quinonez L S	LB115	33.90	95-08	WallysChoice1151 GoldenGlen1121½ Cryptograph1186½	Best stride in time	11
24Oct04-9Wds	fst	1 1/16	:243 :48 1:134 1:453	WdsDerby25k	76	6	57 55 2hd 1hd 13¼	Robletto L C	LB121	4.20	88-17	*WllysChoice*1213¼ Rorofvictory121no NickMissed121nk	5 wide, drove clear	7
6Sep04-6Cby	gd	6½f	:23 :461 1:113 1:181	®MTAStalLad42k	54	1	4 31 4nk 41¼ 44½	Escobar M	LB120	*.40	81-15	Vasant120½ Sahab1204 Gopher This One120hd	Pressed rail, gave way	4
22Aug04-10Cby	fst	1 1/16	:234 :47 1:112 1:413	3↑ⓈMinnClscCh40k	86	5	45½ 23 2½ 2hd 12½	Escobar M	LB117	*1.10	111 -	WllysChoice1172½ AdroitlySuprb1222¼ *BluDncr*11711	Steady bid, prevailed	6
31Jly04-9Cby	fst	170	:231 :471 1:121 1:423	ⓈMinnDerby62k	81	5	98¼ 78 44½ 31 11¾	Escobar M	LB120	4.30	88-19	*Wally's Choice*1201¾ Lt. Sampson1201¾ *Carl*1207¾	Broke in air, rallied	10
10Jly04-6Cby	fst	6f	:223 :46 :574 1:093	ⓈVSMyersJr40k	72	3	5 32½ 41½ 42 46	Escobar M	LB120	4.00	90-09	Lt. Sampson120¾ *Vazandar*1204½ Sir Tricky120¾	Inside, no late bid	6
11Jun04-4Cby	sly	1 ⊗	:232 :471 1:12 1:363	3↑Alw 21284N3L	78	6	46 36½ 23 13 16¾	Escobar M	LB114	5.50	103-05	WllysChoc1146¾ ThJudgJos1181½ PlumSobr1151½	Steady advance,driving	8
15May04-8Cby	fst	5½f	:22 :452 :574 1:041	3↑Alw 17857N3L	68	3	4 42¼ 52¾ 54½ 34	Escobar M	LB115	*1.50e	90-12	AcesofGold120½ MythicHero1203½ *WllysChoice*1151	Broke in, bumped foe	7

Weigelia

Own: Balsamo Joseph J

B. c. 4 (Feb)
Sire: Safely's Mark (Danzig) $3,000
Dam: Turning North (Obligato)
Br: Shelley Huber (Fla)
Tr: Azpurua Manuel J(0 0 0 0 .00) 2004:(309 39 .13)

Life	17	6	4	3	$480,710	109
2004	12	4	3	3	$447,790	109
2003	5	2	1	0	$32,920	86
	0	0	0	0	$0	–
D.Fst	15	6	4	2	$468,450	109
Wet(380)	2	0	0	1	$12,260	91
Turf(316*)	0	0	0	0	$0	–
Dst(0)	0	0	0	0	$0	–

Date/Race	Cond	Dist	Fractions	Race	Spd	PP	Calls	Jockey	Med/Wt	Odds	Fig	Top Finishers	Comment	Fld
27Dec04-10Crc	fst	5½f	:22 :451 :573 1:042	3↑Mint40k	97	1	5 33 21½ 21½ 31	Velazquez J R	L113	*.40	98-11	AllHailStormy113½ SwiftReplica115½ Weigelia1132¼	Steadied backstretch	6
18Dec04-10Crc	fst	7f	:221 :45 1:093 1:223	3↑KenyNoeJrH100k	81	1	8 1hd 2hd 34½ 714¾	Bailey J D	L116	*1.00	88-11	Medallist1144½ ParadiseDancer113¾ HastyKris1151¾	Battled, inside, faded	10
13Nov04-11Crc	fst	6f	:214 :444 :571 1:101	3↑ⓈJDudlySprH150k	109	3	5 31½ 31 1hd 11	Velazquez J R	L116	*.90	98-10	Weigelia1161 Onebadshark1163 Love That Moon1162	All out, prevailed	10
14Oct04-8Kee	my	*7f	:224 :452 1:093 1:25	Perryville112k	91	5	1 21½ 21½ 22½ 37½	Albarado R J	L123	*1.40	93-11	*Commentator*1177 Eurosilver123½ *Weigelia*123nk	Chased,4w,weakened	7
28Aug04-10Sar	fst	7f	:22 :443 1:082 1:204	KngsBshp-G1	105	5	2 3½ 3½ 2hd 21½	Velazquez J R	L121	7.70	98-04	Pomeroy1211½ Weigelia1211 Ice Wynnd Fire1174¼	Carried out, gamely	8
7Aug04-8Sar	fst	6f	:214 :443 :564 1:092	Amstrdam-G2	99	2	4 53¼ 4¾ 43 32¾	Toribio A Jr	L123	7.20	92-13	Bwana Charlie123¾ *Pomeroy*1232 Weigelia123½	Stumbled start, inside	7
10Jly04-9Crc	fst	6f	:212 :442 :57 1:102	CarryBck-G3	108	4	4 4¾ 3½ 1hd 1½	Toribio A Jr	L117	10.50	97-09	Weigelia117½ Classy Migration1124 *Bwana Charlie*1194	All out, prevailed	11
29May04-3Crc	fst	6f	:222 :453 :574 1:11	3↑PoncheH75k	97	4	2 2½ 2hd 2½ 24¼	Toribio A Jr	L114	*1.10	90-13	Built Up1164¼ *Weigelia*1142 Bernard's Candy114½	Vied, no match	5
9May04-3Crc	fst	6f	:212 :441 :564 1:093	WstrnBrdrs40k	104	4	2 31 21 2½ 1¾	Toribio A Jr	L122	2.10	101-14	Weigelia122¾ Classy Migration1195 Baronage119hd	Wore down rival late	6
4Apr04-6Tam	fst	7f	:223 :454 1:11 1:242	Sophomore83k	86	4	3 2hd 1hd 1hd 1hd	Toribio A Jr	L116	4.10	91-16	*Weigelia*116hd *Avid Skier*1164¾ Spirit of Montreal116½	Dueled,brushd,all out	10
14Feb04-10GP	fst	7f	:213 :433 1:084 1:221	Hutchesn-G2	80	2	9 85½ 75 77¾ 58½	Penalba C	L116	51.70	82-07	*Limehouse*1222¼ DeputyStorm1181¾ *SartogCounty*116¾	Slow st, no menace	10
25Jan04-5GP	fst	7f	:223 :45 1:092 1:23	Alw 36000N2X	87	1	5 1hd 1hd 1½ 2¾	Penalba C	L120	4.80	86-13	Frisky Spider122¾ Weigelia1203 Orphan Brigade118½	Hit gate, outgamed	6

Well Fancied

Own: Goldfarb Sanford, Hoffman, Stewart an

B. g. 7 (Mar)
Sire: Prosper Fager (Mr. Prospector) $2,500
Dam: Patty's Fancy Tric (Tricky Creek)
Br: Seymour Cohn (NY)
Tr: Dutrow R E Jr(0 0 0 0 .00) 2004:(603 166 .28)

Life	30	12	4	4	$828,176	110	D.Fst	28 11 3 4 $784,576 110
2004	3	2	0	0	$189,070	110	Wet(286)	2 1 1 0 $43,600 107
2003	8	4	1	1	$350,164	109	Turf(218)	0 0 0 0 $0 –
	0	0	0	0	$0	–	Dst(0)	0 0 0 0 $0 –

10Apr04-9Aqu fst 7f :213 :432 1:072 1:201 3↑CarterH-G1 **88** 7 2 42 45½ 69¼ 812¼ Coa E M L116 4.50 92-04 *PicoCentrl*1171½ StrongHope1192 EyeoftheTigr114¾ Chased outside, tired 9
13Mar04-8Aqu fst 7f :222 :45 1:092 1:22 3↑ToboggnH-G3 **110** 7 4 22½ 22½ 1hd 12 Coa E M L118 *1.50 95-17 Well Fancied1182 *Gators N Bears*115nk Don Six1131¾ Speed outside, clear 10
16Feb04-9Lrl fst 7f :223 :452 1:10 1:222 3↑GenGrgeH-G2 **109** 6 1 11 11 11 11 Prado E S L115 3.00 98-17 *WellFncid*1151 UnforgttblMx114¾ GtorsNBrs116hd Well rated 2wd,driving 9

Western Ransom

Own: Chandler Dr. John A

Dk. b or b. f. 4 (Feb)
Sire: Red Ransom (Roberto) $47,962
Dam: Western Wind (Gone West)
Br: Dr. John A. Chandler (Ky)
Tr: Dickinson Michael W(0 0 0 0 .00) 2004:(190 39 .21)

Life	9	4	3	1	$229,290	91	D.Fst	2 0 1 1 $7,430 57
2004	7	4	2	0	$221,860	91	Wet(326)	1 1 0 0 $18,000 74
2003	2	M	1	1	$7,430	57	Turf(339)	6 3 2 0 $203,860 91
	0	0	0	0	$0	-	Dst(0)	0 0 0 0 $0 -

25Sep04-9Pim fm 1 1/16 Ⓣ:233 :472 1:112 1:431 ⒻMWashBC-G3 **91** 6 87¾ 810 88¾ 45 1hd Fogelsonger R L122 *2.10 86-14 Western Ransom122hd Plenty115nk *With Affection*1153¾ 6 wide, up 12
3Jly04-6Hol fm 1¼ Ⓣ:49 1:14 1:381 2:012 ⒻAmrcnOks-G1 **86** 9 21½ 21 42 45 106½ Santiago Javier LB121 20.40 78-13 TckrTp1211 DncnthMood1212 HollywodStry121½ Stalked pace, weakened 13
12Jun04-7CD yl 1⅛ Ⓣ:493 1:142 1:39 1:512 ⒻRegret-G3 **85** 1 32½ 31½ 42½ 32 23¾ Day P L120 *2.50 72-25 Sister Star1163¾ Western Ransom120hd Jinny's Gold1181¼ 5w bid,all out 7
8May04-9Pim fm 1 1/16 Ⓣ:23 :472 1:12 1:431 ⒻHilltop50k **89** 5 78 65½ 43½ 31½ 1¾ Fogelsonger R L115 *1.00 86-14 WesternRansom115¾ ArtFan1153¾ StrofAnziyn1151½ Swung wide, driving 11
14Apr04-8Kee gd 1 Ⓣ:241 :483 1:13 1:372 ⒻApplachian113k **91** 6 42½ 31½ 2hd 11½ 2hd Bejarano R L116 7.00 85-15 LcfrsSton120hd *WstrnRnsom*1164¼ HnyRydr116hd Exch bumps outfinished 9
24Feb04-7FG wf 1 1/16 ⊗:24 :483 1:13 1:462 ⒻOC 50k/n1x-N **74** 4 48 39 38½ 2hd 11½ Melancon L L119 f *1.50 78-16 Western Ransom1191½ Plaid1178¾ Greygoosegal119nk Loomed, clear late 4
24Jan04-10FG fm *1 Ⓣ:241 :491 1:15 1:392 ⒻMd Sp Wt 28k **75** 4 77 74¾ 85½ 43½ 11¼ Melancon L L119 *1.90 83-19 *Western Ransom*1191¼ Storm Stream119½ *Oblivious*119½ Big finish, clear 12

Where We Left Off (GB)

Own: Moyglare Stud Farm Ltd

Ch. f. 5 (Feb)
Sire: Dr Devious*Ire (Ahonoora*GB) $12,210
Dam: Rekindled Affair*Ire (Rainbow Quest)
Br: Moyglare Stud Farm Ltd (GB)
Tr: Clement Christophe(0 0 0 0 .00) 2004:(344 68 .20)

Life	13	7	3	0	$291,039	96	D.Fst	0	0	0	0	$0	-
2004	7	4	2	0	$194,480	96	Wet(193)	0	0	0	0	$0	-
2003	6	3	1	0	$96,559	90	Turf(322)	13	7	3	0	$291,039	96
	0	0	0	0	$0	-	Dst(0)	0	0	0	0	$0	-

22Oct04-8Med gd 1 1/16 Ⓣ:243 :482 1:1131:412 3↑ⒻVioletH-G3 **92** 1 42½ 36 36 35 43¾ Bravo J L118 6.30 87-12 ChngingWorld113¼ HighCourt117hd OcenDriv1212½ Inside,chased,evenly 7
5Sep04-7Sar fm 1⅜ 🅃:5011:16 1:4012:151 3↑ⒻGlenFlsH-G3 **93** 4 32 31½ 31 2hd 2½ Prado E S L116 *.90 92-06 Humit114½ WhereWLftOff1161¼ Svdbythlight1152 Saved ground, gamely 9
Run in divisions
8Aug04-9Mth fm 1⅛ Ⓣ:4811:122 1:3631:484 3↑ⒻMatchmkr-G3 **96** 7 76 75½ 83¼ 33½ 11 Nakatani C S L118 2.50 86-12 WhereWeLftOff1181 MrsM1181¾ SpinControl1161 Inside,closed strongly 9
21Jly04-7Bel fm 1 Ⓣ:231 :462 1:1031:351 4↑ⒻOC 100k/c-N **96** 1 52½ 41½ 31½ 1½ 12½ Samyn J L L120 *1.85 84-16 *WhereWeLeftOff*1202½ FeistyBull116no Ktzn118hd Drew clear when roused 7
3Jly04-9Pha fm 1 1/16 Ⓣ:24 :483 1:13 1:434 3↑ⒻDrJPennyMH100k **94** 8 66 55 52¼ 2½ 2no Samyn J L L117 *1.90 93-07 LdyofthFtr117no *WhrWLftOff*1172 *CghtnthRn*1161 Between upper,lost bob 10
12Jun04-10Suf fm *170 Ⓣ 1:44 3↑ⒻMyFairLady40k **90** 8 31 21 2hd 12 11¼ Hampshire J F Jr LB120 *1.10 95-07 WhereWeLeftOff1201¼ *LredoLil*1172 HlysClssic117no 2wd trip, mild str drv 9
25Apr04-8GP fm 1 1/16 Ⓣ:233 :474 1:1131:411 4↑ⒻOC 100k/N3x-N **91** 7 52½ 43 32 3nk 1hd Bravo J L117 *.90 91-13 *WhereWeLeftOff*117hd *ValintAnn*1171¾ NnniesSword117¾ Clear late, lasted 7

Wildcat Heir

Own: New Farm

B. h. 5 (Feb)
Sire: Forest Wildcat (Storm Cat) $35,000
Dam: Penniless Heiress (Pentelicus)
Br: New Farm (Fla)
Tr: Perkins B W Jr(0 0 0 0 .00) 2004:(174 27 .16)

Life	10	5	4	0	$364,460	110	D.Fst	9	5	3	0	$357,050	110
2004	7	4	2	0	$305,860	110	Wet(342)	1	0	1	0	$7,410	91
2003	1	0	1	0	$9,400	99	Turf(305)	0	0	0	0	$0	-
	0	0	0	0	$0	-	Dst(0)	0	0	0	0	$0	-

20Nov04-10Pim fst 6f :223 :452 :5711:092 3↑DeFrncsM-G1 **109** 8 1 3½ 31 12 1nk Elliott S L119f 16.00 98-13 WildcatHeir119nk MidsEyes1231½ ClockStopper119¾ Tracked 3wd, dug in 10
8Oct04-7Kee fst 6f :21 :434 :56 1:083 3↑PhoenxBC-G3 **110** 4 10 31½ 31½ 2½ 41¼ •Albarado R J L118f 8.10 97-08 Champli122¾ GoldStorm118nk ClockStopper118nk Well placed,empty late 11
6Sep04-9Mth fst 6f :213 :441 :5631:091 3↑Icecapade60k **102** 5 2 31½ 3½ 11½ 14 Velez J A Jr L117f *2.00 94-15 WildctHir1174 SingMBckHom119¾ HrsZlous1151¾ Outside bid,ridden out 7
8Aug04-10Mth fst 6f :214 :443 :5631:09 3↑TeddyDrone100k **101** 1 5 43½ 43 34 21 Day P L117f *1.90 94-11 CndinFrontier1221 *WildctHir*1172 HrsZlous1152¾ Late momentum,fin well 7
21Jly04-8Bel fst 6f :22 :45 :5641:083 3↑Alw 47000N2x **96** 4 5 2hd 2½ 12 13¾ Luzzi M J L121f *2.05 96-12 WildcatHeir1213¾ *Evesdropper*121½ *CleverElectricin*1213½ Vied inside, clear 6
26Jun04-6Mth fst 6f :22 :45 :5711:093 3↑Alw 39000N1x **93** 3 3 31½ 1hd 11 14¼ Coa E M L119 *.30 92-09 *WildcatHeir*1194¼ Belichick119nk PioneerEmpire1143¼ Widened,ridden out 6
31May04-7Mth gd 6f :211 :434 :56 1:084 3↑Alw 39000N1x **91** 3 7 63¼ 44 35½ 22 Coa E M L119 *.80 94-09 Choose1152 *Wildcat Heir*119½ Golden Gator1136 Bumped start,got 2nd 9

Wilko
Own: Reddam J. Paul and Roy, Susan

Ch. c. 3 (Jan) KEESEP03 $75,000
Sire: Awesome Again (Deputy Minister) $125,000
Dam: Native Roots*Ire (Indian Ridge*Ire)
Br: Ro Parra (Ky)
Tr: Dollase Craig(0 0 0 0 .00) 2004:(191 35 .18)

Life	12	3	2	5	$934,074	98	D.Fst	2	1	0	1	$833,580 98
2004	12	3	2	5	$934,074	98	Wet(378)	0	0	0	0	$0 –
2003	0	M	0	0	$0	–	Turf(300)	10	2	2	4	$100,494 –
	0	0	0	0	$0	–	Dst(0)	0	0	0	0	$0 –

18Dec04–8Hol fst $1\frac{1}{16}$:23^2 :46 1:10 1:41^3 HolFut-G1 **94** 1 3^1 $4^{1\frac{1}{2}}$ 2^{hd} 2^1 3^1 Nakatani C S **LB**121 2.80 92– 11 Declan's Moon121^1 Giacomo121^{no} Wilko121^2 Bid inside,lost 2nd 7

Previously trained by Noseda Jeremy

30Oct04–7LS fst $1\frac{1}{16}$:23^2 :47^2 1:11^1 1:42 BCJuvnle-G1 **98** 8 3^2 3^2 $4^{\frac{3}{4}}$ 4^1 $1^{\frac{3}{4}}$ Dettori L **L**122 28.30 92– 02 Wilko$122^{\frac{3}{4}}$ Afleet Alex122^{nk} Sun King$122^{1\frac{1}{4}}$ 3-4w,came again,gamely 8

25Sep04 Ascot (GB) gf 1 Ⓣ RH 1:41^4 Royal Lodge Stakes-G2 Hcp 180000 $3^{2\frac{3}{4}}$ Ahern E 123 7.00 Perfectperformance$123^{1\frac{1}{2}}$ Scandinavia$123^{1\frac{1}{4}}$ *Wilko*$123^{\frac{1}{2}}$ 8
Timeform rating: 105+ *Wide in 4th,dueled & in tight 2f out,checked,up for 3rd*

10Sep04 Doncaster (GB) gf 7f Ⓣ Str 1:23^1 Champagne Stakes-G2 Stk 179000 $4^{4\frac{1}{4}}$ Ahern E 122 16.00 Etlaala$122^{\frac{1}{2}}$ Iceman$127^{2\frac{1}{2}}$ Oude$122^{1\frac{1}{4}}$ 10
Timeform rating: 100 *Rated in 7th,progress 2-1/2f out,up for 4th*

13Aug04 Newbury (GB) gs 7f Ⓣ Str 1:28^2 Washington Singer Stakes (Lstd) Stk 46000 $2^{\frac{1}{2}}$ Ahern E 123 1.85 Kings Quay$123^{\frac{1}{2}}$ Wilko123^1 Subyan Dreams$119^{2\frac{1}{2}}$ 5
Timeform rating: 100 *Tracked winner,outpaced 1-1/2f out,came again*

4Aug04 Yarmouth (GB) gf 7f Ⓣ Str 1:28^3 Custom Kitchens Novice Stakes Alw 9400 $1^{\frac{1}{2}}$ Ahern E 131 *.10 Wilko$131^{\frac{1}{2}}$ Shrine Mountain$121^{2\frac{1}{2}}$ *Linngari*$120^{1\frac{3}{4}}$ 4
Timeform rating: 96? *Tracked leader,led 170y out,readily*

28Jly04 Goodwood (GB) gd 7f Ⓣ RH 1:27^2 Vintage Stakes-G2 Stk 127000 $2^{2\frac{1}{2}}$ Ahern E 123 7.00 *Shamardal*$123^{2\frac{1}{2}}$ *Wilko*$123^{1\frac{1}{4}}$ Fox123^{no} 10
Timeform rating: 105 *Tracked in 5th,bid 1-1/2f out,held by winner*

8Jly04 Newmarket (GB) gs 7f Ⓣ Str 1:26^2 Superlative Stakes-G3 Stk 73900 $3^{\frac{3}{4}}$ Ahern E 123 11.00 *Dubawi*$123^{\frac{1}{2}}$ Henrik123^{nk} Wilko$123^{1\frac{1}{4}}$ 12
Timeform rating: 105+ *Rated at rear,angled right 1-1/2f out,gaining late*

19Jun04 Ascot (GB) fm 7f Ⓣ Str 1:29^2 Chesham Stakes (Listed) Stk 73500 $3^{3\frac{1}{2}}$ Ahern E 126 16.00 Whazzat$119^{3\frac{1}{2}}$ Brecon Beacon126^{hd} Wilko126^2 11
Timeform rating: 101 *Towards rear,mild late gain in traffic*

2Jun04 Yarmouth (GB) fm 6f Ⓣ Str 1:11^4 EBF Vauxhall Holiday Pk Novice Stks Alw 13500 1^1 Ahern E 124 3.50 Wilko124^1 Dance Anthem$128^{2\frac{1}{2}}$ Speed Dial Harry124^{nk} 7
Timeform rating: 86+ *Rank twrds rear,rallied to lead 200y out,drifted late*

12May04 York (GB) sf 6f Ⓣ Str 1:18 EBF Maiden Stakes Stk 13300 $7^{4\frac{1}{4}}$ Ahern E 126 3.50 Pivotal Flame$126^{\frac{3}{4}}$ *Crimson Sun*$126^{\frac{1}{2}}$ Capable Guest126^{hd} 11
Timeform rating: 75 *Led or dueled to 1-1/2f out,weakened*

3May04 Kempton (GB) hy 5f Ⓣ Str 1:06^1 EBF Sharp Minds Betfair Mdn Stks Maiden 14600 $3^{11\frac{1}{2}}$ Ahern E 125 3.00 Turnkey126^{11} Planet Tomato$126^{\frac{1}{2}}$ Wilko126^3 8
Timeform rating: 69 *Tracked leaders,weakened 1-1/2f out*

Wimbledon
Own: McIngvale James

Gr/ro. c. 4 (Feb) FTFFEB03 $425,000
Sire: Wild Rush (Wild Again) $10,000
Dam: Strawberry Clover (Darn That Alarm)
Br: Sabine Stables (Ky)
Tr: Baffert Bob(0 0 0 0 .00) 2004:(562 105 .19)

Life	7	2	3	0	$430,980	101	D.Fst	7	2	3	0	$430,980 101
2004	4	2	1	0	$412,400	101	Wet(371)	0	0	0	0	$0 –
2003	3	M	2	0	$18,580	84	Turf(223)	0	0	0	0	$0 –
	0	0	0	0	$0	–	Dst(0)	0	0	0	0	$0 –

3Apr04–8SA fst 1⅛ :46⁴1:11 1:36²1:49¹ SADerby-G1 **87** 3 4³ 4²¾ 3ⁿᵏ 5³¾ 5⁹½ Santiago Javier LB122 2.60 78–09 Castledle122ʰᵈ D RockHrdTen122² Imperilism122¹ Bid 3wd btwn,wkened 7
7Mar04–9FG fst 1¹⁄₁₆ :22² :45¹ 1:10³1:42³ LaDerby-G2 **101** 3 8¹² 7¹⁰ 6⁶ 2¹½ 1²¼ Santiago Javier L122 7.20 97–07 Wimbledon122²¼ Borrego122ʰᵈ *Pollard's Vision*122¾ 4-w rally, going away 11
8Feb04–1SA fst 1 :22² :46¹ 1:10³1:36¹ Md Sp Wt 46k **98** 4 5⁵ 3¹½ 1½ 1³½ 1⁸ Santiago Javier LB120 *.70 90–13 *Wimbledon*120⁸ *Melanyhsthеppers*120⁵ WildShmn120³ Drew off, ridden out 6
18Jan04–6SA fst 1¹⁄₁₆ :22² :46 1:10¹1:42 Md Sp Wt 49k **87** 3 1ʰᵈ 1ʰᵈ 1ʰᵈ 2¹½ 2³½ Stevens G L LB120 b *1.40 91–13 QntonsGoldRsh120³½ *Wmbldon*120⁶½ Onvryclct120³½ Btwn,inside,2nd best 12

Winter Garden
Own: Di Giulio F D Jr

B. m. 5 (Mar)
Sire: Roy (Fappiano) $10,000
Dam: Hillsburgh Rumors (Bold Ruckus)
Br: Anomaly Investments LP (Ky)
Tr: Tiller Robert P(0 0 0 0 .00) 2004:(282 69 .24)

Life	18	12	3	2	$902,788	99	D.Fst	15	11	2	2	$833,446 99
2004	6	4	2	0	$353,460	99	Wet(384)	3	1	1	0	$69,342 86
2003	9	6	1	2	$470,826	93	Turf(267)	0	0	0	0	$0 –
	0	0	0	0	$0	–	Dst(0)	0	0	0	0	$0 –

6Nov04–8WO fst 6f :22¹ :44³ :57 1:10¹ 3↑Ⓕ OntFashnH137k **94** 1 5 4¹ 1ʰᵈ 1¹ 1¹¾ Clark D L122 *.90 89–16 Winter Garden122¹¾ El Prado Essence118¾ Big Cheque113¹¼ Rail,driving 8
11Sep04–8WO fst 7f :22² :45¹ 1:09²1:22¹ 3↑Ⓕ Seaway-G3 **93** 4 7 7⁷½ 7⁵¾ 4⁵ 2²¼ Clark D L119 *1.60 94–13 BrssinPocket119²¼ *WintrGrdn*119²¼ ElPrdoEssnc117¹ Brk in air,4w,rallied 7
22Aug04–7WO fst 6½f :22² :44⁴ 1:09 1:15² 3↑Ⓕ Alw 76100NC **96** 6 2 1ʰᵈ 2½ 1½ 1¾ Clark D L118 *.40 101–10 WinterGrden118¾ ElPrdoEssence117⁷ SpnishDecre116¾ Rebid top stretch 7
6Jun04–4WO fst 7f :23 :46 1:10²1:23⁴ 3↑Ⓕ SwtBriarTo108k **93** 2 4 1½ 1¹ 1¹½ 1¾ Clark D L122 *.30 88–10 *Winter Garden*122¾ Spanish Decree116¹ Miss Santa Anita117¹ Ridden out 7
16May04–8WO fst 6½f :22² :45¹ 1:09⁴1:16³ 4↑Ⓕ GCHndriH-G3 **99** 5 1 3½ 3ⁿᵏ 1²½ 1³ Clark D L122 1.80 95–14 *Winter Garden*122³ Spanish Decree115ⁿᵏ Handpainted119² Bid 3-wide,drvg 5
18Apr04–9WO my 6f :22⁴ :46 :58 1:10¹ 4↑Ⓕ Whimsical139k **86** 3 1 2¹ 2² 2²½ 2²¾ Clark D L123 1.50 86–15 HolyBubbette114²¾ *WinterGrden*123³ MilleFeville115ʰᵈ No match,2nd best 6

Wonder Again
Own: Phillips Racing Partnership

B. m. 6 (Feb)
Sire: Silver Hawk (Roberto) $75,000
Dam: Ameriflora (Danzig)
Br: Phillips Racing Partnership & John Phillips (Ky)
Tr: Toner James J(0 0 0 0 .00) 2004:(112 19 .17)

Life	19	7	2	3	$1,111,682	110	D.Fst	1	0	0	0	$0 47
2004	5	2	0	1	$611,767	110	Wet(284)	1	0	0	1	$4,840 49
2003	6	1	1	1	$176,075	103	Turf(386)	17	7	2	2	$1,106,842 110
	0	0	0	0	$0	–	Dst(0)	0	0	0	0	$0 –

30Oct04–6LS yl 1⅜ Ⓣ :52²1:18² 1:42¹2:18¹ 3↑Ⓕ BCF&MTrf-G1 **105** 12 11⁹½ 11⁹ 10⁶ 4² 3¹¾ Prado E S L123 10.70 96–07 Ouija Board118¹½ Film Maker123ⁿᵏ Wonder Again123²¾ Rail move turn 12
2Oct04–7Bel yl 1¼ [T] :52²1:17⁴ 1:41²2:04³ 3↑Ⓕ FlwrBlIv-G1 **99** 4 2½ 2¹ 2¹ 5¹½ 6¹¾ Prado E S L123 *.95 69–25 Riskvrs118¾ *Commrcnt*118ʰᵈ MoscowBurnng120ⁿᵏ With pace, no response 8
31Jly04–7Sar yl 1⅛ Ⓣ :47³1:11³ 1:36³1:48⁴ 3↑Ⓕ DianaH-G1 **110** 4 3⁵½ 3⁷½ 4²½ 1⁵ 1⁵¾ Prado E S L120 3.10 86–14 WonderAgain120⁵¾ Riskverse118²¼ *OcenDrive*118²¼ Found room on hedge 7
5Jly04–9Bel sf 1¼ [T] :50 1:15 1:40²2:05³ 3↑Ⓕ NewYorkH-G2 **103** 3 3¹½ 2¹½ 2ʰᵈ 1⁵ 1³¼ Prado E S L115 3.95 66–34 *WonderAgin*115³¼ *StyForever*115ⁿᵒ SpicIslnd118⁶½ Drew clear when roused 7
5Jun04–8Bel fm 1 Ⓣ :23³ :46⁴ 1:10¹1:33¹ 3↑Ⓕ JsAGmBCH-G2 **95** 5 5¹½ 6¹¾ 7³¼ 7⁴½ 6³¾ Prado E S L116 10.30 90–06 Intercontinental118¹¼ Vngurdi113½ EtoileMontnte121¾ Wide trip, no rally 8

Wynn Dot Comma

Own: Cherry Martin L

Ch. c. 4 (May)
Sire: Struggler*GB (Night Shift) $2,500
Dam: I Like Punch (Two Punch)
Br: T. Wynn Jolley & Harry Hoglander (Fla)
Tr: Wolfson Martin D(0 0 0 0 .00) 2004:(176 39 .22)

Life	8	6	1	0	$298,525	96	D.Fst	8	6	1	0	$298,525	96
2004	3	2	0	0	$159,000	96	Wet(287)	0	0	0	0	$0	–
2003	5	4	1	0	$139,525	95	Turf(200)	0	0	0	0	$0	–
	0	0	0	0	$0	–	Dst(0)	0	0	0	0	$0	–

Date/Race	Cond	Dist	Fractions	Race	Fig	PP	St	1c	2c	Str	Fin	Jockey	Med/Wt	Odds	Speed	Top Finishers	Comment	Fld
13Mar04-10GP	fst	7f	:22 :44^3 1:09^2 1:22^4	Swale-G3	**96**	2	4	2½	2hd	1 1½	1hd	Prado E S	L120	4.00	88–13	WynnDotComm120hd Eroslvr120 4¼ DshbordDrmmr120 1	Clear, just lasted	5
14Feb04-10GP	fst	7f	:21^3 :43^3 1:08^4 1:22^1	Hutchesn-G2	**89**	6	6	4 2½	5 2½	5 5½	4 4¾	Bravo J	L122	*2.30	86–07	*Limehouse*122 2¼ DeputyStorm118 1¾ *SaratogCounty*116¾	Lacked room turn	10
10Jan04-8GP	fst	6f	:22^2 :45^4 :58^1 1:10^3	SpectBid-G3	**95**	4	2	6 3¼	5 1¼	4 1½	1 1¼	Bravo J	L120	*1.70	89–20	WynnDotComm120 1¼ SrtogCounty116¾ GhostMontn120½	Up late, driving	7

Yearly Report

Own: Golden Eagle Farm

B. f. 4 (Jan) BARMAY03 $95,000
Sire: General Meeting (Seattle Slew) $10,000
Dam: Fiscal Year (Half a Year)
Br: Mr. & Mrs. John C. Mabee (Cal)
Tr: Baffert Bob(0 0 0 0 .00) 2004:(562 105 .19)

Life	9	6	2	0	$835,900	109	D.Fst	8	6	2	0	$798,400	109
2004	7	5	1	0	$787,500	109	Wet(340)	1	0	0	0	$37,500	95
2003	2	1	1	0	$48,400	100	Turf(327)	0	0	0	0	$0	–
	0	0	0	0	$0	–	Dst(0)	0	0	0	0	$0	–

Date/Race	Cond	Dist	Fractions	Race	Fig	PP	St	1c	2c	Str	Fin	Jockey	Med/Wt	Odds	Speed	Top Finishers	Comment	Fld
29Oct04-10LS	fst	7f	:21^4 :43^4 1:08^1 1:20^3	Ⓕ Stonerside150k	**109**	7	3	21	2½	16	1 9¼	Bailey J D	L123	*.40	101–12	YerlyReport123 9¼ *Homemker*119 2½ AngelicSlw117 4¼	Drew away, ridden out	8
16Oct04-3SA	fst	1 1/16	:23^1 :46^3 1:10^3 1:42^1 3↑	Ⓕ Ⓢ CalCupMatH150k	**103**	5	42	4 2½	31	1hd	2no	Nakatani C S	LB120	*.80	94–11	DrmfSmmr12 no *YrlRprt*120 6 SmrWndDncr122½	4wd move, led, outgamed	6
21Aug04-10Sar	sly	1¼	:47^1 1:11^2 1:36^2 2:02^3	Ⓕ Alabama-G1	**95**	1	2hd	2hd	43	42	4 8¼	Bailey J D	L121	4.70	86–18	SocietySelection121 2½ *StellarJayne*121½ *Ashado*121 5¼	Between rivals, tired	8
17Jly04-8Del	fst	1 1/16	:24^1 :48^1 1:12^3 1:43^4	Ⓕ DelOaks-G2	**99**	4	2½	2hd	1hd	1½	11	Bailey J D	L122	*.40	93–14	YerlyReport122 1 EndrsSistr119 8 ALuluOfMnif115 2	Repulsed bid, prevaild	8
14May04-10Pim	fst	1⅛	:49^3 1:13^4 1:39^2 1:52^3	Ⓕ BlkEySsn-G2	**87**	5	3 1½	3nk	2½	2hd	1 1½	Bailey J D	L122	*.50	81–17	*YerlyReport*122 1½ PwynePrincess115nk RrGift115 1½	3-4w, duel, strong drive	7
24Apr04-3Hol	fst	1 1/16	:22^3 :45^4 1:09^4 1:41^3	Ⓕ Ⓢ Melair200k	**98**	1	2½	31	1½	1 2½	14	Nakatani C S	LB119	*.10e	93–05	*YerlyReport*119 4 *WstrnHmisphr*114 5½ NicolndBn114 1½	Rail, strong hand ride	8
19Jan04-5SA	fst	7f	:22 :44^1 1:08^2 1:21	Ⓕ SntaYnez-G2	**107**	3	6	42	21	1hd	14	Bailey J D	LB114	2.10	100–07	*YerlyReport*114 4 *HouseofFortune*121 4½ *PptoKinzie*115 3	Stalked, bid, led, clear	8

Yessirgeneralsir
Own: Jackson James D

B. g. 5 (Jan)
Sire: Patton (Lord At War*Arg) $3,000
Dam: Honeydoon (My Favorite Moment)
Br: Jim D. Jackson (Tex)
Tr: Keen Dallas E(0 0 0 0 .00) 2004:(139 23 .17)

Life	12	3	1	2	$302,555	107
2004	7	2	0	1	$278,250	107
2003	5	1	1	1	$24,305	78
	0	0	0	0	$0	–

D.Fst	9	3	1	1	$270,805	107
Wet(247)	2	0	0	1	$31,750	101
Turf(279)	1	0	0	0	$0	89
Dst(0)	0	0	0	0	$0	–

26Sep04–9LaD gd 1 1/16 Ⓣ :24 :481 1:122 1:432 3↑LaDBCH150k **89** 8 11 11½ 2½ 34 76 Meche L J L115 3.30 85–13 Warleigh118½ Waupaca1163 Gentlemen J J114nk Comfortable pace,faded 9

4Sep04–8Sar fst 7f :221 :444 1:09 1:221 3↑ForegoH-G1 **88** 4 6 11½ 2hd 36 811½ Albarado R J L114 39.00 81–19 Midas Eyes1171¾ Clock Stopper1141¼ Gygistar114no Set pace, tired 9

7Aug04–9Sar fst 1⅛ :451 1:084 1:344 1:482 3↑WhitneyH-G1 **91** 3 1½ 1½ 12½ 52¾ 814 Figueroa O L113 49.00 79–14 *RosesinMy*114no PerfctDrift1172¼ BowmnsBnd114no Pace, clear, gave way 9

10Jly04–9Hol fst 1¼ :464 1:102 1:344 2:003 3↑HolGldCp-G1 **100** 4 12½ 1hd 11½ 2hd 45¾ Figueroa O LB124 8.00 93 - TotlImpct1241¼ Olmodvor124½ EventheScore1244 Inside,btwn 1/8,wkened 7

31May04–9LS fst 1 1/16 :224 :453 1:082 1:411 3↑LSParkH-G3 **104** 6 11½ 11½ 15 16 12¼ Figueroa O L114 11.60 96–08 Yssirgnrlsir1142¼ SonicWst1171 SpnishEmpr117nk Drew off 2nd turn,held 6

24Apr04–8LS sly 1 :231 :461 1:10 1:353 3↑TexsMile-G3 **101** 6 12 12 12 22½ 36¾ Figueroa O L114 14.20 88–22 Kela1195¼ Supah Blitz1161½ *Yessirgeneralsir*114nk Headed 3/16, tired 8

4Mar04–9FG fst 140 :23 :462 1:111 1:382 4↑Alw 30000N1X **107** 3 11½ 11 11 14 110 Albarado R J L117 7.60 102–11 Yessirgeneralsir11710 *Nakeeb*1181¾ Autopscot117nk Set pace, drew away 7

Yougottawanna
Own: Peter Redekop B. C. Ltd

Ch. g. 6 (Feb)
Sire: Candi's Gold (Yukon) $3,500
Dam: Chapel's Sister (Midway Circle)
Br: Halo Farms (Cal)
Tr: Hollendorfer Jerry(0 0 0 0 .00) 2004:(1300 308 .24)

Life	30	9	7	4	$574,124	103
2004	11	5	3	1	$223,008	103
2003	9	0	1	2	$35,031	95
	0	0	0	0	$0	–

D.Fst	21	8	6	1	$485,510	103
Wet(283)	2	0	1	0	$15,375	90
Turf(262)	7	1	0	3	$73,239	93
Dst(0)	0	0	0	0	$0	–

26Nov04–8GG fst 1 1/16 :223 :462 1:104 1:42 3↑FortyNinrH82k **97** 1 2½ 1hd 11 12½ 1nk Schvaneveldt C P LB118 fb 5.90 93–20 Yougottwnn118nk Adremisborn1193½ MyCred1141 Alternated 2w, gamely 9

16Oct04–8SA fst 1⅛ :461 1:10 1:344 1:473 3↑ⓈCalCpClscH250k **57** 4 42 85 1010 914 830¾ Baze R A LB120 fb 7.50 65–11 *Cozy Guy*117¾ Lava Man1125 *Anziyan Royalty*1164 Gave way, eased 10

28Aug04–8Sac fst 1⅛ :471 1:104 1:36 1:481 3↑GovernorsH60k **92** 7 31½ 22 21½ 2hd 11½ Baze R A LB120 fb *.80 98–11 Yougottawanna1201½ Sanger1172¼ Snoopy Cat1171½ Stalked, pulled away 7

7Aug04–11SR fst 1 1/16 :233 :471 1:103 1:411 3↑JTGraceH97k **98** 4 12 12 11½ 11½ 2¾ Baze R A LB119 fb *.40 99–12 CalkinsRoad115¾ *Yougottawnn*1199 PeteskisChrm1103 Broke slow, caught 4

1Jly04–9Hst fst 1⅛ :463 1:111 1:353 1:49 3↑LtGovrnH-G3 **84** 4 54 52½ 53 79¼ 79¼ Alvarado P V L122 fb *1.10 91–06 Royal Place119nk Lord Nelson1234¼ Roscoe Pito119hd Steadied early 8

31May04–3BM fst 1 1/16 :231 :46 1:092 1:40 3↑SbsctBCH-G3 **103** 4 11 11 11 12 1¾ Baze R A LB116 fb *1.30 107–05 Yougottawanna116¾ Gold Ruckus1153 Snorter118½ 2wide trip, driving 5

22Apr04–3BM fst 1 1/16 :232 :47 1:104 1:402 3↑OC c-80k/N3X **102** 5 21 2½ 2hd 13 16 Carr D LB118 fb *.40 105–08 *Yougottawanna*1186 Boss Ego1182½ Debonair Joe1182½ 3w rally, handily 5

Claimed from Kenton, Michael, Martin, John F. and O'Connor, Patrick for $80,000, Martin John F Trainer 2004(as of 4/22): (146 36 26 16 0.25)

27Mar04–7GG fst 1 :224 :46 1:094 1:334 3↑BrklyBCH-G3 **100** 2 11 11 1½ 1hd 21 Carr D LB116 fb 2.20 99–09 Snorter1161 *Yougottawanna*116nk TsteofPrdise116hd Pace off rail, gamely 5

28Feb04–3GG fst 1 1/16 :224 :454 1:094 1:403 4↑OC c-50k/N2X **102** 4 33 42 21 14 18 Carr D LB117 fb *1.80 100–11 Yougottawanna1178 Honegle1163 MrinMinister1161 Rallied 3w,ridden out 6

Claimed from Halo Farms and Craig, Sidney H. for $50,000, Hollendorfer Jerry Trainer 2003: (1216 282 211 193 0.23)

7Feb04–4GG fst 1 :222 :454 1:092 1:35 4↑OC 50k/N2X **96** 2 11 11 2hd 2hd 2hd Carr D LB117 fb *2.30e 94–16 *Jets Fan*116hd *Yougottawanna*1171 Debonair Joe1181 Gave way grudgingly 10

18Jan04–1GG sf 1 1/16 Ⓣ :242 :502 1:152 1:461+4↑OC 50k/N2X **85** 4 21 21 31 42 32 Carr D LB117 fb 1.70 77–21 ClbFortyOn118¾ ConstntThndr1171¼ Yogottwnn117no 3w,brushed, evenly 5

Zakocity
Own: Pompa P P Jr

B. c. 4 (May)
Sire: Precocity (Aferd) $3,000
Dam: Zakcat (Vilzak)
Br: John Franks (Fla)
Tr: Reynolds Patrick L(0 0 0 0 .00) 2004:(186 25 .13)

Life	23	4	4	5	$341,970	103	D.Fst	16	3	1	4	$277,168	103
2004	14	3	3	3	$240,967	103	Wet(332)	4	1	3	0	$56,860	99
2003	9	1	1	2	$101,003	87	Turf(254*)	3	0	0	1	$7,942	71
	0	0	0	0	$0	-	Dst(0)	0	0	0	0	$0	-

Date/Race	Trk	Dist	Fractions	Race	Fig	PP	St	1C	2C	Str	Fin	Jockey	Wt	Odds	Pace	Top Finishers	Comment	Fld
4Dec04- 8Aqu	fst	1 3/16 ⊡	:474 1:122 1:38 1:57	3↑ QeensCoH-G3	**101**	9	31	32	31	33	51¾	Castellano J J	L115 b	8.30	92- 18	Classic Endeavor117¾ EveningAttire123½ Colita115no	Leveled off final 1/8	9
27Oct04- 8Aqu	fst	1⅛	:484 1:131 1:371 1:493	DiscvryH-G3	**103**	7	1½	1½	11	14½	13½	Castellano J J	L116 b	6.50	91- 16	Zakocity1163½ Stolen Time113¾ Mahzouz115½	Set pace, drew clear	8
1Oct04- 7Med	fst	1⅛	:464 1:103 1:353 1:482	Pegasus-G3	**95**	1	31½	4¾	1hd	31	33¾	Castellano J J	L118 b	6.20	86- 11	Pies Prospect118nk *Eddington*1183½ *Zakocity*118hd	Steadied first turn	8
30Aug04- 7Sar	gd	1⅛	:463 1:111 1:354 1:482	3↑ Alw 50000N2x	**99**	1	21½	21½	2hd	12½	11¾	Castellano J J	L115 b	1.70	93- 06	Zakocity1151¾ *BroadwyView*1156 DrRockett1151¼	Drew clear when roused	9
14Aug04- 3Sar	gd	1⅛	:471 1:111 1:36 1:49	3↑ Alw 50000N2x	**93**	5	43	42½	32	22½	22¼	Castellano J J	L116 b	6.50	88- 14	Tales of Glory1172¼ *Zakocity*1164¾ Stratostar1241¼	Steadied, steadied	6
17Jly04- 9Mth	fst	1 1/16	:23 :462 1:10 1:432	LBrnchBC-G3	**84**	1	43	43	43½	58	510¼	Coa E M	L114	24.90	78- 19	*LionHert*116hd MySnookisBoy1155½ RoylAssult1223½	4-path,no stretch bid	7
22Jun04- 8Del	fst	1 1/16	:233 :471 1:114 1:434	FloorShow55k	**84**	4	63½	53¾	52¼	64	38	Alvarado R Jr	L117 f	6.00	85- 22	Pies Prospect1175½ Gmork1172½ Zakocity117½	Steadied, mild rally	8
5Jun04- 1Bel	fst	1 1/16	:233 :47 1:113 1:43	3↑ Alw 58000N2x	**87**	4	61¾	41½	44	44½	34½	Santos J A	L115	7.90	80- 10	Seek Gold1211½ [D]Spite the Devil118no Zakocity115no	Carried out stretch	10
Placed second through disqualification																		
22May04- 8Bel	fst	1⅛	:46 1:10 1:35 1:474	PeterPan-G2	**88**	3	53	52	63	68¾	612	Santos J A	L115 b	44.75	80- 24	Purge1156¾ *Swingforthefences*1151¼ MsterDvid1152¼	Inside run turn, tired	10
Previously trained by Wolfson Martin D																		
3Apr04- 11GP	fst	1 1/16	:234 :481 1:122 1:443	Aventura250k	**87**	1	85½	85½	55	56	45¼	Gryder A T	L122 b	2.70	81- 15	Kaufy Mate1224½ Humorously122nk Baronage122½	Checked early, 3 wide	8
14Mar04- 11Tam	fst	1 1/16	:233 :473 1:114 1:434	TampaDby-G3	**95**	7	75	72¾	62½	42	43	Santos J A	L116 b	9.00	96- 10	Limehouse116nk Mustnfr1161 Swingforthefencs1161¾	Rated,looped,wknd	8
21Feb04- 10Tam	fst	1 1/16	:232 :474 1:123 1:443	SamFDavis100k	**85**	9	63½	41¾	32	3½	33¼	Castanon J L	L118 b	4.80	92- 15	Kaufy Mate1161¾ The Cliff's Edge1161½ Zakocity1182	Bid 4w, hung late	11
18Jan04- 10GP	sly	1 1/16 ⊗	:241 :484 1:13 1:454	DaveFeldmn66k	**83**	4	52	52	62¼	32	2hd	Santos J A	L120 b	2.40	80- 25	Tap Day118hd Zakocity1202¾ Commendation1222	Inside rally, missed	8
3Jan04- 6GP	fst	1 1/16	:231 :473 1:122 1:45	Alw 34000N1x	**83**	10	53	52¼	52	31½	11	Santos J A	L118 b	*2.60	84- 13	Zakocity1181 BattleHero122nk NightmareAffair1181¼	Steadied,long drive	12

Records of 2004 Leaders

Owners
Trainers
Jockeys

(Money and Races Won)

Annual Leaders

(Money and Races Won)

Lifetime Records of Leading Jockeys

Leading Owners in 2004 by Money Won

Owner	St	1st	2d	3d	Purses
Michael J. Gill	2,885	487	432	345	$10,835,561
Someday Farm	12	7	2	0	*7,584,305
Stronach Stables	507	109	81	74	7,193,867
Ramsey, Kenneth L. and Sarah K.	361	84	63	42	5,855,964
Sam-Son Farms	260	47	36	38	4,830,939
Melnyk, Eugene and Laura	453	93	68	63	4,447,689
Juddmonte Farms, Inc.	113	35	20	7	3,454,794
Gary A. Tanaka	136	21	22	16	3,112,187
Lewis, Robert B. and Beverly J.	263	50	41	35	3,069,130
Robert D. Bone	353	113	66	49	3,015,251
Heiligbrodt Racing Stable	312	75	53	41	2,997,977
Starlight Stables LLC, Saylor, Paul and Martin, Johns	16	7	3	1	2,672,374
Edmund A. Gann	68	20	16	8	2,639,725
Richard A. Englander	514	104	81	63	2,510,037
Jay Em Ess Stable	142	34	22	16	2,290,203
Overbrook Farm	367	54	60	49	2,256,719
Darley Stable	204	31	34	28	2,235,777
Flying Zee Stable	507	79	78	78	2,218,064
Gumpster Stable LLC	512	114	90	84	2,142,198
Golden Eagle Farm	260	43	48	37	2,105,726
Rosendo G. Parra	419	71	54	67	2,103,999
Smith, Derrick and Tabor, Michael	48	13	15	7	2,097,526
Everest Stables, Inc.	321	32	36	31	2,036,755
Pin Oak Stable LLC	183	45	21	38	2,013,577
Paraneck Stable	434	45	46	60	2,004,251
Dale Baird	1,055	128	152	128	2,002,813
Robert V. LaPenta	74	14	14	9	2,001,302
Maggi Moss	503	98	86	65	1,986,173
Edward P. Evans	251	38	52	33	1,984,817
Live Oak Plantation	234	47	39	34	1,959,052
Buckram Oak Farm	291	48	55	45	1,919,336
Michael B. Tabor	54	18	14	4	1,877,867
Padua Stables	198	41	26	28	1,847,253
Tracy Farmer	102	30	11	15	1,823,046
Dogwood Stable	280	46	38	32	1,786,556
Ogden Mills Phipps	63	19	15	7	1,780,647
Wygod, Mr. and Mrs. Martin J.	117	24	21	13	1,753,972
Frank D. Di Giulio, Jr.	125	27	23	16	1,748,615
Stan E. Fulton	214	34	28	28	1,726,957
Diamond A Racing Corporation	36	6	8	4	1,640,876
Marylou Whitney Stables	68	15	9	5	1,628,890
Blahut Stables LLC, Kagele Brothers, Tepper, Allen, et al	4	3	1	0	1,612,150
Stonerside Stable LLC	165	40	25	17	1,560,389
Augustin Stable	245	38	35	42	1,517,857
Godolphin Racing, Inc.	9	2	1	0	1,504,632
Steven M. Asmussen	441	122	67	70	1,490,707
Broman, Sr., Mary and Chester	187	24	22	25	1,487,891
Amerman Racing Stables LLC	93	20	16	12	1,454,199
Bruno Schickedanz	626	101	86	70	1,453,748
Mrs. E Paul Robsham	142	32	31	25	1,420,947
Louis D. O'Brien	796	230	149	133	1,408,259
James McIngvale	73	15	12	16	1,396,671
Allen E. Paulson Living Trust	75	11	12	11	1,396,642
K. K. Sangara	156	36	30	20	1,371,131
Dominion Bloodstock, Ball, Derek and Galbraith, Hugh	193	27	22	23	1,370,014
Willmott Stables, Inc.	104	16	15	19	1,352,569
John D. Gunther	83	15	19	5	1,350,580
Chiefswood Stable	72	13	9	9	1,335,774
Jim Ford, Inc., Pearson, Deron and Sweesy, Jack	44	7	5	5	1,306,670
Little Red Feather Racing	24	5	5	4	1,302,310
Frank Carl Calabrese	301	83	47	42	1,301,613
B. Wayne Hughes	173	31	31	20	1,269,571
Edgewood Farm	27	8	7	2	1,262,124
Franks Farms	238	37	43	29	1,260,812
Cowan, Marge and Irving M.	48	12	13	6	1,256,319
Danny J. Chen	675	110	97	80	1,216,464
Tucci Stables	113	27	22	12	1,198,671
Moss, Mr. and Mrs. Jerome S.	203	33	30	29	1,185,965
Klaravich Stables, Inc.	73	20	10	8	1,178,597
Kelynack Racing Stable, Inc.	135	18	24	22	1,175,422
Alpine Stable Ltd.	222	39	23	27	1,166,006
Peter Vegso	172	31	20	25	1,165,741
Jay Manoogian	43	14	5	7	1,143,031
John D. Murphy, Sr.	273	41	43	51	1,140,793
J. Paul Reddam	125	22	17	13	1,140,168
Edward E. Turner	271	60	56	53	1,136,940
Sackatoga Stable	23	4	2	4	1,109,593
Harris Farms, Inc.	169	27	38	26	1,103,810
Puglisi Stables	115	24	26	14	1,101,587
Jayeff B Stables	199	34	31	26	1,100,004
Fox Ridge Farm, Inc.	69	9	10	13	1,076,606
Bushwood Racing Partners	8	2	2	0	1,076,400
G. Watts Humphrey, Jr.	229	30	25	36	1,073,816
The Two Bit Racing Stable	7	4	3	0	1,060,790
William S. Farish	113	24	23	12	1,044,381
Phipps, Ogden Mills, et al	41	13	4	11	1,020,649
Equils, James W. and Marcia S.	298	38	44	50	995,369
Klein, Richard, Bertram and Elaine	163	29	29	19	991,126
Turf Express, Inc.	266	66	40	31	990,830
Team Block	122	17	21	16	979,018
T N T Stud	61	14	15	8	977,625
Monarch Stables, Inc.	350	77	42	44	976,254
Runnin Horse Farm, Inc.	226	41	35	27	972,398
Michael H. Sherman	418	64	49	53	963,078
Jones, Aaron U. and Marie D.	72	20	11	7	960,621
Gustav Schickedanz	80	15	12	9	954,606
Spendthrift Farm LLC, Kidder, Chuck, Cole, Nancy and Strong, Nick	12	3	2	2	947,476
Martin S. Schwartz	72	16	8	17	942,640
Brushwood Stable	41	9	5	2	939,675
New Farm	106	27	13	17	929,275
Stonecrest Farm	65	4	13	7	926,546
Mercedes Stables LLC	89	16	14	18	923,998
J D Farms	154	21	24	20	920,455
Gary Owens	440	78	67	66	918,582
Peachtree Stable	108	28	17	11	913,993
Robert L. Cole, Jr.	178	50	18	33	911,799
Wertheimer and Frere	80	8	17	16	902,836
Anstu Stables, Inc.	58	15	10	7	898,747
Knighton, Jeri and Sam	18	6	5	2	889,600
Hollendorfer, Jerry and Todaro, George	259	57	51	35	884,705
Gilbert G. Campbell	165	41	26	18	881,045
Valene Farms	150	32	31	21	858,357
Joseph V. Shields, Jr.	93	19	15	14	835,148
Reddam, J. Paul and Roy, Susan	2	1	0	1	833,580
Courtlandt Farms	96	19	16	10	816,645
Joseph Allen	63	10	13	10	816,586
Barry K. Schwartz	147	25	14	21	809,844
Erdenheim Farm	121	20	20	19	807,398
Cappuccitti, Audre and Gordon	148	12	22	25	804,069
Jack J. Armstrong	382	69	65	43	798,903
Al Kabeer, Sultan Mohammed Saud and Bridport, S. A.	10	1	5	2	793,430
Red Oak Stable	103	11	20	16	785,840
Claiborne Farm	79	10	16	12	781,450
Aguirre, Paul G. and Aldabbagh, Omar	20	5	4	3	777,283
Shadwell Stable	108	15	16	13	774,189
Nelson Bunker Hunt	165	23	26	20	771,365

Owner	St	1st	2d	3d	Purses
Mercedes Stables LLC and Paulson, Madeleine	11	3	2	1	771,240
Sheikh Maktoum bin Rashid Al Maktoum	39	10	5	2	770,550
WinStar Farm LLC	160	26	29	13	768,546
M. Y. Stables, Inc.	386	73	58	57	767,259
Cash is King LLC	13	6	6	1	763,190
Kagele Brothers, Inc.	129	51	29	11	760,393
C D and G Stable	294	38	52	42	750,630
Kinsman Stable	110	22	13	16	745,352
West Point Stable	95	16	15	9	742,076
Glen Hill Farm	114	24	20	13	734,532
Lord Derby	1	1	0	0	733,200
Naify, Marsha and Woodside Farms LLC	24	6	3	4	727,753
Acclaimed Racing Stable	190	40	36	28	721,945
Pyrite Stables	365	40	37	58	716,682
John Alecci Stable, Inc.	134	40	16	18	714,541
Prestonwood Farm LLC	19	7	4	2	713,174
Santa Cruz Ranch, Inc.	112	13	13	9	712,343
Tommy Town T'breds LLC	133	25	18	13	711,363
Silverton Hill LLC	149	26	22	17	709,448
Jacks or Better Farm, Inc.	193	21	30	17	709,102
Plumstead Stables	294	38	51	40	704,622
Steve Taub	26	6	1	7	703,410
Charles E. Fipke	47	7	8	4	703,036
Hwy 1 Racing Stable LLC	425	55	73	34	702,419
Charlton Baker	149	45	25	20	695,566
William L. Clifton, Jr.	117	19	15	13	690,301
Taylor Mountain Farm LLC	156	23	25	20	690,091
Moore, Susan and John	56	9	13	8	688,178
Kuehne Racing	86	16	10	12	687,649
Edwin Thomas Broome	134	24	27	17	686,183
William A. Sorokolit, Sr.	103	10	6	15	683,945
Paul P. Pompa, Jr.	143	15	24	15	680,153
Lloyd Madison Farms, IV LLC	13	6	1	1	674,680
Karakorum Farm	131	24	16	15	671,883
Centaur Farms, Inc.	169	19	23	24	668,344
Fred F. Bradley	28	4	7	2	667,066
Craig, Sidney H. and Jenny	106	17	22	15	664,800
Sumaya Us Stables	22	3	7	3	652,777
Russell L. Reineman Stable, Inc.	100	27	13	11	651,780
TradeWinds Stable	151	37	25	25	644,924
Patricia A. Generazio	226	18	21	29	643,680
Daniel M. Ryan	174	36	24	23	643,404
Dare To Dream Stable LLC	158	28	26	17	642,884
Haras Santa Maria de Araras	119	12	19	13	642,459
Robert J. Amendola	95	27	14	13	641,278
Home Team Stables	197	42	47	31	636,909
Warren, Jr., Mr. and Mrs. William K.	14	2	2	3	636,098
William Stiritz	176	37	22	23	635,309
Vincent S. Scuderi	67	20	11	13	634,783
Bruce Lunsford	37	7	1	7	633,639
Ken Murphy T'breds, Ltd.	219	44	39	28	633,036
Baskin, Bonnie and Sy	31	7	5	6	630,583
Falourd, Alain, Guy, Hubert and Trussell, Robert	4	2	1	0	630,000
Peter F. Karches	81	16	14	14	621,829
Kupferberg, Saul J. and Max	172	30	19	28	621,739
Lakeside Farms LLC	16	2	2	2	618,435
Joseph J. Balsamo	65	12	10	14	614,031
Naveed Chowhan	21	6	5	2	613,848
Bruno Brothers Farms	43	10	4	3	613,425
Arnold Zetcher	44	6	7	5	609,995
Lael Stables	90	10	15	15	607,169
Wilson, David W. and Holly F.	112	20	15	16	605,329
Winchell Thoroughbreds LLC	100	15	14	19	603,156
Dennis E. Weir	148	35	32	21	602,656
Attfield, Roger L. and Werner, William	64	8	6	11	602,127
Vetter, Linda and Wira, Richard and Yvette	7	2	2	1	598,905
Panic Stable LLC	117	39	17	11	597,549
Knob Hill Stable	92	13	19	7	596,778
Margaret Squires	29	7	1	8	594,970
Liberty Stable	33	11	7	1	592,000
River Ridge Ranch	217	27	19	35	590,939
Asiel Stable	120	15	17	18	590,930
Earle I. Mack	81	13	11	12	583,714
Evelyn M. Pollard	75	11	8	13	582,520
Diamond Oak Stable	95	26	20	9	582,372
David J. Lanzman Racing Stable, Inc.	73	20	5	8	581,652
Equirace.Com LLC	37	4	3	4	579,720
Martin L. Cherry	65	15	12	6	578,184
William A. Carl	93	17	18	6	577,142
Janis R. Whitham	73	10	22	7	576,700
Charles, Ronald L. and Clear Valley Stables	94	18	13	6	576,371
Hobeau Farm	99	16	10	20	576,101
Molinaro Stable	134	18	18	17	574,127
Noctis LLC, Papiano, Neil and Taub, Steve	29	6	4	3	568,852
C R K Stable	54	12	6	10	565,457
Francis C. McDonnell	179	37	28	17	562,543
Rose Family Stable	272	23	24	27	561,198
Jeffrey Sengara	72	15	17	14	559,764
Michael Barkowski	209	40	43	28	559,558
West, Gary L. and Mary E.	67	17	8	8	559,112
Arthur I. Appleton	104	21	18	17	559,067
John Cardella	113	17	13	19	558,747
La Marca Stable	124	24	17	23	558,553
John C. Oxley	86	12	14	13	558,444
Lanning, Curt and Lila	206	24	44	35	556,443
Sondra D. Bender	112	16	20	13	555,995
Schwartz, Herbert T. and Carol A.	158	7	19	28	555,461
Fox Hill Farms, Inc.	85	18	12	10	554,633
C. R. Trout	132	21	16	23	554,479
Zuckerman, Donald S. and Roberta Mary	65	11	9	11	553,657
Gary and Mary West Stables, Inc.	68	20	14	5	551,845
Phillips, Joan G. and John W.	14	5	0	0	549,957
Team Valor Stables LLC	75	12	15	8	549,295
Orion Stables	308	25	32	31	547,208
Herbert Washington Chambers	206	19	14	21	544,908
Worcester Stable	218	31	35	22	544,778
Roddy J. Valente	72	19	17	5	543,260
Williams, Mr. and Mrs. Larry D.	87	17	14	8	540,834
Char-Mari Stable	59	9	7	10	540,586
Vivian, Barbara and Vittese, Dominic	32	8	5	2	540,150
Our Sugar Bear Stable	101	18	15	9	536,914
Beal, Jr., Richard T. and Ramsey-Brog, Lana	10	4	2	1	536,540
Tom R. Durant	174	25	16	19	535,838
Wild Horse Stable	208	40	33	27	534,383
J B Stables, Inc.	190	32	22	13	532,201
Alex G. Campbell, Jr.	114	22	9	10	530,703
Mark E. Casse	71	11	11	17	530,188
Danny A. Limongelli	236	34	38	26	528,976
Cohen, Philip and Marcia	31	5	6	3	527,208
Mac Fehsenfeld	132	13	16	30	526,405
The Elkstone Group LLC	243	24	37	31	524,349
Jerry Hollendorfer	174	54	33	21	523,567
George Krikorian	53	10	5	4	521,717
Joseph S. Parisi	121	15	15	16	518,212
Michael Bello	23	7	3	3	517,190
Green Lantern Stables LLC	28	6	10	6	514,526

Owner	St	1st	2d	3d	Purses
Ocean Front Property and Asmussen, Keith	71	17	15	12	512,812
Weatherwatch Farm and Valente, Roddy	43	14	6	5	511,761
Mrs. John Magnier	4	0	0	3	510,000
Cartagena, Julio and Feinberg, Robert	113	35	17	10	509,121
Carlo D'Amato	176	15	17	14	508,243
Scarberry, Howard and Penny	160	18	23	13	507,970
Nickolas DeToro	123	18	11	18	505,738
Ed Friendly	24	7	0	7	505,630
S J B Stable	134	20	15	14	505,434
William C. Schettine	66	10	9	8	503,344
Ronald Winchell	12	2	1	1	503,201
J. Mack Robinson	183	16	23	21	503,066
Vinery Stables	66	18	10	8	500,690
Deckert, Robert, Jr. and Robert, Sr.	115	16	17	11	497,500
Fan, Peter and Ward, Wesley	6	4	1	1	496,180
R. A. Marcello	25	9	3	3	494,914
Michael E. Pegram	79	12	5	7	492,401
Michael House	43	10	7	4	491,195
Preferred Pals Stable	47	9	6	6	488,395
Michael Dubb	127	17	20	16	484,558
Minshall Farms	104	8	13	12	482,443
Wags Nags LLC	198	32	22	27	481,613
E and G Stables	127	37	29	18	480,842
Grant, Mary and Joseph and Kelly, Thomas J.	33	2	6	4	480,505
Audre Cappuccitti	146	16	11	13	480,329
James L. Ingalls	262	42	30	25	478,352
The Merv Griffin Ranch Co.	51	15	9	4	478,101
Foxwood Plantation, Ltd.	90	20	10	14	473,888
Morris Bailey	92	20	13	18	472,072
L. T. B., Inc. and Williams, R. A.	33	11	6	7	470,880
Timber Bay Farm and Walsh, Mrs. Thomas J.	8	5	1	0	467,578
Chandler, Dr. John A.	32	13	4	2	466,604
Parsley, Ken and Pettifer, Rick	15	4	3	4	466,255
Ivan Dalos	93	13	12	12	466,158
Vincent Papandrea	62	11	13	9	465,001
Steel Your Face Stables	45	12	8	9	464,996
Lazy Lane Farms, Inc.	58	14	12	10	464,636
Kirkwood, Al and Saundra S.	56	7	2	3	464,537
Nick Sanna Stables, Inc.	107	26	19	10	464,475
Robert J. Costigan	14	3	3	1	463,649
John H. Peace	86	14	12	13	463,630
Tabor, Michael and Magnier, Mrs. John	6	0	1	2	461,000
Stony Oak Farm LLC	105	16	17	8	460,419
Bar None Ranches	218	41	24	29	458,214
Nico Nierenberg	56	10	11	11	455,946
G Racing, VanBurger, Carl F. and Vaughn, Landon	13	3	4	0	455,920
Colebrook Farms	187	22	22	22	454,069
Dennis A. Drazin	109	17	15	15	452,767
Michel A. Ward, II	259	21	31	25	452,387
Kelly, Jon, Scott, Brad, Ralls and Foster, LLC, et al	6	0	5	0	452,190
James B. Tafel	71	17	2	7	451,744
George Farr	25	5	6	3	450,704
Lyons, Frank and Knee, Greg	3	1	0	0	450,000
Keith I. Asmussen	99	23	19	9	448,914
Cohen, Philip and Marcia and Klesaris, Steve	54	17	9	7	447,318
Tulip Hill Farm	128	27	20	15	446,229
Billy Hays	404	55	49	71	444,066
Lewis G. Lakin	32	12	2	3	443,906
Iron County Farms, Inc.	39	8	7	6	441,070
Fly Racing LLC	46	10	5	11	440,515
R Bar S Thoroughbreds LLP	34	5	6	5	440,307
Andrena Van Doren	53	7	9	10	440,300
Leo S. Nechamkin, II	41	8	6	8	440,000
R. Gary Patrick	440	53	51	52	439,642
Donald R. Dizney	134	23	19	13	439,087
Di Giulio, Jr., Frank and Tiller, R. P.	24	9	8	2	435,937
Team Solaris Stable	23	7	3	1	434,899
Sanford J. Goldfarb	50	14	6	5	434,898
Ocean View Stables	124	10	13	8	434,719
Crawford, Jerry, Gannon, Matt and Grask, Charlie	10	3	1	1	434,634
Daniel Franko	217	29	24	30	434,346
Come By Chance Stable	74	5	7	8	433,430
Steel Your Face Stables and Emily Racing Stables	33	13	7	6	432,366
Nancy A. Vanier	102	14	14	13	432,202
Raymond W. Makarovich, Jr.	74	25	13	14	432,046
Buddy Lee Racing Stable	276	66	46	41	430,782
D. J. Stable LLC	124	24	12	17	430,124
Fog City Stable	30	5	6	1	426,710
Earnhardt, III, Patti and Hal J.	33	8	4	5	426,508
Richard Malouf	81	20	8	16	426,315
Bohemia Stable	77	11	8	11	426,106
Cobra Farm, Inc.	67	18	8	6	425,169
Timothy Cunningham	88	12	17	18	423,429
Wexler Racing Stables, Inc.	200	21	20	25	423,297
Mark Yagour, Inc.	462	48	50	38	420,726
George Brunacini	87	11	8	12	420,120
Benjamin C. Warren	124	11	13	12	417,049
Jayaraman, Kalarikkal K. and Vilasini D.	109	19	18	17	415,707
S and B Stable	9	4	2	2	414,813
Kaaren J. Biggs	128	25	22	19	414,715
Madeline Auerbach	39	7	10	6	414,129
Frank J. Regalbuto	117	21	14	16	413,765
La Canada Stable LLC	109	23	15	9	413,327
Lothenbach Stables, Inc.	31	3	5	4	412,551
G. Chris Coleman	43	11	7	7	412,265
Fitzhugh LLC	63	14	12	10	411,887
Scott A. Lake	67	15	13	7	411,681
M.A.D. Racing Stables and Gonzalez, Martha	22	8	6	3	409,995
Golden, Bruce and Lake, Scott	51	13	11	8	409,971
Raymond Dweck	49	7	9	8	409,752
Hardwicke Stable	72	10	9	6	409,354
Whitbred, Howard T. and Brennan, Christine	31	9	8	2	407,272
Carl F. Pollard	60	8	8	9	406,756
Raymond H. Cottrell, Sr.	9	4	3	1	405,946
Stone Spire LLC	35	5	8	4	405,497
Sovereign Stable and Gatsas Stables	67	10	12	10	404,041
William M. Rickman	156	32	24	22	403,497
Richard Otto Stables, Inc.	40	8	4	4	403,097
Mrs. S. K. Johnston, Jr.	101	15	13	6	401,639
Star Track Farms	124	13	8	20	401,136
Ben Barnow	122	17	8	21	400,964
McKee Stables, Inc.	66	14	10	10	400,890
Kagele Brothers, Inc., Leatherman, Ty and Leib, Mark A.	7	3	2	2	400,740
Daniel A. Herrmann	32	11	7	7	400,145
Fieldstone Farms	68	8	6	5	399,248
James T. Hines, Jr.	165	27	21	19	397,507
Patricia B. Blass	65	7	17	10	397,315
Namcook Stables LLC	93	13	13	9	395,881
Loren G. Cox	236	27	37	18	395,449
Lee Lewis	56	12	11	5	394,786
Stuart S. Janney, III	67	8	10	11	392,511

Owner	St	1st	2d	3d	Purses
Tricar Stable, Inc.	210	19	24	33	392,120
Win and Place Stable	85	16	17	13	390,946
Kinross Farm	71	13	10	15	390,540
Destiny Farm LLC	131	17	22	16	390,468
William M. Backer	97	13	7	12	390,323
George A. Wolff	51	10	18	8	389,757
Coast To Coast Racing Fund LLC	79	19	15	14	389,528
Norseman Racing Stable	53	13	2	2	389,215
Albert Fried, Jr.	103	14	13	11	387,009
Phillips Racing Partnership	33	4	6	5	386,625
Shadwell Farm LLC	31	9	6	2	386,266
O'Sullivan Farms LLC	43	10	8	10	384,939
David Beard	65	12	9	10	384,575
Claiborne Farm and Dilschneider, Adele B.	26	4	6	2	383,664
John R. Parker	34	8	11	1	383,534
Bushwood Stables	7	2	2	1	382,190
Flaxman Holdings, Ltd.	18	4	3	2	382,110
John D. McKee	215	20	20	25	381,617
Jane M. Freed	56	16	9	5	381,479
Robert H. Shepard	128	13	16	20	381,377
Jack L. Boggs	145	29	26	14	380,835
Ersoff Racing Stable Inc.	120	20	18	18	380,330
Mrs. Frank P. Wright	109	11	21	13	379,694
Max H. Pearson	81	11	15	9	379,466
Green Hills Farm	21	9	4	2	378,899
Rainbow Stable	108	17	25	13	377,713
Larry R. Teague	10	6	1	1	377,179
Ron Crockett, Inc.	103	18	27	19	377,073
Michael G. Weatherly	116	28	19	11	375,626
Rey Wan Racing	137	20	22	23	375,350
John Castro	101	16	13	20	374,425
J. Jeps Stable	204	30	22	26	374,075
Peter Redekop B. C., Ltd.	44	11	4	9	374,067
E. A. Ranches	68	6	12	12	373,180
The Nonsequitur Stable LLC	63	16	8	9	372,985
Dapple Stables LLC	60	10	6	12	372,015
Toby Roth	96	12	26	13	371,029
Harry J. Aleo	53	18	7	8	370,676
Glen C. Warren	84	12	9	13	370,582
Wimp Free Racing Stables	79	25	17	9	370,170
Rodney C. Faulkner	345	56	52	31	368,268
Linda S. Gaudet	96	15	17	8	366,620
Poston, Bill and Vicki	41	6	5	10	366,600
Donamire Farm	53	9	7	7	366,295
J. Michael Baird	125	30	24	10	366,203
D D Stable	176	26	20	30	365,625
Robert Bakerman	161	17	20	17	364,624
Doneson, Mark and Dubb, Michael	113	21	19	15	364,611
Southern Equine Stable LLC	109	10	18	18	362,553
Armando Lage	143	25	21	15	361,741
Moyglare Stud Farm, Ltd.	10	6	1	0	361,580
Goldmart Farms	107	12	12	14	361,448
Scatuorchio, James T., Pletcher, Jake and Wetterman, Pete	9	6	1	1	360,899
A. Stevens Miles, Jr.	14	4	4	3	360,825
Oxenberg, Bea and Plesa, Laurie	7	4	0	1	360,710
West Point Thoroughbreds LLC	43	9	6	6	360,063
Stride Rite Racing Stable, Inc.	48	11	6	14	360,060
James C. Spence	41	8	4	5	360,051
Kjell H. Qvale	171	24	26	27	359,326
John L. Stahlin	141	19	27	20	359,144
Donald E. Souder	185	15	25	25	358,301
Harry C. and Tom O. Meyerhoff LLC	91	19	14	11	358,160
Jam Jar Racing Stable	69	10	8	8	357,849
Ronald C. Waranch	36	8	5	4	357,675
Lynne M. Scace	186	37	22	30	356,460
William Dorminy	36	15	5	4	355,767
Manfred Roos	105	20	22	15	355,272
Maine, J. and Baker, R.	28	4	5	7	354,297
CJZ Racing Stable	38	10	13	2	353,210
Buckingham Farm	40	10	0	4	353,192
Dresden Farm	124	19	20	17	353,009
Charles J. Cella	52	7	8	7	352,726
Mariani, Jeffrey J., Nentwig, Michael and Van Kempen, Dallas	7	2	2	1	352,600
Howard Roberts Farm	95	13	8	15	352,430
Llers Corporation	27	3	4	5	352,042
Azalea Stables LLC	8	2	2	1	350,978
Rudina Stable	47	8	6	3	349,722
Stanley B. Seelig	45	8	8	4	349,128
Daniel J. Lopez	84	19	20	10	348,845
901 Racing Stables LLC	93	28	15	9	348,639
Kaster, Nancy R. and Richard S.	77	11	9	5	348,230
Ryehill Farm	88	9	17	11	347,875
Camelia J. Casby	119	16	17	13	346,878
K and K Racing Stable LLC	27	3	1	5	346,127
Kelly, Jon and Sarah	26	7	3	6	345,831
Laurence I. Foggle	54	13	9	8	345,550
Jpf Investments I LLC	70	8	8	9	344,897
Charles P. Hukill	229	26	32	30	344,361
Windhaven Farm	19	5	2	2	341,259
Thomas Vanderhyde	126	25	24	24	341,178
Canyon Farms	55	6	11	5	341,157
David E. Garner	24	3	2	6	340,836
Joseph Clark Faulkner	360	68	46	50	340,810
Skeedattle Stable	3	1	1	1	340,000
Jer-Mar Stable LLC	68	20	9	12	339,502
Toscano, III, John T., Corrado, Kim and Carlat, Yamile	5	2	1	0	338,866
Goldish, Marc D. and Savoy Stable	80	16	18	9	337,140
Robert N. Clay	21	5	1	2	336,988
Oxbow Racing LLC	86	13	11	14	335,850
Hickory Plains	100	10	16	14	334,717
Monty Roberts	4	2	0	0	334,000
P.T.K., LLC	161	11	22	24	333,867
Hendrickson Farms LLC	111	17	7	16	333,240
Lori Goodz	45	19	5	2	332,776
Thunderbolt Racing LLC	100	27	19	10	332,075
Timber Creek Farms	58	16	16	5	329,062
Kevin J. Joy	104	20	16	9	328,727
Darrell R. Sapp	203	22	30	27	328,638
Whippoorwill Farm, Inc.	65	8	11	11	328,037
Jerry Jamgotchian	94	14	9	12	327,882
Don Eberts	85	23	6	9	327,609
Michael A. Lecesse	124	27	18	20	327,279
Domino Stud of Lex LLC	45	5	5	9	326,901
Finish Line Racing Stable	74	22	11	13	325,610
Hayes, Mr. and Mrs. Jeff, Higman, Jerome, et al	12	5	2	1	325,579
O'Brien, P. and F.	21	4	0	0	324,764
Dale K. S. Lucas	74	13	16	13	323,943
Terra Farm	55	6	3	9	322,731
Carey K. Miller	43	13	4	10	322,182
Charles Cono	37	6	7	6	321,960
Diamond G Ranch, Inc.	152	29	27	15	321,855
Winn, Mrs. James A.	24	6	4	5	321,710
Peter G. Angelos	7	3	1	0	320,964
Robert S. Mitchell Trust	114	14	18	17	319,814
Steeplechase Farm	57	12	10	12	319,810
Ted Taylor	119	16	14	17	319,786
S L U, Inc.	85	7	4	17	319,751
Carl C. Icahn	45	10	12	4	319,076
Startin Small Racing Stable, Ltd. and Ante Up Stable	56	9	12	7	318,805

Owner	Starts	1st	2d	3d	Purses
Francis J. Paolangeli	84	19	3	16	318,194
Lawrence Goichman	49	8	6	9	317,961
Stephen A. Richardson	181	31	23	21	317,784
William R. Scott	12	5	3	1	317,740
William S. Farish, Jr.	28	6	5	6	316,826
J. and G. Murphy Holdings, Ltd.	110	17	7	13	314,709
Rodriguez, Lorraine and Rod	64	5	9	8	314,672
Edward Clouston	207	28	26	21	313,775
Beclawat Stable	55	7	3	6	313,477
Walter Family Trust	101	12	13	15	313,466
Silver Diamond T'breds, Inc.	116	17	10	9	311,458
Kim Noble Hart	97	19	20	8	310,983
Southern Nevada Racing Stables, Inc.	105	24	15	14	310,673
Calmar Stables and Ranch	77	13	11	16	310,383
John C. Sessa	77	10	17	7	310,117
Grasshopper Stable	11	7	3	1	309,974
Rowell Enterprises, Inc.	55	13	9	5	309,580
Jim Dandy Stable	28	5	6	2	309,486
Fishelberg, Leonard and Yolanda	37	10	7	4	309,295
James Weigel	4	4	0	0	309,000
Thomas F. Van Meter, II	12	2	2	3	307,937
Doro J. Stable, Inc.	231	38	35	31	306,845
Jim H. Plemmons	88	12	11	9	306,438
Flatbird Stable	41	7	4	6	305,710
Rolph A. Davis	8	3	2	0	305,223
Richter, Kristine and John	89	16	11	10	305,152
David A. Ross	105	14	13	17	304,676
Grand Slam Racing Stable	129	48	20	20	304,405
Trillium Stable	17	4	4	0	304,173
Jarvis, Michael, Margolis, Gary, Smole, Ken, et al	12	2	0	2	303,145
Tom Mankiewicz	25	4	4	2	302,902
Eldon Farm LLC	30	5	3	3	302,828
Humphrey, Jr., Louise I. and G. Watts	35	8	5	5	302,663
Henry E. Pabst	44	7	5	7	302,630
James D. Jackson	21	4	0	4	301,695
Spraberry, Hassel R. and Bonnie V.	7	2	2	1	301,627
Stud TNT and Slack, Mrs. M.	2	1	0	0	300,000
Turf Syndikat 2001	1	0	1	0	300,000
James R. Lewis, Jr.	80	10	7	10	299,979
Sapara, James and Alice	32	7	1	4	299,236
James T. Scatuorchio	33	7	5	2	298,830
Volar Corporation	163	38	26	22	297,445
Vickie L. Krantz	14	7	1	0	296,945
Heinz Steinmann	56	11	10	10	296,340
Joseph W. Gerrity, Jr.	84	8	8	9	295,861
Walts David Stable LLC	35	8	3	7	295,215
Coming Home Stables, Inc.	98	11	11	17	294,750
Carl R. Moore Management LLC	65	11	16	5	294,653
Turf Express, Inc. and Darrell and Evelyn Yates, Ltd.	5	2	2	0	294,640
Kaufman, Robert and Weiss, Roger and Stephen M.	3	1	0	0	294,500
Bridgette Sipp	304	38	33	31	294,305
Daniel J. Ljoka	92	8	7	12	293,766
Elaine M. Gross	593	49	66	70	293,589
Stix-N-Stones Stable and Miller, Thomas	200	35	23	32	293,557
Centennial Farms	50	10	6	7	293,501
C. K. Woods Stable	21	3	2	2	292,207
Goldfarb, Sanford, Carney, C. L., Fleisig, J., Rosenfeld, N. and Hochman, J.	13	5	3	2	291,725
Rich Meadow Farm	32	9	7	5	291,707
Porter Racing Stable LLC	89	16	4	8	291,320
Michael Jawl	35	7	8	7	291,156
Richard Lueck	37	12	5	6	291,034
Robert S. Evans	56	9	6	10	290,834
McCarty Racing	75	19	12	13	290,420
So Madcapt Stable	22	5	2	3	290,341
Triple B Farms	33	6	5	3	290,164
Canino, Michael and Phyllis, Werner, William and Attfield, Roger	8	3	2	0	290,060
Dreabon Copeland	31	11	8	2	289,064
William R. Harris	150	18	19	19	288,287
B. and B. Stable and Penny, W.	34	4	4	5	287,973
Heiligbrodt Racing Stable and Burning Day Farm	5	3	0	0	287,390
A. Kales Company	57	10	4	15	287,270
McCaffery, Trudy and Toffan, John A.	43	3	3	9	287,148
Gerald F. Sleeter	58	5	13	4	285,599
Country Life Farm	50	10	11	4	285,305
Our Blue Streaks Stable	95	10	10	12	285,094
Steven Peskoff	51	8	4	4	285,052
Ciresa, Edward and Papapandrea, Vincent	8	3	4	0	285,040
Linwood Stables	76	12	9	5	284,768
Ruberto Racing Stable, Inc.	64	19	13	6	284,369
Michael W. Jester	53	13	16	7	283,233
N. Eddie Householder	78	11	7	15	283,231
Thomas F. Metzger, Sr.	21	7	3	3	282,960
Terry Bruner	110	14	17	15	282,809
Candy Stables	54	11	2	5	282,808
Seven Oaks Farm	69	13	10	12	282,800
Windways Farm and Quinn Stable	39	5	9	3	282,275
Tanourin Stable	46	7	11	4	282,200
Dany Dion	119	17	18	21	281,673
Padua Stables and Manoogian, Jay	6	2	0	0	280,835
Mount Joy Stables, Inc.	64	11	11	6	280,715
Confetti Farms, Inc.	81	14	18	14	280,502
Ferro Family Trust and Bonde, Jeff	22	4	4	4	279,225
Blackjack Thoroughbreds	96	13	18	13	278,859
Elaine C. Bassford	35	12	7	4	278,120
Cecil N. Peacock	58	6	7	6	278,079
Kay Hale	81	16	11	8	277,715
Mast Thoroughbreds LLC	83	11	13	12	277,232
IEAH Stables	75	15	14	9	276,786
Diglett Stable	75	19	12	8	275,708
Daniel M. Borislow	75	10	10	6	275,609
Samuel F. Bayard	27	7	1	5	275,260
Stubbs Investment, Inc.	50	5	11	5	273,891
John W. Baird	139	19	15	19	273,856
Stewart Mather Madison	27	8	4	1	273,602
Robert Perez	68	10	5	8	273,098
Greenoaks Farm	91	17	12	10	272,743
Brereton C. Jones	70	11	13	7	272,112
Sea Soft Stable	20	4	3	1	271,996
Shelly R. Radosevich	279	44	35	47	271,515
Cuchna, John R., Jim Ford, Inc. and Pearson, Deron	16	1	3	2	270,458

*Includes $5,000,000 bonus

Snapshot Facts: There were 265 owners whose horses earned $500,000 or more in 2004. There were 86 whose horses earned $1 million or more.

Leading Owners in 2004 by Races Won

Owner	St	1st	2d	3d	Purses
Michael J. Gill	2,885	487	432	345	$10,835,561
Louis D. O'Brien	796	230	149	133	1,408,259
Dale Baird	1,055	128	152	128	2,002,813
Steven M. Asmussen	441	122	67	70	1,490,707
Gumpster Stable LLC	512	114	90	84	2,142,198
Robert D. Bone	353	113	66	49	3,015,251
Danny J. Chen	675	110	97	80	1,216,464
Stronach Stables	507	109	81	74	7,193,867
Richard A. Englander	514	104	81	63	2,510,037
Bruno Schickedanz	626	101	86	70	1,453,748
Maggi Moss	503	98	86	65	1,986,173
Melnyk, Eugene and Laura	453	93	68	63	4,447,689
Ramsey, Kenneth L. and Sarah K.	361	84	63	42	5,855,964
Frank Carl Calabrese	301	83	47	42	1,301,613
Flying Zee Stable	507	79	78	78	2,218,064
Gary Owens	440	78	67	66	918,582
Monarch Stables, Inc.	350	77	42	44	976,254
Heiligbrodt Racing Stable	312	75	53	41	2,997,977
M. Y. Stables, Inc.	386	73	58	57	767,259
Rosendo G. Parra	419	71	54	67	2,103,999
Jack J. Armstrong	382	69	65	43	798,903
Joseph Clark Faulkner	360	68	46	50	340,810
Turf Express, Inc.	266	66	40	31	990,830
Buddy Lee Racing Stable	276	66	46	41	430,782
Michael H. Sherman	418	64	49	53	963,078
Edward E. Turner	271	60	56	53	1,136,940
Hollendorfer, Jerry and Todaro, George	259	57	51	35	884,705
Rodney C. Faulkner	345	56	52	31	368,268
Hwy 1 Racing Stable LLC	425	55	73	34	702,419
Billy Hays	404	55	49	71	444,066
Overbrook Farm	367	54	60	49	2,256,719
Jerry Hollendorfer	174	54	33	21	523,567
R. Gary Patrick	440	53	51	52	439,642
Kagele Brothers, Inc.	129	51	29	11	760,393
Lewis, Robert B. and Beverly J.	263	50	41	35	3,069,130
Robert L. Cole, Jr.	178	50	18	33	911,799
Elaine M. Gross	593	49	66	70	293,589
Buckram Oak Farm	291	48	55	45	1,919,336
Mark Yagour, Inc.	462	48	50	38	420,726
Grand Slam Racing Stable	129	48	20	20	304,405
Sam-Son Farms	260	47	36	38	4,830,939
Live Oak Plantation	234	47	39	34	1,959,052
Dogwood Stable	280	46	38	32	1,786,556
My Way Stable	338	46	50	52	229,886
Pin Oak Stable LLC	183	45	21	38	2,013,577
Paraneck Stable	434	45	46	60	2,004,251
Charlton Baker	149	45	25	20	695,566
Ken Murphy T'breds, Ltd.	219	44	39	28	633,036
Shelly R. Radosevich	279	44	35	47	271,515
Golden Eagle Farm	260	43	48	37	2,105,726
Home Team Stables	197	42	47	31	636,909
James L. Ingalls	262	42	30	25	478,352
Padua Stables	198	41	26	28	1,847,253
John D. Murphy, Sr.	273	41	43	51	1,140,793
Runnin Horse Farm, Inc.	226	41	35	27	972,398
Gilbert G. Campbell	165	41	26	18	881,045
Bar None Ranches	218	41	24	29	458,214
Stonerside Stable LLC	165	40	25	17	1,560,389
Acclaimed Racing Stable	190	40	36	28	721,945
Pyrite Stables	365	40	37	58	716,682
John Alecci Stable, Inc.	134	40	16	18	714,541
Michael Barkowski	209	40	43	28	559,558
Wild Horse Stable	208	40	33	27	534,383
Alpine Stable Ltd.	222	39	23	27	1,166,006
Panic Stable LLC	117	39	17	11	597,549
Edward P. Evans	251	38	52	33	1,984,817
Augustin Stable	245	38	35	42	1,517,857
Equils, James W. and Marcia S.	298	38	44	50	995,369
C D and G Stable	294	38	52	42	750,630
Plumstead Stables	294	38	51	40	704,622
Doro J. Stable, Inc.	231	38	35	31	306,845
Volar Corporation	163	38	26	22	297,445
Bridgette Sipp	304	38	33	31	294,305
Franks Farms	238	37	43	29	1,260,812
TradeWinds Stable	151	37	25	25	644,924
William Stiritz	176	37	22	23	635,309
Francis C. McDonnell	179	37	28	17	562,543
E and G Stables	127	37	29	18	480,842
Lynne M. Scace	186	37	22	30	356,460
K. K. Sangara	156	36	30	20	1,371,131
Daniel M. Ryan	174	36	24	23	643,404
Juddmonte Farms, Inc.	113	35	20	7	3,454,794
Dennis E. Weir	148	35	32	21	602,656
Cartagena, Julio and Feinberg, Robert	113	35	17	10	509,121
Stix-N-Stones Stable and Miller, Thomas	200	35	23	32	293,557
James L. Nicholson	216	35	34	31	258,397
Blackjack Stables LLC	265	35	38	40	189,830
Jay Em Ess Stable	142	34	22	16	2,290,203
Stan E. Fulton	214	34	28	28	1,726,957
Jayeff B Stables	199	34	31	26	1,100,004
Danny A. Limongelli	236	34	38	26	528,976
Stephen M. Zimmerman	165	34	22	29	251,496
Slick 1 Racing	157	34	22	26	227,439
Oak Tree Stables, Inc. and Cheyenne Stable LLC	114	34	12	15	208,319
Moss, Mr. and Mrs. Jerome S.	203	33	30	29	1,185,965
Everest Stables, Inc.	321	32	36	31	2,036,755
Mrs. E Paul Robsham	142	32	31	25	1,420,947
Valene Farms	150	32	31	21	858,357
J B Stables, Inc.	190	32	22	13	532,201
Wags Nags LLC	198	32	22	27	481,613
William M. Rickman	156	32	24	22	403,497
Adam Sobczak	218	32	44	21	249,142
Darley Stable	204	31	34	28	2,235,777
B. Wayne Hughes	173	31	31	20	1,269,571
Peter Vegso	172	31	20	25	1,165,741
Worcester Stable	218	31	35	22	544,778
Stephen A. Richardson	181	31	23	21	317,784
Tracy Farmer	102	30	11	15	1,823,046
G. Watts Humphrey, Jr.	229	30	25	36	1,073,816
Kupferberg, Saul J. and Max	172	30	19	28	621,739
J. Jeps Stable	204	30	22	26	374,075
J. Michael Baird	125	30	24	10	366,203
Klein, Richard, Bertram and Elaine	163	29	29	19	991,126
Daniel Franko	217	29	24	30	434,346
Jack L. Boggs	145	29	26	14	380,835
Diamond G Ranch, Inc.	152	29	27	15	321,855
Peachtree Stable	108	28	17	11	913,993
Dare To Dream Stable LLC	158	28	26	17	642,884
Michael G. Weatherly	116	28	19	11	375,626
901 Racing Stables LLC	93	28	15	9	348,639
Edward Clouston	207	28	26	21	313,775
Frank D. Di Giulio, Jr.	125	27	23	16	1,748,615
Dominion Bloodstock, Ball, Derek and Galbraith, Hugh	193	27	22	23	1,370,014
Tucci Stables	113	27	22	12	1,198,671
Harris Farms, Inc.	169	27	38	26	1,103,810
New Farm	106	27	13	17	929,275
Russell L. Reineman Stable, Inc.	100	27	13	11	651,780
Robert J. Amendola	95	27	14	13	641,278
River Ridge Ranch	217	27	19	35	590,939
Tulip Hill Farm	128	27	20	15	446,229
James T. Hines, Jr.	165	27	21	19	397,507
Loren G. Cox	236	27	37	18	395,449
Thunderbolt Racing LLC	100	27	19	10	332,075
Michael A. Lecesse	124	27	18	20	327,279

Owner	St	1st	2d	3d	Purses
WinStar Farm LLC	160	26	29	13	768,546
Silverton Hill LLC	149	26	22	17	709,448
Diamond Oak Stable	95	26	20	9	582,372
Nick Sanna Stables, Inc.	107	26	19	10	464,475
D D Stable	176	26	20	30	365,625
Charles P. Hukill	229	26	32	30	344,361
Barry K. Schwartz	147	25	14	21	809,844
Tommy Town T'breds LLC	133	25	18	13	711,363
Orion Stables	308	25	32	31	547,208
Tom R. Durant	174	25	16	19	535,838
Raymond W. Makarovich, Jr.	74	25	13	14	432,046
Kaaren J. Biggs	128	25	22	19	414,715
Wimp Free Racing Stables	79	25	17	9	370,170
Armando Lage	143	25	21	15	361,741
Thomas Vanderhyde	126	25	24	24	341,178
British Mist Racing	164	25	22	28	163,482
Wygod, Mr. and Mrs. Martin J.	117	24	21	13	1,753,972
Broman, Sr., Mary and Chester	187	24	22	25	1,487,891
Puglisi Stables	115	24	26	14	1,101,587
William S. Farish	113	24	23	12	1,044,381
Glen Hill Farm	114	24	20	13	734,532
Edwin Thomas Broome	134	24	27	17	686,183
Karakorum Farm	131	24	16	15	671,883
La Marca Stable	124	24	17	23	558,553
Lanning, Curt and Lila	206	24	44	35	556,443
The Elkstone Group LLC	243	24	37	31	524,349
D. J. Stable LLC	124	24	12	17	430,124
Kjell H. Qvale	171	24	26	27	359,326
Southern Nevada Racing Stables, Inc.	105	24	15	14	310,673
Rolf Obrecht	177	24	26	25	246,534
Widman, Larry and Hansen, Russell	109	24	19	19	195,640
Jim Bausch	233	24	24	21	193,399
Meyaard, Jim and Logan, Terry E.	132	24	18	22	113,688
Varue Wilson	113	24	22	12	45,549
Nelson Bunker Hunt	165	23	26	20	771,365
Taylor Mountain Farm LLC	156	23	25	20	690,091
Rose Family Stable	272	23	24	27	561,198
Keith I. Asmussen	99	23	19	9	448,914
Donald R. Dizney	134	23	19	13	439,087
La Canada Stable LLC	109	23	15	9	413,327
Don Eberts	85	23	6	9	327,609
Roger Davis	63	23	8	10	256,879
Lorraine E. Barberino	105	23	9	7	218,675
Anjo Racing, Inc.	131	23	19	13	163,290
J. Paul Reddam	125	22	17	13	1,140,168
Kinsman Stable	110	22	13	16	745,352
Alex G. Campbell, Jr.	114	22	9	10	530,703
Colebrook Farms	187	22	22	22	454,069
Darrell R. Sapp	203	22	30	27	328,638
Finish Line Racing Stable	74	22	11	13	325,610
Herb Riecken	150	22	19	26	236,013
Robert E. Roussel	127	22	7	11	212,016
Delphine Miller	101	22	15	16	176,092
Stevark Stable, Inc.	118	22	18	6	156,786
William J. Amos	99	22	16	17	156,532
Henry Aversa	103	22	19	16	153,536
Richaleen Turpin	154	22	21	22	144,194
Gary A. Tanaka	136	21	22	16	3,112,187
J D Farms	154	21	24	20	920,455
Jacks or Better Farm, Inc.	193	21	30	17	709,102
Arthur I. Appleton	104	21	18	17	559,067
C. R. Trout	132	21	16	23	554,479
Michel A. Ward, II	259	21	31	25	452,387
Wexler Racing Stables, Inc.	200	21	20	25	423,297
Frank J. Regalbuto	117	21	14	16	413,765
Doneson, Mark and Dubb, Michael	113	21	19	15	364,611
Doris Hebert	119	21	22	18	268,390
Roos, Manfred and Rigattieri, John	62	21	9	2	201,581
Peggy Faulkner	111	21	23	15	147,495
Edmund A. Gann	68	20	16	8	2,639,725
Amerman Racing Stables LLC	93	20	16	12	1,454,199
Klaravich Stables, Inc.	73	20	10	8	1,178,597
Jones, Aaron U. and Marie D.	72	20	11	7	960,621
Erdenheim Farm	121	20	20	19	807,398
Vincent S. Scuderi	67	20	11	13	634,783
Wilson, David W. and Holly F.	112	20	15	16	605,329
David J. Lanzman Racing Stable, Inc.	73	20	5	8	581,652
Gary and Mary West Stables, Inc.	68	20	14	5	551,845
S J B Stable	134	20	15	14	505,434
Foxwood Plantation, Ltd.	90	20	10	14	473,888
Morris Bailey	92	20	13	18	472,072
Richard Malouf	81	20	8	16	426,315
John D. McKee	215	20	20	25	381,617
Ersoff Racing Stable Inc.	120	20	18	18	380,330
Rey Wan Racing	137	20	22	23	375,350
Manfred Roos	105	20	22	15	355,272
Jer-Mar Stable LLC	68	20	9	12	339,502
Kevin J. Joy	104	20	16	9	328,727
James A. Michael	147	20	22	24	268,468
Leonard Liberto	95	20	19	9	263,219
Dream Walkin Farms, Inc.	108	20	14	14	250,460
STD Racing Stable	124	20	12	24	232,922
Bruce D. Anderson	150	20	20	32	207,929
Barbara Rehbein	163	20	22	19	203,646
Shane M. Spiess	240	20	27	31	182,770
Martin Brothers, Inc.	157	20	20	28	176,605
Jerry L. Balo	79	20	6	4	163,482
Larry A. Byer	122	20	19	13	163,125
Paul H. Horton	120	20	12	12	158,327
Diamond J Ranch	134	20	21	13	128,465
Kenneth Collins	71	20	11	7	126,773
Charles David Nielsen	84	20	14	9	124,766
Jim Hill	65	20	10	8	118,227
Charles Lawson	165	20	26	29	108,296
Homer Thoroughbreds	111	20	20	14	53,263
Ogden Mills Phipps	63	19	15	7	1,780,647
Joseph V. Shields, Jr.	93	19	15	14	835,148
Courtlandt Farms	96	19	16	10	816,645
William L. Clifton, Jr.	117	19	15	13	690,301
Centaur Farms, Inc.	169	19	23	24	668,344
Herbert Washington Chambers	206	19	14	21	544,908
Roddy J. Valente	72	19	17	5	543,260
Jayaraman, Kalarikkal K. and Vilasini D.	109	19	18	17	415,707
Tricar Stable, Inc.	210	19	24	33	392,120
Coast To Coast Racing Fund LLC	79	19	15	14	389,528
John L. Stahlin	141	19	27	20	359,144
Harry C. and Tom O. Meyerhoff LLC	91	19	14	11	358,160
Dresden Farm	124	19	20	17	353,009
Daniel J. Lopez	84	19	20	10	348,845
Lori Goodz	45	19	5	2	332,776
Francis J. Paolangeli	84	19	3	16	318,194
Kim Noble Hart	97	19	20	8	310,983
McCarty Racing	75	19	12	13	290,420
Ruberto Racing Stable, Inc.	64	19	13	6	284,369
Diglett Stable	75	19	12	8	275,708
John W. Baird	139	19	15	19	273,856
Murphy, Timothy and Brown, Dave E.	219	19	21	28	269,764
Eugene E. Weymouth	100	19	11	17	243,206
Red Ron Farms	95	19	15	11	181,595
Ricky Faulkner	160	19	19	26	148,100
Hammond, Everett and Cox, Robert L.	97	19	18	12	129,923

Owner	Starts	1st	2d	3d	Purses
S. T. C. Racing	106	19	11	12	128,196
C. Les Hogg	65	19	8	10	117,354
Yo Racing	100	19	20	18	63,768
Redbird Farm	44	19	5	8	38,890
Michael B. Tabor	54	18	14	4	1,877,867
Kelynack Racing Stable, Inc.	135	18	24	22	1,175,422
Patricia A. Generazio	226	18	21	29	643,680
Charles, Ronald L. and Clear Valley Stables	94	18	13	6	576,371
Molinaro Stable	134	18	18	17	574,127
Fox Hill Farms, Inc.	85	18	12	10	554,633
Our Sugar Bear Stable	101	18	15	9	536,914
Scarberry, Howard and Penny	160	18	23	13	507,970
Nickolas DeToro	123	18	11	18	505,738
Vinery Stables	66	18	10	8	500,690
Cobra Farm, Inc.	67	18	8	6	425,169
Ron Crockett, Inc.	103	18	27	19	377,073
Harry J. Aleo	53	18	7	8	370,676
William R. Harris	150	18	19	19	288,287
Joseph P. Morey, Jr. Revocable Trust	76	18	16	10	263,024
Walter T. Bates	87	18	12	15	260,835
Victory Thoroughbreds LLC	72	18	10	8	257,327
Michael L. Reavis	81	18	13	8	252,245
Efrain T. Garcia	150	18	15	17	249,434
Peruvian Glass and More, Inc.	193	18	11	28	223,564
Gold N. Z. Stable	48	18	4	7	202,665
Indian Mills Stock Farm	114	18	15	14	196,339
Clifford W. Sise, Jr.	97	18	13	13	180,034
David C. George	150	18	13	18	167,044
Boyce K. Gooch	139	18	23	15	153,290
Zimbler, Bettie L. and Gary A.	67	18	10	10	94,234
Christy R. Johnson	96	18	11	12	80,652
Jaqueline Smith	80	18	17	9	42,887
Gabriel Road Stables	51	18	4	6	33,552
Team Block	122	17	21	16	979,018
Craig, Sidney H. and Jenny	106	17	22	15	664,800
William A. Carl	93	17	18	6	577,142
West, Gary L. and Mary E.	67	17	8	8	559,112
John Cardella	113	17	13	19	558,747
Williams, Mr. and Mrs. Larry D.	87	17	14	8	540,834
Ocean Front Property and Asmussen, Keith	71	17	15	12	512,812
Michael Dubb	127	17	20	16	484,558
Dennis A. Drazin	109	17	15	15	452,767
James B. Tafel	71	17	2	7	451,744
Cohen, Philip and Marcia and Klesaris, Steve	54	17	9	7	447,318
Ben Barnow	122	17	8	21	400,064
Destiny Farm LLC	131	17	22	16	390,468
Rainbow Stable	108	17	25	13	377,713
Robert Bakerman	161	17	20	17	364,624
Hendrickson Farms LLC	111	17	7	16	333,240
J. and G. Murphy Holdings, Ltd.	110	17	7	13	314,709
Silver Diamond T'breds, Inc.	116	17	10	9	311,458
Dany Dion	119	17	18	21	281,673
Greenoaks Farm	91	17	12	10	272,743
Walnut View Farms Inc.	64	17	13	10	262,970
Authors Stable LLC	120	17	20	18	240,215
Carrol S. Langley	155	17	22	22	235,979
Covenant Stable	122	17	15	17	230,558
Terry Eoff	94	17	18	10	213,655
Blue Streak Stable	105	17	14	13	207,614
Paul J. Matties, Jr.	93	17	12	9	197,231
Jose A. Martinez	180	17	30	25	169,709
Richard T. Beal, Jr.	81	17	13	12	156,322
M. Anthony Ferraro	124	17	17	13	153,889
Rosebud Stable, Inc. and Leonard, III, George	107	17	10	18	138,929
Mast Thoroughbreds LLC and Gorham, Robert M.	74	17	12	4	134,389
Lathrop, David and Priscilla	110	17	14	14	133,252
Dick Cappellucci	63	17	5	12	132,271
Ronnie Duke	131	17	13	15	89,869
Willmott Stables, Inc.	104	16	15	19	1,352,569
Martin S. Schwartz	72	16	8	17	942,640
Mercedes Stables LLC	89	16	14	18	923,998
West Point Stable	95	16	15	9	742,076
Kuehne Racing	86	16	10	12	687,649
Peter F. Karches	81	16	14	14	621,829
Hobeau Farm	99	16	10	20	576,101
Sondra D. Bender	112	16	20	13	555,995
J. Mack Robinson	183	16	23	21	503,066
Deckert, Robert, Jr. and Robert, Sr.	115	16	17	11	497,500
Audre Cappuccittl	146	16	11	13	480,329
Stony Oak Farm LLC	105	16	17	8	460,419
Win and Place Stable	85	16	17	13	390,946
Jane M. Freed	56	16	9	5	381,479
John Castro	101	16	13	20	374,425
The Nonsequitur Stable LLC	63	16	8	9	372,985
Camelia J. Casby	119	16	17	13	346,878
Goldish, Marc D. and Savoy Stable	80	16	18	9	337,140
Timber Creek Farms	58	16	16	5	329,062
Ted Taylor	119	16	14	17	319,786
Richter, Kristine and John	89	16	11	10	305,152
Porter Racing Stable LLC	89	16	4	8	291,320
Kay Hale	81	16	11	8	277,715
C. L. Nix	151	16	16	17	269,960
Robert D. Nash	88	16	10	14	264,577
Yasou Stable Trust	88	16	18	11	254,716
Broadwall Farm	103	16	23	14	240,957
Steven Dwoskin	96	16	17	10	239,252
Harry L. Veruchi	89	16	11	17	239,241
Anthony Barbanti	76	16	15	13	230,018
Two C Stables	107	16	16	13	229,304
Barry R. Ostrager	87	16	10	12	227,539
Timber Creek Farm	162	16	20	17	217,892
One and Won Stable	102	16	15	12	215,326
Johnny A. Butler	100	16	12	20	209,072
Six Brothers Stable	122	16	16	13	202,148
Bluestem Farm, Inc.	101	16	12	13	199,916
Lloyd W. Lockhart	140	16	16	9	192,505
Pecoraro Racing Stable	128	16	17	23	190,199
Versatile Thoroughbreds LLC and Lawson, Russell	88	16	8	10	190,004
Equest Racing Stable LLC	79	16	11	9	185,271
KAT Racing Stable	56	16	11	7	177,073
R.E.V. Racing	115	16	27	6	156,444
J. D. Riker	68	16	14	10	129,109
M. C. R. Stable	57	16	10	11	107,236
James R. Compton	82	16	15	14	78,727
David C. Anderson	54	16	7	9	62,096
Marylou Whitney Stables	68	15	9	5	1,628,890
James McIngvale	73	15	12	16	1,396,671
John D. Gunther	83	15	19	5	1,350,580
Gustav Schickedanz	80	15	12	9	954,606
Anstu Stables, Inc.	58	15	10	7	898,747
Shadwell Stable	108	15	16	13	774,189
Paul P. Pompa, Jr.	143	15	24	15	680,153
Winchell Thoroughbreds LLC	100	15	14	19	603,156
Asiel Stable	120	15	17	18	590,930
Martin L. Cherry	65	15	12	6	578,184
Jeffrey Sengara	72	15	17	14	559,764
Joseph S. Parisi	121	15	15	16	518,212
Carlo D'Amato	176	15	17	14	508,243
The Merv Griffin Ranch Co.	51	15	9	4	478,101
Scott A. Lake	67	15	13	7	411,681
Mrs. S. K. Johnston, Jr.	101	15	13	6	401,639
Linda S. Gaudet	96	15	17	8	366,620
Donald E. Souder	185	15	25	25	358,301
William Dorminy	36	15	5	4	355,767

Owner	Starts	1st	2d	3d	Purses
IEAH Stables	75	15	14	9	276,786
Annecchini, Frank and D'Alimonte Holdings, Inc.	99	15	8	6	268,790
Amestoy, Pierre Jean and Leslie A.	71	15	12	3	234,049
Michael De Saye	84	15	12	14	232,543
Crown Valley Stable	65	15	6	11	230,003
Leland P. Cook	98	15	13	18	228,932
Eutrophia Farm	68	15	8	11	223,273
Lara Racing Stables, Ltd.	123	15	12	11	208,149
Charles W. Everett	103	15	12	22	207,326
Par 3 Stables	71	15	10	14	207,235
McClay, Thomas and Nye, Harry	54	15	5	8	204,832
Olympia Stables	87	15	8	13	187,345
Gentry Farms	106	15	15	16	184,164
Dennis G. Punches	86	15	16	15	183,080
Darryl B. Jackson	30	15	5	2	178,921
Scarlet Stable	82	15	9	7	178,336
Joel Slavens Racing Stable	107	15	24	13	178,256
Joseph E. Asbell	114	15	17	10	176,471
Driver, Ywachetta H. and James Travis	54	15	6	11	175,790
One Pond Stable	65	15	4	5	175,674
Wafer T'bred Ranch, Inc.	85	15	10	6	169,855
Herman Sarkowsky	44	15	6	7	166,822
Michael J. Clare	81	15	9	10	164,704
P and G Stable and C D and G Stable	34	15	5	4	161,850
Green River Stable	112	15	8	11	157,470
Wire To Wire Stable, Inc.	68	15	12	12	154,484
James S. Acquilano	65	15	7	8	150,268
Eilers, Marilyn and Larry J.	143	15	16	25	142,756
Sun Stable	63	15	13	10	141,312
Novak, Marshall L. and Suzanne	81	15	11	15	132,759
Ken Russell	39	15	5	6	124,974
H. Joseph Allen	66	15	5	6	115,854
Bryant H. Prentice, III	59	15	3	9	115,033
Mary Ann Thomas	116	15	16	26	89,476
Pamela D. Hall	51	15	7	8	79,224
Larry J. Cronin	86	15	8	13	78,669
James F. Yaegel	107	15	14	12	70,093
Grenier, Dennis and Norine	59	15	8	7	69,726
Myron D. Kumke	92	15	16	14	69,163
Robert V. LaPenta	74	14	14	9	2,001,302
Jay Manoogian	43	14	5	7	1,143,031
T N T Stud	61	14	15	8	977,625
Weatherwatch Farm and Valente, Roddy	43	14	6	5	511,761
Lazy Lane Farms, Inc.	58	14	12	10	464,636
John H. Peace	86	14	12	13	463,630
Sanford J. Goldfarb	50	14	6	5	434,898
Nancy A. Vanier	102	14	14	13	432,202
Fitzhugh LLC	63	14	12	10	411,887
McKee Stables, Inc.	66	14	10	10	400,890
Albert Fried, Jr.	103	14	13	11	387,009
Jerry Jamgotchian	94	14	9	12	327,882
Robert S. Mitchell Trust	114	14	18	17	319,814
David A. Ross	105	14	13	17	304,676
Terry Bruner	110	14	17	15	282,809
Confetti Farms, Inc.	81	14	18	14	280,502
Martha T. Gallaway	89	14	20	9	268,844
Prosser, Eric and Kathy	108	14	15	22	265,534
Circle S Ranch, Inc.	124	14	27	16	257,798
Cynthia E. O'Bannon	203	14	15	21	249,542
Paul M. Steckel	50	14	12	9	247,490
John Charles Zimmerman	59	14	4	6	245,221
Belvoir, Howard, Corby, Dan and Hoppe, Harley	103	14	11	16	242,773
Casino Royale Farm, Inc.	68	14	6	6	236,247
Lloyd DeBruycker	110	14	21	11	223,918
Girdner, Paul K. and Jones, Reginald C.	95	14	11	7	223,682
Mast Thoroughbreds LLC, Bieke, Ron and Gorham, Robert M.	101	14	17	20	223,139
Gilmore, Gene and Phyllis	63	14	14	13	221,608
Against The Wind	90	14	11	7	212,402
Tangarae Farms LLP	127	14	23	16	210,383
Well-Being Stable	71	14	15	13	208,850
Prime Time Stable	91	14	13	9	198,724
Fast Forward Racing Stable LLC	40	14	8	3	196,611
Anita Racing Stable	114	14	24	13	183,759
Martha K. Struthers	115	14	17	27	166,501
Lathrop G. Hoffman	60	14	12	6	165,575
East Coast Stables LLC	121	14	24	16	162,042
James E. Hess	42	14	5	8	160,135
Donald L. Griffin	66	14	14	13	146,966
Larry H. Carlton	67	14	8	6	136,388
Shrum Racing, Inc.	103	14	19	9	132,922
Rosebud Stable	88	14	10	10	114,490
R-W Racing Stable, Inc.	103	14	14	17	114,259
Gwen Reading	79	14	13	12	103,888
Alan Booge Racing, Inc.	64	14	7	6	100,721
Theresa Anderson	95	14	13	14	82,069
Suits Me Farm LLC	70	14	7	8	75,730
Chad M. Ferguson	76	14	9	8	62,563
John W. Layton	58	14	2	8	41,007
Jim Gilmour	88	14	10	6	36,608
Lowell N. Bunyard	72	14	9	13	29,720
Smith, Derrick and Tabor, Michael	48	13	15	7	2,097,526
Chiefswood Stable	72	13	9	9	1,335,774
Phipps, Ogden Mills, et al	41	13	4	11	1,020,649
Santa Cruz Ranch, Inc.	112	13	13	9	712,343
Knob Hill Stable	92	13	19	7	596,778
Earle I. Mack	81	13	11	12	583,714
Mac Fehsenfeld	132	13	16	30	526,405
Chandler, Dr. John A.	32	13	4	2	466,604
Ivan Dalos	93	13	12	12	466,158
Steel Your Face Stables and Emily Racing Stables	33	13	7	6	432,366
Golden, Bruce and Lake, Scott	51	13	11	8	409,971
Star Track Farms	124	13	8	20	401,136
Namcook Stables LLC	93	13	13	9	395,881
Kinross Farm	71	13	10	15	390,540
William M. Backer	97	13	7	12	390,323
Norseman Racing Stable	53	13	2	2	389,215
Robert H. Shepard	128	13	16	20	381,377
Howard Roberts Farm	95	13	8	15	352,430
Laurence I. Foggle	54	13	9	8	345,550
Oxbow Racing LLC	86	13	11	14	335,850
Dale K. S. Lucas	74	13	16	13	323,943
Carey K. Miller	43	13	4	10	322,182
Calmar Stables and Ranch	77	13	11	16	310,383
Rowell Enterprises, Inc.	55	13	9	5	309,580
Michael W. Jester	53	13	16	7	283,233
Seven Oaks Farm	69	13	10	12	282,800
Blackjack Thoroughbreds	96	13	18	13	278,859
Veranda Farm, Inc.	54	13	6	6	263,129
Carolyn K. Friedberg	57	13	10	8	243,614
Thomas G. McClay	62	13	9	7	235,871
Arnold Heppner	37	13	3	5	233,286
Donald H. Mensh	54	13	9	11	221,225
Donald R. Cox	79	13	16	7	212,961
S. A. Partnership	83	13	4	6	211,821
Baker, Charlton and Frankel, Richard	57	13	13	13	208,563
William T. Reed	104	13	9	9	202,469
Script R Farm	73	13	6	10	200,425
Quadrun Farm LLC	71	13	12	15	199,410

Owner	Starts	1st	2d	3d	Purses
Mrs. James B. Moseley	72	13	8	12	198,871
Tae Shin	71	13	10	10	195,368
Deep Rock Farm	71	13	16	4	194,860
Debra E. Kachel	47	13	8	8	187,703
Billingsley Creek Ranch	55	13	10	8	186,453
Patrick Q. Maguire	60	13	7	7	185,163
R Legacy Racing, Inc. and Stokes, Lonnie	44	13	12	6	179,737
Horky, Theresa and Shelansky, Keith	90	13	13	11	164,806
Carrol Castille	50	13	8	5	162,619
Stacey Moak	52	13	9	3	161,242
William R. Yeagley III	77	13	7	9	160,513
Sandra Hall Trust	64	13	9	17	158,259
Greg Frye	54	13	4	7	153,200
Scooter Davis	61	13	9	8	152,187
Florence Gemma Siravo	177	13	21	23	148,909
Fred A. Nemann	88	13	13	8	147,894
Stephen R. Baker	99	13	16	13	145,707
Georgeades, James and Dasher, Gregge	70	13	8	3	143,693
Karen M. Kunes	92	13	8	15	138,348
F and S Stables, Inc.	69	13	8	4	135,330
Agnes J. Perdue	97	13	12	14	129,193
Big Bad Thoroughbreds, Inc.	54	13	6	10	127,143
Israel Flores	113	13	16	14	126,686
American T'bred Stable LLC	41	13	6	1	125,181
Gilley, Bob and Quinn, James	42	13	6	5	125,121
Al J. Horton	98	13	11	17	118,248
L and D Farm	119	13	7	10	116,845
Jami C. Poole	90	13	7	12	108,387
Michael Newell	203	13	21	19	108,313
Dona M. Albright	104	13	14	14	104,842
Robert M. Gorham	75	13	17	9	92,390
Leavitt Thoroughbreds LLC	81	13	8	10	92,364
Chris Powell	144	13	6	15	91,037
Gary Page	83	13	13	10	72,548
Robert D. Lawrence	85	13	8	14	66,444
Bruce W. Williams	47	13	6	7	52,017
Linda Grace	36	13	5	4	23,474
Cowan, Marge and Irving M.	48	12	13	6	1,256,319
Cappuccitti, Audre and Gordon	148	12	22	25	804,069
Haras Santa Maria de Araras	119	12	19	13	642,459
Joseph J. Balsamo	65	12	10	14	614,031
C R K Stable	54	12	6	10	565,457
John C. Oxley	86	12	14	13	558,444
Team Valor Stables LLC	75	12	15	8	549,295
Michael E. Pegram	79	12	5	7	492,401
Steel Your Face Stables	45	12	8	9	464,996
Lewis G. Lakin	32	12	2	3	443,906
Timothy Cunningham	88	12	17	18	423,429
Lee Lewis	56	12	11	5	394,786
David Beard	65	12	9	10	384,575
Toby Roth	96	12	26	13	371,029
Glen C. Warren	84	12	9	13	370,582
Goldmart Farms	107	12	12	14	361,448
Steeplechase Farm	57	12	10	12	319,810
Walter Family Trust	101	12	13	15	313,466
Jim H. Plemmons	88	12	11	9	306,438
Richard Lueck	37	12	5	6	291,034
Linwood Stables	76	12	9	5	284,768
Elaine C. Bassford	35	12	7	4	278,120
James H. Stone	48	12	5	5	258,763
Shotwell Farm	124	12	13	15	255,380
Triple AAA Ranch	84	12	13	11	253,908
Arthur B. Hancock, III	63	12	13	6	244,266
Kamikaze Stable	111	12	24	18	242,474
Barr Three LLC	116	12	12	8	237,491
William J. Hartwell	65	12	9	9	236,252
Robert Corrado	134	12	17	9	232,721
Wam Stable	127	12	14	18	230,382
Grunwald Racing LLC	45	12	7	11	223,656
Donald D. Orbovich	84	12	11	8	219,557
Emmanuel Tzortzakis	58	12	9	11	216,555
Drumlanrig Farm	41	12	8	3	214,635
Hidden Lane Farms, Inc.	46	12	8	4	214,076
High Mesa Racing LLC	56	12	6	8	211,986
K 5 Stables	95	12	22	11	210,647
Roger A. Nickol	98	12	9	11	210,430
James A. Griffin	58	12	9	8	209,707
Old Coach Farm	106	12	20	13	207,517
Taylor, Kenneth, et al	65	12	10	16	206,325
Joseph F. Orseno	65	12	5	11	204,141
Woodvale Farm	135	12	16	21	203,189
Winfred L. Hess, Jr.	50	12	4	5	202,362
Michael F. Buccina	81	12	10	8	194,081
Hugh H. Robertson	50	12	9	6	192,100
Charles Moneypenny	38	12	6	6	189,285
Tony Schuler	51	12	9	2	188,477
Evans, Marty and Jimmy T.	58	12	6	12	187,339
Sunshine Hill Farm	100	12	18	20	186,070
Rafter L Stables	57	12	12	2	183,389
R. Sidney Brown, II	55	12	6	7	175,055
Jeremy J. Gassman	45	12	9	6	172,648
Rick Wiest	63	12	8	3	169,083
Tbd Owners LLC	159	12	14	26	160,579
A. A. C. Stables	68	12	15	10	158,279
Todd M. Beattie	26	12	6	2	149,356
Dennis J. Federico	39	12	5	8	144,185
David W. Geist	89	12	17	12	135,202
Carl T. Bowling	43	12	4	4	127,615
Win Stable	44	12	6	8	117,040
Warwick Stable	51	12	11	4	115,721
Anne L. Walsh	79	12	6	13	113,272
Red Top Racing Stable	57	12	11	6	113,161
A. B. Chevy Stable	71	12	10	6	110,201
Denis Cluley	47	12	4	7	107,477
JON Stable	110	12	11	9	107,019
Robert Calhoun	58	12	14	7	105,228
Gary Marrone	97	12	12	12	104,891
Cynthia K. Bayley	65	12	7	9	103,495
Lori L. Lockhart	90	12	5	10	90,245
Double D Farm Corp.	56	12	6	6	87,074
Team Cobra	41	12	7	5	84,001
Seawind Stables LLC	95	12	9	13	81,097
Gerald R. Richards	62	12	12	5	75,755
Nancy Wood	67	12	16	11	73,938
John C. Rupert	65	12	13	7	70,843
Jamison, Michael, et al	46	12	9	4	66,789
Beverly Hamilton	38	12	5	5	60,372
Alex A. Moretti	38	12	4	7	59,917
Gregory W. Biddell	61	12	11	3	57,732
Sandra Lee Smith	59	12	9	8	55,793
Daniel Miller	33	12	13	3	34,582

Snapshot Facts: There were 36 owners whose horses won 50 or more races in 2004. Seventeen owners won more than 75 races and 10 won more than 100.

Annual Leading Owner – Money Won

Year	Owner	Earnings
1902	Green B. Morris	$98,350
1903	William C. Whitney	102,569
1904	H.B. Duryea	200,107
1905	James R. Keene	228,724
1906	James R. Keene	155,519
1907	James R. Keene	397,342
1908	James R. Keene	282,342
1909	Samuel C. Hildreth	159,112
1910	Samuel C. Hildreth	152,645
1911	Samuel C. Hildreth	47,473
1912	John W. Schorr	58,225
1913	Harry Payne Whitney	55,056
1914	John W. Schorr	85,326
1915	L.S. Thompson	104,106
1916	H. Guy Bedwell	71,100
1917	A. King Macomber	68,578
1918	J.K.L. Ross	99,179
1919	J.K.L. Ross	209,303
1920	Harry Payne Whitney	270,675
1921	Rancocas Stable (Harry F. Sinclair)	263,500
1922	Rancocas Stable (Harry F. Sinclair)	239,503
1923	Rancocas Stable (Harry F. Sinclair)	438,849
1924	Harry Payne Whitney	240,193
1925	Glen Riddle Farm Stable (Samuel D. Riddle)	199,143
1926	Harry Payne Whitney	407,139
1927	Harry Payne Whitney	328,769
1928	Edward B. McLean	234,640
1929	Harry Payne Whitney	362,305
1930	C.V. Whitney	385,972
1931	C.V. Whitney	422,923
1932	C.V. Whitney	403,681
1933	C.V. Whitney	241,292
1934	Brookmeade Stable (Mrs. Dodge Soane)	251,138
1935	A.G. Vanderbilt	303,605
1936	Milky Way Farm (Mrs. Ethel V. Mars)	206,450
1937	Mrs. Charles S. Howard	214,559
1938	H. Maxwell Howard	226,495
1939	Belair Stud (William Woodward)	284,250
1940	Charles S. Howard	334,120
1941	Calumet Farm (Warren Wright)	475,091
1942	Greentree Stable (Mrs. Payne Whitney)	414,432
1943	Calumet Farm (Warren Wright)	267,915
1944	Calumet Farm (Warren Wright)	601,660
1945	Maine Chance Farm (Mrs. Elizabeth N. Graham)	589,170
1946	Calumet Farm (Warren Wright)	564,095
1947	Calumet Farm (Warren Wright)	1,402,436
1948	Calumet Farm (Warren Wright)	1,269,710
1949	Calumet Farm (Warren Wright)	1,128,942
1950	Brookmeade Stable (Mrs. Dodge Sloane)	651,399
1951	Greentree Stable (Mrs. C.S. Payne & J.H. Whitney)	637,242
1952	Calumet Farm (Mrs. Gene Markey)	1,283,197
1953	A.G. Vanderbilt	987,306
1954	King Ranch (Robert J. Kleberg Jr.)	837,615
1955	Hasty House Farm (Mr. & Mrs. A.E. Reuben)	832,879
1956	Calumet Farm (Mrs. Gene Markey)	1,057,383
1957	Calumet Farm (Mrs. Gene Markey)	1,150,910
1958	Calumet Farm (Mrs. Gene Markey)	946,262
1959	Cain Hoy Stable (H.F. Guggenheim)	742,081
1960	C.V. Whitney	1,039,091
1961	Calumet Farm (Mrs. Gene Markey)	759,856
1962	Ellsworth Stable (Rex C. Ellsworth)	1,154,454
1963	Ellsworth Stable (Rex C. Ellsworth)	1,096,863
1964	Wheatley Stable (Mrs. Henry C. Phipps)	1,073,572
1965	Marion H. Van Berg	895,246
1966	Wheatley Stable (Mrs. Henry C. Phipps)	1,225,861
1967	Hobeau Farm (J.J. Dreyfus Jr.)	1,120,143
1968	Marion H. Van Berg	1,105,388
1969	Marion H. Van Berg	1,453,679
1970	Marion H. Van Berg	1,347,289
1971	Sigmund Sommer	1,523,508
1972	Sigmund Sommer	1,605,896
1973	Dan R. Lasater	1,498,785
1974	Dan R. Lasater	3,022,960
1975	Dan R. Lasater	2,894,726
1976	Dan R. Lasater	2,894,074
1977	Elmendorf (Max Gluck)	2,309,200
1978	Harbor View Farm	2,097,443
1979	Harbor View Farm	2,701,741
1980	Harbor View Farm	2,207,576
1981	Elmendorf (Max Gluck)	1,928,102
1982	Viola Sommer	2,182,626
1983	John Franks	2,643,251
1984	John Franks	3,070,225
1985	Mr. & Mrs. Eugene V. Klein	5,451,201
1986	John Franks	4,463,375
1987	Mr. & Mrs. Eugene V. Klein	5,746,334
1988	Ogden Phipps	5,858,168
1989	Ogden Phipps	5,438,034
1990	Kinghaven Farms	5,041,280
1991	Sam-Son Farm	6,881,902
1992	Golden Eagle Farm	5,479,484
1993	John Franks	5,682,786
1994	John Franks	4,518,083
1995	Allen Paulson	7,238,800
1996	Overbrook Farm	7,008,802
1997	Allen Paulson	5,259,107
1998	Stronach Stable	7,221,416
1999	Stronach Stable	6,221,147
2000	Stronach Stable	11,198,225
2001	Richard A. Englander	9,783,472
2002	Stronach Stable	8,349,249
2003	Michael J. Gill	9,236,530
2004	Michael J. Gill	10,835,561

Annual Leading Owner – Races Won

Year	Owner	Amount Won	Races Won
1905	E. Corrigan	$41,465	100
1906	B. Schreiber	85,713	120
1907	B. Schreiber	68,068	105
1908	B. Schreiber	88,329	110
1909	B. Schreiber	54,475	143
1910	R.F. Carman	64,440	105
1911	W.B. Carson	16,690	74
1912	H. Guy Bedwell	47,452	103
1913	H. Guy Bedwell	40,475	80
1914	H. Guy Bedwell	50,465	87
1915	H. Guy Bedwell	59,530	123
1916	H. Guy Bedwell	71,100	136
1917	H. Guy Bedwell	38,790	65
1918	R.D. &P.J. Williams	55,831	77
1919	K. Spence	40,080	67
1920	J.K.L. Ross	250,586	118
1921	J.K.L. Ross	167,642	88
1922	J.K.L. Ross	169,134	78
1923	C.B. Irwin	104,054	147
1924	H. Guy Bedwell	106,580	86
1925	G. Frank Croissant	112,081	86
1926	Harry Payne Whitney	407,139	122
1927	Seagram Stable (E. F. Seagram)	254,922	95
	Audley Farm Stable (M. & B. B. Jones)	148,183	95
1928	Audley Farm Stable (B. B. Jones)	188,106	83
	Seagram Stable (E.F., N. & T. W.Seagram)	173,558	83
1929	Seagram Stable (E.F., N. & T. W.Seagram)	155,945	88
1930	C.V. Whitney	385,972	120
1931	C.V. Whitney	422,923	105
1932	C.V. Whitney	413,361	119
1933	C.V. Whitney	241,292	136
1934	B. B. Stable (Beebe-Byers)	74,295	92
1935	Mrs. A.M. Creech	103,260	107
1936	Mrs. Ethel D. Jacobs	137,859	149
1937	Mrs. Ethel D. Jacobs	115,329	102
1938	Medway Stable (J. E. Smallman)	78,062	99
1939	Mrs. Emil Denemark	108,520	88
1940	Mrs. Emil Denemark	115,207	112
1941	Mrs. Emil Denemark	123,109	111
1942	Calumet Farm (Warren Wright)	315,005	72
1943	Mrs. Ethel D. Jacobs	141,775	81
1944	C. V. Whitney	172,434	64
1945	Mrs. Lottie Wolf	238,361	127
1946	Willian Helis	458,060	89
1947	Calumet Farm (Warren Wright)	1,402,436	100
1948	Calumet Farm (Warren Wright)	1,269,710	92
1949	William Hal Bishop	235,901	129
1950	William Hal Bishop	218,689	127
1951	William Hal Bishop	232,622	117
1952	Marion H. Van Berg	311,560	140
1953	W. H. Bishop Stable, Inc.	360,514	153
1954	W. H. Bishop Stable, Inc.	334,305	119
1955	Marion H. Van Berg	348,580	127
1956	T. A. Grissom	335,137	118
	Mr. and Mrs. Marion H. Van Berg	315,945	118
1957	T. A. Grissom	430,506	139
1958	W. H. Bishop Stable, Inc.	670,864	165
1959	W. H. Bishop Stable, Inc.	626,149	160
1960	Marion H. Van Berg	642,607	221
1961	Marion H. Van Berg	556,732	192
1962	Marion H. Van Berg	597,625	205
1963	Marion H. Van Berg	670,367	201
1964	Marion H. Van Berg	822,305	258
1965	Marion H. Van Berg	895,246	270
1966	Marion H. Van Berg	897,794	277
1967	Marion H. Van Berg	1,001,568	268
1968	Marion H. Van Berg	1,105,388	339
1969	Marion H. Van Berg	1,453,679	393
1970	Marion H. Van Berg	1,347,289	391
1971	Audley Farm (J. F. Edwards)	1,400,258	370
1972	Audley Farm (J. F. Edwards)	1,175,343	302
1973	Audley Farm (J. F. Edwards)	1,162,438	266
1974	Dan R. Lasater	3,022,960	494
1975	Dan R. Lasater	2,894,726	459
1976	Dan R. Lasater	2,894,074	404
1977	Dan R. Lasater	1,647,107	263
1978	Dale Baird	309,685	162
1979	Dale Baird	415,045	234
1980	Dale Baird	409,836	230
1981	Dale Baird	503,021	293
1982	Dale Baird	445,650	259
1983	John Franks	2,643,251	183
1984	John Franks	3,070,225	172
1985	Dale Baird	377,542	202
1986	John Franks	4,463,115	250
1987	John Franks	3,445,736	235
1988	John Franks	3,834,908	232
1989	John Franks	3,852,813	255
1990	Dale Baird	365,639	197
1991	Dalc Baird	424,072	246
1992	Dale Baird	395,496	222
1993	Dale Baird	397,194	225
1994	Dale Baird	428,314	201
1995	Dale Baird	614,535	251
1996	Dale Baird	923,807	278
1997	Dale Baird	1,129,787	275
1998	Dale Baird	1,434,265	264
1999	Dale Baird	2,122,900	308
2000	Dale Baird	2,327,230	241
2001	Richard A. Englander	9,783,472	405
2002	Richard A. Englander	7,515,562	278
2003	Michael J. Gill	9,236,530	425
2004	Michael J. Gill	10,835,561	487

Leading Trainers in 2004 by Money Won

Trainer	Starts	1st	2d	3d	Pct.	Purses
Todd A. Pletcher	948	240	154	125	0.253	$17,511,923
Robert J. Frankel	491	135	94	60	0.275	15,605,911
Steven M. Asmussen	2,293	555	361	348	0.242	14,003,202
John C. Servis	284	68	38	38	0.239	*8,922,686
Bob Baffert	562	105	75	74	0.187	7,627,913
Richard E. Dutrow, Jr.	603	166	117	87	0.275	7,576,986
Scott A. Lake	1,688	374	297	251	0.222	7,420,036
Dale L. Romans	580	109	87	87	0.188	7,081,653
Doug O'Neill	938	170	132	124	0.181	7,004,827
Nicholas P. Zito	452	86	68	52	0.190	6,967,792
Jeff Mullins	538	140	98	65	0.260	6,910,572
Jerry Hollendorfer	1,300	308	261	186	0.237	6,005,484
William I. Mott	680	116	106	98	0.171	5,730,530
D. Wayne Lukas	577	67	87	70	0.116	5,567,299
Kiaran P. McLaughlin	462	84	81	56	0.182	5,525,744
Mark R. Frostad	269	49	36	41	0.182	4,912,015
H. Allen Jerkens	374	72	44	56	0.193	4,447,047
H. Graham Motion	424	81	65	43	0.191	4,358,674
Claude R. McGaughey III	254	48	48	39	0.189	4,208,832
Mark Shuman	987	159	134	138	0.161	4,183,826
Mark A. Hennig	516	72	100	66	0.140	3,957,058
Robert P. Tiller	282	69	48	33	0.245	3,939,642
Sid C. Attard	315	76	55	38	0.241	3,844,401
Mike R. Mitchell	391	97	67	45	0.248	3,834,120
Cole Norman	894	250	169	98	0.280	3,730,732
Thomas M. Amoss	484	140	88	68	0.289	3,617,785
Bruce N. Levine	432	107	84	65	0.248	3,541,853
Christophe Clement	344	68	58	51	0.198	3,541,781
Bernard S. Flint	575	124	82	64	0.216	3,513,351
Kenneth G. McPeek	413	74	71	49	0.179	3,418,225
Patrick L. Biancone	130	29	24	19	0.223	3,397,917
Julio C. Canani	186	42	31	22	0.226	3,364,545
Steve Klesaris	482	97	95	60	0.201	3,205,571
Richard E. Mandella	160	24	25	30	0.150	3,083,102
Timothy A. Hills	585	103	86	68	0.176	3,075,524
Allen Iwinski	506	98	69	64	0.194	3,004,795
Timothy F. Ritchey	414	86	87	55	0.208	2,991,693
John W. Sadler	396	65	59	58	0.164	2,976,823
Mark E. Casse	323	48	45	46	0.149	2,946,340
Stanley M. Hough	259	53	56	39	0.205	2,918,862
Reade Baker	274	44	45	40	0.161	2,844,159
Vladimir Cerin	339	59	52	61	0.174	2,796,647
Roger L. Attfield	292	35	36	35	0.120	2,777,942
W. Bret Calhoun	714	148	124	93	0.207	2,733,984
Carl A. Nafzger	358	54	52	52	0.151	2,732,948
Gary C. Contessa	537	75	91	60	0.140	2,730,527

Trainer	Starts	1st	2d	3d	Pct.	Purses
Robert E. Holthus	364	72	54	55	0.198	2,635,551
Neil D. Drysdale	180	37	26	22	0.206	2,630,399
James M. Cassidy	157	18	19	18	0.115	2,580,222
John Charles Zimmerman	773	193	113	115	0.250	2,554,139
Michael Machowsky	154	23	25	22	0.149	2,529,347
James A. Jerkens	207	43	40	22	0.208	2,480,146
Ronald L. McAnally	249	26	41	34	0.104	2,479,531
Guadalupe Preciado	602	118	102	88	0.196	2,464,075
Dale Capuano	649	136	93	111	0.210	2,452,257
Art Sherman	611	152	102	84	0.249	2,353,216
Barclay Tagg	235	32	25	32	0.136	2,335,781
Donnie K. Von Hemel	479	91	84	77	0.190	2,285,398
Ronney W. Brown	708	131	119	81	0.185	2,269,499
Michael Stidham	369	81	58	41	0.220	2,228,860
Richard A. Violette, Jr.	249	41	34	24	0.165	2,213,779
Daniel J. Vella	223	37	35	29	0.166	2,198,573
Dallas Stewart	295	49	53	35	0.166	2,170,555
John F. Martin	487	125	98	64	0.257	2,153,411
Hugh H. Robertson	469	100	82	71	0.213	2,133,342
Patrick J. Kelly	238	21	27	37	0.088	2,120,689
Dale Baird	1,109	131	158	132	0.118	2,063,884
John C. Kimmel	281	34	32	37	0.121	2,055,898
Michael W. Dickinson	190	39	27	31	0.205	2,036,362
David R. Bell	217	36	22	32	0.166	2,019,903
Gregory D. Foley	283	66	42	43	0.233	2,017,295
Jennifer Pedersen	423	44	46	59	0.104	2,015,485
Michael V. Pino	458	108	85	72	0.236	1,992,141
Josie Carroll	250	43	26	37	0.172	1,990,780
Wesley A. Ward	447	75	82	68	0.168	1,975,167
Craig Dollase	191	35	23	26	0.183	1,951,256
Neil J. Howard	173	37	30	26	0.214	1,938,175
Michael R. Matz	214	32	33	33	0.150	1,928,354
George Weaver	401	46	50	52	0.115	1,925,813
Paulo H. Lobo	118	22	18	13	0.186	1,923,033
Michael E. Gorham	442	66	72	74	0.149	1,903,968
Jeff C. Runco	599	104	96	65	0.174	1,899,518
Abraham R. Katryan	295	32	55	46	0.108	1,895,649
Kristin Mulhall	154	23	18	18	0.149	1,883,697
Patrick Gallagher	220	39	35	33	0.177	1,883,313
Wallace A. Dollase	111	21	19	18	0.189	1,866,307
Michael E. Hushion	306	53	48	44	0.173	1,853,071
Edward Plesa, Jr.	397	56	60	51	0.141	1,830,409
William Spawr	287	64	57	37	0.223	1,826,342
Jonathan E. Sheppard	423	58	58	70	0.137	1,821,893
Marcelo Polanco	245	26	26	26	0.106	1,810,533
Keith L. Bourgeois	711	132	104	79	0.186	1,789,609
Kevin J. Joy	607	117	75	73	0.193	1,762,880
Paul J. McGee	290	49	44	42	0.169	1,758,830

Trainer	Starts	1st	2d	3d	Pct.	Purses
Frank J. Kirby	539	76	68	53	0.141	1,746,292
Bobby C. Barnett	407	48	45	46	0.118	1,712,929
Martin D. Wolfson	176	39	32	15	0.222	1,710,249
Rafael Becerra	258	36	34	46	0.140	1,708,343
David Cotey	247	32	33	31	0.130	1,680,885
William P. White	361	73	55	50	0.202	1,667,257
Benjamin M. Feliciano, Jr.	317	69	53	52	0.218	1,665,721
Laura De Seroux	98	8	16	17	0.082	1,664,329
Catherine Day Phillips	88	15	13	12	0.170	1,654,688
Scott H. Fairlie	304	48	32	39	0.158	1,648,951
Doris Hebert	536	102	87	81	0.190	1,614,269
Edward T. Allard	348	86	51	40	0.247	1,596,655
Danny Pish	623	121	99	80	0.194	1,594,907
Chris M. Block	298	51	48	43	0.171	1,592,782
Henry Dominguez	446	85	78	70	0.191	1,568,023
Wayne M. Catalano	335	84	52	38	0.251	1,563,353
Paul G. Aguirre	159	29	22	28	0.182	1,532,835
Donald Chatlos, Jr.	76	12	9	6	0.158	1,528,196
Chris J. Englehart	650	149	114	101	0.229	1,520,898
A. Ferris Allen III	553	78	98	73	0.141	1,507,701
Steve Knapp	436	50	54	65	0.115	1,507,223
Saeed bin Suroor	9	2	1	0	0.222	1,504,632
Hamilton A. Smith	456	66	66	68	0.145	1,498,140
Gerald S. Bennett	586	117	109	96	0.200	1,475,786
Philip M. Serpe	227	30	33	25	0.132	1,472,803
W. Elliott Walden	207	33	34	15	0.159	1,454,424
John A. Shirreffs	182	23	18	25	0.126	1,453,958
Dick R. Clark	475	97	86	52	0.204	1,445,356
Anthony L. Reinstedler	201	31	27	22	0.154	1,435,674
Jack Carava	325	55	48	44	0.169	1,435,136
Gamaliel Vazquez	309	55	48	32	0.178	1,415,285
John Rigattieri	427	122	67	53	0.286	1,412,568
Ralph Martinez	796	230	149	133	0.289	1,408,259
Anthony W. Dutrow	249	49	53	40	0.197	1,402,416
Linda Rice	288	38	40	27	0.132	1,389,239
Emanuel Tortora	410	58	55	49	0.141	1,381,375
Patricia Farro	479	80	66	52	0.167	1,365,040
Bruce M. Kravets	942	164	127	114	0.174	1,363,168
David R. Vance	260	35	27	44	0.135	1,347,291
Harry F. Thompson, Jr.	819	125	118	102	0.153	1,342,794
Eric Coatrieux	71	13	9	9	0.183	1,335,774
Jeff Bonde	303	47	51	46	0.155	1,333,438
Flint W. Stites	642	101	106	78	0.157	1,329,400
Charlton Baker	377	93	59	58	0.247	1,325,775
David M. Carroll	157	33	22	21	0.210	1,324,580
Ronald W. Ellis	121	24	16	19	0.198	1,322,251
Layne S. Giliforte	406	73	65	45	0.180	1,316,280
Dominic G. Galluscio	305	39	41	41	0.128	1,297,843

Trainer	Starts	1st	2d	3d	Pct.	Purses
Audre Cappuccitti	298	28	34	38	0.094	1,293,288
John J. Robb	386	66	63	38	0.171	1,290,425
Vito Armata	223	42	22	29	0.188	1,285,037
Merrill R. Scherer	281	55	31	38	0.196	1,282,508
Michael L. Reavis	400	76	52	53	0.190	1,281,314
Michael P. DePaulo	202	29	22	24	0.144	1,279,814
Albert M. Stall, Jr.	319	46	56	45	0.144	1,279,031
H. James Bond	191	34	22	23	0.178	1,279,019
Martin F. Jones	176	30	26	27	0.170	1,276,513
James J. Toner	112	19	5	15	0.170	1,276,282
Malcolm Pierce	182	23	28	23	0.126	1,273,698
Manuel J. Azpurua	309	39	38	49	0.126	1,272,120
George R. Arnold, II	189	24	25	28	0.127	1,270,678
Henry Collazo	445	59	62	51	0.133	1,269,953
Michael J. Maker	200	31	28	10	0.155	1,236,295
Donald S. Reeder	484	80	76	66	0.165	1,233,717
Bruce Headley	134	22	19	20	0.164	1,232,704
Samuel Breaux	392	70	60	53	0.179	1,231,147
David G. Donk	291	25	30	56	0.086	1,230,912
Clifford W. Sise, Jr.	358	57	49	49	0.159	1,227,779
Brian J. Koriner	288	57	38	37	0.198	1,220,298
Todd M. Beattie	352	88	66	45	0.250	1,219,926
Justin J. Nixon	158	43	34	30	0.272	1,213,172
Phil Schoenthal	373	61	68	40	0.164	1,204,822
Troy Young	218	44	43	41	0.202	1,201,649
Michael Keogh	103	14	7	8	0.136	1,198,873
Howard E. Wolfendale	283	75	62	46	0.265	1,193,210
Alan E. Goldberg	200	33	31	25	0.165	1,185,591
Gary Capuano	230	47	44	32	0.204	1,182,311
Dale Angelle	372	90	66	45	0.242	1,180,918
Darrell Vienna	162	17	20	24	0.105	1,170,636
Kathleen A. Demasi	544	61	66	56	0.112	1,170,534
J. Larry Jones	189	35	33	26	0.185	1,167,990
Edwin Thomas Broome	259	49	40	36	0.189	1,167,863
Timothy Ritvo	486	46	51	66	0.095	1,165,953
Walter M. Bindner, Jr.	109	18	20	12	0.165	1,138,357
Benjamin W. Perkins, Jr.	174	27	26	27	0.155	1,137,210
Ronny W. Werner	242	46	45	35	0.190	1,133,292
Ernest M. Haynes	276	61	57	34	0.221	1,122,273
Kelly R. Von Hemel	334	63	40	57	0.189	1,118,883
Norman R. Pointer	287	45	40	37	0.157	1,118,012
Armando Lage	612	84	62	82	0.137	1,117,136
William E. Morey	383	86	75	43	0.225	1,115,343
Larry Robideaux, Jr.	295	51	38	40	0.173	1,101,264
Richard W. Small	181	39	28	27	0.215	1,099,148
Ross Armata	280	46	38	32	0.164	1,094,862
Richard P. Hazelton	291	36	34	45	0.124	1,091,075
Jason Servis	223	40	30	33	0.179	1,088,949

Trainer	Starts	1st	2d	3d	Pct.	Purses
Patrick L. Reynolds	186	25	29	29	0.134	1,078,403
Anthony Adamo	351	56	41	37	0.160	1,073,430
Macdonald Benson	93	13	13	9	0.140	1,072,838
Thomas Albertrani	65	11	13	7	0.169	1,046,365
Juan J. Garcia	263	21	25	45	0.080	1,044,666
David R. Brownlee	183	23	26	22	0.126	1,044,510
Thomas F. Tomillo	612	58	87	75	0.095	1,042,626
Aidan P. O'Brien	12	0	1	5	0.000	1,037,300
Barry Abrams	253	22	33	44	0.087	1,037,140
Kathleen O'Connell	537	59	74	65	0.110	1,035,666
Murray W. Johnson	87	4	16	6	0.046	1,033,915
Steven B. Flint	157	30	29	20	0.191	1,032,822
Michael A. Lecesse	400	80	57	59	0.200	1,030,953
David E. Hofmans	102	16	10	11	0.157	1,028,050
William Bradley	229	24	28	21	0.105	1,027,462
Ron K. Smith	348	68	54	44	0.195	1,026,602
Christine K. Janks	213	46	40	19	0.216	1,021,255
Ted H. West	142	30	28	20	0.211	1,020,284
Jeffrey A. Radosevich	535	98	90	61	0.183	1,020,173
Mark Fusco	456	72	68	70	0.158	1,018,544
Jason R. Orman	53	8	7	8	0.151	1,017,685
Del W. Carroll, II	135	20	18	16	0.148	1,014,973
Thomas M. Bush	130	26	19	13	0.200	1,006,603
Rodney Jenkins	245	45	45	44	0.184	1,001,290

* Includes $5,000,000 bonus.

Leading Trainers in 2004 by Races Won

Trainer	Starts	1st	2d	3d	Pct.	Purses
Steven M. Asmussen	2,293	555	361	348	0.242	14,003,202
Scott A. Lake	1,688	374	297	251	0.222	7,420,036
Jerry Hollendorfer	1,300	308	261	186	0.237	6,005,484
Cole Norman	894	250	169	98	0.280	3,730,732
Todd A. Pletcher	948	240	154	125	0.253	17,511,923
Ralph Martinez	796	230	149	133	0.289	1,408,259
John Charles Zimmerman	773	193	113	115	0.250	2,554,139
Doug O'Neill	938	170	132	124	0.181	7,004,827
Richard E. Dutrow, Jr.	603	166	117	87	0.275	7,576,986
Bruce M. Kravets	942	164	127	114	0.174	1,363,168
Mark Shuman	987	159	134	138	0.161	4,183,826
Art Sherman	611	152	102	84	0.249	2,353,216
Chris J. Englehart	650	149	114	101	0.229	1,520,898
W. Bret Calhoun	714	148	124	93	0.207	2,733,984
Jeff Mullins	538	140	98	65	0.260	6,910,572
Thomas M. Amoss	484	140	88	68	0.289	3,617,785
Dale Capuano	649	136	93	111	0.210	2,452,257
Robert J. Frankel	491	135	94	60	0.275	15,605,911
Keith L. Bourgeois	711	132	104	79	0.186	1,789,609
Ronney W. Brown	708	131	119	81	0.185	2,269,499
Dale Baird	1,109	131	158	132	0.118	2,063,884
John F. Martin	487	125	98	64	0.257	2,153,411
Harry F. Thompson, Jr.	819	125	118	102	0.153	1,342,794
Bernard S. Flint	575	124	82	64	0.216	3,513,351
John Rigattieri	427	122	67	53	0.286	1,412,568
Danny Pish	623	121	99	80	0.194	1,594,907
Guadalupe Preciado	602	118	102	88	0.196	2,464,075
Kevin J. Joy	607	117	75	73	0.193	1,762,880
Gerald S. Bennett	586	117	109	96	0.200	1,475,786
William I. Mott	680	116	106	98	0.171	5,730,530
Dale L. Romans	580	109	87	87	0.188	7,081,653
Michael V. Pino	458	108	85	72	0.236	1,992,141
Bruce N. Levine	432	107	84	65	0.248	3,541,853
Bob Baffert	562	105	75	74	0.187	7,627,913
Jeff C. Runco	599	104	96	65	0.174	1,899,518
Timothy A. Hills	585	103	86	68	0.176	3,075,524
Doris Hebert	536	102	87	81	0.190	1,614,269
Flint W. Stites	642	101	106	78	0.157	1,329,400
Hugh H. Robertson	469	100	82	71	0.213	2,133,342
Allen Iwinski	506	98	69	64	0.194	3,004,795
Jeffrey A. Radosevich	535	98	90	61	0.183	1,020,173
Mike R. Mitchell	391	97	67	45	0.248	3,834,120
Steve Klesaris	482	97	95	60	0.201	3,205,571
Dick R. Clark	475	97	86	52	0.204	1,445,356
Kim Hammond	567	97	81	85	0.171	784,344
Rodney C. Faulkner	622	96	94	66	0.154	683,836
David C. Anderson	395	94	61	48	0.238	481,940
Charlton Baker	377	93	59	58	0.247	1,325,775

Trainer	Starts	1st	2d	3d	Pct.	Purses
Donnie K. Von Hemel	479	91	84	77	0.190	2,285,398
Dale Angelle	372	90	66	45	0.242	1,180,918
Todd M. Beattie	352	88	66	45	0.250	1,219,926
Nicholas P. Zito	452	86	68	52	0.190	6,967,792
Timothy F. Ritchey	414	86	87	55	0.208	2,991,693
Edward T. Allard	348	86	51	40	0.247	1,596,655
William E. Morey	383	86	75	43	0.225	1,115,343
Henry Dominguez	446	85	78	70	0.191	1,568,023
Joseph Clark Faulkner	460	85	59	66	0.185	448,662
Kiaran P. McLaughlin	462	84	81	56	0.182	5,525,744
Wayne M. Catalano	335	84	52	38	0.251	1,563,353
Armando Lage	612	84	62	82	0.137	1,117,136
Gary L. Johnson	741	83	87	79	0.112	822,439
Jose A. Martinez	727	82	114	113	0.113	823,557
H. Graham Motion	424	81	65	43	0.191	4,358,674
Michael Stidham	369	81	58	41	0.220	2,228,860
Patricia Farro	479	80	66	52	0.167	1,365,040
Donald S. Reeder	484	80	76	66	0.165	1,233,717
Michael A. Lecesse	400	80	57	59	0.200	1,030,953
Michael W. Nance	428	80	60	63	0.187	801,191
Steve Manley	459	79	84	64	0.172	569,917
A. Ferris Allen III	553	78	98	73	0.141	1,507,701
Timothy C. Kreiser	270	78	40	38	0.289	783,038
Barbara I. McBride	375	77	68	53	0.205	719,970
Reid Gross	741	77	82	82	0.104	408,058
Sid C. Attard	315	76	55	38	0.241	3,844,401
Frank J. Kirby	539	76	68	53	0.141	1,746,292
Michael L. Reavis	400	76	52	53	0.190	1,281,314
Gary C. Contessa	537	75	91	60	0.140	2,730,527
Wesley A. Ward	447	75	82	68	0.168	1,975,167
Howard E. Wolfendale	283	75	62	46	0.265	1,193,210
David W. Geist	520	75	83	76	0.144	909,385
Troy Bainum	311	75	54	47	0.241	761,085
Kenneth G. McPeek	413	74	71	49	0.179	3,418,225
Stanley W. Roberts	561	74	85	50	0.132	894,578
Don J. Mills	291	74	56	35	0.254	731,497
William P. White	361	73	55	50	0.202	1,667,257
Layne S. Giliforte	406	73	65	45	0.180	1,316,280
J. Michael Baird	373	73	61	36	0.196	961,956
Ronald J. Dandy	367	73	52	57	0.199	784,364
H. Allen Jerkens	374	72	44	56	0.193	4,447,047
Mark A. Hennig	516	72	100	66	0.140	3,957,058
Robert E. Holthus	364	72	54	55	0.198	2,635,551
Mark Fusco	456	72	68	70	0.158	1,018,544
Raymond E. Stifano	407	72	73	55	0.177	820,064
Robert M. Gorham	425	71	69	57	0.167	947,343
Thomas M. Agosti	371	71	74	43	0.191	844,762
Jake S. Radosevich	454	71	51	67	0.156	427,159
Samuel Breaux	392	70	60	53	0.179	1,231,147

Trainer	Starts	1st	2d	3d	Pct.	Purses
Luis Albert Palacios	347	70	56	55	0.202	738,228
Robert P. Tiller	282	69	48	33	0.245	3,939,642
Benjamin M. Feliciano, Jr.	317	69	53	52	0.218	1,665,721
Ronald D. Allen, Sr.	314	69	44	47	0.220	756,125
Eddie M. Essenpreis	424	69	83	62	0.163	670,906
John C. Servis	284	68	38	38	0.239	*8,922,686
Christophe Clement	344	68	58	51	0.198	3,541,781
Ron K. Smith	348	68	54	44	0.195	1,026,602
Joseph R. Martin	435	68	57	63	0.156	804,266
Scooter Davis	358	68	47	34	0.190	773,589
Jesus Nunez	489	68	65	57	0.139	482,433
Bill Brashears	327	68	53	47	0.208	308,524
D. Wayne Lukas	577	67	87	70	0.116	5,567,299
Gregory D. Foley	283	66	42	43	0.233	2,017,295
Michael E. Gorham	442	66	72	74	0.149	1,903,968
Hamilton A. Smith	456	66	66	68	0.145	1,498,140
John J. Robb	386	66	63	38	0.171	1,290,425
Ramon O. Gonzalez	373	66	48	48	0.177	933,141
John G. Locke	480	66	66	75	0.138	909,082
John W. Sadler	396	65	59	58	0.164	2,976,823
William Spawr	287	64	57	37	0.223	1,826,342
John W. Baird	402	64	41	43	0.159	900,886
Kelly R. Von Hemel	334	63	40	57	0.189	1,118,883
Philip T. Aristone	458	63	64	48	0.138	750,442
Keith Bennett	200	63	31	29	0.315	505,847
Phil Schoenthal	373	61	68	40	0.164	1,204,822
Kathleen A. Demasi	544	61	66	56	0.112	1,170,534
Ernest M. Haynes	276	61	57	34	0.221	1,122,273
Timothy Mark Gleason	433	61	64	67	0.141	689,280
Jon G. Arnett	380	61	62	42	0.161	583,562
Andrew Konkoly	370	61	67	33	0.165	477,865
Chad Hassenpflug	269	60	44	32	0.223	774,158
Frank Lucarelli	369	60	50	51	0.163	570,508
Vladimir Cerin	339	59	52	61	0.174	2,796,647
Henry Collazo	445	59	62	51	0.133	1,269,953
Kathleen O'Connell	537	59	74	65	0.110	1,035,666
Jonathan E. Sheppard	423	58	58	70	0.137	1,821,893
Emanuel Tortora	410	58	55	49	0.141	1,381,375
Thomas F. Tomillo	612	58	87	75	0.095	1,042,626
Dan L. McFarlane	323	58	62	45	0.180	787,750
Clifford W. Sise, Jr.	358	57	49	49	0.159	1,227,779
Brian J. Koriner	288	57	38	37	0.198	1,220,298
Angel C. Salinas	356	57	40	47	0.160	879,330
Ralph D'Alessandro	289	57	44	32	0.197	817,057
J. Eric Kruljac	282	57	38	39	0.202	742,199
Michael S. Ferraro	327	57	46	35	0.174	635,896
Leroy Hellman	319	57	38	51	0.179	433,965
Craig W. Robertson	171	57	26	26	0.333	360,050
Edward Plesa, Jr.	397	56	60	51	0.141	1,830,409

Trainer	Starts	1st	2d	3d	Pct.	Purses
Anthony Adamo	351	56	41	37	0.160	1,073,430
Paula S. Capestro	272	56	44	35	0.206	902,324
David Van Winkle	310	56	56	45	0.181	764,336
Tommie T. Morgan	355	56	40	33	0.158	637,592
Rinzy Nocero	416	56	59	62	0.135	290,729
Jack Carava	325	55	48	44	0.169	1,435,136
Gamaliel Vazquez	309	55	48	32	0.178	1,415,285
Merrill R. Scherer	281	55	31	38	0.196	1,282,508
Joel H. Marr	281	55	40	37	0.196	853,723
Richard R. Rettele	312	55	61	49	0.176	677,380
Oscar S. Barrera, Jr.	309	55	53	54	0.178	593,985
Carl A. Nafzger	358	54	52	52	0.151	2,732,948
Gary W. Cross	250	54	35	34	0.216	886,219
Julio R. Cartagena	220	54	30	27	0.245	812,746
Daniel C. Hurtak	334	54	46	53	0.162	702,855
M. Anthony Ferraro	386	54	59	43	0.140	575,184
Marvin A. Johnson	300	54	29	35	0.180	278,126
Stanley M. Hough	259	53	56	39	0.205	2,918,862
Michael E. Hushion	306	53	48	44	0.173	1,853,071
Ramon Preciado	274	53	43	33	0.193	816,865
Carmelo Mendoza	251	53	32	36	0.211	391,722
Jim Fergason	230	53	33	31	0.230	254,149
Martin Lozano	298	52	44	51	0.174	719,836
Bernell B. Rhone	413	52	59	45	0.126	658,802
James T. Wright	236	52	30	26	0.220	545,682
Samuel J. Keyrouze	404	52	47	50	0.129	431,214
Burton K. Sipp	401	52	54	44	0.130	418,260
Chris M. Block	298	51	48	43	0.171	1,592,782
Larry Robideaux, Jr.	295	51	38	40	0.173	1,101,264
Timothy E. Salzman	313	51	47	51	0.163	950,253
Anthony Correnti	360	51	57	45	0.142	946,166
Robert J. Seeger	397	51	64	51	0.128	941,098
Tim McCanna	286	51	43	49	0.178	643,474
Bart G. Hone	252	51	47	38	0.202	528,561
Randall R. Russell	398	51	51	62	0.128	425,806
Roger F. Engel	180	51	23	24	0.283	331,120
Steve Knapp	436	50	54	65	0.115	1,507,223
Kearney Segura	340	50	39	39	0.147	753,155
Dale L. Saunders	280	50	44	33	0.179	696,580
L. Craig Cox	313	50	49	46	0.160	695,154
Michael Lenzini	499	50	58	68	0.100	556,518
Jami C. Poole	275	50	21	36	0.182	553,479
Michael W. Salvaggio, Jr.	267	50	59	47	0.187	541,343
Clayton C. Hurt	304	50	59	27	0.164	436,802

* Includes $5,000,000 bonus.

Annual Leading Trainers – Money Won

Year	Trainer	Amount Won	Strts*	No. of Wins
1908	J. Rowe	$284,335		50
1909	S. C. Hildreth	123,942		73
1910	S. C. Hildreth	148,010		84
1911	S. C. Hildreth	49,418		67
1912	J. F. Schorr	58,110		63
1913	J. Rowe	45,936		18
1914	R. C. Benson	59,315		45
1915	J. Rowe	75,596		19
1916	S. C. Hildreth	70,950		39
1917	S. C. Hildreth	61,698		23
1918	H. G. Bedwell	80,296		53
1919	H. G. Bedwell	208,728		63
1920	L. Feustal	186,087		22
1921	S. C. Hildreth	262,768		85
1922	S. C. Hildreth	247,014		74
1923	S. C. Hildreth	392,124		75
1924	S. C. Hildreth	255,608		77
1925	G. R. Thompkins	199,245		30
1926	S. P. Harlan	205,681		21
1927	W. H. Bringloe	216,563		63
1928	J. F. Schorr	258,425		65
1929	J. Rowe Jr	314,881		25
1930	J Fitzsimmons	397,355		47
1931	J. W. Healy	297,300		33
1932	J. Fitzsimmons	266,650		68
1933	R. A. Smith	135,720		53
1934	R. A. Smith	249,938		43
1935	J. H. Stotler	303,005		87
1936	J. Fitzsimmons	193,415		42
1937	R. McGarvey	209,925		46
1938	E. H. Sande	226,495		15
1939	J. Fitzsimmons	266,205		45
1940	T. Smith	269,200		14
1941	B. A. Jones	475,318		70
1942	J. M. Gaver	406,547		48
1943	B. A. Jones	267,915		73
1944	B. A. Jones	601,660		60
1945	T. Smith	510,655		52
1946	H. Jacobs	560,077		99
1947	H. A. Jones	1,334,805		85
1948	H. A. Jones	1,118,670		81
1949	H. A. Jones	978,587		76
1950	P. M. Burch	637,754		96
1951	J. M. Gaver	616,392		42
1952	B. A. Jones	662,137		29
1953	H. Trotsek	1,028,873		54
1954	W. Molter	1,107,860		136
1955	J. Fitzsimmons	1,270,055		66
1956	W. Molter	1,227,402		142

Year	Trainer	Amount Won	Strts*	No. of Wins
1957	H. A. Jones	1,150,910		70
1958	W. Molter	1,116,544		69
1959	W. Molter	847,290		71
1960	H. Jacobs	748,349		97
1961	H. A. Jones	759,856		62
1962	M. A. Tenney	1,099,474		58
1963	M. A. Tenney	860,703	192	40
1964	W. C. Winfrey	1,350,534	287	61
1965	H. Jacobs	1,331,628	610	91
1966	E. A. Neloy	2,456,250	282	93
1967	E. A. Neloy	1,776,089	262	72
1968	E. A. Neloy	1,233,101	212	52
1969	Elliott Burch	1,067,936	156	26
1970	C. Whittingham	1,302,354	551	82
1971	C. Whittingham	1,737,115	393	77
1972	C. Whittingham	1,734,020	429	79
1973	C. Whittingham	1,865,385	423	85
1974	F. Martin	2,408,419	846	166
1975	C. Whittingham	2,437,244	487	93
1976	J. Van Berg	2,976,196	2,362	496
1977	L. S. Barrera	2,715,848	781	127
1978	L. S. Barrera	3,307,164	592	100
1979	L. S. Barrera	3,608,517	492	98
1980	L. S. Barrera	2,969,151	559	99
1981	C. Whittingham	3,993,302	376	74
1982	C. Whittingham	4,587,457	410	63
1983	D. Wayne Lukas	4,267,261	595	78
1984	D. Wayne Lukas	5,835,921	805	131
1985	D. Wayne Lukas	11,155,188	1,140	218
1986	D. Wayne Lukas	12,345,180	1,510	259
1987	D. Wayne Lukas	17,502,110	1,735	343
1988	D. Wayne Lukas	17,842,358	1,500	318
1989	D. Wayne Lukas	16,103,998	1,398	305
1990	D. Wayne Lukas	14,508,871	1,396	267
1991	D. Wayne Lukas	15,942,223	1,497	289
1992	D. Wayne Lukas	9,806,436	1,349	230
1993	Robert Frankel	8,883,252	346	79
1994	D. Wayne Lukas	9,250,591	693	147
1995	D. Wayne Lukas	12,858,429	840	194
1996	D. Wayne Lukas	15,967,608	1,007	192
1997	D. Wayne Lukas	10,355,154	854	175
1998	Bob Baffert	16,660,880	721	167
1999	Bob Baffert	14,266,707	500	134
2000	Bob Baffert	11,831,605	678	146
2001	Robert J. Frankel	14,607,446	390	101
2002	Robert J. Frankel	17,748,340	480	117
2003	Robert J. Frankel	19,143,289	411	114
2003	Todd A. Pletcher	17,511,923	948	240

*Starts unavailable until 1963

Annual Leading Trainers – Races Won

Year	Trainer	Amount Won	Strts*	No. of Wins
1907	J. Rowe	397,342		70
1908	A. J. Boyner	170,775		71
1909	H. G. Bedwell	64,943		122
1910	F. Ernest	64,525		105
1911	W. B. Carson	16,250		72
1912	H. G. Bedwell	42,595		84
1913	H. G. Bedwell	42,895		87
1914	H. G. Bedwell	49,430		84
1915	H. G. Bedwell	51,015		97
1916	H. G. Bedwell	70,545		123
1917	H. G. Bedwell	47,585		66
1918	K. Spence	35,303		58
1919	K. Spence	67,352		96
1920	K. Spence	94,674		74
	S. A. Clopton	152,312		74
1921	S.C. Hindreth	262,768		85
1922	H. McDaniel	169,134		78
	J. A. Parsons	40,465		78
1923	C. B. Irwin	104,054		147
1924	J. A. Parsons	42,566		93
1925	J. J. Duggan	49,830		70
1926	W. Perkins	127,753		82
1927	S.C. Hindreth	161,569		72
1928	J. F. Schorr	258,425		65
	J. Reed	63,795		65
1929	L. Gentry	65,821		74
1930	C. B. Irwin	70,411		92
1931	J. C. Mikel	49,770		72
1932	G. Alexandra	55,890		76
1933	H. Jacobs	76,965		116
1934	H. Jacobs	113,055		127
1935	H. Jacobs	95,155		114
1936	H. Jacobs	155,789		177
1937	H. Jacobs	142,474		134
1938	H. Jacobs	116,609		109
1939	H. Jacobs	100,907		106
1940	D. Womeldorff	112,137		108
1941	H. Jacobs	165,964		123
1942	H. Jacobs	186,371		133
1943	H. Jacobs	210,775		128
1944	H. Jacobs	306,821		117
1945	S. Liepiec	228,361		127
1946	W. Molter	329,725		122
1947	W. Molter	833,970		155
1948	W. Molter	1,015,547		184
1949	W. Molter	686,184		129
	W. H. Bishop	236,131		129
1950	R. H. McDaniel	441,590		156
1951	R. H. McDaniel	539,204		164
1952	R. H. McDaniel	573,837		168
1953	R. H. McDaniel	751,957		211
1954	R. H. McDaniel	834,390		206
1955	F. H. Merrill Jr.	298,794		154
1956	V. R. Wright	532,344		177
1957	V. R. Wright	527,271		192
1958	F. H. Merrill Jr.	320,827		171
1959	V. R. Wright	534,319		172
1960	F. H. Merrill Jr.	344,459		143
1961	V. R. Wright	442,650		178
1962	W. H. Bishop	544,261		162
1963	H. Jacobson	730,418	688	140
1964	H. Jacobson	801,869	730	169
1965	H. Jacobson	863,721	886	200
1966	L. Cavalaris Jr.	763,201	635	175
1967	E. Hammond	325,905	996	200
1968	Jack C. Van Berg	776,330	1,152	256
1969	Jack C. Van Berg	952,207	1,092	239
1970	Jack C. Van Berg	974,818	1,312	282
1971	Dale Baird	290,553	1,130	245
1972	Jack C. Van Berg	1,381,067	1,342	286
1973	Dale Baird	416,592	1,558	305
1974	Jack C. Van Berg	1,567,418	1,712	329
1975	R. E. Dutrow	1,840,041	1,419	352
1976	Jack C. Van Berg	2,976,196	2,362	496
1977	K. T. Leatherbury	1,702,112	1,475	322
1978	K. T. Leatherbury	1,512,048	1,488	304
1979	Dale Baird	554,333	1,908	316
1980	Dale Baird	542,259	1,964	306
1981	Dale Baird	592,929	1,983	349
1982	Dale Baird	477,136	1,763	276
1983	Jack C. Van Berg	3,212,318	1,740	258
1984	Jack C. Van Berg	4,163,118	1,638	250
1985	Dale Baird	453,038	1,670	249
1986	Jack C. Van Berg	5,536,478	1,841	266
1987	D. Wayne Lukas	17,502,110	1,735	343
1988	D. Wayne Lukas	17,842,358	1,500	318
1989	D. Wayne Lukas	16,103,998	1,398	305
1990	D. Wayne Lukas	14,508,871	1,396	267
1991	Dale Baird	499,475	1,626	296
1992	Dale Baird	461,626	1,592	256
1993	Dale Baird	475,294	1,673	269
1994	Mario Beneito	1,440,880	1,108	247
1995	Dale Baird	699,146	1,485	286
1996	Dale Baird	1,077,565	1,520	330
1997	Dale Baird	1,237,322	1,479	300
1998	Dale Baird	1,575,592	1,378	290
1999	Dale Baird	2,091,769	1,297	304
2000	Scott Lake	5,736,002	1,045	337
2001	Scott Lake	7,817,856	1,566	407
2002	Steven M. Asmussen	10,246,910	1,810	407
2003	Scott Lake	9,152,959	2,009	454
2004	Steven M. Asmussen	14,003,202	2,293	555

*Starts unavailable until 1963

Leading North American Trainers – Lifetime Wins

The list below includes the top 50 winning trainers since 1911 and their records through Dec. 31, 2004. It includes wins and earnings from Thoroughbred races in the United States and Canada. Trainer statistics from seasons prior to 1963 include only wins and earnings and exclude trainers which did not saddle at least 10 winners during the year. Statistics prior to 1911 are not available.

Trainer	1st	Purses
Dale Baird	9,019	$29,277,186
Jack C. Van Berg	6,343	80,353,864
King T. Leatherbury	6,052	52,485,435
Richard P. Hazelton	4,593	36,722,343
D. Wayne Lukas	4,299	240,229,394
Jerry Hollendorfer	4,246	75,194,063
Frank H. Merrill, Jr.	3,974	16,980,632
Richard E. Dutrow, Sr.	3,665	36,189,085
Grover G. Delp	3,636	40,017,326
Hirsch Jacobs	3,593	15,356,904
H. Allen Jerkens	3,579	87,377,893
Everett Hammond	3,425	7,781,650
William I. Mott	3,283	134,697,056
Frank Martin, Sr.	3,172	45,044,683
Robert J. Frankel	3,128	173,587,987
Jere R. Smith, Sr.	3,108	28,865,426
William H. Bishop	3,058	10,337,050
David R. Vance	2,910	30,406,895
Bruce M. Kravets	2,896	18,110,176
Bernard S. Flint	2,890	44,556,137
Jerome C. Meyer	2,746	20,552,518
Steven M. Asmussen	2,715	63,136,615
Mario Beneito	2,695	11,038,092
Scott A. Lake	2,653	44,079,769
Robert E. Holthus	2,618	35,523,580
Harry F. Thompson, Jr.	2,560	15,103,656
Charles E. Whittingham	2,534	109,215,527
Robert R. Hilton	2,512	6,000,312
Jonathan E. Sheppard	2,470	48,221,025
Don Von Hemel	2,455	27,663,987
Gerald S. Bennett	2,452	18,302,261
Ronald L. McAnally	2,424	112,842,508
Dale Capuano	2,372	36,567,688
Henry P. Mercer	2,365	6,994,981
Bob E. Arnett	2,358	6,594,854
Ronald J. Dandy	2,326	17,984,207
Philip G. Johnson	2,315	47,519,937
Frank L. Brothers	2,274	43,834,881
Lazaro S. Barrera	2,269	49,932,176
Michael S. Ferraro	2,268	12,536,241
Edward T. Allard	2,246	26,253,146
Del W. Carroll	2,224	19,059,524
Ron K. Smith	2,208	14,658,703
James Sunny Fitzsimmons	2,176	12,981,615
Jeff C. Runco	2,169	15,000,558
Robert L. Martin	2,146	17,305,495
Charles W. Walker	2,141	11,953,492
Glenn L. Hild	2,139	22,486,361
John H. Forbes	2,124	29,791,856
Robert P. Klesaris	2,122	29,562,130

Leading North American Trainers – Lifetime Earnings

The list below includes the top 50 earning trainers since 1911 and their records through Dec. 31, 2004. It includes records from Thoroughbred races in the United States and Canada. Trainer statistics from seasons prior to 1963 include only wins and earnings and exclude trainers which did not saddle at least 10 winners during the year. Statistics prior to 1911 are not available.

Trainer	Starters	1st	2nd	3rd	Purses
D. Wayne Lukas	23,963	4,299	3,547	3,040	$240,229,394
Robert J. Frankel	15,149	3,128	2,547	2,118	173,587,987
William I. Mott	15,420	3,283	2,540	2,127	134,697,056
Ronald L. McAnally	16,291	2,424	2,243	2,043	112,842,508
Charles E. Whittingham	13,805	2,534	1,868	1,706	109,215,527
Bob Baffert	6,760	1,448	1,085	962	106,398,390
Richard E. Mandella	9,332	1,654	1,467	1,383	98,343,926
H. Allen Jerkens	18,912	3,579	2,571	2,256	87,377,893
Claude R. McGaughey III	5,998	1,411	1,068	924	86,939,859
Jack C. Van Berg	38,500	6,343	5,325	4,680	80,353,864
Jerry Hollendorfer	18,070	4,246	3,071	2,570	75,194,063
Neil D. Drysdale	5,635	1,115	856	826	71,291,047
Todd A. Pletcher	5,506	1,149	889	686	66,936,953
Nicholas P. Zito	10,916	1,366	1,307	1,246	65,319,329
Steven M. Asmussen	12,984	2,715	2,174	1,865	63,136,615
Roger L. Attfield	7,543	1,412	1,158	1,018	63,033,160
Flint S. Schulhofer	8,765	1,328	1,208	1,102	54,657,686
Woodford C. Stephens	8,208	1,937	1,173	983	53,014,814
Gary F. Jones	7,900	1,465	1,107	981	52,672,611
King T. Leatherbury	33,296	6,052	4,862	4,268	52,485,435
Melvin F. Stute	14,878	1,913	1,912	1,877	52,263,999
Lazaro S. Barrera	13,201	2,269	1,864	1,729	49,932,176
Jonathan E. Sheppard	14,802	2,470	2,226	2,123	48,221,025
Philip G. Johnson	14,066	2,315	1,784	1,829	47,519,937
W. Elliott Walden	5,531	1,001	842	715	45,146,868
Frank Martin, Sr.	17,664	3,172	2,465	2,329	45,044,683
Bernard S. Flint	15,794	2,890	2,316	1,957	44,556,137
Scott A. Lake	11,689	2,653	2,049	1,666	44,079,769
Frank L. Brothers	9,881	2,274	1,544	1,221	43,834,881
Mark A. Hennig	5,083	815	803	663	43,795,712
Darrell Vienna	7,176	1,110	999	924	43,625,860
James E. Day	6,878	1,138	1,013	898	43,059,429
Carl A. Nafzger	7,531	991	966	1,000	41,768,624
George R. Arnold, II	8,288	1,293	1,261	1,093	40,182,031
John C. Kimmel	4,961	935	801	675	40,039,437
Grover G. Delp	17,665	3,636	2,791	2,449	40,017,326
Gasper S. Moschera	8,910	1,546	1,355	1,310	40,004,972
Harvey L. Vanier	14,042	1,979	1,832	1,739	39,547,101
David E. Hofmans	5,487	868	721	686	39,177,935
Christophe Clement	3,650	679	607	485	39,158,938
Mike R. Mitchell	9,377	1,957	1,478	1,126	38,194,309
Thomas M. Amoss	6,693	1,569	1,138	915	37,718,488
Richard P. Hazelton	24,439	4,593	3,718	3,376	36,722,343
Dale Capuano	11,964	2,372	1,966	1,654	36,567,688
Mark R. Frostad	2,450	483	356	340	36,252,666
Neil J. Howard	4,599	965	739	634	36,230,163
Richard E. Dutrow, Sr.	18,996	3,665	3,009	2,514	36,189,085
Jerry M. Fanning	12,670	1,544	1,534	1,535	35,873,029
John W. Sadler	7,735	1,155	1,135	964	35,560,971
Robert E. Holthus	18,125	2,618	2,290	2,182	35,523,580

Leading Jockeys in 2004 by Money Won

Jockey	Starts	1st	2d	3d	Purses
John R. Velazquez	1,327	335	222	181	$22,248,661
Edgar S. Prado	1,445	281	249	204	18,342,106
Victor Espinoza	1,336	240	244	185	15,933,757
Stewart Elliott	1,363	262	211	177	*14,533,061
Jerry D. Bailey	641	148	113	99	14,503,844
Javier Castellano	1,283	212	204	197	13,038,943
Corey S. Nakatani	1,080	220	194	146	12,466,557
Rafael Bejarano	1,922	455	355	280	12,210,087
Ramon A. Dominguez	1,353	383	231	216	11,507,889
Cornelio H. Velasquez	1,593	240	260	241	11,098,689
Pat Day	798	172	134	105	10,882,222
Todd Kabel	686	156	109	77	10,637,082
Robby Albarado	1,309	213	223	197	10,371,173
Tyler Baze	1,399	239	187	205	10,181,132
Kent J. Desormeaux	696	109	108	104	8,729,543
Rene R. Douglas	1,297	242	194	182	8,495,434
David Romero Flores	874	123	102	128	8,365,977
Joe Bravo	1,153	214	188	160	8,169,405
Richard Migliore	873	149	122	109	8,058,110
Alex O. Solis	555	119	96	80	7,954,851
Mike E. Smith	692	111	112	75	7,863,942
Eibar Coa	1,015	210	149	116	7,799,508
Jose A. Santos	984	137	108	129	7,601,843
Patrick Husbands	748	141	115	114	7,432,199
Pablo Fragoso	1,181	164	201	180	7,167,990
Shaun Bridgmohan	1,265	153	178	178	7,093,424
Shane J. Sellers	698	146	97	94	6,531,304
Eddie Castro	1,552	270	249	226	6,109,838
John McKee	1,444	210	219	200	6,062,316
Emile Ramsammy	935	94	135	116	6,009,954
James McAleney	682	110	91	91	5,981,418
Jono C. Jones	670	91	90	83	5,978,103
Russell A. Baze	1,182	321	246	174	5,771,940
Eddie M. Martin, Jr.	1,300	225	190	172	5,658,957
Jose Valdivia, Jr.	761	76	98	98	5,648,352
Jorge F. Chavez	932	119	131	109	5,286,952
Abel Castellano, Jr.	1,209	201	203	180	5,077,531
Aaron T. Gryder	971	113	111	115	4,716,004
Gerard Melancon	1,267	205	182	187	4,711,881
Michael J. Luzzi	781	114	111	108	4,695,488
Jon Kenton Court	771	82	117	102	4,606,598
Jeremy Rose	885	165	136	127	4,550,917
Ryan Fogelsonger	1,065	217	174	179	4,525,877
Brian Joseph Hernandez, Jr.	1,466	243	210	191	4,401,867
Christopher A. Emigh	1,193	176	173	141	4,312,720
Eusebio Razo, Jr.	985	160	144	116	4,301,244
Mario G. Pino	922	156	145	144	4,300,470
Norberto Arroyo, Jr.	831	109	131	141	4,274,888
Javier Santiago	642	88	72	74	4,237,653
Julian Pimentel	747	116	107	102	4,236,205
Dana G. Whitney	1,428	267	214	196	4,184,757
Manoel R. Cruz	1,198	203	173	201	4,151,816
Robert C. Landry	529	58	66	64	4,144,957
Calvin H. Borel	1,062	115	124	127	4,001,877
Charles C. Lopez	658	107	100	104	3,990,297
Brice Blanc	554	65	73	69	3,984,038
Mark Guidry	785	120	97	93	3,900,613
Roberto Alvarado, Jr.	909	167	137	118	3,863,571
Slade Callaghan	555	73	68	69	3,772,048
Deshawn L. Parker	1,606	238	270	194	3,751,116
Angel R. Quinones	1,208	199	178	128	3,736,142
Martin A. Pedroza	828	139	113	103	3,731,447
Willie Martinez	1,058	152	137	109	3,638,700
Manuel Aguilar	1,272	170	176	172	3,625,226
Corey J. Lanerie	1,096	165	179	149	3,602,925
Steven Ronald Bahen	544	69	63	54	3,578,698
Gary L. Stevens	266	49	38	42	3,546,284
Carlos H. Marquez, Jr.	765	119	101	94	3,508,554
Roberto M. Gonzalez	966	163	141	139	3,469,182
Lonnie Meche	925	199	136	119	3,417,018
Ronald J. Warren, Jr.	928	170	145	129	3,350,617
Travis L. Dunkelberger	895	160	128	111	3,310,367
Mick Ruis	1,054	172	136	133	3,305,019
Timothy T. Doocy	1,029	187	183	143	3,259,729
Dennis Carr	939	170	163	150	3,215,657
Steve D. Hamilton	1,129	164	178	163	3,209,208
Roman Chapa	956	214	148	129	3,205,914
Constant Montpellier	592	62	66	82	3,199,444
Monte Clifton Berry	1,191	234	176	162	3,180,955
Kendrick Carmouche	1,146	159	128	137	3,180,600
Horacio Karamanos	956	135	151	144	3,166,819
Dino Luciani	461	67	54	67	3,164,150
J. D. Acosta	1,303	148	156	185	3,154,370
Larry J. Sterling, Jr.	787	125	98	106	3,119,216
Anthony Mawing	1,174	127	147	141	3,113,379
Jesse M. Campbell	970	119	146	119	3,067,883
Larry Melancon	619	85	63	77	3,019,547
Chad K. Murphy	861	157	120	110	2,985,318
Jose C. Caraballo	711	106	106	108	2,961,983
Edwin L. King, Jr.	837	90	108	120	2,894,221
James Graham	1,066	135	116	125	2,887,325
Gary Boulanger	919	128	131	126	2,874,748
Guy Smith	1,008	154	129	128	2,827,674
Ken S. Tohill	829	194	138	127	2,824,550
David Clark	429	55	42	46	2,818,626
Clinton L. Potts	872	125	128	115	2,789,972
Chance J. Rollins	934	139	154	156	2,781,325
Harry Vega	873	177	127	112	2,765,434
Alex Bisono	859	83	92	94	2,754,974
T. D. Houghton	1,524	285	270	210	2,754,284
Jose A. Velez, Jr.	517	60	86	72	2,749,866
John Jacinto	1,139	202	162	131	2,747,169
Steve J. Bourque	888	178	128	116	2,728,241
Jozbin Z. Santana	750	131	108	80	2,667,243
Chad Phillip Schvaneveldt	589	144	90	85	2,662,325
Casey T. Lambert	925	151	106	132	2,640,814
Frank T. Alvarado	981	117	163	163	2,612,235
Ramsey Zimmerman	1,295	326	227	181	2,597,941
Jesus Lopez Castanon	1,008	142	151	131	2,579,835
Rodney A. Prescott	1,789	251	233	233	2,572,852
Oswald M. Pereira	1,284	159	188	156	2,569,745
Luis S. Quinonez	1,140	148	165	174	2,567,843
Jose L. Espinoza	711	49	58	69	2,525,380
Fernando Jara	732	70	64	73	2,496,412
Brandon Whitacre	918	141	125	113	2,414,794
Corey Fraser	475	67	63	57	2,401,102
Christopher P. DeCarlo	449	66	53	61	2,395,994

Jockey	Starts	1st	2d	3d	Purses
Gerald Almodovar	939	139	132	110	2,372,230
Jamie Theriot	937	139	126	93	2,369,411
Jeremy Beasley	914	128	122	98	2,343,436
Anthony S. Black	670	149	111	93	2,330,382
Gerry Olguin	415	44	49	44	2,325,902
David Cora	892	122	117	104	2,325,367
Jose Luis Flores	931	178	129	132	2,317,433
Lanfranco Dettori	13	3	1	2	2,312,900
Quincy Welch	794	173	135	124	2,274,600
Terry J. Thompson	638	109	87	97	2,244,212
Michael C. Baze	797	99	112	91	2,229,363
Pedro V. Alvarado	533	130	85	87	2,216,447
Aurelio Toribio, Jr.	784	92	96	104	2,199,798
Alan Garcia	651	66	79	71	2,197,428
Carl James Woodley	884	157	142	97	2,180,834
Glenn W. Corbett	833	157	133	100	2,152,719
Oliver Castillo	839	89	107	103	2,151,370
Dean A. Sarvis	1,280	256	160	157	2,150,493
Eurico Rosa Da Silva	524	49	52	60	2,149,351
Elvis Joseph Perrodin	550	86	77	78	2,140,481
Jake Barton	751	108	124	110	2,133,705
Nick Santagata	954	124	140	128	2,111,271
Richard Anthony Dos Ramos	364	35	33	47	2,107,596
Francisco Duran	870	132	126	110	2,102,356
Carlos H. Silva	733	86	75	94	2,098,110
David G. Lopez	916	123	134	153	2,068,830
Jesus Sanchez	918	104	92	98	2,062,597
Kerwin John	597	50	62	76	2,053,203
Erick D. Rodriguez	823	102	112	114	2,023,780
Oscar Flores	751	100	89	65	2,019,988
Felipe F. Martinez	701	54	73	101	2,013,725
Shane Laviolette	938	93	100	129	2,007,063
Josiah Francis Hampshire, Jr.	954	176	105	138	1,985,642
Winston Albert Thompson	1,068	183	181	147	1,982,528
Na Somsanith	416	56	52	49	1,960,404
Ricardo Jaime	677	89	93	93	1,951,946
Seth B. Martinez	674	114	114	96	1,911,756
Richard Monterrey	764	101	114	87	1,910,556
Raymond Brian Sabourin	373	38	35	49	1,899,112
Carlos L. Castro	887	95	117	93	1,887,684
Rajiv Maragh	796	78	88	93	1,883,289
Patrick A. Valenzuela	202	45	26	39	1,864,873
Huber Villa-Gomez	974	178	143	133	1,849,748
Omar Figueroa	485	49	51	57	1,846,330
Jason P. Lumpkins	701	90	83	97	1,840,622
Rickey Walcott	702	138	114	106	1,835,637
Dyn Panell	723	159	99	91	1,819,451
Craig Perret	226	33	29	34	1,809,832
Eduardo O. Nunez	740	86	100	95	1,801,905
Victor H. Molina	665	105	101	91	1,791,385
Julio A. Garcia	417	76	54	52	1,773,518
Jorge Martin Bourdieu	676	95	102	85	1,771,807
Jillian Scharfstein	437	35	44	49	1,767,394
Abdiel Toribio	497	80	68	78	1,761,540
Scott A. Stevens	862	142	144	143	1,757,294
Timothy Thornton	505	69	63	79	1,756,059
Emanuel Cosme	910	101	110	103	1,754,380
Frankie Pennington	1,154	140	155	156	1,750,364
William D. Troilo	881	96	80	104	1,746,569

Jockey	Starts	1st	2d	3d	Purses
Sunny Singh	565	42	85	64	1,741,026
Donald R. Pettinger	474	72	54	76	1,716,614
Tracy J. Hebert	761	113	100	90	1,706,146
Thomas Clifton	909	183	122	113	1,700,822
Eduardo E. Perez	557	78	63	72	1,686,806
Scott Spieth	897	181	121	100	1,686,680
Perry Compton	928	146	131	125	1,673,500
Edwin Perez	864	91	117	113	1,662,407
Alex Birzer	1,002	127	122	143	1,662,355
Luis Garcia	790	93	111	118	1,656,247
Alfredo J. Juarez, Jr.	652	119	105	83	1,645,983
Bobby J. Walker, Jr.	510	93	73	49	1,635,833
Eric Camacho	660	111	106	83	1,626,091
Justin Shepherd	759	71	86	82	1,624,163
Cruz Contreras	583	84	82	74	1,618,810
Neil Poznansky	560	89	68	81	1,614,614
Alcibiades C. Cortez	666	87	76	76	1,612,286
Jose E. Lopez	721	91	87	90	1,612,005
Perry Wayne Ouzts	1,454	212	191	178	1,592,472
Casey Fusilier	670	88	98	83	1,582,951
David Wilson	577	80	88	78	1,582,686
Pedro A. Rodriguez	725	143	96	96	1,579,076
Randall A. Meier	637	70	76	82	1,569,440
Emilio Flores	1,295	160	187	167	1,567,387
Juan Umana	869	99	100	111	1,564,377
Martin Ramos Ramirez	675	83	86	73	1,563,430
Real E. Simard	723	112	92	77	1,562,267
Mary Elizabeth Doser	721	128	133	110	1,555,537
Derek C. Bell	678	115	102	84	1,550,470
Jeffery Burningham	1,109	118	123	141	1,531,111
Larry Taylor	952	118	107	124	1,523,579
Rosemary B. Homeister, Jr.	536	65	67	81	1,517,995
Heberto Castillo, Jr.	439	32	34	32	1,498,263
Marlon St. Julien	866	94	114	77	1,494,346
Eddie Zuniga	1,039	122	123	121	1,493,663
Leanne M. Painter	725	98	108	104	1,492,727
John R. Davila, Jr.	722	137	112	81	1,490,318
Ricky J. Faul	839	110	87	103	1,488,917
Andrew R. Ramgeet	720	90	89	94	1,486,634
Danny Sorenson	290	38	32	34	1,479,067
Kevin Leon Cogburn	1,004	114	172	146	1,474,260
Ricky Frazier	599	111	90	90	1,472,387
Frank Lovato, Jr.	469	44	51	50	1,471,891
Elvis Trujillo	534	55	75	73	1,463,099
Francine Villeneuve	391	67	55	48	1,457,356
David Mello	939	107	128	121	1,452,290
Joe M. Castro	445	76	63	84	1,447,396
Donnie J. Meche	432	59	58	53	1,446,659
Carlos Gonzalez	552	84	73	76	1,438,465
Macario Rodriguez	835	109	123	119	1,428,888
Miguel A. Perez	592	84	68	90	1,425,303
Sunday Diaz	625	76	79	82	1,402,937
Vladimir Diaz	1,030	143	161	134	1,399,696
Leroy Nelson	722	82	79	102	1,379,963
Paul R. Toscano	456	52	42	39	1,375,523
Larry C. Reynolds	488	49	67	54	1,374,944
Matt S. Garcia	406	39	36	62	1,372,915
Luis Antonio Gonzalez	878	144	114	103	1,372,312
Pedro Luis Cotto, Jr.	436	35	49	53	1,371,631

Jockey	Starts	1st	2d	3d	Purses
Martin Escobar	940	106	121	96	1,369,401
Joe Stokes	988	134	129	133	1,368,772
Jill E. Kinsey	921	94	114	100	1,367,597
Thomas L. Pompell	958	139	114	124	1,366,950
Julia Brimo	406	39	47	35	1,363,246
Ted D. Gondron	549	93	80	69	1,359,087
Rui M. Pimentel	284	39	26	34	1,358,016
Mark E. Rosenthal	568	65	62	56	1,356,647
Vernon Bush	842	97	86	107	1,354,102
William P. Otero	994	172	134	151	1,351,632
Chantal Sutherland	363	31	39	47	1,348,269
Simon P. Husbands	349	32	36	25	1,345,475
Terry A. Stanton	868	119	97	123	1,340,692
Christopher VanHassel	700	90	84	100	1,340,484
James McKnight	210	25	21	23	1,339,398
Brian Todd Bochinski	495	66	82	64	1,324,641
Adalberto Diaz Lopez	787	93	111	115	1,320,277
Greta Kuntzweiler	502	36	42	49	1,319,779
Garrett K. Gomez	261	36	46	40	1,314,941
Rex A. Stokes, III	709	97	74	77	1,313,235
Jean-Luc Samyn	368	22	27	32	1,311,895
Federico Mata	889	136	112	119	1,311,037
Wilson Omar Dieguez	945	188	135	125	1,306,281
Joseph C. Judice	765	108	108	88	1,303,800
Cecilio Penalba	607	73	66	68	1,302,407
James Lopez	612	67	87	67	1,301,176
Paul Albert Nicol, Jr.	520	88	76	81	1,291,848
Felix L. Ortiz	566	49	56	70	1,285,760
Orlando Mojica	952	110	123	95	1,283,454
Quincy Hamilton	873	137	128	106	1,281,674
Anthony J. D'Amico	440	53	58	55	1,280,991
Isaias D. Enriquez	455	43	55	50	1,274,978
Rodrigo Madrigal, Jr.	504	59	91	65	1,273,913
Kirk Paul LeBlanc	648	65	80	80	1,265,382
Roberto A. Perez	820	127	107	116	1,260,517
Joe M. Johnson	682	58	69	77	1,257,724
Dean P. Butler	667	73	81	69	1,257,065
Taylor M. Hole	778	115	130	117	1,256,986
Tammi Piermarini	778	117	128	95	1,256,177
Jose C. Ferrer	408	46	45	40	1,251,854
Jose R. Martinez, Jr.	576	46	42	62	1,243,337
Alfredo V. Clemente	434	32	51	53	1,234,467
Pedro Mercado	611	72	98	79	1,226,873
Kieren Fallon	11	4	3	0	1,226,640
Kevin Radke	344	66	56	48	1,224,181
Gary A. Birzer	618	75	81	83	1,214,008
Orlando Bocachica	670	105	100	92	1,188,348
Ricardo A. Valdes	432	55	51	52	1,175,924
Alfredo Clemente	791	98	104	84	1,171,511
Jeff Johnston	716	90	103	71	1,170,902
Perry A. Winters	615	79	72	73	1,167,266
Marco A. Ccamaque	1,298	200	196	181	1,165,398
Chin C. Yang	775	79	91	85	1,163,415
Sebastian O. Madrid	467	54	71	53	1,161,040
Joseph Rocco	545	51	76	52	1,158,689
Weldon T. Cloninger, Jr.	720	115	109	86	1,155,609
Ricardo Feliciano	647	85	81	96	1,146,352
Hiram G. Rivera	525	64	67	63	1,141,239
Julio E. Felix	886	118	137	112	1,133,033
Ignacio Puglisi	438	43	42	56	1,132,074
Hector L. Rosario, Jr.	986	154	132	135	1,128,888
Joel Campbell	686	121	89	91	1,127,173
Jason R. Eads	658	72	69	85	1,126,344
Leslie Mawing	754	68	94	97	1,121,441
Donald Edward Simington	679	69	94	86	1,120,808
Brian Joseph Hernandez	618	81	74	64	1,118,260
Russell W. Woolsey	818	93	125	99	1,114,137
Pedro Monterrey, Jr.	554	64	62	71	1,109,618
John A. Grabowski	566	100	94	74	1,093,348
Jose Riquelme	912	66	81	95	1,084,537
Todd Glasser	420	71	51	67	1,080,517
Ivan R. Gonzalez	1,004	179	135	129	1,072,509
Parker R. Buckley	650	104	85	75	1,070,795
Christopher Griffith	454	51	63	57	1,051,606
Curtis Kimes	888	142	125	93	1,048,944
Uriel A. Lopez	711	56	68	74	1,048,198
Enrique M. Jurado	336	53	45	35	1,046,324
Francisco Perez Fuentes	369	46	51	46	1,045,101
Shannon Campbell	715	56	57	56	1,039,976
Juan Ortega	626	44	59	76	1,036,024
Frank Albert Gonsalves	629	82	83	76	1,034,103
E. T. Baird	379	46	60	37	1,031,358
Brian Dale Peck	305	28	34	23	1,027,766
Jennie Roche	477	65	56	47	1,021,909
Lester Cash Knight	587	92	82	88	1,021,728
Jamie P. Spencer	15	0	1	5	1,015,900
Victor Carrero	616	70	66	80	1,012,225

*Includes $5,000,000 bonus.

North American earnings only

Leading Jockeys in 2004 by Races Won

Jockey	Starts	1st	2d	3d	Purses
Rafael Bejarano	1,922	455	355	280	$12,210,087
Ramon A. Dominguez	1,353	383	231	216	11,507,889
John R. Velazquez	1,327	335	222	181	22,248,661
Ramsey Zimmerman	1,295	326	227	181	2,597,941
Russell A. Baze	1,182	321	246	174	5,771,940
T. D. Houghton	1,524	285	270	210	2,754,284
Edgar S. Prado	1,445	281	249	204	18,342,106
Eddie Castro	1,552	270	249	226	6,109,838
Dana G. Whitney	1,428	267	214	196	4,184,757
Stewart Elliott	1,363	262	211	177	*14,533,061
Dean A. Sarvis	1,280	256	160	157	2,150,493
Rodney A. Prescott	1,789	251	233	233	2,572,852
Brian Joseph Hernandez, Jr.	1,466	243	210	191	4,401,867
Rene R. Douglas	1,297	242	194	182	8,495,434
Victor Espinoza	1,336	240	244	185	15,933,757
Cornelio H. Velasquez	1,593	240	260	241	11,098,689
Tyler Baze	1,399	239	187	205	10,181,132
Deshawn L. Parker	1,606	238	270	194	3,751,116
Monte Clifton Berry	1,191	234	176	162	3,180,955
Eddie M. Martin, Jr.	1,300	225	190	172	5,658,957
Corey S. Nakatani	1,080	220	194	146	12,466,557
Ryan Fogelsonger	1,065	217	174	179	4,525,877
Joe Bravo	1,153	214	188	160	8,169,405
Roman Chapa	956	214	148	129	3,205,914
Robby Albarado	1,309	213	223	197	10,371,173
Javier Castellano	1,283	212	204	197	13,038,943
Perry Wayne Ouzts	1,454	212	191	178	1,592,472
Eibar Coa	1,015	210	149	116	7,799,508
John McKee	1,444	210	219	200	6,062,316
Gerard Melancon	1,267	205	182	187	4,711,881
Manoel R. Cruz	1,198	203	173	201	4,151,816
John Jacinto	1,139	202	162	131	2,747,169
Abel Castellano, Jr.	1,209	201	203	180	5,077,531
Marco A. Ccamaque	1,298	200	196	181	1,165,398
Angel R. Quinones	1,208	199	178	128	3,736,142
Lonnie Meche	925	199	136	119	3,417,018
Ken S. Tohill	829	194	138	127	2,824,550
Wilson Omar Dieguez	945	188	135	125	1,306,281
Timothy T. Doocy	1,029	187	183	143	3,259,729
Winston Albert Thompson	1,068	183	181	147	1,982,528
Thomas Clifton	909	183	122	113	1,700,822
Scott Spieth	897	181	121	100	1,686,680
Ivan R. Gonzalez	1,004	179	135	129	1,072,509
Steve J. Bourque	888	178	128	116	2,728,241
Jose Luis Flores	931	178	129	132	2,317,433
Huber Villa-Gomez	974	178	143	133	1,849,748
Harry Vega	873	177	127	112	2,765,434
Christopher A. Emigh	1,193	176	173	141	4,312,720
Josiah Francis Hampshire, Jr.	954	176	105	138	1,985,642
Quincy Welch	794	173	135	124	2,274,600
Pat Day	798	172	134	105	10,882,222
Mick Ruis	1,054	172	136	133	3,305,019
William P. Otero	994	172	134	151	1,351,632
Manuel Aguilar	1,272	170	176	172	3,625,226
Ronald J. Warren, Jr.	928	170	145	129	3,350,617
Dennis Carr	939	170	163	150	3,215,657
Roberto Alvarado, Jr.	909	167	137	118	3,863,571
Jeremy Rose	885	165	136	127	4,550,917
Corey J. Lanerie	1,096	165	179	149	3,602,925
Pablo Fragoso	1,181	164	201	180	7,167,990
Steve D. Hamilton	1,129	164	178	163	3,209,208
Roberto M. Gonzalez	966	163	141	139	3,469,182
Eusebio Razo, Jr.	985	160	144	116	4,301,244
Travis L. Dunkelberger	895	160	128	111	3,310,367
Emilio Flores	1,295	160	187	167	1,567,387
Kendrick Carmouche	1,146	159	128	137	3,180,600
Oswald M. Pereira	1,284	159	188	156	2,569,745
Dyn Panell	723	159	99	91	1,819,451
Chad K. Murphy	861	157	120	110	2,985,318
Carl James Woodley	884	157	142	97	2,180,834
Glenn W. Corbett	833	157	133	100	2,152,719
Todd Kabel	686	156	109	77	10,637,082
Mario G. Pino	922	156	145	144	4,300,470
Guy Smith	1,008	154	129	128	2,827,674
Hector L. Rosario, Jr.	986	154	132	135	1,128,888
Shaun Bridgmohan	1,265	153	178	178	7,093,424
Willie Martinez	1,058	152	137	109	3,638,700
Casey T. Lambert	925	151	106	132	2,640,814
Richard Migliore	873	149	122	109	8,058,110
Anthony S. Black	670	149	111	93	2,330,382
Jerry D. Bailey	641	148	113	99	14,503,844
J. D. Acosta	1,303	148	156	185	3,154,370
Luis S. Quinonez	1,140	148	165	174	2,567,843
Shane J. Sellers	698	146	97	94	6,531,304
Perry Compton	928	146	131	125	1,673,500
Chad Phillip Schvaneveldt	589	144	90	85	2,662,325
Luis Antonio Gonzalez	878	144	114	103	1,372,312
Pedro A. Rodriguez	725	143	96	96	1,579,076
Vladimir Diaz	1,030	143	161	134	1,399,696
Jesus Lopez Castanon	1,008	142	151	131	2,579,835
Scott A. Stevens	862	142	144	143	1,757,294
Curtis Kimes	888	142	125	93	1,048,944
Juan M. Gutierrez	806	142	137	141	904,865
Patrick Husbands	748	141	115	114	7,432,199
Brandon Whitacre	918	141	125	113	2,414,794
Frankie Pennington	1,154	140	155	156	1,750,364
Martin A. Pedroza	828	139	113	103	3,731,447
Chance J. Rollins	934	139	154	156	2,781,325
Gerald Almodovar	939	139	132	110	2,372,230
Jamie Theriot	937	139	126	93	2,369,411
Thomas L. Pompell	958	139	114	124	1,366,950
Robert Dean Williams	903	139	100	99	964,827
Rickey Walcott	702	138	114	106	1,835,637
Jose A. Santos	984	137	108	129	7,601,843
John R. Davila, Jr.	722	137	112	81	1,490,318
Quincy Hamilton	873	137	128	106	1,281,674
Federico Mata	889	136	112	119	1,311,037
Horacio Karamanos	956	135	151	144	3,166,819
James Graham	1,066	135	116	125	2,887,325
Joe Stokes	988	134	129	133	1,368,772
Francisco Duran	870	132	126	110	2,102,356
Jozbin Z. Santana	750	131	108	80	2,667,243
Pedro V. Alvarado	533	130	85	87	2,216,447
Gary Boulanger	919	128	131	126	2,874,748
Jeremy Beasley	914	128	122	98	2,343,436
Mary Elizabeth Doser	721	128	133	110	1,555,537
Anthony Mawing	1,174	127	147	141	3,113,379
Alex Birzer	1,002	127	122	143	1,662,355
Roberto A. Perez	820	127	107	116	1,260,517
Larry J. Sterling, Jr.	787	125	98	106	3,119,216
Clinton L. Potts	872	125	128	115	2,789,972
Nick Santagata	954	124	140	128	2,111,271
David Romero Flores	874	123	102	128	8,365,977
David G. Lopez	916	123	134	153	2,068,830
David Cora	892	122	117	104	2,325,367
Eddie Zuniga	1,039	122	123	121	1,493,663
Joel Campbell	686	121	89	91	1,127,173
Esteban Angel Gomez	826	121	130	99	823,045
Mark Guidry	785	120	97	93	3,900,613
Alex O. Solis	555	119	96	80	7,954,851
Jorge F. Chavez	932	119	131	109	5,286,952
Carlos H. Marquez, Jr.	765	119	101	94	3,508,554
Jesse M. Campbell	970	119	146	119	3,067,883
Alfredo J. Juarez, Jr.	652	119	105	83	1,645,983
Terry A. Stanton	868	119	97	123	1,340,692
Jeffery Burningham	1,109	118	123	141	1,531,111
Larry Taylor	952	118	107	124	1,523,579

Jockey	Starts	1st	2d	3d	Purses
Julio E. Felix	886	118	137	112	1,133,033
Frank T. Alvarado	981	117	163	163	2,612,235
Tammi Piermarini	778	117	128	95	1,256,177
Julian Pimentel	747	116	107	102	4,236,205
Calvin H. Borel	1,062	115	124	127	4,001,877
Derek C. Bell	678	115	102	84	1,550,470
Taylor M. Hole	778	115	130	117	1,256,986
Weldon T. Cloninger, Jr.	720	115	109	86	1,155,609
Michael J. Luzzi	781	114	111	108	4,695,488
Seth B. Martinez	674	114	114	96	1,911,756
Kevin Leon Cogburn	1,004	114	172	146	1,474,260
Aaron T. Gryder	971	113	111	115	4,716,004
Tracy J. Hebert	761	113	100	90	1,706,146
Real E. Simard	723	112	92	77	1,562,267
Mike E. Smith	692	111	112	75	7,863,942
Eric Camacho	660	111	106	83	1,626,091
Ricky Frazier	599	111	90	90	1,472,387
Daniel Centeno	776	111	93	98	861,079
James McAleney	682	110	91	91	5,981,418
Ricky J. Faul	839	110	87	103	1,488,917
Orlando Mojica	952	110	123	95	1,283,454
Kent J. Desormeaux	696	109	108	104	8,729,543
Norberto Arroyo, Jr.	831	109	131	141	4,274,888
Terry J. Thompson	638	109	87	97	2,244,212
Macario Rodriguez	835	109	123	119	1,428,888
Jake Barton	751	108	124	110	2,133,705
Joseph C. Judice	765	108	108	88	1,303,800
Charles C. Lopez	658	107	100	104	3,990,297
David Mello	939	107	128	121	1,452,290
Jose C. Caraballo	711	106	106	108	2,961,983
Martin Escobar	940	106	121	96	1,369,401
Victor H. Molina	665	105	101	91	1,791,385
Orlando Bocachica	670	105	100	92	1,188,348
Jesus Sanchez	918	104	92	98	2,062,597
Parker R. Buckley	650	104	85	75	1,070,795
Christian Rojas	753	103	89	91	626,762
Erick D. Rodriguez	823	102	112	114	2,023,780
Travis Wayne Hightower	508	102	67	72	897,521
Richard Monterrey	764	101	114	87	1,910,556
Emanuel Cosme	910	101	110	103	1,754,380
Dennis Michael Collins	699	101	109	99	629,467
Oscar Flores	751	100	89	65	2,019,988
John A. Grabowski	566	100	94	74	1,093,348
Miguel Luis Gaeta Hernandez	783	100	131	111	952,430
Ben Russell	446	100	78	57	912,399
Michael C. Baze	797	99	112	91	2,229,363
Juan Umana	869	99	100	111	1,564,377
Leanne M. Painter	725	98	108	104	1,492,727
Alfredo Clemente	791	98	104	84	1,171,511
Armando Martinez	792	98	66	87	594,228
Vernon Bush	842	97	86	107	1,354,102
Rex A. Stokes, III	709	97	74	77	1,313,235
Amanda L. Crandall	957	97	93	100	988,629
William D. Troilo	881	96	80	104	1,746,569
Carlos L. Castro	887	95	117	93	1,887,684
Jorge Martin Bourdieu	676	95	102	85	1,771,807
Emile Ramsammy	935	94	135	116	6,009,954
Marlon St. Julien	866	94	114	77	1,494,346
Jill E. Kinsey	921	94	114	100	1,367,597
Shane Laviolette	938	93	100	129	2,007,063
Luis Garcia	790	93	111	118	1,656,247
Bobby J. Walker, Jr.	510	93	73	49	1,635,833
Ted D. Gondron	549	93	80	69	1,359,087
Adalberto Diaz Lopez	787	93	111	115	1,320,277
Russell W. Woolsey	818	93	125	99	1,114,137
Paul M. Nolan	873	93	134	125	946,004
Aurelio Toribio, Jr.	784	92	96	104	2,199,798
Lester Cash Knight	587	92	82	88	1,021,728
Edilberto Rodriguez	729	92	91	95	799,658

Jockey	Starts	1st	2d	3d	Purses
Luis A. Belmonte	760	92	107	87	792,006
Jono C. Jones	670	91	90	83	5,978,103
Edwin Perez	864	91	117	113	1,662,407
Jose E. Lopez	721	91	87	90	1,612,005
Lorenzo Castane Lopez	801	91	87	109	571,730
Edwin L. King, Jr.	837	90	108	120	2,894,221
Jason P. Lumpkins	701	90	83	97	1,840,622
Andrew R. Ramgeet	720	90	89	94	1,486,634
Christopher VanHassel	700	90	84	100	1,340,484
Jeff Johnston	716	90	103	71	1,170,902
Justin Kravets	684	90	68	60	728,049
Jorge Tipa	601	90	67	68	650,464
Oliver Castillo	839	89	107	103	2,151,370
Ricardo Jaime	677	89	93	93	1,951,946
Neil Poznansky	560	89	68	81	1,614,614
Joel Santiago	908	89	120	131	844,406
Kelly Bridges	592	89	99	80	697,610
Javier Santiago	642	88	72	74	4,237,653
Casey Fusilier	670	88	98	83	1,582,951
Paul Albert Nicol, Jr.	520	88	76	81	1,291,848
Alcibiades C. Cortez	666	87	76	76	1,612,286
Elvis Joseph Perrodin	550	86	77	78	2,140,481
Carlos H. Silva	733	86	75	94	2,098,110
Eduardo O. Nunez	740	86	100	95	1,801,905
Jose J. Delgado	743	86	88	79	855,796
Alberto R. Higuera	772	86	98	114	654,389
Larry Melancon	619	85	63	77	3,019,547
Ricardo Feliciano	647	85	81	96	1,146,352
Twyla Beckner	524	85	110	85	296,077
Cruz Contreras	583	84	82	74	1,618,810
Carlos Gonzalez	552	84	73	76	1,438,465
Miguel A. Perez	592	84	68	90	1,425,303
Nena Matz	686	84	89	99	966,789
Alex Bisono	859	83	92	94	2,754,974
Martin Ramos Ramirez	675	83	86	73	1,563,430
Gallyn Vick Mitchell	441	83	73	73	868,460
Sandi Lee Gann	479	83	82	65	831,793
Jon Kenton Court	771	82	117	102	4,606,598
Leroy Nelson	722	82	79	102	1,379,963
Frank Albert Gonsalves	629	82	83	76	1,034,103
Brian Joseph Hernandez	618	81	74	64	1,118,260
James Christopher Herrell	784	81	68	90	670,673
Deborah Hoonan	595	81	89	81	628,796
Abdiel Toribio	497	80	68	78	1,761,540
David Wilson	577	80	88	78	1,582,686
Jerome Carkeek	846	80	98	130	513,467
Edgar Paucar	605	80	56	75	495,684
Perry A. Winters	615	79	72	73	1,167,266
Chin C. Yang	775	79	91	85	1,163,415
Jeffrey Skerrett	779	79	83	82	876,549
Yuri Yaranga	927	79	96	117	487,293
Rajiv Maragh	796	78	88	93	1,883,289
Eduardo E. Perez	557	78	63	72	1,686,806
Juan G. Rivera	753	78	83	84	707,298
Jorge Carreno	601	78	87	64	537,315
Shannon Beauregard	604	77	93	90	994,979
Ken A. Shino	565	77	71	73	877,803
Jose Valdivia, Jr.	761	76	98	98	5,648,352
Julio A. Garcia	417	76	54	52	1,773,518
Joe M. Castro	445	76	63	84	1,447,396
Sunday Diaz	625	76	79	82	1,402,937
Jeremias Flores	515	76	70	65	732,934
David Garcia	601	76	76	73	597,830
Gary A. Birzer	618	75	81	83	1,214,008
Sidney P. LeJeune, Jr.	813	75	85	91	952,119
Irwin J. Rosendo	721	75	107	85	869,003
Jose Luis Calo	707	75	94	81	447,609

*Includes $5,000,000 bonus.
North American starts only

Leading Jockeys in 2004 by Stakes Earnings

Jockey	Starts	1st	2d	3d	Purses
John R. Velazquez	248	56	49	38	$13,485,981
Jerry D. Bailey	191	44	33	31	10,559,278
Edgar S. Prado	235	50	35	31	10,480,485
Stewart Elliott	139	29	18	14	*9,567,184
Victor Espinoza	193	39	28	24	8,703,610
Javier Castellano	162	27	17	27	5,874,291
Corey S. Nakatani	168	33	28	20	5,642,497
Pat Day	184	26	36	28	5,594,209
Todd Kabel	99	36	13	13	5,497,303
Kent J. Desormeaux	134	17	20	16	4,964,237
Robby Albarado	171	29	26	22	4,712,718
Ramon A. Dominguez	132	27	19	22	4,624,915
Mike E. Smith	139	17	29	17	4,443,831
Alex O. Solis	103	27	14	14	4,348,546
Cornelio H. Velasquez	199	20	35	25	4,312,432
David Romero Flores	148	20	12	26	4,201,693
Rafael Bejarano	145	31	16	18	4,129,334
Jose A. Santos	156	20	14	24	3,569,123
Eibar Coa	170	43	18	19	3,542,121
Richard Migliore	127	18	24	12	3,482,745
Shane J. Sellers	105	24	17	10	3,332,731
Tyler Baze	163	18	26	18	3,121,840
Rene R. Douglas	119	14	16	17	2,999,552
Jose Valdivia, Jr.	113	15	18	15	2,887,748
Joe Bravo	138	19	24	21	2,687,090
Lanfranco Dettori	10	3	1	0	2,303,000
Jono C. Jones	62	8	12	13	2,167,229
Emile Ramsammy	89	13	11	11	2,100,071
Gary L. Stevens	82	10	11	13	2,010,780
Brice Blanc	90	15	12	10	1,914,178
Patrick Husbands	84	10	10	13	1,886,429
Jon Kenton Court	87	8	15	12	1,875,899
Eddie Castro	119	18	17	22	1,848,858
Jorge F. Chavez	127	8	13	18	1,679,634
Robert C. Landry	60	4	9	10	1,661,893
Gerard Melancon	111	22	17	18	1,638,184
Eddie M. Martin, Jr.	100	18	18	10	1,632,216
James McAleney	68	8	10	12	1,616,415
Shaun Bridgmohan	110	7	17	23	1,586,735
John McKee	93	12	10	14	1,468,462
Javier Santiago	81	5	7	11	1,376,054
Pablo Fragoso	86	10	10	14	1,259,258
Russell A. Baze	69	16	15	11	1,220,632
Abel Castellano, Jr.	80	15	13	7	1,199,139
Ryan Fogelsonger	72	15	9	12	1,172,648
Kieren Fallon	6	2	1	0	1,148,995
Steven Ronald Bahen	31	9	8	2	1,148,886
Jeremy Rose	61	6	11	8	1,119,309
Christopher P. DeCarlo	71	18	8	5	1,097,351
Charles C. Lopez	63	6	14	12	1,085,665
Calvin H. Borel	71	5	11	11	1,060,178
Carlos H. Marquez, Jr.	66	12	10	6	1,049,606
Willie Martinez	54	6	8	4	1,037,324
Aaron T. Gryder	82	11	11	11	1,028,395
Mario G. Pino	63	13	13	11	1,019,437
Jamie P. Spencer	11	0	1	5	1,013,300
Michael J. Luzzi	63	9	7	8	956,650
Manuel Aguilar	91	9	13	13	940,771
Manoel R. Cruz	104	13	9	20	930,461
Roberto M. Gonzalez	46	11	4	7	923,925
Mark Guidry	70	7	5	9	917,616
Norberto Arroyo, Jr.	72	11	5	14	915,991
Corey J. Lanerie	106	8	17	16	886,145
Eusebio Razo, Jr.	66	6	11	7	852,862
Ken S. Tohill	71	18	12	14	849,010
Lonnie Meche	81	16	11	8	833,840
Julian Pimentel	81	11	10	14	832,724
Ricardo Jaime	63	5	12	14	799,680
David Clark	28	7	4	2	787,116
Roman Chapa	64	11	5	10	781,910
Donald R. Pettinger	51	8	9	14	765,313
Jose A. Velez, Jr.	87	4	14	12	765,010
Slade Callaghan	40	2	7	8	745,457
Elvis Joseph Perrodin	73	12	8	9	732,252
Jorge Martin Bourdieu	69	16	10	9	723,477
Jeremy Beasley	56	8	10	8	716,681
Larry Melancon	66	4	6	9	715,421
Timothy T. Doocy	56	15	6	8	715,191
Richard Anthony Dos Ramos	40	5	2	3	708,124
Heberto Castillo, Jr.	45	9	2	2	705,319
Terry J. Thompson	33	7	7	8	684,075
Martin A. Pedroza	54	10	5	9	676,839
Julio A. Garcia	68	8	9	5	675,183
Greta Kuntzweiler	25	3	5	4	648,017
Guy Smith	55	9	10	10	642,579
Omar Figueroa	36	8	0	5	629,805
Ronald J. Warren, Jr.	46	13	5	5	611,025
Ricky Frazier	36	9	8	3	607,705
Jozbin Z. Santana	49	9	7	3	602,076
Aurelio Toribio, Jr.	61	9	8	2	601,425
Monte Clifton Berry	68	6	11	10	598,771
Craig Perret	48	4	4	8	597,070
Donnie J. Meche	45	7	4	7	591,907
Patrick A. Valenzuela	20	3	3	6	582,303
Pedro V. Alvarado	39	9	7	8	572,034
Mary Elizabeth Doser	27	8	7	2	542,068
Chance J. Rollins	42	7	4	7	537,220
John Jacinto	63	12	10	4	533,776
Scott A. Stevens	87	15	17	14	532,456
Christopher A. Emigh	57	4	8	6	524,077
Horacio Karamanos	62	4	6	14	512,678
Larry J. Sterling, Jr.	39	6	4	6	510,117
Casey T. Lambert	55	6	4	8	505,392
Paul R. Toscano	36	5	5	1	496,566
Dino Luciani	34	3	4	6	483,013
Chad K. Murphy	26	6	6	5	479,300
Jesus Lopez Castanon	41	8	2	6	478,294
Raymond Brian Sabourin	26	3	6	6	477,931
Jesse M. Campbell	47	6	4	5	474,957
T. D. Houghton	51	6	11	3	473,526
Gary Boulanger	84	4	8	13	468,198
Mick Ruis	59	8	7	2	467,541
Jillian Scharfstein	16	4	2	3	462,194
Jose L. Espinoza	40	5	5	1	436,808
Roberto Alvarado, Jr.	36	5	2	6	436,789
Quincy Welch	48	8	9	8	429,884
Steve J. Bourque	36	9	6	4	427,500
Glenn W. Corbett	61	6	10	7	427,178
Danny Sorenson	35	4	0	5	424,125
Kerwin John	36	2	1	4	419,870
David Wilson	45	4	11	8	419,552
Tracy J. Hebert	40	6	5	9	416,395
Jean-Luc Samyn	32	3	3	3	416,128
Gerry Olguin	23	3	2	3	415,919
Carlos H. Silva	29	7	2	2	409,825
Abdiel Toribio	56	7	6	8	407,950
Constant Montpellier	41	1	3	7	406,800
Jamie Theriot	39	5	7	3	406,750
Garrett K. Gomez	33	2	4	6	400,497
Harry Vega	40	5	3	4	397,953
Luis S. Quinonez	65	5	6	11	394,230
Francisco Perez Fuentes	35	10	4	2	389,864
Jose C. Caraballo	34	5	2	7	388,173
Jake Barton	39	4	6	7	385,589
Edwin L. King, Jr.	72	2	9	10	377,237
Real E. Simard	44	7	5	4	366,900
Wilson Omar Dieguez	58	11	14	10	361,708
Alfredo J. Juarez, Jr.	64	11	6	5	358,762
Travis L. Dunkelberger	37	7	7	5	358,660
Larry C. Reynolds	21	6	3	4	355,028
Anthony S. Black	29	7	2	4	352,257
Frank Lovato, Jr.	41	3	3	4	352,103
Larry Taylor	38	6	3	4	347,781
Steve D. Hamilton	43	4	6	3	347,200
Seth B. Martinez	34	8	8	4	345,326
Eurico Rosa Da Silva	21	2	1	3	335,294
Huber Villa-Gomez	39	8	7	5	332,525
Joel Campbell	57	10	2	5	332,208
Jason P. Lumpkins	28	4	7	2	331,297
Ariel Smith	18	5	0	0	328,597
Leanne M. Painter	39	7	7	5	328,106
Matthew Otis McCarron	23	6	1	1	327,413
Ramsey Zimmerman	35	7	4	4	326,956

Jockey	Starts	1st	2d	3d	Purses
James McKnight	18	2	0	3	326,051
Chad Phillip Schvaneveldt	32	5	4	4	324,950
Rosemary B. Homeister, Jr.	42	4	9	5	322,075
Miguel Luis Gaeta Hernandez	62	13	8	7	317,134
Erick D. Rodriguez	28	5	2	8	315,295
James Graham	54	4	4	6	307,054
Derek C. Bell	43	4	8	13	302,013
David C. Nuesch	15	1	4	1	301,772
James Lopez	36	4	6	2	298,310
Brian Dale Peck	18	2	5	0	296,818
Brian Joseph Hernandez, Jr.	34	4	3	7	295,775
Francine Villeneuve	15	4	4	2	283,825
Jose E. Lopez	28	4	3	6	283,000
Richard Harvey Hamel	34	8	2	1	280,450
Rickey Walcott	40	5	8	7	278,390
Frank T. Alvarado	36	3	3	8	275,960
Vince J. Guerra	44	9	3	5	274,660
Adalberto Diaz Lopez	33	5	2	5	273,743
Dennis Carr	38	1	9	5	272,200
Roberto A. Perez	25	7	2	3	270,527
Tony Noguez	20	6	1	0	269,578
Alex Bisono	30	2	4	1	269,544
Justin Shepherd	31	3	2	1	268,468
Sandi Lee Gann	37	6	4	6	267,893
Eduardo O. Nunez	46	3	3	2	266,250
Sebastian O. Madrid	44	1	11	2	266,000
Phil Teator	22	3	2	2	264,700
David Bentley	24	6	3	3	263,964
Chad Hoverson	28	3	4	2	261,493
Victor H. Molina	21	5	1	3	258,236
Gallyn Vick Mitchell	30	6	7	5	258,060
Richard Monterrey	26	3	6	3	256,800
Isaias D. Enriquez	27	3	5	2	255,669
Oliver Castillo	42	1	8	2	252,430
Eric Saint-Martin	17	3	3	0	250,085
Joe M. Castro	26	3	5	4	249,370
Perry Compton	50	6	6	6	247,994
Neil Poznansky	22	5	2	2	247,850
Federico Mata	39	5	2	5	247,491
J. D. Acosta	25	5	4	2	245,866
Chin C. Yang	12	2	2	1	244,370
Chris Loseth	36	4	4	6	244,068
Robert V. Skelly	24	3	6	1	242,174
William D. Troilo	38	5	2	5	240,992
Travis Wayne Hightower	28	7	7	1	237,245
Dean A. Sarvis	28	4	2	3	235,191
Weldon T. Cloninger, Jr.	24	5	1	3	233,952
Carlos Olivero	12	3	1	1	232,000
Jason R. Eads	36	7	4	1	223,242
Perry A. Winters	35	4	8	5	222,060
Felipe F. Martinez	28	2	2	2	218,207
Felipe Valdez	31	6	5	3	218,130
Donald Edward Simington	35	3	7	3	213,120
Anthony J. D'Amico	18	2	3	3	211,800
Corey Fraser	11	1	3	1	211,764
Ricardo Feliciano	26	4	3	5	209,825
Shannon Uske	13	3	2	1	209,260
Jose C. Ferrer	40	4	3	0	205,525
Dana G. Whitney	21	4	1	4	205,425
Casey Fusilier	19	3	6	2	204,778
Jose R. Martinez, Jr.	30	1	2	3	204,598
Ted D. Gondron	25	3	5	4	204,449
Dale V. Beckner	24	1	6	0	201,546
Kelly Bridges	50	6	9	6	201,069
Andrasch Starke	2	0	1	1	200,000
Carlos D. Madeira	37	3	5	9	197,930
Joseph C. Judice	32	0	8	3	196,601
Danush Sukie	17	4	3	2	196,204
Joseph Rocco, Jr.	18	4	3	2	195,380
Luis Garcia	27	2	3	1	193,539
Matt S. Garcia	25	2	2	1	192,818
Alex Birzer	33	4	1	7	192,015
Frank Albert Gonsalves	26	3	3	4	191,462
Ken Hendricks	19	4	7	1	191,249
Rick Wilson	11	3	3	1	191,000
Nick Santagata	24	3	5	6	189,259
Carlos Gonzalez	38	2	5	6	189,150
Chantal Sutherland	15	0	5	0	187,920
Winston Albert Thompson	25	4	3	5	186,510
Martin Ramos Ramirez	13	4	2	0	183,750
Cecilio Penalba	34	4	4	2	182,350
Tom Foley	17	5	3	0	180,670
Hector L. Rosario, Jr.	23	4	2	5	180,600
Michael Phillip Iammarino	33	4	1	8	180,470
Carlos Montalvo	11	2	3	1	180,191
Hiram G. Rivera	19	3	3	0	179,280
Na Somsanith	14	0	3	3	177,944
Curtis Kimes	37	6	3	5	177,136
Bobby J. Walker, Jr.	16	2	5	2	177,100
G. F. Almeida	13	1	3	1	173,607
Eduardo E. Perez	26	3	2	4	172,340
Thomas L. Pompell	27	5	4	2	170,244
Pat Smullen	2	1	0	0	170,000
Filemon T. Rodriguez	19	2	2	3	169,360
Michael Dennis Clark	8	1	1	1	169,249
Christopher Read	7	3	0	3	168,810
Dyn Panell	27	4	6	2	168,800
Josiah Francis Hampshire, Jr.	20	6	1	2	166,000
Robert Walsh	14	3	4	1	165,916
Desmond Bryan	25	3	2	2	162,800
Earlie Fires	18	1	1	3	157,121
Robert W. Johnson	17	3	0	0	157,015
Esteban Angel Gomez	56	5	8	5	156,178
Terry A. Stanton	36	1	5	10	156,150
Kevin Radke	16	2	0	2	155,125
Luis Antonio Gonzalez	26	3	6	2	154,725
Tony Farina	15	1	2	2	153,913
Ben Russell	28	2	5	2	152,593
Kendrick Carmouche	23	1	3	2	151,786
John A. Grabowski	8	3	1	1	151,066
Marlon St. Julien	32	1	3	3	150,770
Yutaka Take	2	0	1	0	150,000
Ricky J. Faul	30	3	1	5	148,700
Paul Albert Nicol, Jr.	14	3	2	2	147,988
Jeff Johnston	22	2	4	4	145,850
Rui M. Pimentel	14	0	2	2	145,512
Brian James Theriot	25	6	3	3	144,540
Kelly Michael Murray	28	3	2	5	142,379
Kevin Krigger	25	3	3	2	140,338
Enrique M. Jurado	20	2	2	3	139,350
Rodney A. Prescott	26	3	5	4	139,262
Simon P. Husbands	12	1	1	0	137,620
Alberto R. Higuera	45	4	8	11	136,832
Thomas Clifton	16	2	3	2	136,763
Tom G. Turner	12	3	0	0	135,300
Anthony Mawing	33	0	5	6	134,799
Kevin Leon Cogburn	32	3	3	3	134,751
Pedro A. Rodriguez	21	2	1	5	134,288
Martin Escobar	30	3	2	3	132,998
Nena Matz	30	1	4	4	132,040
Francisco Duran	22	2	3	2	131,679
Armando Martinez	42	8	5	3	131,379
Perry S. Whetstone	31	2	4	3	131,149
Juan M. Gutierrez	42	6	4	8	130,818
Lester Cash Knight	15	4	3	0	130,086
Joseph J. Steiner	9	1	1	0	129,160
Russell Vicchrilli	24	4	9	3	129,005
Travis Wales	23	5	2	3	127,570
Ignacio Puglisi	32	1	2	5	126,558
Carl James Woodley	33	0	8	4	125,422
Gus M. Brown	17	1	3	2	123,980
Miguel A. Perez	13	2	1	2	123,545
Anthony Stephen	23	2	0	3	120,714
Berkley R. Packer	30	13	4	4	120,387
Russell W. Woolsey	24	2	2	6	118,910
Blair Waterman	14	3	3	2	118,164
Clark E. Jones	21	2	5	2	117,191
Bobby L. Johnson	28	3	5	8	117,069
Paul Leacock	17	3	3	2	115,241

* Includes $5,000,000 bonus.

Leading Jockeys in 2004 by Stakes Won

Jockey	Starts	1st	2d	3d	Purses
John R. Velazquez	248	56	49	38	$13,485,981
Edgar S. Prado	235	50	35	31	10,480,485
Jerry D. Bailey	191	44	33	31	10,559,278
Eibar Coa	170	43	18	19	3,542,121
Victor Espinoza	193	39	28	24	8,703,610
Todd Kabel	99	36	13	13	5,497,303
Corey S. Nakatani	168	33	28	20	5,642,497
Rafael Bejarano	145	31	16	18	4,129,334
Stewart Elliott	139	29	18	14	*9,567,184
Robby Albarado	171	29	26	22	4,712,718
Javier Castellano	162	27	17	27	5,874,291
Ramon A. Dominguez	132	27	19	22	4,624,915
Alex O. Solis	103	27	14	14	4,348,546
Pat Day	184	26	36	28	5,594,209
Shane J. Sellers	105	24	17	10	3,332,731
Gerard Melancon	111	22	17	18	1,638,184
Cornelio H. Velasquez	199	20	35	25	4,312,432
David Romero Flores	148	20	12	26	4,201,693
Jose A. Santos	156	20	14	24	3,569,123
Joe Bravo	138	19	24	21	2,687,090
Richard Migliore	127	18	24	12	3,482,745
Tyler Baze	163	18	26	18	3,121,840
Eddie Castro	119	18	17	22	1,848,858
Eddie M. Martin, Jr.	100	18	18	10	1,632,216
Christopher P. DeCarlo	71	18	8	5	1,097,351
Ken S. Tohill	71	18	12	14	849,010
Kent J. Desormeaux	134	17	20	16	4,964,237
Mike E. Smith	139	17	29	17	4,443,831
Russell A. Baze	69	16	15	11	1,220,632
Lonnie Meche	81	16	11	8	833,840
Jorge Martin Bourdieu	69	16	10	9	723,477
Jose Valdivia, Jr.	113	15	18	15	2,887,748
Brice Blanc	90	15	12	10	1,914,178
Abel Castellano, Jr.	80	15	13	7	1,199,139
Ryan Fogelsonger	72	15	9	12	1,172,648
Timothy T. Doocy	56	15	6	8	715,191
Scott A. Stevens	87	15	17	14	532,456
Rene R. Douglas	119	14	16	17	2,999,552
Emile Ramsammy	89	13	11	11	2,100,071
Mario G. Pino	63	13	13	11	1,019,437
Manoel R. Cruz	104	13	9	20	930,461
Ronald J. Warren, Jr.	46	13	5	5	611,025
Miguel Luis Gaeta Hernandez	62	13	8	7	317,134
Berkley R. Packer	30	13	4	4	120,387
John McKee	93	12	10	14	1,468,462
Carlos H. Marquez, Jr.	66	12	10	6	1,049,606
Elvis Joseph Perrodin	73	12	8	9	732,252
John Jacinto	63	12	10	4	533,776
Aaron T. Gryder	82	11	11	11	1,028,395
Roberto M. Gonzalez	46	11	4	7	923,925
Norberto Arroyo, Jr.	72	11	5	14	915,991
Julian Pimentel	81	11	10	14	832,724
Roman Chapa	64	11	5	10	781,910
Wilson Omar Dieguez	58	11	14	10	361,708
Alfredo J. Juarez, Jr.	64	11	6	5	358,762
Gary L. Stevens	82	10	11	13	2,010,780
Patrick Husbands	84	10	10	13	1,886,429
Pablo Fragoso	86	10	10	14	1,259,258
Martin A. Pedroza	54	10	5	9	676,839
Francisco Perez Fuentes	35	10	4	2	389,864
Joel Campbell	57	10	2	5	332,208
Jay Conklin	26	10	5	1	105,389
Steven Ronald Bahen	31	9	8	2	1,148,886
Michael J. Luzzi	63	9	7	8	956,650
Manuel Aguilar	91	9	13	13	940,771
Heberto Castillo, Jr.	45	9	2	2	705,319
Guy Smith	55	9	10	10	642,579
Ricky Frazier	36	9	8	3	607,705
Jozbin Z. Santana	49	9	7	3	602,076
Aurelio Toribio, Jr.	61	9	8	2	601,425
Pedro V. Alvarado	39	9	7	8	572,034
Steve J. Bourque	36	9	6	4	427,500
Vince J. Guerra	44	9	3	5	274,660
Scott Sterr	39	9	12	5	74,287
Jono C. Jones	62	8	12	13	2,167,229
Jon Kenton Court	87	8	15	12	1,875,899
Jorge F. Chavez	127	8	13	18	1,679,634
James McAleney	68	8	10	12	1,616,415
Corey J. Lanerie	106	8	17	16	886,145
Donald R. Pettinger	51	8	9	14	765,313
Jeremy Beasley	56	8	10	8	716,681
Julio A. Garcia	68	8	9	5	675,183
Omar Figueroa	36	8	0	5	629,805
Mary Elizabeth Doser	27	8	7	2	542,068
Jesus Lopez Castanon	41	8	2	6	478,294
Mick Ruis	59	8	7	2	467,541
Quincy Welch	48	8	9	8	429,884
Seth B. Martinez	34	8	8	4	345,326
Huber Villa-Gomez	39	8	7	5	332,525
Richard Harvey Hamel	34	8	2	1	280,450
Armando Martinez	42	8	5	3	131,379
Serge R. Rocheleau	15	8	5	1	49,080
Shaun Bridgmohan	110	7	17	23	1,586,735
Mark Guidry	70	7	5	9	917,616
David Clark	28	7	4	2	787,116
Terry J. Thompson	33	7	7	8	684,075
Donnie J. Meche	45	7	4	7	591,907
Chance J. Rollins	42	7	4	7	537,220
Carlos H. Silva	29	7	2	2	409,825
Abdiel Toribio	56	7	6	8	407,950
Real E. Simard	44	7	5	4	366,900
Travis L. Dunkelberger	37	7	7	5	358,660
Anthony S. Black	29	7	2	4	352,257
Leanne M. Painter	39	7	7	5	328,106
Ramsey Zimmerman	35	7	4	4	326,956
Roberto A. Perez	25	7	2	3	270,527
Travis Wayne Hightower	28	7	7	1	237,245
Jason R. Eads	36	7	4	1	223,242
Peter McAleney	22	7	3	0	39,246
Brooke Mellish	29	7	3	5	35,716
Jeremy Rose	61	6	11	8	1,119,309
Charles C. Lopez	63	6	14	12	1,085,665
Willie Martinez	54	6	8	4	1,037,324
Eusebio Razo, Jr.	66	6	11	7	852,862
Monte Clifton Berry	68	6	11	10	598,771
Larry J. Sterling, Jr.	39	6	4	6	510,117
Casey T. Lambert	55	6	4	8	505,392
Chad K. Murphy	26	6	6	5	479,300
Jesse M. Campbell	47	6	4	5	474,957
T. D. Houghton	51	6	11	3	473,526
Glenn W. Corbett	61	6	10	7	427,178
Tracy J. Hebert	40	6	5	9	416,395
Larry C. Reynolds	21	6	3	4	355,028
Larry Taylor	38	6	3	4	347,781
Matthew Otis McCarron	23	6	1	1	327,413
Tony Noguez	20	6	1	0	269,578
Sandi Lee Gann	37	6	4	6	267,893
David Bentley	24	6	3	3	263,964
Gallyn Vick Mitchell	30	6	7	5	258,060
Perry Compton	50	6	6	6	247,994
Felipe Valdez	31	6	5	3	218,130
Kelly Bridges	50	6	9	6	201,069
Curtis Kimes	37	6	3	5	177,136
Josiah Francis Hampshire, Jr.	20	6	1	2	166,000
Brian James Theriot	25	6	3	3	144,540
Juan M. Gutierrez	42	6	4	8	130,818
Daniel P. Vergara	21	6	2	1	97,337
Daniel Lee Beck	29	6	5	4	93,590
Twyla Beckner	40	6	9	3	69,126
Shannon Wippert	14	6	2	1	14,854
Javier Santiago	81	5	7	11	1,376,054
Calvin H. Borel	71	5	11	11	1,060,178
Ricardo Jaime	63	5	12	14	799,680
Richard Anthony Dos Ramos	40	5	2	3	708,124
Paul R. Toscano	36	5	5	1	496,566
Jose L. Espinoza	40	5	5	1	436,808
Roberto Alvarado, Jr.	36	5	2	6	436,789
Jamie Theriot	39	5	7	3	406,750
Harry Vega	40	5	3	4	397,953
Luis S. Quinonez	65	5	6	11	394,230
Jose C. Caraballo	34	5	2	7	388,173
Ariel Smith	18	5	0	0	328,597
Chad Phillip Schvaneveldt	32	5	4	4	324,950

Jockey	Starts	1st	2d	3d	Purses
Erick D. Rodriguez	28	5	2	8	315,295
Rickey Walcott	40	5	8	7	278,390
Adalberto Diaz Lopez	33	5	2	5	273,743
Victor H. Molina	21	5	1	3	258,236
Neil Poznansky	22	5	2	2	247,850
Federico Mata	39	5	2	5	247,491
J. D. Acosta	25	5	4	2	245,866
William D. Troilo	38	5	2	5	240,992
Weldon T. Cloninger, Jr.	24	5	1	3	233,952
Tom Foley	17	5	3	0	180,670
Thomas L. Pompell	27	5	4	2	170,244
Esteban Angel Gomez	56	5	8	5	156,178
Travis Wales	23	5	2	3	127,570
Dennis Michael Collins	31	5	5	5	91,729
Melissa Peery	26	5	2	5	45,687
Robert C. Landry	60	4	9	10	1,661,893
Jose A. Velez, Jr.	87	4	14	12	765,010
Larry Melancon	66	4	6	9	715,421
Craig Perret	48	4	4	8	597,070
Christopher A. Emigh	57	4	8	6	524,077
Horacio Karamanos	62	4	6	14	512,678
Gary Boulanger	81	4	8	13	468,198
Jillian Scharfstein	16	4	2	3	462,194
Danny Sorenson	35	4	0	5	424,125
David Wilson	45	4	11	8	419,552
Jake Barton	39	4	6	7	385,589
Steve D. Hamilton	43	4	6	3	347,200
Jason P. Lumpkins	28	4	7	2	331,297
Rosemary B. Homeister, Jr.	42	4	9	5	322,075
James Graham	54	4	4	6	307,054
Derek C. Bell	43	4	8	13	302,013
James Lopez	36	4	6	2	298,310
Brian Joseph Hernandez, Jr.	34	4	3	7	295,775
Francine Villeneuve	15	4	4	2	283,825
Jose E. Lopez	28	4	3	6	283,000
Chris Loseth	36	4	4	6	244,068
Dean A. Sarvis	28	4	2	3	235,191
Perry A. Winters	35	4	8	5	222,060
Ricardo Feliciano	26	4	3	5	209,825
Jose C. Ferrer	40	4	3	0	205,525
Dana G. Whitney	21	4	1	4	205,425
Danush Sukie	17	4	3	2	196,204
Joseph Rocco, Jr.	18	4	3	2	195,380
Alex Birzer	33	4	1	7	192,015
Ken Hendricks	19	4	7	1	191,249
Winston Albert Thompson	25	4	3	5	186,510
Martin Ramos Ramirez	13	4	2	0	183,750
Cecilio Penalba	34	4	4	2	182,350
Hector L. Rosario, Jr.	23	4	2	5	180,600
Michael Phillip Iammarino	33	4	1	8	180,470
Dyn Panell	27	4	6	2	168,800
Alberto R. Higuera	45	4	8	11	136,832
Lester Cash Knight	15	4	3	0	130,086
Russell Vicchrilli	24	4	9	3	129,005
Robert Dean Williams	39	4	9	2	113,554
Cliff James Miyashiro	29	4	5	7	46,969
Carl Hebert	30	4	3	9	40,643
Victor G. Navarro	8	4	1	0	22,230
Russell David Kingrey	14	4	4	1	18,974
Lanfranco Dettori	10	3	1	0	2,303,000
Greta Kuntzweiler	25	3	5	4	648,017
Patrick A. Valenzuela	20	3	3	6	582,303
Dino Luciani	34	3	4	6	483,013
Raymond Brian Sabourin	26	3	6	6	477,931
Jean-Luc Samyn	32	3	3	3	416,128
Gerry Olguin	23	3	2	3	415,919
Frank Lovato, Jr.	41	3	3	4	352,103
Frank T. Alvarado	36	3	3	8	275,960
Justin Shepherd	31	3	2	1	268,468
Eduardo O. Nunez	46	3	3	2	266,250
Phil Teator	22	3	2	2	264,700
Chad Hoverson	28	3	4	2	261,493
Richard Monterrey	26	3	6	3	256,800
Isaias D. Enriquez	27	3	5	2	255,669
Eric Saint-Martin	17	3	3	0	250,085
Joe M. Castro	26	3	5	4	249,370
Robert V. Skelly	24	3	6	1	242,174
Carlos Olivero	12	3	1	1	232,000
Donald Edward Simington	35	3	7	3	213,120
Shannon Uske	13	3	2	1	209,260
Casey Fusilier	19	3	6	2	204,778
Ted D. Gondron	25	3	5	4	204,449
Carlos D. Madeira	37	3	5	9	197,930
Frank Albert Gonsalves	26	3	3	4	191,462
Rick Wilson	11	3	3	1	191,000
Nick Santagata	24	3	5	6	189,259
Hiram G. Rivera	19	3	3	0	179,280
Eduardo E. Perez	26	3	2	4	172,340
Christopher Read	7	3	0	3	168,810
Robert Walsh	14	3	4	1	165,916
Desmond Bryan	25	3	2	2	162,800
Robert W. Johnson	17	3	0	0	157,015
Luis Antonio Gonzalez	26	3	6	2	154,725
John A. Grabowski	8	3	1	1	151,066
Ricky J. Faul	30	3	1	5	148,700
Paul Albert Nicol, Jr.	14	3	2	2	147,988
Kelly Michael Murray	28	3	2	5	142,379
Kevin Krigger	25	3	3	2	140,338
Rodney A. Prescott	26	3	5	4	139,262
Tom G. Turner	12	3	0	0	135,300
Kevin Leon Cogburn	32	3	3	3	134,751
Martin Escobar	30	3	2	3	132,998
Blair Waterman	14	3	3	2	118,164
Bobby L. Johnson	28	3	5	8	117,069
Paul Leacock	17	3	3	2	115,241
Nathan J. Chaves	16	3	1	2	113,125
Juan G. Rivera	28	3	3	3	101,119
Francisco C. Torres	10	3	0	0	95,340
Beth S. Butler	16	3	3	4	94,455
Jason Leacock	22	3	1	5	91,882
Rita M. Helton	6	3	0	0	91,500
Randy Schacht	10	3	1	1	88,830
Ashton Fitzpatrick	7	3	0	2	80,166
Fernando S. Rojas	16	3	1	4	72,543
Luis Robletto	14	3	2	2	71,648
Yuri Yaranga	11	3	1	0	42,803
Cameron Colledge	26	3	4	5	41,589
Richard M. Vasquez	19	3	3	3	40,766
Angelle Wilson	27	3	5	5	36,548
Joe A. Crispin	15	3	6	3	24,102
Jackie Smith	23	3	1	4	21,120
Janet Leah Wilson	8	3	0	0	18,189
Duane Lee D'Amico	14	3	1	6	18,158
Shawna Barber	14	3	1	1	17,867
Scot A. Schindler	6	3	0	1	14,178
Ivan Ortiz, Jr.	17	3	2	2	13,416
Roger Butterfly	6	3	0	0	11,509
Kieren Fallon	6	2	1	0	1,148,995
Slade Callaghan	40	2	7	8	745,457
Kerwin John	36	2	1	4	419,870
Garrett K. Gomez	33	2	4	6	400,497
Edwin L. King, Jr.	72	2	9	10	377,237
Eurico Rosa Da Silva	21	2	1	3	335,294
James McKnight	18	2	0	3	326,051
Brian Dale Peck	18	2	5	0	296,818
Alex Bisono	30	2	4	1	269,544
Chin C. Yang	12	2	2	1	244,370
Felipe F. Martinez	28	2	2	2	218,207
Anthony J. D'Amico	18	2	3	3	211,800
Luis Garcia	27	2	3	1	193,539
Matt S. Garcia	25	2	2	1	192,818
Carlos Gonzalez	38	2	5	6	189,150
Carlos Montalvo	11	2	3	1	180,191
Bobby J. Walker, Jr.	16	2	5	2	177,100
Filemon T. Rodriguez	19	2	2	3	169,360
Kevin Radke	16	2	0	2	155,125
Ben Russell	28	2	5	2	152,593
Jeff Johnston	22	2	4	4	145,850
Enrique M. Jurado	20	2	2	3	139,350
Thomas Clifton	16	2	3	2	136,763
Pedro A. Rodriguez	21	2	1	5	134,288
Francisco Duran	22	2	3	2	131,679
Perry S. Whetstone	31	2	4	3	131,149

* Includes $5,000,000 bonus.

Apprentice Jockeys – Money Won in 2004

Jockey	Mts.	1st	2d	3d	Pct.	Purses
Hernandez, Jr., Brian J.	1457	241	208	189	.165	$4,344,432
Quinones, Angel R.	1208	199	178	128	.165	3,736,142
Ruis, Mick	839	125	103	111	.149	2,901,163
Fragoso, Pablo	438	84	82	83	.192	2,855,825
Bisono, Alex	740	76	79	78	.103	2,438,746
Whitacre, Brandon	918	141	125	113	.154	2,414,794
Fraser, Corey	475	67	63	57	.141	2,401,102
Almodovar, Gerald	939	139	132	110	.148	2,372,230
Maragh, Rajiv	796	78	88	93	.098	1,883,289
Baze, Michael C.	683	81	88	80	.119	1,817,302
Jara, Fernando	481	58	41	60	.121	1,814,085
Thornton, Timothy	505	69	63	79	.137	1,756,059
Graham, James	654	92	78	78	.141	1,742,309
Scharfstein, Jillian	379	35	40	40	.092	1,644,031
Camacho, Eric	660	111	106	83	.168	1,626,091
Singh, Sunny	480	39	78	59	.081	1,603,687
Pennington, Frankie	953	121	131	129	.127	1,446,443
Contreras, Cruz	493	77	67	63	.156	1,424,178
Cotto, Jr., Pedro Luis	433	34	49	53	.079	1,344,519
VanHassel, Christopher	700	90	84	100	.129	1,340,484
Cosme, Emanuel	736	82	88	89	.111	1,332,853
Mello, David	837	93	116	114	.111	1,276,180
Nelson, Leroy	656	77	72	92	.117	1,262,963
Kinsey, Jill E.	832	92	106	90	.111	1,262,484
Hamilton, Quincy	834	130	121	102	.156	1,224,186
Brimo, Julia	326	34	41	29	.104	1,214,086
Monterrey, Jr., Pedro	554	64	62	71	.116	1,109,618
Perez, Edwin	285	32	33	37	.112	1,057,927
Campbell, Shannon	715	56	57	56	.078	1,039,976
Roche, Jennie	477	65	56	47	.136	1,021,909
Beauregard, Shannon	604	77	93	90	.127	994,979
Vaz, Eriluis	595	64	53	66	.108	971,027
Morris, Liz	595	47	73	58	.079	910,421
Crandall, Amanda L.	850	88	81	90	.104	882,691
Shepherd, Justin	390	39	45	40	.100	814,452
Lezcano, Jose	314	26	26	43	.083	781,738
Gomez, Oscar	409	27	28	37	.066	770,733
Espitia, Jorge	403	45	58	50	.112	746,069
Agilar, Trey	502	43	68	58	.086	688,596
Garcia, Alan	207	14	30	27	.068	677,786
Medina, Luis	435	41	57	37	.094	667,458
Cohen, David	244	27	22	29	.111	648,179
Olmo, Christian J.	360	45	32	47	.125	644,889
Hernandez, Rafael M.	539	57	50	65	.106	643,015
Fusilier, Casey	267	35	43	32	.131	637,736
Castillo, Elaine	523	63	57	58	.120	605,623
Delorme, Larren	456	66	78	64	.145	541,395
Fong, Jr., Freddy	355	31	31	27	.087	518,661
Lopez, Jose E.	263	33	27	25	.125	498,655
Uske, Shannon	126	9	11	19	.071	465,134
Ando, Happy H.	327	21	25	36	.064	440,851
Garcia, Luis	172	24	23	25	.140	384,580
Ramos, Ramon	422	28	37	48	.066	380,108
Romero, Hector R.	271	26	38	34	.096	375,653
Santana, Daniel	269	37	33	28	.138	361,179
Hill, Channing	293	25	31	30	.085	343,357
Molina, Jr., Juan F.	240	19	33	26	.079	339,332
Perez, Cristian Yermay	569	38	54	72	.067	337,606
Bentley, David	71	11	8	12	.155	329,974
Rivera, Jr., Jose Luis	364	31	27	44	.085	311,593
Fitzpatrick, Ashton	313	27	26	32	.086	302,458
Beckon, Chad	267	15	17	26	.056	281,140
Kaenel, Kyle	235	40	28	29	.170	276,136
Monterrey, Richard	137	19	22	18	.139	269,725
Offutt, Leigh	98	15	15	10	.153	267,708
Rodriguez, Ruben	187	15	20	23	.080	258,048
Terry, Dominic M.	268	15	23	26	.056	242,122
Torres, Jose	328	13	39	51	.040	219,785
Walsh, Robert	61	8	15	3	.131	204,911
Ning, Stan	226	17	32	30	.075	200,678
Read, Christopher	26	5	3	7	.192	199,560
Ignacio, Rodolfo	166	12	15	19	.072	198,284
Nicholls, Keveh	283	21	22	33	.074	191,498
McDaid, Joanne	280	14	23	30	.050	190,406
Sharp, Joe	199	18	37	25	.090	186,077
Raghunath, Raymond	189	9	17	17	.048	183,313
Perez, Melvin L.	146	13	8	17	.089	179,594
Saenz, Diego	256	18	30	22	.070	177,837
Schmidt, Jennifer	352	16	35	30	.045	175,827
Lee, Katie	241	18	19	23	.075	173,457
Baez, Jose	288	16	13	27	.056	166,405
Diaz, Renzo	178	14	11	17	.079	164,696
Schneider, Joseph	136	6	5	16	.044	164,619
Avila, Juan	202	10	13	18	.050	158,721
Rojas, Ruben	227	17	16	17	.075	156,206
Torres, Carlos	196	9	13	15	.046	148,004
Hodsdon, Danielle	39	10	5	8	.256	146,978
Williams, Justin L.	216	15	16	12	.069	145,796
Young, Paddy	66	6	7	9	.091	142,585
Aizpuru, Xavier	24	7	4	3	.292	136,487
Mendez, Emmanuel	164	13	19	19	.079	130,005
Kewin, Steve	221	13	12	15	.059	128,163
Colon, Sammy	159	16	16	20	.101	125,134
Betancourt, Jose R.	134	7	13	12	.052	121,697
Laurente, Godofredo	153	11	19	18	.072	119,973
Ore, Zarella	154	13	14	12	.084	117,637
Smith, Cherell	214	6	12	16	.028	114,296
Petty, Jody	36	5	6	6	.139	106,700
King, Dallas	144	8	17	16	.056	104,397
Torbit, Renee	219	16	28	18	.073	99,587
Mena, Miguel	83	7	9	11	.084	94,960
O'Donnell, Kristin	197	19	33	28	.096	94,762
Russell, Chris	117	9	10	11	.077	94,742
Camaque, Cesar	192	7	8	24	.036	93,515
Thomas, Michael	307	9	9	24	.029	91,957
Miller, Zach	25	9	2	4	.360	88,550
Sanguinetti, Anne	106	11	12	14	.104	81,291
Wilson, Emma Jayne	31	4	3	4	.129	80,295
Michael, Stephen	65	3	8	7	.046	79,304
Farrell, Jaleina	152	5	10	16	.033	78,181
Carter, Maggie	91	11	12	19	.121	74,069
Murphy, Jeff	50	3	7	5	.060	71,858
Irion, Heather	55	8	13	8	.145	58,208
Martinez, Catalino	19	1	2	5	.053	57,690
Zambrana, Eddie Joe	103	10	11	14	.097	53,601
Repp, Kate M.	58	1	10	8	.017	53,111
Covington, Raina	101	3	9	12	.030	52,109
Gray, Akili	180	5	9	14	.028	52,059
Vazquez, Manuel A.	96	2	7	9	.021	50,585
Stein, Justin	40	4	6	5	.100	49,841
Fewster, Emily	68	4	4	4	.059	49,627
Cadeddu, Lisa	34	4	3	4	.118	49,276
MacLaren, Jeff	27	4	1	3	.148	49,084
Rice, Jessica	49	1	10	0	.020	47,000
Creary, Chris	65	2	7	7	.031	45,209
Itschner, Christine	128	3	5	13	.023	44,394
Hunter, Michele L.	7	1	2	1	.143	42,800
Seesequasis, Danny	144	16	14	14	.111	42,532

Leading Apprentice Jockeys – Races Won in 2004

Jockey	Mts.	1st	2d	3d	Pct.	Purses
Hernandez, Jr., Brian J.	1457	241	208	189	.165	$4,344,432
Quinones, Angel R.	1208	199	178	128	.165	3,736,142
Whitacre, Brandon	918	141	125	113	.154	2,414,794
Almodovar, Gerald	939	139	132	110	.148	2,372,230
Hamilton, Quincy	834	130	121	102	.156	1,224,186
Ruis, Mick	839	125	103	111	.149	2,901,163
Pennington, Frankie	953	121	131	129	.127	1,446,443
Camacho, Eric	660	111	106	83	.168	1,626,091
Mello, David	837	93	116	114	.111	1,276,180
Graham, James	654	92	78	78	.141	1,742,309
Kinsey, Jill E.	832	92	106	90	.111	1,262,484
VanHassel, Christopher	700	90	84	100	.129	1,340,484
Crandall, Amanda L.	850	88	81	90	.104	882,691
Fragoso, Pablo	438	84	82	83	.192	2,855,825
Cosme, Emanuel	736	82	88	89	.111	1,332,853
Baze, Michael C.	683	81	88	80	.119	1,817,302
Maragh, Rajiv	796	78	88	93	.098	1,883,289
Contreras, Cruz	493	77	67	63	.156	1,424,178
Nelson, Leroy	656	77	72	92	.117	1,262,963
Beauregard, Shannon	604	77	93	90	.127	994,979
Bisono, Alex	740	76	79	78	.103	2,438,746
Thornton, Timothy	505	69	63	79	.137	1,756,059
Fraser, Corey	475	67	63	57	.141	2,401,102
Delorme, Larren	456	66	78	64	.145	541,395
Roche, Jennie	477	65	56	47	.136	1,021,909
Monterrey, Jr., Pedro	554	64	62	71	.116	1,109,618
Vaz, Eriluis	595	64	53	66	.108	971,027
Castillo, Elaine	523	63	57	58	.120	605,623
Jara, Fernando	481	58	41	60	.121	1,814,085
Hernandez, Rafael M.	539	57	50	65	.106	643,015
Campbell, Shannon	715	56	57	56	.078	1,039,976
Morris, Liz	595	47	73	58	.079	910,421
Espitia, Jorge	403	45	58	50	.112	746,069
Olmo, Christian J.	360	45	32	47	.125	644,889
Agilar, Trey	502	43	68	58	.086	688,596
Medina, Luis	435	41	57	37	.094	667,458
Kaenel, Kyle	235	40	28	29	.170	276,136
Singh, Sunny	480	39	78	59	.081	1,603,687
Shepherd, Justin	390	39	45	40	.100	814,452
Perez, Cristian Yermay	569	38	54	72	.067	337,606
Santana, Daniel	269	37	33	28	.138	361,179
Scharfstein, Jillian	379	35	40	40	.092	1,644,031
Fusilier, Casey	267	35	43	32	.131	637,736
Cotto, Jr., Pedro Luis	433	34	49	53	.079	1,344,519
Brimo, Julia	326	34	41	29	.104	1,214,086
Lopez, Jose E.	263	33	27	25	.125	498,655
Perez, Edwin	285	32	33	37	.112	1,057,927
Fong, Jr., Freddy	355	31	31	27	.087	518,661
Rivera, Jr., Jose Luis	364	31	27	44	.085	311,593
Ramos, Ramon	422	28	37	48	.066	380,108
Gomez, Oscar	409	27	28	37	.066	770,733
Cohen, David	244	27	22	29	.111	648,179
Fitzpatrick, Ashton	313	27	26	32	.086	302,458
Lezcano, Jose	314	26	26	43	.083	781,738
Romero, Hector R.	271	26	38	34	.096	375,653
Hill, Channing	293	25	31	30	.085	343,357
Garcia, Luis	172	24	23	25	.140	384,580
Ando, Happy H.	327	21	25	36	.064	440,851
Nicholls, Keveh	283	21	22	33	.074	191,498
Molina, Jr., Juan F.	240	19	33	26	.079	339,332
Monterrey, Richard	137	19	22	18	.139	269,725
O'Donnell, Kristin	197	19	33	28	.096	94,762
Sharp, Joe	199	18	37	25	.090	186,077
Saenz, Diego	256	18	30	22	.070	177,837
Lee, Katie	241	18	19	23	.075	173,457
Ning, Stan	226	17	32	30	.075	200,678
Rojas, Ruben	227	17	16	17	.075	156,206
Schmidt, Jennifer	352	16	35	30	.045	175,827
Baez, Jose	288	16	13	27	.056	166,405
Colon, Sammy	159	16	16	20	.101	125,134
Torbit, Renee	219	16	28	18	.073	99,587
Seesequasis, Danny	144	16	14	14	.111	42,532
Beckon, Chad	267	15	17	26	.056	281,140
Offutt, Leigh	98	15	15	10	.153	267,708
Rodriguez, Ruben	187	15	20	23	.080	258,048
Terry, Dominic M.	268	15	23	26	.056	242,122
Williams, Justin L.	216	15	16	12	.069	145,796
Garcia, Alan	207	14	30	27	.068	677,786
McDaid, Joanne	280	14	23	30	.050	190,406
Diaz, Renzo	178	14	11	17	.079	164,696
Torres, Jose	328	13	39	51	.040	219,785
Perez, Melvin L.	146	13	8	17	.089	179,594
Mendez, Emmanuel	164	13	19	19	.079	130,005
Kewin, Steve	221	13	12	15	.059	128,163
Ore, Zarella	154	13	14	12	.084	117,637
Ignacio, Rodolfo	166	12	15	19	.072	198,284
Bentley, David	71	11	8	12	.155	329,974
Laurente, Godofredo	153	11	19	18	.072	119,973
Sanguinetti, Anne	106	11	12	14	.104	81,291
Carter, Maggie	91	11	12	19	.121	74,069
Avila, Juan	202	10	13	18	.050	158,721
Hodsdon, Danielle	39	10	5	8	.256	146,978
Zambrana, Eddie Joe	103	10	11	14	.097	53,601
Uske, Shannon	126	9	11	19	.071	465,134
Raghunath, Raymond	189	9	17	17	.048	183,313
Torres, Carlos	196	9	13	15	.046	148,004
Russell, Chris	117	9	10	11	.077	94,742
Thomas, Michael	307	9	9	24	.029	91,957
Miller, Zach	25	9	2	4	.360	88,550
Cosgriff, Katie Jo	107	9	9	10	.084	26,409
Walsh, Robert	61	8	15	3	.131	204,911
King, Dallas	144	8	17	16	.056	104,397
Irion, Heather	55	8	13	8	.145	58,208
Stinn, Caroline	37	8	9	7	.216	18,785
Aizpuru, Xavier	24	7	4	3	.292	136,487
Betancourt, Jose R.	134	7	13	12	.052	121,697
Mena, Miguel	83	7	9	11	.084	94,960
Camaque, Cesar	192	7	8	24	.036	93,515
Smith, Nate	93	7	5	15	.075	22,796
Black, Nikeela	56	7	4	8	.125	16,573
Schneider, Joseph	136	6	5	16	.044	164,619
Young, Paddy	66	6	7	9	.091	142,585
Smith, Cherell	214	6	12	16	.028	114,296
Olesiak, Jake	121	6	5	6	.050	41,454
Read, Christopher	26	5	3	7	.192	199,560
Petty, Jody	36	5	6	6	.139	106,700
Farrell, Jaleina	152	5	10	16	.033	78,181
Gray, Akili	180	5	9	14	.028	52,059
Elsner, Drew	111	5	16	17	.045	28,242
Wilson, Emma Jayne	31	4	3	4	.129	80,295
Stein, Justin	40	4	6	5	.100	49,841
Fewster, Emily	68	4	4	4	.059	49,627
Cadeddu, Lisa	34	4	3	4	.118	49,276
MacLaren, Jeff	27	4	1	3	.148	49,084
Dohnalova, Nadia	72	4	6	4	.056	41,830
Charles, Maria	45	4	3	5	.089	40,011
Michael, Stephen	65	3	8	7	.046	79,304
Murphy, Jeff	50	3	7	5	.060	71,858

Annual Leading Jockeys – Money Won

Jockey	Mts.	1st	2d	3d	Pct.	Purses
1908 Notter, J.	872	249	178	140	.29	$464,322
1909 Dugan, E.	631	143	123	86	.23	166,355
1910 Shilling, C. H.	506	172	96	64	.34	176,030
1911 Koerner, T.	813	162	133	112	.20	88,308
1912 Butwell, J.	684	144	122	110	.21	79,843
1913 Buxton, M.	887	146	131	136	.16	82,552
1914 McCahey, J.	824	155	157	130	.19	121,845
1915 Garner, M.	775	151	118	90	.19	96,628
1916 McTaggart, J.	832	150	137	119	.18	155,055
1917 Robinson, F.	731	147	125	108	.20	148,057
1918 Luke, L.	756	178	123	108	.24	210,864
1919 Loftus, J.	177	65	36	24	.37	252,707
1920 Krummer, C.	353	87	79	48	.25	292,376
1921 Sande, E.	340	112	69	59	.33	263,043
1922 Johnson, A.	297	43	57	40	.14	345,054
1923 Sande, E.	430	122	89	79	.28	569,394
1924 Parke, I.	844	205	175	121	.24	290,395
1925 Fator, L.	315	81	54	44	.26	305,775
1926 Fator, L.	511	143	90	86	.28	361,435
1927 Sande, E.	179	49	33	19	.27	277,877
1928 McAtee, L.	235	55	43	25	.23	301,295
1929 Garner, M.	274	57	39	33	.21	314,975
1930 Workman, R.	571	152	88	79	.27	420,438
1931 Kurtsinger, C.	519	93	82	79	.18	392,095
1932 Workman, R.	378	87	48	55	.23	385,070
1933 Jones, R.	471	63	57	70	.13	226,285
1934 Wright, W. D.	919	174	154	114	.19	287,185
1935 Coucci, S.	749	141	125	103	.19	319,760
1936 Wright, W. D.	670	100	102	73	.15	264,000
1937 Kurtsinger, C.	765	120	94	106	.16	384,292
1938 Wall, N.	658	97	94	82	.15	385,161
1939 James, B.	904	191	165	105	.21	353,333
1940 Arcaro, E.	783	132	143	112	.17	343,661
1941 Meade, D.	1,164	210	185	158	.18	398,627
1942 Arcaro, E.	687	123	97	89	.18	481,949
1943 Longden, J.	871	173	140	121	.20	573,276
1944 Atkinson, T.	1,539	287	231	213	.19	899,101
1945 Longden, J.	778	180	112	100	.23	981,977
1946 Atkinson, T.	1,377	233	213	173	.17	1,036,825
1947 Dodson, D.	646	141	100	75	.22	1,429,949
1948 Arcaro, E.	726	188	108	98	.26	1,686,230
1949 Brooks, S.	906	209	172	110	.23	1,316,817
1950 Arcaro, E.	888	195	153	144	.22	1,410,160
1951 Shoemaker, W.	1,161	257	197	161	.22	1,329,890
1952 Arcaro, E.	807	188	122	109	.23	1,859,591
1953 Shoemaker, W.	1,683	485	302	210	.29	1,784,187
1954 Shoemaker, W.	1,251	380	221	142	.30	1,876,760
1955 Arcaro, E.	820	158	126	108	.19	1,864,796
1956 Hartack, W.	1,387	347	252	184	.25	2,343,955
1957 Hartack, W.	1,238	341	208	178	.28	3,060,501
1958 Shoemaker, W.	1,133	300	185	137	.26	2,961,693
1959 Shoemaker, W.	1,285	347	230	159	.27	2,843,133
1960 Shoemaker, W.	1,227	274	196	158	.22	2,123,961
1961 Shoemaker, W.	1,256	304	186	175	.24	2,690,819
1962 Shoemaker, W.	1,126	311	156	128	.28	2,916,844
1963 Shoemaker, W.	1,203	271	193	137	.22	2,526,925
1964 Shoemaker, W.	1,056	246	147	133	.23	2,649,553
1965 Baeza, B.	1,245	270	200	201	.22	2,582,702
1966 Baeza, B.	1,341	298	222	190	.22	2,951,022
1967 Baeza, B.	1,064	256	184	127	.24	3,088,888
1968 Baeza, B.	1,089	201	184	145	.18	2,835,108
1969 Velasquez, J.	1,442	258	230	204	.18	2,542,315
1970 Pincay, L. Jr.	1,328	269	208	187	.20	2,626,526
1971 Pincay, L. Jr.	1,627	380	288	214	.23	3,784,377
1972 Pincay, L. Jr.	1,388	289	215	205	.21	3,225,827
1973 Pincay, L. Jr.	1,444	350	254	209	.24	4,093,492
1974 Pincay, L. Jr.	1,278	341	227	180	.27	4,251,060
1975 Baeza, B.	1,190	196	208	180	.16	3,674,398
1976 Cordero, A. Jr.	1,534	274	273	235	.18	4,709,500
1977 Cauthen, S.	2,075	487	345	304	.23	6,151,750
1978 McHargue, D. G.	1,762	375	294	263	.21	6,188,353
1979 Pincay, L. Jr.	1,708	420	302	261	.25	8,183,535
1980 McCarron, C. J.	1,964	405	318	282	.20	7,661,000
1981 McCarron, C. J.	1,494	326	251	207	.22	8,397,604
1982 Cordero, A. Jr.	1,838	397	338	227	.22	9,702,520
1983 Cordero, A. Jr.	1,792	362	296	237	.20	10,116,807
1984 McCarron, C. J.	1,565	356	276	218	.23	12,038,213
1985 Pincay, L. Jr.	1,409	289	246	183	.21	13,415,049
1986 Santos, J. A.	1,636	329	237	222	.20	11,329,297
1987 Santos, J. A.	1,639	305	268	208	.19	12,407,355
1988 Santos, J. A.	1,867	370	287	265	.20	14,877,298
1989 Santos, J. A.	1,459	285	238	220	.20	13,847,003
1990 Stevens, G. L.	1,504	283	245	202	.19	13,881,198
1991 McCarron, C. J.	1,440	265	228	206	.18	14,456,073
1992 Desormeaux, K. J.	1,568	361	260	208	.23	14,193,006
1993 Smith, M. E.	1,510	343	235	214	.23	14,008,148
1994 Smith, M.E.	1,483	317	250	196	.21	15,979,820
1995 Bailey, J.D.	1,265	287	193	144	.23	16,308,230
1996 Bailey, J.D.	1,185	297	189	165	.25	17,064,409
1997 Bailey, J.D.	1,144	272	186	178	.24	15,946,282
1998 Stevens, G.L.	839	171	141	118	.20	18,884,352
1999 Bailey, J.D.	972	242	164	135	.25	17,530,905
2000 Day, P.	1,219	267	206	186	.22	17,479,838
2001 Bailey, J. D.	910	226	194	137	.25	18,997,720
2002 Bailey, J. D.	832	213	139	118	.26	19,271,814
2003 Bailey, J. D.	776	206	149	97	.27	23,354,960
2004 Velazquez, J.R.	1,327	335	222	181	.25	22,248,661

Annual Leading Jockeys – Races Won

Year	Jockey	Mts.	1st	2d	3d	Unplc.	Pct.
1895	Perkins, J.	762	192	177	129	264	.25
1896	Scherrer, J.	1,093	271	227	172	423	.24
1897	Martin, H.	803	173	152	116	362	.21
1898	Burns, T.	973	277	213	149	334	.28
1899	Burns, T.	1,064	273	173	266	352	.26
1900	Mitchell, C	874	195	140	139	380	.23
1901	O'Connor, W.	1,047	253	221	192	381	.24
1902	Ranch, J.	1,069	276	205	181	407	.26
1903	Fuller, G. C.	918	229	152	122	415	.25
1904	Hildebrand, E.	1,169	297	230	171	471	.25
1905	Nicol, D.	861	221	143	136	861	.26
1906	Miller, W	1,384	388	300	199	497	.28
1907	Miller, W	1,194	334	226	170	464	.28
1908	Powers, V.	1,260	324	204	185	547	.26
1909	Powers, V.	704	173	121	114	296	.25
1910	Garner, G.	947	200	188	153	406	.20
1911	Koerner, T.	813	162	133	112	406	.20
1912	Hill, P.	967	168	141	129	529	.17
1913	Buxton, M.	887	146	131	136	474	.16
1914	McTaggart, J.	787	157	132	106	392	.20
1915	Garner, M.	775	151	118	90	416	.19
1916	Robinson, F.	791	178	131	124	358	.23
1917	Crump, W.	803	151	140	101	411	.19
1918	Robinson, F.	864	185	140	108	431	.21
1919	Robinson, C.	896	190	145	126	435	.21
1920	Butwell, J.	721	152	129	139	301	.21
1921	Lang, C.	696	135	110	105	346	.19
1922	Fator, M.	859	188	153	116	402	.22
1923	Parke, I.	718	173	105	95	345	.24
1924	Parke, I.	844	205	175	121	343	.24
1925	Mortensen, A.	987	187	145	138	517	.19
1926	Jones, R.	1,172	190	163	152	667	.16
1927	Hardy, L.	1,130	207	192	151	580	.18
1928	Inzelone, J.	1,053	155	152	135	610	.15
1929	Knight, M.	871	149	132	133	547	.17
1930	Riley, H.R.	861	177	145	123	416	.21
1931	Roble, H.	1,174	173	173	155	673	.15
1932	Gilbert, J.	1,050	212	144	160	534	.20
1933	Westrope, J.	1,224	301	235	166	522	.25
1934	Peters, M.	1,045	221	179	147	498	.21
1935	Stevenson, C.	1,099	206	169	146	578	.19
1936	James, B.	1,106	245	196	161	505	.22
1937	Adams, J.	1,265	260	186	177	642	.21
1938	Longden, J.	1,150	236	168	171	575	.21
1939	Meade, D.	1,284	255	221	180	628	.20
1940	Dew, E.	1,377	287	201	180	709	.21
1941	Meade, D.	1,164	210	185	158	611	.18
1942	Adams, J.	1,120	245	185	150	540	.22
1943	Adams, J.	1,069	228	159	171	511	.21
1944	Atkinson, T.	1,539	287	231	213	808	.19
1945	Jessop, J. D.	1,085	290	182	168	445	.27
1946	Atkinson, T.	1,377	233	213	173	758	.17
1947	Longden, J.	1,327	316	250	195	566	.24
1948	Longden, J.	1,197	319	223	161	494	.27
1949	Gilson, G	1,347	270	217	181	679	.20
1950	Culmone, J.	1,676	388	283	218	787	.23
	Shoemaker, W.	1,640	388	266	230	756	.24

Year	Jockey	Mts.	1st	2d	3d	Unplc.	Pct.
1951	Burr, C.	1,319	310	232	192	585	.24
1952	DeSpirito, A.	1,482	390	247	212	633	.26
1953	Shoemaker, W.	1,683	485	302	210	686	.29
1954	Shoemaker, W.	1,251	380	221	142	508	.30
1955	Hartack, W.	1,702	417	298	215	772	.25
1956	Hartack, W.	1,387	347	252	184	604	.25
1957	Hartack, W.	1,238	341	208	178	511	.28
1958	Shoemaker, W.	1,133	300	185	137	511	.26
1959	Shoemaker, W.	1,285	347	230	159	549	.27
1960	Hartack, W.	1,402	307	247	190	658	.22
1961	Sellers, J.	1,394	328	212	227	627	.24
1962	Ferraro, R.	1,755	352	252	226	925	.20
1963	Blum, W.	1,704	360	286	215	843	.21
1964	Blum, W.	1,577	324	274	170	809	.21
1965	Davidson, J.	1,502	310	228	190	816	.20
1966	Gomez, A.	996	318	173	142	363	.32
1967	Velasquez, J.	1,939	438	315	270	916	.23
1968	Cordero Jr., A.	1,662	345	278	219	820	.21
1969	Snyder, L.	1,645	352	290	243	760	.21
1970	Hawley, S.	1,908	452	313	265	878	.24
1971	Pincay Jr., L.	1,627	380	288	214	745	.23
1972	Hawley, S.	1,381	367	269	200	545	.27
1973	Hawley, S.	1,925	515	336	292	782	.27
1974	McCarron, C. J.	2,199	546	392	297	964	.25
1975	McCarron, C. J.	2,194	468	389	305	1,032	.21
1976	Hawley, S.	1,634	413	245	201	778	.25
1977	Cauthen, S.	2,075	487	345	304	939	.23
1978	Delahoussaye, E.	1,666	384	285	238	759	.23
1979	Gall, D.	2,146	479	396	326	945	.22
1980	McCarron, C. J.	1,964	405	318	282	959	.20
1981	Gall, D.	1,917	376	305	297	939	.20
1982	Day, P.	1,870	399	326	255	890	.21
1983	Day, P.	1,725	454	321	251	699	.26
1984	Day, P.	1,694	399	296	259	740	.24
1985	Antley, C. W.	2,335	469	371	288	1,208	.20
1986	Day, P.	1,417	429	246	202	540	.30
1987	Desormeaux, K. J.	2,207	450	370	294	1,093	.20
1988	Desormeaux, K. J.	1,897	474	295	276	852	.25
1989	Desormeaux, K. J.	2,312	598	385	309	1,021	.26
1990	Day, P.	1,421	364	265	222	575	.26
1991	Day, P.	1,405	430	256	213	506	.31
1992	Baze, R. A.	1,691	433	296	237	725	.25
1993	Baze, R. A.	1,579	410	297	225	647	.26
1994	Baze, R. A.	1,587	415	310	266	605	.26
1995	Baze, R. A.	1,537	448	312	233	544	.29
1996	Baze, R. A.	1,465	415	297	201	552	.28
1997	Prado, E. S.	2,046	536	388	307	815	.26
1998	Prado, E. S.	1,969	470	377	285	837	.24
1999	Prado, E. S.	1,902	402	307	276	917	.21
2000	Baze, R.A.	1,513	412	252	239	610	.27
2001	Dominguez, R. A.	1,864	431	368	278	786	.23
2002	Baze, Russell A.	1,508	431	302	219	556	.29
2003	Dominguez, R.A.	1,627	453	316	252	606	.28
2004	Bejarano, R.	1,922	455	355	280	832	.24

Leading North American Jockeys – Lifetime Wins

The list below includes the most prolific winning jockeys in racing history and their records through Dec. 31, 2004. It includes any jockey with 1,900 career victories in Thoroughbred races. Statistics are based on U.S. and Canadian starts. If the jockey retired, the last year of competition is indicated.

Jockeys	Last Rode	Mounts	1st	2d	3d	Win %	Purses
Pincay, Jr. Laffit A.	2003	48,486	9,530	7,784	6,650	19.7%	$237,120,625
Shoemaker William	1990	40,350	8,833	6,136	4,987	21.9%	123,375,524
Baze Russell A.		40,118	8,805	6,812	5,716	21.9%	130,896,395
Day Pat		40,151	8,777	6,833	5,666	21.9%	296,164,696
Gall David A.	1999	41,775	7,396	6,525	6,131	17.7%	24,972,821
McCarron Chris J.	2002	34,239	7,141	5,670	4,672	20.9%	263,985,505
Cordero, Jr. Angel	1995	38,656	7,057	6,136	5,359	18.3%	164,561,227
Velasquez Jorge	1997	40,852	6,795	6,178	5,755	16.6%	125,544,379
Hawley Sandy	1998	31,455	6,449	4,825	4,159	20.5%	88,681,292
Snyder Larry	1996	35,681	6,388	5,030	3,440	17.9%	47,207,289
Delahoussaye Eddie J.	2002	39,213	6,384	5,676	5,586	16.3%	195,884,940
Gambardella Carl	1994	39,018	6,349	5,953	5,353	16.3%	29,389,041
Fires Earlie		43,986	6,331	5,423	5,245	14.4%	82,479,309
Longden John	1966	32,413	6,032	4,914	4,273	18.6%	24,665,800
Bailey Jerry D.		30,168	5,719	4,442	3,834	19.0%	277,476,725
Pino Mario G.		33,858	5,461	4,978	4,653	16.1%	87,222,324
Vasquez Jacinto	1996	37,337	5,228	4,714	4,510	14.0%	85,754,115
Ardoin Ronald D.	2003	32,335	5,226	4,298	3,793	16.2%	58,908,059
Prado Edgar S.		27,308	5,224	4,455	3,876	19.1%	148,871,708
Wilson Rick	2004	24,681	4,939	4,250	3,461	20.0%	77,303,270
Baez Rodolfo	1999	28,609	4,875	4,291	4,103	17.0%	30,474,225
Black Anthony S.		31,746	4,847	4,193	4,074	15.3%	54,814,021
Stevens Gary L.		27,107	4,794	4,303	3,896	17.7%	211,940,679
Arcaro Eddie	1961	24,092	4,779	3,807	3,302	19.8%	30,039,543
Ouzts Perry Wayne		36,909	4,702	4,571	4,498	12.7%	26,540,211
Guidry Mark		29,037	4,658	4,138	3,887	16.0%	81,278,158
Brumfield Don	1989	33,223	4,573	4,076	3,758	13.8%	43,567,861
Desormeaux Kent J.		22,605	4,477	3,695	3,156	19.8%	174,736,297
Doocy Timothy T.		29,323	4,475	3,947	3,651	15.3%	54,428,696
Brooks Steve	1975	30,330	4,451	4,219	3,658	14.7%	18,239,817
Smith Mike E.		26,652	4,439	3,797	3,424	16.7%	168,674,746
Perret Craig		27,114	4,408	3,888	3,606	16.3%	113,327,453
Maple Eddie	1998	33,974	4,398	4,516	4,335	12.9%	105,338,573
Blum Walter	1975	28,673	4,382	3,913	3,350	15.3%	26,497,189
Romero Randy P.	1999	26,091	4,294	3,743	3,313	16.5%	75,264,198
Lloyd Jeffrey Scott	2000	31,296	4,276	4,318	4,179	13.7%	34,199,413
Hartack William	1975	21,535	4,272	3,370	2,871	19.8%	26,466,758
Sibille Ray		36,859	4,264	4,346	4,367	11.6%	68,880,807
Solis Alex O.		27,715	4,160	3,850	3,918	15.0%	179,192,880
Gomez Avelino	1980	17,028	4,081	2,947	2,405	24.0%	11,777,297
Sellers Shane J.	2004	23,778	4,069	3,504	2,976	17.1%	122,429,944
Dittfach Hugo	1989	33,905	4,000	4,092	6,113	11.8%	13,506,052
Rowland Michael F.		26,713	3,997	3,666	3,244	15.0%	28,637,371
Chavez Jorge F.		23,372	3,992	3,327	2,890	17.1%	142,582,745
Grove Philip	1997	26,901	3,991	3,761	3,580	14.8%	16,511,842
Borel Calvin H.		26,794	3,990	3,621	3,111	14.9%	72,169,563
Colton Robert E.	2002	24,932	3,982	3,561	3,395	16.0%	40,779,163
Migliore Richard		26,806	3,980	3,534	3,356	14.8%	134,306,238
Santos Jose A.		24,347	3,870	3,448	3,393	15.9%	174,651,966
Meier Randall A.		30,398	3,840	3,697	3,543	12.6%	52,706,743
Santagata Nick		33,980	3,819	3,777	3,846	11.2%	67,616,059
Hulet Leslie	1999	25,286	3,816	3,589	3,293	15.1%	17,847,169

Jockeys	Last Rode	Mounts	1st	2d	3d	Win %	Purses
Williams Robert Dean		25,608	3,802	3,330	3,188	14.8%	27,738,176
Atkinson Ted	1959	23,661	3,795	3,300	2,913	16.0%	17,449,360
Whited D. E.	1990	28,036	3,795	3,602	3,374	13.5%	25,206,767
Neves Ralph	1964	25,334	3,772	3,547	3,352	14.9%	13,786,239
Gonzalez Roberto M.		27,431	3,772	3,546	3,308	13.8%	51,040,591
Moyers Leroy	1992	26,040	3,770	3,529	3,190	14.5%	21,491,585
Baird R. L.	1985	24,822	3,749	3,281	2,912	15.1%	12,592,611
Krone Julie A.		21,411	3,704	3,261	2,912	17.3%	90,122,764
Weiler Dan	1995	27,706	3,694	3,362	3,213	13.3%	12,225,344
Hansen Ron D.	1993	20,430	3,693	3,204	2,839	18.1%	42,635,184
Neff Steve	1995	27,951	3,685	3,384	3,299	13.2%	15,526,196
Loseth Chris		25,980	3,654	3,418	3,122	14.1%	32,461,865
Ussery Robert	1974	20,593	3,611	3,941	2,427	17.5%	22,714,074
Valenzuela Patrick A.		23,661	3,588	3,559	3,049	15.2%	127,655,330
Powell Jim Paul	2001	27,455	3,587	3,400	3,403	13.1%	15,997,565
Toro Fernando	1990	27,496	3,555	3,507	3,484	12.9%	56,299,765
Pierce Don	1985	28,740	3,546	3,655	3,617	12.3%	39,018,422
Bracciale, Jr. Vincent	1995	20,291	3,545	3,003	2,712	17.5%	37,817,349
Bravo Joe		19,509	3,543	3,131	2,657	18.2%	81,862,049
Passmore William J.	1984	29,409	3,531	3,143	2,994	12.0%	22,992,805
Antley Chris W.	2000	19,723	3,480	2,881	2,494	17.6%	92,261,894
Lively John	1991	26,134	3,468	3,033	3,073	13.3%	32,573,504
Dlugopolski Anthony R.	2001	25,428	3,453	3,146	2,900	13.6%	10,582,479
Rocco Joseph		25,941	3,452	3,407	3,331	13.3%	48,552,770
Thornburg Buck	1989	27,258	3,433	3,208	3,163	12.6%	22,876,221
Elliott Stewart		22,056	3,430	2,858	2,678	15.6%	47,214,410
Tejeira Jorge Enrique	2001	21,987	3,419	3,050	2,826	15.6%	28,146,870
Houghton T. D.		19,651	3,404	2,908	2,522	17.3%	28,100,210
Davis Robbie G.	2002	24,260	3,382	3,365	3,108	13.9%	115,732,836
Baze Gary		22,457	3,354	2,962	2,775	14.9%	27,448,932
Bourque Steve J.		22,571	3,354	2,896	2,700	14.9%	22,605,287
Stevens Scott A.		23,962	3,348	3,238	3,206	14.0%	23,186,158
Burton John E.	1999	20,511	3,336	2,816	2,821	16.3%	7,782,602
Hinojosa Herbert	1998	25,160	3,334	3,349	3,246	13.3%	17,962,176
Iliescu Arnold	1996	25,972	3,324	3,026	3,139	12.8%	14,840,887
Warren, Jr. Ronald J.		22,362	3,300	3,221	3,164	14.8%	58,086,192
Whitley Kevin	2001	19,189	3,275	2,580	2,345	17.1%	19,271,837
Adams John	1958	20,159	3,270	2,704	2,635	16.2%	9,743,109
Flores Jose Luis		18,766	3,259	2,864	2,432	17.4%	28,287,824
Platts Robin	2000	20,442	3,245	2,835	2,570	15.9%	39,266,629
Ferrer Jose C.		21,959	3,226	2,924	2,716	14.7%	49,684,763
Silva Carlos H.		26,316	3,217	3,087	3,119	12.2%	52,931,292
Compton Perry		23,083	3,207	2,963	2,670	13.9%	21,893,326
Pettinger Donald R.		19,672	3,205	2,674	2,576	16.3%	41,532,697
Dupuy Larry A.	2000	18,855	3,204	2,780	2,477	17.0%	10,990,706
Judice Joseph C.		21,695	3,202	2,977	2,833	14.8%	32,463,135
Rivera, Jr. Heriberto	2000	22,110	3,183	3,010	2,825	14.4%	24,110,789
Hampshire, Jr. Josiah F.		17,965	3,170	2,575	2,439	17.6%	27,315,468
Diaz Juvenal Lopez	2000	20,808	3,164	2,797	2,570	15.2%	41,589,019
Castaneda Marco	1997	27,053	3,163	3,192	3,329	11.7%	53,068,587
Krasner Samuel B.		19,747	3,157	2,893	2,536	16.0%	23,761,563
Velazquez John R.		18,301	3,149	2,670	2,400	17.2%	141,973,493
Baeza Braulio	1976	17,239	3,140	2,730	2,422	18.2%	36,150,142
Bourque Curt C.		21,023	3,131	2,595	2,427	14.9%	36,602,138
Boulanger Gary		20,462	3,102	2,860	2,759	15.2%	55,897,317
Lopez Charles C.		20,755	3,097	2,699	2,545	14.9%	55,490,992

Jockeys	Last Rode	Mounts	1st	2d	3d	Win %	Purses
Johnston Mark T.		18,820	3,085	2,844	2,642	16.4%	56,750,060
York Ray	2000	25,159	3,082	2,911	2,740	12.3%	14,206,054
Knight Lester Cash		21,292	3,078	3,118	3,086	14.5%	23,291,307
Faul Ricky J.		23,626	3,070	2,844	2,827	13.0%	23,846,349
McCauley W. Herbert	1998	20,129	3,049	2,892	2,552	15.1%	71,391,327
McKnight James		21,622	3,046	2,835	2,724	14.1%	37,074,744
D'Amico Anthony J.		21,802	3,044	2,769	2,514	14.0%	36,314,663
Morgan Michael R.		21,905	3,043	2,757	2,659	13.9%	26,126,155
Davidson Jesse	1988	18,433	3,035	2,440	2,264	16.5%	10,727,089
Turcotte Ron	1978	20,281	3,032	2,897	2,559	14.9%	28,606,490
Reynolds Larry C.		20,106	3,022	2,873	2,517	15.0%	38,157,257
Albarado Robby		19,001	3,018	2,774	2,542	15.9%	91,277,677
Madden Darrel	1974	20,822	3,000	2,607	2,618	14.4%	7,374,831
Douglas Rene R.		19,735	2,995	2,902	2,593	15.2%	76,311,998
Rincon Rudy	1999	23,559	2,975	2,860	2,804	12.6%	9,252,809
Court Jon Kenton		23,910	2,965	2,827	2,726	12.4%	53,261,908
Salvaggio Mark V.	2003	18,564	2,956	2,750	2,514	15.9%	17,265,491
Vargas Jorge L.		19,629	2,952	2,771	2,622	15.0%	22,221,163
Nicol, Jr. Paul Albert		17,930	2,928	2,638	2,516	16.3%	24,963,428
Baltazar Chuck	1997	22,618	2,912	2,497	2,405	12.9%	23,902,514
Kabel Todd		15,778	2,908	2,500	2,121	18.4%	82,663,742
Rotz John L.	1973	20,288	2,907	2,495	2,288	14.3%	22,991,932
McCarthy Michael J.	2002	17,180	2,907	2,654	2,493	16.9%	44,677,863
Velez, Jr. Jose A.		21,349	2,897	2,874	2,648	13.6%	57,217,440
Culmone Joe	1972	16,307	2,868	2,496	2,183	17.6%	12,010,447
Woods, Jr. Charles R.	2003	21,086	2,860	2,601	2,534	13.6%	36,644,771
Vega Harry		16,378	2,849	2,347	2,215	17.4%	32,899,652
Kutz Dean	2002	21,860	2,835	2,682	2,609	13.0%	33,691,225
Miller, Jr. Donald A.	1996	18,113	2,830	2,580	2,595	15.6%	37,018,336
Munsell George R.	1999	23,931	2,822	2,762	2,697	11.8%	8,157,106
Martin, Jr. Eddie M.		20,981	2,809	2,751	2,547	13.4%	47,814,768
Nakatani Corey S.		16,461	2,808	2,492	2,299	17.1%	150,219,779
Perrodin Elvis Joseph		19,596	2,803	2,586	2,504	14.3%	32,929,795
Feliciano Bennie R.	1999	17,566	2,802	2,572	2,370	16.0%	14,063,084
Sellers John	1977	18,636	2,787	2,500	2,371	15.0%	18,359,523
Boulmetis Sam	1966	15,512	2,783	2,308	2,069	17.9%	15,425,953
Hebert Tracy J.		19,010	2,781	2,364	2,162	14.6%	30,197,510
Mercier Norman	1992	21,275	2,769	2,621	2,524	13.0%	9,004,650
Barrera Carlos	1997	19,670	2,762	2,510	2,506	14.0%	18,486,045
Grabowski John A.		14,395	2,760	2,306	2,021	19.2%	19,980,461
MacBeth Donald	1986	22,415	2,755	2,822	2,924	12.3%	40,859,309
Dupuy Allen C.	2003	18,309	2,755	2,350	2,150	15.0%	14,135,559
Flores David Romero		18,878	2,743	2,557	2,447	14.5%	102,271,889
Gryder Aaron T.		21,296	2,736	2,694	2,765	12.8%	82,683,986
Pineda Alvaro	1975	18,007	2,731	2,418	2,165	15.2%	15,327,910
Craig, Jr. H. A.	1976	17,454	2,719	2,308	1,984	15.6%	5,138,364
Guerin Eric	1977	20,131	2,712	2,557	2,408	13.5%	17,305,136
Cave Roy	1984	19,937	2,711	2,458	2,469	13.6%	4,305,341
Melancon Gerard		19,348	2,709	2,635	2,465	14.0%	34,085,975
Ecoffey Fred	1984	17,522	2,683	2,471	2,181	15.3%	6,045,127
Coa Eibar		13,716	2,671	2,145	1,752	19.5%	65,305,143
Winters Perry A.		17,206	2,670	2,448	2,350	15.5%	18,386,855
Shuk Nick	1981	23,206	2,669	2,586	2,456	11.5%	11,286,518
Hinojosa Emede	1990	15,418	2,665	2,188	1,898	17.3%	4,667,134
Trosclair Angelo Jean	1998	20,776	2,660	2,470	2,407	12.8%	24,798,012
Delgado Alberto		21,948	2,656	2,633	2,666	12.1%	35,173,111

Jockeys	Last Rode	Mounts	1st	2d	3d	Win %	Purses
Lapensee Michel		19,769	2,650	2,526	2,381	13.4%	12,040,131
Fell Jeff	1990	15,165	2,649	2,204	1,954	17.5%	38,742,852
Lewis, Jr. William R.		18,137	2,644	2,410	2,343	14.6%	7,587,843
Woodhouse Hedley	1972	21,442	2,642	2,376	2,401	12.3%	14,483,558
Melancon Larry		19,105	2,637	2,497	2,441	13.8%	52,815,991
Barrow Thomas	1991	21,061	2,627	2,578	2,515	12.5%	12,816,323
Landing Ray	1983	21,164	2,620	2,692	2,463	12.4%	4,919,246
LeBlanc Kirk Paul		20,749	2,613	2,672	2,542	12.6%	30,223,202
Lopez Ricardo D.	2002	17,995	2,612	2,668	2,476	14.5%	24,819,034
Frazier Ricky		21,153	2,606	2,566	2,496	12.3%	31,788,508
Bush Vernon		19,534	2,603	2,474	2,418	13.3%	17,622,998
Manganello Mike	1990	16,773	2,598	2,184	2,042	15.5%	8,946,751
Houghton Rick L.	2003	19,573	2,595	2,585	2,469	13.3%	11,136,223
Saumell Francisco	1979	18,231	2,591	2,298	2,204	14.2%	3,499,032
Chapman Thomas M.	1996	20,575	2,587	2,554	2,621	12.6%	36,788,641
Maple Sam	1996	20,211	2,578	2,495	2,366	12.8%	29,091,687
Meza Rafael Q.	2001	19,923	2,573	2,403	2,226	12.9%	48,865,366
McHargue D. G.	1988	15,712	2,553	2,154	1,927	16.2%	39,609,526
Licata Frank	1999	16,826	2,546	2,302	2,235	15.1%	9,629,846
Valenzuela Ismael	1980	21,203	2,545	2,494	2,346	12.0%	20,122,760
Lambert Jerry	1996	16,564	2,535	2,371	2,249	15.3%	20,933,326
Molina Victor H.		17,378	2,532	2,314	2,100	14.6%	33,846,917
Dunkelberger Travis L.		12,147	2,531	1,885	1,662	20.8%	29,371,981
Pedroza Martin A.		21,374	2,531	2,542	2,484	11.8%	63,347,985
Clark David		17,605	2,528	2,314	2,176	14.4%	59,090,588
McDowell Michael	1992	19,337	2,517	2,290	2,274	13.0%	16,734,420
St. Leon Gene	1999	18,482	2,514	2,373	2,215	13.6%	24,508,230
Potts Clinton L.		14,696	2,514	2,103	1,935	17.1%	24,339,273
Luzzi Michael J.		18,958	2,511	2,291	2,425	13.2%	67,347,522
Diaz Antonio L.	1992	19,081	2,501	2,209	2,056	13.1%	20,525,336
Walker, Jr. Bobby J.		18,543	2,489	2,290	2,100	13.4%	27,267,050
Guillory David	2002	20,649	2,482	2,564	2,429	12.0%	26,706,082
Graell Antonio	2000	18,982	2,481	2,217	2,202	13.1%	22,016,374
Spieth Scott		17,013	2,478	2,292	2,232	14.6%	22,014,719
Woodley Carl James		18,456	2,475	2,241	2,179	13.4%	18,482,951
Samyn Jean-Luc		21,857	2,469	2,527	2,704	11.3%	85,651,485
Westrope Jack	1958	17,497	2,467	2,406	2,166	14.1%	8,226,677
Bourque Kenneth	1999	19,873	2,467	2,312	2,270	12.4%	20,422,060
Berry Monte Clifton		17,898	2,462	2,352	2,209	13.8%	23,277,401
Martinez Luis Jeronimo		16,794	2,454	2,134	2,128	14.6%	17,694,446
Howard Donald Lee	2001	18,209	2,450	2,219	2,192	13.5%	26,774,427
Johnson Brian G.	2001	16,279	2,445	2,054	2,095	15.0%	16,420,346
Rini Anthony	1975	18,716	2,438	2,429	2,221	13.0%	10,879,825
Martinez Willie		17,610	2,424	2,257	1,993	13.8%	54,871,936
Duffy Lloyd	1996	21,339	2,419	2,549	2,579	11.3%	24,047,045
Agnello Anthony	1993	15,691	2,414	2,104	1,912	15.4%	10,851,294
Cruguet Jean	1996	20,636	2,407	2,419	2,524	11.7%	51,557,267
McCarron Gregg	1995	20,595	2,403	2,316	2,407	11.7%	27,268,536
Pruitt Jerry		18,028	2,401	2,364	2,250	13.3%	7,615,609
Guerra Vince J.		18,973	2,394	2,319	2,305	12.6%	12,279,495
LaGue Larry	2001	21,287	2,380	2,352	2,440	11.2%	10,210,209
Patterson G.	1990	17,202	2,376	2,214	2,114	13.8%	17,649,667
Ycaza Manuel C.	1970	10,563	2,367	1,749	1,515	22.4%	19,935,226
Attard Larry	1997	19,126	2,366	2,342	2,382	12.4%	34,206,895
Thompson Winston A.		16,187	2,341	2,297	2,192	14.5%	19,522,314
Zook Dana	1997	23,515	2,336	2,690	2,660	9.9%	8,783,561

Jockeys	Last Rode	Mounts	1st	2d	3d	Win %	Purses
Meyers Tommy		13,991	2,320	2,036	1,776	16.6%	12,278,489
Hendricks Ken		14,563	2,320	2,012	1,925	15.9%	8,902,423
Sayler Bernon	2001	26,016	2,302	2,393	2,420	8.8%	11,859,582
Lopez Adalberto Diaz		15,134	2,299	2,273	1,937	15.2%	29,359,889
Gonsalves Frank Albert		17,895	2,298	2,291	2,175	12.8%	14,653,082
Sanchez Herson A.	1998	18,313	2,289	2,182	2,117	12.5%	11,048,856
Bartram Brent E.	2002	16,806	2,280	2,211	2,216	13.6%	35,113,773
Solomone Mickey	1990	17,174	2,276	1,846	1,776	13.3%	18,176,887
Vigliotti Matthew J.	1996	16,555	2,268	2,216	2,180	13.7%	23,027,131
Guajardo Alonzo		18,018	2,253	2,029	1,907	12.5%	12,574,063
Campbell Ronald J.	1993	13,874	2,245	1,926	1,706	16.2%	9,403,215
Montoya Daryl		19,547	2,242	2,213	2,236	11.5%	22,490,750
Avant James E.		13,049	2,241	1,788	1,545	17.2%	10,533,853
Lumpkins Jason P.		11,461	2,234	1,673	1,504	19.5%	26,296,318
Aviles Rudy	1997	14,180	2,216	1,970	1,847	15.6%	9,663,913
McGregor Christopher H.	2002	13,608	2,214	2,029	2,029	16.3%	12,844,009
Steinberg Patrick W.	1993	13,884	2,210	1,903	1,681	15.9%	15,698,892
Dominguez Ramon A.		9,936	2,191	1,776	1,476	22.1%	54,285,237
Freeman Wayne	2001	17,952	2,188	2,177	2,057	12.2%	4,625,840
Whited Daniel W.	1999	18,343	2,182	2,024	1,928	11.9%	9,062,031
Gomez Esteban Angel		16,069	2,179	2,132	1,996	13.6%	12,459,875
Scocca Dante		18,199	2,172	2,199	2,036	11.9%	13,240,845
Razo, Jr. Eusebio		18,950	2,169	2,408	2,196	11.4%	42,481,341
Troilo William D.		17,572	2,168	1,983	2,045	12.3%	21,916,383
Bruin James Edward		22,588	2,162	2,226	2,259	9.6%	25,127,691
Alvarado Pedro V.		12,425	2,155	1,982	1,686	17.3%	15,552,206
Small Stanley	1992	18,088	2,149	2,075	2,118	11.9%	4,453,100
Allen, Jr. Ronald Dale	2002	16,734	2,147	2,047	1,963	12.8%	15,647,606
Seymour Don James	1994	11,626	2,141	1,759	1,577	18.4%	31,440,583
Lanerie Corey J.		14,989	2,137	2,071	1,949	14.3%	37,572,517
Cooksey Patricia J.	2004	18,267	2,137	2,185	2,120	11.7%	19,890,479
Messina Robert		14,092	2,134	1,969	1,816	15.1%	15,277,859
Baker Christopher John		18,128	2,123	2,442	2,416	11.7%	13,316,808
Verge Mario E.		17,247	2,122	2,104	2,072	12.3%	31,038,939
Lambert Casey T.		17,244	2,101	2,049	1,983	12.2%	20,556,584
Saumell Larry	1999	17,379	2,098	2,025	1,909	12.1%	24,876,170
Thomas Douglas Bruce	1997	18,026	2,092	2,103	2,199	11.6%	21,173,003
Markham, Jr. Richard L.		18,896	2,087	2,074	1,917	11.0%	4,815,868
Moran Michael		15,992	2,082	1,979	2,115	13.0%	11,948,894
Corbett Glenn W.		14,687	2,074	1,948	1,793	14.1%	20,227,346
Gomez Garrett K.		13,147	2,071	1,919	1,726	15.8%	61,627,772
Edwards James W.	1991	15,202	2,057	1,928	1,898	13.5%	18,456,759
Castillo, Jr. Heberto		16,622	2,055	1,961	1,983	12.4%	45,601,084
Shino Ken A.		13,685	2,053	1,819	1,798	15.0%	14,081,165
Quinonez Luis S.		15,039	2,051	1,998	1,962	13.6%	25,182,258
Boland William N.	1969	17,233	2,049	1,895	1,922	11.9%	14,856,095
Vergara Euclides B.	1994	13,449	2,049	1,949	1,843	15.2%	12,501,317
Hutton Greg W.		15,640	2,047	1,914	1,692	13.1%	28,247,109
Kaenel Jack Leroy	2003	15,250	2,046	1,831	1,794	13.4%	24,423,893
Emigh Christopher A.		16,926	2,042	2,128	1,967	12.1%	33,430,514
Valovich Christopher Jon	2002	14,351	2,034	1,804	1,661	14.2%	19,655,653
Clark Kerwin D.		17,176	2,033	2,049	1,925	11.8%	26,297,581
Mitchell Gallyn Vick		13,718	2,032	1,875	1,884	14.8%	13,224,043
Romero Shane P.		15,594	2,029	1,723	1,600	13.0%	21,574,665
Phelps Billy	1996	16,970	2,026	2,176	1,988	11.9%	8,294,797
Martinez Orlando A.		16,349	2,025	1,954	1,927	12.4%	12,755,264

Jockey	Year	Mounts	1st	2nd	3rd	Win %	Earnings
Marquez, Jr. Carlos H.		15,574	2,021	1,952	1,916	13.0%	39,207,893
Simonetti Frank	1995	16,593	2,016	2,009	1,956	12.1%	3,696,461
Caballero Raul	1995	16,676	2,002	1,927	1,946	12.0%	9,273,564
Gale Michael Allen		15,327	1,993	2,141	2,027	13.0%	10,311,356
Rivas Carlos		14,100	1,992	1,744	1,726	14.1%	8,253,449
Ernst Phil	1998	17,430	1,988	2,055	2,026	11.4%	5,195,796
Martinez Joe A.		12,569	1,985	1,796	1,694	15.8%	10,639,775
Munar Luis H.		11,426	1,983	1,645	1,466	17.4%	12,814,281
Maese Alex	1998	18,575	1,981	1,992	2,133	10.7%	8,673,676
Best Frank	1999	15,564	1,977	2,012	1,860	12.7%	7,613,461
Murphy Glen		15,590	1,970	2,074	1,925	12.6%	19,675,814
Castro Joe M.		14,123	1,968	1,877	1,817	13.9%	20,781,241
Simington Donald E.		18,002	1,950	2,007	1,999	10.8%	21,113,072
Kato Akifumi		18,440	1,946	2,009	2,107	10.6%	5,394,943
Grant Howard	1984	10,327	1,944	1,506	1,339	18.8%	12,120,579
King, Jr. Edwin L.		17,449	1,942	2,161	2,360	11.1%	31,506,105
Walker Mark K.	2000	13,219	1,935	1,803	1,620	14.6%	12,844,094
Torres Cesar A.		12,034	1,920	1,662	1,547	16.0%	13,959,031
Martinez, III Flavio	1998	15,512	1,918	1,857	1,768	12.4%	9,715,487
Nelson Eldon	1975	14,415	1,917	1,682	1,535	13.3%	10,084,711
Gondron Ted D.		13,039	1,915	1,693	1,553	14.7%	13,120,573
Thompson Clifford Ray	1995	14,832	1,914	1,856	1,834	12.9%	3,590,178
Dos Ramos Richard A.		16,090	1,907	2,025	1,957	11.9%	47,374,384
Saul Dennis	2000	17,819	1,906	2,022	2,294	10.7%	10,385,284
Schvaneveldt Chad P.		14,408	1,905	1,840	1,771	13.2%	25,028,712
Caraballo Jose C.		13,088	1,901	1,806	1,755	14.5%	22,948,823

World's Leading Jockey – Laffit Pincay Jr.

A legendary career came to an end in 2003 when Laffit Pincay Jr., world's leading jockey with 9,530 winning rides to his credit, retired in the aftermath of an accident at Santa Anita Park.

Pincay, born in Panama on Dec. 29, 1946, started his U.S. riding career in 1966, after winning nearly 450 races in Panama. Within 10 years, he had risen to the height of his profession in North America, leading all jockeys in money won from 1970 through 1974 and earning an Eclipse Award in 1971, 1973 and 1974. His spectacular success warranted election into the Hall of Fame in 1975.

Such success would be sustained. Pincay earned two more Eclipse Awards, in 1979 and 1985, years that again saw him lead all jockeys in earnings.

During his lengthy career, Pincay won the Kentucky Derby in 1984 aboard Swale and rode three consecutive winners of the Belmont, with the Woody Stephens-trained trio of Conquistador Cielo, Caveat and Swale in 1982-1984. He would win seven Breeders' Cup events, including the 1986 Classic aboard Skywalker. Pincay's other Breeders' Cup victories came aboard Bayakoa in the Distaff in 1989 and 1990; with Tasso, Capote and Is It True in the 1985, 1986 and 1988 runnings of the Juvenile, respectively; and Phone Chatter in the 1993 Juvenile Fillies.

The Southern California-based Pincay frequently appeared aboard luminaries such as Affirmed, John Henry, Bayakoa, Susan's Girl, Ancient Title and many others.

Laffit Pincay Jr.

Pincay won over 150 Grade 1 events, including victories in the Arlington Million, Jockey Club Gold Cup, Woodward, Spinster, Metropolitan Handicap, Travers, Florida Derby and Washington D.C. International away from his California home base. He was a dominant force in southern California, winning the Hollywood Gold Cup nine times, the Santa Anita Derby seven times and the Santa Anita Handicap on five occasions.

On Dec. 10, 1999, Pincay surpassed Bill Shoemaker's previous standard of 8,833 winning rides to become racing's all-time leading rider.

Laffit Pincay Jr. Year-by-Year

Before 1976, US and Foreign

Mts	1st	2nd	3rd	Earnings
13,677	3,106	2,298	1,942	$28,740,923

1976 and Later, US and Foreign

Year	Mts	1st	2nd	3rd	Earnings
1976	1,435	386	263	173	$4,377,961
1977	1,329	295	247	200	4,385,951
1978	1,428	287	253	205	4,132,993
1979	1,707	420	302	260	8,182,260
1980	1,419	289	222	222	6,390,355
1981	1,511	301	286	229	7,914,392
1982	1,478	302	240	221	9,076,024
1983	1,421	299	246	192	8,813,456
1984	1,407	299	235	192	10,909,948
1985	1,409	289	246	183	13,315,049
1986	1,318	252	208	161	10,168,428
1987	1,463	313	272	199	11,838,196
1988	1,102	198	159	145	8,575,377
1989	1,594	298	224	212	11,361,610
1990	1,079	150	122	137	6,546,989
1991	1,433	218	200	173	8,323,411
1992	1,283	193	189	128	7,320,773
1993	1,214	164	171	167	6,697,141
1994	1,211	157	171	172	6,828,999
1995	1,270	156	187	185	6,181,225
1996	979	129	122	135	4,160,355
1997	718	75	94	82	2,520,342
1998	730	103	101	112	3,917,084
1999	1,112	170	158	141	6,662,689
2000	1,090	202	186	136	8,490,360
2001	1,252	225	180	152	10,049,166
2002	1,189	205	168	163	9,572,037
2003	229	49	34	31	1,967,131
Totals:	**48,487**	**9,530**	**7,784**	**6,650**	**$237,420,625**

Graded Stakes Events Won By Laffit Pincay Jr.

Year	Stakes Name	Winner
1973	Santa Susana	Belle Marie
1973	Demoiselle	Chris Evert
1973	Golden Rod	Chris Evert
1973	Santa Anita H.	Cougar II
1973	Hollywood Express H.	Crimson Saint
1973	Selima	Dancealot
1973	Stymie H.	Forage
1973	Hollywood Inv H.	Life Cycle
1973	San Miguel	Linda's Chief
1973	Lexington H.	London Company
1973	Manhattan H.	London Company
1973	Santa Anita Derby	Sham
1973	Hollywood Lassie	Special Goddess
1973	Delaware H.	Susan's Girl
1973	Santa Barbara H.	Susan's Girl
1973	Santa Margarita Inv H.	Susan's Girl
1973	Santa Maria H.	Susan's Girl
1973	Susquehanna H.	Susan's Girl
1973	San Marcos H.	Tuqui II
1973	Pasadena	Windy's Daughter
1974	Charles H. Strub	Ancient Title
1974	Los Angeles H.	Ancient Title
1974	Palos Verdes H.	Ancient Title
1974	San Fernando	Ancient Title
1974	Argonaut H.	Battery E.
1974	Baldwin	Battery E.
1974	Santa Maria H.	Convenience
1974	Brighton Beach H.	Crafty Khale
1974	Beldame	Desert Vixen
1974	Matchmaker	Desert Vixen
1974	Hol Juv Champ	Dimaggio
1974	Blue Grass	Judger
1974	Florida Derby	Judger
1974	Adirondack	Laughing Bridge
1974	Sequoia H.	Lt.'s Joy
1974	Hollywood Oaks	Miss Musket
1974	Cygnet	Miss Tokyo
1974	Junior League	Miss Tokyo
1974	Frizette	Molly Ballantine
1974	American H.	Plunk
1974	San Antonio	Prince Dantan
1974	San Carlos H.	Royal Owl
1974	Carleton F. Burke H.	Tallahto
1974	Oak Tree Invitational	Tallahto
1974	Santa Barbara H.	Tallahto
1974	Vanity H.	Tallahto
1974	Whitney	Tri Jet
1974	San Bernardino H.	Wichita Oil
1974	Westchester	Windy Whisper
1975	Californian	Ancient Title
1975	Hol Gold Cup Inv H.	Ancient Title
1975	San Carlos H.	Ancient Title
1975	Los Angeles H.	Big Band
1975	California Derby	Diabolo
1975	Demoiselle	Free Journey
1975	Remsen	Hang Ten
1975	Maskette H.	Let Me Linger
1975	San Luis Obispo H.	Madison Palace
1975	Spinster	Susan's Girl
1976	Santa Anita Derby	An Act
1976	San Luis Rey	Avatar
1976	Beverly Hills H.	Bastonera II
1976	Milady H.	Bastonera II
1976	San Jacinto	Bold Forbes
1976	Thanksgiving Day H.	Classy Surgeon
1976	Del Mar Oaks	Go March
1976	Will Rogers H.	Madera Sun
1976	San Carlos H.	No Bias
1976	Anoakia	Telferner
1976	Del Mar Debutante	Telferner
1976	Volante H.	Today 'n Tomorrow
1976	Del Mar Futurity	Visible
1976	Hollywood Lassie	Wavy Waves
1977	Hol Juv Champ	Affirmed
1977	Century H.	Anne's Pretender
1977	Cinema H.	Bad 'n Big
1977	El Dorado H.	Bad 'n Big
1977	Californian	Crystal Water
1977	Hol Gold Cup H.	Crystal Water
1977	Santa Anita H.	Crystal Water
1977	Honeymoon H.	Joyous Ways
1977	San Fernando	Kirby Lane
1977	Santa Ynez	Wavy Waves
1978	Santa Anita Derby	Affirmed
1978	Thanksgiving Day H.	Always Gallant
1978	American H.	Effervescing
1978	Las Palmas H.	Grenzen
1978	Santa Barbara H.	Kittyluck
1978	Volante H.	Wayside Station
1979	Californian	Affirmed
1979	Charles H. Strub	Affirmed
1979	Hol Gold Cup H.	Affirmed
1979	Jockey Club Gold Cup	Affirmed
1979	Santa Anita H.	Affirmed
1979	Woodward	Affirmed
1979	Jamaica H.	Belle's Gold
1979	Ramona H.	Country Queen
1979	Wilshire H.	Country Queen
1979	Yellow Ribbon	Country Queen
1979	Arcadia H.	Fluorescent Light
1979	San Luis Obispo H.	Fluorescent Light
1979	Demoiselle	Genuine Risk
1979	Santa Maria H.	Grenzen
1979	Santa Monica H.	Grenzen
1979	Ruffian H.	It's in the Air
1979	Native Diver H.	Life's Hope

Year	Stakes Name	Winner
1979	Del Mar Derby H.	Relaunch
1979	La Jolla Mile	Relaunch
1979	Bel Air H.	Sirlad
1979	San Bernardino H.	Star Spangled
1979	Santa Ynez	Terlingua
1979	Paterson H.	Valdez
1979	Rutgers H.	Valdez
1979	Silver Screen H.	Valdez
1979	Swaps	Valdez
1980	Los Angeles H.	Beau's Eagle
1980	Beverly Hills H.	Country Queen
1980	Metropolitan H.	Czaravich
1980	Del Mar Derby H.	Exploded
1980	San Carlos H.	Handsomeness
1980	Frizette	Heavenly Cause
1980	Selima	Heavenly Cause
1980	El Encino	It's in the Air
1980	Vanity H.	It's in the Air
1980	Oak Tree Invitational	John Henry
1980	Hol Juv Champ	Loma Malad
1980	Hollywood Lassie	Native Fancy
1980	San Gabriel H.	Premiere Ministre
1980	Santa Barbara H.	Sisterhood
1980	San Pasqual H.	Valdez
1980	Arl-Wash Futurity	Well Decorated
1981	Anoakia	A Kiss for Luck
1981	Acorn	Heavenly Cause
1981	Fantasy	Heavenly Cause
1981	Kentucky Oaks	Heavenly Cause
1981	Hollywood Inv H.	John Henry
1981	San Luis Obispo H.	John Henry
1981	San Luis Rey	John Henry
1981	Santa Anita H.	John Henry
1981	Swaps	Noble Nashua
1981	Arcadia H.	Premier Ministre
1981	Santa Margarita Inv H.	Princess Karenda
1981	Santa Ana H.	Queen to Conquer
1981	Malibu	Raise a Man
1981	El Dorado H.	Seafood
1981	Bay Meadows H.	Super Moment
1981	Hol Juv Champ	The Captain
1982	Gamely H.	Ack's Secret
1982	Santa Barbara H.	Ack's Secret
1982	Santa Margarita Inv H.	Ack's Secret
1982	Belmont	Conquistador Cielo
1982	Californian	Erins Isle
1982	Hollywood Inv H.	Exploded
1982	San Pasqual H.	Five Star Flight
1982	Del Mar Derby	Give Me Strength
1982	Malibu	Island Whirl
1982	Volante H.	Lamerok
1982	Anoakia	Landaluce
1982	Del Mar Debutante	Landaluce
1982	Hollywood Lassie	Landaluce
1982	Oak Leaf	Landaluce
1982	Santa Anita Derby	Muttering
1982	Arcadia H.	Perrault
1982	Hol Gold Cup H.	Perrault
1982	San Luis Rey	Perrault
1982	Linda Vista H.	Skillful Joy
1982	San Marcos H.	Super Moment
1982	Hollywood Oaks	Tango Dancer
1983	Del Mar Debutante	Althea
1983	Del Mar Futurity	Althea
1983	Hol Juv Champ	Althea
1983	Hollywood Starlet	Althea
1983	Belmont	Caveat
1983	Longacres Mile H.	Chinook Pass
1983	Fountain of Youth	Copelan
1983	Hollywood Inv H.	Erins Isle
1983	S Juan Capistrano Inv H.	Erins Isle
1983	San Luis Rey	Erins Isle
1983	Del Mar Oaks	Heartlight No. One
1983	Hollywood Oaks	Heartlight No. One
1983	Ruffian H.	Heartlight No. One
1983	Santa Maria H.	Sangue
1983	Super Derby	Sunny's Halo
1983	Malibu	Time to Explode
1984	Delaware H.	Adored
1984	Milady H.	Adored
1984	Santa Susana	Althea
1984	San Gabriel H.	Beldale Lustre
1984	Santa Ynez	Boo la Boo
1984	Travers	Carr de Naskra
1984	San Carlos H.	Danebo
1984	San Pasqual H.	Danebo
1984	Del Mar Debutante	Fiesta Lady
1984	Matron	Fiesta Lady
1984	Oak Leaf	Folk Art
1984	AKS Omaha Gold Cup	Gate Dancer
1984	Super Derby	Gate Dancer
1984	Princess	Gene's Lady
1984	Santa Ynez	Gene's Lady
1984	Century H.	Interco
1984	S Juan Capistrano Inv H.	Load the Cannons
1984	Rothmans Int	Majesty's Prince
1984	Santa Maria H.	Marisma
1984	Flower Bowl H.	Rossard
1984	Futurity	Spectacular Love
1984	Belmont	Swale
1984	Florida Derby	Swale
1984	Kentucky Derby	Swale
1984	Eddie Read H.	Ten Below
1984	Silver Screen H.	Tights
1984	Wilshire H.	Triple Tipple
1984	Will Rogers H.	Tsunami Slew
1985	Hawthorne H.	Adored
1985	Milady H.	Adored

Year	Stakes Name	Winner
1985	Santa Maria H.	Adored
1985	Spinster	Dontstop Themusic
1985	Arl-Wash Lassie	Family Style
1985	Frizette	Family Style
1985	Las Flores H.	Foggy Notion
1985	Californian	Greinton
1985	Hol Gold Cup H.	Greinton
1985	San Bernardino H.	Greinton
1985	San Felipe H.	Image of Greatness
1985	Hillsborough H.	Justicara
1985	Alibhai H.	Nostalgia's Star
1985	Nat Sprint Champ	Pancho Villa
1985	Silver Screen H.	Pancho Villa
1985	Santa Anita Derby	Skywalker
1985	Jersey Derby	Spend a Buck
1985	Monmouth H.	Spend a Buck
1985	Dwyer	Stephan's Odyssey
1985	Jim Dandy	Stephan's Odyssey
1985	Breeders' Cup Juv	Tasso
1985	Breeders' Futurity	Tasso
1985	Del Mar Futurity	Tasso
1986	Breeders' Cup Juv	Capote
1986	Norfolk	Capote
1986	Hawthorne H.	Dontstop Themusic
1986	Santa Anita H.	Greinton
1986	San Antonio H.	Hatim
1986	Native Diver H.	Hopeful Word
1986	Princess	Melair
1986	San Carlos H.	Phone Trick
1986	Breeders' Cup Classic	Skywalker
1986	Longacres Mile H.	Skywalker
1986	Mervyn Leroy H.	Skywalker
1986	San Diego H.	Skywalker
1986	Bel Air H.	Super Diamond
1986	Goodwood H.	Super Diamond
1986	Hol Gold Cup H.	Super Diamond
1987	American H.	Clever Song
1987	Jockey Club Gold Cup	Creme Fraiche
1987	Meadowlands Cup H.	Creme Fraiche
1987	San Gorgonio H.	Frau Altiva
1987	Sorrento	Hasty Pasty
1987	Washington D. C., Int	Le Glorieux
1987	Del Mar Futurity	Lost Kitty
1987	El Camino Real Derby	Masterful Advocate
1987	San Rafael	Masterful Advocate
1987	San Gabriel H.	Nostalgia's Star
1987	Carleton F. Burke H.	Rivlia
1987	S Juan Capistrano Inv H.	Rosedale
1987	Eddie Read H.	Sharrood
1987	Cinema H.	Something Lucky
1987	Will Rogers H.	Something Lucky
1987	Boojum H.	Sun Master
1987	San Diego H.	Super Diamond
1987	Hollywood Futurity	Tejano
1987	San Fernando	Variety Road
1987	Affirmed H.	W.D. Jacks
1987	Mervyn Leroy H.	Zabaleta
1988	California Derby	All Thee Power
1988	Rancho Bernardo H.	Clabber Girl
1988	Riva Ridge	Evening Kris
1988	Haskell Invitational	Forty Niner
1988	La Canada	Hollywood Glitter
1988	Breeders' Cup Juv	Is It True
1988	Malibu	Oraibi
1988	Railbird	Sheesham
1988	Frizette	Some Romance
1988	San Pasqual H.	Super Diamond
1989	Apple Blossom H.	Bakayoa
1989	Breeders' Cup Distaff	Bayakoa
1989	Hawthorne H.	Bayakoa
1989	Milady H.	Bayakoa
1989	Ruffian H.	Bayakoa
1989	Santa Margarita Inv H.	Bayakoa
1989	Spinster	Bayakoa
1989	Vanity H.	Bayakoa
1989	Sorrento	Cheval Volant
1989	Affirmed H.	Exploding Prospect
1989	San Vicente	Gum
1989	Bay Shore	Houston
1989	Derby Trial	Houston
1989	Las Virgenes	Kool Arrival
1989	Rancho Bernardo H.	Kool Arrival
1989	Malibu	Music Merci
1989	Will Rogers H.	Notorious Pleasure
1989	Del Mar Bud BC H.	On the Line
1989	Sierra Madre H.	Oraibi
1989	Mervyn Leroy H.	Ruhlmann
1989	San Bernardino H.	Ruhlmann
1989	Los Angeles H.	Sam Who
1989	San Antonio H.	Super Diamond
1989	San Marcos H.	Trokhos
1989	Arl-Wash Lassie	Trumpet's Blare
1989	Las Flores H.	Very Subtle
1989	San Gabriel H.	Wretham
1990	Breeders' Cup Distaff	Bayakoa
1990	Chula Vista H.	Bayakoa
1990	Hawthorne H.	Bayakoa
1990	Milady H.	Bayakoa
1990	Spinster	Bayakoa
1990	Budweiser Int H.	Fly Till Dawn
1990	Col. F. W. Koester H.	Notorious Pleasure
1990	Silver Screen H.	Stalwart Charger
1990	Hollywood Turf H.	Steinlen
1990	Del Mar Derby	Tight Spot
1991	Rancho Bernardo BC H.	Cascading Gold
1991	Citation H.	Fly Till Dawn
1991	San Marcos H.	Fly Till Dawn
1991	Gamely H.	Miss Josh

Year	Stakes Name	Winner
1991	Matchmaker	Miss Josh
1991	River Cities Bud BC	Miss Josh
1991	Linda Vista H.	Nice Assay
1991	Citation H.	Notorious Pleasure
1991	Triple Bend H.	Robyn Dancer
1991	Rolling Green H.	Shotiche
1991	Palomar H.	Somethingmerry
1991	American H.	Tight Spot
1991	Arlington Million	Tight Spot
1991	Eddie Read H.	Tight Spot
1991	Inglewood H.	Tight Spot
1992	Golden Gate H.	Algenib
1992	San Diego H.	Another Review
1992	Chula Vista H.	Exchange
1992	El Encino	Exchange
1992	La Canada	Exchange
1992	Arcadia H.	Fly Till Dawn
1992	San Luis Rey	Fly Till Dawn
1992	Laurel Dash	Glen Kate
1992	NYRA Mile H.	Ibero
1992	Palos Verdes H.	Individualist
1992	Silver Screen H.	Natural Nine
1992	Hollywood Futurity	River Special
1992	River Cities Bud BC	Sacque
1992	Lazaro Barrera H.	Star Recruit
1992	Louisiana Downs H.	Stark South
1992	San Francisco Mile H.	Tight Spot
1993	Swaps	Devoted Brass
1993	Malibu	Diazo
1993	Pegasus H.	Diazo
1993	Santa Ana H.	Exchange
1993	Santa Barbara H.	Exchange
1993	Metropolitan H.	Ibero
1993	Breeders' Cup Juv F	Phone Chatter
1993	Oak Leaf	Phone Chatter
1993	Sorrento	Phone Chatter
1993	Hollywood Futurity	Valiant Nature
1994	San Marcos H.	Bien Bien
1994	Lazaro Barrera H.	College Town

Year	Stakes Name	Winner
1994	Strub	Diazo
1994	Matriarch	Exchange
1994	San Gorgonio H.	Hero's Love
1994	Del Mar Inv Derby	Ocean Crest
1994	Senorita BC	Rabiadella
1994	Volante H.	Run Softly
1995	Arcadia H.	College Town
1995	Orchid H.	Exchange
1995	Del Mar Inv H.	Royal Chariot
1995	Oak Leaf	Tipically Irish
1997	Los Angeles H.	Men's Exclusive
1998	Hollywood Futurity	Tactical Cat
1999	Las Flores H.	Enjoy the Moment
1999	Hollywood Turf Cup	Lazy Lode
1999	Beverly Hills H.	Virginie
2000	Sorrento	Give Praise
2000	Hawthorne Derby	Hymn
2000	Vernon O. Underwood	Men's Exclusive
2000	Native Diver H.	Sky Jack
2000	Hol Juv Champ	Squirtle Squirt
2000	Rancho Bernardo H.	Theresa's Tizzy
2001	Hollywood Gold Cup	Aptitude
2001	Hollywood Prevue	Fonz's
2001	Arcadia H.	Lazy Lode
2001	Palos Verdes H.	Men's Exclusive
2001	Vernon O. Underwood	Men's Exclusive
2001	Toyota Blue Grass	Millennium Wind
2001	Buena Vista H.	Rare Charmer
2001	Frank E. Kilroe Mile H.	Road to Slew
2001	Cinema H.	Sligo Bay
2001	Bel Air H.	Smile Again
2001	Del Mar H.	Timboroa
2002	Monrovia H.	Lil Sister Stich
2002	San Felipe	Medaglia d'Oro
2002	Native Diver H.	Piensa Sonando
2002	Hollywood Gold Cup	Sky Jack
2002	Mervyn LeRoy H.	Sky Jack
2002	Desert Stormer H.	Slewsbox
2002	Hollywood Turf Cup	Sligo Bay

Baze's Isaac Murphy Award monopoly ended by Dominguez

An unbroken streak ended in 2004 when Ramon Dominguez supplanted Russell Baze as the recipient of the Isaac Murphy Award, which is awarded annually to the jockey with the highest win percentage (with a minimum of 500 mounts) during the year. The award, inaugurated in 1995 to honor the legendary black jockey of the 19th century who won 44 percent of his races, had never previously gone to anyone but Baze. The Isaac Murphy Award is presented by the National Turf Writers Association.

Fourth in 2002 with 23.2 percent winners and second in 2003 with 27.8 percent winners, Dominguez climbed to the top in 2004 with 383 winners from 1,354 mounts for 28.3 percent winners. Baze held on for second place, with 27.2 percent winners.

Through Dec. 31, 2004, he had ridden 2,191 winners in his career for an overall win rate of 22.1 percent. The nation's leader in races won in both 2001 and 2003, Dominguez had another strong year overall in 2004, finishing second in races won.

Leading Jockeys of 2004 (by percent wins, with at least 500 rides)

Jockey	Percent Wins
Ramon Dominguez	28.3
Russell A. Baze	27.2
John Velazquez	25.2
Ramsey Zimmerman	25.2
Chad Schvaneveldt	24.5
Pedro Alvarado	24.4
Rafael Bejarano	23.7
Ken Tohill	23.4
Jerry Bailey	23.1
Todd Kabel	22.7

Previous Isaac Murphy Award Statistics

Year	Winner	Percent Wins
1995	Russell Baze	29.1
1996	Russell Baze	28.3
1997	Russell Baze	28.3
1998	Russell Baze	27.6
1999	Russell Baze	28.1
2000	Russell Baze	27.2
2001	Russell Baze	28.1
2002	Russell Baze	28.6
2003	Russell Baze	30.2
2004	Ramon Dominguez	28.3

Leading Female Jockey – Julie Krone

In 2000, Julie Krone became the first woman inducted into North American thoroughbred racing's Hall of Fame, a crowning achievement in a career filled with superlatives and firsts.

Born July 24, 1963, in Benton Harbor, Mich., Krone rode her first winner at Tampa Bay Downs on Jan. 30, 1981.

She proved an immediate success in New Jersey, where she won numerous riding titles at Atlantic City, Meadowlands and Monmouth Park beginning in the early 1980s.

In 1993, Krone became the first woman to ride the winner of a U.S. classic race when she piloted Colonial Affair to victory in the Belmont. Ten years later, she became the first female jockey to win a Breeders' Cup event, winning the Juvenile Fillies aboard eventual champion Halfbridled.

Julie Krone

Other major horses Krone has won aboard include Classy Mirage, Gaily Gaily, Lite the Fuse, Peaks and Valleys, Rubiano and Spectacular Tide.

Krone is the winningest female rider in history, both in wins and earnings. Through the end of 2004, she is credited with 3,704 wins. Her mounts have won over $90 million. On both measures, she has a daunting lead over her nearest pursuers.

Bad racing luck was a constant shadow during the last 10 years of Krone's career. Serious accidents in 1993 and 1995 kept her out of the saddle for months at a time, leading to a temporary retirement in 1999. In late 2002, she returned to race riding but suffered significant injuries early and late in 2003. In between, however, she had a tremendous partial season, riding the winners of over $8 million including Halfbridled and Candy Ride, but it was likely to be her last hurrah as a jockey. After a December 2003 accident, she rode but three more times. Off-track, she has been a spokesperson and broadcast personality.

Julie Krone Year-by-Year

Year	Mts	1st	2nd	3rd	Earnings	Year	Mts	1st	2nd	3rd	Earnings
1981	747	124	106	120	$796,773	1993	1,012	212	171	136	6,417,269
1982	1,049	155	150	146	1,238,161	1994	570	101	85	79	3,981,939
1983	1,024	151	140	138	1,095,662	1995	866	147	141	111	7,763,310
1984	801	108	95	121	785,982	1996	998	141	121	140	5,243,877
1985	1,041	106	140	119	1,060,352	1997	905	175	128	124	4,202,631
1986	1,442	199	208	182	2,357,136	1998	762	137	114	116	3,998,045
1987	1,698	324	270	247	4,511,391	1999	425	82	61	61	2,308,509
1988	1,958	363	331	273	7,770,314	2002	133	20	17	11	814,473
1989	1,673	368	287	235	8,031,445	2003	806	139	103	93	8,198,327
1990	634	142	120	81	2,577,727	2004	3	0	0	0	1,456
1991	1,416	231	229	188	7,751,363						
1992	1,448	279	244	191	9,216,622	**Totals:**	**21,411**	**3,704**	**3,261**	**2,912**	**$90,122,764**

Jockeys with 6 or more wins on a single day, 1891–2004

Jockey	Date	Total Wins	Wins	Mts	Track
Antley, C.W.	31-Oct-87	9	4	6	AQU
			5	8	MED
Dunkelberger, Travis L.	30-Mar-00	8	7	8	CT
			1	2	PIM
Shino, Ken A.	2-Apr-00	8	8	10	FON
Umana, Juan	5-Mar-93	8	4	7	GS
			4	8	PHA
Day, P	13-Sep-89	8	8	9	AP
Loseth, C.	9-Apr-84	8	8	10	EP
Williams, R.D.	29-Sep-84	8	8	10	LNN
Gall, D	18-Oct-78	8	8	10	CKA
Tejeira, J.	16-Jun-76	8	3	6	KEY
			5	6	ATL
Jones, H.S.	11-Jun-44	8	8	13	AC
Bejarano Rafael	12-Mar-04	7	7	11	TP
Welch Quincy	14-Aug-04	7	7	10	NP
Douglas, Rene R.	24-Jul-03	7	7	9	AP
Pino, Mario G.	7-Jul-02	7	7	10	CNL
Pompell, Thomas L.	19-Jul-02	7	7	9	FP
Karamanos, Horatio	26-Oct-02	7	7	11	LRL
Lanci, Howard L.	30-Jun-01	7	7	9	BF
Moccasln, Tim	25-Aug-01	7	7	7	MD
Valdez, Felipe	23-Dec-01	7	7	9	PM
Compton, Perry	19-Feb-00	7	7	10	FON
Dunkelberger, Travis L.	30-Aug-00	7	7	9	TIM
Houghton, T. D.	19-Jul-98	7	7	9	DET
Rocheleau, Serge R.	16-Aug-98	7	7	9	MD
Andrews, Maureen E.	17-Nov-97	7	7	10	MNR
Bailey, Jerry D.	11-Mar-95	7	7	10	GP
Lovelace, Austin K.	10-Dec-94	7	7	10	HOU
Martinez, Willie	6-Jul-93	7	7	10	ELP
Wash, Jack	22-Jul-93	7	7	9	MD
Baze, Russell A.	16-Apr-92	7	7	9	GG
Baez, Rodolfo	27-Sep-91	7	7	10	RKM
Reynolds, Larry C.	7-Jun-91	7	4	9	CT
			2	3	PIM
			1	1	TRM
Vergara, E.B.	31-Jul-88	7	7	11	DET
Pincay, L. Jr.	14-Mar-87	7	7	8	SA
Fires, E.	25-May-87	7	7	8	AP
Vergara, E.B.	28-Aug-87	7	7	10	DET
Enriquez, H.	26-Jan-86	7	7	11	AC
Gall, D	9-Oct-86	7	7	10	FP
Day, P	20-Jun-84	7	7	8	CD
Frazier, R.L.	27-Oct-84	7	7	11	LAD
Nicol, P.A. Jr.	8-Jun-83	7	7	9	PIM
Fires, E.	16-Aug-83	7	7	8	AP
Wentz, M.	17-Dec-83	7	7	11	TUP
Delgado, A.	16-Aug-82	7	5	6	DEL
			2	2	TIM
Gall, D	26-Sep-81	7	7	11	FP
DePass, R.	15-Mar-80	7	7	7	FD
Gall, D	2-May-80	7	7	9	CKA
Gall, D	6-Jun-79	7	7	9	CKA
Noguez, A.	9-Oct-77	7	7	10	AC
Sorenson, J.	23-Jun-76	7	7	9	ASD
Hawley, S.	10-Oct-74	7	7	9	WO
Pierce, L.	20-May-72	7	7	8	LGA
Hawley, S.	22-May-72	7	7	9	WO
York, R.	14-Jan-70	7	7	10	TUP
Baltazar, C.	15-Dec-69	7	7	8	LRL
Grubb, R.	16-May-67	7	7	8	WO
Moyers, L.	4-Jul-67	7	7	8	SUF
Diaz, J.P.	18-Nov-67	7	7	11	AC
Heath, M.	12-Oct-63	7	7	9	FNO
Heckmann, J.	1-Oct-56	7	7	8	HAW
Turnbull, W.	31-Jul-42	7	7	9	RKM
Sylvester, J.	18-Oct-30	7	7	8	RAV
Bejarano Rafael	2-Jan-04	6	6	10	TP
Martin, Jr. Eddie M.	18-Jan-04	6	6	8	FG
Bejarano Rafael	28-Feb-04	6	6	9	TP
Albarado Robby	11-Mar-04	6	6	9	FG
Compton Perry	10-Apr-04	6	6	8	FON
Kimes Curtis	30-Apr-04	6	6	8	FON
Mojica Orlando	7-May-04	6	4	7	IND
			2	4	RD
Prescott Rodney A.	8-May-04	6	4	8	IND
			2	6	RD
Whitacre Brandon	14-May-04	6	5	8	CT
			1	3	PIM
Bejarano Rafael	19-Jun-04	6	3	9	CD
			3	6	IND
Williams Robert Dean	2-Jul-04	6	6	8	LNN
Fogelsonger Ryan	18-Sep-04	6	6	8	PIM
Bejarano Rafael	21-Sep-04	6	6	8	KD
Knight Lester Cash	19-Nov-04	6	6	10	HOO
Compton, Perry	19-Apr-03	6	6	8	FON
Prescott, Rodney A.	03-May-03	6	6	9	IND
Martinez, Armando	29-Aug-03	6	6	9	CLS
Nuttall, Todd J.	21-Sep-03	6	6	7	SJ
Monterrey, Richard	01-Oct-03	6	4	6	CT
			2	5	PIM
Dominguez, Ramon A.	03-Oct-03	6	6	7	MED
Berry, Monte Clifton	24-Oct-03	6	6	9	RP
Pino, Mario G.	25-Oct-03	6	6	9	LRL
Garcia, Luis	20-Nov-03	6	3	6	CT
			3	7	LRL
Gutierrez, Juan M.	01-Dec-03	6	6	9	PM
Lumpkins, Jason P.	21-Apr-02	6	6	8	BM
Carkeek, Jerome	26-Apr-02	6	6	10	FON
Pino, Mario G.	11-May-02	6	6	10	PIM
Bravo, Joe	18-May-02	6	6	8	MTH
Thompson, Terry J.	20-May-02	6	6	9	PRM
Houghton, T. D.	26-May-02	6	6	9	GLD
Clark, Kerwin David	19-Aug-02	6	6	7	EVD
Radke, Kevin	2-Sep-02	6	6	10	EMD
Chapa, Roman	4-Sep-02	6	6	9	RET
Fogelsonger, Ryan	18-Sep-02	6	5	10	PIM
			1	5	CT
Cora, David	18-Oct-02	6	6	8	PEN
Shino, Ken A.	2-Nov-02	6	6	8	WDS
Bourque, Steven Joseph	15-Nov-02	6	6	8	DED
Velasquez, Cornelio H.	24-Nov-02	6	6	10	CRC
Berry, Monte Clifton	30-Sep-01	6	6	9	RP
Dominguez, Ramon A.	13-Dec-01	6	3	6	CT
			3	6	LRL

***NOTE:** Data on six-win days when there were more than nine mounts that day was not published in the American Racing Manual prior to recent editions and such riding feats that occurred prior to 1991 are not included.*

Jockey	Date	Total Wins	Wins	Mts	Track
Dunkelberger, Travis L.	12-Apr-01	6	1	3	CT
			5	7	PIM
Dunkelberger, Travis L.	20-Sep-01	6	1	3	CT
			5	7	
Dunkelberger, Travis L.	27-Sep-01	6	4	7	CT
			2	2	
Lovato, Anthony J.	3-Jul-01	6	6	7	LS
Lumpkins, Jason P.	19-May-01	6	6	9	BM
Messina, Robert	23-Nov-01	6	6	6	FL
Pino, Mario G.	9-Jul-01	6	6	7	CNL
Potts, Clinton L.	8-Feb-01	6	6	8	PEN
Prather, Kris	11-Feb-01	6	6	10	TP
Ramos, Jr., Walter W.	7-Jul-01	6	6	6	MD
Rowland, Michael F.	21-Oct-01	6	1	2	MNR
			5	6	TDN
Thompson, Terry J.	13-Oct-01	6	6	9	HOO
Thompson, Terry J.	20-Oct-01	6	6	9	HOO
Thompson, Terry J.	18-Nov-01	6	6	8	HOO
Thompson, Terry J.	25-Nov-01	6	6	9	HOO
Velazquez, John R.	3-Sep-01	6	6	10	SAR
Wilson, David	8-Jul-01	6	6	8	HST
Avant, James E.	10-Jul-00	6	6	8	EVD
Ayers, Lance K.	18-Jun-00	6	6	9	BOI
Bailey, Jerry D.	11-Mar-00	6	6	9	GP
Bush, Vernon	10-Sep-00	6	6	7	NMP
Castellano, Javier	31-Dec-00	6	6	11	CRC
Compton, Perry	22-Apr-00	6	4	6	FON
			2	4	PRM
Court, Jon Kenton	6-Aug-00	6	6	9	ELP
Dunkelberger, Travis L.	29-Apr-00	6	2	3	CT
			4	9	PIM
Dunkelberger, Travis L.	4-Sep-00	6	6	9	TIM
Dunkelberger, Travis L.	30-Nov-00	6	3	8	CT
			3	5	LRL
Grabowski, John A.	1-Apr-00	6	6	10	FL
Lopez, Lorenzo Castane	21-Oct-00	6	6	8	PM
Nakatani, Corey S.	23-Apr-00	6	6	8	SA
Santos, Felipe J.	25-Sep-00	6	6	9	GLD
Baze, Russell A.	30-Jan-99	6	6	8	BM
Baze, Russell A.	21-Aug-99	6	6	8	BMF
Bielby, James A.	31-May-99	6	6	8	FP
Carkeek, Jerome	26-Jun-99	6	6	9	LNN
Castellano, Javier	9-Dec-99	6	6	8	CRC
Chavez, Jorge F.	13-Feb-99	6	6	10	GP
Day, Pat	13-May-99	6	6	8	CD
Doser, Mary Elizabeth	21-Jun-99	6	6	7	GLD
Gann, Sandi Lee	17-Apr-99	6	6	8	TUP
Gonzalez, Carlos	5-Nov-99	6	6	11	LAD
Houghton, T. D.	5-Jul-99	6	6	8	GLD
Howarth, Jr., Albert	12-Sep-99	6	6	10	NMP
Morgan, Michael R.	5-Dec-99	6	6	10	HOO
Potts, Clinton L.	1-May-99	6	6	12	CT
Prado, Edgar S.	18-Nov-99	6	4	8	AQU
			2	6	MED
Rollins, Chance J.	22-Dec-99	6	6	10	TUP
Rowland, Michael F.	19-Oct-99	6	6	7	TDN
Rowland, Michael F.	27-Dec-99	6	6	7	MNR
Shino, Ken A.	28-Feb-99	6	6	9	FON
Shino, Ken A.	2-Oct-99	6	1	3	PRM
			5	8	WDS

Jockey	Date	Total Wins	Wins	Mts	Track
Whitney, Dana G.	25-Jul-99	6	6	9	MNR
Bridgmohan, Shaun	15-Feb-98	6	6	9	AQU
Clark, David	17-Jul-98	6	6	9	WO
Coa, Eibar	7-Sep-98	6	6	9	CRC
Court, Jon Kenton	12-Sep-98	6	6	10	HOO
Court, Jon Kenton	24-Nov-98	6	6	9	HOO
Dunkelberger, Travis L.	21-Nov-98	6	6	8	CT
Guillory, David	17-Jul-98	6	6	8	LAD
McCarthy, Michael J.	20-May-98	6	6	6	DEL
Melancon, Gerard	8-Aug-98	6	6	9	EVD
Prado, Edgar S.	23-Oct-98	6	6	10	LRL
Reynolds, Larry C.	11-Dec-98	6	5	7	CT
			1	4	LRL
Ardoin, Ronald	17-Jul-97	6	6	7	LS
Baez, Rodolfo	30-May-97	6	6	9	SUF
Bailey, Jerry D.	15-Feb-97	6	6	9	GP
Birzer, Alex	15-Aug-97	6	6	8	CLS
Carkeek, Jerome	26-Oct-97	6	6	10	ATO
Casallas, Eduardo	28-Sep-97	6	6	11	YD
Houghton, T. D.	4-Jul-97	6	6	9	DET
Houghton, T. D.	18-Nov-97	6	6	9	DET
Krasner, Samuel B.	18-Apr-97	6	6	7	HST
McCarthy, Michael J.	2-Nov-97	6	6	9	DEL
Melancon, Kevin Lee	22-Mar-97	6	5	8	DED
			1	1	FG
Prado, Edgar S.	2-Aug-97	6	6	10	LRL
Rowland, Michael F.	20-Oct-97	6	3	5	MNR
			3	5	TDN
Shino, Ken A.	5-Apr-97	6	6	10	FON
Baze, Russell A.	2-May-96	6	6	7	GG
Chavez, Jorge F.	18-Feb-96	6	6	9	AQU
Crispin, Joe A.	6-Jul-96	6	6	9	BOI
Dlugopolski, Anthony R.	29-Apr-96	6	6	7	MNR
Freeman, Wayne	27-Jul-96	6	6	9	GF
Hampshire, Jr., Josiah F.	8-Sep-96	6	6	8	RKM
Houghton, T. D.	26-Jul-96	6	6	9	DET
Houghton, T. D.	27-Oct-96	6	6	11	DET
Ma, Henry C.H.	1-Sep-96	6	6	8	NMP
McCarthy, Michael J.	6-Dec-96	6	3	7	MED
			3	8	PHA
Messina, Robert	4-May-96	6	6	8	FL
Shino, Ken A.	26-May-96	6	6	8	LNN
Avant, James E.	14-Aug-95	6	6	7	EVD
Baez, Rodolfo	19-Aug-95	6	6	9	RKM
Baez, Rodolfo	15-Oct-95	6	6	10	RKM
Day, Pat	20-Feb-95	6	6	8	OP
Delgado, Alberto	30-Aug-95	6	6	9	TIM
Dominguez, Carlos V.	6-Nov-95	6	6	9	FL
Douglas, Rene R.	15-Jul-95	6	6	9	CRC
Houghton, T. D.	28-Apr-95	6	6	9	DET
Hulet, Leslie	21-Nov-95	6	6	10	FL
Jordan, Jimmy	3-Jun-95	6	6	7	ATO
LeBlanc, Kirk Paul	5-Aug-95	6	6	10	EVD
Mitchell, Gallyn Victor	13-Aug-95	6	6	10	YM
Schaefer, Gregory Allen	5-Mar-95	6	6	11	FON
Black, Kenneth	25-Sep-94	6	6	7	MEP
Bravo, Joe	31-Aug-94	6	6	10	MTH
Houghton, T. D.	21-Aug-94	6	6	10	DET
Houghton, T. D.	2-Oct-94	6	6	8	DET

Jockey	Date	Total Wins	Wins	Mts	Track
LaGue, Larry	22-Jan-94	6	6	8	BEU
Loseth, Chris	14-Sep-94	6	6	8	HST
Schaefer, Gregory Allen	12-Aug-94	6	6	9	CLS
Schaefer, Gregory Allen	12-Sep-94	6	6	9	CLS
Toscano, Paul R.	29-Jul-94	6	6	9	SR
Vergara, Euclides B.	2-Jun-94	6	6	10	DET
Anderson, Chad W.	16-Apr-93	6	6	9	FON
Bayer, Jason Dwayne	10-Mar-93	6	6	9	YM
Baze, Gary	5-Sep-93	6	6	8	YM
Bergsrud, Scott Alan	11-Jul-93	6	6	8	PLA
Bergsrud, Scott Alan	19-Sep-93	6	6	10	PLA
Black, Kenneth	26-Sep-93	6	6	11	MEP
Borel, Calvin H.	2-May-93	6	6	10	LAD
Day, Pat	11-Mar-93	6	6	8	OP
Doocy, Timothy T.	5-Dec-93	6	6	10	RP
Douglas, Rene R.	8-Dec-93	6	6	7	CRC
Martin, Christopher	6-Sep-93	6	6	10	CT
Umana, Juan	20-Mar-93	6	1	7	GS
			5	9	PHA
Vergara, Euclides B.	15-Jul-93	6	6	10	DET
Winnett, Jr., Buddy G.	6-Nov-93	6	6	9	EP
Ardoin, Ronald	7-Sep-92	6	6	7	LAD
Barnett, Wayne A.	18-Oct-92	6	6	9	CT
Black, Anthony S.	31-Jul-92	6	4	4	ATL
			2	2	PHA
Day, Pat	10-Jun-92	6	6	8	CD
Desormeaux, Kent J.	3-Jul-92	6	6	9	HOL
Doocy, Timothy T.	21-Jun-92	6	6	10	LGA
Flores, David Romero	20-Sep-92	6	6	9	FPX
Flores, David Romero	30-Sep-92	6	6	8	FPX
Green, Brian D.	6-Jun-92	6	6	9	BRD
Guidry, Mark	20-Mar-92	6	6	10	SPT
Guidry, Mark	5-Apr-92	6	6	10	SPT
Guidry, Mark	25-Apr-92	6	6	10	SPT
Jensen, Loren Dale	26-Jun-92	6	6	9	ATO
Pedroza, Martin A.	31-Oct-92	6	6	7	SA
Simard, Real E.	21-Oct-92	6	6	9	STP
Smith, Mike E.	13-Jan-92	6	6	8	AQU
Smith, Mike E.	30-Jan-92	6	6	7	AQU
Whitley, Kevin	21-Aug-92	6	6	8	FL
Aragon, Vicky Ann	24-Nov-91	6	6	7	YM
Borel, Calvin H.	23-Aug-91	6	6	9	LAD
Boulanger, Gary	22-May-91	6	6	9	LGA
Bourque, Curt C.	4-May-91	6	6	8	EVD
Bourque, Curt C.	23-Jun-91	6	6	8	EVD
Day, Pat	30-May-91	6	6	8	CD
Day, Pat	3-Aug-91	6	6	9	AP
Lopez, Adalberto Diaz	16-Mar-91	6	6	8	AC
Lopez, Adalberto Diaz	5-May-91	6	6	10	AC
Lopez, Adalberto Diaz	26-May-91	6	6	10	AC
Romero, Shane P.	10-Feb-91	6	6	10	FG
Romero, Shane P.	24-Feb-91	6	6	8	FG
Rowland, Michael F.	29-Mar-91	6	6	9	TDN
Sellers, Shane J.	6-Sep-91	6	6	9	AP
Sellers, Shane J.	4-Oct-91	6	6	8	AP
Shino, Ken A.	10-Nov-91	6	6	8	CLS
Torres, Hector	12-Aug-91	6	1	4	DMR
			5	9	LA
Winters, Perry A.	15-Aug-91	6	6	10	NP
Elliott, S.	18-Mar-90	6	6	7	RKM

Jockey	Date	Total Wins	Wins	Mts	Track
Salvaggio, M.V.	31-Mar-90	6	6	9	PEN
Romero, R.P.	7-Apr-90	6	6	9	KEE
Perret, C.	18-Apr-90	6	6	7	KEE
Hansen, R.D.	21-Apr-90	6	6	9	GG
Elliott, S.	2-May-90	6	6	8	RKM
Jensen, L.D.	23-Jul-90	6	6	9	CLS
Desormeaux, K.J.	17-Feb-89	6	6	9	LRL
Perret, C.	19-Mar-89	6	6	7	HIA
Vega, H.	1-Apr-89	6	6	9	RKM
Fires, E.	19-Jun-89	6	6	6	HAW
Ardoin, R.	4-Jul-89	6	6	8	LAD
Krone, J.	16-Sep-89	6	6	8	MED
Vega, H.	21-Dec-89	6	6	8	RKM
Desormeaux, K.J.	26-Apr-88	6	6	8	PIM
Valenzuela, P.A.	21-Oct-88	6	6	9	SA
Desormeaux, K.J.	12-May-87	6	6	8	PIM
Baze, M.B.	28-Jun-87	6	6	7	PLA
Grove, P.	28-Aug-87	6	6	8	CT
Steinberg, P.W.	6-Dec-87	6	6	9	TUP
Day, P.	17-Feb-86	6	6	7	OP
Martinez, L.	7-May-86	6	6	8	DET
Knight, L.C.	18-Sep-86	6	6	9	DET
Diaz, J.L.	4-Dec-86	6	6	9	BML
Romero, R.P.	8-May-85	6	6	8	CD
DePass, R.	22-Jun-85	6	6	8	DET
Romero, R.P.	8-Feb-84	6	6	8	FG
Miller, D.A. Jr.	17-Feb-84	6	6	9	BOW
Garcia, J.R.	27-Apr-84	6	6	6	PEN
Edwards, J.W.	28-May-84	6	6	9	DEL
Antley, C.W.	30-Jul-84	6	6	9	MTH
Snyder, L.	19-Aug-84	6	6	6	LAD
Baze, R.A.	1-Sep-84	6	6	7	BMF
Santage, J.L.	22-May-83	6	6	8	DET
Markham, R.L. Jr.	4-Jul-83	6	6	9	WAT
Moreno, O.	24-Jul-83	6	6	7	CT
Mills, B.L.	28-Aug-83	6	6	8	TDN
Whitley, K.	20-Jun-82	6	6	8	FL
Petro, N.	21-Nov-82	6	6	9	SUF
Pincay, L. Jr.	4-Mar-81	6	6	8	SA
Platts, R.	3-May-81	6	6	7	WO
Velasquez, J.	9-Jul-81	6	6	6	BEL
Delgadillo, C.	5-Sep-81	6	6	8	AC
Sibille, R.	23-Jun-80	6	6	7	AP
Cantagallo, G.J.	28-Jun-80	6	6	8	ATL
Lopez, R.D.	9-Aug-80	6	6	8	HP
Seldomridge, A.	19-Aug-80	6	6	9	POC
Graell, A.	14-Nov-80	6	6	9	TDN
Hulet, L.	14-Apr-79	6	6	8	FL
Diaz, A.L.	25-Apr-79	6	6	6	GG
Creighton, R.L.	30-Apr-79	6	6	8	EP
McHargue, D.G.	25-Oct-79	6	6	7	SA
Perrodin, E.J.	18-Nov-79	6	6	9	FG
Noguez, A.	11-Mar-78	6	6	9	AC
Mercado, V.V.	1-Apr-78	6	6	8	AC
Orona, W.	11-Jun-78	6	6	9	PJ
Feliciano, B.R.	18-Jun-78	6	6	9	TDN
Pincay, L. Jr.	29-Jul-78	6	6	8	DMR
Cauthen, S.	22-Jan-77	6	6	9	AQU
Cauthen, S.	7-Apr-77	6	6	9	AQU
Gomez, G.J.	12-May-77	6	6	9	CRC

Jockey	Date	Total Wins	Wins	Mts	Track
Edwards, J.W.	24-May-77	6	6	7	ATL
Fann, B.	28-May-77	6	6	9	HAW
Maple, S.	23-Jul-77	6	6	9	AKS
Stahlbaum, G.	5-Aug-77	6	6	6	FE
Noguez, A.	10-Sep-77	6	6	9	AC
Hollingsworth, R.	1-Oct-77	6	6	9	YM
Meaux, C.	2-Oct-77	6	6	6	FP
Cauthen, S.	29-Nov-77	6	6	8	AQU
Hawley, S.	20-Feb-76	6	6	9	SA
Graell, A.	21-Feb-76	6	6	9	TDN
Passmore, W.J.	5-Mar-76	6	6	6	BOW
Turcotte, R.	5-Mar-76	6	6	9	AQU
Cordero, A. Jr.	12-Mar-75	6	6	8	AQU
Mucciolo, J.	14-Apr-75	6	6	8	KEY
Wash, J.	20-Jul-75	6	6	8	PJ
Baze, R.	10-Sep-75	6	6	9	LGA
McCarron, G.	6-Jul-74	6	6	8	DEL
Hawley, S.	4-Aug-74	6	6	7	FE
McCarron, C.J.	11-Aug-74	6	6	9	PIM
Hawley, S.	11-Aug-74	6	6	9	FE
McCarron, C.J.	27-Sep-74	6	6	9	BOW
McCarron, C.J.	23-Nov-74	6	6	7	LRL
McCarron, C.J.	7-Dec-74	6	6	8	PEN
McCarron, C.J.	15-Dec-74	6	6	8	PEN
Pincay, L. Jr.	17-Feb-73	6	6	8	SA
Bracciale, V. Jr.	5-Mar-73	6	6	7	BOW
Menard, N.	3-Apr-73	6	6	8	JND
Kirby, C.	30-Sep-73	6	6	8	SAL
Valdez, S.	15-Oct-73	6	6	9	SA
Snyder, L.	27-Oct-73	6	6	9	DET
Hawley, S.	26-May-72	6	6	9	WO
Snyder, L.	26-May-72	6	6	9	HP
Lively, J.	12-Jul-72	6	6	7	AKS
Cave, R.	9-Sep-72	6	6	9	PIT
Hinojosa, H.	4-Feb-71	6	6	8	LIB
Hawley, S.	2-May-71	6	6	9	FE
Lively, J.	4-Jun-71	6	6	9	AKS
Stewart, R.	16-Jun-71	6	6	8	ASD
Cox, R.	7-Aug-71	6	6	8	FL
Tranchina, P.	22-Aug-71	6	6	7	BOI
Hawley, S.	1-Sep-71	6	6	9	FE
Platts, R.	8-Sep-71	6	6	9	WO
Mitchell, M.	12-Sep-71	6	6	8	PJ
Snyder, L.	25-Oct-71	6	6	7	HP
Shoemaker, W.	24-Jun-70	6	6	7	HOL
Niblick, D.	7-Aug-70	6	6	9	ELP
Agnello, A.	27-Aug-70	6	6	9	WAT
Dur'usseau, L.J.	14-Mar-69	6	6	8	TUP
Snyder, L.	1-Apr-69	6	6	8	OP
Frey, P.	31-May-69	6	6	9	LGA
Perez, A	21-Jun-69	6	6	7	PJ
Dur'usseau, L.J.	3-Jul-69	6	6	8	AKS
Dur'usseau, L.J.	4-Jul-69	6	6	9	AKS
Dur'usseau, L.J.	5-Jul-69	6	6	9	AKS
Rosales, R.	6-Sep-69	6	6	9	DMR
Maffeo, C.	20-Sep-69	6	6	8	NAR
Bowcut, D.	20-Sep-69	6	6	8	POC
Turcotte, Rudy	2-Dec-69	6	6	8	AQU
Cordero, A. Jr.	28-Feb-68	6	6	8	HIA
Pincay, L. Jr.	27-Apr-68	6	6	9	HOL
Cusimano, G.	16-Jul-68	6	6	9	DEL
Ecoffey, F.	5-Aug-68	6	6	7	LNN
Hinojosa, H.	17-Aug-68	6	6	9	RKM
Blum, W.	19-Oct-68	6	6	8	GS
Ecoffey, F.	30-Oct-68	6	6	9	ATO
Vasquez, J.	9-Aug-67	6	6	8	ATL
Velasquez, J.	30-Aug-67	6	6	7	ATL
Madden, D.	9-Sep-67	6	6	8	LD
Whited, D.E.	26-Sep-67	6	6	8	DET
Marquez, C.	20-Jul-66	6	6	7	RD
Fires, E.	6-Sep-66	6	6	7	AP
Bowlds, J.P.	11-Mar-65	6	6	8	FG
Baze, J.	12-Apr-65	6	6	8	GG
Barrera, C.	15-May-65	6	6	8	MEX
Fires, E.	17-Jun-65	6	6	9	MP
Frey, P.	3-Sep-65	6	6	9	LGA
Velasquez, J.	16-Nov-65	6	6	7	GS
Green, F.	5-Jun-64	6	6	9	WAT
Rollins, B.	4-Jul-64	6	6	9	CEN
Witmer, R.	10-Oct-64	6	6	7	HAG
Venezia, M.	7-Dec-64	6	6	9	AQU
Hinojosa, H.	13-May-63	6	6	9	WAS
Coy, A.	6-Jul-63	6	6	7	BB
Silva, G.	10-Jul-63	6	6	7	RD
Reynolds, L.	17-Jul-63	6	6	8	MAR
Whited, D.W.	8-Sep-63	6	6	9	RUI
Carrozzella, M.	11-Sep-63	6	6	9	LD
Shoemaker, W.	23-Feb-62	6	6	7	SA
Reynolds, L.	3-Aug-62	6	6	9	BLR
Lucas, W.D.	10-Aug-62	6	6	7	RD
Davidson, J.	24-Aug-62	6	6	8	SHD
Davidson, J.	1-Oct-62	6	6	9	SHD
Blum, W.	19-Jun-61	6	6	8	MTH
Weiler, D.	12-Aug-61	6	6	8	TDN
Neves, R.	24-Oct-61	6	6	8	BM
Barnett, R.L.	7-May-60	6	6	8	SPT
Reynolds, L.	1-Oct-60	6	6	9	HAG
Grant, H.	16-Mar-59	6	6	8	BOW
Shoemaker, W.	4-Apr-59	6	6	8	JAM
Dixon, G.	11-Jun-59	6	6	7	PM
Hunt, G.	19-Jun-59	6	6	9	PM
North't, J.F. Jr.	7-Sep-59	6	6	8	CT
Coy, A.	25-Apr-58	6	6	7	FE
Nelson, E.	20-Jun-58	6	6	7	DEL
Dittfach, H.	1-Sep-58	6	6	8	CEG
Ycaza, M.	7-Apr-57	6	6	9	MEX
Ycaza, M.	16-May-57	6	6	8	MEX
Morris, B.	18-Jul-57	6	6	7	MAD
Bravo, J.	1-Apr-56	6	6	7	MEX
Seller, J.	28-Jul-56	6	6	9	HP
Gaudreau, R.	31-Jul-56	6	6	8	CLS
Hartack, W.	25-Apr-55	6	6	7	LRL
Shoemaker, W.	16-Aug-55	6	6	7	WAS
Hartack, W.	5-Nov-55	6	6	8	LRL
Gomez, A.	21-Mar-54	6	6	7	MEX
Lumm, R.	9-Apr-54	6	6	8	AD
Gomez, A.	11-Apr-54	6	6	7	MEX
Harmatz, W.	23-Apr-54	6	6	7	BM
Padron, R.	13-Jun-54	6	6	9	HAV
Shoemaker, W.	4-Sep-54	6	6	8	DMR

Meaux, C.	6-Oct-54	6	6	8	CKA
Burr, C.	30-Mar-53	6	6	6	GP
Shoemaker, W.	4-Apr-53	6	6	8	TAN
Shoemaker, W.	20-Jun-53	6	6	8	HOL
Knisley, C.	3-Sep-53	6	6	6	HO
Hartack, W.	6-Oct-53	6	6	8	WAT
Shoemaker, W.	10-Oct-53	6	6	9	GG
DeSpirito, A.	10-Oct-53	6	6	8	RKM
Kaelin, F.	18-Aug-52	6	6	8	WHE
DeSpirito, A.	20-Aug-52	6	6	8	RKM
Rossall, R.	26-Oct-52	6	6	8	AC
Knowles, L.	20-Apr-51	6	6	7	AD
Craig, H.	2-Jul-51	6	6	8	WAT
Coppernoll, K.	11-Sep-51	6	6	8	EP
Shoemaker, W.	13-Oct-50	6	6	8	BM
Keene, H.	24-Oct-50	6	6	8	SPT
Keene, H.	4-Nov-50	6	6	9	SPT
Culmone, J.	27-Nov-50	6	6	9	BOW
Gomez, A.	22-Jun-49	6	6	8	ASC
Brooks, S.	15-May-48	6	6	8	CD
Florio, A.	19-Aug-47	6	6	6	MF
Roy, E.	22-Aug-47	6	6	7	EDM
Longden, J.	22-Nov-47	6	6	7	BM
Plesa, E.	3-Oct-46	6	6	7	PLA
Jessop, J.D.	9-Aug-45	6	6	7	DAD
Jessop, J.D.	16-Aug-45	6	6	7	DAD
Siverwright, J.	21-Jul-44	6	6	7	BRG
Atkinson, J.E.	28-Sep-44	6	6	7	GMP
McCadden, W.P.	26-Jun-43	6	6	8	FM
Adams, John	2-Sep-42	6	6	8	TDN
Robertson, A.	9-Oct-41	6	6	7	JAM
Fonte, C.	23-Sep-39	6	6	7	HAV
Adams, J.	7-Apr-38	6	6	7	BM
James, B.	3-May-38	6	6	7	TAN
Robertson, A.	19-Feb-33	6	6	7	HAV
Haas, B.	28-Aug-33	6	6	7	TDN
Adams, A.	11-Sep-30	6	6	6	MAR
Sande, E.	17-Sep-19	6	6	7	HDG
Phillips, H.	5-Jul-16	6	6	6	REN
Turner, C	9-Apr-12	6	6	7	CHA
Lee, J.	5-Jun-07	6	6	6	CD
Overton, W.	7-10-1891	6	6	6	OWP

Track Abbreviations for Tracks Not Listed Elsewhere

The following are track abbreviations used in the preceding list which are not found on pages 1100 and 1101. Most of these tracks are closed.

AC	Aqua Caliente
AD	Arizona Downs
AKS	Ak-Sar-Ben
ASC	Ascot Park
ATO	Atokad Park
BB	Blue Bonnets
BLR	Bel Air
BML	Balmoral
BOW	Bowie Race Course
BRG	Brighouse Park
CEG	Victoria Park
CEN	Centennial Race Track
CHA	Charleston
CKA	Cahokia Downs
DAD	Dade Park
DET	Detroit Race Course
EDM	Edmonton
EP	Exhibition Park
FD	Florida Downs
FM	Fort Miami
GMP	Gresham Park
GS	Garden State Park
HAG	Hagerstown
HAV	Oriental Park
HDG	Havre de Grace
HIA	Hialeah Park
HO	Hamilton (Ohio)
HP	Hazel Park
JAM	Jamaica
JND	Jefferson Downs
KEY	Keystone
LD	Lincoln Downs
LGA	Longacres
LIB	Liberty Bell Park
MAD	Madison Downs
MAR	Marlboro
MEP	MetraPark
MF	Marshfield Fair
MP	Miles Park
NAR	Narragansett Park
OWP	Old Washington Park
PIT	Pitt Park
PJ	Park Jefferson
PLA	Playfair
POC	Pocono Downs
RAV	Ravenna Park
REN	Reno
SHD	Shenandoah Downs
SJ	Apache County Fair
TAN	Tanforan
WAS	Washington Park
WAT	Waterford Park
WHE	Wheeling Downs

Top Money–Winning Jockeys and Trainers, by Meet, in 2004

Track	Meet dates		Starts	1st	2d	3d	Win %	Earnings
ALB	9/10 - 9/26	Jockey	Starts	1st	2d	3d	Win %	Earnings
		Ken S. Tohill	27	11	2	5	41	142,190
		Alfredo J. Juarez, Jr.	40	8	8	2	20	99,651
		Jorge Martin Bourdieu	38	5	9	4	13	66,640
		Carlos D. Madeira	21	7	3	4	33	63,779
		Clark E. Jones	18	3	4	3	17	63,772
ALB	9/10 - 9/26	Trainer	Starts	1st	2d	3d	Win %	Earnings
		Henry Dominguez	20	5	4	1	25	72,112
		Joel H. Marr	13	5	4	3	38	63,356
		Gary W. Cross	6	2	1	3	33	57,376
		Todd W. Fincher	14	3	3	1	21	51,046
		Jose R. Gonzalez	5	2	2	0	40	40,682
ALB	4/9 - 7/5	Jockey	Starts	1st	2d	3d	Win %	Earnings
		Ken S. Tohill	123	31	26	19	25	324,423
		Jorge Martin Bourdieu	73	13	13	8	18	241,398
		Ricardo Jaime	102	20	12	13	20	193,632
		Tony Noguez	59	15	5	8	25	168,918
		Brian James Theriot	112	14	13	9	13	143,304
ALB	4/9 - 7/5	Trainer	Starts	1st	2d	3d	Win %	Earnings
		Henry Dominguez	69	13	11	13	19	171,940
		Gary W. Cross	65	12	9	10	18	159,239
		H. Ray Ashford, Jr.	27	7	5	2	26	97,921
		Jon G. Arnett	60	9	14	7	15	94,555
		Fred I. Danley	36	6	7	4	17	89,861
ANF	7/16 - 7/25	Jockey	Starts	1st	2d	3d	Win %	Earnings
		Dustin W. Williams	19	5	8	2	26	18,780
		Richard M. Vasquez	16	7	2	4	44	17,583
		Thomas Wellington	4	2	0	0	50	12,120
		Gary L. Worst	11	1	2	2	9	9,495
		Terry Bennett	13	2	1	4	15	4,620
ANF	7/16 - 7/25	Trainer	Starts	1st	2d	3d	Win %	Earnings
		Joe Frederick Thomas, Sr.	17	4	2	2	24	22,768
		Tyrone Gleason	10	1	5	1	10	11,505
		Donald G. Black	6	3	3	0	50	7,070
		Ellis Pugh	3	2	0	0	67	4,700
		J. Sue Hunt	4	2	0	1	50	4,485
AP	5/14 - 9/19	Jockey	Starts	1st	2d	3d	Win %	Earnings
		Rene R. Douglas	504	125	84	83	25	3,232,485
		Eusebio Razo, Jr.	496	86	68	63	17	2,386,270
		Christopher A. Emigh	504	71	73	63	14	1,911,260
		Carlos H. Marquez, Jr.	374	62	51	53	17	1,888,790
		James Graham	469	57	49	59	12	1,355,493
AP	5/14 - 9/19	Trainer	Starts	1st	2d	3d	Win %	Earnings
		Chris M. Block	147	29	26	15	20	917,338
		Michael Stidham	111	25	18	14	23	758,709
		Frank J. Kirby	236	32	25	26	14	696,151
		Steven M. Asmussen	141	31	24	23	22	691,151
		Hugh H. Robertson	112	22	19	17	20	653,405
AQU	10/27 - 12/31	Jockey	Starts	1st	2d	3d	Win %	Earnings
		Pablo Fragoso	236	29	44	31	12	1,441,897
		Norberto Arroyo, Jr.	229	36	38	27	16	1,377,264
		Shaun Bridgmohan	222	28	37	37	13	1,370,677
		Rafael Bejarano	162	33	21	25	20	1,207,781
		Javier Castellano	125	19	15	19	15	939,689
AQU	10/27 - 12/31	Trainer	Starts	1st	2d	3d	Win %	Earnings
		Richard E. Dutrow, Jr.	95	29	20	14	31	1,098,328
		Todd A. Pletcher	77	11	8	9	14	788,843
		Kiaran P. McLaughlin	64	9	12	6	14	564,703
		Gary C. Contessa	86	15	14	10	17	528,842
		Jennifer Pedersen	65	14	7	9	22	514,129
AQU	3/10 - 5/2	Jockey	Starts	1st	2d	3d	Win %	Earnings
		Javier Castellano	155	37	25	26	24	1,508,233
		Shaun Bridgmohan	184	30	28	25	16	1,204,950
		Michael J. Luzzi	159	28	25	23	18	1,006,889
		Pablo Fragoso	163	28	29	29	17	953,431
		Richard Migliore	120	23	26	9	19	944,506

Track	Dates	Name	Starts	1st	2d	3d	Win %	Earnings
AQU	3/10 - 5/2	Trainer	Starts	1st	2d	3d	Win %	Earnings
		Todd A. Pletcher	50	15	9	6	30	800,072
		H. Allen Jerkens	50	16	5	8	32	679,091
		Richard E. Dutrow, Jr.	73	17	11	16	23	659,713
		Gary C. Contessa	96	19	18	9	20	607,982
		Michael W. Dickinson	5	2	1	0	40	484,450
AQU	1/1 - 3/7	Jockey	Starts	1st	2d	3d	Win %	Earnings
		Pablo Fragoso	296	59	57	56	20	1,983,223
		Shaun Bridgmohan	252	42	43	29	17	1,362,391
		Javier Castellano	184	32	38	22	17	1,246,653
		Michael J. Luzzi	203	34	33	26	17	1,224,101
		Richard Migliore	141	31	18	22	22	1,024,388
AQU	1/1 - 3/7	Trainer	Starts	1st	2d	3d	Win %	Earnings
		Richard E. Dutrow, Jr.	90	32	26	6	36	1,111,968
		Jennifer Pedersen	79	14	18	14	18	671,173
		Bruce N. Levine	77	19	13	14	25	547,103
		Scott A. Lake	85	16	19	12	19	499,068
		Michael E. Hushion	71	13	10	12	18	435,191
ARP	7/3 - 9/6	Jockey	Starts	1st	2d	3d	Win %	Earnings
		Travis Wales	161	40	24	29	25	305,413
		Russell Vicchrilli	170	33	39	27	19	304,152
		Fernando S. Rojas	186	37	31	33	20	276,657
		Bobby L. Johnson	134	15	27	34	11	194,708
		Carl Mel Kutz	172	27	20	20	16	179,772
ARP	7/3 - 9/6	Trainer	Starts	1st	2d	3d	Win %	Earnings
		Kenneth Gleason	151	22	36	24	15	283,176
		Ramon O. Gonzalez	89	22	11	17	25	189,561
		Temple D. Rushton	153	27	32	37	18	186,590
		Jon G. Arnett	104	31	22	12	30	160,086
		James E. Jones	62	21	9	12	34	134,085
ASD	5/2 - 10/3	Jockey	Starts	1st	2d	3d	Win %	Earnings
		Travis Wayne Hightower	456	98	67	63	21	849,761
		Vince J. Guerra	389	52	49	50	13	573,483
		Larren Delorme	456	66	78	64	14	541,395
		Beth S. Butler	398	57	62	57	14	500,586
		Jason Leacock	400	53	52	57	13	468,629
ASD	5/2 - 10/3	Trainer	Starts	1st	2d	3d	Win %	Earnings
		Emile J. Corbel	192	34	18	14	18	351,752
		Ardell Sayler	234	40	30	26	17	307,205
		Clayton Gray	161	17	36	25	11	272,467
		Chad Torevell	172	24	28	23	14	250,295
		Gary Danelson	171	29	26	31	17	244,527
ATL	5/5 - 5/19	Jockey	Starts	1st	2d	3d	Win %	Earnings
		Gus M. Brown	7	2	3	1	29	43,700
		Richard A. Bracho	12	2	3	1	17	41,740
		Stewart Elliott	10	3	0	0	30	37,910
		F. Bruce Miller, Jr.	8	1	1	0	13	36,850
		Danielle Hodsdon	6	3	0	1	50	27,350
ATL	5/5 - 5/19	Trainer	Starts	1st	2d	3d	Win %	Earnings
		F. Bruce Miller	9	1	1	1	11	43,650
		Jonathan E. Sheppard	9	3	0	3	33	40,260
		Thomas H. Voss	11	3	2	2	27	38,350
		Patricia Farro	5	2	0	1	40	28,970
		Linda M. Brown	6	1	1	0	17	27,300
ATO	9/17 - 9/19	Jockey	Starts	1st	2d	3d	Win %	Earnings
		Dennis Michael Collins	17	4	3	2	24	38,206
		Perry Compton	17	4	4	1	24	37,481
		Armando Martinez	17	3	2	4	18	31,735
		Daniel Lee Beck	16	3	2	3	19	30,380
		Lee Sensenbach	17	1	2	1	6	18,520
ATO	9/17 - 9/19	Trainer	Starts	1st	2d	3d	Win %	Earnings
		David C. Anderson	7	3	1	0	43	19,505
		David Grimes	4	2	1	0	50	15,240
		Daniel Coughlin	6	2	0	2	33	14,131
		Paul Linafelter	3	2	1	0	67	13,800
		Herb Riecken	7	1	0	1	14	12,300

Track	Dates	Name	Starts	1st	2d	3d	Win %	Earnings
BEL	9/10 - 10/24	Jockey	Starts	1st	2d	3d	Win %	Earnings
		John R. Velazquez	201	58	27	26	29	3,623,363
		Javier Castellano	203	32	29	28	16	2,568,362
		Edgar S. Prado	179	31	39	16	17	2,443,263
		Cornelio H. Velasquez	235	33	31	51	14	2,266,358
		Jose A. Santos	142	22	15	21	15	1,704,454
BEL	9/10 - 10/24	Trainer	Starts	1st	2d	3d	Win %	Earnings
		Todd A. Pletcher	90	23	12	12	26	1,690,737
		Robert J. Frankel	52	13	11	5	25	1,674,573
		Patrick L. Biancone	16	7	2	2	44	847,661
		Richard E. Dutrow, Jr.	54	16	9	6	30	781,079
		Patrick J. Kelly	34	4	4	5	12	699,086
BEL	5/5 - 7/25	Jockey	Starts	1st	2d	3d	Win %	Earnings
		John R. Velazquez	346	77	55	51	22	3,896,779
		Edgar S. Prado	318	73	48	49	23	3,634,432
		Jerry D. Bailey	171	44	34	22	26	2,608,893
		Javier Castellano	310	50	56	44	16	2,315,369
		Jose A. Santos	268	37	37	36	14	1,822,367
BEL	5/5 - 7/25	Trainer	Starts	1st	2d	3d	Win %	Earnings
		Todd A. Pletcher	142	33	28	22	23	2,092,122
		Robert J. Frankel	49	17	11	7	35	1,359,286
		Nicholas P. Zito	59	14	7	7	24	1,212,600
		H. Allen Jerkens	103	20	14	14	19	1,119,763
		Kiaran P. McLaughlin	82	10	11	9	12	845,019
BEU	9/18 - 12/21	Jockey	Starts	1st	2d	3d	Win %	Earnings
		Marco A. Ccamaque	407	84	65	66	21	411,910
		Ivan R. Gonzalez	339	57	45	40	17	326,999
		Hector L. Rosario, Jr.	194	35	22	16	18	244,237
		Perry Wayne Ouzts	231	39	35	24	17	192,541
		Paul M. Nolan	332	29	43	51	9	175,829
BEU	9/18 - 12/21	Trainer	Starts	1st	2d	3d	Win %	Earnings
		Luis Albert Palacios	75	18	11	10	24	175,878
		Jake S. Radosevich	192	26	25	25	14	128,008
		Joseph Clark Faulkner	127	33	21	14	26	127,613
		Reid Gross	163	31	19	19	19	112,885
		Rinzy Nocero	140	17	22	26	12	86,171
BEU	1/10 - 5/1	Jockey	Starts	1st	2d	3d	Win %	Earnings
		Marco A. Ccamaque	403	65	68	54	16	388,937
		Ivan R. Gonzalez	341	75	56	57	22	370,199
		Christian Rojas	343	66	56	34	19	299,989
		Jose Luis Calo	361	48	49	49	13	239,233
		Ramon Luna	336	34	38	30	10	187,631
BEU	1/10 - 5/1	Trainer	Starts	1st	2d	3d	Win %	Earnings
		Jake S. Radosevich	138	33	18	28	24	138,896
		Reid Gross	178	23	19	20	13	100,811
		Jerry L. Balo	57	20	8	6	35	94,551
		Luis Albert Palacios	42	16	7	3	38	92,768
		William D. Cowans	58	18	16	6	31	86,063
BM	9/3 - 11/7	Jockey	Starts	1st	2d	3d	Win %	Earnings
		Russell A. Baze	283	92	52	49	33	1,429,386
		Dennis Carr	247	41	43	35	17	877,229
		Ronald J. Warren, Jr.	236	39	46	36	17	865,393
		Francisco Duran	241	40	44	33	17	666,809
		Roberto M. Gonzalez	218	31	34	34	14	617,220
BM	9/3 - 11/7	Trainer	Starts	1st	2d	3d	Win %	Earnings
		Jerry Hollendorfer	209	47	42	36	22	993,978
		John F. Martin	99	25	25	16	25	508,927
		Art Sherman	102	31	18	11	30	478,590
		Armando Lage	125	21	11	19	17	270,591
		Brian J. Koriner	57	12	7	8	21	262,679
BM	4/7 - 6/20	Jockey	Starts	1st	2d	3d	Win %	Earnings
		Russell A. Baze	287	90	59	30	31	1,391,016
		Chad Phillip Schvaneveldt	234	51	39	34	22	956,040
		Ronald J. Warren, Jr.	235	44	30	33	19	904,016
		Chance J. Rollins	289	30	54	47	10	747,048
		Roberto M. Gonzalez	233	37	33	29	16	745,530

Track	Dates	Name	Starts	1st	2d	3d	Win %	Earnings
BM	4/7 - 6/20	Trainer	Starts	1st	2d	3d	Win %	Earnings
		Jerry Hollendorfer	256	64	53	36	25	1,421,161
		Art Sherman	148	37	17	27	25	558,509
		John F. Martin	97	22	20	9	23	407,958
		Charles J. Jenda	60	12	11	10	20	278,078
		Brian J. Koriner	65	14	13	5	22	266,325
BMF	8/11 - 8/23	Jockey	Starts	1st	2d	3d	Win %	Earnings
		Dennis Carr	52	14	8	9	27	179,872
		Ronald J. Warren, Jr.	48	13	6	5	27	166,385
		David G. Lopez	47	11	10	9	23	137,233
		Chance J. Rollins	52	8	9	9	15	133,913
		Francisco Duran	55	13	9	9	24	133,719
BMF	8/11 - 8/23	Trainer	Starts	1st	2d	3d	Win %	Earnings
		John F. Martin	17	7	2	1	41	101,002
		Jerry Hollendorfer	34	6	5	6	18	100,075
		William E. Morey	18	6	2	2	33	70,080
		Armando Lage	36	6	5	3	17	64,166
		Art Sherman	19	4	3	5	21	46,790
BOI	5/1 - 8/15	Jockey	Starts	1st	2d	3d	Win %	Earnings
		Berkley R. Packer	210	63	35	36	30	210,832
		Jay Conklin	137	46	28	18	34	162,361
		Cameron Colledge	208	55	36	32	26	132,199
		Casey Greene	156	20	22	26	13	50,567
		Matt Williams	132	11	21	14	8	37,962
BOI	5/1 - 8/15	Trainer	Starts	1st	2d	3d	Win %	Earnings
		Kenneth E. McReynolds	48	20	6	10	42	69,032
		Dru S. Hall	38	10	3	6	26	56,680
		Kevin Knudsen	123	22	23	25	18	54,836
		Farrell Christoffersen	21	7	3	2	33	53,816
		Cindy Rodgers	48	13	5	6	27	49,999
BRD	8/6 - 11/8	Jockey	Starts	1st	2d	3d	Win %	Earnings
		Fernando Camacho	44	4	8	8	9	20,345
		Bryan Ernst	41	4	6	6	10	12,911
		Stephen Randle	28	5	5	0	18	11,798
		Adam Wade Roughley	35	4	6	5	11	11,317
		Joel William Allen	39	5	3	3	13	10,800
BRD	8/6 - 11/8	Trainer	Starts	1st	2d	3d	Win %	Earnings
		Jim Dale Brooks	27	3	6	5	11	12,724
		Clifton D. Brooks	21	5	4	1	24	10,090
		Britt G. Cranford	17	2	5	4	12	8,999
		Marty R. Ireland	9	3	3	2	33	8,620
		Kevin Macon	11	1	0	1	9	5,879
BRD	2/21 - 5/1	Jockey	Starts	1st	2d	3d	Win %	Earnings
		Janet Leah Wilson	67	13	11	9	19	40,225
		Wendell John Hilburn	45	8	5	5	18	22,799
		Bryan Ernst	45	5	7	3	11	13,978
		Jorge L. Fontanez	49	3	6	6	6	13,291
		Joel William Allen	37	6	3	7	16	13,116
BRD	2/21 - 5/1	Trainer	Starts	1st	2d	3d	Win %	Earnings
		John Clark Garvin	11	5	2	2	45	14,805
		Clifton D. Brooks	22	10	0	3	45	14,697
		J. Alan Williams	19	5	1	2	26	9,322
		Kevin Macon	10	2	0	2	20	8,945
		James M. Limbaugh	24	4	2	3	17	8,764
BRN	9/11 - 9/12	Jockey	Starts	1st	2d	3d	Win %	Earnings
		Nikeela Black	9	3	1	1	33	4,515
		Tim Neal	12	2	2	2	17	4,405
		Twyla Beckner	12	2	1	4	17	4,275
		Jim Bob Whiteside	9	1	3	1	11	3,800
		Jaime Martinez	11	1	4	1	9	3,627
BRN	9/11 - 9/12	Trainer	Starts	1st	2d	3d	Win %	Earnings
		Marion Stitzel	8	3	1	0	38	5,446
		Steve Duschka	5	2	1	0	40	2,710
		Don D. Young	7	1	2	1	14	2,476
		Bill Hof	8	1	1	1	13	2,345
		Raymond Wilson	5	1	1	1	20	1,830

Track	Dates	Name	Starts	1st	2d	3d	Win %	Earnings
CBY	5/14 - 9/6	Jockey	Starts	1st	2d	3d	Win %	Earnings
		Derek C. Bell	384	92	75	48	24	1,183,094
		Seth B. Martinez	375	74	68	62	20	1,089,277
		Martin Escobar	382	59	59	39	15	829,201
		Scott A. Stevens	303	48	43	52	16	747,967
		Paul M. Nolan	396	57	66	50	14	660,274
CBY	5/14 - 9/6	Trainer	Starts	1st	2d	3d	Win %	Earnings
		Hugh H. Robertson	181	53	32	29	29	866,805
		Michael E. Biehler	157	32	28	26	20	603,763
		David Van Winkle	212	40	44	31	19	584,616
		Bernell B. Rhone	299	43	45	34	14	565,089
		Todd M. Hoffrogge	118	20	16	13	17	306,191
CD	10/31 - 11/27	Jockey	Starts	1st	2d	3d	Win %	Earnings
		Pat Day	103	23	20	9	22	1,115,617
		John McKee	166	27	24	20	16	1,106,274
		Eddie M. Martin, Jr.	152	22	16	16	14	1,091,871
		Brice Blanc	107	18	12	10	17	885,118
		Brian Joseph Hernandez, Jr.	176	23	24	30	13	811,050
CD	10/31 - 11/27	Trainer	Starts	1st	2d	3d	Win %	Earnings
		Steven M. Asmussen	67	14	13	11	21	631,146
		Dale L. Romans	63	10	8	10	16	628,252
		Robert E. Holthus	32	11	5	7	34	472,634
		Carl A. Nafzger	56	9	11	9	16	472,290
		Kenneth G. McPeek	34	11	3	3	32	417,801
CD	4/24 - 7/5	Jockey	Starts	1st	2d	3d	Win %	Earnings
		Stewart Elliott	2	1	0	0	50	5,884,800
		Rafael Bejarano	417	81	71	54	19	2,966,656
		Pat Day	208	54	38	29	26	2,702,948
		Robby Albarado	319	46	49	48	14	2,068,681
		Cornelio H. Velasquez	295	48	55	53	16	1,780,387
CD	4/24 - 7/5	Trainer	Starts	1st	2d	3d	Win %	Earnings
		John C. Servis	2	1	0	0	50	5,884,800
		Steven M. Asmussen	150	35	22	25	23	1,326,722
		Dale L. Romans	154	32	28	27	21	1,281,954
		D. Wayne Lukas	98	20	18	12	20	950,628
		Thomas M. Amoss	86	29	14	8	34	913,912
CLS	7/23 - 9/12	Jockey	Starts	1st	2d	3d	Win %	Earnings
		Jerome Carkeek	198	27	29	29	14	145,857
		Armando Martinez	167	29	17	17	17	132,515
		Dennis Michael Collins	154	26	24	25	17	127,781
		Filmer Munaylla	119	32	17	15	27	126,548
		Daniel Lee Beck	182	21	21	18	12	110,497
CLS	7/23 - 9/12	Trainer	Starts	1st	2d	3d	Win %	Earnings
		David C. Anderson	88	24	10	9	27	104,194
		Marvin A. Johnson	43	12	5	4	28	47,344
		Gene Deroin	46	11	6	6	24	42,054
		James R. Compton	48	9	4	7	19	36,807
		David Grimes	58	7	5	13	12	33,511
CNL	6/11 - 7/26	Jockey	Starts	1st	2d	3d	Win %	Earnings
		Ryan Fogelsonger	204	53	44	38	26	1,008,710
		Horacio Karamanos	183	36	23	33	20	652,284
		Steve D. Hamilton	232	25	38	45	11	583,190
		Edgar S. Prado	8	3	1	1	38	479,620
		Christopher VanHassel	204	31	23	28	15	467,770
CNL	6/11 - 7/26	Trainer	Starts	1st	2d	3d	Win %	Earnings
		Hamilton A. Smith	89	14	19	13	16	358,535
		Phil Schoenthal	83	22	14	9	27	329,220
		Dale L. Romans	1	1	0	0	100	300,000
		Jonathan E. Sheppard	70	16	10	7	23	289,450
		H. Graham Motion	27	5	4	4	19	229,030
CPW	6/12 - 6/27	Jockey	Starts	1st	2d	3d	Win %	Earnings
		B. Buck Harris	30	8	8	8	27	11,463
		Frank La Forge	25	6	5	2	24	7,295
		Herman Fennell	31	3	2	9	10	6,340
		Shannon Wippert	17	5	4	2	29	6,037
		Donald D. Herber, Jr.	24	4	2	0	17	4,325

Track	Dates	Name	Starts	1st	2d	3d	Win %	Earnings
CPW	6/12 - 6/27	Trainer	Starts	1st	2d	3d	Win %	Earnings
		David Gourneau	8	6	1	0	75	5,245
		Kelly Kaelberer	14	2	6	2	14	4,462
		Wally Decoteau	11	2	2	3	18	3,486
		Bob Mitchell	13	3	1	2	23	3,373
		Kenneth Olson	13	1	4	0	8	2,807
CRC	10/24/04 - 1/2/05	Jockey	Starts	1st	2d	3d	Win %	Earnings
		Eddie Castro	416	83	79	60	20	1,464,365
		Manoel R. Cruz	286	60	44	47	21	1,113,230
		Cornelio H. Velasquez	151	32	25	31	21	815,260
		Manuel Aguilar	301	39	47	47	13	794,370
		Eibar Coa	131	34	16	15	26	694,980
CRC	10/24/04 - 1/2/05	Trainer	Starts	1st	2d	3d	Win %	Earnings
		Todd A. Pletcher	34	10	2	6	29	405,260
		David R. Brownlee	49	8	3	3	16	288,585
		Angel C. Salinas	108	18	13	17	17	282,740
		William P. White	84	14	11	12	17	271,140
		Daniel C. Hurtak	115	21	13	22	18	265,380
CRC	4/26 - 10/23	Jockey	Starts	1st	2d	3d	Win %	Earnings
		Eddie Castro	772	154	131	120	20	3,321,885
		Manuel Aguilar	733	109	108	100	15	2,425,385
		Manoel R. Cruz	646	120	100	117	19	2,358,290
		Abdiel Toribio	420	72	60	60	17	1,581,520
		Gary Boulanger	413	65	67	60	16	1,528,680
CRC	4/26 - 10/23	Trainer	Starts	1st	2d	3d	Win %	Earnings
		Edward Plesa, Jr.	183	31	29	28	17	1,085,910
		William P. White	189	48	30	30	25	1,011,305
		Manuel J. Azpurua	144	22	17	24	15	729,675
		Emanuel Tortora	201	32	26	23	16	694,320
		Henry Collazo	212	30	36	25	14	656,478
CT	10/1 -12/31	Jockey	Starts	1st	2d	3d	Win %	Earnings
		Angel R. Quinones	414	62	64	40	15	1,200,050
		Kendrick Carmouche	347	56	44	43	16	1,149,507
		Oscar Flores	268	49	26	21	18	863,223
		David Cora	337	46	46	35	14	853,580
		J. D. Acosta	351	38	41	47	11	852,208
CT	10/1 -12/31	Trainer	Starts	1st	2d	3d	Win %	Earnings
		Jeff C. Runco	185	47	20	25	25	750,896
		Ronney W. Brown	227	40	37	23	18	741,058
		Anthony Adamo	224	35	23	21	16	668,786
		Kevin J. Joy	223	42	24	27	19	633,470
		Ernest M. Haynes	90	21	18	9	23	313,065
CT	7/1 - 9/30	Jockey	Starts	1st	2d	3d	Win %	Earnings
		Angel R. Quinones	297	59	47	39	20	1,006,389
		J. D. Acosta	327	37	45	39	11	755,121
		Travis L. Dunkelberger	198	35	28	24	18	734,406
		Carlos L. Castro	231	35	35	22	15	648,027
		Gerald Almodovar	220	36	30	28	16	614,676
CT	7/1 - 9/30	Trainer	Starts	1st	2d	3d	Win %	Earnings
		Kevin J. Joy	95	28	14	11	29	423,200
		Ronney W. Brown	147	26	19	16	18	397,057
		Mark Shuman	59	16	10	10	27	327,507
		Jeff C. Runco	120	14	27	12	12	289,380
		Harry F. Thompson, Jr.	78	15	8	8	19	240,800
CT	4/1 - 6/30	Jockey	Starts	1st	2d	3d	Win %	Earnings
		Brandon Whitacre	280	65	48	26	23	1,184,764
		Angel R. Quinones	324	50	48	33	15	1,108,916
		Gerald Almodovar	348	47	46	47	14	894,140
		Anthony Mawing	306	38	25	39	12	877,395
		David Cora	294	39	39	35	13	847,794
CT	4/1 - 6/30	Trainer	Starts	1st	2d	3d	Win %	Earnings
		Ronney W. Brown	161	34	33	12	21	643,709
		Jeff C. Runco	143	23	18	13	16	444,885
		Ernest M. Haynes	56	19	14	9	34	404,320
		Mark Shuman	73	15	12	9	21	369,680
		Kevin J. Joy	103	21	16	11	20	360,625

Track	Dates	Jockey/Trainer	Starts	1st	2d	3d	Win %	Earnings
CT	1/1 - 3/31	Jockey	Starts	1st	2d	3d	Win %	Earnings
		Anthony Mawing	358	55	59	48	15	1,197,216
		Travis L. Dunkelberger	266	54	38	27	20	1,009,766
		J. D. Acosta	311	43	43	53	14	845,365
		Kendrick Carmouche	298	36	30	41	12	718,160
		Mark E. Rosenthal	196	34	22	16	17	641,048
CT	1/1 - 3/31	Trainer	Starts	1st	2d	3d	Win %	Earnings
		Ronney W. Brown	169	30	30	29	18	483,775
		Mark Shuman	114	23	14	9	20	411,685
		Jeff C. Runco	137	19	29	12	14	392,490
		Kevin J. Joy	71	15	6	11	21	195,576
		Steve Klesaris	21	9	1	4	43	189,438
DED	10/31/03 - 3/27/04	Jockey	Starts	1st	2d	3d	Win %	Earnings
		Steve J. Bourque	516	120	76	80	23	2,138,344
		Guy Smith	482	79	64	64	16	1,479,056
		Carlos Gonzalez	355	71	55	48	20	1,185,153
		Carl James Woodley	434	66	67	50	15	1,132,833
		Casey Fusilier	442	59	66	53	13	989,813
DED	10/31/03 - 3/27/04	Trainer	Starts	1st	2d	3d	Win %	Earnings
		Doris Hebert	261	58	45	46	22	1,013,795
		Keith L. Bourgeois	311	61	54	40	20	899,876
		Steve Wren	2	1	1	0	50	620,000
		Dale Angelle	167	29	40	26	17	573,472
		Steven M. Asmussen	61	17	12	11	28	512,620
DEL	4/24 - 11/7	Jockey	Starts	1st	2d	3d	Win %	Earnings
		Ramon A. Dominguez	636	198	106	97	31	4,347,105
		Roberto Alvarado, Jr.	630	130	110	86	21	3,151,186
		Mario G. Pino	565	104	88	91	18	2,936,991
		Jeremy Rose	539	100	87	89	19	2,706,196
		Jose C. Caraballo	586	91	87	92	16	2,552,673
DEL	4/24 - 11/7	Trainer	Starts	1st	2d	3d	Win %	Earnings
		Scott A. Lake	366	91	79	51	25	1,872,540
		Timothy F. Ritchey	288	68	63	36	24	1,734,386
		Michael V. Pino	235	63	48	39	27	1,162,913
		Steve Klesaris	129	27	33	18	21	1,028,420
		Michael E. Gorham	201	37	34	35	18	916,379
DG	4/10 - 4/18	Jockey	Starts	1st	2d	3d	Win %	Earnings
		Charles Lyn McClellan	17	3	2	3	18	4,327
		Stephen Michael Karr	14	3	2	0	21	4,146
		Terry Lee Gard	17	2	3	3	12	4,146
		Fernando Manuel Gamez	18	1	5	1	6	3,203
		Flavio Lozano	17	2	1	2	12	2,953
DG	4/10 - 4/18	Trainer	Starts	1st	2d	3d	Win %	Earnings
		Wiley Aker	6	2	1	1	33	2,941
		Gene K. Wilson	9	2	1	1	22	2,363
		Clyde W. England	2	2	0	0	100	1,728
		Roy V. Ronquillo	3	1	0	0	33	1,472
		B. Odell Reidhead	3	1	1	1	33	1,230
DMR	7/21 - 9/8	Jockey	Starts	1st	2d	3d	Win %	Earnings
		Corey S. Nakatani	212	54	37	30	25	2,927,069
		Victor Espinoza	247	44	51	33	18	2,851,839
		Tyler Baze	286	52	42	37	18	2,693,254
		David Romero Flores	186	29	25	27	16	1,774,715
		Kent J. Desormeaux	146	21	21	19	14	1,442,074
DMR	7/21 - 9/8	Trainer	Starts	1st	2d	3d	Win %	Earnings
		Jeff Mullins	93	24	16	15	26	1,330,045
		Julio C. Canani	41	11	10	4	27	1,297,042
		Bob Baffert	89	17	10	20	19	1,035,401
		Doug O'Neill	126	28	12	15	22	1,024,398
		Mike R. Mitchell	77	16	15	5	21	935,018
DUN	3/13 - 3/21	Jockey	Starts	1st	2d	3d	Win %	Earnings
		Charles Lyn McClellan	20	4	3	3	20	6,399
		Todd J. Nuttall	18	3	4	4	17	5,405
		Alfredo Torres	15	2	1	1	13	5,062
		Stephen Michael Karr	18	4	1	3	22	4,866
		Anna M. Barrio	19	3	4	5	16	4,768

Track	Dates	Name	Starts	1st	2d	3d	Win %	Earnings
DUN	3/13 - 3/21	Trainer	Starts	1st	2d	3d	Win %	Earnings
		Charlie Bauerelen	2	2	0	0	100	4,039
		Laurie Jones	10	3	1	2	30	3,888
		Gene K. Wilson	11	1	4	2	9	2,626
		Eddy Lenard May	9	2	1	0	22	2,466
		William H. Mahan	8	2	0	1	25	2,268
ELK	8/28 - 9/6	Jockey	Starts	1st	2d	3d	Win %	Earnings
		Nathan R. Condie	33	16	5	4	48	34,158
		Casey Greene	30	7	4	6	23	18,717
		Matt Williams	28	3	5	8	11	11,817
		Casey Sherman	14	4	4	0	29	7,715
		Brett W. Anderson	21	2	4	3	10	6,941
ELK	8/28 - 9/6	Trainer	Starts	1st	2d	3d	Win %	Earnings
		Shawn H. Davis	17	6	1	2	35	18,799
		Steve Duschka	18	4	2	2	22	8,060
		Blake L. Cragun	7	4	2	1	57	7,390
		Brice Underdahl	4	2	0	1	50	7,103
		R. Mike Scudder	10	1	3	2	10	7,075
ELP	7/7 - 9/6	Jockey	Starts	1st	2d	3d	Win %	Earnings
		Rafael Bejarano	317	85	74	44	27	1,193,517
		John McKee	266	45	42	37	17	783,011
		Willie Martinez	261	47	40	29	18	682,621
		Jesus Lopez Castanon	225	30	35	33	13	543,561
		Mark Guidry	86	21	13	16	24	543,473
ELP	7/7 - 9/6	Trainer	Starts	1st	2d	3d	Win %	Earnings
		Dale L. Romans	49	7	14	10	14	327,043
		Robert E. Holthus	61	9	7	7	15	272,788
		Bobby C. Barnett	73	13	15	9	18	260,654
		William I. Mott	36	11	6	3	31	248,734
		Thomas M. Amoss	29	12	5	6	41	217,882
EMD	4/16 - 9/20	Jockey	Starts	1st	2d	3d	Win %	Earnings
		Ricky Frazier	555	109	86	85	20	1,208,018
		Ben Russell	445	100	78	56	22	909,374
		Gallyn Vick Mitchell	438	83	73	72	19	861,960
		Adalberto Diaz Lopez	489	70	78	70	14	752,855
		Juan M. Gutierrez	484	65	75	68	13	640,642
EMD	4/16 - 9/20	Trainer	Starts	1st	2d	3d	Win %	Earnings
		Tim McCanna	256	50	40	45	20	614,419
		Jim Penney	191	47	29	32	25	551,098
		Frank Lucarelli	271	52	40	39	19	488,576
		Sharon Ross	228	46	35	36	20	429,765
		Grant T. Forster	158	35	27	13	22	427,364
EUR	5/1 - 7/4	Jockey	Starts	1st	2d	3d	Win %	Earnings
		Richard M. Vasquez	53	19	8	9	36	34,756
		Thomas Wellington	19	9	2	3	47	15,166
		Mike J. Bishop	40	7	8	6	18	14,722
		Gary L. Worst	44	4	7	7	9	10,530
		Dustin W. Williams	32	3	8	4	9	9,458
EUR	5/1 - 7/4	Trainer	Starts	1st	2d	3d	Win %	Earnings
		Joe Frederick Thomas, Sr.	31	9	6	9	29	17,910
		John W. Layton	15	10	0	2	67	16,650
		Jeffrey T. Rutland	8	3	1	1	38	5,818
		Gary Sharpe	15	3	2	0	20	5,657
		Cresencio Arceo	19	2	3	5	11	5,477
EVD	4/1 - 9/6	Jockey	Starts	1st	2d	3d	Win %	Earnings
		Brian Joseph Hernandez, Jr.	431	99	63	57	23	970,954
		Steve J. Bourque	418	76	65	45	18	895,098
		Carl James Woodley	367	73	53	39	20	797,235
		Tracy J. Hebert	436	68	56	52	16	727,885
		Jamie Theriot	396	58	40	45	15	717,652
EVD	4/1 - 9/6	Trainer	Starts	1st	2d	3d	Win %	Earnings
		Keith L. Bourgeois	312	60	44	27	19	679,078
		Dale Angelle	200	55	30	23	28	566,183
		Doris Hebert	198	38	40	26	19	483,280
		Samuel Breaux	168	30	31	25	18	390,678
		Donald J. Cormier, Sr.	255	17	26	31	7	301,904

			Starts	1st	2d	3d	Win %	Earnings
FAR	8/6 - 9/6	Jockey	Starts	1st	2d	3d	Win %	Earnings
		Chris R. Fiegen	63	12	12	11	19	47,942
		Joe Sharp	65	12	16	14	18	45,885
		Anne Von Rosen	48	15	10	8	31	43,337
		Scot A. Schindler	49	15	12	7	31	42,277
		Jimmy Jordan	50	6	9	9	12	25,997
FAR	8/6 - 9/6	Trainer	Starts	1st	2d	3d	Win %	Earnings
		John Ness	54	16	9	8	30	46,115
		Craig Bonn	28	9	6	3	32	27,519
		Chad Torevell	2	2	0	0	100	25,000
		Kenneth Olson	33	9	8	2	27	20,519
		Kelly Kaelberer	29	5	3	4	17	15,501
FE	5/1 - 9/6	Jockey	Starts	1st	2d	3d	Win %	Earnings
		Neil Poznansky	405	71	44	64	18	1,335,527
		Martin Ramos Ramirez	394	67	60	45	17	1,152,900
		Brian Todd Bochinski	415	63	74	55	15	1,141,149
		Jake Barton	353	52	65	47	15	1,107,341
		Francine Villeneuve	333	57	50	41	17	1,053,048
FE	5/1 - 9/6	Trainer	Starts	1st	2d	3d	Win %	Earnings
		Thomas M. Agosti	129	27	22	15	21	436,200
		Layne S. Giliforte	135	23	24	17	17	382,988
		Debra E. Rombis	144	20	20	14	14	358,247
		Daryl G. Ezra	121	13	12	17	11	354,742
		Ross Armata	131	26	18	16	20	347,368
FER	8/12 - 8/22	Jockey	Starts	1st	2d	3d	Win %	Earnings
		Victor G. Navarro	23	9	6	3	39	41,400
		Victor Miranda	27	9	5	5	33	38,812
		Ryan Morris	29	5	8	6	17	28,217
		Robert Boyce	23	3	4	5	13	18,318
		Elliott Demesme	21	2	3	0	10	12,738
FER	8/12 - 8/22	Trainer	Starts	1st	2d	3d	Win %	Earnings
		Dennis Hopkins	27	5	8	5	19	31,575
		Karen Haverty	12	4	1	2	33	20,033
		John McDevitt	33	2	3	3	6	17,565
		Santiago C. Rodriguez	9	4	3	0	44	13,455
		Ron E. White	10	3	2	1	30	11,195
FG	11/27/03 - 3/28/04	Jockey	Starts	1st	2d	3d	Win %	Earnings
		Robby Albarado	452	106	101	65	23	3,084,990
		Shane J. Sellers	351	84	55	48	24	1,894,756
		Gerard Melancon	534	76	80	83	14	1,811,806
		Corey J. Lanerie	473	71	75	70	15	1,799,197
		Eddie M. Martin, Jr.	489	78	74	65	16	1,698,140
FG	11/27/03 - 3/28/04	Trainer	Starts	1st	2d	3d	Win %	Earnings
		Steven M. Asmussen	247	63	41	37	26	1,388,645
		Thomas M. Amoss	137	32	25	22	23	680,230
		W. Bret Calhoun	134	32	27	17	24	625,692
		Neil J. Howard	54	16	14	8	30	587,020
		Richard R. Scherer	60	10	9	7	17	521,695
FL	4/16 - 11/27	Jockey	Starts	1st	2d	3d	Win %	Earnings
		John R. Davila, Jr.	640	136	108	74	21	1,462,125
		Pedro A. Rodriguez	589	130	82	82	22	1,373,543
		John A. Grabowski	491	78	78	67	16	980,181
		Chin C. Yang	566	63	77	66	11	967,162
		Parker R. Buckley	531	91	76	66	17	936,341
FL	4/16 - 11/27	Trainer	Starts	1st	2d	3d	Win %	Earnings
		Chris J. Englehart	589	136	110	93	23	1,342,832
		Michael A. Lecesse	380	79	57	55	21	982,808
		Charlton Baker	250	67	40	36	27	774,848
		Ralph D'Alessandro	287	56	44	32	20	665,807
		Michael S. Ferraro	313	56	46	33	18	613,112
FLG	7/2 - 7/5	Jockey	Starts	1st	2d	3d	Win %	Earnings
		Lorenzo Castane Lopez	18	4	1	2	22	14,944
		Charles Lyn McClellan	15	3	4	2	20	13,901
		Stephen Michael Karr	17	3	1	4	18	12,218
		Daniel P. Vergara	8	3	3	0	38	11,675
		Janna Sorrells	11	2	5	0	18	10,791

Track	Dates	Name	Starts	1st	2d	3d	Win %	Earnings
FLG	7/2 - 7/5	Trainer	Starts	1st	2d	3d	Win %	Earnings
		George Wern	4	2	2	0	50	7,844
		Jon Phil Zimmerman	5	2	1	1	40	7,025
		B. Odell Reidhead	4	2	0	2	50	6,717
		Sandra Ehret	6	1	3	0	17	5,736
		Wiley Aker	2	2	0	0	100	5,596
FMT	5/27 - 7/25	Jockey	Starts	1st	2d	3d	Win %	Earnings
		Curtis Kimes	114	31	18	15	27	312,907
		Randy R. Wilson	73	14	8	9	19	144,843
		Kerry D. Kretzer	83	9	9	12	11	119,603
		Tonja A. Arruda	88	9	13	10	10	116,345
		Larry D. Payne	28	5	5	4	18	113,585
FMT	5/27 - 7/25	Trainer	Starts	1st	2d	3d	Win %	Earnings
		Mike R. Teel	42	14	8	6	33	121,425
		Debbie Holland Dyer	23	5	4	2	22	81,442
		Robert L. Listen	11	2	2	1	18	55,750
		Robert L. Roughton	11	5	2	0	45	46,510
		Joe S. Offolter	21	4	2	2	19	46,386
FNO	10/6 - 10/17	Jockey	Starts	1st	2d	3d	Win %	Earnings
		Macario Rodriguez	45	11	19	3	24	92,385
		Modesto Linares	39	13	2	5	33	73,285
		Victor Miranda	44	7	6	7	16	53,228
		Victor G. Navarro	38	5	6	8	13	44,668
		Joy Marie Scott	28	2	2	2	7	40,645
FNO	10/6 - 10/17	Trainer	Starts	1st	2d	3d	Win %	Earnings
		Michael Lenzini	41	4	6	11	10	61,992
		Dennis Hopkins	39	6	6	3	15	47,038
		Rene Amescua	18	4	2	4	22	27,512
		Clifford DeLima	15	4	1	3	27	25,010
		W. R. Whitehouse	14	3	5	1	21	22,530
FON	2/14 - 5/8	Jockey	Starts	1st	2d	3d	Win %	Earnings
		Perry Compton	294	80	57	46	27	403,114
		Curtis Kimes	327	69	59	33	21	347,220
		Dennis Michael Collins	294	32	44	43	11	239,562
		Armando Martinez	263	30	17	27	11	176,896
		Robert Dean Williams	170	23	21	24	14	147,519
FON	2/14 - 5/8	Trainer	Starts	1st	2d	3d	Win %	Earnings
		David C. Anderson	126	31	22	16	25	149,471
		Marvin A. Johnson	108	28	11	6	26	115,236
		Brian M. Roberts	59	12	7	11	20	92,267
		Boyd Caster	62	12	7	11	19	65,784
		Steve L. Hall	52	11	8	11	21	63,537
FP	3/26 - 9/18	Jockey	Starts	1st	2d	3d	Win %	Earnings
		Ramsey Zimmerman	613	180	119	94	29	973,547
		Michael Allen Gale	354	61	57	62	17	514,148
		Joel Santiago	529	70	81	98	13	492,250
		Gilbert Concha	474	67	73	69	14	436,433
		Thomas L. Pompell	246	55	41	39	22	393,262
FP	3/26 - 9/18	Trainer	Starts	1st	2d	3d	Win %	Earnings
		Ralph Martinez	513	143	96	91	28	748,716
		Eddie M. Essenpreis	299	55	62	48	18	452,832
		Steve Manley	298	54	58	43	18	334,728
		Carmelo Mendoza	210	44	27	33	21	256,034
		Leroy Hellman	181	28	20	31	15	204,696
FPX	9/10 - 9/26	Jockey	Starts	1st	2d	3d	Win %	Earnings
		Martin A. Pedroza	134	51	25	14	38	1,000,142
		Omar Figueroa	72	14	12	9	19	496,257
		Alex Bisono	44	6	7	9	14	199,328
		Ignacio Puglisi	49	7	3	9	14	195,854
		Garrett K. Gomez	30	4	7	9	13	187,249
FPX	9/10 - 9/26	Trainer	Starts	1st	2d	3d	Win %	Earnings
		Doug O'Neill	45	16	5	3	36	361,490
		Jeff Mullins	23	8	4	3	35	312,952
		William Spawr	16	6	2	2	38	169,494
		Mike R. Mitchell	15	3	2	3	20	135,440
		Paul G. Aguirre	16	4	3	5	25	122,623

Track	Dates	Jockey/Trainer	Starts	1st	2d	3d	Win %	Earnings
GCF	10/2 - 10/10	Jockey	Starts	1st	2d	3d	Win %	Earnings
		Alfredo Torres	22	8	3	4	36	10,257
		Anna M. Barrio	20	7	1	3	35	8,670
		Terry Lee Gard	21	0	7	7	0	3,973
		Steve Hancock	22	1	4	3	5	3,702
		Angel Felix	17	1	4	1	6	3,225
GCF	10/2 - 10/10	Trainer	Starts	1st	2d	3d	Win %	Earnings
		Gene K. Wilson	11	6	1	1	55	6,827
		Guillermo Jimenez, Sr.	5	3	0	0	60	3,076
		Laurie Jones	10	2	0	4	20	2,908
		Pablo C. Figueroa, Sr.	2	2	0	0	100	2,290
		William H. Mahan	10	1	1	0	10	1,853
GF	7/3 - 8/1	Jockey	Starts	1st	2d	3d	Win %	Earnings
		Ivan Ortiz, Jr.	45	8	13	4	18	20,381
		Joe Holmes, Sr.	47	9	6	10	19	18,310
		Carl Hebert	43	6	9	8	14	15,764
		B. Buck Harris	34	10	5	5	29	14,907
		Russell David Kingrey	35	6	4	4	17	11,953
GF	7/3 - 8/1	Trainer	Starts	1st	2d	3d	Win %	Earnings
		Doug Johnson	23	5	4	1	22	9,979
		Mark Buckley	19	4	5	7	21	9,350
		Mel Berkram	25	4	5	5	16	8,294
		Bryan Krone	24	2	5	5	8	8,214
		Janis D. Schoepf	18	6	2	2	33	8,179
GG	11/5/03 - 4/4/04	Jockey	Starts	1st	2d	3d	Win %	Earnings
		Kevin Radke	474	89	72	69	19	1,658,369
		Chance J. Rollins	491	80	67	89	16	1,566,314
		Chad Phillip Schvaneveldt	328	76	47	49	23	1,432,856
		Russell A. Baze	335	71	68	52	21	1,421,354
		Dennis Carr	422	75	85	67	18	1,349,497
GG	11/5/03 - 4/4/04	Trainer	Starts	1st	2d	3d	Win %	Earnings
		Jerry Hollendorfer	449	88	83	61	20	2,026,353
		Art Sherman	222	58	43	28	26	844,019
		John F. Martin	183	52	32	24	28	775,300
		Armando Lage	316	34	40	44	11	618,294
		Brian J. Koriner	120	28	19	22	23	474,098
GIL	7/3 - 8/29	Jockey	Starts	1st	2d	3d	Win %	Earnings
		Salvador Perez	18	6	5	1	33	29,328
		Santos Carrizales	20	3	4	2	15	15,458
		W. Bill McClaran	15	4	2	3	27	14,910
		Russell Brown	13	1	3	1	8	7,086
		Isaac Chapa	13	1	1	1	8	6,218
GIL	7/3 - 8/29	Trainer	Starts	1st	2d	3d	Win %	Earnings
		Danny Pish	1	1	0	0	100	10,080
		Marvin Hayes	4	2	0	2	50	6,840
		Gabe Newman	4	2	0	1	50	5,778
		O. S. Carlton III	8	1	2	1	13	5,612
		M. Shawn Finch	8	1	0	0	13	5,532
GLD	4/25 - 10/30	Jockey	Starts	1st	2d	3d	Win %	Earnings
		T. D. Houghton	784	196	159	111	25	1,650,108
		Mary Elizabeth Doser	620	119	114	95	19	1,355,940
		Roberto A. Perez	666	118	92	98	18	1,087,584
		Federico Mata	534	98	82	82	18	854,363
		Felipe J. Santos	481	57	79	71	12	575,990
GLD	4/25 - 10/30	Trainer	Starts	1st	2d	3d	Win %	Earnings
		Gerald S. Bennett	417	94	77	76	23	1,106,712
		Robert M. Gorham	289	57	51	40	20	692,413
		Richard R. Rettele	312	55	61	49	18	677,380
		Ronald D. Allen, Sr.	173	46	28	28	27	450,745
		Randall R. Russell	395	51	51	62	13	425,500
GP	1/3 - 4/25	Jockey	Starts	1st	2d	3d	Win %	Earnings
		John R. Velazquez	276	78	60	33	28	2,789,414
		Edgar S. Prado	383	68	56	54	18	2,064,850
		Joe Bravo	412	68	60	58	17	1,992,862
		Jerry D. Bailey	144	32	26	20	22	1,811,811
		Cornelio H. Velasquez	408	64	68	46	16	1,761,846

Track	Dates	Trainer/Jockey	Starts	1st	2d	3d	Win %	Earnings
GP	1/3 - 4/25	Trainer	Starts	1st	2d	3d	Win %	Earnings
		Todd A. Pletcher	145	42	30	16	29	1,968,860
		John C. Kimmel	50	10	4	7	20	862,710
		Christophe Clement	60	13	8	11	22	778,280
		William I. Mott	122	24	18	15	20	728,201
		Kiaran P. McLaughlin	37	16	4	1	43	662,340
GPR	7/9 - 8/22	Jockey	Starts	1st	2d	3d	Win %	Earnings
		Scott Sterr	56	14	11	9	25	46,608
		Angelle Wilson	46	10	12	8	22	35,758
		Brooke Mellish	54	8	9	8	15	34,052
		Jackie Smith	47	8	7	10	17	31,548
		Peter McAleney	35	6	4	0	17	26,266
GPR	7/9 - 8/22	Trainer	Starts	1st	2d	3d	Win %	Earnings
		Pete Dubois	19	6	4	3	32	21,345
		Stan Marks	16	8	1	2	50	20,038
		William Bud Matier	12	3	4	0	25	14,077
		Amanda Fogle	21	4	4	2	19	13,744
		W. R. Brigden	20	3	3	2	15	13,329
GRP	5/15 - 7/5	Jockey	Starts	1st	2d	3d	Win %	Earnings
		Twyla Beckner	105	28	27	29	27	55,292
		Joe A. Crispin	115	22	27	25	19	47,810
		Duane Lee D'Amico	72	19	17	11	26	35,694
		Darlene Braden	113	17	10	15	15	34,925
		Ty Dangerfield	80	17	13	14	21	33,272
GRP	5/15 - 7/5	Trainer	Starts	1st	2d	3d	Win %	Earnings
		John McDevitt	47	7	7	11	15	14,890
		Vannessa Hunt	30	5	5	9	17	14,144
		Robert Beckner	29	8	3	9	28	12,866
		Judi Yearout	25	8	5	3	32	12,660
		Jaqueline Smith	20	7	6	2	35	12,418
HAW	9/24/04 - 1/2/05	Jockey	Starts	1st	2d	3d	Win %	Earnings
		Christopher A. Emigh	450	69	63	47	15	1,462,111
		Jesse M. Campbell	322	39	55	36	12	1,049,232
		Larry J. Sterling, Jr.	240	47	26	34	20	1,043,164
		Eusebio Razo, Jr.	264	35	35	27	13	910,172
		Carlos H. Silva	287	32	30	32	11	732,017
HAW	9/24/04 - 1/2/05	Trainer	Starts	1st	2d	3d	Win %	Earnings
		Brian Williamson	87	19	17	7	22	534,616
		Frank J. Kirby	179	26	25	14	15	495,054
		Michael J. Maker	1	1	0	0	100	450,000
		Michael L. Reavis	130	25	11	20	19	368,169
		Steven M. Asmussen	94	24	10	14	26	353,946
HAW	2/27 - 5/11	Jockey	Starts	1st	2d	3d	Win %	Earnings
		Cruz Contreras	291	47	45	36	16	840,486
		Eusebio Razo, Jr.	193	36	35	25	19	806,276
		Christopher A. Emigh	214	32	30	33	15	801,028
		Larry J. Sterling, Jr.	175	32	16	25	18	753,372
		Jesse M. Campbell	201	32	26	29	16	690,267
HAW	2/27 - 5/11	Trainer	Starts	1st	2d	3d	Win %	Earnings
		Richard P. Hazelton	87	17	15	16	20	510,967
		Thomas F. Tomillo	154	19	29	20	12	353,772
		Pat Cuccurullo	80	25	13	11	31	326,833
		Frank J. Kirby	113	18	12	13	16	308,326
		Todd A. Pletcher	1	1	0	0	100	300,000
HOL	11/3 - 12/20	Jockey	Starts	1st	2d	3d	Win %	Earnings
		Victor Espinoza	157	31	26	19	20	1,414,636
		Rene R. Douglas	188	37	26	31	20	1,209,326
		Tyler Baze	189	35	24	22	19	1,032,456
		Corey S. Nakatani	130	23	30	18	18	1,024,674
		Jon Kenton Court	135	18	27	24	13	863,877
HOL	11/3 - 12/20	Trainer	Starts	1st	2d	3d	Win %	Earnings
		Robert J. Frankel	32	5	9	5	16	1,030,640
		Doug O'Neill	120	17	22	17	14	674,388
		Neil D. Drysdale	30	8	5	2	27	480,280
		Bob Baffert	58	14	9	5	24	449,280
		Ronald W. Ellis	14	3	3	4	21	393,420

Track	Dates	Jockey/Trainer	Starts	1st	2d	3d	Win %	Earnings
HOL	4/21 - 7/18	Jockey	Starts	1st	2d	3d	Win %	Earnings
		Alex O. Solis	210	40	41	30	19	2,875,455
		Victor Espinoza	309	55	50	51	18	2,819,421
		Corey S. Nakatani	236	48	42	27	20	2,271,965
		Tyler Baze	311	59	39	48	19	2,134,667
		Mike E. Smith	141	26	29	17	18	2,063,167
HOL	4/21 - 7/18	Trainer	Starts	1st	2d	3d	Win %	Earnings
		Doug O'Neill	217	32	34	36	15	1,477,291
		Jeff Mullins	119	37	21	11	31	1,316,403
		Vladimir Cerin	79	18	9	15	23	1,252,414
		Bob Baffert	116	20	17	15	17	1,228,135
		Robert J. Frankel	48	12	5	7	25	890,337
HOO	9/2 - 11/21	Jockey	Starts	1st	2d	3d	Win %	Earnings
		Lester Cash Knight	524	89	79	83	17	985,598
		Ramsey Zimmerman	329	92	51	51	28	869,514
		Rodney A. Prescott	412	72	60	43	17	753,660
		Jose J. Delgado	302	32	39	51	11	365,183
		Billy Charles Patin	232	33	28	25	14	337,226
HOO	9/2 - 11/21	Trainer	Starts	1st	2d	3d	Win %	Earnings
		Ralph Martinez	197	62	34	27	31	436,436
		William Bradley	1	1	0	0	100	306,780
		Kim Hammond	148	28	16	24	19	247,396
		Claude R. McGaughey III	1	1	0	0	100	243,780
		Barbara I. McBride	96	22	15	8	23	198,172
HOU	10/23/03 - 4/10/04	Jockey	Starts	1st	2d	3d	Win %	Earnings
		Jeremy Beasley	451	100	67	56	22	1,207,058
		John Jacinto	502	76	72	57	15	777,020
		Terry A. Stanton	411	65	47	61	16	634,311
		Kerwin D. Clark	349	55	44	43	16	541,703
		Donald Edward Simington	384	50	54	49	13	535,131
HOU	10/23/03 - 4/10/04	Trainer	Starts	1st	2d	3d	Win %	Earnings
		Steven M. Asmussen	210	60	40	25	29	927,605
		Danny Pish	269	53	45	37	20	499,416
		Michael Stidham	59	20	7	8	34	344,003
		W. Bret Calhoun	100	34	12	9	34	265,069
		Charles P. Hukill	121	20	22	16	17	257,830
HPO	7/15 - 7/18	Jockey	Starts	1st	2d	3d	Win %	Earnings
		Perry Compton	16	3	2	2	19	108,519
		Robert Dean Williams	16	4	4	1	25	88,055
		Daniel Lee Beck	12	3	1	1	25	60,625
		Armando Martinez	13	2	1	1	15	47,880
		Filmer Munaylla	13	1	3	0	8	33,000
HPO	7/15 - 7/18	Trainer	Starts	1st	2d	3d	Win %	Earnings
		Frank J. Kirby	1	1	0	0	100	57,000
		Herb Riecken	9	2	1	1	22	45,396
		David C. Anderson	13	1	3	0	8	35,725
		Steve Hobby	1	1	0	0	100	23,700
		Kim Veerhusen	4	1	1	0	25	19,625
HST	4/17 - 11/28	Jockey	Starts	1st	2d	3d	Win %	Earnings
		Pedro V. Alvarado	533	130	85	87	24	2,216,447
		David Wilson	562	79	87	76	14	1,539,392
		Francisco Perez Fuentes	369	46	51	46	12	1,045,101
		Chris Loseth	405	51	49	47	13	943,710
		Chad Hoverson	327	33	50	36	10	770,876
HST	4/17 - 11/28	Trainer	Starts	1st	2d	3d	Win %	Earnings
		David Forster	112	19	18	12	17	676,391
		Dino K. Condilenios	194	37	26	22	19	650,697
		Harold J. Barroby	273	36	45	38	13	591,592
		Barbara Heads	218	34	33	22	16	525,921
		Gary E. Demorest	135	32	23	22	24	475,702
IND	4/16 - 6/20	Jockey	Starts	1st	2d	3d	Win %	Earnings
		Rodney A. Prescott	368	74	63	52	20	623,493
		Joe Stokes	337	54	47	48	16	449,190
		Eddie Zuniga	271	48	41	33	18	421,789
		Orlando Mojica	246	40	35	26	16	361,841
		Jose J. Delgado	285	38	33	21	13	317,058

			Starts	1st	2d	3d	Win %	Earnings
IND	4/16 - 6/20	Trainer	Starts	1st	2d	3d	Win %	Earnings
		R. Gary Patrick	204	30	34	25	15	231,967
		Barbara I. McBride	66	21	15	16	32	156,373
		Lori A. Smock	64	11	9	8	17	99,142
		Robert Zahl	50	10	8	4	20	96,353
		Joseph R. Martin	68	12	10	14	18	96,139
KAM	8/8 - 9/5	Jockey	Starts	1st	2d	3d	Win %	Earnings
		Ronald Joseph Bilodeau	7	1	1	2	14	8,705
		Pamela M. Peaker	3	1	2	0	33	4,324
		Shelley Friesen	3	1	1	1	33	3,790
		Caroline Stinn	8	1	1	2	13	3,622
		Cliff James Miyashiro	3	2	1	0	67	3,555
KAM	8/8 - 9/5	Trainer	Starts	1st	2d	3d	Win %	Earnings
		Marlon Stitzel	3	1	0	0	33	7,440
		Vicki Pozzobon	1	1	0	0	100	3,150
		Frank R. Wilson	2	0	1	0	0	2,784
		Charles Butch McDonald	2	1	1	0	50	2,355
		Bruce Hattori	4	1	0	0	25	1,662
KAM	5/30 - 7/4	Jockey	Starts	1st	2d	3d	Win %	Earnings
		Angelle Wilson	14	6	1	3	43	8,480
		Caroline Stinn	15	3	4	3	20	6,420
		Laurina Bugeaud	17	3	2	5	18	6,060
		Robert Stein	9	2	4	0	22	4,420
		Ronald Joseph Bilodeau	7	1	2	2	14	2,680
KAM	5/30 - 7/4	Trainer	Starts	1st	2d	3d	Win %	Earnings
		Frank R. Wilson	8	3	1	0	38	4,320
		Vicki Pozzobon	6	3	0	2	50	4,100
		Dale Schaffrick	7	2	1	1	29	3,200
		Kathy Dean	4	1	1	2	25	2,040
		Jim Hille	5	1	1	0	20	1,900
KD	9/18 - 9/28	Jockey	Starts	1st	2d	3d	Win %	Earnings
		Rafael Bejarano	35	12	8	4	34	298,390
		Brice Blanc	18	2	1	5	11	168,876
		James Graham	27	3	5	4	11	88,871
		Mark Guidry	5	2	0	0	40	87,250
		Jesus Lopez Castanon	22	3	3	4	14	82,122
KD	9/18 - 9/28	Trainer	Starts	1st	2d	3d	Win %	Earnings
		Tim Yakteen	1	1	0	0	100	124,000
		Charles Simon	6	1	3	0	17	82,300
		Anthony L. Reinstedler	5	1	1	2	20	72,100
		Jonathan E. Sheppard	4	1	1	2	25	69,000
		Lynn S. Whiting	1	1	0	0	100	62,000
KEE	10/8 - 10/30	Jockey	Starts	1st	2d	3d	Win %	Earnings
		Rafael Bejarano	128	26	17	30	20	1,771,064
		Pat Day	79	20	13	13	25	1,456,504
		Robby Albarado	104	9	16	15	9	1,072,484
		Brian Joseph Hernandez, Jr.	101	20	11	9	20	605,807
		Calvin H. Borel	83	9	7	6	11	557,004
KEE	10/8 - 10/30	Trainer	Starts	1st	2d	3d	Win %	Earnings
		D. Wayne Lukas	34	5	7	5	15	805,991
		Robert J. Frankel	5	2	2	0	40	514,507
		Nicholas P. Zito	27	11	4	4	41	440,353
		Steven M. Asmussen	46	11	2	7	24	406,808
		Carl A. Nafzger	35	7	3	7	20	354,562
KEE	4/2 - 4/23	Jockey	Starts	1st	2d	3d	Win %	Earnings
		Shane J. Sellers	85	15	10	10	18	1,145,560
		Pat Day	82	21	13	13	26	1,061,364
		Jerry D. Bailey	43	12	4	7	28	916,424
		Robby Albarado	115	13	15	24	11	852,048
		Edgar S. Prado	37	9	8	3	24	587,904
KEE	4/2 - 4/23	Trainer	Starts	1st	2d	3d	Win %	Earnings
		Nicholas P. Zito	33	4	8	5	12	684,627
		Todd A. Pletcher	26	7	7	4	27	638,029
		Steven M. Asmussen	44	9	8	8	20	570,068
		Kenneth G. McPeek	30	7	1	5	23	313,973
		Frank L. Brothers	2	1	0	0	50	310,000

Track	Dates	Name	Starts	1st	2d	3d	Win %	Earnings
KIN	7/11 - 8/1	Jockey	Starts	1st	2d	3d	Win %	Earnings
		Roger Butterfly	10	4	1	1	40	12,742
		Caroline Stinn	14	4	4	2	29	8,743
		Robert Stein	5	2	1	1	40	4,955
		Ronald Joseph Bilodeau	12	2	2	5	17	4,910
		Ty Dangerfield	7	2	3	1	29	4,565
KIN	7/11 - 8/1	Trainer	Starts	1st	2d	3d	Win %	Earnings
		Garry Saitz	6	4	1	0	67	7,425
		Marion Stitzel	2	2	0	0	100	7,200
		Wade Hardie	6	0	3	1	0	4,305
		Dave Desautel	6	3	0	1	50	4,200
		John Stabenfeldt	4	1	1	1	25	2,225
KSP	8/20 - 8/29	Jockey	Starts	1st	2d	3d	Win %	Earnings
		Carl Hebert	13	4	2	4	31	5,866
		Joe Holmes, Sr.	14	3	3	4	21	5,184
		Russell David Kingrey	5	3	2	0	60	4,182
		Nate Smith	14	1	3	3	7	3,292
		Roger Butterfly	9	2	2	0	22	2,443
KSP	8/20 - 8/29	Trainer	Starts	1st	2d	3d	Win %	Earnings
		Mel Berkram	7	3	1	2	43	3,888
		Janis D. Schoepf	7	1	1	0	14	2,421
		Harlan Bird Rattler	12	1	0	4	8	2,102
		Jaqueline Smith	4	1	2	1	25	1,965
		Andrew Schildt	5	1	1	0	20	1,452
LA	12/26/03 - 12/19/04	Jockey	Starts	1st	2d	3d	Win %	Earnings
		Guillermo R. Gutierrez	309	58	58	48	19	367,427
		Agapito Delgadillo	215	56	40	35	26	274,014
		Antonio Lopez Castanon	255	37	45	32	15	250,662
		Baltazar Contreras	251	43	30	29	17	242,096
		Alex Bautista	176	36	19	34	20	200,336
LA	12/26/03 - 12/19/04	Trainer	Starts	1st	2d	3d	Win %	Earnings
		Jesus Nunez	388	66	56	50	17	382,924
		Craig W. Robertson	127	47	22	18	37	254,819
		Charles S. Treece	226	39	41	39	17	231,677
		Christopher G. O'Dell	64	9	15	13	14	76,976
		Fidencio L. Jimenez	71	12	5	17	17	67,176
LAD	5/14 - 10/31	Jockey	Starts	1st	2d	3d	Win %	Earnings
		Lonnie Meche	648	158	104	85	24	2,390,166
		Gerard Melancon	553	101	81	83	18	2,125,549
		John Jacinto	590	118	89	72	20	1,732,255
		Luis S. Quinonez	733	113	106	118	15	1,708,964
		Corey J. Lanerie	512	80	90	76	16	1,525,969
LAD	5/14 - 10/31	Trainer	Starts	1st	2d	3d	Win %	Earnings
		Cole Norman	391	111	72	43	28	1,481,209
		Steven M. Asmussen	224	49	29	32	22	803,265
		Troy Young	104	25	23	19	24	608,724
		Patrick Mouton	145	23	30	15	16	507,705
		Larry Robideaux, Jr.	147	26	24	25	18	489,534
LBG	9/4 - 10/31	Jockey	Starts	1st	2d	3d	Win %	Earnings
		Scott Sterr	135	28	26	26	21	137,894
		Cliff James Miyashiro	99	23	19	18	23	105,467
		Angelle Wilson	100	12	14	17	12	78,093
		Nate Smith	111	15	17	11	14	77,352
		Janine Stianson	91	14	11	13	15	65,351
LBG	9/4 - 10/31	Trainer	Starts	1st	2d	3d	Win %	Earnings
		Phil Wiest	35	11	7	6	31	43,848
		Allan Brown	20	7	3	6	35	36,627
		Ron David	30	7	6	8	23	35,142
		Rick Wiest	20	5	7	3	25	33,194
		Stan Marks	36	4	9	5	11	31,365
LBG	5/1 - 7/4	Jockey	Starts	1st	2d	3d	Win %	Earnings
		Peter McAleney	95	24	21	11	25	92,646
		Scott Sterr	95	18	18	11	19	73,746
		Carl Hebert	97	11	15	16	11	57,908
		Amber Dickinson	48	17	7	10	35	56,299
		Janine Stianson	93	10	15	20	11	55,058

Track	Dates	Trainer	Starts	1st	2d	3d	Win %	Earnings
LBG	5/1 - 7/4	Jason Homer	50	17	12	5	34	63,621
		Jim Meyaard	42	15	5	9	36	45,978
		Kevin Oberholtzer	33	6	9	3	18	33,597
		Stan Marks	35	9	3	2	26	32,618
		Mel Berkram	39	4	7	8	10	22,266

Track	Dates	Jockey	Starts	1st	2d	3d	Win %	Earnings
LNN	5/14 - 7/11	Robert Dean Williams	238	70	35	30	29	307,098
		Dennis Michael Collins	220	39	37	28	18	208,207
		Armando Martinez	202	29	20	23	14	160,918
		Daniel Lee Beck	181	24	18	31	13	153,116
		Jerome Carkeek	231	27	28	45	12	150,695

Track	Dates	Trainer	Starts	1st	2d	3d	Win %	Earnings
LNN	5/14 - 7/11	David C. Anderson	125	29	17	17	23	146,195
		Herb Riecken	57	15	8	9	26	95,767
		Marvin A. Johnson	80	11	9	16	14	65,451
		Steve L. Hall	32	14	4	1	44	56,565
		James R. Compton	51	14	11	9	27	54,914

Track	Dates	Jockey	Starts	1st	2d	3d	Win %	Earnings
LRL	1/1 - 3/28	Ramon A. Dominguez	326	88	59	63	27	1,532,780
		Abel Castellano, Jr.	272	46	48	41	17	934,370
		Jeremy Rose	259	53	36	26	20	836,795
		Mario G. Pino	183	25	29	26	14	555,975
		Jozbin Z. Santana	199	34	27	21	17	543,980

Track	Dates	Trainer	Starts	1st	2d	3d	Win %	Earnings
LRL	1/1 - 3/28	John J. Robb	172	36	24	18	21	523,010
		Dale Capuano	136	33	24	25	24	500,515
		Mark Shuman	94	19	16	15	20	398,410
		Phil Schoenthal	92	17	18	13	18	332,695
		John V. Alecci	40	16	5	4	40	269,610

Track	Dates	Jockey	Starts	1st	2d	3d	Win %	Earnings
LS	10/1 - 10/31	John R. Velazquez	11	3	4	0	27	3,300,200
		Javier Castellano	3	2	0	0	67	2,140,000
		Jerry D. Bailey	10	3	3	2	30	1,594,000
		Ramon A. Dominguez	3	1	0	1	33	1,186,600
		David Romero Flores	4	1	1	0	25	886,300

Track	Dates	Trainer	Starts	1st	2d	3d	Win %	Earnings
LS	10/1 - 10/31	Robert J. Frankel	7	1	0	0	14	2,111,800
		Todd A. Pletcher	6	3	1	0	50	1,761,200
		H. Graham Motion	3	1	1	0	33	1,352,000
		Dale L. Romans	2	0	2	0	0	1,200,000
		Donald Chatlos, Jr.	1	1	0	0	100	873,600

Track	Dates	Jockey	Starts	1st	2d	3d	Win %	Earnings
LS	4/15 - 7/11	Eddie M. Martin, Jr.	415	87	76	64	21	1,684,025
		Monte Clifton Berry	394	78	55	53	20	1,389,270
		Jeremy Beasley	330	41	39	32	12	850,483
		Casey T. Lambert	280	40	34	36	14	766,969
		Kevin Leon Cogburn	344	26	45	50	8	566,485

Track	Dates	Trainer	Starts	1st	2d	3d	Win %	Earnings
LS	4/15 - 7/11	Steven M. Asmussen	342	82	66	42	24	1,859,727
		Cole Norman	202	59	46	25	29	791,320
		W. Bret Calhoun	160	26	30	28	16	680,200
		Donnie K. Von Hemel	111	14	15	17	13	411,790
		Danny Pish	185	21	22	26	11	393,908

Track	Dates	Jockey	Starts	1st	2d	3d	Win %	Earnings
MAF	7/24 - 7/25	Shannon Wippert	5	2	1	0	40	3,687
		Joe Holmes, Sr.	7	2	2	2	29	3,062
		Ivan Ortiz, Jr.	6	2	0	1	33	2,371
		Carl Hebert	7	1	2	1	14	2,333
		Terrance Birdrattler	1	1	0	0	100	880

Track	Dates	Trainer	Starts	1st	2d	3d	Win %	Earnings
MAF	7/24 - 7/25	Janis D. Schoepf	2	1	1	0	50	2,332
		Mel Berkram	6	1	2	1	17	2,221
		Jim Depew	2	1	0	0	50	1,611
		Cleo Medicine Horse, Jr.	4	1	0	2	25	1,526
		Harlan Bird Rattler	4	1	1	0	25	1,344

Track	Dates	Jockey	Starts	1st	2d	3d	Win %	Earnings
MAN	2/28 - 4/25	Jockey	Starts	1st	2d	3d	Win %	Earnings
		Santos Carrizales	38	7	7	7	18	37,109
		James Bo White	33	8	2	5	24	35,710
		Charlotte Bronstad	41	6	6	4	15	33,144
		Randy B. Edison	39	4	10	3	10	24,332
		Rick L. Knott	29	4	5	3	14	20,867
MAN	2/28 - 4/25	Trainer	Starts	1st	2d	3d	Win %	Earnings
		Bobby A. Jenkins	10	4	4	0	40	21,912
		Bradley C. Bolen	10	2	2	2	20	17,591
		Gabe Newman	10	3	1	1	30	14,210
		Robert Fitzpatrick	11	2	2	1	18	10,410
		M. Shawn Finch	14	1	2	3	7	9,350
MC	5/9 - 5/16	Jockey	Starts	1st	2d	3d	Win %	Earnings
		Shaunda L. Larsen	8	4	0	0	50	7,146
		Shannon Wippert	5	2	2	0	40	4,318
		Zack Kelsey	6	0	3	2	0	2,310
		Shann Nomee	3	1	1	0	33	1,460
		Frank La Forge	3	1	0	0	33	834
MC	5/9 - 5/16	Trainer	Starts	1st	2d	3d	Win %	Earnings
		Bryan Krone	12	5	0	1	42	8,861
		Edward Buxbaum	9	0	2	4	0	2,297
		Amber Flom	3	1	1	0	33	2,150
		Cleo Medicine Horse, Jr.	4	1	1	0	25	1,460
		Janis D. Schoepf	4	0	3	0	0	1,260
MD	5/28 - 9/11	Jockey	Starts	1st	2d	3d	Win %	Earnings
		Serge R. Rocheleau	188	56	31	24	30	148,106
		Haniff Emamalie	177	38	40	33	21	108,316
		Rennie Latchman	182	22	32	31	12	78,676
		Danny Seesequasis	144	16	14	14	11	42,532
		Janice Seesequasis	131	9	19	20	7	42,466
MD	5/28 - 9/11	Trainer	Starts	1st	2d	3d	Win %	Earnings
		Hubert Pilon	76	19	19	10	25	80,836
		Don Bjarnarson	47	19	5	10	40	39,740
		Judy Hunter	28	11	8	3	39	36,506
		Fern Zdunick	46	10	6	6	22	34,064
		Russell Gardipy	49	18	4	5	37	33,060
MDA	10/2 - 10/11	Jockey	Starts	1st	2d	3d	Win %	Earnings
		Tim Moccasin	22	8	11	2	36	9,243
		Cameron Campbell	22	7	3	4	32	7,745
		Danny Seesequasis	14	4	3	1	29	4,277
		Danielle Beischer	17	2	4	4	12	3,692
		Doug T. Jones	7	1	1	3	14	1,729
MDA	10/2 - 10/11	Trainer	Starts	1st	2d	3d	Win %	Earnings
		Mike Tourangeau	18	2	5	6	11	3,835
		Brad Ball	10	4	1	3	40	3,743
		James R. Ross	10	3	2	3	30	3,222
		Elton Keshane	11	2	3	1	18	3,094
		Dana T. Keshane	8	2	5	0	25	2,925
MDA	5/8 - 5/16	Jockey	Starts	1st	2d	3d	Win %	Earnings
		Bernie Tourangeau	18	5	6	2	28	6,012
		Sheldon Chickeness	17	4	3	5	24	4,935
		Hector Rabbitskin	16	3	5	2	19	4,345
		Danielle Beischer	8	4	1	2	50	3,666
		Norbert Keshane	9	2	3	2	22	2,860
MDA	5/8 - 5/16	Trainer	Starts	1st	2d	3d	Win %	Earnings
		Elton Keshane	13	5	2	2	38	4,998
		Mike Tourangeau	10	3	5	0	30	3,731
		Brad Ball	8	4	1	2	50	3,679
		Irene Britton	12	2	1	6	17	2,746
		Joseph Vandane	4	1	2	0	25	1,391
MED	10/1 - 11/13	Jockey	Starts	1st	2d	3d	Win %	Earnings
		Stewart Elliott	170	37	23	21	22	1,056,567
		Joe Bravo	135	28	22	24	21	1,029,557
		Eibar Coa	108	22	25	12	20	791,770
		Rajiv Maragh	185	28	25	27	15	746,181
		Julian Pimentel	114	20	18	12	18	701,785

Track	Dates	Name	Starts	1st	2d	3d	Win %	Earnings
MED	10/1 - 11/13	Trainer	Starts	1st	2d	3d	Win %	Earnings
		Todd A. Pletcher	27	6	4	4	22	556,730
		Mark Shuman	49	7	8	8	14	293,520
		Mark A. Hennig	22	4	6	3	18	285,460
		Edwin Thomas Broome	47	9	7	6	19	278,831
		Patricia Farro	51	11	10	5	22	252,974
MIL	7/1 - 7/2	Jockey	Starts	1st	2d	3d	Win %	Earnings
		Scott Sterr	5	1	2	2	20	5,634
		Peter McAleney	5	1	1	0	20	4,214
		Nate Smith	5	1	0	2	20	3,568
		Laurina Bugeaud	4	1	1	0	25	3,457
		Brooke Mellish	5	1	0	0	20	2,967
MIL	7/1 - 7/2	Trainer	Starts	1st	2d	3d	Win %	Earnings
		Marlon Draper	2	2	0	0	100	5,088
		Nellie Opal Pigeau	3	1	1	0	33	3,334
		Ron David	3	1	0	2	33	3,325
		Barry R. Price	1	1	0	0	100	2,147
		Robert Allen	3	0	1	0	0	1,474
MNR	10/1 - 12/28	Jockey	Starts	1st	2d	3d	Win %	Earnings
		Dana G. Whitney	346	59	45	43	17	939,170
		Deshawn L. Parker	375	49	66	46	13	850,912
		Oswald M. Pereira	378	55	59	41	15	841,323
		Chad K. Murphy	168	35	21	22	21	736,791
		Rex A. Stokes, III	287	47	28	31	16	608,552
MNR	10/1 - 12/28	Trainer	Starts	1st	2d	3d	Win %	Earnings
		Dale Baird	223	29	26	26	13	453,747
		Bernard S. Flint	36	15	4	2	42	382,854
		John W. Baird	102	24	13	12	24	304,415
		J. Michael Baird	92	21	13	11	23	262,869
		Jami C. Poole	90	20	6	7	22	221,949
MNR	7/1 - 9/30	Jockey	Starts	1st	2d	3d	Win %	Earnings
		Deshawn L. Parker	468	79	75	54	17	1,194,181
		Dana G. Whitney	441	60	69	70	14	1,103,920
		Oswald M. Pereira	401	47	59	60	12	796,988
		Chad K. Murphy	239	37	37	30	15	787,890
		Bobby J. Walker, Jr.	153	34	25	12	22	560,555
MNR	7/1 - 9/30	Trainer	Starts	1st	2d	3d	Win %	Earnings
		Dale Baird	263	39	39	36	15	599,709
		Nicholas P. Zito	1	1	0	0	100	363,000
		J. Michael Baird	105	26	17	14	25	329,399
		Bernard S. Flint	37	9	10	5	24	279,223
		John W. Baird	105	18	12	12	17	278,815
MNR	4/1 - 6/30	Jockey	Starts	1st	2d	3d	Win %	Earnings
		Dana G. Whitney	498	107	83	64	21	1,606,646
		Deshawn L. Parker	470	70	69	60	15	1,103,604
		Chad K. Murphy	305	55	38	38	18	976,517
		Gary A. Birzer	384	45	52	52	12	756,293
		Oswald M. Pereira	308	35	43	31	11	574,607
MNR	4/1 - 6/30	Trainer	Starts	1st	2d	3d	Win %	Earnings
		Dale Baird	310	32	38	39	10	606,934
		Bernard S. Flint	40	15	4	8	38	285,410
		Wayne M. Catalano	59	22	8	7	37	278,369
		Paula S. Capestro	77	24	13	11	31	264,511
		Scooter Davis	117	21	14	11	18	246,963
MNR	1/3 - 3/31	Jockey	Starts	1st	2d	3d	Win %	Earnings
		Deshawn L. Parker	238	34	50	27	14	536,242
		Dana G. Whitney	135	39	16	18	29	473,791
		Chad K. Murphy	144	30	22	19	21	425,720
		Oswald M. Pereira	191	21	26	24	11	338,737
		David J. McFadden	115	18	17	11	16	266,239
MNR	1/3 - 3/31	Trainer	Starts	1st	2d	3d	Win %	Earnings
		Dale Baird	149	12	31	16	8	274,804
		Scooter Davis	67	22	5	4	33	189,542
		Jeffrey A. Radosevich	44	7	7	4	16	106,336
		J. Michael Baird	29	7	5	3	24	106,276
		John W. Baird	68	8	6	9	12	103,718

Track	Dates	Category	Starts	1st	2d	3d	Win %	Earnings
MOF	5/8 - 5/16	Jockey	Starts	1st	2d	3d	Win %	Earnings
		Stephen Michael Karr	16	4	5	4	25	7,428
		Charles Lyn McClellan	17	4	3	6	24	6,928
		Terry Lee Gard	8	3	1	0	38	4,111
		Anna M. Barrio	14	1	2	1	7	2,941
		Rick Oliver	14	2	0	2	14	2,899
MOF	5/8 - 5/16	Trainer	Starts	1st	2d	3d	Win %	Earnings
		Wiley Aker	6	2	1	1	33	3,270
		Eddy Lenard May	7	1	5	1	14	3,175
		Lyndel G. Rutherford	10	2	1	1	20	2,810
		Juan Pablo Silva	4	2	1	0	50	2,693
		Ira Price	4	2	0	0	50	2,201
MPM	5/1 - 9/26	Jockey	Starts	1st	2d	3d	Win %	Earnings
		Julie Fritz	39	8	9	6	21	21,090
		Lee Gates	36	5	5	8	14	15,350
		Dale Berryhill	28	4	7	4	14	13,465
		Mike Simpson	26	4	3	6	15	11,135
		Ronald Alan Louchart	9	5	1	2	56	8,250
MPM	5/1 - 9/26	Trainer	Starts	1st	2d	3d	Win %	Earnings
		Reid Gross	34	7	11	6	21	19,530
		Larry O. Smith	29	6	8	2	21	16,020
		Denis Cluley	21	5	5	6	24	12,995
		David N. Gates	21	4	0	5	19	9,030
		Ron Raper	20	2	4	1	10	6,970
MTH	5/29 - 9/26	Jockey	Starts	1st	2d	3d	Win %	Earnings
		Joe Bravo	414	96	79	53	23	3,790,542
		Stewart Elliott	517	82	72	75	16	2,960,737
		Eibar Coa	368	85	56	41	23	2,870,235
		Charles C. Lopez	341	65	65	56	19	2,327,506
		Julian Pimentel	336	57	47	51	17	2,040,975
MTH	5/29 - 9/26	Trainer	Starts	1st	2d	3d	Win %	Earnings
		Timothy A. Hills	182	36	29	26	20	1,161,244
		Gamaliel Vazquez	171	27	27	20	16	825,660
		Patrick L. Biancone	11	6	1	1	55	811,940
		Todd A. Pletcher	79	14	11	13	18	771,610
		Richard E. Dutrow, Jr.	79	24	12	16	30	762,220
NMP	9/3 - 9/19	Jockey	Starts	1st	2d	3d	Win %	Earnings
		Willie Belmonte	65	16	10	6	25	37,455
		Edgar Paucar	42	16	9	6	38	35,215
		Jesse Hall	70	10	11	17	14	30,760
		Keturah E. Obed	60	8	7	8	13	23,810
		Marino Carlos	59	7	10	8	12	23,515
NMP	9/3 - 9/19	Trainer	Starts	1st	2d	3d	Win %	Earnings
		Samuel J. Keyrouze	63	8	9	8	13	25,330
		Tom Crowley	26	5	2	7	19	12,540
		Anthony Tamburino	35	2	5	6	6	10,690
		Jason G. Grudzien	10	6	1	1	60	10,360
		William E. Hamer, Sr.	20	4	4	0	20	10,120
NP	6/25 - 10/30	Jockey	Starts	1st	2d	3d	Win %	Earnings
		Quincy Welch	474	108	84	68	23	1,469,512
		Rickey Walcott	428	88	67	66	21	1,157,460
		Real E. Simard	448	67	61	41	15	963,458
		Leanne M. Painter	428	55	73	56	13	913,796
		Shannon Beauregard	420	61	65	71	15	783,199
NP	6/25 - 10/30	Trainer	Starts	1st	2d	3d	Win %	Earnings
		Ron K. Smith	214	39	36	27	18	635,441
		Joan Petrowski	219	29	21	27	13	457,236
		Dale L. Saunders	153	30	30	17	20	425,143
		Rick Hedge	92	17	8	9	18	315,025
		Stuart C. Simon	140	19	18	21	14	305,977
OP	1/23 - 4/10	Jockey	Starts	1st	2d	3d	Win %	Earnings
		John McKee	384	71	69	51	18	1,694,028
		Timothy T. Doocy	351	52	51	42	15	1,063,268
		Terry J. Thompson	341	46	39	44	13	926,892
		Jamie Theriot	253	49	46	24	19	806,694
		Stewart Elliott	5	3	0	1	60	781,500

Track	Dates	Name	Starts	1st	2d	3d	Win %	Earnings
OP	1/23 - 4/10	Trainer	Starts	1st	2d	3d	Win %	Earnings
		Robert E. Holthus	117	27	21	16	23	866,538
		John C. Servis	29	4	3	3	14	855,550
		Cole Norman	205	56	36	21	27	818,742
		Steven M. Asmussen	79	33	12	13	42	744,870
		Donnie K. Von Hemel	94	16	15	17	17	470,720
OTC	3/15	Jockey	Starts	1st	2d	3d	Win %	Earnings
		Cornelio H. Velasquez	3	1	1	0	33	81,500
		Edgar S. Prado	5	2	0	1	40	74,500
		Frank Lovato, Jr.	1	1	0	0	100	60,000
		Pat Day	3	1	1	1	33	39,000
		Patrick Husbands	2	1	0	0	50	32,800
OTC	3/15	Trainer	Starts	1st	2d	3d	Win %	Earnings
		Edward Plesa, Jr.	3	1	1	1	33	60,000
		Rebecca Maker	1	1	0	0	100	60,000
		William P. White	1	1	0	0	100	60,000
		Mark E. Casse	2	1	0	0	50	30,000
		Philip A. Gleaves	1	1	0	0	100	24,000
PEN	1/2 - 12/30	Jockey	Starts	1st	2d	3d	Win %	Earnings
		Emilio Flores	1148	150	174	144	13	1,320,152
		Thomas Clifton	833	166	114	103	20	1,299,170
		William P. Otero	959	166	127	146	17	1,245,886
		Vladimir Diaz	939	131	145	124	14	1,136,789
		Luis A. Belmonte	749	92	105	86	12	778,266
PEN	1/2 - 12/30	Trainer	Starts	1st	2d	3d	Win %	Earnings
		Bruce M. Kravets	783	145	110	97	19	995,904
		John Charles Zimmerman	350	110	45	48	31	767,860
		Jose A. Martinez	651	73	100	102	11	600,886
		David W. Geist	401	63	68	58	16	592,653
		Harry F. Thompson, Jr.	551	84	91	69	15	569,504
PHA	6/23 - 12/31	Jockey	Starts	1st	2d	3d	Win %	Earnings
		Anthony S. Black	496	109	82	72	22	1,607,923
		Harry Vega	469	101	58	69	22	1,409,136
		Jose Luis Flores	542	107	73	69	20	1,324,414
		Nick Santagata	478	65	78	60	14	1,066,004
		Victor H. Molina	355	56	57	49	16	991,630
PHA	6/23 - 12/31	Trainer	Starts	1st	2d	3d	Win %	Earnings
		Scott A. Lake	251	71	46	35	28	821,625
		Guadalupe Preciado	213	41	35	32	19	702,041
		Anthony Correnti	188	30	32	19	16	490,985
		John C. Servis	122	32	18	16	26	470,369
		Edward T. Allard	130	34	12	12	26	432,515
PHA	1/1 - 6/22	Jockey	Starts	1st	2d	3d	Win %	Earnings
		Stewart Elliott	467	106	92	61	23	1,377,969
		Harry Vega	322	62	62	34	19	811,525
		Jose Luis Flores	335	61	47	59	18	760,609
		Victor H. Molina	253	43	38	37	17	655,057
		David Mello	367	48	62	61	13	605,212
PHA	1/1 - 6/22	Trainer	Starts	1st	2d	3d	Win %	Earnings
		Scott A. Lake	286	65	52	52	23	746,553
		Guadalupe Preciado	186	44	36	21	24	543,473
		Anthony Correnti	127	20	19	19	16	365,800
		Ramon Preciado	107	27	14	19	25	362,116
		Edward T. Allard	98	28	21	13	29	348,404
PIM	9/9 - 12/31	Jockey	Starts	1st	2d	3d	Win %	Earnings
		Ryan Fogelsonger	383	83	54	58	22	1,666,435
		Steve D. Hamilton	287	46	41	41	16	910,765
		Abel Castellano, Jr.	210	32	26	34	15	828,940
		Eric Camacho	297	53	50	38	18	743,780
		Luis Garcia	282	31	36	54	11	670,435
PIM	9/9 - 12/31	Trainer	Starts	1st	2d	3d	Win %	Earnings
		Richard W. Small	77	19	17	12	25	485,010
		Dale Capuano	139	30	12	19	22	478,765
		Mark Shuman	122	17	13	18	14	413,020
		Rodney Jenkins	84	21	17	12	25	380,530
		Edmond D. Gaudet	81	15	17	16	19	369,580

Track	Dates	Name	Starts	1st	2d	3d	Win %	Earnings
PIM	7/31 - 8/27	Jockey	Starts	1st	2d	3d	Win %	Earnings
		Erick D. Rodriguez	101	16	14	23	16	302,970
		Horacio Karamanos	89	14	19	15	16	281,010
		Steve D. Hamilton	95	11	13	8	12	277,445
		Christopher VanHassel	83	16	12	9	19	204,625
		Richard Monterrey	93	9	17	8	10	200,715
PIM	7/31 - 8/27	Trainer	Starts	1st	2d	3d	Win %	Earnings
		Hamilton A. Smith	23	4	5	4	17	110,100
		Dale Capuano	37	6	5	9	16	103,910
		Richard W. Small	18	2	1	3	11	97,405
		Timothy J. Tullock, Jr.	15	3	2	1	20	95,705
		Benjamin M. Feliciano, Jr.	16	4	2	4	25	92,420
PIM	3/31 - 6/6	Jockey	Starts	1st	2d	3d	Win %	Earnings
		Ryan Fogelsonger	244	46	45	48	19	937,202
		Abel Castellano, Jr.	253	40	42	42	16	892,244
		Steve D. Hamilton	282	49	48	32	17	867,093
		Ramon A. Dominguez	104	27	20	14	26	841,272
		Jozbin Z. Santana	163	36	21	23	22	709,099
PIM	3/31 - 6/6	Trainer	Starts	1st	2d	3d	Win %	Earnings
		John C. Servis	7	1	2	0	14	680,750
		Dale Capuano	84	25	17	11	30	382,305
		John J. Robb	73	14	12	7	19	322,250
		Michael Machowsky	1	1	0	0	100	300,000
		Mark Shuman	51	13	3	7	25	296,205
PLN	6/30 - 7/11	Jockey	Starts	1st	2d	3d	Win %	Earnings
		Chad Phillip Schvaneveldt	34	8	6	6	24	183,503
		Russell A. Baze	48	10	10	4	21	180,679
		Frank T. Alvarado	52	7	12	8	13	175,223
		Chance J. Rollins	58	6	14	7	10	164,268
		Joe M. Castro	33	9	5	6	27	116,950
PLN	6/30 - 7/11	Trainer	Starts	1st	2d	3d	Win %	Earnings
		Jerry Hollendorfer	40	6	10	5	15	176,433
		Brian J. Koriner	15	3	1	3	20	81,200
		Art Sherman	28	4	4	2	14	76,630
		John F. Martin	20	1	7	5	5	60,650
		Don J. Mills	14	2	2	3	14	44,690
PM	10/18/03 - 4/26/04	Jockey	Starts	1st	2d	3d	Win %	Earnings
		Juan M. Gutierrez	410	105	76	83	26	361,924
		Twyla Beckner	376	53	64	51	14	230,584
		Joe A. Crispin	329	73	49	47	22	228,645
		Duane Lee D'Amico	326	51	48	38	16	165,217
		Melissa Peery	301	46	47	29	15	157,461
PM	10/18/03 - 4/26/04	Trainer	Starts	1st	2d	3d	Win %	Earnings
		Jim Fergason	206	50	41	36	24	165,300
		Jonathan Nance	195	40	38	25	21	159,532
		Ben Root	166	32	29	20	19	132,970
		Delmer L. Webb	103	28	19	9	27	110,232
		Jim Keen	210	27	25	35	13	88,015
PRM	7/9 - 9/25	Jockey	Starts	1st	2d	3d	Win %	Earnings
		Timothy T. Doocy	245	54	48	44	22	809,131
		Glenn W. Corbett	223	49	28	31	22	635,076
		James Lopez	234	34	39	27	15	566,621
		Alex Birzer	226	32	38	33	14	562,040
		Jason R. Eads	151	14	23	13	9	297,262
PRM	7/9 - 9/25	Trainer	Starts	1st	2d	3d	Win %	Earnings
		Dick R. Clark	191	43	25	21	23	582,076
		Timothy Mark Gleason	131	26	31	21	20	342,459
		David D. McShane	110	20	13	17	18	289,323
		Kelly R. Von Hemel	80	16	9	11	20	275,103
		Ray E. Tracy, Jr.	72	9	14	4	13	184,082
PRM	4/16 - 7/4	Jockey	Starts	1st	2d	3d	Win %	Earnings
		Timothy T. Doocy	402	78	80	53	19	1,295,717
		Terry J. Thompson	290	61	47	51	21	956,120
		Glenn W. Corbett	321	58	64	40	18	921,239
		Alex Birzer	369	55	39	59	15	742,367
		Ken A. Shino	253	47	32	32	19	543,022

Track	Dates	Name	Starts	1st	2d	3d	Win %	Earnings
PRM	4/16 - 7/4	Trainer	Starts	1st	2d	3d	Win %	Earnings
		Dick R. Clark	250	52	56	27	21	792,090
		Kelly R. Von Hemel	134	32	15	27	24	530,039
		Stanley W. Roberts	181	35	44	19	19	397,226
		Don Von Hemel	66	16	14	14	24	352,301
		Paul M. Pearson	95	12	10	21	13	337,990
PRV	7/7 - 7/10	Jockey	Starts	1st	2d	3d	Win %	Earnings
		Joe A. Crispin	24	10	4	3	42	19,415
		Ty Dangerfield	21	3	9	1	14	10,438
		Roger Butterfly	21	3	2	1	14	8,210
		Twyla Beckner	21	2	4	7	10	8,083
		Tim Neal	19	3	2	6	16	7,634
PRV	7/7 - 7/10	Trainer	Starts	1st	2d	3d	Win %	Earnings
		Scott Nance	7	3	1	2	43	5,798
		Tom Farrell	5	2	1	1	40	4,045
		Jaqueline Smith	4	2	1	0	50	3,800
		Judi Yearout	4	2	0	0	50	3,300
		Lyle Perry, Sr.	3	1	2	0	33	3,150
RD	6/27 - 9/6	Jockey	Starts	1st	2d	3d	Win %	Earnings
		Dean A. Sarvis	352	83	53	44	24	438,681
		Perry Wayne Ouzts	366	66	49	55	18	434,868
		Hector L. Rosario, Jr.	279	49	41	38	18	361,487
		Jeff Johnston	169	30	34	16	18	280,959
		Mathieu G. Adam	238	27	31	35	11	224,760
RD	6/27 - 9/6	Trainer	Starts	1st	2d	3d	Win %	Earnings
		Timothy E. Hamm	25	10	4	2	40	169,410
		Michael W. Dickinson	1	1	0	0	100	120,000
		Luis Albert Palacios	77	13	12	9	17	111,191
		Bernard S. Flint	4	2	1	0	50	100,000
		Joe Woodard	75	14	8	12	19	81,006
RD	4/9 - 6/26	Jockey	Starts	1st	2d	3d	Win %	Earnings
		Dean A. Sarvis	326	84	50	49	26	519,506
		Perry Wayne Ouzts	360	67	65	60	19	426,303
		Rodney A. Prescott	185	28	22	31	15	189,600
		Hector L. Rosario, Jr.	229	29	32	40	13	187,902
		Mathieu G. Adam	213	20	28	28	9	152,698
RD	4/9 - 6/26	Trainer	Starts	1st	2d	3d	Win %	Earnings
		James E. Morgan	43	14	9	3	33	116,001
		Luis Albert Palacios	74	12	16	17	16	104,330
		Kris Nemann	45	11	7	8	24	100,906
		Joe Woodard	86	16	15	11	19	81,875
		Lori Grace	8	5	1	1	63	56,073
RET	7/23 - 9/25	Jockey	Starts	1st	2d	3d	Win %	Earnings
		Roman Chapa	210	58	36	40	28	589,230
		Casey T. Lambert	132	31	18	24	23	393,735
		Terry A. Stanton	159	30	24	24	19	306,485
		Amanda L. Crandall	214	34	25	31	16	267,850
		Jeremy Beasley	105	10	25	11	10	255,350
RET	7/23 - 9/25	Trainer	Starts	1st	2d	3d	Win %	Earnings
		Danny Pish	145	41	35	22	28	389,050
		Steven M. Asmussen	57	9	10	16	16	224,910
		John G. Locke	114	18	15	16	16	210,445
		Tommie T. Morgan	76	16	14	7	21	141,735
		R. Paul Duhon	51	8	8	6	16	123,025
RIL	1/17 - 2/29	Jockey	Starts	1st	2d	3d	Win %	Earnings
		Fernando Manuel Gamez	60	13	11	12	22	22,418
		Stephen Michael Karr	66	11	13	8	17	20,386
		Todd J. Nuttall	66	12	12	10	18	19,998
		James Daniel Schwartz	51	15	4	8	29	19,543
		Anna M. Barrio	44	9	5	7	20	14,878
RIL	1/17 - 2/29	Trainer	Starts	1st	2d	3d	Win %	Earnings
		Bill K. Earle	26	8	4	6	31	13,139
		Gene K. Wilson	30	4	8	6	13	8,040
		Laurie Jones	31	4	4	4	13	7,099
		Eddie Tellez	20	2	8	3	10	5,852
		Ceasar J. Lopez	13	4	3	0	31	5,698

Track	Dates	Jockey/Trainer	Starts	1st	2d	3d	Win %	Earnings
RKM	9/5	Jockey	Starts	1st	2d	3d	Win %	Earnings
		Orlando Bocachica	3	2	1	0	67	22,700
		Edwin Molinari	3	1	0	0	33	7,750
		Jill Ann Jellison	2	0	1	0	0	3,400
		Tammi Piermarini	3	0	1	0	0	3,400
		Alfredo Clemente	3	0	0	2	0	2,850
RKM	9/5	Trainer	Starts	1st	2d	3d	Win %	Earnings
		George R. Handy	2	2	0	0	100	20,400
		Lucy Delgado	1	1	0	0	100	6,900
		Robert A. Raymond	1	0	1	0	0	3,400
		Thomas J. Ryan	2	0	1	0	0	3,400
		Thomas S. McCooey, Jr.	2	0	0	1	0	2,550
RP	8/6 - 12/5	Jockey	Starts	1st	2d	3d	Win %	Earnings
		Monte Clifton Berry	344	91	63	41	26	738,383
		Quincy Hamilton	445	94	66	53	21	692,647
		Nena Matz	402	65	71	62	16	606,255
		Kevin Leon Cogburn	336	43	58	57	13	433,820
		Curtis Kimes	412	38	48	42	9	336,472
RP	8/6 - 12/5	Trainer	Starts	1st	2d	3d	Win %	Earnings
		Donnie K. Von Hemel	144	35	28	17	24	406,274
		Roger F. Engel	92	36	12	12	39	202,625
		Joe S. Offolter	158	25	19	15	16	186,816
		Rick S. Engel	73	14	17	9	19	155,753
		Ricky J. Gustafson	47	14	9	6	30	152,375
RUI	5/28 - 9/6	Jockey	Starts	1st	2d	3d	Win %	Earnings
		Alfredo J. Juarez, Jr.	131	34	20	27	26	333,149
		Jorge Martin Bourdieu	167	27	35	24	16	306,062
		Carlos D. Madeira	145	34	18	25	23	267,130
		Perry S. Whetstone	157	22	30	25	14	254,060
		Oscar Ceballos	137	22	19	21	16	167,327
RUI	5/28 - 9/6	Trainer	Starts	1st	2d	3d	Win %	Earnings
		Todd W. Fincher	52	17	14	10	33	247,886
		O. Dwain Grissom	83	16	14	7	19	172,443
		Ralph W. Black, Jr.	97	16	18	16	16	152,734
		Joel H. Marr	83	18	10	14	22	149,778
		Henry Dominguez	79	15	14	18	19	144,286
SA	9/29 - 10/31	Jockey	Starts	1st	2d	3d	Win %	Earnings
		Corey S. Nakatani	88	21	18	13	24	1,430,982
		Rene R. Douglas	111	18	20	14	16	1,076,590
		David Romero Flores	96	12	11	20	13	957,061
		Victor Espinoza	112	19	19	14	17	861,007
		Tyler Baze	102	19	12	15	19	848,020
SA	9/29 - 10/31	Trainer	Starts	1st	2d	3d	Win %	Earnings
		Robert J. Frankel	30	10	5	3	33	1,089,140
		Doug O'Neill	71	11	11	9	15	640,150
		Mike R. Mitchell	30	13	4	4	43	448,412
		John W. Sadler	44	9	5	4	20	392,125
		Bob Baffert	45	5	9	5	11	381,833
SA	12/26/03 - 4/18/04	Jockey	Starts	1st	2d	3d	Win %	Earnings
		Victor Espinoza	509	89	99	70	17	5,590,929
		Alex O. Solis	332	79	56	49	24	4,121,001
		Tyler Baze	497	71	69	83	14	3,268,818
		Corey S. Nakatani	381	67	60	53	18	2,899,433
		Kent J. Desormeaux	233	48	34	38	21	2,859,620
SA	12/26/03 - 4/18/04	Trainer	Starts	1st	2d	3d	Win %	Earnings
		Jeff Mullins	166	45	34	16	27	2,419,818
		Robert J. Frankel	130	34	27	21	26	2,247,987
		Bob Baffert	166	27	18	21	16	1,655,344
		Doug O'Neill	241	42	37	29	17	1,644,961
		Michael Machowsky	52	7	7	10	13	1,582,147
SAC	8/25 - 9/6	Jockey	Starts	1st	2d	3d	Win %	Earnings
		Victor Miranda	52	12	7	4	23	106,344
		David G. Lopez	39	12	4	9	31	103,479
		Ryan Morris	64	10	2	13	16	95,776
		Macario Rodriguez	53	6	12	3	11	74,165
		Berkley R. Packer	56	6	5	8	11	67,647

Track	Dates	Name	Starts	1st	2d	3d	Win %	Earnings
SAC	8/25 - 9/6	Trainer	Starts	1st	2d	3d	Win %	Earnings
		Michael Lenzini	64	6	4	12	9	73,065
		Dennis Hopkins	42	6	7	7	14	67,185
		Rene Amescua	23	8	4	3	35	58,922
		Jerry Hollendorfer	3	1	0	1	33	46,755
		Art Sherman	2	1	1	0	50	30,910
SAF	3/27 - 4/4	Jockey	Starts	1st	2d	3d	Win %	Earnings
		Justin Vanderwoude	9	5	0	2	56	7,236
		Stephen Michael Karr	13	3	3	3	23	6,379
		Anna M. Barrio	14	3	2	0	21	5,688
		Todd J. Nuttall	12	2	2	1	17	4,279
		Rick Oliver	9	1	1	3	11	3,813
SAF	3/27 - 4/4	Trainer	Starts	1st	2d	3d	Win %	Earnings
		William H. Mahan	7	1	3	1	14	3,465
		Ceasar J. Lopez	3	2	0	1	67	3,320
		Brittany Rogers	2	1	0	0	50	2,239
		Adalberto G. Romero	1	1	0	0	100	2,108
		Eddie Tellez	2	1	0	1	50	2,024
SAR	7/28 - 9/6	Jockey	Starts	1st	2d	3d	Win %	Earnings
		Edgar S. Prado	242	39	50	32	16	3,839,977
		John R. Velazquez	227	65	28	30	29	3,565,318
		Cornelio H. Velasquez	213	26	35	24	12	1,853,127
		Jerry D. Bailey	131	29	24	23	22	1,801,956
		Javier Castellano	220	29	31	40	13	1,585,758
SAR	7/28 - 9/6	Trainer	Starts	1st	2d	3d	Win %	Earnings
		Todd A. Pletcher	120	35	19	15	29	2,155,688
		Nicholas P. Zito	59	10	8	3	17	1,275,753
		Robert J. Frankel	43	15	8	5	35	969,725
		H. Allen Jerkens	33	5	2	6	15	876,758
		D. Wayne Lukas	76	4	15	10	5	747,036
SJ	9/18 - 9/26	Jockey	Starts	1st	2d	3d	Win %	Earnings
		Anna M. Barrio	13	8	1	0	62	9,575
		Carl S. Williams	22	3	7	8	14	7,484
		Terry Lee Gard	22	3	5	8	14	7,083
		Alfredo Torres	22	3	4	3	14	6,283
		Javier A. Ortega	9	3	1	0	33	3,611
SJ	9/18 - 9/26	Trainer	Starts	1st	2d	3d	Win %	Earnings
		Gene K. Wilson	10	5	3	0	50	6,356
		Lowell N. Bunyard	6	3	1	0	50	3,901
		Ernest R. Williams	11	2	2	4	18	3,694
		Mike D. Thomas	3	3	0	0	100	3,254
		Guillermo Jimenez, Sr.	7	2	0	1	29	2,780
SOL	7/14 - 7/26	Jockey	Starts	1st	2d	3d	Win %	Earnings
		Chance J. Rollins	54	10	8	8	19	155,222
		Chad Phillip Schvaneveldt	25	10	2	2	40	127,455
		Russell A. Baze	37	10	10	4	27	117,670
		Francisco Duran	52	8	5	7	15	107,265
		Joe M. Castro	33	5	7	6	15	99,100
SOL	7/14 - 7/26	Trainer	Starts	1st	2d	3d	Win %	Earnings
		Jerry Hollendorfer	20	7	5	2	35	122,005
		Dennis Hopkins	15	3	2	2	20	43,685
		Armando Lage	14	4	3	2	29	43,340
		Wesley A. Ward	10	2	3	4	20	38,198
		Art Sherman	15	4	3	1	27	37,975
SON	4/24 - 5/2	Jockey	Starts	1st	2d	3d	Win %	Earnings
		Stephen Michael Karr	16	4	1	4	25	5,734
		Alfredo Torres	12	1	3	1	8	4,528
		Charles Lyn McClellan	15	2	3	1	13	4,334
		Anna M. Barrio	17	2	3	2	12	4,253
		Flavio Lozano	13	3	2	1	23	4,039
SON	4/24 - 5/2	Trainer	Starts	1st	2d	3d	Win %	Earnings
		Pablo C. Figueroa, Sr.	2	2	0	0	100	3,724
		Ceasar J. Lopez	3	2	0	0	67	2,297
		Lowell N. Bunyard	4	2	0	1	50	2,158
		Robert M. Pledge	4	1	1	0	25	2,022
		Guillermo Jimenez, Sr.	4	1	0	2	25	1,757

Track	Dates	Jockey/Trainer	Starts	1st	2d	3d	Win %	Earnings
SR	7/28 - 8/9	Jockey	Starts	1st	2d	3d	Win %	Earnings
		Russell A. Baze	61	15	14	10	25	250,903
		Chad Phillip Schvaneveldt	34	12	2	4	35	213,326
		Frank T. Alvarado	33	5	3	11	15	128,065
		Ronald J. Warren, Jr.	26	8	5	4	31	124,193
		Francisco Duran	43	7	5	6	16	115,425
SR	7/28 - 8/9	Trainer	Starts	1st	2d	3d	Win %	Earnings
		Jerry Hollendorfer	32	8	7	6	25	190,320
		John F. Martin	18	8	1	2	44	94,431
		Greg Gilchrist	9	5	0	1	56	72,900
		John A. Shirreffs	1	1	0	0	100	55,085
		Keith Bennett	8	3	2	2	38	54,405
SRP	8/2 - 11/2	Jockey	Starts	1st	2d	3d	Win %	Earnings
		Ken S. Tohill	164	50	33	27	30	453,468
		Frank Albert Gonsalves	147	19	25	21	13	274,916
		Brian James Theriot	110	17	18	16	15	137,991
		Alfredo J. Juarez, Jr.	55	15	10	5	27	122,179
		Robert W. Johnson	111	12	21	11	11	109,783
SRP	8/2 - 11/2	Trainer	Starts	1st	2d	3d	Win %	Earnings
		Gary W. Cross	48	16	9	4	33	140,682
		Dan H. Dennison	39	17	7	4	44	127,923
		H. Ray Ashford, Jr.	48	10	13	5	21	118,786
		Patricia K. Shirley	27	9	5	1	33	99,340
		Mitch T. Lane	37	7	5	10	19	90,085
STK	6/16 - 6/27	Jockey	Starts	1st	2d	3d	Win %	Earnings
		Ken S. Tohill	52	14	11	10	27	118,961
		Macario Rodriguez	56	11	8	9	20	98,122
		Carlos Ignacio Silva	36	7	9	5	19	70,570
		Ryan Morris	52	3	5	9	6	60,894
		Hector R. Romero	16	5	4	1	31	50,798
STK	6/16 - 6/27	Trainer	Starts	1st	2d	3d	Win %	Earnings
		Michael Lenzini	30	2	2	4	7	29,486
		Barry Holmes	5	5	0	0	100	27,815
		Art Sherman	9	2	3	1	22	25,501
		Craig W. Robertson	8	2	1	1	25	25,410
		William E. Morey	14	2	2	2	14	20,723
STP	4/2 - 6/20	Jockey	Starts	1st	2d	3d	Win %	Earnings
		Quincy Welch	314	65	51	56	21	803,249
		Rickey Walcott	273	50	47	40	18	678,177
		Leanne M. Painter	294	43	35	47	15	578,191
		Desmond Bryan	260	43	34	31	17	542,812
		Real E. Simard	271	43	31	36	16	514,809
STP	4/2 - 6/20	Trainer	Starts	1st	2d	3d	Win %	Earnings
		Ron K. Smith	131	29	18	16	22	387,161
		Dale L. Saunders	126	20	14	16	16	271,437
		Joan Petrowski	127	17	20	12	13	264,001
		Ron Grieves	83	15	12	12	18	199,893
		Rodney Haynes	99	18	16	16	18	199,689
SUD	4/3 - 5/2	Jockey	Starts	1st	2d	3d	Win %	Earnings
		Jay Conklin	35	10	8	7	29	15,742
		Mark Allen Boag	34	8	5	8	24	12,478
		David Deforest Brown	37	7	7	6	19	11,479
		Ronald Joseph Bilodeau	36	7	8	3	19	11,276
		Peter McAleney	22	3	4	4	14	5,758
SUD	4/3 - 5/2	Trainer	Starts	1st	2d	3d	Win %	Earnings
		Robert L. Lawrence	16	7	4	2	44	9,960
		James R. Craig	28	8	3	4	29	9,776
		A. Lynn Homer	31	7	4	3	23	9,372
		Marion Stitzel	22	3	2	4	14	6,084
		Tracy Lebret	26	4	4	2	15	5,610
SUF	5/1 - 11/30	Jockey	Starts	1st	2d	3d	Win %	Earnings
		Winston Albert Thompson	742	154	139	114	21	1,556,866
		Josiah Francis Hampshire, Jr.	634	143	83	93	23	1,541,825
		Dyn Panell	535	127	75	70	24	1,417,086
		Tammi Piermarini	727	114	120	88	16	1,195,044
		Orlando Bocachica	527	75	82	74	14	843,494

Track	Dates	Name	Starts	1st	2d	3d	Win %	Earnings
SUF	5/1 - 11/30	Trainer	Starts	1st	2d	3d	Win %	Earnings
		John Rigattieri	306	93	51	40	30	1,078,468
		Ronald J. Dandy	274	62	42	38	23	636,728
		Raymond E. Stifano	290	58	49	39	20	583,453
		Burton K. Sipp	390	51	50	44	13	409,225
		Kevin G. Clark	234	30	38	32	13	321,514
SUN	11/25/03 - 4/11/04	Jockey	Starts	1st	2d	3d	Win %	Earnings
		Ken S. Tohill	337	68	56	53	20	1,480,242
		Ricardo Jaime	343	43	40	48	13	1,448,484
		Casey T. Lambert	371	67	44	50	18	1,142,996
		Jorge Martin Bourdieu	327	43	37	43	13	980,775
		Isaias D. Enriquez	275	31	37	29	11	709,453
SUN	11/25/03 - 4/11/04	Trainer	Starts	1st	2d	3d	Win %	Earnings
		Henry Dominguez	218	40	28	23	18	1,030,811
		Steven M. Asmussen	191	53	28	35	28	1,014,708
		Joel H. Marr	135	23	15	17	17	559,110
		Ramon O. Gonzalez	176	29	26	16	16	529,364
		Fred I. Danley	98	13	11	15	13	433,023
TAM	12/13/03 - 5/2/04	Jockey	Starts	1st	2d	3d	Win %	Earnings
		Jesus Lopez Castanon	523	87	75	73	17	1,202,216
		T. D. Houghton	686	82	103	90	12	1,024,498
		Joseph C. Judice	391	69	50	40	18	768,213
		Juan Umana	456	63	63	58	14	762,376
		Russell W. Woolsey	486	61	80	53	13	703,288
TAM	12/13/03 - 5/2/04	Trainer	Starts	1st	2d	3d	Win %	Earnings
		Ronald D. Allen, Sr.	128	23	16	18	18	330,264
		Lynne M. Scace	149	25	25	22	17	298,309
		Kirk Ziadie	45	19	3	3	42	280,073
		Layne S. Giliforte	130	23	21	15	18	242,797
		Don R. Rice	171	17	17	24	10	238,307
TDN	10/7 - 12/31	Jockey	Starts	1st	2d	3d	Win %	Earnings
		Scott Spieth	244	57	38	29	23	395,385
		Huber Villa-Gomez	250	39	46	35	16	335,240
		Julio E. Felix	221	40	43	26	18	311,175
		Luis Antonio Gonzalez	229	32	29	22	14	246,546
		Daniel Centeno	200	26	27	24	13	205,862
TDN	10/7 - 12/31	Trainer	Starts	1st	2d	3d	Win %	Earnings
		Jeffrey A. Radosevich	137	32	17	11	23	190,925
		Jerry Hollendorfer	68	18	15	7	26	179,053
		Rodney C. Faulkner	130	24	22	15	18	162,883
		Rodrigo Madrigal, Sr.	48	12	8	4	25	126,150
		Timothy E. Hamm	45	7	4	10	16	97,207
TDN	7/25 - 10/6	Jockey	Starts	1st	2d	3d	Win %	Earnings
		Luis Antonio Gonzalez	250	44	35	36	18	380,502
		Scott Spieth	198	44	23	21	22	343,517
		Huber Villa-Gomez	213	38	28	28	18	325,881
		Weldon T. Cloninger, Jr.	159	33	27	17	21	284,264
		Daniel Centeno	231	31	26	29	13	232,838
TDN	7/25 - 10/6	Trainer	Starts	1st	2d	3d	Win %	Earnings
		Jerry Hollendorfer	64	20	11	7	31	159,704
		Rodney C. Faulkner	117	24	20	12	21	157,668
		Miguel A. Feliciano	75	10	10	9	13	157,575
		Andrew Konkoly	71	17	16	8	24	120,494
		Jeffrey A. Radosevich	77	14	18	15	18	118,880
TDN	5/15 - 7/24	Jockey	Starts	1st	2d	3d	Win %	Earnings
		Luis Antonio Gonzalez	189	38	26	22	20	343,854
		Huber Villa-Gomez	225	45	31	30	20	316,501
		Weldon T. Cloninger, Jr.	205	39	35	23	19	306,065
		Willie Martinez	2	2	0	0	100	237,000
		Scott Spieth	192	28	21	21	15	228,651
TDN	5/15 - 7/24	Trainer	Starts	1st	2d	3d	Win %	Earnings
		William Bradley	1	1	0	0	100	210,000
		Timothy E. Hamm	59	10	17	7	17	184,135
		Joseph R. Martin	58	12	9	12	21	159,465
		Rodney C. Faulkner	115	24	26	8	21	145,276
		Gary L. Johnson	142	22	14	11	15	130,355

Track	Dates	Name	Starts	1st	2d	3d	Win %	Earnings
TDN	4/8 - 5/14	Jockey	Starts	1st	2d	3d	Win %	Earnings
		Huber Villa-Gomez	118	30	13	18	25	219,152
		Luis Antonio Gonzalez	113	18	11	13	16	153,350
		Scott Spieth	107	18	14	6	17	126,613
		Ricardo Feliciano	83	11	11	13	13	110,691
		Luis J. Martinez, Jr.	91	13	9	8	14	107,897
TDN	4/8 - 5/14	Trainer	Starts	1st	2d	3d	Win %	Earnings
		Rodrigo Madrigal, Sr.	30	7	6	4	23	80,588
		Gary L. Johnson	92	12	12	11	13	78,757
		Jeffrey A. Radosevich	49	12	10	4	24	73,700
		Rodney C. Faulkner	60	10	9	11	17	63,954
		Jerry Hollendorfer	24	12	3	2	50	52,275
TIL	8/12 - 8/14	Jockey	Starts	1st	2d	3d	Win %	Earnings
		Jaime Martinez	13	5	3	2	38	7,956
		Kevin C. Murray	14	5	3	2	36	7,950
		Twyla Beckner	16	3	5	3	19	6,699
		Darlene Braden	17	2	3	4	12	5,383
		Jose M. Rivera, Jr.	11	2	1	1	18	3,345
TIL	8/12 - 8/14	Trainer	Starts	1st	2d	3d	Win %	Earnings
		Judi Yearout	6	2	2	0	33	3,632
		Don D. Young	5	2	2	0	40	3,060
		Donald L. Lawrence	2	2	0	0	100	2,475
		James C. Harrell	6	1	2	1	17	2,415
		Bill Hof	6	1	2	1	17	2,320
TIM	8/28 - 9/6	Jockey	Starts	1st	2d	3d	Win %	Earnings
		Erick D. Rodriguez	48	12	13	7	25	141,755
		Eric Camacho	46	12	6	6	26	131,030
		Luis Garcia	47	5	11	4	11	89,205
		Travis L. Dunkelberger	13	4	2	3	31	77,580
		Larry C. Reynolds	22	4	4	0	18	59,520
TIM	8/28 - 9/6	Trainer	Starts	1st	2d	3d	Win %	Earnings
		Gary Capuano	9	4	1	1	44	74,040
		Benjamin M. Feliciano, Jr.	13	3	5	1	23	39,825
		Kenneth M. Cox	6	4	1	0	67	38,745
		Timothy E. Salzman	10	2	2	1	20	32,485
		Lawrence E. Horning, Jr.	1	1	0	0	100	30,000
TP	11/28 - 12/31	Jockey	Starts	1st	2d	3d	Win %	Earnings
		Dean A. Sarvis	173	39	27	22	23	438,056
		Ramsey Zimmerman	183	24	38	11	13	324,150
		William D. Troilo	109	17	12	17	16	209,973
		Rodney A. Prescott	146	16	15	17	11	183,458
		Willie Martinez	83	13	12	10	16	180,622
TP	11/28 - 12/31	Trainer	Starts	1st	2d	3d	Win %	Earnings
		Bernard S. Flint	36	7	6	5	19	144,729
		Wayne D. Mogge	20	7	5	3	35	68,985
		David R. Vance	17	3	3	2	18	64,986
		W. Elliott Walden	9	4	4	0	44	63,480
		Paul J. McGee	18	5	5	2	28	61,123
TP	9/8 - 10/7	Jockey	Starts	1st	2d	3d	Win %	Earnings
		Rafael Bejarano	146	35	29	25	24	570,987
		John McKee	124	23	22	21	19	423,121
		Willie Martinez	124	27	18	15	22	377,781
		Mark Guidry	42	10	8	11	24	257,397
		John R. Velazquez	3	1	0	0	33	231,500
TP	9/8 - 10/7	Trainer	Starts	1st	2d	3d	Win %	Earnings
		Dale L. Romans	23	5	5	3	22	328,712
		Robert E. Holthus	20	9	1	1	45	215,273
		D. Wayne Lukas	10	2	0	3	20	139,920
		Steven M. Asmussen	15	3	2	1	20	116,235
		Carl A. Nafzger	19	2	9	0	11	110,524
TP	1/1 - 4/1	Jockey	Starts	1st	2d	3d	Win %	Earnings
		Rafael Bejarano	472	150	99	65	32	2,008,233
		Jason P. Lumpkins	270	40	41	39	15	707,543
		Anthony J. D'Amico	172	29	24	29	17	665,175
		Eddie Zuniga	296	44	29	37	15	577,315
		Perry Wayne Ouzts	359	34	35	23	9	414,859

Track	Dates	Name	Starts	1st	2d	3d	Win %	Earnings
TP	1/1 - 4/1	Trainer	Starts	1st	2d	3d	Win %	Earnings
		Gregory D. Foley	71	24	13	10	34	481,950
		Bernard S. Flint	87	16	14	10	18	350,048
		John T. Toscano, Jr.	1	1	0	0	100	300,000
		Dale L. Romans	49	12	7	8	24	293,211
		S. Joseph Cain	72	17	10	7	24	207,057
TUP	9/26/03 - 5/16/04	Jockey	Starts	1st	2d	3d	Win %	Earnings
		Scott A. Stevens	610	110	97	97	18	1,087,922
		Esteban Angel Gomez	755	107	118	90	14	877,580
		Glenn W. Corbett	464	99	75	63	21	855,587
		Mick Ruis	596	132	91	80	22	825,286
		Wilson Omar Dieguez	684	115	81	93	17	822,467
TUP	9/26/03 - 5/16/04	Trainer	Starts	1st	2d	3d	Win %	Earnings
		J. Eric Kruljac	202	54	26	39	27	518,986
		Troy Bainum	255	79	50	44	31	465,964
		Don J. Mills	216	65	42	22	30	436,339
		Kevin Lewis	204	35	39	32	17	423,505
		Molly J. Pearson	204	47	29	38	23	393,638
UN	6/11 - 6/13	Jockey	Starts	1st	2d	3d	Win %	Earnings
		Jim Bob Whiteside	16	6	3	3	38	10,883
		Roger Butterfly	14	2	2	1	14	4,902
		Ronald Joseph Bilodeau	11	2	2	3	18	4,701
		David Deforest Brown	9	1	4	0	11	3,418
		Ty Dangerfield	5	2	1	0	40	3,293
UN	6/11 - 6/13	Trainer	Starts	1st	2d	3d	Win %	Earnings
		Marion Stitzel	9	3	0	1	33	5,426
		Brook Mobley	7	2	1	2	29	3,737
		Patrick Stitzel	3	2	1	0	67	3,010
		Lyle Perry, Sr.	2	2	0	0	100	2,640
		Robert L. Lawrence	4	1	2	0	25	2,282
WDS	9/20 - 10/31	Jockey	Starts	1st	2d	3d	Win %	Earnings
		Alex Birzer	157	30	23	26	19	157,636
		Kelly Michael Murray	174	22	27	28	13	140,624
		Jason R. Eads	80	15	13	12	19	122,386
		Russell Vicchrilli	105	14	15	11	13	105,343
		Ken A. Shino	102	16	19	18	16	94,126
WDS	9/20 - 10/31	Trainer	Starts	1st	2d	3d	Win %	Earnings
		Kenneth Gleason	75	11	16	9	15	114,548
		James B. McCoy	47	9	8	7	19	105,605
		Timothy Mark Gleason	72	19	11	12	26	91,321
		Leroy Hellman	36	15	6	2	42	79,191
		Temple D. Rushton	58	9	5	5	16	40,078
WMF	8/10 - 8/15	Jockey	Starts	1st	2d	3d	Win %	Earnings
		Russell David Kingrey	28	11	7	3	39	22,134
		Ivan Ortiz, Jr.	35	9	6	5	26	20,987
		Shannon Wippert	23	7	2	2	30	15,453
		Joe Holmes, Sr.	35	2	9	10	6	14,039
		Carl Hebert	34	3	6	9	9	14,013
WMF	8/10 - 8/15	Trainer	Starts	1st	2d	3d	Win %	Earnings
		John Stabenfeldt	4	4	0	0	100	6,710
		Bryan Krone	11	1	2	4	9	5,932
		Mark Buckley	11	3	1	2	27	5,781
		Doug Johnson	14	2	1	2	14	5,626
		Edward Buxbaum	9	2	3	2	22	5,340
WO	4/17 - 12/12	Jockey	Starts	1st	2d	3d	Win %	Earnings
		Todd Kabel	681	156	108	76	23	10,467,572
		Patrick Husbands	713	136	114	107	19	7,176,319
		James McAleney	668	109	89	90	16	5,790,603
		Jono C. Jones	663	90	88	81	14	5,613,667
		Emile Ramsammy	726	74	111	94	10	5,036,317
WO	4/17 - 12/12	Trainer	Starts	1st	2d	3d	Win %	Earnings
		Mark R. Frostad	176	39	22	21	22	4,343,853
		Robert P. Tiller	277	68	45	33	25	3,877,986
		Sid C. Attard	311	73	55	38	23	3,573,181
		Mark E. Casse	293	45	45	44	15	2,878,630
		Reade Baker	249	40	41	37	16	2,545,411

Track	Dates	Jockey	Starts	1st	2d	3d	Win %	Earnings
WYO	6/26 - 8/22	Jockey	Starts	1st	2d	3d	Win %	Earnings
		Travis Hamilton	24	6	5	5	25	10,190
		Melissa Marshall	19	5	3	3	26	8,316
		Tony F. Guymon	25	3	4	7	12	7,484
		Layne Davis	26	3	6	5	12	6,671
		Chris Bowen	6	2	2	1	33	4,525
WYO	6/26 - 8/22	Trainer	Starts	1st	2d	3d	Win %	Earnings
		Mike D. Taylor	15	5	4	1	33	10,248
		Terrill Gibbs	18	5	1	8	28	7,720
		Zane G. Alder	9	2	2	1	22	4,706
		Tawnja Elison	1	1	0	0	100	3,300
		Daren K. Jones	18	2	4	3	11	2,942
YAV	5/29 - 9/7	Jockey	Starts	1st	2d	3d	Win %	Earnings
		Daniel P. Vergara	202	41	42	30	20	194,877
		Wilson Omar Dieguez	184	46	35	29	25	174,030
		Lorenzo Castane Lopez	203	37	27	33	18	173,163
		Alberto R. Higuera	215	35	46	32	16	173,121
		Esteban Angel Gomez	191	38	27	31	20	164,172
YAV	5/29 - 9/7	Trainer	Starts	1st	2d	3d	Win %	Earnings
		Bill Brashears	131	39	18	21	30	126,622
		Jerry Atkin	81	17	17	14	21	81,514
		Dennis T. Sowers	51	13	11	9	25	68,196
		Jon Phil Zimmerman	76	13	15	16	17	59,463
		George Wern	60	11	9	10	18	53,866
YD	9/5 - 9/26	Jockey	Starts	1st	2d	3d	Win %	Earnings
		Russell David Kingrey	14	5	3	2	36	15,743
		Kym Espy	34	5	8	6	15	14,040
		Dan Karr	33	3	10	3	9	13,448
		Ivan Ortiz, Jr.	35	7	2	2	20	12,086
		Chad Benjamin	24	6	0	4	25	10,971
YD	9/5 - 9/26	Trainer	Starts	1st	2d	3d	Win %	Earnings
		Doug Johnson	18	3	7	1	17	11,138
		Leroy G. Coombs	3	3	0	0	100	10,085
		Edward Buxbaum	23	4	7	3	17	9,606
		Kenneth Olson	13	3	1	5	23	6,380
		Cleo Medicine Horse, Jr.	22	1	2	2	5	5,698
YKT	7/3 - 7/10	Jockey	Starts	1st	2d	3d	Win %	Earnings
		Danielle Beischer	8	2	2	1	25	2,304
		Bernie Tourangeau	9	1	3	1	11	2,020
		Frank La Forge	10	1	1	4	10	1,820
		Norbert Keshane	3	1	1	0	33	1,532
		Chad Keshane	4	1	1	1	25	1,248
YKT	7/3 - 7/10	Trainer	Starts	1st	2d	3d	Win %	Earnings
		Dana T. Keshane	6	4	1	0	67	3,692
		Mike Tourangeau	9	2	2	3	22	2,724
		Brad Ball	6	1	2	1	17	1,464
		James R. Ross	4	1	1	0	25	1,224
		William Keshane	2	1	0	1	50	888

Top Race–Winning Jockeys and Trainers, by Meet, in 2004

Track	Meet dates		Starts	1st	2d	3d	Win %	Earnings
ALB	9/10 - 9/26	Jockey	Starts	1st	2d	3d	Win %	Earnings
		Ken S. Tohill	27	11	2	5	41	142,190
		Alfredo J. Juarez, Jr.	40	8	8	2	20	99,651
		Carlos D. Madeira	21	7	3	4	33	63,779
		Jorge Martin Bourdieu	38	5	9	4	13	66,640
		Ricardo Jaime	33	4	7	3	12	56,565
ALB	9/10 - 9/26	Trainer	Starts	1st	2d	3d	Win %	Earnings
		Joel H. Marr	13	5	4	3	38	63,356
		Henry Dominguez	20	5	4	1	25	72,112
		Jose A. Gonzalez	6	4	0	1	67	11,545
		Todd W. Fincher	14	3	3	1	21	51,046
		H. Ray Ashford, Jr.	6	3	0	1	50	21,024
ALB	4/9 - 7/5	Jockey	Starts	1st	2d	3d	Win %	Earnings
		Ken S. Tohill	123	31	26	19	25	324,423
		Ricardo Jaime	102	20	12	13	20	193,632
		Tony Noguez	59	15	5	8	25	168,918
		Frank Albert Gonsalves	105	14	13	14	13	134,632
		Brian James Theriot	112	14	13	9	13	143,304
ALB	4/9 - 7/5	Trainer	Starts	1st	2d	3d	Win %	Earnings
		Henry Dominguez	69	13	11	13	19	171,940
		Gary W. Cross	65	12	9	10	18	159,239
		Jon G. Arnett	60	9	14	7	15	94,555
		Priscilla Leon	20	8	2	4	40	45,254
		Johnny R. Montes, Jr.	33	7	8	3	21	45,869
ANF	7/16 - 7/25	Jockey	Starts	1st	2d	3d	Win %	Earnings
		Richard M. Vasquez	16	7	2	4	44	17,583
		Dustin W. Williams	19	5	8	2	26	18,780
		Terry Bennett	13	2	1	4	15	4,620
		Megan Ludlow	9	2	1	0	22	3,850
		Thomas Wellington	4	2	0	0	50	12,120
ANF	7/16 - 7/25	Trainer	Starts	1st	2d	3d	Win %	Earnings
		Joe Frederick Thomas, Sr.	17	4	2	2	24	22,768
		Donald G. Black	6	3	3	0	50	7,070
		J. Sue Hunt	4	2	0	1	50	4,485
		Ellis Pugh	3	2	0	0	67	4,700
		Tyrone Gleason	10	1	5	1	10	11,505
AP	5/14 - 9/19	Jockey	Starts	1st	2d	3d	Win %	Earnings
		Rene R. Douglas	504	125	84	83	25	3,232,485
		Eusebio Razo, Jr.	496	86	68	63	17	2,386,270
		Christopher A. Emigh	504	71	73	63	14	1,911,260
		Carlos H. Marquez, Jr.	374	62	51	53	17	1,888,790
		James Graham	469	57	49	59	12	1,355,493
AP	5/14 - 9/19	Trainer	Starts	1st	2d	3d	Win %	Earnings
		Frank J. Kirby	236	32	25	26	14	696,151
		Steven M. Asmussen	141	31	24	23	22	691,151
		Chris M. Block	147	29	26	15	20	917,338
		Thomas M. Amoss	82	27	16	13	33	553,596
		Michael Stidham	111	25	18	14	23	758,709
AQU	10/27 - 12/31	Jockey	Starts	1st	2d	3d	Win %	Earnings
		Norberto Arroyo, Jr.	229	36	38	27	16	1,377,264
		Rafael Bejarano	162	33	21	25	20	1,207,781
		Pablo Fragoso	236	29	44	31	12	1,441,897
		Shaun Bridgmohan	222	28	37	37	13	1,370,677
		Aaron T. Gryder	171	22	17	22	13	829,647
AQU	10/27 - 12/31	Trainer	Starts	1st	2d	3d	Win %	Earnings
		Richard E. Dutrow, Jr.	95	29	20	14	31	1,098,328
		Scott A. Lake	68	16	4	13	24	473,015
		Gary C. Contessa	86	15	14	10	17	528,842
		Jennifer Pedersen	65	14	7	9	22	514,129
		Michael E. Hushion	50	13	6	7	26	321,155
AQU	3/10 - 5/2	Jockey	Starts	1st	2d	3d	Win %	Earnings
		Javier Castellano	155	37	25	26	24	1,508,233
		Shaun Bridgmohan	184	30	28	25	16	1,204,950
		Pablo Fragoso	163	28	29	29	17	953,431
		Michael J. Luzzi	159	28	25	23	18	1,006,889
		Richard Migliore	120	23	26	9	19	944,506

Track	Dates	Name	Starts	1st	2d	3d	Win %	Earnings
AQU	3/10 - 5/2	Trainer	Starts	1st	2d	3d	Win %	Earnings
		Gary C. Contessa	96	19	18	9	20	607,982
		Richard E. Dutrow, Jr.	73	17	11	16	23	659,713
		Bruce N. Levine	47	16	6	7	34	398,475
		H. Allen Jerkens	50	16	5	8	32	679,091
		Todd A. Pletcher	50	15	9	6	30	800,072
AQU	1/1 - 3/7	Jockey	Starts	1st	2d	3d	Win %	Earnings
		Pablo Fragoso	296	59	57	56	20	1,983,223
		Shaun Bridgmohan	252	42	43	29	17	1,362,391
		Michael J. Luzzi	203	34	33	26	17	1,224,101
		Javier Castellano	184	32	38	22	17	1,246,653
		Richard Migliore	141	31	18	22	22	1,024,388
AQU	1/1 - 3/7	Trainer	Starts	1st	2d	3d	Win %	Earnings
		Richard E. Dutrow, Jr.	90	32	26	6	36	1,111,968
		Bruce N. Levine	77	19	13	14	25	547,103
		Scott A. Lake	85	16	19	12	19	499,068
		Gary C. Contessa	102	16	17	12	16	431,075
		Jennifer Pedersen	79	14	18	14	18	671,173
ARP	7/3 - 9/6	Jockey	Starts	1st	2d	3d	Win %	Earnings
		Travis Wales	161	40	24	29	25	305,413
		Fernando S. Rojas	186	37	31	33	20	276,657
		Russell Vicchrilli	170	33	39	27	19	304,152
		Carl Mel Kutz	172	27	20	20	16	179,772
		Don Lee Frazier	151	26	18	20	17	133,795
ARP	7/3 - 9/6	Trainer	Starts	1st	2d	3d	Win %	Earnings
		Jon G. Arnett	104	31	22	12	30	160,086
		Temple D. Rushton	153	27	32	37	18	186,590
		Kenneth Gleason	151	22	36	24	15	283,176
		Ramon O. Gonzalez	89	22	11	17	25	189,561
		James E. Jones	62	21	9	12	34	134,085
ASD	5/2 - 10/3	Jockey	Starts	1st	2d	3d	Win %	Earnings
		Travis Wayne Hightower	456	98	67	63	21	849,761
		Larren Delorme	456	66	78	64	14	541,395
		Beth S. Butler	398	57	62	57	14	500,586
		Jerry Pruitt	361	57	47	49	16	436,527
		Jason Leacock	400	53	52	57	13	468,629
ASD	5/2 - 10/3	Trainer	Starts	1st	2d	3d	Win %	Earnings
		Ardell Sayler	234	40	30	26	17	307,205
		Emile J. Corbel	192	34	18	14	18	351,752
		Gary Danelson	171	29	26	31	17	244,527
		Blair A. Miller	149	25	25	21	17	233,912
		Chad Torevell	172	24	28	23	14	250,295
ATL	5/5 - 5/19	Jockey	Starts	1st	2d	3d	Win %	Earnings
		Danielle Hodsdon	6	3	0	1	50	27,350
		Stewart Elliott	10	3	0	0	30	37,910
		Gus M. Brown	7	2	3	1	29	43,700
		Richard A. Bracho	12	2	3	1	17	41,740
		Cyril Murphy	5	2	0	2	40	19,600
ATL	5/5 - 5/19	Trainer	Starts	1st	2d	3d	Win %	Earnings
		Thomas H. Voss	11	3	2	2	27	38,350
		Jonathan E. Sheppard	9	3	0	3	33	40,260
		Patricia Farro	5	2	0	1	40	28,970
		Paul Douglas Fout	6	2	0	0	33	16,700
		F. Bruce Miller	9	1	1	1	11	43,650
ATO	9/17 - 9/19	Jockey	Starts	1st	2d	3d	Win %	Earnings
		Perry Compton	17	4	4	1	24	37,481
		Dennis Michael Collins	17	4	3	2	24	38,206
		Armando Martinez	17	3	2	4	18	31,735
		Daniel Lee Beck	16	3	2	3	19	30,380
		Lee Sensenbach	17	1	2	1	6	18,520
ATO	9/17 - 9/19	Trainer	Starts	1st	2d	3d	Win %	Earnings
		David C. Anderson	7	3	1	0	43	19,505
		David Grimes	4	2	1	0	50	15,240
		Paul Linafelter	3	2	1	0	67	13,800
		Daniel Coughlin	6	2	0	2	33	14,131
		Andrew H. Johnson	3	1	1	0	33	11,095

Track	Dates	Name	Starts	1st	2d	3d	Win %	Earnings
BEL	9/10 - 10/24	Jockey	Starts	1st	2d	3d	Win %	Earnings
		John R. Velazquez	201	58	27	26	29	3,623,363
		Cornelio H. Velasquez	235	33	31	51	14	2,266,358
		Javier Castellano	203	32	29	28	16	2,568,362
		Edgar S. Prado	179	31	39	16	17	2,443,263
		Richard Migliore	145	28	19	20	19	1,183,947
BEL	9/10 - 10/24	Trainer	Starts	1st	2d	3d	Win %	Earnings
		Todd A. Pletcher	90	23	12	12	26	1,690,737
		Bruce N. Levine	45	17	9	2	38	525,123
		Richard E. Dutrow, Jr.	54	16	9	6	30	781,079
		Robert J. Frankel	52	13	11	5	25	1,674,573
		Claude R. McGaughey III	28	10	5	5	36	478,075
BEL	5/5 - 7/25	Jockey	Starts	1st	2d	3d	Win %	Earnings
		John R. Velazquez	346	77	55	51	22	3,896,779
		Edgar S. Prado	318	73	48	49	23	3,634,432
		Javier Castellano	310	50	56	44	16	2,315,369
		Jerry D. Bailey	171	44	34	22	26	2,608,893
		Jose A. Santos	268	37	37	36	14	1,822,367
BEL	5/5 - 7/25	Trainer	Starts	1st	2d	3d	Win %	Earnings
		Todd A. Pletcher	142	33	28	22	23	2,092,122
		Richard E. Dutrow, Jr.	97	21	14	17	22	778,453
		William I. Mott	84	20	19	9	24	837,100
		H. Allen Jerkens	103	20	14	14	19	1,119,763
		Robert J. Frankel	49	17	11	7	35	1,359,286
BEU	9/18 - 12/21	Jockey	Starts	1st	2d	3d	Win %	Earnings
		Marco A. Ccamaque	407	84	65	66	21	411,910
		Ivan R. Gonzalez	339	57	45	40	17	326,999
		Perry Wayne Ouzts	231	39	35	24	17	192,541
		Hector L. Rosario, Jr.	194	35	22	16	18	244,237
		Paul M. Nolan	332	29	43	51	9	175,829
BEU	9/18 - 12/21	Trainer	Starts	1st	2d	3d	Win %	Earnings
		Joseph Clark Faulkner	127	33	21	14	26	127,613
		Reid Gross	163	31	19	19	19	112,885
		Jake S. Radosevich	192	26	25	25	14	128,008
		Luis Albert Palacios	75	18	11	10	24	175,878
		Rinzy Nocero	140	17	22	26	12	86,171
BEU	1/10 - 5/1	Jockey	Starts	1st	2d	3d	Win %	Earnings
		Ivan R. Gonzalez	341	75	56	57	22	370,199
		Christian Rojas	343	66	56	34	19	299,989
		Marco A. Ccamaque	403	65	68	54	16	388,937
		Jose Luis Calo	361	48	49	49	13	239,233
		Ramon Luna	336	34	38	30	10	187,631
BEU	1/10 - 5/1	Trainer	Starts	1st	2d	3d	Win %	Earnings
		Jake S. Radosevich	138	33	18	28	24	138,896
		Reid Gross	178	23	19	20	13	100,811
		Jerry L. Balo	57	20	8	6	35	94,551
		William D. Cowans	58	18	16	6	31	86,063
		Rinzy Nocero	103	18	11	20	17	80,539
BM	9/3 - 11/7	Jockey	Starts	1st	2d	3d	Win %	Earnings
		Russell A. Baze	283	92	52	49	33	1,429,386
		Dennis Carr	247	41	43	35	17	877,229
		Francisco Duran	241	40	44	33	17	666,809
		Ronald J. Warren, Jr.	236	39	46	36	17	865,393
		Roberto M. Gonzalez	218	31	34	34	14	617,220
BM	9/3 - 11/7	Trainer	Starts	1st	2d	3d	Win %	Earnings
		Jerry Hollendorfer	209	47	42	36	22	993,978
		Art Sherman	102	31	18	11	30	478,590
		John F. Martin	99	25	25	16	25	508,927
		Armando Lage	125	21	11	19	17	270,591
		William E. Morey	85	20	17	8	24	259,978
BM	4/7 - 6/20	Jockey	Starts	1st	2d	3d	Win %	Earnings
		Russell A. Baze	287	90	59	30	31	1,391,016
		Chad Phillip Schvaneveldt	234	51	39	34	22	956,040
		Ronald J. Warren, Jr.	235	44	30	33	19	904,016
		Roberto M. Gonzalez	233	37	33	29	16	745,530
		Dennis Carr	194	31	34	38	16	655,842

Track	Dates	Name	Starts	1st	2d	3d	Win %	Earnings
BM	4/7 - 6/20	Trainer	Starts	1st	2d	3d	Win %	Earnings
		Jerry Hollendorfer	256	64	53	36	25	1,421,161
		Art Sherman	148	37	17	27	25	558,509
		John F. Martin	97	22	20	9	23	407,958
		William E. Morey	87	19	17	8	22	218,790
		Armando Lage	133	17	14	19	13	219,265
BMF	8/11 - 8/23	Jockey	Starts	1st	2d	3d	Win %	Earnings
		Dennis Carr	52	14	8	9	27	179,872
		Francisco Duran	55	13	9	9	24	133,719
		Ronald J. Warren, Jr.	48	13	6	5	27	166,385
		David G. Lopez	47	11	10	9	23	137,233
		Chance J. Rollins	52	8	9	9	15	133,913
BMF	8/11 - 8/23	Trainer	Starts	1st	2d	3d	Win %	Earnings
		John F. Martin	17	7	2	1	41	101,002
		Jerry Hollendorfer	34	6	5	6	18	100,075
		Armando Lage	36	6	5	3	17	64,166
		William E. Morey	18	6	2	2	33	70,080
		Art Sherman	19	4	3	5	21	46,790
BOI	5/1 - 8/15	Jockey	Starts	1st	2d	3d	Win %	Earnings
		Berkley R. Packer	210	63	35	36	30	210,832
		Cameron Colledge	208	55	36	32	26	132,199
		Jay Conklin	137	46	28	18	34	162,361
		Casey Greene	156	20	22	26	13	50,567
		Dirk Crane	90	13	13	15	14	33,168
BOI	5/1 - 8/15	Trainer	Starts	1st	2d	3d	Win %	Earnings
		Kevin Knudsen	123	22	23	25	18	54,836
		Kenneth E. McReynolds	48	20	6	10	42	69,032
		Steve Duschka	88	15	18	10	17	35,611
		Gary Simpson	57	13	11	5	23	33,342
		Cindy Rodgers	48	13	5	6	27	49,999
BRD	8/6 - 11/8	Jockey	Starts	1st	2d	3d	Win %	Earnings
		Stephen Randle	28	5	5	0	18	11,798
		Joel William Allen	39	5	3	3	13	10,800
		Joyce Epsteen	23	5	1	2	22	8,244
		Fernando Camacho	44	4	8	8	9	20,345
		Bryan Ernst	41	4	6	6	10	12,911
BRD	8/6 - 11/8	Trainer	Starts	1st	2d	3d	Win %	Earnings
		Clifton D. Brooks	21	5	4	1	24	10,090
		Jim Dale Brooks	27	3	6	5	11	12,724
		Marty R. Ireland	9	3	3	2	33	8,620
		Robert L. Roughton	10	3	2	0	30	4,940
		Jose M. Gonzalez	8	3	0	2	38	4,968
BRD	2/21 - 5/1	Jockey	Starts	1st	2d	3d	Win %	Earnings
		Janet Leah Wilson	67	13	11	9	19	40,225
		Wendell John Hilburn	45	8	5	5	18	22,799
		William Thomas Thomason	31	7	2	1	23	12,481
		Joel William Allen	37	6	3	7	16	13,116
		Bryan Ernst	45	5	7	3	11	13,978
BRD	2/21 - 5/1	Trainer	Starts	1st	2d	3d	Win %	Earnings
		Clifton D. Brooks	22	10	0	3	45	14,697
		John Clark Garvin	11	5	2	2	45	14,805
		J. Alan Williams	19	5	1	2	26	9,322
		James M. Limbaugh	24	4	2	3	17	8,764
		Ron Moquett	6	3	0	0	50	3,768
BRN	9/11 - 9/12	Jockey	Starts	1st	2d	3d	Win %	Earnings
		Nikeela Black	9	3	1	1	33	4,515
		Tim Neal	12	2	2	2	17	4,405
		Twyla Beckner	12	2	1	4	17	4,275
		Joe S. Holmes, Jr.	7	2	0	0	29	3,316
		Jaime Martinez	11	1	4	1	9	3,627
BRN	9/11 - 9/12	Trainer	Starts	1st	2d	3d	Win %	Earnings
		Marion Stitzel	8	3	1	0	38	5,446
		Steve Duschka	5	2	1	0	40	2,710
		Don D. Young	7	1	2	1	14	2,476
		Bill Hof	8	1	1	1	13	2,345
		Raymond Wilson	5	1	1	1	20	1,830

Track	Dates	Name	Starts	1st	2d	3d	Win %	Earnings
CBY	5/14 - 9/6	Jockey	Starts	1st	2d	3d	Win %	Earnings
		Derek C. Bell	384	92	75	48	24	1,183,094
		Seth B. Martinez	375	74	68	62	20	1,089,277
		Martin Escobar	382	59	59	39	15	829,201
		Paul M. Nolan	396	57	66	50	14	660,274
		Scott A. Stevens	303	48	43	52	16	747,967
CBY	5/14 - 9/6	Trainer	Starts	1st	2d	3d	Win %	Earnings
		Hugh H. Robertson	181	53	32	29	29	866,805
		Bernell B. Rhone	299	43	45	34	14	565,089
		David Van Winkle	212	40	44	31	19	584,616
		Michael E. Biehler	157	32	28	26	20	603,763
		Jamie Ness	205	29	35	32	14	292,573
CD	10/31 - 11/27	Jockey	Starts	1st	2d	3d	Win %	Earnings
		John McKee	166	27	24	20	16	1,106,274
		Brian Joseph Hernandez, Jr.	176	23	24	30	13	811,050
		Pat Day	103	23	20	9	22	1,115,617
		Eddie M. Martin, Jr.	152	22	16	16	14	1,091,871
		Brice Blanc	107	18	12	10	17	885,118
CD	10/31 - 11/27	Trainer	Starts	1st	2d	3d	Win %	Earnings
		Steven M. Asmussen	67	14	13	11	21	631,146
		Robert E. Holthus	32	11	5	7	34	472,634
		Kenneth G. McPeek	34	11	3	3	32	417,801
		Dale L. Romans	63	10	8	10	16	628,252
		Carl A. Nafzger	56	9	11	9	16	472,290
CD	4/24 - 7/5	Jockey	Starts	1st	2d	3d	Win %	Earnings
		Rafael Bejarano	417	81	71	54	19	2,966,656
		Pat Day	208	54	38	29	26	2,702,948
		Cornelio H. Velasquez	295	48	55	53	16	1,780,387
		Robby Albarado	319	46	49	48	14	2,068,681
		Mark Guidry	291	40	38	35	14	1,352,536
CD	4/24 - 7/5	Trainer	Starts	1st	2d	3d	Win %	Earnings
		Steven M. Asmussen	150	35	22	25	23	1,326,722
		Dale L. Romans	154	32	28	27	21	1,281,954
		Thomas M. Amoss	86	29	14	8	34	913,912
		D. Wayne Lukas	98	20	18	12	20	950,628
		Gregory D. Foley	84	15	9	17	18	490,548
CLS	7/23 - 9/12	Jockey	Starts	1st	2d	3d	Win %	Earnings
		Filmer Munaylla	119	32	17	15	27	126,548
		Armando Martinez	167	29	17	17	17	132,515
		Jerome Carkeek	198	27	29	29	14	145,857
		Dennis Michael Collins	154	26	24	25	17	127,781
		Daniel Lee Beck	182	21	21	18	12	110,497
CLS	7/23 - 9/12	Trainer	Starts	1st	2d	3d	Win %	Earnings
		David C. Anderson	88	24	10	9	27	104,194
		Marvin A. Johnson	43	12	5	4	28	47,344
		Gene Deroin	46	11	6	6	24	42,054
		James R. Compton	48	9	4	7	19	36,807
		Dale Burns	35	7	6	3	20	30,184
CNL	6/11 - 7/26	Jockey	Starts	1st	2d	3d	Win %	Earnings
		Ryan Fogelsonger	204	53	44	38	26	1,008,710
		Horacio Karamanos	183	36	23	33	20	652,284
		Christopher VanHassel	204	31	23	28	15	467,770
		Richard Monterrey	144	30	25	16	21	438,437
		Steve D. Hamilton	232	25	38	45	11	583,190
CNL	6/11 - 7/26	Trainer	Starts	1st	2d	3d	Win %	Earnings
		Phil Schoenthal	83	22	14	9	27	329,220
		Jonathan E. Sheppard	70	16	10	7	23	289,450
		Hamilton A. Smith	89	14	19	13	16	358,535
		Vincent L. Blengs	38	12	9	7	32	152,335
		A. Ferris Allen III	79	10	16	15	13	167,294
CPW	6/12 - 6/27	Jockey	Starts	1st	2d	3d	Win %	Earnings
		B. Buck Harris	30	8	8	8	27	11,463
		Frank La Forge	25	6	5	2	24	7,295
		Shannon Wippert	17	5	4	2	29	6,037
		Donald D. Herber, Jr.	24	4	2	0	17	4,325
		Gilbert D. Rivera	18	4	1	0	22	4,238

Track	Dates	Name	Starts	1st	2d	3d	Win %	Earnings
CPW	6/12 - 6/27	Trainer	Starts	1st	2d	3d	Win %	Earnings
		David Gourneau	8	6	1	0	75	5,245
		Bob Mitchell	13	3	1	2	23	3,373
		Kelly Kaelberer	14	2	6	2	14	4,462
		Wally Decoteau	11	2	2	3	18	3,486
		Joe Thorne	10	2	2	1	20	2,714
CRC	10/24/04 - 1/2/05	Jockey	Starts	1st	2d	3d	Win %	Earnings
		Eddie Castro	416	83	79	60	20	1,464,365
		Manoel R. Cruz	286	60	44	47	21	1,113,230
		Manuel Aguilar	301	39	47	47	13	794,370
		Gary Boulanger	193	38	27	25	20	649,725
		Eibar Coa	131	34	16	15	26	694,980
CRC	10/24/04 - 1/2/05	Trainer	Starts	1st	2d	3d	Win %	Earnings
		Daniel C. Hurtak	115	21	13	22	18	265,380
		Angel C. Salinas	108	18	13	17	17	282,740
		Emanuel Tortora	92	15	13	11	16	243,140
		William P. White	84	14	11	12	17	271,140
		Henry Collazo	105	13	10	15	12	253,260
CRC	4/26 - 10/23	Jockey	Starts	1st	2d	3d	Win %	Earnings
		Eddie Castro	772	154	131	120	20	3,321,885
		Manoel R. Cruz	646	120	100	117	19	2,358,290
		Manuel Aguilar	733	109	108	100	15	2,425,385
		Abdiel Toribio	420	72	60	60	17	1,581,520
		Gary Boulanger	413	65	67	60	16	1,528,680
CRC	4/26 - 10/23	Trainer	Starts	1st	2d	3d	Win %	Earnings
		William P. White	189	48	30	30	25	1,011,305
		Angel C. Salinas	199	37	21	23	19	521,525
		Kathleen O'Connell	250	34	34	23	14	574,010
		Emanuel Tortora	201	32	26	23	16	694,320
		Edward Plesa, Jr.	183	31	29	28	17	1,085,910
CT	10/1 -12/31	Jockey	Starts	1st	2d	3d	Win %	Earnings
		Angel R. Quinones	414	62	64	40	15	1,200,050
		Kendrick Carmouche	347	56	44	43	16	1,149,507
		Oscar Flores	268	49	26	21	18	863,223
		David Cora	337	46	46	35	14	853,580
		J. D. Acosta	351	38	41	47	11	852,208
CT	10/1 -12/31	Trainer	Starts	1st	2d	3d	Win %	Earnings
		Jeff C. Runco	185	47	20	25	25	750,896
		Kevin J. Joy	223	42	24	27	19	633,470
		Ronney W. Brown	227	40	37	23	18	741,058
		Anthony Adamo	224	35	23	21	16	668,786
		Ernest M. Haynes	90	21	18	9	23	313,065
CT	7/1 - 9/30	Jockey	Starts	1st	2d	3d	Win %	Earnings
		Angel R. Quinones	297	59	47	39	20	1,006,389
		J. D. Acosta	327	37	45	39	11	755,121
		Gerald Almodovar	220	36	30	28	16	614,676
		Carlos L. Castro	231	35	35	22	15	648,027
		Travis L. Dunkelberger	198	35	28	24	18	734,406
CT	7/1 - 9/30	Trainer	Starts	1st	2d	3d	Win %	Earnings
		Kevin J. Joy	95	28	14	11	29	423,200
		Ronney W. Brown	147	26	19	16	18	397,057
		Mark Shuman	59	16	10	10	27	327,507
		Harry F. Thompson, Jr.	78	15	8	8	19	240,800
		Jeff C. Runco	120	14	27	12	12	289,380
CT	4/1 - 6/30	Jockey	Starts	1st	2d	3d	Win %	Earnings
		Brandon Whitacre	280	65	48	26	23	1,184,764
		Angel R. Quinones	324	50	48	33	15	1,108,916
		Gerald Almodovar	348	47	46	47	14	894,140
		David Cora	294	39	39	35	13	847,794
		Anthony Mawing	306	38	25	39	12	877,395
CT	4/1 - 6/30	Trainer	Starts	1st	2d	3d	Win %	Earnings
		Ronney W. Brown	161	34	33	12	21	643,709
		Jeff C. Runco	143	23	18	13	16	444,885
		Kevin J. Joy	103	21	16	11	20	360,625
		Ernest M. Haynes	56	19	14	9	34	404,320
		Mark Shuman	73	15	12	9	21	369,680

Track	Dates	Name	Starts	1st	2d	3d	Win %	Earnings
CT	1/1 - 3/31	Jockey	Starts	1st	2d	3d	Win %	Earnings
		Anthony Mawing	358	55	59	48	15	1,197,216
		Travis L. Dunkelberger	266	54	38	27	20	1,009,766
		J. D. Acosta	311	43	43	53	14	845,365
		Kendrick Carmouche	298	36	30	41	12	718,160
		Mark E. Rosenthal	196	34	22	16	17	641,048
CT	1/1 - 3/31	Trainer	Starts	1st	2d	3d	Win %	Earnings
		Ronney W. Brown	169	30	30	29	18	483,775
		Mark Shuman	114	23	14	9	20	411,685
		Jeff C. Runco	137	19	29	12	14	392,490
		Kevin J. Joy	71	15	6	11	21	195,576
		Ernest M. Haynes	58	11	9	2	19	168,262
DED	10/31/03 - 3/27/04	Jockey	Starts	1st	2d	3d	Win %	Earnings
		Steve J. Bourque	516	120	76	80	23	2,138,344
		Guy Smith	482	79	64	64	16	1,479,056
		Carlos Gonzalez	355	71	55	48	20	1,185,153
		Carl James Woodley	434	66	67	50	15	1,132,833
		Brian Joseph Hernandez, Jr.	376	60	67	45	16	975,461
DED	10/31/03 - 3/27/04	Trainer	Starts	1st	2d	3d	Win %	Earnings
		Keith L. Bourgeois	311	61	54	40	20	899,876
		Doris Hebert	261	58	45	46	22	1,013,795
		Chad Hassenpflug	155	37	29	18	24	504,770
		Kearney Segura	153	32	20	17	21	470,242
		Dale Angelle	167	29	40	26	17	573,472
DEL	4/24 - 11/7	Jockey	Starts	1st	2d	3d	Win %	Earnings
		Ramon A. Dominguez	636	198	106	97	31	4,347,105
		Roberto Alvarado, Jr.	630	130	110	86	21	3,151,186
		Mario G. Pino	565	104	88	91	18	2,936,991
		Jeremy Rose	539	100	87	89	19	2,706,196
		Clinton L. Potts	664	92	91	85	14	2,245,399
DEL	4/24 - 11/7	Trainer	Starts	1st	2d	3d	Win %	Earnings
		Scott A. Lake	366	91	79	51	25	1,872,540
		Timothy F. Ritchey	288	68	63	36	24	1,734,386
		Michael V. Pino	235	63	48	39	27	1,162,913
		Michael E. Gorham	201	37	34	35	18	916,379
		Howard E. Wolfendale	113	36	27	21	32	647,210
DG	4/10 - 4/18	Jockey	Starts	1st	2d	3d	Win %	Earnings
		Charles Lyn McClellan	17	3	2	3	18	4,327
		Stephen Michael Karr	14	3	2	0	21	4,146
		Terry Lee Gard	17	2	3	3	12	4,146
		Flavio Lozano	17	2	1	2	12	2,953
		Shannon Wippert	12	2	1	0	17	2,536
DG	4/10 - 4/18	Trainer	Starts	1st	2d	3d	Win %	Earnings
		Wiley Aker	6	2	1	1	33	2,941
		Gene K. Wilson	9	2	1	1	22	2,363
		Clyde W. England	2	2	0	0	100	1,728
		B. Odell Reldhead	3	1	1	1	33	1,230
		Craig W. Gentry	2	1	1	0	50	1,152
DMR	7/21 - 9/8	Jockey	Starts	1st	2d	3d	Win %	Earnings
		Corey S. Nakatani	212	54	37	30	25	2,927,069
		Tyler Baze	286	52	42	37	18	2,693,254
		Victor Espinoza	247	44	51	33	18	2,851,839
		David Romero Flores	186	29	25	27	16	1,774,715
		Kent J. Desormeaux	146	21	21	19	14	1,442,074
DMR	7/21 - 9/8	Trainer	Starts	1st	2d	3d	Win %	Earnings
		Doug O'Neill	126	28	12	15	22	1,024,398
		Jeff Mullins	93	24	16	15	26	1,330,045
		Bob Baffert	89	17	10	20	19	1,035,401
		Mike R. Mitchell	77	16	15	5	21	935,018
		William Spawr	56	13	15	4	23	448,733
DUN	3/13 - 3/21	Jockey	Starts	1st	2d	3d	Win %	Earnings
		Charles Lyn McClellan	20	4	3	3	20	6,399
		Stephen Michael Karr	18	4	1	3	22	4,866
		Anna M. Barrio	19	3	4	5	16	4,768
		Todd J. Nuttall	18	3	4	4	17	5,405
		Rick Oliver	13	3	0	1	23	3,728

			Starts	1st	2d	3d	Win %	Earnings
DUN	3/13 - 3/21	Trainer	Starts	1st	2d	3d	Win %	Earnings
		Laurie Jones	10	3	1	2	30	3,888
		Eddy Lenard May	9	2	1	0	22	2,466
		William H. Mahan	8	2	0	1	25	2,268
		Wiley Aker	5	2	0	1	40	2,041
		Charlie Bauerelen	2	2	0	0	100	4,039
ELK	8/28 - 9/6	Jockey	Starts	1st	2d	3d	Win %	Earnings
		Nathan R. Condie	33	16	5	4	48	34,158
		Casey Greene	30	7	4	6	23	18,717
		Casey Sherman	14	4	4	0	29	7,715
		Matt Williams	28	3	5	8	11	11,817
		Brett W. Anderson	21	2	4	3	10	6,941
ELK	8/28 - 9/6	Trainer	Starts	1st	2d	3d	Win %	Earnings
		Shawn H. Davis	17	6	1	2	35	18,799
		Steve Duschka	18	4	2	2	22	8,060
		Blake L. Cragun	7	4	2	1	57	7,390
		Farrell Christoffersen	10	2	3	3	20	6,375
		Ronald P. Carter	4	2	1	1	50	2,910
ELP	7/7 - 9/6	Jockey	Starts	1st	2d	3d	Win %	Earnings
		Rafael Bejarano	317	85	74	44	27	1,193,517
		Willie Martinez	261	47	40	29	18	682,621
		John McKee	266	45	42	37	17	783,011
		Rodney A. Prescott	343	32	42	42	9	398,153
		Jesus Lopez Castanon	225	30	35	33	13	543,561
ELP	7/7 - 9/6	Trainer	Starts	1st	2d	3d	Win %	Earnings
		Bobby C. Barnett	73	13	15	9	18	260,654
		Barbara I. McBride	69	13	13	7	19	129,915
		Bernard S. Flint	73	12	12	9	16	212,030
		Thomas M. Amoss	29	12	5	6	41	217,882
		William I. Mott	36	11	6	3	31	248,734
EMD	4/16 - 9/20	Jockey	Starts	1st	2d	3d	Win %	Earnings
		Ricky Frazier	555	109	86	85	20	1,208,018
		Ben Russell	445	100	78	56	22	909,374
		Gallyn Vick Mitchell	438	83	73	72	19	861,960
		Adalberto Diaz Lopez	489	70	78	70	14	752,855
		Juan M. Gutierrez	484	65	75	68	13	640,642
EMD	4/16 - 9/20	Trainer	Starts	1st	2d	3d	Win %	Earnings
		Frank Lucarelli	271	52	40	39	19	488,576
		Tim McCanna	256	50	40	45	20	614,419
		Jim Penney	191	47	29	32	25	551,098
		Sharon Ross	228	46	35	36	20	429,765
		Grant T. Forster	158	35	27	13	22	427,364
EUR	5/1 - 7/4	Jockey	Starts	1st	2d	3d	Win %	Earnings
		Richard M. Vasquez	53	19	8	9	36	34,756
		Thomas Wellington	19	9	2	3	47	15,166
		Mike J. Bishop	40	7	8	6	18	14,722
		Gary L. Worst	44	4	7	7	9	10,530
		Dustin W. Williams	32	3	8	4	9	9,458
EUR	5/1 - 7/4	Trainer	Starts	1st	2d	3d	Win %	Earnings
		John W. Layton	15	10	0	2	67	16,650
		Joe Frederick Thomas, Sr.	31	9	6	9	29	17,910
		Gary Sharpe	15	3	2	0	20	5,657
		Jim Dale Brooks	5	3	2	0	60	3,725
		Jeffrey T. Rutland	8	3	1	1	38	5,818
EVD	4/1 - 9/6	Jockey	Starts	1st	2d	3d	Win %	Earnings
		Brian Joseph Hernandez, Jr.	431	99	63	57	23	970,954
		Steve J. Bourque	418	76	65	45	18	895,098
		Carl James Woodley	367	73	53	39	20	797,235
		Tracy J. Hebert	436	68	56	52	16	727,885
		Ricky J. Faul	478	61	55	56	13	691,685
EVD	4/1 - 9/6	Trainer	Starts	1st	2d	3d	Win %	Earnings
		Keith L. Bourgeois	312	60	44	27	19	679,078
		Dale Angelle	200	55	30	23	28	566,183
		Doris Hebert	198	38	40	26	19	483,280
		Samuel Breaux	168	30	31	25	18	390,678
		Kearney Segura	141	21	14	17	15	246,246

Track	Dates	Name	Starts	1st	2d	3d	Win %	Earnings
FAR	8/6 - 9/6	Jockey	Starts	1st	2d	3d	Win %	Earnings
		Scot A. Schindler	49	15	12	7	31	42,277
		Anne Von Rosen	48	15	10	8	31	43,337
		Joe Sharp	65	12	16	14	18	45,885
		Chris R. Fiegen	63	12	12	11	19	47,942
		Jimmy Jordan	50	6	9	9	12	25,997
FAR	8/6 - 9/6	Trainer	Starts	1st	2d	3d	Win %	Earnings
		John Ness	54	16	9	8	30	46,115
		Kenneth Olson	33	9	8	2	27	20,519
		Craig Bonn	28	9	6	3	32	27,519
		Kelly Kaelberer	29	5	3	4	17	15,501
		Robert E. Partridge	15	3	3	1	20	7,035
FE	5/1 - 9/6	Jockey	Starts	1st	2d	3d	Win %	Earnings
		Neil Poznansky	405	71	44	64	18	1,335,527
		Martin Ramos Ramirez	394	67	60	45	17	1,152,900
		Brian Todd Bochinski	415	63	74	55	15	1,141,149
		Francine Villeneuve	333	57	50	41	17	1,053,048
		Jennie Roche	323	53	39	32	16	700,889
FE	5/1 - 9/6	Trainer	Starts	1st	2d	3d	Win %	Earnings
		Thomas M. Agosti	129	27	22	15	21	436,200
		Ross Armata	131	26	18	16	20	347,368
		Donald C. MacRae	66	26	9	9	39	282,244
		Layne S. Giliforte	135	23	24	17	17	382,988
		Debra E. Rombis	144	20	20	14	14	358,247
FER	8/12 - 8/22	Jockey	Starts	1st	2d	3d	Win %	Earnings
		Victor G. Navarro	23	9	6	3	39	41,400
		Victor Miranda	27	9	5	5	33	38,812
		Ryan Morris	29	5	8	6	17	28,217
		Robert Boyce	23	3	4	5	13	18,318
		Elliott Demesme	21	2	3	0	10	12,738
FER	8/12 - 8/22	Trainer	Starts	1st	2d	3d	Win %	Earnings
		Dennis Hopkins	27	5	8	5	19	31,575
		Santiago C. Rodriguez	9	4	3	0	44	13,455
		Karen Haverty	12	4	1	2	33	20,033
		Glen Stanley Wasson	8	3	3	0	38	11,078
		Ron E. White	10	3	2	1	30	11,195
FG	11/27/03 - 3/28/04	Jockey	Starts	1st	2d	3d	Win %	Earnings
		Robby Albarado	452	106	101	65	23	3,084,990
		Shane J. Sellers	351	84	55	48	24	1,894,756
		Eddie M. Martin, Jr.	489	78	74	65	16	1,698,140
		Gerard Melancon	534	76	80	83	14	1,811,806
		Corey J. Lanerie	473	71	75	70	15	1,799,197
FG	11/27/03 - 3/28/04	Trainer	Starts	1st	2d	3d	Win %	Earnings
		Steven M. Asmussen	247	63	41	37	26	1,388,645
		W. Bret Calhoun	134	32	27	17	24	625,692
		Thomas M. Amoss	137	32	25	22	23	680,230
		Merrill R. Scherer	83	28	7	10	34	466,495
		Ronny W. Werner	88	21	13	8	24	347,755
FL	4/16 - 11/27	Jockey	Starts	1st	2d	3d	Win %	Earnings
		John R. Davila, Jr.	640	136	108	74	21	1,462,125
		Pedro A. Rodriguez	589	130	82	82	22	1,373,543
		Parker R. Buckley	531	91	76	66	17	936,341
		John A. Grabowski	491	78	78	67	16	980,181
		Jeremias Flores	505	74	70	63	15	721,996
FL	4/16 - 11/27	Trainer	Starts	1st	2d	3d	Win %	Earnings
		Chris J. Englehart	589	136	110	93	23	1,342,832
		Michael A. Lecesse	380	79	57	55	21	982,808
		Charlton Baker	250	67	40	36	27	774,848
		Michael S. Ferraro	313	56	46	33	18	613,112
		Ralph D'Alessandro	287	56	44	32	20	665,807
FLG	7/2 - 7/5	Jockey	Starts	1st	2d	3d	Win %	Earnings
		Lorenzo Castane Lopez	18	4	1	2	22	14,944
		Charles Lyn McClellan	15	3	4	2	20	13,901
		Daniel P. Vergara	8	3	3	0	38	11,675
		Stephen Michael Karr	17	3	1	4	18	12,218
		Janna Sorrells	11	2	5	0	18	10,791

Track	Dates		Starts	1st	2d	3d	Win %	Earnings
FLG	7/2 - 7/5	Trainer	Starts	1st	2d	3d	Win %	Earnings
		George Wern	4	2	2	0	50	7,844
		Jon Phil Zimmerman	5	2	1	1	40	7,025
		B. Odell Reidhead	4	2	0	2	50	6,717
		Wiley Aker	2	2	0	0	100	5,596
		Sandra Ehret	6	1	3	0	17	5,736
FMT	5/27 - 7/25	Jockey	Starts	1st	2d	3d	Win %	Earnings
		Curtis Kimes	114	31	18	15	27	312,907
		Randy R. Wilson	73	14	8	9	19	144,843
		Wendell John Hilburn	55	10	4	4	18	97,585
		Tonja A. Arruda	88	9	13	10	10	116,345
		Kerry D. Kretzer	83	9	9	12	11	119,603
FMT	5/27 - 7/25	Trainer	Starts	1st	2d	3d	Win %	Earnings
		Mike R. Teel	42	14	8	6	33	121,425
		Debbie Holland Dyer	23	5	4	2	22	81,442
		Jory Ferrell	12	5	2	2	42	38,685
		Robert L. Roughton	11	5	2	0	45	46,510
		Joe S. Offolter	21	4	2	2	19	46,386
FNO	10/6 - 10/17	Jockey	Starts	1st	2d	3d	Win %	Earnings
		Modesto Linares	39	13	2	5	33	73,285
		Macario Rodriguez	45	11	19	3	24	92,385
		Victor Miranda	44	7	6	7	16	53,228
		Victor G. Navarro	38	5	6	8	13	44,668
		John Rochabrun	21	4	2	2	19	25,415
FNO	10/6 - 10/17	Trainer	Starts	1st	2d	3d	Win %	Earnings
		Dennis Hopkins	39	6	6	3	15	47,038
		Michael Lenzini	41	4	6	11	10	61,992
		Rene Amescua	18	4	2	4	22	27,512
		Clifford DeLima	15	4	1	3	27	25,010
		W. R. Whitehouse	14	3	5	1	21	22,530
FON	2/14 - 5/8	Jockey	Starts	1st	2d	3d	Win %	Earnings
		Perry Compton	294	80	57	46	27	403,114
		Curtis Kimes	327	69	59	33	21	347,220
		Dennis Michael Collins	294	32	44	43	11	239,562
		Armando Martinez	263	30	17	27	11	176,896
		Alonzo Guajardo	253	23	23	29	9	129,064
FON	2/14 - 5/8	Trainer	Starts	1st	2d	3d	Win %	Earnings
		David C. Anderson	126	31	22	16	25	149,471
		Marvin A. Johnson	108	28	11	6	26	115,236
		Brian M. Roberts	59	12	7	11	20	92,267
		Boyd Caster	62	12	7	11	19	65,784
		Steve L. Hall	52	11	8	11	21	63,537
FP	3/26 - 9/18	Jockey	Starts	1st	2d	3d	Win %	Earnings
		Ramsey Zimmerman	613	180	119	94	29	973,547
		Joel Santiago	529	70	81	98	13	492,250
		Gilbert Concha	474	67	73	69	14	436,433
		Michael Allen Gale	354	61	57	62	17	514,148
		Thomas L. Pompell	246	55	41	39	22	393,262
FP	3/26 - 9/18	Trainer	Starts	1st	2d	3d	Win %	Earnings
		Ralph Martinez	513	143	96	91	28	748,716
		Eddie M. Essenpreis	299	55	62	48	18	452,832
		Steve Manley	298	54	58	43	18	334,728
		Carmelo Mendoza	210	44	27	33	21	256,034
		Jerry Hammond	229	38	30	44	17	192,894
FPX	9/10 - 9/26	Jockey	Starts	1st	2d	3d	Win %	Earnings
		Martin A. Pedroza	134	51	25	14	38	1,000,142
		Omar Figueroa	72	14	12	9	19	496,257
		Casey Fusilier	51	7	12	9	14	148,028
		Ignacio Puglisi	49	7	3	9	14	195,854
		Isaias D. Enriquez	62	6	7	10	10	167,284
FPX	9/10 - 9/26	Trainer	Starts	1st	2d	3d	Win %	Earnings
		Doug O'Neill	45	16	5	3	36	361,490
		Jeff Mullins	23	8	4	3	35	312,952
		Wesley A. Ward	23	8	3	5	35	118,748
		Jack Carava	14	6	3	0	43	84,860
		William Spawr	16	6	2	2	38	169,494

Track	Dates	Jockey/Trainer	Starts	1st	2d	3d	Win %	Earnings
GCF	10/2 - 10/10	Jockey	Starts	1st	2d	3d	Win %	Earnings
		Alfredo Torres	22	8	3	4	36	10,257
		Anna M. Barrio	20	7	1	3	35	8,670
		Javier A. Ortega	4	2	0	0	50	2,007
		Steve Hancock	22	1	4	3	5	3,702
		Angel Felix	17	1	4	1	6	3,225
GCF	10/2 - 10/10	Trainer	Starts	1st	2d	3d	Win %	Earnings
		Gene K. Wilson	11	6	1	1	55	6,827
		Guillermo Jimenez, Sr.	5	3	0	0	60	3,076
		Laurie Jones	10	2	0	4	20	2,908
		Pablo C. Figueroa, Sr.	2	2	0	0	100	2,290
		William H. Mahan	10	1	1	0	10	1,853
GF	7/3 - 8/1	Jockey	Starts	1st	2d	3d	Win %	Earnings
		B. Buck Harris	34	10	5	5	29	14,907
		Joe Holmes, Sr.	47	9	6	10	19	18,310
		Ivan Ortiz, Jr.	45	8	13	4	18	20,381
		Carl Hebert	43	6	9	8	14	15,764
		Russell David Kingrey	35	6	4	4	17	11,953
GF	7/3 - 8/1	Trainer	Starts	1st	2d	3d	Win %	Earnings
		Janis D. Schoepf	18	6	2	2	33	8,179
		Doug Johnson	23	5	4	1	22	9,979
		Mark Buckley	19	4	5	7	21	9,350
		Mel Berkram	25	4	5	5	16	8,294
		Sid M. Billingsley	13	4	0	4	31	5,367
GG	11/5/03 - 4/4/04	Jockey	Starts	1st	2d	3d	Win %	Earnings
		Kevin Radke	474	89	72	69	19	1,658,369
		Chance J. Rollins	491	80	67	89	16	1,566,314
		Chad Phillip Schvaneveldt	328	76	47	49	23	1,432,856
		Dennis Carr	422	75	85	67	18	1,349,497
		Russell A. Baze	335	71	68	52	21	1,421,354
GG	11/5/03 - 4/4/04	Trainer	Starts	1st	2d	3d	Win %	Earnings
		Jerry Hollendorfer	449	88	83	61	20	2,026,353
		Art Sherman	222	58	43	28	26	844,019
		John F. Martin	183	52	32	24	28	775,300
		Armando Lage	316	34	40	44	11	618,294
		William E. Morey	154	29	31	25	19	431,464
GIL	7/3 - 8/29	Jockey	Starts	1st	2d	3d	Win %	Earnings
		Salvador Perez	18	6	5	1	33	29,328
		W. Bill McClaran	15	4	2	3	27	14,910
		Santos Carrizales	20	3	4	2	15	15,458
		Russell Brown	13	1	3	1	8	7,086
		David C. Elston	6	1	1	2	17	5,116
GIL	7/3 - 8/29	Trainer	Starts	1st	2d	3d	Win %	Earnings
		Marvin Hayes	4	2	0	2	50	6,840
		Gabe Newman	4	2	0	1	50	5,778
		O. S. Carlton III	8	1	2	1	13	5,612
		Edelmiro Carrizales	10	1	2	1	10	5,358
		Edward D. Cross	4	1	1	2	25	4,800
GLD	4/25 - 10/30	Jockey	Starts	1st	2d	3d	Win %	Earnings
		T. D. Houghton	784	196	159	111	25	1,650,108
		Mary Elizabeth Doser	620	119	114	95	19	1,355,940
		Roberto A. Perez	666	118	92	98	18	1,087,584
		Federico Mata	534	98	82	82	18	854,363
		Luis Jeronimo Martinez	345	63	38	60	18	569,221
GLD	4/25 - 10/30	Trainer	Starts	1st	2d	3d	Win %	Earnings
		Gerald S. Bennett	417	94	77	76	23	1,106,712
		Robert M. Gorham	289	57	51	40	20	692,413
		Richard R. Rettele	312	55	61	49	18	677,380
		Randall R. Russell	395	51	51	62	13	425,500
		Ronald D. Allen, Sr.	173	46	28	28	27	450,745
GP	1/3 - 4/25	Jockey	Starts	1st	2d	3d	Win %	Earnings
		John R. Velazquez	276	78	60	33	28	2,789,414
		Joe Bravo	412	68	60	58	17	1,992,862
		Edgar S. Prado	383	68	56	54	18	2,064,850
		Cornelio H. Velasquez	408	64	68	46	16	1,761,846
		Rene R. Douglas	407	48	52	44	12	1,604,037

Track	Dates	Name	Starts	1st	2d	3d	Win %	Earnings
GP	1/3 - 4/25	Trainer	Starts	1st	2d	3d	Win %	Earnings
		Todd A. Pletcher	145	42	30	16	29	1,968,860
		Allen Iwinski	102	25	14	7	25	473,650
		William I. Mott	122	24	18	15	20	728,201
		Dale L. Romans	76	20	5	12	26	461,020
		Timothy A. Hills	117	19	21	8	16	413,130
GPR	7/9 - 8/22	Jockey	Starts	1st	2d	3d	Win %	Earnings
		Scott Sterr	56	14	11	9	25	46,608
		Angelle Wilson	46	10	12	8	22	35,758
		Brooke Mellish	54	8	9	8	15	34,052
		Jackie Smith	47	8	7	10	17	31,548
		Antonio Ramirez	49	6	7	11	12	26,153
GPR	7/9 - 8/22	Trainer	Starts	1st	2d	3d	Win %	Earnings
		Stan Marks	16	8	1	2	50	20,038
		Pete Dubois	19	6	4	3	32	21,345
		Amanda Fogle	21	4	4	2	19	13,744
		Brant Laczo	22	3	4	4	14	12,955
		Stan Webb	8	3	4	1	38	11,367
GRP	5/15 - 7/5	Jockey	Starts	1st	2d	3d	Win %	Earnings
		Twyla Beckner	105	28	27	29	27	55,292
		Joe A. Crispin	115	22	27	25	19	47,810
		Duane Lee D'Amico	72	19	17	11	26	35,694
		Ty Dangerfield	80	17	13	14	21	33,272
		Darlene Braden	113	17	10	15	15	34,925
GRP	5/15 - 7/5	Trainer	Starts	1st	2d	3d	Win %	Earnings
		Judi Yearout	25	8	5	3	32	12,660
		Robert Beckner	29	8	3	9	28	12,866
		John McDevitt	47	7	7	11	15	14,890
		Jaqueline Smith	20	7	6	2	35	12,418
		Sally M. Reid	15	6	4	3	40	9,849
HAW	9/24/04 - 1/2/05	Jockey	Starts	1st	2d	3d	Win %	Earnings
		Christopher A. Emigh	450	69	63	47	15	1,462,111
		Larry J. Sterling, Jr.	240	47	26	34	20	1,043,164
		Jesse M. Campbell	322	39	55	36	12	1,049,232
		Shane Laviolette	294	36	30	43	12	724,075
		Eusebio Razo, Jr.	264	35	35	27	13	910,172
HAW	9/24/04 - 1/2/05	Trainer	Starts	1st	2d	3d	Win %	Earnings
		Frank J. Kirby	179	26	25	14	15	495,054
		Michael L. Reavis	130	25	11	20	19	368,169
		Steven M. Asmussen	94	24	10	14	26	353,946
		Thomas F. Tomillo	167	23	26	18	14	313,376
		Roger A. Brueggemann	87	23	12	11	26	296,430
HAW	2/27 - 5/11	Jockey	Starts	1st	2d	3d	Win %	Earnings
		Cruz Contreras	291	47	45	36	16	840,486
		Eusebio Razo, Jr.	193	36	35	25	19	806,276
		Christopher A. Emigh	214	32	30	33	15	801,028
		Jesse M. Campbell	201	32	26	29	16	690,267
		Larry J. Sterling, Jr.	175	32	16	25	18	753,372
HAW	2/27 - 5/11	Trainer	Starts	1st	2d	3d	Win %	Earnings
		Pat Cuccurullo	80	25	13	11	31	326,833
		Thomas F. Tomillo	154	19	29	20	12	353,772
		Frank J. Kirby	113	18	12	13	16	308,326
		Richard P. Hazelton	87	17	15	16	20	510,967
		Michael L. Reavis	82	14	10	12	17	261,512
HOL	11/3 - 12/20	Jockey	Starts	1st	2d	3d	Win %	Earnings
		Rene R. Douglas	188	37	26	31	20	1,209,326
		Tyler Baze	189	35	24	22	19	1,032,456
		Victor Espinoza	157	31	26	19	20	1,414,636
		Corey S. Nakatani	130	23	30	18	18	1,024,674
		Jon Kenton Court	135	18	27	24	13	863,877
HOL	11/3 - 12/20	Trainer	Starts	1st	2d	3d	Win %	Earnings
		Doug O'Neill	120	17	22	17	14	674,388
		Bob Baffert	58	14	9	5	24	449,280
		Mike Harrington	36	12	4	4	33	208,310
		Jeff Mullins	62	10	8	9	16	295,780
		John W. Sadler	57	9	6	8	16	296,288

Track	Dates	Jockey	Starts	1st	2d	3d	Win %	Earnings
HOL	4/21 - 7/18	Tyler Baze	311	59	39	48	19	2,134,667
		Victor Espinoza	309	55	50	51	18	2,819,421
		Corey S. Nakatani	236	48	42	27	20	2,271,965
		Alex O. Solis	210	40	41	30	19	2,875,455
		Mick Ruis	280	36	26	40	13	1,243,275

Track	Dates	Trainer	Starts	1st	2d	3d	Win %	Earnings
HOL	4/21 - 7/18	Jeff Mullins	119	37	21	11	31	1,316,403
		Doug O'Neill	217	32	34	36	15	1,477,291
		Mike R. Mitchell	106	29	19	12	27	882,142
		Bob Baffert	116	20	17	15	17	1,228,135
		Vladimir Cerin	79	18	9	15	23	1,252,414

Track	Dates	Jockey	Starts	1st	2d	3d	Win %	Earnings
HOO	9/2 - 11/21	Ramsey Zimmerman	329	92	51	51	28	869,514
		Lester Cash Knight	524	89	79	83	17	985,598
		Rodney A. Prescott	412	72	60	43	17	753,660
		Billy Charles Patin	232	33	28	25	14	337,226
		Jose J. Delgado	302	32	39	51	11	365,183

Track	Dates	Trainer	Starts	1st	2d	3d	Win %	Earnings
HOO	9/2 - 11/21	Ralph Martinez	197	62	34	27	31	436,436
		Kim Hammond	148	28	16	24	19	247,396
		Barbara I. McBride	96	22	15	8	23	198,172
		R. Gary Patrick	197	19	16	26	10	182,335
		Michael W. Nance	43	14	6	6	33	132,940

Track	Dates	Jockey	Starts	1st	2d	3d	Win %	Earnings
HOU	10/23/03 - 4/10/04	Jeremy Beasley	451	100	67	56	22	1,207,058
		John Jacinto	502	76	72	57	15	777,020
		Terry A. Stanton	411	65	47	61	16	634,311
		Kerwin D. Clark	349	55	44	43	16	541,703
		Donald Edward Simington	384	50	54	49	13	535,131

Track	Dates	Trainer	Starts	1st	2d	3d	Win %	Earnings
HOU	10/23/03 - 4/10/04	Steven M. Asmussen	210	60	40	25	29	927,605
		Danny Pish	269	53	45	37	20	499,416
		W. Bret Calhoun	100	34	12	9	34	265,069
		John G. Locke	216	28	27	30	13	250,595
		Jim Bausch	165	22	18	26	13	168,452

Track	Dates	Jockey	Starts	1st	2d	3d	Win %	Earnings
HPO	7/15 - 7/18	Robert Dean Williams	16	4	4	1	25	88,055
		Perry Compton	16	3	2	2	19	108,519
		Daniel Lee Beck	12	3	1	1	25	60,625
		Armando Martinez	13	2	1	1	15	47,880
		Filmer Munaylla	13	1	3	0	8	33,000

Track	Dates	Trainer	Starts	1st	2d	3d	Win %	Earnings
HPO	7/15 - 7/18	Herb Riecken	9	2	1	1	22	45,396
		David C. Anderson	13	1	3	0	8	35,725
		Kim Veerhusen	4	1	1	0	25	19,625
		James R. Compton	3	1	1	0	33	19,125
		Milton M. Gaede	4	1	0	1	25	17,200

Track	Dates	Jockey	Starts	1st	2d	3d	Win %	Earnings
HST	4/17 - 11/28	Pedro V. Alvarado	533	130	85	87	24	2,216,447
		David Wilson	562	79	87	76	14	1,539,392
		Chris Loseth	405	51	49	47	13	943,710
		Francisco Perez Fuentes	369	46	51	46	12	1,045,101
		Jorge Espitia	361	45	55	46	12	725,413

Track	Dates	Trainer	Starts	1st	2d	3d	Win %	Earnings
HST	4/17 - 11/28	Dino K. Condilenios	194	37	26	22	19	650,697
		Harold J. Barroby	273	36	45	38	13	591,592
		Barbara Heads	218	34	33	22	16	525,921
		Gary E. Demorest	135	32	23	22	24	475,702
		Richard Kamps	106	23	19	21	22	361,812

Track	Dates	Jockey	Starts	1st	2d	3d	Win %	Earnings
IND	4/16 - 6/20	Rodney A. Prescott	368	74	63	52	20	623,493
		Joe Stokes	337	54	47	48	16	449,190
		Eddie Zuniga	271	48	41	33	18	421,789
		Orlando Mojica	246	40	35	26	16	361,841
		Jose J. Delgado	285	38	33	21	13	317,058

Track	Dates		Starts	1st	2d	3d	Win %	Earnings
IND	4/16 - 6/20	Trainer	Starts	1st	2d	3d	Win %	Earnings
		R. Gary Patrick	204	30	34	25	15	231,967
		Barbara I. McBride	66	21	15	16	32	156,373
		Kim Hammond	69	12	14	10	17	95,746
		Joseph R. Martin	68	12	10	14	18	96,139
		Lori A. Smock	64	11	9	8	17	99,142
KAM	8/8 - 9/5	Jockey	Starts	1st	2d	3d	Win %	Earnings
		Cliff James Miyashiro	3	2	1	0	67	3,555
		Pamela M. Peaker	3	1	2	0	33	4,324
		Ronald Joseph Bilodeau	7	1	1	2	14	8,705
		Caroline Stinn	8	1	1	2	13	3,622
		Shelley Friesen	3	1	1	1	33	3,790
KAM	8/8 - 9/5	Trainer	Starts	1st	2d	3d	Win %	Earnings
		Charles Butch McDonald	2	1	1	0	50	2,355
		Marion Stitzel	3	1	0	0	33	7,440
		Vicki Pozzobon	1	1	0	0	100	3,150
		Bruce Hattori	4	1	0	0	25	1,662
		Kathy Dean	2	1	0	0	50	1,260
KAM	5/30 - 7/4	Jockey	Starts	1st	2d	3d	Win %	Earnings
		Angelle Wilson	14	6	1	3	43	8,480
		Caroline Stinn	15	3	4	3	20	6,420
		Laurina Bugeaud	17	3	2	5	18	6,060
		Robert Stein	9	2	4	0	22	4,420
		Ronald Joseph Bilodeau	7	1	2	2	14	2,680
KAM	5/30 - 7/4	Trainer	Starts	1st	2d	3d	Win %	Earnings
		Frank R. Wilson	8	3	1	0	38	4,320
		Vicki Pozzobon	6	3	0	2	50	4,100
		Dale Schaffrick	7	2	1	1	29	3,200
		Kathy Dean	4	1	1	2	25	2,040
		Bruce Hattori	3	1	1	1	33	1,840
KD	9/18 - 9/28	Jockey	Starts	1st	2d	3d	Win %	Earnings
		Rafael Bejarano	35	12	8	4	34	298,390
		Brian Joseph Hernandez, Jr.	15	4	2	0	27	71,119
		James Graham	27	3	5	4	11	88,871
		Jesus Lopez Castanon	22	3	3	4	14	82,122
		Calvin H. Borel	28	3	2	1	11	68,633
KD	9/18 - 9/28	Trainer	Starts	1st	2d	3d	Win %	Earnings
		W. Elliott Walden	8	3	0	2	38	42,050
		Merrill R. Scherer	9	3	0	1	33	30,327
		Eric R. Reed	5	3	0	0	60	57,000
		Dallas Stewart	4	2	1	0	50	37,535
		Thomas M. Amoss	8	2	0	1	25	28,117
KEE	10/8 - 10/30	Jockey	Starts	1st	2d	3d	Win %	Earnings
		Rafael Bejarano	128	26	17	30	20	1,771,064
		Pat Day	79	20	13	13	25	1,456,504
		Brian Joseph Hernandez, Jr.	101	20	11	9	20	605,807
		Robby Albarado	104	9	16	15	9	1,072,484
		Calvin H. Borel	83	9	7	6	11	557,004
KEE	10/8 - 10/30	Trainer	Starts	1st	2d	3d	Win %	Earnings
		Nicholas P. Zito	27	11	4	4	41	440,353
		Steven M. Asmussen	46	11	2	7	24	406,808
		Carl A. Nafzger	35	7	3	7	20	354,562
		D. Wayne Lukas	34	5	7	5	15	805,991
		Dale L. Romans	31	5	4	3	16	226,310
KEE	4/2 - 4/23	Jockey	Starts	1st	2d	3d	Win %	Earnings
		Pat Day	82	21	13	13	26	1,061,364
		Shane J. Sellers	85	15	10	10	18	1,145,560
		Robby Albarado	115	13	15	24	11	852,048
		Jerry D. Bailey	43	12	4	7	28	916,424
		Edgar S. Prado	37	9	8	3	24	587,904
KEE	4/2 - 4/23	Trainer	Starts	1st	2d	3d	Win %	Earnings
		Steven M. Asmussen	44	9	8	8	20	570,068
		Todd A. Pletcher	26	7	7	4	27	638,029
		Kenneth G. McPeek	30	7	1	5	23	313,973
		Nicholas P. Zito	33	4	8	5	12	684,627
		Thomas M. Amoss	17	4	3	3	24	156,580

		Jockey	Starts	1st	2d	3d	Win %	Earnings
KIN	7/11 - 8/1	Caroline Stinn	14	4	4	2	29	8,743
		Roger Butterfly	10	4	1	1	40	12,742
		Ty Dangerfield	7	2	3	1	29	4,565
		Ronald Joseph Bilodeau	12	2	2	5	17	4,910
		Robert Stein	5	2	1	1	40	4,955

		Trainer	Starts	1st	2d	3d	Win %	Earnings
KIN	7/11 - 8/1	Garry Saitz	6	4	1	0	67	7,425
		Dave Desautel	6	3	0	1	50	4,200
		Marion Stitzel	2	2	0	0	100	7,200
		John Stabenfeldt	4	1	1	1	25	2,225
		Robert D. Schmidt	1	1	0	0	100	1,800

		Jockey	Starts	1st	2d	3d	Win %	Earnings
KSP	8/20 - 8/29	Carl Hebert	13	4	2	4	31	5,866
		Joe Holmes, Sr.	14	3	3	4	21	5,184
		Russell David Kingrey	5	3	2	0	60	4,182
		Roger Butterfly	9	2	2	0	22	2,443
		Jack Cano, Jr.	9	2	0	0	22	2,052

		Trainer	Starts	1st	2d	3d	Win %	Earnings
KSP	0/20 - 8/29	Mel Berkram	7	3	1	2	43	3,888
		Jaqueline Smith	4	1	2	1	25	1,965
		Janis D. Schoepf	7	1	1	0	14	2,421
		Andrew Schildt	5	1	1	0	20	1,452
		Marcie Riley	3	1	1	0	33	1,295

		Jockey	Starts	1st	2d	3d	Win %	Earnings
LA	12/26/03 - 12/19/04	Guillermo R. Gutierrez	309	58	58	48	19	367,427
		Agapito Delgadillo	215	56	40	35	26	274,014
		Baltazar Contreras	251	43	30	29	17	242,096
		Antonio Lopez Castanon	255	37	45	32	15	250,662
		Alex Bautista	176	36	19	34	20	200,336

		Trainer	Starts	1st	2d	3d	Win %	Earnings
LA	12/26/03 - 12/19/04	Jesus Nunez	388	66	56	50	17	382,924
		Craig W. Robertson	127	47	22	18	37	254,819
		Charles S. Treece	226	39	41	39	17	231,677
		Fidencio L. Jimenez	71	12	5	17	17	67,176
		Jose Antonio Flores	42	10	1	7	24	43,940

		Jockey	Starts	1st	2d	3d	Win %	Earnings
LAD	5/14 - 10/31	Lonnie Meche	648	158	104	85	24	2,390,166
		John Jacinto	590	118	89	72	20	1,732,255
		Luis S. Quinonez	733	113	106	118	15	1,708,964
		Gerard Melancon	553	101	81	83	18	2,125,549
		Corey J. Lanerie	512	80	90	76	16	1,525,969

		Trainer	Starts	1st	2d	3d	Win %	Earnings
LAD	5/14 - 10/31	Cole Norman	391	111	72	43	28	1,481,209
		Steven M. Asmussen	224	49	29	32	22	803,265
		Morris G. Nicks	75	29	11	6	39	373,107
		Sam B. David, Jr.	114	27	20	12	24	425,810
		Larry Robideaux, Jr.	147	26	24	25	18	489,534

		Jockey	Starts	1st	2d	3d	Win %	Earnings
LBG	9/4 - 10/31	Scott Sterr	135	28	26	26	21	137,894
		Cliff James Miyashiro	99	23	19	18	23	105,467
		Nate Smith	111	15	17	11	14	77,352
		Janine Stianson	91	14	11	13	15	65,351
		Angelle Wilson	100	12	14	17	12	78,093

		Trainer	Starts	1st	2d	3d	Win %	Earnings
LBG	9/4 - 10/31	Phil Wiest	35	11	7	6	31	43,848
		Ron David	30	7	6	8	23	35,142
		Allan Brown	20	7	3	6	35	36,627
		Mel Berkram	38	6	4	6	16	25,154
		Rick Wiest	20	5	7	3	25	33,194

		Jockey	Starts	1st	2d	3d	Win %	Earnings
LBG	5/1 - 7/4	Peter McAleney	95	24	21	11	25	92,646
		Scott Sterr	95	18	18	11	19	73,746
		Amber Dickinson	48	17	7	10	35	56,299
		Cliff James Miyashiro	75	12	11	8	16	48,832
		Carl Hebert	97	11	15	16	11	57,908

Track	Dates	Name	Starts	1st	2d	3d	Win %	Earnings
LBG	5/1 - 7/4	Trainer	Starts	1st	2d	3d	Win %	Earnings
		Jason Homer	50	17	12	5	34	63,621
		Jim Meyaard	42	15	5	9	36	45,978
		Stan Marks	35	9	3	2	26	32,618
		Kevin Oberholtzer	33	6	9	3	18	33,597
		Mel Berkram	39	4	7	8	10	22,266
LNN	5/14 - 7/11	Jockey	Starts	1st	2d	3d	Win %	Earnings
		Robert Dean Williams	238	70	35	30	29	307,098
		Dennis Michael Collins	220	39	37	28	18	208,207
		Armando Martinez	202	29	20	23	14	160,918
		Jerome Carkeek	231	27	28	45	12	150,695
		Filmer Munaylla	203	26	24	21	13	134,057
LNN	5/14 - 7/11	Trainer	Starts	1st	2d	3d	Win %	Earnings
		David C. Anderson	125	29	17	17	23	146,195
		Herb Riecken	57	15	8	9	26	95,767
		James R. Compton	51	14	11	9	27	54,914
		Steve L. Hall	32	14	4	1	44	56,565
		Marvin A. Johnson	80	11	9	16	14	65,451
LRL	1/1 - 3/28	Jockey	Starts	1st	2d	3d	Win %	Earnings
		Ramon A. Dominguez	326	88	59	63	27	1,532,780
		Jeremy Rose	259	53	36	26	20	836,795
		Abel Castellano, Jr.	272	46	48	41	17	934,370
		Jozbin Z. Santana	199	34	27	21	17	543,980
		Steve D. Hamilton	222	32	35	36	14	525,145
LRL	1/1 - 3/28	Trainer	Starts	1st	2d	3d	Win %	Earnings
		John J. Robb	172	36	24	18	21	523,010
		Dale Capuano	136	33	24	25	24	500,515
		John Rigattieri	73	21	8	6	29	216,495
		Mark Shuman	94	19	16	15	20	398,410
		Phil Schoenthal	92	17	18	13	18	332,695
LS	10/1 - 10/31	Jockey	Starts	1st	2d	3d	Win %	Earnings
		Roman Chapa	107	24	12	10	22	450,465
		Monte Clifton Berry	94	15	20	14	16	276,885
		Larry Taylor	94	15	8	15	16	209,240
		Casey T. Lambert	88	15	6	12	17	271,405
		Donnie J. Meche	86	14	22	11	16	289,340
LS	10/1 - 10/31	Trainer	Starts	1st	2d	3d	Win %	Earnings
		Steven M. Asmussen	125	24	32	14	19	603,425
		Danny Pish	58	17	7	3	29	308,960
		W. Bret Calhoun	35	9	5	6	26	152,005
		Cody Autrey	29	8	9	3	28	154,970
		Gamaliel Vazquez	40	8	4	3	20	165,280
LS	4/15 - 7/11	Jockey	Starts	1st	2d	3d	Win %	Earnings
		Eddie M. Martin, Jr.	415	87	76	64	21	1,684,025
		Monte Clifton Berry	394	78	55	53	20	1,389,270
		Jeremy Beasley	330	41	39	32	12	850,483
		Casey T. Lambert	280	40	34	36	14	766,969
		Larry Taylor	329	35	32	39	11	499,431
LS	4/15 - 7/11	Trainer	Starts	1st	2d	3d	Win %	Earnings
		Steven M. Asmussen	342	82	66	42	24	1,859,727
		Cole Norman	202	59	46	25	29	791,320
		W. Bret Calhoun	160	26	30	28	16	680,200
		Danny Pish	185	21	22	26	11	393,908
		Tommie T. Morgan	123	19	11	8	15	266,332
MAF	7/24 - 7/25	Jockey	Starts	1st	2d	3d	Win %	Earnings
		Joe Holmes, Sr.	7	2	2	2	29	3,062
		Shannon Wippert	5	2	1	0	40	3,687
		Ivan Ortiz, Jr.	6	2	0	1	33	2,371
		Carl Hebert	7	1	2	1	14	2,333
		Terrance Birdrattler	1	1	0	0	100	880
MAF	7/24 - 7/25	Trainer	Starts	1st	2d	3d	Win %	Earnings
		Mel Berkram	6	1	2	1	17	2,221
		Janis D. Schoepf	2	1	1	0	50	2,332
		Harlan Bird Rattler	4	1	1	0	25	1,344
		Cleo Medicine Horse, Jr.	4	1	0	2	25	1,526
		Sid M. Billingsley	2	1	0	1	50	1,076

Track	Dates	Name	Starts	1st	2d	3d	Win %	Earnings
MAN	2/28 - 4/25	Jockey	Starts	1st	2d	3d	Win %	Earnings
		James Bo White	33	8	2	5	24	35,710
		Santos Carrizales	38	7	7	7	18	37,109
		Charlotte Bronstad	41	6	6	4	15	33,144
		Danny J. Lavergne	25	5	0	3	20	16,163
		Randy B. Edison	39	4	10	3	10	24,332
MAN	2/28 - 4/25	Trainer	Starts	1st	2d	3d	Win %	Earnings
		Bobby A. Jenkins	10	4	4	0	40	21,912
		Gabe Newman	10	3	1	1	30	14,210
		Roy J. Ragland, Jr.	8	2	3	0	25	7,780
		Bradley C. Bolen	10	2	2	2	20	17,591
		Robert Fitzpatrick	11	2	2	1	18	10,410
MC	5/9 - 5/16	Jockey	Starts	1st	2d	3d	Win %	Earnings
		Shaunda L. Larsen	8	4	0	0	50	7,146
		Shannon Wippert	5	2	2	0	40	4,318
		Shann Nomee	3	1	1	0	33	1,460
		Frank La Forge	3	1	0	0	33	834
		Zack Kelsey	6	0	3	2	0	2,310
MC	5/9 - 5/16	Trainer	Starts	1st	2d	3d	Win %	Earnings
		Bryan Krone	12	5	0	1	42	8,861
		Amber Flom	3	1	1	0	33	2,150
		Cleo Medicine Horse, Jr.	4	1	1	0	25	1,460
		Jan Ibach	2	1	0	0	50	918
		Janis D. Schoepf	4	0	3	0	0	1,260
MD	5/28 - 9/11	Jockey	Starts	1st	2d	3d	Win %	Earnings
		Serge R. Rocheleau	188	56	31	24	30	148,106
		Haniff Emamalie	177	38	40	33	21	108,316
		Rennie Latchman	182	22	32	31	12	78,676
		Danny Seesequasis	144	16	14	14	11	42,532
		David A. Karn	114	14	9	12	12	39,992
MD	5/28 - 9/11	Trainer	Starts	1st	2d	3d	Win %	Earnings
		Hubert Pilon	76	19	19	10	25	80,836
		Don Bjarnarson	47	19	5	10	40	39,740
		Russell Gardipy	49	18	4	5	37	33,060
		Mike Tourangeau	80	12	11	10	15	28,590
		Alphonse Lavallee	56	11	12	13	20	31,498
MDA	10/2 - 10/11	Jockey	Starts	1st	2d	3d	Win %	Earnings
		Tim Moccasin	22	8	11	2	36	9,243
		Cameron Campbell	22	7	3	4	32	7,745
		Danny Seesequasis	14	4	3	1	29	4,277
		Danielle Beischer	17	2	4	4	12	3,692
		Doug T. Jones	7	1	1	3	14	1,729
MDA	10/2 - 10/11	Trainer	Starts	1st	2d	3d	Win %	Earnings
		Brad Ball	10	4	1	3	40	3,743
		James R. Ross	10	3	2	3	30	3,222
		Mike Tourangeau	18	2	5	6	11	3,835
		Dana T. Keshane	8	2	5	0	25	2,925
		Elton Keshane	11	2	3	1	18	3,094
MDA	5/8 - 5/16	Jockey	Starts	1st	2d	3d	Win %	Earnings
		Bernie Tourangeau	18	5	6	2	28	6,012
		Sheldon Chickeness	17	4	3	5	24	4,935
		Danielle Beischer	8	4	1	2	50	3,666
		Hector Rabbitskin	16	3	5	2	19	4,345
		Norbert Keshane	9	2	3	2	22	2,860
MDA	5/8 - 5/16	Trainer	Starts	1st	2d	3d	Win %	Earnings
		Elton Keshane	13	5	2	2	38	4,998
		Brad Ball	8	4	1	2	50	3,679
		Mike Tourangeau	10	3	5	0	30	3,731
		Irene Britton	12	2	1	6	17	2,746
		Joseph Vandane	4	1	2	0	25	1,391
MED	10/1 - 11/13	Jockey	Starts	1st	2d	3d	Win %	Earnings
		Stewart Elliott	170	37	23	21	22	1,056,567
		Rajiv Maragh	185	28	25	27	15	746,181
		Joe Bravo	135	28	22	24	21	1,029,557
		Eibar Coa	108	22	25	12	20	791,770
		Julian Pimentel	114	20	18	12	18	701,785

			Starts	1st	2d	3d	Win %	Earnings
MED	10/1 - 11/13	Trainer	Starts	1st	2d	3d	Win %	Earnings
		Patricia Farro	51	11	10	5	22	252,974
		Edwin Thomas Broome	47	9	7	6	19	278,831
		Scott A. Lake	24	8	2	4	33	200,285
		Mark Shuman	49	7	8	8	14	293,520
		Timothy A. Hills	59	7	8	5	12	190,025
MIL	7/1 - 7/2	Jockey	Starts	1st	2d	3d	Win %	Earnings
		Scott Sterr	5	1	2	2	20	5,634
		Peter McAleney	5	1	1	0	20	4,214
		Laurina Bugeaud	4	1	1	0	25	3,457
		Nate Smith	5	1	0	2	20	3,568
		Brooke Mellish	5	1	0	0	20	2,967
MIL	7/1 - 7/2	Trainer	Starts	1st	2d	3d	Win %	Earnings
		Marlon Draper	2	2	0	0	100	5,088
		Nellie Opal Pigeau	3	1	1	0	33	3,334
		Ron David	3	1	0	2	33	3,325
		Barry R. Price	1	1	0	0	100	2,147
		Robert Allen	3	0	1	0	0	1,474
MNR	10/1 - 12/28	Jockey	Starts	1st	2d	3d	Win %	Earnings
		Dana G. Whitney	346	59	45	43	17	939,170
		Oswald M. Pereira	378	55	59	41	15	841,323
		Deshawn L. Parker	375	49	66	46	13	850,912
		Rex A. Stokes, III	287	47	28	31	16	608,552
		Chad K. Murphy	168	35	21	22	21	736,791
MNR	10/1 - 12/28	Trainer	Starts	1st	2d	3d	Win %	Earnings
		Dale Baird	223	29	26	26	13	453,747
		John W. Baird	102	24	13	12	24	304,415
		J. Michael Baird	92	21	13	11	23	262,869
		Jami C. Poole	90	20	6	7	22	221,949
		John R. Semer	72	17	14	5	24	187,662
MNR	7/1 - 9/30	Jockey	Starts	1st	2d	3d	Win %	Earnings
		Deshawn L. Parker	468	79	75	54	17	1,194,181
		Dana G. Whitney	441	60	69	70	14	1,103,920
		Oswald M. Pereira	401	47	59	60	12	796,988
		Chad K. Murphy	239	37	37	30	15	787,890
		Rex A. Stokes, III	249	37	26	31	15	502,609
MNR	7/1 - 9/30	Trainer	Starts	1st	2d	3d	Win %	Earnings
		Dale Baird	263	39	39	36	15	599,709
		J. Michael Baird	105	26	17	14	25	329,399
		John W. Baird	105	18	12	12	17	278,815
		Jami C. Poole	74	14	7	14	19	160,442
		Scooter Davis	90	13	15	13	14	184,044
MNR	4/1 - 6/30	Jockey	Starts	1st	2d	3d	Win %	Earnings
		Dana G. Whitney	498	107	83	64	21	1,606,646
		Deshawn L. Parker	470	70	69	60	15	1,103,604
		Chad K. Murphy	305	55	38	38	18	976,517
		Gary A. Birzer	384	45	52	52	12	756,293
		Oswald M. Pereira	308	35	43	31	11	574,607
MNR	4/1 - 6/30	Trainer	Starts	1st	2d	3d	Win %	Earnings
		Dale Baird	310	32	38	39	10	606,934
		Paula S. Capestro	77	24	13	11	31	264,511
		Wayne M. Catalano	59	22	8	7	37	278,369
		Scooter Davis	117	21	14	11	18	246,963
		Bernard S. Flint	40	15	4	8	38	285,410
MNR	1/3 - 3/31	Jockey	Starts	1st	2d	3d	Win %	Earnings
		Dana G. Whitney	135	39	16	18	29	473,791
		Deshawn L. Parker	238	34	50	27	14	536,242
		Chad K. Murphy	144	30	22	19	21	425,720
		Oswald M. Pereira	191	21	26	24	11	338,737
		David J. McFadden	115	18	17	11	16	266,239
MNR	1/3 - 3/31	Trainer	Starts	1st	2d	3d	Win %	Earnings
		Scooter Davis	67	22	5	4	33	189,542
		Dale Baird	149	12	31	16	8	274,804
		John W. Baird	68	8	6	9	12	103,718
		Loren G. Cox	42	8	5	2	19	94,239
		Jeffrey A. Radosevich	44	7	7	4	16	106,336

Track	Dates		Starts	1st	2d	3d	Win %	Earnings
MOF	5/8 - 5/16	Jockey	Starts	1st	2d	3d	Win %	Earnings
		Stephen Michael Karr	16	4	5	4	25	7,428
		Charles Lyn McClellan	17	4	3	6	24	6,928
		Terry Lee Gard	8	3	1	0	38	4,111
		Rick Oliver	14	2	0	2	14	2,899
		Alfredo Torres	17	1	2	2	6	2,897
MOF	5/8 - 5/16	Trainer	Starts	1st	2d	3d	Win %	Earnings
		Wiley Aker	6	2	1	1	33	3,270
		Lyndel G. Rutherford	10	2	1	1	20	2,810
		Juan Pablo Silva	4	2	1	0	50	2,693
		Ira Price	4	2	0	0	50	2,201
		Eddy Lenard May	7	1	5	1	14	3,175
MPM	5/1 - 9/26	Jockey	Starts	1st	2d	3d	Win %	Earnings
		Julie Fritz	39	8	9	6	21	21,090
		Lee Gates	36	5	5	8	14	15,350
		Ronald Alan Louchart	9	5	1	2	56	8,250
		Ruben Pizarro	9	5	1	2	56	7,745
		Dale Berryhill	28	4	7	4	14	13,465
MPM	5/1 - 9/26	Trainer	Starts	1st	2d	3d	Win %	Earnings
		Reid Gross	34	7	11	6	21	19,530
		Larry O. Smith	29	6	8	2	21	16,020
		Denis Cluley	21	5	5	6	24	12,995
		David N. Gates	21	4	0	5	19	9,030
		Tom D. Dunlap	5	3	0	1	60	4,750
MTH	5/29 - 9/26	Jockey	Starts	1st	2d	3d	Win %	Earnings
		Joe Bravo	414	96	79	53	23	3,790,542
		Eibar Coa	368	85	56	41	23	2,870,235
		Stewart Elliott	517	82	72	75	16	2,960,737
		Charles C. Lopez	341	65	65	56	19	2,327,506
		Julian Pimentel	336	57	47	51	17	2,040,975
MTH	5/29 - 9/26	Trainer	Starts	1st	2d	3d	Win %	Earnings
		Timothy A. Hills	182	36	29	26	20	1,161,244
		Edwin Thomas Broome	145	29	24	22	20	683,707
		Gamaliel Vazquez	171	27	27	20	16	825,660
		Richard E. Dutrow, Jr.	79	24	12	16	30	762,220
		Joseph F. Orseno	130	20	16	18	15	460,810
NMP	9/3 - 9/19	Jockey	Starts	1st	2d	3d	Win %	Earnings
		Willie Belmonte	65	16	10	6	25	37,455
		Edgar Paucar	42	16	9	6	38	35,215
		Jesse Hall	70	10	11	17	14	30,760
		Keturah E. Obed	60	8	7	8	13	23,810
		Marino Carlos	59	7	10	8	12	23,515
NMP	9/3 - 9/19	Trainer	Starts	1st	2d	3d	Win %	Earnings
		Samuel J. Keyrouze	63	8	9	8	13	25,330
		Jason G. Grudzien	10	6	1	1	60	10,360
		Tom Crowley	26	5	2	7	19	12,540
		William E. Hamer, Sr.	20	4	4	0	20	10,120
		Ed Connelly	7	4	2	1	57	7,470
NP	6/25 - 10/30	Jockey	Starts	1st	2d	3d	Win %	Earnings
		Quincy Welch	474	108	84	68	23	1,469,512
		Rickey Walcott	428	88	67	66	21	1,157,460
		Real E. Simard	448	67	61	41	15	963,458
		Shannon Beauregard	420	61	65	71	15	783,199
		Leanne M. Painter	428	55	73	56	13	913,796
NP	6/25 - 10/30	Trainer	Starts	1st	2d	3d	Win %	Earnings
		Ron K. Smith	214	39	36	27	18	635,441
		Dale L. Saunders	153	30	30	17	20	425,143
		Joan Petrowski	219	29	21	27	13	457,236
		Pam McDougall	88	23	10	19	26	216,063
		Dale Greenwood	155	20	21	23	13	296,225
OP	1/23 - 4/10	Jockey	Starts	1st	2d	3d	Win %	Earnings
		John McKee	384	71	69	51	18	1,694,028
		Timothy T. Doocy	351	52	51	42	15	1,063,268
		Jamie Theriot	253	49	46	24	19	806,694
		Roman Chapa	225	49	28	23	22	780,680
		Terry J. Thompson	341	46	39	44	13	926,892

Track	Dates	Jockey/Trainer	Starts	1st	2d	3d	Win %	Earnings
OP	1/23 - 4/10	Trainer	Starts	1st	2d	3d	Win %	Earnings
		Cole Norman	205	56	36	21	27	818,742
		Steven M. Asmussen	79	33	12	13	42	744,870
		Robert E. Holthus	117	27	21	16	23	866,538
		Donnie K. Von Hemel	94	16	15	17	17	470,720
		Stanley W. Roberts	169	15	10	18	9	213,492
OTC	3/15	Jockey	Starts	1st	2d	3d	Win %	Earnings
		Edgar S. Prado	5	2	0	1	40	74,500
		Pat Day	3	1	1	1	33	39,000
		Cornelio H. Velasquez	3	1	1	0	33	81,500
		Frank Lovato, Jr.	1	1	0	0	100	60,000
		Patrick Husbands	2	1	0	0	50	32,800
OTC	3/15	Trainer	Starts	1st	2d	3d	Win %	Earnings
		Edward Plesa, Jr.	3	1	1	1	33	60,000
		Rebecca Maker	1	1	0	0	100	60,000
		William P. White	1	1	0	0	100	60,000
		Mark E. Casse	2	1	0	0	50	30,000
		Philip A. Gleaves	1	1	0	0	100	24,000
PEN	1/2 - 12/30	Jockey	Starts	1st	2d	3d	Win %	Earnings
		William P. Otero	959	166	127	146	17	1,245,886
		Thomas Clifton	833	166	114	103	20	1,299,170
		Emilio Flores	1148	150	174	144	13	1,320,152
		Vladimir Diaz	939	131	145	124	14	1,136,789
		Luis A. Belmonte	749	92	105	86	12	778,266
PEN	1/2 - 12/30	Trainer	Starts	1st	2d	3d	Win %	Earnings
		Bruce M. Kravets	783	145	110	97	19	995,904
		John Charles Zimmerman	358	110	45	48	31	767,860
		Harry F. Thompson, Jr.	551	84	91	69	15	569,504
		Jose A. Martinez	651	73	100	102	11	600,886
		Timothy C. Kreiser	205	67	27	27	33	509,745
PHA	6/23 - 12/31	Jockey	Starts	1st	2d	3d	Win %	Earnings
		Anthony S. Black	496	109	82	72	22	1,607,923
		Jose Luis Flores	542	107	73	69	20	1,324,414
		Harry Vega	469	101	58	69	22	1,409,136
		Nick Santagata	478	65	78	60	14	1,066,004
		Frankie Pennington	536	64	77	75	12	955,306
PHA	6/23 - 12/31	Trainer	Starts	1st	2d	3d	Win %	Earnings
		Scott A. Lake	251	71	46	35	28	821,625
		Guadalupe Preciado	213	41	35	32	19	702,041
		Donald S. Reeder	207	35	29	31	17	406,152
		Edward T. Allard	130	34	12	12	26	432,515
		John C. Servis	122	32	18	16	26	470,369
PHA	1/1 - 6/22	Jockey	Starts	1st	2d	3d	Win %	Earnings
		Stewart Elliott	467	106	92	61	23	1,377,969
		Harry Vega	322	62	62	34	19	811,525
		Jose Luis Flores	335	61	47	59	18	760,609
		David Mello	367	48	62	61	13	605,212
		Victor H. Molina	253	43	38	37	17	655,057
PHA	1/1 - 6/22	Trainer	Starts	1st	2d	3d	Win %	Earnings
		Scott A. Lake	286	65	52	52	23	746,553
		Guadalupe Preciado	186	44	36	21	24	543,473
		Donald S. Reeder	148	29	36	19	20	308,948
		Philip T. Aristone	197	29	27	25	15	304,442
		Edward T. Allard	98	28	21	13	29	348,404
PIM	9/9 - 12/31	Jockey	Starts	1st	2d	3d	Win %	Earnings
		Ryan Fogelsonger	383	83	54	58	22	1,666,435
		Eric Camacho	297	53	50	38	18	743,780
		Steve D. Hamilton	287	46	41	41	16	910,765
		Ramon A. Dominguez	110	33	31	15	30	582,250
		Abel Castellano, Jr.	210	32	26	34	15	828,940
PIM	9/9 - 12/31	Trainer	Starts	1st	2d	3d	Win %	Earnings
		Dale Capuano	139	30	12	19	22	478,765
		Scott A. Lake	102	25	16	16	25	351,560
		Rodney Jenkins	84	21	17	12	25	380,530
		Kenneth M. Cox	101	20	12	14	20	293,880
		Richard W. Small	77	19	17	12	25	485,010

PIM	7/31 - 8/27	Jockey	Starts	1st	2d	3d	Win %	Earnings
		Erick D. Rodriguez	101	16	14	23	16	302,970
		Christopher VanHassel	83	16	12	9	19	204,625
		Horacio Karamanos	89	14	19	15	16	281,010
		Steve D. Hamilton	95	11	13	8	12	277,445
		Ryan Fogelsonger	49	10	5	10	20	174,635
PIM	7/31 - 8/27	Trainer	Starts	1st	2d	3d	Win %	Earnings
		Dale Capuano	37	6	5	9	16	103,910
		Hamilton A. Smith	23	4	5	4	17	110,100
		Rodney Jenkins	11	4	3	2	36	76,260
		Benjamin M. Feliciano, Jr.	16	4	2	4	25	92,420
		Edmond D. Gaudet	13	4	2	3	31	58,600
PIM	3/31 - 6/6	Jockey	Starts	1st	2d	3d	Win %	Earnings
		Steve D. Hamilton	282	49	48	32	17	867,093
		Ryan Fogelsonger	244	46	45	48	19	937,202
		Abel Castellano, Jr.	253	40	42	42	16	892,244
		Jozbin Z. Santana	163	36	21	23	22	709,099
		Ramon A. Dominguez	104	27	20	14	26	841,272
PIM	3/31 - 6/6	Trainer	Starts	1st	2d	3d	Win %	Earnings
		Dale Capuano	84	25	17	11	30	382,305
		John J. Robb	73	14	12	7	19	322,250
		Benjamin M. Feliciano, Jr.	42	13	9	3	31	224,239
		Mark Shuman	51	13	3	7	25	296,205
		Julio R. Cartagena	32	12	5	2	38	141,335
PLN	6/30 - 7/11	Jockey	Starts	1st	2d	3d	Win %	Earnings
		Russell A. Baze	48	10	10	4	21	180,679
		Roberto M. Gonzalez	42	9	6	6	21	112,877
		Joe M. Castro	33	9	5	6	27	116,950
		Chad Phillip Schvaneveldt	34	8	6	6	24	183,503
		Frank T. Alvarado	52	7	12	8	13	175,223
PLN	6/30 - 7/11	Trainer	Starts	1st	2d	3d	Win %	Earnings
		Jerry Hollendorfer	40	6	10	5	15	176,433
		Art Sherman	28	4	4	2	14	76,630
		William E. Morey	8	3	2	1	38	24,180
		Armando Lage	20	3	1	5	15	38,062
		Brian J. Koriner	15	3	1	3	20	81,200
PM	10/18/03 - 4/26/04	Jockey	Starts	1st	2d	3d	Win %	Earnings
		Juan M. Gutierrez	410	105	76	83	26	361,924
		Joe A. Crispin	329	73	49	47	22	228,645
		Twyla Beckner	376	53	64	51	14	230,584
		Duane Lee D'Amico	326	51	48	38	16	165,217
		Melissa Peery	301	46	47	29	15	157,461
PM	10/18/03 - 4/26/04	Trainer	Starts	1st	2d	3d	Win %	Earnings
		Jim Fergason	206	50	41	36	24	165,300
		Jonathan Nance	195	40	38	25	21	159,532
		Ben Root	166	32	29	20	19	132,970
		Delmer L. Webb	103	28	19	9	27	110,232
		Jim Keen	210	27	25	35	13	88,015
PRM	7/9 - 9/25	Jockey	Starts	1st	2d	3d	Win %	Earnings
		Timothy T. Doocy	245	54	48	44	22	809,131
		Glenn W. Corbett	223	49	28	31	22	635,076
		James Lopez	234	34	39	27	15	566,621
		Alex Birzer	226	32	38	33	14	562,040
		Kelly Michael Murray	165	18	17	27	11	287,305
PRM	7/9 - 9/25	Trainer	Starts	1st	2d	3d	Win %	Earnings
		Dick R. Clark	191	43	25	21	23	582,076
		Timothy Mark Gleason	131	26	31	21	20	342,459
		David D. McShane	110	20	13	17	18	289,323
		Kelly R. Von Hemel	80	16	9	11	20	275,103
		Stanley W. Roberts	95	13	22	5	14	160,728
PRM	4/16 - 7/4	Jockey	Starts	1st	2d	3d	Win %	Earnings
		Timothy T. Doocy	402	78	80	53	19	1,295,717
		Terry J. Thompson	290	61	47	51	21	956,120
		Glenn W. Corbett	321	58	64	40	18	921,239
		Alex Birzer	369	55	39	59	15	742,367
		Ken A. Shino	253	47	32	32	19	543,022

			Starts	1st	2d	3d	Win %	Earnings
PRM	4/16 - 7/4	Trainer	Starts	1st	2d	3d	Win %	Earnings
		Dick R. Clark	250	52	56	27	21	792,090
		Stanley W. Roberts	181	35	44	19	19	397,226
		Kelly R. Von Hemel	134	32	15	27	24	530,039
		Ray E. Tracy, Jr.	114	18	14	12	16	219,706
		Don Von Hemel	66	16	14	14	24	352,301
PRV	7/7 - 7/10	Jockey	Starts	1st	2d	3d	Win %	Earnings
		Joe A. Crispin	24	10	4	3	42	19,415
		Ty Dangerfield	21	3	9	1	14	10,438
		Tim Neal	19	3	2	6	16	7,634
		Roger Butterfly	21	3	2	1	14	8,210
		Darlene Braden	20	3	1	1	15	7,100
PRV	7/7 - 7/10	Trainer	Starts	1st	2d	3d	Win %	Earnings
		Scott Nance	7	3	1	2	43	5,798
		Tom Farrell	5	2	1	1	40	4,045
		Jaqueline Smith	4	2	1	0	50	3,800
		Judi Yearout	4	2	0	0	50	3,300
		Brian Tschirgi	5	1	2	1	20	2,700
RD	6/27 - 9/6	Jockey	Starts	1st	2d	3d	Win %	Earnings
		Dean A. Sarvis	352	83	53	44	24	438,681
		Perry Wayne Ouzts	366	66	49	55	18	434,868
		Hector L. Rosario, Jr.	279	49	41	38	18	361,487
		James Christopher Herrell	256	31	24	26	12	212,265
		Jeff Johnston	169	30	34	16	18	280,959
RD	6/27 - 9/6	Trainer	Starts	1st	2d	3d	Win %	Earnings
		Joe Woodard	75	14	8	12	19	81,006
		Luis Albert Palacios	77	13	12	9	17	111,191
		Dennis T. Moore	53	11	6	11	21	66,611
		Rinzy Nocero	83	10	16	9	12	60,528
		Timothy E. Hamm	25	10	4	2	40	169,410
RD	4/9 - 6/26	Jockey	Starts	1st	2d	3d	Win %	Earnings
		Dean A. Sarvis	326	84	50	49	26	519,506
		Perry Wayne Ouzts	360	67	65	60	19	426,303
		Hector L. Rosario, Jr.	229	29	32	40	13	187,902
		Rodney A. Prescott	185	28	22	31	15	189,600
		Ivan R. Gonzalez	156	26	18	16	17	151,297
RD	4/9 - 6/26	Trainer	Starts	1st	2d	3d	Win %	Earnings
		Joe Woodard	86	16	15	11	19	81,875
		James E. Morgan	43	14	9	3	33	116,001
		Luis Albert Palacios	74	12	16	17	16	104,330
		Kris Nemann	45	11	7	8	24	100,906
		Rinzy Nocero	61	8	10	5	13	45,578
RET	7/23 - 9/25	Jockey	Starts	1st	2d	3d	Win %	Earnings
		Roman Chapa	210	58	36	40	28	589,230
		Amanda L. Crandall	214	34	25	31	16	267,850
		Casey T. Lambert	132	31	18	24	23	393,735
		Terry A. Stanton	159	30	24	24	19	306,485
		Larry Taylor	191	27	26	21	14	248,295
RET	7/23 - 9/25	Trainer	Starts	1st	2d	3d	Win %	Earnings
		Danny Pish	145	41	35	22	28	389,050
		John G. Locke	114	18	15	16	16	210,445
		Tommie T. Morgan	76	16	14	7	21	141,735
		Amos Laborde	58	13	11	7	22	104,630
		Tim D. Garner	48	13	7	6	27	79,220
RIL	1/17 - 2/29	Jockey	Starts	1st	2d	3d	Win %	Earnings
		James Daniel Schwartz	51	15	4	8	29	19,543
		Fernando Manuel Gamez	60	13	11	12	22	22,418
		Todd J. Nuttall	66	12	12	10	18	19,998
		Stephen Michael Karr	66	11	13	8	17	20,386
		Justin Vanderwoude	44	9	7	5	20	14,419
RIL	1/17 - 2/29	Trainer	Starts	1st	2d	3d	Win %	Earnings
		Bill K. Earle	26	8	4	6	31	13,139
		Gene K. Wilson	30	4	8	6	13	8,040
		Laurie Jones	31	4	4	4	13	7,099
		Ceasar J. Lopez	13	4	3	0	31	5,698
		Lowell N. Bunyard	13	4	1	2	31	5,070

Track	Dates	Jockey/Trainer	Starts	1st	2d	3d	Win %	Earnings
RKM	9/5	Jockey	Starts	1st	2d	3d	Win %	Earnings
		Orlando Bocachica	3	2	1	0	67	22,700
		Edwin Molinari	3	1	0	0	33	7,750
		Jill Ann Jellison	2	0	1	0	0	3,400
		Tammi Piermarini	3	0	1	0	0	3,400
		Alfredo Clemente	3	0	0	2	0	2,850
RKM	9/5	Trainer	Starts	1st	2d	3d	Win %	Earnings
		George R. Handy	2	2	0	0	100	20,400
		Lucy Delgado	1	1	0	0	100	6,900
		Robert A. Raymond	1	0	1	0	0	3,400
		Thomas J. Ryan	2	0	1	0	0	3,400
		James E. Hartley	1	0	1	0	0	2,300
RP	8/6 - 12/5	Jockey	Starts	1st	2d	3d	Win %	Earnings
		Quincy Hamilton	445	94	66	53	21	692,647
		Monte Clifton Berry	344	91	63	41	26	738,383
		Nena Matz	402	65	71	62	16	606,255
		Kevin Leon Cogburn	336	43	58	57	13	433,820
		Curtis Kimes	412	38	48	42	9	336,472
RP	8/6 - 12/5	Trainer	Starts	1st	2d	3d	Win %	Earnings
		Roger F. Engel	92	36	12	12	39	202,625
		Donnie K. Von Hemel	144	35	28	17	24	406,274
		Joe S. Offolter	158	25	19	15	16	186,816
		Frederico Villafranco	72	18	14	10	25	107,822
		Richard L. Harper	135	15	12	12	11	95,315
RUI	5/28 - 9/6	Jockey	Starts	1st	2d	3d	Win %	Earnings
		Alfredo J. Juarez, Jr.	131	34	20	27	26	333,149
		Carlos D. Madeira	145	34	18	25	23	267,130
		Jorge Martin Bourdieu	167	27	35	24	16	306,062
		Perry S. Whetstone	157	22	30	25	14	254,060
		Oscar Ceballos	137	22	19	21	16	167,327
RUI	5/28 - 9/6	Trainer	Starts	1st	2d	3d	Win %	Earnings
		Joel H. Marr	83	18	10	14	22	149,778
		Todd W. Fincher	52	17	14	10	33	247,886
		Ralph W. Black, Jr.	97	16	18	16	16	152,734
		O. Dwain Grissom	83	16	14	7	19	172,443
		Henry Dominguez	79	15	14	18	19	144,286
SA	9/29 - 10/31	Jockey	Starts	1st	2d	3d	Win %	Earnings
		Corey S. Nakatani	88	21	18	13	24	1,430,982
		Victor Espinoza	112	19	19	14	17	861,007
		Tyler Baze	102	19	12	15	19	848,020
		Rene R. Douglas	111	18	20	14	16	1,076,590
		Garrett K. Gomez	95	15	20	7	16	418,942
SA	9/29 - 10/31	Trainer	Starts	1st	2d	3d	Win %	Earnings
		Mike R. Mitchell	30	13	4	4	43	448,412
		Doug O'Neill	71	11	11	9	15	640,150
		Robert J. Frankel	30	10	5	3	33	1,089,140
		John W. Sadler	44	9	5	4	20	392,125
		Jack Carava	40	8	8	5	20	160,844
SA	12/26/03 - 4/18/04	Jockey	Starts	1st	2d	3d	Win %	Earnings
		Victor Espinoza	509	89	99	70	17	5,590,929
		Alex O. Solis	332	79	56	49	24	4,121,001
		Tyler Baze	497	71	69	83	14	3,268,818
		Corey S. Nakatani	381	67	60	53	18	2,899,433
		Mike E. Smith	299	52	40	33	17	2,474,687
SA	12/26/03 - 4/18/04	Trainer	Starts	1st	2d	3d	Win %	Earnings
		Jeff Mullins	166	45	34	16	27	2,419,818
		Doug O'Neill	241	42	37	29	17	1,644,961
		Robert J. Frankel	130	34	27	21	26	2,247,987
		Mike R. Mitchell	122	30	24	16	25	964,408
		Bob Baffert	166	27	18	21	16	1,655,344
SAC	8/25 - 9/6	Jockey	Starts	1st	2d	3d	Win %	Earnings
		Victor Miranda	52	12	7	4	23	106,344
		David G. Lopez	39	12	4	9	31	103,479
		Ryan Morris	64	10	2	13	16	95,776
		Modesto Linares	31	7	5	3	23	57,048
		Macario Rodriguez	53	6	12	3	11	74,165

Track	Dates	Name	Starts	1st	2d	3d	Win %	Earnings
SAC	8/25 - 9/6	Trainer	Starts	1st	2d	3d	Win %	Earnings
		Rene Amescua	23	8	4	3	35	58,922
		Dennis Hopkins	42	6	7	7	14	67,185
		Michael Lenzini	64	6	4	12	9	73,065
		John F. Martin	10	4	1	2	40	29,160
		Efrain Miranda	12	3	3	1	25	24,192
SAF	3/27 - 4/4	Jockey	Starts	1st	2d	3d	Win %	Earnings
		Justin Vanderwoude	9	5	0	2	56	7,236
		Stephen Michael Karr	13	3	3	3	23	6,379
		Anna M. Barrio	14	3	2	0	21	5,688
		Todd J. Nuttall	12	2	2	1	17	4,279
		Fernando Manuel Gamez	11	2	1	2	18	3,580
SAF	3/27 - 4/4	Trainer	Starts	1st	2d	3d	Win %	Earnings
		Ceasar J. Lopez	3	2	0	1	67	3,320
		Lowell N. Bunyard	3	2	0	0	67	1,734
		William H. Mahan	7	1	3	1	14	3,465
		Gary Duke	3	1	0	2	33	1,912
		Eddie Tellez	2	1	0	1	50	2,024
SAR	7/28 - 9/6	Jockey	Starts	1st	2d	3d	Win %	Earnings
		John R. Velazquez	227	65	28	30	29	3,565,318
		Edgar S. Prado	242	39	50	32	16	3,839,977
		Javier Castellano	220	29	31	40	13	1,585,758
		Jerry D. Bailey	131	29	24	23	22	1,801,956
		Cornelio H. Velasquez	213	26	35	24	12	1,853,127
SAR	7/28 - 9/6	Trainer	Starts	1st	2d	3d	Win %	Earnings
		Todd A. Pletcher	120	35	19	15	29	2,155,688
		Robert J. Frankel	43	15	8	5	35	969,725
		Nicholas P. Zito	59	10	8	3	17	1,275,753
		Mark Shuman	59	10	6	9	17	363,266
		William I. Mott	69	9	12	8	13	575,033
SJ	9/18 - 9/26	Jockey	Starts	1st	2d	3d	Win %	Earnings
		Anna M. Barrio	13	8	1	0	62	9,575
		Carl S. Williams	22	3	7	8	14	7,484
		Terry Lee Gard	22	3	5	8	14	7,083
		Alfredo Torres	22	3	4	3	14	6,283
		Javier A. Ortega	9	3	1	0	33	3,611
SJ	9/18 - 9/26	Trainer	Starts	1st	2d	3d	Win %	Earnings
		Gene K. Wilson	10	5	3	0	50	6,356
		Lowell N. Bunyard	6	3	1	0	50	3,901
		Mike D. Thomas	3	3	0	0	100	3,254
		Ernest R. Williams	11	2	2	4	18	3,694
		Guillermo Jimenez, Sr.	7	2	0	1	29	2,780
SOL	7/14 - 7/26	Jockey	Starts	1st	2d	3d	Win %	Earnings
		Russell A. Baze	37	10	10	4	27	117,670
		Chance J. Rollins	54	10	8	8	19	155,222
		Chad Phillip Schvaneveldt	25	10	2	2	40	127,455
		Macario Rodriguez	49	9	8	9	18	90,964
		Francisco Duran	52	8	5	7	15	107,265
SOL	7/14 - 7/26	Trainer	Starts	1st	2d	3d	Win %	Earnings
		Jerry Hollendorfer	20	7	5	2	35	122,005
		John F. Martin	12	5	1	0	42	34,507
		Armando Lage	14	4	3	2	29	43,340
		Art Sherman	15	4	3	1	27	37,975
		Don J. Mills	13	4	2	2	31	36,993
SON	4/24 - 5/2	Jockey	Starts	1st	2d	3d	Win %	Earnings
		Stephen Michael Karr	16	4	1	4	25	5,734
		Flavio Lozano	13	3	2	1	23	4,039
		Anna M. Barrio	17	2	3	2	12	4,253
		Charles Lyn McClellan	15	2	3	1	13	4,334
		Shannon Wippert	10	2	2	2	20	3,839
SON	4/24 - 5/2	Trainer	Starts	1st	2d	3d	Win %	Earnings
		Lowell N. Bunyard	4	2	0	1	50	2,158
		Pablo C. Figueroa, Sr.	2	2	0	0	100	3,724
		Ceasar J. Lopez	3	2	0	0	67	2,297
		Gary Duke	3	1	1	1	33	1,598
		Wiley Aker	4	1	1	1	25	1,493

SR	7/28 - 8/9	Jockey	Starts	1st	2d	3d	Win %	Earnings
		Russell A. Baze	61	15	14	10	25	250,903
		Chad Phillip Schvaneveldt	34	12	2	4	35	213,326
		Roberto M. Gonzalez	31	9	4	3	29	114,015
		Ronald J. Warren, Jr.	26	8	5	4	31	124,193
		Chance J. Rollins	39	7	8	6	18	98,267
SR	7/28 - 8/9	Trainer	Starts	1st	2d	3d	Win %	Earnings
		Jerry Hollendorfer	32	8	7	6	25	190,320
		John F. Martin	18	8	1	2	44	94,431
		Gil Matos	9	5	1	0	56	26,940
		Greg Gilchrist	9	5	0	1	56	72,900
		Keith Bennett	8	3	2	2	38	54,405
SRP	8/2 - 11/2	Jockey	Starts	1st	2d	3d	Win %	Earnings
		Ken S. Tohill	164	50	33	27	30	453,468
		Frank Albert Gonsalves	147	19	25	21	13	274,916
		Brian James Theriot	110	17	18	16	15	137,991
		Alfredo J. Juarez, Jr.	55	15	10	5	27	122,179
		Robert W. Johnson	111	12	21	11	11	109,783
SRP	8/2 - 11/2	Trainer	Starts	1st	2d	3d	Win %	Earnings
		Dan H. Dennison	39	17	7	4	44	127,923
		Gary W. Cross	48	16	9	4	33	140,682
		H. Ray Ashford, Jr.	48	10	13	5	21	118,786
		Henry Dominguez	36	10	8	7	28	79,348
		Patricia K. Shirley	27	9	5	1	33	99,340
STK	6/16 - 6/27	Jockey	Starts	1st	2d	3d	Win %	Earnings
		Ken S. Tohill	52	14	11	10	27	118,961
		Macario Rodriguez	56	11	8	9	20	98,122
		Carlos Ignacio Silva	36	7	9	5	19	70,570
		Alfredo Miranda	27	6	3	2	22	45,936
		Hector R. Romero	16	5	4	1	31	50,798
STK	6/16 - 6/27	Trainer	Starts	1st	2d	3d	Win %	Earnings
		Barry Holmes	5	5	0	0	100	27,815
		Andy Mathis	6	3	1	1	50	19,335
		Efrain Miranda	13	3	0	1	23	20,622
		Art Sherman	9	2	3	1	22	25,501
		Michael Lenzini	30	2	2	4	7	29,486
STP	4/2 - 6/20	Jockey	Starts	1st	2d	3d	Win %	Earnings
		Quincy Welch	314	65	51	56	21	803,249
		Rickey Walcott	273	50	47	40	18	678,177
		Leanne M. Painter	294	43	35	47	15	578,191
		Desmond Bryan	260	43	34	31	17	542,812
		Real E. Simard	271	43	31	36	16	514,809
STP	4/2 - 6/20	Trainer	Starts	1st	2d	3d	Win %	Earnings
		Ron K. Smith	131	29	18	16	22	387,161
		Dale L. Saunders	126	20	14	16	16	271,437
		Rodney Haynes	99	18	16	16	18	199,689
		Joan Petrowski	127	17	20	12	13	264,001
		Ernie J. Keller	99	17	7	20	17	182,258
SUD	4/3 - 5/2	Jockey	Starts	1st	2d	3d	Win %	Earnings
		Jay Conklin	35	10	8	7	29	15,742
		Mark Allen Boag	34	8	5	8	24	12,478
		Ronald Joseph Bilodeau	36	7	8	3	19	11,276
		David Deforest Brown	37	7	7	6	19	11,479
		Peter McAleney	22	3	4	4	14	5,758
SUD	4/3 - 5/2	Trainer	Starts	1st	2d	3d	Win %	Earnings
		James R. Craig	28	8	3	4	29	9,776
		A. Lynn Homer	31	7	4	3	23	9,372
		Robert L. Lawrence	16	7	4	2	44	9,960
		Tracy Lebret	26	4	4	2	15	5,610
		Marion Stitzel	22	3	2	4	14	6,084
SUF	5/1 - 11/30	Jockey	Starts	1st	2d	3d	Win %	Earnings
		Winston Albert Thompson	742	154	139	114	21	1,556,866
		Josiah Francis Hampshire, Jr.	634	143	83	93	23	1,541,825
		Dyn Panell	535	127	75	70	24	1,417,086
		Tammi Piermarini	727	114	120	88	16	1,195,044
		Orlando Bocachica	527	75	82	74	14	843,494

Track	Dates	Name	Starts	1st	2d	3d	Win %	Earnings
SUF	5/1 - 11/30	Trainer	Starts	1st	2d	3d	Win %	Earnings
		John Rigattieri	306	93	51	40	30	1,078,468
		Ronald J. Dandy	274	62	42	38	23	636,728
		Raymond E. Stifano	290	58	49	39	20	583,453
		Burton K. Sipp	390	51	50	44	13	409,225
		Robert A. Raymond	263	34	29	23	13	295,594
SUN	11/25/03 - 4/11/04	Jockey	Starts	1st	2d	3d	Win %	Earnings
		Ken S. Tohill	337	68	56	53	20	1,480,242
		Casey T. Lambert	371	67	44	50	18	1,142,996
		Ricardo Jaime	343	43	40	48	13	1,448,484
		Jorge Martin Bourdieu	327	43	37	43	13	980,775
		Alfredo J. Juarez, Jr.	264	39	34	24	15	682,717
SUN	11/25/03 - 4/11/04	Trainer	Starts	1st	2d	3d	Win %	Earnings
		Steven M. Asmussen	191	53	28	35	28	1,014,708
		Henry Dominguez	218	40	28	23	18	1,030,811
		Ramon O. Gonzalez	176	29	26	16	16	529,364
		Joel H. Marr	135	23	15	17	17	559,110
		Gary W. Cross	100	20	15	15	20	422,147
TAM	12/13/03 - 5/2/04	Jockey	Starts	1st	2d	3d	Win %	Earnings
		Jesus Lopez Castanon	523	87	75	73	17	1,202,216
		T. D. Houghton	686	82	103	90	12	1,024,498
		Joseph C. Judice	391	69	50	40	18	768,213
		Juan Umana	456	63	63	58	14	762,376
		Russell W. Woolsey	486	61	80	53	13	703,288
TAM	12/13/03 - 5/2/04	Trainer	Starts	1st	2d	3d	Win %	Earnings
		Lynne M. Scace	149	25	25	22	17	298,309
		Layne S. Giliforte	130	23	21	15	18	242,797
		Ronald D. Allen, Sr.	128	23	16	18	18	330,264
		Duane Knipe	120	20	11	13	17	204,671
		Thomas M. Agosti	108	19	22	9	18	144,933
TDN	10/7 - 12/31	Jockey	Starts	1st	2d	3d	Win %	Earnings
		Scott Spieth	244	57	38	29	23	395,385
		Julio E. Felix	221	40	43	26	18	311,175
		Huber Villa-Gomez	250	39	46	35	16	335,240
		Luis Antonio Gonzalez	229	32	29	22	14	246,546
		Daniel Centeno	200	26	27	24	13	205,862
TDN	10/7 - 12/31	Trainer	Starts	1st	2d	3d	Win %	Earnings
		Jeffrey A. Radosevich	137	32	17	11	23	190,925
		Rodney C. Faulkner	130	24	22	15	18	162,883
		Jerry Hollendorfer	68	18	15	7	26	179,053
		Joseph R. Martin	61	12	10	12	20	85,205
		Rodrigo Madrigal, Sr.	48	12	8	4	25	126,150
TDN	7/25 - 10/6	Jockey	Starts	1st	2d	3d	Win %	Earnings
		Luis Antonio Gonzalez	250	44	35	36	18	380,502
		Scott Spieth	198	44	23	21	22	343,517
		Huber Villa-Gomez	213	38	28	28	18	325,881
		Weldon T. Cloninger, Jr.	159	33	27	17	21	284,264
		Daniel Centeno	231	31	26	29	13	232,838
TDN	7/25 - 10/6	Trainer	Starts	1st	2d	3d	Win %	Earnings
		Rodney C. Faulkner	117	24	20	12	21	157,668
		Joseph Clark Faulkner	91	22	10	9	24	113,801
		Jerry Hollendorfer	64	20	11	7	31	159,704
		Andrew Konkoly	71	17	16	8	24	120,494
		Jeffrey A. Radosevich	77	14	18	15	18	118,880
TDN	5/15 - 7/24	Jockey	Starts	1st	2d	3d	Win %	Earnings
		Huber Villa-Gomez	225	45	31	30	20	316,501
		Weldon T. Cloninger, Jr.	205	39	35	23	19	306,065
		Luis Antonio Gonzalez	189	38	26	22	20	343,854
		Scott Spieth	192	28	21	21	15	228,651
		Daniel Centeno	180	26	23	24	14	176,769
TDN	5/15 - 7/24	Trainer	Starts	1st	2d	3d	Win %	Earnings
		Rodney C. Faulkner	115	24	26	8	21	145,276
		Gary L. Johnson	142	22	14	11	15	130,355
		Jerry Hollendorfer	51	22	12	7	43	122,956
		Andrew Konkoly	50	18	15	5	36	113,803
		Joseph Clark Faulkner	105	17	13	18	16	103,689

Track	Dates	Jockey/Trainer	Starts	1st	2d	3d	Win %	Earnings
TDN	4/8 - 5/14	Jockey	Starts	1st	2d	3d	Win %	Earnings
		Huber Villa-Gomez	118	30	13	18	25	219,152
		Scott Spieth	107	18	14	6	17	126,613
		Luis Antonio Gonzalez	113	18	11	13	16	153,350
		Julio E. Felix	104	15	15	11	14	106,346
		Daniel Centeno	99	15	14	14	15	96,947
TDN	4/8 - 5/14	Trainer	Starts	1st	2d	3d	Win %	Earnings
		Gary L. Johnson	92	12	12	11	13	78,757
		Jeffrey A. Radosevich	49	12	10	4	24	73,700
		Jerry Hollendorfer	24	12	3	2	50	52,275
		Rodney C. Faulkner	60	10	9	11	17	63,954
		Rodrigo Madrigal, Sr.	30	7	6	4	23	80,588
TIL	8/12 - 8/14	Jockey	Starts	1st	2d	3d	Win %	Earnings
		Jaime Martinez	13	5	3	2	38	7,956
		Kevin C. Murray	14	5	3	2	36	7,950
		Twyla Beckner	16	3	5	3	19	6,699
		Darlene Braden	17	2	3	4	12	5,383
		Jose M. Rivera, Jr.	11	2	1	1	18	3,345
TIL	8/12 - 8/14	Trainer	Starts	1st	2d	3d	Win %	Earnings
		Judi Yearout	6	2	2	0	33	3,632
		Don D. Young	5	2	2	0	40	3,060
		Donald L. Lawrence	2	2	0	0	100	2,475
		Gary Peters	2	2	0	0	100	2,200
		James C. Harrell	6	1	2	1	17	2,415
TIM	8/28 - 9/6	Jockey	Starts	1st	2d	3d	Win %	Earnings
		Erick D. Rodriguez	48	12	13	7	25	141,755
		Eric Camacho	46	12	6	6	26	131,030
		Christian J. Olmo	26	7	3	4	27	58,950
		Luis Garcia	47	5	11	4	11	89,205
		Larry C. Reynolds	22	4	4	0	18	59,520
TIM	8/28 - 9/6	Trainer	Starts	1st	2d	3d	Win %	Earnings
		Gary Capuano	9	4	1	1	44	74,040
		Kenneth M. Cox	6	4	1	0	67	38,745
		Benjamin M. Feliciano, Jr.	13	3	5	1	23	39,825
		Hamilton A. Smith	12	3	1	3	25	26,490
		Howard E. Wolfendale	8	3	1	2	38	28,155
TP	11/28 - 12/31	Jockey	Starts	1st	2d	3d	Win %	Earnings
		Dean A. Sarvis	173	39	27	22	23	438,056
		Ramsey Zimmerman	183	24	38	11	13	324,150
		William D. Troilo	109	17	12	17	16	209,973
		Rodney A. Prescott	146	16	15	17	11	183,458
		Juan F. Molina, Jr.	116	13	15	17	11	169,547
TP	11/28 - 12/31	Trainer	Starts	1st	2d	3d	Win %	Earnings
		Bernard S. Flint	36	7	6	5	19	144,729
		Wayne D. Mogge	20	7	5	3	35	68,985
		George Leonard, III	30	7	2	3	23	45,703
		Ralph Martinez	21	6	6	2	29	41,533
		Paul J. McGee	18	5	5	2	28	61,123
TP	9/8 - 10/7	Jockey	Starts	1st	2d	3d	Win %	Earnings
		Rafael Bejarano	146	35	29	25	24	570,987
		Willie Martinez	124	27	18	15	22	377,781
		John McKee	124	23	22	21	19	423,121
		Dean A. Sarvis	142	21	11	15	15	219,200
		Brian Joseph Hernandez, Jr.	86	11	13	10	13	147,281
TP	9/8 - 10/7	Trainer	Starts	1st	2d	3d	Win %	Earnings
		Robert E. Holthus	20	9	1	1	45	215,273
		Bernard S. Flint	33	8	2	3	24	87,570
		Dale L. Romans	23	5	5	3	22	328,712
		Gregory D. Foley	20	5	4	3	25	82,291
		Akiko M. Gothard	11	4	1	1	36	53,025
TP	1/1 - 4/1	Jockey	Starts	1st	2d	3d	Win %	Earnings
		Rafael Bejarano	472	150	99	65	32	2,008,233
		Eddie Zuniga	296	44	29	37	15	577,315
		Jason P. Lumpkins	270	40	41	39	15	707,543
		Perry Wayne Ouzts	359	34	35	23	9	414,859
		Anthony J. D'Amico	172	29	24	29	17	665,175

Track	Dates	Category	Starts	1st	2d	3d	Win %	Earnings
TP	1/1 - 4/1	Trainer	Starts	1st	2d	3d	Win %	Earnings
		Gregory D. Foley	71	24	13	10	34	481,950
		S. Joseph Cain	72	17	10	7	24	207,057
		Bernard S. Flint	87	16	14	10	18	350,048
		Kim Hammond	63	16	9	8	25	119,898
		Dale L. Romans	49	12	7	8	24	293,211
TUP	9/26/03 - 5/16/04	Jockey	Starts	1st	2d	3d	Win %	Earnings
		Mick Ruis	596	132	91	80	22	825,286
		Wilson Omar Dieguez	684	115	81	93	17	822,467
		Scott A. Stevens	610	110	97	97	18	1,087,922
		Esteban Angel Gomez	755	107	118	90	14	877,580
		Joel Campbell	511	102	64	64	20	777,697
TUP	9/26/03 - 5/16/04	Trainer	Starts	1st	2d	3d	Win %	Earnings
		Troy Bainum	255	79	50	44	31	465,964
		Don J. Mills	216	65	42	22	30	436,339
		J. Eric Kruljac	202	54	26	39	27	518,986
		Keith Bennett	112	48	20	11	43	255,731
		Michael Lenzini	316	47	38	30	15	379,192
UN	6/11 - 6/13	Jockey	Starts	1st	2d	3d	Win %	Earnings
		Jim Bob Whiteside	16	6	3	3	38	10,883
		Ronald Joseph Bilodeau	11	2	2	3	18	4,701
		Roger Butterfly	14	2	2	1	14	4,902
		Ty Dangerfield	5	2	1	0	40	3,293
		David Deforest Brown	9	1	4	0	11	3,418
UN	6/11 - 6/13	Trainer	Starts	1st	2d	3d	Win %	Earnings
		Marion Stitzel	9	3	0	1	33	5,426
		Brook Mobley	7	2	1	2	29	3,737
		Patrick Stitzel	3	2	1	0	67	3,010
		Lyle Perry, Sr.	2	2	0	0	100	2,640
		Robert L. Lawrence	4	1	2	0	25	2,282
WDS	9/20 - 10/31	Jockey	Starts	1st	2d	3d	Win %	Earnings
		Alex Birzer	157	30	23	26	19	157,636
		Kelly Michael Murray	174	22	27	28	13	140,624
		Ken A. Shino	102	16	19	18	16	94,126
		Don Lee Frazier	114	16	9	7	14	70,755
		Jason R. Eads	80	15	13	12	19	122,386
WDS	9/20 - 10/31	Trainer	Starts	1st	2d	3d	Win %	Earnings
		Timothy Mark Gleason	72	19	11	12	26	91,321
		Leroy Hellman	36	15	6	2	42	79,191
		Kenneth Gleason	75	11	16	9	15	114,548
		James B. McCoy	47	9	8	7	19	105,605
		Temple D. Rushton	58	9	5	5	16	40,078
WMF	8/10 - 8/15	Jockey	Starts	1st	2d	3d	Win %	Earnings
		Russell David Kingrey	28	11	7	3	39	22,134
		Ivan Ortiz, Jr.	35	9	6	5	26	20,987
		Shannon Wippert	23	7	2	2	30	15,453
		Carl Hebert	34	3	6	9	9	14,013
		Jack Cano, Jr.	11	3	4	0	27	7,176
WMF	8/10 - 8/15	Trainer	Starts	1st	2d	3d	Win %	Earnings
		John Stabenfeldt	4	4	0	0	100	6,710
		Mark Buckley	11	3	1	2	27	5,781
		Edward Buxbaum	9	2	3	2	22	5,340
		Bill C. Schmitt	9	2	2	1	22	4,267
		William Cheff	7	2	2	1	29	4,037
WO	4/17 - 12/12	Jockey	Starts	1st	2d	3d	Win %	Earnings
		Todd Kabel	681	156	108	76	23	10,467,572
		Patrick Husbands	713	136	114	107	19	7,176,319
		James McAleney	668	109	89	90	16	5,790,603
		Jono C. Jones	663	90	88	81	14	5,613,667
		Emile Ramsammy	726	74	111	94	10	5,036,317
WO	4/17 - 12/12	Trainer	Starts	1st	2d	3d	Win %	Earnings
		Sid C. Attard	311	73	55	38	23	3,573,181
		Robert P. Tiller	277	68	45	33	25	3,877,986
		Mark E. Casse	293	45	45	44	15	2,878,630
		Scott H. Fairlie	259	41	31	34	16	1,562,333
		Reade Baker	249	40	41	37	16	2,545,411

Track	Dates	Jockey	Starts	1st	2d	3d	Win %	Earnings
WYO	6/26 - 8/22	Travis Hamilton	24	6	5	5	25	10,190
		Melissa Marshall	19	5	3	3	26	8,316
		Antonio Perez	24	4	2	3	17	4,074
		Layne Davis	26	3	6	5	12	6,671
		Tony F. Guymon	25	3	4	7	12	7,484

Track	Dates	Trainer	Starts	1st	2d	3d	Win %	Earnings
WYO	6/26 - 8/22	Mike D. Taylor	15	5	4	1	33	10,248
		Terrill Gibbs	18	5	1	8	28	7,720
		Cory Hackford	6	3	0	1	50	2,534
		Daren K. Jones	18	2	4	3	11	2,942
		Kevin D. Newby	14	2	3	3	14	2,774

Track	Dates	Jockey	Starts	1st	2d	3d	Win %	Earnings
YAV	5/29 - 9/7	Wilson Omar Dieguez	184	46	35	29	25	174,030
		Daniel P. Vergara	202	41	42	30	20	194,877
		Esteban Angel Gomez	191	38	27	31	20	164,172
		Lorenzo Castane Lopez	203	37	27	33	18	173,163
		Alberto R. Higuera	215	35	46	32	16	173,121

Track	Dates	Trainer	Starts	1st	2d	3d	Win %	Earnings
YAV	5/29 - 9/7	Bill Brashears	131	39	18	21	30	126,622
		Jerry Atkin	81	17	17	14	21	81,514
		Jon Phil Zimmerman	76	13	15	16	17	59,463
		Dennis T. Sowers	51	13	11	9	25	68,196
		George Wern	60	11	9	10	18	53,866

Track	Dates	Jockey	Starts	1st	2d	3d	Win %	Earnings
YD	9/5 - 9/26	Ivan Ortiz, Jr.	35	7	2	2	20	12,086
		Chad Benjamin	24	6	0	4	25	10,971
		Kym Espy	34	5	8	6	15	14,040
		Russell David Kingrey	14	5	3	2	36	15,743
		Shannon Wippert	19	4	2	4	21	7,868

Track	Dates	Trainer	Starts	1st	2d	3d	Win %	Earnings
YD	9/5 - 9/26	Edward Buxbaum	23	4	7	3	17	9,606
		Doug Johnson	18	3	7	1	17	11,138
		Mel Yelvington	12	3	3	1	25	5,505
		Kenneth Olson	13	3	1	5	23	6,380
		Adlai Falls Down	11	3	1	1	27	5,276

Track	Dates	Jockey	Starts	1st	2d	3d	Win %	Earnings
YKT	7/3 - 7/10	Danielle Beischer	8	2	2	1	25	2,304
		Bernie Tourangeau	9	1	3	1	11	2,020
		Frank La Forge	10	1	1	4	10	1,820
		Chad Keshane	4	1	1	1	25	1,248
		Norbert Keshane	3	1	1	0	33	1,532

Track	Dates	Trainer	Starts	1st	2d	3d	Win %	Earnings
YKT	7/3 - 7/10	Dana T. Keshane	6	4	1	0	67	3,692
		Mike Tourangeau	9	2	2	3	22	2,724
		Brad Ball	6	1	2	1	17	1,464
		James R. Ross	4	1	1	0	25	1,224
		William Keshane	2	1	0	1	50	888

General Statistics of 2004

Trend of Racing

Mutuel Handle

Number of Races and Purses

Races by State or Province

Locations of North American

Alb – Albuquerque, NM
AP – Arlington Park, IL- (Arlington Int'l Race Course)
Aqu – Aqueduct, NY
ArP – *Arapahoe Park, CO -
AsD – *Assiniboia Downs, Man, Canada -
Atl – Atlantic City, NJ
Bel – Belmont Park, NY
Beu – Beulah Park, OH
BM – Bay Meadows, CA
Bmf – Bay Meadows Fair, CA
Boi – *Boise, ID (Les Bois Park)
BRD – *Blue Ribbon Downs, OK
Cby – Canterbury Park, MN
CD – Churchill Downs, KY
Cls – *Columbus, NE
Cnl – Colonial Downs,VA
Crc – Calder Race Course, FL
CT – *Charles Town, WV
DeD – *Delta Downs, LA
DeP – *Desert Park, BC, Canada
Del – Delaware Park, DE
Dmr – Del Mar, CA
ElP – Ellis Park, KY
EmD – Emerald Downs, WA
EvD – *Evangeline Downs, LA
Fai – Fair Hill, MD
FE – Fort Erie, Ont, Canada
Fer – *Ferndale, CA
FG – Fair Grounds, LA
FL – Finger Lakes, NY
FMT – *Fair Meadows, OK (Tulsa State Fair)
Fno – Fresno, CA
Fon – *Fonner Park, NE
FP – Fairmount Park, IL
Fpx – *Fairplex (Pomona), CA
Fs – *Flagstaff, AZ
GBF – Great Barrington Fair, MA
GF – *Great Falls, MT
GG – Golden Gate Fields, CA
Gil – *Gillespie County Fair, TX
GLD – Great Lakes Downs, MI
GP – Gulfstream Park, FL (Includes Breeders' Cup)
GrP – *Grants Pass, OR
HaP – *Harbor Park, WA
Haw – Hawthorne, IL
Hia – Hialeah Park, FL
Hol – Hollywood Park, CA
Hoo – Hoosier Park, IN
Hou – Sam Houston Race Park, TX
HPO – Horsmen's Park, NE
Hst – *Hastings Park, BC, Canada (Formerly Exhibition Park)
Ind – Indiana Downs, IN
Kam – *Kamloops, BC, Canada
KD – Kentucky Downs (Formerly Deuling Grounds)
Kee – Keeneland, KY
Kin – *Kin Park, BC, Canada
LA – *Los Alamitos, CA
LaD – Louisana Downs, LA
LnN – *Lincoln State Fair, NE
Lrl – Laurel Park, MD
LS – Lone Star Park, TX
MD – *Marquis Downs, Sask, Canada
Med – Meadowlands, NJ
Mex – *Mexico City, Mexico (Hipodromo de las Americas)

Thoroughbred Race Tracks

TRENDS IN THOROUGHBRED RACING

General statistics for race meetings that ended in 2004. The statistics on the following pages include race meets scheduled for 2004 and 2005 along with comparisons of total races, purses, numbers of starters, average size of field, and average purse for 2004 by states.

			Meetings Ending in 2004						Avg. Overnight	Avg Purses	2005 Dates	
State	Track	Days	First Day	Last Day	Races	Starters	Favwins	Fwinpct	Purses	. w/Stks	First Day	Last Day
AR	OP	55	01/23/04	04/10/04	558	4,858	204	37	$165,760	$238,487	01/21/05	04/16/05
AR	**Totals**	**55**			**558**	**4,858**	**204**	**37**				
AZ	DG	4	04/10/04	04/18/04	19	144	3	16	$4,750	$4,750	04/16/05	04/24/05
AZ	DUN	4	03/13/04	03/21/04	24	174	5	21	$5,750	$6,000	03/12/05	03/20/05
AZ	FLG	4	07/02/04	07/05/04	23	157	11	48	$5,750	$5,750	07/01/05	07/04/05
AZ	GCF	4	10/02/04	10/10/04	22	152	5	23	$5,500	$5,500	10/01/05	10/09/05
AZ	MOF	4	05/08/04	05/16/04	18	113	5	28	$4,000	$4,500	05/14/05	05/22/05
AZ	RIL	14	01/17/04	02/29/04	82	617	36	44	$6,000	$6,214	01/22/05	03/06/05
AZ	SAF	4	03/27/04	04/04/04	17	114	9	53	$4,250	$4,250	04/02/05	04/10/05
AZ	SJ	4	09/18/04	09/26/04	23	127	10	43	$5,750	$5,750	09/17/05	09/25/05
AZ	SON	4	04/24/04	05/02/04	17	123	9	53	$3,500	$4,250	04/30/05	05/08/05
AZ	TUP	165	09/26/03	05/16/04	1,463	12,109	529	36	$55,551	$70,525	10/01/04	05/22/05
AZ	YAV	56	05/29/04	09/07/04	354	2,634	123	35	$26,204	$30,123	05/28/05	09/06/05
AZ	**Totals**	**267**			**2,062**	**16,464**	**745**	**36**				
CA	BM	55	04/07/04	06/20/04	464	3,239	168	36	$133,967	$154,604	02/02/05	05/08/05
CA	BM	49	09/03/04	11/07/04	414	2,875	158	38	$128,886	$149,294	09/03/05	10/16/05
CA	BMF	12	08/11/04	08/23/04	97	644	35	36	$107,333	$107,333	08/10/05	08/22/05
CA	DMR	43	07/21/04	09/08/04	371	3,064	117	32	$298,744	$469,674	07/20/05	09/07/05
CA	FER	10	08/12/04	08/22/04	34	188	18	53	$12,610	$16,810	08/11/05	08/21/05

State	Track	Days	First Day	Last Day	Races	Starters	Favwins	Fwinpct	Avg. Overnight Purses	Avg Purses . w/Stks	2005 Dates First Day	Last Day
			Meetings Ending in 2004									
CA	FNO	10	10/06/04	10/17/04	62	520	23	37	$46,318	$53,591	10/05/05	10/16/05
CA	FPX	17	09/10/04	09/26/04	161	1,289	62	39	$162,118	$236,235	09/09/05	09/25/05
CA	GG	109	11/05/03	04/04/04	920	6,546	338	37	$133,768	$152,438	05/11/05	12/31/05
CA	GG	59	11/10/04	01/30/05	491	3,517	173	35	$131,878	$143,742		
CA	HOL	65	04/21/04	07/18/04	558	4,459	177	32	$257,415	$396,800	04/22/05	07/17/05
CA	HOL	36	11/03/04	12/20/04	308	2,321	104	34	$221,861	$331,014	11/09/05	12/19/05
CA	LA	189	12/26/03	12/19/04	386	2,903	143	37	$13,164	$13,164	12/26/04	12/18/05
CA	PLN	11	06/30/04	07/11/04	91	706	24	26	$108,000	$129,818	06/29/05	07/10/05
CA	SA	84	12/26/03	04/18/04	726	5,842	277	38	$277,726	$438,857	12/26/04	04/18/05
CA	SA	26	09/29/04	10/31/04	222	1,772	85	38	$219,923	$407,423	09/28/05	11/06/05
CA	SAC	11	08/25/04	09/06/04	89	677	33	37	$78,727	$88,727	08/24/05	09/05/05
CA	SOL	11	07/14/04	07/26/04	94	752	40	43	$96,545	$109,273	07/13/05	07/25/05
CA	SR	12	07/28/04	08/09/04	97	748	36	37	$97,542	$122,542	07/27/05	08/08/05
CA	STK	10	06/16/04	06/27/04	74	576	27	36	$70,840	$70,840	06/15/05	06/26/05
CA	**Totals**	**819**			**5,659**	**42,638**	**2,038**	**36**				
CN	ASD	71	05/02/04	10/03/04	583	4,634	210	36	$59,169	$77,310	05/01/05	09/25/05
CN	FE	81	05/01/04	09/06/04	799	6,796	270	34	$156,080	$181,574	05/01/05	10/31/05
CN	GPR	21	07/09/04	08/22/04	62	396	14	23	$8,017	$12,384	07/08/05	08/21/05
CN	HST	71	04/17/04	11/28/04	691	5,381	226	33	$124,982	$161,672	04/16/05	11/27/05
CN	KAM	5	05/30/04	07/04/04	17	87	7	41	$6,800	$6,800	08/06/05	09/04/05
CN	KAM	3	08/08/04	09/05/04	8	38	3	38	$4,000	$9,417		
CN	KIN	3	07/11/04	08/01/04	15	70	7	47	$9,500	$14,583	07/09/05	07/30/05
CN	LBG	25	05/01/04	07/04/04	121	846	38	31	$23,454	$25,750	05/07/05	07/03/05
CN	LBG	26	09/04/04	10/31/04	147	1,074	42	29	$23,515	$31,607	09/03/05	10/30/05
CN	MD	29	05/28/04	09/11/04	205	1,463	71	35	$16,603	$21,713	05/27/05	09/17/05

State	Track	Days	Meetings Ending in 2004 First Day	Last Day	Races	Starters	Favwins	Fwinpct	Avg. Overnight Purses	Avg Purses . w/Stks	2005 Dates First Day	Last Day
CN	MDA	4	05/08/04	05/16/04	18	84	9	50	$5,825	$5,825	05/05/05	05/22/05
CN	MDA	5	10/02/04	10/11/04	24	117	7	29	$6,240	$6,240	09/24/05	10/09/05
CN	MIL	2	07/01/04	07/02/04	5	29	1	20	$12,275	$17,525	07/01/05	07/01/05
CN	NP	72	06/25/04	10/30/04	626	4,886	200	32	$91,715	$120,465	06/24/05	10/29/05
CN	STP	46	04/02/04	06/20/04	403	3,124	121	30	$96,145	$107,847	04/01/05	06/19/05
CN	WO	167	04/17/04	12/12/04	1,529	13,140	498	33	$363,608	$493,668	04/16/05	12/11/05
CN	YKT	3	07/03/04	07/10/04	10	45	4	40	$3,600	$4,267	06/18/05	07/03/05
CN	**Totals**	**634**			**5,263**	**42,210**	**1,728**	**33**				
CO	ARP	37	07/03/04	09/06/04	252	1,721	98	39	$39,731	$52,820	06/04/05	08/28/05
CO	**Totals**	**37**			**252**	**1,721**	**98**	**39**				
DE	DEL	134	04/24/04	11/07/04	1,202	8,891	457	38	$205,615	$247,096	04/30/05	11/13/05
DE	**Totals**	**134**			**1,202**	**8,891**	**457**	**38**				
FL	CRC	123	04/26/04	10/23/04	1,281	10,071	444	35	$179,952	$238,599	04/25/05	12/31/05
FL	CRC	55	10/24/04	01/02/05	596	4,730	208	35	$171,009	$236,827		
FL	GP	91	01/03/04	04/25/04	899	7,858	321	36	$212,141	$302,522	01/03/05	04/24/05
FL	OTC	1	03/15/04	03/15/04	6	58	0	0	$0	$380,000	03/21/05	03/21/05
FL	TAM	93	12/13/03	05/02/04	992	9,863	295	30	$123,617	$144,854	12/11/04	05/08/05
FL	**Totals**	**363**			**3,774**	**32,580**	**1,268**	**34**				
IA	PRM	49	04/16/04	07/04/04	461	3,671	172	37	$129,456	$167,926	04/21/05	07/04/05
IA	PRM	47	07/09/04	09/25/04	285	2,288	97	34	$68,938	$89,683	07/08/05	09/24/05
IA	**Totals**	**96**			**746**	**5,959**	**269**	**36**				

State	Track	Days	First Day	Last Day	Races	Starters	Favwins	Fwinpct	Avg. Overnight Purses	Avg Purses . w/Stks	2005 Dates First Day	Last Day
			Meetings Ending in 2004									
ID	BOI	46	05/01/04	08/15/04	274	1,792	99	36	$11,428	$18,149	05/04/05	08/14/05
ID	**Totals**	**46**			**274**	**1,792**	**99**	**36**				
IL	AP	96	05/14/04	09/19/04	896	7,405	294	33	$196,505	$266,036	05/13/05	09/18/05
IL	FP	101	03/26/04	09/18/04	960	6,869	320	33	$53,739	$58,641	03/25/05	09/17/05
IL	HAW	47	02/27/04	05/11/04	444	3,508	162	36	$181,766	$224,957	02/25/05	05/10/05
IL	HAW	66	09/24/04	01/02/05	620	5,726	194	31	$179,888	$211,082	09/23/05	01/01/06
IL	**Totals**	**310**			**2,920**	**23,508**	**970**	**33**				
IN	HOO	59	09/02/04	11/21/04	642	5,574	255	40	$112,413	$138,413	09/03/05	11/25/05
IN	IND	48	04/16/04	06/20/04	434	3,643	149	34	$79,267	$85,933	04/15/05	06/18/05
IN	**Totals**	**107**			**1,076**	**9,217**	**404**	**38**				
KS	ANF	6	07/16/04	07/25/04	21	124	9	43	$3,883	$11,550	07/15/05	07/24/05
KS	EUR	21	05/01/04	07/04/04	55	350	29	53	$4,552	$4,910	05/07/05	07/10/05
KS	WDS	30	09/20/04	10/31/04	203	1,846	81	40	$33,017	$40,683	09/24/05	10/29/05
KS	**Totals**	**57**			**279**	**2,320**	**119**	**43**				
KY	CD	53	04/24/04	07/05/04	537	4,565	200	37	$323,309	$458,687	04/30/05	07/10/05
KY	CD	21	10/31/04	11/27/04	217	2,137	70	32	$357,190	$489,324	10/30/05	11/26/05
KY	ELP	54	07/07/04	09/06/04	540	4,321	201	37	$147,746	$167,191	07/13/05	09/05/05
KY	KD	6	09/18/04	09/28/04	44	456	10	23	$131,167	$227,833	09/17/05	09/27/05
KY	KEE	15	04/02/04	04/23/04	142	1,186	47	33	$382,600	$634,267	04/08/05	04/29/05
KY	KEE	17	10/08/04	10/30/04	156	1,399	56	36	$324,765	$599,765	10/07/05	10/29/05
KY	TP	79	11/30/03	04/01/04	780	7,124	299	38	$140,100	$162,259	11/28/04	04/07/05
KY	TP	22	09/08/04	10/07/04	220	1,866	71	32	$130,223	$179,086	09/07/05	10/06/05
KY	**Totals**	**267**			**2,636**	**23,054**	**954**	**36**				

			Meetings Ending in 2004						Avg. Overnight	Avg Purses	2005 Dates	
State	Track	Days	First Day	Last Day	Races	Starters	Favwins	Fwinpct	Purses	. w/Stks	First Day	Last Day
LA	DED	86	10/31/03	03/27/04	890	7,985	319	36	$147,491	$193,828	10/01/04	04/02/05
LA	EVD	92	04/01/04	09/06/04	918	8,661	301	33	$107,705	$114,499	04/07/05	09/05/05
LA	FG	80	11/27/03	03/28/04	796	6,578	316	40	$182,075	$252,200	11/25/04	03/27/05
LA	LAD	102	05/14/04	10/31/04	1,081	9,020	389	36	$143,525	$178,378	04/29/05	10/09/05
LA	**Totals**	**360**			**3,685**	**32,244**	**1,325**	**36**				
MA	NMP	9	09/03/04	09/19/04	71	520	27	38	$24,230	$25,730	09/02/05	09/18/05
MA	SUF	119	05/01/04	11/29/04	1,109	8,836	418	38	$99,413	$112,579	04/30/05	11/19/05
MA	**Totals**	**128**			**1,180**	**9,356**	**445**	**38**				
MD	LRL	117	10/08/03	03/28/04	1,041	8,238	386	37	$146,898	$182,589	01/22/05	04/17/05
MD	PIM	48	03/31/04	06/06/04	413	3,115	159	38	$143,333	$223,021	08/10/05	08/26/05
MD	PIM	16	07/31/04	08/27/04	142	1,183	40	28	$149,156	$169,469	09/09/04	01/17/05
MD	PIM	67	09/09/04	12/20/04	588	4,434	200	34	$141,846	$188,610	04/20/05	06/12/05
MD	TIM	8	08/28/04	09/06/04	75	532	24	32	$119,438	$131,938	08/27/05	09/05/05
MD	**Totals**	**256**			**2,259**	**17,502**	**809**	**36**				
MI	GLD	118	04/25/04	10/30/04	1,008	7,512	364	36	$66,916	$81,184	04/25/05	11/05/05
MI	MPM	28	05/01/04	09/26/04	42	237	11	26	$3,832	$3,832	05/07/05	09/25/05
MI	**Totals**	**146**			**1,050**	**7,749**	**375**	**36**				
MN	CBY	67	05/14/04	09/06/04	578	4,704	203	35	$90,149	$118,825	05/07/05	09/05/05
MN	**Totals**	**67**			**578**	**4,704**	**203**	**35**				
MT	GF	9	07/03/04	08/01/04	52	355	15	29	$10,156	$13,367	07/04/05	07/31/05
MT	KSP	3	08/20/04	08/29/04	16	89	8	50	$7,925	$8,600	08/19/05	08/28/05

State	Track	Days	First Day	Last Day	Races	Starters	Favwins	Fwinpct	Avg. Overnight Purses	Avg Purses . w/Stks	2005 Dates First Day	Last Day
			Meetings Ending in 2004									
MT	MAF	2	07/24/04	07/25/04	8	46	1	13	$4,600	$6,750	07/23/05	07/24/05
MT	MC	3	05/09/04	05/16/04	8	47	3	38	$4,633	$6,400	05/15/05	05/22/05
MT	WMF	6	08/10/04	08/15/04	41	266	17	41	$13,067	$19,238	08/09/05	08/14/05
MT	YD	9	09/05/04	09/26/04	41	270	10	24	$10,144	$12,144	08/19/05	09/25/05
MT	**Totals**	**32**			**166**	**1,073**	**54**	**33**				
ND	CPW	6	06/12/04	06/27/04	33	222	15	45	$7,375	$8,658	06/04/05	06/26/05
ND	FAR	14	08/06/04	09/06/04	70	460	38	54	$12,514	$19,707	08/05/05	09/05/05
ND	**Totals**	**20**			**103**	**682**	**53**	**51**				
NE	ATO	3	09/17/04	09/19/04	18	163	9	50	$68,333	$68,333	09/16/05	09/18/05
NE	CLS	25	07/23/04	09/12/04	217	1,832	67	31	$39,734	$43,434	07/28/05	09/11/05
NE	FON	37	02/14/04	05/08/04	362	3,192	134	37	$47,918	$58,444	02/11/05	05/07/05
NE	HPO	4	07/15/04	07/18/04	16	149	8	50	$62,500	$125,000	07/21/05	07/24/05
NE	LNN	33	05/14/04	07/11/04	281	2,364	110	39	$43,798	$48,210	05/13/05	07/17/05
NE	**Totals**	**102**			**894**	**7,700**	**328**	**37**				
NH	RKM	1	09/05/04	09/05/04	3	29	0	0	$45,500	$45,500	09/04/05	09/04/05
NH	**Totals**	**1**			**3**	**29**	**0**	**0**				
NJ	ATL	4	05/05/04	05/19/04	30	280	8	27	$139,750	$152,250	04/28/05	05/12/05
NJ	MED	33	10/01/04	11/13/04	311	2,371	118	38	$247,106	$339,924	09/30/05	11/12/05
NJ	MTH	87	05/29/04	09/26/04	846	6,746	320	38	$255,724	$344,805	05/14/05	09/25/05
NJ	**Totals**	**124**			**1,187**	**9,397**	**446**	**38**				

State	Track	Days	First Day	Last Day	Races	Starters	Favwins	Fwinpct	Avg. Overnight Purses	Avg Purses . w/Stks	2005 Dates First Day	Last Day
			Meetings Ending in 2004									
NM	ALB	53	04/09/04	07/05/04	244	2,118	85	35	$35,687	$48,920	04/02/05	06/12/05
NM	ALB	16	09/10/04	09/26/04	69	517	33	48	$23,213	$49,957	09/09/05	09/25/05
NM	RUI	57	05/28/04	09/06/04	261	1,996	104	40	$29,311	$42,168	05/27/05	09/05/05
NM	SRP	44	08/02/04	11/02/04	231	1,847	74	32	$40,884	$53,290	07/02/05	09/05/05
NM	SUN	80	11/25/03	04/11/04	566	5,543	187	33	$127,199	$164,136	11/05/04	04/03/05
NM	**Totals**	**250**			**1,371**	**12,021**	**483**	**35**				
NV	ELK	6	08/28/04	09/06/04	36	213	21	58	$11,183	$17,483	08/27/05	09/05/05
NV	**Totals**	**6**			**36**	**213**	**21**	**58**				
NY	AQU	61	12/03/03	03/07/04	542	4,534	176	32	$289,783	$327,101	01/01/05	03/06/05
NY	AQU	38	03/10/04	05/02/04	345	2,629	130	38	$301,590	$385,436	03/09/05	05/01/05
NY	AQU	25	10/27/04	11/28/04	218	1,768	80	37	$307,800	$439,000	11/02/05	12/31/05
NY	BEL	60	05/05/04	07/25/04	550	4,420	186	34	$331,150	$486,067	05/04/05	07/24/05
NY	BEL	33	09/10/04	10/24/04	312	2,544	120	38	$334,455	$660,667	09/09/05	10/30/05
NY	FL	157	04/16/04	11/27/04	1,416	11,963	514	36	$97,945	$106,003	04/15/05	11/29/05
NY	SAR	36	07/28/04	09/06/04	343	2,943	130	38	$354,056	$633,778	07/27/05	09/05/05
NY	**Totals**	**410**			**3,726**	**30,801**	**1,336**	**36**				
OH	BEU	70	01/10/04	05/01/04	566	4,898	180	32	$41,785	$44,185	01/08/05	05/07/05
OH	BEU	67	09/18/04	12/21/04	493	4,708	156	32	$39,824	$43,704	09/24/05	12/20/05
OH	RD	122	04/09/04	09/06/04	892	7,587	328	37	$46,237	$53,389	04/08/05	09/05/05
OH	TDN	182	04/08/04	12/31/04	1,337	12,071	512	38	$58,554	$66,281	04/08/05	12/23/05
OH	**Totals**	**441**			**3,288**	**29,264**	**1,176**	**36**				

State	Track	Days	Meetings Ending in 2004 First Day	Last Day	Races	Starters	Favwins	Fwinpct	Avg. Overnight Purses	Avg Purses . w/Stks	2005 Dates First Day	Last Day
OK	BRD	23	02/21/04	05/01/04	75	626	26	35	$6,526	$8,087	02/19/05	05/07/05
OK	BRD	26	08/06/04	11/08/04	58	534	19	33	$4,373	$5,251	08/06/05	10/30/05
OK	FMT	28	05/27/04	07/25/04	135	1,272	58	43	$56,310	$62,310	06/09/05	07/30/05
OK	RP	65	08/06/04	12/05/04	589	5,525	222	38	$64,220	$80,758	08/05/05	11/27/05
OK	**Totals**	**142**			**857**	**7,957**	**325**	**38**				
OR	BRN	2	09/11/04	09/12/04	13	83	6	46	$13,800	$15,050	09/10/05	09/11/05
OR	GRP	19	05/15/04	07/05/04	135	789	45	33	$13,611	$15,517	05/14/05	07/04/05
OR	PM	80	10/18/03	04/26/04	636	4,672	248	39	$25,049	$29,258	10/16/04	04/24/05
OR	PRV	4	07/07/04	07/10/04	25	171	14	56	$15,125	$17,000	07/06/05	07/09/05
OR	TIL	3	08/12/04	08/14/04	20	110	8	40	$13,000	$14,167	08/11/05	08/13/05
OR	UN	3	06/11/04	06/13/04	16	89	8	50	$12,567	$12,567	06/10/05	06/12/05
OR	**Totals**	**111**			**845**	**5,914**	**329**	**39**				
PA	PEN	196	01/02/04	12/30/04	1,740	15,054	611	35	$69,545	$71,261	01/05/05	12/30/05
PA	PHA	216	01/01/04	12/31/04	2,071	16,213	733	35	$120,627	$131,676	01/01/05	12/31/05
PA		**412**			**3,811**	**31,267**	**1,344**	**35**				
TX	GIL	8	07/03/04	08/29/04	21	179	4	19	$11,900	$13,775	07/02/05	08/28/05
TX	HOU	89	10/23/03	04/10/04	853	7,555	316	37	$81,339	$104,261	11/17/04	04/10/05
TX	LS	63	04/15/04	07/11/04	613	5,680	219	36	$148,381	$189,625	04/14/05	07/17/05
TX	LS	19	10/01/04	10/31/04	186	1,638	72	39	$142,711	$962,447		
TX	MAN	16	02/28/04	04/25/04	48	418	11	23	$13,988	$16,224	02/26/05	04/24/05
TX	RET	39	07/23/04	09/25/04	327	2,904	111	34	$68,551	$92,397	08/05/05	10/15/05
TX	**Totals**	**234**			**2,048**	**18,374**	**733**	**36**				

State	Track	Days	First Day	Last Day	Races	Starters	Favwins	Fwinpct	Avg. Overnight Purses	Avg Purses .w/Stks	2005 Dates First Day	Last Day
			Meetings Ending in 2004									
VA	CNL	34	06/11/04	07/26/04	342	2,968	124	36	$156,485	$200,309	06/17/05	08/09/05
VA	**Totals**	**34**			**342**	**2,968**	**124**	**36**				
WA	EMD	90	04/16/04	09/20/04	813	5,893	274	34	$72,805	$95,805	04/15/05	10/16/05
WA	SUD	10	04/03/04	05/02/04	48	291	16	33	$7,700	$8,325	04/02/05	05/01/05
WA	**Totals**	**100**			**861**	**6,184**	**290**	**34**				
WV	CT	231	01/01/04	12/31/04	2,489	22,983	813	33	$217,455	$227,573	01/01/05	12/31/05
WV	MNR	219	01/03/04	12/28/04	2,149	19,625	713	33	$160,389	$171,584	01/15/05	12/27/05
WV	**Totals**	**450**			**4,638**	**42,608**	**1,526**	**33**				
WY	WYO	18	06/26/04	08/22/04	36	259	11	31	$1,978	$3,561	06/25/05	08/21/05
WY	**Totals**	**18**			**36**	**259**	**11**	**31**				

NOTES: Meet Days are days counted on which at least one official Thoroughbred race occurred;

Races are official Thoroughbred Races

Avg. Daily Overnight Purse excl. Stakes is the amount of Daily Overnight Purses excl. Stakes Races divided by Entry Days

Avg. Daily Overnight Purse incl. Stakes is the amount of Daily Overnight Purses incl. Stakes Races divided by Entry Days

PARI-MUTUEL HANDLE

Pari-mutuel handle wagered on thoroughbred racing in the United States during 2004 declined .5%, the first decrease in 11 years, while combined US and Canadian handle slipped .7%. The off-track sector accounted for 87.7% of US handle, up slightly from the year before.

TOTAL NORTH AMERICAN HANDLE 2001-2004

	2001		2002		2003		2004	
	Total*	% of total	Total*	% of total	Total*	% of total	Total*	% of total
On Track	$2,273	14.8	$2,190	13.81	$2,049	12.85	$1,997	12.80
Off Track	13,082	85.2	13,668	86.19	13,890	87.14	13,603	87.20
TOTAL	15,355	(+2.1)	15,858	(+3.3)	15,940	(+0.5)	**15,600	

UNITED STATES

	2001		2002		2003		2004	
	Total	* %of total	Total*	%of total	Total*	%of total	Total*	% of total
On Track	$2,112	14.5	$2,029	13.47	$1,902	12.53	$1,860	12.32
Off Track	12,487	85.5	13,033	86.53	13,278	87.47	13,239	87.68
TOTAL	14,599	(+1.9)	15,062	(+3.2)	15,180	(+.8)	15,099	(-.5)

CANADA

	2001		2002		2003		2004	
	Total*	%of total	Total*	%of total	Total*	% of total	Total*	% of total
On Track	$153	28.3	$153	26.98	$139	26.03	$137	27.29
Off Track	387	71.7	414	73.02	394	73.78	364	72.51
TOTAL	540	(+13.7)	567	(+5.0)	534	(-6.2)	502	(-6.4)

PUERTO RICO

	2001		2002		2003		2004	
	Total	* %of total	Total*	%of total	Total*	%of total	Total*	% of total
On Track	$8	3.7	$8	3.49	$8	3.54	NA	
Off Track	208	96.3	221	96.51	218	96.46	NA	
TOTAL	216	(-13.9)	229	(+6.0)	226	(-1.3)	NA	

• All Dollars in Millions. ** 2004 figures include US and Canada only

PARI MUTUEL HANDLE FROM 1988 THROUGH 2000

Year	United States	% change from prior year	Canada	Total
1988	$8,935,978,600	(+7.3%)	$719,365,900	$9,655,344,500
1989	9,285,509,800	(+3.9%)	772,675,600	10,058,185,400
1990	9,385,072,100	(+1.1%)	823,280,300	10,208,352,400
1991	9,393,460,600	(+0.1%)	804,442,500	10,197,903,100
1992	9,638,864,200	(+2.6%)	770,080,900	10,408,945,100
1993	9,600,545,400	(-0.4%)	730,876,000	10,331,421,400
1994	9,897,028,600	(+3.1%)	680,960,500	10,577,989,100
1995	10,428,822,300	(+5.4%)	794,877,000	11,223,699,300
1996	11,627,000,000	(+11.5%)	**642,000,000	12,269,000,000
1997	12,542,000,000	(+7.9)	527,000,000	13,327,000,000
1998	13,115,000,000	(+4.6)	498,000,000	13,805,000,000
1999	13,724,000,000	(+4.7)	439,000,000	14,408,000,000
2000	14,321,000,000	(+4.4)	475,000,000	14,796,000,000

*-figures in millions of dollars **-includes Breeders' Cup Day

Sources: The Jockey Club; Equibase Company LLC; California Horse Racing Information Management Systems, Association of Racing Commissioners International and El Comandante.

Gross Purses in North America

Gross purses in the United States reached record levels in 2004, rebounding +3.5% from 2003 when purses sustained their first decline in 10 years. Driving this growth was the introduction of alternative gaming at Evangeline Downs and Finger Lakes Racetrack, as well as expansion of slot operations at Charles Town Races. Accordingly, the states showing the largest percentage of increases in available purse money in 2004 were Louisiana (+23.5%) and West Virginia (+21.4%). With its expanding purse structure, West Virginia ranked only behind California and New York in total purse money available..

YEAR	US*	(% CHANGE)	CANADA*	PUERTO RICO*	STARTERS	TOTAL*
1990	714.5	(+1.1%)	69.6	12.4	90,938	$796.5
1991	698.7	(-2.2%)	65.2	12.6	88,189	$776.5
1992	709.6	(+1.6%)	68.4	13.6	84,755	$791.6
1993	692.1	(-2.5%)	63.2	14.4	80,238	$769.7
1994	718.4	(+3.8%)	64	14.8	76,539	$797.2
1995	761.6	(+6.0%)	74.7	15.9	73,870	$852.2
1996	792.7	(+4.1%)	**86.3	18	71,982	$897.0
1997	851.5	(+7.4%)	68.7	18.2	70,370	$938.4
1998	904	(+6.2%)	74.3	15.2	70,291	$993.5
1999	962.9	(+6.5%)	87.7	16.1	70,284	$1,066.7
2000	1,030.9	(+7.1%)	114.9	18.8	70,869	$1,164.6
2001	1,067.5	(+3.6%)	131.9	19.5	71,278	$1,218.9
2002	1,074.2	(+0.6%)	149.1	19.1	74,288	$1,242.4
2003	1,055.5	(-1.7%)	150.4	18.7	75,347	$1,224.6
2004	1,092.1	(+3.5%)	136.0	18.9	75,627	$1,246.9

* Dollars in Millions...

** Includes Breeders' Cup Day at Woodbine

Purses include monies not won and returned to state breeder or other funds, but do not include retroactive payments. In Puerto Rico, retroactive payments represent a significant part of total prize money distributed.

Sources: Equibase Company LLC and Racing Sport Administration of Puerto Rico.

Snapshot Facts: The +3.5% rebound in purse growth in 2004 after a decline in 2003 was similiar to the +3.8% rebound following the last year of decline, 1993.

TWO-YEAR-OLD RACING

With a smaller population of 2-year-olds in 2004 due to the effects of MRLS on the foal crop of 2002, races for 2-year-olds represented just 7.3% of all races run in North America. Two-year-olds today run less frequently than ever before, with the majority of all 2-year-old starters doing so little more than three times during their brief preparatory season.

Year	2YO Starters	2YO Starts	Avg Sts.	All starters	%all starters	2YO races	All races	%all races	2YO Purses
1988	14,976	59,988	4	90,486	16.6	6,410	78,270	8.2	86,762,000
1989	14,907	57,956	3.9	91,436	16.3	6,280	81,400	7.7	87,680,400
1990	14,685	57,538	3.9	89,716	16.4	6,189	79,971	7.7	90,028,524
1991	14,631	58,305	4	86,937	16.8	6,361	79,303	8	89,021,900
1992	13,561	55,020	4.1	83,404	16.3	6,167	77,712	7.9	89,672,800
1993	12,471	47,562	3.9	78,740	15.9	5,362	72,342	7.4	81,970,300
1994	11,838	45,066	3.8	74,955	15.8	5,275	70,699	7.5	83,261,500
1995	11,415	42,517	3.7	72,399	15.7	4,963	68,245	7.3	91,472,723
1996	10,977	40,757	3.7	70,450	15.6	4,750	64,388	7.4	96,372,058
1997	10,906	39,573	3.6	69,056	15.8	4,701	63,487	7.4	101,129,962
1998	11,056	39,588	3.6	68,697	16.1	4,639	61,293	7.6	106,820,755
1999	10,936	38,603	3.5	68,678	15.9	4,554	60,182	7.6	116,157,359
2000	11,292	39,745	3.5	69,569	16.2	4,743	60,872	7.8	126,795,123
2001	11,519	40,119	3.5	71,278	16.2	4,731	60,738	7.8	128,371,786
2002	11,964	40,827	3.4	72,825	16.4	4,791	59,896	8	131,477,440
2003	11,559	38,360	3.3	73,918	15.6	4,514	59,001	7.7	130,872,472
2004	10,843	35,797	3.3	74,206	14.6	4,313	58,858	7.3	129,568,288

Above figures include US and Canada only Source: The Jockey Club and Equibase.

SIZE OF FIELD AND STARTS PER HORSE 1950–2004

Average field size underwent a persistent decline throughout the 1990s, but increases in the annual registered foal crop in the late 1990s and early 2000s, coupled with fewer races, has helped stabilize average field size in recent years. Average number of starts per runner, however, continues to decline steadily, with the average starts per runner in 2004 once again the lowest on record.

YEAR	STARTERS	RACES	STARTS	AVG. FIELD	AVG. STARTS PER RUNNER
1950	22,388	26,932	244,343	9.07	10.91
1955	25,924	31,757	287,775	9.06	11.1
1960	29,798	37,661	337,060	8.95	11.31
1965	37,386	47,335	406,646	8.59	10.88
1970	47,778	56,676	488,326	8.62	10.22
1975	58,816	68,210	601,780	8.82	10.23
1980	64,506	68,243	593,849	8.7	9.21
1985	82,548	75,687	683,667	9.03	8.28
1990	89,716	79,971	712,494	8.91	7.94
1991	86,937	79,303	693,614	8.75	7.98
1992	83,404	77,712	669,967	8.62	8.03
1993	78,740	72,342	618,974	8.56	7.86
1994	74,955	70,699	587,404	8.31	7.84
1995	72,399	68,245	559,669	8.2	7.73
1996	70,450	64,388	534,861	8.31	7.59
1997	69,056	63,487	520,880	8.2	7.54
1998	68,697	61,293	500,710	8.17	7.29
1999	68,678	60,182	493,926	8.21	7.19
2000	69,569	60,872	493,682	8.11	7.1
2001	71,278	60,738	496,604	8.18	6.97
2002	72,825	59,896	495,228	8.27	6.80
2003	73,918	59,001	489,503	8.30	6.62
2004	74,206	58,858	487,428	8.28	6.57

Above figures include US and Canada only. Data provided by Equibase and The Jockey Club

THOROUGHBRED RACING AND BREEDING WORLDWIDE

Today's world of the thoroughbred reaches to the four corners of the Earth, transcending geographical boundaries. While the following statistics demonstrate the overall strength of horse racing and breeding in the United States in comparison with other countries, they only hint at the tremendous contribution made by the US to the thoroughbred industries of other countries.

Country	Races	Purses*	Handle*	Mares	Foals	Starts	Starters
Algeria	527	1.56	17.02	200	168	6,851	***
Argentina	7,295	42.96	324.91	12,024	6,631	53,726	12,735
Australia	20,847	249.34	8,791.62	25,155	15,300	203,311	31,639
Austria	88	0.56	***	96	53	685	212
Bahrein	152	0.63	▼▼	102	64	***	267
Belgium	360	0.80	30.03	92	74	2,768	629
Brazil	5,143	10.07	104.58	4,575	3,238	41,120	6,449
Canada	5,498	150.39	533.58	3,571	2,425	43,233	7,355
Chad	180	0.07	***	0	0	1,980	423
Chile	6,662	19.73	182.98	2,393	1,716	63,062	4,105
Cyprus	930	10.19	125.84	789	462	9,043	1,225
Czech Republic	482	1.02	1.31	675	368	4,998	1,319
Denmark	284	2.36	***	210	138	3,980	560
France	6,612	238.18	9,162.84	8,503	4,402	70,645	13,261
Germany	2,135	31.85	230.86	2,298	1,242	20,602	3,627
Great Britain	8,028	114.64	18,390.94	8,988	5,429	83,063	16,904
Greece	1,196	20.78	404.61	653	389	11,368	1,412
Hong Kong	697	86.97	8,385.08	0	0	8,994	1,227
Hungary	310	0.62	6.47	807	254	2,677	422
India	3,016	11.95	205.01	2,767	1,372	22,512	3,679
Ireland	2,166	31.91	2,728.21	16,938	10,574	28,902	6,977
Israel	***	***	***	83	41	***	***
Italy	5,635	118.64	***	2,992	2,093	46,723	7,272
Japan	21,402	1075.33	32,371.12	11,304	8,488	230,293	28,843
Kenya	209	0.36	0.51	165	108	2,000	278
Lebanon	365	1.10	13.23	0	0	2,724	380
Macau	1,100	32.23	655.61	0	0	12,719	1,111
Madagascar	121	0.01	4.50	7	5	***	83
Malaysia/Singapore	1,273	30.89	1,228.39	84	37	15,568	2,397
Mauritius	232	2.14	67.90	0	0	2,150	368
Mexico	1,456	6.93	21.59	490	311	11,367	1,561
Morocco	431	2.11	185.80	211	119	4,960	690
Netherlands	155	0.51	42.94	32	29	1,135	241
New Zealand	2,791	22.63	436.69	8,964	4,750	30,766	5,564
Norway	278	3.36	360.11	79	50	2,817	607
Oman	119	0.42	▼▼	45	14	***	144
Peru	2,216	3.86	21.91	703	420	22,956	1,524
Poland	383	1.04	7.11	901	432	2,724	516
Portugal	48	0.14	***	40	6	516	100
Qatar	185	2.36	▼▼	34	15	1,727	283
Russia	1,346	0.35	***	954	445	7,523	2,699

Saudi Arabia	305	3.37	▼▼	***	***	3,982	1,293
Slovakia	170	0.51	0.97	257	95	1,410	441
South Africa	3,933	29.12	***	4,161	2,493	43,805	6,945
South Korea	1,106	62.06	4,722.72	1,611	1,053	11,909	1,727
Spain	398	3.11	***	230	190	3,583	706
Sweden	701	9.09	1,464.91	404	355	6,573	1,450
Switzerland	208	1.69	90.27	169	52	1,893	423
Thailand	500	4.15	82.27	677	127	3,765	902
Tunisia	380	2.20	***	157	97	5,000	520
Turkey	3,022	105.63	862.95	2,110	1,307	32,917	3,347
United Arab Emer.	357	26.39	▼▼	141	54	4,076	1,026
United States	53,503	1,055.50	15,180.11	58,285	34,025	446,250	68,249
Total	176,936	3,633.81	107,447.50	186,126	111,510	1,647,351	256,117

* All totals in millions of US dollars and where applicable they include a conversion from Euro Dollars at 1.00 Euro at US $ 1.209.

Some handle figures in some countries include sums wagered via legal bookmaking firms and some betting handle figures include Harness racing.

*** Not reported. . . . ▼▼ No wagering.

Snapshot Fact: Among countries which reported the number of starters and the total number of starts that they made during the season, Chile and Peru showed the highest average starts per starter, with each starter averaging over 15 starts during the season.

Statistics provided by The Jockey Club and are based based on 2003 totals made available by the International Statistical Survey of Horse Racing and 2003 statistics, as compiled by the International Federation of Horseracing Authorities and presented at the 38th International Conference of Racing Authorities, Paris, France, Oct. 4, 2004.

TRENDS IN DISTRIBUTION OF RACES BY PURSES AND DISTANCES

Since 1994, in spite of a substantial reduction in the number of races run, the distribution of races for 3-year-olds and up has remained relatively stable. During this period, the percentage of races over six furlongs and under a mile declined from 15.2% of all races to 14.8%, while the percentage of races between one mile and a mile and a quarter increased from 34.4% of all races to 34.9%. Increasing average purse money in the three major categories continues to favor longer distances.

Year	Races 6F, under	Avg. Purses	Races over 6f, under 1M	Avg. Purses	Races 1 Mile-1 1/4 Mi.	Avg. Purses	Races over 1 1/4 mi.	Avg. Purses
1989	38,304	6,319	11,487	8,400	24,770	12,563	559	41,126
1990	36,398	6,483	11,662	8,587	25,175	12,970	547	40,050
1991	36,370	6,316	11,289	8,665	24,760	13,188	523	40,551
1992	34,971	6,583	11,200	8,799	24,832	13,342	542	39,087
1993	32,031	7,045	10,069	9,272	23,346	13,811	534	36,642
1994	32,422	7,600	9,930	9,539	22,498	14,252	574	34,861
1995	31,482	8,345	9,117	11,060	22,107	16,268	576	37,615
1996	29,266	9,317	8,744	11,920	21,076	18,176	552	41,060
1997	28,738	10,124	8,451	12,580	21,053	18,949	544	41,919
1998	27,798	11,271	8,134	13,934	20,236	20,827	486	48,069
1999	27,137	12,302	8,330	15,535	19,717	22,533	444	60,399
2000	27,904	13,126	8,110	17,651	19,650	24,478	465	61,335
2001	27,767	14,000	8,074	18,290	19,736	25,718	430	62,953
2002	27,135	14,403	8,308	19,391	19,248	26,404	414	64,315
2003	26,959	14,208	8,091	20,113	19,037	26,435	400	65,063
2004	27,024	14,661	8,053	20,277	19,048	26,898	420	63,549

Above figures include US and Canada only. Excludes all two-year-old racing

Source: Equibase Company LLC

Snapshot Facts: Since 1989, purses for races longer than six furlongs and less than a mile saw the greatest increase in average, climbing from its 1989 average of $8,400 over 240% to $20,277. The relatively rare events longer than 10 furlongs saw the least increase in average over the same time period, showing a 155% increase from $41,146 to $63,549.

FOAL CROPS BY STATE

UNITED STATES

Kentucky annually leads the list of states producing registered thoroughbred foals but, after peaking at more than 10,100 foals in 2000, the state's foal crop has come under pressure from the effects of MRLS and lucrative breeder incentive programs in other states. Nevertheless, Kentucky is one of five states among the top 12 foal producers to increase its registered foal production since 1993, with New York showing the largest percentage increase.

State by 2003 Ranking	1993 Reg. Foals	Per Cent US Crop	2002 Reg. Foals	Per Cent US Crop	2003 Reg. Foals	Per Cent US Crop	% Change 1993–03
Kentucky	7,008	20.7	8,226	25.2	8,641	26.4	23.3
Florida	3,527	10.4	4,383	13.4	4,394	13.4	24.6
California	3,860	11.4	3,798	11.6	3,745	11.5	-3.0
New York	1,388	4.1	1,809	5.5	1,927	5.9	38.8
Texas	2,386	7.1	1,924	5.9	1,733	5.3	-27.4
Louisiana	1,558	4.6	1,473	4.5	1,516	4.6	-2.7
Pennsylvania	877	2.6	868	2.7	986	3.0	12.4
Maryland	1,387	4.1	986	3.0	980	3.0	-29.3
Oklahoma	1,592	4.7	950	2.9	900	2.8	-43.5
Illinois	1,397	4.1	948	2.9	897	2.7	-35.8
New Mexico	572	1.7	671	2.1	707	2.2	23.6
Washington	1,235	3.7	792	2.4	699	2.1	-43.4
Ohio	832	2.5	626	1.9	576	1.8	-30.8
Indiana	94	0.3	547	1.7	505	1.5	437.2
Virginia	623	1.8	454	1.4	483	1.5	-22.5
West Virginia	398	1.2	388	1.2	438	1.3	10.1
Iowa	155	0.5	459	1.4	415	1.3	167.7
Arizona	327	1.0	311	1.0	337	1.0	3.1
Michigan	435	1.3	370	1.1	329	1.0	-24.4
New Jersey	462	1.4	389	1.2	328	1.0	-29.0
Arkansas	465	1.4	324	1.0	285	0.9	-38.7
Minnesota	242	0.7	253	0.8	259	0.8	7.0
Colorado	226	0.7	246	0.8	251	0.8	11.1
Oregon	230	0.7	272	0.8	236	0.7	2.6
Nebraska	417	1.2	145	0.4	163	0.5	-60.9
Idaho	281	0.8	180	0.6	162	0.5	-42.3
Kansas	259	0.8	99	0.3	107	0.3	-58.7
Montana	271	0.8	77	0.2	101	0.3	-62.7
Massachusetts	119	0.4	84	0.3	80	0.2	-32.8
Georgia	102	0.3	71	0.2	66	0.2	-35.3
Alabama	101	0.3	59	0.2	63	0.2	-37.6
South Carolina	109	0.3	62	0.2	57	0.2	-47.7
South Dakota	68	0.2	65	0.2	56	0.2	-17.6
North Dakota	58	0.2	43	0.1	52	0.2	-10.3
Utah	209	0.6	56	0.2	49	0.2	-76.6
Missouri	154	0.5	53	0.2	35	0.1	-77.3
North Carolina	121	0.4	43	0.1	35	0.1	-71.1
Tennessee	85	0.3	40	0.1	34	0.1	-60.0
Mississippi	40	0.1	30	0.1	25	0.1	-37.5
Wyoming	36	0.1	24	0.1	17	0.1	-52.8
Nevada	40	0.1	18	0.1	12	0.0	-70.0
Wisconsin	35	0.1	16	0.1	8	0.0	-77.1
Alaska	1	0.0	0	0.0	3	0.0	200.0
New Hampshire	10	0.0	5	0.0	2	0.0	-80.0
Vermont	3	0.0	3	0.0	2	0.0	-33.3
Maine	1	0.0	1	0.0	2	0.0	100.0
Connecticut	16	0.0	6	0.0	1	0.0	-93.8
Virgin Islands	2	0.0	1	0.0	1	0.0	-50.0
Delaware	2	0.0	1	0.0	0	0.0	-100.0
Hawaii	4	0.0	1	0.0	0	0.0	-100.0
Total US	**33,819**		**32,650**		**32,700**		**-3.3**
Canada	2,713		2,452		2,479		-8.6
Puerto Rico	605		519		498		-17.7
Total Crop	**37,137**		**35,621**		**35,677**		**-3.9**

Snapshot Facts: In 1993, New York, the state posting the largest percentage increase in foal production during the last decade, ranked eighth, behind Kentucky, California, Florida, Texas, Oklahoma, Louisiana and Illinois.

DISTRIBUTION OF ACTIVE STALLIONS AND MARES BRED

State by 2004 Ranking	2002 Stallions	2002 Mares Bred	2002 Avg. Book	2003 Stallions	2003 Mares Bred	2003 Avg. Book	2004 Stallions	2004 Mares Bred	2004 Avg. Book
California	407	5,827	14.3	397	5,819	14.7	376	5,661	15.1
Kentucky	387	19,664	50.8	381	19,881	52.2	352	20,024	56.9
Texas	433	3,623	8.4	393	3,200	8.1	319	2,869	9.0
Florida	289	7,161	24.8	258	6,663	25.8	228	6,797	29.8
Louisiana	210	2,304	11.0	223	2,742	12.3	228	3,047	13.4
Oklahoma	226	1,768	7.8	212	1,587	7.5	171	1,477	8.6
New Mexico	158	1,474	9.3	161	1,521	9.4	148	1,515	10.2
New York	155	2,532	16.3	157	2,741	17.5	142	2,557	18.0
Illinois	121	1,236	10.2	112	1,136	10.1	111	1,055	9.5
Pennsylvania	109	1,026	9.4	115	1,020	8.9	109	996	9.1
Washington	107	1,159	10.8	100	1,148	11.5	94	1,151	12.2
Indiana	113	885	7.8	102	857	8.4	86	681	7.9
Ohio	107	881	8.2	108	660	6.1	83	512	6.2
West Virginia	66	917	13.9	82	1,020	12.4	77	1,042	13.5
Arkansas	77	645	8.4	66	579	8.8	68	592	8.7
Maryland	105	1,844	17.6	92	1,651	17.9	67	1,583	23.6
Colorado	84	473	5.6	85	495	5.8	62	425	6.9
Michigan	72	522	7.3	73	527	7.2	57	540	9.5
Arizona	71	548	7.7	65	563	8.7	53	485	9.2
Virginia	81	548	6.8	71	455	6.4	53	386	7.3
Oregon	45	390	8.7	53	432	8.2	46	447	9.7
Idaho	62	305	4.9	53	298	5.6	45	307	6.8
Iowa	61	669	11.0	49	627	12.8	45	505	11.2
Montana	43	243	5.7	41	194	4.7	41	179	4.4
Nebraska	39	340	8.7	44	354	8.0	36	357	9.9
Minnesota	39	313	8.0	37	341	9.2	32	340	10.6
Utah	35	151	4.3	34	123	3.6	27	216	8.0
Alabama	22	99	4.5	23	121	5.3	25	135	5.4
Kansas	31	188	6.1	32	184	5.8	25	189	7.6
New Jersey	42	456	10.9	36	324	9.0	25	257	10.3
South Carolina	33	176	5.3	24	150	6.3	24	140	5.8
Georgia	33	135	4.1	21	119	5.7	20	114	5.7
North Dakota	12	106	8.8	17	75	4.4	19	110	5.8
Massachusetts	29	119	4.1	24	93	3.9	17	67	3.9
Missouri	37	164	4.4	32	107	3.3	17	72	4.2
North Carolina	24	72	3.0	19	73	3.8	17	61	3.6
Mississippi	16	75	4.7	16	69	4.3	14	72	5.1
Tennessee	30	112	3.7	23	89	3.9	13	56	4.3
South Dakota	17	154	9.1	15	127	8.5	9	108	12.0
Wisconsin	16	38	2.4	15	56	3.7	7	22	3.1
Nevada	6	12	2.0	8	18	2.3	6	15	2.5
Wyoming	12	36	3.0	14	33	2.4	6	19	3.2
Vermont	5	11	2.2	2	2	1.0	3	4	1.3
Alaska	1	1	1.0	1	2	2.0	1	3	3.0
Connecticut	0	0	0	0	0	0	1	1	1.0
Rhode Island	0	0	0	2	2	1.0	1	1	1.0
Delaware	1	5	5.0	1	1	1.0	0	0	0
New Hampshire	1	6	6.0	1	1	1.0	0	0	0
Maine	2	3	1.5	2	5	2.5	0	0	0
TOTALS	**4,072**	**59,416**	**14.6**	**3,892**	**58,285**	**15.0**	**3,406**	**57,192**	**16.8**

* Initial returns only (as of 02/01/05); ranked by number of stallions. Source: The Jockey Club

Takeout Percentages in North America by State

The following are the pari-mutuel takeout percentages for each state in which legal wagering was conducted in 2004. The breakdown includes the differing percentages for various wagering formats as well as for the type of race meet and/or racing breed involved.

Arizona – 20% on win-place-show, 21% on Daily Double, Quinella and Exacta, 25% on Trifecta, Superfecta, and Pick 3.

Arkansas – 17% on single wagers and 21% on multiple wagers.

California – 15.43 % Win-place-show takeout for Thoroughbred and Quarter Horse meetings; 16% for Harness, Mixed and Fair meetings. Additional takeout on exotic wagering is 5.25% for Thoroughbred, Quarter Horse and Fair meetings; 6.75% for Mixed meetings and 7.75% for Harness meetings.

Colorado – 18.5% on straight wagers, 25% on exotics.

Delaware – For Thoroughbreds, 17% on straight wagers; additional 2% on Daily Doubles and Exactas, plus an additional 8% on other exotic wagers. For Harness, 18% on straight wagers, 20% on multiple wagers on 8-horse field, 25% on multiple wagers with 9 or more horses in the field.

Florida – Individual tracks allowed to determine the level of total takeout.

Idaho – 20% on straight wagers, 20.75% on exotics.

Illinois – 17% on win-place-show, 20.5% on Exacta, Quinella and Daily Double, 25% on Trifecta, Pick 3, Pick 4 and Superfecta.

Indiana – 18% on straight wagers, 21.5% on exotics.

Iowa – 16% on win-place-show, 19% on on two-horse wagers, 22% on other forms of wagering.

Kansas – 18% on win-place-show, up to 22% on multiple wagers if authorized by racing commission.

Kentucky – For Thoroughbred tracks over $1,200,000 daily average, 16% on straight wagers and 19% on exotics; at tracks under $1,200,000 daily average, 17.5% on straight wagers and 22% on exotics. For Harness, 18% on straight wagers and 25% on exotics. For Quarter Horse, Appaloosa and Arabian, 18% on straight wagers and 25% on exotics.

Louisiana – 17% on win-place-show, 20.5% on two-horse wagers, 25% on three horse wagers, 25% on Pick 4 and Pick 6.

Maine – 18% on straight wagers, 26% on exotics.

Maryland – At Thoroughbreds tracks, 18% on straight wagers, 21% on two-horse multiples, 25.75% on three-horse multiples, 14% on Pick 4. At the Fair Hill hunt meeting, 22% on all wagers. At Harness tracks over $600,000 daily, 17% on straight wagers, 19% on two-horse multiplesand 25% on three-horse multiples. At Harness tracks under $600,000 daily,18.75% on straight wagers, 20.75% on two-horse wagers and 26.75% on three-horse wagers.

Massachusetts – 19% win-place-show wagers, 26% on exotics, 19% at fairs.

Michigan – 17% on straight wagers, 20.5% on two race multiples and 25% on multiples involving three or more races.

Minnesota – Not to exceed 17% on win-place-show wagering, 23% on exotic wagering.

Montana – 20% on straight wagers and up to 25% on exotics.

Nebraska – Not less than 15% or more than 18% on straight wagers, up to and including 23% on exotic wagers.

New Hampshire – For Thoroughbreds, 19% on win-place-show wagers, 26% on multiple wagers. For Harness, 19% on win-place-show wagers, 25% on multiple wagers.

New Jersey – 17% straight wagers, 19% on two-horse selections, 25% on three or more horse selections regardless of number of races involved, 15% Pick 4.

New Mexico – For Class A tracks, 19% on win-place-show, 21%-25% on exotic wagers. For Class B tracks, 18.75% to 25% on win-place-show, 21% to 30% on exotic wagers. 21% on Exacta and Daily Double, 25% on trifecta and superfecta.

New York – At NYRA tracks, 14% on straight wagers, 17.5% on Daily Double, Quinella and Exacta, 25% on Trifecta, Pick 3, Pick 4 and Superfecta, 25% on Pick 6 (15% on non-carryover days). For Harness, 18% on straight wagers, 20% on multiple, 25% on exotics and 34% on super exotics. For Quarter Horse, 17% on straight wagers, 19% on multiple, 25% on exotic and 36% on super exotics. Takeout is the same at Off-Track-Betting facilities, but an additional surcharge of 5% is charged by most OTBs on winning straight wagers, and 6% on winning multiples and exotics.

Ohio – 18% on win-place-show wagers, 22.5% on all other wagers.

Oklahoma – 18% on win-place-show wagers, 20% on multiple-horse wagers and up to three-race wagers, 25% on multiple race wagers involving four or more races.

Oregon – For commercial meets, 18% on win-place-show, 22% on wagers with two or more wagering interests. At fairs and non-profit meets, up to 22%.

Pennsylvania – Philadelphia Park: 17% on win-place-show wagers, 20% on Daily Double and Exactas, 26% on Pick 3, 30% on Trifecta and Superfecta. Penn National: 17% on win-place-show wagers, 20% on Daily Double, 22% on Exacta, 26% on Pick 3, 28% on Pick 4, 31% on Trifecta and Superfecta.

Texas – 18% on regular wagers, 21% on Daily Double, Exacta, Quinella, Trifecta, 25% on superfectas, 12% on Pick Three.

Virginia – 18% on straight wagers, 22% on all other wagers.

Washington – 16.1% on win-place-show wagers, 22.1% on all other wagers, (21.1% for non-profit meetings of less than 10 days).

West Virginia – 17.25% on win-place-show wagers, 19% on two-horse wagers, 25% on wagers on three horses or more.

North American Racetracks

AQUEDUCT

New York Racing Association Inc.,

President and CEO: Charles Hayward; Co-Chairman: Peter F. Karches; Co-Chairman: C. Steven Duncker; Senior Vice President: William A Nader; Racing Secretary and Handicapper: Michael S. Lakow.

Street Address: 110th Street and Rockaway Blvd., Jamaica, New York 11417
12 miles from Times Square in New York City
Nearest Airport: John F. Kennedy Int l., 1/2 mile from track

Mailing: P.O. Box 90, Jamaica, New York 11417
Phone: (718) 641-4700; Results: (718) 976-3333
Fax: (718) 322-3814
Web Site: www.nyra.com

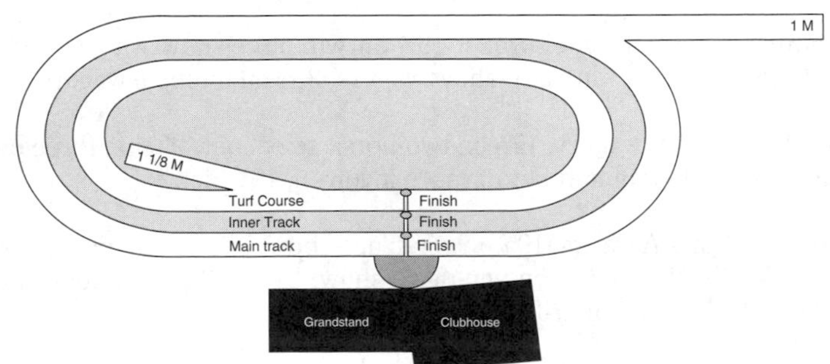

Track Data: Main Course, 1 1/8-mile oval, sandy loam; 100 feet wide, with one-mile chute. Length of stretch, 1,155.6 feet. Winterized, inner dirt course, one mile. Inner turf course, seven furlongs plus 43 feet with 1 1/8-mile diagonal chute. Stable accommodations: 547 horses; Seating capacity: 27,000. Total capacity: 90,000. Parking capacity, approximately 16,000 cars.

Opened September 14, 1959, Aqueduct conducts live racing from the fall through late spring, using the one mile, winterized inner dirt track from December to mid-March. During the 2003-2004 winter meet, daily purses still were pegged at $327,000, including stakes. For the 25-day fall 2004 meet purses were $439,000 per day.

TRACK RECORDS

4 1/2 furs.	About to Burst	2	117	:51.60	Apr. 26, 1984
5 furs.	Bazaar	2		:57.00	Jan. 1, 1963
5 1/2 furs.	Raise a Native	2	124	1:02.60	Jul. 17, 1963
6 furs.	Captain Red	6	111	107.80	Feb. 26, 2003
6 1/2 furs.	Coronado s Quest	2	122	1:14-1/5	Oct. 26, 1997
7 furs.	Artax	4	114	1:20.04	May 2, 1999
7-1/2 furs.	Imafavoritetrick	3	122	1:28.54	Nov. 27, 2004
1 mile	Easy Goer	3	123	1:32-2/5	Apr. 8, 1989
1-1/8 m	Riva Ridge	4	130	1:47	Oct. 15, 1973
1-3/16 m	Riva Ridge	4	127	1:52-2/5	Jul. 4, 1973
1-1/4 m	Damascus	4	130	1:59-1/5	Jul. 20, 1968
1-5/16 m	Gold Star Deputy	5	116	2:07.32	Apr. 10, 1999
1-3/8 m	Demi s Bret	4	116	2:12.31	Oct. 26, 1997
1-1/2 m	Going Abroad	4	116	2:26-1/5	Oct. 12, 1964
1-5/8 m	Sharp Gary	4	116	2:40-2/5	Dec. 13, 1975
1-3/4 m	Malmo	5	114	2:53.73	Mar. 30, 1996
1-7/8 m	Erin Bright	5	118	3:12-4/5	Apr. 18, 1985
2 miles	Kelso	7	124	3:19-1/5	Oct. 31, 1964
2 -1/4 m	Paraje	7	113	3:47-4/5	Dec. 15, 1973

Inner Dirt

4 furs.	Native Moment	2	122	:53.40	Apr. 2, 1979
4-1/2 furs.	Call Me Up	2	115	:52.29	Apr. 16, 1998
6 furs.	Captain Red	6	111	1:07.93	Feb. 26, 2003
1 mile	Tejano Couture	6	116	1:35.79	March 9, 2000
1 m 70 yds	Carry My Colors	4	114	1:38.92	Feb. 5, 2000
1-1/16 m	Autoroute	3	115	1:41.06	Dec. 19, 1992
1-1/8 m	Conveyor	5	111	1:47.33	Mar. 6, 1993
1-3/16 m	Victoriously	5	119	1:54-2/5	Jan. 25, 1998
1-1/4 m	Transient Trend	3	111	2:01.53	Dec. 21, 1995
1-1/2 m	Piling	5	122	2:29-3/5	Mar. 13, 1983
1-5/8 m	Relaxing	4	120	2:42-2/5	Dec. 13, 1980
1-3/4 m	Sophie s Friend	5	113	2:56-3/5	Feb. 10, 1996
2 miles	Charlie Coast	4	122	3:24-4/5	Feb. 21, 1979
2-1/16 m	Rollix	4	105	3:38-4/5	Feb. 3, 1983
2-1/8 m	Peat Moss	6	128	3:40-3/5	Jan. 31, 1981
2-1/4 m	Field Cat	4	110	3:51-4/5	Dec. 31, 1981

Turf Course

1 mile	Tax Dodge*	4	116	1:34-3/5	Nov. 1, 1985
	Possible Mate*	4	116	1:34-3/5	Nov. 1, 1985
1-1/16 m	Spindrift	5	118	1:40.88	May 6, 2000
1-1/8 m	Slew The Dragon	3	117	1:47	Nov. 3, 1985
1 1/4 m	Fluorescent Light	4	115	2:14-1/5	Nov. 7, 1978
1-1/2 m	Pebbles	4	123	2:27	Nov. 2, 1985
2 miles	Putting Green	4	112	3:30-2/5	Nov. 23, 1984

* Dead Heat.

Leading Jockey, inner track, winter, 2004: Pablo Fragoso, 59 wins; Leading Trainer, inner track, winter, 2004: Richard E. Dutrow Jr, 32 wins

Leading Jockey, spring meet, 2004: Javier Castellano, 37 wins

Leading Trainer, spring meet, 2004: Gary C. Contessa, 19 wins

Leading Jockey, fall-winter, 2004: Norberto Arroyo Jr, 36 wins; Leading Trainer, fall-winter, 2004: Richard E. Dutrow Jr, 29 wins

Record Attendance: 73, 435, May 31, 1965. Record Handle: $8, 171, 520, Nov 2, 1985. (Breeders' Cup Day): $26, 941, 288 November 2, 1985, (Breeders' Cup Day, all sources.)

ARAPAHOE PARK

26000 E Quincy Avenue, Aurora, CO 80016
(303) 690-2400, Fax: (303) 690-6730
Free Results (303) 227-4726

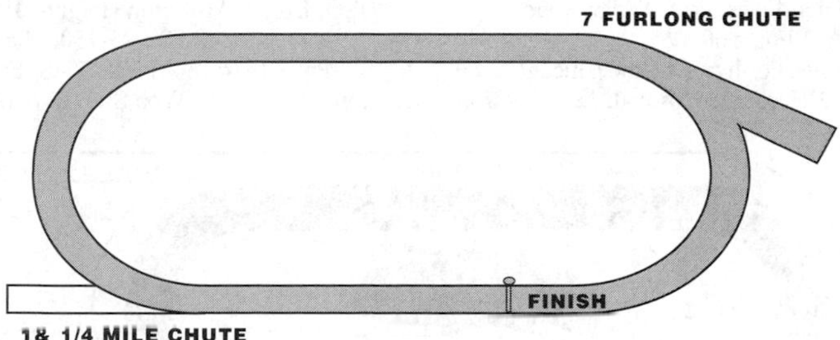

One mile oval, two chutes, seven furlongs and 1-1/4 miles. Distance from last turn to finish 1,029 feet. Seating capacity 2,000. Stable capacity 1,500, Parking for 2,200 cars.

Opened May 24, 1984. Located in Northeastern Colorado, operates the only pari-mutuel racetrack in that state and offered mixed breed racing from July 3 to September 6 in 2004, with total daily purses of almost $53,000 per day including stakes funded significantly through Year-round simulcasting.

TRACK RECORDS

4 furs.	Et Tu Brutus	3	120	:44.60	Jul. 26, 2004	1 m 70 yds	Naskra s Advocate	5	118	1:38-1/5	July 23, 1993
4-1/2 furs.	V.G s Catch	2	116	:50.40	June 23, 2002	1-1/16 m	Run at Night	4	116	1:42.20	Aug. 14, 2004
5 furs.	Nycity	2	118	:56.00	July 13, 2002	1-1/8 m	Maysville Slew	6	124	1:49.00	Sept. 1, 2002
5-1/2 furs.	Ribot Line	5	118	1:02.20	June 30, 2002	1-1/4 m	Builder s Boy	6	119	2:05-2/5	June 26, 1992
6 furs.	Absolutely True	4	118	1:08.20	Jul. 11, 2004	1-1/2 m	Calgary Classic	6	122	2:33-1/5	July 24, 1993
6-1/2 furs.	Pray For Booger	3	116	1:18-3/5	Aug. 25, 1995	1-3/4 m	Read My Mind	6	112	3:02	Aug. 9, 1992
7 furs.	Daring Pegasus	5	118	1:21.00	July 4, 2003	2 miles	Little Reeves	6	116	3:28-2/5	Aug. 27, 1994
1 mile	Honor Bright	5	116	1:35-1/5	Aug. 7, 1993						

Leading Jockey in 2004: Travis Wales, 40 wins
Leading Trainer in 2004: Jon G. Arnett, 31 wins

ARLINGTON PARK

Churchill Downs, Inc.

Chairman: Richard L. Duchossois; President: Clifford Goodrich; Vice President of Operations: Ted G. Nicholson; Senior Vice President of Racing: William A. Thayer; Executive Vice President of Racing and Racing Secretary: Frank G. Gabriel, Jr.; Senior Director Marketing & Sales: Keith Darby; Director of Communications: Dan Leary, (847) 385-7754.

Street Address: Euclid Avenue & Wilke Road
Arlington Heights, Illinois 60006
Arlington is 26 miles northwest of the Chicago Loop
Nearest Airport: O'Hare International, 12 miles from Arlington

P.O. Box 7, Arlington Heights, Illinois 60006-0007
(847) 385-7500. Fax: (847) 385-7251
Press Box: (847) 385-7548; Fax (847) 870-6727
Web Site: www.arlingtonpark.com

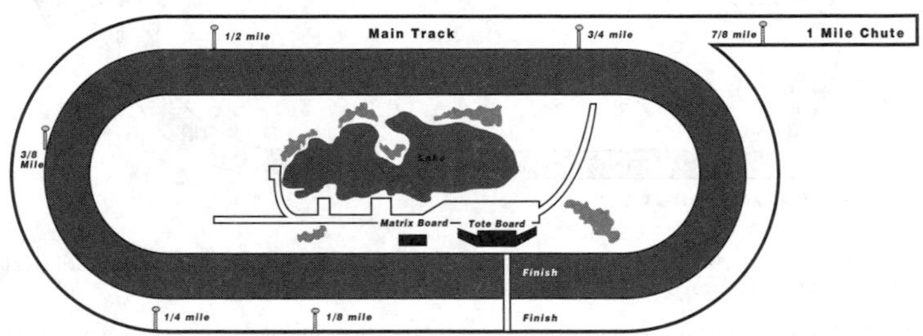

Track Data: 1 1/8-mile oval, sandy loam. One-mile chute. One-mile turf course. five-eighths mile training track. Stalls: 2,140. Seating capacity: 14,000, parking for 8,500 cars.

Originally opened October 13, 1927 and after a crushing fire destroyed the plant in 1985, reopened as Arlington International Racecourse with a spectacular, ultra modern facility on June 28, 1989, only to close in 1997 after dispute over pari-mutuel takeout percentages with the state government. In 2000, Arlington returned, with live racing and more than $290,000 in daily average purses. In 2001, the track changed its name back to 'Arlington Park', complete with a new logo that includes the Twin Spires of Churchill Downs to symbolize the union between the two tracks. . .The 96-day meet in 2004 ran from May 14 to Sept. 19 and included the prestigious Arlington Million, one of the premier grass races in the world. Daily average purses excluding the rich stakes schedule were in excess of $215,000 per day.

TRACK RECORDS

4-1/2 furs.	Wheat Penny	2	119	:51.64	Jun. 8, 2000
	Bold America	2	120	:51.64	Jun. 28, 2002
5 furs.	Staunch Avenger	2	119	:57-1/5	Jun. 29, 1970
	Heisanative	2	118	:57-1/5	Jun. 12, 1971
	Shecky Greene	2	118	:57-1/5	Jun. 12, 1972
5-1/2 furs.	Hey That s Great	5	113	1:02-3/5	Jun. 27, 1992
6 furs.	Taylor s Special	5	118	1:08	Aug. 22, 1986
6-1/2 furs.	Pentelicus	6	115	1:14-1/5	Jul. 14, 1990
7 furs.	Tumiga	4	120	1:20-2/5	Jul. 13, 1968
7-1/2 furs.	I ll Raise You One	3	112	1:28-4/5	Aug. 3, 1987
1 mile	Dr. Fager	4	134	1:32-1/5	Aug. 24, 1968
Abt 1-1/16 m	Ashleigh s Jet	4	120	1:44.10	Jun. 14, 2001
1-1/16 m	Kindly Manner	4	114	1:41-2/5	Aug. 22, 1977
	Mojave	3	109	1:41-2/5	Jun. 30, 1981
1-1/8 m	Spectacular Bid	4	130	1:46-1/5	Jul. 19, 1980
1-3/16m	Tenpins	4	116	1:55.07	Sep. 29, 2002
1-1/4 m	Private Thoughts	4	117	1:59-2/5	Aug. 20, 1977
1-5/16 m	Rush Home	5	115	2:10	Aug. 7, 1971
1-1/2 m	El Misterio	5	112	2:28-1/5	Sep. 5, 1960
1-5/8 m	Fool s Robbery	4	111	2:45-3/5	Jul. 5, 1973
1-3/4 m	Deux-Moulins	8	119	2:59-2/5	Jul. 14, 1955
2 miles	Swede of Norfolk	6	127	3:26-2/5	Aug. 15, 1970

Turf Course

Abt. 5 furs.	Nicole s Dream	3	120	:56.38	Sep. 18, 2003
5 furs.	Distinctive Mr. B	5	122	:56.36	Sep. 15, 2001
Abt. 5-1/2 F.	Loco Kid	4	112	1:01-3/5	May 28, 1969
5-1/2 furs.	Marley s Revenge	3	116	1:02.44	Sep. 19, 2004
Abt 1 Mile.	Soaking Smoking	6	113	1:34.92	Jul. 24, 1991
1 Mile	Gee Can He Dance	6	113	1:34.50	Sep. 4, 1995
Abt.1m70y	Elegant Heir	5	116	1:41-2/5	Aug. 22, 1970
1 m 70 yds	Pass the Brandy	7	114	1:38-4/5	Jul. 25, 1970
Abt 1-1/16 m	Top Floor	4	118	1:40-2/5	Jun. 18, 1969
	Crafty Bee	5	103	1:40-2/5	Jun. 21, 1969
1-1/16 m	Zeeruler	4	113	1:41	Sep. 7, 1992
Abt 1-1/8 m	Lotus Pool	4	116	1:47.22	Aug. 1, 1991
1-1/8 m	Mr. Leader	4	116	1:47-2/5	Jul. 4, 1970
	World Class Splash	3	113	1:47.40	Jul. 11, 1992
Abt.1-3/16m	Duckaroo	5	117	1:57.51	Jun. 10, 1992
1-3/16 m	Reluctant Guest	4	123	1:53-1/5	Sep. 1, 1990
1-1/4 m	Awad	5	126	1:58.69	Aug. 27, 1995
Abt.1-1/2 m	Noble Savage	5	112	2:22.37	Jul. 20, 1991
1-1/2 m	Cetewayo	8	118	2:27.50	Jul. 6, 2002
Abt 1-5/8 m	Roman Leader	8	108	2:51	Aug. 19, 1972

Jumps

2-1/8 m	Invest West	6	142	4:00.62	Sep. 10, 2000
2-3/8 m	Double Reefed	5	137	4:44	Aug. 29, 1981
3 miles	Shy Donald	9	152	5:47	Aug. 29, 1982

Leading Jockey in 2004: Rene R. Douglas, 125 wins; Leading Trainer in 2004: Frank J. Kirby, 32 wins

Record attendance: 50,568, July 4, 1941. Record handle: $116,059,574 – October 26, 2002 (Breeders' Cup Day). Record handle, non–Breeders' Cup Day: $17,913,433 – August 14, 2004.

ASSINIBOIA DOWNS

Manitoba Jockey Club Inc.

President: Harvey Warner; General Manager: Sharon Gulyas; Racing Secretary: Ray Miller; Director Media and Corporate Relations: Ernie Nairn; Director of Operations: Darren Dunn.

3975 Portage Avenue, Winnipeg, Manitoba, R3K 2E9

(204) 885-3330 Fax: (204) 831-5348; Free scratch line (204) 889-5137 Free result line (204) 831-0321

E-mail: info@assiniboiadowns.com

Web Site: www.assiniboiadowns.com

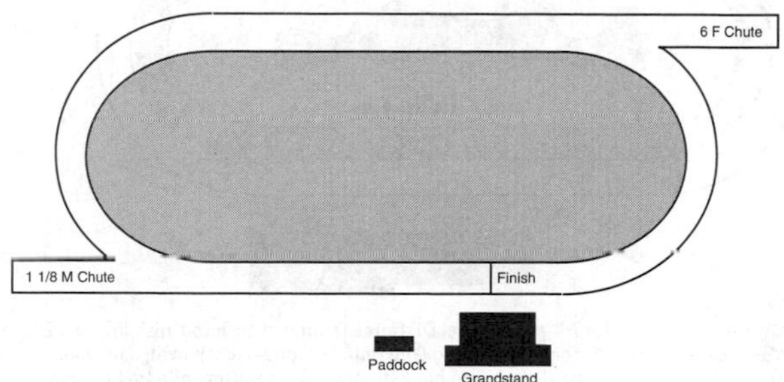

Track: Six and a half furlong oval. Training track four furlongs, with two chutes, six furlongs and 1 1/8 miles. Width of track 80 feet; Distance from last turn to finish 990 feet. Seating capacity 5,000; Stable accommodations 950.

Opened June 10, 1958...Operated a 71-day meet in 2004, May 2 to Oct. 3. The 2005 live thoroughbred season will again feature a 75-day meet. Live racing will begin on Sunday, May 1, 2005, and the meet will conclude on Sunday, Sept. 25, 2005.

TRACK RECORDS

Distance	Horse	Age	Wt.	Time	Date
Abt 3 furs.	Apart	2	120	:29	May 8, 1972
4 furs.	Northern Spike	5	119	:44-2/5	Apr. 23, 1982
4-1/2 furs.	Astral Moon	9	115	:50-4/5	May 1, 1982
5 furs.	Northern Spike	5	120	:56-2/5	Sep. 5, 1982
5-1/2 furs.	Sunny Famous	5	120	1:02-4/5	Sep. 19, 1992
Abt 6 furs.	Lone Spruce	7	122	1:12	Jun. 24, 1984
6 furs.	Nephrite	5	122	1:09	Oct. 8, 1989
Abt 7 furs.	Proven Reserve	4	121	1:23-3/5	Jul. 9, 1986
7 furs.	Victor s Pride	6	118	1:23-1/5	Aug. 16, 1978
7-1/2 furs.	Iron Vigors	4	122	1:31	Oct. 9, 1989
1 mile	Gladiatore II	5	114	1:35-4/5	Jul. 7, 1972
1-1/16 m	Goa	4	118	1:41-3/5	Jul. 23, 1988
1-1/8 m	Overskate	3	126	1:47-3/5	Sep. 9, 1978
1-1/4 m	Nifty	4	124	2:05	Sep. 20, 1986
1-5/16 m	Scarlet Rich	6	124	2:15-4/5	Oct. 21, 1981
1-3/8 m	Island Fling	6	123	2:16-4/5	Oct. 29, 1977
1-1/2 m	Baron Hudec	6	119	2:32	Sep. 9, 1978
1-5/8 m	Northern Kip	6	118	2:46-4/5	Oct. 30, 1978
1-11/16 m	Hi Executor	8	116	2:56-4/5	Sep. 30, 1984
1-3/4 m	Just As Sunny	7	118	3:01-2/5	Oct. 14, 1989
2-1/4 miles	Fremarcton	8	124	3:58-1/5	Aug. 15, 1960

Leading Jockey in 2004: Travis Wayne Hightower, 102 wins

Leading Trainer in 2004: Ardell Sayler, 40 wins

Record attendance: 13,276, August 6, 1979. Record handle $753, 122, July 5, 1981 (16 race–double program.)

ATLANTIC CITY RACE COURSE

Located 14 miles west of Atlantic City
Nearest Airport: Atlantic City International in Pomona, 5 miles from track

4501 Black Horse Pike, Mays Landing, NJ 08330
(609) 641-2190; Fax: (609) 645-8309
Simulcasting: (609) 383-0859

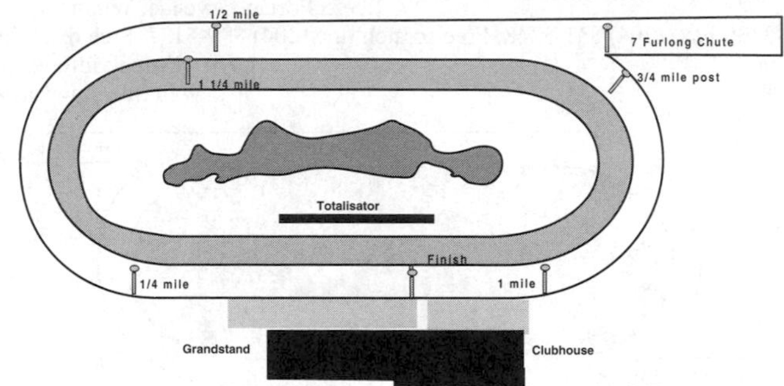

Track data: One and one-eighth mile, oval, with 7/8-mile chute. Distance from last turn to finish line, 947.29 feet; width 100 feet. One mile turf course, width also 100 feet. Both courses lit for night racing One mile and one-eighth oval; sandy loam with seven-furlong chute. Length of homestretch, 947.29 feet. Width of homestretch and backstretch, 100 feet. One mile turf course 100 feet in width. Stable accommodations for 1,602. Seating Capacity 16,000, parking for 4,500. Admission Free.

Opened July 22, 1946 by a virtual "Who's Who" of personalities including Bob Hope and Frank Sinatra. John B. Kelly Sr., Olympic gold medalist and father of the late Princess Grace, was Atlantic City's first president. After more than 50 years of summer racing, AC ran six nights of turf racing in 1999 and 2000, to maintain its simulcast license and was bought by the Greenwood Racing Corp. In 2001 the meet was expanded to 10 dates but in 2002, Atlantic City only was open on May 10, for a one day meet of seven turf races while conducting its nine other racing days at Monmouth Park. After a four-day meets in 2003 and 2004, the latter featuring purses of just over $150,000, the 2005 meet is set to run April 28 through May 12.

TRACK RECORDS

4-1/2 furs.	Jo Jo s Sparkle	2	117	:51-2/5	Jun. 22, 1988	1-1/16 m	Prince of Truth	7	121	1:41	Jun. 28, 1975
5 furs.	Dark Tzarina	5	117	:56-2/5	Jul. 16, 1988	1-1/8 m	World Appeal	3	118	1:46-3/5	Jul. 16, 1983
5-1/2 furs.	Aeronotic	5	119	1:02-3/5	Jul. 4, 1986	1-3/16 m	Mississippi Mud	4	119	1:54-1/5	Aug. 6, 1977
6 furs.	Margerine	5	110	1:08-1/5	Aug. 27, 1988	1-1/4 m	Greek Ship	4	119	2:01-4/5	Sep. 29, 1951
6-1/2 furs.	Zartarian	7	122	1:15-4/5	Jun. 26, 1994	1-3/4 m	Abdallati	6	119	3:06-2/5	Nov. 22, 1973
7 furs.	Mexican General	4	114	1:20-2/5	Jul. 4, 1977						

Turf Course

Abt 5 furs.	Bald Smile	7	119	:57-1/5	Aug. 8, 1996	Abt 1-1/8 m	Emptor	7	117	1:49-4/5	Jun. 9, 1993
5 furs.	Hostility	4	116	:55.86	May 13, 2004	1-1/8 m	Marco Bay	4	114	1:46-4/5	Jun. 10, 1994
Abt 5-1/2 f	Mr. Mink	4	118	1:02-3/5	Sep. 8, 1967	Abt 1-3/16m	Grey Lord II	7	111	1:56-3/5	Sep. 30, 1969
5-1/2 furs.	Legal Justice	5	119	1:01-4/5	Jul. 12, 1989	1-3/16 m	Steinlen	7	124	1:52	Jul. 21, 1990
Abt 1 mile	Silvino	5	119	1:36-4/5	Jun. 8, 1988	Abt 1-1/2 m	Northern Nights	7	115	2:31-4/5	Jul. 10, 1996
1 mile	Canal	6	120	1:34-1/5	Aug. 19, 1967	1-1/2 m	Advocator	5	115	2:27-1/5	Sep. 21, 1968
Abt 1m40yds	First Grade Reader	5	106	1:40-4/5	Jun. 7, 1991	Abt 1-1/16m	Misty Model	4	115	3:08-3/5	Aug. 19, 1977
1m 40 yds	Castaneto-Ar	7	115	1:38	Jun. 28, 1991	Abt 2 miles	Pier	7	120	3:35-4/5	Sep. 2, 1977
1-1/16 m	Road At Sea	3	120	1:41-1/5	Sep. 23, 1967	Abt 2-1/16m	Bangguster	4	117	3:45-4/5	Jul. 6, 1995
	Chiati	6	118	1:41-1/5	Jul. 6, 1979	2-1/16 m	Sticktoitive	8	117	3:42-4/5	Aug. 25, 1993
Abt 1-1/16m	Home Front	5	112	1:43-2/5	Jun. 12, 1976						

Jumps

2-1/8 m	Fighting Star	5	152	3:58.14	Apr. 23, 2003

Leading Jockeys in 2004: Danielle Hodsdon & Stewart Elliott, 3 wins (tie)

Leading Trainers in 2004: Thomas H. Voss & Jonathan E. Sheppard, 3 wins (tie)

Record attendance: 33,404, Sept 7, 1953. Record handle $3,168, 229, August 12,1967

ATOKAD

P.O.Box 518, South Sioux City, Nebraska, 68776
(402) 494-5722

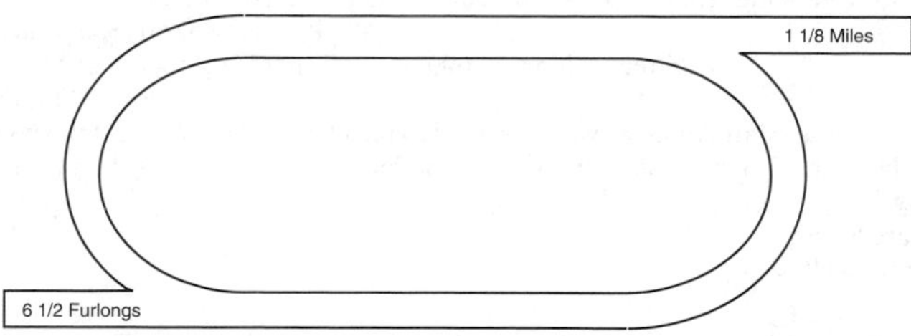

Track data: Five-eighths-mile oval, with two chutes, 6 1/2 furlongs and 1 1/8 miles. Distance from last turn to finish, 660 feet. Width 68 feet. Stable accommodations: 850; Seating capacity: 3,112.

Opened September 20, 1956. In most years since, Atokad has operated a late summer race meet in the Northwest corner of Nebraska near the South Dakota border. In recent years, Atokad has had short live race meets of one to three days, with three days of racing in 2004. Racing is scheduled for 2005 on Sept. 16 through Sept. 18.

TRACK RECORDS

Abt 4 furs.	Classy Fleet	3	114	:43-4/5	Nov. 19, 1977	1m 70 yds	No Mystery	7	117	1:42-1/5	Nov. 5, 1976
4 furs.	Shining Sea	6	117	:44-2/5	Jun. 28, 1992	1-1/16 m	Great Commander	4	120	1:43-3/5	Nov. 3, 1973
5-1/2 furs.	Slipped in Space	4	115	1:05-1/5	Oct. 24, 1976	1-1/8 m	Reason To Explode	6	114	1:50-1/5	Jul. 13, 1991
Abt 6 furs.	Urgent Valentine	4	121	1:16.40	Jul. 20, 2003	1-3/8 m	Barker s Tip	5	111	2:20	Oct. 17, 1964
6 furs.	Don Rivers	3	122	1:11-2/5	Oct. 28, 1966	1-7/16	Echo Bar	5	117	2:28	Oct.30, 1968
Abt 6-1/2 f	What About David	5	120	1:15.80	Sep. 19, 2004	Abt.1-7/16 m	Duke of Badgerland	7	115	2:29-3/5	Nov. 6, 1996
6-1/2 furs.	Spanish Key	7	123	1:16-2/5	Oct. 24, 1970	2 miles	Navy Grey	5	115	3:30-1/5	Oct. 30, 1962
1 mile	Quilla Sue	7	120	1:38	Oct. 30, 1973		Middle Road	5	122	3:30-1/5	Nov. 21, 1976

Leading Jockeys in 2004: Perry Compton & Dennis Michael Collins, 4 wins (tie)
Leading Trainer in 2004: David C. Anderson, 3 wins
Record Attendance: 6,200, October18, 1958.Record handle: $483,486, November 9, 1980

BAY MEADOWS
and SAN MATEO COUNTY FAIR

Magna Entertainment

Chairman & Director: Frank Stronach; General Manager, Administration: Bernie Thurman; General Manager, Operations: Mike Ziegler; Vice President of Operations: Mike Scalzo; Racing Secretary: Tom Doutrich; Coordinator of Racing: Richard Lewis; Publicity Manager: Tom Ferrall.

P.O. Box 5050, San Mateo, California 94402.
Street Address: 2600 South Delaware Street, San Mateo, California 94403.
(650) 574-7223; Fax: (650) 573-4632.
E-Mail Address: webmaster@baymeadows.com; Web Site: www.baymeadows.com.
Nearest Airports: San Francisco International Airport, 7 miles; San Carlos (private), 5 miles.

San Mateo County Fair
2600 South Delaware Street
San Mateo, California 94403
(650) 574-3247

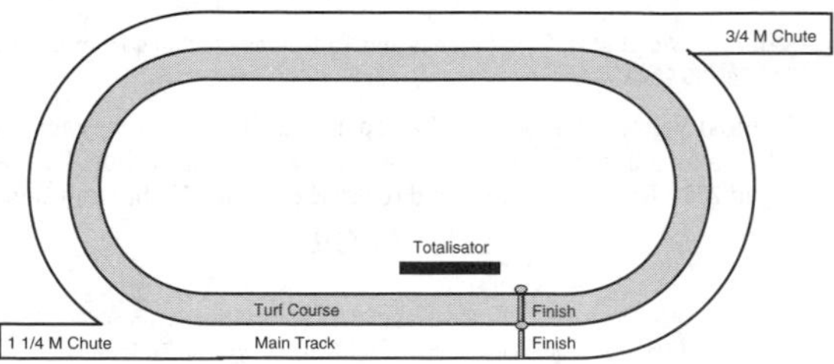

One-mile dirt track with six-furlong and 1 1/4-mile chutes. Length of stretch, 990 feet. Seven-furlong turf course. Stable accommodations, 900 horses. Seating: Grandstand and Infield, 10,000; Club House, 1,500; Turf Club, 1,200. Children's recreational areas in Grandstand and Infield Park. Parking for 5,000 cars.

Opened November 3, 1934. Introduced the totalizator and photo finish camera to United States racing at inaugural meet in 1934. The Bay Meadows Handicap, run since the first Bay Meadows season, is the oldest continuously run stakes in California. Two Thoroughbred meets in 2004 alternating with Golden Gate Fields throughout the major track season in the region. Bay Meadows also plays host annually to the mixed breed, San Mateo County Fair dates (BMf-meet) in August and offers year-round simulcasting. In 2004, purses, including stakes, averaged at least $149,000 per day during the two BM meets and over $107,000 during the BMf meet.

TRACK RECORDS

2 furs.	Royalette	2	118	:21.11	Apr. 12, 2002	1 m 70 yds	Redress	4	105	1:41-3/5	Dec. 10, 1934
3-1/2 furs.	Harrogate	2	115	:40-4/5	Mar. 16, 1935	1-1/16 m	Hoedown s Day	5	119	1:38-2/5	Oct. 23, 1983
4 furs.	Ina Dear	2	112	:46-2/5	Apr. 2, 1935	1-1/8 m	Super Moment	3	116	1:46-1/5	Dec. 13, 1980
4-1/2 furs.	Metatron	2	118	:50.59	May 24, 2001		See the King	4	114	1:46-1/5	Oct. 23, 1983
5 furs.	Trickey Trevor	5	117	:56.01	Oct. 28, 2004	1-3/16 m	Force of Reason	5	117	1:52-4/5	Nov. 5, 1983
5-1/2 furs.	Rio Oro	6	117	1:01.60	Oct. 7, 2001	1-1/4 m	Ask Father	7	112	2:00-2/5	Sep. 28, 1968
6 furs.	Black Jack Road	6	116	1:07-1/5	Oct. 28, 1990	1-1/2 m	Cattle Creek	3	114	2:27-3/5	Dec. 8, 1979
7-1/2 furs.	Lookabout	3	107	1:30-2/5	Nov. 26, 1936	1-5/8 m	Rag King	4	115	2:43-1/5	Dec. 15, 1990
1 mile	Aristocratical	6	113	1:33-3/5	Sep. 10, 1983	1-3/4 m	Tornillo	3	108	2:57-3/5	Nov. 21, 1936

Turf Course

4-1/2 furs.	Santano	4	123	:50.38	May 17, 2001	1-1/8 m	Ocean Queen	3	110	1:47.80	Oct. 12, 1996
5 furs.	Excessive Barb	4	117	:56.32	May 30, 2004	Abt. 1-1/8 m	Mula Gula	3	117	1:45.34	Sep. 25, 1999
7 furs.	First Flyer	4	119	1:24.35	Sep. 25, 1997	1-3/8 m	Peu a Peu	4	115	2:16.39	May 18, 2002
7-1/2 furs.	Hegemony	4	119	1:28.80	Oct. 12, 1985	Abt. 1-3/8 m	Handsome Weed	4	122	2:17.10	Nov. 24, 1991
1 mile	Position s Best	7	116	1:34-3/5	Sep. 6, 1987	1-1/2 m	Swiss Connection	4	124	2:31.46	Oct. 12, 1998
1-1/16 m	Dreamer	5	118	1:40.21	Aug. 17, 1997						

Leading Jockey in 2004: Russell Baze, at both BM meets, with 90 and 92 wins, respectively
Leading Trainer in 2004: Jerry Hollendorfer, at both BM meets, with 64 and 47 wins, respectively
Leading Jockey BMf in 2004: Dennis Carr, 14 wins
Leading Trainer BMf in 2004: John F. Martin, 7 wins
Record attendance:29, 300, April 17, 1948; Record handle: $8,660, 396, Nov 6, 1999

BELMONT PARK

New York Racing Association Inc.
President and CEO: Charles Hayward; Co-Chairman: Peter F. Karches; Co-Chairman: C. Steven Duncker; Senior Vice President: William A Nader; Racing Secretary and Handicapper: Michael S. Lakow.
Street Address: 2150 Hempstead Turnpike
Elmont, New York 11003
Nearest Airports: John F. Kennedy International Airport, six miles south west of track and Laguardia Airport, 12 miles west of track.
P.O. Box 90, Jamaica, New York 11417
Telephone: (718) 641-4700; (516) 488-6000
Fax: (516) 352-0919; Results: (718) 976-3333
Email: info@nyrainc.com
Web Site: www.nyra.com

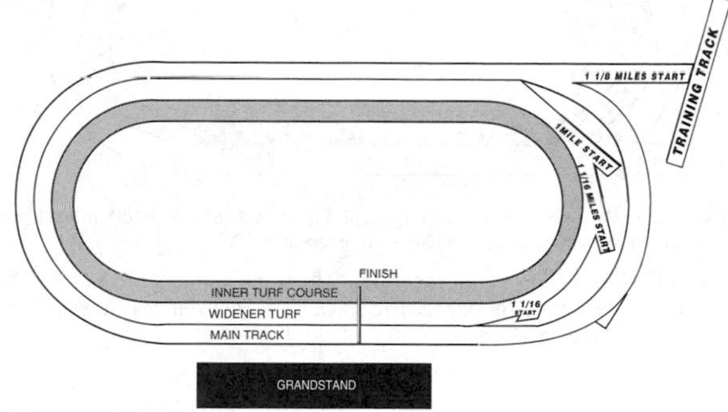

Track Data: 1 1/2-mile oval, sandy surface, length of stretch, 1,097 feet; Widener Turf Course, 1 5/16 miles plus 27 feet with two chutes, one mile and 1 1/16 miles; Inner Turf Course, 1 3/16 miles plus 103 feet, with one chute 1 1/16 miles. Seating 30,000; Capacity: 85-90,000. Parking for 18,500 cars.

Inaugural meet May 4, 1905 and permanent home of the 1 1/2-mile Belmont Stakes, the climax to the world famous Triple Crown series. Also has played host to three of the 20 Breeders' Cup Championships through 2004, including BC VII in 1990, BC XII in 1995, and BC XVIII on Oct. 27, 2001. Purses during the 60-day spring meet in 2004 averaged in excess of $486,000 per day, while purses averaged over $660,000 per day during the 33-day Fall Championship meeting. Belmont's 1 1/2-mile main oval is the largest in North America.

TRACK RECORDS

5 furs.	Kelly Kip	2	114	:55-3/5	Jun. 21, 1996	1-1/16 m	Rock and Roll	3	112	1:39.51	Jun. 13, 1998
5-1/2 furs.	Mike s Classic	5	119	1:02.26	Jun. 20, 2004	1-1/8 m	Secretariat	3	124	1:45-2/5	Sep. 15, 1973
6 furs.	Artax	4	120	1:07.66	Oct. 16, 1999	1-3/16 m	Rock Hall	4	109	1:56.	May 26, 1986
6-1/2 furs.	Bear Fan	5	121	1:14.46	Jun. 5, 2004	1-1/4 m	In Excess-Ir	4	119	1:58-1/5	Jul. 4, 1991
7 furs.	Left Bank	5	121	1:20.17	Jul. 4, 2002	1-3/8 m	Victoriously	4	118	2:14-3/5	Oct. 16, 1997
7-1/2 furs.	Commentator	3	119	1:27.44	Sep. 24, 2004	1-1/2 m	Secretariat	3	126	2:24	Jun. 9, 1973
1 mile	Najran	4	113	1:32.24	May 7, 2003	1-5/8 m	Kelso	3	124	2:40.80	Sep. 28, 1960

Widener Turf Course

6 furs.	Masterclass	4	114	1:07-1/5	May 24, 1992	1-1/4 m	Honey Dear	4	112	2:03-4/5	Oct. 10, 1962
7 furs.	Official Permission	7	112	1:19.88	Jul. 23, 2000	1-3/8 m	Influent	6	120	2:11	Jul. 13, 1997
1 mile	Elusive Quality	5	117	1:31.63	Jul. 4, 1998	1-1/2 m	Fantastic Light	5	126	2:24.35	Oct. 27, 2001
1-1/16 m	Fortitude	4	112	1:38.53	Sep. 6, 1997	2 miles	King s General	5	112	3:20-2/5	Jul. 4, 1983

Inner Turf Course

1-1/16 m	Roman Envoy	4	117	1:39.38	May 23, 1992	1-1/4 m	Paradise Creek	5	124	1:57-3/5	Jun. 11, 1994
1-1/8 m	Artie Schiller	3	123	1:45.50	Sep. 26. 2004	1-3/8 m	With Approval	4	118	2:10-1/5	Jun. 17, 1990

Jumps

2 miles	Rio Claro	5	148	3:34-4/5	Jun. 10, 1988	2-5/8 m	Flatterer	6	170	4:51-1/5	Oct. 11, 1985
2-1/2 m	Sur la Tete	6	154	4:36.53	Jun. 3, 2004	3 miles	High Patches	5	144	5:39-3/5	Jun. 12, 1970

Leading Jockey in 2004 Spring meet: John R. Velazquez, 77 wins
Leading Trainer in 2004 Spring meet: Todd A. Pletcher, 33 wins
Leading Jockey in 2004 Fall meet: John R. Velazquez, 58 wins
Leading Trainer in 2004 Fall meet: Todd A. Pletcher, 23 wins

Spring Meet: Record attendance: 103,222 June 7, 2002; Record handle: $10,035,906, June 6, 1999. Fall meet: Record attendance: 63,605, Sep 7, 1970; Record handle: $10,577, 736, October 27, 1990 (Breeders Cup): $98, 711, 413, October 27, 2001, (Breeders' Cup, all sources.)

BEULAH PARK

Heartland Jockey Club Ltd.

President: Charles J. Ruma; General Manager: Michael Weiss; Director of Publicity: Vic Mason; Racing Secretary: Ed Vomacka. pressbox@beulahpark.com
Street Address: 3664 Grant Avenue P.O. Box 850, Grove City, Ohio 43123-0850
Grove City, Ohio 43123 (614) 871-9600; Fax: (614) 871-0433
Website: www.beulahpark.com Racing Office: (614) 871-1938

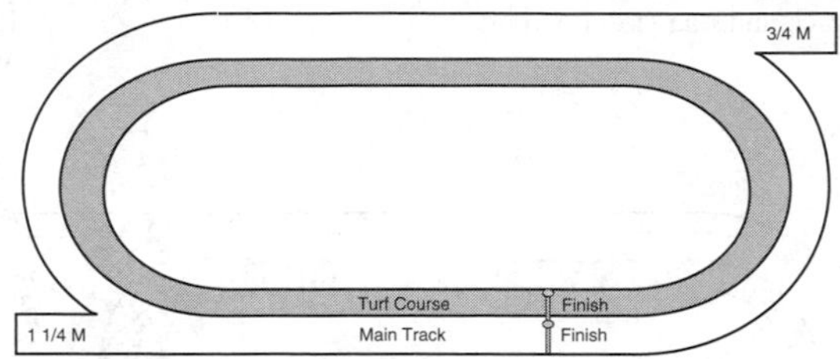

Track Data: One mile oval. Two chutes, six furlongs and 1 1/4 miles. Width of stretch: 80 feet; width of backstretch, 75 feet; distance from last turn to finish line, 1,100 feet.Stable Accommodations: 1,200; Seating capacity 7,200.

Opened April 21, 1923, Beulah Park was Ohio's first racetrack. The track conducts live racing from September to May, split into two meets, with only a short break between. The track is open seven days a week for full-card simulcasting. Purses per day average over $40,000 for both meets.

TRACK RECORDS

2 furs.	Go Chop	2	112	:21-3/5	May 7, 1989	1-3/16 m	World of Magic	4	119	1:55	Sep. 21, 1991
4 furs.	Float Away	2	117	:46-2/5	May 12, 1938	1-1/4 m	On the Scent	4	122	2:00-1/5	Oct. 19, 1991
4-1/2 furs.	Last Rebel	8	116	:50.96	Apr. 18, 2003	1-1/2 m	Doctor s Romance	6	117	2:29-2/5	Mar. 26, 1994
5 furs.	Love Poppa Mucci	5	117	:56-3/5	Feb. 11, 1994	1-5/8 m	Big Beans	4	113	2:46	Oct. 5, 1957
5-1/2 furs.	North and South	8	116	1:02.52	Feb. 1, 2004	1-3/4 m	Dot Your Eye	4	123	2:57-3/5	Oct. 20, 1971
6 furs.	Devil Time	7	125	1:08.32	Apr. 10, 2004	2 miles	Whipall	4	108	3:27-2/5	Sep. 29, 1951
1 mile	Appygolucky	6	116	1:35.47	Jan. 17, 2003	2 m 70 yds	Benomen	5	119	3:29-4/5	Nov. 20, 1993
1 m 70 yds.	King s Wailea	5	111	1:40	Nov. 19, 1993	2-1/16 m	She Looks Great	3	122	3:41-2/5	Nov. 28, 1983
1-1/16 m	Din s Dancer	5	122	1:40-4/5	Nov. 3, 1990	2-1/8 m	Second City	4	114	3:48-4/5	Nov. 25, 1984
1-1/8 m	Lord Try On	4	114	1:48-4/5	Sep. 26, 1992	2-1/4 m	Hallay s Pride	6	115	3:48-4/5	May 4, 1991

Turf Course

Abt. 6 Furs	Brent s Gail	4	114	1:07	Sep. 1, 1986	Abt.1-3/8 m	Spend Ten	4	113	2:12-4/5	Oct. 8, 1988
Abt. 1 Mile	Khal Me Sir	7	116	1:38-3/5	Oct. 4, 1992	1-3/8 m	Syncospin	4	115	2:12-3/5	Sep. 25, 1987
1 mile	Gaelic Cross	7	115	1:35-2/5	Sep. 23, 1987	1-5/8 m	Nigilik	5	121	2:48-1/5	Oct. 24, 1986
Abt 1m 70y	Nail s McNally	4	119	1:40-2/5	Oct. 1, 1988	Abt 2 m	Persian Jig	5	124	3:23-2/5	May 17, 1987
1 m 70 yds	Twin To Win	3	108	1:41	Oct. 24, 1986						

Jumps

2 miles	Bet Your Silver	4	152	3:45-3/5	Oct. 23, 1988

Leading Jockey in 2004 Spring meet: Marco Ccamaque
Leading Trainer in 2004 Spring meet: Jake S. Radosevich
Leading Jockey in 2004 Fall meet: Marco Ccamaque
Leading Trainer in 2004 Fall meet: Joseph Clark Faulkner

Record attendance: 11, 772, May 15, 1954; Record handle: $1,095, 950, March 5, 1980; Record handle with simulcasting: $1,478,038, October 5, 2000.

BLUE RIBBON DOWNS

Backstretch, LLC
General Manager: Frank Deal; Assistant General Manager: Blaine Story; Racing Secretary: Shirley Ellis; Director of Marketing: Robin Akers.
Mailing: PO Box 489, Sallisaw, OK 74955-0788 3700 West Cherokee, Sallisaw, OK 74955
Phone: (918) 775-7771 Fax: (918) 775-5805 Web Site: www.blueribbondowns.net

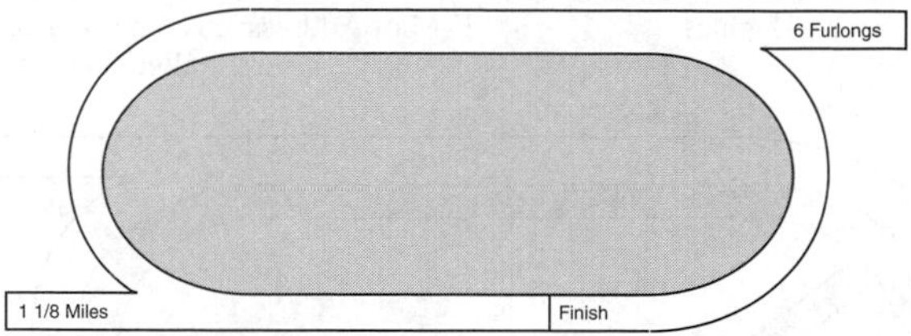

Track Data: Seven-eighth mile plus 30 yards oval, with 6-furlong and 1 1/8-mile chutes. Distance from last turn to finish 845 feet; width 72 feet. Stable accommodations 1,200. Seating capacity 3,500.

Opened August 30, 1984. Live mixed breed race meet on weekends. 2005 dates: Feb. 19 to May 7 and Aug. 6 to Oct. 30.

TRACK RECORDS

Distance	Horse	Age	Wt.	Time	Date
4 furs.	Iwontbeback	7	120	:44-3/5	Jul. 3, 1995
4-1/2 furs.	Rebel s Jon	4	121	:50.69	Jun. 29, 1996
5 furs.	Pow Wow Al	5	121	:56.86	May 27, 1996
5-1/2 furs.	Rebel s Jon	3	118	1:02-2/5	Oct. 1, 1995
6 furs.	Rebel s Jon	3	119	1:08.92	Jul. 9, 1995
7 furs.	Pretentious Chief	7	118	1:23	Sep. 10, 1995
7-1/2 furs.	Karate Kick	6	126	1:29.70	Sep. 17, 1994
1 mile	Staged Attraction	5	122	1:36-1/5	Jun. 10, 1989
	Tasca	3	120	1:36-1/5	Oct. 6, 1990
1-1/16 m	Just Ask Rudy	6	119	1:43.25	Apr. 6, 1996
1-1/8 m	Long On Rowdy	6	120	1:49.76	Jul. 17, 1994
Abt 1-1/4 m	Indio Jo	6	117	2:09-2/5	Nov. 10, 1985
1-1/4 m	Dare More	6	121	2:03.66	Aug. 28, 1994
1-3/8 m	Say It All	5	121	2:17-1/5	Oct. 1, 1995
1-1/2 m	Mr. Sanhedrin	6	119	2:32.78	Nov. 14, 1993
Abt 1-5/8 m	Chivas Elf	4	120	2:50	Nov. 30, 1986
1-5/8 m	Askherout	4	118	2:47	Nov. 26, 1989

Leading Jockey in 2004 Spring Meet: Janet Leah Wilson, 13 wins
Leading Trainer in 2004 Spring Meet: Clifton D. Brooks, 10 wins
Leading Jockeys in 2004 Fall Meet: Stephen Randle & Joel W. Allen & Joyce Epsteen, 5 wins (tie)
Leading Trainer in 2004 Fall Meet: Clifton D. Brooks, 5 wins
Record attendance 10,169, August 30, 1984; Record handle $1,152, 006, May 2, 1987.

CALDER RACE COURSE

Calder Race Course, Inc.

Chairman and CEO: Thomas H. Meeker; President: C. Kenneth Dunn; Vice President & General Manager: Michael Abes; Racing Secretary: Robert D. Umphrey; Simulcast Director: Diane Stoess; Director of Publicity: Michele Blanco.

Street Address: 21001 NW 27th Avenue
Miami, Florida 33056
Nearest Airports: Ft. Lauderdale-Hollywood Intl., 8 miles; Miami International, 15 miles

P.O. Box 1808, Miami, Florida 33055-0808
(305) 625-1311 (Dade Co.); (954) 523-4324 (Broward Co.)
Fax: (305) 620-2569; Publicity (305) 624-6284
E-Mail Address: customerservice@calderracecourse.com
Web Site: www.calderracecourse.com

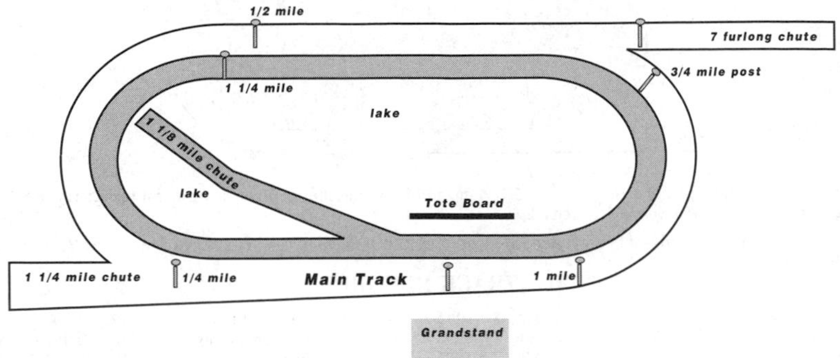

Track Data: One-mile oval. Two chutes: quarter mile, 7 furlongs. Length of stretch: 990 feet. 7-furlong turf course with 1 1/8-mile diagonal chute. Seating for 15,585; Parking for 10,000 cars; Stable Accommodations: 1,850.

Calder Race Course in Miami has grown through its 32 years of existence to become a foundation for the thoroughbred racing industry in south Florida. The track, which opened in 1971 and was acquired by Churchill Downs Incorporated in April of 1999, is located adjacent to Pro Player Stadium, the home of the Miami Dolphins and Florida Marlins. The track annually conducts eight months of live racing, with the Calder meet that runs from late April through late October and the Tropical Park-at-Calder meet that runs from late October to early January. In 2005, the Calder meet runs from April 25 through Oct. 16 and the Tropical-at-Calder meet is set for Oct. 17 through Jan. 2, 2006. Highlights of the racing season include the Festival of the Sun and Summit of Speed.

TRACK RECORDS

Distance	Horse	Age	Wt.	Time	Date
2 furs.	Baby Shark	2	122	:20.81	Jul. 13, 2002
4-1/2 furs.	Gold Phantom	2	118	:51.86	Sep. 16, 2001
5 furs.	Honest	3	117	:57.61	Jul. 1, 1996
5-1/2 furs.	Bernard s Candy	3	118	1:04.39	Aug. 9, 2002
6 furs.	Forty One Carats	4	116	1:08.95	Oct. 7, 2000
6-1/2 furs.	Tour of the Cat	4	119	1:15.99	Aug. 17, 2002
7 furs.	Constant Escort	4	114	1:21.82	Sep. 28, 1996
1 mile	High Ideal	3	118	1:36.25	Sep. 15, 2001
1 m 70 yds	Halo s Image	4	115	1:41.78	Oct. 31, 1995
1-1/16 m	Castlebrook	4	118	1:42.55	Sep. 15, 2001
1-1/8 m	Jumping Hill	6	117	1:50	Dec. 30, 1978
1-3/16 m	Arctic Honeymoon	4	114	1:59-3/5	Jan. 3, 1987
1-1/4 m	Wicapi	4	114	2:05.08	Jun. 24, 1996
1-1/2 m	Lead m Home	3	111	2:32-3/5	Dec. 31, 1977
1-5/8 m	Timberlea Tune	5	111	2:50-1/5	Oct. 16, 1971
1-3/4 m	Detective II	7	113	3:03-1/5	Oct. 23, 1971
2 miles	Detective II	7	130	3:30-1/5	Nov. 11, 1971

Turf Course

Distance	Horse	Age	Wt.	Time	Date
5 furs.	Whenthedoveflies	4	115	:54.78	May 23, 2004
7 furs.	Carterista	4	119	1:22.36	Jun. 19, 1993
7-1/2 furs.	Court Lark	6	115	1:26.54	Jul. 16, 1994
1 mile	Dillonmyboy	3	119	1:33.66	Oct. 30, 2000
1-1/16 m	He s Crafty	5	117	1:39.27	Dec. 28, 2004
1-1/8 m	The Vid	5	120	1:44.99	Nov. 25, 1995
1-3/8 m	King s Design	3	114	2:13.18	Jul. 23, 1999
1-1/2 m	Flag Down	5	116	2:24.11	Dec. 16, 1995
2 miles	Skate On Thin Ice	9	117	3:21.89	Jan. 2, 1996

Jumps

Distance	Horse	Age	Wt.	Time	Date
2-1/4 m	Pompeyo	6	158	4:08.84	Dec. 9, 2000

Leading Jockey in 2004 Calder meet: Eddie Castro, 154 wins
Leading Trainer in 2004 Calder meet: William P. White, 48 wins
Leading Jockey in 2004-2005 Tropical Park meet: Eddie Castro, 83 wins
Leading Trainer in 2004-2005 Tropical Park meet: Daniel C. Hurtak, 21 wins

Record attendance: (Calder meet) 23, 103, May 4, 1985 (Derby Day); (Tropical meet) 17,671, January 14, 1978; Record on-track handle: (Calder meet) : $2,954,162 – May 7, 1988 (Derby Day); (Tropical meet) $2,793,767 – January 7, 1989 (Tropical Park Derby Day); Record handle, including simulcasting: (Calder meet) $10,843,994 – July 10, 2004 (Summit of Speed); (Tropical meet) $9,461,604, December 29, 2001 (Grand Slam II Day)

CANTERBURY PARK

Canterbury Park Holding Corp.
Chairman of the Board: Curtis Sampson; President and CEO: Randall Sampson; Director of Racing/Racing Secretary: Douglas Schoepf. Media Relations Manager: Joe Anderson.

Nearest Airport: Twin Cities International, 15 minutes east of track.

1100 Canterbury Road, Shakopee, MN 55379
Telephone: (952) 445-7223; (800) 340-6361
Publicity/Press Box (952) 496-6408; Fax: (952) 496-6476
Web Site: www.canterburypark.com

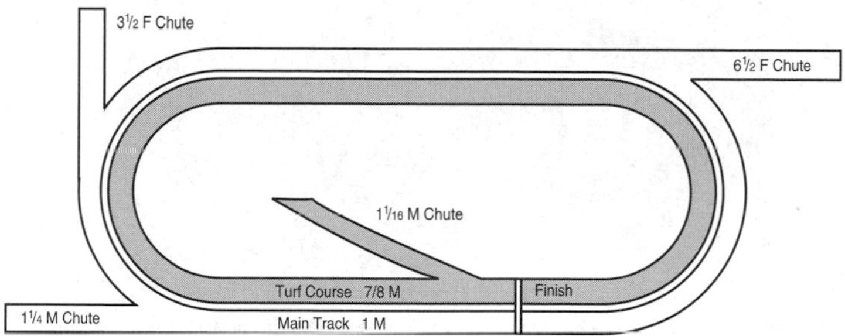

Track Data: One-mile dirt oval, six and one half furlong chute; 7/8-mile turf oval. Stable accommodations, 1,600 horses. Grandstand Capacity, 16,000; Parking for 7,500 cars.

Opened June 26, 1985. After multiple closings into the early 1990's, Canterbury was reopened as Canterbury Park under new management including local horsemen in 1994. In 2005, Canterbury Park will host the seventh renewal of the seven-race, $650,000 Claiming Crown, to be held July 16. In addition to its regular May to September race meet, Canterbury purses have doubled to about $120,000 per day in the years since introducing the first racetrack-based poker facility in the Midwest.

TRACK RECORDS

Abt 3-1/2 f	Bye For Now	3	115	:40	Jun. 30, 1985	1 mile	Minneapple	5	121	1:35-1/5	Sep. 27, 1987
3-1/2 furs.	In Moderation	2	118	:39.11	May 26, 1997	1m-70 yds	Come Summer	3	112	1:40-1/5	Aug. 18, 1985
4-1/2 furs.	Gallapiat s Song	2	120	:51.27	Jun. 23, 1991	1-1/16 m	Wally s Choice	3	117	1:41.74	Aug. 22, 2004
5 furs.	Tonight Rainbow	5	117	:57.11	May 31, 2004	1-1/8 m	Olympio	3	123	1:46.47	Jul. 7, 1991
5-1/2 furs.	Nickel Slot	4	116	1:02-4/5	May 17, 1989	1-1/4 m	John Bullit	6	122	2:04-3/5	Jul. 25, 1986
6 furs.	So Long Seoul	3	114	1:08-3/5	May 6, 1990	1-1/2 m	Loustros	5	116	2:32-3/5	Aug. 28, 1987
	Iwazza Bad Boy	4	112	1:08-3/5	Aug. 18, 1996	1-3/4 m	Luciole	5	118	2:59-4/5	Oct. 12, 1985
6-1/2 furs.	Don s Irish Melody	5	115	1:14	Jun. 12, 1988	2 miles	My Tulles Free	4	116	3:25-3/5	Sep. 1, 1986

Turf Course

5 furs.	Win the Crown	5	118	:56.31	Aug. 21, 2004	Abt 1-1/16 m	Diplomat s Reward	4	116	1:41.34	Jul. 17, 1999
Abt 7-1/2 f	Kiltartan Cross	3	113	1:27.82	Aug. 11, 1991	1-1/16 m	Little Bro Lantis	7	118	1:40-1/5	Jun. 17, 1995
7-1/2 furs.	Honor the Hero	7	122	1:28	Jun. 18, 1995	Abt 1-3/8 m	Le Fabulous Song	4	112	2:14.93	Oct. 20, 1991
Abt 1 mile	Kiltartan Cross	3	112	1:33.44	Jul. 10, 1991	1-3/8 m	Treizieme	5	114	2:12-3/5	Aug. 3, 1986
1 Mile	Go Go Jack	4	112	1:33-2/5	Jun. 3, 1995	Abt 1-7/8 m	Mark of Strength	7	118	3:11.53	Sep. 12, 1992
Abt 1m 70y	Tainer s Toy	8	109	1:39.30	Aug. 10, 1991	1-7/8 m	John Bullit	7	120	3:11-2/5	Sep. 26, 1987
1 m 70 yds	Numchuek	6	114	1:39-1/5	Jul. 6, 1988						

Leading Jockey in 2004: Derek C. Bell, 92 wins
Leading Trainer in 2004: Hugh H. Robertson, 53 wins
Record attendance: 27,439, April 24, 1987; Record handle: $3,560,228, July 19, 2003

CHARLES TOWN RACES AND SLOTS

PNGI Charles Town Races & Slots, LLC

Senior Vice President of Regional Operations: John V. Finamore; General Manager: Albert T. Britton; General Manager, Racing Operations: Richard L. Moore; Director of Racing/Racing Secretary: James E. Hammond, Jr.; Publicity Manager: Jeff Gilleas.

PO Box 551, Charles Town, WV 25414

Phone: (304) 725-7001; Racing Secretary s Office Fax: (304) 724-4326; Free results: (304) 724-4284

E-Mail Address: jeff.gilleas@pngaming.com; Web Site: www.charlestownraces.com

Track data: six-furlong oval, with two chutes, 4 1/2 furlongs and 1 5/16 miles. Distance from last turn to finish, 660 feet. Stable accommodations 1,050; seating capacity 6,000.

Charles Town Races opened on Dec. 2, 1933, and was the first northern track to operate during the winter season. Charles Town Races was home to the first black female trainer to be licensed in the United States and featured the first woman jockey to win a pari-mutuel race. Home of the West Virginia Breeders Classics founded by NFL Hall of Fame member, Sam Huff. In 1997, a referendum passed to approve video lottery machines. At present there are 3,800 slots machines. Features a covered parking garage. Charles Town is open year-round for simulcast wagering and slots. Wednesday through Sunday for live night racing, post time is 7:15 pm with Sunday's post at 1 pm. Live racing in 2005 from January to December, split into four seasonal meets totaling approximately 245 racing days, with daily purses of almost $220,000.

TRACK RECORDS

Abt 4 furs.	Lawrenceville	4	120	:46-2/5	Dec. 30, 1990
4 furs.	Choctaw Ridge	6	117	:44.86	Oct. 8. 2004
4-1/2 furs.	It s Only Money	4	117	:50.36	Jul. 4, 1999
6-1/2 furs.	Jet Appeal	5	109	1:17	Jan. 6, 1976
Abt 7 furs.	Morgan s Grove	2	117	1:27-3/5	Nov. 5, 1988
7 furs.	Ohmylove	5	109	1:24	Jan. 7, 1976
1-1/16 m	My Sister Pearl	5	111	1:43.83	Jan. 4, 2001
1-1/8 m	Lexington Park	6	126	1:50.20	Sep. 21, 1973
1-1/4 m	Belle d Amour	3	112	2:05-3/5	Jun. 28, 1941
1-5/16 m	Jim-A-Mike	3	114	2:14	Dec. 3, 1966
1-1/2 m	Guasave Breeze	3	118	2:34	Jun. 9, 1972
1-9/16 m	Allen Caid	6	115	2:40	Dec. 10, 1941
1-5/8 m	Cincpac	5	121	2:49-2/5	Nov. 13, 1970
1-13/16 m	Crafty Chris	3	111	3:11-2/5	Nov. 20, 1970
1-7/8 m	Gustav II	5	116	3:16-3/5	Nov. 25, 1972

Leading Jockey in 2004: Angel R. Quinones

Leading Trainer in 2004: Ronney Brown

Record attendance: 21,480 September17, 1981; Record handle: $2,148,451 May 1, 2004

CHURCHILL DOWNS

Churchill Downs Incorporated.

President and CEO of Churchill Downs Inc.: Thomas H. Meeker; Chairman: Carl F. Pollard; President of Churchill Downs: Steve Sexton; Vice President Racing Communication: John S. Asher; Director of Racing, Racing Secretary: Doug Bredar; Vice President of Operations: David Sweazy; Vice President of Administration: Jim Gates; Vice President Track Superintendent: Raymond Butch Lehr.

700 Central Avenue
Louisville, Kentucky 40208-1200
Nearest Airport: Louisville International, 3 miles from track.

(502) 636-4400; Racing, (502) 636-4470; Fax: (502) 636-4430
Publicity: (502) 636-4460 Fax: (502) 636-4469
Trackside (simulcasting), (502) 962-2210
Kentucky Derby Museum: (502) 637-1111
Web Site: www.churchilldowns.com

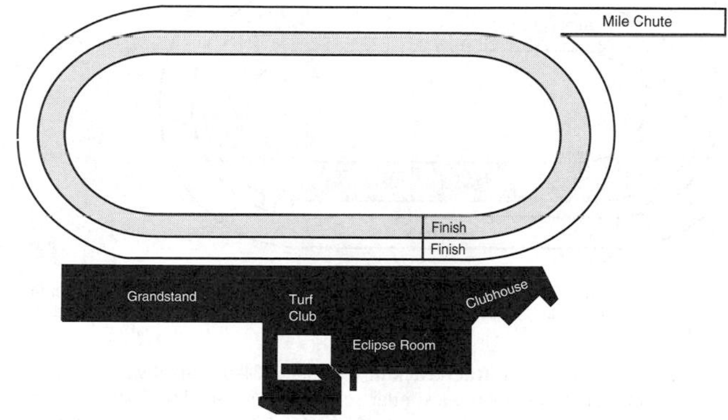

Track Data: One-mile oval, sandy loam with chute for one-mile races. Length of stretch, 1,234 1/2 feet. Matt Winn Turf Course: seven furlongs. Stable capacity, 1,400. Seating for 48,500, capacity 155,000 with infield; Parking for 5,000 cars, with many private lots in surrounding area. NOTE: Derby Day and Oaks seats are sold on an request basis. Derby and Oaks Ticket requests should be directed to Special Events Department, Churchill Downs, 700 Central Avenue, Louisville, Kentucky 40208.

Opened May 17, 1875. The legendary home of the Kentucky Derby and the Kentucky Derby Museum, Churchill Downs is a registered National Historic Landmark. The world-famous Twin Spires were unveiled on Derby Day, May 6, 1895. Churchill also is the oldest North American track with continuous annual racing and daily average purses in 2004 were more than $461,573 during the 52 day spring meet which annually begins with Kentucky Derby week. In 2002, a $121 million Master Plan, more comprehensive than any other construction project in the history of the track, was begun. The first of two phases, 64 luxury suites, was completed in 2003. The second phase began in 2003 and will open April 30, 2005 with the beginning of Derby week. The facility will feature a long list of improvements and enhancements including more luxury suites; a new Millionaire's Row; a new, expanded Turf Club, premium indoor and outdoor box seating; new dining and entertainment areas and a year-round area for hosting simulcasting wagering. 2005 Dates: April 30 through July 10; Oct. 30 through Nov. 26.

TRACK RECORDS

4 furs.	Fair Phantom	2	114	:46-3/5*	May 7, 1921	1-1/16 m	Yes Sir	5	110	1:41-3/5	Nov. 25, 1970
4-1/2 furs.	Chilukki	2	118	:51.00	Apr. 28, 1999	1-1/8 m	Victory Gallop	4	120	1:47.28	Jun. 12, 1999
5 furs.	Put Me In	4	121	:56.61	Jun. 10, 2004	1-3/16 m	Bonnie Andrew	5	110	1:58-3/5	Nov. 14, 1942
5-1/2 furs.	Cashier's Dream	2	118	1:02.52	Jul. 7, 2001	1-1/4 m	Secretariat	3	126	1:59-2/5	May 5, 1973
6 furs.	Kona Gold	6	126	1:07.77	Nov. 4, 2000	1-3/8 m	Elliott	6	109	2:20-3/5	Oct. 15, 1906
6-1/2 furs.	Love At Noon	3	121	1:14.34	May 5, 2001	1-1/2m	A Storm Is Brewing	4	112	2:32.02	Jun. 17, 2001
7 furs.	Alannan	5	116	1:20.50	May 5, 2001	1-5/8 m	Tupolev	5	112	2:49-2/5	Jul. 23, 1983
7-1/2 furs.	Miss Lodi	3	113	1:28.08	Jun. 1, 2002	1-3/4 m	Caslon Bold	7	114	2:59.64	Jul. 4, 1995
1 mile	Chilukki	3	116	1:33.57	Nov. 4, 2000	2 miles	Libertarian	4	113	3:22.26	Nov. 28, 1998
1 m 20 yds	Frog Legs	4	107	1:39	May 13, 1913	2-1/16 m	Hi Neighbor	8	117	3:40-4/5	Nov. 11, 1949
1 m 50 yds	Hodge	5	120	1:41-4/5	Oct. 4, 1916	2-1/4 m	Raincoat	3	90	3:53	Oct. 7, 1915
1 m 70 yds	The Porter	4	110	1:41-3/5	May 30, 1919	3 miles	Ten Broeck	4	104	5:26-1/2	Sep. 3, 1876
1 m 100 yds	The Caxton	4	101	1:49-1/5	May 16, 1902	4 miles	Sotemia	5	119	7:10-4/5	Oct. 7, 1912

Turf Course

5 furs.	Are You Down	4	111	:55.57	May 14, 2003	1-1/8 m	Lure	4	123	1:46.34	Apr. 30, 1993
1 mile	Jaggery John	4	113	1:33.78	Jul. 4, 1995	1-3/8 m	Snake Eyes	7	123	2:13.00	May 22, 1997
1-1/16m	Ever With You	3	115	1:40.82	Nov. 7, 2001	1-1/2 m	Tikkanen	3	122	2:26.50	Nov. 5, 1994

Leading Jockey in 2004 Spring meet: Rafael Bejarano, 81 wins

Leading Trainer in 2004 Spring meet: Steven M. Asmussen, 35 wins

Leading Jockey in 2004 Fall meet: John McKee, 27 wins; Leading Trainer in 2004 Fall meet: Steven M. Asmussen, 14 wins

Spring meet: Record attendance: May 4, 1974 (Derby Day) 163,628. Record handle: May 3, 2003 (Derby Day) $20,583,143 (on-track), May 1, 2004 (Derby Day) $141,088,445 (all sources). Fall meet: Record attendance: November 7, 1998 (Breeders' Cup) 80,452. Record handle: Nov. 4, 2000(Breeders' Cup) $13,579,798.

COLONIAL DOWNS

Colonial Downs Holdings, Inc.

Chief Executive Officer & Board Chairman: Jeff Jacobs; President and CFO: Ian Stewart; General Manager: John E. Mooney (Pres. MD-VA Racing Circuit, Inc.); Racing Secretary: Clayton Beck.

10515 Colonial Downs Parkway, New Kent, Virginia 23124
(804) 966-7223 or (888) 482-8725; Fax: (804) 966-1565. Free results: (888) 482-8722
Web Site: www.colonialdowns.com.; E-Mail Address: codowns@erols.com

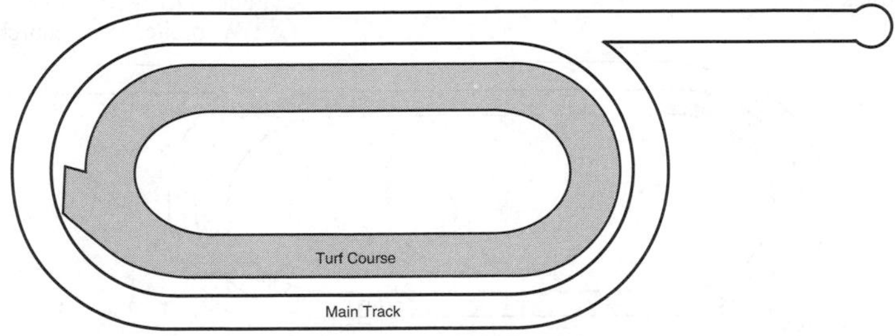

Track Data: 1 1/4 mile dirt track with chute for one-mile races; 7 1/2 furlongs to 1 1/8-mile turf track, depending on rail position, 180 feet wide. Stabling Capacity: 1,050; Seating capacity 6,000 capacity; Parking for 4,000 cars. Operates Virignia OTB facilities in Richmond, Chesapeake, Hampton, Vinton and Alberta.

Opened September 1, 1997 as the first pari-mutuel track in Virginia. A 34-day meet was run from June 11 through July 26 in 2004, with a strong accent on turf racing and a similar schedule is planned for 2005. Colonial also operates OTB facilities in Richmond, Chesapeake, Hampton, Vinton and Alberta, which contribute to the purse structure of over $200,000 per day. At 1-1/4 miles in circumference, the main dirt track is the second largest in North America. 2005 dates: June 17 to Aug. 9.

TRACK RECORDS

5 furs.	Timothy Mac	5	122	:55.74	Jul. 1, 2003	1 mile	Mt. Carson	4	119	1:35.07	Jun. 26, 2004
5-1/2 furs.	Bid Wild	6	117	1:02.68	Jul. 1, 2003	1-1/16 m	Gold Token	5	115	1:41.09	Sep. 13, 1998
6 furs.	Satan s Code	6	119	1:08.48	Jun. 27, 2004	1-1/8 m	Our Toby	3	114	1:48.95	Oct. 4, 1997
6-1/2 furs.	Cool Ken Jane	5	115	1:16-3/5	Sep. 7, 1997	1-1/4 m	Macgyver	3	114	2:03.54	Sep. 1, 1997
7 furs.	Sky Watch	4	117	1:20.87	Sep. 1, 1997	1-1/2 m	Lord Mendelson	3	118	2:30.13	Sep. 4, 2000

Turf Course

5 furs.	Bop	5	117	:55.85	Jun. 22, 2002	1-1/8 m	Kerfoot Corner	7	117	1:47.40	Sep. 26, 1998
5-1/2 furs.	Devereaux	6	115	1:01.93	Sep. 24, 1999	1-3/16 m	Jacksonzac	8	119	1:54.41	Oct. 10, 1998
6 furs.	Tyaskin	5	122	1:08.11	Sep. 20, 1998	1-1/4 m	Phi Beta Doc	3	117	1:59.97	Oct. 2, 1999
1 mile	La Reine s Terms	3	115	1:34.24	Sep. 17. 1998	1-1/2 m	Winsox	7	117	2:27.04	Sep. 28, 1998
1-1/16 m	Grass Roots	5	117	1:41.01	Oct. 8, 1999	1-5/8 m	Our Game	4	122	2:44.82	Sep. 24, 1999

Jumps

1-7/8 m	Moneytrain	5	148	3:22.83	Jun. 13, 2004	2-1/4 m	Dynamite Vic	4	150	3:58-4/5	Oct. 6, 2000

Leading Jockey in 2004: Ryan Fogelsonger, 53 wins
Leading Trainer in 2004: Phil Schoenthal, 22 wins

COLUMBUS RACES

822 15th Street, Columbus, NE 68601
Phone: (402) 564-0133 Fax: (402) 564-0990
Web Site: www.agpark.com

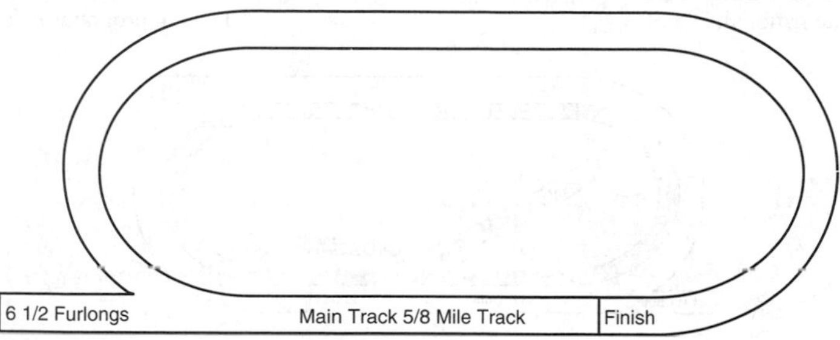

Track data: five-furlong oval with a 6 1/2-furlong chute Distance from last turn to finish, 720 feet, width of stretch 75 feet. Stable accommodations 900. Seating capacity 4,000.

Opened in the 1940's and usually runs a summer meet of about 25 days with about $40,000 in daily purses.

TRACK RECORDS

3-1/2 furs.	Timetoprofit	6	124	39.60	Aug. 24, 2002	1-1/16 m	Foreign Intent	3	114	1:44-2/5	Sep. 21, 1974
5-1/2 furs.	Foreign Flag	3	114	1:05-1/5	Sep. 30, 1978	1-5/16 m	Too Little Man	4	116	2:19-1/5	Sep. 6, 1969
6 furs.	Evas Choice	5	117	1:10-2/5	Aug. 27, 1994	1-3/8 m	In Doc s Honor	6	116	2:18-2/5	Sep. 3, 1994
6-1/2 furs.	Jae Ranch	4	114	1:17	Aug. 12, 1984	1-1/2 m	Skeeter Do	7	117	2:27-4/5	Sep. 12, 1994
1 m 70 yds	Ilatan	7	118	1:41-3/5	Sep. 9, 1984	2 miles	Blazing Don	7	111	3:36-3/5	Sep. 26, 1982

Leading Jockey in 2004: Filmer Munaylla, 32 wins
Leading Trainer in 2004: David C. Anderson, 24 wins
Record attendance, 8,856, September 3, 1973. Record handle $719, 725 September 3, 1984.

DELAWARE PARK

Delaware Racing Association

Chairman of the Board: William M. Rickman Sr.; President and Chief Executive Officer: William M. Rickman Jr.; Chief Operating Officer: William Fasy; Racing Secretary: Sam Abbey.

777 Delaware Park Blvd.
Wilmington, Delaware 19804
Nearest Airport: New Castle County Airport, 4 miles;
Philadelphia International, 20 miles.

(302) 994-2521; Free Results: (302) 998-0110
Web site: http://www.delawarepark.com
E-mail: programs@delawarepark.com

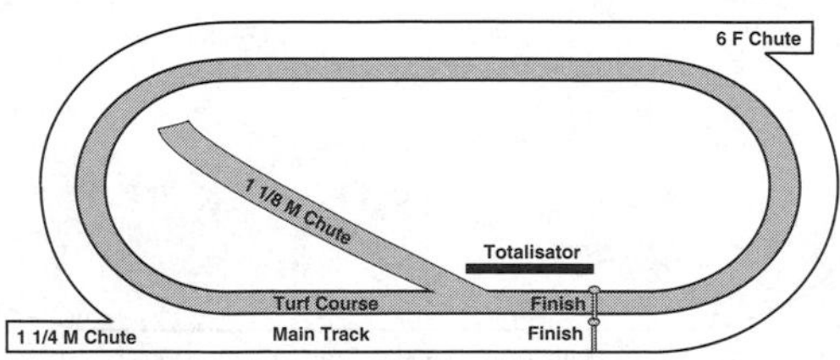

Track Data: One mile sandy loam oval with six-furlong and 1 1/4 mile chutes. Distance from last turn to finish, 995 feet; width 100 feet. Turf course: 7-furlongs. Stable accommodations 1,450. Must be 21 years or older to enter VLT area.

Opened June 26, 1937. Acquired in 1983 by William Rickman, Sr., a Rockville, Md. developer, Delaware Park has enjoyed a major rebirth since video lottery machines were included in the mix on December 29, 1995. In 2004, the season included 134 racing days from April to November with purses in excess of $247,000 including stakes. Highlights included the Delaware Handicap Festival of racing in late July and the prestigious Delaware Handicap. The 2005 live racing season is scheduled for April 30 through Nov. 13. In addition to its two full floors of slot machines, Delaware Park offers full-card, multi-track simulcasting 7 days a week except Christmas and Easter.

TRACK RECORDS

2 furs.	Glitter River	6	133	:21.60	Sep. 5, 2000	1-1/8 m	Victoria Park	3	122	1:47-2/5	Jun. 18, 1960
4 furs.	Star Event	2	118	:47.02	May 5, 1997	1-3/16 m	Gold Star Deputy	5	114	1:56.72	Oct. 31, 1999
4-1/2 furs.	Erlton	2	118	:51-4/5	May 5, 1998	1-1/4 m	Coup De Fusil	5	114	1:59-4/5	Jul. 25, 1987
5 furs.	Milky Way Gal	5	116	:56-1/5	Jul. 29, 1989	1-1/2 m	Bam	5	115	2:31	Jun. 26, 1948
5-1/2 furs.	Dontcloseyoureyes	4	122	1:03	Oct. 14, 1990	1-5/8 m	Flying Retsina Run	5	121	2:45.52	Sep. 4, 2000
6 furs.	Damitrius	5	115	1:08-1/5	Sep. 2, 1980	1-3/4 m	Cer Vantes	6	118	2:56-2/5	Jun. 27, 1951
1 mile	Ashlar	4	117	1:35-1/5	Jun. 25, 1960	2 miles	Dixies Act	5	118	3:29-2/5	Aug. 10, 1975
1 m 70 yds	Distinct Vision	3	115	1:39.20	Aug. 25, 2003	2 m 70yds	Wolfe Tone	6	114	3:34.16	Nov. 7, 1993
1-1/16 m	Lies Of Omission	6	116	1:41.52	Jul. 4, 1998	2-1/4 m	Sanguine Sword	8	114	3:58-3/5	Jul. 2, 1986

Turf Course

Abt 5 furs.	Incredible Revenge	4	116	:56.15	Sep. 4, 1996	Abt. 1-3/8m	King James	5	116	2:15.62	Jun. 21, 1997
5 furs.	Mujado	4	116	:56.16	Jul. 27, 2002	1-3/8 m	Cool Prince	5	114	2:12-2/5	Jul. 3, 1965
Abt 1 m	Big Warning	4	122	1:35-2/5	Jul. 22, 1990	Abt 1-1/2 m	Yield	4	116	2:29.98	Aug. 26, 1997
1 mile	Hanover Hollywood	5	118	1:34.74	Aug. 3, 2002	1-1/2 m	Revved Up	5	116	2:26.46	Jul. 20, 2003
Abt 1-1/16 m	My Sweet Lord	4	116	1:41.54	Jul. 7, 1996	Abt 2 m	Peace Peace Peace	6	141	3:21.98	Jul. 18, 1993
1-1/16 m	Charabanc	5	108	1:40-4/5	Jul. 20, 1963	2 miles	Verdance	4	113	3:24-2/5	Sep. 21, 1986
Abt 1-1/8 m	I m A Lil Devil	5	114	1:48.25	Jul. 19, 1992	2-3/8 m	Lively London	5	113	4:09	Jul. 25, 1986
1-1/8 m	Foufa s Warrior	3	115	1:47.44	Jul. 20, 2003	2-7/8 m	Call Louis	4	107	5:08-1/5	Aug. 24, 1986

Jumps

2 miles	Castleworth	6	148	3:38.33	Jul. 19, 1992

Leading jockey in 2004: Ramon A. Dominguez, 198 wins
Leading trainer in 2004: Scott A. Lake, 91 wins
Record attendance: 35,473, July 5, 1954. Record handle: $4,837,856 – July 21, 2002

DEL MAR

Del Mar Thoroughbred Club

President and General Manager, Joe Harper; Executive Vice President, Craig Fravel; Senior VP & CFO, Mike Ernst; Vice President, Marketing, Craig Dado; Vice President, Racing/Racing Secretary, Tom Robbins; Director of Media, Dan Smith; Director of Operations, Tim Read; Director of Mutuels, Bill Navarro.

Street Address: 2260 Jimmy Durante Blvd.
Del Mar, CA 92014
Nearest Airports: Lindbergh Field, 18 miles south of the track in San Diego. Private planes and helicopters may land at Palomar Airport, 12 miles to the north

Mailing Address: P.O. Box 700, Del Mar, CA 92014
(858) 755-1141; Fax: (858) 792-1477
Free scratches, results and stretch calls: (858) 793-5544
Web Site: www.delmarracing.com. E-mail: marys@dmtc.com

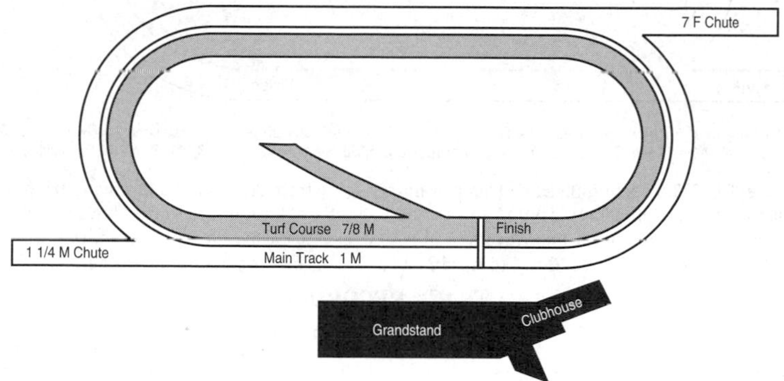

Track Data: One-mile oval with seven-furlong and 1 1/4-mile chutes. Distance from last turn to finish, 919 feet. Jimmy Durante Turf Course, seven-furlong oval, with one-eighth-mile diagonal chute. 350-acre Del Mar fairgrounds includes one-half-mile training track.
Stable accommodations: 2,100.
Seating capacity 14,304; Parking for 10,000 cars.

Opened July 3, 1937 with Bing Crosby collecting tickets at the main gate. Crosby and several of his Hollywood pals were among Del Mar's original investors. The inaugural meeting also featured the first photo-finish camera (invented by Lorenzo del Riccio, an optical engineer at Paramount Pictures). During the 2004 season, which ran from July 21 through Sept. 8, Del Mar's purses averaged a record $559,349 per day. In 2005, Del Mar's prestigious 43-day meet will run from July 20 to Sept. 7. "Daybreak at Del Mar" - breakfast watching workouts trackside - every weekend 7:30 to 9:30 a.m. First post daily at 2 p.m. with exception of "Four O'Clock Fridays."

TRACK RECORDS

5 furs.	Soldier Girl	3	116	:56-2/5	Aug. 13, 1964	1 mile	Precisionist	7	114	1:33-1/5	Aug. 1, 1988
5-1/2 furs.	Ack Ack	4	124	1:02-1/5	Sep. 12, 1970	1-1/16 m	Windy Sands	5	122	1:40	Aug. 4, 1962
	Lakeside Trail	5	117	1:02-1/5	Aug. 18, 1974		Native Diver	6	131	1:40	Aug. 7, 1965
	Little Mustard	4	114	1:02-1/5	Sep. 5, 1974		Matching	4	116	1:40	Aug. 18, 1982
	King s Sea Rullah	4	115	1:02-1/5	Aug. 12, 1977	1-1/8 m	Latin Touch	4	109	1:46	Sep. 1, 1979
	World Pleasure	4	122	1.02-1/5	Aug. 24, 1977	1-3/16 m	Four by Five	7	118	1:56-2/5	Aug. 16, 1954
6 furs.	King Of Cricket	6	115	1:07-3/5	Aug. 22, 1973	Abt 1-1/4 m	Ancient Title	7	123	1:55-2/5	Sep. 5, 1977
6-1/2 furs.	Native Paster	4	117	1:13-3/5	Sep. 4, 1988	1-1/4 m	Candy Ride	4	124	1:59.11	Aug. 24, 2003
7 furs.	Solar Launch	3	122	1:20	Aug. 10, 1990	1-1/2 m	Spring Boy	5	116	2:29-2/5	Aug. 16, 1958

Turf Course

5 furs.	Maria s Mirage	4	119	:55.06	Jul. 28, 2003	1-1/16 m	Allover	4	121	1:39.84	Aug. 27, 2003
7-1/2 furs.	Syncopate	6	115	1:27-4/5	Aug. 24, 1981	1-1/8 m	Special Ring	6	117	1:45.87	Jul. 27, 2003
1 mile	Touch of the Blues	6	122	1:32.22	Aug. 2, 2003	1-3/8 m	Crazy Ensign	7	121	2:12.07	Aug. 29, 2003

Leading Jockey in 2004: Corey S. Nakatani, 54 wins
Leading Trainer in 2004: Doug O Neill, 28 wins
Record Attendance: 44, 181, August 10, 1996. Record Handle: $5,657, 840 August 15, 1987 (on track). $22,857, 782 August 15, 1998 (all sources)

DELTA DOWNS

Delta Downs Racetrack & Casino

Owner: Boyd Gaming Corporation; General Manager: Jack Bernsmeier.

PO Box 175, Vinton, LA 70668-0175
(337) 589-7441 Fax: (337) 589-2399
Web Site: www.deltadowns.com;

Track data: six-furlong oval with two chutes, five furlongs and 1 1/16 miles. Distance from last turn to finish line 660 feet. Width of stretch 80 feet; backstretch and turns 70 feet. Stable accommodations 1,320. Seating capacity 3,400; Parking for 3,000 cars.

Opened September 20, 1973. Thoroughbred and quarter horse racing from January to March and from October to late December in 2004 with year round simulcasting and a casino on the track grounds. Purses have increased steadily during the four years of casino operation, with a new high of over $193,000 per day registered from October 2003 through March 2004. Dates for 2004-05: Oct. 1 to April 2 and a similar meeting beginning in the fall.

TRACK RECORDS

2-1/2 furs.	Mrs. Deville	2	112	:27	Feb. 19, 1976	1-1/16 m	Norms Promise	4	125	1:43-1/5	Mar. 23, 1975
	Cajun s Two Step	2	115	:27	Feb. 10, 1985	1-1/8 m	Lemon Mousse	4	117	1:56-1/5	Nov. 22, 1992
4 furs.	Rock Afire	5	119	:46-1/5	Dec. 10 1994	1-3/16 m	Ponderosa Lark	5	114	2:03-3/5	Oct. 31, 1975
4-1/2 furs.	Raisable Adversary	4	120	:51	Feb. 15, 1992	1-1/4 m	Shy Bull	5	122	2:10-1/5	Nov. 3, 1974
5 furs.	Britt s Jules	2	117	57.49	Nov. 5, 2003	1-5/16 m	Gentleman Mike	4	115	2:17-3/5	Dec. 1, 1974
6-1/2 furs.	Chief Okie Dokie	6	118	1:18.76	Feb. 8, 2002	1-3/8 m	Surrogate s Irish	8	118	2:23.52	Mar. 22, 2003
7 furs.	No Its Not	5	123	1:24.31	Jan. 24, 2003	1-1/2 m	Art Work	6	122	2:41-1/5	Jan. 11, 1974
7-1/2 furs.	Junior Gent	4	108	1:33-1/5	Mar. 14, 1974	1-9/16 m	Golden Foil	7	118	2:46.86	Mar. 27, 2004
1 mile	Freon Flier	4	118	1:37.52	Mar. 10, 2002	2 miles	Can Em	5	118	3:43-4/5	Dec. 10, 1988
1 m 70 yds	Thriller	6	117	1:42-2/5	Sep. 27, 1973						

Leading Jockey in 2004: Steve J. Bourque, 120 wins

Leading Trainer in 2004: Keith L. Bourgeois, 61 wins

Record attendance: 10, 824, December 30, 1990; Record handle: $2,477,000, December 5. 2003

THE DOWNS AT ALBUQUERQUE

201 California St. NE, Albq. NM 87108
PO Box 8510, Albuquerque, NM 87198-8510
(505) 266-5555 Fax: (505) 268-1970
E-Mail Address: michaell@abqdowns.com
Web Site: www.abqdowns.com

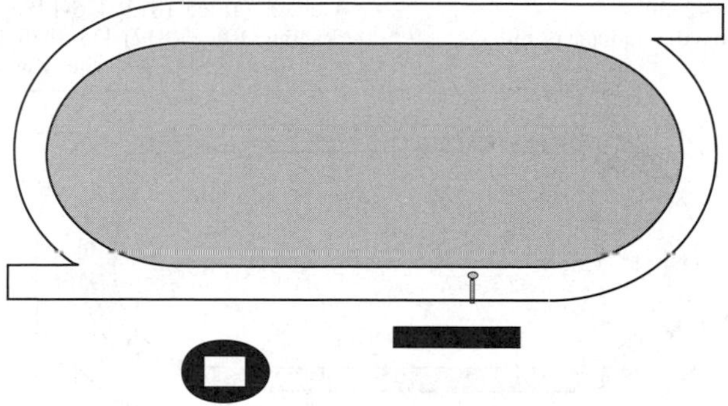

Track data: One-mile oval with 1/4-mile and seven-furlong chutes. Distance from last turn to finish 1,114; width 90 feet. Stable accommodations 1,700.

Opened October of 1938, along old Route 66, as a single-story structure. There are three stories now, all glass enclosed. A casino contributes a percentage of its revenue to the daily purses, which averaged about $50,000 including stakes in 2004. The Downs will run two mixed-breed meets in 2005: Spring, April 2 through June 12; New Mexico State Fair, Sept. 9 through Sept. 25. The Spring meet features The Lineage, a day of racing dedicated to New Mexico-bred horses on a complete card of 10 races, each with a $40,000 purse.

TRACK RECORDS

4 furs.	Chipper J.	2	118	:45.76	May 6, 2000
4-1/2 furs.	Silver Matt	2	115	:51.22	Jun. 17, 2000
5 furs.	Scout Revolt	3	120	:56.35	Dec. 12, 1998
5-1/2 furs.	Yulla Yulla	5	119	1:01.60	Sep. 23, 2000
6 furs.	Huggin the Rail	6	119	1:08.44	Sep. 29, 1996
6-1/2 furs.	Ben Told	8	120	1:14.59	May 10, 2002
7 furs.	Star Smasher			1:21.01*	Jun. 9, 2002
1 mile	Curve Ball	6	120	1:35.57	Apr. 27, 2003
1 m 70 yds	Fire Knight	6	112	1:41.60	Sep. 26, 1959
1-1/16 m	Ciento	3	120	1:40.60	Sep. 22, 2001
1-1/8 m	Moro Grande	8	114	1:48.42	Jun. 8, 2003
1-3/16 m	Savage Wind	7	114	2:05-4/5	Oct. 6, 1985
1-1/4 m	Luedke	8	119	2:03.69	Apr. 14, 1996
1-1/2 m	Luedke	6	116	2:33.73	Sep. 25, 1994
1-3/4 m	Prince De-Or	8	111	2:59.20	Sep. 25, 1966
1-13/16 m	Vermejo	6	118	3:05-2/5	Sep. 27, 1970
2 miles	Betty Falcon	5	109	3:28-3/5	Oct. 7, 1956

Leading Jockey in spring meet, 2004: Ken S. Tohill, 31 wins
Leading Trainer in spring meet, 2004: Henry Dominguez, 13 wins
Leading Jockey in fall meet, 2004: Ken S. Tohill, 11 wins
Leading Trainers in fall meet, 2004: Joel H. Marr & Henry Dominguez, 5 wins (tie)
Record attendance: 13, 979 September 16, 1990. Record handle: $1,050,700, September 16, 1990, (includes simulcasting.)

ELLIS PARK

Churchill Downs, Inc.

Chairman: Thomas H. Meeker; President: Steve Sexton; General Manager: Paul D. Kuerzi; Racing Secretary and Director of Racing: Doug Bredar; Director of Publicity: Luke Kruytbosch; Marketing Director: Jennifer Ray.

Street Address: 3300 U.S. Highway 41 North
Henderson, Kentucky 42420
Nearest Airport: Evansville, Indiana (8 miles)

P.O. Box 33, Henderson, Kentucky 42419-0033
General Office: (812) 425-1456; Fax (812) 425-0146
Racing Office: (812) 435-8940; Fax: (812) 425-3725
Web site: www.ellisparkracing.com

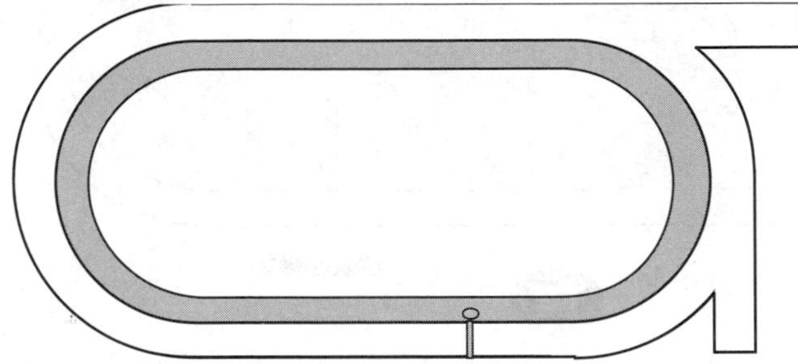

Track Data: One mile and one-eighth sandy loam oval with seven-furlong and one-mile chutes. Distance from last turn to finish, 1,175 feet; width 100 feet in stetch, 85 feet in backstretch.. One-mile turf course; Stable accommodations for 1,290 stalls; training facilities also available at Kentucky Horse Center in Lexington, (606) 293-1853. Seating for 7,750; Parking for 6,000 cars.

Opened November 8, 1922 and operated by James C. Ellis from 1924 to his death in 1956. Acquired by Churchill Downs in 1998. Several improvements to the facility were made in 2001. In 2004, purses including stakes averaged over $167,000. For 2005, Ellis Park offers year-round Clubhouse Simulcasting. Live racing Wednesday through Sunday and Labor Day Monday from July 13-Sept. 5, a total of 41 racing d ays.

TRACK RECORDS

5 furs.	White Image	2	119	:57-3/5	Jul. 9, 1988	1-1/4 m	Won Du Loup	4	115	2:03	Sep. 4, 1988
5-1/2 furs.	Relentless Seller	3	114	1:03.37	Aug.16, 2002	1-3/8 m	Ramona Jay	4	102	2:23	Aug. 24, 1985
6 furs.	Stubilem	4	117	1:09	Jul. 1, 1982	1-1/2 m	Unaccountable	5	115	2:29-3/5	Jul. 23, 1988
6-1/2 furs.	American Chance	5	113	1:15	Jul. 16, 1994	1-5/8 m	Sir Lightning	7	112	2:45-4/5	Aug. 9, 1992
7 furs.	Josh s Madelyn	3	112	1:21.37	Sep. 5, 2004	1-3/4 m	Bondi	5	115	3:00	Aug. 27, 1966
Abt 7-1/2 f	Illbeastar	4	113	1:35-1/5	Jul. 1, 1977	2 miles	Classic Deal	6	119	3:25-3/5	Aug. 21, 1988
1 mile	Still Waving	5	118	1:34-3/5	Aug. 13, 1988	2-1/4 m	Bondi	5	115	3:54	Sep. 5, 1966
1-1/8 m	Lt. Lao	4	123	1:47-3/5	Aug. 27, 1988						

Turf Course

5-1/2 furs.	Bettybird	3	112	1:00.52	Aug. 21, 2002	1-1/8 m	Yaqthan	6	113	1:44-3/5	Sep. 2, 1996
1 mile	Slewper Imp	5	115	1:32-3/5	Jul. 16, 1995	1-1/4 m	Ye Slew	7	112	1:59-3/5	Aug. 6, 1994
	Suffragette	3	112	1:32-3/5	Jul. 24, 1999	1-1/2 m	Our Forbes	4	115	2:25-2/5	Aug. 10, 1994
1-1/16 m	Stay Sound	3	115	1:38-4/5	Jul. 20, 1998	2 miles	Irish Harbour	6	113	3:20-1/5	Sep. 2, 1996

Leading Jockey in 2004: Rafael Bejarano, 85 wins

Leading Trainers in 2004: Bobby C. Barnett & Barbara I. McBride, 13 wins (tie)

Record attendance: 15,500 estimated, September 4, 1967.

EMERALD DOWNS

Northwest Racing Associates, LP
President: Ronald D. Crockett.

Street address: 2300 Emerald Downs Dr.Auburn, Wa., 98001
PO Box 617, Auburn, WA 98071-0617 ; (253) 288-7000 Fax: (253) 288-7010
Web Site: www.emdowns.com

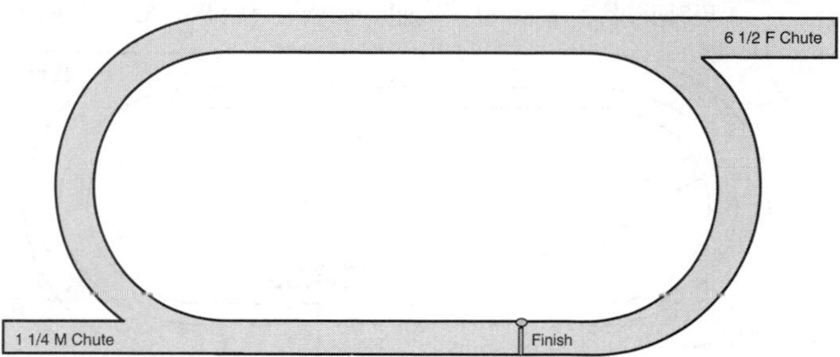

Track data: One-mile oval with two chutes, 1 1/4 miles and 6 1/2 furlongs. Distance from last turn to finish 990 feet.

Opened in 1996 to replace the void left in Seattle area by the termination of racing at Longacres. The 2004 meet featured more than $95,000 in purses, including stakes during a 90-day session from mid-April to mid-September. 2005 dates: April 15 through Oct. 16.

TRACK RECORDS

Distance	Horse	Age	Wt.	Time	Date
2 furs.	Midnight Cruiser	2	118	:21.40	May 4, 2000
	Adventure Man	2	118	:21.40	May 10, 2000
4-1/2 furs.	I. M. Adevil	2	118	:50-3/5	May 30, 1999
	Pacificat	2	118	:50.60	May 21, 2000
5 furs.	Jazzy Mac	5	98	:55.40	Aug. 20, 2000
	Victor Slew	4	115	:55.40	Aug. 24, 2003
5-1/2 furs.	Willie the Cat	5	118	1:01.20	Apr. 16, 2004
6 furs.	Blue Tejano	8	119	1:07.60	Jun. 7, 2002
6-1/2 furs.	Best on Tap	4	119	1:13.60	May 31, 2004
1 mile	Sky Jack	7	123	1:33.00	Aug. 24, 2003
1-1/16 m	Kid Katabatic	5	123	1:39-3/5	Jul. 26, 1998
1-1/8 m	Flying Notes	3	122	1:45.40	Sep. 2, 2002
1-1/4 m	Rapid Stream	7	118	2:01-4/5	Aug. 15, 1998
1-1/2 m	Keen Line	9	120	2:30-3/5	Sep. 6, 1997
2 miles	Horatio	5	115	3:22.60	Sep. 20, 2004

Leading Jockey in 2004: Ricky Frazier, 109 wins
Leading Trainer in 2004: Frank Lucarelli, 52 wins
Record handle: August 22, 1999, $1,217,590; August 22, 1999 $2,731,852, all sources

EVANGELINE DOWNS

Old Evangeline Downs, LLC

GM: Mike Howard; Executive Director of Racing Operations: David A. Yount; Racing Secretary: Jason M. Boulet; Publicity Director, Sean D. Beirne.

2235 Creswell Lane Ext, Opelousas, LA 70570
(337) 594-3000 Fax: (337) 594-3174
E-Mail Address: info@evangelinedowns.com; Web Site: www.evangelinedowns.com

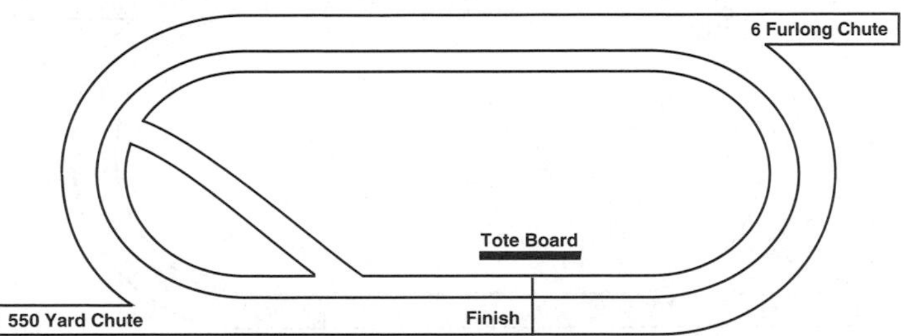

Track data: One-mile oval, with six-furlong and 1 1/4-mile chutes, seven-furlong turf course (expected opening: 2006). Distance from last turn to finish 1,035 feet; width 80 feet. Stable accommodations approximately 1,000

Original facility opened April 28, 1966. The new facility in Opelousas, La., marks the 40th anniversary of racing at Evangeline Downs with a thoroughbred race meeting April 7 through Labor Day, Sept. 5, 2005, and a newly added five-week spring Quarter Horse meeting, Feb. 5 through March 27. Fall Quarter horse racing is also planned with dates to be announced in April 2005. Year-round simulcasting is available at Evangeline Downs Racetrack and Casino and also its off-track betting sites in New Iberia and Port Allen (several new sites expected in 2005). Evangeline Downs Racetrack and Casino opened on Dec. 19, 2003. Purses for the 2005 season will increase from the $120,000 range in 2004 to over $150,000 per day in 2005. Evangeline has been the starting point for some of the best jockeys currently in the sport, including recently retired Hall of Famer Eddie Delahoussaye and Randy Romero, a winner of 4,292 races. The great gelding John Henry won his first stakes at Evangeline Downs. On June 3, 2000, the filly Hallowed Dreams won her 14th consecutive race with a defeat, an American record for thoroughbred fillies.

TRACK RECORDS

(FROM OLD FACILITY; 2005 IS THE FIRST SEASON FOR THE NEW COURSE AND RECORDS WILL START OVER.)

2-1/2 furs.	Flutter Butterfly	2	118	:27.00	Jul. 10, 2004
4 furs.	Rare Trip	2	118	:46-3/5	May 20, 1977
4-1/2 furs.	Bag In Hand	5	116	:51.60	Aug. 28, 2000
5 furs.	Hallowed Dreams	2	117	:57.40	Jul. 3, 1999
5-1/2 furs.	Money Is the Key	3	117	1:03.40	Aug. 26, 2004
6 furs.	Rail	6	121	1:09.20	Jul. 22, 1995
7-1/2 furs.	Top Silk	4	117	1:31.40	Jun. 2, 1991
1 mile	Selma s Boy	6	124	1:36-3/5	Jul. 12, 1981
	Winning Connection	4	115	1:36.60	Aug. 19, 2000
1 m 40 yds	Mr. D s Prank	7	119	1:43.60	Jul. 11, 1983
1 m 70 yds	State Commander	5	117	1:42.10	Apr. 22, 1991
1-1/16 m	Nin s Pick	3	116	1:43-2/5	Jun. 19, 1977
1-1/8 m	Report to Glory	4	117	1:50.80	Aug. 9, 1993
1-3/16 m	Pasquale G.	8	120	2:01.40	Jul. 31, 1977
1-7/16 m	Paw Paw s Pride	5	122	2:28.40	Jul. 19, 2002
1-1/2 m	Just For Charlie	5	117	2:41.40	Sep. 15, 1986
1-5/8 m	Lucky Man	6	119	2:48.20	Aug. 2, 2002
1-7/8 m	Concho County	6	122	3:19.40	Aug. 18, 2000
2 miles	Gray Gardner	5	122	3:31.60	Aug. 27, 1990

Leading Jockey in 2004: Brian Joseph Hernandez Jr., 99 wins
Leading Trainer in 2004: Keith L. Bourgeois, 60 wins

FAIR GROUNDS

Fair Grounds Corp.
President and General Manager: Randall Soth; Racing Secretary: Ben Huffman.

Street Address: 1751 Gentilly Blvd.
New Orleans, Louisiana 70119

P.O. Box 52529, New Orleans, LA 70152
Telephone: (504) 944-5515; Fax: (504) 944-2511
E-mail Address: webmaster@fgno.com
Web Site: http://www.fairgroundsracecourse.com

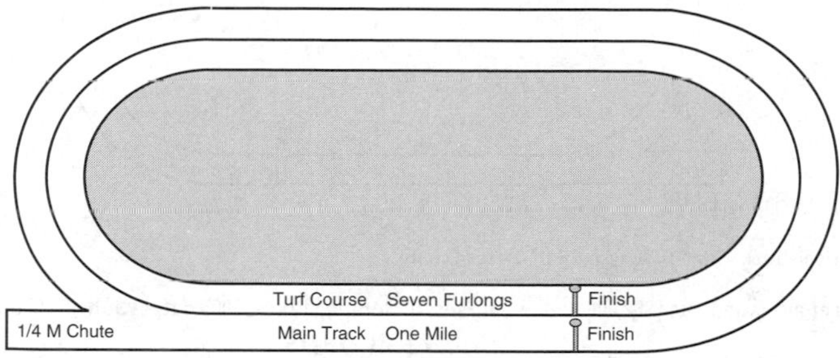

Track Data: One-mile oval, sandy loam. Seven-furlong turf course. One chute, one quarter mile schooling chute. Length of stretch, 1,346 feet. Width of home stretch, 75 feet; backstretch, 70 feet; turns, 75 feet. Stable accommodations, 1,950. Seating capacity 6,500, total capacity 20,000. Parking for 5,000 cars.

Opened April 12, 1872. Suffered a major fire in 1993. After four years of successful meets using tents to replace the burned down grandstand, Fair Grounds opened with a new grandstand in 1997 and has enjoyed some of its most successful meetings in history, averaging more than $250,000 in daily purses each of the last six years. The $600,000 Louisiana Derby is the track's flagship race. Dates for 2004-2005 season: Nov. 25, 2004 through March 27, 2005. Year-round simulcasting, phone betting and Internet wagering.

TRACK RECORDS

3 furs.	Henry s Baby	2	112	:33-4/5	Feb. 15, 1971
	It s the Law	2	119	:33-4/5	Feb. 18, 1976
4-1/2 furs.	Debs Mini Bars	2	112	:52-1/5	Mar. 8, 1971
5 furs.	Posse	3	118	:57.35	Feb. 10, 2003
5-1/2 furs.	Toby s Success	4	122	1:03.20	Jan. 26. 2004
6 furs.	Mountain General	4	118	1:08.03	Nov. 28, 2002
1 mile	Kitwe	4	112	1:35.94	Mar. 26, 1998
1 m 40 yds	Total Rage	4	117	1:38.52	Mar. 23, 1997
1-1/16 m	Pie in Your Eye	5	117	1:42.02	Mar. 19, 1994
1-1/8 m	Phantom On Tour	4	114	1:48.13	Mar. 8, 1998
1-3/16 m	Half Magic	4	109	1:56-1/5	Mar. 21, 1977
1-1/4 m	It s the One	4	124	2:01-4/5	Mar. 21, 1982
	Westheimer	4	112	2:01-4/5	Mar. 24, 1985
	Herat	4	116	2:01-4/5	Mar. 16, 1986
1-9/16 m	Retintin	7	117	2:42-4/5	Mar. 28, 1970
1-3/4 m	Aladdin Prince	8	113	3:01-2/5	Apr. 5, 1981
4 miles	Major Mansir	6	112	8:04.60	Mar. 21, 1903

Turf Course

Abt 5-1/2 f	My Lord	5	118	1:02.90	Mar. 27, 2004
Abt 7-1/2 f	Northcote Road	5	121	1:29.26	Mar. 7, 2000
Abt 1 mile	Great Bloom	6	117	1:35.57	Mar. 20, 2004
Abt 1-1/16 m	Dixie Poker Ace	7	119	1:42.00	Jan. 8, 1994
Abt 1-1/8 m	Mystery Giver	6	120	1:48.29	Mar. 21, 2004
Abt 1-3/8 m	Present The Colors	5	111	2:17-1/5	Apr. 4, 1982
Abt 1-1/2 m	Palace Panther	5	116	2:32	Apr. 6, 1986
Abt 1-9/16m	To the Floor	7	114	2:40.26	Mar. 29, 1999

Leading Jockey in 2003-2004 meet: Robby Albarado, 106 wins

Leading Trainer in 2003-2004 meet: Steven M. Asmussen, 63 wins

Record attendance: 23, 662, November 27, 1969. Record handle: $9,080,419, March 12, 2000

FAIR MEADOWS

Tulsa State Fairgrounds

P.O. Box 4735 Tulsa, Oklahoma
918-743-7223; Fax (918) 743-8053

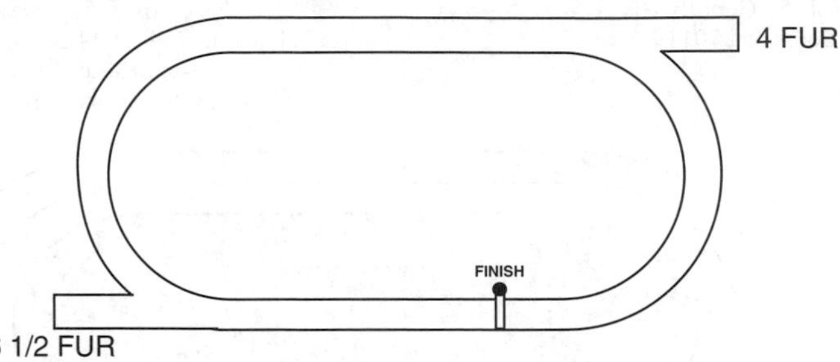

Track data: five-furlong track with 4-furlong and 6 1/2-furlong chutes.

A 28-day 2004 meet averaged over $62,000 in daily purses, including stakes. 2005 dates: June 9 through July 30.

TRACK RECORDS

4 furs.	Only Cash	5	118	:44-2/5	May 30, 1997	1-1/16 m	Stop the Bluffing	5	124	1:45.60	May 29, 2003
5-1/2 furs.	Double Jack	5	124	1:03-4/5	Aug. 1, 2001	1-1/8 m	Demascus Slew	4	118	1:51.80	May 30, 1998
6 furs.	Carsoni	6	122	1:10-4/5	Aug. 3, 1995	1-3/8 m	Second Avie	5	115	2:20	Aug. 5, 1995
6-1/2 furs.	Tic Tic	4	120	1:16-3/5	Jul. 10, 1998	1-5/8 m	Phantom Cottage	9	118	2:51-4/5	Aug. 1, 1992
1 mile	Judge North	6	124	1:37	Aug. 5, 1995						

Leading Jockey in 2004: Curtis Kimes, 31 wins
Leading Trainer in 2004: Mike R. Teel, 14 wins

FAIRMOUNT PARK

Ogden-Fairmount, Inc.

President, CEO; and General Manager: Brian Zander; Racing Secretary: Robert Pace; Simulcasting Director: Gregory Graves.

Located on the Illinois side of the Mississippi River near St. Louis, Missouri

9301 Collinsville Rd., Collinsville, IL 62234
(618) 345-4300 Fax: (618) 344-8218
E-Mail Address: fmtpark@fairmountpark.com
Web Site: www.fairmountpark.com

Track data: One-mile oval with 3/4-mile and 1 1/4-mile chutes. Distance from last turn to finish 1,050 feet; width 80 feet stretch and turns, 70 feet in backstretch. Stable accommodations 1,000. Seating capacity 5,500.

Opened September 26, 1925. The 2004 meet ran 101 dates, from March 26 to Sept. 18, with purses at about $58,000 per day. Dates are scheduled for 2005 from March 25 through Sept. 17. Trainer Ralph Martinez, the leading trainer at every Fairmount Park meet since 2000, owns the Fairmount meet record with 157 victories, which he set in 2001. Night racing and extensive simulcasting.

TRACK RECORDS

2 furs.	Glit	8	122	:20.80	May 3, 2003	1-1/4 m	Leaddrop	4	116	2:03	Jul. 22, 1989
4 furs.	Aledo	5	120	:45-3/5	Jun. 2, 1994	1-1/2 m	Firth of Tay	5	105	2:33	Sep. 21, 1927
4-1/2 furs.	Vague Promise	4	122	:51-3/5	May 19, 1978	1-5/8 m	Monthazar	8	120	2:48	Nov. 3, 1973
5 furs.	Slight in the Rear	2	118	:56-4/5	Jul. 25, 1989	1-3/4 m	Lightin Bill	8	110	3:02-4/5	Oct. 14, 1939
5-1/2 furs.	Sarof Jr.	4	120	1:03-2/5	Jun. 5, 1980	2 miles	East Royalty	4	120	3:32-3/5	Dec. 1, 1991
6 furs.	Ye Country	3	112	1:08-3/5	Nov. 26, 1977	2 m 70 yds	King Boogie	5	119	3:33-3/5	Sep. 1, 1984
1 mile	Dusty Appeal	7	116	1:37-2/5	Jun. 20, 1992	2-1/16 m	Tim Trefle	5	113	3:38-4/5	Sep. 10, 1983
1 m 70 yds	Dusty Appeal	4	116	1:39-4/5	Jul. 30, 1989	2-1/8 m	Lucrest	5	115	3:46-1/5	Sep. 24, 1983
1-1/16 m	Lt. Lao	5	118	1:40-4/5	Jul. 22, 1989	2-1/4 m	Baye Dawn	5	117	4:00	Oct. 8, 1983
1-1/8 m	Andover Man	3	113	1:47-3/5	Aug. 26, 1989	2-1/2 m	Cat Walk	4	114	4:29	Oct. 22, 1983

Leading Jockey in 2004: Ramsey Zimmerman, 180 wins

Leading Trainer in 2004: Ralph Martinez, 143 wins

Record attendance: 13,898 September 7, 1953. Record handle: $1,380,880, May 5, 1990

FAIRPLEX PARK

Street Address: 1101 West McKinley Avenue
Pomona, CA 91768

P.O. Box 2250, Pomona, CA 91769
(909) 623-3111 Fax: (909) 865-3602
E-Mail Address: info@fairplex.com
Web Site: www.fairplex.com

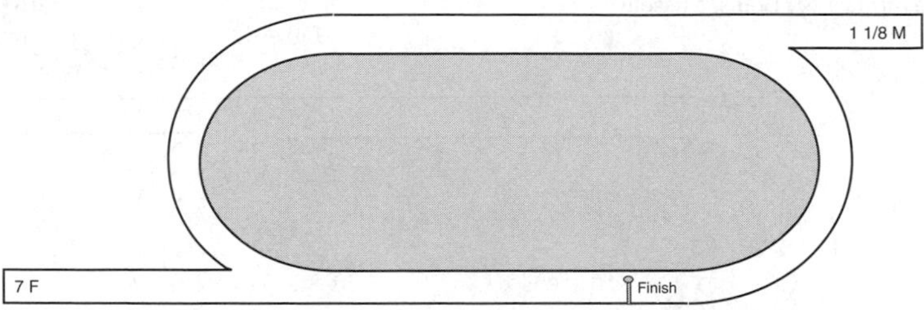

Track data: five-furlong oval with 1/4-mile and 1 1/8-mile chutes. Distance from last turn to finish 757, width 70 feet. Stable accommodations 850. Seating capacity 10,000, parking for 30,000 cars on county fairgrounds.

Opened September 1933. Runs the three-week Pomona County Fair meet immediately after Del Mar. In 2004, daily average purses were $236,000 including stakes. Part of the California County Fair system that features numerous short meets throughout the state and has a simulcast pavilion open throughout the year. 2005 dates: Sept. 9 through Sept. 25, with no dark days.

TRACK RECORDS

Abt. 4 furs.	Quemado	3	120	:44.79	Sep. 25, 2003
6 furs.	Drouilly s Boy	4	116	1:09-1/5	Sep. 19, 1989
6-1/2 furs.	Bundle Of Iron	4	116	1:15-1/5	Sep. 23, 1986
7 furs.	Magical Dust	3	116	1:22.53	Sep. 26, 2004
1-1/16 m	Monte Parnes-Ar	5	121	1:41-3/5	Sep. 29, 1990
Abt 1-1/8 m	Dachi s Folly	3	114	1:48-2/5	Sep. 29, 1990
1-3/8 m	Mummy s Pleasure	7	120	2:15	Sep. 28, 1986

Leading Jockey in 2004: Martin A. Pedroza, 51 wins
Leading Trainer in 2004: Doug O Neill, 16 wins
Record attendance: 28,300 September 25, 1948. Record Handle: $9,455,278 September19, 1998

FERNDALE

P.O.Box 637
Ferndale, California, 95536
(707) 786-9511

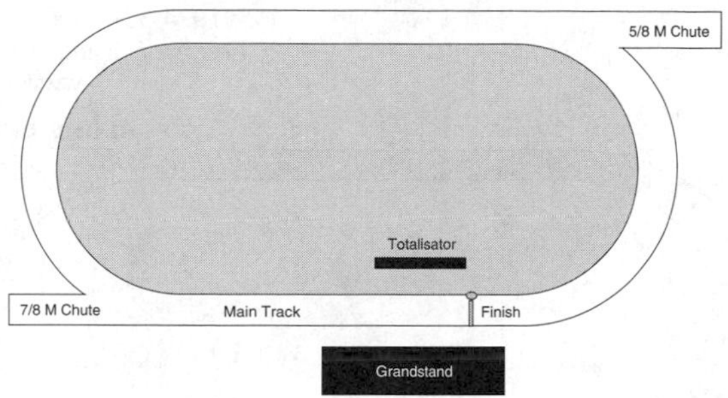

One-half-mile oval with two chutes, five furlongs and 7 furlongs. Distance from last turn to finish 530 feet. Width of track 50 feet.

Opened in the 1950's and runs an annual short meet during August in a true county fair setting in the redwood forest region of Northern California, near the Oregon border. During 2004, purses averaged almost $17,000 per day for 34 total Thoroughbred races on 10 daily cards. 2005 meet: Aug. 11 to Aug. 21.

TRACK RECORDS

3 furs.	Distance Power	5	123	:33.73	Aug. 19, 2004	1-1/16 m	Skipper Sam,	6	115	1:43-2/5	Aug. 4, 1969
5 furs.	Fight for Silver	5	118	:57.18	Aug. 11, 2002	1-1/8 m	Daytime Bargain	3	120	1:53-1/5	Aug. 22, 1987
6-1/2 furs.	Rumbita's Lad	5	116	1:19-2/5	Aug. 20, 1992	1-3/8 m	Timnocrea	6	119	2:23	Aug. 20, 1960
7 furs.	Never Miss T.V.	8	116	1:24-1/5	Aug. 14, 1992	1-5/8 m	Prince Aglo	4	122	2:44-3/5	Aug. 21, 1994

Leading Jockeys in 2004: Victor G. Navarro & Victor Miranda, 9 wins (tie)
Leading Trainer in 2004: Dennis Hopkins, 5 wins
Record attendance: 7, 142, July 28, 1979. Record handle: $287,548, August 17, 1985

FINGER LAKES

Finger Lakes Racing Association, Inc.

President and General Manager: Christian Riegle; Racing Secretary: Joe Colasacco; Publicity and Media: Steve Martin; Director of Simulcasting: Patrick Placito.

5857 Rte. 96, Farmington, New York 14425
Mailing address: P.O. Box 25250, Farmington, New York 14425
(585) 924-3232; Fax: Publicity: (585) 924-7275
Free scratch and results line: (585) 935-5252
www.fingerlakesracetrack.com

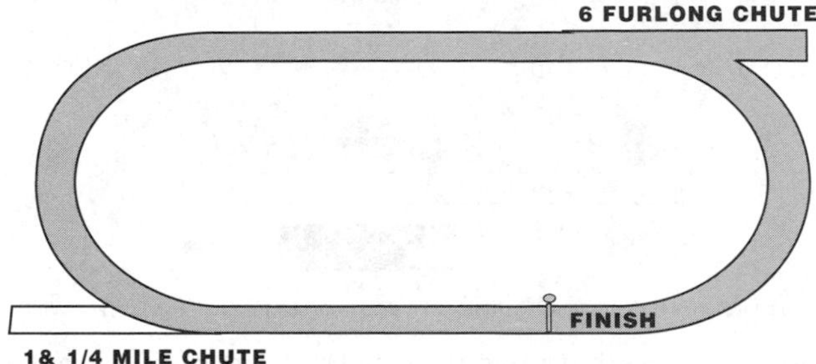

Track Data: One-mile oval; sandy loam. Six-furlong and 1 1/4-mile chutes; length of stretch, 960 feet. Stable accommodations, 1,214. Seating for 6,000; Parking for 4,000 cars.

Opened May 23, 1962 in the picturesque Finger Lakes region and has become the home base for many owners and trainers with New York bred stock. Finger Lakes' daily average purses exceeded $100,000 per day in 2004 for 157 racing days including stakes. A similar meet in 2005 will run from April 15 through November 29.

TRACK RECORDS

Distance	Horse	Age	Wt.	Time	Date
2 furs.	Broadway Blondie	5	116	:21-4/5	Apr. 3, 1998
4 furs.	Valley Cat	9	120	:46-2/5	Apr. 15, 1994
4-1/2 furs.	Top End	7	115	:50-3/5	Apr. 8, 1998
5 furs.	Wonderous Wise	6	115	:57-1/5	Apr. 11, 1989
	Bobby s Code	6	116	:57-1/5	Apr. 8, 1998
5-1/2 furs.	Hilary Star	6	111	1:02-4/5	Apr. 16, 1989
	With It	5	115	1:02-4/5	Jun. 12, 1994
	What a Rollick	3	117	1:02-4/5	Dec. 12, 1994
6 furs.	Kelly Kip	4	119	1:08-1/5	Jun. 20, 1998
Abt 7 furs.	Jerri Prince	7	114	1:26-4/5	Oct. 11, 1976
1 mile	Transact	4	119	1:36-1/5	Aug. 29, 1994
1 m 40 yds	Gallant Tiger	4	119	1:40-1/5	Jun. 22, 1975
1 m 70 yds	C B Account	4	116	1:40	Jul. 6, 1997
1-1/16 m	Fit For Royalty	9	119	1:43	May 19, 1997
1-1/8 m	Copper Mount	3	119	1:48-4/5	Aug. 27, 1994
1-3/16 m	North Warning	10	113	1:58-2/5	Jul. 10, 1994
1-1/4 m	Caramba	6	114	2:05-1/5	Jul. 11, 1987
1-1/2 m	Brave Beast	6	124	2:33-3/5	Sep. 22, 1991
1-9/16 m	Poor Man s Friend	5	116	2:44	Oct. 16, 1976
1-5/8 m	North Warning	10	119	2:46-3/5	Sep. 4, 1994
1-11/16 m	Prime Example	6	117	2:58	Nov. 23, 1974
1-3/4 m	Win Eddie	6	122	3:05-1/5	Aug. 28, 1977
2 miles	Brier Spirit	8	108	3:47-4/5	Oct. 26, 1980
2 m 40 yds	Black Lodge	3	113	3:41	Oct. 5, 1974
2 m 70 yds	Eastern Promise	5	112	3:42-3/5	Oct. 14, 1972
2-1/16 m	Tabula	4	110	3:44-3/5	Oct. 13, 1973
2-1/8 m	Eastern Promise	5	116	3:51	Oct. 21, 1972
2-3/16 m	Blazing Cedar	4	113	4:04-1/5	Nov. 10, 1973
2-1/4 m	Amber Dare	3	109	4:11-3/5	Oct. 20, 1973
2-9/16 m	Diamond Platter	7	116	4:50	Oct. 12, 1974
2-5/8 m	Amber Dare	3	115	5:12-2/5	Nov. 17, 1973
2-11/16 m	Polo Prince	3	107	5:14-3/5	Oct. 28, 1972
2-3/4 m	Fourth Flight	7	116	5:35-2/5	Nov. 24, 1973
3 m 70 yds	Count Mafosta	7	116	5:39-1/5	Oct. 27, 1973
3-1/16 m	Dauntless Pride	4	111	5:45-2/5	Oct. 19, 1974
3-1/4 m	Dauntless Pride	4	117	6:15-2/5	Oct. 26, 1974
4 m 70 yds	Gloria Dream	6	113	8:01	Nov. 4, 1972
4-1/16 m	Amber Dare	3	113	8:12-2/5	Nov. 3, 1973
4-1/8 m	Victory Tour	4	115	8:08	Nov. 2, 1974

Leading Jockey in 2004: John R. Davila, Jr, 136 wins
Leading Trainer in 2004: Chris J. Englehart, 136 wins
Record attendance: 15, 334, September 3, 1962. Record handle: $765,580, September 24, 1978.

FONNER PARK

Hall County Livestock Improvement Association, Inc.
President: Gary Rosacker; Executive Vice President and CEO: Hugh M. Miner, Jr.; COO: Bruce A. Swihart; Racing Secretary: Doug Schoepf.
Street Address: 700 East Stolley Park Road
Grand Island, Nebraska 68801.
Nearest Airport: Hall County Regional Airport
3 miles north of track, 150 miles from Omaha
P.O. Box 490, Grand Island, Nebraska 68802-0490
(308) 382-4515; Fax: (308) 384-2753
Email: fonnerpark@aol.com
Web Site: www.fonnerpark.com

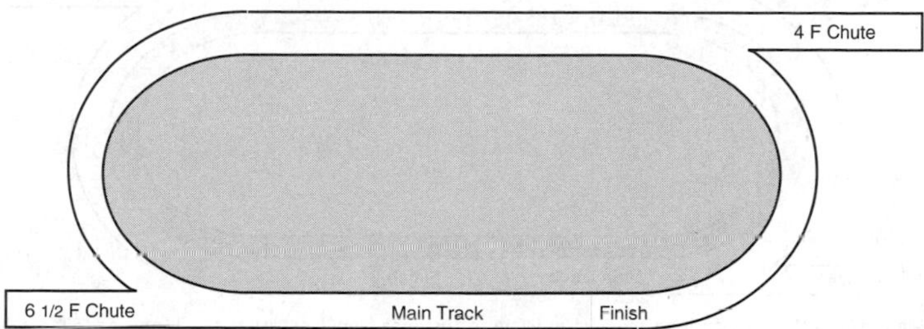

Track Data: five-furlong oval, sandy loam. Distance from last turn to finish line, 700 feet. 6 1/2-furlong and 4-furlong chutes. Width of track 70 feet. Stable accommodations for 1,200. Seating for 5,766; Parking for 5,000 cars.

Opened April 29, 1954. Fonner Park is the home of the Hall County Fair and many livestock shows. Construction has started on a new 6,000-seat multi-purpose civic center at Fonner Park. The Heartland Events Center is scheduled for completion in July 2006. The new facility, adjacent to the Fonner grandstand, will offer many different types of entertainment and sporting events and will host trade shows and conventions. Glass enclosed heated grandstand; extensive simulcasting, 6-7 days per week and the 2005 meet will run Feb. 11 through May 7.

TRACK RECORDS

4 furs.	Leaping Plum	5	122	:44-1/5	Feb. 17, 1996	1 m 70 yds	Shamtastic	6	116	1:40	Apr. 26, 1986
5-1/2 furs.	Little L. M.	6	115	1:04-2/5	Apr. 12, 1975	1-1/16 m	Sahara King	7	116	1:43	Apr. 27, 1996
6 furs.	Orphan Kist	5	123	1:10	Apr. 8, 1989	1-1/8 m	Potro	5	117	1:51-2/5	Apr. 25, 1993
6-1/2 furs.	Majority Of One	5	119	1:17	Mar. 18, 1989	1-3/8 m	Meat Loaf	5	114	2:22-2/5	Apr. 29, 1970
1 mile	Brian s Star	4	112	1:36-3/5	Apr. 9, 1986						

Leading Jockey in 2004: Perry Compton, 80 wins

Leading Trainer in 2004: David C. Anderson, 31 wins

Record Handle: $1,285,011 April 28, 1990. Record Attendance: 10,930 March 17, 1990

FORT ERIE RACETRACK

Director of Operations: Herb McGirr; Racing Secretary: Tom Gostlin.

Street Address: 230 Catherine Street
Fort Erie, Ontario, Canada.

P.O.Box 1130, Fort Erie, Ontario, CA,L2A5N9
(905) 871-3200; (800) 295-3770; Fax (905) 994-3629,
Web site:www.forterieracing.com;E-mail: femedia@forterieracetrack.com

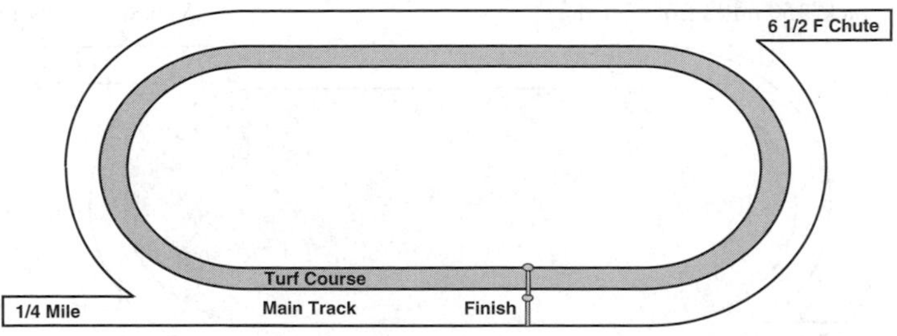

Track Data: One-mile oval with a 6 1/2-furlong and 1 1/4-mile chute. Distance from last turn to finish, about 1,060 feet. Width of stretch 85 feet, backstretch 65 feet; 7-furlong turf course. Stable accommodations for 1,150; seating capacity, 10,700. Parking for 8,500 cars.

Opened June 16, 1897, this beautifully appointed track is home to the Prince of Wales Stakes, second jewel of the Canadian Triple Crown. Fort Erie operated its 107th live race meet in 2004 with 81 racing days from May 1 through Sept. 6. About 1,200 slot machines helped boost purses sharply from $107,000 in 2000 to more than $180,000 in 2004. In 2005, the meet will run from May 1 through Oct. 31. Located across the Niagara River from Buffalo, N.Y., in close proximity to Niagara Falls...Year-round simulcasting.

TRACK RECORDS

2 furs.	Leisure Road	5	120	:21.20	Sep. 5, 1998	1-3/16 m	Bruce s Mill	3	126	1:53-4/5	Jul. 31, 1994
4-1/2 furs.	Island Mission	6	117	:52.02	Apr. 29, 2000	1-1/4 m	Do s Vigil	3	110	2:03-2/5	Aug. 14, 1974
5 furs.	Dart for Dough	5	114	:56.50	Oct. 6, 2003		French Tambourine	5	115		Aug. 10, 1975
5-1/2 furs.	Just a Lord	4	113	1:03-3/5	Jun. 15, 1991	1-1/2 m	Itshouldbesoeasy	5	116	2:32.57	Aug. 10, 1999
6 furs.	Deputy Carson	5	122	1:08.80	Sep. 9, 2001	1-5/8 m	Gay Story	4	112	2:48-3/5	Aug. 27, 1956
6-1/2 furs.	Muzledick	3	115	1:15-4/5	Aug. 10, 1968	1-3/4 m	Brave Zappa	5	107	2:59	Jul. 9, 1984
1 m 70yds	Myrtle Irene	5	111	1:39-4/5	Aug. 26, 1994	1-13/16 m	Captain Charisma	5	121	3:09-2/5	Aug. 12, 1984
1-1/16 m	Act of Courage	3	119	1:42-1/5	Aug. 7, 1971	1-7/8 m	Frost Prince	7	119	3:22.60	Aug. 20, 1999
	Dimanno	4	118	1:42.20	Sep. 11, 2001	2 m yds	Devils Gold	6	115	3:33	Oct. 6, 1997
1-1/8 m	Lauries Dancer	4	108	1:48	Aug. 23, 1972						

Turf Course

5 furs.	Oh Mar	6	120	:56.99	Sep. 9, 2002	1-1/2 m	Norwick	4	120	2:28	Aug. 21, 1983
Abt 7 furs.	Native Vigil	5	118	1:22	Jul. 2, 1991	1-3/4 m	Ahead of the Best	4	119	2:56-3/5	Sep. 10, 1991
1 mile	Fifth and a Jigger	3	115	1:34-1/5	Jun. 10, 1991	Abt 1-7/8 m	Regal Admiral	7	112	3:19-4/5	Aug. 7, 1974
1-1/16 m	Road Of War	4	112	1:40-4/5	Jun. 19, 1994	1-7/8 m	Medlaw	5	123	3:16-1/5	Sep. 30, 1985
1-3/8 m	Lord Vancouver	4	126	2:15	Jul. 30, 1972						

Leading Jockey in 2004: Neil Poznansky, 71 wins
Leading Trainer in 2004: Thomas M. Agosti, 27 wins
Record Attendance. 17,379 April 8,1961. Record Handle. $1,934,407 Oct 2, 1995.

FRESNO FAIR

1121 S. Chance Avenue, Fresno, CA 93702
(559) 650-3247 Fax: (559) 650-3226
E-Mail Address: info@fresnofair.com; Web Site: www.fresnofair.com

Track data: One-mile oval with 2-furlong and 6-furlong chutes. Distance from last turn to finish 979 feet. Stable accommodations 900; Seating capacity 6,000, parking for 10,000 cars on county fairgrounds.

Opened September 25, 1935. Runs an 10-day meet in October as part of Northern California Fair circuit and daily average purses were pegged at just over $50,000 during the 2004 meet. The 2005 meet: Oct. 5 to Oct. 16 with year round simulcasting in the pavilion.

TRACK RECORDS

4 furs.	Nellie s Girl	3	127	:44-4/5	Oct. 7, 1978	1 mile	The Ayes Have It	5	113	1:33-4/5	Nov. 11, 1986
	King Stephen	2	127	:44-4/5	Oct. 7, 1978	1-1/16 m	Dimaggio	4	116	1:39-4/5	Oct. 16, 1976
4-1/2 furs.	Lovin Laurie	3	118	:51.14	Oct. 8, 2003	1-1/8 m	Minutes Away	3	114	1:46-2/5	Nov. 20, 1985
5 furs.	Big Volume	4	120	:55-2/5	Nov. 15, 1977	1-1/4 m	Capt. Quicksilver	6	114	1:59-4/5	Oct. 18, 1992
5-1/2 furs.	Knight In Savannah	3	113	1:01-2/5	Nov. 13, 1990	1-1/2 m	El Maduro	5	111	2:30-2/5	Sep. 17, 1980
Abt. 6 furs.	Tia Ping	5	113	1:10-1/5	Oct. 11, 1963	1-11/16 m	Bull Patch	4	111	2:56	Oct. 5, 1954
6 furs.	Two out of Three	4	121	1:07.50	Oct. 8, 2004	2 miles	Nina s Flag	4	120	3:29-2/5	Oct. 9, 1954

Leading Jockey in 2004: Modesto Linares, 13 wins

Leading Trainer in 2004: Dennis Hopkins, 6 wins

Record attendance 15, 596, October 6, 1979.

GOLDEN GATE FIELDS

A Magna Entertainment Facility

Chairman and Director: Frank Stronach; Vice-President and General Manager: Michael Scalzo; Racing Secretary: Sean Greely; Coordinator of Racing Operations: Richard Lewis; Publicity Manager: Tom Ferrall.

25 miles Northwest of San Francisco Airport

PO Box 6027, Albany, CA 94706-0027
(510) 559-7300 Fax: (510) 559-7465
Web Site: www.goldengatefields.com

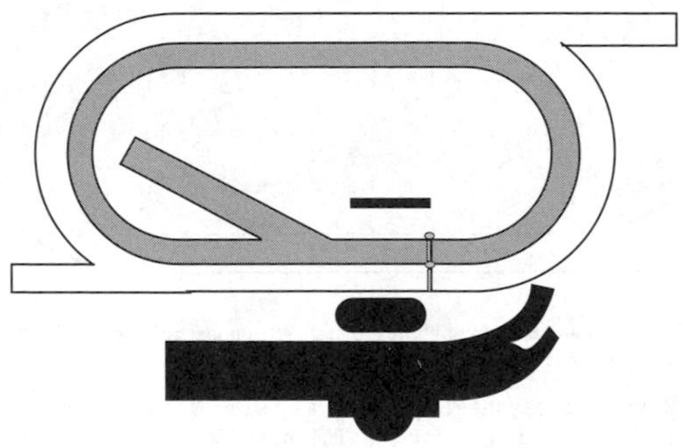

Track data: One-mile oval, with 3/4- and 1 1/4-mile chutes. Distance from last turn to finish 1,000 feet; width of stretch 78 feet, backstretch 75 feet. Turf course: Seven furlongs and 132 feet. Stable accommodations 1,323; Seating capacity Grandstand, 8,000; Club House, 5,200; Turf Club, 1,200. Parking for 4,723 cars.

Opened February 1, 1941. Bought by Frank Stronach's Magna Entertainment Inc. in 1999. The 2003-2004 racing season featured 109 days of racing and was held Nov. 5, 2003, through April 4, 2004. Purses averaged over $152,000. The track offers year-round simulcasting. Jerry Hollendorfer saddled 88 winners during the 2003-2004 season to earn his 24th straight training title at GGF.

TRACK RECORDS

2 furs.	Extra Kick	2	118	:21.09	Mar. 27, 2003	1-1/16 m	Restless Con	4	118	1:39.50	Jun. 24, 1991
4-1/2 furs.	Victory Found	2	117	:50.30	Apr. 30, 1992	1-1/8 m	Simply Majestic	4	114	1:45	Apr. 2, 1988
5 furs.	Contradiction	4	118	:56.12	Jan. 1, 2003	1-3/16 m	Fleet Bird	4	123	1:52-3/5	Oct. 24, 1953
5-1/2 furs.	Linear Lights	4	119	1:01.99	Feb. 25, 2004	1-1/4 m	Noor	5	127	1:58-1/5	Jun. 24, 1950
6 furs.	Smoke Till Dawn	4	117	1:07.45	Dec.17, 2003	1-1/2 m	Bo Donna	5	120	2:29-2/5	Jun. 8, 1979
1 mile	Caros Love	4	117	1:33	Feb. 13, 1988		Tabular	6	116	2:29-2/5	Jun. 6, 1987

Turf Course

4-1/2 furs.	Stuttgart	6	119	:49.86	Mar. 29, 2003	1 mile	Don Alberto	5	114	1:33-2/5	Mar. 22, 1980
5 furs.	Black Tornado	5	119	:56	May 10, 1975	1-1/16 m	Announcer	5	115	1:40-2/5	Apr. 16, 1977
	L Natural	4	114	:56	May 28, 1977	1-3/8 m	John Henry	9	125	2:13	May 6, 1984
	Neat Claim	4	113	:56	May 30, 1977	1-1/2 m	Silveyville	6	121	2:27-2/5	Jun. 10, 1984
	Goldie s Goldian	4	115	:56	May 27, 1978		Kings Island	4	116	2:27-2/5	Jun. 9, 1985
7-1/2 furs.	Struttin George	5	122	1:28	May 5, 1979		Val Danseur	6	119	2:27-2/5	Jun. 8, 1986
	His Honor	6	118	1:28	Apr. 25, 1981	1-7/8 m	Paired And Painted	4	114	3:12-1/5	Jun. 28, 1987
	Clever Song	4	122	1:28	May 25,1986	2-3/8 m	Situada	7	115	4:10-4/5	Jun. 25, 1990

Turf Course (from the diagonal, infield chute)

1-1/16 m	Gum	6	116	1:41.23	Apr. 11, 1992	2 miles	Never-Rust	8	114	3:25-3/5	Jun. 26, 1988
1-1/8 m	Blues Traveller	4	112	1:47-3/5	May 14, 1994						

Leading Jockey in 2003-2004 meet: Kevin Radke, 89 wins

Leading Trainer in 2003-2004 meet: Jerry Hollendorfer, 88 wins

Record attendance 34,967, May 5, 1990. Record handle $8,723,810 May 2, 1998 (includes simulcasts).

GRANTS PASS DOWNS

PO Box 282, Grants Pass, OR 97526
Phone: (541) 476-3215

Track data: One-half-mile oval with a 400-yard chute in the homestretch.

Opened June 21, 1979. Usually runs two and/or three day weekend racing cards from mid-May into July. Simulcasting. 2005 dates: May 14 to July 4.

TRACK RECORDS

4-1/2 furs.	Sizzlin Cisco	6	124	:51.40	Jun. 27, 2004	6-1/2 furs.	Teri Time	3	128	1:17.20	May 16, 2004
5 furs.	Primecat	3	119	:58.20	Jul. 3, 2004	1-1/16 m	Handy Man Jeff	7	121	1:45.40	Jul. 6, 2003
5-1/2 furs.	Tickles Prince	5	119	1:04.14	May 22, 1999	1 3/16 m	Tyonek	4	119	2:01.25	Jun. 19, 1994
Abt 6 furs.	Lucky May Babe	6	123	1:08-2/5	Jun. 25, 1995	1-5/16 m	A Shot at Fame	6	124	2:14.60	Jul. 4, 2000
6 furs.	Honest Sea	5	119	1:09-4/5	Jul. 4, 1983	1-3/8 m	Summers Comin	5	122	2:16-2/5	Jul. 4, 1989
Abt 6-1/2 f	Toll Free	4	122	1:23-3/5	Jun. 30, 1979	1-5/8 m	Moes Cat	5	122	2:52-2/5	Jul. 8, 1990

Leading Jockey in 2004: Twyla Beckner, 28 wins

Leading Trainers in 2004: Judi Yearout & Robert Beckner, 8 wins (tie)

Record attendance: 2,540, May 28, 1990. Record handle: $185, 121, July 4, 1987

GREAT FALLS
Montana State Fair Race Meet

PO Box 2810, Great Falls, MT 59403
(406) 727-8900 Fax: (406) 452-8955

Track data: One half mile oval, 5/8- and 7/8-mile chutes. Distance from last turn to finish, 410.1 feet; Width of track 60 feet. Distance from last turn to finish 979 feet. Stable accommodations for 900. Seating capacity 6,000.

Opened in the 1940's as part of the Montana State Fair and has conducted a three week pari-mutuel meet in most years since. Ran nine days from July 3 through Aug. 1 in 2004, with a similar meet scheduled in 2005 starting July 4.. .Extensive simulcasting.

TRACK RECORDS

3 furs.	My Squeaky Ruler	2	122	:34-2/5	Jun. 8, 1986	Abt. 6-1/2 f	Charmhersweet	5	122	1:19-4/5	Jul. 30, 1978
Abt. 4 furs.	Midnight Mackee	4	125	:53-2/5	Jun. 16, 1991	7 furs.	Diamond Eagle	6	125	1:24.60	Aug. 4, 2000
4-1/2 furs.	Gay Deil	2	118	:55-2/5	Aug. 7, 1946	1 mile	Timpanogos	5	128	1:41-3/5	Aug. 9, 1947
5 furs.	Tiger Sam	4	112	:57-4/5	Jul. 27, 1970	1 m70yds	Proud Barbarian	7	115	1:44.80	Jul. 31, 1986
Abt. 5 furs.	Happy Vixen	5	110	:56-4/5	Aug. 5, 1946	1-1/16 m	Im Bay	4	122	1:47-4/5	Aug. 3, 1986
Abt. 5-1/2 f	Crown Butte	4	119	1:04.40	Jun. 20, 1999	1-1/8 m	Prince of Queens	4	122	1:52.80	Jul. 26, 1997
6 furs.	Gallantsia	6	108	1:14-2/5	Aug. 6 1946	Abt. 1-1/8 m	Copper Guard	8	103	1:51	Aug. 10, 1946
6-1/2 furs.	Lightning Rose	3	114	1:24-1/5	May 28, 1984						

Leading Jockey in 2004: B. Buck Harris, 10 wins

Leading Trainer in 2004: Janis D. Schoepf, 6 wins

Record attendance: 6,597, July 28, 1985. Record handle: $193, 036, August 3, 1985.

GREAT LAKES DOWNS

Magna Entertainment Company

4800 Harvey St., Muskegon, MI 49444
(231) 799-2400 Fax: (231) 798-3120
E-Mail Address: glweb@greatlakesdowns.com
Web Site: www.greatlakesdowns.com

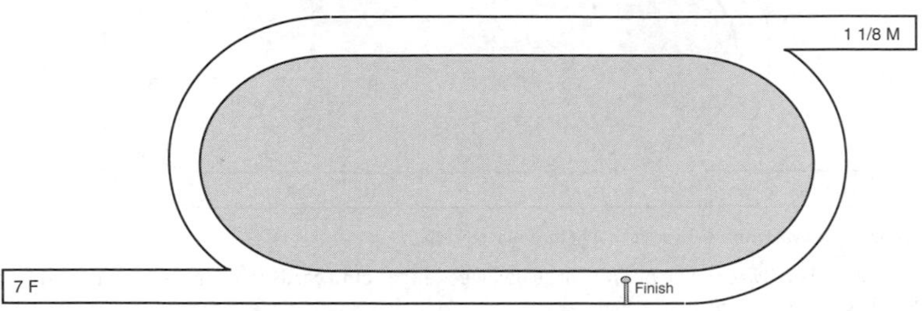

Track data: Five-eighths mile oval, with distance from last turn to finish, 580 feet.

Opened April 23, 1999 and filled the void left by the demise of Detroit Racecourse. The 2005 meet is scheduled to run from Apr. 25 to Nov. 5. . .Year-round simulcasting.

TRACK RECORDS

2 furs.	Skirt in the Wind	6	110	:23.52	Jun. 22, 1999	1 mile	Override Battle	5	114	1:40.14	Oct. 31, 2000
4 furs.	Dinner Band	4	114	:45.87	May 15, 2001		Secret Romeo	3	120	1:40.14	Oct. 29, 2001
5-1/2 furs.	Ambitious Buster	4	115	1:05.37	Sep. 26, 2003	1 m 70 yds	Secret Romeo	2	122	1:49.50	Nov. 4, 2000
6 furs.	Native Ruck	5	112	1:11.86	Oct. 11, 2003	1-1/16 m	That Monetary	6	115	1:47.28	Aug. 27, 2001
6-1/2 furs.	Native Ruck	4	113	1:19.43	Jul. 28, 2002	1-1/8 m	The Bold Bruiser	4	114	1:54.11	Oct. 28, 2000
7 furs.	Secret Romeo	3	120	1:24.77	Sep. 2, 2001	1-5/16 m	You redusty	5	120	2:22.81	Sep. 8, 2004

Leading Jockey in 2004: T.D. Houghton, 196 wins
Leading Trainer in 2004: Gerald S. Bennett, 94 wins

Record attendance 4,427, May 6, 2000. Record handle $966,732, May 15, 2000

GULFSTREAM PARK

Magna Entertainment Corp.

Chairman of the Board: Frank Stronach; President and Chief Executive Officer: Jim McAlpine; Track President and General Manager: Scott Savin; Director of Racing: David Bailey.

Nearest Airport: Ft. Lauderdale/Hollywood International

Mailing Address: 901 South Federal Highway
Hallandale Beach, Florida 33009
(954) 454-7000; (800) 771-8873; Fax: (954) 454-7827
Web Site: www.gulfstreampark.com

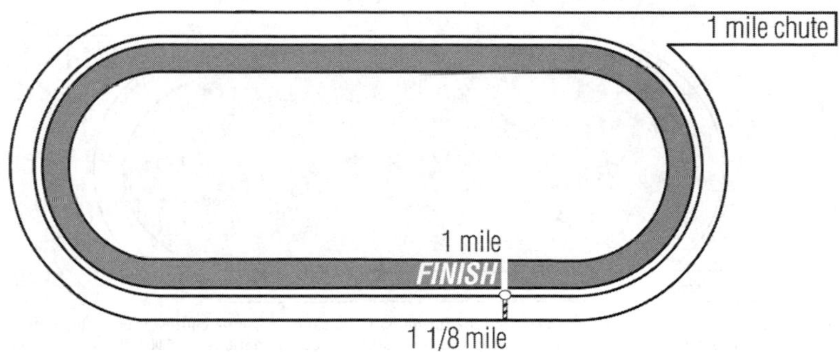

Track Data: One an 1/8th-mile oval. Stable accommodations for 1,024; Permanent facilities to be completed by 2006.

Gulfstream opened Feb. 1, 1939. Gulfstream was purchased by Frank Stronach's Magna Entertainment Corp. in September 1999. Gulfstream hosted the Breeders' Cup three times. Gulfstream's 2005 racing dates are Jan. 3 through April 24. The highlights of the meeting were the Sunshine Millions Day, the Grade 1 Florida Derby and the Grade 1 Donn Handicap. A renovation project began after the completion of the 2004 meet. An enlarged nine-furlong track, with an expanded turf course, was complete in time for the 2005 meet. New clubhouse and grandstand facilities are expected to be completed by January 2006.

TRACK RECORDS

(FOR OLD COURSES; 2005 IS THE FIRST SEASON FOR THE NEW COURSES AND RECORDS WILL START OVER.)

Distance	Horse	Age	Wt.	Time	Date
2-1/2 furs.	Sonnyhero	2	116	:28.05	Apr. 5, 2000
3 furs.	El Macho	2	118	:32-1/5	Feb. 26, 1974
4-1/2 furs.	Iron Rail	2	119	:51-2/5	Apr. 6, 1960
5 furs.	Boston Brat	6	120	:56.35	Jan. 17, 2003
5-1/2 furs.	Boston Brat	6	122	1:02.47	Feb. 3, 2003
6 furs.	Mr. Prospector	3	119	1:07-4/5	Mar. 31, 1973
6-1/2 furs.	Federal Hill	3	122	1:15	Mar. 25, 1957
7 furs.	Elusive Quality	4	119	1:20.17	Feb. 21, 1997
1 m 70 yds	Blacksburg	5	122	1:39.19	Feb. 6, 1994
Abt 1-1/16m	Search the Shadows	3	120	1:48.10	Mar. 1, 1991
1-1/16 m	Saxony Warrior	7	107	1:40-1/5	Mar. 6, 1976
1-1/8 m	Jumping Hill	7	122	1:46-2/5	Feb. 3, 1979
1-1/4 m	Mat Boy	5	118	1:59	Mar. 24, 1984
1-1/2 m	Buffalo Lark	5	120	2:27-3/5	Apr. 12, 1975
2 miles	Undue Influence	6	117	3:25.73	Mar. 16, 1997

Turf Course

Distance	Horse	Age	Wt.	Time	Date
Abt. 5 furs.	Desirable Moment	5	120	:55.61	Mar. 28, 2004
5 furs.	Bop	6	124	:55.10	Apr. 12, 2003
Abt.1 mile	Volochine	6	119	1:33.84	Feb. 28, 1997
1 mile	Lure	3	122	1:32.90	Oct. 31, 1992
Abt.1-1/16m	Deep Dive	4	122	1:40.53	Feb. 21, 1999
1-1/16 m	Garbu	5	113	1:39.33	Mar. 13, 1999
1-1/8 m	Proud Man	6	120	1:45.69	Jan. 24, 2004
Abt.1-3/8 m	Rice	5	117	2:13.80	Mar. 3, 1997
1-3/8 m	Yagli	6	121	2:10.73	Feb. 6, 1999
Abt. 1-1/2 m	Doctor Disaster	6	117	2:26.25	Mar. 5, 1995
1-1/2 m	Unite s Big Red	5	114	2:23.15	Mar. 6, 1999
Abt 2 miles	Practitioner	5	121	3:18-1/5	May 6, 1978
2 miles	Sabinus	4	115	3:22-2/5	Apr. 17, 1971

Turf Course (infield chute)

Distance	Horse	Age	Wt.	Time	Date
Abt.1 mile	Z. Bengal Tiger	4	116	1:35.68	Mar. 8, 1992
1 mile	Sunny Prince	5	112	1:35.53	Mar. 1, 1992
Abt1-1/16m	Weekend Madness	5	113	1:40.39	Feb. 12, 1995
1-1/16 m	Federal Trial	5	115	1:39.08	Feb. 19, 2000
Abt 1-1/8 m	Scannapieco	5	117	1:47.35	Feb. 24, 1995
Abt 2 miles	Charle s Quest	7	117	3:30.41	Mar. 16, 2000

Leading Jockey in 2004: John R. Velazquez, 78 wins

Leading Trainer in 2004: Todd A. Pletcher, 42 wins

Record attendance: 51, 342, November 4, 1989, Breeders' Cup Day. Record handle: $100, 336, 230, November 6, 1999 Breeders' Cup Day, all sources, all races

HASTINGS RACECOURSE

Hastings Entertainment Inc.

Vice President and COO: Michael Brown; Director of Racing: Lorne Mitchell.

Nearest Airport: Vancouver International Airport, 15 miles

Mailing Address: Hastings Racecourse
Vancouver, B.C., Canada V5K 3N8
Race Office: (604) 255-8823; (800) 677-7702; Fax: (604) 251-0428
Free scratch and results line: (888) 675-6337
Web Site: www.hastingsracecourse.com

Track Data: Main Course five-furlong, 208-foot oval with 6 1/2 furlongs, 1 1/16- and 1 1/8-mile chutes; four-furlong inner training track; distance from last turn to finish line, 513 feet; width of track, 65 feet. Stable accommodations for 1,000. Seating Capacity 5,600. Parking for 2,500 cars.

Hastings Racecourse will celebrate its 116th anniversary in 2005. On May 1, 2002, Hastings Racecourse was purchased by Woodbine Entertainment Group and became known as Hastings Entertainment Inc doing business as Hastings Racecourse. Hastings Entertainment Inc. (HEI) is a wholly owned subsidiary of Woodbine Entertainment Group (WEG), which also owns and operates Ontario's Woodbine and Mohawk racetracks and the Champions Off-Track wagering teletheatre network. For 2004, the Hastings meet ran from April 17 through Nov. 28 with purses averaging $161,000 per day including stakes. 2005 dates: April 16 through Nov. 27.

TRACK RECORDS

Distance	Horse	Age	Wt.	Time	Date
Abt 3-1/2 f	Turn to Knight	2	117	:41-1/5	May 27, 1990
3-1/2 furs.	Flying Memo	2	116	:39.40	Oct. 26, 2003
Abt 6 furs.	Count The Green	6	123	1:10-4/5	Apr. 17, 1971
6 furs.	Great Descretion	4	117	1:10-2/5	May 10, 1969
6-1/2 furs.	Torque Converter	6	116	1:15	Jul. 1, 1996
1 m 70 yds	Westbury Road	6	124	1:40-2/5	Jul. 29, 1967
1-1/16 m	Coral Isle	5	119	1:42-1/5	Jul. 28, 1973
	No Time Flat	3	119	1:42-1/5	Sep. 12, 1987
	Timely Stitch	3	118	1:42-1/5	Jul. 6, 1996
1-1/8 m	Artic Son	4	116	1:46-4/5	Aug. 3, 1998
1-3/8 m	Irish Bear	3	122	2:14-2/5	Oct. 17, 1987
1-7/16 m	Who s In Command	5	111	2:23	Aug. 10, 1987
1-1/2 m	Lucky Son	4	117	2:29	Aug. 25, 1995
1-11/16 m	Glen Gower	4	114	2:51-1/5	Sep. 9, 1987
1-3/4 m	Glen Gower	4	119	2:59	Sep. 23, 1987
2-1/16 m	Laddie s Prince	4	116	3:30	Oct. 7, 1987
2-1/8 m	Mr. Chancellor	4	111	3:38-4/5	Oct. 18, 1987

Leading Jockey in 2004: Pedro V. Alvarado, 130 wins

Leading Trainer in 2004: Dino K. Condilenios, 37 wins

Record attendance: 21,156, July 9, 1982.Record handle: $2,612,316 July 9, 1982.

HAWTHORNE RACE COURSE

Hawthorne Race Course, Inc.

President and General Manager: Thomas F. Carey Jr.; Director of Operations: Thomas F. Carey III; Racing Secretary: Gary M. Duch; Director of Publicity: Jim Miller; Simulcast Director: Lorene Heninger.

Mailing Address: 3501 S. Laramie Avenue, Stickney/Cicero, Illinois 60804
(708) 780-3700 and Fax: (708) 780-3677
Web Site: www.hawthorneracecourse.com
Nearest Airport: Midway Airport, 2 miles.

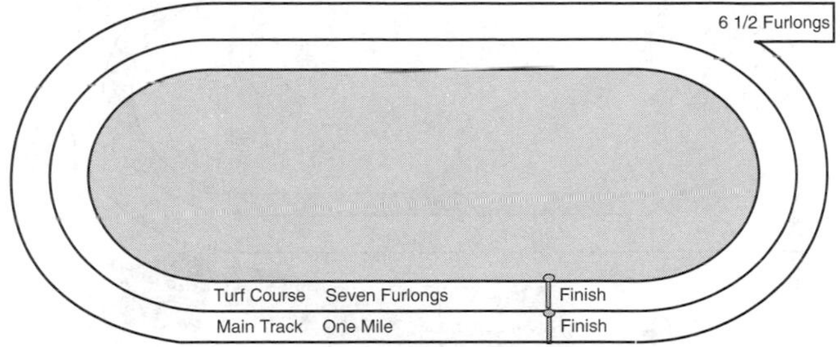

Track Data: Main Course one-mile oval with 6 1/2 furlongs chute; Turf Course, seven furlongs, 184 feet; Distance from last turn to wire 1,320 feet. Stall capacity, (including Sportsman's) 2,400; Seating capacity 18,000; Parking for 7,000 cars.

Opened May 20, 1891. The fifth oldest track in North America, Hawthorne was first owned by Ed Corrigan, who sold to the Carey Family in 1909. Reopened in 1980 after a devastating fire in 1977 and extensively renovated for the 1998 meeting. Took over Sportsman's meet in 2003. In 2004, the two meets offered 113 combined days of racing with purses well in excess of $200,000 per day, including stakes. 2005 dates: Feb 25 through May 10 and Sept. 23 through Jan. 1, 2006.

TRACK RECORDS

2 furs.	Minty Flavors	2	118	:20.88	May 14, 1999	Abt. 1-1/8 m	Crafty Oak	5	114	1:46.69	May 15, 1999
4-1/2 furs.	Joanies Bella			:51.80	May, 28, 2001	1-3/16 m	Lindy s Lad	5	115	1:59-2/5	Nov. 12, 1980
5 furs.	De La Concorde	3	119	:57	Nov. 11, 1992		Steal The Account	5	114	1:59-2/5	Aug. 28, 1999
5-1/2 furs.	Bold Tactics	3	122	1:02-2/5	Oct. 7, 1966	1-1/4 m	Gladwin	4	115	1:58-4/5	Oct. 1, 1970
6 furs.	Coach Jimi Lee	3	118	1:07.27	Dec. 12, 2003	1-1/2 m	David II	5	113	2:29-3/5	Oct. 1, 1969
6-1/2 furs.	Dee Lance	3	115	1:14-2/5	Jul. 27, 1988	1-5/8 m	Viale	6	118	2:47.02	Dec. 10, 2000
Abt.6-1/2 f	Sharp Carleen	3	111	1:18-4/5	Sep. 24, 1986	1-3/4 m	America Fore	4	110	3:02-1/5	Oct. 2, 1943
1 m 70 yds	Soldat Bleu	6	116	1:39-1/5	Jul. 27, 1988	2 m 70 yds.	Sun N Shine	4	113	3:30-2/5	Oct. 19, 1974
1-1/16 m	Sensitive Prince	3	118	1:39-3/5	Sep. 23, 1978	2-1/16 m	Revoque	8	113	3:35-2/5	Oct. 5, 1963
1-1/8 m	Zografos	6	119	1:46-3/5	Oct. 9, 1974	2-1/8 m	Hallandale	3	113	3:41-4/5	Oct. 12, 1963

Turf Course

5 furs.	Sulemark	5	119	:56	Oct. 25, 1992	Abt.1-1/16m	Galic Boy			1:41.48	May 5, 2001
	Magic Doe	4	119	:56.19	Oct. 28, 1999	1-1/16 m	Janeian	5	118	1:49-4/5	Oct. 11, 2003
Abt. 5 furs.	Lady Gin	3	114	:56.19	Oct. 22, 2000	1-1/8 m	Rainbows for Life	3	122	1:44-3/5	Oct. 13, 1991
Abt. 7 furs.	Point Guard	5	114	1:24-2/5	May 31, 1986	Abt.1-1/8 m	Color by d'Or			1:48.44	May 20, 2001
7 furs.	Zenobia Empress	5	123	1:22-4/5	Jul. 27, 1986	1-3/16 m	Perth Drummer	7	123	1:57-1/5	Jul. 19, 1986
Abt.7-1/2 f	Jack s Kingdom	5	119	1:30-3/5	Sep. 1, 1988	Abt.1-1/4 m	Sharp Swinger	5	117	2:08-1/5	Oct. 30, 1987
7-1/2 furs.	Joey Jr.	3	118	1:27-1/5	Nov. 5, 1989	1-1/4 m	Pass The Line	5	117	2:01	Aug. 2, 1986
Abt.1 mile	Hi Dee Ho Coyote			1:35.62	May 20, 2001	1-3/8 m	Shayzari	6	118	2:15-1/5	Sep. 3, 1988
1 mile	Niccolo Polo	5	119	1:33-3/5	Sep. 5, 1988	1-1/2 m	Lord Comet	6	117	2:26.87	Oct. 10, 1999
	Sean's Sunshine	5	114	1:36-1/5	Sep. 26, 1999						

Leading Jockey in 2004 Spring meet: Cruz Contreras, 47 wins
Leading Trainer in 2004 Spring meet: Pat Cuccurullo, 25 wins
Leading Jockey in 2004 Fall meet: Christopher A. Emigh, 69 wins
Leading Trainer in 2004 Fall meet: Frank J. Kirby, 26 wins

Record attendance: 39,033 May 30, 1946 (Lincoln Fields meeting), 37,792, September 6, 1937 (Regular Hawthorne meeting)
Record handle: $11,225,769, October 25, 2003

HOLLYWOOD PARK

Churchill Downs California Company

President: Frederick M. Baedeker Jr.; General Manager: Eual G. Wyatt, Jr.; Racing Secretary: Martin Panza; Public Relations Director: Michael Mooney; Vice President, Marketing: Allen Gutterman.

1050 S. Prairie Ave, Inglewood, CA 90301-4197
(310) 419-1500 Fax: (310) 671-4460 Free Results and Scratches: (310) 242-2150
Web site: www.hollywoodpark.com

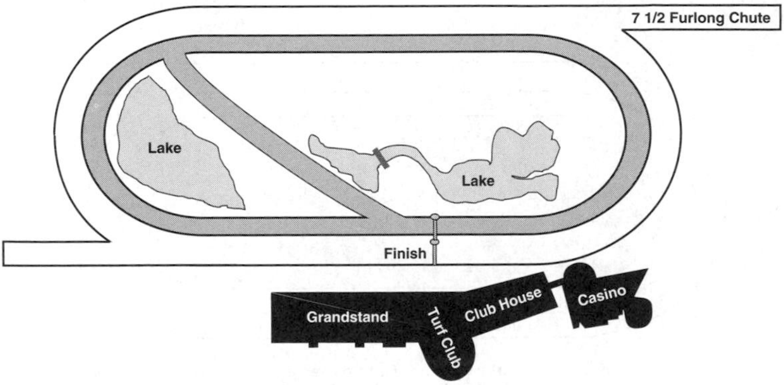

7 1/2 Furlong Chute
Lake
Lake
Finish
Grandstand
Turf Club
Club House
Casino

Track data: 1 1/8-mile oval, with one-mile chute. Distance from last turn to finish 1,321 feet. Width of stretch 90 1/2 feet, backstretch 80 1/2 feet. Turf course: One mile and 145 feet, with diagonal straightaway. Stable accommodations for 2,008; Seating capacity 35,000; Parking for 10,000.

Opened June 19, 1938. Was owned and operated by Marje Everett from the 1960's until R.D. Hubbard acquired the track in the early 1990's. Now owned and operated by Churchill Downs, Inc. and has a card casino on the grounds built in the early 1980's. Hollywood has hosted the Breeders' Cup three times, in the inaugural year, 1984, 1987, and 1997. Now hosts two meets each year. The Spring meet in 2004 ran from April 21 through July 18 with just under $400,000 in daily purses, while the 36-day fall meet ran from Nov. 3 through Dec. 20, with $331,000 in purses. The 2005 meets are respectively scheduled for April 22 through July 17 and from Nov. 9 through December 19.

TRACK RECORDS

Distance	Horse	Age	Wt.	Time	Date	Distance	Horse	Age	Wt.	Time	Date
4-1/2 furs.	Bridge of Royalty	2	117	:50.59	May 4, 1995	1 mile	Greinton	4	119	1:32-3/5	Jun. 9, 1985
5 furs.	Diligent Prospect	2	119	:56.29	May 30, 2004	1-1/16 m	Power Forward	4	115	1:40	Dec. 19, 1987
5-1/2 furs.	Hombre Rapido	5	118	1:01.67	Dec. 20, 2002	1-1/8 m	Gentlemen	4	121	1:45.35	Dec. 22, 1996
6 furs.	Apalachee Ridge	3	114	1:07.52	Dec. 12, 1997	1-3/16 m	Dig for It	6	118	1:54.85	May 30, 2001
	Tough Game	4	119	1:07.52	Nov. 15, 2003	1-1/4 m	Greinton	4	120	1:58-2/5	Jun. 23, 1985
6-1/2 furs.	Lucky Forever	6	118	1:13.24	May 20, 1995	1-3/8 m	Golden Ticket	4	116	2:13.42	Dec. 21, 2002
7 furs.	Mazel Trick	4	115	1:19.97	Jun. 27, 1999	1-5/8 m	Ol Henry	5	115	2:42.50	Jun. 27, 1997
7-1/2 furs.	Awesome Daze	5	119	1:26.26	Nov. 23, 1997	1-3/4 m	Roman Cuzzin	4	113	2:56.77	Jul. 21, 1997

Turf Course

Distance	Horse	Age	Wt.	Time	Date	Distance	Horse	Age	Wt.	Time	Date
5 furs.	Excusabull	2	119	:58.28	Jun. 20, 2004	1-1/8 m	Fastness	5	120	1:44.78	Nov. 25, 1995
5-1/2 furs.	Pembroke	5	120	1:00.46	Jul. 15, 1995	1-3/16 m	Kudos	4	123	1:51.99	Apr. 25, 2001
6 furs.	Answer Do	4	115	1:07	Dec. 15, 1990	1-1/4 m	Bien Bien	4	119	1:57.75	May 31, 1993
1 mile	Megan s Interco	5	119	1:32.64	May 22, 1994	1-1/2 m	Talloires	6	116	2:23.55	Jul. 21, 1996
1-1/16 m	Leroidesanimaux	4	114	1:38.45	May 1, 2004	Abt 1-3/4 m	Big Warning	4	117	2:50-2/5	Dec. 22, 1990
Abt-1/8 m	Zoffany	5	116	1:44-4/5	Nov. 16, 1985						

Leading Jockey in 2004 Spring-summer meet: Tyler Baze, 59 wins
Leading Trainer in 2004 Spring-summer meet: Jeff Mullins, 37 wins
Leading Jockey in 2004 Fall meet: Rene R. Douglas, 37 wins
Leading Trainer in 2004 Fall meet: Doug O Neill, 17 wins

Record attendance: 80,340, May 4, 1980. Record handle: $14, 352, 515, Nov 8, 1987 (Breeders' Cup Day), $73, 897, 276, November 8, 1997 (Breeders' Cup Day, all sources).

HOOSIER PARK

A Churchill Downs Company

Chairman: Thomas Meeker (Churchill Downs, president and CEO.); President, General Manager: Richard Moore; Racing Secretary: Raymond Butch Cook; Vice President, Operations and Communications: Thomas Bannon; Vice President, Finance: Steven L. Wilkening; Vice President, Marketing: Donna Smith.

4500 Dan Patch Circle, Anderson, IN 46013
(765) 642-7223 Fax: (765) 644-0467
E-Mail: info@hoosierpark.com; Web Site: www.hoosierpark.com

Track data: Seven-eighths mile oval, with a six furlong chute. Distance from last turn to finish 1,255 feet.

Opened Sept. 1, 1994. Runs thoroughbred and harness dates. A controlling interest in the track is owned by Hoosier Park, LP, a subsidiary of Churchill Downs. In 2004, offered 59 racing days featuring average daily purses of over $138,000 including stakes. The 2005 dates are Sept. 3 through Nov. 25.

TRACK RECORDS

5 furs.	Jimmy Jones	7	123	:58.39	Oct. 9, 2004	1-1/8 m	Henbane s Cat	4	118	1:54.47	Oct. 2, 2004
5-1/2 furs.	Moro Oro	3	119	1:02-1/5	Sep. 20, 1996	1-1/2 m	Got Brass	5	118	2:36.88	Oct. 30, 2004
	Chukker Creek	5	118	1:02.-1/5	Nov. 24, 1996	1-9/16 m	Our Forbes	7	119	2:39-1/5	Nov. 7, 1997
6 furs.	Moro Oro	3	122	1:07-2/5	Nov. 16, 1996	1-5/8 m	Open Space	6	114	2:41.20	Nov. 16, 1996
1 mile	Vic s Rebel	4	122	1:33.99	Oct. 13, 1998	1-7/8 m	Raw New	6	121	3:16.20	Dec. 1, 2000
1-1/16 m	Alydar s Rib	5	120	1:41	Nov. 1, 1996						

Leading Jockey in 2004: Ramsey Zimmerman, 92 wins

Leading Trainer in 2004: Ralph Martinez, 62 wins

Record Attendance: 10,827, October 7, 2000. Handle Record $2,207,621, November14, 2003

HORSEMEN'S PARK

6303 Q Street, Omaha, Nebraska 68117
Telephone: (402) 731-2900; Fax: (402) 731-5122 and (402) 731-5416

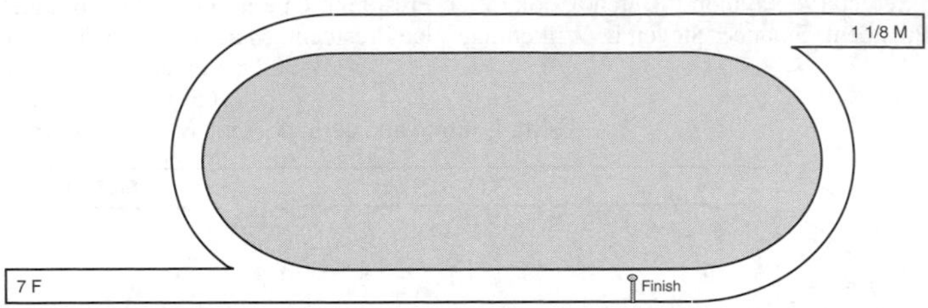

Track Data: 5/8 mile oval. distance from last turn to finish line, 757 feet. Seating capacity, 2800.

Opened July 1998 with two days of two races each by the Nebraska Horsemen's Benevolent and Protective Association. While mostly a simulcast facility, a short four-day live meet with purses worth in excess of $125,000 per day was run in 2004 with a similar meet scheduled for July 21 through July 24 in 2005. Year-round simulcasting of 15-18 tracks per day.

TRACK RECORDS

6 furs.	Pretty Boy Pete	1:10.20	Jul. 20, 2001	1 Mile	Sure Shot Biscuit			1:35.80	Jul. 22, 2001
	Come a Stridin	1:10.20	Jul. 21, 2001	1-3/8 m	Aly Aly Oxen Free	7	119	2:18.00	Jul. 21, 2002

Leading Jockey in 2004: Robert Dean Williams, 4 wins
Leading Trainer in 2004: Herb Riecken, 2 wins

INDIANA DOWNS

Oliver Racing, LLC; LHT Capital, LLC

General Manager, Jon Schuster; Director of Racing, Jim Ewart; Thoroughbred Racing Secretary, Butch Cook; Human Resource Manager/Marketing Coordinator, Julie Metz.

4200 N. Michigan Rd.
Shelbyville, IN 46176
(317) 421-0000; Fax, (317) 421-0100
Race Office, (866) 478-7223
www.indianadowns.com

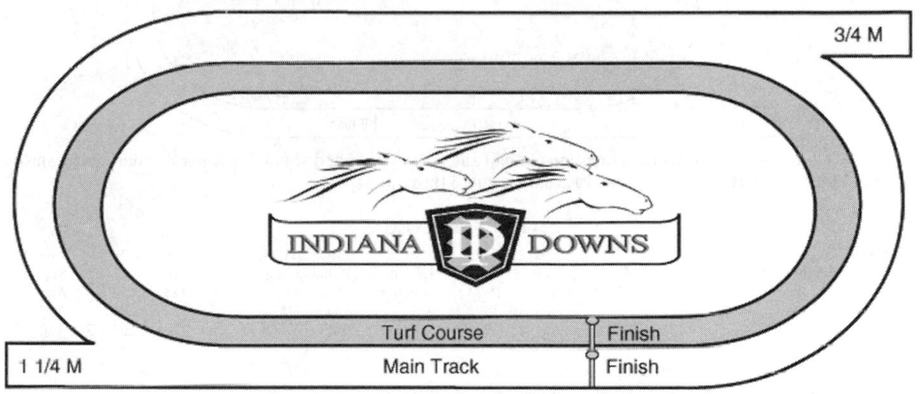

Track Data: One mile dirt track and seven-furlong turf course. Indoor seating 3,000.

Opened in December 2002 for harness racing, with first thoroughbred meet commencing on April 11, 2003. In 2004, a meet of 48 days was conducted from April 16 through June 20, featuring purses of over $85,000. Conducts live racing of thoroughbreds, Quarter Horses and standardbreds. Offers year-round full-card simulcasting of thoroughbred and harness racing. An off-site wagering facility is located in Evansville with a second facility in Clarksville due to open in 2004.

TRACK RECORDS

4-1/2 furs.	Cat Tracks	5	123	:50.75	May 10, 2003	1 m 70 yds	K K Avey	3	114	1:41.56	May 7, 2003
5 furs.	Roll the Gold	4	118	:57.85	May 6, 2004	1-1/16 m	Roberto Royale	7	118	1:44.00	Jun. 16, 2004
5-1/2 furs.	Savoya on Ice	5	118	1:03.30	Jun. 11, 2004	1-1/8 m	A Secret Scoop	4	117	1:50.62	May 15, 2003
6 furs.	Lx Commander	3	117	1:09.89	May 26, 2003	1-1/4 m	High Chieftain	6	117	2:06.31	May 26, 2003
1 mile	Way Fleeter	4	123	1:37.74	May 19, 2004						

Turf Course

Abt. 5 furs.	Fit to Keep	4	118	:58.64	Jun. 11, 2004	1 mile	If I Were You	5	116	1.36.51	May 23, 2004
5 furs.	Captain Larkin	5	115	:57.14	Jun. 4, 2004	1-1/16 m	Luckymata	4	119	1:42.34	May 22, 2004
7-1/2 furs.	Crackerbox Palace	5	123	1:29.89	Jun. 4, 2004	1-3/8 m	Parisky	7	118	2:11.37	Jun. 20, 2004
Abt. 1 mile	Dashing Princess	5	123	1:39.73	Jun. 11, 2004						

Leading Jockey in 2004: Rodney A. Prescott, 74 wins
Leading Trainer in 2004: R. Gary Patrick, 30 wins

KAMLOOPS

479 Chilcotin Road
Kamloops, British Columbia V2H 1G4
(604) 828-3590; Fax (606) 828-0836

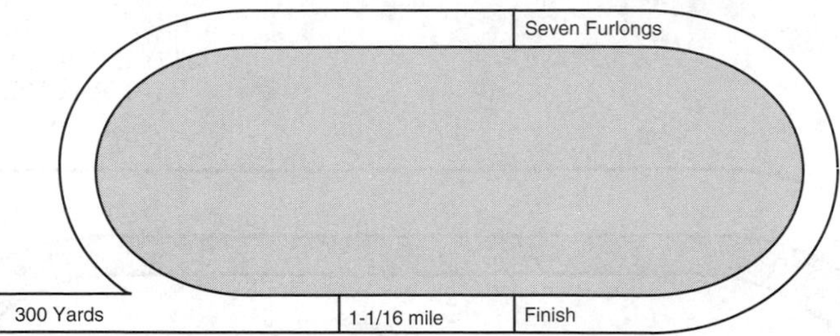

Ran separate three- and five-day race meetings in **2004** and purses averaged about **$6,800** per day during the spring meet and **$9,400** during the summer meet. **2005** dates: Aug. **6** through Sept. **4**

TRACK RECORDS

3-1/2 furs.	Spooks Classy Lady	2	123	:39-3/5	May 23, 1993	1 Mile	Just Like Light	7	126	1:36.60	Aug. 9, 1998
4 furs.	Rampaging Alf	2	122	:47	Aug. 8, 1999	1-1/8 m	Winning Edge	6	120	1:51-4/5	Sep. 7, 1992
Abt 4-1/2 f	War Of Aces	4	126	:48-2/5	Jun. 6, 1992	1-3/16 m	Mondo Key	6	123	1:58	Aug. 29, 1993
6-1/2 furs.	Gate Hand	7	127	1:17	Aug. 16, 1992	Abt 1-1/4 m	Sidero	6	117	2:07	Aug. 18, 1991
7 furs.	McBrat	4	123	1:23	Aug. 25, 1991	1-1/4 m	Native Winter	6	126	2:07-1/5	Aug. 29, 1992

Leading Jockey in 2004 Spring meet: Angelle Wilson, 6 wins
Leading Trainers in 2004 Spring meet: Frank R. Wilson & Vicki Pozzobon, 3 wins (tie)
Leading Jockey in 2004 Summer meet: Cliff James Miyashiro, 2 wins
Leading Trainer in 2004 Summer meet: No trainers had more than one win

KEENELAND

Keeneland Association, Incorporated.

President and CEO: Nick Nicholson; Director of Racing: W.B. Rogers Beasley; Racing Secretary: Ben Huffman; Director of Communications: Jim Williams: (859) 288-4220; fax: (859) 288-4254.

Street Address: 4201 Versailles Road
Lexington, Kentucky 40510
Nearest Airport: Blue Grass Field, next to track

P.O. Box 1690, Lexington, Kentucky 40588-1690
(859) 254-3412; (800) 456-3412; Fax: (859) 288-4348
E-mail: keeneland@keeneland.com
Web Site: www.keeneland.com.

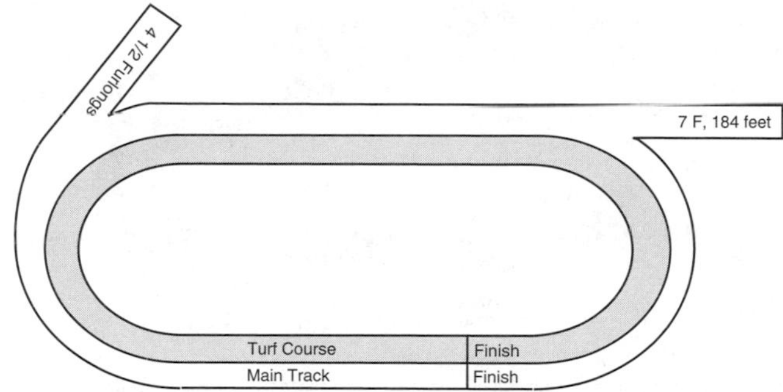

Track Data: Main track, 1 1/16 miles, sandy loam, with 4 1/2- and seven-furlong chutes. Stretch length, 1,174 feet. Turf course, 7 1/2 furlongs. Training Track, five furlongs, polytrack. Stable accommodations for 1,852. Seating capacity: 8,500; Parking for 10,000 cars.

Opened October 15, 1936, to provide a forum for horses bred in Kentucky and/or bought at the famous Keeneland Yearling sales. Keeneland remains a National Historic Landmark. Its dual live meets – three weeks in April and three more weeks in October – are among the classiest in the sport with purses to match, including numerous Graded stakes and daily average purses nearing $600,000. The Keeneland library, one of the finest Thoroughbred research libraries in the world, is open Monday through Friday with Daily Racing Form archives among the important reference material. Provides announced coverage of workouts on Saturday mornings with trackside breakfast. The 2005 Spring meet is scheduled for April 8 through Apr. 29 and the fall meet from Oct. 7 through Oct. 29. Simulcasting throughout the year.

TRACK RECORDS

4-1/2 furs.	Quick Swoon	2	121	:51	Apr. 20, 1966	1-1/8 m	Midway Road	4	116	1:46.78	Apr. 22, 2004
	Royality Note	2	114	:51	Apr. 23, 1968	1-3/16 m	Arch	3	123	1:53.87	Oct. 11, 1998
	Bend The Times	2	117	:51	Apr. 8, 1980	1-1/4 m	Political Fact	4	112	2:02.21	Oct. 15, 1993
6 furs.	Anjiz	5	114	1:07.78	Oct. 9, 1993	1-5/8 m	Put-in-Bay	4	113	2:45	Oct. 13, 1967
6-1/2 furs.	Number One Sheikh	3	116	1:14.70	Oct. 11, 2000		Mr. Copy Chief	3	118	2:45	Oct. 20, 1971
7 furs.	Binalong	4	112	1:20.39	Oct. 13, 1993						
Abt 7 furs.	Lamb Chop	3	118	1:24-3/5	Oct. 10, 1963						
1-1/16 m	Din s Dancer	5	123	1:40-4/5	Oct. 9, 1990						

Turf Course

5-1/2 furs.	Chris s Thunder	5	123	1:01.72	Oct. 8, 2000	1-3/16 m	Happyanunoit	4	119	1:53.91	Oct. 15, 1999
1 mile	Perfect Soul	6	116	1:33.54	Apr. 9, 2004	1-1/2 m	Bursting Forth	5	114	2:27.54	Apr. 22, 1999
1-1/16 m	Quiet Resolve	5	116	1:40.30	Apr. 27, 2000	1-5/8 m	Royal Strand	5	117	2:38.68	Oct. 24, 1999
1-1/8 m	Memories of Silver	3	121	1:45.81	Oct. 5, 1996	About distances no longer run over this turf course.					

Jumps

2 miles	Hotspur	5	156	3:52-2/5	Apr. 26, 2002	2-1/2 m	Pompeyo	7	158	4:34-2/5	Apr. 27, 2001

Leading Jockey in 2004 Spring meet: Pat Day, 21 wins

Leading Trainer in 2004 Spring meet: Steven M. Asmussen, 9 wins

Leading Jockey in 2004 Fall meet: Rafael Bejarano, 26 wins

Leading Trainers in 2004 Fall meet: Nicholas P. Zito & Steven M. Asmussen, 11 wins (tie)

Record attendance: 31,028, Aprll 17, 2004. Record handle: $3,516,621 April 13, 2002, $17,076,993 April 14, 2001 includes simulcasting.

KENTUCKY DOWNS

Kentucky Downs, LLC.
General Manager: Ryan Driscoll

PO Box 405, Franklin, KY 42134
(270) 586-7778 Fax: (502) 586-8080
Web site:www.turfwaypark.com

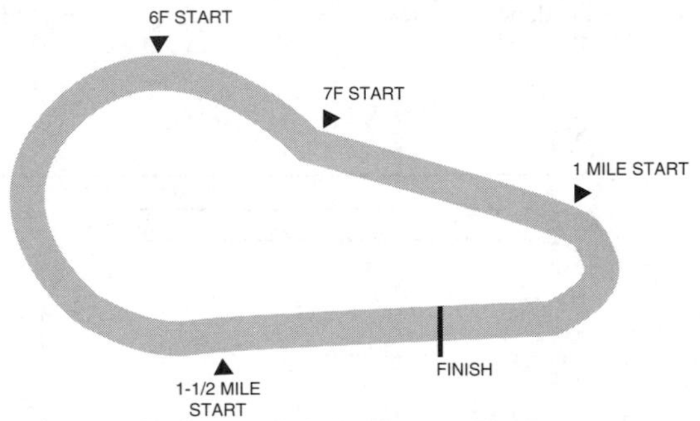

Track data: 1-3/8 miles European turf course in a pear shape that features a sharp first turn and a wide, bulging second turn.

Opened as Dueling Grounds April 22, 1990, and was bought in 1997 by a consortium that included Churchill Downs and Turfway Park. Now managed by Turfway, ran a six-day fall meeting in 2004 with several stakes races over its European style turf course, offering just over $227,000 in daily purses. A similar meet is scheduled from Sept. 17 to Sept. 27 in 2005. Year-round simulcasting.

TRACK RECORDS

6 furs.	Morluc	4	116	1:09.66	Sep. 23, 2000	1 Mile	Rob n Gin	4	119	1:35.00	Sep. 19, 1998
7 furs.	Slew of Deuces	5	116	1:22.77	Sep. 18, 2000	1-1/2 m	Yaqthan	8	115	2:27.60	Sep. 19, 1998
					Jumps						
2-1/8 m	Lord Zada	7	144	3:48.62	Sep. 23, 2000	2-3/4 m	Grabel	7	151	5:29	Apr. 22, 1990

Leading Jockey in 2004: Rafael Bejarano, 12 wins
Leading Trainers in 2004: W. Elliott Walden & Merrill R. Scherer & Eric R. Reed, 3 wins (tie)

Record attendance: 2,191, May 1999. Record handle: $585,762

KIN PARK

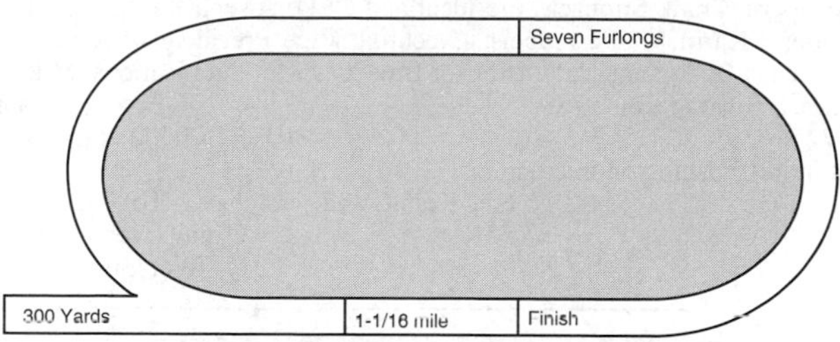

A 3-day, summer meet in 2004 and a similar meet in 2005.

TRACK RECORDS

Abt 3 furs.	Mcnoonie	2	122	:34	Jun. 26, 1994
3 furs.	Rejected Frenchman	3	122	:32-1/5	Aug. 1, 1993
Abt 4 furs.	Tammy Star	5	116	:44.33	Jul. 11, 2004
5-1/2 furs.	Tim O Hara	6	123	1:03-1/5	Sep. 20, 1992
6 furs.	Diplomatic Eagle	3	118	1:10.60	Jul. 10, 1994
Abt 6 furs.	Detective M	5	126	1:09.60	Aug. 7, 1994
Abt 6-1/2 f	Little Duke	4	131	1:19.00	Jul. 30, 2000
Abt 7 furs.	Mexican Macho Man	4	126	1:21.00	Jul. 19, 1998
7 furs.	Gate Hand	6	123	1:22	Jul. 28, 1991
1-1/16 m	Wicked Advances	7	122	1:45.40	Aug. 7, 1993
Abt 1-1/16m	Gavotte	5	126	1:44.20	Jul. 31, 1999
1-1/8 m	Ninja Warrior	11	120	1:47-2/5	Jul. 16, 1995
Abt. 1-1/8 m	Conversano	3	134	1:50.80	Jul. 30, 2000
1-1/4 m	Prospector Bobby	4	123	1:59-1/5	Sep. 29, 1991

Leading Jockeys in 2004: Caroline Stinn & Roger Butterfly, 4 wins (tie)
Leading Trainer in 2004: Gary Saitz, 4 wins

LAUREL PARK

Magna Entertainment Corp.

Chairman of the Board: Frank Stronach; President and CEO: Joseph A. De Francis; COO: Lou Raffetto; Executive Vice President: Karin M. De Francis; Executive Vice President of Racing Operations: James L. Gagliano; Racing Secretary: Georganne Hale; Director Broadcast Communications: Mike Gathagan.

Street Address: Racetrack Road & Route 198
Laurel, Maryland 20725
Nearest Airport: Baltimore-Washington International (BWI), 12 miles

Box 130, Laurel, Maryland 20725
(301) 725-0400 or (410) 792-7775 (Baltimore)
Fax: (410) 792-4877
Free Results and scratches: (410) 792-0278 and (301) 470-3056
E-mail: webmaster@marylandracing.com
Web Site: www.marylandracing.com

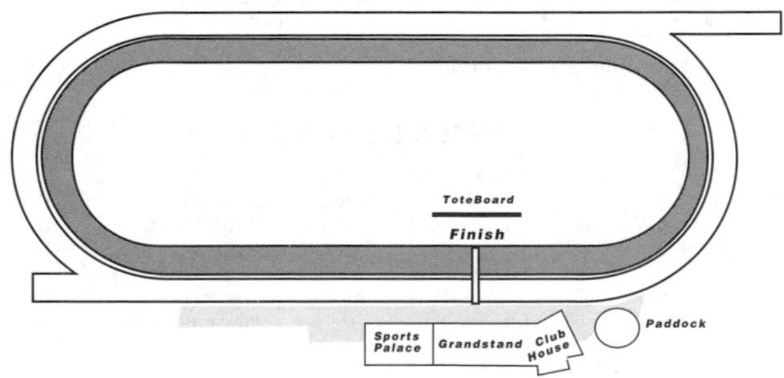

Track Data: 1 1/8-mile loam oval. 7-furlong chute. Length of stretch from last turn to finish line, 1,344 feet.Width of dirt course, 95 feet. One-mile turf course. Width of turf course, 142 feet. Stable accommodations:880. Seating capacity: 5,200; Parking for 8,000 cars.

Opened October 2, 1911, Laurel Park has been the sister track of Pimlico Racecourse during the two decades it was opened and operated by the DeFrancis family. In 2003, Magna Entertainment Corp. purchased a 58 percent stake in Laurel and a 51 percent stake in Pimlico Race Course, which are both owned and operated by the Maryland Jockey Club. Purses including stakes averaged over $182,000 for a meet that ran from Oct. 8, 2003, through March 28, 2004. Dates for 2005 season: Jan. 22 through April 17; Aug. 10 through Aug. 27; and Sept. 7 through Dec. 31.

5 furs.	Dave s Friend	5	119	:57	Nov. 21, 1980	1 mile	Skipper s Friend	4	122	1:34-2/5	Dec. 6, 1980
5-1/2 furs.	Crossing Point	5	117	1:02.45	Nov. 1, 2002	1-1/16 m	Willard Scott	4	115	1:41-4/5	Nov. 16, 1985
6 furs.	Richter Scale	6	123	1:07.95	Jul. 15, 2000	1-1/8 m	Pyramid Peak	4	122	1:47.63	Jul. 6, 1996
6-1/2 furs.	Ebonizer	3	115	1:15-2/5	Nov. 23, 1990	1-3/16 m	Testing	7	121	1:54.51	Oct. 21, 2000
7 furs.	Tappiano	5	123	1:21-2/5	Feb. 12, 1989	1-1/4 m	Ritchie the Coach	5	118	1:59.96	Nov. 23, 1996
7-1/2 furs.	Tidal Surge	4	117	1:29.52	Mar. 12, 1994	1-3/4 m	Asserche	6	116	2:58.51	Feb. 13, 1994

Turf Course

5-1/2 furs.	Pal Joey	5	119	1:02.20	Nov. 9, 2000	1-3/16	Gilded Youth	10	117	1:53.70	Jun. 27, 1998
6 furs.	Texas Glitter	4	115	1:08.00	Oct. 28, 2000	1-1/4 m	Dynamic Trick	5	114	1:58.42	Oct. 22, 2000
1 mile	Portsmouth	3	116	1:34	Oct. 30, 1965	1-1/2 m	Kelso	7	126	2:23-4/5	Nov. 11, 1964
	Flaming Emperor	4	116	1:34	Jul. 4, 1990	1-5/8 m	Copper Prospect	4	122	2:47.99	Jul. 31, 1993
1-1/16 m	Warning Glance	4	117	1:39.35	Jun. 18, 1995	2 miles	Summer Ensign	4	118	3:23.64	Jun. 15, 1993
1-1/8 m	La Reine s Terms	7	122	1:46.04	Aug. 11, 2002						

Jumps

2-1/8 m	Joli s Summer	5	151	4:02.10	Jun. 22, 1995

Leading Jockey in 2004: Ramon A. Dominguez, 88 wins
Leading Trainer in 2004: John J. Robb, 36 wins

LES BOIS PARK

5610 Glenwood Rd., Boise, ID 83714
(208) 376-7223 Fax: (208) 376-7227

Track data: six-furlong oval, with five-furlong and one-mile chutes, the latter also used for two-furlong straightaway races. Distance from last turn to finish 660 feet; width 80 feet.. Stable accommodations 834, Seating capacity 3,300.

Opened May 15, 1970, ran a 46 day meet in 2004, with $18,000 in daily average purses. The 2005 meet is scheduled for May 4 through August 14.

TRACK RECORDS

2 furs.	Rare n to Syn	4	124	:21.40	May 4, 2003
3 furs.	Big Order	6	117	:33-4/5	May 30, 1970
4 furs.	We Go Easy	4	123	:45-2/5	Jun. 27, 1976
4-1/2 furs.	C. K. s Orphan	5	122	:50-3/5	May 25, 1987
5 furs.	Lord Goodoon	4	122	:55-4/5	May 25, 1987
6 furs.	Shilne	5	119	1:12-1/5	Jul. 25, 1971
6-1/2 furs.	Stretch the Truth	4	122	1:17	Jul. 12, 1997
7 furs.	Pride of Kent	5	122	1:22.60	Jul. 10, 1998
7-1/2 furs.	Joyous Gard	4	122	1:28.80	Jun. 17, 1998
1 mile	Barsotti	3	122	1:35.60	Jul. 24, 1999
1-1/8 m	Song Festival	7	122	1:50	Jun. 15, 1991
1-3/16 m	Standup Comedian	8	117	1:58-1/5	Jun. 27, 1987
1-1/4 m	Talent To Amuse	7	122	2:02	Aug. 11, 1996
1-3/8 m	Chikara	4	119	2:17-3/5	Aug. 13, 1988
1-1/2 m	Uncle Maurice	5	122	2:35-3/5	Aug. 12, 1979
1-3/4 m	Final K.	4	120	2:48-1/5	Sep. 1, 1975
1-7/8 m	Chikara	5	127	2:59-2/5	Jul. 29, 1989

Leading Jockey in 2004: Berkley R. Packer, 63 wins
Leading Trainer in 2004: Kevin Knudsen, 22 wins

LINCOLN
(Nebraska State Fair Park)

Box 81223, Lincoln, NE 68501-1223
(402) 474-5371 Fax: (402) 473-4114
Web Site: www.statefair.org

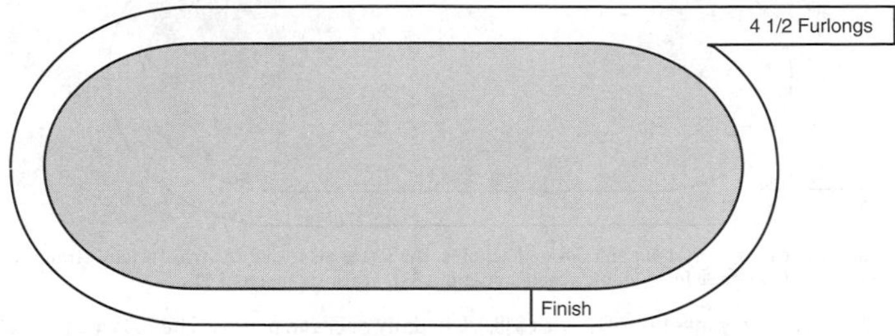

Track data: Five-eighths mile oval, with 4 1/2-furlong chute. Distance from last turn to finish 480 feet. Stable accommodations 1,200. Seating capacity 5,800. Parking for 9,000 cars on the fairgrounds.

Live racing is scheduled in 2005 from May 13 to July 17; a similar meet in 2004 featured purses of about $48,000 per day fueled by year round simulcasting.

TRACK RECORDS

4 furs.	Mr. Mayor	4	120	:46-4/5	Aug. 1, 1975	1-3/16 m	Speedy Rick	6	110	1:54-1/5	Aug. 13, 1977
4-1/2 furs.	Leaping Plum	4	122	:50	Sep. 17, 1995	1-5/16 m	Famous Event	5	122	2:18-3/5	Oct. 22, 1995
6 furs.	Genuine Lass	4	120	1:10.20	Jun. 20, 2002	1-3/8 m	Trumpty Dumpty	8	120	2:17.80	Jun. 17, 2001
1 mile	Sensitive Ghost	8	116	1:36.00	Jul. 14, 2002	1-5/8 m	Hunters Soup	6	120	2:45-4/5	Nov. 5, 1989
1 m 70yds	High Dice	6	122	1:39.40	Jun. 24, 2001	2 miles	Step n Ring	5	116	3:25	Jul. 13, 1996
1-1/16 m	Old n Bold	4	121	1:42-3/5	Aug. 25, 1979	2 3/8 m	Naughty Nipper	5	119	4:34-1/5	Nov. 13, 1983
1-1/8 m	Prince Hedstart	6	122	1:49-4/5	Aug. 1, 1982	3 miles	Hunters Soup	6	121	5:18-3/5	Nov. 19, 1989

Leading Jockey in 2004: Robert Dean Williams, 70 wins
Leading Trainer in 2004: David C. Anderson, 29 wins
Record attendance: 10, 107, August 19, 1978.

LONE STAR PARK

Magna Entertainment Corp.

Chairman: Frank Stronach; CEO: Jim McAlpine; President: Corey S. Johnsen; Vice President and General Manager: Jeffrey Greco; Vice President of Finance: Paula Dowell; Vice President of Marketing and Sales: G.W. Hail; Director of Media Relations: Darren Rogers.

Nearest Airport: Dallas-Fort Worth Int l. Airport, 10 miles .

1000 Lone Star Parkway, Grand Prairie, Texas 75050
(972) 263-7223; Fax: (972) 262-5622
Web Site: www.lonestarpark.com

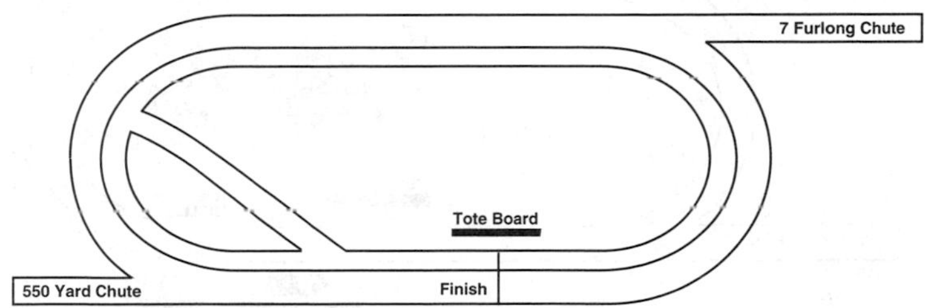

Track Data: One-mile dirt track with a seven-furlong chute. Distance from last turn to finish, 930 feet; width 90 feet. Turf: 7/8-miles with 1 1/8-mile infield chute; width 70 feet. 550-yard Quarter Horse chute. Seating for 12,000; capacity 50,000; Parking for 6,000 cars.

Opened April 1997, Lone Star Park has been the most successful pari-mutuel track in Texas. In 2004, it hosted the Breeders' Cup. The track plays host to the annual NTRA All-Star Jockey Championship. Scheduled dates for 2005: Apr. 14 to July 17.

TRACK RECORDS

2-1/2 furs.	Yes He Will	4	124	:26.53	Nov. 7, 1997	1-1/16 m	Dixie Dot Com	6	118	1:40.53	May 28, 2001
4-1/2 furs.	Ruby Be Mine	2	118	:51.30	Apr. 30, 2004	1-1/8 m	Ashado	3	119	1:48.26	Oct. 30, 2004
5 furs.	Joyful Tune	4	116	:56.25	May 5, 2002	1-3/16 m	Moosekabear	7	117	1:56.21	May 10, 1997
5-1/2 furs.	That Tat	5	123	1:01.88	Apr. 11, 2003	1-1/4 m	Ghostzapper	4	126	1:59.02	Oct. 30, 2004
6 furs.	Savorthetime	5	117	1:07.82	May 31, 2004	1-5/16	Gabriel s Pat	6	119	2:12.34	Oct. 22, 2004
6-1/2 furs.	Spiritbound	5	117	1:14.16	May 3, 1997	1-1/2 m	Tali Hai	7	120	2:32.57	Jul. 5, 1997
7 furs.	Yearly Report	3	123	1:20.67	Oct. 29, 2004	1-3/4 m	Sir Moon Dancer	5	114	3:00.46	Jul. 19, 1998
1 mile	Isitingood	6	123	1:34.44	Apr. 20, 1997						

Turf Course

Abt.5 furs.	Brenda Stahr	5	117	:54.17	Jun. 14, 1998	1 mile	Kiraday	6	116	1:33.56	Jul. 4, 1997
5 furs.	Caro s Royalty	4	122	:55.60	Jul. 20, 1997	1-1/16 m	Sharpest Image	6	115	1:40.05	Jun. 12, 1998
Abt.7-1/2 f	Sweet Eleanor	4	112	1:28.97	Jul. 24, 1997	1-1/8 m	Yaqthan	8	116	1:45.54	May 25, 1998
7-1/2 furs.	Special Moments	5	119	1:28.20	May 24, 1998	1-3/8 m	Rugged Bugger	7	114	2:13.53	May 10, 1998
Abt.1 mile	Royalty Case	3	117	1:34.79	Jul. 20, 1997	1-1/2 m	Final Val	5	114	2:28.20	Jul. 4, 1998

Leading Jockey in 2004 Spring-Summer meet: Eddie M. Martin Jr., 87 wins
Leading Trainer in 2004 Spring-Summer meet: Steven M. Asmussen, 82 wins
Leading Jockey in 2004 Fall meet: Roman Chapa, 24 wins
Leading Trainer in 2004 Fall meet: Steven M. Asmussen, 24 wins
Record attendance 53,717, October 30, 2004 (Breeders' Cup). Record handle: $13,326,726, October 30, 2004 (Breeders' Cup).

LOS ALAMITOS RACE COURSE

Los Alamitos

President: Edward C. Allred; Racing Secretary: Ron Church; Marketing Director: Orlando Gutierrez.

4961 Katella Ave. Los Alamitos, CA 90720
(714) 820-2800 Fax: (714) 236-4534 Free Scratches and Results (714) 995-2222
E-Mail Address: larace@losalamitos.com; Web Address: www.losalamitos.com

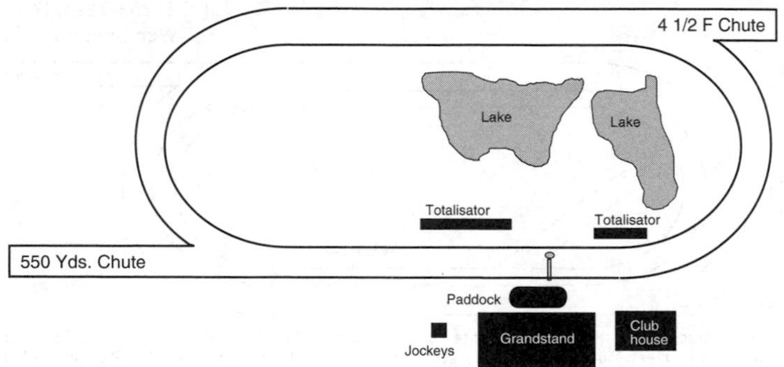

Track data: Five-eighths mile oval, with 4 1/2-furlong and 550-yard straight course. Distance from last turn to finish 558 feet. Width 100 feet in stretch, 90 feet in backstretch and on turns; 6.9 feet banking on turns. Stable accommodations for 1,438. Seating capacity 7,500.

Los Alamitos runs a virtually year-round mixed-breed meet. The 2005 meet is scheduled for Dec. 26, 2004, through Dec. 18, 2005.

THOROUGHBRED TRACK RECORDS

4-1/2 furs.	Valiant Pete	4	121	:49-1/5	Aug. 11, 1990

Leading Jockey in 2004: Guillermo R. Gutierrez, 58 wins
Leading Trainer in 2004: Jesus Nunez, 66 wins
All time single day attendance 19,970 May 6. 1983. All time single day handle $2,127,758 June 30, 1995

LOUISIANA DOWNS

Harrah s Entertainment

Senior Vice President and General Manager: Ted Bogich; Vice President Racing: Ray A. Tromba.

Street Address: 8000 East Texas Ave.
Bossier City, Louisiana 71111
Nearest Airport: Shreveport Regional Airport, 12 Miles

P.O. Box 5519, Bossier City, Louisiana 71171-5519
(318) 742-5555; Fax: (318) 741-2615
Web Site: www.ladowns.com

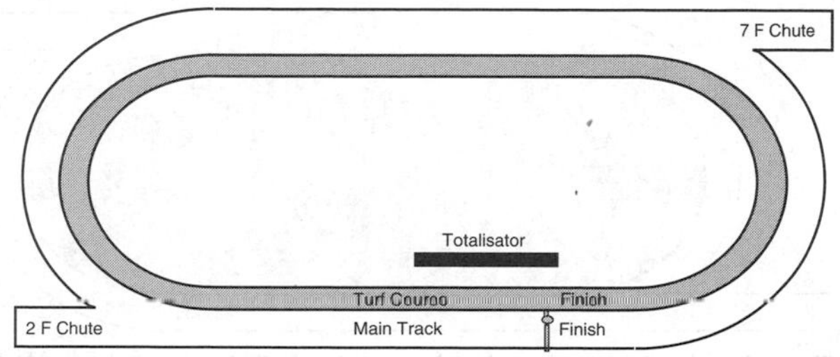

Track Data: One-mile, sandy loam; seven-furlong and 1 1/4-mile chutes; Distance from last turn to finish, 1,010 feet; Width of stretch and backstretch, 80 feet; Turf course: 7 furlongs and 50 feet, distance from last turn to finish, 940 feet, width 70 feet. Stable accommodations for 1,360. Seating capacity 17,000; Parking for 4,000 cars.

Opened October, 30, 1974, Louisiana Downs annually runs from spring through fall. Home of the Super Derby. Slot machines were introduced May 21, 2003, and purses in 2004 averaged almost $180,000 a day. The 2005 meet is scheduled for April 29 through Oct. 9.

TRACK RECORDS

4 furs.	A Lady For Junius	5	123	:45.43	Oct. 9, 1997
4-1/2 furs.	Sondor	2	119	:51-3/5	May 16, 1984
5 furs.	Joyful Tune	4	124	:56.90	Sep. 7, 2002
5-1/2 furs.	Fighting K	4	122	1:02.84	Sep. 11, 1993
6 furs.	Tangent	4	123	1:08-2/5	Apr. 28, 1984
6-1/2 furs.	Prince Of The Mt.	5	117	1:14.98	May 23, 1996
7 furs.	Carrysport	3	116	1:21-3/5	Jul. 4, 1984
1 m 70 yds	Country Jim	4	111	1:39-2/5	Jul. 4, 1982
1-1/16 m	Nelson	6	113	1:41.44	Aug. 15, 1993
1-1/8 m	Mocha Express	5	118	1:48.14	Jul. 24, 1999
1-3/16 m	Jungle Pocket	7	118	1:57-2/5	Aug. 15, 1984
1-1/4 m	Tiznow	3	124	1:59.84	Sep. 30, 2000
1-1/2 m	Frankie s Pal	6	110	2:31-4/5	Sep. 3, 1990
1-3/4 m	Frankie s Pal	6	113	2:58-4/5	Oct. 14, 1990
1-13/16 m	Stage Door Joey	5	113	3:09.91	Sep. 20, 1992
2 miles	Vain Lass	11	110	3:35-1/5	Nov. 16, 1975
2-1/8 m	Woodtie	5	123	3:44-1/5	Oct. 22, 1989
2-1/4 m	Eulogize	4	117	3:58-4/5	Nov. 11, 1990

Turf Course

Abt.5 furs.	Top Commander	4	124	:54.96	Jul. 22, 2004
5 furs.	Sunshine Classic	5	119	:55.79	Aug. 31, 2002
Abt.7-1/2 f	Home In Front	4	112	1:27-2/5	Aug. 22, 1987
7-1/2 furs.	Chuck N Luck	6	113	1:28-2/5	Aug. 5, 1989
Abt.1 mile	Dressy Time	7	114	1:33-2/5	Sep. 1, 1984
1 mile	Cherokee Circle	4	116	1:34-1/5	Jul. 24, 1983
Abt.1-1/16m	Inevitable Leader	7	116	1:40	May 26, 1986
	Vaguely Crafty	6	114	1:40	Jul. 22, 1989
1-1/16 m	Clever Song	3	120	1:40-1/5	Aug. 11, 1985
Abt.1-1/8m	Highly Attractive	4	115	1:42	Jun. 17, 1990
Abt.1-1/4 m	Tali Hai	6	121	2:04.19	Aug. 31, 1996
1-1/4 m	Alystorm	4	115	2:05.03	Oct. 1, 1999
Abt.1-3/8 m	Symbol Of Pride	5	113	2:16-1/5	Jul. 20, 1986
1-3/8 m	Semillero	5	116	2:13-1/5	Oct. 12, 1985
Abt.1-1/2 m	Comely Dancer	7	117	2:29-3/5	Aug. 12, 1990
Abt.1-13/16	Alamance	6	122	3:05.12	Sep. 4, 1993
Abt.1-7/8m	Gisela s Dancer	5	128	3:14.59	Sep. 18, 1993
Abt.1-15/16	Woodtie	5	122	3:19	Oct. 8, 1989

Leading Jockey in 2004: Lonnie Meche, 158 wins

Leading Trainer in 2004: Cole Norman, 111 wins

Record attendance: 26,513, May 26, 86. Record handle: $4,371,781, September 27, 1987; $6,773,009, September 20, 2003, all sources.

MARQUIS DOWNS RACECOURSE

Box 6010, Saskatoon, Sask, CAN S7K 4E4
(306) 931-7149 Fax: (306) 931-7886
Web Site: www.saskatoonex.com

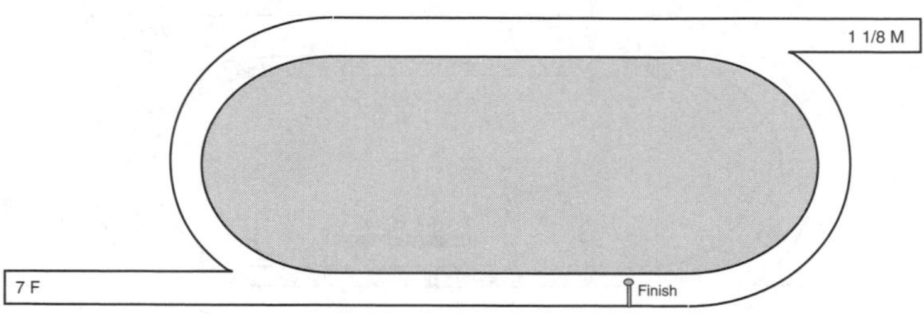

Five-eighths mile oval, 7-furlong and 1 1/8-mile chutes. Distance from last turn to finish 660 feet; width 90 feet. Stable accommodations for 750. Seating capacity 3,027.

Opened August 18, 1969 and runs a mixed breed meet on weekends throughout the summer with (with approximately 200 total Thoroughbred races) for a daily average of about $22,000 per day in purses. 2005 dates: May 27 through Sept. 17.

TRACK RECORDS

3-1/2 furs.	Kid Dynamo	2	120	:40-2/5	Jun. 20, 1977	1 mile	Three for You	5	124	1:37-1/5	Jun. 12, 1981
Abt.4 furs.	Royal Alibi	9	124	:45-1/5	May 20, 1978	1-1/16 m	Little Bo	4		1:42.00	Sep. 1, 1984
4 furs.	Zizzilin	4	116	:45	May 8, 1981	Abt 1-1/8	Easy Riser	4	119	1:49-2/5	Aug. 25, 1980
5-1/2 furs.	Mickey s Mark	5	124	1:04-2/5	Jul. 28, 1980	1-1/8 m	Zance	6	124	1:49-3/5	Oct. 10, 1988
6 furs.	Shotgun Annie	6	119	1:10-2/5	Aug. 7, 1981	1-5/16m	Extrapolate	6	118	2:13	Aug. 29, 1993
Abt.6-1/2 f	Shona Rae	5	120	1:17-4/5	Jun. 11, 1992	1-3/8 m	Secret Cipher	4	127	2:18	Oct. 15, 1983
6-1/2 furs.	Christmas Country	4	124	1:18-3/5	Aug. 1, 1994	Abt.1-1/2 m	Spring Sunsation	3	115	2:35	Sep. 26, 1993
Abt.7 furs.	Graceful Klinchit	5	122	1:23-3/5	Aug. 31, 1991	1-5/8 m	Bright Bern	4	115	2:48	Jul. 31, 1976
7 furs.	Party in the Park	4	121	1:25.35	Aug. 6, 2004	1-3/4 m	Lloyd s Admiral	5	122	3:01-2/5	Oct. 19, 1986

Leading Jockey in 2004: Serge R. Rocheleau, 56 wins
Leading Trainers in 2004: Hubert Pilon and Don Bjarnarson, 19 wins (tie)

THE MEADOWLANDS

New Jersey Sports & Exposition Authority

President & Chief Executive Officer: George R. Zoffinger; Senior Vice President/Racing: Dennis O. Dowd; Vice President/Racing Operations: Christopher McErlean; Racing Secretary: Mike Dempsey; Director of Media Relations: Carol Hodes.

Meadowlands Racetrack, 50 Route 120, East Rutherford, New Jersey 07073
(201) 935-8500; (201) 843-2446; Fax:(201) 460-4244
Media/Public Relations, (201) 460-4050. Free scratches & results: (201) 843-2446
E-mail: cmcerlean@njsea.com; Web Site: www.thebigm.com
Nearest Airport: Newark International, 10 miles from track

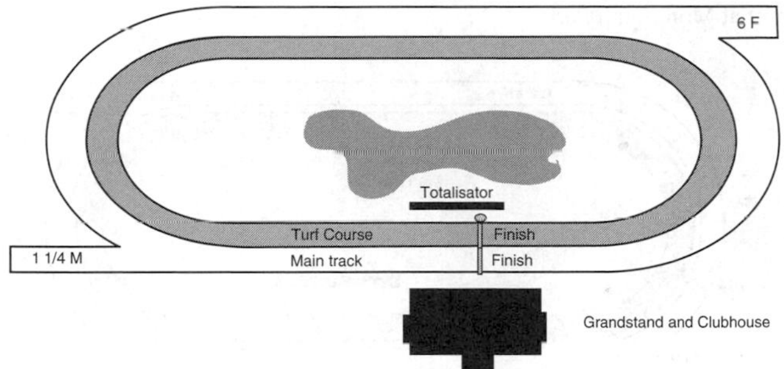

Track Data: One-mile oval, limestone screening and loam with 6-furlong and 1 1/4-mile chutes. Distance from last turn to finish line 990 feet. Width of homestretch , 90 feet; backstretch, 80 feet. Turf course: 7 furlongs. Stable accommodations for 1,760 horses. Seating capacity 6,000; parking for 20,000 cars.

The Meadowlands Racetrack debuted its first nighttime thoroughbred meet on Sept. 6, 1977, a year after the track opened for business in the Meadowlands Sports Complex, eight miles from Manhattan and across a parking lot from the home field for a pair of NFL franchises, the Giants and the Jets. The 2004 meet, 32 programs from Oct. 8 through Nov. 13, featured the track's signature stakes, the $500,000, Grade 2 Meadowlands Breeders' Cup which was won by the Anstu Stable's Balto Star by half-length over 6-5 favorite Dynever. Purses for the short but sweet meet averaged $290,000. New Jersey Account Wagering began on Oct. 28, 2004.

TRACK RECORDS

5 furs.	Stu s Choice	3	119	:55-4/5	Sep. 6, 1996	1-1/16 m	Black Forest	4	113	1:40.39	Sep. 26, 1998
5-1/2 furs.	Red Hot Spot	4	122	1:02.33	Oct. 14, 2003	1-1/8 m	Forty One Carats	3	120	1:45-2/5	Oct. 29, 1999
6 furs.	Sweet Beast	4	122	1:07-4/5	Nov. 18, 1994	1-3/16 m	Key Lory	5	117	1:53-4/5	Nov. 20, 1999
	Purple Peopleater	8	119	1:07-4/5	Sep. 24, 1999		With Anticipation	5	119	1;53-4/5	Nov. 18, 2000
1 mile:	On The Tour	4	116	1:34-2/5	Nov. 10, 1999	1-1/4 m	Alysheba	4	127	1:58-4/5	Oct. 14, 1988
1 m 70 yds	Schedule	3	115	1:37.90	Oct. 15, 2004						

Turf Course

5 furs.	Special Occasion	6	117	:55.17	Sep. 4, 2000	Abt. 1-70y	Pyrite Search			1:44.01	Oct. 24, 2002
Abt. 5 furs.	Tangier Sound			:59.05	Nov. 4, 2002	1-1/16 m	Wanderkin	5	118	1:39-2/5	Sep. 30, 1988
1 mile	Beckon the King	5	113	1:33.88	Oct. 19, 2001	1-3/8 m	Rice	6	126	2:12.00	Sep. 25, 1998
Abt. 1 mile	Onasilverplatter	4	119	1:38.96	Oct. 23, 2002						
1 m 70 yds	Cape Playhouse	3	115	1:38	Oct. 25, 1978						

Jumps

2 miles	Romeo Lima	4	140	3:43-3/5	Sep. 23, 1980

Leading Jockey in 2004: Stewart Elliott, 37 wins
Leading Trainer in 2004: Patricia Farro, 11 wins
Record attendance: 44, 462, September 16, 1981. Record handle: $5,025,645 October 14, 1994

MONMOUTH PARK

New Jersey Sports and Exposition Authority

President & Chief Executive Officer: George Zoffinger.; Senior Executive Vice President/Racing: Bruce Garland; Vice President/Thoroughbred Racing: Robert J. Kulina; Racing Secretary: Mike Dempsey; Marketing and Media Manager: Bill Knauf.

Monmouth Park, 175 Oceanport Avenue, Oceanport, New Jersey 07757
(732) 222-5100; Fax: (732) 571-8658
Free scratches & results: (732) 222-2917
Web Site: www.monmouthpark.com

Nearest Airport: Monmouth County Airport, 12 miles from track; Newark International Airport, 40 miles from track; private heliport at Monmouth Park.

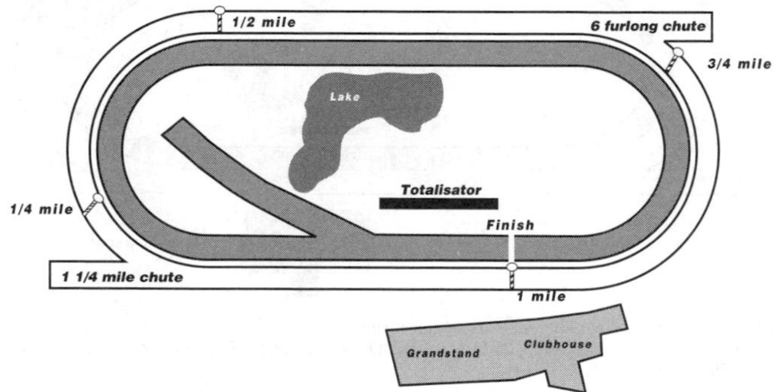

Track Data: One-mile oval, with six-furlong and 1 1/4-mile chutes. Distance from last turn to finish 985 feet; width in stretch 100 feet; backstretch 90 feet. Turf course, 7 furlongs; 90 feet wide, with diagonal chute. Steeplechase racing on turf course. Stable accommodations for 1,550. Seating capacity 18,000. Parking for 14,000.

Opened July 4, 1870 in nearby Long Branch, New Jersey. After being closed for five decades approaching the turn of the century due to state wide anti-gambling legislation, Monmouth was rebuilt in 1946 at its present location in Oceanport, where it has conducted summer racing every year since. In 2004, Monmouth Park had an 87-day meet with purses pegged at almost $345,000 per day, including stakes. The 2005 meet is set for May 14 through Sept. 25.

TRACK RECORDS

5 furs.	L.B. on Tour	4	120	:56.16	Aug. 21, 1999
5-1/2 furs.	American Royale	2	115	1:02.96	Jul. 21, 1991
6 furs.	Gilded Time	2	122	1:07.84	Aug. 8, 1992
1 mile	Forty Niner	3	114	1:33-4/5	Jul. 16, 1988
1 m 70 yds	Presidentialaffair	5	115	1:38.85	Jul. 5, 2004
1-1/16 m	Formal Gold	4	121	1:40.20	Aug. 23, 1997
1-1/8 m	Spend A Buck	3	118	1:46-4/5	Aug. 17, 1985
	Jolie s Halo	5	116	1:46-4/5	Aug. 8, 1992
1-1/4 m	Carry Back	4	124	2:00-2/5	Jul. 14, 1962
	Majestic Light	4	124	2:00-2/5	Aug.30, 1977
1-1/2 m	Chappys Joy	6	112	2:34-1/5	Aug. 5, 1989

Turf Course (On Hedge – Exact Distances)

5 furs.	Klassy Briefcase	6	115	:54.97	Jun. 8, 1991
1 mile	Inkatha	7	114	1:33.95	May 31, 1999
1-1/16 m	Mi Narrow	5	113	1:39.40	Jul. 11, 1999
1-1/8 m	Batique	5	113	1:46.19	Jun. 16, 2001
1-3/16 m	Doreinne	5	105	2:01	Jun. 30, 1953
1-1/4 m	Muzzle	7	122	2:08-2/5	Jul. 10, 1953
1-3/8 m	Balto Star	5	117	2:12.78	Jul. 5, 2003

Turf Course (On Hedge – Exact Distances – Chute)

1-1/16 m	Double Booked	4	117	1:41-1/5	Jul.3, 1989

Jumps

2 miles	Summer Colony	5	151	3:33-3/5	Jun.22, 1988
2-1/4 m	Ninepins	5	148	4:13.92	Sep. 7, 1992

Leading Jockey in 2004: Joe Bravo, 96 wins

Leading Trainer in 2004: Timothy A. Hills, 36 wins

Record attendance: 53,638, August 3, 2003. Record handle: $12,536,345, August 5, 2003

MOUNTAINEER RACE TRACK & GAMING RESORT

MTR Gaming, Inc.
President & CEO: Edson Arneault.
PO Box 358, Chester, WV 26034; (800) 804-0468 Fax: (304) 387-8303
E-Mail Address: info@mtrgaming.com; Web Site: www.mtrgaming.com

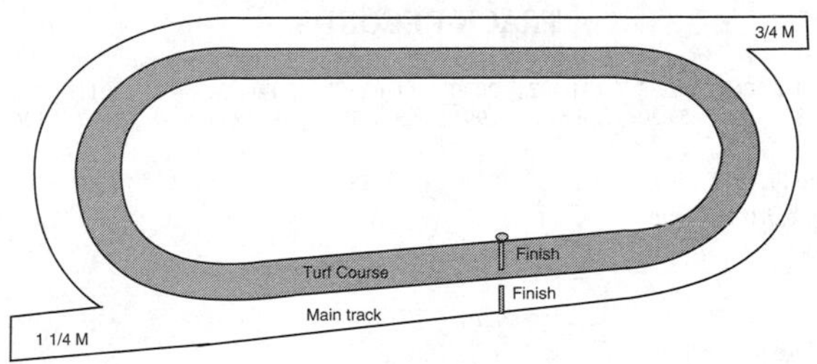

Track data: One-mile oval, with six-furlong and 1 1/4-mile chutes. Distance from last turn to finish 905.31 feet; width, 80 feet. Turf course: 7 furlongs. Stable accommodations for 1,234. Seating capacity 7,400.

Opened as Waterford Park May 19, 1951 when operated by the Charles Town Jockey Club. Renamed Mountaineer Park in 1987 and was a relatively obscure racing venue until slots were legalized in 1993. Live racing five nights a week now is conducted from January to December with extensive simulcasting and 3,220 slot machines on the premises that have boosted purses to over $171,000 per day. Home of the Grade 3, $600,000 West Virginia Derby, the state's only graded stakes.

TRACK RECORDS

2 furs.	Promised Cruise	6	120	:21.00	Jun. 23, 1990	1-1/8 m	Soto	3	111	1:46.29	Aug. 9, 2003
4-1/2 furs.	Ameri Brilliance	5	118	:50.16	Aug. 7, 2004	1-3/16 m	Game Bird	7	115	1:56.66	May 17, 2003
5 furs.	Mayor Steve	8	115	:55.92	Aug. 31, 2003	Abt.1-1/4 m	Grain	5	119	2:08	May 29, 1974
5-1/2 furs.	The Dancer	4	121	1:02.24	Dec. 29, 2000	1-1/4 m	Georgie Porgie	4	114	2:03.3	Aug. 6, 1995
6 furs.	Hustler	6	113	1:07.81	Aug. 11, 2001	1-1/2 m	Pete s Skianno	4	115	2:31.43	Jun. 10, 2000
Abt.1 mile	Mr. Pantop	4	116	1:36.20	Jun. 26, 1970	1-5/8 m	Prince Swivel	7	119	2:45	Sep. 8, 1973
1 mile	Find The Mine	5	114	1:33.86	Jul. 4, 2000	1-3/4 m	Chased Again	9	115	2:58.4	Jul. 18, 1959
1 m 40 yds.	Ski Sez	5	115	1:39.4	Mar. 9, 1996	Abt. 2 miles	Dark Ajax	7	119	3:27.4	Jun. 9, 1973
1 m 70 yds.	Mort	4	121	1:38.81	Apr. 1, 2000	2 miles	Pleasant Company	4	121	3:30.57	Sep. 1, 2003
1-1/16 m	Be Like Mike	4	110	1:41.15	Aug. 9, 2003	2-1/16 m	Sovereign M.D.	7	121	3:28.40	Dec. 30, 2000

Turf Course

4-1/2 furs.	Cake N Steak	8	118	:50	Aug. 9, 1993	Abt.1-1/16 m	Black Eye	4	119	1:40.1	Jun. 28, 1958
Abt. 5 furs.	Skindles Hotel	6	111	:55.1	Jul. 26, 1960	Abt.1-1/4 m	King Haigler	5	120	2:09.3	Jul. 4, 1983
5 furs.	Fina Dur	5	121	:55.52	Sep. 6, 1999	Abt. 1-5/16 m	Ruff Mack	5	114	2:06	Aug. 25, 1962
7 furs.	On to Richmond	4	121	1:21.40	Jun. 16, 2002	1-3/8 m	Sunset Party	5	113	2:13.23	Sep. 26, 1999
7-1/2 furs.	Magical Madness	5	115	1:27.48	May 27, 2002	Abt. 1-1/2 m	Revenooer	7	116	2:29	Jul. 4, 1959
1 mile	La Reine s Terms			1:33.49	Sep. 2, 2002	1-1/2 m	Guild Hall	5	135	2:33.1	Jun. 20, 1969
1 m 70 yds.	Fast And Friendly	8	121	1:43	Sep. 7, 1964	1-3/4 m	Pleasant Company	5	113	2:55.11	Aug. 15, 2004
	Poteau	7	120	1:43	Jul. 25, 1982	1-7/8 m	Code s Best	6	121	3:08.23	Sep. 4, 2000

Leading Jockeys in 2004: Dana G. Whitney won three of four meets and Deshawn L. Parker won the remaining meet
Leading Trainers in 2004: Dale R. Baird won three of four meets and Scooter Davis won the remaining meet
Record attendance: 17,934, – August 10, 2002. Record Handle: $2,513,911 – August 9, 2003

MOUNT PLEASANT MEADOWS

PO Box 220, Mt. Pleasant, MI 48858
(989) 773-0012

A mixed breed meet of 28 days spread out between May 1 and Sept. 26 in 2004, with a total of 42 Thoroughbred races. 2005 dates: May 7 through Sept. 25.

TRACK RECORDS

4 furs.	Bad Boy Eric			:48.35	Aug. 25, 2001	5-1/2 furs.	Comedy Routine	7		1:05.40	Jul. 31, 1994
4-1/2 furs.	Wildcat Express	4	126	:52.35	May 21, 2000	6 furs.	Tate Express	11	126	1:13.78	Jun. 7, 2003
5 furs.	My Friend Charlie	8		:59.30	Jun. 29, 1991	1m 70 yds	Halover	7	126	1:51.61	Jul. 6, 2003

Leading Jockey in 2004: Julie Fritz, 8 wins
Leading Trainer in 2004: Reid Gross, 7 wins

NORTHAMPTON FAIR

Hampshire, Franklin & Hampden Agricultural Society
PO Box 305, Northampton, MA 01061-0305
(413) 584-2237 Fax: (413) 648-5214

Track Data: Half-mile oval with banked turns. Distance from last turn to finish 431 feet; width, 50 feet. Stable accommodations for 450. Seating capacity 13,000.

Opened September 1943 and annually conducts a nine- or 10-day late summer meet in the Berkshire region of western Massachussetts. 2005 dates: Sept. 2 through Sept. 18; in 2004, purses averaged approximately $26,000 per day.

TRACK RECORDS

Abt.5 furs.	Sweetest Music	6	117	:54-4/5	Sep. 2, 1957	Abt.1-1/8 m	Congress Inn	6	119	1:49-1/5	Sep. 10, 1966
Abt.6-1/2 F	Northern Puppy	4	122	1:20-3/5	Sep. 8, 1992	Abt.1-5/8 m	Boss Man Jarett	10	122	2:46.18	Sep. 13, 1999

Leading Jockeys in 2004: Edgar Paucar and Willie Belmonte, 16 wins (tie)

Leading Trainer in 2004: Samuel J. Keyrouze, 8 wins

Record attendance: 30,000 (estimated), September 4, 1972. Record handle to come.

NORTHLANDS PARK

Northlands Park
General Manager: Les Butler; Racing Secretary: Fred Hilts; Marketing and Communications Manager: Stephanie Gosselin; Communications Coordinator: Jonathan Huntington.
PO Box 1480, Edmonton, Alb, CAN T5J 2N5
(780) 471-7210 Fax: (780) 471-8195
E-Mail: info@northlands.com; Web Site: www.northlands.com

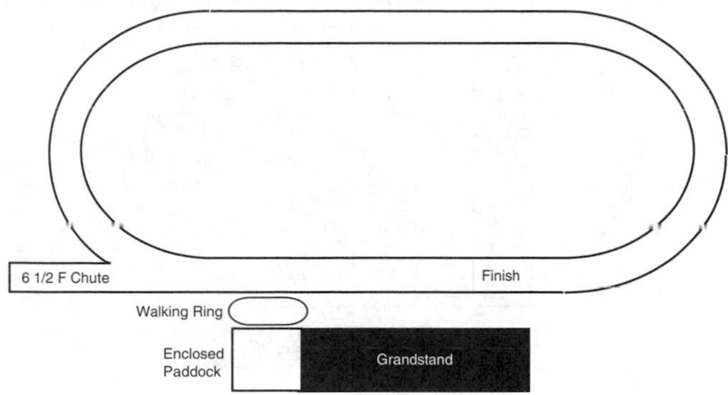

Track data: Five-eighths mile oval with 6 1/2-furlong chute. Distance from last turn to finish 625 feet; width 70 feet. Stable accommodations for 1,100. Seating capacity 9,000.

Opened July 1925 as Edmonton Racetrack, renamed Northlands Park in January 1964. Live racing from June through October, plus extensive simulcasting. In 2004, the 72-day meet averaged purses of over $120,000. 2005 dates: June 24 through Oct. 29.

TRACK RECORDS

3-1/2 furs.	Steel Penny Black	2	115	:38-1/5	Jun. 14, 1984	1-1/16 m	Chilcoton Blaze	4	119	1:42-3/5	Aug. 4, 1984
5-1/2 furs.	So Long Fellas	5	115	1:04-2/5	Aug. 16, 1975	1-1/4 m	Arctic Laur	7	116	2:09	Aug. 20, 1995
6 furs.	Lynn s Dream	4	115	1:09.80	Jul. 8, 2000	1-3/8 m	Slyly Gifted	3	126	2:15-4/5	Aug. 30, 1986
6-1/2 furs.	Timely Ruckus			1:15-2/5	Jun. 26, 1999	1-5/8 m	Dancers Nugget	6	117	2:45.20	Sep. 21, 2001
1 mile	Bagfull	5	115	1:35-4/5	May 16, 1981						

Leading Jockey in 2004: Quincy Welch, 108 wins

Leading Trainer in 2004: Ron K. Smith, 39 wins

Record attendance: 15, 922, August 25, 1973; Record handle: $1,652, 940, August 16, 1990.

OAKLAWN PARK

Oaklawn Jockey Club

President: Charles J. Cella; General Manager: R. Eric Jackson; Racing Secretary: Patrick J. Pope; Media Relations Director: Terry Wallace; Director of Wagering and Simulcast: Bobby Geiger.

Street Address: 2705 Central Avenue
Hot Springs, Arkansas 71902

Mailing Address: P.O. Box 699, Hot Springs, Arkansas 71902
(501) 623-4411 or (800) 625-5296; Fax: (501) 624-4950
E-mail: winning@oaklawn.com; Web Site: www.oaklawn.com

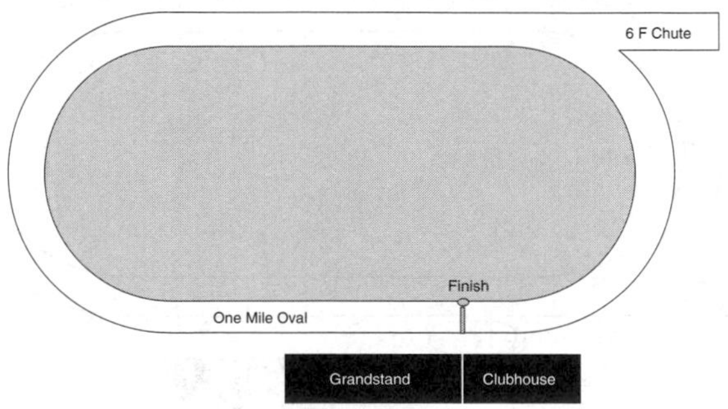

Track Data: One-mile sandy loam oval. Distance from last turn to finish, 1,155 feet; Width, 70 feet on straightaways, 80 feet on turns; Stable accommodations for 1,600. Seating capacity 26,200; Parking for 5,000 cars.

Built in 1904 and opened February 15, 1905, Oaklawn remains the number one tourist attraction in Arkansas. Purses in 2004 exceeded $238,000 per day. The January - April meet annually concludes with the famed Racing Festival of the South, with over $2.6 million in purses for stakes events over a period of one week. Oaklawn offers three major products while it is open 12 months of the year. In addition to the live racing season, the simulcast season runs from May through January. Oaklawn also offers Instant Racing, the innovative pari-mutuel electronic gaming system, which has provided over $1 million in purses since it was introduced in 2000.

TRACK RECORDS

4 furs.	Crimson Saint	2	119	:44-4/5	Apr. 1, 1971	1-1/16 m	Heatherten	5	116	1:40-1/5	Apr. 18, 1984
5 furs.	Miss Brendy	3	107	:57-3/5	Feb. 22, 1966	1-1/8 m	Snow Chief	4	123	1:46-3/5	Apr. 17, 1987
5-1/2 furs.	Sis Pleasure Fager	4	115	1:02-3/5	Feb. 15, 1984	1-3/16 m	Brassy	5	112	1:57-2/5	Mar. 29, 1952
6 furs.	Karen s Tom	3	120	1:07-4/5	Apr. 16, 1990	1-1/2 m	Dapper	6	111	2:31-3/5	Mar. 30, 1957
1 mile	Whitebrush	3	119	1:34-2/5	Mar. 10, 1984	1-3/4 m	Flag Carrier	4	116	2:58	Apr. 18, 1987
1 m 70 yds	Win Stat	7	112	1:38-2/5	Mar. 7, 1984						

Leading Jockey in 2004: John McKee, 71 wins
Leading Trainer in 2004: Cole Norman, 56 wins
Record attendance: 71,203, April 19, 1986. Record handle: $15,133,537, April 15, 2000

OCALA TRAINING CENTER

TRACK RECORDS

5 furs.	Hana Highway	5	122	:56.40	Mar. 17, 2003
6 furs.	Lucky Livi	3		1:09.00	Mar. 20, 2000
1-1/16 m	The Name s Bond	3	122	1:44.20	Mar. 17, 2003

Leading Jockey in 2004: Edgar S. Prado, 2 wins
Leading Trainer in 2004: No trainer won more than one race

PENN NATIONAL RACE COURSE

Penn National Gaming Inc.
Chairman of the Board, President: Peter M. Carlino; General Manager: Richard T. Schnaars; Director of Publicity: Frederick D. Lipkin.

Street Address: Interstate 81, Exit 80
Grantville, Pennsylvania 17028
Nearest Airport: Harrisburg International,
15 miles from the track

P.O. Box 32, Grantville, Pennsylvania 17028
(717) 469-2211; Fax: (717) 469-2910. (717) 469 0921
E-Mail Address: fred.lipkin@pngaming.com
Web Site: www.pnrc.com

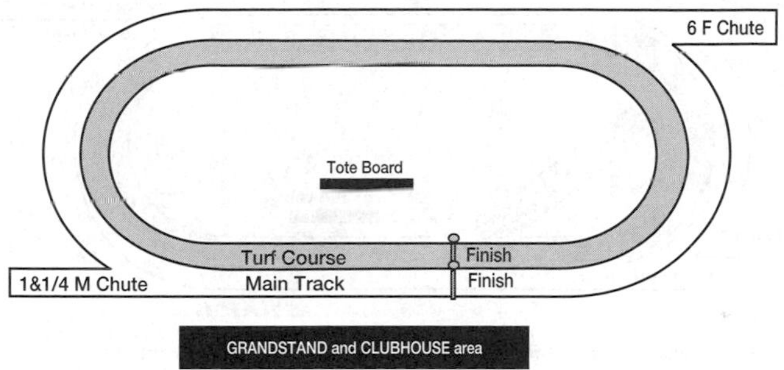

Track Data: One mile, sandy loam with 1/4-mile and 3/4-mile chutes. Distance from last turn to finish, 990 feet. Turf course: 7-furlongs. Stable accommodations, 1,200 horses. Seating capacity: 9,570, Parking for 5,000 cars.

Opened August 30, 1972, Penn National is located 12 1/2 miles Northeast of the Pennsylvania state capital of Harrisburg, Pa. In recent years, including 2004, Penn National has operated approximately 200 days from January to December with purses in 2004 averaging more than $71,000 per day. But that is only a small part of the picture. In 1982, Penn National Gaming Inc. inaugurated telephone account wagering and soon afterward introduced cable television broadcasts of its races throughout the state. In the early 1990's the parent, public company was formed (Penn National Gaming, Inc.) and began to operate several OTB sites in Pennsylvania while expanding its horizons to own and operate Charles Town racetrack in West Virginia, Pocono Downs in eastern Pennsylvania, and other racing related enterprises and casinos in other states.

TRACK RECORDS

2 furs.	Pensglitter	7	119	:20.71	Oct. 9, 2004	1 m 70yds	Wee Thunder	6	115	1:39-3/5	Jul. 13, 1996
4 furs.	Gross	2	118	:46-1/5	Apr. 13, 1973	1-1/16 m	A Letter To Harry	4	117	1:41-1/5	Sep. 10, 1978
4-1/2 furs.	Rita's Best			:50.67	Apr. 27, 2001	1-1/8 m	Collection Agent	4	121	1:49-4/5	Aug. 22, 1987
5 furs.	On The Phone	4	117	:56-3/5	Jul. 13, 1996	1-3/16 m	Bar Tab	8	114	1:55-2/5	Oct. 14, 1972
5-1/2 furs.	Cortan	4	113	1:03-1/5	May 29, 1978	1-1/4 m	Adda Nickell	4	122	2:03-3/5	Oct. 30, 1976
	Flaming Emperor				Jun. 26, 1994	1-1/2 m	Holly Holme	5	118	2:31-2/5	Sep. 29, 1973
	Hunter s Ridge				May 1, 1996	1-5/8m	New Episode	8	119	2:48.15	May 18, 2001
6 furs.	Holiday Music			1:08.89*	May 4, 2002	1-3/4 m	Chasqui	7	119	3:00	Jun. 21, 1980
1 mile	Vambourine	5	122	1:36 1/5	Jun. 12, 1977	2 miles	Finny Flyer	6	111	3:28	May 25, 1974
	Agate Bay				Mar 22, 1981						

Turf Course

5 furs.	Bop	5	121	:54.61	Aug. 3, 2002	1-1/16 m	Told	4	123	1:38	Sep. 14, 1980
1 mile	The Very One	4	110	1:33-1/5	Jul. 15, 1979	1-1/2 m	Coalitioncandidate	5	113	2:27	May 27, 1991
1 m 70yds	Aborigine	6	119	1:37-1/5	Aug. 20, 1978						

Leading Jockeys in 2004: William P. Otero & Thomas Clifton, 166 wins (tie)
Leading Trainer in 2004: Bruce M. Kravets, 145 wins
Record attendance: 15, 442, April 19,1986. Record handle: $2,173,921, December 26, 1998.

PHILADELPHIA PARK

Greenwood Racing

Chief Executive Officer: Harold G. Handel; Director of Phonebet: Kimberly Smith; Director of Racing and Racing Secretary: Sal Sinatra; Simulcast Director: Geri Mercer; Director of Public Relations: Keith Jones.

Street Address: 3001 Street Road
Bensalem, Pennsylvania 19020
Nearest Airports: Philadelphia Int l. 16 miles;
Northeast (private) 3 miles

P.O. Box 1000, Bensalem, Pennsylvania 19020-2096
(215) 639-9000; Fax: (215) 639-0337
E-Mail: hhandel@philadelphiapark.com
Web-Site: www.philadelphiapark.com

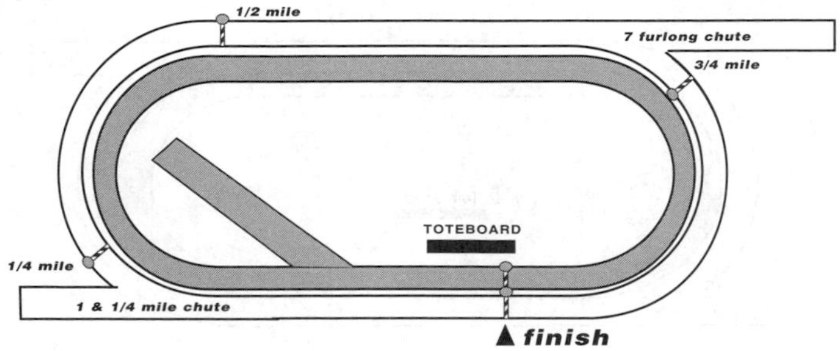

Track Data: One mile, sand, clay and loam, with 7-furlong and 1 1/4-mile chutes. Distance from last turn to finish, 974 feet. Width, 80 ft. Turf Course: 7/8 of a mile oval with 1 & 1/8 mile chute. 1,400 stalls. Seating capacity: 8,400; Parking for 5,500.

Opened November 4, 1974, as Keystone Racetrack, changed name in 1984 when acquired by Robert Brennan, owner at the time of newly rebuilt Garden State Park, who was forced out of the racing business in 1990 due to several failed racing related investments. Acquired by present owners Greenwood Racing, a British-based bookmaking operation which has upgraded the facility and stabilized its financial standing. In 2004, Philadelphia Park operated a total of 216 racing days, from January through December, with daily average purses in excess of $131,000 per day including stakes. Like Penn National Gaming, Philadelphia Park operates its own off-track betting parlors in Pennsylvania and telephone wagering accounts.

TRACK RECORDS

2 furs.	Queen Millie	7	116	:21.32	Jan. 30, 1994	1-1/4 m	It s Always Archie	5	116	2:02	Nov. 23, 1974
4 furs.	Heres A Tip	2	120	:45	Jun. 11, 1982	1-1/2 m	Laugh a Minute	6	117	2:31	Jan. 4, 1992
4-1/2 furs.	Distinctive Hat	4	114	:51.48	May 2, 1994	1-9/16 m	Laugh a Minute	6	122	2:40.85	Jan. 18, 1992
5 furs.	My Favorite Grub	5	119	:56.06	Sep. 7, 1998	1-5/8 m	River Wolf	4	120	2:46-2/5	Oct. 13, 1990
5-1/2 furs.	Saint Verre	2	118	1:02.65	Jul. 17, 2000	1-11/16 m	Laugh a Minute	5	112	2:53-1/5	Dec. 21, 1991
6 furs.	Iron Punch	6	114	1:07.89	Jul. 29, 2000	1-3/4 m	Johnny s Silencer	3	109	2:57-4/5	Dec. 17, 1988
6-1/2 furs.	Tricky Mister	4	117	1:14.40	Jun. 21, 1998	1-13/16 m	Fire North	6	111	3:04-4/5	Mar. 14, 1992
7 furs.	Flaming Bridle	4	119	1:20.61	Sep. 28, 1999	1-7/8 m	Haberdasher	5	116	3:13-3/5	Oct. 17, 1987
1 mile	Regal Count	3	116	1:34-4/5	Dec. 5, 1985	2 miles	Perfect To A Tee	4	120	3:25.87	Sep. 2, 1996
1 m 70 yds	Tragedy	4	114	1:38.70	Dec. 12, 1995	2-1/8 m	Heavy Medal Man	5	114	3:39.59	Apr. 25, 1992
1-1/16 m	Cool Spring Park	3	109	1:40-4/5	Nov. 4, 1974	2-1/4 m	Transfer Ticket	4	111	3:56	Dec. 31, 1988
1-1/8 m	Selari Spirit	4	116	1:47	Nov. 30, 1974	2-1/2 m	Half Chance	5	111	4:24.15	May 25, 1992
1-3/16 m	Southern Shade	5	113	1:56-2/5	Oct. 20, 1984						

Turf Course

Abt.5 furs.	Sport d Hiver	9	120	:56.61	Aug. 26, 2001	1-1/16 m	Whatever For	4	117	1:40-2/5	Jun. 22, 1986
5 furs.	Lou s Bucks	4	117	:56.07	Sep. 20, 1998	Abt 1-1/8 m	Brenton Reef	7	114	1:50-1/5	Aug. 6, 1989
Abt.7-1/2 f	Mount Bleu	3	109	1:33.73	Aug. 27, 1994	1-1/8 m	Whatever For	4	113	1:46-1/5	Sep. 1, 1986
7-1/2 furs.	Here Comes Scott	4	116	1:30.85	Sep. 10, 1994	Abt.1-3/8 m	Quality Affirmed	8	120	2:18.89	Jul. 30, 2002
Abt.1 mile	Speak Compelling	3	107	1:39.77	Jul. 24, 2000	1-3/8 m	Juanca	8	117	2:16-2/5	Sep. 1, 1986
1 mile	Lake Cecebe	3	111	1:35-3/5	Jun. 28, 1986	Abt 1-1/2 m	Mort the Sport	4	118	2:31	Aug. 22, 1989
Abt.1m70yds	Vin Rouge	5	112	1:41.38	Jul. 17, 1994	1-1/2 m	Lord Zada	7	115	2:28.38	Jun. 10, 2000
1 m 70 yds	Rolfe s Ruby	6	122	1:39-2/5	Jun. 21, 1986	Abt 2 miles	Proctor s Image	5	114	3:27-2/5	Oct. 15, 1988
	Marlish	4	116	1:39-2/5	Aug. 13, 1986	2 miles	Chippenham Park	4	113	3:28-4/5	Sep. 1, 1990
Abt.1-1/16m	Mount Bleu	3	108	1:43.26	Oct. 4, 1994						

Jumps

2-1/16 m	Frecuente	5	154	3:41.15	Oct. 12, 2003

Leading Jockey in 2004, Winter-Spring meet: Stewart Elliot, 106 wins
Leading Trainer in 2004, Winter-Spring meet: Scott A. Lake, 65 wins
Leading Jockey in 2004, Summer-Fall-Winter meet: Anthony S. Black, 109 wins
Leading Trainer in 2004, Summer-Fall-Winter meet: Scott A. Lake, 71 wins

PIMLICO

Magna Entertaiment Corp.

Chairman of the Board: Frank Stronach; President and CEO: Joseph A. De Francis; COO: Lou Raffetto; Executive Vice President: Karin M. De Francis; Executive Vice President of Racing Operations: James L. Gagliano; Racing Secretary: Georganne Hale; Director Broadcast Communications: Mike Gathagan.

Street Address: Hayward and Winner Avenues, Baltimore, MD 21215
Nearest Airport, BWIA, 12 miles south on Washington Baltimore Parkway.

Maryland Jockey Club, Pimlico Race Course
Baltimore, Maryland 21215
Telephone: (410) 542-9400; Fax: (410) 466-2521
Media Relations: (410) 466-5622
Free Results and scratches: (410) 792-0278 and (301) 470-3056
E-mail: webmaster@marylandracing.com Web Site: www.marylandracing.com

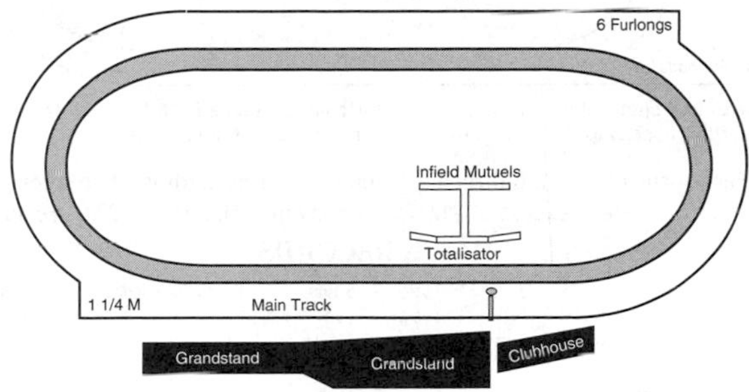

Track Data: One-mile oval with 6-furlong and 1 1/4-mile chutes. Distance from last turn to finish, 1,162 feet, 70 feet wide. Turf course: 7 furlongs. Stable accommodations for 794. Seating capacity: 25,000; total capacity 125,000 with infield on Preakness Day. Parking for 8,000 cars with many private lots in neighborhood. All seats reserved on Preakness Day, mail orders recommended.

Opened October 25, 1870, in Baltimore by the Maryland Jockey Club that was formed in May 1743, in Annapolis, Maryland. The MJC is the nation's oldest sporting organization and Pimlico is the second-oldest track in the United States. Home of the Grade 1 Preakness Stakes, the middle jewel in the Triple Crown, and the Grade 1 Pimlico Special. In 2004, purses during the spring meet averaged over $223,000.

TRACK RECORDS

Distance	Horse	Age	Wt.	Time	Date
4-1/2 furs.	Countess Diana	2	119	:51.50	Jun. 6, 1997
5 furs.	Kingmaker	4	119	:56.46	Sep. 27, 2003
5-1/2 furs.	Higher Strata	5	119	1:02.46	Jul. 29, 1995
6 furs.	Northern Wolf	4	120	1:09.00	Aug. 18, 1990
1 Mile	Jun. Grass	4	110	1:37-3/5	May 2, 1923
1 m 70 yds	Sabotage	3	117	1:41-2/5	Dec. 17, 1958
1-1/16 m	Deputed Testamony	4	123	1:40-4/5	May 19, 1984
	Knight s Devotion	3	112	1:40-4/5	Jul.24, 1986
	Finder s Choice	4	115	1:40-4/5	May 6, 1989
1-1/8 m	Private Terms	4	122	1:47-1/5	May 27, 1989
1-3/16 m	Farma Way	4	119	1:52.55	May 11, 1991
1-1/4 m	Manzotti	5	116	2:01-4/5	Mar. 19, 1988
1-3/8 m	Narwhal	5	120	2:16-2/5	Dec. 16, 1962

Turf Course

Distance	Horse	Age	Wt.	Time	Date
5 furs.	Yankee Wildcat	6	119	:55.99	Jun. 4, 2004
1 mile	North East Bound	4	115	1:33.42	May 7, 2000
1-1/16m	Air Attack	6	109	1:40.33	May 27, 1991
1-1/8 m	Mr O Brien	5	119	1:46.34	May 15, 2004
1-1/2 m	Fort Marcy	6	124	2:27-2/5	May 9, 1970
	Uptown Swell	4	117	2:27-2/5	May 10, 1986

Jumps

Distance	Horse	Age	Wt.	Time	Date
2 miles	Age Of Flight	5	146	3:38.52	Jun. 18, 1997

Leading Jockey in 2004 Spring meet: Steve D. Hamilton, 49 wins
Leading Trainer in 2004 Spring meet: Dale Capuano, 25 wins
Leading Jockey in 2004 Fall meet: Ryan Fogelsonger, 83 wins
Leading Trainer in 2004 Fall meet: Dale Capuano, 30 wins

Record attendance: 118,926, May 19, 2001 (Preakness Day). Record handle: $7,357,961 (On track). $71,468,223, May 18, 2002 (all sources)

PLEASANTON

4501 Pleasanton Ave., Pleasanton, CA 94566
(925) 426-7600 Fax: (925) 426-7599
E-Mail Address: info@alamedacountyfair.com; Web Site: www.alamedacountyfair.com

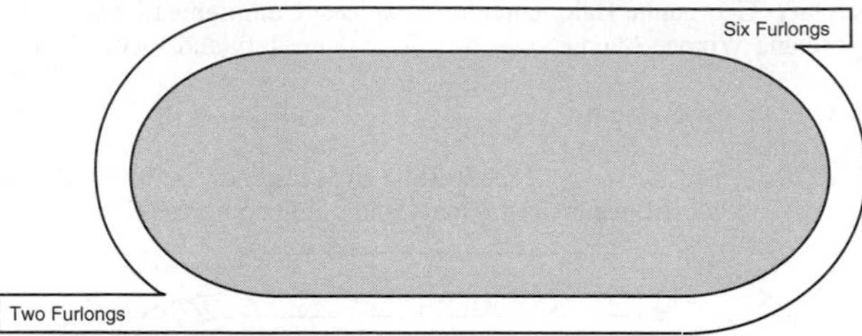

Track data: One-mile oval with two chutes, two furlongs and six furlongs. Distance from last turn to finish, 1085 feet, width 60 feet. Stable accomodations 700; seating capacity 6,808; Parking for 15,000 cars on county fair grounds.

Opened August 10, 1939. Part of the northern California County Fair circuit. Runs a two week mixed breed meet every summer and offered a purse structure in excess of $129,000 per day in 2004. Dates in 2005 are June 29 through July 10.

TRACK RECORDS

4-1/2 furs.	French Invader	3	115	:51-1/5	Jun. 27, 1996		6 furs.	Black Jack Road	8	118	1:08-1/5	Jul. 10, 1993
5 furs.	Wind Water	2	116	:56.20	Jul. 4, 2004		1 m 70 yds	Call It	4	122	1:38.01	Jul. 5, 2003
5-1/2 furs.	Boundary Ridge	4	117	1:02	Jun. 29, 1993		1-1/16 m	Marwood	4	117	1:40.04	Jul. 5, 2004

Leading Jockey in 2004: Russell A. Baze, 10 wins

Leading Trainer in 2004: Jerry Hollendorfer, 6 wins

Record attendance: 21, 334–July 4, 1989; Record handle: $3,464, 612 July 9, 1989 (includes Quarter Horse racing.)

PORTLAND MEADOWS

Magna Entertaiment Corp..

General Manager: Christopher Dragone; Director of Operations and Publicity: Patrick Kerrison.

1001 N. Schmeer Rd., Portland, Oregon 97217
(503) 285-9144; Fax: (503) 286-9763
E-Mail Address: pkerrison@portlandmeadows.com
Web Site: www.portlandmeadows.com

Track data: One-mile oval; with 3/4-mile and 1 1/4-mile chutes. Distance from last turn to finish 990 feet. Seating capacity 6,500.

Opened September 14, 1946, with the first night time racing in America, under direction of William P. Kyne who also built Bay Meadows. Rebuilt in 1971 after a devastating fire, The 'New Portland Meadows, Incorporated' operated the track since from 1991 for 10 years until Magna Entertainment Inc. acquired it in 2001. Live, mixed-breed racing now is the standard with over $29,000 in Thoroughbred purses per day for its annual meet from October through April. 2004-05 dates: Oct. 16 to April 24.

TRACK RECORDS

Distance	Horse	Age	Wt.	Time	Date
4 furs.	Wayne S.	2	120	:47	May 22, 1947
4-1/2 furs.	Star Expresso	7	122	:51.84	Apr. 3, 1999
5 furs.	Pajone s Hostess	5	120	:58	Jan. 6, 1977
	Sweet Shooter	7	120	:58	Jan. 8, 1977
	Bob Seldom Dances	4	120	:58	Dec. 29, 1978
5-1/2 furs.	My Runaway	4	120	1:02-4/5	Jan. 6, 1977
6 furs.	Lethal Grande	4	122	1:09.06	Mar. 30, 2003
1 mile	Star of Kuwait	7	122	1:36-1/5	May 11, 1975
1 m 70yds	Beau Julian	3	120	1:41-1/5	May 14, 1972
1-1/16 m	Me Brave	5	120	1:43-1/5	May 5, 1969
	Rockey s Crest	5		1:43-1/5	May 24, 1969
	Pancheta s Will	5	123	1:43-1/5	May 22, 1977
1-1/8 m	Hannibal Khal	4	119	1:48-4/5	Dec. 30, 1978
1-3/16 m	Kitsap Kid	6	121	1:58-2/5	Apr. 27, 1968
1-1/4 m	True Enough	8	122	2:03.12	Apr. 9, 1994
1-1/2 m	Martins Lemon	4	116	2:32	May 13, 1973
1-3/4-m	Moribana	7	124	2:58-3/5	May 27, 1972
2 miles	Martins Lemon	4	120	3:27-3/5	May 20, 1973

Leading Jockey in 2004: Juan M. Gutierrez, 105 wins
Leading Trainer in 2004: Jim Fergason, 50 wins
Attendance record: 12,635, February 6, 1971

PRAIRIE MEADOWS

Prairie Meadows Racetrack and Casino

President, CEO, and General Manager: Robert Farinella; Director of Racing: Derron Heldt; Racing Secretary, Thoroughbred meeting: Daniel Doocy; Simulcast Coordinator: Mike Jacobsen; Media Communications: Mary Lou Coady.

Street Address: 1 Prairie Meadows Drive,
Altoona, Iowa 50009
Nearest Airports: Des Moines International,
(15 miles from track), Ankeny Aviation,
(private charter, 11 miles from track)

P.O. Box 1000, Altoona, Iowa 50009
(515) 967-1000 or (800) 325-9015
Fax: (515) 967-1344; Media, (515) 967-8247
Fax on Demand: (515) 967-8576; Results Line: (515) 967-8585
E-mail: webmaster@prairiemeadows.com
Web Site: www.prairiemeadows.com

6 Furlongs
2 Furlongs
Finish

Track Data: One-mile oval, 6-furlong and 1 1/4-mile chutes. Distance from last turn to finish 1,033 feet. Stable accommodations for 1400. Seating Capacity: 7,000; Parking for 3,600 cars.

Opened March 1, 1989, and after suffering financial difficulties in the early 1990s, has become one of the most successful tracks in the Midwest, with purses fueled by slots that were legalized in 1995. Two meets involved thoroughbreds in 2004. The 49-day season from April 16 through July 4 offered average daily purses in excess of $173,700 including supplement and breeder awards. Following was a mixed-breed season, 47 days, from July 9 through Sept. 25 offering more than $98,100 in average daily purses plus supplement and breeder awards. Thoroughbred purses during 2004, including supplement and breeder awards, totaled $13,128,097.

TRACK RECORDS

Distance	Horse	Age	Wt.	Time	Date	Distance	Horse	Age	Wt.	Time	Date
2 furs.	Dashboard Drummer	2	117	:22.20	May 9, 2003	1 m 70 yds	Northwest Hill	5	123	1:39.69	Jul. 4, 2003
4 furs.	Straight Fever	2	117	:46-1/5	Jul. 16, 1993	1-1/16 m	Excessivepleasure	3	122	1:40.82	Jul. 5, 2003
4-1/2 furs.	Southern Alert	2	118	:51.24	May 7, 2002	1-1/8 m	Beboppin Baby	5	114	1:46.62	Jul. 4, 1998
5 furs.	Dayjob	5	114	:56	May 1, 1999	1-1/4 m	Famous Event	5	119	2:02-3/5	Jun. 23, 1995
5-1/2 furs.	Leaping Plum	6	122	1:02.50	Aug. 5, 1997	1-1/2 m	Famous Event	5	123	2:32	Jul. 9, 1995
6 furs.	Coach Jimi Lee	4	117	1:07.85	Jul. 4, 2004	1-5/8 m	Sir Star	9	118	2:44-3/5	May 12, 1989
1 mile	Tartine	4	117	1:35.00	Aug. 11, 1998	2 miles	Gritti Marco	6	114	3:26	Jul. 28, 1995

Leading Jockey in 2004 early meet: Timothy T. Doocy, 78 wins
Leading Trainer in 2004 early meet: Dick R. Clark, 52 wins
Leading Jockey in 2004 late meet: Timothy T. Doocy, 54 wins
Leading Trainer in 2004 late meet: Dick R. Clark, 43 wins
Highest Live Handle – On-Track: May 5, 1990 – $488,070 Highest Live Handle – Off-Track: June 2, 1999 – $1,658,931

REMINGTON PARK

Magna Entertrainment Corp.

Chairman: Frank Stronach; President: Corey Johnsen; General Manager: R. D. Logan; Director of Racing and Racing Secretary: Fred Hutton; Director of Media Relations and Marketing: Dale Day.

Nearest Airport: Will Rogers World Airport, 12 miles

One Remington Place, Oklahoma City, Oklahoma 73111
(405) 424-1000; Fax: (405) 425-3297; Press Box (405) 425-3221
Web Site: www.remingtonpark.com

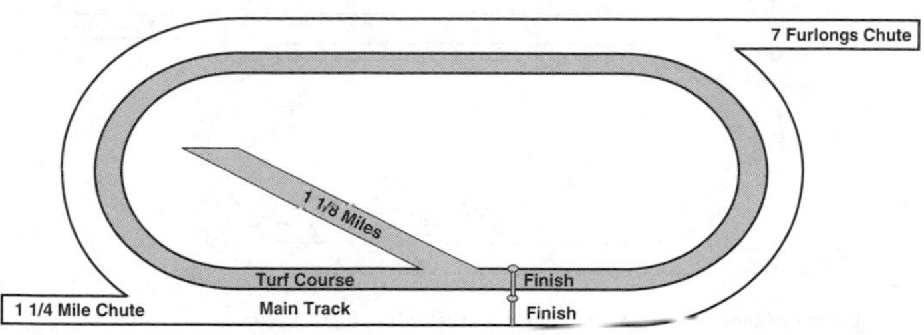

Track Data: One-mile oval, with a seven furlong and a 1 1/4-mile chute that also is used for straightaway, up to 3-furlong mixed-breed racing. Distance from last turn to finish 975 feet. Stable accommodations for 1,340. Seating capacity: 8,300; Capacity 24,000. Parking for 6,000 cars.

Opened Sept. 1, 1988, by the DeBartolo corporation and acquired in 1999 by Magna Entertainment., Inc. Remington Park conducted 65 thoroughbred dates in 2004, with average daily purses of $83,000, as well as 28 days of mixed-breed racing. In 2005, there are 67 days of racing scheduled from Aug. 5 through Nov. 27, with 32 days of mixed-breed racing scheduled for March 19 through June 5.

TRACK RECORDS

3 furs.	Raisable Adversary	11	119	:31.20	Aug. 29, 1999	1 m 70 yds	Marked Tree	3	117	1:39-3/5	Mar. 13, 1993
4-1/2 furs.	Payday Two	8	117	:52.20	Feb. 26, 2000	1-1/16 m	Valid Bonnet	3	123	1:41-1/5	Jul. 26, 1997
5 furs.	Highland Ice	6	122	:57.20	Dec. 3, 1999	1-1/8 m	Classic Cat	3	124	1:48	Aug. 30, 1998
5-1/2 furs.	Run Johnny	5	116	1:02	Sep. 6, 1997	1-3/16 m	Wild Rush	3	121	1:53-3/5	Aug. 10, 1997
6 furs.	Smoke of Ages	5	115	1:08.10	Sep. 29, 1991	1-1/4 m	Double Platinum	4	117	2:03-2/5	Oct. 10, 1999
6-1/2 furs.	Kangaroo King	4	119	1:14.40	Jul. 26, 1997	1-3/8 m	Wild and Comfy	5	117	2:17.96	Oct. 18, 2002
7 furs.	Golden Gear	4	114	1:20-2/5	Mar. 18, 1995	1-1/2 m	Bid the Zeal	4	122	2:31-2/5	Oct. 24, 1998
1 mile	White Wheels	5	116	1:35-2/5	Aug. 17, 1997	2 miles	Saavedra	7	114	3:26-4/5	Dec. 10, 1989

Turf Course

5 furs.	Otro Mambo	8		:55.85	Oct. 5, 2001	1-1/2 m	Cumulus	5	120	2:38.38	Nov. 8, 2004
7-1/2 furs.	Foreign Justice	3	112	1:27.46	Aug. 27, 2004	1-3/8 m	Vergennes	5	114	2:13.15	Sep. 3, 2000
1 mile	No More Hard Times	6	118	1:33.80	Sep. 20, 1992	2 miles	Big Notice	6	119	3:29	Nov. 20, 1993
1-1/16 m	Burbank	4	115	1:39-1/5	Aug. 30, 1997						
1-1/8 m	Major Rhythm	5	116	1:46.22	Sep. 6, 2004						

Leading Jockey in 2004: Quincy Hamilton, 94 wins

Leading Trainer in 2004: Roger F. Engel, 36 wins

Record attendance: 26,411 February 29,1992. Record handle: $2, 808, 243, February24, 1990

RETAMA PARK

Retama Entertainment Group
Chairman: Joe Straus Jr.; Chief Executive Officer: Bryan Brown; General Manager: Robert W. Pollock; Director of Racing: Larry Craft; Director of Marketing/Publicity: Doug Vair.
PO Box 47535, San Antonio, TX 78265-7535
(210) 651-7000 Fax: (210) 651-7097
E-Mail: run@retamapark.com; Web Site: www.retamapark.com

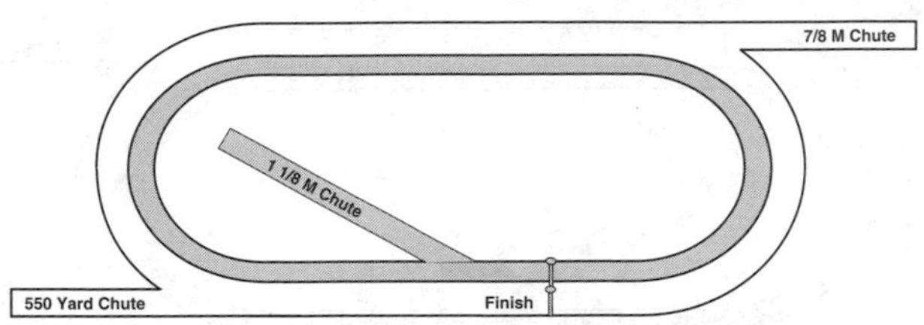

Track data: One-mile oval, with distance from last turn to finish 990 feet. 7 furlong turf course.

Opened April 1995. After financial difficulties that led to bankruptcy protection in 1996, it was acquired by present management in 2001. . .In 2004, held a 39-day meet from July 23 through Sept. 25 with purses averaging over $92,000 per day.

TRACK RECORDS

2-1/2 furs.	Texas Hope	4	107	:28.20	Jun. 28, 1998	7 furs.	Bucharest	5	120	1:22.05	May 24, 1995
4-1/2 furs.	Raise a Tab	3	117	:51.06	Aug. 1, 1998	1 mile	Mr. Pappion	7	120	1:36.90	May 11, 1995
5 furs.	Play The Jazz	4	115	:57.26	Aug. 23, 1998	1-1/16 m	Heavily Armed	5	120	1:43.20	Sep. 20, 1997
5-1/2 furs.	Bailando	5	122	1:02.90	May 13, 1995	1-1/8 m	Fletchers Pride	5	116	1:51.43	Aug. 14, 1998
6 furs.	Bucharest	5	117	1:08.82	May 10, 1995	1-1/4 m	Call Me Wild	6	120	2:04.01	Sep. 3, 1995
6-1/2 furs.	Heavily Armed	5	123	1:15.30	Aug. 30, 1997	1-5/16 m	Opening Remark	7	114	2:13.99	Sep. 5, 1996

Turf Course

Abt. 5 furs.	Mine Glow	4	119	:56.20	Sep. 6, 2002	1-1/16 m	Fly Slama Jama	5	115	1:40.79	Oct. 4, 2003
5 furs.	Beach Heat	5	119	:55.69	Aug. 24, 2003	1-1/8 m	Untraceable	5	115	1:48.13	Aug. 10, 1996
7-1/2 furs.	Call Me Wild	6	122	1:28.43	Sep. 17, 1995	1-3/8 m	Point Click	4	119	2:18.09	Oct. 18, 2003
1 mile	Eagle Lake	5	122	1:34.54	Oct. 4, 2003	1-13/16 m	Misting Rain	8	115	3:13.22	Sep. 28, 1996

Leading Jockey in 2004: Roman Chapa, 58 wins
Leading Trainer in 2004: Danny Pish, 41 wins

RIVER DOWNS

River Downs Investment Company

General Manager: Jack Hanessian; Racing Secretary: Ed Vomacka; Public Relations Director: John Engelhardt.

6301 Kellogg Avenue, Cincinnati, OH 45230
(513) 232-8000 Fax: (513) 232-1412
E-Mail Address: johne@riverdowns.com; Web Site: www.riverdowns.com

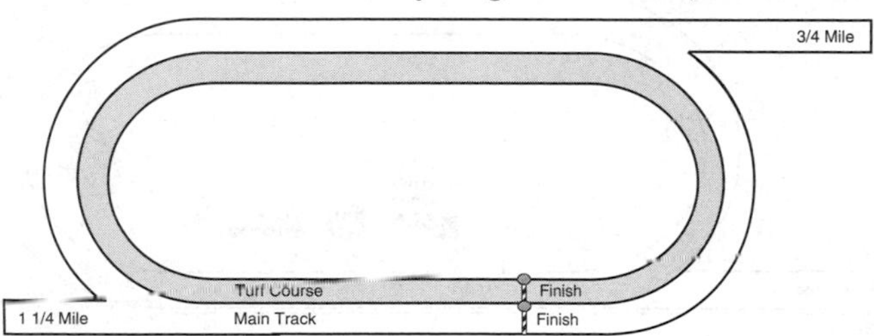

Track data: One-mile oval with six furlongs and 1 1/4-mile chutes. Distance from last turn to finish 1,117 feet, width 80 feet. Turf course: 7-furlongs. Stable accommodations 1,350. Seating capacity 11,000.

Opened July 6, 1925. Operates at least 120 live racing dates each year with 2004 purses at more than $53,000 per day and often offers seven races in tandem with Beulah Park as both tracks swap simulcast signals to complete a statewide 14-race program. The 2005 dates: April 8 through Sept. 5.

TRACK RECORDS

4-1/2 furs.	One Bad Dude	7	117	:52.20	Jul. 9, 2004	1-1/8 m	Brown Sugar	3	114	1:49	Sep. 2, 1925
5 furs.	Banker s Forbes	5	117	:57-3/5	Jun. 7, 1994	1-1/4 m	Crusader	3	126	2:02	Jul. 24, 1926
5-1/2 furs.	Tazua	3	120	1:03	Aug. 1, 1964	1-1/2 m	South Dakota	8	116	2:30-3/5	Jul. 1, 1950
6 furs.	Francine M.	5	124	1:08-3/5	Jul. 4, 1969	1-5/8 m	Sada	8	115	2:45-3/5	Oct. 13, 1934
1 mile	Alladin Rib	3	119	1:36-1/5	Aug. 8, 1988	1-11/16 m	Distribute	9	109	2:51-3/5	Sep. 7, 1940
1 m 70 yds	South Dakota	3	122	1:40	Aug. 4, 1945	1-3/4 m	Brigler	6	109	2:59-3/5	Oct. 19, 1940
1-1/16 m	Irish Dude	5	126	1:41-4/5	Jul. 5, 1969	1-7/8 m	Shot Bills	7	113	3:26-3/5	Aug. 19, 1979

Turf Course

4-1/2 furs.	Adena	4	110	:50-4/5	May 26, 1977	1-1/16 m	Franchise Player	5	112	1:40-3/5	Jun. 12, 1994
5 furs.	Hobbs	4	122	:56.30	Sep. 1, 1991	1-3/8 m	Hi Rise	4	122	2:15.60	Aug. 15, 2000
7-1/2 furs.	Stormy Deep	3	117	1:28-2/5	Aug. 15, 1990	1-7/16 m	Dina s Playmate	11	120	2:25	Aug. 30, 1969
	Sheer Speed	5	116	1:28-2/5	Aug. 18, 1998	1-1/2 m	Rebel Thunder	4	116	2:28	Jun. 28, 1996
1 mile	Bad News Blues	3	119	1:34-1/5	Jul. 23, 1994	1-7/8 m	Big Bettor	5	122	3:10-1/5	May 31, 1986

Leading Jockey in 2004 Spring meet: Dean A. Sarvis, 84 wins
Leading Trainer in 2004 Spring meet: Joe Woodard, 16 wins
Leading Jockey in 2004 Summer meet: Dean A. Sarvis, 83 wins
Leading Trainer in 2004 Summer meet: Joe Woodard, 14 wins
Record attendance 13, 768 May 30, 1956.

RUIDOSO DOWNS RACE TRACK & CASINO

Ruidoso Downs Race Track & Casino
Chairman: R.D. Hubbard; President.

1200 Futurity Dr., Ruidoso Downs, NM 88346
(505) 266-5555
Website: www.ruidownsracing.com

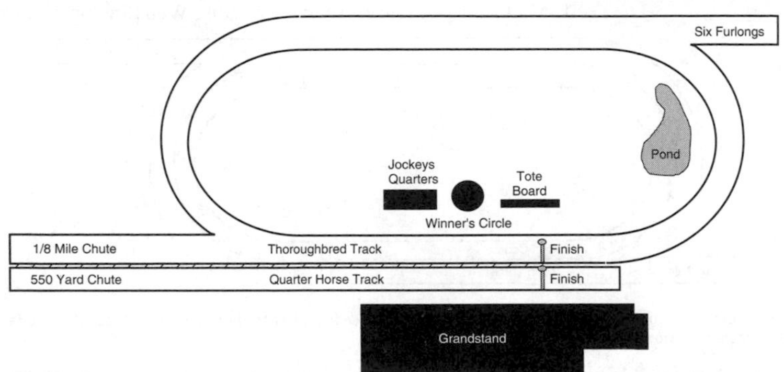

Track data: Seven furlong oval, with 6 furlong and 1-1/8 miles chutes. Distance from last turn to finish 656 feet; width 75 feet. Stable accommodations for 2,000. Seating capacity 7,000, parking for 14,000 cars.

Opened July 1, 1947 and has been the home of the All American Futurity, the richest Quarter Horse race in the world, with a purse worth approximately $2 million. In addition, Ruidoso also more than 250 Thoroughbred races during its 50-60 annual racing dates, from late May through Labor Day, when the All American is run.

TRACK RECORDS

2-1/2 furs.	Crafty Number	5	119	:27.40	Aug. 18, 2001
4-1/2 furs.	Becca s Shoulder	2	124	:52.00	Jun. 25, 2004
5 furs.	Twilight Diamond	4	122	:56.60	Jul. 17, 2004
5-1/2 furs.	Rocky Gulch	2	120	1:02.00	Jul. 13, 2003
6 furs.	Jack Wilson	4	120	1:08.80	Aug. 16, 1992
6-1/2 furs.	Mr. Tattoo	4	121	1:17.60	Jul. 4, 1973
7 furs.	Fill Mackis Cup	6	121	1:24.40	Jul. 15, 1984
7-1/2 furs.	Caliban	6	117	1:29.40	Jul. 19, 2003
1 mile	Set Records	4	121	1:37.00	Jul. 28, 1995
	Strong Arm Robbery	5	122	1:37.00	Sep. 1, 2001
1 m 70yds	Brogander	4	115	1:45.20	Jul. 31, 1954
1-1/16 m	Lucky Bluff	3	122	1:43.40	Sep. 2, 2001
1-1/8 m	Brownburough	5	119	1:51-2/5	Jun. 28, 1964
1-1/4 mile	Pentelipiano	6	122	2:07.60	Sep. 1, 2003
1-3/8 m	Start Jumpin	8	122	2:24.20	Aug. 18, 1990
1-1/2 m	Decidedly Henry C.	6	115	2:37.00	Aug. 19, 1989
1-5/8 m	More Than Glory	4	114	2:52.80	Aug. 15, 1992

Leading Jockeys in 2004: Alfredo J. Juarez Jr. & Carlos D. Madeira, 34 wins (tie)
Leading Trainer in 2004: Joel H. Marr, 18 wins
Record Attendance: 13,526 on September 4, 1999. Record Handle: $1,318,233 on September 4, 1999

SACRAMENTO

1600 Exposition Blvd. Sacramento, CA 95815
(916) 263-3000 Fax: (916) 263-3198
Web Site: www.bigfun.org

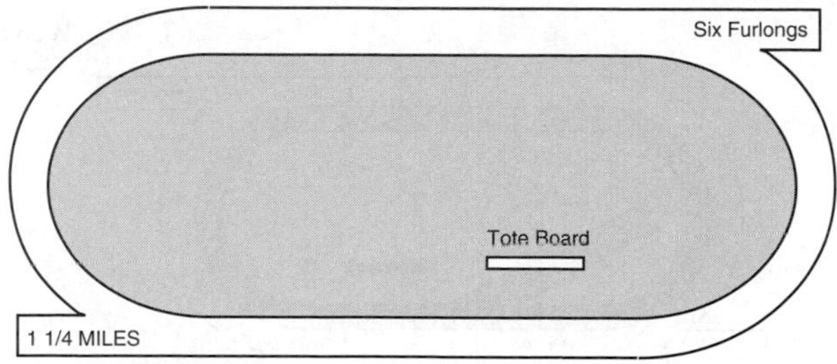

One mile oval, two chutes, six furlongs and 1-1/4 miles. Distance from last turn to finish 990 feet. Width of stretch 80 feet. Seating capacity 6,000; Parking for 12,000 cars on county fair grounds.

Opened September 2, 1935. Annually conducts mixed-breed race meets as part of the California Fair circuit in late August through early September. In 2004, purses were pegged in excess of $88,000 per day for its daily dose of seven-eight Thoroughbred races.

TRACK RECORDS

5 furs.	Maui Lyphcor D	6	116	:55-4/5	Sep. 3, 1990
5-1/2 furs.	Super Donna	4	116	1:01-2/5	Aug. 26, 1990
6 furs.	Passing Game	8	121	1:07-3/5	Sep. 4, 1993
1 mile	Makaleha	4	116	1:33-3/5	Aug. 23, 1991
1-1/16 m	Stan s Lad	3	122	1:40-2/5	Aug. 26, 1990
1-1/18 m	Make Him Famous	4	112	1:46-1/5	Sep. 6, 1982
1-1/4 m	Schuss II	7	121	2:01	Sep. 23, 1987
1-1/2 m	Classy Dame	4	107	2:31-4/5	Sep. 7, 1971
	Nordic Chief	8	113	2:31-4/5	Sep. 4, 1979
1-3/4 m	Money Buck	5	108	2:56	Aug. 30, 1987

Leading Jockeys in 2004: Victor Miranda & David G. Lopez, 12 wins (tie)
Leading Trainer in 2004: Rene Amescua, 8 wins
Record attendance 18,722–September 1, 1975. Record handle $1,257, 787, September 7, 1981.

SAM HOUSTON RACE PARK

Sam Houston Race Park, Ltd.

President and General Manager: Robert L. Bork; Vice President of Operations: Ann McGovern.

7575 North Sam Houston Pkwy. West, Houston, Texas 77064.

(281) 807-8700; Fax: (281) 807-8777

Web Site: www.shrp.com

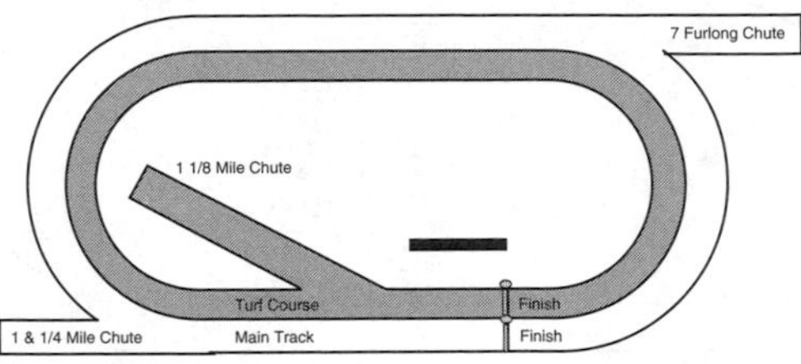

Track Data: One-mile dirt oval; 7/8-mile turf oval. Distance from last turn to finish, 966 feet. Stall accommodations for 1,250; Seating capacity 14,000, including simulcast pavilion; Parking for 6,000 cars.

Opened April 29, 1994 as the first Class-1, pari-mutuel track in Texas, home state for fabled King Ranch, but a state that had outlawed pari-mutuel wagering since the Depression. Built and owned by Houston businessman Charles Hurwitz's Maxxam Inc., Sam Houston racetrack suffered through two difficult seasons until Robert Bork was hired as general manager in 1995 and turned the program around with the help of legislative concessions that led to expanded simulcasting revenue and higher purses. In 2003-04, there were 89 days of racing from late October into April, with average daily purses including stakes of over $100,000. 2004-05 dates: Nov. 17 to April 10.

TRACK RECORDS

4-1/2 furs.	Prime Time Man	7	118	:51.70	Feb. 12, 2004	1 m 70 yds	Capt. Tiff's Beau	5	116	1:40.52	Oct. 24, 1998
5 furs.	Endofthestorm	4	118	:57.21	Oct. 25, 2003	1-1/16 m	Desert Air	4	124	1:42.74	Feb. 13, 1999
5-1/2 furs.	Bucharest	6	118	1:02.92	Apr. 13, 1996	1-1/8 m	Lost Soldier	7	120	1:48.75	May 3, 1997
6 furs.	Bucharest	4	122	1:08.91	May 11, 1994	1-1/4 m	Sauvage Isn't Home	3	114	2:04.75	Dec. 29, 1995
6-1/2 furs.	Brass Jacks	3	113	1:15.77	May 21, 1994	1-1/2 m	Final Val	5	119	2:32.99	Feb. 20, 1998
7 furs.	Bucharest	6	118	1:21.29	May 4, 1996	1-3/4 m	Final Val	5	122	3:01.50	Mar. 13, 1998
1 mile	Catalissa	3	122	1:36.33	Mar. 8, 2003	2 miles	Final Val	5	122	3:31.29	Apr. 3, 1998

Turf Course

5 furs.	Go Scotty	5	115	:56.93	Mar. 6, 1999	1-1/8 m	Chorwon	6	117	1:47.65	Mar. 6, 1999
1 mile	Solo Attack	5	118	1:36.16	Mar. 17, 2001	1-1/2 m	Commander Calhoun	5	113	2:32.56	Oct. 3, 1996
1-1/16 m	Luna Delight	4	116	1:43.24	Dec. 4, 1998						

Leading Jockey in 2004: Jeremy Beasley, 100 wins

Leading Trainer in 2004: Steven M. Asmussen, 60 wins

Record attendance: 24,316, July 4, 2003. Record handle: $5,740,955 (Live, Host and Guest) – December 7, 2002; $5,083,955 (Live and Host) – December 7, 2002

SANTA ANITA PARK

A Magna Entertainment Corporation Facility. Los Angeles Turf Club, Incorporated.
Directors: Chairman: Frank Stronach; Racing Secretary: Rick Hammerle.
Street Address: 285 W. Huntington Dr. P.O. Box 60014, Arcadia, California 91066-6014
Arcadia, California 91007 (626) 574-7223
Fax: (626) 821-1514; Results (626) 446-8501
E-mail: info@santaanita.com; Web Site: www.santaanita.com
Nearest Airports: Hollywood-Burbank, 15 miles. Private planes may land at nearby El Monte Airport.

Oak Tree Racing Association.
Same mailing, street address and Internet site. (626) 574-7223; Fax: (626) 446-9565; Marketing/ Publicity: (626) 574-5074; Executive Vice President: Sherwood Chillingworth; Racing Secretary: Mike Harlow, (626) 574-6472.

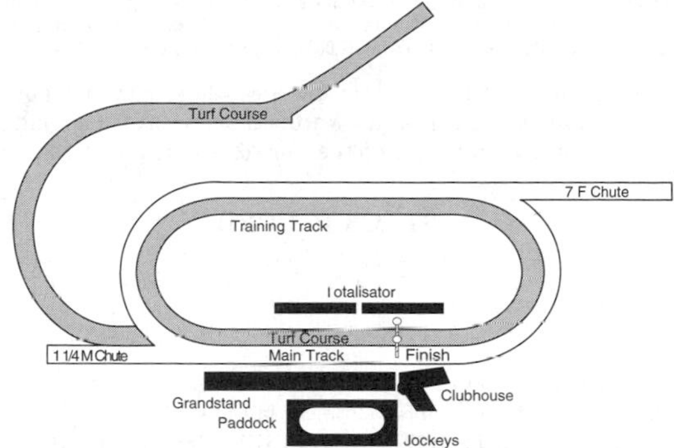

Track Data: One-mile dirt track with seven-furlong and 1 1/4-mile chutes. Distance from last turn to finish, 900 feet; width 85 feet. Turf course: 7 furlongs, plus the downhill chute, 1,408.45 yards from top of the hill to the finish. Stable accommodations for 2,000. Seating Capacity: 19,200. Total capacity with infield 85,000. Parking for 22,000 cars.

Opened December 25, 1934 and built by Charles H. Strub, after races had been conducted without pari-mutuel wagering on virtually the same site north of Los Angeles in the valley of the San Gabriel mountain range where a public one-mile course had been built by E. J. Baldwin in 1907. In more recent times, Santa Anita hosted the Breeders' Cup three times (1986, 1993 and 2003) during the fall dates leased by the Oak Tree Racing Association. During the track's regular winter-spring meet, it is home for the $1 million Santa Anita Handicap, the nation's oldest, continuously run $100,000 race. Santa Anita also features a European style, hillside turf course and was the site for 1984 Olympic Equestrian events. . .In December 1998, the track was purchased by Frank Stronach's Magna Entertainment, Inc. and Stronach has stated plans to expand the entertainment aspects of the facility. In 2004, Santa Anita had two meets, the 'Oak Tree' meet and regular winter-spring meet that annually begins on Dec. 26. Purses also are among the highest in the nation, pegged at almost $439,000 per day in the spring and $407,000 at the Oak Tree meet. Enhancing the Santa Anita experience are public workouts with breakfast served 7:30 to 9:30 AM on racing days at 'Clocker's Corner'; an infield playground with picnic areas for families and Tram Tours of the stable area on weekends.

TRACK RECORDS

2 furs.	Whatsthenameman	2	118	:21.09	Apr. 15, 2004	7 furs.	Spectacular Bid	4	126	1:20	Jan. 5, 1980
4-1/2 furs.	Willy Float	2	118	:51-2/5	Mar. 23, 1972	1 mile	Ruhlmann	4	118	1:33-2/5	Mar. 5, 1989
5 furs.	Zero Henry	2	120	:57.78	Oct. 23, 1996	1-1/16 m	Efervescente	5	118	1.39.18	Jan. 6, 1993
5-1/2 furs.	Kona Gold	5	119	1:01.74	Jan. 3, 1999	1-1/8 m	Star Spangled	5	117	1:45-4/5	Mar. 24, 1979
6 furs.	Sunny Blossom	4	115	1:07-1/5	Dec. 30, 1989	1-1/4 m	Spectacular Bid	4	126	1:57-4/5	Feb. 3, 1980
6-1/2 furs.	Son Of A Pistol	6	114	1:13.71	Apr. 4, 1998	1-1/2 m	Queen s Hustler	4	112	2:27-1/5	Feb. 19, 1973

Turf Course

Abt.6-1/2 f	Lennyfromalibu	5	123	1:11.13	Jan. 22, 2004	Abt.1-1/2 m	Practicante	6	118	2:26-2/5	Feb. 21, 1972
1 Mile	Atticus	5	117	1:31.89	Mar. 1, 1997	1-1/2 m	Hawkster	3	121	2:22-4/5	Oct. 14, 1989
1-1/8 m	Kostroma	5	117	1:43.92	Oct. 20, 1991	Abt.1-3/4 m	Bienamado	5	122	2:42.96	Apr. 14, 2001
1-1/4 m	Double Discount	4	116	1:57-2/5	Oct. 9, 1977						

Leading Jockey SA 2002-2003 meet: Victor Espinoza, 89 wins. Leading Trainer SA 2002-2003 meet: Jeff Mullins, 45 wins
Leading Jockey 2003 Oak Tree meet: Corey S. Nakatani, 21 wins. Leading Trainer 2003 Oak Tree meet: Mike Mitchell, 13 wins.
Record attendance: 85, 529, March 3, 1985. Record handle: $17,171,465, October 25, 2003 (Breeders' Cup Day); $120,788,128, all sources (Breeders' Cup Day)

SANTA ROSA

PO Box 1536, Santa Rosa, CA 95402
(707) 545-4200 Fax: (707) 573-9342
Web Site: www.sonomacountyfair.com

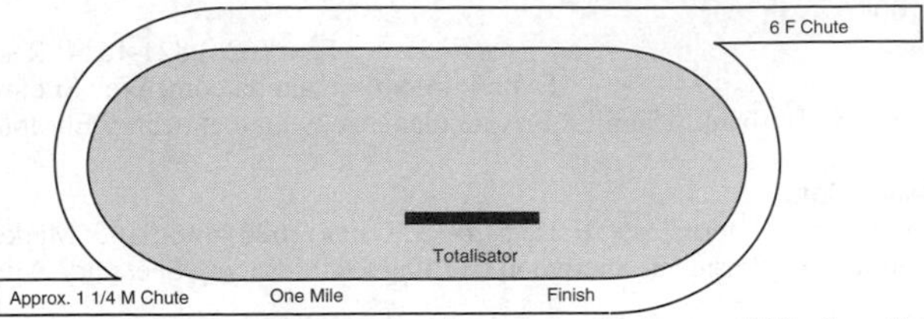

Track data: About one-mile oval (132.6 feet short of one mile), with two chutes, 6 furlongs and 1 1/4 miles, which also is used for two-furlong straightaway races for Quarter Horses. Distance from last turn to finish 1,145.8 feet, width 80 feet, except for first turn, 60 feet. Stable accommdations 1,022. Seating capacity 8,181. Parking for 12,000 cars on the fairgrounds.

Opened October 8, 1936. Runs a picturesque, two week, mixed-breed meet in the heart of the northern California wine country during late July into early August as part of the Northern California fair circuit. In 2004, purses averaged in excess of $122,000 for the seven Thoroughbred races on the daily 12- and 13-race cards. Year-round simulcasting. 2005 dates: July 27 to August 8.

TRACK RECORDS

4-1/2 furs.	Westwood Rhythm	5	117	:50.39	Jul. 24, 2003	1 mile	Magaki	3	115	1:34.40	Jul. 26, 1984
5 furs.	Valid Redress	5	117	:56.20	Aug. 1, 2003	1-1/16 m	Castle Tweed	4	114	1:39.80	Aug. 2, 1986
5-1/2 furs.	Truely Rude	6	114	1:02.20	Aug. 8, 1982	1-1/8 m	Diplomat Ruler	5	115	1:47.40	Jul. 27, 1985
6 furs.	Royalty	6	120	1:07.80	Aug. 4, 2000	Abt 1-1/4 m	River Lad	6	113	1:58.00	Jul. 24, 1976

Leading jockey in 2004: Russell A. Baze, 15 wins
Leading Trainers in 2004: Jerry Hollendorfer & John F. Martin, 8 wins (tie)
Record attendance: 19, 208, July 28, 1990. Record handle: $1,056,543, August 8, 1987; $3,967,973, August 7, 1999, all sources.

SARATOGA RACE COURSE

New York Racing Association Inc.

President and CEO: Charles Hayward; Co-Chairman: Peter F. Karches; Co-Chairman: C. Steven Duncker; Senior Vice President: William A Nader; Racing Secretary and Handicapper: Michael S. Lakow.

New York Racing Association Inc.
P.O. Box 90
Jamaica, New York 11417

P.O. Box 564, Saratoga Springs, New York 12866.
Street Address: 267 Union Avenue, Saratoga Springs, New York 12866
(518) 584-6200; or (718) 641-4700; Results: (900) 443-1111
E-mail: info@nyrainc.com; Web Site: www.nyra.com

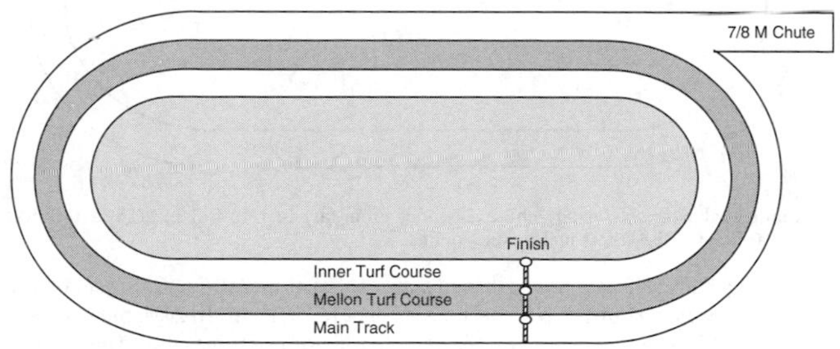

Track data: One and one eighth miles, oval, with a seven furlong chute. Distance from last turn to finish, 1,144. Width of main track 100 feet; Two turf courses: (A: One mile plus 98 feet, and (B: an inner course at 7-furlongs and 304 feet and both turf courses are used for steeplechase racing on a limited basis. Stable accommodations 1,825; Seating capacity 10,000, plus 12,000 outside benches; total capacity 65,000. Parking for 4,000 cars, with many private lots nearby.

Opened August 2, 1864, Saratoga Race Course is a National Landmark, the oldest track in America and one of the most spectacular and historic venues in the racing world. Located in picturesque Saratoga Springs in the Adirondack Mountains of upstate New York-where the Philadelphia Orchestra and the New York City Ballet are in summer residence-Saratoga Racetrack operates six weeks from late July to Labor Day, with an unmatched graded stakes menu. This pushed daily average purses to over $633,000 per day...In 2005, the Grade 1 Travers for 3-year-olds will be run for the 135th time on August 27. The dates for the 2005 meet: July 27 through Sept. 5...Please note that most reserved seats for all dates are sold out months in advance via mail.

TRACK RECORDS

5 furs.	Fabulous Force	2	118	:56-3/5	Aug. 18, 1993	1-1/8 m	Left Bank	5	118	1:47.04	Aug. 3, 2002
5-1/2 furs.	Mayakovsky	2	118	1:03.32	Jul. 25, 2001	1-3/16 m	Winter s Tale	6	117	1:54-3/5	Aug. 21, 1982
6 furs.	Spanish Riddle	3	113	1:08	Aug. 18, 1972	1-1/4 m	General Assembly	3	126	2:00	Aug. 18, 1979
6-1/2 furs.	Topsider	5	115	1:14-2/5	Aug. 1, 1979	1-5/8 m	Green Highlander	5	117	2:43-2/5	Aug. 15, 1991
7 furs.	Darby Creek Road	3	113	1:20-2/5	Aug. 8, 1978	2 miles	James Boswell	5	116	3:26	Aug. 11, 1983
1 mile	Key Contender	4	115	1:34-3/5	Aug. 9, 1992						

Turf Course

1-1/16 m	Fourstardave	6	115	1:38-4/5	Jul. 29, 1991	1-5/8 m	Tom Swift	5	110	2:37	Aug. 23, 1978
1-1/8 m	Tentam	4	118	1:45-2/5	Aug. 10, 1973	2-1/16 m	Popular Victory	7	120	3:31-2/5	Aug. 23, 1979
1-3/16 m	Phi Beta Doc	3	118	1:51.61	Sep. 1, 1999						

Inner Turf Course

1 mile	L Oiseau d Argent	5	118	1:33.42	Aug. 5, 2004	1-3/8 m	Babinda	4	114	2:12	Jul. 26, 1997
1-1/16 m	Roman Envoy	4	119	1:39-4/5	Aug. 3, 1992	1-1/2 m	Awad	7	117	2:23-1/5	Aug. 9, 1997
1-1/8 m	Amarettitorun	5	115	1:46-1/5	Jul. 26, 1997						

Jumps

2-1/16 m	Equistar	5	153	3:36.28	Aug. 22, 2002
2-3/8 m	Hokan	5	142	4:12.04	Aug. 27, 1998
	It s a Giggle	7	142	4:12.04	Aug. 30, 2001

Leading jockey in 2004: John R. Velazquez, 65 wins
Leading trainer in 2004: Todd A. Pletcher, 35 wins
Record attendance: 77,337, August 17, 2003. Record handle: $9,390,934, August 23, 2003; $39,489,786, August 23, 2003, (all sources, Travers Day)

SOLANO (Vallejo)

900 Fairgrounds Drive, Vallejo, CA 94589
Phone: (707) 551-2000
Web Address: www.scfair.org

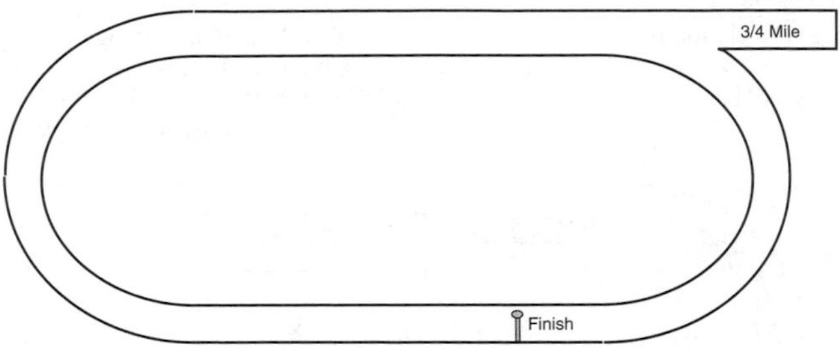

Track data: Seven-eighths mile oval, with six-furlong chute. Distance from last turn to finish, 1,085 feet. Stable accommodations for 1,004. Seating capacity, 6,500. Parking for 10,000 cars on the fairgrounds.

Opened June 16, 1951 , annually runs a 10 day, mixed-breed summer meet in Vallejo, California on the northeastern corner of the San Francisco Bay as part of the Northern California fair circuit. In 2004, purses were in excess of $109,000 per day for seven-eight Thoroughbred races per day. Year round simulcasting. The dates for the 2005 meet: July 13 through July 25.

TRACK RECORDS

4-1/2 furs.	Genuine Sparky			:51.38	Jul. 20, 2002	1-1/16 m	Hoedown s Day	5	113	1:39-4/5	Jul. 24, 1983
5 furs.	One Bad Shark	2	118	:56.60	Jul. 14, 2002	1-1/8 m	Baffi s Eagle	7	114	1:48-2/5	Jul. 17, 1984
5-1/2 furs.	Ridgewood High	5	119	1:02-1/5	Jul. 18, 1982	1-1/4 m	Super Sonet	5	113	2:03-2/5	Jun. 20, 1974
6 furs.	Salta s Pride	6	116	1:07-4/5	Jul. 13, 1996	1-3/8 m	Rain Storm	6	119	2:15-4/5	Jun. 22, 1973
1 mile	Kamalii King	6	107	1:34-4/5	Jul. 18, 1982	1-1/2 m	Always King	5	113	2:32-3/5	Jun. 24, 1978

Leading Jockeys in 2004: Russell A. Baze & Chance J. Rollins & Chad Philip Schvaneveldt, 10 wins (tie)
Leading Trainer in 2004: Jerry Hollendorfer, 7 wins
Record attendance 18, 127, June 14, 1980.

STAMPEDE PARK

Box 1060, Calgary, Alberta, CAN T2P 2K8
(403) 261-0214 Fax: (403) 265-7009 Race results: (403) 974-7223
Web Site: www.stampede-park.com

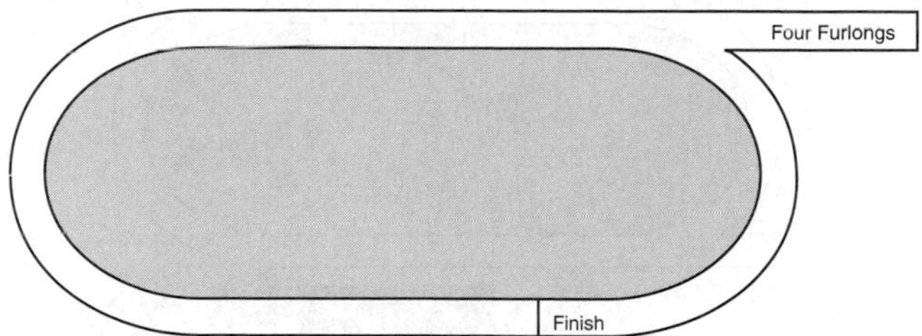

Track data: five-eighths mile oval, with a 4-furlong chute. Distance from last turn to finish, 660 feet; width 70 feet. Stable accommodations for 1,300. Seating capacity 17,800.

Originally opened as Victoria Park in July 1925, renamed Stampede Park in 1973. Current track and grounds rebuilt and reopened June 20, 1974. Runs a 40-50 day spring meet in most years and with a boost from slots, purses reached a new record of almost $108,000 per day in 2004.

TRACK RECORDS

3-1/2 furs.	Wild After Dark	2	116	:39-3/5	Jun. 2, 2000	1-1/16 m	Pilotson	7	115	1.42-1/5	Oct. 8, 1988
4 furs.	Adventuresome Love	7	115	:43-4/5	Apr. 3, 1993	1-1/8 m	Steady Power	3	126	1;47-4/5	Sep. 19, 1987
5-1/2 furs.	Malawi s Champ	5	108	1:03-4/5	Oct. 29, 1978	1-5/16 m	Postell Man	3	124	2:10-1/5	Oct. 18, 1986
6 furs.	Classic Rock	3	120	1:09-2/5	Sep. 19, 1981	1-3/8 m	Two Ticky	4	123	2:16-1/5	Oct. 29, 1995
6-1/2 furs.	Blue Bouncer	3	115	1:19-2/5	Jun. 22, 1974	1-5/8 m	Whiskey Wisker	4	114	2:46-3/5	Oct. 25, 1987
7 furs.	Edie s Prize	5	115	1:24	Jun. 22, 1974	1-3/4 m	Jubal Tee	4	115	2:59	Nov. 9, 1981
1 mile	Roll On Briartic	4	123	1:35-4/5	May 21, 1989	2 miles	Grandin Park	9	118	3:29	Oct. 13, 1979

Leading Jockey in 2004: Quincy Welch, 65 wins

Leading Trainer in 2004: Ron K. Smith, 29 wins

Record attendance: 6, 167, August 15, 1981.

STOCKTON

1658 S. Airport Way, Stockton, CA 95206
Phone: (209) 466-5041 Fax: (209) 466-5739
Website: www.sanjoaquinfair.com

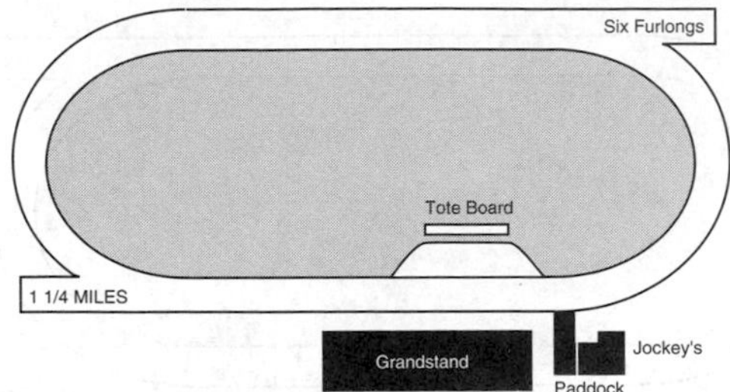

Track data: One-mile oval, with two chutes, 6 furlongs and 1 1/4 miles. Distance from last turn to finish 1,003 feet, width 80 feet. Stable accommodations for 756; Seating capacity 5,660.

Opened in the 1880's, but the first pari-mutuel meet was in August 1934. . .Runs a 10-day, mixed-breed meet in June as part of the Northern California Fair circuit with year-round simulcasting. Thoroughbred purses were pegged at about $70,000 per day. Dates for 2005: June 15 to June 26.

TRACK RECORDS

5 furs.	Shining Prince	6	121	:55-4/5	Jun. 26, 1994	1-1/16 m	Athenia Green-En	6	118	1:40-2/5	Jun. 28, 1992
5-1/2 furs.	Sandy s Era	3	117	1:02-1/5	Jun. 14, 1997	1-1/8 m	Episodic	4	118	1:49-1/5	Jun. 27, 1993
6 furs.	Lynn s Notebook	4	117	1:07-4/5	Jun. 25, 1995	1-1/4 m	Ali Kato	7	112	2:01-3/5	Aug. 17, 1986
1 mile	Flying Cuantal	6	117	1:33-2/5	Jun. 15, 1997						

Leading Jockey in 2004: Ken S. Tohill, 14 wins
Leading Trainer in 2004: Barry Holmes, 5 wins

SUFFOLK DOWNS

Sterling Suffolk Racecourse LLC

Chairperson: Patricia Moseley; Chief Operating Officer: Robert O Malley; Assistant General Manager: Joseph Fatalo; Racing Secretary: Jim Pambianchi.

111 Waldemar Ave., East Boston, MA 02128
Phone: (617) 567-3900 Fax: (617) 567-7511
Web Site: www.suffolkdowns.com

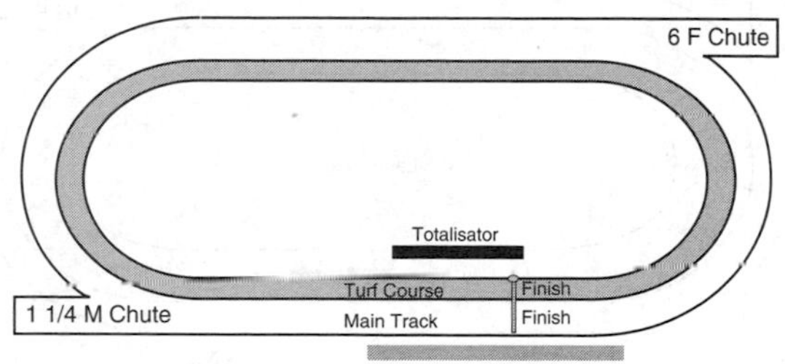

Track data: One-mile oval with six-furlong and 1 1/4-mile chutes. Distance from last turn to finish, 1,030 feet, width in stretch, 90 feet, width in backstretch 70 feet. Turf course: About 7 furlongs. Stable accommodations for 1,300. Seating capacity 12,000.

Opened in July 1935...Dates for 2005: 150-day meet, April 30 to Nov. 19. Year-round simulcasting.

TRACK RECORDS

2 furs.	Adriano s Girl	2	120	:21.94	Jun. 4, 1997	1-1/8 m	Skip Away	5	130	1:47.27	May 30, 1998
4 furs.	Crimson Streak	2	120	:45-2/5	Apr. 6, 1970	1-3/16 m	Shut Out	3	126	1:55-2/5	Jul. 4, 1942
4-1/2 furs.	Lovely Gypsy	2	116	:51-4/5	May 7, 1965	1-1/4 m	Helioscope	4	126	2:01	May 19, 1955
	Happy Voter	2	118	:51-4/5	May 16, 1966	1-1/2 m	Connie Rab	6	112	2:30-3/5	May 15, 1954
5 furs.	Rene Depot	3	124	:57-2/5	Jun. 25, 1972	1-5/8 m	Count Fire	4	113	2:45-2/5	Jun. 23, 1962
5-1/2 furs.	Four Cards Too	5	121	1:04.11	May 1, 2004	2 m 70 yds	On The Square	5	119	3:39-4/5	Apr. 16, 1973
6 furs.	Canal	5	123	1:08-1/5	May 14, 1966	2-1/16 m	Bold Fencer	6	114	3:35-4/5	Apr. 18, 1983
1 mile	Back Bay Brave	5	115	1:35-1/5	Jul. 12, 1986	2-1/4 m	Fundy Bay	6	119	3:54-1/5	Dec. 9, 1973
1 m 70 yds	Half Breed	6	115	1:40	May 23, 1964						
1-1/16 m	Talent Show	7	112	1:41-4/5	May 12, 1962						
	Bear the Palm	3	112	1:41-4/5	Jul. 3, 1977						

Turf Course

Abt.5 furs.	Bishop Ridley	7	118	:57-1/5	Jul. 19, 1987	Abt.1-3/8 m	Graybrook Swan	5	110	2:20-4/5	Jul. 18, 1970
Abt.7-1/2 f	Times Ahead	6	116	1:32-2/5	Sep. 3, 1988		Chompion	5	108	2:20-4/5	Jul. 18, 1970
Abt.1 mile	Diablo Reigns	5	119	1:39.35	Sep. 15, 2003	Abt.1-1/2 m	Akbar Khan	5	120	2:30-3/5	Jun. 17, 1957
Abt.1m70yds	Alphabetical	5	121	1:42.07	Jun. 30, 2004	Abt 1-15/16m	Jamf	9	112	3:11-1/5	Jul. 4, 1975
Abt.1-1/16 m	Landing Court	6	116	1:44.91	Oct. 26, 1994	Abt.2 miles	Jean-Pierre	5	113	3:19-4/5	Jun. 28, 1969

Jumps

2-1/4 m	Brigade of Guards	5	155	4:24.36	Jun. 1, 1997

Leading Jockey in 2004: Winston Albert Thompson, 154 wins
Leading Trainer in 2004: John Rigattieri, 93 wins
Record attendance: 52, 726, August 10, 1935 Record handle: $2, 175, 836, May 30, 1960. $5, 867, 414, May 31, 1997, Mass. Cap Day, (Includes simulcasting)

SUN DOWNS

PO Box 6662, Kennewick, WA 99336
(509) 582-5434 Fax: (509) 586-9780

Track data: Five-eighths mile oval, with a 6 1/2-furlong chute. Stable accommodations for 365. Seating capacity 3,800.

Opened September 12, 1981 and operated 10 days during in 2004 spread out between April 3 and May 2 A similar meet is scheduled for 2005.
Leading Jockey in 2004: Jay Conklin, 10 wins
Leading Trainer in 2004: James R. Craig, 8 wins

SUNLAND PARK RACETRACK & CASINO

1200 Futurity Drive Sunland Park, NM 88063
(505) 874-5200 Fax: (505) 589-1518
E-Mail Address: sunlandinfo@sunland-park.com.com
Web Site: www.sunland-park.com

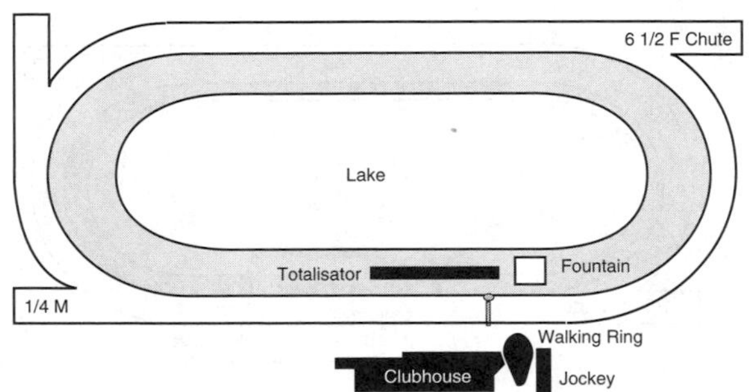

Track data: One-mile oval, with two chutes, 6 1/2 furlongs and 1 1/4 miles, which also is used for straightaway Quarter Horse races. Distance from last turn to finish, 990 feet; width 80 feet. Stable accommodations for 1,600. Seating capacity 5,710.

Opened Sept. 12, 1981 and typically holds a Winter-Spring meet from November through early April. . .Bolstered by casino revenue, purses at Sunland were up to over $164,000 per day for the 2003-2004 meet. A similar meet is scheduled to run from Nov. 5, 2004, through April 3, 2005.

TRACK RECORDS

2 furs.	Bekky s Star	2	115	:21-1/5	Feb. 12, 1968	1 mile	Mr. Trieste	3	119	1:35.38	Dec. 7, 2004
3 furs.	Sara Dier	2	118	:33-3/5	Mar. 31, 1962	1-1/16 m	Butte City	5	116	1:41.92	Dec. 12, 2004
4 furs.	Tamran s Jet	2	118	:44-4/5	Mar. 22, 1968	1-1/8 m	Winsham Lad	5	121	1:48-1/5	Jan. 8, 1961
4-1/2 furs.	Bold Liz	2	118	:50-2/5	Mar. 19, 1972	1-3/16 m	Mickey J.	8	115	1:58-1/5	Nov. 14, 1970
5 furs.	Jimmy Jones	7	118	:55.90	Feb. 7, 2004	1-1/4 m	Curribot	7	124	2:01-2/5	May 6, 1984
5-1/2 furs.	Treasure Hunt	7	116	1:02.39	Jan. 28, 2003	1-3/8 m	Hot Deck	5	117	2:19-2/5	Jan. 10, 1970
6 furs.	Yet Anothernatalie	5	120	1:08.24	Dec. 11, 2004	1-1/2 m	Houston Blaze	6	118	2:33-1/5	May 3, 1964
6-1/2 furs.	Bang	4	122	1:14.29	Mar. 6, 2004	1-5/8 m	Rush Line	6	120	2:47-3/5	Apr. 6, 1969

Leading Jockey in 2003-2004: Ken S. Tohill, 68 wins
Leading Trainer in 2003-2004: Steven M. Asmussen, 53 wins

SUNRAY PARK & CASINO

39 Road 5568, Farmington, NM 87401
(505) 326-4551
Web Site: www.sunraygaming.com

Track data: A six-furlong oval with two chutes, 4 1/2 furlongs and one mile.

Opened in 1984 and located in the northwestern corner of New Mexico, offered mixed breed racing on a limited basis with minimum financial success until closed in 1993. Reopened in 1999 with slot machines to boost purses and in 2004 had 44 racing dates from August through November, with Thoroughbred purses over $50,000 per day. 2005 Dates: July 2 through Sept. 5.

TRACK RECORDS

4 furs.	Absolutely True	3	117	:44.60	Nov. 16, 2003	7 furs.	Oh Gracie	5	119	1:22.60	Sep. 25, 2000
4-1/2 furs.	Sky Diver	6	123	:49.80	Oct. 10, 2003	7-1/2 furs.	Dalt s Kingpin	4	123	1:28.60	Nov. 17, 2003
6 furs.	Unbridled Set	3	122	1:11.40	Oct. 11, 1999	1 mile	Ben Told	6	118	1:35.60	Oct. 15, 2000
6-1/2 furs.	Herecomesthemannow	3	116	1:15.60	Sep. 22, 2003	1-1/8 m	Line Gauge	6	118	1:48.80	Nov. 21, 1999

Leading Jockey in 2004: Ken S. Tohill, 50 wins
Leading Trainer in 2004: Dan H. Dennison, 17 wins

TAMPA BAY DOWNS

Tampa Bay Downs, Inc.

President and Treasurer: Stella F. Thayer; Vice President and General Manager: Peter N. Berube; Director of Public Relations: Margo Flynn.

Street Address: 11225 Racetrack Rd., Tampa, Florida 33626
Nearest Airport: Tampa International Airport, 8 miles from track.

P.O. Box 2007, Oldsmar, Florida 34677
(813) 855-4401; Fax: (813) 854-3539
Web Site: www.tampadowns.com

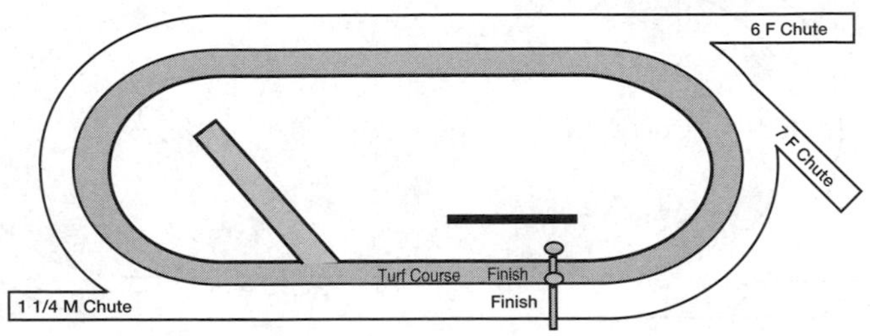

Track Data: One-mile track, 3/8-mile and 7/8-mile chutes; distance from last turn to finish, 976 feet; Turf Course: 7/8-mile with a 1/4-mile chute located inside main track. Stable accommodations for 1,400 horses. Seating Capacity: 6,000; Parking for 5,000 cars.

Originally opened as Tampa Downs on Feb. 18, 1926, the racetrack has amassed a long and colorful history. It was renamed Sunshine Park in 1947 and in 1965, the track was acquired by a group of Tampa sportsmen and renamed Florida Downs. Finally, in 1980, during another change in ownership, the track was renamed again as Tampa Bay Downs. Present ownership assumed the reins just prior to the 1986-1987 season and the facility has been in a state of constant improvement since. In 2003, Tampa Bay Downs launched a state of the art golf practice and wagering facility. The 2004 meet saw the debut of the Silks Card Room, a poker room operating during live racing days from noon to midnight. The 2004 meet also featured a new commingled record handle of over $4.2 million.

TRACK RECORDS

Distance	Horse	Age	Wt.	Time	Date
2 furs.	Silver Dollar Boy	2	120	:21-4/5	Jan. 18, 1980
3 furs.	Hot Star	2	117	:33-2/5	Feb. 14, 1980
	Wynn Dot Comma	2	118	:33.40	Apr. 21, 2003
4 furs.	Camp Izard	2	122	:46-4/5	May 1, 1993
4-1/2 furs.	Geronimo J.	2	120	:52-4/5	Mar. 16, 1984
5 furs.	Arion Fair	4	116	:57-1/5	Mar. 20, 1982
5-1/2 furs.	Schmoopy	4	116	1:03.55	Mar. 17, 2000
6 furs.	Bootlegger s Pet	4	112	1:09	Jan. 26, 1974
6-1/2 furs.	O Malley	5	116	1:16.99	Dec. 31, 2004
7 furs.	Oh So Striking	8	114	1:22-3/5	Apr. 5, 1997
1 m 40yds	Mistum	5	113	1:41-1/5	Mar. 21, 1981
1-1/16 m	Sunny Prospector	6	119	1:43-2/5	Mar. 29, 1989
1-1/8 m	Position Leader	4	122	1:50-3/5	Apr. 9, 1989
1-3/16 m	Warning Flag	8	126	1:59-3/5	Jan. 25, 1986
1-1/4 m	Finale Puer	6	119	2:07-2/5	Mar. 7, 1959
1-3/8 m	Rugged Zeal	6	120	2:20.68	Apr. 23, 2002
1-1/2 m	Royal Jacopo	6	118	2:33	Mar. 12, 1955
1-5/8 m	Most Valiant	11	110	2:48-1/5	Mar. 29, 1997
1-3/4 m	Our Day	4	119	3:00-2/5	Mar. 20, 1957
1-7/8 m	Best Hearted	5	118	3:18-3/5	Mar. 22, 1986
2 miles	Boss Man Jarett	10	118	3:30.30	Apr. 24, 1999
2-1/16 m	Mystic Fox	5	116	3:37-3/5	Mar. 27, 1988

Turf Course

Distance	Horse	Age	Wt.	Time	Date
Abt. 5 furs.	Whenthedoveflies	4	116	:57.23	Apr. 20, 2004
5 furs.	Nicole s Dream	3	113	:56.06	Mar. 16, 2003
Abt. 1 mile	Dieago	4	120	1:36.86	Jan. 17, 1999
1 mile	Lucky J J	3	115	1:33.79	Feb. 12, 2000
Abt.1-1/16m	Ben s Quixote	5	116	1:41.23	Dec. 28, 1999
1-1/16 m	Legs Galore	4	122	1:39.65	Feb. 20, 1999
Abt. 1-1/8 m	Guardianofthegate	5	116	1:47.90	May 5, 2001
1-1/8 m	Lilys Cousin	6	115	1:46.34	May 6, 2000
Abt. 1-3/8 m	Galic Boy	9	116	2:17.40	Mar. 9, 2004
1-3/8 m	Earnest Storm	5	123	2:17.40	Mar. 11, 2003
Abt. 1-1/2 m	Top Senor	6	118	2:31.60	Feb. 26, 2002

Jumps

Distance	Horse	Age	Wt.	Time	Date
2-1/16 m	Red Classic	6	154	3:43.82	May 4, 2000

Leading jockey in 2004: Jesus Lopez Castanon, 87 wins
Leading Trainer in 2004: Lynne M. Scace, 25
Record handle: $4,722,986, all sources.

THISTLEDOWN

Magna Entertainment Corp.

Chairman: Frank Stronach; President & CEO: Tom Hodgson; General Manager: William D. Murphy; Director of Racing: William Couch; Director of Communications: Heather McColloch; Director, Simulcasting: Greg Davis.

Street Address: 21501 Emery Road, North Randall, Ohio, 44128
Nearest Airport: Cleveland Hopkins International, 15 miles (216) 662-8600; Fax: (216) 662-5339
Web Site: www.thistledown.com

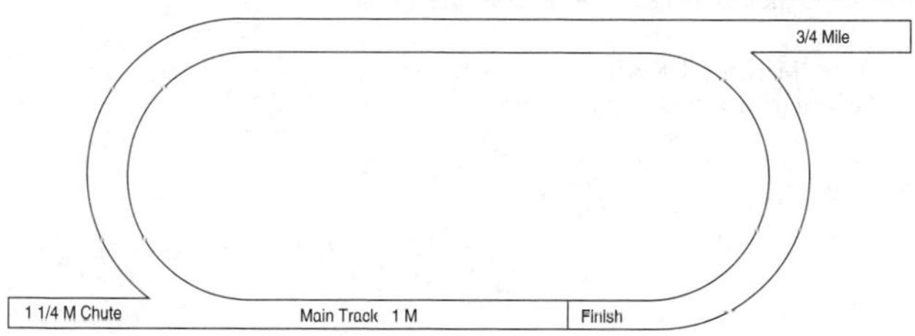

Track Data: One mile oval, six-furlong and 1 1/4 mile chutes; distance from last turn to finish, 978 feet; width 95 feet in the stretch, 75 feet backstretch. Stable accommodations for 1,560. Seating capacity: 6,400; Parking for 6,000 cars.

Opened July 20, 1925, and owned by the DeBartolo Corporation since 1959, Thistledown was acquired in 1999 by Frank Stronach's Magna Entertainment Corp., a spin-off of Magna International, Inc. In 2005, will run 187 dates from April to December, plus extensive simulcasting. Note: The CRANWOOD, RANDALL and SUMMIT RACING CLUB race meets were incorporated into Thistledown's regular meet during the DeBartolo years at Thistledown. In 2004, purses were in excess of $66,000 per day. The dates for 2005: April 8 through Dec. 23.

TRACK RECORDS

2 furs.	Onion Roll	7	111	:20-4/5	Sep. 27, 1993	1 m 70 yds	Wisdom Seeker	5	122	1:40-4/5	Jul. 22, 1995
4 furs.	Ifufeelfroggyleap	4	122	:45.30	Oct. 8, 2004	1-1/16 m	Entitled to Star	5	112	1:41-1/5	Nov. 25, 1995
4-1/2 furs.	Onion Roll	6	118	:51-2/5	Nov. 20, 1992	1-1/8 m	Smarten	3	124	1:47-2/5	Jun. 17, 1979
5 furs.	Jet Bupers	7	118	:57-2/5	Jun. 4, 1978	1-3/16 m	Smoke Screen	5	116	1:55-3/5	Jul. 17, 1954
	Great Allegiance	5	116		May 18, 1997	1-1/4 m	Pert Near	6	117	2:03	Dec. 1, 1979
	Regal Diamond	5	116		Mar. 22, 1997	1-1/2 m	Martha s Wave	6	115	2:31-4/5	Jun. 18, 1955
5-1/2 furs.	Down Thepike Mike	4	116	1:03-1/5	Aug. 10, 1998	1-5/8 m	Alsang	3	101	2:46	Aug. 8, 1936
6 furs.	Fancy Threat	5	115	1:08-2/5	Nov. 21, 1987	1-3/4 m	Mala Kee	4	116	2:57-3/5	Jul. 17, 1957
1 mile	Setting Limits	5	118	1:35-3/5	Nov. 19, 1989	2 miles	Likely Advice	5	115	3:27	Dec. 15, 1980
1 m 40 yds	Ifthisbe Britches	5	116	1:38-3/5	Dec. 8, 1989	2 m 70 yds	Lonely Cloud	8	118	3:41-3/5	May 13, 1990
	North Island	4	119	1:38.60	Dec. 9, 1989	2-1/16 m	Bunker	8	112	3:32-4/5	Jul. 13, 1955

Leading Jockey in 2004: Huber Villa-Gomez, 152 wins
Leading Trainer in 2004: Rodney C. Faulkner, 82 wins

TILLAMOOK COUNTY FAIR

Tillamook County Fairgrounds

Fair Board President and racing director: Mel Tupper. General Manager: Jerry Underwood.

4603 E Third Street, Tillamook, Oregon.
(503) 842-2272
Website: wcn.net@tillamookfair
or tillamookfair@wcn.net for any racing information.

Runs a three day mixed-breed during August as part of the Tillamook County Fair with $14,000 in daily Thoroughbred purses. Total purses for the 20 thoroughbred races in 2004 was $42,500.

Leading Jockeys in 2004: Jaime Martinez & Kevin C. Murray, 5 wins (tie)
Leading Trainer in 2004: Several trainers tied with two wins

TIMONIUM

Maryland State Fair & Agricultural Society, Inc.

F. Grove Miller, Chairman of the Board; Howard Max Mosner, Jr., President and General Manager; Racing Secretary: Georganne Hale

Street Address: 2200 York Road,
Timonium, Maryland 21094

Mailing Address: Maryland State Fair, P.O. Box 188
Timonium, Maryland 21094
Telephone: Office and Track: (410) 252-0200
Free Scratch and Results: (410) 792-0278 and/or (301) 470-3056
E-Mail Address: msfair@msn.com; Web Site: www.bcpl.lib.md.us/~mdstfair
Nearest Airport: Baltimore-Washington International, 25 miles from track.

Track Data: Five-eighths mile, with 4-furlong and 6 1/2-furlong chutes. Distance from last turn to finish, 700 feet. Stable accommodations, 600. Seating capacity 5,000; Parking for 5,000 cars.

Opened September 1887, Timonium is operated by the Maryland State Fair & Agricultural Society, Inc. The 8-day Fair & Race meeting attracts more than 500,000 fans and concludes on Labor Day. Profits are for the Fair, 4-H Club awards and improvements.

TRACK RECORDS

4 furs.	Ameri Brilliance	4	121	:43.76	Aug. 23, 2003	1 m 70 yds	One More Snooze	4	117	1:42	Aug. 31, 1984
Abt.6-1/2f	Dontcloseyoureyes	5	119	1:15	Aug. 25, 1991	1-1/16 m	Valley Command	4	117	1:42-1/5	Aug. 28, 1990
6-1/2 furs.	Weather Vane	3	122	1:16-3/5	Sep. 1, 1997	Abt.1-1/16m	Groom s Reckoning	4	117	1:49-1/5	Sep. 2, 1992
1 mile	Count Off	8	113	1:36-4/5	Aug. 26, 1981	1-1/8 m	Count Disco	4	114	1:49-1/5	Jul. 30, 1983

Leading Jockeys in 2004: Erick Rodriguez & Eric Camacho, 12 wins (tie)
Leading Trainers in 2004: Gary Capuano & Kenneth M. Cox, 4 wins (tie)
Record Attendance: 17,306, September, 4, 1967. Record handle: $2,452,514, August 29, 1998

TURF PARADISE

Turf Paradise, Inc.

President and General Manager: Randy Fozzard; Racing Secretary/Director of Racing: Shawn Swartz; Viec President and Assistant General Manager: Dave Johnson; Director of Marketing: Vince Francia.

1501 West Bell Road, Phoenix, AZ 85023
(602) 942-1101 Fax: (602) 942-8659
E-Mail Address: turf@turfparadise.net; Web Site: www.turfparadise.com

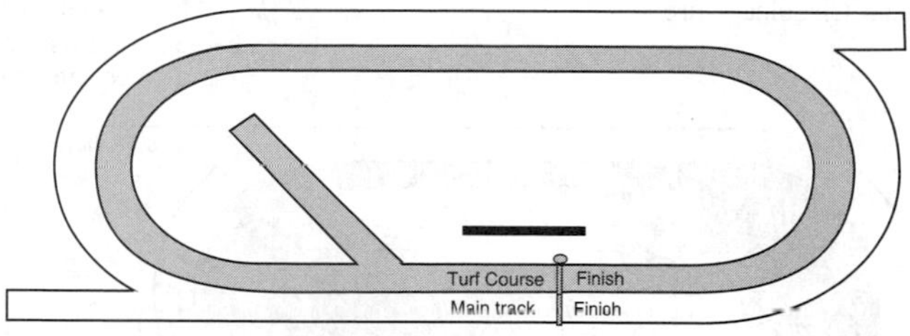

Track data: One-mile oval, with two chutes: 3/8 miles and 6 1/2 furlongs. Distance from last turn to finish, 990 feet. Width 80 feet in stretch, 70 feet in backstretch, 100 feet on turns. Turf course: 7/8 miles, with 1/8 miles infield chute. Stable accommodations for 1,700. Seating capacity 7,284.

Opened January 7, 1956 and after several ownership changes has consistently run an extended Fall-Winter-Spring meet of 160 or more days in recent seasons. During the 165-day session in 2003-2004, purses averaged more than $70,000 per day. Dates in 2005: Oct. 1, 2004 through May 22, 2005.

TRACK RECORDS

2 furs.	Wandering Boy	6	118	:21-1/5	Dec. 5, 1965	1-1/16 m	Down The Isle	8	117	1:39-1/5	Feb. 11, 1987
3 furs.	Never Shamed	2	118	:31-3/5	Apr. 1, 1996	1-1/8 m	Our Forbes	6	116	1:47-3/5	Nov. 29, 1996
4-1/2 furs.	Jazz Hot	2	115	:50.20	Apr. 18, 1995	1-1/4 m	Truly a Pleasure	8	121	2:01-2/5	Mar. 26, 1995
5 furs.	Zip Pocket	3	122	:55-2/5	Apr. 22, 1967	1-3/8 m	Bloom N Character	4	114	2:15-2/5	Apr. 12, 1980
5-1/2 furs.	Plenty Zloty	5	118	1:01.10	Apr. 18, 1995	1-5/8 m	Masked Rider	6	119	2:44.40	Feb. 10, 2002
6 furs.	G Malleah	4	120	1:06-3/5	Apr. 8, 1995	1-3/4 m	Arsenal	7	121	2:55-2/5	Feb. 7, 1971
6-1/2 furs.	Lost in the Fog	2	119	1:13.55	Dec. 26, 2004	2 miles	Vermejo	5	114	3:24	Apr. 20, 1969
1 mile	Mr. Pappion	5	118	1:33-1/5	Jan. 30, 1993						

Turf Course

4-1/2 furs.	Dan s Groovy	7	120	:49.26	Apr. 13, 2003	Abt.1-1/16m	Charging Pete	4	116	1:43-2/5	Apr. 21, 1998
Abt.5 furs.	J. Zac	5	114	:57-4/5	Feb. 18, 1990	1-1/16 m	Caesour	5	120	1:40-2/5	Feb. 5, 1995
5 furs.	Amersham			56.29	Feb. 2, 2002	Abt.1-1/8m	Flying Rebel	5	114	1:51	Mar. 28, 1997
Abt.7 furs.	Faro	4	119	1:25-1/5	Nov. 23, 1986	1-1/8 m	Narghile	5	116	1:48	Feb. 1, 1987
7 furs.	Bristolville	5	119	1:28.60	Nov. 3, 2001	Abt.1-3/8m	Doctor Trotter	6	121	2:16-4/5	Apr. 18, 1998
Abt.7-1/2 f	Balboa Park	4	119	1:30.40	Dec. 19, 2001	1-3/8 m	Free Corona	5	126	2:15.17	Apr. 27, 2003
7-1/2 furs.	Black Bart	5	122	1:27.54	Nov. 6, 2004	Abt.1-1/2 m	Estonia	7	121	2:34	Apr. 5, 1997
Abt.1 mile	Oblomov	5	121	1:37-3/5	Apr. 19, 1998	1-1/2 m	Senator McGuire	6	117	2:29-3/5	May 22, 1988
1 mile	Prose	6	118	1:34.60	Mar. 27, 2001	Abt.1-7/8 m	Amapour	8	115	3:15-1/5	May 18, 1986

Leading Jockey in 2003-2004: Mick Ruis, 132 wins
Leading Trainer in 2003-2004: Troy Bainum, 79 wins
Record attendance: 16,000 estmated, March 18, 1984

TURFWAY PARK

Turfway Park LLC.
President and CEO: Robert N. Elliston; General Manager/Director of Operations: Greg Schmitz; |Racing Secretary: Richard S. Leigh; Director of Marketing/Communications: To be announced.
Street Address: 7500 Turfway Road, Florence, Kentucky 41042
Nearest Airport: Greater Cincinnati Airport (2 miles from track)
P.O. Box 8, Florence, Kentucky 41022
(859) 371-0200, (800) 733-0200; Fax: (859) 647-4730
Media Relations: (859) 647-4842
E-Mail Address: info@turfway.com
Web Site: www.turfway.com

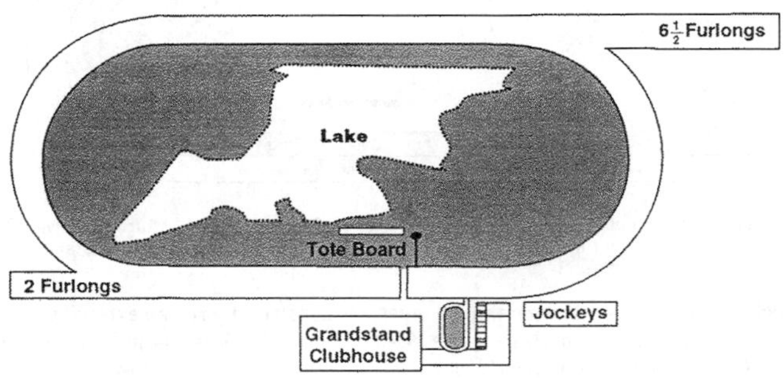

Track Data: One-mile oval with 6 1/2-furlong and 1 1/4-mile chutes. Distance from last turn to finish, 970 feet. Stable accommodations for 1,200. Seating capacity 8,000; Parking for 6,500 cars.

Opened August 27, 1959 and purchased in 1999 by Keeneland Association; Dreamport, Inc., a subsidiary of the GTECH Corporation; and Harrah's Entertainment Inc. Turfway operates three meets each year and is home to the $500,000 Grade 2 Lane's End Stakes, an early prep for the Kentucky Derby, and the Kentucky Cup Day of Champions, five stakes races (four graded) pointing toward the Breeders' Cup. 2005 race dates: Winter/Spring Meet, Jan. 1 through April 7; Fall meet, Sept. 7 through Oct. 6; Holiday Meet, Nov. 27 through Dec. 31. Lane's End Stakes: March 26. Kentucky Cup Day: Sept. 17.

TRACK RECORDS

2 furs.	Sizzling Lisa	2	108	:21-3/5	Apr. 2, 1979	1-1/16 m	Anet	3	115	1:40-3/5	Mar. 29, 1997
3 furs.	Cut Glass	2	11	:34-3/5	Mar. 27, 1976	1-1/8 m	Hansel	3	121	1:46-3/5	Mar. 30, 1991
5 furs.	Cindy s Hobby	7	122	:56.93	Jan. 7, 2004	1-1/4 m	Executor	7	117	2:03.82	Dec. 29, 2000
Abt. 5 furs.	Blazing Genius	7	129	1:03.20	Aug. 30, 2003	1-1/2 m	Fast Dish	5	111	2:29.19	Mar. 26, 2004
5-1/2 furs.	Da White Judge	4	119	1:03-2/5	Sep. 29, 1979	1-5/8 m	Bluegrass Warrior	6	115	2:46-3/5	Feb. 23, 1991
6 furs.	Appealing Skier	3	118	1:08-1/5	Sep. 21, 1996	1-11/16 m	Sestos	9	116	2:56-1/5	Jan. 1, 1969
Abt 6-1/2 f	Billy Genn	3	113	1:19-2/5	Sep. 12, 1990	1-3/4 m	Bluegrass Warrior	5	111	2:59	Mar. 10, 1990
6-1/2 furs.	Boone s Mill	3	120	1:14-1/5	Dec. 30, 1995	2 miles	Bluegrass Warrior	6	119	3:23-4/5	Mar. 30, 1991
1 mile	Secreto s Hideaway	5	119	1:34	Mar. 5, 1994						

Leading Jockeys in 2004: Rafael Bejarano won two of three meets and Dean A. Sarvis won the remaining meet
Leading Trainer in 2004: Gregory D. Foley and Robert E. Holthus each won one meet and the remaining meet ended in a tie between Bernard S. Flint, Wayne D. Mogge and George Leonard 3d

Record Attendance: 22, 480, April 25, 2000. Record Handle: $3,223,778, April 2, 1994.

WOODBINE

Woodbine Entertainment Group

Honorary Chairman: Jake Howard; Chairman and CEO: David Willmot; Vice President and COO.: James Ormiston; Racing Secretary: Steve Lym; Vice Pres. of Media and Community Relations: Glenn Crouter.

Street Address: 555 Rexdale Blvd.,
Rexdale, Ontario, Canada, M9W 5L2
Nearest Airport: Lester B. Pearson Int l.,
3 kilometers from track

P.O. Box 156, Toronto, Ontario, Canada, M9W 5L2
(416) 675-7223; Fax: (416) 213-2129; Publicity: (416) 213-2122
Web site: www.woodbineentertainment.com;
e-mail: jss@woodbineentertainment.com

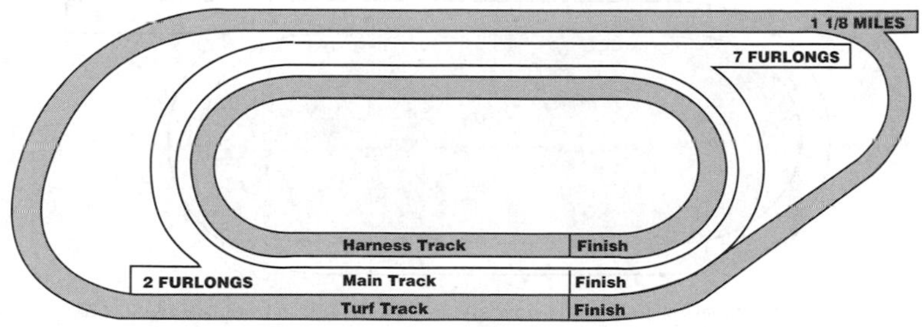

Track Data: One-mile dirt track, with two chutes, 1/4 mile and 7 furlongs. Distance from last turn to finish, 975 feet, width 85 feet in the stretch. Turf course: 1 1/2 miles. Distance from last turn to finish, 1,440 feet, width 100 feet. Also has 7/8-mile Harness track,. Stable accommodations for 1,650. Seating Capacity: 13,500; Parking for 14,700 cars.

The original Woodbine opened in 1874 on the far-eastern outskirts of Toronto, which became Toronto downtown. The name was changed to Old Woodbine in 1956 and Greenwood in 1963. The present facility opened on June 12, 1956. The E.P. Taylor Turf course, unveiled in 1995, is the only 1 1/2-mile grass course in North America and features the longest stretch run in American racing at 1,440 feet. It also rings the one mile dirt track, with a stretch run of 975 feet. . .In 1996, Woodbine became the first track outside the United States to host the Breeders' Cup and in 2004 with nearly 1,800 slot machines on site, purses for 167 racing dates were more than $490,000, to place Woodbine among the leaders in that category in North America. Dates for 2005: April 16 to Dec. 11.

TRACK RECORDS

3 furs.	Noble Herod	2	115	:33-3/5	May 5, 1978	1-1/16 m	Kiridashi	4	121	1:40-4/5	Aug. 17, 1996
4-1/2 furs.	Hallmarked	4	118	:50-2/5	Mar. 24, 1996	1-1/8 m	Glorious Song	5	125	1:48	Jul. 1, 1981
	Written Approval	4	118	:50-2/5	Mar. 25, 1996	1-3/16 m	Runnin Roman	3	114	1:55-4/5	Sep. 15, 1974
5 furs.	Jack and Emma	4	118	:55.95	Apr. 5, 2003	1-1/4 m	Alphabet Soup	5	126	2:01	Oct. 26, 1996
5-1/2 furs.	Uncle Woger	4	119	1:02.70	Apr. 4, 1999	1-3/8 m	Lovely Sunrise	3	112	2:17	Oct. 26, 1974
6 furs.	Chris s Bad Boy	6	118	1:08.05	Nov. 29, 2003	1-1/2 m	Norcliffe	4	122	2:29-1/5	Oct. 29, 1977
6-1/2 furs.	Chris s Bad Boy	7	120	1:14.27	Aug. 7, 2004	1-5/8 m	Eugenia II	4	123	2:43-2/5	Oct. 27, 1956
7 furs.	Oronero	3	114	1:20-3/5	Dec. 6, 1995	1-3/4 m	Major Pots	5	115	2:52.60	Dec. 8, 1994
1 m 70 Yds	Regal Courser	5	121	1:39-3/5	Aug. 8, 1998	1-7/8 m	Flying Commander	3	112	3:13.29	Dec. 2, 2001

Turf Course

6 furs.	Wild Zone	6	119	1:07-3/5	Jul. 7, 1996	Abt 1-1/4 m	Desert Waves	5	117	2:02-2/5	Jun. 24, 1995
6-1/2 furs.	Chris s Bad Boy	7	120	1:14.27	Aug. 7, 2004		Murad	5	115	2:02-2/5	Jun. 4, 1998
7 furs.	Soaring Free	5	126	1:19.38	Jul. 24, 2004	1-1/4 m	Arbalest	4	115	2:01	Jun. 15, 1995
1 mile	Royal Regalia	6	120	1:31.84	Jul. 1, 2004		Set Ablaze	4	109	2:01	Jul. 5, 1996
1-1/16 m	Jet Freighter	4	119	1:39-1/5	Jun. 4, 1995	Abt 1-3/8 m	Chief Bearhart	3	109	2:16	Jul. 25, 1996
	Honolulu Gold	4	117	1:39-1/5	Jul. 11, 1996	1-3/8 m	Shoal Water	4	116	2:12.37	Jul. 25, 2004
	Western Express	9	115	1:39-1/5	Jul. 12, 1998	Abt 1-1/2 m	Mr. Lucky Junction	5	116	2:29-3/5	Jul. 26, 1995
Abt 1-1/8 m	Surging River	4	118	1:42.87	Aug. 8, 2004	1-1/2 m	Raintrap	4	126	2:25-3/5	Oct. 16, 1994
1-1/8 m	Bold Ruritana	5	117	1:45-1/5	Jun. 18, 1995	Abt 1-5/8 m	Moon Bow	6	114	2:46	Sep. 11, 1998

Leading Jockey in 2004: Todd Kabel, 156 wins

Leading Trainer in 2004: Sid Attard, 73 wins

Record attendance: 42, 243, October 26, 1996, (Breeders' Cup Day). Record handle: $6, 884, 357 October 26, 1996: $67, 738, 890, October 26, 1996, (All sources).

THE WOODLANDS

Kansas Racing, LLC

Vice President: Bruce Schmitter; General Manager: Jim Gartland; Racing Secretary: Doug Schoepf; PR/Marketing Director: Connie Loebsack.

9700 Leavenworth Road
Kansas City, KS 66112-0036
(913) 299-9797 Fax: (913) 299-9804
Web Site: www.woodlandskc.com
E-Mail Address: info@woodlandskc.com;larocca@woodlandskc.com;cloebsack@woodlandskc.com

Track data: One-mile oval with 6-furlong chute. Distance from last turn to finish, 1,030 feet. Seating capacity 4,250.

Opened May 24, 1990 for Thoroughbred racing after a year of Greyhound racing which continues to be offered on a separate track in the Woodlands complex. Now runs a one month, mixed-breed meet in the fall with about $50,000 in daily purses. Year-round simulcasting. Dates for 2005: Sept. 24 to Oct. 29. (12 races per day, on Saturday-Wednesday.)

TRACK RECORDS

4 furs.	King of Diamonds	5	119	:45.80	Oct. 10, 2001	1-1/16 m	Shatter the Stars	3	114	1:43	Jul. 21, 1991
4-1/2 furs.	Lanyons Star	2	117	:51-2/5	Jun. 29, 1990	1-1/8 m	Model Age	6	119	1:49-4/5	Jul. 18, 1990
5 furs.	Tim Dougan	2	118	:57-4/5	Jun. 30, 1991	1-3/16 m	Old Man s Delite	7	124	1:58.00	Oct. 21, 2003
5-1/2 furs.	Axe Age	6	116	1:03-1/5	Aug. 15, 1993	1-1/4 m	Midway Mail	5	122	2:03-1/5	Sep. 10, 1993
6 furs.	Great Immunity	4	116	1:08-2/5	Jun. 30, 1991	1-1/2 m	He s a Valentine	4	116	2:33.20	Oct. 14, 1994
1 mile	French Fritter	4	114	1:36	Jun. 1, 1991	1-3/4 m	Mark of Strength	8	116	3:04-3/5	Sep. 26, 1993
1 m 70 Yds	Holly s Wind	4	120	1:40-2/5	Jun. 24, 1990						

Leading Jockey in 2004: Alex Birzer, 30 wins
Leading Trainer in 2004: Timothy Mark Gleason, 19 wins
Record attendance: 22,015, July 22, 1990

WYOMING DOWNS

Wyoming Horseracing, Inc.

President: Eric Nelson; General Manager and Director of Racing: Dale Parker; Assistant General Manager: Brody Johnson; Director of Operations: Joan Ramos; Controller: Lorie Anderson.

Physical Address:
10180 Highway 89 North
Evanston, WY, 82930
(866) 681-7223

Mailing Address:
PO Box 1607, Evanston, WY, 82931
(307) 789-0511; (Fax): (307) 789-9439
E-Mail Address: info@wydowns.com
Web Site: www.wyomingdowns.com

Track data: Seven and one half furlong oval with two chutes. 6 1/2 furlongs and 550 yards for Quarter Horse and mixed-breed races. Distance from last turn to finish, 1,050 feet. Stable accommodations for 860. Seating capacity 2,100.

Opened May 25, 1985, and is scheduled for a summer meet in 2005 on Saturdays and Sundays from June 25 to Aug. 21. Year-round simulcasting at off-track betting facilities located in Casper, Cheyenne, Evanston and Rock Springs.

TRACK RECORDS

4 furs.	Mister To You	2	122	:46-2/5	Sep. 1, 1991	7-1/2 furs.	Become A Lord	6	116	1:29-3/5	Jul. 14, 1990
Abt. 4-1/2 f	Mackay Man	5	126	:52.01	Aug. 8, 2004	1 mile.	Rapt	5	122	1:36	Aug. 9, 1987
4-1/2 furs.	Truly a Habit	7	124	:51.20	Jul. 22, 2000	1-1/16 m	Running Razor	6	114	1:42-4/5	Sep. 3, 1990
5 furs.	Briefly Noted	4	122	:56-2/5	Sep. 2, 1990	1-1/8 m	Mud Dancer	9	119	1:49-4/5	Aug. 22,1992
5-1/2 furs.	Beat the Latch	7	124	1:01.80	Aug. 21, 1999	1-1/4 m	Prowlin Time	5	122	2:13-1/5	Sep. 2, 1985
6 furs.	Speed Fancier	4	124	1:08	Aug. 20, 1995	Abt.1-1/4 m	Lurky	6	122	2:03	Aug. 26,1990

Leading Jockey in 2004: Travis Hamilton, 6 wins

Leading Trainers in 2004: Mike D. Taylor & Terrill Gibbs, 5 wins (tie)

Record attendance: 9,200 September 2, 1985. Record handle $324, 878, September 2, 1985.

YAVAPAI DOWNS

Yavapai County Fair Association
General Manager: James M. Grundy.

10401 Highway 89 A
Prescott Valley, AZ 86312-6557
(928) 775-8000 Fax: (928) 445-0408
Web Site: http://www.yavapaidownsatpv.com

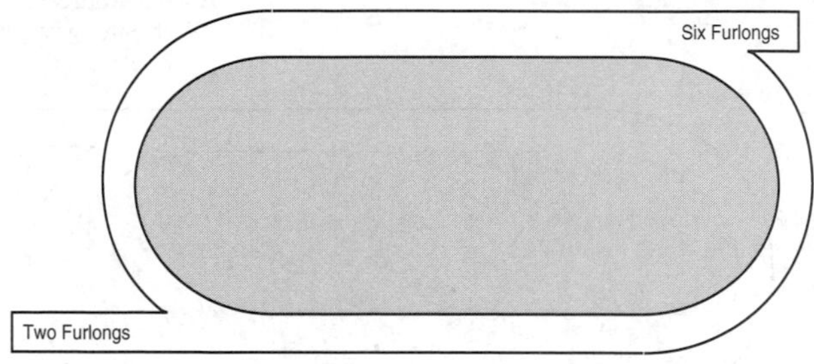

Track data: One-mile oval with 2-furlong and 6-furlong chutes. Distance from last turn to finish 1,020 feet.

Opened May 26, 2001... Located in Prescott Valley, Arizona, 15 miles from the old historic Prescott Downs. The 90-year history of racing in the area continues. The dates for 2005: May 28 though Sept. 6 with thoroughbred purses averaging $30,000 per day.

TRACK RECORDS

Distance	Horse	Age	Wt.	Time	Date	Distance	Horse	Age	Wt.	Time	Date
Abt. 4-1/2 f	Half Penny	4	120	:49.60	Jul. 25, 2004	1 mile	Heightenedinterest			1:35.01	Jun. 3, 2002
4-1/2 furs.	Red Spark	4	123	:50.20	Sep. 7, 2004	1-1/16 m	Gusto Forzado			1:42.63	Jun. 24, 2002
5 furs.	Canyon s Wildcat	8	123	:56.40	Aug. 9, 2004	1-1/8 m	Moonray			1:49.40	Jun. 25, 2002
5-1/2 furs.	Hemandan			1:02.36	Aug. 13, 2002	1-1/4 m	Cajun Bound	5	126	2:03.20	Aug. 18, 2003
6 furs.	Miss Pixie			1:08.12	Aug. 24, 2002						

Leading Jockey in 2004: Wilson Omar Dieguez, 46 wins
Leading Trainer in 2004: Bill Brashears, 39 wins
Record attendance: 35,000 – May 26, 2001. Record handle $1,386,000 – June 8, 2002.

YELLOWSTONE DOWNS

PO Box 1138, Billings, MT 59103
(406) 869-5251

Held 9 days of mixed-breed racing between Sept. 5 and Sept. 26 in 2004, with average daily Thoroughbred purses of over $12,000. 2005 dates: Aug. 19 through Sept. 25.
Leading Jockey in 2004: Ivan Ortiz, 7 wins
Leading Trainer in 2004: Edward Buxbaum, 4 wins

Puerto Rico

EL COMMANDANTE

Hipodromo El Comandante
COO and Executive Vice President: Alejandro Fuentes Fernandez.

El Commandante Management Co LLC
PO Box 1675, Canovanas, PR 00729
787-641-6060 Fax: 787-876-5170
Web Site: www.elcomandantepr.com

Track data: One-mile oval, with seven-furlong chute. Width of stretch 85 feet; width of backstretch 75 feet; distance from last turn to finish 900 feet. Stable accommodations for 1,200. Seating capacity 11,000; parking for 4,000 cars.

Opened November 17, 1976. Unsettled racing schedule, pending seasonal weather and other factors. Year round simulcasting.

Record attendance: 20,429, December 10, 1978.

Racing Organizations

National and State Organizations

International Organizations

The American Stud Book

Prominent Racing Organizations in North America

NATIONAL THOROUGHBRED RACING ASSOCIATION

NTRA is a tax-exempt membership organization and trade association, formed in 1998 to increase the popularity of Thoroughbred racing and improve economic conditions in the industry. NTRA member contributions, as well as funds from sponsorships and other marketing alliances, are reinvested in programs to grow the horse racing and breeding industries. That reinvestment takes many forms, including marketing, advertising, promotions, television, national consumer research, publicity, economic programs, sponsorship sales and legislative advocacy.

Three years after its founding, NTRA combined operations with Breeders' Cup Limited through a 10-year licensing and operating agreement under which the corporations retained their separate legal identities, Breeders' Cup programs were licensed to the NTRA to manage, and BCL personnel became NTRA employees. The result was one virtual corporation to generate new interest and participation in Thoroughbred racing and its culminating event, the Breeders' Cup World Thoroughbred Championships.

Since its founding, NTRA has developed several subsidiaries, which now include NTRA Productions, NTRA Investments, NTRA Purchasing and NTRA Charities, as well as the NTRA Creative Services program, an in-house marketing agency.

NTRA and Breeders' Cup operate under a single budget, with a combined staff headquartered in Lexington, Ky., and an office of media and sponsorships located in New York City.

2004 NTRA Board of Directors

The 15-member NTRA Board of Directors consists of the NTRA Commissioner and seven representatives each for racetracks and for horsemen, owners and breeders. For a complete listing of NTRA Directors visit the NTRA Web site, NTRA.com, or contact the NTRA at (800) 792-NTRA to request its current Annual Report.

NTRA Commissioner and Chief Executive Officer and Breeders' Cup President

D.G. Van Clief, Jr.

Mr. Van Clief was appointed NTRA Commissioner and Chief Executive Officer in September 2004, after serving as NTRA Vice Chairman since January 2001 in addition to that of Breeders' Cup President. He is also a Breeders' Cup representative on the NTRA Board.

NTRA
800 Third Avenue
Suite 901
New York, NY 10022
Tel (212) 230-9500
Fax (212) 752-3093

NTRA
2525 Harrodsburg Road
Fifth Floor
Lexington, KY 40504
Tel (859) 223-5444
Fax (859) 223-3945

Internet: ntra.com
E-mail: ntra@ntra.com

THOROUGHBRED RACING ASSOCIATIONS OF NORTH AMERICA, INC.

Organization of member racetracks and racing associations that was created in 1942, to serve as a unified voice of the Thoroughbred racing industry, to work under a code of Standards and By-Laws. Mission statement: To place maximum emphasis on the integrity of racing and act with other pari-mutuel industries to promote legislation and provide assistance to member tracks in their relationships with State, Federal or Provincial legislatures. To provide statistical and informational services to all members and to assist in the promotion of racing. To co-sponsor annually, with the National Turf Writers Association and Daily Racing Form, the Eclipse Awards program. To recommend support for organizations and institutions, which engage in equine research, provide formal educational programs designed to produce racetrack management personnel and the protection and promotion of the entire horse industry.

To maintain liaison with other segments of the Thoroughbred industry, and with organizations and associations of other horse breeds. To explore possibilities of group insurance, printing, generic TV commercials, etc. To maintain a register of available part-time personnel such as racing officials, management, publicity, etc.

420 Fair Hill Drive,
Suite 1 Elkton, Maryland 21921-2573
Tel: (410) 392-9200
Fax: (410) 398-1366
E-mail: info@tra-online.com
Web Site: www.tra-online.com

Officers:
Corey S. Johnsen, President
C. Kenneth Dunn, Vice President
David S. Willmot, Vice President
Robert L. Bork, Secretary
William I. Fasy, Treasurer
Christopher N. Scherf, Executive Vice President

Directors:
Don Amos, Portland Meadows
Charles W. Bidwill III
Robert L. Bork
Michael Brown, Hastings Park
Thomas F. Carey III
Charles J. Cella
Sherwood C. Chillingworth
Joseph A. De Francis
Dennis Dowd, Monmouth
C. Steven Duncker, NYRA
C. Kenneth Dunn
Robert N. Elliston
Robert A. Farinella
James L. Gagliano
William Gallo, Jr.
Clifford C. Goodrich
Robert W. Green
Harold G. Handel
Joe Harper
Charles E. Hayward, NYRA
Corey S. Johnsen
Peter F. Karches, NYRA
Robert P. Levy
F. Jack Liebau
James McAlpine
Christopher McErlean, Meadowlands
Hugh M. Miner, Jr.
Jerry M. Monahan
Richard E. Moore
Howard M. Mosner, Jr
Nick Nicholson
Louis J. Raffetto, Jr.
William M. Rickman, Jr.
Charles J. Ruma
Randall D. Sampson
Christopher N. Scherf
Richard T. Schnaars
Steven P. Sexton
Randall E. Soth
Ronald A. Sultemeier

Stella F. Thayer
Ray A. Tromba
David S. Willmot

Alternate Directors:
Michael Abes
Rogers Beasley
Patricia M. Bidwill
Peter M. Carlino
Richard L. Duchossois
William I. Fasy
Howell L. Ferguson
John Finamore
Craig R. Fravel
Jeffrey Greco
Eric Halstrom
Derron Heldt
William E. Hogwood
R. Eric Jackson
Robert Kulina
R. D. Logan
Jack McDaniel
Peter D. McGivney
Ann McGovern
F. Grove Miller
Jim Miller
John E. Mooney
William D. Murphy
William A. Nader
Louis J. Raffetto, Jr.
Clifford A. Reed
Christian Riegle
Dr. Jack K. Robbins
Scott Savin
Sal Sinatra
Bruce A. Swihart
Bernie Thurman
Ray A. Tromba
Michael Weiss
Scott Wells
Joseph Wilson
Iain F. Woolnough

Directors Emeriti:
James E. "Ted" Bassett III
Baird C. Brittingham
Robert S. Gunderson
Lynn Stone

Former Presidents:
1942-1943 John C. Clark
1944-1946 Henry A. Parr III
1947-1948 James E. Dooley
1949-1950 Donald P. Ross
1951-1952 Alfred G. Vanderbilt
1953-1954 John A. Morris

1955-1956 Amory L. Haskell
1957-1958 James D. Stewart
1959-1960 John G. Cella
1961-1962 E. E. Dale Shaffer
1963-1964 Robert P. Strub
1965-1966 Edward P. Taylor
1967-1968 L. L. Haggin III
1969-1970 John D. Schapiro
1971-1973 James E. Brock
1973-1975 Frank M. Basil
1975-1976 Charles J. Cella
1977-1978 Baird C. Brittingham
1979-1980 Robert S. Gunderson
1981-1982 Lynn Stone
1983-1984 Morris J. Alhadeff
1985-1986 James E. Bassett III
1987-1988 Gerard J. McKeon
1989-1990 Robert P. Levy
1991-1992 Thomas H. Meeker
1993-1994 David M. Vance
1995-1996 Clifford C. Goodrich
1997-1998 Harold G. Handel
1999-2000 Stella F. Thayer
2001-2002 Bryan G. Krantz
2003-2004 Joe Harper

THOROUGHBRED RACING PROTECTIVE BUREAU
A wholly owned subsidiary of TRA formed in 1946. Bureau of investigation and inter state security for the racing industry.

420 Fair Hill Drive, Suite 2
Elkton, Maryland 21921-2573
Telephone: (410) 398-2261
Fax: (410) 398-1499
E-Mail: trpbinfo@trpb.com
Web Site: http://www.trpb.com

Officers:
Franklin J. Fabian, President & Treasurer
James P. Gowen, Vice President & Secretary

Board Of Directors:
John E. Mooney - Chairman Colonial Downs
Bryan G. Krantz - Vice Chairman Fair Grounds
Robert L. Bork, Sam Houston Race Park
Charles J. Cella, Oaklawn Park
Sherwood C. Chillingworth, Oak Tree Racing Association
James L. Gagliano, Magna Entertainment Corp.
C. Kenneth Dunn, Calder
Christopher McErlean, Meadowlands
Terence J. Meyocks, NTRA
Nick Nicholson, Keeneland Association
Richard T. Schnaars, Penn National
Stella F. Thayer, Tampa Bay Downs

Equibase Company LLC.
Established in 1991 as a general partnership between the Thoroughbred Racing Associations of North America (TRA) and The Jockey Club, Equibase maintains the industry owned, Official database for North American racing. That database is the source material from which Daily Racing Form produces its result charts and comprehensive past performance lines.

821 Corporate Drive
Lexington, Kentucky 40503-2794
Telephone: (859) 224-2860 or (800) 333-2211
Fax: (859) 224-2811
www.equibase.com

Officers:
Chairman, Alan Marzelli
Secretary, Christopher N. Scherf

Management Committee:
Sherwood C. Chillingworth, The Jockey Club
C. Steven Duncker, The Jockey Club
Dan Fick, The Jockey Club
Craig R. Fravel, Del Mar Thoroughbred Club
Alan Marzelli, The Jockey Club
Jim McAlpine, Magna Entertainment Corporation
Bill Nader, New York Racing Association
Nick Nicholson, Keeneland
Ogden Mills Phipps, The Jockey Club
Steve Sexton, Churchill Downs
Ray Tromba, Louisiana Downs
Michael Weiss, Beulah Park

Executive Staff:
Phillip T. O'Hara, Jr., President and Chief Executive Officer
Hank Zeitlin, Executive Vice President and Chief Operating Officer
Chuck Scaravilli, Vice President, Track and Field

Fred Russell-Grantland Rice TRA Sports Writing Scholarship
Begun in 1956, originally named to honor the late Grantland Rice, a Vanderbilt alumnus and one of the best known sports writers of the 20th century. In 1986, the name was changed to also honor Fred Russell, another Vanderbilt alumnus and columnist for the Atlanta Constitution who helped guide the scholarship and its recipients throughout his career. A $500,000 grant was made on behalf of the TRA in 1986 to ensure the future of this valuable stipend. The scholarship, worth $40,000 over 4 years of study, is co-sponsored by Vanderbilt. It is awarded annually to students with special interest and potential in the field of sports writing. The deadline for applying is January 1st each year. High school seniors may obtain a scholarship application form and further information from: Coordinator of Special Scholarships, Undergraduate Admission, Vanderbilt University, 2305 West End Avenue, Nashville, TN 37203-1727; (615) 322-2561.
E-Mail: admissions@vanderbilt.edu
Web Site: http://www.vanderbilt.edu/Admissions

Among previous winners were nationally prominent sports writers Roy A. Blount, Mill River, Mass, (1959) and 1970 Skip Bayless, Dallas, Tex. The last four winners were:

2001 Robert Craig Murray III, Brentwood, Tennessee
2002 Byron Patrick Dubow, Alphretta, Georgia
2003 Matthew Collins McDavid, Bethesda, Maryland
2004 Christopher Fielding Callaway, Atlanta, Georgia

THE JOCKEY CLUB

The Jockey Club was originally formed as the Board of Control in 1891 and ratified its first charter as The Jockey Club, February 9, 1894. Through its 110 years, The Jockey Club has served as the official Thoroughbred breed registry for North America and with its family of companies, remains dedicated to the improvement of Thoroughbred breeding and racing. Responsibilities of The Jockey Club consist primarily of maintaining The American Stud Book in a manner that insures integrity of the Thoroughbred in the United States, Canada, and Puerto Rico. In 1996, The Jockey Club began to implement Interactive Registration™, a free service used by approximately 18,000 owners and breeders to fulfill the requirements for registration and naming of Thoroughbreds over the Internet, including submission of digital foal identification photos. The program includes an online 'Names Book' which puts users in direct electronic contact with The Jockey Club's database of names in active use. The Registry also replaced blood-typing with DNA-typing for Thoroughbred parentage verification, beginning with the 2001 foal crop. In addition, The Jockey Club founded Equibase Company in partnership with the Thoroughbred Racing Associations in 1990.

New York Office:
40 East 52nd Street,
New York, New York 10022
(212) 371-5970 Fax (212) 371-6123
Web site: http://www.jockeyclub.com

Kentucky Office:
821 Corporate Drive
Lexington, Kentucky 40503-2794
(859) 224-2700 Fax (859) 224-2710
Web site: http://www.jockeyclub.com

Officers:
Ogden Mills Phipps, Chairman
William S. Farish, Vice Chairman
James C. Brady, Secretary-Treasurer
Alan Marzelli, President and Chief Operating Officer
Dan Fick, Executive Vice President and Executive Director
Laura Barillaro, Executive Vice President and Chief Financial Officer

Members:
Josephine E. Abercrombie, Helen C. Alexander, Joe L. Allbritton, John Ed Anthony, William Backer, Charles Baker, * John Barr, James E. Bassett III, Rollin W. Baugh, John A. Bell III, Reynolds Bell, Jr., Gary Biszantz, Edward S. Bonnie, Frank A. Bonsal, Jr., * James C. Brady, Nicholas F. Brady, Dr. Larry Bramlage, Michael C. Byrne, Alexander G. Campbell, Jr., Thomas R. Capehart, Charles J. Cella, Mrs. Alice H. Chandler, Helen B. Chenery, Sherwood C. Chillingworth, Robert N. Clay, F. Eugene Dixon, Jr., * Donald R. Dizney, Allan R. Dragone, Jack J. Dreyfus, Jr., Richard L. Duchossois, Duke of Devonshire CBE, C. Steven Duncker, Allaire duPont, William duPont III, Edward P. Evans, Robert S. Evans, * William S. Farish, William S. Farish, Jr., Hugh A. Fitzsimons, Jr., Martha F. Gerry, John K. Goodman, Louis L. Haggin III, Lucy Young Hamilton, Arthur B. Hancock III, * Dell Hancock, Seth W. Hancock, Joseph W. Harper, John C. Harris, John Hettinger, E. Edward Houghton, * G. Watts Humphrey, Jr., * Stuart S. Janney III, Richard I. G. Jones, Russell B. Jones, Jr., Peter F. Karches, Dr. A. Gary Lavin, Robert B. Lewis, F. Jack Liebau, William C. MacMillen, Jr., Harry T. Mangurian, Jr., Frank L. Mansell, J.W.Y. Martin, Jr., James K. McManus, Robert McNair, Robert E. Meyerhoff, Leverett Miller, MacKenzie Miller, Nick Nicholson, Kenneth Noe Jr., Charles Nuckols, Jr., J. Michael O'Farrell, Jr., * John C. Oxley, John H. Peace, John W. Phillips, * Ogden Mills Phipps, Dr. Hiram C. Polk, Jr., Carl Pollard, David P. Reynolds, Reuben F. Richards, Dr. J. David Richardson, Dr. Jack K. Robbins, J. Mack Robinson, Timothy H. Sams, Richard Santulli, Peter G. Schiff, Barry Schwartz, Joseph V. Shields, Jr., Mace Siegel, Viola Sommer, Robert S. Strauss, George Strawbridge, Jr., Shirley H. Taylor, Stella Thayer, Oakleigh B. Thorne, Donald J. Valpredo, Daniel G. Van Clief, Jr., Frank "Scoop" Vessels III, Joseph Walker, Jr., Charlotte C. Weber, Wheelock Whitney, David Willmot, Martin Wygod, William T. Young, Jr.
* Stewards

THE JOCKEY CLUB INFORMATION SYSTEMS, INC. (TJCIS)

TJCIS, incorporated in 1989, is a wholly owned subsidiary of The Jockey Club. All profits from TJCIS activities are reinvested in the Thoroughbred industry, funding many industry projects which would otherwise lack financial support.

Operations of the multimedia information and service provider include equineline.com, the Internet-based information network for Thoroughbred and American Quarter Horse industry professionals; catalogue pages for North American Thoroughbreds sold at public auction; and software sales and consulting. Equineline.com features a reports service that provides instant access to pedigrees and race records; as well as a portfolio service that allows owners and breeders to create a personal profile of their equine interests which is updated with real-time information. The equineline.com web site also includes a 'trainer program' to help professional horsemen and their assistants streamline or automate the business-related details associated with training horses; and a 'farm program' to help farms organize all of the billing, health care, breeding and foaling records upon which successful operation of their business depends. In addition to its equineline.com services, TJCIS also offers Veterinary Management™ Software to help equine veterinary practices organize all of its health and billing records; and the Horse Farm Management HealthBook™, which enables farm personnel to collect and record reproductive and herd health information in the field through a lightweight Tablet PC.

821 Corporate Drive, Lexington, KY 40503
Toll free (800) 333-1778
(859) 224-2800. . .Fax: (859) 224-2810
http://www.equineline.com
Chairman & Chief Executive Officer: Carl Hamilton

InCompass

As part of a November 2001 corporate restructuring at The Jockey Club family of companies, McKinnie Systems, Inc., the software company that specialized in racing office and horsemen's bookkeeper applications, was re-named InCompass. The re-named entity is a technology solutions company that has centralized the software applications and systems that serve North American racetracks. Leveraging the power of a centralized database to deliver a wide array of re-engineered solutions, InCompass is helping racetracks achieve operational efficiencies, reduce costs and enhance marketing efforts and business analysis, while improving the accuracy, comprehensiveness and timeliness of racing information for the entire industry.

821 Corporate Drive, Lexington, KY 40503
(859) 296-3000. . .Fax: (859) 296-3010
http://www.incompass-solutions.com
President: David Haydon

The Jockey Club Technology Services, Inc.

The Jockey Club Technology Services, Inc. (TJCTS) was formed out of the November 2001 corporate restructuring at The Jockey Club family of companies when the business unit that served as the information technology group for The Jockey Club and a technology consultant for the industry at large was spun-off into a wholly-owned subsidiary of The Jockey Club. TJCTS provides infrastructure support services for The Jockey Club family of companies, as well as software design and programming services at the request of other industry organizations.
821 Corporate Drive, Lexington, KY 40503
(859) 224-2700. . .Fax: (859) 224-2777
http://www.tjctechnology.com
President: Robert A. Burch

Grayson-Jockey Club Research Foundation, Inc.

The Grayson Foundation was established in 1940, to raise support for the promotion and funding of equine veterinary research. In 1989, resources were combined with those of The Jockey Club Research Foundation. Since 1983, the Foundation has contributed more than $11 million toward projects aimed at enhancing the health and safety of horses.
During the year 2004, the Foundation allocated $850,888 for 20 projects at 12 universities continent-

wide, confirming its position as a leading source of private funding for equine veterinary research. Contributions in support of the Foundation may be addressed to:

The Grayson-Jockey Club Research Foundation
821 Corporate Drive, Lexington, KY 40503
(859) 224-2850. . .Fax: (859) 224-2853
http://www.grayson-jockeyclub.org
President: Edward L. Bowen

The Jockey Club Foundation
Founded in 1943, The Jockey Club Foundation is a charitable trust created to provide relief to needy members of the Thoroughbred industry and their families.

Administered by a Board of Trustees, comprised of members of The Jockey Club, financial aid is extended either through a monthly assistance program or on a one-time lump-sum basis, and includes extensive contributions to other benevolent organizations in the Thoroughbred industry. Since 1985, the Foundation has been able to help thousands of individuals and their families with approximately $11 million in support. Grants from the Foundation totaled approximately $590,000 in 2004. Contributions in support of the Foundation may be addressed to:

The Jockey Club Foundation
40 East 52nd Street
New York, NY 10022.
(212) 521-5305.Fax: (212) 371-6123
http://www.tjcfoundation.org

Trustees:
C. Steven Duncker
John Hettinger
D.G. Van Clief, Jr.
Treasurer: Laura Barillaro
Executive Director: Nancy Kelly

OTHER RACING ORGANIZATIONS

AMERICAN ASSOCIATION OF EQUINE PRACTITIONERS
Mailing Address: 4075 Iron Works Parkway,
Lexington, KY 40511
Phone: (859) 233-0147 Fax: (859) 233-1968
E-Mail: aaepoffice@aaep.org
President: Scott E. Palmer V.M.D.; Executive Director: David L. Foley

AMERICAN HORSE COUNCIL
Mailing Address: 1616 H. St. NW, 7th floor Washington, D.C. 20006
Phone: (202) 296-4031 Fax: (202) 296-1970
E-Mail: ahc@horsecouncil.org
Chairman: James F. Barton
President: James J. Hickey, Jr.

AMERICAN QUARTER HORSE ASSOCIATION
Mailing Address: P.O. Box 200,
Amarillo, TX 79168
Phone: (806) 376-4811 Fax: (806) 349-6402
E-Mail: racing@aqha.org
Executive Vice President: Bill Brewer

ASSOCIATION OF RACING COMMISSIONERS INTERNATIONAL, INC.
Mailing Address: 2343 Alexandria Drive, Suite 200,
Lexington, KY 40504-3276
Phone: (859) 224-7070 Fax: (859) 224-7071
E-Mail: support@arci.com
Chairman: Timothy "Ted" Connors (2005) Replaces Frank Zanzuccki
President and CEO: Edward J. Martin

BREEDERS' CUP LIMITED
Mailing Address: 2525 Harrodsburg Road, Suite 500,
Lexington, KY 40504-3359
Phone: (859) 223-5444 Fax: (859) 223-3945
E-Mail: breederscup@breederscup.com
President: D.G. Van Clief, Jr.
Media Relations Director: James Gluckson, (212) 230-9512

HARNESS TRACKS OF AMERICA
Mailing Address: 4640 East Sunrise, Suite 200,
Tucson, AZ 85718
Phone: (520) 529-2525 Fax: (520) 529-3235
E-Mail: info@harnesstracks.com
President: Jeffrey Smith;
Executive Vice President: Stanley F. Bergstein
General Counsel and Secretary: Paul J. Estok

THE JOCKEYS' GUILD, INC.
Mailing Address: P.O. Box 150, Monrovia, CA 91017
Phone: 866-GOJOCKS (465-6257) or (626) 305-5605 Fax: (626) 305-5615
E-Mail: info@jockeysguild.com
President: L. Wayne Gertmenian
Chairman: Tomey Jean Swan
Vice President: Albert Fiss

NATIONAL HORSEMEN'S BENEVOLENT & PROTECTIVE ASSOCIATION
4063 Ironworks Parkway, B2,
Lexington, KY 40511-8905
Email: racing@hbpa.org
Phone: (859) 259-0451
Fax: (859) 259-0452
President: John Roark
Executive Director: Remi Bellocq

NATIONAL RACING COMPACT
Mailing Address: 2343 Alexandria Drive
Lexington, KY 40504
Phone: (877) 457-2538
Fax: (804) 966-7422
E-Mail: nrcsupport@racinglicense.com
Chairman: Robin Williams

NATIONAL TURF WRITERS ASSOCIATION
1244 Meadow Lane
Frankfort, Kentucky, 40601
(502) 875-4864
President: Mike Kane, 2004 – 2006
Secretary: Dan Liebman
Email:dliebman@bloodhorse.com

NORTH AMERICAN PARI-MUTUEL REGULATORS ASSOCIATION
Mailing Address:
120 North Third Street Suite 100 Bismarck, ND 58501
Phone: (701) 221-2142 Fax: (701) 255-7979
E-Mail: pbowlinger@napraonline.com
Executive Director: Paul Bowlinger

RACE TRACK CHAPLAINCY OF AMERICA
Mailing Address: PO Box 91640, Los Angeles, CA 90009
Phone: (310) 419-1640
Fax: (310) 419-1642
Email: etorres@racetrackchaplaincy.org
President: Ed Smith
Executive Director: Dr. Enrique Torres

THOROUGHBRED HORSEMEN'S ASSOCIATIONS, INC.
Mailing Address: 10500 Little Patuxent Pkwy,
Suite 650 Columbia, MD, 21044
Phone: (410) 740-4900 Fax: (410) 740-0800
Email: thassoc@erols.com
Chairman of the Board & CEO: Alan M. Foreman
President: Richard Violette, Jr.

THOROUGHBRED OWNERS & BREEDERS ASSOCIATION
Mailing Address: P.O. Box 4367, Lexington, KY 40544-4367
Phone: (859) 276-2291 Fax: (859) 276-2462
E-mail: info@toba.org
Chairman of the Board: Gary E. Biszantz
President: Daniel J. Metzger

TRIPLE CROWN PRODUCTIONS LLC
Mailing Address: 700 Central Avenue,
Louisville, KY 40208-1200
Phone: (502) 636 4405 Fax: (502) 638-3894
E-Mail: triplecrown@kyderby.com
President: Thomas H. Meeker
Executive Vice-President: Edward P. Seigenfeld

PHONE AND WEB SITES FOR RACING COMMISSIONS IN NORTH AMERICA

ASSOCIATION OF RACING COMMISSIONERS INTERNATIONAL, INC
2343 Alexandria Drive, Suite 200
Lexington, Kentucky, 40504-3276
859/224-7070 Fax: 859/224-7071
Web site: www.arci.com
Contact: Timothy "Ted" Connors

NORTH AMERICAN PARI-MUTUEL REGULATORS ASSOCIATION
120 North Third Street Suite 100
Bismarck, ND 58501
701/221-2142; Fax 701/255-7979
http://www.napraonline.com
Email: pbowlinger@napraonline.com
Executive Director: Paul Bowlinger

ALABAMA: BIRMINGHAM RACING COMMISSION
2101 6th Avenue North Suite 725
Birmingham, 35203
205/328-7223

ARIZONA DEPARTMENT OF RACING
1110 West Washington, Suite 260
Phoenix, 85007
602/364-1700; Fax: 602/364-1703
http://www.raccom.state.az.us/

ARKANSAS RACING COMMISSION
1515 West 7th, Suite 505
P.O. Box 3076
Little Rock, 72203
501/682-1467, Fax: 501/682-5273
http://www. accessarkansas.org/dfa/racing/

BRITISH COLUMBIA RACING COMMISSION
408-4603 Kingsway Avenue
Burnaby, B.C., Canada V5H 4M4
604/660-7400; Fax: 604/660-7414
http://www.pssg.gov.bc.ca/gaming/commercial/tracks.htm

CALIFORNIA HORSE RACING BOARD
1010 Hurley Way, Suite 300
Sacramento, 95825
916/263-6000; Fax: 916/263-6042
http://www.chrb.ca.gov/

CANADIAN PARI-MUTUEL AGENCY
1130 Morrison Drive
Ottawa, Ontario K2H 9N6
613/949-0735; Fax: 613/949-0750
http://www.cpma-acpm.gc.ca/cpma_e.html

COLORADO DIVISION OF RACING EVENTS
1881 Pierce Street, Suite 108
Lakewood, 80214
303/205-2990; Fax: 303/205-2950
http://www.revenue.state.co.us/racing_dir/home.asp

DELAWARE THOROUGHBRED RACING COMMISSION
2320 South DuPont Highway
Dover, 19901
302/698-4500; Fax: 302/697-6287
http://www.state.de.us/deptagri/thoroughbred/index.htm

FLORIDA DIVISION OF PARI-MUTUEL WAGERING
1940 North Monroe Street,
Tallahassee, 32399-1035
850/488-9130, Fax: 850/488-0550
http://www.state.fl.us/dbpr/pmw/index.shtml

HORSE RACING ALBERTA
9707 110th Street, Suite 720
Edmonton, Alberta, T5K 2L9, Alberta
780/415-5432
http://www.thehorses.com

IDAHO STATE POLICE RACING COMMISSION
PO Box 700
Meridian, 83680-0700
208/884-7080; Fax: 208/884-7098
http://www.isp.state.id.us/race/index.html

ILLINOIS RACING BOARD
100 West Randolph Street, Suite 7-701
Chicago, 60601
312/814-2600
http://www.state.il.us/agency/irb/

INDIANA HORSE RACING COMMISSION
ISTA Center, Suite 530
150 West Market Street
Indianapolis, 46204
317/233-3119, Fax: 317/233-4470
http://www.in.gov/ihrc/

IOWA RACING AND GAMING COMMISSION
717 East Court Avenue, Suite B
Des Moines, 50309
515/281-7352; Fax: 515/242-6560
http://www3.state.ia.us/irgc/

JAMAICA RACING COMMISSION
P.O. Box 309, Kingston 10, Jamaica
876/926-2718;Fax: 876/926-2207

KANSAS RACING AND GAMING COMMISSION
700 Southwest Harriso Suite 420
Topeka, 66603
785/296-5800; Fax: 785/296-0900
http://www.accesskansas.org/krc/

KENTUCKY HORSE RACING AUTHORITY
4063 Iron Works Parkway, Building B,
Lexington, 40511
859/246-2040; Fax: 859/246-2039
http://www.state.ky.us/agencies/cppr/krc/

LOUISIANA RACING COMMISSION
320 North Carrollton Avenue, Suite 2-B,
New Orleans, 70119
504/483-4000; Fax: 504/483-4898
http://horseracing.la.gov/

MANITOBA HORSE RACING COMMISSION
PO Box 46086 RPO Westdale
Winnipeg, MB R3R 3S3
204/885-7770; Fax: 204/831-0942
http://www.manitobahorsecomm.org/

MARYLAND RACING COMMISSION
500 North Calvert Street, Second Floor, Room 201
Baltimore, 21202-3651
410/230-6330; Fax: 410/333-8308
http://www.dllr.state.md.us/racing/

MASSACHUSETTS STATE RACING COMMISSION
One Ashburton Place, Room 1313
Boston, 02108
617/727-2581; Fax: 617/727-6062
http://www.state.ma.us/src/

MICHIGAN: THE OFFICE OF RACING COMMISSIONER
37650 Professional Center Drive, Suite 105A,
Livonia, 48154-1100
734/462-2400
http://www.michigan.gov/mda/

MINNESOTA RACING COMMISSION
P.O. Box 630
Shakopee, 55379
952/496-7950, Fax: 952/496-7954
http://www.mnrace.commission.state.mn.us/

MISSOURI GAMING COMMISSION
P.O. Box 1847, 3417 Knipp Drive
Jefferson City, 65102-1847
573/526-4080; Fax: 573/526-1999
http://www.mgc.state.mo.us/horse.html

MONTANA BOARD OF HORSE RACING
PO Box 200512
Helena, 59620
406/444-4287 Fax 406/444-4305
http://www.discoveringmontana.com/liv/HorseRacing/Index.asp

NEBRASKA STATE RACING COMMISSION
301 Centennial Mall South, 6th floor
Lincoln, 68509
402/471-4155; Fax 402/471-2339
http://horseracing.state.ne.us

NEVADA GAMING COMMISSION AND STATE GAMING CONTROL BOARD
555 E. Washington Ave., Suite 2600
Las Vegas, 89101
702/486-2000; Fax: 702/486-2045
http://gaming.nv.gov/

NEW HAMPSHIRE PARI-MUTUEL COMMISSION
78 Regional Drive Building 2
Concord, 03301
603/271-2158; 603/271-3381
http://www.nh.gov/nhpmc/

NEW JERSEY RACING COMMISSION
140 East Front Street, 4th Floor PO Box 088
Trenton, 08625
609/292-0613; Fax: 609/599-1785
http://www.njrconline.com/

NEW MEXICO RACING COMMISSION
300 San Mateo Boulevard N.E. Suite 110
Albuquerque, 87108
505/841-6400; Fax: 505/841-6413
http://nmrc.state.nm.us/

NEW YORK STATE RACING AND WAGERING BOARD
1 Watervliet Avenue Extension, Suite 2
Albany, 12206
Phone: 518/453-8460
http://www.racing.state.ny.us/

NORTH DAKOTA RACING COMMISSION
500 North 9th Street
Bismark, 58501-4509
701/328-4633; Fax 701/328-4280
http://www.ndracingcommission.com/

OHIO STATE RACING COMMISSION
77 South High Street, 18th Floor
Columbus, 43215-6108
614/466-2757; Fax: 614/466-1900
http://www.racing.ohio.gov/

OKLAHOMA HORSE RACING COMMISSION
Shepherd Mall, 2401 NW 23rd St Suite 78
Oklahoma City, 73107
405/943-6472; Fax: 405/943-6474
http://www.ohrc.org/intro.html

ONTARIO RACING COMMISSION
9th Floor, 20 Dundas Street West,
Toronto, Ontario M5G 2C2
416/327-0520; Fax: 416/325-3478

OREGON RACING COMMISSION
800 NE Oregon Street #11, Suite 310
Portland, 97232
503/731-4052; Fax: 503/731-4053
http://www.orednet.org/~orc/

PENNSYLVANIA STATE HORSE RACING COMMISSION
Agriculture Building, Room 304
2301 North Cameron Street
Harrisburg, 17110
717/787-1942; Fax 717/346-1546
http://www.state.pa.us/ Subject Search: "horse racing commission"

PUERTO RICO RACING SPORT ADMINISTRATION
Racing Board-c/o Junta Hipica de Puerto Rico,
Apartado, 30229,
San Juan, 00929-1229
787/762-5210; Fax: 787/762-5377

RHODE ISLAND DEPT. OF BUSINESS REGULATION
Div. of Racing & Athletics
223 Richmond Street
Providence, 02903
401/222-2246; Fax: 401/222-6098
http://www.dbr.state.ri.us/

SASKATCHEWAN LIQUOR AND GAMING AUTHORITY
2500 Victoria Avenue, P.O. Box 5054
Regina, SK S4P 3M3
306/787-4213
http://www.slga.gov.sk.ca/

SOUTH DAKOTA COMMISSION ON GAMING
425 East Capitol Avenue
Pierre, 57501
605/773-6050; Fax: 605/773-6053
http://www.state.sd.us/drr2/reg/gaming/

TEXAS RACING COMMISSION
8505 Cross Park Drive, Suite 110
Austin, 78754
512/833-6699; Fax: 512/833-6907
http://txrc6.txrc.state.tx.us/

TRINIDAD & TOBAGO RACING AUTHORITY
Santa Rosa Park, Churchill Roosevelt Highway,
O'Meara, Arima,
Trinidad, W.I.
868/646-2004; Fax: 868/646-0103

VERMONT RACING COMMISSION
128 Merchants Row
Rutland, 05701
802/786-5050; Fax: 802/786-5051

VIRGINIA RACING COMMISSION
10700 Horsemen's Road
New Kent, 23124
804/966-7400; Fax: 804/966-7418
http://www.vrc.state.va.us/

WASHINGTON HORSE RACING COMMISSION
6326 Martin Way E, Suite 209
Olympia, 98516
360/459-6462; Fax: 360/459-6461
http://www.whrc.wa.gov/

WEST VIRGINIA RACING COMMISSION
106 Dee Drive, Suite 2
Charleston, 25311
304/558-2150; Fax: 304/558-6319
http://www.wvf.state.wv.us/racing/

WISCONSIN DEPARTMENT OF ADMINISTRATION
Division Of Gaming
2005 West Beltline Highway, Suite 201
P.O. Box 8979
Madison, 53708-8979
608/270-2555; Fax: 608/270-2564
http://www.doa.state.wi.us/gaming/index.asp

WYOMING PARI-MUTUEL COMMISSION
2515 Warren Avenue, Suite 301
Cheyenne, 82002
307/777-5928; Fax: 307/777-3681
http://parimutuel.state.wy.us/

European and South American Horse Racing Bureaus:

International Racing Bureau
Alton House, 117 High Street,
Newmarket, Suffolk, CB8 9WL England
(44) 1 63866 8881
http://www.irbracing.com/

Jockey Club of Buenos Aires
Buenos Aires, Republica Argentina
http://www.jockeyclub.com.ar/english/

Phone and Internet Directory of Thoroughbred Racing Organizations

North American listings below include phone numbers for the vast majority of active racetracks, county fairs, horsemen's groups, sales companies, breeding and racing organizations, horse rescue and retirement foundations, lobbying groups and select educational institutions with racetrack management programs and/or Veterinary programs.
Foreign listings that follow include the most prominent ruling body of the sport in each country or province and selected racing organizations.

THE UNITED STATES

ALABAMA

Birmingham Racing Commission	Birmingham	(205) 328-7223

ARIZONA

Apache County Fair	St. Johns	(928) 337-4469
Arizona Department of Racing	Phoenix	(602) 364-1700
Arizona Racing Commission	Phoenix	(602) 364-1700
Arizona State Horsemens Association	Cave Creek	(602) 390-6806
Arizona Thoroughbred Breeders Association	Phoenix	(602) 942-1310
Cochise County Fair	Douglas	(520) 364-3819
Coconino Fair	Flagstaff	(928) 774-5139
Gila County Fair	Globe	(928) 425-0348
Graham County Fair	Safford	(928) 428-6240
Greenlee County Fair	Duncan	(928) 359-2032
Horsemen's Benevolent & Protective Association	Phoenix	(602) 942-3336
Mohave County Fair	Kingman	(928) 753-8383
Race Track Industry Program	Tucson	(520) 621-5660
Rillito Park	Tucson	(520) 293-5011
Santa Cruz County Fair	Sonoita	(520) 455-5553
Turf Paradise	Phoenix	(602) 942-1101
Yavapai Downs	Prescott Valley	(928) 775-8000
Yuma County Fair	Yuma	(928) 726-4420

ARKANSAS

Arkansas Horse Council	Jasper	(870) 446-6226
Arkansas State Racing Commission	Little Rock	(501) 682-1467
Arkansas Thoroughbred Breeders' and Horsemen's Assoc	Hot Springs	(501) 624-6328
Horsemen's Benevolent & Protective Association	Hot Springs	(501) 623-7641
Oaklawn Park	Hot Springs	(800) 625-5296

CALIFORNIA

Barretts Equine Sales	Pomona	(909) 629-3099
Bay Meadows	San Mateo	(650) 574-7223
Bay Meadows Fair	San Mateo	(650) 574-3247
California Assn. of Thoroughbred Racetracks, LLC	Sacramento	(916) 449-6820
California Authority of Racing Fairs	Sacramento	(916) 263-3340
California Horse Racing Board	Sacramento	(916) 263-6000
California State Horsemen's Assoc.	Clovis	(559) 325-1055

California Thoroughbred Breeders Association	Arcadia	(626) 445-7800
California Thoroughbred Sales	Arcadia	(626) 445-7753
California Thoroughbred Trainers	Arcadia	(626) 447-2145
Del Mar	Del Mar	(858) 755-1141
Fairplex Park	Pomona	(909) 623-3111
Ferndale/Humboldt	Ferndale	(707) 786-9511
Fresno	Fresno	(559) 650-3247
Golden Gate Fields	Albany	(510) 559-7300
Hollywood Park	Inglewood	(310) 419-1500
Los Alamitos	Los Alamitos	(714) 820-2800
Oak Tree Racing Association	Arcadia	(626) 574-7223
Pleasanton/Alameda	Pleasanton	(925) 426-7600
Sacramento/Cal Expo	Sacramento	(916) 263-3000
Santa Anita Park	Arcadia	(626) 574-7223
Santa Rosa/Sonoma	Santa Rosa	(707) 545-4200
Solano/Vallejo	Vallejo	(707) 551-2000
Stockton/San Joaquin	Stockton	(209) 466-5041
Thoroughbred Owners of California	Arcadia	(626) 574-6620

COLORADO

Arapahoe Park	Aurora	(303) 690-2400
Colorado Division of Racing Events	Lakewood	(303) 205-2990
Colorado Horse Council	Denver	(303) 292-4981
Colorado Horsemen's Council	Arvada	(303) 279-4546
Colorado Thoroughbred Breeders Association	Denver	(303) 294-0260
Horsemen's Benevolent & Protective Association	Aurora	(303) 690-5919

CONNECTICUT

Connecticut Division of Special Revenue	Newington	(860) 594-0500
Connecticut Horse Council	Durham	(860) 282-0468

DELAWARE

Delaware Equine Council	Harrington	(302) 875-7869
Delaware Park	Wilmington	(800) 417-5687
Delaware Thoroughbred Horsemen's Association	Wilmington	(302) 994-2521
Delaware Thoroughbred Racing Commission	Dover	(302) 698-4500

FLORIDA

Calder Race Course	Miami	(305) 625-1311
Fasig-Tipton Florida	Miami	(352) 368-6623
Florida Division of Pari-Mutuel Wagering	Tallahassee	(850) 488-9130
Florida Thoroughbred Breeders & Owners Association	Ocala	(352) 629-2160
Gulfstream Park	Hallandale Beach	(954) 454-7000
Horsemen's Benevolent & Protective Association	Opa Locka	(305) 625-4591
Horsemen's Benevolent & Protective Association (Tampa)	Oldsmar	(800) 200-4434
Ocala Breeders' Sales Co.	Ocala	(352) 237-2154
Sunshine State Horse Council, Inc.	Brandon	(813) 651-5953
Tampa Bay Downs	Oldsmar	(813) 855-4401

GEORGIA

Georgia Horse Council	Conyers	(770) 922-3350
Georgia Thoroughbred Owners & Breeders Association	Atlanta	(866) 664-8622

IDAHO

Cassia County Fair	Burley	(208) 678-8610
Eastern Idaho State Fair	Blackfoot	(208) 785-2480
Gem County	Emmett	(208) 365-5560
Horsemen's Benevolent & Protective Association	Boise	(208) 939-0650
Idaho Horse Council	Boise	(208) 323-8148
Idaho State Racing Commission	Meridian	(208) 884-7080
Idaho Thoroughbred Assoc.	Boise	(208) 375-5930
Les Bois Park	Boise	(208) 376-7223
Oneida County Fair	Malad	(208) 766-2247
Pocatello Downs	Pocatello	(208) 238-1721
Rupert Fairgrounds	Rupert	(208) 436-4793
Sandy Downs - Teton Racing	Rigby	(208) 529-0671

ILLINOIS

Arlington Park	Arlington Heights	(847) 385-7500
Fairmount Park	Collinsville	(618) 345-4300
Hawthorne Race Course	Stickney/Cicero	(708) 780-3700
Horsemen's Benevolent & Protective Assn. (Chicago)	Barrington	(847) 382-3484
Horsemen's Benevolent & Protective Assn. (Illinois)	Caseyville	(618) 345-7724
Horsemen's Council of Illinois	Springfield	(217) 585-1600
Illinois Dept. of Agriculture Horse Racing Programs	Springfield	(217) 782-2172
Illinois Racing Board	Chicago	(312) 814-2600
Illinois Thoroughbred Breeders & Owners Foundation	Caseyville	(618) 344-3427
Illinois Thoroughbred Horsemen's Association	Cicero	(708) 652-2201

INDIANA

Hoosier Park	Anderson	(765) 642-7223
Horsemen's Benevolent & Protective Association	Anderson	(812) 256-3221
Indiana Downs	Shelbyville	(317) 421-0000
Indiana Horse Council	Indianapolis	(317) 692-7115
Indiana Horse Racing Commission	Indianapolis	(317) 233-3119
Indiana Thoroughbred Owners and Breeders Association	Carmel	(800) 450-9895

IOWA

Horsemen's Benevolent & Protective Association	Altoona	(515) 967-4804
Iowa Racing & Gaming Commission	Des Moines	(515) 281-7352
Iowa Thoroughbred Breeders and Owners Association	Altoona	(800) 577-1097 and (515) 957-3002
Prairie Meadows	Altoona	(800) 325-9015

KANSAS

Horsemen's Benevolent & Protective Association	Zenda	(316) 243-6641
Kansas Horse Council	Manhattan	(785) 776-0662
Kansas Thoroughbred Association	Fredonia	(620) 378-4772
Kansas Racing Commission	Topeka	(785) 296-5800
The Woodlands	Kansas City	(913) 299-9797

KENTUCKY

Churchill Downs	Louisville	(502) 636-4400
Ellis Park	Henderson	(812) 425-1456
Fasig-Tipton Company, Inc.	Lexington	(859) 255-1555
Horsemen's Benevolent & Protective Association	Louisville	(502) 363-1077
Keeneland Association, Inc.	Lexington	(859) 254-3412
Kentucky Derby Museum	Louisville	(502) 637-1111
Kentucky Downs	Franklin	(270) 586-7778
Kentucky Horse Council	Lexington	(859) 367-0509
Kentucky Horse Park	Lexington	(859) 233-4303
Kentucky Horse Racing Authority	Lexington	(859) 246-2040
Kentucky Thoroughbred Association	Lexington	(859) 381-1414
Kentucky Thoroughbred Owners & Breeders	Lexington	(859) 259-1643
Stallion Access/Fasig-Tipton	Lexington	(859) 255-1555
Turfway Park Race Course	Florence	(859) 371-0200
University of Louisville Equine Industry Program	Louisville	(502) 852-6440

LOUISIANA

Breeders Sales Co. of Louisiana	New Orleans	(504) 947-4676
Delta Downs	Vinton	(800) 589-7441
Evangeline Downs	Opelousas	(337) 594-3000
Fair Grounds	New Orleans	(504) 944-5515
Horsemen's Benevolent & Protective Association	New Orleans	(504) 945-1555
Louisiana Downs	Bossier City	(318) 742-5555
Louisiana Racing Commission	New Orleans	(504) 483-4000
Louisiana Thoroughbred Breeders Association	New Orleans	(504) 943-7556
Louisiana Thoroughbred Breeders Sales Co.	Carencro	(337) 896-6152

MARYLAND

Fasig-Tipton Midlantic, Inc.	Elkton	(410) 392-5555
Laurel Race Course	Laurel	(410) 792-7775
Maryland Horse Breeders Association	Timonium	(410) 252-2100
Maryland Horse Breeders Foundation	Timonium	(410) 252-2100
Maryland Horse Council, Inc.	Lisbon	(410) 489-7826
Maryland Million, Ltd.	Timonium	(410) 252-2100
Maryland Racing Commission	Baltimore	(410) 230-6330
Maryland Thoroughbred Horsemen's Association	Baltimore	(410) 265-6842
National Steeplechase Association	Elkton	(410) 392-0700
Pimlico Race Course	Baltimore	(410) 542-9400
Timonium	Timonium	(410) 252-0200

MASSACHUSETTS		
Horsemen's Benevolent & Protective Assn. (New England)	Revere	(617) 567-3900
Massachusetts State Racing Commission	Boston	(617) 727-2581
Massachusetts Thoroughbred Breeders Association, Inc.	Cambridge	(617) 492-7217
Northampton Fair	Northampton	(413) 584-2237
Suffolk Downs	East Boston	(617) 567-3900
MICHIGAN		
Great Lakes Downs	Muskegon	(231) 799-2400
Horsemen's Benevolent & Protective Association	Muskegon	(231) 798-2250
Michigan Horse Council	Lansing	(231) 821-2487
Michigan - Office of the Racing Commissioner	Livonia	(734) 462-2400
Michigan Thoroughbred Owners & Breeders Assn.	Muskegon	(231) 798-7721
Mount Pleasant Meadows	Mt. Pleasant	(989) 773-0012
MINNESOTA		
Canterbury Park	Shakopee	(952) 445-7223
Horsemen's Benevolent & Protective Association	Shakopee	(952) 496-6442
Minnesota Horse Council	Coon Rapids	(763) 755-7729
Minnesota Racing Commission	Shakopee	(952) 496-7950
Minnesota Thoroughbred Association	Shakopee	(952) 496-3770
MISSISSIPPI		
Mississippi Thoroughbred Breeders & Owners Association	Madison	(601) 856-8293
MISSOURI		
Missouri Equine Council	Fulton	(800) 313-3327
Missouri Gaming Commission	Jefferson City	(573) 526-4080
MONTANA		
Great Falls State Fair	Great Falls	(406) 727-8900
Horsemen's Benevolent & Protective Association	Vaughn	(406)452-2135
Marias Fair	Shelby	(406) 337-3600
Miles City	Miles City	(406) 232-1210
Northwest Montana Fair	Kalispell	(406) 758-5810
State of Montana Board of Horse Racing	Helena	(406) 444-4287
Western Montana Fair	Missoula	(406) 721-3247
Yellowstone Downs	Billings	(406) 869-5251
NEBRASKA		
Atokad Downs	South Sioux City	(402) 494-5722
Columbus	Columbus	(402) 564-0133
Fonner Park	Grand Island	(308) 382-4515
Horsemen's Benevolent & Protective Association	Omaha	(402) 438-4684
Horsemen's Park	Omaha	(402) 731-2900
Lincoln	Lincoln	(402) 474-5371
Nebraska State Racing Commission	Lincoln	(402) 471-4155
Neb. Thoroughbred Breeders' Assoc.	Grand Island	(308) 384-4683

NEVADA		
Nevada Gaming Commission	Las Vegas	(702) 486-2000
NEW HAMPSHIRE		
New Hampshire Pari-Mutuel Comm.	Concord	(603) 271-2158
NEW JERSEY		
Atlantic City Racing Association	Atlantic City	(609) 641-2190
Monmouth Park	Oceanport	(732) 222-5100
New Jersey Horse Council	Moorestown	(856) 231-0771
New Jersey Racing Commission	Trenton	(609) 292-0613
New Jersey Thoroughbred Horsemen's Assoc. Inc.	Colts Neck	(908) 389-0804
The Meadowlands	East Rutherford	(201) 843-2446
Thoroughbred Breeders' Association of New Jersey	Long Branch	(732) 870-9718
NEW MEXICO		
New Mexico Horse Breeders' Assoc.	Albuquerque	(505) 262-0224
New Mexico Horse Council	Albuquerque	(505) 345-8959
New Mexico Racing Commission	Albuquerque	(505) 841-6400
Ruidoso Downs	Ruidoso Downs	(505) 378-4431
SunRay Park	Farmington	(505) 326-4551
Sunland Park	Sunland Park	(505) 874-5200
The Downs at Albuquerque	Albuquerque	(505) 266-5555
NEW YORK		
Aqueduct Race Track	Jamaica	(718) 641-4700
Belmont Park	Elmont	(516) 488-6000
Capital Regional OTB	Schenectady	(518) 370-5151
Catskill Regional OTB	Pomona	(888) 386-2238
Fasig-Tipton Saratoga	Saratoga Springs	(516) 584-4700
Finger Lakes	Farmington	(585) 924-3232
Genesee Valley Breeders Association	Shortsville	(585) 289-8524
Horsemen's Benevolent & Protective Assn. (Finger Lakes)	Farmington	(585) 924-3004
Nassau Downs OTB	Hempstead	(516) 572-2800
New York City Off-Track Betting Corp.	New York	(212) 704-5642
New York State Horse Council	Westport	(518) 962-2316
New York State Racing & Wagering Board	Albany	(518) 453-8460
New York State Thoroughbred Breeding & Dev. Fund Corp.	Saratoga Springs	(518) 580-0100
New York Thoroughbred Breeders	Saratoga Springs	(518) 587-0777
New York Thoroughbred Horsemens Association	Jamaica	(718) 641-4700
Saratoga Race Course	Saratoga Springs	(518) 584-6200
Suffolk Regional OTB	Hauppauge	(631) 853-1000
Western Regional OTB	Batavia	(585)343-1423
NORTH CAROLINA		
North Carolina Horse Council	Raleigh	(919) 854-1990
North Carolina Thoroughbred Breeders Assoc.	Hillsborough	(919) 471-0131
NORTH DAKOTA		
North Dakota Racing Commission	Bismarck	(701) 328-4633

OHIO

Beulah Park	Grove City	(614) 871-9600
Horsemen's Benevolent & Protective Association	Grove City	(614) 875-1269
Ohio Horseman's Council	Logan	(740) 385-5306
Ohio State Racing Commission	Columbus	(614) 466-2757
Ohio Thoroughbred Breeders & Owners	Cincinnati	(513) 574-0440
River Downs	Cincinnati	(513) 232-8000
Thistledown	North Randall	(216) 662-8600

OKLAHOMA

Blue Ribbon Downs	Sallisaw	(918) 775-7771
Fair Meadows at Tulsa	Tulsa	(918) 743-7223
Heritage Place Sales Company	Oklahoma City	(405) 682-4551
Horsemen's Benevolent & Protective Association	Oklahoma City	(405) 427-8753
Oklahoma Horsemen's Association	Oklahoma City	(405) 843-8333
Oklahoma Horse Racing Commission	Oklahoma City	(405) 943-6472
Oklahoma Thoroughbred Association	Edmond	(405) 330-1006
Remington Park	Oklahoma City	(405) 424-1000

OREGON

Grants Pass Downs	Grants Pass	(541) 476-3215
Horsemen's Benevolent & Protective Association	Portland	(503) 285-4941
Klamath County Fairgrounds	Klamath Falls	(541) 883-3796
Oregon Racing Commission	Portland	(503) 731-4052
Oregon Thoroughbred Breeders' Association	Portland	(503) 285-0658
Portland Meadows	Portland	(503) 285-9144
Tillamook County Fairgrounds	Tillamook	(503) 842-2272

PENNSYLVANIA

Horsemen's Benevolent & Protective Assn (Penn National)	Grantville	(717) 469-2970
Penn National	Grantville	(717) 469-2211
Pennsylvania Equine Council	York	(717) 840-1985
Pennsylvania Horse Breeders' Assoc.	Kennett Square	(610) 444-1050
Philadelphia Park	Bensalem	(215) 639-9000
Philadelphia Thoroughbred Horsemen's Association	Bensalem	(215) 638-2012
State Horse Racing Commission	Harrisburg	(717) 787-1942

RHODE ISLAND

R.I. Dept. of Business Reg., Div. of Racing & Athletics	Providence	(401) 222-2246

SOUTH CAROLINA

South Carolina Department of Agriculture	Columbia	(803) 734-2210
South Carolina Horsemen's Council	Lexington	(803) 356-4535

SOUTH DAKOTA

South Dakota Commission on Gaming	Pierre	(605) 773-6050

TENNESSEE

Tennessee Department of Agriculture, Marketing Division	Nashville	(615) 837-5103
Tennessee Horse Council	Murfreesboro	(615) 217-3113

TEXAS

Fasig-Tipton Texas	Grand Prairie	(972) 262-0000
Gillespie County Fair	Fredericksburg	(830) 997-2359
Lone Star Park	Grand Prairie	(972) 263-7223
Manor Downs	Austin	(512) 272-5581
Retama Park	Selma	(210) 651-7000
Sam Houston Race Track	Houston	(281) 807-8700
Texas Horse Council	Houston	(713) 463-6666
Texas Horsemen's Partnership LLP	Austin	(512) 467-9799
Texas Racing Commission	Austin	(512) 833-6699
Texas Thoroughbred Association	Austin	(512) 458-6133

VERMONT

Vermont Horse Council	Braintree	(802) 728-6303
Vermont Racing Commission	Rutland	(802) 786-5050

VIRGINIA

Colonial Downs	New Kent	(804) 966-7223
Horsemen's Benevolent & Protective Association	Warrenton	(540) 347-0033
Virginia Horse Council	Mineral	(888) 467-7382
Virginia Horse Industry Board	Richmond	(804) 786-5842
Virginia Horsemen's Association	Warrenton	(540) 349-4600
Virginia Racing Commission	New Kent	(804) 966-7400
Virginia Thoroughbred Association	Warrenton	(540) 347-4313

WASHINGTON

Emerald Downs	Auburn	(253) 288-7000
Horsemen's Benevolent & Protective Association	Auburn	(253) 804-6822
Horsemen's Benevolent & Protective Assn. (Inland NW)	Spokane	(509) 536-5123
Sun Downs	Kennewick	(509) 582-5434
Walla Walla Racetrack	Walla Walla	(509) 527-3247
Washington Horse Racing Commission	Olympia	(360) 459-6462
Washington Thoroughbred Breeders Association	Auburn	(253) 288-7878

WEST VIRGINIA

Charles Town Races	Charles Town	(800) 795-7001
Horsemen's Benevolent & Protective Assn. (Charles Town)	Charles Town	(304) 725-1535
Horsemen's Benevolent & Protective Assn. (Mountaineer Pk)	Chester	(304) 387-9772
Mountaineer Park	Chester	(800) 804-0468
West Virginia Racing Commission	Charleston	(304) 558-2150
West Virginia Thoroughbred Breeders Association	Charles Town	(304) 728-6868

WISCONSIN

Wisconsin Dept of Administration - Division of Gaming	Madison	(608) 270-2555
Wisconsin State Horse Council	Columbus	(920) 623-0393

WYOMING

Wyoming Downs	Evanston	(307) 789-0511
Wyoming Pari-Mutuel Commission	Cheyenne	(307) 777-5928

PUERTO RICO and CANADA

PUERTO RICO

El Comandante	San Juan	(787) 641-6060
Puerto Rico Racing Sport Administration	San Juan	(787) 762-5210
Puerto Rico Thoroughbred Breeders Association	San Juan	(787) 725-8715

CANADA

Canadian Thoroughbred Horse Society (National Office)	Rexdale, Ont.	(416) 675-3602
The Jockey Club of Canada	Etobicoke, Ont.	(416) 675-7756

ALBERTA

Canadian Thoroughbred Horse Society (Alberta Division)	Calgary	(403) 229-3609
Horsemen's Benevolent & Protective Association (Alberta)	Calgary	(403) 261-0415
Horse Racing Alberta	Edmonton	(780) 415-5432
Northlands Park	Edmonton	(780) 471-7210
Stampede Park	Calgary	(403) 261-0214

BRITISH COLUMBIA

British Columbia Racing Commission	Burnaby	(604) 660-7400
Canadian Thoroughbred Horse Society (B.C. Division)	Surrey	(604) 574-0145
Hastings Racecourse	Vancouver	(604) 254-1631
Horsemen's Benevolent & Protective Association	Vancouver	(604) 647-2211

MANITOBA

Assiniboia Downs	Winnipeg	(204) 885-3330
Canadian Thoroughbred Horse Society (Manitoba Division)	Winnipeg	(204) 832-1702
Manitoba Horse Racing Commission	Winnipeg	(204) 885-7770

ONTARIO

Canadian Thoroughbred Horse Society (Ontario Division)	Rexdale	(416) 675-3602
Fort Erie	Fort Erie	(905) 871-3200
Horsemen's Benevolent & Protective Association	Rexdale	(416) 747-5252
Ontario Racing Commission	Toronto	(416) 327-0520
Woodbine	Rexdale	(416) 675-7223

QUEBEC

Canadian Thoroughbred Horse Society (Quebec Division)	Lac Guindon	(450) 475-8648
Quebec Racing Commission	Quebec	(418) 646-1632

SASKATCHEWAN

Canadian Thoroughbred Horse Society (Saskatchewan Div.)	Saskatoon	(306) 955-3870
Horsemen's Benevolent & Protective Association (Sask.)	Saskatoon	(306) 668-4243
Marquis Downs	Saskatoon	(306) 242-6100
Saskatchewan Liquor & Gaming Auth.	Regina	(306) 787-4213

AUSTRALIA, EUROPE, ASIA, SOUTH AMERICA and AFRICA

Country	Code	Telephone	Fax
AUSTRALIA			
Australian Jockey Club (Randwick)	(61)	2 9663 8400	2 9662 6292
Australian Stud Book (Randwick)	(61)	2 9663 8411	2 9663 4718
Racing Services Bureau (Flemington)	(61)	3 9258 4700	3 9258 4715
Racing Victoria Ltd (Flemington)	(61)	3 9258 4258	3 9258 4707
BRITAIN			
Tattersalls (Newmarket)	(44)	1 63866 5931	1 63866 0850
The Jockey Club (London)	(44)	2 07486 4921	2 07935 8703
Weatherbys (Wellingborough)	(44)	1 93344 0077	1 93344 0807
GERMANY			
Direktorium Fur Vollblutzucht und Rennen (Cologne)	(49)	221 7498 13	221 7498 68
HONG KONG			
Hong Kong Jockey Club (Happy Valley)	(852)	2966 8111	2966 7000
IRELAND			
Goffs Bloodstock Sales Ltd. (Kill)	(353)	45-886600	45-877119
Horse Racing Ireland (Dublin)	(353)	45-842800	45-842801
Tattersalls (Ireland) Ltd. (Ratoath)	(353)	1 886 4300	1 886 4303
The Turf Club (The Curragh)	(353)	45-445600	45-445601
Weatherbys (Ireland) Ltd. (Naas)	(353)	45-879979	45-879691
ITALY			
U.N.I.R.E. (Rome)	(39)	06.518971	6 58.33.09.21
NEW ZEALAND			
New Zealand T'bred Racing (Wellington)	(64)	4 576-6240	4 568-8866
SOUTH AFRICA			
Jockey Club of South Africa (Turffontein)	(27)	11 683-9283	11 683-5548
TRINIDAD & TOBAGO RACING AUTHORITY			
Trinidad & Tobago Racing Authority	(868)	646-2004	(868) 646-0103
UNITED ARAB EMIRATES			
The Emirates Racing Association (Dubai)	(971)	4 3313311	4 3313322

FOREIGN RACING WEBSITES

ARGENTINA

www.studbook.com.ar News, stakes results and statistics of Argentine racing. Includes a link to Peruvian racing. In Spanish.
www.monti.com News and results of racing in Argentina. In English.

AUSTRALIA

www.racingvictoria.net.au Official website of the Victoria Racing Club (Flemington).
www.ajc.org.au Official website of the Australian Jockey Club (Randwick).
www.stc.com.au Official website of the Sydney Turf Club (Rosehill).

BRAZIL

www.jcb.com.br Official website of the Jockey Club Brasileiro. Entries and results of racing in Brazil. In Portuguese.

BRITAIN

www.racingpost.com Racing Post, British racing daily. News, tips, statistics, entries and results for all British and Irish races, plus results of French races on the Parisian circuit, European group races and major stakes races in Asia and North America.
www.sportinglife.com Entries and quick results of British and Irish races, racing news, plus general British and European sports news.

CHILE

www.hipodromo.cl News, entries and results of racing at the Hipodromo Chile, the dirt track in Santiago, Chile. In Spanish.
www.clubhipico.cl News, entries and results of racing at Club Hipico, the turf track in Santiago, Chile. In Spanish.

FRANCE

www.france-galop.com Official website of France-Galop, the French Jockey Club. Nominations, entries and results for all French meetings, plus jockey, trainer and owner stats and descriptions of all French racecourses. In French.
www.paris-turf.com Paris-Turf, French racing daily. News, entries and results for all race in France. Paid subscription necessary for entries and results service. In French.

GERMANY

www.galopp-sport.de Official website of the Direktorium fur Vollblutzucht & Rennen (German Jockey Club). News, entries and results for all races in Germany. In German.
www.horses.de News, entries and results for all German races. In German.

HONG KONG

www.hkjc.com/english/index.asp Official website of the Hong Kong Jockey Club. News entries and results of all races in Hong Kong at both Sha Tin and Happy Valley. In English.

IRELAND

www.irish-field.com Irish Field, Irish racing weekly. News, entries and results of all races in Ireland.

ITALY

www.hippoweb.it News, entries and results for all races in Italy. In Italian.
www.trenno.it News, entries and results for all races in Milan (San Siro). In Italian.

JAPAN

www.jair.jrao.ne.jp Official website of the Japan Racing Association and the National Association of Racing. News of Japanese racing. Results of stakes races. Descriptions of all Japanese racecourses. In English.

NEW ZEALAND

www.nzracing.co.nz News, entries and results of racing in New Zealand.

UNITED ARAB EMIRATES

www.emiratesracing.com Official website of the Emirates Racing Association. News, entries and results for all races in the United Arab Emirates. In English.

CORRECTIONS: Please submit information about corrections, deletions or additions to the Phone and Internet directory to arm2005@drf.com.

THE AMERICAN STUD BOOK

Principal Rules and Requirements

RULES FOR REGISTRATION, DNA/BLOODTYPING AND PARENTAGE VERIFICATION

1. ELIGIBILITY FOR FOAL REGISTRATION

A. These rules apply to horses foaled in the United States, Puerto Rico and Canada, provided Rules 11 and 12 apply to horses foaled outside of the United States, Puerto Rico or Canada.

B. Foals must be genetically typed and qualified by parentage verification by a laboratory approved and authorized by The Jockey Club.

C. A foal is eligible for registration provided it is shown to the satisfaction of the Stewards of The Jockey Club that the foal's pedigree authentically traces in all its lines to horses recorded in The American Stud Book or a Foreign Stud Book approved by The Jockey Club and the International Stud Book Committee and if it satisfies all other requirements set forth in these rules. No horse foaled in the United States, Puerto Rico or Canada may be registered unless both its sire and dam have been previously registered in The American Stud Book. The only exception to this rule is a foal imported in utero whose dam is properly registered in The American Stud Book and whose sire was not imported but is properly registered in an approved Foreign Stud Book.

A dead horse is not eligible for registration.

D. To be eligible for registration, a foal must be the result of a stallionís Breeding with a broodmare (which is the physical mounting of a broodmare by a stallion with intromission of the penis and ejaculation of semen into the reproductive tract). As an aid to the Breeding, a portion of the ejaculate produced by the stallion during such mating may immediately be placed in the uterus of the broodmare being bred. A natural gestation must take place in, and delivery must be from, the body of the same broodmare in which the foal was conceived. Without limiting the above, any foal resulting from or produced by the processes of Artificial Insemination, Embryo Transfer or Transplant, Cloning or any other form of genetic manipulation not herein specified, shall not be eligible for registration.

E. If a broodmare is bred to two or more stallions during the same breeding season, The Jockey Club will make every effort to eliminate the incorrect stallion or stallions including:

1. Genetic typing and parentage qualification;

2. Calculation of gestation period; and

3. Applying the principles of two-coat color inheritance, that is, a chestnut sire and a chestnut dam must produce a chestnut or, in some instances, a palomino foal; and a gray/roan foal must have at least one gray/roan parent.

In the case of double qualifying sires, the name of each sire must be recorded as the sire of the foal in the same order that they were bred to the dam. A valid Service Certificate must be supplied with respect to the services of each qualifying sire.

F. A foal is not eligible for registration unless all requirements to register that foal as set forth in Rule 2 are met within one year of the actual foaling date; provided however, under certain limited circumstances, a foal may be eligible for late registration providing the applicant completes all registration requirements, submits the appropriate late registration fee (see Fee Schedule) and The Jockey Club determines that the applicant has sufficiently demonstrated mistake, inadvertence, excusable neglect or other circumstances which justify late registration.

G. A foal is not eligible for registration unless its sire and dam have been genetically typed, as required under Rule 5, provided however, if the sire or dam died prior to being genetically typed, a foal may still be eligible for registration if a notarized statement is submitted by the stallion owner or breeder reporting the death, explaining why the sire or dam was not genetically typed, and requesting that the Stewards of The Jockey Club waive this requirement for the registration of the resulting foal. The deceased sire or dam's Certificate of Foal Registration must also be returned to The Jockey Club (see Rule 16).

If a foal's sire or dam has been blood typed and dies before being DNA typed, it may be necessary to DNA and blood type the foal in order to qualify its parentage.

H. When an application is made to register a foal by an unnamed but registered sire or out of an unnamed but registered dam, the unnamed sire or dam must be named before the registration of the foal can be completed. A fee may be required to claim a name for an unnamed, but registered, sire or dam (see Fee Schedule).

2. REGISTRATION, GENETIC TYPING AND PARENTAGE VERIFICATION OF FOALS

A. A preprinted Live Foal/No Foal Report will be sent to the owner of record of each broodmare listed on a Report of Mares Bred form. If for any reason a breeder does not receive a preprinted Live Foal/No Foal Report by the time the foal is born, the breeder should contact The Jockey Club immediately. The Live Foal/No Foal Report serves a dual purpose; it is used to report the birth of a live foal or to report the status of a broodmare which did not produce a live foal. This report may be submitted through Interactive RegistrationTM at registry.jockeyclub.com.

B. To begin the registration process, each Live Foal Report should be fully completed, signed and returned to The Jockey Club no later than 30 days following the birth of the foal.

If reporting no live foal, submit the No Foal Report within 30 days of the intended birth of the foal. If the mare was not bred submit the No Foal Report in January.

C. A genetic typing kit and a preprinted Registration Application will be sent to the person specified on the Live Foal Report. If the genetic typing kit and preprinted Registration Application are not received within 180 days (6 months) of the foaling date, contact The Jockey Club immediately to request a genetic typing kit.

D. Within 45 days of receipt, the genetic typing kit should be used and the sample sent to the laboratory. The fully completed and signed Registration Application, along with a set of four color photographs of the foal (front, both sides and rear views) clearly showing the color and the markings (or lack of markings) on the head, legs and body, should be submitted to The Jockey Club along with the prescribed fee and a valid service certificate (see Rule 14C). The Registration Application may also be submitted through Interactive RegistrationTM at registry.jockeyclub.com. If either of these requirements are not met, the foal owner may be required to restart the process by obtaining a new genetic typing kit from The Jockey Club and an additional restart fee may be assessed (see Fee Schedule).

E. To correctly identify the foal, a Registration Application must be fully completed and signed each time a genetic sample is submitted.

F. In the case of twins, each twin must be registered separately. The fact that the foal is the product of a twin birth must be reported on the Live Foal Report (see Rule 15). If both twins are alive, the birth of each twin must be reported separately on a Live Foal Report. When submitting the Registration Applications for twins, attach a photocopy of the Service Certificate to the second Registration Application.

G. Upon the completion of all registration requirements within the specified deadlines, and if the foal qualifies as an offspring of its reported sire and dam, a Certificate of Foal Registration will be issued.

If a foal does not qualify as an offspring of its reported sire and/or dam, additional genetic typing may be required. Based on the results of the genetic typing and any other relevant information available, The Jockey Club will make a determination regarding the registration of the foal.

It is the registration applicantís responsibility to resolve doubts regarding parentage.

3. RACING PERMIT

A. The Stewards of The Jockey Club, in their discretion and for good cause, may issue a Racing Permit for any horse which has been genetically typed and parentage analyzed and whose dam qualified, but whose sire did not qualify. The Stewards may consider any other relevant factors in their determination and may require the owner and/or breeder to provide additional information which the Stewards deem necessary. A horse issued a Racing Permit cannot be considered a Thoroughbred for breeding purposes and cannot be entered into The American Stud Book. The term "Racing Permit" must always accompany the name of the horse in any trade journal or racetrack program. Any horse receiving a Racing Permit will never be entitled to receive a Certificate of Foal Registration.

B. To apply for a Racing Permit, the owner must submit a written request to the Stewards.

4. FEES TO REGISTER, GENETIC TYPE AND PARENTAGE VERIFY A FOAL

A. Foal registration fees are assessed according to a Registry Office Fee Schedule. Copies of this Fee Schedule are available from The Jockey Club Registry Office and are periodically included in Registry Office mailings and on The Jockey Club web site.

B. The fee to register a foal as stated in the current Fee Schedule will also cover:

1. Naming, provided a valid attempt to claim a name is received prior to February 1 of the two year old year;

2. The correction of a Certificate of Foal Registration, within six months of the date of issue, if necessary.

3. Subsequent transfers of ownership: and

4. Reissuance of a genetic typing kit for untestable samples.

C. Fees are not refundable, unless a foal dies and the death is reported prior to the issuance of a Certificate of Foal Registration. In this case, a fee will be charged for the genetic typing kit and processing, and upon written request, the remainder of the fee will be refunded (see Fee Schedule).

5. GENETIC TYPING REQUIREMENTS FOR STALLIONS, MARES AND EXPORTED HORSES

A. In addition to genetic typing and parentage verification of all foals as outlined in Rule 2, the following horses must be genetically typed:

1. All stallions and broodmares if not previously genetically typed.

2. All stallions and broodmares for foal crops of 2001 and thereafter must be DNA typed, either from DNA samples extracted from a blood sample already on file with the genetic laboratories or, if none is available, from DNA samples submitted in accordance with this Rule;

3. Foals of 2001 and thereafter that enter the stud for the first time as stallions must be re-DNA typed; and

4. All horses applying for an Export Certificate that have not been previously genetically typed (see Rule 10).

B. To apply for a blood typing kit, complete a Request for a Blood Typing Kit form and submit it to The Jockey Club, along with:

1. A check or money order payable to The Jockey Club for the prescribed fee (see Fee Schedule); and

2. The Certificate of Foal Registration (copies are not acceptable).

DNA typing kits can be obtained from The Jockey Club by request.

C. Within 45 days of receipt, the genetic typing kit should be used and the sample sent to the laboratory. The fully completed Identification form, along with a set of four color photographs of the horse (front, both sides and rear views) clearly showing the color and markings (or lack of markings) on the head, legs and body, must be submitted to The Jockey Club. If either of these requirements are not timely met, the owner may be required to restart the process by obtaining a new genetic typing kit from The Jockey Club, and a restart fee may be assessed (see Fee Schedule).

D. To correctly identify a horse, an Identification form must be fully completed each time a genetic sample is submitted.

E. The Jockey Club shall have the right to require that any horse be genetically typed or re-genetically typed at any time to establish or investigate a horse's identity or pedigree. If at any time The Jockey Club determines that the genetic type of a horse is inconsistent with the genetic type of either or both of its reported parents, The Jockey Club will notify the owner and the Certificate of Foal Registration will be revoked unless the owner provides an explanation satisfactory to the Registrar (or any other person designated by the President of The Jockey Club) within 30 days of notice. In the event that an explanation from the owner is timely received and establishes parentage to the satisfaction of The Jockey Club, a corrected Certificate of Foal Registration may be issued.

F. The Jockey Club will not respond to inquiries, other than pursuant to legal process, Court Order, approved Foreign Stud Book Authorities, recognized State Racing Commissions, Racetrack Authorities or law enforcement agencies with respect to genetic typing information as to specific horses, except upon written request, from a person whose name appears in The Jockey Club records as having an ownership interest in that horse, stating why this information is needed. In these instances, The Jockey Club will state in writing, if requested, whether, based upon information on file, the horse qualifies as an offspring of its reputed parents.

6. NAMING

A. A name may be claimed on the Registration Application, on a Name Claiming Form or through Interactive RegistrationTM at registry.jockeyclub.com. Name selections should be listed in order of preference. Names will be assigned based upon availability and compliance with the naming rules as stated herein. Names may not be claimed or reserved by telephone. When a foreign language name is submitted, an English translation must be furnished to The Jockey Club. An explanation must accompany "coined" or "made-up" names that have no apparent meaning. Horses that were born in the United States, Puerto Rico or Canada and currently reside in another country must be named by The Jockey Club through the Stud Book Authority of their country of residence.

B. If a valid attempt to name a foal is submitted to The Jockey Club by February 1 of the foal's two year old year and such a name is determined not eligible for use, no additional fee is required for a subsequent claim of name for that foal. If a valid attempt to name a foal is not submitted to The Jockey Club by February 1 of the foal's two year old year, a fee is required to claim a name for such a foal (see Fee Schedule).

C. A reserved name must be used within one year from the day it was reserved. Reserved names cannot be used until notification requesting the assignment of the name to a specific horse is received by the Registry Office. If the reserved name is not used within one year from its reservation, it will become available for any horse. A fee is required to reserve a name for a foal (see Fee Schedule).

D. A foal's name may be changed at any time prior to starting in its first race. Ordinarily, no name change will be permitted after a horse has started in its first race or has been used for breeding purposes. However, in the event a name must be changed after a horse has started in its first race, both the old and new names must be used until the horse has raced three times following the name change. The prescribed fee (see Fee Schedule) and the Certificate of Foal Registration must accompany any request to the Registry Office for a change of name.

E. Names of horses over ten years old may be eligible if they are not excluded under Rule 6(F) and have not been used during the preceding five years either in breeding or racing.

Names of geldings and horses that were never used for breeding or racing may be available five years from the date of their death as reported.

F. The following classes of names are not eligible for use:

1. Names consisting of more than 18 letters (spaces and punctuation marks count as letters);

2. Initials such as C.O.D., F.O.B., etc.;

3. Names ending in "filly," "colt," "stud," "mare," "stallion," or any similar horse-related term;

4. Names consisting entirely of numbers. Numbers above thirty may be used if they are spelled out.

5. Names ending with a numerical designation such as "2nd" or "3rd," whether or not such a designation is spelled out;

6. Names of persons unless written permission to use their name is on file with The Jockey Club;

7. Names of "famous" people no longer living unless approval is granted by the Board of Stewards of The Jockey Club;

8. Names of "notorious" people;

9. Names of racetracks or graded stakes races;

10. Recorded names such as assumed names or stable names;

11. Names clearly having commercial significance, such as trade names;

12. Copyrighted material, titles of books, plays, motion pictures, popular songs, etc., unless the applicant furnishes The Jockey Club with proof that the copyright has been abandoned or that such material has not been used within the last five years;

13. Names that are suggestive or have a vulgar or obscene meaning; names considered in poor taste; or names that may be offensive to religious, political or ethnic groups.

14. Names that are currently active either in the stud or on the turf, and names similar in spelling or pronunciation to such names, see 6(E);

15. Permanent names and names similar in spelling or pronunciation to permanent names. The list of criteria to establish a permanent name is as follows:

a. Horses in racing's Hall of Fame;

b. Horses that have been voted Horse of the Year;

c. Horses that have won an Eclipse Award;

d. Horses that have won a Sovereign Award (Canadian Champions);

e. Annual leading sire and broodmare sire by progeny earnings;

f. Cumulative money winners of $2 million or more;

g. Horses that have won the Kentucky Derby, Preakness, Belmont Stakes, The Jockey Club Gold Cup, the Breeders' Cup Classic or the Breeders' Cup Turf; and

h. Horses included in the International List of Protected Names.

G. In addition to the provisions of this Rule 6, the Registrar of The Jockey Club reserves the right of approval on all name claiming requests.

7. TRANSFER AND REPORT OF OWNERSHIP: OWNERSHIP DISPUTES

A. The transfer of ownership for all registered Thoroughbreds may be reported to The Jockey Club by completing a Transfer of Ownership form or through Interactive RegistrationTM at registry.jockeyclub.com.

B. The ownership of all Thoroughbred stallions and broodmares must be reported to The Jockey Club each year. For stallions, ownership must be reported by submitting a Report of Mares Bred form (see Rule 14). In the case of a broodmare, ownership must be reported by submitting a Live Foal/No Foal Report (see Rules 2(A), (B), and 15). Based on the ownership reported on the respective forms, The Jockey Club will record any transfer of ownership. If a Thoroughbred stallion or broodmare is sold or otherwise transferred after submitting a Report of Mares Bred Form or Live Foal/No Foal Report, the new ownership must be reported by submitting a Transfer of Ownership Form as in Rule 7(A).

C. If The Jockey Club becomes aware of conflicting information with respect to the ownership of a horse, or other rights in or related to a horse ("Ownership Issues"), The Jockey Club may request additional information and The Jockey Club may defer action related to the horse until the interested parties agree to resolve the Ownership Issues or The Jockey Club may take action based upon Court Order (see Rule 21(F)) or other factors it deems appropriate in its discretion. The Jockey Club shall have no obligation to any party arising out of its decision to defer action or to take action.

In addition, the failure of an owner to submit a valid service certificate pursuant to Rule 2(D) may be considered evidence of an ownership issue to be resolved as set forth above, but in the event action is deferred by The Jockey Club it will process but not issue the Certificate of Foal Registration until a valid service certificate is submitted to The Jockey Club and all other requirements of Rule 2 are satisfied.

D. The Jockey Club will not respond to inquiries, other than pursuant to legal process, Court Order, approved Foreign Stud Book Authorities, recognized State Racing Commissions, Racetrack Authorities or law enforcement agencies with respect to ownership information as to a specific horse, except upon written request, from a person whose name appears in The Jockey Club records as having an ownership interest in that horse.

E. It is advisable that no one complete the purchase of a Thoroughbred until the Certificate of Foal Registration has been transferred by the previous owner. Before completing the sale, the new owner should compare the description on the Certificate of Foal Registration with the actual markings, including cowlicks, found on the horse.

8. CORRECTION OF CERTIFICATE OF FOAL REGISTRATION

A. To obtain a Corrected Certificate of Foal Registration, the following must be submitted to the Registry Office:

1. A check or money order payable to The Jockey Club covering the prescribed fee (see Fee Schedule).

2. A set of four color photographs of the horse (front, both sides, and rear views) clearly showing the color, markings (or lack of markings) on the head, legs and body, and showing any discrepancies, if possible, with the existing Certificate of Foal Registration;

3. A completed and signed Corrected Certificate Form containing the written description of the markings as they now appear on the horse, including the exact location of the head and neck cowlicks; and

4. The Certificate of Foal Registration.

B. Nothing in this rule shall preclude the use of genetic typing information for the purpose of reidentifying any horse at any time. If the identity or pedigree of any horse is in question, The Jockey Club may require genetic typing and/or parentage verification to ensure proper identity or pedigree.

9. DUPLICATE CERTIFICATE OF FOAL REGISTRATION

A. If a Certificate of Foal Registration has been lost or destroyed, a Duplicate Certificate of Foal Registration may be issued by the Registry Office upon submission of the following:

1. A check or money order payable to The Jockey Club covering the prescribed fee (see Fee Schedule);

2. A set of four color photographs of the horse (front, both sides, and rear views) clearly showing the color, and the markings (or lack of markings) on the head, legs and body;

3. A completed and signed Duplicate Certificate Form containing the written description of the markings on the horse, including the exact location of the head and neck cowlicks;

4. A notarized statement from the owner or his authorized agent describing the circumstances under which the Certificate of Foal Registration was lost or destroyed;

5. Proof of ownership of that specific horse (for example, a bill of sale or cancelled check including the name or pedigree of the horse, date of sale and the name of the new owner); and

6. Any further evidence and assurances as The Jockey Club may require, such as genetic typing and/or parentage verification.

B. Except as expressly provided in this Rule 9, a Duplicate Certificate of Foal Registration will not be issued as long as the original Certificate of Foal Registration is known to be in existence; provided however, in the event of a sheriff's (or similar) sale or under a non-appealable Court Order, a Duplicate Certificate of Foal Registration will be issued if the Certificate of Foal Registration cannot be obtained from the previous owner only after a good faith effort to recover it is made by the seller and/or the new owner, and in either case, the requirements of Rule 9(A) 1, 2, 3, 5 and 6 must be met and an opinion must be submitted to The Jockey Club from an attorney or an official representative of the court, indicating that the sale (if applicable) was conducted in accordance with the laws of the state and providing such other information as The Jockey Club may request regarding the circumstances and validity of the sale or court order.

C. Once a Duplicate Certificate of Foal Registration is issued, the original Certificate of Foal Registration becomes null and void, and if located, must be returned to the Registry Office.

10. EXPORT REQUIREMENTS

A. When a horse is to be exported to a country outside of the United States, Puerto Rico or Canada, a Certificate of Exportation and passport must be obtained from The Jockey Club within 60 days of exportation. If for any reason the requirements are not completed within 60 days of exportation, the Certificate of Exportation may be obtained only after approval by the Stewards of The Jockey Club and the payment of an additional fee (see Fee Schedule).

B. To obtain a Certificate of Exportation and passport, a horse must be genetically typed, or be in the process of being genetically typed (samples must have arrived at the laboratory in a testable condition) unless the horse was genetically typed previously. If genetic typing is required, a genetic typing kit must be obtained as set forth in Rule 5(B) and the following must be completed and submitted to The Jockey Club by the time of the horse's departure:

1. A check or money order payable to The Jockey Club covering the prescribed fee (see Fee Schedule);

2. A set of four color photographs of the horse (front, both sides and rear views) clearly showing the color and the markings (or lack of markings) on the head, legs and body;

3. A completed Export Identification form. The form must be signed by the owner (or owner's authorized agent) and must also indicate the country of destination, name of broker, date of shipment, and ownership of the horse. This form may also be submitted through Interactive RegistrationTM at registry.jockeyclub.com;

4. The Certificate of Foal Registration, 30-Day Racing Permit or Certificate of Foreign Registration;

5. A valid Service Certificate for all mares in foal. If a Service Certificate is not available at the time of shipment, it must be submitted to The Jockey Club as soon as it is received by the owner.

C. The Jockey Club will forward directly to the appropriate Foreign Stud Book Authority the Certificate of Exportation and any other necessary documents as may be reasonably requested by that Stud Book Authority.

D. If a horse is exported to a country whose Stud Book is not approved and then returns to the United States, Puerto Rico or Canada, the owner (or owner's authorized agent) must satisfy all of the requirements of Rule 10(A) and (B), and the horse must be genetically typed and identified within 60 days of its return. No progeny foaled or conceived in a country whose Stud Book is not approved will be eligible for registration in The American Stud Book.

E. Any horse exported without receiving a Certificate of Exportation that returns to the United States, Puerto Rico or Canada must be re-identified, genetically typed, obtain a Certificate of Exportation and pay an additional fee (see Fee Schedule) before The Jockey Club will reissue the Certificate of Foal Registration.

F. Any horse imported into the United States, Puerto Rico or Canada whose sire or dam was not exported properly in accordance with Rule 10 will not receive a Certificate of Foreign Registration until that sire or dam has fulfilled the export requirements.

G. If a horse is imported into the United States, Puerto Rico or Canada and its sire or dam was not exported in accordance with Rule 10, and has since died, The Jockey Club will issue a Certificate of Foreign Registration only upon written application and approval of the Stewards of The Jockey Club to waive the export requirements.

11. IMPORT REQUIREMENTS

A. Horses bred outside of the United States, Puerto Rico or Canada must satisfy the eligibility requirements of Rules 1(C) and 1(D) and must obtain a Certificate of Foreign Registration from The Jockey Club when imported into the United States, Puerto Rico or Canada.

B. To obtain a Certificate of Foreign Registration, the owner or broker must cause the exporting country's registry to submit directly to The Jockey Club within 60 days of arrival of the horse in the United States, Puerto Rico or Canada the following:

1. The Stud Book Certificate or Export Certificate containing the written description and diagrams of the markings on the horse including the exact location of the head and neck cowlicks;

2. A certified copy of the horse's complete racing record. Racing records from the World Hub may also be accepted if available; and

3. A valid Service Certificate if the imported broodmare is in foal.

C. In addition, within 60 days of arrival of the horse in the United States, Puerto Rico or Canada, the owner or broker of the horse must submit the following to The Jockey Club Registry office:

1. A check or money order payable to The Jockey Club covering the prescribed fee (see Fee Schedule);

2. A completed and signed Import Registration Form containing the written description and diagrams of the markings on the horse including the exact location of the head and neck cowlicks. This form may also be submitted through Interactive RegistrationTM at registry.jockeyclub.com.

3. Four color photographs of the horse (front, both sides, and rear views) taken in this country clearly showing the color and the markings (or lack of markings) on the head, legs and body; and

4. The Passport Book, if applicable.

D. If for any reason, the requirements are not completed within 60 days of arrival, the Certificate of Foreign Registration may be obtained only after approval of the Stewards of The Jockey Club and the payment of an additional fee (see Fee Schedule). A horse is not eligible for a Certificate of Foreign Registration unless all requirements, including the appropriate fee (see Fee Schedule), are received by The Jockey Club within one year of the date of arrival in the United States, Puerto Rico or Canada; provided however, the Stewards may, under limited circumstances, grant late registration to a horse that has been in the United States, Puerto Rico, or Canada for more than one year since its arrival provided the following conditions are met:

1. The applicant sets forth in writing to The Jockey Club the reasons the applicant believes he should be relieved from the one year registration requirement; and

2. The Stewards of The Jockey Club determine that the applicant has sufficiently demonstrated mistake, inadvertence, excusable neglect or other circumstances which justify late registration; and

3. The horse had been genetically typed in its country of birth and/or its identity can be established to the satisfaction of the Stewards of The Jockey Club; and

4. The applicant completes all registration requirements, including genetic typing, and submits a late registration fee (see Fee Schedule).

12. 30-DAY FOREIGN RACING PERMIT

A. A 30-Day (Foreign) Racing Permit is a permit issued by the Registry Office of The Jockey Club entitling foreign Thoroughbreds to race in the United States, Puerto Rico or Canada for a period of not longer than 30 days.

B. To obtain a 30-Day (Foreign) Racing Permit, the owner or broker must cause the exporting country's registry to submit directly to The Jockey Club:

1. The Stud Book Certificate or Export Certificate containing the written description of the markings on the horse including the exact location of the head and neck cowlicks, or if neither of these documents are available at that time, a written confirmation of the identity of the horse from the exporting country's Stud Book Authority; and a certified copy of the horse's complete racing record.

C. The owner or broker of the horse must submit the following directly to The Jockey Club Registry Office:

1. A check or money order payable to The Jockey Club covering the prescribed fee (see Fee Schedule);

2. A completed and signed Import Registration Form containing the written description and diagrams of the markings on the horse, including the exact location of the head and neck cowlicks;

3. Four color photographs of the horse (front, both sides and rear views) clearly showing the color and the markings (or lack of markings) on the head, legs and body; and

4. The Passport Book, if applicable.

D. A 30-Day Foreign Racing Permit shall expire upon the expiration date on the permit or earlier if the Thoroughbred leaves the country prior to the expiration date.

E. In the event a Thoroughbred remains in the United States, Puerto Rico or Canada more than 30 days, the owner or authorized agent must apply for a Certificate of Foreign Registration and all import requirements must be satisfied as stated in Rule 11.

13. LEASES AND FOAL-SHARING AGREEMENTS

When a Thoroughbred, through contract or agreement, is leased or entered into foal-sharing, it must be reported to The Jockey Club each year. The lease of a stallion should be reported by checking the lessee box on the Report of Mares Bred form. For a broodmare, a lease or foal-sharing agreement must be reported by checking the lessee or foal-sharing box on the Live Foal Report.

14. STALLION REPORTS (REPORT OF MARES BRED)

A. All stallion owners must report each Thoroughbred broodmare that was bred to their stallion(s) on the Report of Mares Bred form which must be sent to The Jockey Club no later than August 1 of each breeding year. This form may also be submitted through Interactive RegistrationTM at registry.jockeyclub.com. Failure to comply with this deadline will result in delays in the issuance of Service Certificates. Mares bred on Southern Hemisphere time must be reported as soon as possible.

B. A separate Report of Mares Bred form must be completed yearly for each stallion and must be signed by the stallion owner, lessee or authorized agent.

If the stallion was leased, check the appropriate box provided on the Report of Mares Bred form. If the stallion has died since the last stallion report, a Report of Deaths form should also be submitted.

C. Based on the information on the Report of Mares Bred form submitted by August 1, The Jockey Club will forward to the stallion owner, lessee or authorized agent a preprinted Service Certificate for each broodmare bred, including the name of the stallion, the name of the broodmare, the name of the dam of the broodmare, and the date of the last cover. When the stallion owner, lessee or authorized agent receives the preprinted Service Certificate, it should be examined for accuracy, signed by the stallion owner, lessee or authorized agent and forwarded to the breeder of the foal or submitted to The Jockey Club through Interactive RegistrationTM at registry.jockeyclub.com. The Service Certificate is required to register a foal. Service Certificates will not be issued unless a Report of Mares Bred form is on file at The Jockey Club and until genetic or re-DNA typing of the stallion has been completed (see Rule Five).

D. If the preprinted Service Certificates are lost, duplicate Service Certificates will be issued upon request of the stallion owner, lessee or authorized agent.

15. LIVE FOAL/NO FOAL REPORTS (MARE REPORTS)

A. The breeding status of all Thoroughbred broodmares must be reported yearly to The Jockey Club by submitting a Live Foal/No Foal Report indicating either live foal information or no foal information. This report may also be submitted through Interactive RegistrationTM at registry.jockeyclub.com.

B. In case of a live foal, a fully completed and signed Live Foal Report must be submitted to The Jockey Club within 30 days of the birth of the foal as required in Rule 2.

C. In the case of no foal to be registered, the breeder should submit to The Jockey Club a fully completed and signed No Foal Report within 30 days of the intended birth of the foal. If the mare was not bred submit the No Foal Report in January.

16. DEATH REPORTS

The death of a registered Thoroughbred, or foal for which registration is pending, should be reported to The Jockey Club Registry Office within 30 days of the death by submitting a completed Report of Deaths Form, or through Interactive RegistrationTM at registry.jockeyclub.com and returning the Certificate of Foal Registration, if issued.

17. GELDING REPORTS

If a Colt or Horse has been gelded, the owner or his authorized agent should promptly report that information to The Jockey Club Office by submitting a completed Gelding Report or by furnishing the information through registry.jockeyclub.com. Additionally, The Jockey Club will accept gelding reports from a racetrack recognized by The Jockey Club.

18. SOLD WITHOUT PEDIGREE

A. Any owner who desires a horse no longer to be considered a Thoroughbred for racing or breeding purposes must promptly surrender the Certificate of Foal Registration to The Jockey Club within 60 days of the date of sale with an accompanying notation that the horse was transferred or sold "without pedigree." The notation must be signed by the owner or authorized agent and indicate the date of disposition. In the event the owner or his authorized agent surrenders the Certificate of Foal Registration to The Jockey Club in the above manner more than 60 days after the date of transfer or sale, then the new owner or transferee must also submit a statement that the horse was purchased or received without pedigree.

B. Upon receipt in The Jockey Club Registry Office, the respective Certificate of Foal Registration will be canceled. Once the registration is canceled, the horse cannot be reinstated into the registry, and a Duplicate Certificate of Foal Registration will not be issued.

C. Notations upon a Certificate of Foal Registration which do not clearly indicate transferred or sold without pedigree, including notations such as "not to be raced," shall not result in cancellation of the Certificate of Foal Registration. Such notations could be regarded as defacing the Certificate of Foal Registration and, submission to The Jockey Club of any such defaced Certificate of Foal Registration, may cause a Corrected Certificate of Foal Registration to be issued.

19. DECEPTIVE PRACTICES

A. Any person or entity (collectively "Person") may be denied any or all of the privileges of The American Stud Book in the event:

1. That Person either knowingly misrepresents or aids or abets the misrepresentation of the identity, name, age, appearance, pedigree, genetic type, eligibility for registration or any other information in, or in connection with, any communication to The Jockey Club;

2. That Person steals, counterfeits, forges or alters a certificate or document issued by The Jockey Club or knowingly receives a stolen, counterfeited, forged or altered certificate or document issued by The Jockey Club;

3. That Person intentionally violates any of the Principal Rules and Requirements of The American Stud Book; or

4. There is a final determination by a court (whether civil, criminal or administrative), an official tribunal or an official racing body that such Person: (a) knowingly misrepresented or aided or abetted the misrepresentation of a horse's identity, name, age, appearance, pedigree, genetic type or any other information in connection with either entry in a race or the racing of any horse; (b) knowingly misrepresented or aided or abetted the misrepresentation of a horse's eligibility for registration or any other matter related to The American Stud Book; (c) stole, counterfeited, forged or altered a certificate or document issued by The Jockey Club or knowingly received a stolen, counterfeited, forged or altered certificate or document issued by The Jockey Club; or (d) killed, abandoned, mistreated, neglected or abused, or otherwise committed an act of cruelty to a horse.

B. In the event the Registrar has a reasonable basis upon which to conclude that any of the circumstances identified in subparagraphs (1) through (4) above may apply, the Registrar shall notify such Person in writing (the "Rule 19 Notification"): (i) of the specific subpart(s) of this rule which apply; (ii) of the basis upon which the Registrar believes that the subparts apply; (iii) of the Registrar's proposed action; and (iv) that the Person has the right, within 30 days of the date that Person receives the Rule 19 Notification, either to submit to the Board of Stewards of The Jockey Club ("Stewards") written information to be considered in their determination of the matter or to request a hearing by submitting to the Stewards a written request for a hearing, briefly stating the reasons why that Person asserts that this rule does not apply and/or that the proposed action is not appropriate ("Rule 19 Hearing Request").

C. If a hearing is requested, a non-refundable administrative fee of one thousand dollars ($1,000.00) must be submitted with the Rule 19 Hearing Request.

If no hearing is requested, then all information submitted by the Registrar and the Person shall be considered by the Stewards at their next meeting, at which time the Stewards shall make a final determination as to whether to deny the Person any or all of the privileges of The American Stud Book and the nature and extent of any such denial. The Stewards' determination shall be promptly reduced to writing, stating the decision made and briefly stating the reasons for such decision, and delivered to the Person (and his counsel, if any) and to the Registrar.

If a hearing is requested, then all further proceedings shall be conducted in accordance with the procedures set forth in Rule 20(C).

D. Any Person who receives a Rule 19 Notification may request an expedited determination by submitting a written request to the Stewards with a detailed explanation as to why an expedited determination is warranted.

The authority of the Stewards under this rule and of any Hearing Officer appointed under Rule 20 to hear a matter pursuant to a Rule 19 Hearing Request shall be limited to considering (i) whether a denial of any or all of the privileges of The American Stud Book is warranted under the criteria in this rule and (ii) the nature and extent of any denial of those privileges.

Any determination of the Stewards made pursuant to this Rule 19 shall be final.

20. APPEALS AND HEARINGS

A. Any person or entity ("Person") wishing to object to any action or decision of the Registrar or other officer of The Jockey Club (collectively "Registrar/Officer") (other than Rule 19 Notifications and Rule 19 final determinations) in the application of the Rules to such Person or to such Person's horses(s), may, within 30 days of being advised of such action or decision, submit to the Board of Stewards of The Jockey Club ("Stewards") a written statement ("Statement") including:

1. The specific nature and basis for objecting to the action or decision of the Registrar/Officer;

2. A brief statement of the facts and any documents, affidavits or other written material which that Person believes will be helpful in considering the matter; and

3. If a hearing is desired, a specific request for a hearing.

If a hearing is requested, a non-refundable administrative fee of one thousand dollars ($1,000.00) must be submitted with the Statement.

B. If no hearing is requested, then all information submitted by the Person and the Registrar shall be considered by the Stewards at their next meeting after receipt of the Statement, at which time the Stewards shall make a final determination. That determination shall be promptly reduced to writing, stating the decision made and briefly stating the reasons for such decision, and delivered to the Person (and his counsel, if any) and the Registrar/Officer.

C. If a hearing is requested under either Rule 20(A) or Rule 19 then, within 10 days after receiving the Statement or the Rule 19 Hearing Request, whichever applies, the designee of the Chairman of the Stewards shall provide written notice to the Person of the name, address and telephone number of the individual Steward or independent hearing officer (collectively "Hearing Officer') appointed to hear the matter.

Within 15 days after the date of the appointment of the Hearing Officer, the Hearing Officer shall conduct a telephonic prehearing conference for the purpose of ruling on preliminary matters, clarifying and narrowing the issues, entering into stipulations, scheduling the hearing and considering other issues as may aid in the disposition of the matter. The final hearing shall be scheduled no less than 15 and no more than 30 days after the date of the prehearing conference unless the parties otherwise agree. All hearings shall take place at the offices of The Jockey Club, 821 Corporate Drive, Lexington, Kentucky 40503.

Any Person requesting a hearing may appear personally, if such Person is an individual, or with counsel authorized to act on such Person's behalf and may present witnesses and other evidence. The Registrar/Officer of The Jockey Club may appear with counsel and may testify and present witnesses and other evidence. Any other person having an interest in the subject matter may appear at the hearing if the Hearing Officer determines that such person might materially assist in the determination of the matter.

All testimony at the hearing shall be under oath and stenographically recorded. The Hearing Officer shall not be bound by technical rules of evidence and may receive any evidence which he considers to be reliable and relevant, if not unduly repetitious, including testimony which would be hearsay if presented in a court of law.

The Hearing Officer shall, within 45 days after the close of the hearing, submit written factual findings and recommendations to the Stewards and provide a copy of those findings and recommendations to the Person (and his counsel, if any) and to counsel for the Registrar/Officer. The Stewards shall, no later than the next meeting of the Stewards after the findings and recommendations are made, make a final determination of the matter. The Stewards may accept or reject the findings and/or recommendations in whole or in part. The determination of the Stewards shall then be promptly reduced to writing, stating the decision made and briefly stating the reasons for such decision, and delivered to the Person (and his counsel, if any) and to counsel for the Registrar/Officer.

A Person who has requested a hearing may subsequently waive the right to a hearing by submitting to the Hearing Officer a written statement waiving the right to hearing, in which case, the matter shall proceed under Rule 20(B) or Rule 19, whichever applies, as if no hearing had been requested. Any requests for postponement of a scheduled hearing must be made in writing showing good cause why the postponement should be granted and must actually be received by the Hearing Officer at least 3 business days prior to the scheduled date of the hearing, absent extreme exigent circumstances.

If a Person requests a hearing but fails to appear on the scheduled date, the matter shall proceed under Rule 20(B) or Rule 19, whichever applies, as if no hearing had been requested.

D. Any person submitting a Statement under this rule may request an expedited determination by submitting a written request to the Stewards with a detailed explanation as to why an expedited determination is warranted.
The authority of the Stewards and any Hearing Officer appointed to hear any matter initiated under Rule 20(A) shall be limited to considering whether the Registrar/Officer acted in accordance with the Principal Rules and Requirements of The American Stud Book and any applicable policies of The Jockey Club.

Any determination of the Stewards made pursuant to this Rule 20 shall be final.

21. GENERAL RULES

A. Owners, breeders and authorized agents are responsible for being familiar with the Principal Rules and Requirements of The American Stud Book. Amendments and new rules are available on The Jockey Club web site at jockeyclub.com.

B. Notwithstanding any other provisions in these Rules, it is the responsibility of each applicant to obtain from The Jockey Club all necessary forms and to submit all completed forms and other requirements by the applicable deadlines.

C. Certificates of Foal Registration are issued on the basis of information submitted to The Jockey Club by the applicant and are subject to revocation and cancellation if further information is received by The Jockey Club indicating improper or erroneous issuance. In the event of cancellation or revocation of a Certificate of Foal Registration, that Certificate must be promptly returned to The Jockey Club Registry Office.

D. For the purpose of determining whether a deadline has been met, any document or other material submitted to The Jockey Club shall be deemed to have been submitted to and/or received by The Jockey Club only upon: (1) actual receipt in the appropriate office of The Jockey Club; or (2) if transmitted by United States Mail or other recognized mail carrier, the date such carrier received the material from the sender if that date is noted by the carrier on the outside of the container.

E. Any notices or other material sent by The Jockey Club to any person, including any owner or authorized agent, shall be mailed to the last known address on file with The Jockey Club for the horse which is the subject of the notice or other material regardless of whether the same person has other addresses on file with The Jockey Club for other horses. Change of Address Forms are available from The Jockey Club and may be submitted by the horse owner or authorized agent to notify The Jockey Club of a change of address for mailing notices or other material for any specified horse(s).

F. Notwithstanding any other provisions in these rules, The Jockey Club may require any party(ies) who requests action or inaction from The Jockey Club arising out of or relating to a dispute or controversy with a third party(ies) to settle that dispute in a court of competent jurisdiction and The Jockey Club may defer a decision concerning the matter pending resolution of the dispute as aforesaid. The Jockey Club shall have no obligation to any party arising out of any decision to defer action or to take action under any provision of these Rules.

G. The Jockey Club may decline to process any material received from an owner or breeder not in good standing with The Jockey Club. An owner or breeder will be considered not in good standing if the owner or breeder has any outstanding fees owed to The Jockey Club for any horse including, but not limited to, fees related to registration, genetic typing, naming, imports, exports, duplicates or corrections.

H. Subject to the rules requiring payment of late fees, all fees are due at the time of the submittal of the applicable form or request to The Jockey Club. The Fee Schedule sets forth each submittal to The Jockey Club for which there is a fee and the amount of each fee. In the event any person fails to pay a fee owed to The Jockey Club, then The Jockey Club shall apply any payment subsequently received from that person to the outstanding fees owed by that person to The Jockey Club.

GLOSSARY OF TERMS

The American Stud Book

The American Stud Book is the registry maintained by The Jockey Club for all Thoroughbreds foaled in the United States, Puerto Rico and Canada and for all Thoroughbreds imported into the United States, Puerto Rico and Canada from countries that have a registry recognized by The Jockey Club and the International Stud Book Committee.

Age of a Horse

Foal: A young horse of either sex in its first year of life.

Suckling: A foal of any sex in its first year of life while it is still nursing.

Weanling: A foal of any sex in its first year of life after being separated from its dam.

Yearling: A colt, filly or gelding in its second calendar year of life (Beginning January 1 of the year following its birth).

Two-Year-Old: A colt, filly or gelding in its third calendar year of life (Beginning January 1 of the year following its yearling year).

Breeding Practices Not Approved by The Jockey Club

Artificial Insemination: The process of depositing semen into the reproductive tract of a broodmare in order to get a broodmare in foal (pregnant) without the physical mounting by a stallion.

Cloning: Any method by which the genetic material of an unfertilized egg or an embryo is (i) removed, (ii) replaced by genetic material taken from another organism, (iii) added to with genetic material from another organism, or (iv) otherwise modified by any means in order to produce a live foal.

Embryo Transfer (Transplants): The method whereby a developing embryo or unfertilized egg is removed from its natural dam and implanted into the reproductive tract of either the natural dam or a host dam for a portion of the gestation period in order to produce a live foal.

Breeding Terminology

Bred (Mated): Any filly or mare that has undergone the physical act of breeding (mating).

Bred (Area Foaled): The term "bred" is sometimes used to describe the location where a foal was born, i.e., Kentucky Bred, New York Bred, etc.

Breeder: The breeder of a foal is the owner of the dam at the time of foaling, unless the dam was under a lease or foal-sharing agreement at the time of foaling. In that case, the person(s) specified by the terms of the agreement is (are) the breeder of the foal.

Stallion: A male horse that is used to produce foals.

Sire: A male horse that has produced, or is producing, foals.

Broodmare: A filly or mare that has been bred (mated) and is used to produce foals.

Dam: A female horse that has produced, or is producing, foals.

Maiden: A filly or mare that has never been bred (mated).

In Foal (Pregnant) Broodmare: A filly or mare that was bred (mated), conceived and is currently in foal (pregnant).

Aborted: A term used to describe a broodmare that has been pronounced in foal (pregnant) based on an examination of 42 days or more post breeding (mating) and lost her foal prematurely; or a broodmare from whom an aborted fetus has been observed.

Barren (Not Pregnant): A term used to describe a filly or mare, other than a maiden mare, that was bred (mated) and did not conceive during the last breeding season.

Breeding (Mating): The physical act of a stallion mounting a broodmare with intromission of the penis and ejaculation of semen into the reproductive tract.

Sex

Colt: An entire male horse four-years-old or younger.

Horse: When reference is made to sex, a "horse" is an entire male five-years-old or older.

Ridgling ("rig"): A lay term used to describe either a monorchid or cryptorchid.

Cryptorchid: A male horse of any age that has no testes in his scrotum but was never gelded (the testes are undescended).

Monorchid: A male horse of any age that has only one testicle in his scrotum - the other testicle was either removed or is undescended.

Gelding: A male horse of any age that is unsexed - had both testicles removed.

Filly: A female horse four-years-old or younger.

Mare: A female horse five-years-old or older.

Thoroughbred

A Thoroughbred is a horse which has satisfied the rules and requirements set forth herein and is registered in The American Stud Book or in a Foreign Stud Book recognized by The Jockey Club and the International Stud Book Committee.

United States

The United States includes the 50 states, the District of Columbia, and the insular territories and possessions of the United States of America.

Interactive RegistrationTM

An internet site where breeders, owners and authorized agents can submit registration forms, check registration status and browse the online names book.

Genetic Typing

The process of determining the genetic factors present in a blood or DNA sample.

COLOR GUIDE

The following colors are recognized by The Jockey Club:

Bay: The entire coat of the horse may vary from a yellow-tan to a bright auburn. The mane, tail and lower portion of the legs are always black, unless white markings are present.

Black: The entire coat of the horse is black, including the muzzle, the flanks, the mane, tail and legs, unless white markings are present.

Chestnut: The entire coat of the horse may vary from a red-yellow to a golden-yellow. The mane, tail and legs are usually variations of the coat color, unless white markings are present.

Dark Bay/Brown: The entire coat of the horse will vary from a brown, with areas of tan on the shoulders, head and flanks, to a dark brown, with tan areas seen only in the flanks and/or muzzle. The mane, tail and lower portion of the legs are always black, unless white markings are present.

Gray/Roan: The Jockey Club has combined these colors into one color category. This does not change the individual definitions of the colors for gray and roan and in no way impacts on the two-coat color inheritance principle as stated in Rule 1(E).

Gray: The majority of the coat of the horse is a mixture of black and white hairs. The mane, tail and legs may be either black or gray, unless white markings are present.

Roan: The majority of the coat of the horse is a mixture of red and white hairs or brown and white hairs. The mane, tail and legs may be black, chestnut or roan, unless white markings are present.

Palomino: The entire coat of the horse is golden-yellow, unless white markings are present. The mane and tail are usually flaxen.

White: A rare color not to be confused with the colors gray or roan. The entire coat, including the mane, tail and legs, is white and no other color should be present.

LOCATION OF OFFICES & AVAILABILITY OF FORMS AND INFORMATION

Executive Office:
The Jockey Club
40 East 52nd Street
New York, New York 10022
Telephone: (212) 371-5970
FAX: (212) 371-6123

Registry Office:
The Jockey Club
821 Corporate Drive
Lexington, Kentucky 40503-2794
Telephone: (859) 224-2700
Registration Services: (800) 444-8521
FAX: (859) 224-2710

Canada:
The Jockey Club of Canada
P.O. Box 156
Rexdale, Ontario M9W 5L1
Telephone: (416) 675-7756
FAX: (416) 675-4573
Availability of forms and information only.

All Registry Office forms and current Fee Schedules are available from the Registration Services Department in the Lexington, Kentucky office.

Top Priced North American Yearlings Since 1980

Sale	Horse	Sex	Sire	Dam	Buyer	Sale price
KEE JUL SEL YRLG 85	Seattle Dancer	C	Nijinsky II	My Charmer	BBA (England)	$13,100,000
KEE JUL SEL YRLG 83	Snaafi Dancer	C	Northern Dancer	My Bupers	Aston Upthorpe Stud	10,200,000
KEE JUL SEL YRLG 84	Imperial Falcon	C	Northern Dancer	Ballade	BBA (England)	8,250,000
KEE SEP YRLG 04		C	Storm Cat	Welcome Surprise	Hideyuki Mori	8,000,000
KEE JUL SEL YRLG 84	Jareer	C	Northern Dancer	Fabuleux Jane	Darley Stud Management	7,100,000
KEE JUL SEL YRLG 85	Laa Etaab	C	Nijinsky II	Crimson Saint	Gainsborough Farm	7,000,000
KEE SEP YRLG 00	Tasmanian Tiger	C	Storm Cat	Hum Along	Demi O'Byrne	6,800,000
KEE JUL SEL YRLG 84	Amjaad	C	Seattle Slew	Desiree	Darley Stud Management	6,500,000
KEE SEP YRLG 01	Van Nistelrooy	C	Storm Cat	Halory	Demi O'Byrne	6,400,000
KEE SEP YRLG 01	Alajwad	C	Storm Cat	La Affirmed	John Ferguson Bloodstock	5,500,000
KEE JUL SEL YRLG 84	Obligato	C	Northern Dancer	Truly Bound	BBA (Ireland)	5,400,000
KEE SEP YRLG 00	King's Consul	C	Kingmambo	Battle Creek Girl	John Ferguson Bloodstock	5,300,000
KEE JUL SEL YRLG 84	Wassl Touch	C	Northern Dancer	Queen Sucree	Darley Stud Management	5,100,000
KEE JUL SEL YRLG 84	Professor Blue	C	Northern Dancer	Mississippi Mud	BBA (England)	4,600,000
FTN YRLG SAR 84	Parlando	C	Northern Dancer	Bubbling	BBA (Ireland)	4,600,000
KEE SEP YRLG 00	Shah Jehan	C	Mr. Prospector	Voodoo Lily	Demi O'Byrne	4,400,000
KEE SEP YRLG 00	Moon's Whisper	F	Storm Cat	East of the Moon	Shadwell Estate Co.	4,400,000
KEE JUL SEL YRLG 82	Empire Glory	C	Nijinsky II	Spearfish	BBA (Ireland)	4,250,000
KEE JUL SEL YRLG 83	Foxboro	C	Northern Dancer	Desert Vixen	BBA (England)	4,250,000
FTN SEL YRLG SAR 00	Distinction	C	Seattle Slew	Omi	David J. Shimmon	4,200,000
KEE JUL SEL YRLG 83	Gallant Archer	C	Nijinsky II	Belle of Dodge Me	Aston Upthorpe Stud	4,100,000
FTN YRLG SAR 84	Elnawaagi	C	Roberto	Gurkhas Band	Darley Stud Management	4,000,000
KEE SEP YRLG 00	Showlady	F	Theatrical (IRE)	Claxton's Slew	John Ferguson Bloodstock	4,000,000
KEE JUL YRLG 01	Warhol	C	Saint Ballado	Charm a Gendarme	Demi O'Byrne	4,000,000
KEE JUL YRLG 98	Fusaichi Pegasus	C	Mr. Prospector	Angel Fever	Fusao Sekiguchi	4,000,000
KEE SEP YRLG 99	Dubai to Dubai	C	Kris S.	Mr. P's Princess	John Ferguson Bloodstock	3,900,000
KEE SEP YRLG 03	Hashimiya	F	Gone West	Touch of Greatness	John Ferguson	3,800,000
KEE SEP YRLG 01	Hoyer	C	Mr. Prospector	Destination Mir	John Ferguson Bloodstock	3,800,000
KEE JUL SEL YRLG 84	Alchaasibiyeh	F	Seattle Slew	Fine Prospect	Darley Stud Management	3,750,000
KEE JUL YRLG 01	Virtuosa	F	Seeking the Gold	Escena	Reynolds Bell Jr., agent	3,700,000
KEE JUL SEL YRLG 87	Warrshan	C	Northern Dancer	Secret Asset	Darley Stud Management	3,700,000
KEE JUL YRLG 00	Born Perfect	F	Mr. Prospector	Molly Girl	Padua Stables	3,600,000
KEE SEP YRLG 00	America's Storm	C	Storm Cat	Lilly Capote	Padua & Gaines-Gentry	3,600,000
KEE JUL SEL YRLG 86	Northern State	C	Northern Dancer	South Ocean	Darley Stud Management	3,600,000
KEE JUL YRLG 01	Act of Duty	C	Mr. Prospector	Nuryette	John Ferguson Bloodstock	3,600,000
KEE SEP YRLG 03	Olympic	C	Danzig	Queena	Demi O'Byrne	3,600,000
KEE JUL SEL YRLG 88	Royal Academy	C	Nijinsky II	Crimson Saint	M V O Brien	3,500,000
KEE JUL SEL YRLG 81	Ballydoyle	C	Northern Dancer	South Ocean	BBA (Ireland)	3,500,000
KEE JUL YRLG 00	Sophisticat	F	Storm Cat	Serena's Song	Demi O'Byrne	3,400,000
KEE JAN ALL AGES 98	Inkling	F	Seeking the Gold	Number	Demi O'Byrne	3,400,000
KEE SEP YRLG 04	Blessed Storm	C	Storm Cat	Bless	Hideyuki Mori	3,400,000
KEE SEP YRLG 01	Newfoundland	C	Storm Cat	Clear Mandate	Demi O'Byrne	3,300,000
KEE JUL SEL YRLG 81	Shareef Dancer	C	Northern Dancer	Sweet Alliance	Aston Upthorpe Stud	3,300,000
KEE JUL YRLG 00	Authenticate	C	Gone West	Lakeway	Padua Stables	3,300,000
FTN SEL YRLG SAR 01	Habayeb	C	Storm Cat	Gone to Venus	John Ferguson Bloodstock	3,300,000
KEE SEP YRLG 00	Full Mandate	C	A.P. Indy	Clear Mandate	Padua Stables	3,200,000
KEE JUL SEL YRLG 86	Dancing Groom	C	Nijinsky II	Blush With Pride	BBA (Ireland)	3,200,000
KEE SEP YRLG 04		C	Kingmambo	Zuri	John Ferguson	3,100,000
KEE JUL YRLG 02	One Cool Cat	C	Storm Cat	Tacha	Demi O'Byrne	3,100,000
KEE SEP YRLG 04		C	A.P. Indy	Sahara Gold	John Ferguson	3,100,000
FTN YRLG SAR 83	Immortal Dancer	C	Spectacular Bid	Farouche	Aston Upthorpe Stud	3,000,000
KEE JUL YRLG 99	Norway	C	Storm Cat	Weekend Surprise	Demi O'Byrne	3,000,000
KEE JUL YRLG 01	Ustoura	F	Storm Cat	Inca Legacy	John Ferguson Bloodstock	3,000,000
FTN SEL YRLG SAR 01	Royal Walk	C	Mr. Prospector	Stone Flower	Bob Baffert, agent	3,000,000
FTN SEL YRLG SAR 01	Russia	C	Kingmambo	Seattle Way	Demi O'Byrne	3,000,000
KEE JUL SEL YRLG 84	Woodman	C	Mr. Prospector	Playmate	BBA (England)	3,000,000
FTN SEL YRLG SAR 99	Ochoco	C	Mr. Prospector	Eaves	Aaron and Marie Jones	3,000,000

Snapshot Facts: Storm Cat's 13 yearlings at $3 million or more surpasses celebrated grandsire Northern Dancer's 12.

Top Priced North American Yearlings in 2004

Sale	Horse	Sex	Sire	Dam	Buyer	Sale price
KEE SEP YRLG 04		C	Storm Cat	Welcome Surprise	Hideyuki Mori	$8,000,000
KEE SEP YRLG 04	Blessed Storm	C	Storm Cat	Bless	Hideyuki Mori	3,400,000
KEE SEP YRLG 04		C	Kingmambo	Zuri	John Ferguson	3,100,000
KEE SEP YRLG 04		C	A.P. Indy	Sahara Gold	John Ferguson	3,100,000
KEE SEP YRLG 04		C	Kingmambo	Crown of Crimson	Shadwell Estate Co.	2,850,000
KEE SEP YRLG 04		C	Unbridled's Song	Cruising Haven	Demi O'Byrne	2,800,000
KEE SEP YRLG 04		C	Danzig	Scads	Demi O'Byrne	2,000,000
KEE SEP YRLG 04		C	Forestry	Clever Bertie	Buzz Chace, agent	1,900,000
KEE SEP YRLG 04		C	Galileo (IRE)	Regina Maria	Demi O'Byrne	1,900,000
FTN SEL YRLG SAR 04	Fairbanks	C	Giant's Causeway	Alaska Queen	Team Valor	1,850,000
KEE SEP YRLG 04		C	Seeking the Gold	Angel Fever	Hideyuki Mori	1,800,000
KEE SEP YRLG 04		F	Storm Cat	Warm Mood	John Ferguson	1,700,000
FTN SEL YRLG SAR 04		F	A.P. Indy	Seebe	W.S. Farish	1,500,000
KEE SEP YRLG 04		C	Danehill	Fiji (GB)	Demi O'Byrne	1,500,000
KEE SEP YRLG 04	Sense of Class	F	Fusaichi Pegasus	Golden Oriole	Skara Glen Stables	1,500,000
FTN SEL YRLG SAR 04		F	Storm Cat	Jewel Princess	Roger King	1,400,000
KEE SEP YRLG 04		C	Danzig	Shouldnt Say Never	John Ferguson	1,400,000
KEE SEP YRLG 04	A. P. Warrior	C	A.P. Indy	Warrior Queen	Fleetwood/N.W. Mgmt	1,300,000
KEE SEP YRLG 04		F	Storm Cat	Strategic Maneuver	Reynolds Bell Jr., agent	1,300,000
KEE SEP YRLG 04		C	Grand Slam	Sheza Honey	Demi O'Byrne	1,300,000
KEE SEP YRLG 04	Tawfeer	C	Storm Cat	Program Pick	Shadwell Estate Co.	1,250,000
KEE SEP YRLG 04		F	Unbridled's Song	Towering Success	Brushwood Stable	1,250,000
FTN SEL YRLG SAR 04	Wicked B. Havior	C	Unbridled's Song	Mesmerized	William B. Haines	1,150,000
KEE SEP YRLG 04	Joe Hirsch	C	Giant's Causeway	Statuette	Demi O'Byrne	1,150,000
KEE SEP YRLG 04	King Shooting Star	F	Storm Cat	Gone to the Moon	Roger King	1,100,000
KEE SEP YRLG 04		C	Forestry	Christmas in Aiken	John Ferguson	1,100,000
KEE SEP YRLG 04		C	Rahy	Crystal Crossing (IRE)	John Ferguson	1,050,000
KEE SEP YRLG 04		F	Giant's Causeway	Touch of Greatness	Reynolds Bell Jr., agent	1,050,000
KEE SEP YRLG 04		C	A.P. Indy	Million Gift (JPN)	Mike Ryan, agent	1,000,000
FTN SEL YRLG SAR 04		C	Storm Cat	Gone to Venus	R B and B J Lewis	1,000,000
KEE SEP YRLG 04		C	Giant's Causeway	Smokey Mirage	John Ferguson	1,000,000
KEE SEP YRLG 04		C	Kingmambo	Possibly Perfect	John Ferguson	950,000
KEE SEP YRLG 04		C	Forestry	Concentric	John Ferguson	950,000
KEE SEP YRLG 04		F	Seattle Slew	Pleasant Temper	Lael Sta, Nicoma Bldstk, agt	950,000
FTK SUM YRLG 04		C	Elusive Quality	Cercida	John Ferguson	950,000
KEE SEP YRLG 04		C	Kingmambo	String Quartet (IRE)	Shadwell Estate Co.	950,000
KEE SEP YRLG 04		F	Seeking the Gold	Corona Lake	Buzz Chace, agent	925,000
KEE SEP YRLG 04		F	Gone West	England's Rose	John Ferguson	900,000
KEE SEP YRLG 04	Pulpiteer	C	Pulpit	Mountain Girl	John Ferguson	900,000
FTN SEL YRLG SAR 04	Bisbee Slam	C	Grand Slam	Bisbee	Fleetwood/N.W. Mgmt	900,000
FTN SEL YRLG SAR 04		F	Kingmambo	Sweet and Ready	Narvick International	900,000
KEE SEP YRLG 04		C	War Chant	Safely Kept	Narvick International	900,000
KEE SEP YRLG 04		C	Giant's Causeway	Serape	John Ferguson	875,000
KEE SEP YRLG 04		C	Elusive Quality	First Glimmer	Buzz Chace, agent	850,000
KEE SEP YRLG 04		F	Storm Cat	Pennant Fever	Edward Evans	850,000
KEE SEP YRLG 04		C	Giant's Causeway	Devine Beauty	Demi O'Byrne	850,000
KEE SEP YRLG 04		F	Storm Cat	Nannerl	John Ferguson	850,000
FTK SUM YRLG 04	Ratibor	C	Cozzene	Avie's Fancy	Lane's End Bloodstock, agt	825,000
KEE SEP YRLG 04		C	Rahy	Balistroika	Shadwell Estate Co.	825,000
KEE SEP YRLG 04	Gray Star	C	Giant's Causeway	Fountain Lake	R Baker & W Mack	825,000
FTK SUM YRLG 04		C	Fusaichi Pegasus	Regent's Walk	Demi O'Byrne	800,000
KEE SEP YRLG 04		C	Point Given	Classic Threat	R B and B J Lewis	800,000
KEE SEP YRLG 04	Doubleshot of Gold	F	Touch Gold	Arches of Gold	B. Wayne Hughes	800,000
KEE SEP YRLG 04		C	A.P. Indy	Ring of Fire	John Ferguson	800,000
KEE SEP YRLG 04		C	Giant's Causeway	Sweeping Story	John Ferguson	800,000
FTN SEL YRLG SAR 04		C	Deputy Minister	Horsafire	B. Wayne Hughes	800,000
KEE SEP YRLG 04	Daniele Beautiful	F	A.P. Indy	Kelli Cat	Buzz Chace, agent	800,000
KEE SEP YRLG 04	Ski Seattle	F	Seattle Slew	Ski Dancer	B. Wayne Hughes	800,000

Snapshot Facts: Welcome Surprise, dam of the year's most expensive yearling, is a half-sister by Seeking the Gold to A.P. Indy, the top-priced yearling of 1990 who went on to be a classic-winning Horse of the Year and leading stallion.

Status of Top Priced North American Yearlings of 2002
(3–Year–Olds of 2004)

Led by $3.1 million purchase One Cool Cat, a list of the 27 most expensive yearlings bought at public auction in North America in 2002 is presented below, along with their tabulated race record through 12/31/2004. North American starts are tabulated separately of all foreign starts, as are starts at 2 and 3. If a horse raced more than one season, or both in North America and overseas, a total is given. Stakes winners are indicated in capitalized, bold-face type, while stakes-placed horses are shown in mixed case, bold-face type.

Most successful to date of the top-priced yearlings of 2002 was One Cool Cat, winner of the Phoenix and National stakes at 2, both Group 1 events in Ireland, as well as two Group 3 events. One Cool Cat won a Cartier Award as top 2-year-old colt. The other stakes winner from this select group of sales yearlings, through the conclusion of their 3-year-old season, was Antonius Pius.

Sale	Horse (Sire - Dam) Year	Country	Sts	1st	2d	Sale Price 3rd	Earnings	Buyer (US Dollars)
KEE JUL YRLG 02	**ONE COOL CAT** (Storm Cat - Tacha)					$3,100,000	Demi O'Byrne
	2003	Foreign	5	4	0	0	$461,878
	2004	Foreign	5	1	0	1	$106,208
		Total	10	5	0	1	$568,086
KEE JUL YRLG 02	Platinum Heights (Storm Cat - Amelia Bearhart)					$2,800,000	Eugene Melnyk
	2004	USA/CAN	4	1	1	0	$29,800
KEE SEP YRLG 02	**The Mighty Tiger** (Storm Cat- Clear Mandate)					$2,500,000	Demi O'Byrne
	2003	Foreign	4	1	1	2	$54,540
KEE SEP YRLG 02	Offenbach (Danzig - Aquilegia)					$2,400,000	D. Wayne Lukas, agent
	2003	Foreign	1	1	0	0	$14,996
KEE SEP YRLG 02	Necropolis (Seeking the Gold - Gioconda)					$2,150,000	Demi O'Byrne
	Unraced						
KEE JUL YRLG 02	Intimidator (Gone West - Colonial Play)					$2,100,000	Buzz Chace, agent
	2004	USA/CAN	7	1	2	1	$46,637
KEE JUL YRLG 02	Possession (Belong to Me - Tomisue's Delight)					$2,000,000	John Ferguson Bloodstock
	2003	USA/CAN	2	1	1	0	$35,000
KEE JUL YRLG 02	Ensenada (Seeking the Gold - Desert Stormer)					$1,800,000	Reynolds Bell Jr., agent
	2003	USA/CAN	1	0	0	0	$1,350
	2004	USA/CAN	8	2	2	1	$66,055
		Total	9	2	2	1	$67,405
KEE JUL YRLG 02	Great Exhibition (Gone West - Touch of Greatness)					$1,800,000	John Ferguson Bloodstock
	2003	Foreign	2	0	1	1	$6,486
	2004	Foreign	5	0	2	1	$5,680
		Total	7	0	3	2	$12,166
KEE SEP YRLG 02	Maastricht (Deputy Minister - Highest Glory)					$1,650,000	John Ferguson Bloodstock
	2004	USA/CAN	3	0	0	0	$1,800
KEE SEP YRLG 02	Lutyens (Dixieland Band - Hidden Garden)					$1,600,000	John Ferguson Bloodstock
	2004	USA/CAN	1	0	0	1	$4,680
KEE JUL YRLG 02	Destination Dubai (Kingmambo - Mysterial)					$1,500,000	John Ferguson Bloodstock
	2003	Foreign	2	0	2	0	$6,183
	2004	Foreign	6	2	0	1	$40,265
		Total	8	2	2	1	$46,448
KEE SEP YRLG 02	**ANTONIUS PIUS** (Danzig - Catchascatchcan (GB))					$1,500,000	Demi O'Byrne
	2003	Foreign	3	2	0	0	$103,618
	2004	Foreign	8	0	0	2	$124,158
	USA/CAN		1	0	1	0	$336,000
		Total	12	2	1	2	$563,776

Sale	Horse (Sire - Dam) Year	Country	Sts	1st	2d	Sale Price 3rd	Earnings	Buyer (US Dollars)
KEE SEP YRLG 02	Rosberg (A.P. Indy - Bosra Sham)					$1,500,000		John Ferguson Bloodstock
	2003	USA/CAN	2	1	0	0	$26,180	
KEE SEP YRLG 02	Speed Succeeds (Gone West - Daijin)					$1,450,000		Live Oak Plantation
	Unraced							
KEE SEP YRLG 02	Stenka Rasin (Pulpit - Marshesseaux)					$1,400,000		Kazuko Yoshida
	2003	Foreign	2	1	0	0	$46,505	
	2004	Foreign	8	1	1	1	$128,759	
		Total	10	2	1	1	$175,264	
KEE JUL YRLG 02	Mystified (Gone West - Primedex)					$1,350,000		R.B. & B.J. Lewis and Overbrook Farm
	2003	USA/CAN	4	0	0	4	$19,800	
	2004	USA/CAN	4	0	0	2	$11,360	
		Total	8	0	0	6	$31,160	
FTN SEL YRLG SAR 02	Dossier (Storm Cat - Sacahuista)					$1,300,000		John Sikura
	2004	USA/CAN	2	1	0	0	$14,100	
KEE JUL YRLG 02	Line of Departure (A.P. Indy - Ballerina Princess)					$1,250,000		B. Wayne Hughes
	2004	USA/CAN	1	0	0	1	$5,520	
KEE SEP YRLG 02	**Path of Thunder** (Thunder Gulch - Drina)					$1,200,000		Demi O'Byrne
	2003	USA/CAN	2	0	0	2	$10,010	
	2004	USA/CAN	7	3	3	0	$106,700	
		Total	9	3	3	2	$116,710	
KEE SEP YRLG 02	**Hippocrates** (Hennessy - Altair)					$1,100,000		Demi O'Byrne
	2003	Foreign	1	0	0	0	$0	
	2003	USA/CAN	1	0	0	0	$980	
	2004	USA/CAN	6	1	0	2	$49,058	
		Total	8	1	0	2	$50,038	
KEE JAN ALL AGES 02	**Value Plus** (Unbridled's Song - Roll Over Baby)					$1,100,000		Buzz Chace, agent
	2003	USA/CAN	4	1	1	0	$87,000	
	2004	USA/CAN	5	1	1	0	$220,900	
		Total	9	2	2	0	$307,900	
KEE SEP YRLG 02	Turbo Storm (Storm Cat - Scoop the Gold)					$1,000,000		John Ferguson Bloodstock
	Unraced							
FTN SEL YRLG SAR 02	Everwood (Unbridled's Song - Wanda's Dream)					$1,000,000		Aaron & Marie Jones, Buzz Chace, agt
	2004	USA/CAN	3	0	0	2	$9,090	
KEE SEP YRLG 02	Civilize (A.P. Indy - Wild Planet)					$1,000,000		Reynolds Bell Jr., agent
	2004	USA/CAN	6	0	2	1	$19,530	
KEE SEP YRLG 02	Beaufort Scale (Storm Cat - Unbridled Wind)					$1,000,000		Mrs. M.J. Dance Jr.
	2003	USA/CAN	3	0	0	0	$390	
KEE SEP YRLG 02	Seeking the Best (Ire) (Seeking the Gold - Mackie)					$1,000,000		Kazuko Yoshida
	2004	Foreign	2	0	0	0	$0	

Top Priced Weanlings Sold in North America Since 1980

Sale	Horse	Sex	Sire	Dam	Buyer	Sale Price
* NEWSTEAD FARM FTK 85	Magic of Life	F	Seattle Slew	Larida	BBA (England)	$2,500,000
KEE NOV BRDG 03		C	Storm Cat	Spain	Dromoland Farm	2,400,000
* WARNER JONES KEE 87	Ghashtah	F	Nijinsky II	My Charmer	Shadwell Estates	2,300,000
KEE NOV BRDG 98	King Charlemagne	C	Nureyev	Race the Wild Wind	Demi O'Byrne	1,500,000
KEE NOV BRDG 01	Teeming	F	Storm Cat	Better Than Honour	Josham Farms	1,500,000
KEE NOV BRDG 98	Juniper	C	Danzig	Montage	Demi O'Byrne	1,450,000
KEE NOV BRDG 03	Secret Thyme	F	Storm Cat	Garden Secrets	Brushwood Stable	1,400,000
KEE NOV BRDG 96	Winthrop	C	Storm Cat	Tinnitus	Demi O'Byrne	1,400,000
KEE NOV BRDG 03	Serena's Cat	F	Storm Cat	Serena's Tune	Dell Ridge Farm	1,400,000
KEE NOV BRDG 99	Restoration	C	Sadler's Wells	Madame Est Sortie (FR)	M.W. Miller III, agent	1,400,000
KEE NOV BRDG 99	New Trieste	C	A.P. Indy	Lovlier Linda	Paul Shanahan	1,300,000
KEE NOV BRDG 00	She's a Beauty	F	Storm Cat	Now That's Funny	T. Hyde	1,200,000
KEE NOV BRDG 98	Tide Cat	F	Storm Cat	Maytide	505 Farms, Brad Martin, agent	1,200,000
KEE NOV BRDG 89	Net Dancer	F	Nureyev	Doubles Partner	E. Hudson	1,200,000
* WARNER JONES KEE 87	Razeen	C	Northern Dancer	Secret Asset	Darley Stud Management	1,175,000
KEE NOV BRDG 04		F	Unbridled's Song	Helsinki (GB)	John Sikura	1,150,000
KEE NOV BRDG 00	A. P. Petal	F	A.P. Indy	Golden Petal	D. Wayne Hughes	1,150,000
* NEWSTEAD FARM FTK 85	Worood	F	Vaguely Noble	Farouche	BBA (England)	1,100,000
KEE NOV BRDG 00	Hold That Tiger	C	Storm Cat	Beware of the Cat	Demi O'Byrne	1,100,000
* WARNER JONES KEE 87	Seaside Attraction	F	Seattle Slew	Kamar	Hinton, Monty	1,050,000
KEE NOV BRDG 00	Wildcat Queen	F	Storm Cat	Jetapat	Bradley and Bowden, agents	1,050,000
KEE NOV BRDG 98	Lemon Tart	F	Deputy Minister	Lemon Dove	Brushwood Stable	1,000,000
KEE NOV BRDG 89	Swiss Desert	C	Danzig	Strictly Raised	Gainsborough Farm	1,000,000
KEE NOV BRDG 98	Malibu Karen	F	Seeking the Gold	Regent's Walk	B. Wayne Hughes	1,000,000
KEE NOV BRDG 96	Blissful	F	Mr. Prospector	Angel Fever	J. B. & B. Stables	1,000,000
KEE NOV BRDG 98	Princess Atoosa	F	Gone West	Kooyonga (IRE)	Brushwood Stable	1,000,000
KEE NOV BRDG 00	Baltic Nations	F	Seattle Slew	Baltic Sea	B. Wayne Hughes	975,000
KEE NOV BRDG 00	Perfect Story	F	Tale of the Cat	Turko's Turn	John C. Oxley	975,000
KEE NOV BRDG 89	Khazar	C	Nureyev	Kathleen's Girl	Darley Stud Management	975,000
KEE NOV BRDG 01	Tizdubai	F	Cee's Tizzy	Cee's Song	John Ferguson Bloodstock	950,000
* NEWSTEAD FARM FTK 85	Allen's Alydar	C	Alydar	Kittiwake	Paulson, Allen E.	950,000
KEE NOV BRDG 89	Machikane Aida	F	Alydar	Lady's Secret	Muirfield East	950,000
KEE NOV BRDG 97	Bernstein	C	Storm Cat	La Affirmed	Demi O'Byrne	925,000
KEE NOV BRDG 89	Bevel	F	Mr. Prospector	Bev Bev	Darley Stud Management	900,000
KEE NOV BRDG 99	Costume Party	F	Storm Cat	Now That's Funny	G. Watts Humphrey Jr.	900,000
KEE NOV BRDG 99	Trial by Jury	C	Deputy Minister	Fantastic Ways	Robert B. and Beverly J. Lewis	900,000
KEE NOV BRDG 99	Dubai Tiger	C	Storm Cat	Toga Toga Toga	Tim Hyde	900,000
KEE NOV BRDG 99	Lethal Temper	F	Seattle Slew	Shy Princess	LML	875,000
KEE NOV BRDG 98	Lucrative	F	Seeking the Gold	Banker's Lady	John Ferguson Bloodstock	850,000
KEE NOV BRDG 98	Paynes Bay	C	Mr. Prospector	Embellished	Mayfield Equine	825,000
KEE NOV BRDG 03		C	Thunder Gulch	Turko's Turn	Chestnut Valley Farm	800,000
KEE NOV BRDG 02	Council Member	C	Seattle Slew	Zoe Montana	John Ferguson Bloodstock	800,000
KEE NOV BRDG 89	Fair American	C	Mr. Prospector	Win Nona	Curragh Bloodstock Agency	800,000
KEE NOV BRDG 00	Patriot's Pride	C	A.P. Indy	Windmill Point	Kentucky Properties	800,000
KEE NOV BRDG 99	Sky Legend	F	Deputy Minister	Sky Beauty	Tracy Farmer	800,000
* NEWSTEAD FARM FTK 85	Mrs. Nijinsky	F	Nijinsky II	Mrs. Warren	Delta Thoroughbreds, Inc.	800,000
KEE NOV BRDG 98	Talk Is Money	C	Deputy Minister	Isle Go West	Smithfield Investments	785,000
KEE NOV BRDG 98	Fiddlin Devon	F	Deputy Minister	La Chaposa (PER)	Jane M. Schosberg	775,000
KEE NOV BRDG 99	Wiseman's Ferry	C	Hennessy	Emmaus	Indian Hill Farm	775,000
KEE NOV BRDG 99	Nutcase	F	Forest Wildcat	Raise the Standard	Wertheimer et Frere	775,000
KEE NOV BRDG 99	Sports Hero	C	Mr. Prospector	Alysoft	High Mills Farm	775,000
KEE NOV BRDG 99	Tricky Indy	F	A.P. Indy	Bag of Tricks	B. Wayne Hughes	775,000
KEE NOV BRDG 98	Black Minnaloushe	C	Storm Cat	Coral Dance (FR)	Demi O'Byrne	750,000
KEE NOV BRDG 83	Clef En Or	F	Alydar	Irish Trip	BBA (England)	750,000
KEE NOV BRDG 93	K. G. Beauty	F	Private Account	Maplejinsky	Morio Sakurai	750,000
KEE NOV BRDG 99	Battle Tough	C	Hennessy	Princess Alydar	Chestnut Valley Farm	735,000
KEE NOV BRDG 02	Scandinavia	C	Fusaichi Pegasus	Party Cited	John McCormack Bloodstock	725,000
KEE NOV BRDG 99	Nijinsky's Crown	C	Gone West	Nijinsky's Lover	R.A. Adkinson	725,000
KEE NOV BRDG 98	Stellar Slew	F	Seattle Slew	Crown of Love	Karen Taylor, agent	725,000
KEE NOV BRDG 91	Suave Tern	C	Arctic Tern	Suavite	Henri Chalhoub	725,000

* A dispersal sale

Snapshot Facts: Seventeen of the 26 weanlings sold in North America for $1 million or more since 1980 were fillies.

Highest Priced Weanlings Sold at Public Auction in 2004

Only includes Weanlings sold in North America

Sale	Horse	Sex	Sire	Dam	Buyer	Sale Price
KEE NOV BRDG 04		F	Unbridled's Song	Helsinki (GB)	John Sikura	$1,150,000
KEE NOV BRDG 04		F	Gone West	Dance Swiftly	M.W. Miller III, agent	700,000
KEE NOV BRDG 04	Heavenly Vision	C	Grand Slam	Heavenly Cat	Glen Hill Farm	650,000
KEE NOV BRDG 04		F	War Chant	Dissemble (GB)	Stewart L. Armstrong	625,000
KEE NOV BRDG 04		F	Giant's Causeway	Halo America	Sir Robert Ogden	575,000
KEE NOV BRDG 04		F	Pulpit	Mila	Lael Sta, Nicoma Bldstk, agt	575,000
KEE NOV BRDG 04		C	Elusive Quality	Barbara Sue	John Ferguson Bloodstock	550,000
KEE NOV BRDG 04		C	Fusaichi Pegasus	Gracie Lady (IRE)	Foxtale Farm	535,000
KEE NOV BRDG 04		C	Elusive Quality	Silver Tornado	John Ferguson Bloodstock	500,000
KEE NOV BRDG 04		C	Elusive Quality	Valid Warning	John Ferguson Bloodstock	450,000
KEE NOV BRDG 04		C	Giant's Causeway	Esther Rose	Dromoland Farm	450,000
KEE NOV BRDG 04		C	Mr. Greeley	Hard Knocker	Eldon Farm Equine	440,000
KEE NOV BRDG 04	Miss Abita	F	Dixie Union	Be a Prospector	Robert E. Courtney Jr., agt	400,000
FTK FALL MIX NOV 04		F	Giant's Causeway	Million Stories	Gus Bell, agent	385,000
KEE NOV BRDG 04		F	Fusaichi Pegasus	Silent Eskimo	Frederic Sauque, agent	375,000
KEE NOV BRDG 04		F	Giant's Causeway	Lemon Dove	Sunrise Stable	360,000
KEE NOV BRDG 04		C	Cozzene	Forest Key	ClassicStar	340,000
KEE NOV BRDG 04		F	Unbridled's Song	Goodness	Never Tell Farm	340,000
KEE NOV BRDG 04		C	Tale of the Cat	Dayclear	Bloodstock Services	330,000
KEE NOV BRDG 04		F	Giant's Causeway	Rose Frances	Fleetwood Bloodstock	325,000
KEE NOV BRDG 04		C	Came Home	Cristalline (CHI)	DOC Bloodstock	310,000
KEE NOV BRDG 04		F	Giant's Causeway	Slide	Athens Woods	285,000
KEE NOV BRDG 04		F	Street Cry (IRE)	Chelsey Dancer	Olin Gentry, agent	285,000
KEE NOV BRDG 04		F	Elusive Quality	Affair With Aflair	Irving Cowan	285,000
KEE NOV BRDG 04		C	Johannesburg	Attasliyah (IRE)	Indian Hill Farm	280,000
KEE NOV BRDG 04		C	Awesome Again	J. D. Flowers	Marty and Pam Wygod	260,000
KEE NOV BRDG 04		C	Distorted Humor	Game Trick	WinStar Farm	260,000
KEE NOV BRDG 04		C	Tale of the Cat	Prosper	DOC Bloodstock	260,000
KEE NOV BRDG 04		C	Johannesburg	Tune in to the Cat	Indian Hill Farm	260,000
KEE NOV BRDG 04		C	Pulpit	Dynasty	Dapple Bloodstock	250,000
KEE NOV BRDG 04		F	Orientate	Ms. Strike Zone	Brushwood Stable	250,000
KEE NOV BRDG 04		F	Awesome Again	Country Garden (GB)	Frederic Sauque, agent	250,000
KEE NOV BRDG 04		C	Orientate	Haleys Fury	Athens Woods	250,000
KEE NOV BRDG 04		F	Mr. Greeley	Miss Hot Salsa	Orchard Lane	230,000
KEE NOV BRDG 04	Optari	C	Diesis (GB)	Desert Sky (IRE)	Thomas B. Breen	225,000
KEE NOV BRDG 04		C	Rahy	Roza Robata	B.B.A. (Ireland)	225,000
KEE NOV BRDG 04		F	Elusive Quality	Swearingen	Classic Oaks Farm	220,000
KEE NOV BRDG 04		C	Mr. Greeley	Fair and Lively	Roman Bloodstock	220,000
KEE NOV BRDG 04		C	Distorted Humor	Snow County Honey	JC Bloodstock	220,000
KEE NOV BRDG 04		C	Dixie Union	Stylish Storm	CDJ Bloodstock	220,000
KEE NOV BRDG 04		F	Fusaichi Pegasus	Angelica Tree	G. Watts Humphrey Jr.	220,000
FTK FALL MIX NOV 04		F	Orientate	Harry's Charm (SAF)	Mike Ryan	210,000
KEE NOV BRDG 04		C	Victory Gallop	Hennessy Waltz	WinStar Farm	210,000
KEE NOV BRDG 04		C	Yonaguska	Jetazelle	Bloodstock Services	210,000
KEE NOV BRDG 04		F	El Prado (IRE)	Smooth Swinger	Phillip F. McCarthy, agent	200,000
KEE NOV BRDG 04		C	Buddha	Barbed Wire	Bloodstock Services	200,000
KEE NOV BRDG 04		F	Yonaguska	Gate Swinger	Vinery	200,000
KEE NOV BRDG 04		F	Thunder Gulch	Added Elegance	Springhill Farm	200,000
KEE NOV BRDG 04		C	Johannesburg	Danzerella	Chestnut Valley Farm	200,000
KEE NOV BRDG 04		F	Gone West	Miznah (IRE)	Wertheimer et Frere	200,000
KEE NOV BRDG 04		C	Distorted Humor	Madame Saddam	Occidental Tbreds, agt	195,000
KEE NOV BRDG 04		C	Silver Deputy	Copperfield	Classic Oaks Farm	190,000
KEE NOV BRDG 04		C	Mr. Greeley	Peaks Mill	Bloodstock Services	190,000
KEE NOV BRDG 04		C	Thunder Gulch	Lite Light	Edward Evans	190,000
KEE NOV BRDG 04		C	Distorted Humor	Cozzena	Gulf Coast Farm	180,000
KEE NOV BRDG 04		C	Stormy Atlantic	I'll Be Along	Barry Berkelhammer, agt	180,000
KEE NOV BRDG 04		C	Tale of the Cat	Love U Fran	Twin Spires, agent	180,000
KEE NOV BRDG 04		F	Stormy Atlantic	I'm No Pussycat	Farmer, Kern/Lillingston, agt	180,000
KEE NOV BRDG 04		C	Carson City	Act Devoted	Farmer, Kern/Lillingston, agt	180,000

Snapshot Facts: The top-priced weanling of 2004 is the highest-priced weanling by a Raise a Native-line stallion ever sold at auction in North America.

Average and Median Price Per Yearling

Representing half the dollar volume of the auction sales market, the yearling market is generally accepted as being a true barometer of the health of the Thoroughbred breeding industry. The yearling auction market in 2004 recorded strong gains across the board in terms of number sold, gross sales, average price and median price.

Year	Sale yearlings	Percent change	Yearling sales gross	Percent change	Avg. price	Percent change	Median price	Percent change
1980	7,079	(+11.9)	210,128,000	(+34.1)	29,683	(+19.8)	10,000	(+25.0)
1981	7,949	(+12.3)	279,376,221	(+33.0)	35,146	(+18.4)	11,500	(+15.0)
1982	8,174	(+2.8)	269,376,805	(-3.5)	32,991	(-6.1)	8,116	(-29.4)
1983	8,705	(+6.5)	359,148,103	(+33.2)	41,258	(+25.1)	8,500	(+4.7)
1984	9,268	(+6.5)	383,659,326	(+6.8)	41,396	(+0.3)	6,500	(-23.5)
1985	8,420	(-9.1)	347,842,155	(-9.3)	41,311	(-0.2)	6,800	(+4.6)
1986	8,206	(-2.5)	281,358,236	(-19.1)	34,285	(-17.0)	6,000	(-11.7)
1987	8,845	(+7.8)	313,477,421	(+11.4)	35,441	(+3.3)	6,500	(+8.3)
1988	9,083	(+2.7)	283,845,192	(-9.5)	31,250	(-11.8)	5,500	(-15.0)
1989	8,564	(-5.7)	281,806,185	(-0.7)	32,905	(+5.3)	7,000	(+27.3)
1990	8,760	(+2.3)	257,342,967	(-8.7)	29,377	(-10.7)	7,000	0.0
1991	8,154	(-6.9)	213,905,856	(-16.9)	26,233	(-10.7)	6,028	(-13.9)
1992	7,908	(-3.0)	180,232,617	(-15.7)	22,791	(-13.1)	7,000	(+16.1)
1993	7,413	(+12.0)	188,598,650	(+4.6)	25,442	(+11.6)	8,000	(+14.3)
1994	7,706	(+4.0)	210,336,433	(+11.5)	27,295	(+7.3)	9,162	(+14.5)
1995	7,882	(+2.3)	242,778,829	(+15.4)	30,801	(+12.8)	10,000	(+9.2)
1996	8,025	(+1.8)	277,224,816	(+14.2)	34,539	(+12.1)	9,500	(-5.0)
1997	8,014	(-0.1)	307,607,857	(+11.0)	38,384	(+11.1)	11,500	(+21.1)
1998	8,275	(+3.3)	354,058,332	(+15.1)	42,787	(+11.5)	11,500	0.0
1999	8,738	(+5.6)	440,078,922	(+24.3)	50,364	(+17.7)	12,000	(+4.3)
2000	9,530	(+9.1)	519,443,808	(+18.0)	54,506	(+8.2)	11,500	(-4.2)
2001	9,002	(-5.5)	473,044,553	(-8.9)	52,549	(-3.6)	9,000	(-21.7)
2002	8,941	(-0.7)	390,714,442	(-17.4)	43,699	(-16.8)	11,000	(+22.2)
2003	8,843	(-1.1)	425,251,514	(+8.8)	48,089	(+10.0)	12,000	(+9.1)
2004	9,412	(+6.4)	497,153,983	(+16.9)	52,821	(+9.8)	13,200	(+10.0)

Average and Median Price Per Weanling

Year	Sale weanlings	Percent change	Weanling sales gross	Percent change	Avg. price	Percent change	Median price	Percent change
1980	1,480	(+24.9)	21,130,450	(+62.0)	14,277	(+29.7)	N/A	N/A
1981	1,723	(+16.4)	23,944,919	(+13.3)	13,897	(-2.7)	N/A	N/A
1982	1,770	(+2.7)	21,631,160	(-9.7)	12,221	(-12.1)	N/A	N/A
1983	1,656	(-6.4)	24,750,636	(+14.4)	14,946	(+22.3)	N/A	N/A
1984	1,509	(-8.9)	15,609,855	(-36.9)	10,345	(-30.8)	N/A	N/A
1985	1,441	(-4.5)	25,556,965	(+63.7)	17,736	(+71.4)	3,000	N/A
1986	1,432	(-0.6)	22,354,648	(-12.5)	15,611	(-12.0)	3,200	(+6.7)
1987	1,488	(+3.9)	34,660,720	(+55.0)	23,293	(+49.2)	4,200	(+31.3)
1988	1,362	(-8.5)	21,852,247	(-37.0)	16,044	(-31.1)	3,500	(-16.7)
1989	1,475	(+8.3)	35,088,817	(+60.6)	23,789	(+48.3)	5,200	(+48.6)
1990	1,565	(+6.1)	28,406,636	(-19.0)	18,151	(-23.7)	5,500	(+5.8)
1991	1,430	(-8.6)	29,201,455	(+2.8)	20,420	(+12.5)	6,500	(+18.2)
1992	1,505	(+5.2)	23,979,536	(-17.9)	15,933	(-22.0)	6,500	0.0
1993	1,536	(+2.1)	36,244,725	(+51.1)	23,597	(+48.1)	9,000	(+38.5)
1994	1,897	(+23.5)	41,376,763	(+14.2)	21,811	(-7.6)	8,500	(-5.6)
1995	2,000	(+5.4)	52,233,042	(+26.2)	26,111	(+19.7)	11,000	(+29.4)
1996	2,163	(+8.2)	61,083,609	(+16.9)	28,240	(+8.2)	8,500	(-22.7)
1997	2,107	(-2.6)	67,564,249	(+10.6)	32,067	(+13.6)	12,000	(+41.2)
1998	2,282	(+8.3)	89,350,261	(+32.2)	39,154	(+22.1)	12,000	0.0
1999	2,290	(+0.4)	98,109,089	(+9.8)	42,842	(+9.4)	15,000	(+25.0)
2000	2,346	(+2.4)	83,758,024	(-14.6)	35,702	(-16.6)	10,000	(-33.34)
2001	1,933	(-17.6)	52,534,780	(-37.3)	27,178	(-23.9)	7,000	(-30.0)
2002	1,575	(-18.5)	49,061,493	(-6.6)	31,150	(+14.6)	10,000	(+42.9)
2003	1,706	(+8.3)	68,058,938	(+38.7)	39,386	(+26.4)	12,000	(+20.0)
2004	1,952	(+14.4)	71,730,989	(+5.4)	36,747	(-7.2)	15,000	(+25.0)

Top Priced 2-Year-Olds Sold in North America Since 1980

Sale	Horse	Sex	Sire	Dam	Buyer	Sale Price
FTF FEB SEL 2YO TRN 04	Fusaichi Samurai	C	Fusaichi Pegasus	Hidden Storm	Fusao Sekiguchi	$4,500,000
KEE APR 2YO KY 04	Chekhov	C	Pulpit	In My Cap	Demi O'Byrne	3,300,000
FTF FEB SEL 2YO TRN 04	Dubai Dreamer	C	Stephen Got Even	Blacktie Bid	John Ferguson	3,100,000
BAR MAR 2YO TRN 03	Diamond Fury	R	Sea of Secrets	Swift Spirit	Charles Fipke	2,700,000
KEE APR 2YO KY 99	La Salle Street	C	Not For Love	Three Grand	Demi O'Byrne	2,000,000
BAR MAR 2YO TRN 04	Dubai Escapade	F	Awesome Again	Sassy Pants	John Ferguson Bloodstock	2,000,000
BAR MAR 2YO TRN 00	Gotham City	C	Saint Ballado	What a Reality	David J. Shimmon	2,000,000
BAR MAR 2YO TRN 99	Morocco	C	Brocco	Roll Over Baby	The Thoroughbred Corp.	2,000,000
FTF FEB SEL 2YO TRN 00	Yonaguska	C	Cherokee Run	Marital Spook	Demi O'Byrne	1,950,000
BAR MAR 2YO TRN 02	Atlantic Ocean	F	Stormy Atlantic	Super Chef	The Thoroughbred Corp.	1,900,000
FTF FEB SEL 2YO TRN 00	Harmony Lodge	F	Hennessy	Win Crafty Lady	Eugene Melnyk	1,650,000
OBS SEL 2YO CAL 04	Mutanabi	C	Wild Rush	Freudenau	John Ferguson	1,600,000
FTF FEB SEL 2YO TRN 04	Timsaah	C	Rubiano	Magari	John Ferguson	1,500,000
FTF FEB SEL 2YO TRN 03	Lion Heart	C	Tale of the Cat	Satin Sunrise	Demi O'Byrne	1,400,000
BAR MAR 2YO TRN 95	Unbridled's Song	C	Unbridled	Trolley Song	Hiroshi Fujita	1,400,000
KEE APR 2YO KY 04	Radetzky	C	Dixie Union	Sneaky Quiet	Demi O'Byrne	1,400,000
*NEWSTEAD FARM FTK 05	Minstress	F	The Minstrel	Fleet Victress	Farish, W. S.	1,300,000
KEE APR 2YO KY 99	Lochlin Slew	F	Seattle Slew	Lochlin	B. Wayne Hughes	1,250,000
FTF FEB SEL 2YO TRN 00	Le Chat	C	Storm Cat	Adorable Micol	John Moynihan, agent	1,250,000
BAR MAR 2YO TRN 99	Dance Master	C	Gone West	Nijinsky's Lover	Padua Stables	1,200,000
KEE JAN ALL AGES 98	Task	F	Mr. Prospector	Department	Course Investment	1,200,000
OBS SEL 2YO CAL 03	Chapel Royal	C	Montbrook	Cut Class Leanne	Demi O'Byrne	1,200,000
BAR MAR 2YO TRN 97	Scatmandu	C	Storm Cat	Princess Alydar	John C. Kimmel, agent	1,100,000
KEE APR 2YO KY 99	I'm Persuaded	C	Deputy Minister	The Way We Were	Narvick International	1,100,000
FTF FEB SEL 2YO TRN 99	Prather	C	Brocco	Dazzling Dixie	Aaron and Marie Jones	1,100,000
OBS OPN 2YO 01	Warners	C	Dehere	Sweet Gold	Eugene Melnyk	1,050,000
FTF FEB SEL 2YO TRN 04	Storm Cat Johnny	C	Storm Cat	Add	Robert V. LaPenta	1,050,000
BAR MAR 2YO TRN 03	This Is That	C	El Prado (IRE)	Ask Anita	S Tsujimoto & W Schettine	1,000,000
FTF FEB SEL 2YO TRN 03	Storm Away	F	Storm Cat	Sun Blush	LeRoy Jolley, agent	1,000,000
BAR MAR 2YO TRN 99	Satin Cat	F	Storm Cat	Mended Heart	The Thoroughbred Corp.	1,000,000
FTF FEB SEL 2YO TRN 02	Dawson Trail	G	Seeking the Gold	Bounteous (IRE)	Demi O'Byrne	1,000,000
KEE JAN ALL AGES 98	Measure	F	Seeking the Gold	Number	Demi O'Byrne	1,000,000
FTF FEB SEL 2YO TRN 01	Rosetti	C	Seattle Slew	Chic Shirine	Demi O'Byrne	1,000,000
FTF FEB SEL 2YO TRN 98	Awesome Cat	C	Storm Cat	Pookette	Chester Broman	1,000,000
BAR MAR 2YO TRN 97	Something Else	F	Seeking the Gold	Rythmical	The Thoroughbred Corp.	1,000,000
FTF FEB SEL 2YO TRN 00	Songandaprayer	C	Unbridled's Song	Alizea	Robert and Leslie Hurley	1,000,000
BAR MAR 2YO TRN 98	Public Figure	C	Clever Trick	Belle of Killarney	The Thoroughbred Corp.	1,000,000
BAR MAR 2YO TRN 97	Marie J	F	Mr. Prospector	In My Cap	John Ferguson Bloodstock	1,000,000
OBS SPR 2YO 04	Woodford Gale	C	Distorted Humor	Zuppardo Ardo	John Ferguson, agent	975,000
KEE APR 2YO KY 03	Work	C	Menifee	Pacific City	M & M Racing	950,000
BAR MAR 2YO TRN 98	Debit Account	F	Mr. Prospector	Awesome Account	Demi O'Byrne	950,000
FTF FEB SEL 2YO TRN 99	Brave Quest	C	Miswaki	Cousin Margaret	John C. Oxley	950,000
FTF FEB SEL 2YO TRN 99	Significant	C	Unbridled	Remarkably Easy	R B and B J Lewis	950,000
BAR MAR 2YO TRN 99	Barrage	G	Tabasco Cat	Allouette	R Waxman, J.C. Kimmel, agt	950,000
FTF FEB SEL 2YO TRN 01	Bella Bellucci	F	French Deputy	Blue Avenue	Demi O'Byrne	925,000
BAR MAR 2YO TRN 00	Fun and Sun	C	Southern Halo	Cause I'm Special	Target Bloodstock	900,000
OBS SEL 2YO CAL 01	Max's Buddy	C	Irish River (FR)	Exposed	Buzz Chace, agent	900,000
BAR MAR 2YO TRN 97	Liquid Gold	C	Woodman	Shirley L.	The Thoroughbred Corp.	900,000
BAR MAR 2YO TRN 96	Sharp Cat	F	Storm Cat	In Neon	The Thoroughbred Corp.	900,000
FTF FEB SEL 2YO TRN 03	Forest Danger	C	Forestry	Starry Ice	Buzz Chace, agent	900,000
BAR MAR 2YO TRN 97	Malibu Wesley	C	Storm Cat	La Spia	B. Wayne Hughes	900,000
BAR MAR 2YO TRN 97	Clarinova	F	Danzig	Life At the Top (GB)	Demi O'Byrne	900,000
FTF FEB SEL 2YO TRN 02	Atswhatimtalknbout	C	A.P. Indy	Lucinda K	B. Wayne Hughes	900,000
FTF FEB SEL 2YO TRN 04	Daddy Joe	C	Unbridled's Song	Vennila Cream	Buzz Chace, agent	900,000
BAR MAR 2YO TRN 95	El Paso Danzig	C	Danzig	Lady in Silver	Hiroshi Fujita	900,000
BAR MAR 2YO TRN 96	Native Storm	C	Storm Bird	Aquakiss (FR)	B. Wayne Hughes	900,000
KEE APR 2YO KY 03	Temescal Ridge	C	Unbridled's Song	Belonging	R B and B J Lewis	875,000
BAR MAR 2YO TRN 97	Majestic Beauty	F	Danzig	Sister Dot	B. Wayne Hughes	875,000
FTF FEB SEL 2YO TRN 99	Chilukki	F	Cherokee Run	Song of Syria	Stonerside Stable	875,000
FTF FEB SEL 2YO TRN 96	Speed World	C	Woodman	Gray Tab	Heatherway	875,000

* A dispersal sale.

Snapshot Facts: Of the 38 2-year-olds sold in North America for $1 million or more since 1980, eight were sold in 2004. The next most productive year for seven-figure 2-year-olds was 1999, with seven.

Highest Priced 2-Year-Olds Sold at Public Auction in 2004

Only includes 2-Year-Olds sold in North America

Sale	Horse	Sex	Sire	Dam	Buyer	Sale Price
FTF FEB SEL 2YO TRN 04	Fusaichi Samurai	C	Fusaichi Pegasus	Hidden Storm	Fusao Sekiguchi	$4,500,000
KEE APR 2YO KY 04	Chekhov	C	Pulpit	In My Cap	Demi O'Byrne	3,300,000
FTF FEB SEL 2YO TRN 04	Dubai Dreamer	C	Stephen Got Even	Blacktie Bid	John Ferguson	3,100,000
BAR MAR 2YO TRN 04	Dubai Escapade	F	Awesome Again	Sassy Pants	John Ferguson Bloodstock	2,000,000
OBS SEL 2YO CAL 04	Mutanabi	C	Wild Rush	Freudenau	John Ferguson	1,600,000
FTF FEB SEL 2YO TRN 04	Timsaah	C	Rubiano	Magari	John Ferguson	1,500,000
KEE APR 2YO KY 04	Radetzky	C	Dixie Union	Sneaky Quiet	Demi O'Byrne	1,400,000
FTF FEB SEL 2YO TRN 04	Storm Cat Johnny	C	Storm Cat	Add	Robert V. LaPenta	1,050,000
OBS SPR 2YO 04	Woodford Gale	C	Distorted Humor	Zuppardo Ardo	John Ferguson, agent	975,000
FTF FEB SEL 2YO TRN 04	Daddy Joe	C	Unbridled's Song	Vennila Cream	Buzz Chace, agent	900,000
FTF FEB SEL 2YO TRN 04	Fusaichi Rock Star	C	Wild Wonder	Grannies Feather	Fusao Sekiguchi	825,000
KEE APR 2YO KY 04	She's a Devil Slew	F	Seattle Slew	She's a Devil Due	Fleetwood/N.W. Mgmt	800,000
FTF FEB SEL 2YO TRN 04	Deputy Grant	C	Deputy Minister	Win Crafty Lady	B. Wayne Hughes	800,000
KEE APR 2YO KY 04	Coach Kent	C	Fusaichi Pegasus	Rokeby Rosie	A&M Jones, B Chace, agt	750,000
FTF FEB SEL 2YO TRN 04	Backchat	C	Distorted Humor	Dare to Be Me	John Ferguson	750,000
FTF FEB SEL 2YO TRN 04	War Plan	C	Fusaichi Pegasus	Li Law	Brian Morgan, agent	700,000
FTF FEB SEL 2YO TRN 04	One Smart Deputy	C	Silver Deputy	Awful Smart	Roger Attfield	700,000
OBS SPR 2YO 04	Collegiate Honor	C	Double Honor	Camptown Miss	William J. Condren	675,000
OBS OPN 2YO 04	Notable Tiger	C	Tiger Ridge	Notable Girl	John Ferguson	650,000
FTF FEB SEL 2YO TRN 04	Rachel's Song	F	Tale of the Cat	Too too Divine	Mike Ryan, agent	650,000
FTF FEB SEL 2YO TRN 04	Fashion Cat	F	Forest Wildcat	Hold to Fashion	Bar S Ranch	630,000
FTF FEB SEL 2YO TRN 04	Pulpit Exchange	C	Pulpit	Silent Greeting	Mike Ryan, agent	625,000
BAR MAR 2YO TRN 04	Should Be Royalty	F	Pine Bluff	Malley	Demi O'Byrne	600,000
BAR MAR 2YO TRN 04	Swissle Stick	C	Swiss Yodeler	Miss Soft Sell	R B and B J Lewis	600,000
FTF FEB SEL 2YO TRN 04	Nasema's Slam	F	Grand Slam	Nasema	Fleetwood/N.W. Mgmt	600,000
FTF FEB SEL 2YO TRN 04	Going Wild	C	Golden Missile	Pola	R B and B J Lewis	600,000
BAR MAR 2YO TRN 04	True Integrity	C	Honour and Glory	Defer West	Narvick International	575,000
OBS OPN 2YO 04	Yankee Million	F	Yankee Victor	Betamillion Bock	Narvick International	575,000
FTF FEB SEL 2YO TRN 04	For All We Know	F	Stephen Got Even	Over All	John C. Oxley	550,000
FTF FEB SEL 2YO TRN 04	Happy as Larry	C	Yes It's True	Don't Be Blue	John Ferguson	525,000
FTF FEB SEL 2YO TRN 04	Play Ballado	F	Saint Ballado	Piccolo Player	John C. Oxley	525,000
FTF FEB SEL 2YO TRN 04	Devil At Sea	C	Devil His Due	Atlantique du Nord	John H. Peace	500,000
FTF FEB SEL 2YO TRN 04	Quiet Money	C	Seattle Slew	Discreet Account	R.A. Violette	500,000
BAR MAR 2YO TRN 04	Jim's Smokin Pinot	C	Victory Gallop	Buck's Lady	Never Tell Farm	500,000
BAR MAR 2YO TRN 04	Ridges in Time	C	Tiger Ridge	Winning Journey	Bruno DeBerdt, agent	500,000
KEE APR 2YO KY 04	Brazilian	F	Stravinsky	Golden Pond (IRE)	John Fort	500,000
OBS SEL 2YO CAL 04	Spanish Chestnut	C	Horse Chestnut (Saf)	Baby Rabbit	Demi O'Byrne	500,000
KEE APR 2YO KY 04	Blitzen	F	Siphon (BRZ)	Misty Music	A&M Jones, B Chace, agt	500,000
KEE APR 2YO KY 04	Fusaichi Forza	C	Polish Numbers	Student Wife	Fusao Sekiguchi	500,000
OBS SEL 2YO CAL 04	Siphon City	C	Siphon (BRZ)	Carsona	Demi O'Byrne	500,000
OBS SPR 2YO 04	Western Acres	C	West Acre	Y'All Sing	Kaaren Biggs	500,000
FTF FEB SEL 2YO TRN 04	Materialism	C	Not For Love	Gala Goldie's Best	John Ferguson	500,000
FTF FEB SEL 2YO TRN 04	Storm Silk	C	Stormin Fever	Carpenter's Lace	John Ferguson	500,000
OBS SPR 2YO 04	Afrashad	C	Smoke Glacken	Flo White	John Ferguson, agent	500,000
KEE APR 2YO KY 04	Malheur	C	Saint Ballado	Sapphire Beads	A&M Jones, B Chace, agt	475,000
KEE APR 2YO KY 04	Theschemeofthings	F	Grand Slam	Schematic	Never Tell Farm	460,000
OBS OPN 2YO 04	Compulsive	C	Chief Seattle	Helen's Pick	James McIngvale	450,000
FTF FEB SEL 2YO TRN 04	Buddy Got Even	C	Stephen Got Even	Gem Treck	Fleetwood/N.W. Mgmt	450,000
OBS OPN 2YO 04	Proud Accolade	C	Yes It's True	Proud Ciel	Padua Stables	450,000
OBS OPN 2YO 04	Writer's Walk	C	Yankee Victor	Mesmerized	Joseph Brocklebank, agt	450,000
BAR MAR 2YO TRN 04	Deputy Kris	C	Kissin Kris	In Reverence	La Cresta Farm	450,000
KEE APR 2YO KY 04	Desert Breeze	C	Deputy Minister	Date Stone	David Moore	450,000
BAR MAR 2YO TRN 04	Paragon Queen	F	Lord Carson	Storm Struck	R B and B J Lewis	450,000
FTI SPR 2YO TRN 04	Lady H	F	Silver Deputy	Livia B	C & M Hesse, B Chace, agt	450,000
OBS OPN 2YO 04	Magic Belle	F	Gold Case	Magical Thinking	Puglisi Sta, S Klesaris, agt	425,000
OBS OPN 2YO 04	Maidanni	C	Private Terms	Carley's Birthday	John Ferguson	425,000
OBS SEL 2YO CAL 04	Upscaled	C	Sir Cat	Limestone Landing	Todd A. Pletcher, agent	425,000
FTF FEB SEL 2YO TRN 04	Maddalena	F	Good and Tough	Two Foxie	Demi O'Byrne	425,000

Snapshot Facts: The high-priced colt and filly of 2004 both set overall records for their gender for 2-year-olds sold at auction in North America.

Top Priced Broodmares Sold at Public Auction Since 1980

Sale	Horse	Age	Sire	Dam	Buyer	Sale Price
KEE NOV BRDG 03	Cash Run	6	Seeking the Gold	Shared Interest	John Magnier	$7,100,000
KEE NOV BRDG 98	Korveya	16	Riverman	Konafa	Reynolds Bell Jr., agent	7,000,000
* NEWSTEAD FARM FTK 85	Miss Oceana	4	Alydar	Kittiwake	Foxfield	7,000,000
KEE NOV BRDG 03	Windsharp	12	Lear Fan	Yes She's Sharp	John Ferguson Bloodstock	6,100,000
FTK SEL FALL MIX 84	Priceless Fame	9	Irish Castle	Comely Nell	Darley Stud Management	6,000,000
KEE NOV BRDG 85	Princess Rooney	5	Verbatim	Parrish Princess	Wichita Equine, Inc.	5,500,000
KEE NOV BRDG 86	Life's Magic	5	Cox's Ridge	Fire Water	E. V. Klein	5,400,000
KEE NOV BRDG 03	Spain	6	Thunder Gulch	Drina	Dromoland Farm	5,300,000
KEE NOV BRDG 83	Producer	7	Nashua	Marion	BBA (England)	5,250,000
FTK FALL MIX NOV 04	I'll Get Along	12	Smile	Dont Worry Bout Me	Gaines-Gentry Tbreds	5,000,000
KEE JAN ALL AGES 00	Mackie	7	Summer Squall	Glowing Tribute	Britton House Stud	5,000,000
KEE NOV BRDG 00	Jewel Princess	8	Key to the Mint	Jewell Ridge	John Magnier	4,900,000
KEE NOV BRDG 04	Santa Catarina	4	Unbridled	Purrfectly	Eaton Sales, agent	4,800,000
KEE NOV BRDG 00	Catchascatchcan (GB)	5	Pursuit of Love	Catawba	Lyons Demesne	4,700,000
KEE NOV BRDG 99	Dance Design (IRE)	6	Sadler's Wells	Elegance in Design (Ire)	Hugo Lascelles, agent	4,700,000
KEE NOV BRDG 00	Myhrr	3	Mr. Prospector	Miesque	Reynolds Bell Jr., agent	4,600,000
KEE NOV BRDG 99	Winglet	11	Alydar	Highest Trump	John Magnier	4,600,000
KEE NOV BRDG 84	It's in the Air	8	Mr. Prospector	A Wind Is Rising	Darley Stud Management	4,600,000
KEE NOV BRDG 83	Two Rings	13	Round Table	Allofthem	Due Process Stable	4,500,000
KEE NOV BRDG 85	Estrapade	5	Vaguely Noble	Klepto	A. E. Paulson	4,500,000
KEE NOV BRDG 04	Unbridled Elaine	6	Unbridled's Song	Carols Folly	John Ferguson Bloodstock	4,400,000
FTK STARS 87	Life's Magic	6	Cox's Ridge	Fire Water	Shadwell Estates	4,400,000
KEE NOV BRDG 04	Take Charge Lady	5	Dehere	Felicita	Eaton Sales, agent	4,200,000
KEE NOV BRDG 00	Magical Allure	5	General Meeting	Rare Lady	Shadwell Estate Co.	4,200,000
KEE NOV BRDG 84	Sangue (IRE)	6	Lyphard	Prodice (FR)	N. B. Hunt	4,100,000
KEE NOV BRDG 84	Love Sign	7	Spanish Riddle	Native Nurse	Arthur I. Appleton	4,100,000
* NEWSTEAD FARM FTK 85	Larida	6	Northern Dancer	Kittiwake	Foxfield	4,000,000
KEE NOV BRDG 02	Bless	3	Mr. Prospector	Angel Fever	ClassicStar	4,000,000
KEE NOV BRDG 00	Blissful	4	Mr. Prospector	Angel Fever	John Magnier	4,000,000
KEE NOV BRDG 01	Twenty Eight Carat	11	Alydar	Voo Doo Dance	Brushwood Stable	4,000,000
KEE NOV BRDG 04	Helsinki (GB)	11	Machiavellian	Helen Street (GB)	Christy Grassick	3,900,000
KEE NOV BRDG 82	Royal Honoree	9	Round Table	Matriarch	Seth W. Hancock, agent	3,800,000
* NEWSTEAD FARM FTK 85	Kittiwake	17	Sea-Bird	Ole Liz	Mint Tree Stable	3,800,000
KEE NOV BRDG 89	Lady's Secret	7	Secretariat	Great Lady M.	Fares Farm	3,800,000
KEE NOV BRDG 83	Prayers'n Promises	5	Foolish Pleasure	Luiana	Three Chimneys Farm	3,750,000
KEE NOV BRDG 00	Squeak (GB)	6	Selkirk	Santa Linda	John Ferguson Bloodstock	3,700,000
KEE NOV BRDG 85	Barb's Bold	7	Bold Forbes	Goofed	Due Process Stable	3,650,000
KEE NOV BRDG 04	Dessert	4	Storm Cat	Windsharp	Shadwell Farm	3,600,000
KEE NOV BRDG 04	Stellar Jayne	3	Wild Rush	To the Hunt	John Ferguson Bloodstock	3,600,000
KEE NOV BRDG 03	Composure	3	Touch Gold	Party Cited	John Ferguson Bloodstock	3,600,000
KEE JAN ALL AGES 02	Desert Stormer	12	Storm Cat	Breezy Stories	Live Oak Stud	3,600,000
KEE NOV BRDG 01	Phone Chatter	10	Phone Trick	Passing My Way	John Magnier	3,600,000
DISP GENTRY 86	Crimson Saint	17	Crimson Satan	Bolero Rose	Dorsey, John E.	3,450,000
KEE NOV BRDG 03	Golden Apples (IRE)	5	Pivotal (GB)	Loon (FR)	Shadwell Estate Co.	3,400,000
* ALAN CLORE FTK 88	Triptych	6	Riverman	Trillion	Patrick Biancone	3,400,000
KEE JAN ALL AGES 00	Claxton's Slew	16	Seattle Slew	Nutmeg Native	John Magnier	3,300,000
KEE JAN ALL AGES 99	Escena	6	Strawberry Road (Aus)	Claxton's Slew	Reynolds Bell Jr., agent	3,250,000
KEE NOV BRDG 99	Advancing Star	6	Soviet Star	Fair Advantage	Summer Wind Equine	3,200,000
KEE NOV BRDG 83	Avum	10	Umbrella Fella	Avle	M. H. Goodbody	3,200,000
KEE NOV BRDG 83	Priceless Fame	8	Irish Castle	Comely Nell	Jeffry Morris, agent	3,200,000
KEE NOV BRDG 03	Purrfectly	9	Storm Cat	Perfect Example	Courtlandt Farm	3,150,000
KEE NOV BRDG 03	Sharp Cat	9	Storm Cat	In Neon	John Ferguson Bloodstock	3,100,000
KEE NOV BRDG 00	Caress	9	Storm Cat	La Affirmed	John Ferguson Bloodstock	3,100,000
KEE NOV BRDG 02	Fiji (GB)	8	Rainbow Quest	Island Jamboree	Brushwood Stable	3,100,000
* NEWSTEAD FARM FTK 85	White Star Line	10	Northern Dancer	Fast Line	Darley Stud Management	3,000,000
BAR 505 DISP 00	Manistique	5	Unbridled	Astaire Step	Aaron and Marie Jones	3,000,000
KEE NOV BRDG 01	Dancing Mahmoud	11	Topsider	Execution	Reynolds Bell Jr., agent	3,000,000
KEE NOV BRDG 00	Bright Tiara	11	Chief's Crown	Expressive Dance	John Ferguson Bloodstock	3,000,000
KEE JAN ALL AGES 86	Lucky Lucky Lucky	5	Chieftain	Just One More Time	Shadwell Farm, Inc.	3,000,000
KEE NOV BRDG 83	Solar	7	Halo	Sex Appeal	Due Process Stable	3,000,000

* A dispersal sale

Snapshot Facts: Of the 30 broodmares sold for $4 million or more since 1980, only two were older than 12-year-old I'll Get Along, high-priced broodmare of 2004, at the time of their sale.

Top Priced Broodmares Sold at Public Auction in 2004

Only broodmares sold in North America included

Sale	Horse Name	Age	Sire	Dam	Buyer	Sale Price
FTK FALL MIX NOV 04	I'll Get Along	12	Smile	Dont Worry Bout Me	Gaines-Gentry Tbreds	$5,000,000
KEE NOV BRDG 04	Santa Catarina	4	Unbridled	Purrfectly	Eaton Sales, agent	4,800,000
KEE NOV BRDG 04	Unbridled Elaine	6	Unbridled's Song	Carols Folly	John Ferguson Bloodstock	4,400,000
KEE NOV BRDG 04	Take Charge Lady	5	Dehere	Felicita	Eaton Sales, agent	4,200,000
KEE NOV BRDG 04	Helsinki (GB)	11	Machiavellian	Helen Street (GB)	Christy Grassick	3,900,000
KEE NOV BRDG 04	Dessert	4	Storm Cat	Windsharp	Shadwell Farm	3,600,000
KEE NOV BRDG 04	Stellar Jayne	3	Wild Rush	To the Hunt	John Ferguson Bloodstock	3,600,000
KEE NOV BRDG 04	Cat Fighter	4	Storm Cat	Strategic Maneuver	Live Oak Stud	2,300,000
KEE NOV BRDG 04	Storm Beauty	9	Storm Cat	Stick to Beauty	Brushwood Stable	2,200,000
KEE NOV BRDG 04	Be Gentle	3	Tale of the Cat	Gentlelilstar	Diamond A Farms	2,100,000
KEE NOV BRDG 04	Better Than Honour	8	Deputy Minister	Blush With Pride	B.B.A. (Ireland)	2,000,000
KEE NOV BRDG 04	Miss Lodi	5	Mr. Greeley	Firtide	Skara Glen Stables	2,000,000
KEE NOV BRDG 04	Dimitrova	4	Swain (IRE)	The Caretaker (IRE)	Abbott Bloodstock	2,000,000
KEE NOV BRDG 04	Blithe	3	Unbridled	Angel Fever	Reynolds Bell Jr., agent	2,000,000
KEE NOV BRDG 04	Words of War	15	Lord At War (ARG)	Right Word	Malibu Farm	1,950,000
KEE NOV BRDG 04	Gaviola	7	Cozzene	Forest Key	ClassicStar	1,900,000
KEE NOV BRDG 04	Golden Sonata	5	Mr. Prospector	Elissa Beethoven (GB)	Skara Glen Stables	1,900,000
KEE NOV BRDG 04	Elloluv	4	Gilded Time	Currency Quest	Frank Stronach	1,750,000
KEE NOV BRDG 04	Happily Unbridled	6	Unbridled	Spire	Frederic Sauque, agent	1,700,000
KEE NOV BRDG 04	Profit Column	11	Private Account	Ballet de France	ClassicStar	1,600,000
KEE NOV BRDG 04	Renaissance Lady	3	A.P. Indy	Storm Beauty	Summer Wind Farm	1,600,000
KEE NOV BRDG 04	Stylish	6	Thunder Gulch	Miss Lenora	Malibu Farm	1,500,000
KEE NOV BRDG 04	Got Koko	5	Signal Tap	Baby North	Narvick International	1,500,000
KEE NOV BRDG 04	Halo America	14	Waquoit	Ameriangel	John Sikura	1,450,000
KEE NOV BRDG 04	Unbridled Beauty	3	Unbridled's Song	Dreamscape	Forging Oaks Farm	1,400,000
KEE NOV BRDG 04	Fashion Star	12	Chief's Crown	Miss Ivor	Summer Wind Farm	1,300,000
KEE NOV BRDG 04	Silver Tornado	6	Maria's Mon	Silvery Swan	B.B.A. (Ireland)	1,250,000
KEE NOV BRDG 04	Smok'n Frolic	5	Smoke Glacken	Cherokyfrolicflash	Adena Springs Farm	1,250,000
KEE NOV BRDG 04	Dublino	5	Lear Fan	Tuscoga	Cheveley Park Stud	1,200,000
KEE NOV BRDG 04	Fairest Cape	2	Storm Cat	Myth	Skara Glen Stables	1,200,000
KEE NOV BRDG 04	Nonsuch Bay	5	Mr. Greeley	Brighter Than Gold	Never Tell Farm	1,150,000
KEE NOV BRDG 04	She's a Beauty	4	Storm Cat	Now That's Funny	Manganaro Stable	1,100,000
KEE NOV BRDG 04	Mer de Corail (IRE)	5	Sadler's Wells	Miss Tahiti (IRE)	Fr Pur-Sang & 6C Stallions	1,050,000
KEE NOV BRDG 04	Mila	6	Unbridled	Incha (GB)	Claiborne Farm	1,000,000
KEE NOV BRDG 04	Rubywood	4	Woodman	Ruby Slippers	Reynolds *Bell Jr., agent	1,000,000
KEE NOV BRDG 04	Star Begonia (GB)	9	Sadler's Wells	Alexandrie	Shadai Farm	975,000
KEE NOV BRDG 04	Tropical Blossom	6	Thunder Gulch	Barbara Sue	Katsumi Yoshida	950,000
KEE NOV BRDG 04	Nevermore	4	Unbridled	Teewinot	Vin Cox Bloodstock	950,000
KEE NOV BRDG 04	Megans Bluff	7	Pine Bluff	Cozzena	Eldon Farm Equine	900,000
KEE NOV BRDG 04	Carib Lady (IRE)	5	Sadler's Wells	Belle Passe (IRE)	Shadai Farm	900,000
KEE NOV BRDG 04	Fordyce	10	Cox's Ridge	Foresta	Diamond A Farms	875,000
FTK FALL MIX NOV 04	Zonk	6	Farma Way	In Concert	J. Fred Miller III	875,000
KEE JAN ALL AGES 04	Beckys Shirt	13	Cure the Blues	Thundertee	B.B.A. (Ireland)	850,000
FTK FALL MIX NOV 04	Avie's Fancy	13	Lord Avie	Fancy Pan	ClassicStar	850,000
KEE NOV BRDG 04	Ms. Strike Zone	10	Deputy Minister	Bat Prospector	Shadai Farm	850,000
KEE NOV BRDG 04	Silent Eskimo	9	Eskimo	Slide Out Front	ClassicStar	850,000
KEE NOV BRDG 04	Reina Blanca (GB)	6	Darshaan (GB)	Reine d'Beaute (GB)	B.B.A. (Ireland)	850,000
KEE NOV BRDG 04	Lindy Wells	4	A.P. Indy	Luna Wells (IRE)	Narvick International	825,000
KEE JAN ALL AGES 04	Luna Wells (IRE)	11	Sadler's Wells	Lunadix (FR)	John McCormack Bldstk	800,000
KEE NOV BRDG 04	Miss Firefly	10	Salt Lake	Glomo	Nesco II	800,000
KEE JAN ALL AGES 04	La Galerie (ARG)	8	Southern Halo	Aquarelle	B Mabee, Hopewell Farm, agt	800,000
KEE NOV BRDG 04	Transcendental	6	Mt. Livermore	Ladies Cruise	Frank Stronach	800,000
KEE NOV BRDG 04	Ballado's Halo	5	Saint Ballado	Goulash	ClassicStar	800,000
KEE JAN ALL AGES 04	Spring Meadow	5	Meadowlake	Go for It Lady	Live Oak Stud	800,000
KEE NOV BRDG 04	Bella Mi Amore	4	Storm Cat	Claxton's Slew	Narvick International	800,000
KEE NOV BRDG 04	Desert Queen	11	Wavering Monarch	Seen and Silent	ClassicStar	775,000
KEE NOV BRDG 04	Fluid Move	10	Nureyev	From Sea to Sea	Narvick International	775,000
KEE NOV BRDG 04	North Lake Jane	7	Meadowlake	Cassowary	ClassicStar	775,000

Snapshot Facts: There were four broodmares by Unbridled that brought prices of $1 million or more at North American auctions in 2004. Not since 2000 has a broodmare sired by Unbridled brought $1 million or more at such auctions.

Top–Priced Horses of Racing Age Since 1980

Sale	Horse Name	Sex	Age	Sire	Dam	Buyer	Sale Price
FTK STARS 87	Lady's Secret	F	5	Secretariat	Great Lady M.	Fasig-Tipton Bldstk, agt	$5,400,000
KEE NOV BRDG 89	Open Mind	F	3	Deputy Minister	Stage Luck	Kazuo Nakamura	4,600,000
FTF FEB SEL 2YO TRN 04	Fusaichi Samurai	C	2	Fusaichi Pegasus	Hidden Storm	Fusao Sekiguchi	4,500,000
KEE NOV BRDG 89	Winning Colors	F	4	Caro (IRE)	All Rainbows	Gainesway Bldstk Services	4,100,000
KEE NOV BRDG 04	Stellar Jayne	F	3	Wild Rush	To the Hunt	John Ferguson Bloodstock	3,600,000
FTK FALL MIX NOV 04	Toccet	C	4	Awesome Again	Cozzene's Angel	Castleton Lyons	3,350,000
KEE NOV BRDG 86	Midway Lady	F	3	Alleged	Smooth Bore	BBA (Ireland)	3,300,000
KEE APR 2YO KY 04	Chekhov	C	2	Pulpit	In My Cap	Demi O'Byrne	3,300,000
KEE JAN ALL AGES 99	Escena	M	6	Strawberry Road (Aus)	Claxton's Slew	Reynolds Bell Jr., agent	3,250,000
KEE NOV BRDG 84	Hail Bold King	C	3	Bold Bidder	Inca Queen	Due Process Stable	3,200,000
FTF FEB SEL 2YO TRN 04	Dubai Dreamer	C	2	Stephen Got Even	Blacktie Bid	John Ferguson	3,100,000
BAR 505 DISP 00	Manistique	M	5	Unbridled	Astaire Step	Aaron and Marie Jones	3,000,000
FTN 2YO TRN HRA 92	Strike the Gold	C	4	Alydar	Majestic Gold	W J Condren & J Cornacchia	2,900,000
BAR MAR 2YO TRN 03	Diamond Fury	C	2	Sea of Secrets	Swift Spirit	Charles Fipke	2,700,000
BAR 505 DISP 00	David Copperfield	C	3	Halo	Bannockburn	Visionary Corp.	2,600,000
KEE NOV BRDG 04	Cat Fighter	F	4	Storm Cat	Strategic Maneuver	Live Oak Stud	2,300,000
DISP WOLFSON FTF 83	Royal Roberto	C	4	Roberto	Princess Roycraft	R.L. Cuchossois	2,200,000
BAR MAR 2YO TRN 04	Dubai Escapade	F	2	Awesome Again	Sassy Pants	John Ferguson Bloodstock	2,000,000
KEE NOV BRDG 04	Dimitrova	F	4	Swain (IRE)	The Caretaker (IRE)	Abbott Bloodstock	2,000,000
BAR MAR 2YO TRN 00	Gotham City	C	2	Saint Ballado	What a Reality	David J. Shimmon	2,000,000
BAR MAR 2YO TRN 99	Morocco	C	2	Brocco	Roll Over Baby	The Thoroughbred Corp.	2,000,000
KEE APR 2YO KY 99	La Salle Street	C	2	Not For Love	Three Grand	Demi O'Byrne	2,000,000
FTF FEB SEL 2YO TRN 00	Yonaguska	C	2	Cherokee Run	Marital Spook	Demi O'Byrne	1,950,000
BAR MAR 2YO TRN 02	Atlantic Ocean	F	2	Stormy Atlantic	Super Chef	The Thoroughbred Corp.	1,900,000
KEE NOV BRDG 01	Jostle	F	4	Brocco	Moon Drone	Pete Wittmann	1,700,000
FTF FEB SEL 2YO TRN 00	Harmony Lodge	F	2	Hennessy	Win Crafty Lady	Eugene Melnyk	1,650,000
OBS SEL 2YO CAL 04	Mutanabi	C	2	Wild Rush	Freudenau	John Ferguson	1,600,000
KEE RYEHILL DISP 88	Homebuilder	C	4	Mr. Prospector	Smart Heiress	John Franks	1,600,000
KEE JAN ALL AGES 99	J J'sdream	M	6	Glitterman	Thwack	Robert E. Courtney, agent	1,600,000
FTK STARS 87	Family Style	F	4	State Dinner	Sharp Kitty	Brushwood Stable	1,550,000
FTF FEB SEL 2YO TRN 04	Timsaah	C	2	Rubiano	Magari	John Ferguson	1,500,000
KEE NOV BRDG 04	Got Koko	M	5	Signal Tap	Baby North	Narvick International	1,500,000
FTN HRA SAR 83	Fast Gold	C	4	Mr. Prospector	Flack Attack	J.C. Meyer	1,500,000
KEE NOV BRDG 01	Sequoyah (IRE)	F	3	Sadler's Wells	Brigid	Bill Farish	1,400,000
FTF FEB SEL 2YO TRN 03	Lion Heart	C	2	Tale of the Cat	Satin Sunrise	Demi O'Byrne	1,400,000
BAR MAR 2YO TRN 95	Unbridled's Song	C	2	Unbridled	Trolley Song	Hiroshi Fujita	1,400,000
KEE APR 2YO KY 04	Radetzky	C	2	Dixie Union	Sneaky Quiet	Demi O'Byrne	1,400,000
BAR MAR 2YO TRN 04	Cat Fighter	F	4	Storm Cat	Strategic Maneuver	John G. Sikura	1,350,000
* NEWSTEAD FARM FTK 85	Minstress	F	2	The Minstrel	Fleet Victress	Farish, W. S.	1,300,000
* ALAN CLORE FTK 88	River Memories	F	4	Riverman	Le Vague a l'Ame	Patrick Biancone	1,300,000
CTS FALL MIX 89	Kool Arrival	F	3	Relaunch	Irish Arrival	Pete Valenti	1,250,000
FTF FEB SEL 2YO TRN 00	Le Chat	C	2	Storm Cat	Adorable Micol	John Moynihan, agent	1,250,000
FTK STARS 87	Pine Tree Lane	F	5	Apalachee	Carealot	Prather, John B.	1,250,000
KEE APR 2YO KY 99	Lochlin Slew	F	2	Seattle Slew	Lochlin	B. Wayne Hughes	1,250,000
FTK STARS 87	North Sider	F	5	Topsider	Back Ack	Mare Haven Farm	1,225,000
FTK SEL FALL MIX 82	Carefully Hidden	F	3	Caro (IRE)	Treasure Chest	King Ranch, Inc.	1,215,000
KEE JAN ALL AGES 98	Task	F	2	Mr. Prospector	Department	Course Investment	1,200,000
OBS SEL 2YO CAL 03	Chapel Royal	C	2	Montbrook	Cut Class Leanne	Demi O'Byrne	1,200,000
BAR MAR 2YO TRN 99	Dance Master	C	2	Gone West	Nijinsky's Lover	Padua Stables	1,200,000
CTS FALL MIX 87	Very Subtle	F	3	Hoist the Silver	Never Scheme	Ben Rochelle	1,200,000
KEE NOV BRDG 04	Fairest Cape	F	2	Storm Cat	Myth	Skara Glen Stables	1,200,000
FTK SEL FALL MIX 82	Secrettame	F	4	Secretariat	Tamerett	Mare Haven Farm	1,150,000
KEE NOV BRDG 89	Some Romance	F	3	Fappiano	Zippy Do	Skara Glen Stables	1,150,000
BAR MAR 2YO TRN 97	Scatmandu	C	2	Storm Cat	Princess Alydar	John C. Kimmel, agent	1,100,000
FTK STARS 87	Life At the Top	F	4	Seattle Slew	See You At the Top	Eaton, Lee, agent	1,100,000
FTF FEB SEL 2YO TRN 99	Prather	C	2	Brocco	Dazzling Dixie	Aaron and Marie Jones	1,100,000
KEE APR 2YO KY 99	I'm Persuaded	C	2	Deputy Minister	The Way We Were	Narvick International	1,100,000
KEE NOV BRDG 02	Nasty Storm	F	4	Gulch	A Stark Is Born	Frank Stronach	1,075,000
FTN NOV HRA BEL 83	Luminaire	F	4	Al Hattab	Margaret's Number	Kenneth F. Johnston	1,055,000
FTF FEB SEL 2YO TRN 04	Storm Cat Johnny	C	2	Storm Cat	Add	Robert V. LaPenta	1,050,000
OBS OPN 2YO 01	Warners	R	2	Dehere	Sweet Gold	Eugene Melnyk	1,050,000

* A dispersal sale

Snapshot Facts: Five of the six horses of racing age sold in North America for more than $3 million since 1989 were sold in 2004.

Top–Priced Horses of Racing Age in 2004

(North American sales only)

Sale	Horse Name	Sex	Age	Sire	Dam	Buyer	Sale Price
FTF FEB SEL 2YO TRN 04	Fusaichi Samurai	C	2	Fusaichi Pegasus	Hidden Storm	Fusao Sekiguchi	$4,500,000
KEE NOV BRDG 04	Stellar Jayne	F	3	Wild Rush	To the Hunt	John Ferguson Bloodstock	3,600,000
FTK FALL MIX NOV 04	Toccet	C	4	Awesome Again	Cozzene's Angel	Castleton Lyons	3,350,000
KEE APR 2YO KY 04	Chekhov	C	2	Pulpit	In My Cap	Demi O'Byrne	3,300,000
FTF FEB SEL 2YO TRN 04	Dubai Dreamer	C	2	Stephen Got Even	Blacktie Bid	John Ferguson	3,100,000
KEE NOV BRDG 04	Cat Fighter	F	4	Storm Cat	Strategic Maneuver	Live Oak Stud	2,300,000
BAR MAR 2YO TRN 04	Dubai Escapade	F	2	Awesome Again	Sassy Pants	John Ferguson Bloodstock	2,000,000
KEE NOV BRDG 04	Dimitrova	F	4	Swain (IRE)	The Caretaker (IRE)	Abbott Bloodstock	2,000,000
OBS SEL 2YO CAL 04	Mutanabi	C	2	Wild Rush	Freudenau	John Ferguson	1,600,000
FTF FEB SEL 2YO TRN 04	Timsaah	C	2	Rubiano	Magari	John Ferguson	1,500,000
KEE NOV BRDG 04	Got Koko	M	5	Signal Tap	Baby North	Narvick International	1,500,000
KEE APR 2YO KY 04	Radetzky	C	2	Dixie Union	Sneaky Quiet	Demi O'Byrne	1,400,000
BAR MAR 2YO TRN 04	Cat Fighter	F	4	Storm Cat	Strategic Maneuver	John G. Sikura	1,350,000
KEE NOV BRDG 04	Fairest Cape	F	2	Storm Cat	Myth	Skara Glen Stables	1,200,000
FTF FEB SEL 2YO TRN 04	Storm Cat Johnny	C	2	Storm Cat	Add	Robert V. LaPenta	1,050,000
OBS SPR 2YO 04	Woodford Gale	C	2	Distorted Humor	Zuppardo Ardo	John Ferguson, agent	975,000
KEE NOV BRDG 04	Nevermore	F	4	Unbridled	Teewinot	Vin Cox Bloodstock	950,000
FTF FEB SEL 2YO TRN 04	Daddy Joe	C	2	Unbridled's Song	Vennila Cream	Buzz Chace, agent	900,000
FTF FEB SEL 2YO TRN 04	Fusaichi Rock Star	C	2	Wild Wonder	Grannies Feather	Fusao Sekiguchi	825,000
FTF FEB SEL 2YO TRN 04	Deputy Grant	C	2	Deputy Minister	Win Crafty Lady	B. Wayne Hughes	800,000
KEE APR 2YO KY 04	She's a Devil Slew	F	2	Seattle Slew	She's a Devil Due	Fleetwood/N.W. Mgmt	800,000
KEE APR 2YO KY 04	Ecclesiastic	C	3	Pulpit	Starry Dreamer	Joe Allen	775,000
KEE APR 2YO KY 04	Coach Kent	C	2	Fusaichi Pegasus	Rokeby Rosie	A & M Jones, B Chace, agt	750,000
FTF FEB SEL 2YO TRN 04	Backchat	C	2	Distorted Humor	Dare to Be Me	John Ferguson	750,000
FTF FEB SEL 2YO TRN 04	War Plan	C	2	Fusaichi Pegasus	Li Law	Brian Morgan, agent	700,000
KEE NOV BRDG 04	Lucifer's Stone	F	3	Horse Chestnut (Saf)	Ladue	Nesco II	700,000
BAR MAR 2YO TRN 04	Atlantic Ocean	F	4	Stormy Atlantic	Super Chef	Never Tell Farm	700,000
FTF FEB SEL 2YO TRN 04	One Smart Deputy	C	2	Silver Deputy	Awful Smart	Roger Attfield	700,000
OBS SPR 2YO 04	Collegiate Honor	C	2	Double Honor	Camptown Miss	William J. Condren	675,000
OBS OPN 2YO 04	Notable Tiger	C	2	Tiger Ridge	Notable Girl	John Ferguson	650,000
FTF FEB SEL 2YO TRN 04	Rachel's Song	F	2	Tale of the Cat	Too too Divine	Mike Ryan, agent	650,000
FTF FEB SEL 2YO TRN 04	Fashion Cat	F	2	Forest Wildcat	Hold to Fashion	Bar S Ranch	630,000
FTF FEB SEL 2YO TRN 04	Pulpit Exchange	C	2	Pulpit	Silent Greeting	Mike Ryan, agent	625,000
KEE NOV BRDG 04	Sand Springs	F	4	Dynaformer	Lovely Martha	B.B.A. (Ireland)	625,000
KEE NOV BRDG 04	Soldera	F	4	Polish Numbers	La Pepite	Wertheimer et Frere	600,000
FTF FEB SEL 2YO TRN 04	Going Wild	C	2	Golden Missile	Pola	R B and B J Lewis	600,000
FTF FEB SEL 2YO TRN 04	Nasema's Slam	F	2	Grand Slam	Nasema	Fleetwood/N.W. Mgmt	600,000
BAR MAR 2YO TRN 04	Should Be Royalty	F	2	Pine Bluff	Malley	Demi O'Byrne	600,000
BAR MAR 2YO TRN 04	Swissle Stick	C	2	Swiss Yodeler	Miss Soft Sell	R B and B J Lewis	600,000
OBS OPN 2YO 04	Yankee Million	F	2	Yankee Victor	Betamillion Bock	Narvick International	575,000
BAR MAR 2YO TRN 04	True Integrity	C	2	Honour and Glory	Defer West	Narvick International	575,000
FTF FEB SEL 2YO TRN 04	For All We Know	F	2	Stephen Got Even	Over All	John C. Oxley	550,000
FTF FEB SEL 2YO TRN 04	Happy as Larry	C	2	Yes It's True	Don't Be Blue	John Ferguson	525,000
FTF FEB SEL 2YO TRN 04	Play Ballado	F	2	Saint Ballado	Piccolo Player	John C. Oxley	525,000
BAR MAR 2YO TRN 04	Word of Mouth	F	4	Saint Ballado	Katies (IRE)	R.D. Hubbard	525,000
BAR MAR 2YO TRN 04	Honest Answer	F	4	Tale of the Cat	Cup of Honey	Never Tell Farm	510,000
FTF FEB SEL 2YO TRN 04	Devil At Sea	C	2	Devil His Due	Atlantique du Nord	John H. Peace	500,000
OBS SPR 2YO 04	Western Acres	C	2	West Acre	Y'All Sing	Kaaren Biggs	500,000
FTF FEB SEL 2YO TRN 04	Quiet Money	C	2	Seattle Slew	Discreet Account	R.A. Violette	500,000
BAR MAR 2YO TRN 04	Ridges in Time	C	2	Tiger Ridge	Winning Journey	Bruno DeBerdt, agent	500,000
BAR MAR 2YO TRN 04	Jim's Smokin Pinot	C	2	Victory Gallop	Buck's Lady	Never Tell Farm	500,000
KEE APR 2YO KY 04	Fusaichi Forza	C	2	Polish Numbers	Student Wife	Fusao Sekiguchi	500,000
KEE APR 2YO KY 04	Blitzen	F	2	Siphon (BRZ)	Misty Music	A & M Jones, B Chace, agt	500,000
KEE APR 2YO KY 04	Brazilian	F	2	Stravinsky	Golden Pond (IRE)	John Fort	500,000
OBS SEL 2YO CAL 04	Spanish Chestnut	C	2	Horse Chestnut (Saf)	Baby Rabbit	Demi O'Byrne	500,000
KEE NOV BRDG 04	Guana (FR)	M	5	Sillery	Great Connection	Doug Hendrickson	500,000
OBS SEL 2YO CAL 04	Siphon City	C	2	Siphon (BRZ)	Carsona	Demi O'Byrne	500,000
OBS SPR 2YO 04	Afrashad	C	2	Smoke Glacken	Flo White	John Ferguson, agent	500,000
FTF FEB SEL 2YO TRN 04	Storm Silk	C	2	Stormin Fever	Carpenter's Lace	John Ferguson	500,000
KEE NOV BRDG 04	Cat Alert	F	4	Tabasco Cat	Gold n Delicious	Never Tell Farm	500,000
FTF FEB SEL 2YO TRN 04	Materialism	C	2	Not For Love	Gala Goldie's Best	John Ferguson	500,000

Snapshot Facts: There were more horses of racing age sold for **$1,000,000** or more (15) in North America in **2004** than there were in **2001, 2002** and **2003** combined.

Leading Breeders in 2004 by Money Won

Breeder	Starters	Starts	1st	2d	3d	Purses
Adena Springs	373	2,473	384	367	323	$14,133,631
Franks, John	540	4,194	531	546	488	10,210,103
Farnsworth Farms	408	3,459	447	426	434	8,500,254
Someday Farm	2	11	6	1	0	*7,563,853
Mabee, John, C. Mr. & Mrs.	204	1,322	201	205	193	5,063,818
Appleton, Arthur, I.	124	851	158	124	108	5,016,808
Juddmonte Farms	62	283	55	35	36	4,989,627
Kenneth L. Ramsey & Sarah K. Ramsey	102	648	110	90	82	4,796,483
Sam-Son Farm	53	317	51	39	47	4,782,501
Evans, Edward, P.	139	989	134	147	121	4,717,408
Sez Who Thoroughbreds	182	1,228	164	161	153	4,340,206
Jones, Brereton, C.	237	1,503	212	184	165	4,190,937
Aaron U. Jones & Marie D. Jones	25	145	30	25	19	4,033,129
Everest Stables Inc.	111	764	98	102	95	3,913,268
Wygod, Martin, J. Mr. & Mrs.	116	686	105	104	95	3,109,849
Paulson, Allen, E.	65	419	69	58	48	3,082,697
Overbrook Farm	132	691	102	109	88	3,079,050
WinStar Farm, LLC	76	467	74	62	63	3,069,372
Mockingbird Farm, Inc.	164	1,410	166	205	166	3,007,061
Campbell, Gilbert, G.	153	1,122	179	137	164	2,865,742
Wimborne Farm, Inc.	48	317	49	42	47	2,812,351
Stonerside Stable, LLC	70	373	53	47	51	2,643,617
Charles Nuckols Jr. & Sons	108	786	115	105	103	2,562,735
Harris Farms Inc.	101	731	106	130	92	2,554,661
Parra, Ro	97	612	82	84	79	2,336,683
Live Oak Stud	79	505	83	63	64	2,259,520
J D Farms	100	733	90	102	96	2,213,965
Pin Oak Stud, LLC	55	324	64	42	53	2,098,583
Margaux Farm LLC	9	93	21	16	9	1,937,135
Farish, W., S.	59	384	67	50	43	1,929,239
Phipps Stable	16	81	19	12	17	1,849,454
Frazier, D., W. Dr.	109	926	112	109	119	1,747,125
Hill 'N' Dale Farm	51	348	42	52	56	1,743,197
Robert H. Roberts & Bea Roberts	49	419	57	49	46	1,629,181
Tommy Town Thoroughbreds, LLC	83	488	77	71	64	1,591,302
Foxwood Plantation, Inc.	63	471	65	57	58	1,573,737
Beclawat Stable	20	131	18	18	14	1,569,669
Flying Zee Stables	68	426	61	69	52	1,564,002
The Thoroughbred Corp.	56	311	52	36	34	1,527,330
Sabine Stable	31	201	23	36	27	1,520,533
Gomez, Ron, E.	46	366	51	58	46	1,512,428
Haras Don Alberto	14	111	12	20	16	1,510,017
Firmamento	18	128	15	21	18	1,509,506
Thomas/Lakin	40	226	37	28	29	1,481,351
Marylou Whitney Stables	16	112	18	14	18	1,480,547
Kinghaven Farms Limited	40	267	43	33	24	1,475,008
Melnyk, Eugene	39	201	37	31	21	1,455,796
Clovelly Farms	11	69	12	12	9	1,421,112
Adcock, J	101	614	84	72	77	1,417,127
Schickedanz, Gustav	38	251	38	39	31	1,415,871
McGinnes, Charles Mr. & Mrs.	34	238	45	40	32	1,409,433
Foxfield	59	365	61	43	43	1,406,454
Ocala Stud Farm	55	384	64	56	52	1,406,171
Humphrey, G., Watts Jr.	39	273	32	34	36	1,403,414
Chester Broman & Mary R. Broman	33	186	25	19	24	1,386,411
Dizney, Donald, R.	84	626	81	92	70	1,385,019
Brylynn Farm, Inc.	55	367	54	50	42	1,355,990
Hargus Sexton & Sandra Sexton	72	436	61	51	42	1,310,799
Liberation Farm & Oratis Thoroughbreds	67	450	65	62	53	1,307,453
Shadwell Farm, LLC	32	193	32	33	16	1,283,909

Breeder	Starters	Starts	1st	2d	3d	Purses
Claiborne Farm	50	271	28	35	34	1,273,630
Phipps, Ogden, Mills	21	143	29	19	22	1,268,176
Gunther, John, D.	19	133	21	28	14	1,252,717
Strawbridge, George Jr.	55	272	34	29	32	1,234,407
Chiefswood Stables Limited	11	60	12	7	7	1,207,701
Meadowbrook Farms, Inc.	57	420	60	56	51	1,202,571
Hermitage Farm LLC	67	476	61	65	62	1,194,522
Disler Farms Ltd	2	9	3	2	1	1,193,221
Haras Santa Maria de Araras	54	352	44	48	42	1,191,223
Shields, J., V. Jr.	33	291	40	35	43	1,183,277
Mt. Brilliant Farm LLC	31	193	35	26	23	1,159,176
Car Colston Hall Stud	1	10	5	3	1	1,159,075
Jacks or Better Farm Inc.	46	296	30	48	27	1,146,671
Haras Fronteira P.A.P.	3	19	8	1	3	1,145,972
Glen Hill Farm	50	328	52	47	37	1,139,626
SLU, Inc.	40	257	28	29	48	1,121,882
Flaxman Holdings Ltd.	27	129	28	20	19	1,116,382
Glory Days Breeding, Inc.	34	200	33	19	26	1,109,337
Wind Hill Farm	13	102	12	7	12	1,101,341
Gulf Coast Farms Bloodstock LP	39	237	38	34	35	1,098,432
Hancock, Arthur, B. III	70	493	54	78	67	1,091,047
Dr. William A. Reed & Stonecrest Farm	11	72	4	14	8	1,080,872
Santa Cruz Ranch Inc.	52	327	36	40	36	1,078,742
Wertheimer & Frere	25	115	13	21	16	1,071,015
Stonewall Farm	50	321	42	22	30	1,067,995
E & D Enterprises	72	511	56	64	79	1,066,203
TAC Holdings, Inc.	32	206	35	22	24	1,053,139
Newchance Farm	13	74	4	3	3	1,050,026
La Quebrada	43	230	36	25	28	1,049,289
Applebite Farms	44	240	44	27	40	1,048,636
Minshall Farms	41	349	38	36	50	1,047,666
Kinsman Farm	50	320	45	50	36	1,043,654
Meyerhoff, Robert, E.	48	309	48	47	47	1,039,166
Hunter, Barbara	68	417	56	49	49	1,036,020
Smith, Charles, A.	2	16	5	5	2	1,032,045
McKee Stables Inc	23	136	20	13	17	1,016,962
John Toffan & Trudy McCaffery	53	290	32	36	46	1,016,950
Cypress Farms 1991	15	120	25	23	15	1,015,269
Marjorie Cowan & Irving Cowan	3	26	6	6	3	1,012,705
Four Horsemen's Ranch	30	191	24	19	26	1,001,919
Highland Farms, Inc.	77	470	54	54	58	994,643
Sondra Bender & Howard M. Bender	40	264	36	43	32	987,648
Tri-County Farms LLC	10	57	9	8	10	983,266
Plummer, S., David	55	351	47	46	32	980,014
Paulson, Madeleine, A.	9	62	13	5	8	959,138
Vegso Racing Stable	14	105	21	15	12	940,627
Donald & R. Mary Zuckerman, as Tenants by the Entireties	32	227	23	20	33	938,543
Marablue Farm	70	491	47	59	59	938,325
Glencrest Farm LLC	61	414	48	42	47	935,201
Centaur Farms, Inc.	35	234	39	28	32	929,632
Ryehill Farm	48	324	38	40	42	927,363
Knob Hill Stable	25	155	24	21	23	924,452
Toffolon, Roger	48	381	54	50	50	915,887
Jayeff B Stables	38	146	33	23	20	905,937
Phillips Racing Partnership	33	204	37	26	30	901,546
Casey, James, W.	51	287	29	38	40	900,544
The Niarchos Family	1	1	1	0	0	900,000
Old English Rancho	39	291	44	31	40	899,128
R Bar S Thoroughbreds LLP	64	419	52	44	54	879,662
Fox Ridge Farm Inc	8	45	4	5	9	859,385
Burning Daylight Farms, Inc.	33	189	33	35	28	858,847

Breeder	Starters	Starts	1st	2d	3d	Purses
Hopewell Investments LLC	19	109	24	16	12	857,069
McDonnell, Francis	46	346	59	46	42	850,955
Schickedanz, Bruno	48	385	56	52	37	849,435
Naify, Valerie	7	52	13	6	6	842,599
Moloney & Thompson	11	68	17	7	14	841,710
Seaman, Casey	40	296	47	39	32	836,473
Wakefield Farm	30	244	34	25	32	829,654
Bassett, Lucy, G.	14	72	12	12	13	808,811
Vanier, Harvey, L. Mr. & Mrs.	49	328	35	41	34	804,859
L. T. Smith Enterprises	39	307	45	39	34	804,519
Byrne, Michael, C.	27	205	20	31	30	802,313
Plemmons, Jim, H.	50	291	32	41	34	799,592
Winchell, Verne, H.	30	200	22	33	26	794,625
Calumet Farm	47	238	32	37	29	794,328
Robsham, E., Paul	43	294	29	36	35	792,821
Cobleskill College Found	6	52	8	11	7	792,323
Iron County Farms Inc.	34	243	32	38	28	791,180
Lussky, William	29	246	36	38	30	786,535
Gardiner Farms Limited	34	216	28	36	28	785,288
New Farm	22	89	20	8	14	784,760
Robert H Walter Family Trust	40	272	37	46	42	782,802
Hettinger, John	42	291	31	30	39	776,304
Malmuth, Marvin	25	174	32	22	26	753,104
Irish Acres Farm	58	512	49	65	46	751,175
Generazio, Patricia	37	322	28	30	56	745,991
J. B. Stables Inc.	41	290	41	36	29	742,866
Moss, J., S. Mr. & Mrs.	30	180	25	24	30	739,118
Jones, John, T. L. Jr.	56	338	35	35	44	738,120
Stanley Estate and Stud Co.	1	1	1	0	0	733,200
Montanari, Marion, G.	22	164	21	21	25	727,997
Lazy E Ranch Inc	24	184	28	19	20	727,248
Whitham, Janis, R.	24	134	15	28	12	723,607
Gainesway Thoroughbreds Ltd.	41	202	34	21	30	722,056
Robinson, J., Mack	39	262	32	41	28	720,225
Schettine, William, C.	26	162	20	24	13	719,997
Nolan, Chris	11	70	9	7	6	718,328
Richter Family Trust	33	233	41	29	30	713,599
Ersoff, Stanley, M.	54	401	42	45	45	713,567
Triple AAA Ranch	49	362	63	49	45	710,715
Darley	13	51	3	5	9	705,618
McDowell Farm	51	368	55	38	36	705,425
Jan Siegel, Mace Siegel & Samantha Siegel	13	67	11	8	11	701,557
Silvertand, John, Martin	4	16	5	2	1	698,180
Bradley, Fred, F.	3	23	6	7	5	697,530
Borislow, Dan	34	252	34	29	28	696,274
Justice Farm, Greg Justice & Steve Justice	46	323	36	35	35	695,277
Harris Farms, Inc. & Ken Maddy Trust	2	23	4	5	5	693,120
Farish, William, S. Jr.	13	83	15	12	9	691,497
South River Ranch Inc.	47	420	74	56	54	687,054
Brunacini, George	24	146	21	14	16	685,824
Sorokolit, William	15	101	10	6	15	683,051
Lazy Lane Stables, Inc.	30	191	31	28	30	680,539
Teague, Larry, R.	13	87	18	16	7	676,860
Southern Nevada Racing Stables Inc	45	360	56	39	47	675,627
Rainbow Stables	21	199	35	36	26	673,998
Cobra Farm	20	137	29	16	16	672,283
Carl Rosen Associates	4	26	4	5	6	670,551
Billingsley Creek Ranch	35	224	44	35	27	663,211
Marshall Naify Revocable Trust	34	184	45	25	17	661,261
Brushwood Stable	12	89	17	13	16	660,755
Prestonwood Farm, LLC	30	268	29	38	26	658,321

Breeder	Starters	Starts	1st	2d	3d	Purses
Colebrook Farms	41	292	41	37	30	655,756
duPont, Richard, C. Mrs.	26	214	23	19	32	655,298
Dreyfuss, Donald, S. Dr.	51	394	51	47	43	654,529
Willmott Stable	16	116	16	22	16	653,364
Heiligbrodt Racing Stable	32	203	31	30	18	652,301
Rooker, John, W.	15	96	9	15	12	650,261
Rutherford, Mike, G. Sr.	30	208	26	28	38	642,757
Weir, Dennis, E.	42	283	51	45	45	637,195
Jones, Brenda	8	69	7	11	10	636,310
Phillips Racing Partnership & John Phillips	3	13	3	1	1	634,899
Har. De Bernesq & S.C. Ecurie Ouaki Fabien	2	12	2	2	1	632,190
Smith, Paul	5	34	6	3	1	626,537
Price, Sandy, Lynn Dr.	12	86	13	13	9	625,858
Cherry Valley Farm LLC	7	54	12	10	4	625,728
Fahrhof, Stiftung, Gestut	4	19	7	2	0	619,806
River Ridge Ranch	35	331	35	41	55	619,750
Scott E. Ricker & Richard S. Kaster	25	229	34	33	30	615,854
Goichman, Lawrence	21	121	15	11	15	613,761
Baker, Reade	13	70	12	10	10	606,993
Tricar Stables Inc	43	346	38	43	54	605,352
Jerkens, Elisabeth, R.	23	182	20	22	21	602,272
Richard Wira, Yvette Wira, Linda Vetter & Deborah Penny	1	7	2	2	1	598,905
Squires, Margaret	3	29	7	1	8	594,970
Allen, Joseph	15	90	14	15	12	593,267
McMaster, Marilyn	36	260	29	40	32	593,019
Pacelco S.A.	7	29	5	4	3	592,692
Amestoy, Pierre	26	182	30	31	20	592,508
Sleeter, Carolyn	20	136	15	24	15	591,848
Camac, Robert, W.	10	74	10	7	9	591,774
Devonia Stud, Inc.	18	170	22	15	11	590,601
Tony Bowling & Bobby Dodd	23	167	25	35	16	582,455
Loch Lea Farm, Inc.	21	124	17	16	14	581,938
James Arnold & Marcia Arnold	40	318	55	32	39	580,596
Curtin, Cheryl, A.	15	78	12	12	10	579,552
Windways Farm Limited	16	117	17	16	18	578,935
Evans, R., S.	21	154	28	23	25	578,172
Watral, Michael	33	282	34	38	37	577,940
Porter, John, B.	20	147	26	16	21	577,320
Colts Ltd	15	105	24	11	12	576,353
Drazin, Dennis	25	157	21	15	26	573,416
Nielsen, Gerald Mr. & Mrs.	15	93	12	15	9	573,264
Paraneck Stallions	22	153	16	17	21	566,822
Tracy Farmer	1	9	4	1	1	566,105
David Block & Patricia Block	4	30	4	9	4	561,618
Scott, John, S.	28	216	41	27	29	561,546
Ridgely, Brice	4	19	6	2	5	558,218
Hugel, Max	18	132	15	15	12	550,878
North Wales LLC	23	151	19	19	20	550,072
Adkins, Jerry, R.	24	178	29	24	24	549,997
Eberts, Donald	24	153	35	20	19	548,428
Hidden Point Farm Inc.	34	213	26	21	32	546,962
Wachtel, Edwin	39	301	40	38	31	546,246
Ward, Wesley	2	11	5	2	2	546,220
Schwartz, Herbert, T.	19	198	17	31	32	546,023
Jim Tafel, LLC	13	79	18	5	7	544,605
Palides Investments N. V. Inc	15	83	16	16	8	542,726
Timber Creek Farm	52	348	36	38	39	542,631
Jack Ronan and des Vere Hunt Farm Co	2	15	3	3	1	540,010
Needham/ Betz Thoroughbreds & James Blackburn	1	5	4	0	1	536,400
Tall Oaks Farm	25	156	17	15	19	535,050
Landes, William, L. S. III	22	192	30	27	31	533,481

Breeder	Starters	Starts	1st	2d	3d	Purses
Hechavarria, Luis, de	31	265	35	39	24	529,284
Schoenborn, Gus Jr.	25	191	21	22	27	528,669
Kilroy Thoroughbred Partnership	10	55	13	10	11	527,275
Hurstland Farm	27	192	29	28	34	527,224
Mills, Randy	44	378	38	39	55	524,426
Hobeau Farm Ltd.	34	188	24	15	30	524,004
Haras San Patricio	1	5	4	1	0	521,780
Scott, C., G. DVM	3	24	8	3	5	519,806
Ackerman, Bob	5	39	6	7	5	518,946
Double D Farm Corp.	77	510	45	60	48	517,486
Clover Leaf Farms II, Inc.	26	169	26	22	14	512,881
Mereworth Farm	44	302	31	21	37	512,865
Woodlynn Farm Inc	21	135	20	24	18	511,985
Hines, James, T. Jr.	38	277	41	32	29	506,540
James D. Conway & Thomas C. Mueller	1	11	4	3	3	505,900
Fuller, Peter	31	264	35	34	37	505,865
Haras Bage Do Sul	4	29	9	1	3	505,677
Mangurian, Jr., Harry, T.	50	377	23	57	54	504,955
Swettenham Stud	18	109	19	13	15	504,843
Robert Norman & Patricia Norman	34	282	36	28	36	504,507
John R Mulholland & Martha Jane Mulholland	8	55	10	13	7	504,113
Mabee, John, C. Mrs.	25	70	10	11	6	502,280
King, Betty	27	161	26	20	23	499,437
Buckingham Farm	11	83	18	8	9	496,593
Bruno Brothers Farms	5	35	9	2	1	492,540
Dr. & Mrs. T. Bowman, Mr. & Mrs. T. Sutton & M.P. Higgins III	1	5	3	1	0	491,500
Sentinel Thoroughbred Farms	11	99	19	15	18	491,213
G. Watts Humphrey Jr. & Louise I. Humphrey	25	127	15	12	16	491,133
Tee N Jay Farm	15	121	13	15	12	491,036
Orion Stables	38	275	24	25	31	489,621
Oldenburg Farms, LLC	2	9	1	1	1	489,336
Whisper Hill Farm	37	214	24	28	24	489,219
Canyon Farms	26	142	19	20	20	488,865
Pacelco S.A. & Chelston Ireland, Ltd.	4	22	5	5	4	488,575
France Weiner & Irwin J. Weiner	7	38	3	8	7	488,400
Paxson, Henry, D. Mrs.	23	199	30	25	23	488,246
Domino Stud of Lexington, LLC	22	116	16	16	13	488,157
Mitchell, Nancy, W.	11	78	14	12	6	487,987
Huckabay, Jackie, D. MD	22	144	14	15	13	484,743
Bennett, R., J. Mr. & Mrs.	47	301	41	27	39	483,905
Few, Ed	39	279	33	35	32	483,730
Peace, John, H.	14	105	17	19	17	483,336
H. E. Pabst & T. J. Pabst	2	15	8	3	3	483,260
Dinesh Maniar & Getaway Farms	36	258	44	35	28	481,556
Thomas J. Kelly & Joseph M. Grant	3	33	2	6	4	480,505
Perez, Robert	33	203	23	22	23	480,267
Cheveley Park Stud Ltd	6	31	4	5	6	479,231
Mills, Alice, du Pont	4	39	8	6	4	474,937
Gordon Wootton & Mary Lou Wootton	3	16	4	1	2	474,820
Copeland, Dreabon	13	105	27	18	11	474,405
Hidden Point Farm, Inc.	30	215	30	23	23	473,000
Swifty Farms Inc.	60	363	36	41	36	472,243
Chandler, John, A. Dr.	9	44	14	11	4	472,145
Seeger, Roberta	23	187	21	33	18	471,467
Wright, Frank, P. Mrs.	22	150	16	23	24	471,415
Green Lantern Stables, LLC	11	44	5	10	7	470,241
Farnsworth Farms & Locust Valley Corp.	31	280	44	32	36	469,353
Jon S. Kelly, C. Beau Greely, Dr. Sam Bradley & Brad Scott	2	20	1	8	2	467,908
Haras Du Mezeray S.A.	1	8	5	1	0	467,578
Twin Hopes Farm, Inc.	21	102	19	9	13	467,322
Hughes, B., Wayne	19	110	13	24	12	466,433

Breeder	Starters	Starts	1st	2d	3d	Purses
Hager,, David, E. II	16	117	21	15	15	465,862
Bee Bee Stables Inc & Equitor, Inc	2	23	2	7	2	464,540
Buckram Oak Farm	16	91	15	22	13	463,718
Sampson, Curtis, A.	16	99	19	9	10	463,558
White Cross Farm	28	271	44	34	38	463,054
Heiligbrodt, L., William	15	97	11	17	10	462,540
Blazing Meadows Farm	24	229	26	30	27	462,532
Halo Farms	30	206	24	21	27	461,952
Berkshire Stud	13	78	14	15	8	461,490
Auerbach, Madeline	7	60	8	12	10	461,410
Nichols, Thomas, L.	12	124	26	22	16	461,077
Ostrager, Barry, R.	29	188	23	20	21	459,099
Edition Farm	13	88	16	10	4	458,770
Madison, Stewart	8	71	16	10	7	457,682
Huber, Shelley	2	23	5	5	3	457,231
Asiel Stable, L.C.	15	115	15	16	24	456,377
Whitbred, H., T.	5	51	13	11	4	455,690
Highclere Inc.	24	169	21	21	17	455,252
Zamora, John	4	39	10	5	4	454,460
Lister, Richard, L.	9	64	8	8	2	452,936
Howard Scarberry & Penny Scarberry	21	127	14	19	10	451,820
Adv a P Joubert	1	1	1	0	0	450,000
Gigginstown House Stud	1	3	1	0	0	450,000
Oxley, John, C.	24	135	21	17	13	449,847
Blum, Peter, E.	21	133	11	21	18	446,610
C. S. Tateson	1	7	2	1	1	446,180
Casino Royale Farms Inc.	11	98	21	8	7	445,463
Maynard, Richard, D.	5	32	4	4	2	444,884
Sapp, Darrell, R.	36	262	31	39	33	444,754
Haley, James, D.	12	78	8	13	13	443,666
Sun Valley Farm	32	231	23	36	22	443,253
Lake, Richard	6	42	4	6	8	443,196
Gainsborough Farm LLC	5	12	2	1	1	442,420
De La Pomme	16	161	24	19	21	441,919
Stud TNT	7	20	3	7	2	440,191
Anstu Stables Inc	2	14	3	4	2	439,557
Sugar Maple Farm	25	157	18	19	18	439,330
Albert Bell & Joyce Bell	5	31	4	5	6	438,826
Fried,, Albert Jr.	17	117	15	15	12	437,916
Valentino, John	15	124	17	6	8	437,809
Tackett, Bill	47	354	42	42	52	437,374
Dresden Farm	17	137	25	28	14	437,313
Ironwater Farms Joint Venture	24	143	15	12	24	437,300
Bakerman, Robert	24	224	25	28	21	437,081
Bertolino, Frank	23	177	27	19	16	437,059
Lothenbach, Robert	3	23	3	3	5	436,836
Hickory Tree Farm Inc.	11	62	13	10	10	436,655
Al Profitt & Larry Demeritte	1	10	3	1	1	434,634
Williamson, Garland, E.	8	52	8	2	8	434,349
R. Alex Rankin & Louis Wright	8	62	11	9	2	434,241
Farfellow Farms Ltd.	20	116	16	15	14	434,059
Blass, Patricia	10	75	12	17	12	433,858
Parrish Hill Farm	17	148	28	20	12	432,228
Stronach, Andy	22	136	13	16	15	431,148
Diamond A Racing Corporation	15	63	11	11	4	431,057
Shuford, Nancy, C.	37	248	21	31	30	430,735
Edmond A. Hudon & Sharon Hudon	19	145	21	16	23	430,399

*Includes $5,000,000 bonus

Snapshot Facts: There were 265 breeders whose horses earned $500,000 or more in 2004. There were 100 breeders whose horses earned more than $1 million and 28 breeders with $2 million.

Leading Breeders in 2004 by Races Won

Breeder	Starters	Starts	1st	2d	3d	Purses
Franks, John	540	4,194	531	546	488	$10,210,103
Farnsworth Farms	408	3,459	447	426	434	8,500,254
Adena Springs	373	2,473	384	367	323	14,133,631
Jones, Brereton, C.	237	1,503	212	184	165	4,190,937
Mabee, John, C. Mr. & Mrs.	204	1,322	201	205	193	5,063,818
Campbell, Gilbert, G.	153	1,122	179	137	164	2,865,742
Mockingbird Farm, Inc.	164	1,410	166	205	166	3,007,061
Sez Who Thoroughbreds	182	1,228	164	161	153	4,340,206
Appleton, Arthur, I.	124	851	158	124	108	5,016,808
Evans, Edward, P.	139	989	134	147	121	4,717,408
Charles Nuckols Jr. & Sons	108	786	115	105	103	2,562,735
Frazier, D., W. Dr.	109	926	112	109	119	1,747,125
Kenneth L. Ramsey & Sarah K. Ramsey	102	648	110	90	82	4,796,483
Harris Farms Inc.	101	731	106	130	92	2,554,661
Wygod, Martin, J. Mr. & Mrs.	116	686	105	104	95	3,109,849
Overbrook Farm	132	691	102	109	88	3,079,050
Everest Stables Inc	111	764	98	102	95	3,913,260
J D Farms	100	733	90	102	96	2,213,965
Adcock, J	101	614	84	72	77	1,417,127
Live Oak Stud	79	505	83	63	64	2,259,520
Parra, Ro	97	612	82	84	79	2,336,683
Dizney, Donald, R.	84	626	81	92	70	1,385,019
Tommy Town Thoroughbreds, LLC	83	488	77	71	64	1,591,302
WinStar Farm, LLC	76	467	74	62	63	3,069,372
South River Ranch Inc.	47	420	74	56	54	687,054
Paulson, Allen, E.	65	419	69	58	48	3,082,697
Farish, W., S.	59	384	67	50	43	1,929,239
Foxwood Plantation, Inc.	63	471	65	57	58	1,573,737
Liberation Farm & Oratis Thoroughbreds	67	450	65	62	53	1,307,453
Pin Oak Stud, LLC	55	324	64	42	53	2,098,583
Ocala Stud Farm	55	384	64	56	52	1,406,171
Triple AAA Ranch	49	362	63	49	45	710,715
Flying Zee Stables	68	426	61	69	52	1,564,002
Foxfield	59	365	61	43	43	1,406,454
Hargus Sexton & Sandra Sexton	72	436	61	51	42	1,310,799
Hermitage Farm LLC	67	476	61	65	62	1,194,522
Meadowbrook Farms, Inc.	57	420	60	56	51	1,202,571
McDonnell, Francis	46	346	59	46	42	850,955
Robert H. Roberts & Bea Roberts	49	419	57	49	46	1,629,181
E & D Enterprises	72	511	56	64	79	1,066,203
Hunter, Barbara	68	417	56	49	49	1,036,020
Schickedanz, Bruno	48	385	56	52	37	849,435
Southern Nevada Racing Stables Inc	45	360	56	39	47	675,627
Juddmonte Farms	62	283	55	35	36	4,989,627
McDowell Farm	51	368	55	38	36	705,425
James Arnold & Marcia Arnold	40	318	55	32	39	580,596
Brylynn Farm, Inc.	55	367	54	50	42	1,355,990
Hancock, Arthur, B. III	70	493	54	78	67	1,091,047
Highland Farms, Inc.	77	470	54	54	58	994,643
Toffolon, Roger	48	381	54	50	50	915,887
Stonerside Stable, LLC	70	373	53	47	51	2,643,617
The Thoroughbred Corp.	56	311	52	36	34	1,527,330
Glen Hill Farm	50	328	52	47	37	1,139,626
R Bar S Thoroughbreds LLP	64	419	52	44	54	879,662
Sam-Son Farm	53	317	51	39	47	4,782,501
Gomez, Ron, E.	46	366	51	58	46	1,512,428
Dreyfuss, Donald, S. Dr.	51	394	51	47	43	654,529
Weir, Dennis, E.	42	283	51	45	45	637,195
Wimborne Farm, Inc.	48	317	49	42	47	2,812,351
Irish Acres Farm	58	512	49	65	46	751,175
Meyerhoff, Robert, E.	48	309	48	47	47	1,039,166
Glencrest Farm LLC	61	414	48	42	47	935,201

Breeder	Starters	Starts	1st	2d	3d	Purses
Plummer, S., David	55	351	47	46	32	980,014
Marablue Farm	70	491	47	59	59	938,325
Seaman, Casey	40	296	47	39	32	836,473
Phenix, Harold	35	259	46	34	29	381,148
McGinnes, Charles Mr. & Mrs.	34	238	45	40	32	1,409,433
Kinsman Farm	50	320	45	50	36	1,043,654
L. T. Smith Enterprises	39	307	45	39	34	804,519
Marshall Naify Revocable Trust	34	184	45	25	17	661,261
Double D Farm Corp.	77	510	45	60	48	517,486
Haras Santa Maria de Araras	54	352	44	48	42	1,191,223
Applebite Farms	44	240	44	27	40	1,048,636
Old English Rancho	39	291	44	31	40	899,128
Billingsley Creek Ranch	35	224	44	35	27	663,211
Dinesh Maniar & Getaway Farms	36	258	44	35	28	481,556
Farnsworth Farms & Locust Valley Corp.	31	280	44	32	36	469,353
White Cross Farm	28	271	44	34	38	463,054
Byer, Larry	45	295	44	40	29	416,577
Kinghaven Farms Limited	40	267	43	33	24	1,475,008
Hill 'N' Dale Farm	51	348	42	52	56	1,743,197
Stonewall Farm	50	321	42	22	30	1,067,995
Ersoff, Stanley, M.	54	401	42	45	45	713,567
Tackett, Bill	47	354	42	42	52	437,374
J. B. Stables Inc.	41	290	41	36	29	742,866
Richter Family Trust	33	233	41	29	30	713,599
Colebrook Farms	41	292	41	37	30	655,756
Scott, John, S.	28	216	41	27	29	561,546
Hines, James, T. Jr.	38	277	41	32	29	506,540
Bennett, R., J. Mr. & Mrs.	47	301	41	27	39	483,905
Shields, J., V. Jr.	33	291	40	35	43	1,183,277
Wachtel, Edwin	39	301	40	38	31	546,246
Centaur Farms, Inc.	35	234	39	28	32	929,632
Schickedanz, Gustav	38	251	38	39	31	1,415,871
Gulf Coast Farms Bloodstock LP	39	237	38	34	35	1,098,432
Minshall Farms	41	349	38	36	50	1,047,666
Ryehill Farm	48	324	38	40	42	927,363
Tricar Stables Inc	43	346	38	43	54	605,352
Mills, Randy	44	378	38	39	55	524,426
Gentry Farms	45	318	38	35	38	366,053
Sunrise Stable South	35	244	38	30	28	364,048
Thomas/Lakin	40	226	37	28	29	1,481,351
Melnyk, Eugene	39	201	37	31	21	1,455,796
Phillips Racing Partnership	33	204	37	26	30	901,546
Robert H Walter Family Trust	40	272	37	46	42	782,802
Santa Cruz Ranch Inc.	52	327	36	40	36	1,078,742
La Quebrada	43	230	36	25	28	1,049,289
Sondra Bender & Howard M. Bender	40	264	36	43	32	987,648
Lussky, William	29	246	36	38	30	786,535
Justice Farm, Greg Justice & Steve Justice	46	323	36	35	35	695,277
Timber Creek Farm	52	348	36	38	39	542,631
Robert Norman & Patricia Norman	34	282	36	28	36	504,507
Swifty Farms Inc.	60	363	36	41	36	472,243
Mt. Brilliant Farm LLC	31	193	35	26	23	1,159,176
TAC Holdings, Inc.	32	206	35	22	24	1,053,139
Vanier, Harvey, L. Mr. & Mrs.	49	328	35	41	34	804,859
Jones, John, T. L. Jr.	56	338	35	35	44	738,120
Rainbow Stables	21	199	35	36	26	673,998
River Ridge Ranch	35	331	35	41	55	619,750
Eberts, Donald	24	153	35	20	19	548,428
Hechavarria, Luis, de	31	265	35	39	24	529,284
Fuller, Peter	31	264	35	34	37	505,865
Strawbridge, George Jr.	55	272	34	29	32	1,234,407
Wakefield Farm	30	244	34	25	32	829,654
Gainesway Thoroughbreds Ltd.	41	202	34	21	30	722,056
Borislow, Dan	34	252	34	29	28	696,274

Breeder	Starters	Starts	1st	2d	3d	Purses
Scott E. Ricker & Richard S. Kaster	25	229	34	33	30	615,854
Watral, Michael	33	282	34	38	37	577,940
Glory Days Breeding, Inc.	34	200	33	19	26	1,109,337
Jayeff B Stables	38	146	33	23	20	905,937
Burning Daylight Farms, Inc.	33	189	33	35	28	858,847
Few, Ed	39	279	33	35	32	483,730
Northwest Farms	35	210	33	23	18	414,172
Jacobi, Charles	21	165	33	15	18	397,262
Humphrey, G., Watts Jr.	39	273	32	34	36	1,403,414
Shadwell Farm, LLC	32	193	32	33	16	1,283,909
John Toffan & Trudy McCaffery	53	290	32	36	46	1,016,950
Plemmons, Jim, H.	50	291	32	41	34	799,592
Calumet Farm	47	238	32	37	29	794,328
Iron County Farms Inc.	34	243	32	38	28	791,180
Malmuth, Marvin	25	174	32	22	26	753,104
Robinson, J., Mack	39	262	32	41	28	720,225
Sutherland Farm, Inc	39	209	32	26	18	150,133
Hettinger, John	42	291	31	30	39	776,304
Lazy Lane Stables, Inc.	30	191	31	28	30	680,539
Heiligbrodt Racing Stable	32	203	31	30	18	652,301
Mereworth Farm	44	302	31	21	37	512,865
Sapp, Darrell, R.	36	262	31	39	33	444,754
Roberts, Guy, C. Mr. & Mrs.	33	255	31	41	36	394,659
Hollis Cotton Oil Mill Inc.	51	283	31	24	28	188,681
Aaron U. Jones & Marie D. Jones	25	145	30	25	19	4,033,129
Jacks or Better Farm Inc.	46	296	30	48	27	1,146,671
Amestoy, Pierre	26	182	30	31	20	592,508
Landes, William, L. S. III	22	192	30	27	31	533,481
Paxson, Henry, D. Mrs.	23	199	30	25	23	488,246
Hidden Point Farm, Inc.	30	215	30	23	23	473,000
Bluestem Farm Inc.	30	241	30	24	27	363,790
Phipps, Ogden, Mills	21	143	29	19	22	1,268,176
Casey, James, W.	51	287	29	38	40	900,544
Robsham, E., Paul	43	294	29	36	35	792,821
Cobra Farm	20	137	29	16	16	672,283
Prestonwood Farm, LLC	30	268	29	38	26	658,321
McMaster, Marilyn	36	260	29	40	32	593,019
Adkins, Jerry, R.	24	178	29	24	24	549,997
Hurstland Farm	27	192	29	28	34	527,224
Emerald Pastures Corp.	24	194	29	21	15	382,691
Vessels Stallion Farm LLC	25	164	29	29	23	360,489
Pabst, Frederick, L. Mr. & Mrs.	28	145	29	25	17	352,981
Clarkland Farm	30	210	29	17	18	332,420
Claiborne Farm	50	271	28	35	34	1,273,630
SLU, Inc.	40	257	28	29	48	1,121,882
Flaxman Holdings Ltd.	27	129	28	20	19	1,116,382
Gardiner Farms Limited	34	216	28	36	28	785,288
Generazio, Patricia	37	322	28	30	56	745,991
Lazy E Ranch Inc	24	184	28	19	20	727,248
Evans, R., S.	21	154	28	23	25	578,172
Parrish Hill Farm	17	148	28	20	12	432,228
Asmussen, Keith, I.	27	165	28	24	21	417,520
Elliott, James, R.	31	229	28	29	26	359,627
Copeland, Dreabon	13	105	27	18	11	474,405
Bertolino, Frank	23	177	27	19	16	437,059
Newport Farm	16	139	27	24	20	429,719
Scharbauer, Clarence Jr.	23	157	27	18	22	404,874
Winemiller, Becky	26	188	27	19	23	317,475
Rutherford, Mike, G. Sr.	30	208	26	28	38	642,757
Porter, John, B.	20	147	26	16	21	577,320
Hidden Point Farm Inc.	34	213	26	21	32	546,962
Clover Leaf Farms II, Inc.	26	169	26	22	14	512,881
King, Betty	27	161	26	20	23	499,437
Blazing Meadows Farm	24	229	26	30	27	462,532

Breeder	Starters	Starts	1st	2d	3d	Purses
Nichols, Thomas, L.	12	124	26	22	16	461,077
Granger, J., Weldon	30	219	26	30	28	415,503
Shortleaf Stable	28	195	26	24	32	363,862
Heinlein, Herman	25	187	26	15	25	360,803
Bonita Farm	24	205	26	31	17	353,648
McAllister, Norman, J.	42	230	26	17	29	337,142
Purdy, Patricia, Staskowski	27	190	26	14	15	303,339
Riecken, Herb, L.	19	185	26	28	24	258,787
Allaire Farms	26	158	26	26	20	247,908
Chester Broman & Mary R. Broman	33	186	25	19	24	1,386,411
Cypress Farms 1991	15	120	25	23	15	1,015,269
Moss, J., S. Mr. & Mrs.	30	180	25	24	30	739,118
Tony Bowling & Bobby Dodd	23	167	25	35	16	582,455
Dresden Farm	17	137	25	28	14	437,313
Bakerman, Robert	24	224	25	28	21	437,081
Green Willow Farms	25	168	25	20	24	410,071
Robert Miller & Delphine Miller	20	163	25	24	29	245,140
Root, Jack, B. Dr. & Mrs. Jr.	32	235	25	27	35	157,837
Four Horsemen's Ranch	30	191	24	19	26	1,001,919
Knob Hill Stable	25	155	24	21	23	924,452
Hopewell Investments LLC	19	109	24	16	12	857,069
Colts Ltd	15	105	24	11	12	576,353
Hobeau Farm Ltd.	34	188	24	15	30	524,004
Orion Stables	38	275	24	25	31	489,621
Whisper Hill Farm	37	214	24	28	24	489,219
Halo Farms	30	206	24	21	27	461,952
De La Pomme	16	161	24	19	21	441,919
Plumley, Harold, J.	30	150	24	14	23	427,737
Horne, Steve	31	203	24	27	24	423,319
Murphy, John, D.	25	179	24	18	28	396,216
Santen, J., D.	20	134	24	17	21	382,685
Burbach, Willard	23	111	24	17	20	351,490
Farnsworth Farms & Jack T. Hammer	18	153	24	17	20	348,096
Rickman, William, M.	26	179	24	20	21	330,301
Hukill, Charles	24	197	24	24	27	299,591
Carl Cannata & Olivia Cannata	33	231	24	27	34	256,447
Horton, Al, J.	17	132	24	15	19	221,477
Patrick, Gary	23	202	24	21	20	196,160
Jensen, Luella, M.	21	147	24	16	24	150,875
Sabine Stable	31	201	23	36	27	1,520,533
D. & R.M. Zuckerman, as Tenants by the Entireties	32	227	23	20	33	938,543
duPont, Richard, C. Mrs.	26	214	23	19	32	655,298
Mangurian, Jr., Harry, T.	50	377	23	57	54	504,955
Perez, Robert	33	203	23	22	23	480,267
Ostrager, Barry, R.	29	188	23	20	21	459,099
Sun Valley Farm	32	231	23	36	22	443,253
Brambly Lane Farm	21	143	23	26	15	401,358
Marty Hershe & Carol Hershe	18	159	23	26	23	371,847
George Waggoner Stables Inc.	17	136	23	25	13	359,669
McKee, Ronald, E.	15	104	23	15	16	334,887
Cashmark Farm	30	179	23	29	23	311,506
Bachman, Thomas, W.	26	165	23	27	18	307,788
Allred, Edward	20	118	23	14	14	299,127
White, Dan, W. Dr.	24	183	23	26	18	271,718
Smart, Bruce	11	92	23	14	6	212,047
Winchell, Verne, H.	30	200	22	33	26	794,625
Devonia Stud, Inc.	18	170	22	15	11	590,601
Sharp, Bayard	17	97	22	15	11	419,754
Grousemont Farm	17	108	22	17	13	392,736
R. C. Durr & George Budig	14	104	22	16	9	391,038
Paul R. and Mary Anne Denes	13	115	22	22	12	364,719
Prentice, Bryant, H. III	18	136	22	14	17	299,957
Glen Ridge Farm LLC	25	205	22	27	26	272,910

Breeder	Starters	Starts	1st	2d	3d	Purses
Ron Crockett Inc.	17	114	22	17	12	210,091
Willow Ridge Farms, Inc.	25	127	22	12	16	153,598
Gerald Schneider & Gail Schneider	15	86	22	12	10	145,423
Margaux Farm LLC	9	93	21	16	9	1,937,135
Gunther, John, D.	19	133	21	28	14	1,252,717
Vegso Racing Stable	14	105	21	15	12	940,627
Montanari, Marion, G.	22	164	21	21	25	727,997
Brunacini, George	24	146	21	14	16	685,824
Drazin, Dennis	25	157	21	15	26	573,416
Schoenborn, Gus Jr.	25	191	21	22	27	528,669
Seeger, Roberta	23	187	21	33	18	471,467
Hager,, David, E. II	16	117	21	15	15	465,862
Highclere Inc.	24	169	21	21	17	455,252
Oxley, John, C.	24	135	21	17	13	449,847
Casino Royale Farms Inc.	11	98	21	8	7	445,463
Shuford, Nancy, C.	37	248	21	31	30	430,735
Edmond A. Hudon & Sharon Hudon	19	145	21	16	23	430,399
Madera Thoroughbreds	27	165	21	27	27	415,501
Lotz, Nicholas, M	24	135	21	8	28	414,372
Regalbuto, Frank	16	117	21	14	16	413,765
West, R., Smiser Dr. & Mrs.	24	150	21	17	13	393,034
Ramsey, Linda, L.	14	125	21	20	22	381,466
Jesiak, Ralph	15	125	21	16	18	369,396
Granja Vista Del Rio	26	156	21	18	20	349,379
O H Wienges & Son	28	161	21	21	30	344,350
Our Farm Inc	44	352	21	34	39	309,771
Jeanne F Clagett & Hal C. B. Clagett	18	120	21	12	9	302,105
Richland Ranch & Sue Cook	28	166	21	22	25	277,708
Bourke, W., John	22	172	21	18	27	267,037
Kaaren Biggs & Hays Biggs	11	99	21	16	14	266,032
Classen, T., F. Dr.	19	161	21	27	21	263,819
Kitchen, C., Harold	15	119	21	13	18	261,641
Tod Mtn Thoroughbred	27	163	21	21	27	231,018
Diamond G Ranch, Inc.	27	173	21	27	16	211,330
Smith, R., K.	13	82	21	11	16	198,066
McKee Stables Inc	23	136	20	13	17	1,016,962
Byrne, Michael, C.	27	205	20	31	30	802,313
New Farm	22	89	20	8	14	784,760
Schettine, William, C.	26	162	20	24	13	719,997
Jerkens, Elisabeth, R.	23	182	20	22	21	602,272
Woodlynn Farm Inc	21	135	20	24	18	511,985
Jockey Club Farm	19	121	20	16	13	403,254
Hart Farm, Inc.	34	208	20	31	29	387,173
McFadden, Neal	40	277	20	29	27	382,089
McKathan Farms	23	175	20	20	19	380,257
Horses of Course Inc.	20	149	20	23	22	375,550
John A Nerud Revocable Trust	19	145	20	26	10	367,851
Silverleaf Farms, Inc.	17	94	20	13	4	365,713
Hidden Lane Farms Inc.	12	96	20	14	13	340,591
Cuprill, Charles, A. Mr. & Mrs.	24	238	20	27	34	337,637
Scott Dudley & Diane Dudley	13	111	20	16	23	336,198
Houghton, Ronald, B. Mrs.	15	130	20	10	17	334,676
Castle Rock Stud Inc	12	126	20	22	23	329,325
Campbell, D., Mike	19	130	20	14	16	312,282
Murray, E., Allen Mr. & Mrs. Jr.	14	123	20	16	15	300,308
Cardiff Farm Management Corp.	17	132	20	16	15	295,775
Berger, Robert, B.	13	119	20	17	11	292,290
O'Meara, John	15	130	20	25	22	290,295
Fares Farm Inc	28	166	20	14	16	270,627
Karutz, W., S. Dr.	19	130	20	13	14	264,378
Hillis, Larry, O.	23	165	20	29	23	195,488
Jerry D. Woods & Peggy F. Woods	27	134	20	17	21	194,911
Lockhart, Lloyd, W.	17	148	20	11	18	174,332
Hoover, John, C.	26	169	20	20	16	169,048

Breeder	Starters	Starts	1st	2d	3d	Purses
Moler, C., Bruce	25	184	20	26	26	132,374
Phipps Stable	16	81	19	12	17	1,849,454
North Wales LLC	23	151	19	19	20	550,072
Swettenham Stud	18	109	19	13	15	504,843
Sentinel Thoroughbred Farms	11	99	19	15	18	491,213
Canyon Farms	26	142	19	20	20	488,865
Twin Hopes Farm, Inc.	21	102	19	9	13	467,322
Sampson, Curtis, A.	16	99	19	9	10	463,558
Al Noren & Bunny Noren	30	163	19	21	28	375,107
Jones, Russell, B. Jr.	13	96	19	17	12	360,120
Dahlberg Farms LLC	12	107	19	12	15	346,710
Shewchuk, Johnnie, P.	24	163	19	18	22	326,286
Stautberg, G., J. Mr. & Mrs.	25	151	19	20	13	307,197
Haras El Palenque & Earl McNeil	21	187	19	11	32	291,926
Tackett, Paul	19	143	19	20	20	263,298
Qvale, Kjell, H.	14	122	19	29	22	249,832
K 5 Stables, Inc.	23	154	19	29	20	248,954
Weymouth, Eugene	14	112	19	16	14	246,788
Meeks, Mike	22	132	19	12	16	226,041
August Moon Farm	12	106	19	9	14	224,756
Paulson Bros Ranch	10	82	19	12	17	204,709
Parris, Mary, Anne	19	147	19	16	10	197,031
James, John	12	112	19	17	9	190,919
Center Hills Farm	26	132	19	19	13	158,688
Johnson, Marvin, A.	19	129	19	8	19	90,524
Beclawat Stable	20	131	18	18	14	1,569,669
Marylou Whitney Stables	16	112	18	14	18	1,480,547
Teague, Larry, R.	13	87	18	16	7	676,860
Jim Tafel, LLC	13	79	18	5	7	544,605
Buckingham Farm	11	83	18	8	9	496,593
Sugar Maple Farm	25	157	18	19	18	439,330
Spence, James, C.	11	102	18	13	12	428,571
Youngman, Patricia	21	100	18	10	12	413,159
Carey, John	26	181	18	16	25	397,720
Freed, Jane, M.	7	79	18	10	6	397,144
White Fox Farm	24	134	18	14	12	393,413
Devenport, Roger	17	105	18	12	14	373,432
Hubert Pilcher & Docia Pilcher	27	235	18	35	20	356,747
Virginia Tech Foundation Inc.	12	106	18	13	14	351,041
Payson Stud Inc	23	138	18	15	20	306,279
Morreale, Jake, V.	30	207	18	19	10	268,603
Croley, Thomas, L. Dr.	11	90	18	6	12	257,191
Fair Winds Farm	15	112	18	5	16	235,025
Farnsworth Farms & Gerald Robins	15	107	18	17	8	233,690
St. George's Farm	16	99	18	13	14	213,126
Miller, Maurice	10	98	18	17	13	211,452
Whiting, Ronald, J.	9	102	18	16	19	180,957
Littleton, B., L.	23	157	18	15	21	175,986

Snapshot Facts: There were 58 breeders whose horses won 50 races or more in 2004. There were 16 breeders whose horses won 100 races or more.

Annual Leading Breeder – Money Won

Year	Breeder	Sts.	1st	2d	3d	Purses
1923	John E. Madden		419	366	323	$623,630
1924	Harry Payne Whitney		272	201	235	482,865
1925	John E. Madden		383	374	376	535,790
1926	Harry Payne Whitney		351	322	308	715,790
1927	Harry Payne Whitney		271	306	234	718,144
1928	Harry Payne Whitney		234	291	269	514,832
1929	Harry Payne Whitney		278	284	234	825,374
1930	Harry Payne Whitney		294	295	281	698,280
1931	Harry Payne Whitney		264	241	244	582,970
1932	Harry Payne Whitney Estate		244	236	217	560,803
1933	Harry Payne Whitney & Cornelius V. Whitney		282	276	320	342,866
1934	Harry Payne Whitney & Cornelius V. Whitney		310	295	287	320,955
1935	Arthur B. Hancock		392	245	252	359,218
1936	Arthur B. Hancock		310	271	265	362,762
1937	Arthur B. Hancock		279	279	223	416,558
1938	Harry Payne Whitney & Cornelius V. Whitney		154	170	169	374,049
1939	Arthur B. Hancock		242	240	261	345,503
1940	Joseph E. Widener		184	161	153	317,961
1941	Calumet Farm (Warren Wright)		124	127	110	528,211
1942	Mrs. Payne Whitney (Greentree Stable)		175	161	163	536,173
1943	Arthur B. Hancock		346	330	315	619,049
1944	Calumet Farm (Warren Wright)		253	227	231	990,612
1945	E. E. Dale Shaffer (Coldstream Stud)		227	147	142	791,477
1946	Meresworth Farm		341	352	344	962,677
1947	Calumet Farm (Warren Wright)		266	207	168	1,807,432
1948	Calumet Farm (Warren Wright)		227	189	160	1,559,850
1949	Calumet Farm (Warren Wright)		270	206	209	1,515,181
1950	Calumet Farm (Warren Wright)		243	219	231	1,090,286
1951	Calumet Farm (Mrs. Gene Markey)		260	180	217	1,198,107
1952	Calumet Farm (Mrs. Gene Markey)		256	217	209	2,060,590
1953	Calumet Farm (Mrs. Gene Markey)		236	168	169	1,573,803
1954	Calumet Farm (Mrs. Gene Markey)		201	145	176	1,139,609
1955	Calumet Farm (Mrs. Gene Markey)		203	175	148	999,737
1956	Calumet Farm (Mrs. Gene Markey)		208	156	163	1,528,727
1957	Calumet Farm (Mrs. Gene Markey)		178	157	124	1,469,473
1958	Claiborne Farm (A. B. Hancock Sr. & A. B. Hancock Jr.		146	128	133	1,414,355
1959	Claiborne Farm (A. B. Hancock Jr.)		147	144	138	1,322,595
1960	Cornelius V. Whitney		108	106	92	1,193,181
1961	Calumet Farm (Mrs. Gene Markey)		156	120	144	1,078,894
1962	Rex C. Ellsworth		185	181	155	1,678,769
1963	Rex C. Ellsworth	1,468	194	166	150	1,465,069
1964	Bieber-Jacobs Stable (I. Bieber and H. Jacobs)	2,282	271	271	256	1,301,677
1965	Bieber-Jacobs Stable (I. Bieber and H. Jacobs)	2,233	259	278	269	1,994,649
1966	Bieber-Jacobs Stable (I. Bieber and H. Jacobs)	1,785	216	238	217	1,575,027
1967	Bieber-Jacobs Stable (I. Bieber and H. Jacobs)	1,702	183	182	219	1,515,414
1968	Claiborne Farm (A. B. Hancock Jr.)	797	147	116	95	1,493,189
1969	Claiborne Farm (A. B. Hancock Jr.)	728	111	96	98	1,331,485
1970	Harbor View Farm (L. Wolfson)	2,856	366	342	323	1,515,861
1971	Harbor View Farm (L. Wolfson)	3,160	394	348	358	1,739,214
1972	Leslie Combs II	1,693	240	191	203	1,578,851
1973	Elmendorf Farm Max Gluck)	1,604	220	173	175	2,128,080
1974	Edward P.Taylor	2,480	329	326	314	1,926,937
1975	Edward P.Taylor	2,604	344	366	310	2,369,145
1976	Edward P.Taylor	2,718	356	381	313	3,022,181
1977	Edward P.Taylor	2,968	409	417	401	3,414,169
1978	Edward P.Taylor	2,869	442	417	381	3,387,945
1979	Edward P.Taylor	2,671	353	356	360	3,001,108
1980	Edward P.Taylor	2,194	305	270	266	3,111,006
1981	Elmendorf Farm (Max Gluck)	1,179	149	137	145	2,736,029
1982	Elmendorf Farm (Max Gluck)	1,210	143	146	122	3,049,444
1983	Edward P.Taylor	1,813	227	247	206	3,472,128
1984	Claiborne Farm (A. B. Hancock Jr.)	514	87	82	55	5,554,012
1985	Edward P.Taylor	1,691	241	217	189	4,492,453
1986	N. B. Hunt (Bluegrass Farm)	2,481	281	274	284	5,013,667
1987	N. B. Hunt (Bluegrass Farm)	2,855	324	337	298	5,095,050
1988	O. Phipps	249	47	27	32	6,031,305
1989	O. Phipps	166	33	34	17	5,568,537
1990	Tartan Farms	1,081	170	145	113	6,930,043
1991	Sam-Son Farms	648	117	86	78	6,922,993
1992	Mr. & Mrs John C. Mabee	1,805	282	244	217	7,026,627
1993	John Franks	3,967	541	490	471	6,485,545
1994	Allen E. Paulson	1,526	236	187	167	5,776,308
1995	Allen E. Paulson	1,850	283	249	236	10,975,247
1996	Allen E. Paulson	1,986	295	267	230	9,757,559
1997	Allen E. Paulson	1,762	249	229	210	7,728,812
1998	Mr./Mrs. John C. Mabee	1,610	270	219	230	8,225,102
1999	Harry T. Mangurian Jr..	2,779	457	401	369	10,445,981
2000	Harry T. Mangurian Jr..	2,989	455	403	401	10,347,975
2001	Mockingbird Farm, Inc.	2,309	347	311	346	9,155,451
2002	Mockingbird Farm, Inc.	3,279	516	415	456	11,175,975
2003	Adena Springs	1,936	296	308	238	11,542,871
2004	Adena Springs	2,473	384	367	323	14,133,631

Starts tabulation began in 1963*

Annual Leading Breeder – Races Won

Year	Breeder	Races Won
1918	John E. Madden	213
1919	John E. Madden	311
1920	John E. Madden	313
1921	John E. Madden	424
1922	John E. Madden	366
1923	John E. Madden	419
1924	John E. Madden	318
1925	John E. Madden	383
1926	John E. Madden	368
1927	John E. Madden	362
1928	Himyar Stud	331
1929	Himyar Stud	335
1930	Audley Farm	318
1931	Audley Farm	359
1932	Himyar Stud	267
1933	Harry Payne Whitney & Cornelius V. Whitney	282
1934	Harry Payne Whitney & Cornelius V. Whitney	310
1935	Arthur B. Hancock	292
1936	Arthur B. Hancock	314
1937	Arthur B. Hancock	279
1938	Arthur B. Hancock	300
1939	Willis Sharp Kilmer	269
1940	Arthur B. Hancock	302
1941	Willis Sharp Kilmer	256
1942	Arthur B. Hancock	333
1943	Arthur B. Hancock	346
1944	Arthur B. Hancock	322
1945	Mereworth Farm	307
1946	Mereworth Farm	350
1947	Mereworth Farm	358
1948	Mereworth Farm	330
1949	Mereworth Farm	347
1950	Mereworth Farm	313
1951	Mereworth Farm	299
1952	Mereworth Farm	270
1953	Mereworth Farm	246
1954	Calumet Farm	201
1955	Henry H. Knight	223
1956	Henry H. Knight	293
1957	Henry H. Knight	284
1958	Henry H. Knight	260
1959	King Ranch	227
1960	Edward P. Taylor	267
1961	Edward P. Taylor	265
1962	Edward P. Taylor	263
1963	Edward P. Taylor	300
1964	Edward P. Taylor	305
1965	Edward P. Taylor	290
1966	Edward P. Taylor	310
1967	Edward P. Taylor	288
1968	Edward P. Taylor	280
1969	Edward P. Taylor	302
1970	Harbor View Farm	366
1971	Harbor View Farm	394
1972	Harbor View Farm	326
1973	Rex C. Ellsworth	365
1974	Rex C. Ellsworth	415
1975	Rex C. Ellsworth	402
1976	Rex C. Ellsworth	361
1977	Edward P. Taylor	409
1978	Edward P. Taylor	442
1979	Edward P. Taylor	353
1980	Edward P. Taylor	305
1981	Edward P. Taylor	242
1982	Edward P. Taylor	233
1983	Edward P. Taylor	227
1984	Edward P. Taylor	261
1985	Edward P. Taylor	241
1986	N. B. Hunt (Bluegrass Farm)	281
1987	N. B. Hunt (Bluegrass Farm)	324
1988	John Franks	414
1989	John Franks	486
1990	John Franks	451
1991	John Franks	491
1992	John Franks	584
1993	John Franks	541
1994	John Franks	432
1995	John Franks	399
1996	John Franks	360
1997	Farnsworth Farms	360
1998	Farnsworth Farms	369
1999	Harry T. Mangurian Jr.	457
2000	Harry T. Mangurian Jr.	455
2001	Farnsworth Farms	358
2002	Mockingbird Farm, Inc.	516
2003	Farnsworth Farms	475
2004	John Franks	531

Breeders of Winners of $1 Million or More in America

Horse	Sex	Born	Sts	1st	2d	3d	Earnings
Abolengo							
Empress Club (ARG)	M	1988	26	16	2	1	1,155,235
Adena Springs							
Ghostzapper	C	2000	10	8	0	1	2,996,120
Perfect Sting	M	1996	21	14	3	0	2,202,042
Macho Uno	H	1998	14	6	1	3	1,851,803
Red Bullet	H	1997	14	6	2	2	1,161,920
Agrovista Hermosa C.A.							
My Own Business (Ven)	H	1997	50	37	5	1	1,016,908
Airlie Stud							
Sangue (IRE)	M	1978	30	13	6	3	1,272,086
White Muzzle (GB)	H	1990	17	6	3	2	1,060,443
Mohammed al Maktoum							
Singspiel (IRE)	H	1992	20	9	8	0	5,952,825
Sheikh Mohammed bin Rashid al Maktoum							
Street Cry (IRE)	H	1998	12	5	6	1	5,150,837
Swain (IRE)	H	1992	22	10	4	6	3,797,566
In the Wings (GB)	H	1986	11	7	1	0	1,562,335
Sheikh Mohammed Obaid Al Maktoum							
High-Rise (IRE)	H	1995	13	5	2	2	1,871,726
Alexander & Aykroyd & Groves							
Althea	M	1981	15	8	4	0	1,275,255
Herbert Allen & Ray Stark							
Subordination	H	1994	21	11	3	1	1,221,068
J. Allen							
Slew City Slew	H	1984	42	11	10	6	1,166,296
High Brite	H	1984	45	15	7	9	1,150,519
Allez France Stables							
Steinlen (GB)	H	1983	45	20	10	7	3,297,169
Arcangues	H	1988	19	6	2	2	1,981,423
Volga (IRE)	M	1998	19	7	5	2	1,141,759
E.C. Allred & Crystal Springs Farm & Robert Moore							
Deputy Commander	H	1994	13	4	3	2	1,906,640
Simoes de Almeida Armenio							
Silic (FR)	H	1995	15	8	2	0	1,422,299
Happy Alter							
Pistols and Roses	H	1989	44	10	4	6	1,680,506
American Livestock Insurance Co & Foxfield							
Helmsman	H	1992	22	6	7	3	1,132,142
Amerigroup Leasing							
Dear Doctor (FR)	H	1987	32	8	7	4	1,742,671
Amherst Stable							
Volponi	H	1998	31	7	12	5	3,187,232
Angmering Park Stud							
Timboroa (GB)	H	1996	25	10	3	3	1,397,228
Anstu Stables Inc							
Balto Star	G	1998	38	12	7	3	2,363,780
Arthur I. Appleton							
Southern Image	C	2000	8	6	1	1	1,843,750
Forbidden Apple	H	1995	31	8	6	9	1,680,640
Jolie's Halo	H	1987	20	8	0	2	1,218,120
M. Arbib							
Strategic Choice	H	1991	33	5	5	5	1,126,735
A. Arculli							
River Verdon (IRE)	G	1987	26	16	4	2	1,574,735
Mr & Mrs Roy L. Ash							
Fruits of Love	H	1995	23	5	3	5	1,089,543
Ashford Stud							
Mystic Lady	M	1998	27	10	8	2	1,170,390

Horse	Sex	Born	Sts	1st	2d	3d	Earnings
Ashford Stud & Worswick							
Indian Skimmer	M	1984	16	10	1	3	1,469,299
R. & M. Aubert							
Volochine (IRE)	H	1991	45	8	12	9	1,205,580
Audley Farm Inc							
Mandy's Gold	M	1998	24	11	4	6	1,081,744
Peggy Augustus & Keswick Stables							
Simply Majestic	H	1984	44	18	4	7	1,667,713
Azienda Agricola Francesca							
Falbrav (IRE)	H	1998	26	13	5	5	5,825,517
John W. Backer							
Dispersal	H	1986	22	12	3	2	1,511,137
Sanford Bacon							
Say Florida Sandy	H	1994	98	33	17	12	2,085,408
Howard J. Baker							
Serena's Song	M	1992	38	18	11	3	3,283,388
Ballylinch Stud Ltd							
River Keen (IRE)	H	1992	42	11	5	5	1,642,385
Ballymacoll Stud Farm Ltd							
Pilsudski (IRE)	H	1992	22	10	6	2	4,080,297
Golan (IRE)	H	1998	11	4	2	1	1,623,376
Fastness (IRE)	H	1990	24	9	6	1	1,581,165
Islington (IRE)	M	1999	15	6	0	4	1,553,043
Mrs Thomas M. Bancroft							
Damascus	H	1964	32	21	7	3	1,176,781
Anna Marie Barnhart							
Skip Away	H	1993	38	18	10	6	9,616,360
Lucy G. Bassett							
Adoration	M	1999	20	8	3	1	2,051,160
Beall & French Jr							
Tejano	H	1985	21	5	6	3	1,428,177
Robert L. Beall							
Dave's Friend	H	1975	76	35	16	8	1,079,915
Beclawat Stable							
A Bit O'Gold	G	2001	11	7	3	0	1,290,819
Richard Bendit							
Ten Keys	H	1984	54	21	8	4	1,209,211
Jeanne F. Begg							
Victor Cooley	G	1993	39	13	12	3	1,320,475
Belair Stud							
Nashua	H	1952	30	22	4	1	1,288,565
Albert Bell & Joyce Bell							
Medaglia d'Oro	H	1999	17	8	7	0	5,754,720
Biddestone Stud							
Mutamam (GB)	H	1995	21	11	2	1	1,388,410
Ela Athena (GB)	M	1996	17	3	7	2	1,125,252
Bieber-Jacobs Stable							
Allez France	M	1970	21	13	3	1	1,262,801
David Block & Patricia Block							
Mystery Giver	G	1998	33	11	7	2	1,165,900
Blue Diamond Ranch							
Snow Chief	H	1983	24	13	3	5	3,383,210
Blue Seas Music Inc							
Soul of the Matter	H	1991	16	7	4	2	2,302,818
Afternoon Deelites	H	1992	12	7	3	0	1,061,193
Bluegrass Farm							
Dahar	H	1981	29	7	6	4	1,207,286
Rivlia	H	1982	41	9	2	8	1,005,041

Horse	Sex	Born	Sts	1st	2d	3d	Earnings
Peter E. Blum							
Devil His Due	H	1989	41	11	12	3	3,920,405
Richard M. Bonze							
Fourstardave	G	1985	100	21	18	16	1,636,737
Fourstars Allstar	H	1988	59	14	14	9	1,596,760
Bonnie Heath Farm							
Honor Glide	H	1994	38	11	5	2	1,397,187
Clydene Boots							
Richter Scale	H	1994	25	12	2	0	1,139,958
C. Bowling & C. Thompson							
Western Pride	H	1998	32	10	4	1	1,289,929
Peter M. Brant							
Gulch	H	1984	32	13	8	4	3,095,521
Thunder Gulch	H	1992	16	9	2	2	2,915,086
Track Barron	H	1981	21	12	3	1	1,353,674
Peter M. Brant & Haras Santa Maria de Araras							
Wallenda	H	1990	33	7	5	5	1,205,929
Brick Kiln Stud & Lariston Apartments Ltd							
Labeeb (GB)	H	1992	20	8	3	4	1,464,950
David Brillembourg							
Windsharp	M	1991	29	11	7	3	1,293,075
Bronson Stable							
Megan's Interco	G	1989	36	16	11	0	1,062,465
Brushwood Stable							
High Yield	H	1997	14	4	4	3	1,170,196
Frau N. Bscher							
Epalo (GER)	H	1999	21	8	8	2	1,419,259
Buckland Farm							
Sir Beaufort	H	1987	34	10	10	4	1,149,130
Martha H. Buckner							
Dixie Dot Com	H	1995	23	8	6	1	1,332,775
Calbourne Farm							
Brown Bess	M	1982	36	16	8	6	1,300,920
Mr & Mrs C.D. Callaway III							
Farma Way	H	1987	23	8	5	1	2,897,175
Calumet Farm							
Strike the Gold	H	1988	31	6	8	5	3,457,026
Agnes World	H	1995	20	8	6	1	3,365,680
Criminal Type	H	1985	24	10	5	3	2,351,274
Elmhurst	G	1990	51	8	11	6	1,100,567
Citation	H	1945	45	32	10	2	1,085,760
Alex G. Campbell Jr							
Mr Purple	H	1992	21	6	3	5	1,133,538
Gilbert G. Campbell							
Marlin	H	1993	26	9	3	5	2,448,880
Blazing Sword	G	1994	45	11	7	7	1,184,055
Carl & Olivia Cannata							
Gourmet Girl	M	1995	33	9	7	10	1,255,373
Car Colston Stud Hall							
Ticker Tape (GB)	F	2001	18	7	6	2	1,267,426
Cardiff Stud Farm							
Letthebighossroll	G	1988	60	18	14	6	1,014,377
Carelaine Farm							
Annoconnor	M	1984	29	12	7	5	1,002,420
Carelaine Farm & Vintage Meadow Farm							
Golden Pheasant	H	1986	22	7	4	3	2,453,958
Carondelet Farm & Vinery							
Artax	H	1995	25	7	9	3	1,685,840

Horse	Sex	Born	Sts	1st	2d	3d	Earnings
Carpinelli & Henwood Brothers							
Zoffany	H	1980	36	15	10	2	1,225,569
James S. Carrion							
Meadow Star	M	1988	20	11	1	2	1,445,740
Cutlass Reality	H	1982	66	14	12	9	1,405,660
Recoup the Cash	G	1990	74	23	6	3	1,098,920
Norman E. Casse & Harry Katz							
Isitingood	H	1991	24	11	3	4	1,219,430
Ben S. Castleman							
Seattle Slew	H	1974	17	14	2	0	1,208,726
Chadds Ford Stable							
Keeper Hill	M	1995	21	4	7	5	1,661,281
John A. Chandler							
Cetewayo	H	1994	37	11	5	4	1,170,258
Cherokee Farms Inc							
Smok'n Frolic	M	1999	33	9	8	2	1,534,720
Cheveley Park Stud Ltd							
Megahertz (GB)	M	1999	28	10	5	5	1,481,594
Soviet Line (IRE)	G	1990	48	16	8	6	1,450,130
K. Chong, G. Fong & W. Kwok							
Surfers Paradise (NZ)	G	1987	57	17	5	0	1,419,964
Christiana Stables							
Go for Wand	M	1987	13	10	2	0	1,373,338
Cisley Stable & R.P. Levy							
North Sider	M	1982	36	15	7	5	1,126,400
Citadel Stud							
Tobougg (IRE)	H	1998	12	3	2	2	1,079,901
Hal C.B. Clagett							
Little Bold John	G	1982	105	38	16	14	1,956,406
Claiborne Farm							
Slew o' Gold	H	1980	21	12	5	1	3,533,534
Forty Niner	H	1985	19	11	5	0	2,726,000
Round Table	H	1954	66	43	8	5	1,749,869
Swale	H	1981	14	9	2	2	1,583,660
Royal Glint	H	1970	52	21	9	4	1,004,816
Claiborne Farm & The Gamely Corp							
Lure	H	1989	25	14	8	0	2,515,289
A.G. & R.N. Clay & Hermitage Inc							
Gorgeous	M	1986	14	8	4	1	1,171,370
Albert G. Clay							
Albert the Great	H	1997	22	8	6	4	3,012,490
Catesby W. Clay & Runnymede Farm							
Tejano Run	H	1992	21	8	4	6	1,166,842
J.E. Clay							
It's the One	H	1978	28	9	7	9	1,038,444
Clear Creek & Highclere Inc							
Silverbulletday	M	1996	23	15	3	1	3,093,207
Violet Cleveland & Frank J. Zureick							
Urbane	M	1992	18	8	4	4	1,018,568
William L. Clifton Jr							
Rhythm Band	G	1996	18	5	2	2	1,349,066
Clovelly Farms							
Pleasantly Perfect	H	1998	18	9	3	2	7,789,880
Pay the Butler	H	1984	40	5	5	5	1,934,140
James B. Cody							
Polar Expedition	G	1991	49	20	5	7	1,491,071
E.M. Conjuango Jr							
Manila	H	1983	18	12	5	0	2,692,799

Horse	Sex	Born	Sts	1st	2d	3d	Earnings
J.D. Corcoran							
Happyanunoit (NZ)	M	1995	21	9	6	2	1,582,118
S. Coughlan							
High Chaparral (IRE)	H	1999	13	10	1	2	5,331,231
Ridgewood Pearl (GB)	M	1992	8	6	1	1	1,179,301
Courtney & Congleton							
Fit to Fight	H	1979	26	14	3	3	1,042,075
Mr & Mrs Robert E. Courtney							
Dollar Bill	H	1998	22	4	5	5	1,225,546
Marjorie Cowan & Irving Cowan							
Hollywood Wildcat	M	1990	21	12	3	3	1,432,160
War Chant	H	1997	7	5	1	0	1,130,600
Society Selection	F	2001	12	5	3	1	1,256,700
E.A. Cox Jr							
Ecton Park	H	1996	23	6	4	6	1,503,825
Edward I. Cox Jr							
Marquetry	H	1987	36	10	9	4	2,857,886
Joe Crowley and Mr And Mrs A. P. O'Brien							
Rock of Gibraltar (IRE)	H	1999	13	10	2	0	1,888,048
Cuadra T Y T Inc							
Luthier Fever	H	1991	25	6	5	6	1,160,852
Cypress Farms 1991							
Kela	H	1998	25	8	6	0	1,011,527
Cypress Farms 1991 & Vessels Stallion Farm LLC							
Excessivepleasure	G	2000	16	5	5	1	1,054,970
Constance DaParma & Flying M Acres							
Flying Pidgeon	H	1981	56	12	9	13	1,154,337
Bud Dardi							
Echo Eddie	G	1997	28	10	7	3	1,044,354
Darley Stud Management Co Ltd							
Annus Mirabilis (FR)	H	1992	30	9	7	6	1,541,938
Noverre	H	1998	21	5	7	4	1,429,344
State City	H	1999	17	6	0	3	1,375,993
Shantou	H	1993	14	6	2	4	1,132,399
State Shinto	H	1996	38	9	7	2	1,078,174
D.B. Davidson							
Beau Genius	H	1985	42	19	7	4	1,055,600
W.R. Davis							
Gate Dancer	H	1981	28	7	8	7	2,501,705
Dayton Ltd							
All Along (FR)	M	1979	21	9	4	2	2,125,828
Paul de Moussac							
Subotica (FR)	H	1988	15	6	4	1	1,856,255
Apple Tree (FR)	H	1989	26	7	4	5	1,388,260
Austin Delaney							
Irish Linnet	M	1988	62	19	16	10	1,220,180
Delta Thoroughbreds Inc							
Cardmania	G	1986	76	16	12	20	1,503,780
Julian DeMarco & Mr & Mrs Scott E. Ricker							
North East Bound	G	1996	50	12	7	3	1,363,228
Pamela duPont & S. Darmstadt							
Go for Gin	H	1991	19	5	7	2	1,380,866
Derry Meeting Farm							
Yankee Affair	H	1982	55	22	14	8	2,282,156
Charles H. Deters							
Down the Aisle	H	1993	21	9	5	5	1,007,988
Frank Digiulio & Frank Digiulio, Jr.							
Brass in Pocket	M	1999	24	14	3	2	1,146,023
Dinwiddie Farm							
King Cugat	H	1997	16	7	7	1	1,293,782
Disler Farms Ltd							
Singletary	C	2000	16	6	5	2	1,439,732
Donald R. Dizney							
Wekiva Springs	H	1991	21	10	4	2	1,512,575
DMD Properties & Samara Fm							
Forever Silver	H	1985	47	8	9	9	1,001,974
Double D Farm Corp.							
Harlan's Holiday	H	1999	22	9	6	1	3,632,664
Double J Farm							
Star of Cozzene	H	1988	38	14	8	5	2,308,923
Catherine Dubois							
Starine (FR)	M	1997	33	10	12	1	1,674,491
Due Process Stable							
Open Mind	M	1986	19	12	2	2	1,844,372
Tavner Dunlap Jr							
Mi Selecto	H	1985	40	9	7	9	1,475,762
Mrs Richard C. duPont							
Kelso	G	1957	63	39	12	2	1,977,896
Shine Again	M	1997	34	14	10	7	1,271,840
Richard E. Dutrow							
Lite the Fuse	H	1991	21	9	4	6	1,036,882
Echo Valley Horse Farm Inc							
Winning Colors	M	1985	19	8	3	1	1,526,837
James Egan & David Hanley							
Golden Apples (IRE)	M	1998	16	6	6	2	1,672,583
Elcee-H Stable & Breeding Farm Inc							
Island Whirl	H	1978	34	11	6	6	1,144,010
J. Elkins & W.S. Farish & W.T. Webber Jr							
Secret Status	M	1997	19	8	3	4	1,053,705
James Elkins & William S. Farish							
Tomisue's Delight	M	1994	20	7	5	4	1,207,537
Elmendorf Farm							
Flying Continental	H	1986	51	12	15	10	1,815,938
Honor Medal	H	1981	87	19	13	19	1,347,073
Alphabatim	H	1981	22	7	3	5	1,313,175
Top Corsage	M	1983	53	15	7	9	1,110,028
Super Moment	H	1977	47	10	8	5	1,017,940
Antespend	M	1993	24	10	4	2	1,011,954
Mrs C.W. Engelhard							
Exceller	H	1973	33	15	5	6	1,674,587
Robert W. Entenmann							
Victory Speech	H	1993	27	9	2	5	1,289,020
Equigroup Thoroughbreds							
Corporate Report	H	1988	10	3	5	0	1,067,908
Edward P. Evans							
Gold Mover	M	1998	31	13	9	5	1,523,010
Raging Fever	M	1998	26	11	7	3	1,458,198
Summer Colony	M	1998	24	10	5	1	1,448,930
Freefourinternet	H	1998	34	8	3	6	1,050,275
Robert S. Evans							
Sewickley	H	1985	32	11	9	4	1,017,517
Thomas M. Evans							
Pleasant Variety	H	1984	58	8	10	11	1,123,783
Pleasant Tap	H	1987	32	9	9	5	2,721,169
Colonial Waters	M	1985	32	6	12	3	1,112,847
Everest Stables Inc							
Island Fashion	F	2000	17	6	2	0	1,727,970

Horse	Sex	Born	Sts	1st	2d	3d	Earnings
Famille Niarchos							
Six Perfections (FR)	F	2000	14	6	6	1	1,811,179
Fares Farm Inc							
Da Hoss	G	1992	20	12	5	2	1,931,558
Janet (GB)	M	1997	27	8	4	6	1,027,237
William S. Farish & William S. Kilroy							
Lemon Drop Kid	H	1996	24	10	3	3	3,245,370
A.P. Indy	H	1989	11	8	0	1	2,979,815
Bien Bien	H	1989	26	9	8	1	2,331,875
Summer Squall	H	1987	20	13	4	0	1,844,282
Stephen Got Even	H	1996	11	5	1	1	1,019,200
William S Farish & Parrish Hill Farm							
Charismatic	H	1996	17	5	2	4	2,038,064
William S. Farish Jr							
Burning Roma	H	1998	36	13	5	7	1,500,200
W.S. Farish & E.J. Hudson							
Bet Twice	H	1984	26	10	6	4	3,308,599
W.S. Farish & G.W. Humphrey Jr							
Sacahuista	M	1984	21	6	7	2	1,298,842
W.S. Farish & O.M. Phipps							
Storm Song	M	1994	12	4	1	2	1,020,050
W.S. Farish, James Elkins & W.T. Webber Jr.							
Mineshaft	H	1999	18	10	3	1	2,283,402
Farnsworth Farm							
Beautiful Pleasure	M	1995	25	10	5	2	2,734,078
Mecke	H	1992	40	12	7	9	2,470,550
Jewel Princess	M	1992	29	13	4	7	1,904,060
Frisk Me Now	H	1994	36	12	5	6	1,727,707
Fawn Leap Farm Inc							
Editor's Note	H	1993	31	6	4	3	1,601,394
F. Feeney							
April Run (IRE)	M	1978	18	8	2	4	1,182,819
Finney & Taylor							
Peeping Tom	G	1997	49	14	7	9	1,398,547
C. Fipke							
Perfect Soul (IRE)	H	1998	21	7	5	1	1,527,764
Mr & Mrs Bertram R. Firestone							
Paradise Creek	H	1989	25	14	7	1	3,401,416
Theatrical (IRE)	H	1982	22	10	4	2	2,940,036
Chief Honcho	H	1987	34	10	6	3	1,265,719
Myrna Firestone & Mr & Mrs P. O'Dell							
The Very One	M	1975	71	22	12	9	1,104,623
Pamela H. Firman & G. Watts Humphrey							
Creme Fraiche	G	1982	64	17	12	13	4,024,727
Clear Mandate	M	1992	31	10	6	4	1,085,588
Mr & Mrs Weston L. Fitzpatrick							
Continental Red	G	1996	64	7	14	13	1,180,358
Flaxman Holdings Ltd							
Miesque	M	1984	16	12	3	1	2,070,163
Denon	H	1998	22	6	4	3	1,744,025
Aldebaran	H	1998	25	8	12	3	1,739,186
Spinning World	H	1993	14	8	3	1	1,734,477
Good Journey	H	1996	16	7	5	3	1,733,058
Floors Farming & Side Hill Stud							
Brave Act (GB)	H	1994	27	13	6	2	1,546,269
D.G. Foley							
Taylor's Special	H	1981	41	21	7	2	1,065,805
Forest Retreat Farms Inc & Miller							
Roo Art	H	1982	27	10	4	5	1,011,723
D.J. Foster							
Sunny's Halo	H	1980	20	9	3	2	1,247,791
Fountainebleau Farm Inc							
El Senor	H	1984	44	12	7	5	1,769,215
Ski Paradise	M	1990	20	6	8	1	1,470,588
Four Horsemen's Ranch Inc							
Val's Prince	G	1992	52	13	12	5	2,118,785
Fourth Estate Stables & Keswick Stable							
Sabin	M	1980	25	18	0	2	1,098,341
Ahmed M. Foustok							
In Excess (ire)	H	1987	25	11	2	3	1,736,733
Fox Ridge Farm Inc							
Riskaverse	M	1999	27	8	6	4	1,717,706
Francis A. Genter Stable							
Smile	H	1982	27	14	4	3	1,664,027
Tappiano	M	1984	34	17	2	4	1,305,522
Frankfurt Stables							
Temperate Sil	H	1984	19	6	2	1	1,113,775
John Franks							
Sharp Cat	M	1994	22	15	3	0	2,032,575
Royal Anthem	H	1995	12	6	3	1	1,876,876
Kissin Kris	H	1990	35	4	8	5	1,616,936
Halo America	M	1990	40	15	8	2	1,460,992
Littlebitlively	H	1994	33	10	9	5	1,303,343
Lady Tak	F	2000	18	10	4	1	1,155,682
Kiss a Native	G	1997	40	14	5	3	1,109,022
Silent Eskimo	M	1995	31	9	4	9	1,039,485
Daniel W. Frazier							
Anet	H	1994	19	8	5	0	1,189,873
Carl M. Freeman							
Miss Alleged	M	1987	15	5	4	3	1,757,342
Albert Fried Jr							
Affirmed Success	G	1994	42	17	10	6	2,285,315
Fulmer Farms							
Slew of Damascus	G	1988	48	16	9	8	1,420,350
Gainesway Thoroughbreds Ltd							
Orientate	H	1998	19	10	3	0	1,716,950
Gainsborough Farm Inc							
Fantastic Light	H	1996	25	12	5	3	8,486,957
Hatoof	M	1989	21	9	4	1	1,841,070
Irish Prize	G	1996	28	10	4	2	1,242,364
Gainsborough Stud Management Ltd							
Touch of the Blues (FR)	H	1997	35	8	6	5	1,655,358
Storming Home (GB)	H	1998	24	8	4	3	1,536,704
Sayyedati (GB)	M	1990	22	6	5	3	1,408,616
Galbreath & Phillips Racing Partnership							
Memories of Silver	M	1993	19	9	3	5	1,448,715
Soaring Softly	M	1995	16	9	1	3	1,270,433
John W. Galbreath							
Sunshine Forever	H	1985	23	8	6	3	2,084,800
Mrs John W. Galbreath							
Proud Truth	H	1982	21	10	4	0	2,198,895
Garrison & Hundley							
Fly So Free	H	1988	33	12	5	3	2,330,954
Tom Gentry							
Judge Angelucci	H	1983	22	10	4	2	1,582,535
George G Farm Inc							
Cryptoclearance	H	1984	44	12	10	7	3,376,327

Horse	Sex	Born	Sts	1st	2d	3d	Earnings
George Waggoner Stables Inc							
Yes It's True	H	1996	22	11	2	3	1,080,700
Gestut Ammerland							
Borgia (GER)	M	1994	22	6	7	2	1,697,771
Gestut Hof Ittlingen							
Lando (GER)	H	1990	24	10	3	1	3,438,727
Mrs W. Gilmour & Mrs W.M. Jason							
Spectacular Bid	H	1976	30	26	2	1	2,781,608
Josephine T. Gleis							
Fly Till Dawn	H	1986	27	10	5	4	1,556,525
Glen Hill Farm							
One Dreamer	M	1988	25	12	6	2	1,266,067
Glen Oak Farm							
Dancing Brave	H	1983	10	8	1	0	1,435,434
Randie L. Glosson							
Vivace	M	1993	40	20	4	6	1,037,671
Golden Chance Farm Inc							
John Henry	G	1975	83	39	15	9	6,591,860
Golden Orb Farm & K. David Schwartz							
Unbridled Elaine	M	1998	11	6	2	1	1,770,740
Glitter Woman	M	1994	23	10	9	3	1,256,805
Sir J. Goldsmith							
Montjeu (IRE)	H	1996	16	11	2	0	3,178,177
Janet Gomez							
Bet On Sunshine	G	1992	47	22	7	10	1,449,882
Grand Stud							
Preeminence (JPN)	M	1997	50	13	9	7	5,042,956
Thomas A. Graul							
Our New Recruit	H	1999	19	6	7	2	1,470,915
Frau R. Grunewald							
Kazzia (GER)	M	1999	7	5	0	0	1,094,206
Ron Guidolin, Sr., Ron Guidolin Jr., and Steven Guidolin							
Krz Ruckus	G	1997	39	15	8	4	1,040,036
H & Y Bloodstock							
Taiki Blizzard	H	1991	23	6	8	2	5,523,549
Kurofune Mystery	M	1990	21	6	5	4	1,009,342
Cleo & Vivian Hall							
Judy's Red Shoes	M	1983	83	25	13	12	1,085,668
Halo Farms							
King Glorious	H	1986	9	8	1	0	1,175,650
Arthur B. Hancock III							
Menifee	H	1996	11	5	4	1	1,732,000
Arthur B. Hancock III & Stonerside							
Fusaichi Pegasus	H	1997	9	6	2	0	1,994,400
Hancock III & Peters							
Risen Star	H	1985	11	8	2	1	2,029,845
Gato Del Sol	H	1979	39	7	9	7	1,340,107
Haras Abolenga							
Different (ARG)	M	1992	19	9	3	5	1,349,802
Haras Comalal							
Algenib (ARG)	H	1987	21	7	5	2	1,042,299
Haras de la Pomme							
Gentlemen (ARG)	H	1992	24	13	4	2	3,608,558
Haras de St. George Ltd							
Al Mamoon	H	1981	32	11	7	3	1,249,906
Haras D'Ecouves							
Jim and Tonic (FR)	G	1994	39	13	13	4	4,975,807
Haras Don Alberto							
Total Impact (CHI)	H	1998	22	5	8	2	1,586,778
Haras Don Yayo							
Festin (ARG)	H	1986	24	9	4	4	2,256,295
Haras El Tio							
Carnegie (IRE)	H	1991	13	7	1	1	1,458,787
Haras Figuron							
Lido Palace (CHI)	H	1997	23	11	7	2	2,705,865
Haras Fronteira PAP							
Pico Central (BRZ)	H	1999	15	9	0	3	1,183,145
Haras General Cruz							
Cougar II	H	1966	50	20	7	17	1,172,625
Haras Karen Sissy							
Trinycarol (VEN)	M	1979	29	18	3	1	2,644,392
Haras Mocito Guapo							
Malek (CHI)	H	1993	23	10	7	2	2,382,623
Haras Old Friends							
Hard Buck (BRZ)	H	1999	19	9	5	0	1,073,674
Haras Principal							
Bayakoa (ARG)	M	1984	39	21	9	0	2,861,701
Haras Rosa del Sur							
Leger Cat (ARG)	H	1986	53	16	5	7	1,211,402
Haras San Ignacio de Loyola							
Ibero (ARG)	H	1987	34	10	7	4	1,345,199
Lazy Lode (ARG)	H	1994	29	8	4	6	1,296,740
Haras Santa Ana do Rio Grande							
Redattore (BRZ)	H	1995	32	15	2	6	1,799,883
Riboletta (BRZ)	M	1995	28	13	3	3	1,555,103
Haras Santa Maria de Araras							
Troyanos (BRZ)	H	1985	13	10	1	1	1,038,083
Haras Santa Olga							
Puerto Madero (CHI)	H	1994	24	11	3	2	1,361,626
Haras Sao Jose da Serra							
Sandpit (BRZ)	H	1989	40	14	11	6	3,812,597
Haras Sao Jose E Expedictus							
Siphon (BRZ)	H	1991	25	12	6	2	3,136,428
Haras Vacacion							
Paseana (ARG)	M	1987	36	19	10	2	3,317,427
Odalea (ARG)	M	1986	21	8	7	2	1,674,812
Harbor View Farm							
Flawlessly	M	1988	28	16	4	3	2,572,536
Affirmed	H	1975	29	22	5	1	2,393,818
Outstandingly	M	1982	28	10	4	3	1,412,206
Zoman	H	1987	24	7	5	3	1,040,372
Mort Hardy							
Mysterious Affair	M	1997	37	12	9	6	1,059,971
Harper & Irish Hill Farm							
Spend a Buck	H	1982	15	10	3	2	4,220,689
W.R. Hawn							
Real Connection	M	1991	72	7	14	7	1,225,018
Mr & Mrs D. Hayden							
Safely Kept	M	1986	31	24	2	3	2,194,206
Highclere Inc & Louie Roussel III							
Star Standard	H	1992	25	7	4	3	1,121,512
Highclere Stud Ltd							
Sheikh Albadou (GB)	H	1988	15	6	4	1	1,229,702
Highview Stud Bloodstock Partnership No 3							
Let's Elope (NZ)	M	1987	26	11	0	5	2,528,902
Hill 'N' Dale Farm							
Hawk Wing	H	1999	12	5	5	0	1,610,604
One for Rose	M	1999	22	12	4	2	1,047,243

Horse	Sex	Born	Sts	1st	2d	3d	Earnings
Hill 'n Dale Farm & Holtsinger Inc & Star Stable							
Touch Gold	H	1994	15	6	3	1	1,679,907
His Highness The Aga Khan's Studs S.C.							
Daliapour (IRE)	H	1996	26	7	3	3	2,123,763
Lashkari (GB)	H	1981	13	5	2	2	1,127,658
Daylami (IRE)	H	1994	21	11	3	4	4,614,762
Kalanisi (IRE)	H	1996	11	6	4	1	2,148,836
Manndar (IRE)	H	1996	20	4	6	3	1,128,835
Timarida (IRE)	M	1992	16	10	2	2	1,116,186
Hobeau Farm Ltd							
Kelly Kip	H	1994	31	15	3	4	1,157,142
Georgia E. Hofmann							
Heritage of Gold	M	1995	28	16	2	4	2,381,762
Louis Quatorze	H	1993	18	7	5	1	2,054,434
Holly Ridge Farms Inc							
Exbourne	H	1986	14	8	5	1	1,000,198
Fred W. Hooper							
Precisionist	H	1981	46	20	10	4	3,485,398
Diplomatic Jet	H	1992	51	9	5	9	1,267,202
Susan's Girl	M	1969	63	29	14	11	1,251,668
Al J. Horton							
Silver Goblin	G	1991	26	16	4	3	1,083,895
G. Watts Humphrey Jr & Joe Pierce Jr							
Morluc	H	1996	40	11	9	5	1,045,758
G. Watts Humphrey Jr. & W. S. Farish							
Misil	H	1988	36	14	8	3	1,296,417
G. Humphrey Jr., J. Pierce Jr., A. Gilman & K. Koontz							
Gaily Magnum	G	1993	24	8	2	2	1,218,578
Cyril Humphris							
Halling	H	1991	18	12	1	0	1,332,651
Nelson B. Hunt							
Estrapade	M	1980	30	12	5	5	1,937,142
Lively One	H	1985	36	9	7	5	1,544,100
Dahlia	M	1970	48	15	3	7	1,489,105
N.B. Hunt & E. Stephenson							
Triptych	M	1982	41	14	5	11	2,318,946
Valerie Hunter							
Defensive Play	H	1987	26	6	4	5	1,688,631
International Thoroughbred Breeders Inc							
On the Line	H	1984	37	14	7	2	1,125,810
Irish Acres Farm							
Buck's Boy	G	1993	30	16	5	2	2,750,148
Iron County Farms Inc							
Nuclear Debate	G	1995	52	11	8	10	1,234,054
Bare Necessities	M	1999	26	8	4	7	1,062,251
Jack Syndicate							
Spook Express (SAF)	M	1994	22	11	2	3	1,016,744
Jamm Ltd							
Strut the Stage	H	1998	23	10	2	3	1,496,986
Mr & Mrs S.S. Janney Jr							
Private Terms	H	1985	17	12	0	0	1,243,947
Stuart S. Janney III							
Coronado's Quest	H	1995	17	10	2	0	2,046,190
Janus Bloodstock Inc							
Riviera (FR)	H	1994	21	10	4	3	1,018,535
Walter M. Jeffords Jr							
Lonesome Glory	G	1988	44	24	5	6	1,325,868
John R. Gaines Thoroughbreds LLC & De De McGehee							
Imperial Gesture	M	1999	11	6	2	1	1,419,140

Horse	Sex	Born	Sts	1st	2d	3d	Earnings
Jonabell Farm Inc et al							
Essence of Dubai	H	1999	13	5	1	2	2,001,058
Aaron U. Jones							
Lemhi Gold	H	1978	22	8	3	1	1,131,355
Aaron U. Jones and Marie Jones							
Speightstown	H	1998	16	10	2	2	1,258,256
Ashado	F	2001	14	9	3	2	2,870,440
Brereton C. Jones							
Southjet	H	1983	30	5	7	2	1,040,483
Brereton C. Jones & Warnerton Farm							
Desert Wine	H	1980	25	8	8	3	1,618,043
John T.L. Jones, Jr. & H. Smoot Fahlgren							
Cajun Beat	G	2000	17	7	3	0	1,159,100
Juddmonte Farms							
Sightseek	M	1999	20	12	5	0	2,445,216
Skimming	H	1996	20	8	5	1	2,286,601
Polish Summer (GB)	H	1997	27	6	10	0	2,277,871
Empire Maker	C	2000	8	4	3	1	1,985,800
Aptitude	H	1997	15	5	4	2	1,965,410
Chester House	H	1995	21	6	4	4	1,944,545
Tinners Way	H	1990	27	7	6	4	1,846,546
Banks Hill (GB)	M	1998	15	5	5	3	1,824,008
Beat Hollow (GB)	H	1997	12	7	2	2	1,814,481
Quest for Fame (GB)	H	1987	19	5	4	4	1,790,417
Running Stag	H	1994	40	7	11	2	1,663,227
Tates Creek	M	1998	17	11	3	0	1,471,674
Ryafan	M	1994	10	7	1	0	1,342,142
Savinio	G	1990	48	11	11	8	1,321,860
Raintrap (GB)	H	1990	28	9	4	2	1,283,707
Wandesta (GB)	M	1991	21	7	3	5	1,255,145
Brian Boru (GB)	C	2000	18	4	4	3	1,209,054
Powerscourt (GB)	C	2000	17	4	5	3	1,200,917
Dushyantor	H	1993	20	5	5	2	1,197,570
Heat Haze (GB)	M	1999	14	7	2	2	1,183,696
Public Purse	H	1994	14	7	1	4	1,103,324
Flute	M	1998	8	4	3	0	1,101,504
Urgent Request (IRE)	H	1990	25	7	4	1	1,035,339
Richard S. Kaster							
Countess Diana	M	1995	14	7	2	0	1,117,185
KCV Stable							
Lottsa Talc	M	1990	65	21	10	12	1,206,248
Mrs Joan Keaney							
Yavana's Pace (IRE)	G	1992	74	16	14	11	1,199,409
H.B. Keck							
Ferdinand	H	1983	29	8	9	6	3,777,978
Mr & Mrs Rodes Kelly							
Formal Gold	H	1993	16	8	4	1	1,533,600
Thomas J. Kelly & Joseph M. Grant							
Evening Attire	G	1998	39	11	12	3	2,373,010
Ken-Mort Stables							
Maxzene	M	1993	23	11	5	0	1,175,259
Kennelot Stables Ltd							
Stephan's Odyssey	H	1982	16	6	4	1	1,255,328
Danzig Connection	H	1983	17	6	5	4	1,002,620
Mrs D.K. Kerr							
King's Swan	H	1980	107	31	19	18	1,924,845
Keswick Stables							
Alwuhush	H	1985	22	5	4	7	1,012,423

Horse	Sex	Born	Sts	1st	2d	3d	Earnings
Miss Christine Kiernan							
Phoenix Reach (IRE)	C	2000	10	4	1	1	2,075,669
Kilcarn Stud							
Snurge (IRE)	H	1987	30	7	10	5	1,674,441
J. Howard King							
Very Subtle	M	1984	29	12	6	4	1,608,360
Kinghaven Farms Ltd							
With Approval	H	1986	23	13	5	1	2,863,540
Izvestia	H	1987	21	11	2	2	2,702,527
Exchange	M	1988	30	15	7	4	1,287,795
Carotene	M	1983	41	12	8	5	1,287,232
Present Value	H	1984	42	15	5	3	1,153,853
Steady Power	G	1984	70	13	19	9	1,132,197
Kinghaven Farms Ltd & D. Granite							
Cozzene's Prince	G	1987	68	16	10	10	1,270,057
Kinsman Farm							
Dream Supreme	M	1997	16	9	2	2	1,007,680
Kinsman Stud Farm							
Concerto	H	1994	21	10	4	2	1,308,118
Mr & Mrs William Kirkland							
Ancient Title	H	1970	57	24	11	9	1,252,791
Edgar Kitchen							
Track Robbery	M	1976	59	22	12	7	1,098,537
Knob Hill Stables							
Thornfield	G	1994	19	6	1	3	1,206,074
Benburb	G	1989	22	7	2	4	1,159,949
Mr & Mrs R. Koerber							
Sunny Sunrise	G	1987	63	18	12	9	1,367,268
Jean-Luc Lagardere							
Val Royal (FR)	H	1996	12	7	2	0	1,186,687
Rene & Margie Lambert							
Sky Jack	G	1996	18	10	2	2	1,115,127
Landon & Mary A. Sullivan							
Kiri's Clown	H	1989	62	16	6	8	1,005,469
Roger Laubach							
Captain Steve	H	1997	25	9	3	7	6,828,356
Mel Lawson							
Ginger Gold	M	1999	25	7	6	2	1,065,448
Lazy E. Ranch Inc							
Voodoo Dancer	M	1998	21	11	4	2	1,427,052
Lazy F Ranch							
Forego	G	1970	57	34	9	7	1,938,957
Lazy Lane Stables Inc							
Seeking the Pearl	M	1994	21	8	2	3	4,021,716
Gerald W. Leigh							
Barathea (IRE)	H	1990	16	5	4	0	1,189,181
Blanche P. Levy & Murphy Stable							
Housebuster	H	1987	22	15	3	1	1,229,696
Henry C.B. Lindh							
Grecian Flight	M	1984	40	21	6	3	1,320,215
Lin-Drake Farm							
Grand Canyon	H	1987	8	4	3	0	1,019,540
Lin-Drake Farm & Pierce & Pierce Inc							
Friendly Lover	H	1988	66	22	13	12	1,247,670
Little Hill Farm							
Real Quiet	H	1995	20	6	5	6	3,271,802
Marvin Little Jr							
Hansel	H	1988	14	7	2	3	2,936,586

Horse	Sex	Born	Sts	1st	2d	3d	Earnings
W.P. Little							
Wild Again	H	1980	28	8	7	4	2,204,829
Lawrence I Littmann							
Lil E. Tee	H	1989	13	7	4	1	1,437,506
Live Oak Stud							
Sultry Song	H	1988	23	9	3	5	1,616,276
Solar Splendor	G	1987	42	11	3	6	1,386,468
Loblolly Stable							
Pine Bluff	H	1989	13	6	1	3	2,255,884
Prairie Bayou	G	1990	12	7	3	0	1,450,621
Vanlandingham	H	1981	19	10	3	3	1,409,476
De Roche	G	1986	28	5	8	7	1,078,200
Loblolly Stable & A. Hochner Jr							
Lost Mountain	H	1988	36	5	6	8	1,004,939
Mrs E. Longton							
Saumarez (GB)	H	1987	9	5	1	0	1,275,719
Lord Porchester							
Ibn Bey (GB)	H	1984	28	10	3	4	1,626,059
Lowquest Ltd							
Timber Country	H	1992	12	5	1	4	1,560,400
Bruce W. Lunsford							
Golden Missile	H	1995	25	7	7	4	2,194,510
Vision and Verse	H	1996	21	4	3	5	1,030,330
Lyonstown Stud							
Dr Devious (IRE)	H	1989	15	6	4	0	1,484,230
W.G. Lyster III							
Lu Ravi	M	1995	26	11	8	3	1,819,781
W.G. Lyster III & Jayeff 'B' Stables							
Johannesburg	H	1999	10	7	1	0	1,014,585
Mr & Mrs John C. Mabee							
Best Pal	G	1988	47	18	11	4	5,668,245
General Challenge	G	1996	21	9	3	1	2,877,178
Dramatic Gold	G	1991	39	9	13	6	2,567,630
Nostalgia's Star	H	1982	59	9	17	13	2,154,827
Excellent Meeting	M	1996	20	8	5	3	1,402,396
Early Pioneer	G	1995	33	9	9	5	1,156,815
Full Moon Madness	G	1995	46	15	11	12	1,097,805
Event of the Year	H	1995	9	5	2	1	1,095,200
Captain J. Macdonald-Buchanan							
In the Groove (GB)	M	1987	21	7	4	4	1,336,783
Frank E. Mackle Jr							
Waquoit	H	1983	30	19	4	3	2,225,360
Angus M. MacLean							
Twice the Vice	M	1991	23	12	6	1	1,447,064
Preston Madden							
Alysheba	H	1984	26	11	8	2	6,679,242
Mamakos & Stubbin							
Fali Time	H	1981	15	5	4	2	1,033,179
Mandysland Farm							
Unbridled's Song	H	1993	12	5	4	0	1,311,800
Harry T. Mangurian Jr							
Swept Overboard	H	1997	20	8	5	3	1,137,767
Mareinvest-83 Ltd							
Lost Code	H	1984	27	15	5	2	2,085,396
Margaux Farm LLC							
Roses in May	C	2000	11	7	3	0	1,795,187
J.D. Marsh							
Majesty's Prince	H	1979	43	12	10	10	2,077,796

Horse	Sex	Born	Sts	1st	2d	3d	Earnings
Marylou Whitney Stables							
Birdstone	C	2001	9	5	0	0	1,575,600
Marystead Farm							
Urban Sea	M	1989	23	8	4	3	1,704,553
Talloires	H	1990	28	5	8	3	1,423,949
Robert E. Masterson							
Pleasant Breeze	G	1995	36	10	8	6	1,271,680
Maylands Stud Farm							
Trempolino	H	1984	11	4	3	3	1,369,233
Dernier Empereur	H	1990	30	8	5	4	1,152,425
Richard D. Maynard							
Chief Bearhart	H	1993	26	12	5	3	3,381,557
McKee Stables Inc							
Champali	C	2000	22	11	2	4	1,073,794
P. McLean Sr, P. McLean Jr., M. McLean & P. Feringa Jr							
Xtra Heat	M	1998	35	26	5	2	2,389,635
Don McNeill							
Clever Trevor	G	1986	30	15	5	2	1,388,841
Mr Ross	G	1995	44	18	6	10	1,091,046
Meadow Stud Inc							
Secretariat	H	1970	21	16	3	1	1,316,808
Riva Ridge	H	1969	30	17	3	1	1,111,497
Meadowbrook Farm Inc							
Prized	H	1986	17	9	2	3	2,262,555
Ladies Din	G	1995	37	12	6	6	1,966,754
Brocco	H	1991	8	4	2	0	1,003,550
Paul Mellon							
Sea Hero	H	1990	24	6	3	4	2,929,869
Java Gold	H	1984	15	9	3	1	1,908,832
Fort Marcy	G	1964	75	21	18	14	1,109,791
Meon Valley Stud							
Opera House (GB)	H	1988	18	8	4	3	1,397,456
Robert E. Meyerhoff							
Concern	H	1991	30	7	7	11	3,079,350
Broad Brush	H	1983	27	14	5	5	2,656,793
Include	H	1997	20	10	1	4	1,659,560
Valley Crossing	H	1988	48	8	13	8	1,616,490
Lee Miller							
Heatherten	M	1979	53	21	7	4	1,022,699
Mr & Mrs M. Miller & Mr & Mrs R.S. West							
Lite Light	M	1988	26	8	4	4	1,231,596
Mimika Financicia & Warren Hill Stud							
Pebbles (GB)	M	1981	15	8	4	0	1,419,632
Aubrey W. Minshall							
Mt. Sassafras	G	1992	47	8	7	14	1,382,985
Kiridashi	H	1992	44	14	9	8	1,201,981
Bold Ruritana	M	1990	44	14	10	6	1,140,163
Moira & W.S. Tanaka							
Silveyville	H	1978	56	19	11	8	1,282,880
T. J. Monaghan							
Ezzoud (IRE)	H	1989	22	6	5	2	1,171,885
Moor M.P.J.							
Ipi Tombe (ZIM)	M	1998	14	12	2	0	1,529,799
Nancy Penn Morgan							
Skip Trial	H	1982	38	16	7	2	1,837,451
Dolphus C. Morrison							
You	M	1999	23	9	8	2	2,101,353
Mr & Mrs J.S. Moss							
Kudos	G	1997	24	7	5	4	1,238,935
Moyglare Stud Farm Ltd							
Twilight Agenda	H	1986	32	13	5	4	2,174,529
Refuse To Bend (IRE)	C	2000	15	7	0	1	1,350,034
Thomas C. Mueller							
Chorwon	G	1993	44	13	7	8	1,161,795
Muirfield Ventures							
Dimitrova	F	2000	14	4	2	1	1,142,696
Murifield Ventures & Jayeff B Stables							
Mutafaweq	H	1996	19	7	1	3	1,800,800
William F. Murphy							
Silver Ending	H	1987	37	8	1	9	1,073,420
David Nagle							
Petite Ile (IRE)	M	1986	14	6	3	4	1,281,665
Ed Nahem							
Bertrando	H	1989	24	9	6	2	3,185,610
Marshall Naify							
Manistique	M	1995	15	11	1	1	1,311,800
Valerie Naify							
Kicken Kris	C	2000	19	6	3	3	1,326,600
Audrey Narducci							
Squirtle Squirt	H	1998	16	8	4	0	1,112,220
J.A. Nerud							
Clabber Girl	M	1983	39	8	12	6	1,006,261
Newchance Farm							
Peace Rules	C	2000	19	9	2	2	3,084,278
Newgate Stud Co							
Moon Ballad (IRE)	H	1999	14	5	3	1	4,364,791
Newhaven Park Stud Ltd							
Prowl (AUS)	G	1995	22	5	2	2	1,082,344
Newstead Farm							
Miss Oceana	M	1981	19	11	6	1	1,010,385
The Niarchos Family							
Sulamani (IRE)	H	1999	17	9	3	1	5,252,368
S. Niarchos							
Hernando (FR)	H	1990	20	7	4	1	2,081,978
Greinton (GB)	H	1981	22	10	8	0	1,943,605
Dream Well (FR)	H	1995	14	4	4	4	1,439,441
Gerard A. Nielsen							
Capades	M	1986	27	11	9	2	1,051,006
Joanne H. Nor							
Behrens	H	1994	27	9	8	3	4,563,500
North Central Bloodstock							
Tranquility Lake	M	1995	27	11	7	3	1,662,390
North Ridge Farm							
Ruhlmann	H	1985	27	10	3	4	1,824,154
Blushing John	H	1985	19	9	1	2	1,548,081
North Wales LLC							
Elloluv	F	2000	16	5	3	2	1,297,075
Charles Nuckols Jr & Sons							
War Emblem	H	1999	13	7	0	0	3,491,000
Nuckols Brothers							
Fighting Fit	H	1979	49	14	7	8	1,004,174
Oak Cliff Thoroughbreds Ltd							
Sunday Silence	H	1986	14	9	5	0	4,968,554
Skywalker	H	1982	20	8	3	3	2,226,750
Ocala Stud Farms Inc							
Shake You Down	G	1998	42	17	6	4	1,277,164
Bolshoi Boy	G	1983	58	16	7	8	1,039,702
Queen Alexandra	M	1982	46	19	8	5	1,034,144

Horse	Sex	Born	Sts	1st	2d	3d	Earnings
Gay O'Callaghan							
Earl of Barking (IRE)	H	1990	37	9	3	10	1,230,519
George L. Onett							
Cherokee Run	H	1990	28	13	5	5	1,531,818
Orpendale							
Ballingarry (IRE)	H	1999	23	6	1	6	1,741,049
Orpendale & John R. Gaines Thoroughbreds							
Caller One	G	1997	21	10	3	3	3,190,000
Orpendale & Michael Tabor							
Giant's Causeway	H	1997	13	9	4	0	3,078,989
C. Ostermann-Richter							
Paolini (GER)	H	1997	28	5	6	4	3,253,469
Overbrook Farm							
Cat Thief	H	1996	30	4	9	8	3,951,012
Boston Harbor	H	1994	8	6	1	0	1,934,605
Surfside	M	1997	15	8	3	2	1,852,987
Mountain Cat	H	1990	11	6	2	0	1,478,901
Grindstone	H	1993	6	3	2	0	1,224,510
Honour and Glory	H	1993	17	6	5	2	1,202,942
Overbrook Farm & David Reynolds							
Tabasco Cat	H	1991	18	8	3	2	2,347,671
The Overbury Stud							
Caitano (GB)	H	1994	44	9	6	7	2,137,459
Ovidstown Bloodstock Ltd							
Kooyonga (IRE)	M	1988	18	9	4	1	1,476,193
OWD Inc.							
A Fleets Dancer	H	1995	45	12	6	8	1,036,649
Bea Oxenberg							
Best of the Rest	H	1995	32	16	8	2	1,407,796
J. Pantos							
Strawberry Road (AUS)	H	1979	50	21	7	9	1,655,678
Mr & Mrs Parrish & D.C. Parrish III							
Life's Magic	M	1981	32	8	11	6	2,255,218
Allen E. Paulson							
Cigar	H	1990	33	19	4	5	9,999,815
Azeri	M	1998	24	17	4	0	4,079,820
Escena	M	1993	29	11	9	3	2,962,639
Fraise	H	1988	34	10	5	6	2,613,105
Geri	H	1992	19	9	4	3	1,707,980
Yagli	H	1993	27	10	6	3	1,702,121
Astra	M	1996	16	11	1	2	1,378,424
Hap	H	1996	20	10	2	2	1,329,210
Ajina	M	1994	17	7	3	2	1,327,915
Eliza	M	1990	12	5	2	2	1,095,316
Payson Stud Inc							
Farda Amiga	M	1999	8	4	1	0	1,282,302
Virginia Kraft Payson							
L'Carriere	G	1991	23	8	4	3	1,726,175
Salem Drive	H	1982	46	13	7	10	1,046,065
John H. Peace							
West by West	H	1989	30	10	3	7	1,038,123
Pedigree Farms Inc							
License Fee	M	1995	43	16	7	6	1,200,416
Pelican Stable							
Holy Bull	H	1991	16	13	0	0	2,481,760
Oscar T. Penn Jr							
Mercedes Won	H	1986	52	12	7	12	1,087,435
Carlos Perez							
Kona Gold	G	1994	30	14	7	2	2,293,384

Horse	Sex	Born	Sts	1st	2d	3d	Earnings
Stephen D. Peskoff							
Black Tie Affair (IRE)	H	1986	45	18	9	6	3,370,694
Petra Bloodstock Agency Ltd							
Falcon Flight (FR)	H	1996	20	5	2	3	1,428,849
Mr & Mrs J.W. Phillips							
Brian's Time	H	1985	21	5	2	6	1,001,269
Phillips Racing Partnership & John Phillips							
Wonder Again	M	1999	19	7	2	3	1,111,682
Cynthia Phipps							
Versailles Treaty	M	1988	20	9	9	2	1,271,154
Mrs O. Phipps							
My Big Boy	G	1983	50	10	12	10	1,196,102
Ogden Phipps							
Easy Goer	H	1986	20	14	5	1	4,873,770
Seeking the Gold	H	1985	15	8	6	0	2,307,000
Heavenly Prize	M	1991	18	9	6	3	1,825,940
Personal Ensign	M	1984	13	13	0	0	1,679,880
Dancing Spree	H	1985	35	10	6	9	1,470,484
Buckpasser	H	1963	31	25	4	1	1,462,014
Personal Flag	H	1983	24	8	4	4	1,258,924
Polish Navy	H	1984	12	7	1	3	1,118,076
Ogden Mills Phipps							
Inside Information	M	1991	17	14	1	2	1,641,806
Rhythm	H	1987	20	6	3	4	1,592,532
My Flag	M	1993	20	6	3	4	1,557,057
Educated Risk	M	1990	23	11	6	4	1,163,717
Dispute	M	1990	19	9	4	4	1,106,907
Phipps Stable							
Storm Flag Flying	F	2000	14	7	3	3	1,951,828
Pin Oak Stud Inc							
Peaks and Valleys	H	1992	16	9	3	2	1,589,270
Ward C. Pitfield							
Wild Rush	H	1994	16	8	0	3	1,386,302
Jim H. Plemmons							
Precocity	H	1994	33	9	7	5	1,835,798
Ten Most Wanted	C	2000	13	5	3	1	1,718,460
Michael Poland							
King's Theatre (IRE)	H	1991	19	5	3	4	1,154,329
A.F. Polk Jr							
Temperence Hill	H	1977	31	11	4	2	1,567,650
Ronald Popely							
Hever Golf Rose (GB)	M	1991	66	17	11	10	1,020,328
William Powell & Bates Newton							
Drum Taps	H	1986	31	15	5	2	1,140,788
Prestonwood Farm Inc							
Jostle	M	1997	20	8	5	2	1,389,932
J.A. Price							
Carry Back	H	1958	62	21	11	11	1,241,165
Kenneth L. Ramsey & Sarah K. Ramsey							
Kitten's Joy	C	2001	12	8	3	0	1,705,911
W. Kenan Rand Jr							
Candid Glen	G	1997	40	11	10	6	1,239,330
Rathbarry Stud							
Alpride (IRE)	M	1991	26	11	4	4	1,048,270
Raven Brook Farm Inc							
Not Surprising	G	1990	61	23	4	5	1,112,301
H.E. Reed							
Men's Exclusive	G	1993	48	11	16	4	1,451,126

Horse	Sex	Born	Sts	1st	2d	3d	Earnings
Dr. William A. Reed & Stonecrest Farm							
Perfect Drift	G	1999	27	9	8	3	3,168,963
William O. Reed							
Goodbye Halo	M	1985	24	11	5	4	1,706,702
Bonapaw	G	1996	48	18	7	4	1,158,752
P. Ribes							
Fieldy (IRE)	M	1983	54	19	9	8	1,212,168
The Richter Family Trust							
Bien Nicole	M	1998	26	12	8	2	1,074,620
B.J. Ridder							
Flying Paster	H	1976	27	13	7	2	1,127,460
Ridgeley Farm							
Grey Memo	H	1997	54	8	4	10	1,736,683
B. & T. Roach							
Princess Rooney	M	1980	21	17	2	1	1,343,339
Robert H. Roberts & Bea Roberts							
Request for Parole	H	1999	34	9	7	3	1,205,892
Corbin J. Robertson							
Turkoman	H	1982	22	8	8	3	2,146,924
G. Robins & T.H. Sams							
Tasso	H	1983	23	9	4	4	1,207,884
Lance K. Robinson							
Crafty Shaw	H	1998	42	15	7	7	1,040,440
M.T. Robinson							
Groovy	H	1983	26	12	4	1	1,346,956
Mrs I.M. Roddick							
Rough Habit (NZ)	G	1986	66	28	16	7	2,861,579
Mrs Julian G. Rogers & Swettenham Stud							
John W. Rooker							
Bowman's Band	H	1998	34	7	11	6	1,315,774
Harold Rose							
Hal's Hope	H	1997	33	9	5	3	1,098,422
Rosemont Farm Inc							
River Bay	H	1993	20	8	3	3	1,167,970
C. Rosen							
Chief's Crown	H	1982	21	12	3	3	2,191,168
Morton Rosenthal							
Fit for a Queen	M	1986	51	13	14	9	1,226,429
Warren W. Rosenthal							
Mubtaker	H	1997	20	9	6	3	1,007,998
Cecilia Straub Rubens							
Tiznow	H	1997	15	8	4	2	6,427,830
Budroyale	G	1993	52	17	12	2	2,840,810
Angela Rugnetta							
Gander	G	1996	60	15	10	9	1,824,011
Rutledge Farm							
Colonial Affair	H	1990	20	7	4	3	1,635,228
B.L. Ryan							
Royal Heroine (IRE)	M	1980	21	10	4	2	1,229,449
Ryehill Farm							
Awad	H	1990	70	14	10	11	3,270,131
Homebuilder	H	1984	60	11	11	17	1,172,153
Sabine Stable							
Lion Heart	C	2001	10	5	3	0	1,390,800
Graeme Hall	H	1997	22	7	7	1	1,147,441
R. Sahm							
Super Diamond	H	1980	37	16	5	5	1,469,233
Peter W. Salmen III							
Bourbon Belle	M	1995	40	16	11	5	1,152,223

Horse	Sex	Born	Sts	1st	2d	3d	Earnings
Sam-Son Farm							
Sky Classic	H	1987	29	15	6	1	3,320,398
Dance Smartly	M	1988	17	12	2	3	3,263,835
Quiet Resolve	G	1995	31	10	6	4	2,346,768
Soaring Free	G	1999	22	13	3	0	1,917,544
Dancethruthedawn	M	1998	16	7	2	3	1,609,643
Wilderness Song	M	1988	37	15	12	2	1,482,03
Regal Classic	H	1985	27	8	8	3	1,456,584
Desert Waves	G	1990	63	15	9	6	1,241,295
Rainbows for Life	H	1988	36	15	5	3	1,105,926
Regal Intention	H	1985	41	14	7	10	1,083,103
R.L. Sanford							
Maysville Slew	G	1996	69	17	11	7	1,046,409
Herman Sarkowsky							
Dixie Union	H	1997	12	7	3	0	1,233,190
F.H. Sasse & A.D. Shead							
Perrault (GB)	H	1977	25	9	5	5	1,536,103
Scott C. Savin							
Richman	H	1988	33	14	5	5	1,314,360
SCEA de Maulepaire							
Tuzla (FR)	M	1994	26	12	6	1	1,332,587
SCEA Haras du Mezeray							
Lassigny	H	1991	28	8	2	5	1,318,371
E.A. Scheib							
Fran's Valentine	M	1982	34	13	4	5	1,375,465
William Schettine							
Take Charge Lady	M	1999	22	11	7	0	2,480,377
Bruno Schickedanz							
Wake At Noon	H	1997	51	19	7	6	1,601,829
Gustav Schickedanz							
Wando	C	2000	19	11	2	1	2,543,229
Mobil	C	2000	23	11	5	1	1,507,924
K.C. Schlich							
Sefa's Beauty	M	1979	52	25	7	8	1,171,628
Barry Schwartz							
Peteski	H	1990	11	7	2	1	1,287,866
Herbert T. Schwartz							
Critical Eye	M	1997	38	14	4	3	1,060,984
Selective Seasons							
Family Style	M	1983	35	10	8	7	1,537,118
E.A. Seltzer							
Tank's Prospect	H	1982	14	5	2	2	1,355,645
Shadai Farm							
Dance in the Mood (Jpn)	F	2001	10	4	3	0	2,931,889
Shadwell Estate Company Limited							
Almutawakel (GB)	H	1995	19	4	4	1	3,643,021
Shadwell Farm Inc							
Dumaani	H	1991	26	7	3	3	1,079,098
Sakhee	H	1997	14	8	3	1	3,253,253
Shady Bend TB							
Sure Shot Biscuit	G	1996	54	23	10	11	1,025,480
Mr & Mrs L.K. Shapiro							
Native Diver	H	1959	81	37	7	12	1,026,500
Johnnie P. Shewuck							
Parose	G	1994	92	21	22	15	1,089,156
Shockey & Willow Wood Farm							
Thirty Six Red	H	1987	20	4	3	5	1,094,310
Karen Silva							
Express Tour	H	1998	14	5	1	1	1,767,515

Horse	Sex	Born	Sts	1st	2d	3d	Earnings
Robert C. Sims							
Hawkster	H	1986	23	6	3	4	1,510,942
J.B. Singer							
Videogenic	M	1982	73	20	9	10	1,154,360
Charles A. Smith							
Pollard's Vision	C	2001	17	5	5	3	1,075,311
T. Smith							
Frost King	H	1978	55	27	10	3	1,196,954
A.L. Smollin							
Sir Bear	G	1993	71	19	12	14	2,538,422
Hal Snowden Jr & Raymond Simpson							
Two Item Limit	M	1998	28	7	3	5	1,060,585
Hal Snowden Jr.							
Mr Epperson	G	1995	70	19	11	12	1,079,851
Someday Farm							
Smarty Jones	C	2001	9	8	1	0	7,613,155
Shawnna Sorenson							
Unshaded	G	1997	20	6	3	3	1,318,492
Southeast Associates							
Alphabet Soup	H	1991	24	10	3	6	2,990,270
Spendthrift Farm							
Interco	H	1980	21	10	4	3	1,070,688
Robert Spiegel							
Milwaukee Brew	H	1997	24	8	4	5	2,879,612
R.H. Spreen							
Lady's Secret	M	1982	45	25	9	3	3,021,325
J.D. Squires							
Monarchos	H	1998	10	4	1	3	1,720,830
Stack & Valerio Ltd							
Kostroma (IRE)	M	1986	26	12	2	3	1,200,088
T. Stack							
Corwyn Bay (IRE)	H	1986	15	6	4	0	1,018,749
Stackallan Stud							
Erins Isle (IRE)	H	1978	33	9	9	3	1,233,889
Kathleen D. Standridge							
J J'sdream	M	1993	40	13	11	7	1,022,217
Stanley Estate and Stud Co							
Ouija Board (GB)	F	2001	8	5	0	3	1,671,768
F. & R. Stark							
Cacoethes	H	1986	14	4	3	3	1,169,064
Beverly R. Steinman							
Colstar	M	1996	18	11	2	1	1,053,056
E.L. Stephenson							
Nasr El Arab	H	1985	16	6	2	2	1,198,585
Stetchworth Park Stud Ltd							
User Friendly (GB)	M	1989	16	8	1	2	1,764,938
Stiftung Gestut Fahrhof							
Silvano (GER)	H	1996	18	7	2	2	2,321,024
Stonerside Stable							
Congaree	H	1998	25	12	2	4	3,267,490
The Cliff's Edge	C	2001	13	4	5	2	1,265,258
Stratford Place Stud							
Sarafan	G	1997	44	10	12	4	2,588,671
George Strawbridge Jr							
With Anticipation	G	1995	48	15	9	8	2,660,543
Tikkanen	H	1991	17	4	2	3	1,599,335
Music Merci	G	1986	35	12	7	4	1,500,710

Horse	Sex	Born	Sts	1st	2d	3d	Earnings
Frank H. Stronach							
Awesome Again	H	1994	12	9	0	2	4,374,590
Nite Dreamer	H	1995	37	5	10	6	1,149,788
Basqueian	G	1991	37	13	10	2	1,094,767
Stud TNT							
Lundy's Liability (BRZ)	C	2000	7	4	1	0	1,553,930
Sugar Maple Farm Inc							
Itsallgreektome	G	1987	29	8	10	2	1,994,618
Sky Beauty	M	1990	21	15	2	2	1,336,000
Summa Stable							
Frankly Perfect	H	1985	22	6	6	4	1,272,957
Swettenham Stud							
Missionary Ridge (GB)	H	1987	42	8	5	8	1,864,498
Lit de Justice	H	1990	36	10	8	6	1,397,649
Rodrigo de Triano	H	1989	13	9	0	0	1,354,192
Single Empire (IRE)	H	1994	23	5	5	3	1,110,889
Swettenham Stud and Partners							
Northern Spur (IRE)	H	1991	15	6	4	3	1,614,425
Symboli Bokujo							
Symboli Rudolf (JPN)	H	1981	16	13	1	1	2,764,980
Paul Tackett							
Hopeful Word	H	1981	43	18	12	3	1,073,051
James B. Tafel							
Banshee Breeze	M	1995	18	10	5	2	2,784,798
Tall Oaks Farm							
Victory Gallop	H	1995	17	9	5	1	3,505,895
Tartan Farm Corporation							
Unbridled	H	1987	24	8	6	6	4,489,475
Equalize	H	1982	43	13	9	8	1,455,298
Primal	G	1985	45	17	11	7	1,209,530
Dr. Fager	H	1964	22	18	2	1	1,002,642
Edward P. Taylor							
Glorious Song	M	1976	34	17	9	1	1,004,534
Taylor Made Farm Inc							
Repent	H	1999	10	5	3	1	1,255,660
The Thoroughbred Corporation							
Point Given	H	1998	13	9	3	0	3,968,500
Spain	M	1997	35	9	9	7	3,540,542
Johar	H	1999	16	6	4	2	1,494,496
Third Kirsmith Racing Associates							
Rubiano	H	1987	28	13	6	1	1,252,817
Ralph Todd & Aury Todd							
The Tin Man	G	1998	21	7	4	2	1,097,860
John A. Toffan & Trudy McCaffery							
Free House	H	1994	22	9	5	3	3,178,971
Came Home	H	1999	12	9	0	0	1,835,940
Bienamado	H	1996	16	8	3	0	1,261,089
Tri-County Farms LLC							
Magistretti	C	2000	16	4	6	0	1,264,117
D Tsui and Orpendale							
Galileo (IRE)	H	1998	8	6	1	0	2,245,373
Mr & Mrs H.L. Vanier							
Western Playboy	H	1986	45	8	7	7	1,128,449
Vintage Meadow Stable							
Classic Cat	H	1995	20	6	3	5	1,221,300
Joseph Vitello							
Tenpins	H	1998	17	9	3	2	1,133,449
Waldemar Farms							
Foolish Pleasure	H	1972	26	16	4	3	1,216,705

Robert H. Walter

Cavonnier..........G 1993 23 8 3 2 1,254,165

Robert H. Walter Family Trust

Tout Charmant..........M 1996 29 9 9 1 1,781,879

Lazy Slusan..........M 1995 47 12 7 10 1,150,410

Warner L Jones Farm Inc

Tap to Music..........M 1995 21 6 4 4 1,052,526

Marvin L. Warner

Stalwars..........H 1985 79 17 17 8 1,211,556

Fred Watarida

Native Desert..........G 1993 74 21 13 17 1,828,177

James B. Watriss

Great Communicator..H 1983 56 14 10 7 2,922,615

Georges Wegliszewski

Celtic Arms (FR)..........H 1991 23 5 2 3 1,102,806

R.G. Wehle

Win..........G 1980 44 14 10 3 1,408,980

Irwin Weiner & France Weiner

Maltese Superb..........M 1997 35 4 7 4 1,145,491

Welcome Farm

Bessarabian..........M 1982 37 18 5 4 1,032,640

Wertheimer et Frere

Kotashaan (FR)..........H 1988 22 10 5 2 2,812,114

Dare and Go..........H 1991 22 7 7 5 1,608,972

Atticus..........H 1992 18 7 3 1 1,205,933

Mr & Mrs R.S. West & Mr & Mrs M. Miller

Chilukki..........M 1997 17 11 3 0 1,201,828

Murray D. West

Freedom Cry (GB)..........H 1991 12 5 5 0 1,089,080

White Fox Farm

Fleetstreet Dancer..........G 1998 25 5 7 3 1,704,806

Janis R. Whitham

Affluent..........M 1998 23 8 5 4 1,497,651

Wickfield Stud Ltd

Hawksley Hill (IRE)....G 1993 46 14 12 6 1,730,922

Konrad Widmer

Thunder Rumble..........H 1989 19 8 0 1 1,047,552

Edward Wiest

Captain Bodgit..........H 1994 12 7 1 4 1,014,849

Scott S. Willis

Scott's Scoundrel..........H 1992 50 22 4 8 1,270,052

Catherine Wills

Dynever..........C 2000 16 4 6 1 1,408,714

Charles T. Wilson

Hodges Bay..........G 1985 51 7 15 3 1,050,363

Ralph C. Wilson Jr

Arazi..........H 1989 14 9 1 1 1,212,351

Wimborne Farm Inc

John's Call..........G 1991 40 16 11 3 1,571,267

Better Talk Now..........G 1999 25 8 5 2 1,744,437

J.D. Wimpfheimer

Opening Verse..........H 1986 30 10 7 2 1,669,357

Bounding Basque..........H 1980 40 10 4 6 1,256,258

Win Star Farm LLC

Funny Cide..........G 2000 21 8 4 5 3,174,485

Verne H. Winchell

Tight Spot..........H 1987 21 12 3 1 1,566,100

Olympio..........H 1988 17 9 4 0 1,456,315

V.H. Winchell & Katalpa Farm

Sea Cadet..........H 1988 29 10 6 5 1,807,150

Wind Hill Farm

Stellar Jayne..........F 2001 18 6 2 3 1,111,244

Starrer..........M 1998 20 6 5 3 1,043,033

Windfields Farm

Flag Down..........H 1990 43 11 11 8 1,699,711

Mrs J.A. Winn

Proper Reality..........H 1985 19 10 3 1 1,701,650

Mr & Mrs Robert Witt

Possibly Perfect..........M 1990 18 11 2 4 1,377,634

Wood & Woodhaven Farms

Pine Tree Lane..........M 1982 38 19 4 4 1,150,561

Mr & Mrs M.L. Wood

Favorite Trick..........H 1995 16 12 0 1 1,726,793

Personal Rush..........C 2001 10 5 0 1 1,234,820

Woodcrest

Del Mar Dennis..........G 1990 26 10 1 4 1,023,373

Forty Niner Days..........G 1987 45 9 9 3 1,009,625

Woodlynn Farm Inc

Guided Tour..........G 1996 31 12 8 1 1,964,253

More Than Ready..........H 1997 17 7 4 1 1,026,229

Mary Lou Wootton

Silver Charm..........H 1994 24 12 7 2 6,944,369

Mrs R.W. Worthington

Jameela..........M 1976 58 27 15 6 1,038,704

John Youngblood & Fletcher Gray

Left Bank..........H 1997 24 14 2 0 1,402,806

Julius H. Zolezzi

Big Jag..........G 1993 30 13 5 3 1,800,329

Donald Zuckerman & R. Mary Zuckerman

Kalookan Queen..........M 1996 25 11 8 4 1,044,474

Edward N. Zurek

The Wicked North..........H 1989 17 8 4 1 1,180,750

This section includes all horses with at least $1 million in career earnings that had at least one start in North America. It includes any foreign earnings and bonus money awarded for racing performance that was reported to *Daily Racing Form*.

Highest Stud Fees in North America for 2004

Stallion	Stud Fee
Storm Cat	$500,000
A.P. Indy	300,000
Kingmambo	225,000
Seeking the Gold	150,000
Gone West	125,000
Unbridled's Song	125,000
Broad Brush	100,000
Deputy Minister	100,000
Empire Maker	100,000
Mineshaft	100,000
Fusaichi Pegasus	85,000
Rahy	80,000
Awesome Again	75,000
Dynaformer	75,000
El Prado (IRE)	75,000
Giant's Causeway	75,000
Grand Slam	75,000
Point Given	75,000
Tale of the Cat	75,000
Theatrical (IRE)	75,000
Cozzene	60,000
War Chant	60,000
Aldebaran	50,000
Distorted Humor	50,000
Dixieland Band	50,000
Elusive Quality	50,000
Forestry	50,000
Gulch	50,000
Lemon Drop Kid	50,000
Mr. Greeley	50,000
Thunder Gulch	50,000
Touch Gold	50,000
Vindication	50,000
Came Home	40,000
Cherokee Run	40,000
Forest Wildcat	40,000
Silver Deputy	40,000
Stravinsky	40,000
Carson City	35,000
Cat Thief	35,000
Hennessy	35,000
Maria's Mon	35,000
Mt. Livermore	35,000
Pulpit	35,000
Quiet American	35,000
Capote	30,000
Deputy Commander	30,000
Diesis (GB)	30,000
Dixie Union	30,000
Johannesburg	30,000
Langfuhr	30,000
Red Bullet	30,000
Sky Mesa	30,000
Street Cry (IRE)	30,000
Tiznow	30,000
Victory Gallop	30,000
Aptitude	25,000
Belong to Me	25,000
Cape Town	25,000
Golden Missile	25,000
High Yield	25,000
In Excess	25,000
Monarchos	25,000
Orientate	25,000
Phone Trick	25,000
Silver Charm	25,000
Smart Strike	25,000
Smoke Glacken	25,000
Stormin Fever	25,000
Swain (IRE)	25,000
Two Punch	25,000
Woodman	25,000

Editor's Note: Some high-profile horses at stud do not have published stud fees and are priced according to individual contracts via private arrangements.

Top North American Sires in 2004 – Money Won

Sire	Perfs	Win Perfs	Starts	1st	2nd	3rd	Unpl	Purses
Elusive Quality	131	77	751	119	111	92	429	$10,700,039
A.P. Indy	162	87	898	149	120	117	512	8,359,685
El Prado (IRE)	173	94	1,222	169	155	163	735	7,987,415
Storm Cat	103	56	461	91	69	63	238	6,709,124
Saint Ballado	156	82	879	129	121	140	489	6,614,013
Smart Strike	128	80	791	150	109	105	427	6,464,274
Awesome Again	104	58	536	103	83	67	283	6,312,464
Tale of the Cat	170	98	956	162	155	127	512	6,031,213
Unbridled's Song	152	76	831	141	110	112	468	5,853,286
Carson City	174	96	1,089	161	160	120	648	5,577,819
Not For Love	179	102	1,201	195	169	137	700	5,439,082
Langfuhr	173	95	1,236	167	173	153	743	5,402,570
Dynaformer	141	60	785	91	87	104	503	5,380,967
Devil His Due	190	100	1,325	183	171	173	798	5,243,659
Alphabet Soup	173	99	1,232	181	151	140	760	5,099,550
Wild Rush	123	73	835	132	107	112	484	5,063,397
Grand Slam	152	84	859	138	128	93	500	4,970,163
Distorted Humor	120	71	738	131	106	93	408	4,947,035
Smoke Glacken	143	95	1,123	179	160	180	604	4,777,548
Silver Deputy	158	85	1,038	154	155	123	606	4,206,718
Kris S.	84	40	458	72	66	63	257	4,172,340
Belong to Me	135	76	895	136	130	110	519	4,003,212
Roar	144	91	1,132	174	173	167	618	3,991,395
Quiet American	146	83	1,034	163	134	132	605	3,955,954
Gulch	102	61	667	95	104	107	361	3,949,278
Gold Fever	132	79	971	137	135	150	549	3,936,290
In Excess (IRE)	109	60	607	109	83	62	353	3,913,762
Sky Classic	144	68	914	106	99	112	597	3,896,069
Unbridled	104	46	467	68	68	58	273	3,873,111
Pulpit	98	50	528	80	72	65	311	3,846,835
Cherokee Run	163	95	1,046	152	140	145	609	3,824,103
Hennessy	141	75	803	127	92	95	489	3,758,224
Jules	109	58	658	104	77	67	410	3,712,521
Petionville	116	62	829	107	111	106	505	3,711,026
Valid Expectations	131	81	954	159	130	144	521	3,693,552
Storm Boot	174	96	1,167	182	142	153	690	3,637,687
Forest Wildcat	165	89	936	130	131	116	559	3,538,680
American Chance	119	57	867	122	132	101	512	3,527,691
Grindstone	96	48	563	87	81	86	309	3,518,346
Halo's Image	110	60	767	113	103	96	455	3,484,769
Crafty Prospector	132	81	1,050	146	134	143	627	3,410,437
Indian Charlie	95	65	663	138	105	107	313	3,392,633
Allen's Prospect	193	103	1,341	165	159	181	836	3,378,387
Skip Away	121	77	880	142	118	122	498	3,368,862
Tabasco Cat	102	57	745	102	113	92	438	3,362,777
Runaway Groom	161	93	1,181	155	153	153	720	3,347,556
Glitterman	142	78	994	146	138	123	587	3,329,448
Polish Numbers	132	72	848	128	97	125	498	3,221,466
Touch Gold	128	58	723	85	86	86	466	3,194,085
Gone West	86	45	473	80	58	55	280	3,179,564
Boston Harbor	129	77	755	127	97	90	441	3,139,694
Regal Classic	142	73	1,086	120	137	142	687	3,120,289
Cryptoclearance	214	107	1,596	161	189	210	1,036	3,107,485
Royal Academy	114	59	620	96	97	71	356	3,089,478
Wild Again	111	56	762	99	111	91	461	3,083,844
With Approval	147	78	952	138	104	103	607	3,076,229
Gilded Time	145	77	939	134	113	142	550	3,070,001
General Meeting	92	51	540	80	84	61	315	3,061,344
Honour and Glory	167	87	916	141	120	116	539	3,041,134
Honor Grades	136	63	834	115	109	100	510	3,018,364
West by West	147	81	1,237	156	146	161	774	3,002,281
Souvenir Copy	122	68	780	115	136	117	412	2,991,615
Jade Hunter	108	57	760	106	65	89	500	2,988,455
Lit de Justice	111	62	938	117	131	104	586	2,965,855
Dixie Brass	113	67	844	120	121	124	479	2,958,921

Sire	Perfs	Win Perfs	Starts	1st	2nd	3rd	Unpl	Purses
Stormy Atlantic	123	66	679	118	83	92	386	2,929,520
Peaks and Valleys	169	94	1,209	151	172	157	729	2,920,548
Holy Bull	136	71	849	110	82	113	544	2,912,741
Two Punch	132	78	919	134	101	126	558	2,875,021
Maria's Mon	163	84	1,026	133	126	107	660	2,864,607
A. P Jet	146	76	920	120	135	114	551	2,858,564
Southern Halo	146	68	984	127	126	123	608	2,858,080
Numerous	118	50	898	94	113	117	574	2,852,231
Mr. Greeley	162	83	998	123	124	135	616	2,839,027
Northern Afleet	64	45	460	75	72	70	243	2,829,201
Mt. Livermore	144	73	971	120	159	124	568	2,808,984
Out of Place	147	75	1,062	132	141	136	653	2,805,290
Bold Executive	88	45	612	82	69	74	387	2,800,055
Victory Gallop	85	49	531	81	79	91	280	2,784,293
Dixieland Band	137	51	766	76	92	116	482	2,782,135
Deputy Minister	124	58	594	81	81	78	354	2,779,601
Whiskey Wisdom	77	42	528	69	65	63	331	2,745,065
French Deputy	90	56	602	93	83	92	334	2,744,403
Pleasant Colony	45	23	297	39	43	42	173	2,728,433
Judge T C	115	62	983	113	135	131	604	2,719,835
Formal Gold	107	69	699	125	95	90	389	2,707,994
Coronado's Quest	82	38	404	59	47	57	241	2,700,964
Marquetry	148	78	1,018	127	150	143	598	2,689,881
Montbrook	126	72	838	122	107	101	508	2,688,969
Sultry Song	99	46	674	76	89	87	422	2,685,573
Deputy Commander	132	63	832	101	118	111	502	2,674,917
Pioneering	106	63	816	127	109	121	459	2,674,521
Rubiano	132	67	895	111	114	126	544	2,663,036
Louis Quatorze	142	69	863	117	89	98	559	2,660,975
Smokester	136	83	939	150	136	119	534	2,651,586
Gold Case	127	76	812	129	113	98	472	2,641,759
Kissin Kris	140	76	1,049	147	125	120	657	2,623,396
Pleasant Tap	133	68	917	126	116	115	560	2,620,987
Silver Ghost	136	71	808	120	88	98	502	2,570,419
Bertrando	136	74	672	123	95	84	370	2,566,291
Roy	88	58	662	96	99	95	372	2,546,396
Mutakddim	98	50	667	114	95	92	366	2,545,324
Arch	75	48	475	87	75	70	243	2,541,487
Defrere	119	70	845	140	90	119	496	2,525,480
End Sweep	139	72	1,101	134	162	154	651	2,516,558
Boundary	98	50	537	89	83	63	302	2,510,713
Cozzene	88	48	517	76	60	60	321	2,507,742
Slew City Slew	136	72	1,020	114	123	119	664	2,506,545
Storm Creek	159	76	1,098	130	138	130	700	2,502,450
Formal Dinner	137	83	1,192	156	158	125	753	2,490,309
High Brite	128	80	986	158	147	134	547	2,484,565
Cape Town	87	53	509	80	80	68	281	2,476,375
Theatrical (IRE)	77	35	341	62	40	30	209	2,447,149
Forestry	65	33	315	57	53	36	169	2,445,702
Salt Lake	147	82	867	143	124	109	491	2,425,995
Tomorrows Cat	119	55	691	83	77	78	453	2,422,843
Thunder Gulch	123	48	567	81	83	88	315	2,419,702
Dance Brightly	115	70	799	118	96	108	477	2,364,046
Pentelicus	148	86	1,192	166	158	146	722	2,305,476
Notebook	116	69	852	122	139	107	484	2,300,806
Sword Dance (IRE)	138	69	981	135	116	138	592	2,279,344
Pine Bluff	99	55	603	100	70	73	360	2,248,850
Tactical Advantage	144	73	1,093	129	154	156	654	2,240,866
Lite the Fuse	108	61	738	111	89	91	447	2,234,366
Distant View	58	32	395	65	49	59	222	2,230,256
Siberian Summer	85	50	572	92	64	67	349	2,176,034
Sir Cat	119	74	781	122	94	112	453	2,162,388
Patton	117	71	922	128	91	103	600	2,158,848
Suave Prospect	99	56	858	119	95	113	531	2,142,040
Double Honor	114	66	817	126	90	106	495	2,135,142
Fortunate Prospect	102	63	909	134	126	125	524	2,132,040
Rahy	88	47	565	73	91	75	326	2,118,832

Sire	Perfs	Win Perfs	Starts	1st	2nd	3rd	Unpl	Purses
Wekiva Springs	130	79	956	127	120	114	595	2,113,529
Afternoon Deelites	120	56	750	101	100	84	465	2,113,444
Broad Brush	95	43	506	66	66	68	306	2,089,083
Robyn Dancer	123	62	951	114	117	106	614	2,083,990
Summer Squall	71	38	509	71	55	58	325	2,074,850
Is It True	97	57	683	106	84	96	397	2,047,878
Take Me Out	97	58	737	105	75	91	466	2,043,087
Seeking the Gold	73	34	341	52	55	45	189	2,026,886
Conquistador Cielo	111	67	800	102	104	103	491	2,013,900
Cee's Tizzy	107	59	583	108	83	67	325	2,002,145
Candy Stripes	69	36	477	61	58	45	313	1,980,865
Prized	76	40	563	75	70	75	343	1,978,375
Phone Trick	120	67	792	106	105	92	489	1,978,184
Archers Bay	56	29	293	42	41	33	177	1,954,905
Helmsman	81	47	628	94	94	83	357	1,947,037
Unusual Heat	49	25	343	57	57	51	178	1,932,697
Partner's Hero	94	50	692	94	87	96	415	1,928,686
Lost Soldier	129	62	879	102	106	100	571	1,918,241
Miswaki	60	34	413	65	57	57	234	1,912,607
Citidancer	79	45	581	86	90	82	323	1,911,287
Wheaton	101	64	755	136	102	102	415	1,910,402
Capote	92	43	532	70	65	51	346	1,908,113
Kiridashi	72	35	492	59	56	73	304	1,906,365
Malibu Moon	70	35	365	56	51	36	222	1,900,933
Fit to Fight	112	66	862	121	127	120	494	1,886,785
Dove Hunt	99	57	741	110	83	103	445	1,884,365
Tour d'Or	129	67	1,017	120	138	114	645	1,879,527
Swiss Yodeler	98	56	624	102	78	95	349	1,873,892
Line In The Sand	154	72	1,272	119	145	155	853	1,868,655
Silver Charm	75	32	368	49	55	55	209	1,864,055
Mazel Trick	77	38	416	65	61	48	242	1,855,552
Exploit	85	45	494	75	64	55	300	1,833,610
Mecke	83	38	626	67	87	69	403	1,808,795
Menifee	59	34	284	58	33	37	156	1,807,034
Lord Carson	122	61	714	97	100	99	418	1,804,029
Wild Zone	140	69	866	106	102	104	554	1,803,514
Pembroke	112	64	855	139	122	96	498	1,790,804
Friendly Lover	122	56	934	98	118	118	600	1,788,419
Kingmambo	75	33	386	54	56	37	239	1,780,330
Talkin Man	25	10	169	17	23	18	111	1,778,782
Spend a Buck	59	22	322	38	36	34	214	1,773,629
Danehill	27	9	95	17	11	6	61	1,770,378
Meadowlake	102	52	645	83	90	86	386	1,768,052
Will's Way	66	35	496	68	64	52	312	1,751,595
Benchmark	77	39	465	64	73	70	258	1,745,504
Memo (CHI)	86	50	452	90	70	62	230	1,734,700
Artax	72	37	421	52	45	57	267	1,730,613
Red Ransom	80	33	383	60	47	47	229	1,724,279
Successful Appeal	20	15	76	31	13	10	22	1,724,080
Twining	85	44	736	98	98	87	453	1,707,533
Bold Badgett	72	30	460	48	49	90	273	1,698,327
Diesis (GB)	29	13	153	19	26	14	94	1,696,790
Ide	86	52	672	88	99	84	401	1,694,378
Personal Flag	109	49	877	93	99	116	569	1,690,776
Siphon (BRZ)	132	48	696	79	74	81	462	1,689,495
Charismatic	88	39	464	58	50	53	303	1,683,095
Unaccounted For	112	49	723	94	90	84	455	1,680,609
Demidoff	81	55	716	110	103	79	424	1,673,839
Lucky Lionel	88	50	632	73	91	68	400	1,665,073
Unreal Zeal	118	69	985	114	129	112	630	1,653,357
Beau Genius	106	57	874	114	105	103	552	1,645,410
Editor's Note	106	50	791	80	109	87	515	1,645,305
Open Forum	105	47	709	80	92	87	450	1,644,627
Valid Wager	86	49	669	90	95	74	410	1,644,122
Doneraile Court	73	46	533	71	71	78	313	1,630,449
Danzig	38	18	126	29	22	12	63	1,627,345
Distinctive Pro	95	42	673	74	89	90	420	1,603,868

Sire	Perfs	Win Perfs	Starts	1st	2nd	3rd	Unpl	Purses
Rizzi	110	63	829	111	98	96	524	1,602,243
Lord Avie	83	41	560	77	60	69	354	1,594,956
Slewdledo	141	82	806	128	110	109	459	1,586,607
Tactical Cat	55	29	328	54	45	58	171	1,569,377
Cobra King	77	45	546	82	67	79	318	1,567,522
Concorde's Tune	73	43	525	74	68	75	308	1,565,361
Vying Victor	106	50	657	84	105	90	378	1,564,244
Favorite Trick	89	49	586	85	84	70	347	1,562,394
Lac Ouimet	99	57	725	92	80	77	476	1,548,974
Valley Crossing	68	33	517	69	73	48	327	1,544,862
Cartwright	94	50	656	92	81	73	410	1,529,175
Diligence	54	31	403	70	48	50	235	1,529,029
Mister Jolie	83	54	637	107	97	83	350	1,523,221
Appealing Skier	76	49	582	88	79	66	349	1,521,637
Crafty Friend	83	41	478	60	55	61	302	1,507,561
Sea Hero	85	47	622	80	80	78	384	1,498,232
Banker's Gold	86	46	636	81	85	90	380	1,490,215
Skywalker	97	48	524	77	51	63	333	1,489,889
Clever Trick	99	54	726	96	90	85	455	1,488,281
Halory Hunter	67	43	654	78	99	93	384	1,482,621
Go for Gin	74	32	519	67	62	67	323	1,479,828
Captain Bodgit	111	49	815	78	115	135	487	1,472,039
Sefapiano	80	46	645	89	106	70	380	1,465,924
Sandpit (BRZ)	98	55	782	85	93	92	512	1,461,719
Cat's Career	103	54	743	108	78	91	466	1,456,434
Concerto	59	37	480	69	76	64	271	1,454,515
Rodeo	80	39	501	66	45	52	338	1,444,428
Jeblar	72	41	556	68	77	55	356	1,430,404
Alydeed	92	44	623	73	71	72	407	1,426,386
Yes It's True	40	15	141	25	12	31	73	1,424,382
Press Card	78	43	578	88	66	70	354	1,422,222
Stormin Fever	83	38	471	55	68	55	293	1,421,609
Explosive Red	90	49	730	88	73	91	478	1,413,113
Our Emblem	82	46	552	82	58	55	357	1,409,837
Old Trieste	64	27	296	46	33	40	177	1,404,244
Ghazi	84	48	582	85	77	79	341	1,402,041
Demaloot Demashoot	82	51	719	107	109	87	416	1,395,026
Dehere	70	37	461	63	57	79	262	1,393,746
Gold Legend	78	43	558	83	85	66	324	1,384,923
Matty G	39	25	375	51	41	51	232	1,381,853
Joyeux Danseur	75	35	463	64	61	50	288	1,378,647
Tejano Run	51	28	409	44	68	71	226	1,378,199
Stuka	37	22	278	30	39	40	169	1,362,895
Seattle Slew	60	29	297	42	40	29	186	1,352,871
Carnivalay	78	41	577	70	70	78	359	1,352,146
Subordination	62	39	424	64	54	53	253	1,338,992
Evansville Slew	71	37	413	62	58	53	240	1,329,124
Sadler's Wells	20	4	60	5	4	9	42	1,326,568
Moscow Ballet	61	27	366	47	53	54	212	1,322,892
Waquoit	73	37	511	60	63	67	321	1,319,279
Count the Time	83	49	575	90	82	80	323	1,313,333
Williamstown	74	37	561	60	63	70	368	1,311,405
Tethra	62	27	391	44	36	58	253	1,305,850
Lear Fan	60	28	354	36	42	39	237	1,302,555
Ascot Knight	74	27	397	46	39	35	277	1,300,819
In Case	97	50	664	81	70	65	448	1,299,267
K. O. Punch	76	37	506	78	64	80	284	1,298,403
Private Terms	89	43	709	78	78	101	452	1,289,020
Cahill Road	75	40	479	79	58	59	283	1,281,070
Colony Light	72	36	527	62	76	65	324	1,276,748
Wild Event	48	27	300	46	38	37	179	1,267,433
Skip Trial	74	34	490	62	58	62	308	1,261,917
$Royal Applause (GB)	7	3	38	7	6	2	23	1,260,745
Prospect Bay	82	46	550	76	74	69	331	1,256,458
Hernando (FR)	4	2	13	4	3	2	4	1,255,518
Labeeb (GB)	54	27	381	39	36	67	239	1,245,033
Flying Continental	115	55	904	108	109	107	580	1,244,806

Sire	Perfs	Win Perfs	Starts	1st	2nd	3rd	Unpl	Purses
Birdonthewire	64	29	392	49	56	59	228	1,244,302
Gold Token	52	25	375	48	41	41	245	1,244,135
Mountain Cat	86	41	582	80	82	61	359	1,244,079
Victory Speech	78	36	546	79	71	53	343	1,239,615
Proud and True	66	36	530	75	70	64	321	1,234,178
Foxtrail	41	17	219	27	30	22	140	1,233,873
Excavate	96	48	662	68	58	76	460	1,212,311
Devil's Bag	75	35	399	63	40	50	246	1,208,492
Real Quiet	70	33	411	50	51	36	274	1,207,167
Caller I. D.	93	45	655	81	87	72	415	1,199,148
Gold Alert	56	29	497	56	75	45	321	1,192,780
King of Kings (IRE)	77	26	475	46	48	55	326	1,191,134
Bold n' Flashy	57	16	347	26	45	46	230	1,190,760
Zarbyev	70	35	503	54	63	64	322	1,187,828
Signal Tap	76	34	593	56	72	76	389	1,174,077
Diamond	55	32	368	62	47	48	211	1,166,495
Kipper Kelly	86	40	663	87	76	75	425	1,151,073
Bag	106	44	675	71	71	89	444	1,143,638
You and I	92	41	543	61	66	64	352	1,141,570
Regal Intention	81	46	520	75	78	65	302	1,137,671
War Deputy	45	27	352	49	39	44	220	1,135,654
Hadif	93	60	752	102	102	106	442	1,127,112
Family Calling	77	40	570	69	74	79	348	1,117,930
Way West (FR)	71	41	480	71	40	54	315	1,116,773
Stravinsky	46	23	238	32	26	34	146	1,116,507
Roanoke	79	41	686	73	66	97	450	1,116,093
Private Interview	55	24	390	37	48	44	261	1,115,543
Outflanker	60	38	432	72	47	54	259	1,115,443
Affirmed	52	21	292	34	32	39	187	1,108,572
Game Plan	88	54	544	91	101	86	266	1,107,468
Norquestor	52	26	401	54	43	46	258	1,106,657
Miner's Mark	87	41	706	82	89	82	453	1,105,926
Larrupin'	54	30	425	52	66	57	250	1,097,158
Olympio	93	40	516	62	62	65	327	1,095,841
Good and Tough	45	31	304	55	49	42	158	1,091,717
On Target	79	43	529	81	81	74	293	1,082,474
Yarrow Brae	55	29	400	51	62	57	230	1,082,194
Stage Colony	46	30	402	68	43	71	220	1,082,131
Announce	87	47	584	75	69	78	362	1,080,636
Master Bill	51	27	450	62	69	59	260	1,077,922
Silver Hawk	27	10	105	15	10	9	71	1,072,911
Lil's Lad	65	36	387	53	47	59	228	1,069,894
Bianconi	54	29	310	50	36	38	186	1,060,632
Spinning World	40	20	229	33	32	35	129	1,056,279
All Gone	63	34	594	69	82	69	374	1,051,911
Tricky Creek	82	44	618	74	82	83	379	1,051,028
Tamayaz	85	36	677	62	69	90	456	1,050,070
Prospector Jones	59	28	396	53	51	39	253	1,049,973
Lord At War (ARG)	22	13	173	33	23	19	98	1,049,938
Eastern Echo	78	43	585	77	57	59	392	1,039,669
Katahaula County	70	34	492	55	70	78	289	1,035,173
Accelerator	77	39	538	52	58	62	366	1,031,557
Candi's Gold	60	34	449	65	57	63	264	1,021,351
Strodes Creek	50	32	448	66	68	64	250	1,017,087
Concern	69	38	491	60	68	52	311	1,015,257
Native Regent	51	28	422	50	45	44	283	1,005,766
Free House	47	22	275	33	46	37	159	1,005,675
Abaginone	63	31	384	52	41	45	246	1,004,882
Marked Tree	99	48	632	86	85	75	386	1,000,041

The above list includes only North American earnings
* Foreign based stallion with North American starters
Statistics provided by Equibase

Top North American Sires in 2004 – Races Won

Sire	Perfs	Win Perfs	Starts	1st	2nd	3rd	Unpl	Purses
Not For Love	179	102	1,201	195	169	137	700	$5,439,082
Devil His Due	190	100	1,325	183	171	173	798	5,243,659
Storm Boot	174	96	1,167	182	142	153	690	3,637,687
Alphabet Soup	173	99	1,232	181	151	140	760	5,099,550
Smoke Glacken	143	95	1,123	179	160	180	604	4,777,548
Roar	144	91	1,132	174	173	167	618	3,991,395
El Prado (IRE)	173	94	1,222	169	155	163	735	7,987,415
Langfuhr	173	95	1,236	167	173	153	743	5,402,570
Pentelicus	148	86	1,192	166	158	146	722	2,305,476
Allen's Prospect	193	103	1,341	165	159	181	836	3,378,387
Quiet American	146	83	1,034	163	134	132	605	3,955,954
Tale of the Cat	170	98	956	162	155	127	512	6,031,213
Carson City	174	96	1,089	161	160	120	648	5,577,819
Cryptoclearance	214	107	1,596	161	189	210	1,036	3,107,485
Valid Expectations	131	81	954	159	130	144	521	3,693,552
High Brite	128	80	986	158	147	134	547	2,484,565
West by West	147	81	1,237	156	146	161	774	3,002,281
Formal Dinner	137	83	1,192	156	158	125	753	2,490,309
Runaway Groom	161	93	1,181	155	153	153	720	3,347,556
Silver Deputy	158	85	1,038	154	155	123	606	4,206,718
Cherokee Run	163	95	1,046	152	140	145	609	3,824,103
Peaks and Valleys	169	94	1,209	151	172	157	729	2,920,548
Smart Strike	128	80	791	150	109	105	427	6,464,274
Smokester	136	83	939	150	136	119	534	2,651,586
A.P. Indy	162	87	898	149	120	117	512	8,359,685
Kissin Kris	140	76	1,049	147	125	120	657	2,623,396
Crafty Prospector	132	81	1,050	146	134	143	627	3,410,437
Glitterman	142	78	994	146	138	123	587	3,329,448
Salt Lake	147	82	867	143	124	109	491	2,425,995
Skip Away	121	77	880	142	118	122	498	3,368,862
Unbridled's Song	152	76	831	141	110	112	468	5,853,286
Honour and Glory	167	87	916	141	120	116	539	3,041,134
Defrere	119	70	845	140	90	119	496	2,525,480
Pembroke	112	64	855	139	122	96	498	1,790,804
Grand Slam	152	84	859	138	128	93	500	4,970,163
Indian Charlie	95	65	663	138	105	107	313	3,392,633
With Approval	147	78	952	138	104	103	607	3,076,229
Gold Fever	132	79	971	137	135	150	549	3,936,290
Belong to Me	135	76	895	136	130	110	519	4,003,212
Wheaton	101	64	755	136	102	102	415	1,910,402
Sword Dance (IRE)	138	69	981	135	116	138	592	2,279,344
Gilded Time	145	77	939	134	113	142	550	3,070,001
Two Punch	132	78	919	134	101	126	558	2,875,021
End Sweep	139	72	1,101	134	162	154	651	2,516,558
Fortunate Prospect	102	63	909	134	126	125	524	2,132,040
Maria's Mon	163	84	1,026	133	126	107	660	2,864,607
Wild Rush	123	73	835	132	107	112	484	5,063,397
Out of Place	147	75	1,062	132	141	136	653	2,805,290
Distorted Humor	120	71	738	131	106	93	408	4,947,035
Forest Wildcat	165	89	936	130	131	116	559	3,538,680

Sire	Perfs	Win Perfs	Starts	1st	2nd	3rd	Unpl	Purses
Storm Creek	159	76	1,098	130	138	130	700	2,502,450
Saint Ballado	156	82	879	129	121	140	489	6,614,013
Gold Case	127	76	812	129	113	98	472	2,641,759
Tactical Advantage	144	73	1,093	129	154	156	654	2,240,866
Polish Numbers	132	72	848	128	97	125	498	3,221,466
Patton	117	71	922	128	91	103	600	2,158,848
Slewdledo	141	82	806	128	110	109	459	1,586,607
Hennessy	141	75	803	127	92	95	489	3,758,224
Boston Harbor	129	77	755	127	97	90	441	3,139,694
Southern Halo	146	68	984	127	126	123	608	2,858,080
Marquetry	148	78	1,018	127	150	143	598	2,689,881
Pioneering	106	63	816	127	109	121	459	2,674,521
Wekiva Springs	130	79	956	127	120	114	595	2,113,529
Pleasant Tap	133	68	917	126	116	115	560	2,620,987
Double Honor	114	66	817	126	90	106	495	2,135,142
Formal Gold	107	69	699	125	95	90	389	2,707,994
Mr. Greeley	162	83	998	123	124	135	616	2,839,027
Bertrando	136	74	672	123	95	84	370	2,566,291
American Chance	119	57	867	122	132	101	512	3,527,691
Montbrook	126	72	838	122	107	101	508	2,688,969
Notebook	116	69	852	122	139	107	484	2,300,806
Sir Cat	119	74	781	122	94	112	453	2,162,388
Fit to Fight	112	66	862	121	127	120	494	1,886,785
Regal Classic	142	73	1,086	120	137	142	687	3,120,289
Dixie Brass	113	67	844	120	121	124	479	2,958,921
A. P Jet	146	76	920	120	135	114	551	2,858,564
Mt. Livermore	144	73	971	120	159	124	568	2,808,984
Silver Ghost	136	71	808	120	88	98	502	2,570,419
Tour d'Or	129	67	1,017	120	138	114	645	1,879,527
Elusive Quality	131	77	751	119	111	92	429	10,700,039
Suave Prospect	99	56	858	119	95	113	531	2,142,040
Line In The Sand	154	72	1,272	119	145	155	853	1,868,655
Stormy Atlantic	123	66	679	118	83	92	386	2,929,520
Dance Brightly	115	70	799	118	96	108	477	2,364,046
Lit de Justice	111	62	938	117	131	104	586	2,965,855
Louis Quatorze	142	69	863	117	89	98	559	2,660,975
Honor Grades	136	63	834	115	109	100	510	3,018,364
Souvenir Copy	122	68	780	115	136	117	412	2,991,615
Mutakddim	98	50	667	114	95	92	366	2,545,324
Slew City Slew	136	72	1,020	114	123	119	664	2,506,545
Robyn Dancer	123	62	951	114	117	106	614	2,083,990
Unreal Zeal	118	69	985	114	129	112	630	1,653,357
Beau Genius	106	57	874	114	105	103	552	1,645,410
Halo's Image	110	60	767	113	103	96	455	3,484,769
Judge T C	115	62	983	113	135	131	604	2,719,835
Rubiano	132	67	895	111	114	126	544	2,663,036
Lite the Fuse	108	61	738	111	89	91	447	2,234,366
Rizzi	110	63	829	111	98	96	524	1,602,243
Holy Bull	136	71	849	110	82	113	544	2,912,741
Dove Hunt	99	57	741	110	83	103	445	1,884,365
Demidoff	81	55	716	110	103	79	424	1,673,839

Top North American Sires in 2004 – Winning Performers

Sire	Perfs	Win Perfs	Starts	1st	2nd	3rd	Unpl	Purses
Cryptoclearance	214	107	1,596	161	189	210	1,036	$3,107,485
Allen's Prospect	193	103	1,341	165	159	181	836	3,378,387
Not For Love	179	102	1,201	195	169	137	700	5,439,082
Devil His Due	190	100	1,325	183	171	173	798	5,243,659
Alphabet Soup	173	99	1,232	181	151	140	760	5,099,550
Tale of the Cat	170	98	956	162	155	127	512	6,031,213
Carson City	174	96	1,089	161	160	120	648	5,577,819
Storm Boot	174	96	1,167	182	142	153	690	3,637,687
Langfuhr	173	95	1,236	167	173	153	743	5,402,570
Smoke Glacken	143	95	1,123	179	160	180	604	4,777,548
Cherokee Run	163	95	1,046	152	140	145	609	3,824,103
El Prado (IRE)	173	94	1,222	169	155	163	735	7,987,415
Peaks and Valleys	169	94	1,209	151	172	157	729	2,920,548
Runaway Groom	161	93	1,181	155	153	153	720	3,347,556
Roar	144	91	1,132	174	173	167	618	3,991,395
Forest Wildcat	165	89	936	130	131	116	559	3,538,680
A.P. Indy	162	87	898	149	120	117	512	8,359,685
Honour and Glory	167	87	916	141	120	116	539	3,041,134
Pentelicus	148	86	1,192	166	158	146	722	2,305,476
Silver Deputy	158	85	1,038	154	155	123	606	4,206,718
Grand Slam	152	84	859	138	128	93	500	4,970,163
Maria's Mon	163	84	1,026	133	126	107	660	2,864,607
Quiet American	146	83	1,034	163	134	132	605	3,955,954
Mr. Greeley	162	83	998	123	124	135	616	2,839,027
Smokester	136	83	939	150	136	119	534	2,651,586
Formal Dinner	137	83	1,192	156	158	125	753	2,490,309
Saint Ballado	156	82	879	129	121	140	489	6,614,013
Salt Lake	147	82	867	143	124	109	491	2,425,995
Slewdledo	141	82	806	128	110	109	459	1,586,607
Valid Expectations	131	81	954	159	130	144	521	3,693,552
Crafty Prospector	132	81	1,050	146	134	143	627	3,410,437
West by West	147	81	1,237	156	146	161	774	3,002,281
Smart Strike	128	80	791	150	109	105	427	6,464,274
High Brite	128	80	986	158	147	134	547	2,484,565
Gold Fever	132	79	971	137	135	150	549	3,936,290
Wekiva Springs	130	79	956	127	120	114	595	2,113,529
Glitterman	142	78	994	146	138	123	587	3,329,448
With Approval	147	78	952	138	104	103	607	3,076,229
Two Punch	132	78	919	134	101	126	558	2,875,021
Marquetry	148	78	1,018	127	150	143	598	2,689,881
Elusive Quality	131	77	751	119	111	92	429	10,700,039
Skip Away	121	77	880	142	118	122	498	3,368,862
Boston Harbor	129	77	755	127	97	90	441	3,139,694
Gilded Time	145	77	939	134	113	142	550	3,070,001
Unbridled's Song	152	76	831	141	110	112	468	5,853,286
Belong to Me	135	76	895	136	130	110	519	4,003,212
A. P Jet	146	76	920	120	135	114	551	2,858,564
Gold Case	127	76	812	129	113	98	472	2,641,759
Kissin Kris	140	76	1,049	147	125	120	657	2,623,396
Storm Creek	159	76	1,098	130	138	130	700	2,502,450
Hennessy	141	75	803	127	92	95	489	3,758,224

Sire	Perfs	Win Perfs	Starts	1st	2nd	3rd	Unpl	Purses
Out of Place	147	75	1,062	132	141	136	653	2,805,290
Bertrando	136	74	672	123	95	84	370	2,566,291
Sir Cat	119	74	781	122	94	112	453	2,162,388
Wild Rush	123	73	835	132	107	112	484	5,063,397
Regal Classic	142	73	1,086	120	137	142	687	3,120,289
Mt. Livermore	144	73	971	120	159	124	568	2,808,984
Tactical Advantage	144	73	1,093	129	154	156	654	2,240,866
Polish Numbers	132	72	848	128	97	125	498	3,221,466
Montbrook	126	72	838	122	107	101	508	2,688,969
End Sweep	139	72	1,101	134	162	154	651	2,516,558
Slew City Slew	136	72	1,020	114	123	119	664	2,506,545
Line In The Sand	154	72	1,272	119	145	155	853	1,868,655
Distorted Humor	120	71	738	131	106	93	408	4,947,035
Holy Bull	136	71	849	110	82	113	544	2,912,741
Silver Ghost	136	71	808	120	88	98	502	2,570,419
Patton	117	71	922	128	91	103	600	2,158,848
Defrere	119	70	845	140	90	119	496	2,525,480
Dance Brightly	115	70	799	118	96	108	477	2,364,046
Formal Gold	107	69	699	125	95	90	389	2,707,994
Louis Quatorze	142	69	863	117	89	98	559	2,660,975
Notebook	116	69	852	122	139	107	484	2,300,806
Sword Dance (IRE)	138	69	981	135	116	138	592	2,279,344
Wild Zone	140	69	866	106	102	104	554	1,803,514
Unreal Zeal	118	69	985	114	129	112	630	1,653,357
Sky Classic	144	68	914	106	99	112	597	3,896,069
Souvenir Copy	122	68	780	115	136	117	412	2,991,615
Southern Halo	146	68	984	127	126	123	608	2,858,080
Pleasant Tap	133	68	917	126	116	115	560	2,620,987
Dixie Brass	113	67	844	120	121	124	479	2,958,921
Rubiano	132	67	895	111	114	126	544	2,663,036
Conquistador Cielo	111	67	800	102	104	103	491	2,013,900
Phone Trick	120	67	792	106	105	92	489	1,978,184
Tour d'Or	129	67	1,017	120	138	114	645	1,879,527
Stormy Atlantic	123	66	679	118	83	92	386	2,929,520
Double Honor	114	66	817	126	90	106	495	2,135,142
Fit to Fight	112	66	862	121	127	120	494	1,886,785
Indian Charlie	95	65	663	138	105	107	313	3,392,633
Wheaton	101	64	755	136	102	102	415	1,910,402
Pembroke	112	64	855	139	122	96	498	1,790,804
Honor Grades	136	63	834	115	109	100	510	3,018,364
Deputy Commander	132	63	832	101	118	111	502	2,674,917
Pioneering	106	63	816	127	109	121	459	2,674,521
Fortunate Prospect	102	63	909	134	126	125	524	2,132,040
Rizzi	110	63	829	111	98	96	524	1,602,243
Petionville	116	62	829	107	111	106	505	3,711,026
Lit de Justice	111	62	938	117	131	104	586	2,965,855
Judge T C	115	62	983	113	135	131	604	2,719,835
Robyn Dancer	123	62	951	114	117	106	614	2,083,990
Lost Soldier	129	62	879	102	106	100	571	1,918,241
Gulch	102	61	667	95	104	107	361	3,949,278
Lite the Fuse	108	61	738	111	89	91	447	2,234,366
Lord Carson	122	61	714	97	100	99	418	1,804,029

Top 10 Sires and Their Progeny

Elusive Quality, B H (1993)
By Gone West – Touch of Greatness, by Hero's Honor

131 Performers, 77 winning performers, $10,700,039 total earnings

Progeny	Mare	Age	Sts	1st	2d	3d	Money Won
Actaeon	Love to Fight	3	5	0	1	1	14,368
Adopted Daughter	Special Test	4	5	1	3	1	66,805
Ann Summers Two	Lakeland	3	5	1	1	1	36,980
Ann's Quality	Serna	3	5	0	0	1	3,258
Another Elusive	Another Anita	4	8	1	1	0	14,038
Appas Tappas	Barzana	4	5	0	1	2	23,618
Avalanche Express	Dafnah	3	3	0	0	0	201
Baba Gonzo	Meadowlake Mist	3	12	3	1	1	48,810
Battledress	Silver Wing	3	8	0	2	1	22,960
Best Quality	Jovan's Lady	4	15	2	2	2	37,000
Best to Be Elusive	Bestofbothaccounts	3	7	0	1	2	6,740
Better Quality	Better Be Sure	3	2	0	1	0	2,050
Brushpopper	Pumpkin Hill	3	5	1	0	0	6,630
Buzzy Bee	K. J. Ma Kate	3	3	1	1	0	6,785
Cabo Sunrise	Miss Dreamland	4	2	0	0	2	7,260
California Heart	Honey Sipper	3	1	1	0	0	22,200
Camp Nagawicka	Teddy Bear Tears	4	10	2	2	2	58,220
Can't Buy Class	Zigabout	3	11	0	5	2	39,710
Caribbean Sun	Scotch Mist	2	1	0	0	0	274
Chet Minty	Carolina Mint	3	7	1	0	0	4,118
Cookie Bight Cove	Big Truffle	3	7	1	0	2	10,603
Cosmic Train	Starpiece	4	4	0	1	0	6,305
Courageous King	Pleas Write	3	4	1	0	2	25,500
Deadly Weapon	Hawiian Sunburst	4	7	0	1	1	7,813
Draw Fire	Beyond the Storm	4	10	1	2	2	59,570
Election Night	Cameo Performance	4	17	1	3	1	8,399
Electric Guitar	New Wave	4	5	0	0	2	2,990
Elusive A. C.	Doedee	4	3	2	1	0	64,780
Elusive Aussie	Diamonds n Frills	3	8	1	0	0	16,560
Elusive Chris	Kara's Heart	2	6	2	3	0	122,570
Elusive City	Star of Paris	4	1	0	0	0	0
Elusive Dawn	Soft Dawn	3	4	1	1	1	34,785
Elusive Diva	Taj Alre	3	9	3	1	2	221,470
Elusive Figure	Flawless Figure	4	7	1	1	1	15,220
Elusive Gal	Hollow Gal	3	1	1	0	0	10,004
Elusive Glory	Dau Dau de Dau	3	5	1	0	1	26,882
Elusive Honey	Honey Sipper	4	8	1	2	2	45,610
Elusive Indian	Personal Lady	4	15	3	1	1	26,285
Elusive Jo Jo	Bye Bye	4	2	0	0	0	878
Elusive Jordan	Gold Premieress	3	8	2	1	1	40,208
Elusive Joy	Fun Bound	3	4	0	1	0	5,191
Elusive King	Storm of Glory	3	8	1	1	2	16,680
Elusive Knight	Duchess Zea	3	9	1	2	1	71,942
Elusive Magic	Lucy's Magic	4	8	2	1	0	18,840
Elusive Princess	Senora Tiara	4	2	0	0	1	4,420
Elusive Project	Pray Lady	3	7	0	3	0	25,100
Elusive Queen	Highway Queen	3	4	1	0	0	15,090
Elusive Road	Bridlewood Road	4	8	1	1	0	17,750
Elusive Smile	Smile On Saratoga	3	5	1	2	0	36,100
Elusive Speed	Nice Life	3	12	1	3	1	15,153
Elusive Thought	Closerthanyouthink	4	2	0	0	0	1,115
Elusive Time	Silver Graphics	3	8	1	1	1	21,360
Elusive Toga	Saratoga Sweetie	2	1	0	0	0	0
Elusive Touch	Residential	3	10	0	0	3	15,310
Elusively	Cozelia	3	3	1	0	0	9,000
Enhanced Edition	Pageantry	3	9	1	0	1	25,835
Evasive	Stephanie's Road	3	3	1	2	0	38,840
Excellent Payback	Norene's Nemesis	3	9	1	1	0	10,870
Exclusively Wild	Holy Bolla	3	5	2	0	0	62,356
Extensive Quality	New Reference (GB)	4	3	1	0	0	6,155
Factory Reject	Cookie Factory	3	12	1	4	2	40,301
Faith of the West	Mystery of Faith	3	12	2	2	1	22,721
Fine Quality	Double Exposure	3	2	0	0	1	2,531
Foryourearsonly	L'Enjolady	4	1	0	0	0	78
Frankiefourfingers	Citi Sounds	4	6	1	0	2	25,502
Gimmeawink	Miss Alethia	4	4	0	1	2	15,330
Girl Warrior	Qhazeenah (GB)	3	3	2	0	0	56,340
Governor Bennett	Follow the Music	4	11	2	1	1	64,320
Great Notion	Evening Primrose	4	2	0	0	0	748
Hawk in Flight	Nasty But Worth It	3	2	0	0	0	0
Heavy Traffic	Mount Helena (GB)	3	1	0	0	0	780
High Descent	Labeled Lady	4	1	1	0	0	36,000
Irish Quality	Irish Moment	3	4	1	1	2	39,320
Jamaica Bay	A. M. Sully	2	2	0	0	0	4,850
Kid Red	Mysti's Poem	3	7	1	0	0	35,280
L C Mystery	Lea Carter	3	3	0	0	0	2,255
La La Boom	Cherry Creek	2	1	0	0	0	195
Lake Kiowa	Single Set	3	8	1	1	0	12,200
Lusi Pond	Tina Pond	3	14	2	2	2	67,384
Madonna Lily	Mi Louisa	3	2	0	0	0	455
Marshon	Coax Me Dear	3	2	1	0	1	33,245
Maryfield	Sly Maid	3	2	1	0	0	19,581
Megara	Dance for Jan	4	2	1	0	1	5,765
Merchant Banker	Sacagawea	3	10	2	0	1	11,291
Miss Elusive	Impassion	3	11	2	1	1	53,710
Missing Silks	Elusive Bird	4	11	4	1	0	23,205
Moss Rose	Prying (ARG)	3	8	2	1	1	70,750
Mr. Elusive	Capote's Joy	4	6	0	1	0	6,105
Nattitude	Love to Fight	4	7	2	1	1	55,635
New Wind Blowin'	T. V. Jingles	3	2	0	0	0	2,880
Night Charger	Smashing Pumpkin	3	7	1	2	0	9,985
Noble Silence	Dark Heat	4	3	0	0	0	1,040
Novice	Pleasant Key	4	1	0	0	0	0
Omega Code	Tin Oaks	4	3	0	0	0	727
Pair of Wings	Elegant Champagne	4	3	0	0	0	1,260
Point Clear	Fight to Love	4	1	0	0	0	360
Prayer Chain	Sambra	4	5	2	1	0	21,860
Pretty Cagey	Pretty Crafty	4	15	3	0	4	45,420
Priceless Quality	Catumbella	4	4	2	0	0	40,590
Pure Quality	T. N. T. Lady	3	5	0	1	0	1,810
Quality Armor	Aromacor	3	6	0	0	1	6,180
Quality Hero	Sweet Roberta	4	7	0	5	0	10,615
Roads West	On Her Merit	4	8	0	0	2	4,391
Rocketeering	Highway Queen	4	5	1	0	1	19,040
Rodney Bay	Count Tootsies	3	2	0	0	0	499
Ruby's Prize	Ruby Surprise	2	2	0	1	0	9,525
Runingforpresident	Neatie	3	7	2	2	1	75,624
Runnin' On Nitro	Explosive Meg	4	9	1	4	0	43,110
Sara Margaret	Kinda Beau	4	1	0	1	0	5,315
Shandy	Sweet Claire Bear	4	8	2	1	2	116,680
Smarty Jones	I'll Get Along	3	7	6	1	0	7,563,535
Smarty Me	Adios	3	4	1	0	0	14,700
Smoking Quality	Splashing Girl	3	7	1	0	2	19,640
Social Virtue	Mercury Direct	2	3	1	1	1	57,280
Sound Judgement	Safe and Sound	2	1	0	0	0	300
Speedjama	Lhotse	3	5	0	1	2	17,634
Tap'n Tango	Song for Par Ci	3	8	0	4	0	38,445
Three Coconuts	Cherokee Twiggy	2	1	0	0	1	2,523
Tino Rossi	Smash That Phone	3	10	1	1	0	13,849
Torre and Zin	Loose Park	4	12	3	0	0	34,641
Touch of Quality	Adelaide	3	17	2	3	3	17,799
Tributetothatcher	Mylittlegeneral	4	1	0	0	0	300
Trickey Mickey	Dancelikethedevil	4	8	3	0	2	14,075
Trulips	Lip Sing	3	4	0	0	0	1,201
Tsu's Aplenty	Tsu's Delta	4	7	1	2	2	28,400
Volatile Vickie	Explosive Meg	3	12	2	4	0	104,680
Weatherfield	Big Truffle	2	3	1	0	0	15,786
Western Royalty	Ariadne's Crown	3	5	2	0	1	40,945
Whale	Coziness	3	1	0	0	0	184
Wild Evasion	Judys Wild Rose	3	2	0	1	0	4,550
Wren	Speedy Tweetie	4	1	0	0	0	320

A.P. Indy, Dk B H (1989)
By Seattle Slew – Weekend Surprise, by Secretariat

162 Performers, 87 winning performers, $8,359,685 total earnings

Progeny	Mare	Age	Sts	1st	2d	3d	Money Won
A. P. Adventure	Nataliano	3	5	2	0	2	268,080
A. P. Aspen	Gone for Gusto	5	4	0	0	0	0
Addicks	Don't Read My Lips	5	14	1	0	2	15,520
Adrenalin Running	Harda Arda	3	8	1	4	0	35,010
Alchemist	Aldiza	4	11	1	4	1	95,488
Alleged Ruler	La Nana (FR)	3	11	3	2	1	140,594
Alluring	Educated Risk	5	3	0	0	0	3,860
Alumni Hall	Private Status	5	10	4	2	1	191,045
Anasheed	Flagbird	4	4	0	0	0	1,959
Appleby Gardens	Larkwhistle	4	4	0	0	1	18,155
Apprentice	Woodyousmileforme	2	2	1	0	1	32,100
Apt	Liable	3	1	0	0	0	2,250
Arbiter	Poolesta (IRE)	7	14	1	2	3	55,480
Arturo	Digit	4	3	1	0	1	26,740
Ashoka	Gallanta (FR)	4	2	1	0	0	31,200
Aztec Pearl	Aurora	5	5	0	2	2	38,080
Bayou Breeze	Bayou Storm	2	1	0	0	0	118
Big Country	Flanders	4	4	0	0	0	1,108
Bold Stock	Dance With Grace	3	6	0	2	0	19,860
Brands Hatch	Watch Out	3	7	1	0	0	41,556
Brazen n' Bold	Go for Bold	5	9	1	1	2	22,744
Bridger	Wakonda	10	1	0	0	0	390
Brother Indy	Alghuzaylah (IRE)	5	3	0	2	0	800
Bubba's Colors	Two Altazano	6	17	3	4	3	54,341
Campionessa	Pacific Squall	2	2	0	0	0	2,760
Capital Spending	Starlet Storm	4	12	2	4	1	107,515
Cat On a Wire	Coldheartedcat	2	3	0	0	0	720
Catalindy	Catalina Court	3	3	1	0	0	30,780
Caught in the Act	Creaking Board (GB)	3	5	0	0	0	6,030
Chic Joy	Chic Corine	4	6	0	2	0	20,090
Chivalric	Ivor Jewel	3	9	2	1	1	48,289
Civilize	Wild Planet	3	6	0	2	1	19,530
Clasp	Hitch	7	16	2	3	2	14,874
Cleft	Choir	2	2	0	0	0	800
Compound	Biding Time	3	8	0	1	1	9,314
Congrats	Praise	4	6	2	0	1	160,832

Progeny	Mare	Age	Sts	1st	2d	3d	Money Won
Connie's Magic	Connie's Gift	8	15	4	1	3	80,860
Crocker Road	Gallanta (FR)	3	4	1	2	0	43,792
Dance With Ravens	Dance Smartly	2	3	1	1	1	223,820
Dancinandsingin	Scoot Yer Boots	3	9	2	0	4	60,680
Dawn Exodus	Grey Parlo	9	10	1	1	1	14,428
Daydreaming	Get Lucky	3	8	5	1	1	483,180
Decision	Gana	6	2	0	0	0	0
Delta Princess	Lyphard's Delta	5	9	2	1	0	109,312
Deputy Indy	Pemaquid	2	1	1	0	0	27,000
Destin	Ocean Cat	3	1	0	0	0	0
Diamond Indy	Adel	3	3	1	0	0	31,400
Domestic Crime	Homewrecker	4	1	0	0	0	250
Elshaan	Thawakib (IRE)	3	1	0	1	0	9,200
Endemaj	Miss Union Avenue	4	2	0	0	0	0
Ender's Shadow	Gold Rush Queen	4	5	1	1	0	86,816
Ender's Sister	Gold Rush Queen	3	7	2	3	1	317,580
Extra	Everhope	4	6	0	0	0	3,360
Fantastic Voyage	Chateaubaby	4	5	2	0	1	31,140
Fashion Sense	Donna Karan (CHI)	4	1	0	0	0	340
Fircroft	Pemaquid	4	7	1	1	1	56,687
Fisher Pond	Chipeta Springs	5	6	1	0	0	42,035
Flying Passage	Chic Shirine	4	2	0	0	0	680
Fragrance	Esther Rose	3	2	0	0	0	1,050
Friends Lake	Antespend	3	4	1	0	1	611,800
Fully Confident	Successfully	3	2	0	0	0	640
Game Box	Aucilla	4	11	1	0	3	22,770
Gold Magic	Run for Lassie	3	2	0	0	0	640
Gradepoint	Class Kris	3	3	2	0	0	108,000
Grat	Likeable Style	2	4	1	1	0	37,515
Handpainted	Daijin	4	6	2	0	2	119,596
High Octane	Bright Candles	2	2	0	0	0	2,280
Highgate Park	High Heeled Hope	3	4	1	1	0	40,609
Hope's Triumph	Clever Monique	3	2	0	0	0	1,260
Icanseeclearlynow	Ifyoucouldseemenow	5	8	2	0	1	19,810
Idealism	Sovereign Kitty	4	10	2	3	1	27,565
Impetuous Fling	Impetuous Image	4	1	0	0	0	1,521
India Sun	Sultry Sun	3	8	1	0	0	18,486
Indiana Express	Merit Wings	4	4	0	0	0	717
Indies (GB)	Cinnamon Sugar (IRE)	3	3	0	0	0	1,800
Indixie	Dixie Accent	6	8	5	0	1	82,570
Indy Charmer	Dancing Mirage	3	8	2	0	1	55,430
Indy Dancer	Dance With Grace	4	4	0	0	1	15,080
Indy Five Hundred	Lyphard's Delta	4	2	0	0	0	5,260
Indy Future	Everhope	3	8	1	2	0	53,247
Indy Groove	Niner's Home	4	10	3	2	1	160,545
Indy Lead	Court Hostess	6	7	0	1	2	28,950
Indy Minstrel	Minstrella	3	5	0	0	0	1,400
Indy Moon	Autumn Moon	2	3	1	0	0	30,080
Indy Snow (GB)	November Snow	3	6	1	0	1	20,768
Indy Storm	Unbridled Wind	2	1	1	0	0	11,400
Indy Thunder	Lucky Souvenir	4	6	1	1	1	12,565
Indy Zone	One Dreamer	4	1	0	0	0	125
Indy's Treasure	Treasure Mine	4	12	1	2	3	24,295
Indygal	Garimpeiro	3	3	1	0	0	29,660
Ivory Coast	Catch Me by Nine	3	5	1	0	1	25,520
Kentucky Pride	Voodoo Lily	4	12	1	4	2	64,116
King's Honor	Great Lady M.	8	9	3	0	0	4,122
La Reina	Queena	3	5	1	1	0	85,922
Lady Margot	Jeano	4	3	0	0	0	1,485
Leading the Parade	My Flag	3	7	1	0	2	38,292
Leif Erikson	Sigrun	3	5	1	1	1	11,150
Lethal Litigator	Vinista	3	1	0	0	0	0
Light From Above	Very Special Lite	2	1	0	0	0	0
Line of Departure	Ballerina Princess	3	1	0	0	1	5,520
Listen Indy	Ecoute	4	7	0	2	2	41,300
Liz On Polk Street	Silver Maiden	3	6	3	1	1	77,480
Lovely Rafaela	Campagnarde (ARG)	3	6	1	1	0	125,535
Lunar Colony	Solar Colony	4	1	0	1	0	6,000
Lunar Perigee	Meteor Colony	4	13	2	2	1	55,081
Mach Speed	Bay Harbor	3	1	0	0	0	0
Mingun	Miesque	4	1	0	0	0	24,000
Miss Hellie	Puestera	5	6	0	1	1	46,448
Mithaal	Zakiyya	3	9	2	0	0	51,500
Monarchoftheglen	Milliardaire	5	6	0	2	1	10,926
Mostly	Smolensk	3	2	0	0	0	3,460
Mrs. Bassett	Ice Cream Cone	3	9	1	0	1	11,899
Munchkin	Honoria	4	3	1	1	0	41,090
Mymich	Dixie Ghost	4	13	3	3	1	132,952
Nasheet	Ma-Arif (IRE)	2	4	0	0	0	2,730
Nor'wester	Pacific Squall	3	9	0	1	3	28,220
Olmodavor	Corrazona	5	6	1	2	1	367,000
Open Flirt	With a Wink	3	3	0	0	1	4,534
Pagosa Springs	Cahill Kate	3	3	0	0	1	6,040
Parrott Bay	Agotaras	7	15	3	2	2	155,802
Passing Shot	Aucilla	5	6	1	1	2	185,460
Patriot Act	Classic Value	2	4	0	2	1	114,885
Perfect Cut	Crystal Shard	4	7	1	0	1	33,372
Pinlochle	Whist (GB)	3	4	0	0	2	11,000
Political Risk	Two Altazano	4	3	1	1	1	29,120
Possibility	Personal Ensign	4	5	0	0	2	14,928
Quick Temper	Halo America	3	11	1	4	1	87,675
Race On Green	Grab the Green	6	9	0	1	1	15,670
Raceready	Esther Rose	2	4	0	0	1	2,640
Racey Dreamer	Dahlia's Dreamer	5	4	4	0	0	112,500
Red Wing Evan	Envied	5	3	2	0	0	31,430
Renaissance Lady	Storm Beauty	3	3	0	2	0	20,200
Romantic Comedy	Zagora	4	7	3	1	0	67,085
Royal Box	Private Status	3	5	0	0	3	10,350
Sa Ad	Zakiyya	7	1	0	0	0	1,150
Safe Haven	Missed the Storm	3	1	1	0	0	15,000
Schwarzwald	Foret Noire	3	9	1	0	1	18,347
Scipion	Strawberry Reason	2	3	1	0	1	47,000
Seattle Weekend	Lassie's Lady	3	2	0	0	0	2,429
Seeking the Glory	Seeking Regina	4	4	1	1	0	37,700
Selection	Mine Only	3	11	0	1	1	5,728
Shake Off	Shake the Yoke (GB)	3	10	2	0	2	104,763
Shanghied	Fleet Road	3	7	4	0	1	98,433
Shaniko	Sapphire n' Silk	3	7	2	2	0	64,320
Sharps 'n Flats	Nine Keys	5	6	0	1	1	8,406
Sheer Luck	Vegas Prospector	3	2	0	0	0	3,840
Sign of Love	Fran's Valentine	4	5	0	1	1	11,260
Silent Moccasins	Quiet Cleo	2	3	0	0	0	0
Snake Mountain	Coup de Genie	6	6	1	0	2	58,210
Spin Control	Prospinsky	4	5	1	0	1	34,352
Steel Buns	Miss Dahlia	2	2	0	1	0	5,840
Strategy	Educated Risk	3	8	2	3	1	93,680
Suave	Urbane	3	11	2	2	2	448,328
Sungold	Queen's Word	2	5	0	1	1	6,293
Teenage Temper	Pleasant Temper	3	8	2	0	1	62,975
Tell J	Prospinsky	5	9	0	1	1	3,689
Trident House	Amizette	4	8	2	0	1	48,930
Two Mile Hill	Flat Fleet Feet	4	11	4	2	1	165,747
Twoindytoo	Two Altazano	5	1	0	0	0	154
U. S. Indy	Top Secret	4	2	0	0	0	640
Under Caution	Coldheartedcat	3	3	0	1	0	2,200
Yell	Wild Applause	4	6	0	2	1	157,826

El Prado, Gr H (1989)
By Sadler's Wells – Lady Capulet, by Sir Ivor

173 Performers, 94 winning performers, $7,987,415 total earnings

Progeny	Mare	Age	Sts	1st	2d	3d	Money Won
Aliado	Alison Sez	2	1	0	0	0	795
Alie's Del Prado	Highland Strike	3	2	0	1	1	11,920
Andalusian	Perfect Pearl	2	2	0	0	0	3,762
Are You Home	Mi Louisa	4	10	0	2	2	26,940
Artie Schiller	Hidden Light	3	8	5	1	0	467,578
Arty	Trust in Me	3	7	0	0	1	3,770
Avenida Lady	Saturn's Image	5	3	0	1	0	3,386
Babypaws	Hazel Wand	5	12	1	0	0	6,003
Baccarat Babe	Family Enterprize	2	1	0	0	0	184
Baena	Big City Dream	2	4	1	0	0	19,460
Barcelona Beauty	Holy Blitz	2	1	0	0	1	2,500
Bermuda Isle	Gone for Gusto	3	2	1	0	0	9,120
Big Gold Martini	Javelin Catcher	7	2	0	0	0	106
Blue Guru	Ruffle My Feathers	6	13	1	0	5	55,690
Border Blues	Miss the Blues	4	12	2	4	2	96,597
Borrego	Sweet as Honey	3	8	0	5	0	452,190
Bright and Shiny	Sunburst (GB)	3	8	1	0	1	41,664
Bruheria	Miss Witchcraft	4	1	0	0	0	0
Captiva Bay	Capotiva	2	2	0	0	0	1,585
Catchaser	Do Not Panic	6	3	0	0	1	1,600
Chameleon	Polly's Rumor	4	12	1	3	5	55,060
Checkthisgroove	Flora Spring	4	4	0	0	1	5,040
Chindi	Rousing	10	10	0	2	6	43,217
Christina Sanchez	Cope's Light	4	1	0	0	0	0
Chuckie's in Love	Crusie	4	13	2	3	0	63,632
Clever Crawford	Remda	5	8	0	2	1	2,392
Cloakof Vagueness	Moving Picture	4	10	1	4	0	126,691
Corning	Painted Portrait	5	2	0	1	0	960
Cowpet Bay	Keeling	3	8	0	0	1	1,854
Crimson and Roses	Flower Garden	4	5	0	1	0	16,880
Crown Pacific	Runaway Royalty	4	8	1	0	0	16,830
Destiny's Design	Lady Brigand	4	8	1	2	2	27,828
Donna's Hope	Lil's Crown	3	7	2	0	1	17,979
Double Haul	Preachersnightmare	3	2	0	0	0	310
Dr. Bombay	Valid Design	4	5	0	0	0	585
Driftwood Lodge	Luke's Drifter	4	6	0	1	1	11,130
Dwendi	Stately Lady	6	4	0	0	0	1,641
Dyna's Legacy	Dynanite	5	4	0	0	0	3,378
El Baby Grand	Piano	3	6	0	1	0	7,310
El Brette	L and n Bride	5	8	0	0	1	5,292
El Case	Miss Mauna Lisa	5	17	3	2	1	32,720
El Charro	Peanut Cowgirl	3	2	0	0	0	480
El Cisc	Bazzie	4	13	1	3	4	52,138
El Crusader	Flying Relaunch	5	8	1	2	3	14,471
El Damien	Souffle (GB)	3	5	1	0	1	22,030
El General	Valid Victress	5	3	2	0	1	48,000
El Giuliani	Eileen Dover	5	6	1	1	2	2,295
El Prado Diamond	Diamonds Again	4	12	1	2	3	10,627

Progeny	Mare	Age	Sts	1st	2d	3d	Money Won
El Prado Essence	Quadrahope	7	4	0	3	1	90,035
El Prado in Action	Gold Action	6	4	0	0	1	4,520
El Prado Rob	Jurisprudence	3	9	0	0	0	37,714
El Prado's Boy	Shes Got the Facts	3	4	1	1	1	19,750
El Prado's Gal	Cazzy B.	3	6	1	0	1	33,101
El Prado's Plata	Diamondsandrubys	4	6	0	0	0	1,600
El Prados Treasure	Racing Treasure	6	10	2	1	0	2,636
El Soprano	Pat Wolsh	5	3	0	0	1	7,700
El Trickster	Weed It Out	3	5	0	0	0	2,751
Elle Runaway	Runaway Venus	2	5	1	1	0	31,962
Eugapae	Revolution Leader	4	6	2	0	1	23,730
Exaggerate This	Palana	3	12	2	4	0	105,794
Exceptionally	Swingin Nickel	3	10	3	0	4	96,621
Exclusive Hopper	Eurobid	4	12	0	4	1	26,955
Ferene	Rapid Rosa	7	1	0	0	0	75
Fleet Selena	Fleet Wahine	3	2	0	0	1	6,270
Fort Prado	Fort Pond	3	10	3	2	0	125,692
Frisco Belle	Runaway Ashleigh	4	8	1	0	3	48,350
Game Day	Figi Bidders	4	9	4	2	0	45,890
Garden Dance	Clearthedancefloor	5	7	2	0	0	40,440
Gavro	Bunbeg	4	4	1	0	0	40,680
Gun Barrel	Wild Warning	9	12	2	1	1	9,733
Halloween Fun	On Hand	4	9	2	1	0	24,295
High Volt Jolt	Bold Blast	4	5	1	2	0	57,000
Humberto	Sweets for All	8	13	3	1	1	28,525
Image	Shared Reflections	6	12	2	1	2	48,210
Julie's Prize	Julie Mis	4	7	2	1	1	127,594
Just Four Austin	All Ability	5	7	1	2	1	21,002
Kenny Run	Regal Gentry	3	10	2	2	1	42,380
Kitten's Joy	Kitten's First	3	8	6	2	0	1,625,796
Kristine's King	Santa Cristina	4	13	3	1	3	88,540
La Prada	Amarata	5	8	0	2	2	7,129
La Prado	Crama	5	5	0	0	0	1,590
Lady Drama	Proper Darling	5	18	1	5	1	16,233
Lady Livingston	Vienna Knickers	3	12	1	2	3	30,740
Last Crown	Six Crowns	3	0	0	1	0	8,978
Leaf Treader	Stately Lady	3	7	0	0	0	2,850
Little Miss Pamela	Top Tip	4	4	0	1	1	17,594
Longhorn Blues	Explosive Ele	4	5	1	0	1	7,480
Louie's Luck	Miss Livi	3	3	0	0	0	1,185
Lusty Latin	Scarlet Ann	5	10	3	1	2	182,040
Magnolia Park	Her Name in Lights	5	7	0	0	1	3,323
Master Barry	Kiwi Mint	2	2	0	0	0	0
McKinney	La Milibucks	6	1	0	0	1	3,500
Meadow Slipper	Aliata	3	5	1	0	1	12,192
Medaglia d'Oro	Cappucino Bay	5	1	1	0	0	300,000
Memorial Bridge	Devil's Orchid	3	6	1	0	2	16,646
Mexican Moonlight	Nellie Custis	4	12	1	3	1	77,500
Middleworth Bay	Runaway Ashleigh	8	5	0	0	0	880
Mona Lisa Lady	Artful Player	5	3	0	0	1	1,891
Mr. Livingston	Vienna Knickers	7	4	1	0	0	21,460
Ms. Monica	Pearl Essence	3	2	0	0	0	165
Mt. Ouray	Fay Morgan	7	12	1	2	0	23,564
My Amandari	Madame Adolphe	3	3	0	0	0	3,320
Mybrowneyedgal	Misbinnhaven	2	2	0	0	1	1,540
Natural Image	Natural Elegance	4	7	1	0	0	21,900
Nives	Certainly a Star	2	4	0	1	1	18,370
Odie	Radiation Delight	5	1	0	0	0	60
Onella	Perfect Red	4	8	1	0	0	7,977
Our Joy	Landholder	3	6	0	2	1	10,952
P J Prado	Silk Pajamas	4	3	0	0	0	0
Paco El Prado	Accadia Rocket	7	9	2	3	1	31,427
Palatine	Slide by (GB)	4	13	1	4	3	35,258
Phillies Dream	Blossom Time	5	11	5	3	1	73,980
Point of Flight	V Formation	3	10	1	0	2	49,231
Power of Elprado	Lovers Power	7	7	1	1	1	6,994
Prado Lady	Jaded Lady	4	6	1	1	0	15,280
Prado Maximus	Copelan's Charm	4	5	1	0	0	18,440
Prado Power	Stage Baby	7	17	4	3	4	50,860
Prado Wells	New Season	9	4	0	0	0	691
Prado's Lass	Leary Lass	4	11	1	1	0	16,800
Prado's Picture	Losthepicture	4	4	3	0	0	19,120
Pranna	Anna's Halo	4	15	1	0	3	7,645
Precious Prado	Practice	5	9	0	0	0	666
Prince Prado	Hardi Lady	4	9	3	1	1	122,263
Princess Cooney	Runaway Royalty	2	2	0	0	0	1,359
Princess Pelona	Peachtree City	4	8	2	0	1	61,531
Pro Prado	Mama's Pro	3	6	1	0	3	183,530
Proper Prado	Proper Banner	3	6	1	3	0	70,180
Pyrite Lady	Carol Jane	5	8	1	2	4	25,405
Quizzle	Glory's Ghost	4	3	1	0	0	19,890
Rainy Parade	September Rain	5	19	3	4	3	41,655
Remagen Bridge	Fine Impression	6	17	1	2	2	14,860
Rhonesquarterswish	Pertinent Wish	9	2	0	0	0	225
Richochet	Attach	3	4	0	0	0	4,880
Royalton	Miss Sanmar	5	2	0	0	0	960
Ruggles Road	Rivermaid Dancing	4	6	0	1	0	5,540
Run to the Border	Pixies Lass	5	10	5	0	2	79,467
Sayitlikeumeanit	Bounding Boldly	4	13	0	1	1	3,929
Senor Prado	Forbes Sparkler	7	10	3	1	2	6,100
Senor Swinger	Smooth Swinger	4	10	4	0	1	418,178
Shaconage	Carita Tostada (CHI)	4	11	2	1	3	256,340
Shamus Shea	Renewable	7	1	0	0	1	3,750
Shaunavon	Sweet and Steady	3	7	4	0	0	136,320
She's Got It	Hanque Bankque	5	7	0	2	0	4,019
Shires Reflection	Shared Reflections	4	6	0	1	0	3,860
Sidetrack	Dream Away	2	2	0	0	0	600
Silverbulletrocket	Seemslikeoldtimes	2	4	0	0	0	617
Simmer	Hotunderthecollar	8	5	1	1	1	27,920
Simmerette	Hotunderthecollar	3	3	0	0	0	615
Sinister Lady	Bridal Wings	3	4	0	2	0	18,240
Sir Prado	Regally Refined (IRE)	6	10	1	0	0	5,687
Soo Much	Smile and Cry	5	8	3	1	2	40,705
Spanish Artist	Summer Sketches	4	22	2	1	4	51,312
Spanish Eyes	Bedford Street	6	7	0	1	2	5,112
Spanish Johnny	It's Windy	5	12	0	1	1	7,666
Spanish Secrets	Secret Vista	3	13	3	2	0	27,290
Summer of Seventy	Almost Saintly	3	2	0	0	0	0
Superfines Prado	Commercial Diamond	6	3	0	0	0	824
Tell No One	Rashas Warning	3	2	0	0	1	4,440
The Gray Spur	Soft Reply	6	13	1	1	2	9,216
The Plains	Jennifer Elaine	4	3	0	0	0	1,345
This Is That	Ask Anita	3	5	1	0	1	14,645
Timo	Elocat's Burglar	3	6	2	1	1	253,308
Tomadache	Too Loud	8	7	0	0	0	345
Tomprado	Crystal Woods	5	13	2	3	3	26,150
Toogie too Shoes	Toogie Too	4	8	1	2	0	27,750
Top Hill	Hill Fifty Four	3	13	2	1	4	70,823
Town Ghost	Tough Case	7	16	0	1	1	2,350
Undisputed Terms	Wendys Terms	5	5	0	0	0	248
Vencer	La Gueriere	3	4	1	0	0	29,020
Whytwocayman	Cayman Queen	5	8	2	1	0	17,239
Willing Coalition	Nabla	3	3	1	0	1	18,600
Winspear	Nay Nay Renay	4	12	1	3	5	44,251
Zach Slim and Eddy	Natalie Natalie	3	15	2	2	2	40,444

Storm Cat, Dk B H (1983)
By Storm Bird – Terlingua, by Secretariat

103 Performers, 56 winning performers, $6,709,124 total earnings

Progeny	Mare	Age	Sts	1st	2d	3d	Money Won
Air Adair	Beyrouth	4	6	2	0	1	51,260
Al Mukhtar	Miss Henderson Co.	3	3	0	1	1	11,710
Ambitious Cat	Lilac Garden	3	4	1	2	0	61,425
American Liberty	Love From Mom	4	6	2	2	0	76,640
Big Top Cat	Golden Attraction	2	2	0	0	0	225
British Blue	Memories of Silver	4	4	1	1	0	22,415
Burmese Cat	Timely Broad	2	2	0	1	0	5,300
Cabaret Star	Pike Place Dancer	2	4	0	0	0	1,925
Captain Thunder	Especially	4	4	0	1	0	11,300
Cat Fighter	Strategic Maneuver	4	5	1	1	3	206,060
Cat On a Rail	Train Robbery	3	1	1	0	0	24,600
Catascatcan	Colcon	3	4	0	2	1	17,160
Clarins	Shell Ginger (IRE)	3	3	1	1	0	33,240
Coffee House	Coffee Springs	2	3	0	0	2	5,720
Cold Front	Ho Baby	3	4	1	0	0	22,700
Connie Belle	Minister's Melody	2	2	0	0	0	4,350
Consolidator	Good Example (FR)	2	7	2	1	1	480,260
Dark Lightning	Secret's Halo	3	4	1	1	1	24,180
Delmonico Cat	Glass Ceiling	5	2	1	0	0	60,000
Denebola	Coup de Genie	3	1	0	0	0	0
Dossier	Sacahuista	3	2	1	0	0	14,100
Dream Time	Fantastic Find	2	1	1	0	0	25,800
Encore	Cash Run	2	1	0	0	0	0
Erin's Storm	Shannkara (IRE)	4	5	0	0	0	4,104
Everydayissaturday	India Divina (CHI)	3	10	3	1	0	130,909
Exotic Elegance	Exotic Wood	3	2	0	0	1	6,860
Fantasticat	Lotta Dancing	3	14	3	4	2	418,400
Fifth Edition	Hiaam	3	5	1	1	0	38,776
Final Round	Profit Column	4	7	2	0	2	102,476
Gata Bella	Capote Belle	3	2	0	1	1	8,680
Good Reward	Heavenly Prize	3	8	3	1	2	444,353
Grand Reward	Serena's Song	3	1	0	0	0	0
Guard Cat	Secretly	6	2	0	0	0	295
Habayeb	Gone to Venus	4	4	0	0	1	2,035
Hell Roaring Creek	Dance Colony	3	4	0	1	0	11,510
Home Court	Jewel Princess	3	3	1	0	2	46,675
Irish Legacy	Ingot Way	5	14	2	2	4	24,046
Kaseh	Magical Allure	3	1	0	0	0	2,500
Katablastic	Lady Lingafelter	4	7	0	2	1	21,844
Major Storm	Next Fall	5	1	0	0	0	2,150
Marino Marini	Halo America	4	5	0	2	1	87,025
Metro Cat	Ruby City	2	2	2	0	0	19,800
Mr. Mabee	Young Flyer	3	4	1	2	0	45,260
Native Vitality	Bountiful Native	5	10	1	2	0	15,950
Nebraska Tornado	Media Nox (GB)	4	1	0	0	0	0
Newfoundland	Clear Mandate	4	9	2	3	1	523,750
Old Deuteronomy	Jewel in the Crown	3	5	1	1	0	48,255
One Nice Cat	Jewel Princess	4	12	1	1	3	55,015
One Stormy Mama	Wicked Mama	2	4	0	1	1	13,130

Progeny	Mare	Age	Sts	1st	2d	3d	Money Won
Our Cat	Lady Lingafelter	3	4	0	0	0	5,040
Ozzie Cat	Hopespringsforever	4	2	1	0	0	25,800
Pasketty	Towering Success	4	6	2	1	2	64,610
Penny's Fortune	Lovlier Linda	3	9	3	2	0	141,609
Phantom Wind	Ryafan	3	1	0	0	0	25,000
Platinum Heights	Amelia Bearhart	3	4	1	1	0	29,800
Pride of Cats	Alpride (IRE)	6	3	0	0	0	600
Prof. McGonagall	Rootentootenwooten	4	7	2	0	3	79,400
Prowling	Miner's Game	5	12	2	2	2	16,035
Pvt. Lynch	Sky Beauty	3	3	0	1	0	9,400
Quick as a Cat	Pearl City	3	2	0	0	0	690
Quick Silver Dream	Tennis Lady	3	5	0	0	0	2,477
Reason This	Low Tolerance	4	7	1	0	0	7,590
Roar of the Tiger	Mariah's Storm	5	4	1	0	1	37,850
Roaring Fever	Pennant Fever	4	9	1	2	3	83,649
Sensational Choice	Oh What a Windfall	3	2	0	0	0	3,400
Sequoia Grove	Lilly Capote	2	3	1	1	0	19,501
Shawnee Warrior	Shawnee Country	3	1	0	0	0	0
Show Me the Roses	Myth	3	2	0	0	0	1,660
Some Kind of Tiger	Morning Devotion	4	7	2	0	0	63,641
Spellmaker	Sofitina	4	6	1	0	0	26,800
Stone Cat	Miss Caerleona (FR)	4	2	1	0	1	17,320
Storm Bowl	Powder Bowl	5	5	1	1	1	21,680
Storm Breaking	Sigrun	4	6	2	1	2	52,070
Storm Commander	Picco Bello	5	6	1	1	0	43,200
Storm Flag Flying	My Flag	4	8	3	2	3	963,248
Storm Legacy	Inca Legacy	3	10	2	1	1	77,220
Storm Minstrel	Colonial Minstrel	3	11	4	4	1	152,420
Storm Signal	Glass Ceiling	7	3	0	0	0	0
Storm Soaring	Soaring Softly	3	2	0	0	0	1,670
Storm Surge	Especially	2	7	4	1	0	192,770
Storm Uprising	Hidden Lake	3	3	0	0	1	5,385
Storm Warning	Let	2	4	1	1	0	44,150
Stormed	Liteup My Life	5	3	0	0	0	400
Stormica	Lovlier Linda	4	7	2	2	1	99,120
Storming Pride	Alpride (IRE)	2	1	0	0	0	400
Stormy Season	Timely Broad	3	11	1	2	3	48,830
Stormy Weather	Bay Harbor	2	4	0	0	0	690
Subtle Breeze	Morning Devotion	3	1	0	0	0	55
Summer Wind Storm	Ingot Way	4	3	0	0	1	3,108
Sweet Catomine	Sweet Life	2	4	3	1	0	799,800
Swift Attraction	Golden Attraction	3	5	1	0	1	41,500
T S Eliot	Gold Sunrise	4	2	1	0	0	17,435
Terrific Storm	Twenty One A. C.	3	7	1	2	1	56,115
Thunder Ridge	City Band	2	2	0	0	0	2,379
Timber Legend	Lady Vixen	5	2	0	0	0	0
Tonitruant	Soundings	4	3	0	0	3	14,475
Tropical Storm	Pearl City	4	3	1	0	0	29,570
Turn of the Tide	Vana Turns	4	2	0	0	0	205
War Trace	Memories of Silver	3	6	3	0	0	86,420
Weather Alert	China Bell	2	3	0	0	0	129
Wildcat Queen	Jetapat	4	2	0	0	0	2,395
With Distinction	Extravagant Woman	3	6	2	1	0	56,245
World Trade	Daring Bidder	5	1	0	0	0	0

Saint Ballado, Dk B H (1989)
By Halo – Ballade, by Herbager

156 Performers, 82 winning performers, $6,614,013 in total earnings

Progeny	Mare	Age	Sts	1st	2d	3d	Money Won
African Skyline	Why Go On Dreaming	5	8	2	1	1	39,300
Angelica Slew	Slewzig	3	8	4	2	2	92,820
Arcola Lane	Star Actress	5	5	1	1	0	7,196
Ashado	Goulash	3	8	5	2	1	2,259,640
Athlete	Pulsatilla	4	5	0	0	2	13,280
Axis	Moscow Tap	5	10	0	0	0	4,555
Bahama John	Rhythm of Life	4	6	2	1	1	65,760
Balladeer	Roman Nile	6	14	1	4	1	16,137
Ballado	Tenga	2	1	0	0	0	140
Ballado Breeze	Wild Royal	3	4	0	0	1	6,950
Ballado Hill	Hill Fifty Four	4	2	0	0	0	509
Ballado Melody	Oh So Sharp	5	4	0	0	1	2,657
Ballado's Baby	Dusty's Mirage	6	5	0	1	0	8,570
Ballado's Cat	Wonder Cat	3	3	0	1	0	9,040
Ballado's Devil	Seashore Miss	6	3	0	0	1	1,262
Ballado's Halo	Goulash	5	1	0	0	1	5,000
Ballence	Excellence	4	7	0	0	1	3,750
Base Stealer	Vennila Cream	4	9	1	0	1	34,089
Battle Red	Royal Fit	3	2	0	0	1	3,120
Biting Feather	Highest Carol	3	6	1	0	0	17,520
Blossum	Single Flower	5	1	0	0	0	0
Bowery Care	Fit to Scout	3	4	0	0	0	2,006
Braytonville	Mission Park	3	4	1	0	2	21,980
Cajole	Common Threads	4	10	2	4	2	62,320
Candlebrook	Lil Cozette	3	4	0	0	0	0
Cartage Agent	Imaginary Number	3	5	0	2	0	18,687
Comanche Star	Deceit Princess	3	11	1	2	5	72,450
Continuum	Charlies Paradise	4	3	1	0	0	16,560
Coverly	Mended Heart	4	1	0	0	0	320
Dance Quiet	Quiet Dance	2	2	0	0	0	430
Deflation	Sunyata	3	6	1	0	2	37,198
Defy Logic	Clever Monique	4	6	2	2	0	49,700
Devine Will	In the Will	2	2	0	1	0	11,250
Divorce Lawyer Jay	Wishing Mood	4	15	2	2	4	28,424
Dr. Tony	Dr. Velvet	4	13	6	1	2	60,749
Dreamers Point	Dance With Bees	7	11	0	0	0	3,173
Drill Hall	Stephanie's Road	5	4	1	1	0	9,120
Eastside Ballad	Eastside Westside	4	1	0	0	1	5,880
Ecumenical	Inca Sun	4	3	0	0	0	450
Evangelizer	Religiosity	3	3	1	1	0	36,140
Exit Laughing	Bolshoi Comedy	4	8	1	1	1	27,526
Family Business	Company Binness	3	12	2	4	2	108,645
Feather Boa	Runaway Spy	4	4	0	2	1	19,678
Fleet Ballado	Afleet Francais	3	4	0	1	0	5,031
Flirting With Fate	Biogio's Baby	3	7	1	1	1	26,580
Future Saint	Prospective	2	1	1	0	0	15,625
Gethsemani	Bottle Top	3	8	0	0	1	19,091
Gimme Shelter	Efficiently	3	2	0	0	0	272
Golden Tango	Dixie Fine	3	6	2	0	0	28,980
Gotta Ballado	Gotta Be Classi	6	16	6	4	1	45,516
Grace Course	Lady Vernalee	5	2	0	1	0	9,000
Halo Hallo	Halloween Joy	3	2	0	0	0	85
Handzz Up	Great Escape	4	6	0	0	1	1,160
Hard Quality	Sweetsoutherncross	4	4	0	0	0	1,424
Harts Gap	Special Test	5	10	1	2	3	51,210
Heavenly Bound	Flowing Melody	3	13	3	1	3	68,820
Heros Among Us	Lady Ling (ARG)	3	2	0	0	0	1,020
Hold the Lime	Coming Out Party	5	9	0	1	2	8,311
Holy Ground	La Ville Rouge	2	1	1	0	0	12,300
Hooloomooloo	Broad Expectations	3	1	1	0	0	8,400
Horse Hill	Mt. Cuba	4	7	1	3	0	31,006
How Little We Know	Sophisticatedcielo	4	13	1	2	4	25,288
I Love a Tru Saint	True Love	3	9	1	1	2	11,716
I'm Just a Peach	I'm a Raisin	7	3	0	0	0	433
Ideal Scenario	Perfect Isn't Easy	3	5	0	0	0	2,935
In Rome	Our Shopping Spree	3	3	0	0	0	1,429
Jangled	Arising	5	6	0	0	1	537
Jettin to Heaven	Jettin Diplomacy	3	1	0	0	0	400
Joe Perfect	Vashon	2	2	0	0	0	75
Joyful Ballad	Bring Me Joy	4	9	2	0	4	56,410
Judge of Character	Fanny's Frolic	5	3	1	0	0	9,887
Justintime G	Miss Valid Pache	2	1	0	0	0	0
Kid Ballado	Red Dynasty	6	3	1	0	0	4,500
Klassy Katlyn	Chicken Delight	3	5	0	0	1	6,080
Lights On	Chicken Delight	5	6	0	0	0	13,370
Lindsay Jean	Colony Bay	6	1	0	0	0	0
Lindt	Harpa	6	14	1	2	0	9,502
Lord of the Game	She's a Winner	3	1	1	0	0	6,300
Lord Ofthe Thunder	Astarte	5	5	1	1	1	56,554
Lottaballado	Truffles Royale	8	6	0	0	0	186
Mad Donna	Marchtothemine	4	3	0	1	2	3,380
Malheur	Sapphire Beads	2	4	1	1	1	42,988
Media Saint	Mediation (IRE)	3	7	2	0	0	25,683
Melody Maiden	Lake Placid (IRE)	3	4	0	2	0	15,500
Mikey's Magic	Shift Surprise	2	1	0	0	0	0
Mille Feville	Captivant	5	9	0	0	3	48,894
Minstrel's Melody	Glorious Minstrel	4	9	0	0	2	6,620
Nine Ballads	Nine Flags	3	4	0	0	1	3,743
Northern Ballad	Sloane Street	3	9	1	1	0	25,780
Ocho Negro	Dolce Amore	3	3	0	0	0	0
Omaha Brave	Mamselle Bebette	3	11	2	3	4	48,020
Orlean	Nidd	3	3	1	1	0	22,400
Paddington	Painted Portrait	3	5	0	0	1	17,540
Paint Ballado	Donusa	3	11	0	2	1	24,447
Parnell Square	Smart Lady Too	4	3	0	1	1	14,450
Pawyne Princess	Scottische	3	7	3	2	1	117,230
Popular Delusions	Pretty Flame	2	2	0	0	0	1,530
Preach It	Arrested Dreams	3	12	1	2	1	54,479
Primo Primo	Divine Dixie	4	7	1	1	0	14,175
Prospective Saint	A. B. Prospect	3	7	2	1	0	87,393
Queens Village	Annie Imp	6	8	3	3	0	15,358
Roused	With Every Wish	3	4	0	0	0	1,020
Royal Duke	Dark Sapphire (IRE)	4	10	1	1	3	13,268
Royal Parade	Deputy Royal	3	7	1	1	0	17,330
Royal Saint	Deputy Royal	2	1	0	0	0	300
Running Saint	Chadra North	3	7	1	1	2	43,295
Rutledge Ballado	Gold From the West	2	2	1	1	0	20,480
Saint Appeal	Nanerpeal	5	2	0	0	0	0
Saint Buddy	Heart of America	4	10	1	3	3	196,120
Saint Cali	Cali	2	3	1	0	0	25,320
Saint Chrisjon	California Rush	3	3	1	0	0	18,535
Saint Damien	Wife Begone	6	20	4	6	4	63,035
Saint Liam	Quiet Dance	4	5	2	2	1	618,760
Saint Lorenzo	Twochindordor	4	4	3	1	0	77,760
Saint Martin	Hope's Ahead	3	9	2	1	1	105,826
Saint Ray	High Heeled Hope	2	3	0	0	0	1,410
Saint Sabates	Island Splendour	4	1	0	0	0	218
Saint Stephen	Goulash	4	6	1	1	1	40,040
Saint Waki	Mollywaki	4	12	1	0	3	43,140
Saint's Play	Colonial Play	2	1	0	0	0	205

Progeny	Mare	Age	Sts	1st	2d	3d	Money Won
Sainted Colony	Probable Colony	4	13	1	5	2	48,125
Saintlike	Lady Lodger (GB)	4	4	2	0	0	37,925
Saintly Action	Act	5	6	0	1	2	57,450
Saintly Look	Sensational Eyes	4	10	1	0	3	31,470
Saintly Persuasion	Private Persuasion	4	2	0	0	1	9,520
Saints a Plenty	Plenty of Sunshine	4	5	1	1	1	13,785
Santa Croce	Broad Dynamite	4	5	2	2	1	74,500
Santa Rosalia	Sugar Is Gold	3	8	0	2	3	33,024
Santo Pio	La Ice Queen	3	4	0	0	0	3,950
Savedbythelight	Wild Royal	4	7	0	2	1	76,440
She Ain't No Saint	Jolie's Valentine	3	2	0	0	0	440
Silverlado	Silver Clover	3	3	0	0	0	900
Silview	Tanwi (IRE)	4	3	1	0	1	13,351
Sinners N Saints	Navarra	3	2	0	0	0	1,436
Slant	To Be a Lover	3	6	1	1	1	22,090
Smiling Eyes	Western Lady	4	3	1	0	0	26,200
Special Ballad	Special Mistress	5	14	1	4	6	28,087
Spirited Maiden	Pacific City	5	4	0	2	0	27,450
St Averil	Avie's Fancy	3	4	1	1	0	140,000
St Ballado's Image	Sugar's Image	3	10	1	1	2	31,530
St. Kilda	Call Catherine	3	9	1	0	1	17,480
Stacie's Ballado	Storm Minister	3	7	2	0	4	58,990
Stuck by Eddie	Packet	3	3	1	0	1	8,987
Sweet Blessing	Sweet Alabastar	4	12	0	1	0	1,627
Sweet Kassidy	Dear Sweet	3	1	1	0	0	14,250
Sweet Melody	Interpretive Mood	3	1	0	0	1	2,470
Tequesta	Bodacious Tatas	3	3	1	0	1	25,250
Theo's Saint	Fancy Pan	4	6	1	1	1	12,945
Top Gate	Nimble Feet	3	2	1	0	0	31,945
Upswing	Rewarding	3	4	0	0	0	281
Vagabond Saint	Queens n Vagabonds	3	9	0	0	4	16,476
Wadena	Ammy Hils	3	8	1	0	1	51,538
Whatasaint	Whatamiss	5	4	1	1	1	18,510
Wild Horses	Waltzing With Deb	5	5	3	0	0	49,885
Windham Flash	Ameritop	4	5	2	1	0	20,560
Worthing	With Every Wish	4	5	0	0	3	6,060

Smart Strike, B H (1992)
By Mr. Prospector – Classy 'n Smart, by Smarten

128 Performers, 80 winning performers, $6,464,274 in total earnings

Progeny	Mare	Age	Sts	1st	2d	3d	Money Won
A's Anchorman	Ropa Usada	5	10	1	2	1	10,435
Acklen	Exotic Dancer	3	5	0	0	2	3,245
Added Edge	Sweet Nostalgia	4	8	3	1	2	170,075
American Strike	Americarr	5	5	0	1	0	2,943
Ask Dorothy	Psychic Spirit	5	1	0	0	0	825
Asp	Cleopatra's Pearl	4	4	0	1	0	1,993
Bastione	Hear the Sea	4	4	1	1	1	11,340
Beach Club	Pelican Reef	4	4	1	1	2	18,980
Beached	Pelican Reef	5	7	2	3	2	35,930
Burst of Fire	Quiet Cheer	3	11	4	2	2	290,765
Buzz Strikes	Courtly Attire	2	1	0	0	0	205
Byback	Eastern Connection	5	12	2	2	1	36,982
Cal's Baby	Silver Dollar Kate	6	5	1	1	3	16,430
Chief Black Hawk	Silver Trainor	5	11	0	2	0	4,715
Classy Strike	Auxiliary	5	9	3	1	0	17,751
Clever Greek	Dixie Heiress	3	2	2	0	0	22,800
Coastal Strike	Costa Rica	2	2	2	0	0	89,520
Coconut Popsicle	Time Crisis	2	7	1	0	2	38,795
Colonial Strike	Colonial Reef	2	6	0	0	1	9,790
Crosslander	Inthefastlane	3	5	1	1	0	23,230
Dance With Lance	Mi Hush Puppy	2	1	0	0	0	200
Deputy Strike	Political Process	6	5	2	2	0	94,375
Don't Strike Out	Classy n' Sassy	4	11	4	2	0	42,342
E. B. Striker	Miss Owens	2	6	0	1	0	6,955
English Channel	Belva	2	1	1	0	0	27,600
Eye of the Sphynx	Queen of Egypt	3	7	4	2	0	688,340
Fine Strike	Perle Fine	3	9	0	4	1	30,800
Fire Strike	Cape Fire	3	11	1	3	0	20,600
Fleetstreet Dancer	Street Ballet	6	1	0	0	1	30,000
Fly Smartly	Spinnakers Flying	6	7	1	0	3	42,008
Forever Smart	Champagne Forever	2	3	0	1	1	12,640
Free Hit	Wainee	3	6	0	1	0	6,620
Free Strike	Free City	3	14	1	1	1	11,741
Fresh Thunder	Fresh Air	5	12	2	1	0	28,552
Get Smarter	Regal Feeling	4	1	0	0	0	360
Gold Strike	Brassy Gold	2	3	2	1	0	51,592
Good Luck Strikes	Lucky Minister	3	3	0	0	0	0
Grand Marshall	Icy Anne	2	1	0	0	0	0
Guaranteed Victory	Peaches On Ice	2	2	0	0	0	3,340
Hard Edge	Countus In	5	13	2	1	1	115,110
Hatpin	Lafayette's Lady	2	1	1	0	0	35,280
Hellacious Curve	Regency Island	4	9	1	0	2	5,145
Hestosmartforyou	Polish Spirit	6	1	0	0	0	80
High Alert	Apalachee Princess	5	5	1	0	1	19,330
High Strike Zone	Danzig Island	4	9	4	2	2	98,710
Intimidating	Pretty Ribbons	2	1	0	0	0	1,881
It's So Simple	Kaylem Ho	6	14	5	0	4	108,260
It's Vodka Talking	Twin Voice (JPN)	2	1	0	0	1	1,920
Joyjoyjoy	Corking	3	5	0	1	2	15,810
Jrsoutofcontrol	Chic Chanel	6	9	1	1	1	18,706
Just a Little Jet	Just a Little Kiss	2	2	0	1	1	11,100
K Girl	Checkmeout First (GB)	2	3	0	0	1	3,307
Kait Can't Wait	Handmade	4	8	1	0	0	11,471
Kalookan Lass	Fascinate	3	2	1	0	0	27,860
Kim the Brat	Whow	4	2	0	0	0	680
Kristina's Wish	On Kris's Wings	4	15	5	2	3	88,926
Longship	Spinnakers Flying	4	9	2	0	5	106,998
Luckyandsmart	Call Her	2	3	1	0	1	19,198
Matched	Call Her	5	12	3	5	2	32,880
McKee's Gallery	Art Gallery	4	3	1	0	0	37,375
Miss Smart Strike	Atlantra	4	6	3	1	0	47,585
Moonlight Duel	Countus In	3	6	1	1	0	27,045
Mr. J. T. L.	Star Reputation	3	11	1	2	0	52,444
Mr. Technique	Reassert	4	2	0	1	0	7,500
My Lucky Strike	Launch Time	5	12	1	2	2	105,396
Parasail	Dancing With Wings	4	4	1	1	0	51,740
Party Maker	Meu Paixao (ARG)	2	2	1	1	0	49,826
Pat the Winner	Karakorum (IRE)	4	9	1	2	0	35,730
Pelham Bay	Brazen	2	7	3	0	2	126,777
Poison Oak Camp	Erina	5	17	1	1	0	7,091
Poydras	Debra C.	4	2	0	1	0	6,460
Precision Strike	Affordable Fantasy	2	2	0	0	0	630
Prospectors Strike	Zuri	5	12	2	0	1	24,121
Red Haze	Doc's Scarlet	3	2	0	1	0	8,568
Reine des Neiges	Miss Snowflake	5	3	0	0	0	3,765
Roman Peace	Queen of Egypt	5	3	0	2	1	15,300
Run Sarah Run	Breech	4	11	2	1	2	73,230
Sapphire Hill	Dark Sapphire (IRE)	6	10	2	0	2	33,900
Say Cousin Lenny	Lolli Lucka Lolli	5	8	1	3	0	57,340
Shadow Cast	Daily Special	3	12	4	1	4	267,480
Shadow Steele	Miss Vice	6	3	1	0	1	3,470
She'samystery Girl	Mory's Cups	3	5	0	0	0	4,410
Shining Strike	Raj Dancer	5	2	1	0	0	25,800
Shoal Water	Puffin Island	4	5	2	1	1	336,414
Slumber Party	Just Us Girls	4	13	2	3	3	28,936
Smart Agenda	Agenda	5	13	6	2	1	55,165
Smart Ana	Ana Belen (CHI)	5	10	1	2	4	30,544
Smart Coup	Offshore Account	5	6	0	0	1	2,987
Smart N Classy	Teenage Queen	4	9	3	4	0	134,444
Smart N Sassy	Marsh Cat	5	3	0	0	0	2,406
Smart N Smooth	Wide Country	5	8	2	2	1	53,200
Smart October	October Beauty	5	11	2	1	2	50,219
Smart Skater	Crystal Skater	3	11	3	3	1	65,348
Smart Thought	Opentotheright	3	4	2	0	1	31,080
Smartest Thing	Alycheer	2	3	1	2	0	99,020
Soaring Free	Dancing With Wings	5	8	6	0	0	1,113,862
Soaring Strike	Dancing With Wings	2	2	1	0	0	15,900
Somebody Smart	Somebody Else	2	3	0	0	0	0
Sosella	Mosella	3	5	0	1	1	6,741
Strategic Strike	Larking	4	13	2	0	1	30,726
Strike a Star	Scoutingforastar	3	3	0	0	0	1,517
Strike and Run	Great Girlfriend	3	6	1	0	1	46,029
Strike Breaker	Maria Candela (CHI)	4	3	0	0	0	233
Strike Em Hard	Crying Out Loud	3	11	0	1	2	75,074
Strike Island	Picnic Island	3	10	1	2	0	17,900
Strike Me Lucky	Chickapee	3	5	0	0	1	6,850
Strike Point	Point of Honor	4	9	2	2	0	22,802
Strike Rate	Harda Arda	4	11	3	1	2	95,236
Strike the Moment	Angry Moment	3	6	1	1	2	19,876
Strikeapromise	Promiseville	5	1	0	0	0	0
Striking Flames	Flaming Gold	5	10	0	0	1	1,729
Striking T	Rather Be Dancing	3	15	2	1	1	17,250
Strikingly	Torrent	4	12	1	0	1	28,546
Sunnyridge Sam	Know B's	4	6	1	1	0	33,546
Sunup	Streets of Rio	4	8	1	4	1	59,490
Superior Cat	Ira's Cat	2	2	0	0	2	2,415
Talk the Walk	Sunset Strip	3	5	2	1	0	47,300
Tenpins	Maid's Broom	6	1	0	1	0	12,000
Threeandoh	Lady Clever Trick	2	1	0	0	0	274
Walls of Jericho	Dancer's Gate	4	5	1	1	0	55,014
Well Struck	Summer Fantasy	5	5	0	0	1	5,580
Westmoorings	Creole	2	3	1	0	0	24,624
Whiletheiron'shot	No More Ironing	5	4	0	0	1	11,043
Whisper Bay	Senita Lane	3	2	1	0	0	28,920
Windstruck	Wilderness Hush	3	3	0	0	1	9,888
Winning Approach	Chateau Rossi	5	6	0	0	1	2,984
Wishful Splendor	Kaylem Ho	5	1	1	0	0	60,000
With Assurance	Queen of Egypt	4	9	1	0	2	20,713

Awesome Again, B H (1994)
By Deputy Minister – Primal Force, by Blushing Groom

104 Performers, 58 winning performers, $6,312,464 in total earnings

Progeny	Mare	Age	Sts	1st	2d	3d	Money Won
Always Awesome	Anzille	4	5	2	0	1	95,000
Amazing Again	Crystal Shard	3	2	0	0	1	5,000

Progeny	Mare	Age	Sts	1st	2d	3d	Money Won
Aristocrat	Baby Zip	2	1	0	0	0	2,250
Awesome Action	Opinionated Lady	4	7	2	1	2	142,238
Awesome Alarm	Belle de Soleil	3	3	0	1	1	5,630
Awesome Anew	Aisle Seeya	3	14	1	3	3	29,240
Awesome Cannonball	Splash Em Baby	4	4	1	0	0	25,610
Awesome Charm	Reet Petite	4	8	0	1	1	17,490
Awesome Dancing	Lulu	4	1	1	0	0	14,750
Awesome Deduction	Taxable Deduction	3	9	1	2	2	38,005
Awesome Dividend	Bluff's Dividend	4	5	3	1	0	63,520
Awesome Doe	Roobels	2	9	1	1	1	17,550
Awesome for Sure	Woodsy Meadow	4	5	2	1	0	22,423
Awesome Frances	Frances in the Sky	4	4	1	1	1	22,860
Awesome Powers	Jill Miner	4	13	3	3	2	72,430
Awesome Pro	Fickle Fate	2	1	0	0	0	205
Awesome Punch	Joustabout	4	4	0	0	0	0
Awesome Reef	Colonial Reef	4	7	3	2	0	31,120
Awesome Rush	Rose Diamond	4	3	0	2	0	25,120
Awesome Sign	Hekeepsmesinging	2	1	0	0	0	400
Awesome Takeover	On the Tree Top	3	3	0	0	0	660
Awesome Time	Slew Boyera	4	1	0	0	0	240
Awesome Touch	Baby Millie	4	4	1	1	1	28,620
Awesome Venture	Forever Land	2	2	0	0	0	4,500
Awesome Victory	Sarabi	2	2	0	0	0	720
Awesomebabyawesome	Takeover Target	3	10	1	0	1	7,160
Awesomely	Phone the Doctor	3	2	0	0	0	431
Awesomeness	Glory in Motion	3	7	2	0	0	58,171
Awesomewithbroads	Aggressive Broad	3	8	1	1	4	35,400
Awestruck	My Heart Sez Yes	3	4	0	0	0	306
Ball Girl	Bal d'Argent	2	2	1	1	0	36,600
Brush the Law Agin	Brush With the Law	4	14	2	3	1	17,273
Cajun Dawn	Pat's Reward	3	2	0	0	0	161
Call Me Awesome	Pagofire	3	4	0	1	1	14,312
Carolina Sunrise	Stylish Star	4	3	1	0	1	7,017
Clays Awesome	Our Shopping Spree	4	1	0	1	0	5,670
Comealong	Dark Hours	2	1	0	0	0	0
Cupid's Arrow	Cupids Revenge	3	10	2	2	2	67,885
Dashing Deputy	Ms. Copelan	3	9	1	0	3	26,084
Dealing With Daisy	Campaign Worker	4	7	0	2	3	26,794
Destined to Win	Designatoree	4	7	2	1	1	46,570
Diamond Bullet	Po Po Au Pooh	4	16	4	4	3	59,880
Diane Again	Dianes Halo	2	5	1	0	1	17,280
Easy Cruiser	Desert Radiance	4	7	1	0	5	70,569
Echeverria	Evil's Pic	4	2	0	0	0	113
Encore Encore	Honolulu Honey	3	3	0	0	0	2,288
Enterprise Coast	Eye Catching	3	1	0	0	0	975
Europe Again	Europa	3	3	0	1	0	9,250
Expressly	Rapid Selection	3	4	0	0	0	105
Extra Exclusive	Prominent Feather	2	2	1	1	0	10,100
Final Marriage	Society Column	3	4	0	0	0	1,900
Formalities Aside	Well Dressed	2	5	1	1	1	38,089
Ghostzapper	Baby Zip	4	4	4	0	0	2,590,000
Glorious Again	Family Enterprize	4	9	3	3	2	86,148
Goofball	Letting Loose	2	3	0	2	0	4,360
Guildhall	Earth Song	2	3	0	1	0	4,362
He's a Hunk	Fanny's Flying	4	10	2	2	3	58,760
He's Awesome	Sister Queen	4	5	1	0	0	9,979
Headline News	Printing Press	4	3	1	0	0	6,760
Hillbilly Bandit	Diablo's Peace	2	6	1	0	2	19,180
Hillside Dreamer	Nikita Moon	3	3	1	0	0	14,050
Hotstufanthensome	Don't Read My Lips	4	10	5	2	0	143,200
I'm an Awesome Cat	I'm No Pussycat	4	15	4	2	2	22,822
I'm Awesome	Valid Dorothy	3	1	0	0	0	0
I'm Awesome Again	Imaglee	3	11	2	0	1	45,645
In Love Again	Dhaka	4	2	0	0	0	2,241
Jennie R.	Petrouchka	3	5	2	2	0	48,800
Justa Lil Awesome	Gratify	3	1	0	0	0	0
Kaysome	McKaymackenna	3	7	1	1	1	13,255
King Mustang	Feeling Easy	2	2	0	0	0	580
Magoo's Magic	Slew the Queen	2	4	2	1	0	70,358
Mantova Run	Tassa	2	6	1	1	0	22,600
Miney's Awesome	Mine Tonight	4	6	1	2	0	32,731
Naked Again	Naked Glory	2	3	0	1	0	2,800
Not Acclaim	Eurobid	3	6	2	0	1	20,170
Orange Power	A Dream Above	3	8	1	1	0	9,050
Personal Legend	Highland Legend	4	8	3	2	1	224,330
Pink Champagne	Turkappeal	3	9	0	1	0	13,257
Poker Game	Stormy Blues	3	4	0	2	1	15,010
Post Its Awesome	Post It	4	8	3	2	0	23,798
Prince Awesome	Pure Red	3	1	0	0	0	0
Queen Kennelot	Le Grand Epic	3	1	0	0	0	0
Rock Again	Track Gal	4	2	1	0	1	57,329
Rockin' Again	Touch Dial	3	9	2	2	0	70,922
Rolling Benz	Fighting Jet	4	5	2	0	0	38,640
Rousing Again	Rousing	4	7	3	2	0	62,660
Royal Force	Indy Ama	3	9	0	1	2	10,525
Rumor Has It	Garden Secrets	3	1	0	0	0	0
Snorter	Retiro Park	4	6	2	0	1	125,100
Spun Sugar	Irish Cherry	2	1	0	1	0	9,000
Strictly Business	Lets Do Lunch	4	15	1	2	3	41,523
Supah Sensation	Supah Gem	3	5	2	0	0	47,256
Symmetron	Valid Symmetry	4	3	1	0	1	49,476
Thunder Fox	Astas Foxy Lady	3	5	1	3	0	35,460
Toccet	Cozzene's Angel	4	8	0	2	0	83,597
Triple J	Triple Strike	4	6	0	2	0	13,250
Tyne	Banantyne	4	3	0	0	0	1,180
Up and Again	Up an Eighth	3	6	0	0	0	2,530
Valid Again	Valid Way	3	10	3	0	0	86,331
Vallelunga	Brushing Gloom	3	4	1	0	1	8,195
Welcome Again	Alda's Will	2	2	0	1	0	5,700
Wilko	Native Roots (IRE)	2	2	1	0	1	833,580
Win Again	Valid Approval	2	1	0	0	0	0
Xtra Awesome	Woofy	2	1	0	0	0	0

Tale of the Cat, Dk B H (1994)
By Storm Cat – Yarn, Mr. Prospector

(170 Performers, 98 winning performers, $6,031,213 in total earnings.)

Progeny	Mare	Age	Sts	1st	2d	3d	Money Won
Adage	Firey Affair	3	3	0	0	0	816
American Saga	Louisiana Flash	4	1	0	0	0	880
Ancient Myth	Pleasant Oasis	3	5	1	2	0	27,360
Aristocat	Mended Fences	4	2	0	0	1	4,680
Artemus Sunrise	Eggs Binnedict	3	12	4	3	0	124,620
Arwa	Woman of Quality	3	4	1	0	0	16,630
Barbara Orr	Forli's Slew	4	4	1	1	0	59,140
Belmont Babe	Arizona Star	3	11	2	1	2	29,991
Black Tie Classic	Black Tie M. D.	3	4	0	0	1	810
Blazing Purrsuit	Blazing Kadie	3	3	1	0	2	35,200
Blushingkittentale	Blushing Issue	3	7	2	2	0	28,190
Boom a Cat a Boom	Lovely Sebeecha	3	10	2	2	0	50,440
Call Me Shane	Maeslady	3	3	1	0	0	24,995
Canadian Gem	Izara	2	6	2	2	0	125,580
Captain Prudent	Widow Women	3	4	1	0	2	10,759
Captiva Cat	Donna Says So	4	1	0	0	0	230
Casual Cat	Cyane's Slippers	3	1	0	0	1	2,860
Cat Buster	Big Dreams	3	6	2	1	1	72,315
Cat Patrol	Miss Evans	4	7	0	2	2	25,460
Cat Sound	Sound It	3	10	1	1	4	14,119
Cat Story	My Trim	4	5	0	0	0	2,710
Cat's Account	Miner's Match	3	5	1	0	1	29,850
Cat's At Bat	The Babe	4	2	0	0	0	0
Catalissa	Lissa	4	7	2	1	0	63,380
Catboat	Northern Fleet	3	12	6	3	1	184,598
Catlike Dancer	Meadow Flyer	4	7	4	1	0	53,180
Catmeifyoucan	Seattle Starlet	2	7	2	2	0	39,820
Catsgotninelives	Sea Abyss	3	7	0	3	1	38,000
Cattail Lake	Lake Travis	2	1	0	0	0	100
Catzinga	Hunzinga	4	10	4	3	0	55,444
Cavans Lane	L'Insatiable	3	7	1	1	0	42,780
Chez Black	Dam Clever	4	8	1	0	0	7,473
Chocolate Tale	Shamrock Time	3	5	1	2	0	10,385
Cielo's Cat	Cielo's Dance	3	5	1	2	0	9,100
Civility Cat	Civility (GB)	4	1	0	0	0	0
Crockett	Shared Magic	3	3	1	0	0	6,683
Crouching Tiger	Berkshire Shopper	4	13	0	0	2	12,208
Cry of the Cat	Crying Out Loud	4	8	1	2	0	21,047
Cunning Cat	Bet Birdie	3	5	1	0	1	20,485
Curiosity	My Big Sis	4	12	1	1	2	81,722
Eleventh Street	Afleet's Gold	2	5	0	2	2	31,664
Endless Dream	Conquistador Blue	2	3	0	1	0	13,270
Epic	Wigwam	4	4	0	0	1	9,396
Ernie Cat	Dreaming Time	2	5	2	1	0	26,690
Feline Story	Shappy	3	9	2	4	2	224,985
Fire Path	Stirling Bridge	2	4	1	0	0	16,550
Fleeting Feline	Fleeting Fable	4	3	0	0	1	4,810
Frat Party	Estate Sale	3	9	1	2	0	17,855
Full Cooler	P. D. Tobin	4	2	1	0	0	11,485
Gallant Tale	Perla Fina	4	8	2	0	0	17,559
Gatito Fuerte	Financial Lady	2	7	3	3	0	63,990
Gattina Bella	Exclusive Hold	2	9	2	1	2	32,540
Glamour Cat	Turk Machine	3	5	0	2	2	26,960
Go Kitty Go	Miami Margie	3	11	2	3	0	102,602
Green Eyes	Sheza Honey	3	1	0	0	0	400
Haughty Lady	Birchfrost	4	5	1	2	2	20,900
Haunted House	Bungalow	2	1	0	0	1	2,860
Heaven's Cat	Debs Angel	3	8	1	0	2	23,140
Honest Answer	Cup of Honey	4	1	0	0	0	3,600
Hypercat	Regent n'Flashy	4	1	0	0	0	0
Ignition	Scapegoat	4	2	1	1	0	27,880
Iolanda	Teddy Bear Tears	2	1	1	0	0	16,200
Itawtisawaputtytat	Rubies for Alicia	3	4	0	2	0	20,670
Jack of Clubs	Regal Ruby	3	7	0	2	3	23,684
Jones Tale	Jones Time Machine	4	4	0	2	2	28,760
Kalens Jet	Thruthelookinglass	4	5	0	0	1	2,945
Kat's Fairy Tale	Woodman's Diplomat	2	1	0	0	0	2,050
Key to the Cat	Key to Paradise	3	13	2	4	3	109,706
Krakowviak	Queen of Women	4	8	1	2	1	19,565
Last Oasis	Southern Letters	2	1	1	0	0	13,800
Legend	Halo Queen	2	3	1	2	0	20,210
Legendary Squire	A Shaky Queen	3	4	1	0	0	27,874
Lest We Forget	Kay Bee Bee (IRE)	4	2	2	0	0	58,200

Lil Gary Too	She's Family	3	13	0	4	4	40,460
Lion Cat	Maryland Parkway	2	3	0	1	0	10,180
Lion Heart	Satin Sunrise	3	7	2	3	0	1,080,000
Lonesomenumberone	Mime (IRE)	3	3	1	0	0	7,626
Lord of the Cats	Energise	3	12	1	1	2	29,310
Macann's Promise	Bearly Smiling	3	5	0	0	0	3,488
Maltese Baby	With Cheer	4	4	0	2	0	10,550
Matching Sox	Silver and Bronze	3	3	0	0	0	1,077
Matt Daddy	Twirl	2	2	0	0	2	7,370
Max's Tale	Walking Stick	4	2	0	0	0	0
McGeever	Jovi San	4	8	1	0	2	7,678
Minstrel Show	Proud Minstrel	2	3	0	1	0	8,845
Miss Cat Tail	Miss Winver	3	4	0	0	0	570
Miss Tale Cat	Fleet Line Lady	4	10	2	4	0	33,810
Missmaybe	May We	3	6	3	0	1	71,010
My Kitty Cat	My Oooo Aah	3	2	0	0	1	3,520
My Trusty Cat	Entrusted	4	10	3	3	0	311,290
My Turbeau Cat	My Turbulent Beau	3	7	1	0	1	21,862
Mysterious Dream	Ms Jaguar Type	3	1	0	0	0	1,230
Neon Magic	Star of Light	4	14	3	1	4	54,930
Never Ending Tale	Departing Ms. S.	3	8	1	0	0	8,673
Northern Tales	Tres Norte	2	1	0	0	0	450
One Lucky Storm	Shameem	3	12	2	0	2	27,580
Oneverycoolcat	Kowloon	3	2	0	0	1	10,380
Our Josephina	Ropa Usada	4	10	3	2	2	179,414
Perfect Story	Turko's Turn	4	2	0	0	0	380
Pixie Dust	Estate Sale	2	1	1	0	0	9,000
Point Hidden	Rose of Cimarron (FR)	3	5	1	1	2	41,353
Preacher's Tale	Preachersnightmare	2	3	0	2	0	17,323
Prospector's Bride	Correoso	2	2	1	0	0	19,740
Pussycat Pussycat	Dancing Rhythm	2	3	0	0	1	8,607
Queen Isabel	Scherzando	4	1	0	0	0	640
Red Earthquake	Zuppa	3	12	2	1	2	48,190
Relato Del Gato	Sole	3	5	1	1	0	15,380
Remarqable Tale	Marquetry Road	3	5	1	2	2	44,250
Resplendency	Doppio Espresso	3	4	2	1	1	121,080
Risky Cat	Calling Ann	4	9	1	0	0	13,730
Rocket Launcher	Regal Consort	3	2	0	0	0	400
Rollmeaseven	Fordyce	2	2	0	0	0	348
Royal Epic	Your Ladyship	2	5	0	2	0	21,560
Satawa Cat	Satawa	3	2	0	0	0	150
Seismic Cat	Tremulous	4	10	1	1	0	9,200
Shenanigan Cat	Cool Slate	3	5	1	0	0	5,940
Shoalihs Tale	Shoalih	4	8	1	1	2	32,782
Six Pack Sally	Sara Six Pack	4	3	0	0	1	1,884
Smart Tale	Smart Angle	4	12	1	2	3	10,752
Snappy Tale	Snappy Time	4	5	0	0	0	1,440
Song of the Cat	Strum the Banjo	2	1	0	0	0	125
Sophie's Cat	Oh Miss Sophie	4	2	0	0	0	875
Speak Easy	Donna Says So	3	9	2	3	0	71,530
Spellbinder	Thorough Fair	3	3	1	0	1	39,000
St. Joe's Cat	White Corners	3	3	0	0	1	1,700
Stalkerazzi	Haze	3	10	1	1	2	43,372
Starlet Cat	Shining Starlet	4	16	2	3	4	21,826
Storied Cat	Celestial Crown	2	5	2	2	0	80,602
Storm At Sunset	Holly Sunset	3	2	1	0	0	11,400
Storm Glory	Glorious Purple	4	3	0	0	0	0
Story of the Cat	With Brilliance	3	5	0	0	0	0
Sultry Cat	Hello Mom	4	10	1	0	1	16,200
Sunny Isles Beauty	Iron and Silver	2	7	1	0	0	26,700
Supreme Tale	Supreme Excellence	4	2	0	0	0	714
Swing the Cat (NZ)	Awave (NZ)	4	3	1	1	1	21,840
Sydneyleigh	Noble Dream Maker	3	6	0	0	1	3,412
Symphony in C	Paris Operetta	3	3	1	1	0	29,390
Tack Room	Previewed	4	2	0	0	0	297
Tailwind Flyer	Flying Code	3	5	0	1	2	17,376
Tale of a Dream	Graceful Manor	4	7	1	1	0	67,630
Tale of the Hills	Out of the Hills	2	1	0	0	0	400
Tale of Woe	Robyns Tune	3	7	2	0	1	56,722
Taleofdistinction	Nuance (IRE)	4	2	0	0	0	215
Taleofthewampuscat	Gracious Reason	3	13	3	2	2	63,550
Tales to Tell	Snappy Time	3	4	1	0	0	13,100
Tango Tales	Tango's Mambo	3	5	1	2	1	44,490
Taxicat	Kowloon	4	12	2	0	3	51,080
Tempered Steel	Cruise Line (GB)	4	7	2	2	1	105,289
Tencies Cat	Mimi's Brett	3	5	1	2	0	16,920
That Darn Cat	Alyrida	4	17	4	3	3	48,600
The Cat's Tail	Safe T Matches	3	11	0	2	0	4,603
The Cheetah's Tale	Artful Player	3	2	0	0	2	6,400
Theatrical Cat	Theatre Flight	4	4	1	0	1	31,260
Thong	Intimate Moments	4	16	3	2	1	59,935
Tomo	Charette	4	5	0	1	0	4,520
Total Commitment	Coming Out Party	4	2	1	0	0	9,600
Touchwood	Tears	4	6	2	0	1	13,070
Truecat	Bravada	3	4	0	0	0	4,046
Turkocat	La Turka	4	2	0	0	0	193
Uppity Kitty	Princess Harriet	3	3	0	0	1	11,520
West Side Cat	Prime Plus One	3	6	0	0	1	2,425
Whale of a Tale	Sunriseonsaratoga	3	9	0	5	1	20,320
Whoopi Cat	Whoopi (NZ)	3	6	0	3	1	51,220
Wild Tale	Young and Wild	3	12	4	2	1	82,780
Will's Cat	Miss Blanche	4	8	0	0	3	7,180
Winitformom	Colonial Feast	3	11	3	1	3	19,891
Winter Tide	Winthrop Arms	3	11	3	3	1	86,568
Woodford Cat	Conquistas Jessica	2	2	1	0	0	12,470
Wrapped Up in You	Rose Ransom	2	1	0	0	0	370
Zipcody	Rosekris	3	10	1	2	1	36,215

Unbridled's Song, Gr/Ro H (1993)
By Unbridled – Trolley Song, by Caro

152 Performers, 76 winning performers, $5,853,286 in total earnings

Progeny	Mare	Age	Sts	1st	2d	3d	Money Won
Adventure	Palace Weekend	3	6	2	0	1	57,370
All of Me	Bold and Gorgeous	5	2	1	0	0	27,150
Alpha Mama	Desert Queen	5	1	0	0	0	2,940
Ambition Unbridled	Retained	3	9	4	1	2	140,286
American Song	Rose Jade	4	5	1	1	1	30,360
Annabelle's Song	Ascloseasitgets	3	7	1	1	1	29,614
Appealing Bride	Regally Appealing	2	3	2	0	1	19,035
Arthur's Ring	Camlan	4	1	0	0	1	1,000
Asong for Billy	Adarling	5	4	1	0	0	28,000
Awesome Alec	La Lucky Strike	5	6	3	2	0	11,709
Awesome Song	Phone Caller	4	5	0	1	0	6,110
Be Like Mike	Thiscatsforcaryl	5	3	0	1	1	17,740
Blazing Song	Crystal Blaze	4	16	1	6	1	80,173
Bluegrass Belle	Breeze Lass	4	1	0	0	0	2,250
Bombay Blues	Assisi	5	12	1	0	3	19,830
Brand Name	Nocciolina	3	4	1	0	2	45,700
Bridle On	Exceptional Jan	3	11	1	1	1	35,626
Bush's Song	Bushy's Pride	3	6	0	1	0	14,340
Buzz Song	Buzzovertomyhouse	2	3	2	0	1	92,100
Cleito	Jungle Woman	3	4	0	0	0	827
Code Song	Two Fer Boston	3	2	0	0	0	2,040
Cojet	Airhart	5	7	0	0	4	29,205
Colt Python	Wind Drinker	4	11	2	3	2	94,870
Confirmed	Eric Dearie	3	11	3	6	1	154,137
Conjurer	Magical Holiday	3	2	0	1	0	7,280
Consistent	Arctic Valley	3	1	0	0	1	4,200
Crafty Song	Crafty Casa	4	3	1	0	1	33,915
Crazy Song	Misako Togo	5	5	1	0	0	30,293
Cry of the Wild	Haunting	3	6	0	2	0	25,080
Daddy Joe	Vennila Cream	2	5	1	1	1	42,600
Danesbury	Whatamiss	3	4	0	0	0	6,907
Decibel	Incircle Miss	3	8	1	1	2	34,710
Deep South	Southern Delicacy	3	4	0	1	1	7,110
Delivering Speed	Vaguely Regal (IRE)	3	1	0	0	0	940
Desnuda	Proper Form	3	4	0	0	0	1,580
Dogleg Left	Bugs Rabbit	3	10	0	2	0	4,675
Domestic Dispute	Majestical Moment	4	6	1	2	0	293,428
Drivingthelane	Dial Tone	3	6	0	1	0	15,005
Dusti's Tune	Rare Bird	5	4	0	0	0	5,832
Ecology	Gdansk's Honour	3	2	0	0	0	0
Elijah's Song	Toda Una Dama (ARG)	3	1	0	0	0	320
Endless Song	La Finale	6	1	0	0	0	110
Eurosilver	Russian Tango	3	4	1	2	0	90,860
Even the Score	Ashtabula	6	4	2	0	2	343,272
Everwood	Wanda's Dream	3	3	0	0	2	9,090
Flame Song	Flaming Gold	6	4	1	0	0	34,370
Forest Music	Defer West	3	7	3	0	3	188,590
Frank the Tank (AUS)	Fairy Tree	4	3	1	1	1	45,770
Freedom Land (AUS)	Avietwo (IRE)	6	3	0	0	1	1,540
Fullbridled	Constantia	3	2	0	1	0	10,040
Fully Engaged	Star Actress	3	2	1	0	0	20,232
Funk	Verbal Volley	2	5	2	1	1	74,960
Giant's Song	She's So Dixie	3	5	0	0	1	1,045
Glory Lane	Power Play	3	1	1	0	0	13,680
Going Commando	Regal Miss Copelan	4	3	0	0	0	1,155
Golden Unbridled	Golden Spell	4	4	0	1	0	5,140
Grey Beard	Danzig Darling	5	13	1	3	0	82,093
Greygoosegal	Regal Approval	3	4	0	0	1	5,602
Habiboo	Blushing Ogygian	3	10	3	0	3	115,520
Hamaaly	Jazzalong	4	19	2	4	2	25,200
He's of Royalty	She's of Royalty	3	3	0	1	0	4,000
Hennie's Song	Zama Hummer	4	2	0	0	0	0
Heroic Moment	Call Me Up	3	11	1	1	1	48,150
Higher and Higher	Graceful Minister	2	1	0	0	1	1,260
I'm Rial	I'm Splendid	3	2	0	0	0	517
Illucination	Golden Par	3	8	1	0	0	18,141
In the Weeds	Marfisa	3	7	3	0	0	48,148
Instinctively	Jetting Angel	2	1	0	0	0	400
Irish Melody	Irish Coco	3	9	3	1	1	88,595
Jonathan Quick	Clever Tide	2	2	0	0	0	1,650
Kid Carrots	Scholar	4	11	1	5	2	39,129
Lacy Gray	Field Point Road	3	1	0	0	0	0
Last Song	Queen of Spirit	3	11	3	1	2	254,253
Lexa's Song	Lexa (FR)	3	6	0	0	1	6,065
Lloydminster	Born Twice	3	9	2	2	2	56,647
Lonnies Song	Carefree Flyer	4	7	1	1	0	4,150
Marylebone	Desert Queen	3	3	0	2	0	24,800

Progeny	Mare	Age	Sts	1st	2d	3d	Money Won
Melissa's Luv Song	Miss Ali King	3	10	2	2	2	31,630
My Very Own Muggle	Finite E. F.	4	2	0	0	0	480
Nanys Lullaby	Valid Nany	3	4	1	0	1	8,280
Naughty Nae	Rockaroller	3	1	0	0	1	4,300
Net Force	Noble House	4	1	0	0	0	134
Notacheapsong	V Formation	4	8	1	1	2	17,132
Open Session	Private Session	5	3	0	0	0	976
Opera Box	Center Box	3	6	1	0	1	27,740
Opera Song	Misty Dancer	3	3	0	0	0	764
Our Song	Shesmineallmine	5	7	4	0	1	40,638
Paul B. Jones	October Beauty	3	5	1	0	2	19,650
Pete Shure	My Real Star	6	18	0	3	2	6,608
Presto Cavallo	Sleeplessnseattle	4	7	2	0	1	23,845
Pure	Nueces Strip	3	14	2	5	3	70,510
Quarter Time	Quarteira	4	13	1	1	3	16,060
Rare Gift	Rare Blend	3	8	2	1	4	161,220
Rationalexuberance	Alizea	2	2	0	1	0	8,380
Reaching Up	Going Up	4	5	3	0	0	62,311
Rebridled Dreams	Key Cents	4	9	0	0	0	10,567
River Kenmare	Wisla	2	3	0	1	0	4,800
Rockport Harbor	Regal Miss Copelan	2	4	4	0	0	210,300
Scene Maker	Walk in Time	3	4	0	0	1	3,090
Scenic Wonder	Mimi Kat	4	4	0	0	2	9,115
Seducer's Song	Seducer	3	8	4	1	1	239,760
Self Esteem	My Turbulent Miss	6	7	0	0	2	3,461
Sing D Song	Winnie D.	4	9	1	1	0	8,500
Skip's Song	Flowing Melody	2	5	1	2	0	22,705
Song Dancer	Lizeality	6	15	6	2	1	53,321
Song Du Jour (AUS)	Tamari	4	4	1	0	1	16,730
Song of the Sword	Appealing Ms Sword	3	10	4	2	1	258,600
Space Age	Stellar Cat	5	5	0	1	0	2,760
Splendid Blended	Valid Blend	2	4	3	1	0	327,400
Spring Tide	Chicken Delight	2	1	0	0	0	184
Stokowski	Precious Tiffini	6	2	0	0	0	0
Straphanger	Cheerful Spree	5	9	0	0	0	3,100
Streetmusic	Sentinelle	5	4	1	0	1	10,555
Superfine Song	Pawsitivly Purrfec	3	2	0	0	0	570
Swaggering	Yamuna	3	9	2	1	1	30,300
Sweetness Song	Sugar and Spice	5	1	0	0	0	0
The Coffin	If Bald Music	6	7	5	0	1	32,520
The Man	Nifty Fifty	4	9	0	3	0	12,100
Thefull Circle	Highland Vixen	5	5	0	0	2	14,050
Tigerline	Silken Cat	2	1	0	0	1	5,000
Tina's Love	Danara	3	4	0	0	1	5,800
Towering Palace (GB)	Palace Weekend	2	1	0	0	0	132
Trolley Belle	Crafty Casa	2	2	2	0	0	31,075
Twice Unbridled	Lady Millicent	2	5	0	0	2	11,140
Unbridels King	Love Avie	4	7	2	1	3	103,610
Unbridled America	Airhart	4	12	2	1	2	93,065
Unbridled Aria	Astaire Case	3	5	0	0	0	1,920
Unbridled Contessa	Wende	3	6	0	2	1	23,092
Unbridled Drive	Stretch Drive	4	6	1	0	0	30,652
Unbridled Echo	A. P. Indy's Lady	3	6	2	0	0	31,121
Unbridled Energy	Ataentsic	2	1	1	0	0	15,625
Unbridled Game	Starlet Minister	4	2	0	0	0	154
Unbridled Mate	Bishop's Mate	4	8	3	2	1	53,645
Unbridled Nan	Queen Tutta	3	3	0	1	0	4,780
Unbridled Resolve	Miss Pop Carn	4	7	0	1	0	3,975
Unbridled Rose	Rosa Eterna	3	8	0	2	0	9,718
Unbridled Sidney	Baltic Sea	3	6	2	2	0	69,020
Unbridled's Comet	Rainbow Promise	4	2	0	0	1	6,020
Unbridled's Lady	Sumija	4	1	0	0	0	172
Unbridled's Storm	Stormy Krissy	5	5	0	0	0	1,704
Unchecked Melody	Madam Sandie	3	5	0	0	0	1,011
Ungoverned	Fashion Dynasty	5	20	2	5	3	39,210
Uninhibited Song	Special Mistress	3	7	3	0	0	71,371
Up Periscope	Dust Bucket	4	1	0	0	0	188
Value Plus	Roll Over Baby	3	5	1	1	0	220,900
Warrior Song	La Gueriere	2	1	0	0	0	1,560
Werblin	Roll Over Baby	5	3	0	0	0	720
Western Legacy	Silveroo	5	6	1	0	0	7,408
Western Song	Cats Meow	3	7	1	1	1	28,250
Whistlin a Song	Aintjustwhistlin'	3	4	0	0	0	5,124
White Mercedes	Windrifter	4	8	1	0	1	12,957
Zawzooth	Lady Blockbuster	5	6	1	0	2	67,560

Carson City, Ch H (1987)

By Mr. Prospector – Blushing Promise, by Blushing Groom

174 Performers, 96 winning performers, $5,577,819 in total earnings

Progeny	Mare	Age	Sts	1st	2d	3d	Money Won
A. P. Carson	Auto Alarm	3	6	1	1	1	16,880
Absolute Nectar	Hear the Sea	3	8	1	1	2	47,750
Allready	Saucy Maisie	5	7	3	2	0	21,549
Andrew the Man	Storm in Sight	7	11	2	0	2	20,942
Another Chapter	Grandeur	4	10	1	3	0	27,320
Aphonic	Matinee Mimic	4	13	3	1	1	32,038
Around the Cape	Song of Africa	2	2	0	1	1	8,400
Arrive	Miss Jo	3	8	0	0	0	225
Auto City	Saucy Maisie	4	6	0	1	1	17,750
Avaricity	Avarice	3	12	2	1	1	49,744
B. Carson	Cazzy B.	4	6	0	0	0	640
Baby Let's Roll	Silver Spirit	4	2	1	0	0	9,480
Bada in Nevada	Suspicions	3	7	1	1	1	22,060
Bella Sierra	Louise's Ridge	4	3	1	0	0	5,490
Belle City Boy	Belle Evon	3	7	1	1	0	19,970
Big City Spender	Speedy Spender	3	7	3	1	2	117,343
Black Jack Attack	Moondust Mink	3	4	0	0	1	3,950
Black Springs	Andriana B.	2	2	0	0	0	0
Bohemian Lady	Weekend in Indy	3	6	2	1	1	121,682
Bonaparte	True Blue Story	4	5	0	2	0	14,399
Boomanji	Mombasa	2	2	0	0	0	4,860
Breach of Promise	Green Pompadour	5	8	3	0	2	46,658
C. C. Seven	Mimosa Cocktail	3	4	0	0	0	644
Callheracitygirl	Your Call	3	3	0	0	0	235
Capitalina	Granja Realeza	4	2	0	0	0	50
Captain Paul	Little Fuzzy	3	1	0	0	0	400
Cargi	Fleet Road	7	7	3	2	0	33,888
Carlea	De Puntillas (GB)	2	2	0	1	0	14,820
Carrington	Inch Marlowe	3	6	1	0	0	24,608
Carson Beach	Aquaplane	9	6	1	1	0	18,150
Carson City Kid	Classy and Quick	10	17	3	5	2	34,052
Carson City Star	Star of Albion (GB)	4	6	1	1	0	15,812
Carson Cove	Hidden Cove	4	4	1	0	0	24,000
Carson Guy	Funny Girl	3	9	1	1	1	16,378
Carson Kit	Manhattan Vice	2	2	0	0	1	9,690
Carson Unleashed	Unlaced	3	14	2	1	4	52,080
Carson's Angel	Solitary Angel	2	1	0	0	0	363
Carson's Bridge	Bridge to Cross	2	2	1	0	0	29,532
Carson's Star	Jaramar Miss	2	5	0	1	1	8,530
Carsonic	Hidden Trail	9	3	0	0	0	0
Castletown	Sweet Nostalgia	5	8	0	0	0	646
Cat Carson	Marsh Cat	3	5	2	0	1	64,040
Celophane Man	La Princesa	3	13	3	1	0	25,280
City Blues	Imia	4	8	1	2	1	35,530
City Circle	Fairy Circle	10	6	0	1	1	1,585
City Clerk	Le Clerc	8	4	1	1	0	3,605
City Code	Valid Affect	2	5	2	0	2	52,040
City Fear	Elkin	5	7	1	0	0	6,682
City Fire	Gillingham	4	8	1	1	1	54,835
City Forum	Distinguish Forum	2	1	0	0	0	115
City Island	Glorious Minstrel	6	9	1	1	1	7,783
City Jewel	Dixie Jewel	2	1	0	0	0	624
City Kid	Letakia	6	11	1	1	1	8,375
City News	Princess Tru	4	13	2	1	2	38,620
City of Peace	Creeksider	7	1	0	0	0	0
City Prince	Plum Thicket	3	19	1	2	2	19,980
City Rain	Rainy Night	4	2	1	1	0	26,200
City Rapid	Zili	5	1	0	0	0	0
City Sister	Demi Souer	4	3	0	0	0	3,160
City Sleeper	Slept Thru It	4	5	0	1	3	22,987
City Sprint	Fay Morgan	2	2	0	0	0	0
City Styling	Cara Carissima	4	1	0	0	0	906
City Weekend	Weekend Storm	2	1	0	0	0	150
Classic Elegance	Taegu	2	6	3	0	1	204,006
Cold Claim	Vice On Ice	6	3	0	0	0	680
Country Only	Only Maisie	7	6	0	0	1	5,096
Cripple Creek	Cally	5	6	1	1	1	33,590
Cuvee	Christmas Star	3	3	0	2	0	41,340
Debt to Equity	Ten Cents a Kiss	5	18	2	2	2	18,380
Degenerate Gambler	Cosa Lucinante	3	12	0	2	1	16,165
Desert Girl	Desert Angel	4	2	0	0	0	214
Dont Tell the Kids	Smile n Molly	7	9	1	1	1	14,520
Double Down	Penny's Valentine	3	9	2	0	0	20,486
Dream City	Dream Motel	5	1	0	0	0	110
Driana	Andriana B.	5	1	0	0	0	360
Exciting Metro	Excitations	3	2	1	0	0	30,895
Fantino	Deeds Speak	3	13	1	4	2	72,941
Fire Fox	Incinerate	6	6	0	0	2	6,587
Fitting Tribute	Silky Oaks	3	12	2	2	4	41,430
Fort Point	Ocean Queen	5	7	0	0	0	235
Game Effort	Connecting Link	6	12	3	2	2	59,775
Go to the City	Lemhi Go	2	5	1	1	1	23,050
Golden Victress	Amber Gem	3	7	0	2	0	16,230
Hear No Evil	Nizy	4	10	0	3	1	182,500
Hey Chub	Donna Doo	4	10	2	6	1	126,327
High Button Shoes	Marianka	2	2	1	0	0	43,695
Hot Slot	Hot Option	5	5	1	0	0	11,886
Irish Gambler	Love of Ireland	4	4	0	2	1	15,960
Itchetucknee	Midway Squall	4	12	1	3	0	21,533
Ivy League Miss	Yesterdays Gone	2	3	0	1	0	7,320
Jaclini	Contagious Love	5	7	0	0	0	2,234
Jazz Society	Dixieland Gold	2	2	0	0	0	568
Kalamazoo	Offshore Account	6	2	1	0	0	11,040
Keeping Cool	Madam Chairman	4	10	1	2	1	11,210
King Zonic	Molly O'Horton	5	7	1	0	3	27,710
Kitty Carson	Top o' the Cat	4	3	0	1	0	6,783
Knox City	Ellen's Ad	10	2	0	0	0	1,010
Kuanyan	Plate Queen	4	9	2	2	2	85,132
Late Carson	Can't Be Late	8	12	0	3	0	8,228

Limited Entry	Grand Betty	2	3	1	1	0	52,780
Little Nicky Regs	Sister Explodent	3	12	4	4	1	101,488
Lorenzon	Encorevous	3	4	1	0	2	11,348
Lorraine's Secret	Three Secrets	6	14	0	2	3	9,205
Lovely R R	Lolabell	3	7	1	1	0	18,460
Lucky Frolic	Lindsay Frolic	2	8	2	0	2	60,620
Manosh	Uforia	3	2	0	0	0	800
Miss Quick City	Seattle Wave	4	2	1	0	0	9,240
Molto Vita	Princess Polonia	4	8	3	2	0	220,730
Moonlight Sonata	Wheatly Way	4	7	1	0	2	25,243
Ms. Executive City	Rare Executive	3	8	0	1	2	11,392
Mystic Night	Lady Becker	6	3	3	0	0	20,700
National City	Paper Money	8	15	0	6	2	8,787
Needarunner	Trumpet's Blare	3	12	1	1	1	7,328
Nevada Miss	Jaramar Miss	4	4	0	2	0	17,460
Nevada Strip	Picabo Street	7	8	0	2	0	3,793
Nevada Sunrise	Radiant Megan	3	8	1	1	2	38,440
Nighttimeinthecity	Turn Off the Light	3	18	3	4	2	39,990
No Luck in Reno	Dance Time	10	1	0	0	0	0
Nomoreskoal	Danza Regio	7	14	3	3	1	17,443
Obtuse	Openstock	3	2	0	0	0	1,400
Ole Rebel	Velvet Tulip	5	12	5	2	1	178,500
Perspicacity	Not So Careless	3	2	0	0	0	170
Piano Bar	Hidden Pleasure	2	2	0	0	1	2,640
Plumlake Lady	Second Degree	3	7	3	2	1	71,265
Pollard's Vision	Etats Unis	3	11	4	4	1	1,022,020
Premier Rocket	Creeksider	4	2	0	0	0	0
Prevalent	Lethal Leta	3	2	1	0	0	28,180
Private City	Privately	4	9	1	0	1	44,760
Promenade Girl	Promenade Colony	2	1	1	0	0	12,000
Promising Storm	Stormy Texan Girl	2	6	0	1	1	7,313
Proper Carson	Proper Banner	2	3	1	0	1	32,970
Quick Action	Indian Sunset	3	11	2	2	1	133,140
Rach Three	Tomorrow's Song	6	12	0	3	2	20,150
Ran D Scott	Stolie	6	5	1	1	1	9,620
Rich City Girl	Great Lady Slew	4	8	2	3	1	64,770
Ring City	Ring Star	2	7	1	1	0	63,869
Rooster Rudy	Dial Tone	2	2	0	0	0	320
Rose City	Roses In The Snow (IRE)	2	1	0	0	0	2,040
Royal Fudge	Chocolate Fudge	2	7	1	0	1	47,770

Sacred Feather	Marianna's Girl	2	5	1	0	0	17,011
Salt Wells	Grassy Springs	4	6	1	0	2	17,200
Samba City	Samba Rhythm	2	4	0	1	0	4,630
Seeinsbelieven	Coragil	2	1	1	0	0	29,395
Shine Forth	Sister Crown	5	3	0	0	0	1,281
Show Me the Town	Khalifa of Kushog	2	6	1	3	0	36,943
Silicon City	One Fine Day	4	2	0	0	0	800
Silver Traffic	Adored Slew	4	1	0	0	0	400
Small Promises	Promiseville	6	10	1	1	0	43,057
Smart Set	Kris' Dear Deby	7	1	0	1	0	1,160
Smile N Carson	Smile n Molly	3	8	1	2	1	18,677
Sock Hop	Arashi Dancer	7	2	0	0	0	144
Song'n Dance	Song for Par Ci	2	2	0	0	1	4,720
Southwest City	Mercedes Miss	3	5	0	1	2	13,580
Sparkler	Coragil	3	6	0	0	0	492
Speciality	Special Feeling	4	2	0	0	0	660
Sprucity	Sprucory	8	6	1	0	0	5,160
Storm City Blues	Musical Cat	3	9	1	3	0	41,592
Strength and Honor	Dame Avie	5	9	5	0	2	183,145
Strike Three	Otoka	7	13	0	2	5	26,390
Sultry City	Sultry Lass	2	2	0	0	0	1,333
Sutter Street	Buttercup	4	8	2	4	0	49,035
Sweet Carson	Apreciada	4	1	0	0	0	380
Talbot County	Artistic	3	4	1	1	1	11,580
Tex and the City	Shepherd's Moon	3	14	2	1	1	33,629
Tiger Mania	Slew Kitty Slew	6	16	0	1	0	2,113
Top Call	Colonial Stage	6	2	0	0	0	114
Tough Kid	Tough Broad	3	10	2	1	1	22,945
Tracibee	Tea Cozzy	2	2	1	1	0	22,000
Tucson City	Buy the Cat	4	10	2	1	2	24,023
Vive Bene	Alya	4	2	0	0	0	0
Who's News	Shufflin n Seatle	5	1	0	0	0	135
Wholehearted	Stolen Beauty	3	7	1	2	0	44,766
Wild Bill Hiccup	Storm Attack	4	14	5	0	2	61,040
Z B's Carson City	Mz. Zill Bear	5	15	1	0	0	5,434

Annual Leading Sire – Money Won

Year	Sire	Perfs.	Races Won	Amount Won
1914	Broomstick	31	90	99,043
1915	Broomstick	47	108	94,387
1916	Star Shoot	87	218	138,163
1917	Star Shoot	81	167	131,674
1918	Sweep	33	69	139,057
1919	Star Shoot	55	108	197,233
1920	Fair Play	27	72	269,102
1921	Celt	52	124	206,167
1922	McGee	57	125	222,491
1923	The Finn	16	31	285,759
1924	Fair Play	45	84	296,204
1925	Sweep	65	185	237,564
1926	Man o' War	26	49	408,137
1927	Fair Play	45	84	296,204
1928	High Time	55	109	307,631
1929	Chicle	41	88	289,123
1930	Sir Gallahad III	16	49	422,200
1931	St. Germans	15	47	315,585
1932	Chatterton	47	93	210,040
1933	Sir Gallahad III	49	78	136,428
1934	Sir Gallahad III	55	92	180,165
1935	Chance Play	38	88	191,465
1936	Sickle	48	128	209,800
1937	The Porter	45	104	292,262
1938	Sickle	48	128	209,800
1939	Challenger II	42	99	316,281
1940	Sir Gallahad III	63	102	305,610
1941	Blenheim II	30	64	378,981
1942	Equipoise	36	82	437,141
1943	Bull Dog	75	172	372,706
1944	Chance Play	71	150	431,100
1945	War Admiral	26	59	591,352
1946	Mahmoud	47	101	638,025
1947	Bull Lea	61	128	1,259,718
1948	Bull Lea	63	147	1,334,027
1949	Bull Lea	73	165	991,842
1950	Heliopolis	77	167	852,292
1951	Count Fleet	64	124	1,160,847
1952	Bull Lea	65	136	1,630,655
1953	Bull Lea	56	107	1,155,846
1954	Heliopolis	76	148	1,406,638
1955	Nasrullah	40	69	1,433,660
1956	Nasrullah	50	106	1,462,413
1957	Princequillo	75	147	1,698,427
1958	Princequillo	65	110	1,394,540
1959	Nasrullah	69	141	1,434,543
1960	Nasrullah	64	122	1,419,683
1961	Ambiorix	73	148	936,976
1962	Nasrullah	62	107	1,474,831
1963	Bold Ruler	26	56	917,531
1964	Bold Ruler	44	88	1,457,156
1965	Bold Ruler	51	90	1,091,924
1966	Bold Ruler	51	107	2,306,523
1967	Bold Ruler	63	135	2,249,272
1968	Bold Ruler	57	99	1,988,427
1969	Bold Ruler	59	90	1,357,144
1970	Hail to Reason	53	82	1,400,839
1971	Northern Dancer	44	93	1,288,580
1972	Round Table	65	98	1,199,933
1973	Bold Ruler	41	74	1,488,622
1974	T.V. Lark	98	121	1,242,000
1975	What a Pleasure	90	101	2,011,878
1976	What a Pleasure	85	108	1,622,159
1977	Dr. Fager	79	124	1,593,079
1978	Exclusive Native	63	106	1,969,867
1979	Exclusive Native	71	104	2,872,605
1980	Raja Baba	108	149	2,483,352
1981	Nodouble	92	115	2,800,884
1982	His Majesty	56	86	2,675,823
1983	Halo	69	86	2,773,637
1984	Seattle Slew	46	49	5,361,259
1985	Buckaroo	49	50	4,145,272
1986	Lyphard	50	49	4,051,985
1987	Mr. Prospector	81	104	5,877,385
1988	Mr. Prospector	82	106	8,986,790
1989	Halo	93	114	7,520,142
1990	Alydar	98	111	6,378,760
1991	Danzig	68	109	6,214,669
1992	Danzig	62	83	5,873,773
1993	Kris S.	110	142	4,822,888
1994	Broad Brush	92	72	5,403,999
1995	Palace Music	44	22	5,313,060
1996	Forty Niner		110	4,820,916
1997	Deputy Minister		104	8,519,155
1998	Deputy Minister	92	96	8,517,482
1999	Storm Cat	104	117	9,657,579
2000	Storm Cat	102	99	6,833,882
2001	Thunder Gulch	92	82	7,699,918
2002	El Prado (Ire)	173	154	6,609,533
2003	A.P. Indy	162	153	8,827,360
2004	Elusive Quality	131	119	10,700,039

Annual Leading Sire – Races Won

Year	Sire	Perfs.	Winning Performers	Races Won
1999	Allen's Prospect	184	105	217
2000	Allen's Prospect	199	125	231
2001	Allen's Prospect	223	132	256
2002	Allen's Prospect	205	129	248
2003	End Swep	201	135	253
2004	Not for Love	179	102	195

Sires of Winners of $1 Million or More in America

Horse	Sex	Born	Sts	1st	2d	3d	Earnings
A.P. Indy							
Mineshaft	H	1999	18	10	3	1	2,283,402
Golden Missile	H	1995	25	7	7	4	2,194,510
Aptitude	H	1997	15	5	4	2	1,965,410
Lu Ravi	M	1995	26	11	8	3	1,819,781
Tomisue's Delight	M	1994	20	7	5	4	1,207,537
Secret Status	M	1997	19	8	3	4	1,053,705
Stephen Got Even	H	1996	11	5	1	1	1,019,200
Acatenango (GER)							
Lando (GER)	H	1990	24	10	3	1	3,438,727
Borgia (GER)	M	1994	22	6	7	2	1,697,771
Accordion							
Yavana's Pace (IRE)	G	1992	74	16	14	11	1,199,409
Ack Ack							
Broad Brush	H	1983	27	14	5	5	2,656,793
Aferd							
Precocity	H	1994	33	9	7	5	1,835,798
Affirmed							
Flawlessly	M	1988	28	16	4	3	2,572,536
Quiet Resolve	G	1995	31	10	6	4	2,346,768
Affirmed Success	G	1994	42	17	10	6	2,285,315
Affluent	M	1998	23	8	5	4	1,497,651
Peteski	H	1990	11	7	2	1	1,287,866
The Tin Man	G	1998	21	7	4	2	1,097,860
Zoman	H	1987	24	7	5	3	1,040,372
Afleet							
Preeminence (JPN)	M	1997	50	13	9	7	5,042,956
Gaily Magnum	G	1993	24	8	2	2	1,218,578
A Fleets Dancer	H	1995	45	12	6	8	1,036,649
Ahmad (ARG)							
Paseana (ARG)	M	1987	36	19	10	2	3,317,427
Ahonoora (GB)							
Dr Devious (IRE)	H	1989	15	6	4	0	1,484,230
Air Forbes Won							
Mercedes Won	H	1986	52	12	7	12	1,087,435
Al Nasr (FR)							
Nasr El Arab	H	1985	16	6	2	2	1,198,585
Alhaarth (IRE)							
Phoenix Reach (IRE)	C	2000	10	4	1	1	2,075,669
Alleged							
Miss Alleged	M	1987	15	5	4	3	1,757,342
Shantou	H	1993	14	6	2	4	1,132,399
Strategic Choice	H	1991	33	5	5	5	1,126,735
Alphabet Soup							
Our New Recruit	H	1999	19	6	7	2	1,470,915
Alydar							
Alysheba	H	1984	26	11	8	2	6,679,242
Easy Goer	H	1986	20	14	5	1	4,873,770
Strike the Gold	H	1988	31	6	8	5	3,457,026
Criminal Type	H	1985	24	10	5	3	2,351,274
Turkoman	H	1982	22	8	8	3	2,146,924
Dare and Go	H	1991	22	7	7	5	1,608,972
Althea	M	1981	15	8	4	0	1,275,255
Cacoethes	H	1986	14	4	3	3	1,169,064
Miss Oceana	M	1981	19	11	6	1	1,010,385
Clabber Girl	M	1983	39	8	12	6	1,006,261
Alysheba							
Desert Waves	G	1990	63	15	9	6	1,241,295
Alzao							
Alpride (IRE)	M	1991	26	11	4	4	1,048,270

Horse	Sex	Born	Sts	1st	2d	3d	Earnings
Amerigo							
Fort Marcy	G	1964	75	21	18	14	1,109,791
Apalachee							
Pine Tree Lane	M	1982	38	19	4	4	1,150,561
Arazi							
Congaree	H	1998	25	12	2	4	3,267,490
At the Threshold							
Lil E. Tee	H	1989	13	7	4	1	1,437,506
Avatar							
Honor Medal	H	1981	87	19	13	19	1,347,073
Awesome Again							
Ghostzapper	C	2000	10	8	0	1	2,996,120
Bahri							
Sakhee	H	1997	14	8	3	1	3,253,253
Bailjumper							
Skip Trial	H	1982	38	16	7	2	1,837,451
Barachois							
Win	G	1980	44	14	10	3	1,408,980
Barathea (IRE)							
Tobougg (IRE)	H	1998	12	3	2	2	1,079,901
Batonnier							
Cavonnier	G	1993	23	8	3	2	1,254,165
Baynoun (IRE)							
Sandpit (BRZ)	H	1989	40	14	11	6	3,812,597
Be My Native							
River Verdon (IRE)	G	1987	26	16	4	2	1,574,735
Believe It							
Al Mamoon	H	1981	32	11	7	3	1,249,906
Best Turn							
High Brite	H	1984	45	15	7	9	1,150,519
Bet Big							
Bet On Sunshine	G	1992	47	22	7	10	1,449,882
Richman	H	1988	33	14	5	5	1,314,360
Bien Bien							
Bienamado	H	1996	16	8	3	0	1,261,089
Bien Nicole	M	1998	26	12	8	2	1,074,620
Big Spruce							
Super Moment	H	1977	47	10	8	5	1,017,940
Bikala							
Apple Tree (FR)	H	1989	26	7	4	5	1,388,260
Black Tie Affair (IRE)							
Evening Attire	G	1998	39	11	12	3	2,373,010
Formal Gold	H	1993	16	8	4	1	1,533,600
License Fee	M	1995	43	16	7	6	1,200,416
Blushing Groom (FR)							
Blushing John	H	1985	19	9	1	2	1,548,081
Sky Beauty	M	1990	21	15	2	2	1,336,000
Arazi	H	1989	14	9	1	1	1,212,351
Bold Bidder							
Spectacular Bid	H	1976	30	26	2	1	2,781,608
Bold Reasoning							
Seattle Slew	H	1974	17	14	2	0	1,208,726
Bold Ruckus							
Kiridashi	H	1992	44	14	9	8	1,201,981
Bold Ruritana	M	1990	44	14	10	6	1,140,163
Beau Genius	H	1985	42	19	7	4	1,055,600
Krz Ruckus	G	1997	39	15	8	4	1,040,036
Bold Ruler							
Secretariat	H	1970	21	16	3	1	1,316,808

Horse	Sex	Born	Sts	1st	2d	3d	Earnings
Bolger							
Sea Cadet	H	1988	29	10	6	5	1,807,150
Bounding Basque							
Basqueian	G	1991	37	13	10	2	1,094,767
Broad Brush							
Concern	H	1991	30	7	7	11	3,079,350
Include	H	1997	20	10	1	4	1,659,560
Farda Amiga	M	1999	8	4	1	0	1,282,302
Brocco							
Jostle	M	1997	20	8	5	2	1,389,932
Buckaroo							
Spend a Buck	H	1982	15	10	3	2	4,220,689
Lite the Fuse	H	1991	21	9	4	6	1,036,882
Roo Art	H	1982	27	10	4	5	1,011,723
Buckfinder							
Track Barron	H	1981	21	12	3	1	1,353,674
Bucksplasher							
Buck's Boy	G	1993	30	16	5	2	2,750,148
Bull Lea							
Citation	H	1945	45	32	10	2	1,085,760
Busted (GB)							
Erins Isle (IRE)	H	1978	33	9	9	3	1,233,889
Cabrini Green							
Mr. Epperson	G	1995	70	19	11	12	1,079,851
Cadeaux Genereux (GB)							
Touch of the Blues (FR)	H	1997	35	8	6	5	1,655,358
Caerleon							
Missionary Ridge (GB)	H	1987	42	8	5	8	1,864,498
Kostroma (IRE)	M	1986	26	12	2	3	1,200,088
Volga (IRE)	M	1998	19	7	5	2	1,141,759
Corwyn Bay (IRE)	H	1986	15	6	4	0	1,018,749
Candy Stripes							
Lundy's Liability (BRZ)	C	2000	7	4	1	0	1,553,930
Different (ARG)	M	1992	19	9	3	5	1,349,802
Cape Cross (IRE)							
Ouija Board (GB)	F	2001	8	5	0	3	1,671,768
Capote							
Boston Harbor	H	1994	8	6	1	0	1,934,605
Caro (IRE)							
With Approval	H	1986	23	13	5	1	2,863,540
Golden Pheasant	H	1986	22	7	4	3	2,453,958
Winning Colors	M	1985	19	8	3	1	1,526,837
Tejano	H	1985	21	5	6	3	1,428,177
Carr de Naskra							
L'Carriere	G	1991	23	8	4	3	1,726,175
Carson City							
State City	H	1999	17	6	0	3	1,375,993
Pollard's Vision	C	2001	17	5	5	3	1,075,311
Caucasus							
Videogenic	M	1982	73	20	9	10	1,154,360
Caveat							
Awad	H	1990	70	14	10	11	3,270,131
Cee's Tizzy							
Tiznow	H	1997	15	8	4	2	6,427,830
Budroyale	G	1993	52	17	12	2	2,840,810
Gourmet Girl	M	1995	33	9	7	10	1,255,373
Celtic Swing (GB)							
Six Perfections (FR)	F	2000	14	6	6	1	1,811,179

Horse	Sex	Born	Sts	1st	2d	3d	Earnings
Cherokee Run							
Chilukki	M	1997	17	11	3	0	1,201,828
Chief's Crown							
Chief Bearhart	H	1993	26	12	5	3	3,381,557
Concerto	H	1994	21	10	4	2	1,308,118
Chief Honcho	H	1987	34	10	6	3	1,265,719
Chieftain							
Fit to Fight	H	1979	26	14	3	3	1,042,075
Cinco Grande							
Ibero (ARG)	H	1987	34	10	7	4	1,345,199
Citidancer							
Urbane	M	1992	18	8	4	4	1,018,568
Clever Trick							
Anet	H	1994	19	8	5	0	1,189,873
Kurofune Mystery	M	1990	21	6	5	4	1,009,342
Codex							
Lost Code	H	1984	27	15	5	2	2,085,396
Comic Blush							
Spook Express (SAF)	M	1994	22	11	2	3	1,016,744
Common Grounds							
Earl of Barking (IRE)	H	1990	37	9	3	10	1,230,519
Compliance							
Fourstardave	G	1985	100	21	18	16	1,636,737
Fourstars Allstar	H	1988	59	14	14	9	1,596,760
Comrade in Arms							
Celtic Arms (FR)	H	1991	23	5	2	3	1,102,806
Conquistador Cielo							
Marquetry	H	1987	36	10	9	4	2,857,886
Forty Niner Days	G	1987	45	9	9	3	1,009,625
Consultant's Bid							
Bayakoa (ARG)	M	1984	39	21	9	0	2,861,701
Cool Victor							
Victor Cooley	G	1993	39	13	12	3	1,320,475
Copelan							
Recoup the Cash	G	1990	74	23	6	3	1,098,920
Cormorant							
Gander	G	1996	60	15	10	9	1,824,011
Go for Gin	H	1991	19	5	7	2	1,380,866
Grecian Flight	M	1984	40	21	6	3	1,320,215
Coronado's Quest							
Society Selection	F	2001	12	5	3	1	1,256,700
Cougar II							
Gato Del Sol	H	1979	39	7	9	7	1,340,107
Cox's Ridge							
Life's Magic	M	1981	32	8	11	6	2,255,218
Sultry Song	H	1988	23	9	3	5	1,616,276
Cardmania	G	1986	76	16	12	20	1,503,780
Vanlandingham	H	1981	19	10	3	3	1,409,476
De Roche	G	1986	28	5	8	7	1,078,200
Lost Mountain	H	1988	36	5	6	8	1,004,939
Cozzene							
Alphabet Soup	H	1991	24	10	3	6	2,990,270
Star of Cozzene	H	1988	38	14	8	5	2,308,923
Running Stag	H	1994	40	7	11	2	1,663,227
Tikkanen	H	1991	17	4	2	3	1,599,335
Rhythm Band	G	1996	18	5	2	2	1,349,066
Cozzene's Prince	G	1987	68	16	10	10	1,270,057
Maxzene	M	1993	23	11	5	0	1,175,259
Chorwon	G	1993	44	13	7	8	1,161,795

Horse	Sex	Born	Sts	1st	2d	3d	Earnings
Crafty Prospector							
Crafty Shaw	H	1998	42	15	7	7	1,040,440
Crested Wave							
Surfers Paradise (NZ)	G	1987	57	17	5	0	1,419,964
Crozier							
Precisionist	H	1981	46	20	10	4	3,485,398
Crusader Sword							
Isitingood	H	1991	24	11	3	4	1,219,430
Cryptoclearance							
Victory Gallop	H	1995	17	9	5	1	3,505,895
Volponi	H	1998	31	7	12	5	3,187,232
Crystal Glitters							
Dear Doctor (FR)	H	1987	32	8	7	4	1,742,671
Cure the Blues							
Wake At Noon	H	1997	51	19	7	6	1,601,829
Cutlass							
Cutlass Reality	H	1982	66	14	12	9	1,405,660
Friendly Lover	H	1988	66	22	13	12	1,247,670
D'Accord							
North East Bound	G	1996	50	12	7	3	1,363,228
Damascus							
Desert Wine	H	1980	25	8	8	3	1,618,043
Dancing Brave							
White Muzzle (GB)	H	1990	17	6	3	2	1,060,443
Danehill							
Rock of Gibraltar (IRE)	H	1999	13	10	2	0	1,888,048
Banks Hill (GB)	M	1998	15	5	5	3	1,824,008
Danzig							
Agnes World	H	1995	20	8	6	1	3,365,680
Dance Smartly	M	1988	17	12	2	3	3,263,835
Lure	H	1989	25	14	8	0	2,515,289
Pine Bluff	H	1989	13	6	1	3	2,255,884
Chief's Crown	H	1982	21	12	3	3	2,191,168
Versailles Treaty	M	1988	20	9	9	2	1,271,154
Stephan's Odyssey	H	1982	16	6	4	1	1,255,328
War Chant	H	1997	7	5	1	0	1,130,600
Polish Navy	H	1984	12	7	1	3	1,118,076
Dispute	M	1990	19	9	4	4	1,106,907
Dumaani	H	1991	26	7	3	3	1,079,098
Danzig Connection	H	1983	17	6	5	4	1,002,620
Darby Creek Road							
Salem Drive	H	1982	46	13	7	10	1,046,065
Darn That Alarm							
Pistols and Roses	H	1989	44	10	4	6	1,680,506
Darshaan (GB)							
Kotashaan (FR)	H	1988	22	10	5	2	2,812,114
Mutamam (GB)	H	1995	21	11	2	1	1,388,410
Deerhound							
Countess Diana	M	1995	14	7	2	0	1,117,185
Dehere							
Take Charge Lady	M	1999	22	11	7	0	2,480,377
Graeme Hall	H	1997	22	7	7	1	1,147,441
Deputy Commander							
Ten Most Wanted	C	2000	13	5	3	1	1,718,460
Deputy Minister							
Awesome Again	H	1994	12	9	0	2	4,374,590
Deputy Commander	H	1994	13	4	3	2	1,906,640
Open Mind	M	1986	19	12	2	2	1,844,372
Flag Down	H	1990	43	11	11	8	1,699,711
Touch Gold	H	1994	15	6	3	1	1,679,907
Keeper Hill	M	1995	21	4	7	5	1,661,281
Go for Wand	M	1987	13	10	2	0	1,373,338
Victory Speech	H	1993	27	9	2	5	1,289,020
Mr Purple	H	1992	21	6	3	5	1,133,538
Clear Mandate	M	1992	31	10	6	4	1,085,588
Desert Classic							
Native Desert	G	1993	74	21	13	17	1,828,177
Determined King							
Queen Alexandra	M	1982	46	19	8	5	1,034,144
Devil His Due							
Roses in May	C	2000	11	7	3	0	1,795,187
Devil's Bag							
Devil His Due	H	1989	41	11	12	3	3,920,405
Twilight Agenda	H	1986	32	13	5	4	2,174,529
Dewan							
It's the One	H	1978	28	9	7	9	1,038,444
Diesis (GB)							
Halling	H	1991	18	12	1	0	1,332,651
Magistretti	C	2000	16	4	6	0	1,264,117
Din's Dancer							
Ladies Din	G	1995	37	12	6	6	1,966,754
Distant View							
Sightseek	M	1999	20	12	5	0	2,445,216
Distorted Humor							
Funny Cide	G	2000	21	8	4	5	3,174,485
Dixie Brass							
Dixie Dot Com	H	1995	23	8	6	1	1,332,775
Dixieland Band							
Bowman's Band	H	1998	34	7	11	6	1,315,774
Dixie Union	H	1997	12	7	3	0	1,233,190
Drum Taps	H	1986	31	15	5	2	1,140,788
Del Mar Dennis	G	1990	26	10	1	4	1,023,373
Dixieland Heat							
Xtra Heat	M	1998	35	26	5	2	2,389,635
Djakao							
Perrault (GB)	H	1977	25	9	5	5	1,536,103
Domasca Dan							
Brass in Pocket	M	1999	24	14	3	2	1,146,023
Double Bed (FR)							
Jim and Tonic (FR)	G	1994	39	13	13	4	4,975,807
Doyoun (IRE)							
Daylami (IRE)	H	1994	21	11	3	4	4,614,762
Kalanisi (IRE)	H	1996	11	6	4	1	2,148,836
Manndar (IRE)	H	1996	20	4	6	3	1,128,835
Dr. Carter							
Benburb	G	1989	22	7	2	4	1,159,949
Dynaformer							
Perfect Drift	G	1999	27	9	8	3	3,168,963
Riskaverse	M	1999	27	8	6	4	1,717,706
Dynever	C	2000	16	4	6	1	1,408,714
Mystery Giver	G	1998	33	11	7	2	1,165,900
Critical Eye	M	1997	38	14	4	3	1,060,984
Starrer	M	1998	20	6	5	3	1,043,033
Eagle Eyed							
Peeping Tom	G	1997	49	14	7	9	1,398,547
Easy Goer							
My Flag	M	1993	20	6	3	4	1,557,057

Horse	Sex	Born	Sts	1st	2d	3d	Earnings
Efisio							
Hever Golf Rose (GB)	M	1991	66	17	11	10	1,020,328
El Gran Senor							
Lit de Justice	H	1990	36	10	8	6	1,397,649
Rodrigo de Triano	H	1989	13	9	0	0	1,354,192
Candid Glen	G	1997	40	11	10	6	1,239,330
Helmsman	H	1992	22	6	7	3	1,132,142
El Prado (IRE)							
Medaglia d'Oro	H	1999	17	8	7	0	5,754,720
Kitten's Joy	C	2001	12	8	3	0	1,705,911
Nite Dreamer	H	1995	37	5	10	6	1,149,788
Ela-Mana-Mou (IRE)							
Snurge (IRE)	H	1987	30	7	10	5	1,674,441
Elusive Quality							
Smarty Jones	C	2001	9	8	1	0	7,613,155
Emperor Jones							
Janet (GB)	M	1997	27	8	4	6	1,027,237
End Sweep							
Swept Overboard	H	1997	20	8	5	3	1,137,767
Eskimo							
Silent Eskimo	M	1995	31	9	4	9	1,039,485
Eternal Prince							
Val's Prince	G	1992	52	13	12	5	2,118,785
Exclusive Native							
Affirmed	H	1975	29	22	5	1	2,393,818
Outstandingly	M	1982	28	10	4	3	1,412,206
Men's Exclusive	G	1993	48	11	16	4	1,451,126
Explodent							
Mi Selecto	H	1985	40	9	7	9	1,475,762
Exchange	M	1988	30	15	7	4	1,287,795
Exbourne	H	1986	14	8	5	1	1,000,198
Ezzoud (IRE)							
Ela Athena (GB)	M	1996	17	3	7	2	1,125,252
Fairy King							
Falbrav (IRE)	H	1998	26	13	5	5	5,825,517
Faliraki (IRE)							
Fali Time	H	1981	15	5	4	2	1,033,179
Fappiano							
Unbridled	H	1987	24	8	6	6	4,489,475
Cryptoclearance	H	1984	44	12	10	7	3,376,327
Defensive Play	H	1987	26	6	4	5	1,688,631
Tappiano	M	1984	34	17	2	4	1,305,522
Rubiano	H	1987	28	13	6	1	1,252,817
Tasso	H	1983	23	9	4	4	1,207,884
Grand Canyon	H	1987	8	4	3	0	1,019,540
Far North							
The Wicked North	H	1989	17	8	4	1	1,180,750
Farnesio (ARG)							
Empress Club (ARG)	M	1988	26	16	2	1	1,155,235
First Landing							
Riva Ridge	H	1969	30	17	3	1	1,111,497
Fit to Fight							
Fit for a Queen	M	1986	51	13	14	9	1,226,429
Fly So Free							
Captain Steve	H	1997	25	9	3	7	6,828,356
Flying Continental							
Continental Red	G	1996	64	7	14	13	1,180,358

Horse	Sex	Born	Sts	1st	2d	3d	Earnings
Flying Paster							
Flying Continental	H	1986	51	12	15	10	1,815,938
Letthebighossroll	G	1988	60	18	14	6	1,014,377
Foolish Pleasure							
Kiri's Clown	H	1989	62	16	6	8	1,005,469
Forceten							
Heatherten	M	1979	53	21	7	4	1,022,699
Forli							
Forego	G	1970	57	34	9	7	1,938,957
Forty Niner							
Coronado's Quest	H	1995	17	10	2	0	2,046,190
Editor's Note	H	1993	31	6	4	3	1,601,394
Ecton Park	H	1996	23	6	4	6	1,503,825
French Deputy							
Left Bank	H	1997	24	14	2	0	1,402,806
Friend's Choice							
Dave's Friend	H	1975	76	35	16	8	1,079,915
Full Pocket							
Fighting Fit	H	1979	49	14	7	8	1,004,174
Gallantsky							
Puerto Madero (CHI)	H	1994	24	11	3	2	1,361,626
Geiger Counter							
Nuclear Debate	G	1995	52	11	8	10	1,234,054
General Meeting							
General Challenge	G	1996	21	9	3	1	2,877,178
Excellent Meeting	M	1996	20	8	5	3	1,402,396
Gilded Time							
Elloluv	F	2000	16	5	3	2	1,297,075
Mandy's Gold	M	1998	24	11	4	6	1,081,744
Glitterman							
Balto Star	G	1998	38	12	7	3	2,363,780
Glitter Woman	M	1994	23	10	9	3	1,256,805
Champali	C	2000	22	11	2	4	1,073,794
J J'sdream	M	1993	40	13	11	7	1,022,217
Go for Gin							
Albert the Great	H	1997	22	8	6	4	3,012,490
Gold Fever							
Gold Mover	M	1998	31	13	9	5	1,523,010
A Bit O'Gold	G	2001	11	7	3	0	1,290,819
Gold Legend							
Heritage of Gold	M	1995	28	16	2	4	2,381,762
Golden Gear							
Ginger Gold	M	1999	25	7	6	2	1,065,448
Gone West							
Da Hoss	G	1992	20	12	5	2	1,931,558
Came Home	H	1999	12	9	0	0	1,835,940
Johar	H	1999	16	6	4	2	1,494,496
Lassigny	H	1991	28	8	2	5	1,318,371
Speightstown	H	1998	16	10	2	2	1,258,256
West by West	H	1989	30	10	3	7	1,038,123
Grand Slam							
Cajun Beat	G	2000	17	7	3	0	1,159,100
Graustark							
Proud Truth	H	1982	21	10	4	0	2,198,895
Great Above							
Holy Bull	H	1991	16	13	0	0	2,481,760
Great Nephew (GB)							
Carotene	M	1983	41	12	8	5	1,287,232

Horse	Sex	Born	Sts	1st	2d	3d	Earnings
Green Dancer							
Greinton (GB)	H	1981	22	10	8	0	1,943,605
Green Desert							
Sheikh Albadou (GB)	H	1988	15	6	4	1	1,229,702
Heat Haze (GB)	M	1999	14	7	2	2	1,183,696
Grey Dawn II							
Bounding Basque	H	1980	40	10	4	6	1,256,258
Grindstone							
Birdstone	C	2001	9	5	0	0	1,575,600
Gulch							
Thunder Gulch	H	1992	16	9	2	2	2,915,086
The Cliff's Edge	C	2001	13	4	5	2	1,265,258
Wallenda	H	1990	33	7	5	5	1,205,929
Gummo							
Ancient Title	H	1970	57	24	11	9	1,252,791
Flying Paster	H	1976	27	13	7	2	1,127,460
Habitat							
Steinlen (GB)	H	1983	45	20	10	7	3,297,169
Habitony							
Best Pal	G	1988	47	18	11	4	5,668,245
Richter Scale	H	1994	25	12	2	0	1,139,958
Half a Year							
Full Moon Madness	G	1995	46	15	11	12	1,097,805
Halo							
Sunday Silence	H	1986	14	9	5	0	4,968,554
Goodbye Halo	M	1985	24	11	5	4	1,706,702
Lively One	H	1985	36	9	7	5	1,544,100
Sunny's Halo	H	1980	20	9	3	2	1,247,791
Jolie's Halo	H	1987	20	8	0	2	1,218,120
Present Value	H	1984	42	15	5	3	1,153,853
Glorious Song	M	1976	34	17	9	1	1,004,534
Halo's Image							
Southern Image	C	2000	8	6	1	1	1,843,750
Hansel							
Guided Tour	G	1996	31	12	8	1	1,964,253
Fruits of Love	H	1995	23	5	3	5	1,089,543
Harlan							
Harlan's Holiday	H	1999	22	9	6	1	3,632,664
Menifee	H	1996	11	5	4	1	1,732,000
Hawkin's Special							
Taylor's Special	H	1981	41	21	7	2	1,065,805
Hennessy							
Johannesburg	H	1999	10	7	1	0	1,014,585
Hernando (FR)							
Sulamani (IRE)	H	1999	17	9	3	1	5,252,368
High Estate (IRE)							
High-Rise (IRE)	H	1995	13	5	2	2	1,871,726
His Majesty							
Majesty's Prince	H	1979	43	12	10	10	2,077,796
Tight Spot	H	1987	21	12	3	1	1,566,100
Cetewayo	H	1994	37	11	5	4	1,170,258
Hoist the Silver							
Very Subtle	M	1984	29	12	6	4	1,608,360
Hold Your Tricks							
Judy's Red Shoes	M	1983	83	25	13	12	1,085,668
Holy Bull							
Macho Uno	H	1998	14	6	1	3	1,851,803
Honest Pleasure							
Judge Angelucci	H	1983	22	10	4	2	1,582,535
Honor Grades							
Adoration	M	1999	20	8	3	1	2,051,160
Honor Glide	H	1994	38	11	5	2	1,397,187
Horatius							
Safely Kept	M	1986	31	24	2	3	2,194,206
Housebuster							
Morluc	H	1996	40	11	9	5	1,045,758
Icecapade							
Izvestia	H	1987	21	11	2	2	2,702,527
Wild Again	H	1980	28	8	7	4	2,204,829
Ile de Bourbon							
Petite Ile (IRE)	M	1986	14	6	3	4	1,281,665
Imbros							
Native Diver	H	1959	81	37	7	12	1,026,500
In Excess (IRE)							
Excessivepleasure	G	2000	16	5	5	1	1,054,970
In Reality							
Proper Reality	H	1985	19	10	3	1	1,701,650
Smile	H	1982	27	14	4	3	1,664,027
In the Wings (GB)							
Singspiel (IRE)	H	1992	20	9	8	0	5,952,825
Indian Ridge (IRE)							
Ridgewood Pearl (GB)	M	1992	8	6	1	1	1,179,301
Interco							
Megan's Interco	G	1989	36	16	11	0	1,062,465
Intrepid Hero							
Interco	H	1980	21	10	4	3	1,070,688
Irish River (FR)							
Paradise Creek	H	1989	25	14	7	1	3,401,416
Hatoof	M	1989	21	9	4	1	1,841,070
Irish Prize	G	1996	28	10	4	2	1,242,364
River Bay	H	1993	20	8	3	3	1,167,970
Is It True							
Yes It's True	H	1996	22	11	2	3	1,080,700
Itajara							
Siphon (BRZ)	H	1991	25	12	6	2	3,136,428
Jade Hunter							
Azeri	M	1998	24	17	4	0	4,079,820
Yagli	H	1993	27	10	6	3	1,702,121
Jaklin Klugman							
Sky Jack	G	1996	18	10	2	2	1,115,127
Java Gold							
Kona Gold	G	1994	30	14	7	2	2,293,384
John Alden							
Little Bold John	G	1982	105	38	16	14	1,956,406
Jolie's Halo							
Hal's Hope	H	1997	33	9	5	3	1,098,422
Judge T C							
Request for Parole	H	1999	34	9	7	3	1,205,892
Jules							
Peace Rules	C	2000	19	9	2	2	3,084,278
Kalaglow							
Timarida (IRE)	M	1992	16	10	2	2	1,116,186
Keen (GB)							
River Keen (IRE)	H	1992	42	11	5	5	1,642,385
Key to the Kingdom							
Great Communicator	H	1983	56	14	10	7	2,922,615
Key to the Mint							
Java Gold	H	1984	15	9	3	1	1,908,832
Jewel Princess	M	1992	29	13	4	7	1,904,060

Horse	Sex	Born	Sts	1st	2d	3d	Earnings
Kingmambo							
Lemon Drop Kid	H	1996	24	10	3	3	3,245,370
Voodoo Dancer	M	1998	21	11	4	2	1,427,952
King Cugat	H	1997	16	7	7	1	1,293,782
King's Bishop							
King's Swan	H	1980	107	31	19	18	1,924,845
Kipper Kelly							
Kelly Kip	H	1994	31	15	3	4	1,157,142
Kissin Kris							
Kiss a Native	G	1997	40	14	5	3	1,109,022
Kleven							
Big Jag	G	1993	30	13	5	3	1,800,329
Kodiack							
Polar Expedition	G	1991	49	20	5	7	1,491,071
Kris (GB)							
Single Empire (IRE)	H	1994	23	5	5	3	1,110,889
Riviera (FR)	H	1994	21	10	4	3	1,018,535
Kris S.							
Prized	H	1986	17	9	2	3	2,262,555
Kissin Kris	H	1990	35	4	8	5	1,616,936
Hollywood Wildcat	M	1990	21	12	3	3	1,432,160
Kicken Kris	C	2000	19	6	3	3	1,326,600
Soaring Softly	M	1995	16	9	1	3	1,270,433
Kudos	G	1997	24	7	5	4	1,238,935
Brocco	H	1991	8	4	2	0	1,003,550
Lando (GER)							
Paolini (GER)	H	1997	28	5	6	4	3,253,469
Epalo (GER)	H	1999	21	8	8	2	1,419,259
Langfuhr							
Wando	C	2000	19	11	2	1	2,543,229
Mobil	C	2000	23	11	5	1	1,507,924
Imperial Gesture	M	1999	11	6	2	1	1,419,140
Last Tycoon (IRE)							
Ezzoud (IRE)	H	1989	22	6	5	2	1,171,885
Lear Fan							
Sarafan	G	1997	44	10	12	4	2,588,671
Labeeb (GB)	H	1992	20	8	3	4	1,464,950
Ryafan	M	1994	10	7	1	0	1,342,142
Windsharp	M	1991	29	11	7	3	1,293,075
L'Enjoleur							
Scott's Scoundrel	H	1992	50	22	4	8	1,270,052
Little Missouri							
Prairie Bayou	G	1990	12	7	3	0	1,450,621
Lively One							
Littlebitlively	H	1994	33	10	9	5	1,303,343
Lode							
Lazy Lode (ARG)	H	1994	29	8	4	6	1,296,740
Logical							
Leger Cat (ARG)	H	1986	53	16	5	7	1,211,402
Lomitas (GB)							
Silvano (GER)	H	1996	18	7	2	2	2,321,024
Lord At War (ARG)							
John's Call	G	1991	40	16	11	3	1,571,267
Lost Code							
Kalookan Queen	M	1996	25	11	8	4	1,044,474
Louis Quatorze							
Repent	H	1999	10	5	3	1	1,255,660
Lt. Stevens							
Sefa's Beauty	M	1979	52	25	7	8	1,171,628
Lyphard							
Manila	H	1983	18	12	5	0	2,692,799
Ski Paradise	M	1990	20	6	8	1	1,470,588
Dancing Brave	H	1983	10	8	1	0	1,435,434
Sangue (IRE)	M	1978	30	13	6	3	1,272,086
Dahar	H	1981	29	7	6	4	1,207,286
Rainbows for Life	H	1988	36	15	5	3	1,105,926
Sabin	M	1980	25	18	0	2	1,098,341
Lypheor (GB)							
Royal Heroine (IRE)	M	1980	21	10	4	2	1,229,449
Machiavellian							
Street Cry (IRE)	H	1998	12	5	6	1	5,150,837
Almutawakel (GB)	H	1995	19	4	4	1	3,643,021
Storming Home (GB)	H	1998	24	8	4	3	1,536,704
Majestic Light							
Simply Majestic	H	1984	44	18	4	7	1,667,713
Solar Splendor	G	1987	42	11	3	6	1,386,468
Lite Light	M	1988	26	8	4	4	1,231,596
Manila							
Bien Bien	H	1989	26	9	8	1	2,331,875
Manshood (GB)							
Ipi Tombe (ZIM)	M	1998	14	12	2	0	1,529,799
Marauding (NZ)							
Prowl (AUS)	G	1995	22	5	2	2	1,082,344
Marfa							
Farma Way	H	1987	23	8	5	1	2,897,175
Maria's Mon							
Monarchos	H	1998	10	4	1	3	1,720,830
Marquetry							
Artax	H	1995	25	7	9	3	1,685,840
Squirtle Squirt	H	1998	16	8	4	0	1,112,220
Mat-Boy (ARG)							
Festin (ARG)	H	1986	24	9	4	4	2,256,295
Maudlin							
Beautiful Pleasure	M	1995	25	10	5	2	2,734,078
Mecke	H	1992	40	12	7	9	2,470,550
Primal	G	1985	45	17	11	7	1,209,530
Meadowlake							
Meadow Star	M	1988	20	11	1	2	1,445,740
Medieval Man							
Not Surprising	G	1990	61	23	4	5	1,112,301
Mehmet							
On the Line	H	1984	37	14	7	2	1,125,810
Memo (CHI)							
Grey Memo	H	1997	54	8	4	10	1,736,683
Mendocino							
Starine (FR)	M	1997	33	10	12	1	1,674,491
Mill Reef							
Ibn Bey (GB)	H	1984	28	10	3	4	1,626,059
Lashkari (GB)	H	1981	13	5	2	2	1,127,658
Miracle Heights							
Sure Shot Biscuit	G	1996	54	23	10	11	1,025,480
Mister Frisky							
Frisk Me Now	H	1994	36	12	5	6	1,727,707
Miswaki							
Black Tie Affair (IRE)	H	1986	45	18	9	6	3,370,694
Urban Sea	M	1989	23	8	4	3	1,704,553
Misil	H	1988	36	14	8	3	1,296,417

Horse	Sex	Born	Sts	1st	2d	3d	Earnings
Mocito Guapo							
Malek (CHI)	H	1993	23	10	7	2	2,382,623
Montbrook							
Shake You Down	G	1998	42	17	6	4	1,277,164
Mountain Cat							
Classic Cat	H	1995	20	6	3	5	1,221,300
Mr. Leader							
Ruhlmann	H	1985	27	10	3	4	1,824,154
Mr. Prospector							
Gulch	H	1984	32	13	8	4	3,095,521
Forty Niner	H	1985	19	11	5	0	2,726,000
Seeking the Gold	H	1985	15	8	6	0	2,307,000
Fusaichi Pegasus	H	1997	9	6	2	0	1,994,400
Chester House	H	1995	21	6	4	4	1,944,545
Aldebaran	H	1998	25	8	12	3	1,739,186
Dancethruthedawn	M	1998	16	7	2	3	1,609,643
Rhythm	H	1987	20	6	3	4	1,592,532
Tank's Prospect	H	1982	14	5	2	2	1,355,645
Homebuilder	H	1984	60	11	11	17	1,172,153
Educated Risk	M	1990	23	11	6	4	1,163,717
Mt. Livermore							
Orientate	H	1998	19	10	3	0	1,716,950
Peaks and Valleys	H	1992	16	9	3	2	1,589,270
Mt. Sassafras	G	1992	47	8	7	14	1,382,985
Housebuster	H	1987	22	15	3	1	1,229,696
Subordination	H	1994	21	11	3	1	1,221,068
Luthier Fever	H	1991	25	6	5	6	1,160,852
Eliza	M	1990	12	5	2	2	1,095,316
Mutakddim							
Lady Tak	F	2000	18	10	4	1	1,155,682
Mysterious Vice							
Mysterious Affair	M	1997	37	12	9	6	1,059,971
Naevus							
King Glorious	H	1986	9	8	1	0	1,175,650
Nashwan							
Swain (IRE)	H	1992	22	10	4	6	3,797,566
Wandesta (GB)	M	1991	21	7	3	5	1,255,145
Naskra							
Olympio	H	1988	17	9	4	0	1,456,315
Nasrullah							
Nashua	H	1952	30	22	4	1	1,288,565
Nassipour							
Let's Elope (NZ)	M	1987	26	11	0	5	2,528,902
Night Shift							
In the Groove (GB)	M	1987	21	7	4	4	1,336,783
Nijinsky II							
Ferdinand	H	1983	29	8	9	6	3,777,978
Sky Classic	H	1987	29	15	6	1	3,320,398
Dancing Spree	H	1985	35	10	6	9	1,470,484
Niniski							
Caitano (GB)	H	1994	44	9	6	7	2,137,459
Hernando (FR)	H	1990	20	7	4	1	2,081,978
No Robbery							
Track Robbery	M	1976	59	22	12	7	1,098,537
Norcliffe							
Groovy	H	1983	26	12	4	1	1,346,956
Northern Baby							
Possibly Perfect	M	1990	18	11	2	4	1,377,634
Northern Fling							
Yankee Affair	H	1982	55	22	14	8	2,282,156
Northern Jove							
Equalize	H	1982	43	13	9	8	1,455,298
Northfields							
Fieldy (IRE)	M	1983	54	19	9	8	1,212,168
Northjet (IRE)							
Southjet	H	1983	30	5	7	2	1,040,483
Nostalgia							
Nostalgia's Star	H	1982	59	9	17	13	2,154,827
Numerous							
Kela	H	1998	25	8	6	0	1,011,527
Nureyev							
Theatrical (IRE)	H	1982	22	10	4	2	2,940,036
Skimming	H	1996	20	8	5	1	2,286,601
Miesque	M	1984	16	12	3	1	2,070,163
Spinning World	H	1993	14	8	3	1	1,734,477
Good Journey	H	1996	16	7	5	3	1,733,058
Atticus	H	1992	18	7	3	1	1,205,933
Alwuhush	H	1985	22	5	4	7	1,012,423
Annoconnor	M	1984	29	12	7	5	1,002,420
Oak Dancer (GB)							
Algenib (ARG)	H	1987	21	7	5	2	1,042,299
Ole Bob Bowers							
John Henry	G	1975	83	39	15	9	6,591,860
One for All							
The Very One	M	1975	71	22	12	9	1,104,623
Opening Verse							
Colstar	M	1996	18	11	2	1	1,053,056
Our Emblem							
War Emblem	H	1999	13	7	0	0	3,491,000
Our Hero							
My Big Boy	G	1983	50	10	12	10	1,196,102
Our Native							
Zoffany	H	1980	36	15	10	2	1,225,569
Overskate							
Capades	M	1986	27	11	9	2	1,051,006
Pago Pago							
Island Whirl	H	1978	34	11	6	6	1,144,010
Palace Music							
Cigar	H	1990	33	19	4	5	9,999,815
Pampabird							
Subotica (FR)	H	1988	15	6	4	1	1,856,255
Panoramic (GB)							
Tuzla (FR)	M	1994	26	12	6	1	1,332,587
Parlay Me							
Parose	G	1994	92	21	22	15	1,089,156
Partholon (GB)							
Symboli Rudolf (JPN)	H	1981	16	13	1	1	2,764,980
Pass the Glass							
Super Diamond	H	1980	37	16	5	5	1,469,233
Peaks and Valleys							
Dollar Bill	H	1998	22	4	5	5	1,225,546
Pepenador							
Odalea (ARG)	M	1986	21	8	7	2	1,674,812
Perrault (GB)							
Frankly Perfect	H	1985	22	6	6	4	1,272,957
Persian Bold (IRE)							
Brave Act (GB)	H	1994	27	13	6	2	1,546,269
Kooyonga (IRE)	M	1988	18	9	4	1	1,476,193
Falcon Flight (FR)	H	1996	20	5	2	3	1,428,849

Horse	Sex	Born	Sts	1st	2d	3d	Earnings
Personal Flag							
Say Florida Sandy	H	1994	98	33	17	12	2,085,408
Petionville							
Island Fashion	F	2000	17	6	2	0	1,727,970
Petrone							
Brown Bess	M	1982	36	16	8	6	1,300,920
Silveyville	H	1978	56	19	11	8	1,282,880
Phone Trick							
Caller One	G	1997	21	10	3	3	3,190,000
Favorite Trick	H	1995	16	12	0	1	1,726,793
Pivotal (GB)							
Golden Apples (IRE)	M	1998	16	6	6	2	1,672,583
Megahertz (GB)	M	1999	28	10	5	5	1,481,594
Play Fellow							
Western Playboy	H	1986	45	8	7	7	1,128,449
Pleasant Colony							
Pleasantly Perfect	H	1998	18	9	3	2	7,789,880
Behrens	H	1994	27	9	8	3	4,563,500
Pleasant Tap	H	1987	32	9	9	5	2,721,169
Denon	H	1998	22	6	4	3	1,744,025
Forbidden Apple	H	1995	31	8	6	9	1,680,640
Colonial Affair	H	1990	20	7	4	3	1,635,228
Sir Beaufort	H	1987	34	10	10	4	1,149,130
Pleasant Variety	H	1984	58	8	10	11	1,123,783
Colonial Waters	M	1985	32	6	12	3	1,112,847
State Shinto	H	1996	38	9	7	2	1,078,174
Pleasant Tap							
Pleasant Breeze	G	1995	36	10	8	6	1,271,680
Tap to Music	M	1995	21	6	4	4	1,052,526
Polish Navy							
Sea Hero	H	1990	24	6	3	4	2,929,869
Polish Precedent							
Pilsudski (IRE)	H	1992	22	10	6	2	4,080,297
Polish Summer (GB)	H	1997	27	6	10	0	2,277,871
Princequillo							
Round Table	H	1954	66	43	8	5	1,749,869
Private Account							
Personal Ensign	M	1984	13	13	0	0	1,679,880
Inside Information	M	1991	17	14	1	2	1,641,806
Valley Crossing	H	1988	48	8	13	8	1,616,490
Personal Flag	H	1983	24	8	4	4	1,258,924
Private Terms	H	1985	17	12	0	0	1,243,947
Public Purse	H	1994	14	7	1	4	1,103,324
Corporate Report	H	1988	10	3	5	0	1,067,908
Private Terms							
Soul of the Matter	H	1991	16	7	4	2	2,302,818
Afternoon Deelites	H	1992	12	7	3	0	1,061,193
Pulpit							
Essence of Dubai	H	1999	13	5	1	2	2,001,058
Quadrangle							
Susan's Girl	M	1969	63	29	14	11	1,251,668
Quiet American							
Real Quiet	H	1995	20	6	5	6	3,271,802
Rahy							
Fantastic Light	H	1996	25	12	5	3	8,486,957
Serena's Song	M	1992	38	18	11	3	3,283,388
Hawksley Hill (IRE)	G	1993	46	14	12	6	1,730,922
Tranquility Lake	M	1995	27	11	7	3	1,662,390
Tates Creek	M	1998	17	11	3	0	1,471,674
Noverre	H	1998	21	5	7	4	1,429,344
Early Pioneer	G	1995	33	9	9	5	1,156,815

Horse	Sex	Born	Sts	1st	2d	3d	Earnings
Rainbow Quest							
Quest for Fame (GB)	H	1987	19	5	4	4	1,790,417
Raintrap (GB)	H	1990	28	9	4	2	1,283,707
Saumarez (GB)	H	1987	9	5	1	0	1,275,719
Urgent Request (IRE)	H	1990	25	7	4	1	1,035,339
Raja Baba							
Sacahuista	M	1984	21	6	7	2	1,298,842
Rambunctious							
Jameela	M	1976	58	27	15	6	1,038,704
Red Ransom							
Perfect Sting	M	1996	21	14	3	0	2,202,042
Reflected Glory							
Snow Chief	H	1983	24	13	3	5	3,383,210
Relaunch							
With Anticipation	G	1995	48	15	9	8	2,660,543
Skywalker	H	1982	20	8	3	3	2,226,750
Waquoit	H	1983	30	19	4	3	2,225,360
One Dreamer	M	1988	25	12	6	2	1,266,067
Honour and Glory	H	1993	17	6	5	2	1,202,942
Restless Con							
Echo Eddie	G	1997	28	10	7	3	1,044,354
Rich Cream							
Creme Fraiche	G	1982	64	17	12	13	4,024,727
Rich Man's Gold							
Lido Palace (CHI)	H	1997	23	11	7	2	2,705,865
Risen Star							
Star Standard	H	1992	25	7	4	3	1,121,512
Riverman							
Triptych	M	1982	41	14	5	11	2,318,946
Rivlia	H	1982	41	9	2	8	1,005,041
Roberto							
Sunshine Forever	H	1985	23	8	6	3	2,084,800
Brian's Time	H	1985	21	5	2	6	1,001,269
Robin des Bois							
Gentlemen (ARG)	H	1992	24	13	4	2	3,608,558
Roi Normand							
Redattore (BRZ)	H	1995	32	15	2	6	1,799,883
Riboletta (BRZ)	M	1995	28	13	3	3	1,555,103
Roman Diplomat							
Diplomatic Jet	H	1992	51	9	5	9	1,267,202
Roughcast							
Rough Habit (NZ)	G	1986	66	28	16	7	2,861,579
Rough'n Tumble							
Dr. Fager	H	1964	22	18	2	1	1,002,642
Round Table							
Royal Glint	H	1970	52	21	9	4	1,004,816
Rousillon							
Fastness (IRE)	H	1990	24	9	6	1	1,581,165
Royal Academy							
Val Royal (FR)	H	1996	12	7	2	0	1,186,687
Royal Applause (GB)							
Ticker Tape (GB)	F	2001	18	7	6	2	1,267,426
Rubiano							
Burning Roma	H	1998	36	13	5	7	1,500,200
Run the Gantlet							
April Run (IRE)	M	1978	18	8	2	4	1,182,819
Runaway Groom							
Cherokee Run	H	1990	28	13	5	5	1,531,818
Wekiva Springs	H	1991	21	10	4	2	1,512,575
Down the Aisle	H	1993	21	9	5	5	1,007,988

Horse	Sex	Born	Sts	1st	2d	3d	Earnings
Ruritania							
Frost King	H	1978	55	27	10	3	1,196,954
Sabona							
Bonapaw	G	1996	48	18	7	4	1,158,752
Sadler's Wells							
High Chaparral (IRE)	H	1999	13	10	1	2	5,331,231
Montjeu (IRE)	H	1996	16	11	2	0	3,178,177
Galileo (IRE)	H	1998	8	6	1	0	2,245,373
Daliapour (IRE)	H	1996	26	7	3	3	2,123,763
Beat Hollow (GB)	H	1997	12	7	2	2	1,814,481
Ballingarry (IRE)	H	1999	23	6	1	6	1,741,049
Northern Spur (IRE)	H	1991	15	6	4	3	1,614,425
In the Wings (GB)	H	1986	11	7	1	0	1,562,335
Islington (IRE)	M	1999	15	6	0	4	1,553,043
Perfect Soul (IRE)	H	1998	21	7	5	1	1,527,764
Carnegie (IRE)	H	1991	13	7	1	1	1,458,787
Dream Well (FR)	H	1995	14	4	4	4	1,439,441
Opera House (GB)	H	1988	18	8	4	3	1,397,456
Refuse To Bend (IRE)	C	2000	15	7	0	1	1,350,034
Brian Boru (GB)	C	2000	18	4	4	3	1,209,054
Powerscourt (GB)	C	2000	17	4	5	3	1,200,917
Dushyantor	H	1993	20	5	5	2	1,197,570
Barathea (IRE)	H	1990	16	5	4	0	1,189,181
King's Theatre (IRE)	H	1991	19	5	3	4	1,154,329
Sagace (FR)							
Arcangues	H	1988	19	6	2	2	1,981,423
Saggy							
Carry Back	H	1958	62	21	11	11	1,241,165
Saint Ballado							
Ashado	F	2001	14	9	3	2	2,870,440
Captain Bodgit	H	1994	12	7	1	4	1,014,849
Salse							
Timboroa (GB)	H	1996	25	10	3	3	1,397,228
Saros (GB)							
Fran's Valentine	M	1982	34	13	4	5	1,375,465
Sea-Bird							
Allez France	M	1970	21	13	3	1	1,262,801
Seattle Slew							
Taiki Blizzard	H	1991	23	6	8	2	5,523,549
Slew o' Gold	H	1980	21	12	5	1	3,533,534
A.P. Indy	H	1989	11	8	0	1	2,979,815
Surfside	M	1997	15	8	3	2	1,852,987
Swale	H	1981	14	9	2	2	1,583,660
Slew City Slew	H	1984	42	11	10	6	1,166,296
Flute	M	1998	8	4	3	0	1,101,504
Event of the Year	H	1995	9	5	2	1	1,095,200
Seattle Song							
Irish Linnet	M	1988	62	19	16	10	1,220,180
Secretariat							
Lady's Secret	M	1982	45	25	9	3	3,021,325
Risen Star	H	1985	11	8	2	1	2,029,845
Tinners Way	H	1990	27	7	6	4	1,846,546
Seeking the Gold							
Seeking the Pearl	M	1994	21	8	2	3	4,021,716
Heavenly Prize	M	1991	18	9	6	3	1,825,940
Dream Supreme	M	1997	16	9	2	2	1,007,680
Shadeed							
Sayyedati (GB)	M	1990	22	6	5	3	1,408,616
Sharpen Up (GB)							
Pebbles (GB)	M	1981	15	8	4	0	1,419,632
Trempolino	H	1984	11	4	3	3	1,369,233
Shot Gun Scott							
Vivace	M	1993	40	20	4	6	1,037,671
Siberian Express							
In Excess (IRE)	H	1987	25	11	2	3	1,736,733
Sillery							
Silic (FR)	H	1995	15	8	2	0	1,422,299
Silver Buck							
Silver Charm	H	1994	24	12	7	2	6,944,369
Forever Silver	H	1985	47	8	9	9	1,001,974
Silver Deputy							
Silverbulletday	M	1996	23	15	3	1	3,093,207
Bare Necessities	M	1999	26	8	4	7	1,062,251
Silver Ghost							
Silver Goblin	G	1991	26	16	4	3	1,083,895
Silver Hawk							
Mutafaweq	H	1996	19	7	1	3	1,800,800
Hawkster	H	1986	23	6	3	4	1,510,942
Memories of Silver	M	1993	19	9	3	5	1,448,715
Wonder Again	M	1999	19	7	2	3	1,111,682
Silver Ending	H	1987	37	8	1	9	1,073,420
Mubtaker	H	1997	20	9	6	3	1,007,998
Singspiel (IRE)							
Moon Ballad (IRE)	H	1999	14	5	3	1	4,364,791
Sir Ivor Again							
Ten Keys	H	1984	54	21	8	4	1,209,211
Sir Leon							
Sir Bear	G	1993	71	19	12	14	2,538,422
Skip Trial							
Skip Away	H	1993	38	18	10	6	9,616,360
Best of the Rest	H	1995	32	16	8	2	1,407,796
Sky Classic							
Thornfield	G	1994	19	6	1	3	1,206,074
Skywalker							
Bertrando	H	1989	24	9	6	2	3,185,610
Slew City Slew							
Maysville Slew	G	1996	69	17	11	7	1,046,409
Slew o' Gold							
Dramatic Gold	G	1991	39	9	13	6	2,567,630
Gorgeous	M	1986	14	8	4	1	1,171,370
Thirty Six Red	H	1987	20	4	3	5	1,094,310
Slewacide							
Slew of Damascus	G	1988	48	16	9	8	1,420,350
Clever Trevor	G	1986	30	15	5	2	1,388,841
Mr Ross	G	1995	44	18	6	10	1,091,046
Slewvescent							
Tout Charmant	M	1996	29	9	9	1	1,781,879
Lazy Slusan	M	1995	47	12	7	10	1,150,410
Slip Anchor (GB)							
User Friendly (GB)	M	1989	16	8	1	2	1,764,938
Smart Strike							
Soaring Free	G	1999	22	13	3	0	1,917,544
Fleetstreet Dancer	G	1998	25	5	7	3	1,704,806
Tenpins	H	1998	17	9	3	2	1,133,449
Smoke Glacken							
Smok'n Frolic	M	1999	33	9	8	2	1,534,720

Horse	Sex	Born	Sts	1st	2d	3d	Earnings
Smokester							
Free House	H	1994	22	9	5	3	3,178,971
Southern Halo							
More Than Ready	H	1997	17	7	4	1	1,026,229
Sovereign Dancer							
Gate Dancer	H	1981	28	7	8	7	2,501,705
Louis Quatorze	H	1993	18	7	5	1	2,054,434
Itsallgreektome	G	1987	29	8	10	2	1,994,618
Bolshoi Boy	G	1983	58	16	7	8	1,039,702
Soviet Star							
Soviet Line (IRE)	G	1990	48	16	8	6	1,450,130
Volochine (IRE)	H	1991	45	8	12	9	1,205,580
Freedom Cry (GB)	H	1991	12	5	5	0	1,089,080
Spectrum (IRE)							
Golan (IRE)	H	1998	11	4	2	1	1,623,376
Spend a Buck							
Pico Central (BRZ)	H	1999	15	9	0	3	1,183,145
Hard Buck (BRZ)	H	1999	19	9	5	0	1,073,674
Antespend	M	1993	24	10	4	2	1,011,954
Sportin' Life							
Bet Twice	H	1984	26	10	6	4	3,308,599
Stalwart							
Stalwars	H	1985	79	17	17	8	1,211,556
Star de Naskra							
Sewickley	H	1985	32	11	9	4	1,017,517
State Dinner							
Family Style	M	1983	35	10	8	7	1,537,118
Steady Growth							
Steady Power	G	1984	70	13	19	9	1,132,197
Stop the Music							
Temperence Hill	H	1977	31	11	4	2	1,567,650
Music Merci	G	1986	35	12	7	4	1,500,710
Storm Bird							
Summer Squall	H	1987	20	13	4	0	1,844,282
Indian Skimmer	M	1984	16	10	1	3	1,469,299
Storm Boot							
Bourbon Belle	M	1995	40	16	11	5	1,152,223
Storm Cat							
Cat Thief	H	1996	30	4	9	8	3,951,012
Giant's Causeway	H	1997	13	9	4	0	3,078,989
Tabasco Cat	H	1991	18	8	3	2	2,347,671
Sharp Cat	M	1994	22	15	3	0	2,032,575
Storm Flag Flying	F	2000	14	7	3	3	1,951,828
Mountain Cat	H	1990	11	6	2	0	1,478,901
Raging Fever	M	1998	26	11	7	3	1,458,198
High Yield	H	1997	14	4	4	3	1,170,196
Vision and Verse	H	1996	21	4	3	5	1,030,330
Strawberry Road (AUS)							
Escena	M	1993	29	11	9	3	2,962,639
Fraise	H	1988	34	10	5	6	2,613,105
Ajina	M	1994	17	7	3	2	1,327,915
Stuka							
Total Impact (CHI)	H	1998	22	5	8	2	1,586,778
Sultry Song							
Singletary	C	2000	16	6	5	2	1,439,732
Summer Squall							
Charismatic	H	1996	17	5	2	4	2,038,064
Summer Colony	M	1998	24	10	5	1	1,448,930
Storm Song	M	1994	12	4	1	2	1,020,050

Horse	Sex	Born	Sts	1st	2d	3d	Earnings
Sunday Silence							
Dance in the Mood (JPN)	F	2001	10	4	3	0	2,931,889
Sunny's Halo							
Dispersal	H	1986	22	12	3	2	1,511,137
Sunny Sunrise	G	1987	63	18	12	9	1,367,268
Swain (IRE)							
Dimitrova	F	2000	14	4	2	1	1,142,696
Swing Till Dawn							
Fly Till Dawn	H	1986	27	10	5	4	1,556,525
Sword Dance (IRE)							
Marlin	H	1993	26	9	3	5	2,448,880
Blazing Sword	G	1994	45	11	7	7	1,184,055
Sword Dancer							
Damascus	H	1964	32	21	7	3	1,176,781
Tabasco Cat							
Freefourinternet	H	1998	34	8	3	6	1,050,275
Talc							
Lottsa Talc	M	1990	65	21	10	12	1,206,248
Tale of the Cat							
Lion Heart	C	2001	10	5	3	0	1,390,800
Tale of Two Cities							
Cougar II	H	1966	50	20	7	17	1,172,625
Talkin Man							
Better Talk Now	G	1999	25	8	5	2	1,744,437
Targowice							
All Along (FR)	M	1979	21	9	4	2	2,125,828
Tejano							
Tejano Run	H	1992	21	8	4	6	1,166,842
Tejano Run							
One for Rose	M	1999	22	12	4	2	1,047,243
Temperence Hill							
Temperate Sil	H	1984	19	6	2	1	1,113,775
The Minstrel							
Opening Verse	H	1986	30	10	7	2	1,669,357
Savinio	G	1990	48	11	11	8	1,321,860
Theatrical (IRE)							
Royal Anthem	H	1995	12	6	3	1	1,876,876
Geri	H	1992	19	9	4	3	1,707,980
Strut the Stage	H	1998	23	10	2	3	1,496,986
Astra	M	1996	16	11	1	2	1,378,424
Hap	H	1996	20	10	2	2	1,329,210
Thunder Gulch							
Point Given	H	1998	13	9	3	0	3,968,500
Spain	M	1997	35	9	9	7	3,540,542
Mystic Lady	M	1998	27	10	8	2	1,170,390
Thunder Puddles							
Thunder Rumble	H	1989	19	8	0	1	1,047,552
Time for a Change							
Fly So Free	H	1988	33	12	5	3	2,330,954
Tom Fool							
Buckpasser	H	1963	31	25	4	1	1,462,014
Topsider							
North Sider	M	1982	36	15	7	5	1,126,400
Top Corsage	M	1983	53	15	7	9	1,110,028
Tour d'Or							
Express Tour	H	1998	14	5	1	1	1,767,515
Transworld							
Lonesome Glory	G	1988	44	24	5	6	1,325,868

Horse	Sex	Born	Sts	1st	2d	3d	Earnings
Trempolino							
Talloires	H	1990	28	5	8	3	1,423,949
Dernier Empereur	H	1990	30	8	5	4	1,152,425
Twining							
Two Item Limit	M	1998	28	7	3	5	1,060,585
Unbridled							
Banshee Breeze	M	1995	18	10	5	2	2,784,798
Empire Maker	C	2000	8	4	3	1	1,985,800
Unshaded	G	1997	20	6	3	3	1,318,492
Manistique	M	1995	15	11	1	1	1,311,800
Unbridled's Song	H	1993	12	5	4	0	1,311,800
Grindstone	H	1993	6	3	2	0	1,224,510
Red Bullet	H	1997	14	6	2	2	1,161,920
Unbridled's Song							
Unbridled Elaine	M	1998	11	6	2	1	1,770,740
Upper Case							
Flying Pidgeon	H	1981	56	12	9	13	1,154,337
Vacilante (ARG)							
Troyanos (BRZ)	H	1985	13	10	1	1	1,038,083
Vaguely Noble							
Estrapade	M	1980	30	12	5	5	1,937,142
Exceller	H	1973	33	15	5	6	1,674,587
Dahlia	M	1970	48	15	3	7	1,489,105
Lemhi Gold	H	1978	22	8	3	1	1,131,355
Val de l'Orne (FR)							
Pay the Butler	H	1984	40	5	5	5	1,934,140
Valdez							
El Senor	H	1984	44	12	7	5	1,769,215
Velvet Cap							
Trinycarol (VEN)	M	1979	29	18	3	1	2,644,392
Verbatim							
Princess Rooney	M	1980	21	17	2	1	1,343,339
Alphabatim	H	1981	22	7	3	5	1,313,175
Hopeful Word	H	1981	43	18	12	3	1,073,051
Vice Regent							
Regal Classic	H	1985	27	8	8	3	1,456,584
Twice the Vice	M	1991	23	12	6	1	1,447,064
Regal Intention	H	1985	41	14	7	10	1,083,103
Bessarabian	M	1982	37	18	5	4	1,032,640

Horse	Sex	Born	Sts	1st	2d	3d	Earnings
Vigors							
Real Connection	M	1991	72	7	14	7	1,225,018
Hodges Bay	G	1985	51	7	15	3	1,050,363
Voyageur							
My Own Business (VEN)	H	1997	50	37	5	1	1,016,908
Waquoit							
Halo America	M	1990	40	15	8	2	1,460,992
Warning (GB)							
Annus Mirabilis (FR)	H	1992	30	9	7	6	1,541,938
Way West (FR)							
Western Pride	H	1998	32	10	4	1	1,289,929
What a Pleasure							
Foolish Pleasure	H	1972	26	16	4	3	1,216,705
Whiskey Road							
Strawberry Road (AUS)	H	1979	50	21	7	9	1,655,678
Wild Again							
Milwaukee Brew	H	1997	24	8	4	5	2,879,612
Wilderness Song	M	1988	37	15	12	2	1,482,033
Wild Rush	H	1994	16	8	0	3	1,386,302
Shine Again	M	1997	34	14	10	7	1,271,840
Elmhurst	G	1990	51	8	11	6	1,100,567
Wild Rush							
Personal Rush	C	2001	11	5	0	1	1,234,820
Stellar Jayne	F	2001	18	6	2	3	1,111,244
With Approval							
Maltese Superb	M	1997	35	4	7	4	1,145,491
Woodman							
Hansel	H	1988	14	7	2	3	2,936,586
Hawk Wing	H	1999	12	5	5	0	1,610,604
Timber Country	H	1992	12	5	1	4	1,560,400
Yachtie (AUS)							
Happyanunoit (NZ)	M	1995	21	9	6	2	1,582,118
You and I							
You	M	1999	23	9	8	2	2,101,353
Your Host							
Kelso	G	1957	63	39	12	2	1,977,896
Zinaad (GB)							
Kazzia (GER)	M	1999	7	5	0	0	1,094,206

This section includes all horses with at least $1 million in career earnings that had at least one start in North America. It includes any foreign earnings and bonus money awarded for racing performance that was reported to *Daily Racing Form.*

Top Juvenile Sires in 2004 – Money Won

Sire	Perfs.	Winning Perfs.	Starts	1st	2nd	3rd	Unplaced	Purses
Successful Appeal	20	15	76	31	13	10	22	$1,724,080
Storm Cat	18	7	56	14	7	4	31	1,616,329
Yes It's True	40	15	141	25	12	31	73	1,424,382
Awesome Again	23	9	65	10	12	6	37	1,100,214
Valid Expectations	33	17	133	32	19	24	58	1,074,026
In Excess (IRE)	12	6	27	11	5	2	9	1,019,531
Petionville	26	8	97	13	10	15	59	950,910
Fusaichi Pegasus	22	7	54	14	8	9	23	923,385
Thunder Gulch	50	15	153	20	20	20	93	916,731
Malibu Moon	27	9	84	18	6	8	52	872,112
Unbridled's Song	19	9	50	18	7	8	17	870,306
Cape Canaveral	30	11	106	18	25	12	51	864,072
More Than Ready	34	17	134	24	23	18	69	837,567
Northern Afleet	13	8	51	12	10	4	25	814,430
Carson City	35	15	108	19	13	14	62	806,117
A. P Jet	46	16	145	20	20	13	92	772,446
Whiskey Wisdom	14	9	42	13	7	5	17	759,611
Foxtrail	24	8	91	15	11	12	53	739,773
Wild Event	17	9	86	15	11	10	50	696,800
Dixie Union	21	11	93	15	21	12	45	695,666
Precise End	27	11	98	12	20	17	49	689,598
Victory Gallop	25	8	93	11	18	16	48	653,377
Smart Strike	26	11	69	15	7	12	35	632,789
Tale of the Cat	30	14	96	21	22	8	45	629,414
Timber Country	4	1	10	3	3	0	4	623,056
Swiss Yodeler	37	15	151	20	19	24	88	611,810
Wheaton	39	21	138	33	16	18	71	610,032
Peaks and Valleys	31	13	96	19	12	14	51	608,262
Afternoon Deelites	31	12	110	17	19	20	54	600,556
Double Honor	37	20	177	30	17	26	104	575,537
Stormy Atlantic	43	16	152	21	20	24	87	558,563
Silver Charm	30	10	100	13	13	16	58	556,645
A.P. Indy	19	7	50	7	6	6	31	547,981
Forest Wildcat	28	15	101	18	13	15	55	547,562
Maria's Mon	38	14	126	15	21	6	84	546,303
Menifee	25	10	66	16	6	7	37	540,178
Cherokee Run	29	13	101	17	8	13	63	530,736
Bernstein	18	11	60	17	18	6	19	525,467
Smoke Glacken	22	14	90	19	13	17	41	519,737
Tiger Ridge	25	11	82	13	15	7	47	517,686
Running Stag	33	10	107	15	13	14	65	516,682
Wild Rush	22	8	90	14	14	14	48	514,205
Wild Zone	42	15	159	21	25	25	88	499,683
Old Topper	19	10	76	15	20	11	30	498,815
Lord Carson	34	16	118	17	16	22	63	498,791
Sweetsouthernsaint	23	11	106	19	15	10	62	494,024
Charismatic	37	10	112	11	7	10	84	491,531
Southern Halo	12	5	38	11	6	3	18	490,571
Honour and Glory	46	15	130	18	14	26	72	488,491
Indian Charlie	14	8	71	13	13	14	31	488,045
Gilded Time	24	14	90	17	11	15	47	478,366
Rubiano	31	11	108	15	15	14	64	464,271
Cape Town	20	12	76	16	14	10	36	456,305
Robyn Dancer	38	11	165	18	22	19	106	455,740
Catienus	31	19	120	23	13	11	73	451,551
Distorted Humor	28	11	87	14	12	13	48	451,206

Sire	Perfs.	Winning Perfs.	Starts	1st	2nd	3rd	Unplaced	Purses
Devil His Due	38	14	128	17	20	19	72	430,551
Leestown	32	10	108	17	13	16	62	430,376
Doneraile Court	21	11	81	13	14	7	47	423,669
Meadow Monster	26	13	109	19	17	17	56	423,620
Bartok (IRE)	32	13	114	21	19	9	65	422,829
Allen's Prospect	40	11	130	14	21	20	75	414,045
Straight Man	33	12	105	15	18	16	56	413,206
Stormin Fever	31	11	103	13	16	12	62	402,948
Slew City Slew	18	7	75	9	8	14	44	401,619
Lucky Lionel	26	9	106	11	19	10	66	401,009
Yankee Victor	27	12	86	13	15	8	50	399,274
Grand Slam	25	9	63	13	14	7	29	396,762
Silver Ghost	22	8	57	10	6	7	34	392,942
Lion Hearted	13	9	40	12	5	7	16	391,917
Western Expression	20	7	60	8	9	7	36	384,961
Dance Master	7	4	25	7	5	7	6	383,496
Vying Victor	23	11	90	16	13	8	53	382,110
Lite the Fuse	26	6	63	7	8	12	36	377,573
Pulpit	23	6	54	7	11	7	29	374,406
Touch Gold	31	9	83	10	8	7	58	372,643
Bold Executive	9	2	26	4	6	1	15	366,015
American Chance	23	7	79	13	8	11	47	365,335
Suave Prospect	19	11	116	18	13	20	65	364,177
Mt. Livermore	18	6	60	6	12	10	32	363,303
Dixieland Band	14	5	36	6	5	6	19	361,835
Souvenir Copy	15	4	46	7	7	9	23	361,335
Slew Gin Fizz	34	18	138	20	13	20	85	353,556
Boundary	12	4	31	7	4	6	14	353,237
Citidancer	6	3	21	7	4	5	5	347,410
Archers Bay	19	7	50	7	6	5	32	346,801
Parade Ground	22	6	84	9	12	9	54	345,732
Coronado's Quest	16	5	54	8	11	4	31	343,170
Lemon Drop Kid	16	6	46	7	11	10	18	342,983
Formal Gold	20	9	77	10	12	19	36	340,695
Mud Route	15	6	70	9	12	12	37	339,717
Deputy Minister	17	6	49	8	5	7	29	336,459
Golden Missile	24	6	66	7	7	5	47	332,496
Boston Harbor	19	8	59	10	8	8	33	332,388
Sword Dance (IRE)	27	13	132	18	9	11	94	330,070
Chester House	25	9	67	11	9	7	40	326,963
Cee's Tizzy	15	7	49	8	8	4	29	326,067
Good and Tough	15	7	44	11	8	6	19	321,588
Rizzi	28	12	112	17	10	14	71	318,113
Fortunate Prospect	22	12	99	17	8	9	65	315,093

Top Juvenile Sires in 2004 – Races Won

Sire	Perfs.	Winning Perfs	Starts	1st	2nd	3rd	Unplaced	Purses
Wheaton	39	21	138	33	16	18	71	$610,032
Valid Expectations	33	17	133	32	19	24	58	1,074,026
Successful Appeal	20	15	76	31	13	10	22	1,724,080
Double Honor	37	20	177	30	17	26	104	575,537
Yes It's True	40	15	141	25	12	31	73	1,424,382
More Than Ready	34	17	134	24	23	18	69	837,567
Catienus	31	19	120	23	13	11	73	451,551
Tale of the Cat	30	14	96	21	22	8	45	629,414
Stormy Atlantic	43	16	152	21	20	24	87	558,563
Wild Zone	42	15	159	21	25	25	88	499,683
Bartok (IRE)	32	13	114	21	19	9	65	422,829
Thunder Gulch	50	15	153	20	20	20	93	916,731
A. P Jet	46	16	145	20	20	13	92	772,446
Swiss Yodeler	37	15	151	20	19	24	88	611,810
Slew Gin Fizz	34	18	138	20	13	20	85	353,556
Carson City	35	15	108	19	13	14	62	806,117
Peaks and Valleys	31	13	96	19	12	14	51	608,262
Smoke Glacken	22	14	90	19	13	17	41	519,737
Sweetsouthernsaint	23	11	106	19	15	10	62	494,024
Meadow Monster	26	13	109	19	17	17	56	423,620
Malibu Moon	27	9	84	18	6	8	52	872,112
Unbridled's Song	19	9	50	18	7	8	17	870,306
Cape Canaveral	30	11	106	18	25	12	51	864,072
Forest Wildcat	28	15	101	18	13	15	55	547,562
Honour and Glory	46	15	130	18	14	26	72	488,491
Robyn Dancer	38	11	165	18	22	19	106	455,740
Suave Prospect	19	11	116	18	13	20	65	364,177
Sword Dance (IRE)	27	13	132	18	9	11	94	330,070
In Excessive Bull	26	13	96	18	13	9	56	277,363
Afternoon Deelites	31	12	110	17	19	20	54	600,556
Cherokee Run	29	13	101	17	8	13	63	530,736
Bernstein	18	11	60	17	18	6	19	525,467
Lord Carson	34	16	118	17	16	22	63	498,791
Gilded Time	24	14	90	17	11	15	47	478,366
Devil His Due	38	14	128	17	20	19	72	430,551
Leestown	32	10	108	17	13	16	62	430,376
Rizzi	28	12	112	17	10	14	71	318,113
Fortunate Prospect	22	12	99	17	8	9	65	315,093
Bertrando	21	12	73	17	5	6	45	311,089
Menifee	25	10	66	16	6	7	37	540,178
Cape Town	20	12	76	16	14	10	36	456,305
Vying Victor	23	11	90	16	13	8	53	382,110
Line In The Sand	32	11	163	16	17	24	106	312,371
Foxtrail	24	8	91	15	11	12	53	739,773
Wild Event	17	9	86	15	11	10	50	696,800
Dixie Union	21	11	93	15	21	12	45	695,666
Smart Strike	26	11	69	15	7	12	35	632,789
Maria's Mon	38	14	126	15	21	6	84	546,303
Running Stag	33	10	107	15	13	14	65	516,682
Old Topper	19	10	76	15	20	11	30	498,815
Rubiano	31	11	108	15	15	14	64	464,271
Straight Man	33	12	105	15	18	16	56	413,206
Storm Cat	18	7	56	14	7	4	31	1,616,329
Fusaichi Pegasus	22	7	54	14	8	9	23	923,385
Wild Rush	22	8	90	14	14	14	48	514,205
Distorted Humor	28	11	87	14	12	13	48	451,206
Allen's Prospect	40	11	130	14	21	20	75	414,045

Sire	Perfs.	Winning Perfs.	Starts	1st	2nd	3rd	Unplaced	Purses
Basket Weave	18	12	69	14	7	6	42	156,826
Petionville	26	8	97	13	10	15	59	950,910
Whiskey Wisdom	14	9	42	13	7	5	17	759,611
Silver Charm	30	10	100	13	13	16	58	556,645
Tiger Ridge	25	11	82	13	15	7	47	517,686
Indian Charlie	14	8	71	13	13	14	31	488,045
Doneraile Court	21	11	81	13	14	7	47	423,669
Stormin Fever	31	11	103	13	16	12	62	402,948
Yankee Victor	27	12	86	13	15	8	50	399,274
Grand Slam	25	9	63	13	14	7	29	396,762
American Chance	23	7	79	13	8	11	47	365,335
Exploit	32	10	125	13	12	14	86	310,082
Magic Cat	29	11	101	13	13	11	64	279,934
Fit to Fight	15	8	60	13	9	5	33	270,763
Family Calling	25	11	118	13	15	25	65	242,885
Tour d'Or	22	10	118	13	21	8	76	221,980
Subordination	16	10	75	13	7	12	43	189,197
Free At Last	22	10	72	13	7	9	43	131,396
Northern Afleet	13	8	51	12	10	4	25	814,430
Precise End	27	11	98	12	20	17	49	689,598
Lion Hearted	13	9	40	12	5	7	16	391,917
Montbrook	23	9	90	12	12	4	62	297,486
Untuttable	14	7	64	12	10	7	35	263,005
Hadif	18	10	92	12	18	12	50	175,285
Danjur	12	7	35	12	5	6	12	120,297
In Excess (IRE)	12	6	27	11	5	2	9	1,019,531
Victory Gallop	25	8	93	11	18	16	48	653,377
Charismatic	37	10	112	11	7	10	84	491,531
Southern Halo	12	5	38	11	6	3	18	490,571
Lucky Lionel	26	9	106	11	19	10	66	401,009
Chester House	25	9	67	11	9	7	40	326,963
Good and Tough	15	7	44	11	8	6	19	321,588
Colony Light	16	6	84	11	18	11	44	308,347
Concorde's Tune	18	8	79	11	10	9	49	307,907
High Yield	27	8	74	11	4	13	46	299,331
Cartwright	24	10	88	11	8	7	62	270,254
High Brite	19	10	72	11	13	14	34	268,656
Lost Soldier	28	10	88	11	10	10	57	223,330
Louis Quatorze	35	10	98	11	8	12	67	222,588
Twin Spires	16	8	78	11	8	7	52	206,056
Formal Dinner	15	9	66	11	11	6	38	180,033
Awesome Again	23	9	65	10	12	6	37	1,100,214
Silver Ghost	22	8	57	10	6	7	34	392,942
Touch Gold	31	9	83	10	8	7	58	372,643
Formal Gold	20	9	77	10	12	19	36	340,695
Boston Harbor	19	8	59	10	8	8	33	332,388
Chief Seattle	24	9	74	10	9	12	43	304,361
Forestry	16	7	48	10	5	2	31	278,063
Tomorrows Cat	26	9	92	10	12	8	62	273,430
Seneca Jones	11	7	44	10	6	6	22	179,725
Mister Jolie	9	7	45	10	5	6	24	174,224
Confide	12	7	45	10	6	4	25	171,361
Moro Oro	8	7	37	10	3	10	14	168,480
Blumin Affair	13	7	38	10	0	4	24	162,875
Quaker Ridge	8	7	44	10	12	5	17	151,914

Top Juvenile Sires in 2004 – Winning Performers

Sire	Perfs.	Winning Perfs	Starts	1st	2nd	3rd	Unplaced	Purses
Wheaton	39	21	138	33	16	18	71	$610,032
Double Honor	37	20	177	30	17	26	104	575,537
Catienus	31	19	120	23	13	11	73	451,551
Slew Gin Fizz	34	18	138	20	13	20	85	353,556
Valid Expectations	33	17	133	32	19	24	58	1,074,026
More Than Ready	34	17	134	24	23	18	69	837,567
A. P Jet	46	16	145	20	20	13	92	772,446
Stormy Atlantic	43	16	152	21	20	24	87	558,563
Lord Carson	34	16	118	17	16	22	63	498,791
Successful Appeal	20	15	76	31	13	10	22	1,724,080
Yes It's True	40	15	141	25	12	31	73	1,424,382
Thunder Gulch	50	15	153	20	20	20	93	916,731
Carson City	35	15	108	19	13	14	62	806,117
Swiss Yodeler	37	15	151	20	19	24	88	611,810
Forest Wildcat	28	15	101	18	13	15	55	547,562
Wild Zone	42	15	159	21	25	25	88	499,683
Honour and Glory	46	15	130	18	14	26	72	488,491
Tale of the Cat	30	14	96	21	22	8	45	629,414
Maria's Mon	38	14	126	15	21	6	84	546,303
Smoke Glacken	22	14	90	19	13	17	41	519,737
Gilded Time	24	14	90	17	11	15	47	478,366
Devil His Due	38	14	128	17	20	19	72	430,551
Peaks and Valleys	31	13	96	19	12	14	51	608,262
Cherokee Run	29	13	101	17	8	13	63	530,736
Meadow Monster	26	13	109	19	17	17	56	423,620
Bartok (IRE)	32	13	114	21	19	9	65	422,829
Sword Dance (IRE)	27	13	132	18	9	11	94	330,070
In Excessive Bull	26	13	96	18	13	9	56	277,363
Afternoon Deelites	31	12	110	17	19	20	54	600,556
Cape Town	20	12	76	16	14	10	36	456,305
Straight Man	33	12	105	15	18	16	56	413,206
Yankee Victor	27	12	86	13	15	8	50	399,274
Rizzi	28	12	112	17	10	14	71	318,113
Fortunate Prospect	22	12	99	17	8	9	65	315,093
Bertrando	21	12	73	17	5	6	45	311,089
Basket Weave	18	12	69	14	7	6	42	156,826
Cape Canaveral	30	11	106	18	25	12	51	864,072
Dixie Union	21	11	93	15	21	12	45	695,666
Precise End	27	11	98	12	20	17	49	689,598
Smart Strike	26	11	69	15	7	12	35	632,789
Bernstein	18	11	60	17	18	6	19	525,467
Tiger Ridge	25	11	82	13	15	7	47	517,686
Sweetsouthernsaint	23	11	106	19	15	10	62	494,024
Rubiano	31	11	108	15	15	14	64	464,271
Robyn Dancer	38	11	165	18	22	19	106	455,740
Distorted Humor	28	11	87	14	12	13	48	451,206
Doneraile Court	21	11	81	13	14	7	47	423,669
Allen's Prospect	40	11	130	14	21	20	75	414,045
Stormin Fever	31	11	103	13	16	12	62	402,948
Vying Victor	23	11	90	16	13	8	53	382,110
Suave Prospect	19	11	116	18	13	20	65	364,177
Line In The Sand	32	11	163	16	17	24	106	312,371
Magic Cat	29	11	101	13	13	11	64	279,934
Family Calling	25	11	118	13	15	25	65	242,885
Silver Charm	30	10	100	13	13	16	58	556,645
Menifee	25	10	66	16	6	7	37	540,178
Running Stag	33	10	107	15	13	14	65	516,682
Old Topper	19	10	76	15	20	11	30	498,815

Sire	Perfs.	Winning Perfs.	Starts	1st	2nd	3rd	Unplaced	Purses
Charismatic	37	10	112	11	7	10	84	491,531
Leestown	32	10	108	17	13	16	62	430,376
Exploit	32	10	125	13	12	14	86	310,082
Cartwright	24	10	88	11	8	7	62	270,254
High Brite	19	10	72	11	13	14	34	268,656
Lost Soldier	28	10	88	11	10	10	57	223,330
Louis Quatorze	35	10	98	11	8	12	67	222,588
Tour d'Or	22	10	118	13	21	8	76	221,980
Subordination	16	10	75	13	7	12	43	189,197
Hadif	18	10	92	12	18	12	50	175,285
Free At Last	22	10	72	13	7	9	43	131,396
Awesome Again	23	9	65	10	12	6	37	1,100,214
Malibu Moon	27	9	84	18	6	8	52	872,112
Unbridled's Song	19	9	50	18	7	8	17	870,306
Whiskey Wisdom	14	9	42	13	7	5	17	759,611
Wild Event	17	9	86	15	11	10	50	696,800
Lucky Lionel	26	9	106	11	19	10	66	401,009
Grand Slam	25	9	63	13	14	7	29	396,762
Lion Hearted	13	9	40	12	5	7	16	391,917
Touch Gold	31	9	83	10	8	7	58	372,643
Formal Gold	20	9	77	10	12	19	36	340,695
Chester House	25	9	67	11	9	7	40	326,963
Chief Seattle	24	9	74	10	9	12	43	304,361
Montbrook	23	9	90	12	12	4	62	297,486
Storm Creek	38	9	113	9	15	12	77	294,201
Vicar	29	9	86	9	9	12	56	278,996
Tomorrows Cat	26	9	92	10	12	8	62	273,430
Phone Trick	17	9	68	9	15	7	37	257,481
Formal Dinner	15	9	66	11	11	6	38	180,033
Regal Intention	26	9	87	9	15	12	51	179,553
Petionville	26	8	97	13	10	15	59	950,910
Northern Afleet	13	8	51	12	10	4	25	814,430
Foxtrail	24	8	91	15	11	12	53	739,773
Victory Gallop	25	8	93	11	18	16	48	653,377
Wild Rush	22	8	90	14	14	14	48	514,205
Indian Charlie	14	8	71	13	13	14	31	488,045
Silver Ghost	22	8	57	10	6	7	34	392,942
Boston Harbor	19	8	59	10	8	8	33	332,388
Concorde's Tune	18	8	79	11	10	9	49	307,907
High Yield	27	8	74	11	4	13	46	299,331
Concerto	12	8	54	9	4	9	32	290,756
Belong to Me	16	8	44	9	8	6	21	280,775
Fit to Fight	15	8	60	13	9	5	33	270,763
Cat Thief	19	8	57	8	8	7	34	238,135
Twin Spires	16	8	78	11	8	7	52	206,056
Crafty Friend	27	8	95	8	9	17	61	201,732
Skywalker	24	8	72	9	14	6	43	185,578
Artax	25	8	76	8	5	7	56	144,093

Top 10 Juvenile Sires and Their Progeny

Successful Appeal, Dk B H (1996)
By Valid Appeal – Successful Dancer, by Fortunate Prospect

20 Performers, 15 winning performers, $1,724,080 in total earnings

Progeny	Mare	Age	Sts	1st	2d	3d	Money Won
Accountforthegold	Accountess	2	3	1	1	1	103,325
Brillant Success	Brillant Way	2	3	1	1	0	15,332
Classy Choice	Cecilia's Choice	2	6	3	1	1	66,360
Closing Argument	Mrs. Greeley	2	5	2	2	1	421,984
Double D Appeal	Wicked Diablo	2	3	2	0	1	73,530
Hostile Witness	Diablo's Blend	2	7	2	1	2	59,530
Loni's Appeal	Loni Girl	2	1	0	0	0	860
Looking for Loot	Dance Naturally	2	4	1	1	0	14,380
Lunarpal	Quiet Eclipse	2	5	4	0	0	284,677
Mr. Meridian	Notable Crusader	2	1	0	0	0	580
One El of a Lady	Crafty El	2	2	1	0	0	10,320
Palacios Appeal	Wild Devil	2	5	1	2	0	37,000
Power Link	Linking	2	2	1	0	0	24,805
Prolific Appeal	No Holding David	2	1	0	0	0	0
Punch Appeal	Okanagan Dawn	2	9	6	0	1	389,840
She's a Jewel	Binawin	2	5	2	0	1	70,600
Still Guilty	Oh Jay	2	2	1	1	0	32,600
Successful Affair	Private Pouf	2	1	0	0	0	137
Successfully Sweet	Princess Meadowlak	2	4	3	1	0	104,650
Sun Appeal	Sun Creme	2	7	0	2	2	13,570

Storm Cat, Dk B H, (1983)
By Storm Bird – Terlingua, by Secretariat

18 Performers, 7 winning performers, $1,616,329 in total earnings

Progeny	Mare	Age	Sts	1st	2d	3d	Money Won
Big Top Cat	Golden Attraction	2	2	0	0	0	225
Burmese Cat	Timely Broad	2	2	0	1	0	5,300
Cabaret Star	Pike Place Dancer	2	4	0	0	0	1,925
Coffee House	Coffee Springs	2	3	0	0	2	5,720
Connie Belle	Minister's Melody	2	2	0	0	0	4,350
Consolidator	Good Example (FR)	2	7	2	1	1	480,260
Dream Time	Fantastic Find	2	1	1	0	0	25,800
Encore	Cash Run	2	1	0	0	0	0
Metro Cat	Ruby City	2	2	2	0	0	19,800
One Stormy Mama	Wicked Mama	2	4	0	1	1	13,130
Sequoia Grove	Lilly Capote	2	3	1	1	0	19,501
Storm Surge	Especially	2	7	4	1	0	192,770
Storm Warning	Let	2	4	1	1	0	44,150
Storming Pride	Alpride (IRE)	2	1	0	0	0	400
Stormy Weather	Bay Harbor	2	4	0	0	0	690
Sweet Catomine	Sweet Life	2	4	3	1	0	799,800
Thunder Ridge	City Band	2	2	0	0	0	2,379
Weather Alert	China Bell	2	3	0	0	0	129

Yes It's True, B H (1996)
By Is ItTrue – Clever Monique, by Clever Trick

40 Performers, 15 winning performers, $1,424,382 in total earnings

Progeny	Mare	Age	Sts	1st	2d	3d	Money Won
A True Star	Plano Star	2	5	0	0	1	11,250
B. B. Best	Bold Juana	2	7	4	0	1	360,710
Bushwacked	Launch Site	2	1	0	0	1	1,560
Chandtrue	Chandelle	2	4	4	0	0	182,970
Fab Four	Three's Perfect	2	3	0	1	0	3,300
Hallie Lyn	Semilla Besada	2	2	0	0	0	357
Hollow Sky	Hollow Miss	2	1	0	0	0	1,410
It's Not So	Alinda	2	1	0	0	0	300
Its True Atlast	Joyatlast	2	3	1	0	0	12,500
Its True Its True	Poms Rising Star	2	3	1	0	0	9,030
J. J. Dancer	Flunky Dancer	2	1	0	0	0	230
Krissy C.	Aunt Pia	2	2	0	0	0	4,200
Lotsa Yes	Lotsa Pasta	2	3	0	0	2	4,295
Loud Enough	Speak Up	2	1	0	0	0	78
Maes Gift	Madeleine's Gift	2	3	0	1	0	3,240
Midtown Miss	Van Nic	2	7	2	3	0	51,230
Missile Bay	Saint La Petit	2	7	1	1	3	42,570
Mr. Fourth of July	Illumination	2	1	0	0	0	129
Mrs. Ripley	Sam's Reality	2	2	0	0	0	240
Mz. Winjum	Dyna Performer	2	5	1	1	1	28,860
Palace Intrigue	Time for a Crown	2	1	0	0	0	1,290
Proud Accolade	Proud Ciel	2	5	3	0	0	364,130
Qureall	Sisters Creek	2	2	1	0	0	19,800
R U Sure	Grand Corsage	2	2	0	0	0	1,525
Say It Isn't Sold	Strikingperfection	2	7	0	0	3	9,120
Shoot the Bugler	Sinful Devotion	2	7	1	0	2	39,839
Spider Joe	Josefina	2	6	1	0	2	25,920
Sporty McGee	An A. Forel	2	3	0	0	2	5,290
Suny's Boy	Evanna	2	4	0	1	0	10,773
Tax Considerations	Safety Deposit	2	4	1	0	0	23,451
Testingonetwothree	Notatinkertoy	2	7	0	0	4	4,605
Thanks Fox	Wild Harem	2	5	0	0	2	4,500
True Tails	Cocktail	2	4	2	1	1	51,930
Truly False	Highland Park Ms	2	3	0	0	1	3,260
Wishing for You	Ocean Apart	2	1	0	0	0	1,200
Yes He's a Pistol	Maggies Pistol	2	4	1	0	0	22,780
Yes I'm a Lady	Jellied Madrilene	2	2	0	0	0	270
Yes It's Gold	Maid of Gold	2	7	1	1	4	102,800
Yes Its You	Ice Folly	2	4	0	1	1	5,740
Yes Yes Yes	Daring Doone (GB)	2	1	0	1	0	7,700

Awesome Again, B H (1994)
By Deputy Minister – Primal Force, by Blushing Groom

23 Performers, 9 winning performers, $1,100,214 in total earnings

Progeny	Mare	Age	Sts	1st	2d	3d	Money Won
Aristocrat	Baby Zip	2	1	0	0	0	2,250
Awesome Doe	Roobels	2	9	1	1	1	17,550
Awesome Pro	Fickle Fate	2	1	0	0	0	205
Awesome Sign	Hekeepsmesinging	2	1	0	0	0	400
Awesome Venture	Forever Land	2	2	0	0	0	4,500
Awesome Victory	Sarabi	2	2	0	0	0	720
Ball Girl	Bal d'Argent	2	2	1	1	0	36,600
Comealong	Dark Hours	2	1	0	0	0	0
Diane Again	Dianes Halo	2	5	1	0	1	17,280
Extra Exclusive	Prominent Feather	2	2	1	1	0	10,100
Formalities Aside	Well Dressed	2	5	1	1	1	38,089
Goofball	Letting Loose	2	3	0	2	0	4,360
Guildhall	Earth Song	2	3	0	1	0	4,362
Hillbilly Bandit	Diablo's Peace	2	6	1	0	2	19,180
King Mustang	Feeling Easy	2	2	0	0	0	580
Magoo's Magic	Slew the Queen	2	4	2	1	0	70,358
Mantova Run	Tassa	2	6	1	1	0	22,600
Naked Again	Naked Glory	2	3	0	1	0	2,800
Spun Sugar	Irish Cherry	2	1	0	1	0	9,000
Welcome Again	Alda's Will	2	2	0	1	0	5,700
Wilko	Native Roots (IRE)	2	2	1	0	1	833,580
Win Again	Valid Approval	2	1	0	0	0	0
Xtra Awesome	Woofy	2	1	0	0	0	0

Valid Expectations, B H (1993)
By Valid Appeal – Mepache, by Iron Constitution

33 Performers, 17 winning performers, $1,074,026 in total earnings

Progeny	Mare	Age	Sts	1st	2d	3d	Money Won
Appealing Air	Funky Diva	2	1	0	0	0	0
Big Doc	My Grande	2	2	0	0	0	360
Butterfly Bloom	Flying Katuna	2	3	1	0	2	30,435
Chance Five	Capture the Market	2	1	0	0	1	1,622
Expect Lace	Just Like Lace	2	1	0	0	1	1,210
Expect Will	Amazing Trace	2	10	6	2	0	251,496
Expect Wings	Jovial Wings	2	4	1	1	1	49,848
Just Validation	Just Lace	2	8	3	0	0	30,900
Leaving On My Mind	Sudden Attraction	2	13	5	2	3	299,873
Legal Force	Just Wanna Dance	2	3	0	0	1	1,255
Lonestar Rocket	Celebrate Life	2	1	0	0	1	825
Martys Expectation	Personal Fantasy	2	8	1	2	3	29,305
Mickey's Hope	Chris's Gal	2	3	0	0	0	3,420
Oh I See	Cynwyd	2	4	0	2	1	11,180
Pip	I'mararebird	2	5	1	2	0	26,438
Rasm	Limit Pusher	2	3	0	0	1	3,500
Red Birds Big Hart	Patient Saint	2	7	1	0	2	8,196
Robbeau	City Hideaway	2	6	1	3	1	62,570
Rocky Joseph Pm	Eightress	2	1	0	0	0	78
Ruffled Up	Forever Ruffles	2	3	0	0	0	0
Security Code	Excess Loot	2	4	2	0	0	19,725
Smoke Pit	Dame's Rocket	2	2	0	1	0	5,420
Social Validation	Social Desire	2	4	1	0	1	9,405
Substantiate	Counting Halos	2	5	1	2	0	29,405
Super Expectations	Diable Rose	2	5	1	0	2	10,660
Texas Trouble	Saucy and Sweet	2	2	0	1	0	5,000
Total Expectations	Tellif	2	4	2	0	1	13,070
Tuned In	Charlie Fepp	2	4	2	1	1	105,500
Valid Echo	A. J. Echo	2	5	0	0	0	750
Valid Freeze	Celtic Twang	2	2	0	0	0	165
Valid Virtue	Iron's Advance	2	5	2	0	0	44,164
Validalia	National Account	2	2	1	0	1	17,585
Winninexpectations	Temperence Valley	2	2	0	0	0	666

In Excess, Dk B H (1987)
By Siberian Express – Kantado, by Saulingo

12 Performers, 6 winning performers, $1,019,531 in total earnings

Progeny	Mare	Age	Sts	1st	2d	3d	Money Won
Enchanting Lady	Sharp Looking Lady	2	1	0	1	0	7,000
Excessively Nice	House of Soviet's	2	2	1	0	1	50,220

Excessiveobsession	Letthemoondancerap	2	2	0	0	0	2,500
Miss January	Pure Pleasure	2	2	1	1	0	50,800
Moorea	Beautiful Isle	2	1	0	0	0	400
Mr Charlie D	Scrod	2	2	1	1	0	33,020
Mr Magic	Royal Malt (IRE)	2	7	2	0	1	9,606
Only in Reno	Filaree	2	1	0	1	0	8,800
Point Luck	Moscow Minute	2	1	0	0	0	2,583
Texcess	Danish Alamode	2	4	3	1	0	725,427
Turbo Kick	Lip Service	2	1	0	0	0	400
Uncle Denny	Gift to the World	2	3	3	0	0	128,775

Petionville, Dk B H (1992)
By Seeking the Gold – Vana Turns, by Wavering Monarch

26 Performers, 8 winning performers, $950,910 in total earnings

Progeny	Mare	Age	Sts	1st	2d	3d	Money Won
Big Slew	Slewtress	2	3	0	0	1	3,765
Blue Heaven	Dynablue	2	7	0	1	1	6,788
Casual Cash	Cool Million	2	4	0	0	1	2,940
Culture Clash	Antonia Bin (IRE)	2	4	1	0	0	41,400
Danse Kongo	Out of Step	2	2	0	0	0	1,420
Doctor Voodoo	Go Ahead and Cry	2	7	3	1	2	109,745
Good as Gold	Wow Ittsa Pleasure	2	5	1	0	1	47,411
Iron Gene	Unbroken Chain	2	2	0	0	0	250
Island Escape	Royal Deception	2	5	1	1	1	43,500
Island Myth	Enchanted Spirit	2	2	0	0	0	360
Mastercraft	Future Dispersal	2	2	0	1	0	3,663
Mother Superior	Stricter Sister	2	5	0	0	1	3,600
Petion's Shadow	Valid Play	2	1	0	0	0	100
Petionce	Miss Cynthia	2	1	0	0	0	0
Pitch and Toss	Frivolous Sal	2	3	0	1	0	4,450
Roust About	Better Look Twice	2	3	1	1	1	24,290
Runway Model	Ticket to Houston	2	10	4	2	2	580,598
She Sings	Karaoke Kid	2	5	1	0	1	31,520
Shush	It's Silent	2	4	1	0	0	22,200
Slap Shot	Playful Valentine	2	5	0	0	1	4,490
So Still	Hushed	2	4	0	0	1	3,240
Spearsville	Fancy Forbes	2	1	0	0	0	0
Successville	Secreto's Success	2	1	0	0	0	0
Take a Chance	Wing It	2	4	0	0	0	3,700
Three Elevens	In Triplacate	2	4	0	0	0	1,600
Trigger Fish Lane	Gold Medallion	2	3	0	2	1	9,880

Fusaichi Pegasus, B H (1997)
By Mr. Prospector – Angel Fever, by Danzig

22 Performers, 7 winning performers, $923,385 in total earnings

Progeny	Mare	Age	Sts	1st	2d	3d	Money Won
Andromeda's Hero	Marozia	2	2	1	0	1	17,300
Bandini	Divine Dixie	2	1	0	0	0	180
Boardroom Scandal	Synformer	2	1	0	0	0	118
Candy Striper (GB)	Nurse Goodbody	2	2	0	0	1	4,750
Easterly Breeze	Nakiska Wind	2	3	0	1	1	13,650
Every Other Memory	Frozen Rope	2	6	1	1	1	26,680
Fusaichi Samurai	Hidden Storm	2	1	1	0	0	21,000
Killenaule	Tipically Irish	2	9	4	3	2	198,540
Massasoit	Fancy Clancy	2	1	0	0	1	3,740
Nevsky Prospekt	Northern Hilite	2	1	0	0	0	0
Orezza	Oyster Catcher (IRE)	2	1	0	0	0	2,160
Patience Pays	Mamselle Bebette	2	4	1	0	1	29,830
Princess Medusa	Bet Twice Princess	2	2	0	0	0	600
Princess Pegasus	Shy Princess	2	4	0	0	0	4,250
Roman Ruler	Silvery Swan	2	5	3	1	0	330,800
Scalator	From Time to Time	2	2	0	1	0	3,895
Scandinavia	Party Cited	2	1	0	0	0	0
South Bay Cove	Fantasy Lake	2	4	3	0	0	256,897
Spirited Way	Pacheca	2	1	0	0	0	400
War Plan	Li Law	2	1	0	1	0	3,895
Winged Wishes	Slewzig	2	1	0	0	1	4,700
Witten	Word o' Ransom	2	1	0	0	0	0

Thunder Gulch, CH H (1992)
By Gulch – Line of Thunder, by Storm Bird

50 Perfomers, 15 winning performers, $916,731 in total earnings

Progeny	Mare	Age	Sts	1st	2d	3d	Money Won
Ace On the River	Squawk	2	2	0	0	0	491
Afeher	Isleworth	2	5	0	0	0	700
Alice's Thunder	Cool Alice	2	3	0	0	0	400
Bachelor's Gulch	Cosa Lucinante	2	5	0	2	0	20,930
Beyond Thunder	Beyond Temptation	2	2	0	1	0	2,040
California Thunder	Tilbury	2	2	0	0	1	6,780
Call the Thunder	Record the Call	2	1	0	1	0	9,000
Come With Thunder	Boldly Extravagant	2	4	0	2	2	14,030
Crack the Sky	Heaven to Earth	2	7	1	0	2	13,785
Daisy's Secret	Don't Tell Maisie	2	1	0	0	0	1,200
Drina's Thunder	Crafty Queen	2	1	0	0	0	0
Elusive Thunder	Be Elusive	2	7	2	1	0	75,420
Escapist	Offshore Account	2	1	0	0	0	0
Flagstaff	Beautiful Moment	2	5	0	2	2	29,600
Forever Bertie	Alltheway Bertie	2	2	0	0	0	2,835
Glorieta Pass	Morgan J.	2	1	0	0	0	0
Glorious Thunder	Winloc's Glorious	2	4	0	0	0	1,484
Jenkim	Satin and Lace	2	1	0	0	0	161
Just Thunder	Cochet Cochet	2	5	1	0	1	13,380
La Balladar	Ballasecret (GB)	2	4	0	1	2	18,615
Legal Control	Miss Legality	2	6	3	1	1	95,782
Miss Thunderella	Lady Danz	2	2	0	0	0	330
Mr. Morley	Exuberine (FR)	2	1	0	0	0	300
Peg's Thunder	Peg's Puffin	2	3	0	0	0	175
Pleasant Thunder	Caroline's Dance	2	6	1	1	1	9,713
Power of Thunder	Costa	2	5	0	0	0	0
Rachele R's Angel	Pass the School	2	2	0	0	0	222
Regal Approach	Regal Approval	2	6	1	1	1	26,082
Reverberate	Peggibonsi	2	3	1	0	1	34,785
Sense of Style	Save Me the Waltz (IRE)	2	5	3	0	0	369,000
Shorty Knudtson	Tuzia	2	2	1	0	0	29,200
Steal Your Thunder	Jewel Thief	2	2	1	1	0	28,200
Stock Tip	Cookingwithmartha	2	1	0	0	0	180
Superior Gulch	Campfire	2	1	0	1	0	1,980
Sussex County	Gail's Brush	2	4	1	0	0	7,484
Sweet Dee's	G. U. Dancer	2	1	1	0	0	21,000
Thunder Again	Disclaimed	2	2	0	0	0	0
Thunder Belle	Rangoon Belle	2	1	0	0	1	1,560
Thunder Cloud	Hopi	2	1	0	0	0	0
Thunder E. O. G.	Rare Pick	2	7	1	1	1	9,735
Thunder Lady	Embrace Lauren	2	2	0	0	1	6,300
Thunder Maker	Degree	2	1	0	0	1	4,200
Thunder Point	Stormy Jewel	2	1	0	0	0	307
Thunderchaser	Ascloseasitgets	2	5	1	2	0	24,475
Thunderous Summer	Stormy Squall	2	5	0	0	0	7,175
Tracy Arm	Silver Hiawatha	2	4	0	1	0	2,935
Valdini	Halholah	2	2	0	0	2	9,720
Wantagh Warrior	Shine Up	2	5	0	0	0	1,140
What's That Sound	Fairway Dynasty	2	3	0	1	0	5,800
Young Thunder	Dream Team	2	1	1	0	0	8,100

Malibu Moon, B H (1997)
By A.P. Indy – Macoumba, by Mr. Prospector

27 Perfomers, 9 winning performers, $916,731 in total earnings

Progeny	Mare	Age	Sts	1st	2d	3d	Money Won
Blondes	Marilyn	2	3	0	0	0	300
Blue Crush	Gretel's Chore	2	2	0	0	0	1,860
Carmel Valley Moon	Keep Tabs	2	2	0	0	0	700
Cerulean Moon	Thru the Night	2	6	2	0	1	30,580
Declan's Moon	Vee Vee Star	2	4	4	0	0	507,300
Fire Drill	Dr. Nunn	2	1	0	0	0	360
Golden Malibu	Golden Press	2	5	3	0	1	87,610
Halawa Moon	Halawa	2	6	2	0	0	21,450
Hello Jerry	Wood Nymph	2	2	0	1	0	10,200
Keystone Malibu	Habar's Mystery	2	2	0	1	0	9,100
Kite Hawk	Greenback Blues	2	5	1	0	0	17,550
Little Big Moon	Dittany	2	3	0	0	1	5,520
Lower Shore	See Sea Sara	2	8	0	1	1	9,360
Luna La Estrellas	Skip'n Anda Jump'n	2	1	0	0	0	570
Lunar Ruler	Sovereign Nation	2	2	0	0	0	288
Malibu Maybe	Get Real	2	1	0	0	0	0
Malibu Moonshine	Time to Coast	2	6	3	0	0	65,280
Malibu Sun	Walking in Da Sun	2	2	1	0	0	17,820
Momma's Eyes	Raging Smart	2	2	0	0	0	720
Monday's Moon	Stormy Monday	2	1	0	0	0	2,580
Moonshine Man	Proud Cosmah	2	2	1	0	0	16,200
Mysto's	I Have an Idea	2	2	0	2	0	12,400
Noonday Idol	Out Burst	2	7	0	0	2	4,760
Pocomoonshine	Summell	2	1	0	0	0	600
Prairie Heat	Sean's Gold	2	2	0	0	1	3,430
Shenandoah Harley	Shenandoah Lady	2	4	0	1	1	16,174
Starleena	Clever Rache	2	2	1	0	0	29,400

Annual Leading Juvenile Sire – Money Won

Year	Sire	Winning Perfs.	Races Won	Amount Won
1914	*Ogden	19	56	$339,911
1915	Broomstick	11	38	178,546
1916	Olambala	5	16	56,289
1917	Peter Quince	6	18	48,537
1918	Sweep	12	39	97,947
1919	Fair Play	4	17	90,002
1920	Peter Pan	7	30	92,965
1921	Runnymede	7	23	128,195
1922	*Allumeur	1	5	94,847
1923	Black Toney	11	37	115,745
1924	Ultimus	10	31	104,349
1925	*Sun Briar	1	7	121,630
1926	*Wrack	12	22	112,504
1927	Luke McLuke	1	6	111,905
1928	High Time	18	44	229,100
1929	Mad Hatter	10	24	77,735
1930	Pennant	5	17	182,950
1931	*Dis Donc	13	34	247,916
1932	Pompey	11	28	141,025
1933	*Royal Minstrel	8	16	102,395
1934	Chance Shot	8	17	94,900
1935	*Sir Gallahad III	13	31	102,670
1936	Pompey	6	11	87,150
1937	Pharamond II	22	41	105,875
1938	John P. Grier	7	20	95,535
1939	Black Toney	1	6	135,090
1940	*Bull Dog	14	28	100,676
1941	Good Goods	6	24	118,425
1942	*Bull Dog	8	26	221,332
1943	*Bull Dog	14	33	178,344
1944	Case Ace	10	28	230,525
1945	*Sickle	7	13	188,150
1946	*Mahmoud	18	40	283,983
1947	Bull Lea	11	31	420,940
1948	War Admiral	6	23	346,260
1949	Roman	18	38	227,604
1950	War Relic	14	35	272,182
1951	Menow	6	13	247,700
1952	Polynesian	12	28	341,730
1953	Roman	15	33	550,966
1954	*Nasrullah	14	31	625,692
1955	*Nirgal	12	24	293,800
1956	*Nasrullah	10	30	422,573
1957	Jet Jewel	3	8	360,402
1958	*Turn-To	8	25	463,280
1959	Determine	6	14	411,765
1960	*My Babu	9	18	437,240
1961	Bryan G	9	25	428,810
1962	*Nasrullah	9	17	574,231
1963	Bold Ruler	9	17	343,585
1964	Bold Ruler	11	36	967,814
1965	Tom Fool	5	15	592,871
1966	Bold Ruler	9	24	941,493
1967	Bold Ruler	12	34	1,126,844
1968	Bold Ruler	11	27	609,243
1969	Prince John	5	11	418,183
1970	Hail to Reason	9	16	473,244
1971	First Landing	9	17	551,120
1972	Bold Ruler	6	14	541,990
1973	Raise a Native	7	18	311,002
1974	What a Pleasure	13	21	387,748
1975	What a Pleasure	16	25	611,071
1976	Raja Baba	13	26	419,872
1977	In Reality	8	16	432,596
1978	Secretariat	5	12	600,617
1979	Mr. Prospector	14	26	529,665
1980	Raja Baba	9	19	807,335
1981	Hoist The Flag	12	12	680,753
1982	Olden Times	7	16	948,900
1983	Alydar	4	19	1,136,063
1984	Danzig	10	10	2,146,530
1985	Fappiano	8	16	1,232,408
1986	Rajab	4	9	950,335
1987	Mr. Prospector	9	21	1,566,919
1988	Seattle Slew	7	15	911,567
1989	Fappiano	9	15	1,416,884
1990	Habitony	5	11	1,083,588
1991	Capote	15	20	1,160,237
1992	Storm Cat	4	13	1,668,559
1993	Storm Cat	14	29	1,514,992
1994	Seeking The Gold	19	11	1,170,201
1995	Storm Cat	28	16	1,252,266
1996	Capote	31	14	2,694,604
1997	Phone Trick	38	16	1,692,737
1998	Storm Cat	24	10	1,408,473
1999	Storm Cat	20	12	1,389,759
2000	Honour and Glory	22	30	1,439,824
2001	Valid Expectations	27	40	1,393,897
2002	Storm Cat	16	11	1,455,651
2003	Tale of the Cat	24	34	1,918,383
2004	Successful Appeal	15	31	1,724,080

* Denotes Foreign-bred. Note: Prior to 1962, amount won included earnings only from juvenile winning performers.

Top Broodmare Sires in 2004 – Money Won

Broodmare Sire	Perf	Winning Perf	Mares	Starts	1st	2nd	3rd	Unplaced	Purses
Dixieland Band	325	182	187	2,197	326	299	305	1,267	$11,556,169
Relaunch	323	186	183	2,200	297	283	262	1,358	9,442,575
Deputy Minister	313	170	187	1,933	292	256	245	1,140	9,035,408
Smile	76	41	48	561	83	65	54	359	8,828,709
Mr. Prospector	252	131	155	1,512	236	185	188	903	8,447,383
Bold Ruckus	229	130	135	1,696	246	258	216	976	6,883,093
Storm Bird	243	132	139	1,531	210	207	177	937	6,801,246
Danzig	176	96	119	1,061	166	164	121	610	6,762,695
Kris S.	221	118	144	1,463	212	211	203	837	6,471,678
Valid Appeal	302	164	168	1,968	284	256	257	1,171	5,939,964
Clever Trick	307	156	179	2,051	256	252	260	1,283	5,913,450
Affirmed	225	125	132	1,539	217	196	194	932	5,613,315
Seattle Slew	220	98	143	1,257	179	179	153	746	5,579,573
Storm Cat	221	105	139	1,274	175	173	165	761	5,309,637
Pleasant Colony	221	120	123	1,570	213	222	229	906	5,271,283
Vice Regent	237	120	135	1,623	227	205	213	978	5,229,968
Woodman	207	122	123	1,422	212	182	174	854	5,095,320
Crafty Prospector	281	154	165	1,908	280	248	262	1,118	5,054,773
Conquistador Cielo	267	137	157	1,090	240	247	200	1,141	5,014,327
Sovereign Dancer	213	116	114	1,552	195	191	222	944	4,995,786
Miswaki	244	128	150	1,490	224	204	171	891	4,940,625
Alleged	175	88	119	1,069	144	143	121	661	4,862,754
Wild Again	247	129	155	1,559	209	210	197	943	4,800,658
Star de Naskra	179	94	112	1,193	164	155	156	718	4,783,238
Cox's Ridge	229	119	144	1,564	206	215	195	948	4,696,972
Private Account	228	116	138	1,468	190	198	207	873	4,678,004
Green Dancer	198	90	113	1,288	169	137	186	796	4,631,856
Cure the Blues	235	121	137	1,575	205	184	208	978	4,624,546
Nureyev	109	59	76	650	98	83	79	390	4,615,323
Regal Classic	152	82	85	1,078	151	148	137	642	4,614,148
Halo	258	134	146	1,623	214	206	189	1,014	4,409,242
Smarten	175	87	112	1,249	155	155	154	785	4,316,654
Spectacular Bid	180	100	123	1,160	164	145	133	718	4,267,865
Seeking the Gold	126	69	84	704	102	109	89	404	4,263,103
Phone Trick	229	119	146	1,464	196	200	176	892	4,207,981
Saratoga Six	181	93	111	1,157	169	136	152	700	4,192,898
Forty Niner	162	90	95	948	147	123	120	558	4,129,967
Mr. Leader	188	86	109	1,263	148	149	171	795	4,117,753
Majestic Light	234	114	140	1,587	196	155	196	1,040	3,914,370
Naskra	111	44	70	801	78	100	98	525	3,871,669
Mari's Book	82	45	51	555	94	75	79	307	3,846,576
Copelan	175	94	100	1,054	155	150	125	624	3,795,622
Broad Brush	176	100	112	1,177	182	153	184	658	3,791,890
Alydar	175	80	112	1,111	143	153	143	672	3,752,801
Dynaformer	139	68	88	923	111	114	110	588	3,723,250
Mt. Livermore	209	97	127	1,373	171	185	155	862	3,705,649
Baldski	130	62	82	874	106	94	124	550	3,694,905
Carson City	136	76	91	815	146	138	101	430	3,679,408
Strawberry Road (AUS)	145	91	86	907	144	142	122	499	3,653,252
Rahy	164	74	100	890	122	130	81	557	3,652,309
Devil's Bag	210	99	123	1,323	169	192	175	787	3,648,570
Lost Code	191	105	118	1,313	183	162	184	784	3,597,852
Two Punch	144	78	93	1,000	128	113	108	651	3,572,566
Stalwart	173	93	105	1,264	171	183	149	761	3,536,014
Lear Fan	128	64	77	859	108	98	110	543	3,529,599
Caveat	162	84	83	1,177	137	152	137	751	3,488,226
Nijinsky II	129	60	86	820	112	113	114	481	3,475,440
Silver Deputy	110	62	80	694	120	113	64	397	3,439,722
Meadowlake	203	104	123	1,208	163	164	151	730	3,424,222
Topsider	147	87	82	1,087	148	143	125	671	3,418,305
Fit to Fight	188	92	109	1,294	173	164	156	801	3,391,358
Gone West	126	58	86	795	117	92	101	485	3,390,287
Secretariat	199	90	129	1,433	148	174	168	943	3,377,668
Silver Hawk	136	61	82	799	94	102	97	506	3,369,215
Capote	167	83	105	1,050	140	125	129	656	3,334,613
Afleet	153	78	92	989	144	119	118	608	3,290,637
Slew o' Gold	148	70	100	970	124	132	140	574	3,249,892
Our Native	164	82	97	1,136	152	148	139	697	3,195,432
Chief's Crown	145	67	90	839	127	95	98	519	3,059,997
Jade Hunter	115	64	79	798	116	105	83	494	3,018,913
Allen's Prospect	154	85	105	1,141	160	154	124	703	2,979,095
Fappiano	145	78	92	943	129	118	115	581	2,924,854
Fortunate Prospect	147	80	87	1,103	139	162	126	676	2,923,488

Broodmare Sire	Perf	Winning Perf	Mares	Starts	1st	2nd	3rd	Unplaced	Purses
Red Ransom	130	77	87	833	127	104	101	501	2,919,416
Well Decorated	192	108	112	1,413	180	170	175	888	2,857,505
Premiership	162	83	92	1,165	164	138	150	713	2,833,038
Runaway Groom	183	76	117	1,219	132	133	173	781	2,826,309
His Majesty	152	71	91	1,111	136	125	134	716	2,765,756
Hold Your Peace	106	59	58	745	109	92	85	459	2,750,125
Black Tie Affair (IRE)	155	83	93	1,159	131	170	157	701	2,726,369
Cryptoclearance	172	81	107	1,168	138	135	125	770	2,715,593
Great Above	152	70	99	980	135	147	116	582	2,703,321
Bates Motel	137	67	78	1,010	118	125	128	639	2,687,374
Gate Dancer	124	68	76	819	131	112	112	464	2,654,235
Irish Tower	154	72	96	1,070	125	150	122	673	2,621,982
Key to the Mint	150	72	101	957	128	101	101	627	2,600,585
Theatrical (IRE)	150	67	96	885	115	119	104	547	2,591,247
Known Fact	137	66	84	824	113	128	106	477	2,571,695
Flying Paster	158	82	92	1,016	124	125	141	626	2,566,040
Sunny's Halo	166	84	96	1,172	147	158	159	708	2,559,719
Mining	138	71	86	836	120	104	116	496	2,537,422
Air Forbes Won	145	88	85	1,037	150	138	127	622	2,524,849
Housebuster	95	52	63	556	93	67	69	327	2,445,409
Spend a Buck	130	61	77	778	98	100	107	473	2,425,094
Pirate's Bounty	193	90	139	1,262	160	151	164	787	2,390,020
Personal Flag	120	72	74	952	132	132	121	567	2,368,422
Magesterial	91	43	56	592	85	86	58	363	2,358,603
Cormorant	120	57	76	755	103	87	87	478	2,349,042
With Approval	107	48	66	700	82	89	89	440	2,349,032
Lord Avie	158	72	101	959	124	128	119	588	2,345,193
Apalachee	169	79	110	1,112	141	143	119	709	2,338,088
Ogygian	132	63	87	845	110	85	107	543	2,301,378
Lucky North	94	43	51	673	97	89	70	417	2,291,862
Silver Buck	137	68	92	1,022	124	113	116	669	2,268,801
Northern Baby	130	62	81	884	103	121	113	547	2,262,377
Gulch	111	62	71	753	120	105	106	422	2,238,772
Distinctive Pro	121	63	79	833	112	100	118	503	2,228,002
Stop the Music	183	83	111	1,232	132	156	130	814	2,205,563
Northern Jove	148	72	88	1,079	116	122	126	715	2,199,639
Lyphard	105	48	70	639	83	72	85	399	2,193,775
Waquoit	89	49	59	640	95	97	89	359	2,191,630
Cozzene	134	59	85	905	114	94	105	592	2,182,400
Notebook	85	54	55	566	93	78	74	321	2,175,524
Alysheba	111	48	65	751	88	102	102	459	2,159,666
Corporate Report	69	36	44	428	50	51	63	264	2,145,264
Wolf Power (SAF)	142	66	90	947	119	142	106	580	2,142,233
Irish River (FR)	130	58	83	729	93	94	78	464	2,135,819
Salt Lake	89	41	59	551	71	68	61	351	2,126,399
Easy Goer	45	26	28	255	46	38	35	136	2,088,667
Time for a Change	161	76	102	979	126	116	110	627	2,086,343
Geiger Counter	117	49	79	737	74	86	91	486	2,085,606
Houston	106	51	68	752	77	81	96	498	2,071,071
General Assembly	91	56	51	648	105	74	79	390	2,064,082
D'Accord	112	59	65	790	104	108	105	473	2,022,331
Unreal Zeal	77	43	47	606	98	80	67	361	2,018,292
Seattle Dancer	96	44	58	581	78	89	75	339	2,014,307
It's Freezing	144	73	76	1,022	118	142	133	629	1,998,442
Danzig Connection	128	68	79	918	131	102	115	570	1,989,552
Wavering Monarch	123	64	77	805	107	89	101	508	1,980,966
Vigors	140	74	84	1,038	130	121	95	692	1,967,966
Quiet American	60	28	39	347	54	38	45	210	1,962,337
Beau Genius	91	42	56	582	80	67	71	364	1,956,216
Fred Astaire	76	38	48	509	75	57	67	310	1,948,309
Explodent	162	69	100	1,074	108	143	96	727	1,939,368
Temperence Hill	164	75	99	1,117	122	115	138	742	1,938,017
Unbridled	78	34	57	458	58	44	61	295	1,912,790
Seattle Song	85	41	55	523	77	56	85	305	1,906,699
Buckaroo	137	61	82	940	117	124	114	585	1,901,246
Blushing Groom (FR)	68	39	46	400	61	48	41	250	1,854,869
The Minstrel	106	50	66	639	81	68	80	410	1,847,676
Lord Gaylord	87	42	53	565	79	61	66	359	1,837,494
Slewpy	104	54	73	641	95	85	81	380	1,836,628
Pentelicus	94	52	60	586	82	71	73	360	1,828,557
Eastern Echo	78	44	45	522	74	73	72	303	1,828,237
Turkoman	103	45	72	665	81	85	75	424	1,827,348
Lord At War (ARG)	108	46	69	574	85	77	69	343	1,826,609
Pancho Villa	124	62	74	927	106	130	128	563	1,816,808

Half a Year	64	35	45	362	59	47	46	210	1,816,062
Dayjur	57	32	34	354	62	42	47	203	1,799,823
Skywalker	98	49	58	574	85	81	77	331	1,791,007
John Alden	68	29	38	476	61	50	62	303	1,789,119
Horatius	95	45	59	569	81	75	57	356	1,777,998
Far North	132	56	78	863	96	100	94	573	1,771,203
Speak John	6	2	6	24	6	2	2	14	1,759,223
Ascot Knight	73	37	52	506	65	66	62	313	1,751,818
Far Out East	101	54	64	772	94	112	109	457	1,732,523
Groovy	90	48	57	629	92	85	80	372	1,729,809
Talc	107	54	60	761	96	88	104	473	1,723,061
Sadler's Wells	47	23	36	257	35	29	37	156	1,719,400
Desert Wine	108	58	65	656	99	68	86	403	1,718,578
Slewacide	91	34	55	541	50	49	57	385	1,710,093
El Gran Senor	74	37	44	476	61	68	52	295	1,703,153
Dr. Blum	79	44	50	543	75	78	75	315	1,686,267
Manila	82	40	55	578	65	70	53	390	1,671,892
Citidancer	44	28	33	290	54	31	31	174	1,636,928
Summer Squall	75	37	45	510	65	70	60	315	1,625,731
Rare Performer	97	55	64	710	96	93	118	403	1,625,133
Damascus	97	44	60	599	73	77	79	370	1,623,591
Rainbow Quest	30	11	25	134	21	13	19	81	1,608,527
*Grey Dawn II	110	60	69	830	90	95	99	546	1,607,803
Oh Say	101	57	62	709	100	85	91	433	1,606,669
Polish Navy	91	47	49	573	79	99	67	328	1,606,200
Silver Ghost	102	50	71	647	88	71	87	401	1,605,595
Northern Prospect	90	48	65	631	85	70	98	378	1,600,401
Skip Trial	85	53	52	640	94	81	73	392	1,595,209
Ahonoora (GB)	10	5	10	42	12	5	0	25	1,594,271
Moscow Ballet	120	53	80	696	79	92	106	419	1,585,473
World Appeal	86	52	49	646	94	90	77	385	1,574,318
Riverman	118	46	84	688	80	76	86	446	1,570,322
Criminal Type	60	32	37	441	63	50	44	284	1,564,145
Believe It	127	66	87	867	104	118	112	533	1,551,879
Olympio	37	19	24	218	29	26	28	135	1,549,502
Kennedy Road	87	45	50	561	80	73	67	341	1,535,633
Drone	76	39	47	528	63	55	61	349	1,532,823
Fast Play	86	48	50	564	90	63	80	331	1,531,437
Raise a Native	97	43	67	630	76	92	64	398	1,521,238
Tunerup	80	40	47	551	61	75	64	351	1,520,887
L'Enjoleur	110	60	66	880	112	100	105	563	1,496,202
Hawkster	49	23	37	374	44	48	45	237	1,484,573
Java Gold	81	42	42	587	74	62	83	368	1,472,422
Silent Screen	121	66	74	819	103	74	91	551	1,466,555
Private Terms	116	54	70	771	85	86	85	515	1,462,160
Marshua's Dancer	96	48	56	658	83	84	84	407	1,448,724
Strike Gold	93	41	58	505	68	62	59	316	1,444,821
Risen Star	78	39	46	502	69	62	68	303	1,440,003
Roberto	79	40	47	506	67	68	61	310	1,426,933
Staff Writer	100	58	59	728	106	96	117	409	1,425,945
Septieme Ciel	64	30	44	425	55	58	46	266	1,419,610
Nasty and Bold	93	43	61	560	73	75	76	336	1,411,110
Secreto	70	36	41	493	58	62	81	292	1,407,283
Slew City Slew	71	40	45	588	75	94	75	344	1,381,594
Jeblar	80	45	52	577	90	70	65	352	1,371,082
Carr de Naskra	85	36	54	535	57	68	81	329	1,359,385
Alydeed	41	23	35	246	39	40	24	143	1,355,424
Marfa	103	47	67	693	85	88	75	445	1,341,941
Prospectors Gamble	78	38	47	560	72	67	65	356	1,340,760
Alwuhush	87	41	55	600	72	67	77	384	1,331,843
At the Threshold	47	27	27	347	48	51	54	194	1,325,626
Tri Jet	108	46	69	623	67	74	85	397	1,323,997
Trempolino	48	22	37	326	40	44	49	193	1,322,579
Lomond	48	33	30	378	73	36	53	216	1,308,143
Foolish Pleasure	95	47	64	625	73	66	69	417	1,306,854
Rubiano	66	26	47	375	42	61	58	214	1,300,743
Jolie's Halo	47	27	31	289	48	39	37	165	1,298,781
Assert (IRE)	56	21	34	314	36	41	39	198	1,293,004
Al Nasr (FR)	50	28	35	397	51	53	53	240	1,289,663
Big Spruce	79	44	54	544	81	55	53	355	1,287,758
Cutlass	106	49	63	666	78	84	69	435	1,286,883
Shadeed	60	35	37	427	50	52	49	260	1,286,589
Norquestor	53	24	34	377	47	53	48	229	1,283,988
Polish Numbers	68	32	47	411	62	53	52	244	1,283,258
Icecapade	94	44	58	645	90	69	76	410	1,281,572
Proud Truth	78	45	53	629	78	78	77	396	1,269,331

Broodmare Sire	Perf	Winning Perf	Mares	Starts	1st	2nd	3rd	Unplaced	Purses
Bucksplasher	94	49	60	638	74	76	67	421	1,256,626
Crusader Sword	69	36	41	476	57	54	70	295	1,249,324
Regal Intention	51	24	30	327	44	51	39	193	1,243,821
Timeless Moment	107	51	71	733	73	100	89	471	1,229,990
Sauce Boat	114	53	71	784	106	81	120	477	1,229,138
Herat	66	35	35	488	84	54	61	289	1,213,799
Vanlandingham	64	31	42	457	56	62	53	286	1,210,683
Island Whirl	94	44	59	692	73	89	81	449	1,205,941
Fire Dancer	97	46	66	701	84	77	81	459	1,203,493
Blushing John	105	47	68	668	79	62	71	456	1,201,873
A.P. Indy	57	27	42	316	35	44	37	200	1,200,576
High Brite	92	46	56	616	79	76	62	399	1,198,836
Bold Forbes	88	51	54	711	82	85	82	462	1,196,920
Imperial Falcon	75	35	45	599	68	79	66	386	1,180,472
Sky Classic	61	31	43	410	45	62	41	262	1,176,562
Green Forest	97	43	60	581	67	65	67	382	1,174,246
Farma Way	77	39	50	519	56	55	62	346	1,173,375
Linkage	79	33	50	546	68	80	56	342	1,169,736
Bailjumper	55	26	40	350	42	42	40	226	1,166,444
Diablo	47	28	36	275	45	40	40	150	1,163,563
Tejano	63	32	39	456	64	61	61	270	1,163,190
Son of Briartic	79	41	52	493	61	80	71	281	1,161,061
Darn That Alarm	46	21	35	312	38	42	41	191	1,156,375
Proper Reality	75	39	51	514	60	68	63	323	1,155,287
Carnivalay	85	34	64	577	58	57	64	398	1,155,128
Caro (IRE)	63	26	41	389	41	45	50	253	1,153,132
Tsunami Slew	89	44	55	615	79	53	69	414	1,151,623
Hatchet Man	92	43	54	649	79	71	79	420	1,139,279
Purple Mountain	1	1	1	7	5	0	2	0	1,139,000
On to Glory	85	37	51	665	69	79	77	440	1,135,046
Bold Executive	39	17	27	242	26	30	24	162	1,128,687
Diesis (GB)	70	33	50	381	48	48	38	247	1,124,949
Tank's Prospect	75	34	48	510	48	50	64	348	1,123,410
Buckfinder	74	43	56	501	73	63	58	307	1,123,136
Native Prospector	65	32	42	420	61	57	48	254	1,120,074
Procida	67	40	35	511	68	65	76	302	1,111,811
Greinton (GB)	77	43	41	488	72	57	61	298	1,108,782
Cahill Road	46	30	34	273	54	28	45	146	1,106,621
No Louder	42	21	21	309	44	35	45	185	1,106,098
Knights Choice	119	68	61	750	109	99	118	424	1,103,536
What Luck	63	33	43	480	57	76	66	281	1,101,308
Gold Alert	66	36	40	496	61	57	75	303	1,101,191
Regal and Royal	55	30	33	375	53	56	50	216	1,099,800
Blue Ensign	92	45	63	658	85	80	79	414	1,097,993
Golden Act	87	37	52	568	55	74	63	376	1,090,200
In Reality	86	37	53	577	77	67	65	368	1,086,720
Great Gladiator	58	25	33	372	36	52	49	235	1,085,621
Strike the Gold	36	16	27	247	32	40	30	145	1,079,646
Coastal	84	38	51	600	69	57	74	400	1,071,618
Full Pocket	67	37	45	487	64	65	62	296	1,067,678
Plugged Nickle	65	34	37	472	64	45	48	315	1,064,457
Val de l'Orne (FR)	74	33	44	498	54	56	60	328	1,061,581
Yukon	67	31	34	441	44	56	50	291	1,055,170
Hooched	63	34	34	452	60	64	46	282	1,047,419
Time to Explode	69	37	41	484	55	59	54	316	1,046,464
Palace Music	72	34	36	449	61	49	55	284	1,042,167
Sir Ivor	75	36	48	565	67	58	71	369	1,027,095
Deputed Testamony	50	31	34	327	48	34	42	203	1,007,852
Naevus	78	37	51	463	63	58	66	276	1,007,132
Quack	71	31	47	426	53	51	56	266	1,000,908

Top Broodmare Sires in 2004 – Races Won

Broodmare Sire	Perf	Winning Perf	Mares	Starts	1st	2nd	3rd	Unplaced	Purses
Dixieland Band	325	182	187	2,197	326	299	305	1,267	$11,556,169
Relaunch	323	186	183	2,200	297	283	262	1,358	9,442,575
Deputy Minister	313	170	187	1,933	292	256	245	1,140	9,035,408
Valid Appeal	302	164	168	1,968	284	256	257	1,171	5,939,964
Crafty Prospector	281	154	165	1,908	280	248	262	1,118	5,054,773
Clever Trick	307	156	179	2,051	256	252	260	1,283	5,913,450
Conquistador Cielo	267	137	157	1,896	248	247	260	1,141	5,014,327
Bold Ruckus	229	130	135	1,696	246	258	216	976	6,883,093
Mr. Prospector	252	131	155	1,512	236	185	188	903	8,447,383
Vice Regent	237	120	135	1,623	227	205	213	978	5,229,968
Miswaki	244	128	150	1,490	224	204	171	891	4,940,625
Affirmed	225	125	132	1,539	217	196	194	932	5,613,315
Halo	258	134	146	1,623	214	206	189	1,014	4,409,242
Pleasant Colony	221	120	123	1,570	213	222	229	906	5,271,283
Kris S.	221	118	144	1,463	212	211	203	837	6,471,678
Woodman	207	122	123	1,422	212	182	174	854	5,095,320
Storm Bird	243	132	139	1,531	210	207	177	937	6,801,246
Wild Again	247	129	155	1,559	209	210	197	943	4,800,658
Cox's Ridge	229	119	144	1,564	206	215	195	948	4,696,972
Cure the Blues	235	121	137	1,575	205	184	208	978	4,624,546
Phone Trick	229	119	146	1,464	196	200	176	892	4,207,981
Majestic Light	234	114	140	1,587	196	155	196	1,040	3,914,370
Sovereign Dancer	213	116	114	1,552	195	191	222	944	4,995,786
Private Account	228	116	138	1,468	190	198	207	873	4,678,004
Lost Code	191	105	118	1,313	183	162	184	784	3,597,852
Broad Brush	176	100	112	1,177	182	153	184	658	3,791,890
Well Decorated	192	108	112	1,413	180	170	175	888	2,857,505
Seattle Slew	220	98	143	1,257	179	179	153	746	5,579,573
Storm Cat	221	105	139	1,274	175	173	165	761	5,309,637
Fit to Fight	188	92	109	1,294	173	164	156	801	3,391,358
Mt. Livermore	209	97	127	1,373	171	185	155	862	3,705,649
Stalwart	173	93	105	1,264	171	183	149	761	3,536,014
Green Dancer	198	90	113	1,288	169	137	186	796	4,631,856
Saratoga Six	181	93	111	1,157	169	136	152	700	4,192,898
Devil's Bag	210	99	123	1,323	169	192	175	787	3,648,570
Danzig	176	96	119	1,061	166	164	121	610	6,762,695
Star de Naskra	179	94	112	1,193	164	155	156	718	4,783,238
Spectacular Bid	180	100	123	1,160	164	145	133	718	4,267,865
Premiership	162	83	92	1,165	164	138	150	713	2,833,038
Meadowlake	203	104	123	1,208	163	164	151	730	3,424,222
Allen's Prospect	154	85	105	1,141	160	154	124	703	2,979,095
Pirate's Bounty	193	90	139	1,262	160	151	164	787	2,390,020
Smarten	175	87	112	1,249	155	155	154	785	4,316,654
Copelan	175	94	100	1,054	155	150	125	624	3,795,622
Our Native	164	82	97	1,136	152	148	139	697	3,195,432
Regal Classic	152	82	85	1,078	151	148	137	642	4,614,148
Air Forbes Won	145	88	85	1,037	150	138	127	622	2,524,849
Mr. Leader	188	86	109	1,263	148	149	171	795	4,117,753
Topsider	147	87	82	1,087	148	143	125	671	3,418,305
Secretariat	199	90	129	1,433	148	174	168	943	3,377,668
Forty Niner	162	90	95	948	147	123	120	558	4,129,967
Sunny's Halo	166	84	96	1,172	147	158	159	708	2,559,719
Carson City	136	76	91	815	146	138	101	430	3,679,408
Alleged	175	88	119	1,069	144	143	121	661	4,862,754

Broodmare Sire	Perf	Winning Perf	Mares	Starts	1st	2nd	3rd	Unplaced	Purses
Strawberry Road (AUS)	145	91	86	907	144	142	122	499	3,653,252
Afleet	153	78	92	989	144	119	118	608	3,290,637
Alydar	175	80	112	1,111	143	153	143	672	3,752,801
Apalachee	169	79	110	1,112	141	143	119	709	2,338,088
Capote	167	83	105	1,050	140	125	129	656	3,334,613
Fortunate Prospect	147	80	87	1,103	139	162	126	676	2,923,488
Cryptoclearance	172	81	107	1,168	138	135	125	770	2,715,593
Caveat	162	84	83	1,177	137	152	137	751	3,488,226
His Majesty	152	71	91	1,111	136	125	134	716	2,765,756
Great Above	152	70	99	980	135	147	116	582	2,703,321
Runaway Groom	183	76	117	1,219	132	133	173	781	2,826,309
Personal Flag	120	72	74	952	132	132	121	567	2,368,422
Stop the Music	183	83	111	1,232	132	156	130	814	2,205,563
Black Tie Affair (IRE)	155	83	93	1,159	131	170	157	701	2,726,369
Gate Dancer	124	68	76	819	131	112	112	464	2,654,235
Danzig Connection	128	68	79	918	131	102	115	570	1,989,552
Vigors	140	74	84	1,038	130	121	95	692	1,967,966
Fappiano	145	78	92	943	129	118	115	581	2,924,854
Two Punch	144	78	93	1,000	128	113	108	651	3,572,566
Key to the Mint	150	72	101	957	128	101	101	627	2,600,585
Chief's Crown	145	67	90	839	127	95	98	519	3,059,997
Red Ransom	130	77	87	833	127	104	101	501	2,919,416
Time for a Change	161	76	102	979	126	116	110	627	2,086,343
Irish Tower	154	72	96	1,070	125	150	122	673	2,621,982
Slew o' Gold	148	70	100	970	124	132	140	574	3,249,892
Flying Paster	158	82	92	1,016	124	125	141	626	2,566,040
Lord Avie	158	72	101	959	124	128	119	588	2,345,193
Silver Buck	137	68	92	1,022	124	113	116	669	2,268,801
Rahy	164	74	100	890	122	130	81	557	3,652,309
Temperence Hill	164	75	99	1,117	122	115	138	742	1,938,017
Silver Deputy	110	62	80	694	120	113	64	397	3,439,722
Mining	138	71	86	836	120	104	116	496	2,537,422
Gulch	111	62	71	753	120	105	106	422	2,238,772
Wolf Power (SAF)	142	66	90	947	119	142	106	580	2,142,233
Bates Motel	137	67	78	1,010	118	125	128	639	2,687,374
It's Freezing	144	73	76	1,022	118	142	133	629	1,998,442
Gone West	126	58	86	795	117	92	101	485	3,390,287
Buckaroo	137	61	82	940	117	124	114	585	1,901,246
Jade Hunter	115	64	79	798	116	105	83	494	3,018,913
Northern Jove	148	72	88	1,079	116	122	126	715	2,199,639
Theatrical (IRE)	150	67	96	885	115	119	104	547	2,591,247
Cozzene	134	59	85	905	114	94	105	592	2,182,400
Known Fact	137	66	84	824	113	128	106	477	2,571,695
Nijinsky II	129	60	86	820	112	113	114	481	3,475,440
Distinctive Pro	121	63	79	833	112	100	118	503	2,228,002
L'Enjoleur	110	60	66	880	112	100	105	563	1,496,202
Dynaformer	139	68	88	923	111	114	110	588	3,723,250
Ogygian	132	63	87	845	110	85	107	543	2,301,378
Hold Your Peace	106	59	58	745	109	92	85	459	2,750,125
Knights Choice	119	68	61	750	109	99	118	424	1,103,536
Lear Fan	128	64	77	859	108	98	110	543	3,529,599
Explodent	162	69	100	1,074	108	143	96	727	1,939,368
Wavering Monarch	123	64	77	805	107	89	101	508	1,980,966

Top Broodmare Sires in 2004 – Winning Performers

Broodmare Sire	Perf	Winning Perf	Mares	Starts	1st	2nd	3rd	Unplaced	Purses
Relaunch	323	186	183	2,200	297	283	262	1,358	$9,442,575
Dixieland Band	325	182	187	2,197	326	299	305	1,267	11,556,169
Deputy Minister	313	170	187	1,933	292	256	245	1,140	9,035,408
Valid Appeal	302	164	168	1,968	284	256	257	1,171	5,939,964
Clever Trick	307	156	179	2,051	256	252	260	1,283	5,913,450
Crafty Prospector	281	154	165	1,908	280	248	262	1,118	5,054,773
Conquistador Cielo	267	137	157	1,896	248	247	260	1,141	5,014,327
Halo	258	134	146	1,623	214	206	189	1,014	4,409,242
Storm Bird	243	132	139	1,531	210	207	177	937	6,801,246
Mr. Prospector	252	131	155	1,512	236	185	188	903	8,447,383
Bold Ruckus	229	130	135	1,696	246	258	216	976	6,883,093
Wild Again	247	129	155	1,559	209	210	197	943	4,800,658
Miswaki	244	128	150	1,490	224	204	171	891	4,940,625
Affirmed	225	125	132	1,539	217	196	194	932	5,613,315
Woodman	207	122	123	1,422	212	182	174	854	5,095,320
Cure the Blues	235	121	137	1,575	205	184	208	978	4,624,546
Pleasant Colony	221	120	123	1,570	213	222	229	906	5,271,283
Vice Regent	237	120	135	1,623	227	205	213	978	5,229,968
Cox's Ridge	229	119	144	1,564	206	215	195	948	4,696,972
Phone Trick	229	119	146	1,464	196	200	176	892	4,207,981
Kris S.	221	118	144	1,463	212	211	203	837	6,471,678
Sovereign Dancer	213	116	114	1,552	195	191	222	944	4,995,786
Private Account	228	116	138	1,468	190	198	207	873	4,678,004
Majestic Light	234	114	140	1,587	196	155	196	1,040	3,914,370
Well Decorated	192	108	112	1,413	180	170	175	888	2,857,505
Storm Cat	221	105	139	1,274	175	173	165	761	5,309,637
Lost Code	191	105	118	1,313	183	162	184	784	3,597,852
Meadowlake	203	104	123	1,208	163	164	151	730	3,424,222
Spectacular Bid	180	100	123	1,160	164	145	133	718	4,267,865
Broad Brush	176	100	112	1,177	182	153	184	658	3,791,890
Devil's Bag	210	99	123	1,323	169	192	175	787	3,648,570
Seattle Slew	220	98	143	1,257	179	179	153	746	5,579,573
Mt. Livermore	209	97	127	1,373	171	185	155	862	3,705,649
Danzig	176	96	119	1,061	166	164	121	610	6,762,695
Star de Naskra	179	94	112	1,193	164	155	156	718	4,783,238
Copelan	175	94	100	1,054	155	150	125	624	3,795,622
Saratoga Six	181	93	111	1,157	169	136	152	700	4,192,898
Stalwart	173	93	105	1,264	171	183	149	761	3,536,014
Fit to Fight	188	92	109	1,294	173	164	156	801	3,391,358
Strawberry Road (AUS)	145	91	86	907	144	142	122	499	3,653,252
Green Dancer	198	90	113	1,288	169	137	186	796	4,631,856
Forty Niner	162	90	95	948	147	123	120	558	4,129,967
Secretariat	199	90	129	1,433	148	174	168	943	3,377,668
Pirate's Bounty	193	90	139	1,262	160	151	164	787	2,390,020
Alleged	175	88	119	1,069	144	143	121	661	4,862,754
Air Forbes Won	145	88	85	1,037	150	138	127	622	2,524,849
Smarten	175	87	112	1,249	155	155	154	785	4,316,654
Topsider	147	87	82	1,087	148	143	125	671	3,418,305
Mr. Leader	188	86	109	1,263	148	149	171	795	4,117,753
Allen's Prospect	154	85	105	1,141	160	154	124	703	2,979,095
Caveat	162	84	83	1,177	137	152	137	751	3,488,226
Sunny's Halo	166	84	96	1,172	147	158	159	708	2,559,719
Capote	167	83	105	1,050	140	125	129	656	3,334,613
Premiership	162	83	92	1,165	164	138	150	713	2,833,038

Broodmare Sire	Perf	Winning Perf	Mares	Starts	1st	2nd	3rd	Unplaced	Purses
Black Tie Affair (IRE)	155	83	93	1,159	131	170	157	701	2,726,369
Stop the Music	183	83	111	1,232	132	156	130	814	2,205,563
Regal Classic	152	82	85	1,078	151	148	137	642	4,614,148
Our Native	164	82	97	1,136	152	148	139	697	3,195,432
Flying Paster	158	82	92	1,016	124	125	141	626	2,566,040
Cryptoclearance	172	81	107	1,168	138	135	125	770	2,715,593
Alydar	175	80	112	1,111	143	153	143	672	3,752,801
Fortunate Prospect	147	80	87	1,103	139	162	126	676	2,923,488
Apalachee	169	79	110	1,112	141	143	119	709	2,338,088
Two Punch	144	78	93	1,000	128	113	108	651	3,572,566
Afleet	153	78	92	989	144	119	118	608	3,290,637
Fappiano	145	78	92	943	129	118	115	581	2,924,854
Red Ransom	130	77	87	833	127	104	101	501	2,919,416
Carson City	136	76	91	815	146	138	101	430	3,679,408
Runaway Groom	183	76	117	1,219	132	133	173	781	2,826,309
Time for a Change	161	76	102	979	126	116	110	627	2,086,343
Temperence Hill	164	75	99	1,117	122	115	138	742	1,938,017
Rahy	164	74	100	890	122	130	81	557	3,652,309
Vigors	140	74	84	1,038	130	121	95	692	1,967,966
It's Freezing	144	73	76	1,022	118	142	133	629	1,998,442
Irish Tower	154	72	96	1,070	125	150	122	673	2,621,982
Key to the Mint	150	72	101	957	128	101	101	627	2,600,585
Personal Flag	120	72	74	952	132	132	121	567	2,368,422
Lord Avie	158	72	101	959	124	128	119	588	2,345,193
Northern Jove	148	72	88	1,079	116	122	126	715	2,199,639
His Majesty	152	71	91	1,111	136	125	134	716	2,765,756
Mining	138	71	86	836	120	104	116	496	2,537,422
Slew o' Gold	148	70	100	970	124	132	140	574	3,249,892
Great Above	152	70	99	980	135	147	116	582	2,703,321
Seeking the Gold	126	69	84	704	102	109	89	404	4,263,103
Explodent	162	69	100	1,074	108	143	96	727	1,939,368
Dynaformer	139	68	88	923	111	114	110	588	3,723,250
Gate Dancer	124	68	76	819	131	112	112	464	2,654,235
Silver Buck	137	68	92	1,022	124	113	116	669	2,268,801
Danzig Connection	128	68	79	918	131	102	115	570	1,989,552
Knights Choice	119	68	61	750	109	99	118	424	1,103,536
Chief's Crown	145	67	90	839	127	95	98	519	3,059,997
Bates Motel	137	67	78	1,010	118	125	128	639	2,687,374
Theatrical (IRE)	150	67	96	885	115	119	104	547	2,591,247
Known Fact	137	66	84	824	113	128	106	477	2,571,695
Wolf Power (SAF)	142	66	90	947	119	142	106	580	2,142,233
Believe It	127	66	87	867	104	118	112	533	1,551,879
Silent Screen	121	66	74	819	103	74	91	551	1,466,555
Lear Fan	128	64	77	859	108	98	110	543	3,529,599
Jade Hunter	115	64	79	798	116	105	83	494	3,018,913
Wavering Monarch	123	64	77	805	107	89	101	508	1,980,966
Ogygian	132	63	87	845	110	85	107	543	2,301,378
Distinctive Pro	121	63	79	833	112	100	118	503	2,228,002
Baldski	130	62	82	874	106	94	124	550	3,694,905
Silver Deputy	110	62	80	694	120	113	64	397	3,439,722
Northern Baby	130	62	81	884	103	121	113	547	2,262,377
Gulch	111	62	71	753	120	105	106	422	2,238,772
Pancho Villa	124	62	74	927	106	130	128	563	1,816,808

Top 10 Broodmare Sires and Their Progeny

Dixieland Band, B H (1980)

By Northern Dancer – Mississippi Mud, by Delta Judge

325 Performers, 182 winning performers, $11,556,169 total earnings

Mare	Progeny (Sire)	Age	Sts	1st	2d	3d	Money Won
A Touch of Brass	Wishbone Kid (Canyon Creek (IRE))	3	7	1	0	1	45,642
Abbeville	Apple Waites (Lord Carson)	2	2	0	1	0	2,300
Abbeville	Bert's Bar (Go for Gin)	4	4	0	0	0	802
Adorable Slew	Exceptional Ride (Chester House)	2	8	3	0	2	106,303
Aintjustwhistlin'	Whistlin a Song (Unbridled's Song)	3	4	0	0	0	5,124
All Sweets	Colita (Grindstone)	4	7	2	3	1	120,330
All Sweets	Dixie's Band (Twining)	6	19	3	3	4	27,950
All Sweets	Thunder Boot (Storm Boot)	5	7	0	1	1	13,650
Allison's Pride	Penobscot Bay (Is It True)	4	6	0	2	2	19,440
Allison's Pride	Sudden Flame (Stravinsky)	2	5	1	1	1	32,355
Allison's Pride	The Pride of Dixie (Editor's Note)	3	5	0	2	1	5,210
Amore E Baci	Amo Ebaci (Avenue of Flags)	4	11	2	1	2	37,536
Attitude Dancer	Stuka's Dancer (Stuka)	8	16	1	3	2	8,430
Attitude Dancer	Tatie Dancer (Unaccounted For)	4	5	1	0	1	10,290
Ava Singstheblues	Glitteration (Glitterman)	3	7	0	3	1	37,380
Backwater Blues	Backwater Hope (Chilito)	4	5	1	0	0	6,675
Bandral	Bandito (Lord Carson)	4	2	0	0	0	342
Bandral	North Potomac (Not For Love)	2	3	0	1	0	6,930
Bandral	Speckled Band (Cobra King)	3	11	1	0	1	7,733
Banjo Lady	Bomber Beau (Lucky Lionel)	4	14	1	2	0	8,389
Banjo Lady	Lady of the Press (Press Card)	7	12	1	1	1	22,070
Banjo Lady	Sultry Sound (Demaloot Demashoot)	5	4	2	1	0	21,800
Battle Ofthe Bands	Band of Reflection (Codex's Reflection)	6	8	0	1	0	1,415
Battle Ofthe Bands	Midnight Explosion (Pyramid Peak)	3	7	1	3	0	26,655
Beal Street Blues	Koloszar (Pulpit)	3	1	0	0	0	320
Belle of the Band	Band Director (Gold Regent)	2	5	0	3	1	11,220
Besame Mucho	Kiss'n Dyna (Dynaformer)	3	10	0	0	4	19,680
Big Band Singer	Secret Rush (Marquetry)	5	4	1	2	0	33,299
Big Band Singer	Tiverton (Unaccounted For)	2	1	0	0	0	225
Bourbon Street Gal	King of Mardi Gras (Smoke Glacken)	3	16	3	0	2	52,887
Bourbon Street Gal	Sophiecallingsara (Parade Ground)	2	3	0	0	0	3,420
Bourbon Street Gal	Southern Smoke (Smoke Glacken)	4	3	0	0	2	3,450
Box Office Gold	Air Jones (Skywalker)	3	2	0	1	0	7,400
Box Office Gold	Basic Concern (Concern)	7	6	0	2	0	5,643
Box Office Gold	Golden Concern (Concern)	6	3	0	0	0	253
Box Office Gold	New York Gold (Gold Token)	4	11	4	2	3	56,219
Bundleofstars	Irguns Star (Irgun)	2	4	1	0	2	8,400
Bundleofstars	Star's Kandi Kane (Evansville Slew)	3	10	1	1	2	21,340
C. C. Overdrive	Good Power (Falstaff)	3	2	0	0	0	0
C. C. Overdrive	Humoresque (Falstaff)	5	10	0	2	0	2,250
C. C. Overdrive	Summer Special (Siberian Summer)	4	13	3	3	1	27,787
Cacophony	Cat Striker (Tactical Cat)	3	11	1	3	1	51,751
Cajun Colors	Golden Ellen (Gold Fever)	4	9	0	0	1	6,560
Cheerio Charmer	El Galante (Fly So Free)	3	3	0	1	0	7,800
Chordette	Operatic (Gilded Time)	4	7	2	0	1	40,245
Cincinnati Pops	Jacobs Smile (Ops Smile)	4	11	3	1	3	54,930
Cincinnati Pops	Jolie Louise (Mister Jolie)	3	7	1	1	2	24,700
Cincinnati Pops	Lucky Pops (Truluck)	2	5	0	2	0	2,910
Cincinnati Pops	Twist and Pop (Oliver's Twist)	5	10	6	3	0	167,440
Coastal Wave	Cross the Infield (Mr. Greeley)	5	10	0	0	0	744
Coastal Wave	The Nth Degree (Distorted Humor)	3	11	2	3	3	56,241
Coastal Wave	Typical Situation (Distorted Humor)	4	2	0	0	0	225
College Band	Current Miss (Comet Shine)	3	6	0	1	2	4,720
Courtin' Dixie	Terras Terry (Monetary Gift)	4	7	1	0	2	4,806
Cue Girl	Mr. Novak (Mr. Roberts)	5	12	1	3	1	11,306
Dancin Dixie Miss	Dream Deliverer (Sea Hero)	4	11	1	1	2	17,797
Dancin Dixie Miss	Espresso Oro (Java Gold)	9	9	1	0	1	9,943
Dancin Dixie Miss	Fox Drive (Sea Hero)	6	5	0	0	0	2,070
Dancin Dixie Miss	Norwellian (Precise End)	2	2	1	0	0	9,730
Dazzling Dixie	Dazzling Dr. Cevin (Cutlass Fax)	2	6	2	2	2	38,010
Dazzling Dixie	Dazzling Rubies (Rubiano)	5	10	1	3	1	51,240
Desaucered	Sold (Kris S.)	4	10	1	1	2	21,680
Diamond Star	Starship Diligence (Diligence)	4	11	2	0	2	16,540
Divine Dixie	Bandini (Fusaichi Pegasus)	2	1	0	0	0	180
Divine Dixie	Divine Lady (Kris S.)	3	2	0	1	1	13,800
Divine Dixie	Primo Primo (Saint Ballado)	4	7	1	1	0	14,175
Dixie Accent	Indixie (A.P. Indy)	6	8	5	0	1	82,570
Dixie Accent	Jazz Legend (Silver Deputy)	3	8	3	2	0	88,990
Dixie Band	Cielo Girl (Conquistador Cielo)	5	4	1	0	1	35,527
Dixie Belle	Sweetjudyblueeyes (Proud and True)	4	8	2	0	0	11,730
Dixie Belle	Wild Boy (Wild Wonder)	2	1	0	0	0	150
Dixie Blue	Blue Grey (With Approval)	8	6	0	0	1	4,210
Dixie Blue	Mister Blues (Mr. Greeley)	7	1	0	0	0	0
Dixie Chimes	Freefourinternet (Tabasco Cat)	6	9	2	1	0	527,693
Dixie Daf	Dixie Gemstone (Grindstone)	2	2	1	0	1	17,750
Dixie Dash	Dash Home (Two Punch)	4	5	0	0	0	1,050
Dixie Dash	Gold Sensation (Prized)	7	3	0	0	0	130
Dixie Daylight	Boca Beacon (Kingmambo)	3	1	0	0	0	600
Dixie de Kay	Lethimrun (Roy)	6	6	1	2	2	22,400
Dixie Derby	Dixie Law (Martial Law)	8	5	0	0	2	16,080
Dixie Derby	Shades of Dixie (Alyshadeed)	4	2	0	0	0	3,340
Dixie Distinction	Numerous Lady (Numerous)	4	11	1	4	3	29,947
Dixie Distinction	Proud Diligence (Diligence)	2	3	0	0	0	3,240
Dixie Distinction	Wishing Dixie (Lycius)	3	1	0	0	0	130
Dixie Echo	Greg's Syrah (Cape Town)	4	10	3	1	1	63,235
Dixie Favor	Kiralik (GB) (Efisio)	4	5	0	0	0	1,960
Dixie Favor	River Belle (GB) (Lahib)	3	4	2	0	2	202,613
Dixie Flash	Discipline (Stuka)	7	7	0	0	0	780
Dixie Flash	Dixie Stripes (Candy Stripes)	5	13	2	3	1	16,914
Dixie Glory	Dixiecrat (Lil Tyler)	3	4	1	0	1	10,225
Dixie Glory	Lil Bit Glamorous (Lil Tyler)	7	2	0	0	0	100
Dixie Guide	Grin (Geri)	5	7	2	3	0	38,050
Dixie Heiress	Clever Greek (Smart Strike)	3	2	2	0	0	22,800
Dixie Highway	A Demi (Demidoff)	3	9	0	3	2	6,451
Dixie Highway	Out At Home (Take Me Out)	4	7	3	1	0	54,309
Dixie Highway	Scarlett'sprospect (Native Prospector)	6	9	0	1	0	1,495
Dixie Holiday	Holiday Runner (Meadowlake)	4	2	0	1	0	10,000
Dixie Holiday	Jazzy Letters (Alphabet Soup)	3	13	1	2	2	7,885
Dixie Honey	Old Dixie Home (Home At Last)	4	10	1	0	1	18,555
Dixie Honey	Victory Voodoo (Victory Gallop)	2	1	0	0	0	0
Dixie Jewel	City Jewel (Carson City)	2	1	0	0	0	624
Dixie Lane	Neenamusha (Sandpit (BRZ))	4	18	2	3	5	18,219
Dixie Luck	Crafty Luck (Crafty Prospector)	5	1	0	0	0	1,475
Dixie Maintenance	Marathon Man (Capote)	4	5	0	0	0	760
Dixie Maintenance	Miss Fairfield (Hennessy)	3	6	2	1	2	23,800
Dixie Melody	Joe Six Pack (Silver Deputy)	3	4	0	0	1	19,890
Dixie Pearl	Cupar (Broad Brush)	3	2	0	0	1	3,840
Dixie Pirate	Captain Craig (Texas City)	10	10	3	0	3	9,819
Dixie Pirate	Hickory Doc (Two Punch)	4	11	0	1	1	5,185
Dixie Pirate	Ms. Dixie Time (Gilded Time)	3	3	0	0	1	1,487
Dixie Pirate	Prospecting Dixie (Allen's Prospect)	5	10	0	1	4	12,941
Dixie Pirate	Sugar Ray Silver (Two Punch)	6	13	2	4	1	23,170
Dixie Rouge	Albert and Baby (Defrere)	4	11	1	0	1	9,146
Dixie Rouge	Lilah (Defrere)	7	6	3	0	1	75,740
Dixie Slippers	Playa Maya (Arch)	4	3	2	0	1	45,941
Dixie Step	Dixie's Irish (Proud Irish)	4	10	2	1	1	8,290
Dixie Sunrise	A Bag of Gold (Abaginone)	3	8	1	0	3	22,225
Dixie Sunrise	Dixie Two Thousand (Private Interview)	6	10	0	3	1	55,035
Dixie Time	Dixie Melinda (Half Term)	2	2	0	0	0	0
Dixieland Bandit	Hamlet (Roaring Camp)	4	7	2	2	0	20,020
Dixieland Belle	Bad Dog (Allen's Prospect)	8	10	1	1	3	7,390
Dixieland Blues	Comeon Dixie (Mr. Greeley)	4	2	0	0	0	640
Dixieland Blues	Limehouse (Grand Slam)	3	5	2	0	1	367,000
Dixieland Dream	Fantasy Valley (Gulch)	6	5	1	1	1	6,239
Dixieland Fantasy	Admiration (Marquetry)	5	16	1	1	2	16,505
Dixieland Fantasy	Currituck Springs (Wekiva Springs)	4	7	0	4	0	14,423
Dixieland Fantasy	Dixie High (Anet)	3	1	0	0	1	30,000
Dixieland Gal	Tales of Glory (Honour and Glory)	3	10	3	3	3	145,150
Dixieland Gold	Dixieland Gulch (Gulch)	4	1	0	0	0	1,800
Dixieland Gold	Jazz Society (Carson City)	2	2	0	0	0	568
Dixieland Gold	Yellowstone Lady (Crafty Prospector)	5	13	2	2	1	43,249
Dixieland Queen	Cheverly Gold (Formal Gold)	4	5	1	2	0	23,480
Dixieland Queen	She's a Rebel Too (Two Punch)	3	7	2	1	1	60,650
Dixieland Queen	Two Punch Sonny (Two Punch)	8	1	0	0	0	0
Dixieland Special	Jazz Music (Jules)	4	12	2	1	1	10,492
Dixity Do Dah	Dixie Meister (Holzmeister)	2	8	1	0	2	50,150
Dixity Do Dah	Foxhole (Digging In)	6	11	0	0	0	1,296
Dixity Do Dah	Woodmeister (Holzmeister)	3	17	3	2	4	57,022
Donnan's Holly	Conservation (Tamayaz)	4	11	2	1	3	82,046
Donnan's Holly	Two Hollys (Two Punch)	3	14	3	1	0	76,694
Donttellthefluff	Eldixie (Eltish)	3	8	1	0	1	6,081
Donttellthefluff	Eye Pea Oh (With Approval)	8	8	3	1	2	74,280
Donttellthefluff	Sultry Fluff (Sultry Song)	5	8	1	0	1	24,026
Dootsie	Jacksonian (Pleasant Tap)	2	1	0	0	0	205
Down South	Swell (Rage)	2	6	1	0	0	28,648
Dutchess of Dixie	Good Boy Duke (Mr. Integrity)	10	4	0	0	0	0
Dutchess of Dixie	Meet Me in Dixie (General Meeting)	7	3	0	1	0	2,800
Etats Unis	Pollard's Vision (Carson City)	3	11	4	4	1	1,022,020
Fairytale Ending	Cash Marquet (Marquetry)	4	8	3	0	1	10,185
Fairytale Ending	Fairy Tale Dream (Lord Carson)	2	7	1	0	2	37,800
Fluffkins	Sword of Lords (Crafty Prospector)	3	9	1	0	2	12,155
For Dixie	Mittens Mambo (Kingmambo)	4	2	1	0	0	7,940
For Dixie	Vicarage (Vicar)	2	4	1	0	0	34,470
Force Majeure	Distinctively R C (Distinctive Pro)	3	8	0	1	0	2,318
Force Majeure	R Cs Slew (Slewacide)	6	2	0	0	0	372
Golden Tiy	Ammalu (Boston Harbor)	4	2	0	1	0	7,380
Golden Wave Band	Leslie's Last (Crafty Friend)	3	6	1	2	0	17,574
Goldheartedmonica	Goldhearted Kris (Kris S.)	4	1	0	0	1	1,567
Gunner Lil	Perfect Lil (Perfect)	5	2	0	0	0	0
Gunner Lil	Ragtime Gunner (Cryptoclearance)	6	2	0	0	1	687
Gunner Lil	Zarb's Gunner (Zarbyev)	2	7	1	2	0	29,830
Hatchet Band	Baltic Hydra (Torrential)	3	5	0	0	2	4,590
Hatchet Band	Baltic Maria (Maria's Mon)	4	11	0	3	2	19,295
Hatchet Band	Baltic Marque (Marquetry)	7	8	1	0	2	2,986
Hear the Sea	Absolute Nectar (Carson City)	3	8	1	1	2	47,750
Hear the Sea	Bastione (Smart Strike)	4	4	1	1	1	11,340
Hekeepsmesinging	Awesome Sign (Awesome Again)	2	1	0	0	0	400
Holy Land Band	Betty's Wish (Gold Case)	4	1	0	0	1	6,000
Holy Land Band	Geronimo Joe (Indian Charlie)	3	3	1	1	0	8,445
Holy Land Band	R. Dixie Chick (Pioneering)	6	1	0	0	0	83
Hug'm	Smokehouse (Smoke Glacken)	5	6	0	0	0	748
Hum Dixie	Sans Win (Double Honor)	3	8	3	1	0	20,860
Hum Dixie	Southern Honoree (Double Honor)	4	9	0	0	1	3,617
Igotrhythm	Gone Musical (Gone West)	5	1	0	0	0	450
Igotrhythm	Gone to War (Gone West)	4	6	0	1	2	17,996

Mare	Progeny (Sire)	Age	Sts	1st	2d	3d	Money Won
Igotrhythm	Native Rhythm (Woodman)	6	6	0	0	1	2,602
Illusive Note	Captain Greybeard (Runaway Groom)	4	2	0	0	1	1,155
J. D. Flowers	Vase (Rahy)	4	1	0	1	0	6,600
Jazz Rags	Blades of Silver (Old Trieste)	2	1	0	0	0	205
Jazz Rags	Ragtime Request (Coronado's Quest)	3	5	1	0	0	21,770
Jazzability	Glitter Baby (Glitterman)	6	11	0	2	0	6,118
Jazzalong	Hamaaly (Unbridled's Song)	4	19	2	4	2	25,200
Jazzitup	Spin Jazz Baby (Spinning World)	2	3	2	0	0	16,800
Jazzy	Count Basic (Slewacide)	6	10	1	1	1	5,093
Jazzy	Ms Bessie (Pleasant Tap)	3	10	2	1	3	38,785
Kicker Dancin'	Late to the Dance (With Approval)	5	10	1	0	3	10,597
Kicker Dancin'	Musashi (Supremo)	7	16	3	1	3	20,870
Kutira	Triptips (Regal Classic)	4	7	1	1	2	7,683
L'Abidjanaise	Dynabid (Dynaformer)	3	4	0	0	0	2,628
L'Abidjanaise	Ponta Das Canas (Woodman)	2	2	0	0	0	3,040
Lady of Tralee	Columbia Gorge (Red Ransom)	9	13	1	0	3	4,520
Lady of Tralee	Velvets and Silks (Southern Halo)	4	10	2	2	3	31,456
Landholder	Our Joy (El Prado (IRE))	3	6	0	2	1	10,952
Lizzie Toon	Hot Dancer (Will's Way)	4	1	0	0	0	180
Lizzie Toon	Willy o'the Valley (Will's Way)	3	9	3	3	1	112,823
Lookaway Dixie	Precise Motion (Precise End)	2	2	1	0	0	24,805
Lookaway Dixie	Swinging Ghost (Silver Ghost)	3	7	3	0	2	95,240
Love That Jazz	Society Selection (Coronado's Quest)	3	9	3	3	1	929,700
Magic in the Music	Tune Lender (Banker's Gold)	3	8	3	2	2	28,826
Magic Music	Cool Runnings (Pleasant Tap)	3	12	1	2	1	5,340
Mason Dixie	Wood Dixie Dance (Woodman)	3	8	2	0	3	27,860
Masquerade Lady	Freedom Roar (Roar)	5	12	3	1	3	24,180
Masquerade Lady	Girl Fever (Gold Fever)	4	9	2	0	1	36,940
Masquerade Lady	Up Jump the Devil (Devil His Due)	6	14	3	2	3	18,534
Matika	Mattie's Luck (Lucky So n' So)	3	5	2	1	0	11,500
Metalmark	Honorable Mark (Double Honor)	3	10	0	1	2	5,583
Metalmark	Pepesqueez (Judge T C)	5	17	4	0	2	29,325
Miss Blush	Nova Scotia Norma (Salt Lake)	2	2	1	0	1	3,921
Miss Blush	Strodee (Strodes Creek)	5	13	3	2	0	17,345
Mission Park	Braytonville (Saint Ballado)	3	4	1	0	2	21,980
Mission Park	Broad Acres (Quiet American)	2	6	0	1	1	10,390
Mrs. K.	Biddy Biddy (Bet Twice)	10	8	0	1	1	2,410
Mrs. K.	Last Waltz (Ghazi)	3	5	1	0	1	38,275
Mrs. K.	Lethal Agenda (Twilight Agenda)	6	3	0	0	0	0
Musical Delight	Killing M Softly (Lac Ouimet)	3	9	1	3	0	35,620
Musical Delight	Smugglers Basin (Mr. Greeley)	5	10	1	4	3	45,200
Musical Flight	Sapphireontherocks (Go for Gin)	5	10	0	3	0	10,718
Mustbeabeauty	Mustbeamarlin (Marlin)	3	8	1	0	0	10,954
Needlepoint	Dyna Girl (Dynaformer)	3	15	3	1	0	47,260
Needlepoint	Justa Old Love (Pleasant Tap)	2	3	0	0	0	0
Needlepoint	Sir Rubi (Rubiano)	4	6	1	2	0	5,274
Never Binn Better	Relative Strength (Twining)	6	11	1	0	0	14,562
Newhall Road	Bayfront (Prospect Bay)	3	5	2	0	1	41,920
No Fairytales	Shybynature (Blushing John)	8	3	0	0	1	2,200
No Need to Party	Carouse (Cure the Blues)	5	15	3	3	5	36,802
Nocciolina	Brand Name (Unbridled's Song)	3	4	1	0	2	45,700
Nocciolina	Railway (Catrail)	6	18	0	1	2	4,176
Northern Dixie	Major Alliance (Crafty Friend)	3	9	1	4	1	20,589
Northern Dixie	Mister Misty (Mister Baileys (GB))	4	9	1	1	0	7,709
O. K. Mom	Perfect Ride (Cherokee Run)	5	5	3	0	0	78,651
O. K. Mom	Yes Beth (Deputy Commander)	2	2	0	0	1	4,265
One More Flag	Robyn's Pal (Unaccounted For)	3	10	3	0	0	20,161
One More Flag	Wistano (Waquoit)	2	3	0	1	0	4,427
Pas de Problem	Sweet Problem (Is It True)	3	10	4	2	1	249,205
Play the Scale	Natrona (Lord Avie)	5	3	0	0	0	1,302
Play the Scale	Whistle Dixie (With Approval)	3	9	3	3	0	30,125
Pleasant Dixie	Southern Image (Halo's Image)	4	4	3	1	0	1,612,150
Pray Lady	Elusive Project (Elusive Quality)	3	7	0	3	0	25,100
Pray Lady	Sierra Kitty (Mountain Cat)	4	1	0	0	0	88
Preakness Lady	Will Belong (Belong to Me)	5	13	0	4	1	6,113
Quite a Rapper	My Friend Bruce (Dance Brightly)	3	2	0	0	0	670
Radioactivity	Champali (Glitterman)	4	8	4	1	1	634,398
Radioactivity	Drexel Monorail (Glitterman)	5	5	1	1	0	48,570
Radioactivity	Shorewalk Drive (Formal Gold)	3	8	1	0	0	22,867
Ragtimely	Siward (Distant View)	6	6	2	1	0	10,475
Ragtimely	Timely Minister (Mane Minister)	7	11	0	0	4	9,146
Ragtimely	Tribe (Cherokee Run)	4	7	0	1	2	8,160
Raise the Band	Matchless Hunter (Jade Hunter)	8	7	1	0	1	5,501
Rampart Street	Charmeleon (Smokester)	6	16	1	2	4	6,475
Rampart Street	Tatooma (Lycius)	2	1	1	0	0	24,600
Randy Nance	Graceful Nancy (Maria's Mon)	2	3	1	0	0	38,250
Rebel Account	Torquay (Deputy Commander)	2	1	0	0	0	3,528
Regal Band	Mon Belle (Maria's Mon)	2	1	1	0	0	15,625
Regal Band	Montaraz (Numerous)	4	4	0	0	1	4,760
Regal Band	My Man Gus (Supremo)	5	8	2	1	1	17,660
Regal Band	Resurgence (Black Tie Affair (IRE))	7	8	2	3	0	53,734
Regal Band	Siphonophora (Siphon (BRZ))	3	1	0	0	0	0
Rekindled	Dyna King (Dynaformer)	7	15	3	2	2	5,006
Rhapsodic	Bossa Rio (Red Ransom)	3	2	0	1	1	7,275
Rockaroller	Aspen Tree (Holy Bull)	2	3	1	2	0	47,061
Rockaroller	Naughty Nae (Unbridled's Song)	3	1	0	0	1	4,300
Rockaroller	Phone Tech (Favorite Trick)	4	1	0	0	0	0
Satchmo's Lady	Red Seattle (Septieme Ciel)	8	13	6	1	3	29,940
Satchmo's Lady	Sssh It'sa Secret (Sea of Secrets)	3	12	1	1	1	6,996
Satin Promise	Baldwin County (Prized)	6	8	2	3	0	62,820
Satin Promise	Promise of War (Lord At War (ARG))	8	11	4	4	3	98,080
Satin Promise	Turtle Beach (Out of Place)	4	3	0	1	0	3,350
Sazarac Jazz	Orison (Pulpit)	2	2	0	0	1	4,330
Scorched	Burning Marque (Marquetry)	8	13	2	1	2	30,177
Sea Jamie Win	Dowry (Belong to Me)	4	4	1	1	0	27,330
Sea Jamie Win	Summerfield (Affirmed)	5	1	0	0	0	0
Sea Jamie Win	The Herc (Lord Carson)	3	7	0	1	0	11,267
Sehna	C C's Last Stand (Conquistador Cielo)	3	12	1	1	0	9,702
She's So Dixie	Giant's Song (Unbridled's Song)	3	5	0	0	1	1,045
Sheshallhavemusic	No Music (Miner's Mark)	5	6	0	1	0	6,738
Shoe Band	Joseph George (Rubiano)	7	9	1	3	2	3,190
Showemyourclass	Act Classy (Noactor)	3	10	1	1	0	7,667
Showemyourclass	Actalot (Noactor)	7	7	1	0	0	3,798
Showemyourclass	Actceed (Noactor)	5	3	0	1	0	828
Showemyourclass	Josie'slil'actress (Noactor)	4	23	0	0	0	2,181
Simple Dreams	Table of Contents (Event of the Year)	3	4	1	0	3	19,560
Sing and Swing	Got That Swing (With Approval)	9	2	0	0	0	115
Skat Girl	Andiamo (Rubiano)	3	7	3	1	0	65,460
Smile n Molly	Dont Tell the Kids (Carson City)	7	9	1	1	1	14,520
Smile n Molly	Smile N Carson (Carson City)	3	8	1	2	1	18,677
So Jazzy	Brite Future (High Brite)	7	11	1	3	1	16,782
So Jazzy	So Alive (Siberian Summer)	4	5	1	1	1	19,165
Song of Dixie	Singing Siren (Maria's Mon)	2	5	0	1	0	4,650
Sorority Jazz	Slewrenity (Dr. Caton)	4	4	2	1	1	20,630
Southern Day	Seney (Repriced)	2	1	0	0	0	100
Southern Day	Southernengagement (Broad Brush)	3	8	2	0	1	53,305
Southern Sound	Uncle Walter (Tabasco Cat)	3	3	0	0	0	860
Southern Swing	Erinsouthernman (Eltish)	4	6	2	1	0	37,956
Southern Swing	Mr. Pee Vee (Eltish)	3	4	3	0	0	81,260
Starlight Cove	Frosty Starlight (Sharp Frosty)	7	15	1	0	3	11,160
Street Corner Jive	Bigger Wagner (Stolen Gold)	3	9	1	3	1	15,038
Street Corner Jive	Vilma Bankey (Lear Fan)	4	10	1	0	3	7,356
Sunset Song	J J Thedotcom Man (Private Terms)	6	18	1	5	3	5,025
Sunshine Again	Spirit Woman (Crafty Friend)	2	3	0	0	0	450
Sunshine Again	Sunshine Lake (Meadowlake)	3	12	1	2	0	24,562
Supreme Dixieland	Sayville (Slew City Slew)	4	7	1	0	0	11,881
Sweet Bayou Blues	Sing Me No Blues (Lion Cavern)	2	1	0	0	0	0
Swingin' Sister	Bunt (Cherokee Run)	3	2	0	0	0	388
Swingin' Sister	Flaming Fire (Smoke Glacken)	4	20	1	1	7	20,333
Swingin' Sister	Take the A Train (Smoke Glacken)	5	2	0	0	0	1,170
Tajannub	Almungid (Thunder Gulch)	5	13	1	4	2	15,851
Targhee	Dixie Deputy (French Deputy)	3	2	0	0	2	1,800
That's a Plenty	El Progreso (Latin American)	6	10	0	1	0	16,770
That's a Plenty	Jenny Bean Girl (Sefapiano)	2	3	0	0	0	3,150
That's a Plenty	Thats Private (Private Interview)	3	5	0	0	0	1,200
Timeless Tempo	Dekay (Exploit)	3	5	1	0	0	10,230
Tiny's Teardrop	Don't Cry for Me (Siyah Kalem)	5	1	0	0	1	3,360
Tiny's Teardrop	Irish Dodger (Helmsman)	2	1	0	1	0	7,365
Tiny's Teardrop	Nut Lovin (Avenue of Flags)	3	8	1	1	0	19,550
Tortuga Band	Lightsnatcher (Wild Zone)	2	8	0	4	2	8,420
Trust in Dixie	Boston Gold (Boston Harbor)	4	2	0	1	0	9,000
Trust in Dixie	Dixie Tea Party (Boston Harbor)	2	2	0	0	0	2,160
Trust in Dixie	Midnight Miner (Miner's Mark)	8	6	2	1	0	16,699
Trust in Dixie	Red Band Run (Red Ransom)	3	2	0	0	0	1,450
Twigazuri	Futural (Future Storm)	8	8	0	2	2	16,128
Twigazuri	Justastorm (Storm Creek)	5	1	0	0	0	340
Twigazuri	Talara (Hennessy)	4	12	4	1	4	25,990
Unending Love	Amoramente (Repriced)	2	2	0	1	0	7,450
Unending Love	Mon T. Hauls (Mahogany Hall)	5	12	1	2	6	4,636
Wrong Delivery	Heart of Jules (Jules)	3	11	3	1	0	58,920

Relaunch, Gr H (1976)
By In Reality – Foggy Note, by The Axe II

323 Performers, 186 winning performers, $9,442,575 total earnings

Mare	Progeny (Sire)	Age	Sts	1st	2d	3d	Money Won
A Little Reality	A Real Runaround (Run Softly)	4	10	1	0	0	1,407
A Little Reality	Who You Gonna Call (Ghost Ranch)	3	8	0	0	0	4,929
Admat	Apollo Won (Apollo)	4	3	0	0	1	3,080
Advertising	Advantage (CHI) (Repriced)	7	3	0	0	0	143
Aerosilver	Lake Silver (Meadowlake)	6	11	1	0	3	11,153
All Systems Go	Caller Junction (Caller I. D.)	7	1	0	0	0	0
All Systems Go	Florida Recount (Grindstone)	5	2	0	0	0	1,710
All Systems Go	Go for Diamonds (Grindstone)	3	3	1	1	0	7,448
All Systems Go	Online (Unaccounted For)	2	1	0	0	0	276
Appian Road	Liberty Creek (Bertrando)	5	4	0	0	1	1,877
Arena Blanca	Boss Nass (Video Ranger)	3	3	1	1	0	45,080
Ascloseasitgets	Annabelle's Song (Unbridled's Song)	3	7	1	1	1	29,614
Ascloseasitgets	Thunderchaser (Thunder Gulch)	2	5	1	2	0	24,475
Attractive Missile	Rocket Royale (Roy)	4	9	2	2	0	27,560
Attractive Missile	Smokey Diplomacy (Dynaformer)	3	7	2	0	2	45,980
Aucilla	Game Box (A.P. Indy)	4	11	1	0	3	22,770
Aucilla	Passing Shot (A.P. Indy)	5	6	1	1	2	185,460
Authorized Staff	Dayton's Bluff (Lord At War (ARG))	7	7	0	3	1	4,603
Authorized Staff	Morgan's Charm (Silver Charm)	3	2	1	0	0	4,237
Baby Bar	Paster's Baby (Paster's Caper)	5	8	0	0	0	2,489
Baby Zip	Aristocrat (Awesome Again)	2	1	0	0	0	2,250
Baby Zip	Ghostzapper (Awesome Again)	4	4	4	0	0	2,590,000
Barbaloot	Daulide (ARG) (Numerous)	4	1	0	0	0	400
Beauty Supply	Beautybeyondbasics (Numerous)	3	15	1	0	2	18,875

Beauty Supply	Farma Way Jr. (Farma Way)	4	6	0	1	0	1,166
Before the Wind	Good as Her Word (Alphabet Soup)	3	11	3	1	4	92,837
Before the Wind	Miles for Mickey (Judge T C)	5	9	1	0	1	4,012
Beguiled	Cunningly (Lit de Justice)	3	4	1	0	0	24,720
Besmirched	Texas Swing (Rodeo)	3	8	1	0	1	14,150
Big Idea	Goodbye Big Cat (Goodbye Doeny)	4	7	1	3	0	21,843
Big Idea	Miss Moolah (Spend a Buck)	3	3	1	1	0	13,946
Bill Back	House Party (French Deputy)	4	3	1	1	0	80,000
Breech	Run Sarah Run (Smart Strike)	4	11	2	1	2	73,230
Breech	Unpeteable (Peteski)	7	6	3	0	1	31,630
Bundle of Energy	Reenergize (Repriced)	4	10	1	2	1	9,637
Cabernet Queen	Arbitration (Event of the Year)	3	2	0	0	0	150
Cape Fire	Fire Strike (Smart Strike)	3	11	1	3	0	20,600
Cape Fire	Foxy Allure (Foxhound)	4	18	1	2	3	20,129
Cape Fire	Miss Alexis (Dehere)	5	1	0	0	0	0
Cardo	Eurhrates (Helmsman)	5	5	0	2	1	3,301
Cardo	Sand Save (Line In The Sand)	3	12	0	0	0	519
Careful Approach	My Nina Rose (Lucky Roberto)	3	14	1	2	1	52,781
Careful Approach	Shaky Town (Peaks and Valleys)	4	5	1	1	1	26,707
Cash Cow	Mikes Westwaypride (Way West (FR))	4	1	0	0	0	140
Cash Cow	Sendek (Way West (FR))	3	11	3	0	1	20,330
Casual Aside	Youthful Comment (Lil's Lad)	3	1	0	1	0	4,340
Celestial Bliss	River to Heaven (Irish River (FR))	7	10	1	0	1	4,910
Cents Off	Pfenning (Cox's Ridge)	6	1	0	0	0	0
Cents Off	Tententwotwenty (Phone Trick)	4	13	2	0	3	68,810
Ciro's Seductress	Casper Peterson (Victory Speech)	4	10	3	3	0	112,430
Ciro's Seductress	Glaciers End (Clever Trick)	5	2	1	0	0	26,520
Ciro's Seductress	Sea Squirrel (Private Terms)	6	16	4	1	0	28,825
Classy Women	Fleeting Glance (Charismatic)	3	13	2	3	1	18,657
Classy Women	Polish Pianist (Forty Niner)	8	15	3	1	2	27,856
Cocktail	Sean's Pride (Pentelicus)	4	6	1	0	1	13,250
Cocktail	True Tails (Yes It's True)	2	4	2	1	1	51,930
Colors Inthe Storm	Princesscassandra (Valid Expectations)	4	2	0	0	0	413
Constant Companion	Constant Thunder (Thunder Gulch)	5	5	0	1	0	9,255
Constant Companion	Favorite Companion (Favorite Trick)	4	17	2	3	0	11,570
Constantia	Fullbridled (Unbridled's Song)	3	2	0	1	0	10,040
Controllable	Control the Devil (Devil His Due)	3	2	0	0	0	470
Controllable	Cyndi's Beauty (The Deputy (IRE))	2	5	0	0	1	2,123
Cut 'n Set	Acacian Song (Sultry Song)	8	2	0	0	0	146
Cut Test	Marsh Harbour (Labeeb (GB))	4	15	0	0	2	5,389
Darling Sola	Lasserre (Phone Trick)	6	12	2	1	2	10,602
Darling Sola	Malalco (Meadowlake)	5	9	3	2	1	16,782
Darling Sola	Ola Docura (Meadowlake)	3	9	1	1	2	24,117
Dawn Launch	Puck (Mr. Greeley)	5	4	0	0	0	240
Deep Discount	Final Discount (Repriced)	4	6	0	0	2	11,948
Definition	Let's Dance Nance (Judge T C)	5	15	1	4	1	23,664
Definition	Redefined (Labeeb (GB))	3	7	1	0	2	36,160
Diane's Girl	Code Found (Lost Code)	9	5	0	2	1	3,410
Diane's Girl	Last Intention (End Sweep)	5	7	1	1	4	68,829
Dolce Amore	Noir Et Rouge (Quiet American)	4	17	3	3	3	54,720
Dolce Amore	Ocho Negro (Saint Ballado)	3	3	0	0	0	0
Double Down Eleven	Artie Takes Two (Artema (IRE))	3	8	0	0	0	1,240
Double Down Eleven	Onda Ray (On Target)	4	12	2	3	4	23,575
Double Norm	Spy Shark (Spy Signal)	8	9	0	0	0	488
Double the Pot	One Eyed Gambler (Notebook)	3	4	0	1	1	2,681
Dream Launch	Wouldn't We All (Woodman)	10	7	2	1	1	23,469
Dream Motel	Dream City (Carson City)	5	1	0	0	0	110
Dreamsport	Wildly (Wild Wonder)	3	6	1	1	2	42,706
Due Bill	Salty Beach (Meadowlake)	2	6	1	2	1	25,274
Due Bill	Truly a Legend (Mr. Greeley)	5	3	0	2	1	12,085
Especially Aly	A Ps Special Jet (A. P Jet)	2	2	1	0	0	9,480
Especially Aly	Especially Royal (General Royal)	3	7	1	1	1	8,085
Especially Aly	Freedom Forever (Will's Way)	4	8	3	1	0	13,240
Evening Launch	Cloudy Mist (Twining)	5	2	0	0	0	0
Evening Launch	Doctor Price (Flag Down)	4	10	1	0	0	7,294
Existentialist	Governor Hickel (Gulch)	5	2	0	0	0	540
Existentialist	Oration (Deputy Minister)	7	13	1	2	3	49,260
Existentialist	Philosophy (Gone West)	2	3	0	0	1	4,997
Fenimore	Earmark (Personal Flag)	8	5	1	2	0	18,400
Fenimore	Happy Acres (Phone Trick)	7	2	0	0	0	83
Fenimore	Joethehorse (Runaway Groom)	3	3	0	0	1	1,725
Fenimore	With the Works (With Approval)	5	4	1	1	0	13,720
Firma	Firm Reality (Roy)	4	11	2	1	1	46,533
Firma	Relaunch Star (Opening Verse)	6	9	1	0	0	52,872
First Spot	Bull Head (Holy Bull)	4	5	0	0	1	1,605
First Spot	Minerveeni (Afternoon Deelites)	5	9	1	1	3	38,140
First Spot	Tom the River Rat (Virginia Rapids)	6	7	1	1	1	20,510
First Stage	Jones Arena (Seneca Jones)	2	1	0	0	0	0
First Stage	Stage Clearance (Cryptoclearance)	4	2	0	0	1	671
Flirted	Gypsy Chief (Polish Numbers)	3	3	0	0	0	480
Flirted	Pipes of Pan (Theatrical (IRE))	2	1	0	0	0	0
Flycatcher	C. G's Dollar (Ghostly Moves)	2	6	1	1	0	17,869
Flycatcher	Iron Cloud (Little Missouri)	6	12	1	2	3	8,116
Flying Galoshes	Billybeck (Anees)	2	6	2	1	0	37,337
Flying Galoshes	Diamond Heirloom (Pembroke)	4	10	3	2	0	34,400
Flying Galoshes	Hello Pepper (Ide)	5	10	1	1	1	6,577
Flying Galoshes	Mike the Navy Man (Out of Place)	3	7	2	1	0	40,850
Flying Relaunch	El Crusader (El Prado (IRE))	5	8	1	2	3	14,471
Flying Relaunch	Flick Creek (El Mayaguezano)	6	9	0	3	1	9,294
Flying Relaunch	Gold Will (Formal Gold)	3	10	2	0	6	37,230
Foegal	Gray Black N White (Quiet American)	3	7	1	2	1	34,760
Foggy Note Medley	Mr. Piano Man (Rubiano)	3	14	1	1	1	14,542
Free Launch	Ralph's Launch (Crowning Decision)	5	2	0	0	0	0
Fulla Finesse	S. S. Finesse (Blue Ensign)	8	12	1	1	0	10,735
Fulla Finesse	S. S. Spitfire (Blue Ensign)	7	12	1	1	2	5,822
Gatefold	Enemy Mine (Sir Cat)	3	7	1	2	0	15,205
Gatefold	Isabel's Pride (Binalong)	5	14	2	2	2	16,121
Gatefold	Rumsfeld (Pembroke)	4	1	0	0	0	0
Global Star	C. C.'s Cash (High Yield)	2	2	0	0	0	0
Global Star	Cairne (Gilded Time)	3	15	2	6	2	81,710
Good Response	Competitive Edge (Tactical Advantage)	4	1	1	0	0	4,740
Good Response	Core Idea (Breeders Bonus)	10	3	0	1	0	1,680
Good Response	Restage (Repriced)	5	5	3	0	1	101,185
Gray Cashmere	Astor Street (Pulpit)	4	18	2	1	1	23,739
Gray Cashmere	Purple Hills (Dynaformer)	5	2	0	0	0	480
Gray Mood	Look Out Joe (Dehere)	5	5	0	0	1	1,816
Great Escape	Ceely's Classic (Always a Classic)	5	6	1	1	0	20,766
Great Escape	Handzz Up (Saint Ballado)	4	6	0	0	1	1,160
Harps and Wings	Battle (Glitterman)	6	3	0	0	1	1,680
Heavenly Launch	Bug in a Bottle (Birdonthewire)	5	12	3	2	2	15,662
Heavenly Launch	Crimson Wave (Ocean Crest)	4	3	0	0	0	377
Heavenly Launch	Idle Dreamer (T. H. Fappiano)	3	3	0	0	0	240
Heavenly Launch	Sky Hunter (Distant View)	6	8	0	2	2	38,133
Heavenly Times	Grindtime (Grindstone)	4	3	1	0	0	28,950
Heavenly Times	Western Times (Mr. Greeley)	3	12	3	1	3	80,900
Herbs and Spices	Fast Spot (Unbridled)	5	17	3	1	1	27,846
Herbs and Spices	Three Charms (Silver Charm)	2	2	0	0	0	590
Here for Glory	Owyee (Major Impact)	6	3	0	1	0	1,116
Here for Glory	Tricks of Glory (Favorite Trick)	3	1	0	0	0	165
Hidden Valley	Won Arm Bandit (Air Forbes Won)	4	1	0	0	0	0
High Share	Revitalized (Repriced)	2	1	0	0	0	0
Honeycomb Honey	Maysville (Notebook)	2	2	2	0	0	24,450
If At First	Bandana (Academy Award)	7	12	3	0	2	29,567
If At First	Marquet First (Marquetry)	4	8	3	1	2	31,913
Instore	Ravishly (Gold Case)	3	3	0	0	0	2,177
Instore	Souvenier Biz (Souvenir Copy)	4	7	0	2	0	37,524
Investment Spend	Quintons Relaunch (Alphabet Soup)	2	5	2	0	0	12,014
Investment Spend	Sahara Sound (Gold Case)	3	7	1	1	1	31,199
Investment Spend	Silver Gun (Lit de Justice)	4	9	3	0	3	99,864
Jah	Uncanny (Unbridled)	4	5	0	1	0	8,085
Jah	Western Bulldog (Charismatic)	2	1	0	0	0	120
Jo Ann's Gal	Rubiano Star (Rubiano)	4	6	1	0	0	3,660
Judaea	Asserted (Affirmed)	4	11	1	1	0	9,459
Just Rumors	Just Gossip (Affirmed)	5	9	1	0	3	35,880
Kitty Hawk	Paragon John (Marked Tree)	4	4	0	0	0	0
La Luminosa	Hurricane Bay (Hurricane State)	3	8	1	3	1	26,520
La Luminosa	Luminous Lady (Partner's Hero)	2	5	0	0	0	1,698
Laun Shaw	Memphis (Hennessy)	6	2	1	0	0	8,250
Laun Shaw	Servant King (Cobra King)	5	11	4	0	2	16,687
Launch Light Tek	Taos Gold (Gulch)	3	3	0	0	1	6,140
Launch Site	Bushwacked (Yes It's True)	2	1	0	0	1	1,560
Launch Site	Vigilant Site (Diplomatic Jet)	4	5	0	0	3	4,640
Launch the Clan	Atagirl Genius (Beau Genius)	2	5	0	0	1	4,098
Launch the Clan	Corcovado (Dixieland Band)	7	7	1	0	0	4,880
Launch the Clan	Diamond Dawn (Dehere)	5	14	4	1	3	49,775
Launch the Clan	Free Rocket (Free House)	3	3	0	0	1	9,780
Launch Time	My Lucky Strike (Smart Strike)	5	12	1	2	2	105,396
Launchable	Compelling Launch (Compelling Sound)	7	5	0	0	1	2,185
Launchette	Renumbered (Polish Numbers)	5	4	1	0	1	10,924
Launchique	Swim Or Sink (Greenwood Lake)	2	5	0	0	1	2,625
Liquid Fill	Can't Stop James (Stop the Music)	6	14	2	2	0	26,170
Liquid Fill	Lil Charlie Too (Stop the Music)	8	11	1	2	2	18,560
Little Fogger	Foggerinthevalley (Peaks and Valleys)	4	9	1	0	0	8,587
Little Zip	Zip Gun (Oh Say)	4	18	1	1	3	27,561
Little Zip	Zip Zip Boom (Jeblar)	3	11	2	4	1	30,505
Lollypalooza	Alipalooza (Supremo)	4	11	2	2	0	11,575
Lollypalooza	Ocean Commotion (Ocean Crest)	5	6	1	0	0	4,050
Lollypalooza	Party Case (Gold Case)	3	5	0	0	1	1,327
Lonely Girl	Kilkea Castle (Pleasant Colony)	4	7	2	2	1	77,466
Lonely Girl	Power Wing (Sovereign Dancer)	10	7	1	1	3	11,225
Lonely Girl	Solitary (Rahy)	3	14	1	7	0	26,480
Luthier's Launch	Gassan Rock (Cape Town)	3	7	3	0	1	52,640
Magnolia Springs	She's a Mugs (Doneraile Court)	3	8	3	2	0	111,187
Main Gain	Bar Leah (Bartok (IRE))	2	5	0	0	0	4,476
Main Gain	Prismatic (Bertrando)	5	1	1	0	0	34,320
Market News	Bobski (Petionville)	3	2	0	0	0	653
Market News	Dinkers Good News (Yeti)	4	14	1	5	2	13,501
Marketplace	Gamble Monger (Labeeb (GB))	3	10	2	2	0	52,298
Marketplace	Package Store (Mister Baileys (GB))	6	1	0	0	0	245
Mary Roland	Army Man (Patton)	4	9	2	2	0	12,900
Mary Roland	Captain Red (Mr. Greeley)	7	3	0	0	0	2,130
Me and Myun	Revolver (Laabity)	5	8	0	1	0	3,130
Me and Myun	Sweet Cane (Laabity)	4	16	1	1	1	26,832
Milk Toast	Barrington Lady (Will's Way)	3	13	1	6	2	21,605
Milk Toast	French Toast (Storm Boot)	4	3	0	0	0	0
Milk Toast	Toast the Ghost (Silver Ghost)	2	3	0	0	0	1,260
Misty Launch	Leading Lioness (Lion Cavern)	3	4	0	0	0	3,000
Ms. Cuvee Napa	Deb's Charm (Silver Charm)	3	3	0	1	0	12,190
Ms. Cuvee Napa	Harve de Grace (Boston Harbor)	4	3	1	0	0	12,990
Native Connection	Presumption (Acceptable)	3	5	1	0	0	30,180
Native Connection	The Jean Genie (Glitterman)	4	3	1	1	0	9,375
O K Three Wire	Ok Monsoon (Maria's Mon)	3	9	1	1	0	17,860

On the Aisle	Diablo's Aisle (Diablo)	5	6	0	2	1	6,315
One Dreamer	Foreseeable (Unbridled)	3	1	0	0	0	135
One Dreamer	Indy Zone (A.P. Indy)	4	1	0	0	0	125
One Hot Minute	Doubleback (Gentlemen (ARG))	4	4	1	1	0	12,100
One Hot Minute	Headbanger (Conquistador Cielo)	3	11	2	1	1	17,845
One Hot Minute	Man Apart (Scatmandu)	2	3	0	1	0	5,322
Onesta	Joan's Gray Beauty (Cat's Career)	4	7	0	1	1	7,940
Paperback Romance	Ferriday (Roar)	4	12	1	2	2	9,348
Parioli's Gift	Parioli's Legacy (Maria's Mon)	3	1	0	0	0	795
Party On Deck	I Miss You (You and I)	4	2	0	0	0	0
Peaceable Mood	Siphonette (Siphon (BRZ))	3	12	1	1	1	30,900
Perfect Launch	Bolido (Kissin Kris)	2	4	1	2	0	15,650
Perfect Launch	Power Launch (Premiership)	3	12	1	1	1	6,952
Perky Wonder	Anniversary Bonus (Bonus Money (GB))	3	4	0	0	1	6,538
Perky Wonder	Any Wonder (Walter Willy (IRE))	5	2	0	0	0	100
Photo Please	Jeramiah John (Mercer Mill)	3	14	1	2	2	15,170
Photo Please	The Potters Hand (Bound by Honor)	4	14	2	2	2	20,504
Planet Eros	Jakob Teddy (All Gone)	3	13	1	3	1	12,860
Poker Nell	B's Big Boy (Double Honor)	4	8	0	0	1	1,487
Poker Nell	Long Since Past (Hunting Hard)	3	10	0	0	1	7,814
Poker Nell	Mystical Allure (Concern)	5	13	3	3	2	33,200
Prematurely Gray	Decoding the Gray (Cryptoclearance)	8	4	2	0	1	5,515
Prematurely Gray	Gray's Tee (Lil E. Tee)	3	1	0	0	0	35
Prematurely Gray	Queen's Triomphe (Cure the Blues)	5	2	0	0	0	3,288
Proper Reflection	Crafty Reflection (Crafty Prospector)	4	12	1	2	0	23,355
Proper Reflection	Proper Conquest (Conquistador Cielo)	7	5	1	1	0	9,820
Proper Reflection	Proper Prospector (Crafty Prospector)	3	11	0	2	2	7,965
Proper Reflection	Proper Wildcat (Forest Wildcat)	2	4	1	0	2	17,240
Proper Valentine	Bia Valentine (Bianconi)	3	7	2	0	1	40,391
Pure Wool	Pure American (Quiet American)	3	7	1	2	0	45,860
Purple Rose	Flamingo Flash (Manzotti)	5	10	1	1	1	12,589
Purple Rose	Relaunchy Bid (Aggressive Bid)	4	5	0	0	0	1,389
Quarry Hill	Bartus Christian (Doneraile Court)	3	7	0	2	3	13,661
Quarry Hill	Concrete Block (Sky Classic)	4	1	0	0	0	910
Quarry Hill	Mountain Eagle (Sky Classic)	6	16	1	0	4	22,337
Quarry Hill	Stonington (Always a Classic)	5	4	1	0	0	43,296
Rayelle	Erik's the Charm (Silver Charm)	3	5	1	1	0	35,800
Real Orphan	Real Gallant (Feeling Gallant)	6	1	0	0	0	0
Realahta	Really Something (Ormsby)	5	14	2	0	0	11,949
Realahta	Sheila Defrere (Defrere)	3	16	1	6	2	31,330
Really an Angel	Shining Angel (Dance Brightly)	3	10	0	2	2	14,710
Rearrived	Forgiving (Ole')	3	1	0	0	0	840
Rebow	Bowkeen (Rakeen)	6	5	1	1	0	30,221
Rebow	Pam's Grey Girl (Partner's Hero)	3	7	0	1	0	7,020
Rebow	Retam (Tamayaz)	4	7	0	1	1	11,230
Rebow	Two Bows (Two Punch)	5	20	3	1	1	21,748
Reclass	Cut Class (Cutlass Reality)	5	13	4	3	2	27,992
Reclass	Last Class (Steinlen (GB))	3	1	0	0	0	400
Reilette	Lettet Rumble (Pembroke)	7	10	2	2	2	12,932
Rejoyced	Pincay (Diesis (GB))	3	11	1	0	0	32,488
Rekindled Romance	Silvery Crown (Lord Carson)	3	11	3	0	1	41,630
Relasure	Eagles Hill (Boundary)	4	5	0	0	0	2,382
Relasure	Takkat (Horse Chestnut (SAF))	3	6	1	0	1	20,200
Relax and Smile	Five to Four (Metfield)	6	9	0	0	0	780
Relax and Smile	Justified Attack (Hawk Attack)	5	6	0	0	1	5,015
Relax and Smile	Miracle Mets (Metfield)	7	8	2	1	1	6,620
Relax and Smile	Rideitout (Stormy Atlantic)	3	2	1	0	0	14,787
Relaxer	Profusion (Northern Spur (IRE))	5	1	0	0	0	2,208
Reliant	Whereisspringfield (Pembroke)	7	15	1	6	0	34,535
Remittance	Humor the Rumor (Devil's Cry)	5	2	0	0	0	0
Renewed Delight	Chinoe (A. P Jet)	2	3	1	0	0	6,000
Renewed Delight	Never Take Risk (A. P Jet)	4	11	2	0	1	9,468
Renewed Delight	Vault (Gold Case)	5	5	1	0	0	9,720
Resubmit	Hannaboy (Repriced)	4	13	2	1	3	9,987
Rocket Launch	Rockin Regent (Gold Regent)	2	4	1	3	0	70,000
Rose Cafe	Tricks Not Treats (Favorite Trick)	3	11	1	5	1	38,350
Royal Launch	Fred's Passion (Numerous)	5	2	0	0	1	594
Sally's Spirit	Emma Renee (Defrere)	3	4	0	0	0	4,911
Sally's Spirit	Ice Girl (Devil On Ice)	4	10	2	0	1	64,590
Samba Rhythm	Samba City (Carson City)	2	4	0	1	0	4,630
Scatter Buy	Amazing Buy (High Yield)	2	1	0	0	1	4,100
Set to Fly	Historic Speech (Pulpit)	5	1	0	1	0	1,900
Set to Fly	Stealth Flier (Quiet American)	3	13	2	1	2	39,452
Shabanu	Jet Wash (A. P Jet)	2	4	1	1	1	32,708
Shabanu	Shabanu's Jet (A. P Jet)	3	3	1	0	0	4,590
Shrewd Idea	Cutshin (Forest Wildcat)	4	9	0	1	1	4,436
Shrewd Idea	Shrewd Maria (Maria's Mon)	3	8	2	0	1	16,800
Si Se Puede	Nino Dorado (Man From Eldorado)	6	9	0	2	2	5,057
Skilaunch	Catlaunch (Noble Cat)	3	13	3	2	2	29,988
Skilaunch	Jet Ski (Wavering Monarch)	9	13	2	2	2	8,865
Skilaunch	Mercer's Launch (Mercer Mill)	5	8	4	1	1	77,680
Skilaunch	Scioto Bootski (Storm Boot)	6	5	3	1	0	37,720
Smart Launch	Ghost Launcher (Silver Ghost)	3	10	1	1	0	8,759
So Re So	Banker's Note (Banker's Gold)	3	5	0	1	1	5,600
So Re So	Bold Banker (Banker's Gold)	4	3	0	0	0	2,520
Social Launch	Relaunch the Fever (Luthier Fever)	4	5	0	0	0	612
Solamente Un Vez	Ticklemyfancy (Fastness (IRE))	5	5	0	1	1	8,500
Space Flower	Yimmy (Good and Tough)	3	11	1	2	0	16,125
Splendid Launch	Splendid Prospect (Prospect Bay)	4	11	0	0	1	3,657
Springtique	Kaceysexpelled (Expelled)	3	3	0	0	0	0
Steamy Recipe	Guidebook (Notebook)	4	6	3	1	0	72,590
Steamy Recipe	Peak Performance (Major Impact)	3	18	0	5	2	10,793
Stock Price	Super Fund (Jules)	4	8	0	1	3	10,089
Sweet Relaunch	Apache Flyer (Marquetry)	3	3	2	0	0	12,985
Sweet Relaunch	Patron Hombre (Allen's Prospect)	2	1	0	0	0	0
Sweet Relaunch	Sweet Country Girl (Roy)	4	4	0	0	0	1,390
Sweet Surprise	Blown Surprise (Valid Expectations)	4	10	1	1	1	25,680
Sweet Surprise	Expect a Surprise (Valid Expectations)	3	6	1	0	1	15,054
Tacomolly	Taquito (Fly Till Dawn)	3	3	0	0	0	800
Taras Way	Wholesale (Repriced)	3	6	1	0	1	11,950
Tengo Prisa	Estrella Prisa (Star de Naskra)	8	4	1	0	1	3,330
Tengo Prisa	Hombre Rapido (Falstaff)	7	5	0	0	3	59,250
Tengo Prisa	Remonte (Flying Continental)	4	9	1	1	1	49,440
Tengo Prisa	Sombrio (Siberian Summer)	5	1	0	0	0	740
Tengo Prisa	Velocista (Artax)	2	3	1	0	1	12,280
That Kind I Want	Final Goal (Half Term)	2	2	1	0	0	6,600
That Kind I Want	Kind Lena (Seneca Jones)	3	6	1	1	0	18,220
To the Hunt	Stellar Jayne (Wild Rush)	3	13	3	2	3	992,169
Two Dreamer	Indian Dreamer (Numerous)	4	2	0	0	0	900
Two Dreamer	Tactical Blast (Tactical Cat)	3	15	3	4	4	46,914
We Have Lift Off	Kondoa Way (Press Card)	5	8	1	0	1	11,070
We Have Lift Off	Press My Bet (Press Card)	4	6	0	2	0	10,470
Whateverlolawants	Aloha Lola (Aloha Prospector)	4	9	2	1	3	8,176
Whateverlolawants	Golden Proposition (Aloha Prospector)	3	2	0	0	0	567
Whateverlolawants	Whateveralohawants (Aloha Prospector)	2	1	1	0	0	9,000
Whats Doin	You're Up (Silver Charm)	3	2	0	1	0	9,080
Wonderwhyme	Account for Me (Unaccounted For)	6	13	2	6	2	92,226

Deputy Minister, Dk B H (1979)
By Vice Regent – Mint Copy, by Bunty's Flight

313 Performers, 170 winning performers, **$9,035,408** total earnings

Mare	Progeny (Sire)	Age	Sts	1st	2d	3d	Money Won
Accent On Gold	American Jewel (NZ) (Rodrigo de Triano)	6	10	3	1	1	25,493
Action Lil	Sailin Windswept (Joker)	4	2	0	0	0	150
Adorable Minister	Absolutely Joe (Rodeo)	3	6	1	0	2	50,370
Adorable Minister	Gratiaen (Cure the Blues)	7	1	0	0	0	220
Altar Guild	Sky Deputy (Sky Classic)	7	3	0	0	0	2,820
Alya	Joyful Chaos (Rahy)	3	9	1	2	2	55,478
Alya	Vive Bene (Carson City)	4	2	0	0	0	0
Anthem	Naval Salute (Cryptoclearance)	2	3	0	0	0	1,940
Anthem	Southern Sensation (Southern Halo)	4	13	2	4	1	38,977
Apex Princess	Kiawah (Rahy)	4	7	1	1	1	15,901
Approve	Victorious Slam (Grand Slam)	3	6	0	0	0	1,163
Approve	Xtra Heart (Favorite Trick)	4	2	0	0	0	2,820
Arbitrary Risk	Boogie Woogie Man (Rhythm)	4	8	5	1	0	31,755
Arbitrary Risk	Maladyscat (Sir Cat)	5	5	1	2	1	8,062
Arbitrary Risk	Pleasant Risk (Pleasant Tap)	3	10	1	2	2	18,986
Astarte	Dummy (Souvenir Copy)	4	4	0	0	1	1,139
Astarte	Lord Ofthe Thunder (Saint Ballado)	5	5	1	1	1	56,554
Auxiliary	Classy Strike (Smart Strike)	5	9	3	1	0	17,751
Barnie Fife	Neville (Miswaki)	4	17	2	1	2	13,103
Beaty Sark	Ivanavinalot (West Acre)	4	2	0	0	0	6,000
Beaty Sark	Johnnies Wagon (Wheaton)	6	9	6	0	0	26,275
Beaty Sark	What a Lady (West Acre)	3	3	1	0	0	13,900
Border Wish	Colonial Trust (Hadif)	6	12	1	0	1	3,486
Border Wish	U Go Hugo (Capote's Prospect)	3	14	0	1	1	3,612
Border Wish	Villa Roja (Pancho Villa)	4	10	1	2	1	3,198
Brief Interlude	Brief Contact (Bertrando)	3	2	0	0	0	4,958
Brief Interlude	Ran for the Dough (Bertrando)	4	10	2	3	1	101,520
Bring Me Joy	Joyful Ballad (Saint Ballado)	4	9	2	0	4	56,410
Butter Cream	Crypto Cream (Cryptoclearance)	5	4	1	1	1	10,670
Butterflies	Celestialbutterfly (Affirmed)	8	4	0	0	0	800
Calamitous Jen	Country Jeweler (Judge T C)	6	4	0	0	0	192
Capital Coverup	Gold Scammer (Gold Tribute)	5	12	2	2	2	28,756
Capital Coverup	Thelionshare (Menifee)	3	11	0	2	1	16,114
Capricorn Moon	Princess Godiva (Swain (IRE))	2	2	0	0	0	2,580
Captivant	Mille Feville (Saint Ballado)	5	9	0	0	3	48,894
Captivant	Noisette (Broad Brush)	4	7	2	3	0	147,764
Captivant	Pour La Paix (Cozzene)	2	1	0	0	0	2,350
Choral Minister	Honest Grade (Honor Grades)	4	1	0	0	0	0
Choral Minister	R McLennen (Roy)	6	8	4	0	0	52,575
Clear Mandate	Newfoundland (Storm Cat)	4	9	2	3	1	523,750
Coastal Minister	Maytown (Menifee)	3	4	1	2	0	45,315
Coastal Minister	Minister of Note (Editor's Note)	5	10	1	0	0	14,419
Coastal Minister	Mountain Minister (Mountain Cat)	4	11	1	0	0	6,155
Consolata	Chicka Hermosa (Crusader Sword)	5	6	3	2	0	26,360
Consolata	Humorous Type (Distorted Humor)	3	12	2	0	2	30,570
Consolata	Monologue (Opening Verse)	7	13	0	2	3	5,871
Continental Divide	Vision of Division (Private Terms)	5	1	0	0	0	0
Daijin	Handpainted (A.P. Indy)	4	6	2	0	2	119,596
Daijin	Shadow Hawk (Mr. Prospector)	5	5	1	1	1	57,280
Dave's Deacon	Bruno the Dog (Chief Prospect)	9	13	0	0	2	2,136
Dave's Deacon	Hear Come Peanut (Chief Prospect)	4	12	1	2	3	15,748
Dave's Deacon	Who On First (Dance Brightly)	2	1	0	0	0	164
Debra C.	Cocoa Mio (Horse Chestnut (SAF))	3	6	0	0	1	2,875
Debra C.	Poydras (Smart Strike)	4	2	0	1	0	6,460
Delagating	Mudslide Slim (Crafty Prospector)	7	5	0	1	0	5,134
Deputation	Embarkation (Coronado's Quest)	3	2	0	1	0	6,935
Deputy Clerk	Humble Deputy (Humble Eleven)	2	1	1	0	0	7,200

Deputy Dancer	Best Foot Forward (Bien Bien)	5	13	1	3	2	31,801
Deputy Dancer	Gilded Deputy (Gilded Time)	4	2	0	0	1	686
Deputy Darlin	Cambaco (Menifee)	3	4	1	0	0	24,480
Deputy Darlin	Paint It Black (Mt. Livermore)	4	9	2	1	4	79,840
Deputy Dear	Bond Arbitrage (Forest Wildcat)	3	4	0	0	0	1,085
Deputy Dear	Storm Thief (Cat Thief)	2	2	1	1	0	33,600
Deputy Double	Thegamemustgoon (Fly So Free)	2	3	0	0	0	5,931
Deputy Double	Twice Removed (Unaccounted For)	3	9	0	0	1	1,785
Deputy Envoy	Holy Envoy (Holy Bull)	2	1	0	0	0	230
Deputy Envoy	Recollection (Cherokee Run)	4	2	0	0	0	680
Deputy Miss	Another One (Miswaki)	4	5	0	0	0	280
Deputy Miss	Eventually (Affirmed)	3	4	0	0	0	976
Deputy Royal	Royal Parade (Saint Ballado)	3	7	1	1	0	17,330
Deputy Royal	Royal Saint (Saint Ballado)	2	1	0	0	0	300
Deputy Snoop	Polish Snoop (Polish Pro)	6	1	0	0	0	73
Deputy Snoop	Snoopy Blues (Cure the Blues)	5	4	0	0	0	317
Deputy Snoop	Take Me Out Deputy (Take Me Out)	3	9	1	2	0	8,070
Deputy's Mistress	Crimson Courtier (Montreal Red)	6	5	0	0	2	15,536
Deputy's Mistress	Wild Mistress (Forest Wildcat)	3	1	0	0	0	340
Desiray	Romeo Tango (Rubiano)	4	4	1	0	0	6,375
Deux Danseuses	King Harvest (Affirmed)	3	9	1	3	0	11,920
Diablerie	Devilment (Peaks and Valleys)	2	2	1	1	0	22,200
Diablerie	Glory Me (Rahy)	3	2	0	0	0	265
Diva's Debut	Maestro's Debut (Woodman)	7	9	1	2	0	19,070
Doyenne	Dolce Diva (Maria's Mon)	2	7	0	2	0	16,055
Earth	Tabor Boy (Two Punch)	3	3	0	0	0	672
El Diabla	Hemlock (King of Kings (IRE))	4	11	0	0	1	2,800
Electric Brae	Darby Lane (Top Account)	5	18	4	1	0	29,130
Emmy Lou	Luxury Line (Major Impact)	4	4	0	0	0	316
Emmy Lou	Major Jonathan (Major Impact)	3	1	0	0	1	4,100
Emmy Lou	Redraw (Repriced)	5	13	2	0	2	27,175
Endless Devotion	Bertrando's Babe (Bertrando)	2	5	2	0	0	31,920
Epistolary	Deputy Lad (Mecke)	4	11	3	2	2	72,600
Epistolary	Galarus (Notebook)	5	2	0	0	0	160
Fancy Minister	Nici's Gold (Skip Trial)	3	7	0	0	1	1,140
Field of Vision	Hidden Image (Cherokee Run)	3	4	1	1	1	19,400
Field of Vision	Revealed (Old Trieste)	2	1	1	0	0	21,000
Fire the Deputy	Brush Up (Broad Brush)	4	16	1	2	2	28,540
Fire the Deputy	Southern Fire (Southern Halo)	3	3	0	0	0	4,095
Fire the Deputy	Ten Alarm Fire (Tabasco Cat)	5	1	0	0	1	1,430
Fly Butterfly	Fly Borboleta (Pulpit)	5	1	0	0	0	380
Fly Butterfly	Flying Pulpit (Pulpit)	4	6	1	0	0	18,680
Flying Minister	Charlie Whiskey (Cryptoclearance)	4	11	1	0	3	32,170
Flying Minister	Lifting Fog (Wild Again)	5	4	0	0	1	1,171
Flying Minister	Planets Aligned (Gold Fever)	3	3	1	0	0	25,578
For The King	King's Cloak (Capote)	8	1	0	0	0	113
Forever Rainbows	Garrison Hill (Cozzene)	5	11	3	1	3	53,498
Foxy Deputy	Krisco Kid (Taj Alriyadh)	6	21	2	1	6	21,059
Frannie Frantic	Crypto Gal (Cryptoclearance)	4	15	2	2	1	22,977
Frannie Frantic	Debi's Sportscar (Gold Tribute)	5	6	2	0	0	20,923
Frannie Frantic	Effrene (Evansville Slew)	6	5	0	0	0	870
Frannie Frantic	What a Strike (Strike the Gold)	8	5	0	0	1	1,551
Full Approval	Lisa's Approval (Farma Way)	6	11	1	2	1	15,988
Full Approval	Spac (Semoran)	4	12	1	1	3	13,805
Garfield Holme	Coal Inmy Stocking (Benny the Dip)	4	10	1	0	0	6,729
Garfield Holme	Garfield's Bluff (Pine Bluff)	3	2	0	0	0	340
Gentle Minister	Cat in the Box (Capote's Prospect)	2	2	0	1	0	5,840
Gentle Minister	Italian Riviera (Cozzene)	3	8	1	2	1	28,860
Geraldine	Dixie Preacher (Dixie Brass)	4	4	2	1	0	62,028
Good Cents	Count Centavos (Miesque's Son)	6	12	6	0	3	28,215
Good Cents	Fifth of Hennessy (Hennessy)	4	7	2	0	1	23,215
Good Secretary	Del Mar Ticket (Bertrando)	3	5	1	0	1	36,836
Good Secretary	Mister Bingbangboo (Bertrando)	4	2	0	1	0	9,000
Graceful Minister	Higher and Higher (Unbridled's Song)	2	1	0	0	1	1,260
Graceful Minister	Uncontrollable (Wild Again)	3	3	0	2	0	18,360
Grandeur	Another Chapter (Carson City)	4	10	1	3	0	27,320
Grechelle	Reverend Du (Pulpit)	2	5	0	0	0	226
Half Queen	Halfbridled (Unbridled)	3	2	0	2	0	110,000
Hanto Yo	High Speed Travel (Bold Ruckus)	7	8	1	1	2	65,005
Hanto Yo	Red Hot Flyer (Slew o' Gold)	8	2	0	0	0	363
Hanto Yo	Snake Pit (Kiridashi)	4	2	0	0	0	0
Henlopen	Messerschmitt (Sky Classic)	3	7	2	0	2	19,000
Henlopen	Shining Beacon (Diesis (GB))	4	6	0	0	0	3,420
House of Love	Fly Beside Me (Flying Continental)	6	5	1	0	0	7,615
House of Love	Not a Dollar Off (Marquetry)	5	11	2	1	1	2,847
Icanseeyounow	Not You Me (Dynaformer)	4	17	1	1	3	18,663
Icanseeyounow	You Can't Hide (Alphabet Soup)	3	8	0	3	0	16,194
Intriguing	Lady Pamela (Charismatic)	3	5	0	0	1	6,420
Kay Bee Bee (IRE)	Home Tour (Souvenir Copy)	3	9	1	2	2	38,520
Kay Bee Bee (IRE)	Lest We Forget (Tale of the Cat)	4	2	2	0	0	58,200
Kissie	Slate Run (Hennessy)	4	6	2	0	1	54,967
Knight Minstress	New Opposition (Slew the Surgeon)	3	11	3	2	1	52,627
Kristen's Treat	Beautiful Bay (Arch)	3	1	1	0	0	26,400
La Deputay	Keoni (Rakeen)	6	6	0	0	0	1,290
La Deputay	Never Delay (Press Card)	5	7	0	3	1	16,140
Lady Allaire	Turbo Bullet (Sky Classic)	6	11	2	2	2	15,394
Lady Go Faster	Little Wing (Allen's Prospect)	6	14	2	2	1	17,988
Langara	Timely Action (Gilded Time)	5	5	0	0	5	28,240
Leisurely	Vino Tinto (Boundary)	3	3	0	0	0	0
Letthemagicbegin	Reggie's Magic (Confide)	4	4	0	1	1	3,660
Likely Minister	Top Cappelletti (Capote)	4	7	4	0	0	26,224
Lilac Charm	Ecstatic (Rahy)	5	1	0	0	0	3,900
Lilac's Star	Atticus Star (Atticus)	4	2	1	0	0	27,784
Lilac's Star	On the River (Grand Slam)	2	2	0	1	1	12,300
Lilac's Star	Stars and Spice (Tabasco Cat)	3	4	1	0	0	26,901
Love From the Air	Lovers Bend (Arch)	3	7	1	0	0	11,330
Love From the Air	Migwaki (Miswaki)	8	10	8	0	1	46,276
Love Me Dearly	Pyramid's Gal (Pyramid Peak)	2	4	0	0	0	310
Madam Chairman	Chairman's Agenda (Souvenir Copy)	3	3	0	1	0	6,400
Madam Chairman	Keeping Cool (Carson City)	4	10	1	2	1	11,210
Madame Deputy	Funny Honey (Distorted Humor)	3	6	0	1	3	23,077
Madison's Quest	Request for Parole (Judge T C)	5	10	3	2	0	757,100
Magical Maze	Flagship Mission (Bertrando)	2	6	0	0	0	2,200
Maid's Broom	It's a Sweep (Jade Hunter)	8	4	0	0	0	250
Maid's Broom	Tenpins (Smart Strike)	6	1	0	1	0	12,000
Malley	Should Be Royalty (Pine Bluff)	2	2	1	1	0	36,400
Minister of Music	Jim's Super Bonus (Bonus Money (GB))	3	18	1	2	1	6,921
Minister of Music	Toppers Lil Trick (Old Topper)	2	2	0	1	1	2,000
Minister Wife	Bertolucci (GB) (Bertrando)	3	6	0	0	1	770
Minister's Flag	Graziella (Honour and Glory)	4	3	0	1	0	8,408
Minister's Melody	Connie Belle (Storm Cat)	2	2	0	0	0	4,350
Ministrada	Classic Advantage (Tactical Advantage)	3	4	0	2	0	10,970
Ministrada	Galaxy Lady (Rizzi)	2	4	0	1	1	7,525
Miraloma	Traditional (Gone West)	5	9	1	2	3	45,110
Mispillion	Trick Shot Artist (Favorite Trick)	3	1	0	0	0	1,280
Miss Jo	Arrive (Carson City)	3	8	0	0	0	225
Miss Katie C.	C the Minister (Gulch)	4	1	0	0	0	0
Miss Katie C.	Cold Stone Steve (Gulch)	5	6	1	1	0	6,500
Mission Hill	Malone (Affirmed)	5	3	0	0	1	935
Ms. Strike Zone	Dream Out Loud (Stravinsky)	3	2	0	0	0	0
Ms. Strike Zone	Magistretti (Diesis (GB))	4	4	1	2	0	764,000
Musical Minister	Minister Eric (Old Trieste)	3	6	1	1	2	54,851
My Last Alibi	Western Princess (Gone West)	2	3	1	0	1	34,073
Northern Mynx	Northern Request (Urgent Request (Ire))	5	8	1	0	1	3,563
Nuts About You	Princess Itron (Itron)	3	11	1	2	1	17,085
Nuts About You	Super Itron (Itron)	2	11	1	2	2	26,800
One for Hebe	Call Me Glitter (Glitterman)	2	2	0	1	1	3,850
One for Hebe	Hebe a Genius (Beau Genius)	3	8	1	2	1	9,834
One for Hebe	Litter the Glitter (Glitterman)	4	7	3	1	1	29,825
One for Hebe	Two for Hebe (Farma Way)	9	7	1	0	1	2,696
Open House	Homemaker (Afternoon Deelites)	3	6	2	1	1	64,368
Open Marriage	Affair in the Air (A P Jet)	6	12	0	3	2	37,512
Particular Style	Diplomat (Black Tie Affair (IRE))	9	15	0	6	2	19,024
Pemaquid	Broad Base (Broad Brush)	3	5	1	0	1	37,863
Pemaquid	Deputy Indy (A.P. Indy)	2	1	1	0	0	27,000
Pemaquid	Fircroft (A.P. Indy)	4	7	1	1	1	56,687
Perfect Copy	Copyco (Cozzene)	2	3	1	0	0	26,350
Picabo Street	Nevada Strip (Carson City)	7	8	0	2	0	3,793
Picabo Street	Thataintnomarlin (Holy Bull)	5	9	1	3	1	10,545
Pixie Rose	Fromheretobrazil (Rubiano)	4	4	1	1	0	3,475
Pixie Rose	Lively Minister (Lively One)	8	11	2	0	2	39,650
Pixie Rose	With Roses (With Approval)	5	10	2	0	2	16,015
Plenty of Sunshine	Saints a Plenty (Saint Ballado)	4	5	1	1	1	13,785
Plenty of Sunshine	Shiny Emblem (Our Emblem)	3	7	1	1	2	25,850
Policy Setter	Resolution (Pulpit)	2	2	0	1	0	9,900
Policy Setter	Southern Leader (Dixieland Band)	3	7	0	0	0	3,405
Political Process	Deputy Strike (Smart Strike)	6	5	2	2	0	94,375
Possible Consort	Consort Music (Prospector's Music)	5	2	0	0	1	15,040
Possible Consort	Marina Minister (Rubiano)	4	17	2	6	2	102,975
Possible Consort	Possibly Silver (Silver Ghost)	3	1	0	0	0	125
Prayer Colony	Atlas Peak (Pyramid Peak)	3	5	1	2	0	15,945
Precious One	Anxiously Awaiting (More Than Ready)	2	2	0	0	0	2,500
Presence Galore	Elijah M. (Labeeb (GB))	2	4	0	0	0	980
Presence Galore	Madame Galore (Fantastic Fellow)	3	5	0	0	0	0
Presence Galore	Road Town (Announce)	4	12	3	1	1	70,760
Presence Galore	Roberto's Minister (Royal Roberto)	7	3	0	0	0	120
Presence Galore	Runaway Victor (Runaway Groom)	8	11	1	3	4	73,192
President's Girl	Conservationist (Forestry)	3	7	2	1	0	76,752
Pretty Keane	Freedom Fair (Honour and Glory)	3	8	2	1	1	6,730
Prime Affair	True to Slew (Capote)	4	2	0	0	0	153
Prime Affair	Without a Ring (Phone Trick)	2	3	0	0	0	1,464
Prime Investor	Miss Moses (Gulch)	3	10	3	2	2	102,870
Primedex	Mystified (Gone West)	3	4	0	0	2	11,360
Primedex	Primerica (Mr. Greeley)	6	3	1	0	0	26,950
Promiscuous Angel	Winewomenandsong (Cape Town)	4	9	1	2	0	38,580
Promise Promise	Striped (Tiger Ridge)	2	4	0	0	0	790
Proper Form	Desnuda (Unbridled's Song)	3	4	0	0	0	1,580
Propose to Me	Barbarian (Mazel Trick)	3	2	0	0	0	0
Psychic Spirit	Ask Dorothy (Smart Strike)	5	1	0	0	0	825
Psychic Spirit	Fly Me Ali (Grand Slam)	3	11	4	0	2	66,320
Puppet Show	Fear Factory (Gold Case)	4	2	0	1	0	3,105
Puppet Show	Sparkman (Lit de Justice)	3	7	2	0	2	51,386
Queen of Spirit	Last Song (Unbridled's Song)	3	11	3	1	2	254,253
Queen of Spirit	Tetrahedron (High Yield)	2	2	0	0	0	0
Racemedowntheaisle	Miles of Aisles (Favorite Trick)	4	3	0	0	0	1,414
Rebs Odyssey (IRE)	Rebs Agenda (Twilight Agenda)	3	8	1	1	0	8,125
Red Mistress	Carmen Rouge (Prospectors Gamble)	3	4	0	0	2	4,750
Red Mistress	Trenchtown (Cape Town)	4	9	1	0	0	5,045
Regina's Vice	Early Snow (Souvenir Copy)	4	5	1	0	1	39,888
Regina's Vice	Funny Copy (Event of the Year)	3	2	0	1	1	8,240
Return of Mom	Taps Return (Pleasant Tap)	3	2	0	2	0	5,600
Rhythm of Life	Bahama John (Saint Ballado)	4	6	2	1	1	65,760

Mare	Progeny (Sire)	Age	Sts	1st	2d	3d	Money Won
Rhythm of Life	Sarava (Wild Again)	5	7	0	0	0	76,980
Rhythm of Life	Tropic Rhythm (Dynaformer)	3	1	0	0	0	720
Rhythm of Life	Wild Rocket (Wild Again)	6	8	0	2	2	5,968
Rooneys Princess	Notable Act (Exploit)	3	11	3	0	2	49,705
Sabbath Song	Sirona Gold (Gold Case)	4	8	2	2	0	74,503
Scottische	Pawyne Princess (Saint Ballado)	3	7	3	2	1	117,230
Second Bloom	Molto Bene (Jules)	5	4	0	0	0	1,141
Second Bloom	Orsay (Lycius)	3	4	1	2	0	58,508
See Moon	Nault (Woodman)	4	1	0	0	0	900
Seoul	Rush Bay (Cozzene)	2	4	1	2	1	87,755
Seoul	Seoul Wild (Wild Again)	3	5	1	0	0	6,435
Share the Fun	Cape Good Hope (Cape Town)	4	10	1	3	1	58,314
Share the Space	Chasing Skirts (K. O. Punch)	4	9	1	0	0	3,024
Share the Space	Copy Bien (Bien Bien)	5	4	0	0	0	0
Sharp Minister	Fancy Rose (Joyeux Danseur)	3	3	0	0	0	475
Sharp Minister	Sharp Writer (Capote)	2	7	1	2	2	37,208
Shaunlee	Banshee Brad (Candy Stripes)	6	15	4	2	2	75,994
Shaunlee	Cuba (Not For Love)	3	9	2	1	2	78,220
Shaunlee	Ruby Brad (Rubiano)	7	9	2	2	3	62,559
Shaunlee	Runaway Twins (Runaway Groom)	5	7	2	0	1	22,245
Shaunlee	Tell Me I'm Pritt (Peaks and Valleys)	4	14	2	2	3	42,770
Sheena	Gold Search (Seeking the Gold)	4	2	0	2	0	8,680
Sherriff's Deputy	Ms Deep Cover (Excellent Secret)	2	1	0	0	1	2,750
Shining Through	Litigasion (Miesque's Son)	6	4	0	2	0	4,935
Shining Through	Strong Hope (Grand Slam)	4	4	1	1	1	185,100
Social Director	Dream About (Cherokee Run)	3	2	0	0	0	11,033
Special Mistress	Mariatom (Irish Tower)	10	14	2	2	0	12,111
Special Mistress	Special Ballad (Saint Ballado)	5	14	1	4	6	28,087
Special Mistress	Special Way (Runaway Groom)	9	6	0	0	1	2,755
Special Mistress	Twilight Time (Twilight Agenda)	7	12	4	1	0	67,810
Special Mistress	Uninhibited Song (Unbridled's Song)	3	7	3	0	0	71,371
Stanley's Girl	Addie's Adventure (Gilded Time)	4	1	0	0	0	300
Star Deputy	License Free (Miswaki)	3	5	0	0	1	4,380
Star Minister	Exploding Star (Exploit)	3	2	0	1	0	6,400
Starlet Minister	Moonlet Minister (Chimes Band)	5	2	0	0	0	452
Starlet Minister	Unbridled Game (Unbridled's Song)	4	2	0	0	0	154
Stately Event	Stately Deputy (Miswaki)	4	1	0	0	0	215
Stolen Beauty	Wholehearted (Carson City)	3	7	1	2	0	44,766
Storm Minister	Stacie's Ballado (Saint Ballado)	3	7	2	0	4	58,990
Story Book	Skip a Page (Skip Trial)	6	6	0	0	2	7,570
Story Book	Story Grinder (Grindstone)	4	6	2	0	0	20,960
Sunset Service	Database (Known Fact)	5	5	1	0	1	33,990
Sunset Service	Service Medal (Our Emblem)	3	1	0	0	0	0
Sunset Service	Vespers (Known Fact)	6	9	1	1	4	62,034
Sweet Carolina	Carolina Ties (Quiet American)	4	9	1	1	0	7,770
Tin Oaks	Omega Code (Elusive Quality)	4	3	0	0	0	727
Tin Oaks	Wild Success (Forest Wildcat)	5	6	0	0	0	41
Triple Bright	Affirm the Light (Affirmed)	3	6	0	0	0	1,116
True Mood	Denimsanddiamonds (Private Terms)	4	11	2	1	2	36,600
Twenty One A. C.	Terrific Storm (Storm Cat)	3	7	1	2	1	56,115
Vandra	Crafty Joanne (Prospect Bay)	6	11	1	2	0	5,720
Vandra	Wild in the Forest (Forest Wildcat)	3	1	0	0	1	4,100
Very Popular	Citadella (Slew City Slew)	3	11	2	3	0	19,698
Very Popular	Seattlespectacular (Seattle Slew)	4	7	1	1	2	66,122
Victory Minister	Fair Minister (Farragut)	3	3	0	0	1	975
Victory Minister	Furious Victory (Furiously)	8	9	1	0	4	2,421
Viva Girl	Editiorial (Editor's Note)	4	9	3	2	0	44,410
Vivalita	Big Bad Louie (Loup Sauvage)	3	10	2	3	2	35,860
Vivalita	Friend of a Friend (Crafty Friend)	2	3	1	0	0	12,500
Vivalita	Monster Move (Meadow Monster)	4	8	1	1	0	27,730
Waltzing Beauty	Gold Ginny (Gold Legend)	3	11	3	2	0	73,590
Waltzing Beauty	Queen of Wands (Wekiva Springs)	4	7	2	2	0	17,958
Wedding March	Marching (Coronado's Quest)	3	1	0	0	0	320
Wedding Photo	Poison Cake (Formal Gold)	3	5	2	0	0	13,260
Wheres the Rainbow	Doppler Radar (Runaway Groom)	5	9	4	2	2	49,830
Wheres the Rainbow	Fofie's Pooka (Runaway Groom)	4	10	2	3	2	13,578
Wheres the Rainbow	Mr. Carpe Diem (Good and Tough)	3	17	2	5	3	25,181
Wonders to Come	Many Ministers (Numerous)	6	8	2	0	2	7,211
Wonders to Come	Miss Crafty Pal (Crafty Friend)	3	10	1	2	2	29,450
Xanadu	Big Profit (Woodman)	2	1	0	1	0	2,700
Xanadu	First Comes Love (Grindstone)	3	7	1	3	1	22,910
Xanadu	Twisted (Twining)	6	7	0	0	0	1,657
Zonda	Tail Number (Lear Fan)	5	5	1	1	0	9,062
Zonda	This N That (Cryptoclearance)	4	2	1	0	1	20,640

Smile, Dk B H (1982)
By In Reality – Sunny Smile, by Boldnesian

76 Performers, 41 winning performers, $8,828,709 total earnings

Mare	Progeny (Sire)	Age	Sts	1st	2d	3d	Money Won
Awesome Grin	Awesome Jason (Ray's Word)	3	7	0	0	0	0
Awesome Grin	Cool and Calm (Northstar Prospect)	4	6	2	0	0	7,980
Awesome Grin	I Know You (Alleged Stardom)	5	18	1	1	4	13,712
Barbara's Smile	Turbulent Tigress (Turbulent Kris)	3	5	1	0	2	1,710
Bearly Smiling	Beat the Chalk (Valid Wager)	2	5	2	1	0	88,630
Bearly Smiling	Macann's Promise (Tale of the Cat)	3	5	0	0	0	3,488
Besmirk	Got a Ticket (Deposit Ticket)	6	8	0	0	1	1,124
Besmirk	Our Olivia (Captain Bodgit)	3	4	0	0	1	1,762
Billie's Grin	Havana Anna (Never Wavering)	3	12	1	3	2	13,426
Billie's Grin	Ms. Bluebird (Never Wavering)	4	5	1	0	0	13,270
Blythe Smile	White Wedding Day (Crimson Guard)	4	1	0	0	0	60
Bourbon Miss	Bubble Dourbon (Lived It Up)	4	7	3	0	2	39,377
Candy's Smile	Sweet 'n Fiesty (Fit to Fight)	5	6	0	0	0	884
Certam de May	Certam Sweep (End Sweep)	4	7	0	0	0	4,330
Certam de May	Diablo for Certain (Diablo)	7	4	0	0	0	270
Certam de May	May Expectations (Valid Expectations)	5	10	1	2	3	39,608
Cherished Times	Timely Jeff (Avenue of Flags)	4	8	3	1	2	92,320
Consentida	Prospector's Smile (Suave Prospect)	4	11	1	1	0	9,474
Corelate	Cometes (Indy Mood)	4	8	0	1	0	2,983
Dazzling Smile	Awesome Allen (Allen's Prospect)	3	17	2	3	3	34,065
Dazzling Smile	Only Love (Not For Love)	5	5	0	0	0	600
Dazzling Smile	Smile as I Go By (Line In The Sand)	7	8	1	0	0	6,060
Delie Smiles	Byasmile (Society Max)	8	11	1	1	3	4,463
Delie Smiles	Delies Delight (Chanate)	2	4	0	1	0	1,558
Delie Smiles	Nuevo (Society Max)	5	8	2	1	2	8,204
Desireable Smile	La Paramour (Not For Love)	5	1	0	0	0	0
Dimples	Emolument (Tactical Advantage)	6	6	0	0	0	1,021
Evil Little Grin	Cheap Talk N Wine (Dreamfield)	3	9	2	2	1	10,584
Evil Little Grin	Dr. Dreamsteamer (J. P. Brother)	5	8	1	0	2	4,337
Evil Little Grin	Smokey Busted (Jim Nui)	4	6	0	0	0	957
Gana	Decision (A.P. Indy)	6	2	0	0	0	0
Guilty Grin	Allys Golden Smile (Gold Tribute)	2	3	1	0	1	20,080
Happy Looker	Look'n Smile (Announce)	4	12	2	5	2	6,860
Happy Looker	River Monster (Meadow Monster)	5	25	6	5	4	51,823
Hey Judith	Ruth's Sisu (Exetera)	4	6	1	0	0	3,155
Hidden Grin	Coax No More (Coax Me Chad)	4	3	0	0	0	207
Hidden Grin	Hidden Zone (Wild Zone)	3	1	0	0	0	90
I'll Get Along	Smarty Jones (Elusive Quality)	3	7	6	1	0	7,563,535
Iron Maiden	Wannagoto Court (Doneraile Court)	3	7	1	0	0	6,780
Jubilant Nature	Dragon the Pot (Slew City Slew)	2	12	1	2	0	13,520
Just for Grins	Whoopsy Doopsy (Czar Nijinsky)	3	3	0	0	0	180
Kaaren's Smile	Tyger Mam (Devon Lane)	3	1	0	0	0	75
Kaaren's Smile	Tyger Smiles (Haymarket (GB))	6	3	0	1	0	2,112
Kiss the Wind	Kiss 'n a Smile (Jeblar)	3	2	0	1	0	1,596
Kiss the Wind	Windy Zeal (Unreal Zeal)	5	13	2	0	2	8,564
Lavender	Sea Heather (Coronado's Quest)	2	5	0	1	0	7,000
Majestic Smile	Simsimmer (Mi Cielo)	6	12	0	0	0	0
Mia Smiling	Mr. Digger (Allen's Prospect)	3	11	1	1	0	23,560
Milliondollarsmile	Just Gabi (Devil His Due)	4	8	1	2	1	53,550
Not to Be Outdone	Signs and Wonders (Artax)	3	3	1	0	0	25,057
Not to Be Outdone	Smilesallaround (Peaks and Valleys)	5	5	0	0	1	2,050
Pentium Chip	Five Star Award (Marquee Star)	6	8	0	3	0	8,074
Private Smile	Ambers Smile (Rinka Das)	5	5	0	0	0	790
Pyrite Smile	But I'm Innocent (Skip Trial)	4	4	0	0	0	755
Pyrite Smile	Smile Dinners Here (Formal Dinner)	3	10	2	1	1	24,190
Pyrite Smile	World Class Smile (World Stage (IRE))	5	16	2	3	2	15,574
Reallysmiling	Hepdaboyout (Aide Memoire)	3	4	0	0	0	60
Seattle Smiles	Shemakesmesmile (Allied Forces)	3	3	0	0	0	352
Seattle Smiles	Three Ladies Man (Pembroke)	5	13	2	3	2	17,800
Shoot the Breeze	Kiss the Blarney (Grand Jewel)	4	11	3	1	1	17,580
Shotgun Romance	Maysville Slew (Slew City Slew)	8	14	3	2	0	208,440
Shotgun Romance	Rosieville (Boston Harbor)	3	8	1	1	1	19,060
Smile With a Smile	Star of Sahm (Sahm)	3	7	2	0	1	38,173
Smile With a Smile	Transcendent (Muhtafal)	5	16	7	1	1	82,394
Smilin' Through	Katana Girl (Crusader Sword)	5	8	0	0	0	1,065
Smilin' Through	Skipper (Westminster)	3	10	2	5	0	53,040
Smilin' Through	Smilin' Minster (Westminster)	4	9	5	0	1	29,480
Smiling Cop	Historic Countess (Historic)	3	4	1	0	0	19,320
Smiling Cop	Smiling Skip (Hickman Creek)	4	4	0	1	0	2,120
Smokem N Smile	Happy to Smokem (Happy Intentions)	4	7	0	2	0	4,807
Smokem N Smile	Smokemmakemehappy (Happy Intentions)	3	2	0	0	0	315
Susie Smile	Katy Smiles (Limit Out)	2	2	1	1	0	11,200
Susie Smile	Snowbird (Appealing Skier)	3	7	1	2	1	14,800
Ticklin' Toni	Toni T (Defrere)	4	12	0	0	3	17,759
Whos Smiling Now	Smile Away (Irish Open)	4	10	3	2	1	45,510
Yu Hu Stewardess	Smokin' Six (Smokester)	5	3	0	0	0	0

Mr. Prospector, B H (1970)
By Raise a Native – Gold Digger, by Nashua

252 Performers, 131 winning performers, $8,447,383 total earnings

Mare	Progeny (Sire)	Age	Sts	1st	2d	3d	Money Won
A Real Native	Nature's Power (Kris S.)	8	11	0	3	4	14,502
Abrade	Berry Good (Arch)	3	7	1	0	1	8,659
Abrade	Forty Nine Deeds (Alydeed)	5	13	1	2	1	20,249
Abrade	Wear (Arch)	4	9	1	2	2	35,364
Act	Saintly Action (Saint Ballado)	5	6	0	1	2	57,450
Aliata	Ferrazzi (Arazi)	6	13	2	3	0	34,506
Aliata	Meadow Slipper (El Prado (IRE))	3	5	1	0	1	12,192
Allusion	Dixieland Gem (Dixieland Band)	2	1	0	0	0	0
Allusion	Rag Time Dancer (Dixieland Band)	3	9	1	0	1	12,080
Alqwani	Fehr (Dumaani)	4	5	0	1	0	6,900
Art's Prospector	Harangue (Theatrical (IRE))	3	4	1	1	0	11,555
Art's Prospector	Lendy (Theatrical (IRE))	8	4	0	0	0	166
Artemisia	Tricktor (Favorite Trick)	3	4	0	0	0	1,220
Autumn Moon	Cycle of Life (Spinning World)	4	7	0	0	0	1,492
Autumn Moon	Indy Moon (A.P. Indy)	2	3	1	0	0	30,080
Ballerina Princess	Line of Departure (A.P. Indy)	3	1	0	0	1	5,520

Ballerina Princess	Peak Dancer (Mt. Livermore)	7	1	0	0	0	0
Bat Prospector	Bat Runner (Broad Brush)	6	5	0	1	2	5,285
Bat Prospector	Cherokee Prospect (Cherokee Run)	7	10	4	3	1	57,120
Bat Prospector	Holy Prospect (Holy Bull)	3	5	0	0	0	3,020
Bat Prospector	On Exhibit (Cherokee Run)	4	13	1	2	1	20,729
Be a Prospector	Mr Forestrey (Forestry)	2	5	1	0	0	9,443
Be a Prospector	Rich Find (Exploit)	3	11	3	1	0	84,622
Beau Prospector	Abu Leil (Chief's Crown)	8	20	3	4	4	21,825
Beautiful Gem	Max Jones (Capote)	6	5	0	0	1	1,350
Bejat	Glick (Theatrical (IRE))	8	8	3	2	0	160,960
Blazing Alarmiss	Advance to Go (Reprized)	3	9	1	1	0	15,025
Blazing Alarmiss	Lucky Alarm (Eltish)	2	3	2	0	0	25,260
Blue Jean Baby	Blue Jean Racer (Silver Hawk)	8	7	1	1	1	10,920
Brenda Lagrange	Bugsy N Tuff (Fly So Free)	6	8	3	1	0	5,215
Brenda Lagrange	Forever Hopeful (State Craft)	2	2	0	0	0	0
Brenda Lagrange	Overnight Delivery (Mountain Cat)	5	11	0	4	0	17,624
Brenda Lagrange	Wilful (Ops Smile)	3	8	1	3	1	19,667
Carol's Prospector	Mary's Prospector (Loup Sauvage)	4	10	0	0	0	1,575
Chere Amie	Desert Anger (Gb) (Cadeaux Genereux (Gb))	3	4	1	0	1	30,744
Chic Shirine	Flying Passage (A.P. Indy)	4	2	0	0	0	680
Chic Shirine	Temple Owl (Deputy Minister)	9	3	0	0	1	2,100
Classic Event	Easy Elegance (General Meeting)	3	5	0	0	1	10,360
Connie's Prospect	Dos Reyes (Southern Halo)	4	2	0	2	0	2,040
County Fair	Celtic County (Boston Harbor)	4	4	1	0	0	5,115
Coup de Genie	Denebola (Storm Cat)	3	1	0	0	0	0
Coup de Genie	Snake Mountain (A.P. Indy)	6	6	1	0	2	58,210
Crystal Shard	Amazing Again (Awesome Again)	3	2	0	0	1	5,000
Crystal Shard	Clear Destiny (Deputy Minister)	5	3	0	0	1	9,855
Crystal Shard	Perfect Cut (A.P. Indy)	4	7	1	0	1	33,372
Dabble	Blame It On Beau (Beau Genius)	5	13	2	0	0	12,975
Dance With Grace	Bold Stock (A.P. Indy)	3	6	0	2	0	19,860
Dance With Grace	Dance With Kelly (Devil's Bag)	8	2	0	0	0	107
Dance With Grace	Indy Dancer (A.P. Indy)	4	4	0	0	1	15,080
Danseuse	Valbon (Belong to Me)	3	3	0	0	0	726
Debt	Tennesee Burbin (Hennessy)	4	12	2	0	0	33,493
Delta Love	Delta Guard (Old Trieste)	3	2	0	0	0	575
East Cape	Ottawa Chief (Forestry)	3	4	0	0	0	1,508
East Cape	Printemps (Royal Anthem)	2	4	0	0	1	4,560
Educated Risk	Alluring (A.P. Indy)	5	3	0	0	0	3,860
Educated Risk	Strategy (A.P. Indy)	3	8	2	3	1	93,680
Envied	Close to Perfect (Stravinsky)	3	5	0	2	1	13,965
Envied	Pantages (Louis Quatorze)	4	7	1	0	0	7,658
Envied	Red Wing Evan (A.P. Indy)	5	3	2	0	0	31,430
Especially	Boston Common (Boston Harbor)	5	6	3	1	0	141,960
Especially	Captain Thunder (Storm Cat)	4	4	0	1	0	11,300
Especially	Special Tactics (Tactical Cat)	3	10	1	0	6	53,265
Especially	Storm Surge (Storm Cat)	2	7	4	1	0	192,770
Fabulous Prospect	Chum (Fortunate Prospect)	5	9	1	2	1	13,564
Fabulous Prospect	Fabulous Fortune (Fortunate Prospect)	6	18	4	4	2	40,125
Fabulous Prospect	Ghetto (Line In The Sand)	3	6	0	0	0	540
Faith's Folly	Maid's Folly (Maria's Mon)	5	3	0	1	0	1,020
Fantastic Find	Dream Time (Storm Cat)	2	1	1	0	0	25,800
Fantastic Find	Grand Gala (Dixieland Band)	3	1	0	0	0	430
Foolish Gold	Cymbidium (Heaven's Wish)	4	1	0	0	0	700
Garimpeiro	Indygal (A.P. Indy)	3	3	1	0	0	29,660
Garimpeiro	Stage Shy (Theatrical (IRE))	4	4	3	0	0	111,480
Gay Chiffon	Commander's Flag (Spinning World)	5	4	1	0	0	48,150
Gay Chiffon	Knight Affair (Black Tie Affair (IRE))	9	12	0	1	0	4,124
Get Lucky	Daydreaming (A.P. Indy)	3	8	5	1	1	483,180
Gild	Fungee (Dixieland Band)	3	7	0	1	0	15,480
Gild	Poker Brad (Go for Gin)	6	6	2	2	0	87,745
Gilded Dancer	Valentine Dancer (In Excess (IRE))	4	3	1	0	0	287,000
Glittering Legend	Legendary Run (Runaway Groom)	5	4	1	0	0	4,845
Gold Hearted	Benny the Lip (Benny the Dip)	6	6	0	0	1	2,010
Gold Hearted	Encanto Oro (Charismatic)	3	2	0	0	0	150
Gold Hearted	Goldharbor Express (Boston Harbor)	4	14	4	2	3	20,227
Gold Heist	Churchhill (The Prime Minister)	4	3	1	0	1	9,695
Gold Heist	Prime Jewel (The Prime Minister)	5	10	2	0	3	34,920
Gold Seal	Fixed Image (Halo's Image)	5	7	0	0	0	1,116
Gold Seal	Island Chancellor (Island Whirl)	2	5	1	1	0	16,390
Gold Shadow	Day Trade (Dixieland Band)	8	15	2	0	1	12,447
Gold Shadow	Keys to the Heart (Wild Again)	5	7	1	2	0	100,800
Gold Shadow	Shadow of Mine (Belong to Me)	3	8	0	0	1	13,886
Gold Whirl	Whirley (Summer Squall)	7	11	0	0	4	5,215
Golden Attraction	Big Top Cat (Storm Cat)	2	2	0	0	0	225
Golden Attraction	Swift Attraction (Storm Cat)	3	5	1	0	1	41,500
Golden Petal	Golden Glen (Forestry)	3	10	3	2	1	112,301
Golden Reef	Delightful Reef (Pleasant Colony)	8	5	0	1	0	1,240
Goldminess	Crimson Caper (Red Ransom)	3	3	0	0	0	1,260
Goldminess	Gold Bull (Holy Bull)	6	1	0	0	0	0
Grass Skirt	Flaming Dixie (Dixieland Band)	3	11	2	6	1	75,840
Grass Skirt	Straw Hat (Dixie Union)	2	9	1	3	2	57,345
Hard to Copy	Andover Lady (Kris S.)	4	6	1	1	1	54,196
Hard to Copy	Teton National (Forestry)	3	2	0	0	0	400
Here I Go	Summerly (Summer Squall)	2	3	1	0	1	53,035
Hidden Garden	Lutyens (Dixieland Band)	3	1	0	0	1	4,680
Hidden Reserve	Defer (Danzig)	2	3	2	1	0	108,000
Hidden Reserve	Leaveminthedust (Danzig)	4	3	0	1	1	13,360
Hidden Reserve	Philanthropist (Kris S.)	3	6	2	1	1	71,850
Hollywood Gold	I Testify (Lit de Justice)	4	12	4	2	1	87,173
Hollywood Gold	Quintons Gold Rush (Wild Rush)	3	9	3	0	0	322,235
Hopespringsforever	Giant Hope (Giant's Causeway)	2	2	0	1	0	5,010
Hopespringsforever	Ozzie Cat (Storm Cat)	4	2	1	0	0	25,800
Hot Match	Bogangles (Joyeux Danseur)	3	7	0	1	1	22,870
Hot Match	Danseur Chaud (Joyeux Danseur)	2	4	0	1	0	4,050
Ikhteyaar	Jovial Joshua (Bahri)	3	6	2	0	0	10,372
Illicit	Double Jeopardy (Horse Chestnut (SAF))	3	2	0	0	0	1,422
Im a Star Prospect	Star Raider (Belong to Me)	4	9	1	1	1	16,044
Impetuous Image	Fusaichi Towani (Hennessy)	3	4	1	0	1	19,610
Impetuous Image	Hallucinogin (Go for Gin)	7	1	0	0	0	44
Impetuous Image	Impetuous Fling (A.P. Indy)	4	1	0	0	0	1,521
In the Till	Gingham and Lace (Kris S.)	3	3	1	1	0	43,740
In the Till	Incorrigible (Mt. Livermore)	5	2	1	0	0	3,600
Jordanesque	Rosegate (Cherokee Run)	2	5	0	1	0	9,360
Julia Jane	Vancouver Vice (Vice Regent)	9	4	0	2	0	3,250
Kalinka	Claridges (With Approval)	6	1	0	0	0	0
Kalinka	Kamoya (Dayjur)	4	7	0	2	0	3,220
Kettle Ridge	Four Corners (Salt Lake)	5	9	1	1	2	14,455
Key to My Heart	Fusaichi Donight (Kris S.)	3	1	0	0	0	300
Kydall	Vertical Ascent (Lear Fan)	4	3	0	0	0	1,680
Lady Bequest	Romeo's Bequest (Proudest Romeo)	2	1	0	0	0	900
Lady Isa Tramp (IRE)	Privateer (ARG) (Private Terms)	6	19	6	3	4	43,884
Lit'l Rose	Big Bud (Dr. Caton)	2	4	1	0	0	10,290
Lit'l Rose	Handsome Hunk (Hennessy)	5	10	1	1	2	16,920
Looking for Gold	Stunning Image (IRE) (Kris S.)	4	8	0	2	3	24,891
Lost Lode	Eye of the Wind (Stravinsky)	3	3	0	0	1	2,624
Lost Lode	Silver Diablo (Holy Bull)	4	10	2	0	0	20,000
Louis d'Or	Diplomatic Bag (Devil's Bag)	4	1	1	0	0	90,000
Louis d'Or	Royal Stamp (With Approval)	5	1	1	0	0	34,800
Love From Mom	American Liberty (Storm Cat)	4	6	2	2	0	76,640
Macoumba	Somethingdangerous (Danzig)	6	12	1	5	1	57,565
Marie J	Sisti's Pride (Forestry)	3	4	0	0	0	6,362
Mary's Spirit	Tavacat (Tabasco Cat)	4	5	0	0	0	1,185
Mine Only	Selection (A.P. Indy)	3	11	0	1	1	5,728
Miner's Game	Prowling (Storm Cat)	5	12	2	2	2	16,035
Miner's Game	Survivalist (Danzig)	2	2	1	0	0	28,950
Miss Du Bois	Film Maker (Dynaformer)	4	6	1	2	1	470,430
Miss Du Bois	Sazerac Song (Phone Trick)	3	6	1	0	1	33,780
Mission Pass	Coast Line (Boston Harbor)	3	3	3	0	0	67,400
Mission Pass	Harbor Pass (Boston Harbor)	5	1	0	0	0	0
More Flags	Dixiemore (Dixieland Band)	7	18	3	4	8	76,750
More Flags	More Bands (Dixieland Band)	4	4	0	0	0	0
More Flags	Wildest (Wild Again)	6	13	0	0	1	2,872
Nortena	Cherry Tree Hill (Red Ransom)	6	2	0	0	1	5,850
Nortena	Flower Forest (Kris S.)	4	2	1	0	0	42,396
O My Darling	Black Cove (Kris S.)	8	12	2	4	1	12,697
O My Darling	Bullistic Flight (Holy Bull)	5	12	1	1	0	15,575
On Final	Final Attack (Hadif)	4	10	3	1	0	23,914
On Final	Fleet Final (Hadif)	5	19	1	3	4	11,156
On Final	Magic Uno (Magic Cat)	2	6	1	1	0	12,930
On Final	Off the Screen (Hadif)	6	10	0	0	2	1,919
On Final	Radar Trap (Hadif)	8	15	1	1	5	10,909
Onaga	Yarico's Pond (IRE) (Seattle Slew)	4	3	0	0	0	390
Onyx	Classic Onyx (Sky Classic)	6	3	0	0	1	760
Onyx	Holmdel (Housebuster)	8	2	0	0	1	484
Our Millie	Winlocs Grama Rose (Anjiz)	7	1	0	0	0	109
Pedicure	Masseuse (Dynaformer)	2	3	0	0	1	6,650
Pedicure	Second Performance (Theatrical (IRE))	3	11	2	0	4	106,260
Pennant Champion	Swinging (Wild Again)	3	5	2	0	0	57,272
Pent	Boarded Hall (Red Ransom)	4	2	0	1	0	4,400
Perfect Probe	Core Sample (Forestry)	3	11	0	2	1	17,520
Praise	Congrats (A.P. Indy)	4	6	2	0	1	160,832
Praise	Gigger (Go for Gin)	2	1	1	0	0	12,300
Private View	Savor (Hennessy)	3	4	0	0	0	1,830
Propositioning	American Band (Dixieland Band)	5	4	0	0	0	222
Prospect Digger	Hecandigit (Marlin)	5	13	2	2	0	75,520
Prospective	Charismatic Rob (Charismatic)	3	9	0	0	0	7,187
Prospective	Dixie Drummer (Dixieland Band)	6	7	3	1	1	54,170
Prospective	Future Saint (Saint Ballado)	2	1	1	0	0	15,625
Prospective Wife	Besttobeabachelor (Kris S.)	9	11	1	3	2	8,004
Prospective Wife	Ride 'Em Rags (Rahy)	8	12	0	1	1	9,451
Prospective Wife	Tomoka Bound (Boundary)	3	3	0	0	0	1,600
Prospector's Fable	Old Liar (Old Trieste)	3	1	0	0	0	170
Prospector's Fire	Royal Alchemist (Royal Academy)	4	1	0	0	0	0
Prospector's First	Pancho Pete (Pancho Villa)	9	3	0	1	0	2,445
Prospector's Punch	Battle Ghost (Battle Launch)	7	4	0	0	0	244
Prospector's Queen	High Rank (Gentlemen (ARG))	4	15	2	0	3	15,151
Prospector's Queen	Rahy Rhythm (Rahy)	7	9	0	0	1	6,140
Prosperity Found	Our Freya (Skip Away)	4	11	2	0	2	36,688
Prosperity Found	Prospect Green (Green Dancer)	6	8	1	2	3	35,820
Prospinsky	Spin Control (A.P. Indy)	4	5	1	0	1	34,352
Prospinsky	Tell J (A.P. Indy)	5	9	0	1	1	3,689
Pueblo	Cherokee Trail (Seattle Slew)	5	1	0	0	0	72
Pueblo	Maryneill (Belong to Me)	3	4	0	1	1	7,000
Queena	La Reina (A.P. Indy)	3	5	1	1	0	85,922
Race Artist	Almost Holy (Holy Bull)	4	12	2	2	3	29,000
Race Artist	Eye of the Artist (Old Trieste)	3	3	0	0	0	0
Realm	Play With Fire (Boundary)	2	5	1	0	2	107,000
Reckless Star	Lightninginabottle (Lightning Leap)	7	1	0	0	0	0
Regal Grant	Gold Cluster (Formal Gold)	3	14	4	0	1	61,090
Rhineland	Palatinate (Out of Place)	3	1	0	0	0	217
Ridan Prospector	Polish Account (Polish Numbers)	4	1	0	0	0	0

Ridan Prospector	Ridan's Mon (Maria's Mon)	5	9	0	1	4	26,880
Rock On Now	Intimate Music (Private Terms)	6	9	3	0	2	37,080
Ryn	Aisle Light (Bertrando)	4	2	2	0	0	40,398
Ryn	I've Decided (Bertrando)	7	5	0	0	0	388
Ryn	Lord Albion (Lord At War (ARG))	6	19	7	4	0	50,038
Ryn	Merryvale (Bertrando)	3	3	1	0	0	27,000
Safe Return	Never Left (Seattle Slew)	4	3	1	0	1	14,940
Safe Return	Welcome Home (Dixieland Band)	3	6	2	2	1	66,560
San Angelo	Old Lodge (Lure)	8	7	0	0	2	4,300
Sayedat Alhadh	Musaa Ed (Deputy Minister)	5	10	2	1	1	28,405
Scrape	Gin and Tea (Go for Gin)	2	1	0	0	0	120
Scrape	Sobriquet (Hennessy)	3	5	0	0	1	7,736
Sealed Bid	Lejos (Charismatic)	3	11	1	2	2	13,870
Shake Hand	Loving Cup (JPN) (Brian's Time)	4	4	1	1	0	33,200
Sierra Madre	Sierra Crossing (Boston Harbor)	3	5	1	1	0	26,400
Sierra Madre	Sun Cat (Tabasco Cat)	7	3	0	0	0	1,740
Sigh Ho	Ascribe (Lil E. Tee)	3	5	0	1	0	2,671
Silver Discovery	Discover the Glory (Honour and Glory)	4	5	1	1	0	34,814
Silver Discovery	Holy Silver (Holy Bull)	2	3	0	1	0	10,129
Silver Valley	Buzzy's Gold (Touch Gold)	4	8	2	1	2	83,507
Sometimesadiamond	Diamond Blues (Dixieland Band)	3	3	0	0	0	1,680
Sometimesadiamond	Sky Diamond (Sky Classic)	4	13	5	1	2	196,348
Soundings	Tonitruant (Storm Cat)	4	3	0	0	3	14,475
Special Strike	Beware Avalanche (Mt. Livermore)	8	16	2	2	1	42,650
Special Strike	Mary's Special (Atticus)	3	3	1	0	0	8,640
Spring Morning	Silverado Trail (Silver Charm)	2	3	1	1	1	43,445
Spring Morning	Spring Training (Cherokee Run)	3	8	1	3	2	20,260
Sugar Gold	Quite Continental (Joyeux Danseur)	3	7	0	0	0	4,000
Sweetheart	Sweet Band (Dixieland Band)	5	1	0	0	0	0
Takreem	Spinning Tales (Spinning World)	5	10	1	2	2	24,990
Tappity Tap	Click Here (Red Ransom)	3	3	0	0	0	690
Tenga	Ballado (Saint Ballado)	2	1	0	0	0	140
Tenga	Gannett Peak (Mt. Livermore)	3	2	0	0	1	3,520
Tenga	Startac (Theatrical (IRE))	6	1	0	0	1	6,430
Tersa	Donald David (Kris S.)	4	5	0	0	1	3,860
Tersa	Rock Hard Ten (Kris S.)	3	8	4	1	1	790,380
Thirst for Gold	Funshine (Deputy Commander)	3	2	0	0	0	0
Thirst for Gold	It's About Me (Belong to Me)	2	2	1	0	1	16,110
Unbeatable Foe	Full Force Gale (Mt. Livermore)	7	7	2	0	4	23,620
Utr	Zurich (IRE) (Giant's Causeway)	2	4	0	3	0	22,213
Vantive	Private Opinion (Deputy Minister)	3	5	2	1	0	57,256
Vue	Vision of Beauty (Danzig)	3	4	2	2	0	103,040
Watch Out	Brands Hatch (A.P. Indy)	3	7	1	0	0	41,556
Water Saver	Trinity River (River Special)	7	9	1	0	1	9,905
Wayage	Crystal Castle (Gilded Time)	6	1	0	0	0	8,482
Wayage	Teresa Ann (Boston Harbor)	5	1	0	0	0	2,475
Wayward Bound	Orchid Island (Broad Brush)	3	3	0	0	0	584
Wayward Bound	Way to Trieste (Old Trieste)	2	5	0	0	2	7,250
Whist (GB)	Pinlochle (A.P. Indy)	3	4	0	0	2	11,000
Wind Capers	Capable Capers (Native Factor)	5	12	3	3	2	32,765
Wind Capers	Wind Factor (Native Factor)	4	11	3	2	0	18,957
Winloc's Millie	Winlocs Glory Days (Belong to Me)	3	8	2	2	0	81,320
Winze	Gildmore (Gilded Time)	5	10	2	0	0	18,660
Withallprobability	With Probability (Wild Again)	3	7	2	1	0	59,158

Bold Ruckus, Dk B H (1976)
By Boldnesian – Raise a Ruckus, by Raise a Native

229 Performers, 130 winning performers, $6,883,093 total earnings

Mare	Progeny (Sire)	Age	Sts	1st	2d	3d	Money Won
Accadia Rocket	Gotta Jiboo (Tactical Advantage)	5	15	3	2	5	46,267
Accadia Rocket	Paco El Prado (El Prado (IRE))	7	9	2	3	1	31,427
Ada Ruckus	Quite a Ruckus (Richter Scale)	2	4	1	1	0	110,653
Africo	Roar of Africa (Roar)	3	11	2	2	1	40,600
Air Walker	Air Driver (K. O. Punch)	4	6	1	0	2	20,460
Air Walker	Overtime Bid (Lord Carson)	3	5	0	1	1	4,039
Allegro Dancer	Weekend Ruckus (Weekend Guest)	3	1	0	0	0	340
Andrea Ruckus	Bold Trader (Forest Wildcat)	3	9	2	1	1	41,534
Andrea Ruckus	Captivating (Arch)	2	1	0	0	0	0
Andrea's Bestgirl	Chris's Counter (Grey Counter)	6	2	0	0	0	228
Annie's Ruckus	La Vitesse (Joe Spatts)	8	5	3	0	1	44,403
Antique Ruckus	Rare Antique (Always a Classic)	5	14	0	0	0	3,572
Arctiana	Niota (Dumaani)	3	1	0	0	0	0
Arctiana	Ossabaw (Brunswick)	4	11	0	2	0	4,644
Aromacor	Corenn (Hennessy)	4	15	3	1	1	45,180
Aromacor	Quality Armor (Elusive Quality)	3	6	0	0	1	6,180
Bald Ruckus	Ruby's Ruby (Mutakddim)	3	7	2	2	1	13,938
Ballybeg	Curlew Road (Parade Ground)	2	5	0	1	3	19,930
Beautiful Feeling	Citi Feeling (Citidancer)	2	1	0	0	0	3,420
Bellarose	Son of the North (Foxtrail)	2	8	1	2	3	51,193
Bellarose	Super Gal (Tejabo)	5	10	0	2	2	5,404
Bellarose	Tejabelle (Tejabo)	6	9	2	1	2	13,771
Blind Trust	Gwynedd (Old Trieste)	2	3	0	0	0	0
Blind Trust	Quiet Motivator (Quiet American)	3	10	2	2	1	38,864
Bodust	Bo's a Ten (Patton)	4	8	1	0	1	7,365
Bodust	Tubby Cat (Personal Flag)	7	7	1	0	0	4,702
Body Works	Body Image (Go for Gin)	5	3	0	0	0	200
Body Works	Golden Works (Banker's Gold)	4	7	2	3	0	14,520
Bold and Stormy	Maristen (Dr. Caton)	2	2	0	0	0	125
Bold and Stormy	Quiet Ruckus (Friendly Lover)	3	10	1	3	2	12,682
Bold Blast	High Volt Jolt (El Prado (IRE))	4	5	1	2	0	57,000
Bold Blast	Major Blast (Crafty Prospector)	3	5	1	2	1	23,410
Bold Brise	Scher Bold (Scherando)	3	6	3	1	0	22,840
Bold Connie	Bold Al (Jeblar)	3	11	0	1	1	8,707
Bold Connie	Bold Kissin Kris (Kissin Kris)	2	3	0	0	0	240
Bold Lady	Ring of Gold (Formal Gold)	3	9	3	0	1	8,910
Bold Ruritana	Raw Power (Rahy)	4	9	1	2	1	62,810
Bold Vevila	Saucy Viv (Dr. Adagio)	4	9	0	2	2	15,480
Boldly	Bravely (Tejabo)	5	2	0	0	0	3,881
Boldly Extravagant	Come With Thunder (Thunder Gulch)	2	4	0	2	2	14,030
Boldly Extravagant	Hypertension (Salt Lake)	3	1	1	0	0	34,200
Boldly Extravagant	Promenade Road (Dance Brightly)	4	11	1	2	2	41,923
Bounding Ruckus	Bound to Be Sunny (Sunny's Halo)	3	1	1	0	0	3,060
Bounding Ruckus	Kentucky Ruckus (Alphabet Soup)	5	8	1	0	0	9,387
Broadway Ruckus	Good Knight Story (Ascot Knight)	4	11	1	1	1	11,146
Broadway Ruckus	Hollywood Ending (Eagle Eyed)	6	15	4	4	1	197,174
Bucki Ruckus	J W's Ruckus (Catillac)	3	5	0	0	0	546
Buckys Red Ruckus	Run for Bucky (Foxtrail)	2	5	0	0	0	1,908
Buxton Spice	Spice Rack (Sea Wall)	3	13	1	2	3	43,322
Camomille	Capucine (Dance Brightly)	3	12	2	1	0	22,301
Candid Colours	Orphan Lover (Friendly Lover)	5	10	1	1	1	22,705
Carenage	Deputy O'Neal (Deputy Diamond)	2	3	0	0	0	1,590
Carenage	Goodbye Beautiful (Goodbye Doeny)	3	10	2	1	1	28,375
Carenage	Legs O'Neal (Nelson)	4	9	1	2	2	63,167
Carenage	Silent Ruckus (Silent King)	5	8	1	1	0	7,818
Carenage	Sutter's Ruckus (Sutter's Prospect)	6	2	0	1	0	3,884
Carolina Ruckus	Blind River Fox (Foxtrail)	2	5	0	1	1	11,499
Carolina Ruckus	Set to Sparkle (Lite the Fuse)	4	8	3	0	1	70,780
Castlemania	Battlements (Sea Wall)	4	8	0	0	2	23,546
Castlemania	Coastal Fortress (Sea Wall)	2	6	2	1	1	165,309
Castlemania	Strike the Harp (Sea Wall)	3	6	0	0	0	2,397
Cause a Ruckus	Levada (Jambalaya Jazz)	3	9	0	2	0	14,619
Cause a Ruckus	Peakaboo Peak (Pyramid Peak)	4	8	1	0	1	25,080
Celmis	Cassique (Alphabet Soup)	3	6	0	1	1	5,095
Celmis	El Sloridno (Souvenir Copy)	2	3	0	0	1	6,468
Celmis	Rheaxthus (Cozzene)	6	15	2	3	1	27,156
Celtic Harp	Faxamillion (Islefaxyou)	5	7	1	0	0	8,761
Celtic Harp	Harpist (Gold Regent)	3	11	3	0	1	33,311
Chi Sa	Appealing Ruckus (Appealing Skier)	3	5	1	1	0	9,005
Chi Sa	Lady Helma (Helmsman)	4	5	1	0	2	32,835
Clerical Crisis	Canterra (Arctic Blitz)	3	2	0	0	0	0
Coastal Ruckus	A Diligent Ruckus (Diligence)	4	14	5	4	1	33,437
Coastal Ruckus	Red Hot Tequila (Time Bandit)	3	7	2	1	0	21,570
Courageously	Attitude E. Ree (Character (GB))	4	15	0	4	2	11,582
D'Or Ruckus	Lucky Ride (Sultry Song)	6	9	3	0	3	28,678
Darley's Ruckus	Sayitain'tso Joe (Dr. Adagio)	4	6	2	3	0	41,707
Deli Cat	Slice of Glory (Langfuhr)	2	3	0	1	0	14,820
Delightful	Landler (Langfuhr)	5	4	1	0	1	22,630
Devoted Angel	Eclipsing (Comet Shine)	3	6	0	1	1	1,635
Diamond Lane	Eclipse Winner (Event of the Year)	3	9	1	3	0	25,046
Douce Douce	Dillinger (Sea Wall)	5	7	1	2	0	93,060
Douce Douce	Ease Your Mind (Allen's Prospect)	2	5	1	1	0	21,500
Douce Douce	Hands On (Friendly Lover)	3	9	1	1	4	54,080
Douce Douce	Piersixer (Sea Wall)	4	9	2	1	1	93,998
Duck Legs	Legs Legs Legs (Consigliere (GB))	3	4	1	0	0	2,970
Embur Sunshine	Embattle (Phone Trick)	5	8	1	1	0	33,381
Embur Sunshine	Texas (Meadowlake)	2	1	0	0	0	0
Fearless Vixen	Moe's Mon (Maria's Mon)	5	6	1	1	2	13,500
Florisa	Big Bloke (Trempolino)	5	5	1	2	1	17,810
Florisa	Langfleur (Langfuhr)	4	5	2	0	0	75,770
Founder's First	Sweet Share (Danzatore)	4	10	1	0	3	11,240
Francesca's Ruckus	Frank's Approval (With Approval)	8	6	0	0	0	389
Francesca's Ruckus	Scabbard (Dayjur)	3	4	0	0	1	2,760
Francesca's Ruckus	Urban Space (Barkerville)	4	9	0	0	0	1,249
Gallant Uproar	Foxtracker (Foxtrail)	2	6	0	0	0	230
Gallant Uproar	Jade's in Uproar (I Can't Believe)	3	5	1	2	0	7,200
Good Pharlap	Good Company (Quite Special)	7	12	0	2	0	10,410
Good Pharlap	Jolie Good (Mister Jolie)	4	16	5	3	1	42,588
Hillsburgh Rumors	Winter Garden (Roy)	4	6	4	2	0	353,460
Holly Ruckus	Slewpy Ruckus (Slew of Angels)	4	7	0	1	0	5,270
Holly Ruckus	Slewth Slayer (Slew of Angels)	5	4	0	0	1	1,275
Inaruckus	Brocco Bob (Brocco)	6	13	3	4	1	38,750
Indiana Jane	Dazzling Jane (Dazzling Falls)	5	2	0	1	0	4,590
Indiana Jane	Fort Ruckus (Fort Chaffee)	3	5	0	0	1	2,475
Indiana Jane	Sharp Jane (Champagneforashley)	2	1	0	0	0	0
Josella	Josey Hill (Archers Bay)	3	3	0	0	0	0
Josella	Tenantry Road (Tejano Run)	4	7	1	0	3	8,625
Julie's Ruckus	Johnnie's Crowner (Strike the Gold)	5	10	1	1	2	5,783
Julie's Ruckus	Kiss for Julie (Kissin Kris)	4	15	4	2	2	37,518
Kennisis Bold Magi	Brass Ruckus (Brass Minister)	5	4	0	0	0	104
Kennisis Bold Magi	Gusso (Editor's Note)	2	2	1	0	0	11,473
Lady Summerhill	Alyswell (Alysheba)	9	17	1	0	2	13,364
Lady Summerhill	Gastown (Ghazi)	3	11	3	2	0	65,442
Laetare	Fortunate Buy (Fortunate Prospect)	3	15	2	2	0	49,850
Lahaina Pearl	Back to Work (Signal Tap)	4	14	3	0	3	37,930
Last Reagent	Bright Reagent (Dance Brightly)	3	13	1	5	2	48,924
Last Reagent	Solina (Wild Rush)	4	2	0	1	0	6,620
Last Reagent	Wild Dare (Dare and Go)	6	12	2	2	2	25,166
Lemons Ain't Limes	Limone Forte (Dixie Brass)	4	10	2	0	1	47,505
Lemons Ain't Limes	Skyloper (Skywalker)	2	3	0	1	0	9,882

Little Star Vicky	Stark (Langfuhr)	3	5	0	1	0	6,960
Little Star Vicky	Stello (Trempolino)	4	5	1	0	1	23,128
Louvemeorleaveme	Bold Lover (Petionville)	4	6	2	1	0	12,290
Louvemeorleaveme	Friendly Departure (Friendly Lover)	5	7	2	0	2	14,682
Lucky Minister	Becky Sharp (Favorite Trick)	2	2	0	1	1	17,670
Lucky Minister	Good Luck Strikes (Smart Strike)	3	3	0	0	0	0
Lucky Minister	Lucky Tec (Technology)	6	14	3	1	3	130,569
Lucky Minister	Meadow Minister (Meadowlake)	4	6	2	0	0	67,758
Majestic Ruckus	Gold Ruckus (Gold Alert)	6	12	1	2	4	139,920
Majestic Ruckus	Majestic Deputy (Byars)	3	9	2	1	1	33,231
Majestic Ruckus	Majestic Kris (Kissin Kris)	4	7	4	1	2	45,164
Maragin	Manjrekar (Storm Creek)	3	6	0	1	0	2,965
Miss Blue Bell	Bell's Lass (Tethra)	3	7	1	1	2	64,395
Miss Traffic	Caught in Traffic (Flare Dancer)	2	1	0	0	0	78
Miyoshi	Celebrated Anna (Salt Lake)	3	1	0	0	0	0
Miyoshi	Southern Celebrity (Southern Halo)	4	8	1	0	3	10,144
Moonlit	Accra (Always a Classic)	5	11	3	0	2	25,180
Moonlit	Moonlit Romance (Romanov (IRE))	4	11	3	2	2	54,860
Most Inviting	Cattolica (Lycius)	3	19	0	1	2	5,295
Most Inviting	Don Peso (Rubiano)	2	9	0	1	1	10,400
My Intended	My Vintage Port (Porto Foricos)	3	9	2	1	4	383,302
My Intended	Swooshel (Barbeau)	6	14	3	4	0	45,867
My Sweet Country	Deputy Country (Silver Deputy)	6	10	6	0	0	171,250
My Sweet Country	Homeland (Silver Deputy)	3	2	0	0	0	960
Newest Edition	Repeat Edition (Ascot Knight)	2	3	0	1	1	14,480
No More Ruckus	Inspired Ruckus (Inspired Prospect)	2	6	0	0	0	1,634
Noon At Tom's	Noon Star (Lit de Justice)	3	0	0	1	0	3,264
Numberonetreasure	Hope On the Run (Porto Foricos)	2	1	0	0	1	6,270
Opening Bid	La Grande Mamma (Compadre)	3	5	1	1	0	65,380
Opening Bid	Master Carver (Barbeau)	4	19	2	1	2	19,044
Peek a Boo Ruckus	Deputy Ruckus (War Deputy)	4	5	0	0	0	0
Peek a Boo Ruckus	Peek a Boo Sara (Great Gladiator)	6	2	0	0	0	3,696
Petite Duchess	Bold Nxs (In Excessive Bull)	3	8	0	1	2	8,843
Petite Duchess	Silver Ace (Silver Deputy)	7	7	0	1	1	3,228
Playing Catch Up	Fortune Catcher (Fortunate Prospect)	3	16	1	2	1	20,076
Playing Catch Up	Fourtimesaruler (Formal Dinner)	4	12	2	3	3	36,410
Politely Streaking	Bella Corona (Crown Attorney)	3	10	1	1	1	21,591
Politely Streaking	Stop Looking (Dr. Adagio)	4	9	2	2	0	82,264
Positively Stompin	By the Bay (Sea Wall)	4	13	1	1	5	17,162
Praise the Lady	Devoted Lover (Friendly Lover)	3	11	1	3	2	35,740
Praise the Lady	Shout to the North (Old Topper)	2	5	2	1	0	132,292
Precocious Queen	Alghero (Unaccounted For)	4	13	3	2	3	22,119
Precocious Queen	Avellino (Premiership)	6	1	0	0	0	0
Princess Revenue	Princess Love (Friendly Lover)	4	7	0	1	0	5,970
Prone to Ruckus	Ascot Devil (Ascot Knight)	3	1	0	0	0	0
Quick Observation	Midnight Velvet (Game Plan)	3	7	0	4	1	22,460
Rainbow Memories	Dr. Mo (Maudlin)	5	9	1	3	1	31,088
Rambuckus	Howard B. (Real Quiet)	3	3	0	2	1	16,040
Reason to Ruckus	Judge Ruckus (Judge T C)	4	10	1	3	1	22,860
Reason to Ruckus	Reason for Justice (Judge T C)	5	4	0	0	0	368
Renee's Reflection	Blazing Deputy (Silver Deputy)	5	1	0	0	0	0
River Ruckus	Gold Honey (On Target)	3	1	0	0	0	0
Rolicking Rachel	Rachels Rocket (Eltish)	3	2	0	0	0	150
Rolicking Rachel	Rolickandroll (Kelly Kip)	2	3	0	0	0	1,020
Roshenara	California Kiss (Barbeau)	5	10	2	2	2	20,666
Roshenara	Real Souvenir (Crown Attorney)	3	11	1	0	3	10,194
Ruck's Beauty	Native Ruck (Native Factor)	6	13	3	3	2	31,311
Ruckin Angel	Ruckus in Court (Doneraile Court)	3	13	3	3	3	138,775
Ruckin Angel	Wings True (Is It True)	5	12	4	1	4	41,662
Ruckleberry	Believable Nemo (I Can't Believe)	2	1	0	0	0	0
Ruckleberry	Believer's Lucky (I Can't Believe)	5	9	2	1	2	45,473
Ruckleberry	Believer's Ruckus (I Can't Believe)	3	5	0	0	0	2,276
Ruckus Pette	Ruckus in Rio (Flying Down to Rio)	3	1	0	0	0	0
Ruckus Pette	Whatta Big Ruckus (Big Wig)	5	11	0	0	0	2,003
Ruckus Ridge	Mighty Ruckus (West by West)	3	5	0	0	0	317
Ruckus Ridge	Paradise Dancer (Langfuhr)	4	11	1	3	4	75,160
Ruckus Town	Rozalyn Ruckus (Siberian Summer)	4	4	0	0	0	1,600
Ruffled Rose	Prowling Wolf (Wolf Power (SAF))	3	11	1	1	1	33,591
Ruffled Rose	Rose's Echo (Eastern Echo)	4	12	0	1	1	3,931
Sarannah	Hot Little Redhead (Line In The Sand)	2	4	0	0	0	1,530
Sarannah	Maximum Degree (Jeblar)	5	13	0	0	0	657
Sarannah	Nautilus (Jeblar)	6	3	0	0	0	2,170
Sassy Ruler	Sassy Lear (Cat's Career)	3	15	2	3	4	26,561
Sassytoga	Colebrook Creek (Tricky Creek)	8	12	3	3	0	21,000
Seattle Cyrina	Action Attraction (Wild Escapade)	5	17	4	7	2	83,750
Sissy Ruckus	Doran (Dr. Schwartzman)	10	2	0	0	0	766
Slick Prospector	Sassy and Blue (Dance Brightly)	4	8	2	0	1	21,836
Soiled Dove	Obliquity (Ascot Knight)	4	7	2	0	1	98,751
South Ocean Lane	Ariel's Melody (Sea Wall)	5	8	0	2	0	29,908
Spritely Strain	Champion Ri (Distorted Humor)	4	5	1	0	1	32,610
Spritely Strain	Montana Deputy (French Deputy)	3	10	2	3	1	85,260
Spritely Strain	Tudor Court (Lord Carson)	5	5	0	0	0	1,311
Stanhope Magic	Haliburton Eva (Foxtrail)	2	6	2	1	0	56,454
Stanhope Magic	Inspired Magic (Inspired Prospect)	3	13	2	5	2	82,988
Stanhope Magic	Magic's Delight (Barbeau)	4	3	0	1	0	3,841
Studio Affair	Italian Accent (Bianconi)	3	3	0	1	0	6,460
Studio Affair	Leavethestudio (Sea Wall)	6	9	0	1	3	9,575
Studio Affair	Speak Out (Victory Speech)	4	12	3	4	3	75,930
Summer Ruckus	Excess Summer (In Excess (IRE))	4	6	1	1	2	228,200
Sweet and Silent	Not Again Dan (Green Dancer)	3	4	0	1	1	18,228
This Weeks Special	Oklahoma Natural (Northern Jay)	3	7	1	1	2	12,509
This Weeks Special	Outrider (Northern Jay)	6	9	1	1	2	6,133
Tobie Ruckus	Charming Ruckus (Silver Charm)	2	4	1	2	0	52,160
Tobie Ruckus	Psych (Mazel Trick)	3	4	0	2	2	25,270
Tobie Ruckus	Tobie Lang (Langfuhr)	4	10	2	3	2	39,976
Unique Gal	Unique Devil (Devil His Due)	5	17	0	5	2	10,695
Unique Gal	Unique Sky (Sky Classic)	3	6	0	0	0	3,762
Vin Du Paradis	Ellerbeck Street (Porto Foricos)	2	1	0	0	0	0
Voile Rouge	Fle'che Rouge (Mr. Greeley)	5	9	1	1	0	7,867
Voile Rouge	Foggia (Unaccounted For)	4	11	5	2	1	86,170
Voile Rouge	Voile Soar (Roar)	3	7	1	1	1	19,843
What'salltheruckas	Sweet Bay (Archers Bay)	3	13	1	1	1	28,022
Wolfe Island	Cypress Hill (Tri Line)	4	2	0	2	0	5,420
Yousurearebold	Afterdinnerthunder (Formal Dinner)	3	15	1	4	1	11,162
Zadracarta	Carta Gold (Touch Gold)	3	1	0	0	0	140
Zadracarta	Major Zee (Dayjur)	11	5	3	0	0	69,640
Zadracarta	Zacharov (Cool Victor)	10	10	0	4	2	22,615
Zandalusia	Cee's Irish (Cee's Tizzy)	2	5	2	2	0	93,960
Zandalusia	Zanda's Bonus (Bonus Money (GB))	3	10	3	3	0	44,125

Storm Bird, B H (1978)

By Northern Dancer – South Ocean, by New Providence

243 Performers, 132 winning performers, $6,801,246 total earnings

Mare	Progeny (Sire)	Age	Sts	1st	2d	3d	Money Won
Alydar's Storm	Two Retired Tires (Friendly Lover)	2	1	0	0	0	140
Andrea Gail	Areyoutalkintome (Smokester)	3	11	4	5	1	268,352
Andrea Gail	Call Sign Maverick (Free House)	2	8	0	1	1	9,680
April Starlight	Plunkit (Lemon Drop Kid)	2	2	0	0	0	800
Ardor	Circle Z (Wild Gold)	4	6	1	2	0	15,662
Auction Cat	Livestock Auction (Marlin)	3	6	0	0	1	1,650
Baby Sips	Gone an Done It (Wouldn't We All)	2	1	0	0	0	0
Balanchine	Gulf News (Woodman)	5	2	0	0	0	1,250
Bay Colony	Guy Getaway (Meadowlake)	3	13	1	3	3	63,020
Bay Colony	Mazel Power (Mazel Trick)	2	2	0	0	1	2,100
Beauty Coat	Punch and Beauty (Two Punch)	3	8	2	0	0	48,550
Beauty Coat	Tucan (Two Punch)	2	2	1	0	0	10,929
Beebrush	Bee a Gold Mine (Strike Gold)	6	3	2	0	0	9,270
Beebrush	My Bee Bop Baby (My Memoirs (GB))	5	6	1	0	0	8,371
Bering South	Oxford Joy (Lord Carson)	2	3	1	0	0	10,920
Big B's Secretary	Big B's Prospect (Capote's Prospect)	2	2	1	0	0	15,780
Big B's Secretary	Spanish Rioja (Patton)	3	13	0	0	1	1,650
Bird Dance	High Rhode (Rhodes)	6	4	0	0	0	368
Bird Dance	Stormy Honor (Bound by Honor)	4	10	0	1	3	3,318
Bird Dance	The Storm Trackerr (Covered Wagon)	5	2	0	0	1	561
Bird to the Wire	Tick to the Wire (Supremo)	4	3	1	0	0	4,164
Bluegrass Queen	Stormy Queen (Western Fame)	2	10	0	2	3	8,296
Boom Bird	Higher Impact (Fly Till Dawn)	9	2	1	0	0	2,460
Boom Bird	Kakapo (Silver Charm)	3	7	0	2	2	11,659
Boom Bird	Mauk Eight (Capote)	4	6	0	2	1	9,873
Bruces Blue Lou	All American Blue (Phone Trick)	4	11	0	1	2	15,677
Brutally Honest	Then Today Always (Miswaki)	3	11	1	1	1	25,628
Cent Nouvelles	Ann Dear (Grand Slam)	4	2	0	0	0	342
Centennial Time	Academy Lass (Royal Academy)	3	1	0	0	0	0
Centennial Time	Clay Time (Two Punch)	5	3	2	0	0	10,684
Centennial Time	Finisterre Rock (Miner's Mark)	8	18	1	1	1	13,179
Chimes Bird	Hawaiin Gold (Wild Rush)	3	12	3	0	2	28,484
Chimes Bird	Ringading (Gilded Time)	4	3	1	0	0	11,400
Classy Mirage	Golden Prospect (Mr. Prospector)	4	1	0	0	0	1,600
Classy Mirage	Mickey's Mirage (Deputy Minister)	3	7	1	0	0	16,810
Classy Mirage	Mike's Classic (Seeking the Gold)	5	5	3	0	1	111,200
Cruise Ticket (GB)	Welcome Aboard (Avenue of Flags)	5	12	4	1	1	22,735
Curlew	High Bird (High Brite)	3	5	0	3	0	9,647
Deanna's Special	Ashleys Art (Theatrical (IRE))	3	11	1	4	0	38,870
Deanna's Special	Corrigan (Pleasant Colony)	5	2	0	0	1	3,300
Dear Birdie	Birdstone (Grindstone)	3	6	3	0	0	1,236,600
Dear Birdie	Brave All the Way (Cryptoclearance)	9	9	1	0	2	5,500
Dear Birdie	Cviano (Rubiano)	7	6	0	1	0	1,814
Dear Birdie	So Long Birdie (Pioneering)	2	2	1	0	0	21,400
Demi Souer	City Sister (Carson City)	4	3	0	0	0	3,160
Demi Souer	Fast Decision (Gulch)	5	8	1	1	3	46,186
Demi Souer	Treasure Seeker (Gold Fever)	3	4	1	0	1	23,425
Elusive Bird	Missing Silks (Elusive Quality)	4	11	4	1	0	23,205
Encorevous	Lorenzon (Carson City)	3	4	1	0	2	11,348
Endless Storm	Ana's Lady Bird (Lord Carson)	3	2	0	0	1	6,640
Endless Storm	Endless Torrential (Torrential)	6	1	0	0	0	0
Endless Storm	Endofthestorm (Lord Carson)	5	13	2	5	2	31,430
Endless Storm	Macho Image (Clever Trick)	4	4	0	1	0	2,856
Endymion Maid	Mr. Barracuda (Rubiano)	2	4	1	1	0	22,935
Eurostorm	Man O'Mystery (Diesis (GB))	7	2	0	1	0	3,600
Exclusive Bird	Gone Exclusive (Gone West)	4	3	1	0	0	21,600
Exclusive Bird	Private Ryan (Quiet American)	7	9	1	1	1	19,537
Exclusive Bird	She's Exclusive (Pyramid Peak)	3	5	1	0	0	16,559
Extraterrestral	Alienated (Gone West)	5	2	0	0	0	1,500
Falconette	Big Head Phil (Stalwars)	5	7	2	1	0	8,588
Falconette	Win Suite (Winthrop)	3	5	0	1	0	2,165
First Flurries	Cool Days (American Chance)	2	3	1	1	0	33,500
Fixin to Storm	Barometric (Kris S.)	5	3	0	0	1	10,800
Fixin to Storm	Miffed (Artax)	3	8	1	3	1	55,002

Fixin to Storm	Northern Storm (Arch)	2	3	0	0	0	470
Flaming Gold	Flame Song (Unbridled's Song)	6	4	1	0	0	34,370
Flaming Gold	Golder Than Gold (Formal Gold)	2	5	1	1	1	31,820
Flaming Gold	Key West Sunset (Silver Deputy)	4	12	1	1	2	11,340
Flaming Gold	Striking Flames (Smart Strike)	5	10	0	0	1	1,729
Flamingo's Pride	Expert Design (Event of the Year)	3	7	1	0	4	16,779
Flamingo's Pride	Pride of the Group (General Meeting)	7	7	0	1	0	1,353
Flip the Bird	Mr. Charisma (Charismatic)	2	2	1	0	0	6,600
Flying Lauren	Jackdaw (Gulch)	3	6	1	1	0	26,347
Foufa	Certantee (Known Fact)	7	1	0	1	0	5,600
Foufa	Foufa's Warrior (Jade Hunter)	4	8	1	2	2	113,140
Foufa	Full Brush (Broad Brush)	9	4	0	1	0	4,700
Give a Toast	Juventus (Mazel Trick)	3	4	1	0	0	15,360
Good Taste	A Spire a Dream (Marquetry)	3	14	1	3	0	15,715
Good Taste	Good and Crafty (Crafty Prospector)	2	5	0	0	2	7,100
Halcyon Bird (IRE)	Miss Paranoid (Honor Grades)	3	7	1	1	3	20,095
Highland Legend	Hanover Hollywood (Gulch)	7	2	0	0	0	281
Highland Legend	High Potential (Pleasant Colony)	5	1	0	0	1	1,812
Highland Legend	Personal Legend (Awesome Again)	4	8	3	2	1	224,330
Honolua Bay	Honolua Storm (Old Trieste)	3	10	3	0	2	161,157
Indian Ocean	Snowball Flannagan (Affirmed)	9	4	2	1	0	67,250
Indian Sunset	Quick Action (Carson City)	3	11	2	2	1	133,140
Indian Sunset	Space Hero (Cape Canaveral)	2	3	0	3	0	23,400
Jo Go Dancer	Barry Line (Botanic)	7	2	0	0	0	684
Just a Bird	Dynamite Flyer (Dynaformer)	3	4	3	0	0	73,564
Karri Valley	Trebizond (IRE) (Sadler's Wells)	8	6	0	0	0	5,200
Knoosh	Anja (Gulch)	4	6	1	1	0	14,934
Lady for Two	Casual Fashion (General Meeting)	3	8	1	0	3	19,100
Lady for Two	Deep Thunder (Gulch)	5	10	1	1	0	7,206
Lady of Choice	Decided (Coronado's Quest)	3	4	0	2	1	3,880
Lady of Choice	Dr. Walsh (Gulch)	4	15	2	3	1	60,222
Lady of Choice	Lemon Lady (Lemon Drop Kid)	2	4	0	0	0	3,254
Lady of Choice	Multiple Choice (Mt. Livermore)	6	14	1	4	1	123,008
Lady of Mine	Chairman of Vice (Woodman)	4	3	0	0	0	189
Line of Thunder	Delacroix (Gulch)	4	6	1	1	0	39,723
Louisiana Band	Branded in Gold (Formal Gold)	2	6	2	1	1	40,400
Louisiana Band	Golden Louisia (Formal Gold)	4	6	2	0	0	11,010
Louisiana Band	Music City Girl (Formal Gold)	3	10	1	1	1	8,440
Lovely Martha	Port Henry (Conquistador Cielo)	6	18	2	4	4	50,625
Lovely Martha	Sand Springs (Dynaformer)	4	7	1	1	1	143,756
Low Pressure	Cedar Summer (Souvenir Copy)	3	10	1	0	3	39,210
Maremaid	Glitter Maid (Glitterman)	4	10	3	3	0	31,360
Maremaid	Maid for Speed (Phone Trick)	2	8	1	4	1	33,390
Maremaid	Tea Is Served (Boston Harbor)	3	3	0	0	0	0
Mariscal	Catch Confide (Confide)	3	2	0	0	0	210
Marozia	Andromeda's Hero (Fusaichi Pegasus)	2	2	1	0	1	17,300
Middle Course	Aurora Gold (Mutakddim)	4	11	1	1	3	8,661
Middle Course	Sanskrit (Pancho Villa)	11	6	0	3	0	3,510
Middle Course	Tonyrony (Marquetry)	6	15	1	2	3	12,867
Midway Squall	British Attitude (Broad Brush)	2	1	0	0	0	0
Midway Squall	Itchetucknee (Carson City)	4	12	1	3	0	21,533
Migrate	Honorable Path (Honour and Glory)	2	3	1	0	1	14,532
Miss Madisyn Rose	Christian Gulch (Gulch)	4	15	0	1	1	8,170
Miss Popularity	Go Go Wild (Wild Event)	3	1	0	0	0	154
Miss Popularity	Paralegal (Skip Trial)	7	4	0	0	1	1,030
Miss Tenenholtz	Class Ack (Sky Classic)	2	2	0	0	1	4,420
Miss Tenenholtz	Extra Check (Chequer)	5	8	0	2	2	20,136
Miss Tenenholtz	Extra Fit (Fit to Fight)	4	15	2	5	1	76,070
Miss Tenenholtz	Margie Golden (Golden Gear)	3	4	0	0	0	142
Moon Tide	Lemon Bar (Lemon Drop Kid)	2	2	1	1	0	24,680
Namaqua	Goodnight Trail (Gulch)	7	4	1	1	1	6,395
Namaqua	Kaskazi (Kris S.)	3	5	1	0	0	30,367
Olympic Storm	Olympic Emblem (Our Emblem)	3	6	2	1	0	35,340
Olympic Storm	Storm Gulch (Gulch)	4	15	2	2	3	27,465
Oogie Poogie	Dial for Dollars (Woodman)	8	14	1	1	2	7,151
Oogie Poogie	I'm a Goer (Favorite Trick)	4	3	0	0	0	340
Oogie Poogie	Oogie (Mazel Trick)	3	3	0	1	0	950
Outsource	Call Me Chief (Chief Seattle)	2	5	0	1	0	4,690
Outsource	Commentator (Distorted Humor)	3	5	5	0	0	180,692
Pacific Squall	Campionessa (A.P. Indy)	2	2	0	0	0	2,760
Pacific Squall	Nor'wester (A.P. Indy)	3	9	0	1	3	28,220
Pacific Squall	Sea Storm (Gulch)	7	12	2	1	1	27,866
Pacific Squall	Wind Sand n' Stars (Gone West)	4	4	0	0	0	192
Pasque Flower	Wolf Running (Wolf Power (SAF))	3	4	0	0	0	440
Pasque Flower	Wood Lily (American Chance)	7	15	2	3	2	21,910
Pay Bird	Sea Swallow (Houston)	2	3	0	0	0	540
Petit Oiseau	Samsville (Barkerville)	4	24	3	1	2	5,051
Petit Oiseau	Stormin Scooter (Canvas)	2	5	0	0	2	1,617
Petit Oiseau	Stormin' Oiseau (Pioneering)	6	9	1	4	2	10,020
Petit Oiseau	Sure Delite (Petionville)	3	3	0	0	0	105
Pocket Beauty	Northern Concorde (Concorde's Tune)	2	5	1	1	0	32,450
Precious Parrot	Birdland (Hazaam)	4	14	2	1	2	18,380
Precious Parrot	Johnny Tornado (Lycius)	3	9	0	0	1	7,419
Queen's Visit	Sandylikethebeach (Tomorrows Cat)	3	5	0	1	1	2,685
Rainy Day Woman	Party Boy (Go for Gin)	5	4	0	1	0	2,120
Rajas Secret	C C Ryder (American Chance)	2	1	0	0	0	126
Raven Runner	Crafty Runner (Crafty Prospector)	7	10	1	1	1	8,665
Red Rock Lake	Method Actor (De Niro)	4	8	1	0	0	7,897
Red Rock Lake	Waconda Lake (Fantastic Fellow)	3	3	0	0	0	990
Red Soul	My Muchacha (Honour and Glory)	2	5	0	1	1	9,582
Red Soul	Paris Sunrise (Cape Town)	4	3	0	1	0	11,450
Rewarding	Gift Wrap (Pleasant Colony)	4	3	0	0	0	2,327
Rewarding	Upswing (Saint Ballado)	3	4	0	0	0	281
Rogatien	Glacken Bird (Smoke Glacken)	2	8	0	0	1	5,055
Rosebird	Peekaboo Cat (Crafty Prospector)	3	5	0	0	0	1,560
Samba Storm	Kinnelon (Our Emblem)	5	5	2	0	1	23,145
Samba Storm	Seneca Storm (Seneca Jones)	2	1	0	0	0	0
Savannah's Honor	Grand Storm (Grand Slam)	3	5	1	0	1	11,690
Secret Harbor	Charming Jim (Silver Charm)	3	13	2	3	2	70,630
Secret Harbor	Downtime (Favorite Trick)	4	11	1	2	2	28,740
Shared Emotion	Golden Authority (Acceptable)	4	12	1	0	2	11,713
Shared Emotion	Logansport (Rahy)	3	9	1	2	2	16,264
Sooty Tern	Logan Field (Boston Harbor)	5	10	1	1	0	9,494
Star Bird	Bizzy Trick (Mazel Trick)	2	8	2	1	0	49,730
Star Bird	The Editor's Son (Mr. Greeley)	5	10	2	3	2	51,930
Starfire	Fever Fire (Gold Fever)	3	14	1	0	3	12,580
Starlet Storm	Capital Spending (A.P. Indy)	4	12	2	4	1	107,515
Steady Gaze	Raise the Stripes (Pembroke)	4	3	0	1	0	8,910
Stone Flower	Lucky Ransom (Red Ransom)	2	1	0	0	0	161
Stone Flower	Royal Walk (Mr. Prospector)	4	1	0	0	0	400
Storm Alley	Twister Alley (Comstock Lode)	3	7	0	2	3	16,860
Storm Attack	Center (Gulch)	5	8	1	4	1	24,906
Storm Attack	Raid (Pioneering)	3	4	0	0	0	114
Storm Attack	Wild Bill Hiccup (Carson City)	4	14	5	0	2	61,040
Storm Berry	Black Ties Ferrari (Black Tie Affair (Ire))	8	4	0	0	0	186
Storm Berry	Stormin Tammy (Tamayaz)	5	2	0	0	0	0
Storm Bride	Distant Venture (Geiger Counter)	9	1	0	0	0	0
Storm in Sight	Andrew the Man (Carson City)	7	11	2	0	2	20,942
Storm o' Fire	Fiery Diablo (Diablo)	6	7	2	3	0	59,400
Storm o' Fire	Wha'pa (Victory Gallop)	3	5	0	1	1	6,960
Storm Riding	Audrey Hep (Crafty Prospector)	4	7	1	0	3	50,865
Storm Struck	Paragon Queen (Lord Carson)	2	7	1	4	0	85,540
Storm Struck	Savannah's Gold (Gold Fever)	3	6	1	0	0	5,580
Storm Teal	Gold Storm (Seeking the Gold)	4	8	3	1	2	207,300
Storm's Award	Stormy Conquest (Conquistador Cielo)	5	10	1	1	3	17,516
Storm's Honor	Rocaco (Geiger Counter)	7	3	1	2	0	19,160
Stormfeather	Devils Disciple (Devil His Due)	2	5	3	2	0	161,800
Stormfeather	Girl Gone Crazy (Roar)	3	4	0	0	0	315
Stormin Diamond A	Jake Skate (Arch)	4	10	3	4	2	139,320
Stormin Diamond A	Katestormedthebird (Out of Place)	3	4	2	0	0	41,900
Stormin Diamond A	Rotunda Beauty (Phone Trick)	5	11	2	2	0	11,209
Storming Up	Caiman (Malibu Moon)	3	16	2	1	1	80,732
Stormwilhit	Sir Norman (Brentwood Style)	5	5	0	0	0	125
Stormy Agreement	Risky Agreement (King of Kings (IRE))	2	2	0	0	0	0
Stormy Bend	Candybedandy (Holy Bull)	4	11	3	2	3	101,700
Stormy Bend	Minnie's Meadow (Affirmed)	3	11	1	0	1	28,239
Stormy Bend	Speedy Ransom (Red Ransom)	5	5	0	0	0	925
Stormy Divorce	False Promises (Jules)	4	7	0	1	1	37,346
Stormy Divorce	Time to Divorce (Halo's Image)	2	6	2	3	1	42,141
Stormy Jewel	Thunder Point (Thunder Gulch)	2	1	0	0	0	307
Stormy Lass	Astutely (Crafty Friend)	3	5	0	0	0	1,400
Stormy Lass	Savethebestforlass (Crafty Friend)	2	4	1	1	1	21,300
Stormy Moment	Cherokee's Moment (Cherokee Run)	3	1	0	1	0	1,600
Stormy Moment	Navesink View (Holy Bull)	5	4	1	0	1	10,500
Stormy Moment	No Approval Needed (Lasting Approval)	4	9	0	2	0	3,134
Stormy Moud	American Moud (Quiet American)	3	10	1	0	1	9,516
Stormy Moud	American Ruler (Quiet American)	2	4	2	0	0	13,145
Stormy Reflection	Flip Side (Devil His Due)	2	5	1	1	1	9,214
Stormy Squab	Stormsabrewin (Rahy)	4	5	0	0	0	1,222
Stylish Storm	Stylish N Adorable (Grand Slam)	3	5	2	1	1	30,170
Suddenly Sydney	Buckeye Bound (Bound by Honor)	2	4	0	0	0	1,383
Suddenly Sydney	Distorted Humor Jr (Distorted Humor)	4	1	0	0	0	0
Sunward Soaring	Mr. Marquet Maker (Marquetry)	2	3	0	0	0	236
Suspicious Storm	Hanover Storm (Raffie's Majesty)	3	5	0	2	0	5,570
Suspicious Storm	Raffie's Storm (Raffie's Majesty)	4	6	0	1	0	13,310
Sweet Tease	Bucyrus (Rahy)	3	11	2	0	2	30,540
Umbrella	Cotinga (Silver Hawk)	2	1	0	0	0	0
Umbrella	Parachute (Polish Numbers)	3	6	0	0	1	3,234
Victoriana	Vicereine (GB) (Zamindar)	4	4	0	1	1	16,438
Wajibird	Mel's Marque (Marquetry)	7	11	2	0	0	15,438
Wajibird	No Regular Cat (Cat Doctor)	3	12	2	2	1	10,982
Wander Storm	Glitter Storm (Glitterman)	4	3	0	0	0	144
Wander Storm	Wander Time (Gilded Time)	3	6	1	1	0	11,540
Water Street	Miss Adams (Quiet American)	3	11	2	1	2	28,963
Water Street	Pontoosuc (Coronado's Quest)	2	2	0	0	0	840
Weekend Storm	City Weekend (Carson City)	2	1	0	0	0	150
Weekend Storm	Storm Strip (Comic Strip)	3	2	0	0	2	9,200
Westwood	Clapton (Fly So Free)	8	8	1	0	1	14,402
Westwood	Less Talk (Crafty Friend)	2	3	1	0	0	6,300
Westwood	Spring's Glory (Honour and Glory)	3	4	1	2	0	24,200
Westwood	Stormy Surprise (Mr. Greeley)	5	9	1	1	1	9,341
Windmill Point	Exclamation (Capote)	3	1	0	0	0	400
Windmill Point	Sugar Mags (Miswaki)	7	8	1	2	0	18,834
Wings of a Storm	Cryptic Storm (Cryptoclearance)	5	12	0	3	2	3,828
Wings of a Storm	Mistys Dark Angel (Traitor)	4	7	0	0	0	2,557
Winterland	Dee's Little Dee (Gulch)	2	2	0	0	0	1,350
Youwantmetodowhat	Dr Silver Packet (Artax)	3	9	1	0	0	10,480
Youwantmetodowhat	In the Wildzone (Wild Zone)	6	4	0	0	0	450
Youwantmetodowhat	Paparazzi (Press Card)	5	7	4	0	1	56,520

Danzig, B H (1977)

By Northern Dancer – Pas de Nom, by Admiral's Voyage

176 Performers, 96 winning performers, $6,762,695 total earnings

Mare	Progeny (Sire)	Age	Sts	1st	2d	3d	Money Won
A Dancing Fable	Tincan Too (Barkerville)	4	8	0	2	1	20,140
A Dancing Fable	Took Out (Barkerville)	5	7	1	1	1	32,710
Absolute Trust	Quies (Quiet American)	3	6	1	1	1	43,900
Adelphi	She's the Ticket (Conquistador Cielo)	4	9	3	0	3	30,410
Agneshka	Miss Delia (Out of Place)	4	10	0	1	1	12,275
Agneshka	Wild Chase (Wild Event)	3	2	0	0	0	280
Ameriflora	Wonder Again (Silver Hawk)	5	5	2	0	1	611,767
Amirati	Amber Myth (Holy Bull)	4	1	0	0	0	145
Anarine	Archer County (Temperence Hill)	9	5	0	0	0	0
Anarine	Roar Like a Lion (Roar)	3	8	2	1	0	12,626
Anna Sterz	Matt's a Giant (Giant's Causeway)	2	2	0	0	0	1,440
Atuf	Golazo (Sahm)	3	5	1	0	0	10,825
Atuf	Ingles (Kayrawan)	4	10	5	2	1	67,235
Aurora	Aztec Pearl (A.P. Indy)	5	5	0	2	2	38,080
Aurora	Mukhtaser (Kris S.)	4	3	0	0	0	2,887
Bahrain Star	Woodman's Star (Woodman)	3	12	0	3	0	18,123
Baltic Sea	Caller One (Phone Trick)	7	1	0	0	1	5,500
Baltic Sea	Unbridled Sidney (Unbridled's Song)	3	6	2	2	0	69,020
Battle Hymn	Glory Hymn (Mr. Prospector)	4	6	1	1	0	15,410
Bering Cruise	Lieutenant Danz (Gold Fever)	2	4	2	0	1	36,080
Black Tie Kiss	Argento (More Than Ready)	2	2	0	0	0	258
Bravalma	Sweet Go (Dare and Go)	3	3	0	1	0	3,100
Cash Deal	Casmon (Maria's Mon)	2	3	0	1	0	5,750
Cielo's Dance	Cielo's Cat (Tale of the Cat)	3	5	1	2	0	9,100
Cielo's Dance	Cute Operator (Phone Trick)	2	4	1	2	0	33,940
Cluster	Urban Warrior (Cape Town)	3	3	0	0	0	810
Contredance	North Place (Out of Place)	3	8	0	0	2	5,452
Danara	Danaslam (Grand Slam)	2	1	0	0	0	370
Danara	Tina's Love (Unbridled's Song)	3	4	0	0	1	5,800
Dance Smartly	Dance to Destiny (Mr. Prospector)	5	2	0	1	1	11,880
Dance Smartly	Dance With Ravens (A.P. Indy)	2	3	1	1	1	223,820
Dance Swiftly	Paiota Falls (Kris S.)	3	5	4	1	0	177,354
Dancing Party	Crafty Boo (Crafty Friend)	3	3	0	0	0	324
Dancing Reef	Silver Illusion (Silver Ghost)	5	4	0	0	0	0
Dancing Style	Dance for Fun (Devil His Due)	6	1	1	0	0	3,720
Dancing Style	Keep 'Em Up There (Avenue of Flags)	3	9	0	0	1	8,471
Dancing Style	Stylish Sensation (Half a Year)	7	11	1	1	3	2,912
Dancing With Wings	Parasail (Smart Strike)	4	4	1	1	0	51,740
Dancing With Wings	Soaring Free (Smart Strike)	5	8	6	0	0	1,113,862
Dancing With Wings	Soaring Strike (Smart Strike)	2	2	1	0	0	15,900
Dans l'Argent	Silver Plata (Conquistador Cielo)	2	2	1	0	0	23,550
Dans l'Argent	Silver Shine (Gold Fever)	5	13	2	1	4	29,550
Danzig Darling	Grey Beard (Unbridled's Song)	5	13	1	3	0	82,093
Danzig Island	High Strike Zone (Smart Strike)	4	9	4	2	2	98,710
Danzig's Beauty	Secret Quest (Coronado's Quest)	3	1	0	0	0	130
Danzig's Bride	Lost Bride (Pioneering)	3	12	6	0	1	133,785
Danzig's Bride	Tropical Heatwave (Twining)	4	2	0	0	0	1,090
Danzig's Juliette	Sabre Rattling (Valid Expectations)	3	9	1	1	1	18,015
Danzig's Peach	Polly Peabody (Hadif)	3	5	0	0	1	2,125
Danzig's Song	Carmalley (Miner's Mark)	4	6	1	0	1	6,810
Danzig's Song	Cryptologic (Cryptoclearance)	6	15	1	1	1	6,038
Danzing Crown	House of Danzing (Chester House)	2	2	0	1	0	9,940
Dazzling Bright	Ms Freddie Bright (Peruvian)	4	11	2	3	1	17,939
Dispute	Disrupt (Deputy Minister)	4	1	0	0	0	0
Doubles Match	Up to Date News (Unbridled)	4	5	1	1	1	8,955
Doubles Match	Varian (Gulch)	7	16	2	3	4	16,377
Dream Scheme	Perfect Timing (Deputy Minister)	4	5	0	0	1	8,730
Dual Blessing	Mark's Miner (Miner's Mark)	6	2	0	0	0	480
Elhasna	Karis Makaw (Charismatic)	3	5	2	2	1	45,623
Elhasna	Taraf (Deputy Minister)	5	3	0	0	1	1,275
Erandel	Runspastum (Woodman)	7	2	0	0	0	1,180
Everhope	Extra (A.P. Indy)	4	6	0	0	0	3,360
Everhope	Indy Future (A.P. Indy)	3	8	1	2	0	53,247
Exultation	Find the Mine (Geiger Counter)	9	5	0	0	0	1,458
Fabulous Babs	Fabulous Fraser (Fraser River)	5	11	1	1	0	2,490
Fabulous Babs	Nitro Chip (Finest Hour)	3	7	2	0	3	99,420
Flora Danica	Alnbill (Miesque's Son)	5	11	1	1	1	5,359
Flora Danica	Escapade (Tactical Cat)	3	10	3	1	2	18,064
Free City	Free Strike (Smart Strike)	3	14	1	1	1	11,741
Freedom of Speech	Serene Place (Out of Place)	3	8	1	3	2	28,983
Freedom of Speech	T. D. Vance (Rahy)	2	2	1	0	0	20,610
Freedom of Speech	Unalienable Right (Irish River (FR))	7	4	0	1	1	7,900
Gdansk's Honour	Ecology (Unbridled's Song)	3	2	0	0	0	0
Gear	Auto Pilot (Kingmambo)	3	6	1	0	0	31,580
George Sand	Ima Gentleman (Gentlemen (ARG))	4	2	0	0	0	354
George Sand	Valentine Parade (Parade Ground)	2	2	1	0	0	3,190
Giles' Girl	John's Dixie Chic (Seattle Sleet)	2	1	0	0	0	0
Hang the Moon	Atria (Atticus)	3	4	1	0	0	22,590
Harbor Island	Hasty Star (Woodman)	5	11	0	1	1	5,015
Honoria	Colonial Power (Pleasant Colony)	10	2	0	0	0	0
Honoria	Munchkin (A.P. Indy)	4	3	1	1	0	41,090
Jode	Schedule (GB) (Brian's Time)	3	8	2	3	0	102,240
Just About Enough	Go On Forever (Metfield)	7	6	0	1	1	4,312
Juta's Fame	Skake Em (Miner's Mark)	6	16	2	3	1	38,521
Juta's Fame	Special Fame (Exploit)	3	5	0	1	0	6,870
Juta's Fame	Tracemark (Conquistador Cielo)	5	13	2	1	1	16,400
Lady Danz	Miss Thunderella (Thunder Gulch)	2	2	0	0	0	330
Le Grand Epic	Queen Kennelot (Awesome Again)	3	1	0	0	0	0
Linguist	Speechmaker (Benchmark)	4	4	0	1	1	3,660
Lotka	Indolent (Conquistador Cielo)	3	1	0	0	0	0
Lotka	Ravine Rose (Gulch)	4	2	0	0	1	2,750
Lucky Port	Cut Me In (Seeking the Gold)	6	9	0	1	0	8,770
Mahasin	Haasil (IRE) (Machiavellian)	6	6	1	1	0	18,320
Mariuka	Lydgate (Pulpit)	4	5	1	2	0	97,374
Mariuka	Mystic Speed (Miswaki)	3	2	0	0	0	0
Midnight Polka	Capability (Acceptable)	3	1	1	0	0	16,240
Midnight Polka	Four Pennies (Gulch)	5	1	0	0	0	0
Min Elreeh	Silvermin (Silver Deputy)	4	14	2	3	1	20,435
Moments of Magic	Red Rabbit Run (Red Ransom)	2	7	0	1	1	5,050
Mount Helena (GB)	Heavy Traffic (Elusive Quality)	3	1	0	0	0	780
My Fling	Grafton (Rahy)	4	8	2	1	3	105,900
My Fling	Poise (Sword Dance (IRE))	5	9	3	1	1	41,123
Nimble Feet	Top Gate (Saint Ballado)	3	2	1	0	0	31,945
Our Honoree	Backhaul (Relaunch)	7	6	1	1	1	7,287
Pamzig	Carr Queen (Carr de Naskra)	7	10	2	2	1	33,257
Peg's Puffin	Peg's Thunder (Thunder Gulch)	2	3	0	0	0	175
Personal Colors	Jenkins' Ferry (Miswaki)	4	9	1	3	2	21,385
Pledge the Fifth	Mixed Message (Gulch)	3	1	0	0	0	1,980
Pledge the Fifth	Pledge for Allen (Allen's Prospect)	2	2	1	0	0	11,970
Polish Dame	Zig's Quiet Lady (Quiet American)	6	11	0	3	2	10,630
Polish Holiday	Broadway Johnny (Miswaki)	6	14	1	2	0	12,670
Polish Maid	T E Jones (Grand Slam)	4	4	1	0	0	20,680
Polish Treaty	Hot to Tango (Kingmambo)	5	9	1	1	0	11,420
Poundzig	Wood Pound (Woodman)	8	7	1	2	0	16,110
Pride of Darby	Five Straight (Roy)	7	14	3	2	0	12,948
Princess Polonia	Molto Vita (Carson City)	4	8	3	2	0	220,730
Queen of Bermuda	Azure (Bright Launch)	6	8	2	0	2	23,726
Queen of Bermuda	Mr. Word (Mongol Warrior)	3	11	1	1	1	5,665
Radiola	Makewayforbighoss (Apalachee)	9	7	4	2	0	5,079
Recital	Silent Majority (Real Quiet)	3	8	2	1	0	22,381
Redzig	In Sync (Gilded Time)	7	4	0	3	0	7,068
Rim	Flange (Unbridled)	3	3	0	1	0	5,096
Ropa Usada	A's Anchorman (Smart Strike)	5	10	1	2	1	10,135
Ropa Usada	Our Josephina (Tale of the Cat)	4	10	3	2	2	179,414
Royal Jubilation	Bell Court (Chester House)	2	1	0	0	0	184
Rumoosh	Right Revved (Rahy)	10	6	0	1	3	5,736
Sawara (GB)	Japanese Whisper (UAE) (Machiavellian)	3	1	1	0	0	5,520
Sawara (GB)	Maiden Tower (GB) (Groom Dancer)	4	1	0	0	0	3,000
Scipio	Tax (Artax)	2	3	1	0	0	13,800
Selling Sunshine	Sunrise Slew (Seattle Slew)	4	4	1	0	1	14,410
Ship n' Shore	Governor's Pride (Housebuster)	7	10	3	1	1	56,750
Ship n' Shore	Xtreamotion (Marquetry)	3	5	0	0	1	10,470
Silent Classic	Classic Boom (Boone's Mill)	4	10	0	0	1	1,694
Silent Classic	Classic Home (Home At Last)	3	6	1	1	0	3,912
Sir Line	Escalade (Broad Brush)	7	12	2	4	3	10,457
Sister Crown	Shine Forth (Carson City)	5	3	0	0	0	1,281
Smolensk	Mostly (A.P. Indy)	3	2	0	0	0	3,460
Subtle Blend	Force One (Cahill Road)	2	1	0	0	0	0
Subtle Blend	Illusive Force (Yoonevano)	4	10	2	3	2	137,217
Sudden Sun	House Alarm (Chester House)	2	2	0	0	1	1,100
Sudden Sun	Soaring (Boston Harbor)	3	12	2	3	2	23,176
Sugar Nipper	Gilded Nip (Gilded Time)	5	7	0	0	4	25,520
Sugar Nipper	Irish Nip (Irish River (FR))	8	14	3	1	3	31,930
Sweet Lexy May	Dixie Boy (Southern Halo)	3	16	2	3	3	72,480
Sweet Lexy May	Fortune Writers (Kris S.)	4	3	1	1	0	39,050
Tension Point	Vinotech (Smoke Glacken)	2	3	2	1	0	39,400
Tension Point	Your Add (Tactical Advantage)	4	1	0	0	0	0
Tomisue's Dancer	Our Friend Timmy (Stephen Got Even)	2	5	1	0	1	37,420
Tomisue's Dancer	Stand United (Gulch)	4	19	2	6	0	20,115
Tomisue's Girl	Toscanini (Charismatic)	3	11	1	0	0	5,021
Valiant Sweetheart	Always Valiant (Home At Last)	4	9	2	1	1	21,185
Valiant Sweetheart	Be Valiant (Lord Avie)	8	10	0	2	1	7,084
Valiant Sweetheart	Valiant King (Home At Last)	5	3	1	1	0	20,660
Valiant Sweetheart	Valiant Queen (Lord Avie)	3	6	1	0	1	22,745
Versailles Treaty	Negotiation (Coronado's Quest)	4	7	0	0	2	8,388
Versailles Treaty	Saarland (Unbridled)	5	4	0	2	0	39,550
Warta	Dynawave (Dynaformer)	5	3	0	1	0	2,530
Warta	Miss Memento (Souvenir Copy)	3	3	1	2	0	24,400
Why Go On Dreaming	African Skyline (Saint Ballado)	5	8	2	1	1	39,300
Why Go On Dreaming	Duke Wilson (Defrere)	3	5	0	0	0	106
Winters' Love	Campaigner (Gulch)	5	11	2	2	1	22,580
Wisla	Confirmed Temper (Kris S.)	3	2	0	1	0	1,770
Wisla	Glimmer Twin (Kris S.)	4	6	0	1	1	10,520
Wisla	River Kenmare (Unbridled's Song)	2	3	0	1	0	4,800
Zigabout	Can't Buy Class (Elusive Quality)	3	11	0	5	2	39,710
Zigabout	Edith Prickley (Cape Canaveral)	2	4	0	1	0	33,780
Zigabout	It's About Silver (Silver Deputy)	5	7	0	1	2	16,253
Zigember	John N Tom (Gulch)	6	1	0	0	0	300
Zigember	The Cliff's Edge (Gulch)	3	8	1	4	2	1,010,000
Zigland	Affordability (Unbridled)	4	3	1	1	0	20,526
Zigland	Favorite Times (Souvenir Copy)	3	6	3	3	0	54,930
Zignut	Canyon Dan (Gulch)	3	2	0	0	0	176
Zigor	Chickaroo (Indian Charlie)	4	17	3	2	3	24,220
Zigor	He's in the House (Out of Place)	3	1	1	0	0	11,970
Zuri	Cartoonist (Comic Strip)	3	1	0	0	1	4,600
Zuri	Prospectors Strike (Smart Strike)	5	12	2	0	1	24,121

Kris S., Dk B H (1977)
By Roberto – Sharp Queen, by Princequillo

221 Performers, 118 winning performers, $6,471,678 total earnings

Mare	Progeny (Sire)	Age	Sts	1st	2d	3d	Money Won
Aleyna's Love	We All Love Aleyna (Nines Wild)	3	14	6	1	1	188,020
Aleyna's Love	Who's Aleyna (Star of Valor)	2	6	0	1	3	16,320
Alie S	Krismas (Siyah Kalem)	4	5	0	0	0	3,040
All Hat	Countinonamiracle (Silver Ghost)	3	1	0	0	0	0
And Guess What	Seapoint (Crafty Friend)	2	1	0	0	0	400
Annora Springs	Spring Stroll (Skywalker)	3	3	0	1	1	11,400
Appealing Kris	Gentleman Player (Gentlemen (ARG))	3	3	0	0	0	550
Appealing Kris	Rahys' Appeal (Rahy)	2	4	1	1	0	38,206
Ballerina Queen	Ballet King (Cryptoclearance)	3	7	1	0	1	19,556
Bird Cage	Caged Glory (Honour and Glory)	2	1	0	0	0	0
Bird Cage	Greedy Executive (Siphon (BRZ))	3	18	3	1	4	26,011
Blessed Kris	Chronicle S. (Notebook)	9	5	2	0	0	9,520
British Bauble	Royal Place (Out of Place)	4	10	2	1	2	137,696
British Bauble	She's Booked (Notebook)	3	14	1	3	4	27,540
Calamity	Ra Der Dean (Rahy)	4	15	1	4	2	22,010
Canadian Kris	Krissbequick (Dumaani)	3	11	0	2	1	13,860
Cartakris	Cadenhead (Iskandar Elakbar)	7	10	1	2	3	38,580
Cartakris	Highland Gardens (Cool Victor)	8	4	1	0	0	4,288
Cartakris	Roman Romance (San Romano)	6	10	1	0	2	103,750
Chauffeurette	Grooms Trouble (Groomstick)	2	7	1	0	1	20,930
Class Kris	Gradepoint (A.P. Indy)	3	3	2	0	0	108,000
Class Kris	Student Council (Kingmambo)	2	3	0	0	0	2,758
Clean Up Kris	Nashua's Launch (Bright Launch)	4	5	1	0	0	8,450
Clean Up Kris	Ohbeegeewhyen (Doc's Leader)	3	8	1	0	0	33,067
Cristina	Polar Sparkel (Quiet American)	3	9	0	0	1	5,473
Crossing Over	Formal Pass (Formal Dinner)	3	12	2	1	4	50,440
Crossing Over	No More Chads (Atticus)	5	12	2	2	6	76,700
Cruising Kris	Bold Kris (Bold Executive)	5	14	1	0	0	44,748
Cruising Kris	Cruising Executive (Bold Executive)	4	10	0	0	1	14,500
Cruising Kris	Cruising for Gold (Strike a Gold Mine)	3	2	0	0	0	0
Cruising Kris	Stormy Kristine (Storm Creek)	2	2	0	0	0	0
Dancin Kris	Aggressive Dixie (Dixie Power)	5	7	1	1	3	9,614
Dancin Kris	Showmesomelove (Montbrook)	3	11	2	0	5	71,430
Departing Ms. S.	Hang Up Call (Phone Trick)	4	4	3	0	0	25,528
Departing Ms. S.	Never Ending Tale (Tale of the Cat)	3	8	1	0	0	8,673
Diane G	Mollyputthepeaches (Dance Brightly)	3	2	0	0	0	1,185
Doe River	Immediately (Broad Brush)	3	4	0	0	0	1,593
Doe River	Ugotta (Seattle Slew)	2	5	1	1	0	15,510
Empress of China	China Princess (Corslew)	4	7	1	1	2	37,452
Empress of China	Chinese Checkers (Game Plan)	2	3	2	0	0	32,448
Empress of China	San Miguel Boy (Corslew)	3	8	1	0	0	12,654
Empress of China	Tewkin (Corslew)	6	15	0	2	2	8,502
Episode	Path (Coronado's Quest)	4	1	0	0	0	360
Erie Dearie	Confirmed (Unbridled's Song)	3	11	3	6	1	154,137
Erie Dearie	Passionate Dancer (Cat Thief)	2	1	0	0	1	4,700
Ever Hasty	Get the Doc (Unreal Zeal)	5	1	0	0	0	0
Ever Hasty	Irish Freckles (Unreal Zeal)	3	8	0	0	0	2,380
F Sharp	Mendham (Meadow Flight)	6	5	2	2	0	18,920
Fair Kris	Fairly Crafty (Crafty Prospector)	4	15	3	3	2	142,144
Firey Prospect	Burning Fever (Stormin Fever)	3	2	1	0	1	26,270
Flowers Kris S.	Allen's Dream (Exploit)	2	2	1	0	0	13,240
Flowers Kris S.	Harboringfugitives (Boston Harbor)	3	2	0	0	0	324
French Kriss	Miss Dakota (Never Wavering)	4	4	0	1	0	2,720
Gandhara	Okaya (Lycius)	3	9	2	2	1	29,208
Gotta Wear Shades	Alotacherokee (Cherokee Run)	3	6	1	2	1	14,520
Gotta Wear Shades	Macho Bean (French Deputy)	5	5	0	1	1	2,815
Gotta Wear Shades	Me in Shades (Belong to Me)	4	9	2	1	0	48,880
Gravel Queen	Absolute Rocks (Doneraile Court)	3	8	0	1	0	8,035
Great Lady Mary	Giant Slam (Grand Slam)	4	4	2	1	0	15,795
Gris Gris Gal	Sea Scout (Once a Sailor)	4	4	0	0	1	1,410
Hail Kris	Hailey (Petionville)	3	1	0	0	1	977
Haunting	Cry of the Wild (Unbridled's Song)	3	6	0	2	0	25,080
Haunting	Monkton Miss (Out of Place)	4	6	0	2	1	13,347
Hello Kris	Bite N Red (Explosive Red)	4	5	3	0	0	3,825
Her Best Ever	Granby (Larrupin')	4	3	1	0	0	14,430
Her Best Ever	Nanden (Second Childhood)	5	6	0	0	1	5,100
Her Best Ever	Trego (Meadow Monster)	2	5	1	1	0	13,560
High Hatted	Blue Chapeau (Miswaki)	5	11	2	4	0	13,629
High Noon Gal	From Mike's Heart (For Uncle Mike)	5	5	0	0	0	900
Hollywood Baldcat	White Aura (Rahy)	2	1	0	1	0	10,200
Hollywood Wildcat	Ministers Wild Cat (Deputy Minister)	4	9	1	2	1	73,072
Hong Kong Gold	Judge Spada (Sea Salute)	6	11	3	2	2	30,182
Imagination	Orlik (Cozzene)	3	12	1	4	0	44,720
Iman	Honor Prayer (Honor Grades)	3	7	1	0	0	22,650
Iman	Noite (Runaway Groom)	4	11	0	5	2	60,642
In the District	Voteforhennessy (Hennessy)	4	7	0	3	1	20,615
Into Temptation	Touch of Splendor (Charismatic)	2	3	0	0	1	2,390
Istinad	Coquinerie (Sahm)	3	10	1	2	0	50,523
Iwannakawana	Deference (Sky Classic)	2	2	1	0	0	9,450
Iwannakawana	Regal Kawana (Regal Classic)	3	4	0	0	0	1,122
Jandi Lee	Miracle Maker (Out of Place)	2	1	1	0	0	25,800
Jandi Lee	Owns the Place (Out of Place)	3	8	1	1	3	46,210
Jandi Lee	Run Willa Run (Candy Stripes)	5	7	2	1	0	22,674
Jesshaw	Big Sugar (Ranger (FR))	3	10	0	1	0	2,176
Jeunesse Doree	Kris Creek (Storm Creek)	2	4	0	0	3	2,965
Jewel of the East	Jewel's Dream (King of Kings (IRE))	4	13	3	0	1	21,849
Joey's Love	Phone Back (Phone Roberto)	2	1	0	0	0	400
Karen S.	Coin Trick (Favorite Trick)	4	2	0	0	2	2,420
Kiffi	Assemblyman (Crowd Pleaser)	2	4	1	0	1	15,530
King's Kristine	Erica J (Not For Love)	3	12	1	2	2	21,869
King's Kristine	Wrinkle Free (Mt. Livermore)	8	13	0	4	0	3,293
King's Mate	Mt. Livermate (Mt. Livermore)	2	3	0	1	0	6,213
Komprised	Outsmart (Out of Place)	4	14	1	1	4	14,115
Kris Is It	Wise Investor (Belong to Me)	2	5	1	1	1	46,808
Kris' Dear Deby	Ruby Red Slippers (Rubiano)	5	5	0	0	1	1,936
Kris' Dear Deby	Smart Set (Carson City)	7	1	0	1	0	1,160
Kris' Song	Kris'stalwart (Stalwart)	2	2	0	0	0	330
Kris's Destiny	Christopher Robyn (Robb)	2	6	1	0	1	13,070
Kris's Destiny	Edge of Destiny (Standing On Edge)	3	15	2	0	1	9,800
Kris's Destiny	I Have Wings (Always Fair)	4	9	0	1	1	4,303
Kris's Destiny	Kris Taylor (Ocean Crest)	5	16	2	1	2	52,425
Kris's Doll	Lavaca (Mystery Storm)	6	13	2	5	2	29,272
Kris's Intention	All Trumps (Grand Slam)	2	3	1	0	0	31,682
Kris's Intention	Kangaroo Jack (Victory Gallop)	3	8	0	1	2	4,955
Kris's Kiss	Country Judge (Judge T C)	4	12	3	5	3	149,840
Kris's Kiss	T C Kiss (Judge T C)	6	8	0	0	1	10,950
Kris's Krissy	General George S (Patton)	3	11	2	1	1	8,920
Kris's Peach	Pale Peach (Din's Dancer)	2	3	0	1	0	2,500
Kris's Stan	Bosox Babe (Michael's Flyer)	3	2	0	0	1	1,370
Krisharp	Fair Lady Camille (Captain Bodgit)	5	9	0	1	1	5,506
Krisharp	Magic Ink (Captain Bodgit)	4	2	0	0	0	222
Kristening	Naragansett (Personal Flag)	3	2	0	0	0	258
Kristening	The Falcon (Mughtanim)	5	5	1	0	2	34,398
Kristopher Street	On the Course (Spinning World)	4	9	5	0	1	133,195
Kristopher Street	Tisket a Tasket (Broad Brush)	3	6	2	2	0	55,140
Kute Kris	Capt. Smooth (Awad)	3	3	0	0	0	0
Ladies Double	Dinner At Ago's (Star of Valor)	3	12	3	0	1	31,041
Lady Semi	Semi Broke (Pembroke)	4	6	1	0	2	13,993
Lady Semi	Semi Lost (Lost Soldier)	3	8	3	2	0	163,070
Laurie's Folly	Try a Thing (Worldly Manner)	2	2	0	0	0	215
Lil Cozette	Candlebrook (Saint Ballado)	3	4	0	0	0	0
Lil Cozette	Cosmic Kris (Storm Creek)	2	3	0	1	0	6,680
Lyin to the Moon	Bayou the Moon (Dixieland Band)	6	2	0	1	0	6,087
Main Squeeze	Big Squeeze (Petionville)	3	8	1	1	0	43,820
Mary Kris	Extreme Hero (Traitor)	3	4	0	1	1	4,275
Mary Kris	Melanie's Smile (Cobra King)	4	9	1	0	2	2,790
Melegant	See Alice (Distorted Humor)	2	6	1	0	1	12,265
Merry Kris Miss	Grinch (Salt Lake)	3	9	2	2	1	83,530
Merry Kris Miss	Riding the Pine (Pine Bluff)	4	2	0	1	0	1,995
Minority Dater	Date More Minors (Mt. Livermore)	6	2	0	0	0	64
Missbourboncounty	Aquaduck (Basket Weave)	5	7	2	2	3	20,255
Missbourboncounty	Ratafee (Tough Knight)	3	4	0	0	1	290
Mistress S.	Decker (Crafty Prospector)	5	3	1	0	1	4,550
Mistress S.	Feverish Affair (Stormin Fever)	2	6	1	1	0	37,440
Momma Dear	Mister Ma (Mister Jolie)	5	2	0	0	0	0
Nimble Kris	Duce's Image (Halo's Image)	3	14	1	4	2	36,325
Office Fire	Kindling (Boundary)	2	1	0	0	0	145
Office Fire	Office Ghost (Silver Ghost)	4	9	1	1	1	25,200
Office Fire	Tinder (Cherokee Run)	3	17	2	4	2	31,869
On Kris's Wings	Kristina's Wish (Smart Strike)	4	15	5	2	3	88,926
Our Dear Krissy	Golden Oak (Conveyor)	5	14	2	1	1	23,789
Our Dear Krissy	Sedition (Dispersal)	6	1	0	0	0	150
Outcross	Exempt (Exploit)	2	6	0	1	2	11,780
Past Kris Ms.	Speaks Volumes (Urgent Request (IRE))	5	8	2	2	1	35,937
Patmos	Charles Harbor (Harbor Man)	4	11	2	2	3	44,500
Patmos	Chip's Diamond (Diamond)	3	6	1	1	1	22,930
Pecan Park	Rameses (Golden Legend)	5	4	0	0	0	189
Pecan Park	Sierra Bella (Montbrook)	2	9	0	3	2	11,040
Pink Mitten	Gorin (Private Terms)	3	16	2	3	6	22,423
Polywolydoodle	Sanfran (Sandpit (BRZ))	2	2	1	0	0	5,525
Pot of Coffee	Decaf (D'Hallevant)	5	6	0	2	1	13,760
Pot of Coffee	Quick Blend (Wised Up)	2	4	1	1	1	25,550
Princess Kali	Belvedere Belle (Hennessy)	3	2	0	0	1	4,900
Princess Kali	Sabella (Atticus)	4	6	0	0	0	653
Princess Sara P.	Babe's Baby (Wolf Power (SAF))	3	6	0	0	0	504
Princess Sara P.	My Gamblin Lady (Prospectors Gamble)	5	3	0	0	0	159
Proper Kris	Proper Dancer (Dance Brightly)	3	5	1	1	0	15,580
Queen Tutta	Unbridled Nan (Unbridled's Song)	3	3	0	1	0	4,780
Rare Fling	Hawking (Defrere)	3	5	1	0	2	21,200
Rare Fling	Presidential Fling (Wallenda)	7	7	1	0	0	10,970
Reality Will Be	Gallant Princess (Slew Gin Fizz)	2	6	1	0	2	27,036
Resilient Kris	It Is What It Is (Forest Wildcat)	6	5	1	1	1	29,440
Resilient Kris	Uphill Skier (Appealing Skier)	4	5	2	0	1	104,400
Rising Reason	Super Moe (Supremo)	4	1	0	0	0	0
Rising Reason	Superfly Girl (Good and Tough)	3	6	0	1	3	13,810
Ritzy Blitz	Titanius (Halo's Image)	3	12	3	0	3	77,210
Rosekris	Thebigbrushoff (Schossberg)	4	16	6	3	3	56,005
Rosekris	Zipcody (Tale of the Cat)	3	10	1	2	1	36,215
Royal Jubilee	French Jubilee (French Deputy)	3	7	0	0	1	1,510
Royal Jubilee	Seasoned Salt (Salt Lake)	2	2	0	0	0	720
Rumors Are Flying	Idle Rumor (Belong to Me)	3	2	0	0	0	320
Sealedwithakriss	Exploiting (Exploit)	3	8	3	1	1	17,390
Sealedwithakriss	Herecomesbrice (Hennessy)	4	5	1	1	1	11,013
Shannon Ashley	Mae East (Sharkey)	3	2	0	0	0	0
She Is Here	Lotta Light (Colony Light)	3	13	2	2	2	35,970

Mare	Progeny (Sire)	Age	Sts	1st	2d	3d	Money Won
She Is Here	Santee Light (Colony Light)	2	3	0	3	0	7,840
Sienna	Backbone (Peaks and Valleys)	4	10	2	0	0	18,345
Sienna	Joe Domino (Out of Place)	2	3	0	1	0	4,080
Sienna	Sienna's Honor (Honor Grades)	3	11	2	2	0	16,595
Smart Kris	Smarter Than Kris (Icy Glow)	5	24	2	1	6	25,608
Smarten Up Kris	Marjan (Cappuccio)	4	13	2	4	2	18,929
Smooth Swinger	Senor Swinger (El Prado (IRE))	4	10	4	0	1	418,178
Smooth Swinger	Swinging Sammi (Honour and Glory)	5	2	1	0	0	6,504
Snowy Egret	Snow Glitter (Glitterman)	2	1	0	0	0	205
Soaring Softly	Storm Soaring (Storm Cat)	3	2	0	0	0	1,670
Solo Karen	Fantastic Finish (Formal Dinner)	8	9	1	1	0	11,668
Solo Karen	Moon Warrior (Migrating Moon)	3	12	1	3	1	42,090
Sonata Style	Starlight Sonata (Bertrando)	2	2	0	0	0	800
Soontobspectacular	Soon to Be Family (Family Calling)	3	12	0	2	3	6,071
Sophisticatedbagel	Public Defender (Judge T C)	3	2	0	0	0	0
Spirit of Kris	Delmar Annie (Star of Valor)	2	4	1	0	1	20,060
St. Kristine	Blue Crane (Cape Town)	2	3	0	0	0	500
St. Kristine	Twisted Kris (Twining)	6	1	0	0	0	450
Stage Door Canteen	Naturelle's Way (Skip Away)	3	14	1	4	3	40,280
Sugar Kris	Hickory Pete (Ordway)	3	11	3	0	2	86,140
Sugar Kris	Juniper Kris (Go for Gin)	4	10	2	1	0	43,730
Sugar Kris	Sugar Date (Out of Place)	2	1	0	1	0	5,600
Surely Kris	Brijetta Light (Colony Light)	2	10	0	2	3	14,555
Surely Kris	Heather Light (Colony Light)	7	3	0	0	2	7,850
Surely Kris	Old Scudder (Colony Light)	3	16	3	2	1	26,700
Surely Kris	Strolling Kris (Whitney Tower)	4	10	2	3	1	21,200
Sweet Choice	Astros Choice (Astro)	4	1	0	1	0	2,100
Sweet Choice	Just Another Fact (Known Fact)	3	10	1	2	3	28,062
Sweet Kris	Angelic Aura (Concerto)	4	5	3	0	1	138,100
Sweet Kris	Secret Messenger (Montbrook)	3	7	0	4	2	30,805
Sweet Life	Sweet Catomine (Storm Cat)	2	4	3	1	0	799,800
Sweet Little Kris	Sweet Little Avie (Lord Avie)	4	13	3	4	1	76,060
Sweet Snob	Cowboy Up (Capote's Prospect)	2	1	0	0	0	0
Tess' Krissmiss	Providence (Meadowlake)	4	1	0	0	0	696
Tidal Reach	Innit (IRE) (Distinctly North)	6	1	0	0	0	4,252
Trufulla Rose	Starview's Rose (Din's Dancer)	4	7	0	1	0	4,030
Urus	Adobe Gold (Touch Gold)	3	12	4	3	0	130,288
Urus	Dizzy Spell (Spinning World)	4	4	0	1	1	11,070
Valid Krissy	Clever Blonde (Clever Trick)	5	6	0	0	0	1,675
Vertigineux	Where's Bailey (Aljabr)	2	5	3	0	0	35,200
Vex	Condeleezza S. (Alydeed)	4	2	0	0	0	110
Vex	Sort It Out (Out of Place)	2	6	1	1	0	49,085
Vex	Vexation (Out of Place)	3	7	0	0	1	4,568
Water Kris	Cardinal Rule (Maria's Mon)	3	5	0	3	0	25,532
Water Kris	Nonno Guido (Nicholas)	5	4	0	1	0	1,416
Wicked Kris	Eastern Bay (Marquetry)	3	12	2	3	2	44,770

Valid Appeal, B H (1972)
By In Reality – Desert Trial, by Moslem Chief

302 Performers, 164 winning performers, $5,939,964 total earnings

Mare	Progeny (Sire)	Age	Sts	1st	2d	3d	Money Won
A Lady With Appeal	El Condor (Birdonthewire)	5	10	1	4	1	49,820
A Lady With Appeal	Lady Bella (Notebook)	2	3	0	0	0	11,320
A Lady With Appeal	Lady Gwen (Alphabet Soup)	4	6	1	2	1	42,550
A Lady With Appeal	Valid Rush (Wild Rush)	3	1	0	0	0	1,560
A Little Bit Valid	Golden Dewdrop (Gold Case)	3	4	1	1	0	12,360
A Little Bit Valid	Little Missile (Golden Missile)	2	3	0	0	0	615
Absence of Malice	Macy's Grey (Open Forum)	2	2	0	0	0	112
All You All	Lovey Lovey Lovey (Danzig Connection)	10	2	0	0	0	396
All You All	Short Cat (Tomorrows Cat)	2	1	0	0	0	0
All You All	Signal Tapper (Signal Tap)	5	7	0	0	0	1,067
Always Asking	Aguara (End Sweep)	4	12	2	2	5	38,831
Alwaysinlove	Hasse (Wayne's Crane)	5	1	0	0	0	0
Amavalidhope	Hope for Love (Fortunate Prospect)	4	1	0	0	0	1,350
Amavalidhope	Kohut (Fortunate Prospect)	2	5	1	2	1	44,020
Angel's Appeal	Looks Bold (He's a Looker)	6	8	0	0	0	2,575
Appealing Andover	Grace the Stage (Pembroke)	4	3	1	1	1	8,200
Appealing Andover	Megan's Appeal (Gold Case)	3	8	0	1	0	16,154
Appealing Beauty	Triple Shot (Helmsman)	3	4	1	2	0	16,579
Appealing Blues	Brooker B. Tee (Fortunate Prospect)	2	3	1	1	0	26,149
Appealing Brunette	Forty Sweeps (End Sweep)	4	9	0	0	3	3,347
Appealing Brunette	Sharp Brunette (Crusader Sword)	3	9	1	0	2	40,575
Appealing Es	At Ease Diablo (Diablo)	5	6	0	1	1	3,395
Appealing Es	Es Muy Stormy (Storm Creek)	4	9	1	1	3	9,315
Appealing Es	Stars On the Water (Marquetry)	3	10	1	1	6	10,969
Appealing Gal	Open to Appeal (Open Forum)	2	1	0	1	0	1,615
Appealing Gypsy	L S Gypsyannio (Giuseppe)	3	10	2	0	0	15,540
Appealing Gypsy	Ls Storming Gypsy (Bag)	4	9	2	2	1	16,442
Appealing Jeanne	Mackenzie Nicole (Royal Academy)	2	3	1	1	0	17,460
Appealing Jeanne	Pull Over Please (Glitterman)	5	10	3	3	1	24,590
Appealing Jeanne	Wild for Jeanne (Wild Zone)	3	2	0	0	0	0
Appealing Kanska	Karroo (Cape Town)	4	9	2	2	3	32,721
Appealing Kanska	Mr. Heartbreaker (French Parliament)	2	3	0	0	2	9,800
Appealing Look	Special Matter (River Special)	6	9	2	0	2	149,920
Appealing Miss	Dr. Miller (My Prince Charming)	4	3	0	0	0	1,145
Appealing Miss	Prince Peapa (My Prince Charming)	2	6	0	1	0	5,318
Appealing Miss	Soes Bandit (Buckaroo)	8	17	3	1	0	29,210
Appealing Miss	What's That (My Prince Charming)	3	7	1	0	1	11,635
Appealing Miss Cox	Stormy Appeal (Storm Creek)	5	5	0	0	0	0
Appealing Nany	Victory Wanted (Victory Gallop)	2	4	2	0	0	16,039
Appealing Sam	Appealing Lauren (Double Cash)	4	9	1	1	2	19,734
Appealing Sam	Appealing Saint (Sweetsouthernsaint)	2	3	0	0	0	5,280
Appealing Sam	Appealing Secret (Sea of Secrets)	3	12	2	2	2	27,391
Appealing Sara	Dear to Me (Mister Baileys (GB))	4	1	0	0	1	1,800
Appealing Slew	Appealing Jet (Jessie Jet)	6	6	1	0	0	9,600
Appealing Slew	Fort Seattle (Fort Wayne)	2	6	0	0	1	3,825
Appealing Slew	Slewbe Jet (Jessie Jet)	3	4	0	1	2	15,750
Appealing Slew	Spring Jet (Jessie Jet)	7	20	1	0	3	9,460
Appealing Spirit	Spiritually (French Deputy)	3	14	1	0	1	14,155
Appealing Storm	Former Stormer (Dynaformer)	3	8	0	0	1	2,715
Appealing Story	Diablo's Fable (Diablo)	6	6	0	0	0	0
Appealing Style	Nindawayma (Ascot Knight)	6	13	2	1	2	16,999
Appealing Susie	Strike Your Colors (Dynaformer)	2	5	1	0	1	14,380
Applepeal	Apple Appeal (Sunrise Shower)	4	9	1	0	0	3,906
Applepeal	Chilipin (Sunrise Shower)	6	11	2	1	1	17,545
Applepeal	Peal Out (Sunrise Shower)	5	10	2	2	1	7,812
Applepeal	Zee Bull (Repriced)	3	1	0	1	0	1,600
Belle's Appeal	Harbour Gate (Boston Harbor)	3	6	1	1	0	31,755
Beth's Appeal	Explosive Appeal (Explosive Red)	4	4	1	2	1	12,810
Beth's Appeal	Marlindsey (Sweetsouthernsaint)	2	4	0	0	0	2,710
Boldly Appealing	Bold Explorer (Open Forum)	3	7	1	1	1	11,590
Call	Makena North (Regal Search)	4	2	1	0	0	4,575
Call	Mekena South (Skip Trial)	6	10	1	2	1	18,545
Chelly M.	Hitchcock's Best (Bates Motel)	4	2	0	0	0	0
Chief Appeal	Cozzene Appeal (Cozzene)	6	9	0	0	0	2,115
Chief Appeal	Unbridled Appeal (Unbridled)	3	4	0	1	1	14,700
Counselor Deb	Take Me Outahere (Take Me Out)	3	3	0	0	0	560
Cozily	Cozy (Wallenda)	7	6	0	0	2	12,000
Cozily	Getcozywithkaylee (Zafarrancho (ARG))	3	16	5	2	2	78,455
Danielle's Jewel	Despina (A. P Jet)	2	2	0	0	0	255
Dara's Appeal	Nine's Appealagain (Nines Wild)	6	9	0	0	0	1,295
Dara's Appeal	Quackers Appeal (Quaker Ridge)	3	13	4	4	0	72,315
Dara's Appeal	Ruffles and Ridges (Quaker Ridge)	2	10	3	3	1	53,820
Dara's Appeal	Wild Romeo (Wild Syn)	4	9	0	0	0	1,170
Di's Song	Hunting Hillbilly (Dove Hunt)	3	13	3	0	3	71,810
Discover Silver	Sleep Away (Skip Away)	4	13	1	5	3	23,413
Elgin Lady	Mr. Snippington (Roar)	2	7	1	2	1	42,660
Elgin Lady	Uncle Ack (Housebuster)	5	17	2	4	2	14,122
Elgin Lady	York Hills (Fit to Fight)	6	4	1	1	0	9,668
Enjoy the Silence	Silent Embrace (Twining)	4	8	0	0	0	1,415
Enjoy the Silence	Silver Silence (Rubiano)	6	6	2	0	0	20,239
Expensive Glue	Kalt Cafe (In Excessive Bull)	4	2	0	0	0	1,344
Few Choice Words	Commander Benno (Deputy Commander)	4	3	0	0	0	510
Few Choice Words	County (Menifee)	2	1	0	0	0	1,020
Five Hundred S. L.	Mercedes Mystery (Mystery Storm)	4	3	0	0	1	4,530
Flood Warning	Valid Afleet (Rizzi)	3	9	2	2	0	12,270
Fortune Cookie	Bugatti's Booty (Bugatti Reef (IRE))	3	4	0	0	0	375
French Appeal	Home James (Whitney Tower)	4	8	1	1	1	4,960
Gee Thanks	If I Were You (Defrere)	5	12	2	0	2	23,631
Gee Thanks	Miss Susan (Defrere)	4	14	3	3	1	16,575
Gee Thanks	Thank You Mom (Holzmeister)	3	1	0	1	0	1,500
Go Again Valid	Dynappeal (Dynaformer)	2	3	0	0	0	860
Heavenly Shadow	Kimberley Regiment (Lost Soldier)	4	5	1	1	2	18,669
Hidden Desire	Cometary (Comet Shine)	5	18	1	2	1	4,860
Hidden Desire	Dale Evans (Rodeo)	2	2	0	0	0	528
Hidden Desire	Sheilas Desire (Rodeo)	4	10	2	1	2	16,314
Ice Pop	Grifton (Roaring Camp)	4	1	0	1	0	3,000
Ice Pop	Valid Roar (Roaring Camp)	3	1	0	0	0	620
In Pay	Good Bidness (Crafty Dude)	4	3	1	0	0	4,669
Joyatlast	Its True Atlast (Yes It's True)	2	3	1	0	0	12,500
Joyatlast	Rocky Robyn (Robyn Dancer)	9	5	2	1	0	23,540
Kind of Appealing	Shadow Government (Reincarnate)	4	10	0	0	0	749
Law N Order	Gambler's Law (Prospectors Gamble)	3	12	2	2	2	18,162
Light Rain	Sexy Appeal (Colonial Affair)	5	5	0	0	1	2,530
Little Sister	Spoiled (Wild Again)	3	2	0	1	0	13,102
Mary's Appeal	Scobey (Proud Birdie)	9	13	5	2	1	23,674
Mate's Appeal	Paul's Lil Mate (Lil E. Tee)	3	11	2	4	2	16,634
Midnight Appeal	Family Appeal (Family Calling)	2	9	1	0	2	17,090
Milky Way Gal	Cosmic Snowman (Frosty the Snowman)	8	3	0	0	0	244
Milky Way Gal	Jujuba (Jules)	5	6	2	0	2	12,902
Milky Way Gal	Milky Way Guy (Skip Trial)	6	14	7	2	1	115,600
Miss Bold Appeal	Jersey Boy (Danzig)	4	3	1	0	1	24,480
Miss Bold Appeal	Partition (Danzig)	3	5	1	2	0	35,390
Miss Valdance	Hammerlane (Editor's Note)	3	3	0	0	1	938
Miss Valid Match	Carnival Match (Carnivalay)	6	11	0	0	0	690
Miss Valid Match	Ms. Sofia Ann (Tour d'Or)	3	6	1	0	1	23,478
Miss Valid Moment	Flying Moment (Northern Afleet)	3	1	0	1	0	1,408
Miss Valid Pache	Justintime G (Saint Ballado)	2	1	0	0	0	0
Miss Valid Pache	Zuni Gold (Coronado's Quest)	3	11	1	2	1	36,410
Miz United States	American Joe (Silver Charm)	2	5	0	1	1	7,540
My Jenny	Palm Avenue (Broad Brush)	2	4	1	0	1	42,180
My Jenny	Park Ranger (Forestry)	3	1	0	0	0	135
Nanerpeal	As You Like It (Belong to Me)	3	1	0	0	0	400
Nanerpeal	Saint Appeal (Saint Ballado)	5	2	0	0	0	0
Naughty Nora	Don't Ignore Her (Slewdledo)	7	7	2	2	0	10,949
Naughty Nora	Don't Ignore Me (Petersburg)	2	2	0	0	0	870
Not My Cup of Tea	Go Not Whoa (Tilt Up)	9	11	1	3	5	22,561
Oedy's Appeal	Eyes On Eddy (Touch Gold)	2	2	1	0	1	21,500
Oedy's Appeal	Oedy's Riches (Rizzi)	6	1	0	0	0	153

Oedy's Appeal	Stormin Oedy (Mystery Storm)	7	13	0	2	3	27,650
Peace Rose	Heart in Hand (Notebook)	7	3	0	0	0	450
Perfect Exchange	Cauy (Maria's Mon)	6	2	0	0	0	0
Perfect Exchange	Honeycomb Gus (Is It True)	2	2	1	0	1	12,330
Perfect Exchange	Perfect Miss (Diligence)	4	1	0	0	0	0
Personal Line	Erotico (Lost Soldier)	3	12	3	3	3	29,180
Personal Line	Storm's Lining (Storm Creek)	6	12	1	1	0	5,990
Piney Woods	My Limit (Wagon Limit)	3	12	6	0	0	101,660
Pisces Appeal	Brilliant Man (Straight Man)	2	4	1	1	0	17,070
Pisces Appeal	Frankeneddie (Open Forum)	3	20	3	2	2	24,250
Plea	Pazhalsta (Moscow Ballet)	6	4	0	2	1	7,775
Plea	Pleas Deal (Delineator)	4	12	1	4	3	18,078
Proud n' Precious	Matsui (Double Honor)	3	7	2	2	1	71,903
Proud n' Precious	Mooji Moo (Jeblar)	5	5	1	2	0	203,500
Quiet Talk	K. P. Express (Captain Bodgit)	4	12	2	0	1	10,851
Quiet Talk	Soundless (Red Ransom)	2	7	0	1	2	10,031
Radical Appeal	Devil Shade (Devil His Due)	2	3	0	0	0	181
Radical Appeal	Lau Mor's Glitter (Glitterman)	3	7	0	2	0	5,255
Radical Appeal	Sunny Stutz (Stutz Blackhawk)	9	7	0	0	0	1,339
Really Appealing	Note Appeal (Notebook)	3	9	1	0	0	9,290
Really Appealing	Picata (Rizzi)	2	3	1	0	1	10,050
Really Appealing	Real Forum (Open Forum)	5	6	1	0	0	7,620
Regally Appealing	Appealing Bride (Unbridled's Song)	2	3	2	0	1	19,035
Rivkah	Dan's Jet (Unbridled Jet)	2	10	0	3	1	7,744
Say Please	Priceless Jet (Mahogany Hall)	4	1	0	0	0	206
Sedna	Goldscheider (The Deputy (IRE))	2	2	1	0	0	6,510
Silk Appeal	Concorde's Appeal (Concorde's Tune)	5	4	1	0	0	7,000
Silk Appeal	Silk Notebook (Notebook)	3	1	0	0	0	75
Silk Appeal	Silk Splendor (Pentelicus)	4	4	0	1	1	6,400
Snubs	Snub the Devil (Devil's Bag)	3	9	3	1	0	81,380
Sober Appeal	Cheer Girl (Blumin Affair)	2	4	1	0	1	19,500
Sober Appeal	Plum Sober (Blumin Affair)	3	9	1	2	2	47,692
Squarely Appealing	Racing Tiger (Tiger Ridge)	2	4	1	0	0	5,085
Striking Move	Golden Move (Golden Missile)	2	2	0	0	0	2,435
Sugar's Image	St Ballado's Image (Saint Ballado)	3	10	1	1	2	31,530
Sugar's Image	Unbridled's Image (Unbridled)	4	10	0	1	0	6,425
Sweet Message	Sea of Sweets (Sea of Secrets)	3	8	0	1	0	3,000
Sweet Message	Show Killer (Banker's Gold)	4	3	1	0	0	4,692
Sweet Reality	Starship Garnet (Unzipped)	5	16	3	3	1	28,982
Tashmo Joe	Appealing Greeley (Mr. Greeley)	5	8	1	2	2	10,500
Tashmo Joe	Viasec Son (D'Accord)	7	18	2	1	4	25,116
Temporary Appeal	Temporary Zone (Wild Zone)	2	7	2	2	1	45,400
Temptous	Tempest Run (Alydeed)	4	1	0	0	0	74
Tracy V.	American Challenge (You and I)	4	4	1	1	1	22,640
True Melody	Hot Melody (Unusual Heat)	2	1	0	0	0	400
True Melody	Miss Guts (American Chance)	5	6	0	2	0	8,140
Unchained Appeal	Skip Son (Skip Trial)	3	16	3	3	2	44,793
Uniquely Appealing	Cryptos' Best (Cryptoclearance)	3	7	1	1	1	46,020
Uniquely Appealing	Great Power (Devil Power)	2	14	1	2	0	36,479
Uniquely Appealing	Joyous Appeal (Devil His Due)	4	15	0	5	4	45,185
Uniquely Appealing	Lazar (Exemplary Leader)	8	3	1	0	0	5,085
Uniquely Appealing	Mr. Bo Jo (Devil His Due)	5	8	0	0	0	561
Unlimited Pleasure	Show Stomper (Slew Gin Fizz)	2	1	0	1	0	3,600
Valid Affect	City Code (Carson City)	2	5	2	0	2	52,040
Valid Affect	Intrinsic Worth (Red Ransom)	3	6	3	0	0	80,450
Valid Allure	Liberation (Green Dancer)	5	12	1	3	1	20,695
Valid and True	Gold Wings (Our Emblem)	6	9	2	0	3	36,865
Valid and True	Unbridled Gamble (Unbridled)	8	1	1	0	0	3,300
Valid Approval	Fierce Knight (Birdonthewire)	3	9	1	4	2	62,880
Valid Approval	Sand Burner (Touch Gold)	4	14	2	3	4	48,585
Valid Approval	Win Again (Awesome Again)	2	1	0	0	0	0
Valid Attraction	Pat's Blast O. (Explosive Red)	6	4	0	0	0	924
Valid Blend	Alex's Sister (Storm Creek)	4	1	0	1	0	1,500
Valid Blend	Splendid Blended (Unbridled's Song)	2	4	3	1	0	327,400
Valid Bonnet	Little Bonnet (Coronado's Quest)	4	4	0	0	2	10,590
Valid Carnauba	Any Reason (Unbridled)	5	1	0	0	0	150
Valid Carnauba	Ebony Breeze (Belong to Me)	4	9	2	3	1	255,360
Valid Carnauba	Valid Chief (Belong to Me)	3	2	0	0	0	228
Valid Coins	Jewel Creek (Storm Creek)	4	6	1	0	1	4,585
Valid Coins	Moneybackguarantee (Commendable)	2	9	2	0	2	13,229
Valid Coins	Rich Coins (Rizzi)	6	11	0	2	2	9,474
Valid Coins	Valid Skip (Skip Trial)	3	8	0	1	3	8,000
Valid Dawn	Rupert Haint (Haint)	4	3	0	0	0	205
Valid Dawn	Rupert's Hazaam (Hazaam)	3	4	0	0	1	2,040
Valid Dawn	Ruperts Valid Dawn (Sasha's Prospect)	2	3	2	0	0	16,435
Valid Dawn	Valid Flight (Meadow Flight)	6	2	0	0	0	240
Valid Design	Dr. Bombay (El Prado (IRE))	4	5	0	0	0	585
Valid Design	Heaven (Septieme Ciel)	7	5	1	0	1	4,810
Valid Doge	Shock the World (World Stage (IRE))	3	15	0	0	0	1,862
Valid Dorothy	I'm Awesome (Awesome Again)	3	1	0	0	0	0
Valid Dream	Brogans Shield (Brogan)	4	7	1	0	1	14,042
Valid Dream	Fun Maggie (Brogan)	3	19	2	3	2	17,057
Valid Eloquence	Rarest Love (Not For Love)	5	16	3	1	5	24,926
Valid Evidence	Anna's Cat (Storm Creek)	4	10	2	0	0	16,670
Valid Expression	Rich Expression (Rizzi)	5	9	0	0	0	1,486
Valid Fixation	More Influence (Southern Halo)	6	13	4	2	3	37,970
Valid Funding	Itsanewday (Wheaton)	3	18	2	4	2	18,484
Valid Gem	Madison's Wish (Eltish)	3	5	1	1	0	33,850
Valid Goddess	Broad Sanctions (Broad Brush)	4	8	1	2	2	30,290
Valid Goddess	Valid (Broad Brush)	5	3	0	0	0	186
Valid Goddess	Valid Concern (Concern)	2	1	0	0	0	480
Valid Joy	Bubba's Last (Bianconi)	2	4	0	0	1	1,848
Valid Joy	Roar of Joy (Roar)	3	3	0	0	0	1,710
Valid Lassie	Valid Chad (Fuzziano)	4	14	0	1	6	8,490
Valid Lesson	Actcellent (Noactor)	4	5	1	0	3	38,621
Valid Lesson	Actxpedite (Noactor)	3	6	0	1	1	9,240
Valid Lesson	Valid Action (Noactor)	5	7	3	1	1	12,744
Valid Linda	Amazon River (River Special)	6	9	0	0	1	9,925
Valid Looker	Bye Bye Beylen (Fort Chaffee)	5	15	1	3	6	31,100
Valid Looker	Cullen (Repriced)	3	9	1	0	1	16,420
Valid Looker	Jaycejace (You and I)	4	2	0	0	0	165
Valid Miss	Cowboy Cumbia (Kentucky Jazz)	6	7	1	1	0	5,056
Valid Miss	Lil Cowboy (Kentucky Jazz)	3	1	0	0	0	0
Valid Miss	Olympia Prince (Fire Maker)	5	10	0	2	1	5,820
Valid Miss Zenda	Seattle Appeal (Hubble)	8	6	1	0	0	8,450
Valid Ms Cherokee	Waltz King (Leo Castelli)	6	13	1	1	1	12,766
Valid Nany	Bull Leave It (Holy Bull)	6	9	3	0	1	8,668
Valid Nany	Lullaby League (Rubiano)	5	2	0	0	1	1,750
Valid Nany	Nanys Lullaby (Unbridled's Song)	3	4	1	0	1	8,280
Valid Obsession	Dark Torment (Devil's Bag)	5	1	0	0	0	125
Valid Obsession	Endless Obsession (End Sweep)	7	9	0	2	2	7,031
Valid Obsession	Lost Obsession (Out of Place)	2	1	0	0	0	105
Valid Obsession	Soul Obsession (Diablo)	6	9	5	2	0	17,090
Valid Obsession	Unbridledobsession (Unbridled)	3	4	1	0	1	8,615
Valid Pache	Staci Got Bowleggs (Laabity)	2	3	0	0	0	271
Valid Pache	Valid Hero (Sea Hero)	4	6	1	1	0	6,433
Valid Peak	Josie's Peak (Regal Search)	4	15	1	4	4	14,262
Valid Peak	Kissintobeclever (Kissin Kris)	3	8	1	0	1	11,370
Valid Precision	Fred's Notebook (Notebook)	4	6	0	0	1	1,575
Valid Precision	Transcribe (Notebook)	3	12	1	1	2	10,878
Valid Pride	Case of Pride (Gold Case)	5	11	2	0	2	22,974
Valid Pride	Father Tom (Sweetsouthernsaint)	2	1	0	0	0	230
Valid Pride	Mc Meese (Notebook)	4	5	0	0	0	664
Valid Proclamation	Jeanie Sue (Level Sands)	5	5	0	2	0	12,564
Valid Risk	Risk It (Majesty's Imp)	5	8	1	0	2	3,438
Valid Search	Rich Search (Rizzi)	6	1	0	0	0	0
Valid Silk	Rocky River (Concorde's Tune)	2	3	2	0	0	61,680
Valid Silk	Valid Pro (Polish Pro)	4	1	0	0	0	143
Valid Storm	Riverbrook (Montbrook)	3	6	2	0	3	49,180
Valid Storm	Storm Forcast (Slew Gin Fizz)	2	6	1	0	2	15,865
Valid Storm	Storm in Philly (Smoke Glacken)	5	6	1	1	1	15,895
Valid Storm	Sweep in Philly (End Sweep)	4	9	5	1	1	55,100
Valid Story	Pretty Toni (Bold Anthony)	4	6	3	1	0	23,380
Valid Success	Outlandishlady (Lucky North)	5	12	0	4	1	8,721
Valid Sweetheart	Son of Appeal (Miesque's Son)	2	7	1	0	2	15,465
Valid Sylvia	Up the Volume (Stop the Music)	6	8	3	1	2	13,126
Valid Symmetry	La Reine Victoria (Touch Gold)	3	6	0	4	0	33,802
Valid Symmetry	Symmetron (Awesome Again)	4	3	1	0	1	49,476
Valid Tenet	Appealing Wayz (Truckee)	4	1	0	0	0	0
Valid Tenet	Rainman's Request (Urgent Request (Ire))	5	8	1	1	0	13,300
Valid Tenet	White Pine (Truckee)	2	1	0	0	0	0
Valid Trade	Valid Jet (Diplomatic Jet)	5	15	0	4	2	8,540
Valid Triumph	Cut Trail (Malek (CHI))	2	1	0	0	0	400
Valid Triumph	Smoke 'n Triumph (Smokester)	3	7	2	0	0	22,040
Valid Victress	El General (El Prado (IRE))	5	3	2	0	1	48,000
Valid Warning	Unbridled Ashley (Unbridled)	4	1	0	0	0	340
Valid Way	Sweeping Way (End Sweep)	6	11	0	2	3	4,423
Valid Way	Valid Again (Awesome Again)	3	10	3	0	0	86,331
Valid Wind	Doubly Appealing (Unbridled Jet)	2	1	0	0	0	460
Valid Witness	Golden Witness (Golden Missile)	2	1	0	0	0	135
Validated	Randaroo (Gold Case)	4	3	2	0	1	181,365
Validated	Unleashedthedragon (Belong to Me)	3	3	0	3	0	21,090
Validated	Valid Charmer (Silver Charm)	2	2	0	0	0	1,935
Valley Vixen	Secret Command (West by West)	5	5	2	0	0	14,310
Valley Vixen	Top Appeal (Glitterman)	2	2	0	0	0	140
Valley Vixen	Wildcata (Forest Wildcat)	4	4	0	0	0	2,280
Velvet Tulip	Cloud Walker (Phone Trick)	4	7	4	0	1	106,844
Velvet Tulip	Cronenbold (Exploit)	3	5	0	1	2	21,760
Velvet Tulip	Ole Rebel (Carson City)	5	12	5	2	1	178,500
Vennila Cream	Base Stealer (Saint Ballado)	4	9	1	0	1	34,089
Vennila Cream	Carefree (Unbridled)	7	8	1	2	1	9,180
Vennila Cream	Daddy Joe (Unbridled's Song)	2	5	1	1	1	42,600
Vennila Cream	Kazoo (Tabasco Cat)	6	6	1	2	0	54,920
Very Appealing	Power Appeal (Wolf Power (SAF))	7	7	0	1	1	1,200
Very Appealing	Very Gifted (Gift of Gib)	4	12	2	5	0	24,917
Vivio Appeal	La Chunk (Prospector's Halo)	5	15	0	4	2	23,887
Wellingtons Choice	Exploit Choice (Exploit)	3	12	1	1	1	15,594
Wellingtons Choice	Gadir (Sejm)	7	1	0	0	0	192
Worldly Possession	Montezuma's Gold (Red Ransom)	8	1	0	0	0	0
Worldly Possession	Super Case (Gold Case)	4	5	1	1	0	71,524
You'll B Impressed	Clif's Storm (Storm Creek)	2	3	1	1	1	22,110
You'll B Impressed	I Am Impressed (Mecke)	5	15	3	2	0	15,363
You'll B Impressed	Moon Bird (Meadow Flight)	6	9	1	1	0	18,747
You'll B Impressed	Seductive Lady (Langfuhr)	3	1	0	0	0	240

Annual Leading Broodmare Sires – Money Won

Year	Sire	Mares	Perfs.	Sts.	1st	2d	3d	Amt. Won
1937	Sweep	85	140		271	217	278	$382,744
1938	Fair Play	76	129		254	260	230	408,369
1939	Sir Gallahad III*	55	95		168	149	156	480,018
1940	High Time	70	134		247	255	236	335,807
1941	Sweep	65	115		217	197	236	462,587
1942	Chicle*	66	113		205	166	196	533,572
1943	Sir Gallahad III*	110	195		365	334	311	703,301
1944	Sir Gallahad III*	129	236		447	432	387	1,024,290
1945	Sir Gallahad III*	138	236		362	364	335	1,020,235
1946	Sir Gallahad III*	153	276		475	470	466	1,529,393
1947	Sir Gallahad III*	152	273		465	407	432	1,458,309
1948	Sir Gallahad III*	156	302		433	462	456	1,468,648
1949	Sir Gallahad III*	165	317		537	519	502	1,393,104
1950	Sir Gallahad III*	178	345		542	568	507	1,376,629
1951	Sir Gallahad III*	176	341		587	607	578	1,707,823
1952	Sir Gallahad III*	173	344		567	575	569	1,656,221
1953	Bull Dog*	114	234		490	449	429	1,941,345
1954	Bull Dog*	116	243		459	430	379	1,780,267
1955	Sir Gallahad III*	170	336		591	534	587	1,499,162
1956	Bull Dog*	110	228		420	408	381	1,683,908
1957	Mahmoud*	92	171		283	247	260	2,593,782
1958	Bull Lea	89	172		252	211	227	1,645,812
1959	Bull Lea	104	189		335	335	280	1,479,375
1960	Bull Lea	102	196		352	333	298	1,915,881
1961	Bull Lea	99	196		364	303	333	1,632,559
1962	War Admiral	94	120		348	295	263	1,654,396
1963	Count Fleet	114	205	2,287	332	265	232	1,866,809
1964	War Admiral	109	212	2,757	351	338	323	2,928,459
1965	Roman	118	217	2,572	368	333	309	2,394,944
1966	Princequillo*	111	191	2,074	287	268	243	2,007,184
1967	Princequillo*	118	215	2,079	323	270	238	2,311,709
1968	Princequillo*	131	219	2,179	299	285	264	2,116,648
1969	Princequillo*	129	215	2,027	275	264	213	2,196,327
1970	Princequillo*	133	209	2,026	261	243	257	2,454,097
1971	Double Jay	105	202	2,263	290	319	266	2,051,296
1972	Princequillo*	134	238	2,262	297	267	269	2,722,783
1973	Princequillo*	149	241	2,237	322	246	265	3,071,322
1974	Olympia	103	174	2,058	297	254	235	2,300,121
1975	Double Jay	131	238	2,651	329	341	358	2,233,642
1976	Princequillo*	118	202	2,027	266	250	274	2,778,695
1977	Double Jay	130	233	2,325	300	321	279	2,696,490
1978	Crafty Admiral	95	172	1,848	260	220	220	2,295,375
1979	Prince John	133	207	1,764	281	226	213	2,895,534
1980	Prince John	132	210	1,875	282	258	223	3,434,042
1981	Double Jay	90	153	1,509	187	193	180	3,471,976
1982	Olden Times	119	185	1,598	256	229	179	3,235,590
1983	Buckpasser	72	114	796	117	111	86	3,482,059
1984	Buckpasser	72	108	794	104	87	117	5,140,500
1985	Speak John	74	122	987	127	96	108	5,189,390
1986	Prince John	140	214	1,825	236	222	217	4,440,027
1987	Hoist the Flag	69	103	664	111	86	73	5,533,406
1988	Graustark	99	157	1,229	182	153	145	7,736,657
1989	Buckpasser	95	150	1,190	181	174	151	9,164,291
1990	Grey Dawn II	146	252	2,161	285	237	264	6,003,127
1991	Diplomat Way	129	216	1,908	232	213	201	5,283,778
1992	Secretariat	135	239	1,864	259	215	205	6,665,607
1993	Nijinsky II	131	215	1,487	206	179	170	6,363,743
1994	Nijinsky II	121	214	1,544	223	211	207	7,059,431
1995	Seattle Slew	82	142	941	149	125	104	7,762,384
1996	Mr. Prospector	162	267	1,922	294	226	269	7,095,747
1997	Mr. Prospector	159	275	1,950	297	256	251	8,708,618
1998	Mr. Prospector	175	275	1,897	303	244	255	8,175,483
1999	Mr. Prospector	160	286	1,945	286	262	244	8,869,556
2000	Mr. Prospector	153	292	1,909	270	267	220	8,472,649
2001	Mr. Prospector	179	295	1,764	253	238	215	8,944,180
2002	Deputy Minister	159	270	1,668	241	235	223	8,774,040
2003	Deputy Minister	176	316	2,036	311	273	266	11,645,931
2004	Dixieland Band	187	325	2,197	326	299	305	11,556,169

**Foreign-bred*

Top Freshman Sires in 2004 – Money Won

Sire	Perfs.	Winning Perfs.	Starts	1st	2nd	3rd	Unplaced	Purses
Successful Appeal	20	15	76	31	13	10	22	$1,724,080
Yes It's True	40	15	141	25	12	31	73	1,424,382
Fusaichi Pegasus	22	7	54	14	8	9	23	923,385
Cape Canaveral	30	11	106	18	25	12	51	864,072
More Than Ready	34	17	134	24	23	18	69	837,567
Dixie Union	21	11	93	15	21	12	45	695,666
Precise End	27	11	98	12	20	17	49	689,598
Bernstein	18	11	60	17	18	6	19	525,467
Tiger Ridge	25	11	82	13	15	7	47	517,686
Running Stag	33	10	107	15	13	14	65	516,682
Old Topper	19	10	76	15	20	11	30	498,815
Sweetsouthernsaint	23	11	106	19	15	10	62	494,024
Catienus	31	19	120	23	13	11	73	451,551
Straight Man	33	12	105	15	18	16	56	413,206
Yankee Victor	27	12	86	13	15	8	50	399,274
Lion Hearted	13	9	40	12	5	7	16	391,917
Western Expression	20	7	60	8	9	7	36	384,961
Dance Master	7	4	25	7	5	7	6	383,496
Lemon Drop Kid	16	6	46	7	11	10	18	342,983
Golden Missile	24	6	66	7	7	5	47	332,496
Chester House	25	9	67	11	9	7	40	326,963
Stephen Got Even	22	7	76	8	6	13	49	314,967
War Chant	14	7	38	8	4	5	21	306,168
Chief Seattle	24	9	74	10	9	12	43	304,361
High Yield	27	8	74	11	4	13	46	299,331
Anees	19	5	55	6	4	7	38	280,239
Magic Cat	29	11	101	13	13	11	64	279,934
Vicar	29	9	86	9	9	12	56	278,996
Untuttable	14	7	64	12	10	7	35	263,005
Cat Thief	19	8	57	8	8	7	34	238,135
Intidab	4	1	13	3	1	4	5	232,834
Littlebitlively	21	6	93	6	14	14	59	216,700
Richter Scale	14	5	38	5	3	3	27	204,013
Greenwood Lake	14	7	68	8	8	8	44	175,395
Wised Up	13	5	57	6	9	6	36	173,748
Meadow Prayer	6	2	15	5	0	2	8	168,542
Storm and a Half	12	5	42	6	9	7	20	166,425
Devonwood	15	5	46	8	8	9	21	153,358
Muqtarib	8	3	28	4	6	4	14	149,932
Unbridled Jet	26	2	84	2	11	11	60	133,071
Deputy Diamond	25	7	94	7	6	8	73	127,081
Kelly Kip	11	3	38	3	11	2	22	118,053
Elnadim	3	3	10	4	1	0	5	117,110
Giant's Causeway	17	2	29	2	5	1	21	113,805
Commendable	14	6	45	7	3	7	28	113,743
Karen's Cat	6	3	17	7	1	1	8	109,430
Brave Act (GB)	1	1	2	1	0	0	1	106,380
Untold Gold	3	2	12	3	4	1	4	100,917
Badge	8	3	30	4	6	3	17	100,581
Crowning Storm	13	2	36	2	8	3	23	97,897
The Deputy (IRE)	16	5	57	5	6	9	37	89,025
Robb	5	3	34	3	2	6	23	85,482
Fiend	2	1	11	2	1	2	6	85,305
Sasha's Prospect	7	3	27	6	3	1	17	83,155
Malek (CHI)	12	1	36	1	8	8	19	81,757
King of Scat	12	6	37	8	3	6	20	79,732
Royal Anthem	17	2	42	2	3	3	34	74,392
Sea Twister	3	2	15	6	1	2	6	72,960

Sire	Perfs.	Winning Perfs.	Starts	1st	2nd	3rd	Unplaced	Purses
Makula King	3	3	15	5	3	1	6	70,330
Behrens	6	3	23	3	4	1	15	70,045
Close Up	5	2	14	3	0	0	11	69,500
B. J.'s Mark	4	1	9	3	0	1	5	69,345
Crowd Pleaser	19	3	54	3	4	8	39	68,567
Brushed On	7	1	29	1	3	6	19	68,190
Best of Luck	27	2	86	2	4	5	75	67,958
Aljabr	5	3	10	5	0	0	5	65,945
Millions	5	2	17	3	1	3	10	63,767
Fine n' Majestic	8	3	79	3	7	7	62	57,180
Commitisize	7	2	29	3	1	6	19	57,066
Adcat	9	2	41	2	5	6	28	56,720
Joe Who (BRZ)	8	4	45	4	8	3	30	55,177
Gone Hollywood	2	2	9	3	3	1	2	53,206
Wind Whipper	10	5	42	5	4	3	30	51,896
Downtown Seattle	3	1	15	2	1	4	8	51,743
Gen Stormin'norman	4	3	14	3	4	0	7	48,960
Malibu Wesley	7	2	23	2	1	5	15	47,382
Star Programmer	12	2	29	2	2	3	22	46,398
Sinndar (IRE)	1	1	1	1	0	0	0	45,000
Rob 'n Gin	5	1	14	1	3	1	9	44,330
Truluck	4	1	14	2	2	1	9	43,941
Maghnatis	4	2	20	4	2	1	13	42,475
Burbank	5	2	20	3	0	2	15	40,570
Seattle Pattern	2	2	12	2	3	2	5	39,995
K One King	6	1	16	3	1	5	7	39,830
Maximum Wager	1	1	10	2	2	1	5	39,742
Go West	2	1	8	1	1	0	6	39,400
Down the Aisle	11	2	37	2	1	6	28	39,220
Paramour	4	2	30	2	5	4	19	39,012
Matricule	9	4	34	4	2	5	23	38,479
Impeachment	6	2	17	2	2	2	11	37,417
Devil Power	1	1	14	1	2	0	11	36,479
Adonis	7	1	20	1	2	3	14	33,774
Red Hammer Red	1	1	6	1	1	1	3	32,522
Tidehaven	3		18	0	3	3	12	31,477
Misnomer	1	1	7	1	0	1	5	30,990
Phonetics	5	1	13	1	1	1	10	30,980
Oly Ogy	3		12	0	3	3	6	30,130
Mantles Star (GB)	5	2	10	3	1	1	5	29,490
Twin Halo	4	1	13	1	3	0	9	28,055
Mighty	12		30	0	3	3	24	26,778
Rod and Staff	2	1	7	1	2	1	3	25,380

Top Freshman Sires in 2004 – Races Won

Sire	Perfs.	Winning Perfs.	Starts	1st	2nd	3rd	Unplaced	Purses
Successful Appeal	20	15	76	31	13	10	22	$1,724,080
Yes It's True	40	15	141	25	12	31	73	1,424,382
More Than Ready	34	17	134	24	23	18	69	837,567
Catienus	31	19	120	23	13	11	73	451,551
Sweetsouthernsaint	23	11	106	19	15	10	62	494,024
Cape Canaveral	30	11	106	18	25	12	51	864,072
Bernstein	18	11	60	17	18	6	19	525,467
Dixie Union	21	11	93	15	21	12	45	695,666
Running Stag	33	10	107	15	13	14	65	516,682
Old Topper	19	10	76	15	20	11	30	498,815
Straight Man	33	12	105	15	18	16	56	413,206
Fusaichi Pegasus	22	7	54	14	8	9	23	923,385
Tiger Ridge	25	11	82	13	15	7	47	517,686
Yankee Victor	27	12	86	13	15	8	50	399,274
Magic Cat	29	11	101	13	13	11	64	279,934
Precise End	27	11	98	12	20	17	49	689,598
Lion Hearted	13	9	40	12	5	7	16	391,917
Untuttable	14	7	64	12	10	7	35	263,005
Chester House	25	9	67	11	9	7	40	326,963
High Yield	27	8	74	11	4	13	46	299,331
Chief Seattle	24	9	74	10	9	12	43	304,361
Vicar	29	9	86	9	9	12	56	278,996
Western Expression	20	7	60	8	9	7	36	384,961
Stephen Got Even	22	7	76	8	6	13	49	314,967
War Chant	14	7	38	8	4	5	21	306,168
Cat Thief	19	8	57	8	8	7	34	238,135
Greenwood Lake	14	7	68	8	8	8	44	175,395
Devonwood	15	5	46	8	8	9	21	153,358
King of Scat	12	6	37	8	3	6	20	79,732
Dance Master	7	4	25	7	5	7	6	383,496
Lemon Drop Kid	16	6	46	7	11	10	18	342,983
Golden Missile	24	6	66	7	7	5	47	332,496
Deputy Diamond	25	7	94	7	6	8	73	127,081
Commendable	14	6	45	7	3	7	28	113,743
Karen's Cat	6	3	17	7	1	1	8	109,430
Anees	19	5	55	6	4	7	38	280,239
Littlebitlively	21	6	93	6	14	14	59	216,700
Wised Up	13	5	57	6	9	6	36	173,748
Storm and a Half	12	5	42	6	9	7	20	166,425
Sasha's Prospect	7	3	27	6	3	1	17	83,155
Sea Twister	3	2	15	6	1	2	6	72,960
Richter Scale	14	5	38	5	3	3	27	204,013
Meadow Prayer	6	2	15	5	0	2	8	168,542
The Deputy (IRE)	16	5	57	5	6	9	37	89,025
Makula King	3	3	15	5	3	1	6	70,330
Aljabr	5	3	10	5	0	0	5	65,945
Wind Whipper	10	5	42	5	4	3	30	51,896
Muqtarib	8	3	28	4	6	4	14	149,932
Elnadim	3	3	10	4	1	0	5	117,110
Badge	8	3	30	4	6	3	17	100,581
Joe Who (BRZ)	8	4	45	4	8	3	30	55,177
Maghnatis	4	2	20	4	2	1	13	42,475
Matricule	9	4	34	4	2	5	23	38,479
Intidab	4	1	13	3	1	4	5	232,834
Kelly Kip	11	3	38	3	11	2	22	118,053
Untold Gold	3	2	12	3	4	1	4	100,917
Robb	5	3	34	3	2	6	23	85,482
Behrens	6	3	23	3	4	1	15	70,045

Sire	Perfs.	Winning Perfs.	Starts	1st	2nd	3rd	Unplaced	Purses
Close Up	5	2	14	3	0	0	11	69,500
B. J.'s Mark	4	1	9	3	0	1	5	69,345
Crowd Pleaser	19	3	54	3	4	8	39	68,567
Millions	5	2	17	3	1	3	10	63,767
Fine n' Majestic	8	3	79	3	7	7	62	57,180
Commitisize	7	2	29	3	1	6	19	57,066
Gone Hollywood	2	2	9	3	3	1	2	53,206
Gen Stormin'norman	4	3	14	3	4	0	7	48,960
Burbank	5	2	20	3	0	2	15	40,570
K One King	6	1	16	3	1	5	7	39,830
Mantles Star (GB)	5	2	10	3	1	1	5	29,490
Unbridled Jet	26	2	84	2	11	11	60	133,071
Giant's Causeway	17	2	29	2	5	1	21	113,805
Crowning Storm	13	2	36	2	8	3	23	97,897
Fiend	2	1	11	2	1	2	6	85,305
Royal Anthem	17	2	42	2	3	3	34	74,392
Best of Luck	27	2	86	2	4	5	75	67,958
Adcat	9	2	41	2	5	6	28	56,720
Downtown Seattle	3	1	15	2	1	4	8	51,743
Malibu Wesley	7	2	23	2	1	5	15	47,382
Star Programmer	12	2	29	2	2	3	22	46,398
Truluck	4	1	14	2	2	1	9	43,941
Seattle Pattern	2	2	12	2	3	2	5	39,995
Maximum Wager	1	1	10	2	2	1	5	39,742
Down the Aisle	11	2	37	2	1	6	28	39,220
Paramour	4	2	30	2	5	4	19	39,012
Impeachment	6	2	17	2	2	2	11	37,417
Kipling	13	2	24	2	3	2	17	24,753
King of the Hunt	3	2	14	2	1	5	6	24,261
Part the Waters	3	2	12	2	2	3	5	22,270
Go Gary Go	5	1	13	2	1	1	9	20,504
Kessem Power (NZ)	7	2	16	2	1	0	13	18,817
Classic Cat	3	2	14	2	1	1	10	17,795
Brave Act (GB)	1	1	2	1	0	0	1	106,380
Malek (CHI)	12	1	36	1	8	8	19	81,757
Brushed On	7	1	29	1	3	6	19	68,190
Sinndar (IRE)	1	1	1	1	0	0	0	45,000
Rob 'n Gin	5	1	14	1	3	1	9	44,330
Go West	2	1	8	1	1	0	6	39,400
Devil Power	1	1	14	1	2	0	11	36,479
Adonis	7	1	20	1	2	3	14	33,774
Red Hammer Red	1	1	6	1	1	1	3	32,522
Misnomer	1	1	7	1	0	1	5	30,990
Phonetics	5	1	13	1	1	1	10	30,980
Twin Halo	4	1	13	1	3	0	9	28,055
Rod and Staff	2	1	7	1	2	1	3	25,380
Shawaf	2	1	10	1	3	1	5	24,690
True Confidence	13	1	43	1	2	4	36	24,561
Why Change	4	1	20	1	3	1	15	24,407
Pulling Punches	12	1	24	1	3	1	19	23,775
Comeonmom	2	1	6	1	0	1	4	21,080
Reparations	1	1	1	1	0	0	0	20,580
Sllic (FR)	5	1	17	1	2	2	12	18,053
Silk Song	2	1	4	1	1	1	1	17,879
Secret Firm	5	1	17	1	1	3	12	17,321
Tropic Lightning	3	1	6	1	2	1	2	15,798
Cascadian	5	1	10	1	2	2	5	15,661
Captain Collins (IRE)	3	1	14	1	0	0	13	15,226
Ground Stroke	4	1	11	1	1	1	8	14,898

Top Freshman Sires in 2004 – Winning Performers

Sire	Perfs.	Winning Perfs.	Starts	1st	2nd	3rd	Unplaced	Purses
Catienus	31	19	120	23	13	11	73	$451,551
More Than Ready	34	17	134	24	23	18	69	837,567
Successful Appeal	20	15	76	31	13	10	22	1,724,080
Yes It's True	40	15	141	25	12	31	73	1,424,382
Straight Man	33	12	105	15	18	16	56	413,206
Yankee Victor	27	12	86	13	15	8	50	399,274
Cape Canaveral	30	11	106	18	25	12	51	864,072
Dixie Union	21	11	93	15	21	12	45	695,666
Precise End	27	11	98	12	20	17	49	689,598
Bernstein	18	11	60	17	18	6	19	525,467
Tiger Ridge	25	11	82	13	15	7	47	517,686
Sweetsouthernsaint	23	11	106	19	15	10	62	494,024
Magic Cat	29	11	101	13	13	11	64	279,934
Running Stag	33	10	107	15	13	14	65	516,682
Old Topper	19	10	76	15	20	11	30	498,815
Lion Hearted	13	9	40	12	5	7	16	391,917
Chester House	25	9	67	11	9	7	40	326,963
Chief Seattle	24	9	74	10	9	12	43	304,361
Vicar	29	9	86	9	9	12	56	278,996
High Yield	27	8	74	11	4	13	46	299,331
Cat Thief	19	8	57	8	8	7	34	238,135
Fusaichi Pegasus	22	7	54	14	8	9	23	923,385
Western Expression	20	7	60	8	9	7	36	384,961
Stephen Got Even	22	7	76	8	6	13	49	314,967
War Chant	14	7	38	8	4	5	21	306,168
Untuttable	14	7	64	12	10	7	35	263,005
Greenwood Lake	14	7	68	8	8	8	44	175,395
Deputy Diamond	25	7	94	7	6	8	73	127,081
Lemon Drop Kid	16	6	46	7	11	10	18	342,983
Golden Missile	24	6	66	7	7	5	47	332,496
Littlebitlively	21	6	93	6	14	14	59	216,700
Commendable	14	6	45	7	3	7	28	113,743
King of Scat	12	6	37	8	3	6	20	79,732
Anees	19	5	55	6	4	7	38	280,239
Richter Scale	14	5	38	5	3	3	27	204,013
Wised Up	13	5	57	6	9	6	36	173,748
Storm and a Half	12	5	42	6	9	7	20	166,425
Devonwood	15	5	46	8	8	9	21	153,358
The Deputy (IRE)	16	5	57	5	6	9	37	89,025
Wind Whipper	10	5	42	5	4	3	30	51,896
Dance Master	7	4	25	7	5	7	6	383,496
Joe Who (BRZ)	8	4	45	4	8	3	30	55,177
Matricule	9	4	34	4	2	5	23	38,479
Muqtarib	8	3	28	4	6	4	14	149,932
Kelly Kip	11	3	38	3	11	2	22	118,053
Elnadim	3	3	10	4	1	0	5	117,110
Karen's Cat	6	3	17	7	1	1	8	109,430
Badge	8	3	30	4	6	3	17	100,581
Robb	5	3	34	3	2	6	23	85,482
Sasha's Prospect	7	3	27	6	3	1	17	83,155
Makula King	3	3	15	5	3	1	6	70,330
Behrens	6	3	23	3	4	1	15	70,045
Crowd Pleaser	19	3	54	3	4	8	39	68,567
Aljabr	5	3	10	5	0	0	5	65,945
Fine n' Majestic	8	3	79	3	7	7	62	57,180
Gen Stormin'norman	4	3	14	3	4	0	7	48,960
Meadow Prayer	6	2	15	5	0	2	8	168,542
Unbridled Jet	26	2	84	2	11	11	60	133,071

Sire	Perfs.	Winning Perfs.	Starts	1st	2nd	3rd	Unplaced	Purses
Giant's Causeway	17	2	29	2	5	1	21	113,805
Untold Gold	3	2	12	3	4	1	4	100,917
Crowning Storm	13	2	36	2	8	3	23	97,897
Royal Anthem	17	2	42	2	3	3	34	74,392
Sea Twister	3	2	15	6	1	2	6	72,960
Close Up	5	2	14	3	0	0	11	69,500
Best of Luck	27	2	86	2	4	5	75	67,958
Millions	5	2	17	3	1	3	10	63,767
Commitisize	7	2	29	3	1	6	19	57,066
Adcat	9	2	41	2	5	6	28	56,720
Gone Hollywood	2	2	9	3	3	1	2	53,206
Malibu Wesley	7	2	23	2	1	5	15	47,382
Star Programmer	12	2	29	2	2	3	22	46,398
Maghnatis	4	2	20	4	2	1	13	42,475
Burbank	5	2	20	3	0	2	15	40,570
Seattle Pattern	2	2	12	2	3	2	5	39,995
Down the Aisle	11	2	37	2	1	6	28	39,220
Paramour	4	2	30	2	5	4	19	39,012
Impeachment	6	2	17	2	2	2	11	37,417
Mantles Star (GB)	5	2	10	3	1	1	5	29,490
Kipling	13	2	24	2	3	2	17	24,753
King of the Hunt	3	2	14	2	1	5	6	24,261
Part the Waters	3	2	12	2	2	3	5	22,270
Kessem Power (NZ)	7	2	16	2	1	0	13	18,817
Classic Cat	3	2	14	2	1	1	10	17,795
Intidab	4	1	13	3	1	4	5	232,834
Brave Act (GB)	1	1	2	1	0	0	1	106,380
Fiend	2	1	11	2	1	2	6	85,305
Malek (CHI)	12	1	36	1	8	8	19	81,757
B. J.'s Mark	4	1	9	3	0	1	5	69,345
Brushed On	7	1	29	1	3	6	19	68,190
Downtown Seattle	3	1	15	2	1	4	8	51,743
Sinndar (IRE)	1	1	1	1	0	0	0	45,000
Rob 'n Gin	5	1	14	1	3	1	9	44,330
Truluck	4	1	14	2	2	1	9	43,941
K One King	6	1	16	3	1	5	7	39,830
Maximum Wager	1	1	10	2	2	1	5	39,742
Go West	2	1	8	1	1	0	6	39,400
Devil Power	1	1	14	1	2	0	11	36,479
Adonis	7	1	20	1	2	3	14	33,774
Red Hammer Red	1	1	6	1	1	1	3	32,522
Misnomer	1	1	7	1	0	1	5	30,990
Phonetics	5	1	13	1	1	1	10	30,980
Twin Halo	4	1	13	1	3	0	9	28,055
Rod and Staff	2	1	7	1	2	1	3	25,380
Shawaf	2	1	10	1	3	1	5	24,690
True Confidence	13	1	43	1	2	4	36	24,561
Why Change	4	1	20	1	3	1	15	24,407
Pulling Punches	12	1	24	1	3	1	19	23,775
Comeonmom	2	1	6	1	0	1	4	21,080
Reparations	1	1	1	1	0	0	0	20,580
Go Gary Go	5	1	13	2	1	1	9	20,504
Silic (FR)	5	1	17	1	2	2	12	18,053
Silk Song	2	1	4	1	1	1	1	17,879
Secret Firm	5	1	17	1	1	3	12	17,321
Tropic Lightning	3	1	6	1	2	1	2	15,798
Cascadian	5	1	10	1	2	2	5	15,661
Captain Collins (IRE)	3	1	14	1	0	0	13	15,226
Ground Stroke	4	1	11	1	1	1	8	14,898

Top 10 Freshman Sires and Their Progeny

Successful Appeal, Dk B H (1996)
By Valid Appeal – Successful Dancer, by Fortunate Prospect

20 Performers, 15 winning performers, $1,724,080 in total earnings.

Progeny	Mare	Age	Sts	1st	2d	3d	Money Won
Accountforthegold	Accountess	2	3	1	1	1	103,325
Brillant Success	Brillant Way	2	3	1	1	0	15,332
Classy Choice	Cecilia's Choice	2	6	3	1	1	66,360
Closing Argument	Mrs. Greeley	2	5	2	2	1	421,984
Double D Appeal	Wicked Diablo	2	3	2	0	1	73,530
Hostile Witness	Diablo's Blend	2	7	2	1	2	59,530
Loni's Appeal	Loni Girl	2	1	0	0	0	860
Looking for Loot	Dance Naturally	2	4	1	1	0	14,380
Lunarpal	Quiet Eclipse	2	5	4	0	0	284,677
Mr. Meridian	Notable Crusader	2	1	0	0	0	580
One El of a Lady	Crafty El	2	2	1	0	0	10,320
Palacios Appeal	Wild Devil	2	5	1	2	0	37,000
Power Link	Linking	2	2	1	0	0	24,805
Prolific Appeal	No Holding David	2	1	0	0	0	0
Punch Appeal	Okanagan Dawn	2	9	6	0	1	389,840
She's a Jewel	Binawin	2	5	2	0	1	70,600
Still Guilty	Oh Jay	2	2	1	1	0	32,600
Successful Affair	Private Pouf	2	1	0	0	0	137
Successfully Sweet	Princess Meadowlak	2	4	3	1	0	104,650
Sun Appeal	Sun Creme	2	7	0	2	2	13,570

Yes It's True, B H (1996)
By Is It True – Clever Monique, by Clever Trick

40 Performers, 15 winning performers, $1,424,382 in total earnings

Progeny	Mare	Age	Sts	1st	2d	3d	Money Won
A True Star	Plano Star	2	5	0	0	1	11,250
B. B. Best	Bold Juana	2	7	4	0	1	360,710
Bushwacked	Launch Site	2	1	0	0	1	1,560
Chandtrue	Chandelle	2	4	4	0	0	182,970
Fab Four	Three's Perfect	2	3	0	1	0	3,300
Hallie Lyn	Semilla Besada	2	2	0	0	0	357
Hollow Sky	Hollow Miss	2	1	0	0	0	1,410
It's Not So	Alinda	2	1	0	0	0	300
Its True Atlast	Joyatlast	2	3	1	0	0	12,500
Its True Its True	Poms Rising Star	2	3	1	0	0	9,030
J. J. Dancer	Flunky Dancer	2	1	0	0	0	230
Krissy C.	Aunt Pia	2	2	0	0	0	4,200
Lotsa Yes	Lotsa Pasta	2	3	0	0	2	4,295
Loud Enough	Speak Up	2	1	0	0	0	78
Maes Gift	Madeleine's Gift	2	3	0	1	0	3,240
Midtown Miss	Van Nic	2	7	2	3	0	51,230
Missile Bay	Saint La Petit	2	7	1	1	3	42,570
Mr. Fourth of July	Illumination	2	1	0	0	0	129
Mrs. Ripley	Sam's Reality	2	2	0	0	0	240
Mz. Winjum	Dyna Performer	2	5	1	1	1	28,860
Palace Intrigue	Time for a Crown	2	1	0	0	0	1,290
Proud Accolade	Proud Ciel	2	5	3	0	0	364,130
Qureall	Sisters Creek	2	2	1	0	0	19,800
R U Sure	Grand Corsage	2	2	0	0	0	1,525
Say It Isn't Sold	Strikingperfection	2	7	0	0	3	9,120
Shoot the Bugler	Sinful Devotion	2	7	1	0	2	39,839
Spider Joe	Josefina	2	6	1	0	2	25,920
Sporty McGee	An A. Forel	2	3	0	2	0	5,290
Suny's Boy	Evanna	2	4	0	1	0	10,773
Tax Considerations	Safety Deposit	2	4	1	0	0	23,451
Testingonetwothree	Notatinkertoy	2	7	0	0	4	4,605
Thanks Fox	Wild Harem	2	5	0	0	2	4,500
True Tails	Cocktail	2	4	2	1	1	51,930
Truly False	Highland Park Ms	2	3	0	0	1	3,260
Wishing for You	Ocean Apart	2	1	0	0	0	1,200
Yes He's a Pistol	Maggies Pistol	2	4	1	0	0	22,780
Yes I'm a Lady	Jellied Madrilene	2	2	0	0	0	270
Yes It's Gold	Maid of Gold	2	7	1	1	4	102,800
Yes Its You	Ice Folly	2	4	0	1	1	5,740
Yes Yes Yes	Daring Doone (GB)	2	1	0	1	0	7,700

Fusaichi Pegasus, B H (1997)
By Mr. Prospector – Angel Fever, by Danzig

22 Performers, 7 winning performers, $923,385 in total earnings.

Progeny	Mare	Age	Sts	1st	2d	3d	Money Won
Andromeda's Hero	Marozia	2	2	1	0	1	17,300
Bandini	Divine Dixie	2	1	0	0	0	180
Boardroom Scandal	Synformer	2	1	0	0	0	118
Candy Striper (GB)	Nurse Goodbody	2	2	0	0	1	4,750
Easterly Breeze	Nakiska Wind	2	3	0	1	1	13,650
Every Other Memory	Frozen Rope	2	6	1	1	1	26,680
Fusaichi Samurai	Hidden Storm	2	1	1	0	0	21,000
Killenaule	Tipically Irish	2	9	4	3	2	198,540
Massasoit	Fancy Clancy	2	1	0	0	1	3,740
Nevsky Prospekt	Northern Hilite	2	1	0	0	0	0
Orezza	Oyster Catcher (IRE)	2	1	0	0	0	2,160
Patience Pays	Mamselle Bebette	2	4	1	0	1	29,830
Princess Medusa	Bet Twice Princess	2	2	0	0	0	600
Princess Pegasus	Shy Princess	2	4	0	0	0	4,250
Roman Ruler	Silvery Swan	2	5	3	1	0	330,800
Scalator	From Time to Time	2	2	0	1	0	3,895
Scandinavia	Party Cited	2	1	0	0	0	0
South Bay Cove	Fantasy Lake	2	4	3	0	0	256,897
Spirited Way	Pacheca	2	1	0	0	0	400
War Plan	Li Law	2	1	0	1	0	3,895
Winged Wishes	Slewzig	2	1	0	0	1	4,700
Witten	Word o' Ransom	2	1	0	0	0	0

Cape Canaveral, Dk B H (1997)
By Mr. Prospector – Seaside Attraction, by Seattle Slew

30 Performers, 11 winning performers, $864,072 in total earnings.

Progeny	Mare	Age	Sts	1st	2d	3d	Money Won
Adriad's Cape	Ariadne's Crown	2	3	0	2	0	20,630
Anariel	Queen Excess	2	1	0	0	0	400
Angel Trumpet	Tricki Mae	2	8	3	3	1	146,456
Apollo Jones	Sister Jones	2	6	1	1	1	44,240
Beyond the Blue	Hot Salsa	2	2	0	0	1	6,897
Byeseeyouchow	Wishmiss	2	3	0	0	0	1,764
Canapuddlejump	Puddlejump	2	5	1	1	0	21,920
Cape Cosmo	Cosmo Topper	2	7	1	3	0	34,250
Cape County	Wheatly Special	2	1	0	0	0	1,230
Cape Kennedy	Dark Jewel	2	1	0	0	0	400
Cape Love	Forbidden Love	2	2	0	0	0	1,272
Cyalady	Miz Riz	2	2	0	1	0	5,250
Edith Prickley	Zigabout	2	4	0	1	0	33,780
Galaxy	Closerthanyouthink	2	6	1	3	1	109,504
J C and Me	White Ice Cream	2	3	0	0	0	1,760
Kitty and Boo	Kitty Car	2	4	1	0	0	17,045
Lady Canaveral	Lady Zip	2	1	0	0	0	161
Lisa the Great	Reach	2	2	0	0	0	400
Megascape	Bigger Half	2	5	3	0	1	161,740
Miss Rocket Jag	Puddy Cat	2	5	1	0	1	9,780
Mr. P D Q	Danzing Tori	2	2	0	0	0	0
Ralitsa	Lucky Lucky Lady	2	10	0	3	2	6,840
Riverman Jack	Jacqueline Alice	2	2	1	0	1	5,120
Roving Angel	Angelinahalo	2	5	3	0	1	120,536
Space Cruise	Engaging	2	1	0	0	0	2,500
Space Hero	Indian Sunset	2	3	0	3	0	23,400
Space Watch	Cat Appeal	2	2	0	0	0	573
Starlits Mission	Starlit Hour	2	4	2	1	0	35,695
Susur	Twochindordor	2	3	0	2	1	41,049
Whistling Straits	Dynamic Broad	2	3	0	1	1	9,480

More Than Ready, Dk B H (1997)
By Southern Halo – Woodman's Girl, by Woodman

34 Performers, 17 winning performers, $837,567 in total earnings.

Progeny	Mare	Age	Sts	1st	2d	3d	Money Won
Anxiously Awaiting	Precious One	2	2	0	0	0	2,500
Argento	Black Tie Kiss	2	2	0	0	0	258
Ask Molly	Chinook Gale	2	6	0	1	1	9,525
Belknap County	Las Manitas	2	8	0	1	1	13,348
Blue Warbler	Meadow Flyer	2	10	0	3	5	52,935
Daytime Delight	Sinfully Delicious	2	5	1	1	0	14,885
Diana's Ready	Madiana	2	6	1	2	0	13,880
Flight Ready	Unbridled Bird	2	2	0	1	1	12,600
Imreadyimready	Micheline	2	3	0	0	1	3,755
Just as Ready	Maybe in May	2	1	0	0	0	205
Lucky Sherman	Special Feeling	2	6	1	1	0	24,780
Merchant Prince	Changing Seasons	2	1	0	0	0	400
Miss Copley Hall	Cup of Cheers	2	1	0	1	0	7,400
More Moonlight	Miss Moonlight	2	5	2	0	1	72,880
More Than Perfect	Pawsitivly Purrfec	2	7	1	0	0	17,880
More Than Promised	Sacred Promise	2	4	2	1	0	38,000
More Than Tricky	Sand Trick	2	5	0	1	2	8,520
More Than Wild	Tell Margie	2	6	2	2	1	56,890
Nawras	Marquetry Road	2	1	0	0	0	0
No More Politics	Office Politics	2	2	2	0	0	23,400
Obsidian	Laday	2	3	0	0	1	2,850
Pevny	Psalms	2	3	1	0	1	18,950
Portsea	Out With the Old	2	3	1	1	0	31,730
Readiness	Batty Dualidad (ARG)	2	4	1	0	0	4,940
Ready Ruler	Reina Victoriosa (ARG)	2	7	2	2	2	114,470
Ready to Flee	Fleet Cherokee	2	4	0	1	0	5,215
Ready to Live	Viva La Viva	2	7	2	3	0	79,500
Ready to Snap	Snappy Time	2	2	1	0	0	7,095
Ready to Swing	Swing	2	2	0	0	0	0
Ready's Gal	Exquisite Mistress	2	3	2	1	0	155,200

Progeny	Mare	Age	Sts	1st	2d	3d	Money Won
Readyfortheweekend	Miss Friday Nite	2	4	1	0	0	15,000
Recommend	Private Seductress	2	3	0	0	0	476
Snow More	Miss Snowflake	2	2	0	0	0	0
Stand Ready	Dame Avie	2	4	1	0	1	28,100

Dixie Union, Dk B H (1997)
By Dixieland Band – She's Tops, by Capote

21 Performers, 11 winning performers, $695,666 in total earnings.

Progeny	Mare	Age	Sts	1st	2d	3d	Money Won
Al Johnstan	Bandeira Nativa	2	2	0	0	1	4,613
Bubble N Squeak	Fiscal Gold	2	7	1	3	0	35,530
Carson's Band	Sharp Tradition	2	3	0	0	0	734
Comacina	Lake Palace	2	6	1	0	3	55,902
Cupid's Dixie	Cary Grove	2	2	0	0	2	7,840
Dixie Boom	Pleasant Boom	2	2	0	1	0	9,180
Elke	Call to the Post	2	7	2	3	1	110,800
Golden Union	Gold Streamer	2	7	1	1	1	29,753
Hanging Chads	Chadra North	2	2	1	1	0	36,000
Im a Dixie Girl	Im Out First	2	9	3	1	1	150,200
J P Jewel	Easy 'n Gold	2	5	1	1	0	42,994
Kim's Grace	Klassy Kim	2	3	0	0	0	1,200
Megaphone	Promised Trial	2	3	0	1	0	7,160
Qadar	Wife for Life	2	1	0	0	0	150
Rascal	April Squall	2	1	0	0	0	0
Snitch	Yousaidamouthful	2	3	0	2	0	4,800
Spikes	Safe At the Plate	2	7	1	0	1	13,709
Straw Hat	Grass Skirt	2	9	1	3	2	57,345
Trooping the Color	Runup the Colors	2	2	0	0	0	0
Union Train	Bries Golden Girl	2	3	1	1	0	32,360
United	Robyns Tune	2	9	2	3	0	95,396

Precise End, Dk B H (1997)
By End Sweep – Precisely, by Summing

27 Performers, 11 winning performers, $689,598 in total earnings

Progeny	Mare	Age	Sts	1st	2d	3d	Money Won
Accurate	Love Destiny	2	6	2	0	1	115,688
Big Apple Daddy	Clever Actress	2	6	1	3	0	100,394
Boggy Creek Dancer	Radon Dancer	2	5	0	0	1	4,902
Bold Decision	Houston Tune	2	1	1	0	0	24,600
Champagne Ending	Dark Champagne	2	3	0	1	0	9,778
Daylights End	Delta Daylight	2	2	0	1	1	12,300
Dynamo Hum	Precious Choice	2	7	1	2	0	45,804
Fixed Amount	Gringo Money	2	2	1	0	1	28,900
Freddy the Cap	Farma Speech	2	5	1	2	0	61,426
Gold Ending	Made for Satin	2	4	0	2	1	8,450
Hoosick Falls	Aaron's Terms	2	4	1	2	0	41,454
Jomarkel	Chap Slewy	2	3	0	1	0	8,169
Look At Me Go Now	Far Away Lady	2	5	0	1	2	8,863
Mr. Rainmaker	Truth and Beauty	2	1	0	0	0	120
Musical Finale	Musical Diablo	2	2	0	0	0	3,280
Naomi's Hope	Lipsia	2	2	0	0	1	4,264
Norwellian	Dancin Dixie Miss	2	2	1	0	0	9,730
Pain and Glory	Strong Little Girl	2	4	0	2	0	17,025
Precise Motion	Lookaway Dixie	2	2	1	0	0	24,805
Precise Star	Arizona Star	2	1	0	1	0	3,690
Precision Perfect	Afleet Closer	2	8	1	1	3	47,976
Quite Precise	C B Carm	2	1	0	0	0	0
Reddy for Rubys	Diamondsandrubys	2	3	1	0	1	80,234
Sweet Hours	Minutes Into Hours	2	4	0	0	1	1,911
Sybelee	Miss Angel Too	2	6	0	0	0	1,855
Taylor D	Jolie Britt	2	3	0	0	1	2,040
The End Is Clear	Clear Vision	2	6	0	1	3	21,940

Bernstein, B H (1994)
By Storm Cat – La Affirmed, by Affirmed

18 Perfomers, 11 winning performers, $525,467 in total earnings.

Progeny	Mare	Age	Sts	1st	2d	3d	Money Won
Bad Little Bernie	Lady Criminal	2	4	1	3	0	34,226
Berbatim	Word Harvest	2	4	2	1	0	56,120
Bernice	Leslie's Jet	2	1	0	0	0	164
Bernie Blue	Blue Sword	2	2	2	0	0	16,320
Bernie's Baby	Jet Ready	2	4	1	1	1	13,620
Bernstein's Babe	The Babe	2	5	0	3	0	38,521
Bernt Out	Outlandish	2	4	2	0	0	15,468
Crafty Kitty	Spotted Prospector	2	2	0	0	0	0
Gilgal	Trista	2	1	0	1	0	2,320
Lady Bernadett	Lefty's Dollbaby	2	1	0	0	0	195
Lenny	Glowing Gal	2	5	1	2	1	23,000
Leonard's Winner	Slipper	2	1	0	1	0	1,500
Miss Bernstein	Kate Carson	2	1	0	1	0	2,565
Prescriptionneeded	Wires Crossed	2	3	1	1	0	20,775
Rugula	Skygusty	2	2	2	0	0	32,400

Progeny	Mare	Age	Sts	1st	2d	3d	Money Won
Sweet Solairo	Sweetascake	2	7	1	4	1	133,683
Toll Taker	Tappanzee	2	6	3	0	1	114,240
Zone Stopper	Dynazone	2	7	1	0	2	20,350

Tiger Ridge, Dk B H (1996)
By Storm Cat – Weekend Surprise, by Secretariat

25 Performers, 11 winning performers, $517,686 in total earnings

Progeny	Mare	Age	Sts	1st	2d	3d	Money Won
Anthony J.	Sly Stylist	2	5	1	1	1	213,630
Apalachee Tiger	Indian Saint	2	2	0	1	0	10,200
Catch That Tiger	Inmusicalflight	2	1	0	0	0	300
Chapel Ridge	Tri Me Later	2	3	1	0	1	7,062
Crystal Tiger	Sky Crystal	2	1	0	1	0	8,200
Destination Heaven	Stop the Rest	2	4	1	0	1	14,430
G P's Black Knight	Ample Time	2	7	2	2	1	89,500
I'll Prey for You	Nasty Sabina	2	2	0	2	0	17,200
June the Tiger	Artic Experience	2	3	1	0	0	31,094
Lookstoogood	Spectacular Image	2	5	1	1	0	17,950
Mail Car Johnny	Princess of Attica	2	6	0	2	0	6,020
Man of Danger	Cope Lady	2	2	1	0	0	20,400
Ms. Tiger Beat	Emeralds and Rubys	2	1	0	1	0	4,600
North Rim	Grainne Waile	2	1	0	0	0	1,150
Racing Tiger	Squarely Appealing	2	4	1	0	0	5,085
Raging Tiger	Mykato	2	7	0	1	1	5,170
Rhea of Villanova	Fab Dancer	2	8	2	1	0	28,410
Striped	Promise Promise	2	4	0	0	0	790
Stud Cat	East Pacemont	2	2	0	0	0	235
Sweet Mercy	Lighting Cielo	2	6	1	1	0	6,980
Taming the Tiger	Archangel Wind	2	1	0	0	1	2,160
Tiger Belle	Sanctioned	2	3	1	0	0	16,980
Tiger Fever	Fuzzy Risque	2	1	0	1	0	6,600
Tiger Lace	Silvery Lace	2	1	0	0	1	1,620
Tiger Rose	Fifty Percent	2	2	0	0	0	1,920

Running Stag, B H (1994)
By Cozzene – Fruhligstag, by Orsini II

33 Performers, 10 winning performers, $516,682 in total earnings

Progeny	Mare	Age	Sts	1st	2d	3d	Money Won
Amandine	Out Out Out	2	1	0	0	0	1,025
Ballari	Pretoria	2	6	0	0	1	2,332
Canadian Cowboy	First Canadian	2	3	0	0	1	4,430
Crafty Stag	Crafty Siren	2	1	0	0	0	0
Dakota Scout	Meadow Melody	2	1	0	0	0	135
Do Run Run	Bobbysoxaroo	2	9	1	1	2	27,510
Enchanted Stag	Bonnies First Lady	2	1	0	0	0	184
Feistee Deer	Oh Tee	2	2	1	0	0	34,200
Gallardo	Motel Time	2	3	0	0	1	5,240
Get On Track	Big Fins	2	3	0	0	1	2,905
Hassayampa	Jametta	2	4	2	0	1	63,209
Hot Shot Luke	Silverdew	2	1	0	0	0	0
Just Jenn	One Smooth Dancer	2	2	0	0	0	350
Miss Oatie May	Most Studious	2	1	0	0	0	0
Nicky Santoro	Corporate Vision	2	1	0	1	0	9,800
Our Sonny Boy	Sea Art	2	5	0	0	1	1,290
Quick Lil Lady	Taft Lil Queen	2	4	1	0	0	8,820
Renga	Alpine Aster	2	3	1	0	0	21,540
Running Bobcats	Backatem	2	8	4	2	1	108,680
Running Deniro	Lady Deniro	2	5	0	1	0	4,495
Running Edition	Rachel's Edition	2	3	0	0	1	3,040
Running Facts	Know the Facts	2	5	0	2	1	14,835
Running Jin	Fleta Kalem	2	2	0	1	0	5,962
Running Surprise	Spring Loose	2	4	1	0	0	16,055
Seacrumbs	Mad 'bout You	2	7	1	0	1	18,880
Send the Facts	Facts of Winning	2	6	1	3	1	60,431
Sidcup	Nice Change	2	3	0	0	1	3,685
Spred Satin	Fleur de Talc	2	1	0	0	0	0
Stag Dancer	Fast Lover	2	2	0	0	0	247
Stag Nation	Class	2	6	2	1	0	92,652
Tik Tak Doe	Nicky Tiki	2	2	0	0	0	1,710
Velocity	Tina Fleet	2	1	0	0	0	100
Why Not Run	My Sainted Aunt	2	1	0	1	0	2,940

Annual Leading Freshman Sire – Money Won

Year	Sire	Winning Perfs.	Races Won	Amount Won
1958	Turn-to	8	25	$463,280
1959	Determine	6	14	411,765
1960	Pappa Fourway	3	11	283,073
1961	Traffic Judge	10	23	264,354
1962	Bold Ruler	10	26	170,643
1963	Cohoes	8	14	201,397
1964	Petare	8	21	543,594
1965	Better Bee	9	21	107,140
1966	Windy Sands	7	11	122,811
1967	Never Bend	5	11	216,212
1968	Northern Dancer	8	20	194,960
1969	Native Charger	3	6	257,717
1970	Tom Rolfe	5	10	362,279
1971	Buckpasser	5	13	498,566
1972	What a Pleasure	11	21	162,147
1973	Drone	9	17	115,012
1974	Dust Commander	6	14	196,742
1975	Al Hattab	11	18	121,146
1976	Raja Baba	13	26	419,872
1977	Roberto	5	13	237,638
1978	Mr. Prospector	8	15	308,311
1979	Tri Jet	6	10	193,282
1980	Foolish Pleasure	7	15	536,783
1981	Turn and Count	11	19	283,279
1982	Seattle Slew	4	11	666,755
1983	Alydar	4	15	1,136,063
1984	Danzig	10	22	2,146,530
1985	Fappiano	8	16	1,232,408
1986	Sportin' Life	8	12	781,734
1987	Crafty Prospector	8	17	349,405
1988	Secreto	3	5	515,284
1989	Moscow Ballet	10	15	541,810
1990	Meadowlake	3	10	1,025,600
1991	Capote	15	20	1,160,237
1992	Silver Deputy	6	13	571,702
1993	Seeking the Gold	8	16	835,792
1994	Red Ransom	11	19	666,658
1995	Farma Way	13	23	819,711
1996	Salt Lake	13	20	850,956
1997	Gilded Time	12	16	722,072
1998	End Sweep	31	42	935,638
1999	Cherokee Run	17	26	1,369,126
2000	Honour and Glory	22	30	1,439,824
2001	Valid Expectations	27	40	1,393,897
2002	Distorted Humor	15	27	1,300,602
2003	Victory Gallop	11	14	914,179
2004	Successful Appeal	15	31	1,724,080

Prior to 1962, amount won included earnings only from winning performers.

Prior to 1965, earnings only include money earned in the United States, Canada, Mexico and Puerto Rico.

From 1965 through 1994, earnings only include money earned in the United States, Canada and Mexico.

After 1994, earnings only include the United States and Canada.

World Records

DIST	HORSE	AGE	WT	TRACK	DATE	TIME
2f	Pensglitter	7	116	Penn National	9-Oct-04	:20.71
2 1/2f	Nice Choice	7	121	Nuevo Laredo	25-Sep-83	:26-1/5
3f	Raisable Adversary	11	119	Remington Park	29-Aug-99	:31.20
3 1/2f	Steel Penny Black	2	115	Northlands Park	14-Jun-84	:38.20
4f	Ameri Brilliance	4	121	Timonium	23-Aug-03	:43.76
4 1/2f	Valiant Pete	4	121	Los Alamitos	11-Aug-90	:49.20
5f (T)	General Express	5	114	Monmouth	8-Jul-00	:54.60
5 1/2f (T)	Pembroke	5	120	Hollywood Park	15-Jul-95	1:00.46
6f	G Malleah	4	120	Turf Paradise	8-Apr-95	1:06.60
6 1/2f	Lucky Forever	6	118	Hollywood Park	20-May-95	1:13.24
7f (T)	Soaring Free	5	126	Woodbine	24-Jul-04	1:19.38
7 1/2f	Awesome Daze	5	119	Hollywood Park	23-Nov-97	1:26.26
1 mile(T)	Elusive Quality	5	117	Belmont Park	4-Jul-98	1:31.63
1m40 (T)	Castaneto	7	115	Atlantic City	28-Jun-91	1:38.08
1m70(T)	Aborigine	6	119	Penn National	20-Aug-78	1:37.20
1 1/16m (T)	Told	4	123	Penn National	14-Sep-80	1:38
1 1/8m(T)	Kostroma	5	117	Santa Anita	20-Oct-91	1:43.92
1 3/16m(T)	Toonerville	5	120	Hialeah Park	7-Feb-76	1:51.40
1 1/4m(T)	Double Discount	4	116	Santa Anita	6-Oct-77	1:57.40
1 5/16m(T)	Roberto	3	122	York (England)	15-Aug-72	2:07
1 3/8(T)	With Approval	4	118	Belmont Park	17-Jun-90	2:10.20
1 7/16m	Who's in Command	5	111	Ellis Park	10-Aug-87	2:23
1 1/2(T)	Hawkster	3	121	Santa Anita	14-Oct-89	2:22.80
1 9/16m	Well Lit	5	120	Sportsman's Park	25-Apr-92	2:35.77
1 5/8m(T)	Tom Swift	5	110	Saratoga	23-Aug-78	2:37
1 11/16m	Glen Gower	4	114	Exhibition Park	9-Sep-87	2:51.20
1 3/4m	Major Pots	5	115	Woodbine	8-Dec-94	2:52.60
1 7/8m(T)	Code's Best	6	121	Mountaineer Racetrack	4-Sep-00	3:08.23
2 m(T)	Petrone	5	124	Hollywood Park	23-Jul-69	3:18
2 1/16m	Midafternoon	4	126	Jamaica	15-Nov-56	3:29.60
2 1/8m	Mr Chancellor	4	111	Exhibition Park	18-Oct-87	3:38.80
2 3/16m	Santiago	5	112	Narragansett	27-Sep-41	3:51.20
2 1/4m	Fenelon	4	119	Belmont Park	4-Oct-41	3:47
2 5/16m	Heiress Marie	3	101	Fairmount Park(Cahokia)	16-Jul-60	4:07.20
2 1/2m	Miss Grillo	6	118	Pimlico	12-Nov-48	4:14.60
3 miles	Farragut	5	113	Agua Caliente, (Mexico)	9-Mar-41	5:15
4 miles	Sotemia	5	119	Churchill Downs	7-Oct-12	7:10.80

Editor's note: All above records are for exact distances and none shorter than 3 1/2 furlongs were set on straight courses. (T) designates turf. Most times were set in .20 intervals. Exact times in hundredths are noted when available.

North American Dirt Records

	HORSE	AGE	WT	TRACK	DATE	TIME
2f	Pensglitter	7	116	Penn National	9-Oct-04	:20.71
2 1/2f	Nice Choice	7	121	Nuevo Laredo	25-Sep-83	:26-1/5
3f	Raisable Adversary	11	119	Remington Park	29-Aug-99	:31.20
3 1/2f	Steel Penny Black	2	115	Northlands Park	14-Jun-84	:38-1/5
	Spiderwoman	5	122	Douglas	23-Apr-00	:38.20
4f	Ameri Brilliance	4	121	Timonium	23-Aug-03	:43.76
4 1/2f	Valiant Pete	4	121	Los Alamitos	11-Aug-90	:49.20
5f	Chinook Pass	3	113	Longacres	17-Sep-82	:55-1/5
5 1/2f	Plenty Zloty	5	118	Turf Paradise	18-Apr-95	1:01.10
6f	G Malleah	4	120	Turf Paradise	08-Apr-95	1:06.60
6 1/2f	Lucky Forever	6	118	Hollywood Park	20-May-95	1:13.24
7f	Rich Cream	5	118	Hollywood Park	28-May-80	1:19-2/5
	Time To Explode	3	117	Hollywood Park	26-Jun-82	1:19-2/5
7 1/2f	Awesome Daze	5	119	Hollywood Park	23-Nov-97	1:26.26
1 mile	Dr. Fager	4	134	Arlington	24-Aug-68	1:32 1/5
	Najran	4	113	Belmont Park	07-May-2003	1:32.24
1 1/16m	Hoedown's Day	5	119	Bay Meadows Fair	23-Oct-83	1:38 2/5
1 1/8m	Simply Majestic	4	114	Golden Gate Fields	02 Apr-88	1:45.
1 3/16m	Riva Ridge	4	127	Aqueduct	04-Jul-73	1.52-2/5
	Farma Way	4	119	Pimlico	11-May-91	1:52-2/5
1 1/4m	Spectacular Bid	4	126	Santa Anita Park	03-Feb-80	1:57-4/5
1 5/16m	Gold Star Deputy	5	116	Aqueduct	10-Apr-99	2:07.32
1 3/8m	Demi's Bret	4	116	Aqueduct	26-Oct-97	2.12.31
1 7/16m	Who's In Command	5	111	Hastings Park	10-Aug-87	2:23.00
1 1/2m	Secretariat	3	126	Belmont Park	09-Jun-73	2:24.00
1 9/16m	Well Lit	5	120	Sportsman's Park	25-Apr-92	2:35.77
1 5/8m	Swaps	4	130	Hollywood Park	25-Jul-56	2:38.20

DIST	HORSE	AGE	WT	TRACK	DATE	TIME
1 11/16m	Glen Gower	4	114	Hastings Park	09-Sep-87	2:51-1/5
1 3/4m	Paper Junction	4	123	Lincoln State Fair	10-Nov-85	2:50-2/5
1 13/16m	Fire North	6	111	Philadelphia Park	14-Mar-92	3:04-4/5
1 7/8m	Asserche	6	123	Laurel Park	20-Mar-94	3:11.56
1 15/16m	Chased Again	10	117	Shenandoah Downs	17-Sep-60	3:24-3/5
2 miles	Kelso	7	124	Aqueduct	31-Oct-64	3:19-1/5
2 1/8m	Laddie's Prince	4	116	Hastings Park	07-Oct-87	3:30
2 1/4m	Paraje	7	113	Aqueduct	15-Dec-73	3:47-4/5
2 5/16m	Heiress Marie	3	101	Cahokia Downs	16-Jul-60	4:07-1/5
2 3/8m	Naughty Nipper	5	119	Lincoln State Fair	13-Nov-83	4:34-1/5
2 1/2m	Miss Grillo	6	118	Pimlico	12-Nov-48	4:14-3/5
2 9/16m	Diamond Platter	7	116	Finger Lakes	12-Oct-74	4:50
2 5/8m	Amber Dare	3	115	Finger Lakes	17-Nov-73	5:12-2/5
2 11/16m	Bea Beauty	8	122	Thistledown	08-Sep-73	4:47-4/5
2 3/4m	Fourth Flight	7	116	Finger Lakes	24-Nov-73	5:35-2/5
3 miles	Farragut	5	113	Agua Caliente	09-Mar-41	5:15
3m 40y	Bea Beauty	8	128	Thistledown	22-Sep-73	5:31-4/5
3m 70y	Gloria Dream	6	110	River Downs	09-Aug-72	5:32-2/5
3 1/16m	Dauntless Pride	4	111	Finger Lakes	19-Oct-74	5:45-2/5
3 1/4m	Dauntless Pride	4	117	Finger Lakes	26-Oct-74	6:15-2/5
3 5/8m	Eastern Promise	6	120	Thistledown	06-Oct-73	6:49-3/5
4 miles	Sotemia	5	119	Churchill Downs	07-Oct-22	7:10-4/5
4m 70y	Gloria Dream	6	113	Finger Lakes	04-Nov-72	8:01
4 1/16m	Amber Dare	3	113	Finger Lakes	03-Nov-73	8:12-2/5
4 1/8m	Victory Tour	4	115	Finger Lakes	02-Nov-74	8:08

Editor's Note: Only exact distances are included in this listing, no 'About' distances.

North American Turf Records

DIST	HORSE	AGE	WT	TRACK	DATE	TIME
4f	Fine Tassles	5	122	Rillito	30-Jan-94	:46.-3/5
4 1/2f	Dan's Groovy	7	120	Turf Paradise	13-Apr-03	:49.26
5f	General Express	5	114	Monmouth Park	08-Jul-00	:54.-3/5
	Bop	5	121	Penn National	03-Aug-02	:54.61
5 1/2f	Pembroke	5	120	Hollywood Park	15-Jul-95	1:00.46
6f	Answer Do	4	115	Hollywood Park	15-Dec-90	1:07.00
6 1/2f	Chris's Bad Boy	7	120	Woodbine	7-Aug-04	1:14.27
7f	Soaring Free	5	126	Woodbine	24-Jul-04	1.19.38
7 1/2f	Court Lark	6	115	Calder Race Course	16-Jul-94	1:26-2/5
1 mile	Elusive Quality	5	117	Belmont Park	04-Jul-98	1:31.63
1 1/16m	Told	4	123	Penn National	14-Sep-80	1:38.00
1 1/8m	Kostroma	5	117	Santa Anita Park	20-Oct-91	1:43.92
1 3/16m	Toonerville	4	120	Hialeah Park	07-Feb-76	1:51-2/5
1 1/4m	Double Discount	4	116	Santa Anita Park	09-Oct-77	1:57-2/5
1 5/16m	Ruff Mack	5	114	Mountaineer Park	25-Aug-62	2:06
1 3/8m	With Approval	4	118	Belmont Park	17-Jun-90	2:10.20
1 7/16m	Dina's Playmate	11	120	River Downs	30-Aug-69	2:25.00
1 1/2m	Hawkster	3	121	Santa Anita Park	14-Oct-89	2:22-4/5
1 5/8m	Tom Swift	5	110	Saratoga	23-Aug-78	2:37.00
1 3/4m	Pleasant Company	5	119	Mountaineer	15-Aug-04	2:55.11
1 13/16m	Misting Rain	8	115	Retama Park	28-Sep-96	3:13.22
1 7/8m	Code's Best	6	121	Mountaineer Park	04-Sep-00	3:08.23
2 miles	Petrone	5	124	Hollywood Park	23-Jul-69	3:18
2 1/16m	Deux-Moulins	8	124	Arlington	28-Jul-55	3:30-4/5
2 1/4m	Buteo	6	122	River Downs	03-Sep-90	3:48.40
2 3/8m	Lively London	5	113	Delaware Park	25-Jul-86	4:09.00
2 13/16	Augustus Bay	8	142	Camden	16-Nov-74	5:24.00
2 7/8m	Call Louis	4	107	Delaware Park	24-Aug-86	5:08-1/5

Editor's note: All records are exact distances. No 'About' distances included.

Canadian Dirt Records

DIST	HORSE	AGE	WT	TRACK	DATE	TIME
2f	Leisure Road	5	120	Fort Erie	5-Sep-98	:21 1/5
3f	Rejected Frenchman	3	122	Kin Park	1-Aug-93	:32 1/5
3 1/2f	Steel Penny Black	2	115	Northlands Park	14-Jun-84	:38 1/5
4f	Adventuresome Love	8	115	Stampede Park	3-Apr-93	:43 4/5
4 1/2f	Canadian Silver	4	119	Greenwood	22-Mar-92	:50
5f	Jack and Emma	4	118	Woodbine	5-Apr-03	:55.95
5 1/2f	Uncle Woger	4	119	Woodbine	4-Apr-99	1:02 3/5
6f	Great Defender	3	114	Woodbine	27-Nov-99	1:08
6 1/2f	Fair Juror	4	105	Woodbine	17-Oct-61	1:14 3/5
7f	Oronero	3	114	Woodbine	6-Dec-95	1:20 3/5
7 1/2f	Iron Vigors	4	122	Assiniboia Downs	9-Oct-89	1:31
1 mile	Twist The Snow	3	117	Greenwood	2-Dec-89	1:34
1m 1/16	Kiridashi	4	121	Woodbine	17-Aug-96	1:40 4/5
1m 1/8	Artic Son	5	117	Hastings Park	3-Aug-98	1:46 4/5
1m 3/16	Bruce's Mill	3	126	Fort Erie	31-Jul-94	1:53 4/5
1m 1/4	Alphabet Soup	5	126	Woodbine	26-Oct-96	2:01
1m 5/16	Arctic Laur	7	116	Northlands Park	20-Aug-95	2:09
1m 3/8	Irish Bear	3	122	Hastings Park	17-Oct-87	2:14 2/5
1m 7/16	Who's In Command	5	111	Hastings Park	10-Aug-87	2:23
1m 1/2	Lucky Son	4	117	Hastings Park	25-Aug-95	2:29
1m 9/16	Eagle's Game	4	123	Kamloops Ex.	6-Sep-92	2:41
1m 5/8	Eugenia II	4	123	Woodbine	27-Oct-56	2:43 2/5
1m 11/16	Glen Gower	4	114	Hastings Park	9-Sep-87	2:51 1/5
1m 3/4	Major Pots	5	115	Woodbine	8-Dec-94	2:52 3/5
1m 13/16	Captain Charisma	5	121	Fort Erie	12-Aug-84	3:09 2/5
1m 7/8	Flying Commander	3	112	Woodbine	2-Dec-01	3:13 1/5
2 miles	Grandin Park	9	118	Stampede Park	13-Oct-79	3:29
2m 1/16	Laddie's Prince	4	116	Hastings Park	7-Oct-87	3:30
2m 1/4	Fremarcton	8	124	Assiniboia Downs	15-Aug-60	3:58 1/5

Editor's note: Only exact distances included on this list, no 'About' distances. Some records were set on tracks that no longer exist.

Canadian Turf Records

DIST	HORSE	AGE	WT	TRACK	DATE	TIME
5f	Oh Mar	6	120	Fort Erie	9-Sep-02	56:99
6f	Wild Zone	6	119	Woodbine	7-Jul-96	1:07 3/5
6.5f	Chris's Bad Boy	7	120	Woodbine	7-Aug-04	1:14.27
7f	Soaring Free	5	126	Woodbine	24-Jul-04	1:19.38
1 mile	Royal Regalia	6	120	Woodbine	1-Jul-04	1:31.84
1m 1/16	Bravest Shot	6	114	Woodbine	1-Jun-90	1:38 4/5
1m 1/8	Bold Ruritana	5	117	Woodbine	18-Jun-95	1:45 1/5
1m 1/4	Mill Native	9	126	Woodbine	20-Aug-88	2:00
1m 3/8	Shoal Water	4	116	Woodbine	25-Jul-04	2:12.37
1m 1/2	Raintrap	4	126	Woodbine	16-Oct-94	2:25 3/5
1m 5/8	Dahlia	4	123	Woodbine	27-Oct-74	2:40
1m 3/4	Desperado Dan	4	115	Woodbine	22-Jul-84	2:56 2/5
1m 7/8	Medlaw	5	123	Fort Erie	30-Sep-85	3:16 1/5
2 miles	Sir Axton	4	117	Woodbine	23-Oct-65	3:56 4/5

Editor's note: Only exact distances included, no 'About' distances.

Track	Surf.	Abt.	Distance	Win Time	Date

The Downs at Albuquerque

Track	Surf.	Abt.	Distance	Win Time	Date
ALB	D		5F	:56.79	4/24/04
ALB	D		5 1/2F	1:02.56	4/9/04
ALB	D		6F	1:08.44	5/2/04
ALB	D		6 1/2F	1:15.41	5/1/04
ALB	D		7F	1:22.11	9/24/04
ALB	D		1M	1:35.84	5/23/04
ALB	D		1 1/16M	1:44.24	6/12/04
ALB	D		1 1/8M	1:49.30	9/26/04
ALB	D		1 1/2M	2:34.34	7/5/04
ALB	D		1 13/16M	3:10.04	9/26/04
ALB	NO TURF				

Anthony Fair

Track	Surf.	Abt.	Distance	Win Time	Date
ANF	D		4 1/2F	:56.46	7/17/04
ANF	D		5F	1:01.39	7/25/04
ANF	D	A	5F	1:01.72	7/18/04
ANF	D		6 1/2F	1:21.54	7/25/04
ANF	D		7F	1:31.93	7/17/04
ANF	D		1 1/16M	1:53.42	7/24/04
ANF	D	A	1 1/16M	1:54.54	7/17/04
ANF	NO TURF				

Arlington Park

Track	Surf.	Abt.	Distance	Win Time	Date
AP	D		4 1/2F	:52.51	5/31/04
AP	D		5F	:57.33	7/9/04
AP	D		5 1/2F	1:04.29	8/8/04
AP	D		6F	1:08.65	8/28/04
AP	D		6 1/2F	1:15.59	6/11/04
AP	D		7F	1:22.25	5/20/04
AP	D		7 1/2F	1:28.81	9/15/04
AP	D		1M	1:35.28	7/4/04
AP	D		1 1/8M	1:49.46	7/10/04
AP	D		1 3/16M	1:56.87	7/31/04
AP	D		1 1/4M	2:07.17	9/18/04
AP	D		1 1/2M	2:33.37	6/12/04

AP Turf

Track	Surf.	Abt.	Distance	Win Time	Date
AP	T	A	5F	:57.10	8/13/04
AP	T		5F	:57.17	8/8/04
AP	T		5 1/2F	1:02.44	9/19/04
AP	T		1M	1:35.84	8/1/04
AP	T	A	1M	1:36.53	8/13/04
AP	T	A	1 1/16M	1:42.32	6/30/04
AP	T		1 1/16M	1:42.57	9/18/04
AP	T		1 1/8M	1:48.63	9/18/04
AP	T	A	1 1/8M	1:48.84	7/30/04
AP	T		1 3/16M	1:54.93	7/24/04
AP	T		1 1/4M	1:59.65	8/14/04
AP	T	A	1 1/2M	2:29.34	8/13/04
AP	T		1 1/2M	2:33.52	7/25/04

Aqueduct

Track	Surf.	Abt.	Distance	Win Time	Date
AQU	D		4 1/2F	:53.01	4/8/04
AQU	D		6F	1:08.81	10/30/04
AQU	D		6 1/2F	1:15.96	11/27/04
AQU	D		7F	1:20.22	4/10/04
AQU	D		7 1/2F	1:28.54	11/27/04
AQU	D		1M	1:33.46	11/27/04
AQU	D		1M 70Y	1:41.28	2/12/04
AQU	D		1M 70Y	1:41.28	3/5/04
AQU	D		1 1/16M	1:42.13	1/17/04
AQU	D		1 1/8M	1:48.33	4/7/04
AQU	D		1 3/16M	1:56.57	3/26/04
AQU	D		1 1/4M	2:04.76	12/10/04
AQU	D		1 5/16M	2:09.63	4/10/04
AQU	D		1 5/8M	2:43.95	12/29/04

Aqu Turf

Track	Surf.	Abt.	Distance	Win Time	Date
AQU	T		1M	1:35.27	5/1/04
AQU	T		1 1/16M	1:42.47	4/24/04
AQU	T		1 1/8M	1:49.95	10/30/04
AQU	T		1 3/8M	2:16.68	10/27/04
AQU	T		1 1/2M	2:31.51	11/6/04

Arapahoe Park

Track	Surf.	Abt.	Distance	Win Time	Date
ARP	D		4F	:44.60	7/26/04
ARP	D		4 1/2F	:50.40	7/19/04
ARP	D		5F	:56.60	8/16/04
ARP	D		5 1/2F	1:02.20	9/4/04
ARP	D		6F	1:08.20	7/11/04
ARP	D		7F	1:21.40	8/1/04
ARP	D		1M	1:36.00	7/31/04
ARP	D		1M 70Y	1:42.80	8/7/04
ARP	D		1 1/16M	1:42.20	8/14/04
ARP	D		1 1/8M	1:50.80	8/29/04
ARP	D		1 1/2M	2:35.60	9/6/04
ARP	NO TURF				

Assiniboia Downs

Track	Surf.	Abt.	Distance	Win Time	Date
ASD	D		4 1/2F	:53.40	7/1/04
ASD	D		5F	:59.20	7/23/04
ASD	D		5F	:59.20	8/6/04
ASD	D		5 1/2F	1:05.80	6/4/04
ASD	D		6F	1:11.00	9/18/04
ASD	D		6F	1:11.00	9/24/04
ASD	D		7 1/2F	1:32.20	7/18/04
ASD	D		1M	1:38.20	8/2/04
ASD	D		1 1/16M	1:44.60	7/11/04
ASD	D		1 1/8M	1:51.80	8/29/04
ASD	NO TURF				

Atlantic City Racecourse

Track	Surf.	Abt.	Distance	Win Time	Date
ATL	NO DIRT				
ATL	T		5F	:55.86	5/13/04
ATL	T		5 1/2F	1:02.39	5/13/04
ATL	T		1M	1:36.73	5/13/04
ATL	T		1 1/16M	1:43.87	5/13/04
ATL	T		1 1/2M	2:28.10	5/5/04

Atokad

Track	Surf.	Abt.	Distance	Win Time	Date
ATO	D		6F	1:11.80	9/17/04
ATO	D	A	6 1/2F	1:15.80	9/19/04
ATO	D		1M	1:42.00	9/17/04
ATO	D		1M 70Y	1:45.20	9/17/04
ATO	D		1M 70Y	1:45.20	9/18/04
ATO	D		1 1/16M	1:47.60	9/18/04
ATO	NO TURF				

Belmont Park

Track	Surf.	Abt.	Distance	Win Time	Date
BEL	D		5F	:57.12	6/6/04
BEL	D		5 1/2F	1:02.26	6/20/04
BEL	D		6F	1:08.04	6/5/04
BEL	D		6 1/2F	1:14.46	6/5/04
BEL	D		7F	1:20.42	7/4/04
BEL	D		7 1/2F	1:27.44	9/24/04
BEL	D		1M	1:34.80	10/1/04
BEL	D		1 1/16M	1:40.02	7/11/04
BEL	D		1 1/8M	1:46.30	6/12/04
BEL	D		1 1/4M	1:59.52	7/3/04
BEL	D		1 1/2M	2:27.50	6/5/04

Bel Turf

Track	Surf.	Abt.	Distance	Win Time	Date
BEL	T		6F	1:10.02	7/11/04
BEL	T		7F	1:20.84	10/11/04
BEL	T		1M	1:32.46	6/17/04
BEL	T		1M	1:32.46	7/10/04
BEL	T		1 1/16M	1:38.64	7/3/04
BEL	T		1 1/8M	1:45.50	9/26/04
BEL	T		1 1/4M	1:59.34	6/5/04
BEL	T		1 3/8M	2:12.19	7/17/04
BEL	T		1 1/2M	2:29.91	10/16/04

Beulah Park

Track	Surf.	Abt.	Distance	Win Time	Date
BEU	D		4 1/2F	:51.29	4/6/04
BEU	D		5F	:57.30	12/16/04
BEU	D		5 1/2F	1:02.52	2/1/04
BEU	D		6F	1:08.32	4/10/04
BEU	D		1M	1:37.20	12/16/04
BEU	D		1M 70Y	1:42.53	1/24/04
BEU	D		1 1/16M	1:46.08	5/1/04
BEU	D		1 1/8M	1:52.63	1/17/04
BEU	D		1 3/16M	2:01.56	2/15/04
BEU	D		1 1/4M	2:06.18	11/21/04
BEU	D		1 1/2M	2:37.18	11/9/04
BEU	D		1 3/4M	3:05.88	11/30/04
BEU	D		2M	3:31.97	12/21/04
BEU	D		2 1/4M	4:02.17	5/1/04
BEU	NO TURF				

Bay Meadows

Track	Surf.	Abt.	Distance	Win Time	Date
BM	D		2F	:21.69	4/22/04
BM	D		4 1/2F	:51.81	6/13/04
BM	D		5F	:56.01	10/27/04
BM	D		5 1/2F	1:02.88	4/16/04
BM	D		6F	1:07.41	9/11/04
BM	D		1M	1:34.51	9/12/04
BM	D		1 1/16M	1:40.08	5/31/04
BM	D		1 1/8M	1:47.95	4/17/04

BM Turf

Track	Surf.	Abt.	Distance	Win Time	Date
BM	T		5F	:56.32	5/30/04
BM	T		7 1/2F	1:29.66	4/17/04
BM	T		1M	1:35.16	4/24/04
BM	T		1 1/16M	1:41.46	4/10/04
BM	T	A	1 1/8M	1:46.55	10/2/04
BM	T		1 1/8M	1:50.40	5/5/04
BM	T		1 3/8M	2:20.01	10/15/04

Bay Meadows Fair

Track	Surf.	Abt.	Distance	Win Time	Date
BMF	D		5F	:59.04	8/11/04
BMF	D		5 1/2F	1:03.10	8/13/04
BMF	D		6F	1:09.01	8/21/04
BMF	D		1M	1:35.80	8/19/04
BMF	D		1 1/16M	1:43.65	8/18/04

BMF Turf

Track	Surf.	Abt.	Distance	Win Time	Date
BMF	T		5F	:56.43	8/11/04
BMF	T		7 1/2F	1:30.31	8/13/04
BMF	T		1M	1:35.16	8/15/04
BMF	T		1 1/16M	1:43.29	8/14/04

Les Bois Park

Track	Surf.	Abt.	Distance	Win Time	Date
BOI	D		4 1/2F	:53.20	7/4/04
BOI	D		5F	:56.60	6/27/04
BOI	D		6 1/2F	1:17.60	7/11/04
BOI	D		7F	1:23.80	7/11/04
BOI	D		7 1/2F	1:31.80	7/4/04
BOI	D		1M	1:38.00	7/31/04
BOI	D		1M	1:38.00	7/31/04
BOI	D		1 1/4M	2:06.60	8/15/04
BOI	NO TURF				

Blue Ribbon Downs

Track	Surf.	Abt.	Distance	Win Time	Date
BRD	D		4F	:46.13	3/14/04
BRD	D		4 1/2F	:52.30	8/15/04
BRD	D		5F	:58.87	2/22/04
BRD	D		5 1/2F	1:03.88	10/17/04
BRD	D		6F	1:11.00	4/18/04
BRD	D		7 1/2F	1:33.60	10/17/04
BRD	D		1M	1:39.78	11/7/04
BRD	NO TURF				

Harney County Fair

Track	Surf.	Abt.	Distance	Win Time	Date
BRN	D		5F	1:00.60	9/12/04
BRN	D		7F	1:29.60	9/11/04
BRN	D		1 1/8M	1:57.00	9/12/04
BRN	NO TURF				

Track	Surf.	Abt.	Distance	Win Time	Date

Canterbury Park

Track	Surf.	Abt.	Distance	Win Time	Date
CBY	D		3 1/2F	:39.63	5/29/04
CBY	D		5F	:57.11	5/31/04
CBY	D		5 1/2F	1:03.15	8/20/04
CBY	D		6F	1:08.85	8/15/04
CBY	D		6 1/2F	1:15.56	7/17/04
CBY	D		1M	1:35.30	8/14/04
CBY	D		1M 70Y	1:40.59	8/13/04
CBY	D		1 1/16M	1:41.74	8/22/04
CBY	D		1 1/8M	1:49.62	7/17/04

Cby Turf

Track	Surf.	Abt.	Distance	Win Time	Date
CBY	T		5F	:56.31	8/21/04
CBY	T	A	7 1/2F	1:29.62	7/29/04
CBY	T		7 1/2F	1:29.91	9/2/04
CBY	T	A	1M	1:35.36	7/23/04
CBY	T		1M	1:35.55	6/20/04
CBY	T		1M	1:35.55	8/22/04
CBY	T		1 1/16M	1:41.89	6/19/04
CBY	T	A	1 1/16M	1:42.00	8/13/04
CBY	T		1 3/8M	2:20.64	9/6/04

Churchill Downs

Track	Surf.	Abt.	Distance	Win Time	Date
CD	D		4 1/2F	:51.29	4/29/04
CD	D		5F	:56.61	6/10/04
CD	D		5 1/2F	1:03.94	7/3/04
CD	D		6F	1:08.67	6/9/04
CD	D		6 1/2F	1:15.63	7/4/04
CD	D		7F	1:21.38	5/1/04
CD	D		7 1/2F	1:28.26	4/29/04
CD	D		1M	1:35.05	11/7/04
CD	D		1 1/16M	1:42.44	5/8/04
CD	D		1 1/8M	1:49.66	6/10/04
CD	D		1 1/4M	2:03.71	5/8/04
CD	D		1 1/2M	2:32.84	7/4/04

CD Turf

Track	Surf.	Abt.	Distance	Win Time	Date
CD	T		5F	:55.97	6/23/04
CD	T		1M	1:34.15	7/3/04
CD	T		1 1/16M	1:41.51	5/23/04
CD	T		1 1/8M	1:46.75	6/26/04
CD	T		1 3/8M	2:16.71	5/6/04

Columbus

Track	Surf.	Abt.	Distance	Win Time	Date
CLS	D		3 1/2F	:41.00	7/23/04
CLS	D		6F	1:13.40	8/14/04
CLS	D		6F	1:13.40	8/14/04
CLS	D		6F	1:13.40	9/11/04
CLS	D		6 1/2F	1:19.40	9/4/04
CLS	D		1M 70Y	1:44.60	9/3/04
CLS	D		1 1/16M	1:49.40	8/13/04
CLS	NO TURF				

Colonial Downs

Track	Surf.	Abt.	Distance	Win Time	Date
CNL	D		5F	:56.66	6/28/04
CNL	D		5 1/2F	1:03.85	7/24/04
CNL	D		6F	1:08.48	6/27/04
CNL	D		7F	1:22.90	7/13/04
CNL	D		1M	1:35.07	6/26/04
CNL	D		1 1/16M	1:42.90	7/26/04
CNL	D		1 1/8M	1:49.68	6/25/04

Cnl Turf

Track	Surf.	Abt.	Distance	Win Time	Date
CNL	T		5F	:56.95	7/2/04
CNL	T		5 1/2F	1:03.67	7/5/04
CNL	T		1M	1:37.32	7/6/04
CNL	T		1 1/16M	1:43.14	7/2/04
CNL	T		1 1/8M	1:50.08	7/10/04
CNL	T		1 3/16M	1:58.37	7/23/04
CNL	T		1 1/4M	2:01.22	7/10/04

Chippewa Downs

Track	Surf.	Abt.	Distance	Win Time	Date
CPW	D	A	2F	:19.80	6/20/04
CPW	D		2 1/2F	:32.80	6/12/04
CPW	D		4 1/2F	:59.40	6/27/04
CPW	D		5F	1:02.20	6/27/04
CPW	D		5 1/2F	1:09.20	6/19/04
CPW	D		6 1/2F	1:22.80	6/20/04
CPW	D		1M 70Y	1:51.80	6/27/04
CPW	NO TURF				

Calder Race Course

Track	Surf.	Abt.	Distance	Win Time	Date
CRC	D		2F	:21.65	7/10/04
CRC	D		4 1/2F	:52.27	8/21/04
CRC	D		5F	:58.06	11/25/04
CRC	D		5 1/2F	1:04.50	12/27/04
CRC	D		6F	1:09.64	5/9/04
CRC	D		6 1/2F	1:17.18	12/18/04
CRC	D		7F	1:22.62	12/18/04
CRC	D		1M	1:38.28	6/7/04
CRC	D		1M 70Y	1:46.30	10/2/04
CRC	D		1 1/16M	1:45.46	7/9/04
CRC	D		1 1/8M	1:50.74	12/18/04
CRC	D		1 1/4M	2:10.37	6/28/04
CRC	D		1 1/2M	2:40.55	6/5/04

Crc Turf

Track	Surf.	Abt.	Distance	Win Time	Date
CRC	T		5F	:54.78	5/23/04
CRC	T		7 1/2F	1:27.89	12/16/04
CRC	T		1M	1:34.18	7/11/04
CRC	T		1 1/16M	1:39.27	12/28/04
CRC	T		1 1/8M	1:45.74	12/4/04
CRC	T		1 3/8M	2:24.53	7/19/04
CRC	T		1 1/2M	2:26.60	12/18/04

Charles Town

Track	Surf.	Abt.	Distance	Win Time	Date
CT	D		4F	:44.86	10/8/04
CT	D		4 1/2F	:50.85	8/1/04
CT	D		6 1/2F	1:18.38	10/27/04
CT	D		7F	1:25.05	12/26/04
CT	D		1 1/16M	1:46.12	5/1/04
CT	D		1 1/8M	1:52.95	7/18/04
CT	NO TURF				

Delta Downs

Track	Surf.	Abt.	Distance	Win Time	Date
DED	D		4 1/2F	:52.98	3/19/04
DED	D		5F	:57.91	1/14/04
DED	D		6 1/2F	1:19.21	1/2/04
DED	D		7F	1:25.86	11/12/04
DED	D		7 1/2F	1:35.84	1/15/04
DED	D		1M	1:38.21	3/27/04
DED	D		1 1/16M	1:45.00	3/27/04
DED	D		1 1/4M	2:13.49	12/22/04
DED	D		1 3/8M	2:28.12	2/20/04
DED	D		1 9/16M	2:46.86	3/27/04
DED	NO TURF				

Delaware Park

Track	Surf.	Abt.	Distance	Win Time	Date
DEL	D		4 1/2F	:52.56	5/24/04
DEL	D		5F	:57.87	9/19/04
DEL	D		5 1/2F	1:03.56	9/4/04
DEL	D		6F	1:08.99	6/15/04
DEL	D		1M	1:36.62	5/8/04
DEL	D		1M 70Y	1:41.19	7/20/04
DEL	D		1 1/16M	1:43.00	8/21/04
DEL	D		1 1/8M	1:48.43	9/11/04
DEL	D		1 3/16M	1:57.73	10/2/04
DEL	D		1 1/4M	2:02.74	5/18/04
DEL	D		1 1/2M	2:35.73	7/18/04

Del Turf

Track	Surf.	Abt.	Distance	Win Time	Date
DEL	T		5F	:56.26	9/13/04
DEL	T	A	5F	:57.17	9/27/04
DEL	T		1M	1:36.69	9/8/04
DEL	T	A	1M	1:39.36	8/23/04
DEL	T		1 1/16M	1:41.73	9/13/04
DEL	T	A	1 1/16M	1:43.48	7/4/04
DEL	T		1 1/8M	1:48.90	9/12/04
DEL	T	A	1 1/8M	1:51.88	9/25/04
DEL	T		1 3/8M	2:20.07	7/17/04

Cochise County Fair

Track	Surf.	Abt.	Distance	Win Time	Date
DG	D	A	3F	:38.00	4/11/04
DG	D		5 1/2F	1:05.00	4/18/04
DG	D		6F	1:11.20	4/17/04
DG	D		7F	1:25.20	4/18/04
DG	D		1M	1:40.20	4/18/04
DG	NO TURF				

Del Mar

Track	Surf.	Abt.	Distance	Win Time	Date
DMR	D		5F	:58.82	7/25/04
DMR	D		5 1/2F	1:03.48	9/6/04
DMR	D		6F	1:08.25	9/6/04
DMR	D		6 1/2F	1:14.98	8/21/04
DMR	D		7F	1:21.17	8/15/04
DMR	D		1M	1:35.09	9/3/04
DMR	D		1 1/16M	1:42.00	7/25/04
DMR	D		1 1/8M	1:51.09	8/5/04
DMR	D		1 1/4M	2:01.17	8/22/04

Dmr Turf

Track	Surf.	Abt.	Distance	Win Time	Date
DMR	T		5F	:55.10	8/12/04
DMR	T		1M	1:33.25	8/28/04
DMR	T		1 1/16M	1:39.93	8/20/04
DMR	T		1 1/8M	1:45.90	7/25/04
DMR	T		1 3/8M	2:12.71	8/29/04

Greenlee County Fair

Track	Surf.	Abt.	Distance	Win Time	Date
DUN	D		5F	1:00.40	3/20/04
DUN	D		5 1/2F	1:06.00	3/21/04
DUN	D	A	6F	1:10.80	3/13/04
DUN	D		7F	1:27.20	3/21/04
DUN	D		7F	1:27.20	3/21/04
DUN	NO TURF				

Elko

Track	Surf.	Abt.	Distance	Win Time	Date
ELK	D		5 1/2F	1:06.00	9/4/04
ELK	D		6F	1:12.00	9/5/04
ELK	D		6 1/2F	1:19.80	9/4/04
ELK	D		7F	1:25.00	9/5/04
ELK	D		1M	1:38.60	9/6/04
ELK	D		1 5/16M	2:19.40	9/6/04
ELK	NO TURF				

Ellis Park

Track	Surf.	Abt.	Distance	Win Time	Date
ELP	D		5F	:58.19	9/6/04
ELP	D		5 1/2F	1:03.79	8/26/04
ELP	D		6F	1:09.38	8/25/04
ELP	D		6 1/2F	1:16.06	7/11/04
ELP	D		7F	1:21.37	9/5/04
ELP	D		1M	1:35.34	8/28/04
ELP	D		1 1/8M	1:49.54	8/7/04

ELP Turf

Track	Surf.	Abt.	Distance	Win Time	Date
ELP	T		5 1/2F	1:00.84	7/15/04
ELP	T		1M	1:33.71	9/5/04
ELP	T		1 1/16M	1:39.22	9/6/04
ELP	T		1 1/8M	1:49.28	8/20/04
ELP	T		1 1/4M	2:03.88	8/29/04
ELP	T		1 1/2M	2:40.86	7/11/04

Emerald Downs

Track	Surf.	Abt.	Distance	Win Time	Date
EMD	D		2F	:22.40	4/25/04
EMD	D		4 1/2F	:51.40	6/3/04
EMD	D		4 1/2F	:51.40	6/18/04
EMD	D		5F	:56.00	4/24/04
EMD	D		5F	:56.00	8/22/04
EMD	D		5 1/2F	1:01.20	4/16/04
EMD	D		6F	1:07.80	4/25/04
EMD	D		6 1/2F	1:13.60	5/31/04
EMD	D		1M	1:33.80	5/30/04
EMD	D		1 1/16M	1:40.60	9/19/04
EMD	D		1 1/8M	1:46.60	7/25/04
EMD	NO TURF				

Eureka

Track	Surf.	Abt.	Distance	Win Time	Date
EUR	D		4F	:45.53	6/6/04
EUR	D		6F	1:13.65	6/26/04
EUR	D		7F	1:29.37	6/12/04
EUR	NO TURF				

Evangeline Downs

Track	Surf.	Abt.	Distance	Win Time	Date
EVD	D		2 1/2F	:27.00	7/10/04
EVD	D		4 1/2F	:52.00	6/3/04
EVD	D		5F	:57.40	4/24/04
EVD	D		5 1/2F	1:03.40	8/26/04
EVD	D		6F	1:10.00	6/25/04
EVD	D		7 1/2F	1:31.40	4/2/04
EVD	D		1M	1:37.80	8/14/04
EVD	D		1M 70Y	1:43.60	4/10/04
EVD	D		1 1/16M	1:46.00	5/1/04
EVD	NO TURF				

North Dakota Horse Park

Track	Surf.	Abt.	Distance	Win Time	Date
FAR	D		4F	:48.60	8/29/04
FAR	D		5F	1:00.00	9/4/04
FAR	D		5F	1:00.00	9/5/04
FAR	D		5 1/2F	1:06.60	8/21/04
FAR	D		6F	1:13.00	8/14/04
FAR	D		7F	1:28.60	8/28/04
FAR	D		1M	1:41.40	9/6/04
FAR	D		1 1/2M	2:40.60	9/6/04
FAR	NO TURF				

Fort Erie

Track	Surf.	Abt.	Distance	Win Time	Date
FE	D		2F	:21.61	8/3/04
FE	D		5F	:57.31	6/12/04
FE	D		6F	1:10.26	7/1/04
FE	D		6 1/2F	1:16.12	8/21/04
FE	D		1M 70Y	1:42.42	8/2/04
FE	D		1 1/16M	1:43.49	6/15/04
FE	D		1 1/8M	1:53.12	8/16/04
FE	D		1 3/16M	1:57.69	7/18/04
FE	D		1 1/4M	2:09.57	7/24/04
FE	D		1 3/4M	3:08.50	8/10/04
FE	D		2M 70Y	3:40.05	9/5/04

FE Turf

Track	Surf.	Abt.	Distance	Win Time	Date
FE	T		5F	:58.12	7/25/04
FE	T	A	5F	:59.07	8/27/04
FE	T	A	7F	1:22.76	6/29/04
FE	T		1M	1:37.82	9/4/04
FE	T	A	1M	1:39.82	7/1/04
FE	T		1 1/16M	1:43.39	6/28/04
FE	T	A	1 1/16M	1:45.91	7/13/04
FE	T	A	1 3/8M	2:21.53	7/1/04

Ferndale

Track	Surf.	Abt.	Distance	Win Time	Date
FER	D		3F	:33.73	8/19/04
FER	D		5F	:58.23	8/21/04
FER	D		6 1/2F	1:19.15	8/14/04
FER	D		7F	1:24.96	8/16/04
FER	D		1 1/16M	1:46.67	8/21/04
FER	D		1 5/8M	2:47.04	8/22/04
FER	NO TURF				

Fair Ground

Track	Surf.	Abt.	Distance	Win Time	Date
FG	D		5 1/2F	1:03.20	1/26/04
FG	D		6F	1:08.83	3/14/04
FG	D		1M	1:36.71	2/19/04
FG	D		1M 40Y	1:38.53	3/4/04
FG	D		1 1/16M	1:42.71	3/7/04
FG	D		1 1/8M	1:48.61	2/29/04

FG Turf

Track	Surf.	Abt.	Distance	Win Time	Date
FG	T	A	5 1/2F	1:02.90	3/27/04
FG	T	A	7 1/2F	1:30.12	3/28/04
FG	T	A	1M	1:35.57	3/20/04
FG	T	A	1 1/16M	1:43.58	3/26/04
FG	T	A	1 1/8M	1:48.29	3/21/04

Finger Lakes

Track	Surf.	Abt.	Distance	Win Time	Date
FL	D		4 1/2F	:51.68	4/16/04
FL	D		5F	:57.84	4/30/04
FL	D		5 1/2F	1:03.52	8/22/04
FL	D		6F	1:09.02	8/21/04
FL	D		1M	1:40.21	4/24/04
FL	D		1M 70Y	1:41.15	8/27/04
FL	D		1 1/16M	1:44.53	9/6/04
FL	D		1 1/8M	1:53.63	7/4/04
FL	D		1 1/4M	2:09.32	9/10/04
FL	NO TURF				

Flagstaff

Track	Surf.	Abt.	Distance	Win Time	Date
FLG	D	A	3F	:39.60	7/3/04
FLG	D		5 1/2F	1:09.00	7/4/04
FLG	D		5 1/2F	1:09.00	7/4/04
FLG	D		6F	1:14.80	7/2/04
FLG	D		6 1/2F	1:22.80	7/4/04
FLG	D		7F	1:26.80	7/4/04
FLG	D		1M	1:43.60	7/4/04
FLG	NO TURF				

Fair Meadows

Track	Surf.	Abt.	Distance	Win Time	Date
FMT	D		4F	:44.60	6/19/04
FMT	D		5 1/2F	1:05.20	6/25/04
FMT	D		6F	1:11.40	7/10/04
FMT	D		6 1/2F	1:18.60	6/25/04
FMT	D		6 1/2F	1:18.60	7/9/04
FMT	D		1M	1:38.40	6/12/04
FMT	NO TURF				

Fresno

Track	Surf.	Abt.	Distance	Win Time	Date
FNO	D		5F	:56.79	10/9/04
FNO	D		5 1/2F	1:03.53	10/14/04
FNO	D		6F	1:07.50	10/8/04
FNO	D		1M	1:34.79	10/16/04
FNO	D		1 1/8M	1:48.09	10/9/04
FNO	NO TURF				

Fonner Park

Track	Surf.	Abt.	Distance	Win Time	Date
FON	D		4F	:45.20	2/14/04
FON	D		4F	:45.20	2/21/04
FON	D		6F	1:11.60	3/13/04
FON	D		6F	1:11.60	4/9/04
FON	D		6 1/2F	1:18.20	5/1/04
FON	D		1M	1:38.80	5/8/04
FON	D		1M 70Y	1:44.00	5/7/04
FON	D		1M 70Y	1:44.00	5/8/04
FON	D		1 1/16M	1:46.80	4/24/04
FON	D		1 1/8M	1:52.40	5/8/04
FON	NO TURF				

Fairmount Park

Track	Surf.	Abt.	Distance	Win Time	Date
FP	D		4F	:47.40	3/26/04
FP	D		4 1/2F	:53.20	3/26/04
FP	D		4 1/2F	:53.20	3/27/04
FP	D		5F	:58.60	8/28/04
FP	D		5 1/2F	1:04.40	5/4/04
FP	D		5 1/2F	1:04.40	5/14/04
FP	D		6F	1:09.20	5/1/04
FP	D		1M	1:38.00	5/4/04
FP	D		1M 70Y	1:41.20	5/13/04
FP	D		1 1/4M	2:04.40	8/20/04
FP	NO TURF				

Fairplex Park

Track	Surf.	Abt.	Distance	Win Time	Date
FPX	D	A	4F	:44.79	9/13/04
FPX	D		6F	1:10.03	9/25/04
FPX	D		6 1/2F	1:15.42	9/21/04
FPX	D		7F	1:22.53	9/26/04
FPX	D		1 1/16M	1:42.48	9/11/04
FPX	D	A	1 1/8M	1:48.95	9/25/04
FPX	D		1 3/8M	2:17.34	9/26/04
FPX	NO TURF				

Gila County Fair

Track	Surf.	Abt.	Distance	Win Time	Date
GCF	D		3F	:35.00	10/10/04
GCF	D		5F	1:01.20	10/9/04
GCF	D		5 1/2F	1:08.00	10/2/04
GCF	D		6F	1:15.40	10/2/04
GCF	D		6F	1:15.40	10/9/04
GCF	D		7F	1:33.60	10/10/04
GCF	D		1 1/16M	1:55.60	10/10/04
GCF	NO TURF				

Great Falls

Track	Surf.	Abt.	Distance	Win Time	Date
GF	D		5F	:59.60	7/30/04
GF	D	A	5F	1:04.80	7/18/04
GF	D	A	5 1/4F	1:04.40	8/1/04
GF	D	A	5 1/4F	1:04.40	8/1/04
GF	D		7F	1:26.40	8/1/04
GF	D		7F	1:26.40	8/1/04
GF	D		1M 70Y	1:46.20	8/1/04
GF	NO TURF				

Golden Gate Fields

Track	Surf.	Abt.	Distance	Win Time	Date
GG	D		2F	:21.75	3/26/04
GG	D		5F	:56.34	1/10/04
GG	D		5 1/2F	1:01.99	2/25/04
GG	D		6F	1:07.56	2/20/04
GG	D		1M	1:33.92	3/27/04
GG	D		1 1/16M	1:40.67	2/28/04
GG	D		1 1/8M	1:49.14	12/5/04

GG Turf

Track	Surf.	Abt.	Distance	Win Time	Date
GG	T		4 1/2F	:50.25	4/2/04
GG	T		1M	1:35.78	3/18/04
GG	T		1 1/16M	1:41.94	3/20/04
GG	T		1 1/8M	1:48.48	3/14/04

Gillespie County Fair

Track	Surf.	Abt.	Distance	Win Time	Date
GIL	D		5 1/2F	1:09.19	8/28/04
GIL	D		6F	1:16.30	7/18/04
GIL	D		7F	1:29.61	8/29/04
GIL	NO TURF				

Great Lakes Downs

Track	Surf.	Abt.	Distance	Win Time	Date
GLD	D		4F	:46.90	6/25/04
GLD	D		5 1/2F	1:07.57	4/25/04
GLD	D		6F	1:12.65	6/12/04
GLD	D		6 1/2F	1:21.32	10/2/04
GLD	D		7F	1:27.63	8/29/04
GLD	D		1M	1:42.82	6/1/04
GLD	D		1 1/16M	1:49.95	9/17/04
GLD	D		1 1/8M	1:57.63	10/9/04
GLD	D		1 5/16M	2:22.81	9/8/04
GLD	NO TURF				

Gulfstream Park

Track	Surf.	Abt.	Distance	Win Time	Date
GP	D		3F	:33.38	4/24/04
GP	D		5F	:56.48	3/3/04
GP	D		5 1/2F	1:03.29	2/11/04
GP	D		6F	1:08.30	1/8/04
GP	D		6 1/2F	1:15.55	3/7/04
GP	D		7F	1:21.42	2/8/04
GP	D		7F	1:21.42	2/14/04
GP	D		1M 70Y	1:41.96	4/16/04
GP	D		1 1/16M	1:42.39	1/3/04
GP	D		1 1/8M	1:47.68	2/7/04
GP	D		1 1/4M	2:02.80	4/3/04

GP Turf

Track	Surf.	Abt.	Distance	Win Time	Date
GP	T	A	5F	:55.61	3/28/04
GP	T		5F	:56.16	4/11/04
GP	T		1M	1:33.38	2/21/04
GP	T	A	1M	1:36.11	1/29/04
GP	T		1 1/16M	1:40.50	1/3/04
GP	T	A	1 1/16M	1:42.15	4/7/04
GP	T		1 1/8M	1:45.69	1/24/04

Track	Surf.	Abt.	Distance	Win Time	Date
GP	T	A	1 1/8M	1:48.58	3/12/04
GP	T		1 3/8M	2:11.56	2/22/04
GP	T	A	1 3/8M	2:19.14	3/19/04
GP	T		1 1/2M	2:26.27	2/22/04
GP	T	A	1 1/2M	2:34.65	3/1/04

Grande Prairie

Track	Surf.	Abt.	Distance	Win Time	Date
GPR	D		4F	:47.20	8/1/04
GPR	D		5 1/2F	1:07.60	7/16/04
GPR	D		5 1/2F	1:07.60	8/1/04
GPR	D		5 1/2F	1:07.60	8/15/04
GPR	D		5 1/2F	1:07.60	8/22/04
GPR	D		6F	1:13.40	8/7/04
GPR	D		6F	1:13.40	8/20/04
GPR	D		6 1/2F	1:20.00	8/13/04
GPR	D		7F	1:25.40	8/15/04
GPR	D		1M	1:40.60	8/14/04
GPR	D		1 1/16M	1:50.40	7/25/04
GPR	D		1 1/8M	1:55.00	8/22/04
GPR	NO TURF				

Grants Pass

Track	Surf.	Abt.	Distance	Win Time	Date
GRP	D		4 1/2F	:51.40	6/27/04
GRP	D		5F	:58.20	7/3/04
GRP	D		5 1/2F	1:04.40	5/15/04
GRP	D		6 1/2F	1:17.20	5/16/04
GRP	NO TURF				

Hawthorne

Track	Surf.	Abt.	Distance	Win Time	Date
HAW	D		4 1/2F	:53.53	5/4/04
HAW	D		6F	1:08.97	12/5/04
HAW	D		6 1/2F	1:15.99	12/11/04
HAW	D		1M 70Y	1:41.77	3/26/04
HAW	D		1 1/16M	1:43.25	12/4/04
HAW	D		1 1/8M	1:49.54	4/17/04
HAW	D		1 1/4M	2:03.34	10/2/04

Haw Turf

Track	Surf.	Abt.	Distance	Win Time	Date
HAW	T		1M	1:34.51	10/9/04
HAW	T		1 1/16M	1:41.10	5/2/04
HAW	T		1 1/8M	1:47.89	10/16/04

Hollywood Park

Track	Surf.	Abt.	Distance	Win Time	Date
HOL	D		4 1/2F	:50.83	4/29/04
HOL	D		5F	:56.29	5/30/04
HOL	D		5 1/2F	1:02.19	12/12/04
HOL	D		6F	1:08.04	12/5/04
HOL	D		6 1/2F	1:14.30	11/3/04
HOL	D		7F	1:20.69	12/18/04
HOL	D		7 1/2F	1:27.30	11/13/04
HOL	D		1 1/16M	1:40.69	12/20/04
HOL	D		1 1/8M	1:47.06	12/11/04
HOL	D		1 1/4M	2:00.72	7/10/04

Hol Turf

Track	Surf.	Abt.	Distance	Win Time	Date
HOL	T		5F	:58.28	6/20/04
HOL	T		5 1/2F	1:00.60	4/23/04
HOL	T		1M	1:32.81	5/31/04
HOL	T		1 1/16M	1:38.45	5/1/04
HOL	T		1 1/8M	1:46.60	7/4/04
HOL	T		1 1/4M	1:59.04	4/21/04
HOL	T		1 1/2M	2:26.45	5/30/04

Hoosier Park

Track	Surf.	Abt.	Distance	Win Time	Date
HOO	D		5F	:58.39	10/9/04
HOO	D		5 1/2F	1:04.23	10/22/04
HOO	D		6F	1:09.93	9/19/04
HOO	D		1M	1:35.85	11/13/04
HOO	D		1 1/16M	1:43.65	10/1/04
HOO	D		1 1/8M	1:54.47	10/2/04
HOO	D		1 1/2M	2:36.88	10/30/04
HOO	NO TURF				

Sam Houston Racepark

Track	Surf.	Abt.	Distance	Win Time	Date
HOU	D		4 1/2F	:51.70	2/12/04
HOU	D		5F	:57.48	3/4/04
HOU	D		5 1/2F	1:03.42	12/9/04
HOU	D		6F	1:09.61	2/21/04
HOU	D		6 1/2F	1:16.59	12/17/04
HOU	D		7F	1:22.56	3/20/04
HOU	D		1M	1:37.78	11/20/04
HOU	D		1M 70Y	1:42.81	12/4/04
HOU	D		1 1/16M	1:43.74	11/20/04
HOU	D		1 1/8M	1:51.76	1/17/04

Hou Turf

Track	Surf.	Abt.	Distance	Win Time	Date
HOU	T		5F	:57.96	2/28/04
HOU	T		1M	1:38.22	1/10/04
HOU	T		1 1/16M	1:45.44	1/9/04
HOU	T		1 1/8M	1:53.01	4/10/04
HOU	T		1 1/2M	2:39.87	4/9/04

Horsemen's Park

Track	Surf.	Abt.	Distance	Win Time	Date
HPO	D		6F	1:12.40	7/15/04
HPO	D		1M	1:38.60	7/18/04
HPO	D		1 3/8M	2:23.00	7/16/04
HPO	NO TURF				

Hastings

Track	Surf.	Abt.	Distance	Win Time	Date
HST	D		3 1/2F	:39.70	9/11/04
HST	D		6F	1:12.18	4/24/04
HST	D		6F	1:12.18	4/25/04
HST	D		6 1/2F	1:15.74	5/22/04
HST	D		1 1/16M	1:42.41	8/2/04
HST	D		1 1/8M	1:49.08	7/1/04
HST	D		1 3/8M	2:19.05	8/2/04
HST	D		1 1/2M	2:30.91	9/11/04
HST	D		1 3/4M	2:59.47	10/2/04
HST	NO TURF				

Indiana Downs

Track	Surf.	Abt.	Distance	Win Time	Date
IND	D		4 1/2F	:51.20	6/18/04
IND	D		5F	:57.85	5/6/04
IND	D		5 1/2F	1:03.30	6/11/04
IND	D		6F	1:10.17	4/23/04
IND	D		1M	1:37.74	5/19/04
IND	D		1M 70Y	1:41.92	4/16/04
IND	D		1 1/16M	1:44.00	6/16/04
IND	D		1 1/8M	1:52.79	5/31/04
IND	D		1 1/4M	2:06.35	6/9/04

Ind Turf

Track	Surf.	Abt.	Distance	Win Time	Date
IND	T		5F	:57.14	6/4/04
IND	T	A	5F	:58.64	6/11/04
IND	T		7 1/2F	1:29.89	6/4/04
IND	T		1M	1:36.51	5/23/04
IND	T	A	1M	1:39.73	6/11/04
IND	T		1 1/16M	1:41.94	6/6/04
IND	T	A	1 1/16M	1:43.82	6/9/04
IND	T		1 3/8M	2:11.37	6/20/04

Kamloops

Track	Surf.	Abt.	Distance	Win Time	Date
KAM	D	A	4 1/2F	:50.05	5/30/04
KAM	D	A	4 1/2F	:50.05	6/13/04
KAM	D	A	6 1/2F	1:19.37	6/6/04
KAM	D	A	1M	1:38.45	8/15/04
KAM	NO TURF				

Kentucky Downs

Track	Surf.	Abt.	Distance	Win Time	Date
KD	NO DIRT				
KD	T		6F	1:10.49	9/28/04
KD	T		7F	1:23.48	9/21/04
KD	T		1M	1:36.88	9/25/04
KD	T		1 1/2M	2:32.96	9/28/04

Keeneland

Track	Surf.	Abt.	Distance	Win Time	Date
KEE	D		4 1/2F	:51.39	4/16/04
KEE	D		6F	1:08.72	10/8/04
KEE	D		6 1/2F	1:14.96	10/8/04
KEE	D		7F	1:22.44	10/10/04
KEE	D	A	7F	1:25.19	10/14/04
KEE	D		1 1/16M	1:42.61	4/17/04
KEE	D		1 1/8M	1:46.78	4/22/04
KEE	D		1 3/16M	1:57.94	10/10/04
KEE	D		1 1/4M	2:05.37	10/22/04

Kee Turf

Track	Surf.	Abt.	Distance	Win Time	Date
KEE	T		5 1/2F	1:01.78	4/10/04
KEE	T		1M	1:33.54	4/9/04
KEE	T		1 1/16M	1:41.41	4/18/04
KEE	T		1 1/8M	1:47.03	4/9/04
KEE	T		1 3/16M	1:57.08	10/10/04
KEE	T		1 1/2M	2:27.89	4/7/04

Kin Park

Track	Surf.	Abt.	Distance	Win Time	Date
KIN	D	A	4F	:44.33	7/11/04
KIN	D	A	6F	1:11.89	8/1/04
KIN	D	A	6 1/2F	1:20.00	7/18/04
KIN	D		6 1/2F	1:22.20	7/11/04
KIN	D	A	1 1/16M	1:45.62	8/1/04
KIN	NO TURF				

Kalispell

Track	Surf.	Abt.	Distance	Win Time	Date
KSP	D		5F	1:01.80	8/20/04
KSP	D		6F	1:13.60	8/21/04
KSP	D		7F	1:27.60	8/20/04
KSP	NO TURF				

Los Alamitos

Track	Surf.	Abt.	Distance	Win Time	Date
LA	D		4 1/2F	:50.18	2/21/04
LA	NO TURF				

Louisiana Downs

Track	Surf.	Abt.	Distance	Win Time	Date
LAD	D		4 1/2F	:53.20	6/18/04
LAD	D		5F	:57.60	6/25/04
LAD	D		5 1/2F	1:03.45	5/22/04
LAD	D		6F	1:09.22	10/23/04
LAD	D		6 1/2F	1:16.26	8/29/04
LAD	D		7F	1:22.29	5/27/04
LAD	D		1M 70Y	1:41.08	5/23/04
LAD	D		1 1/16M	1:43.20	8/12/04
LAD	D		1 1/8M	1:51.40	9/25/04

LaD Turf

Track	Surf.	Abt.	Distance	Win Time	Date
LAD	T	A	5F	:54.96	7/22/04
LAD	T		5F	:56.05	10/30/04
LAD	T	A	7 1/2F	1:27.88	7/16/04
LAD	T		7 1/2F	1:28.75	5/28/04
LAD	T	A	1M	1:34.21	5/21/04
LAD	T		1M	1:36.11	10/24/04
LAD	T	A	1 1/16M	1:41.38	9/11/04
LAD	T		1 1/16M	1:41.73	7/25/04
LAD	T	A	1 1/4M	2:09.35	8/6/04

Lethbridge

Track	Surf.	Abt.	Distance	Win Time	Date
LBG	D		3F	:35.20	9/11/04
LBG	D		5F	:59.40	6/20/04
LBG	D		5F	:59.40	9/18/04
LBG	D		5 1/2F	1:07.00	6/5/04
LBG	D	A	6F	1:09.20	6/20/04
LBG	D		6F	1:12.20	9/4/04
LBG	D		7F	1:24.40	6/19/04
LBG	D		1 1/16M	1:48.40	10/31/04
LBG	D		1 1/16M	1:48.40	10/31/04
LBG	D		1 1/8M	1:52.20	10/31/04
LBG	D		1 3/16M	2:04.20	10/3/04
LBG	NO TURF				

Lincoln State Fair

Track	Surf.	Abt.	Distance	Win Time	Date
LNN	D		4F	:48.00	6/6/04
LNN	D		4 1/2F	:50.60	5/22/04
LNN	D		6F	1:11.00	5/14/04
LNN	D		1M	1:38.20	5/16/04
LNN	D		1M 70Y	1:41.60	5/16/04
LNN	D		1 1/16M	1:47.80	6/27/04
LNN	D		1 3/8M	2:26.40	6/20/04
LNN	D		2M	3:35.80	7/4/04
LNN	NO TURF				

Laurel Park

Track	Surf.	Abt.	Distance	Win Time	Date
LRL	D		5 1/2F	1:03.33	2/7/04
LRL	D		6F	1:09.28	2/4/04
LRL	D		7F	1:22.49	2/16/04
LRL	D		1 1/16M	1:43.27	1/28/04
LRL	D		1 1/8M	1:49.05	2/14/04
LRL	NO TURF				

Lone Star Park

Track	Surf.	Abt.	Distance	Win Time	Date
LS	D		4 1/2F	:51.30	4/30/04
LS	D		5F	:56.26	5/1/04
LS	D		5 1/2F	1:03.08	5/20/04
LS	D		6F	1:07.82	5/31/04
LS	D		6 1/2F	1:14.94	5/31/04
LS	D		7F	1:20.67	10/29/04
LS	D		1M	1:35.41	10/30/04
LS	D		1 1/16M	1:41.29	5/31/04
LS	D		1 1/8M	1:48.26	10/30/04
LS	D		1 1/4M	1:59.02	10/30/04
LS	D		1 5/16M	2:12.34	10/22/04

LS Turf

Track	Surf.	Abt.	Distance	Win Time	Date
LS	T		5F	:56.09	10/16/04
LS	T		7 1/2F	1:28.24	4/17/04
LS	T		1M	1:35.08	4/15/04
LS	T		1 1/16M	1:41.61	10/1/04
LS	T		1 1/8M	1:48.41	10/3/04
LS	T		1 3/8M	2:18.25	10/30/04
LS	T		1 1/2M	2:29.70	10/30/04

Marias Fair

Track	Surf.	Abt.	Distance	Win Time	Date
MAF	D		5F	1:00.00	7/25/04
MAF	D	A	6F	1:11.00	7/25/04
MAF	D		7F	1:25.80	7/24/04
MAF	D		1M 70Y	1:48.60	7/25/04
MAF	NO TURF				

Manor Downs

Track	Surf.	Abt.	Distance	Win Time	Date
MAN	D		4F	:45.95	2/29/04
MAN	D		4 1/2F	:51.21	4/4/04
MAN	D		5 1/2F	1:04.86	3/20/04
MAN	D		6F	1:10.80	4/24/04
MAN	D		7 1/2F	1:32.12	3/27/04
MAN	D		1M	1:38.92	3/28/04
MAN	NO TURF				

Miles City

Track	Surf.	Abt.	Distance	Win Time	Date
MC	D		5F	1:05.00	5/15/04
MC	D		5 1/2F	1:08.60	5/15/04
MC	NO TURF				

Marquis Downs

Track	Surf.	Abt.	Distance	Win Time	Date
MD	D		4F	:46.53	5/28/04
MD	D		6F	1:12.06	6/26/04
MD	D		6 1/2F	1:22.45	8/21/04
MD	D		7F	1:25.35	8/6/04
MD	D		1M	1:39.53	7/23/04
MD	D		1 1/16M	1:45.45	9/11/04
MD	NO TURF				

Melville District Agripar

Track	Surf.	Abt.	Distance	Win Time	Date
MDA	D		2F	:21.40	5/9/04
MDA	D	A	4 1/2F	:57.00	5/9/04
MDA	D	A	5 1/2F	1:06.60	10/3/04
MDA	D	A	5 1/2F	1:06.60	10/9/04
MDA	D	A	5 1/2F	1:06.60	10/10/04
MDA	D	A	7 1/2F	1:35.40	10/2/04
MDA	D	A	1M	1:42.00	10/10/04
MDA	NO TURF				

The Meadowlands

Track	Surf.	Abt.	Distance	Win Time	Date
MED	D		5F	:56.37	11/5/04
MED	D		5 1/2F	1:04.75	10/9/04
MED	D		6F	1:08.62	10/6/04
MED	D		1M	1:35.17	10/15/04
MED	D		1M 70Y	1:37.90	10/15/04
MED	D		1 1/16M	1:41.83	10/29/04
MED	D		1 1/8M	1:48.57	10/1/04

Med Turf

Track	Surf.	Abt.	Distance	Win Time	Date
MED	T		5F	:56.11	10/8/04
MED	T		1M	1:34.98	10/12/04
MED	T		1M 70Y	1:40.01	10/23/04
MED	T		1 1/16M	1:41.46	10/13/04
MED	T		1 3/8M	2:14.20	10/29/04

Millerville

Track	Surf.	Abt.	Distance	Win Time	Date
MIL	D		5F	1:02.60	7/1/04
MIL	D		7F	1:30.40	7/2/04
MIL	D		7F	1:30.40	7/2/04
MIL	D		1 1/8M	1:54.80	7/1/04
MIL	NO TURF				

Mountaineer Park

Track	Surf.	Abt.	Distance	Win Time	Date
MNR	D		4 1/2F	:50.16	8/7/04
MNR	D		5F	:57.01	2/2/04
MNR	D		5 1/2F	1:03.53	2/2/04
MNR	D		6F	1:09.25	8/16/04
MNR	D		1M	1:36.74	2/16/04
MNR	D		1M 70Y	1:42.25	6/5/04
MNR	D		1 1/16M	1:43.37	8/7/04
MNR	D		1 1/8M	1:49.16	8/7/04

Track	Surf.	Abt.	Distance	Win Time	Date
MNR	D		1 3/16M	2:01.53	5/15/04
MNR	D		1 1/4M	2:06.20	7/31/04
MNR	D		1 1/2M	2:34.72	10/16/04
MNR	D		1 5/8M	2:49.21	10/31/04
MNR	D		1 3/4M	3:06.58	11/16/04
MNR	D		2M	3:34.00	12/7/04

Mnr Turf

Track	Surf.	Abt.	Distance	Win Time	Date
MNR	T		4 1/2F	:50.23	6/21/04
MNR	T		5F	:55.78	9/5/04
MNR	T		7F	1:21.88	6/8/04
MNR	T		7 1/2F	1:28.39	7/11/04
MNR	T		1M	1:34.09	9/6/04
MNR	T		1 3/8M	2:15.86	6/27/04
MNR	T		1 3/4M	2:55.11	8/15/04
MNR	T		1 7/8M	3:10.35	9/6/04

Mohave County Fair

Track	Surf.	Abt.	Distance	Win Time	Date
MOF	D		4F	:44.40	5/15/04
MOF	D		5 1/2F	1:06.20	5/16/04
MOF	D		6F	1:13.60	5/9/04
MOF	D		7F	1:28.00	5/15/04
MOF	D		1 1/16M	1:45.20	5/16/04
MOF	NO TURF				

Mount Pleasant Meadows

Track	Surf.	Abt.	Distance	Win Time	Date
MPM	D		2F	:22.31	7/11/04
MPM	D		4F	:50.22	9/26/04
MPM	D		4 1/2F	:54.79	6/13/04
MPM	D		5F	1:02.28	9/5/04
MPM	D		5 1/2F	1:08.82	8/28/04
MPM	D		1M 70Y	1:53.82	9/12/04
MPM	NO TURF				

Monmouth Park

Track	Surf.	Abt.	Distance	Win Time	Date
MTH	D		5F	:56.34	8/14/04
MTH	D		5 1/2F	1:03.36	6/5/04
MTH	D		6F	1:08.67	8/14/04
MTH	D		1M	1:35.27	7/25/04
MTH	D		1M 70Y	1:38.85	7/5/04
MTH	D		1 1/16M	1:42.18	8/15/04
MTH	D		1 1/8M	1:47.66	8/21/04

Mth Turf

Track	Surf.	Abt.	Distance	Win Time	Date
MTH	T		5F	:55.24	6/26/04
MTH	T		1M	1:33.95	6/19/04
MTH	T		1 1/16M	1:39.88	6/27/04
MTH	T		1 1/8M	1:47.39	6/26/04
MTH	T		1 3/8M	2:13.37	7/3/04

Northampton Fair

Track	Surf.	Abt.	Distance	Win Time	Date
NMP	D	A	5F	:55.82	9/3/04
NMP	D	A	6 1/2F	1:21.03	9/4/04
NMP	D	A	1 1/16M	1:51.34	9/17/04
NMP	NO TURF				

Northlands Park

Track	Surf.	Abt.	Distance	Win Time	Date
NP	D		3 1/2F	:39.40	7/24/04
NP	D		5 1/2F	1:05.80	8/13/04
NP	D		5 1/2F	1:05.80	9/12/04
NP	D		6F	1:11.80	7/24/04
NP	D		6F	1:11.80	8/13/04
NP	D		6F	1:11.80	8/29/04
NP	D		6F	1:11.80	10/8/04
NP	D		6 1/2F	1:17.20	8/2/04
NP	D		6 1/2F	1:17.20	8/7/04
NP	D		6 1/2F	1:17.20	8/15/04
NP	D		1M	1:37.40	8/15/04
NP	D		1 1/16M	1:44.80	8/13/04
NP	D		1 5/16M	2:12.60	8/7/04
NP	D		1 3/8M	2:20.20	9/11/04
NP	D		1 5/8M	2:51.00	10/2/04
NP	NO TURF				

Oaklawn Park

Track	Surf.	Abt.	Distance	Win Time	Date
OP	D		5 1/2F	1:03.67	3/27/04
OP	D		6F	1:08.75	3/10/04
OP	D		1M	1:36.86	4/3/04
OP	D		1 1/16M	1:41.24	4/3/04
OP	D		1 1/8M	1:48.26	4/3/04
OP	D		1 3/16M	1:58.66	3/25/04
OP	D		1 3/4M	3:05.96	4/10/04
OP	NO TURF				

Ocala Training Center

Track	Surf.	Abt.	Distance	Win Time	Date
OTC	D		5F	:57.80	3/15/04
OTC	D		6F	1:10.60	3/15/04
OTC	D		1 1/16M	1:44.20	3/15/04
OTC	D		1 1/16M	1:44.20	3/15/04
OTC	NO TURF				

Penn National Racecourse

Track	Surf.	Abt.	Distance	Win Time	Date
PEN	D		2F	:20.71	10/9/04
PEN	D		4 1/2F	:51.07	11/18/04
PEN	D		5F	:57.52	3/18/04
PEN	D		5 1/2F	1:03.23	11/20/04
PEN	D		6F	1:09.51	11/10/04
PEN	D		1M	1:38.02	5/22/04
PEN	D		1M 70Y	1:42.27	11/17/04
PEN	D		1 1/16M	1:44.98	7/7/04
PEN	D		1 1/8M	1:53.98	3/25/04
PEN	D		1 3/16M	2:00.17	12/16/04
PEN	D		1 1/4M	2:05.10	7/2/04
PEN	D		1 1/2M	2:33.98	5/20/04
PEN	D		1 3/4M	3:02.43	4/22/04
PEN	D		2M	3:35.16	9/4/04

Pen Turf

Track	Surf.	Abt.	Distance	Win Time	Date
PEN	T		5F	:56.06	7/7/04
PEN	T		1M	1:35.36	7/10/04
PEN	T		1M 70Y	1:39.63	7/9/04
PEN	T		1 1/16M	1:41.52	5/27/04

Philadelphia Park

Track	Surf.	Abt.	Distance	Win Time	Date
PHA	D		4 1/2F	:53.87	6/29/04
PHA	D		5F	:56.60	8/17/04
PHA	D		5 1/2F	1:02.79	1/9/04
PHA	D		6F	1:08.11	10/2/04
PHA	D		6 1/2F	1:15.34	1/12/04
PHA	D		7F	1:21.21	1/11/04
PHA	D		1M	1:35.71	1/21/04
PHA	D		1M 70Y	1:40.38	12/18/04
PHA	D		1 1/16M	1:41.68	10/2/04
PHA	D		1 1/8M	1:48.42	9/6/04
PHA	D		1 1/4M	2:06.09	7/27/04

Pha Turf

Track	Surf.	Abt.	Distance	Win Time	Date
PHA	T		5F	:57.53	5/31/04
PHA	T	A	5F	:57.76	9/25/04
PHA	T		7 1/2F	1:32.43	6/22/04
PHA	T	A	7 1/2F	1:36.70	7/10/04
PHA	T		1M	1:38.39	9/26/04
PHA	T	A	1M	1:43.38	8/14/04
PHA	T		1M 70Y	1:42.23	9/25/04
PHA	T	A	1M 70Y	1:46.22	7/17/04
PHA	T		1 1/16M	1:43.80	7/3/04
PHA	T	A	1 1/16M	1:49.11	8/14/04
PHA	T		1 1/8M	1:52.68	9/7/04
PHA	T		1 3/8M	2:19.18	6/28/04
PHA	T		1 1/2M	2:33.32	6/5/04

Pimlico

Track	Surf.	Abt.	Distance	Win Time	Date
PIM	D		4 1/2F	:53.15	6/3/04
PIM	D		5F	:57.20	10/17/04
PIM	D		5 1/2F	1:03.50	10/1/04
PIM	D		6F	1:09.45	11/20/04
PIM	D		1 1/16M	1:42.20	9/10/04
PIM	D		1 1/8M	1:48.23	4/17/04
PIM	D		1 3/16M	1:55.58	10/9/04

Pim Turf

Track	Surf.	Abt.	Distance	Win Time	Date
PIM	T		5F	:55.99	6/4/04
PIM	T		1M	1:35.64	6/3/04
PIM	T		1 1/16M	1:40.85	5/15/04
PIM	T		1 1/8M	1:46.34	5/15/04

Pleasanton

Track	Surf.	Abt.	Distance	Win Time	Date
PLN	D		4 1/2F	:52.28	7/1/04
PLN	D		5F	:56.20	7/4/04
PLN	D		5 1/2F	1:02.34	7/11/04
PLN	D		6F	1:08.09	7/5/04
PLN	D		1M 70Y	1:39.20	7/11/04
PLN	D		1 1/16M	1:40.04	7/5/04
PLN	NO TURF				

Portland Meadows

Track	Surf.	Abt.	Distance	Win Time	Date
PM	D		4 1/2F	:52.41	3/5/04
PM	D		5F	:58.38	10/18/04
PM	D		5 1/2F	1:04.22	10/18/04
PM	D		6F	1:09.76	10/16/04
PM	D		1M	1:38.39	10/18/04
PM	D		1 1/16M	1:46.50	10/30/04
PM	D		1 1/16M	1:46.50	12/4/04
PM	D		1 1/8M	1:53.36	1/24/04
PM	D		1 1/4M	2:09.92	4/5/04
PM	D		1 1/2M	2:37.55	4/24/04
PM	NO TURF				

Prairie Meadows

Track	Surf.	Abt.	Distance	Win Time	Date
PRM	D		4 1/2F	:52.13	5/11/04
PRM	D		5F	:57.05	7/1/04
PRM	D		5 1/2F	1:03.33	5/24/04
PRM	D		6F	1:07.85	7/4/04
PRM	D		1M	1:35.75	5/21/04
PRM	D		1M 70Y	1:40.09	5/30/04
PRM	D		1 1/16M	1:41.44	6/12/04
PRM	D		1 1/8M	1:46.63	7/3/04
PRM	D		1 1/4M	2:03.80	5/30/04
PRM	D		2M	3:32.25	9/25/04
PRM	NO TURF				

Prineville

Track	Surf.	Abt.	Distance	Win Time	Date
PRV	D	A	5F	1:04.00	7/7/04
PRV	D	A	5 1/2F	1:07.10	7/9/04
PRV	D		5 1/2F	1:07.40	7/9/04
PRV	D	A	7F	1:31.40	7/10/04
PRV	D	A	1 1/8M	2:03.20	7/10/04
PRV	NO TURF				

River Downs

Track	Surf.	Abt.	Distance	Win Time	Date
RD	D		4 1/2F	:52.20	7/9/04
RD	D		5F	:57.80	8/21/04
RD	D		5 1/2F	1:04.60	4/27/04
RD	D		6F	1:10.20	8/27/04
RD	D		1M	1:39.40	8/2/04
RD	D		1M	1:39.40	8/27/04
RD	D		1M 70Y	1:44.00	5/13/04
RD	D		1 1/16M	1:45.00	9/6/04
RD	D		1 1/8M	1:53.80	6/13/04
RD	D		1 1/4M	2:08.00	7/11/04
RD	D		1 1/2M	2:40.00	8/30/04
RD	D		1 5/8M	2:52.00	8/10/04

RD Turf

Track	Surf.	Abt.	Distance	Win Time	Date
RD	T		5F	:56.60	6/22/04
RD	T		7 1/2F	1:28.60	7/10/04
RD	T		1M	1:35.80	6/8/04
RD	T		1M	1:35.80	6/29/04
RD	T		1 1/16M	1:42.40	6/8/04
RD	T		1 1/16M	1:42.40	6/20/04
RD	T		1 3/8M	2:16.00	6/27/04
RD	T		1 1/2M	2:30.00	7/25/04
RD	T		1 7/8M	3:10.80	9/6/04

Retama Park

Track	Surf.	Abt.	Distance	Win Time	Date
RET	D		4 1/2F	:51.69	7/24/04
RET	D		5F	:58.38	9/16/04
RET	D		5 1/2F	1:03.82	7/30/04
RET	D		5 1/2F	1:03.82	8/21/04
RET	D		6F	1:10.20	7/23/04
RET	D		6 1/2F	1:16.52	9/25/04
RET	D		7F	1:23.95	9/4/04
RET	D		1M	1:37.64	9/10/04
RET	D		1 1/16M	1:47.45	7/23/04

Ret Turf

Track	Surf.	Abt.	Distance	Win Time	Date
RET	T		5F	:56.04	9/18/04
RET	T		7 1/2F	1:28.77	8/21/04
RET	T		1M	1:35.59	9/25/04
RET	T		1 1/16M	1:41.97	7/31/04

Rillito

Track	Surf.	Abt.	Distance	Win Time	Date
RIL	D		4F	:44.60	1/17/04
RIL	D		5 1/2F	1:04.80	1/31/04
RIL	D		6F	1:10.80	1/18/04
RIL	D		6F	1:10.80	2/21/04
RIL	D		6 1/2F	1:17.00	2/22/04
RIL	D		7F	1:24.20	2/1/04
RIL	D		7F	1:24.20	2/15/04
RIL	D		1 1/16M	1:45.80	1/31/04
RIL	NO TURF				

Rockingham

Track	Surf.	Abt.	Distance	Win Time	Date
RKM	NO DIRT				
RKM	T		1 1/16M	1:46.28	9/5/04
RKM	T	A	1 1/8M	1:50.29	9/5/04

Remington Park

Track	Surf.	Abt.	Distance	Win Time	Date
RP	D		3F	:32.86	8/7/04
RP	D		5F	:57.34	8/27/04
RP	D		5 1/2F	1:03.82	8/14/04
RP	D		6F	1:08.93	8/27/04
RP	D		6 1/2F	1:15.79	11/6/04
RP	D		7F	1:22.45	12/5/04
RP	D		1M	1:37.22	10/30/04
RP	D		1M 70Y	1:41.03	8/29/04
RP	D		1 1/16M	1:43.11	9/25/04
RP	D		1 1/8M	1:50.26	11/21/04
RP	D		1 3/8M	2:19.22	11/26/04

RP Turf

Track	Surf.	Abt.	Distance	Win Time	Date
RP	T		5F	:55.73	9/26/04
RP	T		7 1/2F	1:27.46	8/27/04
RP	T		1M	1:34.93	9/5/04
RP	T		1 1/16M	1:42.33	8/14/04
RP	T		1 1/8M	1:46.22	9/6/04
RP	T		1 3/8M	2:20.00	10/18/04
RP	T		1 1/2M	2:38.38	11/8/04

Ruidoso Downs

Track	Surf.	Abt.	Distance	Win Time	Date
RUI	D		2 1/2F	:27.80	8/29/04
RUI	D		4 1/2F	:52.00	6/25/04
RUI	D		5F	:56.60	7/17/04
RUI	D		5 1/2F	1:02.80	8/1/04
RUI	D		6F	1:08.80	7/18/04
RUI	D		7 1/2F	1:31.40	7/1/04
RUI	D		7 1/2F	1:31.40	8/1/04
RUI	D		1M	1:37.20	6/20/04
RUI	D		1 1/16M	1:44.40	9/5/04
RUI	D		1 1/8M	1:55.60	8/22/04
RUI	D		1 1/4M	2:09.40	9/6/04
RUI	NO TURF				

Santa Anita Park

Track	Surf.	Abt.	Distance	Win Time	Date
SA	D		2F	:21.09	4/15/04
SA	D		5 1/2F	1:02.35	1/1/04
SA	D		6F	1:07.81	1/2/04
SA	D		6 1/2F	1:14.58	9/29/04
SA	D		7F	1:20.11	2/21/04
SA	D		1M	1:34.73	4/16/04
SA	D		1 1/16M	1:41.62	1/17/04
SA	D		1 1/8M	1:47.25	1/31/04
SA	D		1 1/4M	2:01.64	3/6/04

SA Turf

Track	Surf.	Abt.	Distance	Win Time	Date
SA	T	A	6 1/2F	1:11.13	1/22/04
SA	T		1M	1:32.88	1/22/04
SA	T		1 1/8M	1:45.93	3/24/04
SA	T		1 1/4M	1:58.70	10/3/04
SA	T		1 1/2M	2:26.03	3/20/04
SA	T	A	1 3/4M	2:45.98	4/18/04

Sacramento

Track	Surf.	Abt.	Distance	Win Time	Date
SAC	D		5 1/2F	1:02.68	8/29/04
SAC	D		6F	1:08.60	8/29/04
SAC	D		1M	1:35.80	8/27/04
SAC	D		1 1/16M	1:42.57	9/4/04
SAC	D		1 1/8M	1:48.37	8/28/04
SAC	NO TURF				

Safford

Track	Surf.	Abt.	Distance	Win Time	Date
SAF	D		4F	:46.60	3/28/04
SAF	D		5 1/2F	1:08.40	3/28/04
SAF	D		6F	1:14.80	3/27/04
SAF	D		7F	1:27.00	3/28/04
SAF	D		1M	1:46.00	4/4/04
SAF	NO TURF				

Saratoga

Track	Surf.	Abt.	Distance	Win Time	Date
SAR	D		5F	:56.88	8/22/04
SAR	D		5 1/2F	1:04.14	8/26/04
SAR	D		6F	1:08.04	8/14/04
SAR	D		6 1/2F	1:14.82	8/25/04
SAR	D		7F	1:20.99	8/28/04
SAR	D		1 1/8M	1:47.56	8/8/04

Track	Surf.	Abt.	Distance	Win Time	Date
SAR	D		1 3/16M	1:58.37	8/11/04
SAR	D		1 1/4M	2:00.83	8/22/04

Sar Turf

Track	Surf.	Abt.	Distance	Win Time	Date
SAR	T		1M	1:33.42	8/5/04
SAR	T		1 1/16M	1:39.50	8/28/04
SAR	T		1 1/8M	1:47.71	8/9/04
SAR	T		1 3/16M	1:53.11	8/28/04
SAR	T		1 3/8M	2:14.12	9/5/04
SAR	T		1 1/2M	2:28.09	9/6/04
SAR	T		1 5/8M	2:46.29	8/16/04

Saint Johns

Track	Surf.	Abt.	Distance	Win Time	Date
SJ	D		4F	:44.60	9/19/04
SJ	D		5 1/2F	1:06.40	9/19/04
SJ	D		6F	1:13.00	9/19/04
SJ	D		6 1/2F	1:20.80	9/18/04
SJ	D		7F	1:25.60	9/18/04
SJ	NO TURF				

Solano

Track	Surf.	Abt.	Distance	Win Time	Date
SOL	D		4 1/2F	:51.45	7/26/04
SOL	D		5F	:58.12	7/17/04
SOL	D		5 1/2F	1:04.06	7/26/04
SOL	D		6F	1:09.20	7/24/04
SOL	D		1M	1:37.68	7/23/04
SOL	D		1 1/16M	1:45.67	7/25/04
SOL	D		1 1/8M	1:52.96	7/24/04
SOL	NO TURF				

Sonoita

Track	Surf.	Abt.	Distance	Win Time	Date
SON	D		5F	:59.60	5/2/04
SON	D		5 1/2F	1:05.00	5/2/04
SON	D		6F	1:10.40	4/25/04
SON	D		7F	1:28.40	5/1/04
SON	D		1M 70Y	1:47.40	4/24/04
SON	NO TURF				

Santa Rosa

Track	Surf.	Abt.	Distance	Win Time	Date
SR	D		4 1/2F	:51.14	8/5/04
SR	D		5F	:57.68	8/4/04
SR	D		5 1/2F	1:02.78	8/4/04
SR	D		6F	1:08.10	7/31/04
SR	D		1M	1:35.56	7/31/04
SR	D		1 1/16M	1:41.29	8/7/04
SR	NO TURF				

Sun Ray Park

Track	Surf.	Abt.	Distance	Win Time	Date
SRP	D		4 1/2F	:50.40	9/27/04
SRP	D		6 1/2F	1:16.80	8/2/04
SRP	D		7F	1:22.80	8/28/04
SRP	D		7 1/2F	1:32.20	10/25/04
SRP	D		1M	1:36.40	10/19/04
SRP	D		1 1/8M	1:50.40	11/2/04
SRP	NO TURF				

Stockton

Track	Surf.	Abt.	Distance	Win Time	Date
STK	D		4 1/2F	:50.67	6/24/04
STK	D		5F	:57.70	6/16/04
STK	D		5 1/2F	1:02.15	6/16/04
STK	D		6F	1:09.31	6/20/04
STK	D		1M	1:36.01	6/24/04
STK	NO TURF				

Stampede Park

Track	Surf.	Abt.	Distance	Win Time	Date
STP	D		3 1/2F	:41.00	6/19/04
STP	D		4F	:44.00	4/3/04
STP	D		6F	1:09.80	4/21/04
STP	D		6F	1:09.80	6/4/04
STP	D		1M	1:37.60	5/19/04
STP	D		1M	1:37.60	6/2/04
STP	D		1 1/16M	1:44.00	6/4/04
STP	NO TURF				

Sun Downs

Track	Surf.	Abt.	Distance	Win Time	Date
SUD	D		4F	:47.00	5/2/04
SUD	D		6F	1:15.20	5/1/04
SUD	D		6 1/2F	1:22.80	5/2/04
SUD	D		7F	1:27.40	5/2/04
SUD	NO TURF				

Suffolk Downs

Track	Surf.	Abt.	Distance	Win Time	Date
SUF	D		5F	:57.75	7/6/04
SUF	D		5 1/2F	1:04.11	5/1/04
SUF	D		6F	1:09.24	6/19/04
SUF	D		1M	1:37.77	11/23/04
SUF	D		1M 70Y	1:41.76	6/2/04
SUF	D		1 1/16M	1:44.96	7/5/04
SUF	D		1 1/8M	1:49.14	6/19/04
SUF	D		1 1/4M	2:10.59	9/15/04

Suf Turf

Track	Surf.	Abt.	Distance	Win Time	Date
SUF	T	A	5F	:57.80	6/26/04
SUF	T		5F	:59.97	6/26/04
SUF	T	A	7 1/2F	1:32.91	6/19/04
SUF	T	A	1M	1:39.80	7/12/04
SUF	T	A	1M 70Y	1:42.07	6/30/04
SUF	T	A	1 1/16M	1:46.66	9/4/04
SUF	T		1 1/16M	1:49.40	9/27/04

Sunland Park

Track	Surf.	Abt.	Distance	Win Time	Date
SUN	D		2F	:21.86	3/5/04
SUN	D		4 1/2F	:51.92	3/23/04
SUN	D		5F	:55.90	2/7/04
SUN	D		5 1/2F	1:02.70	3/28/04
SUN	D		6F	1:08.24	12/11/04
SUN	D		6 1/2F	1:14.29	3/6/04
SUN	D		1M	1:35.38	12/7/04
SUN	D		1 1/16M	1:41.92	12/12/04
SUN	D		1 1/8M	1:50.15	1/20/04
SUN	D		1 1/4M	2:10.02	4/11/04
SUN	NO TURF				

Tampa Bay Downs

Track	Surf.	Abt.	Distance	Win Time	Date
TAM	D		3F	:36.00	4/25/04
TAM	D		5F	:57.66	2/28/04
TAM	D		5 1/2F	1:04.03	4/20/04
TAM	D		6F	1:10.42	1/3/04
TAM	D		6F	1:10.42	4/24/04
TAM	D		6 1/2F	1:16.99	12/31/04
TAM	D		7F	1:23.78	1/24/04
TAM	D		1 1/16M	1:43.99	3/14/04
TAM	D		1 1/8M	1:52.37	4/19/04
TAM	D		1 3/8M	2:23.09	3/16/04

Tam Turf

Track	Surf.	Abt.	Distance	Win Time	Date
TAM	T		5F	:56.24	4/10/04
TAM	T	A	5F	:57.23	4/20/04
TAM	T		1M	1:35.66	4/10/04
TAM	T	A	1M	1:38.74	4/19/04
TAM	T		1 1/16M	1:41.68	2/14/04
TAM	T	A	1 1/16M	1:44.75	4/18/04
TAM	T	A	1 1/8M	1:48.03	5/1/04
TAM	T		1 1/8M	1:49.79	4/27/04
TAM	T	A	1 3/8M	2:17.40	3/9/04

Thistledown

Track	Surf.	Abt.	Distance	Win Time	Date
TDN	D		4F	:45.30	10/8/04
TDN	D		4 1/2F	:52.44	8/20/04
TDN	D		4 1/2F	:52.44	8/22/04
TDN	D		5F	:58.48	9/30/04
TDN	D		5 1/2F	1:04.58	6/4/04
TDN	D		6F	1:09.28	12/16/04
TDN	D		1M	1:38.96	7/17/04
TDN	D		1M	1:38.96	10/1/04
TDN	D		1M 40Y	1:42.69	4/8/04
TDN	D		1M 70Y	1:41.51	12/16/04
TDN	D		1 1/16M	1:44.60	5/29/04
TDN	D		1 1/8M	1:49.50	6/12/04
TDN	D		1 1/4M	2:05.36	9/6/04
TDN	NO TURF				

Tillamook County Fair

Track	Surf.	Abt.	Distance	Win Time	Date
TIL	D	A	5F	1:03.80	8/14/04
TIL	D	A	1 1/16M	2:04.40	8/14/04
TIL	NO TURF				

Timonium

Track	Surf.	Abt.	Distance	Win Time	Date
TIM	D		4F	:45.76	9/3/04
TIM	D	A	6 1/2F	1:16.41	9/4/04
TIM	D		1M	1:40.16	9/6/04
TIM	D		1 1/16M	1:46.65	9/6/04
TIM	NO TURF				

Turfway Park

Track	Surf.	Abt.	Distance	Win Time	Date
TP	D		5F	:56.93	1/7/04
TP	D		5 1/2F	1:03.75	3/26/04
TP	D		6F	1:08.49	3/26/04
TP	D		6 1/2F	1:15.84	3/28/04
TP	D		1M	1:35.36	3/25/04
TP	D		1 1/16M	1:40.85	3/27/04
TP	D		1 1/8M	1:47.52	12/18/04
TP	D		1 1/4M	2:05.26	2/19/04
TP	D		1 1/2M	2:29.19	3/26/04
TP	NO TURF				

Turf Paradise

Track	Surf.	Abt.	Distance	Win Time	Date
TUP	D		2F	:21.50	3/30/04
TUP	D		4 1/2F	:52.06	5/2/04
TUP	D		5F	:56.26	10/10/04
TUP	D		5 1/2F	1:01.36	4/13/04
TUP	D		6F	1:07.42	2/21/04
TUP	D		6 1/2F	1:13.55	12/26/04
TUP	D		1M	1:33.68	3/1/04
TUP	D		1 1/16M	1:42.07	2/7/04
TUP	D		1 1/8M	1:50.81	12/3/04
TUP	D		1 1/4M	2:03.49	2/10/04
TUP	D		1 5/8M	2:44.40	2/29/04

TuP Turf

Track	Surf.	Abt.	Distance	Win Time	Date
TUP	T		4 1/2F	:50.34	12/17/04
TUP	T		4 1/2F	:50.34	12/26/04
TUP	T		7 1/2F	1:27.54	11/6/04
TUP	T		1M	1:35.05	5/1/04
TUP	T		1 1/16M	1:40.89	2/7/04
TUP	T		1 1/8M	1:48.57	3/29/04
TUP	T		1 3/8M	2:16.12	4/25/04
TUP	T		1 7/8M	3:11.97	5/16/04

Eastern Oregon Livestock Show

Track	Surf.	Abt.	Distance	Win Time	Date
UN	D		5F	1:00.20	6/13/04
UN	D		5 1/2F	1:03.60	6/12/04
UN	D		6 1/2F	1:23.40	6/13/04
UN	D		1 1/16M	1:46.00	6/13/04
UN	NO TURF				

Woodlands

Track	Surf.	Abt.	Distance	Win Time	Date
WDS	D		5F	1:00.00	9/26/04
WDS	D		5 1/2F	1:04.20	10/22/04
WDS	D		6F	1:09.60	9/25/04
WDS	D		1M	1:38.60	9/24/04
WDS	D		1M 70Y	1:44.00	9/26/04
WDS	D		1M 70Y	1:44.00	10/17/04
WDS	D		1M 70Y	1:44.00	10/23/04
WDS	D		1 1/16M	1:45.00	10/10/04
WDS	D		1 1/8M	1:53.00	10/16/04
WDS	D		1 3/4M	3:03.40	10/31/04
WDS	NO TURF				

Western Mountain Fair

Track	Surf.	Abt.	Distance	Win Time	Date
WMF	D		5F	:59.60	8/13/04
WMF	D	A	5F	1:07.00	8/13/04
WMF	D	A	5 1/4F	1:05.00	8/12/04

Track	Surf.	Abt.	Distance	Win Time	Date
WMF	D		6 1/2F	1:22.20	8/15/04
WMF	D		1 1/16M	1:52.20	8/14/04
WMF	D		1 1/8M	1:55.40	8/15/04
WMF	D		1 5/8M	2:57.20	8/14/04
WMF	NO TURF				

Woodbine

Track	Surf.	Abt.	Distance	Win Time	Date
WO	D		4 1/2F	:51.67	5/9/04
WO	D		5F	:57.32	4/30/04
WO	D		5 1/2F	1:03.81	4/30/04
WO	D		6F	1:08.75	4/17/04
WO	D		6 1/2F	1:15.57	8/22/04
WO	D		7F	1:21.81	5/1/04
WO	D		1M 70Y	1:41.08	8/11/04
WO	D		1 1/16M	1:42.74	9/4/04
WO	D		1 1/8M	1:50.98	10/17/04
WO	D		1 3/16M	1:59.23	8/7/04
WO	D		1 1/4M	2:03.34	7/1/04
WO	D		1 1/2M	2:35.49	11/20/04
WO	D		1 3/4M	3:03.52	12/12/04
WO	D		1 7/8M	3:19.50	12/12/04

WO Turf

Track	Surf.	Abt.	Distance	Win Time	Date
WO	T		6F	1:07.83	8/2/04
WO	T		6 1/2F	1:14.27	8/7/04
WO	T		7F	1:19.38	7/24/04
WO	T		1M	1:31.84	7/1/04
WO	T		1 1/16M	1:40.13	8/28/04
WO	T	A	1 1/8M	1:42.87	8/8/04
WO	T		1 1/8M	1:46.68	6/12/04
WO	T		1 1/4M	2:01.68	7/2/04
WO	T	A	1 1/4M	2:04.18	9/12/04
WO	T		1 3/8M	2:12.37	7/25/04
WO	T		1 1/2M	2:25.87	9/6/04
WO	T	A	1 1/2M	2:31.66	9/15/04

Wyoming Downs

Track	Surf.	Abt.	Distance	Win Time	Date
WYO	D	A	4 1/2F	:52.01	8/8/04
WYO	D		4 1/2F	:52.49	7/10/04
WYO	D		5F	:56.77	8/21/04
WYO	D		5 1/2F	1:03.46	8/22/04
WYO	D		6F	1:08.86	8/15/04
WYO	D		7 1/2F	1:31.26	8/7/04
WYO	D		1M	1:38.53	8/22/04
WYO	NO TURF				

Yavapai Downs

Track	Surf.	Abt.	Distance	Win Time	Date
YAV	D	A	4 1/2F	:49.60	7/25/04
YAV	D		4 1/2F	:50.20	9/7/04
YAV	D		5F	:56.40	8/9/04
YAV	D		5 1/2F	1:02.80	6/8/04
YAV	D		5 1/2F	1:02.80	7/11/04
YAV	D		6F	1:08.80	6/27/04
YAV	D		6F	1:08.80	8/2/04
YAV	D		6F	1:08.80	8/22/04
YAV	D		1M	1:36.80	7/24/04
YAV	D		1 1/16M	1:43.80	8/16/04
YAV	D		1 1/8M	1:53.80	6/19/04
YAV	D		1 1/4M	2:06.40	8/9/04
YAV	NO TURF				

Yellowstone Downs

Track	Surf.	Abt.	Distance	Win Time	Date
YD	D		5 1/4F	1:02.40	9/26/04
YD	D		7F	1:27.60	9/19/04
YD	D		1M 70Y	1:47.00	9/26/04
YD	NO TURF				

Yorkton Exh Association

Track	Surf.	Abt.	Distance	Win Time	Date
YKT	D		5F	1:02.20	7/4/04
YKT	D		6 1/2F	1:23.40	7/9/04
YKT	D		1M	1:44.60	7/10/04
YKT	NO TURF				

Fastest Times During 2004

Dirt

Track	Horse	Age	Wt	Distance	Time	Date
PEN	Pensglitter	7	119	2F	:20.71	10/9/04
EVD	Flutter Butterfly	2	118	2 1/2F	:27.00	7/10/04
RP	Desert Wolf Girl	5	113	3F	:32.86	8/7/04
NP	Love's Conquest	2	113	3 1/2F	:39.40	7/24/04
STP	Dance Me Free	5	117	4F	:44.00	4/3/04
MNR	Ameri Brilliance	5	118	4 1/2F	:50.16	8/7/04
SUN	Jimmy Jones	7	118	5F	:55.90	2/7/04
YD	Deadly Talons	2	120	5 1/4F	1:02.40	9/26/04
EMD	Willie the Cat	5	118	5 1/2F	1:01.20	4/16/04
BM	Green Team	5	119	6F	1:07.41	9/11/04
TUP	Lost in the Fog	2	119	6 1/2F	1:13.55	12/26/04
SA	Unfurl the Flag	4	118	7F	1:20.11	2/21/04
HOL	Anziyan Royalty	4	116	7 1/2F	1:27.30	11/13/04
AQU	Lion Tamer	4	115	1M	1:33.46	11/27/04
FG	Yessirgeneralsir	4	117	1M 40Y	1:38.53	3/4/04
MED	Schedule (GB)	3	115	1M 70Y	1:37.90	10/15/04
BEL	Medallist	3	121	1 1/16M	1:40.02	7/11/04
BEL	Seattle Fitz (ARG)	5	116	1 1/8M	1:46.30	6/12/04
PIM	Presidentialaffair	5	126	1 3/16M	1:55.58	10/9/04
LS	Ghostzapper	4	126	1 1/4M	1:59.02	10/30/04
AQU	Angelic Aura	4	119	1 5/16M	2:09.63	4/10/04
FPX	Sigfreto	6	120	1 3/8M	2:17.34	9/26/04
BEL	Birdstone	3	126	1 1/2M	2:27.50	6/5/04
DED	Golden Foil	7	118	*1 9/16M	2:46.86	3/27/04
AQU	Tamburello (CHI)	5	115	1 5/8M	2:43.95	12/29/04
HST	Sea Navigator	6	117	1 3/4M	2:59.47	10/2/04
ALB	Megan's Man	4	116	*1 13/16M	3:10.04	9/26/04
WO	Mr. Perpetuity	7	119	*1 7/8M	3:19.50	12/12/04
EMD	Horatio	5	115	2M	3:22.60	9/20/04
FE	Attonotauto	5	111	*2M 70Y	3:40.05	9/5/04
BEU	Calliehadaprenup	6	112	*2 1/4M	4:02.17	5/1/04

** Only one race run at distance*

Turf

Track	Horse	Age	Wt	Distance	Time	Date
MNR	Long Star	5	121	4 1/2F	:50.23	6/21/04
CRC	Whenthedoveflies	4	115	5F	:54.78	5/23/04
HOL	King Robyn	4	118	5 1/2F	1:00.60	4/23/04
WO	Hour of Justice	4	118	6F	1:07.83	8/2/04
WO	Chris's Bad Boy	7	120	6 1/2F	1:14.27	8/7/04
WO	Soaring Free	5	126	7F	1:19.38	7/24/04
RP	Foreign Justice	3	112	7 1/2F	1:27.46	8/27/04
WO	Royal Regalia	6	120	1M	1:31.84	7/1/04
PEN	Proven Promise	4	116	1M 70Y	1:39.63	7/9/04
HOL	Leroidesanimaux (Brz)	4	114	1 1/16M	1:38.45	5/1/04
BEL	Artie Schiller	3	123	1 1/8M	1:45.50	9/26/04
SAR	Governor Brown	4	121	1 3/16M	1:53.11	8/28/04
SA	Star Over the Bay	6	124	1 1/4M	1:58.70	10/3/04
IND	Parisky	7	118	1 3/8M	2:11.37	6/20/04
WO	Strut the Stage	6	121	1 1/2M	2:25.87	9/6/04
SAR	Spanish Spur (GB)	6	116	*1 5/8M	2:46.29	8/16/04
MNR	Pleasant Company	5	113	1 3/4M	2:55.11	8/15/04
MNR	Pleasant Company	5	121	1 7/8M	3:10.35	9/6/04

** Only one race run at distance*

Fastest Times at Common Distances

6 Furlongs, Dirt (1991–2004)

Horse	Age	Wt	Track	Date	Time
G Malleah	4	120	TUP	4/8/95	1:06.60
Honor the Hero	5	113	TUP	2/21/93	1:06.80
Magical Flyer	4	117	TUP	4/18/95	1:07.00
Ladyteeoff	5	116	TUP	12/19/92	1:07.20
Last Don B.	7	118	TUP	10/22/94	1:07.20
Da Hoss	2	120	TUP	10/30/94	1:07.20
Honor the Hero	7	124	TUP	2/25/95	1:07.20
Left the Latch	4	115	TUP	2/28/95	1:07.20
Honor the Hero	7	115	TUP	3/19/95	1:07.20
Coach Jimi Lee	3	118	HAW	12/12/03	1:07.27
Honor the Hero	5	121	TUP	2/7/93	1:07.40
Last Don B.	7	121	TUP	1/30/94	1:07.40
G Malleah	5	123	TUP	2/24/96	1:07.40
Moro Oro	3	122	HOO	11/16/96	1:07.40
Bay Runner	4	114	SR	7/29/00	1:07.40
Green Team	5	119	BM	9/11/04	1:07.41
Taiaslew	4	119	TUP	2/21/04	1:07.42
Ruff Hombre	6	115	SA	2/6/92	1:07.44
Smoke Till Dawn	4	117	GG	12/17/03	1:07.45
Raving Main E Axe	4	116	RP	2/1/91	1:07.50
Answer Do	5	121	TUP	2/24/91	1:07.50
Two Out of Three	4	121	FNO	10/8/04	1:07.50
Apalachee Ridge	3	114	HOL	12/12/97	1:07.52
Tough Game	4	119	HOL	11/15/03	1:07.52
Kelly Kip	5	123	AQU	4/10/99	1:07.54
El Dorado Shooter	4	114	GG	1/20/01	1:07.55
Twentythreejaybird	5	117	GG	2/20/04	1:07.56
Black Jack Road	8	118	PLN	7/11/92	1:07.57
Marshad	4	114	TUP	2/6/92	1:07.60
Night Glider	5	116	TUP	1/31/93	1:07.60
Passing Game	8	121	SAC	9/4/93	1:07.60
Garabee	4	114	TUP	9/23/94	1:07.60
Plenty Zloty	5	121	TUP	2/12/95	1:07.60
Will Meyers	5	121	SAC	8/24/96	1:07.60
Champ's Star	3	118	SAC	8/30/98	1:07.60
Blue Tejano	8	119	EMD	6/7/02	1:07.60
Kelly Kip	4	117	AQU	4/11/98	1:07.61
Halo Cat	5	118	GG	1/19/03	1:07.62
Artax	4	120	BEL	10/16/99	1:07.66
Mr. Doubledown	6	118	GG	5/13/00	1:07.66
Swept Overboard	4	116	SA	10/6/01	1:07.67
Snow Ridge	4	116	SA	1/27/02	1:07.70
Omega Code	2	117	FNO	10/5/02	1:07.70
Concept Win	4	115	SA	1/30/94	1:07.71
Jetinto Houston	4	119	GG	2/7/03	1:07.71
Kona Gold	6	126	CD	11/4/00	1:07.77
Shake You Down	5	112	AQU	4/26/03	1:07.77
Green Team	5	119	GG	12/11/04	1:07.77
Anjiz	5	114	KEE	10/9/93	1:07.78
Drum Sound	5	118	TUP	12/19/92	1:07.80
Doctor Scott Blurr	5	116	TUP	1/30/93	1:07.80
Smokin Albert	4	116	TUP	3/13/94	1:07.80
Last Don B.	7	125	TUP	4/9/94	1:07.80
Gusto's Marker	6	116	TUP	10/2/94	1:07.80
Bear	3	115	TUP	10/30/94	1:07.80
Boomie's Bravo	4	121	TUP	3/28/95	1:07.80
Lynn's Notebook	4	117	STK	6/25/95	1:07.80
Hooten Harry	3	120	TUP	12/21/95	1:07.80
Left the Latch	5	116	TUP	4/27/96	1:07.80
Salta's Pride	6	116	SOL	7/13/96	1:07.80
Tolemeo	4	114	FNO	10/12/97	1:07.80
Handy N Bold	5	117	EMD	4/30/00	1:07.80
Royalty	6	120	SR	8/4/00	1:07.80
Crowning Meeting	8	117	EMD	4/28/02	1:07.80
Road Afleet	5	118	EMD	4/27/03	1:07.80
Just Outrageous	4	119	EMD	8/31/03	1:07.80
Willie the Cat	5	117	EMD	4/25/04	1:07.80
Hay Cody	4	127	MED	9/6/96	1:07.81
Hustler	6	113	MNR	8/11/01	1:07.81
Amerindio (ARG)	7	121	SA	1/2/04	1:07.81
Savorthetime	5	117	LS	5/31/04	1:07.82
Wild Gold	4	114	GG	2/13/94	1:07.83
Purple Peopleater	8	119	MED	9/24/99	1:07.83
Gilded Time	2	122	MTH	8/8/92	1:07.84
Lexicon	4	116	SA	10/17/99	1:07.84
Presidio Heights	5	119	BM	4/19/03	1:07.84
Avanzado (ARG)	6	116	SA	1/26/03	1:07.85
Coach Jimi Lee	4	117	PRM	7/4/04	1:07.85
True Direction	4	123	BEL	5/24/03	1:07.86
Spanish Eyes	5	122	PLN	7/5/03	1:07.86
Noble Year	5	117	DMR	8/21/95	1:07.87
Trickey Trevor	4	119	GG	1/23/03	1:07.87
Hall of Gold	3	119	GG	11/17/01	1:07.88
Long Range Missile	3	119	SA	10/22/04	1:07.88
Artax	4	126	GP	11/6/99	1:07.89
Iron Punch	6	114	PHA	7/29/00	1:07.89
Romanzo	4	118	GG	1/18/01	1:07.89
Beau's Town	6	118	LS	5/8/04	1:07.89
Plum Twist	7	116	RP	2/3/91	1:07.90
Mr. O. P.	5	115	AC	4/28/91	1:07.90
Forest Gazelle	4	117	HOL	4/28/95	1:07.90
Five Star Day	4	119	KEE	10/14/00	1:07.90
Yankee Gentleman	4	114	DMR	9/6/03	1:07.90
Dat You Miz Blue	4	123	BEL	5/26/01	1:07.92
Captain Red	6	111	AQU	2/26/03	1:07.93
Southern Justice	4	114	SA	1/2/92	1:07.94
Irish Twist	4	119	GG	5/30/93	1:07.94
Sweet Beast	4	122	MED	11/18/94	1:07.94
Blue Tejano	6	117	GG	6/16/00	1:07.94
Delaware Township	4	113	MTH	8/27/00	1:07.94
Lexicon	6	117	BM	9/8/01	1:07.94
Con Quixote	5	117	GG	12/18/03	1:07.94
Crafty Alfel	8	119	AQU	3/30/96	1:07.95
Richter Scale	6	123	LRL	7/15/00	1:07.95
Cajun Beat	3	123	SA	10/25/03	1:07.95
Beau's Town	5	119	DMR	7/26/03	1:07.96
Tres Paraiso	5	116	BM	9/13/97	1:07.98
Amarillo Pride	5	117	GG	1/13/00	1:07.98
Green Team	4	116	SA	11/8/03	1:07.98
Wild 'n Wet	4	122	GG	6/8/00	1:07.99
Presidio Heights	5	117	GG	2/16/03	1:07.99

Many individual performances at 1:08.00

7 Furlongs, Dirt (1991–2004)

Horse	Age	Wt	Track	Date	Time
Mazel Trick	4	115	HOL	6/27/99	1:19.97
Artax	4	114	AQU	5/2/99	1:20.04
Lit de Justice	5	118	DMR	8/19/95	1:20.06
Unfurl the Flag	4	118	SA	2/21/04	1:20.11
Elusive Quality	4	119	GP	2/21/97	1:20.17
Left Bank	5	121	BEL	7/4/02	1:20.17
Pico Central (BRZ)	5	117	AQU	4/10/04	1:20.22
D'Hallevant	4	115	DMR	8/20/94	1:20.25
You and I	3	122	BEL	6/11/94	1:20.33
Binalong	4	112	KEE	10/13/93	1:20.39
Golden Gear	4	114	RP	3/18/95	1:20.40
Early Flyer	3	123	HOL	5/28/01	1:20.42
El Corredor	4	119	DMR	8/12/01	1:20.42
Ghostzapper	4	119	BEL	7/4/04	1:20.42
Mamselle Bebette	3	115	SA	12/28/93	1:20.45
Reality Road	4	121	BEL	6/21/96	1:20.48
Another Star	4	122	HOL	4/25/98	1:20.49
Distorted Humor	5	119	KEE	4/11/98	1:20.50
Alannan	5	116	CD	5/5/01	1:20.50
Memo (CHI)	7	120	HOL	7/2/94	1:20.52
A. P. Assay	4	116	HOL	6/28/98	1:20.53
Limit Out	3	115	AQU	4/11/98	1:20.54
Hal's Pal (GB)	4	116	HOL	11/6/97	1:20.55
Lord Abounding	4	116	GP	3/22/03	1:20.56
Oronero	3	114	WO	12/6/95	1:20.60
Toolighttoquit	4	115	RP	10/19/96	1:20.60
Flaming Bridle	4	119	PHA	9/28/99	1:20.61
Crafty Friend	6	116	BEL	7/4/99	1:20.62
Lord Abounding	4	118	GP	2/28/03	1:20.63
Lion Heart	2	114	HOL	11/15/03	1:20.63
Light of Morn	6	118	GP	10/30/92	1:20.64
Light of Morn	6	116	DMR	8/23/92	1:20.65
Shared Interest	4	111	BEL	10/10/92	1:20.65
Star of the Crop	3	118	SA	12/26/92	1:20.67
Forest Danger	3	116	AQU	4/10/04	1:20.67
Yearly Report	3	123	LS	10/29/04	1:20.67
Indian Country	3	119	HOL	12/18/04	1:20.69
Siphon (BRZ)	4	117	DMR	7/29/95	1:20.70
Dream Supreme	4	120	CD	5/5/01	1:20.70
Gold Land	4	116	HOL	5/3/95	1:20.71
Left Bank	4	126	BEL	9/22/01	1:20.73
The Exeter Man	5	115	HOL	11/7/97	1:20.76
Brutally Frank	6	114	AQU	3/18/00	1:20.77
Alphabet Soup	5	118	DMR	8/17/96	1:20.79
Missy's Mirage	4	119	AQU	4/18/92	1:20.80
Cat's Cradle	4	118	HOL	5/31/96	1:20.80
Western Winter	4	118	BEL	9/19/96	1:20.80
Flaming West	3	114	HOL	11/22/97	1:20.80
Highland Ice	5	121	RP	9/5/98	1:20.80
Hoist the Baba	6	121	RP	9/18/99	1:20.80
Van Patten	7	116	WO	11/23/00	1:20.80
Son of a Pistol	6	118	HOL	6/28/98	1:20.81
Love That Red	3	122	HOL	5/31/99	1:20.81
Now Listen	6	116	HOL	7/3/93	1:20.83
Lady Tak	3	122	SAR	7/26/03	1:20.83
Gold Land	4	117	HOL	5/29/95	1:20.84
Brulay	3	115	HOL	5/17/98	1:20.84
Tough and Rugged	4	109	GP	1/12/93	1:20.86
Binalong	5	117	GP	1/23/94	1:20.86
Sky Watch	4	117	CNL	9/1/97	1:20.87
Sociallyunencumber	4	117	HOL	11/28/97	1:20.88
Darling My Darling	3	117	KEE	10/11/00	1:20.88
Paster's Caper	4	116	HOL	6/22/95	1:20.89
Wouldn't We All	3	119	AQU	4/12/97	1:20.90
Kelleric	4	118	HOL	7/20/97	1:20.90
Lite the Fuse	5	121	BEL	5/5/96	1:20.92
Birdonthewire	4	119	BEL	7/10/93	1:20.93
Twist Afleet	5	122	BEL	5/4/96	1:20.94
Fire Slam	3	123	BEL	6/5/04	1:20.94
Memo (CHI)	6	118	SA	11/6/93	1:20.95
Migrant Worker	5	116	HOL	5/4/94	1:20.95
Wouldn't We All	5	114	AQU	3/14/99	1:20.95
Powis Castle	3	117	SA	12/26/94	1:20.96
Bold Capital	6	116	HOL	5/10/97	1:20.97
Afternoon Deelites	2	115	HOL	11/13/94	1:20.98
Smoke Glacken	3	123	BEL	6/7/97	1:20.98
Clooney	4	118	LS	6/22/01	1:20.98
Collegian	4	117	BEL	6/23/91	1:20.99
Pomeroy	3	121	SAR	8/28/04	1:20.99
Moscow M D	3	114	DMR	8/15/92	1:21.00
Highland Ice	4	118	RP	8/10/97	1:21.00
Ben Told	3	116	ALB	12/19/97	1:21.00
Forestry	3	124	SAR	8/28/99	1:21.00
Daring Pegasus	5	118	ARP	7/4/03	1:21.00
American Chance	5	119	GP	2/10/94	1:21.01
Score Quick	5	113	HOL	6/29/97	1:21.01
Star Smasher	3	123	ALB	6/9/02	1:21.01
Devil of a Trip	3	118	ALB	6/8/03	1:21.01
Le Casque Gris	4	119	HOL	5/8/98	1:21.02
Finder's Fortune	4	117	HOL	6/18/93	1:21.03
Montbrook	3	122	ATL	6/27/93	1:21.04
Banker's Gold	4	115	BEL	7/5/98	1:21.04
Dat You Miz Blue	4	122	AQU	4/7/01	1:21.06
Midas Eyes	3	116	GP	3/15/03	1:21.06
Damar Wayne	5	119	HOL	5/8/04	1:21.06
Pohave	6	116	HOL	7/3/04	1:21.06
Silver Charm	3	120	SA	2/8/97	1:21.07
Exotic Wood	6	121	SA	1/24/98	1:21.07
Richter Scale	6	121	KEE	4/16/00	1:21.07
Bilo	4	123	HOL	12/19/04	1:21.07
Housebuster	4	126	SAR	8/25/91	1:21.08
Capote Belle	3	115	SAR	7/27/96	1:21.08
Concept Win	5	118	HOL	6/24/95	1:21.09
Disturbingthepeace	4	113	HOL	7/6/02	1:21.09
Lady Tak	4	119	SAR	8/29/04	1:21.09
Robyn Dancer	4	118	HOL	6/29/91	1:21.10
Mystery's Edge	4	115	HOL	7/17/92	1:21.10
Orville N Wilbur's	2	119	HOL	12/11/97	1:21.10
Caller One	3	122	HOL	5/29/00	1:21.10
Mass Media	3	113	AQU	10/31/04	1:21.10
I'ma Game Master	3	117	HOL	11/18/94	1:21.11
Van Patten	7	122	WO	9/10/00	1:21.11
Ginzano	5	118	AQU	4/25/03	1:21.11
Yearly Report	3	114	SA	1/19/04	1:21.11
Unbridled	4	122	AP	8/3/91	1:21.12
Private Persuasion	4	116	HOL	6/8/95	1:21.12
Afternoon Deelites	4	124	KEE	4/14/96	1:21.12
Kafwain	3	123	SA	2/1/03	1:21.12

1 Mile, Dirt (1991–2004)

Horse	Age	Wt	Track	Date	Time
Najran	4	113	BEL	5/7/03	1:32.24
Williamstown	3	124	BEL	5/5/93	1:32.79
Honour and Glory	3	110	BEL	5/27/96	1:32.81
Slew of Damascus	5	117	YM	3/28/93	1:33.00
Sky Jack	7	123	EMD	8/24/03	1:33.00
Langfuhr	5	122	BEL	5/26/97	1:33.11
Congaree	4	119	AQU	11/30/02	1:33.11
Mr. Pappion	5	118	TUP	1/30/93	1:33.20
Wild Wonder	4	121	EMD	8/23/98	1:33.20
Edneator	4	111	EMD	8/20/00	1:33.20
Swept Overboard	5	117	BEL	5/27/02	1:33.34
Left Bank	4	120	AQU	11/24/01	1:33.35
Flying Cuantal	6	117	STK	6/15/97	1:33.40
Secret Launch	5	116	EMD	6/16/02	1:33.40
Yankee Victor	4	123	AQU	5/6/00	1:33.45
Lion Tamer	4	115	AQU	11/27/04	1:33.46
Wild Rush	4	119	BEL	5/25/98	1:33.50
French Deputy	3	113	BEL	9/4/95	1:33.53
Chilukki	3	116	CD	11/4/00	1:33.57
Private Music	5	120	STK	6/22/97	1:33.60
Dixie Flag	4	117	AQU	4/18/98	1:33.60
Cat's At Home	4	114	AQU	4/7/01	1:33.60
Rubiano	4	116	AQU	10/26/91	1:33.68
Dixie Brass	3	107	BEL	5/25/92	1:33.68
Black Bart	5	121	TUP	3/1/04	1:33.68
Makaleha	4	116	SAC	8/23/91	1:33.70
Dixie Brass	3	126	BEL	5/6/92	1:33.71
There's Zealous	4	123	AP	8/17/02	1:33.76
Saint Verre	5	117	AQU	4/26/03	1:33.77
Semi Vicious	5	115	TUP	1/19/92	1:33.80
Layton Hill	4	115	TUP	2/3/94	1:33.80
Secret Past	6	121	TUP	1/22/96	1:33.80
Poker Brad	6	119	EMD	5/30/04	1:33.80
B. Charlie	4	114	BM	9/15/95	1:33.83
Slewker	4	117	BM	2/10/96	1:33.86
Find the Mine	5	114	MNR	7/4/00	1:33.86
Colonial Affair	3	110	BEL	5/5/93	1:33.87
Jovial (GB)	6	115	SA	1/1/93	1:33.88
Pacific Fleet	5	114	AQU	4/5/97	1:33.88
Doneraile Court	3	114	BEL	10/11/99	1:33.88
Alexandrina	4	111	WO	6/9/91	1:33.90
Snorter	4	116	GG	3/27/04	1:33.92
Sea Emperor	4	114	BEL	6/20/96	1:33.95
Gold Memory	4	117	AP	7/26/97	1:33.95
Ibero (ARG)	5	117	AQU	10/24/92	1:33.97
Holy Bull	3	112	BEL	5/30/94	1:33.98
I'madrifter	5	115	GG	1/1/03	1:33.98
Count the Time	4	119	AP	8/26/93	1:33.99
Vic's Rebel	4	122	HOO	10/13/98	1:33.99
Bolulight	4	121	LGA	8/23/92	1:34.00
Calgary Classic	6	116	TUP	1/28/93	1:34.00
Nipsy's Son	6	118	TUP	2/7/94	1:34.00
Classy Mirage	4	117	AQU	4/9/94	1:34.00
Bell Vigor	5	117	BM	2/24/96	1:34.00
Stately Star	4	118	HOO	11/23/96	1:34.00
Singing Year	5	120	EMD	6/14/98	1:34.00
Bonapaw	6	121	AP	7/20/02	1:34.00
Lykatill Hil	4	118	DMR	9/11/94	1:34.01
Prenup	5	122	BEL	5/12/96	1:34.01
Subordinated Debt	3	126	BEL	5/8/91	1:34.03
Romeo's Royalty	5	117	GG	5/18/94	1:34.03
Current Worth	4	120	BM	9/7/97	1:34.04
Sir Bear	5	116	AQU	11/28/98	1:34.05
You	3	121	BEL	6/7/02	1:34.05
Wagon Limit	4	114	AQU	4/4/98	1:34.06
Flat Fleet Feet	4	121	AQU	4/6/97	1:34.07
Fusaichi Pegasus	3	124	BEL	9/23/00	1:34.07
Scan	3	117	BEL	9/2/91	1:34.09
Sir Beaufort	5	115	SA	1/2/92	1:34.09
Hello Chicago	3	115	DMR	8/22/94	1:34.09
Trebizond	5	117	SA	1/4/91	1:34.10
Opinionator	3	114	BEL	6/1/91	1:34.10
Bowdoin Street	7	115	BEL	10/3/91	1:34.10
Secreto's Hideaway	5	119	TP	3/5/94	1:34.12
Topsy Robsy	4	115	BEL	9/19/96	1:34.12
Alcaughtup	5	114	AQU	3/29/97	1:34.12
Forest Landing	3	114	CD	5/2/03	1:34.13
Pinfloron (FR)	3	117	BM	12/10/95	1:34.15
Activist	3	118	AQU	4/3/97	1:34.15
I'madrifter	3	114	BM	10/8/01	1:34.15
Harbor Star	4	118	AQU	3/22/03	1:34.15
Aldebaran	5	119	BEL	5/26/03	1:34.15
Touch Gold	4	123	CD	6/28/98	1:34.16
Twilight Agenda	5	122	DMR	9/8/91	1:34.17
Guided Tour	4	122	CD	7/3/00	1:34.17
Affirmed Success	5	118	AQU	11/27/99	1:34.18
Blade Prospector (BRZ)	6	116	GG	3/31/01	1:34.18
Echo of Yesterday	5	115	SA	2/17/94	1:34.19
Stop and Listen	4	119	AQU	4/15/94	1:34.19
Highland Gold	6	116	GG	2/19/01	1:34.19
Furiously	3	113	BEL	9/7/92	1:34.20
Great Energy	7	118	TUP	1/28/94	1:34.20
Want a Winner	4	117	YM	8/14/94	1:34.20
Kemper	7	116	TUP	1/22/95	1:34.20
Brumbeau	7	119	TUP	3/28/95	1:34.20
Passiano	4	118	TUP	10/21/95	1:34.20
Snow Blink	5	116	TUP	4/16/96	1:34.20
Alydar's Rib	5	116	HOO	10/4/96	1:34.20
It's the Wind	7	117	HOO	10/5/96	1:34.20
Bold Zak	7	119	STK	6/11/97	1:34.20
Kid Katabatic	4	113	EMD	8/17/97	1:34.20
You've Got Action	4	117	EMD	6/21/98	1:34.20
Kid Katabatic	6	122	EMD	6/20/99	1:34.20
Doc Art	4	116	TUP	10/26/99	1:34.20
Fleet Pacific	6	120	EMD	8/20/00	1:34.20
Why Change	3	112	BEL	9/15/96	1:34.22
Barrage	4	116	AQU	11/15/01	1:34.22
Crafty Friend	6	115	AQU	4/30/99	1:34.23
Code One	5	118	MNR	12/19/00	1:34.23
Borodislew	5	119	DMR	7/31/95	1:34.24
Bold Assert	3	120	SA	3/6/92	1:34.25
He's Illustrious	6	122	GG	6/12/93	1:34.25
Limited War	5	116	BEL	5/27/96	1:34.25
Awful Smart	4	120	CD	6/1/00	1:34.25
Inside Information	3	121	BEL	5/8/94	1:34.26
How Bout Jose	5	119	BM	5/24/02	1:34.26
Boss Ego	7	116	GG	1/30/03	1:34.26
West by West	3	112	BEL	10/11/92	1:34.27
Red Bullet	3	113	AQU	3/19/00	1:34.27

1 1/16 Miles, Dirt (1991–2004)

Horse	Age	Wt	Track	Date	Time
Efervescente (ARG)	5	118	SA	1/6/93	1:39.18
Restless Con	4	118	GG	6/24/91	1:39.50
Rock and Roll	3	112	BEL	6/13/98	1:39.51
Charts	5	114	GG	4/18/92	1:39.58
O. R. Race Rat	4	117	YM	1/15/93	1:39.60
Kid Katabatic	5	123	EMD	7/26/98	1:39.60
Eagle Mill	4	116	AP	5/31/91	1:39.61
Gateway to Heaven	3	114	FG	12/29/91	1:39.80
Richmond Runner	7	119	BEL	7/16/97	1:39.81
Reality Road	6	115	BM	1/31/98	1:39.85
Master Waco Willie	5	120	YM	3/1/91	1:39.90
Fit to Scout	4	118	GG	3/16/91	1:39.90
Mossflower	4	114	BEL	6/20/98	1:39.90
Key Contender	6	117	BEL	6/11/94	1:39.92
Grand Circus Park	6	117	DET	7/23/94	1:40.00
Medallist	3	121	BEL	7/11/04	1:40.02
Marwood	4	117	PLN	7/5/04	1:40.04
New Journey	4	116	HOL	11/27/97	1:40.06
Jarf	5	115	BEL	6/28/01	1:40.08
Yougottawanna	5	116	BM	5/31/04	1:40.08
Settlers Pub	5	112	TP	2/7/91	1:40.10
Wild Years	4	121	BEL	6/7/02	1:40.11
Bolulight	4	115	GG	6/29/92	1:40.12
Crafty Friend	4	116	HOL	7/12/97	1:40.12
Adreamisborn	5	117	PLN	7/11/04	1:40.14
Hind Most	6	122	PRM	5/14/93	1:40.20
Formal Gold	4	121	MTH	8/23/97	1:40.20
Lord Sterling	4	115	SR	8/5/00	1:40.20
Alfurune	5	117	EMD	7/4/03	1:40.20
Region	5	117	HOL	7/17/94	1:40.21
Flying Chevron	3	112	MED	9/22/95	1:40.27
Event of the Year	3	115	BM	3/7/98	1:40.27
Basqueing Beauty	2	119	TP	9/15/91	1:40.28
Hang On Slewpy	4	119	OP	4/20/91	1:40.30
Twilight Agenda	5	116	HOL	7/13/91	1:40.30
Gondolieri (CHI)	4	116	HOL	5/3/03	1:40.32
Aunt Sophie	5	117	PLN	7/5/03	1:40.34
Riboletta (BRZ)	5	125	BEL	9/16/00	1:40.35
E Dubai	3	121	BEL	7/8/01	1:40.38
Black Forest	4	113	MED	9/26/98	1:40.39
A P Valentine	3	112	HIA	3/24/01	1:40.39
Athenia Green (GB)	6	118	STK	6/28/92	1:40.40
Sneakin Jake	7	120	YM	9/19/94	1:40.40
Secret Past	6	115	TUP	1/1/96	1:40.40
Edneator	4	122	EMD	9/11/00	1:40.40
Jess C's Whirl	3	118	MED	12/10/93	1:40.44
Siphon (BRZ)	5	117	HOL	5/4/96	1:40.44
Snorter	3	117	BEL	5/7/03	1:40.44
Fleet Lady	3	115	GG	12/21/97	1:40.46
Model Dancer	5	117	BEL	5/18/92	1:40.47
The Exeter Man	4	116	HOL	5/17/96	1:40.47
Yougottawanna	5	118	BM	4/22/04	1:40.47
Del Mar Dennis	4	115	HOL	5/15/94	1:40.48
Louis Cyphre (IRE)	5	119	GG	4/14/91	1:40.50
Twilight Agenda	5	114	HOL	6/29/91	1:40.50
Say Dance	5	117	BEL	9/16/93	1:40.52
Berkley Fitz	3	117	BEL	5/9/92	1:40.53
Dixie Dot Com	6	118	LS	5/28/01	1:40.53
Mr. Bluebird	4	118	BEL	9/17/95	1:40.55
My Mogul	3	106	BEL	5/5/93	1:40.56
Regal Rowdy	5	122	HOL	5/12/94	1:40.58
Paseana (ARG)	7	123	DMR	8/28/94	1:40.59
Grand Slam	2	122	BEL	10/18/97	1:40.59
Time to Pass	4	117	LGA	7/4/92	1:40.60
Ibero (ARG)	6	117	HOL	12/19/93	1:40.60
Blare of Trumpets	5	115	BEL	5/7/94	1:40.60
Sky Beauty	4	125	BEL	5/21/94	1:40.60
Alki Joe	5	117	STK	6/18/95	1:40.60
Funny Tale	5	119	EMD	7/20/97	1:40.60
General Royal	5	116	PLN	7/11/99	1:40.60
Feverish	5	122	SR	7/30/00	1:40.60
Reds Superstar	4	114	PLN	7/8/01	1:40.60
Salt Grinder	3	119	EMD	8/11/02	1:40.60
Demon Warlock	4	123	EMD	9/19/04	1:40.60
Hollywood Wildcat	4	124	SA	10/10/94	1:40.61
Admiralty	4	122	BEL	9/7/96	1:40.61
Slew of Damascus	5	116	GG	5/29/93	1:40.62
Worldly Ways (GB)	5	116	GG	6/20/99	1:40.62
Admiralty	5	115	BEL	10/18/97	1:40.63
Ce Flite	3	112	MED	9/6/96	1:40.64
It's So Simple	3	116	BEL	7/8/01	1:40.66
Olanthe	6	117	GG	2/25/95	1:40.67
Raising Havoc	5	119	GG	5/4/97	1:40.67
Jimmy Z	5	115	GG	11/29/02	1:40.67
Yougottawanna	5	117	GG	2/28/04	1:40.67
Mazel Trick	4	117	DMR	8/7/99	1:40.68
River Keen (IRE)	7	115	HOL	7/10/99	1:40.69
Colita	3	115	BEL	5/21/03	1:40.69
Awesome Dividend	4	119	HOL	12/20/04	1:40.69
Sea Cadet	3	117	BM	1/19/91	1:40.70
Lee's Tanthem	4	117	STK	6/23/91	1:40.70
Tossofthecoin	5	118	HOL	5/21/95	1:40.70
Arrivederci Baby	4	113	GG	11/29/96	1:40.72
Anet	3	113	TP	3/29/97	1:40.73
Missy's Mirage	4	116	BEL	5/9/92	1:40.74
Afternoon Deelites	2	121	HOL	12/18/94	1:40.74
Kingdom Found	7	115	SA	1/12/97	1:40.74
Becky's Queen	4	117	FNO	10/11/92	1:40.78
Valiant Nature	2	121	HOL	12/19/93	1:40.78
Cryptodiplomacy	2	117	BEL	10/9/98	1:40.79
Sister Act	4	117	BEL	6/19/99	1:40.79
Military Hawk	7	121	SR	8/7/94	1:40.80
Kiridashi	4	121	WO	8/17/96	1:40.80
Stone Canyon	3	117	BEL	5/7/03	1:40.80
Sapor	5	117	BEL	5/8/96	1:40.81
Will's Way	4	114	BEL	5/15/97	1:40.81
Even the Score	6	116	HOL	5/8/04	1:40.81
Robb	3	112	BEL	5/27/96	1:40.82
Savinio	6	116	DMR	7/27/96	1:40.82
Take Her to Heart	6	115	BM	9/14/97	1:40.82
Musical Gambler	3	111	HOL	12/3/97	1:40.82
Excessivepleasure	3	122	PRM	7/5/03	1:40.82
Goldigger's Dream	3	116	HOL	11/21/93	1:40.83
Poor But Honest	5	117	PIM	9/9/95	1:40.83
General Challenge	3	124	HOL	6/26/99	1:40.83
George Bailey	3	118	HOL	12/20/02	1:40.83
Ayearintime	3	119	GG	12/26/02	1:40.83
Pesci	4	119	HOL	4/30/04	1:40.83

1 1/8 Miles, Dirt (1991–2004)

Horse	Age	Wt	Track	Date	Time
Gentlemen (ARG)	4	121	HOL	12/22/96	1:45.35
Flying Notes	3	122	EMD	9/2/02	1:45.40
Forty One Carats	3	120	MED	10/29/99	1:45.50
Albert the Great	4	120	HIA	3/24/01	1:45.52
Free House	3	122	HOL	7/20/97	1:45.96
Atlanta National	5	116	GP	1/26/91	1:46.00
K. J.'s Appeal	4	112	MED	10/16/98	1:46.06
Riboletta (BRZ)	5	123	BEL	10/14/00	1:46.14
Inside Information	4	123	BEL	10/28/95	1:46.15
Lykatill Hil	6	125	SAC	8/24/96	1:46.20
Sharp Cat	4	123	BEL	10/10/98	1:46.20
Formal Gold	4	119	BEL	6/14/97	1:46.21
Mineshaft	4	126	BEL	9/6/03	1:46.21
Soto	3	111	MNR	8/9/03	1:46.29
Lindsay's Hawk	5	111	RKM	5/3/91	1:46.30
Seattle Fitz (ARG)	5	116	BEL	6/12/04	1:46.30
Lykatill Hil	5	118	BM	12/9/95	1:46.32
Prepo (CHI)	5	115	BM	9/27/97	1:46.32
In Excess (IRE)	4	126	BEL	9/15/91	1:46.33
Seeking Daylight	4	113	BEL	6/15/02	1:46.35
Running Stag	5	117	BEL	6/12/99	1:46.39
Ghostzapper	4	126	BEL	9/11/04	1:46.38
Twice the Vice	6	121	HOL	7/20/97	1:46.41
Doc of the Day	4	119	FNO	10/18/92	1:46.45
Olympio	3	123	CBY	7/7/91	1:46.47
Missouri Ace	6	118	SAC	9/2/91	1:46.50
Hal's Pal (GB)	5	116	BM	9/26/98	1:46.51
Scan	3	119	MED	9/20/91	1:46.53
Old Trieste	4	116	HOL	5/29/99	1:46.55
Volponi	3	114	MED	10/19/01	1:46.55
Lakeway	3	121	BEL	6/12/94	1:46.58
Gator Dancer	4	119	BEL	7/18/97	1:46.58
Strike the Gold	4	116	BEL	6/6/92	1:46.60
Aly's Act	3	119	PLA	10/30/93	1:46.60
Tinners Way	6	116	HOL	6/2/96	1:46.60
Profound Secret	4	114	SAC	8/29/98	1:46.60
Poker Brad	6	118	EMD	7/25/04	1:46.60
Behrens	3	117	MED	9/20/97	1:46.61
Beboppin Baby	5	114	PRM	7/4/98	1:46.62
Twilight Agenda	5	121	MED	10/18/91	1:46.63
Roses in May	4	115	PRM	7/3/04	1:46.63
Subordination	4	114	BEL	6/13/98	1:46.64
The Wicked North	5	120	HOL	6/5/94	1:46.68
Crafty Oak	5	114	HAW	5/15/99	1:46.69
In Excess (IRE)	4	126	SA	1/19/91	1:46.70
Sell Clause	5	118	GG	3/24/91	1:46.70
Hansel	3	121	TP	3/30/91	1:46.70
Devil His Due	5	120	BEL	6/18/94	1:46.71
Bertrando	5	120	SA	10/15/94	1:46.72
Festin (ARG)	5	116	BEL	6/8/91	1:46.75
Wekiva Springs	5	120	BEL	6/15/96	1:46.78
Midway Road	4	116	KEE	4/22/04	1:46.78
Jolie's Halo	5	116	MTH	8/8/92	1:46.80
Artic Son	5	117	HST	8/3/98	1:46.80
Pleasantly Perfect	4	115	SA	10/6/02	1:46.80
Poker Brad	5	115	EMD	7/27/03	1:46.80
Sky Jack	4	118	HOL	12/3/00	1:46.81
Saint Ballado	3	120	AP	6/21/92	1:46.82
Bowman's Band	5	119	MED	10/3/03	1:46.84
River Keen (IRE)	7	126	BEL	9/18/99	1:46.85
Grand Jewel	3	120	KEE	10/10/93	1:46.87
Holy Bull	3	121	BEL	9/17/94	1:46.89
J. T.'s Pet	7	115	SA	3/20/91	1:46.90
Latin American	5	116	HOL	4/24/93	1:46.92
Lakeway	3	121	HOL	7/10/94	1:46.93
Tomorrows Cat	3	113	MED	9/25/98	1:46.95
Saratoga Dew	3	119	BEL	10/10/92	1:46.99
Another Review	4	120	DMR	8/8/92	1:47.00
Athenia Green (GB)	7	116	PLN	7/11/93	1:47.00
Bertrando	4	126	BEL	9/18/93	1:47.00
Indian Charlie	3	120	SA	4/4/98	1:47.00
Moonlight Meeting	7	120	EMD	7/28/02	1:47.00
Yanks Music	3	119	BEL	10/6/96	1:47.02
Seattle Fitz (ARG)	4	119	BEL	9/27/03	1:47.02
Missy's Mirage	4	118	BEL	5/31/92	1:47.03
Alphabet Soup	4	117	HOL	12/23/95	1:47.03
Banshee Breeze	3	119	KEE	10/17/98	1:47.04
Left Bank	5	118	SAR	8/3/02	1:47.04
Ibero (ARG)	5	115	SA	2/15/92	1:47.05
Sultry Song	4	126	BEL	9/19/92	1:47.05
Cigar	6	126	BEL	9/14/96	1:47.06
Old Trieste	3	118	HOL	7/19/98	1:47.06
Truly a Judge	6	115	HOL	12/11/04	1:47.06
Cigar	5	126	BEL	9/16/95	1:47.07
Anshan (GB)	4	115	SA	3/30/91	1:47.10
Ja Ro De	5	117	LGA	6/30/91	1:47.10
Gander	5	114	MED	9/28/01	1:47.11
Event of the Year	3	121	TP	3/29/98	1:47.12
Imperial Gesture	3	117	BEL	9/7/02	1:47.12
Red Sky's	3	118	GG	5/29/99	1:47.16
Jewel Princess	4	120	HOL	7/21/96	1:47.17
Pleasant Breeze	4	110	MED	10/15/99	1:47.17
Diazo	3	117	MED	9/24/93	1:47.18
Keeper Hill	4	123	KEE	10/16/99	1:47.19
Fleet Renee	3	121	BEL	6/30/01	1:47.19
Dispute	3	120	BEL	9/4/93	1:47.20
Military Hawk	7	116	PLN	7/10/94	1:47.20
Heavenly Prize	3	123	BEL	9/4/94	1:47.20
Majestic Nasr	7	113	SAC	9/5/94	1:47.20
Anchor	5	120	FNO	10/14/95	1:47.20
Flirtacious Girl	3	119	EMD	8/21/99	1:47.20
Western Pride	3	113	MNR	8/11/01	1:47.20
Marquetry	6	120	MED	10/15/93	1:47.21
Silver Charm	4	124	SA	10/17/98	1:47.21
Dispute	3	119	BEL	10/16/93	1:47.22
Cigar	5	120	OP	4/15/95	1:47.22
Balto Star	3	121	TP	3/24/01	1:47.23
Mizzen Mast	4	121	SA	2/2/02	1:47.25
Pleasantly Perfect	6	121	SA	1/31/04	1:47.25
Louis Quatorze	3	124	SAR	8/4/96	1:47.26
Del Mar Dennis	5	117	SA	4/2/95	1:47.27
Silver Charm	4	123	SA	2/7/98	1:47.27
Skip Away	5	130	SUF	5/30/98	1:47.27
Victory Gallop	4	120	CD	6/12/99	1:47.28
Sultry Song	4	115	SAR	8/29/92	1:47.29
Serena's Song	3	124	BEL	9/3/95	1:47.29
Skip Away	3	121	KEE	4/13/96	1:47.29

1 1/4 Miles, Dirt (1991–2004)

Horse	Age	Wt	Track	Date	Time
In Excess (IRE)	4	119	BEL	7/4/91	1:58.33
Skip Away	4	126	BEL	10/18/97	1:58.89
Pleasant Tap	5	126	BEL	10/10/92	1:58.95
Lemon Drop Kid	4	122	BEL	7/4/00	1:58.97
Ghostzapper	4	126	LS	10/30/04	1:59.02
Best Pal	4	124	SA	3/7/92	1:59.08
Candy Ride (ARG)	4	124	DMR	8/24/03	1:59.11
Skip Away	4	126	HOL	11/8/97	1:59.16
Albert the Great	3	122	BEL	10/14/00	1:59.24
Urgent Request (IRE)	5	116	SA	3/11/95	1:59.25
Gentlemen (ARG)	5	124	HOL	6/29/97	1:59.26
Tinners Way	4	124	DMR	8/13/94	1:59.43
Cigar	5	126	HOL	7/2/95	1:59.46
Marquetry	4	110	HOL	6/29/91	1:59.50
Cat Thief	3	122	GP	11/6/99	1:59.52
Peace Rules	4	120	BEL	7/3/04	1:59.52
Bertrando	4	124	DMR	8/21/93	1:59.55
Cigar	5	126	BEL	10/28/95	1:59.58
Evening Attire	4	126	BEL	9/28/02	1:59.58
Tinners Way	5	124	DMR	8/13/95	1:59.63
Real Quiet	4	124	HOL	6/27/99	1:59.67
Milwaukee Brew	6	119	SA	3/1/03	1:59.80
Tiznow	3	124	LAD	9/30/00	1:59.84
Capt. Quicksilver	6	114	FNO	10/18/92	1:59.85
Dare and Go	5	124	DMR	8/10/96	1:59.85
Best Pal	3	116	DMR	8/10/91	1:59.86
Pleasantly Perfect	5	126	SA	10/25/03	1:59.88
Best Pal	4	124	SA	2/9/92	1:59.95
Richie the Coach	5	118	LRL	11/23/96	1:59.96
Skimming	5	124	DMR	8/19/01	1:59.96
Monarchos	3	126	CD	5/5/01	1:59.97
Dream of Fame (IRE)	6	116	SA	10/29/92	2:00.12
Dare and Go	4	118	SA	2/5/95	2:00.15
Skip Away	5	124	HOL	6/28/98	2:00.16
Best Pal	5	121	HOL	7/3/93	2:00.17
Stuka	4	115	SA	3/5/94	2:00.17
A.P. Indy	3	121	GP	10/31/92	2:00.20
Big Sky Jim	6	115	HOL	5/24/98	2:00.21
On the Scent	4	122	BEU	10/19/91	2:00.22
Sultry Song	4	113	HOL	6/27/92	2:00.23
Siphon (BRZ)	6	120	SA	3/2/97	2:00.23
Mineshaft	4	126	BEL	9/27/03	2:00.25
Free House	4	124	DMR	8/15/98	2:00.29
Farma Way	4	120	SA	3/9/91	2:00.30
Majestic Dinner	4	122	BEU	10/8/01	2:00.32
Pleasant Tap	5	119	BEL	7/18/92	2:00.33
Diazo	4	120	SA	2/6/94	2:00.33
Mecke	3	126	LAD	9/30/95	2:00.34
Albert the Great	4	123	BEL	7/1/01	2:00.39
Ajina	3	121	BEL	7/19/97	2:00.45
Frisk Me Now	4	118	BEL	7/4/98	2:00.45
Scuffleburg	5	113	GP	3/6/94	2:00.46
Congaree	5	124	HOL	7/13/03	2:00.48
Blessedly Bold	7	117	MNR	6/8/91	2:00.50
Siphon (BRZ)	5	117	HOL	6/30/96	2:00.50
Let's Be Curious	4	116	SA	4/24/95	2:00.51
Lite Light	3	121	BEL	7/6/91	2:00.54
Buck's Boy	4	114	HAW	10/11/97	2:00.54
Sir Beaufort	6	119	SA	3/6/93	2:00.55
Gentlemen (ARG)	5	124	DMR	8/9/97	2:00.56
General Challenge	3	117	DMR	8/29/99	2:00.57
Ecton Park	3	126	LAD	10/2/99	2:00.59
Wagon Limit	4	126	BEL	10/10/98	2:00.62
Duckhorn	4	115	LRL	3/18/01	2:00.62
Tiznow	4	126	BEL	10/27/01	2:00.62
Devoted Brass	3	123	HOL	7/24/93	2:00.64
Concerto	4	120	LRL	11/29/98	2:00.65
Free House	5	123	SA	3/6/99	2:00.67
Festin (ARG)	5	126	BEL	10/5/91	2:00.69
Best Pal	3	116	HOL	7/7/91	2:00.70
Skip Away	3	121	BEL	10/5/96	2:00.70
Total Impact (CHI)	6	124	HOL	7/10/04	2:00.72
Tiznow	3	122	CD	11/4/00	2:00.75
Slew of Damascus	6	117	HOL	7/2/94	2:00.76
Silver Music	3	119	HOL	7/23/94	2:00.76
Guided Tour	5	116	AP	7/21/01	2:00.76
Siberian Summer	4	118	SA	2/7/93	2:00.78
Arcangues	5	126	SA	11/6/93	2:00.83
Evening Attire	6	115	SAR	8/22/04	2:00.83
It's Just Me	3	117	BEU	10/22/94	2:00.85
Missionary Ridge (GB)	5	124	DMR	8/30/92	2:00.87
Defensive Play	4	122	SA	2/10/91	2:00.90
Deputy Commander	3	126	LAD	9/28/97	2:00.92
E Dubai	4	116	BEL	7/6/02	2:00.95
Free Spirit's Joy	3	126	LAD	9/22/91	2:00.96
Olympio	3	126	AP	8/3/91	2:00.99
Thunder Rumble	3	126	SAR	8/22/92	2:00.99
Yourmissinthepoint	4	113	HAW	11/18/95	2:01.00
Alphabet Soup	5	126	WO	10/26/96	2:01.00
Perfect to a Tee	7	122	LRL	11/27/99	2:01.00
Milwaukee Brew	5	115	SA	3/2/02	2:01.02
Jolie's Halo	4	119	GP	3/23/91	2:01.04
Grindstone	3	126	CD	5/4/96	2:01.06
Behrens	5	121	BEL	7/5/99	2:01.06
Truly a Pleasure	8	115	DMR	8/18/95	2:01.09
Running Stag	5	122	SAR	8/29/99	2:01.11
Irish Swap	5	115	HAW	11/21/92	2:01.12
Fusaichi Pegasus	3	126	CD	5/6/00	2:01.12
War Emblem	3	126	CD	5/4/02	2:01.13
Phantom Light	4	115	WO	7/1/03	2:01.15
Pleasantly Perfect	6	124	DMR	8/22/04	2:01.17
Supreme Sound (GB)	5	112	HAW	10/9/99	2:01.19
Funny Cide	3	126	CD	5/3/03	2:01.19
Corporate Report	3	126	SAR	8/17/91	2:01.20
Provins	4	112	SA	3/4/92	2:01.22
Skimming	4	124	DMR	8/26/00	2:01.22
Devil His Due	4	121	BEL	7/4/93	2:01.25
Jean Pierre S	5	119	SA	2/17/94	2:01.27
Thunder Gulch	3	126	CD	5/6/95	2:01.27
Strike Reality	8	116	HAW	12/13/03	2:01.28
Cigar	5	126	BEL	10/7/95	2:01.29
Devil His Due	4	113	GP	3/14/93	2:01.33
Mt. Sassafras	7	113	WO	7/1/99	2:01.38
Volponi	4	126	AP	10/26/02	2:01.39
Truly a Pleasure	8	121	TUP	3/26/95	2:01.40
Firm Dancer	4	115	WO	7/1/97	2:01.40
River Keen (IRE)	7	126	BEL	10/10/99	2:01.40
Early Pioneer	5	124	HOL	7/9/00	2:01.40
Point Given	3	126	SAR	8/25/01	2:01.40

1 Mile, Turf (1991–2004)

Horse	Age	Wt	Track	Date	Time
Elusive Quality	5	117	BEL	7/4/98	1:31.63
Royal Regalia	6	120	WO	7/1/04	1:31.84
Atticus	5	117	SA	3/1/97	1:31.89
Isitingood	6	121	SA	2/5/97	1:32.05
Val Royal (FR)	5	126	BEL	10/27/01	1:32.05
Lucky Coin	4	120	BEL	9/20/97	1:32.17
Touch of the Blues (FR)	6	122	DMR	8/2/03	1:32.22
Volponi	4	115	BEL	7/5/02	1:32.24
Urgent Request (IRE)	6	115	SA	10/5/96	1:32.44
Literary Row	5	122	BEL	6/17/04	1:32.46
Christine's Outlaw	4	113	BEL	7/10/04	1:32.46
Known Ranger (GB)	5	113	BEL	9/9/91	1:32.53
Caress	4	119	BEL	6/11/95	1:32.53
Quake	6	118	SA	9/28/01	1:32.55
Viking King	4	118	WO	6/20/91	1:32.60
Slewper Imp	5	115	ELP	7/16/95	1:32.60
Gilder	6	116	ELP	7/29/97	1:32.60
Suffragette	3	112	ELP	7/24/99	1:32.60
Designed for Luck	6	119	SA	10/5/03	1:32.61
License Fee	6	118	BEL	6/9/01	1:32.62
Megan's Interco	5	119	HOL	5/22/94	1:32.64
Val's Prince	5	114	BEL	6/20/97	1:32.67
Silver Tree	4	123	BEL	6/16/04	1:32.68
Dominant Prospect	4	114	BEL	7/4/94	1:32.69
Antespend	4	117	BEL	5/24/97	1:32.69
Mr O'Brien (IRE)	5	119	BEL	10/9/04	1:32.69
Soviet Line (IRE)	7	115	BEL	6/7/97	1:32.72
Special Ring	5	120	DMR	8/2/02	1:32.72
Soaring Free	5	119	WO	9/19/04	1:32.72
Garbu	4	123	BEL	5/24/98	1:32.73
Fastness (IRE)	6	124	HOL	6/16/96	1:32.74
Pebo's Guy	4	121	BEL	7/15/98	1:32.74
Garbu	6	118	BEL	7/12/00	1:32.75
Spinning World	4	126	HOL	11/8/97	1:32.77
Numerous Times	4	117	WO	9/9/01	1:32.79
Tates Creek	4	119	BEL	9/21/02	1:32.79
Lost Soldier	6	117	WO	7/24/96	1:32.80
Provisions	3	110	ELP	8/24/96	1:32.80
Colcon	4	113	BEL	9/14/97	1:32.80
Oh Nellie	4	116	BEL	10/4/98	1:32.80
Always Sure	3	112	ELP	8/21/99	1:32.80
Rob 'n Gin	5	118	BEL	7/3/99	1:32.81
War Zone	4	117	BEL	7/5/03	1:32.81
Designed for Luck	7	124	HOL	5/31/04	1:32.81
Green Fee	6	120	BEL	6/23/02	1:32.83
Elizabeth Bay	4	114	BEL	6/15/94	1:32.85
Debonair Dan	4	114	BEL	5/25/96	1:32.87
In Frank's Honor	5	116	BEL	6/9/01	1:32.87
Valentine Dancer	3	116	SA	10/12/03	1:32.87
Golden Dragon (GB)	6	119	SA	1/22/04	1:32.88
Journalism	5	114	HOL	4/25/93	1:32.89
Apache Wings	5	118	SA	3/14/03	1:32.89
Lure	3	122	GP	10/31/92	1:32.90
Memories of Silver	4	120	BEL	6/8/97	1:32.90
Alawal	4	121	BEL	7/17/99	1:32.91
Special Ring	5	117	HOL	7/7/02	1:32.91
Valory	3	114	ELP	8/4/01	1:32.93
Night Patrol	6	119	SA	10/5/02	1:32.93
French Lieutenant	4	120	WO	9/4/04	1:32.93
Silic (FR)	4	124	HOL	6/13/99	1:32.95
Tin Smithen	5	116	ELP	7/25/02	1:32.95
Climate	6	116	SA	3/22/02	1:32.98
Keen Runner	7	121	WO	7/19/95	1:33.00
Yaqthan (IRE)	5	114	ELP	7/23/95	1:33.00
Make'n It Happen	4	118	WO	7/28/95	1:33.00
Make'n It Happen	4	115	WO	8/20/95	1:33.00
Camlan	5	117	WO	5/20/96	1:33.00
American Dynasty	3	112	ELP	8/2/97	1:33.00
Labeeb (GB)	6	121	WO	9/20/98	1:33.00
X Country	5	120	ELP	7/20/03	1:33.01
Fourstardave	8	117	BEL	6/26/93	1:33.02
Dalavin	3	118	WO	6/27/04	1:33.02
Dancing Douglas	7	110	BEL	5/31/97	1:33.03
Designed for Luck	6	117	DMR	8/18/03	1:33.04
Star Over the Bay	6	118	HOL	5/16/04	1:33.04
Tradition Rocks	4	123	DMR	8/10/03	1:33.06
Wonder Again	4	117	BEL	9/20/03	1:33.07
Dell Place	5	118	HOL	4/21/04	1:33.07
Draw Shot	4	118	BEL	7/4/97	1:33.08
Odalea (ARG)	6	116	HOL	5/9/92	1:33.09
Rutledge Gold	3	117	ELP	8/25/02	1:33.09
Tarquin Joe	4	118	BEL	7/6/97	1:33.10
Scagnelli	4	119	BEL	6/16/99	1:33.11
Joleur	8	114	ELP	9/3/00	1:33.11
Silver Ticket	3	117	WO	6/5/04	1:33.12
Martessa (GER)	4	118	HOL	5/29/92	1:33.13
Jido	3	108	BEL	9/16/94	1:33.14
Unfinished Symph	4	121	HOL	6/10/95	1:33.14
Denied	5	121	DMR	7/30/03	1:33.14
Crystal Hearted (GB)	5	114	DMR	7/30/99	1:33.15
Pride of Summer	6	117	BEL	6/22/94	1:33.16
Golden Dice	5	119	BEL	6/25/00	1:33.17
Package Store	4	121	BEL	9/14/02	1:33.17
Escorpion (CHI)	5	116	HOL	11/29/96	1:33.18
Riviera (FR)	6	117	WO	9/10/00	1:33.18
Eighties	6	120	ELP	8/5/01	1:33.18
As Expected	5	111	WO	6/4/04	1:33.18
Reluctant Guest	5	119	SA	11/3/91	1:33.19
Quiet Resolve	4	117	WO	9/19/99	1:33.19
Alyzig	6	113	SA	1/25/03	1:33.19
Savethelastdance	3	114	WO	6/30/91	1:33.20
I'da Dance	5	115	ELP	7/29/94	1:33.20
Terremoto	4	121	WO	6/16/95	1:33.20
Bonnie Castle	4	111	WO	8/26/95	1:33.20
Slew Valley	3	114	BEL	7/1/00	1:33.20
Exbourne	6	122	SA	4/12/92	1:33.21
Cat's Cradle	5	116	SA	1/31/97	1:33.21
Lucky Coin	4	123	BEL	10/3/97	1:33.21
Val Royal (FR)	5	119	SA	10/7/01	1:33.21
First Titanium	6	119	DMR	8/11/02	1:33.21
Riskaverse	4	123	BEL	5/18/03	1:33.21
Captive Number	3	113	BEL	7/12/96	1:33.22
Special Ring	5	119	SA	2/21/02	1:33.23
Amarettitorun	5	116	BEL	9/26/97	1:33.24
Strategic Mission	5	122	GP	1/17/00	1:33.24
Special Rate	4	119	DMR	8/28/04	1:33.25
Scott the Great	6	117	BEL	6/27/92	1:33.27
Good Journey	6	121	WO	9/8/02	1:33.27
Moonshine Hall	3	118	WO	6/22/03	1:33.27
Designed for Luck	6	118	DMR	9/10/03	1:33.28

1 1/8 Miles, Turf (1991–2004)

Horse	Age	Wt	Track	Date	Time
Kostroma (IRE)	5	117	SA	10/20/91	1:43.92
Eton Lad (GB)	4	115	SA	10/10/91	1:44.19
Yaqthan (IRE)	6	113	ELP	9/2/96	1:44.60
Rainbows for Life	3	122	HAW	10/13/91	1:44.70
Fastness (IRE)	5	120	HOL	11/25/95	1:44.78
Quilma (CHI)	4	116	SA	10/12/91	1:44.87
Tight Spot	4	117	HOL	5/8/91	1:44.90
Illiquidity	4	117	ELP	9/2/00	1:44.91
Classic Fame	5	116	SA	11/8/91	1:44.96
The Vid	5	120	CRC	11/25/95	1:44.99
Toussaud	4	116	HOL	5/30/93	1:45.07
Leger Cat (ARG)	7	115	HOL	5/9/93	1:45.19
Bold Ruritana	5	117	WO	6/18/95	1:45.20
Majestic Jove	4	117	ELP	8/16/98	1:45.20
Repriced	4	115	HOL	5/22/92	1:45.28
Roxinho (BRZ)	4	114	ELP	9/2/02	1:45.39
Military Shot	4	117	SA	4/4/91	1:45.40
Aboriginal Apex	5	115	ELP	9/7/98	1:45.40
Furiously	4	119	SAR	8/11/93	1:45.46
Artie Schiller	3	123	BEL	9/26/04	1:45.50
Stay Sound	5	117	ELP	9/4/00	1:45.51
Yaqthan (IRE)	8	116	LS	5/25/98	1:45.54
Gentlemen (ARG)	4	119	HOL	11/30/96	1:45.55
Hero's Love	5	118	WO	9/19/93	1:45.60
Mufattish	5	116	HOL	5/21/98	1:45.62
Notorious Pleasure	6	117	HOL	6/14/92	1:45.68
Subordination	3	113	BEL	6/15/97	1:45.69
Proud Man	7	120	GP	1/24/04	1:45.69
Sweetest Thing	4	121	WO	7/6/02	1:45.72
Wolf (CHI)	4	121	SA	10/4/91	1:45.73
Host (CHI)	4	118	CRC	12/4/04	1:45.74
Notorious Pleasure	5	118	HOL	11/30/91	1:45.80
Memories of Silver	3	121	KEE	10/5/96	1:45.81
Astra	4	117	HOL	6/4/00	1:45.81
Political Attack	4	116	CRC	12/6/03	1:45.81
Super Quercus (FR)	3	122	HOL	11/28/99	1:45.82
Hap	4	115	SAR	7/28/00	1:45.82
Jeune Homme	3	114	HOL	11/28/93	1:45.84
Fly Till Dawn	5	119	HOL	11/30/91	1:45.86
Special Ring	6	117	DMR	7/27/03	1:45.87
Sharekann (IRE)	5	116	SA	2/20/97	1:45.90
Subordination	4	121	BEL	9/26/98	1:45.90
Special Ring	7	118	DMR	7/25/04	1:45.90
Slew of Damascus	5	114	BM	10/2/93	1:45.91
Ricky's Shadow	6	114	CRC	7/4/98	1:45.93
Heritage of Gold	4	115	SAR	9/5/99	1:45.93
Little Ghazi	8	118	SA	3/24/04	1:45.93
Fourstardave	7	122	SAR	8/24/92	1:45.94
Gravieres (FR)	5	114	BM	10/9/93	1:45.95
Lazy Lode (ARG)	7	118	SA	3/15/01	1:45.95
Tangazi	4	119	BEL	6/12/99	1:45.97
Fanatic Boy (ARG)	5	116	SA	2/2/92	1:45.99
Tight Spot	4	123	HOL	7/4/91	1:46.00
Thunder Regent	5	113	WO	6/14/92	1:46.00
Allijeba	7	121	ELP	8/14/93	1:46.00
Kiridashi	4	117	WO	6/16/96	1:46.00
Johar	3	118	SA	10/13/02	1:46.00
Madagascar (ARG)	5	123	BEL	6/22/02	1:46.02
Stroll	3	121	BEL	9/21/03	1:46.02
Signal Tap	5	114	HIA	3/31/96	1:46.04
Tranquility Lake	4	119	HOL	6/6/99	1:46.04
La Reine's Terms	7	122	LRL	8/11/02	1:46.04
Fourstars Allstar	4	113	SAR	8/12/92	1:46.06
Kazabaiyn	4	116	SA	3/12/94	1:46.06
Tout Charmant	4	123	HOL	11/26/00	1:46.06
Indy Vidual	6	116	SAR	9/2/00	1:46.07
Marlin	3	122	HOL	12/1/96	1:46.08
Lure	5	125	SAR	8/12/94	1:46.10
Sentimental Moi	7	112	SAR	8/15/97	1:46.11
Stallan	4	115	SAR	8/20/97	1:46.11
Forty Niner Days	5	114	HOL	7/2/92	1:46.13
Finder's Choice	7	117	LRL	10/24/92	1:46.13
Dream Machine (FR)	5	119	SA	10/14/04	1:46.13
Flawlessly	4	123	HOL	11/29/92	1:46.14
Memories of Silver	5	123	SAR	9/6/98	1:46.14
Outta My Way Man	5	114	BEL	6/22/97	1:46.15
Star Connection	5	117	SAR	8/12/99	1:46.16
Hibernian Rhapsody (Ire)	4	114	CRC	11/27/99	1:46.17
Starine (FR)	4	114	SAR	9/3/01	1:46.17
Crazy Ensign (ARG)	7	120	SA	11/9/03	1:46.17
Eternity Range	5	120	HOL	5/20/98	1:46.18
Isle de France	4	116	HOL	5/5/99	1:46.18
Tiffany's Taylor	6	114	SAR	8/24/95	1:46.19
Batique	5	113	MTH	6/16/01	1:46.19
Durham	3	115	ELP	8/7/94	1:46.20
Texas Town	3	105	ELP	7/19/95	1:46.20
Slewper Imp	5	110	ELP	9/4/95	1:46.20
Duck Trap	3	113	ELP	8/18/96	1:46.20
Chief Bearhart	4	119	WO	6/14/97	1:46.20
S'No Business	4	113	ELP	7/9/97	1:46.20
Howell's Poet	5	119	ELP	8/31/97	1:46.20
Colorful Vices	5	118	WO	7/12/98	1:46.20
Think Red	3	114	WO	6/24/00	1:46.20
Candy Ride (ARG)	4	120	HOL	7/4/03	1:46.20
King Chulumbo	4	117	SA	10/2/96	1:46.22
Amarettitorun	5	115	SAR	7/26/97	1:46.22
Yagli	5	121	SAR	7/31/98	1:46.22
Major Rhythm	5	116	RP	9/6/04	1:46.22
Exchange	5	120	SA	3/13/93	1:46.23
Unite's Big Red	4	114	CRC	7/4/98	1:46.24
Distant Mirage (IRE)	3	114	SAR	8/30/98	1:46.26
Amorama (FR)	3	122	DMR	8/21/04	1:46.26
Well Wrapped	4	117	LRL	8/2/91	1:46.27
Medium Cool	3	115	SA	11/6/91	1:46.29
Vaguely Hidden	6	118	SA	4/12/91	1:46.30
Sky Classic	4	119	WO	6/16/91	1:46.30
Happyanunoit (NZ)	4	123	HOL	11/28/99	1:46.30
Promise of War	5	114	ELP	9/3/01	1:46.30
Valentine Dancer	4	118	SA	1/24/04	1:46.31
Signal Tap	4	116	SAR	7/30/95	1:46.32
Floriselli	6	115	BEL	7/1/00	1:46.32
Majestic Nasr	4	118	SA	10/30/91	1:46.33
New Identity	6	118	MTH	7/10/94	1:46.33
Tenski	3	119	SAR	8/26/98	1:46.33
Foggy Day (FR)	5	117	SA	12/29/99	1:46.33
Star Performance	7	116	SA	3/23/00	1:46.33

1 1/4 Miles, Turf (1991–2004)

Horse	Age	Wt	Track	Date	Time
Bequest	5	117	SA	3/31/91	1:57.50
Konba	5	119	SA	10/14/96	1:57.60
Hero's Welcome (IRE)	4	112	SA	10/13/91	1:57.70
Bien Bien	4	119	HOL	5/31/93	1:57.75
Paradise Creek	5	124	BEL	6/11/94	1:57.79
Johar	4	120	SA	1/20/03	1:57.92
Classic Fame	6	120	SA	1/20/92	1:58.02
Who's to Pay	5	117	BEL	9/8/91	1:58.18
Chief Bearhart	5	122	BEL	6/6/98	1:58.25
Boldly Excellent	4	118	SA	10/14/91	1:58.33
Dynamic Trick	5	114	LRL	10/22/00	1:58.42
Dreamer	5	116	SA	2/22/97	1:58.47
Admise (FR)	4	121	SA	10/6/96	1:58.48
Yagli	6	122	BEL	6/5/99	1:58.48
Jungle Pioneer	5	114	SA	4/6/91	1:58.50
Astra	6	124	HOL	6/29/02	1:58.56
Awad	5	121	BEL	6/10/95	1:58.57
Super May	5	117	SA	11/11/91	1:58.58
Janet (GB)	4	123	SA	9/29/01	1:58.64
Fahim (GB)	4	113	LRL	7/4/97	1:58.67
Awad	5	126	AP	8/27/95	1:58.69
Fly Till Dawn	5	120	SA	1/21/91	1:58.70
Star Over the Bay	6	124	SA	10/3/04	1:58.70
Pescagani	4	116	BEL	7/14/94	1:58.71
Sentimental Moi	6	114	BEL	7/7/96	1:58.73
Tombstone (ARG)	6	118	SA	10/13/03	1:58.82
Sweet Return (GB)	4	121	SA	1/19/04	1:58.82
Social Retiree	6	119	LRL	7/11/93	1:58.86
Radevore (GB)	7	118	SA	1/13/00	1:58.86
Hannibal Lad (GB)	7	119	SA	1/16/03	1:58.92
Bienamado	4	121	HOL	6/25/00	1:58.93
Sharp Performance	3	114	BEL	7/15/01	1:58.93
The Tin Man	4	124	SA	10/6/02	1:58.93
Bisbalense (CHI)	5	117	BEL	9/8/94	1:58.95
Big Sky Jim	5	116	SA	4/16/97	1:58.97
Motto	6	118	SA	10/17/01	1:58.97
Quest for Fame (GB)	5	122	HOL	5/25/92	1:58.99
Star of Cozzene	5	118	BEL	6/6/93	1:58.99
Gallant (GB)	7	118	HOL	4/21/04	1:59.04
Aquilegia	4	114	BEL	6/19/93	1:59.05
Lilac Queen (GER)	5	119	SA	1/24/03	1:59.05
Tamhid	5	117	BEL	7/2/98	1:59.06
Mash One (CHI)	5	124	SA	10/3/99	1:59.07
Ops Smile	5	116	BEL	6/7/97	1:59.08
Santovito (IRE)	3	118	SA	10/29/99	1:59.13
Islington (IRE)	4	123	SA	10/25/03	1:59.13
Grand Flotilla	7	116	HOL	5/30/94	1:59.26
Light Jig (GB)	4	123	SA	10/2/04	1:59.28
Correntino	6	114	BEL	7/15/95	1:59.30
Mystic Knight (GB)	5	114	BEL	6/11/98	1:59.31
Happyanunoit (NZ)	5	121	HOL	7/2/00	1:59.32
Free At Last (GB)	5	119	SA	2/29/92	1:59.33
Auntie Mame	4	121	BEL	10/3/98	1:59.33
Special Matter	5	118	SA	10/8/03	1:59.33
Bienamado	5	124	HOL	6/10/01	1:59.34
Meteor Storm (GB)	5	117	BEL	6/5/04	1:59.34
Super Staff	4	123	SA	11/8/92	1:59.36
Incessant (IRE)	5	116	HOL	6/6/92	1:59.37
Six Zero (FR)	4	116	HOL	5/3/98	1:59.37

Horse	Age	Wt	Track	Date	Time
Foresta	5	121	BEL	6/15/91	1:59.38
Geri	5	116	BEL	6/14/97	1:59.39
Barrymore (GB)	5	115	SA	1/19/92	1:59.41
Eternity Range	5	117	SA	4/8/98	1:59.41
The Seven Seas	5	122	HOL	6/3/01	1:59.42
Senure	5	124	SA	9/30/01	1:59.47
Missionary Ridge (GB)	4	117	SA	4/22/91	1:59.50
Auntie Mame	4	118	BEL	7/18/98	1:59.50
Superiority	7	118	SA	10/18/03	1:59.51
Sandpit (BRZ)	7	120	HOL	5/27/96	1:59.52
Spanish Fern	4	123	SA	10/2/99	1:59.52
Chenin Blanc	5	124	BEL	5/24/91	1:59.54
Lech	3	114	BEL	7/21/91	1:59.55
Tight Spot	4	126	AP	9/1/91	1:59.55
Public Purse	6	119	SA	1/22/00	1:59.58
Ye Slew	7	112	ELP	8/6/94	1:59.60
Manndar (IRE)	4	117	BEL	6/10/00	1:59.61
Astra	5	121	HOL	6/24/01	1:59.61
All the Boys	6	115	SA	1/8/03	1:59.61
Kostroma (IRE)	6	121	SA	4/5/92	1:59.63
Paradise Creek	5	126	LRL	10/15/94	1:59.63
Lexa (FR)	5	119	SA	12/30/99	1:59.63
England's Legend (FR)	4	115	BEL	7/14/01	1:59.63
Snow Dance	5	116	BEL	7/4/03	1:59.63
Gassan Royal	4	120	SA	3/25/04	1:59.64
Kitten's Joy	3	123	AP	8/14/04	1:59.65
Polaris Star	6	113	BEL	6/4/94	1:59.67
Nadeszhda (GB)	4	119	SA	10/10/04	1:59.68
You'd Be Surprised	5	118	BEL	7/10/94	1:59.69
Nowrass (GB)	6	116	BEL	7/4/02	1:59.69
Golden Apples (IRE)	4	123	SA	10/5/02	1:59.72
Is Me	4	116	SA	3/13/94	1:59.73
Yashmak	3	114	BEL	10/4/97	1:59.73
Indy Vidual	7	120	BEL	6/27/01	1:59.73
So Sterling	4	117	BEL	6/16/91	1:59.74
Holy Mountain	3	112	BEL	7/17/94	1:59.74
Turkish Tryst	5	121	BEL	7/11/96	1:59.74
Vergennes	3	112	BEL	7/16/98	1:59.74
Academy Award	5	117	BEL	6/7/91	1:59.78
Paradise Creek	5	126	AP	8/28/94	1:59.78
Earl of Barking (IRE)	5	115	HOL	5/29/95	1:59.78
Logia (ARG)	6	115	SA	2/15/97	1:59.79
Le Famo	5	114	BEL	7/22/91	1:59.81
Dowty	5	116	BEL	6/27/97	1:59.81
Owsley	4	114	BEL	7/4/02	1:59.81
Royal Mountain Inn	4	110	BEL	7/18/93	1:59.82
Separated Love	5	113	BEL	10/2/98	1:59.82
Arbiter	5	119	HOL	7/11/02	1:59.82
Lite Approval	4	119	BEL	7/16/97	1:59.83
Dear Doctor (FR)	5	126	AP	9/6/92	1:59.84
Flitch	4	117	LRL	7/4/96	1:59.84
Donna Viola (GB)	5	120	SA	4/19/97	1:59.85
Currency Arbitrage	3	118	BEL	6/28/96	1:59.86
Indy Vidual	3	116	BEL	9/28/97	1:59.86
Storm Trooper	4	118	BEL	6/7/97	1:59.88
Sligo Bay (IRE)	4	118	SA	10/18/02	1:59.88
Horatio Luro	4	115	BEL	9/7/91	1:59.89
Saint Stephen	3	118	BEL	7/6/03	1:59.89
Got the Votes	4	122	SA	10/13/00	1:59.90

1 1/2 Miles, Turf (1991–2004)

Horse	Age	Wt	Track	Date	Time
Unite's Big Red	5	114	GP	3/6/99	2:23.15
Awad	7	117	SAR	8/9/97	2:23.20
Buck's Boy	5	115	GP	3/7/98	2:23.43
Talloires	6	116	HOL	7/21/96	2:23.55
Filago	4	126	SA	10/6/91	2:23.62
Whata Brainstorm	4	114	GP	3/11/01	2:23.75
Coretta (IRE)	5	118	GP	3/7/99	2:23.85
Kotashaan (FR)	5	124	SA	3/21/93	2:23.91
Chief Bearhart	4	126	HOL	11/8/97	2:23.92
With Anticipation	7	120	SAR	8/10/02	2:24.06
Fraise	4	126	GP	10/31/92	2:24.08
Rial (ARG)	6	118	SA	2/18/91	2:24.10
Flag Down	5	116	CRC	12/16/95	2:24.11
Deeliteful Irving	4	113	GP	3/23/02	2:24.14
Diplomatic Jet	4	123	CRC	12/21/96	2:24.20
Dernier Empereur	6	118	SA	11/4/96	2:24.24
High Chaparral (IRE)	4	126	SA	10/25/03	2:24.24
Johar	4	126	SA	10/25/03	2:24.24
Navarone	4	126	SA	10/10/92	2:24.29
Fantastic Light	5	126	BEL	10/27/01	2:24.36
Musgrave	4	119	HOL	5/26/99	2:24.37
Out of the Realm	6	113	HIA	3/26/95	2:24.43
Pleasant Variety	7	126	SA	3/24/91	2:24.50
Sky Classic	5	126	BEL	10/3/92	2:24.50
Shanawi (IRE)	5	111	SA	2/17/97	2:24.51
Fraise	6	124	GP	3/13/94	2:24.65
Down the Aisle	4	115	SAR	8/8/97	2:24.67
Daylami (IRE)	5	126	GP	11/6/99	2:24.73
Colonial Play	4	113	GP	3/8/98	2:24.75
Buck's Boy	7	120	GP	3/4/00	2:24.80
Balto Star	5	121	CRC	12/27/03	2:24.87
Bon Point (GB)	6	117	HOL	5/22/96	2:24.93
Mr. Lucky Junction	7	114	SA	2/9/97	2:25.00
Star Standing	4	114	GP	3/24/91	2:25.02
Kotashaan (FR)	5	124	SA	10/10/93	2:25.06
Bienamado	4	122	HOL	7/23/00	2:25.06
Sandpit (BRZ)	5	124	SA	10/9/94	2:25.12
Best of Music	5	115	SAR	8/26/96	2:25.13
Bombard	4	120	HOL	6/15/00	2:25.14
Kotashaan (FR)	5	126	SA	11/6/93	2:25.16
Royal Chariot	5	126	HOL	12/10/95	2:25.18
Innuendo (IRE)	6	116	GP	3/10/01	2:25.24
Bon Point (GB)	6	121	HOL	7/20/96	2:25.28
Persianlux (GB)	4	120	SA	11/3/00	2:25.28
Dr. Kiernan	4	114	BEL	6/13/93	2:25.30
Storming Home (GB)	5	122	HOL	5/10/03	2:25.31
Heavy Rain	6	116	GP	3/12/94	2:25.33
Mashaallah	6	119	HOL	6/25/94	2:25.37
Marlin	4	120	HOL	7/20/97	2:25.39
Our Forbes	4	115	ELP	8/10/94	2:25.40
Trampoli	5	121	GP	3/16/94	2:25.42
Dr. Root	4	109	BEL	7/20/91	2:25.43
Jahafil (GB)	7	117	HOL	7/1/95	2:25.45
Kiri's Clown	6	114	SAR	7/29/95	2:25.45
Sandpit (BRZ)	6	124	HOL	7/22/95	2:25.50
Wall Street Dancer	4	114	GP	3/15/92	2:25.53
Raintrap (GB)	4	126	WO	10/16/94	2:25.60
Lisieux Rose (IRE)	5	114	GP	3/5/00	2:25.64
Exaltado	8	115	GP	3/5/00	2:25.64
Dexter Drive	5	117	HOL	4/30/00	2:25.65
Frenchpark (GB)	4	126	HOL	12/11/94	2:25.66
Spectacular Tide	4	113	HIA	5/1/93	2:25.67
Bien Bien	4	122	HOL	7/25/93	2:25.69
Marvelous Wonder	6	115	SA	4/13/91	2:25.70
Celtic Arms (FR)	5	115	GP	3/9/96	2:25.71
Fairy Garden	5	115	GP	3/31/93	2:25.79
Public Purse	5	119	SA	10/31/99	2:25.83
Lazy Lode (ARG)	5	126	HOL	12/4/99	2:25.85
Strut the Stage	6	121	WO	9/6/04	2:25.87
Fraise	4	113	SAR	8/8/92	2:25.88
Tikkanen	3	121	BEL	10/8/94	2:25.88
Julie Jalouse	4	114	GP	3/24/02	2:25.89
Sahib's Light	5	116	HOL	6/29/91	2:25.90
Parade Ground	3	121	BEL	9/27/98	2:25.94
Tiger Trap	4	118	SA	4/4/02	2:25.96
Bienamado	4	126	HOL	12/2/00	2:25.98
Barow (FR)	8	113	ELP	8/18/96	2:26.00
Dark Moondancer (GB)	5	122	SA	3/18/00	2:26.00
Meteor Storm (GB)	5	115	SA	3/20/04	2:26.03
Marco Aurelio	5	117	BEL	5/23/92	2:26.04
Square Cut	6	114	SA	2/20/95	2:26.04
Nazirali (IRE)	5	112	SA	2/16/02	2:26.09
Rigamajig	5	114	CRC	1/5/91	2:26.10
Black Monday (GB)	5	112	HOL	7/21/91	2:26.10
Percutant (GB)	6	120	HOL	6/28/97	2:26.10
Cagney (BRZ)	4	116	SA	10/28/01	2:26.10
Polish Admiral (GB)	5	117	HOL	6/22/96	2:26.13
Volga (IRE)	5	119	CRC	12/27/03	2:26.13
Blueprint (IRE)	6	116	HOL	7/15/01	2:26.16
Full of Wonder	4	115	WO	8/31/02	2:26.18
Charley Bates	4	122	HOL	4/23/03	2:26.19
Special Matter	4	118	SA	10/14/02	2:26.21
Skipping (GB)	5	116	HOL	5/19/02	2:26.23
In Hand	4	118	GP	2/22/04	2:26.27
Wicapi	7	114	CRC	12/18/99	2:26.28
Reduit (GB)	5	118	GP	3/1/03	2:26.29
Splendid Career	5	118	SA	4/14/91	2:26.30
Splendid Career	5	123	HOL	6/16/91	2:26.30
Fade to Blue	8	118	SA	3/13/04	2:26.30
Ringaskiddy	5	115	HOL	4/28/01	2:26.32
Grand Flotilla	7	119	HOL	7/24/94	2:26.35
Listen to Ken	5	118	BEL	9/25/98	2:26.35
Single Dawn	6	115	SA	3/12/93	2:26.38
Interim (GB)	4	116	CRC	12/23/95	2:26.38
Auvergne	6	116	HOL	12/8/96	2:26.38
Viernes (BRZ)	5	114	HOL	11/28/02	2:26.38
Charlie's Dewan	3	126	WO	8/20/95	2:26.40
With Anticipation	6	114	SAR	8/11/01	2:26.41
Remonte	4	116	HOL	5/30/04	2:26.45
Shanawi (IRE)	7	122	HOL	7/14/99	2:26.46
Revved Up	5	116	DEL	7/20/03	2:26.46
Fade to Blue	7	116	SA	11/8/03	2:26.46
Quest Star	5	114	GP	3/20/04	2:26.46
Glenbarra	6	119	LRL	6/16/96	2:26.47
River Bay	4	126	HOL	12/14/97	2:26.47
Star Over the Bay	6	113	HOL	7/18/04	2:26.47
Dourbadakan	6	119	HOL	7/10/96	2:26.48
Miss High Blade	6	119	HOL	7/2/94	2:26.49

Triple Crown Facts and Figures

AMERICAN TRIPLE CROWN WINNERS

SIR BARTON - 1919

SIR BARTON
Br: Madden and Gooch (Ky)

		Isonomy
	Isinglass	
		Deadlock
Star Shoot		
		Hermit
	Astrology	
		Stella
		Hindoo
	Hanover	
		Bourbon Belle
Lady Sterling		
		Sterling
	Aquila	
		Eagle

Year	Age	Sts	1st	2nd	3rd	Earnings
1918	2	6	0	1	0	$4,113
1919	3	13	8	3	2	$88,250
1920	4	12	5	2	3	$24,494
Total		31	13	6	5	$116,857

In 1919 Sir Barton, son of the blind Star Shoot, raced to lengthy victories in all three classics, defeating the best 3-year-olds of that year. That Sir Barton could win the 3-year-old championship in a year when such fast horses as Purchase and Eternal were racing was convincing evidence of his quality. He was unfit when defeated by Man o' War in the Kenilworth Gold Cup. However, the latter was undoubtedly superior in any event. Sir Barton was owned by Commander J.K.L. Ross, a Canadian sportsman, and was trained by the veteran H. Guy Bedwell.

At 2: 2nd, Belmont Futurity.
At 3: Won Kentucky Derby, Preakness, Belmont, Withers, Potomac Handicap, Maryland Handicap, Fall Serial # 2, Fall Serial # 3. 2nd, Dwyer. 3rd, Havre de Grace Handicap, Autumn Handicap.
At 4: Won Saratoga Handicap, Dominion Handicap, Merchants and Citizens Handicap, Rennert Handicap. 2nd, Kenilworth Park Gold Cup, Fall Serial #3. 3rd, Laurel Handicap, Fall Serial #2, Marathon Handicap.

GALLANT FOX - 1930

GALLANT FOX
Br: Belair Stud (Ky)

		Ajax
	Teddy	
		Rondeau
Sir Gallahad III		
		Spearmint
	Plucky Liege	
		Concertina
		Commando
	Celt	
		Maid of Erin
Marguerite		
		Radium
	Fairy Ray	
		Seraph

Year	Age	Sts	1st	2nd	3rd	Earnings
1929	2	7	2	2	2	$19,890
1930	3	10	9	1	0	$308,275
Total		17	11	3	2	$328,165

In 1930, Gallant Fox, carrying the silks of Belair Stud, nom de course of William Woodward, New York banker and chairman of The Jockey Club, made racing history when he overcame such rivals as Questionnaire, Whichone and Crack Brigade and stamped himself one of the great thoroughbreds of his time. He was a member of the first crop sired in this country by Sir Gallahad III. The "Fox of Belair," as he was dubbed, was trained through his career by the sagacious James Fitzsimmons.

At 2: Won Junior Champion, Flash. 2nd, United States Hotel. 3rd, Belmont Futurity.
At 3: Won Kentucky Derby, Preakness, Belmont, Jockey Club Gold Cup, Dwyer, Classic, Saratoga Cup, Lawrence Realization, Wood Memorial. 2nd, Travers.

AMERICAN TRIPLE CROWN WINNERS

OMAHA - 1935

OMAHA

Br: Belair Stud (Ky)

Gallant Fox	Sir Gallahad III	Teddy
		Plucky Liege
	Marguerite	Celt
		Fairy Ray
Flambino	Wrack	Robert le Diable
		Samphire
	Flambette	Durbar II
		La Flambee

Year	Age	Sts	1st	2nd	3rd	Earnings
1934	2	9	1	4	0	$3,850
1935	3	9	6	1	2	$142,255
1936	4	4	2	2	0	$8,650
Total		22	9	7	2	$154,755

Omaha was in the first crop of foals sired by Gallant Fox, winner of the title five years previously. After his 3-year-old year in America William Woodward, who bred him and under whose colors he raced, sent him to England in quest of the Ascot Gold Cup. He was defeated by inches in the British classic by the filly Quashed. While abroad he started four times, winning his first two starts - the Victor Wild Stakes and Queens Plate - and finishing second in the Ascot Gold Cup and Princess of Wales Stakes, each time carrying top weight of the field. Shortly after his return to the United States, the colt suffered a recurrence of an old affliction and Woodward retired him to stud.

At 2: 2nd, Champagne, Junior Champion, Sanford.
At 3: Won Kentucky Derby, Preakness, Belmont, Dwyer, Classic. 2nd, Withers. 3rd, Brooklyn Handicap, Wood Memorial.
At 4: Victor Wild, Queen's Plate. 2nd, Ascot Gold Cup, Princess of Wales'.

WAR ADMIRAL - 1937

WAR ADMIRAL

Br: S.D. Riddle (Ky)

Man o' War	Fair Play	Hastings
		Fairy Gold
	Mahubah	Rock Sand
		Merry Token
Brushup	Sweep	Ben Brush
		Pink Domino
	Annette K.	Harry of Hereford
		Bathing Girl

Year	Age	Sts	1st	2nd	3rd	Earnings
1936	2	6	3	2	1	$14,800
1937	3	8	8	0	0	$166,500
1938	4	11	9	1	0	$90,840
1939	5	1	1	0	0	$1,100
Total		26	21	3	1	$273,240

A son of the mighty Man o' War, War Admiral brought many of his illustrious sire's characteristics to the racecourse. Usually a bundle of nerves as he entered the track from the paddock, he was possessed of blazing early speed and ability to carry it over all routes. Undefeated in his 3-year-old season, much of which was spent on the sidelines due to an injury sustained in the Belmont, he had a brilliant season at 4 which was overshadowed by his well-publicized loss to Seabiscuit in the Pimlico Special of that year. Only once in his career did he finish unplaced, that in the mud in the Massachusetts Handicap of 1938.

At 2: Won Eastern Shore Handicap. 2nd, Great American, Richard Johnson. 3rd, National Stallion. (Rated at 121 on Experimental Handicap.)
At 3: Won Kentucky Derby, Preakness, Belmont, Washington Handicap, Chesapeake, Pimlico Special.
At 4: Won Widener Handicap, Jockey Club Gold Cup, Saratoga Cup, Saratoga Handicap, Whitney, Rhode Island Handicap, Wilson, Queens County Handicap. 2nd, Pimlico Special.

AMERICAN TRIPLE CROWN WINNERS

WHIRLAWAY - 1941

WHIRLAWAY
Br: Calumet Farm (Ky)

		Swynford
	Blandford	
		Blanche
Blenheim II		
		Charles O'Malley
	Malva	
		Wild Arum
		Ben Brush
	Sweep	
		Pink Domino
Dustwhirl		
		Superman
	Ormonda	
		Princess Ormonde

Year	Age	Sts	1st	2nd	3rd	Earnings
1940	2	16	7	2	4	$77,275
1941	3	20	13	5	2	$272,386
1942	4	22	12	8	2	$211,250
1943	5	2	0	0	1	$250
Total		60	32	15	9	$561,161

Tough and willful Whirlaway spent the earliest portion of his lengthy career losing races he should have won but nevertheless ranked among the best juveniles of his year and went favored in the Kentucky Derby, which he would win by eight lengths in a track record 2:01 2/5 to start off his Triple Crown sweep. Indeed, he won nine of his next 10 starts after the Derby. At 4, his victories were interspersed more often with losses, but during the season, he displaced Seabiscuit as the sport's leading earner with elan, while winning the Massachusetts Handicap in track-record time. Remarkably, he finished third or better in 48 straight races at 2, 3, 4 and 5 years of age.

At 2: Won Hopeful, Saratoga Special, Breeders' Futurity, Walden. 2nd, United States Hotel, Grand Union Hotel. 3rd, Belmont Futurity, Arlington Futurity, Pimlico Futurity. (Rated at 126 on Experimental Handicap.)
At 3: Won Kentucky Derby, Preakness, Belmont, American Derby, Travers, Lawrence Realization, Dwyer, Saranac Handicap. 2nd, Jockey Club Gold Cup, Classic, Narragansett Special, Blue Grass, Derby Trial.
At 4, Won Jockey Club Gold Cup, Pimlico Special, Massachusetts Handicap, Brooklyn Handicap, Dixie Handicap, Narragansett Special, Washington Handicap, Trenton Handicap, Louisiana Handicap, Governor Bowie Handicap, Clark Handicap. 2nd, Suburban Handicap, Butler Handicap, Riggs Handicap, Manhattan Handicap, Arlington Handicap, Phoenix Handicap. 3rd, Carter Handicap, New York Handicap.

COUNT FLEET - 1943

COUNT FLEET
Br: Mrs J. Hertz (Ky)

		Sundridge
	Sunreigh	
		Sweet Briar II
Reigh Count		
		Count Schomberg
	Contessina	
		Pitti
		Maintenant
	Haste	
		Miss Malaprop
Quickly		
		Stefan the Great
	Stephanie	
		Malachite

Year	Age	Sts	1st	2nd	3rd	Earnings
1942	2	15	10	4	1	$76,245
1943	3	6	6	0	0	$174,055
Total		21	16	4	1	$250,300

The aptly named Count Fleet was one of the fastest horses of his day. Four days before the Futurity, he was credited with a six-furlong workout on the Belmont straightaway in 1:08 1/5, significantly faster than the track record, and though he lost the Futurity, he won the one-mile Champagne in track-record time and equaled the track record in the Pimlico Futurity at an additional half-furlong. At three, nothing got really close to him. In the Preakness, he missed the stakes record by two-fifths of a second and won the Withers in just a fifth off the stakes record. The Belmont was won by 25 lengths in a stakes-record 2:28 1/5, despite suffering a career-ending injury in the running.

At 2: Won Pimlico Futurity, Champagne, Walden, Wakefield. 2nd, Washington Park Futurity, East View. 3rd, Belmont Futurity. (Rated at 132 on Experimental Handicap.)
At 3: Won Kentucky Derby, Preakness, Belmont, Withers, Wood Memorial.

AMERICAN TRIPLE CROWN WINNERS

ASSAULT - 1946

ASSAULT

Br: King Ranch (Tx)

		Swynford
	St. Germans	
		Hamoaze
Bold Venture		
		Ultimus
	Possible	
		Lida Flush
		Pennant
	Equipoise	
		Swinging
Igual		
		Chicle
	Incandescent	
		Masda

Year	Age	Sts	1st	2nd	3rd	Earnings
1945	2	9	2	2	1	$17,250
1946	3	15	8	2	3	$424,195
1947	4	7	5	1	1	$181,925
1948	5	2	1	0	0	$3,250
1949	6	6	1	1	1	$45,900
1950	7	3	1	0	1	$2,950
Total		42	18	6	7	$675,470

Troubled by a foot injured as a youngster, Assault didn't walk like a champion but starting with his 3-year-old season, he ran like one when at his best. A promising 2-year-old, Assault blossomed in the spring at 3 to become a somewhat surprising Triple Crown winner, going to post as favorite only in the Preakness. Though a six-race losing streak separated his springtime glory and late-season recovery, he nevertheless set a single-season earnings record. At 4, he was even better, reigning as the sport's leading earner for a time, but was not right by season's end. When he proved sterile, he eventually was put back in training and though his best was behind him, he did win the 1949 Brooklyn Handicap.

At 2: Won Flash. 3rd, Babylon. (Rated at 116 on Experimental Handicap.)
At 3: Won Kentucky Derby, Preakness, Belmont, Dwyer, Pimlico Special, Westchester Handicap, Wood Memorial, Experimental Handicap #1. 2nd, Roamer Handicap, Jersey Handicap. 3rd, Gallant Fox Handicap, Discovery Handicap, Manhattan Handicap.
At 4: Won Suburban Handicap, Brooklyn Handicap, Butler Handicap, Dixie Handicap, Grey Lag Handicap. 3rd, Gold Cup.
At 6: Won Brooklyn Handicap. 3rd, Edgemere Handicap.

CITATION - 1948

CITATION

Br: Calumet Farm (Ky)

		Teddy
	Bull Dog	
		Plucky Liege
Bull Lea		
		Ballot
	Rose Leaves	
		Colonial
		Gainsborough
	Hyperion	
		Selene
Hydroplane II		
		Hurry On
	Toboggan	
		Glacier

Year	Age	Sts	1st	2nd	3rd	Earnings
1947	2	9	8	1	0	$155,680
1948	3	20	19	1	0	$708,470
1950	5	9	2	7	0	$73,480
1951	6	7	3	1	2	$147,130
Total		45	32	10	2	$1,085,760

Citation concluded his 3-year-old season as one of the most dominating horses the sport had ever seen, having lost just twice in 29 starts - once to an entrymate and once sprinting in the mud. He had won at distances ranging from six furlongs to two miles in seven different states. A diagnosis of osselets followed and his 4-year-old season was lost entirely. When he returned at 5, he had probably lost a step but faced a stern foe in Noor, who simply proved better. In that rival's absence, he ran a world-record mile of 1:33 3/5. By 1951, Noor was retired but Citation pressed on, chasing the million-dollar earnings milestone, which was realized in his final start while winning the Hollywood Gold Cup.

At 2: Won Belmont Futurity, Pimlico Futurity, Elementary. 2nd, Washington Park Futurity. (Rated at 126 on Experimental Handicap.)
At 3: Won Kentucky Derby, Preakness, Belmont, Jockey Club Gold Cup, Gold Cup, American Derby, Pimlico Special, Jersey, Flamingo, Stars and Stripes Handicap, Sysonby Mile, Tanforan Handicap, Derby Trial, Chesapeake, Everglades Handicap, Seminole Handicap. 2nd, Chesapeake Trial.
At 5: Won Golden Gate Mile Handicap. 2nd, Santa Anita Handicap, San Juan Capistrano Handicap, San Antonio Handicap, Golden Gate Handicap, Forty-Niners Handicap.
At 6: Won Hollywood Gold Cup, American Handicap, Century Handicap. 2nd Argonaut Handicap.

AMERICAN TRIPLE CROWN WINNERS

SECRETARIAT - 1973

SECRETARIAT
Br: Meadow Stud Inc (Va)

		Nearco
	Nasrullah	
		Mumtaz Begum
Bold Ruler		
		Discovery
	Miss Disco	
		Outdone
		Prince Rose
	Princequillo	
		Cosquilla
Somethingroyal		
		Caruso
	Imperatrice	
		Cinquepace

Year	Age	Sts	1st	2nd	3rd	Earnings
1972	2	9	7	1	0	$456,404
1973	3	12	9	2	1	$860,404
Total		21	16	3	1	$1,316,808

An equine hero in his day, Secretariat has achieved even more legendary status with the passage of time. His occasional failures are overshadowed with the magnitude of his accomplishments, topped off by track records in the Kentucky Derby, Belmont and Marlboro Cup that still stand decades later. The prodigious 31-length margin of his Belmont victory makes it one of the most remembered thoroughbred performances in history. Displaying versatility, he concluded his career with lengthy victories on the turf against some of the best U.S.-based turf horses. The details of his then-record syndication, determined at the outset of his 3-year-old season, called for his retirement at the conclusion of 1973.

At 2: Won Garden State, Laurel Futurity, Belmont Futurity, Hopeful, Sanford. 2nd, Champagne. (Rated at 129 on Experimental Handicap.)
At 3: Won Kentucky Derby, Preakness, Belmont, Marlboro Cup Invitational Handicap, Canadian International Championship, Arlington Invitational, Man o' War, Gotham, Bay Shore. 2nd, Woodward, Whitney. 3rd, Wood Memorial.

SEATTLE SLEW - 1977

SEATTLE SLEW
Br: Ben S. Castleman (Ky)

		Bold Ruler
	Boldnesian	
		Alanesian
Bold Reasoning		
		Hail to Reason
	Reason to Earn	
		Sailing Home
		Round Table
	Poker	
		Glamour
My Charmer		
		Jet Action
	Fair Charmer	
		Myrtle Charm

Year	Age	Sts	1st	2nd	3rd	Earnings
1976	2	3	3	0	0	$94,350
1977	3	7	6	0	0	$641,370
1978	4	7	5	2	0	$473,006
Total		17	14	2	0	$1,208,726

Questioned for the company he had kept as a 3-year-old and plagued by assorted misfortunes that limited him to just 17 career starts, Seattle Slew never put together a lengthy campaign in any of his three seasons and struggled somewhat for his share of acclaim. Minor injury delayed his 2-year-old debut but once he was on the track, he swept all the way through the Belmont without defeat to become the only horse to win the Triple Crown undefeated. A debacle in the Swaps followed and his 3-year-old season ended on this sour note. Early in 1978, he became ill and nearly died, and later missed several months due to a stall accident. To many of his harshest critics, his finest moment was in gallant defeat in the 1978 Jockey Club Gold Cup.

At 2: Won Champagne. (Rated at 126 on Experimental Handicap.)
At 3: Won Kentucky Derby, Preakness, Belmont, Flamingo, Wood Memorial.
At 4: Won Woodward, Marlboro Cup Handicap, Stuyvesant Handicap. 2nd, Jockey Club Gold Cup, Paterson Handicap.

AMERICAN TRIPLE CROWN WINNERS

AFFIRMED - 1978

AFFIRMED
Br: Harbor View Farm (Fl)

Exclusive Native	Raise a Native	Native Dancer
		Raise You
	Exclusive	Shut Out
		Good Example
Won't Tell You	Crafty Admiral	Fighting Fox
		Admiral's Lady
	Scarlet Ribbon	Volcanic
		Native Valor

Year	Age	Sts	1st	2nd	3rd	Earnings
1977	2	9	7	2	0	$343,477
1978	3	11	8	2	0	$901,541
1979	4	9	7	1	1	$1,148,800
Total		29	22	5	1	$2,393,818

Defined nearly as much by its two-season, 10-race rivalry with Alydar as the Triple Crown in the middle of it, the career of Affirmed was one of sustained quality. Through the end of his 3-year-old season, only one foal from his crop had ever finished in front of him - Alydar, on two occasions. Counting a disqualification in the Travers, he suffered a five-race losing streak through late 1978 and early 1979 but closed his career winning his last seven starts, including one meeting with the year-younger Spectacular Bid. Only once in 29 starts did Affirmed ever finish worse than third, that in the infamous 1978 Jockey Club Gold Cup won by Exceller over Seattle Slew, a race in which Affirmed lost all chance due to equipment trouble.

At 2: Won Laurel Futurity, Belmont Futurity, Hollywood Juvenile Championship, Hopeful, Sanford, Youthful. 2nd, Champagne, Great American. (Rated at 126 on Experimental Handicap.)
At 3: Won Kentucky Derby, Preakness, Belmont, Hollywood Derby, Santa Anita Derby, San Felipe Handicap, Jim Dandy. 2nd, Travers, Marlboro Cup.
At 4: Won Hollywood Gold Cup, Jockey Club Gold Cup, Santa Anita Handicap, Californian, Charles Strub, Woodward. 2nd, San Fernando. 3rd, Malibu.

Kentucky Derby/Preakness winners who failed in the Belmont

Year	Name	Belmont Finish	Beaten Margin	Belmont Winner	Derby Preakness (Finish / Finish)
1944	Pensive	2nd	1/2 length	Bounding Home	DNR/DNR
1958	Tim Tam	2nd	6 lengths	Cavan	DNR/DNR
1961	Carry Back	7th	14 3/4 lengths	Sherluck	5th/5th
1964	Northern Dancer	3rd	6 lengths	Quadrangle	5th/4th
1966	Kauai King	4th	7 3/4 lengths	Amberoid	7th/3rd
1968	*Forward Pass	2nd	1 1/4 lengths	Stage Door Johnny	DNR/DNR
1969	Majestic Prince	2nd	5 1/2 lengths	Arts and Letters	2nd/2nd
1971	Canonero II	4th	4 1/2 lengths	Pass Catcher	DNR/DNR
1979	Spectacular Bid	3rd	3 1/2 lengths	Coastal	DNR/DNR
1981	Pleasant Colony	3rd	1 3/4 lengths	Summing	DNR/DNR
1987	Alysheba	4th	14 1/4 lengths	Bet Twice	2nd/2nd
1989	Sunday Silence	2nd	8 lengths	Easy Goer	2nd/2nd
1997	Silver Charm	2nd	3/4 length	Touch Gold	DNR/4th
1998	Real Quiet	2nd	nose	Victory Gallop	2nd/2nd
1999	Charismatic	3rd	1 1/2 lengths	Lemon Drop Kid	9th/DNR
2002	War Emblem	8th	19 1/2 lengths	Sarava	DNR/DNR
2003	Funny Cide	3rd	5 lengths	Empire Maker	2nd/DNR
2004	Smarty Jones	2nd	1 length	Birdstone	8th/DNR

*** Awarded victory in Derby in disqualification of Dancer's Image** **DNR-Did Not Run**

Burgoo King (1932) and Bold Venture (1936) also won the Kentucky Derby and Preakness, but did not run in the Belmont.

Fillies in the Classics

Year	Race	Name	Finish
1867	**Belmont**	**RUTHLESS**	**1st**
1868	Belmont	Fanny Ludlow	3rd
1869	Belmont	Invercauld	3rd
1869	Belmont	Viola	7th
1870	Belmont	Midday	3rd
1870	Belmont	Nellie James	4th
1870	Belmont	Stamps	6th
1871	Belmont	Nellie Gray	4th
1871	Belmont	Mary Clark	9th
1875	Kentucky Derby	Ascension	10th
1875	Kentucky Derby	Gold Mine	15th
1875	Preakness	Australind	7th
1876	Kentucky Derby	Lizzie Stone	6th
1876	Kentucky Derby	Marie Michon	7th
1877	Kentucky Derby	Early Light	8th
1879	Kentucky Derby	Ada Glenn	7th
1879	Kentucky Derby	Wissahickon	9th
1880	Preakness	Emily F.	3rd
1881	Preakness	Aella	6th
1883	Kentucky Derby	Pike's Pride	6th
1885	Belmont	Miss Palmer	9th
1894	Preakness	Flirt	13th
1895	Preakness	Sue Kittie	3rd
1895	Preakness	Bombazette	7th
1896	Preakness	Intermission	3rd
1896	Preakness	Cassette	4th
1901	Preakness	Sadie S.	2nd
1902	Preakness	Barouche	6th
1902	Preakness	Sun Shower	7th
1903	**Preakness**	**FLOCARLINE**	**1st**
1904	Preakness	Possession	7th
1904	Preakness	Flammula	8th
1905	Preakness	Kiamesha	2nd
1905	Preakness	Coy Maid	3rd
1905	Preakness	Bohemia	5th
1905	Preakness	Iota	9th
1905	**Belmont**	**TANYA**	**1st**
1905	Belmont	Funders	7th
1906	Kentucky Derby	Lady Navarre	2nd
1906	**Preakness**	**WHIMSICAL**	**1st**
1906	Preakness	Content	2nd
1906	Preakness	Flip Flap	7th
1906	Preakness	Fatinitza	8th
1909	Preakness	Hill Top	3rd
1909	Preakness	Arondack	6th
1909	Preakness	Sans Souci II	7th
1909	Preakness	Grania	8th
1911	Kentucky Derby	Round the World	6th
1911	Preakness	Heatherbroom	6th
1912	Kentucky Derby	Flamma	3rd
1912	Preakness	Jeannette B.	5th
1913	Kentucky Derby	Gowell	3rd
1913	Preakness	Cadeau	5th
1913	Belmont	Flying Fairy	3rd
1914	Kentucky Derby	Bronzewing	3rd
1914	Kentucky Derby	Watermelon	7th
1915	**Kentucky Derby**	**REGRET**	**1st**
1915	**Preakness**	**RHINE MAIDEN**	**1st**
1917	Preakness	Fruit Cake	4th
1917	Preakness	Fox Trot	14th
1918	Kentucky Derby	Viva America	3rd
1918	Preakness	Mary Maud	6th
1918	Preakness	Quietude	9th
1918	Preakness*	Kate Bright	3rd
1919	Kentucky Derby	Regalo	9th
1919	Preakness	Milkmaid	8th
1920	Kentucky Derby	Cleopatra	15th
1921	Kentucky Derby	Prudery	3rd
1921	Kentucky Derby	Careful	5th
1921	Preakness	Polly Ann	2nd
1921	Preakness	Careful	12th
1921	Preakness	Lough Storm	13th
1922	Kentucky Derby	Startle	8th
1922	Preakness	Miss Joy	10th
1923	Preakness	Sally's Alley	11th
1923	Belmont	Miss Smith	8th
1924	**Preakness**	**NELLIE MORSE**	**1st**
1925	Preakness	Maid at Arms	11th
1927	Preakness	Fair Star	6th
1927	Belmont	Flambino	3rd
1928	Preakness	Bateau	8th
1929	Kentucky Derby	Ben Machree	18th
1930	Kentucky Derby	Alcibiades	10th
1930	Preakness	Snowflake	3rd
1932	Kentucky Derby	Oscillation	13th
1932	Belmont	Laughing Queen	10th
1934	Kentucky Derby	Mata Hari	4th
1934	Kentucky Derby	Bazaar	9th
1935	Kentucky Derby	Nellie Flag	4th
1935	Preakness	Nellie Flag	7th
1936	Kentucky Derby	Gold Seeker	9th
1937	Preakness	Jewell Dorsett	8th
1939	Preakness	Ciencia	6th
1945	Kentucky Derby	Misweet	12th
1954	Belmont	Riverina	7th
1959	Kentucky Derby	Silver Spoon	5th
1980	**Kentucky Derby**	**GENUINE RISK**	**1st**
1980	Preakness	Genuine Risk	2nd
1980	Belmont	Genuine Risk	2nd
1982	Kentucky Derby	Cupecoy's Joy	10th
1984	Kentucky Derby	Life's Magic	8th
1984	Kentucky Derby	Althea	19th
1988	**Kentucky Derby**	**WINNING COLORS**	**1st**
1988	Preakness	Winning Colors	3rd
1988	Belmont	Winning Colors	6th
1995	Kentucky Derby	Serena's Song	16th
1996	Belmont	My Flag	3rd
1999	Kentucky Derby	Excellent Meeting	5th
1999	Kentucky Derby	Three Ring	19th
1999	Preakness	Excellent Meeting	DNF
1999	Belmont	Silverbulletday	7th

* Preakness run in divisions in 1918.

TRAINERS WITH MORE THAN ONE WIN IN THE KENTUCKY DERBY

SIX WINNERS:

Ben A. Jones – Lawrin (1938), Whirlaway (1941), Pensive (1944), Citation (1948), Ponder (1949), Hill Gail (1952)

FOUR WINNERS:

H. J. Thompson – Behave Yourself (1921), Bubbling Over (1926), Burgoo King (1932), Brokers Tip (1933)
D. Wayne Lukas – Winning Colors (1988), Thunder Gulch (1995), Grindstone (1996), Charismatic (1999)

THREE WINNERS:

James Fitzsimmons – Gallant Fox (1930), Omaha (1935), Johnstown (1939)
Max Hirsch – Bold Venture (1936), Assault (1946), Middleground (1950)
Bob Baffert – Silver Charm (1997), Real Quiet (1998), War Emblem (2002)

TWO WINNERS:

Lazaro Barrera – Bold Forbes (1976), Affirmed (1978)
Henry Forrest – Kauai King (1966), Forward Pass (1968)
LeRoy Jolley – Foolish Pleasure (1975), Genuine Risk (1980)
H. A. "Jimmy" Jones – Iron Liege (1957), Tim Tam (1958)
Lucien Laurin – Riva Ridge (1972), Secretariat (1973)
Horatio Luro – Decidedly (1962), Northern Dancer (1964)
Woodford C. "Woody" Stephens – Cannonade (1974), Swale (1984)
Charles E. "Charlie" Whittingham – Ferdinand(1986), Sunday Silence (1989)
Nicholas "Nick" Zito – Strike the Gold (1991), Go for Gin (1994)

CONSECUTIVE WINNERS:

Bob Baffert – Silver Charm (1997), Real Quiet (1998)
Ben A. Jones – Citation (1948), Ponder (1949)
H.A. "Jimmy" Jones – Iron Liege (1957), Tim Tam (1958)
Lucien Lauren – Riva Ridge (1972), Secretariat (1973)
D. Wayne Lukas – Thunder Gulch (1995), Grindstone (1996)
Herbert John Thompson – Burgoo King (1932), Brokers Tip (1933)

OLDEST TRAINER OF KENTUCKY DERBY WINNER:

Charlie Whittingham, 76 – Sunday Silence (1989)

YOUNGEST TRAINER OF KENTUCKY DERBY WINNER:

James Rowe Sr., 24 – Hindoo (1881)

FATHER-SON WINNING TRAINERS:

James Rowe Sr. (1881/1915)
and James Rowe Jr. (1931)

Ben A. Jones (1938/1941/1944/1948/1949/1952)
and H. A. "Jimmy" Jones (1957/1958)

WINNER AS JOCKEY AND TRAINER:

John Longden – Count Fleet (1943); Majestic Prince (1969)

WOMEN TRAINERS:
Mary Hirsch – No Sir (1937, 13th)
Mrs. Albert Roth – Senecas Coin (1949, pulled up)
Mary Keim – Mr. Pak (1965, 6th)
Dianne Carpenter – Biloxi Indian (1984, 12th) and Kingpost (1988, 14th)
Patti Johnson – Fast Account (1985, 4th)
Shelley Riley – Casual Lies (1992, 2nd)
Kathy Walsh – Hanuman Highway (1998, 7th)
Akiko Gothard – K One King (1999, 8th)
Jenine Sahadi – The Deputy (2000, 14th)
Kristin Mulhall – Imperialism (2004, 3rd)
Jennifer Pedersen – Song of the Sword (2004, 11th)

JOCKEYS WITH MULTIPLE WINS IN THE KENTUCKY DERBY

FIVE WINNERS:
Eddie Arcaro – Lawrin (1938), Whirlaway (1941), Hoop Jr. (1945), Citation (1948), Hill Gail (1952)
Bill Hartack – Iron Liege (1957), Venetian Way (1960), Decidedly (1962), Northern Dancer (1964), Majestic Prince (1969)

FOUR WINNERS:
Bill Shoemaker – Swaps (1955), *Tomy Lee (1959), Lucky Debonair (1965), Ferdinand (1986)

THREE WINNERS:
Isaac Murphy – Buchanan (1884), Riley (1890), Kingman (1891)
Earl Sande – Zev (1923), Flying Ebony (1925), Gallant Fox (1930)
Angel Cordero, Jr. – Cannonade (1974), Bold Forbes (1976), Spend a Buck (1985)
Gary Stevens – Winning Colors (1988), Thunder Gulch (1995), Silver Charm (1997)

TWO WINNERS:
Willie Sims – Ben Brush (1896), Plaudit (1898)
Jimmy Winkfield – His Eminence (1901), Alan-a-Dale (1902)
Johnny Loftus – George Smith (1916), Sir Barton (1919)
Albert Johnson – Morvich (1922), Bubbling Over (1926)
Linus McAtee – Whiskery (1927), Clyde Van Dusen (1929)
Charles Kurtsinger – Twenty Grand (1931), War Admiral (1937)
Conn McCreary – Pensive (1944), Count Turf (1951)
Ismael Valenzuela – Tim Tam (1958), Forward Pass (1968)
Ron Turcotte – Riva Ridge (1972), Secretariat (1973)
Jacinto Vasquez – Foolish Pleasure (1975), Genuine Risk (1980)
Eddie Delahoussaye – Gato Del Sol (1982), Sunny's Halo (1983)
Chris McCarron – Alysheba (1987), Go for Gin (1994)
Jerry Bailey – Sea Hero (1993), Grindstone (1996)
Chris Antley – Strike the Gold (1991), Charismatic (1999)
Kent Desormeaux – Real Quiet (1998). Fusaichi Pegasus (2000)

TWO IN SUCCESSION:
Isaac Murphy (1890-91), Jimmy Winkfield (1901-02), Ron Turcotte (1972-73), and Eddie Delahoussaye (1982-83)

MOST MOUNTS:
Bill Shoemaker rode in 26 Kentucky Derbies, his last in 1988
Pat Day in 22, his most recent in 2004

AFRICAN-AMERICAN JOCKEYS:
Isaac Murphy (Two wins, as above)
Willie Simms (Two wins, as above,)
Jimmy Winkfield. (Two wins, as above)
Oliver Lewis – Aristides (1875)
William Walker – Baden Baden (1877)
George Lewis – Fonso (1880)
Babe Hurd – Apollo (1882)
Erskine Henderson – Joe Cotton (1885)
Isaac Lewis – Montrose (1887)
Alonzo Clayton – Azra (1892)
James "Soup" Perkins – Halma (1895)

APPRENTICE JOCKEYS with victories in the Kentucky Derby:
Ira Hanford – Bold Venture (1936)
William Boland – Middleground (1950)

WOMEN JOCKEYS with mounts in the Derby:
Diane Crump – Fathom (1970), 15th
Patricia Cooksey – So Vague (1984), 11th
Andrea Seefeldt – Forty Something (1991), 16th
Julie Krone – Ecstatic Ride (1992), 14th; Suave Prospect (1995), 11th

OLDEST WINNING JOCKEY:
Bill Shoemaker, 54 – Ferdinand (1986)

YOUNGEST WINNING JOCKEYS:
Alonzo Clayton, 15 – Azra (1892)
James "Soup" Perkins, 15 – Halma (1895)

KENTUCKY/EPSOM DERBY DOUBLE:

Steve Cauthen is the youngest rider, 18, to complete a sweep of the American Triple Crown, the elusive three-race series that has only been completed by 10 other horses since Sir Barton accomplished the feat for the first time in 1919. Cauthen also is the only rider in history to win both the Kentucky Derby and the historic Epsom Derby, the premier classic race for 3-year-olds in Great Britain.

Cauthen won his Kentucky Derby aboard Affirmed in 1978 and won the Epsom Derby twice-in 1985 aboard Slip Anchor and 1987 aboard Reference Point.

FASTEST CLOCKING:
Secretariat – 1973, 1:59.40

LEADING PREAKNESS-WINNING TRAINERS

SEVEN WINNERS:
R.W. Walden – Tom Ochiltree (1875), Duke of Magenta (1878), Harold (1879), Grenada (1880), Saunterer (1881), Vanguard (1882), Refund (1888)
FIVE WINNERS:
Thomas J. Healey – The Parader (1901), Pillory (1922), Vigil (1923), Display (1926), Dr. Freeland (1929),
D. Wayne Lukas – Codex (1980), Tank's Prospect (1985), Tabasco Cat (1994), Timber Country (1995), Charismatic (1999)

FOUR WINNERS:
James Fitzsimmons – Gallant Fox (1930), Omaha (1935), Nashua (1955), Bold Ruler (1957)
H.A. "Jimmy" Jones – Faultless (1947), Citation (1948), Fabius (1956), Tim Tam (1958)
Bob Baffert – Silver Charm (1997), Real Quiet (1998), Point Given (2001), War Emblem (2002)

WOMEN TRAINERS:
Judy Johnson – 1968, Sir Beau, 7th
Judith Zouck – 1980, Samoyed, 6th
Nancy Heil – 1990, Fighting Notion, 5th
Shelley Riley – 1992, Casual Lies, 3rd
Dean Gaudet – 1992, Speakerphone, 14th
Penny Lewis – 1993, Hegar, 9th
Cynthia Reese – 1996, In Contention, 6th
Jean L. Rofe – 1998, Silver's Prospect, 10th
Jennifer Pedersen – 2001, Griffinite, 5th
Nancy Alberts – 2002, Magic Weisner, 2nd
Jennifer Pedersen – 2003, New York Hero, 6th
Lisa Lewis – 2003, Kissin Saint, 10th
Kristin Mulhall – 2004, Imperialism, 5th
Jennifer Pedersen – 2004, Song of the Sword, 9th
Linda Albert – 2004, Water Cannon, 10th

LEADING PREAKNESS-WINNING JOCKEYS

SIX WINNERS:
Eddie Arcaro – Whirlaway (1941), Citation (1948), Hill Prince (1950), Bold (1951), Nashua (1955), Bold Ruler (1957)
FIVE WINNERS:
Pat Day – Tank's Prospect (1985), Summer Squall (1990), Tabasco Cat (1994), Timber Country (1995), Louis Quatorze (1996)

WOMEN RIDERS:
Patricia Cooksey – 1985, 6th
Andrea Seefeldt – 1994, 7th

FASTEST CLOCKING:
Secretariat – 1973, 1:53.40 (DRF timed)
Tank's Prospect – 1985, 1:53.40
Louis Quatorze – 1996, 1:53.40

LEADING BELMONT-WINNING TRAINERS

EIGHT WINNERS:
James Rowe – George Kinney (1883), Panique (1884), Commando (1901), Delhi (1904), Peter Pan (1907), Colin (1908), Sweep (1910), Prince Eugene (1913)

SEVEN WINNERS:
Samuel Hildreth – Jean Bereaud (1899), Joe Madden (1909), Friar Rock (1916), Hourless (1917), Grey Lag (1921), Zev (1923), Mad Play (1924)

SIX WINNERS:
James Fitzsimmons – Gallant Fox (1930), Faireno (1932), Omaha (1935), Granville (1936), Johnstown (1939), Nashua (1955)

FIVE WINNERS:
Woody Stephens – Conquistador Cielo (1982), Caveat (1983), Swale (1984), Creme Fraiche (1985), Danzig Connection (1986)

FOUR WINNERS:
Max Hirsch – Vito (1928), Assault (1946), Middleground (1950), High Gun (1954)
D. Wayne Lukas – Tabasco Cat (1994), Thunder Gulch (1995), Editor's Note (1996) Commendable (2000)
R.W. Walden – Duke of Magenta (1878), Grenada (1880), Saunterer (1881), Bowling Brook (1898)

WOMEN TRAINERS:
Sarah Lundy – 1984, Minstrel Star, 11th
Patricia Johnson – 1985, Fast Account, 4th
Dianne Carpenter – 1988, Kingpost, 2nd
Shelley Riley – 1992, Casual Lies, 5th
Cynthia W. Reese – 1996, In Contention, 9th
Nancy Alberts – 2002, Magic Weisner, 4th
Jennifer Leigh-Pedersen – 2002, Artax Too, 11th
Linda Rice – 2003, Supervisor, 5th

LEADING BELMONT-WINNING JOCKEYS

SIX WINNERS:
James McLaughlin – Forester (1882), George Kinney (1883), Panique (1884), Inspector B. (1886), Hanover (1887), Sir Dixon (1888)
Eddie Arcaro – Whirlaway (1941), Shut Out (1942), Pavot (1945), Citation (1948) One Count (1952), Nashua (1955)

FIVE WINNERS:
Earl Sande – Grey Lag (1921), Zev (1923), Mad Play (1924), Chance Shot (1927) Gallant Fox (1930)
Bill Shoemaker – Gallant Man (1957), Sword Dancer (1959), Jaipur (1962), Damascus (1967), Avatar (1975)

FIRST WOMAN TO WIN THE BELMONT

In 1993, Julie Krone became the only woman to win a Triple Crown race when she guided Colonial Affair to a 2 1/4-length victory in the Belmont Stakes. Krone is the only woman to have ridden in the Belmont. Her other finishes were a ninth aboard Subordinated Debt in 1991, a sixth on Colony Light in 1992 and a second on Star Standard in 1995. In 1996 she rode South Salem, who was eased.

FASTEST CLOCKING:
Secretariat – 1973, 2:24.00

Breeders' Cup Winners

LEADING BREEDERS' CUP CHAMPIONSHIP OWNERS BY MONEY WON

Name	Starters	1st	2nd	3rd	4th	5th	6th	Earnings
Allen E. Paulson*	32	6	2	7	2	1	1	$7,570,000
Stronach Stables (Frank Stronach)*	22	4	0	2	3	4	2	7,538,000
Godolphin Racing Inc.	31	3	2	3	2	5	2	5,004,200
Michael Tabor & Mrs. J. Magnier*	24	3	4	1	1	2	4	4,799,920
Overbrook Farm (W. T. Young)*	28	3	2	4	0	3	1	4,387,000
The T'bred Corp./Universal Stb.*	25	3	5	0	2	3	1	4,234,200
D. Wildenstein/Ecurie Wildenstein	19	2	4	1	2	1	1	3,917,000
Sheikh Mohammed/Darley Stud	25	2	2	5	4	1	1	3,776,800
Ogden Phipps	19	3	5	1	1	0	3	3,611,000
Juddmonte Farms (K. Abdullah)	41	1	3	5	5	2	2	3,443,620
Flaxman Holdings Ltd./Niarchos*	18	5	1	1	1	0	3	3,289,200
Sam-Son Farm	19	2	2	1	3	2	2	3,018,760
Frances A. Genter	8	2	3	1	0	0	0	2,835,000
Diamond A Racing Corp.	3	1	1	1	0	0	0	2,820,000
Robert B. & Beverly J. Lewis*	14	1	5	1	1	1	0	2,642,300
Eugene V. Klein*	17	4	3	1	0	0	1	2,593,000
H.H. Aga Khan	7	2	0	0	2	0	1	2,489,600
M. Cooper & C. Straub-Rubens	1	1	0	0	0	0	0	2,480,400
Edmund A. Gann*	14	0	3	2	2	0	2	2,408,800
Carolyn H. Hine	2	1	0	0	0	0	1	2,288,000
Ogden Mills Phipps	14	3	2	0	3	0	0	2,258,000
Dorothy & Pamela Scharbauer	3	1	1	1	0	0	0	2,133,000
Amherst Stable & Spruce Pond Stable	2	1	0	0	0	0	0	2,080,000
Cee's Stable	1	1	0	0	0	0	0	2,080,000
Ridder Thoroughbred Stable	1	1	0	0	0	0	0	2,080,000
Darby Dan Farm	3	1	1	0	0	0	0	1,800,000
Jeffrey S. Sullivan	3	1	0	1	0	0	0	1,668,000
Augustin Stables	6	1	1	0	0	2	0	1,564,000
La Presle Farm/Wertheimer Bros.	7	2	0	0	0	0	0	1,560,000
Robert E. Meyerhoff	3	1	0	0	0	0	0	1,560,000
Tsurumaki, Farish, Kilroy & Goodman	1	1	0	0	0	0	0	1,560,000
Buckland Farm	9	1	2	0	0	3	1	1,490,000
Golden Eagle Farm	15	0	3	3	2	3	1	1,443,800
Quarter B Farm	3	1	0	1	1	0	0	1,392,000
Black Chip Stable	1	1	0	0	0	0	0	1,350,000
Hancock III, Gaillard & Whittingham	1	1	0	0	0	0	0	1,350,000
Mrs. Elizabeth A. Keck	1	1	0	0	0	0	0	1,350,000
Oak Cliff Stable	4	1	0	0	0	0	0	1,350,000
Marjorie & Irving Cowan	8	2	1	0	0	0	1	1,328,400
Claiborne Farm	4	2	0	0	1	0	0	1,250,000
Starlight Stables, Saylor & Martin	2	1	1	0	0	0	0	1,240,000
Roger J. Devenport	1	1	0	0	0	0	0	1,227,200
Kenneth L. & Sarah K. Ramsey	4	0	2	0	0	0	0	1,200,000
Peter M. Brant	14	1	0	1	3	2	2	1,198,000
Allen E. Paulson Living Trust	4	1	0	0	0	1	0	1,160,000
Amerman Racing	2	1	0	1	0	0	0	1,160,000
Madeleine Paulson*	4	1	0	0	1	0	0	1,152,000
Paraneck Stable	2	2	0	0	0	0	0	1,144,000
Michael E. Pegram	6	1	0	1	0	1	1	1,112,400
John Franks	10	1	0	1	1	0	1	1,100,000
Padua Stables	9	2	0	0	0	0	1	1,076,400

*Does not include earnings in other partnerships

LEADING BREEDERS' CUP CHAMPIONSHIP BREEDERS – MONEY WON

Name	Starters	1st	2nd	3rd	4th	5th	6th	Earnings
Allen E. Paulson	28	6	2	3	2	2	1	$7,854,800
Adena Springs/Frank Stronach	10	4	0	0	1	1	1	6,232,000
Overbrook Farm/W.T. Young	26	3	4	4	1	2	0	4,843,000
Cecilia Straub-Rubens	2	2	0	0	0	0	0	4,560,400
Flaxman Holdings Ltd./Niarchos	26	5	2	2	2	4	3	3,825,600
Ogden Phipps	17	3	5	1	1	0	3	3,611,000
H.H. Aga Khan	10	3	0	0	2	0	1	3,529,600
Sheikh Mohammed/Darley Stud	19	2	2	4	2	1	0	3,423,600
Juddmonte Farms	42	1	3	6	4	2	2	3,381,620
The Thoroughbred Corporation	6	2	2	0	1	0	1	2,732,400
Oak Cliff Thoroughbreds Ltd.	3	2	0	0	0	0	0	2,700,000
Sean Coughlan	3	3	0	0	0	0	0	2,541,600
Clovelly Farms	3	1	0	1	0	0	0	2,520,000
Allez France Stables Ltd.	10	2	1	0	1	1	0	2,332,800
Anna Marie Barnhart	2	1	0	0	0	0	1	2,288,000
Mrs. & Mrs. Bertram Firestone	13	1	4	1	0	0	0	2,240,000
Preston Madden	3	1	1	1	0	0	0	2,133,000
W.S. Farish & W.S. Kilroy	8	1	1	0	0	2	2	2,085,400
Amherst Stable	2	1	0	0	0	0	0	2,080,000
Southeast Associates	1	1	0	0	0	0	0	2,080,000
Sam-Son Farm	15	1	3	1	2	2	0	2,051,760
Ballymacoll Stud Farm Ltd.	6	2	1	1	0	0	1	1,944,800
Aaron U. & Marie Jones	3	2	1	0	0	0	0	1,791,200
Gainsborough Farm Inc.	10	1	1	0	2	3	1	1,744,240
Tartan Farms Corp.	5	1	0	1	0	0	0	1,710,000
Stephen D. Peskoff	3	1	0	1	0	0	0	1,668,000
George Strawbridge Jr.	8	1	1	0	1	2	1	1,634,000
Georgia E. Hofmann	5	0	2	2	1	0	0	1,608,120
Al & Joyce Bell	3	0	2	0	0	0	0	1,600,000
Farnsworth Farms	5	2	0	0	0	0	1	1,560,000
Robert E. Meyerhoff	3	1	0	0	0	0	0	1,560,000
Wertheimer et Frere	10	2	0	0	0	0	0	1,560,000
Mr. & Mrs. John C. Mabee	20	0	3	2	3	3	3	1,555,800
John Franks	11	1	2	1	0	0	0	1,480,000
Mrs. John W. Galbreath	2	1	0	1	0	0	0	1,458,000
Meadowbrook Farm Inc.	3	2	0	0	0	0	0	1,420,000
Ogden Mills Phipps	13	2	1	0	4	0	0	1,408,000
Irish Acres Farm	3	1	0	1	1	0	0	1,392,000
Howard B. Keck	1	1	0	0	0	0	0	1,350,000
W. Paul Little	2	1	0	0	0	0	0	1,350,000
Wimborne Farm	3	1	0	1	0	0	0	1,337,600
Marjorie & Irving Cowan	8	2	1	0	0	0	1	1,328,400
Kinghaven Farms Ltd.	10	0	2	1	2	0	1	1,285,000
Jaime S. Carrion	5	2	0	0	0	0	0	1,230,000
Golden Orb Farm & K. D. Schwartz	1	1	0	0	0	0	0	1,227,200
Thomas M. Evans	10	0	3	0	0	3	2	1,215,000
Richard D. Maynard	3	1	0	0	1	0	0	1,152,000
Claiborne Farm & The Gamely Corp.	7	2	0	1	0	0	0	1,148,000
Frances A. Genter Stable	7	1	3	0	0	0	0	1,125,000
North Ridge Farm	10	1	1	1	0	2	1	1,109,000
Dayton Ltd.	9	0	2	1	0	1	2	1,106,000
Fares Farms Inc.	6	2	0	0	0	1	0	1,060,000

LEADING BREEDERS' CUP CHAMPIONSHIP TRAINERS BY MONEY WON

Name	Starts	1st	2nd	3rd	4th	5th	6th	Purses
D. Wayne Lukas	143	17	20	15	8	12	12	$19,033,900
Robert Frankel	63	3	8	7	9	4	5	9,679,820
William I. Mott	41	5	6	4	3	3	2	8,542,960
Shug McGaughey	47	8	9	1	6	3	3	7,653,560
Richard Mandella	27	6	1	1	4	2	1	7,116,960
Andre Fabre	36	3	4	7	1	2	1	6,435,400
Neil Drysdale	31	6	4	2	4	4	5	6,095,840
Aidan P. O'Brien	30	3	5	4	1	4	4	5,551,020
Bob Baffert	41	3	7	3	6	6	3	5,349,800
Jay M. Robbins	6	2	0	0	2	0	0	4,938,400
Charles Whittingham	24	2	2	3	2	2	2	4,298,000
Saeed Bin Suroor	22	2	1	2	1	5	2	4,099,800
David Hofmans	10	2	0	2	1	2	0	3,731,040
Sir Michael Stoute	24	3	1	3	0	1	6	3,724,600
Patrick Byrne	7	3	0	0	0	0	0	3,718,000
Jack Van Berg	14	1	3	3	1	0	2	3,600,000
Ron McAnally	27	4	3	2	2	1	4	3,518,000
Nick Zito	23	1	4	3	1	5	1	3,336,120
Flint Schulhofer	26	2	2	4	1	6	1	2,841,400
Carl Nafzger	15	1	3	1	1	0	1	2,812,840
Pascal Bary	8	3	0	1	0	1	1	2,601,200
Wallace Dollase	15	1	4	1	1	1	2	2,484,900
Hubert (Sonny) Hine	5	1	0	0	0	0	1	2,288,000
Philip (P. G.) Johnson	4	1	0	0	1	0	1	2,170,000
LeRoy Jolley	16	2	1	0	3	2	2	2,145,000
Joseph Orseno	10	2	0	1	1	3	1	2,049,600
Todd Pletcher	16	2	1	1	0	3	1	2,016,200
John Veitch	5	1	1	1	1	0	0	1,978,000
Jonathan Pease	5	2	1	0	0	0	0	1,812,000
Mark Frostad	9	1	1	0	2	1	0	1,788,760
Francois Boutin	19	3	0	2	1	1	2	1,712,000
Julio Canani	12	3	0	0	1	0	0	1,692,720
Ernie Poulos	3	1	0	1	0	0	0	1,668,000
Richard Small	2	1	0	0	0	0	0	1,560,000
Bruce Headley	11	1	2	3	1	2	0	1,526,640
Jenine Sahadi	7	2	1	1	1	0	1	1,509,600
Jim Day	14	1	2	1	1	1	3	1,455,000
Gary Jones	12	0	2	2	1	1	1	1,439,000
P. Noel Hickey	4	1	0	1	1	0	0	1,392,000
Christopher Speckert	5	1	2	0	0	1	1	1,390,000
H. Graham Motion	3	1	1	0	0	1	0	1,352,000
Michael Whittingham	4	1	0	0	0	0	0	1,350,000
Vincent Timphony	1	1	0	0	0	0	0	1,350,000
Dallas Stewart	5	1	0	0	0	0	2	1,227,200
Christophe Clement	13	0	2	2	1	1	1	1,209,720
Dale Romans	2	0	2	0	0	0	0	1,200,000
Alex Hassinger Jr.	4	2	0	1	0	0	0	1,196,400
Patrick-Louis Biancone	12	0	2	0	2	0	1	1,184,000
Alain de Royer-Dupre	4	1	0	0	2	0	0	1,180,000
Clive E. Brittain	8	1	0	1	1	0	0	1,152,160
Roger Attfield	11	0	2	1	1	1	1	1,095,000
Craig Dollase	7	1	1	0	2	0	0	1,084,000
John T. Ward Jr.	4	1	0	0	0	1	1	1,060,000

LEADING BREEDERS' CUP CHAMPIONSHIP JOCKEYS – MONEY WON

Name	Starts	1st	2nd	3rd	4th	5th	6th	Purses
Pat Day	117	12	17	11	9	11	11	$23,033,360
Jerry Bailey	95	14	11	12	6	8	6	19,069,340
Chris McCarron	101	9	12	7	7	7	13	17,669,600
Gary Stevens	93	8	15	10	7	8	9	13,441,160
Mike Smith	52	10	6	3	4	6	2	10,505,760
Jose Santos	59	7	2	4	6	9	4	8,008,800
Corey Nakatani	56	6	7	7	6	4	3	7,905,280
Eddie Delahoussaye	68	7	3	6	9	8	6	7,775,000
Alex Solis	47	3	7	4	7	6	5	6,827,660
Laffit Pincay Jr.	61	7	4	9	5	3	6	6,811,000
John Velazquez	47	6	4	4	1	6	3	6,361,800
Patrick Valenzuela	46	7	0	3	7	9	3	6,274,280
Lanfranco Dettori	34	4	2	4	5	5	3	6,159,160
Angel Cordero Jr.	48	4	7	7	1	6	8	6,020,000
Kent Desormeaux	50	2	3	6	9	1	6	4,773,200
Michael Kinane	25	3	3	3	1	1	4	4,590,920
Shane Sellers	29	2	3	4	3	1	0	3,960,600
Pat Eddery	30	2	3	3	1	2	1	3,570,000
Jorge Chavez	40	2	2	1	4	1	6	3,438,640
Jorge Velasquez	18	2	5	1	1	0	1	3,353,000
Craig Perret	31	4	2	1	2	1	4	3,205,000
David Flores	19	3	2	1	0	2	1	2,744,800
Edgar Prado	41	0	4	4	3	7	4	2,614,060
Bill Shoemaker	14	1	2	2	1	1	2	2,226,000
Javier Castellano	1	1	0	0	0	0	0	2,080,000
Kieren Fallon	10	2	1	2	0	1	1	1,987,800
Victor Espinoza	19	1	2	0	0	1	1	1,933,200
John Murtagh	5	2	0	0	0	2	0	1,873,800
Walter Swinburn	19	1	1	1	1	2	4	1,714,000
Randy Romero	17	3	0	1	0	3	2	1,648,000
Yves Saint-Martin	4	2	0	0	1	0	0	1,490,000
Olivier Peslier	13	1	1	1	0	0	0	1,362,800
Julie Krone	17	1	2	1	1	0	2	1,285,000
Cash Asmussen	25	1	1	2	1	2	3	1,242,000
Ramon Dominguez	3	1	0	1	0	1	0	1,186,600
Fernando Toro	12	1	0	2	2	0	0	1,162,000
Jacinto Vasquez	12	1	1	1	2	0	1	1,149,000
Walter Guerra	7	2	0	1	1	0	0	1,078,000
Garrett Gomez	8	0	1	1	0	0	0	1,040,000
Eric Legrix	2	1	0	0	0	0	0	1,040,000
Freddie Head	10	2	0	1	0	1	1	1,028,000
Jose Valdivia Jr.	7	1	0	2	1	0	1	982,570
Ray Sibille	1	1	0	0	0	0	0	900,000
Don MacBeth	5	1	0	0	1	1	0	760,000
Richard Quinn	3	0	1	0	0	0	0	675,000
Cornelio Velasquez	8	1	0	0	0	1	0	645,400

LEADING BREEDERS' CUP CHAMPIONSHIP SIRES - MONEY WON

Name	Starters	1st	2nd	3rd	4th	5th	6th	Money Won
Storm Cat	37	4	6	4	3	6	1	$7,136,300
Sadler's Wells	38	6	2	5	2	4	3	6,982,900
Deputy Minister	25	3	1	3	3	2	4	5,370,560
Cee's Tizzy	3	2	1	0	0	0	0	5,360,400
Danzig	42	5	5	3	5	0	3	4,657,320
Seattle Slew	26	3	4	3	0	3	2	4,655,400
Pleasant Colony	20	2	4	1	1	3	2	4,541,320
Alydar	19	1	5	3	0	3	0	4,495,000
Kris S.	13	5	0	1	1	0	1	3,721,900
Cozzene	9	2	1	1	0	0	1	3,468,000
Mr. Prospector	42	3	3	2	5	3	6	3,421,680
Nureyev	23	4	2	2	1	0	3	3,408,400
Fappiano	15	2	2	2	3	3	2	3,386,000
Nijinsky II	12	3	2	2	2	0	1	3,283,000
Sovereign Dancer	11	0	5	3	1	1	0	3,053,000
Relaunch	15	2	1	2	2	2	1	3,004,000
Awesome Again	4	2	0	0	0	0	0	2,860,000
Gone West	16	4	2	0	1	1	3	2,856,000
Strawberry Road (Aus)	8	3	0	1	1	0	0	2,832,000
Unbridled	10	3	2	1	0	1	0	2,576,400
Cox's Ridge	16	3	2	4	0	3	1	2,529,000
Cryptoclearance	3	1	0	0	1	0	0	2,366,720
Doyoun (Ire)	3	2	0	0	0	0	0	2,329,600
Skip Trial	3	1	0	0	0	0	1	2,288,000
Mill Reef	6	1	1	1	2	0	0	2,071,000
Palace Music	2	1	0	1	0	0	0	2,040,000
El Prado (Ire)	5	0	3	0	0	0	1	2,000,000
Thunder Gulch	6	1	2	0	1	0	0	1,969,200
Broad Brush	5	1	1	0	0	0	0	1,960,000
Halo	8	1	0	1	2	0	2	1,888,000
Rahy	15	1	3	0	1	3	0	1,868,480
Miswaki	9	1	0	1	1	1	0	1,758,000
Lyphard	10	1	1	1	1	1	1	1,720,000
Irish River (Fr)	15	0	2	3	2	2	0	1,700,140
Jade Hunter	6	1	1	0	1	1	1	1,672,000
Private Account	10	2	0	2	1	1	2	1,600,000
Sagace (Fr)	2	1	0	0	0	0	0	1,560,000
Seeking the Gold	8	2	2	1	0	0	1	1,560,000
Graustark	2	1	0	1	0	0	0	1,458,000
Dynaformer	16	0	2	1	3	1	3	1,429,040
Bucksplasher	3	1	0	1	1	0	0	1,392,000
Icecapade	4	1	0	0	0	0	1	1,380,000
Sharpen Up (GB)	5	1	1	0	0	1	0	1,370,000
Wild Again	11	1	0	1	1	1	0	1,360,000
Caro (Ire)	6	1	2	2	0	0	0	1,341,000
Mt. Livermore	6	2	0	0	1	0	1	1,336,800
Danehill	8	1	2	1	0	0	0	1,333,200
Phone Trick	11	2	0	1	2	1	0	1,295,600
Alleged	10	1	0	0	1	1	0	1,252,000
Saint Ballado	3	1	1	0	0	0	0	1,240,000

STATUS OF PAST BREEEDERS' CUP WINNERS AS OF FEBRUARY 11, 2005

BREEDERS' CUP CLASSIC

YEAR	WINNER	STATUS
2004	Ghostzapper	Still in Training
2003	Pleasantly Perfect	Stud Prospect, Lane's End Farm, Ky.
2002	Volponi	Stud, Hopewell Farm, Ky.
2001	Tiznow	Stud, WinStar Farm, Ky.
2000	Tiznow	Stud, WinStar Farm, Ky.
1999	Cat Thief	Stud, Overbrook Farm, Ky.
1998	Awesome Again	Stud, Adena Springs Farm, Ky.
1997	Skip Away	Stud, Hopewell Farm, Ky.
1996	Alphabet Soup	Stud, Adena Springs Farm, Ky.
1995	Cigar	Retired, Kentucky Horse Park, Ky.
1994	Concern	Stud, Okla. Equine Lameness Center, Ok.
1993	Arcangues	Stud, Keiba Bokujo, Japan
1992	A.P. Indy	Stud, Lane's End Farm, Ky.
1991	Black Tie Affair (Ire)	Stud, O'Sullivan Farms, Va.
1990	Unbridled	Deceased
1989	Sunday Silence	Deceased
1988	Alysheba	Stud, Janadriya, Saudi Arabia
1987	Ferdinand	Deceased
1986	Skywalker	Deceased
1985	Proud Truth	Stud, Haras Cerro Punta, Panama
1984	Wild Again	Pensioned, Three Chimneys Farm, Ky.

Breeders' Cup Turf

YEAR	WINNER	STATUS
2004	Better Talk Now	Still in Training
2003	High Chaparral (Ire)	Stud, Coolmore, Ireland
2003	Johar	Stud, Mill Ridge Farm, Ky.
2002	High Chaparral (Ire)	Stud, Coolmore, Ireland
2001	Fantastic Light	Stud, Dalham Hall Stud, England
2000	Kalanisi (Ire)	Stud, Gilltown Stud, Ireland
1999	Daylami (Ire)	Stud, Gilltown Stud, Ireland
1998	Buck's Boy	Retired, Quarter B Farm, Il.
1997	Chief Bearhart	Stud, Iburi Stallion Station, Japan
1996	Pilsudski (Ire)	Stud, Anngrove Stud, Ireland
1995	Northern Spur (Ire)	Stud, True North Farm, Ky.
1994	Tikkanen	Stud, Glebe House, Northern Ireland
1993	Kotashaan (Fr)	Stud, Ballycurragh Stud, Ireland
1992	Fraise	Retired, Olympic Club Riding School, Japan
1991	Miss Alleged	Broodmare, Haras de Manneville, France
1990	In the Wings (GB)	Deceased
1989	Prized	Stud, Spendthrift Farm, Ky.
1988	Great Communicator	Deceased
1987	Theatrical (Ire)	Stud, Hill 'N' Dale, Ky.
1986	Manila	Stud, Turkish Jockey Club, Turkey
1985	Pebbles (GB)	Retired, Fukumitsu Farm, Japan
1984	Lashkari (GB)	Deceased

Breeders' Cup Distaff

YEAR	WINNER	STATUS
2004	Ashado	Still in Training
2003	Adoration	Broodmare Prospect, Mill Ridge Farm, Ky.
2002	Azeri	Broodmare Prospect, Ashford Stud, Ky.
2001	Unbridled Elaine	Broodmare, Darley at Jonabell Farm, Ky.
2000	Spain	Broodmare, Location Unknown
1999	Beautiful Pleasure	Broodmare, Fawn Leap Farm, Ky.
1998	Escena	Broodmare, Diamond A Farm, Ky.
1997	Ajina	Broodmare, Stonerside Farm, Ky.
1996	Jewel Princess	Broodmare, Ashford Stud, Ky.
1995	Inside Information	Broodmare, Double Diamond Farm, Fl.
1994	One Dreamer	Broodmare, Glen Hill Farm, Fla.
1993	Hollywood Wildcat	Broodmare, Patchen Wilkes Farm, Ky.
1992	Paseana (Arg)	Broodmare, San Ignacio de Loyola, Argentina
1991	Dance Smartly	Broodmare, Sam-Son Farm, Ontario, Canada
1990	Bayakoa (Arg)	Deceased
1989	Bayakoa (Arg)	Deceased
1988	Personal Ensign	Broodmare, Claiborne Farm, Ky.
1987	Sacahuista	Broodmare, Ashford Stud, Ky.
1986	Lady's Secret	Deceased
1985	Life's Magic	Broodmare, Trackside Farm, Ky.
1984	Princess Rooney	Broodmare, Gentry Bros. Farm, Ky.

Breeders' Cup Filly & Mare Turf

YEAR	WINNER	STATUS
2004	Ouija Board (GB)	Still in Training
2003	Islington (Ire)	Broodmare, Ballymacoll Stud, Ireland
2002	Starine (Fr)	Broodmare, Newsells Park Stud, England
2001	Banks Hill (GB)	Broodmare, Juddmonte Farms, Ky.
2000	Perfect Sting	Broodmare, Adena Springs Farm, Ky.
1999	Soaring Softly	Broodmare, Darby Dan Farm, Ky.

Breeders' Cup Juvenile

YEAR	WINNER	STATUS
2004	Wilko	Still in Training
2003	Action This Day	Stud Prospect, Castleton Lyons, Ky.
2002	Vindication	Stud, Hill 'N' Dale, Ky.
2001	Johannesburg	Stud, Ashford Stud, Ky.
2000	Macho Uno	Stud, Adena Springs South, Fla.
1999	Anees	Deceased
1998	Answer Lively	Deceased
1997	Favorite Trick	Stud, Cloverleaf Farms II, Fl.
1996	Boston Harbor	Stud, Shizunai Stallion Station, Japan
1995	Unbridled's Song	Stud, Taylor Made, Ky.
1994	Timber Country	Stud, Lex Stud, Japan
1993	Brocco	Stud, Slade Farm, New Zealand
1992	Gilded Time	Stud, Vinery, Ky.
1991	Arazi	Stud, Gestut Sohrenhof, Switzerland
1990	Fly So Free	Deceased
1989	Rhythm	Stud, Diamond F Ranch, Ca.
1988	Is it True	Stud, Hartley/DeRenzo Thoroughbreds, Fla.

1987	Success Express	Stud, Vinery, New South Wales, Australia
1986	Capote	Pensioned, Three Chimneys Farm, Ky.
1985	Tasso	Stud, Janadriya, Saudi Arabia
1984	Chief's Crown	Deceased

Breeders' Cup Juvenile Fillies

YEAR	WINNER	STATUS
2004	Sweet Catomine	Still in Training
2003	Halfbridled	Broodmare Prospect, Hagyard Farm, Ky.
2002	Storm Flag Flying	Broodmare Prospect, Claiborne Farm, Ky.
2001	Tempera	Deceased
2000	Caressing	Broodmare, Hermitage Farm, Ky.
1999	Cash Run	Broodmare, Ashford Stud, Ky.
1998	Silverbulletday	Broodmare, Hill 'N' Dale, Ky.
1997	Countess Diana	Broodmare, WinStar Farm, Ky.
1996	Storm Song	Broodmare, Dalham Hall Stud, England
1995	My Flag	Broodmare, Claiborne Farm, Ky.
1994	Flanders	Broodmare, Overbrook Farm, Ky.
1993	Phone Chatter	Broodmare, Ashford Stud, Ky.
1992	Eliza	Broodmare, Ashford Stud, Ky.
1991	Pleasant Stage	Deceased
1990	Meadow Star	Deceased
1989	Go for Wand	Deceased
1988	Open Mind	Deceased
1987	Epitome	Deceased
1986	Brave Raj	Broodmare, Patchen Wilkes Farm, Ky.
1985	Twilight Ridge	Broodmare, Manchester Farm, Ky.
1984	Outstandingly	Deceased

Breeders' Cup Mile

YEAR	WINNER	STATUS
2004	Singletary	Still in Training
2003	Six Perfections (Fr)	Broodmare Prospect, Oak Tree (Lane's End), Ky.
2002	Domedriver (Ire)	Stud, Lanwades Stud, Newmarket, England
2001	Val Royal (Fr)	Stud, Eliza Park Stud, Victoria, Australia
2000	War Chant	Stud, Three Chimneys Farm, Ky.
1999	Silic (Fr)	Stud, Crestwood Farm, Ky.
1998	Da Hoss	Retired, Kentucky Horse Park, Ky.
1997	Spinning World	Stud, Coolmore, Ireland
1996	Da Hoss	Retired, Kentucky Horse Park, Ky.
1995	Ridgewood Pearl (GB)	Deceased
1994	Barathea (Ire)	Stud, Rathbarry Stud, Ireland
1993	Lure	Pensioned, Claiborne Farm, Ky.
1992	Lure	Pensioned, Claiborne Farm, Ky.
1991	Opening Verse	Deceased
1990	Royal Academy	Stud, Ashford Stud, Ky.
1989	Steinlen (GB)	Deceased
1988	Miesque	Broodmare, Oak Tree (Lane's End), Ky.
1987	Miesque	Broodmare, Oak Tree (Lane's End), Ky.
1986	Last Tycoon (Ire)	Stud, Miura Farm, Japan
1985	Cozzene	Stud, Gainesway Farm, Ky.
1984	Royal Heroine (Ire)	Deceased

Breeders' Cup Sprint

YEAR	WINNER	STATUS
2004	Speightstown	Stud Prospect, WinStar Farm, Ky.
2003	Cajun Beat	Still in Training
2002	Orientate	Stud, Gainesway Farm, Ky.
2001	Squirtle Squirt	Stud, Shizunai Stallion Station, Japan
2000	Kona Gold	Retired, Stable Pony, Ca.
1999	Artax	Stud, Metropolitan Stud, NY
1998	Reraise	Retired, Privately Owned, Va.
1997	Elmhurst	Retired, Evergreen Farm, Ky.
1996	Lit de Justice	Stud, Magali Farm, Ca.
1995	Desert Stormer	Broodmare, Claiborne Farm, Ky.
1994	Cherokee Run	Stud, Jonabell Farm, Ky.
1993	Cardmania	Retired, Frosty Acres Ranch, Ca.
1992	Thirty Slews	Retired, Privately Owned, Ca.
1991	Sheikh Albadou (GB)	Deceased
1990	Safely Kept	Broodmare, Lakland Farm, Ky.
1989	Dancing Spree	Broodmare, Chisbury Manor Stud, England
1988	Gulch	Stud, Lane's End Farm, Ky.
1987	Very Subtle	Deceased
1986	Smile	Deceased
1985	Precisionist	Pensioned, Privately Owned, Fairfield, Fl.
1984	Eillo	Deceased

TOTAL SIMULCAST WAGERING

North American simulcast outlets

Year	Outlets	Simulcast Total	Year	Outlets	Simulcast Total
1984	19	$8,009,109	1994	748	68,078,006
1985	37	19,741,113	1995	781	56,484,875
1986	53	19,474,381	1996	875	61,813,421
1987	57	21,662,205	1997	921	72,659,391
1988	92	33,713,296	1998	909	77,793,618
1989	149	45,129,419	1999	917	85,419,282
1990	256	46,220,925	2000	1,071	95,018,338
1991	603	55,642,551	2001	1,070	91,057,372
1992	625	66,961,184	2002	1,110	96,173,455
1993	644	67,601,992	2003	n/a	101,780,683
			2004	n/a	96,648,038

Breeders' Cup Pick 6 History

Year	MinBet	Payoff	No. of Tix	Consolation	No. of Tix	Handle
2004	$2	$0	0	$56,149.00	61	$4,566,837
2003	$2	$2,687,611.20	1	$18,663.00	48	$4,489,454
2002	$2	$0	0	$43,937.60	78	$4,646,289
2001	$2	$262,442.00	11	$1,475.00		$4,811,450
2000	$2	$45,772.00	68	$465.00		$5,123,453
1999	$2	$3,058,138.60	1	$5,996.20		$5,436,691
1998	$2	$34,607.20	114	$335.80	3,906	$6,494,349
1997	$2	$16,417.20	115	$158.20		$3,379,014

Breeders' Cup Pick 7 History

Year	MinBet	Payoff	No. of Tix	Consolation	No. of Tix	Handle
1996	$1	$471,812.00	4	$4,462.00	141	$3,340,945
1995	$1	$22,513.00	81	$205.00	2,959	$3,169,020
1994	$1	$0	0	$66,290.00	54	$4,599,918
1993	$2	$1,549,114.00	2	$251.00	2,054	$5,307,815
1992	$2	$740,115.00	4	$2,800.00	349	$5,104,480
1991	$2	$0	0	$230,250.00	29	$8,526,985

BREEDERS CUP DAY STATISTICS

Race Day	Race Track	Attendance	Wagering*	Weather	Temp
October 30, 2004	Lone Star Park, TX	53,717	$109,838,668	Sunny	79
October 25, 2003	Santa Anita, CA	51,648	107,535,731	Sunny	99
October 26, 2002	Arlington Park, IL	46,118	108,578,049	Cloudy	43
October 27, 2001	Belmont Park, NY.	52,987	98,711,413	Cloudy, windy	50
November 4, 2000	Churchill Downs, KY	76,043	101,283,427	Cloudy	55
November 6, 1999	Gulfstream Park, FL	45,124	96,485,255	Clear	77
November 7, 1998	Churchill Downs, KY	80,452	91,338,477	Clear	54
November 8, 1997	Hollywood Park, CA	51,161	71,639.333	Sunny	74
October 26, 1996	Woodbine, Ontario, Canada	42,243	67,738,890	Sunny	60
October 28, 1995	Belmont Park, NY	37,246	64,075,207	Cloudy	66
November 5, 1994	Churchill Downs, KY	71,671	78,224,530	Clear	75
November 6, 1993	Santa Anita Park, CA	55,130	79,744,742	Sunny	81
October 31, 1992	Gulfstream Park, FL	45,415	76,876,726	Sunny	87
November 2, 1991	Churchill Downs, KY	66,204	67,588,113	Partly Sunny	43
October 27, 1990	Belmont Park, NY	51,236	55,328,195	Sunny	43
November 4, 1989	Gulfstream Park, FL	51,342	55,345,677	Sunny	79
November 5, 1988	Churchill Downs, KY	71,237	42,932,379	Cloudy, Drizzle	50
November 21, 1987	Hollywood Park, CA	57,734	31,864,457	Sunny	73
November 1, 1986	Santa Anita Park, CA	69,155	31,984,490	Sunny	73
November 2, 1985	Aqueduct, NY	42,568	26,941,288	Cloudy	54
November 10, 1984	Hollywood Park, CA	64,254	16,452,179	Sunny	70

* Wagering on Breeders' Cup Championship Races only

HORSES WITH MULTIPLE BREEDERS' CUP CHAMPIONSHIP STARTS

ADJUDICATING
1989 Juvenile 11th
1990 Sprint 4th

AFFIRMED SUCCESS
1998 Sprint 6th
1999 Sprint 12th
2000 Mile 4th
2001 Mile 11th

AFLEET
1987 Classic 10th
1988 Sprint 3rd

AIR DISPLAY
1986 Mile 11th
1987 Mile 11th

AL MAMOON
1985 Mile 2nd
1986 Mile 6th

ALBERT THE GREAT
2000 Classic 4th
2001 Classic 3rd

ALDEBARAN
2002 Mile 11th
2003 Sprint 6th

ALICE SPRINGS
1994 Mile 5th
1995 Turf 7th

ALPHABATIM
1984 Turf 5th
1986 Classic 5th

ALY'S ALLEY
1998 Juvenile 2nd
2000 Turf 9th

ALYSHEBA
1986 Juvenile 3rd
1987 Classic 2nd
1988 Classic 1st

APPEALING SKIER
1995 Juvenile 12th
1996 Sprint 10th

ARAZI
1991 Juvenile 1st
1992 Mile 11th

ASHADO
2003 Juvenile Fillies 2nd
2004 Distaff 1st

AWAD
1995 Turf 6th
1996 Turf 9th
1997 Turf 9th

AZERI
2002 Distaff 1st
2004 Classic 5th

BALTO STAR
2001 Mile 4th
2003 Turf 9th

BANKS HILL
2001 F & M Turf 1st
2002 F & M Turf 2nd

BANSHEE BREEZE
1998 Distaff 2nd
1999 Distaff 2nd

BARATHEA
1993 Mile 5th
1994 Mile 1st

BAYAKOA (Arg)
1989 Distaff 1st
1990 Distaff 1st

BEAUTIFUL PLEASURE
1997 Juvenile Fillies 7th
1999 Distaff 1st
2000 Distaff 6th

BEHRENS
1997 Classic 7th
1999 Classic 7th

BERTRANDO
1991 Juvenile 2nd
1993 Classic 2nd
1994 Classic 6th

BEST PAL
1990 Juvenile 6th
1993 Classic 10th
1994 Classic 5th

BET ON SUNSHINE
1997 Sprint 3rd
2000 Sprint 3rd
2001 Sprint, 13th
2002 Classic 5th

BET TWICE
1986 Juvenile 4th
1988 Mile 8th

BIGSTONE
1993 Mile 6th
1994 Mile 8th

BIRDONTHEWIRE
1993 Sprint 11th
1994 Sprint 6th

BLACK TIE AFFAIR (Ire)
1989 Sprint 9th
1990 Sprint 3rd
1991 Classic 1st

BLUSHING JOHN
1988 Mile 10th
1989 Classic 3rd

BOLD ARRANGEMENT (GB)
1986 Classic 7th
1987 Classic 11th

BONAPARTISTE (FR)
1998 Turf 9th
1999 Turf 6th

BORGIA (Ger)
1997 Turf 2nd
1999 F & M Turf 5th

BRAHMS
1999 Juvenile 7th
2001 Mile 6th

BUCK'S BOY
1997 Turf 4th
1998 Turf 1st
1999 Turf 3rd

CAFE LATTE (Ire)
1999 F&M Turf 4th
2000 F&M Turf 9th

CAJUN BEAT
2003 Sprint 1st
2004 Sprint 5th

CAME HOME
2001 Juvenile 7th
2002 Classic 10th

CAPTAIN STEVE
1999 Juvenile 11th
2000 Classic 3rd

CARDMANIA
1992 Sprint 12th
1993 Sprint 1st
1994 Sprint 3rd

CAT THIEF
1998 Juvenile 3rd
1999 Classic 1st
2000 Classic 7th

CELTIC ARMS
1994 Turf 10th
1995 Turf 10th

CHARGING FALLS
1984 Sprint 6th
1985 Sprint 9th

CHIEF BEARHART
1996 Turf 11th
1997 Turf 1st
1998 Turf 4th

CHIEF'S CROWN
1984 Juvenile 1st
1985 Classic 4th

CIGAR
1995 Classic 1st
1996 Classic 3rd

CITY ZIP
2000 Juvenile 7th
2001 Mile 9th

CLASSIC CROWN
1987 Juvenile Fillies 6th
1988 Distaff 5th

CLEAR MANDATE
1996 Distaff 6th
1997 Distaff 6th

COLONIAL WATERS
1989 Distaff 8th
1990 Distaff 2nd

CONCERN
1994 Classic 1st
1995 Classic 8th

COZZENE
1984 Mile 3rd
1985 Mile 1st

CRYPTOCLEARANCE
1987 Classic 5th
1988 Classic 5th
1989 Classic 5th

CULTURE VULTURE
1991 Juvenile Fillies 9th
1992 Distaff 10th

CUVEE
2003 Juvenile 12th
2004 Sprint 13th

DA HOSS
1995 Sprint 13th
1996 Mile 1st
1998 Mile 1st

DANCE SMARTLY
1990 Juvenile Fillies 3rd
1991 Distaff 1st

DANCING SPREE
1989 Sprint 1st
1990 Sprint 6th

DELAWARE TOWNSHIP
2000 Sprint 10th
2001 Sprint 6th

DERNIER EMPEREUR
1993 Turf 12th
1994 Classic 14th

DEVIL HIS DUE
1993 Classic 8th
1994 Classic 11th

DISPERSAL
1989 Sprint 3rd
1990 Classic 12th

DOLLAR BILL
2000 Juvenile 10th
2002 Classic 6th

DOUBLE FEINT
1986 Mile 4th
1987 Mile 12th

DRAMATIC GOLD
1994 Classic 3rd
1996 Classic 9th

DUSHYANTOR
1996 Turf 7th
1998 Turf 3rd

DYNEVER
2003 Classic 3rd
2004 Classic 8th

EASY GOER
1988 Juvenile 2nd
1989 Classic 2nd

EDITOR'S NOTE
1995 Juvenile 3rd
1996 Classic 12th

EL SENOR
1988 Turf 6th
1989 Turf 7th
1990 Turf 3rd
1991 Turf 9th

ELLOLUV
2003 Distaff 2nd
2004 Distaff 7th

EPITOME
1987 Juvenile Fillies 1st
1988 Distaff 7th

ESCENA
1997 Distaff 3rd
1998 Distaff 1st

EVENING ATTIRE
2002 Classic 4th
2003 Classic 7th

EXCHANGE
1992 Distaff 8th
1994 Distaff 7th

EZZOUD (IRE)
1993 Classic 7th
1994 Classic 7th

FANTASTIC LIGHT
2000 Turf 5th
2001 Turf 1st

FAVORITE TRICK
1997 Juvenile 1st
1998 Mile 8th

FIGHTING FIT
1984 Sprint 3rd
1985 Sprint 4th

FIVE STAR DAY
2000 Sprint 14th
2001 Sprint 8th

FLAG DOWN
1994 Classic 12th
1997 Turf 3rd

FLAWLESSLY
1990 Juvenile Fillies 7th
1993 Mile 9th

FLY SO FREE
1990 Juvenile 1st
1991 Classic 4th
1993 Sprint 9th

FORBIDDEN APPLE
2000 Mile 7th
2001 Mile 2nd
2002 Mile 4th

FOURSTARS ALLSTAR
1992 Mile 9th
1993 Mile 3rd
1995 Mile 7th

FRAISE
1992 Turf 1st
1993 Turf 4th
1994 Turf 11th

FRAN'S VALENTINE
1984 Juvenile Fillies 10th
1985 Distaff 5th
1986 Distaff 2nd

FREEFOURINTERNET
2003 Mile 6th
2004 Classic 13th

FRIENDLY LOVER
1995 Sprint 5th
1996 Sprint 11th

FUNNY CIDE
2003 Classic 9th
2004 Classic 10th

FURLOUGH
1998 Sprint 10th
1999 Sprint 10th

GANDER
2000 Classic 9th
2001 Classic 9th

GATE DANCER
1984 Classic 3rd
1985 Classic 2nd

GILDED TIME
1992 Juvenile 1st
1993 Sprint 3rd

GO AND GO (Ire)
1989 Juvenile 8th
1990 Classic dnf

GO FOR WAND
1989 Juvenile Fillies 1st
1990 Distaff dnf

GOLDEN MISSILE
1999 Classic 3rd
2000 Classic 13th

GOODBYE HALO
1988 Distaff 3rd
1989 Distaff 6th

GRAND SLAM
1997 Juvenile dnf
1998 Sprint 2nd

GREAT COMMUNICATOR
1987 Turf 12th
1988 Turf 1st

GROOVY
1985 Juvenile 10th
1986 Sprint 4th
1987 Sprint 2nd

GUIDED TOUR
2000 Classic 12th
2001 Classic 5th

GULCH
1986 Juvenile 5th
1987 Classic 9th
1988 Sprint 1st

HAP
2000 Mile 9th
2001 Turf 5th

HATOOF
1993 Turf 5th
1994 Turf 2nd

HAWKSLEY HILL (Ire)
1998 Mile 2nd
1999 Mile 5th

HEAVENLY PRIZE
1993 Juvenile Fillies 3rd
1994 Distaff 2nd
1995 Distaff 2nd

HELMSMAN
1996 Mile 6th
1997 Mile 10th

HERITAGE OF GOLD
1999 Distaff 3rd
2000 Distaff 3rd

HERNANDO (FR)
1993 Turf 10th
1994 Turf 6th
1995 Turf 5th

HIGH BRITE
1987 Sprint 5th
1988 Sprint 12th

HIGH CHAPARRAL (IRE)
2002 Turf 1st
2003 Turf 1st-dh

HOLD THAT TIGER
2002 Juvenile 3rd
2003 Classic 5th

HOLLYWOOD STORY
2003 Juvenile Fillies 4th
2004 Distaff 10th

HOLLYWOOD WILDCAT
1993 Distaff 1st
1994 Distaff 6th

HONOR GLIDE
1997 Classic 8th
1999 Turf 8th

HONOUR AND GLORY
1995 Juvenile 4th
1996 Sprint 3rd

IMPERIAL GESTURE
2001 Juv. Fillies 2nd
2002 Distaff 3rd

INTREPIDITY (GB)
1993 Turf 13th
1994 Turf 4th

ISLINGTON (IRE)
2002 F & M Turf 3rd
2003 F & M Turf 1st

ITSALLGREEKTOME
1990 Mile 2nd
1991 Turf 2nd

JEWEL PRINCESS
1996 Distaff 1st
1997 Distaff dnf

JOHANN QUATZ (FR)
1993 Mile 7th
1994 Mile 2nd

JOLIE'S HALO
1991 Mile 6th
1992 Classic 10th

KEEPER HILL
1998 Distaff 3rd
1999 Distaff 4th

KIRBY'S SONG
1997 Juvenile Fillies 5th
1998 Distaff 8th

KONA GOLD
1998 Sprint 3rd
1999 Sprint 2nd
2000 Sprint 1st
2001 Sprint 7th
2002 Sprint 4th

LADY'S SECRET
1985 Distaff 2nd
1986 Distaff 1st

LASHKARI (GB)
1984 Turf 1st
1985 Turf 4th

LEMON DROP KID
1998 Juvenile 5th
1999 Classic 6th
2000 Classic 5th

LIFE'S MAGIC
1984 Distaff 2nd
1985 Distaff 1st

LIT DE JUSTICE
1995 Sprint 3rd
1996 Sprint 1st

LITE LIGHT
1990 Juvenile Fillies 12th
1992 Classic 6th

LIVELY ONE
1988 Classic 8th
1990 Classic 4th

LURE
1992 Mile 1st
1993 Mile 1st
1994 Mile 9th

MACHO UNO
2000 Juvenile 1st
2001 Classic 4th
2002 Classic 5th

MAGELLAN
1997 Mile 6th
1998 Mile 4th

MAGICAL MAIDEN
1992 Distaff 3rd
1993 Distaff 7th

MARQUETRY
1991 Classic 7th
1992 Classic 11th
1993 Classic 4th

MEADOW STAR
1990 Juvenile Fillies 1st
1992 Distaff 7th

MEAFARA
1992 Sprint 2nd
1993 Sprint 2nd

MEDAGLIA D'ORO
2002 Classic 2nd
2003 Classic 2nd

MEGAHERTZ (GB)
2003 F & M Turf 5th
2004 F & M Turf 11th

MI SELECTO
1989 Classic 8th
1990 Classic 9th

MIDAS EYES
2003 Sprint 8th
2004 Sprint 10th

MIESQUE
1987 Mile 1st
1988 Mile 1st

MIGHTY FORUM (GB)
1995 Mile 9th
1996 Mile 13th

MILESIUS
1988 Turf 5th
1989 Turf 10th

MINISTER'S MELODY
1996 Juvenile Fillies 4th
1997 Distaff 5th

MOGAMBO
1985 Juvenile 6th
1986 Classic 9th

MR. NICKERSON
1989 Sprint 12th
1990 Sprint dnf

MUSIC MERCI
1988 Juvenile 4th
1993 Sprint 6th

MUSICAL CHIMES
2003 F & M Turf 11th
2004 Mile 4th

MUTAMAM (GB)
2000 Turf 4th
2001 Turf 11th

MY FLAG
1995 Juvenile Fillies 1st
1996 Distaff 4th

NOSTALGIA'S STAR
1986 Classic 4th
1987 Classic 7th

NOVERRE
2000 Juvenile 11th
2001 Mile 7th

OLYMPIC PROSPECT
1988 Sprint 7th
1989 Sprint 4th

ON THE LINE
1987 Sprint 10th
1989 Sprint dnf

OPEN MIND
1988 Juvenile Fillies 1st
1989 Distaff 3rd

OPENING VERSE
1990 Classic 7th
1991 Mile 1st

ORIENTATE
2001 Classic 12th
2002 Sprint 1st

OUTSTANDINGLY
1984 Juvenile Fillies 1st
1986 Distaff 3rd

PALACE MUSIC
1985 Mile 9th
1986 Mile 2nd

PARADISE CREEK
1992 Mile 2nd
1993 Mile 8th
1994 Turf 3rd

PASEANA (Arg)
1992 Distaff 1st
1993 Distaff 2nd

PERFECT DRIFT
2002 Classic 12th
2003 Classic 6th
2004 Classic 4th

PERFECT SOUL (IRE)
2002 Turf 8th
2003 Mile 9th

PERFECT STING
1999 F&M Turf 6th
2000 F&M Turf 1st

PERSIAN TIARA (Ire)
1984 Turf 7th
1985 Turf 13th

PINE TREE LANE
1986 Sprint 2nd
1987 Sprint 11th

PLEASANT TAP
1989 Juvenile 6th
1990 Turf 8th
1991 Sprint 2nd
1992 Classic 2nd

PLEASANTLY PERFECT
2003 Classic 1st
2004 Classic 3rd

PRECISIONIST
1984 Classic 7th
1985 Sprint 1st
1986 Classic 3rd
1988 Sprint 5th

PRIOLO
1990 Mile 3rd
1991 Mile 5th

PRIVATE TREASURE
1990 Juvenile Fillies 2nd
1991 Distaff 11th

QUEST FOR FAME (GB)
1991 Turf 3rd
1992 Turf 3rd

QUIET RESOLVE
1999 Mile 14th
2000 Turf 2nd
2001 Turf 10th

RHYTHM
1989 Juvenile 1st
1990 Classic 8th

RICHTER SCALE
1997 Sprint 13th
1998 Sprint 12th

RISKAVERSE
2002 F & M Turf 7th
2003 F & M Turf 6th
2004 F & M Turf 8th

ROBYN DANCER
1989 Juvenile 9th
1991 Sprint 3rd

ROYAL ANTHEM
1998 Turf 7th
1999 Turf 2nd

SACAHUISTA
1986 Juvenile Fillies 4th
1987 Distaff 1st

SAFELY KEPT
1989 Sprint 2nd
1990 Sprint 1st

SAVINIO
1995 Mile 5th
1997 Classic 5th

SAYYEDATI (GB)
1993 Sprint 12th
1995 Mile 3rd

SENOR SPEEDY
1990 Sprint 9th
1991 Sprint 4th
1992 Sprint 8th

SERENA'S SONG
1994 Juvenile Fillies 2nd
1995 Distaff 5th
1996 Distaff 2nd

SHARP CAT
1996 Juvenile Fillies 9th
1997 Distaff 2nd

SHEIKH ALBADOU (GB)
1991 Sprint 1st
1992 Sprint 4th

SHOT GUN SCOTT
1989 Juvenile 4th
1990 Mile 11th

SILVERBULLETDAY
1998 Juvenile Fillies 1st
1999 Distaff 6th

SIMPLY MAJESTIC
1988 Mile 3rd
1989 Mile 5th

SIX PERFECTIONS (FR)
2003 Mile 1st
2004 Mile 3rd

SKI PARADISE
1993 Mile 2nd
1994 Mile 10th

SKIP AWAY
1997 Classic 1st
1998 Classic 6th

SKY BEAUTY
1993 Distaff 5th
1994 Distaff 9th

SKY CLASSIC
1990 Turf 11th
1991 Turf 4th
1992 Turf 2nd

SKYWALKER
1986 Classic 1st
1987 Classic 12th

SLEW CITY SLEW
1988 Classic 9th
1989 Classic 6th

SMILE
1985 Sprint 2nd
1986 Sprint 1st

SOARING FREE
2003 Mile 5th
2004 Mile 4th

SOCIETY SELECTION
2003 Juvenile Fillies 10th
2004 Distaff 9th

SOLAR SPLENDOR
1992 Turf dnf
1993 Turf 14th

SONIC LADY
1986 Mile 7th
1987 Mile 3rd

SOUL OF THE MATTER
1994 Classic 4th
1995 Classic 4th

SOVIET LINE (Ire)
1995 Mile 6th
1997 Mile 7th

SPAIN
1999 Juvenile Fillies 4th
2000 Distaff 1st
2001 Distaff 2nd

SPECIAL RING
2003 Mile 8th
2004 Mile 13th

SPINNING WORLD
1996 Mile 2nd
1997 Mile 1st

STARINE (FR)
2001 F & M Turf 10th
2002 F & M Turf 1st

STARRER
2001 Distaff 5th
2002 Distaff 4th

STEINLEN (GB)
1988 Mile 2nd
1989 Mile 1st
1990 Mile 4th

STORM FLAG FLYING
2002 Juvenile Fillies 1st
2004 Distaff 2nd

STRAWBERRY ROAD (Aus)
1984 Turf 4th
1985 Turf 2nd

STRIKE THE GOLD
1991 Classic 5th
1992 Classic 8th

SUCCESSFUL APPEAL
1999 Sprint 5th
2000 Sprint 7th

SULTRY SONG
1991 Mile 14th
1992 Classic 5th

SUNSHINE FOREVER
1988 Turf 2nd
1989 Turf 14th

SUPAH GEM
1992 Juvenile Fillies 4th
1993 Distaff 6th

SURFSIDE
1999 Juvenile Fillies 3rd
2000 Distaff 2nd

SWAIN (Ire)
1996 Turf 3rd
1998 Classic 3rd

SWEPT OVERBOARD
2001 Sprint 4th
2002 Sprint 8th

SYLVAN EXPRESS (Ire)
1987 Sprint 8th
1988 Sprint 8th

TABASCO CAT
1993 Juvenile 3rd
1994 Classic 2nd

TAIKI BLIZZARD
1996 Classic 13th
1997 Classic 6th

TAKE CHARGE LADY
2001 Juvenile Fillies 6th
2002 Distaff 6th
2003 Distaff 6th

TAKE ME OUT
1990 Juvenile 2nd
1991 Sprint 7th

TALLOIRES
1995 Turf 13th
1996 Turf 6th

TAP TO MUSIC
1998 Distaff 5th
1999 Distaff 5th

TAYLOR'S SPECIAL
1986 Sprint 5th
1987 Sprint 6th

THEATRICAL (Ire)
1985 Turf 11th
1986 Turf 2nd
1987 Turf 1st

THIRTY SLEWS
1992 Sprint 1st
1993 Sprint 4th

THE TIN MAN
2002 Turf 4th
2003 Turf 4th

TIZNOW
2000 Classic 1st
2001 Classic 1st

TOCCET
2002 Juvenile 9th
2003 Turf 8th

TOUCH GOLD
1997 Classic 9th
1998 Classic 8th

TOUCH OF THE BLUES (FR)
2002 Mile 10th
2003 Mile 2nd

TRACK BARRON
1984 Classic 4th
1985 Classic 5th

TRACK GAL
1995 Sprint 11th
1997 Sprint 10th

TRANQUILITY LAKE
2000 F&M T 8th
2001 Distaff 9th

TRIPTYCH
1986 Classic 6th
1988 Turf 4th

TSUNAMI SLEW
1984 Mile 5th
1985 Mile 5th

TURKOMAN
1985 Classic 3rd
1986 Classic 2nd

TWILIGHT AGENDA
1991 Classic 2nd
1992 Classic 9th

TWILIGHT RIDGE
1985 Juvenile Fillies 1st
1986 Distaff 6th

TWO ITEM LIMIT
2001 Distaff 3rd
2002 Distaff 7th

UNBRIDLED
1990 Classic 1st
1991 Classic 3rd

VAL DES BOIS
1991 Mile 2nd
1992 Mile 4th

VAL'S PRINCE
1997 Turf 8th
1999 Turf 11th

VERSAILLES TREATY
1991 Distaff 2nd
1992 Distaff 2nd

VERY SUBTLE
1987 Sprint 1st
1988 Sprint 4th

VOLOCHINE
1994 Turf 9th
1996 Mile 8th

VOLPONI
2002 Classic 1st
2003 Classic 10th

WHO'S FOR DINNER
1984 Turf 9th
1985 Turf 9th

WILDERNESS SONG
1990 Juvenile Fillies 8th
1991 Distaff 7th

WITH ANTICIPATION
2001 Turf 7th
2002 Turf 2nd

WINNING COLORS
1988 Distaff 2nd
1989 Distaff 9th

YAGLI
1998 Turf 3rd
1999 Turf 4th

XTRA HEAT
2000 Juvenile Fillies 10th
2001 Sprint 2nd
2002 Sprint 6th

ZAVATA
2002 Juvenile dnf
2003 Sprint 12th

Dams With Multiple Starters in the Breeders' Cup

Baby Grace (Arg)
King Ruckus (1994 Sprint 12th)
Repent (2001 Juvenile 2nd)
Baby Zip
City Zip (2000 Juvenile 7th)
City Zip (2001 Mile 9th)
Ghostzapper (2004 Classic 1st)
Barbs Compact
Green Barb (1989 Turf 8th)
Tsunami Slew (1984 Mile 5th)
Tsunami Slew (1985 Mile 5th)
Beaming Bride
Alwuhush (1990 Turf 4th)
Simply Majestic (1988 Mile 3rd)
Simply Majestic (1989 Mile 5th)
Beware of the Cat
Editor's Note (1995 Juvenile 3rd)
Editor's Note (1996 Classic 12th)
Hold That Tiger (2002 Juvenile 3rd)
Hold That Tiger (2003 Classic 5th)
Blitey
Dancing Spree (1989 Sprint 1st)
Dancing Spree (1990 Sprint 6th)
Furlough (1998 Sprint 10th)
Furlough (1999 Sprint 10th)
Bold Captive
Pac Mania (1984 Sprint 9th)
Skywalker (1986 Classic 1st)
Skywalker (1987 Classic 12th)
Brocade
Barathea (Ire) (1993 Mile 5th)
Barathea (Ire) (1994 Mile 1st)
Gossamer (GB) (2002 F&M T 5th)
Bunting
Mot Juste (GB) (2001 F&M T 12th)
Vision and Verse (1999 Classic 9th)
Vision and Verse (2000 Classic 8th)
Cadeaux d'Amie
Hatoof (1993 Turf 5th)
Hatoof (1994 Turf 2nd)
Irish Prize (2001 Mile 4th)
Cee's Song
Budroyale (1999 Classic 2nd)
Tiznow (2000 Classic 1st)
Tiznow (2001 Classic 1st)
Cheyenne Birdsong
Creston (1993 Juvenile 11th)
Shywing (1986 Distaff 2nd)
Chimes of Freedom
Aldebaran (2002 Mile 11th)
Aldebaran (2003 Sprint 6th)
Good Journey (2002 Mile 3rd)
Clever Miss
Integra (1988 Distaff 9th)
Secret Odds (1992 Juvenile 10th)
Coup de Folie
Coup de Genie (1993 Juv. Fil. 4th)
Exit to Nowhere (1992 Mile 8th)
Crimson Saint
Pancho Villa (1985 Sprint 5th)
Royal Academy (1990 Mile 1st)
Crystal Cup
First Magnitude (Ire) (1999 Turf 14th)
Iktamal (1996 Sprint 6th)
Dahlia
Dahar (1986 Turf 5th)
Dahlia's Dreamer (1994 Turf 12th)
Rivlia (1987 Turf 9th)
Dance Number
Offbeat (1991 Juvenile 4th)
Rhythm (1989 Juvenile 1st)
Rhythm (1990 Classic 8th)
Dancing Tribute
Gold Tribute (1996 Juvenile 6th)
Souvenir Copy (1997 Juvenile 4th)
Danseur Fabuleux
Arazi (1991 Juvenile 1st)
Arazi (1992 Mile 11th)
Noverre (2000 Juvenile 11th)
Noverre (2001 Mile 7th)
Desirable
Dumaani (1996 Mile 12th)
Shadayid (1991 Mile 7th)
Excellent Lady
General Challenge (1999 Classic 10th)
Notable Career (2000 Juv. Fil. 2nd)
Fineza
Golden Gear (1995 Sprint 9th)
Keeper Hill (1998 Distaff 3rd)
Keeper Hill (1999 Distaff 4th)
Flama Ardiente
Magical Wonder (1986 Mile 8th)
Mt. Livermore (1985 Sprint 3rd)
Gentle Hands
Bertrando (1991 Juvenile 2nd)
Bertrando (1993 Classic 2nd)
Bertrando (1994 Classic 6th)
Jade Trade (1987 Juvenile 12th)
Gioconda
Ciro (2000 Turf 6th)
Good Command (1987 Classic 6th)
Graceful Gal
Duluth (1987 Mile 14th)
Real Courage (1985 Juvenile dnf)
Grecian Banner
Personal Ensign (1988 Distaff 1st)
Personal Flag (1988 Classic 6th)
Harbor Springs
Bay Harbor (1997 Juv. Fil. 14th)
Boston Harbor (1996 Juvenile 1st)
Hasili (IRE)
Banks Hill (GB) (2001 F & M Turf 1st)
Banks Hill (GB) (2002 F & M Turf 2nd)
Dansili (GB) (2000 Mile 3rd)
Heat Haze (GB) (2003 F & M Turf 4th)
Hattab Gal
Exetera (1995 Juvenile 2nd)
On Target (1994 Juvenile 4th)

Homewrecker
Honor the Hero (1994 Sprint 7th)
Prenup (1994 Sprint 13th)
Honor an Offer
Sardula (1993 Juv. Fil. 2nd)
Imperial Gesture (2001 Juv. Fil. 2nd)
Imperial Gesture (2002 Distaff 3rd)
Hope (Ire)
Oasis Dream (GB) (2003 Mile 10th)
Zenda (GB) (2003 F & M Turf 8th)
Hunt's Lark
Dove Hunt (1995 Mile 4th)
Lieutenant's Lark (1986 Mile 9th)
In Neon
Royal Anthem (1998 Turf 7th)
Royal Anthem (1999 Turf 2nd)
Sharp Cat (1996 Juv. Fil. 9th)
Sharp Cat (1997 Distaff 2nd)
Star Recruit (1991 Juvenile 9th)
Island Kitty
Hennessy (1995 Juvenile 2nd)
Shy Tom 1990 Turf 10th)
Iza Valentine
Earl's Valentine (1985 Juv. Fil. 10th)
Fran's Valentine (1984 Juv. Fil. 10th)
Fran's Valentine (1985 Distaff 5th)
Fran's Valentine (1986 Distaff 2nd)
Jealous Appeal
Appealing Skier (1995 Juvenile 12th)
Appealing Skier (1996 Sprint 10th)
Jealous Forum (2001 Juv. Fil. 8th)
Trippi (2000 Sprint 9th)
Kamar
Gorgeous1989 Distaff 2nd)
Key to the Moon (1985 Sprint 10th)
La Chaposa (Per)
Chaposa Springs (1996 Mile 14th)
You and I (1995 Sprint 10th)
Louisville
Le Belvedere (1987 Mile 9th)
Louis Le Grand (1987 Turf 5th)
Love From Mom
Fight for Love (1992 Juvenile 11th)
Love That Jazz (1996 Juv. Fil. 2nd)
Navajo Princess
Dancing Brave (1986 Turf 4th)
Jolypha (1992 Classic 3rd)
Never Knock
Go For Gin (1994 Classic 8th)
Pleasant Tap (1989 Juvenile 6th)
Pleasant Tap (1990 Turf 8th)
Pleasant Tap (1991 Sprint 2nd)
Pleasant Tap (1992 Classic 2nd)
Nice Assay
A. P. Assay (1998 Sprint 5th)
Came Home (2001 Juvenile 7th)
Came Home (2002 Classic 10th)
No Class
Regal Classic (1987 Juvenile 2nd)
Sky Classic (1990 Turf 11th)
Sky Classic (1991 Turf 4th)
Sky Classic (1992 Turf 2nd)
North of Eden
Forbidden Apple (2000 Mile 7th)
Forbidden Apple (2001 Mile 2nd)
Forbidden Apple (2002 Mile 4th)
Paradise Creek (1992 Mile 2nd)
Paradise Creek (1993 Mile 8th)
Paradise Creek (1994 Turf 3rd)
Wild Event (1997 Mile 9th)
Nuryette
Northern Afleet (1997 Sprint 2nd)
Tap to Music (1998 Distaff 5th)
Tap to Music (1999 Distaff 5th)
Party Cited
Composure (2002 Juv. Fil. 2nd)
Scandinavia (2004 Juvenile 8th)
Passing Mood
Touch Gold (1997 Classic 9th)
Touch Gold (1998 Classic 8th)
With Approval (1990 Turf 2nd)
Personal Ensign (1988 Distaff 1st)
Miner's Mark (1993 Classic 12th)
My Flag (1995 Juv. Fil. 1st)
My Flag (1996 Distaff 4th)
Our Emblem (1995 Sprint 6th)
Primal Force
Awesome Again (1998 Classic 1st)
Macho Uno (2000 Juvenile 1st)
Macho Uno (2001 Classic 4th)
Macho Uno (2002 Classic 5th)
Primarily
Primaly (1997 Juv. Fil. 3rd)
Whiskey Wisdom (1997 Classic 4th)
Pure Profit
Educated Risk (1992 Juv. Fil. 2nd)
Hidden Reserve 1996 Juv. Fil. 2nd)
Inside Information (1995 Distaff 1st)
Purify
Radu Cool (1997 Distaff 4th)
Chaste (2001 F&M Turf 9th)
Raska
Green Fee (2002 Mile 5th)
Posse (2003 Sprint 4th)
Soul Dream
Dream Well (Fr) (1999 Turf 5th)
Sulamani (Ire) (2003 Turf 5th)
Remote Ruler
Close In (1987 Juv. Fil. 4th)
Mama Mucci (1994 Juv. Fil. 7th)
Repetitious (Ire)
Sarhoob (1988 Turf 8th)
Indian Lodge (Ire) (2000 Mile 13th)
Resolver
Adjudicating (1989 Juvenile 11th)
Adjudicating (1990 Sprint 4th)
Dispute (1993 Distaff 4th)
Rowdy Angel
Demon's Begone (1986 Juvenile 6th)
Pine Bluff (1991 Juvenile 7th)
Safely Home
Partner's Hero (1998 Sprint 8th)
Safely Kept (1989 Sprint 2nd)
Safely Kept (1990 Sprint 1st)

Shared Interest
Cash Run (1999 Juv. Fil. 1st)
Forestry (1999 Sprint 4th)
Sharp Kitty
Family Style (1985 Juv. Fil. 2nd)
Lost Kitty (1987 Juv. Fil. 10th)
Shy Spirit
Izvestia (1990 Classic 6th)
Key Spirit (1991 Sprint 11th)
Silvery Swan
El Corredor (2001 Sprint 12th)
Roman Ruler (2004 Juvenile 5th)
Six Crowns
Chief's Crown (1984 Juvenile 1st)
Chief's Crown (1985 Classic 4th)
Classic Crown (1987 Juv. Fil. 6th)
Classic Crown (1988 Distaff 5th)
Slightly Dangerous
Dushyantor (1996 Turf 7th)
Dushyantor (1998 Turf 3rd)
Warning (GB) (1988 Mile 11th)
Stark Winter
Bien Bien (1993 Turf 2nd)
Dr. Schwartzman (1985 Mile 4th)
Sultry Sun
Solar Splendor (1992 Turf dnf)
Solar Splendor (1993 Turf 14th)
Sultry Song (1991 Mile 14th)
Sultry Song (1992 Classic 5th)
Surgery
Sewickley (1989 Sprint 5th)
Shared Interest (1992 Distaff 11th)
The Brig
He's a Saros (1987 Classic 8th)
Saros Brig (1986 Juv. Fil. 3rd)
Ticket to Houston
Mambo Train (2003 Juvenile 11th)
Runway Model (2004 Juv. Fil. 3rd)
To the Hunt
Starrer (2001 Distaff 5th)
Starrer (2002 Distaff 4th)
Stellar Jayne (2004 Distaff 3rd)
Toussaud (1993 Mile 4th)
Chester House (1999 Classic 4th)
Decarchy ((2003 Mile 12th)
Honest Lady (2000 Sprint 2nd)
Tree of Knowledge
Taiki Blizzard (1996 Classic 13th)
Taiki Blizzard (1997 Classic 6th)
Theatrical (Ire) (1985 Turf 11th)
Theatrical (Ire) (1986 Turf 2nd)
Theatrical (Ire) (1987 Turf 1st)
Trestle
Classy Cathy (1986 Distaff 4th)
Ms. Margi (1987 Distaff 5th)
Turk O Witz
Mr Purple (1994 Juvenile 8th)
Queens Court Queen (1991 Juv. Fil. 13th)
Viviana
Sightseek (2003 Distaff 4th)
Tates Creek (2003 F & M Turf 8th)
Weekend Surprise
A.P. Indy (1992 Classic 1st)
Summer Squall (1991 Classic 9th)
Whakilyric
Hernando (FR) (1993 Turf 10th)
Hernando (FR) (1994 Turf 6th)
Hernando (FR) (1995 Turf 5th)
Johann Quatz (Fr) (1993 Mile 7th)
Johann Quatz (Fr) (1994 Mile 2nd)
White Jasmine
Cinch (1994 Juvenile 7th)
Til Forbid (1991 Distaff 9th)
Willamae
Willa on the Move (1988 Distaff 8th)
Will's Way (1996 Classic 7th)
Zippy Do
Some Romance (1988 Juv. Fil. 6th)
Vilzak (1987 Turf 4th)

HORSES

First horse to win two Breeders' Cup races, **Miesque** – 1987 Mile and 1988 Mile

Other two-time Breeders' Cup race winners
Bayakoa – 1989 Distaff and 1990 Distaff
Da Hoss – 1996 Mile and 1998 Mile
High Chaparral – 2002 Turf and 2003 Turf (dh)
Lure – 1992 Mile and 1993 Mile
Tiznow – 2000 Classic and 2001 Classic

First dead-heat for win in a Breeders' Cup race
High Chaparral and Johar, 2003 Turf

Margin of victory
Inside Information holds the mark for the largest margin of victory in any Breeders' Cup race with a 13 1/2-length triumph in the 1995 Distaff at Belmont.

Unbeaten Breeders' Cup winners
Halfbridled, winner of the Juvenile Fillies in 2003, was the ninth horse to remain undefeated after winning a Breeders' Cup race. The others were **Personal Ensign** ('88 Distaff), **Meadow Star** ('90 Juvenile Fillies), **Gilded Time** ('92 Juvenile), **Flanders** ('94 Juvenile Fillies), **Favorite Trick** ('97 Juvenile) and **Johannesburg** ('01 Juvenile), **Storm Flag Flying** ('02 Juvenile Fillies) and **Vindication** ('02 Juvenile).

Multiple Breeders' Cup starts by one horse
Kona Gold became the first horse to start in a Breeders' Cup race five times when he finished fourth in the 2002 Sprint in his fifth consecutive try at the race. Four other horses – **Affirmed Success, El Senor, Pleasant Tap**, and **Precisionist** – have each made four Breeders' Cup appearances.

Performance of Favorites
Through 2004, post-time betting favorites won 57 of 153 Breeders' Cup races, a 37.3 percent rate.There have been 38 odds-on choices with 17 winners.

Ghostzapper, who won the BC Classic as the 2.50-1 favorite, was the first favorite to win the Classic since 1997, and only the sixth favorite to win the event in 21 years.

Winning Post Positions through 2004.
Post 1 – 15 Winners
Post 2 – 18 Winners
Post 3 – 13 Winners
Post 4 – 17 Winners
Post 5 – 19 Winners
Post 6 – 12 Winners
Post 7 – 5 Winners
Post 8 – 12 Winners
Post 9 – 9 Winners
Post 10 – 8 Winners
Post 11 – 9 Winners
Post 12 – 10 Winners
Post 13 – 2 Winners
Post 14 – 5 Winners

European performances in the Breeders' Cup
In 2004, **Wilko** became the third previously foreign-based colt to win the Breeders' Cup Juvenile. **Arazi** (1991) and **Johannesburg** (2001) were the other two.

In 2004, **Ouija Board** gave Europe its third victory in six runnings of the Filly and Mare Turf. The other winners: **Banks Hill** (2001) and **Islington** (2003).

TRAINERS

In 2004, **Robert Frankel** moved into second place by money won, with an overall Breeders' Cup record of 63-3-8-7 and earnings of $9,679,820. Breeders' Cup Classic winner Ghostzapper was the biggest earner among Frankel's six 2004 starters.

Trainer **D. Wayne Lukas**, the only trainer to saddle at least one starter at every Breeders' Cup, holds the record for in-the-money finishes in one Breeders' Cup race having swept the 1-2-3 finishing positions in the 1988 Juvenile Fillies with Open Mind, Darby Shuffle, and Lea Lucinda. . .Lukas has won the Juvenile Fillies four times, a record for trainers in a single Breeders' Cup race.

Orientate's victory in the 2002 Sprint also gave Lukas a record 17th Breeders' Cup victory. He also leads all trainers with number of starts and money won. Through 2004, Lukas's record is 143-17-20-15 for total earnings of $19,033,900.

Oldest winning Breeders' Cup trainer
P.G. Johnson, at age 77, became the oldest winning trainer of a Breeders' Cup race when Volponi won the 2002 Classic. Whittingham was 76 years old when Sunday Silence won the 1989 Classic.

Youngest winning Breeders' Cup trainer
Craig Dollase, 27, trained **Reraise**, winner of the 1998 Breeders' Cup Sprint.

First woman to train a Breeders' Cup winner
Jenine Sahadi trained Lit de Justice winner of the 1996 Sprint

JOCKEYS

Mike Smith, who did not have a mount at the 2004 Breeders' Cup, has won 10 of 52 starts for a winning percentage of 19.2 percent, highest among jockeys with at least five wins.

Pat Day is the only jockey to have appeared in Breeders' Cup races all 21 years. In 2004, Day's record number of Breeders' Cup mounts increased to 117. Day's career BC mounts have earned a BC record, $23,033,360, almost than $4 million more than **Jerry Bailey**, who moved into second place on the jockey's list in 2004. **Chris McCarron**, who retired in July 2002, is third in career earnings.

Jerry Bailey, who had won a Breeders' Cup race in six consecutive years through 2003, failed to win one in 2004 but finished second or third in five of the six events in which he rode.

Youngest winning jockey
Walter Guerra, 22, rode Outstandingly, winner of the 1984 Juvenile Fillies.

Oldest winning jockey
Bill Shoemaker, 56, rode Ferdinand, winner of the 1987 Breeders' Cup Classic.

BREEDERS and OWNERS

Frank Stronach/Adena Springs bred a Breeders' Cup Classic winner from a homebred Classic winner when Ghostzapper, a son of 1998 Classic winner Awesome Again, won the 2004 event. Awesome Again had another 2004 Breeders' Cup winner with Wilko, winner of the Juvenile.

Breeders' Cup winners that sired Breeders' Cup winners.
A.P. Indy won 1992 Classic; sired Tempera , 2001 Juvenile Fillies.
Awesome Again won 1998 Classic; sired Ghostzapper, 2004 Classic; Wilko, 2004 Juvenile.
Capote won 1986 Juvenile; sired Boston Harbor, 1996 Juvenile.
Chief's Crown won 1984 Juvenile; sired Chief Bearhart,1997 Turf.
Cozzene won 1985 Mile; sired Tikkanen,1994 Turf and Alphabet Soup, 1996 Classic.

Royal Academy won 1990 Mile; sired Val Royal, 2001 Mile.
Unbridled won 1990 Classic; sired Unbridled's Song,1995 Juvenile, Anees,1999 Juvenile and Halfbridled, 2003 Juvenile Fillies.
Unbridled's Song won 1995 Juvenile; sired Unbridled Elaine, 2001 Distaff.
Wild Again won 1984 Classic; sired Elmhurst, 1997 Sprint.

Breeders' Cup winners that produced Breeders' Cup winners
Hollywood Wildcat won 1993 Distaff; produced War Chant 2000 Mile.
Personal Ensign won 1988 Distaff; produced My Flag 1995 Juvenile Fillies.
My Flag won 1995 Juvenile Fillies; produced Storm Flag Flying, 2002 Juvenile Fillies.

Dams that produced multiple Breeders' Cup winners
Primal Force produced Awesome Again, winner of 1998 Classic, and Macho Uno, winner of 2000 Juvenile.
Storm Flag Flying completed a third generation Breeders' Cup triple with her victory in the Juvenile Fillies. Her dam, **My Flag**, won the 1995 Juvenile Fillies at Belmont Park. My Flag's dam, **Personal Ensign**, won the 1988 Distaff at Churchill Downs. With her victory, Storm Flag Flying joined Unbridled Elaine as the second horse to complete a third generation Breeders' Cup triple. Unbridled Elaine's sire, Unbridled's Song, won the 1995 Juvenile. Unbridled, the sire of Unbridled's Song, won the 1990 Breeders' Cup Classic.

RECORD PARIMUTUEL WIN PAYOUTS

Lowest winning payout, **Meadow Star**, $2.40, winner of the 1990 Juvenile Fillies.
Highest winning payout, **Arcangues**, $269.20 winner of the 1993 Classic.

2004 BREEDERS CUP WAGERING INFORMATION

$11,274,036 – On-track handle for Breeders' Cup races
$4,566,837 – Total Pick 6 Handle
$627,664 – Head2Head Handle
$107,570,415 – Total Simulcast Handle

IMPORTANT DATES IN BREEDERS' CUP HISTORY

April 23, 1982, John R. Gaines announces plans for multi-race, multimillion-dollar Breeders' Cup Series at the annual Kentucky Derby Festival 'They're Off' awards luncheon in Louisville, Kentucky.

May 3, 1982, Board of Directors named for Breeders' Cup Limited, the non-profit administrative organization for the Breeders' Cup.

July 27, 1982, Breeders' Cup stakes race program outlined as a one-day, seven-race series with purses totaling $13 million. Series to be known as Racing International's Championship Program.

September 2, 1982, After reviewing proposals from eight different racing associations, Breeders' Cup Track Selection Committee chooses Southern California as locale for inaugural Breeders' Cup Championship in 1984.

February 24, 1983, Hollywood Park in Inglewood, California, selected as site for inaugural Breeders' Cup, November 10, 1984.

April 15, 1983, Nomination of 1,083 stallions, representing more than $10.9 million in fees, announced.

June 8, 1983, $10 million Breeders' Cup Premium Awards Program announced, with allocations slated for 90 racing associations in 22 states and five Canadian provinces.

September 13, 1983, NBC Sports and the Breeders' Cup announce an exclusive, multi-year contract to broadcast all seven Breeders' Cup races live to a worldwide audience in a four-hour television special.

January 2, 1984, The split divisions of the La Prevoyante Handicap at Calder Race Course in Florida become the first races to offer Breeders' Cup Premium Awards.

January 4, 1984, Breeders' Cup Ltd. announces a point system based on first-, second-, and third-place finishes in North American Graded Stakes to be used to determine starters in Breeders' Cup races if any of the races are oversubscribed.

January 17, 1984, The graded stakes panel of the Thoroughbred Owners and Breeders Association announces their unprecedented decision to assign Grade I status to all seven Breeders' Cup races.

February 4, 1984, Ollie Cohen's Eillo, eventual winner of the inaugural Breeders' Cup Sprint, named first Breeders' Cup Horse of the Month.

March 6, 1984, Frank E. Kilroe is named chairman of the five-member Racing Directors / Secretaries Panel, which will select starters for the Breeders' Cup races if fields are oversubscribed.

May 8, 1984, Breeders' Cup Limited announces the official names for the seven Breeders' Cup races, with total purses and nominator awards equaling $10 million, the richest single stakes racing day in racing history.

October 22, 1984, Breeders' Cup unveils its permanent trophy, a 1,850 pound bronze and marble reproduction of the Torrie horse, an ecorche or flayed horse designed by the 16th-century sculptor Giambologna.

October 30, 1984, a total of 77 horses are pre-entered for the seven inaugural Breeders' Cup races.

November 5, 1984, Aqueduct Racetrack in New York is named host track for the 1985 Breeders' Cup, with the races scheduled for November 2, 1985.

November 10, 1984, The inaugural Breeders' Cup is run before 64,254 at Hollywood Park. Chief's Crown wins the first Breeders' Cup race, the Breeders' Cup Juvenile and longshot Wild Again wins the Breeders' Cup Classic in a thrilling, controversial stretch duel with Slew o' Gold and Gate Dancer. After a lengthy inquiry in which NBC television cameras bring the key deliberations and video evidence to the viewing audience in unprecedented detail, the stewards disqualify Gate Dancer from second for interfering with Slew o' Gold in the final furlong.

STATES AND COUNTRIES WHICH PRODUCED BREEDERS' CUP CHAMPIONSHIP WINNERS

CALIFORNIA (2)
Tiznow (C, 2000, 2001)

FLORIDA (18)
Beautiful Pleasure (D, 1999) Brave Raj (JF, 1986) Brocco (J, 1993) Cherokee Run (S, 1994) Cozzene (M, 1985)Eillo (S, 1984) Gilded Time (J, 1992) Hollywood Wildcat (D, 1993) Jewel Princess (D, 1996) Meadow Star (JF, 1990) One Dreamer (D, 1994) Precisionist (S, 1985) Prized (T, 1989) Skip Away (C, 1997) Smile (S, 1986) Tasso (J, 1985) Twilight Ridge (JF, 1985) Unbridled (C, 1990)

ILLINOIS (1)
Buck's Boy (T, 1998)

KENTUCKY (93)
Action This Day (J, 2003) Adoration (D, 2003) Ajina (D, 1997) Alysheba (C, 1988) Anees (J, 1999) Answer Lively (J, 1998) A.P. Indy (C, 1992) Arazi (J, 1991) Arcangues (C, 1993) Artax (S, 1999) Ashado (D, 2004) Azeri (D, 2002) Better Talk Now (T, 2004) Boston Harbor (J, 1996) Cajun Beat (S, 2003) Capote (J, 1986) Cardmania (S, 1993) Caressing (JF, 2000) Cash Run (JF, 1999) Cat Thief (C, 1999) Chief's Crown (J, 1984) Countess Diana (JF, 1997) Da Hoss (M, 1996, 1998) Dancing Spree (S, 1989) Desert Stormer (S, 1995) Eliza (JF, 1992) Elmhurst (S, 1997) Epitome (JF, 1987) Escena (D, 1998), Fantastic Light (T, 2001) Favorite Trick (J, 1997) Ferdinand (C, 1987) Flanders (JF, 1994) Fly So Free (J, 1990) Fraise (T, 1992) Ghostzapper (C, 2004) Great Communicator (T, 1988) Gulch (S, 1988) Halfbridled (JF, 2003) Inside Information (D, 1995)Is It True (J, 1988) Johannesburg (J, 2001) Johar (T, 2003) Kona Gold (S, 2000) Life's Magic (D, 1985) Lit de Justice (S, 1996) Lure (M, 1992) Lure (M, 1993) Macho Uno (J, 2000) Manila (T, 1986) Miesque (M, 1987) Miesque (M, 1988) Miss Alleged (T, 1991) My Flag (JF, 1995) Opening Verse (M, 1991) Orientate (S, 2002) Outstandingly (JF, 1984) Perfect Sting (FMT, 2000) Personal Ensign (D, 1988) Phone Chatter (JF, 1993) Pleasant Stage (JF, 1991) Pleasantly Perfect (C, 2003) Princess Rooney (D, 1984) Proud Truth (C, 1985) Royal Academy (M, 1990) Rhythm (J, 1989) Sacahuista (D, 1987) Silverbulletday (JF, 1998) Singletary (M, 2004) Skywalker (C, 1986) Soaring Softly (FMT, 1999) Spain (D, 2000) Speightstown (S, 2004) Squirtle Squirt (S, 2001) Storm Flag Flying (JF, 2002) Storm Song (JF, 1996) Success Express (J, 1987) Sunday Silence (C, 1989) Sweet Catomine (JF, 2004) Tempera (JF, 2001) Thirty Slews (S, 1992) Timber Country (J, 1994) Unbridled Elaine (D, 2001) Unbridled's Song (J, 1995) Very Subtle (S, 1987) Vindication (J, 2002) Volponi (C, 2002) War Chant (M, 2000),Wild Again (C, 1984) Wilko (J, 2004)

MARYLAND (3)

Cigar (C, 1995) Concern (C, 1994) Safely Kept (S, 1990)

NEW JERSEY (1)
Open Mind (JF, 1988)

OKLAHOMA (1)
Lady's Secret (D, 1986)

PENNSYLVANIA (3)
Alphabet Soup (C, 1996) Go for Wand (JF, 1989) Tikkanen (T, 1994)

CANADA (3)
Awesome Again (C, 1998)Chief Bearhart (T, 1997) Dance Smartly (D, 1991)

ARGENTINA (3)
Bayakoa (ARG) (D, 1989) Bayakoa (ARG) (D, 1990) Paseana (ARG) (D, 1992)

FRANCE (5)
Kotashaan (T, 1993) Silic (M, 1999) Six Perfections (M, 2003) Starine (FMT, 2002) Val Royal (M, 2001)

GREAT BRITAIN (8)
Banks Hill (FMT, 2001) In the Wings (T, 1990) Lashkari (T, 1984) Ouija Board (FMT, 2004) Pebbles (T, 1985) Ridgewood Pearl (M, 1995), Sheikh Albadou (S, 1991) Steinlen (M, 1989)

IRELAND (12)
Barathea (M, 1994) Black Tie Affair (C, 1991) Daylami (T, 1999) Domedriver (M, 2002), High Chaparral (T, 2002, 2003) Islington (FMT, 2003) Last Tycoon (M, 1986) Kalanisi (T, 2000) Northern Spur (T, 1995) Pilsudski (T, 1996) Royal Heroine (M, 1984) Theatrical (T, 1987)
(C-Classic; D-Distaff; J-Juvenile; JF-Juvenile Fillies; M-Mile; S-Sprint; T-Turf; FMT-Filly/Mare Turf)

Reading Daily Racing Form Past Performances

2 Beckon the King
Own:Ramsey Kenneth L & Sarah K
White, Red R, White Band On Red Sleeves,
BAILEY J D (159 40 31 26 .25) 2004:(908 246 .27)

B. g. 5
Sire: Ghazi (Polish Navy) $5,000
Dam: Our Locket(Mr. Leader)
Br: Ramsey Jill D (Ky)
Tr: Mott William I(91 22 14 19 .24) 2004:(733 155 .21)

Date/Race	Trk	Dist	Surf	Fractions	Race	Beyer	PP	Positions	Jockey
11Feb04-6GP	fm	1$\frac{1}{16}$	Ⓣ	:25^1 :50^3 1:14^2 1:43^1+	4↑ OClm 100000(100-90)	**97**	7	3^1 3$^{1\frac{1}{2}}$ 3^1 3^2 3^1	Bailey J D
4Jly03-9CD	fm	1	Ⓣ	:24^2 :47^2 1:10^4 1:35	3↑ FirecrkrBCH-G2	**89**	8	4$^{2\frac{1}{2}}$ 4^2 4^2 6^6 6^6	St Julien M
28May03-8Bel	gd	7f	Ⓣ	:22^4 :45^3 1:09^3 1:21^3	3↑ Jaipur-G3	**88**	8	7 7$^{6\frac{1}{4}}$ 6$^{6\frac{1}{4}}$ 9^7 8$^{6\frac{3}{4}}$	Bailey J D
6May03-8Aqu	fm	1$\frac{1}{16}$	Ⓣ	:23^2 :47^3 1:10^3 1:40^4	3↑ Ft Marcy H-G3	**89**	6	3^4 3^1 4^2 6$^{6\frac{1}{2}}$ 8^9	Castellano J J
11Mar03-8GP	fm	1$\frac{1}{16}$	Ⓣ	:23^2 :46^4 1:10^2 1:40^1+	3↑ Ft Laudrl H-G3	**101**	2	6$^{3\frac{3}{4}}$ 4$^{1\frac{1}{2}}$ 5$^{1\frac{1}{2}}$ 3$^{\frac{1}{2}}$ 1$^{2\frac{1}{4}}$	Bailey J D
17Feb03-9GP	fst	1$\frac{1}{16}$		:24^2 :49 1:12^2 1:43^1	4↑ Alw 38000N3X	**97**	1	3$^{1\frac{1}{2}}$ 3$^{\frac{1}{2}}$ 1$^{\frac{1}{2}}$ 1^3 1$^{3\frac{1}{2}}$	Bailey J D
28Nov02-7Hol	fm	1⅛	Ⓣ	:46^3 1:10^1 1:33^4 1:45^4	Hol Dby-G1	**71**	10	9^4 6$^{4\frac{1}{2}}$ 6$^{4\frac{1}{2}}$ 12^{11} 12^{18}	Bailey J D
Previously trained by Weld Dermot K									
7Nov02-9GP	fm	1	Ⓣ	:22^4 :46^3 1:10^1 1:34	Steinlen200k	**100**	8	8$^{6\frac{1}{2}}$ 8^3 5$^{3\frac{1}{2}}$ 3^1 1$^{1\frac{1}{2}}$	Castellano J J
Claimed from Gold N Z Stable for $100,000, Klesaris Robert P Trainer 2000(as of 7/21):(264 46 35 43 .17)									
29Aug02-6Del	fst	1$\frac{1}{16}$		:23^3 :47^2 1:11^2 1:44	3↑ Alw 33900N2X	**91**	1	3$^{2\frac{1}{2}}$ 4^1 3^1 1$^{\frac{1}{2}}$ 1$^{4\frac{3}{4}}$	Prado E S

WORKS: Feb5 Pay 5f fst 1:05 B *3/5* Jan29 Pay 5f fst 1:04 B *4/16* ●Jan21 Pay 5f fst 1:03 B *1/18* Jan16 Pay 4f fst :52 B *14/24*
TRAINER: Turf(423 .23 $1.61) Alw(324 .25 $1.63)

Owner/Trainer/Jockey: This information appears above the past performances. The record of the jockey at the current meeting and for the current year appears after his/her name. The same information follows the trainer's name. Beckon the King is owned by Kenneth and Sarah Ramsey; a description of the Ramsey stable silks follows their name. He is trained by William Mott and on this day was ridden by Jerry Bailey. Beckon the King has the betting number of 2 in today's race.

Pedigree Information: The top line indicates color, sex and age. The month foaled may follow in parentheses. The second line indicates sire and sire's sire followed by the sire's stud fee where available. The third line indicates the dam and dam's sire. The fourth line indicates the breeder and state bred. Beckon the King is a 6-year-old bay gelding by Ghazi, a son of Polish Navy, out of the Mr. Leader mare Our Locket. He was bred in Kentucky by Jill Ramsey.

Career Box: Indicates lifetime, current year and prior year records and record at track on the left side. Indicates dirt, wet turf and record at the distance on the right side. Beyer Speed Figures following these lines indicate best Beyer on dirt fast tracks (97), turf (101) and today's distance and surface (100). Beckon the King has never run on a wet dirt track, so a dash is displayed. Tomlinson Ratings, measuring a horse's potential to handle turf and muddy/sloppy conditions, are shown in parentheses: 312 for wet tracks, 300 for turf and 312 for today's distance and surface. Previous start statistics always indicate the number of starts, wins, seconds, thirds and earnings; for example, Beckon the King has 17 lifetime starts, of which he has won five, finished second four times and third once, for earnings of $229,400.

Between the pedigree information and the career box is other important information. The large 116 indicates the weight that Beckon the King carries in today's race and the L shows that he is to be treated with furosemide (known commonly as Lasix or Salix). If blinkers were being added or removed, that would be noted above the weight.

Symbols and Abbreviations Used in Past Performances

Colors
B - Bay
Blk - Black
Ch - Chestnut
Dk b or br - Dark Bay or Brown
Gr - Gray
Ro - Roan

Sex
c - colt
f - filly
g - gelding
h - horse
m - mare
r - ridgling

	Life	17	5	4	1	$229,400	101	D.Fst	1	1	0	0	$22,800 97
	2004	1	0	0	1	$5,330	97	Wet(312) 0	0	0	0		$0 –
L 116	2003	5	2	0	0	$82,800	101	Turf(300*) 16	4	4	1		$206,600 101
	GP Ⓣ	3	2	0	1	$185,330	101	DistⓉ(312) 2	1	0	0		$120,000 100

L 118	*2.20	78 – 18	MdivilHro118^{1} IvrsBgPcful120^{no} BckonThKng$118\frac{1}{2}$	3 wide, edged for 2nd	7
L 113	7.20e	94 – 04	Conserve116^{nk} *Riviera*115^{2} King Slayer$115\frac{3}{4}$	Stalked,flattened out	8
L 116	*3.05	85 – 08	Gone Fishin$114^{2\frac{1}{2}}$ Weatherbird$113\frac{3}{4}$ French Envoy113^{nk}	Trapped in traffic	12
L 116 b	*2.15	96 – 01	Spindrift$115^{1\frac{1}{2}}$ Middlesex Drive118^{hd} Wised Up$114^{1\frac{3}{4}}$	Wide trip, tired	9
L 114 b	*2.30	101 – 08	BeckonTheKing$114^{2\frac{1}{4}}$ KettleWon113^{2} Missionry$114^{1\frac{3}{4}}$	Angled out, up late	8
L 117 b	*1.30	92 – 17	*BeckonTheKing*$117^{3\frac{1}{2}}$ KnDoll117^{no} Throwthbooktm$117^{3\frac{3}{4}}$	Strong hand ride	6
LB 122 b	5.50	81 – 07	SuperQuercus122^{2} Mnndr$122^{3\frac{1}{2}}$ FightingFlcon122^{1}	Bobbled start,4–wide	14
L 112 b	19.90	114 – 04	Beckon The King$112^{1\frac{1}{2}}$ *Hap*114^{1} Super Red$116^{1\frac{1}{4}}$	Rallied, up late	11
L 113	*1.00	87 - 13	*BdgrGold*$113^{4\frac{3}{4}}$ *PhblsCd*$118^{1\frac{1}{4}}$ BrklynNck$118^{1\frac{1}{4}}$	3 wide bid, ridden out	8

Jan10 Pay 3f fst :39¹ B *6/16* **●Dec15 Pay 4f fst :50¹ B** *1/9*

Workouts: The latest workouts are printed under each horse's past performances. The *Daily Racing Form* carries up to six works for all horses, with up to 12 for first-time starters. Each workout will include the date, the track or training track where the workout occurred, the distance of the workout, the condition of the track or course, the time of the workout, the manner in which the workout was completed, and a ranking of the workout compared to all others on the same day at the track and distance. A bullet, as seen with Beckon the King's Jan. 21 workout, indicates that this was the best workout of the day at that track and distance. The numbers in italics, such as the 1/18 that follows the Jan. 21 workout, indicate the ranking of the workout; in this example, the five furlongs in 1:03 was the fastest of 18 workouts at this distance.

Trainer Form: Beneath the workouts line are statistics showing the trainer's number of starts, percentage of winners and return on investment (average winnings if a $2 dollar bet were made on each applicable horse) for pertinent race conditions; in this case, Bill Mott's statistics for turf and allowance

Symbols and Abbreviations Used in Past Performances

Dirt Course Conditions
fr - Frozen
fst - Fast
gd - Good
hy - Heavy
my - Muddy
sl - Slow
sly - Sloppy
wf - Wet-Fast

Turf Course Conditions
fm - Firm
gd - Good
hd - Hard
hy - Heavy
sf - Soft
yl - Yielding

Medication
B - Butazolidin
L - Furosemide (Lasix)
L1 - First-time furosemide

Equipment
b - Blinkers
f - Front Bandages
r - Bar Shoes

Margins
hd - Head
nk - Neck
no - Nose

Workouts
B - Breezing
(d) - Worked around dogs
D - Driving
E - Easily
g - Worked from gate
H - Handily
tr.t - Training track

11Feb04- 6GP fm 1 1/16 Ⓣ :25 1 :50 3 1:14 2 1:43 1 + 4↑ OClm 100000 (100-90)

A horse's most recent race always appears first in the past performances, and previous races are shown in reverse chronological order. Observe Beckon the King's last start, shown at the top of his past performances.

Date Race was Run: 11Feb04. This race was run on Feb. 11, 2004.

Race Number, Track: 6GP. This was the sixth race at Gulfstream Park. A complete list of current track abbreviations appears later in this section. A ◆ (diamond symbol) preceding a track name denotes a foreign racetrack.

Track or Course Condition: fm. The course was firm. The Ⓣ symbol indicates the race was run on the turf. A 🅃 symbol indicates the race was run on the inner turf course at a track with more than one turf course.

Distance of Race: 1 1/16. The race was at a mile and a sixteenth (of a mile). Races less than a mile in length are in furlongs; a furlong is one-eighth of a mile. An asterisk (*) before the distance indicates that it was an approximate, or "about," distance.

Fractional Times: :25 1, 50 3, 1:14 2. Three fractional times are given for each race at all distances over 5 furlongs. Races at five furlongs or less only have two fractional times. Fractional times are represented by minutes, seconds and fifths of a second, so 1:14 2 means a time of 1 minute, fourteen seconds and two-fifths of a second. The fractional time is always the time of the leader at a specific point during the running of the race. See the "Points of Call Used for Fractional Times in Past Performances" chart on this page. For example, in this 1 1/16-mile race, the first fraction of :25 1 was after a quarter-mile. Races at foreign tracks do not have internal fractions.

Final Time: 1:43 1. The winning horse stopped the teletimer in 1:43 1. This is always the time of the first horse to cross the finish line, even if the winner is disqualified from first position. The plus sign (+) in this example indicates the race was run out of a chute.

Age conditions: 4↑. This race was for 4-year-olds and upward. If no age condition appears, it means that the race was restricted to horses of a single age.

Type of Race: OClm 100000. This was an optional claiming event, meaning that horses running in it may or may not have been entered to be claimed for a specified price. See the glossary in this section for a detailed discussion of the many types of races.

Class Codes: (100-90). In claiming races, the range of claiming prices is noted. Horses in this race may have been entered to be claimed for $100,000 down to $90,000.

Points of Call Used for Fractional Times in Past Performances

Distance	First Fraction	Second Fraction	Third Fraction	Finish Time
3½f	-	1/4	3/8	finish
4f	-	1/4	3/8	finish
4½f	-	1/4	1/2	finish
5f	-	1/4	1/2	finish
5½f	1/4	1/2	5/8	finish
6f	1/4	1/2	5/8	finish
6½f	1/4	1/2	3/4	finish
7f	1/4	1/2	3/4	finish
7½f	1/4	1/2	3/4	finish
1 mile	1/4	1/2	3/4	finish
1 m70 yds	1/4	1/2	3/4	finish
1 1/16	1/4	1/2	3/4	finish
1⅛	1/2	3/4	mile	finish
1 3/16	1/2	3/4	mile	finish
1¼	1/2	3/4	mile	finish
1⅜	1/2	3/4	mile	finish
1½	1/2	3/4	1 1/4	finish
1⅝	1/2	mile	1 1/4	finish
1¾	1/2	1 1/4	1 1/2	finish
1⅞	1/2	1 1/4	1 1/2	finish
2 miles	1/2	1 1/2	1 3/4	finish
2⅛	1/2	1 1/2	1 3/4	finish

97 7 3¹ 3¹½ 3¹ 3² 3¹ Bailey J D L 118 *2.20

Beyer Speed Figure: 97. Beyer Speed Figures are available exclusively in the *Daily Racing Form.* Every performance by every horse in North America is assigned a number which reflects the time of the race and the inherent speed of the track over which it was run and permits easy comparison of efforts at different distances. A figure of 97 denotes exactly the same quality of performance whether it was earned at Santa Anita or Suffolk Downs.

Post Position: 7. The horse left the starting gate from stall number seven. Post position can differ from the official program number because of late scratches, horses coupled as a betting entry or runners grouped in a mutuel field.

First Call: 3-1. The horse's position at the first call, which, for a 1 1/16-mile race, was a quarter-mile after the start. See the "Points of Call Used for Running Lines in Past Performances" chart on this page. This horse was third, one length behind the leader, after a quarter-mile. The large figure indicates the running position and the smaller figure is the margin behind the leader. If the horse had been in front, the smaller figure would indicate the margin in front of the second horse.

Second Call: 3-1 1/2. The horse was third, a length and a half behind the leader after a half-mile.

Third Call: 3-1. The horse was third, a length behind the leader after three-quarters of a mile.

Stretch Call: 3-2. The horse was third, two lengths behind the leader at the stretch call, which is always one furlong (one-eighth of a mile) from the finish line.

Finish: 3-1. The horse finished third, a length behind the winner.

Jockey: Bailey JD. This horse was ridden by Jerry Bailey. When a small number follows the jockey's name, it indicates the apprentice allowance claimed. Apprentice riders are entitled to weight allowances of 3, 5, 7 or 10 pounds, based on experience and contract rules.

Medication: L. Where rules permit, horses may run on various medications. L indicates that Beckon the King was treated with furosemide.

Weight Carried: 118. The horse carried 118 pounds in this race. This is the weight of the rider and equipment (saddle, lead pads, etc) and includes the apprentice allowance if one is claimed.

Equipment: Beckon the King had no special equipment in this race. In previous races, such as his May 6, 2003, race, he was equipped with blinkers.

Closing Odds: - *2.20. The horse was $2.20 to the dollar. The * symbol preceding the odds indicates that the horse was the betting favorite. The letter "e" following the odds would indicate that the horse was coupled in the betting (an entry) with one or more other horses. The letter "f" in this position would indicate the horse was in the mutuel field.

Points of Call Used for Running Lines in Past Performances

Distance	First Call	Second Call	Third Call	Stretch Call	Finish
3½f	start	1/4	-	str	finish
4f	start	1/4	-	str	finish
4½f	start	1/4	-	str	finish
5f	start	3/16	3/8	str	finish
5½f	start	1/4	3/8	str	finish
6f	start	1/4	1/2	str	finish
6½f	start	1/4	1/2	str	finish
7f	start	1/4	1/2	str	finish
7½f	start	1/4	1/2	str	finish
1 mile	1/4	1/2	3/4	str	finish
1 m70 yds	1/4	1/2	3/4	str	finish
1 1/16	1/4	1/2	3/4	str	finish
1⅛	1/4	1/2	3/4	str	finish
1 3/16	1/4	1/2	3/4	str	finish
1¼	1/4	1/2	mile	str	finish
1⅜	1/4	1/2	mile	str	finish
1½	1/4	1/2	1 1/4	str	finish
1⅝	1/4	1/2	1 3/8	str	finish
1¾	1/2	mile	1 1/2	str	finish
1⅞	1/2	mile	1 5/8	str	finish
2 miles	1/2	mile	1 3/4	str	finish
2⅛	1/2	mile	1 3/4	str	finish

78 - 18 MdivilHro118[1] IvrsBgPcful120[no] BckonThKng118½ 3 wide, edged for 2nd 7

Speed Rating, Track Variant: 78-18. The first number is the speed rating, a comparison of this horse's time with the best time at the distance at that track in the last three years, which is represented by the par value of 100. The second figure, 18, is the track variant which shows how many points below par the times for all races at the distance on the same surface were that day.

First Three Horses at Finish: Medievil Hero 118-1 Ivars Big Peaceful 120-no Beckon the King 118-1/2. The "company line" shows the horses which finished first, second and third in the race, the weight each carried and the margins separating each one from the next horse. Next-out winners - horses that won their next race, such as Riviera, the second-place finisher in Beckon the King's July 4, 2003, race - are italicized in company lines. If any horses from the company lines are entered in today's race, they will be bold-faced.

Comment Line: 3 wide, edged for 2nd. A capsule description of the horse's performance written by the chart caller, with special emphasis on pointing out any trouble encountered.

Number of Starters: 7. There were seven horses in this race.

Other Features

Layoff line: If a significant period of time elapses between races, a layoff line will appear between the two past performance lines. A single line, such as the one between the July 4, 2003, and Feb. 11, 2004, races, indicates a layoff of at least 45 days. A double line would indicate a layoff of a year or more.

Record of "Claimed From" Trainer: If a horse is claimed from another trainer, a note, such as the one beneath the race of Nov. 2, 2002, appears showing the details of the claim and the statistics of the previous trainer.

Previous Trainer: If a horse changes to a new trainer for other reasons, a note, such as the one beneath the race of Nov. 28, 2002, appears.

If a layoff or trainer change has occurred since the last race, the layoff line or trainer change line will appear at the top of the past performances, before the most recent start.

Note: Past performance was altered for illustrative purposes.

Beyer Speed Figures, Speed Rating and Track Variant

Beyer Speed Figures appear exclusively in the *Daily Racing Form*. Every performance by every horse in North America is assigned a Beyer number which reflects the time of the race and the inherent speed of the track over which it was run, permitting easy comparisons of efforts at different distances. A horse who earns a 90 has run faster than one who runs an 80. In this system of numbers, 2 1/2 points are roughly equal to one length in sprints and 2 points to one length in routes.

On the Beyer scale of numbers, the very best stakes horses in the country earn figures in the 120s. Good allowance horses or low-grade stakes horses run around 100. A typical $25,000 claiming race would be run in the low 90s, a $10,000 claiming race in the low to mid 80s. The average winning figure for bottom-level $2,500 claimers at smaller tracks is 57.

Daily Racing Form's Speed Rating and Track Variant provide an "old style" gauge of a horse's speed in a race.

The **Speed Rating** is a comparison of the horse's final time with the best time at the distance at that track in the last three years. The best time is given a rating of 100. One point is deducted for each fifth of a secon by which the horse fails to equal that time. A length is equivalent to a fifth of second. Thus, in a race where the winner equals the best time (a Speed Rating of 100), another horse who is beaten 12 lengths gets a Speed Rating of 88 (100 minus 12).

As a companion to the Speed Rating, *Daily Racing Form*'s **Track Variant** takes into consideration all races run on a particular day under the same conditions of distance and track surface. The Speed Ratings of all winners in each type of race are added together and an average is computed. This average is deducted from the par of 100 and the difference is the Track Variant. (Example: if the average Speed Rating of winners sprinting on the main track is 86, the Track Variant is 14 (par of 100 minus 86). The lower the Track Variant, the faster the track, or the better the overall quality of competition that day.

Conformation of the Horse and Nomenclature of Body Parts

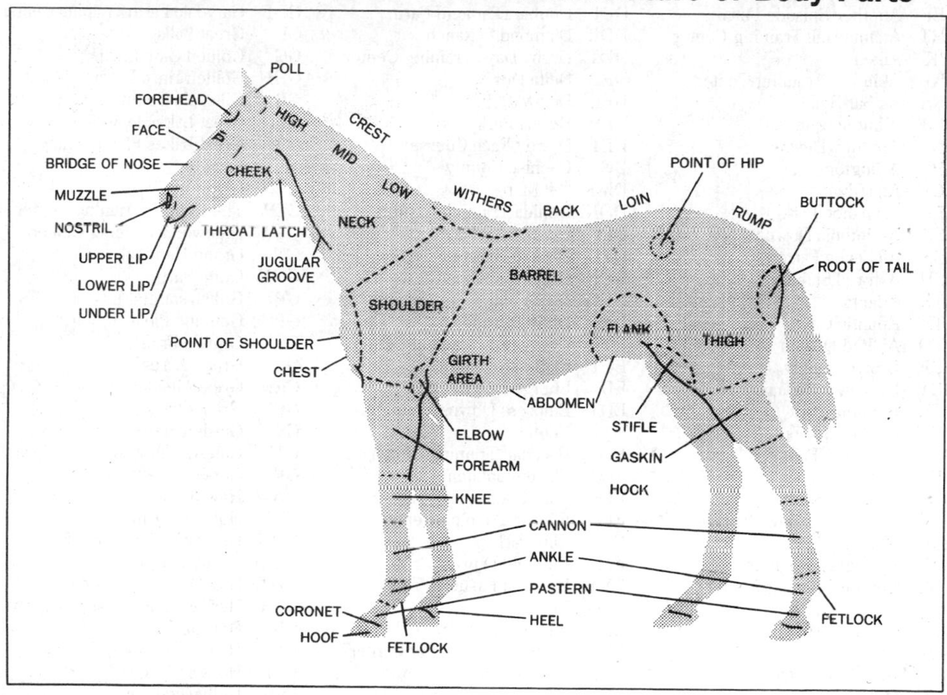

EQUIVALANT VELOCITY RATINGS IN FEET PER SECOND
FOR FRACTIONAL CLOCKINGS and POPULAR RACING DISTANCES

1/4 mile in 23.20 - 56.88 ft. per second
1/2 mile in 46.60 - 56.65 ft. per second
5/8 mile in 58.40 - 56.51 ft. per second
3/4 mile in 1:10.40 - 56.25 ft. per second
7/8 mile in 1:23.80 - 55.13 ft. per second
One mile in 1:37.40 - 54.21 ft. per second
1-1/8 miles 1:50.40 - 53.71 ft. per second
1-1/4 miles 2:04.00 - 53.23 ft. per second
1-1/2 miles 2:29.00 - 53.13 ft. per second

ONE MILE CLOCKINGS AND VELOCITY RATINGS IN FEET PER SECOND.

1:34 - 56.17 ft. per second
1:35 - 55.58 ft. per second
1:36 - 55.00 ft. per second
1:37 - 54.43 ft. per second
1:38 - 53.88 ft. per second
1:39 - 53.33 ft. per second

Abbreviations of Tracks and Training Centers

ABC Abracadabra Farm
ADS Adena Springs
AEF Another Episode Farm
AHT Atlanta Hall Training Center
AIK Aiken
AKI Akindale Training Center
AKS Ak-Sar-Ben
ALB Albuquerque
ANF Anthony Downs
AP Arlington
AQU Aqueduct
ARP Arapahoe Park
ASD Assiniboia Downs
ASF All Seven Farm
ASH Ashwell Stables
ATH Atlanta
ATL Atlantic City
ATO Atokad Downs
BCF Brown County
BDW Bridlewood Farm
BEL Belmont Park
BEU Beulah
BF Brockton Fair
BKF Black Foot
BLS Blaylock South
BLV Belvoir Training Center
BM Bay Meadows
BMF Bay Meadows Fair
BNT Benton Training Center
BOI Les Bois
BON Bonita Farm
BOW Bowie
BRD Blue Ribbon Downs
BRN Harney County
BRO Brookhill Farm
BRS Burns Racing Stable
BTC Braeburn Training Center
CAM Camden
CAS Cassia County
CBQ Chabboquesset
CBT Canyon Breeze Training Center
CBV Cabin View Farm
CBY Canterbury Park
CD Churchill Downs
CDH Cardinal Hill
CDT Churchill Downs Training
CF Chanceland Farm
CHA Charleston
CHL Charlotte
CHM Champagne Farm
CLF Cloverleaf Farms
CLM Clemmons
CLS Columbus
CM Classic Mile
CMB Cumberland County Farigrounds
CMF Calumet Farm Training Center
CNL Colonial Downs
CNR Canyon Road Training Center
CNS Colts Neck Stable
CPW Chippewa Downs
CRC Calder Race Course
CRU Crupis New Castle Farm
CSB Castlebrook Training Center
CT Charles Town
CWF Central Wyoming Fair
CWS Crowns Way South
DAY Dayton
DDF Double Diamond Farm
DDR Diamond D Ranch
DDT Derby Days Training Center
DED Delta Downs
DEL Delaware Park
DEP Desert Park
DET Detroit Race Course
DG Cochise County
DMR Del Mar
DON Donida Training Center
DPF Diamond P Farm
DTD Dare to Dream Farm
DUN Greenelee County
DUQ Du Quoin
DXD Dixie Downs
DYR Derby Run Training Center
ECT East Carolina T C
ED Energy Downs
EDT Empress Downs Training Center
EIS Eisaman Training Center
ELC El Commandante
ELK Elko County Fair
ELL Elloree Training Center
ELP Ellis Park
EMD Emerald Downs
EME Emerald Pastures T C
EMT Emmett
EPF Eagle Point Farm
EPR El Primero Training Center
ETC Eclipse Training Center
EUR Eureka
EVD Evangeline Downs
EVR Evergreen Training Center
EVT Evangeline Training Center
EWT Eddie Woods Training Center
FAI Fair Hill
FAR North Dakota Horse Park
FAX Fairfax
FBF Fox Brown Farm
FCL Faircloth Training Center
FE Fort Erie
FER Ferndale
FFM Folk Farm
FG Fair Grounds
FH Far Hills
FL Finger Lakes
FLG Flagstaff
FMT Fair Meadows Tulsa
FNO Fresno
FOF 505 Farm
FOL Folsom Training Center
FON Fonner Park
FOX Foxboro
FP Fairmount Park
FPF Fort Plains Farm
FPL Fair Play Park
FPX Fairplex Park
FRF Franks Farm
FRN Frontera Training Center
FRO Frost Training Center
FTP Fort Pierre
FX Foxfield
GBF Great Barrington Fair
GCF Gila County Fair
GDC Good Chance Farm
GDF Garydale Farm Training Center
GF Great Falls
GG Golden Gate Fields
GHF Golden Harp Farm
GIL Gillespie County
GLD Great Lakes Downs
GLF Great Lakes Fair Training Facility
GLN Glyndon
GLP The Gallops Training Center
GLW Glenwood Training Center
GN Grand National
GNN Gunn Farm
GP Gulfstream Park
GPF Genuine Pleasure Farm
GPR Grande Prairie
GRA Green Acres
GRM Great Meadow
GRP Grants Pass
GS Garden State
GTW Gateway Downs
GV Genesee Valley
HAW Hawthorne
HBF Hobeau Farm
HBH Hunter Brook Horse Farm
HCF Humboldt County
HDT H & D Training Center
HER Heritage Farm Training Center
HIA Hialeah Park
HLN Helena Downs
HMP Horseman's Park
HOL Hollywood Park
HOO Hoosier Park
HOU Sam Houston
HPO Horsemen's Park
HPT Highpoint Farm and T C
HRF Hawkins Ridge Farm
HST Hastings
HTF Hickory Tree Farm T C
HUF Hunter Farm Training Center
HWK Hawks Ridge Training Center
HYT Hyatt Farm and Training Center
IAF Irish Acres Farm
IND Indiana Downs
ING Ingelside
INT International simulcast
ITC Infields Training Center
JDF Joe Dan Farm
JRM Jerome County
JUB Jubilee Farm
JVR J V Ranch
KAM Kamloops
KD Kentucky Downs
KEE Keeneland
KIN Kin Park
KSP Kalispell
LA Los Alamitos
LAD Louisiana Downs
LBG Lethbridge
LBT Laurel Brown
LEB Lebanon
LEV Little Everglades
LEX Lexington

LLA Llangollen Training Center
LMB Lambholm South Training Center
LNN Lincoln
LRL Laurel Park
LS Lone Star Park
LTC Lubbock Training Center
LXG Ky assoc. Course
MAF Marias Fair
MAL Malvern
MAN Manor Downs
MAR Marlboro
MBF McKathan Brothers Farm
MBK Meadowbrook
MC Miles City
MCU McCutchen Training Center
MD Marquis Downs
MDA Melville District Agripar
MED Meadowlands
MEP MetraPark
MFT McKathan Farm Training Center
MGO Marengo P
MHF Mt Holly Farm Training Center
MID Middleburg
MIH Miami Horsemen's Assoc TC
MIL Millarville
MME Marlyn Meadows
MNR Mountaineer Park
MOF Mohave County
MOG Moment of Glory
MON Monkton
MOR Morven Park
MPM Mt Pleasant Meadows
MRT Martinsville Fairgrounds
MTC Middletown Training Center
MTH Monmouth Park
MTP Montpelier
MTT Middletown Training Track
MTX Minshall Training Center
NAD Nad al Sheba
NBS Niall Brennan Stables
NET New Episode Training Center
NHF New Haven Farm
NJF Nelson Jones Farm and Training Center
NMP Northampton
NP Northlands Park
NPR Napier Training Center
NTC Nobles Training Center
NWF New Farm Training Center
OHC Ocala Horse Farm Complex
OKR Oak Ridge
OLY Olympic Hill Training Center
ONE Oneida County
OP Oaklawn Park
ORT Orting Training Center
OTC Ocala Training Center
OTF Ocala Thoroughbred Farms
OVR Overbrook Training Center
OWT Ocala West
OXF Oxford Training Center
OXM Oxmoor
PAF Paradise Farm T C
PAY Payson Park
PBD Palm Beach Downs
PDA Padua Training Center
PEN Penn National
PER Perfenick Farm
PHA Philadelphia Park
PHT Pleasant Hills Training Center
PIC Picov Downs
PIM Pimlico
PLA Playfair
PLN Pleasanton
PM Portland Meadows
PMM Palm Meadows
PMT Pine Mtn-Calloway Garden
PNS Peninsula Farm
POD Pocatello Downs
POM Pomona
PPX Pleasant Pasture Farm
PRE Prescott Downs
PRM Prairie Meadows
PRO Prospect
PRV Prineville Turf Club
PW Percy Warner
QBY Queensbury Downs
RB Red Bank
RCE Racing Edge Training Center
RD River Downs
RDE Red Earth Training Center
RDM Red Mile
REB Reber Ranch Training Track
RET Retama Park
RIG Rigbie Farm
RIL Rillito
RIS Rising Sun Farm
RKM Rockingham Park
RKV Rocky Valley
RMT Ross Meadows
ROF Red Oak Farm
RP Remington Park
RPD Rossburn Park
RSD Riversude Downs
RSS Rising Sun Stable
RUI Ruidoso Downs
RUP Minidoka County
RVP River Point Training Center
RWD Rollie white Downs
SA Santa Anita
SAB Sabine Farm
SAC Sacramento
SAF Graham County
SAL Salem
SAM Sam-Son Farm
SAN Sandown Park
SAR Saratoga
SBF Shadybrook Farm
SCN Scanlon Training Center
SDY Sandy Downs
SER Serendipity Farm
SFE Santa fe
SFT Sunnyside Farm Training Center
SGC Starting Gate Training Center
SH Strawberry hill
SHD Shenandoah Downs
SHW Shawan Downs
SJ Apache County
SJD San Juan Downs
SJM St. J
SKY Skylight Training Center
SLR San Luis Rey
SMT Summertree Training Center
SND Sunflower Downs
SOL Solano
SON Santa Cruz County
SOP Southern Pines
SOT Silver Oaks Training Center
SPC Starting Point T C
SPT Sportsman's Park
SR Santa Rosa
SRP SunRay Park
SST Sunrise South Stable
SSX Saga and Sand T C
STK Stockton
STN Stoneybrook at Five Points
STO Stony Oak Training Center
STP Stampede Park
SUD Sun Downs
SUF Suffolk Downs
SUN Sunland Park
SWB Sweet Briar T C
SWT Sandy Woods Training Center
SYL Sylmar Farm
TAM Tampa Bay Downs
TAP Tapeta Farm
TBL Timberlake Farm
TDN Thistledown
TIL Tillamook County
TIM Timonium
TP Turfway Park
TRM Trinity Meadows
TRY Tryon
TS Trout Springs
TSF Trackside Farm
TTC The Thoroughbred Center
TUP Turf Paradise
UN Eastern Oregon Livestock Show
UNI Unionville
VAL Valhalla
VHT Victory Haven Training Center
VQF Victory Quest Farm
WAC Washington County Fairgrounds
WAW Wile a Way Farm
WBR Weber Downs
WDB Woodbrook Farm
WDS Woodlands
WFR Wild Falcon Ranch
WIL Willowdale
WMF Western Mt Fair
WND Winding Oaks Farm
WO Woodbine
WOD Woodside Ranch
WPR White Pine
WRD Will Rogers Downs
WRT Windy Ridge Training Center
WSF Wesfield Farm
WTS Waitsburg Race
WW Walla Walla
WXF Wexford Farm
WYO Wyoming Downs
YAV Yavapai Downs
YD Yellowstone Downs
YKT Yorkton Ex Assoc
YM Yakima Meadows
ZIA Zia Park

Glossary of Racing Terms

ACROSS THE BOARD- A bet on a horse to win, place and show. If the horse wins, the player collects three ways; if second, two ways; and if third, one way, losing the win and place bets.
ACTION- A horse's manner of moving.
ADDED MONEY- Money added to the purse of a race by the racing association (or sometimes by a breeding or other fund) to the amount paid by owners in nomination, eligibility, entry and starting fees.
AGENT- A person empowered to transact business of a stable owner or jockey. Also, a person empowered to sell or buy horses for an owner or breeder.
ALL OUT- When a horse extends himself to the utmost.
ALLOWANCE RACE- A race other than claiming for which the racing secretary drafts certain conditions to determine weights.
ALLOWANCES- Weight permitted to be reduced because of the conditions of the race or because an apprentice is on a horse. Also, a weight females are entitled to when racing against males.
ALSO-ELIGIBLE- A horse officially entered, but not permitted to start unless the field is reduced by scratches below a specified number.
ALSO-RAN- A horse who finishes out of the money.
APPRENTICE- Rider who has not ridden a certain number of winners within a specified period of time. Also known as a bug boy.
APPRENTICE ALLOWANCE- Weight concession to an apprentice rider: usually 10 pounds until the fifth winner, seven pounds until the 35th winner and five pounds for one calendar year from the 35th winner.
BABY RACE- A race for 2-year-olds.
BACKSTRETCH- Straight of far side of track between the turns. Also stable area.
BACKSIDE- Stable area
BAD ACTOR- Fractious horse.
BAD DOER- Horse with poor appetite.
BALD (or BALD FACE)- White face of horse, including eyes, nostrils or part of the latter.
BANDAGE- Strips of cloth wound around the lower part of a horse's legs for support or protection against injury.
BAR SHOE- A horse shoe with a rear bar to protect an injured foot; bar shoes may be worn with aluminum pads to protect a bruised frog, or my be worn alone.
BAY- Color of horse varying from yellowish tan (light bay) to brown or dark, rich shade of mahogany (sometimes listed as dark bay or brown) with black points- black mane, tail and shadings of black low on the legs.
BEARING IN (or OUT)- Deviating from a straight course. May be due to weariness, infirmity, punishment by rider or rider's inability to control mount.
BELL- Signal sounded when starter opens the gates or, at some tracks, to mark the close of betting.
BIT- Bar in horse's mouth by which he is guided and controlled.
BLACK- Body, head muzzle, flanks and legs are covered with uniform black hair.
BLACK TYPE- Designation for a stakes winner or stakes-placed horse in sales catalogues.
BRACE (or BRACER)- Rubdown liniment used on a horse after a race or a workout.
BLANKET FINISH- Horses finishing so closely together they could be covered by a blanket.
BLAZE- White patch on face of a horse.
BLEEDER- Horse who bleeds during or after a workout or race due to ruptured blood vessel.
BLIND SWITCH- Being caught in a pocket or such a position behind or between horses that a free course cannot be pursued.
BLINKERS- Device to limit a horse's vision to prevent him from swerving from objects or other horses on either side of him.
BLISTER- Counter-irritant to ease pain or to treat an ailment.
BLOOD WORMS- Parasites that get into the blood stream.
BLOWOUT- A short, final workout, usually a day or two before a race, designed to sharpen a horse's speed.
BOARD- Totalisator board on which odds, betting pools and other information is displayed.
BOBBLE- A bad step away from the starting gate, usually caused by the track breaking away from under a horse's hoof and causing him to duck his head or nearly go to his knees.

BOG SPAVIN- Puffy swelling on the inside and slightly in front of the back, usually caused by overwork or strain.
BOLT- Sudden veering from a straight course.
BOTTOM- Stamina in a horse. Also, sub-surface of racing strip.
BOTTOM LINE- Thoroughbred's breeding on female side. The bottom half of an extended pedigree diagram.
BOWED TENDON (a BOW)- Rupture of the sheath enclosing the tendon from the knee to the fetlock joint.
BREAK (A horse)- To accustom a young horse to racing equipment and methods, and to carry a rider.
BREAKAGE- In pari-mutuel payoffs which are rounded out to a nickel or dime, those pennies that are left over. Breakage is generally split between the track and state and, in some cases, breeding or other funds, in varying proportions.
BREAKDOWN- When a horse suffered an injury; lameness.
BREAK MAIDEN- Horse or rider winning first race of career.
BREATHER- Restraining or easing off on a horse for a short distance in a race to permit him to conserve or renew his strength.
BRED- A horse is bred at the place of his birth. Also, the mating of horses.
BREEDER- Owner of dam at time foal is dropped.
BREEDING FUND- A fund set up by many states to provide bonus prizes for state- breds.
BREEZE- Working a horse at a moderate speed; less effort than handily.
BRIDGE-JUMPER- Someone who makes large show bets on short-priced favorites.
BROODMARE- Female Thoroughbred used for breeding.
BROWN- Sometimes difficult to separate from black or dark bay. This color can usually be distinguished by noting finer tan or brown hairs on the muzzles or flanks.
BUCKED SHINS- Inflammation of front of cannon bone to which young horses are particularly susceptible.
BUG- Apprentice allowance. Apprentice rider.
BULLET (WORK)- The best time for the distance on the work tab for a given day at a track.
BULL RING- Small racetrack; usually less than one mile.
BUTE (or BUTAZOLIDIN)- Trade name for phenylbutazone, a commonly used analgesic for horses.
CALK- Projection bottom of shoe to give horse greater traction, especially on a wet track.
CALL (the)- Running position of horses in a race at various points.
CALLER- One who calls the running positions of horses in a race.
CAPPED HOCK- Injury to hock caused by kicking or rubbing.
CAST- A horse is a cast when he lies down in the stall in such a way that he is too close to the wall, and there is a danger that he may not be able to get up by himself without injury.
CENTER OF DISTRIBUTION- The balance point of speed and stamina influences in a horse's pedigree.
CHART- A statistical "picture" of a race (from which past performances are compiled), which shows the position and margin of each horse at designated points of call (depending on distance of the race), age, weight carried, owner, trainer, purse, conditions, pay-off prices, odds, time and other data.
CHECKED- A horse pulled up by his jockey for an instant because he is cut off or in tight quarters.
CHESTNUT- Varies from light, washy yellow to dark liver color, between which comes red, gold and liver shades. A chestnut never has black points, mane or tail.
CHUTE- Extension of backstretch or homestretch to permit straightaway run from start.
CLAIMING- Buying a horse out of race for entered price.
CLAIMING BOX- Box in which claims are deposited before the race.
CLAIMING RACE- Race in which horses are entered subject to claim for a specified price.
CLASSIC- Race of traditional importance. In the U.S. specifically the Kentucky Derby, Preakness and Belmont stakes for colts, and Coaching Club American Oaks for fillies.
CLERK OF SCALES- An official whose chief duty is to weigh the riders before and after a race to be sure proper weight is carried.
CLIMBING- A fault in a horse's stride in which, instead of reaching out, his action is abnormally high.
CLOCKER- One who times workouts and races.
CLOSER- A horse who runs best in the latter part of the race, coming from off the pace.
CLUBHOUSE TURN- Generally, the turn closest to the clubhouse.

COLORS- Racing silks-jacket and cap-worn by riders to denote the owner(s) of horse.
COLT- Male horse under 5 years of age.
COMPANY- Class of horses in a race. Members of the field.
CONDITION BOOK- Book issued by racing secretary which sets forth conditions of races to be run.
CONDITION RACE- An event with conditions limiting it to a certain class of horse. Such as: Fillies, 3-year-olds, non-winners of two races other than maiden or claiming, etc.
CONFORMATION- A horse's build and general physical structure; the way he is put together.
CONTRACT RIDER- Jockey under contract to a stable.
COOLING OUT- Restoring a horse, usually by walking, to normal temperature after becoming over-heated in a race or workout.
COUGH- Broadly, a cold. More prevalent in spring among young Thoroughbreds.
COUPLED- Two or more horses running as an entry in a single betting unit.
CRIBBER (a WIND SUCKER)- A horse who clings to objects with his teeth and sucks air into his stomach.
CUP- Trophy awarded to owners of winners. Also distance race of a mile and a half or more.
CUP HORSE- One qualified to engage in distance races.
CUPPY (track)- A surface which breaks away under a horse's hoof.
CUSHION- Surface of track or a layer of the track.
DAILY DOUBLE- Type of wager calling for the selection of winners of two consecutive races, usually the first and second.
DAM- Mother of a Thoroughbred.
DAMSIRE (BROODMARE SIRE)- The sire of a broodmare.
DEAD-HEAT- Two or more horses finishing in an exact tie at the wire.
DEAD TRACK- Racing surface lacking resiliency.
DECLARED- In U.S., a horse withdrawn from a stake in advance of scratch time. In Europe, a horse confirmed to start in a race.
DIPLOMA (Earning a...)- Breaking a maiden, winning for the first time.
DISQUALIFICATION- Change of order of finish by officials for an infraction of the rules.
DISTAFF (DISTAFF RACE)- Female. A race for fillies, mares, or both.
DISTANCED- Well beaten, finishing a great distance behind the winner.
DOGS- Wooden barrier (or rubber traffic cones) placed a certain distance out from the inner rail, to prevent horses during workout period, when track is wet, muddy, soft yielding or heavy, from churning the footing along the rail.
DOSAGE DIAGRAM- A diagram showing the number and placement of chefs-de-race in a horse's pedigree.
DOSAGE INDEX- Mathematical reduction of the Dosage Diagram to a number reflecting a horse's potential for speed or stamina.
DQ- Disqualified.
DRIVING- Strong urging by rider.
DROPDOWN- A horse meeting a lower class of rival than he had been running against.
DWELT- Tardy in breaking fromthe gate.
EASED- Chart caller's assessment of a horse that is being deliberately slowed by the jockey to prevent injury or harm to the horse.
EASILY- Running or winning without being pressed by rider or opposition.
EIGHTH- A furlong; 220 yards; 660 feet.
ELIGIBLE- Qualified to start in a race, according to conditions.
ENGAGEMENT- Stake nomination. Riding commitment.
ENTRY- Two or more horses owned by the same stable or (in some cases) trained by the same trainer and thus running as a single betting unit..
EQUIPMENT- Whip, blinkers, etc. Gear carried by a horse in a race.
EQUIVALENT ODDS- Mutuel price horses pay for each $1 bet.
EVENLY- Neither gaining nor losing position or distance during a race.
EXACTA (or PERFECTA)- A wager in which the first two finishers in a race, in exact order of finish, must be picked.
EXCUSED- Withdrawal from a race (sometimes on a veterinarian's recommendation) with consent of stewards.

EXERCISE RIDER- Male or female rider who is aboard a horse in the mornings.
EXTENDED- Forced to run at top speed.
EXTRA WEIGHT (ADDED WEIGHT)- More weight than conditions of race require.
FALTERED- Used for a horse that was in contention early and drops back in the late stages. It is more drastic than weakened but less drastic than stopped.
FALSE FAVORITE- Horse who is bet down to favoritism when others would appear to outclass him on form.
FARRIER- Blacksmith.
FAST TRACK- Footing at best, dry, fast and even.
FEES- Amount paid to rider or the cost of nominating, entering or starting a horse in a stakes race.
FENCE- Sometimes called "outside rail." More properly the barrier between the front of the stands and the racing strip.
FIELD- The horses in a race.
FIELD HORSE (or MUTUEL FIELD)- Two or more starters running as a single betting unit, when there are more entrants than positions on the totalisator board can accommodate.
FILLY- Female horse up to and including the age of 4.
FIRING- Applying a searing instrument, hot iron or electric needle to an injured portion of the leg to promote healing of injury or infirmity.
FIRM- A condition of a turf course corresponding to fast on a dirt track.
FIRST TURN- Bend in the track beyond the starting point.
FLAG- Signal held by man stationed a short distance in front of the gate at exact starting point of race. Official timing starts when flag is dropped to denote proper start.
FLAT RACE- Contested on level ground as opposed to hurdle race or steeplechase.
FLATTEN OUT- When a horse drops his head almost on straight line with body. May indicate exhaustion.
FLOAT- Piece of track equipment dragged over racing strip to squeeze off surface water.
FOAL- Newly born Thoroughbred, or until weaned. Male or female.
FOUNDER- See Laminitis.
FOUR FURLONGS- Half a mile; 880 yards; 2,640 feet.
FRACTIONAL TIME- Interme-diate time recorded in a race, as at the quarter, half, three-quarters, etc.
FRESH (FRESHENED)- A rested horse.
FREE HANDICAP- A race in which no nomination fees.
FRONT-RUNNER- A horse who usually leads (or tries to lead) the field for as far as he can.
FURLONG- One-eighth of a mile; 220 yards; 660 feet.
FUROSEMIDE- Generic term for a medication for the treatment of bleeders. Most common trade name is Lasix.
GAIT- The ways in which a horse can move-walk, trot, canter, gallop, run, etc.
GALLOP- A type of gait, a fast canter. Also, to ride a horse at that gait.
GATE- Starting mechanism.
GELDING- Castrated male horse.
GET- Progeny of sire.
GOOD BOTTOM- Track that is firm under the surface, which may be sloppy or wet.
GOOD TRACK- Condition between fast and slow.
GRAB A QUARTER- To strike the side of a front foot with a hind foot. This is racetrack jargon that would be expressed more clearly by saying that the horse overstepped or overreached and cut himself; reserve grabbed a quarater for direct quotes.
GRADUATE- Winning first time, horse or rider. Also, graduate of the claiming ranks-a horse, that has moved up to allowance, stakes or handicap racing.
GRANDDAM (SECOND DAM)- Grandmother of a horse.
GRANDSIRE- Grandfather of a horse, sire of the horse's dam.
GRAY- A mixture of white and black hairs.
GROOM- A person who cares for a horse in a stable.
GROUP RACE- European equivalent to North American graded races.
HALF- Half a mile, four furlongs; 880 yards; 2,640 feet.
HALF-BROTHER, HALF-SISTER- Horses out of the same dam but by different sires.
HALTER- Like a bridle, but lacing a bit. Used in handling horses around the stable and when not being ridden.

HALTER (TO)- To claim a horse.
HAND- Four inches. Unit used in measuring height of horses from withers to ground.
HANDICAP- Race for which a handicapper assigns weights to be carried. Also, to handicap a race, to make selections on the basis of the past performances.
HANDICAPPER- One who assigns weights for handicap race. Also one who makes selections based on past performances.
HANDICAPPING- One who assigns weights for a handicap race. Also one who makes selctions based on past performances.
HANDILY- Working or racing with moderate effort, but more effort than breezing.
HANDLE- Amount of money wagered in the pari-mutuel on a race, a program, a meeting or a year.
HAND RIDE- Urging a horse with the hands and not using the whip.
HARDBOOT- Kentucky horsemen.
HEAD- A margin between horses. One horse leading another by the length of his head.
HEAD OF THE STRETCH- Beginning of the straight run home.
HEAVY- Condition of track similar to, but even slower than, muddy.
HIGHWEIGHT HANDICAP- Race in which the topweight is assigned no less than 140 pounds.
HOMEBRED- A horse bred by his owner.
HORSE- Broadly, in any Thoroughbred regardless of sex. Specifically, an entire male 5 years old or older.
HORSING- Mare in heat.
HOTWALKER- Person who walks horses to cool them out after workout or races.
HUNG- Horse tiring, but holding position.
HURDLE RACE- Contested over obstacles. A jumping race over lower fences than steeplechase races.
ICING- Standing a horse in a bucket of ice or applying ice packs to the legs to encourage circulation.
IN FOAL- Pregnant mare.
IN THE MONEY- Finishing first, second or third.
INFIELD- Area within the inner rail of the racetrack.
INFIELD RACING (SPORT)- Turf racing.
IN HAND- Running under moderate control, at less than best pace.
IMPOST- Weight carried or assigned.
INTER-STATE (Wagering)- Wagering on a simulcast of a race from another state.
INTER-TRACK (Wagering)- Wagering on a simulcast of a race from another track within the state.
INQUIRY- Reviewing the race to check into a possible infraction of the rules. Also, a sign flashed by officials on tote board on such occasions.
IRONS- Stirrups.
JOCKEY FEE- Sum paid to a rider.
JOG- Slow, easy gait.
JUMPER- Steeplechase or hurdle horse.
JUVENILE- Two-year-old horse.
LAMINITIS- Inflammation under horny wall of foot.
LASIX- See furosemide.
LATE DOUBLE- A second daily double offered on the latter part of the program. (See Daily Double)
LEAD- Strap attached to halter to lead a horse.
LEAD (or LEAD PAD)- Weights carried to make up the difference when a rider weighs less than the poundage a horse is assigned to carry.
LEAD PONY- Horse or pony who heads parade of field from paddock to starting gate. Also a horse or pony who accompanies a starter to post.
LEAKY ROOF CIRCUIT- Minor tracks.
LEG UP- To help a jockey mount his horse. Also a jockey having a mount. Also to strengthen a horse's legs through exercise.
LENGTH- Length of a horse from nose to tail, about 8 feet. Also distance between horses in a race.
LISTED RACE- A European race just below a group race in quality.
LOCK- Slang for a "sure thing" winner.
LUG (in or out)- Action of a tiring horse, bearing in or out.
LUNGE- Horse rearing or plunging.
MAIDEN- A horse who has not won a race. Also applied to non-winning rider.

MAIDEN RACE- A race for non winners.
MAKE A RUN- Charge by a horse in a race.
MARE- Female horse 5 years old or older. Also, female of any age who has been bred.
MASH- Moist mixture, hot or cold, of grain and other feed given to horses.
MEDICATION LIST- A list kept by the track veterinarian and published by the track and Daily Racing Form (when provided by track officials) showing which horses have been treated with phenylbutazone and/or furosemide.
MIDDLE DISTANCE- Broadly from one mile to less than a mile and an eighth.
MINUS POOL- A mutuel pool caused when one horse is so heavily played that, after deductions of state tax and commission, there is not enough money left to pay the legally prescribed minimum on each winning bet. The racing association usually makes up the difference.
MONEY RIDER- A rider who excels in rich races.
MORNING GLORY- Horse who performs well in morning workouts but fails to reproduce that form in races.
MORNING LINE- Approximate odds quoted before wagering determines exact odds. The idea behind the morning line is to serve as an estimate of how the closing odds might shape up. Theoretically, the morning line should be comprised of 119-124 percentage points for all the horses in the race. This includes 100 percentage points distributed to all the horses in the race, plus approximately 19-24 percentage points representing the average takeout and breakage removed from the money wagered in the win pool by the track and state combined. The proper Betting Percentage Table for all odds situations appears below, along with a sample morning line for an eight-horse field.

1-10 90 percentage points
1-5 83 percentage points
2-5 71 percentage points
1-2 66 percentage points
3-5 62 percentage points
4-5 55 percentage points
1-1 50 percentage points
6-5 45 percentage points
7-5 42 percentage points
3-2 40 percentage points
8-5 38 percentage points
9-5 35 percentage points
2-1 33 percentage points
5-2 29 percentage points
3-1 25 percentage points
7-2 22 percentage points
4-1 20 percentage points
9-2 18 percentage points
5-1 16 percentage points
6-1 14 percentage points
8-1 11 percentage points
10-1 9 percentage points
12-1 8 percentage points
15-1 6 percentage points
20-1 4.5 percentage points
25-1 4 percentage points
30-1 3+ percentage points
40-1 2.5 percentage points
50-1 2 percentage points
75-1 1.5 percentage points
99-1 1 percentage point.

A sample morning line:

#1 Secretariat	2-1	(33 percentage points)
#2 Seattle Slew	5-2	(29 percentage points)
#3 Affirmed	3-1	(25 percentage points)
#5 Kelso	9-2	(18 percentage points)
#6 Cigar	15-1	(6 percentage points)
#7 Skip Away	15-1	(6 percentage points)
#8 Alysheba	20-1	(4.5 percentage points)
		121.5 Total percentage points

MUDDY TRACK- Deep condition of racetrack after being soaked with water.
MUDDER- Horse who races well on muddy tracks.
MUDLARK- Superior mudder.
MUZZLE- Nose and lips of a horse. Also a guard placed over a horse's mouth to prevent him from biting or eating.
NAVICULAR DISEASE- Corrosive ulcer on the navicular bone, usually in the fore feet.
NEAR SIDE- Left side of a horse, side on which he is mounted.
NECK- Unit of measurement, about the length of a horse's neck; a quarter of a length.
NERVED- Operation that severs vital nerve to enable horses to race without pain. Illegal in most jurisdictions.
NOD- Lowering of head. Winning in that manner.
NOM DE COURSE- Assumed name of owner or racing partnership.
NOSE- Smallest advantage a horse can win by. In England called a short head.
OAKS- A classic stakes event for 3-year-old fillies.
OBJECTION- Claim of foul lodged by rider, patrol judge or other official. If lodged by official, it is called an inquiry.
ODDS-ON- Odds of less than even money. In England it is simply called "on," thus a horse "5-4 on" is actually at odds of 4-5.
OFFICIAL- Sign displayed when result is confirmed. Also racing official.
OFF SIDE- Right side of horse.
OFF TRACK- An off track refers to a wet racing surface.
OFF-TRACK BETTING- Wagering on horses at legalized betting offices run usually by the state or the tracks, or, in New York, by independent corporations chartered by the state, with wagers commingled with on-track betting pools.
ON THE BIT- When a horse is eager to run.
ON THE BOARD- Finishing among the first four.
ON THE NOSE- Betting a horse to win only.
OSSELETS- Bony growth on the fetlock or ankle joint resulting in inflammation of the enveloping membrane of the bone.
OVER-REACHING- Toe of hind shoe striking forelegs on heel, or back of coronet.
OVERLAND- Racing wide throughout, outside of other horses.
OVERLAY- A horse going off at a higher price than he appears to warrant based on his past performances.
OVERNIGHT LINE- Prices quoted night before the race.
OVERNIGHT RACE- A race in which entries close a specific number of hours before running (such as 48 hours), as opposed to a stakes race for which nominations close weeks and sometimes months in advance.
OVERWEIGHT- Surplus weight carried by a horse when the rider cannot make the required weight.
PADDOCK- Structure or area where horses are saddled and kept before post time.
PADDOCK JUDGE- Official in charge of paddock and saddling routine.
PARIMUTUEL- A form of wagering that originated in France in which all money bet is divided up among those who have winning tickets, after taxes, takeout and other deductions are made.
PAST PERFORMANCES- A compilation in Daily Racing Form of a horse's record, including all pertinent data, as a basis for handicapping.
PATROL JUDGES- Officials who observe progress of race from various vantage points around the track.

PENALTIES- Extra weight a horse must carry, especially in a handicap.
PHOTO FINISH- A result so close it is necessary to use a finish-line camera to determine order of finish.
PICK SIX (or more)- A type of wager in which the winners of all the included races must be selected.
PILL- Small numbered ball drawn to decide post positions.
PINCHED BACK- Horse in close quarters and forced back.
PINHOOKER; PINHOOK- To buy a horse at auction fo r the purpose of reselling him later.
PLACE- Second position at finish.
PLACE BET- Wager on a horse to finish first or second.
PLACING JUDGES- Officials who determine the order in which horses reach the finish line.
PLATTER- Claiming horse. Also a farrier.
PLATES- Shoes horses wear in races. Racing plates.
POCKET- Boxed in, shut off. Running in a position with horses in front and alongside.
POLE- Markers at measured distances around the track, marking the distance from the finish. The quarter pole, for instance, is a quarter of a mile from the finish, not from the start.
POST- Starting point or position in starting gate.
POOL- Mutuel pool. Total sum bet on a race or even, such as the win pool, daily double pool, exacta pool.
POST PARADE- Horses going from paddock to starting gate past the stands.
POST POSITION- Position of stall in starting gate from which a horse starts.
POST TIME- Designated time from race to start.
PREFERRED LIST- Horses with prior rights to starting for various reasons.
PREP (or PREP RACE)- A workout or a race to prepare a horse for a future engagement.
PROP- Refusing to break with field from gate. Standing flat-footed. Also, when a horse suddenly stops running a full speed by extending his forefeet as "brakes."
PUBLIC TRAINER- One whose services are not exclusively engaged by a single stable and who accepts horses from a number of owners.
PURSE- A prize of money to which owners do not contribute.
QUARTER- One-quarter of a mile; 440 yards; 1,320 feet.
QUARTER CRACK- Crack in wall of hoof running downwards from coronet.
QUARTER HORSE- Breed of horse especially fast for a quarter of a mile, from which its name is derived.
QUARTER POLE- Marker one-quarter mile from the finish.
QUINELLA- Wager in which first two finishers must be picked, but payoff is made no matter which of the two wins and which runs second.
RABBIT- A horse that is considered to have little chance of winning a race but is entered purely to ensure a fat pace and tire out the other front-runners, softening up the competition for the benefit of an entrymate.
RACING SECRETARY- Official who drafts conditions of races and assigns weights for handicap events.
RAIL RUNNER- Horse who prefers to run next to inside rail.
RECEIVING BARN- Structure at which horses entered are isolated for a certain period of time before a race.
REFUSE- When a horse will not break from the gate. In jumping races, balking at the jump.
RESERVED- Held for a particular engagement or race. Also, held off the pace.
RIDDEN OUT- Refers to a horse that wins under a vigorous hand ride but is not being whipped.
RIDE SHORT- Using short stirrup leathers.
RIDGLING- A horse with one or both undescended testes.
ROAN- Mixture of white and red (or brown) hairs.
ROARING- Deep, prolonged cough, generally when a horse is galloping.
ROGUE- Ill-tempered horse.
ROMP- Running (or winning) with utmost ease.
ROUTE- Race distance of a mile or longer.
ROUTER- Horse who performs well at distance races.
RUNDOWN- Of a horse, to suffer abrasions on the heels as a result of contact with the dirt and sand of the track surface.

RUNDOWN BANDAGES (or WRAPS)- Bandages on the hind legs, usually with a pad inside, to keep a horse from "burning" or scraping his heels when he races.
RUN-OUT BIT- A special type of bit to prevent a horse from bearing out (or in).
SADDLE CLOTH- Cloth under the saddle on which number (and sometimes horse's name) denoting post position is displayed.
SAVAGE- To bite another horse or a person.
SCALE OF WEIGHTS- Fixed imposts to be carried by horses in a race according to age, distance, sex, and time of year.
SCHOOLING- Accustoming a horse to starting from the gate and to teach him racing practices. In steeplechasing, more particularly to teach a horse to jump.
SCHOOLING LIST- List of horses required by the starter to school at the starting gate before being permitted to race.
SCRATCH- To be taken out of a race.
SECOND CALL- A second engagement of jockey who already is listed for a mount in a race.
SECOND DAM- Grandmother; granddam.
SELLING RACE- A claiming race.
SESAMOID- Sesamoid bones are located at the back of the fetlock, the joint formed by the pastern bone and the cannon bone.
SET- A group of horses working together.
SET DOWN- A suspension. Also, put to a drive, or asked to run by a jockey.
SEVEN FURLONGS- Seven-eighths of a mile; 1,540 yards; 4,620 feet.
SEX ALLOWANCE- Fillies and mares, according to their age and time of year, are allowed to carry three to five pounds less when meeting males.
SHADOW ROLL- Usually a lamb's wool roll half way up the horse's face to keep him from seeing his own shadow.
SHANK- Rope or strap attached to a halter or bridle by which a horse is led.
SHED ROW- Stable area. A row of barns.
SHORT- A horse in need of more work or racing to reach winning form.
SHOW- Third position at the finish.
SHOW BET- Wager on a horse to finish in the money; third or better.
SHUT OFF- Pocketed. Unable to improve position.
SILKS- Jacket and cap worn by riders which designate owner of the horse.
SIMULCAST- Televising a race to other tracks, OTB offices or other outlets for the purpose of wagering.
SIRE- Father of a horse.
SIX FURLONGS- Three-quarter of a mile; 1,320 yards, 3,960 feet.
SIXTEENTH- One-sixteenth of a mile; 110 yards, 330 feet.
SLOPPY- Condition of footing. Wet on surface with firm bottom.
SLOW- Footing that is not fast, between good and heavy.
SNUG- Mild restraining hold by rider.
SOLID HORSE- Contender.
SOPHOMORE- Three-year-old horse.
SPEEDY CUT- Injury to knee or hock caused by a strike from the opposite foot.
SPIT BOX- Receptacle for urine and blood taken from a horse for testing.
SPIT THE BIT- When a horse quits running against the bit, usually because of fatigue; often said disdainfully: "Luck Lady really spit out the bit".
STAKES-PLACED- Finishing first, second or third in a stakes race.
STAKE- A race (usually a feature race) for which owner must pay up a fee to run a horse. The fees can be for nominating, maintaining eligibility, entering and starting, to which the track adds more money to make up the total purse. Some stakes races are by invitation and require no payment or fee.
STAKES HORSE- One capable of competing in such events.
STALLION- Entire male horse.
STALL WALKER- Horse that moves about his stall and frets rather than rests.
STAR- Small patch of white hair on a horse's forehead. Also a credit a horse receives from being forced out of an overcrowded race, giving him priority in future races.

STARTER RACE- An allowance or handicap race restricted to horses who have started for a specific claiming price or less.
STARTING GATE- Mechanical device having partitions (stalls) for horses in which they are confined until the starter releases the doors in front to begin the race.
STATE-BRED- A horse bred in a particular state and thus eligible to compete in special races restricted to state-breds.
STAYER- Stout-hearted horse who can race long distances.
STEADIED- A horse being taken in hand by his rider, usually because of being in close quarters.
STEPS UP- A horse moving up in class to meet better runners.
STEWARDS- Top officials of the meeting responsible for enforcing the rules.
STEEPLECHASE- A jumping race over high obstacles.
STICK- A jockey's whip.
STICKERS- Calks on shoes which give a horse better traction in mud or on soft tracks.
STOCKINGS- White legs below the knees.
STRETCH- Final straight portion of the racetrack to the finish.
STRETCH CALL- Position of horses at the eighth pole, usually about halfway down the stretch.
STRETCH RUNNER- Horse who finishes fast.
STRETCH TURN- Bend of track into homestretch.
STRIDE- Manner of going. Also distance covered after each foot has touched the ground once.
STRIP- Markings of a horse. White hairs running part-way down the face.
STRIPE- A white marking running down a horse's face to bridge of nose or below.
STUD- Male horse used for breeding. Also breeding farm.
STUD BOOK- Registry and genealogical record of the breeding of Thoroughbreds maintained by The Jockey Club.
SUBSCRIPTION- Fee paid by owner to nominate horse for a stakes race or to maintain eligibility for a stakes race.
SUCKLING- Thoroughbred still nursing.
SUSPEND (or SUSPENSION)- Punishment for infraction of rules. Offender denied privileges of race-track for specified period of time. If permanently suspended: Ruled Off.
SWAYBACK- Horse with a dipped backbone.
TACK- Riders' racing equipment. Also applied to stable gear.
TAKE (or TAKEOUT)- Commission deducted from mutuel pools which s shared by the track and local and state governing bodies in the form of tax.
TAKEN UP- A horse pulled up sharply by his rider because of being in close quarters.
TATTOO- A letter and a group of numerals applied to the underside of the upper lip of each registered Thoroughbred.
TELETHEATER- Special facility for showing simulcast races.
THRUSH- Inflammation of the cleft of the frog.
TIGHT- Ready to race.
TIMBER TOPPER- Jumper or steeplechase horse. More properly horses jumping over timber fences.
TONGUE STRAP- Strap or tape bandage used to tie down a horse's tongue to prevent it from choking in a race or workout.
TOP LINE- Thoroughbred's breeding on his sire's side.
TOPWEIGHT- Highest weight assigned or carried in a race.
TOTALISATOR- Machine which sells and records betting tickets and shows odds. Also figures out and displays payoff figures.
TOUT- One who gives tips on racehorses, usually with ecpcetation of some personal reward in return; to give tips.
TRACK BIAS- A racing surface that favors a particular running style or position; horses that run on the lead or on the rail.
TRACK RECORD- Fastest time at various distances recorded at a particular track.
TRIAL- Workout.
TRIFECTA (or TRIPLE)- A wager picking the first three finishers in exact order.
TRIP- A horse's race.
TRIPLE CROWN- In the United States, the Kentucky Derby, Preakness Stakes and Belmont Stakes. In England the 2,000 Guineas, Epsom Derby and St. Leger.

TURF COURSE- Grass course.
TURN DOWN- A protrusion on the bottom of a horseshoe added to give traction.
TWITCH- A device usually consisting of a stick with a loop of rope at one end, which is placed around a horse's nose and upper lip and twisted to curb fractiousness.
UNDER CONTRACT- A trainer or rider formally signed for a specified time and compensation.
UNDERLAY- A horse racing at longer odds than he should.
UNDER PUNISHMENT- Horse being whipped and driven.
UNDER WRAPS- Horse under stout restraint in a race or workout.
UNTRIED- Not raced or tested for speed. Also a stallion who has not been bred.
UNWIND- Gradually withdrawing a horse from intensive training.
VALET- Person who attends riders and keeps their wardrobe and equipment in order.
WALK HOTS- To cool a horse out after a workout or race.
WALKOVER- Race which scratches down to only one starter who merely gallops required distance. A formal gesture required by rules of racing.
WARMING UP- Galloping horse on way to post.
WASHY- Horse breaking out in nervous sweat before race.
WEANLING- A foal that is less than 1-year-old that has been separated from its dam.
WEAVING- Swaying motion in stall, or act of threading way through field in race.
WEIGHT-FOR-AGE- Fixed scale of weights to be carried by horses according to age, sex, distance of race and season of year.
WHIP- Instrument, usually of leather, with which rider strikes horse to increase his speed. Also called bat and gad.
WINDED- Breathing with difficulty after workout or race.
WINNER-TAKES-ALL- Winner receiving all the purse or stakes.
WITHERS- The highest point of a horse's shoulder.
WOBBLER- A neurological disease due to compression of the spinal cord. Seen principally in 2-year-olds and 3-year-olds.
WORK- To exercise a horse. A workout.
YEARLING- Thoroughbred between the first New Year's Day after being foaled and the following January 1.
YIELDING- Condition of turf course with a great deal of moisture.

DRF PRESS HANDICAPPING FEATURE

HANDICAPPING 101 - CHAPTER TWO: FORM

BY BRAD FREE

It was the first truly painful handicapping mistake of my wagering career. It would not be the last. But this one hurt because it resulted from sheer ignorance. Or maybe it was arrogance.

It was June 1991, and I had been a public newspaper handicapper all of five years. Long enough for a know-it-all to cop a cheeky attitude. One spring afternoon, speed was holding on the Hollywood Park main track. Marquetry, the only front-runner in the Hollywood Gold Cup and carrying 12 pounds less than 7-5 favorite Farma Way, raced gate to wire and returned a fat win mutuel of $56.80. I had him. Sort of.

Marquetry was a "single" on a pick-three wager, the only Gold Cup starter on the ticket. To cash, I needed to win the next two races. I had multiple horses in each, including another longshot, 26-1 Saber Six, who won the next race by a nose. Two races down, one to go. With three horses on my ticket in the final leg of the pick three, I was positioned for a jackpot equal to one-fifth my annual salary.

What a genius I was. This game that I learned from my dad was easy. It was my dad who taught me the importance of current form. He said physical condition of racehorses fluctuates. Dad's old-school "form handicapping" concerned analyzing and interpreting the state of a horse's health. Was the horse improving? Or regressing? Sometimes, a racehorse just doesn't fire; other times, he delivers at maximum potential. It was Dad—he started handicapping and betting in the 1950's—who emphasized that one of the most important considerations was current form.

Form handicapping would be a one-step process if horses were machines. A handicapper would only need to view the past performances of the horse's most recent start, and compare the race with the last race of the other horses using basic measurements of class, speed, and pace. But the truth is, horses do change. Trainer Craig Lewis sees it daily.

"People labor under misconceptions. They say, look at that big, strong animal—he's healthy. Well, nothing is further from the truth. There is always something wrong—always. There is a misconception about the saying 'You're as healthy as a horse.' If your doctor ever tells you that, I suggest you immediately check into the hospital and demand a thorough evaluation of your health situation.

"It's not that different from a human. There might be a nice-looking, handsome guy. But he could have cancer, he could have heart disease, he could have a lung infection. There are all kinds of things. It's the same with a horse. That is why betting on horses, you have a much greater chance of [financial] success than owning horses."

Twilight Agenda
Own: MOYGLARE STUD FARM LTD

B. h. 18 (Mar)
Sire: Devil's Bag (Halo) $10,000
Dam: Grenzen (Grenfall)
Br: Moyglare Stud Farm, Ltd. (Ky)
Tr: Lukas D. W(62 0 7 3 .00) 2004:(84 4 .05)

Date/Track	Cond	Dist	Surf	Fractions	Race	Calls	Fin	Jockey	Wt	Odds		Company line	Comment	Field
21Jun91-7Hol	fm	1$\frac{1}{16}$	Ⓣ	:23 :45^4 1:09^2 1:39^3	4↑ ⓇJohnysImag62k	– 1 1½ 1½ 1^1 2½	2^{2}¼	Flores D R	LB113 b	14.60	- -	Super May121^{2}¼ *Twilight Agenda*113^{nk} Laxey Bay118^2	Bore out, held place	8
3Jan91-8SA	sly	6½f		:21^4 :44^1 1:15^1	4↑ Alw 55000NC	– 1 6 3^{1}½ 3^{1}¼ 3^3	3^{5}½	Santos J A	B114 fb	7.00	- -	TankerPort115^1 LurensQuest114^{4}½ TwilightAgend114^{1}¼	Stlk pace; empty	6
26Aug90♦Leopardstwn (Ire)		7f	Ⓣ		Stk 23100		88	Kinane MJ	0	-		Takwim Home Truth Heroes Sash		0
8Aug90♦Phoenix Park (Ire)		7f	Ⓣ		Stk 23100		2	Kinane MJ	0	-		*Norwich* Twilight Agenda Just Three		0
21Jly90♦Leopardstwn (Ire)		7f	Ⓣ		Stk 23100		4	Kinane MJ	0	-		*Norwich* Takwim Kyra		0
20Jun90♦Ascot (GB)	gd	1	Ⓣ		3↑ Hcp 82700		87½	Kinane MJ	131	-		Pontenuovo105^{nk} Curtain Call118^1 Pride of Araby131½		32
11May90♦Phoenix Park (Ire)		7f	Ⓣ		Alw 6200		1	Kinane MJ	0	-		Twilight Agenda Gilt Throne Puissance		0
27Aug89♦Leopardstwn (Ire)		7f	Ⓣ		Stk 22800		1	Kinane MJ	0	-		*Twilight Agenda* Clusette Run to Jenny		0
29Jly89♦Leopardstwn (Ire)		7f	Ⓣ		Hcp 4600		1	Kinane MJ	0	-		*Twilight Agenda He's a Flyer* No Dreaming		0

Of course, on June 29, 1991—Hollywood Gold Cup Day—I was thinking less about current form and more about how to spend the pick-three jackpot I was about to win. With three horses in the final leg of the sequence, I was a lock. The one contender I dismissed was a former European that trainer D. Wayne Lukas was wheeling back just eight days after a fierce comeback effort. I knew enough about current form to expect the horse to regress. You may have heard the expression—Twilight Agenda was going to "bounce." It was a modern concept, and I thought I was a modern handicapper. Certainly I was smarter than Lukas. Figuring as much, and ignoring the fact that Twilight Agenda's comeback race was super, I predicted he would not reproduce his last start. Lukas had not given him enough time to recharge.

Twilight Agenda, of course, performed to Lukas's expectations, not mine. In a minor stakes race, the bay front-runner shot to the lead, set a fast pace, and raced wire to wire. He never looked like a loser. I felt like an idiot, which was quite a change from my self-congratulatory mood minutes earlier. It hurt. Twilight Agenda, who would blossom into one of the country's top handicap runners, reminded me that a smug handicapping novice is asking for trouble when he leaps to premature conclusions. Good trainers know their horses, and what races they belong in. Lukas knew his horse.

I had attempted to make an analysis I was not qualified to make. Handicappers do it all the time. With Twilight Agenda, I had leaped past the fundamentals, to an advanced handicapping concept about which I was under-informed. I expected the horse would bounce even though at the time the only thing I really knew about a bounce was what I had read. Dad was right –current form usually is a matter of logic. Lukas had one reason for pushing Twilight Agenda back just eight days after his comeback. The horse was in good form. He was ready.

The Beginning

The handicapping process always starts with the horse. Some are sharp and healthy, others are dull and disinterested. A sharp horse is "in form," and generally can be relied on to produce an effort that corresponds to previous top efforts. His recent races are strong, his workout pattern is solid, the class level at which he is racing is sensible. A horse that is "off form" has tailed off, or is in the process of tailing off. His recent races are subpar, or his speed figures declining; his workout pattern may be flawed, or the class level at which he is racing unusual. Because of substandard current form, the horse is likely to fall short of prior accomplishments.

Without form, it may not matter that a horse routinely earns faster speed figures than his rivals. Without current condition, pace is less relevant. In the absence of form, class hardly matters. Make no mistake—speed, pace, and class are key, but only in the context of current condition.

The chief premise of handicapping is that horses are likely to do what they have done. But their condition does change, and catches unwary bettors by surprise. Horseplayers often expect horses to remain the same, even when obvious change is imminent. Form fluctuates. The dilemma is determining the direction—up, down, or sideways.

Saratoga Gambler Own: Rock & Warner	B. g. 9 (Mar) Sire: Saratoga Six (Alydar) $3,500 Dam: Cold Buns (Far North) Br: Hillbrook Farm & D. Wayne Lukas (Ky) Tr: Bender M. K(0 0 0 0 .00)	Life 35 8 10 7 $383,105 104 1994 11 3 3 2 $186,430 104 1993 12 3 2 3 $115,025 100 Sa 8 3 3 1 $134,850 103	D.Fst 14 3 4 2 $149,750 103 Wet(354) 6 2 2 2 $88,130 104 Turf(243) 15 3 4 3 $145,225 103 Dst(335) 5 1 2 1 $44,350 99

29Dec94–5SA fst 6½f :21^4 :44^3 1:09^3 1:16 3↑ Clm c-32000 **77** 10 6 10^{6½} 9^{7¾} 8^{5½} 8^{5½} Pedroza M A LB116 fb *1.20 - - Indian School116^{no} Higher Flyer117½ Peak Out116¾ Showed little 11
Claimed from Porter Ken for $32,000, Spawr Bill Trainer 1994(as of 12/29): (-)
10Dec94–9Hol fst 6f :21^2 :43^4 :55^3 1:08^1 3↑ UndrwdBC-G3 **78** 9 8 7^{5¾} 8^{8¾} 9^{12} 9^{10¾} Pedroza M A LB120 fb 10.40 - - *Wekiva Springs*118^{1½} Cardmania120^{no} Gundaghia120¾ Outrun 9
15Oct94–4SA fst 6f :21^3 :44^2 :56^4 1:08^4 3↑ AnTtlBCH-G3 **103** 6 6 7^{5¼} 6^{4¾} 2^{hd} 1^3 Pedroza M A LB113 fb 34.70 - - SrtogGmbler113^3 *UncgedFury*114^{nk} ConceptWin117^{3½} Closed rush 4-wide 8

A blatant example of how horses change—how quickly they can go sour—occurred December 29, 1994, at the start of the 1994-95 winter meet at Santa Anita.

It was only six weeks after Saratoga Gambler had scored a three-length win in the $100,000 Ancient Title Handicap, and trainer Bill Spawr entered him in a $32,000 claiming race. The horse was for sale, and relatively cheap. Something was amiss. Graded stakes winners are not offered up in low-level claiming races without reason. Expectations had been lowered. In a Daily Racing Form story the day of the race, Spawr was quizzed about the maneuver. One did not need to be an expert to read between the lines. The first question was, why run Saratoga Gambler cheap, in a claiming race?

"He's for sale," Spawr said.

Then he must not be as good as he was six weeks earlier.

"No, he's not," Spawr said.

How do you think he will run?

"I think he'll win," Spawr said.

What about his physical condition?

"He's not going to break down," Spawr said.

So how good is he?

"Well, he's not as good as he was, but where do you draw the line?" Spawr said.

Where, indeed? Saratoga Gambler's form was going downhill, as evidenced by Spawr's reduced expectations. Nevertheless, bettors hammered him to odds of 6-5. He was the worst kind of favorite—a good horse going bad. Saratoga Gambler finished eighth, was claimed (purchased by another owner) for $32,000, and never raced again.

Current-condition flaws usually are in black and white in the past performances, and call only for simple interpretation and rational thinking. It is the essence of handicapping—common sense. Anyone could see Saratoga Gambler was dropping in class. But it was an illogical class drop, and usually that means a horse's form is declining.

To find winners, handicappers need to understand why a horse is entered in a particular race. And when possible, project improvement or regression. To bet winners and make money, the change must be projected before it becomes obvious to everyone. That is, while it still has parimutuel value. A trainer's intentions and expectations provide a key determinant in a handicapper's analysis of current form.

Despite Saratoga Gambler's obvious flaw, he started at depressed odds, showing there is hope for skeptical handicappers. Current form refers to the state of a horse's health, and here is one golden rule related to it. Never bet on a horse—at low odds—whose health is declining. Never bet on horses like Saratoga Gambler, or Young Husband.

Trainer Peter Eurton claimed Young Husband for $20,000 in January 1999, waited a month, and ran him back for half the claiming price—$10,000. The horse bore out (horses who drift out often are ailing), and scored an ugly win. Yes, he won. Horses going downhill do win. The example still applies. Young Husband ran twice more, and never ran again. The message was clear. In dropping Young Husband to $10,000, after claiming him for $20,000, Eurton revealed lowered expectations. Take note. No one knows a horse like a trainer. To determine if a horse is in form, the first look should be at the class level at which the horse is placed.

There are enough uncertainties in racing to deal with already; the last thing a bettor needs is to guess about the state of a horse's physical well-being. So do not worry about class, speed, or pace until after considering current form. The good, healthy horses on which you will wager come in different shapes and sizes. Most look obvious.

Different Types

Horses typically fall into one of three categories: those racing regularly, comebackers, and first-time starters. Horses racing regularly comprise the majority of starters. Current form of comebackers (horses returning from layoffs of more than 45 days) and first-time starters (horses who have never raced) is based largely on workout patterns and trainers. Analyzing their form will be the focus later in this chapter. With all three groups, the class level at which a trainer places the horse often answers the issue of condition. Is this horse ready? Is he entered in a race in which he is expected to perform well? How is the horse feeling?

Trainer Vladimir Cerin developed Early Pioneer from a horse he claimed for $62,500 into a Grade 1 winner of the Hollywood Gold Cup. Cerin describes sharp current form.

"You'll hear trainers talk about how a horse is tearing down the barn. They mean that literally as well as figuratively. Because a horse feels so good, he's not really crazy about being confined . . . once he gets done with his exercise in the morning and goes back in his stall, he'll roll, he'll jump up, he'll buck and kick, and sometimes kick the walls just because he feels so good. He wants to go out there into combat. That would be an example of a horse tearing down the barn, of a horse jumping out of his skin."

Horseplayers may not see exactly how a horse behaves at his backstretch stable. But when a horse is feeling that good, it usually is clear from his sharp recent races and the class level at which the trainer places him. If a handicapper can figure out why a horse has been placed in a particular spot, he usually can determine the horse's form. The common-sense approach generally corresponds to the horse's recent races.

A horse that is "in form" typically races at a level corresponding to one it raced well at recently. A class drop below a level of recent success is reason for concern. Typically, a horse that is in form will have produced a competitive effort, or efforts, under circumstances similar to today's race. When a veteran horse is feeling good, a top trainer finds a spot to run him.

"You might as well strike while the iron is hot," explains Jack Carava, consistently one of the leading claiming trainers in Southern California. "These old, sore claiming horses, so many of them do good for such a short period of time, that if you find a little window of opportunity where a horse gives you a sign he's doing well, you try to find any race where they could be halfway competitive. I look at works. If a horse works in 1:03, 1:03, 1:03 . . . then all of a sudden he works in :59 with his neck bowed, I kind of surmise that maybe the horse is doing a bit better than he was before."

An in-form horse usually has raced in the past month. If his last race was more than a month ago, the horse usually will show a workout pattern in the interim. While less important than the actual pattern of works, the workout clocking sometimes can be revealing, particularly if it was extraordinarily fast or slow. This is indicated by the ranking of the workout as shown below. Typically, a horse works out within two weeks of his most recent race. If he does not, there may be reason for concern.

8 Nine Chimes
Own: John J Petre
Pink Green, Pink Bars On Sleeves, Green Cap
GRAHAM J (19 1 2 3 .05) 2003: (303 15 .05)

B. c. 3 (Mar) KEESEP01 $32,000
Sire: Roar (Forty Niner) $5,000
Dam: Eight Bells (Summer Squall)
Br: Redding Family Trust (Ky)
Tr: Thornbury Jeffrey D(5 1 0 2 .20) 2003:(101 17 .17)

L 1097

Life	4	1	1	1	$25,090	89	D.Fst	1 0 1 0	$5,360 74
2003	4	1	1	1	$25,090	89	Wet(392)	2 1 0 1	$19,530 89
2002	0	M	0	0	$0	-	Turf(305)	1 0 0 0	$200 56
Kee	0	0	0	0	$0	-	Dst(367)	2 1 1 0	$22,190 89

26Sep03–8TP fst 6½f :223 :46 1:13 1:20 3↑Alw 26800N1x 74 7 5 6¾ 3½ 1½ 2hd Graham J7 L109 *2.30 77–24 Constitution116hd Nine Chimes109½ Sir Elite113¾ Inside bid, outfinishd 9

22Aug03–8EIP fm 1 Ⓣ:231 :454 1:111 1:362 Alw 30000N1x 56 1 6¾ 710 7½ 6¾ 610¼ Graham J7 L109 4.50 72–23 Justlikedawg116nk Prince Prado1221¾ Captain Amour1163 No rally 9

3Aug03–6EIP gd 6½f :221 :46 1:111 1:173 3↑Md Sp Wt 27k 89 2 8 4¾ 31 1½ 19 Graham J10 L108 21.80 91–18 NinChms1089 *FoundngChrmn*1171 HutchsonSttn111½ 5w,drew off,driving 12

10Jly03–7EIP gd 5½f ⊗:223 :463 :592 1:061 3↑Md Sp Wt 27k 61 2 6 7¾ 5¾ 5½ 3¼ Graham J10 L106 6.40 81–.16 *Devil's Triangle*1164 Libertyville116nk *Nine Chimes*1063 8w lane,minor gain 8

WORKS: ●Oct11 Kee 5f fst 1:001 H *1/22* Sep17 TP 5f fst 1:04 B *9/15* Sep12 TP 4f fst :494 B *6/21* Aug17 EIP 3f fst :361 B *2/12* Jly29 EIP 5f fst 1:023 B *2/5* Jly23 EIP 4f fst :491 Bg *2/25*

TRAINER: Dirt(119 .16 $2.14) Sprint(128 .16 $2.48) Alw(76 .12 $1.97)

Nine Chimes worked five furlongs on October 11, 2003, which was 16 days after his most recent start. Close enough. The bullet in front of the date of the October 11 work indicates it was the fastest work of the day at that distance. The "1/22" designation after the time of the work means it was the fastest of 22 works that day at that distance. His previous work on September 17 was "9/15." The work was ninth-fastest of 15 at the distance.

An in-form horse often will have finished in the money or within three lengths of the winner at a class level similar to today's race. When an in-form horse has won his last race, he usually will move up in class. An in-form horse that lost his last start will typically remain at the same level, or drop one level.

Trainers

A great deal of faith can be placed in good trainers, particularly when evaluating the class level at which they place their horses. Why? Because win percentage has become a paramount concern for trainers. Today, horsemen believe that client-owners are increasingly reliant on win percentage as a means of choosing a trainer. For this reason, trainers are reluctant to waste starts by running horses in spots where they do not belong. So long as horsemen remain concerned about maintaining credible win percentages, handicappers can rely that top horsemen, most of the time, will run their horses in races they can win.

A horse that is in undeniably good form usually has a competent trainer and jockey who win at an acceptable rate, typically above 10 percent. A trainer who wins with less than 10 percent of his starters, or a jockey that wins with less than 10 percent of his mounts, is producing fewer wins than average. The preceding guidelines are purposely liberal, and low. Obviously, a trainer who wins with 15 percent of his starters is more reliable about sending them into the right races. The higher a trainer's win percentage, the more likely his starters are in peak current form and running well. Pretty simple, don't you think?

Finish Position

The definition of "running well" can be wide ranging. For example, if the horse has finished in the top one-third of the field in recent races, it is likely that he is in form. Specifically, the horse should have done so under conditions similar to today's race. If a horse finished in the lower half of the field, without having been competitive at any stage of the race, it probably was a bad race and the horse is likely to be off form. This precludes extenuating circumstances such as traffic trouble or unusual track condition.

Likewise, low finish position can be excused if the horse is a front-runner. He may be in form even if he finished far behind the winner. Front-runners typically race to the point of exhaustion. That is, they race as fast as they can for as far as they can. When a front-runner's energy is spent, he often stops to a virtual walk. Therefore, final finish position may not be an accurate gauge of form. The horse may have been passed late in the race by others who did nothing more than pick up the pieces.

Flying Soldier
Own: Hopkins David, Peters, Todd and Robb,

B. g. 5 (Mar) BARMAR01 $40,000
Sire: Lost Soldier (Danzig) $7,500
Dam: Wing It Baby (Alysheba)
Br: John Franks (Fla)
Tr: Perez Ricardo(0 0 0 0 .00) 2003:(55 3 .05)

Life	12	1	0	0	$13,608	79			
Jumps	0	0	0	0	$0	-			
2004	3	0	0	0	$978	54	Wet	0 0 0 0	$0 -
2003	2	0	0	0	$0	79	Turf	3 0 0 0	$2,340 79

18Sep02–6Fpx fst 7f :213 :444 1:101 1:234 3↑Md 20000 52 9 5 2hd 2½ 3¼ 7¾ Almeida G F LB115 4.00 87–08 Mamone1151¾ *Apollicee*115½ Foxy Johnny1202 Vied,stalked,wkened 10

4Sep02–8Dmr fst 6f :22 :451 :581 1:113 3↑Md 25000(25-22.5) 26 3 5 21 43 6½ 816½ Almeida G F LB119 b 4.90 65–15 FightforFreedom1231½ FabDo1233 *ARealKing*1191½ Stalked inside,wkened 9

24Aug02–2Dmr fst 6f :22 :45 :572 1:104 3↑Md 50000(50-45) 57 5 1 3½ 2½ 4½ 510½ Almeida G F LB119 b 12.50 75–15 OrngeEm1192½ TriblTrick119½ AlohGoodbye1191½ Lunged bit strt,wkened 7

4Nov01–6SA fst 6½f :214 :443 1:093 1:161 Md Sp Wt 40k 44 6 3 105¾ 118 1114 1219 Enriquez I D LB118 b 93.60 68–14 BringemJung1182½ AcdemySpy118no VnRouge1182 Angled in turn,no bid 12

30Sep01–3SA fst 5½f :214 :443 :564 1:031 Md Sp Wt 38k 46 6 4 4½ 4½ 5½ 518 Solis A LB118 b 14.40 74–14 AmericnSystem1181½ Rqusto1182½ *BringmJung*1184½ Angled in, weakened 6

Running Style

A speed horse that has been fading, such as Flying Soldier, often only needs slightly softer foes in order to win. Handicappers can be more forgiving when looking at the finish position of a front-runner. If a speed horse has contended for the lead at the pace call, he is probably in form. The pace call is the next-to-last point of call, before the finish position, as shown below. By the time horses arrive at the pace call, most of their energy has been expended. A horse able to stay in contention to that late stage of the race is generally considered to be in form. Flying Solider dropped into a $20,000 maiden claiming race, the lowest class level in Southern California, and won by 1 1/4 lengths.

Workouts

Regarding a horse's training pattern, his final workout before a race should have been within seven days of the race. A horse with an irregular workout pattern—one who does not have a timed workout in the last week—may be in dubious form, regardless of recent starts. While actual race performance provides most of the information a handicapper requires, there are times when a sketchy workout pattern sends up a warning flag.

Below is an example of a horse with a questionable workout pattern. Hot Weekend was a 2-year-old filly perceived as a standout in the $75,000 Cinderella Stakes on June 8 at Hollywood Park. View the work pattern that followed her winning debut, and try to spot the flaw.

6 Hot Weekend
Own:Soares Michael & Suarez Pablo
Black Royal Blue, Red/yellow Superman
VALENZUELA P A (172 33 28 32 .19) 2003:(637 125 .20)

Dk. b or br f. 2 (Mar) BARMAR03 $50,000
Sire: Summer Squall (Storm Bird) $50,000
Dam: Burning Season(Crafty Prospector)
Br: Winsong Farm (Ky)
Tr: O'Neill Doug(98 22 13 13 .22) 2003:(263 52 .20)

L 116

Life	1	1	0	0	$26,400	84	D.Fst	1	1	0	0	$26,400	84
2003	1	1	0	0	$26,400	84	Wet(330)	0	0	0	0	$0	–
2002	0	M	0	0	$0	–	Turf(285)	0	0	0	0	$0	–
Hol	1	1	0	0	$26,400	84	Dst(320)	0	0	0	0	$0	–

15May03–2Hol fst 4½f :214 :451 :511 ⒻMd Sp Wt 45k 84 1 1 11 12½ 13 Valenzuela P A LB 119 *1.40 99–09 HotWeekend1193 CherishDestiny1194½ HiekiSunris119½ Bit off rail,clear 7
WORKS: Jun3 Hol 4f fst :533 H 17/17 May4 Hol 5f fst :594 H 4/12 ●Apr26 Hol 4f fst :463 H 1/41 Apr19 Hol 3f fst :371 H 11/26 Apr12 Hol 2f fst :242 H 3/9 Apr6 Hol 1f fst :124 H 6/13
TRAINER: 2ndStart(56 .20 $3.18) 2YO(70 .16 $1.70) Dirt(515 .20 $1.88) Sprint(442 .21 $2.10) Stakes(41 .24 $2.17)

Hot Weekend's winning Beyer Speed Figure was 10 points higher than her nearest foe's, which made me think she might be able to win the Cinderella despite her work pattern. Truthfully, I thought she would. I was wrong. Hot Weekend had only one slow workout in the 24 days since she had raced; her condition had to be considered dubious, especially at low odds of 3-2. Note the dissimilarity in workouts before her winning debut, and before the Cinderella. Hot Weekend surrendered at the top of the stretch and finished a weary sixth in the stakes.

A lot goes on behind the scenes to prepare a horse for a race. In order to compete effectively, horses endure rigorous exercise that usually includes a full-speed workout once a week, in addition to standard daily exercise. On a normal day, horses typically gallop a mile and a half to two miles. Although extended gallops provide some benefit, full-speed workouts are what fully activate the aerobic system and simulate the demands that will be placed on a horse during a race. As the Hot Weekend example shows, horses with a workout deficit often come up short.

From A To Z
Own: Kruse David R & Linda
Shocking Pink, Green Golf Emblem On Back
ATKINSON P (20 1 3 0 .05) 2002:(20 2 .10)

B. c. 3 (Apr) OBSMAR01 $17,000
Sire: Alphabet Soup (Cozzene) $30,000
Dam: E. Cherie(Go Step)
Br: Brereton C Jones (Ky)
Tr: Jackson Bruce L(14 1 1 1 .07) 2002:(13 1 .08)

L 120

Life	2	M	0	0	$3,820	80	D.Fst	2	0	0	0	$3,820	80
2002	1	M	0	0	$2,880	74	Wet(279)	0	0	0	0	$0	–
2001	1	M	0	0	$940	80	Turf(267)	0	0	0	0	$0	–
SA	1	0	0	0	$2,880	74	Dist	0	0	0	0	$0	–

17Mar02–4SA fst 6½f :213 :444 1:10 1:164 Md Sp Wt 48k 74 3 5 2hd 1hd 32 44½ Atkinson P LB 120 18.40 84–12 Regiment1201 DoWhtsRight1203½ DoublOption120hd Dueled btwn,lost 3rd 12
19Aug01–4Dmr fst 5½f :22 :444 :564 1:03 Md Sp Wt 47k 80 7 2 21½ 54½ 55½ 57½ Atkinson P LB 118 36.60 89–07 *Sunray Spirit*1182 Requesto1182 Timely Action1182½ Early speed, tired 9
WORKS: Apr2 SA 3f fst :372 H 7/8 Mar26 SA 3f fst :354 H 5/11 Mar10 SA 6f fst 1:133 H 4/17 Mar4 SA 7f fst 1:26 H 1/1 Feb25 SA 6f fst 1:143 H 18/23 Feb19 SA 6f fst 1:13 H 2/31
TRAINER: Dirt(40 .18 $4.37) Sprint(26 .15 $5.68) MdnSpWt(14 .07 $1.57)

Racing Performance

The horse's most recent start—his last running line—provides the greatest indication regarding current form. Horses who are in form typically will have challenged for the lead at a late stage of the race. Regardless of where the horse finished, an in-form horse will have challenged at either the pace call (usually the point in the race with a quarter-mile remaining), or the stretch call (the final call before the finish). The above example of From A to Z is a horse whose last start meets the criteria. He would be considered to be in form. In his next start on April 6, he won a maiden race and paid $58.40.

In referring to the last running line, the issue is determining what it means to "challenge for the lead" or "loom a threat." Some handicappers use fixed rules that mandate eliminating horses that were not within three lengths of the lead at the stretch call in sprint races, or within five lengths of the lead at the stretch call in route races. By those standards, horses not within the guidelines are considered to be off form.

The drawback to specific rules is that they discourage handicappers from thinking for themselves. A horse that was positioned within a reasonable margin of the leader at the pace call can be considered to be in form. A reasonable margin can be within three lengths of the lead at the pace call in a sprint. But what if the horse was within 3 1/2 lengths, then what? Use common sense. The guidelines are not meant to be precise. In routes, the "reasonable margin" guideline might be extended to four lengths at the pace call. Basically, if a horse was relatively competitive deep into the race, then he might be considered to be in form. These general guidelines refer mostly to horses with speed. Come-from-behind types rarely challenge for the lead until the final furlong, when the front-runners are spent. Determining current form of come-from-behinders is more difficult because they often are dependent on a collapse of the pacesetters in order to be competitive.

Late-Runners and Turf Horses

It probably is overly simplistic to abandon late-runners altogether, though in dirt races they do not win their fair share. Dirt racing favors horses with speed. There are times, of course, when a handicapper can anticipate a pace meltdown and seek an opportunistic late-runner to pick up the spoils. An in-form late-runner typically will have finished in the top half of the field in his last start, or a recent start under comparable conditions.

Similar guidelines apply when analyzing the current form of a turf horse. A turf horse whose style is to race close to the lead should have been competitive at the pace call, or stretch call. A turf horse that rallies from behind should have finished in the top half of the field, or within a reasonable margin of the winner.

There are differences in analyzing the current form of a Grade 1 stakes horse such as Cigar, and a $10,000 claiming horse. Current form is considered in light of the class of the horse. Grade 1 horses typically reproduce top form regardless of the 45-day parameter. A Grade 1 horse with a steady work pattern and top trainer can be expected to run well in a Grade 1 even if he has not raced in two months, or longer.

The same is not true with a low-level claiming horse. Cheaper horses should have raced recently if their most recent start is to provide indication of form. Otherwise, the horse might be considered a layoff horse and evaluated accordingly. Claiming horses typically do not go more than a month between starts.

While the issue of current form is the first and foremost consideration for a handicapper, one must use care. This is only the initial stage, after all. Some discretion is required in eliminating horses. There are few worse feelings for a handicapper than prematurely throwing out the ensuing winner without evaluating class, speed, or pace. Consideration of current form is purposely broad, and intended primarily to cast doubt on otherwise logical contenders, or give reason for a closer look at borderline entrants.

The class-level placement of horses works in both directions. A horse dropping in class following a good race may be deteriorating. Conversely, a horse moving up in class after a seemingly nondescript race might be worth extra consideration, particularly if a winning stable is the one employing the raise.

A handicapper places himself in the position of the trainer by asking, what is the reason for this horse to enter this particular race? When an in-form horse is raised in class by a competent trainer, it means expectations have been raised. The horse is moving ahead to face stronger competition, and race for higher purse money, because the trainer believes the horse can handle tougher company. There are few reasons for a top trainer to raise a horse in class if the horse is not up to the challenge. Especially these days, when horsemen are increasingly concerned with win percentage. Strike while the iron is hot.

Heightened expectations of a trainer still produce generous payoff potential. This is such a basic concept that sometimes it can be employed without extensive consideration of speed or pace.

Form and class, however, are closely intertwined, and change radically in short periods. A horse that struggles to hit the board in a $10,000 claiming race may be winning regularly at the $20,000 claiming level or higher only a few weeks later. Horses "get good" for bursts of time, and during those periods, they frequently offer the best bets in racing. When a horse is sharp and getting sharper, the sky is the limit. A hot horse going up the ladder, into virgin class territory, often offers unlimited possibilities.

Early in his career, Bluesthestandard was a $10,000 claiming horse who shifted from one barn to another and raced well for everyone. But he had a fair share of infirmities, which precluded an aggressive workout regimen that could have led to improved performances against better competition. Instead, trainers Susan Weston, Scott Hansen, Mark Glatt, and Ahmad Salih all trained Bluesthestandard delicately, and appropriately. His physical problems were properly managed, and the gelding responded by winning races for every trainer who cared for him.

Then, over time, Bluesthestandard's imperfections waned. The horse began to feel better, and was able to withstand more rigorous training. His racing performances improved along with the stepped-up workout pattern and he gradually rose in class. By the time that Ted H. West claimed him for $50,000 on December 31, 2002, Bluesthestandard had never been better. Up the ladder he continued, responding to aggressive workouts, and winning graded stakes in the spring of his 5-year-old season.

```
8 Bluesthestandard                          B. g. 6 (Apr)                                            Life 26 14 5 3 $571,185 111 | D.Fst 26 14 5 3 $571,185 111
Pink Own: Jeffrey Sengara                   Sire: American Standard (In Reality) $1,500              2003  9  4 1 2 $395,975 111 | Wet(313) 0 0 0 0 $0 -
Hot Pink, Purple Star, Purple Collar        Dam: Bob's Blue (Bob's Dusty)                      L 126 2002 14  7 4 1 $148,810  99 | Turf(226) 0 0 0 0 $0 -
SMITH M E (62 12 7 10 .19) 2003: (754 124 .16)  Br: Terry Brown (Ga)                                 SA   11  7 2 1 $232,715 105 | Dst(306) 9 5 2 2 $135,025 111
                                            Tr: West Ted H(8 0 2 1 .00) 2003:(141 30 .21)

5Oct03-7SA fst 6f :212 :432 :5521:08 3↑AnTtlBCH-G1 103 5 3 32½ 42 32 31½ Smith M E LB115 7.00 96-06 Avnzdo1161½ CptinSquire117hd Blusthstndrd1151½ 3wd into lane,missd 2d 6
17Aug03-8Dmr fst 7f :221 :44 1:0811:212 3↑POBrienH-G2 87 7 4 1½ 2hd 33½ 78¾ Solis A LB117 *1.50 86-09 Dstrbnthpc1162 RshntAltr1174½ FllMnMdnss119½ Dueled btwn,weakened 10
26Jly03-6Dmr fst 6f :214 :44 :5531:074 3↑BCrsbBCH-G2 111 3 4 52½ 52½ 33 31¾ Pedroza M A LB117 9.90 100-07 BeusTown1191½ CptinSquir117nk Blusthstndrd1172 3wd into str,missed 2d 9
5Jly03-8Hol fst 7f :214 :442 1:0821:212 3↑TrBndBCH-G1 101 8 1 41¼ 41½ 21 31½ Pedroza M A LB117 3.90 93-11 JoeyFranco118hd Publiction1161½ [D]Bluesthestndrd1173½ Bid,driftd in 1/8 9
  Disqualified and placed 6th
26May03-8LS fst 1 1/16 :224 :46 1:1011:42 3↑LSParkH-G3 102 8 41½ 43 21 22 22¾ ↓Pedroza M A L120 *1.50 89-08 PNBrgr1172¾ [DH]MysvllSlw114 [DH]Blsthstndrd1201½ Pulled early,no match 8
26Apr03-9LS fst 1 :234 :47 1:1041:353 3↑TexsMile-G3 108 9 21½ 22½ 2½ 12 14 Pedroza M A L120 *1.50 95-16 Bluesthestndrd1204 Bonpw116nk Compendium116½ Drew away,ridden out 9
29Mar03-8SA fst 6½f :212 :44 1:0821:144 4↑PtrGrBCH-G2 105 7 5 32 1hd 1hd 12 Smith M E LB115 f 2.20 99-10 Bluesthestandard1152 JoeyFranco116½ KonaGold1215½ 3wd bid,cleared,held 7
12Mar03-6SA fst 1 1/16 :23 :461 1:1021:43 4↑OClm 100000N 99 6 2½ 1½ 11½ 12 1no Almeida G F LB118 f 3.60 89-13 Blsthstndrd110no BrngHomThgold1181 BnsPyDy1201 3-4 wd, cleared, held 9
17Feb03-9SA fst 6½f :214 :434 1:0921:152 4↑OClm 62500N 104 3 7 1hd 1hd 11½ 14 Krone J A LB119 f 4.10 96-13 Bluesthestandard1194 SunsetPlce1182½ Denied119½ Inside,steady handling 9
31Dec02-4SA fst 6f :212 :441 :5641:093 3↑Clm c-(50-45) 85 7 2 66½ 23 1hd 15½ Pincay L Jr LB121 f *.90 90-13 Bluesthestndrd1215½ MrFreckles115nk Hzctsy119no 5wd to turn,ridden out 7
  Claimed from Cutuli, Joseph, Moran, Michael A. and Sobel, Steven for $50,000 [Glatt Mark Trainer 2002(as of 12/31): (272 44 31 35 0.16)]
13Dec02-6Hol fst 7f :222 :444 1:09 1:212 3↑OClm 80000 91 2 3 31 31½ 22 35½ Pincay L Jr LB120 f 3.80 86-12 Olmodvor1183 FreedomCrest1182½ Bluesthestndrd1204 3wd 1/2,no late bid 5
17Nov02-7GG fst 6f :222 :453 :5741:094 3↑Alw 36712N1x 92 2 9 910 910 74¾ 12 Baze R A LB120 f *.60 88-18 Bluesthestandard1202 Blazing Road120½ Tonco115nk Bold rally, driving 9
12Oct02-7SA fst 6½f :22 :443 1:09 1:152 3↑Alw 45810N1x 95 5 5 31½ 21 21 21½ Pincay L Jr LB118 f 5.30 94-09 SunsetPlace1181½ Bluesthestndrd1182 Primeric1202 Btwn to turn,2nd best 8
31Aug02-2Dmr fst 6½f :222 :452 1:1021:163 3↑Clm 50000(50-45) 89 5 5 51¾ 61½ 3½ 21 Pincay L Jr LB119 f 6.30 91-13 ChampsStar1161 Bluesthestandrd1192 ReEcho1214½ 3wd bid,drfted in,led 7
7Aug02-6Dmr fst 6f :222 :444 :57 1:094 3↑Clm 32000(32-28) 95 2 5 61¾ 32½ 31½ 1no Pincay L Jr LB119 f 5.10 91-13 Bluesthestndrd119no KineticBnd1192½ AlwysGm1191½ Rail bid,just up late 8
7Jly02-7Hol fst 7f :22 :443 1:0931:223 4↑Clm 40000(40-35) 76 5 1 41½ 31 53¾ 48 Pincay L Jr LB118 f *1.80 78-12 Re Echo1202 Divine Spirit1182 B. T. Gotrich1184 4wd into lane,wkened 7
31May02-5Hol fst 6f :221 :45 :57 1:102 4↑Clm 20000(20-18) 99 7 3 53¼ 3½ 12½ 12 Pincay L Jr LB118 f *1.10 88-19 Bluesthestandard1182 Stoney1181 Holy Mackerel1184 3wd bid,led,clear 8
11May02-2Hol fst 6f :222 :45 :57 1:092 4↑Clm 25000(25-22.5) 98 3 5 41½ 42½ 33 23 Gomez G K LB118 f *2.50 90-14 Expressionist1183 Bluesthestandard118no Stoney1184½ Came out, late 2nd 7
20Apr02-8SA fst 6f :212 :443 :5641:093 4↑Clm 20000(20-18) 92 6 3 64¼ 43½ 41¾ 2½ Nakatani C S LB118 f 3.70 89-09 Aggressive118½ Bluesthstndrd1182 BigTmSpirit1182 4wd into lane,willing 8
16Mar02-5SA fst 6½f :22 :452 1:10 1:161 4↑Clm c-10000 89 9 3 31½ 1½ 11½ 11½ Nakatani C S LB122 f *.70 92-12 Blusthstndrd1221½ Mdillothmoon1186½ PicLittl118½ 3wd,steady handling 9
  Claimed from Al Mudarris Salah for $10,000 [Salih Ahmad S Trainer 2002(as of 3/16): (7 3 1 0 0.43)]
17Feb02-6SA fst 7f :224 :46 1:1041:233 4↑Clm c-(16-14) 99 3 5 41½ 31½ 31½ 12 Pincay L Jr LB119 f *1.70 87-16 Bluesthestndrd1192 CMerrillRun1171½ VisulEnrgy1191 Bumped 3/16,rallied 10
  Claimed from Cutuli, Joseph, Moran, Michael A. and Sobel, Steven for $16,000 [Glatt Mark Trainer 2001: (332 39 39 42 0.12)]
2Feb02-10SA fst 7f :223 :46 1:11 1:231 4↑Clm c-10000 94 6 2 21 41½ 12½ 16 Nakatani C S LB121 f *1.00 89-09 Bluesthestandard1216 HotWarsawNights1143 Nikw119½ Rail bid,ridden out 8
  Claimed from Englander Richard A. for $10,000 [Hansen Scott Trainer 2001: (92 13 14 9 0.14)]
1Jan02-3SA fst 6½f :213 :441 1:0921:16 4↑Clm 20000(20-18) 76 3 5 1hd 1hd 21½ 45 Nakatani C S LB119 f 3.00 88-07 NoApollogee1212½ TillisVictor119hd CptinBll1192½ Inside duel, weakened 8
9Dec01-5Hol fst 6½f :222 :45 1:0941:161 3↑Clm 12500(12.5-10.5) 91 9 2 1hd 11 11½ 12 Puglisi I LB118 f 2.60 90-14 Blusthstndrd1182 FlshyFinish118nk HitthBigTim1182 Dueled,clear,driving 9
26May01-2Hol fst 7f :223 :453 1:10 1:224 4↑Clm 10000(10-9) 81 2 4 1½ 1½ 12 12 Puglisi I LB118 f *1.40 85-08 Bluesthestndrd1182 Argolid1204 PririeSwinger1181½ Inside,mild hand ride 5
25Apr01-8Hol fst 6f :221 :452 :58 1:11 3↑Md c-(25-22.5) 73 9 1 3nk 1hd 12½ 11½ Jaime R7 B114 f 9.20 85-16 Bluesthestndrd1141½ Smokevill1235 Flinnopin117nk Dueled 3 wide, driving 9
  Claimed from Weston Susan for $22,500 [Weston Susan Trainer 2001(as of 4/25): (2 1 0 0 0.50)]
WORKS: ●Oct19 SA 4f fst :452 H 1/38 ●Oct12 SA 3f fst :331 B 1/25 ●Sep29 SA 5f fst :58 H 1/41 ●Sep23 Fpx 5f fst :584 H 1/5 ●Sep17 Fpx 4f fst :463 H 1/14 ●Sep12 Fpx 3f fst :34 H 1/9
TRAINER: 2Off45-180(38 .32 $3.26) Dirt(222 .21 $1.79) Sprint(192 .21 $1.82) GrdStk(20 .15 $1.04)
```

While Bluesthestandard's ascent was gradual, improvement that is sudden occurs each spring with 3-year-olds. During the 2003 Santa Anita meet, Jeff Mullins was the hottest trainer in California, winning at a sizzling 35 percent rate (20 percent is considered very good). Mullins entered horses in the proper races, and they consistently delivered. Still, horseplayers are reluctant to back a horse based on non-quantifiable factors. Rather than attribute improvement to simple improved form, they credit it to other factors, such as change of surface or distance. That is what happened with the 3-year-old gelding Buddy Gil, a Mullins-trained longshot in the Grade 2 San Felipe Stakes on March 16.

```
5 Buddy Gil                                  B. g. 3 (Feb)                                           Life 7 3 1 1 $129,455 106 | D.Fst 4 2 1 1 $58,850 95
Green Own:Desperado St & McFadden &Merrill St  Sire: Eastern Echo (Damascus) $3,000                  2003 2 1 0 0  $68,730 106 | Wet(355) 2 0 0 0 $1,875 78
Black, Gold Compass Rose On Back             Dam: Really Rising(For Really)                    L 119 2002 5 2 1 1  $60,725  95 | Turf(260*) 1 1 0 0 $68,730 106
STEVENS G L (65 11 8 9 .17) 2003:(65 11 .17) Br: Billingsley Creek Ranch (Ky)                        SA   0 0 0 0       $0   - | Dst(300) 1 0 0 0 $0 78
                                             Tr: Mullins Jeff(65 20 21 7 .31) 2003:(64 20 .31)

23Feb03-8SA fm *6½f ⓣ :214 :432 1:062 1:122 Baldwin-G3 106 8 2 53½ 52¾ 22½ 12 Stevens G L LB 117 26.70 95-11 BuddyGil1172 KingRobyn1164 FlirtWithFortun1161 5wd into lane,rallied 11
  Previously trained by Jenda Charles J.
11Jan03-8GG my 1 1/16 :221 :452 1:103 1:433 GldnGate DbyG3 78 2 44½ 45½ 42 43½ 74½ Krigger K LB 120 7.70 80-17 Standard Setter120nk Ozzie Cat1201 Pine ForJava120¾ Bid rail, weakened 10
14Dec02-8GG sly 1 :222 :452 1:104 1:381 Gold Rush81k 65 6 1hd 2hd 1hd 44 511 Figueroa O LB 117 f 1.50 68-22 Spensive115hd AlwysRemembr1152½ NturlBlnc1172 Dueled outside, stppd 6
24Nov02-2GG fst 6f :22 :45 :572 1:103 Golden Bear65k 95 4 2 3½ 2½ 13 17½ Figueroa O LB 115 7.30 84-21 BuddyGil1157½ NturlBlnce1172 BsesAreLodd116hd Bid 3w,drew clear drvg 5
17Oct02-6BM fst 1 :231 :47 1:111 1:363 Md Sp Wt 31k 75 3 21 2½ 2hd 1hd 11¼ Lumpkins J LB 118 *1.40 87-10 Buddy Gil1181¼ Onebigbag118½ Winning Stripes113½ Dueled 2w, drvng 8
28Sep02-1BM fst 6f :221 :443 :564 1:094 Md Sp Wt 29k 74 6 4 2hd 2hd 2hd 21¼ Lumpkins J LB 118 2.00 89-11 Quietly Quick1181¼ Buddy Gil1185½ Thanks Dr. G.118½ Hustled, outrun late 7
7Sep02-5BM fst 5½f :211 :441 :564 1:032 Md Sp Wt 28k 64 2 3 44 45½ 34½ 33½ Lumpkins J LB 118 4.60 87-15 Endemaj118½ Attack Force1133 Buddy Gil1186 Svd grnd, gaining 7
WORKS: ●Mar11 SA 5f fst :574 H 1/25 ●Mar5 SA 5f fst :582 H 1/12 Feb15 SA 5f gd 1:043 H 61/68 Feb5 SA ⓣ 5f fm 1:013 H (d)2/3 ●Jan29 SA 4f fst :461 H 1/33 Dec24 GG 4f fst :511 H 69/90
TRAINER: Turf/Dirt(18 .22 $2.50) Sprint/Route(29 .14 $1.23) Dirt(201 .23 $2.29) Routes(91 .19 $2.10) GrdStk(10 .20 $8.60)
```

Buddy Gil had raced three weeks earlier in a turf sprint, his first start since being transferred to Mullins, and woke up with a 26-1 upset. The victory earned him a career-high speed figure. Improved speed figures are a sure indication of improved form. But handicappers still questioned why Buddy Gil had woken up. Conventional reasoning was the surface switch to grass, or the distance switch to sprint. Possibly both. But form analysts offered an alternative. Perhaps, after transferring into Mullins's barn,

Buddy Gil had simply become a better, faster racehorse. That is yet another sign of pending form improvement—a transfer into a winning barn.

A brilliant work pattern following the turf sprint indicated Buddy Gil remained in peak form going into the San Felipe. Buddy Gil was a sharp horse moving up in class. If the reasons for his improvement were surface or distance, he would be exposed. However, if the reason was simple improved form, then 9-1 odds were fat. Buddy Gil, razor sharp, won the San Felipe by a nose and returned $21.60 for $2.

Buddy Gil's example illustrated a number of signs of imminent form improvement. These include:

Improved finish position
Improved speed figures
Faster workouts
Transfer to winning barn

Considering all the above, the only real surprise would have been if Buddy Gil had not run well in the San Felipe.

Charismatic
Own: Lewis Robert B. and Beverly J

Ch. h. 8 (Mar)
Sire: Summer Squall (Storm Bird) $50,000
Dam: Bali Babe (Drone)
Br: Parrish Hill Farm & W. S. Farish (Ky)
Tr: Lukas D. W(18 0 1 1 .00) 2003:(663 71 .11)

Life	17	5	2	4	$2,038,064	108	D.Fst	15	5	2	4	$2,035,934	108
1999	10	4	2	1	$2,007,404	108	Wet(317)	1	0	0	0	$2,130	71
1998	7	1	0	3	$30,660	85	Turf(275)	1	0	0	0	$0	24
Sa	7	1	1	2	$96,610	94	Dst(356)	1	0	0	0	$45,000	94

5Jun99-9Bel	fst	1½	:473 1:12 2:014 2:274	Belmont-G1	**107**	4	2hd	2½	1hd	2½	31½
15May99-10Pim	fst	1 3/16	:451 1:101 1:351 1:551	Preaknss-G1	**107**	6	106	107¾	83¾	13	11½
1May99-8CD	fst	1¼	:474 1:122 1:372 2:031	KyDerby-G1	**108**	16	73½	72¾	31½	2½	1nk
18Apr99-8Kee	fst	1 1/16	:231 :464 1:103 1:41	ClmrLex-G2	**108**	5	65	42½	31½	2hd	12½
3Apr99-5SA	fst	1⅛	:471 1:112 1:361 1:484	SADerby-G1	**94**	8	63½	63¾	64	57	48¼
6Mar99-7BM	fst	1 1/16	:224 :46 1:10 1:431	ElCamRlD-G3	**95**	2	67½	67½	64¾	33½	2hd
19Feb99-6SA	fst	7f	:214 :434 1:081 1:212	Alw 50000N$Y	**94**	2	4	59½	59	36½	25
11Feb99-6SA	fst	6½f	:214 :442 1:102 1:171	Clm 62500(62.5-55)	**80**	8	7	86¼	65	54	2nk
Placed first through disqualification											
31Jan99-8SA	gd	1 1/16	:234 :473 1:12 1:424	StCtlina-G2	**71**	2	52½	54¼	55	57½	513½
16Jan99-5SA	fst	1 1/16	:233 :472 1:114 1:44	Alw 54000N$Y	**78**	8	73¼	75¾	73½	73¼	54

Antley C W	L126	*1.60	103-06	LmonDropKid126hd VisionndVrs1261½ Chrismtic1264¾	Drifted, vanned off	12
Antley C W	L126	8.40	89-09	Charismatic1261½ Menifee126hd *Badge*1262½	5wd mv,drftd 3/16,drvg	13
Antley C W	L126	31.30	89-14	*Charismatic*126nk Menifee126¾ Cat Thief1261¼	5-wide trip,driving	19
Bailey J D	L115	12.10	103-07	*Charismatic*1152½ YnkeeVictor115¾ FindersGold1152	3 wide 2nd turn,drvng	12
Pincay L Jr	LB120	44.30	83-13	GenrlChllng1203½ PrimTimbr1203½ DsrtHro1201¼	Improved position some	8
Warren R J Jr	LB115	10.60	83-24	Cliquot115hd Charismatic1153½ No Cal Bread117¾	Angled out, rallied	7
Pincay L Jr	LB117	17.20	93-08	Apremont1195 Charismatic1172 *Forestry*1197	Finished willingly	5
McCarron C J	LB117	2.70	82-17	[D]What Say You110nk Charismatic117nk ValleyDon1171	Bothered near 1/8	9
Pincay L Jr	LB117	30.10	75-15	GeneralChallenge1173 BuckTrout1201 Brillintly1153½	Bit tight 7/8,wkened	5
Pincay L Jr	LB117	17.90	79-16	Mr. Broad Blade116hd Brilliantly1161 Outstanding Hero1162	Bit tight 3/4	10

Sudden improved form frequently can be accepted at face value, particularly with 3-year-olds early in the season. Form interpretation allows handicappers to delay applications of speed and pace. Instead, it allows one to wager with confidence. After all, what limits are there on improving horses?

When a horse's last start is better than the one before, there is a pretty good chance the horse is getting better. This is common-sense stuff. Charismatic was on the road to nowhere in winter 1999, producing a series of stale, noncompetitive performances. For those reasons, trainer D. Wayne Lukas and owners Bob and Beverly Lewis lowered expectations and dropped the chestnut into a $62,500 claiming race.

Illustrating the meteoric improvement that frequently occurs in spring, Charismatic got good. He crossed the wire second in the claiming race (placed first via disqualification), and was on his way. Runner-up in an allowance race, and again in a Bay Meadows stakes, he followed with a modest fourth in the Santa Anita Derby. Two weeks later, his form bloomed further, as Lukas hinted by where he placed the horse. Raising expectations, Lukas flew Charismatic to Kentucky, where he uncorked a smashing performance in the Lexington Stakes at Keeneland, winning clear and earning a huge speed figure. Charismatic's form was going through the roof.

Two weeks afterward, and less than three months after needing a disqualification to win a claiming race, Charismatic won the Kentucky Derby. His rapid ascension shows how quickly horses can progress, and when a winning horseman reveals heightened expectations, the ride can be thrilling from every perspective. When he won the Derby, Charismatic paid $64.60.

The same thing happens in claiming races, all the time. Trainer Craig Dollase claimed Roncesvalles on January 20, 2000, for $32,000. He ran poorly, finishing last. But three weeks later, new trainer Dollase brought Roncesvalles back at a higher class level. The message? Roncesvalles had improved. Expectations had been raised. Roncesvalles paid $18.

The patterns repeat year after year. In winter 2002, Dollase scored a maiden sprint victory with a filly making her second start. The final time was moderate, but one month later Dollase brought the filly back in the Grade 1 Hollywood Starlet, facing odds-on favorite Composure. Elloluv broke on top, and raced gate to wire. She paid $63.60. Dollase, high percentage throughout his career, does not waste starts. When a good trainer pushes a horse up in class, look out.

Tiznow
Own: Cooper M & Est of C Straub–Rubens

B. c. 3 (Mar)
Sire: Cee's Tizzy (Relaunch) $5,000
Dam: Cee's Song(Seattle Song)
Br: Cecilia Straub Rubens (Cal)
Tr: Robbins Jay M (—) 2000:(60 9 .15)

Life	9	5	3	0	$3,445,950	119
2000	9	5	3	0	$3,445,950	119
1999	0	M	0	0	$0	–
CSC	0	0	0	0	$0	–
D.Fst	9	5	3	0	$3,445,950	119
Wet(345)	0	0	0	0	$0	–
Turf(160)	0	0	0	0	$0	–
Dist	0	0	0	0	$0	–

4Nov00-10CD fst 1¼ :472 1:12 1:36 2:003 3↑ BC Classic-G1 116 12 1hd 1hd 1hd 1hd 1nk McCarron C J L 122 9.20 107 — Tiznow122nk **Gint'sCusewy**122¾ **CptinSteve**122hd Duel,headed,gamely,drv 13
15Oct00-7SA fst 1⅛ :47 1:104 1:35 1:471 3↑ GoodwoodBCH-G2 119 7 11½ 11 1½ 1hd 1½ McCarron C J LB 116 *1.20 99–13 *Tiznow*116½ **Captain Steve**1171½ Euchre1154 Rated, repulsed rival 7
30Sep00-6LaD fst 1¼ :471 1:102 1:351 1:594 Super Derby-G1 114 4 1hd 1½ 11 13 16 McCarron C J L 124 *.80 103–05 *Tiznow*1246 **Commendable**1241 Mass Market1249 Restrained, ridden out 6
26Aug00-8Dmr fst 1¼ :452 1:094 1:35 2:011 3↑ PacificClsc-G1 115 4 32 33½ 21½ 22½ 22 McCarron C J LB 117 4.00 93–14 Skimming1242 *Tiznow*1171¼ Ecton Park124½ Chased,bid, 2nd best 7
23Jly00-6Hol fst 1⅛ :464 1:103 1:352 1:48 Swaps-G1 107 1 41½ 42 41 21½ 22½ Espinoza V LB 118 b 2.90 86–11 **Captain Steve**1202½ Tiznow1181 Spacelink1182 Pulld,trapped rail 3/8 6
1Jly00-8Hol fst 1 1/16 :231 :46 1:101 1:421 Affirmed H-G3 103 3 42 31 3½ 2hd 1nk Espinoza V LB 111 b 10.80 89–18 Tiznow111nk ***Dixie Union***1222 Millencolin1172 Tight rail 7-1/2 & 3/8 6
31May00-4Hol fst 1 1/16 :233 :462 1:104 1:424 3↑ Md Sp Wt 52k 95 5 2½ 2hd 12 14½ 18½ Solis A LB 115 b *1.30 86–21 *Tiznow*1158½ *ColdwterCnyon*1163½ FctulEvidenc115hd Drew off, ridden out 9
11May00-6Hol fst 1 1/16 :232 :47 1:12 1:431 3↑ Md Sp Wt 47k 99 3 73½ 41¼ 42 21 2nk Solis A LB 115 b *2.20 84–15 *SpicyStuff*115nk *Tiznow*1154 ColdwterCnyon116½ Crowded strt,waitd 1/4 9
22Apr00-7SA fst 6f :212 :441 :563 1:10 Md Sp Wt 47k 82 8 5 63¾ 810 78¼ 63 Solis A B 122 bn 13.80 86–13 Mr.Wondrfl1222½ *ProgrmmdAppl*122no CocontWlly122hd Steadied near 3/8 10

Want to understand current form? Watch where good horsemen place their horses. In summer 2000, an unknown California-bred won a maiden race by open lengths. He was entered next in a Grade 3 stakes, an enterprising move by conservative trainer Jay Robbins. Expectations were clear. Robbins said before the race that Tiznow—winner of a single maiden race—was one of the best horses he had trained in more than 30 years at the track.

Handicappers could surmise Robbins's intent simply by viewing the past performances. They showed a recent maiden winner in a graded stakes. Tiznow won the Affirmed Handicap, and paid $23.60. He went on to win the Goodwood, Super Derby, Breeders' Cup Classic, and be named Horse of the Year. For some bettors, Tiznow already was the play of the summer.

This does not mean a handicapper should automatically embrace every horse moving up in class. There must be reasons in the horse's improving performances to support the maneuver. But when the class raise is employed by a good trainer, and the horse's last start was good, a bettor can confidently surmise that the horse is improving.

Negative Drops

Opposite heightened expectations shown by class raises, curious class drops reveal lowered expectations. Wagering on horses whose connections are surrendering is a losing angle, as Saratoga Gambler showed earlier. Illogical class drops are reason to be wary; they send up a red flag regarding current form. The warning signs do not always lead to winning wagers, but they help avoid losing ones.

6 **Chalet Chanteuse**
Black
Own: A & R Stable LLC or Class Racing Stab
Blue, Red And White A/r In White
$25,000
ESPINOZA V (63 11 7 10 .17) 2003: (1076 161 .15)

Ch. f. 2 (Mar)
Sire: Swiss Yodeler (Eastern Echo) $4,000
Dam: Peggy Do (Sharp Victor)
Br: Carol A Turner & Heinz Steinmann (Cal)
Tr: Hines N J(6 0 0 1 .00) 2003:(131 19 .15)

L 118

Life	6	2	1	0	$52,500	71
2003	6	2	1	0	$52,500	71
2002	0	M	0	0	$0	-
SA	0	0	0	0	$0	-
D.Fst	6	2	1	0	$52,500	71
Wet(413)	0	0	0	0	$0	-
Turf(241*)	0	0	0	0	$0	-
Dst(351)	0	0	0	0	$0	-

18Aug03-1Dmr fst 5½f :22 :451 :58 1:05 ⒻClm c-(40-35) 71 4 2 11 11½ 11½ 12 Espinoza V LB118 fb 3.30 90-09 ChaletChnteuse1182 FreesLilLss1207 BongoKitty1181 Inside, held gamely 6
Claimed from Steinmann Heinz for $40,000, Harrington Mike Trainer 2003(as of 8/18): (152 16 20 18 0.11)
9Jly03-1Hol fst 5½f :214 :452 :582 1:06 ⒻClm 55000(62.5-55) 53 4 1 1hd 11 2hd 22½ Espinoza V LB114 b 2.30 75-17 FstSplsh1162½ *ChletChnteuse*1143½ ConclthDl1206½ 4wd,angled in,2nd best 4
8Jun03-7Hol fst 5½f :213 :444 :572 1:042 ⒻCinderella84k 30 4 4 52½ 76 810 818½ Solis A O LB116 b 33.90 67-15 YogisPolrBr1133 SmokBrk1162 OutrgousOystr1162½ Pulled,steadied 4-1/2 9
26May03-1Hol fst 5f :22 :46 :584 ⒻMd 40000(40-35) 68 1 2 12½ 13 12 13 Espinoza V LB119 b 4.00 90-11 ChltChntus1193 ChmpsRockt1194½ Girlsnthoffc1191 Rail,strong hand ride 7
15May03-8Hol fst 4½f :22 :461 :522 ⒻMd 40000(40-35) 50 9 8 77¼ 65¼ 43¼ Espinoza V LB119 10.00 90-09 ConceltheDel1191¼ PpsPickpockt1191 TwistdHumor1191 Late bid outside 10
1May03-8Hol fst 4½f :22 :461 :524 ⒻMd 40000(40-35) 29 7 7 56½ 64 67 Espinoza V LB119 5.00 84-10 OkieDokiKooki1192 HiddnImg1191 ChmpsRockt1192½ Steadied 1/8,no bid 10
WORKS: Oct11 **Hol 5f fst 1:021 H** *30/42* Oct4 **Hol 5f fst 1:053 H** *39/39* Sep19 **Hol 3f fst :374 H** *2/6* Sep9 **Dmr 3f fst :361 H** *5/11* Sep4 **Dmr 4f fst :501 H** *30/33* Aug14 **Dmr 3f fst :361 H** *7/24*
TRAINER: 1stClaim(39 .05 $0.26) 61-180Days(27 .11 $0.92) 2YO(6 .00 $0.00) 31-60Days(121 .11 $1.01) Dirt(236 .12 $1.20) Sprint(175 .11 $1.13)

A good example occurred during the 2003 fall Oak Tree meet at Santa Anita. Chalet Chanteuse was returning from a two-month layoff for a new trainer. Nick Hines had claimed the filly for $40,000—she won the race—but then she did not resurface for two months. And when she did, she was entered for a claiming price of only $25,000. Her new connections were willing to take a loss of $15,000.

Chalet Chanteuse was hammered to even money, and finished a dreadful third in a slow race. The performance was hardly surprising. The filly's current condition was in a state of decline, as shown by the class level at which she was entered.

Avoiding mistakes such as low-odds losers is part of winning. Every horseplayer occasionally goofs. Sometimes, you are just plain wrong. Low-odds horses may attract most of the attention, but to win at the races, a bettor must be cold and shrewd. At very least, bettors must ask, is this horse worth wagering on at low odds? What is he doing in this race, anyway? Horses who have moved from a winning barn into a losing barn also should be treated with skepticism.

Avoid the mistake of betting low-odds runners who have conspicuous flaws, and you will find yourself ahead of horseplayers banging their heads against the wall trying to make sense of something that does not make sense. The current form of horses that have been racing regularly is usually obvious. When their recent races are strong and their form is improving, they usually go up in class. When their form is regressing, they usually are lowered in class, beneath levels of past success. Many times, the only thing a handicapper can surmise is that the horse will run similarly to how it ran last out.

When a low-odds horse is off form, the options are to wager on another horse, or skip the race entirely. Winning often is a matter of not losing—that is, limiting the number of mistakes to as few as possible. The inevitable screw-ups will only kill you if you let them. The idea is to fail fewer times than other bettors. No handicapper is right every single time.

Comebackers and first-time starters offer unique challenges, and a familiar theory applies, particularly with comebackers. The class level at which they return speaks volumes about their current form. Comebackers are horses who have not raced in more than 45 days.

1 Storm Flag Flying
Own:Phipps Ogden Mills
Red Black, Cherry Cap
VELAZQUEZ J R (37 14 4 3 .38) 2003:(372 86 .23)

Dk. b or br f. 3 (Apr)
Sire: Storm Cat (Storm Bird) $500,000
Dam: My Flag(Easy Goer)
Br: Phipps Stable (Ky)
Tr: McGaughey Claude III(10 2 1 0 .20) 2003:(64 18 .28)

L 122

Life	4	4	0	0	$967,000	102	D.Fst	2	2	0	0	$327,000 98
2002	4	4	0	0	$967,000	102	Wet(345)	2	2	0	0	$640,000 102
2001	0	M	0	0	$0	-	Turf(330)	0	0	0	0	$0 -
Aqu	0	0	0	0	$0	-	Dst(330)	1	1	0	0	$120,000 94

26Oct02-4AP gd 1⅛ :461 1:101 1:354 1:493 ⒻB C Juv FillG1 102 3 22 32 21 2hd 1½ Velazquez J R L119 *.80 100 — StormFlagFlying119½ Composure1199¾ *SntCtrin*1192 Headed, very game 10
5Oct02-6Bel fst 1 1/16 :233 :472 1:121 1:441 ⒻFrizette-G1 98 3 31 2½ 2½ 1½ 12 Velazquez J R L120 *.60 79-22 *StrmFlgFln*1202 SntCtrn12011 ApplbGrdns1203 When asked, shown whip 7
15Sep02-6Bel gd 1 :222 :46 1:122 1:382 ⒻMatron-G1 94 2 31½ 32 2hd 13 112¾ Velazquez J R L119 *1.40 77-22 *Storm Flag Flying*11912 Wild Snitch1191 Fircroft1195¼ Greenly, kept busy 7
18Aug02-6Sar fst 6f :221 :453 :58 1:11 ⒻMd Sp Wt 45k 86 3 6 56½ 42 21½ 11 Velazquez J R L119 3.65 87-13 *StrmFlgFlyng*1191 SmthngSlvr1195 OrNncyL1194½ 4 wide move, greenly 9
WORKS: Apr13 Bel 5f fst 1:013 B *4/7* Apr6 Bel 4f fst :471 B *3/19* Mar31 GP 5f fst 1:024 B *6/17* Mar25 GP 4f fst :501 B *12/20* Mar19 GP 5f fst 1:02 B *8/21* Mar13 GP 4f fst :501 B *37/59*
TRAINER: 61-180Days(36 .22 $1.79) Dirt(290 .20 $1.31) GrdStk(52 .17 $1.43)

Comebackers

It had been nearly six months since Storm Flag Flying capped her unbeaten 2-year-old campaign with a stirring triumph in the Breeders' Cup Juvenile Fillies. That autumn day at Arlington, seemingly defeated in midstretch, Storm Flag Flying battled back. She re-rallied when it appeared hope was lost and won by a half-length, delivering one of the most impressive championship performances of the 2002 Breeders' Cup.

But now it was spring, and Storm Flag Flying was returning to battle on April 18. The winter racing season had come and gone, and trainer Shug McGaughey was behind schedule. The season's premier race for 3-year-old fillies was only three weeks away, and Storm Flag Flying was just now returning to action to prepare for the Kentucky Oaks. She returned in the Grade 3 Comely at Aqueduct.

The situation was not ideal, but Storm Flag Flying's spring training pattern had been delayed. With the Kentucky Oaks—the main goal—bearing down, time was running out for a prep race. Despite a six-month hiatus and a formidable rival—Cyber Secret, who was coming off a Grade 3 win—bettors hammered Storm Flag Flying to odds of .25-1.00, even though her ultimate objectives were the more prestigious races ahead on the calendar.

To break even at those odds, a bettor must win four of every five wagers. No handicapper is that good. Storm Flag Flying was the best filly in the Comely, but so what? The facts were clear. She was returning from a six-month layoff, and aiming for a bigger race ahead. For most bettors, the Comely was a mistake, and razor-sharp Cyber Secret, going up in class off a sharp win, rolled home to the tune of a $9 win mutuel.

Bettors who wager on low-odds runners with drawbacks such as Storm Flag Flying's are practically guaranteed to lose over the long haul. Perhaps Storm Flag Flying could have won the Comely despite her layoff and long-range plans. But at depressed odds, the expectations were unreasonable.

When a horse enters a race that is not the main goal, be assured that victory is less important than pure exercise. McGaughey had not prepared Storm Flag Flying for an all-out effort to win a Grade 3. It was only a comeback race.

3 Volponi
Own:Amherst Stable & Spruce Pond Stable
Blue Blue, Pink Yoke, Pink Blocks On Sleeves,
SANTOS J A (2 0 0 1 .00) 2003:(488 74 .15)

B. h. 5
Sire: Cryptoclearance (Fappiano) $20,000
Dam: Prom Knight(Sir Harry Lewis)
Br: Amherst Stable (Ky)
Tr: Johnson Philip G(1 0 1 0 .00) 2003:(52 9 .17)

Blinkers OFF
L 122

Life	23	7	7	3	$2,748,976	116	D.Fst	14	5	5	1	$2,459,670 116
2002	8	3	3	1	$2,389,200	116	Wet(320)	0	0	0	0	$0 -
2001	10	3	2	0	$266,176	113	Turf(240)	9	2	2	2	$289,306 110
Bel	6	2	2	1	$85,470	108	Dst(280)	2	1	1	0	$40,600 105

26Oct02-10AP fst 1¼ :463 1:101 1:352 2:011 3↑ B C Classic-G1 116 2 53½ 54½ 2hd 12½ 16½ Santos J A L126 b 43.50 97 — Volponi1266½ *MedagliaD'oro*121nk MilwukeeBrew1263 Awaited room turn 12
4Oct02-8Med fst 1⅛ :464 1:102 1:353 1:484 3↑ Med Cup H-G2 106 3 64¾ 66 62¼ 31½ 2¾ Bridgmohan S X L116 *2.10 82-19 Burning Roma115¾ *Volponi*1161¼ Windsor Castle112nk 6wd bid,closed 9
14Sep02-6Bel fm 1⅛ Ⓣ :481 1:112 1:35 1:463 3↑ Belmont BCH-G2 103 2 11½ 1½ 1½ 1½ 2¾ Santos J A L117 *.85 95-06 Startac116¾ Volponi1172 Dr. Kashnikow1151¼ Set pace, gamely 6
10Aug02-9Sar fm 1½ Ⓣ :471 1:113 2:002 2:24 3↑ SwordDancrH-G1 106 3 21½ 2½ 1hd 21 32 Santos J A L115 8.70 110-06 *With Anticipation*120hd *Denon*1181¾ Volponi115nk Stayed on gamely 11
26Jly02-8Sar fm 1⅛ Ⓣ :484 1:124 1:362 1:482 3↑ B Baruch H-G2 109 1 11 1½ 1½ 2½ 2nk Bridgmohan S X L116 3.25 96-17 DelMrShow120nk Volponi116no ForbiddenApple1212 Set pace, gamely rail 7
5Jly02-8Bel fm 1 Ⓣ :224 :451 1:081 1:321 3↑ Poker H-G3 110 4 32½ 31½ 3½ 2hd 12¼ Bridgmohan S X L115 9.30 99-05 Volponi1152¼ Saint Verre112nk Navesink117¾ Speed 3 wide, driving 7
30May02-8Bel fst 1 :224 :451 1:091 1:343 4↑ Alw 56000N$mY 95 2 42 42½ 42¾ 47½ 47 Bridgmohan S X L123 b *.40 89-18 OpenSesm116½ WildSummr1163¾ CountryBGold1162¾ 4 wide, no response 7
8May02-6Bel fst 7f :23 :452 1:093 1:222 4↑ Alw 54000C 105 5 3 2½ 2½ 12½ 11 Bridgmohan S X L121 b *.85 91-15 Volponi1211 Cherokee Beau1173½ *Tarek*1155 Speed outside, driving 5
24Nov01-8Aqu fst 1 :232 :453 1:092 1:331 3↑ Cigar MileH-G1 108 8 5¾ 41¾ 52½ 54 45 Bridgmohan S X L115 b 5.60 96-16 *Left Bank*1203¼ Graeme Hall118hd Red Bullet1181¾ Bumped start, chased 9
19Oct01-8Med fst 1⅛ :451 1:084 1:34 1:462 Pegasus H-G2 113 2 42½ 42 41½ 2hd 12¾ Bridgmohan S X L114 b 4.10 95-14 Volponi1142¾ BurningRoma119½ GiantGentlemn1169½ Duel,clear final 1/16 6
6Oct01-2Bel fst 1 :234 :463 1:11 1:361 3↑ Alw 46000N2X 108 4 2½ 2½ 2½ 1½ 13¾ Bridgmohan S X L116 fb 1.50 86-21 *Volponi*1163¾ Pure Prize1202¼ Harley Quinn11911 Bumped start, driving 5
8Sep01-5Bel fst 1 1/16 :23 :451 1:094 1:431 3↑ Alw 46000N2X 93 6 53¼ 42 4¾ 2hd 2no Migliore R L118 b *.80 81-14 *Dayton Flyer*116no *Volponi*1185 Even TheScore118¾ Bumped start, 4 wide 7
WORKS: May5 Bel 4f fst :474 B *11/60* ●Apr28 Bel 5f fst :58 H *1/29* Apr21 Bel 6f fst 1:112 B *1/2* ●Apr14 Bel 5f fst :574 H *1/52* Apr4 Bel tr.t 5f fst 1:013 B *6/18* ●Mar29 Bel tr.t 4f fst :464 B *1/64*
TRAINER: +180Days(14 .07 $0.59) BlinkOff(11 .18 $2.62) Route/Sprint(23 .04 $0.16) Dirt(144 .14 $2.90) Sprint(89 .12 $2.08) Alw(89 .15 $1.37)

It happened again May 9, 2003, at Belmont, when Breeders' Cup Classic winner Volponi returned in an allowance race, his first start in six months. He was the best horse in the race, but the intentions of trainer P. G. Johnson went beyond a mere $56,000 allowance. The rich spring-summer racing season was ahead, and it made little sense for Johnson to have trained Volponi up to a smasher in his first start back. Which is not to say Volponi could not have won. He could have. At odds of 2-5, he made a serious bid, then flattened out and finished second. Bettors who expected him to reproduce his Classic victory following a six-month layoff were foiled. He was 2-5, but lacked current form. How tough is it to wager against horses like that? Or at the very least, to pass the race?

Wagering on low-odds runners who may not be geared up is a road to parimutuel failure. The issue of current form—or lack of current form, regarding Storm Flag Flying and Volponi—must always be a paramount consideration. When the warning signs are out and the odds are low, these horses are to be avoided.

These examples illustrate the pitfalls in backing short-priced top-class comebackers. Horses are laid off for a variety of reasons. They get hurt, tired or sour, or have changed locales and require time to acclimate. Horses need vacations, just like people. When they return, they often return with a fresh attitude, fresh legs, and renewed purpose. But the negative reasons, including injury and form decline, do not lead to high expectations when the horse returns. There are a sufficient number of uncertainties facing bettors anyway, and no reason to compound them by backing layoff horses who may or may not be ready to fire.

Make no mistake, low-odds comebackers do win races. But so what? No bettor is required to wager against them, or on them. When indecision prevails in a race with a low-odds comebacker, there is nothing wrong with simply passing the race. Do not fret. Another wagering opportunity is only minutes away.

Comebackers cover all levels, from maiden claiming to Grade 1. All face the same question—is the horse ready? When a significant period of time has passed since a horse's last race, how can a handicapper know if the horse is primed to deliver a top effort, or if he needs a race or two before returning to form?

Consideration of the class level is first. Does it make sense? When a stakes horse returns in an allowance, the answer is no. There is rarely good reason for a top-caliber horse to deliver maximum effort in a comeback race that is designed solely as a prep. Likewise, when a claiming horse returns in an allowance, the intention is clear. The horse is in a race he is not qualified to win. The purpose is to provide exercise. Following the comeback prep, the horse may be lowered in class into a race where he belongs.

When a comebacker returns at a logical level for a competent trainer, with a credible workout pattern, bettors can feel confident the horse is in form. However, a return above the class level at which he has been competitive in the past suggests the horse is not in the race to win. Rather, he out for exercise. For example, a $16,000 claiming horse who returns from a layoff in a $25,000 claiming race is probably only in for a prep. The purpose in racing the horse at a level above his true value is to protect him from being claimed. Conversely, horses that return from layoffs below their established class level may have lost value since their last start.

Toga Mania
Own: Ward Wesley A

Ch. m. 5
Sire: Saratoga Six (Alydar) $3,500
Dam: Rainbank(Water Bank)
Br: Petrosian Brothers Racing Stables (Ky)
Tr: Ward Wesley A (—) 2001:(46 13 .28)

Life	7	2	2	1	$72,520	91	D.Fst	5	2	1	1	$61,600	91
2001	1	0	0	0	$0	43	Wet(375)	1	0	1	0	$10,000	88
1999	6	2	2	1	$72,520	91	Turf(245)	1	0	0	0	$920	68
CSC	0	0	0	0	$0	-	Dist	3	2	0	0	$45,600	91

30May01- 1Hol fst 6f :22 :452 :574 1:112 4↑ ⒻClm c- (10-9) 43 2 7 3¹½ 2² 4¹½ 79¼ Rodriguez M5 LB 113 fn *.70 74-13 BocDrem118½ NineEst118nk OcenOfStorms118½ Stalked pace, weakened 7
Claimed from Fan Stables & Rikmar Stables for $10,000, Sise Clifford Jr Trainer 2001(as of 05/30): (69 10 11 12 0.14) Previously trained by Dollase Craig
1Aug99- 8Dmr fst 6f :213 :443 :571 1:102 3↑ ⒻAlw 52250N1X 91 5 1 42¾ 2hd 12½ 12 Nakatani C S LB 116 *1.30 88-12 Toga Mania1162 Maria Alana1182 Valdastar1233 Bid,cleared,driving 8
19Jun99- 1Hol fm 5½f Ⓣ :221 :442 :562 1:023 3↑ ⒻAlw 55200N1X 68 1 5 1hd 1½ 2½ 54½ Nakatani C S LB 117 *.90 86-09 DustyHthr116½ *MonyInThSht*122½ BtThDvil1192 Inside duel,wkend late 6
20May99- 7Hol fst 7f :22 :441 1:084 1:213 3↑ ⒻAlw 51000N1X 89 6 2 32½ 22½ 22 24½ Gomez G K LB 115 4.20 89-14 *PennyMarie*1164½ TogaMania1153 KalooknBby1203 Chased, second best 7
25Apr99- 8Hol fst 6½f :214 :444 1:094 1:162 ⒻAlw 57500N1X 82 3 5 31½ 32 31½ 31½ McCarron C J LB 117 *2.00 87-13 Becoming120½ *Miss Chips*1171 Toga Mania1172 Split horses into lane 10
7Apr99- 7SA my 6½f ⊗ :222 :452 1:094 1:161 ⒻAlw 51500N1X 88 5 2 2½ 2½ 2½ 22 Gomez G K LB 118 1.90 85-14 Dianehill1202 Toga Mania1187 Memoranda12210 Dueled, second best 5
3Mar99- 2SA fst 6f :221 :452 :573 1:102 ⒻMd 50000 (50-45) 88 1 5 31½ 2hd 12½ 112 Nakatani C S LB 120 *.60 88-12 Toga Mania12012 Lake Princess1205 Diane G1205 Broke inward, handily 5
WORKS: May21 Hol 6f fst 1:134 H *8/19* May15 Hol 6f fst 1:144 H *6/14* May9 Hol 5f fst 1:02 H *22/29* May3 Hol 5f fst 1:02 H *23/32* Apr27 Hol 4f fst :49 H *8/19* Apr15 Hol 4f fst :491 H *20/33*

Comebackers who return below the level of previous wins can signal trouble, as Toga Mania did at Hollywood Park on May 30, 2001. Toga Mania had been off nearly two years when trainer Cliff Sise brought her back at the lowest level—$10,000 claiming. The message was clear—Sise's expectations were much lower when Toga Mania returned than when she left. You can see what happened. She finished off the board at 3-5, lost once more, and never raced again.

Common sense is the guideline. If a return at a particular level does not make sense—say, the horse returns at two or more levels higher than before, or two or more levels lower—his current condition has to remain suspect.

4 Guiding Force
Own:Beckett Family Trust
Yellow Powder Blue, Dark Blue V-sash, Powder $16,000
PEDROZA M A (73 7 8 11 .10) 2003:(376 49 .13)

Dk. b or br g. 6
Sire: Hollywood Brat (Cannonade) $500
Dam: Eddies Angel(Mo Bay)
Br: James L Beckett (Cal)
Tr: Sadler John W(37 8 5 6 .22) 2003:(136 25 .18)

L 118

Life	11	3	2	0	$133,125	99	D.Fst	10	3	2	0	$133,125	99
2002	3	1	1	0	$42,000	99	Wet(289)	0	0	0	0	$0	-
2001	6	1	1	0	$53,950	96	Turf(225*)	1	0	0	0	$0	69
Hol	4	1	2	0	$65,380	96	Dst(270)	6	1	2	0	$67,605	96

11May02-4Hol fst 6f :221 :443 :564 1:094 3+ Alw 50880N1X 96 4 3 3½ 2½ 22 21½ Krigger K5 LB 118 b 7.60 89-14 *HevenlySerch*1211½ GuidingForce1181 Primeric1211 Stalked,bid,held 2nd 6
10Apr02-4SA fst 6½f :213 :441 1:084 1:153 4+ Clm 40000 (40-35) 99 3 4 1hd 1½ 1hd 11 Espinoza V LB 118 b 5.00 95-12 GuidingForce1181 *Wallahtchie*1181 SingBecuse1173½ Bit off rail, gamely 7
9Feb02-7SA fst 6½f :212 :434 1:094 1:162 4+ Alw 59000N1X 76 3 6 1hd 21 34 68 Espinoza V LB 123 b 4.50 83-16 *Warm April*1231 *Bingo Card*1201½ Wild Roar1201½ Inside duel, weakened 9
3Jun01-4Hol fst 6f :22 :444 :563 1:09 3+ Alw 53000N1X 96 3 2 1hd 11 2½ 21¼ Espinoza V LB 123 bn 4.70 94-10 Mr Freckles1171¼ Guiding Force1233½ Mandola117no Inside lane,2nd best 6
12May01-9Hol fst 6f :22 :444 :57 1:094 3+ Alw 50900N1X 86 1 5 1½ 11 11½ 42½ Espinoza V LB 123 bn 8.50 88-08 RiyadhCity123½ LytleCreek123½ AmericnPstime1171½ Inside,wkened late 6
25Mar01-4SA fm *6½f Ⓣ :222 :443 1:073 1:132 4+ Alw 55120N1X 69 6 1 1hd 2hd 51¾ 77¾ Baze T C LB 122 bn 3.10 85-06 Riverside1201¼ Solarino122nk *Ira S*118¾ Veered out 1/4, tired 7
3Mar01-8SA fst 6f :214 :443 :57 1:101 4+ Alw 89850N1X 85 5 2 11 1hd 2hd 43½ Baze T C LB 122 n 12.30 84-16 FierceHert1221½ Greenbypcker122hd *Significnt*1222 Inside,dueled,wkened 9
28Jan01-5SA fst 6f :212 :44 :562 1:094 4+ ⓈOClm 40000N 89 1 2 1½ 12½ 14½ 1hd Baze T C LB 118 n 21.70 90-12 GuidingForce118hd RetiredHbit1183½ *WrmApril*1193 Inside,clear,just held 8
7Jan01-8SA fst 7f :22 :443 1:094 1:224 4+ ⓈOClm 40000N 29 8 2 11 31 1217 1229¾ Baze T C LB 118 n 7.30 61-14 *FierceHeart*1191¼ It'sAReality119no WrmApril1192¾ Speed,dueled,gave way 12
30Apr00-7Hol fst 6½f :22 :443 1:094 1:161 3+ ⓈMerial60k 96 8 2 11 11 11½ 1½ Chavez J F LB 116 n 6.00 90-11 GuidingForc116½ *KnowSumthn*1162½ IrshMuldoon1232 Kicked clear,held 10
9Apr00-4SA fst 6f :211 :443 :571 1:101 3+ Md Sp Wt 54k 84 7 6 58½ 55 55 55¼ Garcia M S LB 116 n 11.10 83-21 *Matriculate*124nk Sure Man1243 *Martel*1161½ Wide early,rail turn 7
WORKS: May17 Hol 5f fst 1:003 H *8/28* ●May11 Hol 6f fst 1:131 H *1/9* May5 Hol 6f fst 1:152 H *21/22* Apr29 Hol 5f fst 1:02 H *14/20* Apr23 SA 5f fst :593 H *4/31* Apr17 SA 5f fst 1:003 H *4/40*
TRAINER: +180Days(31 .19 $2.68) Dirt(395 .17 $1.65) Sprint(327 .16 $1.64) Claim(157 .18 $1.72)

Good trainers are motivated by fiscal responsibility. When a good trainer drops a horse in class for his comeback, the message is that the horse is not the horse he once was. Sometimes, they win anyway. Guiding Force dropped into a $16,000 claiming race on May 24, 2003, for his first start following a one-year layoff. His class-drop placement suggested he was not the same horse. He won by 3 1/2 lengths and paid $5.20 for a $2 bet. Droppers often start at low odds. A bettor who believes it is possible to generate consistent wagering profit by backing layoff horses at 8-5 is only kidding himself.

Most modern-day trainers are skilled at preparing horses for top races in their first start back. The greater number of horses a trainer has in his barn, the more likely the horses will be ready in their comeback. High-volume trainers typically send out "live" starters. Most top horsemen train horses to deliver a peak effort in their comeback. The exceptions are previously listed. Even when one is handicapping an unfamiliar circuit, the trainer statistics at the bottom of the past performances provide insight to a trainer's specialties and/or weaknesses. The trainer's record with comebackers is directly related to the horse's current form.

A trainer who typically wins with at least 15 percent of his overall starters can be considered "live" in most of the appropriate spots, including comeback races. The past-performance lines also include subcategories of trainer records that can be used to complement the issue of current form.

Revello
Own: Oliver Hal
Black/bronze Quarters, Bronze Dots
MCCARRON C J (45 7 12 2 .16) 2002:(275 52 .19)

B. g. 4
Sire: Memo*Chi (Mocito Guapo)
Dam: Lila Finn(Mamaison)
Br: Palisair Place (Cal)
Tr: Mandella Richard(31 4 9 5 .13) 2002:(138 22 .16)

L 121

Life	2	1	1	0	$28,800	95	D.Fst	2	1	1	0	$28,800	95
2001	2	1	1	0	$28,800	95	Wet(415*)	0	0	0	0	$0	-
2000	0	M	0	0	$0	-	Turf(180*)	0	0	0	0	$0	-
Hol	2	1	1	0	$28,800	95	Dst(340)	2	1	1	0	$28,800	95

1Dec01-1Hol fst 6f :22 :45 :572 1:093 3+ ⓈMd Sp Wt 36k 95 3 5 53 42 2½ 1nk Smith M E LB 120 *.40 92-15 Revello120nk *Eddie Eddie*1207 Treasured Note1202½ 3wd bid,gamely 5
7Nov01-8Hol fst 6f :223 :46 :581 1:102 3+ ⓈMd Sp Wt 36k 91 4 7 74¼ 41¼ 41½ 2½ Smith M E LB 120 4.10 87-16 TakeItOutside120½ *Revello*1201½ TresuredNote1201½ 4wd into lane,rallied 8
WORKS: Jun4 Hol 3f fst :362 H *2/12* May28 Hol 6f fst 1:123 H *2/11* May23 Hol 6f fst 1:143 H *13/17* May17 Hol 6f fst 1:164 H *11/11* May11 Hol 5f fst 1:024 H *22/32* May5 Hol 5f fst 1:033 H *43/44*
TRAINER: +180Days(31 .13 $1.48) Dirt(231 .16 $1.83) Sprint(244 .18 $2.01) Alw(168 .18 $1.59)

For example, the June 7, 2002, past performances of Revello show that trainer Richard Mandella had won with 13 percent of his most recent 31 starters who were away 180 days or more. The win rate was average; the $1.48 return on investment suggests they were frequently overbet.

Thady Quill
Own: Seidler Gary
Dark Green, Green/beige Diagonal
DELAHOUSSAYE E (21 1 7 4 .05) 2001:(493 71 .14)

Ch. c. 4 TATHOU98 $757,777
Sire: Nureyev (Northern Dancer) $125,000
Dam: Alleged Devotion(Alleged)
Br: Orpendale & Barronstown Stud (Ky)
Tr: Frankel Robert(7 2 1 1 .29) 2001:(207 46 .22)

115

Life	7	4	0	1	$124,800	101	D.Fst	0	0	0	0	$0	-
2001	2	2	0	0	$74,400	101	Wet(315)	0	0	0	0	$0	-
2000	2	0	0	0	$5,695	85	Turf(365)	7	4	0	1	$124,800	101
Dmr Ⓣ	0	0	0	0	$0	-	DistⓉ	3	2	0	0	$80,095	101

28Jan01-6SA gd 1 Ⓣ :222 :46 1:112 1:353 4+ OClm 80000N 101 4 59 59½ 41½ 1½ 1hd Delahoussaye E LB 119 2.80 89-17 Thady Quill119hd Entorchado1192½ Duke Of Green1173 Split foes 1/4,held 8
6Jan01-7SA fm 1 Ⓣ :224 :45 1:093 1:334 4+ Alw 60360N2X 100 4 78¾ 712 64½ 32 11 Delahoussaye E LB 117 9.30 90-13 *ThadyQuill*1171 GoodJourney123½ OneForHrry1191½ Split foes 1/8,rallied 11
Previously trained by Byrne Patrick B
5May00-8CD fm 1$\frac{1}{16}$ Ⓣ :232 :464 1:11 1:411 CrwnRylAmTf-G3 — 1 1hd 41 1115 1125 — Albarado R J L 123 8.70 — 02 *King Cugat*1232¾ *Lendell Ray*1163½ Go Lib Go1233¾ Dueled, gave way,eased 11
7Apr00-8Kee fm 1 Ⓣ :224 :46 1:103 1:35 Transylvania113k 85 8 55 66 54 44 45 Sellers S J L 116 3.40 92-09 Field Cat1161½ Lendell Ray1162 Go Lib Go1231½ Bobbled start,no rally 9
Previously trained by O'Brien Aidan P
5Nov99-4GP gd *1⅛ Ⓣ :49 1:14 1:40 1:514+ Prized200k 84 7 2hd 1hd 1hd 21½ 33 O'Donoghue C L 110 *2.70 74-20 *KngCugt*1121¾ *FourOnThFloor*1201¼ ThdyQll1101½ Dueled,weakened,strtch 8
8Jly99♦ Newmarket(GB) gd 7f Ⓣ Str 1:254 Superlative Stakes (Listed) 1no Kinane M J 123 *1.00 Thady Quill123no Full Flow1262 Launfal1261¼ 5
Timeform rating: 93 Stk 28200 *Rank tracking leader,led over 1f out,drifted right,driving*
13Jun99♦ Gowran Park(Ire) gd 7f Ⓣ RH 1:241 Chill Chainnigh EBF Maiden 15½ Kinane M J 128 *.45 Thady Quill1285½ It Happens Now1282 Ezra1285 10
Timeform rating: 98+ Maiden 7900 *Trckd in 4th,rallied to lead over 1-1/2f out,clear 1f out,handily*
WORKS: Jly21 Dmr 6f fst 1:151 H *24/28* Jly15 Hol 6f fst 1:152 H *5/9* Jly7 Hol 6f fst 1:143 H *13/21* Jly1 Hol 6f fst 1:142 H *10/18* Jun23 SA 5f fst 1:01 H *26/54* Jun17 SA 5f fst 1:01 H *22/34*
TRAINER: 61-180Days(84 .20 $1.92) Turf(417 .25 $2.06) Stakes(43 .35 $2.71)

Here is an example with a horse trained by Bobby Frankel. Thady Quill had not raced in six months when he returned July 27, 2001, in a minor stakes race at Del Mar. Frankel's record with horses off more than 180 days showed 20 percent winners from his last 84 runners. The win rate was above average; the $1.92 return on investment also was well above average.

When a horse is laid off following a victory, it often suggests something has gone amiss. When a horse is good, the horse stays in competition. There is little reason to give a horse an extended layoff when he or she has achieved top form. When a horse runs well, look for him to run again soon. If he does not, be suspicious. What is "soon"? You decide what makes sense. For the sake of simplicity, we are using the 45-day layoff line. There are, of course, exceptions. Thady Quill was laid off following a victory, but he returned in a stakes race—high expectations—for a leading barn.

The length of layoff is a consideration. Horses who have been away more than a year do not win their fair share. Horses that have been away that long generally have endured extraordinary setbacks. Eliminate them from consideration, and if they beat you at a short price, what difference does it make? Good handicapping sometimes means nothing more than turning one's back on damaged goods, and daring them to beat you.

The distance and surface at which a comebacker runs are prime considerations, and the "does it make sense?" standard applies. When a horse returns at an unfamiliar distance, it is less likely he will deliver a top race—for example, when a two-turn specialist returns from a layoff in a six-furlong sprint. Surface also is a consideration. When a horse has not run well previously on the surface of today's race, there is less reason to expect him to do so first start back. A dirt horse returning in a grass race is generally not expected to win. Why would a trainer bother racing a dirt horse in a grass race? It could be the grass race is the only race available. The horse needs a prep. He is not expected to win. So why not run him there?

Several criteria should be met to determine if a comebacker is in form. The class, surface, and distance at which he returns should be commensurate with past success. Also, a trainer's statistics reveal how well he does with layoff horses. It is an added benefit if the horse has won previously following layoffs, but not mandatory. The horse's workout pattern should be steady, and increasingly longer in distance. Usually, a horse returning from a layoff will have a short workout as his initial timed work on the comeback trail. The pattern will include perhaps two works at three furlongs, two more at four furlongs, two more at five furlongs, and gradually up.

A sprinter typically has at least two workouts at distances within a furlong of the distance of today's race. For example, a horse returning in a six-furlong sprint should have at least two five-furlong works in order for a handicapper to consider the horse fit enough to deliver first start back.

It is slightly different with route horses. Modern training methods are such that a horse who returns in a mile race does not necessarily require a timed workout at the distance. Thady Quill was returning in a mile race, yet his longest work was six furlongs. He had several of them, of course, so it was logical to believe he was physically fit. It is easier for a comebacker to win a two-turn turf race than a two-turn dirt race, due to the unlike dynamics of the two races. The bottom line: If the workout pattern is consistent, and distances gradually longer, the horse may be physically fit. Workouts as a secondary factor are examined further in Chapter 5.

First-Time Starters

Handicappers who are accustomed to viewing past performances of seasoned veterans may be confused by horses without a racing history. They have no speed figures, cannot be analyzed on pace, and are virtually impossible to evaluate on class. A beginning handicapper might look at horses with no history and admit to utter confusion.

And yet, they are really not so difficult. Despite individual histories that are mere blank pages, first-time starters can be analyzed with as much confidence as veteran campaigners. First and foremost is the question of whether the horse is in form. Rather than base current-form decisions on past performances, one looks to other sources of information. Those include workout pattern, trainer tendency, pedigree, sales price, and where the horse was bred.

A first-time starter can be deemed to be in form if his work pattern is steady, his trainer typically does well with first-time starters, and if his pedigree and sales price make it sensible for him to win this race. The information is available in the past performances.

The primary question is, does the workout pattern imply readiness for a top effort? A positive work pattern with a first-time starter is similar to that of a well-prepared combacker—consistently spaced, and increasingly longer in distance. The actual times of the workouts are less important than their uniformity. Some trainers—Bob Bob Baffert, for example—always work horses fast. Others work them slow. Familiarization with trainers is helpful.

More important than the workout times is that the pattern be regular. If a horse works every five days, he should stay on that five-day pattern. Whatever the pattern is, the horse should adhere to it, be it every six days, or seven days. It is beneficial, though hardly mandatory, for a horse to have a short workout as its final prerace drill. When a trainer conditions a horse up to a big effort first time out, the trainer often sharpens the horse's speed in his final workout before the race. It should be noted that most winning first-time starters are in sprints. Few trainers prepare a horse for a winning debut in a two-turn race. The subject of workout speed will be further examined in the chapter on secondary factors. For now, the idea is to identify a first-time starter who is in form.

As important as workouts are to determine current form, they are considered in the context of the trainer. There may be no trainer-preference category that is as specialized as with first-time starters. The trainer categories at the bottom of the past performances often provide a good indication of whether a first-time starter is in form. A trainer who wins with less than 10 percent of his first-time starters is below par. A trainer who wins with 15 percent is doing well. Anything above 20 percent, and a handicapper has to take notice every time.

The fact that a trainer does well with first-time starters does not mean the horse is necessarily in form. It only increases the likelihood that he is. Trainers whose records show they are inclined to start well-prepared first-timers tend to repeat those inclinations time and time again.

```
Silver Charm                              Gr/ro. h. 5 (Feb)                                     Life 24 12 7 2 $6,944,369 123 | D.Fst     23 11 7 2 $6,644,369 123
Own: Lewis Robert B. and Beverly J        Sire: Silver Buck (Buckpasser) $7,500                 1999  5  1 0 2   $431,363 118 | Wet(310)   1  1 0 0   $300,000 113
                                          Dam: Bonnie's Poker (Poker)                           1998  9  6 2 0 $4,696,506 123 | Turf(235)  0  0 0 0         $0   -
                                          Br: Mary Lou Wootton (Fla)                            Sa    9  5 3 1 $1,234,720 118 | Dst(312)   8  4 2 1 $1,383,339 123
                                          Tr: Baffert Bob(23 5 3 1 .22) 2003:(674 127 .19)

12Jun99-9CD fst 1⅛ :464 1:11 1:352 1:471 3↑SFosterH-G2   104 3 4½ 4½ 4½ 44 48½ Antley C W L123 1.40 98-03 VictoryGllop1205 NiteDremr110¾ Littlbitlivly1152¾ Hopped start,weakened 7
  Previously trained by Baffert Bob
28Mar99♦Nad al Sheba (UAE) fst *1¼ 2:003 4↑Dubai World Cup-G1   614¼ Stevens G 126 - Almutawakel126¾ Malek126¾ Victory Gallop1261½ 8
  Timeform rating: 101                       Stk 5000000      Tracked in 5th,weakened over 2f out.Daylami 5th,Running Stag 7th
  Previously trained by Baffert Bob
6Mar99-5SA fst 1¼ :472 1:112 1:352 2:003 4↑SAH-G1          118 1 3½ 4¼ 4¼ 4½ 31 Stevens G L LB124 *1.00 97-11 FreeHouse123½ EventoftheYer119½ SilvrChrm1243 Came back on outside 6
30Jan99-10GP fst 1⅛ :463 1:102 1:353 1:481 3↑DonnH-G1      106 12 9½ 9¼ 7¾ 6½ 3¼ Stevens G L L126 *.80 91-14 Puerto Madero120¾ Behrens113½ Silver Charm126nk Mild wide rally 12
10Jan99-8SA fst 1 1/16 :242 :472 1:104 1:413 4↑SnPsqalH-G2 109 3 33 3½ 36 31 1¼ Stevens G L LB125 *.30 95-10 Silver Charm125¼ Malek119½ Crafty Friend1182 Rallied,good handling 5
27Nov98-11CD fst 1⅛ :472 1:112 1:361 1:49 3↑ClarkH-G2      113 2 1hd 1hd 2hd 2½ 1hd Stevens G L L124 *.30 99-14 SilverChrm124hd Littlebitlively1131 WildRush117½ Dueled, headed, gamely 8
7Nov98-10CD fst 1¼ :473 1:12 1:371 2:02 3↑BCClasic-G1     115 8 5¼ 41 2½ 1hd 2¾ Stevens G L L126 2.50 94-07 Awesome Again126¾ Silver Charm126nk Swain126no Led, drifted late 10
17Oct98-8SA fst 1⅛ :464 1:101 1:343 1:471 3↑GdwdBCH-G2     111 5 3½ 3½ 3½ 1hd 12½ Stevens G L LB124 *.50 100-07 Silver Charm1242½ Free House1242½ Score Quick1156 Bid 3 wide, driving 6
26Sep98-10TP fst 1⅛ :462 1:10 1:343 1:472 3↑KyCpClH-G3     123 1 32 31 2hd 2hd 117 ♦Stevens G L L123 *.50 100-14 [DH]SilverCharm123 [DH]WildRush11717 Acceptable1175 Long drive, brushed 5
25Jly98-8Dmr fst 1 1/16 :23 :464 1:102 1:41 3↑SnDiegoH-G3   63 4 2½ 21 31 510 527 Stevens G L LB125 *.30 72-09 Mud Route1176 Hal's Pal1135½ Benchmark1175½ Stalked,gave way 5
```

More Warning Signs

It was January 10, 1999, at Santa Anita, and Silver Charm was making the 20th start in a global career. He had won the Kentucky Derby, Preakness, and Dubai World Cup, always with a distinct running style. Silver Charm was always on the attack. He was the most lethal kind of a front-runner, because he could also finish.

But that winter day at Santa Anita, running in the San Pasqual, Silver Charm failed to produce his customary speed. He dropped more than eight lengths off the pace, farther behind than ever. It was as if he had lost interest. The second half of the race, of course, was a different story. Silver Charm blasted home, and won going away. But a skeptical handicapper may have suggested something was not right about Silver Charm's newfangled style. He was losing his speed.

Perhaps Silver Charm was wearing down. He had done something different, and it was not good. Three weeks after the Santa Anita race, Silver Charm was favored at 4-5 in the Donn Handicap at Gulfstream Park. He raced close to the pace, fell back, and lost by more than five lengths. He was defeated three more times at low odds, and was retired.

Silver Charm's loss of speed in one race was reason to question the form of a 20-start veteran. Loss of speed often signals the downside of a form cycle. It did for Silver Charm.

A handicapper who saw the San Pasqual as a signal of potential form regression need not have bothered with other handicapping fundamentals related to Silver Charm when he ran in the Donn. High speed figures and proven Grade 1 class carry less relevance when a horse is losing his form. When a good horse goes bad, there is no way to predict how far he will fall.

Handicappers must take note when a horse does anything different. Successful bettors are able to project form changes before they become obvious. Positive and negative form patterns must be exploited while they still carry parimutuel value. To make money gambling on horses, it is a handicapper's cold-hearted responsibility to identify situations in which low-odds runners are compromised. It happens many ways. Kona Gold went downhill more gradually than Silver Charm. The slide began before Kona Gold's effort in the 2001 Frank J. De Francis Handicap at Laurel.

Kona Gold
Own: Headley Aase, Molasky, Irwin and Mola

B. g. 10 (Mar)
Sire: Java Gold (Key to the Mint) $6,899
Dam: Double Sunrise (Slew o' Gold)
Br: Carlos Perez (Ky)
Tr: Headley Bruce(0 0 0 0 .00) 2003:(138 29 .21)

Life	30	14	7	2	$2,293,384	123				
Jumps	0	0	0	0	$0	-				
2003	4	1	0	1	$95,680	109	Wet	1 0 1 0	$32,310	109
2002	3	1	0	0	$128,340	113	Turf	0 0 0 0	$0	-

Date/Race	Cond	Dist	Fractions	Race	Beyer	PP	St	1C	2C	Str	Fin	Jockey	Med/Wt	Odds	Spd-Var	Top Finishers	Comment	Fld
17Nov01-9Lrl	fst	6f	:21^{2} :44^{1} :56^{2}1:09	3↑DeFrncsM-G1	**106**	7	3	4^{6}	3$^{6\frac{1}{2}}$	4^{3}	4^{4}	Solis A	L125	*2.10	90- 19	DelawareTownship125^{3} EarlyFlyer115$^{\frac{3}{4}}$ *XtrHet*117^{nk}	4wd trip, no response	7
27Oct01-6Bel	fst	6f	:22^{2} :44^{3} :56^{1}1:08^{2}	3↑PnskBCSp-G1	**108**	4	5	11$^{6\frac{3}{4}}$	13$^{7\frac{1}{2}}$	8^{6}	7^{4}	Solis A	L126	*3.50	92- 03	Squirtle Squirt124$^{\frac{1}{2}}$ Xtra Heat121^{nk} Caller One126^{nk}	Inside trip, no rally	14
6Oct01-8SA	fst	6f	:21^{1} :43^{2} :55^{3}1:07^{3}	3↑AnTtlBCH-G1	**115**	6	1	4$^{3\frac{1}{2}}$	4^{5}	2^{1}	2$^{2\frac{1}{2}}$	Solis A	LB127	*.60	98- 12	SweptOverboard116$^{2\frac{1}{2}}$ KonGold127^{3} *ILoveSilver*116^{1}	Led past 1/8,2nd best	6
22Jly01-8Dmr	fst	6f	:22 :44^{1} :55^{4}1:08^{1}	3↑BCrsbBCH-G2	**119**	4	2	2^{5}	2$^{1\frac{1}{2}}$	2$^{1\frac{1}{2}}$	1$^{\frac{3}{4}}$	Solis A	LB126	*.90	99- 07	KonaGold126$^{\frac{3}{4}}$ CllerOne124$^{\frac{1}{2}}$ SweptOverbord115^{5}	Wore down rival,gamely	4
1Apr01-7SA	fst	6½f	:21^{1} :44 1:08^{2}1:15	4↑PtrGrBCH-G2	**112**	2	2	3$^{4\frac{1}{2}}$	3^{2}	2^{hd}	1^{nk}	Solis A	LB126	*.30	93- 12	*Kona Gold*126^{nk} DH Hollycombe114 DH Explicit116^{4}	3wd bid,gamely	4
4Mar01-7SA	fst	7f	:22^{1} :44^{4} 1:08^{4}1:21^{1}	4↑SnCrlosH-G1	**112**	7	3	4$^{1\frac{1}{4}}$	3^{1}	1^{1}	1^{2}	Solis A	LB125	*.30e	99- 12	*KonaGold*125^{2} *BldeProspector*113^{2} GreyMemo115^{hd}	4wd,cut inside,cleared	7
4Nov00-6CD	fst	6f	:20^{4} :43^{2} :55^{1}1:07^{3}	3↑BCSprnt-G1	**114**	10	5	5$^{2\frac{1}{2}}$	2^{2}	2$^{1\frac{1}{2}}$	1$^{\frac{1}{2}}$	Solis A	L126	*1.70	107 -	*KonaGold*126$^{\frac{1}{2}}$ HonestLady123$^{\frac{1}{2}}$ BetOnSunshine126^{2}	Stalked,4w,stiff drive	14
14Oct00-3SA	fst	6f	:21^{4} :44^{2} :56 1:08	3↑AnTtlBCH-G2	**117**	2	3	2$^{2\frac{1}{2}}$	2^{hd}	1$^{1\frac{1}{2}}$	1^{3}	Solis A	LB124	*.30	99- 14	*Kona Gold*124^{3} Regal Thunder117^{no} Elaborate116$^{2\frac{1}{2}}$	Bid betwn, led,driving	4
29Jly00-7Dmr	fst	6f	:22 :44^{3} :56^{3}1:08^{2}	3↑BCrsbBCH-G2	**118**	4	2	3^{4}	2$^{1\frac{1}{2}}$	1^{hd}	1$^{\frac{3}{4}}$	Solis A	LB123	*.60e	98- 10	*Kona Gold*123$^{\frac{3}{4}}$ *Love That Red*118^{7} *Lexicon*117^{1}	Brushed 1/16,gamely	6

Kona Gold's descending Beyer figures were one reason to question his form. Going into the De Francis, his figures had rapidly declined—119 at Del Mar, 115 at Santa Anita, 108 at Belmont. He also had begun to lose his speed, and was falling farther off the pace than early in his career. He did blaze through a pair of blistering three-furlong blowouts November 6 and 12 at Santa Anita, but performance in competition speaks far louder than the quiet of a fast morning workout.

Kona Gold finished fourth as the 2-1 favorite in the De Francis. He won only two of his last eight starts, and was the beaten favorite in six of his last 10. Even the popular old warriors like Kona Gold eventually wear down.

Everything starts with form. Lacking current condition, there is less reason to consider a horse as a likely winner. Handicapping is a tiered process, replete with stipulations. Once current form is satisfied, other considerations such as class, speed, and pace can be regarded.

To determine a horse's current form, a few basic questions might be asked:

Does the horse's presence in this race make sense?
Does the class level suggest improvement, regression, or neither?
Has the horse achieved success in a similar race?
Has the horse recently been competitive under similar conditions, or not?
Are the horse's recent performances good, bad, or indifferent?
Are the horse's speed figures improving, declining, or static?
Is the horse's workout pattern appropriate?

A handicapper cannot always answer every question with unequivocal resolve. One cannot always say for certain a particular horse is in form, or not in form. That's okay. When the issue of form is unclear, simply move on. Handicapping is a process of elimination. If a horse cannot be eliminated on form, do not force it.

Yet because current form is the factor on which everything is contingent, it makes sense that it be the first consideration, even if it is not the ultimate consideration.

A handicapper is asking for trouble by attempting to make an analysis he is not qualified to make. For example, projecting that a horse will "bounce." The theory is valid, and says that when a horse delivers a maximum performance, frequently in his first start following a layoff, the horse needs sufficient time to recover before he runs again. However, the theory applies more to cheap horses and less to top horses. We'll get to that later.

Too bad I misunderstood current form, and the influence of the trainer, way back in spring 1991. That is when I dismissed the chances of razor-sharp Twilight Agenda. I can still see him carrying jockey Corey Nakatani, black and red silks, loose on the lead, strong to the wire. The mistake cost me several thousand dollars. Good horses do not bounce. Twilight Agenda had form.

Did he have sufficient class? That is the subject of Chapter 3.

DRF/NTRA National Handicapping Championship–2004–05

By Noel Michaels

LAS VEGAS - Whoever invented the slogan "What happens in Vegas stays in Vegas" clearly has never been to the Daily Racing Form/NTRA National Handicapping Championship. If they had, the city's advertising slogan instead would have been rephrased, "What happens in Vegas PAYS in Vegas" after horseplayers from across the country took home a tournament record $412,400 in prize money after the two-day handicapping contest.

The sixth annual NHC pitted 214 of North America's top horseplayers against each other at the Bally's race and sports book in Las Vegas on Friday and Saturday, Jan. 21-22. When the dust cleared, Jamie Michelson Jr. walked away with a record first prize of $200,000 and the title of DRF/NTRA Handicapper of the Year for 2005. Michelson is a 39-year-old advertising account director from West Bloomfield, Mich., who describes himself as an occasional weekend horseplayer that primarily enjoys attending Saratoga and playing in handicapping tournaments. Michelson doubled his original NHC bankroll en route to victory, compiling a contest-winning two-day total of $240.40 based on 30 mythical $2 win and place bets at seven tracks. His margin of victory of $31.20 over runner-up Michael Conway of Glencoe, Ill., was a record in the six-year history of the NHC finals.

Michelson, who won an online contest at Youbet.com in order to qualify for the finals, was the most consistent player in the schizophrenic two-day championship. He did well on Day One, which featured many longshots, and also did well on a relatively quiet second day marked by an abundance of favorites that prevented a major reshuffling on the leaderboard.

"To beat all these people is just mind-blowing," Michelson said just minutes after his win was official. "Some days you pick horses and they all run backwards, but this was one of those times when they won. I didn't think I could get lucky two days in a row."

More people than ever before, nearly 100,000 by some estimates, entered preliminary qualifying contests last year, due, in part, to the continued growth of Internet contests. It was out of one of these Internet contests that Michelson qualified. Despite the rise in the amount of people seeking qualifying berths, the finals of NHC VI actually got more exclusive. Due to a rule change limiting the amount of qualifiers per contest from four players to three, the 100,000 preliminary entrants were whittled down to just 214 qualifiers at NHC VI – a drop of 18 percent from NHC V, which featured 261 finalists.

Michelson's $240.40 final score was also the second-highest winning total under the NHC's current format. The only champ ever to compile a higher final total was Michelson's longtime friend Steve Wolfson Jr., who won NHC IV with a record $279.60 bankroll.

Closest rival Conway finished with $208.80. Conway led early in the contest and then again midway on Saturday but could not come up with the late win he needed to catch Michelson. Conway settled for second place but took home an NHC record consolation prize of $75,000, thanks to a new and improved prize structure for 2005's main event.

In addition to his second-place individual prize, Conway also was instrumental in leading his Team Twin Spires Club to a win in the NHC team championship. Players competed in the $15,000 team championship as members of mainly three-person teams based on their qualifying site. The winner take-all prize ($5,000 per player) and the title of NHC VI team champions went to the Twin Spires Club team comprised of Conway and teammates Jason Tudor of Fairdale, Ky. and Bill McAninch from Chicago.

Behind Michelson and Conway in the individual standings was third place finisher Michael Elsass of Anna, Ohio, who earned $30,000. Fourth-place went to Charlie Messina from Slidell, La., just ahead of Damian Roncevich.

The sixth through 10th-place finishers all won $5,000 in prize money. Sixth place went to day one leader Bill Shurman who totaled $200.60 after earning $178.60 on Friday's action alone. Other $5,000 earners were seventh-place finishers (tie) Richard Gaetano and David Kassmier, ninth-place finisher Don Sullivan and tenth-place finisher Calvin Manns.

For the first time ever, the NHC's 11th through 20th-place finishers each earned $2,000 in prize money. They were, in order, defending champion Kent Meyer, Flordeliza Nator, William Haliziw, Larry Moore, Isaac Schultz, Justin Carey, Charlotte Couris, Donald Fritz, Ron Geary and David Gutfreund.

OFFICIAL NTRA/DRF HANDICAPPING CHAMPIONSHIP STANDINGS

TOP 10 FINISHERS	HOME	TOURNAMENT BANKROLL	FINAL PRIZE
1st Jamie Michelson Jr.	West Bloomfield, Mich.	$240.40	$200,000
2nd Michael Conway	Glencoe, Ill.	$208.80	$75,000
3rd Michael Elsass	Anna, Oh.	$205.40	$30,000
4th Charlie Messina	Slidell, La.	$204.20	$17,400
5th Damian Roncevich	Honolulu, Haw.	$202.80	$10,000
6th Bill Shurman	Danville, Calif.	$200.60	$5,000
7thRichard Gaetano (tie)	Waterbury, Conn.	$197.60	$5,000
7thDavid Kassmier (tie)	Wooddale, Ill.	$197.60	$5,000
9th Don Sullivan	Houston, Tex.	$183.60	$5,000
10th Calvin Manns	Raleigh, N.C.	$178.70	$5,000

OFFICIAL 'TEAM' RESULTS

WINNING TEAM	TOTAL	PRIZE
1-Twin Spires Club	$441.60	$15,000

DAY ONE-BONUSES (Awarded for leading first day)

HANDICAPPER	TEAM	TOTAL	PRIZE
1-Bill Shurman	Aqueduct	$178.60	$5,000
2-Damian Roncevich	Del Mar	$171.00	$3,000
3-Michael Conway	Twin Spires	$154.80	$2,000

DAY TWO-BONUSES (Awarded for leading second day)

HANDICAPPER	TEAM	TOTAL	PRIZE
1-Chester Victor Jr.	Golden Gate	$117.00	$5,000
2-Michael Elsass	CD/Louisville Trackside	$115.00	$3,000
3-Justin Carey	TVG	$108.60	$2,000

DRF/NTRA handicapping champion Jamie Michelson Jr. (center) with DRF publisher Steven Crist (left) and Keith Chamblin (right).

2004 Qualifiers for the NTRA-DRF National Handicapping Championship

Finals held at Bally's Hotel in Las Vegas, January 2005.

Qualiying Tournaments	Qualifiers			
Jan. 25- Jul. 10 Prairie Meadows Racetrack	1) Lee Dunham	2) Michael Leeper	3) Patrick Lamoreux	
Feb. 1-Apr. 18 Portland Meadows	1) Sean Felix	2) Nick Lowe	3) Karen Baker	
February 9 Reno Hilton	1) Hesham Ragab	2) Edward De'Ath	3) Richard Kistler	4) Connie Roths
February 9 Sports Haven	1) George Elliot	2) Mike Latella		
Feb. 14-May 1 Canterbury Park	1) Jamie Rau			
February 21 Tampa Bay Downs	1) Charlotte Couris			
February 22 Turfway Park	1) Tim Holland			
Feb. 27-29 Gulfstream Park	1) Tom Quigley	2) Danny Hogan	3) William Guenther	4) Mike Mayo
March 6 Tampa Bay Downs	1) Brynn Gallo			
April 16-17 Bally's Las Vegas	1) Joe Hinson	2) Ron Geary		
Apr. 23-25 Hawthorne Race Course	1) Richard Hoffman	2) Paul Yaffee	3) Robert Lowe	
April 24 Laurel Park	1) Chris Panos	2) Robert Wheeler	3) Peter Kousouris	
April 24-25 www.Brisnet.com	1) Pete Colwell	2) Jeffrey Blaylock	3) Florence Rotman	
Apr. 29-Oct. 30 Publichandicapper.com	1) Dave Stewart	2) Cliff Hartnitt	3) Kim Koran	
May 5-June 23 Churchill Downs	1) Jean Lee	2) William Lenzi	3) Ronald Mitchell	
May 8 Horsemen's Park	1) C.E. Watson			
May 29 Royal River Racing OTB	1) Patrick Gianforte	2) Mary Ann Hartman	3) Mike Labriola	
June 9-Sep. 5 Monmouth	1) Mark Conroy			
June 11 Los Alamitos	1) Rick Adams	2) Salim Ed Hakim	3) Steve Hendricks	
June 12 Suffolk Downs	1) Jerry Goffredo			
June 12 Delaware Park	1) Roger Siple	2) William Burns		
June 12-13 Lone Star Park	1) Jay Johns	2) Roger Warren	3) Bert Cuevas	
June 12-13 Stampede Park	1) Dwight Maisey	2) Albert Wong	3) Al Cameron	
June 26-27 Bradley Teletheater	1) Joe Boyle	2) Paul Shurman		
June 26 Colonial Downs Racetrack	1) William Berkel			
July 10-11 Belmont Park	1) David Gutfreund	2) John Macklin	3) Richard Gaetano	
July 16 Ellis Park Race Course	1) Lee Walker			
July 17 Claiming Crown	1) Calvin Manns	2) Scott Kilbury	3) Arleen Goldman	
July 17 On The Wire	1) Bart Fooden	2) Russell Harris		
July 17 Colonial Downs Racetrack	1) Mariela Biles	2) William Kenney		
July 17-18 River Downs	1) Judy Wagner	2) Gary Russell	3) Eric Isaacson	
July 24 Prairie Meadows Racetrack	1) Judith Gonsulin	2) Ray Fiorda	3) Jerry Brookshire	
July 25 Emerald Downs	1) Mike Brady	2) Larry Kaplan	3) Walter Sommers	
	4) Philip Ziegler	5) Kim Harvick	6 Claude Davey	
	7) Kathy McKee	8) Paul Payne	9) Larry Farhner	
July 26-Sep. 8 Dmr Internet Contest	1) James Loughlin			
July 31-August 1 Sunland Park	1) Ed Barengo	2) John Papa	3) Richard Harris	
July 31-August 1 Del Mar Inv'l	1) Damian Roncevich	2) Tim Maretti	3) Ed Stranger	
	4) Frank Tate	5) James Kimbrall		
August 6 Ellis Park Race Course	1) David Petkovsek			
August 6-7 Bally's Las Vegas	1) Ira Schwartz	2) Robert Bertolucci		
August 7 Suffolk Downs	1) Garry Kaebitzsch			
August 7 Keeneland Association	1) William Smith	2) Jonathan Duncan	3) Richard Grose	
August 14-15 Canterbury Park	1) Rich Nilsen	2) Dave Walczak		
August 21 Youbet.com	1) James Michelson	2) Christopher Larmey	3) David Benning	
August 21 Trackside Louisville	1) August Meyer	2) Melvin Moser	3) Michael Elsass	
August 27 Ellis Park Race Course	1) Jerry Greenwell			

August 28 Horsmen's Park	1) Margo Moline			
August 28 Monmouth	1) Robert Hutt	2) Kevin Engelhard		
August 28 TVG	1) Justin Carey	2) Steve Ussery	3) James Meyers	
Aug. 28-29 Woodbine Racetrack	1) Pat Filipelli	2) Ray Arsenault	3) Joe Rich	
Sept. 2 Cal Exposition & State Fair	1) George Pacheco	2) Glenn Zoslaw	3) Gene Davenport	
September 4 Twin Spires Club	1) Jason Tudor			
September 5-6 AQHA	1) Michael Rea			
Sept. 3-Oct. 23 Bay Meadows	1) Flordeliza Nator	2) Jim Nelson	3) Wayne Atwell	
September 11 Twin Spires Club	1) Bill McAninch			
September 11-12 Fairplex Park	1) Don Beardsworth	2) Louis Constan		
September 18 Twin Spires Club	1) Michael Conway			
September 18-19 Northlands Park	1) Dennis Weller	2) Gary Bain	3) Penny Scott	
September 18-19 Fairplex Park	1) Richard Prozanski	2) Gail Searing		
September 19 Arlington Park	1) Donald Fritz	2) Wendy Jones	3) Michael Rucinski	
September 25-26 Fairplex Park	1) Craig Kaufman	2) Richard Goodall		
September 26 Turfway Park	1) Larry Moore			
Oct. 1-Nov. 13 The Meadowlands	1) Wayne Smeltz			
Oct. 2-Oct. 23 Oak Tree at Santa Anita	1) Sergio Vazquez	2) James Wark	3) Judith Sohl	
October 2 Sam Houston	1) Phil Harrington	2) Steve Lombardo	3) Gwen Quinn	
October 9 Horsmen's Park	1) Jim Bresel	2) Margo Moline	3) Claire Watson	
October 9 Delaware Park	1) Frank Harris	2) Greg Hockman		
October 9 Canterbury Park	1) Dick Mueller	2) Mayer Kanter	3) Jeff Jolley	
October 16 Trackside Louisville	1) Mike Seaton	2) John Edwards	3) Marta Nilsen	
Oct. 23 Harrah's Louisiana Downs	1) Charlie Messina	2) Joe Jackson	3) Glen Love	
October 23 Valley Race Park	1) Gordon Larson	2) Don Sullivan	3) Trey Stiles	
October 23 Youbet.com	1) Dennis Tiernan	2) John Dickson	3) Thomas Watrous	
Nov. 3-Dec. 13 CDSN	1) Joseph Cherichella	2) Jeffrey Daich	3) Noel Pink	
November 6 Thistledown	1) James Michelson, Sr.	2) Andrew Willnus	3) Fred Bamberger	
November 6 AQHA	1) Steve Shalaew			
November 6 The Meadowlands	1) April Scanio	2) Nick Fazzolari		
Nov. 10-Dec. 11 Golden Gate	1) Chester Victor Jr.	2) Arnold Ellis	3) Tiffany Priddy	
November 13-14 Aqueduct	1) Steve Wolfson, Jr.	2) Bill Schurman	3) John Conte	
November 26-28 Hollywood Park	1) Isaac Schultz	2) Philip Rothenberg	3) Marcus Hilton	
Nov. 27-28 Hawthorne Race Course	1) William Haliziw	2) Larry Wood	3) George Smith	
November 27 TVG	1) James Henry	2) Kirby Burkert	3) Walter Rex	4) James Lockwood
November 27 Suffolk Downs	1) Tony Linares Jr.			
November 27 Hoosier Park	1) Tim Yohler	2) Kyle Bowling	3) Tony Fannin	
November 27 Laurel Park	1) Roger Kurrus	2) Tammy Brauer	3) Bob Bandzwolek	
December 4 Keeneland Ass'n	1) Joseph W. Whitacre	2) Tony Garafalo	3) Larry Botkins	
December 4 Delaware Park	1) John Mitchell	2) Michael Harris		
December 4-5 Fair Grounds	1) John Ray	2) Charles Bradshaw	3) Charles Cage	
December 5 Turfway Park	1) Joel Elam			
December 10-11 AQHA	1) Jason Bulger			
December 11 Turf Paradise	1) Tom Leslie	2) Craig Larson	3) David Kassimer	
December 12 Tampa Bay Downs	1) Kevin Matties			
January 19 Bally's Las Vegas	1) Dane Moore	2) Barry Seedman		

2004 Stakes and Graded Stakes Histories

North American Stakes Run in 2004

Stakes	Date	Race	Trk	Dist/Surf		Winner	Jockey	Gross
10,000 Lakes S.	15-May	9	CBY	6F	D	Crocrock	Schacht, R	$40,000
A Gleam Invitational H.-G2	10-Jul	5	HOL	7F	D	Dream of Summer	Smith, ME	150,000
A. C. Kemp H.	22-Sep	8	ALB	7F	D	Railroad	Tohill, KS	33,750
A. J. Foyt S.	20-Jun	11	IND	1 1/16M	T	Red's Honor	Zimmerman, R	44,650
A. L. (Red) Erwin S.	8-Aug	9	LAD	7F	D	Nitro Chip	Meche, DJ	70,000
Accordant H.	30-Oct	8	MED	6F	D	Our Wildcat	Pimentel, J	60,000
Achievement H.	1-Jul	4	WO	6F	D	Twisted Wit	Bahen, SR	159,900
Ack Ack H.	31-May	9	HOL	7 1/2F	D	Taste of Paradise	Court, JK	100,575
Ack Ack H.-G3	31-Oct	9	CD	7 1/2F	D	Sir Cherokee	Borel, CH	165,300
Acorn S.-G1	4-Jun	10	BEL	1M	D	Island Sand	Thompson, TJ	250,000
Adena Springs Matchmaker S.	13-Jun	8	FE	5F	T	Dressed for Action	Sabourin, RB	80,000
Adena Springs Matchmaker Turf Sprint S.	8-Aug	9	RP	5F	T	Fleeta Dif	Helton, RM	41,700
Adena Stallions' Miss Preakness S.-G3	14-May	9	PIM	6F	D	Forest Music	Dominguez, RA	100,000
Adesa Auto Glass H.	25-Jun	7	MD	6F	D	Red Parka Mary	Seesequasis, D	5,000
Aegon Turf Sprint S.-G3	30-Apr	7	CD	5F	T	Lydgate	Day, P	114,700
Affectionately H.-G3	17-Jan	9	AQU	1 1/16M	D	Austin's Mom	Fragoso, P	109,600
Affirmed H.-G3	19-Jun	7	HOL	1 1/16M	D	Boomzeeboom	Espinoza, V	110,200
Afleet S.	29-May	4	WO	6F	D	Cut and Shoot	Husbands, P	106,000
African Prince S.	5-Jun	6	SUF	6F	D	Senor Ladd	Panell, D	40,000
Agassiz S.	21-Aug	6	ASD	1M	D	Gus Again	Guerra, VJ	40,000
Ahwatukee Express S.	23-Oct	8	TUP	6F	D	Wind Flow	Vergara, DP	40,000
Airline S.	5-Jun	8	LAD	6F	D	South Africa	Jacinto, J	50,000
Al Swihart Memorial H.	1-May	9	FON	6 1/2F	D	Southern Alert	Williams, RD	27,500
Alabama Belle S.	10-Sep	6	LAD	6F	D	Comalagold	Melancon, G	55,000
Alabama S.-G1	21-Aug	10	SAR	1 1/4M	D	Society Selection	Velasquez, CH	750,000
Alameda County Fillies and Mares H.	5-Jul	11	PLN	1 1/16M	D	Marwood	Warren, Jr., RJ	50,595
Alamedan H.	11-Jul	11	PLN	1 1/16M	D	Adreamisborn	Baze, RA	50,680
Albany S.	25-Aug	8	SAR	1 1/8M	D	West Virginia	Velazquez, JR	170,250
Albert Dominguez Memorial H.	19-Dec	10	SUN	1 1/16M	D	Rocky Gulch	Bourdieu, JM	104,300
Alberta Bred S.	4-Jul	4	LBG	5 1/2F	D	Guiltybysupiscion	Sterr, S	11,900
Alberta Bred S.	4-Jul	6	LBG	6F	D	Royal Deal	Cano, Jr., J	12,050
Alberta Bred S.	3-Oct	8	LBG	5F	D	Scruffy	Hebert, C	11,900
Alberta Breeders' H.	25-Sep	9	NP	1 1/16M	D	Beau Brass	Simard, RE	75,000
Alberta Derby	19-Jun	9	STP	1 1/16M	D	Fly Esteem	Bryan, D	100,000
Alberta Oaks	25-Sep	4	NP	1M	D	Weekend Ceilidh	Simard, RE	50,000
Alberta Premier's Futurity	25-Sep	8	NP	1M	D	Forever Rascal	Faine, CP	50,000
Alberta Railnet S.	14-Aug	5	GPR	6 1/2F	D	Real Sterling	Smith, J	6,905
Albuquerque Derby	19-Sep	8	ALB	1 1/16M	D	Mr. Trieste	Tohill, KS	34,300
Alex M. Robb H.	31-Dec	8	AQU	1 1/16M	D	Lord Langfuhr	Chavez, JF	84,000
Alfred G. Vanderbilt H.-G2	14-Aug	7	SAR	6F	D	Speightstown	Velazquez, JR	200,000
Algoma S.	5-Sep	4	WO	1 1/16M	D	One for Rose	Ramsammy, E	125,625
All Along Breeders' Cup S.-G3	10-Jul	8	CNL	1 1/8M	T	Film Maker	Prado, ES	200,000
All Brandy S.	14-Aug	9	PIM	1 1/8M	D	True Sensation	Rodriguez, ED	75,000
All Sold Out S.	24-Aug	7	FP	6F	D	Cart's Turn	Molina, T	35,800
Allen Bogan Memorial S.	23-Oct	8	LS	1M	D	Native Annie	Marquez, Jr., CH	75,000
Alma North S.	4-Sep	9	TIM	6 1/2F	D	Ribbon Cane	Dunkelberger, TL	50,000
Alysheba Breeders' Cup S.	2-Oct	9	LS	6F	D	Charming Socialite	Taylor, L	100,000
Alysheba S.	30-Apr	6	CD	1 1/16M	D	Congrats	Velazquez, JR	113,600
Alysheba S.	29-Oct	8	MED	1 1/16M	D	Roaring Fever	Coa, E	65,000
Alyssa H.	1-May	8	BEU	6F	D	Jackie's Hope	Gonzalez, IR	20,000
Alywow S.	13-Jun	5	WO	6 1/2F	T	Sweet Problem	McAleney, J	112,000
Amadevil H.	8-Aug	7	CLS	6F	D	What About David	Carkeek, J	15,700
Ambassador of Luck H.	4-Sep	8	PHA	7F	D	A Vision in Gray	Rose, J	50,000
Amelia Peabody S.	17-Nov	3	SUF	6F	D	Branded in Gold	Hampshire, Jr., JF	40,000
American Beauty S.	7-Feb	9	OP	6F	D	Eternal Cup	Thompson, TJ	50,000
American Derby-G2	24-Jul	5	AP	1 3/16M	T	Simple Exchange (IRE)	Smullen, P	250,000
American H.-G2	4-Jul	8	HOL	1 1/8M	T	Bayamo (IRE)	Flores, DR	150,000
American Oaks-G1	3-Jul	6	HOL	1 1/4M	T	Ticker Tape (GB)	Desormeaux, KJ	750,000
Amsterdam S.-G2	7-Aug	8	SAR	6F	D	Bwana Charlie	Sellers, SJ	150,000
Anark Millwrighting Mechanical S.	15-Aug	6	GPR	7F	D	Lafleur	Mellish, B	4,000
Ancient Title Breeders' Cup H.-G1	10-Oct	8	SA	6F	D	Pt's Grey Eagle	Bisono, A	250,000
Anderson Fowler S.	25-Jul	9	MTH	5F	D	Quick Action	Coa, E	55,000

Stakes	Date	Race	Trk	Dist/Surf		Winner	Jockey	Gross
Angenora S.	24-Apr	7	TDN	6F	D	Gabrieles Princess	Villa-Gomez, H	40,000
Angi Go S.	23-Jun	7	BOI	7F	D	Paradise Wild	Conklin, J	10,965
Angie C. S.	11-Jul	9	EMD	6F	D	Charming Colleen	Mitchell, GV	48,000
Anka Germania S.	19-Jul	3	CRC	1 3/8M	T	Iowa's Image	Aguilar, M	40,000
Ann Arbor S.	13-Aug	8	GLD	1M	D	Gold Ginny	Perez, RA	40,000
Ann Owens Distaff H.	24-Apr	3	TUP	6F	D	Sauceonside	Hernandez, ML	40,000
Anna M. Fisher Debutante S.	21-Aug	9	ELP	7F	D	Kota	McKee, J	100,000
Anne Arundel S.-G3	20-Nov	9	PIM	1 1/8M	D	Essence	Velazquez, JR	100,000
Anoakia S.	24-Oct	7	SA	6F	D	Hello Lucky	Stevens, GL	107,400
Answer Do S.	7-May	8	TUP	6 1/2F	D	King Justin	Gomez, EA	21,700
Anthony Fair H.	25-Jul	9	ANF	6 1/2F	D	Marlin's Ruler	Vasquez, RM	5,000
Anthony Thoroughbred Futurity	25-Jul	13	ANF	5F	D	Slews in Oz Now	Wellington, T	20,500
Appalachian S.	14-Apr	8	KEE	1M	T	Lucifer's Stone	Santos, JA	113,500
Apple Blossom H.-G1	3-Apr	9	OP	1 1/16M	D	Azeri	Smith, ME	500,000
Appleton H.-G3	4-Jan	9	GP	1M	T	Millennium Dragon (GB)	Migliore, R	150,000
Aqueduct H.-G3	17-Jan	4	AQU	1 1/16M	D	Seattle Fitz (ARG)	Gryder, AT	110,100
Arapahoe Park Sprint H.	11-Jul	8	ARP	6F	D	Absolutely True	Wales, T	27,825
Arcadia H.-G2	3-Apr	3	SA	1 1/8M	T	Diplomatic Bag	Flores, DR	150,000
Arcadia S.	13-Jun	9	LAD	6F	D	Skymeister	Meche, L	50,000
Arctic Queen H.	20-Jun	6	FL	6F	D	Travelator	Gryder, AT	50,000
Argent Dixie S.-G2	15-May	10	PIM	1 1/8M	T	Mr O'Brien (IRE)	Dominguez, RA	200,000
Argent Mortgage S.-G3	1-May	7	CD	1M	T	Shaconage	Blanc, B	113,300
Aristides Breeders' Cup H.-G3	19-Jun	9	CD	6F	D	Champali	Bejarano, R	162,150
Arizona Breeders Derby	24-Apr	8	TUP	1 1/16M	D	Overland Road	Campbell, J	48,987
Arizona Breeders' Futurity	4-Dec	6	TUP	6F	D	Missingrbueno	Ruis, M	40,213
Arizona Breeders' Futurity	4-Dec	7	TUP	6F	D	Desert Prospector	Ruis, M	42,384
Arizona County Fair Distance Series S.	16-May	5	MOF	1 1/16M	D	Oil Man	Gard, TL	2,359
Arizona County Fair Speed Series S.	16-May	4	MOF	6F	D	High Riser	Barrio, AM	2,409
Arizona Juvenile S.	26-Dec	7	TUP	6 1/2F	D	Lost in the Fog	Baze, RA	50,000
Arizona Oaks	7-Feb	6	TUP	1 1/16M	D	Very Vegas	Ruis, M	75,000
Arizona Stallion S.	9-Apr	9	TUP	7 1/2F	T	Overland Road	Campbell, J	35,944
Arkansas Derby-G2	10-Apr	9	OP	1 1/8M	D	Smarty Jones	Elliott, S	1,000,000
Ark-La-Tex H.	20-Jun	1	LAD	1 1/16M	D	Pie N Burger	Jacinto, J	50,000
Arlington Breeders' Cup Oaks-G3	21-Aug	9	AP	1 1/8M	D	Lovely Afternoon	Graham, J	150,000
Arlington Breeders' Cup Oaks-G3	21-Aug	9	AP	1 1/8M	D	Catboat	Martin, Jr., EM	150,000
Arlington Breeders' Cup Sprint H.	28-Aug	6	AP	6F	D	Gold Storm	Taylor, L	150,000
Arlington Classic S.-G2	3-Jul	9	AP	1 1/16M	T	Toasted	Douglas, RR	200,000
Arlington H.-G3	24-Jul	7	AP	1 1/4M	T	Senor Swinger	Blanc, B	250,000
Arlington Matron H.-G3	4-Sep	9	AP	1 1/8M	D	Adoration	Espinoza, V	150,000
Arlington Million S.-G1	14-Aug	9	AP	1 1/4M	T	Kicken Kris	Desormeaux, KJ	1,000,000
Arlington-Washington BC Futurity-G3	19-Sep	6	AP	1M	D	Three Hour Nap	Razo, Jr., E	200,000
Arlington-Washington Lassie S.-G3	19-Sep	9	AP	1M	D	Culinary	Marquez, Jr., CH	100,000
Artax H.	27-Mar	11	GP	7F	D	Speightstown	Coa, E	100,000
Arthur I. Appleton Juvenile Turf S.	13-Nov	12	CRC	1 1/16M	T	Turk's Ransom	Velasquez, CH	100,000
Ascot Graduation S.	13-Nov	8	HST	1 1/16M	D	Alabama Rain	Alvarado, PV	122,250
Ashland S.-G1	3-Apr	9	KEE	1 1/16M	D	Madcap Escapade	Douglas, RR	500,000
Ashley T. Cole H.	25-Sep	8	BEL	1 1/8M	T	Provincetown	Farina, T	111,700
Aspen Cup H.	26-Jun	9	RUI	6F	D	Miss Noteworthy	Juarez, Jr., AJ	25,000
Aspen H.	28-Aug	7	ARP	6F	D	Debatable	Johnson, BL	31,000
Aspidistra H.	21-Aug	7	CRC	1M	T	Teak Totem	Nunez, EO	100,000
Aspirant S.	21-Aug	8	FL	6F	D	Caribbean Cruiser	Yang, CC	112,733
Assault S.	23-Oct	9	LS	1 1/16M	D	Goosey Moose	Chapa, R	100,000
Assiniboia Oaks	12-Sep	6	ASD	1 1/16M	D	Ericka's Lass	Guerra, VJ	40,000
Astarita S.-G3	17-Oct	8	BEL	6 1/2F	D	Toll Taker	Coa, E	108,000
Astoria S.	27-Jun	8	BEL	5 1/2F	D	Broadway Gold	Bailey, JD	107,700
ATBA Fall Sales S.	16-Oct	7	TUP	6F	D	Lady Bertrando	Campbell, J	111,241
ATBA Fall Sales S.	16-Oct	8	TUP	6F	D	Power Wave	Hernandez, ML	108,840
ATBA Spring Sales S.	16-May	9	TUP	5F	D	Power Wave	Hernandez, ML	60,282
Atchison Topeka Sante Fe H.	9-Oct	9	WDS	6F	D	Robin Zee	Sukie, D	20,000
Athenia H.-G3	31-Oct	8	AQU	1 1/16M	T	Finery	Fragoso, P	115,700
Atto Mile S.-G1	19-Sep	9	WO	1M	T	Soaring Free	Kabel, T	1,000,000
Au Revior H.	15-Aug	8	BOI	1 1/4M	D	Find My Halter	Packer, BR	6,300
Auburn S.	2-May	7	EMD	6F	D	Crimson Design	Gutierrez, JM	40,000

Stakes	Date	Race	Trk	Dist/Surf		Winner	Jockey	Gross
Audrey Skirball-Kenis S.	7-Nov	8	HOL	1 1/8M	T	Penny's Fortune	Valdivia, Jr., J	80,725
Audubon Oaks	31-Jul	9	ELP	1 1/16M	T	Lenatareese	Blanc, B	75,000
Autotote Derby	31-Oct	10	LBG	1 1/16M	D	Streak a Roani	Hebert, C	16,600
Autumn Classic S.	7-Nov	7	RP	6 1/2F	D	Herecomesthemannow	Kimes, C	40,000
Autumn Daze H.	6-Sep	9	YD	1M 70Y	D	Bobby Naz	Espy, K	4,100
Autumn Leaves H.	4-Sep	8	BM	1M	T	Marwood	Warren, Jr., RJ	71,500
Autumn Leaves S.	28-Sep	9	MNR	1 1/16M	D	Indy Groove	Guidry, M	75,000
Autumn S.	27-Nov	8	CT	7F	D	Lets Just Do It	Dunkelberger, TL	51,550
Aventura S.	3-Apr	11	GP	1 1/16M	D	Kaufy Mate	Cruz, MR	250,000
Azalea Breeders' Cup S.-G3	10-Jul	8	CRC	6F	D	Dazzle Me	Sellers, SJ	300,000
Azalea S.	19-Mar	9	DED	5F	D	Von Braun	Sellers, SJ	50,000
Aztec Oaks	2-Nov	9	SRP	6 1/2F	D	Latenite Special	Tohill, KS	71,000
B Cup S.	16-Oct	5	LBG	6F	D	Special Era	Wilson, A	12,050
B Cup S.	16-Oct	8	LBG	7F	D	Game Princess	Stianson, J	12,200
B Cup S.	16-Oct	9	LBG	7F	D	Silver Sky	Miyashiro, CJ	12,050
B Cup S.	16-Oct	3	LBG	6F	D	Itsaninetyniner	Sterr, S	11,900
B Cup S.	16-Oct	1	LBG	6F	D	I Give Up	Mellish, B	11,750
B Cup S.	16-Oct	7	LBG	5 1/2F	D	Irish Intrigue	Smith, N	12,050
B Cup S.	16-Oct	6	LBG	6F	D	Bizzyweekend	Sterr, S	12,200
B. B. Sixty Rayburn S.	22-May	8	EVD	1M	D	Old Lee	Perrodin, EJ	40,000
B. Thoughtful S.	24-Apr	4	HOL	7F	D	Royally Chosen	Solis, AO	150,000
Bachman S.	28-Feb	8	FON	4F	D	Tee Times Two	Warhol, VL	11,775
Baldwin S.-G3	28-Feb	8	SA	6 1/2F	T	Seattle Borders	Solis, AO	113,350
Ballade S.	30-Jun	7	WO	6F	D	Brass in Pocket	Kabel, T	127,875
Ballerina Breeders' Cup S.-G3	16-Oct	8	HST	1 1/8M	D	See Me Through	Alvarado, PV	197,150
Ballerina H.-G1	29-Aug	9	SAR	7F	D	Lady Tak	Bailey, JD	250,000
Ballston Spa Breeders' Cup H.-G3	30-Aug	8	SAR	1 1/16M	T	Ocean Drive	Velazquez, JR	214,000
Bangles and Beads S.	21-Sep	9	FPX	6 1/2F	D	Madringa	Bisono, A	60,000
Banshee Breeze H.	4-Apr	10	GP	1 1/16M	D	Nonsuch Bay	Coa, E	75,000
Bara Lass S.	20-Nov	9	HOU	7F	D	Snipper Lou	Burningham, J	50,000
Barbara Fritchie H.-G2	14-Feb	9	LRL	7F	D	Bear Fan	Fogelsonger, R	200,000
Barbara Shinpoch S.	28-Aug	9	EMD	1M	D	A Classic Life	Russell, B	55,000
Barb's Dancer S.	13-Jul	7	CRC	6F	D	Petrina Above	Toscano, PR	40,000
Barksdale H.	31-May	10	LAD	1M	T	Waupaca	Lanerie, CJ	50,000
Barona Cup H.	22-Aug	4	DMR	1M	T	Shake Off	Baze, T	98,575
Barretts Debutante S.	18-Sep	11	FPX	6 1/2F	D	Lunar Flight	Gomez, GK	118,800
Barretts Juvenile S.	19-Sep	11	FPX	6 1/2F	D	Beat the Chalk	Pedroza, MA	111,250
Barretts/CTBA Classic S.	24-Jan	6	SA	1 1/8M	D	Southern Image	Espinoza, V	1,000,000
Bashford Manor S.-G3	5-Jul	10	CD	6F	D	Lunarpal	Sellers, SJ	163,200
Battlefield S.	12-Jun	9	MTH	1 1/8M	T	Megantic	Pimentel, J	60,000
Battler Star H.	7-Mar	7	FG	6F	D	Placid Star	Melancon, G	75,000
Baxter S.	20-Mar	9	FON	6 1/2F	D	Mortrump	Beck, DL	17,200
Bay Meadows Breeder's Cup H.-G3	2-Oct	7	BM	1 1/8M	T	Needwood Blade (GB)	Carr, D	150,000
Bay Meadows Breeders' Cup Sprint H.-G3	19-Jun	8	BM	6F	D	Court's in Session	Gonzalez, RM	125,000
Bay Meadows Derby-G3	6-Nov	8	BM	1 1/8M	T	Congressionalhonor	Baze, RA	100,000
Bay Meadows Oaks	12-Jun	3	BM	1 1/16M	T	Crozet	Warren, Jr., RJ	79,950
Bay Shore S.-G3	10-Apr	7	AQU	7F	D	Forest Danger	Velazquez, JR	150,000
Bayakoa H.-G2	12-Dec	8	HOL	1 1/16M	D	Hollywood Story	Espinoza, V	150,000
Bayakoa S.	4-Apr	10	OP	1 1/16M	D	La Reason	Shepherd, J	75,000
Bayou Breeders' Cup H.-G3	28-Feb	9	FG	1 1/8M	T	Bedanken	Pettinger, DR	125,000
Bayou State S.	5-Mar	8	DED	7F	D	Spritely Walker	Sellers, SJ	50,000
BC Cup Classic H.	2-Aug	9	HST	1 1/8M	D	Illusive Force	Wilson, D	72,436
BC Cup Debutante S.	2-Aug	7	HST	6 1/2F	D	Backseat Becka	Wilson, D	54,465
BC cup Distaff H.	2-Aug	8	HST	1 1/8M	D	Dancewithavixen	Valdez, F	55,720
BC Cup Nursery S.	2-Aug	6	HST	6 1/2F	D	Notis Otis	Loseth, C	54,836
BC Cup Sprint H.	2-Aug	4	HST	6 1/2F	D	Five Point Star	Alvarado, PV	55,590
BC Cup Stallion H.	2-Aug	3	HST	1 1/16M	D	Regal Red	Fuentes, FP	55,655
BC Cup Stallion H.	2-Aug	2	HST	1 1/16M	D	Lord Samarai	Wilson, D	55,590
BC Lottery Corp H.	1-Aug	7	KIN	1 1/16M	D	Tender Offer (IRE)	Butterfly, R	10,000
BC Lottery Corporation H.	15-Aug	5	KAM	1M	D	Tender Offer (IRE)	Bilodeau, RJ	12,200
Beau Brummel S.	14-Sep	9	FPX	6 1/2F	D	Forever Foxy	Sorenson, D	60,000
Beaufort S.	25-Sep	3	NP	1 1/16M	D	Royalty Boy	Simard, RE	50,000
Beaugay H.-G3	1-May	9	AQU	1 1/16M	T	Dedication (FR)	Castellano, J	110,000

Stakes	Date	Race	Trk	Dist/Surf		Winner	Jockey	Gross
Beautiful Day S.	12-Jul	8	DEL	6F	D	Humor Me Molly	Pino, MG	54,100
Beck Auto Group Turf Sprint H.	31-May	6	LS	5F	T	Mighty Beau	Sellers, SJ	100,000
Bed o' Roses Breeders' Cup H.-G3	17-Apr	8	AQU	1M	D	Passing Shot	Santos, JA	158,400
Beldame S.-G1	9-Oct	9	BEL	1 1/8M	D	Sightseek	Castellano, J	750,000
Belle Geste S.	10-Oct	4	WO	1 1/8M	T	Mona Rose	Da Silva, ER	104,000
Belle Mahone S.	18-Jul	8	WO	1 1/16M	D	Winning Chance	Kabel, T	107,000
Belle Roberts S.	19-Sep	3	EMD	1 1/16M	D	Aunt Sophie	Gonzalez, RM	50,000
Belmont Breeders' Cup H.-G2	18-Sep	8	BEL	1 1/8M	T	Senor Swinger	Prado, ES	207,300
Belmont S.-G1	5-Jun	11	BEL	1 1/2M	D	Birdstone	Prado, ES	1,000,000
Ben Ali S.-G3	22-Apr	8	KEE	1 1/8M	D	Midway Road	Albarado, R	150,000
Ben Cohen S.	22-May	9	PIM	5F	T	Governor's Pride	Rocco, Jr., J	50,000
Ben Woodward Memorial H.	10-Jul	9	PRV	5 1/2F	D	Larron	Butterfly, R	3,500
Bergen County S.	16-Oct	8	MED	5F	T	All Hail Stormy	Coa, E	55,000
Berkeley Breeders' Cup H.-G3	27-Mar	7	GG	1M	D	Snorter	Baze, RA	100,000
Bernard Baruch H.-G2	30-Jul	8	SAR	1 1/8M	T	Silver Tree	Bailey, JD	150,000
Bernie Dowd H.	18-Jul	6	MTH	6F	D	Something Smith	Lopez, CC	60,000
Bersid S.	17-Oct	3	TUP	1M	D	Arch Lady	Hernandez, ML	21,600
Bertram F. Bongard S.	3 Oct	9	BEL	7F	D	Up Like Thunder	Castellano, J	109,700
Bessarabian H.-G3	28-Nov	8	WO	7F	D	Miss Grindstone	Sabourin, RB	212,750
Bessemer Trust Breeders' Cup Juvenile-G1	30-Oct	7	LS	1 1/16M	D	Wilko	Dettori, L	1,500,000
Best of Ohio Distaff S.	9-Oct	12	TDN	1 1/8M	D	Whitewater Way	Woolsey, RW	50,000
Best of Ohio Endurance S.	9-Oct	14	TDN	1 1/4M	D	Real Echo	Cloninger, Jr., WT	75,000
Best of Ohio Juvenile S.	9-Oct	11	TDN	1 1/16M	D	Fierce Cat	Troilo, WD	60,000
Best of Ohio Sprint S.	9-Oct	10	TDN	6F	D	Ben's Reflection	Johnston, J	50,000
Best of the Rest S.	18-Jul	10	CRC	1 1/16M	D	Super Frolic	Toribio, A	45,000
Best Pal S.-G2	15-Aug	2	DMR	6 1/2F	D	Roman Ruler	Nakatani, CS	150,000
Best Turn S.	21-Feb	9	AQU	6F	D	Redskin Warrior	Migliore, R	81,825
Betsy Ross S.	4-Jul	9	MTH	5F	T	Melody of Colors	Coa, E	60,000
Better Bee S.	3-Jul	5	AP	6F	D	Without a Doubt	Razo, Jr., E	41,250
Bettie Bullock Memorial Derby	22-Aug	8	WYO	5 1/2F	D	Closely Held	Guymon, TF	5,600
Bettors Invitational H.	26-Jun	7	GRP	6 1/2F	D	The Lord Is Eager	Crispin, JA	3,760
Beverly D. S.-G1	14-Aug	8	AP	1 3/16M	T	Crimson Palace (SAF)	Dettori, L	750,000
Beverly Hills H.-G2	27-Jun	8	HOL	1 1/4M	T	Light Jig (GB)	Solis, AO	200,000
Bewitch S.-G3	21-Apr	8	KEE	1 1/2M	T	Meridiana (GER)	Prado, ES	113,400
Bien Bien S.	6-Nov	5	HOL	1M	T	Whilly (IRE)	Martinez, FF	81,325
Bienvenidos S.	1-Oct	9	TUP	1M	D	Cut of Music	Higuera, AR	22,000
Big Country 93.1 XX FM Futurity	21-Aug	7	GPR	5 1/2F	D	John's Magic	Wilson, A	5,540
Big Jag H.	3-Oct	8	BM	6F	D	Onebadshark	Warren, Jr., RJ	71,500
Big Red Mile H.	31-May	8	LNN	1M	D	Grayglen	Yaranga, Y	15,900
Big Sky H.	1-Aug	10	GF	1M 70Y	D	Cabreo	Ortiz, Jr., I	7,550
Bill Callihan H.	5-Sep	8	CLS	6 1/2F	D	Missy Can Do	Sensenbach, L	10,600
Bill Thomas Memorial H.	6-Mar	11	SUN	6 1/2F	D	Bang	Noguez, T	55,100
Bill Wheeler H.	8-Oct	9	MED	1M 70Y	D	Upturn	Coa, E	60,000
Bill Wineberg S.	13-Nov	7	PM	6F	D	Cascadiansasquatch	Beckner, T	20,330
Billy Powell Claiming H.	5-Jul	9	ALB	1 1/2M	D	Hammerin	Tohill, KS	17,350
Billy the Kid Distance Series Final S.	6-Sep	5	RUI	1 1/4M	D	Fin Entertainment	Jones, CE	16,900
Bing Crosby Breeders' Cup H.-G1	25-Jul	2	DMR	6F	D	Kela	Baze, T	250,000
Bird of Pay S.	4-Sep	8	NP	6 1/2F	D	Miss Venturous	Painter, LM	50,000
Birdcatcher S.	6-Sep	8	NP	6 1/2F	D	One Special Hoss	Chaparro, C	50,000
Birdonthewire S.	23-Oct	9	CRC	6F	D	G P's Black Knight	Olivero, C	75,000
Birmingham Maiden S.	12-Jun	7	RD	6F	D	Heatmoney	Rechy, R	22,500
BK Disposal S.	14-Aug	6	GPR	6F	D	Bizzyweekend	Sterr, S	4,340
Black Gold H.	10-Jan	9	FG	7 1/2F	T	Shiloh Bound	Riquelme, J	60,000
Black Mesa S.	24-Oct	9	RP	6F	D	Racing Sundown	Fitzpatrick, A	40,000
Black Swan S.	22-Sep	11	FPX	1 1/16M	D	Kachina Dream	Garcia, MS	60,000
Black Tie Affair H.	10-Jul	9	AP	1 1/8M	D	Alumni Hall	Albarado, R	75,000
Black-Eyed Susan S.-G2	14-May	10	PIM	1 1/8M	D	Yearly Report	Bailey, JD	200,000
Blair's Cove S.	3-Jul	7	CBY	1 1/16M	T	Adroitly Superb	Campbell, J	40,000
Blaze O'Brien S.	15-Mar	9	TUP	1 1/16M	T	Black Bart	Gann, SL	21,800
Blazing Sevens S.	15-Aug	7	FE	7F	T	Baltic Prince	Villeneuve, F	60,000
Bloom n Character S.	10-Feb	8	TUP	1 1/8M	T	Expressionator	Dieguez, WO	21,900
Blue Hen S.	23-Oct	7	DEL	1 1/16M	D	Buzz Song	DeCarlo, CP	100,000
Blue Mountain Juvenile S.	12-Nov	7	PEN	6F	D	Nita Chiquita	Kravets, J	53,000

Stakes	Date	Race	Trk	Dist/Surf		Winner	Jockey	Gross
Blue Norther S.	14-Jan	7	SA	1M	T	Mambo Slew	Smith, ME	98,800
Blue Skies H.	25-Jul	9	LAD	1 1/16M	D	Akanti (IRE)	Meche, L	50,000
Bluebonnet S.	31-Oct	9	LS	1 1/16M	T	My Misty Princess	Theriot, J	100,000
Bluegrass H.	5-Jun	8	LNN	6F	D	Missy Can Do	Collins, DM	11,000
Bob Bryant S.	22-May	8	PRM	6F	D	Hollywood and Wine	Doocy, TT	57,256
Bob Harding S.	5-Sep	10	MTH	1M	T	Stormy Roman	Clemente, AV	60,000
Bob Johnson Memorial S.	3-Jul	8	LS	1M	D	Rare Cure	Martin, Jr., EM	75,000
Bob Slater S.	17-Apr	8	GP	5F	T	Melody of Colors	Coa, E	50,000
Bobbie Bricker Memorial H.	31-Oct	8	BEU	1 1/16M	D	Imahoneytoo	Villa-Gomez, H	40,000
Boeing H.	24-Jul	9	EMD	1 1/16M	D	Cascade Corona	Mitchell, GV	40,000
Boiling Springs S.-G3	12-Sep	9	MTH	1 1/16M	T	Seducer's Song	Bravo, J	150,000
Boise Thoroughbred Derby	11-Aug	7	BOI	1M	D	Silent Snow	Conklin, J	6,050
Bold Accent H.	14-Feb	8	FON	4F	D	Missy Can Do	Warhol, VL	11,750
Bold Ego Thoroughbred H.	3-Jan	10	SUN	5 1/2F	D	Inox (ARG)	Bourdieu, JM	53,950
Bold Ruckus S.	16-Jun	3	WO	6F	T	Dashing Admiral	Kabel, T	133,125
Bold Ruler H.-G3	8-May	7	BEL	6F	D	Canadian Frontier	Castellano, J	107,700
Bold Venture H.	11-Jul	8	WO	6 1/2F	D	I'm the Tiger	Kabel, T	141,250
Bonnie Heath Turf Cup H.	13-Nov	9	CRC	1 1/8M	T	Final Prophecy	Olivero, C	150,000
Bonnie Miss S.-G2	6-Mar	8	GP	1 1/8M	D	Last Song	Prado, ES	200,000
Boomer S.	3-Jul	10	FMT	5 1/2F	D	Frilly Fun	Payne, LD	49,075
Boots 'n Jackie S.	24-May	8	CRC	1 1/16M	D	Gentille Alouette	Penalba, C	40,000
Border Cup S.	2-Aug	7	FE	1 1/16M	D	Olympic Advice	Bochinski, BT	60,000
Borderland Derby	29-Feb	11	SUN	1M	D	Go Kitty Go	Fuentes, MV	105,450
Bosselman/Gus Fonner S.	24-Apr	9	FON	1 1/16M	D	Sonic West	Martinez, W	110,000
Bossier City H.	31-Jul	10	LAD	1 1/16M	T	Alpha Capo	Meche, DJ	50,000
Bourbon County S.	29-Oct	9	KEE	1 1/16M	T	Rey de Cafe	Perret, C	112,200
Bourbonette Breeders' Cup S.	20-Mar	9	TP	1M	D	Class Above	Bailey, JD	150,000
Bouwerie S.	16-May	8	BEL	7F	D	Rodeo Licious	Luzzi, MJ	113,600
Bowling Green H.-G2	17-Jul	8	BEL	1 3/8M	T	Kicken Kris	Prado, ES	150,000
Boyd Gaming's Delta Jackpot S.	4-Dec	8	DED	1 1/16M	D	Texcess	Espinoza, V	1,000,000
Boyd Gaming's Delta Princess S.	4-Dec	6	DED	1M	D	Punch Appeal	Meche, DJ	250,000
Brandywine H.	12-Jun	8	DEL	1 1/16M	D	Loving (BRZ)	Pino, MG	100,600
Brave Raj S.	2-Oct	8	CRC	1M 70Y	D	Dansetta Light	Lopez, JE	100,000
Breeders' Cup Classic (Dodge)-G1	30-Oct	9	LS	1 1/4M	D	Ghostzapper	Castellano, J	4,000,000
Breeders' Cup Distaff (NexTel)-G1	30-Oct	2	LS	1 1/8M	D	Ashado	Velazquez, JR	2,000,000
Breeders' Cup Juvenile Fillies-G1	30-Oct	3	LS	1 1/16M	D	Sweet Catomine	Nakatani, CS	1,000,000
Breeders' Cup Sprint-G1	30-Oct	5	LS	6F	D	Speightstown	Velazquez, JR	1,060,000
Breeders' Gold Cup S.	3-Oct	9	ASD	1 1/8M	D	Deputy Country	Hendricks, K	65,000
Breeders' S.	8-Aug	9	WO	1 1/2M	T	A Bit O'Gold	Jones, JC	500,000
Breeders' Special S.	3-Jul	8	LNN	6F	D	Sheso	Williams, RD	15,600
Brent's Princess S.	22-May	8	TDN	6F	D	Mercer's Launch	Rosario, Jr., HL	40,000
Brickyard S.	24-Oct	9	HOO	6F	D	Mr. Mink	Pompell, TL	40,000
Brighouse Belles H.	19-Jun	3	HST	1 1/16M	D	Victor's Secret	Loseth, C	44,784
British Columbia Breeders' Cup Oaks-G3	25-Sep	8	HST	1 1/8M	D	Summer Symphony	Hoverson, C	192,350
British Columbia Derby-G3	26-Sep	8	HST	1 1/8M	D	Flamethrowintexan	Frazier, R	351,500
Broadway H.	13-Mar	6	AQU	7F	D	Sensibly Chic	Espinoza, JL	84,125
Brooklyn H.-G2	12-Jun	7	BEL	1 1/8M	D	Seattle Fitz (ARG)	Migliore, R	250,000
Brookmeade S.	4-Jul	11	CNL	1 1/16M	D	Bluffie Slew	Rosado, RJ	50,000
Brooks Fields S.	12-Jun	7	CBY	1M	D	Native Hawk	Nolan, PM	40,000
Brother Brown S.	17-Oct	8	RP	5F	T	The Niner Account	Berry, MC	41,500
Brown Bess H.-G3	31-Jan	3	GG	1 1/16M	T	Red Rioja (IRE)	Saint-Martin, E	100,000
Bruce G. Smith Memorial S.	4-Sep	9	SUF	1 1/16M	T	Final Prophecy	Bush, V	40,000
Bucharest S.	31-Jan	8	HOU	6F	D	Jimmy Cracked Corn	Simington, DE	30,000
Buckeye Native S.	15-Aug	12	RD	1 1/16M	T	Hank's Rib	Ouzts, PW	40,000
Buckland S.	3-Jul	9	CNL	5 1/2F	T	Spring Kitten	Kreidel, K	50,000
Buckpasser S.	6-Sep	8	FP	6F	D	Yukon's Gambler	Pompell, TL	25,600
Budweiser Challenger S.	6-Mar	10	TAM	1 1/16M	D	Attack the Books	Bell, DC	75,000
Budweiser Emerald H.	20-Jun	9	EMD	1M	D	Demon Warlock	Lopez, AD	75,000
Buena Vista H.-G2	21-Feb	8	SA	1M	T	Fun House	Stevens, GL	150,000
Bueno S.	17-Dec	8	TUP	6F	D	Corona Del Hielo	Martinez, OA	22,100
Buffalo Bayou S.	27-Nov	8	HOU	1 1/16M	T	Sea Dub	Quinonez, LS	40,000
Buffalo S.	26-Sep	6	ASD	1M	D	Gold Strike	Pruitt, J	41,000
Bull Page S.	9-Oct	6	WO	6F	D	Wholelottabourbon	Clark, D	131,625

Stakes	Date	Race	Trk	Dist/Surf		Winner	Jockey	Gross
Bullys Futurity	30-Oct	2	LBG	6F	D	Itsaninetyniner	Sterr, S	12,200
Bungalow H.	24-Aug	8	FP	1M	D	Princess Paster	Medina, CM	35,700
Bunty Lawless S.	31-Oct	7	WO	1M	T	Millfleet	Scharfstein, J	146,750
Burnaby Breeders' Cup H.	1-Jul	5	HST	1 1/16M	D	Tobe Suave	Alvarado, PV	92,800
Busanda S.	25-Jan	8	AQU	1M 70Y	D	Island Sand	Fragoso, P	84,375
Busher S.	28-Feb	8	AQU	1 1/16M	D	Fond	Gryder, AT	81,600
Bustles and Bows S.	16-Sep	10	FPX	6 1/2F	D	Kash Klip	Figueroa, O	60,000
Buttons and Bows H.	11-Apr	6	SUD	4F	D	Raise a Daughter	Conklin, J	3,050
C. J. Hindley Humboldt County Marathon H.	22-Aug	9	FER	1 5/8M	D	Clip	Navarro, VG	13,295
C. W. Doc Pardee Starter S.	24-Apr	1	TUP	1M	D	Si Ya Dancing	Martinez, OA	15,000
Caballos Del Sol H.	9-Oct	3	TUP	6F	D	Newark	Dieguez, WO	40,000
Cactus Cup S.	12-Mar	8	TUP	6 1/2F	D	Sauceonside	Corbett, GW	40,000
Cactus Flower H.	10-Apr	8	TUP	6F	D	Princess V.	Stevens, SA	40,000
Caesar Rodney H.	16-Oct	8	DEL	1 1/8M	T	B. A. Way	Castellano, Jr., A	200,000
Caesar's Wish S.	24-Apr	8	PIM	1 1/16M	D	He Loves Me	Santana, JZ	75,000
Cajun Express S.	27-Mar	7	DED	5F	D	Zarb's Luck	Gonzalez, C	40,000
Cajun S.	23-Oct	7	LAD	6F	D	Zarb's Dahar	Melancon, G	54,300
Calcasieu S.	13-Nov	7	DED	5F	D	Mr. Excellent	Bourque, SJ	50,000
Calder Derby-G3	23-Oct	10	CRC	1 1/8M	T	Eddington	Coa, E	200,000
Calder Oaks	23-Oct	7	CRC	1 1/8M	T	Hopelessly Devoted	Velasquez, CH	200,000
Calder Turf Sprint H.	10-Jul	7	CRC	5F	T	Whenthedoveflies	Day, P	100,000
California Breeders' Champion S.	26-Dec	4	SA	7F	D	Uncle Denny	Douglas, RR	138,625
California Breeders' Champion S.	27-Dec	7	SA	7F	D	Memorette	Desormeaux, KJ	140,875
California Cup Classic H.	16-Oct	8	SA	1 1/8M	D	Cozy Guy	Nakatani, CS	250,000
California Cup Distaff H.	16-Oct	7	SA	6 1/2F	T	Our Mango	Baze, RA	150,000
California Cup Distance H.	16-Oct	1	SA	1 1/4M	T	Test the Waters	Espinoza, V	100,000
California Cup Juvenile Fillies S.	16-Oct	10	SA	1 1/16M	D	Lady Truffles	Espinoza, V	125,000
California Cup Juvenile S.	16-Oct	4	SA	1 1/16M	D	Texcess	Douglas, RR	125,000
California Cup Matron H.	16-Oct	3	SA	1 1/16M	D	Dream of Summer	Smith, ME	150,000
California Cup Mile H.	16-Oct	9	SA	1M	T	A to the Z	Espinoza, V	175,000
California Cup Sprint H.	16-Oct	6	SA	6F	D	Areyoutalkintome	Nakatani, CS	150,000
California Cup Starter H.	16-Oct	5	SA	1 1/2M	T	Ring of Friendship	Stevens, GL	50,000
California Cup Starter Sprint H.	16-Oct	2	SA	6F	D	Ata Olympio	Gomez, GK	50,000
California Derby	17-Apr	7	BM	1 1/8M	D	Trieste's Honor	Baze, RA	100,000
California Oaks	6-Mar	3	GG	1 1/16M	D	House of Fortune	Warren, Jr., RJ	78,900
California Sprint Championship H.	11-Sep	3	BM	6F	D	Green Team	Baze, RA	100,000
California T'bred Breeders' Association S.	23-Jul	7	DMR	5 1/2F	D	Sterling Cat	Baze, RA	125,000
California Turf Championship H.	6-Sep	8	BM	1M	T	Stage Player	Rollins, CJ	100,000
Californian S.-G2	12-Jun	9	HOL	1 1/8M	D	Even the Score	Flores, DR	250,000
Caltech S.	20-Mar	11	GP	1 1/8M	T	Shakespeare	Santos, JA	67,700
Camelia S.	9-Jan	9	DED	6 1/2F	D	Fuse It	Hernandez, Jr., BJ	50,000
Canad Construction S.	11-Jul	12	GPR	1M	D	Gomka	Mellish, B	5,175
Canada Day S.	1-Jul	6	FE	6F	D	Krz Ruckus	Poznansky, N	100,000
Canada Day S.	1-Jul	7	ASD	1M	D	Pete's Surprise	Hendricks, K	40,000
Canadian Derby-G3	28-Aug	9	NP	1 3/8M	D	Organ Grinder	McAleney, J	250,000
Canadian H.-G2	19-Sep	6	WO	1 1/8M	T	Classic Stamp	Husbands, P	330,500
Canadian Juvenile S.	11-Oct	8	NP	1 1/16M	D	Poor Iggy	Beauregard, S	75,000
Canadian Turf H.-G3	31-Jan	8	GP	1 1/16M	D	Newfoundland	Velazquez, JR	100,000
Candy Eclair S.	6-Sep	11	MTH	5F	T	Ambition Unbridled	Karamanos, H	55,000
Canterbury Park Juvenile S.	11-Jul	7	CBY	5 1/2F	D	Smoke Smoke Smoke	Martinez, SB	40,000
Canterbury Park Lassie S.	11-Jul	6	CBY	5 1/2F	D	Berbatim	Graham, J	40,000
Cape Henlopen S.	18-Jul	8	DEL	1 1/2M	D	Chopper Won	Dominguez, RA	52,900
Capital City H.	20-Aug	2	PEN	1 1/16M	T	Mixed Up	VanHassel, C	40,900
Capitol City Futurity	27-Jun	8	LNN	4 1/2F	D	Slotsfan	Carkeek, J	11,000
Capote Belle S.	21-Apr	8	AQU	6F	D	Kitty Knight	Arroyo, Jr., N	60,550
Capt. Billy Boogie S.	9-May	8	TUP	1M	D	Real Creek	Hernandez, ML	21,700
Captain Condo S.	19-Sep	6	EMD	6F	D	Seattles Best Joe	Krigger, K	40,000
Captain Stanley Harrison H.	2-Jul	6	MD	6F	D	Danzig Ballerina	Rocheleau, SR	5,000
Cardinal H.	26-Jun	8	AP	1 1/16M	T	Runaway Victor	Contreras, C	84,650
Cardinal H.-G3	20-Nov	9	CD	1 1/8M	T	Aud	Blanc, B	173,550
Caressing H.	20-Nov	7	CD	1 1/16M	T	Sweet Talker	Blanc, B	71,700
Carl G. Rose Classic H.	13-Nov	10	CRC	1 1/8M	D	Supah Blitz	Bailey, JD	200,000
Carleton F. Burke H.-G3	23-Oct	9	SA	1 1/2M	T	Habaneros	Flores, DR	100,000

Stakes	Date	Race	Trk	Dist/Surf		Winner	Jockey	Gross
Carlos Salazar S.	12-Jun	8	ALB	7F	D	Shemoveslikeaghost	Tohill, KS	45,000
Carmel H.	12-Sep	8	BM	1M	T	Penny's Fortune	Valdivia, Jr., J	71,850
Carol Wilson Memorial S.	20-Jun	7	GRP	6 1/2F	D	Soup n' Crackers	Braden, D	3,689
Carotene S.	9-Oct	8	WO	1 1/8M	T	Black Rock Road	Kabel, T	165,600
Carousel S.	27-Mar	10	OP	6F	D	Eternal Cup	Thompson, TJ	50,000
Carry Back S.-G3	10-Jul	9	CRC	6F	D	Weigelia	Toribio, Jr., A	300,000
Carson Hollow S.	22-Feb	8	AQU	6F	D	Fit Performer	Pimentel, J	60,250
Carter H.-G1	10-Apr	9	AQU	7F	D	Pico Central (BRZ)	Solis, AO	350,000
Carter McGregor Jr. Memorial S.	31-May	4	LS	6F	D	Term Sheet	Sellers, SJ	50,000
Carterista H.	8-May	8	CRC	1 1/16M	T	Mr. Livingston	Morales, C	75,000
Casey Darnell H.	4-Jul	8	ALB	7F	D	Rocky Gulch	Bourdieu, JM	43,400
Cassidy S.	23-Oct	3	CRC	6F	D	Running Bobcats	Garcia, JA	75,000
Castlebrook S.	21-May	8	CRC	1 1/16M	D	Special Report	Aguilar, M	40,000
Catcharisingstar S.	6-Sep	9	CRC	5F	D	Ragtime Hope	Penalba, C	50,000
Cat's Cradle H.	14-Nov	8	HOL	7 1/2F	D	Royally Chosen	Flores, DR	88,500
Cavonnier Juvenile S.	8-Aug	11	SR	5 1/2F	D	Thresher	Schvaneveldt, CP	54,595
Cavonnier S.	30-Sep	2	SA	7F	D	Swiss Lad	Baze, T	78,975
Centennial H.	24-Jul	11	ANF	5F	D	D D Dot Comm	Worst, GL	10,800
Central Iowa S.	11-Sep	6	PRM	1 1/16M	D	Casual Attitude	Doocy, TT	43,840
Centre Stage Anne S.	6-Sep	7	FE	1 1/16M	T	Clubay	Poznansky, N	60,000
CERF H.	8-Sep	1	DMR	6F	D	Lady Sabrina	Espinoza, V	98,200
Challedon S.	6-Nov	8	PIM	6F	D	Aggadan	Coa, E	75,000
Chamisa H.	16-May	8	ALB	7F	D	Summer Star	Johnson, RW	45,100
Champagne S.-G1	9-Oct	7	BEL	1 1/16M	D	Proud Accolade	Velazquez, JR	500,000
Chandler S.	19-Nov	9	TUP	7 1/2F	T	Muir Beach	Dieguez, WO	40,000
Chantilly S.	12-Jun	7	ASD	6F	D	Ericka's Lass	Iammarino, MP	40,000
Chapel Belle S.	22-May	9	LAD	1M	T	Topango	Perrodin, EJ	50,000
Chaposa Springs H.-G3	31-Dec	10	CRC	7F	D	Expect an Angel	Lopez, JE	100,000
Chariot Chaser H.	4-Jul	7	NP	6 1/2F	D	Kellys Guest	Winters, PA	40,000
Charles H. Hadry S.	20-Nov	8	PIM	1 1/16M	D	Irish Colony	Hamilton, SD	100,000
Charles H. Russell H.	26-Sep	3	BM	6F	D	Jetinto Houston	Lumpkins, JP	71,500
Charles Taylor Derby	3-Jul	8	ALB	1 1/16M	D	Spirit Gulch	Collier, J	42,550
Charles Town Dash H.	4-Jul	7	CT	4 1/2F	D	Fine Stormy	Cora, D	100,000
Charles Whittingham Memorial H.-G1	12-Jun	3	HOL	1 1/4M	T	Sabiango (GER)	Baze, T	350,000
Charlie Barley S.	27-Jun	6	WO	1M	T	Dalavin	Husbands, P	108,000
Charlie Iles Mile H.	23-May	8	ALB	1M	D	Wolfwithintegrity	Bourdieu, JM	44,200
Charlie Palmer H.	14-Aug	8	FER	6 1/2F	D	In Love With Loot	Navarro, VG	7,435
Charon S.	16-Apr	8	GP	7F	D	Fall Fashion	Castro, E	53,500
Checkered Flag S.	31-May	7	IND	1M	T	Cold Water	Zuniga, E	42,400
Chenery S.	24-Jul	9	CNL	5 1/2F	D	Dubleo	Karamanos, H	50,000
Cherokee River Stables Turf Classic S.	4-Apr	11	TAM	1 1/8M	T	Restage	Castanon, JL	84,900
Cherokee Run H.	14-Nov	7	CD	5F	T	Worldwind Romance	Fogelsonger, R	72,100
Cheval S.	31-Jan	10	DED	5F	D	Joyful Tune	Melancon, G	40,000
Chicago Breeders' Cup H.-G3	19-Jun	8	AP	7F	D	My Trusty Cat	Douglas, RR	175,000
Chicagoland H.	10-Apr	6	HAW	6F	D	Shandy	Silva, CH	111,175
Chick Lang Jr. Memorial S.	21-Aug	8	RET	7 1/2F	T	Honorable Pic	Collier, J	40,000
Chief Bearhart S.	30-Oct	9	WO	1 1/4M	T	Last Answer	Jones, JC	108,000
Chief Narbona S.	12-Jun	3	ALB	6F	D	Latenite Special	Tohill, KS	45,000
China Doll S.	18-Mar	7	SA	1M	T	Ticker Tape (GB)	Desormeaux, KJ	96,800
Chinese Cultural Centre S.-G2	25-Jul	8	WO	1 3/8M	T	Shoal Water	Kabel, T	333,300
Chinook Pass Sprint S.	19-Sep	4	EMD	6F	D	Slewicide Cruise	Gann, SL	40,000
Chipiski S.	23-Jul	9	CRC	6F	D	Punch Appeal	Garcia, JA	40,000
Chippewa Downs Open T'bred Futurity S.	27-Jun	8	CPW	4 1/2F	D	Peacefull Sammy	Harris, BB	2,700
Chippewa Downs Open Thoroughbred S.	27-Jun	9	CPW	1M 70Y	D	Stilaferd	Fennell, H	2,700
Chippewa Downs Thoroughbred Derby	26-Jun	8	CPW	6 1/2F	D	Harbour Axe	La Forge, F	2,300
Choice S.	10-Jul	7	MTH	1 1/16M	T	War Trace	DeCarlo, CP	60,000
Chou Croute H.	21-Feb	9	FG	1 1/16M	D	Spectacular Lisa	Albarado, R	100,000
Chris Christian Futurity	2-Jul	6	BOI	5F	D	Shad	Packer, BR	14,175
Chris Thomas Turf Classic S.	1-May	11	TAM	1 1/8M	T	Restage	Castanon, JL	60,000
Christmas S.	26-Dec	9	MNR	6F	D	High Blitz	Stokes, J	75,000
Chuck Taliaferro Memorial S.	15-Aug	8	RP	6F	D	Explosive Count	Berry, MC	41,700
Churchill Downs Distaff H.-G2	7-Nov	10	CD	1M	D	Halory Leigh	Perret, C	230,400
Churchill Downs H.-G2	1-May	5	CD	7F	D	Speightstown	Velazquez, JR	221,800

Stakes	Date	Race	Trk	Dist/Surf		Winner	Jockey	Gross
Cicada S.-G3	20-Mar	9	AQU	7F	D	Bohemian Lady	Prado, ES	109,100
Cigar Mile H.-G1	27-Nov	9	AQU	1M	D	Lion Tamer	Santos, JA	350,000
Cigar S.	14-Aug	10	AP	1M	D	Silver Zipper	Douglas, RR	53,000
Cincinnati Trophy S.	17-Jan	10	TP	6 1/2F	D	Stoneway	Rowland, MF	50,000
Cincinnatian S.	5-Jul	10	RD	1 1/16M	T	Happy Endings Too	Herrell, JC	40,000
Cinderella S.	6-Jun	3	HOL	5 1/2F	D	Souvenir Gift	Smith, ME	99,300
Cinema Breeders' Cup H.-G3	26-Jun	3	HOL	1 1/8M	T	Greek Sun	Solis, AO	162,450
Citation H.-G1	27-Nov	7	HOL	1 1/16M	T	Leroidesanimaux (BRZ)	Court, JK	400,000
City Centre Bingo H.	10-Sep	7	MD	1M	D	Allourwishes	Emamalie, H	5,000
City of Anderson S.	1-Oct	10	HOO	5 1/2F	D	Free Bonus	Zimmerman, R	40,000
City Of Bridges Sophomore S.	7-Aug	6	MD	1M	D	Steel Copy	Rocheleau, SR	6,500
City of Edmonton Distaff H.	28-Aug	2	NP	1 1/16M	D	Ice Girl	Welch, Q	75,000
City of Las Cruces H.	20-Mar	11	SUN	1M	D	Lord Imajones	Bourdieu, JM	103,800
City of Phoenix H.	2-Oct	9	TUP	6F	D	Muir Beach	Dieguez, WO	40,000
City of Roses H.	26-Dec	5	PM	1M	D	Pete's Dolly	Theriot, BJ	10,000
City of Vancouver S.	24-May	9	HST	6 1/2F	D	Mark of Diablo	Valdez, F	44,472
City Zip S.	18-Sep	9	MTH	6F	D	Knight of Darkness	Coa, E	60,000
City Zip S.	18-Dec	7	AQU	6F	D	Pavo	Garcia, A	50,650
Civic Holiday S.	2-Aug	9	FE	1 1/16M	D	Elegant Hunter	Poznansky, N	60,000
Claiming Crown Emerald S.	17-Jul	8	CBY	1 1/16M	T	Stage Player	Baze, T	125,000
Claiming Crown Express S.	17-Jul	5	CBY	6F	D	Chisholm	Campbell, J	50,000
Claiming Crown Glass Slipper S.	17-Jul	6	CBY	6 1/2F	D	Banished Lover	Clifton, T	75,000
Claiming Crown Iron Horse S.	17-Jul	4	CBY	1 1/16M	D	Superman Can	Stevens, SA	50,000
Claiming Crown Jewel S.	17-Jul	9	CBY	1 1/8M	D	Intelligent Male	Martin, Jr., EM	150,000
Claiming Crown Rapid Transit S.	17-Jul	7	CBY	6 1/2F	D	Heroic Sight	Glasser, T	100,000
Claire Marine S.	5-Sep	7	AP	1 1/2M	T	Delicatessa	Campbell, JM	52,800
Clarendon S.	18-Jul	4	WO	5 1/2F	D	Moonshine Justice	Kabel, T	158,700
Clark County S.	21-Oct	8	KEE	5 1/2F	T	Dyna Da Wyna	Day, P	84,450
Clark H.-G2	26-Nov	11	CD	1 1/8M	D	Saint Liam	Prado, ES	558,000
Classic B Cup S.	16-Oct	10	LBG	1 1/8M	D	Candid Remark	Sterr, S	13,200
Classy 'n Smart S.	1-Dec	7	WO	1 1/16M	D	Brass in Pocket	Kabel, T	129,000
Clement L. Hirsch H.-G2	8-Aug	8	DMR	1 1/16M	D	Miss Loren (ARG)	Court, JK	300,000
Clement L. Hirsch Mem Turf Champ S.-G1	3-Oct	5	SA	1 1/4M	T	Star Over the Bay	Baze, T	250,000
Cleveland Gold Cup S.	4-Jul	14	TDN	1 1/8M	D	Crypto's Prospect	Cloninger, Jr., WT	75,000
Cleveland Kindergarten S.	14-Aug	12	TDN	6F	D	Rubius	Felix, JE	40,000
Cliff Hanger H.-G3	15-Oct	8	MED	1 1/16M	T	Dr. Kashnikow	Migliore, R	200,000
Club House Special S.	22-Aug	8	CLS	6F	D	S C King	Munaylla, F	11,100
Cluff Sprint S.	13-Aug	8	WMF	5F	D	Seattle Cue	Hebert, C	4,625
Clyde B. Stephens Memorial S.	20-Mar	10	DED	5F	D	Kim's Gem	Nichols, JE	50,000
Coaching Club American Oaks-G1	24-Jul	8	BEL	1 1/4M	D	Ashado	Velazquez, JR	500,000
Coca-Cola Independence Day H.	4-Jul	4	MNR	1M	T	Missme	Lumpkins, JP	75,000
Cocodrie S.	17-Dec	8	DED	6 1/2F	D	Valid Faith	Smith, G	40,000
Colin S.	31-Jul	7	WO	6F	D	Wholelottabourbon	Villeneuve, F	134,000
Colleen S.	7-Aug	9	MTH	5 1/2F	D	Im a Dixie Girl	Elliott, S	60,000
College of New Jersey S.	13-Nov	6	MED	1M 70Y	D	Paisley Park	DeCarlo, CP	60,000
Colonel E. R. Bradley H.	3-Jan	9	FG	1 1/16M	T	Skate Away	Melancon, G	60,000
Colonel Power H.	11-Jan	9	FG	6F	D	Aloha Bold	Meche, L	60,000
Colorado Derby	15-Aug	8	ARP	1 1/16M	D	Skip and Go	Rojas, FS	26,650
Colts Neck H.	29-Aug	10	MTH	6F	D	Quiet Desperation	Coa, E	100,000
Columbia River S.	27-Nov	8	PM	6F	D	Typhoon Aaron	Theriot, BJ	10,000
Columbine H.	22-Aug	8	ARP	1 1/16M	D	Sideways	Rojas, FS	27,075
Columbus Breeders' Special H.	29-Aug	8	CLS	6 1/2F	D	Sheso	Nguyen, SD	13,200
Columbus Debutante S.	12-Sep	7	CLS	6F	D	Carissa's Shine	Collins, DM	13,000
Columbus Futurity	12-Sep	6	CLS	6F	D	Cork the Barber	Collins, DM	13,100
Come Summer S.	26-Jun	7	CBY	1M	T	Vazandar	Martinez, SB	50,000
Comely S.-G3	9-Apr	8	AQU	1M	D	Society Selection	Chavez, JF	112,000
Comet S.	15-Oct	7	MED	6F	D	Favalora	Vega, H	60,000
Commonwealth Breeders' Cup S.-G2	10-Apr	5	KEE	7F	D	Lion Tamer	Smith, ME	270,250
Commonwealth Turf S.	14-Nov	9	CD	1 1/16M	T	Broadway View	McKee, J	171,150
Con Jackson Claiming H.	26-Sep	9	ALB	1 13/16M	D	Megan's Man	Tohill, KS	15,000
Conifer - General - Buffett Turf S.	30-Oct	10	LS	1 1/8M	T	Royal Regalia	Castellano, J	100,000
Connaught Cup S.-G3	30-May	8	WO	1 1/16M	T	Slew Valley	McAleney, J	164,400
Connie's Magic S.	13-Dec	10	CRC	6 1/2F	D	Alix M	Velasquez, CH	40,000

Stakes	Date	Race	Trk	Dist/Surf		Winner	Jockey	Gross
Conniver S.	7-Mar	8	LRL	7F	D	Bronze Abe	Rodriguez, ED	75,000
Conroe S.	11-Dec	9	HOU	6F	D	Two Down Automatic	Chapa, R	40,000
Continental Mile S.	5-Sep	8	MTH	1M	T	Dubleo	DeCarlo, CP	55,000
Cool Air S.	23-May	5	CRC	5F	T	Whenthedoveflies	Cosme, E	40,000
Coolbythepool S.	11-Jun	3	CRC	1M	D	Dakota Light	Toribio, A	40,000
Coolmore Lexington S.-G2	17-Apr	9	KEE	1 1/16M	D	Quintons Gold Rush	Bailey, JD	325,000
Coors Starter Allowance S.	8-May	10	FON	1 1/8M	D	J. R. Honor	Compton, P	11,500
Copper Top Futurity	11-Apr	13	SUN	4 1/2F	D	Oso Tricky	Johnson, RW	186,384
Cordially S.	27-Sep	8	DEL	1M	D	Thermal Ablasion	Castellano, Jr., A	53,000
Cornucopia H.	9-Oct	9	LAD	1 1/16M	D	Due to Win	Torres, FC	40,000
Coronation Futurity	13-Nov	8	WO	1 1/8M	D	Ablo	Olguin, G	250,000
Correction H.	31-Jan	9	AQU	6F	D	She's Zealous	Luzzi, MJ	82,875
Corte Madera S.	19-Dec	8	GG	1M	D	Cee's Irish	Baze, RA	65,650
Cotillion H.-G2	2-Oct	9	PHA	1 1/16M	D	Ashado	Coa, E	250,000
Count Fleet S.	3-Jan	8	AQU	1M 70Y	D	Smarty Jones	Elliott, S	81,225
Count Fleet Sprint H.-G3	8-Apr	10	OP	6F	D	Shake You Down	Dominguez, RA	150,000
Count Lathum S.	7-Aug	8	NP	1 5/16M	D	Kat Kool	Welch, Q	40,000
Courtship S.	10-Oct	3	BM	6F	D	Tense Wager	Warren, Jr., RJ	71,500
Cover Gal S.	29-Sep	3	SA	7F	D	Short Route	DeAlba, C	81,825
Cover Girl H.	5-Sep	8	HST	6 1/2F	D	Stormented	Espitia, J	44,160
Cowdin S.	17-Oct	7	BEL	6 1/2F	D	Flamenco	Bailey, JD	80,600
Coyote H.	21-Feb	7	TUP	6F	D	Taiaslew	Corbett, GW	40,000
Crank It Up S.	6-Jun	9	MTH	5F	D	Forest Music	Elliott, S	55,000
Creme de la Creme S.	12-Nov	7	DED	5F	D	Indigo Girl	Smith, G	50,000
Crescent City Derby	17-Jan	8	FG	1 1/16M	D	Arcus	Laviolette, S	75,000
Criterium S.	3-Jul	9	CRC	5 1/2F	D	Devils Disciple	Homeister, Jr., RB	100,000
Crooked River Roundup S.	9-Jul	9	PRV	5 1/2F	D	Soup n' Crackers	Braden, D	3,975
Crown Royal American Turf S.-G3	30-Apr	9	CD	1 1/16M	T	Kitten's Joy	Bailey, JD	113,800
Crystal Gail S.	12-Jan	7	TUP	5 1/2F	D	Channing Way	Corbett, GW	21,700
Crystal Water H.	13-Mar	3	SA	1M	T	Lennyfromalibu	Solis, AO	109,000
CTBA Breeders Oaks	7-Aug	7	ARP	1M 70Y	D	Vannacide	Wales, T	27,550
CTBA Derby	4-Sep	9	ARP	1 1/16M	D	Da Boxer	Wales, T	29,025
CTBA Futurity	8-Aug	9	ARP	6F	D	Cajun Pepper	Wales, T	33,325
CTBA Lassie S.	6-Sep	9	ARP	6F	D	Java Jolene	Rojas, FS	30,600
CTBA Marian S.	20-Sep	9	FPX	1 1/16M	D	Drought Breaker	Pedroza, MA	60,000
CTHS Evergreen Park S.	23-Jul	9	GPR	6F	D	Hy Nick	McAleney, P	5,837
CTHS Sales S.	6-Sep	6	ASD	6F	D	Danger Pay	Butler, BS	40,000
CTHS Sales S.	6-Sep	8	ASD	6F	D	Your Excellence	Guerra, VJ	40,000
CTHS Sales S.	11-Sep	7	HST	6 1/2F	D	Run On	Stephen, A	66,396
CTHS Sales S.	11-Sep	9	HST	6 1/2F	D	Backseat Becka	Wilson, D	66,396
Cub Klahr H.	16-Jun	7	BOI	7F	D	Find My Halter	Packer, BR	4,800
Cup and Saucer S.	17-Oct	8	WO	1 1/16M	T	Slew's Saga	Bahen, SR	250,000
Curribot H.	7-Feb	11	SUN	1 1/16M	D	Face the Band	Noguez, T	54,850
Cut the Charm S.	7-May	7	CRC	1 1/16M	D	Secret Request	Garcia, JA	40,000
Cyclones H.	19-Jun	8	PRM	1 1/16M	D	Rubianos Image	Ranilla, L	70,000
Cy-Fair S.	18-Dec	8	HOU	6F	D	Injustice	Quinonez, LS	40,000
Cypress S.	2-Jan	9	DED	6 1/2F	D	Prince Slew	Melancon, G	50,000
Czaria H.	8-Feb	11	SUN	6F	D	Big Score	Enriquez, ID	53,500
D. R. Horton Metroplex Mile S.	30-Oct	1	LS	1M	D	Wishingitwas	Beasley, J	100,000
D. S. Shine Young Memorial Futurity	3-Jul	10	EVD	5F	D	Smilin Fine	Melancon, G	100,000
Da Hoss S.	10-Apr	7	TUP	7 1/2F	T	Zal's Pal	Bridges, K	22,000
Da Hoss S.	26-Jun	9	CNL	1M	D	Mt. Carson	Rocco, Jr., J	50,000
Dade Turf Classic S.	4-Sep	10	ELP	1 1/16M	T	May Gator	Castanon, JL	75,000
Dahlia H.-G3	20-Dec	7	HOL	1 1/16M	D	Festival (JPN)	Sorenson, D	150,000
Daily Courier Inaugural S.	15-May	7	GRP	5 1/2F	D	City Parkway	D'Amico, DL	4,026
Daisycutter H.	30-Jul	7	DMR	5F	T	Icantgoforthat	Steiner, JJ	98,625
Dallas Turf Cup H.	19-Jun	9	LS	1 1/8M	T	Maysville Slew	Berry, MC	200,000
Damon Runyon S.	12-Dec	8	AQU	1 1/16M	D	Naughty New Yorker	Samyn, J	85,725
Dance Smartly H.-G3	17-Jul	4	WO	1 1/8M	T	Mona Rose	Da Silva, ER	212,450
Dancing Count S.	1-Jan	8	LRL	6F	D	Kiowa Prince	Castellano, Jr., A	60,000
Daniel Van Clief S.	17-Jul	9	CNL	1 1/16M	T	Bay Eagle	Jurado, EM	50,000
Danville H.	20-Mar	7	GG	6F	D	More Crafty	Mercado, P	72,100
Danzig S.	14-May	5	PEN	6F	D	Salty Punch	Madrigal, Jr., R	41,400

Stakes	Date	Race	Trk	Dist/Surf		Winner	Jockey	Gross
Darley Alcibiades S.-G2	8-Oct	9	KEE	1 1/16M	D	Runway Model	Bejarano, R	400,000
Darrell Ost Memorial S.	12-Aug	10	WMF	6 1/2F	D	A Step Beyond	Kingrey, RD	5,100
Daryl Wells Sr. Memorial S.	4-Jul	6	FE	6F	D	Roman Romance	Barton, J	100,000
Dating Game S.	30-Oct	4	LBG	7F	D	Temptor Cielo	Miyashiro, CJ	12,200
Dave Feldman S.	18-Jan	10	GP	1 1/16M	D	Tap Day	Boulanger, G	66,300
Davona Dale S.-G2	7-Feb	8	GP	1 1/16M	D	Miss Coronado	Velasquez, CH	150,000
Dayton Andrews Dodge Sophomore Turf S.	4-Apr	7	TAM	1 1/16M	T	Keystone Point	Rocco, Jr., J	85,300
Daytona H.	15-Feb	7	SA	6 1/2F	T	Tsigane (FR)	Flores, DR	92,000
De La Rose S.	11-Aug	6	SAR	1M	T	Personal Legend	Bailey, JD	66,800
De La Rose S.	11-Aug	8	SAR	1M	T	Fast Cookie	Velasquez, CH	67,000
Dear Murray S.	25-Jul	6	CRC	6F	D	Devils Disciple	Homeister, Jr., RB	40,000
Dearly Precious S.	14-Feb	9	AQU	6F	D	Among My Souvenirs	Pino, MG	81,425
Dearly Precious S.	27-Jun	9	MTH	6F	D	Cherish Destiny	Bravo, J	60,000
Deauville S.	22-Dec	6	CRC	7 1/2F	T	Formal Miss	Chavez, JF	40,000
Debutante S.-G3	4-Jul	11	CD	5 1/2F	D	Classic Elegance	Day, P	110,800
Debutante S.	18-Jul	8	ASD	5 1/2F	D	Gold Strike	Hightower, TW	40,000
Decathlon S.	14-Aug	8	MTH	6F	D	Sing Me Back Home	Bravo, J	60,000
Decoration Day H.	31-May	3	MNR	1M	D	Salzurita (ARG)	Walker, Jr., BJ	75,000
Del Mar Breeders' Cup H.-G2	5-Sep	8	DMR	1M	D	Supah Blitz	Espinoza, V	250,000
Del Mar Debutante S.-G1	28-Aug	8	DMR	7F	D	Sweet Catomine	Espinoza, V	250,000
Del Mar Derby-G2	6-Sep	8	DMR	1 1/8M	T	Blackdoun (FR)	Nakatani, CS	400,000
Del Mar Futurity-G2	8-Sep	8	DMR	7F	D	Declan's Moon	Espinoza, V	250,000
Del Mar H.-G2	29-Aug	8	DMR	1 3/8M	T	Star Over the Bay	Baze, T	250,000
Del Mar Oaks-G1	21 Aug	3	DMR	1 1/8M	T	Amorama (FR)	Flores, DR	300,000
Delaware H.-G2	18-Jul	10	DEL	1 1/4M	D	Summer Wind Dancer	Espinoza, V	750,900
Delaware Oaks-G2	17-Jul	8	DEL	1 1/16M	D	Yearly Report	Bailey, JD	500,900
Delta Beau S.	26-Nov	9	DED	5F	D	Blazing Exploit	Smith, G	40,000
Delta Belle S.	20-Nov	9	DED	5F	D	Coronado Rose	Hernandez, BJ	40,000
Delta Colleen H.	26-Sep	6	HST	1 1/16M	D	La Belle Fleur	Hamel, RH	44,056
Delta Mile S.	21-Feb	10	DED	1M	D	Kodema	Bourque, SJ	50,000
Demoiselle S.-G2	27-Nov	7	AQU	1 1/8M	D	Sis City	Velazquez, JR	200,000
Dempsey Gibbons Thoroughbred H.	24-Jul	9	MAF	7F	D	Lost Again	Wippert, S	2,725
Denise Rhudy Memorial S.	10-Jul	8	DEL	1 1/8M	T	Cuyahoga	Castillo, Jr., H	76,500
Deputed Testamony S.	5-Jun	8	PIM	1 1/16M	D	Jane's Luck	Santana, JZ	75,000
Deputy Minister H.-G3	7-Feb	11	GP	6 1/2F	D	Alke	Velazquez, JR	100,000
Deputy Minister S.	20-Oct	7	WO	7F	D	Millfleet	Scharfstein, J	132,500
Derby Trial S.	13-Sep	9	FPX	1 1/16M	D	Lava Man	Figueroa, O	60,000
Derby Trial S.-G3	24-Apr	9	CD	1M	D	Sir Shackleton	Bejarano, R	110,800
Derby Trial S.	11-Jul	8	ASD	1 1/16M	D	Shanghied	Hightower, TW	40,000
Desert Rose H.	15-Aug	9	RUI	6F	D	Yet Anothernatalie	Bourdieu, JM	30,000
Desert Sky H.	1-May	3	TUP	1M	T	Magnificent Val	Stevens, SA	40,000
Desert Stormer H.-G3	5-Jun	1	HOL	6F	D	Coconut Girl	Espinoza, V	106,000
Dessie and Fern Sawyer Futurity	26-Sep	5	ALB	6F	D	Hush's Gold	Juarez, Jr., AJ	62,810
Devil's Honor H.	4-Sep	6	PHA	7F	D	Hero's Glow	Black, AS	50,000
Diamondback S.	27-Jun	6	YAV	6F	D	Red Spark	Vergara, DP	10,200
Diana H.-G1	31-Jul	7	SAR	1 1/8M	T	Wonder Again	Prado, ES	500,000
Diane Kem H.	23-Oct	8	PM	6F	D	Quiz the Maid	Zunino, JL	10,000
Diane Kem S.	19-Sep	8	EMD	6F	D	M K Beck	Chaves, NJ	40,000
Dine S.	2-Nov	5	SRP	6 1/2F	D	Macho Miller	Gonsalves, FA	69,000
Discovery H.-G3	27-Oct	8	AQU	1 1/8M	D	Zakocity	Castellano, J	110,100
Display S.	27-Nov	8	WO	1 1/16M	D	One Smooth Ride	Montpellier, C	137,500
Distaff Breeders' Cup H.-G2	27-Mar	8	AQU	7F	D	Randaroo	Migliore, R	155,400
Distaff H.	1-May	9	BRD	7 1/2F	D	Blonde Okie	Wilson, JL	9,475
Distaff S.	6-Sep	3	ASD	1M	D	Tamorons Blade	Guerra, VJ	40,000
Distorted Humor H.	27-Nov	10	CD	6 1/2F	D	Strength and Honor	Castro, E	72,000
Dixie Belle S.	23-Jan	8	OP	6F	D	Saltwater Runner	McKee, J	50,000
Dixie Miss S.	12-Jun	10	LAD	6F	D	Boston Express	Jacinto, J	50,000
Dixie Poker Ace H.	29-Feb	6	FG	7 1/2F	T	Bebe Garcon	Smith, VL	75,000
Dogwood Breeders' Cup S.-G3	5-Jun	10	CD	1 1/16M	D	Stellar Jayne	Albarado, R	161,400
Dominion Day H.-G3	1-Jul	8	WO	1 1/4M	D	Mobil	Kabel, T	217,200
Don Bernhardt S.	24-Jul	4	ELP	6 1/2F	D	Fire Slam	Day, P	100,000
Don Juan De Onate S.	12-Jun	10	ALB	6F	D	Rocky Gulch	Bourdieu, JM	45,000
Donald LeVine Memorial H.-G3	29-May	9	PHA	6F	D	Peeping Tom	Smith, A	100,000

Stakes	Date	Race	Trk	Dist/Surf		Winner	Jockey	Gross
Donn H.-G1	7-Feb	10	GP	1 1/8M	D	Medaglia d'Oro	Bailey, JD	500,000
Donna Jensen S.	10-Apr	7	PM	1 1/16M	D	Lasting Kiss	D'Amico, DL	10,000
Donna Reed S.	28-Aug	5	PRM	1M 70Y	D	Switch Lanes	Corbett, GW	78,600
Donnie Wilhite Memorial H.	25-Sep	8	LAD	1 1/16M	T	Social King	Perrodin, EJ	50,000
Double Delta S.	20-Jun	8	AP	1M	T	Sahmkindawonderful	Lovato, Jr., F	42,500
Double Your Flavor S.	27-Mar	8	HOU	7F	D	Lady Sonya	Ramos, AB	40,000
Doubledogdare S.	16-Apr	9	KEE	1 1/16M	D	Mayo On the Side	Day, P	114,300
Dover S.	9-Oct	7	DEL	1 1/16M	D	Killenaule	DeCarlo, CP	100,000
Dowd Mile H.	10-Apr	9	FON	1M	D	Getaway Holme	Compton, P	33,000
Dowling S.	14-Aug	6	GLD	1M	D	Rockem Sockem	Houghton, TD	40,000
Down the Isle S.	1-Mar	7	TUP	1M	D	Black Bart	Gann, SL	21,900
Downs at Albuquerque H.	5-Jul	8	ALB	1 1/8M	D	Socko	Theriot, BJ	65,900
Dr. A. B. Leggio Memorial H.	18-Jan	9	FG	5 1/2F	D	Put Me In	Martin, Jr., EM	60,000
Dr. Ernest Benner S.	26-Sep	6	CT	6 1/2F	D	Wild Remarks	Torres, R	41,350
Dr. Fager S.	15-Sep	8	AP	7 1/2F	D	Apt to Be	Razo, Jr., E	43,625
Dr. James Penny Memorial H.	3-Jul	9	PHA	1 1/16M	T	Lady of the Future	Vega, H	100,000
Dr. O. G. Fischer Memorial H.	28-Aug	8	SRP	7F	D	Miss Noteworthy	Juarez, Jr., AJ	31,900
Draw In S.	27-Jun	9	CRC	1 1/16M	D	Firm Reality	Garcia, JA	45,000
Dream Supreme H.	26-Nov	4	CD	6 1/2F	D	Savorthetime	Hernandez, Jr., BJ	71,400
Drumtop S.	14-Aug	9	SUF	1 1/16M	D	Lady Beelzebub	Molinari, E	40,000
DTHA Owners' Day H.	11-Sep	7	DEL	1 1/8M	D	Loving (BRZ)	Pino, MG	75,000
Duchess of York S.	12-Jun	8	STP	1 1/16M	D	Raylene	Walcott, R	40,000
Duchess S.-G3	21-Aug	8	WO	7F	D	Blonde Executive	Dos Ramos, RA	210,650
Duncan Hopeful S.	21-Mar	7	DUN	5 1/2F	D	Two Timing Paul	Torres, A	5,696
Durham Cup H.-G3	16-Oct	8	WO	1 1/8M	D	Norfolk Knight	Scharfstein, J	159,450
Dust Commander S.	21-Feb	9	TP	1M	D	Ask the Lord	Bejarano, R	50,000
Dwight D. Patterson H.	24-Apr	9	TUP	1 1/16M	T	Imdabossau	Vergara, DP	40,000
Dwyer S.-G2	11-Jul	8	BEL	1 1/16M	D	Medallist	Chavez, JF	150,000
E. B. Johnston S.	12-Sep	11	FPX	1 1/16M	D	Shezsospiritual	Figueroa, O	60,000
E. K. Rolfson Mile H.	6-Sep	11	FAR	1M	D	Maddies Blues	Schindler, SA	5,335
E. K. Rolfson Sprint H.	21-Aug	6	FAR	5 1/2F	D	Maddies Blues	Schindler, SA	4,850
E. L. Gaylord Memorial S.	26-Nov	9	RP	6 1/2F	D	Honor the Flag	Kimes, C	41,300
E. P. Taylor S.-G1	24-Oct	6	WO	1 1/4M	T	Commercante (FR)	Velazquez, JR	750,000
E. T. Springer S.	11-Sep	8	ALB	7F	D	Ninety Nine Jack	Bourdieu, JM	32,700
Earlene McCabe Derby	29-Aug	8	SAC	6F	D	Jet West	Duran, F	52,095
Early Times Mint Julep H.-G3	29-May	9	CD	1 1/16M	T	Stay Forever	Castro, E	168,300
Early's Farm And Garden Centre H.	26-Jun	5	MD	6F	D	Double Time	Latchman, R	5,000
East View S.	5-Dec	8	AQU	1 1/16M	D	Successfully Sweet	Smith, A	80,750
Eatontown H.-G3	10-Jul	9	MTH	1 1/16M	T	Ocean Drive	Coa, E	100,000
Eclipse H.-G3	24-May	8	WO	1 1/16M	D	Mark One	Landry, RC	163,350
Eddie Read H.-G1	25-Jul	8	DMR	1 1/8M	T	Special Ring	Espinoza, V	400,000
Edgewood S.	30-Apr	5	CD	1 1/16M	T	Galloping Gal	Prado, ES	116,700
Edmonton Juvenile S.	30-Jul	8	NP	6F	D	Poor Iggy	Walcott, R	40,000
Edward Babst Memorial H.	10-Apr	9	BEU	6F	D	Devil Time	Troilo, WD	40,000
Edward J. Debartolo Sr. Memorial BC H.	6-Sep	8	RP	1 1/8M	T	Major Rhythm	Fires, E	126,700
Eight Thirty S.	31-May	7	DEL	1 1/8M	D	Private Lap	Arroyo, Jr., N	53,300
El Cajon S.	3-Sep	6	DMR	1M	D	Perfect Moon	Nakatani, CS	102,050
El Camino Real Derby-G3	13-Mar	7	GG	1 1/16M	D	Kilgowan	Rollins, CJ	200,000
El Cielo H.	21-Mar	3	SA	6 1/2F	T	Cayoke (FR)	Baze, T	94,000
El Conejo H.-G3	1-Jan	8	SA	5 1/2F	D	Boston Common	Stevens, GL	107,600
El Encino S.-G2	18-Jan	7	SA	1 1/16M	D	Victory Encounter	Smith, ME	150,000
El Paso Times H.	14-Feb	11	SUN	6 1/2F	D	Speedy Falcon	Jaime, R	54,100
Electric City Sprint S.	30-Jul	9	GF	5F	D	Rogan Slew	Ortiz, Jr., I	3,000
Eleven North H.	29-Aug	7	MTH	6F	D	Totally Precious	Bravo, J	100,000
Elge Rasberry S.	7-Aug	10	LAD	7F	D	Happy Ticket	Meche, L	70,000
Elgin S.	5-Sep	7	WO	1 1/16M	D	Just in Case Jimmy	Dos Ramos, RA	134,125
Elie Destruel H.	9-Aug	9	SR	6F	D	Our Mango	Alvarado, FT	54,295
Elkhorn S.-G3	23-Apr	9	KEE	1 1/2M	T	Epicentre	Bailey, JD	150,000
Elko County Thoroughbred Futurity	6-Sep	7	ELK	5 1/2F	D	Handsomchamp	Condie, NR	19,691
Elko Thoroughbred Derby	5-Sep	10	ELK	7F	D	Fanteria	Greene, C	13,650
Elkwood S.	17-Jul	5	MTH	1 1/16M	T	Gulch Approval	Lopez, CC	60,000
Elkwood S.	17-Jul	8	MTH	1 1/16M	T	Spruce Run	Bravo, J	60,000
Ellis Park Breeders' Cup S.	14-Aug	9	ELP	6 1/2F	D	Molto Vita	Melancon, L	103,700

Stakes	Date	Race	Trk	Dist/Surf		Winner	Jockey	Gross
Elmer Heubeck Distaff H.	13-Nov	7	CRC	1 1/16M	D	Hopelessly Devoted	Velasquez, CH	200,000
Elusive Quality S.	6-Oct	8	BEL	1M	T	L'Oiseau d'Argent	Migliore, R	61,100
Emerald Breeders' Cup Distaff H.	22-Aug	9	EMD	1M	D	Aunt Sophie	Gonzalez, RM	100,000
Emerald Downs Breeders' Cup Derby	6-Sep	9	EMD	1 1/8M	D	My Creed	Perez, MA	100,000
Emerald Downs H.	13-Jun	6	HST	6 1/2F	D	Regal Red	Fuentes, FP	44,680
Emerald Express S.	17-Jul	9	EMD	6F	D	Seattles Best Joe	Krigger, K	48,000
Emerald Necklace S.	18-Sep	8	TDN	6F	D	Noon Win	Villa-Gomez, H	40,000
Emergency Nurse S.	19-Sep	10	CRC	1 1/16M	D	Maria's Image	Toribio, Jr., A	40,000
Empire Classic H.	23-Oct	10	BEL	1 1/8M	D	Spite the Devil	Castellano, J	250,000
Endeavour S.	10-Feb	8	TAM	1 1/16M	T	Madeira Mist (IRE)	Prado, ES	100,000
Endine H.-G3	11-Sep	8	DEL	6F	D	Ebony Breeze	Castillo, Jr., H	200,300
Ernest Finley H.	31-Jul	11	SR	6F	D	Halo Cat	Baze, RA	54,030
Ernie Samuel Memorial S.	18-Jul	7	FE	1 1/16M	D	Ginger Gold	Bahen, SR	100,000
Escondido H.	4-Aug	7	DMR	1 3/8M	T	Sarafan	Nakatani, CS	101,500
Essex H.-G3	21-Feb	9	OP	1 1/16M	D	Private Emblem	Doocy, TT	100,000
Estrapade H.	12-Jun	9	AP	1 1/8M	D	Chance Dance	Marquez, Jr., CH	75,000
Eternal Search S.	1-Sep	7	WO	1 1/16M	D	My Vintage Port	Jones, JC	131,125
Eureka Downs Thoroughbred Futurity	20-Jun	6	EUR	4F	D	Slews in Oz Now	Wellington, T	3,952
Evan Shipman H.	25-Jul	8	BEL	1 1/16M	D	Spite the Devil	Prado, ES	108,100
Evangeline Mile H.	14-Aug	8	EVD	1M	D	Pie N Burger	Theriot, J	100,000
Evanston Mayor's Derby	10-Jul	10	WYO	6F	D	Splendid High	House, C	3,800
Evanston Speed H.	10-Jul	6	WYO	4 1/2F	D	Popescu (BRZ)	Marshall, M	3,600
Everett Nevin Alameda County Futurity	4-Jul	11	PLN	5F	D	Wind Water	Alvarado, FT	53,465
Excalibur S.	26-Jun	9	LAD	1M 70Y	D	Britt's Jules	Smith, G	50,000
Excelsior Breeders' Cup H.-G3	3-Apr	8	AQU	1 1/8M	D	Funny Cide	Santos, JA	200,000
Excess Energy S.	26-Nov	9	TUP	5 1/2F	D	Friendofthefamily	Stevens, SA	22,000
Exogenous S.	11-Dec	7	AQU	1M 70Y	D	Our Rite of Spring	Arroyo, Jr., N	60,750
Expedite Plus S.	6-Jun	8	FE	5F	D	Lucky Tec	Ramirez, MR	60,000
Express H.	15-May	9	ALB	5 1/2F	D	Bang	Noguez, T	44,650
Fain Road S.	7-Sep	8	YAV	4 1/2F	D	Red Spark	Vergara, DP	9,900
Fair Grounds Breeders' Cup H.	31-Jan	9	FG	1 1/8M	T	Mystery Giver	Albarado, R	125,000
Fair Grounds Oaks-G2	6-Mar	9	FG	1 1/16M	D	Ashado	Velasquez, CH	300,000
Fair Grounds Sales S.	8-Feb	1	FG	1M	D	Outright Buck	Albarado, R	69,000
Fair Lady S.	2-May	8	HST	6 1/2F	D	Regal Red	Fuentes, FP	44,368
Fair Manager's H.	13-Aug	9	WMF	6 1/2F	D	Northern Master	Wippert, S	4,500
Fair Queen H.	17-Sep	8	ALB	6 1/2F	D	Forward Glance	Tohill, KS	33,200
Fairfield S.	24-Jul	11	SOL	6F	D	Yerevan Star	Castro, JM	54,665
Fairway Fun S.	27-Mar	10	TP	1 1/16M	D	Angela's Love	Guidry, M	50,000
Fall Classic Distaff H.	25-Sep	6	NP	1 1/16M	D	A Shaky Start	Painter, LM	75,000
Fall Highweight H.-G3	28-Nov	9	AQU	6F	D	Thunder Touch	Bejarano, R	111,600
Fall Open S.	6-Sep	7	LBG	7F	D	Lafleur	Mellish, B	11,200
Fall Open S.	6-Sep	7	LBG	7F	D	Royal Group	Huston, HC	11,200
Fall S.	21-Sep	9	MNR	1 1/8M	D	Tour the Hive	Feliciano, R	75,000
Fall S.	11-Sep	8	LBG	6F	D	Real Sterling	Smith, J	11,200
Fall Sprint S.	5-Sep	8	LBG	5 1/2F	D	Highland Road	Smith, J	11,200
Falls Amiss H.	16-Jul	4	HPO	1M	D	Run Around Sue	Martinez, A	29,200
Falls City H.-G2	25-Nov	10	CD	1 1/8M	D	Halory Leigh	Martin, Jr., EM	325,200
Fantango Lady S.	15-Jul	4	HPO	1M	D	Jitterbug Joy	Beck, DL	30,400
Fantasia S.	23-May	8	LAD	6F	D	Shes Dixies Eskimo	Avant, JE	50,000
Fantasy S.-G2	9-Apr	10	OP	1 1/16M	D	House of Fortune	Solis, AO	200,000
Fantasy S.	23-Oct	8	HST	1 1/16M	D	Country Kat	Stephen, A	64,500
Fappie's Notebook S.	13-Jun	9	CRC	6 1/2F	D	Gold Dollar	Toribio, Jr., A	45,000
Farer Belle Lee H.	3-Sep	7	GLD	1 1/16M	D	Dancin for Gold	Doser, ME	50,000
Fashion S.	3-Jun	8	BEL	5F	D	Chocolate Brown	Castellano, J	80,625
Fasig-Tipton Turf Dash S.	6-Sep	12	CRC	5F	D	Monti's Lad	Klinger, CO	50,000
Fayette S.-G3	30-Oct	5	KEE	1 1/8M	D	Midway Road	Borel, CH	161,250
Federal Way H.	16-May	8	EMD	6 1/2F	D	Sariano	Frazier, R	40,000
Federico Tesio S.	17-Apr	9	PIM	1 1/8M	D	Water Cannon	Fogelsonger, R	100,000
Fern Sawyer H.	4-Jul	11	RUI	1M	D	Rubin's Girl	Smallwood, VY	25,000
Fieldy S.	2-Jul	8	BEL	1M	T	Fortunate Damsel	Castellano, J	62,300
Fiesta Mile S.	18-Sep	6	RET	1M	T	Lady Mallory	Boxie, P	40,000
Fifth Season S.-G3	7-Apr	9	OP	1 1/16M	D	Spanish Empire	Martin, Jr., EM	100,000
Fillies and Mares H.	15-Aug	7	BOI	7 1/2F	D	Never Been Caught	Packer, BR	6,350

Stakes	Date	Race	Trk	Dist/Surf		Winner	Jockey	Gross
Fillies and Mares H.	14-Aug	6	BOI	5F	D	Dance for Fun	Cruz, AS	6,200
Filly and Mare S.	12-Jun	7	LBG	6F	D	Choice Slew	McAleney, P	11,050
Filly Sale S.	21-Aug	8	NP	6 1/2F	D	R Lucinda	Welch, Q	60,000
Find H.	21-Aug	9	PIM	1 1/8M	D	Foufa's Warrior	Hamilton, SD	75,000
Finger Lakes Juvenile Fillies S.	2-Oct	8	FL	6F	D	Roving Angel	Grabowski, JA	50,000
Finger Lakes Juvenile S.	23-Oct	8	FL	6F	D	Boston Raider	Rodriguez, PA	50,000
Fire Plug S.	10-Apr	8	PIM	6F	D	Sassy Hound	Castellano, Jr., A	50,000
Firecracker Breeders' Cup H.-G2	3-Jul	8	CD	1M	T	Quantum Merit	Sellers, SJ	287,750
Firecracker H.	4-Jul	3	MNR	1M	T	Passionate Bird	Mawing, L	75,000
First Episode S.	7-Aug	3	SUF	1 1/16M	D	African Princess	Hampshire, Jr., JF	40,000
First Flight H.-G2	30-Oct	4	AQU	7F	D	Bending Strings	Bridgmohan, S	150,000
First Lady H.	19-Jun	9	RUI	6F	D	Yet Anothernatalie	Bourdieu, JM	30,000
First Lady H.-G3	11-Jan	10	GP	6F	D	Harmony Lodge	Migliore, R	100,000
First Lady S.	29-May	2	IND	7 1/2F	T	Speedy Tiffany	Prescott, RA	40,000
First Snowbound S.	23-Aug	5	YAV	5 1/2F	D	Dance for Gold	Gomez, EA	9,800
Fit for a Queen S.	15-May	8	AP	6F	D	Smoke Chaser	Perez, EE	41,875
Flaming Page S.	25-Sep	8	WO	1 1/2M	T	My Pal Lana	Clark, D	109,000
Flash S.-G3	4-Jun	9	BEL	5F	D	Primal Storm	Sellers, SJ	106,300
Flashaway Overnight H.	10-Apr	8	PM	5F	D	Star of Elttaes	Gutierrez, JM	6,500
Flawlessly S.	12-Sep	8	AP	1M	T	Mymich	Razo, Jr., E	44,375
Flawlessly S.	3-Jul	8	HOL	1M	T	Miss Vegas (IRE)	Solis, AO	109,700
Fleet Treat S.	24-Jul	8	DMR	7F	D	Western Hemisphere	Nakatani, CS	100,000
Fleur de Lis H.-G2	12-Jun	8	CD	1 1/8M	D	Adoration	Espinoza, V	439,200
Fleur de Lis S.	30-May	11	LAD	1M 70Y	D	Due to Win	Quinonez, LS	50,000
Fling Ding S.	28-Dec	9	TUP	1M	D	Society Cat	Rivera, JG	21,900
Floor Show S.	22-Jun	8	DEL	1 1/16M	D	Pies Prospect	Arroyo, Jr., N	55,300
Floral Park H.-G3	18-Sep	7	BEL	6F	D	Feline Story	Prado, ES	106,400
Florence Henderson S.	19-Jun	2	IND	1 1/16M	T	Ellens Lucky Star	Bejarano, R	40,000
Florida Breeders' Distaff S.	15-Mar	4	OTC	1 1/16M	D	Doc's Doll	Day, P	40,000
Florida Derby-G1	13-Mar	9	GP	1 1/8M	D	Friends Lake	Migliore, R	1,000,000
Florida Oaks	14-Mar	9	TAM	1 1/16M	D	Ender's Sister	Day, P	150,000
Florida Stallion Affirmed S.	6-Sep	11	CRC	7F	D	Cin Cin	Toribio, A	125,000
Florida Stallion Desert Vixen S.	14-Aug	10	CRC	6F	D	Aclassysassylassy	Aguilar, M	75,000
Florida Stallion Dr. Fager S.	14-Aug	11	CRC	6F	D	B. B. Best	Castro, E	75,000
Florida Stallion In Reality S.	23-Oct	12	CRC	1 1/16M	D	B. B. Best	Castro, E	400,000
Florida Stallion My Dear Girl S.	23-Oct	11	CRC	1 1/16M	D	Aclassysassylassy	Aguilar, M	400,000
Florida Stallion Susan's Girl S.	6-Sep	10	CRC	7F	D	Aclassysassylassy	Aguilar, M	125,000
Florida Thoroughbred Charities S.	15-Mar	3	OTC	5F	D	Vision in Flight	Prado, ES	40,000
Flower Bowl Invitational S.-G1	2-Oct	7	BEL	1 1/4M	T	Riskaverse	Velasquez, CH	750,000
Fly So Free S.	12-Sep	7	BEL	6F	D	Mass Media	Castellano, J	60,550
Flying Concert S.	31-Dec	5	CRC	1 1/8M	D	Vespers	Santos, JA	45,000
Flying Lark S.	31-Jan	9	PM	6F	D	Mythical Road	Barber, S	10,000
Flying Pidgeon H.	9-Oct	7	CRC	1 1/8M	T	Keep Cool	Rivera, II, JA	100,000
Folklore H.	21-Aug	5	LAD	6 1/2F	D	Ole Rebel	Lanerie, CJ	50,000
Fonner Park Special S.	17-Apr	9	FON	6F	D	Thundering Verzy	Martinez, A	30,800
Fonner Park Special S.	18-Apr	9	FON	6F	D	Shesaidsheknowsya	Collins, DM	30,900
Fool the Experts S.	22-Nov	10	TUP	6F	D	Walker	Bridges, K	21,900
Foolish Pleasure S.	2-Oct	10	CRC	1M 70Y	D	Cin Cin	Toribio, A	100,000
Foothill S.	10-Sep	11	FPX	6 1/2F	D	Last Minute Detail	Figueroa, O	60,000
Ford Express S.	8-May	9	LS	6F	D	Beau's Town	Martin, Jr., EM	75,000
Forego H.-G1	4-Sep	8	SAR	7F	D	Midas Eyes	Prado, ES	250,000
Forego H.	31-Jul	8	FP	1M 70Y	D	Moe B Dick	Zimmerman, R	30,600
Forego S.	24-Jan	10	TP	6 1/2F	D	Doc D	Lumpkins, JP	50,000
Forerunner S.	15-Apr	8	KEE	1 1/8M	T	Prince Arch	Blanc, B	111,100
Formal Gold S.	11-Sep	3	MTH	1 1/16M	D	Lion Tamer	Coa, E	65,000
Fort Bend County S.	3-Apr	8	HOU	7F	D	Mr. Devious	Simington, DE	40,000
Fort Marcy H.-G3	24-Apr	8	AQU	1 1/16M	T	Chilly Rooster	Uske, S	111,400
Fort Monmouth S.	30-May	11	MTH	1M	T	High Court (BRZ)	DeCarlo, CP	60,000
Forty One Carats S.	20-Aug	9	CRC	6 1/2F	D	Model Home	Arango, LE	40,000
Forty-Niner H.	26-Nov	8	GG	1 1/16M	D	Yougottawanna	Schvaneveldt, CP	82,650
Forward Pass S.	14-Aug	6	AP	7F	D	Nebraska Moon	Martin, Jr., EM	52,600
Foster City H.	20-Jun	7	BM	1 1/16M	T	Ninebanks	Rollins, CJ	72,400
Fountain of Youth S.-G2	14-Feb	11	GP	1 1/16M	D	Read the Footnotes	Bailey, JD	250,000

Stakes	Date	Race	Trk	Dist/Surf		Winner	Jockey	Gross
Four Seasons H.	7-Nov	7	BRD	1M	D	Royal Chalice	Wilson, JL	9,700
Four Year Olds and Up C & G Sales H.	16-Oct	8	NP	1M	D	Parlay's Prospect	Winters, PA	50,000
Four Year Olds and Up F & MSales H.	15-Oct	7	NP	1M	D	A Shaky Start	Painter, LM	50,000
Fourstardave H.-G2	28-Aug	9	SAR	1 1/16M	T	Nothing to Lose	Velazquez, JR	200,000
Fox Sports Network H.	23-May	8	EMD	6 1/2F	D	Willie the Cat	Frazier, R	40,000
Foxy J. G. S.	17-Jul	9	PHA	7F	D	Defrere's Venture	Diaz, V	53,500
Frances A. Genter S.	27-Nov	8	CRC	7 1/2F	T	R Obsession	Cruz, MR	100,000
Frances Genter S.	10-Jul	7	CBY	6F	D	Shakopee	Escobar, M	41,250
Frances Slocum S.	13-Nov	2	HOO	1 1/16M	D	Senorita Ziggy	Flores, V	40,000
Francis Jock LaBelle Memorial S.	1-May	8	DEL	6F	D	Frisky Spider	King, Jr., EL	75,300
Franfreluche S.	7-Nov	8	WO	6F	D	Simply Lovely	Bahen, SR	165,900
Frank A. Buddy Abadie Memorial S.	5-Jun	9	EVD	1M	D	Placid Star	Melancon, G	40,000
Frank Arnason Sire S.	31-Jul	6	ASD	6F	D	Your Excellence	Guerra, VJ	40,000
Frank E. Kilroe Mile H.-G2	6-Mar	9	SA	1M	T	Sweet Return (GB)	Stevens, GL	350,000
Frank Gall Memorial H.	28-Aug	7	CT	7F	D	Earth Power	Reynolds, LC	76,550
Frank J. De Francis Memorial Dash S.-G1	20-Nov	10	PIM	6F	D	Wildcat Heir	Elliott, S	300,000
Franks Farm Turf S.	24-Jan	10	GP	1 1/8M	T	Proud Man	Douglas, RR	500,000
Fran's Valentine S.	21-Apr	1	HOL	1 1/16M	T	Moscow Burning	Desormeaux, KJ	150,000
Fred Cappy Capossela S.	19-Jan	8	AQU	6F	D	Quick Action	Castillo, Jr., H	81,225
Fred Drysdale Memorial S.	21-Aug	6	GPR	6 1/2F	D	Guiltybysupiscion	Sterr, S	5,500
Fred Mendel Memorial H.	23-Jul	6	MD	1M	D	Beau Ring	Rocheleau, SR	5,000
Fred W. Hooper H.-G3	18-Dec	12	CRC	1 1/8M	D	Pies Prospect	Prado, ES	100,000
Free Press S.	20-Jun	8	ASD	6F	D	Iwoodificould	Guerra, VJ	40,000
Free Spirit H.	27-Jun	9	RUI	6F	D	This Chris	Tohill, KS	30,000
Freedom of the City S.	9-Oct	8	NP	1M	D	Kathern's Cat	Welch, Q	40,000
Friendly Lover H.	19-Sep	9	MTH	6F	D	Upturn	Coa, E	60,000
Frisk Me Now S.	30-May	5	MTH	1M	D	Pretty Wild	Gryder, AT	70,000
Frizette S.-G1	9-Oct	6	BEL	1 1/16M	D	Balletto (UAE)	Nakatani, CS	500,000
Front Range H.	1-Aug	8	ARP	7F	D	Personal Beau	Vicchrilli, R	26,875
Frontier H.	4-Sep	7	GLD	1 1/8M	D	Catch the Dew	Perez, RA	50,000
Frost King S.	27-Oct	7	WO	7F	D	Enough Is Enough	Kabel, T	132,750
Frosty Gardiner Honorary Championship H.	22-Aug	12	WYO	1M	D	Quiet Syns	Conklin, J	5,500
Funallover S.	15-May	8	TUP	6 1/2F	D	Lakesville	Bridges, K	22,100
Funallover S.	27-Dec	8	TUP	6 1/2F	D	Lite Write	Ruis, M	21,800
Funistrada S.	12-Jun	8	BEL	6F	D	She's a Mugs	Nakatani, CS	60,650
Furl Sail H.	23-Dec	9	FG	1 1/16M	D	Chance Dance	Marquez, Jr., CH	60,000
Fury S.	9-May	8	WO	7F	D	Eye of the Sphynx	Kabel, T	163,200
Futurity S.-G2	19-Sep	7	BEL	1M	D	Park Avenue Ball	Castellano, J	300,000
Gala Lil S.	20-Mar	8	LRL	1 1/8M	D	Friel's for Real	Castellano, Jr., A	75,000
Gallant Bloom H.-G2	10-Oct	9	BEL	6 1/2F	D	Lady Tak	Velazquez, JR	150,000
Gallant Bob H.	2-Oct	8	PHA	6F	D	Abbondanza	Coa, E	100,000
Gallant Fox H.	29-Dec	8	AQU	1 5/8M	D	Tamburello (CHI)	Arroyo, Jr., N	82,700
Gallorette H.-G3	15-May	5	PIM	1 1/16M	T	Ocean Drive	Bailey, JD	100,000
Gamely Breeders' Cup H.-G1	31-May	2	HOL	1 1/8M	T	Noches De Rosa (CHI)	Smith, ME	411,250
Garden City Breeders' Cup S.-G1	12-Sep	9	BEL	1 1/8M	T	Lucifer's Stone	Santos, JA	300,000
Garden City Futurity	13-Aug	5	WMF	5F	D	Secret Victory	Brown, DD	4,800
Garden City S.	29-Aug	7	FE	6F	D	Lucky Tec	Ramirez, MR	60,000
Garden Saint S.	10-Oct	7	CRC	1 1/16M	T	Formal Miss	Cruz, MR	40,000
Gardenia H.-G3	7-Aug	10	ELP	1 1/8M	D	Angela's Love	Guidry, M	200,000
Gardenia S.	10-Dec	8	DED	6 1/2F	D	Misty Glo	Kinsey, JE	40,000
Garland of Roses H.	11-Dec	8	AQU	6F	D	Travelator	Arroyo, Jr., N	80,900
Gasparilla S.	31-Jan	8	TAM	7F	D	Crafty Tears	Mata, F	60,000
Gate Dancer S.	21-Aug	8	DEL	1 1/16M	D	Country Be Gold	Alvarado, Jr., R	54,100
Gateway to Glory S.	23-Sep	11	FPX	1 1/16M	D	This Wizard Rocks	Pedroza, MA	60,000
Gaviola S.	8-Oct	8	BEL	1M	T	Noisette	Velasquez, CH	61,250
Gazelle H.-G1	11-Sep	8	BEL	1 1/8M	D	Stellar Jayne	Albarado, R	250,000
GCFA Texas Bred S.	29-Aug	10	GIL	7F	D	Victory Day	Perez, S	16,800
Geisha H.	11-Dec	8	PIM	1 1/8M	D	Silmaril	Castellano, Jr., A	100,000
Gena Stanley Memorial H.	10-Apr	7	BRD	5F	D	Carters Boy	Wilson, JL	10,350
Gene Francis and Associate H.	24-Jul	7	ANF	1 1/16M	D	My Silver Dollar	Williams, DW	5,000
Gene Francis and Associate H.	24-Jul	13	ANF	1 1/16M	D	Overprint	Vasquez, RM	5,440
General Douglas MacArthur H.	10-Sep	8	BEL	7F	D	Clever Electrician	Dominguez, RA	107,100
General George H.-G2	16-Feb	9	LRL	7F	D	Well Fancied	Prado, ES	200,000

Stakes	Date	Race	Trk	Dist/Surf		Winner	Jockey	Gross
Generous Portion S.	1-Sep	7	DMR	6F	D	Coastal Strike	Baze, T	100,000
Generous S.-G3	27-Nov	9	HOL	1M	T	Dubleo	Nakatani, CS	100,000
Genesee Valley Breeders' H.	6-Sep	8	FL	1 1/16M	D	Halo Malone	Davila, Jr., JR	50,000
Genesis S.	3-Jan	9	DED	5F	D	Wacky Patty	Gonzalez, C	40,000
Gentilly H.	20-Mar	9	FG	1M	T	Walk This Way	Lanerie, CJ	100,000
Genuine Risk H.-G2	9-May	8	BEL	6F	D	Bear Fan	Velazquez, JR	150,000
Genuine Risk S.	17-Jul	9	FP	1M 70Y	D	Lady Riss	Gale, MA	30,800
George C. Hendrie H.-G3	16-May	8	WO	6 1/2F	D	Winter Garden	Clark, D	211,250
George Lewis Memorial S.	30-Jul	9	TDN	1 1/8M	D	Majestic Dinner	Spieth, S	45,000
George Maloof Futurity	26-Sep	6	ALB	6F	D	Leon's Bull	Tohill, KS	70,046
George Rosenberger Memorial S.	11-Sep	9	DEL	1 1/16M	T	Mystery Itself	Pino, MG	75,600
George Royal S.	2-May	3	HST	6 1/2F	D	Lord Nelson	Fuentes, FP	44,576
George W. Barker S.	31-May	7	FL	6F	D	Top Shoter	Nicol, Jr., PA	50,000
Georgia Debutante S.	12-Dec	4	CRC	1 1/16M	T	Dansetta Light	Coa, E	50,000
Georgia Peaches S.	1-Aug	5	CRC	1M	T	All the Honor	Castro, E	50,000
Gerry Howard Memorial S.	2-May	8	TUP	6F	D	Expert	Stevens, SA	21,700
Gerry Howard Inaugural H.	29-May	8	YAV	6F	D	Top Boot	Bridges, K	17,500
Gilded Time S.	29-May	8	MTH	5F	D	Smokume	Uske, S	55,000
Ginger Welch H.	2-Jul	7	BOI	1M	D	Never Been Caught	Crane, D	6,350
Girl Powder H.	25-Sep	7	MTH	6F	D	Eastern Gale	Elliott, S	60,000
Glacial Princess S.	27-Nov	8	BEU	1M 70Y	D	Marketable	Rosario, Jr., HL	40,000
Glendale H.	14-Feb	7	TUP	1 1/16M	T	Magnificent Val	Barton, J	50,000
Glens Falls H.-G3	5-Sep	7	SAR	1 3/8M	T	Humaita (GER)	Velasquez, CH	110,400
Glens Falls H.-G3	5-Sep	10	SAR	1 3/8M	T	Arvada (GB)	Velazquez, JR	109,300
Glorious Song S.	21-Nov	8	WO	7F	D	Shout to the North	Ramsammy, E	186,875
Go for Wand H.-G1	1-Aug	9	SAR	1 1/8M	D	Azeri	Day, P	250,000
Go for Wand S.	29-May	7	DEL	1 1/16M	D	Pilfer	Caraballo, JC	100,600
Goddess S.	26-Mar	9	DED	1M	D	Handpainted	Smith, G	75,000
Gold Cup S.	13-Nov	9	DED	1M	D	Witt Ante	Hebert, TJ	100,000
Gold Rush Futurity	5-Sep	9	ARP	6F	D	Railroad	Wales, T	54,000
Gold Rush S.	18-Dec	8	GG	1M	D	Dover Dere	Puglisi, I	65,000
Goldarama S.	2-May	9	CRC	6F	D	Mary Murphy	Velasquez, CH	45,000
Golden Boy S.	11-Jun	8	ASD	6F	D	Shanghied	Hightower, TW	40,000
Golden Circle S.	17-Apr	8	PRM	6F	D	Danieltown	Doocy, TT	50,000
Golden Eagle Farm S.	24-Apr	7	HOL	7F	D	Throw Me a Curve	Espinoza, V	70,000
Golden Gate Breeders' Cup H.-G3	14-Mar	7	GG	1 1/8M	T	Tronare (CHI)	Gonzalez, RM	125,000
Golden Gate Derby-G3	10-Jan	3	GG	1 1/16M	D	Skipaslew	Saint-Martin, E	100,000
Golden Gull Chris Brown Memorial S.	26-Sep	7	CT	4F	D	Weshaam Luck	Dunkelberger, TL	41,400
Golden Horseshoe S.	8-Aug	9	FE	7F	T	Anthonia	Dionne, M	60,000
Golden Or S.	29-Aug	9	CRC	6F	D	Tchula Miss	Toribio, Jr., A	40,000
Golden Or S.	19-Dec	3	CRC	1 1/16M	T	Lentil	Velasquez, CH	45,000
Golden Pond S.	17-Dec	5	CRC	1 1/16M	D	Path of Thunder	DeCarlo, CP	45,000
Golden Poppy H.	23-Oct	8	BM	1M	D	Marwood	Warren, Jr., RJ	55,550
Golden Rod S.-G2	27-Nov	9	CD	1 1/16M	D	Runway Model	Martin, Jr., EM	215,400
Golden State Mile S.	8-Feb	8	GG	1M	D	O. K. Mikie	Lopez, AD	83,175
Golden Sylvia H.	15-Jun	9	MNR	1M	D	Two Mile Hill	Murphy, CK	75,000
Golden Triangle S.	22-Oct	9	DED	1M	D	Baileys Affair	Santos, R	50,000
Goldfinch H.	26-Jun	8	MTH	1M 70Y	D	Firecard	DeCarlo, CP	60,000
Goldfinch S.	16-Apr	8	PRM	6F	D	Saltwater Runner	Doocy, TT	50,000
Goodwood Breeders' Cup H.-G2	2-Oct	8	SA	1 1/8M	D	Lundy's Liability (BRZ)	Flores, DR	500,000
Goss L. Stryker S.	7-Feb	8	LRL	7F	D	White Mountain Boy	Castellano, Jr., A	75,000
Gotham S.-G3	20-Mar	7	AQU	1M	D	Saratoga County	Castellano, J	200,000
Gottstein Futurity	19-Sep	9	EMD	1 1/16M	D	Positive Prize	Frazier, R	100,000
Governor's Buckeye Cup S.	6-Sep	12	TDN	1 1/4M	D	Real Echo	Cloninger, Jr., WT	75,000
Governor's Cup H.	10-Jul	8	WYO	1M	D	Downtown Kid	Hamilton, T	4,000
Governor's Cup H.	15-Sep	10	FPX	6 1/2F	D	Court's in Session	Jauregui, LH	60,000
Governor's H.	26-May	7	BOI	7F	D	Find My Halter	Packer, BR	6,250
Governor's H.	5-Sep	4	ELK	7F	D	Quiet Syns	Williams, M	3,850
Governor's H.	28-Aug	9	ELP	1M	D	Added Edge	Guidry, M	75,000
Governor's H.	28-Aug	8	SAC	1 1/8M	D	Yougottawanna	Baze, RA	60,595
Governor's H.	18-Jul	9	RUI	6F	D	Ninety Nine Jack	Bourdieu, JM	25,000
Governor's H.	8-Aug	9	EMD	6 1/2F	D	Salt Grinder	Mitchell, GV	40,000
Governor's Lady H.	10-Apr	5	HAW	6F	D	Summer Mis	Sterling, Jr., LJ	111,325

Stakes	Date	Race	Trk	Dist/Surf		Winner	Jockey	Gross
Governor's S.	31-May	9	IND	7 1/2F	T	Edgerrin	Troilo, WD	42,400
Governor's Speed S.	27-Mar	6	PM	6F	D	Star of Elttaes	Gutierrez, JM	10,000
Gowell S.	26-Dec	9	TP	6F	D	Angel Trumpet	Bejarano, R	50,000
Graceful Klinchit Distaff H.	27-Aug	6	MD	1 1/16M	D	She's Nifty	Latchman, R	5,000
Graduation S.	28-Jul	7	DMR	5 1/2F	D	Senor Fango	John, K	125,000
Grand Canyon H.	21-Nov	7	CD	1 1/16M	T	Exceptional Ride	Blanc, B	70,420
Grand Prairie Turf Challenge S.	24-Apr	9	LS	1M	D	Cryptograph	Pettinger, DR	75,000
Grasmick H.	21-Feb	8	FON	4F	D	Tonight Rainbow	Kimes, C	11,725
Gravesend H.-G3	19-Dec	8	AQU	6F	D	Don Six	Luzzi, MJ	109,400
Gray's Lake S.	30-May	8	PRM	6F	D	Wild Wild West	Doocy, TT	57,123
Green Carpet S.	29-May	10	RD	1 1/16M	D	Floater	Villa-Gomez, H	45,000
Green Flash H.	18-Aug	7	DMR	5F	T	Geronimo (CHI)	Nakatani, CS	98,400
Green Oaks	27-Feb	9	DED	7F	D	Cryptos' Best	Tervort, J	50,000
Greenwood Cup H.	5-Jun	9	PHA	1 1/2M	T	In Hand	Mojica, Jr., R	100,000
Grey Breeders' Cup S.-G2	11-Oct	8	WO	1 1/16M	D	Dance With Ravens	Kabel, T	270,000
Groomstick H.	31-Jul	9	CRC	6 1/2F	D	Gold Dollar	Lopez, JE	75,000
Groovy S.	20-Nov	3	HOU	7F	D	Expect Will	Meche, DJ	50,000
Gulf Coast Classic S.	27-Mar	8	DED	1 1/16M	D	Kodema	Bourque, SJ	100,000
Gulfstream Park Breeders' Cup H.-G1	22-Feb	11	GP	1 3/8M	T	Hard Buck (BRZ)	Prado, ES	250,000
Gulfstream Park H.-G2	3-Apr	9	GP	1 1/4M	D	Jackpot	Bravo, J	300,000
Gus Grissom S.	3-Oct	9	HOO	1 1/16M	D	Sir Traver	Prescott, RA	40,000
H. A. Hindmarsh S.	10-Jul	8	FE	1 1/16M	D	Kissed by a Prince	Luciani, D	75,000
H. J. Addison Jr. S.	11-Jul	6	FE	1 1/16M	D	Domascas Consort	Robinson, K	75,000
H. Steward Mitchell S.	4-Dec	6	PIM	6F	D	Seeyoubychance	Fogelsonger, R	40,000
H.B.P.A. H.	6-Jun	8	GRP	5 1/2F	D	Jesse Gee	Beckner, T	3,450
Haggin S.	20-Jun	3	HOL	5 1/2F	D	Chandtrue	Nakatani, CS	99,375
Hallowed Dreams S.	15-Aug	9	LAD	6F	D	Leslie's Love	Melancon, G	50,000
Halo America S.	6-Jul	8	CRC	1 1/16M	D	Adobe Gold	Castro, E	45,000
Hal's Hope H.-G3	3-Jan	9	GP	1 1/16M	D	Puzzlement	Chavez, JF	100,000
Halton S.	5-Sep	2	WO	1 1/8M	T	Mobil	Kabel, T	128,750
Hancock County H.	11-May	9	MNR	5F	D	Gabrieles Princess	Villa-Gomez, H	75,000
Hank Mills Sr. Memorial H.	21-Aug	7	WYO	5F	D	Cheese Puff	Hamilton, T	4,300
Hansel S.	20-Mar	10	TP	6F	D	Marley's Revenge	Perez, EE	50,000
Hanshin Cup H.-G3	29-May	9	AP	1M	D	Crafty Shaw	Perret, C	100,000
Harney County Derby	12-Sep	5	BRN	1 1/8M	D	Tender Offer (IRE)	Holmes, Jr., JS	2,500
Harold C. Ramser Sr. H.	11-Oct	8	SA	1M	T	Mea Domina	Stevens, GL	100,000
Harold V. Goodman Sprint S.	31-May	5	LS	6 1/2F	D	Canadian River	Martin, Jr., EM	50,000
Harper County H.	18-Jul	9	ANF	5F	D	Sunset Cruise	Williams, DW	5,000
Harrah's Juvenile S.	25-Sep	12	LAD	1M	T	Major League	Perrodin, EJ	75,000
Harrah's Louisiana Downs Breeders' Cup H.	26-Sep	9	LAD	1 1/16M	T	Warleigh	Meche, DJ	150,000
Harrison E. Johnson Memorial H.	13-Mar	8	LRL	1 1/8M	D	Jorgie Stover	Kreidel, K	75,000
Harry F. Brubaker H.	20-Aug	7	DMR	1 1/16M	T	Cayoke (FR)	Espinoza, V	98,350
Harry Henson S.	21-Apr	7	HOL	5 1/2F	T	Stormin' Lyon	Atkinson, P	99,225
Harry Jeffrey S.	29 Aug	6	ASD	1 1/8M	D	Shanghied	Hightower, TW	40,000
Harry W. Henson H.	4-Apr	11	SUN	1M	D	Academic Angel	Tohill, KS	105,400
Harvest Futurity	10-Oct	9	FNO	6F	D	Air Julie	Scott, JM	40,130
Harvest H.	17-Apr	8	ALB	5 1/2F	D	Ocean Symphony	Jaime, R	44,400
Harvey Arneault Memorial H.	7-Aug	6	MNR	6F	D	Eavesdropper	Castillo, Jr., H	85,000
Haskell Invitational H.-G1	8-Aug	13	MTH	1 1/8M	D	Lion Heart	Bravo, J	1,000,000
Hasta La Vista H.	16-May	10	TUP	1 7/8M	T	Fade to Blue	Dieguez, WO	50,000
Hastings Park H.	9-May	7	EMD	6 1/2F	D	Lasting Code	Baze, G	40,000
Hastings Speed H.	21-Aug	8	HST	6 1/2F	D	Five Point Star	Alvarado, PV	44,524
Hatoof S.	28-Aug	8	AP	1 1/16M	T	Humorous Miss	Graham, J	54,000
Hawkeyes H.	26-Jun	9	PRM	1 1/16M	D	Sharky's Review	Compton, P	70,000
Hawthorne Derby-G3	16-Oct	8	HAW	1 1/8M	T	Cool Conductor	Santos, JA	250,000
Hawthorne Gold Cup H.-G2	2-Oct	7	HAW	1 1/4M	D	Freefourinternet	Kuntzweiler, G	750,000
Hawthorne H.-G3	6-Jun	8	HOL	1 1/16M	D	Summer Wind Dancer	Espinoza, V	108,600
HBPA and WVRC S.	18-Jul	9	CT	1 1/8M	D	Cherokee's Boy	Dunkelberger, TL	51,300
HBPA Au Revoir H.	5-Jul	7	GRP	6 1/2F	D	Nevets	Garcia, Jr., RJ	4,060
HBPA City of Charles Town H.	8-Oct	7	CT	4F	D	Choctaw Ridge	Carmouche, K	51,200
HBPA City of Ranson H.	8-Oct	8	CT	7F	D	Lets Just Do It	Pindell, MD	51,475
HBPA Dash S.	18-Jul	4	CT	4 1/2F	D	Not for Sam	Flores, O	51,250
HBPA Governor's Cup H.	10-Oct	4	CT	1 1/8M	D	Nomorebills	Hernandez, A	51,175

Stakes	Date	Race	Trk	Dist/Surf		Winner	Jockey	Gross
HBPA H.	10-Jul	9	ELP	1M	D	Miss Fortunate	Peck, BD	75,000
HBPA Horsemen's S.	18-Jul	7	CT	4 1/2F	D	Umpateedle	Quinones, AR	51,200
HBPA Sagebrush Downs Derby	22-Aug	6	KAM	6 1/2F	D	Margo Duke	Friesen, S	5,250
HBPA West Virginia S.	18-Jul	8	CT	7F	D	Ribbon Cane	Dunkelberger, TL	51,400
Heavenly Cause S.	30-Oct	10	PIM	6F	D	Golden Malibu	Reynolds, LC	75,000
Helen Anthony Memorial S.	8-Aug	5	YAV	6F	D	Diamondsrbueno	Vergara, DP	12,500
Henry S. Clark S.	1-May	9	PIM	1M	T	Mr O'Brien (IRE)	Wilson, R	50,000
Herald Gold Plate H.	13-Jun	9	STP	1 1/16M	D	Bubblegum Kid	Iammarino, MP	50,000
Herecomesthebride S.-G3	28-Feb	8	GP	1 1/8M	T	Lucifer's Stone	Santos, JA	100,000
Hermosa Beach H.	25-Nov	6	HOL	1 1/2M	T	Uraib (IRE)	Valdivia, Jr., J	80,950
Hidden Light S.	27-Oct	3	SA	1M	T	Conveyor's Angel	Stevens, GL	100,900
High Alexander H.	13-Nov	9	HAW	1 1/16M	D	Home of Stars	Sterling, Jr., LJ	119,025
Hildene S.	30-Oct	5	DEL	6F	D	Joyous Song	Castellano, Jr., A	50,300
Hill 'N' Dale Farms S.	3-Jul	8	WO	1 1/16M	D	My Lordship	Kabel, T	109,500
Hill Prince S.-G3	6-Jun	8	BEL	1 1/8M	T	Artie Schiller	Migliore, R	110,000
Hillsborough H.	25-Sep	3	BM	1 1/16M	T	Uraib (IRE)	Rollins, CJ	72,300
Hillsborough S.-G3	14-Mar	10	TAM	1 1/8M	T	Coney Kitty (IRE)	Santos, JA	100,000
Hillsdale S.	2-Oct	8	HOO	5 1/2F	D	Bruce On the Loose	Knight, LC	40,000
Hilltop S.	8-May	9	PIM	1 1/16M	T	Western Ransom	Fogelsonger, R	50,000
Hirsch Jacobs S.	15-May	6	PIM	6F	D	Abbondanza	Dominguez, RA	100,000
Hoist Her Flag S.	29-May	7	CBY	6F	D	Burning Memories	Schacht, R	40,000
Holiday Inaugural S.	4-Dec	10	TP	6F	D	Revolutionary Act	Patin, BC	50,000
Holiday Inn Express Sprint S.	4-Apr	10	TAM	6F	D	Scrubs	Thompson, WA	81,350
Hollie Hughes H.	15-Feb	8	AQU	6F	D	Papua	Luzzi, MJ	81,675
Holly S.	23-Oct	8	MED	6F	D	More Moonlight	Elliott, S	60,000
Hollywood Breeders' Cup Oaks-G2	12-Jun	4	HOL	1 1/16M	D	House of Fortune	Solis, AO	182,875
Hollywood Derby-G1	28-Nov	9	HOL	1 1/4M	T	Good Reward	Bailey, JD	500,000
Hollywood Futurity-G1	18-Dec	8	HOL	1 1/16M	D	Declan's Moon	Espinoza, V	449,500
Hollywood Gold Cup S.-G1	10-Jul	9	HOL	1 1/4M	D	Total Impact (CHI)	Smith, ME	750,000
Hollywood Juvenile Championship S.-G3	17-Jul	3	HOL	6F	D	Chandtrue	Espinoza, V	106,400
Hollywood Prevue S.-G3	20-Nov	8	HOL	7F	D	Declan's Moon	Espinoza, V	100,000
Hollywood Starlet S.-G1	19-Dec	8	HOL	1 1/16M	D	Splendid Blended	Desormeaux, KJ	390,000
Hollywood Turf Cup S.-G1	4-Dec	7	HOL	1 1/2M	T	Pellegrino (BRZ)	Stevens, GL	250,000
Hollywood Turf Express H.-G3	26-Nov	8	HOL	5 1/2F	T	Cajun Beat	Dominguez, RA	150,000
Hollywood Wildcat Breeder's Cup H.	1-May	5	CRC	1 1/16M	T	Stay Forever	Castro, E	145,500
Holy Bull S.-G3	17-Jan	10	GP	1 1/16M	D	Second of June	Velasquez, CH	100,000
Honest Pleasure S.	1-Aug	8	AP	5 1/2F	D	Straight Line	Emigh, CA	52,600
Honey Bee S.	5-Nov	6	MED	1 1/16M	D	Emerald Earrings	DeCarlo, CP	60,000
Honey Fox H.-G3	3-Jan	11	GP	1 1/16M	T	Delmonico Cat	Bailey, JD	100,000
Honey Jay H.	19-Sep	8	BEU	6F	D	Ben's Reflection	Johnston, J	40,000
Honeybee S.	6-Mar	10	OP	1 1/16M	D	Yoursmineours	Pettinger, DR	75,000
Honeymoon Breeders' Cup H.-G2	5-Jun	8	HOL	1 1/8M	T	Lovely Rafaela	Espinoza, V	188,925
Honeymoon S.	15-May	10	LAD	1M	T	Due to Win Again	LeBlanc, KP	50,000
Hong Kong Jockey Club Sprint H.	23-May	7	HST	6 1/2F	D	Lord Nelson	Fuentes, FP	44,160
Honor the Hero S.	18-Jan	3	TUP	1M	D	Ozoned	Belmonte, W	21,800
Honor the Hero Turf Express S.	31-May	8	CBY	5F	D	Tonight Rainbow	Kimes, C	40,000
Honorable Miss H.-G2	6-Aug	8	SAR	6F	D	My Trusty Cat	Day, P	150,000
Hoofprint on My Heart H.	30-May	8	STP	1M	D	Kat Kool	Welch, Q	40,000
Hoosier Silver Cup S.	17-Oct	7	HOO	6F	D	Slim Justice	Knight, LC	40,000
Hoosier Silver Cup S.	17-Oct	8	HOO	6F	D	Unforgottenpromise	Zimmerman, R	40,000
Hoover S.	24-Jan	8	LRL	6F	D	Gators N Bears	Wilson, R	75,000
Hoover S.	18-Jul	11	RD	5 1/2F	D	Bug Hunter	Rosendo, IJ	40,000
Hopeful S.-G1	21-Aug	9	SAR	7F	D	Afleet Alex	Rose, J	250,000
Horatius S.	21-Mar	8	LRL	6F	D	Basketball Court	Dominguez, RA	60,000
Horizon S.	25-Jul	10	RD	1 1/16M	T	Best Bird	Adam, MG	40,000
Hot Springs S.	21-Mar	10	OP	6F	D	Skeet	McKee, J	50,000
Howard B. Noonan S.	27-Mar	6	BEU	6F	D	Cayenne Red	Ccamaque, MA	40,000
Hubbard Museum Middle Distance Final S.	7-Aug	8	RUI	7 1/2F	D	Highly Suspect	Villa, MA	20,100
Hudson H.	23-Oct	8	BEL	6F	D	Friendly Island	Velazquez, JR	125,000
Humana Distaff H.-G1	1-May	8	CD	7F	D	Mayo On the Side	Day, P	280,250
Humphrey S. Finney S.	11-Sep	8	PIM	1 1/8M	T	Class Concern	Boucher, R	75,000
Huntington S.	14-Nov	8	AQU	6F	D	Magoo's Magic	Castellano, J	82,950
Hurricane Bertie H.	7-Mar	11	GP	6 1/2F	D	House Party	Santos, JA	100,000

Stakes	Date	Race	Trk	Dist/Surf		Winner	Jockey	Gross
Hutcheson S.-G2	14-Feb	10	GP	7F	D	Limehouse	Velazquez, JR	150,000
I. C. Light Memorial Day H.	31-May	4	MNR	1M	D	Gin and Sin	Whitney, DG	75,000
Icecapade S.	6-Sep	9	MTH	6F	D	Wildcat Heir	Velez, Jr., JA	60,000
Idaho Bred Sophomore Distaff S.	5-Jun	7	BOI	6 1/2F	D	Paradise Wild	Conklin, J	8,805
Idaho Bred Sophomore S.	5-Jun	8	BOI	6 1/2F	D	Robs Coin	Colledge, C	9,075
Idaho Cup Claiming S.	31-Jul	2	BOI	7F	D	Sherroyal	Colledge, C	12,078
Idaho Cup Classic S.	31-Jul	10	BOI	1M	D	Crooked Key	Packer, BR	32,099
Idaho Cup Derby	31-Jul	7	BOI	1M	D	Silent Snow	Conklin, J	35,582
Idaho Cup Distaff Derby S.	31-Jul	6	BOI	1M	D	Paradise Wild	Conklin, J	37,323
Idaho Cup Distaff Maturity	31-Jul	8	BOI	1M	D	Thrill After Dark	Packer, BR	28,656
Idaho Cup Juvenile Championship S.	31-Jul	5	BOI	5F	D	Blue Julie	Packer, BR	36,797
Idaho Cup Sprint S.	31-Jul	1	BOI	5F	D	Dun Ringill	Packer, BR	14,796
Illini Princess H.	13-Nov	8	HAW	1 1/16M	D	Cashmere Miss	Silva, CH	122,500
Illinois Derby-G2	3-Apr	7	HAW	1 1/8M	D	Pollard's Vision	Coa, E	500,000
I'm Smokin S.	6-Sep	1	DMR	6F	D	Top Money	Enriquez, ID	100,000
Inaugural H.	2-Aug	8	SRP	6 1/2F	D	Swift for Sure	Zunino, JL	32,500
Inaugural H.	16-Oct	8	PM	6F	D	Slewicide Cruise	Hoonan, D	10,000
Inaugural H.	1-May	7	BOI	6 1/2F	D	Better Choice	Green, P	6,950
Inaugural H.	3-Apr	8	EVD	6F	D	Smalltown Slew	Faul, RJ	50,000
Inaugural H.	26-Jun	10	WYO	6F	D	Restrictions Apply	Bowen, C	4,225
Inaugural S.	3-Jul	9	GF	5F	D	Slew Design	Wippert, S	2,950
Inaugural S.	3-Jul	10	ARP	6F	D	C K Jett	Vicchrilli, R	30,475
Inaugural S.	23-Jul	8	CLS	6F	D	Sheso	Munaylla, F	11,450
Inaugural S.	11-Dec	10	TAM	6F	D	Hostile Witness	Penalba, C	60,000
Incredible Revenge S.	9-Oct	9	MED	5F	T	Tight Spin	Santagata, N	60,000
Independence Day H.	4-Jul	9	EMD	1 1/16M	D	Briartic Gold	Hoonan, D	40,000
Independence H.	4-Jul	9	LAD	1 1/16M	T	Sea Dub	Perrodin, EJ	75,000
Indian Maid Breeders' Cup H.	2-Oct	8	HAW	1 1/16M	T	Beret	Marquez, Jr., CH	122,500
Indiana Breeders' Cup Oaks-G3	1-Oct	9	HOO	1 1/16M	D	Daydreaming	Velazquez, JR	406,300
Indiana Derby-G2	2-Oct	9	HOO	1 1/16M	D	Brass Hat	Martinez, W	511,300
Indiana Futurity	7-Nov	9	HOO	6F	D	Snack	Prescott, RA	40,000
Indiana Stallion S.	20-Nov	9	HOO	6F	D	Free Bonus	Leeds, D	40,000
Indiana Stallion S.	21-Nov	9	HOO	6F	D	Bruce On the Loose	Knight, LC	40,000
Inglewood H.-G3	1-May	6	HOL	1 1/16M	T	Leroidesanimaux (BRZ)	Court, JK	110,900
Ingrid Knotts H.	3-Jul	11	ARP	6F	D	She's Finding Time	Juarez, Jr., AJ	26,575
Instant Racing Breeders' Cup S.	10-Apr	7	OP	1M	D	Tee's Pearl	Day, P	75,000
Interborough H.	1-Jan	8	AQU	6F	D	Fit Performer	Pimentel, J	81,600
International Turf Cup S.	18-Jul	4	FE	1 1/16M	D	Le Cinquieme Essai	Bahen, SR	100,000
Iowa Breeders' Derby	28-Aug	4	PRM	1 1/16M	D	Roarofvictory	Lopez, J	77,530
Iowa Breeders' Oaks	28-Aug	3	PRM	1M 70Y	D	This One for Abbey	Eads, JR	76,300
Iowa Cradle S.	28-Aug	2	PRM	6F	D	Mingo Mohawk	Corbett, GW	75,130
Iowa Derby	2-Jul	7	PRM	1 1/16M	D	Swingforthefences	Bridgmohan, S	250,000
Iowa Distaff Breeders' Cup S.	3-Jul	8	PRM	1 1/16M	D	Wildwood Royal	Sukie, D	125,000
Iowa Oaks-G3	2-Jul	9	PRM	1 1/16M	D	He Loves Me	Santana, JZ	125,000
Iowa Sorority S.	28-Aug	1	PRM	6F	D	Queansco	Doocy, TT	79,630
Iowa Sprint H.	4-Jul	8	PRM	6F	D	Coach Jimi Lee	Perret, C	125,000
Iowa Stallion Futurity	14-Aug	6	PRM	6F	D	Okie Dozer	Doocy, TT	61,880
Iowa Stallion S.	24-Jul	6	PRM	1M 70Y	D	Vazandar	Martinez, SB	63,206
Iowa State Fair S.	21-Aug	6	PRM	6F	D	Sue's Good News	Doocy, TT	40,000
Irish Day H.	13-Jun	9	EMD	1M	D	Swingn' Notes	Lopez, AD	50,000
Irish O'Brien S.	17-Mar	5	SA	6 1/2F	T	Bear Fan	Smith, ME	110,300
Irish Sonnet S.	25-Sep	7	DEL	1M	D	Dance Away Capote	Dominguez, RA	54,350
Iroquois H.	24-Jul	9	PHA	1 1/16M	D	Prince Joseph	Black, AS	52,950
Iroquois H.	23-Oct	6	BEL	7F	D	Sugar Punch	Prado, ES	125,000
Iroquois S.-G3	6-Nov	10	CD	1M	D	Straight Line	Blanc, B	109,600
Irving Distaff S.	17-Apr	9	LS	7 1/2F	T	Janeian (NZ)	Martin, Jr., EM	75,000
Isaac Murphy H.	26-Jun	7	AP	6F	D	Dharma Girl	Silva, CH	85,750
Isadorable S.	19-Jun	3	SUF	6F	D	Glory Be Good	Piermarini, T	40,000
Isi Newborn Memorial S.	12-Jun	10	TDN	6F	D	Cat Singer	Rosario, Jr., HL	45,000
Island Whirl H.	18-Jul	6	LAD	6F	D	That Tat	Jacinto, J	50,000
ITBOA Sales Futurity	17-Jul	6	PRM	5 1/2F	D	Lordslegacy	Lopez, J	42,662
Izvestia S.	21-Aug	4	WO	1 1/16M	D	Refuse to Bend	McKnight, J	104,000
J J'sdream S.	26-Jun	9	CRC	5 1/2F	D	Punch Appeal	Garcia, JA	100,000

Stakes	Date	Race	Trk	Dist/Surf		Winner	Jockey	Gross
J. R. Straus Memorial S.	23-Jul	8	RET	6F	D	Gold Storm	Taylor, L	40,000
J. W. Sifton S.	19-Sep	8	ASD	1 1/8M	D	Coal Smudge	Leacock, P	41,000
J. William (Bill) Petro Memorial H.	12-Jun	15	TDN	1 1/16M	D	Barnsy	Martinez, W	45,000
Jack Betta Be Rite S.	28-Aug	8	FL	1 1/16M	D	French Hideaway	Grabowski, JA	50,000
Jack Diamond Futurity	2-Oct	6	HST	6 1/2F	D	Notis Otis	Loseth, C	107,728
Jack Dudley Sprint H.	13-Nov	11	CRC	6F	D	Weigelia	Velazquez, JR	150,000
Jack Hammer Memorial H.	7-Aug	7	BRD	5F	D	Carters Boy	Camacho, F	8,925
Jack Hardy S.	2-Aug	7	ASD	1M	D	Victory Thrill	Hightower, TW	40,000
Jack Price Juvenile S.	13-Nov	8	CRC	7F	D	Flamenco	Bailey, JD	150,000
Jack Shoemaker Memorial S.	21-Feb	9	RIL	5 1/2F	D	Cyber Move	Oliver, R	3,726
Jackie Wackie S.	24-Jul	10	CRC	1 1/16M	T	Cervelo	Toscano, PR	40,000
Jacques Cartier S.	17-Apr	9	WO	6F	D	Chris's Bad Boy	Jones, JC	135,750
Jaipur H.-G3	30-May	8	BEL	7F	T	Multiple Choice	Castellano, J	112,200
Jamaica H.-G2	26-Sep	9	BEL	1 1/8M	T	Artie Schiller	Migliore, R	200,000
Jameela S.	15-Feb	8	LRL	7F	D	Silmaril	Castellano, Jr., A	75,000
James B. Moseley Breeders' Cup H.	19-Jun	9	SUF	6F	D	Gators N Bears	Lopez, CC	200,000
James C. Ellis Juvenile S.	22-Aug	9	ELP	7F	D	Elusive Chris	McKee, J	100,000
James F. Lyttle Memorial H.	6-Aug	11	SR	1 1/16M	D	My Creed	Perez, MA	54,045
James Leakos Sophomore S.	6-Aug	5	MD	1M	D	Lucky in the Lead	Miyashiro, CJ	6,500
Jammed Lovely S.	14-Nov	8	WO	7F	D	Financingavailable	Kabel, T	160,350
Jane Driggers Debutante S.	11-Dec	5	PM	6F	D	One Tuft Woeman	Neal, T	10,000
Janet Wineberg S.	6-Nov	8	PM	6F	D	One Fast Cowgirl	O'Donnell, K	20,780
Jatski S.	22-Aug	9	CRC	1 1/8M	D	Kristine's King	Morales, C	45,000
Jean Lafitte S.	6-Nov	8	DED	1M	D	Leaving On My Mind	Chapa, R	100,000
Jefferson Cup S.-G3	12-Jun	5	CD	1 1/8M	T	Prince Arch	Blanc, B	226,200
Jefferson Bank West Va Breeders' Classic S.	9-Oct	6	CT	7F	D	Original Gold	Dominguez, RA	250,000
JEH Stallion Station S.	15-May	10	LS	6 1/2F	D	Fleeta Dif	Helton, RM	50,000
Jennings H.	18-Dec	8	PIM	1 1/8M	D	Aggadan	Smith, A	100,000
Jenny Wade H.	6-Aug	2	PEN	5F	T	Desirable Moment	Santagata, N	50,000
Jenny Wiley S.-G3	18-Apr	8	KEE	1 1/16M	T	Intercontinental (GB)	Bailey, JD	110,300
Jerome H.-G2	18-Sep	9	BEL	1M	D	Teton Forest	Bridgmohan, S	150,000
Jerry & Eileen Towslee Memorial H.	14-Aug	6	TIL	5F	D	Larron	Black, N	3,800
Jersey Breeders' Turf Highweight H.	29-Aug	9	MTH	1 1/16M	T	American Freedom	Velez, Jr., JA	100,000
Jersey Derby-G3	31-May	10	MTH	1 1/16M	T	Icy Atlantic	Lopez, CC	100,000
Jersey Girl H.	29-Aug	8	MTH	1M 70Y	D	Uphill Skier	Elliott, S	100,000
Jersey Girl S.	26-May	8	BEL	6F	D	Frenchglen	Velazquez, JR	60,600
Jersey Lilly S.	10-Apr	5	HOU	1 1/16M	T	Sound of Gold	Jacinto, J	40,000
Jersey Shore Breeders' Cup S.-G3	26-Jun	9	MTH	6F	D	Pomeroy	Bravo, J	100,000
Jersey Village S.	21-Feb	8	HOU	1 1/16M	D	Desert Darby	Beasley, J	40,000
Jessamine County S.	28-Oct	8	KEE	1 1/16M	T	Paddy's Daisy	Velazquez, JR	112,600
Jim Coleman Province H.	18-Jul	8	HST	1 1/16M	D	Treasured Friend	Hoverson, C	44,368
Jim Dandy S.-G2	8-Aug	9	SAR	1 1/8M	D	Purge	Velazquez, JR	500,000
Jim Edgar Illinois Futurity	18-Dec	8	HAW	1 1/16M	D	Win Me Over	Emigh, CA	115,350
Jim McKay Breeders' Cup H.	17-Apr	8	PIM	1 1/8M	D	The Lady's Groom	Karamanos, H	150,000
Jim Murray Memorial H.	8-May	7	HOL	1 1/2M	T	Rhythm Mad (FR)	Solis, AO	350,000
Jim Rasmussen Memorial S.	29-May	8	PRM	1 1/16M	D	River Mountain Rd	Doocy, TT	50,000
Jockey Club Gold Cup-G1	2-Oct	10	BEL	1 1/4M	D	Funny Cide	Santos, JA	1,000,000
Joe Hirsch Turf Classic Invitational S.-G1	2-Oct	9	BEL	1 1/2M	T	Kitten's Joy	Velazquez, JR	750,000
Joe O'Farrell Juvenile Fillies S.	13-Nov	5	CRC	7F	D	Aclassysassylassy	Aguilar, M	150,000
John and Kitty Fletcher S.	19-Sep	7	EMD	1M	D	Arco Iris	Mitchell, GV	40,000
John B. Campbell Breeders' Cup H.	14-Feb	8	LRL	1 1/8M	D	Ole Faunty	Luzzi, MJ	150,000
John B. Connally Breeders' Cup Turf H.	10-Apr	7	HOU	1 1/8M	T	Warleigh	Beasley, J	222,000
John Battaglia Memorial S.	28-Feb	10	TP	1 1/16M	D	Silver Minister	Bejarano, R	100,000
John Bullit S.	7-Aug	9	CBY	1 1/16M	T	Dontbotherknocking	Toro, M	50,000
John C. Mabee H.-G1	24-Jul	6	DMR	1 1/8M	T	Musical Chimes	Desormeaux, KJ	400,000
John D. Schapiro Memorial Breeders' Cup H.	18-Sep	9	PIM	1 1/8M	D	Lusty Latin	Fogelsonger, R	150,000
John Deere Breeders' Cup Turf-G1	30-Oct	8	LS	1 1/2M	T	Better Talk Now	Dominguez, RA	2,000,000
John Deere Filly and MareTurf S.	24-Jan	5	SA	1 1/8M	T	Valentine Dancer	Court, JK	500,000
John Franks Juvenile Fillies Turf S.	13-Nov	6	CRC	1 1/16M	T	Rich in Spirit	Castellano, J	100,000
John Franks Memorial S.	14-May	10	LAD	1M	T	Rosecoloredglasses	Romero, SP	50,000
John Franks Memorial Sales S.	31-Jul	8	EVD	5F	D	Grande Diablo	Theriot, J	40,000
John Henry H.	1-May	8	EVD	1 1/16M	D	Kiss a Native	Wright, ML	50,000
John Henry S.	18-Sep	6	AP	1 1/16M	T	Cloudy's Knight	Douglas, RR	44,500

Stakes	Date	Race	Trk	Dist/Surf		Winner	Jockey	Gross
John Henry S.	29-Oct	9	MED	1 3/8M	T	Macaw (IRE)	Bridgmohan, S	60,000
John J. Reilly H.	29-May	9	MTH	6F	D	Trueamericanspirit	Coa, E	60,000
John J. Shumaker H.	30-Jul	7	PEN	6F	D	Lone Traveler	Rivera, HG	40,850
John Kirby S.	20-Nov	6	SUF	1M 70Y	D	Ask Queenie	Perdomo, TA	40,000
John Longden 6000 H.	12-Jun	8	HST	1 1/16M	D	Roscoe Pito	Alvarado, PV	49,680
John McSorley S.	11-Jul	7	MTH	5F	T	Quest of Fate	Bravo, J	60,000
John McSorley S.	11-Jul	7	MTH	5F	T	Shades of Sunny	Elliott, S	60,000
John Morrissey S.	19-Aug	8	SAR	6 1/2F	D	Clever Electrician	Dominguez, RA	66,600
John Patrick H.	23-Jul	6	NP	1M	D	A Shaky Start	Hamel, RH	40,000
John W. Galbreath Memorial S.	9-Oct	13	TDN	1 1/16M	D	Bold Passage	Troilo, WD	60,000
John W. Rooney Memorial H.	5-Jun	8	DEL	1 1/8M	D	Shiny Sheet	Rose, J	100,300
John Wayne S.	15-May	9	PRM	6F	D	Take Me Up	Corbett, GW	60,000
Johnie L. Jamison H.	27-Nov	10	SUN	6 1/2F	D	Rocky Gulch	Bourdieu, JM	132,250
John's Call S.	16-Aug	8	SAR	1 5/8M	T	Spanish Spur (GB)	Velasquez, CH	67,300
Joseph A. Gimma S.	3-Oct	8	BEL	7F	D	Megascape	Velazquez, JR	113,400
Joseph T. Grace H.	7-Aug	11	SR	1 1/16M	D	Calkins Road	Schvaneveldt, CP	100,340
Josephine County S.	31-May	7	GRP	5 1/2F	D	Harvey's Delight	Beckner, T	3,800
Journal H.	26-Jun	8	NP	6 1/2F	D	Deputy Country	Hamel, RH	40,000
Journal Star S.	23-May	8	LNN	6F	D	Thundering Verzy	Martinez, A	11,000
JRA Fillies and Mares H.	23-Oct	9	PIM	1 1/16M	T	With Affection	Monterrey, R	50,000
Juan Gonzalez Memorial S.	3-Jul	11	PLN	5F	D	Timeintown	Schvaneveldt, CP	55,400
Judy's Red Shoes S.	11-Sep	11	CRC	1 1/16M	T	R Obsession	Castro, E	75,000
Junior Champion S.	22-Aug	9	MTH	1M	D	Speedy Deedy	Pimentel, J	55,000
Just a Game Breeders' Cup H.-G2	5-Jun	8	BEL	1M	T	Intercontinental (GB)	Bailey, JD	250,000
Just Smashing S.	26-Sep	10	MTH	6F	D	Mystery's Jules	Pimentel, J	60,000
Justakiss S.	25-Oct	8	DEL	1 1/16M	D	Flower Forest	Dominguez, RA	55,300
Juvenile Mile S.	26-Dec	8	PM	1M	D	Typhoon Aaron	Theriot, BJ	21,550
Juvenile S.	4-Sep	9	FE	6F	D	Wisdomisgold	Callaghan, S	75,000
Juvenile S.	5-Sep	6	FE	6F	D	Highland Warrior	Hemsley, D	75,000
Kachina H.	10-Jan	8	TUP	1M	D	Moonlit Maddie	Higuera, AR	40,000
Kansas Oaks	23-Oct	9	WDS	1M 70Y	D	Lady Riss	Robletto, L	25,000
Kansas Thoroughbred Association Derby	2-Oct	8	WDS	1M 70Y	D	Nick Missed	Vicchrilli, R	20,000
Kansas Thoroughbred Association Derby	3-Oct	9	WDS	1M 70Y	D	Grooms Moka	Vasquez, RM	20,000
Kansas Thoroughbred Association Futurity	17-Oct	9	WDS	5 1/2F	D	Wind Twister	Eads, JR	20,000
Kansas Thoroughbred Association Futurity	17-Oct	8	WDS	5 1/2F	D	Makesyourheadspin	Frazier, DL	20,000
Kansas Thoroughbred Association Futurity	17-Oct	8	WDS	5 1/2F	D	Scarlet Jeff	Eads, JR	20,000
Karl Flaman Memorial S.	10-Jul	5	YKT	1M	D	Makewayforbighoss	Keshane, N	2,000
Katy S.	4-Dec	8	HOU	1 1/16M	T	Key to the Cat	Taylor, L	40,000
Keddies Tack & Western Wear S.	1-Aug	5	GPR	5 1/2F	D	Irish Intrigue	Mellish, B	4,000
Kelly Kip S.	14-May	8	BEL	6 1/2F	D	Indian War Dance	Espinoza, JL	60,850
Kelso Breeders' Cup H.-G2	9-Oct	8	BEL	1M	T	Mr O'Brien (IRE)	Coa, E	350,000
Kelso H.	2-Oct	7	DEL	1 3/16M	D	Lyracist	Petro, NJ	100,300
Ken Kendrick Memorial S.	11-Oct	7	SRP	6 1/2F	D	Gone Western	Olguin, ER	32,200
Ken Maddy Sprint H.	21-Feb	8	GG	6F	D	Giovannetti	Sorenson, D	100,000
Ken Pearson Memorial H.	24-May	8	STP	1M	D	Raylene	Walcott, R	40,000
Kendal Pipeline and Oilfield Services S.	13-Aug	7	GPR	6 1/2F	D	Hy Nick	McAleney, P	6,500
Kenny Noe Jr. H.	18-Dec	10	CRC	7F	D	Medallist	Santos, JA	100,000
Kenora S.	5-Sep	10	WO	6F	D	Forever Grand	Kabel, T	131,375
Kent Breeders' Cup S.-G3	26-Jun	8	DEL	1 1/8M	T	Timo	Migliore, R	250,900
Kent H.	18-Jul	7	EMD	1 1/16M	D	Swingn' Notes	Lopez, AD	40,000
Kentucky Breeders' Cup S.-G3	5-Jun	8	CD	5 1/2F	D	Lunarpal	Sellers, SJ	138,750
Kentucky Cup Classic H.-G2	18-Sep	11	TP	1 1/8M	D	Roses in May	Velazquez, JR	350,000
Kentucky Cup Juvenile Fillies S.	18-Sep	9	TP	1M	D	Punch Appeal	Sellers, SJ	100,000
Kentucky Cup Juvenile S.-G3	18-Sep	10	TP	1 1/16M	D	Greater Good	McKee, J	100,000
Kentucky Cup Ladies Turf S.	25-Sep	12	KD	1M	T	Sand Springs	Guidry, M	100,000
Kentucky Cup Mile S.	25-Sep	9	KD	1M	T	Missme	Bejarano, R	100,000
Kentucky Cup Sprint S.-G3	18-Sep	13	TP	6F	D	Level Playingfield	McKee, J	100,000
Kentucky Cup Turf Dash S.	25-Sep	6	KD	6F	T	Battle Won	Bejarano, R	100,000
Kentucky Cup Turf H.-G3	25-Sep	14	KD	1 1/2M	T	Sabiango (GER)	Blanc, B	200,000
Kentucky Derby-G1 *	1-May	10	CD	1 1/4M	D	Smarty Jones	Elliott, S	6,184,800
Kentucky Jockey Club S.-G2	27-Nov	11	CD	1 1/16M	D	Greater Good	McKee, J	223,200
Kentucky Oaks-G1	30-Apr	10	CD	1 1/8M	D	Ashado	Velazquez, JR	572,000
Ketel One El Joven S.	4-Sep	8	RET	1M	T	Ready Ruler	Beasley, J	100,000

Stakes	Date	Race	Trk	Dist/Surf		Winner	Jockey	Gross
Kevin Goemmer Tah Dah S.	1-Aug	10	RD	5 1/2F	D	Noon Win	Villa-Gomez, H	40,000
King Cotton S.	31-Jan	9	OP	6F	D	Skeet	McKee, J	50,000
King County H.	26-Jun	9	EMD	1M	D	Cascade Corona	Mitchell, GV	40,000
King Edward Breeders' Cup H.-G2	19-Jun	8	WO	1 1/8M	T	Slew Valley	McAleney, J	324,300
Kingarvie S.	12-Dec	4	WO	1 1/16M	D	Enough Is Enough	Kabel, T	134,875
King's Bishop S.-G1	28-Aug	10	SAR	7F	D	Pomeroy	Prado, ES	250,000
King's Court S.	29-May	11	LAD	6F	D	Ole Rebel	Lanerie, CJ	50,000
Kings Point H.	2-May	8	AQU	1 1/8M	D	Gander	Velazquez, JR	80,975
Kingston H.	23-May	8	BEL	1 1/8M	T	Quantum Merit	Migliore, R	114,300
KLAQ H.	7-Nov	10	SUN	5 1/2F	D	Day Trader	Beasley, J	53,700
Klassy Briefcase S.	31-Jul	9	MTH	5F	T	Tangier Sound	Pimentel, J	60,000
Klondike H.	12-Jun	4	HST	6 1/2F	D	Maxwell	Fuentes, FP	44,576
Klondike H.	31-Jul	8	NP	1 1/16M	D	Rindanica	Winters, PA	40,000
Knickerbocker H.-G2	30-Oct	5	AQU	1 1/8M	T	Host (CHI)	DeCarlo, CP	150,000
Kudzu Juvenile S.	10-Dec	2	FG	5 1/2F	D	Pops Return	Meche, DJ	50,000
Ky Alta H.	24-Jul	9	NP	1 1/16M	D	Controlled Meeting	Hamel, RH	40,000
La Brea S.-G1	27-Dec	8	SA	7F	D	Alphabet Kisses	Smith, ME	250,000
La Canada S.-G2	14-Feb	8	SA	1 1/8M	D	Cat Fighter	Solis, AO	200,000
La Coneja H.	11-Dec	10	SUN	5 1/2F	D	Hat Creek	Coates, JR	131,250
La Fiesta H.	9-Apr	8	ALB	5 1/2F	D	Dayjurette	Johnson, RW	43,250
La Habra S.	29-Feb	8	SA	6 1/2F	T	Very Vegas	Ruis, M	111,350
La Jolla H.-G2	14-Aug	8	DMR	1 1/16M	T	Blackdoun (FR)	Nakatani, CS	150,000
La Lorgnette S.	18-Sep	8	WO	1 1/16M	D	Paiota Falls	Castillo, Jr., H	182,625
La Paz S.	21-Nov	8	TUP	6 1/2F	D	Estacada	Stevens, SA	21,800
La Prevoyante H.-G2	18-Dec	9	CRC	1 1/2M	T	Arvada (GB)	Prado, ES	200,000
La Prevoyante S.	26-Sep	8	WO	1M	T	Blonde Executive	Dos Ramos, RA	132,250
La Puente S.	10-Apr	8	SA	1M	T	Toasted	Almeida, GF	110,500
La Quinta S.	19-Jan	8	TUP	1M	D	Pittsburgh Star	Higuera, AR	21,800
La Senora H.	24-Jan	10	SUN	6F	D	Icy Lane	Noguez, T	131,250
La Troienne S.-G3	29-Apr	9	CD	7 1/2F	D	Friendly Michelle	Solis, AO	112,200
La Verendrye S.	13-Jun	8	ASD	6F	D	Remiewaterbluz	Leacock, P	40,000
La Zanzara H.	13-Feb	4	SA	1 1/4M	T	Lady Annaliese (NZ)	Solis, AO	91,875
Labatt Bison City S.	4-Jul	8	FE	1 1/16M	D	Touchnow	Husbands, P	250,000
Labatt Woodbine Oaks	13-Jun	8	WO	1 1/8M	D	Eye of the Sphynx	Kabel, T	500,000
Labeeb S.	7-Nov	4	WO	1M	T	Le Cinquieme Essai	Bahen, SR	106,000
Labor Day H.	6-Sep	3	MNR	1M	T	Freefourinternet	Kuntzweiler, G	75,000
Labor Day H.	6-Sep	8	CLS	6 1/2F	D	Thundering Verzy	Martinez, A	11,625
Ladies H.-G3	18-Dec	8	AQU	1 1/4M	D	Rare Gift	Migliore, R	109,400
Ladnesian S.	17-Jul	1	HST	6 1/2F	D	Notis Otis	Loseth, C	44,784
Lady Angela S.	29-May	8	WO	7F	D	Blonde Executive	Dos Ramos, RA	133,250
Lady Canterbury Breeders' Cup S.	20-Jun	7	CBY	1M	T	Be My Friend	Shepherd, J	100,000
Lady Fingers S.	21-Aug	7	FL	6F	D	Reddy for Rubys	Smith, A	126,133
Lady Hallie S.	10-Apr	8	HAW	6F	D	Slewville	Rivera, HG	117,700
Lady Luck S.	17-Oct	9	LAD	1M	T	Cash Counter	Hebert, TJ	50,000
Lady Razorback Futurity	16-Oct	4	LAD	6F	D	Half a Storm	Hebert, TJ	40,000
Lady Slipper S.	16-May	8	CBY	6F	D	Swasti	Martinez, SB	40,000
Lady's Secret Breeders' Cup H.-G2	3-Oct	6	SA	1 1/16M	D	Island Fashion	John, K	250,000
Lady's Secret H.	23-May	7	BOI	7F	D	Thrill After Dark	Packer, BR	6,900
Lady's Secret H.	7-Aug	7	FP	1M 70Y	D	Moon Shine Time	Pompell, TL	30,700
Lady's Secret S.	8-Aug	8	MTH	1 1/16M	D	Chrusciki	Elliott, S	100,000
Lady's Secret S.	5-Dec	10	RP	7F	D	Casual Attitude	Doocy, TT	41,300
Lafayette H.	1-Jan	8	GG	1M	D	Gold Ruckus	Radke, K	81,000
Lafayette S.-G3	4-Apr	8	KEE	7F	D	Bwana Charlie	Sellers, SJ	109,500
Lafayette S.	6-Sep	9	EVD	6F	D	My Parade	Rodriguez, FT	75,000
Lake George S.-G3	2-Aug	8	SAR	1 1/16M	T	Seducer's Song	Bailey, JD	113,900
Lake Placid H.-G2	23-Aug	8	SAR	1 1/8M	T	Spotlight (GB)	Bailey, JD	150,000
Lakeway S.	7-Aug	8	RET	7F	D	Wacky Patty	Beasley, J	40,000
Lamplighter S.	28-Aug	9	MTH	1M 70Y	D	Gotaghostofachance	Elliott, S	60,000
Land of Enchantment H.	1-Aug	5	RUI	7 1/2F	D	Ninety Nine Jack	Bourdieu, JM	45,000
Land of Jazz S.	20-Aug	7	FER	7F	D	Red Seattle	Navarro, VG	7,160
Land of Lincoln S.	10-Apr	9	HAW	6F	D	Prairie King	Silva, CH	119,350
Landaluce S.-G3	5-Jul	8	HOL	6F	D	Souvenir Gift	Smith, ME	106,800
Lane's End Breeders' Futurity-G1	9-Oct	7	KEE	1 1/16M	D	Consolidator	Bejarano, R	500,000

Stakes	Date	Race	Trk	Dist/Surf		Winner	Jockey	Gross
Lane's End S.-G2	20-Mar	8	TP	1 1/8M	D	Sinister G	Toscano, PR	500,000
Lansing S.	29-May	8	GLD	6F	D	Rockem Sockem	Houghton, TD	40,000
Larkspur H.	11-Jun	6	GLD	6F	D	Charlies Indian	Mata, F	40,000
Larry R. Riviello President's Cup S.	14-Aug	8	PHA	1M 70Y	D	Separato	Rose, J	100,000
Las Cienegas H.-G3	4-Apr	8	SA	6 1/2F	T	Etoile Montante	Santiago, J	112,800
Las Flores H.-G3	22-Feb	8	SA	6F	D	Ema Bovary (CHI)	Gonzalez, RM	107,300
Las Madrinas H.	24-Sep	11	FPX	1 1/16M	D	Tale of a Dream	Pedroza, MA	100,000
Las Palmas H.-G2	31-Oct	8	SA	1 1/8M	T	Theater R. N.	Douglas, RR	150,000
Las Virgenes S.-G1	15-Feb	8	SA	1M	D	A. P. Adventure	Solis, AO	250,000
Lassie H.	22-Aug	9	HST	6 1/2F	D	Slewpast	Fuentes, FP	44,212
Lassie S.	20-Nov	7	PM	5F	D	Bullishdemands	Barber, S	10,000
Last Chance Derby	31-Dec	8	TUP	1 1/16M	D	Aza	Gann, SL	22,000
Last Dance S.	5-Jul	6	SUF	1 1/16M	D	Jini's Jet	Hampshire, Jr., JF	40,000
Last Don B. S.	6-Feb	8	TUP	6 1/2F	D	Icy Tobin	Guerra, VJ	21,800
Laurel Futurity-G3	20-Nov	5	PIM	1 1/16M	D	Defer	Bailey, JD	100,000
Laurel Lane S.	23-Oct	4	LAD	6F	D	The Beter Man Can	Perrodin, EJ	53,600
Lawrence Realization S.-G3	16-Oct	9	BEL	1 1/2M	T	Gunning For	Bravo, J	110,100
Lazaro Barrera Memorial S.-G2	29-May	8	HOL	7F	D	Twice as Bad	Solis, AO	150,000
Leader of the Band S.	28-Aug	8	DEL	1 1/16M	T	Tam's Terms	Caraballo, JC	54,300
LeComte S.-G3	24-Jan	9	FG	1M	D	Fire Slam	Sellers, SJ	100,000
Left the Latch S.	15-May	3	TUP	6 1/2F	D	Swain's Gold	Kato, A	21,800
Legal Light S.	24-Apr	8	DEL	6F	D	Feline Story	Dominguez, RA	75,600
Lenta S.	30-Apr	5	CRC	1 1/16M	D	Special Report	Aguilar, M	40,000
Leonard Richards S.-G3	18-Jul	9	DEL	1 1/16M	D	Pollard's Vision	Bailey, JD	250,600
Les Mackin H.	21-Jun	8	YAV	1M	D	Real Creek	Hernandez, ML	12,500
Les Mademoiselle S.	21-Aug	8	FER	1 1/16M	D	Scattering	Miranda, V	11,220
Lethbridge Oaks	2-Oct	8	LBG	6F	D	Special Era	Wilson, A	12,200
Lewis and Clark Derby	1-Aug	7	GF	7F	D	Streak a Roani	Cano, Jr., J	7,750
Lexington S.-G3	18-Jul	8	BEL	1 1/4M	T	Mustanfar	Santos, JA	111,100
Liberada H.	15-May	4	CRC	1 1/16M	T	Formal Miss	Toribio, Jr., A	40,000
Liberation H.	1-Jul	7	HST	1 1/16M	D	Regal Red	Fuentes, FP	44,368
Lieutenant Governors' H.-G3	1-Jul	9	HST	1 1/8M	D	Royal Place	Olguin, G	110,582
Light Hearted H.	18-Jul	5	DEL	6F	D	Niclie	Dominguez, RA	100,000
Lighthouse S.	19-Sep	7	MTH	1 1/16M	D	Twist and Pop	Trujillo, E	65,000
Lightning Jet H.	13-Nov	5	HAW	6F	D	Silver Bid	Montalvo, C	110,875
Lil E. Tee S.	4-Sep	5	PHA	1 1/16M	D	Prince Joseph	Black, AS	50,000
Lilac H.	4-Jun	8	STP	1M	D	Shy Lil	Wong, PK	40,000
Lincoln H.	1-Aug	11	RUI	6F	D	Shemoveslikeaghost	Tohill, KS	45,000
Lincoln Heritage H.	26-Jun	6	AP	1 1/16M	T	Lighthouse Lil	Marquez, Jr., CH	85,850
Lincroft H.	20-Jun	8	MTH	1M	D	Trueamericanspirit	Coa, E	60,000
Lindsay Frolic S.	6-Sep	5	CRC	1M	D	Dansetta Light	Lopez, JE	50,000
Lineage S.	12-Jun	9	ALB	1 1/16M	D	Ciento	Noguez, T	45,000
Little Ones S.	28-Aug	4	GLD	6F	D	Per Curiam	Rivera, J	45,000
Little Silver S.	5-Jul	10	MTH	1 1/16M	D	Capeside Lady	DeCarlo, CP	60,000
Little Sister S.	9-Aug	6	CRC	7F	D	Silver Lace	Boulanger, G	45,000
Live the Dream H.	8-Sep	6	DMR	1M	T	Statement	Pedroza, MA	98,950
Local Thriller S.	21-Jun	8	DEL	6F	D	Bronze Abe	Pino, MG	54,300
Locust Grove H.-G3	26-Jun	9	CD	1 1/8M	T	Shaconage	Blanc, B	165,750
London Lil S.	30-Dec	5	CRC	1 1/16M	T	High Speed Access	DeCarlo, CP	45,000
Lone Star Oaks	4-Jul	9	LS	1 1/16M	T	America America	Chapa, R	100,000
Lone Star Park H.-G3	31-May	9	LS	1 1/16M	D	Yessirgeneralsir	Figueroa, O	300,000
Lone Star Park Juvenile Fillies S.	28-Oct	8	LS	6F	D	True Tails	Theriot, J	50,000
Lone Star Park Juvenile S.	30-Oct	11	LS	7F	D	Storm Surge	Albarado, R	100,000
Long Branch Breeders' Cup S.-G3	17-Jul	9	MTH	1 1/16M	D	Lion Heart	Bravo, J	100,000
Long Island H.-G2	6-Nov	8	AQU	1 1/2M	T	Eleusis	Santos, JA	150,000
Longacres Mile H.-G3	22-Aug	7	EMD	1M	D	Adreamisborn	Baze, RA	250,000
Longfellow S.	3-Jul	9	MTH	6F	D	Canadian Frontier	Prado, ES	65,000
Lord Juban S.	5-Jun	8	CRC	1M	D	R. Associate	Castro, E	45,000
Lorelei S.	27-Jun	9	LAD	1 1/16M	D	Yoursmineours	Pettinger, DR	50,000
Los Angeles Times H.-G3	8-May	6	HOL	6F	D	Pohave	Court, JK	150,000
Lost Code Breeders' Cup S.	3-Apr	8	HAW	6F	D	Wildcat Shoes	Coa, E	112,500
Louise Kimball S.	6-Nov	3	SUF	1M 70Y	D	Ask Queenie	Thompson, WA	40,000
Louisiana Breeders' Derby	23-Oct	9	LAD	1 1/16M	D	Nitro Chip	Meche, L	81,700

Stakes	Date	Race	Trk	Dist/Surf		Winner	Jockey	Gross
Louisiana Breeders' Oaks	23-Oct	10	LAD	1 1/16M	D	Happy Ticket	Meche, L	82,600
Louisiana Champions Day Classic S.	11-Dec	9	FG	1 1/8M	D	Witt Ante	Hebert, TJ	150,000
Louisiana Champions Day Juvenile S.	11-Dec	5	FG	6F	D	Crimson Stag	Albarado, R	100,000
Louisiana Champions Day Ladies S.	11-Dec	3	FG	1 1/16M	D	Happy Ticket	Meche, L	100,000
Louisiana Champions Day Lassie S.	11-Dec	7	FG	6F	D	Equestrian Girls	Jacinto, J	100,000
Louisiana Champions Day Sprint S.	11-Dec	6	FG	6F	D	Archeval	Meche, DJ	100,000
Louisiana Champions Day Starter H.	11-Dec	4	FG	1 1/16M	D	Setemup Joe	Meche, L	50,000
Louisiana Champions Day Turf S.	11-Dec	8	FG	1 1/16M	T	Mr. Sulu	Albarado, R	100,000
Louisiana Derby-G2	7-Mar	9	FG	1 1/16M	D	Wimbledon	Santiago, J	600,000
Louisiana Futurity	26-Dec	5	FG	6F	D	The Beter Man Can	Perrodin, EJ	85,230
Louisiana Futurity	26-Dec	7	FG	6F	D	Witness to a Fight	Melancon, L	86,430
Louisiana H.	2-Jan	9	FG	1 1/16M	D	Spanish Empire	Martin, Jr., EM	60,000
Louisiana H.	31-Dec	9	FG	1 1/16M	D	Gigawatt	Hernandez, Jr., BJ	60,000
Louisiana Premier Night Bon Temps Starter S.	7-Feb	1	DED	5F	D	Auntie's Bag	Fusilier, C	50,000
Louisiana Premier Night Championship S.	7-Feb	8	DED	1 1/16M	D	Spritely Walker	Sellers, SJ	200,000
Louisiana Premier Night Distaff S.	7-Feb	7	DED	1M	D	Destiny Calls	Sellers, SJ	150,000
Louisiana Premier Night Gentlemen Starter S.	7-Feb	2	DED	1 1/16M	D	Master Jon	Melancon, G	50,000
Louisiana Premier Night Ladies Starter S.	7-Feb	10	DED	1M	D	Witch Revival	Bourque, SJ	50,000
Louisiana Premier Night Matron S.	7-Feb	9	DED	5F	D	Leslie's Love	Melancon, G	100,000
Louisiana Premier Night Prince S.	7-Feb	6	DED	7F	D	Old Lee	Perrodin, EJ	125,000
Louisiana Premier Night Ragin Cajun Starter S.	7-Feb	3	DED	5F	D	Spirit of Malagra	James, MC	50,000
Louisiana Premier Night Sprint S.	7-Feb	4	DED	5F	D	Zarb's Luck	Sellers, SJ	100,000
Louisiana Premier Night Starlet S.	7-Feb	5	DED	7F	D	Placid Star	Melancon, G	125,000
Louisville Breeders' Cup H.-G2	30-Apr	8	CD	1 1/16M	D	Lead Story	Borel, CH	327,000
Louisville H.-G3	31-May	9	CD	1 3/8M	T	Silverfoot	Albarado, R	112,400
Loyalty S.	5-Sep	7	TDN	6F	D	Fierce Cat	Spieth, S	40,000
Luther Burbank H.	1-Aug	11	SR	1 1/16M	D	Marwood	Warren, Jr., RJ	53,810
Lyman Sprint Championship H.	5-Jun	10	PHA	7F	D	Docent	Black, AS	54,700
Lyrique H.	4-Sep	10	LAD	1 1/16M	T	Outright Buck	Melancon, G	50,000
M. R. Jenkins Memorial H.	9-May	7	STP	6F	D	A Shaky Start	Painter, LM	40,000
M. Tyson Gilpin S.	30-Oct	6	DEL	6F	D	Smokin Forest	Castillo, Jr., H	50,300
M2 Technology La Senorita S.	4-Sep	6	RET	1M	T	Malika's Gold	Lambert, CT	100,000
Mac Diarmida H.-G3	25-Jan	10	GP	1 3/8M	T	Request for Parole	Santos, JA	100,000
Mac Diarmida S.	27-Jun	7	BEL	1 1/8M	T	Second Performance	Velazquez, JR	61,800
Mack Hall Starter H.	16-Oct	5	TUP	6 1/2F	D	Fleeting Alliance	Stevens, SA	20,000
Mackinac H.	18-Sep	6	GLD	1 1/16M	D	Do the Impossible	Houghton, TD	50,000
Madamoiselle H.	13-Aug	8	NP	1 1/16M	D	Sweet Monarch	Walcott, R	40,000
Mademoiselle H.	24-Jul	7	MD	1M	D	Picture the Answer	Rocheleau, SR	5,000
Mademoiselle S.	26-Mar	7	DED	5F	D	Light Fling	Bourque, SJ	40,000
Magali Farms S.	24-Apr	2	HOL	6 1/2F	D	Alphabet Kisses	Ruis, M	60,000
Magic City Classic S.	12-Jun	11	RD	6F	D	Chief Tudor	Rechy, R	55,000
Magnolia State H.	28-Mar	1	FG	6F	D	Monster Move	Albarado, R	31,000
Magnolia S.	12-Nov	9	DED	7F	D	Happy Ticket	Meche, L	75,000
Maid of the Mist S.	23-Oct	5	BEL	1M	D	Pelham Bay	Bridgmohan, S	100,000
Majestic Prince S.	11-Sep	9	MTH	1 1/16M	T	Victory Alleged	DeCarlo, CP	60,000
Majorette H.	30-Oct	10	LAD	5F	T	Our Love	Jacinto, J	40,000
Maker's Mark Mile S.-G2	9-Apr	9	KEE	1M	T	Perfect Soul (IRE)	Prado, ES	200,000
Malcolm Anderson S.	13-Jun	8	BM	4 1/2F	D	Whatsthenameman	Sorenson, D	72,750
Malibu S.-G1	26-Dec	8	SA	7F	D	Rock Hard Ten	Stevens, GL	250,000
Mamie Eisenhower S.	8-May	8	PRM	6F	D	Only At Night	Essman, DW	60,000
Mamzelle S.	29-Apr	8	CD	5F	T	Nicole's Dream	Albarado, R	117,700
Man o' War S.-G1	11-Sep	9	BEL	1 3/8M	T	Magistretti	Prado, ES	500,000
Manatee S.	31-Jan	10	TAM	7F	D	Mary Murphy	Rodriguez, PA	60,000
Manhattan Beach S.	30-May	8	HOL	5 1/2F	T	Winendynme	Valdivia, Jr., J	99,750
Manhattan H.-G1	5-Jun	10	BEL	1 1/4M	T	Meteor Storm (GB)	Valdivia, Jr., J	400,000
Manhattan H.	25-Sep	9	WDS	6F	D	Discreetly Irish	Birzer, A	25,000
Manilla S.	4-Nov	8	AQU	1M	D	Infinite Glory	Prado, ES	60,850
Manitoba Lotteries Derby S.	2-Aug	8	ASD	1 1/8M	D	Royalty Boy	Simard, RE	100,000
Manitoba Maturity	10-Jul	6	ASD	1 1/16M	D	Fancy Bru	Hightower, TW	41,000
Manitoba S.	26-Jun	7	ASD	1M	D	Coal Smudge	Leacock, J	40,000
Manor Downs Thoroughbred Futurity	25-Apr	10	MAN	4 1/2F	D	Summer Claim	White, JB	10,000
Manor Downs Thoroughbred Futurity	25-Apr	11	MAN	4 1/2F	D	Kate's Storm	White, JB	10,000
Maple Leaf S.-G3	13-Nov	6	WO	1 1/4M	D	One for Rose	Ramsammy, E	235,850

Stakes	Date	Race	Trk	Dist/Surf		Winner	Jockey	Gross
Marathon Series 2nd Leg S.	31-Oct	11	LBG	1 1/8M	D	Candid Remark	Blinston, RD	11,200
Marathon Series Final S.	29-Feb	7	TUP	1 5/8M	D	Swelter	Stevens, SA	24,900
Marathon Series First Leg S.	2-Oct	10	LBG	1 1/16M	D	Silver Sky	Miyashiro, CJ	11,200
March Madness Starter H.	27-Mar	7	SA	1M	T	La Sorpresa (ARG)	Pedroza, MA	51,850
Mardi Gras H.	24-Feb	9	FG	1M	D	Majestic Thief	Sellers, SJ	50,000
Marfa S.	25-Sep	13	TP	6 1/2F	D	Private Horde	Mojica, O	75,000
Margarita Breeder's Cup H.	24-Jul	8	RET	1 1/16M	T	Cherylville Slew	Stanton, TA	50,000
Mariah's Storm S.	13-Aug	8	AP	1 1/8M	D	Tamweel	Douglas, RR	52,400
Marie G. Krantz Memorial H.	13-Mar	9	FG	6F	D	Put Me In	Martin, Jr., EM	75,000
Marie P. DeBartolo Oaks Breeders' Cup H.	25-Sep	6	LAD	1 1/16M	T	Merry Me in Spring	Desormeaux, KJ	100,000
Marine S.-G3	22-May	8	WO	1 1/16M	D	Judiths Wild Rush	Luciani, D	164,100
Marluel's Troy S.	24-Aug	4	FP	6F	D	Rebel Army	Silva, CH	35,800
Marshland S.	30-Oct	8	DED	1M	D	High Strike Zone	Faul, RJ	50,000
Marshua S.	3-Jan	8	LRL	6F	D	Among My Souvenirs	Pino, MG	60,000
Marshua's River S.	13-Mar	11	GP	1M	T	Dedication (FR)	Prado, ES	67,350
Martanza S.	20-Nov	6	HOU	1M	D	Native Annie	Marquez, Jr., CH	75,000
Martha Washington Breeders' Cup S.-G3	25-Sep	9	PIM	1 1/16M	T	Western Ransom	Fogelsonger, R	150,000
Martha Washington S.	16-Feb	10	OP	1M	D	Turn to Lass	Chapa, R	50,000
Mary Goldblatt S.	6-Mar	8	PM	1M	D	So Happy Together	Gutierrez, JM	10,000
Maryland Breeders' Cup H.-G3	15-May	11	PIM	6F	D	Gators N Bears	Lopez, CC	200,000
Maryland Juvenile Championship S.	31-Dec	8	PIM	1 1/16M	D	Legal Control	Santana, JZ	100,000
Maryland Juvenile Filly Championship S.	30-Dec	8	PIM	1 1/16M	D	Dixie Talking	Castellano, Jr., A	100,000
Maryland Million Classic S.	9-Oct	11	PIM	1 3/16M	D	Presidentialaffair	Elliott, S	200,000
Maryland Million Distaff Sprint H.	9-Oct	8	PIM	6F	D	Merryland Missy	Elliott, S	100,000
Maryland Million Distaff Starter H.	9-Oct	2	PIM	1 1/16M	D	Hunca Munca	Diaz, V	50,000
Maryland Million Ladies S.	9-Oct	10	PIM	1 1/8M	T	Hail Hillary	Pino, MG	100,000
Maryland Million Lassie S.	9-Oct	5	PIM	6F	D	Hear Us Roar	Garcia, L	100,000
Maryland Million Nursery S.	9-Oct	7	PIM	6F	D	What's Up Lonely	Fogelsonger, R	100,000
Maryland Million Oaks	9-Oct	3	PIM	1 1/16M	D	Silmaril	Castellano, Jr., A	100,000
Maryland Million Sprint H.	9-Oct	9	PIM	6F	D	My Poker Player	Fogelsonger, R	100,000
Maryland Million Sprint Starter H.	9-Oct	1	PIM	6F	D	Drum Roll Please	Monterrey, R	25,000
Maryland Million Starter H.	9-Oct	12	PIM	1 1/8M	D	Dixie Colony	Elliott, S	50,000
Maryland Million Turf S.	9-Oct	4	PIM	1 1/8M	T	Dr Detroit	Pino, MG	100,000
Maryland Million Turf Sprint H.	9-Oct	6	PIM	5F	T	Namequest	Turner, TG	100,000
Maryland Racing Media H.	21-Feb	8	LRL	1 1/8M	D	Undercover	Pino, MG	75,000
Massachusetts H.-G2	19-Jun	10	SUF	1 1/8M	D	Offlee Wild	Prado, ES	500,000
Matchmaker H.	19-Jun	8	LNN	1M	D	Irish Flyer	Williams, RD	15,700
Matchmaker S.-G3	8-Aug	9	MTH	1 1/8M	T	Where We Left Off (GB)	Nakatani, CS	100,000
Matriarch S.-G1	28-Nov	7	HOL	1M	T	Intercontinental (GB)	Bailey, JD	500,000
Matron Breeders' Cup S.	2-Oct	7	ASD	1 1/8M	D	Remiewaterbluz	Leacock, P	65,000
Matron H.	4-Sep	9	EVD	1M	D	Due to Win	Torres, FC	50,000
Matron S.-G1	19-Sep	8	BEL	1M	D	Sense of Style	Prado, ES	300,000
Matt Winn S.	8-May	9	CD	6F	D	Fire Slam	Day, P	106,700
Maxine M. Piggott S.	24-Apr	2	TUP	6 1/2F	D	Miss Noteworthy	Hernandez, ML	40,000
Maxxam Gold Cup H.	17-Jan	7	HOU	1 1/8M	D	Sir Cherokee	Thompson, TJ	100,000
Mazarine Breeders' Cup S.-G2	3-Oct	9	WO	1 1/16M	D	Higher World	Husbands, P	278,750
McFadden Memorial S.	21-Feb	9	PM	1 1/16M	D	Northern Baquero	Peery, M	10,000
Meadowlands Breeders' Cup S.-G2	8-Oct	7	MED	1 1/8M	D	Balto Star	Velazquez, JR	500,000
Meafara S.	3-Apr	4	HAW	6F	D	Prevalent	Bejarano, R	42,800
Mecke H.	4-Jul	6	CRC	1 1/8M	T	Unbridels King	Castro, E	100,000
Melair S.	24-Apr	3	HOL	1 1/16M	D	Yearly Report	Nakatani, CS	200,000
Mel's Hope S.	28-Nov	9	CRC	1 1/16M	D	Super Frolic	Castro, E	45,000
Memorial Day H.-G3	31-May	10	CRC	1 1/16M	D	Twilight Road	Teator, P	100,000
Merrillville S.	23-Oct	9	HOO	6F	D	Senorita Ziggy	Herrell, JC	40,000
Merry Time S.	19-Jun	11	TDN	1 1/16M	D	Golden Tour	Meyers, T	45,000
Mervin H. Muniz Jr. Memorial H.-G2	21-Mar	8	FG	1 1/8M	T	Mystery Giver	Albarado, R	500,000
Mervyn LeRoy H.-G2	8-May	9	HOL	1 1/16M	D	Even the Score	Flores, DR	150,000
Mesa H.	18-Dec	4	TUP	6 1/2F	D	Muir Beach	Dieguez, WO	40,000
Metropolitan H.-G1	31-May	9	BEL	1M	D	Pico Central (BRZ)	Solis, AO	750,000
Miami Mile Breeders' Cup H.-G3	11-Sep	7	CRC	1M	T	Twilight Road	Teator, P	150,000
Mia's Hope S.	2-Aug	5	CRC	1 1/16M	D	Adobe Gold	Castro, E	45,000
Michael G. Schaefer Mile S.	13-Nov	3	HOO	1M	D	Added Edge	Zimmerman, R	103,100
Michigan Breeders' H.	17-Jul	7	GLD	1 1/16M	D	Rockem Sockem	Doser, ME	40,000

Stakes	Date	Race	Trk	Dist/Surf		Winner	Jockey	Gross
Michigan Futurity	26-Oct	3	GLD	7F	D	Its His Time	Mata, F	82,500
Michigan Juvenile Fillies S.	25-Oct	3	GLD	7F	D	Musical Factor	Houghton, TD	79,450
Michigan Oaks	17-Sep	8	GLD	1 1/16M	D	Cats Copy	Perez, RA	50,000
Michigan Sire S.	9-Oct	3	GLD	6F	D	Foolininthemeadow	Doser, ME	136,462
Michigan Sire S.	9-Oct	4	GLD	6F	D	Demagoguery	Houghton, TD	137,262
Michigan Slre S.	9 Oct	5	GLD	1 1/16M	D	Circus Du Joy	Doser, ME	136,662
Michigan Sire S.	9-Oct	6	GLD	1 1/16M	D	Exclusivenjoyment	Doser, ME	136,462
Michigan Sire S.	9-Oct	7	GLD	1 1/8M	D	Dancin for Gold	Doser, ME	132,462
Michigan Sire S.	9-Oct	8	GLD	1 1/8M	D	Timely Factor	Martinez, LJ	136,262
Middleground Breeders' Cup S.	3-Oct	7	LS	1M	D	Leaving On My Mind	Chapa, R	100,000
Miesque S.-G3	26-Nov	6	HOL	1M	T	Paddy's Daisy	Nakatani, CS	75,000
Miesque S.-G3	26-Nov	3	HOL	1M	T	Louvain (IRE)	Dominguez, RA	75,000
Mike Lee S.	26-Jun	10	BEL	7F	D	Multiplication	Prado, ES	113,900
Mike Rowland Memorial H.	8-May	8	TDN	6F	D	Hank's Rib	Ouzts, PW	40,000
Milady Breeders' Cup H.-G1	11-Jul	8	HOL	1 1/16M	D	Star Parade (ARG)	Espinoza, V	259,450
Mile Hi H.	31-Aug	5	YAV	1 1/16M	D	Royal Groove	Bridges, K	17,500
Millard Harrell Memorial S.	11-Sep	7	CT	7F	D	Sheckatoo	Dunkelberger, TL	41,250
Millarville Derby	1-Jul	5	MIL	1 1/8M	D	Diamond Passer	McAleney, P	5,500
Miller Genuine Draft Cradle S.-G3	6-Sep	13	RD	1 1/16M	D	Bellamy Road	Castellano, Jr., A	205,000
Miller Lite S.	26-Jun	8	LS	5F	D	Fleeta Dif	Helton, RM	50,000
Milwaukee Avenue H.	10-Apr	7	HAW	1 1/16M	D	Scooter Roach	Campbell, JM	111,400
Minaret S.	3-Jan	10	TAM	6F	D	Sea Span	Castanon, JL	60,000
Minnesota Classic Championship S.	22-Aug	10	CBY	1 1/16M	D	Wally's Choice	Escobar, M	40,000
Minnesota Derby	31-Jul	9	CBY	1M 70Y	D	Wally's Choice	Escobar, M	62,100
Minnesota Distaff Classic Championship S.	22-Aug	8	CBY	1 1/16M	D	A. Caterina	Diego, IV	40,000
Minnesota Distaff Sprint Championship S.	22-Aug	6	CBY	6F	D	Swasti	Martinez, SB	40,000
Minnesota H. B. P. A. Mile S.	5-Jul	8	CBY	1M	T	Sound of Gold	Compton, P	40,000
Minnesota H. B. P. A. Sprint S.	5-Jul	4	CBY	6F	D	Silver Zipper	Martinez, SB	40,000
Minnesota Oaks	31-Jul	8	CBY	1M 70Y	D	Nilini	Martinez, SB	62,250
Minnesota Sprint Championship S.	22-Aug	3	CBY	6F	D	Crocrock	Schacht, R	40,000
Minnesota Turf Championship S.	22-Aug	9	CBY	1M	T	Now Playing	Rivera, JG	40,000
Mint S.	27-Dec	10	CRC	5 1/2F	D	All Hail Stormy	Coa, E	40,000
Miracle Wood S.	28-Feb	8	LRL	1 1/16M	D	Water Cannon	Dominguez, RA	40,000
Miss America H.	10-Apr	7	BM	1 1/16M	T	Hippogator	Gonzalez, RM	83,775
Miss California S.	17-Jan	3	GG	6F	D	Heavenly Humor	Radke, K	78,600
Miss Gibson County S.	10-Dec	3	TUP	5 1/2F	D	Lady Bertrando	Campbell, J	21,700
Miss Grillo S.	24-Oct	7	BEL	1 1/8M	T	Melhor Ainda	Santos, JA	82,200
Miss Indiana S.	6-Nov	12	HOO	6F	D	Free Bonus	LeJeune, Jr., SP	40,000
Miss Indy Anna S.	1-May	8	SUF	6F	D	Quick Smoke	Hampshire, Jr., JF	40,000
Miss Kansas City H.	10-Oct	9	WDS	1 1/16M	D	Wildwood Royal	Sukie, D	25,000
Miss Liberty S.	15-Oct	6	MED	1M 70Y	D	Schedule (GB)	Bravo, J	60,000
Miss Medallion S.	27-Aug	9	CRC	1 1/16M	D	Adobe Gold	Castro, E	45,000
Miss Ohio S.	28-Aug	6	TDN	6F	D	Noon Win	Villa-Gomez, H	40,000
Miss Woodford S.	22-Aug	8	MTH	6F	D	Then She Laughs	Elliott, S	60,000
Mississippi Futurity	4-Dec	2	FG	6F	D	Heart to Heart	Albarado, R	27,100
Missy Good S.	9-Jul	6	PEN	6F	D	Flame of Love	Santagata, N	41,050
Mister Diz S.	7-Aug	9	PIM	5F	T	Yankee Wildcat	Jurado, EM	75,000
Mister Gus S.	31-May	8	AP	1M	D	Intern	Meier, RA	42,375
Mo Bay S.	3-Jul	8	DEL	6F	D	Don Six	Caraballo, JC	52,600
Moccasin S.	21-Nov	8	HOL	7F	D	No Bull Baby	Baze, T	100,000
Mocha Express S.	23-Oct	7	LS	6 1/2F	D	Leaving On My Mind	Chapa, R	50,000
Mockingbird S.	24-Apr	4	GP	3F	D	Shocking Dunn	Homeister, Jr., RB	42,375
Modesty H.-G3	24-Jul	9	AP	1 3/16M	T	Bedanken	Pettinger, DR	150,000
Mohawk H.	23-Oct	7	BEL	1 1/8M	T	Irish Colonial	Velazquez, JR	150,000
Molly Brown H.	25-Jul	7	ARP	6F	D	She's Finding Time	Juarez, Jr., AJ	27,625
Molly Pitcher Breeders' Cup H.-G2	4-Jul	10	MTH	1 1/8M	D	La Reason	Lopez, CC	300,000
Mongo Queen S.	12-Sep	8	MTH	1M 70Y	D	Sis City	Coa, E	60,000
Monmouth Beach S.	13-Jun	9	MTH	1 1/16M	D	Pocus Hocus	Coa, E	70,000
Monmouth Breeders' Cup Oaks-G2	15-Aug	10	MTH	1 1/16M	D	Capeside Lady	DeCarlo, CP	200,000
Monrovia H.	31-Dec	7	SA	6 1/2F	D	Resplendency	Fusilier, C	113,550
Montauk H.	28-Nov	8	AQU	1 1/8M	D	Board Elligible	Fragoso, P	83,275
Montclair State University S.	13-Nov	8	MED	6F	D	Cologny	Gryder, AT	60,000
Moonbeam H.	16-Jul	6	GLD	1M	D	Clever Moon	Perez, RA	40,000

Stakes	Date	Race	Trk	Dist/Surf		Winner	Jockey	Gross
Moonsplash S.	12-Dec	8	TUP	4 1/2F	T	Western Ridge	Barton, J	21,800
Morvich H.-G3	30-Oct	6	SA	6 1/2F	T	Leroidesanimaux (BRZ)	Court, JK	100,000
Mother Goose S.-G1	26-Jun	9	BEL	1 1/8M	D	Stellar Jayne	Albarado, R	300,000
Mount Elbert H.	14-Aug	8	ARP	1 1/16M	D	Run At Night	Johnson, BL	26,575
Mount Royal H.	16-May	7	STP	6F	D	Ericka's Lass	Iammarino, MP	40,000
Mount Vernon H.	20-Jun	6	BEL	1 1/8M	T	Big Tease	Migliore, R	83,700
Mount Vernon H.	20-Jun	8	BEL	1 1/8M	T	Brandala	Espinoza, JL	84,600
Mountain State H.	4-Jul	9	MNR	6F	D	Crossing Point	Murphy, CK	75,000
Mountain Valley S.	24-Jan	9	OP	6F	D	Pro Prado	McKee, J	50,000
Mountaineer Mile H.	13-Nov	9	MNR	1M	D	Discreet Hero	Murphy, CK	100,000
Mr. Prospector H.-G3	3-Jan	10	GP	6F	D	Cajun Beat	Velasquez, CH	100,000
Mrs. Penny S.	4-Sep	9	PHA	1 1/16M	T	Caught in the Rain	Molina, VH	50,000
Mrs. Revere S.-G2	13-Nov	9	CD	1 1/16M	T	River Belle (GB)	Fallon, K	171,150
Ms. S.	7-Feb	8	PM	6F	D	Quiz the Maid	Gutierrez, JM	10,000
Ms. Southern Ohio S.	8-Aug	11	RD	1 1/16M	D	Oh So Easy	Feliciano, R	40,000
Mt. Rainier Breeders' Cup H.	25-Jul	8	EMD	1 1/8M	D	Poker Brad	Frazier, R	100,000
Mt. Sassafras S.	13-Nov	4	WO	7F	D	Wando	Husbands, P	103,000
Mt. St. Helens S.	27-Mar	8	PM	1M	D	Quiz the Maid	Gutierrez, JM	10,000
MTA Stallion Auction Laddie S.	6-Sep	6	CBY	6 1/2F	D	Vasant	Stevens, SA	43,909
MTA Stallion Auction Lassie S.	6-Sep	8	CBY	6 1/2F	D	Nishani	Toro, M	45,160
Muckleshoot Tribal Classic S.	19-Sep	10	EMD	1 1/16M	D	Demon Warlock	Lopez, AD	50,000
Muscogee (Creek) Nation S.	24-Jul	9	FMT	6 1/2F	D	Goldleafed Mirror	Carter, Jr., GR	43,400
Muskoka S.	5-Sep	8	WO	7F	D	Simply Lovely	Bahen, SR	136,000
My Charmer H.-G3	4-Dec	8	CRC	1 1/8M	T	Something Ventured	Velazquez, JR	100,000
My Charmer S.	11-Dec	10	TP	1 1/16M	D	Two Mile Hill	Lopez, J	50,000
My Dear S.	4-Jul	8	WO	5F	D	Quite a Ruckus	McKnight, J	187,625
My Fair Lady S.	12-Jun	10	SUF	1M 70Y	T	Where We Left Off (GB)	Hampshire, Jr., JF	40,000
My Frenchman S.	8-Oct	4	MED	5F	T	Manofglory	Coa, E	60,000
My Frenchman S.	8-Oct	10	MED	5F	T	Worldwind Romance	Fogelsonger, R	60,000
My Juliet S.	26-Jun	9	PHA	6F	D	Ebony Breeze	Castillo, Jr., H	100,000
My Melanie S.	10-Dec	9	CRC	1 1/16M	D	Redoubled Miss	Coa, E	40,000
Mystery Jet S.	31-Jul	3	SUF	6F	D	D D Ruby	Jellison, JA	40,000
Naked Greed S.	18-Jun	8	CRC	5F	T	Gin Rummy Champ	Toribio, Jr., A	40,000
Nanaimo H.	18-Jul	4	HST	1 1/16M	D	Socorro County	Skelly, RV	44,472
Nancy's Glitter H.	17-Jul	9	CRC	1 1/16M	D	Secret Request	Toribio, A	75,000
Nandi S.	8-Aug	6	WO	6F	D	Bosskiri	McAleney, J	131,750
Nashua S.-G3	2-Nov	8	AQU	1M	D	Rockport Harbor	Elliott, S	109,500
Nassau County Breeders' Cup S.-G2	8-May	8	BEL	7F	D	Bending Strings	Bailey, JD	200,000
Nassau S.-G3	5-Jun	8	WO	1 1/16M	T	Inish Glora	Kabel, T	322,250
Natalma S.-G3	12-Sep	8	WO	1M	T	Fearless Flyer (IRE)	Ramsammy, E	227,300
NATC Dash S.	24-Jan	3	SA	6F	D	Saint Afleet	Desormeaux, KJ	250,000
NATC Futurity	4-Sep	8	DEL	6F	D	Closing Argument	Castillo, Jr., H	201,640
NATC Sorority Futurity	4-Sep	7	DEL	6F	D	Swither	Gryder, AT	200,000
National Jockey Club H.-G3	17-Apr	8	HAW	1 1/8M	D	Ten Most Wanted	Flores, DR	250,000
Nat'l Museum of Racing Hall of Fame H.-G2	9-Aug	8	SAR	1 1/8M	T	Artie Schiller	Migliore, R	150,000
Native Dancer S.	27-Jun	8	AP	1M	D	Avid Skier	Lester, RN	41,500
Native Diver H.-G3	11-Dec	7	HOL	1 1/8M	D	Truly a Judge	Pedroza, MA	100,000
Navajo Princess S.	1-Oct	6	MED	1 1/16M	T	Delta Princess	Castillo, Jr., H	60,000
Nearctic H.-G2	24-Oct	3	WO	6F	T	I Thee Wed	McAleney, J	282,750
Nebraska Derby	8-May	9	FON	1M	D	Okie Style	Williams, RD	27,500
Needles S.	28-Aug	7	CRC	1 1/16M	T	Soverign Honor	Aguilar, M	75,000
Nellie Morse S.	31-Jan	9	LRL	1 1/16M	D	City Fire	Castellano, Jr., A	50,000
NetJets Breeders' Cup Mile-G1	30-Oct	4	LS	1M	T	Singletary	Flores, DR	1,680,000
Never Miss T.V. S.	10-Aug	5	YAV	4 1/2F	D	Flarions Flame	Nuttall, TJ	10,000
New Braunfels S.	28-Aug	8	RET	6F	D	Angelica Slew	Lambert, CT	40,000
New Jersey Futurity	5-Nov	7	MED	6F	D	Punch the Odds	Pimentel, J	66,067
New Jersey Futurity	5-Nov	9	MED	6F	D	I'mtoogoodtobetrue	Vega, H	76,481
New Mexico Breeders' Association H.	16-Aug	9	SRP	1M	D	Ciento	Noguez, T	67,600
New Mexico Breeder's Derby	28-Mar	7	SUN	1M	D	Jonnygetachex	Nakatani, CS	102,950
New Mexico Breeders' Distaff H.	21-Aug	9	SRP	6 1/2F	D	Scarzane	Bourdieu, JM	67,500
New Mexico Racing Commission H.	13-Nov	10	SUN	6F	D	Shemoveslikeaghost	Tohill, KS	130,400
New Mexico State Fair H.	26-Sep	8	ALB	1 1/8M	D	Latenite Trick	Montano, M	35,000
New Mexico State Fair T'bred Breeders' Derby	25-Sep	5	ALB	1 1/16M	D	Jonnygetachex	Madeira, CD	46,773

Stakes	Date	Race	Trk	Dist/Surf		Winner	Jockey	Gross
New Mexico State University H.	25-Jan	10	SUN	1M	D	Ciento	Gonzalez, Jr., S	131,806
New Orleans H.-G2	29-Feb	9	FG	1 1/8M	D	Peace Rules	Bailey, JD	500,000
New Providence S.	15-May	8	WO	6F	D	Barbeau Ruckus	Ramsammy, E	134,750
New Westminster H.	22-Aug	6	HST	6 1/2F	D	Alabama Rain	Valdez, F	44,472
New Year's Eve S.	28-Dec	9	MNR	6F	D	Wallop	Goodwin, NG	75,000
New York Breeders' Futurity	6-Sep	9	FL	6F	D	Caribbean Cruiser	Yang, CC	217,359
New York Derby	17-Jul	8	FL	1 1/16M	D	Don Corleone	Frates, DJ	164,000
New York H.-G2	5-Jul	9	BEL	1 1/4M	T	Wonder Again	Prado, ES	250,000
New York Oaks	6-Sep	7	FL	1 1/16M	D	So Sweet a Cat	Grabowski, JA	75,000
New York Stallion Cormorant S.	7-Nov	6	AQU	1M	T	Pa Pa Da	Espinoza, JL	100,000
New York Stallion Fifth Avenue S.	7-Nov	5	AQU	6F	D	Karakorum Splendor	Fragoso, P	125,000
New York Stallion Great White Way S.	7-Nov	7	AQU	6F	D	Accurate	Arroyo, Jr., N	125,000
New York Stallion Park Avenue S.	25-Apr	7	AQU	1M	D	Ihaveadate	Bridgmohan, S	150,000
New York Stallion Perfect Arc S.	7-Nov	8	AQU	1M	T	Kevin's Decision	Prado, ES	100,000
New York Stallion S.	4-Aug	8	SAR	1 1/8M	D	Chowder's First	Prado, ES	250,000
New York Stallion Statue of Liberty S.	5-Aug	8	SAR	1 1/8M	D	So Sweet a Cat	Velazquez, JR	250,000
New York Stallion Times Square S.	25-Apr	8	AQU	1M	D	West Virginia	Velazquez, JR	150,000
Next Move H.-G3	14-Mar	8	AQU	1 1/8M	D	Smok'n Frolic	Migliore, R	108,400
NEXTEL Filly and Mare Sprint S.	24-Jan	4	SA	6F	D	Mooji Moo	Nakatani, CS	300,000
Niagara Breeders' Cup H.-G2	6-Sep	8	WO	1 1/2M	T	Strut the Stage	Kabel, T	324,000
Niagara Falls S.	27-Jun	8	FE	6F	D	Lucky Tec	Ramirez, MR	60,000
Niagara S.	4-Jul	8	FL	6F	D	Camp On Wood	Buckley, PR	50,000
Nick Shuk Memorial S.	6-Jun	8	DEL	1 1/16M	D	Coined for Success	Arroyo, Jr., N	75,300
Nicole S.	8-May	8	HAW	1 1/16M	T	Blue Sky Baby	Razo, Jr., E	43,800
Nijana S.	11-Feb	8	AQU	1 1/16M	D	Exclusively Wild	Castellano, J	60,950
Noble Damsel H.-G3	25-Sep	9	BEL	1M	T	Ocean Drive	Velazquez, JR	150,000
Norfolk S.-G2	3-Oct	7	SA	1 1/16M	D	Roman Ruler	Nakatani, CS	200,000
Norgor Derby	14-Aug	9	RUI	6F	D	Jo Dee Who	Madeira, CD	25,000
Norman Hall S.	27-Nov	5	SUF	6F	D	Reprized Strike	Thompson, WA	40,000
North Dakota Bred Thoroughbred Derby	5-Sep	8	FAR	1M	D	Dakota Dixie	Fiegen, CR	25,000
North Dakota Derby	4-Jul	8	ASD	1M	D	Strike an Image	Leacock, J	20,000
North Dakota First Lady's Cup S.	6-Sep	5	FAR	7F	D	My Statue	Von Rosen, A	12,400
North Dakota Futurity	5-Sep	8	ASD	6F	D	Northrnimprovement	Butler, BS	25,000
North Dakota Open Thoroughbred S.	6-Sep	9	FAR	1M	D	Little Abner	Sharp, J	8,200
North Dakota Stallion S.	30-Jul	6	ASD	1 1/16M	D	Strike an Image	Leacock, J	20,000
North Dakota Stallion S.	22-Aug	7	ASD	6F	D	Doddles	Hightower, TW	30,000
North Randall S.	7-Aug	11	TDN	6F	D	Cayenne Red	Gonzalez, LA	40,000
Northampton S.	5-Sep	6	NMP	6 1/2F	D	Abit Eratic	Perdomo, TA	15,000
Northbound Pride S.	19-Jun	7	CBY	1 1/16M	T	Ghostly Gate	Martinez, SB	40,000
Northern Dancer S.-G3	12-Jun	6	CD	1 1/16M	D	Suave	Bejarano, R	232,400
Northern Dancer S.	27-Nov	8	PIM	1 1/8M	D	Play Bingo	Caraballo, JC	100,000
Northern Lights Debutante S.	22-Aug	7	CBY	6F	D	Wa Wa Windy	Ziegler, MG	56,800
Northern Lights Futurity	22-Aug	4	CBY	6F	D	Careless Navigator	Campbell, J	55,300
Northern Spur Breeders' Cup S.	10-Apr	5	OP	1M	D	Two Down Automatic	Doocy, TT	75,000
Northlands Oaks	25-Jul	8	NP	1M	D	Shy Lil	Wong, PK	40,000
Northwest Stallion Knights Choice S.	1-Aug	9	EMD	6 1/2F	D	Queenledo	Krigger, K	50,000
Northwest Stallion Strong Ruler S.	7-Aug	9	EMD	6 1/2F	D	Indian Weaver	Frazier, R	40,000
Numbered Account S.	31-Mar	8	AQU	1 1/8M	D	Our Tune	Cotto, Jr., PL	60,700
Nursery S.	16-May	8	HOL	5F	D	Double D Appeal	Espinoza, V	101,850
NWMF H.	22-Aug	8	KSP	7F	D	E Mail Trail	Kingrey, RD	2,700
Oak Leaf S.-G2	2-Oct	9	SA	1 1/16M	D	Sweet Catomine	Nakatani, CS	200,000
Oak Tree Breeders' Cup Mile S.-G2	9-Oct	9	SA	1M	T	Musical Chimes	Desormeaux, KJ	250,000
Oak Tree Derby-G2	17-Oct	8	SA	1 1/8M	T	Greek Sun	Prado, ES	150,000
Oakland H.	11-Dec	8	GG	6F	D	Green Team	Gonzalez, RM	65,000
Oaklawn Breeders' Cup S.-G3	13-Mar	10	OP	1 1/16M	D	Golden Sonata	Marquez, Jr., CH	200,000
Oaklawn H.-G2	3-Apr	11	OP	1 1/8M	D	Peace Rules	Bailey, JD	500,000
Oakley S.	20-Jun	9	CNL	1 1/16M	T	Cobbley's Jewel	Hamilton, SD	50,000
Oaks Preview H.	5-Sep	4	HST	1 1/16M	D	Socorro County	Skelly, RV	44,368
Obeah H.	19-Jun	7	DEL	1 1/8M	D	Misty Sixes	Pino, MG	100,300
OBS Championship S.	15-Mar	5	OTC	1 1/16M	D	Tingwithasting	Lovato, Jr., F	100,000
OBS Championship S.	15-Mar	6	OTC	1 1/16M	D	Humorously	Velasquez, CH	100,000
OBS Sprint S.	15-Mar	1	OTC	6F	D	Valid Move	Husbands, P	50,000
OBS Sprint S.	15-Mar	2	OTC	6F	D	Baronage	Prado, ES	50,000

Stakes	Date	Race	Trk	Dist/Surf		Winner	Jockey	Gross
Ocala Breeders' Sales Distaff S.	24-Jan	9	GP	1 1/16M	D	Secret Request	Coa, E	500,000
Ocala Stud Oaks	24-Jan	7	GP	6F	D	Silent Sighs	Flores, DR	250,000
Ocean Place Resort S.	8-Aug	7	MTH	1M	T	Forest Grove	Nakatani, CS	100,000
Oceanport H.-G3	8-Aug	11	MTH	1 1/16M	T	Gulch Approval	Day, P	100,000
Oceanside S.	21-Jul	6	DMR	1M	T	Wild Babe	Flores, DR	85,950
Oceanside S.	21-Jul	8	DMR	1M	T	Blackdoun (FR)	Nakatani, CS	85,450
Office Queen S.	12-Jun	9	CRC	1 1/16M	D	Ladyinareddress	Garcia, JA	100,000
Ogataul H.	13-Mar	9	FON	6F	D	Death Trappe	Martinez, A	25,950
Ogden Phipps H.-G1	19-Jun	9	BEL	1 1/16M	D	Sightseek	Bailey, JD	300,000
Ogle and Company Turf Distaff S.	4-Apr	9	TAM	1 1/16M	T	Skip to Savannah	Castillo, O	84,950
Ogygian S.	9-Jul	8	BEL	5 1/2F	D	Smokume	Uske, S	61,200
Ohio Debutante H.	4-Sep	11	TDN	6F	D	Anna Em	Gonzalez, LA	40,000
Ohio Derby-G2	12-Jun	14	TDN	1 1/8M	D	Brass Hat	Martinez, W	355,000
Ohio Freshman S.	14-Nov	7	BEU	1M	D	Opening Wager	Rosendo, IJ	40,000
Ohio Valley H.	1-Jun	9	MNR	6F	D	Our Josephina	Murphy, CK	75,000
Oilfield H.	25-Jul	10	MAF	1M 70Y	D	Neighborhood Bully	Wippert, S	3,200
Oklahoma Classics Classic S.	25-Sep	8	RP	1 1/16M	D	George Taylor	Matz, N	75,000
Oklahoma Classics Distaff S.	25-Sep	6	RP	1M 70Y	D	Racing Sundown	Fitzpatrick, A	40,000
Oklahoma Classics Filly & Mare Turf S.	25-Sep	7	RP	7 1/2F	T	Wee Okie	Fitzpatrick, A	40,000
Oklahoma Classics Juvenile S.	25-Sep	4	RP	6F	D	Sooner Pride	Cogburn, KL	40,000
Oklahoma Classics Lassie S.	25-Sep	3	RP	6F	D	D Fine Okie	Hamilton, Q	40,000
Oklahoma Classics Sprint S.	25-Sep	2	RP	6F	D	Cheyenne Breeze	Tohill, KS	40,000
Oklahoma Classics Turf S.	25-Sep	5	RP	1M	T	Dance and Dazzle	Berry, MC	40,000
Oklahoma Derby-G3	21-Nov	8	RP	1 1/8M	D	Wally's Choice	Quinonez, LS	168,550
Old Hat S.	14-Feb	8	GP	6F	D	Madcap Escapade	Douglas, RR	100,000
Old Ironsides S.	19-Jun	8	SUF	1M 70Y	T	Gran Cesare (ARG)	Dominguez, RA	40,000
Old Line Policy S.	13-Feb	8	TUP	6F	D	King Justin	Hernandez, ML	21,800
Old South H.	19-Jun	10	LAD	1 1/16M	T	Mexican Moonlight	Perrodin, EJ	50,000
Old Timers S.	15-Aug	7	GPR	7F	D	Aran Island	Sterr, S	4,405
Oliver S.	20-Jun	9	IND	1M	T	Rich Find	Troilo, WD	44,750
Omaha H.	18-Jul	4	HPO	1M	D	Stormy Impact	Compton, P	110,000
Omnibus S.	28-Aug	10	MTH	1 1/16M	T	Coney Kitty (IRE)	Coa, E	60,000
On Trust H.	13-Nov	7	HOL	7 1/2F	D	Anziyan Royalty	Flores, DR	89,200
Ontario Colleen H.	4-Sep	8	WO	1M	T	Emerald Earrings	Barton, J	193,250
Ontario County H.	20-Jun	8	FL	6F	D	House Key	Davila, Jr., JR	50,000
Ontario Damsel S.	10-Jul	9	WO	6 1/2F	T	Velvet Snow	Fraser, C	161,400
Ontario Debutante S.	22-Aug	8	WO	6F	D	South Bay Cove	Kabel, T	190,250
Ontario Derby	10-Oct	8	WO	1 1/8M	D	A Bit O'Gold	Jones, JC	160,050
Ontario Fashion H.	6-Nov	8	WO	6F	D	Winter Garden	Clark, D	186,250
Ontario Jockey Club S.	24-Jul	8	WO	7F	T	Soaring Free	Kabel, T	107,000
Ontario Lassie S.	5-Dec	8	WO	1 1/16M	D	Silver Impulse	Ramsammy, E	163,350
Ontario Matron H.	20-Jun	3	WO	1 1/16M	D	One for Rose	Ramsammy, E	181,250
Open Mind H.	5-Jun	11	MTH	6F	D	Whoop's Ah Daisy	Ortiz, FL	60,000
Open Mind S.	15-May	9	CD	5F	T	Anna Em	Melancon, L	112,300
Open S.	19-Jun	8	LBG	7F	D	Fruit Rapport	Hebert, C	11,200
Open Thoroughbred Inaugural H.	7-Aug	11	FAR	6F	D	Maddies Blues	Schindler, SA	9,400
Opening Verse H.	12-Jun	10	CD	1 1/16M	T	Senor Swinger	Day, P	110,900
Orchid H.-G2	21-Mar	11	GP	1 1/2M	T	Meridiana (GER)	Prado, ES	200,000
Oregon Derby	3-Apr	10	PM	1 1/8M	D	Santiam Top Jazz	Peery, M	20,000
Oregon Distaff Starter H.	11-Dec	4	PM	6F	D	Ashleys Bon Bon	Barber, S	5,475
Oregon Hers S.	11-Dec	7	PM	1M	D	Americas Pride	Valdez, F	10,000
Oregon His S.	11-Dec	8	PM	1 1/16M	D	Might E Man	Theriot, BJ	10,000
Oregon Oaks	17-Apr	8	PM	1 1/16M	D	Kya Jo	Rivera, Jr., JM	10,000
Oregon Starter Sprint H.	11-Dec	6	PM	6F	D	Dusty Slew	Ortega, JA	5,525
Orinda H.	24-Jan	8	GG	6F	D	Ema Bovary (CHI)	Gonzalez, RM	78,700
Orphan Kist H.	6-Mar	9	FON	6F	D	Flaming Night	Collins, DM	25,900
OS West Oregon Futurity	11-Dec	9	PM	1M	D	Wice O Kat	Beckner, T	43,880
Osunitas H.	11-Aug	7	DMR	1 1/16M	T	Voz De Colegiala (CHI)	Baze, T	82,850
OTBA Sales S.	30-Oct	6	PM	6F	D	Eighty Eighty	Peery, M	7,450
OTBA Stallion S.	3-Jan	4	PM	6F	D	Kya Jo	Crispin, JA	10,000
Our Dear Peggy S.	28-Dec	6	CRC	6 1/2F	D	Givememore (BRZ)	Cruz, MR	45,000
Overbrook Spinster S.-G1	10-Oct	8	KEE	1 1/8M	D	Azeri	Day, P	500,000
Overnight S.	17-Jul	9	RUI	5 1/2F	D	Sandias Peppermint	Madeira, CD	19,900

Stakes	Date	Race	Trk	Dist/Surf		Winner	Jockey	Gross
Overskate S.	21-Jul	7	WO	7F	D	Barath	Vega, H	133,000
Ozark Hills H.	14-Mar	7	BRD	4F	D	As de Oro	Eason, CD	9,150
P. G. Johnson S.	23-Oct	7	MED	5F	T	Ms. Trick Or Treat	Elliott, S	55,000
P. G. Johnson S.	23-Oct	9	MED	5F	T	Ambition Unbridled	Gryder, AT	55,000
Pacific Classic S.-G1	22-Aug	8	DMR	1 1/4M	D	Pleasantly Perfect	Bailey, JD	1,000,000
Pacifica H.	31-Oct	8	BM	1 1/16M	T	Ninebanks	Warren, Jr., RJ	72,700
Padua Stables Sophomore S.	4-Apr	6	TAM	7F	D	Weigelia	Toribio, Jr., A	83,300
Padua Stables Sprint S.	24-Jan	8	GP	6F	D	Shake You Down	Luzzi, MJ	300,000
Pago Hop S.	18-Dec	9	FG	1M	T	Shadow Cast	Albarado, R	60,000
Palm Beach S.-G3	21-Feb	11	GP	1 1/8M	T	Kitten's Joy	Bailey, JD	100,000
Palo Alto H.	9-Oct	7	BM	1 1/16M	T	Midwife	Duran, F	72,350
Palo Verde H.	28-Feb	8	TUP	6 1/2F	D	Bold Merit	Gomez, EA	40,000
Palomar Breeders' Cup H.-G2	4-Sep	7	DMR	1 1/16M	T	Etoile Montante	Valdivia, Jr., J	200,000
Palos Verdes H.-G2	1-Feb	7	SA	6F	D	Bluesthestandard	Smith, ME	150,000
Pan American H.-G2	20-Mar	6	GP	1 1/2M	T	Quest Star	Day, P	200,000
Pan Zareta H.	7-Feb	9	FG	6F	D	Handpainted	Melancon, L	60,000
Panhandle H.	1-May	9	MNR	5F	D	Run Zeal Run	Cloninger, Jr., WT	75,000
Panthers S.	5-Jun	9	PRM	1M	D	Josh's Madelyn	Thompson, TJ	50,000
Pappa Riccio S.	29-Aug	5	MTH	1M	D	War's Prospect	Ferrer, JC	75,000
Paradise Creek S.	11-Sep	8	AP	1 1/16M	T	Exploited Storm	Graham, J	44,375
Paradise Mile H.	3-Jan	8	TUP	1M	T	R. Baggio	Drexler, H	50,000
Paradise Valley H.	20-Nov	8	TUP	7 1/2F	T	Cocoa Latte	Stevens, SA	40,000
Parkland Heritage S.	21-Aug	7	MD	1 1/16M	D	Megan's Way	Rocheleau, SR	10,000
Parnitha S.	25-Jul	7	FE	5F	T	Major Zee	Poznansky, N	60,000
Pasadena S.	17-Mar	7	SA	1M	T	Unrivalled (GB)	Ramsammy, E	98,850
Pasco S.	17-Jan	10	TAM	7F	D	Misguided Left	Castanon, JL	60,000
Paseana H.	16-Jan	7	SA	1 1/16M	D	Bare Necessities	Valdivia, Jr., J	98,550
Passing Mood S.	28-Jul	3	WO	7F	T	Blonde Executive	Dos Ramos, RA	131,500
Pat O'Brien Breeders' Cup H.-G2	15-Aug	8	DMR	7F	D	Kela	Baze, T	200,000
Pat Whitworth Illinois Debutante S.	11-Dec	8	HAW	1 1/16M	D	Meadow Bride	Silva, CH	116,175
Patchy Groundfog S.	22-Nov	9	TUP	1M	D	Real Creek	Hernandez, ML	21,900
Paterson S.	8-Oct	8	MED	1 1/16M	T	Grand Heritage	Velasquez, CH	60,000
Paterson S.	8-Oct	6	MED	1 1/16M	T	Forest Grove	Velazquez, JR	60,000
Patrick Wood S.	21-Sep	6	GLD	6F	D	Honorable Class	Perez, RA	50,000
Pattison Canadian International S.-G1	24-Oct	9	WO	1 1/2M	T	Sulamani (IRE)	Dettori, L	1,500,000
Paul Cacci Eel River Sprint S.	15-Aug	8	FER	5F	D	Red Seattle	Navarro, VG	6,510
Paumonok H.	24-Jan	8	AQU	6F	D	Peeping Tom	Smith, A	83,025
Peach of It H.	10-Apr	4	HAW	1 1/16M	D	Julie's Prize	Sterling, Jr., LJ	111,250
Pearl Necklace S.	31-May	8	PIM	1 1/16M	D	He Loves Me	Santana, JZ	75,000
Pebbles S.-G3	11-Oct	9	BEL	1 1/8M	T	Fortunate Damsel	Castellano, J	112,300
Pegasus S.-G3	1-Oct	7	MED	1 1/8M	D	Pies Prospect	Prado, ES	300,000
Pelleteri Breeders' Cup H.	14-Mar	9	FG	6F	D	Cat Genius	Albarado, R	125,000
Pennsylvania Derby-G2	6-Sep	10	PHA	1 1/8M	D	Love of Money	Albarado, R	750,000
Pennsylvania Governor's Cup H.	31-Jul	3	PEN	5F	T	Rudirudy	Rosado, RJ	50,000
Pennsylvania Nursery S.	20-Nov	9	PHA	7F	D	United	Black, AS	55,100
Pennsylvania Oaks	6-Sep	9	PHA	1M 70Y	D	Taittinger Rose	Day, P	100,000
Pennsylvania Oaks	6-Sep	9	PHA	1M 70Y	D	Reforest	Velazquez, JR	100,000
Penny Ridge S.	20-Jun	8	STP	1 1/16M	D	Cypriata	Iammarino, MP	40,000
Pent Up Kiss H.	13-Nov	7	CD	5F	T	Mocha Queen	Blanc, B	72,000
Pepper Oaks Farm S.	24-Apr	5	HOL	6 1/2F	D	Brand Name	Nakatani, CS	60,000
Peppy Addy S.	19-Jun	9	PHA	7F	D	Prince Joseph	Black, AS	53,250
Pepsi Bassinet S.	4-Sep	10	RD	6F	D	Im a Dixie Girl	Martinez, W	105,000
Pepsi Cola H.	17-Jan	10	SUN	6F	D	Rocky Gulch	Clark, MD	128,600
Pepsi Cola H.	31-May	9	EMD	6 1/2F	D	Northwest Attitude	Cedeno, A	40,000
Pepsi S.	3-Apr	9	FON	6F	D	Come On Precious	Kimes, C	17,175
Perryville S.	14-Oct	8	KEE	7F	D	Commentator	Bejarano, R	112,600
Personal Ensign H.-G1	27-Aug	9	SAR	1 1/4M	D	Storm Flag Flying	Velazquez, JR	400,000
Pete Axthelm S.	11-Dec	8	CRC	7 1/2F	T	Wire Bound	Nunez, EO	100,000
Pete Condellone H.	24-Aug	9	FP	1M	D	Road Town	Campbell, JM	35,900
Peter Pan S.-G2	22-May	8	BEL	1 1/8M	D	Purge	Velazquez, JR	200,000
Phil D. Shepherd S.	11-Sep	11	FPX	1 1/16M	D	Verkade	Pedroza, MA	60,000
Philip H. Iselin Breeders' Cup H.-G3	21-Aug	9	MTH	1 1/8M	D	Ghostzapper	Castellano, J	200,000
Phoenix Breeders' Cup S.-G3	8-Oct	7	KEE	6F	D	Champali	Bejarano, R	271,250

Stakes	Date	Race	Trk	Dist/Surf		Winner	Jockey	Gross
Phoenix Gold Cup H.	13-Mar	9	TUP	6F	D	Iron Halo (ARG)	Campbell, J	100,000
Piedra Foundation H.	2-Sep	7	DMR	1M	D	Elloluv	Nakatani, CS	98,500
Pilgrim S.	24-Oct	9	BEL	1 1/8M	T	Crown Point	Espinoza, JL	82,875
Pimlico Breeders' Cup Distaff H.-G3	14-May	8	PIM	1 1/16M	D	Friel's for Real	Castellano, Jr., A	150,000
Pimlico Special H.-G1	14-May	11	PIM	1 3/16M	D	Southern Image	Espinoza, V	500,000
Pin Oak Stud USA S.	31-May	10	LS	1 1/16M	T	No Place Like It	Martin, Jr., EM	200,000
Pinjara S.	29-Oct	3	SA	1M	T	Veiled Speed	Court, JK	101,400
Pinon H.	18-Apr	8	ALB	6 1/2F	D	Shemoveslikeaghost	Tohill, KS	43,000
Pio Pico S.	17-Sep	10	FPX	6 1/2F	D	Market Garden	Pedroza, MA	60,000
Pioneer S.	10-Jul	10	LAD	5 1/2F	D	Crawfish King	Meche, L	50,000
Pippin S.	14-Feb	9	OP	1 1/16M	D	Drexel Monorail	Theriot, J	50,000
Pirate's Bounty H.	6-Sep	6	DMR	6F	D	Our New Recruit	Baze, T	98,825
Pistol Packer H.	7-Aug	9	PHA	1 1/16M	D	Caught in the Rain	Molina, VH	54,600
Plate Trial S.	6-Jun	8	WO	1 1/8M	D	A Bit O'Gold	Jones, JC	166,500
Play the King H.-G3	28-Aug	8	WO	7F	T	Soaring Free	Kabel, T	173,400
Pleasant Temper S.	18-Sep	8	KD	1M	T	Beau Watch	Whitney, DG	40,000
Plymouth S.	2-Jul	5	GLD	7F	D	Gold Ginny	Perez, RA	10,000
Pocahontas S.	6-Nov	8	CD	1M	D	Punch Appeal	Day, P	109,500
Pocahontas S.	25-Nov	10	CRC	6 1/2F	D	D' Wildcat Speed	Toribio, A	45,000
Poker H.-G3	10-Jul	8	BEL	1M	T	Christine's Outlaw	Bridgmohan, S	112,600
Politely S.	20-Jun	9	MTH	1 1/16M	T	Snowdrops (GB)	Bravo, J	60,000
Politely S.	13-Nov	8	PIM	6F	D	Two Punch Gal	Fogelsonger, R	75,000
Polly's Jet S.	7-Aug	8	DEL	6F	D	Baldomera	Alvarado, Jr., R	53,500
Pomona Derby	25-Sep	11	FPX	1 1/8M	D	Semi Lost	Pedroza, MA	100,000
Ponche H.	29-May	3	CRC	6F	D	Built Up	Madrid, SO	75,000
Pony Express S.	12-Jun	6	ALB	5 1/2F	D	Ninety Nine Jack	Bourdieu, JM	45,000
Portland Meadows Mile H.	10-Apr	9	PM	1M	D	Lethal Grande	Webb, R	40,000
Possibly Perfect S.	5-Jul	8	AP	1 1/8M	T	Bedanken	Pettinger, DR	41,875
Potomac H.	10-Apr	4	CT	7F	D	Earth Power	Reynolds, LC	41,250
Potrero Grande Breeders' Cup H.-G2	28-Mar	8	SA	6 1/2F	D	McCann's Mojave	Valdivia, Jr., J	211,400
Powerless H.	13-Nov	4	HAW	6F	D	Synco Peach	Sterling, Jr., LJ	111,700
Prairie Bayou S.	18-Dec	10	TP	1 1/8M	D	Discreet Hero	Sarvis, DA	50,000
Prairie Express S.	1-May	8	PRM	5 1/2F	D	Pie's Lil Brother	Thompson, TJ	50,000
Prairie Gold Juvenile S.	1-Jul	8	PRM	5F	D	Departing Now	Lovato, Jr., F	50,750
Prairie Gold Lassie S.	1-Jul	6	PRM	5F	D	Panorama Valley	Murray, KM	51,500
Prairie Lily Sales S.	4-Sep	3	MD	7F	D	Bleu Royale	Hamel, RH	22,500
Prairie Meadows Cornhusker BC H.-G3	3-Jul	9	PRM	1 1/8M	D	Roses in May	Guidry, M	300,000
Prairie Meadows Debutante S.	4-Sep	6	PRM	6F	D	My Three Sisters	Doocy, TT	40,000
Prairie Meadows Derby	25-Sep	6	PRM	1 1/16M	D	Gamblin	Essman, DW	76,125
Prairie Meadows Freshman S.	6-Sep	6	PRM	6F	D	City Code	Pettinger, DR	41,200
Prairie Meadows H.	31-Jul	6	PRM	1 1/8M	D	Tricky Mocha	Eads, JR	77,250
Prairie Meadows Oaks	18-Sep	6	PRM	1 1/16M	D	Miss Moses	Birzer, A	77,250
Prairie Meadows Sprint S.	7-Aug	6	PRM	6F	D	Shandy	Silva, CH	50,000
Prairie Mile S.	31-May	9	PRM	1M	D	Proper Prado	Doocy, TT	50,000
Prairie Rose S.	24-Apr	8	PRM	6F	D	Surf N Sand	Thompson, TJ	50,875
Prank Call S.	31-May	3	CRC	5F	T	Bourbon N Blues	Toscano, PR	40,000
Preakness S.-G1	15-May	12	PIM	1 3/16M	D	Smarty Jones	Elliott, S	1,000,000
Precious Feather S.	6-Aug	9	CRC	1 1/16M	D	Pampered Princess	Boulanger, G	45,000
Prelude S.	28-Aug	10	LAD	1 1/16M	D	South Africa	Jacinto, J	60,000
Premiere S.	15-Apr	1	LS	1M	D	Agrivating General	Chapa, R	50,000
Premier's H.-G3	17-Oct	8	HST	1 3/8M	D	Blowin in the Wind	Skelly, RV	138,600
President's H.	15-May	8	STP	6F	D	Saw Grass Sabre	Heiler, S	40,000
Preview S.	13-Mar	8	PM	1 1/16M	D	Might E Man	Chaves, NJ	10,000
Prime Rewards S.	23-Jan	10	DED	5F	D	Raymond's Dream	Bourque, SJ	40,000
Prime Rewards S.	31-Dec	8	DED	1M	D	Miss Confusion	Faul, RJ	40,000
Primonetta S.	3-Apr	8	PIM	6F	D	Umpateedle	Dominguez, RA	50,000
Prince of Wales S.	18-Jul	9	FE	1 3/16M	D	A Bit O'Gold	Jones, JC	500,000
Princess Elaine S.	4-Jul	8	CBY	1 1/16M	D	Pandorasconnection	Rivera, JG	40,000
Princess Elizabeth S.	23-Oct	8	WO	1 1/16M	D	Victorious Ami	Ramsammy, E	250,000
Princess H.	6-Nov	10	SUN	6F	D	Coronado Rose	Gondron, TD	52,550
Princess Margaret S.	1-Aug	7	NP	6F	D	Miss Venturous	Painter, LM	40,000
Princess Mora S.	20-Nov	4	CRC	1 1/8M	T	Honey Ryder	Cruz, MR	45,000
Princess of Palms H.	31-Jan	8	TUP	6F	D	Almost Fooled	Guerra, VJ	40,000

Stakes	Date	Race	Trk	Dist/Surf	Winner	Jockey	Gross
Princess Rooney H.-G2	10-Jul	11	CRC	6F D	Ema Bovary (CHI)	Gonzalez, RM	500,000
Princess S.	15-May	8	LNN	6F D	Kerosene Prospect	Martinez, A	11,000
Princeton S.	12-Nov	9	MED	1 1/16M D	Tap Day	Velez, Jr., JA	60,000
Prioress S.-G1	3-Jul	8	BEL	6F D	Friendly Michelle	Nakatani, CS	250,000
Private Terms S.	27-Mar	8	LRL	1 1/16M D	Water Cannon	Dominguez, RA	60,000
Pro Or Con H.	15-Feb	3	SA	1M T	Super High	Baze, T	108,000
Prospectors Gamble H.	29-Aug	8	ARP	1 1/8M D	Personal Beau	Vicchrilli, R	27,075
Proud Puppy H.	17-Jul	7	FL	6F D	Border Bound	Valdes, RA	50,000
Providencia S.	11-Apr	8	SA	1M T	Ticker Tape (GB)	Desormeaux, KJ	113,700
Pucker Up S.-G3	18-Sep	9	AP	1 1/8M T	Ticker Tape (GB)	Desormeaux, KJ	200,000
Punch Line S.	12-Jun	5	CNL	5F T	Native Heir	Fogelsonger, R	50,000
Purple Violet S.	26-Jun	3	AP	1M D	Slewville	Rivera, HG	85,850
Puss n Boots S.	6-Sep	9	FE	1 1/16M T	A Nice Splash	Villeneuve, F	60,000
Queen City Oaks	31-Jul	10	RD	1 1/8M D	Barnsy	Rosario, Jr., HL	75,000
Queen Elizabeth II Challenge Cup S.-G1	16-Oct	8	KEE	1 1/8M T	Ticker Tape (GB)	Desormeaux, KJ	500,000
Queen Lib H.	16-Oct	9	MED	1M 70Y D	Picnic Theme	Pimentel, J	60,000
Queen of the Green H.	27-Nov	8	TUP	1M T	Very Vegas	Ruis, M	50,000
Queen S.	20-Mar	6	TP	6F D	Glorious Miss	Flores, DR	50,000
Queens County H.-G3	4-Dec	8	AQU	1 3/16M D	Classic Endeavor	Gryder, AT	112,100
Queen's H.	17-Jul	3	HPO	1M D	Casual Attitude	Doocy, TT	44,000
Queen's Plate S.	27-Jun	9	WO	1 1/4M D	Niigon	Landry, RC	1,000,000
Queenston S.	8-May	8	WO	7F D	Twisted Wit	Clark, D	166,350
Quick Card S.	8-May	7	DEL	1M D	Max Forever	Rose, J	53,700
Quicken Tree S.	13-Jun	8	HOL	1 1/2M T	Black Bart	Solis, AO	76,800
Quill S.	11-Oct	8	DEL	1 1/8M T	Madeira Mist (IRE)	Dominguez, RA	54,500
R. J. Speers S.	11-Sep	7	ASD	1 1/16M D	Deputy Country	Hendricks, K	40,000
R. R. M. Carpenter Jr. Memorial H.	17-Jul	7	DEL	1 1/16M D	Angelic Aura	Arroyo, Jr., N	100,300
R.C. Anderson S.	3-Jul	7	ASD	1M D	Poppo's Song	Hendricks, K	40,000
Racino Inaugural S.	1-Oct	8	DED	5F D	Believe Im Special	Smith, G	40,000
Raging Fever S.	17-Dec	8	AQU	1M 70Y D	Winning Season	Bejarano, R	50,550
Railbird S.-G3	2-May	8	HOL	7F D	Elusive Diva	Valenzuela, PA	109,600
Rainbow Connection S.	25-Jul	9	FE	5F T	Bold Artic Ice	Olguin, G	125,000
Rainbow Miss S.	28-Mar	9	OP	6F D	K J's Girl	Kuntzweiler, G	50,000
Rainbow S.	28-Mar	7	OP	6F D	Bold Merit	Gomez, EA	50,000
Ralph Hayes S.	28-Aug	6	PRM	1 1/16M D	Cmego	Birzer, A	82,200
Ralph M. Hinds Pomona Invitational H.	26-Sep	11	FPX	1 1/8M D	Hotel Hall (IRE)	Figueroa, O	100,000
Ralph Taylor/Vance Davenport Memorial S.	8-Aug	7	BOI	7 1/2F D	Cam's Cat	Packer, BR	4,400
Rampart H.-G2	14-Mar	6	GP	1 1/8M D	Sightseek	Bailey, JD	200,000
Rancho Bernardo H.-G3	21-Aug	8	DMR	6 1/2F D	Dream of Summer	Smith, ME	150,000
Randy Bailey Memorial H.	22-Feb	7	BRD	7 1/2F D	Doc Senter	Hilburn, WJ	8,925
Rare Treat H.	16-Feb	8	AQU	1 1/8M D	Austin's Mom	Fragoso, P	81,600
Rattlesnake S.	18-Jan	8	TUP	1M D	Kissin Ty	Saint-Martin, E	40,000
Raven Run S.-G2	15-Oct	9	KEE	7F D	Josh's Madelyn	Shepherd, J	224,200
Razorback Futurity	16-Oct	9	LAD	6F D	Stormy But Crafty	Jacinto, J	40,000
Razorback H.-G3	14-Mar	9	OP	1 1/16M D	Sonic West	Martinez, W	100,000
Ready Jet Go S.	2-Oct	8	MED	6F D	Slews Final Answer	Pimentel, J	60,000
Real Good Deal S.	6-Aug	7	DMR	7F D	Areyoutalkintome	Nakatani, CS	100,000
Reappeal S.	3-Oct	9	CRC	6 1/2F D	Love That Moon	Cruz, MR	40,000
Rebel S.	20-Mar	10	OP	1 1/16M D	Smarty Jones	Elliott, S	200,000
Rebel S.	3-Jul	9	LAD	5 1/2F D	Ready to Live	Meche, L	50,000
Red Bank H.-G3	29-May	10	MTH	1M T	Burning Roma	Castanon, JL	100,000
Red Camelia H.	28-Mar	9	FG	1M T	Destiny Calls	Sellers, SJ	100,000
Red Cross S.	18-Jul	9	MTH	6F D	Final Round	DeCarlo, CP	65,000
Red Diamond Express H.	25-Sep	7	NP	6 1/2F D	Sixthirtyjoe	Walcott, R	50,000
Red Hedeman Mile H.	21-Nov	10	SUN	1M D	Sandias Peppermint	Lambert, CT	131,500
Red Smith H.-G2	20-Nov	8	AQU	1 3/8M T	Dreadnaught	Samyn, J	150,000
Regaey Island S.	17-Jul	9	ELP	1M D	Knox	Blanc, B	75,000
Regret S.-G3	12-Jun	7	CD	1 1/8M T	Sister Star	Blanc, B	221,800
Regret S.	8-Aug	12	MTH	6F D	Travelator	Gryder, AT	100,000
Regret S.	28-May	8	GLD	6F D	Cats Copy	Perez, RA	40,000
Remington Green S.	21-Nov	10	RP	1 1/16M D	Zee Oh Six	Lopez, J	51,300
Remington MEC Mile S.	21-Nov	9	RP	1M D	Smooth Bid	Hernandez, Jr., BJ	84,000
Remington Park Oaks	21-Nov	7	RP	1M D	Road to Mandalay	Quinonez, LS	41,300

Stakes	Date	Race	Trk	Dist/Surf		Winner	Jockey	Gross
Remsen S.-G2	27-Nov	8	AQU	1 1/8M	D	Rockport Harbor	Elliott, S	200,000
Restoration S.	19-Jun	9	MTH	1M	T	Frisky Spider	King, Jr., EL	60,000
Retama Park Turf Breeders' Cup H.	31-Jul	8	RET	1 1/16M	T	Fly Slama Jama	Lambert, CT	50,000
Revidere S.	12-Jun	7	MTH	1M	D	Mistda	Ferrer, JC	60,000
Rex's Profile S.	29-Dec	7	CRC	6 1/2F	D	Mr. Pee Vee	Cruz, MR	40,000
Rhododendron S.	15-May	4	CT	7F	D	Pass Me the Salt	Hutton, GW	51,200
Ribbons and Lace H.	25-Apr	8	SUD	6F	D	Raise a Daughter	Conklin, J	3,200
Richard King H.	20-Nov	5	HOU	1 1/8M	T	Late Expectations	Maldonado-Alicea, E	50,000
Richmond Derby Trial H.	6-Sep	9	HST	1 1/16M	D	Rules of War	Ramirez, R	44,368
Richmond H.	14-Feb	8	GG	6F	D	Pheiffer	Warren, Jr., RJ	72,150
Richmond S.	2-Oct	12	HOO	1 1/16M	D	Ellens Lucky Star	Bejarano, R	40,000
Richter Scale BC Sprint Championship H.-G2	6-Mar	11	GP	7F	D	Lion Tamer	Velazquez, JR	200,000
Ricks Memorial S.	5-Sep	7	RP	1M	T	Cherylville Slew	Cogburn, KL	41,700
Riley Allison Futurity	26-Dec	10	SUN	6 1/2F	D	Cajun Pepper	Jimenez, A	161,331
Rio Grande Senor Futurity	1-Aug	8	RUI	5 1/2F	D	Leon's Bull	Tohill, KS	104,670
Rio Grande Senorita Futurity	1-Aug	9	RUI	5 1/2F	D	Hush's Gold	Juarez, Jr., AJ	100,207
Rise Jim S.	29-May	6	SUF	6F	D	Stylish Sultan	Bocachica, O	40,000
Risen Star S.-G3	15-Feb	9	FG	1 1/16M	D	Gradepoint	Albarado, R	150,000
Ritz Cafe S.	22-Aug	9	GPR	5 1/2F	D	Miss Combo	Huston, HC	4,405
Riva Ridge Breeders' Cup S.-G2	5-Jun	9	BEL	7F	D	Fire Slam	Day, P	200,000
River Cities S.	11-Sep	10	LAD	1 1/16M	T	Due to Win Again	Melancon, G	60,000
River City H.-G3	21-Nov	9	CD	1 1/8M	T	G P Fleet	Martinez, Jr., JR	174,300
River Memories S.	6-Nov	5	WO	1M	T	My Pal Lana	Clark, D	112,000
Road Runner H.	1-Aug	1	RUI	5 1/2F	D	Rocky Gulch	Bourdieu, JM	45,000
Robert F. Carey Memorial H.-G3	9-Oct	8	HAW	1M	T	Scooter Roach	Campbell, JM	150,000
Robert G. Dick Memorial Breeders' Cup H.	17-Jul	9	DEL	1 3/8M	T	Alternate	Dominguez, RA	151,500
Robert G. Leavitt Memorial H.	24-Jul	9	CT	7F	D	Brigader	Grafton, DA	76,500
Robert R. Hilton Memorial S.	11-Sep	9	CT	7F	D	Ginger Ale	Acosta, JD	41,250
Robert W. Camac Memorial S.	4-Sep	7	PHA	5F	T	Namequest	Molina, VH	50,000
Rocket Bar S.	20-Dec	4	TUP	6F	D	Cocoa Latte	Stevens, SA	21,700
Rocket Man S.	10-Jul	4	CRC	2F	D	Pembroke Hall	Ramirez, MR	50,000
Rockhill Native S.	22-Sep	8	MTH	6F	D	Doctor Voodoo	Coa, E	60,000
Roger Van Hoozer Memorial S.	26-Sep	4	CT	7F	D	Simon Slew	McGowan, MC	40,650
Rollicking S.	30-Oct	8	PIM	6F	D	Monster Chaser	Monterrey, R	75,000
Roman Colonel S.	26-Jun	8	FP	6F	D	Punch Bag	Gale, MA	30,800
Rood and Riddle Dowager S.	24-Oct	8	KEE	1 1/2M	T	Humaita (GER)	Albarado, R	150,000
Rose Blossom H.	14-Aug	10	WMF	1 1/16M	D	Sarah Oteka	Ortiz, Jr., I	5,500
Rose City S.	20-Jun	8	FE	6F	D	Clubay	Poznansky, N	60,000
Rose DeBartolo Memorial S.	17-Jul	5	TDN	1 1/8M	D	Oh So Easy	Feliciano, R	75,000
Rossi Gold S.	4-Sep	7	AP	1 1/2M	T	On the Course	Marquez, Jr., CH	53,800
Round Table S.	17-Jul	9	AP	1 1/8M	D	Cryptograph	Pettinger, DR	100,000
Route 66 S.	17-Jul	9	FMT	6 1/2F	D	Herecomesthemannow	Payne, LD	49,875
Royal Heroine S.-G3	3-Jul	4	HOL	1M	T	Janeian (NZ)	Desormeaux, KJ	109,700
Royal North H.-G3	2-Aug	8	WO	6F	T	Hour of Justice	Kabel, T	217,550
Royal North S.	3-Apr	6	BEU	6F	D	Salvester	Ccamaque, MA	40,000
Rudy Baez S.	17-Jul	9	SUF	1M 70Y	D	Senor Ladd	Panell, D	40,000
Ruff/Kirchberg Memorial H.	21-Nov	8	BEU	1 1/4M	D	Count On My Word	Oro, E	40,000
Ruffian H.-G1	19-Sep	9	BEL	1 1/16M	D	Sightseek	Velazquez, JR	300,000
Ruffian S.	19-Jun	8	FP	6F	D	Valida	Zimmerman, R	30,800
Ruidoso Mile S.	7-Aug	9	RUI	1M	D	Socko	Theriot, BJ	30,000
Ruidoso Oaks	31-Jul	8	RUI	6F	D	Miss Noteworthy	Juarez, Jr., AJ	25,000
Ruidoso Thoroughbred Championship S.	6-Sep	6	RUI	1 1/16M	D	Stone Canyon	Juarez, Jr., AJ	42,700
Ruidoso Thoroughbred Derby	5-Sep	9	RUI	1 1/16M	D	Southern Twilight	Madrid, NA	30,000
Ruidoso Thoroughbred Sale Futurity	19-Jun	8	RUI	5F	D	Tricky Tactics	Whetstone, PS	92,742
Rumson S.	14-Aug	9	MTH	6F	D	War's Prospect	Ferrer, JC	60,000
Runza H.	10-Apr	8	FON	6F	D	Burning Memories	Compton, P	17,350
Rushaway S.	20-Mar	7	TP	1 1/16M	D	Brass Hat	Lumpkins, JP	100,000
Rushing Man S.	6-Nov	8	MED	6F	D	Choose	Turner, TG	60,000
Ruth C. Funkhouser S.	26-Sep	8	CT	7F	D	White Ice	Grafton, DA	41,250
Ruthless S.	4-Jan	8	AQU	6F	D	Baldomera	Black, AS	79,875
S. W. Randall Plate H.	6-Sep	8	HST	1 1/8M	D	Lord Nelson	Fuentes, FP	44,472
Sabin H.-G3	15-Feb	11	GP	1 1/16M	D	Roar Emotion	Velazquez, JR	100,000
Sabin S.	12-May	8	BEL	1 1/4M	T	Humaita (GER)	Santos, JA	60,800

Stakes	Date	Race	Trk	Dist/Surf		Winner	Jockey	Gross
Sadie Diamond Futurity	2-Oct	8	HST	6 1/2F	D	Avenging Kat	Alvarado, PV	106,818
Sadie Hawkins H.	31-Jul	4	CT	7F	D	Fancy Buckles	Reynolds, LC	76,400
Safely Kept Breeders' Cup S.-G3	2-Oct	9	PIM	6F	D	Bending Strings	Karamanos, H	150,000
Safely Kept H.	10-Jul	8	FP	6F	D	Moon Shine Time	Pompell, TL	30,900
Safely Kept S.	6-Sep	8	AP	6F	D	Souris	Martin, Jr., EM	52,600
Safely Kept S.	20-Nov	7	AQU	6F	D	Storm Minstrel	Fragoso, P	61,050
Saguaro S.	30-Oct	4	TUP	6F	D	Cocoa Latte	Stevens, SA	40,000
Sail On By S.	2-Nov	8	TUP	6F	D	Lead for Speed	Fusilier, C	21,800
Sale S.	21-Aug	9	NP	6 1/2F	D	Blinkanhesgone	Painter, LM	60,000
Salem County S.	2-Oct	9	MED	1M 70Y	T	Paddy's Daisy	DeCarlo, CP	55,000
Salvator Mile H.-G3	25-Jul	10	MTH	1M	D	Presidentialaffair	Elliott, S	100,000
Sam F. Davis S.	21-Feb	10	TAM	1 1/16M	D	Kaufy Mate	Zimmerman, R	100,000
Sam Houston Distaff H.	17-Jan	9	HOU	1 1/16M	D	Spectacular Lisa	Albarado, R	40,000
Sam Houston Oaks	13-Mar	8	HOU	1M	D	Josie G.	Martin, Jr., EM	30,000
Sam Houston Sprint H.	17-Jan	5	HOU	7F	D	Zee Oh Six	Berry, MC	40,000
Sam Houston Texan Juvenile S.	20-Nov	7	HOU	1 1/16M	D	Boggy Creek	Marquez, Jr., CH	150,000
Sam Houston Turf Sprint Cup S.	10-Apr	9	HOU	5F	T	Bold Reply	Cogburn, KL	40,000
Sam J. Whiting Memorial H.	10-Jul	11	PLN	6F	D	Onebadshark	Rollins, CJ	50,595
Sam's Town S.	4-Dec	7	DED	7F	D	Intelligent Male	Hebert, TJ	75,000
Samuel H.	18-Dec	9	BEU	6F	D	Just Michel	Yaranga, Y	25,000
San Antonio H.-G2	31-Jan	8	SA	1 1/8M	D	Pleasantly Perfect	Solis, AO	250,000
San Bernardino H.-G3	3-Apr	10	SA	1 1/8M	D	Dynever	Nakatani, CS	110,600
San Carlos H.	28-Feb	8	GG	1M	D	Jets Fan	Castro, JM	72,000
San Carlos H.-G2	7-Mar	8	SA	7F	D	Pico Central (BRZ)	Flores, DR	150,000
San Clemente H.-G2	31-Jul	4	DMR	1M	T	Sweet Win	Espinoza, V	150,000
San Diego H.-G2	1-Aug	8	DMR	1 1/16M	D	Choctaw Nation	Espinoza, V	250,000
San Felipe S.-G2	14-Mar	5	SA	1 1/16M	D	Preachinatthebar	Santiago, J	250,000
San Fernando Breeders' Cup S.-G2	10-Jan	8	SA	1 1/16M	D	During	Flores, DR	223,800
San Francisco Breeders' Cup Mile H.-G2	24-Apr	3	BM	1M	T	Singletary	Valdivia, Jr., J	150,000
San Gorgonio H.-G2	10-Jan	3	SA	1 1/8M	T	Megahertz (GB)	Solis, AO	150,000
San Jacinto S.	20-Nov	10	HOU	1 1/16M	T	Marfa's Taxes	Lanerie, CJ	50,000
San Jose S.	15-May	3	BM	1 1/16M	D	Heavenly Humor	Warren, Jr., RJ	71,900
San Juan Capistrano Invitational H.-G2	18-Apr	9	SA	1 3/4M	T	Meteor Storm (GB)	Valdivia, Jr., J	250,000
San Juan County Commissioners H.	2-Nov	7	SRP	1 1/8M	D	Pleasant Bend	Gonsalves, FA	52,100
San Luis Obispo H.-G2	16-Feb	9	SA	1 1/2M	T	Puerto Banus	Espinoza, V	200,000
San Luis Rey H.-G2	20-Mar	9	SA	1 1/2M	T	Meteor Storm (GB)	Valdivia, Jr., J	200,000
San Marcos S.-G2	19-Jan	8	SA	1 1/4M	T	Sweet Return (GB)	Stevens, GL	150,000
San Mateo S.	18-Sep	8	BM	6F	D	Wind Water	Alvarado, FT	71,500
San Miguel S.-G3	11-Jan	7	SA	6F	D	Hosco	Baze, T	108,100
San Pasqual H.-G2	3-Jan	7	SA	1 1/16M	D	Star Cross (ARG)	Espinoza, V	150,000
San Pedro S.	27-Mar	3	SA	6 1/2F	D	Courageous Act	Santiago, J	102,975
San Rafael S.-G2	6-Mar	7	SA	1M	D	Imperialism	Espinoza, V	200,000
San Simeon H.-G3	18-Apr	7	SA	6 1/2F	T	Glick	Solis, AO	107,300
San Vicente S.-G2	7-Feb	3	SA	7F	D	Imperialism	Espinoza, V	150,000
Sandia H.	18-Sep	8	ALB	5 1/2F	D	Beyond Brilliant	Juarez, Jr., AJ	33,100
Sandpiper S.	10-Jan	10	TAM	6F	D	Wild Speed	Bell, DC	60,000
Sandra Hall Grand Canyon H.	24-Apr	10	TUP	6F	D	Newark	Dieguez, WO	40,000
Sands Point S.-G3	13-Jun	8	BEL	1 1/8M	T	Mambo Slew	Prado, ES	114,800
Sanford S.-G2	29-Jul	8	SAR	6F	D	Afleet Alex	Rose, J	150,000
Sangue H.	14-Aug	11	LAD	7 1/2F	T	Cherylville Slew	Perrodin, EJ	50,000
Santa Ana H.-G2	27-Mar	9	SA	1 1/8M	T	Katdogawn (GB)	Smith, ME	150,000
Santa Anita Derby-G1	3-Apr	8	SA	1 1/8M	D	Castledale (IRE)	Valdivia, Jr., J	750,000
Santa Anita H.-G1	6-Mar	10	SA	1 1/4M	D	Southern Image	Espinoza, V	1,000,000
Santa Anita Oaks-G1	13-Mar	8	SA	1 1/16M	D	Silent Sighs	Flores, DR	300,000
Santa Barbara H.-G2	17-Apr	9	SA	1 1/4M	T	Megahertz (GB)	Solis, AO	200,000
Santa Catalina S.-G2	17-Jan	7	SA	1 1/16M	D	St Averil	Baze, T	150,000
Santa Clara H.	29-May	3	BM	1M	D	Gonetorule	Baze, RA	72,200
Santa Claus S.	26-Dec	9	CRC	1 1/16M	T	Old Forester	Coa, E	45,000
Santa Lucia H.	4-Apr	7	SA	1 1/16M	D	Hope Rises	Flores, DR	103,725
Santa Margarita Invitational H.-G1	14-Mar	8	SA	1 1/8M	D	Adoration	Smith, ME	300,000
Santa Maria H.-G1	16-Feb	8	SA	1 1/16M	D	Star Parade (ARG)	Espinoza, V	250,000
Santa Monica H.-G1	25-Jan	8	SA	7F	D	Island Fashion	Desormeaux, KJ	250,000
Santa Paula S.	21-Mar	8	SA	6 1/2F	D	Friendly Michelle	Baze, T	103,650

Stakes	Date	Race	Trk	Dist/Surf		Winner	Jockey	Gross
Santa Teresa H.	14-Mar	11	SUN	6 1/2F	D	Big Score	Enriquez, ID	54,050
Santa Ynez S.-G2	19-Jan	5	SA	7F	D	Yearly Report	Bailey, JD	150,000
Santa Ysabel S.-G3	4-Jan	6	SA	1 1/16M	D	A. P. Adventure	Solis, AO	106,800
Sapling S.-G3	28-Aug	11	MTH	6F	D	Evil Minister	Pimentel, J	100,000
Sarah Lane's Oates H.	27-Mar	9	FG	1M	T	Placid Star	Melancon, G	100,000
Saranac H.-G3	6-Sep	10	SAR	1 3/16M	T	Prince Arch	Castellano, J	108,200
Saratoga Breeders' Cup H.-G2	22-Aug	9	SAR	1 1/4M	D	Evening Attire	Velasquez, CH	250,000
Saratoga Dew S.	1-Sep	8	SAR	1 1/8M	D	Fait Accompli	Gryder, AT	66,400
Saratoga H.	22-May	8	BM	6F	D	Onebigbag	Schvaneveldt, CP	72,050
Saskatchewan Derby	11-Sep	7	MD	1 1/16M	D	Noble Dane	Jones, DT	15,000
Saskatchewan Futurity	31-Jul	5	MD	6F	D	Fargo Forbes	Rocheleau, SR	17,800
Saskatoon H.	3-Jul	6	MD	6F	D	Steel Copy	Emamalie, H	5,000
Saylorville S.	4-Jul	6	PRM	6F	D	Summer Mis	Sterling, Jr., LJ	100,000
Scarlet and Gray H.	7-Nov	10	BEU	6F	D	Mercer's Launch	Gonzalez, IR	40,000
Scarlet Carnation S.	12-Jun	6	TDN	6F	D	Codes Preshisone	Gonzalez, LA	45,000
Schenectady H.	26-Sep	8	DEL	6F	D	Sugar Punch	Prado, ES	107,700
Schuylerville S.-G2	28-Jul	9	SAR	6F	D	Classic Elegance	Day, P	150,000
Scotts Highlander H.-G3	27-Jun	4	WO	6F	T	Soaring Free	Kabel, T	219,000
Scott's Scoundrel S.	6-Sep	6	LAD	1 1/16M	T	Spruce's Prince	Meche, L	50,000
Scottsdale H.	27-Mar	2	TUP	1M	T	Church Editor	Stevens, SA	40,000
Scotzanna S.	16-Jul	8	BEL	6F	D	Cologny	Luzzi, MJ	61,200
Sea Emperor S.	9-Sep	8	CRC	7F	D	Swift Replica	Toribio, Jr., A	40,000
Sea O'Erin Breeders' Cup Mile H.	7-Aug	8	AP	1M	T	Herculated	Marquez, Jr., CH	150,000
Seabiscuit Breeders' Cup H.-G3	31-May	3	BM	1 1/16M	D	Yougottawanna	Baze, RA	100,000
Seacliff S.	6-Sep	7	CRC	1M	D	Cherokee Chase	Nunez, EO	50,000
Seagram Cup S.	7-Aug	8	WO	1 1/16M	D	One for Rose	Ramsammy, E	136,750
Seattle H.	25-Apr	8	EMD	6F	D	Willie the Cat	Frazier, R	40,000
Seattle Slew Breeders' Cup H.	31-Jul	9	EMD	1 1/16M	D	Flamethrowintexan	Frazier, R	65,000
Seattle Slew H.	3-Jul	8	FP	6F	D	Living a Dream	Kurek, G	30,500
Seaway S.-G3	11-Sep	8	WO	7F	D	Brass in Pocket	Kabel, T	186,500
Secretariat Memorial S.	1-May	5	SON	6F	D	Speed Pocket	Torres, A	5,054
Secretariat S.-G1	14-Aug	11	AP	1 1/4M	T	Kitten's Joy	Bailey, JD	400,000
Seeking the Gold S.	22-Jul	8	BEL	1 1/16M	D	Free of Love	Luzzi, MJ	61,500
Selene S.-G2	23-May	8	WO	1 1/16M	D	Eye of the Sphynx	Kabel, T	275,000
Selima S.	20-Nov	6	PIM	1 1/16M	D	Hear Us Roar	Elliott, S	100,000
Selma S.	18-Sep	3	RET	5F	T	Seneca Song	Crandall, AL	40,000
Senate Appointee H.	11-Jul	8	HST	1 1/8M	D	Hanselina	Alvarado, PV	44,472
Senator Ken Maddy H.-G3	29-Sep	7	SA	6 1/2F	T	Belleski	Nakatani, CS	100,000
Seneca S.	18-Sep	10	LAD	1 1/16M	T	Happy Ticket	Meche, L	50,000
Senorita S.	24-Jul	10	LAD	1 1/16M	T	Topango	Perrodin, EJ	50,000
Senorita S.-G3	15-May	8	HOL	1M	T	Miss Vegas (IRE)	Solis, AO	108,900
Sensational Star H.	14-Feb	3	SA	6 1/2F	T	McCann's Mojave	Valdivia, Jr., J	109,900
Serena's Song S.	24-Jul	9	MTH	1M 70Y	D	Susan's Angel	Coa, E	60,000
Seton Hall University S.	13-Nov	10	MED	6F	D	Forest Music	Gryder, AT	60,000
Shadwell Turf Mile S.-G1	9-Oct	8	KEE	1M	T	Nothing to Lose	Albarado, R	600,000
Shady Well S.	24-Jul	4	WO	5 1/2F	D	South Bay Cove	Kabel, T	160,350
Shakertown S.-G3	10-Apr	7	KEE	5 1/2F	T	Soaring Free	Sellers, SJ	115,100
Sham S.	8-Feb	8	SA	1 1/8M	D	Master David	Solis, AO	103,900
Shecky Greene S.	6-Nov	8	DEL	1 1/16M	D	Unforgettable Max	Alvarado, Jr., R	54,500
Sheepshead Bay H.-G2	29-May	8	BEL	1 3/8M	T	Moscow Burning	Smith, ME	150,000
Shelby County S.	1-May	8	IND	6F	D	Ellens Lucky Star	Bejarano, R	40,000
Shepperton S.	14-Aug	8	WO	6 1/2F	D	Krz Ruckus	Husbands, P	133,000
Shirley Jones H. G3	8-Feb	11	GP	7F	D	Randaroo	Velazquez, JR	100,000
Shiskabob S.	23-Oct	12	LAD	1 1/16M	T	Screen Idol	Melancon, G	84,350
Shocker T. H.	23-Oct	6	CRC	1 1/16M	D	Redoubled Miss	Coa, E	100,000
Shoemaker Breeders' Cup Mile S.-G1	31-May	7	HOL	1M	T	Designed for Luck	Valenzuela, PA	470,000
Shortgrass Heritage S.	21-Aug	5	MD	1 1/16M	D	Signal to Go	Seesequasis, J	10,000
Showtime Deb S.	13-Nov	6	HAW	6F	D	Bluesbdancing	Montalvo, C	112,400
Shuvee H.-G2	15-May	8	BEL	1M	D	Storm Flag Flying	Velazquez, JR	200,000
Shuvee S.	14-Sep	8	FP	6F	D	Denoun N Deverb	Robletto, L	26,000
Sickle's Image S.	20-Sep	7	GLD	6F	D	Foolininthemeadow	Doser, ME	50,000
Side Bar S.	15-Aug	5	CRC	1M	T	Class of Seventy	Cruz, MR	40,000
Sierra Starlet H.	1-Aug	2	RUI	5 1/2F	D	Latenite Special	Tohill, KS	45,000

Stakes	Date	Race	Trk	Dist/Surf		Winner	Jockey	Gross
Silk Stockings S.	12-Jun	7	YAV	6F	D	Solly's Dolly	Dieguez, WO	9,600
Silver Bells S.	24-Dec	10	CRC	7F	D	Double Scoop	Chavez, JF	45,000
Silver Cup Futurity	15-Aug	7	ARP	5 1/2F	D	Run Do Run	Johnson, BL	25,000
Silver Deputy S.	6-Sep	4	WO	6 1/2F	D	Wholelottabourbon	Villeneuve, F	106,000
Silver Maiden S.	31-Jul	6	AP	5 1/2F	D	Panorama Valley	Murray, KM	54,600
Silver Season S.	7-Aug	6	CRC	7F	D	Caballero Negro	Cruz, MR	45,000
Silver Spur Breeders' Cup S.	1-Oct	9	LS	1M	D	Enduring Will	Meche, L	100,000
Silverado H.	2-May	8	ALB	6F	D	Ninety Nine Jack	Bourdieu, JM	42,550
Silverbulletday S.-G2	14-Feb	9	FG	1 1/16M	D	Shadow Cast	Albarado, R	150,000
Simcoe S.	5-Sep	5	WO	7F	D	Moonshine Justice	Kabel, T	136,125
Simply Majestic S.	22-May	7	CRC	1 1/16M	T	Wire Bound	Garcia, JA	75,000
Sir Barton S.	15-May	9	PIM	1 1/16M	D	Royal Assault	Day, P	100,000
Sir Barton S.	8-Dec	4	WO	1 1/16M	D	Arch Hall	Husbands, P	126,375
Sir Beaufort S.	26-Dec	7	SA	1M	T	Whilly (IRE)	Martinez, FF	112,700
Sir Omni S.	25-Sep	4	CRC	1 1/16M	T	Wire Bound	Cruz, MR	40,000
Sir Winston Churchill H.	25-Sep	6	HST	1 1/8M	D	Metatron	Hoverson, C	44,368
Sissy Woolums Mem Va/South Carolina S.	18-Jul	10	CNL	6F	D	Outstander	Hamilton, SD	40,000
Sixty Sails H.-G3	24-Apr	8	HAW	1 1/8M	D	Allspice	Emigh, CA	250,000
Skip Away H.-G3	13-Mar	13	GP	1 1/16M	D	Newfoundland	Velazquez, JR	100,000
Skip Away S.	5-Jul	5	MTH	1M 70Y	D	Presidentialaffair	Elliott, S	70,000
Skipat S.	29-May	8	PIM	6F	D	Love You Madly	Santana, JZ	50,000
Skunktail S.	18-Jul	3	HPO	1M	D	Mortrump	Beck, DL	29,800
Sky Classic H.-G2	2-Oct	8	WO	1 3/8M	T	Colorful Judgement	Callaghan, S	275,250
Sleepy Hollow S.	23-Oct	4	BEL	1M	D	Galloping Grocer	Velazquez, JR	100,000
Slight in the Rear S.	24-Aug	1	FP	6F	D	Miss Outrageous	Bejarano, R	35,600
Slipton Fell H.	5-Jun	9	MNR	1M 70Y	D	Ask the Lord	Murphy, CK	75,000
Smart Deb S.	14-Aug	3	AP	6F	D	Questionable Past	Marquez, Jr., CH	52,200
Smart Halo S.	4-Apr	9	PIM	6F	D	Spirited Game	Castellano, Jr., A	50,000
Smile Sprint H.-G3	10-Jul	10	CRC	6F	D	Champali	Bailey, JD	500,000
Snow Chief S.	24-Apr	9	HOL	1 1/8M	D	Cheiron	Solis, AO	250,000
Snow White S.	11-Dec	7	CT	7F	D	Smoking Wise	Garcia, L	51,500
Snurb S.	8-Aug	6	CRC	7F	D	Format	Penalba, C	45,000
Soaring Softly S.	11-Nov	8	AQU	1M	T	Right This Way	Prado, ES	61,000
Soft Parade S.	6-Nov	5	CRC	1 1/16M	T	Formal Miss	Cruz, MR	40,000
Soft Parade S.	6-Nov	8	CRC	1 1/16M	T	Beebe Lake	Cruz, MR	45,000
Solana Beach H.	5-Sep	4	DMR	1M	T	Tucked Away	Desormeaux, KJ	125,000
Solano County Juvenile Filly S.	25-Jul	11	SOL	5 1/2F	D	Kelly's Princess	Rollins, CJ	53,400
Solo Haina S.	22-Jun	7	CRC	1M	D	Pampered Princess	Castro, E	45,000
Somethingroyal S.	19-Jun	9	CNL	5 1/2F	T	With Patience	Fogelsonger, R	50,000
Sonny Hine S.	16-Oct	8	PIM	6F	D	Move to Strike	Rodriguez, ED	50,000
Sonoma H.	14-Aug	8	NP	1 1/16M	D	Overact	Welch, Q	100,000
Sophomore Sprint Championship S.	23-Nov	9	MNR	6F	D	Danieltown	Murphy, CK	75,000
Sorority S.	4-Sep	10	MTH	6F	D	Queens Plaza	Elliott, S	100,000
Sorrento S.-G3	7-Aug	8	DMR	6 1/2F	D	Inspiring	Flores, DR	150,000
South Mississippi Owners and Breeders S.	6-Feb	1	FG	6F	D	Ten Times Better	Albarado, R	43,800
South Ocean S.	10-Nov	7	WO	1 1/16M	D	Coastal Fortress	Kabel, T	134,500
Southern Beau S.	29-Aug	7	LAD	5 1/2F	D	Favorite Minit	Bourque, SJ	50,000
Southern Belle S.	22-Aug	8	LAD	5 1/2F	D	Maid in China	Melancon, G	50,000
Southern Belle S.	23-May	9	GRP	5 1/2F	D	Soup n' Crackers	D'Amico, DL	3,760
Southern Oregon Race Horse Assn. S.	3-Jul	7	GRP	5F	D	Primecat	Dangerfield, T	3,290
Southwest S.	28-Feb	9	OP	1M	D	Smarty Jones	Elliott, S	100,000
Soviet Problem H.	21-Mar	7	GG	6F	D	Christmas Time	Baze, RA	71,900
Spangled Jimmy H.	10-Jul	8	NP	1M	D	Deputy Country	Painter, LM	40,000
Spartan S.	3-Jul	5	GLD	7F	D	Rockem Sockem	Houghton, TD	40,000
Spectacular Bid S.-G3	10-Jan	8	GP	6F	D	Wynn Dot Comma	Bravo, J	100,000
Spectacular Bid S.	29-Aug	8	AP	7F	D	Rocky River	Emigh, CA	52,800
Speed H.	22-May	8	LNN	4 1/2F	D	Jack Black and Ice	Beck, DL	11,000
Speed H.	2-Oct	10	LAD	6F	D	Ole Rebel	Melancon, G	40,000
Speed Sprint S.	5-Jun	8	LBG	5 1/2F	D	Lovers Son	McAleney, P	11,200
Speed to Spare S.	11-Sep	10	NP	1 3/8M	D	Beau Brass	Simard, RE	100,000
Spend a Buck H.-G3	23-Oct	13	CRC	1 1/16M	D	Built Up	Coa, E	100,000
Spend a Buck S.	24-Jul	9	FP	1M 70Y	D	It's Lucky	Pompell, TL	30,900
Spicy H.	5-Sep	5	ARP	1 1/16M	D	She's Finding Time	Kutz, CM	26,725

Stakes	Date	Race	Trk	Dist/Surf		Winner	Jockey	Gross
Spinaway S.-G2	20-Aug	8	SAR	7F	D	Sense of Style	Prado, ES	250,000
Spirit of Texas S.	20-Nov	4	HOU	6F	D	Charming Socialite	Taylor, L	50,000
Sport City H.	5-Sep	8	LAD	1 1/16M	T	Northern Scene	Torres, FC	50,000
Sport Page H.-G3	31-Oct	7	AQU	7F	D	Mass Media	Castellano, J	111,200
Sportsman's Paradise S.	13-Mar	10	DED	7F	D	Britt's Jules	Bourque, SJ	50,000
Spring Fever S.	7-Mar	9	OP	5 1/2F	D	Surf N Sand	McKee, J	50,000
Spring S.	20-Mar	8	HOU	7F	D	Catalissa	Gondron, TD	40,000
Springfield S.	26-Jun	5	AP	1M	D	Fort Prado	Campbell, JM	88,050
Springtime S.	24-Apr	8	CT	7F	D	Great Commander	Acosta, JD	51,550
Sprint Championship H.	13-Jun	8	GRP	4 1/2F	D	I'm Yer Hucklebery	Beckner, T	3,660
Spruce Fir H.	24-Jul	8	MTH	1M	D	Uphill Skier	Elliott, S	60,000
Squan Song S.	26-Dec	8	PIM	6F	D	Perilous Night	Santana, JZ	50,000
St. Georges Overnight S.	15-Jun	8	DEL	1 1/16M	D	Becky in Pink	Arroyo, Jr., N	53,700
St. Nick S.	26-Dec	8	CT	7F	D	Malibu Moonshine	Rosenthal, ME	51,150
St. Paul S.	5-Jun	8	CBY	6F	D	Jimmy Cracked Corn	Bell, DC	40,000
Stampede Park Sprint Championship H.	8-May	8	STP	6F	D	Dance Me Free	Bryan, D	40,000
Standard Auto Glass S.	16-Jul	10	GPR	5 1/2F	D	Lafleur	Mellish, B	4,000
Stanford S.	18-Apr	3	BM	6F	D	Allswellthatnswell	Warren, Jr., RJ	72,250
Stanton S.	6-Sep	8	DEL	1 1/8M	T	Gunning For	Alvarado, Jr., R	55,100
Star Ball H.	14-Nov	8	GG	1 1/16M	T	Frisco Belle	Gonzalez, RM	65,750
Star de Naskra S.	25-Apr	8	PIM	6F	D	Move to Strike	Wilson, R	75,000
Star of Texas S.	20-Nov	8	HOU	1 1/16M	D	Goosey Moose	Chapa, R	100,000
Star Shoot S.	25-Apr	9	WO	6F	D	Ontheqt	McAleney, J	183,875
Stardust S.	23-Oct	11	LAD	6F	D	Malanato	St. Julien, M	56,200
Stars and Stripes Breeders' Cup Turf H.-G3	4-Jul	7	AP	1 1/2M	T	Ballingarry (IRE)	Douglas, RR	200,000
Stars and Stripes H.	4-Jul	7	BOI	7 1/2F	D	Reno Bound	Boag, MA	6,550
State Fair Board H.	5-Jul	8	LNN	1M 70Y	D	Grayglen	Yaranga, Y	13,750
State Fair Breeders' Special S.	12-Jun	8	LNN	1M	D	Thundering Verzy	Martinez, A	15,600
State Fair Derby	26-Jun	8	LNN	1M	D	Metts Reward	Beck, DL	13,750
State Fair Futurity	11-Jul	10	LNN	4 1/2F	D	Big Red Fantasy	Beck, DL	15,700
Steady Growth S.	12-Jun	8	WO	1 1/16M	D	Norfolk Knight	Scharfstein, J	129,375
Stefanita S.	20-Nov	7	PIM	6F	D	Sensibly Chic	Dominguez, RA	50,000
Stephen Foster H.-G1	12-Jun	9	CD	1 1/8M	D	Colonial Colony	Bejarano, R	810,750
Steve Van Buren H.	6-Sep	8	PHA	7F	D	Smooth Maneuvers	Dominguez, RA	75,000
Stonehedge Farm Sophomore Fillies S.	4-Apr	8	TAM	7F	D	Chenia	Woolsey, RW	85,100
Stonerside Beaumont S.-G2	8-Apr	8	KEE	7F	D	Victory U. S. A.	Bailey, JD	250,000
Stonerside Forward Gal S.-G2	13-Mar	4	GP	7F	D	Madcap Escapade	Bailey, JD	150,000
Stonerside S.	29-Oct	10	LS	7F	D	Yearly Report	Bailey, JD	150,000
Storm Cat S.	10-Oct	4	KEE	1M	T	Good Reward	Prado, ES	110,600
Storm Cat S.	30-Oct	3	MED	1 1/16M	D	Killenaule	DeCarlo, CP	60,000
Stravinsky S.	17-Apr	7	KEE	5 1/2F	T	Dyna Da Wyna	Day, P	85,575
Strawberry Morn S.	17-Apr	2	HST	6 1/2F	D	Dancewithavixen	Valdez, F	44,680
Strub S.-G2	7-Feb	9	SA	1 1/8M	D	Domestic Dispute	Desormeaux, KJ	300,000
Sturgeon River S.	25-Sep	5	NP	1M	D	Speedy Gone Sally	Winters, PA	50,000
Stuyvesant H.-G3	13-Nov	8	AQU	1 1/8M	D	Classic Endeavor	Prado, ES	109,900
Stymie H.	6-Mar	8	AQU	1 1/8M	D	Ground Storm	Castellano, J	81,625
Subtle Dancer S.	17-Oct	3	CRC	6F	D	Really Royal	Castro, E	40,000
Suburban H.-G1	3-Jul	7	BEL	1 1/4M	D	Peace Rules	Bailey, JD	500,000
Suffolk Downs Oaks	3-Jul	10	SUF	1M 70Y	T	Chenia	Thompson, WA	40,000
Sugar Bowl S.	24-Dec	9	FG	6F	D	Storm Surge	Albarado, R	60,000
Sugar n Spice S.	30-May	6	CRC	6F	D	Mary Murphy	Homeister, Jr., RB	45,000
Summer Classic S.	5-Jun	7	CT	1 1/8M	D	Cherokee's Boy	Rodriguez, ED	51,050
Summer Distaff S.	19-Jun	4	CT	1 1/16M	D	Ribbon Cane	Whitacre, B	51,400
Summer Finale H.	6-Sep	4	MNR	1M	T	Chance Dance	Walker, Jr., BJ	75,000
Summer King S.	22-May	7	DEL	1 1/16M	D	Misty Sixes	Pino, MG	52,700
Summer S.-G2	19-Sep	3	WO	1M	T	Dubleo	Nakatani, CS	277,750
Summertime Promise S.	23-Oct	7	HAW	1 1/16M	D	Code of Ethics	Campbell, JM	43,600
Sumter S.	26-Sep	8	CRC	1 1/16M	D	Tour of the Cat	Cruz, MR	40,000
Sun City H.	13-Mar	8	TUP	1M	T	Aspen Hill	Dieguez, WO	40,000
Sun Devil S.	17-Jan	8	TUP	1M	D	Coke's Melody	Drexler, H	40,000
Sun H.	1-May	8	HST	6 1/2F	D	Dancewithavixen	Valdez, F	44,576
Sun Power S.	13-Nov	7	HAW	6F	D	Humor At Last	Sterling, Jr., LJ	115,225
Sun Sprint Championship H.	2-Aug	8	NP	6 1/2F	D	Deputy Country	Hamel, RH	50,000

Stakes	Date	Race	Trk	Dist/Surf		Winner	Jockey	Gross
Suncoast S.	21-Feb	8	TAM	1 1/16M	D	Ender's Sister	Peck, BD	60,000
Sunflower H.	26-Sep	9	WDS	6F	D	Polar Barron	Murray, KM	25,000
Sunland Park Fall Thoroughbred Derby	14-Nov	10	SUN	6 1/2F	D	Two Down Automatic	Gondron, TD	53,100
Sunland Park H.	10-Apr	11	SUN	1 1/8M	D	A to the Z	Bui, QE	107,950
Sunny Slope S.	23-Oct	8	SA	6F	D	Seattles Best Joe	Espinoza, V	104,025
Sunny's Halo S.	27-Nov	4	WO	6 1/2F	D	Dave the Knave	Bahen, SR	104,000
SunRay Park and Casino S.	9-Aug	8	SRP	6 1/2F	D	Russian Elite	Tohill, KS	32,000
Sunset Gun S.	6-Sep	3	SUF	1 1/16M	T	Sunlit Ridge	Panell, D	40,000
Sunset H.-G2	18-Jul	8	HOL	1 1/2M	T	Star Over the Bay	Baze, T	150,000
Super Bowl S.	24-Jan	8	HOU	6F	D	Lucky Tunnel	Jacinto, J	30,000
Super Derby-G2	25-Sep	10	LAD	1 1/8M	D	Fantasticat	Melancon, G	500,000
Super S.	24-Jan	10	TAM	7F	D	Above the Wind	Mata, F	50,000
Supernaturel H.	24-May	1	HST	6 1/2F	D	Regal Red	Fuentes, FP	44,784
Susan B. Anthony H.	31-May	9	FL	6F	D	Cologny	Nicol, Jr., PA	50,000
Susan's Girl Breeder's Cup S.	19-Jun	8	DEL	1 1/16M	D	Hopelessly Devoted	Alvarado, Jr., R	175,900
Sussex H.	18-Sep	8	DEL	1 1/16M	D	Private Lap	Arroyo, Jr., N	100,000
Suthern Accent S.	6-Jun	9	LAD	6F	D	Leslie's Love	Melancon, G	50,000
Suwannee River H.	31-Jan	11	GP	1 1/8M	D	Wishful Splendor	Santos, JA	100,000
Swale S.-G3	13-Mar	10	GP	7F	D	Wynn Dot Comma	Prado, ES	150,000
Swaps Breeders' Cup S.-G2	10-Jul	7	HOL	1 1/8M	D	Rock Hard Ten	Nakatani, CS	421,300
Sweet and Sassy H.	15-May	7	DEL	6F	D	Bronze Abe	Pino, MG	75,300
Sweet Briar Too S.	6-Jun	4	WO	7F	D	Winter Garden	Clark, D	108,000
Sweetest Chant S.	30-Jul	8	AP	1M	D	Fly Away Angel	McKee, J	54,000
Sweetheart H.	14-Feb	8	PM	1 1/16M	D	Stately's Choice	Crispin, JA	10,000
Sweetheart S.	14-Feb	8	DED	7F	D	Cielo Girl	Bourque, SJ	50,000
Swift S.	24-Jan	8	TUP	5 1/2F	D	Palmerton	Hernandez, ML	40,000
Sword Dancer Invitational S.-G1	14-Aug	8	SAR	1 1/2M	T	Better Talk Now	Dominguez, RA	500,000
Swynford S.	25-Sep	6	WO	7F	D	What's Up Dude	Husbands, P	136,000
Sycamore Breeders' Cup S.-G3	9-Oct	5	KEE	1 1/2M	T	Mustanfar	Santos, JA	162,300
Sydney Gendelman H.	20-Jun	9	RD	1 1/16M	T	Brent's Challanger	Sarvis, DA	45,000
Tacoma H.	27-Jun	7	EMD	1M	D	Random Memo	Mitchell, GV	50,000
Taking Risks S.	6-Sep	9	TIM	1 1/16M	D	Captain Chessie	Hutton, GW	50,000
Tampa Bay Breeders' Cup S.	14-Feb	8	TAM	1 1/16M	T	Burning Roma	Castanon, JL	100,000
Tampa Bay Derby-G3	14-Mar	11	TAM	1 1/16M	D	Limehouse	Day, P	250,000
Tanforan H.	7-Feb	7	GG	1 1/16M	T	Wixoe Express (IRE)	Garcia, MS	84,900
Taylor's Special H.	22-Feb	9	FG	6F	D	Out of My Way	Melancon, G	75,000
Taylor's Special S.	19-Sep	3	AP	5 1/2F	T	Marley's Revenge	Perez, EE	44,125
Ted Theibert Memorial Marathon S.	14-Aug	11	WMF	1 5/8M	D	Neighborhood Bully	Wippert, S	3,450
Teddy Drone S.	8-Aug	10	MTH	6F	D	Canadian Frontier	Coa, E	100,000
Teeworth Plate H.	23-May	8	STP	1M	D	Deputy Country	Hamel, RH	40,000
Tejano Run S.	13-Mar	10	TP	1 1/8M	D	Ask the Lord	Bejarano, R	50,000
Tejas S.	18-Sep	5	RET	5F	T	Charming Socialite	Taylor, L	40,000
Tellike H.	29-May	8	EVD	6F	D	Kylers Midge	Reyes, MJ	40,000
Tempe H.	20-Mar	7	TUP	1M	T	Western Ridge	Dieguez, WO	40,000
Tempe H.	20-Mar	7	TUP	1M	T	Spanish Highway	Campbell, J	40,000
Tempted S.-G3	2-Nov	6	AQU	1M	D	Summer Raven	Elliott, S	106,600
Temptress S.	27-Aug	7	GLD	6F	D	Foolininthemeadow	Doser, ME	45,000
Tenacious H.	4-Dec	9	FG	1 1/16M	D	Midway Road	Albarado, R	60,000
Terpsichorist S.	27-May	8	BEL	1 1/16M	T	Delta Sensation	Chavez, JF	61,000
Test S.-G1	31-Jul	8	SAR	7F	D	Society Selection	Prado, ES	250,000
Testum S.	23-Jun	8	BOI	7F	D	Robs Coin	Colledge, C	13,958
Texas Heritage S.	6-Mar	8	HOU	1M	D	Foxtrot Oscar	Rodriguez, FT	30,000
Texas Horse Racing Hall of Fame S.	18-Sep	8	RET	1 1/16M	T	Rare Cure	Berry, MC	100,000
Texas Mile S.-G3	24-Apr	8	LS	1M	D	Kela	Nuesch, DC	300,000
Texas Stallion S.	11-Jul	9	LS	5 1/2F	D	Expect Will	Beasley, J	125,000
Texas Stallion S.	10-Jul	8	LS	5 1/2F	D	Berdelia	Lambert, CT	125,000
Texas Stallion S.	14-Feb	8	HOU	1 1/16M	D	There Goes Rocket	Perrodin, EJ	75,000
Texas Stallion S.	14-Feb	6	HOU	1 1/16M	D	Native Annie	Albarado, R	75,000
Texas Stallion Two Year Old C & G S.	18-Sep	4	RET	6F	D	Leaving On My Mind	Chapa, R	125,000
Texas Stallion Two Year Old Fillies S.	18-Sep	7	RET	6F	D	Tuned In	Chapa, R	125,000
Tex's Zing S.	24-Aug	6	FP	6F	D	Matthew's Blessing	Santiago, J	35,600
Thanksgiving H.	25-Nov	9	FG	6F	D	Ole Rebel	Lanerie, CJ	60,000
Thanksgiving H.	26-Nov	8	PM	1M	D	Table Me N Saros	Peery, M	10,000

Stakes	Date	Race	Trk	Dist/Surf		Winner	Jockey	Gross
Thats Our Buck S.	26-Apr	8	CRC	7F	D	Twilight Road	Teator, P	45,000
Thats Our Buck S.	26-Apr	6	CRC	7F	D	Sea of Tranquility	Ferrer, JC	45,000
The Very One H.-G3	28-Feb	11	GP	1 3/8M	T	Binya (GER)	Velazquez, JR	100,000
The Very One S.	14-May	12	PIM	5F	T	Go Go Baby Go	Fogelsonger, R	75,000
Thelma S.	3-Jan	8	FG	6F	D	Movant	Borel, CH	60,000
Thomas Edison S.	5-Nov	5	MED	5F	D	Cumby Texas	Bravo, J	60,000
Thomas F. Moran S.	21-Aug	6	SUF	1 1/16M	D	Jini's Jet	Hampshire, Jr., JF	40,000
Thomas J. Malley S.	31-May	8	MTH	5F	D	Hostility	Chavez, LD	60,000
Thoroughbred 3,200 Claiming H.	14-Aug	8	BOI	7 1/2F	D	Hard Hitter	Conklin, J	6,650
Thoroughbred Club of America S.-G3	17-Oct	8	KEE	6F	D	Molto Vita	Bejarano, R	125,000
Thoroughbred Futurity	8-Aug	5	FAR	6F	D	Northrnimprovement	Butler, BS	25,000
Thoroughbred Invitational H.	15-Aug	9	WMF	1 1/8M	D	Staged Reality	Kingrey, RD	4,850
Thoroughbred Maiden Derby	13-Jun	8	BOI	6 1/2F	D	Western Drouilly	Packer, BR	12,010
Thoroughbred Maiden S.	15-May	4	MC	5 1/2F	D	Old Coyote	Larsen, SL	5,300
Thoroughbred Overnight S.	13-Jun	2	RUI	7 1/2F	D	Samurai Nanao	Guajardo, A	15,500
Thoroughbred Overnight S.	24-Jul	8	RUI	6F	D	Tough Pilgrim	Juarez, Jr., AJ	15,800
Thoroughbred Overnight S.	20-Aug	8	RUI	5F	D	Hecamefromaclaim	Juarez, Jr., AJ	15,000
Thoroughbred Overnight S.	6-Sep	9	RUI	7 1/2F	D	Inox (ARG)	Whetstone, PS	15,800
Three Chimneys Juvenile S.	1-May	6	CD	5F	D	Lunarpal	Sellers, SJ	115,400
Three Ring S.	4-Dec	9	CRC	1 1/16M	D	Leona's Knight	Olivero, C	100,000
Three Year Old Sale S.	12-Sep	8	NP	1M	D	Duracat	Hamel, RH	50,000
Three Year Old Sprint H.	6-Jun	7	GRP	5 1/2F	D	Primecat	Dangerfield, T	3,541
Three-Year-Old Filly Sale S.	10-Sep	8	NP	1M	D	View Halloo	Bryan, D	50,000
Thunder Road H.	11-Feb	7	SA	1M	T	Singletary	Espinoza, V	92,350
Ticonderoga H.	23-Oct	9	BEL	1 1/8M	T	On the Bus	Fragoso, P	150,000
Tiffany Lass S.	25-Jan	9	FG	1M	D	Lotta Kim	Albarado, R	100,000
Timber Music S.	17-Jul	7	HST	6 1/2F	D	Fuchsia Gold	Alvarado, PV	44,264
Timeless Prince S.	7-Aug	8	CBY	5 1/2F	D	Careless Navigator	Campbell, J	40,000
Tippett S.	25-Jul	8	CNL	5 1/2F	D	Northern Babe	Camacho, E	50,000
Tiznow S.	24-Apr	6	HOL	7 1/2F	D	Beau Soleil	Espinoza, V	150,000
To Much Coffee S.	14-Nov	9	HOO	1 1/16M	D	Tin Man Commin	Knight, LC	40,000
Toboggan H.-G3	13-Mar	8	AQU	7F	D	Well Fancied	Coa, E	112,200
Toddler S.	4-Dec	9	PIM	6F	D	Golden Malibu	Reynolds, LC	40,000
Tokyo City H.	13-Mar	6	SA	1M	D	Ender's Shadow	Ruis, M	96,300
Tom Bane Starter S.	24-Apr	7	TUP	6F	D	Perfect Fit	Rochabrun, J	15,000
Tom Fool H.-G2	4-Jul	9	BEL	7F	D	Ghostzapper	Castellano, J	150,000
Tomball S.	7-Feb	8	HOU	1 1/16M	D	Prom Date	Cloninger, Jr., WT	40,000
Tomboy S.	15-May	10	RD	1 1/16M	D	Outrageous Queen	Sarvis, DA	45,000
Tondi Budweiser H.	27-Mar	10	FON	6F	D	Abbi's Choice	Birzer, A	27,500
Tony Sanchez Memorial Mile S.	25-Apr	12	MAN	1M	D	Foregone	McClaran, WB	18,000
Toon's H.	28-Aug	6	MD	1 1/16M	D	Rouge Royale	Campbell, C	5,000
Top Flight H.-G2	26-Nov	9	AQU	1M	D	Daydreaming	Bailey, JD	150,000
Top Hat S.	8-Jun	8	YAV	6F	D	Swiss Bounty	Carreno, J	9,700
Topsider S.	6-Sep	9	SUF	6F	D	Senor Ladd	Panell, D	40,000
Toronto Cup H.-G3	17-Jul	8	WO	1 1/8M	T	Silver Ticket	Kabel, T	168,600
Torrey Pines S.	4-Sep	3	DMR	1M	D	Muir Beach	Figueroa, O	101,250
Totah Futurity S.	26-Oct	9	SRP	6 1/2F	D	Geiger Gold	Gonsalves, FA	92,663
Total Rewards S.	31-Oct	9	LAD	5F	T	Beau's Town	Hebert, TJ	40,000
Toyota Blue Grass S.-G1	10-Apr	9	KEE	1 1/8M	D	The Cliff's Edge	Sellers, SJ	750,000
Transylvania S.-G3	2-Apr	9	KEE	1M	T	Timo	Prado, ES	113,400
Travers S.-G1	28-Aug	11	SAR	1 1/4M	D	Birdstone	Prado, ES	1,000,000
Treasure Chest S.	4-Dec	5	DED	7F	D	So Much More	Smith, G	75,000
Treasure State Futurity	31-Jul	5	GF	5F	D	Secret Victory	Brown, DD	8,250
Tremont S.	26-Jun	3	BEL	5 1/2F	D	Gold Joy	Luzzi, MJ	104,900
Trenton S.	1-Aug	9	MTH	5F	D	Smokey Glacken	Bravo, J	55,000
Triple Bend Breeders' Cup Inv'l H.-G1	3-Jul	9	HOL	7F	D	Pohave	Espinoza, V	300,000
Triple Crown Nutrition Breeders' Classic S.	9-Oct	2	CT	4F	D	Weshaam Luck	Dunkelberger, TL	75,000
Triple Sec S.	17-Jan	9	DED	5F	D	Britt's Jules	Smith, G	40,000
Trippi S.	16-May	5	CRC	5F	T	Callthesheriff	Toscano, PR	40,000
Tri-State Futurity	23-Oct	4	CT	7F	D	Jazzy J J	Quinones, AR	73,350
Tri-State H.	6-Sep	10	ELP	1 1/16M	T	G P Fleet	Bejarano, R	75,000
Trooper Seven S.	19-Sep	5	EMD	1M	D	Jazzinarounnightly	Chaves, NJ	40,000
Tropical Park Derby-G3	1-Jan	9	CRC	1 1/8M	T	Kitten's Joy	Bailey, JD	100,000

Stakes	Date	Race	Trk	Dist/Surf		Winner	Jockey	Gross
Tropical Park Oaks	1-Jan	6	CRC	1 1/16M	T	Bobbie Use	Coa, E	100,000
Tropical Turf H.-G3	4-Dec	11	CRC	1 1/8M	T	Host (CHI)	Velazquez, JR	100,000
Troy S.	3-Sep	8	SAR	1M	T	Willard Straight	Velazquez, JR	66,800
True North Breeders' Cup H.-G2	5-Jun	7	BEL	6F	D	Speightstown	Velazquez, JR	211,400
Truly Bound H.	4-Jan	9	FG	1 1/16M	D	Golden Sonata	Melancon, G	60,000
TTA Sales Futurity	12-Jun	8	LS	5F	D	Berdelia	Lambert, CT	129,830
TTA Sales Futurity	12-Jun	9	LS	5F	D	Expect Will	Beasley, J	118,570
Tulsa Dash S.	19-Jun	10	FMT	4F	D	Abbi's Choice	Kimes, C	43,400
Turf Distance Series Final S.	26-Apr	8	TUP	1 3/8M	T	Sargari (IRE)	Stevens, SA	36,350
Turf Monster H.	31-May	9	PHA	5F	T	Abderian (IRE)	Molina, VH	100,000
Turf Paradise Breeders' Cup H.	7-Feb	7	TUP	1 1/16M	T	Irish Warrior	Ramsammy, E	150,000
Turf Paradise Derby	7-Feb	8	TUP	1 1/16M	D	Mambo Train	Ramsammy, E	100,000
Turfway Breeders' Cup S.-G3	18-Sep	12	TP	1 1/16M	D	Susan's Angel	Bejarano, R	175,000
Turfway Park Fall Championship S.-G3	2-Oct	9	TP	1M	D	Cappuchino	Sarvis, DA	100,000
Turfway Prevue S.	3-Jan	10	TP	6 1/2F	D	Silver Minister	Bejarano, R	50,000
Turnback the Alarm H.-G3	6-Nov	9	AQU	1 1/8M	D	Personal Legend	Bailey, JD	110,700
Tuzla H.	28-Jan	7	SA	1M	T	Fudge Fatale	Valdivia, Jr., J	99,350
TVG Khaled S.	24-Apr	8	HOL	1 1/8M	T	Black Bart	Gann, SL	150,000
Twilight Oilfield Derby	14-Aug	8	GPR	1M	D	Ezee Target	McAleney, P	11,080
Twin Lights S.	21-Aug	8	MTH	1 1/8M	D	Richetta	Coa, E	60,000
Twixt S.	31-Jul	8	PIM	1 1/8M	D	He Loves Me	Santana, JZ	100,000
Tyro S.	31-Jul	5	MTH	5 1/2F	D	Park Avenue Ball	Beckner, DV	60,000
U Can Do It H.	18-Sep	11	CRC	6 1/2F	D	Petrina Above	Toribio, A	75,000
U. S. Bank S.	18-Apr	8	EMD	6F	D	Sandia's Flicka	Montoya, D	40,000
Unbridled S.	19-Jun	9	CRC	1 1/16M	D	Mister Fotis	Boulanger, G	100,000
Union Avenue S.	26-Aug	8	SAR	6F	D	Sugar Punch	Prado, ES	66,500
Unique Type S.	13-Aug	9	CRC	5 1/2F	D	Sea Span	Castro, E	40,000
United Nations S.-G1	3-Jul	10	MTH	1 3/8M	T	Request for Parole	Prado, ES	750,000
Vacaville H.	17-Jul	11	SOL	6F	D	Pheiffer	Warren, Jr., RJ	50,510
Vagrancy H.-G2	5-Jun	6	BEL	6 1/2F	D	Bear Fan	Velazquez, JR	150,000
Vague Memory S.	14-Jun	8	CRC	6F	D	French Village	Velasquez, CH	40,000
Valdale S.	21-Feb	10	TP	1M	D	Slewpy's Storm	D'Amico, AJ	50,000
Valedictory H.	12-Dec	8	WO	1 3/4M	D	Daddy Cool	McAleney, J	137,375
Valid Expectations S.	31-May	7	LS	6F	D	Savorthetime	Sellers, SJ	100,000
Valid Leader S.	26-Oct	4	TUP	6 1/2F	D	Arch Lady	Hernandez, ML	21,700
Valley Stream S.-G3	21-Nov	8	AQU	6F	D	Megascape	Velazquez, JR	106,500
Valley View S.-G3	23-Oct	9	KEE	1 1/16M	T	Sister Swank	Day, P	116,300
Valor Farm S.	23-Oct	6	LS	6 1/2F	D	Ms Seneca Rock	Simington, DE	50,000
Vandal S.	15-Aug	8	WO	6F	D	Moonshine Justice	Kabel, T	164,550
Vanity H.-G1	9-May	8	HOL	1 1/8M	D	Victory Encounter	Solis, AO	250,000
Vector Communications S.	30-Jul	7	GPR	6 1/2F	D	Lafleur	Mellish, B	4,300
Vernon Cup H.	1-Aug	5	KIN	1 1/16M	D	Eager Lee	Butterfly, R	5,250
Vernon O. Underwood S.-G3	5-Dec	6	HOL	6F	D	Taste of Paradise	Valdivia, Jr., J	100,000
Via Borghese S.	21-Mar	8	GP	1 1/16M	T	Minge Cove	DeCarlo, CP	68,050
Vice Regent S.	29-Aug	8	WO	1M	T	Archers Bow	Sabourin, RB	131,625
Victor S. Myers Jr. S.	10-Jul	6	CBY	6F	D	Lt. Sampson	Bell, DC	40,600
Victoria Park S.	13-Jun	7	WO	1 1/8M	D	Organ Grinder	Husbands, SP	140,375
Victoria S.	23-Oct	2	LAD	6F	D	Destiny Calls	Meche, L	53,950
Victoria S.	26-Jun	8	WO	5F	D	Flamenco	Landry, RC	139,875
Victorian Queen S.	6-Oct	7	WO	6F	D	Simply Lovely	Bahen, SR	134,500
Victoriana S.	14-Aug	4	WO	1 1/16M	T	Inish Glora	Kabel, T	133,250
Victory Ride S.	28-Aug	8	SAR	6F	D	Smokey Glacken	Bravo, J	76,800
Vigil H.-G3	1-May	8	WO	7F	D	Mobil	Kabel, T	160,800
Vincent A. Moscarelli Memorial H.	24-Jul	8	DEL	6F	D	Don Six	Caraballo, JC	100,000
Vinery Madison S.	7-Apr	8	KEE	7F	D	Ema Bovary (CHI)	Gonzalez, RM	175,000
Violet H.-G3	22-Oct	8	MED	1 1/16M	T	Changing World	Fragoso, P	200,000
Virginia Derby-G3	10-Jul	9	CNL	1 1/4M	T	Kitten's Joy	Prado, ES	500,000
Virginia Oaks	10-Jul	7	CNL	1 1/8M	T	Art Fan	Fogelsonger, R	200,000
Visa Truck Rentals Maturity	13-Aug	6	GPR	7F	D	Mr. Alybro	McAleney, P	5,025
Vivacious H.	22-Aug	11	RD	1 1/16M	T	Oh So Easy	Feliciano, R	45,000
VO5 Breeders' Cup Filly & Mare Turf-G1	30-Oct	6	LS	1 3/8M	T	Ouija Board (GB)	Fallon, K	1,410,000
Voodoo Dancer S.	12-Sep	8	BEL	1M	T	With Patience	Castellano, J	61,450
Vosburgh S.-G1	2-Oct	8	BEL	6F	D	Pico Central (BRZ)	Espinoza, V	500,000
Vulcan S.	26-Mar	2	FG	6F	D	Scotties Abity	Lanerie, CJ	50,000

Stakes	Date	Race	Trk	Dist/Surf		Winner	Jockey	Gross
W. L. McKnight H.-G2	18-Dec	11	CRC	1 1/2M	T	Dreadnaught	Samyn, J	200,000
W. Meredith Bailes Memorial S.	27-Jun	8	CNL	6F	D	Satan's Code	Rocco, Jr., J	50,000
Wade Snapp Memorial Starter S.	5-Jun	6	BOI	7F	D	The Lord Is Eager	Peery, M	9,700
Wadsworth Memorial H.	4-Jul	7	FL	1 1/8M	D	Dulce de Leche	Badamo, JJ	50,000
Wafare Farm S.	22-May	9	LS	6F	D	Everheart	Martin, Jr., EM	50,000
Wagon Yard S.	31-Jul	9	GPR	5 1/2F	D	Captain Carter	Sterr, S	0
Walmac Farm Matchmaker S.	23-Oct	6	LAD	1 1/16M	T	Katlin's Rocket	Jacinto, J	80,750
Walmac Lone Star Derby-G3	29-Oct	7	LS	1 1/16M	D	Pollard's Vision	Velazquez, JR	250,000
Walter R. Cluer Memorial H.	6-Nov	8	TUP	7 1/2F	T	Black Bart	Gann, SL	40,000
Warren's Thoroughbreds S.	24-Apr	10	HOL	7F	D	The Yellow Sheet	Nakatani, CS	70,000
Washington Breeders' Cup Oaks	21-Aug	9	EMD	1 1/8M	D	Bianconi Baby	Russell, B	100,000
Washington Park H.-G2	31-Jul	8	AP	1 3/16M	D	Eye of the Tiger	Razo, Jr., E	350,000
Washington State Legislators H.	6-Jun	9	EMD	6 1/2F	D	Aunt Sophie	Rivera, Jr., JL	40,000
Washington T'bred Breeders' Ass'n Lads S.	29-Aug	9	EMD	1M	D	Positive Prize	Frazier, R	60,000
Waterford Park H.	15-May	9	MNR	6F	D	Cat Genius	Whitney, DG	75,000
Waya S.	13-Aug	8	SAR	1 3/16M	D	Bounding Charm	Bailey, JD	67,000
Wayward Lass S.	28-Feb	10	TAM	1 1/16M	D	Pampered Princess	Castanon, JL	60,000
WEBN S.	7-Feb	9	TP	1M	D	Silver Minister	Bejarano, R	50,000
Weekend Delight S.	11-Sep	9	TP	6F	D	Put Me In	Guidry, M	75,000
Wende S.	20-Apr	9	TUP	7 1/2F	T	Southern Spring	Stevens, SA	21,900
Wende S.	8-Nov	8	TUP	1M	D	Arch Lady	Hernandez, ML	21,900
West Long Branch S.	19-Jun	8	MTH	6F	D	Our Royal Dancer	Velez, Jr., JA	65,000
West Mesa H.	24-Sep	8	ALB	7F	D	Angelica Slew	Jones, CE	33,950
West Point H.	15-Aug	9	SAR	1 1/8M	T	Golden Commander	Castellano, J	114,700
West Va Onion Juice Breeders' Classic S.	9-Oct	5	CT	7F	D	Earth Power	Reynolds, LC	75,000
West Virginia Breeders' Classic S.	9-Oct	7	CT	1 1/8M	D	A Huevo	Dominguez, RA	300,000
West Va Dash for Cash Breeders' Classic S.	9-Oct	4	CT	4F	D	Not for Sam	Flores, O	75,000
West Virginia Derby-G3	7-Aug	8	MNR	1 1/8M	D	Sir Shackleton	Bejarano, R	600,000
WVa Division of Tourism Breeders' Classic S.	9-Oct	3	CT	7F	D	Alaska Ash	Acosta, JD	75,000
West Virginia Futurity	13-Nov	4	CT	7F	D	Bravura	Cortez, AC	52,475
West Virginia Futurity	13-Nov	6	CT	7F	D	Wild Remarks	Acosta, JD	53,325
West Virginia Governor's H.	7-Aug	7	MNR	1 1/16M	D	Wiggins	Bejarano, R	100,000
West Va House of Delegates Speaker's Cup H.	7-Aug	4	MNR	1M	T	Gin and Sin	Bejarano, R	85,000
West Va Legislature Chairman's Cup H.	7-Aug	3	MNR	4 1/2F	D	Ameri Brilliance	Coa, E	85,000
West Virginia Lottery Breeders' Classic S.	9-Oct	8	CT	7F	D	Five Star Account	Ortega, J	75,000
West Virginia Secretary of State H.	7-Aug	2	MNR	6F	D	Put Me In	Coa, E	85,000
West Virginia Senate President's Cup H.	7-Aug	5	MNR	1M	T	Lady of the Future	Vega, H	85,000
West Va VMoscarelli Mem Breeders' Classic S.	9-Oct	1	CT	6 1/2F	D	Mr. Bondsman	Acosta, JD	75,000
Westchester H.-G3	5-May	8	BEL	1M	D	Gygistar	Bravo, J	109,500
Western Borders S.	9-May	3	CRC	6F	D	Weigelia	Toribio, Jr., A	40,000
Western Canada H.	1-Jul	8	NP	6 1/2F	D	Chief Mtn	Simard, RE	40,000
Western Heritage S.	21-Aug	3	MD	6 1/2F	D	Fargo Forbes	Rocheleau, SR	10,000
Western Montana Fair T'bred Maiden Derby	10-Aug	8	WMF	5 1/4F	D	Flying Catman	Wippert, S	4,200
Westerner S.	22-Aug	8	NP	1 5/16M	D	Illusive Force	Welch, Q	40,000
What a Pleasure S.	4-Dec	10	CRC	1 1/16M	D	Better Than Bonds	Blanc, B	100,000
What a Summer S.	17-Jan	8	LRL	6F	D	Bronze Abe	Rodriguez, ED	75,000
Wheat City S.	2-Aug	6	ASD	1M	D	Northern Affair	Simard, RE	40,000
Whimsical S.	18-Apr	9	WO	6F	D	Holy Bubbette	Bravo, J	186,000
Whirlaway H.-G3	1-Feb	8	FG	1 1/16M	D	Olmodavor	Lanerie, CJ	100,000
Whirlaway S.	7-Feb	9	AQU	1 1/16M	D	Little Matth Man	Fragoso, P	82,875
White Carnation S.	5-Jun	5	BEL	1 1/16M	D	Board Elligible	Castellano, J	70,950
White Oak H.	26-Jun	9	AP	6F	D	Silver Bid	Douglas, RR	83,650
Whitney H.-G1	7-Aug	9	SAR	1 1/8M	D	Roses in May	Prado, ES	750,000
Who Doctor Who H.	17-Jul	4	HPO	1M	D	Death Trappe	Martinez, A	31,000
Wickerr H.	31-Jul	8	DMR	1M	T	Statement	Santiago, J	98,825
Wide Country S.	6-Mar	8	LRL	1 1/16M	D	He Loves Me	Santana, JZ	40,000
Wild Flower S.	16-Oct	9	LS	5F	T	Nicole's Dream	Martin, Jr., EM	50,000
Wild Rose H.	3-Jul	5	NP	6 1/2F	D	Sly Lady	Welch, Q	40,000
Wild Rose S.	12-Jun	9	PRM	1 1/16M	D	Wildwood Royal	Sukie, D	50,000
Wildcat H.	25-Apr	8	TUP	1 3/8M	T	Bristolville	Bridges, K	40,000
Will Rogers S.-G3	22-May	8	HOL	1M	T	Laura's Lucky Boy	Valenzuela, PA	109,400
Willard L. Proctor Memorial S.	23-May	8	HOL	5F	D	Chandtrue	Nakatani, CS	101,175
William Almy, Jr. S.	15-May	8	SUF	6F	D	On the Game	Rojas, RI	40,000
William Donald Schaefer H.-G3	15-May	8	PIM	1 1/8M	D	Seattle Fitz (ARG)	Migliore, R	100,000

Stakes	Date	Race	Trk	Dist/Surf		Winner	Jockey	Gross
William Henry Harrison S.	2-May	7	IND	6F	D	Liepers Fork	Mojica, O	40,000
William Kyne H.	24-Jan	9	PM	1 1/8M	D	Yesss	Beckner, T	10,000
Willow Lake H.	24-Jul	8	YAV	1M	D	Sideways	Ortega, JA	12,500
Willowbrook S.	28-Feb	7	HOU	5F	T	Sound of Gold	Jacinto, J	30,000
Willy Fiddle Memorial S.	14-Jul	7	BOI	7 1/2F	D	Quiet Syns	Conklin, J	11,235
Wilshire H.-G3	25-Apr	7	HOL	1M	T	Spring Star (FR)	Solis, AO	110,900
Windsor Ford S.	22-Aug	7	GPR	1 1/8M	D	Moe Boots	Ramirez, A	7,537
Wine Country H.	21-Aug	6	FL	6F	D	Top Shoter	Nicol, Jr., PA	50,000
Winning Colors H.	22-May	9	CD	6F	D	Lady Tak	Sellers, SJ	108,600
Winning Colors S.	9-Jun	7	BOI	7F	D	Thrill After Dark	Packer, BR	10,245
Winnipeg Futurity S.	2-Aug	5	ASD	6F	D	Tuff Justice	Eads, JR	40,000
Winnipeg Sun S.	1-Aug	8	ASD	1 1/16M	D	Maui Money	Guerra, VJ	40,000
Winsham Lad H.	10-Jan	10	SUN	1M	D	Streak of Royalty	Jaime, R	55,250
WinStar Derby	28-Mar	8	SUN	1 1/16M	D	Hi Teck Man	Jaime, R	500,000
WinStar Distaff H.-G3	31-May	8	LS	1M	T	Academic Angel	Sellers, SJ	200,000
WinStar Galaxy S.-G2	10-Oct	6	KEE	1 3/16M	T	Stay Forever	Castro, E	500,000
WinStar/Sunland Park Oaks	27-Mar	8	SUN	1M	D	Speedy Falcon	Jaime, R	261,500
Wintergreen H.	1-May	9	BEU	1 1/16M	D	Floater	Villa-Gomez, H	45,000
Wintergreen S.	12-Mar	9	TP	1M	D	Strike Rate	D'Amico, AJ	50,000
Wishing Well S.	10-Jan	10	TP	6F	D	Saratoga Humor	Bejarano, R	50,000
Witches Brew S.	30-Oct	9	MED	5F	T	Kiss Me Katie	Turner, TG	60,000
With Approval S.	8-Aug	4	WO	1 1/8M	T	Surging River	Kabel, T	104,000
Withers S.-G3	1-May	8	AQU	1M	D	Medallist	Chavez, JF	150,000
Without Feathers S.	25-Sep	9	MTH	1M 70Y	D	Grand Prayer	Coa, E	60,000
Wolf Hill S.	5-Jun	10	MTH	5F	T	Rudirudy	Rivera, Jr., LR	60,000
Wolverine S.	12-Jun	8	GLD	6F	D	Above the Wind	Mata, F	40,000
Wonder Where S.	1-Aug	8	WO	1 1/4M	T	My Vintage Port	Jones, JC	250,000
Wonders Delight S.	11-Jun	8	PEN	6F	D	Defrere's Venture	Clifton, T	41,400
Wood Memorial S.-G1	10-Apr	8	AQU	1 1/8M	D	Tapit	Dominguez, RA	750,000
Woodbine Slots Cup H.-G3	20-Nov	8	WO	1 1/16M	D	Mark One	Landry, RC	157,950
Woodford County S.	22-Oct	9	KEE	5 1/2F	T	Battle Won	Bejarano, R	84,675
Woodford Reserve Turf Classic S.-G1	1-May	9	CD	1 1/8M	T	Stroll	Bailey, JD	453,900
Woodland Heritage S.	21-Aug	1	MD	6 1/2F	D	Sheen Sky	Rocheleau, SR	10,000
Woodlands Derby	24-Oct	9	WDS	1 1/16M	D	Wally's Choice	Robletto, L	25,000
Woodlands H.	30-Oct	9	WDS	1 1/16M	D	Magic Doe	Eads, JR	25,000
Woodlands Juvenile S.	31-Oct	9	WDS	6F	D	Wind Twister	Eads, JR	20,000
Woodlawn S.	15-May	7	PIM	1 1/16M	T	Artie Schiller	Migliore, R	100,000
Woodside H.	2-May	8	BM	6F	D	Christmas Time	Baze, RA	72,000
Woodstock S.	24-Apr	8	WO	6F	D	Nyuk Nyuk Nyuk	Luciani, D	137,375
Woodward S.-G1	11-Sep	10	BEL	1 1/8M	D	Ghostzapper	Castellano, J	500,000
Work the Crowd H.	26-Dec	8	GG	1M	T	Scrofa	Figueroa, O	100,000
Work the Crowd H.	3-Jan	3	GG	1M	D	Super High	Rollins, CJ	100,000
World Appeal S.	1-Oct	8	MED	1M 70Y	T	Elusive Thunder	Elliott, S	55,000
Wynn Dot Comma S.	6-Jun	6	CRC	5F	D	B. B. Best	Aguilar, M	40,000
Yaddo H.	18-Aug	8	SAR	1 1/8M	T	Sabellina	Day, P	114,800
Yankee Affair S.	11-Apr	9	GP	5F	T	True Love's Secret	Garcia, JA	50,000
Yankee Affair S.	9-Oct	9	PHA	1 1/16M	T	Caught in the Rain	Molina, VH	55,100
Yaqthan S.	18-Sep	6	KD	1M	T	Doc D	Whitney, DG	40,000
Yavapai County Arizona Breeders Futurity	27-Jun	8	YAV	5F	D	Cover Now	Vergara, DP	24,943
Yavapai Classic H.	6-Jun	8	YAV	6F	D	Pegalee	Gomez, EA	12,500
Yavapai Downs Derby	23-Aug	7	YAV	1 1/16M	D	His Way	Hernandez, ML	17,500
Yavapai Downs Distance Series S.	9-Aug	4	YAV	1 1/4M	D	Papa's Got Gin	Williams, CS	11,300
Yavapai Downs H.	13-Jul	8	YAV	5 1/2F	D	Jakes Corner	Higuera, AR	12,500
Yavapai Downs Sprint Series S.	9-Aug	6	YAV	6F	D	Padre Murphy	Lopez, LC	11,500
Yavapai Downs TB Futurity	6-Sep	8	YAV	6F	D	Fabulous Fey	Lopez, LC	34,000
Yellow Ribbon S.-G1	2-Oct	4	SA	1 1/4M	T	Light Jig (GB)	Douglas, RR	500,000
Yellow Rose Breeders' Cup S.	3-Oct	8	LS	1 1/8M	T	Aud	Borel, CH	100,000
Yellow Rose S.	20-Nov	2	HOU	6F	D	Countryfide	Meche, L	50,000
Yellowstone Downs Thoroughbred Futurity	26-Sep	4	YD	5 1/4F	D	Deadly Talons	Kingrey, RD	15,000
Yerba Buena Breeders' Cup H.-G3	8-May	3	BM	1 1/8M	T	A B Noodle	Castro, JM	125,000
Zadracarta S.	20-Jun	8	WO	6F	T	Heyahohowdy	Ramsammy, E	108,000
Zip Pocket S.	1-Nov	4	TUP	5 1/2F	D	Newark	Dieguez, WO	21,600
Zydeco S.	9-Oct	9	DED	5F	D	Fuse It	Smith, G	40,000

* Gross includes a $5,000,000 bonus.

Histories of Graded Stakes Events

A GLEAM INVITATIONAL HANDICAP (G2), 7 Furlongs, Fillies and Mares, 3-Year-Olds and Up, Hollywood Park, 2004 Purse: $150,000

Year	Winner	Age	Jockey	Wt.	Second	Wt.	Third	Wt.	Win Value	Time	Beyer
1979	Delice	4	E. Delahoussaye	116	Great Lady M.	117	Sateen	111	25,100	1:08.80	
1980	Great Lady M.	5	P.A. Valenzuela	115	Double Deceit	114	Splendid Girl	122	30,550	1:08.40	
1981	She Can't Miss	4	P.A. Valenzuela	117	Cherokee Frolic	114	Shine High	122	32,050	1:09.00	
1982	Happy Bride	4	W.A. Guerra	113	Lucky Lady Ellen	117	Jones Time Machine	112	30,700	1:08.40	
1983	Matching	5	R. Sibille	121	Sierva	117	Bara Lass	117	31,800	1:22.40	
1984	Lass Trump	4	C.J. McCarron	116	Pleasure Cay	116	Angel Savage	112	39,400	1:21.20	
1985	Dontstop the Music	5	L. Pincay Jr	121	Lovlier Linda	122	Mimi Baker	110	36,500	1:21.20	
1986	Outstandingly	4	G.L. Stevens	120	Eloquack	110	Shywing	120	46,100	1:21.80	
1987	Le L'Argent	5	G.D. McHargue	118	Sari's Heroine	117	Rare Starlet	115	48,650	1:23.00	
1988	Integra	4	G.L. Stevens	118	Behind the Scenes	116	Carol's Wonder	117	46,100	1:23.00	
1989	Daloma	5	C.J. McCarron	115	Survive	116	Winning Colors	123	47,900	1:21.60	
1990	Stormy but Valid	4	G.L. Stevens	120	Hot Novel	121	Tis Juliet	117	61,300	1:21.20	103
1991	Survive	7	R.A. Baze	119	Stormy but Valid	121	Brought to Mind	117	62,400	1:22.00	95
1992	Forest Fealty	5	M.A. Pedroza	116	Brought to Mind	120	Devil's Orchid	120	64,800	1:22.00	99
1993	Bold Windy	4	G.L. Stevens	115	La Spia	115	Bountiful Native	122	65,700	1:21.60	98
1994	Golden Klair	4	C.J. McCarron	117	Cargo	117	Minidar	117	60,400	1:22.00	100
1995	Angi Go	5	G.L. Stevens	117	Desert Stormer	118	Dancing Mirage	115	62,700	1:21.40	100
1996	Igotrhythm	4	E. Delahoussaye	116	Klassy Kim	116	Cat's Cradle	118	63,840	1:21.40	102
1997	Toga Toga Toga	5	G.L. Stevens	119	Our Summer Bid	115	Radu Cool	116	65,040	1:22.60	100
1998	A.P. Assay	4	E. Delahoussaye	116	Exotic Wood	124	Closed Escrow	114	150,000	1:20.40	115
1999	Enjoy the Moment	4	D.R. Flores	117	Snowberg	115	Woodman's Dancer	117	120,000	1:21.20	100
2000	Honest Lady	4	K.J. Desormeaux	121	Seth's Choice	115	Hookedonthefeelin	116	120,000	1:21.47	107
2001	Go Go	4	E. Delahoussaye	124	Kitty On the Track	115	Nany's Sweep	117	120,000	1:22.19	100
2002	Irguns Angel	4	E. Delahoussaye	116	Secret Liaison	116	Kalookan Queen	122	120,000	1:22.50	100
2003	Cee's Elegance	6	V. Espinoza	116	You	121	Affluent	119	150,000	1:21.47	103
2004	Dream of Summer	5	M.E. Smith	114	Tucked Away	116	Elusive Diva	112	90,000	1:21.16	107

Beyer Index: 101.93

ACK ACK HANDICAP (G3), 7 1/2 Furlongs, 3-Year-Olds and Up, Churchill Downs, 2004 Purse: $165,300

Year	Winner	Age	Jockey	Wt.	Second	Wt.	Third	Wt.	Win Value	Time	Beyer
1991	Seven Spades	4	D. Cox	108	Discover		Senator to Be		38,510	1:37.60	100
1994	Lost Pan	4	D. Barton	114	Sir Vixen		Groovy Jett		54,795	1:30.27	108
1995	Mystery Storm	3	C.V. Gonzalez	112	I'm Very Irish		Tarzan's Blade		75,600	1:29.10	109
1996	Western Trader	5	C.H. Borel	113	Top Account		Strategic Intent		70,308	1:29.84	112
1997	Cat's Career	4	W. Martinez.	108	Rare Rock	112	Victor Cooley	122	69,160	1:32.06	104
1998	Distorted Humor	5	C. H. Borel	120	Crafty Friend	113	Chindi	113	68,262	1:29.61	102
1999	Littlebitlively	5	C. H. Borel	119	Run Johnny	117	Tactical Cat	117	71,672	1:28.97	111
2000	Chindi	6	T.T. Doocy	113	Smolderin Heart	113	Millencolin	113	70,494	1:29.30	107
2001	Illusioned	3	P. Day	118	Strawberry Affair	112	Fappie's Notebook	116	70,866	1:28.63	106
2002	Twilight Road	5	P. Day	113	Mountain General	116	Binthebest	113	69,874	1:29.39	105
2003	Cappuchino	4	J.K. Court	117	Pass Rush	116	Twilight Road	116	102,579	1:31.66	99
2004	Sir Cherokee	4	C.H. Borel	114	Fire Slam	117	Slate Run	106	102,486	1:29.48	107

Beyer Index: 105.83

ACORN (G1), 1 Mile, 3-Year-Old Fillies, Belmont Park, 2004 Purse: $250,000

Year	Winner	Age	Jockey	Wt.	Second	Wt.	Third	Wt.	Win Value	Time	Beyer
1931	Baba Kenny	3	W. Cannon	121	Lady Legs	113	Romanesque	113	$3,375	1:41.00	
1932	Top Flight	3	R. Workman	121	Parry	114	Unique	114	12,850	1:39.00	
1933	Iseult	3	H. Mills	114	Edelweiss	114	Illusive	114	10,650	1:40.60	
1934	Fleam	3	J. Stout	109	Dusky Princess	112	Lady Reigh	112	8,575	1:38.00	
1935	Good Gamble	3	S. Renick	112	Guiding Star	109	Sorrow	112	7,325	1:39.20	
1936	Blue Sheen	3	J. Stout	112	High Fleet	112	Split Second	121	10,600	1:39.00	
1937	Dawn Play	3	L. Balaski	109	Royal Raiment	112	Drawbridge	115	10,100	1:38.80	
1938	Handcuff	3	C. Kurtsinger	121	Invoke	121	Catalysis	121	10,325	1:40.40	
1939	Hostility	3	L. Haas	121	Wise Lady	121	Red Eye	121	12,100	1:39.80	
1940	Damaged Goods	3	J. Gilbert	121	Fairy Chant	121	War Beauty	121	12,025	1:37.00	
1941	Proud One	3	W. Eads	121	Cis Marion	121	Up the Hill	121	7,275	1:37.60	
1942	Zaca Rosa	3	C. Wahler	121	Vagrancy	121	Bonnet Ann	121	11,300	1:38.20	
1943	Nellie L.	3	W. Eads	121	La Reigh	121	Stefanita	121	10,320	1:38.60	
1944	Twilight Tear	3	C. McCreary	121	Whirlabout	121	Everget	121	10,815	1:37.00	
1945	Gallorette	3	E. Arcaro	121	Monsoon	121	Recce	121	7,930	1:38.00	
1946	Earshot	3	E. Arcaro	121	Bonnie Beryl	121	Rytina	121	9,480	1:37.20	
1947	But Why Not	3	W. Mehrtens	121	Harmonica	121	Alrenie	121	14,300	1:38.00	

Year	Winner	Age	Jockey	Wt.	Second	Wt.	Third	Wt.	Win Value	Time	Beyer
1948	Watermill	3	E. Arcaro	121	Alablue	121	Pigreeny	121	12,525	1:37.00	
1949	Nell K.	3	D. Dodson	121	Gaffery	121	Adile	121	13,725	1:38.00	
1950	Siama	3	T. Atkinson	121	Next Move	121	Honey's Gal	121	12,600	1:37.20	
1951	Kiss Me Kate	3	W. Mehrtens	121	Wisteria	121	Jacodema	121	16,750	1:36.40	
1951	Nothirdchance	3	B. Green	121	Gorgeous Reded	121	Vulcania	121	16,550	1:38.00	
1952	Parading Lady	3	J.N. Hardinb'l	121	Sufie	121	Lily White	121	18,650	1:38.80	
1953	Secret Meeting	3	J. Nichols	121	Wings o' Morn	121	Tritium	121	18,450	1:39.40	
1954	Riverina	3	W. Boland	121			Question Time	121	10,925	1:38.80	
	Happy Mood	3	P. Moreno	121							
1955	High Voltage	3	E. Arcaro	121	Sometime Thing	121	Hen Party	121	22,900	1:38.80	
1956	Beyond	3	C. McCreary	121			Levee	121	12,650	1:37.80	
	Princess Turia	3	H. Moreno	121							
1957	Bayou	3	R. Ussery	121	Teleran	121	Here and There	121	26,000	1:37.00	
1958	Big Effort	3	P. Anderson	121	Polamby	121	Lopar	121	22,952	1:37.40	
1959	Quill	3	R. Ussery	121	Cobul	121	Hope is Eternal	121	38,075	1:37.60	
1960	Irish Jay	3	H. Woodhouse	121	Airmans Guide	121	Sister Antoine	121	38,293	1:35.80	
1961	Bowl of Flowers	3	E. Arcaro	121	Black Darter	121	Seven Thirty	121	37,537	1:37.40	
1962	Cicada	3	W. Shoemaker	121	Tamarona	121	Upswept	121	37,992	1:35.60	
1963	Spicy Living	3	J. Combest	121	Nalee	121	Lamb Chop	121	39,097	1:37.20	
1964	Castle Forbes	3	J.L. Rotz	121	Sceree	121	Face the Facts	121	39,097	1:37.00	
1965	Ground Control	3	D. Pierce	121	Marshua	121	Up Oars	121	38,220	1:37.20	
1966	Marking Time	3	W. Shoemaker	121	Around the Roses	121	Moccasin	121	38,642	1:36.00	
1967	Furl Sail	3	J. Vasquez	121	Quillo Queen	121	Pepperwood	121	44,330	1:35.60	
1968	Dark Mirage	3	M. Ycaza	121	Another Nell	121	Gay Matelda	121	39,065	1:34.80	
1969	Shuvee	3	J. Davidson	121	Hail to Patsy	121	Big Advance	121	38,707	1:35.60	
1970	Royal Signal	3	G. Patterson	121	Cold Comfort	121	Luci Tee	121	36,969	1:36.20	
1970	Cathy Honey	3	L. Pincay Jr	121	Missile Belle	121	Fast Attack	121	36,969	1:36.00	
1971	Deceit	3	J.L. Rotz	121	Sea Saga	121	Forward Gal	121	38,970	1:36.60	
1972	Susan's Girl	3	V. Tejada	121	Wanda	121	Stacey d'Ette	121	33,720	1:34.60	
1973	Windy's Daughter	3	B. Baeza	121	Poker Night	121	Voler	121	36,540	1:35.40	
1974	Special Team	3	M.A. Rivera	121	Stage Door Betty	121	Raisela	121	33,960	1:35.40	
1974	Chris Evert	3	J. Velasquez	121	Clear Copy	121	Fiesta Libre	121	33,960	1:36.00	
1975	Ruffian	3	J. Vasquez	121	Somethingregal	121	Gallant Trial	121	33,660	1:34.40	
1976	Dearly Precious	3	J. Velasquez	121	Optimistic Gal	121	Tell Me All	121	33,390	1:35.80	
1977	Bring Out the Band	3	D. Brumfield	121	Your Place or Mine	121	Mrs. Warren	121	33,690	1:36.80	
1978	Tempest Queen	3	J. Velasquez	121	Lakeville Miss	121	White Star Line	121	31,920	1:35.40	
1979	Davona Dale	3	J. Velasquez	121	Eloquent	121	Plankton	121	50,130	1:36.00	
1980	Bold 'n Determined	3	E. Delahoussaye	121	Mitey Lively	121	Sugar and Spice	121	50,400	1:36.80	
1981	Heavenly Cause	3	L. Pincay Jr	121	Dame Mysterieuse	121	Expressive Dance	121	50,850	1:35.20	
1982	Cupecoy's Joy	3	A. Santiago	121	Nancy Huang	121	Vestris	121	51,750	1:34.20	
1983	Ski Goggle	3	C.J. McCarron	121	Princess Rooney	121	Thirty Flags	121	69,360	1:35.00	
1984	Miss Oceana	3	E. Maple	121	Life's Magic	121	Proud Clarioness	121	135,720	1:35.80	
1985	Mom's Command	3	A. Fuller	121	Le L'Argent	121	Diplomette	121	113,040	1:35.80	
1986	Lotka	3	J.D. Bailey	121	Dynamic Star	121	Life at the Top	121	113,580	1:35.20	
1987	Grecian Flight	3	C. Perret	121	Fiesta Gal	121	Bound	121	113,580	1:35.20	
1988	Aptostar	3	R.G. Davis	121	Topicount	121	Avie's Gal	121	109,980	1:34.80	
1989	Open Mind	3	A. Cordero Jr	121	Hot Novel	121	Triple Strike	121	111,960	1:35.40	
1990	Stella Madrid	3	A. Cordero Jr	121	Danzig's Beauty	121	Seaside Attraction	121	104,580	1:36.00	95
1991	Meadow Star	3	J.D. Bailey	121	Versailles Treaty	121	Dazzle Me Jolie	121	103,680	1:37.40	98
1992	Prospectors Delite	3	P. Day	121	Pleasant Stage	121	Turnback the Alarm	121	113,400	1:35.00	98
1993	Sky Beauty	3	M.E. Smith	121	Educated Risk	121	In Her Glory	121	90,000	1:35.40	103
1994	Inside Information	3	M.E. Smith	121	Cinnamon Sugar	121	Sovereign Kitty	121	90,000	1:34.20	96
1995	Cat's Cradle	3	C.W. Antley	121	Country Cat	121	Lucky Lavender Gal	121	90,000	1:37.40	92
1996	Star de Lady Ann	3	M.E. Smith	121	Yanks Music	121	Stop Traffic	121	90,000	1:34.60	96
1997	Sharp Cat	3	G.L. Stevens	121	Dixie Flag	121	Ajina	121	90,000	1:34.40	103
1998	Jersey Girl	3	M.E. Smith	121	Santaria	121	Brave Deed	121	90,000	1:36.32	99
1999	Three Ring	3	J.D. Bailey	121	Better Than Honour	121	Madison's Charm	121	120,000	1:36.16	92
2000	Finder's Fee	3	J. Velazquez	121	C'est L'Amour	121	Roxelana	121	120.000	1:37.38	97
2001	Forest Secrets	3	C.J. McCarron	121	Victory Ride	121	Real Cozzy	121	120,000	1:34.92	93
2002	You	3	J.D. Bailey	121	Willa on the Move	121	Bella Bellucci	121	150,000	1:34.05	97
2003	Bird Town	3	E.S. Prado	121	Lady Tak	121	Final Round	121	150,000	1:35.29	96
2004	Island Sand	3	T.J. Thompson	121	Society Selection	121	Friendly Michelle	121	150,000	1:34.89	101

Beyer Index: 97.07

ADIRONDACK (G2), 6 1/2 Furlongs, 2-Year-Old Fillies, Saratoga Race Course, 2003 Purse: $150,000

Year	Winner	Age	Jockey	Wt.	Second	Wt.	Third	Wt.	Win Value	Time	Beyer
1901	Smart Set	2	O'Connor	114	Saturday	112	Leonid	108	4,325	1:16.60	
1902	Molly Brant	2	Odom	109	Wild Thyme	104	Sir Voorhees	112	6,375	1:13.20	
1903	Sweet Gretchen	2	Fuller	102	Leonidas	115	Gold Saint	112	3,025	1:15.80	

Year	Winner	Age	Jockey	Wt.	Second	Wt.	Third	Wt.	Win Value	Time	Beyer
1904	Broadcloth	2	T. Burns	113	Pasadena	112	Blue Coat	98	3,850	1:15.20	
1905	Tangle	2	O'Neill	110	Juggler	111	Ravena	106	3,850	1:13.40	
1906	Salvidere	2	Sewell	128	Don Enrique	110	Aletheuo	108	3,850	1:14.80	
1907	Beaucoup	2	E. Dugan	110	Falcada	104	Fultonville	104	3,850	1:14.00	
1908	Sea Cliff	2	Notter	114	Statesman	114	Con'ght Ranger	109	505	1:15.20	
1909	Scarpia	2	C. Grand	102	Chickasaw	116	Joe Morris	115	1,925	1:13.00	
1910	Zeus	2	Butwell	110	Round the World	120	Iron Mask	124	4,500	1:11.60	
1913	Little Nephew	2	Killingsworth	125	Black Broom	116	Spearhead	106	1,925	1:15.00	
1914	Lady Barbary	2	H. Sunter	114	Trial by Jury	117	Luke	119	2,175	1:14.20	
1915	Friar Rock	2	E. Dugan	116	Achievement	110	Kilmer	102	1,925	1:17.80	
1916	Ultimatum	2	R. Troxler	116	Woodtrap	105	Tragedy	108	2,675	1:14.80	
1917	Happy Go Lucky	2	F. Robinson	109	Matinee Idol	111	Jack Hare Jr.	125	3,750	1:13.60	
1918	Routledge	2	E. Ambrose	111	Daydue	108	Hannibal	125	3,925	1:12.00	
1919	Grayssian	2	T. Nolan	111	Kinnoul	122	Sammy	115	3,925	1:12.80	
1920	Exodus	2	E. Ambrose	125	Jeg	114	Quecreek	110	3,925	1:11.80	
1921	Oil Man	2	E. Haynes	119	Modo	115	Sir Hugh	125	3,925	1:11.80	
1922	Cartoonist	2	C. Kummer	116	Bud Lerner	125	Cherry Pie	122	3,925	1:12.00	
1923	Elvina	2	J. Callahan	112	Sunspero	113	Big Blaze	117	4,350	1:12.00	
	Befuddle finished third but was disqualified										
1924	Cloudland	2	C. Lang	115	Buttin In	110	Pas Seul	118	4,075	1:15.00	
1925	Blockhead	2	A. Johnson	112	Navigator	124	Mar. Militaire	118	3,925	1:13.60	
1926	Friedjof Nansen	2	H. Richards	107	Laddie	116	Easy Money	104	4,525	1:14.60	
1927	One Hour	2	L. Fator	110	Excalibur	110	Glade	108	4,275	1:12.20	
1928	The Worker	2	E. Barnes	107	Sun Worship	116	Hypolux	114	4,225	1:15.40	
1929	War Saint	2	L. McAtee	118	Gold Brook	106	Raccoon	114	5,200	1:12.00	
1930	Ladana	2	L. Fator	120	Chicsu	115	Sovietta	123	4,400	1:12.00	
1931	Brocado	2	M. Garner	120	Mea	114	Pintail	116	3,825	1:14.00	
1932	Speed Boat	2	J. Gilbert	114	Barn Swallow	116	Enactment	112	3,075	1:12.00	
1933	Sun Celtic	2	D. Bellizzi	111	Some Pomp	110	Contessa	109	2,200	1:16.00	
1934	Bird Flower	2	D. Meade	116	Corinne Dailey	111	Pretty Night	114	2,175	1:15.00	
1935	Beanle M.	2	D. Meade	112	Tony's Wife	116	Parade Girl	121	2,300	1:13.80	
1936	Juliet W.	2	D. Brammer	119	Maecloud	123	Swiftply	119	2,550	1:13.00	
1937	Creole Maid	2	H. Richards	120	Miyako	114	Polyata	112	2,275	1:13.20	
1938	Matterhorn	2	J. Longden	105	Grey Nurse	116	Easy Does It	112	4,250	1:15.00	
1939	Rosetown	2	H. Richards	112	Miss Ferdinand	117	Piquet	119	4,800	1:13.60	
1940	Tangled	2	E. Arcaro	121	Dark Discovery	114	Nasca	122	3,675	1:12.00	
1941	Romping Home	2	J. Longden	116	Equipet	120	Horn	114	4,500	1:13.60	
1942	La Reigh	2	J. Longden	123	Navigating	119	Wuskenin	110	3,775	1:12.40	
1943	Fire Sticky	2	H. Lindberg	108	Mrs. Ames	124	Threat o' Gold	116	5,225	1:10.80	
1944	Busher	2	E. Arcaro	123	War Date	114	Leslie Grey	116	7,530	1:11.60	
1945	Rytina	2	C. McCreary	112	Red Shoes	121	Phantasy	111	7,090	1:11.00	
1953	Riant	2	T. Atkinson	111	Case Goods	119	Fascinator	114	8,525	1:05.40	
1954	Hidden Ship	2	J. Nichols	112	Sorceress	119	Bless Pat	114	8,425	1:05.80	
1955	Dark Charger	2	A. DeSpirito	119	Levee	115	First Asking	111	8,875	1:04.40	
1962	Fashion Verdict	2	H. Woodhouse	114	Fast Luck	114	First Nominee	114	15,957	1:12.00	
1963	Petite Rouge	2	J. Sellers	114	Magna Mater	114	Always Modest	114	16,055	1:13.00	
1964	Candalita	2	B. Baeza	114	Queen Empress	123	Marshua	123	15,697	1:10.80	
1965	Lady Dulcinea	2	M. Carrozzella	114	Lovely Gypsy	120	Prides Profile	123	16,542	1:11.60	
1966	Tainted Lady	2	E. Belmonte	115	Intriguing	115	Silver True	115	16,900	1:12.60	
1967	Wildwook	2	H. Gustines	115	Morgaise	123	Syrian Sea	123	16,965	1:11.60	
1968	Process Shot	2	C. Baltazar	123	Fillypasser	115	Big Advance	123	16,575	1:10.60	
1969	Meritus	2	M. Ycaza	115	Cherry Sundae	114	I'm Gorgeous	114	20,085	1:12.60	
1970	Dutiful	2	L. Pincay Jr	114	Forward Gal	122	Patelin	122	19,402	1:10.80	
1971	Debby Deb	2	E. Belmonte	114	Fance Partner	114	Numbered Account	122	20,820	1:10.20	
1972	Faithful Girl	2	C.H. Marquez	120	Behram	120	Bel Sheba	120	16,965	1:11.80	
1973	Talking Picture	2	B. Baeza	120	In Hot Pursuit	120	Bedknob	120	17,625	1:11.00	
1974	Laughing Bridge	2	L. Pincay Jr	120	Stulcer	120	Some Swinger	120	16,950	1:10.80	
1975	Optimistic Gal	2	B. Baeza	120	Glory Glory	120	Against All Fl'gs	120	22,515	1:11.20	
1976	Harvest Girl	2	J. Cruguet	114	Bonnie Empress	114	Drama Critic	119	22,545	1:11.20	
1977	L'Alezane	2	R. Turcotte	121	Sunny Bay	121	Misgivings	114	22,335	1:10.60	
1978	Whisper Fleet	2	J. Cruguet	119	Island Kitty	114	Golferette	114	22,410	1:10.00	
1979	Smart Angle	2	S. Maple	119	Lucky My Way	114	Andrea F.	114	26,835	1:11.00	
1980	Sweet Revenge	2	J. Velasquez	119	Companionship	114	Honey's Appeal	114	34,080	1:10.40	
1981	Thrilld n Delightd	2	J. Velasquez	114	Apalachee Honey	119	Trove	116	35,160	1:10.80	
1982	Jelly Bean Holiday	2	J. Fell	116	Midnight Rapture	114	Flying Lassie	114	34,920	1:10.80	
1983	Buzz My Bell	2	J. Velasquez	114	Upturning	116	Mrs. Flagler	116	33,720	1:12.40	
1984	Contredance	2	E. Maple	114	Outstandingly	114	Oriental	114	53,100	1:10.40	
1985	Nervous Baba	2	J. Velasquez	114	Family Style	114	Steal a Kiss	114	54,450	1:09.60	
1986	Sacahuista	2	C.J. McCarron	119	Collins	114	Release the Lyd	116	53,280	1:11.00	
1987	Over All	2	A. Cordero Jr	121	Flashy Runner	114	Careless Flirt	114	64,890	1:10.60	
1988	Pat Copelan	2	P. Day	114	Channel Three	116	Premier Playmate	116	66,780	1:10.80	
1989	Dance Colony	2	J.A. Santos	116	In Full Cry	114	Saratoga Sizzle	114	52,200	1:11.80	
1990	Really Quick	2	A. Cordero Jr	114	Devilish Touch	119	Ferber's Follies	119	54,270	1:11.40	79

Year	Winner	Age	Jockey	Wt.	Second	Wt.	Third	Wt.	Win Value	Time	Beyer
1991	American Royale	2	A.T. Gryder	119	Bless Our Home	114	Turnbackthe Alarm	119	71,640	1:10.60	
1992	Sky Beauty	2	E. Maple	116	Missed the Storm	114	Distinct Habit	121	70,560	1:10.00	96
1993	Astas Foxy Lady	2	R.P. Romero	119	Footing	114	Casa Eire	119	68,520	1:10.00	89
1994	Seeking Regina	2	J.D. Bailey	114	Changing Ways	119	Phone Bird	114	66,600	1:18.40	72
1995	Flat Fleet Feet	2	M.E. Smith	113	Steady Cat	112	Western Dreamer	120	65,760	1:16.60	95
1996	Storm Song	2	P. Day	113	Last Two States	113	(DH) Larkwhistle	116	84,075	1:17.60	76
1997	Salty Perfume	2	S.J. Sellers	114	Brac Drifter	114	Joustabout	114	90,000	1:17.80	93
1998	Things Change	2	J.A. Santos	114	Extended Applause	117	Brittons Hill	114	90,000	1:18.00	84
1999	Regally Appealing	2	E.S. Prado	114	Miss Wineshine	122	Trump My Heart	114	90,000	1:16.80	92
2000	Raging Fever	2	J.D. Bailey	122	Two Item Limit	117	Secret Lover	117	90,000	1:17.47	101
2001	You	2	E.S. Prado	115	Cashier's Dream	122	Magic Storm	115	90,000	1:15.16	107
2002	Awesome Humor	2	P. Day	122	Stellar	116	Holiday Runner	122	90,000	1:17.75	89
2003	Whoopi Cat	2	E.S. Prado	116	Unbridled Beauty	116	Eye Dazzler	116	90,000	1:17.51	83

Beyer Index: 88.92

Run at 5 1/2 furlongs 1953–55; 6 furlongs 1901–52, 1956–93

AEGON TURF SPRINT (G3), 5 Furlongs (Turf), 3-Year-Olds and Up, Churchill Downs, 2004 Purse: $114,700

Year	Winner	Age	Jockey	Wt.	Second	Wt.	Third	Wt.	Win Value	Time	Beyer
1995	Long Suit	4	W. Martinez	114	Bold N' Flashy		Scottish Fantasy		57,086	:56.90	99
1996	Danjur	4	J.D. Bailey	114	Hello Paradise		Linear		57,281	:56.09	108
1997	Sandtrap	4	A. Solis	123	Appealing Skier		G H's Pleasure		71,734	:56.51	102
1998	Indian Rocket	4	G.L. Stevens	116	G H's Pleasure		Claire's Honor		75,950	:57.32	100
1999	Howbaddouwanit	4	M.E. Smith	123	Mr Festus		Three Card Willie		71,486	:57.03	100
2000	Bold Fact	5	R. Migliore	120	Howbaddouwanit		Fantastic Finish		75,330	:56.37	101
2001	Morluc	5	R.J. Albarado	122	Testify	119	Texas Glitter	122	70,494	:56.60	106
2002	Testify	5	E. Delahoussaye	119	Texas Glitter	122	Gone Fishin	116	75,206	:57.39	104
2003	Fiscally Speaking	4	J.K. Court	114	Morluc	122	Testify	122	71,486	:56.01	102
2004	Lydgate	4	P. Day	114	Mighty Beau	117	Banned in Boston	114	71,114	:56.56	102

Beyer Index: 102.40

AFFECTIONATELY HANDICAP (G3), 1 1/16 Miles, Fillies and Mares, 3-Year-Olds and Up, Aqueduct, 2004 Purse: $109,600

Year	Winner	Age	Jockey	Wt.	Second	Wt.	Third	Wt.	Win Value	Time	Beyer
1976	Proud Delta	4	J. Velasquez	114	Mary Queenofscots	119	Shy Dawn	119	34,650	1:37.40	
1977	Shy Dawn	6	D. Montoya	115	Double Quester	115	Shawi	108	31,620	1:45.20	
1977	Illiterate	5	S. Cauthen	113	Quintas Vicki	113	Secret Lanvin	118	31,770	1:45.20	
1978	One Sum	4	R. Hernandez	117	Keep It Secret	103	Passage Way	113	32,910	1:44.80	
1979	Kit's Double	6	A. Graell	110	Whodatorsay	111	Sue Me Not	116	33,150	1:48.60	
1980	Plankton	4	R. Hernandez	116	Worthy Poise	112	Propitiate	112	35,100	1:45.00	
1981	Plankton	5	R. Hernandez	120	Sweet Maid	114	The Wheel Turns	114	34,380	1:45.40	
1982	Perfect Poppy	5	V.H. Molina	106	Hitting Irish	112	Andover Way	123	33,960	1:48.60	
1983	Adept	4	K.L. Rogers	108	Princess Oola	118	Debonair Dancer	113	32,880	1:43.40	
1983	Polite Rebuff	4	F. Lovato Jr	110	Nafees	107	Cheap Seats	121	32,880	1:43.80	
1984	Am Capable	4	A. Cordero Jr	118	Far Flying	121	Sintrillium	115	59,760	1:46.20	
1985	Descent	5	R.J. Thibeaux J	106	Sweet Missus	112	Bracalena	114	52,110	1:45.60	
1985	Sintrillium	7	R.G. Davis	116	Emphatic	104	Far Flying	116	52,830	1:45.60	
1986	Lady on the Run	4	A. Cordero Jr	118	Satch	112			52,110	1:46.20	
					Squan Song	124					
1987	Squan Song	6	J.A. Santos	124	Clemanna's Rose	107	Ms. Eloise	120	69,840	1:46.20	
1988	Tricky Squaw	5	J.A. Santos	123	With a Twist	111	Seriously	111	52,740	1:45.20	
1989	Rose's Cantina	5	E. Maple	114	Tops in Taps	114	Thirty Eight Go Go	116	54,720	1:42.80	
1990	Naskra's Return	4	M.E. Smith	113	Bold Wench	118	Dreamy Mimi	115	51,480	1:43.80	111
1991	My Treasure	4	C. Lopez	115	Buy the Firm	122	Personal Business	116	54,360	1:44.20	
1992	Get Lucky	4	M.E. Smith	113	My Treasure	114	Haunting	114	52,650	1:46.00	96
1993	Hilbys Brite Flite	4	J.R. Velasquez	111	My Treasure	112	Lady Lear	117	52,470	1:44.60	95
1994	Poolesta	5	Lovato F Jr	115	Hey Baba Lulu	117	Groovy Feeling	123	49,425	1:44.80	96
1995	Sea Ditty	4	Madrid A Jr	113	Beloved Bea	114	Acting Proud	111	50,190	1:46.80	93
1996	Lotta Dancing	5	H. Castillo Jr	120	Winner's Edge	109	Vinista	114	39,024	1:42.40	97
1997	Mil Kilates	4	J.F. Chavez	113	Whaleneck	110	Shoop	120	39,996	1:44.60	96
1998	Sweetzie	6	Pezua J. M.	113	Shoop	116	Gold Colony	112	50,700	1:41.80	102
1999	Biding Time	5	Gryder A. T.	118	Shoop	113	Daily Reflection	112	50,220	1:44.60	111
2000	Theresa the Teacha	5	H. Castillo Jr	114	Roaring Twenties	114	Two Fer Boston	118	51,855	1:46.42	91
2001	Pentatonic	6	A.T. Gryder	117	Strolling Belle	121	Pompei	116	66,300	1:43.17	95
2002	Zonk	4	C.C. Lopez	116	People's Princess	115	Search Party	114	68,040	1:42.58	95
2003	Zonk	5	C.C. Lopez	118	Wishful Splendor	112	Kiss a Miss	113	65,760	1:44.58	94
2004	Austin's Mom	4	P. Fragoso	112	Golden Damsel	114	Consort Music	114	65,760	1:44.02	100

Beyer Index: 98.00

AFFIRMED HANDICAP (G3), 1 1/16 Miles, 3-Year-Olds, Hollywood Park, 2004 Purse: $110,200

Year	Winner	Age	Jockey	Wt.	Second	Wt.	Third	Wt.	Win Value	Time	Beyer
1979	Valdez	3	L. Pincay Jr	119	Pole Position	118	Beau's Eagle	123	37,500	1:47.40	
1980	Score Twenty Four	3	D.G. McHargue	114	First Albert	116			37,200	1:48.20	
					Loto Canada	119					
1981	Stancharry	3	P.A. Valenzuela	117	Dusty Hula	116	Seafood	117	47,150	1:51.00	
1982	Journey at Sea	3	C.J. McCarron	122	Cassaleria	120	Guachan	112	49,600	1:46.80	
1983	My Habitony	3	D. Pierce	115	Tanks Brigade	119	Hyperborean	115	47,250	1:48.60	
1984	Tights	3	L. Pincay Jr	119	M. Double M.	116	Precisionist	121	46,850	1:48.60	
1985	Pancho Villa	3	L. Pincay Jr	118	Proudest Doon	118	Nostalgia's Star	118	64,050	1:33.80	
1986	Melair	3	P.A. Valenzuela	115	Southern Halo	113	Snow Chief	127	220,000	1:32.80	
1987	Candi's Gold	3	G.L. Stevens	116	On the Line	116	The Medic	116	93,000	1:47.60	
1988	Iz a Saros	3	A.T. Gryder	113	Stalwars	119	Bel Air Dancer	117	95,900	1:49.00	
1989	Raise a Stanza	3	C.A. Black	115	Broke the Mold	112	Prized	116	102,200	1:48.40	
1990	Stalwart Charger	3	L. Pincay Jr	120	Toby Jug	112	Kentucky Jazz	120	91,100	1:48.40	104
1991	Compelling Sound	3	G.L. Stevens	118	Best Pal	123	Caliche's Secret	117	91,300	1:47.80	107
1992	Natural Nine	3	L. Pincay Jr	117	Prospect for Four	114	Never Round	117	95,500	1:49.40	94
1993	Codified	3	G.L. Stevens	117	Roman Image	117	Future Storm	118	94,100	1:48.80	99
1994	R Friar Tuck	3	J.D. Bailey	113	Pollock's Luck	114	Wild Invader	115	96,100	1:49.00	95
1995	Mr Purple	3	Nakatani CS	120	Pumpkin House	115	Oncefortheroad	114	77,050	1:42.20	95
1996	Hesabull	3	E. Delahoussaye	117	Benton Creek	116	Semoran	118	61,050	1:43.20	93
1997	Deputy Commander	3	C.S. Nakatani	117	Hello	121	Holzmeister	121	61,500	1:42.80	107
1998	Old Trieste	3	C.J. McCarron	118	Old Topper	117	Kraal	116	62,340	1:41.80	105
1999	General Challenge	3	D.R. Flores	124	Desert Hero	120	Crowning Storm	116	75,000	1:40.83	111
2000	Tiznow	3	C.J. McCarron	111	Dixie Union	122	Millencolin	117	80,550	1:42.40	103
2001	Until Sundown	3	G.L. Stevens	117	Top Hit	114	Bayou the Moon	118	60,000	1:43.10	96
2002	Came Home	3	C.J. McCarron	124	Tracemark	120	Calkins Road	117	64,500	1:41.99	107
2003	Eye of the Tiger	3	A. Solis	119	Ministers Wild Cat	118	Bullistic	115	63,120	1:42.30	107
2004	Boomzeeboom	3	V. Espinoza	115	Twice as Bad	121	Wimplestiltskin	116	66,120	1:42.11	102

Beyer Index: 101.67

ALABAMA (G1), 1 1/4 Miles, 3-Year-Old Fillies, Saratoga Race Course, 2004 Purse: $750,000

Year	Winner	Age	Jockey	Wt.	Second	Wt.	Third	Wt.	Win Value	Time	Beyer
1872	Woodbine	3	Gradwell	107	Nema	107	Sue Rider	107	2,650	2:06.20	
1873	Minnie W.	3	Ponton	107	Sallie Watson	107	Lizzie Lucas	107	3,050	2:01.60	
1874	Regardless	3	Sparling	107	Countess	107	Madge	107	3,100	2:00.20	
1875	Olitipa	3	Evans	107	Invoice	107	Planet Filly	107	2,800	2:00.20	
1876	Merciless	3	Sparling	107	Patience	107	Athlene	107	2,850	2:00.60	
1877	Susquehanna	3	Hayward	107	Zoo Zoo	107	Oriole	107	3,450	1:57.20	
1878	Belle	3	Hayward	113	Balance All	113	Invermoor	113	2,800	1:59.00	
1879	Ferida	3	Hughes	113	Clarissima	113	Scotilla	113	3,300	2:00.60	
1880	Glidelia	3	W. Donohue	113	Kitty J.	113	Bye and Bye	113	2,600	2:00.00	
1881	Thora	3	W. Donohue	113	Bonnie Lizzie	113	Brambaletta	113	1,450	1:59.20	
1882	Belle of Runnymede	3	Stoval	113	Bonella	113	Olivia	113	3,250	2:08.60	
1883	Miss Woodford	3	J. McLaughlin	113	Bessie	113	Vera	113	3,050	1:57.20	
1884	Tolu	3	Blaylock	113	Mittie B	113	Eulogy	113	3,500	2:01.00	
1885	Ida Hope	3	I. Murphy	113	Elizabeth	113	Banana	113	3,225	1:59.00	
1886	Millie	3	J. McLaughlin	113	Molly McCarthy'sLast	113	Charity	113	3,550	1:59.20	
1887	Grisette	3	West	108	Flageoletta	113	Florimore	113	3,000	2:00.20	
1888	Bella B.	3	J. McLaughlin	115	Los Angeles	113	Prose	108	3,675	1:58.00	
1889	Princess Bowling	3	I. Murphy	114	Cotillion	108	Retrieve	113	2,650	2:03.20	
1890	Sinaloa II	3	Barnes	113	Eminence	110	Daisy F.	113	3,750	1:56.20	
1891	Sallie McClelland	3	Anderson	112	Santa Anna	111			2,075	2:05.60	
1892	Ignite	3	Clayton	112	Engarita	117	Miss Dixie	117	2,475	1:57.20	
1897	Poetess	3	C. Thorpe	114	Sunny Slope	121	Partridge	114	1,425	2:01.20	
1901	Morningside	3	N. Turner	116	Reina	121	Sweet Lavender	110	1,900	1:47.80	
1902	Par Excellence	3	Redfern	116	Lux Casta	116	Josepha	116	3,850	1:47.60	
1903	Stamping Ground	3	Fuller	116	Gravina	116	Astarita	124	4,625	1:56.80	
1904	Beldame	3	O'Neill	124	Dimple	116	Ishlana	116	3,850	1:53.60	
1905	Tradition	3	W. Davis	124	Kiamesha	116	Golden Ten	121	4,850	2:16.40	
1906	Running Water	3	W. Miller	116	Brookdale Nymph	124	Comedienne	121	3,850	1:52.40	
1907	Kennyetto	3	Notter	116	Gold Lady	124	Yankee Girl	124	3,850	1:54.20	
1908	Mayfield	3	C.H. Shilling	106	Anonyma	106	Breckon	110	3,850	2:01.00	
	Stamina finished first but was disqualified										
1909	Maskette	3	Scoville	124	Miss Kearney	116	Petticoat	116	3,850	1:59.40	
1910	Ocean Bound	3	C.H. Shilling	124	Cherryola	111	Marigot	111	3,850	1:55.00	
1913	Flying Fairy	3	T. Davies	113	Cadeau	113	Lodona	113	1,455	1:56.20	
1914	Addie M.	3	C. Burlingame	113	Casuarina	117	Early Rose	113	1,740	1:54.40	
1915	Waterblossom	3	E. Martin	126	Lady Rotha	126	Lady Teresa	109	1,160	1:57.60	
1916	Malachite	3	L. Lyke	109	Sprint	109	Jacoba	117	1,720	1:54.60	
1917	Sunbonnet	3	J. Loftus	124	Wistful	124	Fairy Wand	114	3,850	2:07.00	

Year	Winner	Age	Jockey	Wt.	Second	Wt.	Third	Wt.	Win Value	Time	Beyer
1918	Eyelid	3	L. Ensor	117	Enfilade	124	Ballymooney	114	6,575	2:04.20	
1919	Vexatious	3	E. Ambrose	114	Milkmaid	124	Polka Dot	124	7,265	2:09.20	
1920	Cleopatra	3	L. McAtee	126	Ethel Gray	114	Edwina	117	7,275	2:07.80	
1921	Prudery	3	L. Fator	124	Bit of White	121	Chat. Thierry	117	7,275	2:04.20	
1922	Nedna	3	F. Keogh	114	Emotion	114	Prudish	124	8,050	2:08.00	
1923	Untidy	3	E. Sande	124	Sally's Alley	121	Sun Quest	114	8,950	2:05.40	
1924	Priscilla Ruley	3	J. Maiben	117	Princess Doreen	126	Sunayr	117	9,925	2:08.80	
1925	Maid at Arms	3	A. Johnson	124	Lightship	114	Sun Tess	114	10,625	2:07.00	
1926	Rapture	3	L. McAtee	124	Black Maria	126	Ruthenia	117	9,275	2:06.00	
1927	Nimba	3	H. Thurber	124	La Palina	114	Recreation	114	12,925	2:06.80	
1928	Nixie	3	D. McAuliffe	121	Valkyr	114	Darkness	114	11,550	2:10.20	
1929	Aquastella	3	P. Walls	121	Lisa	117	White Veil	117	11,775	2:04.80	
1930	Escutcheon	3	L. McAtee	117	Conclave	117	Flying Gal	121	13,875	2:04.20	
1931	Risque	3	E. Steffen	121	Tambour	126	Allez Vite	117	14,200	2:05.60	
1932	Top Flight	3	R. Workman	126	Parry	116	Laughing Queen	121	12,225	2:06.40	
1933	Barn Swallow	3	D. Meade	124	Swivel	121	Edelweiss	126	11,525	2:06.60	
1934	Hindu Queen	3	L. Humphries	111	Bazaar	121	Fleam	125	11,050	2:05.00	
1935	Alberta	3	S. Coucci	111	Good Gamble	125	Judy O'Grady	111	7,350	2:05.20	
1936	Floradora	3	D. Brammer	111	High Fleet	125	Valse	111	7,525	2:06.60	
1937	Regal Lily	3	H. Richards	123	Recussion	111	Allowance	111	7,475	2:08.20	
1938	Handcuff	3	J. Westrope	125	Black Wave	114	Anaflame	111	8,275	2:07.40	
1939	War Plumage	3	M. Peters	124	Bass Wood	111	Hostility	124	10,100	2:05.00	
1940	Calaminia	3	D. Meade	111	Fairy Chant	124	Piquet	122	9,450	2:04.80	
1941	War Hazard	3	C. McCreary	114	Pomayya	114	Dark Discovery	114	8,975	2:04.80	
1942	Vagrancy	3	J. Stout	126	Smiles	126			8,950	2:05.20	
	Bonnet Ann finished first but was disqualified										
1943	Stefanita	3	C. McCreary	117	Askmenow	124	Tack Room	114	11,425	2:04.40	
1944	Vienna	3	J. Stout	114	Twilight Tear	126	Thread o' Gold	117	18,170	2:03.60	
1945	Sicily	3	T. Atkinson	110	Be Faithful	110	Surosa	110	21,015	2:03.40	
1946	Hypnotic	3	E. Guerin	124	Bridal Flower	124	Alma Mater	108	18,250	2:04.20	
1947	But Why Not	3	E. Guerin	126	Cosmic Missile	122	Bee Ann Mac	112	17,975	2:05.00	
1948	Compliance	3	T. Atkinson	112	Alablue	108	Play Tag	108	16,900	2:06.00	
1949	Adile	3	E. Arcaro	112	Plunder	108	Gaffery	120	17,000	2:04.00	
1950	Busanda	3	R. Permane	108	Next Move	126	Antagonism	108	15,850	2:04.40	
1951	Kiss Me Kate	3	E. Arcaro	126	Vulcania	116	Aunt Jinny	122	15,250	2:05.60	
1952	Lily White	3	T. Atkinson	109	Enchanted Eve	114	Gay Grecque	109	17,000	2:05.80	
1953	Sabette	3	J. Higley	114	Grecian Queen	126	Cherry Fizz	109	18,800	2:06.00	
1954	Parlo	3	E. Arcaro	121	Moonsight	111	Open Sesame	111	20,550	2:06.00	
1955	Rico Monte	3	W. Boland	113	Blue Banner	114	Misty Morn	121	20,750	2:05.80	
1956	Tournure	3	E. Guerin	115	Dotted Line	121	Levee	124	18,600	2:05.40	
1957	Here and There	3	E. Nelson	113	Snow White	113	Outer Space	121	20,450	2:06.40	
1958	Tempted	3	R. Ussery	113	Spar Maid	113	Lopar	114	18,712	2:05.80	
1959	High Bid	3	H. Moreno	113	Miss Blue Gem	113	Rich Tradition	117	37,230	2:05.00	
1960	Make Sail	3	M. Ycaza	118	Clear Road	114	Rash Statement	121	38,205	2:04.00	
1961	Primonetta	3	W. Shoemaker	121	Mighty Fair	114	Bowl of Flowers	124	35,555	2:03.20	
1962	Firm Policy	3	J. Sellers	121	Lincoln Center	114	Cicada	124	37,050	2:06.00	
1963	Tona	3	M. Sorrentino	114	Lamb Chop	124	Prodana Neviesta	114	37,310	2:04.20	
1964	Miss Cavandish	3	H. Grant	124	Beautiful Day	114	Castle Forbes	121	36,530	2:03.20	
1965	What a Treat	3	J.L. Rotz	118	Terentia	114	Discipline	118	41,080	2:03.60	
	Discipline finished second but was disqualified and placed third										
1966	Natashka	3	W. Shoemaker	121	Lady Pitt	124	Prides Profile	114	36,790	2:04.20	
	Lady Pitt finished first but was disqualified and placed second										
1967	Gamely	3	W. Shoemaker	118	Treacherous	114	Muse	114	39,130	2:03.20	
1968	Gay Matelda	3	J.L. Rotz	118	Heartland	114	Miss Ribot	118	36,920	2:04.40	
	Heartland finished first but was disqualified and placed second										
1969	Shuvee	3	J. Davidson	124	Pit Bunny	114	Hail to Patsy	118	35,360	2:06.40	
1970	Fanfreluche	3	R. Turcotte	118	Hunnemannia	114	Office Queen	124	38,415	2:03.80	
1971	Lauries Dancer	3	S. Hawley	118	Alma North	118	Forward Gal	121	35,280	2:03.00	
1972	Summer Guest	3	R. Turcotte	121	Light Hearted	118	Betsy Be Good	114	32,640	2:03.40	
1973	Desert Vixen	3	J. Velasquez	119	Bag of Tunes	119	Summer Festival	116	35,620	2:04.20	
1974	Quaze Quilt	3	H. Gustines	121	Chris Evert	121	Fiesta Libre	121	33,660	2:02.60	
1975	Spout	3	J. Cruguet	121	Aunt Jin	121	Funalon	121	49,170	2:04.00	
1976	Optimistic Gal	3	E. Maple	121	Javamine	121	Moontee	121	48,555	2:01.60	
	Dona Maya finished second but was disqualified and placed fourth										
1977	Our Mims	3	J. Velasquez	121	Sensational	121	Cum Laude Laurie	121	66,060	2:03.00	
1978	White Star Line	3	M. Venezia	121	Summer Fling	121	Tempest Queen	121	64,920	2:04.00	
1979	It's in the Air	3	J. Fell	121	Davona Dale	121	Mairzy Doates	121	64,980	2:01.40	
1980	Love Sign	3	R. Hernandez	121	Weber City Miss	121	Sugar and Spice	121	65,880	2:01.00	
1981	Prismatical	3	E. Maple	121	Banner Gala	121	Discorama	121	66,000	2:02.40	
1982	Broom Dance	3	G. McCarron	121	Too Chic	121	Mademoiselle Forli	121	67,680	2:02.20	
1983	Spit Curl	3	J. Cruguet	121	Lady Norcliffe	121	Sabin	121	65,880	2:02.40	
1984	Life's Magic	3	J. Velasquez	121	Lucky Lucky Lucky	121	Class Play	121	98,100	2:02.60	
1985	Mom's Command	3	A. Fuller	121	Fran's Valentine	121	Foxy Deen	121	8,400	2:03.20	

Year	Winner	Age	Jockey	Wt.	Second	Wt.	Third	Wt.	Win Value	Time	Beyer
1986	Classy Cathy	3	E. Fires	121	Valley Victory	121	Life at the Top	121	138,720	2:04.20	
1987	Up the Apalachee	3	J. Velasquez	121	Without Feathers	121	Fiesta Gal	121	138,240	2:04.00	
1988	Maplejinsky	3	A. Cordero Jr	121	Make Change	121	Willa on the Move	121	136,320	2:01.80	
1989	Open Mind	3	A. Cordero Jr	121	Dearly Loved	121	Dream Deal	121	139,440	2:04.20	
1990	Go for Wand	3	R.P. Romero	121	Charon	121	Pampered Star	121	130,560	2:00.80	111
1991	Versailles Treaty	3	A. Cordero Jr	121	Til Forbid	121	Designated Dancer	121	120,000	2:02.40	96
1992	November Snow	3	C.W. Antley	121	Saratoga Dew	121	Pacific Squall	121	120,000	2:02.60	99
1993	Sky Beauty	3	M.E. Smith	121	Future Pretense	121	Silky Feather	121	120,000	2:03.40	98
1994	Heavenly Prize	3	M.E. Smith	121	Lakeway	121	Sovereign Kitty	121	120,000	2:03.20	111
1995	Pretty Discreet	3	M.E. Smith	121	Friendly Beauty	121	Rogues Walk	121	120,000	2:02.00	110
1996	Yanks Music	3	J.R. Velazquez	121	Escena	121	My Flag	121	150,000	2:03.00	104
1997	Runup the Colors	3	J.D. Bailey	121	Ajina	121	Tomisue's Delight	121	150,000	2:02.20	107
1998	Banshee Breeze	3	J.D. Bailey	121	Lu Ravi	121	Manistique	121	150,000	2:03.41	107
1999	Silverbulletday	3	J.D. Bailey	121	Strolling Belle	121	Gandria	121	240,000	2:02.71	115
2000	Jostle	3	M.E. Smith	121	Secret Status	121	Spain	121	450,000	2:04.72	101
2001	Flute	3	J.D. Bailey	121	Exogenous	121	Two Item Limit	121	450,000	2:01.88	106
2002	Farda Amiga	3	P. Day	121	Allamerican Bertie	121	You	121	450,000	2:04.68	100
2003	Island Fashion	3	J.R. Velazquez	121	Awesome Humor	121	Spoken Fur	121	450,000	2:05.08	101
2004	Society Selection	3	C. Velasquez	121	Stellar Jayne	121	Ashado	121	450,000	2:02.70	107

Beyer Index: 104.87

Distance 1 1/8 miles prior to 1901, in 1904, and from 1906-16; 1 1/16 miles in 1901-02 and on turf in 1903; 1 5/16 miles in 1905

(DARLEY) ALCIBIADES (G2), 1 1/16 Miles, 2-Year-Old Fillies, Keeneland Race Course, 2004 Purse: $400,000

Year	Winner	Age	Jockey	Wt.	Second	Wt.	Third	Wt.	Win Value	Time	Beyer
1952	Sweet Patootie	2	S. Armstrong	119	Good Call	119	Aerolite	119	17,617	1:23.60	
1953	Oil Painting	2	A. Popara	119	Pegeen	119	Queen Hopeful	119	19,390	1:24.40	
1954	Myrtle's Jet	2	W. Blum	119	Lea Lane	119	Gandharva	119	22,718	1:23.00	
1955	Doubledogdare	2	S. Brooks	119	Ament	119	Supple	119	23,039	1:24.20	
1956	Leallah	2	S. Boulmetis	119	Bluebility	119	Nantua	119	25,525	1:27.00	
1957	Moon Glory	2	J. Heckmann	119	My Carrie	119	Carrie Louise	119	26,273	1:27.20	
1958	Fiji	2	J. Nichols	119	Tacking	119	Lindaway	119	28,941	1:28.00	
1959	Rash Statement	2	J.L. Rotz	119	Patty's Song	119	Monarchy	119	21,579	1:25.60	
1960	Little Tumbler	2	R. Broussard	119	Times Two	119	Bright Silver	119	20,685	1:26.60	
1961	Journalette	2	W. Carstens	119	Dulaturee	119	Swoon's Princess	119	21,352	1:27.20	
1962	Abrogate	2	R.L. Baird	119	Sally Ship	119	Village Beauty	119	22,324	1:27.20	
1963	Secret Veil	2	W.D. Lucas	119	Kahgahgee	119	Shama	119	22,054	1:27.40	
1964	Fairway Fun	2	J. Leonard	119	Terentia	119	Kalispell	119	22,324	1:26.40	
1965	Moccasin	2	L. Adams	119	Chalina	119	Hurry Star	119	23,390	1:25.80	
1966	Teacher's Art	2	L. Pincay Jr	119	Thong	119	T.V's Princess	119	31,967	1:28.40	
1967	Lady Tramp	2	I. Valenzuela	119	Sweet Tooth	119	Walk My Lady	119	31,814	1:28.00	
1968	Lil's Bag	2	D. Brumfield	119	Show Off	119	Foolish Miss	119	35,864	1:28.40	
1969	Belle Noire	2	H. Arroyo	119	Song Sparrow	119	Cloudland	119	36,237	1:27.20	
1970	Patelin	2	L. Pincay Jr	119	Bonnie and Gay	119	Secret Retreat	119	34,118	1:27.00	
1971	Mrs. Cornwallis	2	G. Mora	119	La Brisa	119	Stepping High	119	32,068	1:28.40	
1972	Coraggioso	2	D. Brumfield	119	Bag of Tunes	119	Vaguely Familiar	119	34,284	1:27.00	
1973	City Girl	2	E. Fires	119	Fairway Fable	119	Quick Cure	119	44,925	1:27.80	
1974	Hope of Glory	2	J. Nichols	119	Funny Cat	119	Snow Doll	119	54,197	1:27.20	
1975	Optimistic Gal	2	D.G. McHargue	119	Old Goat	119	Answer	119	79,592	1:28.00	
1976	Sans Supplement	2	W. Gavidia	119	Avilion	119	Resolver	119	89,732	1:27.60	
1977	L'Alezane	2	R. Turcotte	119	Robalea	119	No No-Nos	119	80,990	1:27.20	
1978	Angel Island	2	E. Delahoussaye	119	Terlingua	119	Too Many Sweets	119	89,619	1:26.40	
1979	Salud	2	J.C. Espinosa	119	Diorama	119	Sweetest Roman	119	93,503	1:28.20	
1980	Sweet Revenge	2	J. Velasquez	119	Expressive Dance	119	Masters Dream	119	99,190	1:28.00	
1981	Apalachee Honey	2	W. Shoemaker	118	Chilling Thought	118	Casual	118	102,034	1:45.20	
1982	Jelly Bean Hollida	2	D. Brumfield	118	Quarrel Over	118	Issues n' Answers	118	97,825	1:45.80	
1983	Lucky Lucky Lucky	2	J. Vasquez	118	Flippers	118	Geevilla	118	119,675	1:47.00	
1984	Foxy Deen	2	D. Montoya	118	Weekend Delight	118	Dusty Heart	118	117,224	1:45.60	
1985	Silent Account	2	K.K. Allen	118	Steal a Kiss	118	Python	118	132,321	1:46.20	
1986	Zero Minus	2	S. Hawley	118	Bound	118	Desirous	118	125,567	1:45.20	
1987	Terra Incognita	2	D.E. Foster	118	Epitome	118	Pearlie Gold	118	102,996	1:44.60	
1988	Wonders Delight	2	G.L. Stevens	118	Affirmed Classic	118	Seattle Meteor	118	130,000	1:46.40	
1989	Special Happening	2	J.A. Santos	118	Talltalelady	118	Fashion Delight	118	141,375	1:44.60	
1990	Private Treasure	2	J.D. Bailey	118	Through Flight	118	Southern Bar Girl	118	173,420	1:43.80	
1991	Spinning Round	2	J.M. Johnson	118	Queens Court Queen	118	Midnight Society	118	122,200	1:47.20	82
1992	Eliza	2	P.A. Valenzuela	118	Avie's Shadow	118	True Affair	118	122,200	1:43.20	99
1993	Stellar Cat	2	S.J. Sellers	118	Slew Kitty Slew	118	Beau Blush	118	122,200	1:44.60	77
1994	Post It	2	S. Maple	118	Morris Code	118	Cat Appeal	118	66,650	1:46.20	84
1995	Cara Rafaela	2	P. Day	118	Birr	118	Gold Sunrise	118	139,252	1:44.40	90
1996	Southern Playgirl	2	R.P. Romero	118	Screamer	118	Private Pursuit	118	168,330	1:46.80	85

Year	Winner	Age	Jockey	Wt.	Second	Wt.	Third	Wt.	Win Value	Time	Beyer
1997	Countess Diana	2	S.J. Sellers	118	Lily O' Gold	118	Beautiful Pleasure	118	266,600	1:45.20	85
1998	Silverbulletday	2	G.L. Stevens	118	Extended Applause	118	Grand Deed	118	281,976	1:42.40	97
1999	Scratch Pad	2	W.Martinez	118	Rare Beauty	118	Cash Run	118	274,288	1:44.00	82
2000	She's a Devil Due	2	M. Guidry	118	Nasty Storm	118	Cash Deal	118	270,320	1:44.86	83
2001	Take Charge Lady	2	A.J. D'Amico	118	Never Out	118	Cunning Play	118	280,736	1:46.23	93
2002	Westerly Breeze	2	R.J. Albarado	118	Ruby's Reception	118	Final Round	118	276,024	1:46.90	89
2003	Be Gentle	2	C.H. Velasquez	118	Galloping Gal	118	Deb's Charm	118	248,000	1:45.51	81
2004	Runway Model	2	R. Bejarano	118	Sharp Lisa	118	In the Gold	118	248,000	1:44.31	90

Beyer Index: 86.93

Run at about 7 furlongs prior to 1982

ALL ALONG BREEDERS' CUP (G3), 1 1/8 Miles (Turf), Fillies and Mares, 3-Year-Olds and Up, Colonial Downs, 2004 Purse: $200,000

Year	Winner	Age	Jockey	Wt.	Second	Wt.	Third	Wt.	Win Value	Time	Beyer
1988	Ravinella	3	G. Guignard	119	Chapel of Dreams	120	Betty Lobelia	116	150,000	1:49.80	
1989	Lady Winner	3	K.J. Desormeaux	112	Capades	116	Betty Lobelia	116	180,000	1:53.60	
1990	Foresta	4	A. Cordero Jr	120	Miss Josh	120	Vijaya	114	180,000	1:49.40	101
1991	Sha Tha	3	M.E. Smith	113	Julie La Rousse	113	Once in My Life	114	180,000	1:52.40	106
1992	Marble Maiden	3	T. Jarnet	114	Wedding Ring	112	Sheba Dancer	114	180,000	1:49.80	100
1993	Lady Blessington	5	C.A. Black	116	Via Borghese	118	Logan's Mist	116	150,000	1:51.40	102
1994	Alice Springs	4	R.R. Douglas	120	Via Borghese	116	Mz. Zill Bear	116	150,000	1:47.20	107
1996	Another Legend	4	C.O. Klinger	115	Brushing Gloom	119	Short Time	115	60,000	1:58.80	96
1997	Beyrouth	5	D. S. Rice	115	Hero's Pride	117	Palliser Bay	122	67,830	1:49.20	98
1998	Bursting Forth	4	E.S. Prado	122	The Unforgiven	117	Be Elusive	115	60.000	1:48.00	89
2000	Idle Rich	5	A.T. Gryder	115	Emanating	115	Orange Sunset	115	60,000	1:55.95	90
2001	Colstar	5	J.K. Court	121	Lucky Lune	119	Crystal Sea	119	90,000	1:47.53	102
2002	Secret River	5	H.A. Karamanos	117	Golden Corona	117	Cayman Sunset	117	90,000	1:50.76	88
2003	Dress to Thrill	4	E.S. Prado	117	Lady Linda	117	Lady of the Future	117	120,000	1:49.16	95
2004	Film Maker	4	E.S. Prado	119	Noisette	119	Lady Linda	119	120,000	1:50.08	100

Beyer Index: 98.00

AMERICAN DERBY (G2), 1 3/16 Miles (Turf), 3-Year-Olds, Arlington Park, 2004 Purse: $250,000

Year	Winner	Age	Jockey	Wt.	Second	Wt.	Third	Wt.	Win Value	Time	Beyer
1884	Modesty	3	I. Murphy	117	Kosciusko	117	Bob Cook	115	10,700	2:42.75	
1885	Volante	3	I. Murphy	123	Favor	123	Troubadour	123	9,570	2:49.50	
1886	Silver Cloud	3	I. Murphy	121	Blu Wing	121	Sir Joseph	118	8,160	2:37.25	
1887	C.H. Todd	3	Hamilton	118	Miss Ford	113	Wary	116	13,690	2:36.50	
1888	Emperor of Norfolk	3	I. Murphy	123	Falcon	121	Los Angeles	116	14,340	2:40.50	
1889	Spokane	3	T. Kiley	121	Sorrento	118	Retrieve	116	15,400	2:41.25	
1890	Uncle Bob	3	T. Kiley	116	Santiago	118	Ben Kingsbury	109	15,260	2:55.75	
1891	Strathmeath	3	Covington	112	Poet Scout	115	Kingman	129	18,610	2:49.25	
1892	Carlsbad	3	R. Williams	122	Zaldivar	122	Cicero	115	16,930	3:04.25	
1893	Boundless	3	E. Garrison	122	St. Leonards	122	Clifford	122	49,500	2:36.00	
1894	Rey el Santa Anita	3	E. Van Kuren	122	Senator Grady	122	Despot	122	19,750	2:36.00	
1898	Pink Coat	3	W. Martin	127	Warrenton	122	Isabey	122	9,225	2:42.60	
1900	Sidney Lucas	3	J. Bullman	122	James	122	Lieut. Gibson	129	9,425	2:40.20	
1901	Robert Waddell	3	J. Bullman	119	Terminus	127	The Parader	122	19,275	2:33.80	
1902	Wyeth	3	L. Lyne	122	Lucien Appleby	122	Aladdin	122	19,875	2:40.20	
1903	The Picket	3	Helgesen	115	Claude	127	Bernays	122	27,025	2:33.00	
1904	Highball	3	G.C. Fuller	122	Woodson	122	Rapid Water	122	26,325	2:33.00	
1916	Dodge	3	F. Murphy	126	Faux-Col	126	Franklin	122	6,850	2:04.60	
1926	Boot to Boot	3	A. Johnson	121	Display	126	Black Maria	116	89,000	2:30.20	
1927	Hydromel	3	L. McDermott	116	Handy Mandy	111	Buddy Bauer	121	22,750	2:29.00	
1928	Toro	3	E. Ambrose	126	Misstep	126	Solace	126	21,925	2:05.80	
1929	Windy City	3	L. McDermott	118	Naishapur	126	African	118	47,550	2:10.00	
1930	Reveille Boy	3	W. Frank	118	Gallant Knight	121	Zenofol	114	51,300	2:04.80	
1931	Mate	3	G. Ellis	126	Pittsburgher	118	Joey Bibb	118	48,675	2:04.20	
1932	Gusto	3	S. Coucci	118	Osculator	118	Prince Hotspur	118	48,200	2:10.60	
1933	Mr Khayyam	3	P. Walls	121	Head Play	126	Fair Rochester	118	23,410	2:04.20	
1934	Cavalcade	3	M. Garner	126	Discovery	118	Singing Wood	121	23,310	2:04.00	
1935	Black Helen	3	D. Meade	118	Count Arthur	118	Tearout	121	25,025	2:10.40	
1937	Dawn Play	3	L. Balaski	116	Burning Star	118	Dellor	118	25,400	2:05.00	
1940	Mioland	3	J. Adams	123	Sirocco	126	Weigh Anchor	118	44,900	2:05.80	
1941	Whirlaway	3	A. Robertson	126	Bushwhacker	121	Delray	118	44,975	2:04.00	
1942	Alsab	3	G. Woolf	126	With Regards	121	Anticlimax	121	60,850	2:06.60	
1943	Askmenow	3	G. Woolf	115	Bold Captain	117	Famous Victory	117	56,150	2:07.00	
1944	By Jimminy	3	G. Woolf	122	Old Kentuck	118	Nelson Dunstan	118	61,650	2:03.00	

Year	Winner	Age	Jockey	Wt.	Second	Wt.	Third	Wt.	Win Value	Time	Beyer
1945	Fighting Step	3	G. South	118	War Jeep	118	Pot o' Luck	122	68,950	2:02.80	
1946	Eternal Reward	3	R. Campbell	118	Pellicle	118	The Dude	122	83,450	2:02.60	
1947	Fervent	3	D. Dodson	118	Cosmic Bomb	118	Phalanx	126	70,950	2:00.60	
1948	Citation	3	E. Arcaro	126	Free America	118	Volcanic	118	66,450	2:01.60	
1949	Ponder	3	S. Brooks	126	Ky. Colonel	118	Johns Joy	118	66,150	2:00.40	
1950	Hill Prince	3	E. Arcaro	126	All Blue	114	Your Host	126	60,050	2:01.20	
1951	Hall of Fame	3	T. Atkinson	122	Abbe Sting	114	Bernwood	118	61,200	2:01.20	
1952	Mark-Ye-Well	3	E. Arcaro	120	Sub Fleet	114	Marcador	117	103,325	1:49.60	
1953	Native Dancer	3	E. Arcaro	128	Landlocked	120	Precious Stone	114	66,500	1:48.40	
1954	Errard King	3	S. Boulmetis	124	High Gun	124	Hasty Road	124	68,900	1:49.80	
1955	Swaps	3	W. Shoemaker	126	Traffic Judge	119	Parador	113	89,600	1:54.60	
1956	Swoon's Son	3	E. Arcaro	122	The Warrior	116	Toby B.	116	102,600	1:59.20	
1957	Round Table	3	W. Shoemaker	126	Iron Liege	126	Ekaba	120	100,350	1:55.00	
1958	Nadir	3	M. Ycaza	120	Victory Morn	123	Talent Show	120	114,600	1:51.60	
1959	Dunce	3	L.C. Cook	126	Demobilize	120	Little Tytus	120	93,700	1:49.60	
1960	T.V. Lark	3	J. Sellers	123	New Policy	120	Heroshogala	111	70,500	1:47.20	
1961	Beau Prince	3	S. Brooks	112	Editorialist	113	Flutterby	114	71,400	1:51.60	
1962	Black Sheep	3	J. Longden	117	Ridan	123	Jam-Tootin	115	71,250	2:01.60	
1963	Candy Spots	3	W. Shoemaker	126	B. Major	123	Crowdus	114	65,833	2:02.40	
1964	Roman Brother	3	F. Alvarez	122	Lt. Stevens	116	Close By	120	89,300	2:01.40	
1965	Tom Rolfe	3	W. Shoemaker	126	Royal Gunner	112	Mr. Pak	112	83,100	2:00.60	
1966	Buckpasser	3	B. Baeza	128	Jolly Jet	116	Advocator	116	84,100	1:47.00	
1967	Damascus	3	W. Shoemaker	126	In Reality	120	Favorable Turn	112	75,000	1:46.80	
1968	Forward Pass	3	I. Valenzuela	123	Nodouble	116	Poleax	120	70,600	1:48.80	
1969	Fast Hilarious	3	L. Pincay Jr	114	Night Invader	119	Dike	126	55,000	1:48.20	
1970	The Pruner	3	B. Baeza	117	Robin's Bug	114	Coaltown Cat	114	65,300	1:47.80	
1971	Bold Reason	3	L. Pincay Jr	124	Mr. Pow Wow	122	Northfields	119	81,950	1:52.60	
1972	Dubasoff	3	J. Vasquez	123	King's Bishop	122	Tri Jet	116	72,800	1:50.80	
1973	Bemo	3	W.J. Passmore	117	Golden Don	115	Buffalo Lark	109	69,400	1:49.60	
1974	Determined King	3	D. Montoya	112	Orders	114	Sr. Diplomat	111	92,000	1:47.80	
1975	Honey Mark	3	G. Patterson	116	High Steel	112	Go to the Bank	111	93,400	1:44.40	
1976	Fifth Marine	3	R. Turcotte	121	Majestic Light	121	Play the Red	121	93,400	1:49.20	
1977	Silver Series	3	L. Snyder	126	Run Dusty Run	126	Brach's Hilarious	112	68,880	2:02.40	
1978	Nast y and Bold	3	J.L. Samyn	114	Star de Naskra	114	Beau Sham	114	68,100	2:03.40	
1979	Smarten	3	S. Maple	126	Super Hit	114	Weather Tamer	114	63,600	2:05.20	
1980	Hurry Up Blue	3	S. Gallitano	114	Tizon	114	Spruce Needles	123	83,400	2:04.40	
1981	Pocket Zipper	3	H.R. Sibille	120	Fairway Phantom	123	Double Sonic	123	84,000	2:03.80	
1982	Wolfie's Rascal	3	R.A. Hernandez	123	Dew Line	114	Northern Majesty	120	65,100	2:05.60	
1983	Play Fellow	3	P. Day	123	Le Cou Cou	114	Brother	114	65,100	2:04.40	
1984	At the Threshold	3	P. Day	126			Par Flite	114	46,800	2:04.00	
	High Alexander	3	G. Gallitano	120							
1985	Creme Fraiche	3	E. Maple	123	Red Attack	114	Smile	123	96,000	2:01.60	
1987	Fortunate Moment	3	E. Fires	118	Fast Forward	118	Gem Master	118	100,350	2:03.80	
1989	Awe Inspiring	3	C. Perret	126	Dispersal	123	Caesar	114	124,500	2:02.40	
1990	Real Cash	3	P.A. Valenzuela	123	Home at Last	123	Adjudicating	117	180,000	2:02.00	112
1991	Olympio	3	E. Delahoussaye	126	Discover	114	Jackie Wackie	123	180,000	2:00.80	112
1992	The Name's Jimmy	3	P. Day	120	Standiford	114	May I Inquire	114	180,000	1:59.40	101
1993	Explosive Red	3	S.J. Sellers	120	Earl of Barking	120	Newton's Law	114	180,000	1:59.80	103
1994	Overbury	3	S.J. Sellers	115			Star Campaigner	114	120,000	1:55.20	101
	Vaudeville	3	A.D. Lopez	114							
1995	Gold and Steel	3	A.T. Gryder	114	Torrential	120	Unanimous Vote	120	180,000	1:55.00	100
1996	Jaunatxo	3	J.L. Diaz	114	Trail City	120	Marlin	114	180,000	1:55.80	104
	Trail City finished first but was disqualified and placed second										
1997	Honor Glide	3	G.K. Gomez	120	Worldly Ways	120	Daylight Savings	114	120,000	1:55.80	103
2000	Pine Dace	3	E Ahern	114	Hymn	114	Del Mar Show	114	120,000	1:55.46	96
2001	Fan Club's Mister	3	R. Meier	121	Monsieur Cat	116	Royal Spy	123	150,000	2:03.27	97
2002	Mananan McLir	3	R.R. Douglas	116	Jazz Beat	117	Extra Check	116	135,000	1:57.11	95
2003	Evolving Tactics	3	P.J. Smullen	117	Californian	121	Scottago	116	150,000	1:59.04	93
2004	Simple Exchange	3	P.J. Smullen	119	Cool Conductor	119	Toasted	123	150,000	1:54.93	100

Beyer Index: 101.31

AMERICAN HANDICAP (G2), 1 1/8 Miles (Turf), 3-Year-Olds and Up, Hollywood Park, 2004 Purse: $150,000

Year	Winner	Age	Jockey	Wt.	Second	Wt.	Third	Wt.	Win Value	Time	Beyer
1938	Ligaroti	6	N. Richardson	122	Whichcee	122	Frexo	111	6,650	1:50.00	
1939	Kayak II	4	G. Woolf	120	Gosum	107	Olimpo	107	9,800	1:49.80	
1940	Viscounty	4	N. Pariso	115	Hysterical	117	Specify	122	10,700	1:49.00	
1941	Mioland	4	L. Haas	126	Woof Woof	114	Big Pebble	117	15,750	1:49.40	
1944	Paperboy	6	G. Woolf	122	Happy Issue	118	Lou-Bre	112	17,350	1:49.60	
1945	Bull Reigh	7	H. Trent	114	Paperboy	119	Sirde	112	2,600	1:43.40	

Year	Winner	Age	Jockey	Wt.	Second	Wt.	Third	Wt.	Win Value	Time	Beyer
1946	Quick Reward	4	A. Skoronski	120	Olhaverry	111	Autocrat	108	39,750	1:43.20	
1947	Burning Dream	5	J. Londen	112	Cover Up	114	Texas Sandman	115	34,300	1:48.20	
1948	Stepfather	4	G. Pederson	111	Autocrat	112	On Trust	130	32,400	1:50.40	
1949	Double Jay	5	C. Bierman	119	Solidarity	117	Dinner Gong	122	33,250	1:48.60	
1950	Noor	5	J. Longden	132	Dharan	100	Frankly	107	32,500	2:00.20	
1951	Citation	6	S. Brooks	123	Bewitch	106	Sturdy One	112	33,050	1:48.40	
1952	Admiral Drake	5	G. Glisson	113	Sturdy One	115	Intent	127	32,800	1:48.20	
1953	Royal Serenade	5	J. Longden	123	A Gleam	118	Fleet Bird	122	33,350	1:48.60	
1954	Rejected	4	W. Shoemaker	123	High Scud	116	Imbros	126	32,100	1:48.00	
1955	Alidon	4	J. Longden	116	Mister Gus	114	Rejected	118	30,700	1:46.60	
1956	Swaps	4	W. Shoemaker	130	Mister Gus	111	Bobby Brocato	115	57,700	1:46.80	
1957	Find	7	R. Neves	121	Hoop Band	110	Festin	111	32,500	1:48.00	
1958	How Now	5	W. Harmatz	122	Seaneen	116	Eddie Schmidt	120	31,150	1:48.40	
1959	Hillsdale	4	T. Barrow	130	Find	109	Ying and Yang	108	30,600	1:47.20	
1960	Prize Host	5	W. Harmatz	109	Twentyone Guns	108	Bagdad	126	31,150	1:47.60	
1961	Prince Blessed	4	J. Longden	114	Dress Up	112	Sea Orbit	122	33,350	1:47.60	
1962	Prove It	5	H. Moreno	124	Windy Sands	113	Harpie	110	32,850	1:47.60	
1963	Dr. Kacy	4	W. Shoemaker	114	Admiral's Voyage	123	Mr. Consistency	116	34,550	1:48.20	
							Your Alibhai	110			
1964	Colorado King	5	R. York	119	Mustard Plaster	120	Viking Spirit	111	32,700	1:46.40	
1965	Native Diver	6	J. Lamber	125	Tronado	118	Hill Rise	122	31,250	1:47.20	
1966	Travel Orb	4	W. Harmatz	118	Native Diver	128	Real Good Deal	112	34,250	1:47.80	
1967	Pretense	4	J. Sellers	131	Native Diver	123	Biggs	117	32,200	1:47.00	
1968	Pink Pigeon	4	W. Harris	118	Saintex	112	Racing Room	117	34,300	1:47.80	
1969	Figonero	4	L. Pincay Jr	118	Baffle	115	Rivet	113	33,250	1:48.00	
1969	Poleax	4	D. Pierce	120	Bargain Day	114	Revoution	112	31,750	1:48.40	
1970	Fiddle Isle	5	W. Shoemaker	130	Baffle	125	Pinjara	122	31,750	1:47.60	
1971	Ack Ack	5	W. Shoemaker	130	Divide and Rule	121	Figonero	119	45,900	1:47.20	
1972	Buzkashi	5	W. Shoemaker	111	Single Agent	119	Wustenchef	117	49,600	1:48.60	
1973	Kentuckian	4	R. Campas	114	Life Cycle	121	Wing Out	118	50,400	1:48.00	
1974	Plunk	4	L. Pincay Jr	117	Scantling	115	Mr. Cockatoo	114	51,900	1:48.20	
1975	Pass the Glass	4	F. Toro	115	Big Band	116	Against the Snow	114	53,800	1:48.20	
1975	Montmartre	5	F. Toro	115	Top Crowd	115	Ancient Title	128	51,800	1:49.60	
1976	King Pellinore	4	W. Shoemaker	121	Riot in Paris	123	Caucasus	120	59,200	1:48.00	
1977	Hunza Dancer	5	J. Cruguet	120	Anne's Pretender	121	Legendaire	115	68,900	1:47.20	
1978	Effervescing	5	L. Pincay Jr	119	Diagramatic	123	April Axe	113	65,500	1:47.20	
1979	Smoggy	5	D.G. McHargue	114	Dom Alaric	120	Inkerman	119	65,500	1:47.40	
1980	Bold Tropic	5	W. Shoemaker	122	Inkerman	115	Borzoi	117	65,700	1:46.40	
1981	Bold Tropic	6	W. Shoemaker	126	The Bart	117	Don Roberto	112	98,100	1:46.80	
1982	Spence Bay	7	F. Toro	122	The Bart	124	Peter Jones	113	100,300	1:47.20	
1983	John Henry	8	C.J. McCarron	127	Prince Florimund	120	Tonzarun	114	87,100	1:48.40	
1984	Bel Bolide	6	T. Lipham	121	Silveyville	118	Vin St. Bernet	118	123,600	1:46.80	
1985	Tsunami Slew	4	G.L. Stevens	117	Al Mamoon	117	Dahar	123	122,300	1:46.20	
1986	Al Mamoon	5	P.A. Valenzuela	119	Truce Maker	111	Will Dancer	114	107,000	1:09.20	
1987	Clever Song	5	L. Pincay Jr	118	Skip Out Front	114	Barberry	115	127,800	1:45.60	
1988	Skip Out Front	6	C.J. McCarron	115	Steinlen	121	World Court	113	120,800	1:46.40	
1989	Mister Wonderful	6	F. Toro	115	Steinlen	121	Pranke	117	183,600	1:47.20	
1990	Classic Fame	4	E. Delahoussaye	117	Steinlen	125	Pleasant Variety	116	126,800	1:47.80	
1991	Tight Spot	4	L. Pincay Jr	123	Exbourne	122	Super May	118	129,400	1:46.00	111
1992	Man From Eldorado	4	K.J. Desormeaux	114	Bold Russian	116	Golden Pheasant	123	122,000	1:47.00	104
1993	Toussaud	4	K.J. Desormeaux	114	Man From Eldorado	116	Journalism	117	126,000	1:46.80	104
1994	Blues Traveller	4	C.W. Antley	115	Gothland	119	Johann Quatz	116	128,000	1:46.40	106
1995	Silver Wizard	5	G.L. Stevens	118	Romarin	120	Savinio	118	91,900	1:46.00	108
1996	Labeeb	4	E. Delahoussaye	119	Gold And Steel	118	Earl OF Barking	116	66,120	1:45.60	108
1997	El Angelo	5	A. Solis	118	Naninja	114	Wavy Run	117	96,360	1:46.80	100
1998	Magellan	5	G.L. Stevens	116	Bonapartiste	116	Sharekann	112	90,000	1:47.00	106
1999	Takarian	4	G.K. Gomez	114	Montemiro	112	Special Quest	115	90,000	1:47.20	101
2000	Dark Moondancer	5	C.J. McCarron	122	Sardaukar	113	Sunshine Street	119	90,000	1:46.74	106
2001	Takarian	6	G.K. Gomez	114	Fighting Falcon	114	Fateful Dream	116	90,000	1:48.19	101
2002	The Tin Man	4	M.E. Smith	115	Devine Wind	115	Kappa King	116	90,000	1:46.82	105
2003	Candy Ride	4	G.L. Stevens	120	Special Ring	118	Irish Warrior	116	90,000	1:46.20	107
2004	Bayamo	5	D.R. Flores	117	Sarafan	119	Night Patrol	114	90,000	1:46.60	109

Beyer Index: 105.43

AMERICAN OAKS (G1), 1 1/4 Miles (Turf), 3-Year-Old Fillies, Hollywood Park, 2004 Purse: $750,000

Year	Winner	Age	Jockey	Wt.	Second	Wt.	Third	Wt.	Win Value	Time	Beyer
2002	Megahertz	3	A. Solis	121	Dublino	121	Alozaina	121	300,000	2:00.46	95
	Dublino finished first but was disqualified and placed second.										
2003	Dimitrova	3	D.R. Flores	121	Sand Springs	121	Atlantic Ocean	121	450,000	1:59.98	94
2004	Ticker Tape	3	K.J. Desormeaux	121	Dance in the Mood	121	Hollywood Story	121	450,000	2:01.54	98

Beyer Index: 95.67

(CROWN ROYAL) AMERICAN TURF (G3), 1 1/16 Miles (Turf), 3-Year-Olds, Churchill Downs, 2004 Purse: $113,800

Year	Winner	Age	Jockey	Wt.	Second	Wt.	Third	Wt.	Win Value	Time	Beyer
1992	Senor Tomas	3	M.E. Smith	118	Coaxing Matt		Black Question		37,440	1:43.10	94
1993	Desert Waves	3	S.J. Sellers	118	Compadre		Super Snazzle		36,620	1:42.64	84
	Compadre finished first but was disqualified and placed second										
1994	Jaggery John	3	M.Smith	123	Milt's Overture		Zuno Star		56,452	1:45.05	96
1995	Unanimous Vote	3	G.Stevens	120	Nostra		Native Regent		76,700	1:42.07	99
1996	Broadway Beau	3	C.McCarron	114	Trail City	123	Gotcha	114	76,375	1:41.87	99
1997	Royal Strand	3	P.Day	116	Rob 'n Gin	118	Deputy Commander	115	71,796	1:40.93	96
1998	Dernier Croise	3	G.Stevens	116	Tenbyssimo	123	Silver Lord	114	78,120	1:44.28	99
1999	Air Rocket	3	J.Bailey	120	Haus of Dehere	116	Conserve	118	71,548	1:42.65	92
2000	King Cugat	3	J.Bailey	123	Lendell Ray	116	Go Lib Go	123	73,222	1:41.25	99
2001	Strategic Partner	3	J.R. Velazquez	116	Baptize	123	Dynameaux	120	73,098	1:42.89	94
2002	Legislator	3	E.S. Prado	116	Stage Call	123	Orchard Park	123	72,106	1:44.43	92
2003	Senor Swinger	3	P. Day	117	Remind	117	Foufa's Warrior	117	75,268	1:41.38	97
2004	Kitten's Joy	3	J.D. Bailey	123	Prince Arch	123	Capo	117	70,556	1:43.31	93

Beyer Index: 94.92

AMSTERDAM (G2), 6 Furlongs, 3-Year-Olds, Saratoga Race Course, 2004 Purse: $150,000

Year	Winner	Age	Jockey	Wt.	Second	Wt.	Third	Wt.	Win Value	Time	Beyer
1995	Kings Fiction	3	P. Day	112	Lord Carson	115	Ft. Stockton	115	32,250	1:09.60	104
1996	Distorted Humor	3	P. Day	115	Gold Fever	121	Stu's Choice	115	32,820	1:09.00	105
1997	Oro de Mexico	3	C.W. Antley	117	Trafalger	122	Kelly Kip	122	49,275	1:10.80	103
1998	Mint	3	Coa E. M.	119			Southern Bostonion	119	33,060	1:10.20	104
	Secret Firm	3	Prado E. S.	117							
1999	Successful Appeal	3	Prado E. S.	122	Lion Hearted	114	Silver Season	119	50,340	1:10.20	102
2000	Personal First	3	P. Day	120	Disco Rico	123	Trippi	123	66,000	1:09.33	106
2001	City Zip	3	J.F. Chavez	123	Speightstown	118	Smile My Lord	118	81,420	1:11.03	100
2002	Listen Here	3	P. Day	121	Boston Common	123	Bold Truth	115	90,000	1:09.58	98
2003	Zavata	3	J.D. Bailey	119	Great Notion	121	Trust n Luck	123	90,000	1:08.64	112
2004	Bwana Charlie	3	S.J. Sellers	123	Pomeroy	123	Weigelia	123	90,000	1:09.40	106

Beyer Index: 104.00

Formerly run as the Screen King

ANCIENT TITLE BREEDERS' CUP HANDICAP (G1), 6 Furlongs, 3-Year-Olds and Up, Santa Anita, 2004 Purse: $213,000

Year	Winner	Age	Jockey	Wt.	Second	Wt.	Third	Wt.	Win Value	Time	Beyer
1985	Temerity Prince	5	W. Ward	120	Debonaire Junior	124	Bid Us	115	37,150	1:09.20	
1986	Groovy	3	J.A. Santos	123	Rosie's K.T.	117	Sun Master	114	49,450	1:08.20	
1987	Zany Tactics	6	J.L. Kaenel	123	On the Line	116	Carload	117	35,500	1:09.00	
1988	Olympic Prospect	4	L. Pincay Jr	123	Sebrof	118	Reconnoitering	114	55,630	1:09.00	
1989	Sam Who	4	L. Pincay Jr	120	Sunny Blossom	116	Don's Irish Melody	114	46,050	1:08.00	
1990	Corwyn Bay	4	E. Delahoussaye	118	Sensational Star	119	Yes I'm Blue	117	61,375	1:08.40	114
1991	Frost Free	6	C.J. McCarron	118	Answer Do	118	Sir Beaufort	113	61,525	1:08.66	104
1992	Gray Slewpy	4	K.J. Desormeaux	118	Trick Me	114	Light of Morn	117	62,950	1:08.48	103
1993	Cardmania	7	E. Delahoussaye	116	Music Merci	117	Bahatur	114	61,975	1:08.04	109
1994	Saratoga Gambler	6	Pedroza MA	113	Uncaged Fury	114	Concept Win	117	62,500	1:08.87	103
1995	Track Gal	4	Stevens GL	116	Siphon	117	Forest Gazelle	116	59,150	1:08.32	105
1996	Lakota Brave	7	E. Delahoussaye	116	Letthebighossroll	119	Paying Dues	118	93,700	1:08.16	106
	Criollito finished third but was disqualified and placed fourth										
1997	Elmhurst	7	C.S. Nakatani	114	Swiss Yodeler	113	Larry the Legend	116	95,000	1:08.82	100
1998	Gold Land	7	K.J. Desormeaux	117	A.P. Assay	116	Swiss Yodeler	114	94,020	1:08.50	105
1999	Lexicon	4	K.J. Desormeaux	116	Kona Gold	120	Regal Thunder	117	125,400	1:07.84	120
2000	Kona Gold	6	A. Solis	124	Regal Thunder	117	Elaborate	116	123,060	1:08.11	117
2001	Swept Overboard	4	E. Delahoussaye	116	Kona Gold	127	I Love Silver	116	124,260	1:07.67	122
2002	Kalookan Queen	6	A. Solis	119	Crafty C.T.	116	Mellow Fellow	117	125,625	1:08.26	109
2003	Avanzado	6	T. Baze	116	Captain Squire	117	Bluesthestandard	115	81,375	1:08.12	107
2004	Pt's Grey Eagle	3	A. Bisono	109	Pohave	118	Hombre Rapido	114	120,000	1:08.84	104

Beyer Index: 108.53

APPLE BLOSSOM HANDICAP (G1), 1 1/16 Miles, Fillies and Mares, 4-Year-Olds and Up, Oaklawn Park, 2004 Purse: $500,000

Year	Winner	Age	Jockey	Wt.	Second	Wt.	Third	Wt.	Win Value	Time	Beyer
1973	Levee Night	5	D. Gargan	115	Knightly Belle	120	Royal Pussycat	119	12,000	1:11.00	
1974	Big Dare	4	R. Ussery	116	Gallant Davelle	122	Sixty Sails	115	19,050	1:11.80	
1975	Susan's Girl	6	J. Nichols	124	Truchas	113	Matuta	114	36,720	1:42.40	
1976	Summertime Promise	4	D.G. McHargue	119	Baygo	114	Costly Dream	113	35,760	1:40.60	

Year	Winner	Age	Jockey	Wt.	Second	Wt.	Third	Wt.	Win Value	Time	Beyer
1977	Hail Hilarious	4	D. Pierce	121	Kittyluck	112	Summertime Promise	119	82,290	1:41.40	
1978	Northernette	4	D. Brumfield	119	Taisez Vous	124	Cum Laude Laurie	121	74,130	1:42.00	
1979	Miss Baja	4	E. Maple	113	Kit's Double	114	Navajo Princess	121	106,800	1:43.00	
1980	Billy Jane	4	J. Lively	113	Jameela	118	Miss Baja	121	106,290	1:43.60	
1981	Bold 'n Determined	4	E. Delahoussaye	124	La Bonza	111	Karla's Enough	119	131,820	1:44.20	
1982	Track Robbery	6	E. Delahoussaye	124	Andover Way	120	Jameela	123	161,040	1:45.20	
1983	Miss Huntington	6	J. Velasquez	118	Sefa's Beauty	117	Queen of Song	114	172,620	1:44.80	
	Number finished second but was disqualified and placed fourth										
1984	Heatherten	5	S. Maple	116	Try Something New	121	Holiday Dancer	115	167,400	1:40.20	
1985	Sefa's Beauty	6	P. Day	120	Heatherten	127	Life's Magic	123	161,700	1:42.20	
1986	Love Smitten	5	C.J. McCarron	119	Lady's Secret	127	Sefa's Beauty	122	162,180	1:40.40	
1987	North Sider	5	A. Cordero Jr	122	Family Style	120	Queen Alexandra	119	162,300	1:41.20	
1988	By Land By Sea	4	F. Toro	121	Invited Guest	116	Hail a Cab	113	150,000	1:41.20	
1989	Bayakoa	5	L. Pincay Jr	120	Goodbye Halo	125	Invited Guest	116	150,000	1:41.60	
1990	Gorgeous	4	E. Delahoussaye	122	Bayakoa	126	Affirmed Classic	112	210,000	1:40.40	119
1991	Degenerate Gal	6	P. Day	115	Charon	121	Fit to Scout	116	300,000	1:41.20	108
1992	Paseana	5	C.J. McCarron	124	Fit for a Queen	121	Slide out Front	109	300,000	1:42.00	114
1993	Paseana	6	C.J. McCarron	124	Looie Capote	115	Luv Me Luv Me Not	114	300,000	1:41.80	107
1994	Nine Keys	4	M.E. Smith	116	Mamselle Bebette	116	Re Toss	117	300,000	1:42.00	102
1995	Heavenly Prize	4	P. Day	120	Halo America	116	Paseana	122	300,000	1:42.60	104
1996	Twice the Vice	5	C.J. McCarron	117	Halo America	115	Serena's Song	124	300,000	1:41.60	104
1997	Halo America	7	C.H. Borel	117	Jewel Princes	124	Different	121	300,000	1:41.60	114
1998	Escena	5	J.D. Bailey	117	Glitter Woman	119	Toda Una Dama	115	300,000	1:40.95	113
1999	Banshee Breeze	4	J.D. Bailey	122	Sister Act	114	Silent Eskimo	112	300,000	1:41.64	114
2000	Heritage of Gold	5	S.J. Sellers	118	Lu Ravi	114	Bordelaise	113	300,000	1:42.22	107
2001	Gourmet Girl	6	C.H. Borel	113	Lu Ravi	114	Lazy Slusan	116	500,000	1:42.15	110
2002	Azeri	4	M.E. Smith	117	Affluent	118	Miss Linda	118	300,000	1:42.75	110
2003	Azeri	5	M.E. Smith	123	Take Charge Lady	118	Mandy's Gold	116	300,000	1:43.00	105
2004	Azeri	6	M.E. Smith	123	Wild Spirit	119	Star Parade	114	300,000	1:41.24	112

Beyer Index: 109.53

Distance 6 furlongs 1973-74; 1 mile 70 yards from 1975-79

APPLETON HANDICAP (G3), 1 Mile (Turf), 3-Year-Olds and Up, Gulfstream Park, 2004 Purse: $150,000

Year	Winner	Age	Jockey	Wt.	Second	Wt.	Third	Wt.	Win Value	Time	Beyer
1952	Alerted	4	O. Scurlock	116	Why Not Now	116	Going Away	110	7,575	1:43.00	
1953	Battlefield	5	A. Schmidt	122	Golden Gloves	108	Mandingo	106	11,150	1:48.80	
1954	Dr. Stanley	5	H. Woodhouse	112	Count Cain	114	Wise Margin	109	11,500	1:50.00	
1955	Fly Wheel	5	H. Woodhouse	116	Immense	112	Sampan	110	11,250	1:49.20	
1956	Mielleux	4	W. Blum	109	Two Fisted	113	Fabulist	112	11,150	1:49.40	
1957	Bardstown	5	W. Hartack	130	First Served	114	Piecesofeight	110	10,535	1:59.40	
1958	Better Bee	4	S. Boulmetis	112	Go Lightly	103	Oh Johnny	122	9,250	1:47.80	
1959	Better Bee	5	J. Choquette	117	Amerigo	117	Bill's Sky B'y	109	10,475	1:47.40	
1960	Oligarchy	6	J. Sellers	112	Stratmat	115	Tudor Era	123	9,700	1:47.80	
1961	Tudor Way	5	W. Hartack	119	Nickel Boy	117	Derrick	117	10,350	1:48.40	
1962	Beau Purple	5	R. Ussery	114	Trans-Way	113	Garwol	110	10,500	1:48.80	
1963	Key Issue	4	H. Woodhouse	108	Sunrise Flight	119	Jay Fox	115	10,550	1:50.40	
1964	Frankie's nod	4	W. Blum	113	Romancero II	113	Garwol	116	10,150	1:49.80	
1965	Ampose	4	K. Knapp	115	Old Hat	122	Editorialist	115	9,600	1:23.80	
1966	Pollux	5	R. Broussard	120	Country Friend	114	Br'yn Bridge	116	9,675	1:22.60	
1967	Canal	6	W. Boland	114	Tom Poker	112	Chinatowner	113	11,975	1:35.20	
1968	Rego	5	E. Fires	108	Quite an Accent	113	Pistacho II	110	12,100	1:36.00	
1969	Quite an Accent	6	B. Thornburg	113	John Jacob	112	Arundel	110	13,575	1:38.60	
1969	Go Marching	4	M. Ycaza	119	Sea Castle	113	Hespero	112	13,575	1:37.80	
1970	Prevailing	4	C. Baltazar	112	Zarco	112	Great Cohoes	120	26,600	1:37.00	
1971	Rocky Mount	4	J. Vasquez	112	Rouge Chanteur	110	Tudor Rew'rd	113	17,490	1:35.80	
1971	Broker's Tip II	6	M. Hole	113	Lonesome River	111	Barking Steeple	113	17,490	1:36.00	
1972	No No Billy	5	D. MacBeth	114	Droll Role	112	De'ri the Greek	111	16,560	1:23.20	
1972	Mr. Pow Wow	4	J. Vasquez	123	G. Lafayette	109	Speedy Zephyr	119	16,410	1:22.80	
1973	Life Cycle	4	F. Ianelli	112	Roundhouse	108	Hope Eternal	112	16,290	1:35.20	
1973	Windtex	4	J.L. Rotz	113	Getajetholme	112	Pri'e of Tr'h	114	16,140	1:35.20	
1974	Right On	5	E. Maple	112	Rey Maya	112	Rapid Sage	114	21,930	1:37.80	
1975	Duke Tom	5	P.I. Grimm	113	Dartsum	116	Return to Real'ty	110	17,460	1:36.20	
1975	Beau Bugle	5	M. Hole	116	The Grok	114	Mr. Door	115	16,860	1:36.20	
1976	Step Forward	4	M. Solomone	114	Faithful Diplomat	111	Pass'n'te Pete	111	20,775	1:34.00	
1976	Improviser	4	J. Cruguet	113	Odd Man	112	Peppy Addy	113	21,195	1:35.60	
1977	Gay Jitterbug	4	L. Saumell	118	What a Threat	110	Riverside Sam	109	16,185	1:36.40	
1977	Cinteelo	4	B. Thornburg	115	Commanding Lead	110	El Guindo	111	16,335	1:36.20	
1978	Qui Native	4	D. MacBeth	117	All Friends	115	Tablao	114	19,350	1:36.40	
1978	Do Lishus	4	J.D. Bailey	110	Haverty	113	Le'd'r of the B'd	113	19,500	1:37.20	
1979	Fleet Gar	4	J. Fell	114	Romeo	118	Vic's Magic	121	19,005	1:36.40	
1979	Regal and Royal	4	J. Fell	120	North Course	114	Bob's Dusty	121	19,155	1:37.00	

Year	Winner	Age	Jockey	Wt.	Second	Wt.	Third	Wt.	Win Value	Time	Beyer
1980	Morning Frolic	5	A. Cordero Jr	117	Match the Hatch	111	Nar	113	19,365	1:35.40	
1980	Pipe Dreamer	5	J. Cruguet	113	Houdini	119	Once Over Lightly	114	18,915	1:34.40	
1981	North Course	6	B. Thornburg	115	Proctor	120	Royal Centurion	113	23,292	1:34.80	
1981	Drum's Captain	6	A. Gibert	114	Foretake	116	Poverty Boy	114	23,082	1:35.00	
1982	Gleaming Channel	4	C. Perret	116	Double Cadet	111	Victorian Double	112	18,375	1:36.00	
1982	King of Mardi Gr's	6	A. Smith Jr	113	Some One Frisky	114	Explosive Bid	115	18,225	1:36.40	
1983	Northrop	4	J. Velasquez	116	Forkali	114	North Course	113	26,754	1:22.00	
1984	Super Sunrise	5	C. Perret	118	Smart and Sharp	110	Guston	115	23,628	1:34.40	
1984	Great Substance	6	G. St. Leon	113	Dr. Schwartzman	109	Rising Raja	113	23,418	1:35.00	
1985	Smart and Sharp	6	M.L. Russ	117	Amerilad	112	Dr. Schwartzman	117	31,740	1:34.60	
1985	Star Choice	6	J. McKnight	118	Late Act	121	Solidified	114	31,440	1:34.40	
1986	Cool	5	J. Vasquez	116	Dr. Schwartzman	120	Rising Raja	113	39,690	1:39.60	
1987	Regal Flier	6	J. Vasquez	113	Wollaston	112	Hi Ideal	113	27,375	1:35.60	
1987	Racing Star	5	S.B. Soto	111	Trubulare	111	Onyxly	116	27,975	1:35.60	
1988	Yankee Affair	6	R.P. Romero	116	Performing Pappy	114	King's River II	114	60,000	1:35.00	
1989	Fabulous Indian	4	E.O. Nunez	109	Equalize	125	Simply Majestic	121	60,000	1:35.00	
1990	Highland Springs	6	C. Perret	118	Prince Randi	115	Wanderkin	116	60,000	1:35.20	107
1991	Jolie's Halo	4	R. Platts	114	Rowdy Regal	112	Shot Gun Scott	118	60,000	1:40.40	
1992	Royal Ninja	6	J.D. Bailey	112	Archies Laughter	114	Native Boundary	116	60,000	1:42.40	98
1993	Cigar Toss	6	B.G. Moore	112	Bidding Proud	117	Archies Laughter	114	60,000	1:43.40	100
1994	Paradise Creek	5	M.E. Smith	121	Fourstars Allstar	117	Elite Jeblar	111	60,000	1:40.80	106
1995	Dusty Screen	7	W.H. McCauley	116	The Vid	114	Dove Hunt	114	60,000	1:42.60	106
1996	The Vid	6	W.H. McCauley	122	Dove Hunt	120	Montreal Red	114	60,000	1:41.60	111
1997	Montjoy	5	M.E. Smith	116	Mighty Forum	114	Elite Jeblar	114	60,000	1:39.80	106
1998	Sir Cat	5	J. D. Bailley	119	Wild Event	114	Kingcanrunallday	116	60,000	1:42.60	111
1999	Behaviour	7	S.J. Sellers	113	Notoriety	112	Legs Galore	113	60,000	1:45.77	100
2000	Band Is Passing	4	E.M. Coa	115	Hibernian Rhapsody	115	Shamrock City	114	60,000	1:40.11	104
2001	Associate	6	J.F. Chavez	114	Band Is Passing	119	El Mirasol	115	60,000	1:33.69	100
2002	Pisces	5	R.I. Velez	113	North East Bound	117	Capsized	114	90,000	1:39.41	102
2003	Point Prince	4	M.R. Cruz	115	Krieger	115	Red Sea	114	90,000	1:37.84	101
2004	Millennium Dragon	5	R. Migliore	116	Political Attack	118	Proud Man	116	90,000	1:34.40	108

Beyer Index: 104.29

Run on main track in 1999

AQUEDUCT HANDICAP (G3), 1 1/16 Miles, 3-Year-Olds and Up, Aqueduct, 2004 Purse: $110,100

Year	Winner	Age	Jockey	Wt.	Second	Wt.	Third	Wt.	Win Value	Time	Beyer
1902	Glenwater	3	McIerney	117	Andy Williams	110	Carbuncle	116	1,060	1:48.80	
1903	Wild Thyme	3	Redfern	98	Embarrassment	102	Ahumada	98	2,705	1:49.20	
1904	Israelite	3	Shilling	99	Dolly Spanger	120	Agile	97	2,750	1:45.40	
1905	Bedouin	3	O.Neill	114	Coy Maid	108	S. Catalina	106	3,315	1:46.60	
1906	Rye	3	Finn	102	Bad News	109	Oxford	119	3,020	1:46.00	
1907	Brookdale Nymph	4	Notter	116	Monfort	95	Gret.' Green	107	2,760	1:47.00	
1908	Monfort	4	D.McCarthy	100	Royal Tourist	104	The Squire	105	650	1:46.00	
1909	Firestone	4	C.H. Shilling	113	Maskette	126	Olambala	119	1,925	1:48.40	
1917	Roamer	6	A. Schuttinger	127	Manister Toi	108	Runes	101	2,225	1:50.20	
1918	Corn Tassel	4	F. Robinson	113	Ticket	102	Papp	108	2,625	1:52.80	
1919	Lucullite	4	L. Fator	133	Corn Tassel	110	Star Master	122	3,200	1:49.80	
1920	John P. Grier	3	C. Kummer	120	Cleopatra	104			4,550	2:12.00	
1921	Damask	4	L. Penman	108	Mad Hatter	129	Kingdom II	105	4,950	2:11.80	
1922	Prince James	4	E. Taplin	105	Captain Alcock	109	Sedgefield	95	7,600	2:11.00	
1923	My Play	4	A. Schuttinger	121	Sunsini	100	Homest'tch	107	5,150	2:11.60	
1925	Dazzler	4	B. Thompson	98	Dangerous	108	Sunsini	108	5,050	2:12.00	
1926	Black Maria	3	J. Callahan	112	Pompey	118	Dazzler	100	5,950	1:51.40	
1927	Black Maria	4	L. Fator	122	Light Carbine	106	Flippant	107	5,900	1:49.80	
1928	Chance Play	5	H. Thurber	123	Byrd	105	Glade	102	6,550	1:52.00	
1929	Sun Beau	4	F. Coltiletti	116	Diavolo	127	Live Oak	104	5,650	1:50.00	
1930	Black Mammy	3	J. Passero	98	Khara	97	Sun Mission	97	6,100	1:52.20	
1931	Curate	5	M. Garner	114	Blenheim	108	Reveille Boy	126	3,020	1:50.60	
1932	Blenheim	4	T. Malley	120	Apprentice	116			1,700	1:50.40	
1933	Golden Way	3	J. Stout	110	Union	107			1,660	1:45.00	
1934	Coequal	3	E. Litzenberger	102	Indian Runner	120	Go'd Advice	118	3,340	1:45.00	
1935	Good Gamble	3	S. Renick	112	Count Arthur	109	Vicaress	100	5,110	1:43.60	
1936	Action	7	J. Gilbert	116	Rosemont	125	Tatterdem'n	107	4,910	1:44.00	
1937	Caballero II	5	A. Robertson	122	No Dice	106	Thorson	121	5,100	1:43.60	
1938	Isolater	5	J. Longden	114	Idle Miss	113	Fighting Fox	124	4,450	1:43.60	
1939	Volitant	3	D. Meade	113	Stands Alone	110	Opera Hat	115	4,650	1:42.60	
1940	War Dog	4	D. Meade	110	Roman Flag	111	Sickle T.	114	6,200	1:44.00	
1941	Ponty	3	N. Wall	105	Foxbrough	126	Market Wise	114	7,900	1:43.60	
1942	Pictor	5	G. Woolf	114	Blue Pair	110	The Rhymer	114	7,900	1:44.20	
1943	With Regards	4	J. Longden	122	Apache	122	First Fiddle	122	7,850	1:43.60	
1944	Alex Barth	4	F. Zufelt	117	Famous Victory	106	Tex Martin	104	7,535	1:45.00	
1945	New Moon	5	J. Gilbert	112	Eurasian	107	Rick's Raft	109	7,940	1:44.80	

Year	Winner	Age	Jockey	Wt.	Second	Wt.	Third	Wt.	Win Value	Time	Beyer
1946	Coincidence	4	T. Atkinson	118	Lets Dance	112	King Dorsett	126	12,100	1:44.40	
1947	Stymie	6	C. McCreary	132	Gallorette	122	Elpis	114	20,050	1:44.40	
1948	Stymie	7	R. Permane	130	Conniver	117	Double Jay	126	19,750	1:45.40	
1949	Wine List	3	T. Atkinson	114	Riverlane	107	Mount Mary	113	16,625	1:46.00	
1950	Wine List	4	T. Atkinson	108	Steel Blue	105	De Luxe	103	15,975	1:43.60	
1951	Bryan G.	4	J. Nichols	120	Moonrush	118	Post Card	120	15,025	1:44.40	
1952	Bryan G.	5	B. Green	114	Hall of Fame	123	Tocoli	105	19,450	1:44.00	
1953	First Aid	3	A. Catalano	109	Combat Boots	117	Elixir	113	19,050	1:44.60	
1954	Crash Dive	4	E. Guerin	121	G.R. Petersen	106	Level Lea	119	20,200	1:44.40	
1955	Icarian	4	A. Valenzuela	109	Fabulist	116	Paper Tiger	117	19,600	1:44.80	
1959	Hillsdale	4	T. Barrow	132	Bald Eagle	122	Tick Tock	119	37,880	1:36.40	
1960	Bald Eagle	5	M. Ycaza	130	Intentionally	125	Warhead	113	35,930	1:34.80	
1961	Tompion	4	J.L. Rotz	118	Whodunit	121	Black Th'mper	108	36,660	1:47.40	
1962	Crozier	4	B. Baeza	114	Guadalcanal	114	Ridan	123	69,095	1:48.80	
1963	Kelso	6	I. Valenzuela	134	Crimson Satan	129	Garwol	116	71,890	1:49.80	
1964	Kelso	7	I. Valenzuela	128	Gun Bow	128	Saidam	119	70,005	1:48.60	
1965	Malicious	4	R. Ussery	116	Pluck	116	Roman Brother	121	70,330	1:49.00	
1966	Tom Rolfe	4	W. Shoemaker	127	Pluck	114	Big R'ck Candy	110	74,295	1:52.20	
1967	Damascus	3	W. Shoemaker	125	Ring Twice	119	Straight Deal	116	69,420	1:48.20	
1968	Damascus	4	B. Baeza	134	More Scents	114	Fort Drum	114	70,330	1:48.40	
1973	Cannonade	2	P. Anderson	126	Roger's Dandy	112	Flip Sal	116	34,080	1:51.60	
1976	Right Mind	5	R. Turcotte	114	General Beauregard	119	Our Hero	115	34,670	1:38.80	
1977	Magnetizer	4	A. Santiago	112	Turn and Count	126	Due Diligence	112	32,580	1:45.40	
1978	Wise Philip	5	J. Vasquez	117	Gallivantor	119	Vanistorio	112	33,060	1:43.80	
1980	Charlie Coast	5	J. Miranda	112	Pole Position	126	Pirate's Bounty	112	35,400	1:44.80	
1981	Irish Tower	4	J. Fell	114	Dr. Blum	116	Lark Oscillation	108	32,760	1:44.60	
1982	Reef Searcher	5	A. Cordero Jr	114	Deedee's Deal	107	Alla Breva	114	35,760	1:48.40	
1983	Fort Monroe	4	V.H. Molina	108	Lark Oscillation	113	Fabulous Find	116	33,420	1:42.40	
1984	Moro	5	J.L. Samyn	120	Jacksboro	120	Ask Muhammad	117	45,120	1:43.40	
1985	Fight Over	4	A. Cordero Jr	118	Imp Society	113	Verbarctic	112	55,260	1:42.60	
1986	Aggressive Bid	5	M. Venezia	109	Badwagon Harry	120	Carjack	114	50,850	1:43.80	
1987	King's Swan	7	J.A. Santos	118	Raja's Revenge	111	Cost Conscious	112	54,990	1:41.80	
1988	Clever Secret	4	C.W. Antley	112	Proud Debonair	114	Native Wizard	112	54,810	1:45.20	
1989	Lord of the Night	6	W.H. McCauley	114	Its Acedemic	110	True and Blue	113	52,110	1:42.80	
1990	Congeleur	5	A. Cordero Jr	116	Silver Survivor	118	King's Swan	116	52,020	1:44.80	
1991	Sports View	4	J.D. Bailey	115	I'm Sky High	115	Lost Opportunity	112	51,750	1:43.40	109
1992	Formal Dinner	4	A. Cordero Jr	113	Shots are Ringing	113	Island Edition	110	51,750	1:43.60	107
1993	Shots Are Ringing	6	J.R. Velazquez	118	A Call to Rise	111	Federal Funds	110	52,650	1:44.40	100
1994	As Indicated	4	Davis RG	121	Primitive Hall	113	Jacksonport	112	48,690	1:45.60	104
1995	Danzig's Dance	6	Chavez JF	111	Key Contender	115	Golden Larch	112	50,010	1:41.00	112
1996	Mighty Magee	4	M.J. Luzzi	118	May I Inquire	113	More to Tell	115	39,780	1:43.80	109
1997	Pacific Fleet	5	J.F. Chavez	112	More to Tell	116	Admiralty	116	39,924	1:43.40	109
1998	Star of Valor	5	A.T. Gryder	113	Christian Soldier	113	Mr. Sinatra	117	82,875	1:42.40	104
1999	Mr. Sinatra	5	A.T. Gryder	118	Brushing Up	112	Wouldn't We All	117	49,335	1:43.11	106
2000	Sky Approval	6	C. Velasquez	115	Parental Pressure	115	Phone the King	114	49,770	1:44.45	104
2001	Liberty Gold	7	J. Bravo	115	Coyote Lakes	115	Talk Is Cheap	116	66,300	1:42.20	102
2002	Evening Attire	4	S.X. Bridgmohan	116	Ground Storm	115	Tempest Fugit	114	65,520	1:42.69	112
2003	Snake Mountain	5	M.J. Luzzi	120	Ground Storm	117	Cat's at Home	114	64.440	1:44.17	104
2004	Seattle Fitz	5	A.T. Gryder	114	Evening Attire	122	Rogue Agent	112	66,060	1:42.13	111

Beyer Index: 106.64

ARCADIA HANDICAP (G2), 1 1/8 Miles (Turf), 4-Year-Olds and Up, Santa Anita, 2004 Purse: $150,000

Year	Winner	Age	Jockey	Wt.	Second	Wt.	Third	Wt.	Win Value	Time	Beyer
1988	Steinlen	5	G.L. Stevens	117	Political Ambition	120	Neshad	117	88,760	1:34.80	
1989	Political Ambition	5	E. Delahoussaye	121	Patchy Groundfog	118	Steinlen	122	62,600	1:35.60	
1990	Steinlen	7	J.A. Santos	125	Bruho	117	Wonder Dancer	111	63,200	1:33.40	105
1991	Pharisien	4	C.S. Nakatani	113	Exbourne	118	Tartas	112	102,500	1:33.20	105
1992	Exbourne	6	G.L. Stevens	122	Repriced	113	Madjaristan	115	95,000	1:33.20	106
1993	Val des Bois	7	P.A. Valenzuela	118	Star of Cozzene	122	C. Sam Maggio	113	77,750	1:35.00	108
1994	Norwich	7	P.A. Valenzuela	117	Megan's Interco	119	Gothland	118	75,850	1:34.00	109
1995	Savinio	5	C.J. McCarron	116	River Flyer	121	Romarin	120	91,800	1:34.60	108
1996	Tychonic	6	G.L. Stevens	118	Debutant Trick	117	Savinio	117	80,300	1:35.80	108
1997	Labeeb	5	E. Delahoussaye	120	Talloires	118	Pinfloron	115	80,100	1:35.80	106
1998	Hawksley Hill	5	G.L. Stevens	117	Precious Ring	114	Kirkwall	117	100,410	1:49.80	106
1999	Commitisize	4	D.R. Flores	117	Majorien	117	Ladies Din	119	90,000	1:48.20	104
2000	Falcon Flight	4	B. Blanc	114	Bonapartiste	118	Otavalo	114	97,950	1:47.88	102
2001	Lazy Lode	7	L. Pincay Jr	121	Night Patrol	116	Wake the Tiger	114	90,000	1:49.74	111
2002	Seinne	5	C.J. McCarron	115	Irish Prize	122	Kerrygold	116	90,000	1:47.16	104
2003	Century City	4	J. Valdivia Jr	114	Gondolieri	116	Sunday Break	117	90,000	1:47.84	102
2004	Diplomatic Bag	4	D.R. Flores	116	Statement	114	Seinne	115	90,000	1:47.90	103

Beyer Index: 105.80

ARISTIDES BREEDERS' CUP HANDICAP (G3), 6 Furlongs, 3-Year-Olds and Up, Churchill Downs, 2004 Purse: $162,150

Year	Winner	Age	Jockey	Wt.	Second	Wt.	Third	Wt.	Win Value	Time	Beyer
1994	Never Wavering	5	S.Sellers	116	Demaloot Demashoot	119	American Chance	117	53,479	1:17.17	111
1995	Boone's Mill	3	D.Barton	106	Ojai	113	Hot Jaws	118	69,924	1:16.16	105
1996	Lord Carson	4	D.Barton	115	Criollito-Arg.	117	Bet On Sunshine	110	70,525	1:16.16	107
1997	High Stakes Player	5	S.Sellers	119	Traflagar	106	Bet On Sunshine	112	67,580	1:16.16	106
1998	Thisnearlywasmine	4	S.Sellers	115	Partner's Hero	115	El Amante	118	67,518	1:16.16	114
1999	Run Johnny	7	P. Day	116	Squall Valley	112	Neon Shadow	114	68,572	1:16.20	103
2000	Bet On Sunshine	8	F.C. Torres	119	Proven Cure	111	Sun Bull	111	68,014	1:15.11	107
2001	Bet On Sunshine	9	C.H. Borel	120	Alannan	119	Dash for Daylight	110	67,208	1:14.79	113
2002	Orientate	4	R.J. Albarado	118	Binthebest	114	No Armistice	116	66,650	1:14.41	115
2003	Mountain General	5	C.J. Lanerie	116	Beau's Town	123	Pass Rush	118	67,580	1:16.01	102
2004	Champali	4	R. Bejarano	116	Beau's Town	121	Battle Won	114	100,533	1:09.04	105

Beyer Index: 108.00

Run at 6 1/2 furlongs prior to 2004.

ARKANSAS DERBY (G2), 1 1/8 Miles, 3-Year-Olds, Oaklawn Park, 2004 Purse: $1,000,000

Year	Winner	Age	Jockey	Wt.	Second	Wt.	Third	Wt.	Win Value	Time	Beyer
1936	Holl Image	3	H.W. Fischer	117	Understand	117	My Auntie	121	4,110	1:53.40	
1937	Eastport	3	R. Hightshoe	117	Zor	117	Sir Midas	117	4,030	1:50.80	
1938	Tiger	3	A. Robertson	125	Silver Sarah	112	Gov. Chandler	117	4,060	1:50.80	
1939	Ariel Toy	3	L. Hardy	117	Radio Gold	117	Torch Stick	112	3,850	1:52.40	
1940	Super Chief	3	J. Richard	117	Colorado Ore	112	The Fop	117	3,810	1:52.20	
1941	He Rolls	3	P. Mills	117	Oakmont	117	Quizzle	117	3,870	1:52.60	
1942	With Regards	3	J. Longden	120	Cerebus	117	Columbus Day	117	4,080	1:50.00	
1943	Seven Hearts	3	J. Adams	120	Ocean Wave	123	Dove Pie	117	7,170	1:52.20	
1944	Challenge Me	3	A. Skoronski	120	Shut Up	117	Bell-Buzzer	117	7,450	1:50.20	
1946	Bob Murphy	3	W. Eads	117	Cid Play	117	Ariel Ace	120	7,460	1:51.80	
1947	Fleetridge	3	A. Craig	117	Sun Beau Go	117	Mel Van Orman	115	7,550	1:51.40	
1948	Fertile Lands	3	P. Glidewell	117	Lucky Codine	117	Beaukiss	112	7,225	1:51.00	
1949	Cacomo	3	B. Fisk	123	Lyle's First	117	Polly Lass	115	7,100	1:54.60	
1950	Big Ike	3	H. Keene	126	Smoke Screen	117	Virtue	112	7,150	1:52.00	
1951	Ruhe	3	J.D. Jessop	120	Enforcer	120	Good Question	120	7,125	1:51.00	
1952	Gushing Oil	3	A. Popara	120	Lextown	123	Our Challenge	120	7,425	1:49.20	
1953	Curragh King	3	J. Adams	111	Supreme's Bub	111	Wismo	108	7,500	1:49.60	
1954	Timely Tip	3	H. Craig	123	Winning Count	117	Super Devil	120	7,650	1:49.80	
1955	Trim Destiny	3	L.C. Cook	113	Styrunner	117	Shannon Comet	114	7,475	1:49.60	
1956	Johns Chic	3	J.L. Rotz	117	Come on Red	117	Mr. Bob W.	114	7,275	1:51.20	
1957	Kentucky Roman	3	J. Delahoussaye	117	Cosmic Force	114	Lori-El	114	9,200	1:49.60	
1958	Count deBlanc	3	J. Sellers	110	Benedicto	116	Little Hunk	105	14,685	1:53.80	
1959	Al Davelle	3	R. Baldwin	110	Sputnik	116	Am Away	116	14,880	1:48.80	
1960	Spring Broker	3	E. Curry	116	Por Prophet	113	El Zag	122	11,499	1:54.40	
1960	Persian Gold	3	J. Combest	110	Tony Graff	122	Deemster	119	11,628	1:53.00	
1961	Light Talk	3	R. Nono	116	Loyal Son	110	Bass Clef	122	18,639	1:50.20	
1962	Areopolis	3	R.L. Baird	110	Prince Dale	116	Eidolon	119	18,655	1:49.60	
1963	Cosmic Tip	3	R. Mundorf	110	Lemon Twist	116	Snow Fort	113	18,460	1:50.40	
1964	Prince Davelle	3	C. Burr	110	Royal Shuck	110	Goff's Gay	110	19,305	1:51.40	
1965	Swift Ruler	3	L. Spraker	122	Flash Climber	110	Mark-Ye-Royal	113	34,110	1:52.20	
1966	Better Sea	3	J. Sellers	122	Eladio	113	Taipan	116	35,640	1:49.20	
1967	Monitor	3	J. Nichols	116	Ask the Fare	122	Barbs Delight	116	35,520	1:48.60	
1968	Nodouble	3	W. McKeever	116	Te Vega	119	Etony	119	35,220	1:50.00	
1969	Traffic Mark	3	P.I. Grimm	112	King of the Castle	122	Sheik of Bagdad	116	36,600	1:50.60	
1970	Herbalist	3	J. Nichols	116	Don't Stop Me	111	Admiral's Shield	122	35,010	1:50.20	
1971	Twist the Axe	3	G. Patterson	120	Barbizon Streak	123	Bixa	115	38,010	1:49.20	
1972	No Le Hace	3	P. Rubbicco	126	Hassi's Image	120	Great Bear Lake	120	78,660	1:48.80	
1973	Impecunious	3	J. Velasquez	126	Vodika	123	Warbucks	123	74,130	1:49.60	
1974	J.R.'s Pet	3	D.G. McHargue	123	Silver Florin	120	Nick's Folly	120	86,910	1:50.60	
1975	Promised City	3	D.E. Whited	126	Bold Chapeau	117	My Friend Gus	120	82,140	1:51.80	
1976	Elocutionist	3	J. Lively	126	New Collection	117	Klen Klitso	120	81,480	1:49.20	
1977	Clev Er Tell	3	R. Broussard	126	Kodiack	117	Best Person	117	80,520	1:50.60	
1978	Esops Foibles	3	C.J. McCarron	126	Chief of Dixieland	117	Special Honor	120	82,470	1:52.20	
1979	Golden Act	3	S. Hawley	126	Smarten	120	Strike the Main	125	107,280	1:50.00	
1980	Temperence Hill	3	D. Haire	123	Bold 'n Rulling	117	Sun Catcher	120	107,160	1:50.60	
1981	Bold Ego	3	J.L. Lively	123	Top Avenger	120	Woodchopper	123	137,160	1:50.40	
1982	Hostage	3	J. Fell	117	El Baba	126	Bold Style	123	170,580	1:51.60	
1983	Sunny's Halo	3	E. Delahoussaye	126	Caveat	120	Exile King	117	176,340	1:49.40	
1984	Althea	3	P.A. Valenzuela	121	Pine Circle	118	Gate Dancer	118	360,150	1:46.80	
1985	Tank's Prospect	3	G. Stevens	123	Encolure	126	Irish Fighter	115	349,650	1:48.40	
1986	Rampage	3	P. Day	118	Wheatly Hall	115	Family Style	121	300,000	1:48.20	
1987	Demon's Begone	3	P. Day	123	Lookinforthebigone	118	You're No Bargain	115	300,000	1:47.60	

Year	Winner	Age	Jockey	Wt.	Second	Wt.	Third	Wt.	Win Value	Time	Beyer
1988	Proper Reality	3	J.D. Bailey	118	Primal	115	Sea Trek	123	300,000	1:48.40	
1989	Dansil	3	L. Snyder	121	Clevor Trevor	126	Advocate Training	115	240,000	1:49.20	
1990	Silver Ending	3	G.L. Stevens	122	Real Cash	122	Power Lunch	118	300,000	1:48.00	
1991	Olympio	3	E. Delahoussaye	122	Corporate Report	118	Richman	122	300,000	1:47.60	
1992	Pine Bluff	3	J.D. Bailey	122	Lil E. Tee	122	Desert Force	122	300,000	1:49.40	107
1993	Rockamundo	3	C.H. Borel	118	Kissin Kris	122	Foxtrail	122	300,000	1:48.00	103
1994	Concern	3	G.K. Gomez	118	Blumin Affair	118	Silver Goblin	122	300,000	1:48.00	109
1995	Dazzling Falls	3	G.K. Gomez	122	Flitch	118	On Target	122	300,000	1:50.60	95
1996	Zarb's Magic	3	R. Ardoin	122	Grindstone	122	Halo Sunshine	122	300,000	1:49.20	100
1997	Crypto Star	2	P. Day	122	Phantom On Tour	122	Pacificbounty	122	300,000	1:49.20	108
1998	Victory Gallop	3	A. Solis	122	Hanuman Highway	118	Favorite Trick	122	300,000	1:49.80	101
1999	Certain	3	K.J. Desormeaux	122	Torrid Sand	118	Ecton Park	122	300,000	1:49.20	94
	Valhol (101 Beyer) finished first but was subsequently disqualified										
2000	Graeme Hall	3	R.J. Albarado	118	Snuck In	122	Impeachment	118	300,000	1:49.08	104
2001	Balto Star	3	M. Guidry	122	Jamaican Rum	122	Son of Rocket	122	300,000	1:49.04	109
2002	Private Emblem	3	D.J. Meche	122	Wild Horses	118	Windward Passage	122	300,000	1:50.20	100
							Bay Monster	118			
2003	Sir Cherokee	3	T.J. Thompson	118	Eugene's Third Son	118	Christine's Outlaw	118	300,000	1:48.39	106
2004	Smarty Jones	3	S. Elliott	122	Borrego	118	Pro Prado	122	600,000	1:49.41	107

Beyer Index: 103.31

ARLINGTON BREEDERS' CUP OAKS (G3), 1 1/8 Miles, 3-Year-Old Fillies, Arlington Park, 2004 Purse: $150,000

Year	Winner	Age	Jockey	Wt.	Second	Wt.	Third	Wt.	Win Value	Time	Beyer
1930	Alcibiades	3	J. Smith	121	Dustemall	118	Valenciennes	116	12,975	1:52.80	
1931	Canfli	3	P. Dyer	116	Tambour	121	Blind Lane	118	14,875	1:51.80	
1932	Top Flight	3	R. Workman	121	Evening	121	Parry	118	13,475	1:50.80	
1980	Ribbon	3	P. Day	121	Save Wild Life	121	All a Dream	114	50,400	1:50.00	
1981	Sweetest Chant	3	E. Fires	116	Fancy Naskra	114	Contrefaire	115	67,380	1:49.60	
1982	Hurry Renee	3	E. Fires	116	Rose Bouquet	121	Sefa's Beauty	116	50,760	1:50.40	
1983	Choose a Partner	3	K.D. Clark	114	Narrate	116	Bon Gout	121	49,365	1:48.20	
1984	Lucky Lucky Lucky	3	R.G. Davis	121	Mrs. Revere	121	Basie	115	76,590	1:49.80	
1985	Just Anything	3	J.L. Diaz	114	Hope U. Win	116	Front Room	121	49,680	1:50.40	
1986	Top Corsage	3	G. Stevens	120	Lady Gallant	112	Pamela Paul	112	67,500	1:49.40	
1987	Shot Gun Bonnie	3	C.H. Marquez Jr	112	Royal Cielo	112	Acting Sue	114	63,810	1:53.40	
1989	Confirmed Dancer	3	M.E. Smith	112	Etoile Eternelle	112	Flags Waving	112	50,475	1:52.60	
1990	Overturned	3	R.P. Romero	114	Train Robbery	118	Mercedes Miss	116	51,795	1:50.40	89
1991	Til Forbid	3	S.J. Sellers	112	Auto Dial	116	Ms. Aerosmith	116	45,000	1:49.60	
1992	Pleasant Baby	3	G.K. Gomez	111	Low Tolerance	114	Pleasureconnection	116	45,000	1:55.00	89
1993	Added Asset	3	J.S. Sellers	116	Dream Mary	113	Princess Polonia	112	60,000	1:50.00	92
1994	Mariah's Storm	3	R.N. Lester	118	Stellarina	116	Minority Dater	111	60,000	1:49.60	100
1995	Niner's Home	3	T.J. Hebert	111	A Goodlookin Broad	114	Strawberry Reason	114	45,000	1:52.00	79
1996	Cuando Puede	3	R.J. Albarado	113	Ginny Lynn	121	Effectiveness	114	75,000	1:51.20	99
1997	Minister's Melody	3	G.K. Gomez	112	Lady of Blue	113	Dawn's Black Tie	116	60,000	1:51.20	93
2000	Megans Bluff	3	M. Guidry	114	Instinct	115	My Turn Kissin	111	75,000	1:50.20	92
2001	Caressing	3	R.R. Douglas	120	Gal on the Go	120	Scoop	122	75,000	1:50.74	89
2002	Lost at Sea	3	R.R. Douglas	122	See How She Runs	122	Strikes No Spares	116	60,000	1:50.58	91
2003	Sue's Good News	3	T.T. Doocy	120	Keeping the Gold	122	Meet Me at Midnite	118	60,000	1:50.53	90
2004	Lovely Afternoon	3	J. Graham	116			My Time Now	116	60,000	1:51.06	90
	Catboat	3	E.M. Martin Jr	118							

Beyer Index: 91.08

ARLINGTON CLASSIC (G2), 1 1/16 Miles (Turf) 3-Year-Olds, Arlington Park, 2004 Purse: $200,000

Year	Winner	Age	Jockey	Wt.	Second	Wt.	Third	Wt.	Win Value	Time	Beyer
1929	Blue Larkspur	3	M. Garner	126	Live Oak	119	Clyde Van Dusen	126	59,900	2:14.40	
1930	Gallant Fox	3	E. Sande	126	Gallant Knight	123	Ned O.	121	64,750	2:03.80	
1931	Mate	3	A. Robertson	126	Spanish Play	123	Twenty Grand	126	73,650	2:02.40	
1932	Gusto	3	S. Coucci	126	Stepenfetchit	121	Evergold	121	76,600	2:03.60	
1933	Inlander	3	R. Jones	118	Golden Way	118	War Glory	121	32,755	2:12.00	
1934	Cavalcade	3	M. Garner	126	Discovery	121	Hadagal	121	30,325	2:02.80	
1935	Omaha	3	W.D. Wright	126	St. Bernard	121	Bloodroot	113	28,975	2:01.40	
1936	Granville	3	J. Stout	126	Mr. Bones	121	Hollywood	123	28,400	2:03.20	
1937	Flying Scot	3	J. Gilbert	123	Eagle Pass	118	Burning Star	118	27,375	2:05.80	
1938	Nedayr	3	W.D. Wright	121	Bull Lea	121	Cravat	123	27,500	2:06.20	
1939	Challedon	3	H. Richards	126	Sun Lover	121	Johnstown	128	35,600	2:02.00	
1940	Sirocco	3	G. Woolf	121	Gallahadion	126	Bimelech	126	37,935	2:03.00	
1941	Attention	3	C. Bierman	121	Whirlaway	126	Bushwhacker	121	42,450	2:02.80	
1942	Shut Out	3	E. Arcaro	126	Valdina Orphan	126	With Regards	118	69,700	2:01.40	

Year	Winner	Age	Jockey	Wt.	Second	Wt.	Third	Wt.	Win Value	Time	Beyer
1943	Slide Rule	3	F. Zufelt	120	Bourmont	117	Chop Chop	123	53,450	2:04.60	
1944	Twilight Tear	3	L. Haas	114	Old Kentuck	119	Pensive	126	62,050	2:03.60	
1945	Pot o' Luck	3	D. Dodson	119	Air Sailor	119	Fighting Step	119	67,150	2:05.80	
1946	The Dude	3	M. Duhon	119	Sgt. Spence	119	Mighty Story	122	76,950	2:02.60	
1947	But Why Not	3	W. Mehrtens	117	Fervent	122	Cosmic Bomb	118	71,500	2:01.80	
1948	Papa Redbird	3	R.L. Baird	122	Shy Gyu	119	Loujac	119	66,600	2:03.00	
1949	Ponder	3	S. Brooks	126	Admiral Lea	119	Palestinian	126	65,450	2:03.20	
1950	Greek Song	3	O. Scurlock	120	Bed o' Roses	110	Your Host	126	58,950	2:01.80	
1951	Hall of Fame	3	T. Atkinson	120	Battlefield	123	Ruhe	120	62,975	2:03.20	
1952	Mark-Ye-Well	3	E. Arcaro	122	Armageddon	120	Sub Fleet	112	105,375	1:39.20	
1953	Native Dancer	3	E. Guerin	126	Sir Mango	120	Van Crosby	120	97,725	1:38.00	
1954	Errard King	3	S. Boulmetis	120	Helioscope	120	High Gun	123	104,475	1:35.00	
1955	Nashua	3	E. Arcaro	126	Traffic Judge	120	Impromptu	120	91,675	1:35.20	
1956	Swoon's Son	3	D. Erb	120	Ben A. Jones	117	Doubledogdare	112	102,000	1:36.80	
1957	Clem	3	C. McCreary	117	Iron Liege	123	Manteau	117	105,950	1:36.60	
1958	A Dragon Killer	3	J. Combest	117	Talent Show	117	Nadir	120	101,100	1:36.40	
1959	Dunce	3	L.C. Cook	117	On-and-On	117	Intentionally	123	78,700	1:35.00	
1960	T.V. Lark	3	J. Sellers	120	John William	123	Venetian Way	123	85,500	1:36.20	
1961	Globemaster	3	J.L. Rotz	119	Editorialist	113	Crozier	114	72,900	1:35.40	
1962	Ridan	3	A. Gomez	123	Mighty Fennec	114	Admiral's Voyage	123	64,750	1:38.00	
1963	Candy Spots	3	W. Shoemaker	126	Admiral Vic	114	B. Major	123	88,833	1:35.80	
1964	Tosmah	3	S. Boulmetis	115	Lt. Stevens	118	Close By	120	69,000	1:36.20	
1965	Tom Rolfe	3	W. Shoemaker	124	Royal Gunner	118	Sum Up	118	62,500	1:34.80	
1966	Buckpasser	3	B. Baeza	125	Creme Dela Creme	123	He Jr.	116	63,000	1:32.60	
1967	Dr. Fager	3	B. Baeza	120	Lightning Orphan	116	Diplomat Way	118	61,000	1:36.00	
1968	Exclusive Native	3	I. Valenzuela	113	Iron Ruler	116	Good Investment	116	63,000	1:36.00	
1969	Ack Ack	3	B. Baeza	120	King of the Castle	120	Fast Hilarious	120	66,800	1:34.40	
1970	Corn off the Cob	3	E. Belmonte	117	Tenacious Jr.	114	George Lewis	120	64,500	1:36.00	
1971	Son Ange	3	C. Baltazar	114	Mr. Pow Wow	117	Staunch Avenger	117	68,400	1:36.00	
1972	King's Bishop	3	E. Maple	114	Brick Door	117	Gun Tune	114	67,000	1:35.00	
1973	Linda's Chief	3	B. Baeza	123	Blue Chip Dan	114	Golden Don	114	72,200	1:44.60	
1977	Private Thoughts	4	R. Perez	117	Pay Tribute	118	Dragset	114	90,000	1:59.40	
1978	Alydar	3	J. Fell	126	Chief of Dixieland	114	Gordie H.	114	63,000	2:00.40	
1979	Steady Growth	3	B. Swatuk	123	Private Account	114	Third and Lex	114	65,400	2:00.60	
1980	Spruce Needles	3	M.R. Morgan	114	I'ma Hell Raiser	114	Stone Manor	126	81,000	1:49.20	
1981	Fairway Phantom	3	J. Lively	114	Golden Derby	114	Television Studio	117	84,000	1:53.40	
1982	Wolfie's Rascal	3	A. Cordero Jr	114	Drop Your Drawers	114	Dew Line	114	72,600	1:49.00	
1983	Play Fellow	3	P. Day	123	Bet Big	114	Passing Base	114	65,400	1:49.00	
1984	At the Threshold	3	P. Day	126	Par Flite	114	Dugan Knight	114	71,400	1:50.20	
1985	Smile	3	J. Vasquez	117	Red Attack	114	Clever Allemont	123	114,000	1:51.20	
1986	Sumptious	3	R.P. Romero	115	Glow	120	Cheapskate	123	96,720	1:49.40	
1987	Lost Code	3	G. St. Leon	123	Gem Master	120	Avies Copy	120	99,090	1:49.60	
1989	Clever Trevor	3	D.R. Pettinger	126	Bio	114	Western Playboy	126	124,500	1:49.40	
1990	Sound of Cannons	3	P. Day	114	Adjudicating	117	Home at Last	123	150,000	1:47.40	101
1991	Whadjathink	3	J. Velasquez	120	Freezing Dock	114	Character	120	180,000	1:49.00	108
1992	Saint Ballado	3	J.A. Krone	120	Desert Force	114	Star Recruit	117	180,000	1:46.80	104
1993	Boundlessly	3	P. Day	120	Hegar	114	Williamstown	123	78,000	1:49.80	97
1994	Eagle Eyed	3	C.S. Nakatani	120	Mr. Angel	120	Star Campaigner	114	180,000	1:48.40	102
1995	Hawk Attack	3	P. Day	114	Via Lombardia	120	Bryntirion	114	120,000	1:48.00	102
1996	Trail City	3	P. Day	114	More Royal	120	Winter Quarters	114	120,000	1:48.60	104
1997	Honor Glide	3	G.K. Gomez	114	Brave Act	120	Daylight Savings	114	75,000	1:47.40	103
2000	King Cugat	3	R.J. Albarado	123	Boyum	114	El Ballezano	114	90,000	1:48.16	106
2001	Baptize	3	M.Guidry	121	Indygo Shiner	121	Cherokee Kim	116	120,000	1:48.80	99
2002	Mr. Mellon	3	R.R. Douglas	121	Doc Holiday	121	Seainsky	116	105,000	1:41.95	94
2003	Lismore Knight	3	R.R. Douglas	119	Remind	116	Good Day Too	116	105,000	1:42.73	93
2004	Toasted	3	R.R. Douglas	121	Street Theatre	119	Cool Conductor	119	120,000	1:50.91	95

Beyer Index: 100.62

ARLINGTON HANDICAP (G3), 1 1/4 Miles (Turf), 3-Year-Olds and Up, Arlington Park, 2004 Purse: $250,000

Year	Winner	Age	Jockey	Wt.	Second	Wt.	Third	Wt.	Win Value	Time	Beyer
1929	Misstep	4	C. McCrossen	123	Display	115	B'dy Bauer	114	22,075	1:50.40	
1930	Pigeon Hole	5	R. Finnerty	105	Curate	108	The Nut	114	34,400	2:07.60	
1931	Sun Beau	6	C. Phillips	128	Satin Spar	105	Plucky Play	109	27,300	2:03.20	
1932	Plucky Play	5	G. Woolf	111	Equipoise	134	Pittsburger	105	22,000	2:02.20	
1933	Equipoise	5	R. Workman	135	Watch Him	106	Gallant Sir	125	9,260	2:02.60	
1934	Riskulus	3	D. Meade	108	Watch Him	106	Hadagal	114	9,580	2:02.40	
1935	Discovery	4	J. Bejshak	135	Stand Pat	115	Riskulus	116	8,640	2:01.20	
1936	Sun Teddy	3	B. James	98	Where Away	106	Count Morse	102	8,480	2:02.00	
1937	Dellor	3	S. Young	107	Infantry	118	Giant Killer	110	15,375	2:03.20	

Year	Winner	Age	Jockey	Wt.	Second	Wt.	Third	Wt.	Win Value	Time	Beyer
1938	Cardinalis	4	J.G. Wilson	106	Arabs Arrow	112	Grey Gold	118	4,000	2:05.00	
1939	Count d'Or	4	J. Longden	112	Some Count	101	Stands Alone	113	4,050	2:05.00	
1941	Equifox	4	A. Craig	113	Idle Sun	110	Cherry Trifle	100	6,895	1:58.80	
1942	Rounders	3	F.A. Smith	103	Whirlaway	130	Staretor	104	22,000	2:04.00	
1943	Marriage	7	G. Burns	120	Thumbs Up	118	Anticlimax	113	40,950	2:03.60	
1944	War Knight	4	C. Corbett	109	Georgie Drum	121	Daily Trouble	104	37,850	2:02.00	
1945	Busher	3	J. Longden	113	Take Wing	110	Sirde	114	36,900	2:09.80	
1946	Historian	5	O. Scurlock	112	Armed	130	Take Wing	111	38,700	2:01.00	
1947	Armed	6	D. Dodson	130	Bridal Flower	111	Challenge Me	114	37,400	2:02.40	
1948	Stud Poker	5	R.L. Baird	110	Star Reward	113	Fervent	124	38,000	2:04.40	
1949	Coaltown	4	S. Brooks	130	Star Reward	116	Armed	113	36,100	2:03.40	
1950	Ponder	4	S. Brooks	128	Aegina	102	Inseparable	110	46,800	2:01.60	
1951	Cochise	5	O. Scurlock	120	Oil Capitol	108	County Delight	124	98,550	2:03.80	
1952	To Market	4	W. Boland	118	Oil Capitol	113	Ruhe	112	107,150	1:52.20	
1953	Oil Capitol	6	C. McCreary	120	Sub Fleet	118	Brush Burn	108	49,650	2:03.40	
1954	Stan	4	E. Nelson	114	Brush Burn	113	Sir Mango	125	99,050	1:57.00	
1955	Platan	5	J. Adams	117	Impasse	110	Mark-Ye-Well	116	104,650	1:54.60	
1956	Mister Gus	5	I. Valenzuela	118	Summer Tan	122	Sir Tribal	122	97,900	1:54.20	
1957	Manassas	4	D. Dodson	121	Swoon's Son	128	St. Vincent	120	88,800	1:55.40	
1958	Round Table	4	W. Shoemaker	130	Clem	109	St. Vincent	111	54,100	1:54.40	
1959	Round Table	5	W. Shoemaker	132	Manassas	112	Noureddin	109	75,760	1:53.40	
1960	One-Eyed King	6	M. Ycaza	118	King Grail	109	Martini II	109	32,100	1:58.60	
1961	Tudorich	4	S. Hernandez	115	Oink	126	Prince Blessed	118	35,900	1:57.80	
1962	El Bandito	5	R. Broussard	115	Crimson Satan	122	Rablero	109	34,900	1:58.60	
1963	Bounding Main	4	J. Nichols	113	B. Major	115	Hellenic Hero	114	34,300	1:36.20	
1964	Master Dennis	4	D. Brumfield	112	Parka	118	Carteret	116	33,750	1:55.80	
1965	Chieftain	4	W. Shoemaker	123	Suspicious	112	Ampose	122	31,650	1:49.40	
1966	Tronado	6	B. Moreira	114	Hedevar	120	Time Tested	123	31,500	1:35.80	
1967	Stupendous	4	L. Pincay Jr	119	Bold Tactics	116	R. Thomas	113	32,900	1:35.00	
1968	Tumiga	4	W. Blum	120	Info	116	Lightning Orphan	114	20,300	1:20.40	
1972	Cloudy Dawn	3	W. Hartack	116	Viewpoise	109	Our Papa Joe	112	63,350	2:31.00	
1973	Dubasoff	4	J. Vasquez	117	Jogging	114	Red Reality	118	72,750	1:58.60	
1974	Buffalo Lark	4	L. Snyder	118	Royal Glint	112	Spot T.V.	111	91,800	1:54.40	
1975	Royal Glint	5	J. Tejeira	125	Zografos	113	Buffalo Lark	122	87,400	1:55.80	
1976	Victorian Prince	6	R. Platts	118	Improviser	118	Bold Roll	112	90,000	1:58.20	
1977	Cunning Trick	4	B. Fann	110	Vadim	108	No Turning	118	72,480	2:33.80	
1978	Romeo	5	E. Fires	116	Fluorescent Light	118	Improviser	118	73,080	2:32.00	
1979	Bowl Game	5	J. Velasquez	124	Young Bob	110	L've'ntes'nshe	105	79,260	2:32.20	
1980	Yvonand	4	E. Beitia	111	Rossi Gold	120	Lyphard's Wish	121	71,700	2:31.40	
1981	Spruce Needles	4	J.C. Espinoza	115	Summer Advocate	117	Sea Chimes	116	72,060	2:35.00	
1982	Flying Target	5	R. Cox	115	Rossi Gold	125	Don Roberto	118	71,640	2:32.40	
1983	Paliraki	5	W. Shoemaker	116	Rossi Gold	122	Late Act	113	76,200	2:35.80	
1984	Who's for Dinner	5	M. Venezia	109	Nijinsky's Secret	127	Star Choice	112	70,800	2:04.00	
1985	Pass the Line	4	J.L. Diaz	113	The Noble Player	118	Executive Pride	113	82,050	2:00.40	
1986	Mourjane	6	J.A. Santos	117	Will Dancer	115	Clever Song	118	112,350	2:01.40	
1987	Ifrad	5	G. Baze	114	Storm on the Loose	115	Grey Classic	114	90,360	2:12.20	
1989	Unknown Quantity I	4	J. Velasquez	112	Frosty the Snowman	122	Delegant	113	120,000	2:11.20	
1990	Pleasant Variety	6	E. Fires	115	Double Booked	114	Ten Keys	121	180,000	2:04.00	
1991	Filago	4	P.A. Valenzuela	112	Super Abound	113	Izvestia	120	150,000	2:01.40	110
1992	Sky Classic	5	P. Day	125	Buck'roo	112	Glity	116	150,000	2:00.60	102
1993	Evanescent	6	A.T. Gryder	114	Split Run	113	Magesterial Cheer	112	150,000	2:00.80	105
1994	Fanmore	6	P. Day	119	Marastani	114	Split Run	114	150,000	2:00.20	104
1995	Manilaman	4	R.P. Romero	114	Snake Eyes	117	Bluegrass Prince	117	120,000	2:02.80	106
1996	Torch Rouge	5	M.Guidry	116	Sentimental Moi	113	Volochine	115	120,000	2:03.20	105
1997	Wild Event	4	M. Guidry	114	Storm Trooper	114	Chorwon	113	90,000	2:01.40	103
2000	Northern Quest	5	R.J. Albarado	113	Profit Option	112	Where's Taylor	114	90,000	2:02.13	104
2001	Make No Mistake	6	R.J. Albarado	116	Takarian	116	El Gran Papa	115	150,000	2:02.53	101
2002	Falcon Flight	6	R.R. Douglas	115	Kappa King	117	Gretchen's Star	115	135,000	2:03.13	103
2003	Honor in War	4	D.R. Flores	120	Better Talk Now	115	Mystery Giver	118	150,000	2:02.71	100
2004	Senor Swinger	4	B. Blanc	118	Mystery Giver	120	Ballingarry	121	150,000	2:03.38	102

Beyer Index: 103.75

ARLINGTON MATRON HANDICAP (G3), 1 1/8 Miles, Fillies and Mares, 3-Year-Olds and Up, Arlington Park, 2004 Purse: $150,000

Year	Winner	Age	Jockey	Wt.	Second	Wt.	Third	Wt.	Win Value	Time	Beyer
1930	Valenciennes	3	E. Steffen	107	Beaming Over	105	Alcibiades	112	7,900	1:35.80	
1931	Risque	3	E. Steffen	108	Manta	118	Cousin Jo	113	10,850	1:42.20	
1932	Tred Avon	4	J.H. Burke	122	Con Amore	117	Fr. Duchess	98	8,475	1:37.40	
1937	Marica	4	R. Dotter	122	Shatterproof	109	Schoolmom	105	4,810	1:36.80	
1938	Idle Miss	4	P. Ryan	118	Dolly Val	108	Jewell Dorsett	109	5,010	1:42.20	
1939	Flying Lill	3	J. Longden	107	Unerring	108	Lady Maryland	120	4,360	1:36.60	

Year	Winner	Age	Jockey	Wt.	Second	Wt.	Third	Wt.	Win Value	Time	Beyer
1940	Shine O'Night	3	B. Thompson	103	Montsin	110	Ma'nie O'Hara	109	6,565	1:36.20	
1941	Shine O'Night	4	S. Brooks	110	Pink Gal	112	Montsin	112	6,875	1:38.20	
1942	Blue Delight	4	R. Neves	110	Emolument	102	Inscolassie	105	9,960	1:38.40	
1943	Askmenow	3	C. Bierman	109	Mar-Kell	126	Pomayya	118	8,950	1:38.20	
1944	Harriet Sue	3	N. Jemas	103	Traffic Court	112	Happy Issue	114	11,450	1:36.60	
1945	War Date	3	O. Grohs	113	Whirlabout	120	Durazna	117	18,800	1:39.40	
1946	Good Blood	4	N.L. Pierson	120	Jack's Jill	114	Athene	116	22,850	1:36.80	
1947	But Why Not	3	W. Mehrtens	114	Say Blue	111	Camargo	112	24,250	1:37.60	
1948	Four Winds	4	S. Brooks	119	Brownian	111	Happy Issue	114	23,650	1:36.00	
1949	Lithe	3	F.A. Smith	102	Bewitch	121	Danada Gift	112	18,700	1:36.20	
1950	Lithe	4	E. Nelson	108	Wistful	118	Evanstep	107	15,275	1:34.80	
1951	Sickle's Image	3	B. Fisk	120	Aunt Jinny	107	War Talk	109	53,925	1:36.20	
1952	Real Delight	3	E. Arcaro	126	Belle Figura	112	Whirla Lea	113	37,800	1:36.60	
1953	Real Delight	4	E. Arcaro	124	Fulvous	107	Bella Figura	119	25,250	1:35.40	
1954	Lavender Hill	5	C. McCreary	115	Vixen Fixit	105	Rosemary B.	111	20,880	1:36.60	
1955	Arab Actress	5	W.M. Cook	117	Clear Dawn	124	C'ry the News	113	37,100	1:35.80	
1956	Delta	4	S. Brooks	119	Amoret	113	Queen Hopeful	120	34,500	1:36.80	
1957	Pucker Up	4	W. Shoemaker	120	Bornastar	111	Lady Swords	108	34,250	1:37.00	
1958	Estacion	5	J. Combest	109	Munch	116	Rosewood	111	32,400	1:50.40	
1959	Wiggle II	4	R.L. Barnett	116	Honey's Gem	118	Born Rich	111	34,050	1:53.00	
1960	Royal Native	7	W. Hartack	128	Woodlawn	110	Silver Spoon	128	33,750	1:50.40	
1961	Shirley Jones	5	H. Grant	124	Call Card	110	Equifun	111	28,600	1:48.00	
1962	Kootenai	4	W. Shoemaker	116	Shirley Jones	123	Fluoresee	108	33,250	1:52.80	
1963	Smart Deb	3	W. Hartack	116	Solabar	113	Nubile	114	50,500	1:50.00	
1964	Tosmah	3	S. Boulmetis	117	Old Hat	116	Nubile	111	49,050	1:49.40	
1965	Old Hat	6	R. Gallimore	126	Swoonalong	122	Miss Cav'ndish	125	46,200	1:49.40	
1966	Swinging Mood	3	E. Fires	112	Margarethen	124	Amerivan	114	33,250	1:48.60	
1967	May's Guide	5	C. Perret	113	Grand Coulee	111	Gabby Abby	113	26,050	1:49.40	
1967	Swinging Mood	4	E. Fires	121	April Dawn	116	Amerivan	114	25,850	1:49.40	
1968	Ludham	4	J. Vasquez	122	Pattee Canyon	110	Harem Lady	110	31,700	1:52.60	
1969	Pink Pigeon	5	W. Harris	123	Egloga	110	Miss Ribot	118	32,400	1:49.80	
1970	Pattee Canyon	5	D.E. Whited	129	Drumtop	126	Not Too Shy	120	30,900	1:47.60	
1971	Toter Back	4	J.R. Anderson	110	Away	117	Ziba Blue	114	34,300	1:51.20	
1972	Kittiwake	4	R. Woodhouse	122	Blade o' War	110	Barely Even	118	33,200	1:51.20	
1973	Last Home	4	F. Alvarez	112	North Broadway	115	Ziba Blue	114	35,800	1:50.00	
1974	Sixty Sails	4	D.E. Whited	121	Protectora	113	What Will Be	118	46,300	1:50.60	
1975	Polynesienne	4	L. Snyder	110	Princess Grey	110	Pass a Glance	116	45,050	1:51.80	
1975	Sixty Sails	5	L. Snyder	114	Victorian Queen	118	Pr'c's Ormea	110	45,050	1:52.80	
1976	Nicosia	4	W. Gavidia	118	B.J. King	111	H'pe of Glory	109	45,450	1:49.40	
1976	Cycylya Zee	3	H. Arroyo	110	Sugar Plum Time	115	True Reality	109	46,200	1:49.60	
1977	Javamine	4	J. Velasquez	119	Star Ball	110	Ivory Castle	110	52,620	1:53.20	
1978	Rich Soil	4	C.H. Silva	117	Satan's Cheer	112	Sans Arc	113	38,340	1:51.20	
1979	Amerigirl	4	B. Swatuk	115	Frosty Skater	118	Calderina	122	52,800	1:51.20	
1980	Impetuous Gal	5	E. Fires	115	Sal;zburg	112	Liv'nthesunshine	108	67,200	2:01.40	
1981	La Bonzo	5	J. Lively	110	Wistful	123	Weber City Miss	123	66,360	2:02.60	
1982	Sweetest Chant	4	E. Fires	115	Miss Huntington	119	Turnablade	115	48,960	2:02.60	
1983	May Day Eighty	4	J. Vasquez	115	Sefa's Beauty	125	Stay a Leader	113	50,355	2:04.40	
1984	Ch'se a Partner	4	D. Brumfield	116	First Flurry	113	Silvered Silk	117	62,595	2:04.00	
1985	Heatherten	6	R.P. Romero	126	Solo Skater	112	Mr. T.'s Tune	114	49,410	2:04.00	
1986	Queen Alexandra	4	D. Brumfield	122	Mr. T.'s Tune	113	Bessarabian	121	92,220	1:48.40	
1987	Family Style	4	S. Hawley	123	Royal Cielo	113	Tide	114	49,320	1:52.20	
1989	Between the Hedges	5	P.A. Johnson	112	Topicount	116	Stoneleigh's Hope	114	65,010	1:48.60	
1990	Degenerate Gal	5	R.P. Romero	117	Evangelical	115	Confirmed Dancer	113	48,555	1:49.20	
1991	Lucky Lady Lauren	4	J. Velasquez	112	Beth Believes	113	Bungalow	112	45,000	1:49.20	95
1992	Lemhi Go	4	E. Fires	114	Beth Believes	112	Diamond City	112	45,000	1:49.60	99
1993	Erica's Dream	5	W. Martinez	115	Pleasant Jolie	114	Meafara	123	60,000	1:23.00	99
1994	Hey Hazel	4	Pino MG	115	Passing Vice	114	Pennyhill Park	116	60,000	1:49.40	99
1995	Mariah's Storm	4	Lester RN	117	Mysteriously	117	Minority Dater	114	60,000	1:50.80	101
1996	Belle Of Cozzene	4	Pettinger D. R.	115	War Thief	113	Your Ladyship	116	75000	1:49.20	101
1997	Omi	4	Guidry M.	114	Gold Memory	115	Trick Attack	114	60000	1:51.80	100
2000	Megans Bluff	3	C.R. Woods Jr	111	On a Soapbox	115	Tutorial	113	90,000	1:51.41	97
2001	Humble Clerk	4	L. Melancon	114	Maltest Superb	115	Lakenheath	115	90,000	1:51.53	96
2002	Lakenheath	4	C.A. Emigh	115	With Ability	116	Your Out	115	90,000	1:50.78	105
2003	Take Charge Lady	4	S.J. Sellers	123	Lakenheath	116	To the Queen	117	90,000	1:50.19	107
2004	Adoration	5	V. Espinoza	123	Tamweel	116	Indy Groove	116	90,000	1:49.75	97

Beyer Index: 99.67

ARLINGTON MILLION (G1), 1 1/4 Miles (Turf), 3-Year-Olds and Up, Arlington Park, 2004 Purse: $1,000,000

Year	Winner	Age	Jockey	Wt.	Second	Wt.	Third	Wt.	Win Value	Time	Beyer
1981	John Henry	6	W. Shoemaker	126	The Bart	126	Madam Gay	117	600,000	2:07.60	
1982	Perrault	5	L. Pincay Jr	126	Be My Native	118	Motavato	126	600,000	1:58.80	
1983	Tolomeo	3	P. Eddery	118	John Henry	126	Nijinsky's Secret	126	600,000	2:04.40	

Year	Winner	Age	Jockey	Wt.	Second	Wt.	Third	Wt.	Win Value	Time	Beyer
1984	John Henry	9	C.J. McCarron	126	Royal Heroine	122	Gato Del Sol	126	600,000	2:01.40	
1985	Teleprompter	5	T.A. Ives	126	Greinton	126	Flying Pidgeon	126	600,000	2:03.40	
1986	Estrapade	5	F. Toro	122	Divulge	126	Pennine Walk	126	600,000	2:00.80	
1987	Manila	4	A. Cordero Jr	126	Sharrood	126	Theatrical	126	600,000	2:02.40	
1988	Mill Native	4	C.B. Asmussen	126	Equalize	126	Sunshine Forever	126	600,000	2:00.00	
1989	Steinlen	6	J.A. Santos	126	Lady in Silver	117	Yankee Affair	126	600,000	2:03.60	
1990	Golden Pheasant	4	G.L. Stevens	126	With Approval	126	Steinlen	126	600,000	1:59.60	113
1991	Tight Spot	4	L. Pincay Jr	126	Algenib	122	Kartajana	123	600,000	1:59.40	108
1992	Dear Doctor	5	C.B. Asmussen	126	Sky Classic	126	Golden Pheasant	126	600,000	1:59.80	108
1993	Star of Cozzene	5	J.A. Santos	126	Evanescent	126	Johann Quatz	126	600,000	2:07.40	115
1994	Paradise Creek	5	P. Day	126	Fanmore	126	Muhtarram	126	600,000	1:59.60	111
1995	Awad	5	E. Maple	126	Sandpit	126	The Vid	126	600,000	1:58.60	114
1996	Mecke	4	R.G. Davis	126	Awad	126	Sandpit	126	600,000	2:00.40	111
1997	Marlin	4	G.L. Stevens	126	Sandpit	126	Percutant	126	600,000	2:02.40	107
2000	Chester House	5	J.R. Velazquez	126	Manndar	126	Mula Gula	126	1,200,000	2:01.37	110
2001	Silvano	5	A. Suborics	126	Hap	126	Reddatore	126	600,000	2:02.64	118
2002	Beat Hollow	5	J.D. Bailey	126	Sarafan	126	Forbidden Apple	126	600,000	2:02.94	107
2003	Sulamani	4	D.R. Flores	126	Kaieteur	126			600,000	2:02.29	106
					Paolini	126					
	Storming Home finished first but was disqualified and placed fourth										
2004	Kicken Kris	4	K.J. Desormeaux	126	Magistretti	126	Epalo	126	600,000	2:00.08	106
	Powerscourt finished first but was disqualified and placed fourth										

Beyer Index: 110.31

Run at Woodbine in 1988; not run 1998-99

ARLINGTON-WASHINGTON FUTURITY (G3), 1 Mile, 2-Year-Olds, Arlington Park, 2004 Purse: $200,000

Year	Winner	Age	Jockey	Wt.	Second	Wt.	Third	Wt.	Win Value	Time	Beyer
1962	Candy Spots	2	W. Shoemaker	122	Never Bend	122	Rash Prince	122	142,250	1:21.80	
1963	Golden Ruler	2	H. Hinojosa	122	Chieftain	122	Dunfee	122	112,500	1:24.80	
1964	Sadair	2	W. Shoemaker	122	Umbrella Fella	122	Royal Gunner	122	134,925	1:23.40	
1965	Buckpasser	2	B. Baeza	122	Fathers Image	122	Flame Tree	122	190,475	1:23.00	
1966	Diplomat Way	2	W. Shoemaker	122	Wilbur Clark	122	Lightning Orphan	122	195,200	1:22.60	
1967	T.V. Commercial	2	P. Anderson	122	Gin-Rob	122	Royal Cap	122	105,875	1:23.80	
1967	Vitriolic	2	W. Shoemaker	122	Exclusive Native	122	Royal Trace	122	105,875	1:24.00	
1968	Strong Strong	2	D. Gargan	122	King Emperor	122	Night Invader	122	212,850	1:22.80	
1969	Silent Screen	2	J.L. Rotz	122	Insubordination	122	Windy Tide	122	206,075	1:22.60	
1971	Hold Your Peace	2	C. Marquez	122	Heisanative	122	Pokachief	122	45,000	1:11.00	
1971	Governor Max	2	C. Perret	122	Chevron Flight	122	Danahoney	122	45,000	1:11.20	
1972	Shecky Greene	2	C. Marquez	122	Sunny South	122	Sailors Night Out	122	103,020	1:10.40	
1973	Lover Johm	2	R. Ussery	122	Beau Groton	122	Hula Chief	122	97,470	1:11.60	
1974	Greek Answer	2	M. Castaneda	122	Colonel Power	122	The Bagel Prince	122	122,505	1:17.80	
1975	Honest Pleasure	2	D.G. McHargue	122	Khyber King	122	Rule the Ridge	122	140,610	1:18.40	
1976	Run Dusty Run	2	D.G. McHargue	122	Royal Ski	122	Eagletar	122	120,465	1:16.40	
1977	Sauce Boat	2	S. Cauthen	122	Gonquin	122	Forever Casting	122	130,665	1:16.60	
1978	Jose Binn	2	A. Cordero Jr	122	Exuberant	122	Strike Your Colors	122	120,660	1:17.40	
1979	Execution's Reason	2	E. Delahoussaye	122	Preemptive	122	Brent's Trans Am	122	89,790	1:22.40	
1980	Well Decorated	2	L. Pincay Jr	122	Lord Avie	122	Fairway Phantom	122	240,885	1:23.80	
1981	Lets Dont Fight	2	J. Lively	122	Tropic Ruler	122	Music Leader	122	305,385	1:29.20	
1982	Total Departure	2	E. Fires	122	Coax Me Matt	122	Highland Park	122	271,515	1:23.60	
1983	All Fired Up	2	R.D. Evans	122	Holme on Top	122	Smart n Slick	122	330,135	1:27.00	
1984	Spend a Buck	2	C. Hussey	122	Dusty's Darby	122	Viva Maxi	122	355,320	1:38.00	
1985	Meadowlake	2	J.L. Diaz	122	Bar Tender	122	Papal Power	122	286,320	1:16.80	
1986	Bet Twice	2	C. Perret	122	Conquistarose	122	Jazzing Around	122	300,420	1:37.20	
1987	Tejano	2	J. Vasquez	122	Jim's Orbit	122	Native Stalwart	122	247,080	1:36.20	
1989	Secret Hello	2	A.T. Gryder	122	Richard R.	122	Bite the Bullet	122	220,860	1:35.80	
1990	Hansel	2	P. Day	122	Walesa	122	Discover	122	220,440	1:36.40	
1991	Caller I.D.	2	J.D. Bailey	121	Count the Time	121	West by West	121	188,880	1:36.00	91
1992	Gilded Time	2	C.J. McCarron	121	Boundlessly	121	Rockamundo	121	200,580	1:37.80	91
1993	Polar Expedition	2	C.C. Bourque	121	Gimme Glory	121	Delicate Cure	121	120,000	1:39.20	82
1994	Evansville Slew	2	P. Compton	121	Valid Wager	121	Mr Purple	121	120,000	1:37.80	82
1996	Night in Reno	2	M. Guidry	121	Flying With Eagles	121	Thisnearlywasmine	121	120,000	1:36.60	83
1997	Cowboy Dan	2	D. Kutz	121	Captain Maestri	121	Fiamma	121	90,000	1:37.60	90
2000	Trailthefox	2	S.J. Sellers	121	Stabury	121	Blame It On Ruby	121	90,000	1:37.25	91
2001	Publication	2	R. Meier	122	It'sallinthechase	122	Dubai Squire	122	90,000	1:38.78	78
2002	Most Feared	2	M. Guidry	122	Anasheed	122	Unleash the Power	122	90,000	1:37.52	79
2003	Cactus Ridge	2	E.M.Martin Jr	122	Glittergem	117	Texas Deputy	119	90,000	1:35.44	95
2004	Three Hour Nap	2	E. Razo Jr	119	Straight Line	119			120,000	1:38.56	80
					Elusive Chris	122					

Beyer Index: 85.64

ARLINGTON-WASHINGTON LASSIE (G3), 1 Mile, 2-Year-Old Fillies, Arlington Park, 2004 Purse: $100,000

Year	Winner	Age	Jockey	Wt.	Second	Wt.	Third	Wt.	Win Value	Time	Beyer
1929	Capture	2	E. Shropshire	117	Ma Yerkes	117	Thistle Down	124	9,175	1:06.00	
1930	Risque	2	E. Steffen	117	Glidelia	115	Panasette	113	6,650	1:05.80	
1931	Top Flight	2	A. Robertson	120	Modern Queen	113	Princess Camelia	117	19,125	1:05.20	
1932	Hilena	2	R. Workman	119	Edelweiss	117	Swivel	119	17,900	1:10.40	
1933	Mata Hari	2	R. Jones	117	Far Star	119	Dabchick	117	21,670	1:12.00	
1934	Motto	2	R. Workman	119	Toro Nancy	115	Bye Lo	117	22,510	1:13.40	
1935	Forever Yours	2	D. Meade	117	Parade Girl	117	Balcony	117	25,790	1:12.80	
1936	Apogee	2	E. Steffen	122	Jewell Dorsett	117	Oddesa Girl	117	21,020	1:13.20	
1937	Theen	2	I. Anderson	117	Inhale	122	Well Rewarded	122	15,630	1:11.80	
1938	Inscoelda	2	C. Rollins	117	Dinner Date	117	Unerring	119	17,540	1:11.60	
1939	Now What	2	R. Workman	122	War Beauty	117	Piquet	117	18,820	1:13.00	
1940	Blue Delight	2	A. Snider	119	Misty Isle	122	Valdina Myth	122	17,250	1:12.80	
1941	Petrify	2	R. Donoso	117	Lotopoise	117	Court Manners	117	17,200	1:12.60	
1942	Fad	2	A. Craig	117	Askmenow	117	Miss Barbara	117	25,980	1:13.60	
1943	Twilight Tear	2	N. Jemas	113	Miss Keeneland	113	Music Hall	110	26,460	1:13.20	
1944	Expression	2	F. Zufelt	119	Twosy	119	Blue Alibi	119	28,900	1:12.40	
1945	Beaugay	2	J. Adams	119	Enfilade	119	Aladear	119	35,900	1:12.20	
1946	Four Winds	2	I. Anderson	119	Musical Lady	119	War Fan	119	51,000	1:12.00	
1947	Bewitch	2	D. Dodson	119	Boswell Lady	119	Lea Lark	119	47,150	1:10.80	
1948	Pail of Water	2	W. Mehrtens	119	Alsab's Day	119	Stole	119	40,350	1:12.40	
1949	Duchess Peg	2	S. Brooks	119	Baby Comet	119	Bed o' Roses	119	45,125	1:15.60	
1950	Shawnee Squaw	2	A.D. Rivera	119	Red Cross	119	Hasty Request	119	43,865	1:12.00	
1951	Princess Lygia	2	K. Church	119	Hadn't Orter	119	Aesthete	119	45,580	1:11.20	
1952	Fulvous	2	S. Brooks	119	Aerolite	119	Hula	119	53,275	1:13.80	
1953	Queen Hopeful	2	J. Adams	119	Miz Clementine	119	Beanir	119	66,565	1:10.60	
1954	Delta	2	S. Brooks	119	Lea Lane	119	Alspal	119	62,750	1:10.40	
1955	Judy Rullah	2	D. Erb	119	Guard Rail	119	Waikiki	119	57,335	1:13.80	
1956	Leallah	2	W. Hartack	119	Splendored	119	Frank's Flower	119	56,010	1:11.60	
1957	Poly Hi	2	E. Guerin	119	Delnita	119	Hasty Doll	119	65,025	1:10.60	
1958	Dark Vintage	2	J. Heckmann	119	Little Kid	119	Debbie Lorraine	119	64,000	1:10.80	
1959	Monarchy	2	S. Brooks	119	My Dear Girl	119	Heavenly Baby	119	61,950	1:10.00	
1960	Colfax Maid	2	S. Brooks	119	Caps and Bells	119	Apatontheback	119	59,350	1:11.80	
1961	Rudoma	2	W. Hartack	116	Cherry Laurel	116	Song of Glory	116	38,500	1:11.40	
1962	Smart Deb	2	M. Ycaza	119	Honey Bunny	119	Fast Luck	119	44,900	1:16.20	
1963	Sari's Song	2	W. Shoemaker	119	Ye-Cats	119	Castle Forbes	119	61,505	1:18.20	
1964	Admiring	2	W. Hartack	119	Privileged	119	Mr. B's Sister	119	77,815	1:18.00	
1965	Silver Bright	2	J. Nichols	119	Ole Liz	119	Prides Profile	119	111,265	1:18.20	
1966	Mira Femme	2	I. Valenzuela	119	Teacher's Art	119	Woozem	119	96,525	1:16.80	
1967	Shenow	2	L. Pincay Jr	119	Ave Valeque	119	Lucretia Bori	119	92,500	1:18.40	
1968	Process Shot	2	C. Baltazar	119	Kahoolawe	119	Lynne's Orphan	119	80,000	1:17.40	
1969	Clover Lane	2	W. Shoemaker	119	Belle Noire	119	Dixie Wind	119	80,000	1:18.40	
1972	Double Your Fun	2	L. Melancon	119	Crosstie	119	Greek Lovliness	119	35,160	1:12.00	
1972	Natural Sound	2	J. Tejeira	119	Vaguely Familiar	119	Felane	119	35,610	1:11.60	
1973	Special Team	2	A. Pineda	119	Thirty One Jewels	119	Two Timing Lass	119	59,574	1:11.00	
1974	Hot n Nasty	2	D.G. McHargue	119	Sharm a Sheikh	119	Mystery Mood	119	64,386	1:11.40	
1975	Dearly Precious	2	M. Hole	119	Free Journey	119	Head Spy	119	67,938	1:11.20	
1976	Special Warmth	2	S. Maple	119	Wavy Waves	119	Drama Critic	119	68,700	1:10.40	
1977	Stub	2	R. Turcotte	119	Rainy Princess	119	Go Line	119	70,329	1:10.40	
1978	It's in the Air	2	E. Delahoussaye	119	Angel Island	119	Bequa	119	71,394	1:09.60	
1979	Sissy's Time	2	E. Fires	119	Ellie Milove	119	Vogue Folks	119	63,399	1:11.00	
1980	Truly Bound	2	W. Shoemaker	119	Safe Play	119	Masters Dream	119	83,022	1:25.20	
1981	Milingo	2	R. Sibille	119	Maniches	119	Justa Litte One	119	129,798	1:25.20	
1982	For Once'n My Life	2	E. Maple	119	Some Kinda Flirt	119	How Clever	119	106,461	1:23.40	
1983	Miss Oceana	2	E. Maple	119	Life's Magic	119	Bottle Top	119	112,146	1:23.40	
1984	Contredance	2	P. Day	119	Tiltalating	119	Miss Delice	119	211,560	1:26.00	
1985	Family Style	2	L. Pincay Jr	119	Deep Silver	119	Pamela Kay	119	250,200	1:18.00	
1986	Delicate Vine	2	G.L. Stevens	122	Sacahuista	122	Ruling Angel	122	165,660	1:23.40	
1987	Joe's Tammie	2	C. Perret	122	Tomorrow's Child	122	Pearlie Gold	122	186,840	1:25.00	
1989	Trumpet's Blare	2	L. Pincay Jr	122	Special Happening	122	Puffy Doodle	122	128,040	1:38.60	
1990	Through Flight	2	J.M. Johnson	120	Good Potential	120	Wild for Traci	120	138,870	1:39.00	76
1991	Speed Dialer	2	P. Day	119	Cadillac Women	119	Mystic Hawk	119	141,390	1:36.40	79
1992	Eliza	2	P.A. Valenzuela	119	Banshee Winds	119	Tourney	119	134,850	1:39.40	84
1993	Mariah's Storm	2	R.N. Lester	119	Shapely Scrapper	119	Minority Dater	119	90,000	1:38.80	73
1994	Shining Light	2	J.L. Diaz	119	She's a Lively One	119	Alltheway Bertie	119	90,000	1:41.60	68
1996	Southern Playgirl	2	R. P. Romero	119	Leo's Gypsy Dancer	119	Broad Dynamite	119	90,000	1:38.20	79
1997	Silver Maiden	2	B.S. Laviolette	119	Artic Lady	119	So Generous	119	60,000	1:37.40	81
2000	Thunder Bertie	2	J.A. Beasley	119	Caressing	119	Zahwah	119	60,000	1:36.91	87
2001	Joanies Bella	2	M. St. Julien	121	Brief Bliss	121	First Again	121	60,000	1:39.34	80
2002	Moonlight Sonata	2	B.S. Laviolette	121	Parting	121	Souris	121	60,000	1:37.82	76
2003	Zosima	2	P. Day	118	Everyday Angel	116	Cryptos' Best	118	60,000	1:36.02	89
2004	Culinary	2	C.H. Marquez Jr	116	Runway Model	118	Kota	118	60,000	1:36.98	87

Beyer Index: 79.92

ANNE ARUNDEL (G3), 1 1/8 Miles, 3-Year-Old Fillies, Pimlico, 2004 Purse: $100,000

Year	Winner	Age	Jockey	Wt.	Second	Wt.	Third	Wt.	Win Value	Time	Beyer
1974	Pinch Pie	3	C. Baltazar	114	Sailingon	111	Enchanted Native	112	17,595	1:37.40	
1975	My Juliet	3	D.G. McHargue	123	Funny Cat	114	Gala Lil	119	20,070	1:36.80	
1976	What a Summer	3	C.J. McCarron	122	Turn the Guns	114	Avum	114	16,560	1:38.20	
1977	Worrisome Thing	3	H. Hinojosa	112	Northern Sea	121	Luck Penny	121	26,610	1:37.40	
1978	The Very One	3	C. Cooke	110	Silver Ice	121	Dr. Penny Binn	113	26,970	1:40.00	
1979	Jameela	3	W.J. Passmore	123	Sentencia	111	Contrary Rose	111	32,580	1:38.00	
1980	Caught in Amber	3	D.R. Wright	115	Fair Hit	113	Running Around	115	33,330	1:35.60	
1981	Up the Flagpole	3	M.G. Pino	118	Privacy	125	Zvetlana	111	34,080	1:36.20	
1982	Kattegat's Pride	3	D.A. Miller Jr	119	Wedding Party	117	Delicate Ice	115	34,020	1:37.40	
1983	Quixotic Lady	3	G. McCarron	122	Bemissed	119	Batna	117	33,210	1:36.80	
1984	Dowery	3	A.S. Black	118	Basie	115	Dumdedumdedum	114	35,400	1:37.00	
1985	Classy Cut	3	D.A. Miller Jr	116	A Joyful Spray	115	Little Brooks Mesa	106	37,180	1:36.80	
1986	Burt's Dream	3	R. Wilson	114	Now Your Teapottin	110	Vacherie	114	49,900	1:36.00	
1986	Toes Knows	3	D.R. Wright	121	Foot Stone	106	Notches Trace	107	36,400	1:36.40	
1987	Doubles Partner	3	A. Cordero Jr	119	Ruling Angel	122	Arctic Cloud	113	47,330	1:37.20	
1988	Empress Tigere	3	G. McCarron	114	Lost Kitty	119	North Watch	110	58,244	1:49.80	
1989	Misty Ivor	3	M.T. Hunter	115	Under Oath	112	Slew a Native	107	45,000	1:49.60	
1990	McKilts	3	J. Rocco	114	Trumpet's Blare	115	Secreto's Glory	113	32,760	1:50.40	
1991	Devilish Touch	3	M. Castaneda	115	Get Lucky	112	Far Out Nurse	113	30,000	1:24.20	
1992	Avian Assembly	3	L.C. Reynolds	112	Gammy's Alden	117	Singing Ring	115	30,000	1:50.60	
1993	By Your Leave	3	M.G. Pino	114	Tennis Lady	121	Double Sixes	114	33,030	1:52.40	
1994	Miss Slewpy	3	Reynolds LC	114	Cherokee Wonder	114	Churchbell Chimes	121	45,000	1:51.00	
1995	Blue Sky Princess	3	Pino MG	122	Substantial	115	Blonde Actress	115	45,000	1:51.40	
1996	Hay Let's Dance	3	Martinez S. B.	115	Double Stake	115	Mesabi Maiden	122	45,000	1:50.80	91
1997	G. O' Keefe	3	Johnston M. T.	115	Snit	122	Cotton Carnival	122	60,000	1:51.20	97
1998	Merengue	3	Johnston M. T.	122	Queen of Oz	115	Manoa	115	60,000	1:51.80	90
1999	Undermine	3	Melancon L.	115	Gold From the West	115	Batique	115	60,000	1:49.20	100
2000	Gin Talking	3	R.A. Dominguez	122	Tax Affair	115	A.O.L. Hayes	115	60,000	1:50.21	103
2002	Martha's Music	3	S. Elliott	122	Pass the Virtue	122	Shop Till You Drop	115	60,000	1:50.84	92
2003	Smooth Maneuvers	3	M.G. Pino	115	Devotion Unbridled	117	Alchemist	117	60,000	1:51.56	88
2004	Essence	3	J.R. Velazquez	115	Rare Gift	115	Family Business	115	60,000	1:49.37	94

Beyer Index: 94.38

ASHLAND (G1), 1 1/16 Miles, 3-Year-Old Fillies, Keeneland Race Course, 2004 Purse: $485,000

Year	Winner	Age	Jockey	Wt.	Second	Wt.	Third	Wt.	Win Value	Time	Beyer
1937	Drowsy	3	R. Dotter	110	Ann Jones	110	Sparta	115	2,250	1:45.40	
1940	June Bee	3	K. McCombs	115	Flying Jane	115	Miss Co-Ed	112	2,575	1:13.80	
1941	Valdina Myth	3	B. James	121	Laatokka	112	Blue Lily	115	2,600	1:13.00	
1942	The Swallow	3	E. Arcaro	112	Spiral Pass	115	My Choice	115	2,800	1:17.00	
1943	Valdina Marl	3	F. Zufelt	118	Nippy	115	Askmenow	121	2,550	1:14.20	
1944	Harriet Sue	3	J. Higley	115	Darby Delilah	115	Paddle	109	4,275	1:11.80	
1945	Come and Go	3	C.L. Martin	112	Cross Bayou	112	No Blues	110	3,950	1:13.60	
1946	Sweet Caprice	3	F. Zufelt	115	Bogle	110	Tav	115	4,750	1:12.80	
1947	Cosmic Missile	3	W. Balzaretti	121	Ballarita	115	Happiness	109	9,600	1:12.40	
1948	Bewitch	3	N.L. Pierson	121	Silly Gyp	115	Lea Lark	112	8,250	1:12.00	
1949	Tall Weeds	3	C. McCreary	115	Wistful	115	Warsick	115	9,700	1:11.60	
1950	Wondring	3	H. Manifold	112	Famous Shake	115	Radiant	115	10,250	1:11.00	
1951	Sickle's Image	3	B. Fisk	121	Juliets Nurse	118	How	115	8,750	1:18.00	
1952	Free for Me	3	J.D. Jessop	112	Dalal	109	Fancy Step	115	8,972	1:12.80	
1952	Real Delight	3	E. Arcaro	114	Ave	115	Level Sands	115	8,972	1:11.80	
1953	Cerise Reine	3	D. Dodson	115	Bubbley	118	Sweet Patootie	121	13,997	1:12.20	
1954	Jenjay	3	P.J. Bailey	118	Queen Hopeful	121	Siskey	112	13,100	1:11.00	
1955	Insouciant	3	B. Fisk	112	Courtesy	113	Lea Lane	121	13,360	1:10.80	
1956	Doubledogdare	3	S. Brooks	121	Guard Rail	118	Warning Bell	114	12,027	1:11.40	
1957	Jota Jota	3	P. Anderson	114	Lori-El	115	Nile Lily	114	12,000	1:10.80	
1958	Ramadel	3	W. Hartack	115	Bug Brush	114	Fusilade	112	12,455	1:10.00	
1959	Hidden Talent	3	J. Sellers	115	Narissa	115	Tacking	115	13,072	1:09.80	
1960	Tingle	3	H. Hinjosa	112	Airmans Guide	121	Make Sail	118	16,745	1:10.20	
1961	Goldflower	3	S. Brooks	112	My Portrait	115	Ordie	115	16,640	1:10.80	
1962	Windy Miss	3	R.L. Baird	115	Summer Sea	112	Fortunate Isle	115	17,095	1:11.60	
1963	Sally Ship	3	M. Ycaza	113	Bonnie's Girl	118	Myristyl	115	15,632	1:09.00	
1964	Blue Norther	3	W. Shoemaker	121	Silver Dollar	112	Roman Goddess	115	16,347	1:09.00	
1965	Terentia	3	J. Nichols	112	May's Guide	112	Little Gray Pet	115	15,015	1:10.60	
1965	Bright Bauble	3	K. Knapp	115	Saber Dance	118	Respected	121	14,885	1:10.20	
1966	Justakiss	3	R.J. Campbell	121	Prides Profile	121	Champagne Woman	118	19,532	1:10.00	
1967	Dun-Cee	3	W. Harmatz	115	Furl Sail	118	Woozem	121	19,337	1:09.40	
1968	Miss Swapsco	3	D. Richard	115	Moss	112	Fish Net	118	19,597	1:08.80	
1969	Double Delta	3	C.H. Marquez	115	Nutty Donut	121	Bold Heiress	115	19,565	1:10.00	
1970	Gay Missile	3	R. Broussard	116	Kankakee Miss	115	Three Pigeons	118	20,816	1:10.00	

Year	Winner	Age	Jockey	Wt.	Second	Wt.	Third	Wt.	Win Value	Time	Beyer
1971	You All	3	K. Knapp	115	Deceit	121	Silent Beauty	118	20,897	1:11.00	
1972	Barely Even	3	J.L. Rotz	121	Wac	112	La Brisa	115	23,579	1:11.00	
	Happens Song finished first but was disqualified and placed eighth										
1973	Raging Whirl	3	W. Sorez	113	Protest	116	A Little Lovin	110	23,611	1:10.80	
1974	Winged Wishes	3	D. Brumfield	116	Cherished Moment	117	Jay Bar Pet	113	29,786	1:28.80	
1974	Maud Muller	3	D. Brumfield	114	Clemanna	113	Irish Sonnet	119	29,834	1:27.00	
1975	Sun and Snow	3	G. Patterson	116	My Juliet	116	Red Cross	114	39,487	1:26.60	
1976	Optimistic Gal	3	B. Baeza	121	Alvarada	116	Confort Zone	113	37,895	1:26.80	
1977	Sound of Summer	3	F. Toro	118	Mrs. Warren	121	Our Mims	118	40,333	1:26.80	
1978	Mucchina	3	J. Amy	113	Grenzen	121	Bold Rendezvous	118	40,527	1:27.20	
1979	Candy Eclair	3	A.S. Black	121	Himalayan	114	Countess North	115	39,618	1:27.00	
1980	Flos Forum	3	R.P. Romero	112	Cerada Ridge	114	Lady Taurian Peace	116	41,210	1:26.40	
1980	Sugar and Spice	3	J. Fell	113	Nice and Sharp	114	Satin Ribera	116	41,210	1:27.20	
1981	Truly Bound	3	W. Shoemaker	121	Wayward Lass	121	Dame Mysterieuse	121	56,778	1:44.00	
1982	Blush With Pride	3	W. Shoemaker	118	Exclusive Love	116	Delicate Ice	113	83,070	1:45.00	
1983	Princess Rooney	3	J. Vasquez	121	Shamivor	114	Decision	116	74,133	1:45.40	
1984	Enumerating	3	D. Brumfield	114	Miss Oceana	121	Rose of Ashes	113	88,708	1:49.20	
1985	Koluctoo's Jill	3	R.P. Romero	118	Lucy Manette	121	Foxy Deen	121	74,718	1:44.40	
1986	Classy Cathy	3	E. Fires	116	She's a Mystery	116	Patricia J.K.	121	116,513	1:44.00	
1987	Chic Shirine	3	S. Hawley	118	Buryyourbelief	113	Our Little Margie	121	117,683	1:44.60	
1988	Willa on the Move	3	C.J. McCarron	118	On to Royalty	121	Colonial Waters	121	151,125	1:45.80	
1989	Gorgeous	3	E. Delahoussaye	118	Blondeinamotel	115	Some Romance	121	157,430	1:43.20	
1990	Go for Wand	3	R.P. Romero	121	Charon	121	Piper Piper	112	145,665	1:43.60	107
1991	Do It With Style	3	S.J. Sellers	115	Private Treasure	121	Til Forbid	112	182,894	1:43.60	92
1992	Prospectors Delite	3	C. Perret	121	Spinning Round	121	Luv Me Luv Me Not	121	186,063	1:42.60	97
1993	Lunar Spook	3	S.J. Sellers	121	Avie's Shadow	115	Roamin Rachel	115	171,973	1:43.40	95
1994	Inside Information	3	M.E. Smith	121	Bunting	112	Private Status	118	171,197	1:46.80	101
1995	Urbane	3	E. Delahoussaye	115	Conquistadoress	115	Post It	121	207,483	1:43.40	102
1996	My Flag	3	J.D. Bailey	121	Cara Rafaela	121	Mackie	118	335,265	1:42.60	98
1997	Glitter Woman	3	M.E. Smith	121	Anklet	121	Storm Song	121	337,125	1:43.80	104
1998	Well Chosen	3	C.R. Woods Jr	115	Let	115	Banshee Breeze	120	344,410	1:43.00	96
1999	Silverbulletday	3	J.D. Bailey	123	Marley Vale	115	Gold From the West	115	337,280	1:41.72	108
2000	Rings a Chime	3	S.J. Sellers	116	Zoftig	116	Circle of Life	116	341,155	1:44.43	92
2001	Fleet Renee	3	J.R. Velazquez	116	Golden Ballet	123	Latour	120	357,275	1:43.77	104
2002	Take Charge Lady	3	A. D'Amico	123	Take the Cake	118	Belterra	120	345,805	1:43.29	109
2003	Elloluv	3	R.J. Albarado	120	Lady Tak	123	Holiday Lady	116	342,085	1:43.58	105
2004	Madcap Escapade	3	R.R. Douglas	118	Ashado	123	Last Song	120	310,000	1:44.55	98

Beyer Index: 100.53

Distance 6 furlongs from 1941-73; about seven furlongs from 1974-80; for 3-year-olds and up, fillies and mares, prior to 1940; run at Churchill Downs, 1943-45..................

ASTARITA (G3), 6 1/2 Furlongs, 2-Year-Old Fillies, Belmont Park, 2004 Purse: $108,000

Year	Winner	Age	Jockey	Wt.	Second	Wt.	Third	Wt.	Win Value	Time	Beyer
1946	Keynote	2	H. Woodhouse	116	Quarantaine	114	Kai Kai	111	10,325	1:11.20	
1947	Bellsoeur	2	T. May	119	Grey Flight	116	Dusty Legs	111	9,650	1:12.60	
1948	Nell K.	2	D. Dodson	114	Tassel	110	Flying Ship	116	10,275	1:14.60	
1949	Blue Kay	2	T. Atkinson	113	High Frequency	124	Sweetlucybell	115	9,375	1:14.00	
1950	Jacodema	2	R. Permane	113	Self Assurance	116	Ruddy	116	8,950	1:12.00	
1951	Place Card	2	A. Kirkland	111	Landmark	110	Rose Jet	119	9,575	1:12.60	
1952	Grecian Queen	2	E. Guerin	119	Piedmont Lass	116	Flirtatious	122	8,925	1:13.60	
1953	Make a Play	2	B. Green	113	When in Rome	115	Riant	122	8,450	1:13.20	
1954	Two Stars	2	N. Shuk	119	High Voltage	125	My Blue Sky	110	12,800	1:12.80	
1955	Cosmah	2	K. Korte	116	Noors Image	110	Levee	113	12,200	1:11.40	
1956	Alanesian	2	W. Boland	122	Jet's Charm	112	Miss Blue Jay	110	11,450	1:10.00	
1957	Polamby	2	P. Anderson	116	Merry Lark	112	Lopar	114	18,550	1:25.80	
1961	Cicada	2	W. Shoemaker	122	Firm Policy	116	Jazz Queen	112	19,630	1:24.40	
1962	Main Swap	2	B. Baeza	112	Pams Ego	119	Fool's Play	116	19,272	1:23.00	
1963	Petite Rouge	2	J. Sellers	122	Castle Forbes	122	Little Red Belle	112	14,349	1:23.60	
1963	Tosmah	2	S. Boulmetis	119	Beautiful Day	119	Teo Pepi	116	14,511	1:23.00	
1964	I Deceive	2	F. Alvarez	119	Queen Empress	122	Admiring	122	19,955	1:26.60	
1965	Swift Lady	2	H. Gustines	116	Forefoot	114	Lady Diplomat	116	15,697	1:23.60	
1965	Prides Profile	2	D. Pierce	119	....		Destro	116	10,157	1:23.00	
	Lady Pitt	2	R. Turcotte	116							
1966	Irish County	2	B. Baeza	116	Pepperwood	116	Green Glade	116	19,370	1:24.40	
1967	Syrian Sea	2	R. Ussery	119	Good Game	116	Dawn of Tomorrow	112	19,175	1:22.60	
1968	Show Off	2	E. Belmonte	122	Shoo Fly	122	Roundamene	116	14,804	1:25.00	
1968	Dihela	2	R. Turcotte	112	Imbibe	112	Shuvee	112	14,966	1:24.20	
1969	Cherry Sundae	2	J.L. Rotz	116	Corte Madera	116	Royal Picnic	112	19,890	1:24.80	
1970	Deceit	2	R. Turcotte	122	Make Me Laugh	113	Bonnie and Gay	119	19,402	1:23.80	

Year	Winner	Age	Jockey	Wt.	Second	Wt.	Third	Wt.	Win Value	Time	Beyer
1971	Barely Even	2	T. Barrow	119	Miss Gunflint	116	Bridget o' Brick	112	21,120	1:23.40	
1972	Princess Doubleday	2	B. Baeza	114	Tuerta	116	Cherry Jay	114	13,965	1:17.20	
1972	Waltz Fan	2	J. Mallano	117	Behram	114	Fine Tuning	114	14,040	1:17.80	
1973	Raisela	2	R. Turcotte	113	Nancy G	113	Quick Cure	115	17,610	1:16.80	
1974	Stulcer	2	A. Cordero Jr	113	Copernica	113	But Exclusive	116	17,040	1:16.40	
1975	Picture Tube	2	E. Maple	113	La Tamborera	115	Dottie's Doll	113	23,340	1:18.40	
1976	Sensational	2	A. Cordero Jr	112	Tickle My Toes	112	Spy Flag	112	22,185	1:17.40	
1977	Lakeville Miss	2	R. Hernandez	112	Sherry Peppers	116	Tempermental P't	112	21,990	1:17.80	
1978	Fall Aspen	2	R.I. Velez	112	Whisper Fleet	112	Island Kitty	112	25,755	1:17.00	
1979	Royal Suite	2	J. Fell	114	Andrea F.	112	Smart Angle	116	25,815	1:17.20	
1980	Sweet Revenge	2	J. Velasquez	116	Expressive Dance	113	Hagley's Point	112	33,360	1:17.20	
1981	Before Dawn	2	J. Velasquez	119	Betty Money	112	Take Lady Anne	112	33,540	1:16.60	
1982	Wings of Jove	2	W.H. McCauley	112	On the Bench	112	Bammer	112	32,220	1:16.80	
1983	Tina's Ten	2	R. Migliore	112	Masked Barb	112	Upturning	112	34,740	1:19.20	
1984	Mom's Command	2	A. Fuller	116	Self Image	116	Winters' Love	112	54,900	1:17.80	
1985	Guadery	2	A. Cordero Jr	112	Musical Lark	112	I'm Sweets	112	64,800	1:17.00	
1986	Cagey Exuberance	2	J. Nied Jr	116	Sea Basque	113	Maxi Ruler	116	51,300	1:18.20	
1987	Flashy Runner	2	J. Vasquez	112	Tap Your Toes	112	Galway Song	112	70,560	1:16.60	
1988	Channel Three	2	C. Barrera	116	Pat Copelan	119	Mistaurian	112	83,460	1:17.00	
1989	Dance Colony	2	J.A. Santos	119	Charging Fire	114	Trumpet's Blare	114	68,640	1:17.80	
1990	Devilish Touch	2	C. Perret	116	Makin Faces	112	Missy's Mirage	112	71,760	1:18.00	
1991	Easy Now	2	M.E. Smith	112	Stolen Beauty	112	Celeste Cielo	112	69,240	1:22.80	93
1992	Missed the Storm	2	M.E. Smith	119	Dispute	119	Statuette	119	67,920	1:24.80	92
1993	Shapely Scrapper	2	J. Bravo	119	Brighter Course	119	Fashion Maven	119	67,560	1:24.00	77
1994	Miss Golden Circle	2	J.A. Krone	119	Golden Bri	119	Mistress S.	119	64,740	1:23.60	86
1995	Top Secret	2	M.E. Smith	119	Plum Country	119	Mesabi Maiden	119	69,480	1:36.60	84
1996	Broad Dynamite	2	D.W. Cordova	119	Glitter Woman	119	Biding Time	119	63,960	1:24.00	81
1997	Ninth Inning	2	R.G. Davis	119	Salty Perfume	119	Madame Fireplace	119	64,680	1:17.40	83
1998	Paved in Gold	2	J. F. Chavez	119	Blushing Deed	119	Paula's Girl	119	63,780	1:18.80	81
1999	Silentlea	2	R.G. Davis	119	Valerie's Dream	119	Lucky Livi	119	67,620	1:17.40	74
2000	Xtra Heat	2	M.T. Johnston	117	Gold Mover	119	Major Wager	117	66,060	1:16.71	85
2001	Bella Bellucci	2	G.L. Stevens	117	Forest Heiress	120	Speed to Burn	117	63,955	1:16.67	97
2002	Humorous Lady	2	J.D. Bailey	117	Fast Cookie	117	Chimichurri	117	90,000	1:17.76	83
2003	Spectacular Moon	2	J.F. Chavez	117	Feline Story	120	Smokey Glacken	117	90,000	1:17.16	81
2004	Toll Taker	2	E.M. Coa	117	Im a Dixie Girl	120	Summer Raven	117	64,800	1:18.16	79

Beyer Index: 84.00

ATHENIA HANDICAP (G3), 1 1/16 Miles (Turf), Fillies and Mares, 3-Year-Olds and Up, Aqueduct, 2004 Purse: $115,700

Year	Winner	Age	Jockey	Wt.	Second	Wt.	Third	Wt.	Win Value	Time	Beyer
1978	Terpsichorist	3	M. Venezia	114	Consort	110	Bonnie Blue Flag	110	33,300	2:03.20	
1979	Poppycock	3	J. Velasquez	114	Fourdrinier	114	Six Crowns	114	52,470	2:05.60	
1980	Love Sign	3	R. Hernandez	121	Rokeby Rose	111	Classic Curves	111	50,490	2:00.40	
1981	De la Rose	3	E. Maple	125	Noble Damsel	111	Andover Way	113	51,120	2:00.40	
1982	Mintage	3	J.L. Samyn	114	Doodle	119	Street Dance	112	32,790	2:17.80	
1982	Middle Stage	3	J. Miranda	112	Realms Reason	114	Vocal	115	32,790	2:17.40	
1983	Rose Crescent	4	R.G. Davis	108	Lady Norcliffe	111	Infinite	112	34,380	2:22.00	
1984	Key Dancer	3	A. Cordero Jr	111	Surely Georgie's	107	Rossard	123	56,700	2:14.80	
1985	Videogenic	3	J. Cruguet	114	Persian Tiara	119	Key Witness	108	61,020	2:15.40	
1986	Dawn's Curtsey	4	E. Maple	111	Festivity	113	Perfect Point	115	55,440	2:16.00	
1987	Lead Kindly Light	4	J.M. Pezua	110	Barbara's Moment	111	Spectacular Bev	114	70,920	2:23.80	
1988	High Browser	3	P. Day	108	Miss Unnameable	109	Gaily Gaily	110	57,780	2:18.60	
1989	Capades	3	A. Cordero Jr	115	Miss Unnameable	114	Key Flyer	110	54,360	2:13.20	
1990	Buy the Firm	4	J.D. Bailey	111	Rigamajig	111	Igmaar	111	52,650	2:18.20	
1991	Flaming Torch	4	P.A. Valenzuela	113	Plenty of Grace	114	Highland Penny	116	55,800	2:13.80	
1992	Fairy Garden	4	J.A. Krone	112	Passagere du Soir	117	Seewillo	113	52,020	2:13.60	97
1993	Trampoli	4	M.E. Smith	117	Kirov Premiere	110	Dahlia's Dreamer	110	54,000	2:17.00	105
1994	Lady Affirmed	3	Chavez JF	111	Irving's Girl	110	Cox Orange	116	52,245	1:48.60	98
1995	Caress	4	Davis RG	114	Manila Lila	115	Vinista	119	69,340	1:54.00	82
1996	Sixieme Sans	4	J.D. Bailey	116	Rapunzel Runz	115	Fashion Star	113	66660	1:37.80	103
1997	Rapid Selection	4	Bravo J.	113	Dynasty	114	Preachersnightmare	111	65940	1:47.00	105
1998	Tampico	5	Bravo J.	114	Irish Daisy	113	Rumpipumpy	115	51210	1:42.80	96
1999	Antoniette	4	J.F. Chavez	119	Dominique's Joy	113	Prospectress	115	66,840	1:41.89	102
2000	Wild Heart Dancing	4	J.F. Chavez	115	Fickle Friends	114	Silken	114	67,500	1:43.40	95
2001	Verruma	5	J.R. Velazquez	114	Siringas	112	Freefourracing	113	82,725	1:42.09	94
2001	Babae	5	J.F. Chavez	116	Batique	114	Sweet Prospect	110	82,725	1:40.53	108
2002	Babae	6	J.F. Chavez	120	Strawberry Blonde	116	Silver Rail	112	70,020	1:44.90	100
2003	Caught in the Rain	4	R. Migliore	115	Lojo	114	Coney Kitty	113	67,800	1:47.05	93
2004	Finery	4	P. Fragoso	113	Madeira Mist	118	With Patience	114	69,420	1:43.73	96

Beyer Index: 98.14

AZALEA BREEDERS' CUP (G3), 6 Furlongs, 3-Year-Old Fillies, Calder Race Course, 2004 Purse: $300,000

Year	Winner	Age	Jockey	Wt.	Second	Wt.	Third	Wt.	Win Value	Time	Beyer
1972	Mr. Brick's Image	4	J. Salinas	112	First Bloom	122	M's Gunflint	117	16,200	1:46.80	
1976	Forty Nine Sunsets	3	G. St. Leon	122	Head Spy	113	Noble Royalty	113	13,560	1:11.80	
1977	Countess Pruner	3	J.S. Rodriguez	116	Delphic Oracle	113	White Goddess	119	13,440	1:11.20	
1978	Lucy Belle	3	A. Smith Jr	113	We Believe in You	113	Wings of Destiny	122	14,040	1:25.20	
1979	Burn's Return	3	M.A. Rivera	115	Solo Haina	120	Speier's Hope	115	16,860	1:24.00	
1980	She Can't Miss	3	W.A. Guerra	122	Nice and Sharp	115	Karla's Enough	119	16,515	1:11.20	
1981	Ange Gal	3	G. Cohen	113	Float Upstream	115	Whoop It	114	16,515	1:26.00	
1981	Kaylem Ho	3	A. Smith Jr	115	Toga Toga	119	Secret Kingdom	115	16,515	1:25.80	
1982	Here's to Peg	3	J.A. Velez Jr	116	Cut	114	Bad Dancin Rita	116	16,905	1:26.00	
1983	Current Gal	3	E. Cardone	112	Silvered Silk	115	Paris Roulette	115	17,295	1:25.60	
1984	Birdie Belle	3	H.A.Valdivieso	120	Sugar's Image	120	Scorched Panties	120	33,990	1:25.80	
1985	Jackie McCleaf	3	C. Hussey	120	Nahema	118	Nyama	118	33,840	1:25.80	
1986	Classy Tricks	3	M.C. Suckie	112	Janjac	112	Thirty Zip	119	30,410	1:25.40	
1987	My Sweet Replica	3	S.B. Soto	115	Shot Gun Bonnie	114	Ches Pie	116	33,990	1:25.20	
1988	Grand Splash	3	R.N. Lester	114	Myfavorite Charity	114	Hi Maudie	116	46,500	1:25.60	
1989	Princess Mora	3	S. Gaffalione	112	Georgies Doctor	118	Silk Stocks	117	32,790	1:25.60	
1990	Sweet Proud Polly	3	P.A. Rodriguez	115	Highway Lady	115	Bald Cat	112	32,790	1:26.20	
1991	Ranch Ragout	3	E.O. Nunez	113	Parisian Flight	115	Foolishly Wild	110	33,120	1:18.40	
1992	C.C.'s Return	3	R.J. Thibeau Jr	113	Fortune Forty Four	114	Subtle Dancer	113	30,000	1:25.20	90
1993	Kimscountrydiamond	3	J. Vasquez	115	Nijivision	113	Hollywood Wildcat	117	60,000	1:23.40	80
1994	Cut the Charm	3	Castillo H Jr	121	Just a Little Kiss	114	Tasso Bee	112	60,000	1:25.40	83
1995	Lucky Lavender Gal	3	Douglas RR	116	Chaposa Springs	117	Dancin Renee	116	60,000	1:23.40	99
1996	J J's Dream	3	Castillo H. Jr	118	Supah Avalanche	112	Race Artist	114	65100	1:23.80	89
1997	Little Sister	3	Lovato F. Jr	116	Princess Pietrina	112	Maggie Answer	114	120000	1:13.00	98
1998	Cassidy	3	Rivera J. A. II	114	Holy Capote	114	Fantasy Angel	118	75000	1:11.80	98
1999	Show Me the Stage	3	R.J. Courville	116	Could Be	116	Exact	116	75,000	1:11.91	91
2000	Swept Away	3	P. Day	116	Precious Feather	112	Watchfull	116	120,000	1:11.53	103
2001	Hattiesburg	3	M. Guidry	116	Southern Tour	114	Spanish Glitter	116	150,000	1:11.81	93
2002	Bold World	3	C.H. Borel	118	Willa on the Move	114	Tchula Miss	114	105,000	1:10.86	102
2003	Ebony Breeze	3	C. Velasquez	118	Storm Flag	116	Crafty Brat	116	176,025	1:10.82	102
2004	Dazzle Me	3	S.J. Sellers	115	Reforest	114	Boston Express	114	177,000	1:11.40	98

Beyer Index: 94.31

BALDWIN (G3), About 6 1/2 Furlongs (Turf), 3-Year-Olds, Santa Anita, 2004 Purse: $113,350

Year	Winner	Age	Jockey	Wt.	Second	Wt.	Third	Wt.	Win Value	Time	Beyer
1968	Royal Fols	3	W. Harmatz	120	Pinjara	114	Key Rulla	114	9,600	1:12.80	
1968	Fiddle Isle	3	J. Sellers	114	Right or Wrong	117	Baffle	117	9,500	1:13.40	
1969	Tell	3	W. Shoemaker	114	Modern Spirit	114	Might	114	15,200	1:12.80	
1970	Smugglin George	3	J. Lambert	114	Rancho Lejos	120	Cum Shane	114	13,850	1:13.00	
1971	Restless Runner	3	E. Belmonte	117	Triple Bend	120	Long Term	114	18,450	1:13.20	
1972	Finalista	3	L. Pincay Jr	114	Impressive Style	114	Torquemada	114	21,500	1:13.80	
1973	Bensadream	3	D. Pierce	115	Princely Axe	114	Gold Bag	115	21,350	1:14.00	
1974	Battery E.	3	L. Pincay Jr	116	Wedge Shot	117	Ride Off	117	19,150	1:14.00	
1975	Uniformity	3	S. Hawley	114	Crumbs	114	Wine Nipper	114	20,050	1:13.20	
1976	Gaelic Christian	3	R. Rosales	114	El Portugues	117	Grandaries	114	20,750	1:13.60	
1977	Current Concept	3	S. Hawley	120	Bad 'n Big	117	Text	120	24,900	1:13.20	
1978	B.W. Turner	3	D. Pierce	117	O Big Al	120	Princely Lark	114	27,550	1:14.00	
1979	To B. or Not	3	C. Baltazar	114	Debonair Roger	116	Young Driver	114	27,000	1:15.60	
1980	Corvette Chris	3	F. Toro	115	Executive Counsel	114	Moorish Star	114	28,550	1:13.60	
1981	Descaro	3	D.G. McHargue	115	Motivity	120	Steelinctive	114	36,700	1:14.60	
1982	Remember John	3	E. Delahoussaye	117	Time to Explode	120	Crystal Star	114	39,200	1:15.20	
1983	Total Departure	3	L. Pincay Jr	117	Paris Prince	117	Morry's Champ	114	40,950	1:15.20	
1984	Debonaire Junior	3	C.J. McCarron	117	Fortunate Prospect	119	Distant Ryder	117	41,700	1:14.40	
1985	Knighthood II	3	G.L. Stevens	114	Full Honor	117	Infantryman	114	39,900	1:14.80	
1986	Jetting Home	3	D.G. McHargue	116	Royal Treasure	114	El Corazon	114	38,350	1:17.40	
1987	Chime Time	3	P.A. Valenzuela	116	Sweetwater Springs	117	McKenzie Prince	114	40,750	1:15.00	
1988	Exclusive Nureyev	3	E. Delahoussaye	116	Prospectors Gamble	117	Mehmetski	114	39,162	1:14.40	
1988	Dr. Brent	3	A. Solis	117	Accomplish Ridge	117	Glad Music	114	39,262	1:15.00	
1989	Tenacious Tom	3	E. Delahoussaye	119	Mountain Ghost	122	Gum	119	51,900	1:14.80	
1990	Farma Way	3	R. Sibille	115	Iam the Iceman	117	Robyn Dancer	117	52,975	1:13.80	
1991	What a Spell	3	D.R. Flores	117	Broadway's Top Gun	122	Shining Prince	114	49,875	1:16.20	
1992	Reckless Ruckus	3	P.A. Valenzuela	116	Fabulous Champ	114	Slerp	115	49,850	1:17.20	102
1993	Future Storm	3	K.J. Desormeaux	117	Concept Win	119	Siebe	117	51,550	1:15.00	92
1994	Silver Music	3	C.W. Antley	114	Eagle Eyed	117	Makinanhonestbuck	117	48,375	1:13.60	93
1995	Sierra Diablo	3	E. Delahoussaye	116	Raji	117	Huge Gator	116	47,300	1:15.20	96
1996	Sandtrap	3	C.S. Nakatani	114	Strangelove	115	Benton Creek	117	64,300	1:15.00	99
1997	Latin Dancer	3	C.A. Black	117	King of Swing	117	Swiss Yodeler	122	67,850	1:14.40	99
1998	Wrekin Pilot	3	E. Delahoussaye	116	Commitisize	122	Tenbyssimo	117	66,240	1:13.20	101
1999	American Spirit	3	E. Ramsammy	114	Chomper	115	Impressive Grades	119	69,300	1:13.93	89

Year	Winner	Age	Jockey	Wt.	Second	Wt.	Third	Wt.	Win Value	Time	Beyer
2000	Fortifier	3	B. Blanc	114	Performing Magic	116	Joopy Doopy	117	66,870	1:16.79	93
2001	Skip to the Stone	3	C.S. Nakatani	117	Trailthefox	122	Bills Paid	114	66,000	1:16.29	101
2002	Shuffling Kid	3	P.A. Valenzuela	117	Red Briar	116	Dark Sorcerer	114	68,640	1:13.30	89
2003	Buddy Gil	3	G.L. Stevens	117	King Robyn	116	Flirt With Fortune	116	68,730	1:12.56	106
2004	Seattle Borders	3	A. Solis	114	Stalking Tiger	117	Jungle Prince	114	68,010	1:14.09	90

Beyer Index: 96.15

BALLERINA HANDICAP (G1), 7 Furlongs, Fillies and Mares, 3-Year-Olds and Up, Saratoga Race Course, 2004 Purse: $250,000

Year	Winner	Age	Jockey	Wt.	Second	Wt.	Third	Wt.	Win Value	Time	Beyer
1979	Blitey	3	A. Cordero Jr	111	Shukey	116	Bold Rendezvous	116	25,770	1:23.20	
1980	Davona Dale	4	J. Velasquez	119	Misty Gallore	124	It's in the Air	119	33,780	1:22.20	
1981	Love Sign	4	R. Hernandez	119	Jameela	122	Tell a Secret	113	32,400	1:22.60	
1982	Expressive Dance	4	D. MacBeth	122	Tell a Secret	113	Sprouted Rye	113	35,160	1:22.80	
1983	Ambassador of Luck	4	A. Graell	124	Number	119	Broom Dance	122	32,640	1:22.20	
1984	Lass Trump	4	P. Day	122	Adored	122	Sultry Sun	116	51,840	1:21.80	
1985	Lady's Secret	3	D. MacBeth	117	Mrs. Revere	116	Solar Halo	116	67,680	1:22.60	
1986	Gene's Lady	5	R.P. Romero	119	Le Slew	116	Tea Room	110	81,420	1:22.40	
1987	I'm Sweets	4	E. Maple	119	Storm and Sunshine	116	Pine Tree Lane	122	82,260	1:22.60	
1988	Cadillacing	4	A. Cordero Jr	116	Thirty Zip	116	Ready Jet Go	111	69,000	1:21.60	
1989	Proper Evidence	4	C.W. Antley	116	Aptostar	119	Lake Valley	114	73,080	1:23.20	
1990	Feel the Beat	5	J.A. Santos	119	Fantastic Find	116	Proper Evidence	119	71,880	1:22.00	108
1991	Queena	5	M.E. Smith	119	Missy's Mirage	111	Dream Touch	110	72,240	1:22.00	104
1992	Serape	4	C.W. Antley	116	Harbour Club	116	Nannerl	122	71,160	1:21.20	103
1993	Spinning Round	4	J.F. Chavez	119	November Snow	119	Apelia	122	69,120	1:21.40	99
1994	Roamin Rachel	4	P. Day	118	Classy Mirage	123	Twist Afleet	113	65,040	1:21.80	105
1995	Classy Mirage	5	J.A. Krone	119	Inside Information	126	Laura's Pistolette	112	150,000	1:22.40	111
1996	Chaposa Springs	4	S.J. Sellers	120	Capote Belle	117	Broad Smile	114	90,000	1:21.80	107
1997	Pearl City	3	J. Bravo	110	Ashboro	115	Flashy n Smart	112	90,000	1:22.20	107
1998	Stop Traffic	5	S.J. Sellers	118	Runup the Colors	116	U Can Do It	115	120,000	1:22.23	106
1999	Furlough	5	M.E. Smith	114	Bourbon Belle	117	Catinca	121	120,000	1:23.04	103
2000	Dream Supreme	3	P. Day	113	Country Hideaway	117	Bourbon Belle	118	150,000	1:22.97	105
2001	Shine Again	4	J.L. Samyn	113	Country Hideaway	118	Dream Supreme	122	150,000	1:22.33	103
2002	Shine Again	5	J.L. Samyn	116	Raging Fever	121	Mandy's Gold	118	150,000	1:22.26	105
2003	Harmony Lodge	5	R. Migliore	115	Shine Again	120	Gold Mover	118	150,000	1:22.23	100
2004	Lady Tak	4	J.D. Bailey	119	My Trusty Cat	116	Harmony Lodge	119	150,000	1:21.09	102

Beyer Index: 104.53

BALLSTON SPA BREEDERS' CUP HANDICAP (G3), 1 1/16 Miles (Turf), Fillies and Mares, 3-Year-Olds and Up, Saratoga, 2004 Purse: $201,000

Year	Winner	Age	Jockey	Wt.	Second	Wt.	Third	Wt.	Win Value	Time	Beyer
1989	Wakonda	5	A. Cordero Jr	116	Foresta	108	Toll Fee	111	93,900	1:33.80	
1990	Fire the Groom	3	L. Dettori	114	Sally Rous	114	Christiecat	115	95,820	1:35.20	109
1991	Paris Opera	5	G.L. Stevens	116	Daring Doone	114	La Famo	114	94,470	1:37.40	98
1992	Aurora	4	C. Perret	114	Olden Rijn	112	Irish Linnet	113	93,870	1:36.80	96
1993	One Dreamer	5	E. Fires	116	Eenie Meenie Miney	111	Irish Linnet	116	94.440	1:39.20	102
1994	Weekend Madness	5	S.Sellers	115	You'd Be Surprised	120	Heed	111	93,510	1:44.44	104
1995	Weekend Madness	6	S.Sellers	117	Irish Linnet	120	Allez Les Trois	115	93,300	1:40.40	104
1996	Danish	5	J.A. Santos	115	Apolda	121	Caress	113	126,360	1:41.40	105
							Upper Noosh	111	126,360	1:41.40	
1997	Valor Lady	5	J.R. Velazquez	112	Antespend	116	Rumpipumpy	114	130,200	1:39.40	98
1998	Memories of Silver	5	J.D. Bailey	122	Witchful Thinking	118	Ashford Castle	114	126,600	1:40.80	104
1999	Pleasant Temper	5	J.D. Bailey	118	Cuanto Es	113	Lets Get Cozzy	114	124,680	1:41.80	100
2000	License Fee	5	P. Day	116	Pico Teneriffe	116	Hello Soso	114	125,700	1:44.44	99
2001	Penny's Gold	4	J.D. Bailey	118	Babae	114	Chaste	113	126,120	1:40.69	102
2002	Surya	4	J.D. Bailey	114	Shooting Party	118	Solvig	114	126,409	1:52.29	95
2003	Stylish	5	J.R. Velazquez	116	Snow Dance	117	Cozzy Corner	112	120,000	1:41.03	98
2004	Ocean Drive	4	J.R. Velazquez	119	Personal Legend	115	High Court	114	128,400	1:43.92	101

Beyer Index: 101.00

BARBARA FRITCHIE HANDICAP (G2), 7 Furlongs, Fillies and Mares, 3-Year-Olds and Up, Laurel Park, 2004 Purse: $200,000

Year	Winner	Age	Jockey	Wt.	Second	Wt.	Third	Wt.	Win Value	Time	Beyer
1952	Singing Beauty	3	N. Shuk	110	My Nell	102	Chalalette	103	14,875	1:51.60	
1953	Sunshine Nell	5	H. Woodhouse	122	La Corredora	123	Sunny Dale	119	15,075	1:46.20	
1954	Sotto Voce	3	W. Blum	111	Mlle. Loretta	117	Canadiana	118	11,750	1:44.80	
1955	Guayana	4	W. Blum	114	Another World	116	Cerise Reine	124	18,900	1:24.40	
1956	Sometime Thing	4	E. Guerin	124	Searching	122	Myrtle's Jet	124	19,050	1:22.80	
1957	Solar System	6	J. Lynch	113	Scansion	112	Cool Stream	117	18,950	1:12.00	

Year	Winner	Age	Jockey	Wt.	Second	Wt.	Third	Wt.	Win Value	Time	Beyer
1958	Movitave	3	N. Shuk	112	Gay Warbler	116	Derry	114	18,177	1:13.60	
1959	Tinkalero	4	A. Sherman	121	Mlle. Dianne	113	H'sier Honey	118	17,982	1:10.80	
1961	Sun Glint	4	J. Sellers	116	Cherry Flip	106	Miss Orestes	120	17,712	1:40.20	
1962	Call Card	5	J. Culmone	114	Sun Glint	121	Basking	108	14,235	1:25.60	
1963	All Brandy	4	S. Boulmetis	117	Coppahaunk	123	Think Piece	115	17,387	1:10.80	
1964	Pams Ego	4	R. Ferraro	121	Vitamin Shot	114	Srta. Monica	113	21,612	1:24.40	
1965	Basking	7	O. Cutshaw	113	Redpoll	116	County Maid	124	22,360	1:25.00	
1966	Tosmah	5	S. Boulmetis	121	Queen Empress	123	Privileged	111	38,935	1:23.40	
1967	Holly-O	4	F. Lovato	117	Moccasin	120	Lady Diplomat	111	38,935	1:21.80	
1968	Too Bald	4	M. Ycaza	118	Straight Deal	122	Treacherous	121	37,895	1:21.80	
1969	Too Bald	5	M. Ycaza	129	Miss Spin	117	Double Ripple	107	37,115	1:23.80	
1970	Process Shot	4	L. Adams	123	Serica	111	Kushka	113	38,740	1:23.60	
1971	Cold Comfort	4	M. Venezia	114	Take Warning	110	Double Delta	117	38,415	1:23.60	
1973	First Bloom	5	A. Gomez	117	Pas de Nom	116	Winged Affair	111	38,025	1:23.40	
1974	Twixt	5	W.J. Passmore	124	Groton Miss	112	In the Mat's	109	38,350	1:24.40	
1975	Twixt	6	W.J. Passmore	126	Crackerfax	109	Donetta	112	38,350	1:25.40	
1976	Donetta	5	J.W. Moseley	119	Pinch Pie	117	Heydairya	108	37,765	1:24.60	
1977	Mt. Airy Queen	4	D.R. Wright	114	Avum	109	Forty Nine Sunsets	118	36,270	1:23.80	
1978	Bold Brat	5	J.W. Moseley	115	Spot Two	116	Satin Dancer	114	37,375	1:23.40	
1979	Skipat	5	J.W. Edwards	125	Pearl Necklace	122	The Very One	113	53,755	1:22.40	
1980	Misty Gallore	4	D. MacBeth	121	Gladiolus	122	Silver Ice	116	55,770	1:23.60	
1981	Skipat	7	C.B. Asmussen	124	Whispy's Lass	114	Secret Emotion	113	72,865	1:23.00	
1982	Lady Dean	4	D.A. Miller Jr	119	Sweet Revenge	114	Sinister Queen	114	46,768	1:24.20	
1982	The Wheel Turns	5	G. McCarron	121	Island Charm	122	Up the Flagpole	119	46,118	1:23.60	
1983	Stellarette	5	A. Delgado	114	Hoist Emy's Flag	116	Cheap Seats	122	74,100	1:24.40	
1984	Pleasure Cay	4	D.A. Miller Jr	114	Kattegat's Pride	117	Amanti	117	56,325	1:22.80	
1984	Bara Lass	5	D.A. Miller Jr	125	Owned by All	109	Willamae	113	55,025	1:24.00	
1985	Dumdedumdedum	4	D.A. Miller Jr	115	Kattegat's Pride	117	Amanti	117	87,993	1:25.00	
1985	Flip's Pleasure	5	J.L. Samyn	115	Applause	120	Gene's Lady	109	71,793	1:24.00	
1986	Willowy Mood	4	B. Thornbug	115	Aerturas	116	Alabama Nana	119	73,840	1:25.40	
1987	Spring Beauty	4	J.A. Santos	115	Notches Trace	110	Pine Tree Lane	126	88,770	1:25.40	
1988	Psyched	5	K.J. Desormeaux	113	Spring Beauty	116	Kerygma	115	81,250	1:22.60	
1989	Tappiano	5	K.J. Desormeaux	123	Very Subtle	124	Tops in Taps	114	120,000	1:21.40	
1990	Amy Be Good	4	M.E. Smith	112	Channel Three	111	Banbury Fair	110	120,000	1:23.40	95
1991	Fappaburst	4	A. Cordero Jr	114	Devil's Orchid	118	Diva's Debut	116	120,000	1:23.20	104
1992	Wood So	5	M.G. Pino	113	Wide Country	120	W't for the Lady	111	120,000	1:24.40	97
1993	Moon Mist	4	T.G. Turner	112	Ritchie Trail	113	Femma	114	120,000	1:23.40	107
1994	Mixed Appeal	6	A.C. Salazar	111	Known as Nancy	111	Winka	115	120,000	1:23.20	94
1995	Smart 'n Noble	4	M.G. Pino	117	Dust Bucket	114	Gooni Goo Hoo	110	120,000	1:24.00	96
1996	Lottsa Talc	6	F.T. Alvarado	117	Up an Eighth	114	Evil's Pic	116	120,000	1:22.60	97
1997	Miss Golden Circle	5	R. Migliore	118	Lottsa Talc	119	Whaleneck	113	120,000	1:23.00	98
1998	J J'sdream	5	L.C. Reynolds	115	Palette Knife	113	Stylish Encore	114	150,000	1:24.20	102
1999	Passeggiata	6	M.G. Pino	113	Catinca	121	Nothing Special	108	150,000	1:23.40	97
2000	Tap to Music	5	J. Bravo	115	Her She Kisses	114	Di's Time	114	120,000	1:24.75	95
2001	Prized Stamp	4	T.L. Dunkelberger	113	Superduper Miss	114	Tax Affair	113	120,000	1:23.74	94
2002	Xtra Heat	4	H. Vega	128	Prized Stamp	114	Kimbralata	114	120,000	1:22.70	101
2003	Xtra Heat	5	R. Wilson	125	Carson Hollow	119	Spelling	113	120,000	1:24.76	99
2004	Bear Fan	5	R. Fogelsonger	116	Gazillion	116	Bronze Abe	117	120,000	1:23.55	94

Beyer Index: 98.00

LAZARO BARRERA MEMORIAL (G2), 7 Furlongs, 3-Year-Olds, Hollywood Park, 2004 Purse: $150,000

Year	Winner	Age	Jockey	Wt.	Second	Wt.	Third	Wt.	Win Value	Time	Beyer
1953	Perfection	3	W. Shoemaker	118	Laska	112	Speedy Wave	115	10,375	1:23.20	
1954	Milla's Abbey	3	W. Shoemaker	112	Blessed Gal		Hassle		9,475	1:10.80	
1995	Flying Standby	3	C.W. Antley	115	Desert Pirate	119	Boundless Moment	118	40,200	1:09.00	101
1996	Future Quest	3	K.J. Desormeaux	122	Slews Royal Son	119	Tiger Talk	120	35,100	1:15.00	101
1998	Reraise	3	E. Delahoussaye	116	Souvenir Copy	122	Full Moon Madness	117	39,930	1:08.40	115
1999	Love That Red	3	G. Gomez	122	Apremont	118	O'Rey Fantasma	118	56,910	1:20.80	108
2000	Caller One	3	C.S. Nakatani	122	Dixie Union	122	Swept Overboard	122	60,960	1:21.00	116
2001	Early Flyer	3	C.J. McCarron	123	Squirtle Squirt	123	Top Hit	118	65,160	1:20.42	110
2002	Captain Squire	3	C.J. Rollins	123	Fonz's	123	Kamsack	117	90,000	1:21.95	100
2003	Blazonry	3	M.E. Smith	115	Fly to the Wire	116	Jimmy O	115	90,000	1:22.19	99
2004	Twice as Bad	3	A. Solis	116	Wimplestiltskin	116	Don'tsellmeshort	123	90,000	1:21.57	95

Beyer Index: 105.00

Run as the Playa Del Ray prior to 1999. Run at 6 furlongs, 1954, 1995, 1998; at 6 1/2 furlongs 1996

BERNARD BARUCH HANDICAP (G2), 1 1/8 Miles (Turf), 3-Year-Olds and Up, Saratoga Race Course, 2004 Purse: $150,000

Year	Winner	Age	Jockey	Wt.	Second	Wt.	Third	Wt.	Win Value	Time	Beyer
1959	Middle Brother	3	R. Ussery	113	Bagdad	123	Nimmer	114	18,322	1:49.00	
1960	Tompion	3	M. Ycaza	123	Don Rickles	114	Careless John	116	18,127	1:50.00	

Year	Winner	Age	Jockey	Wt.	Second	Wt.	Third	Wt.	Win Value	Time	Beyer
1961	Shield Bearer	6	M. Ycaza	117	Art Market	111	Gawain	110	18,980	1:47.00	
1962	Hitting Away	4	H. Woodhouse	122	Wise Ship	126	Niksar	111	18,752	1:42.20	
1963	Endymion	4	M. Sorrentino	111	Marlin Bay	111	David K.	113	18,980	1:45.80	
1964	Western Warrior	5	R. Ussery	119	Quick Pitch	117	Endymion	109	19,987	1:42.40	
1965	Quick Pitch	5	J. Combest	111	Flag	114	Circus	113	19,337	1:42.60	
1966	Assagai	3	L. Adams	115	Ginger Fizz	114	Northern D'm'n	113	19,727	1:40.00	
1967	Flit-to	4	H. Woodhouse	113	Spoon Bait	113	Flag	115	15,275	1:40.40	
1967	Fort Marcy	3	R. Turcotte	117	Assagai	126	Paoluccio	112	14,950	1:40.40	
1968	Go Marching	3	L. Adams	112	Jollify	109	Ski Lift	109	15,031	1:42.40	
1968	More Scents	4	A. Cordero Jr	126	Grace Born	111	Flit-to	117	14,544	1:42.60	
1969	Larceny Kid	3	L. Pincay Jr	112	Ludham	113	Baitman	110	15,307	1:41.00	
1969	Hawaii	5	M. Ycaza	122	Rhinelander II	113	Mara Lark	113	15,145	1:42.00	
1970	Big Shot II	5	A. Cordero Jr	111	Shelter Bay	111	Pleas'nt H'b'r	112	15,600	1:39.40	
1970	Bailar	5	A. Cordero Jr	112	Chompion	111	Naskra	110	15,762	1:39.80	
1971	Red Reality	5	J. Velasquez	117	Shelter Bay	120	Close Attention	112	21,180	1:42.20	
1972	Scrimsaw	4	R. Woodhouse	109	Maraschino II	111	New Alibhai	115	14,280	1:46.40	
1972	Chrisaway	4	R. Howard	110	North Flight	117	Apollo Nine	112	1,435	1:46.20	
1973	Tentam	4	J. Velasquez	118	Scrims'aw	111	Astray	114	14,265	1:45.40	
1973	Red Reality	7	J. Velasquez	120	Tri Jet	121	Ruritana	113	14,190	1:46.60	
1974	Golden Don	4	V. Bracciale Jr	113	Halo	119	Scantling	117	23,580	1:46.00	
1975	Salt Marsh	5	E. Maple	116			Drollery	112	18,060	1:49.80	
	Ward McAllister	4	D. Montoya	110							
1976	Intrepid Hero	4	E. Maple	123	Modred	118	Erwin Boy	126	22,530	1:50.40	
1977	Majestic Light	4	S. Hawley	126	Alias Smith	112	Clout	114	23,175	1:46.20	
1978	Dominion	6	J.L. Samyn	115	Bill Brill	111	Upper Nile	119	24,480	1:49.00	
1979	Overskate	4	R. Platts	128	Timbo	108	Native Courier	115	35,610	1:51.80	
1980	Premier Ministre	4	R.I. Encinas	116	Great Neck	112	Tiller	126	35,700	2:13.60	
1981	Native Courier	6	E. Maple	114	Manguin	105	Proctor	118	33,450	1:47.40	
1981	Great Neck	5	A. Cordero Jr	119	War of Words	111	Match the Hatch	114	33,690	1:47.60	
1982	Pair of Deuces	4	R. Hernandez	115	Native Courier	117	McCann	112	36,300	1:47.80	
1983	Tantalizing	4	J.D. Bailey	115	Ten Below	115	Acaroid	115	34,140	1:48.80	
1983	Fray Star	5	O. Vergara	114	Fortnightly	113	Who's for Dinner	109	34,380	1:48.40	
1984	Win	4	A. Graell	112	Intensify	113	Cozzene	114	57,510	1:47.40	
1985	Win	5	R. Migliore	124	Cozzene	120	Sitzmark	112	59,400	1:47.00	
1986	Exclusive Partner	4	J. Velasquez	112	I'm a Banker	111	Creme Fraiche	117	82,200	1:50.80	
1987	Talakeno	7	A. Cordero Jr	115	Manila	127	Duluth	114	85,380	1:47.40	
1988	My Big Boy	5	R.P. Romero	113	Steinlen	120	Wanderkin	115	72,600	1:46.80	
1989	Steinlen	6	J.A. Santos	121	Soviet Lad	111	Brian's Time	112	73,920	1:51.00	
1990	Who's to Pay	4	J.L. Samyn	110	Steinlen	126	River of Sin	115	52,920	1:48.40	
1991	Double Booked	6	A. Madrid Jr	122	Who's to Pay	118	Solar Splendor	113	71,400	1:49.00	101
1992	Fourstars Allstar	4	M.E. Smith	113	Lotus Pool	113	Maxigroom	114	70,680	1:46.00	105
1993	Furiously	4	J.D. Bailey	119	Star of Cozzene	123	Royal Mountain Inn	114	70,320	1:45.40	108
1994	Lure	5	M.E. Smith	125	Paradise Creek	126	Fourstardave	114	64,920	1:46.00	112
1995	Fourstars Allstar	7	J.A. Santos	120	Turk Passer	114	Compadre	112	66,240	1:47.60	107
1996	Volochine	5	P. Day	113	Green Means Go	116	Compadre	108	68,700	1:47.40	105
1997	Sentimental Moi	7	C. P. Decarlo	112	Jambalaya Jazz	115	Boyce	120	66,480	1:46.00	105
1998	Yagli	5	J.D. Bailey	121	Tamhid	113	Jambalaya Jazz	115	85,380	1:46.20	105
1999	Middlesex Drive	4	S.J. Sellers	117	Tanghazi	114	Comic Strip	116	90,000	1:46.40	104
2000	Hap	4	J.D. Bailey	115	Inexplicable	115	Draw Shot	114	90,000	1:45.82	104
2001	Hap	5	J.D. Bailey	121	Royal Strand	115	Dr. Kashnikow	114	90,000	1:47.06	107
2002	Del Mar Show	5	J.D. Bailey	120	Volponi	116	Forbidden Apple	121	90,000	1:48.51	110
2003	Trademark	7	R. Migliore	114	Rouvres	116	Slew Valley	113	90,000	1:49.06	110
2004	Silver Tree	4	J.D. Bailey	116	Nothing to Lose	117	Irish Colonial	113	90,000	1:49.66	104

Beyer Index: 106.21

BASHFORD MANOR (G3), 6 Furlongs, 2-Year-Olds, Churchill Downs, 2004 Purse: $163,200

Year	Winner	Age	Jockey	Wt.	Second	Wt.	Third	Wt.	Win Value	Time	Beyer
1902	Von Rouse	2	Winkfield	118	Pericles	113	Captain Arnold	113	1,335	:55.25	
1903	J.P. Mayberry	2	H. Booker	118	Copperfield	113	Paris	118	1,485	:55.00	
1904	Oiseau	2	Munro	121	Florentine	118	Rebounder	113	1,360	:54.50	
1905	George C. Bennett	2	Nicol	118	Charlie Eastman	120	Hermitage	118	1,600	:56.20	
1906	Zal	2	Obert	118	Warner Griswell	118	Fair Fagot	118	1,720	:56.00	
1907	John Marrs	2	Troxler	118	Great Pirate	118	Honest	118	1,570	:54.00	
1908	Fundamental	2	Heidel	118	French Cook	114	Woolwinder	118	1,415	:54.40	
1909	Joe Morris	2	Page	118	King Solomon	118	Donau	118	1,690	:53.40	
1910	La U Mexican	2	E. Griffin	118	Jack Denman	118	Incision	118	1,800	:54.20	
1911	Worth	2	T. Koerner	121	Buckhorn	113	Presumption	115	1,990	:54.80	
1912	Hawthorn	2	Fain	120	Forward	118	Yankee Notions	118	1,940	:54.00	
1913	Little Nephew	2	Loftus	118	Old Rosebud	118	Black Toney	118	700	:53.00	

Year	Winner	Age	Jockey	Wt.	Second	Wt.	Third	Wt.	Win Value	Time	Beyer
1914	Luke	2	W.W. Taylor	121	Marion Goosby	113	Dr. Carmen	113	2,710	:53.00	
1915	Ellison	2	R. Goose	113	Marse Henry	118	Heir Apparent	118	2,350	:54.20	
1916	Harry Kelly	2	G. Garner	121	Sedan	113	Berlin	121	2,190	:53.60	
1917	Escoba	2	J. Hanover	121	Jas. T. Clark	118	Big Enough	118	2,920	:54.00	
1918	Billy Kelly	2	R. Simpson	118	Col. Taylor	118	Col. Livingston	115	2,910	:54.00	
1919	Sam Freedman	2	J. Morys	113	Westwood	113	Best Pal	118	4,680	:54.20	
1920	United Verde	2	L. Ensor	117	Oriole	117	East'eside	122	7,075	:55.60	
1921	Casey	2	D. Connelly	122	Rekab	125	Braedalbane	117	5,900	:55.20	
1922	Triumph	2	A. Johnson	117	Dan E. O'Sullivan	122	Jack Bauer	117	6,980	:53.80	
1923	Black Gold	2	D. Connelly	122	T.S. Jordan	122	Digit	122	7,520	:53.00	
1924	Reputation	2	E. Smallwood	122	Step Along	122	Ocean Current	122	6,280	:53.00	
1925	Take a Chance	2	H. Hamilton	122	Sanction	122	Percentage	117	7,860	:54.00	
1926	Torchilla	2	E. Legere	122	General Haldeman	126	Jock	117	7,740	1:00.60	
1927	Typhoon	2	A. Johnson	122	Toro	122	Misstep	117	7,820	1:00.20	
1928	Roguish Eye	2	J. Heupel	117	The Okah	122	Yermajo	122	7,580	1:00.20	
1929	All Upset	2	R. Zucchini	122	High Foot	122	Sydney	117	7,400	1:00.00	
1930	Back Log	2	H. Fisher	122	Don Leon	125	La Salle	122	7,260	1:00.40	
1931	Proteus	2	J. Smith	125	Liberty Limited	122	Tellico	122	7,030	1:01.00	
1932	In High	2	C. McCrossen	117	Red Whisk	122	Levaal	122	5,710	1:00.40	
1933	Miss Patience	2	G. Elston	119	New Deal	122	Speedy Skippy	122	5,590	1:01.80	
1934	St. Bernard	2	H. Schutte	122	Fraidy Cat	122	Byo Lo	119	3,165	1:00.60	
1935	Coldstream	2	P. Keester	122	Bright Light	125	Lemont	122	3,035	:59.40	
1936	Murph	2	E. Arcaro	122	Foolish Moment	119	Prairie Dog	117	6,015	:59.20	
1937	Sky Larking	2	A. Robertson	122	Teddy's Comet	122	Knee Deep	117	5,460	1:01.60	
1938	Royal Pam	2	I. Hanford	119	Unerring	119	Cherry Jam	122	5,390	:59.00	
1939	Roman	2	W. Yarberry	125	Black Brummel	122	Charitable	122	2,615	:59.40	
1940	Air Brigade	2	T. Marshall	122	My Bill	122	Blue Pair	122	2,525	1:01.20	
1941	Black Raider	2	A. Craig	127	Omathon	122	Bayridge	117	2,655	:59.60	
1942	Navy Cross	2	J. Richard	117	Take Away	122	Hoosier	122	3,045	:59.60	
1943	Black Swan	2	M. Caffarella	122	Civil Liberty	117	Black Badge	117	2,735	1:00.80	
1944	Best Effort	2	M. Caffarella	122	Dockstader	122	Black Pepper	122	3,005	1:01.80	
1945	Fighting Frank	2	G. South	117	Inroc	122	Bold Regard	117	5,050	1:00.40	
1946	Tweet's Boy	2	P. Roberts	125	Colonel O'F	125	Black Knave	122	10,300	1:01.60	
1947	Phar Mon	2	S. Brooks	127	Loujac	122	Circus Clown	122	10,153	1:00.40	
1948	Ky. Colonel	2	S. Brooks	122	Olympia	122	Commodore Lea	122	10,050	1:00.20	
1949	Old Tom	2	J. Duff	122	Curtice	117	Black Sambo	125	10,225	1:00.00	
							Shadows Start	122			
1950	Kings Hope	2	R.L. Baird	122	Robust	122	Pur Sang	122	10,625	1:01.20	
1951	Red Curtice	2	J.D. Jessop	122	Smoke Screen	117	Very Special	117	10,250	:58.80	
1952	Ace Destroyer	2	T. Barrow	122	Prince Marque	122	Happy Carrier	125	9,187	1:01.60	
1953	Mr. Prosecutor	2	J. Adams	122	Everett Jr.	127	Portray	117	13,150	:59.60	
1954	Royal Note	2	H. Moreno	125	Texas Bulldog	117	Prince Eric	122	13,100	1:00.20	
1955	Swoon's Son	2	D. Erb	117	Mr. Jay Gee	122	Night Intruder	117	10,425	1:01.00	
1956	Jet Sub	2	R.L. Baird	122	All Speed	122	Implement	117	13,200	:59.20	
1957	Little Reaper	2	J. Sellers	122	Lord Jan	122	Unique Commando	122	10,650	:58.80	
1958	Tribalove	2	F.A. Smith	117	I Step	122	Wet Back	122	8,812	:58.80	
1959	Maxinkuckee	2	W.B. Williams	122	Pawhuska Sam	122	Dickie Don	122	9,560	:59.00	
1960	He's a Pistol	2	K. Church	122	Ok Chief	122	Arab Road	122	8,634	:58.60	
1961	Mike G.	2	W.M. Cook	122	Jetting Home	122	Loil Roil	117	9,409	:58.40	
1962	Keeper's Choice	2	J. Vasquez	122	Dontstopnow	127	Goer	117	9,100	1:00.40	
1963	Amastar	2	J. Nichols	125	Mom's Request	122	Dancing Brave	122	12,317	:58.20	
1964	Loom	2	J. Nichols	125	Mahjubill	122	Dark Clover	122	12,480	:58.40	
1965	He Jr.	2	J. Fieselman	125	Seaman Sinbad	122	Hard Track	122	12,122	:58.60	
1966	Willow Cage	2	B. Phelps	122	Big Tim	117	Zip Line	122	13,114	:58.60	
1967	T.V. Commercial	2	M. Manganello	125	Royal Exchange	122	Rhythmic	122	12,724	:58.20	
1968	Santiago Road	2	M. Manganello	125	Traffic Mark	125	Campbellsville	122	12,772	:57.80	
1969	Spotted Line	2	D.E. Whited	125	Buptedo	117	Whiskey Romeo	122	12,447	:59.00	
1970	Hook It Up	2	J. Nichols	122	Satan's Story	122	Laughing Dancer	122	16,087	:58.40	
1971	Whitesburg	2	T. Sisum	125	Elmer L. Brown	122	Busted	125	16,315	:58.60	
1972	Pleasure Castle	2	D.E. Whited	122	Gallant Agent	122	Game Lad	122	17,160	:58.20	
1973	Tisab	2	M. Manganello	122	No Advance	122	To the Rescue	122	16,965	:58.80	
1974	Pac Quick	2	G. Patterson	125	Paris Dust	127	Kaanapali	122	16,607	:59.60	
1975	Khyber King	2	E. Delahoussaye	122	Bold Laddie	122	Right on Mike	122	15,632	:58.60	
1976	Judge John Boone	2	E. Delahoussaye	122	Wishem Well	122	Golden Trade	117	14,625	:58.60	
1977	Going Investor	2	B. Sayler	122	Old Jake	117	Chwesboken	122	14,235	:58.40	
1978	Spy Charger	2	G. Mahon	127	Uncle Fudge	122	Vennie Redberry	122	14,089	:58.40	
1979	Rajohn Greco	2	J.C. Espinoza	122	Egg's Dynamite	122	Native Amber	122	19,451	1:00.20	
1980	Golden Derby	2	J.C. Espinoza	117	Wrong Impression	122	Stubilem	117	19,338	:59.00	
1981	T.V. Mark	2	P. Nicolo	122	Shilling	122	Good Ole Master	122	18,103	:59.60	
1982	Willow Drive	2	W.J. Neagle	115	Stepping E.J.	118	Mindboggling	115	20,264	1:05.00	
1983	Betwixt n' Between	2	P. Day	115	Real Sharp Dancer	121	Biloxi Indian	118	22,896	1:05.00	
1984	Jerry F.	2	P. Day	112	Storm Scope	115	Wet My Whistle	115	17,241	1:05.80	
1985	Tile	2	L. Melancon	115	Tug	115	Sir Grandeur	115	30,896	1:04.40	

Year	Winner	Age	Jockey	Wt.	Second	Wt.	Third	Wt.	Win Value	Time	Beyer
1986	Faster Than Sound	2	C. Perret	118	Renumeration	115	Arunti	121	46,648	1:11.20	
1987	Blair's Cove	2	S.J. Sellers	114	Endurance	118	Mr. Igloo	116	37,310	1:11.80	
1988	Bio	2	P.A. Johnson	118	Revive	112	Curtis John	114	37,148	1:11.80	
1989	Summer Squall	2	P. Day	121	Table Limit	118	Appealing Breeze	121	35,068	1:12.20	
1990	To Freedom	2	J.C. Espinoza	121	Richman	121	Discover	116	35,555	1:10.20	
1991	Pick up the Phone	2	J.C. Espinoza	116	Sprintmaster	116	Thanatopsis	112	35,815	1:12.00	78
1992	Mountain Cat	2	C.R. Woods Jr	116	Tempered Halo	121	Storm Flight	116	53,869	1:10.60	85
1993	Miss Ra He Ra	2	W. Martinez	113	Ramblin Guy	116	Riverinn	112	76,180	1:12.80	72
1994	Hyroglyphic	2	Gomez GK	116	Boone's Mill	116	Hobgoblin	116	75,660	1:10.20	91
1995	A.V. Eight	2	Trosclair AJ	115	Aggie Southpaw	115	Seeker's Reward	115	71,630	1:11.40	87
1996	Boston Harbor	2	M.J. Luzzi	115	Prairie Junction	115	Nobel Talent	115	72,150	1:09.80	97
1997	Favorite Trick	2	P. Day	121	Double Honor	115	Cowboy Dan	118	68,696	1:09.80	97
1998	Time Bandit	2	C.R. Woods Jr	115	Yes It's True	121	Haus of Dehere	115	68,262	1:10.60	85
1999	Dance Master	2	B.D. Peck	115	Sky Dweller	115	Snuck In	115	89,280	1:10.20	92
2000	Duality	2	C.H. Borel	115	Strait Cat	114	Take Arms	115	86,258	1:10.09	85
2001	Lunar Bounty	2	F. Lovato Jr	115	Binyamin	115	Storm Passage	115	82,925	1:09.90	80
2002	Lone Star Sky	2	M. Guidry	115	Posse	121	Cooper Crossing	115	84,475	1:09.68	95
2003	Limehouse	2	R.J. Albarado	121	First Money	117	Cuvee	121	100,905	1:10.62	86
2004	Lunarpal	2	S.J. Sellers	121	Storm Surge	117	Maximus C	117	101,184	1:11.54	79

Beyer Index: **86.36**

BAYAKOA HANDICAP (G2), 1 1/16 Miles, Fillies and Mares, 3-Year-Olds and Up, Hollywood Park, 2004 Purse: $150,000

Year	Winner	Age	Jockey	Wt.	Second	Wt.	Third	Wt.	Win Value	Time	Beyer
1993	Golden Klair	3	CJ. McCarron	115	Pacific Squall	118	Cargo	116	63,500	1:41.20	101
1994	Thirst for Peace	5	A. Solis	115	Glass Ceiling	117	Dancing Mirage	119	63,500	1:42.20	101
1995	Pirate's Revenge	4	C.W. Antley	119	Urbane	120	Ashtabula	116	61,900	1:41.80	101
1996	Listening	3	C.J. McCarron	120	Cat's Cradle	120	Belle's Flag	117	64,920	1:42.60	102
1997	Sharp Cat	3	A. Solis	121	WALKOVER				60,000	1:42.60	
1998	Manistique	3	G.L. Stevens	119	India Divina	114	Numero Uno	115	60,000	1:42.40	108
1999	Manistique	4	C.S. Nakatani	124	Snowberg	115	Riboletta	116	90,000	1:43.00	105
2000	Feverish	5	E. Delahoussaye	119	Gourmet Girl	118	Lazy Slusan	117	90,000	1:42.26	104
2001	Starrer	3	J.D. Bailey	118	Queenie Belle	118	Tropical Lady	115	90,000	1:42.52	99
2002	Starrer	4	P.A. Valenzuela	118	Cee's Elegance	113	Angel gift	115	90,000	1:41.74	105
2003	Star Parade	4	V. Espinoza	112	Adoration	121	Bare Necessities	119	90,000	1:41.02	106
2004	Hollywood Story	3	V. Espinoza	115	Royally Chosen	116	A.P. Adventure	117	90,000	1:41.11	97

Beyer Index: **102.64**

BAY MEADOWS BREEDERS' CUP HANDICAP (G3), About 1 1/8 Miles (Turf), 3-Year-Olds and Up, Bay Meadows, 2004 Purse: $112,500

Year	Winner	Age	Jockey	Wt.	Second	Wt.	Third	Wt.	Win Value	Time	Beyer
1934	Time Supply	3	T. Luther	123	Dark Winter	107	Fleam	105	21,100	1:53.80	
1935	Head Play	5	C. Kurtsinger	118	Time Supply	116	Gusto	110	20,300	2:00.60	
1936	Special Agent	4	G. Burns	117	Azucar	124	Uppermost	106	8,100	1:43.00	
1937	Seabiscuit	4	J. Pollard	127	Exhibit	105	Watersplash	103	7,530	1:44.60	
1938	Seabiscuit	5	G. Woolf	133	Gosum	113	Today	112	11,270	1:49.00	
1939	Specify	4	C. Corbett	121	Stands Alone	113	Sweepalot	112	7,150	1:45.80	
1940	Sweepida	3	R. Neves	123	Omelet	115	Mr. Grundy	110	7,380	1:51.60	
1941	No Comp'tion	5	F. Weidaman	115	Mount Vernon II	110	G. M'ager	114	7,710	1:50.80	
1942	Stinging Bee	3	J. Longden	110	Sir Jeffrey	112	Step By	111	7,940	1:54.20	
1943	Put In	4	G. Woolf	115	Jerry Lee	108	Kind Sir	112	12,830	1:50.00	
1944	Okana	3	A. Bassett	126	Shut Up	111	Jade Boy	121	18,450	1:52.00	
1945	No Wrinkles	5	R. Summers	112	Wise Eagle	115	S'my Angott	120	20,930	2:00.80	
1946	Adrogue	6	F. Zufelt	112	Autocrat	113	Olhaverry	120	44,500	1:52.40	
1946	Occupy	5	C. Corbett	124	Mediterranean	112	Stitch Again	124	19,000	1:49.20	
1947	Artillery	4	H. Lindberg	121	Adrogue	115	Happy Issue	113	42,800	1:49.00	
1948	Mafosta	6	J. Longden	126	Faucon	117	Hemet Squaw	109	41,600	1:51.00	
1949	Moonrush	3	B. Pearson	108	Solidarity	120	Colosal	116	40,600	1:49.00	
1950	Frankly	5	W. Shoemaker	122	Coma	108	Sun State	115	12,320	1:49.40	
1951	Moonrush	5	W. Shoemaker	121	Mocopo	110	Be Fleet	121	43,700	1:51.20	
1952	Moonrush	6	R. Neves	115	Two Lea	126	Grantor	118	33,350	2:01.60	
1953	Stranglehold	4	B. Pearson	120	Goose Khal	124	Indian Hemp	117	16,150	1:51.80	
1954	Decorated	4	J. Longden	113	Cyclotron	117	Southarlingt'n	111	16,500	1:43.80	
1955	Arrogate	4	J. Longden	120	Bobby Brocato	117	Bassanio	112	13,700	1:42.00	
1956	Holandes II	3	W. Shoemaker	122	Eugenio	118	Arrogate	122	15,350	1:47.80	
1957	Count Chic	4	M. Volzke	116	Fleet Charge	110	Battle Dance	118	12,700	1:45.60	
1958	Battle Dance	6	R. Neves	121	Ordained	113	More Glory	115	10,150	1:42.20	
1959	Promised Land	5	I. Valenzuela	122	Eddie Schmidt	120	The Searcher	111	16,750	1:48.60	
1960	Prize Host	5	W. Harmatz	112	Sea Orbit	116	Quidico	114	13,100	1:41.40	
1961	Mr. Wag	4	J. Longden	117	Typhoon II	111	Jewelsmith	113	14,450	1:48.00	

Year	Winner	Age	Jockey	Wt.	Second	Wt.	Third	Wt.	Win Value	Time	Beyer
1962	Sea Orbit	6	R. York	129	My Rx	112	Mr. Wag	117	13,050	1:44.80	
1963	Mustard Plaster	4	M. Volzke	112	Dusky Damion	118	Little Juan	115	13,400	1:43.00	
1964	Biggs	4	W. Harmatz	115	Honored Sir	118	Hello Uncle	113	9,125	1:41.60	
1965	Maker's Mark	4	F. Costa	121	Gainstrive	112	By the Way II	112	9,025	1:49.80	
1966	Diamond Lou	4	P. Frey	120	Black Pool	116	Quicken Tree	113	13,425	1:42.80	
1967	No Host	4	A. Maese	116	Aqua Vite	121	Plimenek	117	16,500	1:41.60	
							Father Dino	118			
1968	Praise Jay	4	A. Pineda	114	His Boy II	114	Kings Favor	119	17,650	1:42.40	
1969	Field Master	5	I. Valenzuela	115	Royal Fols	119	True Balcony	114	18,550	1:41.80	
1970	Traffic Beat	5	M. Volzke	115	Try Sheep	110	Dizzy Babe	124	15,650	1:50.60	
1971	Silver Double	5	L. Wall	120	Dagmar's Boy	112	Domineering	114	19,000	1:49.40	
1972	Timoteo	4	F. Alvarez	113	Vitenpost	113	Ipse	114	18,000	1:47.40	
1973	Partner's Hope	4	A.L. Diaz	117	Ipse	116	Woodland Pines	118	17,525	1:43.20	
1974	Indefatigable	4	D. Pierce	117	Star of Kuwait	116	Confederate Yankee	115	31,900	1:41.40	
1975	Bahia Key	5	F. Olivares	122	Fleet Velvet	120	Holding Pattern	120	31,700	1:43.00	
1976	Life's Hope	3	D.G. McHargue	118	Fighting Bill	113	Podium	117	31,400	1:43.40	
1977	Painted Wagon	4	M.S. Sellers	120	Sudanes	117	Mark's Place	123	51,000	1:41.40	
1978	Bywayofchicago	4	F. Toro	122	Noble Bronze	113	As de Copas	119	72,000	1:50.80	
1979	Leonotis	6	M. Gonzalez	118	John Henry	123	Capt. Don	117	69,900	1:49.60	
1980	Super Moment	3	F. Toro	116	Fleet Tempo	114	Mike Fogarty	118	68,600	1:46.20	
1981	Super Moment	4	L. Pincay Jr	124	Tahitian King	121	The Bart	126	98,400	1:53.60	
1982	Super Moment	5	R.A. Baze	120	Buchanette	113	Les Aspres	112	132,400	1:51.60	
1983	Interco	3	J.C. Judice	116	Super Sunrise	116	Floriano	114	179,200	1:55.40	
1984	Scrupules	4	E. Delahoussaye	118	Raami	120	Both Ends Burning	123	178,500	2:17.20	
1985	Drumalis	5	R.Q. Meza	116	Silveyville	121	Talakeno	115	165,000	1:47.00	
1986	Palace Music	5	F. Toro	123	Nugget Point	113	Barberry	116	165,000	1:50.60	
1987	Show Dancer	5	M. Castaneda	113	Skip out Front	114	Exclusive Partner	116	165,000	1:47.80	
1988	Wait Til Monday	4	R. Dominguez	113	Miswaki Tern	113	Skip out Front	117	137,500	1:46.00	
1989	Ten Keys	5	K.J. Desormeaux	118	Colway Rally	116	Nediym	113	137,500	1:46.60	
1990	Robinski	7	J. Velasquez	112	Sekondi	113	Rushing Raj	113	137,500	1:50.80	
1991	French Seventyfive	4	G. Boulanger	112	Forty Niner Days	116	Batshoof	116	137,500	1:49.40	104
1992	Forty Niner Days	5	C.S. Nakatani	115	Bistro Garden	116	Luthier Enchanteur	118	137,500	1:46.40	104
1993	Slew of Damascus	5	T.M. Chapman	114	Fast Cure	115	Lissitki	112	110,000	1:45.80	102
1994	Blues Traveller	4	Stevens GL	116	Fastness	116	Wharf	114	110,000	1:46.00	105
1995	Caesour	5	Baze RA	115	Johann Quatz	115	Canaska Dancer	113	110,000	1:45.40	107
1996	Gentlemen	4	C.S. Nakatani	117	Party Season	116	Petit Poucet	119	110,000	1:45.80	106
1997	El Angelo	5	A. Solis	119	Via Lombardia	115	Dreamer	115	110,000	1:45.40	110
1998	Hawksley Hill	5	A. Solis	120	Magellan	117	Floriselli	114	110,000	1:45.40	109
1999	Kirkwall	5	V. Espinoza	114	Special Quest	115	Game Ploy	113	110,000	1:47.13	100
2000	Devine Wind	4	G.K. Gomez	114	Irish Prize	115	Deploy Venture	117	110,000	1:47.19	103
2001	Super Quercus	5	R.A. Baze	117	Most Likely	112	Sign of Hope	116	55,000	1:47.50	102
2002	David Copperfield	5	J. Lumpkins	117	Ninebanks	115	Little Ghazi	115	110,000	1:48.95	101
2003	Mister Acpen	5	R.M. Gonzalez	116	Fateful Dream	117	Ninebanks	118	55,000	1:46.94	105
2004	Needwood Blade	6	D. Carr	116	Seinne	116	Balestrini	117	55,000	1:46.55	104

Beyer Index: 104.43

BAY MEADOWS BREEDERS' CUP SPRINT HANDICAP (G3), 6 Furlongs, 3-Year-Olds and Up, Bay Meadows, 2004 Purse: $80,000

Year	Winner	Age	Jockey	Wt.	Second	Wt.	Third	Wt.	Win Value	Time	Beyer
1995	Lucky Forever	6	G.Almeida	116	Wild Gold	115	Uncaged Fury	115	117,700	1:08.60	102
1996	Boundless Moment	4	K.Desormeaux	116	Concept Win	115	Paying Dues	119	110,000	1:08.80	102
1997	Tres Paraiso	5	C.Nakatani	116	Mshk's Pride	112	Boundless Moment	117	110,000	1:07.80	107
1998	Musafi	4	D.Flores	116	The Barking Shark	116			110,000	1:08.40	103
					Mr. Doubledown	116					
1999	Big Jag	6	J.Valdivia	118	Men 's Exclusive	115	Lexicon	116	110,000	1:08.80	110
2000	Lexicon	5	R.Baze	115	Men 's Exclusive	115	Dixie Dot Com	116	110,000	1:09.09	105
2001	Lexicon	6	R.A. Baze	117	Swept Overboard	117	You and You Alone	115	82,500	1:07.94	106
2002	Mellow Fellow	7	R.A. Baze	119	Explicit	120	Swept Oveboard	122	110,000	1:08.35	108
2003	El Dorado Shooter	6	C.P. Schvaneveldt	120	Halo Cat	118	Radar Contact	116	82,500	1:08.61	102
2004	Court's in Session	5	R.M. Gonzalez	115	Debonair Joe	117	Hombre Rapido	118	41,250	1:08.91	105

Beyer Index: 105.00

BAY MEADOWS DERBY (G3), About 1 1/8 Miles (Turf), 3-Year-Olds, Bay Meadows, 2004 Purse: $100,000

Year	Winner	Age	Jockey	Wt.	Second	Wt.	Third	Wt.	Win Value	Time	Beyer
1954	Determine	3	R. York	126	Allied	120	Fault Free	114	15,800	1:49.20	
1957	Round Table	3	R. Neves	122	Swirling Abbey	122	Irisher	122	24,375	1:41.60	
1978	Quip	3	T. Lipham	115	Shagbark	115	Kamehameha	123	34,250	1:45.20	
1979	Nain Bleu	3	C. Baltazar	113	Bends Me Mind	118	Gummaka	115	32,300	1:45.40	
1980	Fleet Tempo	3	R.M. Gonzalez	114	Super Moment	123	Aliyoun	112	32,750	1:44.60	

Year	Winner	Age	Jockey	Wt.	Second	Wt.	Third	Wt.	Win Value	Time	Beyer
1981	Silveyville	3	D. Winick	120	Sunshine Swag	113	Tempo's Tiger	117	67,000	1:48.20	
1982	Ask Me	3	F. Toro	120	Water Bank	120	Take the Floor	121	66,100		
1983	Interco	3	J.C. Judice	116	Bang Bang Bang	112	Baron o'Dublin	120	63,500	1:49.60	
1984	Mangaki	3	C. Lamance	115	Refueled	117	Foscarini	120	68,400	1:52.00	
1985	Minutes Away	3	C.R. Hummel	115	Charming Duke	124	Lucky n Green	115	56,800	1:51.40	
1986	Le Belvedere	3	W. Shoemaker	113	Santella Mac	115	Grand Exchange	116	81,300	1:47.60	
1987	Hot and Smoggy	3	J. Vasquez	117	Wolsey	116	Lucky Harold H.	115	66,400	1:48.60	
1988	Coax Me Clyde	3	R.J. Warren Jr	118	Gran Judgement	116	Literati	117	68,500	1:49.00	
1989	Irish	3	M.A. Espindola	115	Polar Boy	115	Two Moccasins	113	55,000	1:48.20	
1990	Sekondi	3	R.M. Gonzalez	114	Courtesy Title	115	Appealing Missy	113	55,000	1:48.80	97
1991	Bistro Garden	3	M. Castaneda	120	Dominion Gold	116	Fraise	115	82,500	1:46.60	102
1992	Star Recruit	3	R.D. Hansen	116	Siberian Summer	116	Fax News	115	55,000	1:49.00	108
1993	Ranger	3	G. Boulanger	114	El Atroz	113	Guide	120	55,000	1:48.80	98
1994	Marvin's Faith	3	Castaneda M	116	Western Trader	116	Turbo Fan	115	55,000	1:48.80	101
1995	Virginia Carnival	3	Warren RJ Jr	115	Helmsman	114	Tabor	116	55,000	1:46.00	100
1996	Ocean Queen	3	J.A. Garcia	110	Mateo	115	Mystic Knight	116	110,000	1:47.80	99
1997	Shellbacks	3	R.Q. Meza	113	Brave Act	122	Zippersup	122	82,500	1:49.00	101
1998	Takarian	3	C.A. Black	116	I.M. Bzy	115	Prevalence	114	82,500	1:46.80	99
1999	Mula Gula	3	R.Q. Meza	117	Miss Chryss	111	Fighting Falcon	120	82,500	1:45.34	100
2000	Walkslikeaduck	3	E. Delahoussaye	122	Jokerman	119	Calamari	115	82,500	1:46.57	101
2001	Blue Steller	3	A. Solis	119	Sir Alfred	116	Sea to See	116	55,000	1:46.81	94
2002	Royal Gem	3	R.A. Baze	119	Aly Bubba	114	Century City	122	55,000	1:48.38	89
2003	Stanley Park	3	E. Saint-Martin	116	Bis Repetitas	118	Kewen	116	55,000	1:48.97	96
2004	Congressionalhonor	3	R.A. Baze	115	Talaris	116	On the Acorn	116	55,000	1:48.92	89

Hendrix finished third but was disqualified and placed 8th

Beyer Index: 98.27

BAY SHORE (G3), 7 Furlongs, 3-Year-Olds, Aqueduct, 2004 Purse: $150,000

Year	Winner	Age	Jockey	Wt.	Second	Wt.	Third	Wt.	Win Value	Time	Beyer
1960	Francis S.	3	H. Moreno	119	Don Rickles	118	Count Amber	116	18,842	1:36.00	
1961	Merry Ruler	3	R.L. Gilbert	115	Hy-Nat	111	Stan the Man	111	18,850	1:36.40	
1962	Duc d'Or	3	I. Valenzuela	113	Sidluck	113	Lucky Uncle	112	14,137	1:36.80	
1962	Western Warrior	3	L. Adams	111	MIster Pitt	110	Dedimoud	112	14,137	1:36.40	
1963	Jet Traffic	3	R. Ussery	120	Top Gallant	112	Bonjour	123	18,322	1:34.20	
1964	Determined Man	3	J. Ruane	110	Lord Date	112	Alphabet	113	18,687	1:23.20	
1965	Flag Raiser	3	I. Valenzuela	114	Turn to Reason	111	Tom Rolfe	120	18,915	1:23.60	
1966	Quinta	3	W. Blum	114	Impressive	128	Buffle	113	18,785	1:22.80	
1967	Damascus	3	W. Shoemaker	115	Disciplinarian	117	Nehoc's Bullet	110	18,590	1:25.80	
1968	Verbatim	3	J.L. Rotz	118	Wellpoised	112	Sir Beau	115	14,576	1:24.20	
1968	Clever Foot	3	J. Culmone	124	Irish Chief	113	Czar Alexander	110	14,576	1:26.00	
1969	Reviewer	3	R. Ussery	130	Hey Good Lookin	113	I Found Gold	111	17,972	1:22.80	
1970	Sunny Tim	3	C. Baltazar	117	Native Royalty	110	Delaware Chief	111	19,435	1:24.20	
1971	Hoist the Flag	3	J. Cruguet	126	Droll Role	117	Jim French	121	20,640	1:21.00	
1972	Explodent	3	M. Venezia	120	Eager Exchange	120	Gay Gallant	112	17,175	1:23.40	
1973	Secretariat	3	R. Turcotte	126	Champagne Charlie	118	Impecunious	126	16,650	1:23.20	
1974	Hudson County	3	M. Miceli	113	Frankie Adams	119	Instead of Roses	116	34,680	1:22.60	
1975	Laramie Trail	3	M. Venezia	113	T.V. Charger	113	Ascetic	121	26,910	1:23.60	
1975	Lefty	3	R. Turcotte	113	Tass	113	Gallant Bob	118	27,360	1:23.80	
1976	Bold Forbes	3	A. Cordero Jr	119	Eustace	121	Full Out	124	33,780	1:20.80	
1977	Cormorant	3	D. Wright	121	Medieval Man	119	Hey Hey J.P.	114	32,460	1:10.80	
1978	Piece of Heaven	3	R. Hernandez	119	Just Right Classi	114	Slap Jack	114	32,460	1:11.00	
1979	Belle's Gold	3	G. Martens	114	Screen King	121	General Assembly	123	32,040	1:21.80	
1980	Colonel Moran	3	J. Velasquez	121	Son of a Dodo	115	Dunham's Gift	114	34,260	1:23.80	
1981	Proud Appeal	3	J. Fell	121	Willow Hour	114	Royal Pavilion	114	32,940	1:22.20	
1982	Shimatoree	3	A. Cordero Jr	114	Big Brave Rock	114	John's Gold	114	33,000	1:23.20	
1983	Strike Gold	3	E. Maple	114	Assault Landing	114	Chas Conerly	114	34,620	1:22.60	
1984	Secret Prince	3	C. Perret	114	The Wedding Guest	126	I'm a Rounder	114	65,580	1:11.20	
1985	Pancho Villa	3	F. Lovato Jr	114	El Basco	114	Spend a Buck	123	97,020	1:22.20	
1986	Zabaleta	3	D.G. McHargue	115	Groovy	117	Belocolus	114	95,250	1:22.00	
1986	Buck Aly	3	N. Santagata	117	Landing Plot	119	Raja's Revenge	119	95,250	1:23.80	
1987	Gulch	3	J.A. Santos	123	High Brite	119	Shawklit Won	114	124,800	1:23.20	
1988	Perfect Spy	3	R.G. Davis	119	Success Express	123	Proud and Valid	117	98,460	1:22.60	
1989	Houston	3	L. Pincay Jr	116	Mr. Nickerson	114	Wee Stark	119	69,000	1:22.40	
1990	Richard R.	3	J.A. Santos	117	For Really	114	Dangerous Dawn	114	70,080	1:22.80	98
1991	Stately Wager	3	J.F. Chavez	119	Mineral Ice	119	Vouch for Me	117	71,040	1:23.80	97
1992	Three Peat	3	C.W. Antley	114	Goldwater	117	Best Decorated	114	75,600	1:21.60	105
1994	Prank Call	3	J.R. Velazquez	113	Mr. Shawklit	117	Popol's Gold	122	65,940	1:09.80	93
1995	Blissful State	3	M.J Luzzi	118	Northern Ensign	113	Pat n Jac	115	64,680	1:23.80	89
1996	Jamies First Punch	3	J.R. Velazquez	115	Gold Fever	115	Firey Jennifer	115	67,200	1:22.00	102
1997	Hawks Landing	3	R. Migliore	114	Adverse	113	Standing on Edge	113	66,480	1:22.00	95

Year	Winner	Age	Jockey	Wt.	Second	Wt.	Third	Wt.	Win Value	Time	Beyer
1998	Limit Out	3	J.L. Samyn	115	Good and Tough	113	Diamond Studs	113	65,460	1:20.40	116
1999	Perfect Score	3	E.S. Prado	118	Royal Ruby	114	Prince Monty	116	66,120	1:22.98	88
2000	Precise End	3	J.F. Chavez	116	Turnofthecentury	114	Port Herman	114	66,000	1:22.27	99
2001	Skip to the Stoe	3	V. Espinoza	120	Multiple Choice	116	Friday's A Comin'	120	90,000	1:22.46	96
2002	Roman Dancer	3	K.J. Desormeaux	120	Warners	116	Monthir	116	90,000	1:22.21	101
2003	Halo Homewrecker	3	J.R. Velazquez	116	Don Six	116	Stanislavsky	116	90,000	1:23.19	96
2004	Forest Danger	3	J.R. Velazquez	116	Abbondanza	116	Indian War Dance	116	90,000	1:20.67	110

Beyer Index: 98.93

BAYOU BREEDERS' CUP HANDICAP (G3), Abt 1 1/8 Miles (Turf), Fillies and Mares, 4-Year-Olds and Up, Fair Grounds, 2004 Purse: $113,500

Year	Winner	Age	Jockey	Wt.	Second	Wt.	Third	Wt.	Win Value	Time	Beyer
1969	Ayuda	5	J. Nichols	119	Copper Canyon	115	Nature II	117	10,850	1:42.80	
1970	Miss Danalee	4	D.E. Whited	121	Maggie's Doll	114	I've Bin Spotted	117	10,650	1:40.80	
1971	Double Delta	5	D.E. Whited	125	Vics Turn	118	Kay Emy	115	11,100	1:39.80	
1972	French Settler	5	K. Bourque	112	Boxing Miss	112	Amber Melody	119	10,775	1:42.60	
1973	Neigh Neigh	4	D. Meade Jr	112	Lyrs Power	115	Daring Jester	114	11,225	1:46.60	
1974	Sixty Sails	4	P. Rubbicco	120	Saucy Bee	116	Knitted Gloves	117	12,050	1:44.40	
1975	Truchas	6	O. Sanchez	115	Big Dare	119	Stylish Genie	115	19,775	1:44.60	
1976	Point in Time	4	A.J. Trosclair	117	Hope She Does	116	Flama Ardiente	124	22,150	1:45.00	
1977	Forlana	4	A.J. Trosclair	118	Hail to El	114	Critical Miss	117	20,550	1:44.60	
1978	Quid Kit	4	D. Copling	115	Famed Princess	118	La Doree	112	30,800	1:45.40	
1979	Lily S.	4	D. Montoya	112	Flaunter	110	Jevalin	114	28,875	2:07.20	
1980	Holy Mount	4	E. Fires	117	Salzburg	118	Fun Worthy	115	35,975	2:04.00	
1981	Royal Saint	4	M. McKnight	118	La Bonzo	122	Vibro Vibes	114	32,075	2:06.00	
1982	Vibro Vibes	5	E.J. Perrodin	114	Lady Offshore	120	Sweetest Sound	113	40,100	2:17.60	
1983	Countess Tully	5	D. Brumfield	114	Full of Reason	114	Valid Bess	115	42,825	2:19.20	
1984	Freeway Folly	5	R.P. Romero	122	Gabfest	113	Erudite II	116	39,025	2:33.00	
1985	Over Your Shoulder	4	G. St. Leon	114	Costa Del Sol	116	Erudite II	113	40,325	2:19.00	
1986	Dancing Slippers	5	J.L. Samyn	113	Costa Del Sol	118	Lock's Dream	114	53,145	2:21.40	
1987	Sastarda	6	K. Bourque	120	Anadia	110	Costa Del Sol	113	21,540	2:22.40	
1988	How I Wish	4	E.J. Perrodin	116	Robertina	117	Vigorous Market	112	16,575	1:48.00	
1989	How I Wish	5	C.H. Borel	120	Factually	112	Profit Island	113	16,815	1:52.00	
1990	Phoenix Sunshine	5	C.J. Woodley	115	Regal Wonder	118	Lyphover	122	16,725	1:53.00	
1991	Phoenix Sunshine	6	V.L. Smith	117	Leering	114	Chore Girl	114	19,755	1:51.40	
1992	Bishops Idea	4	B.E. Poyadou	113	Palace Chill	120	Hero's Love	110	31,545	1:53.80	95
1993	Liz Cee	5	L. Martinez	114	To Be Dazzling	115	Trim Cut	114	32,130	1:52.20	89
1994	Prominent Feather	5	R.D. Ardoin	113	Mystical Path	112	Forever North	116	47,070	1:52.68	83
1995	Lismore Lass	6	J.E. Broussard III	113	Onceinabluemamoon	115	Bendel Bonnet	110	36,000	1:53.97	97
1996	Tough Broad	4	S.P. LeJeune Jr	110	Brushing Gloom	112	Stellarina	114	91,875	1:51.38	98
1997	Maxzene	4	J.A. Krone	116	Flame Valley	112	Tough Broad	114	91,875	1:53.11	102
1998	Cuando	4	W. Martinez	114	Water Street	111	B.A. Valentine	118	52,620	1:53.60	87
1999	Red Cat	4	R.D. Ardoin	113	Swearingen	117	Justenuffheart	115	95,280	1:51.31	106
2000	Histoire Sainte	4	S.J. Sellers	111	Snow Polina	115	Neptune's Bride	115	65,850	1:49.32	102
2001	On a Soapbox	5	M. St. Julien	113	Always Sure	115	Lady Tamworth	111	94,770	1:53.82	96
2002	Katy Kat	4	R.J. Albarado	116	Pretty Gale	113	Temis	109	90,000	1:50.67	103
2003	Quick Tip	5	R.J. Albarado	116	Histoire Sainte	118	Snow Dance	119	90,000	1:54.61	99
2004	Bedanken	5	D.R. Pettinger	121	Due to Win Again	118	Lady Linda	115	75,000	1:52.74	95

Beyer Index: 96.31

Run as Bayou Handicap 1969-1995. Distance 1 mile 40 yards 1969-1972; 1 1/16 miles 1973-1978; 1 1/4 miles 1979-1981; 1 3/8 miles in 1982; about 1 3/8 miles 1983, 1985-1987; 1 1/2 miles in 1984; about 1 1/16 miles in 1988, 1 1/8 miles in 1998, 2002. For 3-year-olds and upward 1973-1978. Run on main track prior to 1982. Off the turf in 1998, 2002.

BEAUGAY HANDICAP (G3), 1 1/16 Miles (Turf), Fillies and Mares, 3-Year-Olds and Up, Aqueduct, 2004 Purse: $110,000

Year	Winner	Age	Jockey	Wt.	Second	Wt.	Third	Wt.	Win Value	Time	Beyer
1978	Shukey	3	J. Velasquez	113	Sans Critique	118	Whodatorsay	109	25,755	1:45.20	
1979	Plankton	3	R. Hernandez	113	Miss Baja	114	Reflection Pool	112	25,612	1:46.00	
1979	Heavenly Ade	3	S. Solomone	114	Propitiate	112	Gladiolus	122	25,612	1:45.60	
1980	Samarta Dancer	4	L. Saumell	114	Plankton	121	Bien Fait	109	33,540	1:43.60	
1981	Andover Way	3	A. Cordero Jr	120	Water Dance	117	Tournament Star	109	34,440	1:44.00	
1982	Cheap Seats	3	A. Cordero Jr	113	Tina Tina Too	115	Fancy Naskra	112	33,780	1:45.20	
1983	Trevita	6	J. Velasquez	119	Beech Island	108	Top of the B'rr'l	105	37,020	1:47.80	
1984	Thirty Flags	4	A. Cordero Jr	113	Jubilous	114	Nany	111	45,840	1:42.00	
1985	Possible Mate	4	J. Vasquez	119	Make the Magic	109	Annie Edge	114	42,600	1:40.60	
1986	Duty Dance	4	J. Cruguet	115	Possible Mate	124	Lucky Touch	109	55,800	1:40.20	
1987	Give a Toast	4	R.G. Davis	111	Videogenic	117	Small Virtue	113	68,940	1:44.20	
1988	Key to the Bridge	4	E. Maple	109	Mrimascus	112	Just Class	115	65,160	1:51.80	
1989	Summer Secretary	4	J.L. Samyn	109	Far East	110	Fieldy	116	56,880	1:43.40	
1990	Fieldy	7	C. Perret	119	Summer Secretary	114	Lady Talc	110	52,740	1:45.80	99

Year	Winner	Age	Jockey	Wt.	Second	Wt.	Third	Wt.	Win Value	Time	Beyer
1991	Summer Secretary	6	J. Velasquez	116	Virgin Michael	113	Christiecat	115	54,270	1:40.00	102
1992	Christiecat	5	J.L. Samyn	116	Metamorphose	113	Navarra	109	56,520	1:46.80	105
1993	McKaymackenna	4	J. Velasquez	113	Aurora	115	Chinese Empress	114	57,240	1:44.80	97
1994	Cox Orange	4	J.D. Bailey	112	Irish Linnet	116	Statuette	116	49,395	1:43.20	99
1995	Caress	4	Davis RG	113	Shir Dar	113	Statuette	116	49,905	1:42.00	101
1996	Christmas Gift	4	J.D. Bailey	118	Caress	119	Aucilla	113	50,805	1:42.80	98
1997	Careless Heiress	4	J. Bravo	116	Song of Africa	113	Gastronomical	115	65,760	1:46.20	100
1998	National Treasure	5	R. Migliore	117	Aspiring	113	Dixie Ghost	111	67,740	1:37.80	90
1999	Tampico	6	J.R. Velazquez	114	U R Unforgetable	115	Shashobegon	114	67,020	1:44.32	101
2000	Perfect Sting	4	J.D. Bailey	119	License Fee	114	Fictitious	114	65,820	1:42.30	101
2001	Gaviola	4	J.D. Bailey	120	Truebreadpudding	113	Efficient Frontier	114	65,940	1:41.74	98
2002	Voodoo Dancer	4	J.D. Bailey	119	Golden Corona	115	Babae	116	67,920	1:43.10	102
2003	Delta Princess	4	M.J. Luzzi	113	Wonder Again	118	Voodoo Dancer	120	67,440	1:42.36	99
2004	Dedication	5	J.J. Castellano	118	Aud	117	Caught in the Rain	114	66,000	1:46.38	97

Beyer Index: 99.27

(STONERSIDE) BEAUMONT (G2), About 7 Furlongs, 3-Year-Old Fillies, Keeneland Race Course, 2004 Purse: $250,000

Year	Winner	Age	Jockey	Wt.	Second	Wt.	Third	Wt.	Win Value	Time	Beyer
1990	Go for Wand	3	R.P. Romero	122	Trumpet's Blare	119	Seaside Attraction	119	53,983	1:26.40	104
1991	Ifyoucouldseemenow	3	M.A. Pedroza	122	Versailles Treaty	114	Ever a Lady	114	54,275	1:27.00	
1992	Fluttery Danseur	3	S.J. Sellers	122	Miss Iron Smoke	119	Spinning Round	122	53,918	1:27.40	89
1993	Roamin Rachel	3	C.W. Antley	122	Added Asset	114	Fit to Lead	122	69,998	1:26.40	98
1994	Her Temper	3	P. Day	112	Lotta Dancing	113	Term Limits	121	67,456	1:28.40	84
1995	Dixieland Gold	3	D. Penna	118	Niner's Home	113	Conquistadoress	118	69,874	1:27.40	94
1996	Golden Gale	3	M.E. Smith	115	Birr	115	Bright Time	115	84,398	1:26.00	96
1997	Screamer	3	R.J. Albarado	112			Move	121	57,041	1:28.00	91
	Make Haste	3	P. Day	112							
1998	Star of Broadway	3	P. Day	119	Santaria	119	Bourbon Belle	119	91,140	1:26.60	99
1999	Swingin On Ice	3	R.J. Albarado	115	Secret Hills	115	Appealing Phylly	123	83,917	1:25.30	95
2000	Sahara Gold	3	J.D. Bailey	123	Swept Away	118	Darling My Darling	116	84,847	1:26.58	97
2001	Xtra Heat	3	R. Wilson	120	Mountain Bird	116	Raging Fever	123	155,000	1:28.79	89
2002	Proper Gamble	3	J.J. Castellano	118	Respectful	116	Vicki Vallencourt	118	155,000	1:28.79	89
2003	My Boston Gal	3	P. Day	120	Bird Town	118	Midnight Cry	118	155,000	1:26.87	101
2004	Victory U.S.A.	3	J.D. Bailey	118	Halfbridled	123	Wildwood Flower	118	155,000	1:27.06	93

Beyer Index: 94.21

BED O' ROSES BREEDERS' CUP HANDICAP (G3), 1 Mile, Fillies and Mares, 3-Year-Olds and Up, Aqueduct, 2004 Purse: $156,900

Year	Winner	Age	Jockey	Wt.	Second	Wt.	Third	Wt.	Win Value	Time	Beyer
1957	Little Pache	4	C. McCreary	121	Gay Life	112	Manotick	118	18,900	1:47.00	
1958	Outer Space	4	W. Boland	113	Lori-El	116	Searching	123	17,575	1:43.80	
1959	Big Effort	4	E. Nelson	122	A Glitter	120	Mlle. Dianne	117	18,257	1:44.20	
1960	Chistosa	5	H. Woodhouse	106	Royal Native	128	Craftiness	110	17,542	1:36.40	
1961	Prince's Gate	4	E. Arcaro	113	Make Sail	117	Teacation	119	18,297	1:36.60	
1962	Seven Thirty	4	L. Adams	121	Epitome	108	Rose O'Neill	121	19,240	1:36.20	
1963	Royal Patrice	4	I. Valenzuela	119	Cyclopavia	117	Nubile	109	18,492	1:39.20	
1964	Spicy Living	4	M. Ycaza	123	Look Ma	108	Oil Royalty	122	13,959	1:38.60	
1964	Beauful	5	W. Mayorga	110	Pams Ego	122	Smart Deb	127	13,959	1:37.80	
1965	Steeple Jill	4	J. Ruane	118	Petticoat	114	Treachery	116	18,590	1:35.80	
1966	Straight Deal	4	R. Ussery	117	What a Treat	126	Queen Empress	123	18,167	1:35.80	
1967	Straight Deal	5	R. Ussery	122	Indian Sunlite	116	Kerensa	110	18,297	1:37.60	
1968	Too Bald	4	M. Ycaza	123	Amerigo Lady	120	Treacherous	114	18,362	1:35.00	
1969	Heartland	4	J.L. Rotz	123	A Pleasant Sort	111	Treacherous	114	18,590	1:35.80	
1970	Watch Fob	5	H. Gustines	111	Process Shot	128	Someday	114	18,525	1:36.80	
1971	Office Queen	4	C. Baltazar	125	Shuvee	127	Royal Fillet	110	19,680	1:36.80	
1972	Red Shoes	4	A. Loguercio	118	Aladancer	119	Dares J.	113	16,680	1:36.40	
1973	Poker Night	3	R. Woodhouse	108	Numbered Account	123	Ferly	114	16,605	1:35.40	
1974	Klepto	4	D. Montoya	123	Ladies Agreement	112	Summer Guest	122	16,410	1:35.40	
1975	Shy Dawn	4	D. Montoya	121	Something Super	118	Flo's Pleasure	115	16,860	1:36.20	
1976	Imminence	4	E. Maple	115	Spring Is Here	108	Land Girl	114	23,040	1:35.40	
1977	Shawi	4	M. Venezia	109	Proud Delta	125	Secret Lanvin	111	25,770	1:45.80	
1978	Fearless Queen	5	M. Venezia	108	Notably	110	One Sum	123	25,785	1:46.20	
1979	Lady Lonsdale	4	C.B. Asmussen	111	Hagany	113	Back to Stay	107	31,980	1:36.80	
1979	One Sum	5	J. Fell	118	Reflection Pool	113	Pearl Necklace	121	31,980	1:37.80	
1980	Misty Gallore	4	D. MacBeth	125	Propitiate	115	Gueniviere	111	33,600	1:36.40	
1981	Chain Bracelet	4	F. Lovato Jr	114	Lady Oakley	116	Contrary Rose	115	33,960	1:35.40	
1982	Who's to Answer	4	E. Beitia	108	Real Prize	114	Faisana	110	33,180	1:36.60	
1983	Broom Dance	4	G. McCarron	118	Adept	109	Viva Sec	112	33,420	1:35.40	
1984	Pleasure Cay	4	R.G. Davis	115	Sweet Missus	103	Sintrillium	113	54,090	1:42.00	

Year	Winner	Age	Jockey	Wt.	Second	Wt.	Third	Wt.	Win Value	Time	Beyer
1985	Nany	5	J. Vasquez	120	Flip's Pleasure	118	Sintrillium	120	50,850	1:36.00	
1986	Chaldea	6	J.L. Samyn	110	Add Mint	112	Lady on the Run	120	75,120	1:36.00	
1987	Ms. Eloise	4	R.G. Davis	115	Spring Beauty	116	Tricky Squaw	115	84,660	1:36.60	
1988	Aptostar	3	J.A. Krone	103	Clabber Girl	117	Psyched	114	70,680	1:35.40	
1989	Banker's Lady	4	A. Cordero Jr	118	Aptostar	118	Avie's Gal	114	68,400	1:35.40	
1990	Survive	6	J.A. Santos	117	Amy Be Good	114	Warfie	111	68,640	1:34.20	
1991	Devil's Orchid	4	R. Baez	120	Colonial Waters	119	Sharp Dance	114	68,520	1:35.80	104
1992	Nannerl	5	J.A. Krone	115	English Charm	111	Spy Leader Lady	115	68,100	1:37.20	102
1992	Lady D'Accord	5	J.F. Chavez	114	My Treasure	112	Crystal Vous	112	68,580	1:37.80	96
1993	Lady D'Accord	6	J.D. Chavez	111	Missy's Mirage	123	Buck Some Belle	106	67,320	1:36.60	96
1994	Classy Mirage	4	R.G. Davis	117	For All Season	115	Dispute	122	64,680	1:34.00	108
1995	Incinerate	5	F. Leon	113	Imah	114	Beckys Shirt	113	63,960	1:35.80	96
1996	Punkin Pie	6	J. Trejo	110	Incinerate	115	Lottsa Talc	121	65,220	1:35.00	95
1997	Flat Fleet Feet	4	M.E. Smith	121	Mama Dean	113	Ashboro	116	95,940	1:34.00	103
1998	Dixie Flag	4	M.J. Luzzi	117	Hidden Reserve	113	U Can Do It	118	96,780	1:33.60	109
1999	Catinca	4	R. Migliore	120	Foil	113	License Fee	113	94,620	1:34.95	99
2000	Ruby Rubles	5	C.C. Lopez	113	Up We Go	114	Go To The Ink	111	65,580	1:36.96	103
2001	Country Hideaway	5	J.R. Velazquez	117	Critical Eye	115	Jostle	117	95,520	1:34.98	102
2002	Raging Fever	4	J.R. Velazquez	121	Atelier	119	Shiny Band	112	94,980	1:34.96	98
2003	Raging Fever	5	A.T. Gryder	119	Smok'n Frolic	120	Nonsuch Bay	117	93,960	1:34.86	101
2004	Passing Shot	5	J.A. Santos	115	Smok'n Frolic	119	Nonsuch Bay	116	95,040	1:35.50	93

Beyer Index: 100.33

BELDAME (G1), 1 1/8 Miles, Fillies and Mares, 3-Year-Olds and Up, Belmont Park, 2004 Purse: $735,000

Year	Winner	Age	Jockey	Wt.	Second	Wt.	Third	Wt.	Win Value	Time	Beyer
1939	Nellie Bly	3	J. Renick	102	Unerring	120	Bala Ormont	115	10,100	1:43.00	
1940	Fairy Chant	3	I. Anderson	119	Dotted Swiss	114	Dolly Val	121	14,050	1:50.80	
1941	Fairy Chant	4	I. Anderson	123	Imperatrice	116	Rosetown	126	14,450	1:51.00	
1942	Barrancosa	7	E. Arcaro	116			Rosetown	126	7,800	1:50.00	
	Vagrancy	3	J. Stout	119							
1943	Mar-Kell	4	B. Thompson	126	Stefanita	116	Vagrancy	122	20,050	1:51.60	
1944	Donitas First	3	T. Atkinson	112	Whirlabout	124	Moon Maiden	114	18,530	1:51.80	
1945	War Date	3	A. Kirkland	119	Letmenow	110	Light of Morn	105	24,100	1:51.00	
1946	Gallorette	4	J. Jessop	126	War Date	113	Kay Gibson	105	39,300	1:51.40	
1946	Bridal Flower	3	A. DeLara	114	Aladear	106	Jupiter Light	108	39,300	1:52.20	
1947	Snow Goose	3	T. Atkinson	106	Gallorette	126	Camargo	112	41,500	1:52.00	
1947	But Why Not	3	E. Arcaro	120	Miss Grillo	126	Elpis	123	42,250	1:51.80	
1948	Conniver	4	D. Dodson	121	Harmonica	114	Gallorette	124	49,700	1:52.40	
1949	Miss Request	4	E. Arcaro	113	Plunder	108	Mother	105	53,600	1:52.80	
	Harmonica finished second but was disqualified										
1950	Next Move	3	N. Combest	116	September	108	Wistful	125	47,400	1:50.20	
1951	Thelma Burger	4	W. Shoemaker	110	Bed o' Roses	124	Kiss Me Kate	119	49,300	1:52.00	
1952	Next Move	5	E. Guerin	125	Renew	117	Nilufer	106	43,400	1:51.00	
1952	Real Delight	3	E. Arcaro	126	Marta	117	La Corredora	112	42,400	1:51.00	
1953	Atalanta	5	H.B. Wilson	121	Miss Traffic	106	La Corredora	119	47,600	1:52.20	
1954	Parlo	3	E. Guerin	116	Open Sesame	110	Clear Dawn	114	45,500	1:49.80	
1955	Lalun	3	H. Moreno	116	Clear Dawn	116	Countess Fleet	116	50,800	1:52.00	
1956	Levee	3	R. Broussard	115	Amoret	114	Searching	123	48,100	1:50.00	
1957	Pucker Up	4	W. Shoemaker	125	Plotter	119	Gay Life	104	51,200	1:49.40	
1958	Outer Space	4	W. Harmatz	117	A Glitter	119	Dotted Line	120	44,595	1:49.40	
1959	Tempted	4	E. Nelson	125	Idun	121	High Bid	113	42,905	1:50.20	
1960	Berlo	3	E. Guerin	119	Royal Native	123	Make Sail	119	57,615	1:49.40	
1961	Airmans Guide	4	H. Grant	123	Craftiness	123	Primonetta	118	62,400	1:49.40	
1962	Cicada	3	W. Shoemaker	118	Shirley Jones	123	Firm Policy	118	57,037	1:48.20	
1963	Oil Royalty	5	M. Ycaza	123	Lamb Chop	118	Smart Deb	118	56,972	1:51.00	
1964	Tosmah	3	S. Boulmetis	118	Miss Cavandish	118	Castle Forbes	118	52,552	1:49.60	
1965	What a Treat	3	J.L. Rotz	118	Steeple Jill	123	Straight Deal	118	53,430	1:49.20	
1966	Summer Scandal	4	W. Blum	123	Straight Deal	123	Lady Pitt	118	55,380	1:49.40	
1967	Mac's Sparkler	5	W. Boland	123	Triple Brook	123	Gamely	118	53,235	1:49.80	
1968	Gamely	4	L. Pincay Jr	123	Politely	123	Amerigo Lady	123	53,202	1:49.60	
1969	Gamely	5	L. Pincay Jr	123	Amerigo Lady	123	Shuvee	118	52,877	1:49.20	
1970	Shuvee	4	R. Turcotte	123	Obeah	123	Cold Comfort	118	54,437	1:48.00	
1971	Double Delta	5	K. Knapp	123	Shuvee	123	Cathy Honey	123	49,710	1:48.60	
1972	Susan's Girl	3	L. Pincay Jr	118	Summer Guest	118	Chou Croute	123	67,680	1:48.40	
1973	Desert Vixen	3	L. Pincay Jr	118	Poker Night	118	Susan's Girl	123	65,880	1:46.20	
1974	Desert Vixen	4	L. Pincay Jr	123	Poker Night	123	Tizna	123	68,760	1:46.60	
1975	Susan's Girl	6	B. Baeza	123	Tizna	123	Pass a Glance	123	67,980	1:48.40	
1976	Proud Delta	4	J. Velasquez	123	Revidere	118	Bastonera II	120	64,920	1:46.80	
1977	Cum Laude Laurie	3	A. Cordero Jr	118	What a Summer	123	Charming Story	118	80,025	2:01.80	
1978	Late Bloomer	4	J. Velasquez	123	Pearl Necklace	123	Cum Laude Laurie	123	78,150	2:02.20	
1979	Waya	5	C.B. Asmussen	123	Fourdrinier	118	Kit's Double	123	97,050	2:06.20	
1980	Love Sign	3	R. Hernandez	118	Misty Gallore	123	It's in the Air	123	93,600	2:02.80	

Year	Winner	Age	Jockey	Wt.	Second	Wt.	Third	Wt.	Win Value	Time	Beyer
1981	Love Sign	4	W. Shoemaker	123	Glorious Song	123			131,100	2:01.80	
					Jameela	123					
1982	Weber City Miss	5	A. Cordero Jr	123	Mademoiselle Forli	118	Love Sign	123	134,100	2:04.20	
1983	Dance Number	4	A. Cordero Jr	123	Heartlight No. One	118	Mochila	123	133,200	2:00.60	
1984	Life's Magic	3	J. Velasquez	118	Miss Oceana	118	Key Dancer	118	158,280	2:03.20	
1985	Lady's Secret	3	J. Velasquez	118	Isayso	123	Kamikaze Rick	118	160,920	2:03.60	
1986	Lady's Secret	4	P. Day	123	Coup de Fusil	123	Classy Cathy	118	189,600	2:01.60	
1987	Personal Ensign	3	R.P. Romero	118	Coup de Fusil	123	Silent Turn	118	182,100	2:04.40	
1988	Personal Ensign	4	R.P. Romero	123	Classic Crown	118	Sham Say	118	199,440	2:01.20	
1989	Tactile	3	R. Migliore	118	Colonial Waters	123	Rose's Cantina	123	170,100	2:05.20	
1990	Go for Wand	3	R.P. Romero	119	Colonial Waters	123	Buy the Firm	123	167,700	1:45.80	120
1991	Sharp Dance	5	M.E. Smith	123	Versailles Treaty	119	Lady D'Accord	123	150,000	1:48.00	101
1992	Saratoga Dew	3	W.H. McCauley	119	Versailles Treaty	123	Coxwold	123	150,000	1:46.80	108
1993	Dispute	3	J.D. Bailey	119	Shared Interest	123	Vivano	123	150,000	1:47.20	107
1994	Heavenly Prize	3	P. Day	119	Educated Risk	123	Classy Mirage	123	150,000	1:48.80	111
1995	Serena's Song	3	G.L. Stevens	119	Heavenly Prize	123	Lakeway	123	150,000	1:48.60	104
1996	Yanks Music	3	J.R. Velazquez	119	Serena's Song	123	Clear Mandate	123	240,000	1:47.00	111
1997	Hidden Lake	4	R. Migliore	123	Ajina	119	Jewel Princess	123	240,000	1:48.20	105
1998	Sharp Cat	4	C.S. Nakatani	123	Tomisue's Delight	123	Pocho's Dream Girl	123	240,000	1:46.20	119
1999	Beautiful Pleasure	4	J.F. Chavez	123	Silverbulletday	119	Catinca	123	300,000	1:47.74	113
2000	Riboletta	5	C.J. McCarron	123	Beautiful Please	123	Pentatonic	123	450,000	1:46.14	115
2001	Exogenous	3	J.J. Castellano	120	Flute	120	Spain	123	450,000	1:49.20	109
2002	Imperial Gesture	3	J.D. Bailey	120	Mandy's Gold	123	Summer Colony	123	450,000	1:50.63	105
2003	Sightseek	4	J.D. Bailey	123	Bird Town	120	Buy the Sport	120	450,000	1:49.27	107
2004	Sightseek	5	J.J. Castellano	123	Society Selection	120	Storm Flag Flying	123	450,000	1:49.60	101

Beyer Index: 109.07

Distance 1 1/16 miles in 1939; 1 1/4 miles from 1977-89; run at Aqueduct from 1939-56, 1959, 1962-68

BELMONT BREEDERS' CUP HANDICAP (G2), 1 1/8 Miles (Turf), 3-Year-Olds and Up, Belmont Park, 2004 Purse: $197,800

Year	Winner	Age	Jockey	Wt.	Second	Wt.	Third	Wt.	Win Value	Time	Beyer
1986	Danger's Hour	4	J.D. Bailey	116	Salem Drive	116	Silver Voice	112	95,280	1:40.80	
1987	Talakeno	7	A. Cordero Jr	117	Lightning Leap	110	Glaros	111	93,090	1:49.40	
1988	Steinlen	5	P. Day	120	Iron Courage	113	Barood	110	93,540	1:43.40	
1989	Highland Springs	5	K.J. Desormeaux	117	Maceo	113	Slew City Slew	118	93,180	1:39.20	
1990	Who's to Pay	4	J.D. Bailey	113	Jalaajel	115	Caltech	120	93,570	1:46.00	
1991	Solar Splendor	4	W.H. McCauley	113	Who's to Pay	118	Jalaajel	114	93,210	1:41.00	106
1992	Roman Envoy	4	C. Perret	113	Lotus Pool	114	Daarik	114	34,800	1:41.40	106
1993	Fourstars Allstar	5	J.A. Santos	116	Lech	115	Cleone	113	92,880	1:39.80	109
1994	A in Sociology	4	Samyn JL	116	Fourstars Allstar	119	Home of the Free	114	34,290	1:40.00	104
1995	Dove Hunt	4	P. Day	121	Fly Cry	116	Unfinished Symph	122	92,970	1:40.00	107
1996	Gentleman Beau	4	J.A. Santos	114	Kiri's Clown	114	Volochine	116	127,140	1:41.00	105
1997	Fortitude	4	R.G. Davis	112	Green Means Go	113	Boyce	118	126,600	1:38.40	104
1998	Subordination	4	D.R. Flores	121	Yagli	122	Bomfim	114	127,020	1:45.80	111
1999	With the Flow	4	J.A. Santos	114	Comic Strip	118	Wised Up	112	127,620	1:49.20	104
2000	Forbidden Apple	5	J.A. Santos	114	Val's Prince	118	Altibr	115	126,000	1:51.73	107
2002	Startac	4	J.D. Bailey	116	Volponi	117	Dr. Kashnikow	115	125,160	1:46.60	105
2003	Della Francesca	4	J.F. Chavez	114	Rouvres	116	Volponi	119	125,760	1:47.48	102
2004	Senor Swinger	4	E.S. Prado	117	Stroll	120	B.A. Way	113	124,680	1:52.72	108

Beyer Index: 106.00

Not run in 2001

BELMONT (G1), 1 1/2 Miles, 3-Year-Olds, Belmont Park, 2004 Purse: $1,000,000

Year	Winner	Age	Jockey	Wt.	Second	Wt.	Third	Wt.	Win Value	Time	Beyer
1867	Ruthless	3	J. Gilpatrick	107	De Courcey	110	Rivoli	110	1,850	3:05.00	
1868	General Duke	3	R. Swim	110	Northumberland	110	Fanny Ludlow	107	2,800	3:02.00	
1869	Fenian	3	C. Miller	110	Glenelg	110	Invercauld	107	3,850	3:04.20	
1870	Kingfisher	3	W. Dick	110	Foster	110	Midday	110	3,750	2:59.20	
1871	Harry Basset	3	W. Miller	110	Stockwood	110	By the Sea	107	5,450	2:56.00	
1872	Joe Daniels	3	J. Rowe	110	Meteor	110	Shylock	110	4,500	2:58.20	
1873	Springbok	3	J. Rowe	110	Count d'Orsay	110	Strachino	110	5,200	3:01.60	
1874	Saxon	3	G. Barbee	110	Grinstead	110	Milner	110	4,450	2:42.20	
1875	Calvin	3	R. Swim	110	Aristides	110	Aaron Penn'ton	110	4,200	2:39.20	
1876	Algerine	3	W. Donohue	110	Fiddlesticks	110	Barricade	110	3,700	2:40.20	
1877	Cloverbrook	3	C. Holloway	110	Loiterer	110	Baden Baden	110	5,200	2:46.00	
1878	Duke of Magenta	3	L. Hughes	118	Bramble	118	Spartan	118	3,850	2:43.20	
1879	Spendthrift	3	S. Evans	118	Monitor	118	Jericho	118	4,250	2:42.60	
1880	Grenada	3	L. Hughes	118	Ferncliffe	118	Turenne	118	2,800	2:47.00	
1881	Saunterer	3	T. Costello	118	Eole	118	Baltic	118	3,000	2:47.00	
1882	Forester	3	J. McLaughlin	118	Babcock	118	Wyoming	115	2,600	2:43.00	

Year	Winner	Age	Jockey	Wt.	Second	Wt.	Third	Wt.	Win Value	Time	Beyer
1883	George Kinney	3	J. McLaughlin	118	Trombone	118	Renegade	118	3,070	2:42.20	
1884	Panique	3	J. McLaughlin	118	Himalaya	118			3,150	2:42.00	
1885	Tyrant	3	P. Duffy	118	St. Augustine	118	Tecumseh	118	2,710	2:43.00	
1886	Inspector B.	3	J. McLaughlin	118	The Bard	118	Linden	118	2,720	2:41.00	
1887	Hanover	3	J. McLaughlin	118	Oneko	118			2,900	2:43.20	
1888	Sir Dixon	3	J. McLaughlin	118	Prince Royal	118			3,440	2:40.20	
1889	Eric	3	W. Hayward	118	Diablo	125	Zephyrus	118	4,960	2:47.00	
1890	Burlington	3	S. Barnes	118	Devotee	115	Padishah	113	8,560	2:07.60	
1891	Foxford	3	E. Garrison	118	Montana	117	Laurestan	112	5,070	2:08.60	
1892	Patron	3	W. Hayward	122	Shellbark	122			6,610	2:17.00	
1893	Comanche	3	W. Simms	117	Dr. Rice	122	Rainbow	119	5,310	1:53.20	
1894	Henry of Navarre	3	W. Simms	117	Prig	119	Assignee	115	6,880	1:56.20	
1895	Belmar	3	F. Taral	119	Counter Tenor	126	Nanki Pooh	126	2,700	2:11.20	
1896	Hastings	3	H. Griffin	122	Handspring	125	Hamilton II	110	3,025	2:24.20	
1897	Scottish Chieftain	3	J. Scherrer	115	On Deck	115	Octagon	122	3,550	2:32.20	
1898	Bowling Brook	3	F. Littlefield	122	Previous	122	Hamburg	122	7,810	2:32.00	
1899	Jean Bereaud	3	R.R. Clawson	122	Half Time	119	Glengar	122	9,445	2:23.00	
1900	Ildrim	3	N. Turner	126	Petruchio	126	Missionary	126	14,790	2:21.20	
1901	Commando	3	H. Spencer	126	The Parader	126	All Green	126	11,595	2:21.00	
1902	Masterman	3	J. Bullman	126	Ranald	126	King Hanover	126	13,220	2:22.20	
1903	Africander	3	J. Bullman	126	Whorler	126	Red Knight	126	12,285	2:23.20	
1904	Delhi	3	G. Odom	126	Graziallo	126	Rapid Water	126	11,575	2:06.60	
1905	Tanya	3	E. Hildebrand	121	Blandy	126	Hot Shot	126	17,240	2:08.00	
1906	Burgomaster	3	L. Lyne	126	The Quail	126	Accountant	126	22,700	2:20.00	
1907	Peter Pan	3	G. Mountain	126	Superman	126	Frank Gill	126	22,765	n/a	
1908	Colin	3	J. Notter	126	Fair Play	126	King James	126	22,765	n/a	
1909	Joe Madden	3	E. Dugan	126	Wise Mason	123	Donald McDonald	123	24,550	2:21.60	
1910	Sweep	3	J. Butwell	126	Duke of Ormonde	126			9,700	2:22.00	
1913	Prince Eugene	3	R. Troxler	109	Rock View	128	Flying Fairy	106	2,825	2:18.00	
1914	Luke McLuke	3	M. Buxton	126	Gainer	126	Charlestonian	123	3,025	2:20.00	
1915	The Finn	3	G. Byrne	126	Half Rock	126	Pebbles	126	1,825	2:18.40	
1916	Friar Rock	3	E. Haynes	126	Spur	126	Churchill	126	4,100	2:22.00	
1917	Hourless	3	J. Butwell	126	Skeptic	126	Wonderful	123	5,800	2:17.80	
1918	Johren	3	F. Robinson	126	War Cloud	126	Cum Sah	126	8,950	2:20.40	
1919	Sir Barton	3	J. Loftus	126	Sweep On	126	Natural Bridge	126	11,950	2:17.40	
1920	Man o' War	3	C. Kummer	126	Donnacona	126			7,950	2:14.20	
1921	Grey Lag	3	E. Sande	126	Sporting Blood	126	Leonardo II	126	8,650	2:16.80	
1922	Pillory	3	C.H. Miller	126	Snob II	126	Hea	126	39,200	2:18.80	
1923	Zev	3	E. Sande	126	Chickvale	126	Rialto	126	38,000	2:19.00	
1924	Mad Play	3	E. Sande	126	Mr. Mutt	126	Modest	126	42,880	2:18.80	
1925	American Flag	3	A. Johnson	126	Dangerous	126	Swope	126	38,500	2:16.80	
1926	Crusader	3	A. Johnson	126	Espino	126	Haste	126	48,550	2:32.20	
1927	Chance Shot	3	E. Sande	126	Bois de Rose	126	Flambino	121	60,910	2:32.40	
1928	Vito	3	C. Kummer	126	Genie	126	Diavolo	126	63,430	2:33.20	
1929	Blue Larkspur	3	M. Garner	126	African	126	Jack High	126	59,650	2:32.80	
1930	Gallant Fox	3	E. Sande	126	Whichone	126	Questionnaire	126	66,040	2:31.60	
1931	Twenty Grand	3	C. Kurtsinger	126	Sun Meadow	126	Jamestown	126	58,770	2:29.60	
1932	Faireno	3	T. Malley	126	Osculator	126	Flag Pole	126	55,120	2:32.80	
1933	Hurryoff	3	M. Garner	126	Nimbus	126	Union	126	49,490	2:32.60	
1934	Peace Chance	3	W.D. Wright	126	High Quest	126	Good Goods	126	43,410	2:29.20	
1935	Omaha	3	W. Saunders	126	Firethorn	126	Rosemont	126	35,480	2:30.60	
1936	Granville	3	J. Stout	126	Mr. Bones	126	Hollyrood	126	29,800	2:30.00	
1937	War Admiral	3	C. Kurtsinger	126	Sceneshifter	126	Vamoose	126	38,020	2:28.60	
1938	Pasteurized	3	J. Stout	126	Dauber	126	Cravat	126	34,530	2:29.40	
1939	Johnstown	3	J. Stout	126	Belay	126	Gilded Knight	126	37,020	2:29.60	
1940	Bimelech	3	F.A. Smith	126	Your Chance	126	Andy K.	126	35,030	2:29.60	
1941	Whirlaway	3	E. Arcaro	126	Robert Morris	126	Yankee Chance	126	39,770	2:31.00	
1942	Shut Out	3	E. Arcaro	126	Alsab	126	Lochinvar	126	44,520	2:29.20	
1943	Count Fleet	3	J. Longden	126	Fairy Manhurst	126	Deseronto	126	35,340	2:28.20	
1944	Bounding Home	3	G.L. Smith	126	Pensive	126	Bull Dandy	126	55,000	2:32.20	
1945	Pavot	3	E. Arcaro	126	Wildlife	126	Jeep	126	52,675	2:30.20	
1946	Assault	3	W. Mehrtens	126	Natchez	126	Cable	126	75,400	2:30.80	
1947	Phalanx	3	R. Donoso	126	Tide Rips	126	Tailspin	126	78,900	2:29.40	
1948	Citation	3	E. Arcaro	126	Better Self	126	Escadru	126	77,700	2:28.20	
1949	Capot	3	T. Atkinson	126	Ponder	126	Palestinian	126	60,900	2:30.20	
1950	Middleground	3	W. Boland	126	Lights Up	126	Mr. Trouble	126	61,350	2:28.60	
1951	Counterpoint	3	D. Gorman	126	Battlefield	126	Battle Morn	126	82,000	2:29.00	
1952	One Count	3	E. Arcaro	126	Blue Man	126	Armageddon	126	82,400	2:30.20	
1953	Native Dancer	3	E. Guerin	126	Jamie K.	126	Royal Bay Gem	126	82,500	2:28.60	
1954	High Gun	3	E. Guerin	126	Fisherman	126	Limelight	126	89,000	2:30.80	
1955	Nashua	3	E. Arcaro	126	Blazing Count	126	Portersville	126	83,700	2:29.00	
1956	Needles	3	D. Erb	126	Career Boy	126	Fabius	126	83,600	2:29.80	
1957	Gallant Man	3	W. Shoemaker	126	Inside Tract	126	Bold Ruler	126	77,300	2:26.60	

Year	Winner	Age	Jockey	Wt.	Second	Wt.	Third	Wt.	Win Value	Time	Beyer
1958	Cavan	3	P. Anderson	126	Tim Tam	126	Flamingo	126	73,440	2:30.20	
1959	Sword Dancer	3	W. Shoemaker	126	Bagdad	126	Royal Orbit	126	93,525	2:28.40	
1960	Celtic Ash	3	W. Hartack	126	Venetian Way	126	Disperse	126	96,785	2:29.60	
1961	Sherluck	3	B. Baeza	126	Globemaster	126	Guadalcanal	126	104,900	2:29.20	
1962	Jaipur	3	W. Shoemaker	126	Admiral's Voyage	126	Crimson Satan	126	109,550	2:28.80	
1963	Chateaugay	3	B. Baeza	126	Candy Spots	126	Choker	126	101,700	2:30.20	
1964	Quadrangle	3	M. Ycaza	126	Roman Brother	126	Northern Dancer	126	110,850	2:28.40	
1965	Hail to All	3	J. Sellers	126	Tom Rolfe	126	First Family	126	104,150	2:28.40	
1966	Amberoid	3	W. Boland	126	Buffle	126	Advocator	126	117,700	2:29.60	
1967	Damascus	3	W. Shoemaker	126	Cool Reception	126	Gentleman James	126	104,950	2:28.80	
1968	Stage Door Johnny	3	H. Gustines	126	Forward Pass	126	Call Me Prince	126	117,700	2:27.20	
1969	Arts and Letters	3	B. Baeza	126	Majestic Prince	126	Dike	126	104,050	2:28.80	
1970	High Echelon	3	J.L. Rotz	126	Needles n Pens	126	Naskra	126	115,000	2:34.00	
1971	Pass Catcher	3	W. Blum	126	Jim French	126	Bold Reason	126	97,710	2:30.40	
1972	Riva Ridge	3	R. Turcotte	126	Ruritania	126	Cloudy Dawn	126	93,540	2:28.00	
1973	Secretariat	3	R. Turcotte	126	Twice a Prince	126	My Gallant	126	90,120	2:24.00	
1974	Little Current	3	M.A. Rivera	126	Jolly Johu	126	Cannonade	126	101,970	2:29.20	
1975	Avatar	3	W. Shoemaker	126	Foolish Pleasure	126	Master Derby	126	116,160	2:28.20	
1976	Bold Forbes	3	A. Cordero Jr	126	McKenzie Bridge	126	Great Contractor	126	117,000	2:29.00	
1977	Seattle Slew	3	J. Cruguet	126	Run Dusty Run	126	Sanhedrin	126	109,080	2:29.60	
1978	Affirmed	3	S. Cauthen	126	Alydar	126	Darby Creek Road	126	110,580	2:26.80	
1979	Coastal	3	R. Hernandez	126	Golden Act	126	Spectacular Bid	126	161,400	2:28.60	
1980	Temperence Hill	3	E. Maple	126	Genuine Risk	121	Rockhill Native	126	176,220	2:29.80	
1981	Summing	3	G. Martens	126	Highland Blade	126	Pleasant Colony	126	170,580	2:29.00	
1982	Conquistador Cielo	3	L. Pincay Jr	126	Gato Del Sol	126	Illuminate	126	159,720	2:28.20	
1983	Caveat	3	L. Pincay Jr	126	Slew o' Gold	126	Barberstown	126	215,100	2:27.80	
1984	Swale	3	L. Pincay Jr	126	Pine Circle	126	Morning Bob	126	310,020	2:27.20	
1985	Creme Fraiche	3	E. Maple	126	Stephan's Odyssey	126	Chief's Crown	126	307,740	2:27.00	
1986	Danzig Connection	3	C.J. McCarron	126	Johns Treasure	126	Ferdinand	126	338,640	2:29.80	
1987	Bet Twice	3	C. Perret	126	Cryptoclearance	126	Gulch	126	1,329,160	2:28.20	
1988	Risen Star	3	E. Delahoussaye	126	Kingpost	126	Brian's Time	126	1,303,720	2:26.40	
1989	Easy Goer	3	P. Day	126	Sunday Silence	126	Le Voyageur	126	413,520	2:26.00	
1990	Go and Go	3	M.J. Kinane	126	Thirty Six Red	126	Baron de Vaux	126	411,600	2:27.20	111
1991	Hansel	3	J.D. Bailey	126	Strike the Gold	126	Mane Minister	126	1,417,480	2:28.00	111
1992	A.P. Indy	3	E. Delahoussaye	126	My Memoirs	126	Pine Bluff	126	458,880	2:26.00	111
1993	Colonial Affair	4	J.A. Krone	126	Kissin Kris	126	Wild Gale	126	444,540	2:29.80	104
1994	Tabasco Cat	3	P. Day	126	Go for Gin	126	Strodes Creek	126	392,280	2:26.80	106
1995	Thunder Gulch	3	G.L. Stevens	126	Star Standard	126	Citadeed	126	415,440	2:32.00	101
1996	Editor's Note	3	R.R. Douglas	126	Skip Away	126	My Flag	121	437,880	2:28.80	106
1997	Touch Gold	3	C.J. McCarron	126	Silver Charm	126	Free House	126	432,600	2:28.80	110
1998	Victory Gallop	3	G.L. Stevens	126	Real Quiet	126	Thomas Jo	126	600,000	2:29.16	110
1999	Lemon Drop Kid	3	J.A. Santos	126	Vision and Verse	126	Charismatic	126	600,000	2:27.88	109
2000	Commendable	3	P. Day	126	Aptitude	126	Unshaded	126	600,000	2:31.19	101
2001	Point Given	3	G.L. Stevens	126	A.P. Valentine	126	Monarchos	126	600,000	2:26.56	114
2002	Sarava	3	E. Prado	126	Medaglia d'Oro	126	Sunday Break	126	600,000	2:29.71	105
2003	Empire Maker	3	J.D. Bailey	126	Ten Most Wanted	126	Funny Cide	126	600,000	2:28.26	110
2004	Birdstone	3	E.S. Prado	126	Smarty Jones	126	Royal Assault	126	600,000	2:27.50	101

Beyer Index: 107.33

Run at Jerome Park prior to 1890; at Morris Park 189-1904; at Aqueduct 1963-67; no time taken 1906-07. Distance 1 5/8 miles prior to 1874; 1 1/4 miles 1890-92, 1895, 1904-05; 1 1/8 miles 1893-94; 1 3/8 miles 1896-903, 1906-25. Value to winner includes $1 million Triple Crown bonus for Bet Twice in 1987; Risen Star in 1988; and Hansel in 1991.

BEN ALI (G3), 1 1/8 Miles, 4-Year-Olds and Up, Keeneland Race Course, 2004 Purse: $150,000

Year	Winner	Age	Jockey	Wt.	Second	Wt.	Third	Wt.	Win Value	Time	Beyer
1917	Colonel Vennie	4	W. Crump	125	Embroidery	108	Marion Goosby	110	1,941	1:46.00	
1918	Opportunity	4	E. Pool	111	Arriet	107	Bribed Voter	104	1,710	1:53.80	
1919	Exterminator	4	J. Morys	124	American Ace	99	Midway	120	2,615	1:50.40	
1920	General Haig	4	M. Garner	110	Regalo	106	Pictor	114	3,460	1:50.00	
1921	Best Pal	4	L. Lyke	116	Ginger	112	Pluribus	107	3,630	1:46.60	
1922	United Verde	4	M. Garner	112	Advocate	108	Rouleau	112	3,280	1:45.60	
1937	Count Morse	4	I. Anderson	117	Dellor	108	White Tie	105	2,700	1:46.20	
1938	Main Man	4	W.F. Yard	120	Old Nassau	110	Galsun	110	2,800	1:45.00	
1939	Burning Star	5	W. Yarberry	120	Birthday	114	Arabs Arrow	117	2,550	1:47.00	
1940	Arabs Arrow	6	C. Bierman	116	Shot Put	106	Easy Mon	122	2,625	1:48.80	
1941	Red Dock	4	A. Bodiou	114	Viscounty	117	Blue Pair	106	2,675	1:46.00	
1942	Steel Heels	6	J. George	116	Aonbarr	116	Get Off	115	2,700	1:46.40	
1943	Aletern	4	J. Adams	112	Valdina Orphan	123	Corydon	113	2,375	1:46.20	
1944	Alquest	4	J. Adams	113	Anticlimax	115	Parasang	110	4,025	1:45.60	
1945	Pot o' Luck	3	D. Dodson	110	Colonel Read	105	Cold Crack	111	3,800	1:46.60	
1946	Bull Play	4	R. Campbell	110	Letmenow	114	South Dakota	116	4,475	1:44.40	

Year	Winner	Age	Jockey	Wt.	Second	Wt.	Third	Wt.	Win Value	Time	Beyer
1947	Pot o' Luck	5	D. Dodson	121	Jack S.L.	112	Bymeabond	115	8,600	1:44.00	
1948	Fervent	4	N.L. Pierson	124	Colosal	116	Star Reward	115	9,350	1:43.80	
1949	Shy Guy	4	C. McCreary	120	Pellicle	106	Free America	114	8,250	1:45.00	
1950	Mount Marcy	5	K. Church	117	Commodore Lea	112	Flying Disc	103	8,850	1:43.80	
1951	Wistful	5	D. Dodson	112	Counterpoint	105	Little Imp	110	8,250	1:45.00	
1952	Seaward	7	S. Brooks	113	Ruhe	114	Hedgewood	110	8,280	1:45.00	
1953	Oil Capitol	6	C. McCreary	119	Seaward	112	Breeze By	104	7,880	1:44.00	
1954	Mister Black	5	J. Adams	122	Second Avenue	113	Greatest	112	8,442	1:27.00	
1955	Sea O Erin	4	S. Brooks	122	Smoke Screen	113	Mister Black	122	8,012	1:27.40	
1956	Timely Tip	5	J.L. Rotz	110	Sea O Erin	124	Breakers	113	8,800	1:27.80	
1957	Star Rover	5	J. Heckmann	118	Sea O Erin	118	Tommy's Jet	113	8,070	1:25.60	
1958	Safe Message	4	D. Dodson	113	Shan Pac	115	Ezgo	121	8,037	1:26.40	
1959	Greek Chief	4	W. Hartack	113	Nadir	125	Gleeman	112	8,395	1:26.60	
1960	Fulcrum	5	S. Brooks	111	Dunce	118	Shan Pac	112	7,591	1:25.40	
1961	Cactus Tom	4	L. Hansman	114	Eight Again	117	Careless John	120	7,979	1:26.80	
1962	Run for Nurse	5	S. Brooks	118	Bluescope	122	Editorialist	122	7,735	1:25.60	
1963	Decidedly	4	J. Nichols	121	Times Roman	115	Gun Glory	114	7,199	1:41.40	
1964	Copy Chief	4	D. Brumfield	117	Choker	118	Lemon Twist	115	11,505	1:42.00	
1965	Gallant Romeo	4	W. Knapp	114	Alphabet	112	Big Brigade	112	14,950	1:42.80	
1966	Swift Ruler	4	L. Spraker	124	Big Brigade	117	Charolero	114	14,690	1:42.80	
1967	Francis U.	4	R.J. Campbell	119	Swift Ruler	120	Moccasin	116	15,080	1:45.00	
1968	Miracle Hill	4	R. Gallimore	121	Gay Flight	114	Air Boat	113	14,300	1:42.60	
1969	Court Recess	4	E. Guerin	116	Miracle Hill	119	Gleaming Sw'd	111	15,015	1:44.60	
1970	Gallant Moment	6	D. Kassen	110	True North	114	Bold Favorite	118	15,047	1:42.60	
1971	Great Mystery	4	P.I. Grimm	117	Early Fall	112	True North	121	14,560	1:41.80	
1972	Knight Counter	4	D. Brumfield	114	No No Billy	115	Tribal Line	117	15,405	1:43.40	
1973	Knight Counter	5	D. Brumfield	120	Guitar Player	118	Introductivo	114	18,785	1:43.00	
1974	Knight Counter	6	E. Fires	119	Model Husband	117	Jim's Alibhi	113	17,647	1:41.80	
1975	Navajo	5	J. Nichols	122	L. Grant Jr.	118	Hasty Flyer	115	19,419	1:43.80	
1976	My Friend Gus	4	D.G. McHargue	114	Packer Captain	116	Dragset	113	18,119	1:42.40	
1977	Honest Pleasure	4	C. Perret	124	Inca Roca	118	Packer Captain	113	18,623	1:42.40	
1978	Prince Majestic	4	E. Delahoussaye	118	Inca Roca	114	All the More	122	21,824	1:41.80	
1979	Kodiack	5	G. Gallitano	114	Hot Words	113	Morning Frolic	115	31,054	1:49.60	
1980	Architect	4	S.A. Spencer	120	Revivalist	116	All the More	116	27,999	1:48.80	
1981	Withholding	4	B. Sayler	113	Summer Advocate	113	Two's a Plenty	115	34,986	1:50.20	
1982	Withholding	5	L. Melancon	121	Aspro	122	Swinging Light	113	35,880	1:49.60	
1983	Aspro	5	V. Bracciale Jr	115	Thirty Eight Paces	116	Rivalero	121	35,588	1:49.60	
1984	Aspro	6	D. Brumfield	116	Play Fellow	123	Jack Slade	115	34,564	1:50.80	
1985	Bello	4	G. Gallitano	116	Silent King	117	Hi Pi	113	35,295	1:48.80	
1986	Czar Nijinsky	4	W.H. McCauley	119	Little Missouri	114	Minneapple	117	43,541	1:50.20	
1987	Intrusion	5	S. Hawley	111	Coaxing Mark	114	Blue Buckaroo	117	34,678	1:49.60	
1988	Homebuilder	4	D. Brumfield	119	Bet Twice	126	Blue Buckaroo	117	52,293	1:51.40	
1989	Classic Account	4	P. Day	114	Regal Classic	117	Brian's Time	121	53,885	1:50.60	
1990	Master Speaker	5	J.D. Bailey	121	Lac Ouimet	114	Silver Survivor	119	54,890	1:49.00	
1991	Sports View	4	C. Perret	119	Bright Again	113	Exemplary Leader	112	53,490	1:49.60	114
1992	Profit Key	5	S. Sellers	119			Out of Place	119	34,210	1:49.80	110
	Loach	4	P.A. Valenzuela	117							
1993	Sunny Sunrise	6	R. Wilson	119	Conte di Savoya	113	Prize Fight	112	50,933	1:48.80	103
1994	Pistols and Roses	5	M.E. Smith	123	Sunny Sunrise	119	Compadre	113	50,251	1:51.60	105
1995	Wildly Joyous	4	Walls MK	114	Danville	117	Powerful Punch	113	50,406	1:49.60	99
1996	Knockadoon	4	J.D. Bailey	112	Halo's Image	117	Thorny Crown	113	66,216	1:48.80	106
1997	Louis Quatorze	4	P. Day	119	Knockadoon	113	King James	113	66,526	1:49.60	115
1998	Storm Broker	4	R.J. Albarado	114	Delay of Game	119	Gator Dancer	114	67,208	1:48.20	106
1999	Jazz Club	4	P. Day	115	Smile Again	115	Early Warning	115	67,456	1:48.16	104
2000	Midway Magistrate	6	S.J. Sellers	116	Liberty Gold	116	Early Warning	118	67,518	1:49.15	101
2001	Broken Vow	4	E.S. Prado	116	Perfect Cat	116	Jadada	116	66,216	1:48.47	116
2002	Duckhorn	5	J.F. Chavez	116	Parade Leader	120	Connected	118	66,464	1:50.18	114
2003	Mineshaft	4	R.J. Albarado	120	American Style	116	Metatron	116	68,386	1:48.52	116
2004	Midway Road	4	R.J. Albarado	116	Evening Attire	116	Sir Cherokee	120	93,000	1:46.78	123

Beyer Index: 109.43

BERKELEY BREEDERS' CUP HANDICAP (G3), 1 Mile, 3-Year-Olds and Up, Golden Gate Fields, 2004 Purse: $94,375

Year	Winner	Age	Jockey	Wt.	Second	Wt.	Third	Wt.	Win Value	Time	Beyer
1981	Head Hawk	5	D. Sorenson	111	His Honor	115	Beau Moro	117	25,750	1:45.60	
1982	Foyt's Ack	7	R.M. Gonzalez	115	Borrego Sun	118	Pleasant Power	112	25,650	1:38.00	
1983	Pleasant Power	5	J.R. Anderson	115	Lord Advocate	117	Red Crescent	119	27,800	1:40.60	
1984	Songhay	5	J.C. Judice	114	Grand Balcony	113	The Jandy Man	113	27,300	1:35.40	
1985	Nak Ack	4	J.C. Judice	114	Holmbury	113	Chum Salmon	116	26,600	1:36.20	
1986	Sun Master	5	M. Castaneda	117	Beldale Lear	123	Prairie Breaker	114	25,400	1:34.60	
1987	Rocky Marriage	7	R. Baze	116	Dormello	115	Bagdad Dawn	112	32,250	1:36.80	
1988	Sanger Chief	5	T.T. Doocy	114	Lucky Harold H.	114	Power Forward	119	31,900	1:35.60	

Year	Winner	Age	Jockey	Wt.	Second	Wt.	Third	Wt.	Win Value	Time	Beyer
1989	Ongoing Mister	4	T.T. Doocy	114	Present Value	113	Lucky Harold H.	110	33,600	1:34.20	
1990	On the Menu	4	C.L. Davenport	112	Crackedbell	116	Ongoing Mister	117	31,600	1:34.80	99
1991	High Energy	4	R. Warren Jr	115	Bold Current	114	Beau's Alliance	115	32,800	1:35.60	90
1992	Music Prospector	5	R.D. Hansen	118	Michael's Flyer	115	Flying Continental	124	31,450	1:35.20	97
1993	Infamous Deed	5	R. Warren Jr	115	Misty Wind	116	J.F. Williams	115	25,960	1:35.67	91
1994	River Special	4	T. Chapman	115	He's Illustrious	116	Misty Wind	114	32,600	1:34.33	106
1995	Double Jab	4	R.Baze	115	Corslew	116	Cleante		49,725	1:35.18	103
1996	Houston Fleet M D	2	D.Carr	118	Slew'a Doop	116	Big Find	116	26,600	1:36.67	86
1998	Wild Wonder	4	R.Baze	115	General Royale	115	March Of Kings	116	51,450	1:35.18	111
1999	Hal's Pal	4	B.Blanc	117	Wild Wonder	122	Worldly Ways	115	75,000	1:34.96	112
2000	Voice Of Destiny	4	R. Meza	113	Mr.Doubledown	115	Twilight Affair	115	75,000	1:35.67	108
2001	Blade Prospector	6	O. Berrio	116	Dixie Dot Com	119	Milkwood	115	55,000	1:34.18	109
2002	Irisheyesareflying	6	J. Valdivia Jr	120	Boss Ego	116	Palmeiro	116	55,000	1:35.41	98
2003	I'madrifter	5	R.M. Gonzalez	115	Palmeiro	117	Skip to the Stone	116	55,000	1:35.13	98
2004	Snorter	4	R.A. Baze	116	Yougottawanna	116	Taste of Paradise	116	55,000	1:33.92	102

Beyer Index: 100.71

For previous runnings, refer to 1980 Manual.

BEST PAL (G2), 6 1/2 Furlongs, 2-Year-Olds, Del Mar, 2004 Purse: $147,000

Year	Winner	Age	Jockey	Wt.	Second	Wt.	Third	Wt.	Win Value	Time	Beyer
1972	Brave Dance	2	F. Toro	120	Groshawk	115	River Lad	118	12,625	1:29.80	
1973	Battery E.	2	W. Harris	115	Jenny's Boy	120	Ma'hen McTavish	115	12,750	1:30.60	
1974	Diabolo	2	W. Shoemaker	120	Trond Sang	114	Neat Claim	114	13,050	1:35.60	
1975	Crazy Channon	2	D. Pierce	115	Classy Surgeon	114	Lexington Laugh	117	15,500	1:37.20	
1976	Visible	2	L. Pincay Jr	117	Habitony	114	Replant	115	16,200	1:35.80	
1977	Spanish Way	2	L. Pincay Jr	117	Tampoy	114	Misrepresentation	114	16,700	1:36.00	
1978	Flying Paster	2	D. Pierce	117	Roman Oblisk	117	Runaway Hit	114	19,500	1:35.60	
1979	Doonesbury	2	S. Hawley	113	Executive Counsel	115	Defiance	115	19,300	1:35.40	
1980	Bold and Gold	2	D.C. Hall	113	Splendid Spruce	115	Sir Dancer	113	22,550	1:37.40	
1981	The Captain	2	L. Pincay Jr	117	Distant Heart	115	Gato del Sol	115	26,400	1:36.60	
1982	Roving Boy	2	E. Delahoussaye	115	Encourager	115	Full Choke	117	30,650	1:35.40	
1983	Party Leader	2	R. Sibille	116	Juliet's Pride	115	Gumboy	116	31,550	1:37.20	
1984	Saratoga Six	2	A. Cordero Jr	120	Private Jungle	117	Indigenous	116	31,650	1:36.80	
1985	Swear	2	E. Delahoussaye	116	Bright Tom	116	Smokey Orbit	114	32,750	1:36.60	
1986	Temperate Sil	2	W. Shoemaker	117	Polar Jet	117	Gold on Green	115	32,250	1:23.00	
1987	Purdue King	2	C.J. McCarron	121	Accomplish Ridge	117	Mixed Pleasure	119	38,500	1:23.20	
1988	Rob an Plunder	2	C.J. McCarron	119	Mountain Ghost	117	Pokarito	117	47,750	1:23.00	
1989	A Sir Dancer	2	E. Delahoussaye	117	Drag Race	115	Patches	113	47,550	1:23.00	
1990	Best Pal	2	P.A. Valenzuela	119	Xray	117	Sunshine Machine	117	46,575	1:22.20	
1991	Scherando	2	F. Mena	121	Star Recruit	117	Prince Wild	119	47,620	1:22.40	92
1992	Devil Diamond	2	K.J. Desormeaux	117	Wheeler Oil	119	Crafty	117	45,900	1:22.60	86
1993	Creston	3	C.A. Black	117	Troyalty	121	Flying Sensation	115	45,900	1:16.20	89
1994	Timber Country	2	Solis A	117	Desert Mirage	115	Supremo	117	46,575	1:16.60	79
1995	Cobra King	2	Baze RA	117	Northern Afleet	117	Desert Native	117	60,350	1:15.80	93
1996	Swiss Yodeler	2	A. Solis	121	Golden Bronze	117	Deeds Not Words	117	65,550	1:16.00	97
1997	Old Topper	2	A. Solis	117	King of the Wild	117	Souvenir Copy	117	68,825	1:16.40	92
1998	Worldly Manner	2	G.L. Stevens	117	Domination	117	Waki American	115	65,580	1:16.60	96
1999	Dixie Union	2	A. Solis	121	Exchange Rate	117	Captain Steve	117	90,000	1:16.40	97
2000	Flame Thrower	2	C.S. Nakatani	117	Trailthefox	121	Legendary Weave	117	90,000	1:16.51	96
2001	Officer	2	V. Espinoza	121	Metatron	117	Essence of Dubai	117	90,000	1:15.08	106
2002	Kafwain	2	V. Espinoza	117	Chief Planner	117	Outta Here	117	90,000	1:17.00	93
2003	Perfect Moon	2	P.A. Valenzuela	122	Capitano	118	Military Mandate	118	90,000	1:16.90	84
2004	Roman Ruler	2	C.S. Nakatani	118	Actxecutive	118	Slewsbag	116	90,000	1:15.93	103

Beyer Index: 93.07

BEVERLY D (G1), 1 3/16 Miles (Turf), Fillies and Mares, 3-Year-Olds and Up, Arlington Park, 2004 Purse: $750,000

Year	Winner	Age	Jockey	Wt.	Second	Wt.	Third	Wt.	Win Value	Time	Beyer
1989	Claire Marine	4	C.J. McCarron	123	Capades	117	Gaily Gaily	123	300,000	2:01.80	
1990	Reluctant Guest	4	R.G. Davis	123	Lady Winner	123	Royal Touch	123	300,000	1:53.20	
1991	Fire the Groom	4	G.L. Stevens	123	Colour Chart	123	Miss Josh	123	300,000	1:53.40	107
1992	Kostroma	6	K.J. Desormeaux	123	Ruby Tiger	123	Dance Smartly	123	300,000	1:54.00	104
1993	Flawlessly	5	C.J. McCarron	123	Via Borghese	123	Let's Elope	123	300,000	1:55.60	103
1994	Hatoof	5	W.R. Swinburn	123	Flawlessly	123	Potridee	123	300,000	1:55.40	104
1995	Possibly Perfect	5	C.S. Nakatani	123	Alice Springs	123	Alpride	123	300,000	1:54.80	105
1996	Timarida	4	J.P. Murtagh	123	Perfect Arc	123	Alpride	123	300,000	1:54.00	109
1997	Memories of Silver	4	J.D. Bailey	123	Maxzene	123	Dance Design	123	300,000	1:54.20	110
2000	Snow Polina	4	J.D. Bailey	123	Happanunoit	123	Country Garden	123	300,000	1:55.87	105
2001	England's Legend	4	C.S. Nakatani	123	The Seven Seas	123	Spook Express	123	420,000	1:56.75	109
2002	Golden Apples	4	P.A. Valenzuela	123	Astra	123	England's Legend	123	420,000	1:54.86	108
2003	Heat Haze	4	J. Valdivia Jr	123	Bien Nicole	123	Riskaverse	123	420,000	1:55.94	104
2004	Crimson Palace	5	L. Dettori	123	Riskaverse	123	Necklace	117	450,000	1:56.58	102

Beyer Index: 105.83

BEVERLY HILLS HANDICAP (G2), 1 1/4 Miles (Turf), Fillies and Mares, 3-Year-Olds and Up, Hollywood Park, 2004 Purse: $200,000

Year	Winner	Age	Jockey	Wt.	Second	Wt.	Third	Wt.	Win Value	Time	Beyer
1938	Brown Jade	4	N. Richardson	115	Rolling Ball	107	Pala Chief	104	4,725	1:45.80	
1939	Bubbling Boy	3	J. Robertson	118	Smoky Snyder	112	Maysette	108	2,110	1:40.20	
1968	Pink Pigeon	4	W. Harris	127	Desert Law	118	Pombal	114	19,700	2:15.20	
1969	Miss Ribot	4	D. Pierce	116	Courageously	111	Princess Endeavour	109	16,850	2:16.40	
1970	Pattee Canyon	5	W. Shoemaker	124	Blow Up II	117	Summer Sorrow	108	32,950	2:13.00	
1971	Manta	5	L. Pincay Jr	127	Typecast	116	Hail the Grey	107	39,400	2:12.20	
1972	Hill Circus	4	W. Shoemaker	115	Manta	116	Typecast	127	37,600	2:13.20	
1973	Le Cle	4	W. Shoemaker	119	Pallisima	115	Convenience	124	49,900	2:14.80	
1974	La Zanzara	4	D. Pierce	120	Mon Miel	114	Dogtooth Violet	116	38,000	2:14.20	
1975	La Zanzara	5	D. Pierce	122	Dulcia	123	Mercy Dee	110	46,500	2:14.80	
1976	Bastonera II	5	L. Pincay Jr	121	Miss Toshiba	124	Miss Tokyo	115	38,800	1:50.20	
1977	Swingtime	5	F. Toro	120	Fortunate Betty	115	Bastonera II	126	25,200	1:48.40	
1978	Swingtime	6	F. Toro	119	Grande Brisa	115	Drama Critic	118	48,000	1:48.40	
1979	Giggling Girl	5	C.J. McCarron	117	Country Queen	123	More So	116	50,100	1:47.60	
1980	Country Queen	5	L. Pincay Jr	122	Wishing Well	122	The Very One	117	50,550	1:47.40	
1981	Track Robbery	5	P.A. Valenzuela	120	Princess Karenda	121	Save Wild Life	115	61,800	1:46.80	
1982	Sangue	4	W. Shoemaker	119	Ack's Secret	123	Miss Huntington	117	64,300	1:47.40	
1983	Absentia	4	F. Toro	115	Latrone	110	Triple Tipple	118	68,500	1:49.00	
1984	Royal Heroine	4	F. Toro	123	Adored	121	Comedy Act	118	93,200	1:47.20	
1985	Johnica	4	G.L. Stevens	115	Estrapade	125	L'Attrayante	118	61,900	1:48.20	
1986	Estrapade	6	F. Toro	122	Treizieme	115	Sauna	117	63,800	1:59.00	
1987	Auspiciante	6	P.A. Valenzuela	117	Reloy	120	Festivity	114	64,600	1:46.20	
1988	Fitzwilliam Place	4	A. Gryder	119	Ladanum	114	Chapel of Dreams	117	98,200	1:47.20	
1989	Claire Marine	4	C.J. McCarron	120	Fitzwilliam Place	121	No Review	116	93,100	1:47.20	
1990	Beautiful Melody	4	K.J. Desormeaux	115			Stylish Star	116	82,300	1:47.00	99
	Reluctant Guest	4	R.G. Davis	116							
1991	Alcando	5	J. Garcia	113	Fire the Groom	120	Countus In	117	130,200	1:46.40	106
1992	Flawlessly	4	C.J. McCarron	122	Kostroma	124	Alcando	113	104,000	1:47.00	103
1993	Flawlessly	5	C.J. McCarron	123	Jolypha	121	Party Cited	117	180,200	1:47.00	108
1994	Corrazona	4	G.L. Stevens	119	Hollywood Wildcat	124	Flawlessly	124	188,400	1:47.40	102
1995	Alpride	4	C.J. McCarron	115	Possibly Perfect	124	Wandesta	119	185,000	1:46.60	108
1996	Different	4	C.J. McCarron	117	Bail Out Becky	118	Flagbird	118	163,800	2:00.60	105
1997	Windsharp	6	C.S. Nakatani	122	Different	121	Donna Viola	122	180,000	2:00.60	108
1998	Squeak	4	G.L. Stevens	115	Sixy Saint	115	Freeport Flight	114	180,000	2:01.56	102
1999	Virginie	5	L. Pincay Jr	118	Tranquility Lake	122	Keeper Hill	118	150,000	2:00.21	108
2000	Happyanunoit	5	B. Blanc	121	Sweet Life	115	Polaire	116	150,000	1:59.32	107
2001	Astra	5	K.J. Desormeaux	121	Happyanunoit	122	Kalypso Katie	116	120,000	1:59.61	107
2002	Astra	6	K.J. Desormeaux	124	Peu a Peu	116	Crazy Ensign	117	150,000	1:58.56	107
2003	Voodoo Dancer	5	C.S. Nakatani	120	Dublino	122	Megahertz	117	120,000	2:00.80	106
2004	Light Jig	4	A. Solis	114	Moscow Burning	117	Noches de Rosa	118	120,000	2:01.52	101

Beyer Index: 105.13

Distance 1 1/16 miles for California foals in 1938; 1 mile for California-foaled 3-year-olds (both sexes) in 1939; 1 3/8 miles 1968–75; 1 1/4 miles in 1986. Run on main course in 1938 and 1939

BEWITCH (G3), 1 1/2 Miles (Turf), Fillies and Mares, 4-Year-Olds and Up, Keeneland Race Course, 2004 Purse: $113,400

Year	Winner	Age	Jockey	Wt.	Second	Wt.	Third	Wt.	Win Value	Time	Beyer
1962	Bonnie's Girl	2	C. Meaux	114	Nalee	111	The Smoocher	114	9,766	:48.20	
1963	Royal Bund	2	A. Gomez	114	Cadabra	114	Vera T.	114	8,547	:49.40	
1964	Mississippi Mama	2	R. Baldwin	114	Swoon's Tune	114	Wing Revoked	114	8,872	:48.20	
1965	Justakiss	2	K. Knapp	114	Hurry Star	114	Balla Fib	114	8,182	:53.00	
1965	Ole Liz	2	W. Shoemaker	119	Champagne Women	114			8,052	:52.40	
					Sturdy Gerty	115					
1966	Shore	2	J. Nichols	115	Lotta Miss	114	Lady Goldie	113	7,735	:52.00	
1966	Furl Sail	2	E. Fires	114	Idle Dreamer	119	Ritanita	114	7,800	:52.60	
1967	Jet to Market	2	G. Overton	119	Blue Carbon	114	Shenow	114	9,051	:51.60	
1968	Royalty Note	2	M. Manganello	114	Alert Princess	114	Artist Johanna	114	15,112	:51.00	
1969	Little Tudor	2	D.E. Whited	114	Glenary	114	Pussy Footing	112	15,242	:52.80	
1970	Fancy Road	2	N. Menard	119	Mistq Joy	114	Holda	111	14,105	:52.20	
1971	Sidle	2	D. Kassen	114	Swing Step	116	Miss Beaustark	114	12,967	:52.20	
1971	Cautious Bidder	2	J. Nichols	115	Apple Jackie	114	Little Queensw're	114	13,032	:52.00	
1972	Gallant Davelle	2	J. Nicholas	119	All in Fun	111	Greek Loveliness	114	13,536	:52.40	
1972	Bosun Strike	2	A. DeSpirito	114	Barrister Girl	114	Say Cheesecake	111	13,731	:53.20	
1973	Me and Connie	2	J. Nichols	121	Lady Bahla	115	Bundler	115	12,603	:52.40	
1974	Dancing Home	2	A. Patterson	116	Semi Princess	119	Spark	116	11,793	:53.60	
1974	Secret's Out	2	D. Brumfield	119	Floral Princess	116	Ain't Easy	119	11,727	:53.20	
1975	Pink Jade	2	E. Delahoussaye	119	Old Goat	119	T.V. Vixen	119	12,139	:51.60	
1976	Olden	2	R. Breen	116	Bagiorix	116	Foreverness	119	11,030	:52.40	

Year	Winner	Age	Jockey	Wt.	Second	Wt.	Third	Wt.	Win Value	Time	Beyer
1976	Fun and Tears	2	L. Melancon	119	Miss Cigarette	119	Every Move	116	11,290	:51.40	
1977	Crystalan	2	G. Patterson	119	No No-Nos	119	Surprise Trip	119	11,947	:53.00	
1978	Twenty One Inch	2	E. Delahoussaye	119	All's Well	119	Satan's Pride	116	11,846	:52.60	
1979	Miss Baja	4	E. Maple	119	Likely Exchange	110	Plains and S'mple	113	23,285	1:43.00	
1980	Jolie Dutch	4	R.P. Romero	113	Miss Baja	112	Mi Muchacha	113	29,039	1:43.00	
1981	Bold 'n Determined	4	E. Delahoussaye	121	Likely Exchange	113	Save Wild Life	110	38,236	1:43.80	
1982	Expressive Dance	4	D. Brumfield	116	Mean Martha	115	Really Royal	116	36,416	1:43.40	
1983	Try Something New	4	P. Day	110	Kattegat's Pride	119	Number	119	37,001	1:44.20	
1984	Heatherten	5	S. Maple	119	Any Spray	110	Marisma	119	36,628	1:45.80	
1985	Sintra	4	K.K. Allen	119	Electric Fanny	110	Switching Trick	110	43,964	1:43.60	
1986	Devalois	4	E. Maple	118	Debutant Dancer	113	Natural Approach	113	35,685	1:54.00	
1987	Gerrie Singer	6	R.L. Frazier	113	Innsbruck	110	Debutant Dancer	110	36,221	1:52.60	
1988	Beauty Cream	5	P. Day	121	Native Mommy	121	Fraulein Lieber	113	55,933	1:51.60	
1989	Gaily Gaily	6	J.A. Krone	122	Chez Chez Chez	114	Bl'ss'm'ngB'ty	113	53,853	1:50.00	
1990	Coolawin	4	J.D. Bailey	122	To the Lighthouse	114	Ann Alleged	122	54,048	1:49.20	
1991	Miss Unnameable	7	P. Day	112	Cheerful Spree	117	The Caretaker	114	56,220	1:50.00	97
1992	La Gueriere	4	B.D. Peck	114	Indian Fashion	117	Plenty of Grace	112	54,430	1:48.20	100
1993	Miss Lenora	4	J.A. Krone	112	Hero's Love	117	Radiant Ring	119	51,367	1:50.60	93
1994	Freewheel	5	P. Day	114	Key Chance	114	Amal Hayati	119	50,871	1:50.20	94
1995	Market Booster	6	P. Day	119	Memories	113	Abigailthewife	114	50,731	2:29.20	101
1996	Memories	5	S.J. Sellers	117	Future Act	117	Curtain Raiser	114	66,030	2:30.00	100
1997	Cymbala	4	P. Day	113	Noble Cause	113	Last Approach	113	69,130	2:28.80	95
1998	Maxzene	5	J.A. Santos	113	Cuando	113	Gastronomical	113	69,626	2:30.40	104
1999	Bursting Forth	5	J.F. Chavez	114	Moments of Magic	114	Pinafore Park	114	68,758	2:27.54	97
2000	The Seven Seas	4	A. Solis	116	Innuendo	116	Hollywood Baldcat	116	70,122	2:29.31	99
2001	Keemoon	5	J.D. Bailey	120	Playact	116	Krisada	116	124,000	2:30.28	99
2002	Sweetest Thing	4	M. Guidry	120	Lapuma	116	Lady Upstage	116	68,634	2:31.97	99
2003	Lilac Queen	5	J.D. Bailey	116	Beyond the Waves	116	San Dare	118	69,503	2:29.70	99
2004	Meridiana	4	E.S. Prado	118	Alternate	116	Binya	118	70,308	2:31.05	97

Beyer Index: 98.14

BLACK-EYED SUSAN (G2), 1 1/8 Miles, 3-Year-Old Fillies, Pimlico, 2004 Purse: $200,0000

Year	Winner	Age	Jockey	Wt.	Second	Wt.	Third	Wt.	Win Value	Time	Beyer
1952	Real Delight	3	E. Arcaro	121	Dinewisely	121	Parading Lady	121	16,500	1:51.80	
1953	Spinning Top	3	C. Burr	121	Milspals	121	Wings o' Morn	121	17,750	1:47.20	
1954	Queen Hopeful	3	J. Adams	121	Gweny G.	121	Walla	121	16,550	1:45.80	
1955	High Voltage	3	E. Arcaro	121	Bless Pat	121	Hen Party	121	1,100	1:46.20	
1956	Princess Turia	3	W. Hartack	121	Beyond	121	Hadareward	121	15,500	1:45.60	
1957	Pillow Talk	3	W. Hartack	121	Jota Jota	121	Woodlawn	121	17,350	1:45.00	
1958	Daumay	3	C. Rogers	121	Movitave	121	Stay Smoochie	121	16,100	1:46.60	
1959	Toulene	3	K. Korte	121	Corvina	121	San Ju Lee	121	15,090	1:48.80	
1960	Airmans Guide	3	W. Harmatz	121	Chalvedele	121	Warlike	121	14,862	1:46.20	
1961	Funloving	3	R, Ussery	121	My Portrait	121	First Sitting	121	15,665	1:45.80	
1962	Batter Up	3	L. Adams	121	Narola	121	Spooky Creature	121	16,347	1:45.80	
1963	Nalee	3	W. Chambers	121	Medici	121	Batteur	121	15,975	1:46.80	
1964	Bold Queen	3	T. Lee	121	Sceree	121	Sabemar	121	15,600	1:47.00	
1965	Sue Baru	3	R. Witmer	121	Wendy's Crown	121	Cavans Rose	121	15,584	1:48.40	
1966	Holly-O	3	J. Culmone	121	Chalina	121	Justakiss	121	18,980	1:44.80	
1967	Farest Nan	3	O. Rosado	111	Back in Paris	111	Devotedly	111	18,882	1:44.00	
1968	Singing Rain	3	G. Patterson	111	Syrian Sea	121	Copper Canyon	111	22,360	1:44.20	
1969	Process Shot	3	C. Baltazar	121	Loyal Ruler	113	Around the Horn	111	22,880	1:44.00	
1970	Office Queen	3	C.H. Marquez	118	Princess Roycraft	116	Artists Proof	116	22,522	1:43.80	
1971	At Arms Length	3	R. Barnes	118	Movette	116	Sew to Bed	114	23,367	1:43.20	
1972	Summer Guest	3	R. Turcotte	114	Twixt	113	Barely Even	121	23,140	1:44.00	
1973	Fish Wife	3	D. Gargan	111	Guided Missile	112	Out Cold	116	2,265	1:44.00	
1974	Blowing Rock	3	A. Agnello	111	Heydairya	111	Shantung Silk	116	22,425	1:43.00	
1975	My Juliet	3	A. Hill	116	Gala Lil	114	Funalon	121	37,635	1:44.00	
1976	What a Summer	3	C.J. McCarron	111	Dearly Precious	121	Artfully	114	37,895	1:42.40	
1977	Small Raja	3	A. Cordero Jr	114	Northern Sea	121	Enthused	116	54,503	1:42.80	
1978	Caesar's Wish	3	D. Wright	121	Jevalin	116	Miss Baja	121	55,120	1:44.20	
1979	Davona Dale	3	J. Velasquez	121	Phoebe's Donkey	118	Plankton	121	72,670	1:42.60	
1980	Weber City Miss	3	V. Bracciale Jr	118	Bishop's Ring	111	Champagne Star	114	74,620	1:44.40	
1981	Dame Mysterieuse	3	E. Maple	121	Wayward Lass	121	Real Prize	121	72,800	1:44.20	
1982	Delicate Ice	3	D. Brumfield	114	Trove	121	Milingo	121	74,945	1:44.60	
1983	Batna	3	L.D. Ruch	121	Lovin Touch	116	Weekend Surprise	121	75,400	1:42.40	
1984	Lucky Lucky Lucky	3	A. Cordero Jr	121	Sintra	116	Duo Disco	121	100,060	1:41.20	
1985	Koluctoo's Jill	3	C.J. McCarron	121	Denver Express	116	A Joyful Spray	116	74,295	1:43.00	
1986	Family Style	3	C.J. McCarron	121	Steel Maiden	121	Firgie's Jule	121	100,385	1:44.60	
1987	Grecian Flight	3	C. Perret	121	Bal du Bois	121	Arctic Cloud	121	101,750	1:44.20	

Year	Winner	Age	Jockey	Wt.	Second	Wt.	Third	Wt.	Win Value	Time	Beyer
1988	Costly Shoes	3	P. Day	121	Thirty Eight Go Go	121	Lost Kitty	121	97,915	1:44.80	
1989	Imaginary Lady	3	G. Stevens	122	Some Romance	122	Moonlight Martini	117	150,000	1:48.20	
1990	Charon	3	C. Perret	122	Valay Maid	122	Bright Candles	122	150,000	1:48.40	95
1991	Wide Country	3	S.N. Chavez	122	John's Decision	117	Nalees Pin	117	150,000	1:51.20	97
1992	Miss Legality	3	C.J. McCarron	122	Known Feminist	114	Diamond Duo	114	150,000	1:51.00	94
1993	Aztec Hill	3	M.E. Smith	122	Traverse City	114	Jacody	117	120,000	1:49.60	103
1994	Calipha	3	R. Wilson	114	Bunting	114	Golden Braids	114	120,000	1:51.00	95
1995	Serena's Song	3	G.L. Stevens	122	Conquistadoress	115	Rare Opportunity	115	120,000	1:48.40	113
1996	Mesabi Maiden	3	M. E. Smith	115	Cara Rafaela	122	Ginny Lynn	122	120,000	1:51.00	93
1997	Salt It	3	C.H. Marquez Jr	117	Buckeye Search	122	Holiday Ball	115	120,000	1:50.40	97
1998	Added Gold	3	J.R. Velazquez	115	Tappin' Ginger	115	Hansel's Girl	117	120,000	1:49.60	95
1999	Silverbulletday	3	G.L. Stevens	122	Dreams Gallore	117	Vee Vee Star	115	120,000	1:47.80	109
2000	Jostle	3	K.J. Desormeaux	122	March Magic	122	Impending Bear	122	120,000	1:52.56	93
2001	Two Item Limit	3	R. Migliore	122	Indy Glory	117	Tap Dance	122	120,000	1:50.84	96
2002	Chamrousse	3	J.D. Bailey	115	Shop Till You Drop	117	Autumn Creek	115	120,000	1:51.61	92
2003	Roar Emotion	3	J.R. Velazquez	122	Fircroft	119	Santa Catarina	117	120,000	1:52.33	93
2004	Yearly Report	3	J.D. Bailey	122	Pawyne Princess	115	Rare Gift	115	120,000	1:52.65	87

Beyer Index: 96.80

(TOYOTA) BLUE GRASS (G1), 1 1/8 Miles, 3-Year-Olds, Keeneland Race Course, 2004 Purse: $750,000

Year	Winner	Age	Jockey	Wt.	Second	Wt.	Third	Wt.	Win Value	Time	Beyer
1911	Governor Gray	3	G. Molesworth	119	Meridian	122	Any Port	122	2,350	1:15.20	
1912	Sprite	3	C.H. Schilling	117	Wheelwright	122	Duval	122	1,447	1:51.20	
1913	Foundation	3	C. Peak	122	Donerail	122	Gowell	117	906	1:51.20	
1914	Bronzewing	3	J.McCabe	117	John Gund	122	Old Ben	119	2,068	1:51.80	
1919	Regalo	3	F. Murphy	117	Under Fire	122	Sennings Park	122	3,005	1:51.60	
1920	Peace Pennant	3	M. Garner	126	Donnacona	126	Damask	126	3,410	1:51.80	
1921	Black Servant	3	N. Barrett	126	Behave Yourself	126	Uncle Velo	126	3,170	1:54.60	
1922	Busy American	3	N. Barrett	126	Bet Mosie	126	Startle	121	3,130	1:55.80	
1923	Bo McMillan	3	D. Connelly	126	Anna M. Humphrey	121	Aspiration	126	3,120	1:56.80	
1924	Altawood	3	L. McDermott	126	Beau Butler	126	Bob Tail	126	3,120	1:51.80	
1925	Step Along	3	E. Pool	126	Broadway Jones	126	Bill Strap	126	3,080	1:51.60	
1926	Bubbling Over	3	E. Legere	126	Boot to Boot	126	Helen's Babe	121	3,090	1:49.60	
1937	Fencing	3	J. Westrope	121	Billionaire	123	Brooklyn	123	6,975	1:57.80	
1938	Bull Lea	3	I. Anderson	121	Menow	123	Redbreast	123	4,855	1:49.60	
1939	Heather Broom	3	B. James	121	Third Degree	121	Viscount	121	5,340	1:54.20	
1940	Bimelech	3	F.A. Smith	123	Roman	123	Bashful Duck	121	5,575	1:51.00	
1941	Our Boots	3	C. McCreary	123	Whirlaway	123	Valdina Paul	121	10,256	1:51.20	
1942	Shut Out	3	E. Arcaro	123	Bless Me	121	Equinox	121	10,042	1:52.40	
1943	Ocean Wave	3	W. Eads	123	Amber Light	123	Crest	121	9,250	1:53.80	
1944	Skytracer	3	M. Cafarella	121	Challenge Me	123	Alorter	123	9,800	1:52.60	
1945	Darby Dieppe	3	M. Calvert	121	Fighting Step	123	Air Sailor	123	9,500	1:53.40	
1946	Lord Boswell	3	E. Arcaro	123	Pellicle	123	In Ernest	121	10,450	1:51.60	
1947	Faultless	3	D. Dodson	126	Riskolater	123	John's Pride	121	11,900	1:51.20	
1948	Coaltown	3	N.L. Pierson	123	Billings	121	Shy Guy	126	12,300	1:49.20	
1949	Halt	3	C. McCreary	121	Johns Joy	126	Wine List	121	16,050	1:52.60	
1950	Mr. Trouble	3	D. Dodson	121	Oil Capitol	126	On the Mark	118	20,300	1:50.40	
1951	Mameluke	3	R. Adair	121	Phil D.	126	Hall of Fame	121	20,750	1:54.40	
1951	Ruhe	3	J.D. Jessop	123	Royal Mustang	121	Counterpoint	121	20,250	1:54.20	
	Sonic finished first but was disqualified and placed fourth										
1952	Gushing Oil	3	S. Brooks	123	Cold Command	121	Smoke Screen	121	19,447	1:52.40	
1953	Correspondent	3	E. Arcaro	121	Straight Face	126	Money Broker	126	19,967	1:49.00	
1954	Goyamo	3	E. Arcaro	123	Hasseyampa	121	Admiral Porter	121	24,290	1:50.60	
	Black Metal finished third but was disqualified and placed fourth										
1955	Racing Fool	3	H. Moreno	121	Jean's Joe	123	Munchausen	123	22,112	1:51.80	
1956	Toby B.	3	R.L. Baird	121	Career Boy	126	Reaping Right	126	21,235	1:51.00	
1957	Round Table	3	R. Neves	126	One-Eyed King	121	Manteau	121	19,600	1:47.40	
1958	Plion	3	D. Erb	126	Warren G.	121	Flamingo	117	21,322	1:52.80	
1959	Tomy Lee	3	W. Shoemaker	126	Dunce	121	Scotland	123	20,607	1:48.60	
1960	Tompion	3	W. Shoemaker	126	Victoria Park	126	Lurullah	121	19,535	1:48.60	
1961	Sherluck	3	B. Baeza	121	Flutterby	126	Mr. Consistency	126	22,250	1:48.60	
1962	Ridan	3	M. Ycaza	126	Decidedly	121	Roman Line	126	21,580	1:47.60	
1963	Chateaugay	3	B. Baeza	121	Get Around	121	Lemon Twist	121	19,695	1:48.00	
1964	Northern Dancer	3	W. Hartack	126	Allen Adair	121	Royal Shuck	121	19,207	1:49.80	
1965	Lucky Debonair	3	W. Shoemaker	126	Swift Ruler	126	Mr. Pak	121	19,760	1:49.00	
1966	Abe's Hope	3	W. Shoemaker	123	Graustark	126	Rehabilitate	123	19,175	1:49.40	
1967	Diplomat Way	3	J. Sellers	126	Proud Clarion	121	Gentleman James	126	20,345	1:49.60	
1968	Forward Pass	3	I. Valenzuela	126	T.V. Commercial	126	Francie's Hat	121	20,995	1:47.80	
1969	Arts and Letters	3	W. Shoemaker	126	Traffic Mark	126	Mr. Coincidence	123	20,182	1:47.80	
1970	Dust Commander	3	M. Manganello	123	Corn Off the Cob	126	Naskra	126	21,434	1:51.20	

Year	Winner	Age	Jockey	Wt.	Second	Wt.	Third	Wt.	Win Value	Time	Beyer
1971	Impetuously	3	E. Guerin	121	Twist the Axe	126	Dynastic	121	22,441	1:49.40	
1972	Riva Ridge	3	R. Turcotte	126	Sensitive Music	121	Thurloe Square	121	32,305	1:49.60	
1973	My Gallant	3	A. Cordero Jr	117	Our Native	123	Warbucks	117	37,765	1:49.60	
							Impecunious	126			
1974	Judger	3	L. Pincay Jr	123	Big Latch	117	Gold and Myrrh	114	42,607	1:49.20	
1975	Master Derby	3	D.G. McHargue	123	Honey Mark	117	Prince Thou Art	123	39,877	1:49.00	
1976	Honest Pleasure	3	B. Baeza	121	Certain Roman	121	Inca Roca	121	73,027	1:49.40	
1977	For the Moment	3	A. Cordero Jr	121	Run Dusty Run	121	Western Wind	121	77,578	1:50.20	
1978	Alydar	3	J. Velasquez	121	Raymond Earl	121	Go Forth	121	77,350	1:49.60	
1979	Spectacular Bid	3	R.J. Franklin	121	Lot O' Gold	121	Bishop's Choice	121	76,657	1:50.00	
1980	Rockhill Native	3	J. Oldham	121	Super Moment	121	Gold Stage	121	84,208	1:50.00	
1981	Proud Appeal	3	J. Fell	121	Law Me	121	Golden Derby	121	120,559	1:51.40	
1982	Linkage	3	W. Shoemaker	121	Gato Del Sol	121	Wavering Monarch	121	127,774	1:48.00	
1983	Play Fellow	3	J. Cruguet	121	Desert Wine	121	Copelan	121	121,924	1:49.40	
	Marfa finished second but disqualified and placed fourth										
1984	Taylor's Special	3	P. Day	121	Silent King	121	Charmed Rook	121	133,883	1:52.20	
1985	Chief's Crown	3	D. MacBeth	121	Floating Reserve	121	Banner Bob	121	127,740	1:47.60	
1986	Bachelor Beau	3	L. Melancon	121	Bolshoi Boy	121	Bold Arrangement	121	171,290	1:51.20	
1987	War	3	W.H. McCauley	121	Leo Castelli	121	Alysheba	121	148,135	1:48.40	
	Alysheba finished first but was disqualified and placed third										
1988	Granacus	3	J. Vasquez	121	Intensive Command	121	Regal Classic	121	190,856	1:52.20	
1989	Western Playboy	3	R.P. Romero	121	Dispersal	121	Tricky Creek	121	185,900	1:51.20	
1990	Summer Squall	3	P. Day	121	Land Rush	121	Unbridled	121	185,006	1:48.60	
1991	Strike the Gold	3	C.W. Antley	121	Fly So Free	121	Nowork All Play	121	260,520	1:48.40	
1992	Pistols and Roses	3	J. Vasquez	121	Conte di Savoya	121	Ecstatic Ride	121	325,000	1:49.00	104
1993	Prairie Bayou	3	M.E. Smith	121	Wallenda	121	Dixieland Heat	121	310,000	1:49.60	96
1994	Holy Bull	3	M.E. Smith	121	Valiant Nature	121	Mahogany Hall	121	310,000	1:50.00	113
1995	Wild Syn	3	R.P. Romero	121	Suave Prospect	121	Tejano Run	121	310,000	1:49.20	109
1996	Skip Away	3	S.J. Sellers	121	Louis Quatorze	121	Editor's Note	121	434,000	1:47.20	113
1997	Pulpit	3	S.J. Sellers	121	Acceptable	121	Stolen Gold	121	434,000	1:49.80	106
1998	Halory Hunter	3	G.L. Stevens	123	Lil's Lad	123	Cape Town	123	465,000	1:47.80	111
1999	Menifee	3	P. Day	123	Cat Thief	123	Vicar	123	465,000	1:48.66	107
2000	High Yield	3	P. Day	123	More Than Ready	123	Wheelaway	123	465,000	1:48.79	106
2001	Millennium Wind	3	L. Pincay Jr	123	Songandaprayer	123	Dollar Bill	123	465,000	1:48.32	114
2002	Harlan's Holiday	3	E. Prado	123	Booklet	123	Ocean Sound	123	465,000	1:51.51	98
2003	Peace Rules	3	E.S. Prado	123	Brancusi	123	Offlee Wild	123	465,000	1:51.73	104
2004	The Cliff's Edge	3	S.J. Sellers	123	Lion Heart	123	Limehouse	123	465,000	1:49.42	111

Beyer Index: 107.08

Run at old Lexington track prior to 1937; run at Churchill Downs 1943–45

BOILING SPRINGS (G3), 1 1/16 Miles (Turf), 3-Year-Old Fillies, Monmouth Park, 2004 Purse: $150,000

Year	Winner	Age	Jockey	Wt.	Second	Wt.	Third	Wt.	Win Value	Time	Beyer
1977	Council House	3	C. Perret	116	Rich Soil	119	Pressing Date	115	28,633	1:42.40	
1977	Critical Cousin	3	A. Cordero Jr	119	Sans Arc	116	Small Raja	123	28,243	1:42.40	
1978	Key to the Saga	3	J.L. Samyn	118	Terpsichorist	117	Amerigirl	112	28,519	1:41.40	
1978	Sisterhood	3	B. Gonzalez	112	Island Kiss	108	White Star Line	122	28,519	1:41.40	
1979	Jameela	3	V. Bracciale Jr	118	Fanny Saperstein	119	Whydidju	119	27,934	1:41.60	
1979	Gala Regatta	3	E. Maple	122	Record Acclaim	114	Tweak	113	27,934	1:41.00	
1980	Champagne Ginny	3	J. Velasquez	114	Qui Royalty	112	Classic Curves	111	26,505	1:42.00	
1980	Refinish	3	C.J. McCarron	113	Keep Off II	111	Cannon Boy	113	26,505	1:41.60	
1981	Irish Joy	3	C.C. Lopez	114	First Approach	113	Dance Forth	114	26,925	1:42.40	
1981	Wings of Grace	3	J. Velasquez	112	Andover Way	114	Pukka Princess	120	26,385	1:41.40	
1982	Sunny Sparkler	3	J.L. Samyn	113	Fact Finder	113	Milingo	117	26,895	1:41.40	
1982	Larida	3	E. Maple	119	Doodle	115	Distinctive Moon	114	27,075	1:41.40	
1983	Sabin	3	E. Maple	124	Aspen Rose	114	Propositioning	117	33,480	1:47.80	
1984	Possible Mate	3	D. MacBeth	116	Distaff Magic	113	Miss Audimar	112	33,930	1:41.80	
1985	Jolly Saint	3	J.A. Santos	114	Miss Hardwick	115	Dawn's Curtsey	115	49,620	1:41.00	
1986	Small Virtue	3	J.A. Santos	114	Sweet Velocity	115	Country Recital	121	47,985	1:41.60	
1986	Small Fir	3	D.B. Thomas	119	Ala Mahlik	116	Spring Innocence	113	47,985	1:41.60	
1987	Rullah Runner	3	W.A. Guerra	109	Tappiano	119	Key Bid	120	35,460	1:41.40	
1988	Siggebo	3	R. Wilson	119	Flashy Runner	115	Lusty Lady	113	51,930	1:43.20	
1989	Darby Shuffle	3	J.A. Krone	116	To the Lighthouse	116	Warranty Applied	115	53,730	1:40.60	
1990	Memories of Pam	3	J.D. Bailey	112	Hot Marshmellow	114	Baltic Chill	118	41,550	1:41.00	
1990	Plenty of Grace	3	J.D. Bailey	112	Southern Tradition	120	Sabina	114	40,950	1:42.20	
1991	Dance o'My Life	3	C.W. Antley	114	Monica Faye	111	Verbasle	115	45,000	1:41.40	97
1992	Captive Miss	3	J. Bravo	120	Logan's Mist	116	Aquilegia	113	45,000	1:40.60	94
1993	Tribulation	3	J.L. Samyn	110	Exotic Sea	114	Bright Penny	115	45,000	1:42.60	92
1994	Avie's Fancy	3	Ferrer JC	119	Teasing Charm	113	Knocknock	115	45,000	1:41.40	98
1995	Christmas Gift	3	W.H. McCauley	116	Ring by Spring	114	Transient Trend	114	48,000	1:43.40	94

Year	Winner	Age	Jockey	Wt.	Second	Wt.	Third	Wt.	Win Value	Time	Beyer
1995	Class Kris	3	Wilson R	118	Twilight Encounter	112	Appointed One	114	48,000	1:43.20	96
1996	Careless Heiress	3	C. Perret	118	Briarcliff	114	Dathuil	115	60,000	1:50.40	94
1997	Stoneleigh	3	J.A. Santos	114	Majestic Sunlight	114	Dancing Water	113	60,000	1:41.00	94
1997	Victory Chime	3	M.E. Smith	114	Miss Pop Carn	111	Colonial Play	113	60,000	1:41.80	87
1998	Mysterious Moll	3	J.L. Espinoza	116	Who Did It and Run	120	Thunder Kitten	116	120,000	1:40.00	99
1999	Wild Heart Dancing	3	J.F. Chavez	116	Confessional	118	Petunia	114	120,000	1:43.08	94
2000	Storm Dream	3	J.L. Samyn	116	Watch	117	Lady Dora	114	60,000	1:47.09	98
2001	Mystic Lady	3	E.M. Coa	120	Shooting Party	114	Plunderthepeasants	114	120,000	1:42.63	94
2002	Showlady	3	E.M. Coa	114	Dreamers Glory	116	With Patience	117	120,000	1:42.27	92
2004	Seducer's Song	3	J. Bravo	119	Go Robin	117	River Belle	117	90,000	1:45.66	93

Beyer Index: 94.40

Run on main track in 2001; Not run in 2003; Run at the Meadowlands prior to 2004.

BOLD RULER HANDICAP (G3), 6 Furlongs, 3-Year-Olds and Up, Belmont Park, 2004 Purse: $107,700

Year	Winner	Age	Jockey	Wt.	Second	Wt.	Third	Wt.	Win Value	Time	Beyer
1976	Chief Tamanaco	3	A. Cordero Jr	114	Relent	114	Jacks'n Square	116	21,750	1:09.80	
1977	Jaipur's Gem	4	J.L. Samyn	113	Expletive Deleted	107	Cojak	126	22,050	1:09.60	
1978	Half High	5	A. Santiago	115	Great Above	121	Cruise on In	110	25,665	1:09.40	
1979	Star de Naskra	4	J. Fell	119	Vencedor	126	Big John Taylor	119	48,420	1:09.20	
1980	Dave's Friend	5	V. Bracciale Jr	123	Tilt Up	121	Double Zeus	121	48,690	1:09.80	
1981	Dave's Friend	6	A.S. Black	123	Naughty Jimmy	119	Fappiano	119	48,510	1:09.60	
1982	Always Run Lucky	4	J. Miranda	123	King's Fashion	119	Band Practice	119	49,050	1:09.40	
1983	Maudlin	5	J.D. Bailey	119	Top Avenger	123	Singh Tu	121	49,500	1:11.60	
1984	Top Avenger	6	A. Graell	121	Believe the Queen	119	Au Point	123	55,350	1:09.80	
1985	Rocky Marriage	5	A. Cordero Jr	119	Entropy	121	Majestic Venture	119	51,390	1:08.80	
1986	Phone Trick	4	J. Velasquez	123	Love That Mac	119	Rexson's Bishop	121	70,680	1:08.80	
1987	Pine Tree Lane	5	A. Cordero Jr	118			Play the King	121	103,680	1:09.00	
1988	King's Swan	8	C.W. Antley	123	Seattle Knight	119	Faster Than Sound	123	103,680	1:10.20	
1989	Pok Ta Pok	4	R. Migliore	121	Teddy Drone	119	Claim	119	67,560	1:09.80	
1990	Mr. Nickerson	4	C.W. Antley	119	Dancing Pretense	119	Diamond Donnie	119	66,240	1:09.20	113
1991	Rousing Past	4	N. Santagata	119	True and Blue	121	Sunshine Jimmy	119	67,200	1:09.80	107
1992	Jolies Appeal	4	W.H. McCauley	119	Reappeal	119	Fiercely	119	67,560	1:09.20	110
1993	Slerp	4	J.A. Santos	119	Argyle Lake	121	Big Jewel	121	70,200	1:09.00	107
1994	Chief Desire	4	Velazquez JR	117	Boom Towner	120	Won Song	112	66,300	1:08.60	107
1995	Rizzi	4	Beckner DV	112	Lite the Fuse	111	Evil Bear	116	64,560	1:08.80	112
1996	Lite the Fuse	5	J.A. Krone	119	Cold Execution	115	Splendid Sprinter	115	64,500	1:09.40	116
1997	Punch Line	7	R.G. Davis	122	Golden Tent	111	Blissful State	116	64,980	1:08.80	103
1998	Kelly Kip	4	J.L. Samyn	117	Say Florida Sandy	111	Johnny Legit	114	66,120	1:07.60	121
1999	Kelly Kip	5	J.L. Samyn	123	Artax	115	Brushed On	115	64,440	1:07.54	120
2000	Brutally Frank	6	S.X. Bridgmohan	115	Kelly Kip	121	Kashatreya	115	65,880	1:08.64	112
2001	Say Florida Sandy	7	J. Bravo	117	Delaware Township	117	Lake Pontchartrain	113	65,520	1:08.67	111
2002	Left Bank	5	J.R. Velazquez	121	Silky Sweep	114	Say Florida Sandy	116	63,646	1:09.30	109
2003	Shake You Down	5	M.J. Luzzi	115	Here's Zealous	114	Peeping Tom	117	65,040	1:08.47	113
2004	Canadian Frontier	5	J.J. Castellano	111	Key Deputy	114	First Blush	113	64,620	1:08.97	107

Beyer Index: 111.20

BONNIE MISS (G2), 1 1/8 Miles, 3-Year-Old Fillies, Gulfstream Park, 2004 Purse: $200,000

Year	Winner	Age	Jockey	Wt.	Second	Wt.	Third	Wt.	Win Value	Time	Beyer
1971	Able Jan	5	R. Breen	113	Director	113	Field Avenue	113	10,035	1:45.20	
1972	Candid Catherine	3	J. Vasquez	117	Barely Even	117	Mrs. Cornwallis	114	21,150	1:23.20	
1973	Fun Palace	4	E. Fires	111	Hasty Jude	119	Viewpoise	113	14,145	1:44.40	
1974	City Girl	3	E. Maple	112	Maud Muller	112	Double Bend	112	21,540	1:22.60	
1975	Cheers Marion	4	M. Castaneda	113	Hinterland	116	Sum'r Sprite	114	10,207	1:42.20	
1975	Diomedia	4	M. Castaneda	116	Gems and Roses	122	Exclusive Lady	113	10,207	1:42.00	
1976	Get Swinging	5	A. Ramos	111	Twenty Six Girl	112	North of B'st'n	114	17,400	1:45.80	
1977	Herecomesthebride	3	L. Saumell	114	Grand Luxe	112	Rich Soil	112	20,970	1:21.80	
1978	Jevalin	3	M. Solomone	114	Raise a Companion	110	Sharp Belle	114	18,600	1:23.80	
1979	Davona Dale	3	J. Velasquez	122	Candy Eclair	122	Prove Me Special	114	17,546	1:21.00	
1980	Lien	3	E. Maple	112	Wistful	115	Champagne Ginny	114	18,510	1:22.00	
1981	Dame Mysterieuse	3	J.L. Samyn	118	Banner Gala	113	Heavenly Cause	121	52,335	1:44.40	
1982	Christmas Past	3	J. Vasquez	121	Norsan	113	Our Darling	112	34,830	1:44.20	
1983	Unaccompanied	3	R. Woodhouse	116	Bright Crocus	114	Dewl Reason	112	58,320	1:45.40	
1984	Miss Oceana	3	E. Maple	121	Enumerating	114	Katrinka	112	70,605	1:42.40	
1985	Lucy Manette	3	C. Perret	121	Outstandingly	121	Micki Bracken	121	72,240	1:44.80	
1986	Patricia J.K.	3	J.A. Santos	121	Noranc	121	Family Style	121	135,570	1:45.20	
1987	Mar Mar	3	W.A. Guerra	121	Super Cook	121	Without Feathers	118	90,000	1:44.60	

Year	Winner	Age	Jockey	Wt.	Second	Wt.	Third	Wt.	Win Value	Time	Beyer
1988	On to Royalty	3	C. Perret	121	Tomorrow's Child	121	Make Change	112	120,000	1:45.60	
1989	Open Mind	3	A. Cordero Jr	121	Seattle Meteor	121	Surging	114	120,000	1:43.80	
1990	Charon	3	E. Fires	121	Trumpet's Blare	121	De La Devil	121	120,000	1:44.60	
1991	Withallprobability	3	C. Perret	117	Fancy Ribbons	117	Outlasting	114	120,000	1:43.20	
1992	Spectacular Sue	3	W.S. Ramos	114	Spinning Round	117	Tricky Cinderella	112	120,000	1:44.00	92
1993	Dispute	3	J.D. Bailey	114	Sky Beauty	114	Lunar Spook	117	120,000	1:43.60	95
1994	Inside Information	3	M.E. Smith	114	Cinnamon Sugar	113	Jade Flush	114	120,000	1:42.80	93
1995	Mia's Hope	3	K.L. Chapman	117	Minister Wife	119	Incredible Blues	117	120,000	1:44.80	91
1996	My Flag	3	J.D. Bailey	117	Escena	114	La Rosa	117	120,000	1:45.60	100
1997	Glitter Woman	3	M.E. Smith	117	Southern Playgirl	119	Dixie Flag	114	120,000	1:43.20	103
1998	Banshee Breeze	3	R.P. Romero	114	Santaria	114	Cotton House Bay	114	120,000	1:46.40	89
1999	Three Ring	3	J.R. Velazquez	122	Olympic Charmer	117	Marley Vale	117	120,000	1:43.60	105
2000	Cash Run	3	J.D. Bailey	119	Deed I Do	114	Bejoyfulandrejoyce	114	120,000	1:44.11	96
2001	Tap Dance	3	J.D. Bailey	122	Halo Reailty	117	Unbridled Lassie	122	120,000	1:52.05	87
2002	Chamrousse	3	J.D. Bailey	115	Shop Till You Drop	117	Autumn Creek	115	120,000	1:51.61	92
2003	Ivanavinalot	3	J.R. Velazquez	122	My Boston Gal	120	Holiday Lady	118	120,000	1:50.72	95
2004	Last Song	3	E.S. Prado	118	Society Selection	120	Rare Gift	116	120,000	1:50.60	92

Beyer Index: 94.62

BOWLING GREEN HANDICAP (G2), 1 3/8 Miles (Turf), 3-Year-Olds and Up, Belmont Park, 2004 Purse: $150,000

Year	Winner	Age	Jockey	Wt.	Second	Wt.	Third	Wt.	Win Value	Time	Beyer
1958	Rafty	6	E. Guerin	124	One-Eyed King	116	Master Boing	122	18,810	2:17.20	
1959	Bell Hop	4	R. Ussery	116	King Grail	109	Pop Corn	120	18,810	2:14.60	
1960	Amber Morn	4	P. Anderson	113	Dunce	123	North Pole II	117	38,010	2:29.20	
1961	Dead Center	4	J. Yother	107	Wolfram	130	Leix	107	25,772	2:29.80	
1962	Royal Record	4	H. Woodhouse	110	Wise Ship	126	S'shine Cake	110	18,752	2:33.20	
1963	Pollingford	4	W. Harmatz	111	Tutankhamen	127	Hunter's Rock	107	18,070	2:45.40	
1964	Cedar Key	4	M. Ycaza	130	Irish Dandy	110	Chicoco	110	18,752	2:41.80	
1965	Or et Argent	4	W. Blum	113	Hot Dust	119	Pr'ce o'Pilsen	112	38,675	2:40.60	
1966	Moontrip	5	L. Adams	112	Flag	113	Knightly Manner	116	38,610	2:38.80	
1967	Poker	4	W. Boland	112	Assagai	127	Buckpasser	135	36,010	2:41.40	
1968	High Hat	4	E. Belmonte	128	Irish Rebellion	125	Ruffled Feathers	119	36,465	2:29.80	
1969	Czar Alexander	4	J. Velasquez	126	Ruffled Feathers	113	Jean-Pierre	115	38,610	2:27.40	
1970	Fort Marcy	6	J. Velasquez	127	Drumtop	120	Hitchcock	118	37,310	2:26.60	
1971	Drumtop	5	C. Baltazar	124	Fort Marcy	128	Practicante	115	34,080	2:25.40	
1972	Run the Gantlet	4	R. Woodhouse	121	king Klig	112	Onandaga	114	33,600	2:27.80	
1973	Summer Guest	4	J. Vasquez	119	Red Reality	124	Astray	113	34,200	2:29.20	
1974	Take Off	5	R. Turcotte	120	Garland of Roses	109	Astray	126	34,260	2:26.40	
1975	Barcas	4	M. Castaneda	113	Drollery	113	Telefonico	124	33,240	2:32.20	
1976	Erwin Boy	5	R. Turcotte	120	Drollery	111	Trumpeter Swan	111	34,740	2:26.00	
1977	Hunza Dancer	5	J. Cruguet	117	Improviser	122	Noble Dancer II	117	68,580	1:58.80	
1978	Tiller	4	J. Fell	117	Proud Arion	111	Bowl Game	124	70,260	2:12.40	
1979	Overskate	4	R. Platts	117	Waya	125	Bowl Game	123	84,525	2:11.40	
1980	Sten	5	J. Fell	117	John Henry	128	Lyphard's Wish	120	86,550	2:13.20	
1981	Great Neck	5	A. Cordero Jr	114	Key to Content	119	Match the Hatch	115	84,450	2:12.00	
1982	Open Call	4	J. Velasquez	124	Johnny Dance	114	Baltimore Canyon	116	89,850	2:24.80	
1983	Tantalizing	4	J. Vasquez	113	Sprink	113	Majesty's Prince	122	105,120	2:14.80	
1984	Hero's Honor	4	J.D. Bailey	120	Nassipour	110	Super Sunrise	123	144,120	2:14.00	
1985	Sharannpour	5	A. Cordero Jr	114	Flying Pigeon	116	Equalize	116	156,300	2:18.20	
1986	Uptown Swell	4	E. Maple	114	Palace Panther	116	Equalize	116	147,690	2:14.80	
1987	Theatrical	5	P. Day	123	Akabir	116	Dance of Life	121	144,960	2:14.00	
1988	Coeur de Lion	4	C. Perret	117	Pay the Butler	112	Milesius	115	151,680	2:13.40	
1989	El Senor	5	W.H. McCauley	117	Coeur de Lion	121	Pay the Butler	116	144,960	2:18.60	
1990	With Approval	4	C. Perret	118	Chenin Blanc	113	El Senor	121	113,280	2:10.20	108
1991	Three Coins Up	3	J.D. Bailey	111	Phantom Breeze	117	Beyond the Lake	115	120,000	2:10.80	105
1992	Wall Street Dancer	4	P. Day	114	Fraise	113	Libor	109	120,000	2:12.80	101
1993	Dr. Kiernan	4	C. Antley	114	Spectacular Tide	111	Lomitas	117	90,000	2:17.60	106
1994	Turk Passer	4	J.R. Velazquez	110	Sea Hero	117	Fraise	124	90,000	2:13.20	109
1995	Sentimental Moi	5	R.B. Perez	111	Awad	121	Proceeded	108	90,000	2:15.40	107
1996	Flag Down	6	J.A. Santos	118	Broadway Flyer	118	Diplomatic Jet	119	90,000	2:13.20	106
1997	Influent	6	J.L.Samyn	120	Flag Down	118	Notoriety	108	90,000	2:11.00	107
1998	Cetewayo	4	J.R. Velazquez	112	Officious	113	Chief Bearhart	124	90,000	2:13.40	106
1999	Honor Glide	5	J.A. Santos	114	Parade Ground	118	Fahris	114	90,000	2:11.00	105
	Federal Trial finished third but was disqualified and placed fourth										
2000	Elhayq	5	S.X. Bridgmohan	113	Yankee Dollar	110	Carpenter's Halo	115	90,000	2:13.81	106
2001	King Cugat	4	J.D. Bailey	119	Slew Valley	112	Man From Wicklow	112	90,000	2:10.62	114
2002	Whitmore's Conn	4	S.X. Bridgmohan	112	Staging Post	115	Moon Solitaire	116	90,000	2:13.43	102
2003	Whitmore's Conn	5	J.L. Samyn	116	Quest Star	117	Macaw	116	90.000	2:15.92	105
2004	Kicken Kris	4	E.S Prado	117	Better Talk Now	115	Gigli	113	90,000	2:12.19	106

Beyer Index: 106.20

(POWERED BY DODGE) BREEDERS' CUP CLASSIC (G1), 1 1/4 Miles, 3-Year-Olds and Up, Lone Star Park, 2004 Purse: $3,668,000

Year	Winner	Age	Jockey	Wt.	Second	Wt.	Third	Wt.	Win Value	Time	Beyer
1984	Wild Again	4	P. Day	126	Slew o' Gold	126	Gate Dancer	122	1,350,000	2:03.40	
	Gate Dancer finished second but was disqualified and placed third										
1985	Proud Truth	3	J. Velasquez	122	Gate Dancer	126	Turkoman	122	1,350,000	2:00.80	
1986	Skywalker	4	L. Pincay Jr	126	Turkoman	126	Precisionist	126	1,350,000	2:00.40	
1987	Ferdinand	4	W. Shoemaker	126	Alysheba	122	Judge Angelucci	126	1,350,000	2:01.40	
1988	Alysheba	4	C.J. McCarron	126	Seeking the Gold	122	Waquoit	126	1,350,000	2:04.80	
1989	Sunday Silence	3	C.J. McCarron	122	Easy Goer	122	Blushing John	126	1,350,000	2:00.20	
1990	Unbridled	3	P. Day	121	Ibn Bey	126	Thirty Six Red	121	1,350,000	2:02.20	116
1991	Black Tie Affair	5	J.D. Bailey	126	Twilight Agenda	126	Unbridled	126	1,560,000	2:02.80	120
1992	A.P. Indy	3	E. Delahoussaye	121	Pleasant Tap	126	Jolypha	118	1,560,000	2:00.20	114
1993	Arcangues	5	J.D. Bailey	126	Bertrando	126	Kissin Kris	122	1,560,000	2:00.80	114
1994	Concern	3	J.D. Bailey	122	Tabasco Cat	122	Dramatic Gold	122	1,560,000	2:02.40	115
1995	Cigar	5	J.D. Bailey	126	L'Carriere	126	Unaccounted For	126	1,560,000	1:59.40	117
1996	Alphabet Soup	5	C.J. McCarron	126	Louis Quatorze	121	Cigar	126	2,080,000	2:01.00	115
1997	Skip Away	4	M.E. Smith	126	Deputy Commander	122	Dowty	126	2,288,000	1:59.00	120
	Whiskey Wisdom finished third but was disqualified and placed fourth										
1998	Awesome Again	4	P. Day	126	Silver Charm	126	Swain	126	2,288,000	2:02.16	116
1999	Cat Thief	3	P. Day	122	Budroyale	126	Golden Missile	126	2,080,000	1:59.52	118
2000	Tiznow	3	C.J. McCarron	122	Giant's Causeway	122	Captain Steve	122	2,438,800	2:00.75	116
2001	Tiznow	4	C.J. McCarron	126	Sakhee	126	Albert the Great	126	2,080,000	2:00.62	117
2002	Volponi	4	J.A. Santos	126	Medaglia d'Oro	121	Milwaukee Brew	126	2,080,000	2:01.39	116
2003	Pleasantly Perfect	5	A. Solis	126	Medaglia d'Oro	126	Dynever	121	2,080,000	1:59.88	119
2004	Ghostzapper	4	J.J. Castellano	126	Roses in May	126	Pleasantly Perfect	126	2,080,000	1:59.02	124

Beyer Index: 117.13

Run at Hollywood, 1984, 1987, 1997; at Aqueduct, 1985; at Santa Anita, 1986, 1993, 2003; at Churchill Downs, 1988, 1991, 1994, 1998, 2000; at Gulfstream Park, 1989, 1992, 1999; at Belmont Park, 1990, 1995, 2001; at Woodbine, 1996; at Arlington Park, 2002

(NEXTEL) BREEDERS' CUP DISTAFF (G1), 1 1/8 Miles, Fillies and Mares, 3-Year-Olds and Up, Lone Star Park, 2004 Purse: $1,834,000

Year	Winner	Age	Jockey	Wt.	Second	Wt.	Third	Wt.	Win Value	Time	Beyer
1984	Princess Rooney	4	E. Delahoussaye	123	Life's Magic	119	Adored	123	450,000	2:02.40	
1985	Life's Magic	4	A. Cordero Jr	123	Lady's Secret	119	Dontstop Themusic	123	450,000	2:02.00	
1986	Lady's Secret	4	P. Day	123	Fran's Valentine	123	Outstandingly	123	450,000	2:01.20	
1987	Sacahuista	3	R.P. Romero	119	Clabber Girl	123	Oueee Bebe	119	450,000	2:02.80	
1988	Personal Ensign	4	R.P. Romero	123	Winning Colors	119	Goodbye Halo	119	450,000	1:52.00	
1989	Bayakoa	5	L. Pincay Jr	123	Gorgeous	119	Open Mind	119	450,000	1:47.40	
1990	Bayakoa	6	L. Pincay Jr	123	Colonial Waters	123	Valay Maid	119	450,000	1:49.20	113
1991	Dance Smartly	3	P. Day	120	Versailles Treaty	120	Brought to Mind	123	520,000	1:50.80	107
1992	Paseana	5	C.J. McCarron	123	Versailles Treaty	123	Magical Maiden	119	520,000	1:48.00	105
1993	Hollywood Wildcat	3	E. Delahoussaye	120	Paseana	123	Re Toss	123	520,000	1:48.20	108
1994	One Dreamer	6	G.L. Stevens	123	Heavenly Prize	120	Miss Dominique	123	520,000	1:50.60	105
1995	Inside Information	4	M.E. Smith	123	Heavenly Prize	123	Lakeway	123	520,000	1:46.00	119
1996	Jewel Princess	4	C.S. Nakatani	123	Serena's Song	123	Different	123	520,000	1:48.40	114
1997	Ajina	3	M.E. Smith	120	Sharp Cat	120	Escena	123	520,000	1:47.20	108
1998	Escena	5	G.L. Stevens	123	Banshee Breeze	120	Keeper Hill	120	1,040,000	1:49.89	105
1999	Beautiful Pleasure	4	J.F. Chavez	123	Banshee Breeze	123	Heritage of Gold	123	1,040,000	1:47.56	109
2000	Spain	3	V. Espinoza	120	Surfside	120	Heritage of Gold	123	1,227,200	1:47.66	108
2001	Unbridled Elaine	3	P. Day	120	Spain	123	Two Item Limit	120	1,227,200	1:49.21	102
2002	Azeri	4	M. E. Smith	123	Farda Amiga	119	Imperial Gesture	119	1,040,000	1:48.64	111
2003	Adoration	4	P.A. Valenzuela	123	Elloluv	119	Got Koko	123	1,040,000	1:49.17	101
2004	Ashado	3	J.R. Velazquez	119	Storm Flag Flying	123	Stellar Jayne	119	1,040,000	1:48.26	102

Beyer Index: 107.80

Run at Hollywood, 1984, 1987, 1997; at Aqueduct, 1985; at Santa Anita, 1986,1993, 2003; at Churchill Downs, 1988, 1991, 1994, 1998, 2000; at Gulfstream Park, 1989, 1992, 1999; at Belmont Park, 1990, 1995, 2001; at Woodbine, 1996; at Arlington Park, 2002; Distance 1 1/4 miles prior to 1988

(VO5) BREEDERS' CUP FILLY AND MARE TURF (G1), 1 3/8 Miles (Turf), Fillies and Mares, 3-Year-Olds and Up, Lone Star Park, 2004 Purse: $1,292,970

Year	Winner	Age	Jockey	Wt.	Second	Wt.	Third	Wt.	Win Value	Time	Beyer
1999	Soaring Softly	4	J.D. Bailey	123	Coretta	123	Zomaradah	123	556,400	2:13.89	105
2000	Perfect Sting	4	J.D. Bailey	123	Tout Charmant	123	Catella	123	629,200	2:13.07	105
2001	Banks Hill	3	O. Peslier	119	Spook Express	123	Spring Oak	119	722,800	2:00.36	112
2002	Starine	5	J. R. Velazquez	123	Banks Hill	123	Islington	118	665,600	2:03.57	109
2003	Islington	4	K. Fallon	123	L'Ancresse	118	Yesterday	118	551,200	1:59.13	109
2004	Ouija Board	3	K. Fallon	118	Film Maker	123	Wonder Again	123	733,200	2:18.25	108

Beyer Index: 108.00

Run at Gulfstream Park, 1999; Churchill Downs, 2000; Belmont Park, 2001; Arlington Park, 2002; Santa Anita, 2003; Distance 1 1/4 miles in 2001–2003.

(BESSEMER TRUST) BREEDERS' CUP JUVENILE (G1), 1 1/16 Miles, 2-Year-Olds, Lone Star Park, 2004 Purse: $1,375,500

Year	Winner	Age	Jockey	Wt.	Second	Wt.	Third	Wt.	Win Value	Time	Beyer
1984	Chief's Crown	2	D. MacBeth	122	Tank's Prospect	122	Spend a Buck	122	450,000	1:36.20	
1985	Tasso	2	L. Pincay Jr	122	Storm Cat	122	Scat Dancer	122	450,000	1:36.20	
1986	Capote	2	L. Pincay Jr	122	Qualify	122	Alysheba	122	450,000	1:43.20	
1987	Success Express	2	J.A. Santos	122	Regal Classic	122	Tejano	122	450,000	1:35.20	
1988	Is It True	2	L. Pincay Jr	122	Easy Goer	122	Tagel	122	450,000	1:46.60	
1989	Rhythm	2	C. Perret	122	Grand Canyon	122	Slavic	122	450,000	1:43.60	
1990	Fly So Free	2	J.A. Santos	122	Take Me Out	122	Lost Mountain	122	450,000	1:43.40	
1991	Arazi	2	P.A. Valenzuela	122	Bertrando	122	Snappy Landing	122	520,000	1:46.40	101
1992	Gilded Time	2	C.J. McCarron	122	It'salilknownfact	122	River Special	122	520,000	1:43.40	87
1993	Brocco	2	G.L. Stevens	122	Blumin Affair	122	Tabasco Cat	122	520,000	1:42.80	97
1994	Timber Country	2	P. Day	122	Eltish	122	Tejano Run	122	520,000	1:44.40	100
1995	Unbridled's Song	2	M.E. Smith	122	Hennessy	122	Editor's Note	122	520,000	1:41.60	103
1996	Boston Harbor	2	J.D. Bailey	122	Acceptable	122	Ordway	122	520,000	1:43.40	99
1997	Favorite Trick	2	P. Day	122	Dawson's Legacy	122	Nationalore	122	520,000	1:41.40	101
1998	Answer Lively	2	J.D. Bailey	122	Aly's Alley	122	Cat Thief	122	520,000	1:44.00	97
1999	Anees	2	G.L. Stevens	122	Chief Seattle	122	High Yield	122	520,000	1:42.29	102
2000	Macho Uno	2	J.D. Bailey	122	Point Given	122	Street Cry	122	556,400	1:42.05	99
2001	Johannesburg	2	M.J. Kinane	122	Repent	122	Siphonic	122	520,000	1:42.27	99
2002	Vindication	2	M. E. Smith	122	Kafwain	122	Hold That Tiger	122	556,400	1:49.61	102
2003	Action This Day	2	D.R. Flores	122	Minister Eric	122	Chapel Royal	122	780,000	1:43.62	92
2004	Wilko	2	L. Dettori	122	Afleet Alex	122	Sun King	122	780,000	1:42.09	98

Beyer Index: 98.36

Run at Hollywood, 1984, 1987, 1997; at Aqueduct, 1985; at Santa Anita, 1986,1993, 2003; at Churchill Downs, 1988, 1991, 1994, 199, 2000; at Gulfstream Park, 1989, 1992, 1999; at Belmont Park, 1990, 1995, 2001; at Woodbine, 1996; at Arlington Park, 2002; Distance 1 mile in 1984, 1985, and 1987; 1 1/8 miles in 2002

BREEDERS' CUP JUVENILE FILLIES (G1), 1 1/16 Miles, 2-Year-Old Fillies, Lone Star Park, 2004 Purse: $917,000

Year	Winner	Age	Jockey	Wt.	Second	Wt.	Third	Wt.	Win Value	Time	Beyer
1984	Outstandingly	2	W.A. Guerra	119	Dusty Heart	119	Fine Spirit	119	450,000	1:37.80	
	Fran's Valentine finished first but was disqualified and placed 10th										
1985	Twilight Ridge	2	J. Velasquez	119	Family Style	119	Steal a Kiss	119	450,000	1:35.80	
1986	Brave Raj	2	P.A. Valenzuela	119	Tappiano	119	Saros Brig	119	450,000	1:43.20	
1987	Epitome	2	P. Day	119	Jeanne Jones	119	Dream Team	119	450,000	1:36.40	
1988	Open Mind	2	R.P. Romero	119	Darby Shuffle	119	Lea Lucinda	119	450,000	1:46.60	
1989	Go for Wand	2	R.P. Romero	119	Sweet Roberta	119	Stella Madrid	119	450,000	1:44.20	
1990	Meadow Star	2	J.A. Santos	119	Private Treasure	119	Dance Smartly	119	450,000	1:44.00	98
1991	Pleasant Stage	2	E. Delahoussaye	119	La Spia	119	Cadillac Women	119	520,000	1:46.40	85
1992	Eliza	2	P.A. Valenzuela	119	Educated Risk	119	Boots 'n Jackie	119	520,000	1:42.80	92
1993	Phone Chatter	2	L. Pincay Jr	119	Sardula	119	Heavenly Prize	119	520,000	1:43.00	95
1994	Flanders	2	P. Day	119	Serena's Song	119	Stormy Blues	119	520,000	1:45.20	92
1995	My Flag	2	J.D. Bailey	119	Cara Rafaela	119	Golden Attraction	119	520,000	1:42.40	95
1996	Storm Song	2	C. Perret	119	Love That Jazz	119	Critical Factor	119	520,000	1:43.60	97
1997	Countess Diana	2	S. Sellers	119	Career Collection	119	Primaly	119	535,600	1:42.00	95
1998	Silverbulletday	2	G.L. Stevens	119	Excellent Meeting	119	Three Ring	119	520,000	1:43.68	101
1999	Cash Run	2	J.D. Bailey	119	Chilukki	119	Surfside	119	520,000	1:43.31	93
2000	Caressing	2	J.R. Velazquez	119	Platinum Tiara	119	She's a Devil Due	119	582,400	1:42.77	92
2001	Tempera	2	D.R. Flores	119	Imperial Gesture	119	Bella Bellucci	119	520,000	1:41.49	107
2002	Storm Flag Flying	2	J. R. Velazquez	119	Composure	119	Santa Catarina	119	520,000	1:49.60	102
2003	Halfbridled	2	J.A. Krone	119	Ashado	119	Victory U.S.A.	119	520,000	1:42.75	99
2004	Sweet Catomine	2	C.S. Nakatani	119	Balletto	119	Runway Model	119	520,000	1:41.65	102

Beyer Index: 96.33

Run at Hollywood, 1984, 1987, 1997; at Aqueduct, 1985; at Santa Anita, 1986,1993, 2003; at Churchill Downs, 1988, 1991, 1994, 1998, 2000; at Gulfstream Park, 1989, 1992, 1999; at Belmont Park, 1990, 1995, 2001; at Woodbine, 1996; at Arlington Park, 2002 Distance 1 mile 1984, 1985, and 1987; 1 1/8 miles in 2002

(NETJETS) BREEDERS' CUP MILE (G1), 1 Mile (Turf), 3-Year-Olds and Up, Lone Star Park, 2004 Purse: $1,540,560

Year	Winner	Age	Jockey	Wt.	Second	Wt.	Third	Wt.	Win Value	Time	Beyer
1984	Royal Heroine	4	F. Toro	123	Star Choice	126	Cozzene	126	450,000	1:32.60	
1985	Cozzene	5	W.A. Guerra	126	Al Mamoon	126	Shadeed	123	450,000	1:35.00	
	Palace Music finished second but was disqualified and placed ninth										
1986	Last Tycoon	3	Y. Saint-Martin	123	Palace Music	126	Fred Astaire	123	450,000	1:35.20	
1987	Miesque	3	F. Head	120	Show Dancer	126	Sonic Lady	123	450,000	1:32.80	
1988	Miesque	4	F. Head	123	Steinlen	126	Simply Majestic	126	450,000	1:38.60	
1989	Steinlen	6	J.A. Santos	126	Sabona	126	Most Welcome	126	450,000	1:37.20	
1990	Royal Academy	3	L. Piggott	122	Itsallgreektome	122	Priolo	122	450,000	1:35.20	111
1991	Opening Verse	5	P.A. Valenzuela	126	Val de Bois	126	Star of Cozzene	123	520,000	1:37.40	110
1992	Lure	3	M.E. Smith	122	Paradise Creek	122	Brief Truce	122	520,000	1:32.80	112
1993	Lure	4	M.E. Smith	126	Ski Paradise	120	Fourstars Allstar	126	520,000	1:33.40	112

Year	Winner	Age	Jockey	Wt.	Second	Wt.	Third	Wt.	Win Value	Time	Beyer
1994	Barathea	4	L. Dettori	126	Johann Quatz	126	Unfinished Symph	123	520,000	1:34.40	109
1995	Ridgewood Pearl	3	J.P. Murtagh	119	Fastness	126	Sayyedati	123	520,000	1:43.60	114
1996	Da Hoss	4	G.L. Stevens	126	Spinning World	122	Same Old Wish	126	520,000	1:35.80	114
1997	Spinning World	4	C.B. Asmussen	126	Geri	126	Decorated Hero	126	572,000	1:32.60	114
1998	Da Hoss	6	J. Velazquez	126	Hawksley Hil	126	Labeeb	126	520,000	1:35.27	114
1999	Silic	4	C.S. Nakatani	126	Tuzla	123	Docksider	126	520,000	1:34.26	110
2000	War Chant	3	G.L. Stevens	123	North East Bound	126	Dansili	126	608,400	1:34.67	108
2001	Val Royal	5	J. Valdivia Jr	126	Forbidden Apple	126	Bach	126	592,800	1:32.05	114
2002	Domedriver	4	T. Thulliez	126	Rock of Gibraltar	122	Good Journey	126	556,400	1:36.92	113
2003	Six Perfections	3	J.D. Bailey	119	Touchoftheblues	126	Century City	126	780,000	1:33.86	105
2004	Singletary	4	D.R. Flores	126	Antonius Pius	122	Six Perfections	123	873,600	1:36.90	109

Beyer Index: 111.27

Run at Hollywood, 1984, 1987, 1997; at Aqueduct, 1985; at Santa Anita, 1986,1993, 2003; at Churchill Downs, 1988, 1991, 1994, 1998, 2000; at Gulfstream Park, 1989, 1992, 1999; at Belmont Park, 1990, 1995, 2001; at Woodbine, 1996; at Arlington Park, 2002

BREEDERS' CUP SPRINT (G1), 6 Furlongs, 3-Year-Olds and Up, Lone Star Park, 2004 Purse: $972,020

Year	Winner	Age	Jockey	Wt.	Second	Wt.	Third	Wt.	Win Value	Time	Beyer
1984	Eillo	4	C. Perret	126	Commemorate	124	Fighting Fit	126	450,000	1:10.20	
1985	Precisionist	4	C.J. McCarron	126	Smile	124	Mt. Livermore	126	450,000	1:08.40	
1986	Smile	4	J. Vasquez	126	Pine Tree Lane	123	Bedside Promise	126	450,000	1:08.40	
1987	Very Subtle	3	P.A. Valenzuela	121	Groovy	126	Exclusive Enough	124	450,000	1:08.80	
1988	Gulch	4	A. Cordero Jr	126	Play the King	126	Afleet	126	450,000	1:10.40	
1989	Dancing Spree	4	A. Cordero Jr	126	Safely Kept	121	Dispersal	124	450,000	1:09.00	
1990	Safely Kept	4	C. Perret	123	Dayjur	123	Black Tie Affair	126	450,000	1:09.60	116
1991	Sheikh Albadou	3	P. Eddery	124	Pleasant Tap	126	Robyn Dancer	126	520,000	1:09.20	113
1992	Thirty Slews	5	E. Delahoussaye	126	Meafara	120	Rubiano	126	520,000	1:08.20	111
1993	Cardmania	7	E. Delahoussaye	126	Meafara	123	Gilded Time	124	520,000	1:08.60	109
1994	Cherokee Run	4	M.E. Smith	126	Soviet Problem	123	Cardmania	126	520,000	1:09.40	114
1995	Desert Stormer	5	K.J. Desormeaux	123	Mr. Greeley	123	Lit de Justice	126	520,000	1:09.00	107
1996	Lit de Justice	6	C.S. Nakatani	126	Paying Dues	126	Honour and Glory	123	520,000	1:08.60	114
1997	Elmhurst	7	C.S. Nakatani	126	Hesabull	126	Bet on Sunshine	126	613,600	1:08.00	111
1998	Reraise	3	C.S. Nakatani	124	Grand Slam	124	Kona Gold	126	572,000	1:09.07	112
1999	Artax	4	J.F. Chavez	126	Kona Gold	126	Big Jag	126	624,000	1:07.89	124
2000	Kona Gold	6	A. Solis	126	Honest Lady	123	Bet on Sunshine	126	520,000	1:07.77	114
2001	Squirtle Squirt	3	J.D. Bailey	124	Xtra Heat	121	Caller One	126	520,000	1:08.41	119
2002	Orientate	4	J. D. Bailey	126	Thunderello	123	Crafty C. T.	126	592,800	1:08.89	114
2003	Cajun Beat	3	C.H. Velasquez	123	Bluesthestandard	126	Shake You Down	126	613,600	1:07.95	120
2004	Speightstown	6	J.R. Velazquez	126	Kela	126	My Cousin Matt	126	551,200	1:08.11	112

Beyer Index: 114.00

Run at Hollywood, 1984, 1987, 1997; at Aqueduct, 1985; at Santa Anita, 1986,1993, 2003; at Churchill Downs, 1988, 1991, 1994, 1998, 2000; at Gulfstream Park, 1989, 1992, 1999; at Belmont Park, 1990, 1995, 2001; at Woodbine, 1996; at Arlington Park, 2002

(JOHN DEERE) BREEDERS' CUP TURF (G1), 1 1/2 Miles (Turf), 3-Year-Olds and Up, Lone Star Park, 2004 Purse: $1,834,000

Year	Winner	Age	Jockey	Wt.	Second	Wt.	Third	Wt.	Win Value	Time	Beyer
1984	Lashkari	3	Y. Saint-Martin	122	All Along	123	Raami	122	900,000	2:25.20	
1985	Pebbles	4	P. Eddery	123	Strawberry Road II	126	Mourjane	126	900,000	2:27.00	
1986	Manila	3	J.A. Santos	122	Theatrical	126	Estrapade	123	900,000	2:25.40	
1987	Theatrical	5	P. Day	126	Trempolino	122	Village Star II	126	900,000	2:24.40	
1988	Great Communicator	5	R. Sibille	126	Sunshine Forever	122	Indian Skimmer	123	900,000	2:35.20	
1989	Prized	3	E. Delahoussaye	122	Sierra Roberta	119	Star Lift	126	900,000	2:28.00	
1990	In the Wings	4	G.L. Stevens	126	With Approval	126	El Senor	126	900,000	2:29.60	113
1991	Miss Alleged	4	E. Legrix	123	Itsallgreektome	126	Quest for Fame	126	1,040,000	2:30.80	111
1992	Fraise	4	P.A. Valenzuela	126	Sky Classic	126	Quest for Fame	126	1,040,000	2:24.00	110
1993	Kotashaan	5	K.J. Desormeaux	126	Bien Bien	126	Luazur	126	1,040,000	2:25.00	111
1994	Tikkanen	3	M.E. Smith	122	Hatoof	123	Paradise Creek	126	1,040,000	2:26.40	112
1995	Northern Spur	4	C.J. McCarron	126	Freedom Cry	126	Carnegie	126	1,040,000	2:42.00	114
1996	Pilsudski	4	W.R. Swinburn	126	Singspiel	126	Swain	126	1,040,000	2:30.20	115
1997	Chief Bearhart	4	J.A. Santos	126	Borgia	119	Flag Down	126	1,040,000	2:23.80	110
1998	Buck's Boy	5	S.J. Sellers	126	Yagli	126	Dushyantor	126	1,040,000	2:28.74	111
1999	Daylami	5	L. Dettori	126	Royal Anthem	126	Buck's Boy	126	1,040,000	2:24.73	118
2000	Kalanisi	4	J.P. Murtagh	126	Quiet Resolve	126	John's Call	126	1,289,600	2:26.96	110
2001	Fantastic Light	5	L. Dettori	126	Milan	126	Timboroa	126	1,112,800	2:24.36	117
2002	High Chaparral	3	M.J. Kinane	121	With Anticipation	126	Falcon Flight	126	1,258,400	2:30.14	111
2003	High Chaparral	4	M.J. Kinane	126			Falbrav	126	763,200	2:24.24	112
	Johar	4	A. Solis	126							
2004	Better Talk Now	5	R.A. Dominguez	126	Kitten's Joy	121	Powerscourt	126	1,040,000	2:29.70	111

Beyer Index: 112.40

Run at Hollywood, 1984, 1987, 1997; at Aqueduct, 1985; at Santa Anita, 1986,1993, 2003; at Churchill Downs, 1988, 1991, 1994, 1998, 2000; at Gulfstream Park, 1989, 1992, 1999; at Belmont Park, 1990, 1995, 2001; at Woodbine, 1996; at Arlington Park, 2002

(LANE'S END) BREEDERS' FUTURITY (G1), 1 1/16 Miles, 2-Year-Olds, Keeneland, 2004 Purse: $500,000

Year	Winner	Age	Jockey	Wt.	Second	Wt.	Third	Wt.	Win Value	Time	Beyer
1910	Housemaid	2	P. Powers	115	Golden Egg	115	Little Oasis	115	2,543	:48.60	
1911	The Manager	2	T. Koerner	115	Bachelor Girl	115	Wheelwright	115	4,848	:48.00	
1912	Helios	2	Molesworth	115	Forward	121	Chris Star	118	4,154	:54.00	
1913	Imperator	2	B. Steele	115	John Gund	118	B. Brother	115	5,803	1:00.60	
1914	Luke	2	W.W. Taylor	118	Chaimers	118	Ed Crump	118	3,800	1:00.60	
1915	Kinney	2	J. Loftus	118	Jacoba	115	Bellita	115	4,259	1:00.80	
1916	Harry Kelly	2	G. Garner	118	Westy Hogan	118	Yeymila	115	3,614	:58.80	
1917	Escoba	2	W. Knapp	123	Atalanta	115	Gipsy Queen	115	7,246	1:10.60	
1918	Colonel Livingston	2	W. Lilley	120	Col. Taylor	118	Ginger	118	5,574	1:09.60	
1919	Blazes	2	C. Robinson	123	Peace Pennant	118	Lorraine	115	6,018	1:09.60	
1920	Believe Idle Hour	2	E. Pool	120	Star Voter	123	Sir T. Kean	118	6,393	1:09.20	
1921	Gentilly	2	H.J. Burke	122	Sayno	114	Jahn Finn	127	12,827	1:11.60	
1922	Donges	2	E. Fator	127	Easter Bells	122	Sweetheart	110	15,018	1:09.80	
1923	Worthmore	2	W. Kelsay	122	Sayno	114	Black Gold	122	16,201	1:11.40	
1924	Candy Kid	2	I. Parke	122	Almadel	122	Annihilator	122	15,984	1:12.20	
1925	Flight of Time	2	J. Malben	127	Bubbling Over	127	Helen's Babe	119	16,527	1:08.80	
1926	Wood Lore	2	J.H. Burke	122	Candy Queen	119	Creek Indian	122	17,899	1:11.00	
1927	Wacker Drive	2	J. Heupel	122	Happy Time	127	Blackwood	122	18,070	1:13.00	
1928	Current	2	E. Pool	124	Windy City	122	Clyde Van Dusen	122	21,231	1:08.80	
1929	Gallant Knight	2	C. McCrossen	122	Busy	122	Galaday	119	19,229	1:12.60	
1930	Mate	2	M. Garner	122	Pennate	122	Blind Bowboy	122	16,975	1:09.20	
1931	The Bull	2	R. Workman	122	Air Pilot	122	Kakapo	119	17,325	1:09.80	
1932	Technique	2	T. Elston	119	The Darb	122	Caterwaul	127	15,099	1:10.40	
1933	Mata Hari	2	H. Schutte	124	Giggling	119	Discovery	122	15,064	1:09.60	
1938	Johnstown	2	J. Stout	119	Allegro	117	Lightspur	117	9,335	1:11.40	
1939	Roman Flag	2	L. Haas	119	Dit	117	Star Chance	117	10,866	1:10.60	
1940	Whirlaway	2	J. Longden	122	Blue Pair	119	Our Boots	122	7,835	1:11.20	
1941	Devil Diver	2	C. McCreary	122	Miss Dogwood	114	Dogpatch	117	7,884	1:11.80	
1942	Occupation	2	L. Haas	122	Amber Light	117	Dove Pie	117	11,140	1:14.00	
1943	Durazna	2	J. Higley	116	Occupy	122	Mr. Rabbit	117	9,886	1:11.60	
1944	Air Sailor	2	L. Haas	119	Bymeabond	117	Be Fearless	117	11,244	1:12.20	
1945	Pellicle	2	S. Brooks	117	Mr. Chairman	117	Warf	117	12,676	1:12.80	
1946	Education	2	S. Brooks	122	John's Pride	117	Turf	117	16,338	1:11.60	
1947	Shy Guy	2	S. Brooks	117	Carrara Marble	117	Pennon	117	20,855	1:11.80	
1948	Olympia	2	W. Garner	122	Johns Joy	122	Fleeting Star	117	27,120	1:11.60	
1949	Oil Capitol	2	K. Church	122	French Admiral	117	Roman Bath	122	28,517	1:12.20	
1950	Big Stretch	2	T. Atkinson	117	Royal Mustang	117	Streaking	117	27,674	1:23.60	
1951	Alladier	2	C. Bierman	117	Ed's Pride	119	Smoke Screen	114	27,052	1:23.80	
1952	Straight Face	2	B. Green	117	Jimminy Baxter	117	Spy Defense	119	27,052	1:23.80	
1953	Hasty Road	2	J. Adams	122	Revolt	119	Homestake	119	32,127	1:23.20	
1954	Brother Tex	2	P. Anderson	122	Traffic Judge	122	Irish Brush	122	37,883	1:24.40	
1955	Jovial Jove	2	D. Dodson	122	Swoon's Son	122	Pester	122	33,606	1:23.60	
1956	Round Table	2	S. Brooks	122	Missile	122	Tranquil	122	38,949	1:26.80	
1957	Fulcrum	2	J. Delahoussaye	122	Can Trust	122	Nunya	122	37,214	1:26.40	
1958	Namon	2	J. Combest	122	Pilot	122	Derrick	122	38,722	1:26.60	
1959	Toby's Brother	2	J.L. Rotz	122	All Hands	122	Malaysia	122	35,527	1:27.20	
1960	He's a Pistol	2	L. Hansman	122	Zebadiah	122	Busher's Beauty	122	33,619	1:27.00	
1961	Roman Line	2	W.M. Cook	122	Times Roman	122	Crafty Actor	122	36,754	1:26.60	
1962	Ornamento	2	J. Lynch	122	Copy Chief	122	No Reprieve	122	35,457	1:26.40	
1963	Duel	2	W.D. Lucas	122	Ishkoodah	122	Bleacherite	122	35,399	1:26.20	
1964	Umbrella Fella	2	J. Nazareth	122	Seafes	122	Florida State	122	35,461	1:26.60	
1965	Tinsley	2	J. Nichols	122	Francis U.	122	Woodford	122	37,554	1:28.40	
1966	Gentleman James	2	J. Nichols	122	Monitor	122	Yorkville	122	39,978	1:28.00	
1967	T.V. Commercial	2	M. Ycaza	122	Family Fun	122	Tampa Trouble	122	39,988	1:26.80	
1968	Dike	2	E. Fires	122	Mr. Leader	122	The Heir	122	40,955	1:26.80	
1969	Hard Work	2	D. Brumfield	122	Toasted	122	Lanyon	122	39,055	1:25.60	
1970	Man of the Moment	2	D. Brumfield	122	Whisk	122	Raja Baba	122	41,574	1:28.80	
1971	Windjammer	2	L. Pincay Jr	122	Central Paris	122	Brilliant Native	122	39,948	1:27.20	
1972	Annihilate 'Em	2	D. Brumfield	122	Rocket Pocket	122	Crimson Falcon	122	38,886	1:27.00	
1973	Provante	2	M. Manganello	122	Training Table	122	Wage Raise	122	48,327	1:27.20	
1974	Packer Captain	2	D. Brumfield	122	Master Derby	122	Ruggles Ferry	122	53,277	1:25.80	
1975	Harbor Springs	2	E. Maple	122	Best Bee	122	Scrutiny	122	82,046	1:27.00	
1976	Run Dusty Run	2	D.G. McHargue	122	Banquet Table	122	Get the Axe	122	84,695	1:27.40	
1977	Gonquin	2	F. Olivares	122	Sunny Songster	122	Jaycean	122	83,866	1:28.00	
1978	Strike Your Colors	2	E. Delahoussaye	122	Lot o' Gold	122	Uncle Fudge	122	92,284	1:26.20	
1979	Gold Stage	2	D. Brumfield	121	Degenerate Jon	121	Tonka Wakhen	121	81,608	1:26.80	
1980	Fairway Phantom	2	J. Lively	121	Total Pleasure	121	Quick Ice	121	94,575	1:28.80	
1981	D'Accord	2	D.G. McHargue	121	Lets Dont Fight	121	Shooting Duck	121	94,575	1:44.40	
1982	Highland Park	2	J.L. Lively	121	Caveat	121	Bright Baron	121	97,825	1:43.60	

Year	Winner	Age	Jockey	Wt.	Second	Wt.	Third	Wt.	Win Value	Time	Beyer
1983	Swale	2	E. Maple	121	Spender	121	Back Bay Barrister	121	108,631	1:44.00	
1984	Crater Fire	2	D. Montoya	121	Nickel Back	121	Cullendale	121	110,474	1:45.80	
1985	Tasso	2	L. Pincay Jr	121	Regal Dreamer	121	Thundering Force	121	122,424	1:46.00	
1986	Orono	2	S. Hawley	121	Alysheba	121	Pledge Card	121	116,711	1:45.20	
1987	Forty Niner	2	E. Maple	121	Hey Pat	121	Sea Trek	121	104,868	1:43.80	
1988	Fast Play	2	A. Cordero Jr	121	Lorenzoni	121	Bio	121	129,350	1:45.20	
1989	Slavic	2	J.A. Santos	121	Top Snob	121	Harry	121	159,770	1:44.60	
1990	Sir Bordeaux	2	W.S. Ramos	121	Wall Street Dancer	121	Fire in Ice	121	145,925	1:44.40	82
1991	Dance Floor	2	C.R. Woods Jr	121	Star Recruit	121	Count the Time	121	122,200	1:44.20	100
1992	Mountain Cat	2	P. Day	121	Living Vicariously	121	Boundlessly	121	122,200	1:45.40	86
1993	Polar Expedition	2	C.C. Bourque	121	Goodbye Doeny	121	Solly's Honor	121	122,200	1:42.20	96
1994	Tejano Run	2	J.D. Bailey	121	Cinch	121	Gold Miner	121	71,548	1:44.60	89
1995	Honour and Glory	2	P. Day	121	City by Night	121	Blushing Jim	121	139,252	1:43.20	101
1996	Boston Harbor	2	J.D. Bailey	121	Blazing Sword	121	Haint	121	168,005	1:45.20	93
1997	Favorite Trick	2	P. Day	121	Time Limit	121	Laydown	121	265,112	1:43.20	100
1998	Cat Thief	2	P. Day	121	Answer Lively	121	Yes It's True	121	272,552	1:44.00	97
1999	Captain Steve	2	G.K. Gomez	121	Graeme Hall	121	Millencolin	121	274,040	1:42.40	95
2000	Arabian Light	2	S.J. Sellers	121	Dollar Bill	121	Holiday Thunder	121	279,744	1:43.18	94
2001	Siphonic	2	C.J. McCarron	121	Harlan's Holiday	121	Metatron	121	281,728	1:43.79	97
2002	Sky Mesa	2	E.S. Prado	121	Lone Star Sky	121	Truckle Feature	121	269,576	1:46.78	93
2003	Eurosilver	2	J. Castellano	121	Tiger Hunt	121	Limehouse	121	248,000	1:43.42	98
2004	Consolidator	2	R. Bejarano	121	Patriot Act	121	Diamond Isle	121	310,000	1:43.67	93

Beyer Index: 94.27

BROOKLYN HANDICAP (G2), 1 1/8 Miles, 3-Year-Olds and Up, Belmont Park, 2004 Purse: $250,000

Year	Winner	Age	Jockey	Wt.	Second	Wt.	Third	Wt.	Win Value	Time	Beyer
1887	Dry Monopole	4	A. McCarthy	106	Blue Wing	112	Hidalgo	115	5,850	2:07.00	
1888	The Bard	5	W. Hayward	125	Hanover	125	Exile	114	6,925	2:13.00	
1889	Exile	7	A. Hamilton	116	Prince Royal	120	Terra Cotta	125	6,900	2:07.50	
1890	Castaway II	4	W. Bunn	100	Badge	114	Eric	110	6,900	2:10.00	
1891	Tenny	5	Barnes	128	Prince Royal	117	Tea Tray	116	14,800	2:10.00	
1892	Judge Morrow	5	A. Covington	116	Pessarra	115	Russell	114	17,750	2:08.75	
1893	Diablo	7	F. Taral	112	Lamplighter	125	Leonawell	110	17,750	2:09.00	
1894	Dr. Rice	4	F. Taral	112	Henry of Navarre	100	Sir Walter	120	17,750	2:07.25	
1895	Hornpipe	4	A. Hamilton	105	Lazzarone	114	Sir Walter	124	7,750	2:11.25	
1896	Sir Walter	6	F. Taral	113	Clifford	125	St. Maxim	108	7,750	2:08.50	
1897	Howard Mann	4	H. Martin	106	Lake Shore	106	Volley	95	7,750	2:09.75	
1898	Ornament	4	T. Sloan	127	Ben Holladay	121	Sly Fox	92	7,800	2:10.00	
1899	Banastar	4	D. Maher	110	Lanky Bob	105	Filigrane	98	7,800	2:06.25	
1900	Kinley Mack	4	P. McCue	122	Raffaello	113	Herbert	99	7,800	2:10.00	
1901	Conroy	3	W. O'Connor	103	Herbert	99	Standing	113	7,800	2:09.00	
1902	Reina	4	W. O'Connor	104	Advance Guard	117	Pentecost	100	7,800	2:07.00	
1903	Irish Lad	3	F. O'Neill	103	Gunfire	111	Heno	113	14,950	2:05.40	
1904	The Picket	4	E. Helgesen	119	Irish Lad	125	Proper	110	15,800	2:06.60	
1905	Delhi	4	T. Burns	124	Ostrich	96	Graziallo	109	15,800	2:06.20	
1906	Tokalon	5	W. Bedell	108	Dandelion	107	The Picket	120	15,800	2:05.60	
1907	Superman	3	W. Miller	99	Beacon Light	100	Nealon	114	15,800	2:09.00	
1908	Celt	3	J. Notter	106	Fair Play	99	Mas Robert	95	19,750	2:04.20	
1909	King James	4	E. Dugan	126	Restigouche	114	Celt	127	3,850	2:04.00	
1910	Fitz Herbert	4	E. Dugan	130	Olambala	116	Pr. Imperial	97	4,800	2:05.60	
1913	Whisk Broom II	6	J. Notter	130	G.M. Miller	106	Sam Jackson	108	3,125	2:03.40	
1914	Buckhorn	5	J. McCahey	113	Ruskin	119	Rock View	128	3,350	2:08.00	
1915	Tartar	5	J. McTaggart	103	Roamer	125	Borrow	128	3,850	1:50.60	
1916	Friar Rock	3	E. Haynes	108	Pennant	123	Slumber II	111	3,850	1:50.00	
1917	Borrow	9	W. Knapp	117	Regret	122	Old Rosebud	120	4,850	1:49.40	
1918	Cudgel	4	L. Lyke	129	Roamer	120	Geo. Smith	122	4,850	1:50.20	
1919	Eternal	3	A. Schuttinger	105	Purchase	117	Questionnaire	100	4,850	1:49.00	
1920	Cirrus	4	L. Esnor	108	Boniface	122	Mad Hatter	115	5,850	1:50.00	
1921	Grey Lag	3	L. Fator	112	John P. Grier	124	Exterminator	129	7,600	1:49.80	
1922	Exterminator	7	A. Johnson	135	Grey Lag	126	Polly Ann	103	7,600	1:50.00	
1923	Little Chief	4	E. Sande	114	Bunting	126	Knobbie	112	7,600	1:50.00	
1924	Hephaistos	5	J. Maiben	106	Susini	102	Enchantment	111	7,600	1:50.80	
1925	Mad Play	4	L. Fator	123	Sting	127	Catalan	107	7,600	1:50.00	
1926	Single Foot	4	C. Turner	123	Peanuts	111	Dangerous	108	11,950	1:50.40	
1927	Peanuts	5	H. Thurber	112	Chance Play	121	Display	112	13,150	1:48.80	
1928	Black Panther	4	J. Maiben	105	Victorian	112	Diavolo	106	13,750	1:51.20	
1929	Light Carbine	6	G. Rose	97	Diavolo	120	Sun Beau	124	14,300	1:50.60	
1930	Sortie	5	P. Walls	111	Jack High	122	Curate	107	10,800	1:49.80	
1931	Questionnaire	4	R. Workman	127	St. Brideaux	104	S. Grant	106	13,900	1:49.00	
1932	Blenheim	4	H. Mills	109	Pari-Mutuel	97	Mate	124	9,800	1:51.00	

Year	Winner	Age	Jockey	Wt.	Second	Wt.	Third	Wt.	Win Value	Time	Beyer
1933	Dark Secret	4	H. Mills	115	Kerry Patch	112	Apprentice	109	3,380	1:51.20	
1934	Discovery	3	J. Bejshak	113	Dark Secret	126	Fleam	108	2,925	1:49.80	
1935	Dicovery	4	J. Bejshak	123	King Saxon	127	Omaha	114	10,200	1:48.20	
1936	Discovery	5	L. Fallon	136	Good Gamble	110	Roman Soldier	126	10,575	1:50.00	
1937	Seabiscuit	4	J. Pollard	122	Aneroid	122	Memory Book	114	18,025	1:50.20	
1938	The Chief	3	J. Longden	105	Stagehand	110	Unfailing	106	18,450	1:48.40	
1939	Cravat	4	B. James	126	Our Ketcham	101	The Chief	112	18,250	1:48.20	
1940	Isolater	7	J. Stout	119	Can't Wait	111	Eight Thirty	130	16,900	2:03.00	
1941	Fenelon	4	J. Stout	119	Dit	110	Your Chance	121	19,250	2:03.60	
1942	Whirlaway	4	G. Woolf	128	Swing and Sway	110	Attention	122	23,650	2:02.60	
1943	Devil Diver	4	S. Brooks	123	Market Wise	128	Don Bingo	113	23,200	2:03.40	
1944	Four Freedoms	4	E. Arcaro	116	Wait a Bit	116	First Fiddle	126	3,720	2:02.80	
1945	Stymie	4	R. Permane	116	Devil Diver	132	Olympic Zenith	110	37,120	2:02.20	
1946	Gallorette	4	J. Jessop	118	Stymie	128	Burning Dream	110	41,100	2:05.00	
1947	Assault	4	E. Arcaro	133	Stymie	124	Larky Day	110	38,100	2:03.60	
1948	Conniver	4	T. Atkinson	114	Gallorette	119	Stymie	130	39,300	2:05.80	
1949	Assault	6	D. Gorman	122	Vulcan's Forge	129	Flying Missel	117	40,600	2:02.80	
1950	My Request	5	T. Atkinson	119	Double Brandy	115	Hypocrite II	103	41,000	2:03.00	
1951	Palestinian	5	S. Boulmetis	121	Sheilas Reward	117	County Delight	124	39,000	2:03.40	
1952	Crafty Admiral	4	E. Guerin	116	County Delight	122	To Market	119	41,700	2:01.80	
1953	Tom Fool	4	T. Atkinson	136	Golden Gloves	110	High Scud	109	37,900	2:04.40	
1954	Invigorator	4	E. Arcaro	114	Find	122	Cold Command	116	40,500	2:03.00	
1955	High Gun	4	E. Arcaro	132	Paper Tiger	107	Straight Face	116	37,900	2:03.40	
1956	Dedicate	4	E. Arcaro	114	Midafternoon	116	Find	119	37,600	1:55.80	
1957	Portersville	5	E. Nelson	116	Admiral Vee	120	Tick Tock	118	37,700	1:55.20	
1958	Cohoes	4	J. Ruane	110	Third Brother	110	Inside Tract	106	36,450	1:55.60	
1959	Babu	5	C. McCreary	112	Sword Dancer	124	Amerigo	117	72,545	1:56.40	
1960	On-and-On	4	I. Valenzuela	118	Greek Star	110	Waltz	113	70,010	2:03.00	
1961	Kelso	4	E. Arcaro	136	Divine Comedy	118	Yorky	122	73,320	2:01.60	
1962	Beau Purple	5	W. Boland	116	Garwol	106	Polylad	114	71,240	2:00.00	
1963	Cyrano	4	R. Ussery	113	Sunrise County	116	Lanvin	108	72,800	2:01.60	
1964	Gun Bow	4	W. Blum	122	Olden Times	122	Sunrise Flight	113	71,500	1:59.60	
1965	Pia Star	4	J. Sellers	121	Roman Brother	121	Kelso	132	69,680	2:00.60	
1966	Buckpasser	3	B. Baeza	120	Buffle	113	Pluck	113	69,615	2:01.80	
1967	Handsome Boy	4	E. Belmonte	116	Buckpasser	136	Mr. Right	113	69,355	2:00.20	
1968	Damascus	4	M. Ycaza	130	Dr. Fager	135	Mr. Right	114	71,110	1:59.20	
1969	Nodouble	4	E. Belmonte	127	Verbatim	120	Dike	114	70,850	2:00.40	
1970	Dewan	5	L. Pincay Jr	118	Pleasure Seeker	117	Hydrologist	114	69,810	2:02.80	
1971	Never Bow	5	R. Ussery	126	Protanto	111	Royal Harmony	111	69,060	2:03.60	
1972	Key to the Mint	3	B. Baeza	112	Autobiography	122	West Coast Scout	114	70,860	1:54.80	
1973	Riva Ridge	4	R. Turcotte	127	True Knight	117	Tentam	119	67,200	1:52.60	
1974	Forego	4	H. Gustines	129	Billy Come Lately	114	Arbees Boy	116	66,600	1:54.80	
1975	Forego	5	H. Gustines	132	Monetary Principle	109	Stop the Music	121	66,780	1:59.80	
1976	Forego	6	H. Gustines	134	Lord Rebeau	114	Foolish Pleasure	126	67,860	2:01.20	
1977	Great Contractor	4	A. Cordero Jr	112	Forego	137	American History	112	66,600	2:26.20	
1978	Nasty and Bold	3	J.L. Samyn	112	Father Hogan	116	Great Contractor	122	63,900	2:26.00	
1979	The Liberal Member	4	R.I. Encinas	114	Bowl Game	119	State Dinner	123	99,000	2:28.80	
1980	Winter's Tale	4	J. Fell	120	State Dinner	121	Ring of Light	114	130,200	2:28.60	
1981	Hechizado	5	R. Hernandez	116	The Liberal Member	113	Peat Moss	111	138,300	2:26.00	
1982	Silver Supreme	5	J. Vasquez	117	Princelet	112	Baltimore Canyon	113	131,700	2:29.40	
1983	Highland Blade	5	J. Vasquez	117	Sing Sing	118	Silver Supreme	113	172,800	2:31.00	
1984	Fit to Fight	5	J.D. Bailey	129	Vision	111	Dew Line	116	201,600	2:27.40	
1985	Bounding Basque	5	A. Graell	111	Life's Magic	114	Pine Circle	115	207,300	2:26.40	
1986	Little Missouri	4	J.L. Samyn	109	Roo Art	118	Creme Fraiche	118	195,900	2:26.40	
1987	Waquoit	4	C.J. McCarron	123	Bordeaux Bob	112	Full Courage	108	249,480	2:28.40	
1988	Waquoit	5	J.A. Santos	121	Personal Flag	120	Creme Fraiche	118	229,740	2:28.80	
1989	Forever Silver	4	J. Vasquez	116	Drapeau Tricolore	112	Jack of Clubs	112	238,560	2:28.60	
1990	Montubio	5	J. Vasquez	113	Mi Selecto	114	De Roche	113	241,920	2:28.60	
1991	Timely Warning	6	M.J. Luzzi	112	Chief Honcho	121	De Roche	115	210,000	2:14.00	107
1992	Chief Honcho	5	R.P. Romero	117	Valley Crossing	113	Lost Mountain	114	210,000	2:16.80	109
1993	Living Vicariously	3	R.G. Davis	111	Michelle Can Pass	116	Jacksonport	111	150,000	2:17.80	107
1994	Devil His Due	5	M.E. Smith	120	Wallenda	118	Sea Hero	119	150,000	1:46.60	116
1995	You and I	4	J.F. Chavez	115	Key Contender	112	Slick Horn	113	150,000	1:49.00	114
1996	Wekiva Springs	5	M.E. Smith	120	Mahogany Hall	114	Admiralty	111	180,000	1:46.60	107
1997	Formal Gold	4	J.D. Bailey	119	Stephanotis	116	Circle of Light	111	180,000	1:46.20	113
1998	Subordination	4	E.M. Coa	114	Sir Bear	118	Mr. Sinatra	114	180,000	1:46.60	109
1999	Running Stag	5	S.J. Sellers	115	Deputy Diamond	113	Sir Bear	119	210,000	1:46.20	118
2000	Lemon Drop Kid	4	E.S. Prado	120	Lager	114	Down the Aisle	112	150,000	1:49.93	115
2001	Albert The Great	4	J.F. Chavez	122	Perfect Cat	115	Top Official	113	150,000	1:47.41	114
2002	Seeking Daylight	4	E.S. Prado	113	Country Be Gold	113	Griffinite	114	150,000	1:46.35	109
2003	Iron Deputy	4	R. Migliore	114	Volponi	122	Saarland	115	150,000	1:47.84	112
2004	Seattle Fitz	5	R. Migliore	116	Dynever	117	Newfoundland	115	150,000	1:46.30	113

Beyer Index: 111.64

BROWN BESS HANDICAP (G3), 1 1/16 Miles (Turf), Fillies and Mares, 4-Year-Olds and Up, Golden Gate, 2004 Purse: 100,000

Year	Winner	Age	Jockey	Wt.	Second	Wt.	Third	Wt.	Win Value	Time	Beyer
1995	Work The Crowd	5	R.Baze	118	Watch Rachel	115	Zoonaqua	120	32,450	1:41.40	107
1996	Traces of Gold	4	R.Baze	115	Luzette	116	Just A Wish	115	55,000	1:42.00	100
1997	Traces of Gold	5	R.Baze	115	Notagoldbrick	115	Princess Kali	115	55,000	1:44.40	100
1998	Traces of Gold	6	R.Baze	118	Taurus Forus	116	La Soberbia	116	55,000	1:43.00	96
1999	Call Me	6	R.Meza	115	Curitibia	115	Plus	115	50,475	1:49.16	95
2000	Guinevere	5	J. Matias	115	Royal Terminal	112	Blended Element	118	55,000	1:47.75	99
2001	Out of Reach	4	R. Baze	115	Miss of Wales	114	Keld	114	55,000	1:46.78	100
2002	Janet	5	D.R. Flores	123	Impeachable	115	Alexine	117	55,000	1:44.14	100
2003	Lindsay Jean	5	C.P. Schvaneveldt	116	Bush Triumph	116	Crazy Ensign	118	55,000	1:44.35	97
2004	Red Rioja	5	E. Saint-Martin	117	Hooked on Niners	117	A B Noodle	116	55,000	1:46.01	87

Beyer Index: 98.10

BUENA VISTA HANDICAP (G2), 1 Mile (Turf), Fillies and Mares, 4-Year-Olds and Up, Santa Anita, 2004 Purse: $150,000

Year	Winner	Age	Jockey	Wt.	Second	Wt.	Third	Wt.	Win Value	Time	Beyer
1988	Davie's Lamb	4	F. Toro	117	Sly Charmer	114	Pen Bal Lady	119	63,050	1:39.00	
1989	Annoconnor	5	C.A. Black	121	Daring Doone	112	Daloma	116	65,800	1:36.40	
1990	Saros Brig	6	P.A. Valenzuela	116	Royal Touch	123	Nikishka	118	68,100	1:34.20	104
1991	Taffeta and Tulle	5	C.J. McCarron	120	Bequest	117	Somethingmerry	114	67,200	1:34.20	101
1992	Gold Fleece	4	A. Solis	114	Elegance	115	Danzante	114	52,100	1:33.40	106
1992	Appealing Missy	5	C.J. McCarron	117	Exchange	120	Re Toss	117	52,100	1:34.20	100
1993	Marble Maiden	4	K.J. Desormeaux	118	Suivi	117	Party Cited	116	65,000	1:36.20	102
1994	Lady Blessington	6	E. Delahoussaye	119	Skimble	118	Hero's Love	121	66,300	1:34.80	103
1995	Lyin to the Moon	6	K.J. Desormeaux	116	Jacodra's Devil	115	Exchange	122	61,700	1:36.60	99
1996	Matiara	4	G.L. Stevens	119	Real Connection	114	Dirca	116	81,800	1:35.60	105
1997	Media Nox	4	C.S. Nakatani	115	Traces Of Gold	115	Grafin	116	85,250	1:33.40	102
1998	Dance Parade	4	K.J. Desormeaux	116	Shake The Yoke	116	Donna Viola	121	101,520	1:36.80	104
1999	Tuzla	5	C.S. Nakatani	120	Supercilious	117	Green Jewel	116	90,000	1:35.60	102
2000	Lexa	6	B. Blanc	115	Here's to You	114	Sierra Virgen	114	97,290	1:36.17	99
2001	Rare Charmer	6	L. Pincay Jr	117	Elegant Ridge	117	Uncharted Haven	116	90,000	1:36.67	97
2002	Blue Moon	5	B. Blanc	113	Queen of Wilshire	116	Old Money	118	90,000	1:35.57	97
2003	Final Destination	5	V. Espinoza	115	Garden in the Rain	115	Embassy Belle	116	90,000	1:35.99	101
2004	Fun House	5	G.L. Stevens	116	Katdogawn	117	Fudge Fatale	116	90,000	1:36.13	97

Beyer Index: 101.19

CARLETON F. BURKE HANDICAP (G3), 1 1/2 Miles (Turf), 3-Year-Olds and Up, Santa Anita, 2004 Purse: $100,000

Year	Winner	Age	Jockey	Wt.	Second	Wt.	Third	Wt.	Win Value	Time	Beyer
1969	Fiddle Isle	4	W. Shoemaker	115	Pink Pigeon	117	Gamelight	110	30,000	1:59.80	
1970	Fiddle Isle	5	W. Shoemaker	129	Daryl's Joy	123	Mickey McGuire	111	30,000	1:58.80	
1971	Kobuk King	5	H. Grant	110	Over the Counter	118	Figonero	115	34,400	1:59.60	
1972	Cougar II	5	D. Pierce	128	Kentuckian	110	Tetrack	114	34,600	2:00.20	
1973	Kentuckian	4	D. Pierce	117	Wing Out	119	Le Cle	116	33,400	1:59.00	
1974	Tallahto	4	L. Pincay Jr	120	High Protein	117	Scantling	117	32,300	1:59.00	
1975	Top Command	4	W. Shoemaker	113	Against the Snow	116	Top Crowd	116	24,875	2:01.20	
1975	Kirrary	5	F. Mena	114	Buffalo Lark	121	Dulcia	117	24,875	2:00.40	
1976	King Pellinore	4	W. Shoemaker	124	Royal Derby II	116	George Navonod	115	33,300	1:57.60	
1977	Double Discount	4	F. Mena	116	No Turning	118	Vigors	120	33,000	1:57.40	
1978	Star of Erin II	4	W. Shoemaker	113	Improviser	115	Mr. Redoy	118	38,400	1:59.00	
1978	Palton	5	H.E. Moreno	122	Star Spangled	118	Lunar Probe	114	38,400	1:59.00	
1979	Silver Eagle	5	F. Toro	115	John Henry	118	Shagbark	118	50,200	1:59.20	
1980	Bold Tropic	5	W. Shoemaker	125	Balzac	121	Shagbark	121	49,300	1:58.20	
1981	Spence Bay	6	F. Toro	120	Providential II	121	Super Moment	121	67,200	2:00.60	
1982	Mehmet	4	E. Delahoussaye	117	Craelius	114	It's the One	124	63,600	1:58.60	
1983	Bel Bolide	5	T. Lipham	122	Travelling Victor	118	Bold Run	118	64,200	2:01.20	
1984	Silveyville	6	C.J. McCarron	117	Gordian	115	Gato del Sol	121	64,100	1:59.60	
1985	Tsunami Slew	4	G.L. Stevens	121	Yashgan	121	Best of Both	115	78,500	1:59.60	
1986	Louis le Grand	4	W. Shoemaker	115	Schiller	114	Silveyville	120	133,700	2:01.20	
1987	Rivlia	5	L. Pincay Jr	121	Captain Vigors	116	Circus Prince	115	102,500	2:03.20	
1988	Nasr el Arab	3	G.L. Stevens	121	Northern Provider	112	Trokhos	115	133,000	2:01.00	
1989	Alwuhush	4	J.A. Santos	120	Frankly Perfect	122	Speedratic	115	134,400	1:58.00	
1990	Ultrasonido	5	C.J. McCarron	114	Rial	118	Eradicate	117	129,400	1:59.80	106
1991	Super May	5	C.S. Nakatani	117	Algenib	121	Pride of Araby	112	103,700	1:58.40	106
1992	Missionary Ridge	5	K.J. Desormeaux	117	Carnival Baby	112	Myrakalu	113	98,000	2:00.80	105
1993	Know Heights	4	K.J. Desormeaux	117	Fanmore	117	Myrakalu	114	96,000	2:00.80	107
1994	Savinio	4	C.J. McCarron	114	Square Cut	114	Sir Mark Sykes	117	95,700	2:02.60	105
1995	Varadavour	6	A. Solis	115	Patio de Naranjos	117	Raintrap	116	90,350	2:30.20	100

Year	Winner	Age	Jockey	Wt.	Second	Wt.	Third	Wt.	Win Value	Time	Beyer
1996	Dernier Empereur	6	C.J. McCarron	118	Bon Point	118	Party Season	116	158,750	2:24.20	108
1997	Prussian Blue	5	K.J. Desormeaux	117	Embraceable You	116	Kessem Power	114	75,000	2:31.20	102
1998	Perim	5	B. Blanc	113	Single Empire	116	Rate Cut	114	75,000	2:29.20	103
1999	Public Purse	5	A. Solis	119	Star Performance	115	Achilles	115	90,000	2:25.83	103
2000	Timboroa	4	D.R. Flores	114	Kerrygold	116			84,990	2:27.91	100
					Res Judicata	115					
2001	Cagney	4	M.E. Smith	116	Kerrygold	116	Northern Quest	118	90,000	2:26.10	105
2002	Special Matter	4	T.C. Baze	110	Alyzig	113	Dance Dreamer	117	90,000	2:28.47	101
2003	Runaway Dancer	4	M.E. Smith	112	Labirinto	116	Senor Swinger	114	83,550	2:28.38	99
2004	Habaneros	5	D.R. Flores	116	Pellegrino	116	Gallant	113	60,000	2:26.91	99

Beyer Index: 103.27

CALDER DERBY (G3), 1 1/8 Miles (Turf), 3-Year-Olds, Calder Race Course, 2004 Purse: $200,000

Year	Winner	Age	Jockey	Wt.	Second	Wt.	Third	Wt.	Win Value	Time	Beyer
1972	First Bloom	4	C. Stone	116	Hickory Gray	117	The Republican	117	6,540	1:25.80	
1973	Wilmar	5	G. St. Leon	122	Sea Phantom	118	Hickory Gray	115	7,020	1:25.20	
1974	Amberbee	6	J. Garrido	117	Enchanted Ruler	112	Seminole Joe	113	14,280	1:46.60	
1975	Rimsky II	4	A. Haldar	116			Plagiarization	121	12,400	1:42.20	
	Strand of Gold	5	P. Nicolo	122							
1976	Chilean Chief	5	J. Imparato	118	El Rosillo	112	L. Grand Jr.	116	17,700	1:45.80	
1977	What a Threat	5	R. Gaffflione	117	Noble Royalty	116	Lightning Thrust	122	17,400	1:42.60	
1978	Ole Wilk	4	L. Jimenez	114	America Behave	110	Classy State	115	18,600	1:42.40	
1979	Breezy Fire	4	M. Rivera	118	Abba Cap	115	Selma's Boy	117	16,665	1:52.00	
1980	J. Rodney G.	5	F. Verardi	113	Two's a Plenty	109	Cherry Pop	125	23,040	1:53.20	
1981	Poking	5	G. Cohen	122	Yosi Boy	114	Pair of Deuces	112	23,415	1:53.40	
1982	Gorious Past	3	A. Smith Jr	115	Court Rebeau	115	Ell's New Canaan	112	19,905	1:45.80	
1983	Opening Lead	3	B. Gonzalez	117	The Cerfer	112	Neutral Player	112	20,640	1:48.20	
1984	Opening Lead	4	J. Santos	114	Ward off Trouble	114	Darn That Alarm	114	34,860	1:47.60	
1985	Gray Haze	3	F. Pennisi	115	Alfred	115	Jeblar	115	33,780	1:46.00	
1986	Annapolis John	3	J. Velez Jr	120	Kid Colin	115	Real Forest	118	28,160	1:46.20	
1987	Schism	3	R. Lester	117	Slewdonza	112	Fabulous Devotion	114	32,640	1:47.20	
1988	Frosty the Snowman	3	D. Valiente	116	In the Slammer	116	Distinctintentions	112	30,750	1:44.40	
1989	Silver Sunsets	3	M. Gonzalez	114	Compuquine	114	Run for Your Honey	111	32,190	1:45.80	
1990	Zalipour	3	D. Acevedo	118	County Isle	115	Rowdy Regal	114	32,580	1:46.60	
1991	Scottish Ice	3	R. Lester	113	Chihuahua	120	Jackie Wackie	121	33,450	1:46.00	
1992	Birdonthewire	3	M. Hunter	112	Shahpour	113	Ponche	111	30,000	1:44.20	106
1993	Medieval Mac	3	M. Russ	113	Raise an Alarm	113	Fight for Love	116	30,000	1:41.60	100
1994	Halo's Image	3	Boulanger G	117	Honest Colors	117	Rocky's Halo	117	90,000	1:52.20	100
1995	Pineing Patty	3	Melancon L	122	Sea Emperor	122	Mucha Mosca	117	60,000	1:51.40	102
1996	Laughing Dan	3	P. Rodriguez	117	Sea Horse	117	Flying Concery	114	66,300	1:50.60	103
1997	Blazing Sword	3	G. Boulanger	117	Topaz Runner	117			90,000	1:53.00	102
					Royal Tuneup	117					
1998	Crowd Pleaser	3	J.L. Samyn	122	Stay Sound	122	The Kaiser	117	120,000	1:47.60	102
1999	Isaypete	3	J.C. Ferrer	122	Rhythmean	117	Phi Beta Doc	122	120,000	1:50.01	92
2000	Whata Brainstorm	3	R.B. Homeister Jr	122	Muntel	122	Womble	117	120,000	1:47.80	98
2001	Western Pride	3	D.G. Whitney	122	Tour of the Cat	113	Built Up	117	120,000	1:51.12	108
2002	Union Place	3	E.M. Coa	115	Miesque's Approval	122	The Judge Sez Who	122	120,000	1:47.76	
2003	Stroll	3	J.D. Bailey	122	Certifiably Crazy	115	Super Frolic	119	120,000	1:48.39	97
2004	Eddington	3	E.M. Coa	114	Bob's Proud Moment	116	Caballero Negro	114	120,000	1:51.25	97

Capias finished third but was disqualified and placed 12th

Beyer Index: 100.58

CALIFORNIAN (G2), 1 1/8 Miles, 3-Year-Olds and Up, Hollywood Park, 2004 Purse: $250,000

Year	Winner	Age	Jockey	Wt.	Second	Wt.	Third	Wt.	Win Value	Time	Beyer
1954	Imbros	4	J. Longden	118	Determine	115	High Scud	114	75,300	1:41.00	
1955	Swaps	3	D. Erb	115	Determine	126	Mister Gus	117	63,700	1:40.40	
1956	Porterhouse	5	I. Valenzuela	118	Swaps	127	Mister Gus	118	63,700	1:40.80	
1957	Social Climber	4	W. Shoemaker	119	Round Table	105	Find	119	71,800	1:40.40	
1958	Seaneen	4	J. Longden	109	Round Table	130	Terrang	115	63,300	1:41.00	
1959	Hillsdale	4	T. Barrow	123	Amerigo	107	Ying and Yang	109	67,900	1:40.80	
1960	Fleet Nasrullah	5	J. Longden	119	Eddie Schmidt	113	Bagdad	123	66,300	1:40.60	
1961	First Balcony	4	E. Burns	115	Prove It	127	Sea Orbit	115	67,700	1:40.40	
1962	Cadiz	6	W. Harmatz	111	Prove It	123	Olden Times	123	71,200	1:41.60	
1963	Winonly	6	J. Leonard	115	Mr. Consistency	111	Harpie	115	77,300	1:41.80	
1964	Mustard Plaster	5	J. Leonard	111	Mr. Consistency	123	Colorado King	123	70,500	1:41.60	
1965	Viking Spirit	5	K. Church	115	Quadrangle	123	Tronado	114	67,900	1:40.80	
1966	Travel Orb	4	W. Harmatz	112	Make Money	112	Sledge	112	75,100	1:41.80	
1967	Biggs	7	W. Harmatz	112	Make Money	112	Pretense	130	74,200	1:41.60	
1968	Dr. Fager	4	B. Baeza	130	Gamely	116	Rising Market	121	74,600	1:40.80	

Year	Winner	Age	Jockey	Wt.	Second	Wt.	Third	Wt.	Win Value	Time	Beyer
1969	Nodouble	4	E. Belmonte	127	Rising Market	121	London Jet	112	70,400	1:40.40	
1970	Baffle	5	J. Lambert	113	Figonero	124	Nodouble	130	62,800	1:40.20	
1971	Cougar II	5	W. Shoemaker	124	Master Hand	112	Fleet Surprise	118	81,100	1:41.20	
1972	Cougar II	6	W. Shoemaker	127	Kennedy Road	119	Miles Tyson	118	76,400	1:39.20	
1973	Quack	4	D. Pierce	126	Royal Owl	125	Tri Jet	118	65,300	1:41.40	
1974	Quack	5	D. Pierce	126	Ancient Title	126	Woodland Pines	120	70,900	1:40.20	
1975	Ancient Title	5	L. Pincay Jr	126	Big Band	117	Century's Envoy	117	73,100	1:40.20	
1976	Ancient Title	6	S. Hawley	127	Pay Tribute	117	Austin Mittler	116	65,300	1:41.20	
1977	Crystal Water	4	L. Pincay Jr	128	Mark's Place	121	Ancient Title	123	65,300	1:41.00	
1978	J.O. Tobin	4	S. Cauthen	126	Replant	120	Cox's Ridge	127	124,550	1:41.00	
1979	Affirmed	4	L. Pincay Jr	130	Syncopate	114	Harry's Love	117	159,900	1:41.20	
1980	Spectacular Bid	4	W. Shoemaker	130	Paint King	115	Caro Bambino	118	184,450	1:45.80	
1981	Eleven Stitches	4	S. Hawley	122	Temperence Hill	130	Kilijaro	123	207,600	1:48.40	
1982	Erins Isle	4	L. Pincay Jr	117	It's the One	128	Major Sport	118	200,200	1:48.00	
1983	The Wonder	5	W. Shoemaker	119	Prince Spellbound	122	Poley	117	192,000	1:48.40	
1984	Desert Wine	4	E. Delahoussaye	121	Interco	126	Sari's Dreamer	116	193,600	1:47.60	
1985	Greinton	4	L. Pincay Jr	119	Precisionist	126	Lord at War	126	179,600	1:32.60	
1986	Precisionist	5	C.J. McCarron	126	Super Diamond	117	Skywalker	121	188,400	1:33.60	
1987	Judge Angelucci	4	G. Baze	118	Iron Eyes	115	Snow Chief	126	193,200	1:48.20	
1988	Cutlass Reality	6	C.J. McCarron	115	Gulch	126	Judge Angelucci	126	180,200	1:47.60	
1989	Sabona	7	C.J. McCarron	115	Blushing John	124	Lively One	118	185,800	1:46.00	
1990	Sunday Silence	4	P.A. Valenzuela	126	Stylish Winner	115	Charlatan III	111	168,400	1:48.00	113
1991	Roanoke	4	E. Delahoussaye	116	Anshan	118	Marquetry	113	175,600	1:48.20	109
1992	Another Review	4	K.J. Desormeaux	119	Defensive Play	120	Ibero	119	119,400	1:48.00	105
1993	Latin American	5	G.L. Stevens	116	Missionary Ridge	116	Memo	118	220,000	1:46.80	111
1994	The Wicked North	5	K.J. Desormeaux	120	Kingdom Found	116	Slew of Damascus	116	165,000	1:46.60	116
1995	Concern	4	M.E. Smith	122	Tossofthecoin	118	Tinners Way	116	160,900	1:47.60	108
1996	Tinners Way	6	E. Delahoussaye	116	Helmsman	122	Mr Purple	122	151,980	1:46.60	113
1997	River Keen	5	K.J. Desormeaux	117	Hesabull	118	Benchmark	118	150,000	1:47.20	112
1998	Mud Route	4	C.J. McCarron	116	Deputy Commander	122	Worldly Ways	117	150,000	1:48.00	109
1999	Old Trieste	4	C.J. McCarron	116	Budroyale	120	Puerto Madero	122	180,000	1:46.40	118
2000	Big Ten	5	A. Solis	116	Early Pioneer	118	Mojave Moon	116	150,000	1:49.22	104
2001	Skimming	5	G.K. Gomez	116	Futural	120	Aptitude	116	300,000	1:48.12	111
2002	Milwaukee Brew	5	K.J. Desormeaux	122	Bosque Redondo	118	Momentum	118	300,000	1:48.06	114
2003	Kudos	6	A. Solis	116	Piensa Sonando	118	Reba's Gold	118	240,000	1:47.91	108
2004	Even the Score	6	D.R. Flores	118	Total Impact	116	Nose the Trade	116	150,000	1:47.64	109

Beyer Index: 110.67

CANADIAN TURF HANDICAP (G3), 1 1/16 Miles (Off the Turf), 3-Year-Olds and Up, Gulfstream Park, 2004 Purse: $100,000

Year	Winner	Age	Jockey	Wt.	Second	Wt.	Third	Wt.	Win Value	Time	Beyer
1967	Chinatower	5	H. Gustines	114	Snow Dance	112	Circus	112	2,300	1:41.20	
1968	Flit-to	5	J. Vasquez				Out the Window	115	15,575	1:41.20	
	War Censor	5	E. Fires	115							
1969	Go Marching	4	M. Ycaza	123	Out the Window	114	Jean-Pierre	112	26,550	1:43.80	
1970	Jungle Cove	4	L. Adams	114	Zarco	112	Elegant Heir	112	34,650	1:52.80	
1971	Broker's Tip II	6	M. Hole	115	Tudor Reward	112	North Flight	110	31,305	1:41.80	
1972	Speedy Zephyr	4	R. Turcotte	117	Knight Counter	113	Mr. Pow Wow	123	43,560	1:43.60	
							Super Sail	112			
1973	Windtex	4	J.L. Rotz	116	Dubasoff	117	Getajetholme	112	23,835	1:41.40	
1973	Life Cycle	4	F. Ianelli	115	Roundhouse	113	Hope Eternal	112	23,415	1:42.80	
1974	Baccalaureate	4	R. Woodhouse	110	Rey Maya	112	Jogging	117	43,800	1:42.20	
1975	Sir Jason	4	M.A. Rivera	113	Westgate Mall	109	Mr. Door	114	30,675	1:40.80	
1976	Step Forward	4	M. Solomone	117	Lord Henham	112	Conesaba	113	40,320	1:40.20	
1977	Gravelines	5	J.D. Bailey	122	Proponent	114	Lord Layabout	112	33,420	1:44.40	
1977	Gay Jitterbug	4	L. Saumell	121	Riverside Sam	110	Blacksmith	110	32,820	1:44.00	
1978	Practitioner	5	J.S. Rodriguez	119	Haverty	112	That's a Nice	116	29,820	1:41.60	
1978	Court Open	4	R. Woodhouse	109	All Friends	114	Oilfield	114	29,520	1:40.80	
1979	Roan Star	6	C. Perret	115	Fleet Gar	117	Family Doctor	113	31,590	1:40.80	
1979	Noble Dancer II	7	J. Vasquez	128	Scythian Gold	118	River Warrior	114	31,290	1:41.00	
1980	Morning Frolic	5	A. Cordero Jr	118	Pearlescent	114	Dickens Hill	122	41,220	1:41.20	
1981	Proctor	4	C. Perret	119	Imperial Dilemma	113	Foretake	115	61,290	1:41.00	
1982	Robsphere	5	D. Brumfield	115	Dom Menotti	111	King of Mardi Gras	115	39,690	1:41.00	
1983	Data Swap	6	M. Solomone	115	Northrop	118	Wicked Will	116	42,105	1:47.20	
1983	Super Sunrise	4	E. Maple	112	Summer Advocate	118	Pin Puller	112	40,755	1:46.60	
1984	Ayman	4	J. Cruguet	112	Smart and Sharp	110	Guston	114	57,555	1:40.00	
1985	Nepal	5	J.D. Bailey	112	Dr. Schwartzman	116	Roving Minstrel	120	61,410	1:40.00	
1986	Amerilad	5	J.A. Velez Jr	113	Flying Pidgeon	119	Uptown Swell	118	57,060	1:40.20	
1986	Vanlandingham	5	D. MacBeth	126	Ends Well	115	Dr. Schwartzman	118	56,460	1:40.00	
1987	Racing Star	5	S.B. Soto	112	Glaros	112	Salem Drive	113	54,420	1:40.80	
1987	New Colony	4	V.H. Molina	109	Tri for Size	110	Trubulare	111	55,020	1:42.00	
1988	Equalize	6	J.D. Bailey	112	Yankee Affair	118	Sans the Shadow	117	99,180	1:41.20	

Year	Winner	Age	Jockey	Wt.	Second	Wt.	Third	Wt.	Win Value	Time	Beyer
1989	Equalize	7	J.A. Santos	126	Sunshine Forever	126	Mi Selecto	116	71,280	1:41.00	
1990	Youmadeyourpoint	4	D. Valiente	114	Wanderkin	116	Maceo	113	60,000	1:44.60	106
1991	Izvestia	4	R. Platts	122	Miss Josh	112	Bye Union Ave.	113	60,000	1:41.40	100
1992	Buckhar	4	J. Cruguet	113	Tin Can Ali	113	Archies L'ghter	114	60,000	1:48.40	102
1993	Stagecraft	6	J.D. Bailey	112	Roman Envoy	121	Carterista	114	60,000	1:47.80	106
1994	Paradise Creek	5	M.E. Smith	123	Glenfiddich Lad	113	Nijinsky's Gold	113	60,000	1:47.80	108
1995	The Vid	5	J.D. Bailey	117	Star of Manila	118	Country Coy	113	60,000	1:47.00	108
1996	The Vid	6	W.H. McCauley	124	Gone for Real	114	Warning Glance	115	60,000	1:47.00	109
1997	Devil's Cup	4	R. Wilson	114	Da Bull	113	Green Means Go	115	60,000	1:47.00	107
1998	Subordination	4	J.D. Bailey	112	Cimarron Secret	117	Tour's Big Red	113	60,000	1:50.80	99
1999	Federal Trial	4	R.G. Davis	114	Deep Dive	114	Unite's Big Red	116	60,000	1:47.90	103
2000	Shamrock City	5	E.S. Prado	114	Rhythmean	113	Sharp Appeal	115	60,000	1:47.15	104
2001	Inexplicable	6	J.A. Santos	115	Band Is Passing	118	David Copperfield	114	90,000	1:39.43	107
2002	North East Bound	6	J.A. Velez Jr	116	Capsized	114	Fyling Avie	116	90,000	1:44.01	101
2003	Political Attack	4	M. Guidry	114	Miesque's Approval	116	Strategic Partner	114	60,000	1:40.43	102
2004	Newfoundland	4	J.R. Velazquez	115	Millennium Dragon	118	Everything to Gain	113	60,000	1:44.90	100

Beyer Index: 104.13

Off the turf in 1998, 2002, 2004

CARDINAL HANDICAP (G3), 1 1/8 Miles (Turf), Fillies and Mares, 3-Year-Olds and Up, Churchill Downs, 2004 Purse: $173,550

Year	Winner	Age	Jockey	Wt.	Second	Wt.	Third	Wt.	Win Value	Time	Beyer
1974	Cut the Talk	3	D. Brown	116	Holding Pattern		Sturdy Steel			1:45.20	
1975	Visier	3	R. Riera	116	Slade's Prospect		Ski Run			1:45.80	
1976	Hope of Glory	4	D. Brumfield	113	Bronze Point		Straignt			1:25.00	
1976	Vivacious Meg	4	R. Breen	113	Regal Gal		Regal Humor			1:25.40	
1977	Likely Exchange	3	J. McKnight	114	My Complements		My Bold Beauty			1:25.80	
1977	Famed Princess	4	C. Ledezma	113	Chatta		Leigh Simms			1:24.80	
1978	Love to Tell	3	E. Delahoussaye	116	Selari's Choice		Bit of Sunshine			1:24.40	
1978	Unreality	4	L. Suire	123	Navajo Princess		Irish Agate			1:24.20	
1979	Impetuous Gal	4	E. Fires	113	Billy Jane		Cookie Puddin			1:24.60	
1979	Gap Axe	4	D. Brumfield	115	Unreality		Honey Blonde			1:24.80	
1980	Vite View	4	D. Brumfield	120	Doing It My Way		Jeanie's Fancy			1:24.60	
1980	Champagne Ginny	3	D. Brumfield	119	Impetuous Gal		Red Chiffon			1:24.80	
1981	Knight's Beauty	4	T. Hightower	115	Deuces Over Seven		Roger's Turn			1:24.80	
1981	Safe Play	3	S. Spencer	122	Lillian Russell		La Vue			1:24.20	
1982	Betty Money	3	B. Sayler	116	Raja's Delight		Mezimica			1:38.80	
1982	Promising Native	3	S. Maple	114	What Glitter		Sweetest Chant			1:39.60	
1983	Charge My Account	4	P. Day	112	Heatherten		Etoile du Matin			1:47.20	
1984	Electric Fanny	3	J. Espinoza	112	Straight Edition		Mickey's Echo			1:48.00	
1985	Mrs. Revere	4	L. Melancon	112	Wealthy and Wise		My Inheritance			1:48.20	
1985	Mr. T's Tune	4	K. Allen	118	Gerrie Singer		Adaptable			1:47.00	
1986	Oriental	4	K. Allen	123	Kapalua Butterflu		Glorious View			1:45.80	
1987	Lake Champlain	4	P. Day	119	Marianna's Girl		Shot Gun Bonnie			1:46.20	
1988	Top Corsage	5	P. Valenzuela	118	Savannah's Honor		Graceful Darby			1:52.40	
1989	Townsend Lass	4	K. Allen	114	Bangkok Lady		Bearly Cooking			1:52.00	
1990	Dance for Lucy	4	D. Penna	113	Betty Lobelia		Phoenix Sunshine		39,270	1:51.80	93
1990	Lady in Silver	4	P. Day	122	Coolawin	121	Splendid Try		38,780	1:51.40	97
1991	Christiecat	4	A. Cordero Jr	118	Super Fan	115	Screen Prospect	113	75,010	1:51.00	99
1992	Auto Dial	4	S.J. Sellers	113	Radiant Ring	119	Red Journey	114	73,125	1:52.04	84
1993	River Ball	7	J.R. Parsley	109	Marshua's River	112	Logan's Mist	118	74,945	1:55.79	99
1994	Bold Ruritana	4	P. Day	116	Eternal Reve	117	Monaassabaat	113	76,375	1:48.25	99
1995	Apolda	4	P. Day	114	Alive With Hope	114	Lady Reiko	115	75,530	1:49.59	100
1996	Miss Caerleona	4	L. Melancon	114	Bail Out Becky	121	Striesen	113	72,850	1:47.81	105
	Bail Out Becky finished first but was disqualified and placed second										
1997	Colcon	4	J.D. Bailey	114	Dancer Clear	112	Sagar Pride	113	108,903	1:51.89	100
1998	B.A. Valentine	5	J.F. Chavez	115	Mingling Glances	112	Cuando	116	111,693	1:48.62	102
1999	Pratella	4	B. Peck	114	Mingling Glances		Uanme		106,299	1:48.88	101
2000	Illiquidity	4	J. Court	115	License Fee	118	Miss of Wales	114	109,182	1:49.72	100
2001	Watch	4	C. Perret	114	Sitka	111	Gino's Spirits	118	104,997	1:49.12	97
2002	Quick Tip	4	R.J. Albarado	114	Sun Dare	114	Bien Nicole	118	107,322	1:51.08	98
2003	Riskaverse	4	C.H. Velasquez	118	Bien Nicole	120	Firth of Lorne	116	108,624	1:50.53	102
2004	Aud	4	B. Blanc	115	May Gator	117	Angela's Love	114	107,601	1:53.94	99

Beyer Index: 98.44

ROBERT F. CAREY MEMORIAL HANDICAP (G3), 1 Mile (Turf), 3-Year-Olds and Up, Hawthorne Race Course, 2004 Purse: $150,000

Year	Winner	Age	Jockey	Wt.	Second	Wt.	Third	Wt.	Win Value	Time	Beyer
1983	Sir Pele	4	O. Vergara	112	John's Gold	120	Energetic King	111	64,800	1:55.00	
1984	Ronbra	4	C. Marquez	115	Grazie	115	Bold Run	115	66,540	2:03.80	

Year	Winner	Age	Jockey	Wt.	Second	Wt.	Third	Wt.	Win Value	Time	Beyer
1985	River Lord	6	R. Meier	112	Harham's Sizzler	118	Attaway to Go	112	63,370	2:06.20	
1986	Pass the Line	5	J.L. Diaz	117	Explosive Darling	117	Salem Drive	116	94,500	2:01.00	
1987	The Sassman	4	K.D. Clark	113	Zaizoom	115	Zuppardo's Love	111	89,130	2:05.40	
1988	New Colony	5	R.R. Douglas	114	Rio's Lark	115	Bank Fast	111	93,900	1:47.60	
1989	Iron Courage	5	D. Penna	121	Saint Oxford	112	Do Loop	109	94,080	1:47.00	
1990	Allijeba	4	K.D. Clark	118	Wave Wise	114	Expensive Decision	118	87,070	1:39.20	
1991	Slew the Slewor	4	G.K. Gomez	114	Jalajel	118	The Great Carl	118	96,090	1:38.60	105
1992	Double Booked	7	J.C. Ferrer	115	Evanescent	113	That's Sunny	114	60,000	1:39.80	98
1993	High Habitation	5	G.C. Retana	114	Beau Fasa	114	Glenfiddich Lad	114	60,000	1:35.20	96
1994	Recoup the Cash	4	J.L. Diaz	119	Road of War	115	Glenfiddich Lad	114	60,000	1:40.80	109
1995	Homing Pigeon	5	R.J. Albarado	114	Gilder	113	Rare Reason	119	60,000	1:38.00	98
1996	Homing Pigeon	6	R.J. Albarado	114	Joker	115	Why Change	115	90,000	1:36.40	104
1997	Trail City	4	J.D. Bailey	119	Power of Opinion	113	Da Bull	114	90,000	1:36.00	105
1998	Soviet Line	8	S.J. Sellers	115	Fun To Run	110	Wild Event	115	90,000	1:33.40	103
1999	Ray's Approval	6	E. Fires	114	Stay Sound	115	Inkatha	115	90,000	1:37.01	103
2000	Where's Taylor	4	C.J. Lanerie	117	Dernier Croise	113	Associate	115	90,000	1:36.31	103
2001	Galic Boy	6	R. Sibille	115	Where's Taylor	121	Good Journey	115	90,000	1:35.10	105
2002	Kimberlite Pipe	6	C.A. Emigh	115	Aslaaf	114	Major Omansky	115	90,000	1:35.94	98
2003	Mystery Giver	5	C.H. Marquez Jr	120	Al's Dearly Bred	118	Major Rhythm	116	90,000	1:34.70	98
2004	Scooter Roach	5	J.M. Campbell	115	Gin and Sin	116	Cloudy's Knight	116	90,000	1:34.51	94

Beyer Index: 101.36

Run at 1 3/16 miles, turf, in 1983; 1 1/4 miles, turf, 1984, 1986-87; 1 1/4 miles, 1985; 1 1/8 miles, turf, 1988-89, 1 mile 70 yards, 1994

CARRY BACK (G3), 6 Furlongs
3-Year-Olds, Calder Race Course, 2004 Purse: $300,000

Year	Winner	Age	Jockey	Wt.	Second	Wt.	Third	Wt.	Win Value	Time	Beyer
1975	Precipitory	2	J. Salinas	116	Chic Ruler	116	Upper Current	119	14,400	1:06.80	
1976	Winner's Hit	2	R. Broussard	119	My Budget	119	Time for Fun	116	14,640	1:07.00	
1977	Chwesboken	2	D. Hidalgo	119	Noon Time Spender	122	Ski's Never Bend	116	13,320	1:05.40	
1978	Admiral Rix	2	T. Barrow	116	Tartan Tam	116	Cherry Pop	116	14,160	1:07.40	
1979	Breezy Fire	4	M. Rivera	120	Cherry Pop	113	Noble Heart	111	16,770	1:24.60	
1980	Diplomatic Note	3	J. Bailey	112	Buck'n Shoe	115	Fast Fast Freddie	113	16,785	1:12.00	
1981	Face the Moment	3	E. Cardone	115	Toga Toga	113	Incredible John	118	16,530	1:11.00	
1982	Rex's Profile	3	E. Cardone	115	Libra Moon	118	Center Cut	123	16,395	1:11.40	
1983	Opening Lead	3	B. Gonzalez	112	El Perico	117	Neutral Player	112	16,785	1:25.80	
1984	Bowmans Express	3	O. Londono	119	Mo Exception	114	No Room	119	19,305	1:25.40	
1985	Smile	3	J. Vasquez	123	Paravon	112	Hickory Hill Flyer	114	46,260	1:23.80	
1986	Kid Colin	3	G. St. Leon	116	Big Jolt	116	Lucky Rebeau	116	38,610	1:25.80	
1987	You're No Bargain	3	O. Londono	117	Right Rudder	112	Jilsie's Gigalo	118	44,010	1:25.60	
1988	In the Slammer	3	M. Gonzalez	114	Lover's Trust	122	Ashmint	115	32,220	1:23.50	
1989	Big Stanley	3	D. Valiente	120	Valid Space	114	Jabotinsky	117	32,610	1:23.60	
1990	Country Isle	3	H. Castillo Jr	114	Run Turn	120	Ultimate Swale	112	33,840	1:24.80	
1991	Ocala Flame	3	R. Lester	113	Sunny and Pleasant	113	Jacquelyn's Groom	113	33,180	1:19.00	
1992	Always Silver	3	M. Lee	116	Appealtothechief	114	Dr Arne	114	30,000	1:25.00	101
1993	Humbugaboo	3	M. Russ	112	Signoir Valery	112	Kassec	113	60,000	1:22.74	98
1994	Score a Birdie	3	H. Castillo Jr	115	Fortunate Joe	112	Ali'Ibito'reality	114	60,000	1:24.09	100
1995	Sonic Signal	3	R. Douglas	115	Leave'm Inthedark	117	Too Great	113	60,000	1:24.79	92
1996	Fortunate Review	3	A. Toribio	117	Betweenhereorthere	115	Night Runner	113	60,000	1:23.27	97
1997	Renteria	3	E. Coa	115	Red	122	Willow Skips Trial	115	120,000	1:11.28	108
1998	Mint	3	E. Coa	115	Diamond Studs	115	Mt. Laurel	112	120,000	1:11.38	110
1999	Silver Season	3	E. Coa	112	Deep Gold	117	Night Patrol	117	120,000	1:11.32	103
2000	Caller One	3	C.S. Nakatani	122	Fappie's Notebook	115	Malagot	115	120,000	1:10.35	116
2001	Illusioned	3	J.F. Chavez	117	Beyond Brilliant	117	Gallant Frolic	115	150,000	1:11.08	102
2002	Royal Lad	3	J.D. Bailey	117	Captain Squire	122	Friendly Frolic	114	150,000	1:10.73	105
2003	Valid Video	3	J. Bravo	122	Cajun Beat	117	Super Fuse	117	177,000	1:10.15	110
2004	Weigelia	3	A Toribio Jr	117	Classy Migration	112	Bwana Charlie	119	177,000	1:10.50	108

Beyer Index: 103.85

Run as Carry Back Handicap, 1981-1993; For 2-year-olds, 1975-1978; For 3-year-olds and up, 1979; At 5 1/2 furlongs, 1975-1978; At 6 1/2 furlongs in 1991; At 7 furlongs in 1979, 1983-1990, 1992-1996

CARTER HANDICAP (G1), 7 Furlongs,
3-Year-Olds and Up, Aqueduct, 2004 Purse: $350,000

Year	Winner	Age	Jockey	Wt.	Second	Wt.	Third	Wt.	Win Value	Time	Beyer
1895	Charade	6	Doggett	100	The Pepper	118	Stephen J.	112	600	2:11.60	
1896	Deerslayer	4	Doggett	100	Charade	105	Lehrman	115	675	1:55.00	
1897	Premier	4	Coylie	114	Storm King	112	Sun Up	116	540	1:49.00	
1898	The Manxman	4	Lewis	114	Don't Care	106	Tabouret	110	1,350	1:29.60	
1899	D. of Middleburg	3	Sullivan	106	Dr. Parker	100	Bannock	118	1,470	1:26.60	
1900	Box	6	Maher	125	Boney Boy	108	The Kentuckian	114	1,560	1:26.00	
1901	Motley	4	Shaw	110	Robert Waddell	99	Pupil	106	1,570	1:28.00	
1902	Ethics	4	H. Cochran	106	Contend	107	Petra	108	1,645	1:28.20	

Year	Winner	Age	Jockey	Wt.	Second	Wt.	Third	Wt.	Win Value	Time	Beyer
1903	Ahumada	3	J. Martin	101	Yellow Tail	106	Illyria	85	2,735	1:33.00	
1904	Beldame	3	F. O'Neill	103	Peter Paul	98	Wotan	100	7,710	1:27.00	
1905	Ormonde's Right	4	W. Davis	110	Roseben	113	Little Em	105	7,140	1:26.80	
1906	Roseben	5	L. Lyne	129	Southern Cross	106	Red Knight	108	7,850	1:26.60	
1907	Glorifier	5	Mountain	119	Roseben	135	Don Diego	108	7,850	1:28.20	
1908	Jack Atkin	4	Musgrave	122	Red River	108	Chapultepec	105	6,850	1:27.80	
1910	Gretna Green	6	G. Burns	105	Alfred Noble	115	Far West	103	1,925	1:27.00	
1914	Roamer	3	M. Buxton	109	Borrow	129	Fl. Fairy	117	1,925	1:24.80	
1915	Phosphor	3	J. Loftus	116	Pomette Bleu	104	Leo. Skolny	105	1,925	1:30.00	
1916	Trial by Jury	4	E. Campbell	121	Ormesdale	105	Sh't Grass	120	1,925	1:25.40	
1917	Old Rosebud	6	A. Schuttinger	130	Bromo	122	The Finn	130	2,825	1:25.80	
1918	Old Koenig	5	G. Byrne	122	Roamer	130	Polymelian	128	2,825	1:23.80	
1919	Naturalist	5	C. Fairbrother	132	Star Master	125	Routledge	104	2,825	1:23.00	
1920	Audacious	4	F. Keogh	117	Constancy	110	Naturalist	124	3,850	1:25.00	
1921	Audacious	5	C. Kummer	126	Sennings Park	113	Idle Dell	96	7,300	1:23.00	
1922	Knobbie	4	L. Fator	120	Careful	115	Bon Homme	109	7,600	1:24.40	
1923	Little Celt	3	C. Turner	116	Knobbie	128	Little Chief	124	7,400	1:25.40	
1924	Sarazen	3	E. Sande	118	Brainstorm	112	Ordinance	115	6,900	1:25.60	
1925	Silver Fox	3	L. Fator	114	Worthmore	128	Candy Kid	106	8,150	1:24.40	
1926	Macaw	3	L. McAtee	123			Extra Dry	99.5	4,750	1:24.60	
	Nedana	4	L. Fator	119							
1927	Happy Argo	4	F. Weiner	119	Black Maria	124	Macaw	124	9,250	1:24.20	
1928	Osmand	4	E. Sande	122	Byrd	110	Happy Argo	129	9,250	1:25.00	
1929	Osmand	5	W. Garner	132	Petee Wrack	123	Distraction	108	8,900	1:26.60	
1930	Flying Heels	3	W. Kelsay	118	Sarazen II	108	Jack High	127	7,650	1:24.40	
1931	Flying Heels	4	C. Kurtsinger	125	Mr. Sponge	116	Hi-jack	130	7,400	1:24.20	
1932	Happy Scot	4	A. Robertson	117	Mr. Sponge	128	Pompeius	111	6,100	1:24.80	
1933	Caterwaul	3	R. Workman	114	Condescend	119	Parry	108	600	1:20.20	
1934	Open Range	3	E. Litzenberger	95	Halcyon	109	Okapi	118	895	1:18.00	
1935	King Saxon	4	C. Rainey	127	Singing Wood	118	Sgt. Byrne	115	6,850	1:23.80	
1936	Clang	4	E. Litzenberger	110	Sation	132	Cycle	112	7,200	1:24.00	
1937	Aneroid	4	C. Rosengarten	123	Deliberator	113	Sgt. Byrne	116	8,875	1:23.60	
1938	Airflame	4	R. Workman	119	Snark	132	Jay Jay	123	7,400	1:23.60	
1939	Fighting Fox	4	J. Stout	119	Can't Wait	112	Rough Time	119	7,600	1:22.80	
1940	He Did	7	G. Woolf	124	Third Degree	124	T.M. Dorsett	113	8,400	1:23.80	
1941	Parasang	4	B. James	114	Harvard Square	120	Omission	117	6,375	1:23.00	
1942	Doublrab	4	B. Thompson	120	Swing and Sway	112	Whirlaway	130	7,250	1:23.00	
1943	Devil Diver	4	G. Woolf	126	Marriage	118	Doublrab	118	7,150	1:24.00	
1944	Bossuet	4	J. Stout	127					3,623	1:23.40	
	Brownie	5	E. Guerin	115							
	Wait a Bit	5	G.L. Smith	118							
1945	Apache	6	J. Stout	130	Wait a Bit	121	First Fiddle	126	7,945	1:24.60	
1946	Flood Town	4	W. Mehrtens	113	King Dorsett	126	Black Swan	112	8,125	1:23.60	
1947	Rippey	4	O. Scurlock	112	Inroc	118	Gallorette	123	19,750	1:23.00	
1948	Gallorette	6	J. Jessop	122	Rippey	132	Skylighter	110	20,550	1:23.40	
1949	Better Self	4	D. Gorman	126	Rippey	123	High Trend	107	20,350	1:25.20	
1950	Guillotine	3	T. Atkinson	109	Noble Impulse	114	Hyphasis	108	16,950	1:23.20	
1951	Arise	5	E. Guerin	122	More Sun	108	Piet	123	16,000	1:23.40	
1952	Northern Star	4	T. Atkinson	115	Crafty Admiral	120	To Market	123	20,250	1:22.00	
1953	Tom Fool	4	T. Atkinson	135	Squared Away	122	Eatontown	113	41,700	1:22.00	
1954	White Skies	5	J. Stout	133	First Aid	115	Royal Vale	126	44,200	1:23.60	
1955	Bobby Brocato	4	R. Broussard	116	Social Outcast	123	Artismo	111	43,000	1:23.40	
1956	Red Hannigan	5	P.J. Bailey	114	Switch On	119	Artismo	111	40,400	1:23.20	
1957	Portersville	5	T. Atkinson	111	Dedicate	126	Jutland	112	40,800	1:23.00	
1958	Bold Ruler	4	E. Arcaro	135	Tick Tock	113	Gallant Man	128	37,620	1:22.60	
1959	Jimmer	4	J. Ruane	108	Tick Tock	122	Nadir	122	37,490	1:22.60	
1960	Yes You Will	4	L. Adams	122	Mail Order	118	Dunce	119	38,205	1:22.40	
1961	Chief of Chiefs	4	J. Leonard	116	April Skies	127	Natural Bid	111	38,805	1:22.80	
1962	Merry Ruler	4	J. Sellers	119	Hitting Away	119	Rullah Red	113	38,545	1:22.00	
1963	Admiral's Voyage	4	R. Broussard	126	For the Road	117	Saidam	112	37,830	1:22.40	
1964	Ahoy	4	H. Grant	133	Red Gar	112	Gun Bow	126	37,505	1:21.60	
1965	Viking Spirit	5	K. Church	123	Cupid	114	Chieftain	125	35,620	1:21.40	
1966	Davis II	6	C. Stone	116	Time Tested	126	Dapper Dan	113	37,440	1:22.80	
1967	Tumiga	3	B. Feliciano	113	Our Michael	120	Indulto	113	36,790	1:23.80	
1968	In Reality	4	J. Velasquez	124	Tumiga	121	Mr. Washington	119	36,270	1:21.80	
1969	Promise	4	R. Ussery	124	Iron Ruler	121	Royal Exchange	121	37,440	1:22.60	
1970	Tyrant	4	R. Ussery	117	Best Turn	118	Fast Hilarious	126	36,010	1:21.40	
1971	Native Royalty	4	J.L. Rotz	112	Cut the Comedy	112	Shut Eye	116	35,280	1:22.80	
	Tyrant finished second but was disqualified and placed last										
1972	Leematt	4	M. Venezia	116	Canonero II	121	Native Royalty	121	34,200	1:22.40	
1973	King's Bishop	4	E. Maple	114	Onion	114	Petrograd	118	35,220	1:20.40	
1974	Forego	4	H. Gustines	129	Mr. Prospector	124	Timeless Moment	113	33,900	1:22.20	
1975	Forego	5	H. Gustines	134	Stop the Music	123	Orders	114	34,860	1:21.60	

Year	Winner	Age	Jockey	Wt.	Second	Wt.	Third	Wt.	Win Value	Time	Beyer
1976	Due Diligence	4	J. Amy	111	Honorable Miss	122	Amerrico	122	33,810	1:22.40	
1977	Quiet Little Table	4	E. Maple	119	Gentle King	110	Full Out	117	21,915	1:22.00	
1977	Soy Numero Uno	4	R. Broussard	126	Barrera	119	Gallant Bob	116	31,770	1:22.20	
1978	Pumpkin Moonshine	4	D.A. Bordern	107	Prefontaine	112	Big John Taylor	113	31,920	1:22.20	
1978	Jaipur's Gem	5	J.L. Samyn	115	Vencedor	111	Half High	118	32,070	1:21.60	
1979	Star de Naskra	4	J. Fell	122	Alydar	126	Sensitive Prince	126	48,690	1:21.20	
1980	Czaravich	4	L. Adams	126	Tanthem	122	Nice Catch	120	49,050	1:21.00	
1981	Amber Pass	4	E. Maple	114	Guilty Conscience	111	Dunham's Gift	116	49,410	1:23.00	
1982	Pass the Tab	4	A. Graell	118	Royal Hierarchy	115	Maudlin	114	52,110	1:22.40	
1983	Vittorioso	4	A. Smith	113	Sing Sing	122	Fit to Fight	116	67,800	1:22.80	
1984	Bet Big	4	J.L. Samyn	115	Cannon Shell	109	A Phenomenon	126	73,200	1:21.80	
1985	Mt. Livermore	4	J.D. Bailey	117	Rocky Marriage	122	Carr de Naskra	125	83,340	1:20.80	
1986	Love That Mac	4	E. Maple	117	Ziggy's Boy	118	King's Swan	120	116,460	1:21.60	
1987	Pine Tree Lane	5	R.P. Romero	119	King's Swan	123	Zany Tactics	119	170,400	1:21.20	
1988	Gulch	4	J.A. Santos	124	Afleet	124	Its Acedemic	108	174,300	1:20.40	
1989	On the Line	5	G.L. Stevens	125	True and Blue	114	Dr. Carrington	110	140,880	1:21.40	
1990	Dancing Spree	5	C.W. Antley	123	Dancing Pretense	115	Sewickley	119	137,280	1:22.00	115
1991	Housebuster	4	C. Perret	122	Black Tie Affair	123	Gervazy	116	120,000	1:21.20	119
1992	Rubiano	5	J.A. Santos	118	Kid Russell	112	In Excess	122	140,640	1:21.40	108
1993	Alydeed	4	C. Perret	122	Loach	112	Argyle Lake	113	90,000	1:22.60	111
1994	Virginia Rapids	4	J.L. Samyn	118	Punch Line	114	Cherokee Run	119	90,000	1:21.40	109
1995	Lite the Fuse	4	R.B. Perez	111	Our Emblem	113	You and I	113	90,000	1:21.40	108
1996	Lite the Fuse	5	J.A. Krone	121	Flying Chevron	115	Placid Fund	114	90,000	1:20.80	111
1997	Langfuhr	5	J.F. Chavez	122	Stalwart Member	113	Western Winter	112	90,000	1:22.80	106
1998	Wild Rush	4	K.J. Desormeaux	117	Banker's Gold	114	Western Borders	115	120,000	1:21.16	115
1999	Artax	4	J.F. Chavez	114	Affirmed Success	119	Western Borders	113	120,000	1:20.04	123
2000	Brutally Frank	6	S.X. Bridgmohan	116	Western Expression	113	Affirmed Success	122	120,000	1:21.66	106
2001	Peeping Tom	4	S.X. Bridgmohan	118	Say Florida Sandy	116	Hook And Ladder	118	180,000	1:21.33	113
2002	Affirmed Success	8	R. Migliore	119	Voodoo	113	Burning Roma	117	210,000	1:21.84	111
2003	Congaree	5	G.L. Stevens	122	Aldebaran	118	Peeping Tom	114	210,000	1:21.48	116
2004	Pico Central	5	A. Solis	117	Strong Hope	119	Eye of the Tiger	114	210,000	1:20.22	116

Beyer Index: 112.47

Distance 1 1/4 miles 1895; 1 1/8 miles, 1896; 1 1/16 miles, 1897; about 7 furlongs (150 feet short), 1898; 6 1/2 furlongs 1899-1902. Run at old Aqueduct, 1895-1945, 1947-55; at Belmont, 1946, 1956-59, 1968-74, 1996

CHAMPAGNE (G1), 1 1/16 Miles, 2-Year-Olds, Belmont Park, 2004 Purse: $500,000

Year	Winner	Age	Jockey	Wt.	Second	Wt.	Third	Wt.	Win Value	Time	Beyer
1867	Sarah B.	2	Washington	97	Lost Cause	97	Boaster	100	1,250	1:45.00	
1868	Cottrill	2	C. Miller	100	Attraction	97			850	1:49.20	
1869	Finesse	2	C. Miller	97	Telegram	100	Cavalier	100	1,200	1:56.00	
1870	Madam Dudley	2	W. Miller	97	Fanchon	97	Barbarian	100	1,350	1:50.20	
1871	Grey Planet	2	Donohue	100	Inverary	104			1,500	1:20.00	
1872	Minnie W.	2	Sparling	97	Delight	97	Survivor	100	1,050	1:19.20	
1873	Grinstead	2	Feakes	100	Dublin	100	Weathercock	100	1,750	1:17.60	
1874	Hyder Ali	2	Donohue	100	James A.	100	Finework	97	1,850	1:20.00	
1875	Virginius	2	W. Clarke	100	Cyclone	97	Tigress	97	2,100	1:19.00	
1876	Bombast	2	Barrett	110	Loiterer	110	Hibernia	107	1,950	1:19.20	
1877	Albert	2	Barbee	110	Maritana	107	Fawn	107	1,900	1:20.60	
1878	Belinda	2	Sparling	107	Boardman	110	Dan Sparling	110	1,275	1:18.00	
1879	Carita	2	Evans	107	Beata	107	Queen's Own	107	2,050	1:18.20	
1880	Lady Rosebery	2	J. McLaughlin	107	Spark	107	Bonnie Lizzie	114	1,175	1:18.20	
1881	Macduff	2	Fisher	110	The Rat	107	Duplex	107	1,150	1:18.20	
1882	Breeze	2	Shauer	108	Cyril	110	Bella	114	1,325	1:20.00	
1883	Leo	2	Shauer	110	Pampero	107	Ecuador	110	1,350	1:18.20	
1884	Eachus	2	J. McLaughlin	115	St. Augustin	115	Unrest	112	1,225	1:19.20	
1885	Dew Drop	2	Olney	122	Inspector B.	115	Lansdowne	115	1,775	1:18.60	
1886	Connemarra	2	A. McCarthy Jr	112	Bessie June	112	Belvidere	115	2,100	1:17.00	
1887	Cascade	2	Church	102	Fordham	122	Blithesome	119	1,875	1:18.20	
1888	Radiant	2	W. Donohue	115	Champagne Charley	115	Stately	119	2,650	1:19.20	
1889	June Day	2	Barnes	118	Successor	113	Rosette	105	1,975	1:17.60	
1890	Hoodlum	2	Covington	106	Peter	108	Russell	118	2,500	1:46.20	
1891	Azra	2	Clayton	108	St. Florian	118	Dagonet	113	3,470	1:30.20	
1892	Ramapo	2	Doggett	111	Prince George	115	Runyon	118	3,780	1:28.00	
1893	Sir Excess	2	Taral	123	Dobbins	128	Rubicon	106	6,320	1:28.60	
1894	Salvation	2	Taral	113	Brandywine	113	Darlen	104	4,880	1:28.20	
1895	Ben Brush	2	Simms	120	Prince Lief	110	Merry Prince	110	2,350	1:27.20	
1896	The Friar	2	Littlefield	118	Rhodesia	105	Divide	110	3,050	1:28.00	
1897	Plaudit	2	R. Williams	125	Lydian	110	San Antonio	112	2,250	1:31.20	
1898	Lothario	2	Maher	108	Filigrane	122	Manuel	122	3,250	1:29.60	
1899	Kilmarnock	2	Odom	112	Montanic	114	Sadducee	109	3,585	1:27.20	
1900	Garry Herrmann	2	Bullman	117	Smile	107	Watercolor	125	2,765	1:27.20	
1901	Endurance by Right	2	O'Connor	119	Yankee	122	Caughnawaga	112	4,375	1:28.00	

Year	Winner	Age	Jockey	Wt.	Second	Wt.	Third	Wt.	Win Value	Time	Beyer
1902	Meltonian	2	Redfern	107	Acefull	122	Grey Friar	119	5,435	1:27.00	
1903	Stalwart	2	W. Hicks	112	Pulsus	122	Wotan	112	6,135	1:26.00	
1904	Oiseau	2	Odom	122	Tradition	119	Pasadena	122	6,600	1:29.00	
1905	Perverse	2	Shaw	119	Whimsical	119	Security	122	6,255	1:23.60	
1906	Kentucky Beau	2	W. Miller	119	W.H. Daniel	122	Ballot	122	5,910	1:23.80	
1907	Colin	2	W. Miller	122	Stamina	119			5,700	1:23.00	
1908	Helmet	2	Notter	122	Selectman	122	Etherial	114	5,625	1:26.00	
1909	Fauntleroy	2	McCahey	122	Kingship	112	Candleberry	107	1,060	1:23.60	
1914	Paris	2	M. Buxton	110	Charter Maid	116	Sharpshooter	110	1,205	1:22.40	
1915	Chicle	2	T. McTaggart	112	Air Man	112	Whimsy	109	1,065	1:24.80	
1916	Vivid	2	A. Schuttinger	105	Woodtrap	110			1,455	1:23.40	
1917	Lanius	2	F. Robinson	110	Matinee Idol	111	Arrah Go On	105	1,650	1:26.20	
1918	War Pennant	2	E. Taplin	106	Terentia	124	Questionnaire	125	2,525	1:25.40	
1919	Cleopatra	2	L. McAtee	107	Upset	125	Dr. Clark	104	3,575	1:24.20	
1920	Grey Lag	2	L. Ensor	112	Banksia	106	Our Flag	115	4,150	1:24.40	
1921	Surf Rider	2	L. Fator	107	Galantman	102	Modo	118	4,400	1:25.40	
1922	Nassau	2	C. Fairbrother	112	Miss Smith	109	Coeur de Lion	112	4,650	1:26.40	
1923	Sarazen	2	E. Sande	112	Aga Khan	107	Sunspero	119	5,225	1:24.60	
1924	Beatrice	2	G. Fields	109	Goldbeater	115	Star Lore	107	6,275	1:26.40	
1925	Bubbling Over	2	A. Johnson	122	Espino	112			4,550	1:26.00	
1926	Valorous	2	L. McAtee	112	Adios	112	Laddie	116	5,750	1:21.60	
1927	Oh Say	2	F. Fields	114	Prate	122	Excalibur	110	6,025	1:22.00	
1928	Healy	2	W. Kelsay	115	Chicatie	115	Marine	115	5,825	1:22.60	
1929	Whichone	2	L. McAtee	127	Gone Away	115	Boojum	130	5,825	1:21.00	
1930	Mate	2	L. Fator	119	Equipoise	132	Sunny Lassie	113	6,050	1:21.80	
1931	Sweeping Light	2	F. Coltiletti	116	Pompeius	116	Cambal	116	5,525	1:20.80	
1932	Dynastic	2	C. Kurtsinger	119	Kerry Patch	116	De Valera	110	4,025	1:20.80	
1933	Hadagal	2	L. Humphries	116	Sgt. Byrne	122	Kawagoe	116	2,170	1:17.40	
1934	Balladier	2	W.D. Wright	124	Omaha	117	Plat Eye	126	3,520	1:16.60	
1935	Brevity	2	W.D. Wright	113	Snark	113	Granville	113	4,875	1:17.40	
1936	Privileged	2	E. Arcaro	122	Dogaway	119	Murph	122	4,200	1:17.00	
1937	Menow	2	C. Kurtsinger	113	Bull Lea	116	Fighting Fox	122	4,225	1:17.20	
1938	Porter's Mite	2	B. James	119	Impound	116	No Competition	122	4,650	1:14.40	
1939	Andy K.	2	J. Longden	124	Calory	113	Strawberry	111	5,875	1:17.00	
1940	Monday Lunch	2	E. Arcaro	110	Bold Irishman	113	Swain	122	9,675	1:37.40	
1941	Alsab	2	C. Bierman	122	Requested	116	Flaught	110	9,500	1:35.40	
1942	Count Fleet	2	J. Longden	116	Blue Swords	119	Attendant	110	9,375	1:34.80	
1943	Pukka Gin	2	T. Atkinson	113	Pressure	106	Pensive	110	10,125	1:38.20	
1944	Pot o' Luck	2	R. Permane	106	Sir Francis	106	Lady's Reward	110	15,950	1:37.40	
1945	Marine Victory	2	D. Padgett	116	Star Pilot	122	Mahout	106	15,665	1:39.20	
1946	Donor	2	J. Jessop	116	Phalanx	110	Jet Pilot	119	20,550	1:37.40	
1947	Vulcan's Forge	2	A. Kirkland	110	Escadru	113	My Request	119	22,650	1:36.60	
1948	Capot	2	T. Atkinson	110	Stone Age	111	Flying Disc	107	24,300	1:37.20	
1949	Theory	2	S. Brooks	113	Androcles	110	Sunglow	110	23,150	1:37.00	
1950	Uncle Miltie	2	H. Woodhouse	122	Battle Morn	122	Nullify	122	24,050	1:36.60	
1951	Armageddon	2	W. Shoemaker	122	Putout	122	Eternal Moon	122	24,050	1:38.20	
1952	Laffango	2	N. Shuk	122	Invigorator	122	Country Coz	122	25,600	1:38.00	
1953	Fisherman	2	H. Woodhouse	122	Best Years	122	War Piper	122	25,700	1:38.60	
1954	Flying Fury	2	H. Moreno	122	Grandpaw	122	Gold Box	122	24,700	1:37.80	
1955	Beau Fond	2	E. Arcaro	122	Head Man	122	Ricci Tavi	122	22,700	1:36.40	
1957	Jewel's Reward	2	W. Shoemaker	122	Misty Flight	122	Rose Trellis	122	84,225	1:37.60	
1958	First Landing	2	E. Arcaro	122	Intentionally	122	Tomy Lee	122	96,870	1:39.40	
	Tomy Lee finished second but was disqualified and placed third										
1959	Warfare	2	I. Valenzuela	122	Tompion	122	Bally Ache	122	138,195	1:35.20	
1960	Roving Minstrel	2	H. Moreno	122	Garwol	122	Bronzerullah	122	108,035	1:35.60	
1961	Donut King	2	M. Ycaza	122	Jaipur	122	Sir Gaylord	122	146,800	1:36.00	
1962	Never Bend	2	M. Ycaza	122	Master Dennis	122	Outing Class	122	129,675	1:36.60	
1963	Roman Brother	2	J.L. Rotz	122	Traffic	122	Bupers	122	152,150	1:38.00	
1964	Bold Lad	2	B. Baeza	122	Royal Gunner	122	Philately	122	116,825	1:36.40	
1965	Buckpasser	2	B. Baeza	122	Our Michael	122	Advocator	122	163,875	1:36.40	
1966	Successor	2	B. Baeza	122	Dr. Fager	122	Proviso	122	148,325	1:35.00	
1967	Vitriolic	2	B. Baeza	122	Iron Ruler	122	Captain's Gig	122	119,500	1:34.60	
1968	Top Knight	2	M. Ycaza	122	Beau Brummel	122	King Emperor	122	110,450	1:35.20	
1969	Silent Screen	2	J.L. Rotz	122	Brave Emperor	122	Toasted	122	128,150	1:37.20	
1970	Limit to Reason	2	J. Velasquez	122	Arctarus	122	Jim French	122	145,025	1:35.40	
	Hoist the Flag finished first but was disqualified last										
1971	Riva Ridge	2	R. Turcotte	122	Chevron Flight	122	Head of the River	122	117,090	1:36.40	
1972	Stop the Music	2	J.L. Rotz	122	Secretariat	122	Step Nicely	122	87,900	1:35.00	
	Secretariat finished first but was disqualified and placed second										
1973	Holding Pattern	2	M. Miceli	122	Green Gambados	122	Hosiery	122	55,425	1:36.00	
1973	Protagonist	2	A. Santiago	122	Prince of Reason	122	Cannonade	122	55,425	1:36.00	
1974	Foolish Pleasure	2	J. Vasquez	122	Harvard Man	122	Ramahorn	122	86,850	1:36.00	
1975	Honest Pleasure	2	B. Baeza	122	Dance Spell	122	Whatsyourpleasure	122	89,625	1:36.40	

Year	Winner	Age	Jockey	Wt.	Second	Wt.	Third	Wt.	Win Value	Time	Beyer
1976	Seattle Slew	2	J. Cruguet	122	For the Moment	122	Sail to Rome	122	82,350	1:34.40	
1977	Alydar	2	J. Velasquez	122	Affirmed	122	Darby Creek Road	122	80,400	1:36.80	
1978	Spectacular Bid	2	J. Velasquez	122	General Assembly	122	Crest of the Wave	122	80,250	1:34.80	
1979	Joanie's Chief	2	R. Hernandez	122	Rockhill Native	122	Googolplex	122	81,750	1:38.20	
1980	Lord Avie	2	J. Velasquez	122	Noble Nashua	122	Sezyou	122	85,350	1:37.20	
1981	Timely Writer	2	J. Fell	122	Before Dawn	119	New Discovery	122	90,150	1:36.40	
1982	Copelan	2	J.D. Bailey	122	Pappa Riccio	122	El Cubanaso	122	144,000	1:37.80	
1983	Devil's Bag	2	E. Maple	122	Dr. Carter	122	Our Casey's Boy	122	142,200	1:34.20	
1984	For Certain Doc	2	M. Zuniga	122	Mighty Appealing	122	Tank's Prospect	122	171,600	1:49.20	
1985	Mogambo	2	A. Cordero Jr	122	Groovy	122	Mr. Classic	122	194,700	1:37.20	
1986	Polish Navy	2	R.P. Romero	122	Demons Begone	122	Bet Twice	122	199,500	1:35.20	
1987	Forty Niner	2	E. Maple	122	Parlay Me	122	Tejano	122	370,800	1:36.80	
1988	Easy Goer	2	P. Day	122	Is It True	122	Irish Actor	122	334,200	1:34.80	
1989	Adjudicating	2	J. Vasquez	122	Rhythm	122	Senor Pete	122	343,200	1:37.60	
1990	Fly So Free	2	J.A. Santos	122	Happy Jazz Band	122	Subordinated Debt	122	381,600	1:35.60	
1991	Tri to Watch	2	A. Cordero Jr	122	Snappy Landing	122	Pine Bluff	122	300,000	1:36.60	94
1992	Sea Hero	2	J.D. Bailey	122	Secret Odds	122	Press Card	122	300,000	1:34.80	99
1993	Dehere	2	C.J. McCarron	122	Crary	122	Amathos	122	300,000	1:35.80	93
1994	Timber Country	2	P. Day	122	Sierra Diablo	122	On Target	122	300,000	1:44.00	100
1995	Maria's Mon	2	R.G. Davis	122	Diligence	122	Devil's Honor	122	300,000	1:42.20	105
1996	Ordway	2	J.R. Velazquez	122	Traitor	122	Gold Tribute	122	240,000	1:42.00	101
1997	Grand Slam	2	G.L. Stevens	122	Lil's Lad	122	Halory Hunter	122	240,000	1:40.40	102
1998	The Groom Is Red	2	C.S. Nakatani	122	Lemon Drop Kid	122	Weekend Money	122	240,000	1:42.91	93
1999	Greenwood Lake	2	J.L. Samyn	122	Chief Seattle	122	High Yield	122	240,000	1:43.70	91
2000	A P Valentine	2	J.F. Chavez	122	Point Given	122	Yonaguska	122	300,000	1:41.45	98
2001	Officer	2	V. Espinoza	122	Jump Start	122	Heavyweight Champ	122	300,000	1:43.39	102
2002	Toccet	2	J.F. Chavez	122	Icecolbeeratreds	122	Erinsouthernman	122	300,000	1:44.45	97
2003	Birdstone	2	J.D. Bailey	122	Chapel Royal	122	Dashboard Drummer	122	300,000	1:44.05	94
2004	Proud Accolade	2	J.R. Velazquez	122	Afleet Alex	122	Sun King	122	300,000	1:42.30	100

Beyer Index: 97.79

Distance 6 furlongs 1871-89; 7 furlongs, 1891-1904; Widener Course (7 furlongs less 165 feet, 1905-32; 6 1/2 furlongs on Widener Course, 1933-39; 1 1/8 miles, 1984; 1 mile, 1940-83, 1985-93. Run at Jerome Park prior to 1890; at Morris Park 1891-1904; Aqueduct, 1959, 1963-67

CHAPOSA SPRINGS HANDICAP (G3), 7 Furlongs, Fillies and Mares, 3-Year-Olds and Up, Calder Race Course, 2004 Purse: $100,000

Year	Winner	Age	Jockey	Wt.	Second	Wt.	Third	Wt.	Win Value	Time	Beyer
1983	Florida Jig	4	R. Danjean	119	Voo Doo Dance	113	Amber's Desire	115	35,340	1:25.60	
1984	Hiusoanso	4	B. Gonzalez	114	Birdie Belle	119	Queen of Song	123	35,550	1:25.00	
1985	Birdie Belle	4	J.A. Santiago	118	Gyspy Prayer	114	Really Flashy	115	35,010	1:24.20	
1986	Jose's Bomb	3	R.N. Lester	114	Algenib	114	Thirty Zip	118	30,570	1:25.60	
1988	Tappiano	4	C. Perret	122	Le L'Argent	117	Easter Mary	111	52,995	1:24.00	
1988	Thirty Zip	5	R. Breen	115	Behind the Scenes	118	Triple Wow	118	66,120	1:25.00	
1990	Love's Exchange	4	H. Castillo Jr	127	Spirit of Fighter	118	Fit for a Queen	114	33,720	1:23.20	
							Ana T.	115			
1990	Ells Once Again	6	M.A. Lee	111	Banbury Fair	113	Storm of Glory	111	52,380	1:24.40	89
1992	Magal	5	R. Hernandez	115	Gene Propp's Dream	113	My Own True Love	113	51,675	1:24.20	100
1993	Maggies Pistol	4	J.A. Bracho	112	My Own True Love	118	Luv Me Luv Me Not	118	45,000	1:23.80	100
1994	Educated Risk	4	M.E. Smith	122	Goldarama	115	Floramera	110	60,000	1:23.00	112
1995	Chaposa Springs	3	J.D. Bailey	119	Investalot	115	Easter Doll	114	60,000	1:25.20	95
1996	Race Artist	4	Boulanger G.	113	La Nina De Orumila	113	Flat Fleet Feet	119	60,000	1:25.20	95
	Chaposa Springs finished first but was disqualified and placed seventh										
1997	Flashy n Smart	4	P. Day	118	U Can Do It	115	Special Request	114	60,000	1:26.60	94
1998	Openstock	6	J.A. Garcia	113	Lily O'Gold	111	U Can Do It	119	60,000	1:24.84	89
2000	Could Be	4	P. Day	115	Extended Applause	114	Class On Class	114	60,000	1:24.97	91
2000	England's Rose	3	J.R. Velazquez	112	Swept Away	118	Sugar N Spice	114	60,000	1:24.82	97
2001	Vague Memory	4	J.A. Garcia	113	Gold Mover	117	Platinum Tiara	114	60,000	1:24.15	90
2002	Chispiski	3	J.A. Garcia	115	Abundantly Blessed	114	Away	117	60,000	1:25.14	86
2003	Barbara O'Brien	4	E. Coa	114	Holy Bubbette	114	Splasha	114	60,000	1:23.51	104
2004	Expect an Angel	4	J.E. Lopez	110	Alix M	120	Habiboo	112	60,000	1:23.66	97

Beyer Index: 95.64

CHICAGO BREEDERS' CUP HANDICAP (G3), 7 Furlongs, Fillies and Mares, 3-Year-Olds and Up, Arlington Park, 2004 Purse: $175,000

Year	Winner	Age	Jockey	Wt.	Second	Wt.	Third	Wt.	Win Value	Time	Beyer
1986	Lazer Show	3	P. Day	115	Balladry	115	Gene's Lady	122	93,360	1:21.40	
1987	Lazer Show	4	P. Day	123	Very Subtle	120	M'nngm McQ'en	111	46,275	1:22.80	
1989	Rose's Record	5	J. Velasquez	114	Sunshine Always	114	Daloma	116	93,120	1:24.60	
1990	Fit for a Queen	4	P. Day	112	Channel Three	113	Sexy Slew	113	94,650	1:23.00	
1991	Safely Kept	5	C. Perret	126	Nurse Dopey	118	Token Dance	114	93,060	1:23.00	102

Year	Winner	Age	Jockey	Wt.	Second	Wt.	Third	Wt.	Win Value	Time	Beyer
1992	Withallprobability	4	G.L. Gomez	115	Fit for a Queen	120	Madam Bear	114	93,450	1:21.20	99
1993	Meafara	4	J.L. Diaz	121	Shared Interest	115	Real Display	114	93,870	1:22.00	100
1994	Minidar	4	Belvoir VT	116	Spinning Round	118	Traverse City	113	93,960	1:22.40	106
1995	Low Key Affair	4	A.T. Gryder	113	Morning Meadow	115	Marina Park	120	93,840	1:24.60	94
1996	Bunbeg	4	M.K. Walls	119	Morris Code	118	Rhapsodic	114	102,990	1:23.80	101
1997	J J'sdream	4	M. Guidry	118	Capote Belle	120	Eseni	117	101,625	1:22.20	106
2000	Saoirse	4	D. Clark	118	The Happy Hopper	115	Dif a Dot	114	102,195	1:23.09	101
2001	Trip	4	C. Perret	114	Hidden Assets	115	Rose of Zollern	115	99,312	1:22.18	97
2002	Mandy's Gold	4	R.R. Douglas	116	Cat and the Hat	116	Caressing	115	98,664	1:22.86	94
2003	For Rubies	4	C. Perret	116	Raging Fever	120	Oglala Sue	113	69,450	1:24.21	95
2004	My Trusty Cat	4	R.R. Douglas	116	Our Josephina	112	Smoke Chaser	116	105,000	1:23.54	97

Beyer Index: 99.33

CHURCHILL DOWNS DISTAFF HANDICAP (G2), 1 Mile, Fillies and Mares, 3-Year-Olds and Up, Churchill Downs, 2004 Purse: $230,400

Year	Winner	Age	Jockey	Wt.	Second	Wt.	Third	Wt.	Win Value	Time	Beyer
1986	Lazer Show	3	C.R. Woods Jr	120	Balladry	116	Mrs. Revere	120	102,473	1:22.60	
1987	Bound	3	E. Maple	113	Miss Bid	115	Intently	114	103,253	1:37.00	
1988	Darien Miss	3	P.A. Johnson	116	Sheena Native	117	Coastal Connection	112	102,928	1:36.80	
1989	Classic Value	3	P. Day	114	Coastal Connection	115	Rose's Record	117	102,960	1:35.40	
1990	Oh My Jessica Pie	3	M.A. Gonzalez	114	Seaside Attraction	115	Sweet Nostalgia	111	102,993	1:36.80	94
1991	Fit for a Queen	5	R.D. Lopez	121	Wilderness Song	118	Summer Matinee	113	100,555	1:38.60	101
1992	Wilderness Song	4	C. Perret	120	Miss Jealski	110	Dance Colony	113	102,440	1:36.20	101
1993	Miss Indy Anna	3	P. Day	111	One Dreamer	115	Deputation	119	141,635	1:37.60	108
1994	Educated Risk	4	P. Day	118	Pennyhill Park	117	Alcovy	116	138,125	1:35.60	114
1995	Lakeway	4	K.J. Desormeaux	122	Alcovy	113	Laura's Pistolette	116	137,280	1:35.80	110
1997	Feasibility Study	5	R.J. Albarado	120	J J'sdream	113	Mama's Pro	115	146,196	1:37.60	100
1996	Fast Catch	4	W. Martinez	109	Serena's Song	125	Bedroom Blues	112	139,624	1:36.20	103
1998	Dream Scheme	5	C.H. Borel	113	Sister Act	111	Beautiful Pleasure	111	138,624	1:34.40	116
1999	Let	4	C.H. Borel	113	Roza Robata	114	Dif A Dot	115	138,880	1:34.40	109
2000	Chilukki	3	G.L. Stevens	116	Reciclada	113	Rose of Zollern	114	154,008	1:33.57	108
2001	Nasty Storm	3	P. Day	115	Forest Secrets	113	Trip	117	137,764	1:35.30	101
2002	Softly	4	J.K. Court	114	Bare Necessities	115	Victory Ride	118	138,632	1:35.07	96
2003	Lead Story	4	C.H. Borel	114	Awesome Humor	118	Born to Dance	113	139,748	1:36.55	98
2004	Halory Leigh	4	C. Perret	115	Lady Tak	123	Susan's Angel	115	142,848	1:35.05	107

Beyer Index: 104.40

Run at 7 furlongs in 1986

CHURCHILL DOWNS HANDICAP (G2), 7 Furlongs, 4-Year-Olds and Up, Churchill Downs, 2004 Purse: $221,800

Year	Winner	Age	Jockey	Wt.	Second	Wt.	Third	Wt.	Win Value	Time	Beyer
1911	Carlton G.	4	Taplin	107	Messenger Boy	92	Star Charter	107	1,990	1:51.80	
1912	Any Port	6	Byrne	103	Mary Davis	105	Star O'Ryan	100	1,580	1:51.60	
1913	Rudolfo	4	Loftus	115	Yankee Notions	106	Gowell	103	700	1:51.80	
1938	Arabs Arrow	4	W.L. Johnson	112	Knee Deep	104	Bacon	116	2,145	1:26.80	
1939	Kings Blue	4	C. Kurtsinger	109	Arabs Arrow	119	Janice	106	1,382	1:24.80	
1940	Arabs Arrow	6	C. Bierman	119	Mucho Gusto	110	Bucking	107	2,285	1:39.80	
1941	My Bill	3	C. McCreary	100	Potranco	116	Betty's B'by	109	2,185	1:36.60	
1942	Royal Crusader	5	A. Craig	111	Aonbarr	115	Moscow II	105	2,270	1:37.60	
1943	Best Seller	5	J. Longden	118	Wishbone	115	Three Clovers	102	2,200	1:38.40	
1944	Traffic Court	6		111	Amber Light	114	Ale'tern	117	4,120	1:36.80	
1945	Equifox	8	A. Bodiou	122	Sigma Kappa	100	Mina J.	100	4,000	1:40.00	
1946	Bull Play	4	R. Campbell	111	Letmenow	110	Sigma Kappa	112	8,175	1:42.40	
1947	Dark Jungle	4	S. Brooks	113	Jack S.L.	114	Joe's Choice	108	8,725	1:25.20	
1948	George Gains	5	A.J. Fernandez	116	Joe's Choice	111	Eternal Reward	115	8,500	1:25.20	
1949	Free America	4	S. Brooks	120	Armed	118	Phar Mon	108	7,750	1:25.00	
1950	Fleeting Star	4	S. Brooks	117	Ol' Skipper	117	Sun Herod	119	8,550	1:24.00	
1951	Johns Joy	5	W.M. Cook	118	Roman Bath	118	Mr. Trouble	115	8,400	1:22.80	
1952	Here's Hoping	5	S. Brooks	113	Futuramatic	107	Air Mail	107	8,100	1:11.00	
1953	Roaming	4	J. Contreras	114	Pomace	110	Pet Bully	120	8,050	1:10.60	
1954	Sunny Dale	6	P.J. Bailey	114	Mon-Pharo	118	Gala Fete	116	8,850	1:11.00	
1955	Torch of War	5	J. Adams	113	Tuosix	115	Vagabond King	115	8,025	1:11.20	
1956	Scrutinized	6	W.M. Cook	110	Styrunner	112	Happy Go L'cky	109	8,700	1:25.40	
1957	Swoon's Son	4	D. Erb	128	Sea O Erin	119	Invalidate	113	8,375	1:24.60	
1958	Shan Pac	4	J. Heckmann	115	Ezgo	120	Dogoon	122	7,447	1:22.00	
1959	Cuvier Boy	4	S. Brooks	113	Greek Chief	116	Yemen	115	7,431	1:22.40	
1960	Little Fitz	5	A.W. Peake	115	Better Bee	118	Aesthetic	110	7,399	1:22.40	
1961	Cactus Tom	4	L. Hansman	118	Eight Again	119	Matthias	115	7,540	1:22.40	
1962	Editorialist	4	W. Shoemaker	125	Weatherton	115	Playgoer	112	7,507	1:22.60	
1963	Editorialist	5	M. Ycaza	128	Bass Clef	111	Times Roman	119	7,394	1:22.40	

Year	Winner	Age	Jockey	Wt.	Second	Wt.	Third	Wt.	Win Value	Time	Beyer
1964	Olden Times	6	W. Shoemaker	124	Piper's Son	113	Lemon Twist	115	7,475	1:21.40	
1965	Little Lu	4	M. Manganello	112	Big Brigade	114	Clem Pac	124	9,100	1:22.40	
1966	Bay Phantom	4	R.J. Campbell	125	Big Brigade	117	Mr. Pak	110	10,627	1:22.00	
1967	Bay Phantom	5	E. Fires	117	Cabildo	122	Slade	112	11,424	1:22.00	
1968	Cabildo	5	J. Combest	122	Tartan Man	114	Gay Flight	115	10,904	1:23.20	
1969	Judge Kilday	4	D.E. Whited	115	Barbs Delight	122	Gr'd Premiere	115	11,180	1:23.60	
1970	True North	4	M. Manganello	113	Advance Party	113	Sh'k of Bagdad	114	11,050	1:22.60	
1971	No No Billy	4	D. MacBeth	111	Great Mystery	119	Rio Bravo	117	15,340	1:23.20	
1972	List	4	J. Nichols	118	Staunch Avenger	116	Tribal Line	117	15,762	1:23.20	
1973	Code of Honor	5	E. Fires	115	Knight Counter	122	Hook It Up	115	15,096	1:23.00	
1974	Barbizon Streak	6	R. Wilson	115	Grocery List	117	Jim's Alibhi	114	15,015	1:25.40	
1975	Navajo	5	J. Nichols	123	Silver Hope	116	Silver Badge	110	14,804	1:24.40	
1976	Yamanin	4	G. Patterson	115	It's Freezing	120	Easter Island	115	14,495	1:23.80	
1977	It's Freezing	5	E. Delahoussaye	120	Buddy Larosa	112	Silver Hope	119	14,528	1:23.40	
1978	To the Quick	4	J. Amy	116	It's Freezing	117	Prince Majestic	121	14,511	1:25.00	
1979	Trimlea	5	J. Velasquez	113	Dr. Riddick	119	Cabrini King	118	19,240	1:24.60	
1980	Dr. Riddick	6	D. Brumfield	114	Cregan's Cap	112	Silent Dignity	119	17,615	1:23.20	
1981	Dreadnought	4	J.C. Espinoza	112	Tiger Lure	113	Turbulence	119	19,874	1:23.60	
1982	Top Avenger	4	R.P. Romero	114	It's a Rerun	110	Shot n' Missed	117	21,662	1:23.00	
1982	Bayou Black	6	R. Ardoin	119	Vodika Collins	118	Prince Crimson	116	23,433	1:22.80	
1983	Shot n' Missed	6	L. Moyers	118	Vodika Collins	112	Gall'nt Gentleman	115	21,239	1:23.60	
1984	Habitonia	4	P. Day	118	Roman Jamboree	114	Euathlos	113	20,914	1:23.00	
1985	Rapid Gray	6	P. Day	120	Roxbury Park	114	Steel Robbing	115	24,391	1:24.00	
1985	Bayou Hebert	4	J. McKnight	111	Harry 'n Bill	117	Never Company	117	24,196	1:23.40	
1986	Sovereign's Ace	4	P. Rubbicco	117	Artichoke	120	Clever Wake	116	21,957	1:22.60	
1987	Sovereign's Ace	5	L. Pincay Jr	117	Sun Master	123	Savings	114	21,236	1:22.00	
1988	Conquer	4	G.L. Stevens	117	Homebuilder	121	Carborundum	115	36,823	1:23.20	
1989	Dancing Spree	4	P. Day	116	Carborundum	117	Broadway Chief	115	38,253	1:24.00	
1990	Beau Genius	5	R.D. Lopez	119	Traskwood	113	Learn by Heart	115	37,830	1:23.20	99
1991	Thirty Six Red	4	J.D. Bailey	117	Private School	113	Bratt's Choice	115	37,635	1:22.00	111
1992	Pleasant Tap	5	E. Delahoussaye	120	Take Me Out	120	Cantrell Road	113	55,526	1:22.20	104
1993	Callide Valley	5	G.L. Stevens	116	Furiously	117	Ojai	110	56,063	1:22.00	106
1994	Honor the Hero	6	Gomez GK	116	Memo	121	Saratoga Gambler	116	71,370	1:23.00	113
1995	Goldseeker Bud	4	Martinez W	109	Level Sands	112	Go for Gin	115	75,205	1:21.60	104
1996	Criollito	5	C.J. McCarron	115	Forty Won	115	Powis Castle	114	74,620	1:22.00	107
1997	Diligence	4	M.F. Smith	114	Victor Cooley	115	Criollito	115	70,432	1:22.20	107
1998	Distorted Humor	5	G.L. Stevens	119	Gold Land	116	El Amante	113	103,509	1:21.00	117
1999	Rock and Roll	5	P. Day	112	Liberty Gold	114	Run Johnny	113	103,137	1:22.80	105
2000	Straight Man	4	J.F. Chavez	112	Mula Gula	114	Patience Game	114	104,904	1:21.53	103
2001	Alannan	5	E.S. Prado	116	Bonapaw	116	Exchange Rate	113	111,321	1:20.50	113
2002	D'wildcat	4	K.J. Desormeaux	115	Snow Ridge	119	Binthebest	113	106,299	1:22.37	102
	Snow Ridge finished first but was disqualified and placed second										
2003	Aldebaran	5	J.D. Bailey	120	Pass Rush	117	Cappuchino	115	144,956	1:21.80	111
2004	Speightstown	6	J.R. Velazquez	115	McCann's Mojave	117	Publication	116	137,516	1:21.38	116

Beyer Index: 107.87

Run as Winnercom Handicap in 2000

CICADA (G3), 7 Furlongs, 3-Year-Old Fillies, Aqueduct, 2004 Purse: $109,100

Year	Winner	Age	Jockey	Wt.	Second	Wt.	Third	Wt.	Win Value	Time	Beyer
1993	Personal Bid	3	J.A. Santos	118	Sheila's Revenge	118	In Excelcis Deo	116	31,800	1:23.40	100
1994	Our Royal Blue	3	Wilson R	113	Sovereign Kitty	118	Princess Joanne	113	48,375	1:22.20	89
1995	Lucky Lavender Gal	3	Davis RG	114	Stormy Blues	118	Dancin Renee	116	48,870	1:23.40	98
1996	J J'sdream	3	G. Boulanger	121	Dahl	114	Mystic Rhythms	118	50,310	1:23.40	98
1997	Vegas Prospector	3	M.J. McCarthy	116	Ormsby County	112	Valid Affect	118	48,375	1:26.20	70
1998	Jersey Girl	3	R. Migliore	116	Vienna Blues	114	Babai Danzig	116	50,175	1:22.80	93
1999	Potomac Bend	3	M.T. Johnston	118	Carleaville	114	Jane	112	48,915	1:23.18	91
2000	Finder's Fee	3	J.D. Bailey	118	Apollo Cat	116	Southern Sandra	121	65,100	1:23.07	92
2001	Xtra Heat	3	R. Wilson	122	Erin Moor	116	Chasm	116	63,770	1:23.39	89
2002	Proper Gamble	3	J.J. Castellano	122	Short Note	118	Forest Heiress	120	65,160	1:23.32	97
2003	Cyber Secret	3	S.X. Bridgmohan	122	Roar Emotion	116	Boxer Girl	118	64,980	1:22.55	88
2004	Bohemian Lady	3	E.S. Prado	116	Whoopi Cat	116	Baldomera	122	65,460	1:23.22	89

Beyer Index: 91.17

CIGAR MILE HANDICAP (G1), 1 Mile, 3-Year-Olds and Up, Aqueduct, 2004 Purse: $350,000

Year	Winner	Age	Jockey	Wt.	Second	Wt.	Third	Wt.	Win Value	Time	Beyer
1988	Forty Niner	3	W.I. Fox Jr	121	Mawsuff	115	Precisionist	124	340,200	1:34.00	
1989	Dispersal	3	A. Cordero Jr	115	Sewickley	120	Speedratic	117	348,600	1:32.80	
1990	Quiet American	4	C.J. McCarron	116	Dancing Spree	119	Sewickley	124	382,800	1:32.80	124
1991	Rubiano	4	J.A. Santos	116	Sultry Song	111	Diablo	112	300,000	1:33.60	110

Year	Winner	Age	Jockey	Wt.	Second	Wt.	Third	Wt.	Win Value	Time	Beyer
1992	Ibero	5	L. Pincay Jr	115	Irish Sweeps	116	Nines Wild	111	300,000	1:32.40	114
1994	Cigar	4	J.D. Bailey	111	Devil His Due	124	Punch Line	112	150,000	1:36.00	115
1995	Flying Chevron	3	R.G. Davis	112	Wekiva Springs	117	Dramatic Gold	120	150,000	1:34.40	112
1996	Gold Fever	3	M.E. Smith	115	Diligence	114	Top Account	117	150,000	1:34.80	108
1997	Devious Course	5	J.F. Chavez	112	Lucayan Prince	114	Basqueian	115	150,000	1:34.80	109
1998	Sir Bear	5	J.D. Bailey	116	Affirmed Success	119	Distorted Humor	116	180,000	1:34.05	111
1999	Affirmed Success	5	J.F. Chavez	118	Adonis	115	Honorifico	113	210,000	1:34.18	109
2000	El Corredor	3	J.D. Bailey	116	Peeping Tom	111	Affirmed Success	120	210,000	1:34.68	112
2001	Left Bank	4	J.R. Velazquez	120	Graeme Hall	118	Red Bullet	118	210,000	1:33.35	118
2002	Congaree	4	J.D. Bailey	119	Aldebaran	116	Crafty C. T.	117	210,000	1:33.11	120
2003	Congaree	5	J.D. Bailey	124	Midas Eyes	115	Toccet	115	210,000	1:34.30	120
2004	Lion Tamer	4	J.A. Santos	115	Badge of Silver	115	Pico Central	123	210,000	1:33.46	111

Beyer Index: 113.79

Run as NYRA Mile Handicap prior to 1997

CINEMA BREEDERS' CUP HANDICAP (G3), 1 1/8 Miles (Turf), 3-Year-Olds, Hollywood Park, 2004 Purse: $153,450

Year	Winner	Age	Jockey	Wt.	Second	Wt.	Third	Wt.	Win Value	Time	Beyer
1946	Honeymoon	3	J. Westrope	128	Don Peppino	107	Eiffel Tower	117	20,050	1:44.00	
1947	Yankee Valor	3	N. Richardson	115	On Trust	129	Stepfather	120	17,750	1:42.80	
1948	Drumbeat	3	O. Webster	112	Belle Jolie	108	Solidarity	122	19,600	1:44.00	
1949	Pedigree	3	J. Longden	124	Rhodes Bull	109	Blue Dart	120	19,250	1:42.80	
1950	Great Circle	3	R. Neves	121	Valquest	115	Akimbo	109	15,150	1:36.00	
1951	Mucho Hosso	3	F. Chojnacki	110	Tuzado	106	Gold Capitol	125	18,450	1:43.60	
1952	A Gleam	3	H. Moreno	124	Alate	115	Horsetrader-Ed	108	17,500	1:42.80	
1953	Ali's Gem	3	W. Shoemaker	120	Rejected	112	Imbros	126	16,350	1:42.00	
1954	Miz Clementine	3	I. Valenzuela	113	Fault Free	116	War Tryst	108	14,050	1:42.60	
1955	Guilton Madero	3	I. Valenzuela	114	Brooksickle	110	Mr. Sullivan	115	15,750	1:41.80	
1956	Social Climber	3	I. Valenzuela	121	Blen Host	109	Terrang	124	16,150	1:48.20	
1957	Round Table	3	W. Shoemaker	130	Joe Price	114	Seaneen	109	26,350	1:47.80	
1958	The Shoe	3	W. Shoemaker	117	Strong Bay	111	El Cajon	108	20,900	1:49.60	
1959	Silver Spoon	3	W. Boland	120	Friar Roach	111	Civic Pride	105	29,990	1:47.60	
1960	New Policy	3	W. Shoemaker	123	Tempestuous	113	T.V. Lark	126	34,450	1:46.60	
1961	Bushel-n-Peck	3	E. Burns	117	Songman	111	Double Lea	114	32,675	1:48.00	
1961	Four-and-Twenty	3	J. Longden	126	Mr. America	122	We're Hoping	110	32,175	1:47.00	
1962	Black Sheep	3	J. Longden	114	Indian Blood	113	Doc Jocoy	125	33,800	1:48.40	
1963	Y Flash	3	E. Burns	120	Missilery	116	Bre'r Rabbit	116	27,075	1:50.00	
1963	Quita Dude	3	J. Leonard	113	Sky Gem	117	Olympiad King	126	27,075	1:49.80	
1964	Close By	3	W. Shoemaker	119	Real Good Deal	122	Pelegrin	114	34,750	1:49.00	
1965	Arksroni	3	W. Hartack	116	Easy Lime	114	Charger's Kin	115	36,000	1:47.80	
1966	Drin	3	W. Shoemaker	115	Tragniew	115	Fleet Host	110	33,800	1:48.80	
1967	Dr. Roy E.	3	W. Mahorney	116	Ruken	123	Tumble Wind	123	35,250	1:48.60	
1968	Pinjara	3	L. Pincay Jr	112	American Tiger	115			32,400	1:49.00	
					Distinctly	112					
1969	Noholme Jr.	3	L. Pincay Jr	117	Tell	128	Makor	113	32,150	1:48.40	
1970	D'Artagnan	3	L. Pincay Jr	113	Top the Market	114	Hanalei Bay	115	33,850	1:47.40	
1971	Niagara	3	F. Toro	114	Crimson Clem	116	Triple Bend	122	40,400	1:48.20	
1972	Finalista	3	L. Pincay Jr	120	Quack	124	Woodland Pines	114	38,300	1:48.00	
1973	Amen II	3	E. Belmonte	115	Kirrary	114	Card Table	110	52,350	1:49.00	
1975	Terrete	3	W. Shoemaker	113	Larrikin	125	Dusty County	117	46,400	1:48.60	
1976	Majestic Light	3	S. Hawley	121	L'Heureux	120	Bynoderm	116	67,200	1:48.20	
1977	Bad 'n Big	3	L. Pincay Jr	121	Iron Constitution	124	Minnesota Gus	112	96,450	1:48.00	
1978	Kamehameha	3	T.M. Chapman	120	El Fantastico	114	Singular	118	102,800	1:47.40	
1979	Beau's Eagle	3	S. Hawley	121	Ibacache	122	Paint King	113	64,500	1:47.00	
1980	First Albert	3	F. Mena	113	Big Doug	115	Kenderboun	117	68,800	1:48.00	
1981	Minnesota Chief	3	C.J. McCarron	119	Stancharry	117	Splendid Spruce	125	69,900	1:40.60	
1982	Give Me Strength	3	J.L. Samyn	121	Journey at Sea	122	Bargain Balcony	118	64,600	1:40.60	
1983	Baron O'Dublin	3	E. Delahoussaye	115	Tanks Brigade	119	Re Ack	116	56,300	1:43.00	
1984	Prince True	3	P.A. Valenzuela	117	M. Double M.	116	Majestic Shore	115	63,700	1:40.20	
1985	Don't Say Halo	3	D.G. McHargue	116	Derby Dawning	115	Emperdori	115	65,800	1:47.60	
1986	Manila	3	F. Toro	117	Vernon Castle	120	Mazaad	121	80,400	1:47.00	
1987	Something Lucky	3	L. Pincay Jr	119	The Medic	117	Savona Tower	115	62,400	1:46.80	
1988	Peace	3	A. Solis	117	Blade of the Ball	113	Roberto's Dancer	115	78,400	1:46.80	
1989	Raise a Stanza	3	L. Pincay Jr	114	Exemplary Leader	116	Notorious Pleasure	120	62,100	1:47.80	
1990	Jovial	3	G.L. Stevens	115	Mehmetori	113	Itsallgreektome	117	67,400	1:47.80	97
1991	Character	3	G.L. Stevens	114	River Traffic	117	Kalgrey	114	62,600	1:47.00	97
1992	Bien Bien	3	C.J. McCarron	114	Fax News	114	Prospect for Four	114	65,600	1:47.00	97
1993	Earl of Barking	3	C.J. McCarron	121	Manny's Prospect	115	Minks Law	113	61,100	1:47.40	95
1994	Unfinished Symph	3	Baze G	118	Vaudeville	115	Fumo di Londra	121	63,100	1:46.40	102
1995	Via Lombardia	3	Delahoussaye E	119	Bryntirion	113	Oncefortheroad	115	65,400	1:47.20	102
1996	Let Bob Do It	3	K.J. Desormeaux	120	Dr. Sardonica	115	Winter Quarters	120	81,660	1:47.40	98
1997	Worldly Ways	3	C.S. Nakatani	115	P.T. Indy	118	Brave Act	120	66,180	1:48.40	97

Year	Winner	Age	Jockey	Wt.	Second	Wt.	Third	Wt.	Win Value	Time	Beyer
1998	Commitisize	3	D.R. Flores	118	Killer Image	115	Lord Smith	116	65,220	1:48.00	100
1999	Fighting Falcon	3	B. Blanc	119	Eagleton	120	Major Hero	113	66,000	1:48.06	98
2000	David Copperfield	3	V. Espinoza	116	Duke of Green	117	Silver Axe	115	64,560	1:47.73	98
2001	Sligo Bay	3	L. Pincay Jr	118	Learing at Kathy	117	Marine	119	65,160	1:48.40	98
2002	Inesperado	3	K.J. Desormeaux	116	Regiment	122	Johar	118	97,560	1:47.63	99
2003	Just Wonder	3	K.J. Desormeaux	117	Bis Repetitas	115	Slew City Citadel	115	98,730	1:47.41	100
2004	Greek Sun	3	A. Solis	120	Laura's Lucky Boy	122	Whilly	117	97,470	1:48.40	96

Beyer Index: 98.27

CITATION HANDICAP (G1), 1 1/16 Miles (Turf), 3-Year-Olds and Up, Hollywood Park, 2004 Purse: $400,000

Year	Winner	Age	Jockey	Wt.	Second	Wt.	Third	Wt.	Win Value	Time	Beyer
1977	Painted Wagon	4	C. Baltazar	117	Legendaire	114	Pay Tribute	118	48,500	1:42.00	
1978	Effevescing	5	L. Pincay Jr	120	Dr. Patches	116	Text	122	62,700	1:40.20	
1979	Text	5	W. Shoemaker	122	Farnesio	117	Bad 'n Big	119	63,600	1:40.40	
1980	Caro Bambino	5	P.A. Valenzuela	118	Life's Hope	116	Island Sultan	114	36,950	1:33.20	
1981	Tahitian King	5	W. Shoemaker	120	King Go Go	115	Cajun Prince	113	136,000	1:48.80	
1982	Caterman	6	C.J. McCarron	121	Cajun Prince	118	Island Whirl	123	45,700	1:41.00	
1983	Beldale Lustre	4	C.J. McCarron	113	The Hague	115	Sir Pele	114	53,000	1:49.40	
1983	Pewter Grey	4	R. Sibille	115	Belmont Bay	119	Lucence	115	53,500	1:49.60	
1984	Lord at War	4	W. Shoemaker	117	Executive Pride	116	Prairie Breaker	116	68,300	1:50.60	
1985	Zoffany	5	E. Delahoussaye	116	Lord at War	125	Foscarini	115	69,100	1:44.80	
1986	Al Mamoon	5	G.L. Stevens	122	Silveyville	118	Will Dancer	115	123,700	1:48.00	
1987	Forlitano	6	P.A. Valenzuela	120	Conquering Hero	115	Ifrad	115	71,500	1:47.40	
1988	Forlitano	7	P.A. Valenzuela	110	Precisionist	121	Skip out Front	117	69,200	1:46.60	
1989	Fair Judgment	5	E. Delahoussaye	117	Quiet Boy	113	Skip out Front	117	63,300	1:50.00	
1990	Colway Rally	6	C.A. Black	114	Exclusive Partner	117	The Medic	116	62,300	1:47.80	97
1991	Notorious Pleasure	5	L. Pincay Jr	118	Somethingdifferent	114	Classic Fame	118	102,600	1:45.80	107
1991	Fly Till Dawn	5	L. Pincay Jr	119	Best Pal	119	Wolf	119	102,600	1:45.80	107
1992	Leger Cat	6	C.S. Nakatani	114	Trishyde	111	Luthier Enchanteur	117	137,500	1:46.40	103
1993	Jeune Homme	3	T. Jarnet	114	Paradise Creek	120	Johann Quatz	120	137,500	1:45.80	110
1994	Southern Wish	5	C.S. Nakatani	115	Square Cut	114	Jeune Homme	118	137,500	2:00.20	108
1995	Fastness	5	G.L. Stevens	120	Earl of Barking	116	Silver Wizard	117	165,000	1:44.60	112
1996	Gentlemen	4	G.L. Stevens	119	Smooth Runner	115	Via Lombardia	116	180,000	1:45.40	108
1997	Geri	5	J.D. Bailey	121	Mufattish	116	Martiniquais	116	180,000	1:48.20	106
1998	Military	4	G.K. Gomez	118	Mr. Lightfoot	117	Worldly Ways	114	180,000	1:50.40	107
1999	Brave Act	5	A. Solis	119	Native Desert	116	Bouccaneer	119	300,000	1:39.60	109
2000	Charge d'Affaires	5	J.A. Santos	116	Ladies Din	122	Native Desert	116	300,000	1:40.30	103
2001	Good Journey	5	C.J. McCarron	115	Decarchy	117	Irish Prize	122	300,000	1:44.30	105
2002	Good Journey	6	P. Day	123	Seinneq	115	White Heart	115	300,000	1:41.45	106
2003	Redattore	8	J.A. Krone	120	Irish Warrior	117	Mister Acpen	116	240,000	1:40.74	106
2004	Leroidesanimaux	4	J.K. Court	117	A to the Z	115	Three Valleys	115	240,000	1:41.36	112

Beyer Index: 106.63

CLARK HANDICAP (G2), 1 1/8 Miles, 3-Year-Olds and Up, Churchill Downs, 2004 Purse: $558,000

Year	Winner	Age	Jockey	Wt.	Second	Wt.	Third	Wt.	Win Value	Time	Beyer
1875	Voltigeur	3	McGrath	110	Calvin	100	Millionaire	100	1,425	3:50.75	
1876	Credmoor	3	W. Williams	100	Vagrant	97	Henry Owings	100	2,150	3:34.75	
1877	McWhirter	3	Miller	100	Vera Cruz	97	Hyena	97	2,000	3:30.50	
1878	Leveller	3	Swim	100	Day Star	100			2,150	3:37.00	
					Solicitor	100					
1879	Falsetto	3	I. Murphy	100	Bucktie	100	Trinidad	100	2,100	3:40.50	
1880	Kinkead	3	J. McLaughlin	105	Aurora's Baby	105	Bye and Bye	102	2,350	3:37.75	
1881	Hindoo	3	J. McLaughlin	105	Alfambra	105	Bootjack	105	3,500	2:10.25	
1882	Runnymede	3	J. McLaughlin	105	Babcock	105	Apollo	102	3,180	2:15.50	
1883	Ascender	3	Stoval	102	Cardinal McCloskey	102	Markland	103	3,270	2:18.00	
1884	Buchanan	3	I. Murphy	110	Loftin	110	Audrain	110	3,230	2:12.00	
1885	Bersan	3	I. Murphy	110	Troubadour	110	Joe Cotton	110	3,420	2:09.25	
1886	Blue Wing	3	Garrison	118	Free Knight	118	Endurer	118	4,190	2:10.00	
1887	Jim Gore	3	L. Jones	118	Libretto	118	Ban Cloche	118	3,630	2:11.25	
1888	Gallifet	3	A. McCarthy	118	White	118	Long Roll	118	3,510	2:15.25	
1889	Spokane	3	Kiley	118	Proctor Knott	118	Once Again	118	3,510	2:12.50	
1890	Riley	3	I. Murphy	118	Robespierre	118	Bill Letcher	118	4,140	2:16.25	
1891	High Tariff	3	Overton	122	Dickerson	122	Milt Young	118	3,370	2:12.00	
1892	Azra	3	A. Clayton	122	Phil Dwyer	122			3,340	2:20.00	
1893	Boundless	3	Kunze	122	Buck McCann	122	Decapod	122	2,300	2:12.00	
1894	Chant	3	W. Martin	122	Pearl Song	122	Buckrene	122	2,730	2:19.50	
1895	Halma	3	Perkins	122	Curator	122			1,720	2:15.50	
1896	Ben Eder	3	Simms	117	Semper Ego	117	Parson	109	3,350	1:56.50	
1897	Ornament	3	A. Clayton	117	Dr. Catlett	117	Panmure	117	3,350	1:55.00	
1898	Plaudit	3	R. Williams	127	Lieber Karl	122			3,350	1:56.50	

Year	Winner	Age	Jockey	Wt.	Second	Wt.	Third	Wt.	Win Value	Time	Beyer
1899	Corsini	3	N. Turner	122	Hapsburg	117	His Lordship	110	3,350	2:01.75	
1900	Lieutenant Gibson	3	Boland	127	Flaunt	117	Dieudonne	107	3,350	1:54.00	
1901	His Eminence	3	Winkfield	127	The Puritan	117	Driscoll	110	3,350	1:55.00	
1902	Death	7	Slack	116	Jim Clark	101	L. Strathm're	108	1,900	1:47.00	
1903	Lover's Labor	6	Scully	100	Harry New	111	Airlight	92	2,150	1:48.00	
1904	Colonial Girl	5	Lyne	109	Monsieur Beaucaire	116	Reservation	116	2,170	1:48.75	
1905	Batts	4	Nicol	104	Early Boy	98	Brancas	109	2,070	1:53.75	
1906	Hyperion II	3	W. McIntyre	103	Envoy	104	Kercheval	108	2,100	1:49.00	
1907	The Minks	4	Nicol	110	Brancas	110	Harry Scott	102	1,820	1:50.80	
1908	Polly Prim	3	V. Powers	117	The Minks	107	Pinkola	105	1,670	1:58.80	
1909	Miami	3	M. McGee	103	Arcite	112	Huck	105	1,820	1:45.20	
1910	King's Daughter	7	T. Koerner	124	T.M. Green	109	Crystal Maid	114	1,600	1:45.60	
1911	Star Charter	3	J. Wilson	105	Countless	132	Joe Morris	108	1,620	1:45.20	
1912	Adams Express	4	C.H. Shilling	122	Mary Davis	100	Cherryola	106	1,900	1:47.80	
1913	Buckhorn	4	Goose	122	Flora Fina	106	Any Port	102	2,080	1:48.20	
1914	Belloc	3	A. Mott	95	Cream	108	Old Ben	92	2,510	1:45.00	
1915	Hodge	4	C. Borel	108	Short Grass	124	B's Choice	112	2,380	1:44.60	
1916	Hodge	5	C. Hunt	120	Ed Crump	120	Dr. Carmen	107	2,520	1:45.40	
1917	Old Rosebud	6	D. Connelly	117	Roamer	128	Embroidery	106	2,230	1:45.20	
1918	Beaverkill	4	O. Willis	104	Fruit Cake	110	Midway	119	2,380	1:48.20	
1919	Midway	5	H. Thurber	117	Beaverkill	109	Hodge	109	436	1:46.60	
1920	Boniface	5	E. Sande	121	Ginger	108	King Gorin	121	10,360	1:45.80	
1921	Ginger	5	T. Murray	112	Upset	122	Dan. Spray	97	9,495	1:45.00	
1922	Exterminator	7	B. Kennedy	133	Lady Madcap	111	Rouleau	107	11,375	1:50.00	
1923	Audacious	7	B. Kennedy	120	Anna M. Humphrey	99	Bon Homme	108	11,200	1:54.60	
1924	Chilhowee	3	B. Harvey	100	Chacolet	124	Hopeless	111	11,200	1:54.40	
1925	Spic and Span	4	G. Fields	103	Son of John	103	Little Celt	117	12,000	1:47.60	
1926	San Utar	5	M. Garner	114	Moonraker	107	Roycrofter	104	13,750	1:45.40	
1927	Helen's Babe	4	W. Lilley	113	Old Slip	114	Percentage	108	12,325	1:46.00	
1928	Jock	4	E. Ambrose	122	Cartago	106	Flat Iron	124	10,925	1:45.00	
1929	Martie Flynn	4	C. Meyer	113	Easter Stockings	111	Cartago	111	10,975	1:46.60	
1930	Stars and Bars	4	L. Jones	108	Easter Stockings	113	Pigeon Hole	106	10,900	1:47.40	
1931	Bargello	5	K. Russell	110	Royal Julian	105	Playtime	109	10,325	1:44.80	
1932	Pittsburgher	4	C. Corbett	112	Spanish Play	115	Canfli	106	4,310	1:50.20	
1933	Osculator	4	S. Coucci	112	The Nut	109	Waylayer	111	4,840	1:45.40	
1934	Esseff	4	L. Humphries	115	Barn Swallow	112	Tick On	114	2,170	1:44.00	
1935	Beaver Dam	3	R. Montgomery	102	Blackbirder	109	Bring Back	108	2,270	1:47.40	
1936	Corinto	4	C. Kurtsinger	114	Ariel Cross	116	Coldstream	109	4,510	1:44.80	
1937	Count Morse	4	I. Anderson	119	Sir Jim James	110	G'nt Killer	112	9,200	1:45.20	
1938	Main Man	4	W.F. Ward	124	Teddy Haslam	109	Old Nassau	112	4,530	1:46.80	
1939	Arabs Arrow	5	C. Bierman	116	Torchy	116	Sortie Star	110	2,130	1:45.80	
1940	Up the Creek	4	G. Wallace	110	Arabs Arrow	120	Shot Put	108	2,175	1:46.00	
1941	Haltal	4	C. McCreary	115	Viscounty	115	Gallahadion	120	2,110	1:44.80	
1942	Whirlaway	4	W. Eads	127	Aonbarr	115	Fairmond	110	2,150	1:44.80	
1943	Anticlimax	4	C. Bierman	112	Corydon	110	Shot Put	108	2,175	1:46.00	
1944	Alquest	4	J. Adams	116	Anticlimax	114	Parasang	108	4,050	1:45.20	
1945	Sentiment Sake	4	F. Wirth	102	Old Kentuck	110	Black Pepper	107	3,910	1:47.20	
1946	Hail Victory	4	D. Dodson	118	Top Reward	111	Bull Play	110	7,775	1:47.80	
1947	Jack S.L.	7	S. Brooks	116	Pellicle	118	Letmenow	110	7,825	1:49.60	
1948	Star Reward	4	S. Brooks	117	Jack S.L.	111	Sun Herod	109	8,175	1:46.60	
1949	Shy Guy	4	C. McCreary	123	Free America	115	Armed	120	7,350	1:45.20	
1950	Mount Marcy	5	S. Brooks	121	Ol' Skipper	114	Dart By	114	8,125	1:44.60	
1951	Wistful	5	D. Dodson	116	Shy Guy	113	Johns Joy	120	7,975	1:44.00	
1952	Seaward	7	K. Church	113	Gay Hunter	102	Hedgewood	110	7,825	1:44.40	
1953	Chombro	6	L.C. Cook	105	Whither	110	Royal Mustang	116	10,887	1:45.60	
1953	Second Avenue	6	C. Bierman	114	Eljay	110	Ad'ms Off Ox	120	10,987	1:45.60	
1954	Bay Bloom	5	J. King	111	Gala Fete	116	Second Avenue	112	11,925	1:44.00	
1955	Happy Go Lucky	6	L.C. Cook	111	Smoke Screen	112	Hasseyampa	121	11,650	1:51.60	
1956	Swoon's Son	3	D. Erb	128	Bernburgoo	111	Mister Black	113	21,925	1:50.60	
1957	Ezgo	3	J. Delahoussaye	114	Aurecolt	111	Styrunner	114	17,957	1:50.80	
1958	My Night Out		E.J. Knapp	116	Shan Pac	116	Praised	108	18,169	1:50.00	
1959	Las Olas	4	F.A. Smith	111	Dru Away	119	Beauguerre	110	17,811	1:48.40	
1960	Counterate	3	J.L. Rotz	114	Little Fitz	118	Cuvier Relic	112	17,925	1:49.00	
1961	Aeroflint	3	E. Curry	116	Neewollah	111	Rev-Up	108	18,785	1:48.40	
1962	Crimson Satan	3	H. Hinojosa	121	Tumble Turbie	116	Bass Clef	117	18,070	1:50.00	
1963	Copy Chief	3	D. Brumfield	117	Lemon Twist	115	Brenner Pass	112	17,842	1:49.20	
1964	Lemon Twist	4	B. Phelps	119	Copy Chief	119	City Line	123	17,842	1:50.60	
1965	Big Brigade	4	J. Nichols	118	Special Prince	110	King of Kentucky	112	18,622	1:50.80	
1966	Flick II	4	H. Pilar	112	Carpenter's Rule	118	King of Kentucky	115	18,574	1:49.60	
1967	Random Shot	4	B. Phelps	114	Maris	116	Backbiter	114	18,639	1:50.80	
1968	Bold Favorite	3	R. Nono	113	Ask the Fare	117	Monitor	116	18,330	1:49.20	
1969	Bold Favorite	4	D. Richard	120	Frederick Street	115	Dorileo	116	18,460	1:50.40	
1970	Watch Fob	5	D. Gargan	114	Spud	113	Dust Commander	118	17,859	1:51.20	

Year	Winner	Age	Jockey	Wt.	Second	Wt.	Third	Wt.	Win Value	Time	Beyer
1971	Sado	4	D. Brumfield	116	French Corners	111	New Round	113	18,850	1:53.60	
1972	Fairway Flyer	3	D.E. Whited	114	Code of Honor	116	Dartsum	113	18,444	1:53.80	
1973	Golden Don	3	M. Manganello	122	Amber Prey	115	Rastaferian	118	22,392	1:52.80	
1974	Mr. Door	3	W. Gavidia	114	Fairway Flyer	116	Cut the Talk	115	17,989	1:52.20	
1975	Warbucks	5	L. Melancon	124	Silver Badge	118	Shoo Dear	111	17,761	1:54.40	
1976	Yamanin	4	G. Patterson	120	Warbucks	115	Play Boy	113	21,661	1:54.40	
1977	Bob's Dusty	3	R. Depass	118	Packer Captain	116	Almost Grown	113	21,889	1:49.80	
1978	Bob's Dusty	4	R. Depass	116	Kodiack	114	Raymond Earl	117	34,629	1:50.20	
1979	Lot o' Gold	3	J.C. Espinoza	123	Poverty Boy	114	Capital Idea	114	38,383	1:50.80	
1980	Sun Catcher	3	D. Brumfield	117	Belle's Ruler	116	Withholding	116	35,636	1:53.40	
1981	Withholding	4	L. Melancon	121	Recusant	111	Hard Up	115	37,213	1:52.00	
1982	Hechizado	6	R.P. Romero	117	Withholding	116	Pleasing Times	115	36,823	1:52.40	
1983	Jack Slade	3	J. McKnight	117	Northern Majesty	122	Cad	118	36,823	1:52.40	
1984	Eminency	6	P. Day	121	Jack Slade	122	Bayou Hebert	114	36,400	1:49.00	
1985	Hopeful Word	4	P. Day	118	Dramatic Desire	113	Big Bobcat	111	49,510	1:51.00	
1986	Come Summer	4	P.A. Johnson	112	Taylor's Special	126	Sumptious	120	47,363	1:49.80	
1987	Intrusion	5	L. Melancon	114	Savings	116	Mister C.	116	47,655	1:51.40	
1988	Balthazar B.	5	K.J. Desormeaux	112	Clever Secret	115	Slew City Slew	123	80,835	1:51.20	
1989	No Marker	5	D.W. Cox	113	Set a Record	114	Stop the Stage	111	75,205	1:51.20	
1990	Secret Hello	3	P. Day	115	Din's Dancer	119	De Roche	121	72,410	1:50.60	
1991	Out of Place	4	W.H. McCauley	119	Echelon's Ice Man	110	British Banker	111	74,230	1:52.20	94
1992	Zeeruler	4	G.K. Gomez	113	Flying Continental	118	Echelon's Ice Man	109	76,050	1:50.00	109
1993	Mi Cielo	3	M.E. Smith	117	Take Me Out	115	Forry Cow How	115	150,540	1:51.40	105
1994	Sir Vixen	6	Kutz D	112	Danville	113	Prize Fight	115	142,480	1:51.20	104
1995	Judge TC	4	Johnson JM	115	Tyus	113	Alphabet Soup	117	153,140	1:49.80	105
1996	Isitingood	5	D.R. Flores	120	Savinio	119	Coup d'Argent	110	174,220	1:48.80	114
1997	Concerto	3	J.D. Bailey	113	Terremoto	114	Rod and Staff	107	284,704	1:49.60	106
1998	Silver Charm	4	G.L. Stevens	124	Littlebitlively	113	Wild Rush	117	275,776	1:49.00	113
1999	Littlebitlively	5	C.H. Borel	118	Pleasant Breeze	112	Nite Dreamer	114	284,456	1:50.80	105
2000	Surfside	3	P. Day	113	Guided Tour	114	Maysville Slew	113	276,272	1:48.75	116
2001	Ubiquity	4	C. Perret	113	Include	120	Mr Ross	114	280,240	1:48.26	106
2002	Lido Palace	5	J.F. Chavez	121	Crafty Shaw	115	Hero's Tribute	114	283,464	1:49.13	112
2003	Quest	4	J. Castellano	114	Evening Attire	118	Aeneas	114	360,840	1:52.42	108
	Evening Attire finished first but was disqualified and placed second										
2004	Saint Liam	4	E.S. Prado	117	Seek Gold	111	Perfect Drift	118	345,960	1:50.81	110

Beyer Index: 107.64

CLIFF HANGER HANDICAP (G3), 1 1/16 Miles (Turf), 3-Year-Olds and Up, The Meadowlands, 2004 Purse: $200,000

Year	Winner	Age	Jockey	Wt.	Second	Wt.	Third	Wt.	Win Value	Time	Beyer
1977	Dan Horn	5	D. MacBeth	125	Shore Patrol	113	Popular Victory	118	34,873	1:43.60	
1978	Mr. Lincroft	4	V. Bracciale Jr	117	Telly Hill	119	Forbidden Isle	109	36,270	1:44.20	
1979	Exclusively Mine	3	W. Nemeti	114	Telly Hill	126	Picturesque	116	34,678	1:44.20	
1980	Quality T.V.	3	J. Velasquez	114	Conservatoire	109	Bill Wheeler	112	32,640	1:43.80	
1981	Bill Wheeler	4	W.H. McCauley	119	Mannerism	113	Brahmin	114	33,510	1:43.60	
1982	Erin's Tiger	4	J. Velasquez	114	Santo's Joe	116	Dew Line	114	26,295	1:44.60	
1982	Acaroid	4	A. Cordero Jr	114	North Course	114	Thirty Eight Paces	116	26,115	1:44.60	
1983	Erin's Tiger	5	J. Velasquez	112	Who's for Dinner	113	Kentucky River	112	33,450	1:41.20	
1984	Late Act	5	E. Maple	113	Sitzmark	112	Quick Dip	112	46,020	1:40.80	
1984	Cozzene	4	W.A. Guerra	115	Ayman	112	Pin Puller	114	45,300	1:40.40	
1985	Late Act	5	E. Maple	113	Silver Surfer	116	Pax Nobiscum	116	47,790	1:45.00	
1986	Explosive Darling	4	R.P. Romero	118	Equalize	114	Lieutenant's Lark	120	48,360	1:40.00	
1987	Foligno	5	J.A. Santos	115	Cost Conscious	116	Air Display	113	46,995	1:41.40	
1987	Silver Comet	4	W.H. McCauley	117	Broadway Tommy	112	Prince Daniel	114	31,830	1:43.80	
1988	Wanderkin	5	R.G. Davis	118	Salem Drive	117	Sans the Shadow	117	53,730	1:39.40	
1989	Ten Keys	5	K.J. Desormeaux	114	Wanderkin	121	Soviet Lad	112	52,290	1:42.40	
1990	Chas' Whim	3	A.T. Stacy	115	Kali High	115	Royal Ninja	112	45,000	1:46.40	
1991	Finder's Choice	6	R.B. Aviles	116	Royal Rue	113	Great Normand	117	45,000	1:40.20	
1992	Roman Envoy	4	C. Perret	116	Futurist	116	Royal Ninja	115	45,000	1:39.80	103
1993	Excellent Tipper	5	C. Perret	117	Rinka Das	115	First and Only	115	45,000	1:43.60	98
1994	Binary Light	5	Samyn JL	112	Brazany	112	Burst of Applause	109	45,000	1:41.40	98
1995	Mighty Forum	4	W.H. McCauley	114	Joker	106	Fourstars Allstar	120	60,000	1:41.00	98
1996	Thorny Crown	5	M.J. Luzzi	115	Ihtiraz	111	Winnetou	112	60,000	1:44.60	100
1997	Dixie Bayou	4	J.R. Velazquez	114	Brave Note	115	Joker	116	60,000	1:39.40	98
1998	Mi Narrow	4	J Bravo	111	Treat Me Doc	114	Boyce	114	60,000	1:43.40	97
1999	Virginia Carnival	7	J.L. Samyn	114	Star Connection	114	Grapeshot	116	90,000	1:42.44	99
2000	North East Bound	4	J.A. Velez Jr	118	Johnny Dollar	114	Swamp	120	90,000	1:41.78	104
2001	Crash Course	5	R. Wilson	114	Solitary Dancer	114	Union One	114	90,000	1:43.14	103
2002	Saint Verre	4	J.L. Samyn	113	Pinky Pizwaanski	116	Spruce Run	115	90,000	1:42.40	106
2004	Dr. Kashnikow	7	R. Migliore	116	Tam's Terms	116	Host	117	120,000	1:42.41	99

Beyer Index: 100.25

Off the turf in 2002; Not run in 2003

COACHING CLUB AMERICAN OAKS (G1), 1 1/4 Miles, 3-Year-Old Fillies, Belmont Park, 2004 Purse: $500,000

Year	Winner	Age	Jockey	Wt.	Second	Wt.	Third	Wt.	Win Value	Time	Beyer
1917	Wistful	3	W.J. O'Brien	124	Battle	120	The Banshee II	115	2,300	1:53.60	
1918	Rose d'Or	3	L. Ensor	111	Eyelid	122	Lady Dorothy	115	5,050	2:06.60	
1919	Polka Dot	3	L. Ensor	111	Passing Shower	121	High Born Lady	111	7,790	2:20.20	
1920	Cleopatra	3	L. McAtee	117	La Rablee	111	Oceanna	111	4,075	2:18.80	
1921	Flambette	3	E. Sande	112	Nancy Lee	121	Ten Buttons	124	4,850	2:17.40	
1922	Prudish	3	L. Morris	111	Emotion	111	King's Fancy	111	11,700	2:18.40	
1923	How Fair	3	A. Johnson	112	Gadfly	114	Untidy	121	11,775	2:18.40	
1924	Princess Doreen	3	H. Stutts	121	Relentless	114	Priscilla Ruley	111	12,875	2:19.20	
1925	Florence Nightingale	3	L. McDermott	111	Gamble	113	Extra Dry	113	13,400	2:17.80	
1926	Edith Cavell	3	F. Coltiletti	117	Black Maria	121	Rapture	117	12,100	2:20.60	
1927	Nimba	3	H. Thurber	111	Frilette	117	Flambino	111	15,775	2:19.80	
1928	Bateau	3	E. Sande	121	Darkness	111	Valkyr	111	14,825	2:24.00	
1929	Sweet Verbena	3	J. Maiben	114	Aquastella	118	Golden Anger	114	16,625	2:18.00	
1930	Snowflake	3	L. Schaefer	121	Red Rag	118	Erin	118	19,600	2:18.40	
1931	Tambour	3	F. Coltiletti	121	Scuttle	114	Allez Vite	114	15,000	2:20.40	
1932	Top Flight	3	R. Workman	121	Argosie	114	Unique	114	15,075	2:20.20	
1933	Edelweiss	3	J. Gilbert	114	Barn Swallow	121	Welcome Gift	114	12,550	2:20.60	
1934	Lady Reigh	3	D. Meade	121	Dusky Princess	111	Hindu Queen	107	9,575	2:18.80	
1935	Black Helen	3	D. Meade	121	Bloodroot	111	Good Gamble	121	7,750	2:18.80	
1936	High Fleet	3	J. Gilbert	111	Split Second	121	Floradora	107	10,575	2:19.60	
1937	Dawn Play	3	L. Balaski	121	Drawbridge	113	Rouge et Noir	107	10,575	2:18.60	
1938	Creole Maid	3	H. Richards	121	Handcuff	121	Gulf Breeze	116	10,425	2:20.80	
1939	War Plumage	3	N. Wall	116	Hostility	121	Wise Lady	121	11,500	2:16.80	
1940	Damaged Goods	3	J. Gilbert	121	Rosetown	121	Dipsy Doodle	121	12,550	2:19.00	
1941	Level Best	3	A. Robertson	121	Dark Discovery	121	Nasca	121	10,275	2:17.60	
1942	Vagrancy	3	T. Malley	121	Mackerel	121	Copperette	121	15,425	2:31.60	
1943	Too Timely	3	G. Woolf	121	Askmenow	121	La Reigh	121	13,250	2:35.00	
1944	Twilight Tear	3	C. McCreary	121	Dare Me	121	Plucky Maud	121	12,495	2:21.00	
1945	Elpis	3	J. Adams	121	Monsoon	121	Segula	121	15,215	2:18.40	
1946	Hypnotic	3	P. Miller	121	Red Shoes	121	Bonnie Beryl	121	21,180	2:18.80	
1947	Harmonica	3	J. Adams	121	Cosmic Missile	121	Snow Goose	121	48,200	2:18.20	
1948	Scattered	3	W. Mehrtens	121	Flitabout	121	Challe Anne	121	43,700	2:18.80	
1949	Wistful	3	S. Brooks	121	Adile	121	Jazz Baby	121	48,700	2:19.60	
1950	Next Move	3	E. Guerin	121	Aegina	121	Busanda	121	44,500	2:15.80	
1951	How	3	E. Arcaro	121	Kiss Me Kate	121	Jacodema	121	46,800	2:16.80	
1952	Real Delight	3	E. Arcaro	121	Lily White	121	Sufie	121	45,100	2:17.80	
1953	Grecian Queen	3	E. Guerin	121	Sabette	121	Ming Yellow	121	45,500	2:18.60	
1954	Cherokee Rose	3	H. Moreno	121	Open Sesame	121	Riverina	121	43,900	2:19.60	
1955	High Voltage	3	T. Atkinson	121	Lalun	121	Manotick	121	45,800	2:17.60	
1956	Levee	3	H. Woodhouse	121	Princess Turia	121	Lady Swords	121	41,100	2:16.60	
1957	Willamette	3	J. Choquette	121	Bayou	121	Woodlawn	121	48,800	2:16.60	
1958	A Glitter	3	I. Valenzuela	121	Spar Maid	121	Craftiness	121	45,792	2:20.00	
1959	Resaca	3	M. Ycaza	121	Quill	121	Czarina	121	58,512	2:02.40	
1960	Berlo	3	E. Guerin	121	Sarcastic	121	Rash Statement	121	55,262	2:04.20	
1961	Bowl of Flowers	3	E. Arcaro	121	Funloving	121	Mighty Fair	121	75,806	2:03.20	
1962	Bramalea	3	R. Ussery	121	Cicada	121	Firm Policy	121	78,081	2:02.60	
1963	Lamb Chop	3	H. Gustines	121	Spicy Living	121	Smart Deb	121	78,244	2:02.80	
1964	Miss Cavandish	3	H. Grant	121	Castle Forbes	121	Sceree	121	79,544	2:04.00	
1965	Marshua	3	R. Broussard	121	What a Treat	121	Terentia	121	84,175	2:02.60	
1966	Lady Pitt	3	W. Blum	121	Prides Profile	121	Help on Way	121	77,919	2:05.00	
	Gentle Rain finished second but was disqualified and placed fourth										
1967	Quillo Queen	3	E. Cardone	121	Muse	121	Pepperwood	121	85,637	2:03.40	
1968	Dark Mirage	3	M. Ycaza	121	Gay Matelda	121	Syrian Sea	121	75,562	2:01.80	
1969	Shuvee	3	J. Davidson	121	Hail to Patsy	121	Secret Verdict	121	77,756	2:03.20	
1970	Missile Belle	3	P. Anderson	121	Cathy Honey	121	Kilts n Kapers	121	87,019	2:03.80	
1971	Our Cheri Amour	3	J. Kurtz	121	Grafitti	121	Inca Queen	121	78,975	2:29.80	
1972	Summer Guest	3	R. Turcotte	121	Wanda	121	Susan's Girl	121	66,360	2:29.40	
1973	Magazine	3	A. Cordero Jr	121	Bag of Tunes	121	Lady Love	121	70,200	2:27.80	
1974	Chris Evert	3	J. Velasquez	121	Fiesta Libre	121	Maud Muller	121	68,520	2:28.80	
1975	Ruffian	3	J. Vasquez	121	Equal Change	121	Let Me Linger	121	66,720	2:27.80	
1976	Revidere	3	J. Vasquez	121	Optimistic Gal	121	No Duplicate	121	68,640	2:28.40	
1977	Our Mims	3	J. Velasquez	121	Road Princess	121	Fia	121	65,880	2:29.40	
1978	Lakeville Miss	3	R. Hernandez	121	Caesar's Wish	121	Tempest Queen	121	63,540	2:29.40	
1979	Davona Dale	3	J. Velasquez	121	Plankton	121	Croquis	121	79,575	2:30.00	
1980	Bold 'n Determined	3	E. Delahoussaye	121	Erin's Word	121	Farewell Letter	121	84,000	2:31.80	
1981	Wayward Lass	3	C.B. Asmussen	121	Real Prize	121	Banner Gala	121	81,750	2:28.20	
	Real Prize finished first but was disqualified and placed second										
1982	Christmas Past	3	J. Vasquez	121	Cupecoy's Joy	121	Flying Partner	121	84,900	2:28.60	
1983	High Schemes	3	J.L. Samyn	121	Spit Curl	121	Lady Norcliffe	121	107,460	2:30.20	
1984	Class Play	3	J. Cruguet	121	Life's Magic	121	Miss Oceana	121	164,520	2:29.80	
1985	Mom's Command	3	A. Fuller	121	Bessarabian	121	Foxy Deen	121	142,560	2:32.00	

Year	Winner	Age	Jockey	Wt.	Second	Wt.	Third	Wt.	Win Value	Time	Beyer
1986	Valley Victory	3	R.P. Romero	121	Life at the Top	121	Lotka	121	166,680	2:28.00	
1987	Fiesta Gal	3	A. Cordero Jr	121	Mint Cooler	121	Run Come See	121	172,500	2:31.00	
1988	Goodbye Halo	3	J. Velasquez	121	Aptostar	121	Make Change	121	170,400	2:32.80	
1989	Open Mind	3	A. Cordero Jr	121	Nite of Fun	121	Rose Diamond	121	170,100	2:32.40	
	Nite of Fun finished first but was disqualified and placed second										
1990	Charon	3	C. Perret	121	Crowned	121	Paper Money	121	172,500	2:02.60	103
1991	Lite Light	3	C.S. Nakatani	121	Meadow Star	121	Car Gal	121	150,000	2:00.40	108
1992	Turnback the Alarm	3	C.W. Antley	121	Easy Now	121	Pleasant Stage	121	150,000	2:03.40	92
1993	Sky Beauty	3	M.E. Smith	121	Future Pretense	121	Silky Feather	121	150,000	2:01.40	96
1994	Two Altazano	3	J.A. Santos	121	Plenty of Sugar	121	Sovereign Kitty	121	150,000	2:02.80	97
1995	Golden Bri	3	J.A. Santos	121	Serena's Song	121	Change Fora Dollar	121	150,000	2:03.80	96
1996	My Flag	3	J.D. Bailey	121	Gold n Delicious	121	Weekend in Seattle	121	180,000	2:04.60	102
1997	Ajina	3	M.E. Smith	121	Tomisue's Delight	121	Key Hunter	121	180,000	2:00.40	102
1998	Banshee Breeze	3	J.D. Bailey	121	Keeper Hill	121	Best Friend Stro	121	180,000	2:31.56	102
1999	On a Soapbox	3	J.D. Bailey	121	Dreams Gallore	121	Strolling Belle	121	210,000	2:29.31	98
2000	Jostle	3	M.E. Smith	121	Resort	121	Secret Status	121	210,000	2:29.99	96
2001	Tweedside	3	J.R. Velazquez	121	Exogenous	121	Unbridled Lassie	121	210,000	2:30.70	93
2002	Jilbab	3	M. Luzzi	121	Tarnished Lady	121	Shop Till You Drop	121	210,000	2:31.48	97
2003	Spoken Fur	3	J.D. Bailey	121	Fircroft	121	Savedbythelight	121	300,000	2:31.02	88
2004	Ashado	3	J.R. Velazquez	121	Stellar Jayne	121	Magical Illusion	121	300,000	2:02.43	106

Beyer Index: 98.40

Distance 1 1/8 miles in 1917; 1 1/4 miles, 1918,1959–70, 1990–97; 1 3/8 miles 1919–41, 1944–58.; 1 1/2 miles 1942–43, 1971– 89, 1998–2003. Run at Aqueduct 1963–67

COMELY (G3), 1 Mile, 3-Year-Old Fillies, Aqueduct, 2004 Purse: $112,000

Year	Winner	Age	Jockey	Wt.	Second	Wt.	Third	Wt.	Win Value	Time	Beyer
1945	Moon Maiden	7	W.D. Wright	113	Darby Delilah	106	Elpis	115	15,615	1:45.40	
1946	Bonnie Beryl	3	H. Woodhouse	114	Hypnotic	114	Bridal Flower	116	16,700	1:44.20	
1947	Elpis	5	L. Hansman	113	Risolator	121	War Date	118	19,225	1:44.20	
1948	Conniver	4	E. Guerin	123	Miss Request	120	Carolyn A.	118	20,200	1:45.00	
1949	Lithe	3	H. Lindberg	107	But Why Not	116	Gaffery	116	20,700	1:45.20	
1950	Siama	3	O Scurlock	112	Antagonism	114	September	118	20,150	1:45.00	
1951	Bed o' Roses	4	E. Guerin	127	Nothirdchance	112	Regal	111	19,500	1:44.60	
1952	Devilkin	3	W. Boland	118	Enchanted Eve	112	Th'lma B'gar	112	20,250	1:44.60	
1953	La Corredora	4	I. Hanford	122	Canadiana	116	Arab Actress	121	19,237	1:45.20	
1953	Home-Made	3	E. Guerin	116	Gay Grecque	116	Sunshine Nell	121	18,987	1:45.20	
1959	Bally Ache	2	D. Erb	122	Tufanhai	122	Progressing	122	11,362	:59.20	
1960	Irish Jay	3	E. Arcaro	121	Improve	115	Staretta	112	18,680	1:23.00	
1961	Seven Thirty	3	H. Woodhouse	112	Apatontheback	115	Shuette	115	15,112	1:24.20	
1962	Upswept	3	B. Baeza	115	First Dark	113	White Gown	114	15,437	1:24.60	
1963	Pams Ego	3	I. Valenzuela	115	Fashion Verdict	115	Vast Scope	112	11,456	1:23.80	
1963	Lamb Chop	3	B. Baeza	118	Spicy Living	112	Fool's Play	115	11,326	1:24.40	
1964	Face the Facts	3	M. Ycaza	118	Petticoat	112	Miss Cavandish	112	18,525	1:23.80	
1965	What a Treat	3	J.L. Rotz	118	Equiria	113	Adorable	112	17,680	1:24.60	
1966	Swift Lady	3	J.L. Rotz	115	Good Queen Bess	113	Tagend	118	18,785	1:23.60	
1967	Gala Honors	3	B. Baeza	113	Just Kidding	118	Lake Chelan	116	18,947	1:25.00	
1968	Best in Show	3	H. Gustines	112	Heartland	113	Gay Matelda	115	19,240	1:22.40	
1969	Ta Wee	3	E. Belmonte	118	Shuvee	121	Hasty Hitter	118	18,492	1:22.60	
1970	Predictable	3	R. Ussery	116	Princess Roycraft	118	Capercaillie	112	14,852	1:24.00	
1970	Royal Signal	3	B. Baeza	118	Office Queen	118	Luci Tee	112	15,015	1:24.00	
1971	Forward Gal	3	M. Hole	121	Sea Saga	118	Deceit	115	20,460	1:23.40	
1972	Stacey d'Ette	3	J. Ruane	115	Numbered Account	121	Candid Catherine	118	16,290	1:21.60	
1973	Java Moon	3	A. Cordero Jr	116	Windy's Daughter	121	Voler	116	17,610	1:22.80	
1974	Clear Copy	3	D. Montoya	113	Shy Dawn	118	Chris Evert	118	17,670	1:24.40	
1975	Ruffian	3	J. Vasquez	113	Aunt Jin	113	Point in Time	113	16,755	1:21.20	
1976	Tell Me All	3	J. Ruane	113	Dearly Precious	121	Worthyana	113	22,080	1:23.20	
1977	Bring out the Band	3	D. Brumfield	118	Cum Laude Laurie	113	Emmy	113	22,650	1:23.60	
1978	Mashteen	3	R. Hernandez	113	Tempest Queen	118	Mucchina	113	25,665	1:23.00	
1979	Countess North	3	A. Cordero Jr	113	Palm Hut	116	Run Cosmic Run	113	25,725	1:23.40	
1980	Cybele	3	C.B. Asmussen	113	Punta Punta	113	Kashan	113	27,225	1:22.60	
1981	Expressive Dance	3	D. MacBeth	113	Tina Tina Too	118	Explosive Kingdom	114	35,220	1:23.40	
1982	Nancy Huang	3	J. Velasquez	113	Broom Dance	113	Dance Number	113	34,860	1:24.40	
1983	Able Money	3	A. Graell	113	Stark Drama	113	Idle Gossip	113	35,580	1:23.80	
1984	Wild Applause	3	P. Day	113	Suavite	113	Proud Clarioness	116	52,110	1:23.20	
1985	Mom's Command	3	A. Fuller	121	Majestic Folly	113	Clocks Secret	121	55,170	1:22.20	
1986	Misty Drone	3	J. Vasquez	113	I'm Splendid	121	Storm and Sunshine	114	59,940	1:24.00	
1987	Devil's Bride	3	R. Meza	116	Oh So Precious	116	Valid Line	114	65,790	1:23.60	
1988	Avie's Gal	3	J. Velasquez	114	Topicount	116	Ready Jet Go	114	53,280	1:22.40	
1989	Surging	3	A. Cordero Jr	118	Nite of Fun	112	Luv That Native	112	52,290	1:23.00	
1990	Fappaburst	3	J. Vasquez	114	Miss Spentyouth	114	Bundle Bits	118	49,770	1:21.60	112

Year	Winner	Age	Jockey	Wt.	Second	Wt.	Third	Wt.	Win Value	Time	Beyer
1991	Meadow Star	3	C.W. Antley	121	Do It With Style	114	I'm a Thriller	118	67,560	1:38.00	95
1992	Saratoga Dew	3	W.H. McCauley	114	City Dance	112	Looking for a Win	114	69,480	1:37.20	93
1993	Private Light	3	R.G. Davis	112	Russian Bride	113	True Affair	118	68,280	1:44.00	91
1994	Dixie Luck	3	Leon F	116	Penny's Reshoot	116	Our Royal Blue	112	66,240	1:37.00	88
1995	Nappelon	3	Chavez JF	112	Stormy Blues	121	Incredible Blues	114	64,440	1:36.20	88
1996	Little Miss Fast	3	J.F. Chavez	118	J J'sdream	118	Stop Traffic	112	65,940	1:36.40	95
1997	Dixie Flag	3	J.L. Samyn	114	Global Star	114	How About Now	114	66,120	1:36.80	94
1998	Fantasy Angel	3	J.F. Chavez	114	Hansel's Girl	116	Best Friend Stro	118	69,300	1:37.40	85
1999	Madison's Charm	3	J.L. Samyn	112	Better Than Honour	121	Oh What a Windfall	121	65,520	1:35.54	92
2000	March Magic	3	R. Migliore	114	Jostle	121	Finder's Fee	121	65,460	1:36.79	92
2001	Two Item Limit	3	R. Migliore	122	Mandy's Gold	118	It All Adds Up	116	66,060	1:36.17	90
	Mandy's Gold (Beyer: 89) finished first but was disqualified and placed second										
2002	Bella Bellucci	3	G.L. Stevens	122	Short Note	116	Nonsuch Bay	116	64,920	1:35.50	103
2003	Cyber Secret	3	S.X. Bridgmohan	122	Storm Flag Flying	122	Bonay	116	64,740	1:35.97	89
2004	Society Selection	3	J.F. Chavez	122	Bending Strings	116	Daydreaming	116	67,200	1:35.89	90

Beyer Index: 93.13

COMMONWEALTH BREEDERS' CUP (G2), 7 Furlongs, 3-Year-Olds and Up, Keeneland Race Course, 2004 Purse: $250,250

Year	Winner	Age	Jockey	Wt.	Second	Wt.	Third	Wt.	Win Value	Time	Beyer
1987	Exclusive Enough	3	M.E. Smith	111	Lazer Show	120	High Brite	120	101,010	1:08.40	
1988	Calestoga	6	D. Brumfield	120	You're No Bargain	117	Carload	120	101,628	1:09.40	
1989	Sewickley	4	R.P. Romero	115	Irish Open	118	Dancing Spree	115	36,368	1:22.40	
1990	Black Tie Affair	4	M. Guidry	121	Shaker Knit	115	Momsfurrari	118	120,608	1:22.00	
1991	Black Tie Affair	5	J.L. Diaz	124	Housebuster	124	Exemplary Leader	115	118,625	1:21.80	106
1992	Pleasant Tap	5	E. Delahoussaye	116	To Freedom	115	Run on the Bank	118	118,138	1:22.40	105
1993	Alydeed	4	C. Perret	115	Binalong	118	Senor Speedy	115	113,057	1:21.40	109
1994	Memo	7	P. Atkinson	118	American Chance	115	British Banker	115	149,900	1:22.20	116
1995	Golden Gear	4	C. Perret	118	Turkomatic	112	Lit de Justice	121	130,758	1:22.00	105
1996	Afternoon Deelites	4	K.J. Desormeaux	124	Western Winter	113	Our Emblem	115	131,068	1:21.00	104
1997	Victor Cooley	4	E.M. Martin Jr	114	Western Winter	112	Appealing Skier	121	129,332	1:22.60	107
1998	Distorted Humor	5	G.L. Stevens	119	El Amante	114	Partner's Hero	121	130,820	1:20.40	116
1999	Good and Tough	4	S.J. Sellers	115	Purple Passion	115	Crucible	115	127,906	1:22.00	107
2000	Richter Scale	6	R. Migliore	121	Son's Corona	117	Deep Gold	117	128,836	1:21.07	114
2001	Alannan	5	E.S. Prado	118	Valiant Halory	118	Liberty Gold	118	170,965	1:22.39	100
2002	Orientate	4	P. Day	120	Aldebaran	118	Twilight Road	118	168,997	1:21.54	109
2003	Smooth Jazz	4	E.S. Prado	118	Crafty C.T.	118	Multiple Choice	120	169,725	1:21.73	117
2004	Lion Tamer	4	M.E. Smith	122	Private Horde	120	Marino Marini	118	167,555	1:23.14	105

Beyer Index: 108.57

COTILLION HANDICAP (G2), 1 1/16 Miles, 3-Year-Old Fillies, Philadelphia Park, 2004 Purse: $250,000

Year	Winner	Age	Jockey	Wt.	Second	Wt.	Third	Wt.	Win Value	Time	Beyer
1969	Shuvee	3	J. Davidson	124	Class Is Out	113	Secret Verdict	114	33,120	1:43.20	
1970	Office Queen	3	J.L. Rotz	123	Ellen Girl	117	Fast Attack	116	34,500	1:44.00	
1971	Alma North	3	F. Lovato	116	Forward Gal	123	Miss Pat R.	110	33,480	1:43.60	
1972	Susan's Girl	3	V. Tejada	125	Groton miss	119	Honestous	115	35,970	1:44.20	
1973	Lilac Hill	3	D. MacBeth	113	Ladies Agreement	114	Suzi Sunshine	114	34,590	1:43.60	
1974	Honky Star	3	D.G. McHargue	121	Special Team	118	Kudara	121	32,910	1:44.00	
1975	My Juliet	3	D. Brumfield	116	Hot n Nasty	116	Gala Lil	118	20,160	1:43.60	
1976	Revidere	3	J. Vasquez	118	Critical Miss	116	Hay Patcher	116	20,190	1:44.00	
1977	Suede Shoe	3	A.S. Black	116	Raise Old Glory	113	Bafflin Lil	116	27,930	1:42.60	
1978	Queen Lib	3	D. MacBeth	121	Silken Delight	116	Sharp Belle	116	28,620	1:43.20	
1979	Alada	3	J. Fell	116	Too Many Sweets	116	Heavenly Ade	118	33,090	1:43.80	
1980	Sugar and Spice	3	G. Martens	116	Pepi Valley	118	Nijit	116	34,800	1:45.00	
1981	Truly Bound	3	R.J. Franklin	121	Pukka Princess	118	Debonair Dancer	118	33,810	1:42.80	
1982	Lady Eleanor	3	C. Perret	122	Smart Heiress	122	Glass House	117	34,800	1:45.00	
1983	Quixotic Lady	3	G. McCarron	122	Lady Hawthorn	117	Springtime Sharon	117	33,180	1:42.80	
1984	Squan Song	3	R.Z. Hernandez	122	Given	122	You're Too Special	113	60,945	1:42.80	
1984	Dowery	3	V. Bracciale Jr	122	Duo Disco	122	Hot Milk	117	60,945	1:42.60	
1985	Koluctoo's Jill	3	W.H. McCauley	119	Overwhelming	115	Tabayour	118	65,520	1:42.80	
1986	Toes Knows	3	D.R. Wright	119	Life at the Top	121	I'm Sweets	119	65,880	1:42.80	
1987	Silent Turn	3	R.P. Romero	118	Sacahuista	119	Single Blade	117	65,280	1:42.80	
1988	Aquaba	3	J. Cruguet	115	Ice Tech	113	Mother of Eight	114	79,320	1:44.40	
1989	Sharp Dance	3	K. Castaneda	115	Misty Ivor	113	Tactile	117	81,900	1:45.80	
1990	Valay Maid	3	L. Saumell	119	Toffeefee	115	Trumpet's Blare	116	81,600	1:43.80	109
1992	Star Minister	3	A.J. Seefeldt	117	Diamond Duo	121	Squirm	116	80,760	1:44.00	95
1993	Jacody	3	T.G. Turner	118	Aztec Hill	121	Cearas Dancer	109	95,520	1:43.20	104
1994	Sovereign Kitty	3	W.H. McCauley	118	Cinnamon Sugar	120	Cavada	116	97,440	1:43.40	95
1995	Clear Mandate	3	J.C. Ferrer	113	Blue Sky Princess	114	Country Cat	118	164,550	1:42.80	98

Year	Winner	Age	Jockey	Wt.	Second	Wt.	Third	Wt.	Win Value	Time	Beyer
1996	Double Dee's	3	F. Leon	111	Ginny Lynn	121	Princess Eloise	113	90,000	1:44.60	90
1997	Snit	3	R. E. Colton	114	Proud Run	116	Salt It	117	90,000	1:43.80	101
1998	Lu Ravi	3	W. Martinez	121	Sister Act	115	Let	117	90,000	1:43.40	100
1999	Skipping Around	3	M.J. McCarthy	114	Strolling Belle	120	Waltz	114	120,000	1:43.40	95
2000	Jostle	3	M.E. Smith	124	Gold For My Gal	112	Prized Stamp	114	120,000	1:42.54	106
2001	Mystic Lady	3	E.M. Coa	121	Zonk	117	Celtic Melody	115	150,000	1:43.86	103
2002	Smok'n Frolic	3	J.A. Velez Jr	118	Pupil	114	Jilbab	120	150,000	1:44.27	96
2003	Fast Cookie	3	N. Santagata	116	Ladyecho	116	Savedbythelight	117	150,000	1:45.83	96
2004	Ashado	3	E.M. Coa	124	Ender's Sister	117	My Lordship	115	150,000	1:41.68	103

Beyer Index: 99.36

COUNT FLEET SPRINT HANDICAP (G3), 6 Furlongs, 4-Year-Olds and Up, Oaklawn Park, 2004 Purse: $150,000

Year	Winner	Age	Jockey	Wt.	Second	Wt.	Third	Wt.	Win Value	Time	Beyer
1974	Barbizon Streak	6	R. Wilson	114	Pleasure Castle	120	Pesty Jay	122	17,370	1:11.00	
1975	Prince Astro	6	D.W. Whited	123	Silver Doctor	117	Faneuil Boy	112	18,030	1:10.00	
1976	Brets Kicker	5	J.D. Bailey	111	Silver Doctor	118	Mr. Barb	110	17,640	1:10.00	
1977	Silver Hope	6	R.L. Turcotte	120	Dr's Enjoy Dollars	116	Brets Kicker	113	18,480	1:10.40	
1978	Last Buzz	5	A. Rini	126	Best Person	110	Sucha Pleasure	118	33,390	1:11.00	
1979	Amadevil	5	T.G. Greer	114	Little Reb	120	Sean's Song	114	34,890	1:11.20	
1980	Silent Dignity	4	S. Maple	114	Gustoso	111	J. Burns	115	34,680	1:11.00	
1981	General Custer	4	L. Snyder	111	Avenging Gossip	111	Be a Prospect	112	34,470	1:10.40	
1982	Sandbagger	4	D. Haire	114	Blue Water Line	117	Lockjaw	116	39,240	1:12.00	
1983	Dave's Friend	8	L. Snyder	124	General Jimmy	117	Liberty Lane	113	70,320	1:10.00	
1984	Dave's Friend	9	E. Delahoussaye	122	All Sold Out	114	Lucky Salvation	114	70,260	1:09.00	
1985	Taylor's Special	4	R.P. Romero	123	Mt. Livermore	119	T.H. Bend	110	98,280	1:08.40	
1986	Mister Gennaro	5	F. Olivares	115	Beveled	114	Charging Falls	125	71,100	1:08.80	
1987	Sun Master	6	G.L. Stevens	117	Rocky Marriage	116	Chhief Steward	118	69,540	1:09.40	
1988	Salt Dome	5	L. Snyder	116	Pewter	113	Bold Pac Man	112	60,000	1:08.60	
1989	Twice Around	4	C.H. Borel	116	Be a Agent	117	Never Forgotten	114	60,000	1:09.20	
1990	Malagra	4	V.L. Smith	117	Pentelicus	115	Sunny Blossom	120	60,000	1:08.80	106
1991	Overpeer	7	P. Day	122	Silent Reflex	113	Peaked	118	60,000	1:08.20	108
1992	Gray Slewpy	4	K.J. Desormeaux	117	Potentiality	116	Hidden Tomahawk	115	60,000	1:08.80	116
1993	Approach	6	P. Day	116	Ponche	113	Never Wavering	110	90,000	1:09.60	109
1994	Demaloot Demashoot	4	M.E. Smith	115	Honor the Hero	117	Sir Hutch	118	90,000	1:08.20	113
1995	Hot Jaws	5	Borel CH	113	Demaloot Demashoot	116	Mr. Cooperative	114	90,000	1:09.40	110
1996	Concept Win	6	G.L. Stevens	116	Roythelittleone	114	Spiritbound	113	90,000	1:09.00	102
1997	High Stakes Player	5	K.J. Desormeaux	120	Capote Belle	116	Victor Avenue	116	90,000	1:08.80	107
1998	Chindi	4	D.R. Pettinger	113	E J Harley	113	Western Fame	115	75,000	1:09.60	104
1999	Reraise	4	C.S. Nakatani	122	Run Johnny	114	E J Harley	115	75,000	1:08.59	109
2000	Show Me the Stage	4	D.R. Flores	116	Smolderin Heart	115	Vinnie's Boy	114	75,000	1:09.62	102
2001	Bonapaw	5	G. Melancon	118	Chindi	114	Bidis	117	75,000	1:08.18	119
2002	Explicit	5	L.J. Meche	116	Entepreneur	115	Junior Deputy	113	90,000	1:08.60	114
2003	Beau's Town	5	H.J. Theriot II	122	Honor Me	116	Sand Ridge	114	90,000	1:09.01	106
2004	Shake You Down	6	R.A. Dominguez	121	Where's the Ring	115	Aloha Bold	114	90,000	1:09.27	102

Beyer Index: 108.47

(MILLER GENUINE DRAFT) CRADLE (G3), 1 1/16 Miles, 2-Year-Olds, River Downs, 2004 Purse: $200,000

Year	Winner	Age	Jockey	Wt.	Second	Wt.	Third	Wt.	Win Value	Time	Beyer
1977	Bolero's Orphan	2	N. Shuk	122	Young Bob	122	Morning Prince	122	26,988	1:10.40	
1978	Noon Shadow	2	J. Harrison	119	Investigate	122	Lawyer's Son	122	30,378	1:12.60	
1979	Ray's Word	2	A.J. Costa	122	Golden Magic	122	Etched in Gold	119	33,375	1:11.60	
1980	Gallant Lt.	2	C. Schwing	122	Hidden Image	122	Those Eyes	122	44,495	1:13.80	
1981	Ashley's Miss	2	E.J. Sipus	119	Marshall Kai	122	Martha's First	122	32,661	1:14.00	
1981	Royal Dan	2	C.R. Woods Jr	122	T.V. Mark	122	Dust off the Mat	122	32,481	1:13.00	
1982	Spare Card	2	G.P. Louviere	122	Tai Power	122	Yandalob	119	60,876	1:14.60	
1983	Coax Me Chad	2	J.C. Espinoza	120	Tall Grass Walker	120	Tah Dah	117	75,000	1:46.60	
1984	Spend a Buck	2	C. Hussey	120	Grand Native	120	Alex's Game	120	75,000	1:45.80	
1985	Go for It Matt	2	C.W. Antley	120	Southern Appeal	120	Steady Effort	120	90,000	1:44.80	
1986	Coaxing Chad	2	S. Neff	120	Grand Rol	120			120,000	1:45.60	
					Win Dusty Win	120					
	David L.'s Rib finished second but was disqualified and placed fourth										
1987	Cannon Dancer	2	M. Manganello	120	Kingpost	120	House Account	120	120,000	1:44.60	
1988	Bravoure	2	M. McDowell	120	Funinthesun	120	Revive	120	120,000	1:45.80	
1989	Table Limit	2	W.H. McCauley	120	On the Scent	120	Stormy Deep	120	120,000	1:45.20	
1990	Wall Street Dancer	2	S.O. Madrid	120	Bobby M.	120	David Michael	120	120,000	1:48.80	
1991	Wolf Brigade	2	S.O. Madrid	120	Seaside Dancer	120	Coax Stardust	120	120,000	1:45.40	
1992	Crosswood	2	J.E. Bruin	120	Nowi'veseenitall	120	Over Spending	120	120,000	1:47.00	71
1993	Moving Van	2	P.J. Cooksey	120	Riverinn	120	Camptown Dancer	120	120,000	1:48.60	74

Year	Winner	Age	Jockey	Wt.	Second	Wt.	Third	Wt.	Win Value	Time	Beyer
1994	Peaks and Valleys	2	P. Day	120	Tejano Run	120	Hold on Josh	120	120,000	1:46.60	86
1995	Devil's Honor	2	A.S. Black	120	City by Night	120	J P Hamer	120	120,000	1:45.00	85
1996	Haint	2	S.J. Sellers	120	Just a Cat	120	Play Waki for Me	120	120,000	1:46.20	91
1997	Cowboy Dan	2	D. Kutz	120	Jigadee	120	Tropic Lightning	120	120,000	1:47.40	93
1998	Mountain Range	2	P. Day	120	Lecture	120	Shake Me Wake Me	120	120,000	1:45.80	91
1999	Deputy Warlock	2	F.A. Arguello Jr	120	Mighty	120	Personal First	120	120,000	1:47.40	83
2000	Mongoose	2	R.J. Albarado	120	Gift of the Eagle	120	Running Rahy	120	120,000	1:46.00	88
2001	Harlan's Holiday	2	A.J. D'Amico	120	Request for Parole	120	Arctic Sand	120	126,300	1:46.40	84
2002	Lone Star Sky	2	M. Guidry	120	Christmas Away	120	Payforaday	120	120,000	1:46.80	83
2003	Tiger Hunt	2	L. Melancon	120	Lightnin n Thunder	120	Blushing Indian	120	120,000	1:49.00	74
2004	Bellamy Road	2	A. Castellano Jr	120	Diamond Isle	120	Scipion	120	120,000	1:45.00	82

Beyer Index: 83.46

Distance 6 furlongs 1977–1982.

BING CROSBY BREEDERS' CUP HANDICAP (G1), 6 Furlongs, 3-Year-Olds and Up, Del Mar, 2004 Purse: $244,000

Year	Winner	Age	Jockey	Wt.	Second	Wt.	Third	Wt.	Win Value	Time	Beyer
1946	War Allies	4	R. Neves	119			Pride of Hy'ro	122	3,250	1:11.40	
	Indian Watch	6	M. Peterson	105							
1947	Be Fearless	5	L. Balaski	121	Barbastel	111	War Valor	108	4,700	1:10.80	
1948	Prevaricator	5	J. Bravo	122	Tape Buster	115	Capt. Flagg	114	6,600	1:11.20	
1949	Cover Up	6	M. Volzke	114	Roman In	115	Barsard	116	6,800	1:10.00	
1950	Imperium	4	W. Shoemaker	122	Akimbo	105	Brave Fox	115	4,500	1:09.80	
1951	Blue Reading	4	B. Pearson	118	Kit Carson	121	Mrs. Fuddy	108	4,450	1:10.40	
1952	Gustaf	9	W. Marsh	107	Blue Reading	123	Trusting	110	4,425	1:10.00	
1953	Ode	6	R. York	111	Big Noise	112	Stranglehold	120	6,200	1:10.20	
1954	Alibhai Lynn	4	J. Phillippi	111	Karim	115	Stranglehold	122	7,100	1:09.60	
1955	One Ton Tony	5	P. Moreno	115	Karim	119	Bobby Brocato	121	6,800	1:09.20	
1956	Colonel Mack	4	R. Neves	122	Poona II	123	Moolah Bux	107	8,700	1:08.80	
1957	How Now	4	R. York	122	Jeddar Ruler	115	Noredski	118	8,725	1:09.20	
1958	How Now	5	W. Harmatz	128	Swirling Abbey	120	Little Moon	110	8,300	1:09.40	
1959	Ole Fols	3	I. Valenzuela	122	Coup de Vent	109	Silky Sullivan	122	8,775	1:08.80	
1960	High Performance	5	R. Campas	110	Little Moon	113	Aliwar	124	8,825	1:09.00	
1961	Ann's Knight	5	R. Mundorf	114	Revel	127	W'nsome Winner	115	8,650	1:08.60	
1962	Sea Orbit	6	R. York	118	Ann's Knight	118	Mr. Wag	114	7,375	1:08.80	
1962	Crazy Kid	4	A. Valenzuela	118	Cadiz	122	Henrijan	118	7,375	1:07.80	
1963	Sledge	4	M. Yanez	117	Testum	119	Gallant Host	114	8,475	1:08.60	
1964	Soldier Girl	3	J. Longden	116	More Megaton	116			8,525	1:09.40	
					Rich Mel	118					
1965	Viking Spirit	5	K. Church	128	Perris	115	Nearco Blue	110	8,500	1:08.60	
1966	Chiclero	4	D. Pierce	119	Traveling Dust	112	Aurelius II	115	8,775	1:08.80	
1967	Kissin' George	4	W. Mahorney	122	Wolfgang	110	Royal Step	114	10,375	1:08.60	
1968	Pretense	5	D. Pierce	122	Kissin' George	125	Dizzy Babe	114	8,500	1:07.80	
1969	Kissin' George	6	W. Mahorney	127	Time to Leave	121	Canterbury Road	119	10,450	1:07.80	
1970	Bargain Day	5	R. Rosales	113	Pinjara	125	Imaginative	117	9,025	1:27.60	
1971	Haveago	4	J. Sellers	115	Long Position	119	Fl't Surprise	123	9,075	1:08.20	
1972	Dominant Star	4	F. Alvarez	112	Restless Runner	114	Crimson Saint	118	9,100	1:08.00	
1973	Pataha Prince	8	W. Shoemaker	114	King of Cricket	114	Rough Night	120	13,700	1:08.00	
1974	Rise High	4	J. Tejeira	113	Tragic Isle	121	Against the Snow	115	13,250	1:09.00	
1975	Messenger of Song	3	J. Lambert	119	Stake Driver	114	Century's Envoy	122	12,450	1:08.80	
1976	Cherry River	6	L. Pincay Jr	120	Sawtooth	111	Fast Spot	115	15,900	1:09.40	
1977	Cherry River	7	L. Pincay Jr	120	Leinster House	111	Mark's Place	124	15,800	1:08.40	
1978	Bad 'n Big	4	W. Shoemaker	124	Amadevil	121	Decoded	115	19,400	1:07.80	
1979	Syncopate	4	S. Hawley	116	White Rammer	122	Fleet Twist	116	22,750	1:08.40	
1980	Reb's Golden Ale	5	S. Hawley	117	Bolger	114	Bad 'n Big	118	24,400	1:08.80	
1981	Syncopate	6	E. Delahoussaye	120	Reb's Golden Ale	119	To B. or Not	122	31,100	1:08.60	
1982	Pencil Point	4	P.A. Valenzuela	114	Terresto's Singer	114	Shanekite	115	32,650	1:09.00	
1983	Chinook Pass	4	L. Pincay Jr	125	Vagabond Song	116	Haughty but Nice	115	32,000	1:08.60	
1984	Night Mover	4	L.E. Ortega	120	Premiership	119	Pac Mania	115	31,800	1:08.60	
1985	My Favorite Mom't	4	E. Delahoussaye	116	Rosie's K.T.	116	Fifty Six Ina Row	119	33,350	1:09.80	
1986	American Legion	6	E. Delahoussaye	119	Bold Brawley	113	Ondarty	112	38,000	1:08.20	
1987	Zany Tactics	6	J.L. Kaenel	120	Bolder Than Bold	118	My Favorite Mom't	115	38,600	1:09.00	
1988	Olympic Prospect	4	A. Solis	121	Faro	118	Sebrof	119	59,410	1:08.80	
1989	On the Line	5	G.L. Stevens	124	Speedratic	117	Cresting Water	115	63,800	1:08.00	
1990	Sensational Star	6	R.Q. Meza	113	Frost Free	116	Timeless Answer	116	60,150	1:08.00	110
1991	Bruho	5	C.S. Nakatani	116	Thirty Slews	115	Due to the King	116	62,900	1:08.20	112
1992	Thirty Slews	5	E. Delahoussaye	116	Slerp	115	Anjiz	114	64,900	1:08.20	106
1993	The Wicked North	4	C.A. Black	116	Thirty Slews	121	Black Jack Road	115	61,200	1:08.40	112
1994	King's Blade	3	Nakatani CS	112	Memo	121	Gundaghia	118	62,400	1:08.60	107
1995	Gold Land	4	Delahoussaye E	116	Lucky Forever	118	G Malleah	116	89,300	1:08.00	112
1996	Lit de Justice	6	C.S. Nakatani	121	Concept Win	116	Gold Land	116	126,750	1:08.00	113

Year	Winner	Age	Jockey	Wt.	Second	Wt.	Third	Wt.	Win Value	Time	Beyer
1997	First Intent	8	R.R. Douglas	115	Boundless Moment	118	High Stakes Player	120	102,000	1:08.80	110
1998	Son of a Pistol	6	A. Solis	120	Gold Land	117	Boundless Moment	116	97,200	1:08.00	118
1999	Christmas Boy	6	C.S. Nakatani	114	Son of a Pistol	123	Expressionist	116	96,360	1:08.00	117
2000	Kona Gold	6	A. Solis	123	Love That Red	118	Lexicon	117	124,200	1:08.50	118
2001	Kona Gold	7	A. Solis	126	Caller One	124	Swept Overboard	115	120,000	1:08.22	119
2002	Disturbingthepeace	4	V. Espinoza	116	Freespool	115	Mellow Fellow	118	90,000	1:09.21	110
2003	Beau's Town	5	P.A. Valenzuela	119	Captain Squire	117	Bluesthestandard	117	120,000	1:07.96	116
2004	Kela	6	T.C. Baze	113	Pohave	118	Hombre Rapido	115	150,000	1:08.51	112

Beyer Index: 112.80

DAHLIA HANDICAP (G3), 1 1/16 Miles (Off the Turf), Fillies and Mares, 3-Year-Olds and Up, Hollywood Park, 2004 Purse: $150,000

Year	Winner	Age	Jockey	Wt.	Second	Wt.	Third	Wt.	Win Value	Time	Beyer
1982	Sangue	4	L. Pincay Jr	122	Star Pastures	118	Pat's Joy	115	31,900	1:41.40	
1982	Milingo	3	T. Lipham	124	Pink Safir	113	Berry Bush	117	33,400	1:42.60	
1983	Geraldine's Store	4	J.L. Samyn	118	Northerly Glow	111	Satin Ribera	115	32,500	1:42.40	
1983	First Advance	4	T. Lipham	114	Absentia	116	Bersid	112	33,500	1:42.00	
1984	Lina Cavalieri	4	E. Delahoussaye	117	Pampas	115	Salt Spring	117	53,050	1:44.20	
1985	Capricorn Belle	4	C.J. McCarron	118	Justicara	118	Solva	115	66,200	1:41.60	
1986	Aberuschka	4	P.A. Valenzuela	122	An Empress	117	Reloy	118	80,740	1:41.60	
1987	Invited Guest	3	W. Shoemaker	114	Secuencia	115	Smooch	117	71,950	1:43.40	
1987	Top Corsage	4	J.A. Santos	118	Any Song	116	Aberuschka	120	48,700	1:43.20	
1988	Balbonella	4	F. Toro	117	Goodbye Halo	120	Pen Bal Lady	117	75,100	1:42.80	
1989	Stylish Star	3	C.J. McCarron	116	Ariosa	113	Sugar Plum Gal	114	51,600	1:40.40	
1989	Saros Brig	5	G.L. Stevens	114	Nikishka	120	Beat	115	49,600	1:40.40	
1990	Petalia	5	K.J. Desormeaux	113	Bequest	117	Island Jamboree	113	48,900	1:41.40	96
1990	Little Brianne	5	J.A. Garcia	119	Stylish Star	119	Girl of France	115	50,900	1:40.60	105
1991	Re Toss	4	C.S. Nakatani	115	Elegance	115	Gaelic Bird	114	70,400	1:40.60	102
1992	Kostroma	6	G.L. Stevens	124	Vijaya	114	Guiza	116	66,500	1:41.40	102
1993	Kalita Melody	5	C.A. Black	115	Vinista	116	Gumpher	116	64,500	1:44.60	99
1994	Skimble	5	E. Delahoussaye	118	Queens Court Queen	118	Shir Dar	115	66,000	1:42.20	100
1995	Didina	3	E. Delahoussaye	115	Dirca	114	Rapunzel Runz	116	68,300	1:45.20	107
1996	Sixieme Sens	4	C.S. Nakatani	115	Grafin	116	Admise	121	66,600	1:42.20	103
1997	Golden Arches	3	C.J. McCarron	117	Sonja's Faith	113	Traces Of Gold	116	60,000	1:41.00	100
1998	Tuzla	4	C.S. Nakatani	119	Sonja's Faith	118	Curitiba	115	60,000	1:41.60	102
1999	Lady At Peace	3	G.K. Gomez	113	Cyrillic	117	Country Garden	115	90,000	1:41.40	98
2000	Follow The Money	4	V. Espinoza	115	Smooth Player	120	Beautiful Noise	117	90,000	1:40.71	98
2001	Verruma	5	G.K. Gomez	115	Vencera	115	Heads Will Roll	117	90,000	1:43.24	99
2002	Tout Charmant	6	A. Solis	119			Honestly Darling	114	60,000	1:44.45	99
	Surya	4	P.A. Valenzuela	118							
2003	Katdogawn	3	M.E. Smith	116	Personal Legend	115	Betty's Wish	117	90,000	1:41.52	97
2004	Festival	5	D. Sorenson	111	Irgunette	113	Belle Ange	114	90,000	1:42.11	90

Beyer Index: 99.81

DAVONA DALE (G2), 1 1/16 Miles, 3-Year-Old Fillies, Gulfstream Park, 2004 Purse: $150,000

Year	Winner	Age	Jockey	Wt.	Second	Wt.	Third	Wt.	Win Value	Time	Beyer
1988	Charming Tigress	5	P. Day	115	Polar Wind		No Doublet		21,069	1:24.60	
1988	Cadillacing	4	R.P. Romero	122	Easter Mary		Saucey Missy		21,429	1:23.00	
1989	Waggley	6	J.L. Samyn	122	Plate Queen		Ataentsic		20,640	1:22.60	
1990	Big Pride	3	E. Fires	112	Crowned		Sonic Gray		21,000	1:26.00	91
1991	Fancy Ribbons	3	C. Perret	118	Hula Pride		Designated Dancer		45,420	1:42.00	92
1992	Miss Legality	3	J.A. Krone	116	November Snow	114	Spectacular Sue	114	30,000	1:42.00	96
1993	Lunar Spook	3	M. Guidry	118	Boots 'n Jackie	121	In Her Glory	118	30,000	1:42.00	99
1994	Cut the Charm	3	J.D. Bailey	118	She Rides Tonite	114	Delightful Bet	113	60,000	1:41.40	82
1995	Mia's Hope	3	Chapman KL	114	Minister Wife	121	Culver City	112	60,000	1:43.20	90
1996	Plum Country	3	P. Day	118	My Flag	118	La Rosa	118	60,000	1:42.00	98
	Rare Blend finished second but was disqualified and placed sixth										
1997	Glitter Woman	3	M.E. Smith	114	City Band	121	Southern Playgirl	121	60,000	1:39.20	108
1998	Diamond On the Run	3	P. Day	112	Uanme	114	Dixie Melody	113	60,000	1:42.60	92
1999	Three Ring	3	J.R. Velazquez	118	Golden Temper	113	Gold From the West	116	60,000	1:41.40	106
2000	Cash Run	3	J.D. Bailey	118	Regally Appealing	116	Secret Status	114	60,000	1:40.37	105
2001	Latour	3	J.R. Velazquez	112	Gold Mover	116	Courageous Maiden	113	60,000	1:45.51	83
2002	Ms Brookski	3	R.B. Homeister	121	Colonial Glitter	117	French Satin	115	60,000	1:45.14	89
2003	Yell	3	J.R. Velazquez	117	Ivanavinalot	121	Gold Player	115	90,000	1:44.96	96
2004	Miss Coronado	3	C.H. Velasquez	117	Eye Dazzler	115	Society Selection	121	90,000	1:44.62	89

Beyer Index: 94.40

Run at 7 furlongs 1988–1990

DEBUTANTE (G3), 5 1/2 Furlongs, 2-Year-Old Fillies, Churchill Downs, 2004 Purse: $110,800

Year	Winner	Age	Jockey	Wt.	Second	Wt.	Third	Wt.	Win Value	Time	Beyer
1895	Amanda	2	N. Turner	120	Marquise	110	Stella	110	1,640	49.40	
1896	Cleophus	2	Simms	110	Eugenia Wickes	110	Ethel Lee	115	1,640	48.00	
1897	Mary Black	2	Corner	110	Sophronia D.	118	Uarda	115	945	50.50	
1898	Rush	2	J. Hill	115	Anna Bain	110	Gay Parisienne	115	945	51.00	
1899	Mollie Newman	2	N. Turner	115	Bab	115	Honeywood	115	945	50.00	
1900	Sinfi	2	Howell	115	Rose Apple	110	Bonnie Lissak	110	945	48.00	
1901	Autumn Leaves	2	Gilmore	110	The Esmond	110	The Boston	116	945	47.60	
1902	Olefiant	2	R. Williams	120	Mary Lavanna	110	Eva Russell	115	1,735	48.75	
1903	White Plume	2	J. Winkfield	110	Nannie Hodge	118	Sararose	110	1,560	48.25	
1904	Miss Inez	2	Helgesen	118	Lady Savoy		Frances Dillon	110	1,530	48.25	
1905	Beautiful Bess	2	Nicol	110	Ohiyesa	118	Lady Carol	110	1,585	50.00	
1906	Lillie Turner	2	D. Austin	118	Wing Ting	118	Alanie	115	1,845	49.60	
1907	Ancient	2	Troxler	115	Woodlane	118	Black Mary	118	1,715	49.40	
1908	Crystal Maid	2	Heidel	110	Elizabeth Harwood	118	Neoga	115	1,455	50.20	
1909	Ethelburg	2	Hannan	115	Placide	110	My Gal	110	1,635	47.80	
1910	Round the World	2	A. Walsh	115	Golden Egg	115	Princess Industry	115	1,440	48.00	
1911	Calisse	2	T. Rice	118	Rose of Jeddah	115	Mary Emily	118	1,990	48.40	
1912	Briar Path	2	Ganz	110	Christmas Star	115	Oneida	115	1,910	48.00	
1913	Robinetta	2	Goose	110	Birdie Williams	115	Aunt Mamie	115	700	47.80	
1914	Climber	2	J. Kederis	120	Waterblossom	115	Aunt Josie	115	2,740	47.40	
1915	Little Sister	2	W. Andress	110	Margaret N.	115	Lucky R.	115	2,590	48.00	
1916	Rosabel	2	F. Cooper	110	Jocular	115	Believe Me Boys	110	2,410	48.40	
1917	Ocean Sweep	2	D. Connelly	110	Violet Bonnie	110	Atalanta	110	2,790	47.80	
1918	Regalo	2	D. Connelly	115	Jap	110	Madras	110	2,610	48.80	
1919	Talisman	2	J. Groth	110	Ruby	111	Busy Signal	112	5,000	47.80	
1920	Bit of White	2	L. Lyke	119	MIss Muffins	122	Miss Fontaine	114	6,115	47.40	
1921	Fair Phantom	2	L. Lyke	114	Martha Fallon	119	Aloft	114	6,770	46.60	
1922	Sympathy	2	B. Kennedy	119	Sweetheart	119	Belphrizonia	114	6,840	48.00	
1923	Edna V.	2	G. Yeargin	122	Paloma	114	Lady Longridge	114	7,200	55.00	
1924	Kitty Pat	2	L. McDermott	119	Little Visitor	119	Cream Puff	119	7,280	53.40	
1925	Epsomite	2	F. Coltiletti	119	Belle	119	Panola	119	8,040	54.00	
1926	Thirteen Sixty	2	E. Legere	119	Ethel Dear	119	Krick	114	8,060	54.00	
1927	Anita Peabody	2	G. Johnson	119	Miss Fire	119	Pink Lily	114	7,700	1:01.80	
1928	Port Harlem	2	H. Thurber	119	Ben Machree	114	That's It	114	7,540	1:03.00	
1929	Alcibiades	2	W. Fronk	119	Lucile	122	Pansy Walker	114	6,920	59.80	
1930	Betty Derr	2	C. McCrossen	119	Purple Lady	119	Martha Jones	114	6,620	1:01.20	
1931	Butter Beans	2	C.E. Allen	119	At Sunrise	119	Princess Ivre	122	6,550	1:00.00	
1938	Dolly Whisk	2	W. Garner	114	Espania	119	Oddesa Beulah	124	2,415	1:01.00	
1939	Downy Pillow	2	J.E. Oros	119	Lynn	114	Drury Lane	119	2,690	59.80	
1940	Wise Moss	2	J.E. Oros	119	Blue Lily	119	Misty Isle	122	2,435	1:01.40	
1941	Royal Martha	2	G. King	119	Valdina Melia	119	My Choice	119	2,535	59.60	
1942	Trustee	2	W. Eads	114	Burgoolette	114	Su nJesting	114	2,740	1:00.60	
1943	Whirlabout	2	J. Adams	114	Miss Valor	114	Red Wonder	119	2,660	1:01.20	
1944	Flyweight	2	R. Eccard	119	Misweet	114	Valdina Jane	119	2,600	1:00.80	
1945	Breezy Louise	2	G. South	114	Calmara	114	Donna M.G.	119	4,810	1:02.00	
1946	Blue Grass	2	D. Padgett	114	Jeannie Pie	119	Gayest	114	10,650	1:02.00	
1947	Bewitch	2	D. Dodson	119	Pelt	114	Loriot	119	9,700	1:00.60	
1948	Acoma	2	W. Garner	119	Blue Note	119	Jetrose	119	9,650	1:01.60	
1949	Aunt Jayne Z.	2	N. Cartwright	119	Lady Marquest	119	Duchess Peg	119	9,700	59.60	
1950	Juliets Nurse	2	K. Church	122	Flyamanita	119	Romanda	114	10,500	59.20	
1951	Crownlet	2	R.L. Baird	122	Mutation	119	Hadn't Orter	119	11,050	59.60	
1952	Bubbley	2	E. Arcaro	119	Biddy Jane	119	Lillal	119	11,125	59.00	
1953	Golly	2	J. Adams	119	Spy Magic	119	Beanir	119	13,350	1:00.00	
1954	Gambetta	2	E. Arcaro	119	Serry	114	Timely Story	119	13,800	:59.20	
1955	Cherry	2	J. Heckmann	119	Babcha	119	Guard Rail	114	13,550	1:00.40	
1956	Delamar	2	K. Church	119	Doris Hart	119	Romanita	119	13,600	58.40	
1957	Margaretta	2	V. Guajardo	119	Errard's Isle	119	Hasty Doll	119	10,925	59.20	
1958	Patty's Choice	2	J. Heckmann	119	Pinecrest Miss	119	Battle Heart	119	8,894	1:00.20	
1959	Airmans Guide	2	E. Gross	119	Greek Top	119	Sandy's Sis W.	119	9,267	58.60	
1960	Bright Silver	2	J.L. Rotz	122	Honey Dear	119	Double Sun	119	8,796	59.80	
1961	Helfersartin	2	J. Bev	119	Volunteer State	119	Miss Sum'r Time	119	9,132	59.80	
1962	Speedwell	2	W. Shoemaker	119	Girl Artist	114	Royal Wayfarer	119	8,905	58.80	
1963	Wood Nymph	2	J.L. Rotz	119	Danville Miss	122	Busy Bird	119	9,230	58.40	
1964	Mississippi Mama	2	W. Shoemaker	122	Amerivan	119	Gracie May	119	9,181	58.20	
1965	Ole Liz	2	W. Shoemaker	122	Justakiss	122	Balafib	119	12,724	58.00	
1966	Furl Sail	2	W. Shoemaker	122	Popping Mary	119	Your It	114	12,642	59.20	
1967	Jet to Market	2	G. Overton	124	Owe Everything	119	Penny Mart	119	12,724	58.80	
1968	Alert Princess	2	I. Valenzuela	119	Royalty Note	122	Jest Come	119	13,292	58.80	
1969	Little Tudor	2	D.E. Whited	122	Dixie Wind	122	Colorado Coed	114	13,000	58.60	
1970	Misty Joy	2	J.L. Rotz	119	Bid High	119	Amber Pudding	119	12,740	59.80	

Year	Winner	Age	Jockey	Wt.	Second	Wt.	Third	Wt.	Win Value	Time	Beyer
1971	Cautious Bidder	2	J. Nichols	122	Excitable Miss	119	Levee Flash	119	16,819	58.80	
1972	Sylva Mill	2	R. Martinez Jr	114	Fish Wife	117	Fairway Fancy	119	17,485	58.60	
1973	Me and Connie	2	J. Nichols	124	Bundler	119	Shanjar	114	16,835	58.20	
1974	Sun and Snow	2	E. Guerin	119	Floral Princess	114	Classy Note	119	17,794	59.40	
1975	Answer	2	M. Hole	119	Pink Jade	122	Turn Over	119	16,282	58.20	
1976	Olden	2	R. Breen	122	Jungle Angel	119	Every Move	114	14,950	58.80	
1977	Sweet Little Lady	2	R. Turcotte	122	Sahsie	119	Crystalan	122	14,706	58.00	
1978	Nervous John	2	C.J. McCarron	122	Porpourie	114	Rainbow Streak	122	14,658	58.40	
1979	Lissy	2	M.S. Sellers	114	Barbizon's Flower	119	Happy Hollie	119	20,426	59.80	
1980	Excitable Lady	2	D. Brumfield	119	Masters Dream	119	Bend the Times	119	19,484	58.60	
1981	Pure Platinum	2	P. Day	119	Miss Preakness	119	Cypress Bay	119	19,939	58.80	
1982	Ice Fantasy	2	P.A. Johnson	115	Wrong Answer	115	Fifth Affair	121	20,735	1:04.60	
1983	Arabizon	2	L. Moyers	115	Ark	115	Starafar	113	22,181	1:05.80	
1984	Knot	2	K.K. Allen	115	Don't Joke	112	Off Shore Breeze	115	22,393	1:06.40	
1985	Tricky Fingers	2	L. Melancon	115	Likker Is Quikker	118	Time for Honor	115	31,013	1:05.20	
1986	Burnished Bright	2	P. Day	121	Before Sundown	118	Shivering Gal	115	46,810	1:11.20	
1987	Bold Lady Anne	2	J. Davidson	118	Over All	118	Penny's Growl	114	25,773	1:11.60	
1987	Dark Silver	2	M. McDowell	116	She's Freezing	116	Saved by Grace	116	26,260	1:12.60	
1988	Seaquay	2	R.M. Ehrlinspie	114	Weekend Spree	118	Coax Chelsie	112	35,718	1:11.20	
1989	Ice Folly	2	K.K. Allen	118	Hard Freeze	118	Lucy's Glory	118	37,993	1:11.20	
1990	Barbara's Nemesis	2	J.C. Deegan	116	Gracielle	112	Cosmic Music	112	36,690	1:12.00	65
1991	Greenhaven Lane	2	K. Tsuchiya	112	Moment of Grace	113	One for Smoke	116	36,950	1:06.20	65
1992	Hollywood Wildcat	2	F.A. Arguello J	116	Cosmic Speed Queen	118	Dixie Band	115	38,480	1:06.02	79
1993	Fly Love	2	B.E. Bertram	116	Miss Ra He Ra	116	Astas Foxy Lady	121	37,635	1:05.23	74
1994	Chargedupsycamore	2	P. Day	121	Phone Bird	116	Our Gem	116	54,405	1:05.24	82
1995	Golden Attraction	2	D.M. Barton	115	Western Dreamer	121	Tipically Irish	115	70,947	1:04.19	82
1996	Move	2	P. Day	121	Sarah's Prospector	115	Live Your Best	115	73,840	1:05.74	78
1997	Love Lock	2	P. Day	115	Countess Diana	115	Quick Lap	115	72,478	1:03.84	92
1998	Silverbulletday	2	W. Martinez	115	The Happy Hopper	115	Mancari's Rose	115	69,502	1:04.71	87
1999	Chilukki	2	W. Martinez	121	Miss Wineshine	112	Cecilia's Crown	115	69,998	1:03.66	98
2000	Gold Mover	2	C. Perret	121	Princess Belle	115	Tricky Elaine	115	69,626	1:03.79	86
2001	Cashier's Dream	2	D.J. Meche	118	Lakeside Cup	115	Colonial Glitter	115	68,510	1:02.52	97
2002	Awesome Humor	2	C.H. Borel	115	Vibs	115	Attemptress	115	67,890	1:03.45	93
2003	Be Gentle	2	C. Velasquez	117	Renaissance Lady	117	Sweet Jo Jo	117	68,758	1:03.96	83
2004	Classic Elegance	2	P. Day	117	Paragon Queen	117	Cool Spell	117	68,696	1:04.18	79

Beyer Index: 82.67

FRANK J. DE FRANCIS MEMORIAL DASH (G1), 6 Furlongs, 3-Year-Olds and Up, Pimlico, 2004 Purse: $300,000

Year	Winner	Age	Jockey	Wt.	Second	Wt.	Third	Wt.	Win Value	Time	Beyer
1990	Northern Wolf	4	M.J. Luzzi	120	Glitterman	124	Sewickley	126	210,000	1:09.00	111
1991	Housebuster	4	C. Perret	126	Clevor Trevor	123	Safely Kept	121	180,000	1:08.60	118
1992	Superstrike	3	D. Sorenson	112	Parisian Flight	114	King Corrie	117	180,000	1:09.80	110
1993	Montbrook	3	C.J. Ladner III	112	Lion Cavern	117	Flaming Emperor	114	180,000	1:08.60	112
1994	Cherokee Run	4	C. Perret	114	Boom Towner	119	Fu Man Slew	107	180,000	1:08.80	114
1995	Lite the Fuse	4	J.A. Krone	119	Crafty Dude	117	Hot JawsBay	119	180,000	1:08.80	109
1996	Lite the Fuse	5	J.A. Krone	117	Meadow Monster	119	Prospect Bay	114	180,000	1:08.80	117
1997	Smoke Glacken	3	C. Perret	113	Wise Dusty	112	Capote Belle	110	180,000	1:09.40	110
1998	Kelly Kip	4	J.L. Samyn	121	Affirmed Success	114	Partner's Hero	114	180,000	1:08.40	119
1999	Yes It's True	3	J.D. Bailey	114	Good and Tough	123	Storm Punch	114	180,000	1:08.67	106
2000	Richter Scale	6	R. Migliore	123	Just Call Me Carl	119	Falkenburg	114	180,000	1:07.95	111
2001	Delaware Township	5	J.D. Bailey	125	Early Flyer	115	Xtra Heat	117	180,000	1:09.00	116
2002	D'wildcat	4	J.F. Chavez	122	Deer Run	118	Sassy Hound	118	180,000	1:10.81	106
2003	A Huevo	7	R.A. Dominguez	119	Shake You Down	123	Gators n Bears	115	180,000	1:08.90	113
2004	Wildcat Heir	4	S. Elliott	119	Midas Eyes	123	Clock Stopper	119	180,000	1:09.45	109

Beyer Index: 112.07

Run at Laurel 1991–2003.

DELAWARE HANDICAP (G2), 1 1/4 Miles, Fillies and Mares, 3-Year-Olds and Up, Delaware Park, 2004 Purse: $750,900

Year	Winner	Age	Jockey	Wt.	Second	Wt.	Third	Wt.	Win Value	Time	Beyer
1937	Rosenna	3	M. Peters	108	Fair Knightess	118	Esposa	123	8,125	1:43.00	
1938	Marica	5	R. Dotter	125	Savage Beauty	109	Esposa	120	8,300	1:45.60	
1939	Shangay Lily	7	R. Donoso	113	Bunny Baby	108	Lady Maryland	118	9,175	1:46.00	
1940	Tedbriar	3	J. Lynch	109	War Beauty	106	Orcades	107	9,625	1:45.20	
1941	Dotted Swiss	4	M. Peters	114	Bala Ormont	116	Fairy Chant	126	8,550	1:49.00	
1942	Monida	5	A. DeLara	112	Rosetown	119	War Hazard	123	8,850	1:45.60	
1944	Everget	3	A. Kirkland	113	Donitas First	110	Anthemion	119	8,975	1:44.80	
1945	Plucky Maud	4	R. Permane	115	Legend Bearer	125	Rampart	111	12,450	1:42.60	
1946	Bridal Flower	3	A. DeLara	111	Surosa	114	Mahmoudess	114	20,200	1:43.80	
1947	Elpis	5	L. Hansman	108	Rampart	111	Bridal Flower	125	22,200	1:46.60	

Year	Winner	Age	Jockey	Wt.	Second	Wt.	Third	Wt.	Win Value	Time	Beyer
1948	Miss Grillo	6	I. Hanford	119	Elpis	119	Rampart	117	20,850	1:49.00	
1949	Allie's Pal	4	R.J. Martin	114	Paddleduck	119	Dobodura	110	19,950	1:46.40	
1950	Adile	4	J. Gilbert	119	The Mater	107	Jazz Baby	109	21,650	1:44.60	
1951	Busanda	4	E. Guerin	126	Leading Home	109	How	115	42,600	2:04.60	
1952	Kiss Me Kate	4	R. Nash	126	Renew	123	My Celeste	113	43,250	2:02.60	
1953	Grecian Queen	3	T. Atkinson	114	Devilkin	120	My Celeste	117	84,600	2:02.80	
1954	Gainsboro Girl	4	A. Catalano	113	Sunshine Nell	126	Lavender Hill	111	101,800	2:02.60	
1955	Parlo	4	E. Guerin	128	Open Sesame	114	Clear Dawn	119	99,900	2:02.40	
1956	Flower Bowl	4	L. Batchellor	112	Manotick	122	Open Sesame	113	104,875	2:03.00	
1957	Princess Turia	4	W. Hartack	119	Pucker Up	117	Little Pache	119	110,875	2:05.00	
1958	Endine	4	E. Nelson	111	Dotted Line	116	Woodlawn	108	106,875	2:03.00	
1959	Endine	5	P.J. Bailey	117	Polamby	114	Tempted	119	98,312	2:03.60	
1960	Quill	4	R. Ussery	125	Royal Native	129	Geechee Lou	110	94,750	2:02.40	
1961	Airmans Guide	4	H. Grant	121	Royal Native	120	Tritoma	118	104,687	2:02.40	
1962	Seven Thirty	4	L. Adams	120	Cicada	114	Bramalea	115	92,375	2:02.60	
1963	Waltz Song	5	S. Mellon	116	Cicada	128	Table Mate	123	112,062	2:04.00	
1964	Old Hat	5	B. Thornburg	113	Miss Cavandish	115	Waltz Song	116	79,254	2:04.00	
1965	Steeple Jill	4	J. Ruane	123	Ho Ho	109	Miss Cavandish	123	80,122	2:02.80	
1966	Open Fire	5	F. Lovato	110	Treachery	110	Discipline	119	79,930	2:00.40	
1967	Straight Deal	5	R. Ussery	125	Malhoa	112	Miss Spin	114	76,879	2:02.20	
1968	Politely	5	A. Cordero Jr	126	Plucky Pan	117	Treacherous	113	76,476	2:02.80	
1969	Obeah	4	J.L. Rotz	113	Double Ripple	111	Pattee Canyon	115	74,168	2:04.20	
1970	Obeah	5	L. Moyers	114	What a Dream	116	Helen J'nnings	114	8,215	2:02.60	
1971	Blessing Angelica	3	J. Vasquez	111	Deceit	115	Cathy Honey	114	80,860	2:03.40	
1972	Blessing Angelica	4	F. Belmonte	114	Grafitti	113	Numbered Account	115	74,100	2:00.60	
1973	Susan's Girl	4	L. Pincay Jr	127	Summer Guest	122	Light Hearted	125	71,305	2:00.60	
1974	Krislin	5	A. Cordero Jr	115	Twixt	124	Summer Guest	114	74,555	2:01.60	
1975	Susan's Girl	6	R. Broussard	125	Pass a Glance	116	Raisela	117	70,915	2:01.80	
1976	Optimistic Gal	3	E. Maple	119	T.V. Vixen	116	Vodka Time	115	65,040	2:01.00	
1977	Our Mims	3	J. Velasquez	117	Mississippi Mud	124	Dottie's Doll	118	70,785	2:01.00	
1978	Late Bloomer	4	J. Velasquez	119	Dottie's Doll	117	Cum Laude Laurie	119	73,938	2:02.20	
1979	Likely Exchange	5	M.S. Sellers	112	Sans Critique	111	Plain and Simple	110	73,938	2:03.40	
1980	Heavenly Ade	4	J.D. Bailey	112	Croquis	112	Blitey	113	93,893	2:00.00	
1981	Relaxing	5	A. Cordero Jr	119	Wistful	121	Lady of Promise	111	75,075	2:01.00	
1982	Jameela	6	J.L. Kaenel	121	Zvetlana	111	Love Sign	125	74,523	2:02.60	
1983	May Day Eighty	4	J. Vasquez	115	Try Something New	116	Broom Dance	119	66,720	2:03.20	
1984	Adored	4	L. Pincay Jr	120	Mademoiselle Forli	114	Weekend Surprise	112	94,680	2:03.20	
1985	Basie	4	J. Cruguet	110	Heatherten	126	Life's Magic	122	93,360	2:02.00	
1986	Shocker T.	4	G. St. Leon	122	Endear	122	Leecoo	112	69,120	2:02.20	
1987	Coup de Fusil	5	A. Cordero Jr	114	Steal a Kiss	113	Catatonic	118	68,760	1:59.80	
1988	Nastique	4	E. Maple	116	Ms. Eloise	117	Lawyer Talk	112	67,410	2:07.60	
1989	Nastique	5	E. Maple	120	Colonial Waters	117	Thirty Eight Go Go	118	64,890	2:01.20	
1990	Seattle Dawn	4	R.E. Colton	115	Warfie	112	Thirty Eight Go Go	115	68,160	2:03.00	
1991	Crowned	4	R. Wilson	117	Naskra's Lady	114	Tia Juanita	113	69,420	2:04.00	94
1992	Brilliant Brass	5	E.S. Prado	117	Train Robbery	111	Risen Colony	113	93,780	2:03.00	101
1993	Green Darlin	4	M.J. Luzzi	113	Girl on a Mission	116	Starry Val	112	96,300	2:03.60	96
1994	With a Wink	4	Migliore R	114	Passing Vice	115	Alphabulous	111	95,130	2:03.20	100
1995	Night Fax	4	Carle JD	108	Cavada	113	It's Personal	114	95,070	2:02.80	96
1996	Urbane	4	A. Solis	117	Alcovy	117	Shoop	115	180,000	2:01.80	114
1997	Power Play	5	L.C. Reynolds	114	Gold n Delicious	115	Effectiveness	113	210,000	2:03.40	106
1998	Amarillo	4	J.A Krone	110	Tuxedo Junction	115	Timely Broad	110	300,000	2:04.20	96
1999	Tap to Music	4	P. Day	116	Keeper Hill	120	Unbridled Hope	114	300,000	2:02.15	107
2000	Lu Ravi	5	P. Day	117	Tap to Music	116	Silverbulletday	119	360,000	2:02.21	107
2001	Irving's Baby	4	R.A. Dominguez	113	Under the Rug	115	Lazy Slusan	121	360,000	2:05.21	98
2002	Summer Colony	5	J.R. Velazquez	118	Your Out	113	Two Item Limit	115	360,000	2:04.52	101
2003	Wild Spirit	4	J.D. Bailey	117	Take Charge Lady	120	Shiny Sheet	112	450,000	2:02.95	110
2004	Summer Wind Dancer	4	V. Espinoza	116	Roar Emotion	117	Misty Sixes	116	450,000	2:03.63	104

Beyer Index: 102.14

Run as New Castle Handicap prior to 1955; run at 1 1/16 miles prior to 1951; run at Saratoga 1983 to 1985

DELAWARE OAKS (G2), 1 1/16 Miles, 3-Year-Old Fillies, Delaware Park, 2004 Purse: $500,900

Year	Winner	Age	Jockey	Wt.	Second	Wt.	Third	Wt.	Win Value	Time	Beyer
1996	Like A Hawk	3	R.Colton	114	Mercedes Song	118	Winter Melody	118	30,000	1:37.00	84
1997	Runup The Colors	3	P.Day	116	Timely Broad	113	City Band	113	90,000	1:44.20	95
1998	Nickel Classic	3	C.Borel	119	Lu Ravi	122	Taffy Davenport	117	120,000	1:42.80	99
1999	Brushed Halory	3	E.Martin, Jr	115	Gold From The West	115	Queen's Word	115	150,000	1:43.42	96
2000	Sincerely	3	M.McCarthy	117	Trip	119	Valleydar	117	150,000	1:43.83	100
2001	Zonk	3	M.J. McCarthy	115	Mystic Lady	122	Lady Andromeda	115	151,000	1:45.27	98
2002	Allamerican Bertie	3	L. Melancon	115	Alternate	117	Pass the Virtue	119	150,000	1:43.81	101
2003	Island Fashion	3	I.L. Puglisi	122	Awesome Humor	115	Ladyecho	115	300,000	1:44.95	94
2004	Yearly Report	3	J.D. Bailey	122	Ender's Sister	119	A Lulu Ofa Menifee	115	300,000	1:43.80	99

Beyer Index: 96.22

Not run 1983–95. For previous runnings, refer to 1983 Manual.

DEL MAR BREEDERS' CUP HANDICAP (G2), 1 Mile, 3-Year-Olds and Up, Del Mar, 2004 Purse: $250,000

Year	Winner	Age	Jockey	Wt.	Second	Wt.	Third	Wt.	Win Value	Time	Beyer
1987	Good Command	4	C.J. McCarron	114	Stop the Fighting	116	Candi's Gold	113	86,250	1:34.80	
1988	Precisionist	7	C.J. McCarron	125	Lively One	114	He's a Saros	116	85,150	1:34.60	
1989	On the Line	5	L. Pincay Jr	124	Good Taste	117	Lively One	125	115,400	1:33.40	
1990	Stalwart Charger	3	R.M. Gonzalez	115	Flying Continental	120	Ruhlmann	123	116,300	1:34.60	
1991	Twilight Agenda	5	K.J. Desormeaux	122	Opening Verse	117	Robyn Dancer	117	116,950	1:34.00	
1992	Reign Road	4	D.R. Flores	114	Sir Beaufort	116	Charmonnier	115	122,000	1:35.20	
1993	Region	4	C.S. Nakatani	115	Lottery Winner	115	L'Express	115	122,100	1:34.80	
1994	Lykatill Hil	4	E. Delahoussaye	118	D'hallevant	117	Stuka	116	62,200	1:34.00	110
1995	Alphabet Soup	4	C.J. McCarron	115	Lykatill Hil	117	Luthier Fever	115	117,150	1:34.20	110
1996	Dramatic Gold	5	K.J. Desormeaux	118	Alphabet Soup	120	Savinio	118	125,650	1:34.60	110
1997	Benchmark	6	E. Delahoussaye	117	Crafty Friend	118	Northern Afleet	120	126,700	1:35.40	107
1998	Old Trieste	3	C.J. McCarron	116	Grajagan	111	Stalwart Tsu	116	123,172	1:35.20	104
1999	Hollycombe	5	G.L. Stevens	116	Flying With Eagles	115	Old Trieste	122	126,060	1:35.40	106
2000	El Corredor	3	V. Espinoza	111	Cliquot	117	Literal Prowler	112	158,160	1:35.05	109
2001	El Corredor	4	V. Espinoza	121	Figlio Mio	113	Performing Magic	116	150,000	1:35.24	114
2002	Congaree	4	M. Smith	119	Kela	117	Reba's Gold	116	150,000	1:36.24	105
2003	Joey Franco	4	P.A. Valenzuela	116	Reba's Gold	116	Grey Memo	117	90,000	1:35.70	104
2004	Supah Blitz	4	V. Espinoza	116	Domestic Dispute	117	During	117	150,000	1:35.14	108

Beyer Index: 107.91

DEL MAR DEBUTANTE (G1), 7 Furlongs, 2-Year-Old Fillies, Del Mar, 2004 Purse: $250,000

Year	Winner	Age	Jockey	Wt.	Second	Wt.	Third	Wt.	Win Value	Time	Beyer
1951	Tonga	2	G. Glisson	112	Nurse O'War	115	Remolacha	112	15,050	1:12.00	
1952	Lap Full	2	H. Moreno	112	Fortune Teller	112	Smart Barbara	112	23,100	1:10.60	
1953	Lady Cover Up	2	W. Shoemaker	113	Dixie Valor	113	Sweet as Honey	113	20,425	1:11.00	
	Frosty Dawn finished first but but was later found to be ineligible and purse was awarded to Lady Cover Up										
1954	Fair Molly	2	W. Shoemaker	116	Madam Jet	113	Solid Rae	113	21,425	1:10.60	
1955	Miss Todd	2	R. York	119	Snoop	113	Edie's sister	113	20,160	1:10.40	
1956	Blue Vic	2	R. Trejos	113	Darling Adelle	119	Market Basket	113	25,120	1:09.00	
1957	Sally Lee	2	P. Moreno	119	Mrs. E.B.	113	Be My Honey	113	26,950	1:10.40	
1958	Khalita	2	R. York	116	Satina	113	Miss Uppity	116	29,120	1:10.60	
1959	Darling June	2	D. Pierce	113	Fair Maggie	113	Cherokee Miss	113	33,710	1:09.20	
1960	Amri-an	2	A. Maese	113	Chicha	113	Annie Alma	113	27,690	1:09.40	
1961	Spark Plug	2	R. Yanez	116	Kabema	113	Savaii	113	36,105	1:09.40	
1962	Brown Berry	2	P. Moreno	113	Star Maggie	113	Golden Curra	113	30,550	1:09.40	
1963	Leisurely Kin	2	J. Lambert	113	Loukahl	113	Go Yala	113	35,900	1:09.20	
1964	Admirably	2	R. York	113	Candyean	116	Real Sweet Deal	116	37,465	1:09.80	
							Music Khal	116			
1965	Century	2	W. Hartack	116	Teton Holiday	113	Premise	119	42,175	1:10.00	
1966	Native Honey	2	R. Campas	113	Louisador	113	Supreme Endeavor	113	42,680	1:10.00	
1967	Fast Dish	2	J. Lambert	113	Time to Leave	113	Equimau Pie	113	40,330	1:09.80	
1968	Fourth Round	2	J. Lambert	113	Singing Surf	113	Love You So	113	41,835	1:10.40	
1969	Atomic Wings	2	D. Pierce	113	Minstrel Miss	114	Regal Wine	113	43,025	1:08.60	
1970	Generous Portion	2	D. Tierney	113	June Darling	119	Ulla Britta	113	50,025	1:09.60	
1971	Impressive Style	2	D. Pierce	113	Miss Lady Bug	119	Chargerette	116	47,770	1:09.20	
1972	Windy's Daughter	2	W. Shoemaker	119	King's Edge	113	Rosalie Mae Wynn	116	50,965	1:09.60	
1973	Fleet Peach	2	D. Pierce	116	Fresno Star	113	Divine Grace	113	46,205	1:09.60	
1974	Bubblewin	2	W. Shoemaker	113	Spout	116	Cut Class	114	57,445	1:36.80	
1975	Queen to Be	2	D. McHargue	116	T.V. Terese	113	Awaken	113	57,805	1:36.80	
1976	Telferner	2	L. Pincay Jr	117	Asterisca	113	Maxine N.	115	65,175	1:37.20	
1977	Extravagant	2	M. Castaneda	113	Foxy Juliana	115	Honey Jar	113	81,490	1:36.40	
1978	Terlingua	2	D. McHargue	119	Beauty Hour	116	Blowin' Wild	113	79,140	1:36.20	
1979	Table Hands	2	W. Shoemaker	119	Hazel R.	116	Arcades Ambo	117	106,770	1:35.00	
1980	Raja's Delight	2	C.J. McCarron	113	Prestigious Lady	115	Native Fancy	119	110,225	1:37.40	
1981	Skillful Joy	2	C.J. McCarron	113	Marl Lee Ann	115	A Kiss for Luck	117	138,310	1:37.40	
1982	Landaluce	2	L. Pincay Jr	119	Issues n Answers	116	Granja Reina	113	124,655	1:35.60	
1983	Althea	2	L. Pincay Jr	119	Diachrony	113	Victorious Joy	113	126,190	1:36.00	
1984	Fiesta Lady	2	L. Pincay Jr	117	Doon's Baby	119	Trunk	115	93,050	1:38.80	
1984	Full O Wisdom	2	C.J. McCarron	113	Pirate's Glow	115	Wayward Pirate	119	91,050	1:37.40	
1985	Arewehavingfunyet	2	P. Valenzuela	120	Python	117	Wee Lavaliere	117	134,210	1:36.00	
1986	Brave Raj	2	C.A. Black	117	Road to Happiness	113	Soft Copy	115	125,325	1:35.80	
1987	Lost Kitty	2	G.L. Stevens	117	Royal Weekend	113	Hasty Pasty	117	128,850	1:36.00	
1988	Lea Lucinda	2	G.L. Stevens	114	Approved to Fly	114	Beware of the Cat	115	193,850	1:36.40	
	Apporved to Fly finished first but was disqualified and placed second										
1989	Rue de Palm	2	R. Baze	115	Dominant Dancer	118	Cheval Volant	118	202,050	1:35.00	
1990	Beyond Perfection	2	A. Solis	114	Lite Light	120	Title Bought	116	191,400	1:34.80	99
1991	La Spia	2	A. Solis	114	Soviet Sojourn	120	Wicked Wit	118	161,000	1:37.00	89
1992	Beal Street Blues	2	G.L. Stevens	116	Fit N Fappy	114	Zoonaqua	120	137,500	1:37.00	84

Year	Winner	Age	Jockey	Wt.	Second	Wt.	Third	Wt.	Win Value	Time	Beyer
1993	Sardula	2	E. Delahoussaye	116	Phone Chatter	119	Ballerina Girl	114	137,500	1:21.60	100
1994	Call Now	2	A. Solis	115	How So Oiseau	119	Ski Dancer	116	137,500	1:21.40	97
1995	Batroyale	2	M. Pedroza	119	Proud Dixie	117	General Idea	117	137,500	1:22.40	88
1996	Sharp Cat	2	R.R. Douglas	115	Desert Digger	119	Broad Dynamite	116	150,000	1:23.80	83
1997	Vivid Angel	2	K.J. Desormeaux	115	Griselle	115	Czarina	117	150,000	1:24.20	78
1998	Excellent Meeting	2	K.J. Desormeaux	115	Antahkarana	115	Colorado Song	115	150,000	1:22.20	98
1999	Chilukki	2	D. Flores	121	Spain	115	She's Classy	116	150,000	1:23.54	88
2000	Cindy's Hero	2	G.K. Gomez	114	Notable Career	119	Euro Empire	119	150,000	1:22.61	99
2001	Habibti	2	V. Espinoza	115	Who Loves Aleyna	116	Tempera	119	150,000	1:22.22	99
2002	Miss Houdini	2	G.L. Stevens	116	Santa Catarina	115	Indy Groove	115	150,000	1:23.43	88
2003	Halfbridled	2	J.A. Krone	116	Hollywood Story	115	Victory U.S.A.	116	150,000	1:22.20	99
2004	Sweet Catomine	2	V. Espinoza	114	Souvenir Gift	120	Hello Lucky	116	150,000	1:24.18	76

Beyer Index: 91.00

Distance 6 furlongs 1951–73; 1 mile, 1974–92

DEL MAR DERBY (G2), 1 1/8 Miles (Turf), 3-Year-Olds, Del Mar, 2004 Purse: $400,000

Year	Winner	Age	Jockey	Wt.	Second	Wt.	Third	Wt.	Win Value	Time	Beyer
1948	Frankly	3	G. Pederson	124	Barsard	118	Smoke Tree	118	11,875	1:42.80	
1949	Bolero	3	J. Westrope	124	Elbutte	118	Dharan	108	12,225	1:42.00	
1950	Great Circle	3	R. Neves	123	Mrs. Fuddy	109	Blue Reading	126	9,400	1:48.40	
1951	Grantor	3	W. Shoemaker	124	Mucho Hosso	116	Oats	122	8,900	1:48.60	
1952	Southarlington	3	R. Summers	108	Blue Trumpeter	109	Arroz	122	9,750	1:48.80	
1953	Apple Valley	3	B. Pearson	109	Smart Barbara	113	Chanlea	122	9,050	1:49.40	
1954	Musselshell	3	W. Shoemaker	115	Spring Count	110	Tussle Patch	110	9,650	1:48.80	
1955	Hi Pardner	3	W. Harmatz	108	Golden Land	119	Count Jac	117	15,500	1:49.00	
1956	Bounty Bay	3	J.R. Adams	113	Lucky G.I.	114	Proselyte	114	17,125	1:48.00	
1957	Mystic Eye	3	W. Skuse	120	Judgar Ruler	115	Seaneen	120	16,275	1:48.20	
1958	The Shoe	3	A. Maese	122	Cowboy Book	110	Sir Ruler	122	15,125	1:48.60	
1959	Mr. Eiffel	3	G. Taniguchi	111	King Ara	122	King o' Turf	112	15,425	1:47.60	
1960	Nagea	3	A. Maese	122	Have Tux	111	Djeddah Pat	109	15,575	1:47.60	
1961	Speak John	3	P. Moreno	121	Shelbyville	122	Aldershot	111	15,425	1:48.00	
1962	Bayou Bourg	3	P. Moreno	114	Sunday Slippers	112	Savail	117	16,475	1:48.20	
1963	Big Raff	3	R. Campas	115	Nevada Battler	118	Real Luck	119	12,425	1:48.00	
1963	Olympiad King	3	J. Longden	126	More Megaton	111	Mary Mel	104	12,425	1:47.80	
1964	Pop's Harmony	3	G. Taniguchi	111	Pelegrin	117	Maker's Mark	112	15,675	1:48.60	
1965	Hasty Trip	3	B. Jennings	113	Terry's Secret	126	Nasharco	119	16,825	1:47.60	
1966	Drin	3	D. Pierce	122	Fleet Host	119	Desert Trial	116	15,325	1:47.40	
1967	Charlie Boots	3	A. Pineda	116	Gentlemans Game	112	Kahl Kabee	120	17,750	1:47.40	
1968	Prince Hemp	3	J. Lambert	114			Fiddle Isle	120	10,087	1:46.60	
	Glory Hallelujah	3	R. Caballero	110							
1969	Commissary	3		116	Commissary	116	Neutral	116	16,500	1:47.40	
1970	War Heim	3	F. Toro	113	Mickey McGuire	113	Freeway Kid	113	13,500	1:49.20	
1970	Mayhedo	3	J. Lambert	114	Sir Wiggle	113	Woodie Can	113	13,750	1:49.20	
1971	Regal Case	3	H. Grant	117	Great Career	113	High and Mighty	114	20,450	1:49.00	
1972	Bicker	3	G. Brogan	113	Oh Hello	113	Queen's Hustler	113	23,750	1:49.00	
1973	Right Honorable	3	J. Lambert	115	Groshawk	119	Dancing Papa	113	28,650	1:10.80	
1974	Lightning Mandate	3	A. Pineda	116	Within Hail	113	Prince Petrone	113	27,900	1:50.00	
1975	Larrikin	3	D. Pierce	116	Messenger of Song	116	Wood Carver	115	28,900	1:48.80	
1976	Montespan	3	D.G. McHargue	115	Dr. Krohn	117	Today 'n Tomorrow	118	26,550	1:48.40	
1977	Text	3	D.G. McHargue	122	Pay the Toll	119	Hill Fox	115	32,750	1:49.40	
1978	Misrepresentation	3	D. Pierce	119	Singular	119	Wayside Station	115	33,450	1:49.60	
1979	Relaunch	3	L. Pincay Jr	121	Kamalii King	112	Pole Position	120	51,450	1:48.80	
1980	Exploded	3	L. Pincay Jr	117	Aristocratical	120	Son of a Dodo	118	70,300	1:49.60	
1981	Juan Barrera	3	F. Toro	115	Buen Chico	114	Rock Softly	115	83,950	1:49.00	
1982	Give Me Strength	3	L. Pincay Jr	123	Water Bank	117	Take the Floor	117	88,350	1:49.00	
1983	Tanks Brigade	3	R.Q. Meza	122	Ansuan	115	Evening M'Lord	117	85,350	1:49.00	
1984	Tsunami Slew	3	E. Delahoussaye	119	Prince True	119	Majestic Shore	115	99,650	1:48.00	
1985	First Norman	3	G.L. Stevens	117	Pretensor	116	Catane	112	82,300	1:48.00	
1986	Vernon Castle	3	G.L. Stevens	117	Prince Bobby B.	119	Mazaad	119	95,500	1:48.40	
1987	Deputy Governor	3	E. Delahoussaye	119	Stately Don	120	The Medic	118	98,700	1:48.40	
1988	Silver Circus	3	R.A. Baze	118	Perfecting	118	Roberto's Dancer	116	127,900	1:49.00	
1989	Hawkster	3	P.A. Valenzuela	121	River Master	119	Lode	116	130,500	1:48.00	
1990	Itsallgreektome	3	L. Pincay Jr	122	Predacessor	122	Pro for Sure	122	165,000	1:49.60	
1991	Eternity Star	3	F.J. Alvarado	122	Stark South	122	June's Reward	122	165,000	1:49.20	100
1992	Daros	3	E. Delahoussaye	122	Smiling and Dancin	122	Major Impact	122	165,000	1:48.80	98
1993	Guide	3	K.J. Desormeaux	122	Future Storm	122	The Real Vaslav	122	165,000	1:49.60	93
1994	Ocean Crest	3	L. Pincay Jr	122	Unfinished Symph	122	Powis Castle	122	165,000	1:48.60	100
1995	Da Hoss	3	R.R. Douglas	122	Lake George	122	Tabor	122	165,000	1:48.00	103
1996	Rainbow Blues	3	C.S. Nakatani	122	The Barking Shark	122	Mateo	122	180,000	1:50.00	99
1997	Anet	3	G.L. Stevens	121	Brave Act	121	Worldly Ways	121	180,000	1:48.40	108

Year	Winner	Age	Jockey	Wt.	Second	Wt.	Third	Wt.	Win Value	Time	Beyer
1998	Ladies Din	3	K.J. Desormeaux	121	Expressionist	121	Scooter Brown	121	180,000	1:48.40	108
1999	Val Royal	3	C.S. Nakatani	121	Fighting Falcon	121	In Frank's Honor	121	180,000	1:48.40	102
2000	Walkslikeaduck	3	E. Delahoussaye	121	Purely Cozzene	121	New Story	118	180,000	1:46.66	107
2001	Romanceishope	3	C.J. McCarron	121	Indygo Shiner	121	Blue Steller	121	180,000	1:47.93	96
2002	Inesperado	3	C.S. Nakatani	121	Johar	121	Rock Opera	121	180,000	1:47.49	102
2003	Fairly Ransom	3	A. Solis	122	Devious Boy	122	Sweet Return	122	180,000	1:46.45	103
2004	Blackdoun	3	C.S. Nakatani	122	Toasted	122	Laura's Lucky Boy	122	240,000	1:46.75	102

Beyer Index: 101.50

DEL MAR FUTURITY (G2), 7 Furlongs, 2-Year-Olds, Del Mar, 2004 Purse: $245,000

Year	Winner	Age	Jockey	Wt.	Second	Wt.	Third	Wt.	Win Value	Time	Beyer
1948	Star Fiddle	2	H. Trent	122	Buddy Hunter	110	Tom's Pride	114	6,825	1:11.80	
1949	Your Host	2	F. Chojnacki	115	Blue Rings	112	Sturdy One	118	31,725	1:10.40	
1950	Patch	2	J. Longden	118	Gay Cavalier	118	Gold Capitol	112	23,700	1:10.60	
1951	Big Noise	2	R. Neves	115	Challtack	115	Arroz	115	26,000	1:10.40	
1952	Hour Regards	2	E. LeBlanc	115	Chanlea	118	Decorated	118	32,200	1:09.80	
1953	Double Speed	2	J. Phillippi	116	James Session	119	For Example	116	29,475	1:10.40	
1954	Blue Ruler	2	W. Shoemaker	119	Colonel Mack	119	Riparlus	116	25,350	1:09.80	
1955	Blen Host	2	R. York	116	Gilding Wings	116	Fortuneway	116	40,440	1:10.60	
1956	Swirling Abbey	2	D. Lewis	116	Mr. Sam S	119	Prince Khaled	116	34,990	1:08.80	
1957	Old Pueblo	2	E. Arcaro	119	Disdainful	116	Strong Bay	116	40,570	1:09.00	
1958	Tomy Lee	2	W. Shoemaker	122	Royal Orbit	116	Bagdad	116	50,980	1:09.20	
1959	Azure's Orphan	2	E. Burns	116	Salatom	116	Warfare	119	50,720	1:09.60	
1960	Short Jacket	2	R. Neves	116	Mr. America	116	Nashua Blue	116	46,760	1:09.00	
1961	Weldy	2	R. York	116	Snappy King	116	Donut King	116	62,390	1:09.20	
1962	Slipped Disc	2	R. Yaka	116	Beekeeper	116	Y Flash	119	56,115	1:09.80	
1963	Perris	2	A. Maese	116	Oldie	116	Harry H.	116	60,200	1:09.40	
1964	Terry's Secret	2	A. Maese	116	Azure Te	116	Ky. Front	116	64,945	1:10.20	
1965	Coursing	2	K. Church	116	Couple o'Quid	116	Ri Tux	116	60,060	1:08.80	
1966	Ruken	2	F. Alvarez	116	Sand Devil	116	Wolfgang	116	66,285	1:09.40	
1967	Baffle	2	W. Blum	119	Broad Shadows	116	Poleax	116	67,050	1:09.60	
1968	Fleet Allied	2	J. Lambert	116	Fleet Kirsch	119	Pellinore	116	57,130	1:08.20	
1969	George Lewis	2	W. Hartack	116	Swarming Bee	116	Atomic Wings	116	63,270	1:08.20	
1970	June Darling	2	W. Mahorney	119	Kfar Tov	119	Bold Joey	116	64,895	1:08.80	
1971	MacArthur Park	2	W. Shoemaker	119	Dorreno	116	Normandy Grey	116	41,975	1:29.00	
1971	D,B. Carm	2	F. Toro	119	Master Ribot	116	Royal Connections	116	41,975	1:29.00	
1972	Groshawk	2	W. Shoemaker	116	Lucky Mike	119	Bottle Brush	116	67,135	1:28.60	
1973	Such a Rush	2	W. Shoemaker	116	Fast Pappa	116	The Gay Greek	116	65,740	1:29.80	
1974	Diabolo	2	W. Shoemaker	116	George Navonod	119	Dimaggio	122	67,120	1:35.40	
1975	Telly's Pop	2	F. Mena	117	Lexington Laugh	114	Body Bend	114	66,275	1:36.00	
1976	Visible	2	L. Pincay Jr	117	Habitony	114	Washoe County	115	74,535	1:35.60	
1977	Go West Young Man	2	F. Olivares	114	Tampoy	114	Spanish Way	117	85,845	1:35.60	
1978	Flying Paster	2	D. Pierce	117	Priority	117	Roman Oblisk	117	100,400	1:34.80	
1979	The Carpenter	2	C.J. McCarron	114	Doonesbury	117	Executive Counsel	114	98,710	1:35.20	
1980	Bold and Gold	2	D.C. Hall	117	Looks Like Rain	114	Sir Dancer	117	129,630	1:36.20	
1981	Gato Del Sol	2	E. Delahoussaye	114	The Captain	120	Ring Proud	115	160,720	1:37.40	
1982	Roving Boy	2	E. Delahoussaye	117	Desert Wine	120	Balboa Native	114	159,945	1:38.80	
1983	Althea	2	L. Pincay Jr	117	Juliet's Pride	115	Gumboy	114	147,865	1:34.80	
1984	Saratoga Six	2	A. Cordero Jr	120	Indigenous	114	Lomax	117	173,440	1:36.00	
1985	Tasso	2	L. Pincay Jr	114	Arewehavingfunyet	117	Snow Chief	117	155,760	1:37.00	
1986	Qualify	2	G.L. Stevens	114	Sacahuista	117	Brevito	116	158,535	1:35.60	
1987	Lost Kitty	2	L. Pincay Jr	117	Bold Second	118	Purdue King	118	174,800	1:36.20	
1988	Music Merci	2	C.J. McCarron	118	Bruho	114	Texian	117	229,300	1:35.40	
1989	Drag Race	2	F. Olivares	114	Rue de Palm	114	Single Dawn	114	241,600	1:35.40	
1990	Best Pal	2	P.A. Valenzuela	120	Pillaring	116	Got to Fly	117	231,600	1:35.40	
1991	Bertrando	2	A. Solis	114	Zurich	114	Star Recruit	115	188,500	1:36.40	84
1992	River Special	2	C.J. McCarron	115	Sudden Hush	120	Seattle Street	114	137,500	1:36.60	88
1993	Winning Pact	2	C.S. Nakatani	115	Ramblin Guy	119	Ferrara	115	137,500	1:22.00	93
1994	On Target	2	A. Solis	115	Supremo	115	Timber Country	119	137,500	1:22.20	90
1995	Future Quest	2	K.J. Desormeaux	115	Othello	115	Cavonnier	117	137,500	1:21.80	94
1996	Silver Charm	2	D.R. Flores	116	Gold Tribute	115	Swiss Yodeler	121	150,000	1:22.80	97
1997	Souvenir Copy	2	C.J. McCarron	115	Old Topper	119	Commitisize	115	150,000	1:23.00	91
1998	Worldly Manner	2	K.J. Desormeaux	119	Daring General	119	Waki American	114	150,000	1:23.00	95
1999	Forest Camp	2	D.R. Flores	116	Dixie Union	121	Captain Steve	115	150,000	1:21.60	106
2000	Flame Thrower	2	J.D. Bailey	119	Street Cry	116	Arabian Light	119	150,000	1:22.00	103
2001	Officer	2	V. Espinoza	121	Kamsack	115	Metatron	116	150,000	1:22.33	99
2002	Icecoldbeeratreds	2	D. Flores	119	Kafwain	119	Chief Planner	115	150,000	1:22.94	94
2003	Siphonizer	2	J.A. Krone	116	Minister Eric	116	Perfect Moon	122	150,000	1:23.10	82
2004	Declan's Moon	2	V. Espinoza	116	Roman Ruler	120	Swiss Lad	116	150,000	1:21.29	107

Beyer Index: 94.50

DEL MAR HANDICAP (G2), 1 3/8 Miles (Turf), 3-Year-Olds and Up, Del Mar, 2004 Purse: $250,000

Year	Winner	Age	Jockey	Wt.	Second	Wt.	Third	Wt.	Win Value	Time	Beyer
1937	Sallys Booster	5	T. Sena	114	Sir Ridgway	107	The Fighter	120	4,225	1:44.80	
1938	Ligaroti	6	W. Moran	128	Capt. Cal	115	Sweepalot	115	3,925	1:43.80	
1939	Wedding Call	3	W.F. Ward	108	Pageboy	107	First Kiss	107	3,975	1:44.00	
1940	Big Flash	3	E. Rodriguez	113	Royal Crusader	107	Woof Woof	110	3,750	1:43.00	
1941	Royal Crusader	4	L. Balaski	113	Wedding Call	112	Lassator	108	6,250	1:43.60	
1945	Texas Sandman	4	M. Peterson	126	Dogpatch	117	Wedding Call	112	10,385	1:43.20	
1946	Olhaverry	7	M. Peterson	116	Adrogue	106	Canina	119	12,100	1:43.20	
1947	Iron Maiden	6	W. Parnell	112	Be Fearless	120	Sierra Fox	115	9,950	1:43.20	
1948	Frankly	3	J. Westrope	112	Hemet Squaw	115			18,350	1:42.40	
					Prevaricator	129					
1949	Top's Boy	5	R. Neves	120	Honeymoon	117	Prevaricator	120	6,450	1:48.80	
1950	Frankly	5	W. Shoemaker	120	Top's Boy	112	Mercenary	112	9,650	1:48.60	
1951	Blue Reading	4	B. Pearson	124	Sturdy One	116	Alderman	117	9,200	1:48.40	
1952	Grantor	4	J. Longden	113	Stormy Cloud	108	Moonrush	117	15,450	1:47.40	
1953	Goose Khal	4	W. Shoemaker	119	Fleet Bird	124	Bernwood	108	14,750	1:48.60	
1954	Stranglehold	5	W. Shoemaker	126	Fleet Khal	109	Blue Tr'peter	108	14,700	1:48.40	
1955	Arrogate	4	J. Longden	116	Bobby Brocato	114	Trigonometry	118	14,800	1:47.40	
1956	Arrogate	5	J. Longden	118	Honeys Alibi	121	Brisk 'n Br't	110	18,050	1:47.00	
1957	How Now	4	R. York	118	Pirnie	109	Windsor Serial	118	18,300	1:47.60	
1958	Noredski	5	D. Pierce	111	Solid Son	112	How Now	126	17,400	1:47.60	
1959	Twentyone Guns	4	G. Taniguchi	118	Mr. Snack	113	Find	122	17,800	1:47.20	
1960	How Now	7	E. Burns	122	Honeys Gem	117	Ying and Yang	113	17,100	1:46.60	
1961	Scotland	5	M. Volzke	112	Nagea	120	Grey Eagle	116	18,000	1:46.80	
1962	Crazy Kid	4	A. Maese	120	Sea Orbit	122	Songman	110	17,950	1:47.60	
1963	Mr. Consistency	5	K. Church	116	Rapido	116	Mr. Wag	113	18,650	1:47.00	
1964	Viking Spirit	4	K. Church	123	Hold Me	119	M're M'g't'n	116	18,700	1:48.00	
1965	Terry's Secret	3	A. Maese	120	Aurelius II	118	Perris	113	18,500	1:47.00	
1966	Old Mose	4	D. Pierce	123	Biggs	115	My Captain	107	18,550	1:47.20	
1967	Native Diver	8	J. Lambert	130	Sharp Decline	109	Quicken Tree	117	23,650	1:46.60	
1968	Quicken Tree	5	W. Hartack	120	Fiddle Isle	113	Rivet	116	17,450	1:46.40	
1969	Figonero	4	A. Pineda	124	Triple Tux	112	Balsamo II	116	27,250	1:46.20	
1970	Daryl's Joy	4	J. Sellers	123	Cougar II	120	Contratodos	110	33,450	2:15.40	
1971	Pinjara	6	W. Shoemaker	121	Makor	110	Great Career	110	51,950	2:15.60	
1972	Hill Circus	4	F. Toro	117	War Heim	116	Wing Out	121	40,000	2:16.00	
1972	Chrisaway	4	R. Howard	112	Marlivam	116	Tetrack	113	40,500	2:16.20	
1973	Red Reality	7	B. Baeza	122	Wing Out	119	Life Cycle	124	60,000	2:17.00	
1974	Redtop III	5	F. Toro	115	My Old Friend	115	Nantwice	111	60,000	2:16.00	
1975	Cruiser II	6	F. Olivares	117	Top Crowd	115	Against the Snow	117	60,000	2:14.40	
1976	Riot in Paris	5	Wl. Shoemaker	122	Avatar	122	Good Report	115	60,000	1:57.40	
1977	Ancient Title	7	D.G. McHargue	123	Painted Wagon	118	Cascapedia	117	60,000	1:55.40	
1978	Palton	5	H.E. Moreno	114	Farnesio	119	Vic's Magic	119	60,000	1:57.40	
1979	Ardiente	4	C.J. McCarron	118	Quick Turnover	122	Sudanes	111	75,000	1:56.80	
1980	G'w'sty'ngman	5	E. Delahoussaye	123	Relaunch	118	Balzac	121	75,000	1:58.20	
1981	Wickerr	6	C.J. McCarron	118	Tahitian King	121	Galaxy Libra	121	82,500	1:57.40	
1982	Muttering	3	W. Shoemaker	117	Regalberto	119	Exploded	121	82,500	1:57.00	
1983	Bel Bolide	5	W. Shoemaker	117	Gato del Sol	123	Egg Toss	117	82,500	1:58.20	
1984	Precisionist	3	C.J. McCarron	116	Pair by Deuces	116	Super Diamond	117	137,000	1:56.80	
1985	Barberstown	5	F. Toro	117	My Habitony	118	First Norman	114	137,000	1:58.00	
1986	Raipillan	4	R.A. Baze	114	Schiller	113	Shulich	113	165,000	2:14.40	
1987	Swink	4	W. Shoemaker	120	Santella Mac	116	Skip Out Front	115	165,000	2:13.80	
1988	Sword Dance	4	C.J. McCarron	114	Great Communicator	120	Baba Karam	115	165,000	2:15.80	
1989	Payant	5	R.G. Davis	118	Saratoga Passage	118	No Review	112	165,000	2:15.20	
1990	Live the Dream	4	A. Solis	118	Mehmetori	107	Soft Machine	113	165,000	2:13.00	104
1991	My Style	4	K.J. Desormeaux	115	Forty Niner Days	118	Super May	117	165,000	2:13.40	109
1992	Navarone	4	P.A. Valenzuela	117	Qathif	117	Stark South	117	137,500	2:15.00	107
1993	Luazur	4	P. Day	116	Kotashaan	123	Myrakalu	114	137,500	2:15.00	108
1994	Navarone	6	P.A. Valenzuela	117	Approach the Bench	116	Sir Mark Sykes	116	137,500	2:14.20	105
1995	Royal Chariot	5	L. Pincay Jr	117	River Rhythm	117	Party Season	116	137,500	2:13.60	104
1996	Dernier Empereur	6	P.A. Valenzuela	116	Talloires	119	Party Season	117	150,000	2:13.80	107
1997	Rainbow Dancer	6	A. Solis	118	Dowty	119	Lord Jain	114	150,000	2:13.80	106
1998	Bonapartiste	4	C.J. McCarron	115	River Bay	123	Military	116	150,000	2:14.00	106
1999	Sayarshan	4	B. Blanc	115	Dancing Place	116	Ladies Din	120	150,000	2:14.20	104
2000	Northern Quest	5	C.J. McCarron	116	Perssonet	114	Alvo Certo	115	150,000	2:12.65	103
	Alvo Certo finished second but was disqualified and placed third										
2001	Timboroa	5	L. Pincay Jr	118	C.J. McCarron	116	Super Quercus	117	150,000	2:12.59	105
2002	Delta Form	6	G. Almeida	115	The Tin Man	117	Blue Stellar	117	150,000	2:12.15	106
2003	Irish Warrior	5	A. Solis	116	Continental Red	117	Continuously	114	150,000	2:12.28	102
2004	Star Over the Bay	6	T.C. Baze	116	Sarafan	121	Moscow Burning	114	150,000	2:12.71	101

Beyer Index: 105.13

DEL MAR OAKS (G1), 1 1/8 Miles (Turf), 3-Year-Old Fillies, Del Mar, 2004 Purse: $300,000

Year	Winner	Age	Jockey	Wt.	Second	Wt.	Third	Wt.	Win Value	Time	Beyer
1957	Royal Rasher	3	I. Valenzuela	118	Vyg	114	Tourbillonte	114	8,524	1:36.20	
1958	Camloc	3	P. Moreno	114	Gleaming Star	114	Mrs. E.B.	114	8,500	1:36.40	
1959	Pie Queen	3	R. Campas	114	Noorette	114	Khalita	114	8,925	1:36.40	
1960	Linita	3	A. Maese	114	Solid Thought	118	Ypres	114	8,575	1:36.00	
1961	Fun House	3	R. Yanez	112	Amri-An	114	Outfield	114	9,075	1:35.20	
1962	Savall	3	W. Harmatz	116	Table Mate	114	Sunday Slippers	114	9,050	1:35.40	
1963	Hi Rated	3	K. Church	114	Poonetta	114	Curious Clover	114	8,900	1:36.20	
1964	Gin Mah	3	J. Longden	121	Loukahl	121	Spoondee	114	8,925	1:36.80	
1965	Alibarb	3	J. Lambert	114	Miss Rincon	114	Glory's Tryst	114	8,725	1:52.40	
1966	Desert Trial	3	A. Maese	114	Ali's Theme	114	April Dawn	121	7,275	1:51.20	
1966	Mikhaless	3	A. Pineda	114	Windy Kate	114	Fleet Treat	121	7,275	1:51.00	
1967	Forgiving	3	A. Pineda	121	Desert Law	114	My Thel	114	9,725	1:50.80	
1968	Greta	3	R. Campas	114	Baby La	114	Grey Cricket	114	8,725	1:50.60	
1969	Commissary	3	A. Pineda	118	Ynez Queen	115	Serica	114	9,500	1:51.60	
1970	Beja	3	W. Shoemaker	113	Likely Lark	113	Sony Gay	114	9,875	1:49.20	
1970	Thoroly Blue	3	F. Toro	118	Word of Honor	113	Dress Me Up	113	9,875	1:50.20	
1971	Turkish Trousers	3	W. Shoemaker	124	Aladancer	117	Shelf Talker	118	14,750	1:50.00	
1972	House of Cards	3	J. Sellers	115	Pallisima	121	Le Cle	118	18,750	1:50.00	
1973	Sandy Blue	3	D. Pierce	121	Sphere	112	Meileur	118	20,850	1:49.40	
1974	Modus Vivendi	3	D. Pierce	113	Move Abroad	116	Heather Road	115	21,850	1:50.20	
1975	Snap Apple	3	F. Mena	113	Mia Amore	115	Miss Francesca	116	21,450	1:50.00	
1976	Go March	3	L. Pincay Jr	116	Pennygown	113	Franmari	116	25,700	1:49.20	
1977	Taisez Vous	3	D. Pierce	121	Drama Critic	114	Giggling Girl	113	31,550	1:48.80	
1978	Country Queen	3	F. Toro	121	B. Thoughtful	124	Donna Inez	113	33,450	1:49.80	
1979	Our Suiti Pie	3	C.J. McCarron	113	Caline	121	Ancient Art	116	52,300	1:49.80	
1980	Movin' Money	3	P.A. Valenzuela	114	Princess Karenda	122	Tobin's Rose	119	71,000	1:49.40	
1981	French Charmer	3	D.G. McHarque	117	Amber Ever	119	Shimmy	119	82,200	1:49.40	
1982	Castilla	3	R. Sibille	122	Avigaition	119	Skillful Joy	119	81,050	1:50.20	
1983	Heartlight No. One	3	L. Pincay Jr	122	Foggy Moon	115	Fabulous Notion	122	84,100	1:50.20	
1984	Fashionably Late	3	C.J. McCarron	119	Lucky Lucky Lucky	125	Auntie Betty	114	92,400	1:49.40	
1985	Savannah Dancer	3	W. Shoemaker	119	Magnificent Lindy	122	Queen of Bronze	115	94,250	1:48.80	
	Pirate's Glow finished second but was disqualified and fourth										
1986	Hidden Light	3	W. Shoemaker	124	Kraemer	114	Shotgun Wedding	119	92,700	1:47.80	
1987	Lizzy Hare	3	G.L. Stevens	114	Chapel of Dreams	114	Down Again	114	104,300	1:50.40	
1988	No Review	3	R.Q. Meza	115	Do So	124	Jungle Gold	115	96,300	1:49.00	
1989	Stylish Star	3	C.J. McCarron	115	Darby's Daughter	119	General Charge	119	97,500	1:48.60	
1990	Slew of Pearls	3	C.A. Black	117	Adorable Emilie	115	Annual Reunion	117	97,900	1:49.80	
1991	Flawlessly	3	C.J. McCarron	120	Seattle Symphony	120	Fowda	120	96,250	1:49.40	97
1992	Suivi	3	A. Solis	120	Race the Wild Wind	120	Alysbelle	120	96,250	1:48.60	94
1993	Hollywood Wildcat	3	E. Delahoussaye	120	Possibly Perfect	120	Miami Sands	120	96,250	1:48.20	102
1994	Twice the Vice	3	G.L. Stevens	120	Malli Star	120	Pharma	120	96,250	1:47.60	100
1995	Bail Out Becky	3	S.J. Sellers	120	Sleep Easy	120	Top Ruhl	120	137,500	1:49.60	97
1996	Antespend	3	C.W. Antley	120	Gastronomical	120	True Flare	120	150,000	1:48.80	100
1997	Famous Digger	3	B. Blanc	120	Golden Arches	121	Seen You Soon	121	150,000	1:49.00	95
1998	Sicy d'Alsace	3	C.S. Nakatani	121	Adel	121	Tranquility Lake	121	150,000	1:48.26	94
	Tranquility Lake finished second but was disqualified and placed third										
1999	Tout Charmant	3	D.R. Flores	121	Smooth Player	121	Sweet Ludy	121	150,000	1:48.64	99
2000	No Matter What	3	V. Espinoza	121	Theoretically	121	Premre Creation	121	150,000	1:50.02	94
2001	Golden Apples	3	G.K. Gomez	121	Affluent	121	Reine de Romance	121	180,000	1:47.98	101
2002	Dublino	3	K.J. Desormeaux	121	Megahertz	121	Alozaina	121	180,000	1:47.16	97
2003	Dessert	3	C.S. Nakatani	122	Solar Echo	122	Personal Legend	122	180,000	1:47.04	95
2004	Amorama	3	D.R. Flores	122	Ticker Tape	122	Sweet Win	122	180,000	1:46.26	99

Beyer Index: 97.43

Distance 1 mile, main course, prior to 1965

DEMOISELLE (G2), 1 1/8 Miles, 2-Year-Old Fillies, Aqueduct, 2004 Purse: $200,000

Year	Winner	Age	Jockey	Wt.	Second	Wt.	Third	Wt.	Win Value	Time	Beyer
1908	Melisande	2	Notter	124	Cotytto	105	Arondack	110	2,720	1:06.40	
1910	Round the World	2	Herbert	122	Horizon	122	Leah	105	1,150	1:08.60	
1914	Couette	2	M. Buxton	119	Comely	126	Brig's Sister	122	1,165	1:07.00	
1915	Celandria	2	M. Buxton	122	Malachite	110	Miss Puzzle	112	1,515	1:07.00	
1916	Tragedy	2	T. Davis	122	Marie Odile	110	Q. o' th' Water	110	1,925	1:07.00	
1917	Wawbeck	2	M. Buxton	113	Rosie O'Grady	125	Quietude	113	2,325	1:09.00	
1918	Lady Rosebud	2	J. Collins	109	Kiss Again	113	Joyful	109	2,325	1:07.60	
1919	Panoply	2	W. Knapp	125	Indiscretion	109	Luke's Pet	114	2,325	1:09.20	
1920	Nancy Lee	2	L. Lyke	112	Pantalette	109	Maiden's Ballet	110	3,170	1:07.80	
1921	My Reverie	2	C. Kummer	119	Penitent	109	Nancy F.	116	3,720	1:07.60	
1922	Cresta	2	L. Penman	119	Suweep	119	Twaddle	109	3,710	1:07.60	
1923	Fluvanna	2	G. Babin	116	Cave Woman	109	Parasol	113	3,715	1:06.40	

Year	Winner	Age	Jockey	Wt.	Second	Wt.	Third	Wt.	Win Value	Time	Beyer
1924	Maud Muller	2	L. McAtee	125	Swinging	113	Extra Dry	107	3,765	1:06.60	
1925	Ethereal	2	F. Coltiletti	109	Hayai	114	Adria	109	3,765	1:07.00	
1926	Pandera	2	L. McAtee	126	Recreation	109	Glen Sprite	109	3,765	1:06.00	
1927	Fair Mist	2	J. Craigmile	105	Giggleorum	110	One Hour	122	3,765	1:07.00	
1928	Toki	2	L. McAtee	109	Ma Mie	105	Ritzy	109	4,425	1:07.60	
1929	The Beasel	2	W. Kelsay	109	Murky Cloud	122	Greyola	109	4,575	1:07.00	
1930	Straying	2	L. McAtee	108	Ladana	122	Double Time	110	4,375	1:06.60	
1931	Straightlace	2	E. Barnes	109	Morden	109	Morush	109	4,175	1:08.40	
1932	Disdainful	2	A. Robertson	127	Teaberry	107	Clare Lee	107	2,325	1:07.00	
1936	Broad Ripple	2	J. Gilbert	113	Drawbridge	113	Sophia Tucker	119	3,585	1:10.60	
1937	Inhale	2	J. Gilbert	122	Miyako	113	Black Wave	113	3,635	1:11.20	
1938	Donita M.	2	W.D. Wright	122	Lady Nicotine	113	Sweet Patrice	122	3,425	1:11.40	
1939	Now What	2	R. Workman	119	Piquet	113	Ponemah	113	3,275	1:09.00	
1940	Level Best	2	B. James	115	Strange Device	122	Tangled	119	6,425	1:09.20	
1941	Pig Tails	2	J. Skelly	107	War Melody	115	Jane Blenheim	112	5,625	1:10.20	
1942	Optimism	2	J. Longden	111	Bras	111	Demolition	111	5,100	1:09.40	
1943	Thread o' Gold	2	J. Stout	111	Boojiana	111	Vietta	106	5,450	1:13.80	
1944	Drumuir	2	R. Permane	115	Safeguard	113	Flyweight	119	9,885	1:13.00	
1945	War Kilt	2	A. Kirkland	115	Phantasy	106	Upper Level	112	8,230	1:12.40	
1946	Carolyn A.	2	E. Arcaro	115	Pipette	119	With Honor	115	33,550	1:12.60	
1947	Ghost Run	2	R. Donoso	114	Bellesoeur	114	Shimmer	114	33,100	1:13.60	
1948	Lithe	2	W. Garner	119	Lady Dorimar	119	Stole	119	47,025	1:48.20	
1949	Bed o' Roses	2	E. Guerin	116	Next Move	119	Rare Perfume	116	38,800	1:45.80	
1950	Aunt Jinny	2	N. Wall	116	Vulcania	119	Rose Fern	119	30,700	1:45.80	
1951	Rose Jet	2	H. Woodhouse	116	Papoose	119	No Store	119	32,600	1:46.20	
1952	Grecian Queen	2	E. Guerin	119	Ballerina	119	Tritium	114	33,325	1:46.60	
1953	O'Alison	2	J. Nichols	119	Parlo	119	Case Goods	119	50,775	1:46.40	
1958	Khalita	2	E. Arcaro	122	Rich Tradition	122	Sybil Brand	116	15,512	1:25.60	
1959	Irish Jay	2	E. Arcaro	122	Rash Statement	113	Space Happy	113	22,595	1:23.60	
1963	Windsor Lady	2	W. Hartack	116	Lovejoy	114	Hem and Haw	112	18,720	1:37.40	
1964	Discipline	2	I. Valenzuela	113	Lay Aft	115	Cordially	112	18,525	1:39.20	
1965	Indian Sunlite	2	W. Boland	114	Lady Pitt	116	Prides Profile	116	19,500	1:38.20	
1966	Woozem	2	K. Knapp	119	On the Carpet	113	Amherst	112	18,785	1:35.60	
1967	Allie's Serenade	2	J.L. Rotz	113	A. Pleasant Sort	112	Wish Well	112	18,167	1:40.40	
1968	Queen's Double	2	B. Baeza	119	Dauntless Dora	112	Mizzle	114	18,720	1:39.20	
1969	Native Fern	2	J. Ruane	114	Luci Tee	116	Grab It	114	18,655	1:38.80	
1970	Inca Queen	2	A. Cordero Jr	112	Deceit	122	Emperors Desire	114	19,532	1:36.40	
1971	Dresden Doll	2	G. St.. Leon	114	Susan's Girl	119	Brenda Beauty	122	21,600	1:35.80	
1972	Protest	2	A. Santiago	114	Flightoletti	116	Rose Chapeau	115	18,405	1:37.60	
1973	Chris Evert	2	L. Pincay	121	Amberalero	116	Khaled's Kaper	116	17,370	1:36.40	
1974	Land Girl	2	J. Vasquez	116	Alpine Lass	121	Funalon	118	35,940	1:36.20	
1975	Free Journey	2	L. Pincay Jr	117	Artfully	112	Dottie's Doll	114	51,210	1:50.20	
1976	Bring out the Band	2	D. Brumfield	116	Our Mims	113	Road Princess	112	49,500	1:50.80	
1977	Caesar's Wish	2	D.R. Wright	116	Lakeville Miss	121	Island Kiss	114	47,565	1:50.60	
1978	Plankton	2	R. Hernandez	112	Distinct Honor	113	Belladora	112	48,465	1:50.00	
1979	Genuine Risk	2	L. Pincay Jr	116	Smart Angle	121	Spruce Pine	112	49,185	1:51.20	
1980	Rainbow Connection	2	A. Cordero Jr	119	De la Rose	116	Tina Tina Too	116	48,870	1:50.80	
1981	Snow Plow	2	A. Cordero Jr	121	Larida	113	Vain Gold	121	49,680	1:52.00	
1982	Only Queens	2	M.A. Rivera	116	Good Spruce	113	National Banner	113	49,680	1:52.00	
1983	Qualique	2	M. Venezia	112	Lucky Lucku Lucky	121	Buzz My Bell	121	65,160	1:51.20	
1984	Diplomette	2	R. Hernandez	112	Golden Silence	114	Koluctoo's Jill	113	72,360	1:54.60	
1985	I'm Sweets	2	E. Maple	121	Family Style	121	Steal a Kiss	112	98,280	1:50.20	
1986	Tappiano	2	J. Cruguet	121	Soaring Princess	112	Graceful Darby	112	131,940	1:53.20	
1987	Goodbye Halo	2	A. Cordero Jr	113	Tap Your Toes	112	Galway Song	119	142,080	1:53.00	
1988	Open Mind	2	A. Cordero Jr	121	Darby's Daughter	119	Gild	121	147,120	1:52.00	
1989	Rootentootenwooten	2	J.D. Bailey	112	Bookkeeper	113	Why Go on Dreaming	113	109,440	1:51.60	
1990	Debutant's Halo	2	C. Perret	116	Private Treasure	121	Slept Thru It	113	69,960	1:53.80	85
1991	Stolen Beauty	2	C.W. Antley	113	Turnback the Alarm	116	Easy Now	116	120,000	1:52.00	92
1992	Fortunate Faith	2	A. Madrid Jr	112	True Affair	116	Our Tomboy	112	120,000	1:53.40	80
1993	Strategic Maneuver	2	J.D. Bailey	116	Sovereign Kitty	112	Bunting	112	120,000	1:53.60	86
1994	Minister Wife	2	J.D. Bailey	121	Miss Golden Circle	118	Special Broad	121	120,000	1:53.40	93
1995	La Rosa	2	J.A. Krone	114	Quiet Dance	114	Escena	112	120,000	1:50.80	89
1996	Ajina	2	P. Day	121	Hidden Reserve	114	Biding Time	114	120,000	1:53.60	83
1997	Clark Street	2	M.E. Smith	121	Soft Senorita	114	Mercy Me	121	120,000	1:53.80	74
1998	Better Than Honour	2	R. Migliore	113	Waltz On By	115	Oh What a Windfall	121	120,000	1:52.60	68
	Tutorial finished first but was disqualified and placed fifth										
1999	Jostle	2	S. Elliott	121	March Magic	112	Shawnee Country	121	120,000	1:51.40	82
2000	Two Item Limit	2	R. Migliore	122	Sweep Dreams	116	Kingsland	116	120,000	1:52.25	88
2001	Smok'n Frolic	2	J.R. Velazquez	121	Lady Shari	121	Proxy Statement	117	120,000	1:50.57	94
2002	Roar Emotion	2	J.R. Velazquez	115	Savedbydaylight	115	Feisty Step	115	120,000	1:51.43	92
2003	Ashado	2	J.D. Bailey	117	La Reina	121	Dr. Kathy	115	120,000	1:52.88	84
2004	Sis City	2	J.R. Velazquez	119	Salute	115	Winning Season	115	120,000	1:50.39	88

Beyer Index: 85.20

DEPUTY MINISTER HANDICAP (G3), 6 1/2 Furlongs, 3-Year-Olds and Up, Gulfstream Park, 2004 Purse: $100,000

Year	Winner	Age	Jockey	Wt.	Second	Wt.	Third	Wt.	Win Value	Time	Beyer
1990	Beau Genius	5	C. Perret	118	The Red Rolls		Joel		30,000	1:23.00	104
1991	Unbridled	4	P. Day	119	Housebuster		Shuttleman		30,000	1:21.80	117
1992	Take Me Out	4	J.D. Bailey	118	Drummond Lane		Frozen Runway		30,000	1:22.60	108
1993	Loach	5	J.A. Santos	114	Hidden Tomahawk		British Banker		30,000	1:22.40	108
1994	I Can't Believe	6	E. Maple	113	Demaloot Demashoot		Devil On Ice		30,000	1:08.00	108
1995	Chimes Band	4	J.Bailey	120	Distinct Reality	112	Ponche	113	30,000	1:09.00	106
1996	Jess C's Whirl	6	J.Krone	115	Buffalo Dan	117	Patton	114	30,000	1:10.60	106
1997	Templado	6	J.Bailey	113	Sea Emperor	114	Punch Line	119	45,000	1:09.60	106
1998	Irish Conquest	5	E.Coa	113	Frisk Me Now		Oro de Mexico		60,000	1:22.40	106
1999	Good And Tough	4	S.Sellers	115	Western Boreders	113	Mint	113	60,000	1:21.60	116
2000	Deep Gold	4	J.R.Velasquez	112	Forty One Carats	116	Klabin's Gold	114	60,000	1:15.89	103
2001	Instintaj	5	J.D. Bailey	118	Fappie's Notebook	113	Fantastic Finish	114	60.000	1:16.08	106
2002	Fappie's Notebook	5	J.F. Chavez	116	Twilight road	113	Binthebest	114	60,000	1:16.19	106
2003	Native Heir	5	C. Velasquez	114	Binthebest	115	Fire and Glory	114	60,000	1:15.17	109
2004	Alke	4	J.R. Velazquez	112	Cajun Beat	123	Coach Jimi Lee	115	60,000	1:15.80	108

Beyer Index: 107.80

DERBY TRIAL (G3), 1 Mile, 3-Year-Olds, Churchill Downs, 2004 Purse: $110,800

Year	Winner	Age	Jockey	Wt.	Second	Wt.	Third	Wt.	Win Value	Time	Beyer
1938	The Chief	3	G. Woolf	117	Lawrin	118	Stagehand	118	2,145	1:35.80	
1939	Viscounty	3	C. Bierman	110	Technician	118	Steel Heels	110	2,150	1:38.40	
1940	Bimelech	3	F.A. Smith	118	Gallahadion	115	Sirocco	112	2,170	1:38.00	
1941	Blue Pair	3	J. Richard	115	Whirlaway	118	Cadmium	110	2,045	1:36.60	
1942	Valdina Orphan	3	C. Bierman	111	Sun Again	118	Alsab	118	23,050	1:36.80	
1943	Ocean Wave	3	W. Eads	112	Slide Rule	115	No Wrinkles	110	2,290	1:38.20	
1944	Broadcloth	3	F. Zufelt	110	Broad Grin	112	Rockwood Boy	110	4,400	1:37.20	
1945	Burning Dream	3	D. Dodson	111	Best Effort	118	Foreign Agent	112	4,570	1:38.20	
1946	Rippey	3	F. Zufelt	110	Spy Song	118	With Pleasure	118	9,775	1:40.20	
1947	Faultless	3	D. Dodson	118	Star Reward	110	Cosmic Bomb	118	9,075	1:37.60	
1948	Citation	3	E. Arcaro	118	Escadru	118	Eagle Look	110	8,525	1:37.40	
1949	Olympia	3	E. Arcaro	118	Ponder	110	Capot	118	9,000	1:37.40	
1950	Black George	3	E. Nelson	112	Middleground	118	Sunglow	118	9,850	1:40.00	
1951	Fanfare	3	D. Dodson	112	Bernwood	110	King Clover	110	10,250	1:36.60	
1952	Hill Gail	3	E. Arcaro	118	Arroz	110	Shag Tails	112	9,775	1:35.40	
1953	Dark Star	3	H. Moreno	115	Money Broker	118	Spy Defense	112	11,650	1:36.00	
1954	Hasty Road	3	J. Adams	118	Determine	118	Allied	115	11,700	1:35.00	
1955	Flying Fury	3	C. McCreary	118	Jean's Joe	118	Nabesna	112	11,200	1:38.00	
1956	Fabius	3	W. Hartack	112	Countermand	118	Head Man	118	13,050	1:36.60	
1957	Federal Hill	3	W. Carstens	122	Gen. Duke	122	Better Bee	116	10,500	1:36.20	
1958	Tim Tam	3	I. Valenzuela	122	Ebony Pearl	116	Flamingo	112	10,380	1:39.60	
1959	Open View	3	K. Korte	116	Finnegan	122	Royal Orbit	119	10,385	1:35.60	
1960	Beau Purple	3	E. Guerin	116	Cuvier Relic	116	Pied d'Or	116	10,770	1:35.60	
1961	Crozier	3	B. Baeza	122	Four-and-Twenty	122	Dr. Miller	116	10,627	1:34.60	
1962	Roman Line	3	J. Combest	122	Lee Town	116	Sharp Count	119	10,432	1:37.20	
1963	Bonjour	3	W. Shoemaker	122	Gray Pet	116	On My Honor	122	10,530	1:36.40	
1964	Hill Rise	3	W. Shoemaker	122	Roman Brother	122	Mr. Moonlight	122	10,432	1:35.20	
1965	Bold Lad	3	W. Hartack	122	Carpenter's Rule	116	Bugler	116	10,237	1:35.20	
1966	Exhibitionist	3	E. Belmonte	122	Duc d'Eclair	116	Williamston Kid	122	10,237	1:36.00	
1967	Barbs Delight	3	W. Hartack	116	Cool Reception	122	Lightning Orphan	122	10,627	1:35.40	
1968	Proper Proof	3	J. Sellers	122	Jig Time	116	Verbatim	116	10,627	1:36.00	
1969	Ack Ack	3	M. Ycaza	122	Indian Emerald	122	Fleet Allied	122	10,432	1:34.40	
1970	Admiral's Shield	3	J. Nichols	119	George Lewis	122	Panicum Repens	117	10,725	1:37.20	
1971	Vegas Vic	3	H. Grant	119	Jr's Arrowhead	116	On the Money	114	13,910	1:37.00	
1972	Key to the Mint	3	B. Baeza	122	No Le Hace	122	Dr. Neale	116	14,560	1:36.20	
1973	Settecento	3	L. Adams	116	Mr. Prospector	116	I'm Guaranteed	119	13,650	1:37.00	
1974	Ga Hai	3	M. Manganello	122	Perfect Aim	122	To the Rescue	116	13,650	1:38.00	
1975	Round Stake	3	M. Hole	122	Rushing Man	116	Naughty Jake	122	13,650	1:36.40	
1976	Justa Bad Boy	3	W. Gavidia	116	Pastry	122	Here Comes Jo	116	13,520	1:38.00	
1977	Kodiack	3	R.L. Turcotte	116	Model Sailor	119	Castle Call	116	13,910	1.25.20	
1978	Braze and Bold	3	J. McKnight	119	Silver Nitrate	122	As in Elbow	116	13,780	1:25.40	
1979	Dreamy Prospect	3	D. Haire	119	Zuppardo's Prince	116	Great Redeemer	112	16,900	1:24.40	
1980	Royal Sporan	3	D. Brumfield	119	Real Emperor	122	Stutz Blackhawk	122	17,290	1:25.60	
1981	What It Is	3	J.C. Espinoza	116	Vodika Collins	119	Cornish Music	119	18,785	1:24.60	
1982	Listcapade	3	D. Haire	116	Star Gallant	122	Royal Roberto	122	40,853	1:30.20	
1983	Caveat	3	L. Pincay Jr	122	Total Departure	122	Pax in Bello	122	39,553	1:37.80	
1984	Devil's Bag	3	E. Maple	122	Biloxi Indian	122	Secret Prince	122	35,425	1:35.60	
1985	Creme Fraiche	3	R.P. Romero	119	Fast Account	122	Nordic Scandal	113	38,285	1:37.40	
1986	Savings	3	P.A. Johnson	113	Trobio	113	Sumptious	113	38,188	1:35.60	

Year	Winner	Age	Jockey	Wt.	Second	Wt.	Third	Wt.	Win Value	Time	Beyer
1987	On the Line	3	P. Day	118	No More Flowers	116	Contractor's Tune	113	36,855	1:36.60	
1988	Jim's Orbit	3	S.P. Romero	122	Kingpost	122	Lover's Trust	119	36,953	1:38.60	
1989	Houston	3	L. Pincay Jr	122	Belek	119	Affirmed's Image	119	54,698	1:36.20	
1990	Housebuster	3	C. Perret	122	Private School	119	Falling Sky	117	54,454	1:37.60	
1991	Alydavid	3	P. Day	114	Honor Grades	117	Formal Dinner	122	57,760	1:36.40	97
1992	Alydeed	3	C. Perret	119	Binalong	117	Dignitas	119	56,200	1:36.20	110
1993	Cherokee Run	3	P. Day	122	Darien Deacon	114	Ground Force	117	56,355	1:37.40	103
1994	Numerous	3	C.J. McCarron	115	Dynamic Asset	114	Exclusive Praline	119	72,540	1:37.20	101
1995	Peaks and Valleys	3	P. Day	122	Our Gatsby	122	Strategic Intent	114	73,515	1:36.40	109
1996	Valid Expectations	3	D.R. Pettinger	119	Great Southern	114	Storm Creek	117	77,025	1:36.81	98
1997	Richter Scale	3	S.J. Sellers	114	Trafalger	122	Precocity	113	70,122	1:36.17	112
1998	Souvenir Copy	3	D.R. Flores	122	Yarrow Brae	114	Black Cash	122	70,246	1:35.80	105
1999	Patience Game	3	C.S. Nakatani	112	Prime Directive	122	Straight Man	114	71,176	1:37.86	105
2000	Performing Magic	3	P. Day	114	Sun Cat	117	Valiant Halory	114	70,680	1:35.99	102
2001	Meetyouathebrig	3	R.J. Albarado	122	Dream Run	114	One By the Knows	119	72,602	1:36.44	98
2002	Sky Terrace	3	C. Perret	114	Cashel Castle	122	Ide Be Spencers	114	69,936	1:36.87	101
2003	Midas Eyes	3	J.D. Bailey	122	Champali	122	Desert Warrior	118	103,788	1:36.22	105
2004	Sir Shackleton	3	R. Bejarano	116	Courageous Act	116	Bwana Charlie	122	68,696	1:37.61	93

Beyer Index: 102.79

DESERT STORMER HANDICAP (G3), 6 Furlongs, Fillies and Mares, 3-Year-Olds and Up, Hollywood Park, 2004 Purse: $106,000

Year	Winner	Age	Jockey	Wt.	Second	Wt.	Third	Wt.	Win Value	Time	Beyer
1997	Advancing Star	4	K.J. Desormeaux	119	Stop Traffic	118	Tiffany Diamond	114	60,000	1:14.20	109
1998	Corona Lake	4	E. Delahoussaye	118	Lavender	116	Grab the Prize	116	64,020	1:14.60	101
1999	A.P. Assay	5	E. Delahoussaye	122	Woodman's Dancer	116	Corona Lake	118	63,600	1:08.60	106
2000	Theresa's Tizzy	6	L. Pincay Jr	118	Hookedonthefeelin	117	Seth's Choice	114	64,980	1:09.30	105
2001	Go Go	4	E. Delahoussaye	122	Kalookan Queen	117	Wired to Fly	113	63,600	1:08.09	113
2002	Slewsbox	5	L. Pincay Jr	117	Kalookan Queen	123	Rolly Polly	117	64,260	1:09.57	104
2003	Madame Pietra	6	P.A. Valenzuela	121	Bear Fan	116	Jetinto Houston	116	64,080	1:09.71	94
2004	Coconut Girl	5	V. Espinoza	115	Ema Bovary	123	Stormica	115	63,600	1:08.91	104

Beyer Index: 104.50

Run at 6 1/2 furlongs, 1997–98

DIANA HANDICAP (G1), 1 1/8 Miles (Turf), Fillies and Mares, 3-Year-Olds and Up, Saratoga Race Course, 2004 Purse: $500,000

Year	Winner	Age	Jockey	Wt.	Second	Wt.	Third	Wt.	Win Value	Time	Beyer
1939	War Regalia	3	D. Meade	110	Flying Lee	104	Sh'gay Lily	126	2,550	1:52.20	
1940	Piquet	3	E. Arcaro	118	Fairy Chant	118	Rosetown	110	2,425	1:52.00	
1941	Rosetown	4	J. Longden	118	Dorimar	119	Fairy Chant	126	2,650	1:53.40	
1942	Pomayya	4	A. Robertson	118	Key Ring	113	Transient	109	2,450	1:53.00	
1943	Bonnet Ann	4	L. Haas	113	Vagrancy	126	Night Glow	112	4,050	1:50.00	
1944	Whirlabout	3	H. Lindberg	118	Good Morning	120	Vienna	115	8,530	1:50.20	
1945	Surosa	3	A. Snider	110	Legend Bearer	113	Letmenow	109	9,020	1:50.80	
1946	Miss Grillo	4	C. McCreary	124	Jackawake	104	Sicily	119	9,150	1:50.20	
1947	Miss Grillo	5	C. McCreary	126	Humaya	106	Rosa Blanca	114	8,850	1:50.40	
1948	Carolyn A.	4	E. Arcaro	114	Miss Grillo	120	Mother	107	8,025	1:51.80	
1949	Spats	4	T. Atkinson	106	Adile	115	Gaffery	115	7,925	1:52.40	
1950	Ouija	3	W. Bolan	110	Jazz Baby	117	Supersonic	110	8,175	1:51.60	
1951	Vulcania	3	R. Bernhardt	108	Marta	115	Adile	111	7,775	1:52.60	
1952	Busanda	5	T. Atkinson	111	Nilufer	106	Valadium	115	7,675	1:53.40	
1953	Sabette	3	J. Higley	114	Canadiana	115	Dinewisely	105	11,250	1:52.60	
1954	Lavender Hill	5	C. McCreary	121	La Corredora	121	Evening Out	116	16,600	1:52.60	
1955	Misty Morn	3	T. Atkinson	115	Carry the News	110	Oil Painting	118	16,150	1:51.20	
1956	Searching	6	W. Hartack	123	Rico Reto	113	Blue Banner	117	18,950	1:52.00	
1957	Pardala	4	H. Woodhouse	111	Searching	125	Rare Treat	118	19,400	1:53.00	
1958	Searching	6	W. Hartack	123	Endine	116	Rare Treat	112	17,412	1:52.20	
1959	Tempted	4	E. Nelson	122	Polamby	116	Spar Maid	110	36,190	1:50.40	
1960	Tempted	5	E. Nelson	124	Quill	128	Aestethic	112	24,430	1:51.40	
1961	Craftiness	6	R. Ussery	117	Sarcastic	120	Linda J.A.	107	18,297	1:49.60	
1962	Waltz Song	4	S. Mellon	113	Seven Thirty	124	Honey Dear	111	17,777	1:49.20	
1963	Frimanaha	6	J. Sellers	113	Waltz Song	119	Upswept	112	17,940	1:50.00	
1964	Prodana Neviesta	4	H. Gustines	108	Fool's Play	111	Tona	118	18,492	1:50.60	
1965	Steeple Jill	4	J. Ruane	126	Straight Deal	113	Ho Ho	109	18,752	1:49.60	
1966	Open Fire	5	F. Lovato	117	Reluctant Pearl	108	Mac's Sparkler	113	18,460	1:48.80	
1967	Prides Profile	4	M. Ycaza	114	Straight Deal	127	Malhoa	111	18,655	1:49.60	
1968	Green Glade	4	K. Knapp	110	Gamely	120	Mount Regina	118	18,622	1:49.60	
1969	Gamely	5	E. Belmonte	127	Obeah	118	Amerigo Lady	123	28,925	1:49.60	
1970	Shuvee	4	R. Turcotte	120	Dark Emerald	109	Native Partner	112	31,915	1:49.60	
1971	Shuvee	5	R. Turcotte	128	Double Delta	126	Cathy Honey	116	26,460	1:50.60	

Year	Winner	Age	Jockey	Wt.	Second	Wt.	Third	Wt.	Win Value	Time	Beyer
1972	Blessing Angelica	4	E. Belmonte	117	Light Hearted	113	Aladancer	115	16,620	1:49.80	
1973	Cathy Baby	4	J. Velasquez	119	Something Super	113	Worlding	111	13,620	1:46.80	
1973	Lightning Lucy	3	R. Turcotte	116	Flying Fur	114	Summer Guest	122	13,545	1:46.60	
1974	Fairway Flyer	5	J. Velasquez	118	North Broadway	117	Brindabella	117	35,070	1:47.20	
1975	Heloise	4	M. Venezia	113	Victorian Queen	118	Princesse Grey	112	35,250	1:47.40	
1976	Glowing Tribute	3	R. Turcotte	116	Fleet Victress	117	Nijana	111	32,910	1:47.60	
1977	Javamine	4	A. Cordero Jr	114	Pearl Necklace	109	Rich Soil	114	32,640	1:48.40	
1978	Waya	4	A. Cordero Jr	115	Pearl Necklace	125	Fia	110	33,240	1:45.40	
1979	Pearl Necklace	5	J. Fell	124	Island Kiss	114	Terpsichorist	119	35,010	1:48.80	
1980	Just a Game II	4	D. Brumfield	123	The Very One	117	Relaxing	113	35,520	1:49.00	
1981	De La Rose	3	E. Maple	114	Rokeby Rose	115	Euphrosyne	112	36,420	1:50.60	
1982	Hush Dear	4	E. Beitia	109	Larida	114	So Pleasantly	109	34,170	1:47.40	
1982	If Winter Comes	4	E. Beitia	110	Canaille II	112	Noble Damsel	114	34,170	1:47.40	
1983	Geraldine's Store	4	J.L. Samyn	108	Trevita	120	Infinite	111	33,840	1:47.20	
1983	Hush Dear	5	J. Vasquez	123	If Winter Comes	113	First Approach	118	34,080	1:48.40	
1984	Wild Applause	3	W. Guerra	109	Pretty Perfect	109	Spit Curl	112	70,650	1:48.20	
1985	Lake Country	4	J. Fell	117	Possible Mate	118	Key Dancer	120	58,230	1:48.40	
1986	Duty Dance	4	J. Cruguet	118	Dismasted	115	Kapalua Butterfly	112	91,380	1:49.80	
1987	Bailrullah	5	J. Cruguet	111	Perfect Point	114	Videogenic	116	91,860	1:46.20	
1988	Glowing Honor	3	P. Day	106	Sunny Roberta	111	Graceful Darby	112	73,680	1:49.40	
1989	Glowing Honor	4	J.D. Bailey	115	Wooing	111	Laugh and Be Merry	114	76,200	1:50.20	
1990	Foresta	4	A. Cordero Jr	113	To the Lighthouse	113	Songlines	111	56,790	1:48.40	105
1991	Christiecat	4	J.L. Samyn	117	Virgin Michael	112	Senora Tippy	111	75,360	1:47.60	104
1992	Plenty of Grace	5	W.H. McCauley	114	Ratings	111	Highland Crystal	115	75,960	1:46.60	99
1993	Ratings	5	J.A. Krone	110	Lady Blessington	118	Garendare	113	72,240	1:49.80	95
1994	Via Borghese	5	J.A. Santos	115	Blazing KAdie	110	Coronation Cup	108	83,010	1:52.00	105
1995	Perfect Arc	3	J.R. Velazquez	113	Danish	118	Tiffany's Taylor	113	85,125	1:46.80	108
1996	Electric Society	5	M.E. Smith	117	Powder Bowl	116	Upper Noosh	110	120,000	1:46.40	103
1997	Rumpipumpy	4	J. A. Santos	114	B. A. Valentine	116	Antespend	117	120,000	1:48.40	100
1998	Memories of Silver	5	J.D. Bailey	123	B.A. Valentine	114	Auntie Mame	122	180,000	1:46.00	105
1999	Heritage Of Gold	4	S.J. Sellers	115	Khumba Mela	114	Mossflower	114	180,000	1:45.80	102
2000	Perfect Sting	4	J.D. Bailey	123	License Fee	116	Hello Soso	113	300,000	1:47.01	102
2001	Starine	4	J.R. Velazquez	114	Babae	114	Penny's Gold	120	300,000	1:46.17	111
2002	Tates Creek	4	J.D. Bailey	117	Voodoo Dancer	120	Snow Dance	117	300,000	1:48.00	102
2003	Voodoo Dancer	5	C.S. Nakatani	120	Heat Haze	118	Pertuisane	115	300,000	1:47.98	106
2004	Wonder Again	5	E.S. Prado	120	Riskaverse	118	Ocean Drive	118	300,000	1:48.99	110

Beyer Index: 103.80

DISCOVERY HANDICAP (G3), 1 1/8 Miles, 3-Year-Olds, Aqueduct, 2004 Purse: $110,100

Year	Winner	Age	Jockey	Wt.	Second	Wt.	Third	Wt.	Win Value	Time	Beyer
1945	War Jeep	3	A. Kirkland	122	Chief Barker	116	Buzfuz	114	20,010	1:51.40	
1946	Mighty Story	3	B. James	115	Mahout	112	Assault	126	20,050	1:51.80	
1947	Cosmic Bomb	3	O. Scurlock	126	Double Jay	115	Phalanx	128	19,750	1:51.20	
1948	Better Self	3	D. Gorman	123	Mount Marcy	117	Loser Weeper	109	20,850	1:53.80	
1949	Prophet's Thumb	3	D. Gorman	113	One Hitter	114	Curandero	109	15,650	1:52.20	
1950	Sunglow	3	D. Dodson	113	Steel Blue	106	Bit o' Fate	104	15,100	1:49.00	
1951	Alerted	3	O. Scurlock	114	Battlefield	126	Vulcania	108	15,225	1:50.40	
1952	Ancestor	3	T. Atkinson	107	Flaunt	107	Marcador	110	19,550	1:50.80	
1953	Level Lea	3	B. Green	112	Dictar	120	Landlocked	126	19,075	1:52.00	
1954	Chevation	3	E. Guerin	122	Kope's Baby	115	Guayana	109	20,500	1:50.00	
1955	Westward Ho	3	C. McCreary	113	Illusionist	111	Power	110	19,300	1:52.80	
1956	Reneged	3	I. Valenzuela	122	Riley	114	Oh Johnny	122	20,600	1:48.20	
1957	Ben Lomond	3	E. Arcaro	116	Harmonizing	110	Bureaucracy	118	21,600	1:49.20	
1958	Warhead	3	E. Arcaro	124	Grey Monarch	118	Backbone	124	19,330	1:51.20	
1959	Middle Brother	3	E. Arcaro	116	Demobilize	117	Intentionally	129	18,777	1:50.60	
1960	Kelso	3	E. Arcaro	124	Careless John	116	Count Amber	116	18,290	1:48.40	
1961	Ambiopoise	3	W. Shoemaker	123	Garwol	112	Wise Flushing	111	18,297	1:48.80	
1962	Comic	3	L. Adams	111	Dedimoud	116	Black Beard	120	19,012	1:48.60	
1963	Quest Link	3	W. Shoemaker	115	Outing Class	123	Hot Dust	117	19,305	1:49.80	
1964	Roman Brother	3	F. Alvarez	125	Lt. Stevens	113	Twice as Gay	109	18,135	1:49.00	
1965	Sammyren	3	H. Gustines	110	Selari	112	Royal Gunner	117	18,492	1:49.00	
1966	Deck Hand	3	W. Shoemaker	114	Yonder	110	Irish Ruler	113	18,557	1:49.60	
1967	Bold Hour	3	W. Shoemaker	119	Successor	119	Gala Performance	118	18,525	1:48.40	
1968	Ardoise	3	E. Belmonte	113	Balustrade	122	Pamir	111	18,557	1:49.20	
1969	Hydrologist	3	D.B. Thomas	111	Red Reality	112	Say Not So	111	18,492	1:47.60	
1970	Burd Alane	3	J. Velasquez	114	Buzkashi	115	Captain Nash	120	18,492	1:47.40	
1971	Autobiography	3	L. Pincay Jr	115	Minsky	114	Boone the Great	109	20,550	1:50.40	
1972	Forage	3	E. Maple	113	Sunny and Mild	120	Festive Mood	112	17,055	1:48.60	
1973	Forego	3	H. Gustines	127	My Gallant	122	Arbees Boy	114	33,300	1:47.20	
1974	Rube the Great	3	A. Cordero Jr	119	Holding Pattern	126	Sharp Gary	118	33,270	1:48.20	

Year	Winner	Age	Jockey	Wt.	Second	Wt.	Third	Wt.	Win Value	Time	Beyer
1974	Green Gambados	3	A. Cordero Jr	120	Best of It	116	Jolly Johu	121	33,570	1:48.20	
1975	Dr. Emil	3	B. Baeza	115	Rushing Man	125	Syllabus	113	33,630	1:48.60	
1976	Wise Phillip	3	D. Montoya	107	Teddy's Courage	115	Patriot's Dream	112	32,460	1:48.60	
1977	Cox's Ridge	3	E. Maple	126	Broadway Forli	123	Papelote	107	32,670	1:48.60	
1978	Sorry Lookin	3	R.I. Velez	110	Silent Cal	115	Judge Advocate	114	31,740	1:49.60	
1979	Belle's Gold	3	A. Cordero Jr	121	Smarten	122	Gallant Best	115	33,270	1:48.00	
1980	Fappiano	3	A. Cordero Jr	114	Reef Searcher	114	Royal Hierarchy	111	35,280	1:50.00	
1981	Princelet	3	E. Maple	113	Accipiter's Hope	118	Pass the Tab	126	33,240	1:51.00	
1982	Trenchant	3	J.L. Samyn	113	Dew Line	113	Exclusive Era	112	32,880	1:50.80	
1983	Country Pine	3	J.D. Bailey	118	Jacque's Tip	115	Father Don Juan	112	33,420	1:49.60	
1984	Key to the Moon	3	D. Beckon	120	Silver Stark	112	Raja's Shark	124	42,300	1:50.00	
1985	Proud Truth	3	J. Velasquez	126	Important Business	113	Romancer	110	51,750	1:49.20	
1986	Moment of Hope	3	M. Venezia	108	Gold Alert	109	Clear Choice	112	54,000	1:49.60	
1987	Parochial	3	J.A. Krone	117	Homebuilder	112	Forest Fair	115	109,620	1:51.20	
1988	Dynaformer	3	A. Cordero Jr	116	Star Attitude	113	Congeleur	112	104,580	1:50.00	
1989	Tricky Creek	3	C. Perret	117	Traskwood	113	Farewell Wave	110	71,280	1:50.00	
1990	Sports View	3	J.A. Santos	113	Chief Honcho	117	Killer Diller	116	52,830	1:48.60	
							Out of Place	112			
1991	Upon My Soul	3	J.L. Samyn	112	Excellent Tipper	114	Honest Ensign	110	75,960	1:49.60	105
1992	New Deal	3	R.G. Davis	111	Offbeat	114	Dodsworth	113	74,880	1:48.00	98
1993	Prospector's Flag	3	J.F. Chavez	114	Virginia Rapids	118	Living Vicariously	114	70,320	1:52.20	103
1994	Serious Spender	3	Chavez JF	113	Unaccounted For	121	Malmo	112	63,540	1:51.20	97
1995	Michael's Star	3	J.A. Krone	112	Hunting Hard	113	Reality Road	114	67,380	1:50.20	99
1996	Gold Fever	3	M.E. Smith	121	Crafty Friend	115	Early Echoes	111	66,720	1:49.00	106
1997	Mr. Sinatra	3	M.E. Smith	116	Concerto	121	Twin Spires	116	64,620	1:49.40	102
1998	Early Warning	3	J.F. Chavez	115	Deputy Diamond	117	Gulliver	115	50,010	1:48.80	111
1999	Adonis	3	J.R. Velazquez	118	Best of Luck	118	Waddaan	113	64,980	1:50.11	103
2000	Left Bank	3	J.R. Velazquez	119	Perfect Cat	114	Open Sesame	115	64,020	1:47.30	103
2001	Evening Attire	3	S.X. Bridgmohan	111	Street Cry	118	Free of Love	115	65,580	1:48.62	103
2002	Saint Marden	3	J.D. Bailey	117	Regency Park	115	No Parole	117	68,400	1:49.13	106
2003	During	3	J.A. Santos	120	Unforgettable Max	114	Inamorato	114	67,080	1:51.18	106
2004	Zakocity	3	J.J. Castellano	116	Stolen Time	116	Mahzouz	115	66,060	1:49.78	103

Beyer Index: 103.21

DISTAFF BREEDERS' CUP HANDICAP (G2), 7 Furlongs, Fillies and Mares, 3-Year-Olds and Up, Aqueduct, 2004 Purse: $147,900

Year	Winner	Age	Jockey	Wt.	Second	Wt.	Third	Wt.	Win Value	Time	Beyer
1954	Mab's Choice	5	A. Valenzuela	109	Sunshine Nell	126	Brazen Brat	125	21,000	1:24.40	
1955	Oil Painting	4	H. Woodhouse	115	Good Child	113	Canadiana	121	20,300	1:24.00	
1956	Blue Banner	4	E. Arcaro	115	Peignoir	108	Myrtle's Jet	123	15,000	1:23.80	
1957	Searching	5	C. McCreary	124	Fanciful Miss	112	Plotter	110	16,700	1:24.40	
1958	Happy Princess	6	H. Woodhouse	116	Outer Space	117	Searching	123	15,675	1:24.00	
1959	Happy Princess	7	H. Woodhouse	114	Mlle. Dianne	115	Idun	125	18,290	1:24.20	
1960	Mommy Dear	4	M. Ycaza	125	Tinkalero	119	Craftiness	115	17,607	1:23.00	
1961	Teacation	4	R. Broussard	117	Sister Antoine	119	Make Sail	117	14,722	1:23.60	
1962	Rose O'Neill	4	I. Valenzuela	118	Seven Thirty	121	Mighty Fair	116	15,015	1:23.80	
1963	Cicada	4	W. Shoemaker	125	Pocosaba	119	Royal Patrice	120	14,527	1:21.60	
1964	Charspiv	4	R. Ussery	117	Look Ma	109	Suiti	112	13,926	1:24.00	
1964	Smart Deb	4	W. Hartack	125	Pams Ego	121	D'c'l C'n'ge	110	13,764	1:25.20	
1965	Affectionately	5	W. Blum	128	Treachery	115	Petticoat	113	18,102	1:24.00	
1966	Sailor Princess	4	G. Mineau	111	Queen Empress	123	Petticoat	112	18,102	1:22.40	
1967	Cologne	4	B. Baeza	113	Lady Diplomat	114	Miss Moona	122	18,070	1:24.20	
1968	Just Kidding	4	J. Velasquez	113	Shirley Heights	111	Serene Queen	107	18,395	1:23.20	
1969	Heartland	4	J.L. Rotz	121	Amerigo Lady	123	C'ms F'ry G'd	113	18,200	1:22.40	
1970	Process Shot	4	C. Baltazar	126	Ta Wee	134	Dedicated to Sue	115	18,037	1:22.80	
1971	Double Delta	5	B. Baeza	116	Cold Comfort	114	I'm for Mama	115	19,980	1:22.80	
1972	Royal Signal	5	C. Baltazar	121	Red Shoes	118	Aladancer	117	16,545	1:24.20	
1973	Ferly	5	R. Turcotte	113	Wakefield Miss	115	Twixt	112	16,920	1:24.00	
1974	Krislin	5	V. Bracciale Jr	113	Batacuda	116	Ladies Agreement	112	16,770	1:22.00	
1975	Something Super	5	J. Cruguet	115	Shy Dawn	121	Second Coming	108	16,995	1:22.20	
1976	Shy Dawn	5	A. Cordero Jr	118	Land Girl	114	Ladies Agreement	114	22,590	1:24.20	
1977	What a Summer	4	E. Maple	118	Secret Lanvin	112	Shy Dawn	120	21,975	1:11.60	
1978	Vandy Sue	4	A.M. Rodriguez	112	Sea Drone	108	Dalton Road	118	22,185	1:12.00	
1979	Skipat	5	J.W. Edwards	122	Sweet Joyce	106	Unpossible	107	32,520	1:10.40	
1980	Misty Gallore	4	D. MacBeth	124	Lady Lonsdale	114	Spanish Fake	112	33,240	1:24.60	
1981	Lady Oakley	4	J. Fell	114	It's in the Air	120	Lovin' Lass	110	33,900	1:25.40	
1982	Lady Dean	4	D.A. Miller Jr	120	Westport Native	114	Raise 'n Dance	107	33,000	1:23.80	
1983	Jones Time Machine	4	A. Cordero Jr	112	Fancy Naskra	113	Adept	111	32,880	1:23.20	
1984	Am Capable	4	A. Cordero Jr	125	Sweet Missus	104	Fissure	107	52,290	1:11.00	
1985	Give Me a Hint	5	W.A. Ward	109	Nany	121	Descent	106	55,080	1:25.20	
1986	Ride Sally	4	W.A. Guerra	118	Willowy Mood	116	Clocks Secret	122	54,540	1:21.60	

Year	Winner	Age	Jockey	Wt.	Second	Wt.	Third	Wt.	Win Value	Time	Beyer
1987	Pine Tree Lane	5	A. Cordero Jr	125	Spring Beauty	117	Gene's Lady	117	52,650	1:22.40	
1988	Cadillacing	4	R.P. Romero	112	Cagey Exuberance	118	Bishop's Delight	111	50,670	1:22.60	
1989	Avie's Gal	4	N. Santagata	112	Haiati	112	Topicount	117	51,660	1:24.00	
1990	Channel Three	4	J.F. Chavez	111	Divine Answer	113	Hedgeabout	112	54,090	1:23.20	
1991	Devil's Orchid	4	R. Baze	117	Your Hope	112	Fappaburst	114	64,080	1:21.00	115
1992	Nannerl	5	M.E. Smith	112	Missy's Mirage	119	Withallprobability	117	68,880	1:24.60	101
1994	Classy Mirage	4	R.G. Davis	114	Jill Miner	114	Air Port Won	109	66,480	1:11.20	100
1995	Recognizable	4	M.E. Smith	120	Beckys Shirt	113	Kurofune Mystery	116	66,540	1:22.80	102
1996	Lottsa Talc	6	F.T. Alvarado	120	Traverse City	120	Dust Bucket	116	75,820	1:24.00	100
1997	Miss Golden Circle	5	R. Migliore	120	Inquisitive Look	110	Punkin Pie	109	65,400	1:24.40	96
1998	Parlay	4	R. Migliore	114	Lucky Marty	113	Green Light	114	67,260	1:24.00	89
1999	Furlough	5	H. Castillo Jr	115	Catinca	121	Tomorrows Sunshine	113	112,260	1:23.20	104
2000	Honest Lady	4	B. Blanc	117	Her She Kisses	115	Tap to Music	118	111,300	1:22.10	103
2001	Dream Supreme	4	A.T. Gryder	119	Folly Dollar	113	Country Hideaway	118	108,960	1:23.66	96
2002	Raging Fever	4	J.R. Velazquez	120	Prized Stamp	114	La Galerie	115	94,680	1:21.78	105
2003	Carson Hollow	4	M.J. Luzzi	120	Raging Fever	118	Bonafide Reason	112	94,740	1:22.42	102
2004	Randaroo	4	R. Migliore	121	Chirimoya	110	Storm Flag Flying	118	93,240	1:22.64	100

Beyer Index: 101.00

(ARGENT MORTGAGE) DISTAFF TURF MILE (G3), 1 Mile (Turf), Fillies and Mares, 3-Year-Olds and Up, Churchill Downs, 2004 Purse: $113,300

Year	Winner	Age	Jockey	Wt.	Second	Wt.	Third	Wt.	Win Value	Time	Beyer
1983	Le Cou Cou		D. Howard	121	High Honors		Common Sense			1:49.60	
1987	Fast Forward		P. Day	115	Sooner Showers		Homebuilder			1:43.20	
	High Honors finished first but was disqualified and placed second										
1988	Buoy		P. Day	123	Frosty the Snowman		Cougarized			1:43.40	
1989	Classic Account	4	P. Day	116	Fast Forward		R.B. McCurry			1:51.20	
1990	Foresta	4	A. Cordero Jr	114	Saros Brig		Bearly Cooking		36,200	1:37.20	103
1991	Foresta	5	A. Cordero Jr	123	Coolawin		Primetime North		38,870	1:36.20	100
1992	Quilma	5	E. Delahoussaye	120	Behaving Dangeer		Raidant Ring		38,200	1:35.36	100
1993	Lady Blessington	5	P. Day	120	You'd Be Surprised		Wassifa		37,570	1:34.96	96
1994	Weekend Madness	4	C. Woods Jr	123	Russian Bride		Suspect Terrain		55,770	1:38.58	98
1995	Bold Ruritana	5	P. Day	123	Icy Warning	114	Rapunzel Runz	116	56,111	1:34.64	101
1996	Apolda	5	J.D. Bailey	123	Country Cat	123	Bold Ruritana	123	55,283	1:36.50	103
1997	B.A. Valentine	4	S.J. Sellers	114	Striesen	116	Romy	123	71.796	1:36.98	100
1998	Witchful Thinking	4	S.J. Sellers	120	Colcon	123	Swearingen	123	74,896	1:37.23	97
1999	Shires End	4	J. Velazquez	118	Ashford Castle	120	Sophie My Love	123	74,152	1:35.43	98
2000	Don't Be Silly	5	J.F. Chavez	116	Really Polish	114	Pricearose	116	71,548	1:34.78	100
2001	Iftiraas	4	J.D. Bailey	118	Gino's Spirits	118	Solvig	120	70,432	1:36.69	100
2002	Sylish	4	J.D. Bailey	116	La Recherche	123	Dianehill	123	71,424	1:35.72	95
2003	Heat Haze	4	J. Valdivia Jr	123	Quick Tip	123	Sentimental Value	121	72,540	1:33.96	99
2004	Shaconage	4	B. Blanc	121	Etoile Montante	123	Chance Dance	117	70,246	1:36.10	95

Beyer Index: 99.00

(ARGENT) DIXIE (G2), 1 1/8 Miles (Turf), 3-Year-Olds and Up, Pimlico Race Course, 2004 Purse: $200,000

Year	Winner	Age	Jockey	Wt.	Second	Wt.	Third	Wt.	Win Value	Time	Beyer
1870	Preakness	3	Hayward	110	Ecliptic	107	Foster	110	6,400	3:47.50	
1871	Harry Bassett		Rowe	110					6,500		
1872	Hubbard	3	McCabe	110	Joe Daniels	110	True Blue	110	13,200	3:36.50	
1873	Tom Bowling	3	Swim	110	Merodac	110	Lizzie Lucas	107	4,000	3:58.00	
1874	Vandalite	3	Houston	107	Madge	107	Brigand	110	13,200	3:35.50	
1875	Tom Ochiltree	3	Evans	110	Viator	107	Joe Cerns	110	4,350	3:42.50	
1876	Vigil	3	Spillman	110	Parole	107	Heretog	110	4,300	3:41.50	
1877	King Faro	3	Walker	110	Major Barker	110	Susquehanna	107	4,450	3:55.00	
1878	Duke of Magenta	3	Hughes	110	Bonnie Wood	107	Spartan	110	4,200	3:41.00	
1879	Monitor	3	Hughes	107	Lord Murphy	110	Harold	110	4,850	3:34.75	
1880	Grenada	3	Hughes	110	Oden	110	Ferncliffe	110	4,200	3:38.00	
1881	Crickmore	3	Hughes	107	Eole	110	Barrett	110	3,550	3:37.00	
1882	Monarch	3	Schauer	110	Hilarity	110	Blenheim	107	3,500	3:44.00	
1883	George Kinney	3	J. McLaughlin	110	Trafalgar	110	Gonfalon	110	3,600	3:56.00	
1884	Loftin	3		113	Blast	110	Thackeray	110	3,595	3:37.75	
1885	East Lynne	3	W. Donahue	115	Richmond	118	Longview	118	3,595	3:49.75	
1886	The Bard	3	W. Hayward	118	Blue Wing	118	Wheatley	115	3,290	3:33.00	
1887	Hanover	3	J. McLaughlin	123	Glenmound	118			4,560	3:51.75	
1902	Adelaide Prince	3	W.L. Powers	113	Potheen	116	Flintlock	113	1,530	3:06.60	
1903	Colonsay	3	W.C. Daly	114					1,750	3:41.40	
1904	The Southerner	3	M. Corbett	116	Ostrich	123	Andrew Mack	116	3,310	3:06.60	
1924	Chacolet	6	M. Garner	116	Martingale	120	Rev. Agent	100	24,840	1:59.20	
1925	Sarazen	4	E. Sande	130	Spot Cash	115	Joy Smoke	104	25,950	2:02.00	

Year	Winner	Age	Jockey	Wt.	Second	Wt.	Third	Wt.	Win Value	Time	Beyer
1926	Sarazen	5	F. Weiner	128	Sun Pal	105	G. Th'tcher	118	24,550	2:00.80	
1927	Mars	4	F. Coltiletti	124	Display	120	Edisto	113	26,375	1:59.40	
1928	Mike Hall	4	H. Richards	110	Scapa Flow	120	Sir Harry	112	24,975	1:59.00	
1929	Diavolo	4	J. Maiben	112	Victorian	122	Display	124	27,600	2:00.00	
1930	Sandy Ford	4	F. Catrone	106	Inception	114	Sir Harry	112	26,025	1:59.20	
1931	Paul Bunyan	5	E. Gianelloni	110	Frisius	112	William T.	110	15,425	2:01.20	
1932	Gallant Knight	5	H. Schutte	121	Sun Meadow	118	Aegis	112	14,550	1:58.00	
1933	Stepenfetchit	4	E. Steffen	112	Keep Out	101	Tred Avon	117	5,100	2:01.80	
1934	Equipoise	6	R. Workman	130	Chatmoss	110	Fla'g Mamie	102	4,190	2:01.80	
1935	Only One	4	R. Merritt	108	Head Play	120	Howard	113	4,520	2:01.80	
1936	Dark Hope	7	R. Jones	113	Good Goods	115	Gallant Mc	109	9,500	1:58.00	
1937	Calumet Dick	5	J. Wagner	108	Finance	118	Aneroid	109	9,450	1:58.40	
1938	Pompoon	4	G. Woolf	118	Busy K.	110	M'ked G'eral	107	20,950	1:56.80	
1939	Sir Damion	5	D. Meade	113	Tatterdemalion	111	Jacola	117	22,025	1:58.60	
1940	Honey Cloud	6	H. Mora	115	Filisteo	112	Aethelwold	107	18,250	1:58.60	
1941	Haltal	4	C. McCreary	110	Mioland	129	Dit	110	19,850	1:58.40	
1942	Whirlaway	4	E. Arcaro	128	Attention	124	Mioland	126	19,275	1:57.00	
1943	Riverland	5	S. Brooks	123	Attention	123	Anticlimax	113	17,775	1:56.40	
1944	Sun Again	5	F.A. Smith	120	Rounders	117	Alquest	106	25,700	1:58.20	
1945	Rounders	6	F. Remerscheid	118	He Rolls	116	Gay Bit	108	25,400	1:56.80	
1946	Armed	5	D. Dodson	130	Stymie	124	Trymenow	117	25,700	1:58.40	
1947	Assault	4	E. Arcaro	129	Rico Monte	120	Talon	115	24,700	1:57.80	
1948	Fervent	4	N.L. Pierson	121	Stymie	127	Incline	107	21,950	2:01.60	
1949	Chains	4	J.D. Jessop	109	Contest	110	Pilaster	120	21,150	1:56.60	
1950	Loser Weeper	5	N. Combest	108	Double Brandy	110	Going Away	106	18,450	1:56.20	
1951	County Delight	4	J. Nichols	114	On the Mark	107	Why Not Now	116	18,650	1:58.80	
1952	Alerted	4	R. Sisto	112	Auditing	111	Hull Down	104	20,400	1:58.00	
1953	Royal Vale	5	J. Westrope	120	Cold Command	115	Crafty Admiral	126	18,800	1:51.80	
1954	Straight Face	4	B. Green	115	Golden Gloves	113	Capeador	116	19,550	1:51.00	
1955	St. Vincent	4	B. James	126	Kaster	120	Maharajah	113	20,250	2:15.40	
1956	Chevation	5	C. Rogers	117	Akbar Khan	111	Maharahah	110	21,000	2:17.40	
1957	Akbar Khan	5	E. Nelson	113	Jabneh	120	Blue Choir	116	19,675	2:16.20	
1958	Pop Corn	4	J. Ruane	110	Master Boing	122	Adare II	110	19,650	2:21.60	
1959	One-Eyed King	5	M. Ycaza	120	Oligarchy	116	Mystic II	110	18,712	2:15.40	
1960	Shield Bearer	5	N. Shuk	114	Harmonizing	126	Mystic II	114	19,070	2:32.40	
1961	Hunter's Rock	3	F. Lovato	111	Shield Bearer	120	Art Market	113	19,857	2:36.20	
1962	Wise Ship	5	H. Gustines	123	Sunshine Cake	108	El Bandito	118	41,437	2:42.40	
1963	Cedar Key	3	T. Lee	110	Mr. Steu	112	Parka	119	40,885	2:32.20	
1964	Will I Rule	4	R. Turcotte	118	Turbo Jet II	132	Your Alibhai	109	40,852	2:40.00	
1965	Or et Argent	4	W. Blum	116	Kentucky Jug	112	Desert Love	109	22,847	2:30.20	
1965	Flag	5	T. Lee	114	Ribot's Fling	109	Lancastrian	111	22,945	2:29.00	
1966	Knightly Manners	5	T. Lee	112	Marchio	110	Paoluccio	112	37,830	2:30.80	
1967	War Censor	4	E. Fires	125	Deck Hand	114	Needle Him	111	38,740	2:36.60	
1968	High Hat	4	R. Broussard	116	Irish Rebellion	117	Royal Mal'bar	112	36,270	2:29.80	
1969	Czar Alexander	4	W. Hartack	122	Taneb	117	Jean-Pierre	115	37,895	2:30.80	
1970	Fort Marcy	6	J. Velasquez	124	War Censor	112	Jungle Cove	114	37,375	2:27.40	
1971	Chompion	6	M. Hole	119	Tudor Reward	114	North Flight	116	36,920	2:34.20	
1972	Onandaga	6	J. Kurtz	110	Star Envoy	116	New Alibhai	112	38,350	2:30.00	
1973	Laplander	6	V. Bracciale Jr	111	Chrisaway	112	Wustenchef	112	38,675	2:30.40	
1974	London Company	4	A. Cordero Jr	122	Scrimshaw	110	Mister Diz	110	38,025	2:28.80	
1975	Bemo	5	C.J. McCarron	114	Outdoors	115	Drollery	114	39,325	2:33.40	
1976	Barcas	5	V. Bracciale Jr	112	One on the Aisle	122	Neapolitan Way	108	37,375	2:29.60	
1977	Improviser	5	M. Rivera	120	Grey Beret	114	Oilfield	118	56,875	2:29.40	
1978	Fluorescent Light	4	V. Bracciale Jr	114	That's a Nice	115	Improviser	118	37,343	2:33.20	
1978	Bowl Game	4	J. Velasquez	120	Oilfield	110	Trumpeter Swan	110	37,993	2:33.40	
1979	The Very One	4	C. Cooke	108	That's a Nice	116	Fluorescent Light	124	72,995	2:28.60	
1980	Marquee Universal	4	H. Pilar	118	The Very One	113	Match the Hatch	115	77,155	2:29.60	
1981	El Barril	5	J. Vasquez	116	Buckpoint	119	Birthday List	108	73,255	2:29.80	
1982	Robsphere	5	J. Velasquez	120	Present the Colors	113	Rich and Ready	115	76,960	2:30.20	
1983	Khatango	4	V. Bracciale Jr	114	London Times	108	Super Sunrise	114	75,075	2:28.60	
1984	Persian Tiara	4	R.L. Shelton	109	Crazy Moon	112	Canadian Factor	118	88,675	2:41.00	
1985	Nassipour	5	V. Bracciale Jr	115	Persian Tiara	113	C'mpters Choce	116	72,800	2:27.80	
1986	Uptown Swell	4	W. Guerra	117	Southern Sultan	112	Castelets	117	92,445	2:27.40	
1987	Akabir	6	C. Perret	115	Little Bold John	117	Vilzak	113	74,360	2:28.60	
1988	Kadial	5	G. Stevens	112	Top Guest	118	Milesius	120	71,045	2:45.00	
1989	Coeur de Lion	5	J. Cruguet	121	Dance Card Filled	115	Dynaformer	118	90,000	2:38.40	
1990	Two Moccasins	4	R.P. Romero	114	My Big Boy	115	Marksmanship	113	90,000	2:35.80	73
1991	Double Booked	6	P. Day	118	Chas' Whim	116	Opening Verse	118	90,000	1:47.00	107
1992	Sky Classic	5	P. Day	122	Fourstars Allstar	116	Social Retiree	112	90,000	1:47.80	105
1993	Lure	4	M.E. Smith	124	Star of Cozzene	119	Binary Light	115	90,000	1:47.60	109
1994	Paradise Creek	5	P. Day	124	Lure	124	Astudillo	115	90,000	1:48.40	102
1995	The Vid	5	J.D. Bailey	119	Pennine Ridge	117	Blues Traveller	115	120,000	1:52.20	111
1996	Gold And Steel	4	A. Solis	121	Same Old Wish	115	Comestock Lode	115	120,000	1:52.80	105

Year	Winner	Age	Jockey	Wt.	Second	Wt.	Third	Wt.	Win Value	Time	Beyer
1997	Ops Smile	5	E.S. Prado	115	Brave Note	115	Sharp Appeal	121	120,000	1:48.20	103
1998	Yagli	5	J.D. Bailey	121	Sky Colony	115	Blazing Sword	115	120,000	1:51.00	105
1999	Middlesex Drive	4	P. Day	115	Sky Colony	115	Divide and Conquer	115	120,000	1:48.60	97
2000	Quiet Resolve	5	R.J. Albarado	117	Haami	117	Holditholditholdit	117	120,000	1:50.42	103
2001	Hap	5	J.D. Bailey	119	Make No Mistake	119	Cynics Beware	119	120,000	1:48.56	101
2002	Strut the Stage	4	R.J. Albarado	117	Del Mar Show	119	Slew the Red	117	120,000	1:51.70	104
2003	Dr. Brendler	5	R.A. Dominguez	117	Perfect Soul	117	Sardaukar	117	120,000	1:57.78	99
2004	Mr O'Brien	5	R.A. Dominguez	119	Millennium Dragon	121	Warleigh	124	120,000	1:46.34	106

Beyer Index: 102.00

DOGWOOD BREEDERS' CUP (G3), 1 1/16 Miles, 3-Year-Old Fillies, Churchill Downs, 2004 Purse: $161,400

Year	Winner	Age	Jockey	Wt.	Second	Wt.	Third	Wt.	Win Value	Time	Beyer
1975	My Juliet	3	A. Hill	121	Snow Dolly	118	Hope She Does	118	14,999	1:24.00	
1976	T.V. Vixen	3	M. Maganello	121	Sunny Romance	116	Old Goat	121	14,154	1:23.40	
1977	Unreality	3	M. Fromin	121	Shady Lou	121	Time for Pleasure	118	15,031	1:25.40	
1978	Bold Rendezvous	3	A. Rini	121	Step in the Circle	118	Timeforaturn	118	14,446	1:23.40	
1979	Split the Tab	3	D. Haire	121	Shawn's Gal	121	Safe	121	19,663	1:24.00	
1980	Quality Corner	3	M.S. Haire	121	Forever Cordial	121	No No Nona	121	19,403	1:24.00	
1981	Savage Love	3	P. Nicolo	116	Westport Native	118	Brian's Babe	116	19,053	1:24.80	
1981	Fancy Naskra	3	J. Lively	118	Contrefaire	121	Solo Disco	118	17,948	1:25.20	
1982	Amazing Love	3	L. Melancon	117	Sefa's Beauty	117	Bold Siren	113	23,546	1:46.60	
1983	Bon Gout	3	P. Day	117	Andthebeatgoeson	112	Workin Girl	112	36,368	1:53.00	
1984	Mrs. Revere	3	L. Melancon	121	Rambling Rhythm	119	Robin's Rob	115	49,510	1:51.20	
1985	Foxy Deen	3	D. Montoya	118	Weekend Delight	120	Clouhalo	112	35,945	1:50.00	
1986	Hail a Cab	3	P.A. Johnson	119	Tall Poppy	111	Marshesseaux	114	46,810	1:46.60	
1987	Lady Gretchen	3	M. McDowell	112	Super Cook	122	Jonowo	122	46,193	1:44.00	
1988	Darien Miss	3	D. Brumfield	121	Stolie	118	Most Likely	116	35,848	1:43.80	
1989	Luthier's Launch	3	P. Day	118	Motion in Limine	116	Dreamy Mimi	121	36,465	1:45.20	
1990	Patches	3	K.K. Allen	118	Mrs. K	116	Mirth	114	34,870	1:46.60	88
1991	Be Cool	3	A.T. Gryder	121	Barri Mac	114	Saratoga Dame	121	36,560	1:46.40	79
1992	Hitch	3	B.E. Bartram	121	Bionic Soul	121	Secretly	114	36,070	1:47.60	83
1993	With a Wink	3	C.R. Woods Jr	114	Lovat's Lady	112	Unlaced	116	36,010	1:44.20	89
1994	Briar Road	3	L.Melancon	114	Stella Cielo		Shadow Miss		53,186	1:44.78	94
1995	Gal In A Ruckus	3	W.McCauley	121	Country Cat	116	Naskra Colors	114	53,527	1:43.88	104
1996	Ginny Lynn	3	L.Melancon	121	Everhope	121	Hidden Lake	114	53,576	1:43.22	99
1997	Leo's Gypsy Dancer	3	P.Day	116	Buckeye Search		Flying Lauren		68,696	1:44.95	93
1998	Really Polish	3	P.Day	116	Beat The Play	114	Victorica	114	67,642	1:44.60	94
	Nickel Classic finished second but was disqualified and placed fifth										
1999	Golden Temper	3	S.J. Sellers	116	Boom Town Girl	121	Honey Hill Lil	116	69.068	1:43.73	94
2000	Welcome Surprise	3	F.C. Torres	112	Lady Melesi	114	Vivid Sunset	114	68,014	1:46.80	86
2001	Nasty Storm	3	L.J. Meche	114	Love at Noon	114	Golly Greeley	116	68,014	1:43.41	98
2002	Take Charge Lady	3	A.J. D'Amico	121	Charmed Gift	116	Allamerican Bertie	114	67,890	1:42.73	98
2003	Golden Marlin	3	S.J. Sellers	115	Double Scoop	114	Throne	114	67,580	1:45.96	91
2004	Stellar Jayne	3	R.J. Albarado	120	Dynaville	114	Ender's Sister	122	100,068	1:43.14	98

Beyer Index: 92.53

DONN HANDICAP (G1), 1 1/8 Miles, 3-Year-Olds and Up, Gulfstream Park, 2004 Purse: $500,000

Year	Winner	Age	Jockey	Wt.	Second	Wt.	Third	Wt.	Win Value	Time	Beyer
1959	One-Eyed King	5	J. Sellers	116	Ekaba	117	General Arthur	126	17,925	2:25.80	
1960	One-Eyed King	6	M. Ycaza	121	North Pole II	114	Rafty	115	17,100	2:27.60	
1961	General Arthur	7	L. Gilligan	111	Civic Guard	112	Merry Top II	113	28,395	2:25.80	
1962	Jay Fox	4	L. Gilligan	116	Nasomo	115	Bigfork	112	26,505	2:28.40	
1963	Tutankhamen	5	W. Shoemaker	124	El Loco	112	Parka	117	27,835	2:26.00	
1964	Cedar Key	4	M. Ycaza	122	Parka	119	Suspicious	115	39,750	2:26.00	
1965	Gun Bow	5	W. Blum	127	Temper	108	Lt. Stevens	119	36,650	1:50.00	
1966	Tronado	6	B. Moreira	112	Just About	116	Selari	113	39,550	1:49.20	
1967	Francis U.	4	R.J. Campbell	111	Sky Guy	111	Quinta	117	41,100	1:50.40	
	Quinta finished second but was disqualified and placed third										
1968	Favorable Turn	4	B. Baeza	122	Rixdal	112	Ring Twice	117	45,500	1:48.20	
1969	Funny Fellow	4	B. Baeza	122	Tropic King II	115	Out the Window	114	44,200	1:49.20	
1970	Twogundan	4	E. Fires	112	Beau Brummel	114	Barely Once	113	39,600	1:51.20	
1971	Judgable	4	W. Blum	113	Snow Sporting	119	The Pruner	114	39,120	1:47.00	
1972	Going Straight	4	M. Solomone	116	Mr. Pow Wow	125	Dot Ed's Bluesky	108	37,140	1:48.20	
1973	Triumphant	4	B. Baeza	114	Second Bar	121	Gentle Smoke	113	37,560	1:47.80	
1974	Forego	4	H. Gustines	125	True Knight	123	Proud and Bold	122	39,000	1:48.60	
1975	Proud and Bold	5	G. St. Leon	118	Holding Pattern	121	Arbees Boy	119	35,280	1:48.00	
1976	Foolish Pleasure	4	B. Baeza	129	Packer Captain	114	Home Jerome	112	37,980	1:21.40	
1977	Legion	7	L. Saumell	113	Logical	114	Yamanin	124	37,440	1:48.80	
1978	Man's Man	4	R. Woodhouse	115	Intercontinent	116	Adriatico	110	39,000	1:42.20	

Year	Winner	Age	Jockey	Wt.	Second	Wt.	Third	Wt.	Win Value	Time	Beyer
1979	Jumping Hill	7	J. Fell	122	Bob's Dusty	120	Silent Cal	121	60,150	1:46.40	
1980	Lot O' Gold	4	D. Brumfield	119	Addison	111	Going Investor	112	54,600	1:48.80	
1981	Hurry Up Blue	4	C. Lopez	116	Tunerup	126	Joanie's Chief	107	51,345	1:49.00	
1982	Joanie's Chief	5	J.L. Samyn	111	Double Sonic	111	Lord Darnley	113	57,330	1:49.00	
1983	Deputy Minister	4	D. MacBeth	122	Key Count	113	Rivalero	121	60,840	1:48.60	
1984	Play Fellow	4	P. Day	122	Courteous Majesty	111	Jack Slade	114	53,955	1:49.00	
1985	Mo Exception	4	R. Breen	115	Dr. Carter	120	Key to the Moon	122	74,280	1:48.60	
1986	Creme Fraiche	4	E. Maple	122	Skip Trial	122	Minneapple	113	77,280	1:51.20	
1987	Little Bold John	5	M.A. Gonzalez	111	Skip Trial	118	Wise Times	117	96,660	1:48.80	
1988	Jade Hunter	4	J.D. Bailey	112	Cryptoclearance	123	Personal Flag	120	120,000	1:48.80	
1989	Cryptoclearance	5	J.A. Santos	121	Slew City Slew	118	Primal	117	120,000	1:50.20	
1990	Primal	5	E. Fires	120	Ole Atocha	111	Western Playboy	119	120,000	1:50.00	
1991	Jolie's Halo	4	R. Platts	114	Sports View	116	Secret Hello	116	300,000	1:47.40	125
1992	Sea Cadet	4	A. Solis	115	Out of Place	114	Sunny Sunrise	115	300,000	1:48.00	116
1993	Pistols and Roses	4	H. Castillo Jr	112	Irish Swap	118	Missionary Ridge	118	240,000	1:50.00	101
1994	Pistols and Roses	5	H. Castillo Jr	113	Eequalsmcsquared	113	Wallenda	118	180,000	1:50.60	110
1995	Cigar	5	J.D. Bailey	115	Primitive Hall	112	Bonus Money	112	180,000	1:49.60	114
1996	Cigar	6	J.D. Bailey	128	Wekiva Springs	117	Heavenly Prize	115	180,000	1:49.00	117
1997	Formal Gold	4	J. Bravo	113	Skip Away	123	Mecke	120	180,000	1:47.40	114
1998	Skip Away	5	J.D. Bailey	126	Unruled	112	Sir Bear	113	180,000	1:50.17	109
1999	Puerto Madero	5	K.J. Desormeaux	120	Behrens	113	Silver Charm	126	300,000	1:48.34	115
2000	Stephen Got Even	4	S.J. Sellers	115	Golden Missile	114	Behrens	121	300,000	1:46.40	120
2001	Captain Steve	4	J.D. Bailey	120	Albert the Great	119	Gander	115	300,000	1:48.95	115
2002	Mongoose	4	E. Prado	114	Kiss a Native	114	Rize	114	300,000	1:49.63	106
	Red Bullet finished second but was disqualified and placed fourth										
2003	Harlan's Holiday	4	J.R. Velazquez	120	Hero's Tribute	114	Puzzlement	114	300,000	1:49.17	113
2004	Medaglia d'Oro	5	J.D. Bailey	122	Seattle Fitz	113	Funny Cide	119	300,000	1:47.68	117

Beyer Index: 113.71

Distance 1 1/2 miles, turf course, prior to 1965; 1 1/16 miles in 1978; 7 furlongs in 1976

DWYER (G2), 1 1/16 Miles, 3-Year-Olds, Belmont Park, 2004 Purse: $150,000

Year	Winner	Age	Jockey	Wt.	Second	Wt.	Third	Wt.	Win Value	Time	Beyer
1918	War Cloud	3	M. Buxton	126	Jack Hare Jr.	124	Johren	127	4,850	1:50.20	
1919	Purchase	3	W. Knapp	118	Sir Barton	127	Crystal Ford	109	4,850	1:52.60	
1920	Man o' War	3	C. Kummer	126	John P. Grier	108			4,850	1:49.20	
1921	Grey Lag	3	E. Sande	123	Sporting Blood	112	Copper Demon	108	7,100	1:49.00	
1922	Ray Jay	3	C. Ponce	117	Letterman	108	Oceanic	108	7,150	1:52.60	
1923	Dunlin	3	C. Lang	123	Moonraker	108	Picketer	112	7,150	1:51.20	
1924	Ladkin	3	J. Maiben	123	Mad Play	123	Aga Khan	108	7,750	1:49.80	
1925	American Flag	3	A. Johnson	126	Dangerous	112	Silver Fox	123	8,900	2:10.60	
1926	Crusader	3	E. Sande	123	Chance Play	120	Espino	108	15,000	2:29.60	
1927	Kentucky II	3	J. Maiben	108	Chance Shot	126	Bois de Rose	108	18,500	2:31.80	
1928	Genie	3	W. Kelsay	110	Sun Beau	110	Ironsides	117	19,600	2:31.60	
1929	Grey Coat	3	S. O'Donnell	117	Blue Larkspur	124	Flag Day	110	19,450	2:34.00	
1930	Gallant Fox	3	E. Sande	126	Xenofol	110	Limbus	110	11,500	2:32.40	
1931	Twenty Grand	3	C. Kurtsinger	126	Blenheim	112	Barometer	110	11,500	2:34.40	
1932	Faireno	3	T. Malley	124	Gusto	122	Sansarica	111	12,200	2:31.40	
1933	War Glory	3	J. Gilbert	118	Jovius	116	Kerry Patch	121	4,250	2:31.80	
1934	Rose Cross	3	S. Coucci	116	Growler	116	Singing Wood	121	4,090	2:32.00	
1935	Omaha	3	W.D. Wright	126	Good Gamble	114	Cheshire	116	92,000	1:49.20	
1936	Mr. Bones	3	J. Gilbert	119	Pullman	116	Memory Book	119	8,500	1:49.80	
1937	Strabo	3	S. Renick	116	Rudie	119	Sceneshifter	116	10,750	1:51.40	
1938	The Chief	3	G. Woolf	119	Mythical King	119	Stagehand	126	8,900	1:48.40	
1939	Johnstown	3	J. Stout	126	Sun Lover	116	Challedon	126	9,250	1:48.40	
1940	Your Chance	3	W.D. Wright	116	Gen'l Manager	116	Andy K.	122	9,650	2:03.80	
1941	Whirlaway	3	E. Arcaro	126	Market Wise	122	Robert Morris	119	8,075	2:04.40	
1942	Valdina Orphan	3	C. Bierman	116	Shut Out	126	Lochinvar	119	21,150	2:01.40	
1943	Vincentive	3	J. Gilbert	111	Famous Victory	110	Princequillo	110	19,600	2:05.00	
1944	By Jimminy	3	T. Atkinson	114	Stir Up	120	Lucky Draw	120	39,170	2:03.40	
1945	Wildlife	3	T. Atkinson	116	Gallorette	116	Esteem	116	38,835	2:05.20	
1946	Assault	3	W. Mehrtens	126	Windfields	116	Lord Boswell	121	40,700	2:06.80	
1947	Phalanx	3	R. Donoso	126	But Why Not	111	Brabancon	116	40,800	2:05.80	
1948	My Request	3	T. Atkinson	121	Better Self	121	Loser Weeper	111	39,200	2:02.00	
1949	Shackleton	3	R. Bernhardt	111	One Hitter	111	Going Away	121	39,200	2:07.80	
1950	Greek Song	3	O. Scurlock	116	Hill Prince	111	LIghts Up	116	27,400	2:03.00	
1951	Battlefield	3	E. Arcaro	121	Alerted	111	Hull Down	111	39,800	2:04.40	
1952	Blue Boy	3	C. McCreary	126	Hitex	114	Golden Gloves	118	39,300	2:01.80	
1953	Native Dancer	3	E. Guerin	126	Guardian II	114	By Zeus	114	38,100	2:05.20	
1954	High Gun	3	E. Guerin	126	Palm Tree	114	Paper Tiger	114	39,300	2:05.00	

Year	Winner	Age	Jockey	Wt.	Second	Wt.	Third	Wt.	Win Value	Time	Beyer
1955	Nashua	3	E. Arcaro	126	Saratoga	122	Mainlander	114	37,200	2:03.80	
1956	Riley	3	T. Atkinson	121	Oh Johnny	123	Bill's Sky Boy	114	30,400	1:57.40	
1957	Bureaucracy	3	W. Boland	114	Little Hermit	107	Tenacious	113	30,500	1:55.40	
1958	Victory Morn	3	E. Guerin	115	Nasco	119	Day Court	112	20,270	1:58.80	
1959	Waltz	3	S. Boulmetis	121	MIddle Brother	113	Hoist Away	110	52,515	1:54.80	
1960	Francis S.	3	P.J. Bailey	119	Irish Lancer	121	Weatherwise	117	34,565	2:03.00	
1961	Hitting Away	3	H. Woodhouse	119	Baldpate	110	Beau Prince	121	54,340	2:03.80	
1962	Cyane	3	E. Nelson	116	Flying Johnnie	111	Noble Jay	119	54,957	2:01.60	
1963	Outing Class	3	R. Ussery	122	Tenacle	108	Chateaugay	129	55,250	2:01.60	
1964	Quadrangle	3	M. Ycaza	126	Malicious	120	Roman Brother	124	53,170	2:01.40	
1965	Staunchness	3	R. Ussery	114	Duc de Great	113	Hail to All	127	53,397	2:01.80	
1966	Mr. Right	3	E. Cardone	110	Exhibitionist	115	Buffle	123	53,527	2:02.80	
1967	Damascus	3	W. Shoemaker	128	Favorable Turn	112	Blasting Charge	116	54,177	2:03.00	
1968	Stage Door Johnny	3	H. Gustines	129	Out of the Way	123	Chompion	110	53,235	2:01.60	
1969	Gleaming Light	3	L. Adams	112	Jay Ray	119	Distray	112	52,747	2:04.00	
1970	Judgable	3	R. Woodhouse	108	Aggressively	112	Needles n Pens	117	54,892	2:02.60	
1971	Jim French	3	A. Cordero Jr	125	Farewell Party	113	Epic Journey	111	49,020	2:01.60	
1972	Cloudy Dawn	3	W. Hartack	118	Ruritana	112	Halo	112	51,525	2:03.20	
1973	Stop the Music	3	H. Gustines	120	Arbees Boy	115	Duc de Fl'n'gan	111	50,625	2:02.60	
1974	Hatchet Man	3	R. Turcotte	114	Rube the Great	124	Kin Run	112	51,120	2:01.20	
1975	Valid Appeal	3	J.S. Long	110	Wajima	118	Hunka Papa	116	50,400	1:48.40	
1976	Quiet Little Table	3	E. Maple	111	Sir Lister	116	Dance Spell	117	50,895	1:49.00	
1977	Bailjumper	3	A. Cordero Jr	116	Lynn Davis	112	Iron Constitution	121	48,870	1:47.60	
1978	Junction	3	J. Fell	120	Buckaroo	127	Darby Creek Road	121	47,025	1:48.80	
1979	Coastal	3	R. Hernandez	126	Private Account	114	Quiet Crossing	119	63,840	1:47.00	
1980	Amber Pass	3	D. MacBeth	114	Tempcrence Hill	129	Comptroller	119	67,440	1:49.00	
1981	Noble Nashua	3	C.B. Asmussen	119	Tap Shoes	126	Silver Express	114	68,160	1:49.20	
1982	Conquistador Cielo	3	E. Maple	126	John's Gold	114	Reinvested	119	67,560	1:46.80	
1983	Au Point	3	J.D. Bailey	114	Potentiate	114	Intention	114	68,640	1:48.20	
1984	Track Barron	3	J. Cruguet	119	Darn That Alarm	123	Slew the Coup	114	99,600	1:47.80	
1985	Stephan's Odyssey	3	L. PIncay Jr	123	Cutlass Reality	114	Important Business	126	88,500	1:49.20	
1986	Ogygian	3	W.A. Guerra	119	Johns Treasure	114	Personal Flag	114	112,680	1:48.40	
1987	Gone West	3	E. Maple	123	Pledge Card	114	Polish Navy	123	138,240	1:48.40	
1988	Seeking the Gold	3	P. Day	123	Evening Kris	119	Gay Rights	123	137,040	1:48.00	
1989	Roi Danzig	3	E. Maple	114	Contested Colors	114	Rampart Road	114	133,680	1:49.20	
1990	Profit Key	3	J.A. Santos	123	Rhythm	123	Graf	114	102,960	1:47.40	
1991	Lost Mountain	3	C. Perret	123	Smooth Performance	114	Fly So Free	126	120,000	1:49.20	102
1992	Agincourt	3	J.F. Chavez	119	Three Peat	119	Windundermywings	114	120,000	1:47.80	106
1993	Cherokee Run	3	P. Day	123	Miner's Mark	123	Silver of Silver	123	120,000	1:47.60	102
1994	Holy Bull	3	M.E. Smith	124	Twining	122	Bay Street Star	119	90,000	1:41.00	119
1995	Hoolie	3	R.G. Davis	117	Reality Road	112	Western Larla	119	90,000	1:42.60	100
1996	Victory Speech	3	J.D. Bailey	117	Gold Fever	119	Robb	117	99,000	1:41.40	109
1997	Behrens	3	J.D. Bailey	117	Glitman	114	Banker's Gold	122	90,000	1:42.20	104
1998	Coronado's Quest	3	M.E. Smith	124	Ian's Thunder	112	Scatmandu	122	90,000	1:42.40	101
1999	Forestry	3	J.D. Bailey	119	Doneraile Court	119	Successful Appeal	122	90,000	1:41.00	104
2000	Albert The Great	3	R. Migliore	115	More Than Ready	119	Red Bullet	123	90,000	1:42.62	108
2001	E Dubai	3	J.D. Bailey	121	Windsor Castle	119	Hero's Tribute	121	90,000	1:40.38	105
2002	Gygistar	3	J.R. Velazquez	121	Nothing Flat	117	American Style	115	90,000	1:42.59	97
2003	Strong Hope	3	J.R. Velazquez	115	Nacheezmo	115	Sky Mesa	119	90,000	1:41.76	110
2004	Medallist	3	J.F. Chavez	121	The Cliff's Edge	123	Sir Shackleton	121	90,000	1:40.02	112

Beyer Index: 105.64

EATONTOWN HANDICAP (G3), 1 1/16 Miles (Turf), Fillies and Mares, 3-Year-Olds and Up, Monmouth Park, 2004 Purse: $100,000

Year	Winner	Age	Jockey	Wt.	Second	Wt.	Third	Wt.	Win Value	Time	Beyer
1971	Flor de Sombra	6	H. Hinojosa	111	Ziba Blue	115	Sea Force	114	18,769	1:43.20	
1972	Telly	4	V. Bracciale Jr	115	Tico's Donna	111	Jolly Fox	114	14,454	1:42.40	
1972	Best Go	4	V. Bracciale Jr	110	Irish Party	115	Joans Paris	112	14,617	1:42.40	
1973	Telly	5	V. Bracciale Jr	113	Lightning Lucy	110	Wire Chief	111	14,763	1:43.60	
1973	Cathy Baby	4	M.A. Rivera	116	Aglimmer	116	Bold Place	117	14,633	1:42.60	
1974	Bird Boots	5	B. Thornburg	119	Belle Marie	117	Shaya	108	19,207	1:46.80	
1975	Hinterland	5	C. Perret	114	Ringmistress	114	Kudara	119	18,135	1:43.60	
1976	Collegiate	4	J.W. Edwards	113	Copano	119	Double Ack	114	14,950	1:43.60	
1976	Stage Luck	4	J.W. Edwards	118	Hinterland	114	D'sse du Val	121	14,787	1:43.20	
1977	Jolly Song	5	J. Nied Jr	112	T.V. Genie	112	All Biz	117	18,590	1:47.20	
1978	Huggle Duggle	4	B. Gonzalez	113	All Biz	118	Navajo Princess	114	22,116	1:42.60	
1979	The Very One	4	C. Cooke	116	Frosty Skater	120	Municipal Bond	113	25,236	1:46.20	
1980	Riddle's Reply	4	E. Cardone	113	Sharp Zone	111	Newmarket Lady	112	20,078	1:44.20	
1980	Nasty Jay	5	R.E. McKnight	111	T.V. Highlights	119	O'Connell Street	113	20,288	1:44.00	
1981	Wayward Lassie	4	D. Montoya	112	Earlham	114	Paris Press	114	16,958	1:44.60	

Year	Winner	Age	Jockey	Wt.	Second	Wt.	Third	Wt.	Win Value	Time	Beyer
1981	Endicotta	5	D. Brumfield	116	Dance Troupe	115	Farewell Letter	113	16,717	1:44.80	
1982	Kuja Happa	4	D.R. Wright	114	Qui Silent	113	Suave Princess	113	27,465	1:44.80	
1983	Doodle	4	J. Miranda	118	Olamic	110	Bright Choice	112	28,410	1:44.00	
1984	Jubilous	4	G. McCarron	118	Maidenhead	113	High Schemes	118	36,060	1:43.40	
1985	Agacerie	4	A. Cordero Jr	116	Meddlin Maggie	115	Naturela Grace	114	34,830	1:44.20	
1986	Mazatleca	6	C. Perret	117	Cope of Flowers	114	Darbrielle	113	27,960	1:43.20	
1986	Bharal	5	J. Velasquez	114	Thirteen Keys	114	Dawn's Curtsey	118	28,200	1:43.80	
1987	Bailrullah	5	N. Santagata	111	Princely Proof	116	Krotz	118	28,590	1:44.00	
1987	Cadabra Abra	4	W.H. McCauley	118	Treasure Map	115	Spruce Fir	121	28,110	1:43.80	
1988	Hear Music	5	M. Castaneda	115	Fancy Pan	112	Antique Mystique	111	34,440	1:49.80	
1989	Highland Penny	4	D. Carr	112	Starofanera	113	River Memories	114	34,770	1:50.00	
1990	Miss Unnameable	6	L. Saumell	113	Lip Service	116	Perfect Coin	112	34,110	1:48.00	
1991	Jacuzzi Boogie	4	N. Santagata	119	Hear the Bells	113	Be Exclusive	113	21,000	1:41.60	
1992	Red Journey	4	N. Santagata	115	Hot Times Are Here	113	Flashing Eyes	113	21,000	1:45.00	89
1993	Topsa	6	L. Rivera Jr	113	Naked Royalty	115	Suspect Terrain	115	21,000	1:46.20	87
1994	Verbal Volley	5	R. Colton	119	Irving's Girl	114	Uptown Show	113	24,000	1:44.60	92
1995	Symphony Lady	5	J. Bravo	119	Cox Orange	122	Grafin	119	30,000	1:43.60	93
1996	Gail's Brush	5	Boulanger G.	116	Plenty Of Sugar	117	Lady Affirmed	116	45,000	1:40.40	96
1997	B. A. Valentine	4	McCarron C. J.	122	Everhope	112	Vashon	112	41,460	1:41.20	96
1998	Gastronomical	5	Stevens G. L.	115	Tampico	117	Dance Clear	112	41,400	1:43.20	100
							Poopsie	114			
1999	Formal Tango	4	J.D. Bailey	113	Proud Owner	115	Natalie Too	122	60,000	1:42.62	99
2000	Reciclada	5	A. Solis	115	Mumtaz	122	Dominique's Joy	117	60,000	1:44.34	104
2001	Cousin Gigi	4	R. Wilson	115	Quidnaskra	116	Crystal Sea	113	60,000	1:47.50	101
2002	Clearly a Queen	5	E.M. Coa	119	Laurica	114	Presumed Innocent	117	60,000	1:44.02	97
2003	Stylish	5	H. Castillo Jr	118	Something Ventured	117	Sweet Deimos	113	60,000	1:41.69	95
2004	Ocean Drive	4	E.M. Coa	120	Honorable Cat	114	Fast Cookie	118	60,000	1:41.79	99

Beyer Index: 96.00

EL CAMINO REAL DERBY (G3), 1 1/16 Miles, 3-Year-Olds, Golden Gate, 2004 Purse: $200,000

Year	Winner	Age	Jockey	Wt.	Second	Wt.	Third	Wt.	Win Value	Time	Beyer
1982	Cassaleria	3	D.G. McHargue	120	Crystal Star	120	Tropic Ruler	120	76,100	1:42.80	
1983	Knightly Rapport	3	F. Toro	120	Croeso	120	Twilight Career	120	96,700	1:44.80	
1984	French Legionaire	3	R.A. Baze	120	Gate Dancer	120	Heavenly Plain	120	126,200	1:42.40	
1985	Tank's Prospect	3	J. Velasquez	120	Right Con	120	Dan's Diablo	120	151,000	1:41.00	
1986	Snow Chief	3	A. Solis	120	Badger Land	120	Darby Fair	120	137,500	1:42.60	
1987	Masterful Advocate	3	L. Pincay Jr	120	Fast Delivery	120	Hot and Smoggy	120	137,500	1:42.40	
1988	Ruhlmann	3	P. Day	117	Havanaffair	117	Chinese Gold	119	137,500	1:39.40	
1989	Double Quick	3	A. Solis	115	Rob an Plunder	119	Hawkster	122	165,000	1:43.60	
1990	Silver Ending	3	G.L. Stevens	115	Individualist I	115	Single Dawn	122	165,000	1:43.00	
1991	Sea Cadet	3	T.M. Chapman	117	General Meeting	118	Mizter Interco	122	165,000	1:40.60	
1992	Casual Lies	3	A. Petterson	117	Seahawk Gold	115	Silver Ray	122	165,000	1:42.00	90
1993	El Atroz	3	R.Q. Meza	117	Offshore Pirate	117	Lykatill Hil	119	110,000	1:43.60	85
1994	Tabasco Cat	3	P. Day	113	Flying Sensation	115	Robannier	115	110,000	1:42.60	90
1995	Jumron	3	G.F. Almeida	113	Snow Kidd'n	115	American Day	114	110,000	1:43.60	103
1996	Cavonnier	3	M.A. Pedroza	115	Sergeant Stroh	113	E C's Dream	115	110,000	1:43.40	90
1997	Pacificbounty	3	K.J. Desormeaux	120	Wild Wonder	115	Carmen's Baby	117	110,000	1:41.80	98
1998	Event of the Year	3	R.A. Baze	115	Post a Note	117	Clover Hunter	120	110,000	1:40.20	105
1999	Cliquot	3	D.R. Flores	115	Charismatic	115	No Cal Bread	117	110,000	1:43.29	95
2000	Remember Sheikh	3	F.T. Alvarado	117	True Confidence	116	Country Coast	115	110,000	1:43.47	92
2001	Hoovergetthekeys	3	R. Warren	120	Startac	120	Mo Mon	115	110,000	1:40.85	103
2002	Yougottawanna	3	J. Lumpkins	120	Danthebluegrassman	117	Lusty Latin	115	110,000	1:43.48	87
2003	Ocean Terrace	3	M.E. Smith	115	Ministers Wild Cat	117	Ten Most Wanted	115	110,000	1:42.26	93
2004	Kilgowan	3	C.J. Rollins	116	Capitano	116			110,000	1:43.87	85
					Seattle Borders	117					

Beyer Index: 93.54

EL CONEJO HANDICAP (G3), 5 1/2 Furlongs, 4-Year-Olds and Up, Santa Anita, 2004 Purse: $107,600

Year	Winner	Age	Jockey	Wt.	Second	Wt.	Third	Wt.	Win Value	Time	Beyer
1981	To B. Or Not	5	P.A. Valenzuela	122	Summer Time Guy	119	Cool Frenchy	115	35,500	1:02.40	
1982	To B. Or Not	6	C.J. McCarron	122	Belfort	116	Terresto's Singer	115	39,350	1:02.20	
1983	Pompeii Court	6	L. Pincay Jr	123	General Jimmy	115	Kangroo Court	120	39,350	1:02.80	
1984	Premiership	4	R.A. Meza	115	Haughty But Nice	116	Chip o' Lark	117	30,425	1:03.40	
1984	Night Mover	4	E. Delahoussaye	117	Dave's Friend	120	Bara Lass	117	30,525	1:03.20	
1985	Debonaire Junior	4	C.J. McCarron	126	Much Fine Gold	112	Fifty Six Ina Row	119	38,950	1:02.60	
1986	Take My Picture	4	G.L. Stevens	119	Rosie's K.T.	119	Five North	114	64,300	1:03.00	

Year	Winner	Age	Jockey	Wt.	Second	Wt.	Third	Wt.	Win Value	Time	Beyer
1988	Sylvan Express	5	E. Delahoussaye	119	Carload	117	High Brite	120	48,100	1:03.80	
1989	Sunny Blossom	4	F.H. Valenzuela	114	Sensational Star	115	Prospector's Gamble	116	47,100	1:04.60	
1990	Frost Free	5	C.J. McCarron	115	Sunny Blossom	119	Prospector's Gamble	114	45,900	1:03.00	
1991	Black Jack Road	7	G.L. Stevens	115	Laurens Quest	110	Lee's Tanthem	117	61,975	1:05.20	
1992	Gray Slewpy	4	K.J. Desormeaux	114	Frost Free	119	Cardmania	116	61,270	1:02.01	111
1993	Fabulous Champ	4	C.J. McCarron	115	Arrowtown	117	Slerp	117	63,800	1:02.66	105
1994	Gundaghia	7	E. Delahoussaye	116	Sir Hutch	114	Davy Be Good	118	64,800	1:02.01	108
1995	Phone Roberto	6	C.J. McCarron	114	Lost Pan	115	Rotsaluck	112	65,000	1:02.34	101
1996	Lit de Justice	6	C.S. Nakatani	119	A.J. Jett	112	Fu Man Slew	116	64,250	1:01.85	114
1997	High Stakes Player	5	C.S. Nakatani	116	Kern Ridge	113	Subtle Trouble	114	63,850	1:02.89	107
1998	The Exeter Man	6	G.K. Gomez	114	Tower Full	117	Red	114	64,020	1:02.23	107
1999	Kona Gold	5	A. Solis	119	Big Jag	117	Mr. Doubledown	118	64,380	1:01.74	115
2000	Freespool	4	C.J. McCarron	114	Mellow Fellow	115	Old Topper	116	64,200	1:03.33	106
2001	Freespool	4	C.J. McCarron	115	Men's Exclusive	117	Lexicon	118	65,220	1:02.50	107
2002	Snow Ridge	4	M.E. smith	114	Explicit	117	Rio Oro	117	65,700	1:03.05	102
2003	Kona Gold	9	A. Solis	123	Radiata	115	No Armistice	116	65,280	1:02.63	109
2004	Boston Common	5	G.L. Stevens	117	Summer Service	112	King Robyn	119	64,560	1:02.35	105

Beyer Index: 107.46

The 2001 running took place in Dec. 2000

EL ENCINO (G2), 1 1/16 Miles, 4-Year-Old Fillies, Santa Anita, 2004 Purse: $150,000

Year	Winner	Age	Jockey	Wt.	Second	Wt.	Third	Wt.	Win Value	Time	Beyer
1968	Hill Shine	4	A. Pineda	119	Aurelius II	117	Khalborough	115	14,650	1:42.60	
1969	Gene's Dancer	4	E. Fires	114	Royal Comedian	122	Injunction	119	15,200	1:43.40	
1971	Efa	5	D. Pierce	114	Crimson Hills	115	M'nt'na W'ds	115	16,900	1:41.80	
1972	Thorn	4	J. Sellers	115	Wildcat Hills	115	Efa	117	19,550	1:42.00	
1973	Class A	5	D. Tierney	122	Sitka D.	119	Cabin	119	18,950	1:44.60	
1974	Wild World	5	W. Shoemaker	118	Class A	115	Proper Escort	112	18,150	1:49.80	
1975	Triggairo	6	D. Pierce	119	Benson	116	Lanquinet	119	19,700	1:49.40	
1976	Fascinating Girl	4	S. Hawley	115	Bold Baby	115	Just a Kick	121	18,850	1:42.40	
1977	Woodsome	4	M. Sellers	115	Lucie Manet	115	Granja Sueno	115	27,450	1:42.20	
1978	Taisez Vous	4	D. Pierce	121	Little Happiness	116	Table the Rumor	121	30,200	1:41.80	
1979	B. Thoughtful	4	D. Pierce	121	Queen Yasma	116	Petron's Love	114	38,200	1:41.40	
1980	It's in the Air	4	L. Pincay Jr	124	Prize Spot	121	Glorious Song	116	38,750	1:41.20	
1981	Princess Karenda	4	E. Delahoussaye	122	Swift Bird	117	Lisawan	114	49,650	1:42.00	
1982	Edge	4	C.B. Asmussen	114	Safe Play	119	Northern Fable	117	68,000	1:41.20	
1983	Beautiful Glass	4	C.J. McCarron	119	Header Card	119	Skillful Joy	122	50,550	1:41.20	
1984	Lovlier Linda	4	W. Shoemaker	117	Weekend Surprise	117	Angel Savage	114	51,250	1:42.00	
1985	Mitterand	4	E. Delahoussaye	119	Percipient	117	Allusion	117	61,600	1:42.00	
1986	Lady's Secret	4	C.J. McCarron	124	Shywing	119	Sharp Ascent	119	65,850	1:41.80	
1987	Seldom Seen Sue	4	W. Shoemaker	114	Miraculous	117	Top Corsage	122	61,850	1:43.00	
1988	By Land By Sea	4	F. Toro	115	Very Subtle	122	Annoconnor	114	64,300	1:41.60	
1989	Goodbye Halo	4	P. Day	124	T.V. of Crystal	117	Savannah's Honor	114	60,200	1:41.80	
1990	Akinemod	4	G.L. Stevens	119	Luthier's Launch	117	Kelly	116	62,900	1:41.20	119
1991	A Wild Ride	4	C.J. McCarron	122	Highland Tide	114	Somethingmerry	117	63,500	1:42.40	103
1992	Exchange	4	L. Pincay Jr	117	Grand Girlfriend	115	Damewood	115	67,000	1:43.20	99
1993	Pacific Squall	4	C.J. McCarron	119	Avian Assembly	117	Magical Maiden	119	63,900	1:45.60	96
1994	Supah Gem	4	C.S. Nakatani	117	Sensational Eyes	117	Stalcreek	119	64,500	1:41.20	100
1995	Klassy Kim	4	K.J. Desormeaux	117	Twice the Vice	119	Crissy Aya	115	61,400	1:42.40	102
1996	Jewel Princess	4	A. Solis	117	Sleep Easy	119	Urbane	119	78,800	1:41.80	104
1997	Belle's Flag	4	C.S. Nakatani	119	Housa Dancer	115	Listening	119	82,650	1:41.60	103
1998	Fleet Lady	4	G.K. Gomez	117	Minister's Melody	117	I Ain't Bluffing	119	96,840	1:43.00	104
	I Ain't Bluffing finished first but was disqualified and placed third										
1999	Manistique	4	G.L. Stevens	119	Gourmet Girl	117	Magical Allure	119	90,000	1:43.20	95
2000	Olympic Charmer	4	C.J. McCarron	119	Her She Kisses	115	Smooth Player	117	97,470	1:42.71	99
2001	Chilukki	4	G.L. Stevens	119	Spain	122	Queenie Belle	119	90,000	1:42.55	96
2002	Affluent	4	E. Delahoussaye	119	Royally Chosen	117	Sea Reel	115	90,000	1:42.60	98
2003	Got Koko	4	A. Solis	119	Bella Bellucci	117	Bare Necessities	119	90,000	1:42.25	107
2004	Victory Encounter	4	M.E. Smith	117	Personal Legend	115	Cat Fighter	115	90,000	1:42.52	90

Beyer Index: 101.00

ELKHORN (G3), 1 1/2 Miles (Turf), 4-Year-Olds and Up, Keeneland Race Course, 2004 Purse: $150,000

Year	Winner	Age	Jockey	Wt.	Second	Wt.	Third	Wt.	Win Value	Time	Beyer
1988	Yankee Affair	6	P. Day	123	Stormonthel'se	118	Blazing Bart	123	56,485	1:49.60	
1989	Exclusive Partner	7	F. Toro	120	Yankee Affair	120	Pappas Swing	120	54,958	1:50.40	
1990	Ten Keys	6	R.P. Romero	123	Yankee Affair	123	Maceo	118	71,460	1:51.80	105

Year	Winner	Age	Jockey	Wt.	Second	Wt.	Third	Wt.	Win Value	Time	Beyer
1991	Itsallgreektome	4	R.A. Baze	123	Pirate Army	113	Spark O'Dan	113	71,143	1:51.20	
1992	Fourstars Allstar	4	J.D. Bailey	113	Slew the Slewor	120	Rainbows for Life	120	79,490	1:47.60	100
1993	Coaxing Matt	4	P. Day	118	Cleone	113	Maxigroom	118	68,572	1:47.60	104
1994	Lure	5	M.E. Smith	123	Buckhar	120	Pride of Summer	120	66,526	1:53.60	109
1995	Marvin's Faith	4	C. Perret	123	Hasten to Add	120	Opera Score	120	70,680	1:47.00	101
1996	Vladivostok	6	P. Day	112	Penn Fifty Three	114	Party Season	119	68,262	2:30.80	102
1997	Chief Bearhart	4	J.A. Santos	114	Snake Eyes	113	Lassigny	122	68,324	2:28.40	104
1998	African Dancer	6	J.D. Bailey	114	Chief Bearhart	122	Chorwon	114	66,712	2:31.60	104
1999	African Dancer	7	J.D. Bailey	114	Magest	114	Chorwon	113	68,138	2:27.84	104
2000	Drama Critic	4	J.D. Bailey	116	Craigsteel	116	Dixie's Crown	116	69,750	2:28.03	101
2001	Williams News	6	R.J. Albarado	116	Gritty Sandie	116	Craigsteel	116	70,308	2:29.13	102
2002	Kim Loves Bucky	5	J.F. Chavez	116	Rochester	116	Cetewayo	118	93,000	2:32.49	98
2003	Kim Loves Bucky	6	K.J. Desormeaux	117	Man From Wicklow	123	Williams News	116	93,000	2:29.39	105
2004	Epicentre	5	J.D. Bailey	116	Rochester	116	Art Variety	116	93,000	2:31.96	99

Beyer Index: 102.71

ENDINE HANDICAP (G3), 6 Furlongs, Fillies and Mares, 3-Year-Olds and Up, Delaware Park, 2004 Purse: $200,300

Year	Winner	Age	Jockey	Wt.	Second	Wt.	Third	Wt.	Win Value	Time	Beyer
1971	Royal Signal	4	M. Hole	119	I'm for Mama	119	Faneuil Hall	112	19,272	1:10.80	
1972	Main Pan	4	W.J. Passmore	114	Alma North	120	Secret Retreat	113	18,850	1:11.20	
1973	Light Hearted	4	E. Neilson	118	Barely Even	125	Levee Night	113	18,525	1:10.00	
1974	Miss Rebound	6	B. Baeza	123	Flo's Pleasure	116	Gallant Davelle	116	19,045	1:10.00	
1975	Honky Star	4	J. Tejeira	119	Laraka	117	Sailingon	114	18,655	1:11.00	
1976	Donetta	5	J.W. Moseley	118	Susie's Last	112	Crackerfax	115	17,145	1:12.00	
1977	My Juliet	5	A.S. Black	127	Debby's Turn	115	Catabias	113	17,973	1:09.60	
1978	Dainty Dotsie	4	B. Phelps	127	Spot Two	123	Debby's Turn	113	21,450	1:09.60	
1979	Quatre Saisons	4	V. Bracciale Jr	115	Shanachie	112	Order in Court	115	21,580	1:12.00	
1980	Candy Eclair	4	J.D. Bailey	126	Wonderous Me	108	Grecian Victory	112	29,803	1:09.80	
1981	Veiled Look	5	W.J. Passmore	120	Rejuvavate	113	Tequila Sheila	109	17,875	1:08.80	
1982	Wading Power	4	H. Pilar	107	Bravo Native	108	Lady Dean	123	14,723	1:10.80	
1996	Hay Hanne	4	J.A. Velez Jr	114	Know B's	116	Ayrial Delight	122	22,770	1:10.20	95
1997	Dancin Renee	3	J.A. Velez Jr	122	Two Punch Lil	122	Ana Belen	113	30,000	1:10.00	101
1998	Soverign Lady	4	M.E. Smith	115	Weather Vane	122	Little Sister	117	45,000	1:09.40	106
1999	Hurricane Bertie	4	P. Day	117	Little Sister	119	Bourbon Belle	119	60,000	1:08.75	109
2000	Superduper Miss	4	T. Turner	114	Debby d'Or	119	Cassidy	119	60,000	1:10.22	95
2001	Xtra Heat	3	R. Wilson	118	Ivy's Jewel	118	Big Bambu	121	90,000	1:09.64	117
2002	Xtra Heat	4	H. Vega	121	Outstanding Info	118	Urban Dancer	118	90,000	1:10.91	100
2003	House Party	3	J.A. Santos	117	Vision in Flight	114	Mooji Moo	115	120,000	1:08.35	108
2004	Ebony Breeze	4	H. Castillo Jr	119	Umpateedle	117	Bronze Abe	119	120,000	1:09.73	101

Beyer Index: 103.56

ESSEX HANDICAP (G3), 1 1/16 Miles 4-Year-Olds and Up, Oaklawn Park, 2004 Purse: $100,000

Year	Winner	Age	Jockey	Wt.	Second	Wt.	Third	Wt.	Win Value	Time	Beyer
1976	Navajo	6	J. Nichols	123	My Friend Gus	121	Bold Trap	113	34,950	1:41.00	
1977	Go to the Bank	5	G. Patterson	111	Romeo	119	Limited Ad't'n	114	37,260	1:42.40	
1978	Cisk	5	G. Patterson	117	Forever Casting	114	Oui Henry	117	36,570	1:41.60	
1980	J. Burns	5	J. McKnight	113	Convenient	114	Dar'ng Damacus	115	35,220	1:42.80	
1981	Prince Majestic	7	G. Patterson	117	Blue Ensign	114	Uncool	117	34,650	1:42.40	
1982	Plaza Star	4	R.P. Romero	118	Vodika Collins	118	Tally Ho the Fox	116	37,950	1:42.80	
1983	Eminency	5	W. Nemeti	121	Dance Pavilion	113	Majestys Prince	125	38,670	1:42.40	
1984	Le Cou Cou	4	D.L. Howard	119	Hi Pi	120	Double Ready	114	36,480	1:41.80	
1985	Star Choice	6	J. McKnight	121	Plaza Star	115	Shamtastic	112	49,260	1:40.60	
1986	Double Ready	6	D.E. Whited	113	Red Attack	112	Kohzaam	112	51,060	1:41.60	
1987	Sun Master	6	R.L. Frazier	116	Royal Troon	112	Lyphard's Ridge	111	36,750	1:41.00	
1988	Savings	5	P.A. Johnson	117	Entitled To	117	Red Attack	115	43,680	1:42.60	
1989	Proper Reality	4	J.D. Bailey	120	Contact Game	111	Lyphard's Ridge	112	34,530	1:44.00	
1990	Forli Light	4	D. Guillory	115	Momsfurrari	115	Traskwood	115	36,930	1:42.80	113
1991	Greydar	4	P. Day	117	Silent Survivor	120	The Great Carl	112	34,770	1:42.00	107
1992	Allijeba	6	P. Day	118	On the Edge	113	Bedeviled	116	34,500	1:43.80	98
1993	Delafield	4	P. Day	113	Famed Devil	117	Yukon Robbery	116	33,900	1:42.00	103
1994	Greatsilverfleet	4	Gomez GK	116	Prize Flight	113	All Gone	111	32,250	1:42.00	106
1995	Silver Goblin	4	Cordova DW	122	Prince of the Mt.	113	Golden Gear	113	33,150	1:42.00	110
1996	Classic Fit	6	C.V. Gonzalez	114	Judge TC	122	Juliannus	113	47,700	1:42.80	107
1997	No Spend No Glow	5	R.N. Lester	113	Illesam	113	Auggie My Dad	111	45,000	1:45.80	100
1998	Relic Reward	4	C.H. Borel	113	Phnatom on Tour	119	Brush With Pride	116	45,000	1:43.80	108
1999	Brush With Pride	7	T.T. Doocy	116	Littlebitlively	115	Treat Me Doc	114	45,000	1:43.26	103

Year	Winner	Age	Jockey	Wt.	Second	Wt.	Third	Wt.	Win Value	Time	Beyer
2000	Maysville Slew	4	L.S. Quinonez	115	Sand Ridge	112	Mr Ross	116	45,000	1:44.12	98
2001	Mr Ross	6	D. Pettinger	117	Remington Rock	114	Maysville Slew	118	45,000	1:43.59	101
2002	Crafty Shaw	4	J. Lopez	116	Kiss of Lion	113	Remington Rock	116	45,000	1:43.14	113
2003	Colorful Tour	4	L.S. Quinonez	116	Ask the Lord	118	Premeditation	117	60,000	1:46.62	99
2004	Private Emblem	5	T.T. Doocy	113	Pie n Burger	118	Crafty Shaw	118	60,000	1:43.66	101

Beyer Index: 104.47

EXCELSIOR BREEDERS' CUP HANDICAP (G3), 1 1/8 Miles, 3-Year-Olds and Up, Aqueduct, 2004 Purse: $196,000

Year	Winner	Age	Jockey	Wt.	Second	Wt.	Third	Wt.	Win Value	Time	Beyer
1903	Blackstock	4	G.C. Fuller	98	Heno	116	Yel. Tail	100	6,730	1:46.60	
1904	Rostand	4	H. Phillips	105	Red Knight	112	Lord Barge	99	6,600	1:45.60	
1905	Santa Catalina	3	W. Miller	95	Rapid Water	119	Sinister	94	6,450	1:46.40	
1906	Merry Lark	4	W. Miller	106	Ormonde's Right	111	Eug. Burch	110	7,350	1:47.20	
1907	Dr. Gardner	4	J. Martin	123	Glorifier	115	Cairngorm	115	7,350	1:48.20	
1908	McCarter	4	J. Notter	113	Jack Atkin	119	Rifleman	111	6,850	1:46.00	
1910	Guy Fisher	4	E. Taplin	100	Fayette	112	Arasee	106	1,925	1:46.00	
1913	Meridian	5	J. Glass	120	Cock o' the Walk	114	Lahore	113	2,575	1:44.60	
1915	Addie M.	3	J. McCahey	97	Stromboli	122	Short Grass	123	1,925	1:45.80	
1916	Sand Marsh	4	J. Butwell	111	Flying Fairy	111	Slumber II	113	2,425	1:46.00	
1917	Roamer	6	A. Schuttinger	123	Borrow	117	Old Koenig	112	2,825	1:45.40	
1918	George Smith	5	W. Kelsay	117	Roamer	120	W. Hogan	122	3,850	1:45.40	
1919	Naturalist	5	C. Fairbrother	122	Star Master	119	Boniface	108	3,850	1:45.40	
1920	Boniface	5	E. Sande	117	Lanius	112	Naturalist	122	4,850	1:45.20	
1921	Blazes	4	T. Rice	118	Exterminator	120	Naturalist	126	8,550	1:47.20	
1922	Sennings Park	6	C. Fairbrother	115	Mad Hatter	129	Vel. Hand	126	5,850	1:44.80	
1923	Grey Lag	5	L. Fator	130	Exodus	111	Prince James	112	5,850	1:45.00	
1924	Rialto	4	J. Corcoran	115	Sunsini	102	Zev	133	5,850	1:46.00	
1925	Sting	4	B. Breuning	106	Cherry Pie	111	Mad Play	124	5,850	1:42.60	
1926	Turf Idol	4	S. Hebert	108	Cherry Pie	107	Wilderness	111	6,400	1:45.60	
1927	Amberjack	4	J. McCoy	102	Cherry Pie	110	Navigator	108	6,200	1:44.00	
1928	Brown Flash	4	V. Peterson	114	Herodian	105	Grey Lag	118	6,200	1:46.40	
1929	Mowlee	4	L. Fator	115	Son o' Battle	106	Mi Vida	108	7,200	1:45.20	
1930	Minotaur	4	C. Kurtsinger	106	Sandy Ford	114	Comstockery	107	5,950	1:45.80	
1931	Mokatam	4	W. Kelsay	126	Flaming	107	Maya	110	5,700	1:46.00	
1932	Pompeius	3	L. Knapp	105	Mountain Elk	114	Light. Bolt	116	4,850	1:45.20	
1934	Watch Him	5	S. Steffen	108	Caesars Ghost	112	Mr. Khayyam	123	2,450	1:46.00	
1935	King Saxon	4	C. Rainey	120	Okapi	109	Coequel	102	5,430	1:43.80	
1936	King Saxon	5	C. Landolt	121	Good Harvest	108	Esposa	102	5,400	1:45.20	
1937	Thorson	5	W. Ray	107	Memory Book	116	Whopper	127	6,950	1:43.80	
1938	Caballero II	6	W.D. Wright	114	Tatterdemalion	112	Teufel	112	6,650	1:45.40	
1939	Thanksgiving	4	R. Workman	120	Fighting Fox	120	Tatterdemalion	114	6,950	1:44.20	
1940	The Chief	5	I. Anderson	112	Sandy Boot	108	Anthology	108	6,200	1:44.20	
1941	Robert Morris	3	N. Wall	100	Olympus	102	Corydon	112	8,275	1:44.60	
1942	Olympus	7	C. Wahler	105	Boysy	114	Sir Jeffrey	106	8,775	1:46.80	
1943	Riverland	5	S. brooks	124	Minee-Mo	108	Marriage	121	9,300	1:44.40	
1944	Alex Barth	4	N. Jemas	105	Grey Wing	109	Boysy	114	7,375	1:46.40	
1945	Saguaro	4	M. Caffarella	108	Dockstader	106	Rounders	113	7,070	1:44.60	
1946	Fighting Step	4	J. Adams	123	King Dorsett	115	Lets Dance	111	12,750	1:45.00	
1947	Coincidence	5	T. Atkinson	115	Polynesian	126	Lets Dance	112	15,900	1:44.00	
1948	Knockdown	5	F. Zufelt	114	Double Jay	125	Stymie	128	20,750	1:46.00	
1949	My Request	4	C. Erickson	126	Vulcan's Forge	123	Nearway	113	16,700	1:44.80	
1950	Arise	4	D. Dodson	116	Olympia	126	Delegate	119	17,200	1:43.80	
1951	Lotowhite	4	E. Arcaro	116	Ferd	123	Great Circle	119	20,750	1:44.20	
1952	Spartan Valor	4	J. Stout	126	Greek Ship	122	Sonic	108	18,950	1:44.60	
1953	First Glance	6	E. Guerin	118	Bryan G.	119	Dark Count	106	20,500	1:44.00	
1954	Find	4	E. Guerin	121	Count Cain	112	Capeador	119	21,250	1:44.00	
1955	Fisherman	4	H. Woodhouse	126	Joe Jones	119	Gold'n Gloves	112	20,450	1:45.00	
1956	Find	6	E. Guerin	116	Joe Jones	119	Fisherman	122	19,800	1:43.20	
1957	Midafternoon	5	E. Arcaro	126	Beam Rider	110	Pylades	112	19,750	1:43.60	
1958	Kingmaker	5	R. Ussery	126	Third Brother	124	Beam Rider	114	18,615	1:43.60	
1959	Whitley	4	S. Boulmetis	116	Mystic II	118	Grey Monarch	118	18,485	1:43.80	
1960	Talent Show	5	R. Broussard	119	Nimmer	115			18,745	1:34.80	
1961	Mail Order	5	L. Adams	120	Disperse	114	All Hands	118	19,110	1:49.20	
1962	Hitting Away	4	R. Ussery	116	Up Scope	113	Manassa Mauler	114	18,557	1:50.00	
1963	Greek Money	4	J.L. Rotz	115	Misty Day	112	Rebellious	108	18,265	1:48.60	
1964	Uppercut	5	J. Sellers	112	Rocky Link	116	Morry E.	115	17,875	1:50.00	
1965	Tenacle	5	W. Mayorga	110	Tibaldo	118	Quita Dude	114	35,750	1:49.40	
1966	Choker	6	R. Ussery	115	Point du Jour	113	Quita Dude	116	36,010	1:49.20	
1968	Peter Piper	5	J. Velasquez	112	Straight Deal	115	Grace Born	112	35,945	1:48.00	

Year	Winner	Age	Jockey	Wt.	Second	Wt.	Third	Wt.	Win Value	Time	Beyer
1969	San Roque	4	H. Gustines	112	Tropic King II	120	Juvenile John	120	37,310	1:49.60	
1970	Hydrologist	4	C. Baltazar	119	Never Bow	119	Gaelic Dancer	118	37,570	1:48.80	
1971	Loud	4	J. Vasquez	116	Personality	126	Knight in Armor	110	34,200	1:50.80	
1972	Autobiography	4	A. Cordero Jr	123	Native Royalty	115	Urgent Message	119	34,860	1:49.00	
1973	Key to the Mint	4	R. Turcotte	126	King's Bishop	115	North Sea	120	32,640	1:47.80	
1974	Everton II	5	M. Castaneda	117	Prince Dantan	123	Three or Less	108	33,840	1:49.00	
1975	Step Nicely	5	A. Cordero Jr	126	Monetary Principle	113	Jolly Johu	119	33,990	1:48.40	
1976	Double Edge Sword	6	A. Cordero Jr	112	Northerly	115	Sharp Gary	119	51,120	1:48.20	
1977	Turn and Count	4	S. Cauthen	123	Festive Mood	115	Gabe Benzur	112	48,150	1:51.00	
1978	Cox's Ridge	4	E. Maple	129	Pumpkin Moonshine	108	Nearly on Time	113	49,005	1:50.60	
1979	Special Tiger	4	G. Martens	113	Mister Brea	125	Coverack	112	63,600	2:03.80	
1980	Ring of Light	5	C.B. Asmussen	114	Silent Cal	122	Rivalero	118	67,560	2:01.40	
1981	Irish Tower	4	J. Fell	127	Ring of Light	113	Relaxing	125	64,680	2:00.80	
1982	Globe	5	M. Venezia	112	Accipiter's Hope	116	Bar Dexter	118	66,480	2:03.40	
1983	Fast Gold	4	J.L. Samyn	114	Turn Bold	107	Sing Sing	124	67,200	2:04.00	
1984	Canadian Factor	4	J. Velasquez	117	Luv a Libra	117	Canadian Calm	108	102,150	2:03.00	
1985	Morning Bob	4	J. Vasquez	112	Lord of the Manor	112	Last Turn	110	67,750	2:04.20	
1986	Garthorn	6	R.Q. Meza	124	Nordance	110	Broadway T'mmy	107	101,340	2:02.40	
1987	Lac Ouimet	4	E. Maple	114	Alioth	113	Proud Debonair	115	106,380	2:02.00	
1988	Lac Ouimet	5	J.D. Bailey	116	Personal Flag	117	Talinum	116	140,880	2:00.20	
1989	Forever Silver	4	J.A. Krone	111	Its Acedemic	113	Jack of Clubs	113	99,720	2:02.60	
1990	Lay Down	6	C.W. Antley	112	Lac Ouimet	113	Doc's Leader	112	100,980	2:02.20	108
1991	Chief Honcho	4	M.E. Smith	117	I'm Sky High	115	Apple Current	115	102,060	2:02.60	113
1992	Defensive Play	5	D.R. Flores	117	Alyten	111	Will to Reign	108	102,780	2:01.80	112
1993	Devil His Due	4	M.E. Smith	117	Exotic Slew	109	Bill of Rights	112	72,120	2:03.00	110
1994	Colonial Affair	4	J.A. Santos	121	Contract Court	109	West by West	116	90,000	1:49.80	110
1995	Iron Gavel	5	J.R. Martinez J	111	Electrojet	114	Danzig's Dance	115	90,000	1:49.20	115
1996	May I Inquire	7	J. Bravo	111	Personal Merit	114	Ormsby	115	120,000	1:50.60	105
1997	Ormsby	5	C.C. Lopez	116	Greatsilverfleet	112	Circle of Light	111	120,000	1:47.60	121
1998	Sir Bear	5	E.M. Jurado	117	K.J.'s Appeal	117	Accelerator	111	120,000	1:49.20	108
1999	Smart Coupons	6	R.R. Douglas	114	Archers Bay	118	Pasay	112	120,000	1:49.71	102
2000	Lager	6	H. Castillo Jr	113	Best of Luck	114	Chester House	117	120,000	1:49.76	109
2001	Cat's at Home	4	F. Leon	115	Top Official	113	Boston Party	115	120,000	1:48.92	112
2002	John Little	4	N. Arroyo Jr	111	Windsor Castle	113	Ground Storm	118	120,000	1:49.25	109
2003	Classic Endeavor	5	C.C. Lopez	113	Balto Star	119	Tempest Fugit	114	90,000	1:48.10	105
2004	Funny Cide	4	J.A. Santos	120	Evening Attire	119	Host	114	120,000	1:49.57	109

Beyer Index: 109.87

FAIR GROUNDS OAKS (G2), 1 1/16 Miles, 3-Year-Old Fillies, Fair Grounds, 2004 Purse: $300,000

Year	Winner	Age	Jockey	Wt.	Second	Wt.	Third	Wt.	Win Value	Time	Beyer
1966	Help on Way	3	L. Gilligan	115	Dutch Maid	115	Ge Ma	115	9,350	1:52.60	
1967	Furl Sail	3	J.R. Lopez	121	Nancy Jr.	118	Filly Folly	115	10,550	1:45.20	
1968	Trapeze	3	J. Nichols	115	Sale Day	115	Le Bijou	115	11,325	1:46.20	
1969	Royal Fillet	3	L. Moyers	121	Around the Horn	115	Scat Kat	115	9,850	1:46.60	
1970	Kay Emy	3	M. Heath	118	Lady Vi-E.	113	Ellen Girl	113	12,075	1:47.60	
1971	Rosemone Bow	3	K. Knapp	121	Cruline	112	Olney's Pet	112	10,925	1:43.40	
1972	My Charmer	3	L. Melancon	112	Color Me Blue	112	Bugle Bow	115	14,350	1:46.00	
1973	Knitted Gloves	3	J.C. Espinoza	118	Fussy Girl	121	Westward	118	14,825	1:46.00	
1974	Bold Rosie	3	P. Rubbicco	118	Trade Me Later	112	Kaye's Co'mander	118	20,625	1:46.60	
1975	Lucky Leslie	3	D. Brumfield	118	Regal Rumor	121	Decanter	118	19,650	1:46.60	
1976	Bronze Point	3	H. Arroyo	118	Little Broadway	118	Confort Zone	118	20,075	1:44.40	
1977	Table the Rumor	3	W. Shoemaker	112	La Doree	112	Ivory Castle	118	57,800	1:52.40	
1978	Shadycroft Lady	3	R. Martinez Jr	109	Miss Baja	117	B'lle of D'ge Me	114	25,738	1:52.60	
1978	La Doree	4	B. Fann	107	Royal Graustark	114	B'rn the M'n'y	107	25,738	1:52.40	
1980	Honest and True	3	A. Guajardo	118	Smart Angle	121	Lady Taurian Peace	118	33,875	1:44.40	
1981	Truly Bound	3	W. Shoemaker	121	Lou's Dance	118	Sunwontshine	112	61,400	1:44.80	
1982	Before Dawn	3	J. Velasquez	121	Girlie	121	Linda North	118	66,400	1:45.40	
1983	Bright Crocus	3	S. Hawley	121	Miss Molly	118	Shamivor	115	66,100	1:45.80	
1984	My Darling One	3	C.J. McCarron	112	Texas Cowgirl Nite	118	Rays Joy	112	101,400	1:44.60	
1985	Marshua's Echelon	3	R.J. Franklin	121	Golden Silence	113	Little Biddy Comet	118	113,400	1:44.80	
1986	Tiffany Lass	3	R.L. Frazier	121	Patricia J.K.	121	Turn and Dance	112	97,400	1:45.00	
1987	Up the Apalachee	3	M.R. Torres	121	Cathy Quick	118	Out of the Bid	121	60,000	1:45.40	
1988	Quite a Gem	3	E.J. Perrodin	115	False Glitter	118	Sable Decor	118	59,580	1:46.40	
1989	Mistaurian	3	D. Valiente	113	Affirmed Classic	121	Exquisite Mistress	118	57,900	1:44.80	
1990	Pampered Star	3	S.P. Romero	112	Windansea	118	Gayla's Pleasure	115	59,520	1:44.60	
1991	Rare Pick	3	P.A. Johnson	112	Nalees Pin	121	Lady Blockbuster	118	65,640	1:46.40	93
1992	Prospectors Delite	3	P. Day	118	Glitzi Bj	118	Desert Radiance	118	63,990	1:44.20	92
1993	Silky Feather	3	E.J. Perrodin	113	She's a Little Shy	121	Sum Runner	121	64,080	1:43.80	87

Year	Winner	Age	Jockey	Wt.	Second	Wt.	Third	Wt.	Win Value	Time	Beyer
1994	Two Altazano	3	Leblanc KP	112	Tricky Code	121	Minority Dater	112	93,840	1:42.40	101
1995	Brushing Gloom	3	Brown JE	112	Kuda	118	Legendary Princess	121	90,000	1:45.00	84
1996	Bright Time	3	L.F. Diaz	112	Mackie	121	Proper Dance	114	90,000	1:45.80	82
1997	Blushing K.D.	3	L. Meche	121	Tomisue's Delight	121	Cozy Blues	112	105,000	1:42.20	102
1998	Lu Ravi	3	W. Martinez	112	Well Chosen	112	Silent Eskimo	112	180,000	1:43.60	89
1999	Silverbulletday	3	G.L. Stevens	121	Runaway Venus	112	Brushed Halory	114	210,000	1:44.80	101
2000	Shawnee Country	3	D.J. Meche	121	Eden Lodge	121	Zoftig	121	210,000	1:44.81	92
2001	Real Cozzy	3	E. Martin Jr	121	Mystic Lady	121	She's a Devil Due	121	210,000	1:44.58	86
2002	Take Charge Lady	3	A.J. D'Amico	121	Lake Lady	121	Chamrousse	121	210,000	1:43.30	107
2003	Lady Tak	3	D.J. Meche	121	Atlantic Ocean	121	Belle of Perintown	121	210,000	1:44.36	95
2004	Ashado	3	C.H. Velasquez	121	Victory U.S.A.	121	Shadow Cast	121	180,000	1:43.07	94

Beyer Index: 93.21

FALL HIGHWEIGHT HANDICAP (G3), 6 Furlongs, 3-Year-Olds and Up, Aqueduct, 2004 Purse: $111,600

Year	Winner	Age	Jockey	Wt.	Second	Wt.	Third	Wt.	Win Value	Time	Beyer
1914	Comely	2	J. McCahey	110	Forum	120	Surprising	124	1,275	1:12.00	
1915	Harmonicon	5	J. Notter	140	Flittergold	128	H. Prynne	124	1,195	1:10.80	
1916	Mount d'Or	5	J. Notter	133	Short Grass	135	Hidden Star	112	1,230	1:13.20	
1917	Ima Frank	4	J. McTaggart	111	Hank O'Day	126	H'wfa	100	1,410	1:11.80	
1918	Hollister	4	J. Loftus	123	Ima Frank	108	Papp	120	2,100	1:10.00	
1919	Naturalist	5	C. Fairbrother	140	Billy Kelly	108	Enfilade	116	2,900	1:11.60	
1920	Lion d'Or	4	E. Sande	134	On Watch	124	Naturalist	145	3,100	1:09.80	
1921	Crocus	3	Coltiletti	122	Krewer	128	Step Lightly	107	2,725	1:11.20	
1922	Careful	4	J. Butwell	126	Prodigious	108	Exodus	128	3,300	1:12.60	
1923	Fair Phantom	4	E. Sande	122	Runviso	115	Dunlin	123	3,275	1:10.40	
1924	Worthmore	3	S. O'Donnell	126	Shuffle Along	125	Sarazen	135	4,225	1:11.60	
1925	Superlette	3	L. Fator	124	Wild Aster	122	McAuliffe	121	3,400	1:12.40	
1926	Powhatan	3	J. Maiben	115	Croydon	117	Pompey	132	3,800	1:12.00	
1927	Happy Argo	4	S. O'Donnell	134	Byrd	118	What'll I Do	116	4,050	1:11.20	
1928	Finite	3	F. Moon	123	Extreme	127	Byrd	120	3,700	1:12.60	
1929	Osmand	5	W. Garner	140	Balko	118	Finite	119	3,600	1:10.60	
1930	Balko	5	J. Bejshak	136	The Heathen	129	Finite	129	3,375	1:09.40	
1931	Mr. Sponge	4	W. Garner	126	Helianthus	115	Balko	138	3,025	1:11.60	
1932	Larranga	3	R. Workman	126	Halcyon	127	Black Jacket	119	2,450	1:10.40	
1933	Microphone	4	S. Coucci	110	Pairbypair	120	B'd Bo'boy	117	1,485	1:11.00	
1934	Miss Merriment	3	E. Steffen	119	Kievex	123	Halcyon	118	2,750	1:10.40	
1935	Sation	5	J. Hunter	140	Whopper	117	Cycle	111	3,075	1:10.20	
1936	Miss Merriment	5	R. Workman	127	Fraidy Cat	113	Cycle	124	3,200	1:09.60	
1937	Preeminent	5	E. Arcaro	128	He Did	130	Crossbow II	130	2,975	1:10.80	
1938	The Fighter	5	R. Workman	131	Go Home	120	Preeminent	140	4,750	1:10.00	
1939	Rough Time	5	F. Faust	129	Golden Voyage	130	Preeminent	120	6,100	1:09.40	
1940	T.M. Dorsett	4	R. Workman	125	Pictor	129	Joe Schenck	126	4,500	1:11.40	
1941	Roman	4	D. Meade	140	Speed to Spare	124	The Chief	120	4,500	1:10.00	
1942	Imperatrice	4	C. McCreary	119	Tola Rose	119	Doublrab	140	5,925	1:10.20	
1943	Cassis	4	T. Atkinson	126	Tellmenow	109	True North	117	6,725	1:11.20	
1944	Ariel Lad	5	E. Arcaro	125	Tellmenow	117	True North	136	7,285	1:08.40	
1945	True North	5	T. Atkinson	140	Armed	135	Breezing Home	120	7,370	1:08.80	
1946	Cassis	7	B. James	116	True North	130	Buzfuz	132	16,750	1:08.80	
1947	Rippey	4	O. Scurlock	131	Pipette	114	Ben Lewis	103	21,300	1:10.80	
1948	First Flight	4	E. Arcaro	123	Big Story	124	Blue Border	124	22,650	1:08.60	
1949	Royal Governor	5	E. Guerin	129	Royal Blood	132	Tea-Maker	127	17,150	1:12.00	
1950	Arise	4	D. Dodson	133	Delegate	128	Royal Governor	129	17,800	1:08.80	
1951	Guillotine	4	T. Atkinson	134	Squared-Away	126	Ferd	128	18,700	1:09.00	
1952	Hitex	3	E. Arcaro	130	Tea-Maker	140	Papoose	117	17,300	1:08.40	
1953	Kaster	4	A. Catalano	121	Jet Master	114	Dutch Lane	118	16,600	1:09.80	
1954	Pet Bully	6	W. Hartack	136	Dutch Lane	117	Dark Peter	125	17,800	1:11.20	
1955	Sailor	3	H. Woodhouse	120	I Appeal	124	Tahiti	130	21,550	1:09.00	
1956	Impromptu	4	C. McCreary	127	Decimal	122	Gay Warrior	114	21,550	1:09.00	
1957	Itobe	4	E. Nelson	124	Commendation	116	Gay Warrior	117	20,600	1:09.40	
1958	Bull Strength	4	E. Arcaro	120	Reneged	136	Cohoes	127	19,135	1:10.00	
1959	Mystic II	5	M. Sorrentino	122	Discard	125	Silver Ship	140	18,095	1:11.00	
1960	Four Lane	3	S. Boulmetis	125	Yes You Will	125	Tick Tock	122	18,192	1:09.00	
1961	Smashing Gail	3	R. Ussery	117	Tick Tock	129	Gyro	122	18,655	1:10.00	
1962	Be on Time	3	P. Anderson	120	Crozier	126	Jets Pat	124	18,752	1:09.40	
1963	Accordant	3	P. Kallai	124	For the Road	132	Merry Ruler	130	14,787	1:10.20	
1964	Delta Judge	4	J.L. Rotz	138	Uppercut	129	Third Martini	137	18,005	1:10.80	
1965	Pack Trip	5	M. Ycaza	131	Determined Man	129	Flag Raiser	140	18,167	1:13.80	
1966	Impressive	3	K. Knapp	132	Brooklyn Bridge	128	Hoist Bar	123	18,752	1:10.40	

Year	Winner	Age	Jockey	Wt.	Second	Wt.	Third	Wt.	Win Value	Time	Beyer
1967	Indulto	4	J.L. Rotz	132	Full of Fun	134	Flag Raiser	137	18,200	1:12.60	
1968	More Scents	4	A. Cordero Jr	136	Gaylord's Feather	133	Taipan	125	18,460	1:11.80	
1969	Ta Wee	3	J.L. Rotz	130	King Emperor	131	Gaylord's Feather	129	18,622	1:10.20	
1970	Ta Wee	4	J.L. Rotz	140	Towzie Tyke	121	Distinctive	134	18,935	1:10.40	
1971	Shut Eye	5	A. Cordero Jr	135	Flight Topic	119	Naskra	124	20,280	1:10.80	
1972	Chou Croute	4	J.L. Rotz	131	Icecapade	135	Saxony Warrior	132	17,340	1:10.00	
1973	King's Bishop	4	E. Maple	129	Shecky Greene	137	Aljamin	125	17,310	1:09.40	
1974	Piamem	4	M.A. Rivera	133	Lonetree	140	Rastaferian	124	22,575	1:10.40	
1975	Honorable Miss	6	W. Shoemaker	130	No Bias	130	Lonetree	132	54,720	1:09.80	
1976	Relent	5	R. Hernandez	120	Kirby Lane	124	Soy Numero Uno	137	39,105	1:09.80	
1976	Honorable Miss	6	W. Shoemaker	130	Lachesis	126	Rush'g Man	129	39,780	1:10.00	
1977	What a Summer	4	J. Vasquez	134	Broadway Forli	123	Piamem	129	50,490	1:10.00	
1978	What a Summer	5	A. Cordero Jr	134	Buckfinder	129	White Rammer	128	48,195	1:09.40	
1979	Whatsyourpleasure	6	A. Cordero Jr	127	Dewan Keys	130	Tilt Up	130	49,095	1:09.60	
1980	King's Fashion	5	J.L. Samyn	136	Double Zeus	135	J.P. Brother	118	51,120	1:10.60	
1981	Piedmont Pete	5	K. Black	128	Miswaki	130	Turbulence	120	50,490	1:10.40	
1982	Gold Beauty	3	D. Brumfield	126	Engine One	131	Osorno	125	50,940	1:09.20	
1983	Chas Conerly	3	J. Miranda	136	Singh Tu	124	Let Burn	134	50,670	1:10.40	
1984	Mamaison	4	C.J. McCarron	130	Timeless Native	138	Muskoka Wyck	131	77,040	1:10.20	
1985	Mt. Livermore	4	J. Velasquez	140	Fighting Fit	139	Ziggy's Boy	134	89,460	1:10.60	
1986	Funistrada	3	R.G. Davis	117	Raja's Shark	137	Love That Mac	133	82,140	1:09.40	
1987	Purple Mountain	5	R. Migliore	123	Banker's Jet	125	Moment of Hope	129	85,500	1:08.80	
1988	Parlay Me	3	R.P. Romero	125	Well Selected	121	High Brite	135	69,000	1:09.60	
1989	Sewickley	4	R.P. Romero	131	Once Wild	129	Dancing Spree	133	68,880	1:09.60	
1990	Senor Speedy	4	J.F. Chavez	131	Sunshine Jimmy	131	Diablo	131	51,030	1:09.80	
1992	Salt Lake	3	M.E. Smith	128	Burn Fair	126	Belong to Me	122	68,520	1:09.00	107
1993	Fly So Free	5	J.D. Bailey	135	Demaloot Demashoot	126	Take Me Out	134	72,360	1:09.40	110
1994	Chimes Band	3	J.D. Bailey	135	Golden Pro	128	Boom Towner	131	65,940	1:11.20	107
1995	Jess C's Whirl	5	J.F. Chavez	126	Classy Mirage	134	Demaloot Demashoot	134	66,180	1:09.80	105
1996	Victor Avenue	3	J.F. Chavez	127	Splendid Sprinter	133	Stalwart Member	128	67,440	1:09.20	109
1997	Royal Haven	5	R. Migliore	136	King Roller	129	Kelly Kip	135	65,820	1:10.60	111
1998	Punch Line	8	J.F. Chavez	136	American Champ	131	Golden Tent	126	66,840	1:10.00	103
1999	Richter Scale	5	J.F. Chavez	134	Aristotle	130	Bought in Dixie	128	66,060	1:09.00	116
2000	Kashatreya	6	O. Vergara	131	Exciting Story	131	Oro de Mexico	130	67,140	1:11.03	92
2001	Yonaguska	3	J.A. Santos	131	Big E E	129	Voodoo	123	67,320	1:09.60	103
2002	True Direction	3	J.J. Castellano	134	Crossing Point	133	Gold I.D.	127	66,960	1:09.62	106
2003	Bossanova	3	E.S. Prado	128	Papua	132	Savoy Special	127	64,980	1:10.06	101
2004	Thunder Touch	3	R. Bejarano	126	Papua	128	Eavesdropper	127	66,960	1:09.83	101

Beyer Index: 105.46

FALLS CITY HANDICAP (G2), 1 1/8 Miles, Fillies and Mares, 3-Year-Olds and Up, Churchill Downs, 2004 Purse: $325,200

Year	Winner	Age	Jockey	Wt.	Second	Wt.	Third	Wt.	Win Value	Time	Beyer
1875	Camargo	3	R. Swim	100	Ascension	100			1,125	1:43.25	
1876	Red Coat	3	Hughes	100	Patriot	100	Leamington	100	975	1:46.00	
1877	Flying Locust	3	B. Walker	100	Commodore Parrisot	100	Kinlock	100	625	1:45.00	
1882	Freeland	3	C. Taylor	104	Katie Creel	104	Anglia	104	800	2:42.50	
1883	Washburn	4	H. Blaylock	114	Silvio	114	McGlinty	97	625	2:49.25	
1884	Chance	3	J. Stoval	109	Hiflight	109	Ascender	118	900	1:55.00	
1892	Wadsworth	3	T. Britton	113	Kindora	97			1,450	1:47.00	
1910	Melisande	4	T. Koerner	121	Jack Atkin	136	Ocean Bound	122	1,440	1:12.00	
1911	High Private	5	G. Taplin	108	Princess Calaway	100	Cherryola	105	1,210	1:51.60	
1912	Buckhorn	3	W. Andress	114	High Private	122	Countless	110	1,180	1:13.20	
1913	Wilhite	4	Borel	109	The Widow Moon	103	K'eburne	110	2,010	1:13.80	
1914	Leochares	4	R. Goose	116	Helen Barbee	116	Governor Hughes	114	1,750	1:13.00	
1915	Prince Hermis	5	E. Pool	108	Vogue	107	Pan Zareta	125	2,060	1:13.20	
1916	Kathleen	3	D. Connelly	117	Bringhurst	117	Vogue	112	2,170	1:13.00	
1917	Vogue	5	J. Callahan	113	Bradley's Choice	108	Pan Zareta	131	1,970	1:13.00	
1918	Last Coin	6	L. Gentry	111	Sedan	111	Ocean Sweep	104	1,885	1:13.00	
1919	King Gorin	6	L. Lyke	118	Jack Hare, Jr.	132	Midway	118	4,485	1:48.00	
1920	Woodtrap	6	D. Connelly	113	Sands of Pleasure	105	Sterling	108	5,080	1:56.60	
1921	Bit of White	3	L. Lyke	110	Rangoon	118	Ginger	108	5,420	1:51.20	
1922	Chatterton	3	B. Kennedy	104	Rockminster	108	Rouleau	109	4,860	1:51.00	
1923	Guest of Honor	3	M. Garner	108	Audacious	122	Cherry Tree	111	5,060	1:53.00	
1924	Princess Doreen	3	H. Stutts	113	Hopeless	107	Just David	102	5,280	1:51.60	
1925	Deeming	3	L. Steinhart	106	Sir Peter	114	Balboa	108	50,000	1:55.00	
1926	Rothermel	4	W. Garner	109	Rhin'ock	112	Longworth	100	4,780	1:55.80	
1927	Rhin'ock	4	C. Hunt	108	Percentage	106	Hydromel	114	4,820	1:52.60	
1941	Misty Isle	3	A. Bodiou	116	Meggy	113	Blue Delight	113	1,975	1:37.60	

Year	Winner	Age	Jockey	Wt.	Second	Wt.	Third	Wt.	Win Value	Time	Beyer
1942	Pig Tails	3	O. Scurlock	108	Meggy	108	Montsin	107	2,025	1:40.60	
1943	Burgoo Maid	3	W. Morrissey	114	Flying Easy	112	Fiddler's Bit	104	2,035	1:37.40	
1944	Traffic Court	6	W. Garner	118	Bold Style	109	S'ttm't Sake	107	3,980	1:39.40	
1945	Jack's Jill	3	A. LoTurco	115	Sigma Kappa	118	Annie's Reply	108	4,220	1:39.20	
1946	Miss Balladier	4	H. Wallace	107	Jack's Jill	119	First Gun	113	7,700	1:39.60	
1947	Say Blue	3	S. Brooks	113	Jack's Jill	112	Be Faithful	119	7,950	1:39.60	
1948	Jack's Jill	6	F.A. Smith	118	Miss Mommy	113	Speedy Lee	117	7,975	1:38.40	
1949	Brownian	5	A.D. Rivera	116	Blue Helen	113	Blue Note	105	6,250	1:38.80	
1950	Our Request	4	T. Barrow	111	Miss Highbrow	116	Here's Hoping	120	5,775	1:39.40	
1951	Dickie Sue	3	H. Craig	110	Our Request	115	Lyceum	113	5,800	1:37.40	
1952	Peu-a-Peu	3	P.A. Ward	108	Gray Challenge	110	Our Request	114	6,125	1:38.40	
1953	Gala Fete	4	A. Kirkland	117	Cajole	107	Belle Rebelle	106	8,350	1:36.60	
1954	Gala Fete	5	A. Kirkland	120	Close Play	106	Vixen Fixit	112	8,250	1:39.00	
1955	Oil Painting	4	D. Dodson	121	Pegeen	112	Jenjay	111	8,525	1:41.20	
1956	Doubledogdare	3	S. Brooks	121	Queen Hopeful	122	Lycka	117	15,175	1:37.00	
1957	Leallah	3	D. Erb	114	Beautillion	118	Lady LaRue	111	14,319	1:36.20	
1958	Bornastar	5	K. Church	122	Little Pache	113	Woodlawn	111	14,416	1:37.20	
1959	Indian Maid	3	J.L. Rotz	122	Lindaway	109	Ruling Beauty	114	14,465	1:35.40	
1960	Indian Maid	4	J. Sellers	124	Gerts Image	113	Chance G'ge	110	14,172	1:37.20	
1961	Indian Maid	5	C. Meaux	120	My Sister Kate	112	Times Two	115	15,145	1:38.00	
1962	Primonetta	4	R.L. Baird	126	Old Hat	113	Fortunate Isle	110	14,739	1:35.60	
1963	Alecee	4	V. Cruz	115	Abrogate	116	Mon Petite	109	15,421	1:36.40	
1964	Old Hat	5	D. Brumfield	128	De Cathy	113	Abrogate	117	10,050	1:35.60	
1965	De Cathy	4	E. Eades	113	Abrogate	117	Really Trying	112	18,216	1:36.00	
1966	Old Hat	7	K. Church	116	Naidni Diam	110	Mac's Sparkler	117	18,184	1:35.00	
1967	Amerigo Lady	3	P. Anderson	116	Gusher	113	Likely Swap	113	18,866	1:36.00	
1968	T.V's Princess	4	E. Fires	111	Frederick Street	112	Pattee Canyon	117	14,649	1:35.80	
1968	Sale Day	3	E. Guerin	119	I've Arrived	112	Drover's Dr'm	107	14,649	1:36.80	
1969	Dedicated to Sue	3	M. Manganello	113	Frederick Street	120	Kelly Keim	111	14,682	1:35.60	
1969	Yes Sir	3	D. Brumfield	115	T.V's Princess	118	Cast Ahead	111	14,682	1:36.00	
1970	Mistong	3	J. Soto	110	Double Delta	123	Yes Sir	111	18,882	1:39.80	
1971	Strider	4	M. Manganello	114	Shee Clachan	115	Golden Circlet	114	18,306	1:37.20	
1971	Magnabid	3	D. Brumfield	113	Hard and Fast	113	Deceit	125	18,143	1:36.00	
1972	Fairway Flyer	3	D.E. Whited	117	Brenda Beauty	116	Turning Bold	112	14,909	1:38.40	
1972	Barely Even	3	R. Broussard	128	Silent Beauty	118	Secret Retr't	116	14,747	1:37.80	
1973	Delta Empress	3	E. Fires	111	Pig Party	113	Fine Tuning	115	15,348	1:37.40	
1973	Fairway Flyer	4	D.E. Whited	115	Nalee's Folly	118	Knitted Gloves	113	15,186	1:37.20	
1974	Susan's Girl	5	W. Gavidia	126	Crystal Stone	114	Enc't Native	112	18,184	1:37.40	
1975	Flama Ardiente	3	B. Fann	119	Costly Dream	120	Go on Dreaming	116	18,622	1:38.20	
1976	Hope of Glory	4	D. Brumfield	118	Hail to El	116	Flama Ardiente	117	21,937	1:48.20	
1977	Time for Pleasure	3	T. Barrow	115	Dear Irish	114	Famed Princess	115	2,084	1:46.20	
1978	Navajo Princess	4	C. Perret	123	Love to Tell	118	Likely Exchange	120	36,043	1:45.40	
1979	Holy Mount	3	M.R. Morgan	112	Impetuous Gal	118	Cup of Honey	115	39,163	1:47.60	
1980	Sweet Audrey	3	C.R. Woods Jr	113	Likely Exchange	123	Impetuous Gal	122	36,156	1:48.20	
1981	Safe Play	3	S.A. Spencer	123	Sweetest Chant	118	Friendly Frolic	112	37,993	1:46.20	
1982	Mezimica	4	D.E. Foster	112	Charge My Account	111	Shade Miss	112	39,910	1:51.40	
1982	What Glitter	4	D. Brumfield	114	Sprite Flight	114	Betty Money	118	36,823	1:52.80	
1983	Narrate	3	M.S. Sellers	117	Queen of Song	116	Promising Native	116	36,335	1:51.60	
1984	Pretty Perfect	4	G. Gallitano	121	Electric Fanny	116	Queen of Song	122	37,115	1:50.80	
1985	Donut's Pride	3	L. Melancon	112	Playful Queen	114	My Inheritance	111	35,743	1:53.20	
1985	Electric Fanny	4	J.C. Espinoza	115	Mrs. Revere	121	Chattahoochee	113	25,780	1:52.60	
1986	Queen Alexandra	4	D. Brumfield	124	Kapalua Butterfly	113	Gerrie Singer	116	49,248	1:51.40	
1987	Royal Cielo	3	K.K. Allen	114	Firgie's Jule	115	Fantasy Lover	113	47,330	1:53.00	
1988	Top Corsage	5	D. Brumfield	121	Epitome	116	Lawyer Talk	111	76,895	1:51.80	
1989	Degenerate Gal	4	L. Melancon	116	Luthier's Launch	113	Blackened	112	72,410	1:52.60	
1990	Screen Prospect	3	P. Day	114	Sleek Feet	110	Degenerate Gal	119	75,920	1:51.40	100
1991	Screen Prospect	4	S.J. Sellers	117	Fit for a Queen	124	Bungalow	112	73,580	1:51.20	105
1992	Bungalow	5	P. Day	118	Wilderness Song	123	Auto Dial	115	70,915	1:52.03	91
1993	Gray Cashmere	4	P. Day	120	Avie's Shadow	110	Princess Polonia	112	142,090	1:51.96	98
1994	Alcovy	4	S.E.Miller	114	Pennyhill Park	115	Hey Hazel	114	141,440	1:51.16	101
1995	Mariah's Storm	4	R.N. Lester	120	Alcovy	112	Heavenliness	112	143,390	1:51.37	106
1996	Halo America	6	C.H. Borel	118	Bedroom Blues	115	Debit My Account	113	171,120	1:49.08	107
1997	Feasibility Study	5	M.E. Smith	122	Omi	114	Naskra Colors	112	170,345	1:50.65	101
1998	Tomisue's Delight	4	S.J. Sellers	121	Top Secret	115	Silent Eskimo	113	171,740	1:51.05	99
1999	Silent Eskimo	4	C.H. Borel	117	Let	116	Pleasant Temper	115	171,585	1:48.85	106
2000	Bordelaise	5	P. Day	117	Spain	122	On a Soapbox	116	168,020	1:50.01	108
2001	Forest Secrets	3	C. Perret	113	Printemps	117	Unbridled Elaine	121	169,570	1:49.49	102
2002	Allamerican Bertie	3	P. Day	117	Take Charge Lady	122	Softly	116	167,400	1:49.60	102
2003	Lead Story	4	C.H. Borel	116	Mayo on the Side	114	Cloakof Vagueness	114	207,204	1:51.23	107
2004	Halory Leigh	4	E.M. Martin Jr	116	Susan's Angel	114	Miss Fortunate	113	201,624	1:51.81	99

Beyer Index: 102.13

FANTASY (G2), 1 1/16 Miles, 3-Year-Old Fillies, Oaklawn Park, 2004 Purse: $200,000

Year	Winner	Age	Jockey	Wt.	Second	Wt.	Third	Wt.	Win Value	Time	Beyer
1973	Knitted Gloves	3	J.C. Espinosa	121	Fussy Girl	121	Westward	118	96,960	1:42.60	
1974	Miss Musket	3	W. Shoemaker	121	Out to Lunch	115	Fairway Fable	118	79,740	1:44.80	
1975	Hoso	3	M. Solomone	121	Luxury	114	Dancers Countess	118	70,830	1:46.00	
1976	T.V. Vixen	3	B. Walt	121	Answer	121	All Rainbows	112	73,170	1:43.40	
1977	Our Mims	3	D. Brumfield	112	Sweet Alliance	118	Meteor Dancer	110	83,970	1:45.00	
1978	Equanimity	3	H.E. Moreno	110	Ba Ba Bee	115	Miss Baja	121	77,850	1:44.60	
1979	Davona Dale	3	J. Velasquez	121	Caline	121	Very Special Lady	110	101,610	1:44.40	
1980	Bold 'n Determined	3	E. Delahoussaye	121	Satin Ribera	115	Honest and True	118	101,940	1:45.20	
1981	Heavenly Cause	3	L. Pincay Jr	121	Nell's Briquette	121	Wayward Lass	121	133,890	1:43.80	
1982	Flying Partner	3	R. Sibille	118	Skillful Joy	121	Before Dawn	121	163,020	1:47.00	
1983	Brindy Brindy	3	K. Jones	115	Fifth Question	115	Choose a Partner	112	169,080	1:44.60	
1984	My Darling One	3	C.J. McCarron	121	Althea	121	Personable Lady	118	160,440	1:41.20	
1985	Rascal Lass	3	R. Sibille	118	Denver Express	113	Little Biddy Comet	114	169,620	1:43.20	
1986	Tiffany Lass	3	G.L. Stevens	121	Lotka	116	Turn and Dance	112	164,640	1:42.00	
1987	Very Subtle	3	C.J. McCarron	121	Up the Apalachee	121	Hometown Queen	116	16,270	1:42.40	
1988	Jeanne Jones	3	W. Shoemaker	118	Fara's Team	112	Costly Shoes	114	150,000	1:42.20	
1989	Fantastic Look	3	C.J. McCarron	113	Imaginary Lady	121	Affirmed Classic	114	150,000	1:43.20	
1990	Silvered	3	D.L. Howard	112	Lonely Girl	114	Fit to Scout	118	150,000	1:44.20	
1991	Lite Light	3	C.S. Nakatani	121	Withallprobability	121	Nalees Pin	121	150,000	1:41.80	100
1992	Race the Wild Wind	3	C.J. McCarron	117	Golden Treat	121	Now Dance	117	150,000	1:43.60	100
1993	Aztec Hill	3	M.E. Smith	121	Adorydar	117	Stalcreek	117	150,000	1:44.20	94
1994	Two Altazano	3	K.P. Leblanc	121	Slide Show	121	Flying in the Lane	121	150,000	1:43.60	91
1995	Cat's Cradle	3	C.W. Antley	121	Forever Cherokee	117	Humble Eight	121	150,000	1:44.20	89
1996	Escena	3	P. Day	117	Antespend	121	Ski Trail	117	150,000	1:43.80	93
1997	Blushing K. D.	3	L.J. Meche	121	Valid Bonnet	121	Ajina	121	150,000	1:42.60	110
1998	Silent Eskimo	3	C.V. Gonzalez	117	Misty Hour	121	Came Unwound	121	150,000	1:43.80	97
1999	Excellent Meeting	3	K.J. Desormeaux	121	The Happy Hopper	121	Dreams Gallore	121	150,000	1:42.60	106
2000	Classy Cara	3	I.L. Puglisi	121	Eden Lodge	117	Gold for My Gal	117	120,000	1:43.95	93
2001	Mystic Lady	3	E.M. Coa	121	Collect Call	121	Mysia Jo	117	120,000	1:43.32	98
2002	See How She Runs	3	D.R. Pettinger	117	:Lake Lady	121	Chamrousse	117	120,000	1:43.80	98
2003	Ruby's Reception	3	T.J. Thompson	121	Harbor Blues	121	Go for Glamour	117	120,000	1:44.61	84
2004	House of Fortune	3	A. Solis	121	Island Sand	121	Stellar Jayne	121	120,000	1:42.62	99

Beyer Index: 96.57

FAYETTE (G3), 1 1/8 Miles, 3-Year-Olds and Up, Keeneland Race Course, 2004 Purse: $161,250

Year	Winner	Age	Jockey	Wt.	Second	Wt.	Third	Wt.	Win Value	Time	Beyer
1959	Terra Firma	4	K. Church	123	Hymient	119	Dru Away	123	10,865	1:51.40	
1960	Little Fitz	5	W.A. Peake	117	Toby's Brother	108	Better Bee	118	11,255	1:49.60	
1961	Zumbador II	4	R. Broussard	116	Bluescope	118	Tompion	126	10,887	1:47.60	
1962	Blue Cro'n	4	N. Cox	117	Gushing Wind	122	Loyal Son	118	11,407	1:48.80	
1963	Choker	3	K. Church	114	Port of Mecca	115	Jet Clipper	114	11,765	1:41.40	
1964	Swoonen	4	K. Knapp	113	City Line	119	Lemon Twist	116	18,590	1:42.00	
1965	Old Hat	6	R. Gallimore	119	Lt. Stevens	122	Big Brigade	114	18,330	1:42.80	
1966	Yumbel	5	H. Pilar	113	Road Hog	109	Come On II	117	18,525	1:43.60	
1967	Swoonaway	6	B. Phelps	119	Hy Frost	116	Miracle Hill	115	19,012	1:42.60	
1968	Yorkville	4	D.E. Whited	119	War Censor	115	Monitor	114	18,362	1:42.00	
1969	Royal Harmony	5	M. Solomone	117	Otomano II	115	Miracle Hill	116	18,557	1:42.60	
1970	Royal Harmony	6	E.J. Knapp	118	Dust Commander	113	Fast Hilarious	122	17,826	1:42.80	
1971	Royal Harmony	7	D.E. Whited	119	New Round	112	Mariuco	111	19,402	1:42.60	
1972	Chou Croute	4	J.L. Rotz	123	Sensitive Music	117	Chateauvira	114	18,899	1:44.00	
1973	Chateauvira	6	G. Gallitano	112	Grocery List	116	O So Big	115	19,094	1:42.80	
1974	Jesta Dream Away	4	A. Rini	115	Super Sail	121	Joyous Jester	112	18,119	1:41.60	
1975	Warbucks	5	J. Nichols	120	Hasty Flyer	119	Mr. Door	114	18,460	1:44.40	
1976	Silver Badge	5	G. Patterson	111	Easy Gallop	117	Topinabee	112	17,981	1:44.60	
1976	Yamanin	4	G. Patterson	114	Run for Clem	111	Faneuil Boy	118	17,899	1:43.20	
1977	Bob's Dusty	3	R. Depass	117	Man's Man	115	Packer Captain	118	18,395	1:42.80	
1978	Silver Series	4	D. Brumfield	121	Buckfinder	121	Romeo	118	20,768	1:41.20	
1979	Architect	3	S.A. Spencer	117	Coverack	121	Trimlea	120	35,699	1:49.60	
1980	Hurry Up Blue	3	G. Gallitano	112	Marcy Road	111	All the More	116	39,423	1:49.00	
1981	Ironworks	3	P. Day	117	Two's a Plenty	116	Sun Catcher	118	39,861	1:49.20	
1982	Rivalero	6	R.P. Romero	115	Cad	114	Recusant	120	35,563	1:50.40	
1982	El Baba	3	D. Brumfield	118	Vodika Collins	120	Hechizado	115	38,813	1:50.20	
1983	Frost King	5	R. Platts	123			Bold Style	120	22,663	1:48.80	
1984	Star Choice	5	J. McKnight	112	Explosive Wagon	117	Bright Baron	113	47,492	1:47.40	
1985	Wop Wop	3	D.E. Foster	112	Banner Bob	117	Exclusive Greer	114	36,530	1:51.40	

Year	Winner	Age	Jockey	Wt.	Second	Wt.	Third	Wt.	Win Value	Time	Beyer
1986	Harham's Sizzler	7	R. Meier	120	Derby Wish	119	Pirate's Skiff	112	34,792	1:49.20	
1987	Good Command	4	D. Brumfield	118	Minneapple	120	Savings	115	73,921	1:46.80	
1988	Homebuilder	4	D. Brumfield	121	Blue Buckaroo	120	Ile de Jinsky	112	68,315	1:51.20	
1989	Drapeau Tricolore	4	J.E. Bruin	114	Air Worthy	116	Blue Buckaroo	118	71,695	1:48.20	
1990	Lac Ouimet	7	R.P. Romero	119	Din's Dancer	121	Secret Hello	116	70,233	1:47.20	111
1991	Summer Squall	4	P. Day	122	Unbridled	122	Secret Hello	115	69,810	1:48.80	109
1992	Barkerville	4	S.J. Sellers	114	Medium Cool	117	Majesterian	114	70,680	1:48.40	112
1993	Grand Jewel	3	J.D. Bailey	120	Split Run	120	Secreto's Hideaway	114	68,634	1:46.80	108
1994	Sunny Sunrise	7	J.D. Carle	120	Key Contender	117	Powerful Punch	117	67,766	1:50.00	111
1995	Judge T C	4	J.M. Johnson	114	Powerful Punch	120	Sir Vixen	114	104,625	1:49.00	109
1996	Isitingood	5	D.R. Flores	120	Distorted Humor	114	Strawberry Wine	117	120,110	1:50.40	110
1997	Whiskey Wisdom	4	W. Martinez	115	City by Night	123	Pyramid Peak	120	101,184	1:48.60	118
1998	Arch	3	S.J. Sellers	123	Touch Gold	115	Wild Tempest	115	98,394	1:53.80	111
1999	Social Charter	4	M. St. Julien	120	Master O Foxhounds	118	Early Warning	118	135,904	1:55.28	100
2000	Jadada	5	S.J. Sellers	118	Mojave Moon	118	Get Away With It	118	214,800	1:54.92	99
2001	Connected	4	M. St. Julien	119	Broken Vow	123	Outofthebox	122	103,509	1:50.05	106
2002	Tenpins	4	C. Perret	123	X Country	119	Crafty Shaw	121	99,789	1:51.17	110
2003	M B Sea	4	C. Perret	119	Tenpins	121	Seattle Fitz	119	101,556	1:50.30	103
							Changeintheweather	119			
2004	Midway Road	4	C.H. Borel	121	Total Impact	125	Alumni Hall	119	99,975	1:50.39	107

Beyer Index: 108.27

Run at 1 1/16 miles, 1963–78; at 1 3/16 miles, 1998–2000

FIFTH SEASON BREEDERS' CUP (G3), 1 1/16 Miles, 4-Year-Olds and Up, Oaklawn Park, 2004 Purse: $100,000

Year	Winner	Age	Jockey	Wt.	Second	Wt.	Third	Wt.	Win Value	Time	Beyer
1994	Nelson	7	S.P. Romero	117	Punch Line	117	Senor Tomas	114	41,640	1:43.00	95
1995	Tyus	6	C. Borel	114	Prince of the Mt.	114	Joseph's Robe	114	26,760	1:42.80	105
1996	No Spend No Glow	5	R. Lester	117	Bucks Nephew	117	Groovy Jett	117	47,880	1:42.80	98
1997	Krigeorj's Gold	5	J. Johnson	119	Bucks Nephew	117	Prince of the Mt.	116	49,500	1:43.20	103
1998	Acceptable	4	A. Solis	117	Littlebitlively	117	Brush With Pride	124	60,000	1:42.40	106
1999	Truluck	4	L. Melancon	114	Slide to the Left	114	Rock and Roll	114	60,000	1:42.20	108
2000	Mr. Ross	5	E. Perner	115	Relic Reward	114	Crimson Classic	114	60,000	1:42.93	106
2001	Remington Rock	7	D.E. Simington	114	Kombat Kat	114	Da Devil	114	45,000	1:43.13	102
2003	Patton's Victory	5	A.E. Birzer	117	Colorful Tour	122	Makors Mark	118	60,000	1:43.26	107
2004	Spanish Empire	4	E.M. Martin Jr	118	Crafty Shaw	122	No Comprende	122	60,000	1:42.50	101

Beyer Index: 103.10

Not run in 2002

FIRECRACKER BREEDERS' CUP HANDICAP (G2), 1 Mile (Turf), 3-Year-Olds and Up, Churchill Downs, 2004 Purse: $287,750

Year	Winner	Age	Jockey	Wt.	Second	Wt.	Third	Wt.	Win Value	Time	Beyer
1993	Cleone	4	C. Perret	115	Magesterial Cheer	113	Harlan	110	74,815	1:35.80	102
1994	First and Only	7	T.J. Hebert	118	Weekend Madness	111	Avid Affection	112	73,580	1:35.20	100
1995	Jaggery John	4	D. Kutz	113	Rare Reason	115	Fly Cry	119	74,360	1:33.60	103
1996	Rare Reason	5	P. Johnson	115	Artema	114	Wavy Run	116	131,950	1:33.80	106
1997	Soviet Line	7	P. Day	114	Volochine	115	Same Old Wish	118	126,077	1:37.60	107
1998	Claire's Honor	4	A.J. D'Amico	109	Soviet Line	115	Optic Nerve	113	177,630	1:35.80	103
1999	Joe Who	6	R.J. Albarado	113	Middlesex Drive	116	Wild Event	121	132,680	1:36.78	107
2000	Conserve	4	S.J. Sellers	116	Riviera	115	King Slayer	115	177,940	1:35.12	102
2001	Irish Prize	5	G.L. Stevens	122	Aly's Alley	117	Where's Taylor	114	175,770	1:34.68	107
2002	Good Journey	6	P.Day	118	Morluc	114	Even the Score	114	181,350	1:34.83	107
	Where's Taylor finished second but was disqualified and placed third										
2003	Tap the Admiral	5	J. McKee	115	Freefourinternet	114	Package Store	114	178,870	1:35.48	100
2004	Quantum Merit	5	S.J. Sellers	117	Perfect Soul	121	Senor Swinger	117	178,405	1:34.15	107
	Senor Swinger finished second but was disqualified and placed third										

Beyer Index: 104.25

FIRST FLIGHT HANDICAP (G2), 7 Furlongs, Fillies and Mares, 3-Year-Olds and Up, Aqueduct, 2004 Purse: $150,000

Year	Winner	Age	Jockey	Wt.	Second	Wt.	Third	Wt.	Win Value	Time	Beyer
1978	What a Summer	5	J. Fell	126	Flying Above	120	Mrs. Warren	113	25,410	1:22.20	
1979	Gladiolus	5	L. Pincay Jr	120	Imarebel	117	Plankton	114	25,740	1:22.40	
1980	Samarta Dancer	4	C.B. Asmussen	112	Jedina	115	Damask Fan	112	33,780	1:25.60	

Year	Winner	Age	Jockey	Wt.	Second	Wt.	Third	Wt.	Win Value	Time	Beyer
1981	Island Charm	4	R. Migliore	120	Tax Holiday	116	Chain Bracelet	123	33,720	1:23.60	
1982	Number	3	E. Maple	112	Lady Dean	123	Privacy	118	34,500	1:22.80	
1983	Pert	4	F. Lovato Jr	112	Pretty Sensible	112	Quixotic Lady	121	34,620	1:25.20	
1984	Shortley	4	M.G. Pino	114	Quixotic Lady	116	Rarely Layte	108	42,060	1:22.60	
1985	Alabama Nana	4	J. Velasquez	121	Gene's Lady	115	Paradies	119	50,040	1:22.20	
1986	Chaldea	6	J.L. Samyn	115	Le Slew	114	Gene's Lady	120	53,100	1:22.40	
1987	Al's Helen	4	J. Velasquez	121	Girl Powder	117	Willowy Mood	118	54,180	1:21.80	
1988	Cagey Exuberance	4	J. Imparato	119	Nasty Affair	114	Intently	111	55,350	1:24.40	
1989	Grecian Flight	5	C. Perret	122	Feel the Beat	121	Dance Teacher	112	51,480	1:22.00	
1990	Queena	4	J.D. Bailey	113	Quick Mischief	115	A Penny Is a Penny	122	51,480	1:22.40	106
1991	Missy's Mirage	3	E. Maple	113	Makin Faces	112	Withallprobability	114	74,160	1:21.80	105
1992	Shared Interest	4	J.D. Bailey	111	Missy's Mirage	121	Nannerl	119	120,000	1:20.60	111
1993	Raise the Heck	5	R.I. Velez	114	Regal Victress	113	Shared Interest	121	69,000	1:23.40	106
1994	Twist Afleet	3	J.D. Bailey	117	Ann Dear	117	Incinerate	113	66,000	1:23.00	98
1995	Twist Afleet	4	G.L. Stevens	121	Igotrhythm	109	Lottsa Talc	116	66,780	1:22.80	101
1996	Thunder Achiever	3	R.G. Davis	112	Miss Golden Circle	117	Call Account	110	81,864	1:21.60	105
1997	Dixie Flag	3	M.J. Luzzi	113	Silent City	113	Aldiza	116	64,800	1:22.80	99
1998	Catinca	3	R. Migliore	116	Glitter Woman	121	Blue Begonia	115	82,260	1:22.00	105
1999	Country Hideaway	3	H. Castillo Jr	114	Harpia	117	Anklet	114	90,000	1:23.00	99
2000	Country Hideaway	4	J.L. Espinoza	117	Go To The Ink	113	Cat Cay	114	90,000	1:22.60	101
2001	Shine Again	4	J.L. Samyn	116	Dream Supreme	121	Kalookan Queen	119	90,000	1:23.21	110
2002	Shine Again	5	J.L. Samyn	117	Redhead Riot	112	Raging Fever	119	90,000	1:23.75	102
2003	Randaroo	3	H. Castillo Jr	115	Shine Again	121	Zawzooth	113	90,000	1:23.65	93
2004	Bending Strings	3	S.X. Bridgmohan	116	Smokey Glacken	115	Passing Shot	118	90,000	1:22.13	98

Beyer Index: 102.60

FIRST LADY HANDICAP (G3), 6 Furlongs, Fillies and Mares, 3-Year-Olds and Up, Gulfstream Park, 2004 Purse: $100,000

Year	Winner	Age	Jockey	Wt.	Second	Wt.	Third	Wt.	Win Value	Time	Beyer
1981	Island Charm	4	J. Velasquez	113	La Voyageuse		Lacey		22,536	1:10.60	
1983	Prime Prospect	5	D. MacBeth	118	Miss Hitch		Mrs. Roberts		28,282	1:10.80	
1985	Nany	5	G. St. Leon	120	Micky's Echo		Birdie Bell		29,352	1:09.80	
1986	Sugar's Image	5	J. Velez Jr	115	Summer Mood		Mr. T's Tune		29,736	1:11.20	
1987	One Fine Lady	5	R. Danjean	114	Fleur de Soleil		Sheer Ice		24,045	1:10.40	
1988	Funistrada	5	W. Guerra	120	Easter Mary		Cadillacing		29,232	1:10.20	
1989	Waggley	6	J.L. Samyn	112	Damality		My Peace		27,288	1:11.00	
1990	Sez Fourty	4	M. Gonzalez	114	Classic Value		Fit for a Queen		22,760	1:11.20	95
1991	Spirit of Fighter	8	J. Velez	118	Mistaurian		Love's Exchange		30,000	1:11.60	
1992	Withallprobability	4	C. Perret	118	Christina Czarina		Spirit of Fighter		30,000	1:11.00	100
1993	Si Si Sezyo	5	R. Hernandez	112	Illeria		Jeano		30,000	1:10.20	97
1994	Santa Catalina	6	J.D. Bailey	114	Insight to Cope	119	Capture the Crown	113	30,000	1:11.20	100
1995	Recognizable	4	M.E. Smith	113	Insight to Cope	114	Maison de Reve	114	30,000	1:09.60	104
1996	Chaposa Springs	4	J.D. Bailey	122	Phone the Doctor	117	Market Slide	113	45,000	1:10.20	98
1997	Chip	4	J. Bravo	113	Phone the Doctor	116	Surprising Fact	113	45,000	1:09.60	101
1998	U Can Do It	5	S.J. Sellers	115	Start at Once	113	Vivace	118	45,000	1:09.80	102
1999	Scotzanna	7	R. Migliore	114	U Can Do It	118	Foil	116	45,000	1:10.17	110
2000	Hurricane Bertie	5	P. Day	118	Marley Vale	118	Cassidy	113	45,000	1:10.22	99
2001	Another	4	E.S. Prado	113	Curious Treasure	114	Dynamite Diablo	115	60,000	1:10.41	90
2002	Raging Fever	4	J.R. Velazquez	118	Cat Cay	118	Mandy's Gold	116	60,000	1:10.36	106
2003	Harmony Lodge	5	J.R. Velazquez	113	Fly Me Crazy	114	Haunted Lass	114	60,000	1:10.31	98
2004	Harmony Lodge	6	R. Migliore	119	House Party	118	Mayo on the Side	115	60,000	1:09.64	106

Beyer Index: 100.43

FLASH (G3), 5 Furlongs, 2-Year-Olds, Belmont Park, 2004 Purse: $104,300

Year	Winner	Age	Jockey	Wt.	Second	Wt.	Third	Wt.	Win Value	Time	Beyer
1981	Ringaro	2	A. Cordero Jr	119	Lead Astray	119	Prince Westport	115	33,300	1:04.60	
1982	Victorious	2	J.D. Bailey	115	Satan's Charger	119	Great Ending	119	33,420	1:04.20	
1999	More Than Ready	2	J.R. Velazquez	119	Diablo's Addition	115	Bevo	115	49,200	:57.00	102
2000	Yonaguska	2	J.D. Bailey	115	The Goo	115	City Zip	115	49,200	:57.80	97
2001	Buster's Daydream	2	E.S. Prado	115	Harmony Hall	115	Huber Woods	115	49,365	:56.93	94
2002	Whywhywhy	2	E.S. Prado	114	Presence	115	Down Play	114	65,460	:57.10	85
2003	Chapel Royal	2	J.R. Velazquez	114	Hasslefree	114	Juventus	114	63,955	:57.02	99
2004	Primal Storm	2	S.J. Sellers	116	Winning Expression	115	Gold Joy	115	63,780	:57.49	84

Beyer Index: 93.50

Run at 5 1/2 furlongs, 1981-1982. Not run from 1972-1980, 1983-1998. For runnings previous to 1972, refer to 1972 Manual.

FLEUR DE LIS HANDICAP (G2), 1 1/8 Miles, Fillies and Mares, 3-Year-Olds and Up, Churchill Downs, 2004 Purse: $439,200

Year	Winner	Age	Jockey	Wt.	Second	Wt.	Third	Wt.	Win Value	Time	Beyer
1975	Bundler	4	J. Nichols	120	Jay Bar Pet	112	Tappahannock	116	14,511	1:39.40	
1976	Pago Hop	4	H. Arroyo	116	Flama Ardiente	122	Prec'us Proof	113	14,056	1:38.40	
1977	Go on Dreaming	5	P. Nicolo	115	B.J. King	114	Kittyluck	117	14,381	1:43.80	
1978	Likely Exchange	4	J. McKnight	113	Time for Pleasure	123	Bold Rendezvous	114	13,894	1:45.40	
1979	Table the Rumor	5	D.E. Whited	118	Likely Exchange	123	Pretty Delight	116	22,864	1:45.20	
1980	Likely Exchange	6	J.S. Sellers	121	Salzburg	116	Smooth Bore	115	23,026	1:45.00	
1981	Forever Cordial	4	D. Haire	114	Salud	114	Passolyn	118	23,205	1:45.40	
1982	Classic Ambition	4	W. Gavidia	112	Beyond Reproof	113	Mean Martha	117	36,855	1:44.80	
1983	Try Something New	4	P. Day	121	Naskra Magic	116	Header Card	117	35,328	1:51.60	
1984	Heatherten	5	S. Maple	124	Satiety	110	Hotsy Totsy	112	35,233	1:51.40	
1985	Straight Edition	5	C.R. Woods Jr	113	Dusty Gloves	110	Del Dun Gee	110	36,108	1:50.80	
1986	Queen Alexandra	4	D. Brumfield	117	Tide	111	Zn'bia Express	119	66,083	1:49.20	
1987	Infinidad	5	M. Solomone	118	Marianna's Girl	117	Queen Alexandra	126	64,815	1:50.60	
1988	Lt. Lao	4	D. Brumfield	116	Lawyer Talk	111	She's a Mystery	111	72,215	1:49.60	
1989	Stoneleigh's Hope	4	J.C. Deegan	112	Way It Should Be	111	Lt. Lao	116	71,435	1:52.60	
1990	A Penny Is a Penny	5	A.T. Gryder	120	Stoneleigh's Hope	115	Lady Hoolihan	112	70,980	1:51.20	91
1991	Maskra's Lady	4	J.M. Johnson	111	Fit for a Queen	116	Under Oath	113	73,515	1:50.40	99
1992	Bungalow	5	F. Torres	114	Til Forbid	113	Beth Believes	112	74,815	1:50.87	94
1993	Quilma	6	R.P. Romero	117	Fappies Cosy Miss	111	Hitch	112	71,240	1:50.80	99
1994	Trishyde	5	C.J. McCarron	117	Eskimo's Angel	115	Ma Guerre	109	107,347	1:51.34	95
1995	Fit to Lead	5	Sellers SJ	117	Pennyhill Park	118	Low Key Affair	112	107,055	1:51.59	102
1996	Serena's Song	4	G.L. Stevens	124	Halo America	117	Alcovy	117	109,493	1:50.30	105
1997	Gold 'n Delicious	4	C.H. Borel	113	Effectiveness	111	Everhope	111	104,718	1:52.87	99
1998	Escena	5	S.J. Sellers	123	One Rich Lady	113	Tomisue's Delight	118	199,020	1:50.19	113
1999	Banshee Breeze	4	R.J. Albarado	124	Silent Eskimo	114	Meadow Vista	109	197,718	1:50.02	110
2000	Heritage of Gold	5	S.J. Sellers	121	Silvebulletday	119	Roza Robata	115	201,252	1:48.26	116
2001	Saudi Poetry	4	V. Espinoza	114	Secret Status	119	Asher	112	206,460	1:49.27	101
2002	Spain	5	J.F. Chavez	121	With Ability	117	Dancethruthedawn	119	204,228	1:49.64	100
2003	You	4	J.D. Bailey	119	Printemps	114	Nonsuch Bay	114	203,298	1:49.12	103
2004	Adoration	5	V. Espinoza	122	Bare Necessities	120	La Reason	110	272,304	1:52.15	94

Beyer Index: 101.40

FLORAL PARK HANDICAP (G3), 6 Furlongs, Fillies and Mares, 3-Year-Olds and Up, Belmont Park, 2004 Purse: $104,400

Year	Winner	Age	Jockey	Wt.	Second	Wt.	Third	Wt.	Win Value	Time	Beyer
1995	Twist Afleet	4	G.L. Stevens	120	For All Reason	115	Regal Solution	113	32,490	1:09.20	109
1996	Lottsa Talc	6	F.T. Alvarado	119	Fresa	113	Culver City	113	38,736	1:09.80	95
1997	Creamy Dreamy	4	R.G. Davis	118	Silent City	113	Secret Prospect	118	47,835	1:10.40	93
1998	Blue Begonia	5	J.F. Chavez	114	Dixie Flag	117	Soverign Lady	116	48,570	1:10.20	100
1999	Positive Gal	3	J.D. Bailey	113	Final Proposal	113	Flamingo Way	113	49,125	1:09.23	102
2000	Big Bambu	3	R.G. Davis	114	Tropical Punch	114	Cash Run	114	64,620	1:09.81	104
2001	Gold Mover	3	E.S. Prado	114	Dat You Miz Blue	119	Finder's Fee	115	65,040	1:10.00	100
2002	Carson Hollow	3	J.R. Velazquez	117	Gold Mover	117	Shiny Band	115	63,955	1:10.25	107
2003	Bauhauser	5	R. Migliore	115	Shine Again	120	Literary Light	113	65,100	1:10.84	94
2004	Feline Story	3	E.S. Prado	114	Cologny	115	Travelator	116	63,840	1:10.69	93

Beyer Index: 99.70

FLORIDA DERBY (G1), 1 1/8 Miles, 3-Year-Olds, Gulfstream Park, 2004 Purse: $1,000,000

Year	Winner	Age	Jockey	Wt.	Second	Wt.	Third	Wt.	Win Value	Time	Beyer
1952	Sky Ship	3	R. Nash	114	Handsome Teddy	117	Sandtop	111	17,550	1:50.80	
1953	Money Broker	3	A. Popara	117	Blaze	111	Jamie K.	117	88,000	1:53.80	
							Slim	117			
1954	Correlation	3	W. Shoemaker	119	Goyamo	119	Big Crest	113	100,000	1:55.20	
1955	Nashua	3	E. Arcaro	122	Blue Lem	113	First Cabin	113	100,000	1:53.20	
1956	Needles	3	E. Erb	117	Count Chic	119	Pintor Lea	113	95,200	1:48.60	
1957	Gen. Duke	3	W. Hartack	122	Bold Ruler	122	Iron Liege	118	73,400	1:46.80	
1958	Tim Tam	3	W. Hartack	122	Lincoln Road	118	Grey Monarch	122	77,900	1:49.20	
1959	Easy Spur	3	W. Hartack	122	Sword Dancer	122	Master Palynch	122	75,300	1:47.20	
1960	Bally Ache	3	R. Ussery	122	Venetian Way	122	Victoria Park	122	79,500	1:47.60	
1961	Carry Back	3	J. Sellers	122	Crozier	122	Beau Prince	122	75,100	1:48.80	
1962	Ridan	3	M. Ycaza	122	Cicada	117	Admiral's Voyage	122	85,800	1:50.40	
1963	Candy Spots	3	W. Shoemaker	122	Sky Wonder	122	Cool Prince	122	74,700	1:50.60	
1964	Northern Dancer	3	W. Shoemaker	122	The Scoundrel	122	Dandy K.	122	76,500	1:50.80	
1965	Native Charger	3	J.L. Rotz	122	Hail to All	122	Gallant Lad	122	79,800	1:51.20	
1966	Williamston Kid	3	R.L. Stevenson	122	Bold and Brave	122	Sky Guy	122	83,400	1:50.60	
	Abe's Hope finished first but was disqualified and placed fourth										
1967	In Reality	3	E. Fires	122	Biller	122	Reason to Hail	122	99,400	1:50.20	

Year	Winner	Age	Jockey	Wt.	Second	Wt.	Third	Wt.	Win Value	Time	Beyer
1968	Forward Pass	3	D. Brumfield	122	Iron Ruler	122	Perfect Tan	118	94,100	1:49.00	
1969	Top Knight	3	M. Ycaza	122	Arts and Letters	122	Al Hattab	122	81,800	1:48.40	
1970	My Dad George	3	R. Broussard	122	Corn off the Cob	122	Cassie Red	122	103,600	1:50.80	
1971	Eastern Fleet	3	E. Maple	118	Executioner	122	Jim French	122	82,680	1:47.40	
1972	Upper Case	3	R. Turcotte	118	Spanish Riddle	122	Gentle Smoke	122	107,760	1:50.00	
1973	Royal and Regal	3	W. Blum	122	Forego	118	Restless Jet	122	78,120	1:47.40	
1974	Judger	3	L. Pincay Jr	118	Cannonade	122	Buck's Bid	118	130,200	1:49.00	
1975	Prince Thou Art	3	B. Baeza	118	Sylvan Place	118	Foolish Pleasure	122	94,440	1:50.40	
1976	Honest Pleasure	3	B. Baeza	122	Great Contractor	122	Proud Birdie	122	94,110	1:47.80	
1977	Coined Silver	3	B. Thornburg	118	Nearly on Time	122	Fort Prevel	122	68,700	1:48.80	
1977	Ruthie's Native	3	C. Perret	122	For the Moment	122	Sir Sir	122	69,900	1:50.20	
1978	Alydar	3	J. Velasquez	122	Believe It	122	Dr. Valeri	122	100,000	1:47.00	
1979	Spectacular Bid	3	R. Franklin	122	Lot o' Gold	122	Fantasy 'n Reality	122	115,000	1:48.80	
1980	Plugged Nickle	3	B. Thornburg	122	Naked Sky	122	Lord Gallant	118	110,000	1:50.20	
1981	Lord Avie	3	C.J. McCarron	122	Akureyri	122	Linnleur	118	147,388	1:50.40	
1982	Timely Writer	3	J. Fell	122	Star Gallant	122	Our Escapade	122	150,000	1:49.60	
1983	Croeso	3	F. Olivares	118	Copelan	122	Law Talk	118	150,000	1:49.80	
1984	Swale	3	L. Pincay Jr	122	Dr. Carter	122	Darn that Alarm	122	180,000	1:47.60	
1985	Proud Truth	3	J. Velasquez	122	Irish Sur	122	Do It Again Dan	122	180,000	1:50.00	
1986	Snow Chief	3	A. Solis	122	Badger Land	122	Mogambo	122	300,000	1:51.80	
1987	Cryptoclearance	3	J.A. Santos	122	No More Flowers	118	Talinum	122	300,000	1:49.60	
1988	Brian's Time	3	R.P. Romero	118	Forty Niner	122	Notebook	122	300,000	1:49.80	
1989	Mercedes Won	3	E. Fires	122	Western Playboy	118	Big Stanley	122	300,000	1:49.60	
1990	Unbridled	3	P. Day	122	Slavic	122	Run Turn	122	300,000	1:52.00	
1991	Fly So Free	3	J.A. Santos	122	Strike the Gold	118	Hansel	122	300,000	1:50.40	
1992	Technology	3	J.D. Bailey	122	Dance Floor	122	Pistols and Roses	122	300,000	1:50.60	101
1993	Bull Inthe Heather	3	W.S. Ramos	122	Storm Tower	122	Wallenda	122	300,000	1:51.20	94
1994	Holy Bull	3	M.E. Smith	122	Ride the Rails	122	Halo's Image	122	300,000	1:47.40	115
1995	Thunder Gulch	3	M.E. Smith	122	Suave Prospect	122	Mecke	122	300,000	1:49.60	101
1996	Unbridled's Song	3	M.E. Smith	122	Editor's Note	122	Skip Away	122	300,000	1:47.80	114
1997	Captain Bodgit	3	A. Solis	122	Pulpit	122	Frisk Me Now	122	300,000	1:50.60	104
1998	Cape Town	3	S.J. Sellers	122	Lil's Lad	122	Halory Hunter	122	450,000	1:49.21	108
	Lil's Lad finished first but was disqualified and placed second										
1999	Vicar	3	S.J. Sellers	122	Wondertross	122	Cat Thief	122	450,000	1:50.83	102
2000	Hal's Hope	3	R.I. Velez	122	High Yield	122	Tahkodha Hills	122	450,000	1:51.49	102
2001	Monarchos	3	J.F. Chavez	122	Outofthebox	122	Imvisible Ink	122	600,000	1:49.95	105
2002	Harlan's Holiday	3	E. Prado	122	Blue Burner	122	Peekskill	122	600,000	1:48.80	101
2003	Empire Maker	3	J.D. Bailey	122	Trust n Luck	122	Indy Dancer	122	600,000	1:49.05	108
2004	Friends Lake	3	R. Migliore	122	Value Plus	122	The Cliff's Edge	122	600,000	1:51.38	92

Beyer Index: 103.62

FLOWER BOWL INVITATIONAL (G1), 1 1/4 Miles (Turf), Fillies and Mares, 3-Year-Olds and Up, Belmont Park, 2004 Purse: $750,000

Year	Winner	Age	Jockey	Wt.	Second	Wt.	Third	Wt.	Win Value	Time	Beyer
1978	Waya	4	A. Cordero Jr	120	Magnificence	108	Leave Me Alone	108	32,490	2:00.60	
1979	Pearl Necklace	5	W. Shoemaker	125	The Very One	112	Terpsichorist	118	68,160	2:02.20	
1980	Just a Game II	4	D. Brumfield	124	Hey Babe	114	Euphrosyne	112	68,640	2:00.80	
1981	Rokeby Rose	4	J. Fell	114	De La Rose	116	Euphrosyne	110	67,200	2:01.60	
1982	Trevita	5	R. Hernandez	117	Hunston	108	Hush Dear	112	71,880	2:01.40	
1983	First Approach	5	J. Velasquez	117	If Winter Comes	113	Mintage	111	68,160	2:00.20	
1984	Rossard	4	L. Pincay Jr	117	Aspen Rose	115	Persian Tiara	116	72,840	2:03.40	
1985	Dawn's Curtsey	3	E. Maple	111	Vers la Caisse	116	Agacerie	117	87,540	2:02.20	
1986	Scoot	3	W. Shoemaker	106			Cope of Flowers	113	65,652	2:00.40	
	Dismasted	4	J.L. Samyn	115							
1987	Slew's Exceller	5	J.A. Santos	113	Videogenic	118	Fiesta Gal	114	91,020	2:02.20	
1988	Gaily Gaily	5	J.A. Krone	109	Love You by Heart	116	Princely Proof	116	76,800	2:02.80	
1989	River Memories	5	P. Day	112	Capades	116	Miss Unnameable	116	74,880	2:06.80	
1990	Laugh and Be Merry	5	W.H. McCauley	115	Foresta	111	Gaily Gaily	117	78,840	2:00.20	105
1991	Lady Shirl	4	R. Migliore	117	Franc Argument	111	Christiecat	120	120,000	2:02.40	106
1992	Christiecat	5	J.L. Samyn	116	Ratings	114	Plenty of Grace	115	120,000	2:01.00	105
1993	Far Out Beast	6	J.L. Samyn	111	Dahlia's Dreamer	110	Lady Blessington	118	90,000	2:03.80	98
1994	Dahlia's Dreamer	5	J.F. Chavez	112	Alywow	114	Danish	113	120,000	2:05.40	113
1995	Northern Emerald	5	R.B. Perez	113	Danish	116	Duda	113	120,000	2:06.60	105
1996	Chelsey Flower	5	R.G. Davis	115	Powder Bowl	116	Electric Society	118	210,000	2:05.80	108
1997	Yashmak	3	C.S. Nakatani	114	Maxzene	123	Memories of Silver	123	240,000	1:59.60	107
1998	Auntie Mame	4	J.R. Velazquez	121	B.A. Valentine	114	Bahr	118	240,000	1:59.33	104
1999	Soaring Softly	4	J.D. Bailey	118	Coretta	118	Mossflower	115	240,000	2:01.41	103
2000	Colstar	4	J.L. Samyn	116	Snow Polina	121	Pico Teneriffe	115	450,000	2:01.78	105
2001	Lailani	3	J.D. Bailey	118	England's Legend	123	Starine	120	450,000	2:01.88	111
2002	Kazzia	3	J.F. Chavez	118	Turtle Bow	115	Mot Juste	118	450,000	2:05.22	103
2003	Dimitrova	3	J.D. Bailey	114	Walzerkoenigin	120	Heat Haze	123	450,000	2:02.74	103
2004	Riskaverse	5	C. Velasquez	118	Commercante	118	Moscow Burning	120	450,000	2:04.65	102

Beyer Index: 105.20

Run on main track in 1987

FOREGO HANDICAP (G1), 7 Furlongs, 3-Year-Olds and Up, Saratoga Race Course, 2004 Purse: $250,000

Year	Winner	Age	Jockey	Wt.	Second	Wt.	Third	Wt.	Win Value	Time	Beyer
1980	Tanthem	5	J. Velasquez	114	Dr. Patches	114	Hold Your Tricks	116	51,030	1:35.00	
1981	Fappiano	4	A. Cordero	119	Herb Water	108	Guilty Conscience	112	50,220	1:33.80	
1982	Engine One	4	R. Hernandez	112	Rise Jim	121	Pass the Tab	120	33,360	1:21.20	
1983	Maudlin	5	A. Cordero Jr	119	Danebo	115	Singh Tu	115	32,580	1:21.60	
1984	Mugatea	4	R.G. Davis	111	Eskimo	108	I Enclose	111	53,370	1:22.40	
1985	Ziggy's Boy	3	A. Cordero Jr	115	Taylor's Special	124	Knight of Armor	112	66,510	1:21.20	
1986	Groovy	3	J.A. Santos	119	Turkoman	124	Innamorato	110	83,820	1:21.20	
1987	Groovy	4	A. Cordero Jr	132	Purple Mountain	113	Sun Master	118	81,060	1:21.80	
1988	Quick Call	4	P. Day	110	Mawsuff	110	High Brite	122	68,520	1:21.00	
1989	Quick Call	5	P. Day	116	Dancing Spree	117	Sewickley	119	67,920	1:21.80	
1990	Lay Down	6	C.W. Antley	113	Quick Call	120	Traskwood	112	51,840	1:22.80	107
1991	Housebuster	4	C. Perret	126	Senor Speedy	112	Clever Trevor	120	69,480	1:21.00	113
1992	Rubiano	5	J.A. Krone	124	Drummond Lane	115	Diablo	114	70,080	1:22.40	110
1993	Birdonthewire	4	M.E. Smith	117	Harlan	110	Senor Speedy	117	73,080	1:21.80	111
1994	American Chance	5	P. Day	113	Evil Bear	114	Go for Gin	117	66,000	1:22.60	108
1995	Not Surprising	5	R.G. Davis	121	Our Emblem	113	Lite the Fuse	123	64,200	1:21.80	120
1996	Langfuhr	4	J.F. Chavez	110	Top Account	115	Lite the Fuse	121	90,000	1:21.40	109
1997	Score A Birdie	6	W.H. McCauley	113	Victor Cooley	120	Royal Haven	120	120,000	1:22.40	111
1998	Affirmed Success	4	J.F. Chavez	115	Receiver	114	Purple Passion	114	120,000	1:21.80	120
1999	Crafty Friend	6	G.L. Stevens	119	Affirmed Success	119	Sir Bear	119	150,000	1:21.20	115
2000	Shadow Caster	4	J.F. Chavez	113	Intidab	118	Successful Appeal	119	150,000	1:15.00	114
2001	Delaware Township	5	J.D. Bailey	116	Left Bank	115	Alannan	117	150,000	1:15.53	109
2002	Orientate	4	J.D. Bailey	122	Aldebaran	115	Multiple Choice	114	150,000	1:15.68	116
2003	Aldebaran	5	J.D. Bailey	123	Najran	114	Gygistar	119	150,000	1:21.26	122
2004	Midas Eyes	4	E.S. Prado	117	Clock Stopper	114	Gygistar	114	150,000	1:22.22	113

Beyer Index: 113.20

Distance 6 1/2 furlongs 2000–2002

FORT MARCY HANDICAP (G3), 1 1/16 Miles (Turf), 3-Year-Olds and Up, Aqueduct, 2004 Purse: $111,400

Year	Winner	Age	Jockey	Wt.	Second	Wt.	Third	Wt.	Win Value	Time	Beyer
1975	Apollo Nine	8	M. Venezia	110	Silver Badge	112	Bold Play	112	24,630	1:23.00	
1975	Beau Bugle	5	J. Cruguet	113	Ribot Grande	112	New Alibhai	112	24,510	1:22.40	
1978	True Colors	4	E. Maple	114	Proud Arion	112	Cinteelo	119	25,410	1:42.80	
1978	Tiller	4	J. Fell	112	Noble Dancer II	127	Arachnoid	111	25,410	1:41.80	
1979	Uncle Pokey	5	J. Cruguet	113	Alias Smith	114	Proud Arion	111	32,550	1:45.60	
1980	Sten	5	C.B. Asmussen	115	Native Courier	126	Told	113	35,460	1:44.00	
1981	Masked Marvel	5	R.I. Encinas	112	Blue Ensign	116	Freeo	113	33,300	1:44.80	
1981	Key to Content	4	J. Fell	117	Ghazwan	114	Contare	107	33,060	1:46.00	
1982	Folge	4	J. Velasquez	110	Johnny Dance	114	St. Brendan	116	36,060	1:42.80	
1983	John's Gold	4	A. Graell	108	Acaroid	115	Beagle	105	36,600	1:47.40	
1984	Hero's Honor	4	J.D. Bailey	115	Super Sunrise	126	Reinvested	113	54,270	1:43.60	
1985	Forzando II	4	J. Velasquez	120	Native Raid	115	Solidified	113	54,180	1:46.00	
1986	Onyxly	5	J.A. Santos	117	Equalize	114	Lieutenant's Lark	117	55,890	1:42.20	
1987	Dance of Life	4	R.P Romero	120	Regal Flier	113	Iroko	113	84,240	1:45.00	
1987	Glaros	5	E. Maple	112	Onyxly	113	Expl'sive Dancer	111	85,200	1:45.00	
1988	Equalize	6	J.A. Santos	115	All Hands on Deck	109	Glaros	111	89,340	1:42.60	
1989	Arlene's Valentine	4	J.A. Krone	112	Fourstardave	113	Sunshine Forever	126	52,920	1:50.20	
1990	Crystal Moment	5	J.F. Chavez	113	Impersonator	112	Wanderkin	117	53,010	1:43.40	
1991	Stage Colony	4	C. Perret	115	Chenin Blanc	114	Scottish Monk	116	54,630	1:42.20	
1992	Maxigroom	4	J.A. Krone	111	Colchis Island	111	Buchman	111	56,460	1:42.60	102
1993	Adam Smith	5	J.L. Samyn	112	Kiri's Clown	114	Casino Magistrate	113	55,260	1:42.20	102
1994	Adam Smith	6	M.E. Smith	118	Halissee	113	Nijinsky's Gold	113	49,650	1:42.40	105
1995	Fourstars Allstar	7	Santos JA	118	Chief Master	112	A in Sociology	118	50,250	1:41.60	105
1996	Warning Glance	5	M.E. Smith	119	Shahid	115	Grand Continental	113	51,690	1:42.40	106
1997	Influent	6	J.L. Samyn	117	Slicious	115	Montjoy	117	67,140	1:47.40	106
1998	Subordination	4	J.F. Chavez	118	Fortitude	116	Crimson Guard	110	67,620	1:35.20	111
1999	Wised Up	4	M.J. Luzzi	112	N B Forrest	116	La-Faah	114	69,660	1:45.03	100
2000	Spindrift	5	J.L. Samyn	115	Middlesex Drive	118	Wised Up	114	67,680	1:40.88	109
2001	Strategic Mission	6	R. Migliore	118	Pine Dance	116	Legal Jousting	114	67,740	1:41.62	104
2002	Pyrus	4	E.S. Prado	113	Proud Man	116	Capsized	113	67,260	1:44.53	98
2003	Saint Verre	5	J.L. Espinoza	117	Windsor Castle	119	Judge's Case	115	70,500	1:33.77	112
2004	Chilly Rooster	4	S. Uske	113	Union Place	113	Slew Valley	119	66,840	1:42.47	99

Beyer Index: 104.54

Off the turf in 2003.

(STONERSIDE) FORWARD GAL (G2), 7 Furlongs, 3-Year-Old Fillies, Gulfstream Park, 2004 Purse: $150,000

Year	Winner	Age	Jockey	Wt.	Second	Wt.	Third	Wt.	Win Value	Time	Beyer
1981	Dame Mysterieuse	3	J.L. Samyn	118	Heavenly Cause	121	Master's Dream	113	26,040	1:22.20	
1982	Trove	3	L. Saumell	116	Here's to Peg	112	Wendy's Ten	113	17,828	1:22.80	
1982	All Manners	3	O.J. Londono	116	Acharmer	114	Smart Heiress	112	17,978	1:23.00	
1983	Unaccompanied	3	R. Woodhouse	114	Lisa's Capital	114	Quixotic Lady	113	28,203	1:23.40	
1984	Miss Oceana	3	E. Maple	121	Katrinka	112	Scorched Panties	121	24,108	1:22.40	
1985	Lucy Manette	3	C. Perret	114	Grand Glory	112	Boldly Dared	112	39,690	1:23.40	
1986	Noranc	3	W.H. McCauley	116	Dancing Danzig	112	I'm Sweets	121	36,000	1:23.80	
1987	Added Elegance	3	J. Vasquez	121	Beau Love Flowers	112	Easter Mary	112	37,380	1:24.60	
1988	On to Royalty	3	C. Perret	114	Social Pro	112	Most Likely	112	37,020	1:23.20	
1989	Open Mind	3	A. Cordero Jr	121	Surging	114	Georgies Doctor	118	36,780	1:24.20	
1990	Charon	3	E. Fires	112	Trumpet's Blare	121	De La Devil	121	36,180	1:24.80	
1991	Withallprobability	3	C. Perret	114	Private Treasure	118	Far Out Nurse	112	48,240	1:22.40	
1992	Spinning Round	3	J.A. Santos	118	Patty's Princess	116	Super Doer	118	44,550	1:24.80	83
1993	Sum Runner	3	E. Fires	118	Boots 'n Jackie	121	Lunar Spook	118	45,250	1:23.60	95
1994	Mynameispanama	3	M. Castaneda	113	Frigid Coed	116	Wonderlan	114	45,960	1:22.80	82
1995	Chaposa Springs	3	H. Castillo Jr	114	Culver City	113	Mackenzie Slew	114	44,580	1:24.00	101
1996	Mindy Gayle	3	J.A. Krone	112	Marfa's Finale	113	Supah Jen	114	45,000	1:24.40	92
1997	Glitter Woman	3	M.E. Smith	114	City Band	121	Southern Playgirl	121	45,000	1:21.60	105
1998	Uanme	3	S.J. Sellers	113	Diamond on the Run	114	Holy Capote	112	45,000	1:24.40	86
1999	China Storm	3	P. Day	114	Three Ring	121	Extended Applause	112	45,000	1:23.69	90
2000	Miss Inquistive	3	T.G. Turner	114	Swept Away	118	Regally Appealing	118	45,000	1:22.25	98
2001	Gold Mover	3	J.D. Bailey	121	Hazino	114	Thunder Bertie	118	60,000	1:22.43	95
2002	Take the Cake	3	R.R. Douglas	117	A New Twist	121	Cherokee Girl	117	60,000	1:25.47	81
2003	Midnight Cry	3	E.S. Prado	117	Final Round	117	Chimichurri	121	60,000	1:22.55	91
2004	Madcap Escapade	3	J.D. Bailey	121	La Reina	121	Frenchglen	115	90,000	1:22.97	95

Beyer Index: 91.85

STEPHEN FOSTER HANDICAP (G1), 1 1/8 Miles, 3-Year-Olds and Up, Churchill Downs, 2004 Purse: $810,750

Year	Winner	Age	Jockey	Wt.	Second	Wt.	Third	Wt.	Win Value	Time	Beyer
1982	Vodika Collins	4	T. Barrow	116	Mythical Ruler	113	Two's a Plenty	115	38,610	1:51.80	
1983	Vodika Collins	5	L. Moyers	118	Mythical Ruler	120	Northern Majesty	114	35,588	1:49.20	
1984	Mythical Ruler	6	J. McKnight	117	Fairly Straight	114	Le Cou Cou	121	34,808	1:49.60	
1985	Vanlandingham	4	P. Day	121	Manantial	112	Sovereign Exchange	113	35,263	1:48.80	
1986	Hopeful Word	5	K.K. Allen	123	Dramatic Desire	114	Ten Gold Pots	122	64,133	1:49.40	
1987	Red Attack	5	J.L. Kaenel	119	Sir Naskra	116	Blue Buckaroo	117	65,254	1:51.20	
1988	Honor Medal	7	L.E. Ortega	123	Outlaws Sham	115	Momsfurrari	109	82,655	1:50.60	
1989	Air Worthy	4	D.J. Soto	115	J.T.'s Pet	115	Present Value	114	73,255	1:49.60	
1990	No Marker	6	A.T. Gryder	115	Western Playboy	117	Lucky Peach	114	72,930	1:49.80	
1991	Black Tie Affair	5	J.L. Diaz	119	Private School	114	Greydar	115	70,915	1:49.80	104
1992	Discover	4	B.E. Bongard	116	Barkerville	113	Classic Seven	113	75,335	1:50.00	111
1993	Root Boy	5	T.G. Turner	113	Discover	114	Flying Continental	117	74,100	1:50.80	99
1994	Recoup the Cash	4	J.L. Diaz	112	Taking Risks	113	Dignitas	113	106,275	1:49.40	108
1995	Recoup the Cash	5	A.T. Gryder	119	Tyus	114	Powerful Punch	114	109,297	1:49.20	105
1996	Tenants Harbor	4	F.C. Torres	112	Pleasant Tango	113	Mt. Sassafras	115	107,933	1:49.80	109
1997	City By Night	4	S.J. Sellers	113	Victor Cooley	115	Semoran	113	101,649	1:50.40	115
1998	Awesome Again	4	P. Day	113	Silver Charm	127	Semoran	115	495,690	1:48.60	118
1999	Victory Gallop	4	J.D. Bailey	120	Nite Dreamer	110	Littlebitlively	115	512,895	1:47.20	118
2000	Golden Missile	5	K.J. Desormeaux	118	Ecton Park	114	Cat Thief	117	502,200	1:49.56	116
2001	Guided Tour	5	L. Melancon	113	Captain Steve	123	Brahms	114	515,220	1:47.74	116
2002	Street Cry	4	J.D. Bailey	120	Dollar Bill	114	Tenpins	115	516,615	1:47.84	116
2003	Perfect Drift	4	P. Day	115	Mineshaft	123	Aldebaran	120	531,030	1:47.55	117
2004	Colonial Colony	6	R. Bejarano	111	Southern Image	122	Perfect Drift	119	502,665	1:50.40	110

Beyer Index: 111.57

FOUNTAIN OF YOUTH (G2), 1 1/16 Miles, 3-Year-Olds, Gulfstream Park, 2004 Purse: $250,000

Year	Winner	Age	Jockey	Wt.	Second	Wt.	Third	Wt.	Win Value	Time	Beyer
1945	Twenty Thirty	2	R. Watson	118	Flag Drill	117	Best Dress	116	3,200	1:45.20	
1947	Atomic Power	3	M. Buxton	116	Skeleton	106	Red Devil	112	6,050	1:40.60	
1947	Tight Squeeze	2	R. Sisto	117	Phar Mon	124	Montayr	115	7,150	1:11.80	
1949	Count-a-Bit	3	J. Robertson	116	Fugitive	113	Top Admiral	114	3,250	1:44.20	
1950	Black George	3	K. Church	110	Theory	123	Erosion	111	3,250	1:23.40	
1951	Alerted	3	W. Cook	114	Pur Sang	118	Blue Speed	115	3,250	1:24.20	

Year	Winner	Age	Jockey	Wt.	Second	Wt.	Third	Wt.	Win Value	Time	Beyer
1953	Ram o' War	3	D. Dodson	115	Slim	112	Dr. Stanley	104	12,150	1:42.60	
1953	Tribe	3	B. Green	120	Sickle's Sound	108	Royal Bay Gem	122	12,300	1:43.40	
1954	Sea O Erin	3	J. Adams	112	Remand	112	Bergeruk	104	11,800	1:48.60	
1955	Nance's Lad	3	J. Choquette	117	First Cabin	117	Blue Lem	116	13,550	1:43.60	
1956	Oh Johnny	3	H. Woodhouse	114	Greek Spy	116	Fabius	118	12,765	1:44.20	
1957	Gen. Duke	3	W. Hartack	119	Iron Liege	113	Better Bee	113	11,560	1:44.00	
1958	Tim Tam	3	W. Hartack	122	Grey Monarch	119	Li'l Fella	122	9,725	1:42.80	
1959	Easy Spur	3	W. Hartack	119	Troilus	122	Rare Rice	116	10,275	1:41.80	
1960	Eagle Admiral	3	M. Ycaza	119	Bally Ache	122	Power Dame	116	10,550	1:41.80	
1961	Beau Prince	3	E. Arcaro	113	Crozier	122	Carry Back	122	10,575	1:43.20	
1962	Sharp Count	3	W. Shoemaker	110	Docot Hank K	110	Good Fight	119	10,400	1:43.20	
1963	Cool Prince	3	J. Combest	110	Hot Dust	111	King Toots	119	10,725	1:45.80	
1964	Dandy K	3	M. Solomone	112	Roman Brother	122	Saltville	111	11,075	1:44.80	
1965	Maribeau	3	S. Boulmetis	111	Hail to All	119	Sparkling Johnny	112	11,275	1:44.60	
1966	Kauai King	3	D. Brumfield	113	Amberoid	112	Abe's Hope	116	11,550	1:43.20	
1967	In Reality	3	E. Fires	122	Biller	122	Reason to Hail	119	15,125	1:44.40	
1968	Wise Exchange	3	E. Belmonte	122	Master Bold	119	Subpet	122	14,925	1:43.80	
	Forward Pass finished second but was disqualified and placed fourth										
1969	Al Hattab	3	R. Broussard	122	Arts and Letters	119	Ad Majora	122	13,925	1:42.60	
1970	Corn Off the Cob	3	A. Cordero Jr	113	Naskra	119	Nehoc's Brother	110	24,950	1:44.60	
1971	Authorize	3	J. Vasquez	112	Northfields	113	Glorioso	114	20,160	1:42.40	
1972	Gentle Smoke	3	W. Blum	113	Native Admiral	112	Tarboosh	112	43,020	1:42.00	
1973	Shecky Greene	3	B. Baeza	122	Twice a Prince	117	My Gallant	112	22,950	1:43.80	
1974	Green Gambados	3	C. Baltazar	112	Judger	115	Eric's Champ	112	46,440	1:42.40	
1975	Greek Answer	3	M. Solomone	122	Decipher	115	Gatch	116	22,650	1:42.80	
1976	Sonkisser	3	B. Baeza	117	Proud Birdie	122	Archie Beamish	113	22,770	1:43.80	
1977	Ruthie's Native	3	C. Perret	122	Steve's Friend	112	Fort Prevel	117	26,010	1:42.00	
	Fort Prevel finished second but was disqualfied and placed third										
1978	Sensitive Prince	3	M. Solomone	114	Believe It	122	Kissing U.	113	22,170	1:41.00	
1979	Spectacular Bid	3	R.J. Franklin	122	Lot O' Gold	117	Bishop's Choice	122	35,880	1:41.20	
1980	Naked Sky	3	J.D. Bailey	112	Joanie's Chief	122	Gold Stage	122	29,820	1:43.80	
1981	Akureyri	3	E. Maple	119	Pleasant Colony	122	Lord Avie	122	47,697	1:44.40	
1982	Star Gallant	3	S. Hawley	117	Distinctive Pro	117	Cut Away	113	54,630	1:43.20	
1983	Highland Park	3	D. Brumfield	122	Thalassocrat	117	Chumming	114	45,338	1:44.60	
1983	Copelan	3	L. Pincay Jr	122	Current Hope	117	Blink	112	44,888	1:43.60	
1984	Darn That Alarm	3	M. Venezia	112	Counterfeit Money	112	Swale	122	73,200	1:43.00	
1985	Proud Truth	3	J. Velasquez	112	Stephan's Odyssey	122	Do It Again Dan	112	106,860	1:43.60	
1986	Ensign Rhythm	3	J. Pezua	112	Jig's Haven	113	Regal Dreamer	117	57,210	1:45.60	
1986	My Prince Charming	3	J.A. Santos	112	Mykawa	117	Papal Power	122	78,060	1:45.00	
1987	Bet Twice	3	C. Perret	122	No More Flowers	112	Gone West	114	100,482	1:43.40	
1988	Forty Niner	3	E. Maple	122	Notebook	122	Buoy	119	98,991	1:43.20	
1989	Dixieland Brass	3	R. Romero	122	Mercedes Won	122	Big Stanley	122	130,000	1:44.60	
1990	Shot Gun Scott	3	D. Penna	122	Smelly	119	Unbridled	117	77,427	1:44.60	99
1991	Fly So Free	3	J.A. Santos	122	Moment of True	117	Subordinated Debt	113	77,737	1:44.20	
1992	Dance Floor	3	C.W. Antley	122	Pistols and Roses	119	Tiger Tiger	112	150,258	1:45.20	98
	Careful Gesture finished second but was disqualified and placed fifth										
1993	Duc d' Sligovil	3	J. Krone	112	Bull Inthe Heather	113	Silver of Silver	122	37,698	1:45.00	94
1993	Storm Tower	3	R. Wilson	112	Great Navigator	117	Kissin Kris	117	37,698	1:44.80	96
1994	Dehere	3	C. Perret	119	Go for Gin		Ride the Rails		120,000	1:44.60	99
1995	Thunder Gulch	3	M.E. Smith	119	Suave Prospect	117	Jambalaya Jazz	119	120,000	1:43.20	105
1996	Built for Pleasure	3	G. Boulanger	112	Unbridled's Song	119	Victory Speech	114	120,000	1:43.60	100
1997	Pulpit	3	S.J. Sellers	112	Blazing Sword	117	Captain Bodgit	117	120,000	1:41.80	104
1998	Lil's Lad	3	J.D. Bailey	112	Coronado's Quest	119	Halory Hunter	112	120,000	1:42.60	113
1999	Vicar	3	S.J. Sellers	114	Cat Thief	119	Certain	117	120,000	1:45.64	97
2000	High Yield	3	P. Day	117	Hal's Hope	117	Elite Mercedes	117	120,000	1:42.56	100
2001	Songandaprayer	3	E.S. Prado	117	Outofthebox	114	City Zip	117	120,000	1:43.48	100
2002	Booklet	3	J.F. Chavez	122	Harlan's Holiday	122	Blue Burner	116	120,000	1:44.49	103
2003	Trust n Luck	3	C. Velasquez	122	Supah Blitz	120	Midway Cat	116	120,000	1:43.33	106
2004	Read the Footnotes	3	J.D. Bailey	122	Second of June	120	Silver Wagon	120	150,000	1:42.71	113

Beyer Index: 101.80

Run twice in 1947. For 2-year-olds in 1945, 1947. Distance 6 furlongs in December 1947; 1 mile 70 yards, March 1947, 1949; 7 furlongs, 1950–51

FOURSTARDAVE HANDICAP (G2), 1 1/16 Miles (Turf), 3-Year-Olds and Up, Saratoga Race Course, 2004 Purse: $200,000

Year	Winner	Age	Jockey	Wt.	Second	Wt.	Third	Wt.	Win Value	Time	Beyer
1988	Sans the Shadow	4	A. Cordero Jr	115	My Big Boy	117	Real Courage	115	56,340	1:40.00	
1989	Steinlen	6	A. Cordero Jr	122	Expensive Decision	117	Sparkling Wit	110	53,955	1:41.00	

Year	Winner	Age	Jockey	Wt.	Second	Wt.	Third	Wt.	Win Value	Time	Beyer
1989	Highland Springs	5	E.S. Prado	122	Fourstardave	122	Soviet Lad	115	53,955	1:41.60	
1990	Fourstardave	5	M.E. Smith	115	Foreign Survivor	119	Wanderkin	119	57,150	1:41.20	
1991	Fourstardave	6	M.E. Smith	115	Who's to Pay	122	Kate's Valentine	117	71,640	1:38.80	
1992	Now Listen	5	J.R. Velazquez	119	Crackedbell	119	Cold Hoist	115	71,640	1:36.60	98
1993	Lure	4	M.E. Smith	122	Fourstardave	122	Scott the Great	115	71,640	1:40.80	108
1994	A in Sociology	4	Samyn JL	115	Namaqualand	113	Fourstars Allstar	120	68,340	1:41.20	107
1995	Pride of Summer	7	Maple E	115	Fourstars Allstar	120	Jaggery John	120	69,240	1:40.80	109
1996	Da Hoss	4	J.R. Velazquez	113	Green Means Go	113	Rare Reason	118	71,100	1:40.40	109
1997	Soviet Line	7	P. Day	118	Val's Prince	114	Outta My Way Man	118	67,500	1:39.80	106
1998	Wild Event	5	M. Guidry	116	Bomfim	114	Rob 'n Gin	119	68,940	1:39.20	108
1999	Comic Strip	4	P. Day	115	Divide and Conquer	114	Bomfim	113	90,000	1:41.76	108
2000	Hap	4	J.D. Bailey	118	Altibr	115	Weatherbird	112	120,000	1:40.24	104
2001	Dr. Kashnikow	4	J.R. Velazquez	113	Tubrok	113	Aly's Alley	117	120,000	1:39.30	104
2002	Capsized	6	J.A. Santos	115	Pure Prize	119	Pyrus	113	120,000	1:50.90	108
2003	Trademark	7	R. Migliore	118	Quest Star	116	Tap the Admiral	115	120,000	1:39.29	109
2004	Nothing to Lose	4	J.R. Velazquez	117	Silver Tree	117	Royal Regalia	114	120,000	1:39.50	107

Beyer Index: 106.54

Run on main track, 2002

FRIZETTE (G1), 1 1/16 Miles, 2-Year-Old Fillies, Belmont Park, 2004 Purse: $500,000

Year	Winner	Age	Jockey	Wt.	Second	Wt.	Third	Wt.	Win Value	Time	Beyer
1945	Bonnie Beryl	2	J. Stout	112	La Liberte	112	Mush Mush	116	8,085	1:11.80	
1946	Bimlette	2	A. DeLara	110	Carolyn A.	122	Pipette	119	14,650	1:12.40	
1947	Slumber Song	2	J. Westrope	113	Grey Flight	112	Watermill	114	14,400	1:12.20	
1948	Our Fleet	2	E. Arcaro	115	Gay Mood	114	Be Sure	114	13,250	1:01.00	
1952	Sweet Patootie	2	T. Atkinson	119	Piedmont Lass	119	Grecian Queen	119	12,050	1:12.40	
1953	Indian Legend	2	T. Atkinson	110	Case Goods	119	Small Favor	115	13,600	1:13.60	
1954	Myrtle's Jet	2	W. Blum	119	Hen Party	119	Sorceress	119	35,000	1:49.20	
1955	Nasrina	2	W. Boland	119	Noors Image	119	Cosmah	119	55,525	1:45.40	
1956	Capelet	2	J. Nichols	119	Light 'n Lovely	119	Romanita	119	58,125	1:45.40	
1957	Idun	2	W. Hartack	119	Lopar	119	Big Fright	119	58,475	1:46.80	
1958	Merry Hill	2	R. Broussard	119	Dance All Night	119	Rich Tradition	119	56,772	1:46.40	
1959	My Dear Girl	2	M.N. Gonzalez	119	Irish Jay	119	Sarcastic	119	59,991	1:40.20	
1960	Bowl of Flowers	2	E. Arcaro	119	Counter Call	119	Good Move	119	69,936	1:35.60	
1961	Cicada	2	W. Shoemaker	119	Firm Policy	119	Jazz Queen	119	83,575	1:36.80	
1962	Pams Ego	2	M. Ycaza	119	Fool;s Play	119	Affectionately	119	73,000	1:38.00	
1963	Tosmah	2	S. Boulmetis	119	Beautiful Day	119	Castle Forbes	119	81,700	1:36.00	
1964	Queen Empress	2	W. Shoemaker	119	Money to Burn	119	Marshua	119	88,875	1:37.40	
	Marshua finished second but was disqualified and finished third										
1965	Priceless Gem	2	W. Blum	119	Lady Pitt	119	Swift Lady	119	85,000	1:36.00	
1966	Regal Gleam	2	M. Ycaza	119	Irish County	119	Pepperwood	119	94,675	1:37.40	
1967	Queen of the Stage	2	B. Baeza	119	Gay Matelda	119	Obeah	119	76,975	1:35.40	
1968	Shuvee	2	J. Davidson	119	Gallant Bloom	119	Dihela	119	93,150	1:37.00	
1969	Tudor Queen	2	A. Gomez	119	Cherry Sundae	119	Repoise	119	100,525	1:38.60	
1970	Forward Gal	2	J. Velasquez	119	Isafloridan	119	Make Me Laugh	119	88,100	1:36.60	
1971	Numbered Account	2	B. Baeza	119	Susan's Girl	119	Barely Even	119	81,525	1:35.60	
1972	La Prevoyante	2	J. LeBlanc	121	Cam Axe	121	Fine Tuning	121	68,640	1:37.40	
1973	Bundler	2	J. Vasquez	121	Chris Evert	121	I'm a Pleasure	121	72,660	1:36.40	
1974	Molly Ballantine	2	L. Pincay Jr	121	Copernica	121	Mystery Mood	121	67,140	1:37.00	
1975	Optimistic Gal	2	B. Baeza	121	Artfully	121	Picture Tube	121	69,360	1:36.80	
1976	Sensational	2	J. Velasquez	119	Northern Sea	119	Mrs. Warren	119	67,740	1:36.20	
1977	Lakeville Miss	2	R. Hernandez	119	Misgivings	119	Itsamaza	119	64,680	1:36.20	
1978	Golferette	2	J. Fell	119	It's in the Air	119	Terlingua	119	63,780	1:35.40	
1979	Smart Angle	2	S. Maple	119	Royal Suite	119	Hardship	119	66,240	1:38.20	
1980	Heavenly Cause	2	L. Pincay Jr	119	Sweet Revenge	119	Prayers'n Promises	119	66,000	1:38.00	
1981	Proud Lou	2	D. Beckon	119	Mystical Mood	119	Chilling Thought	119	70,920	1:38.80	
1982	Princess Rooney	2	J. Fell	119	Winning Tack	119	Weekend Surprise	119	70,080	1:39.00	
1983	Miss Oceana	2	E. Maple	119	Life's Magic	119	Lucky Lucky Lucky	119	68,040	1:36.60	
1984	Charleston Rag	2	D. MacBeth	119	Tiltalating	119	Mom's Command	119	130,860	1:39.00	
1985	Family Style	2	L. Pincay Jr	119	Funistrada	119	Guadery	119	133,200	1:37.20	
1986	Personal Ensign	2	R.P. Romero	119	Collins	119	Flying Katuna	119	161,400	1:36.40	
1987	Classic Crown	2	A. Cordero Jr	119	Tap Your Toes	119	Justsayno	119	215,640	1:37.20	
1988	Some Romance	2	L. Pincay Jr	119	Open Mind	119	Ms. Gold Pole	119	209,520	1:36.80	
1989	Stella Madrid	2	A. Cordero Jr	119	Go for Wand	119	Dance Colony	119	176,700	1:38.80	
1990	Meadow Star	2	J.A. Santos	119	Champagne Glow	119	Flawlessly	119	171,000	1:35.40	
1991	Preach	2	J.A. Krone	119	Vivano	119	Anh Duong	119	150,000	1:37.20	87
1992	Educated Risk	2	J.D. Bailey	119	Standard Equipment	119	Beal Street Blues	119	150,000	1:36.60	84
1993	Heavenly Prize	2	M.E. Smith	119	Facts of Love	119	Footing	119	150,000	1:35.40	94
1994	Flanders	2	P. Day	119	Change Fora Dollar	119	Pretty Discreet	119	150,000	1:43.80	102

Year	Winner	Age	Jockey	Wt.	Second	Wt.	Third	Wt.	Win Value	Time	Beyer
1995	Golden Attraction	2	G.L. Stevens	119	My Flag	119	Flat Fleet Feet	119	150,000	1:42.80	99
1996	Storm Song	2	C. Perret	119	Sharp Cat	119	Aldiza	119	240,000	1:42.40	96
1997	Silver Maiden	2	J.D. Bailey	119	Diamond on the Run	119	Brac Drifter	119	240,000	1:42.60	94
1998	Confessional	2	J.D. Bailey	119	Things Change	119	Pico Teneriffe	119	240,000	1:42.88	93
1999	Surfside	2	P. Day	119	Darling My Darling	119	March Magic	119	240,000	1:43.18	94
2000	Raging Fever	2	J.D. Bailey	120	Out of Sync	120	Western Justice	120	300,000	1:43.57	81
2001	You	2	E.S. Prado	120	Cashier's Dream	120	Riskaverse	120	300,000	1:43.94	99
2002	Storm Flag Flying	2	J. Velazquez	120	Santa Catarina	120	Appleby Gardens	120	300,000	1:44.20	98
2003	Society Selection	2	R. Ganpath	120	Victory U.S.A.	120	Ashado	120	300,000	1:43.95	95
2004	Balletto	2	C.S. Nakatani	120	Ready's Gal	120	Sis City	120	300,000	1:43.52	89

Beyer Index: 93.21

Distance 5 furlongs, 1948; 6 furlongs, 1945-47, 1952-53; 1 mile, 1959-93. Run at Jamaica Race Course prior to 1959; at Aqueduct, 1960-61, 1963-67

FUTURITY (G2), 1 Mile, 2-Year-Olds, Belmont Park, 2004 Purse: $300,000

Year	Winner	Age	Jockey	Wt.	Second	Wt.	Third	Wt.	Win Value	Time	Beyer
1888	Proctor Knott	2	S. Barnes	112	Salvator	108	Galen	115	40,900	1:15.20	
1889	Chaos	2	G. Day	109	St. Carlo	122	Sinaloa II	105	54,500	1:16.80	
1890	Potomac	2	A. Hamilton	115	Masher	108	Strathmeath	124	67,675	1:14.20	
1891	His Highness	2	J. McLaughlin	130	Yorkville Belle	115	Dagonet	108	61,675	1:15.20	
	Huron finished second but was disqualified as a starter by Coney Island Jockey Club										
1892	Morello	2	W. Hayward	118	Lady Violet	118	St. Leonards	115	40,450	1:12.20	
1893	Domino	2	F. Taral	130	Galilee	115	Dobbins	130	48,855	1:12.80	
1894	The Butteflies	2	H. Griffin	112	Brandywine	108	Agitator	110	48,710	1:11.00	
1895	Requittal	2	H. Griffin	115	Silver II	108			53,190	1:11.40	
1896	Ogden	2	F. Turblville	115	Ornament	116	Rodermond	115	43,790	1:10.00	
1897	L'Alouette	2	R. Clawson	115	Uriel	115			34,290	1:11.00	
1898	Martinmas	2	H. Lewis	118	High Degree	113	Mr. Clay	116	36,610	1:12.40	
1899	Chacornac	2	H. Spencer	114	Brigadier	109	Windmere	112	30,630	1:10.40	
1900	Ballyhoo Bey	2	T. Sloan	112	Olympian	112	Tommy Atkins	129	33,580	1:10.00	
1901	Yankee	2	W. O'Connor	119	Lux Casta	109	Barron	112	36,850	1:09.20	
1902	Savable	2	L. Lyne	119	Lord of the Vale	117	Dazzling	116	44,500	1:14.00	
1903	Hamburg Belle	2	G. Fuller	114	Leonidas	123	The Min. Man	122	36,600	1:13.00	
1904	Artful	2	E. Hildebrand	114	Tradition	127	Sysonby	127	40,830	1:11.80	
1905	Ormondale	2	A. Redfern	117	Timber	119	Belmere	117	32,960	1:11.80	
1906	Electioneer	2	W. Shaw	117	Pope Joan	116	De Mund	123	36,880	1:13.60	
1907	Colin	2	W. Miller	125	Bar None	117	Chapultepec	117	26,640	1:11.20	
1908	Maskette	2	J. Notter	118	Sir Martin	127	Helmet	123	26,110	1:11.20	
1909	Sweep	2	J. Butwell	126	Candleberry	117	Grasmere	122	24,100	1:11.80	
1910	Novelty	2	C.H. Shilling	127	Bashti	118	Love Not	114	25,360	1:12.20	
1913	Pennant	2	C. Borel	119	Southern Maid	119	Addie M.	114	15,060	1:15.00	
1914	Trojan	2	C. Burlingame	117	Kaskaskia	120	Harry Junior	122	16,010	1:16.80	
1915	Thunderer	2	J. Notter	122	Bromo	126	Achievement	123	16,590	1:11.80	
1916	Campfire	2	J. McTaggart	125	Rickety	122	Skeptic	122	17,340	1:13.80	
1917	Papp	2	L. Allen	127	Escoba	127	Rosie O'Grady	124	15,600	1:12.00	
1918	Dunboyne	2	A. Schuttinger	127	Sir Barton	117	Purchase	110	23,360	1:12.80	
1919	Man o' War	2	J. Loftus	127	John P. Grier	117	Dominique	122	26,650	1:11.60	
1920	Step Lightly	2	F. Keogh	116	Star Voter	127	Grey Lag	119	35,870	1:12.20	
1921	Bunting	2	F. Coltiletti	117	Galantman	117	D'm of Allah	116	39,700	1:11.40	
1922	Sally's Alley	2	A. Johnson	126	Zev	124	Wilderness	119	47,550	1:11.00	
1923	St. James	2	J. McTaggart	130	Fluvanna	122	Sun Pal	117	64,810	1:10.40	
1924	Mother Goose	2	L. McAtee	114	Stimulus	122	Single Foot	119	67,730	1:10.80	
1925	Pompey	2	L. Fator	127	Canter	120	Chance Play	119	58,480	1:23.00	
1926	Scapa Flow	2	L. Fator	122	Candy Queen	114	Valorous	122	67,980	1:22.00	
1927	Anita Peabody	2	C. Lang	124	Reigh Count	119	Victorian	119	91,790	1:21.80	
1928	High Strung	2	L. McAtee	122	Roguish Eye	125	Jack High	130	97,990	1:19.00	
1929	Whichone	2	R. Workman	125	Hi-Jack	122	Gallant Fox	122	105,730	1:19.60	
1930	Jamestown	2	L. McAtee	130	Equipoise	130	Mate	122	99,600	1:20.60	
1931	Top Flight	2	R. Workman	127	Mad Pursuit	122	Morfair	122	94,780	1:21.00	
1932	Kerry Patch	2	P. Walls	122	Ladysman	130	Dynastic	122	88,690	1:24.40	
1933	Singing Wood	2	R. Jones	122	Sir Thomas	117	Roustabout	122	81,700	1:21.00	
1934	Chance Sun	2	W.D. Wright	122	Balladier	122	Plat Eye	125	77,510	1:17.60	
1935	Tintagel	2	S. Coucci	122	Hollyrood	122	Jean Bart	122	66,450	1:17.40	
1936	Pompoon	2	H. Richards	127	Privileged	125	Flying Cross	122	55,630	1:16.40	
1937	Menow	2	C. Kurtsinger	119	Tiger	126	Fighting Fox	122	56,800	1:15.20	
1938	Porter's Mite	2	B. James	119	Eight Thirty	122	Third Degree	119	57,045	1:16.80	
1939	Bimelech	2	F.A. Smith	126	Calory	119	Call to Colors	119	57,710	1:16.80	
1940	Our Boots	2	E. Arcaro	119	King Cole	122	Whirlaway	126	65,800	1:15.60	
1941	Some Chance	2	W. Eads	119	Devil Diver	126	Caduceus	119	57,900	1:16.80	

Year	Winner	Age	Jockey	Wt.	Second	Wt.	Third	Wt.	Win Value	Time	Beyer
1942	Occupation	2	G. Woolf	126	Askmenow	116	Count Fleet	119	57,890	1:15.20	
1943	Occupy	2	G. Woolf	126	Rodney Stone	122	Platter	114	55,635	1:17.80	
1944	Pavot	2	G. Woolf	126	Alexis	119	Errard	119	53,890	1:15.60	
1945	Star Pilot	2	A. Kirkland	126	Athene	116	Mighty Story	119	52,940	1:17.20	
1946	First Flight	2	E. Arcaro	123	I Will	126	Jet Pilot	122	73,350	1:15.20	
1947	Citation	2	A. Snider	122	Whirling Fox	114	Bewitch	123	78,430	1:15.80	
1948	Blue Peter	2	E. Guerin	126	Myrtle Charm	123	Sport Page	118	88,410	1:14.60	
1949	Guillotine	2	T. Atkinson	122	Theory	122	The Diver	122	87,585	1:15.60	
1950	Battlefield	2	E. Arcaro	122	Big Stretch	122	Rough 'n Tumble	122	81,715	1:15.40	
1951	Tom Fool	2	T. Atkinson	122	Primate	122	Jet's Date	122	86,710	1:17.20	
1952	Native Dancer	2	E. Guerin	122	Tahitian King	122	Dark Star	122	82,845	1:14.40	
1953	Porterhouse	2	W. Boland	122	Artismo	122	Best Years	122	92,875	1:16.00	
1954	Nashua	2	E. Arcaro	122	Summer Tan	122	Royal Coinage	122	88,015	1:15.60	
1955	Nail	2	H. Woodhouse	122	Head Man	122	Polly's Jet	122	100,425	1:16.80	
1956	Bold Ruler	2	E. Arcaro	122	Greek Game	122	Amarullah	122	91,145	1:15.20	
1957	Jester	2	P.J. Bailey	122	Misty Flight	122	Alhambra	122	81,005	1:16.20	
1958	Intentionally	2	W. Shoemaker	122	First Landing	122	Dunce	122	80,690	1:14.60	
1959	Weatherwise	2	E. Arcaro	122	Udaipur	122	All Hands	122	88,470	1:18.60	
1960	Little Tumbler	2	R. Broussard	122	Globemaster	122	Garwol	122	85,191	1:16.60	
1961	Cyane	2	M. Ycaza	122	Jaipur	122	Sir Gaylord	122	86,650	1:17.20	
1962	Never Bend	2	W. Shoemaker	122	Outing Class	122	Pack Trip	122	94,347	1:17.20	
1963	Bupers	2	A. Gomez	122	Black Mountain	122	Count Bud	122	90,974	1:17.40	
1964	Bold Lad	2	B. Baeza	122	Native Charger	122	Tom Rolfe	122	85,566	1:16.00	
1965	Priceless Gem	2	W. blum	119	Buckpasser	122	Indulto	122	93,827	1:17.20	
1966	Bold Hour	2	J.L. Rotz	122	Successor	122	Pinnacle	122	91,084	1:17.60	
1967	Captain's Gig	2	W. Shoemaker	122	Vitriolic	122	Exclusive Native	122	90,493	1:15.80	
1968	Top Knight	2	M. Ycaza	122	True North	122	Never Confuse	122	88,283	1:16.20	
1969	High Echelon	2	J.L. Rotz	122	Tepee Rings	122	Irish Castle	122	92,807	1:18.40	
1970	Salem	2	J.L. Rotz	122	Limit to Reason	122	Frozen Delight	122	99,333	1:16.80	
1971	Riva Ridge	2	R. Turcotte	122	Chevron Flight	122	Hold Your Peace	122	87,636	1:16.60	
1972	Secretariat	2	R. Turcotte	122	Stop the Music	122	Swift Courier	122	83,320	1:16.40	
1973	Wedge Shot	2	J. Vasquez	122	Protagonist	122	Judger	122	82,230	1:17.00	
	Judger finished second but was disqualified and placed third										
1974	Just the Time	2	M. Castaneda	122	High Steel	122	Valid Appeal	122	66,801	1:16.40	
1975	Soy Numero Uno	2	J. Vasquez	122	Jackknife	122	Beau Talent	122	66,408	1:17.80	
1976	For the Moment	2	E. Maple	122	Banquet Table	122	Western Wind	122	67,353	1:23.20	
1977	Affirmed	2	S. Cauthen	122	Alydar	122	Nasty and Bold	122	63,570	1:21.60	
1978	Crest of the Wave	2	J. Cruguet	122	Strike Your Colors	122			75,660	1:24.00	
					Picturesque	122					
	Fuzzbuster finished first but was disqualfied and placed fourth										
1979	Rockhill Native	2	J. Oldham	122	Sportful	122	Gold Stage	122	90,150	1:22.00	
1980	Tap Shoes	2	R. Hernandez	122	Dash o'Pleasure	122	McCracken	122	85,605	1:23.80	
1981	Irish Martini	2	J. Velasquez	122	Herschelwalker	122	Timely Writer	122	103,605	1:24.40	
1982	Copelan	2	J.D. Bailey	122	Satan's Charger	122	Pax in Bello	122	97,110	1:24.20	
1983	Swale	2	E. Maple	122	Shuttle Jet	122	Hail Bold King	122	72,915	1:24.00	
1984	Spectacular Love	2	L. Pincay Jr	122	Chief's Crown	122	Mugzy's Rullah	122	105,900	1:23.20	
1985	Ogygian	2	W.A. Guerra	122	Groovy	122	Mr. Classic	122	81,600	1:22.40	
							Sovereign Don	122			
1986	Gulch	2	A. Cordero Jr	122	Demons Begone	122	Captain Valid	122	82,920	1:22.20	
1987	Forty Niner	2	E. Maple	122	Tsarbaby	122	Crusader Sword	122	80,100	1:22.60	
1988	Trapp Mountain	2	A. Cordero Jr	122	Bio	122	Fast Play	122	74,280	1:23.80	
1989	Senor Pete	2	J.A. Santos	122	Adjudicating	122	Dawn Quixote	122	75,360	1:23.20	
1990	Eastern Echo	2	J.D. Bailey	122	Deposit Ticket	122	Groom's Reckoning	122	69,360	1:22.40	99
1991	Agincourt	2	J.F. Chavez	122	Tri to Watch	122	Pine Bluff	122	73,140	1:23.80	80
1992	Strolling Along	2	C.W. Antley	122	Fight for Love	122	Caponostro	122	72,120	1:23.60	88
1993	Holy Bull	2	M.E. Smith	122	Dehere	122	Prenup	122	69,360	1:23.20	103
1994	Montreal Red	2	J.A. Santos	122	Northern Ensign	122	Wild Escapade	122	66,180	1:36.20	90
1995	Maria's Mon	2	R.G. Davis	122	Louis Quatorze	122	Honour and Glory	122	90,000	1:35.00	101
1996	Traitor	2	J.R. Velazquez	122	Night in Reno	122	Harley Tune	122	90,000	1:35.20	98
1997	Grand Slam	2	G.L. Stevens	122	K.O. Punch	122	Devil's Pride	122	90,000	1:35.60	98
1998	Lemon Drop Kid	2	J.R. Velazquez	122	Yes It's True	122	Medievil Hero	122	90,000	1:37.50	92
1999	Bevo	2	J. Bravo	122	Greenwood Lake	122	More Than Ready	122	90,000	1:36.16	99
2000	Burning Roma	2	R. Wilson	122	City Zip	122	Scorpion	122	120,000	1:37.90	90
	City Zip finished first but was disqualified and placed second										
2002	Whywhywhy	2	E.S. Prado	120	Pretty Wild	120	Truckle Feature	120	120,000	1:36.33	102
2003	Cuvee	2	J.D. Bailey	120	Value Plus	120	El Prado Rob	120	120,000	1:35.75	101
2004	Park Avenue Ball	2	J.J. Castellano	120	Wallstreet Scandal	120	Evil Minister	120	180,000	1:38.84	80

Beyer Index: 94.36

Distance 6 furlongs prior to 1892; from 1902-24; 1,263 yards plus 1 foot from 1892-1901; about 7 furlongs, 1925-33; 6 1/2 furlongs, 1934-75; 7 furlongs, 1976-93. Run at Sheepshead Bay prior to 1910; at Saratoga, 1910, 1913-14; at Aqueduct, 1959-60, 1962-67. Run over old straight course prior to 1926; over Widener Straight Course, 1926-58; not run in 2001.

GALLANT BLOOM HANDICAP (G2), 6 1/2 Furlongs, Fillies and Mares, 3-Year-Olds and Up, Belmont Park, 2004 Purse: $150,000

Year	Winner	Age	Jockey	Wt.	Second	Wt.	Third	Wt.	Win Value	Time	Beyer
1994	Vivano	6	W.H. McCauley	116	Ann Dear	118	Strategic Reward	113	48,255	1:19.80	97
1995	Classy Mirage		J.Bailey	123	Dust Bucket	114	Fantastic Woman	110	48,375	1:17.20	97
1996	Miss Golden Circle	5	R.Migliore	115	J J'sdream	119	Nappelon	117	50,040	1:16.20	97
1997	Top Secret	4	Velazquez J. R.	120	Aldiza	116	Dixie Flag	114	49,260	1:16.00	99
1998	Catinca	3	Migliore R.	114	Dixie Flag	117	Crab Grass	114	50,595	1:15.60	101
1999	Positive Gal	3	Bailey J. D.	116	Flamingo Way	114	Torch	113	65,820	1:16.80	96
2000	Dream Supreme	3	P. Day	118	Finder's Fee	116	Tropical Punch	114	64,380	1:15.86	103
2001	Finder's Fee	4	J.R. Velazquez	113	Cedar Knolls	114	Gold Mover	115	79,928	1:17.60	93
2002	Nasty Storm	4	J.A. Santos	114	Raging Fever	120	Shine Again	118	90,000	1:17.89	100
2003	Harmony Lodge	5	R. Migliore	117	House Party	116	Slews Final Answer	112	90,000	1:16.20	107
2004	Lady Tak	4	J.R. Velazquez	122	Molto Vita	115	Zawzooth	115	90,000	1:16.04	103

Beyer Index: 99.36

GALLORETTE HANDICAP (G3), 1 1/16 Miles (Turf), Fillies and Mares, 3-Year-Olds and Up, Pimlico Race Course, 2004 Purse: $100,000

Year	Winner	Age	Jockey	Wt.	Second	Wt.	Third	Wt.	Win Value	Time	Beyer
1952	La Corredora	3	I. Hanford	112	Kiss Me Kate	123	Marta	117	20,225	1:52.40	
1953	Sabette	3	J. Higley	111	Sunny Dale	117	Canadiana	111	10,075	1:51.60	
1954	Mlle. Lorette	4	A. Catalano	114	Dispute	114	Another World	114	11,900	1:50.20	
1955	Searching	5	D. Erb	117	Brightest Star	111	June Fete	114	10,975	1:53.60	
1956	Little Pache	3	A. Kirkland	112	Blue Banner	117	Searching	120	9,750	1:52.40	
1957	Searching	5	D. Erb	117	Mlle. Dianne	111	Snow White	113	9,725	1:51.20	
1958	Hoosier Honey	4	J. Ruane	117	Alanesian	120	Cousin Con	114	13,790	1:52.40	
1959	High Bid	3	H. Moreno	120	Polamby	115	A Glitter	120	14,660	1:51.00	
1960	Sister Antoine	3	R. York	111	Loyal Lady II	114	My Dear Girl	117	11,329	1:52.80	
1961	Barnesville Miss	3	P. Anderson	114	Colony Flyer	111	Miss Melis'de	114	11,716	1:53.80	
1962	Waltz Song	4	S. Mellon	117	Cyclopavia	114	Royal Patrice	120	19,289	1:52.00	
1963	Double Heritage	4	T. Lee	114	Abby's Crown	114	Doll Ina	117	20,166	1:52.60	
1964	Gay Serenade	4	F. Alvarez	117	Open Fire	111	My Card	117	19,402	1:51.20	
1965	Gold Digger	3	L. Adams	114	Gallarush	111	Lovejoy	114	19,711	1:53.20	
1966	Gold Digger	4	B. Phelps	117	Alondra II	114	Petticoat	114	21,190	1:51.20	
1967	Lady Diplomat	4	F. Toro	112	Straight Deal	126	Indian Sunlite	117	21,612	1:42.60	
1968	Serene Queen	4	F. Lovato	109	Straight Deal	122	Politely	122	21,645	1:44.80	
1969	Back in Paris	5	C. Baltazar	114	Singing Rain	116	Pers'n Intrigue	110	21,385	1:42.80	
1970	Singing Rain	5	F. Lovato	119	Shuvee	122	Miss F'l River	109	21,417	1:43.60	
1971	Cold Comfort	4	M. Venezia	117	Daring Step	114	Lum'n's L'g'n	110	21,222	1:43.40	
1972	Sun Colony	4	C. Jimenez	110	Tico's Donna	109	Alma North	122	21,970	1:45.00	
1973	Deb Marion	3	A. Agnello	107	Groton Miss	115	Aglimmer	115	22,067	1:44.00	
1974	Sarre Green	6	T. Lee	113	Unknown Heiress	103	Out Cold	112	22,295	1:44.60	
1975	Gulls Cry	4	E. Maple	117	Sarah Percy	115	Twixt	127	37,960	1:46.20	
1976	Redundancy	5	R. Broussard	119	Dos a Dos	113	Margravine	112	29,575	1:42.20	
1976	Deesse de Val	5	C. Marquez	119	Summertime Promise	117	Jabot	114	29,835	1:42.20	
1977	Summertime Promise	5	L. Moyers	121	Summer Session	111	Siz Ziz Zit	112	37,050	1:43.60	
1978	Huggle Duggle	4	B. Gonzalez	113	Council House	118	Nanticious	112	37,765	1:44.20	
1979	Calderina	4	C. Perret	121	Dottie O.	105	Warfever	116	56,875	1:44.80	
1980	Jamila Kadir	6	M.G. Pino	109	The Very One	122	Wild Bidder	108	57,428	1:44.40	
1981	Exactly So	4	G. McCarron	112	Crimson April	110	Ernestine	111	55,998	1:47.20	
1982	Island Charm	5	N. Santagata	117	Lovely Lei	112	Vibro Vibes	115	57,168	1:46.40	
1983	Wedding Party	4	C. Perret	119	Sunny Sparkler	122	Bemissed	110	56,648	1:50.00	
1984	Kattegat's Pride	5	D.A. Miller Jr	118	Amanti	114	Bright Choice	110	55,770	1:42.80	
1985	La Reine Elaine	4	G.W. Hutton	115	Stufida	115	Lady Emerald	107	58,013	1:41.60	
1986	Natania	4	J.W. Edwards	114	Scotch Heather	115	Valid Doge	108	71,448	1:45.60	
1987	Scotch Heather	5	M.G. Pino	113	Catatonic	117	Foot Stone	113	54,600	1:44.40	
1988	Just Class	4	C. Perret	115	Landaura	115	Hangin Ona Star	119	54,145	1:42.80	
1989	Dance Teacher	4	J.L. Samyn	115	Arcroyal	114	Fortunate Facts	118	60,000	1:44.00	
1990	Highland Penny	5	R.I. Rojas	116	Saphaedra	112	Channel Three	112	60,000	1:42.40	
							Double Bunctious	113			
1991	Miss Josh	5	E.S. Prado	121	Splendid Try	113	Highland Penny	115	60,000	1:41.80	103
1992	Brilliant Brass	5	E.S. Prado	113	Spanish Dior	112	Stem the Tide	112	60,000	1:44.80	102
1993	You'd Be Surprised	4	J.D. Bailey	113	Captive Miss	117	Dior's Angel	112	60,000	1:43.40	98
1994	Tribulation	4	Samyn JL	117	Mckaymackenna	118	Fleet Broad	115	60,000	1:41.60	96
1995	It's Personal	5	J.A. Krone	112	Churchbell Chimes	112	Open Toe	113	60,000	1:43.60	96
1996	Aucilla	5	M.E. Smith	114	Julie's Brilliance	114	Brushing Groom	114	60,000	1:44.80	88
1997	Palliser Bay	5	C.H. Marquez Jr	113	Elusive	114	Sangria	117	60,000	1:43.80	93
1998	Tresoriere	4	J.A. Santos	113	Bursting Forth	114	Starry Dreamer	114	60,000	1:45.20	100
1999	Winfama	6	E.S. Prado	114	Pleasant Temper	119	Earth to Jackie	119	60,000	1:43.31	101
2000	Colstar	4	A. Delgado	120	Melody Queen	115	Terreavigne	118	60,000	1:43.60	95
2001	License Fee	6	P. Day	118	Starine	114	Crystal Sea	113	60,000	1;42.81	97

Year	Winner	Age	Jockey	Wt.	Second	Wt.	Third	Wt.	Win Value	Time	Beyer
2002	Quidnaskra	7	C.J. McCarron	116	De Aar	111	Step With Style	115	60,000	1:46.73	88
2003	Carib Lady	4	P.A. Valenzuela	116	Affirmed Dancer	113	Lady of the Future	114	60,000	1:50.69	97
2004	Ocean Drive	4	J.D. Bailey	117	Film Maker	120	With Patience	112	60,000	1:40.85	99

Beyer Index: 96.64

GAMELY BREEDERS' CUP HANDICAP (G1), 1 1/8 Miles (Turf), Fillies and Mares, 3-Year-Olds and Up, Hollywood Park, 2004 Purse: $324,250

Year	Winner	Age	Jockey	Wt.	Second	Wt.	Third	Wt.	Win Value	Time	Beyer
1976	Katonka	4	L. Pincay Jr	121	Fascinating Girl	117	Tizna	126	30,750	1:50.40	
1977	Hail Hilarious	4	D. Pierce	123	Cascapedia	118	Swingtime	119	31,250	1:49.60	
1978	Lucie Manet	5	D.G. McHargue	119	Sensational	120	Glenaris	113	38,975	1:48.20	
1978	Star Ball	6	D.G. McHargue	122	Up to Juliet	114	Teisen Lap	116	38,975	1:48.80	
1979	Sisterhood	4	F. Toro	118	Country Queen	118	Camarado	117	50,450	1:47.80	
1980	Wishing Well	5	F. Toro	119	Country Queen	123	Image of Reality	118	69,600	1:47.80	
1981	Kilijaro	5	M. Castaneda	127	Princess Karenda	121	Wishing Well	122	62,900	1:48.20	
1982	Ack's Secret	6	L. Pincay Jr	122	Miss Huntington	117	Vocalist	114	66,100	1:46.80	
1983	Pride of Rosewood	5	E. Delahoussaye	115	Sangue	123	Mademoiselle Forli	119	64,800	1:48.80	
1984	Sabin	4	E. Maple	125	Triple Tipple	116	Fenny Rough	117	65,400	1:47.40	
1985	Estrapade	5	C.J. McCarron	124	Johnica	115	Possible Mate	116	62,500	1:46.60	
1986	La Koumia	4	R. Sibille	118	Estrapade	123	Tax Dodge	115	92,400	1:45.80	
1987	Northern Aspen	5	G.L. Stevens	119	Reloy	121	Frau Altiva	115	89,800	1:47.60	
1988	Pen Bal Lady	4	E. Delahoussaye	120	Chapel of Dreams	117	Galunpe	120	72,800	1:47.00	
1989	Fitzwilliam Place	5	C. Black	119	Claire Marine	119	Ravinella	121	63,700	1:47.80	
1990	Double Wedge	5	R. Davis	112	Stylish Star	116	Beautiful Melody	115	62,700	1:47.80	103
1991	Miss Josh	5	L. Pincay Jr	118	Island Jamboree	116	Fire the Groom	120	68,000	1:47.40	105
1992	Metamorphose	4	G.L. Stevens	114	Guiza	113	Silvered	116	93,300	1:46.40	100
1993	Toussaud	4	K.J. Desormeaux	116	Gold Fleece	114	Bel's Starlet	116	97,700	1:45.00	106
1994	Hollywood Wildcat	4	E. Delahoussaye	122	Mz. Zill Bear	114	Flawlessly	124	92,900	1:46.40	111
1995	Possibly Perfect	5	K.J. Desormeaux	123	Lady Affirmed	114	Don't Read My Lips	115	92,900	1:46.80	103
1996	Auriette	4	K.J. Desormeaux	118	Flagbird	118	Didina	116	128,760	1:46.40	112
1997	Donna Viola	5	G.L. Stevens	121	Real Connection	115	Different	121	120,000	1:47.40	105
1998	Fiji	4	K.J. Desormeaux	123	Kool Kat Katie	119	Squeak	116	158,880	1:47.42	109
1999	Tranquility Lake	4	E. Delahoussaye	119	Midnight Line	117	Green Jewel	117	157,800	1:46.04	112
2000	Astra	4	K.J. Desormeaux	117	Happyanunoit	121	Tout Charmant	119	157,150	1:45.81	107
2001	Happyanunoit	4	B. Blanc	121	Tranquility Lake	124	Beautiful Noise	116	115,710	1:47.34	105
2002	Astra	6	K.J. Desormeaux	123	Starine	122	Voodoo Dancer	119	300,000	1:46.93	105
2003	Tates Creek	5	P.A. Valenzuela	122	Dublino	122	Megahertz	118	263,400	1:46.97	107
2004	Noches de Rosa	6	M.E. Smith	115	Megahertz	122	Quero Quero	115	187,500	1:48.34	96

Beyer Index: 105.73

Run on main course 1978

GARDEN CITY BREEDERS' CUP HANDICAP (G1), 1 1/8 Miles (Turf), 3-Year-Old Fillies, Belmont Park, 2004 Purse: $264,000

Year	Winner	Age	Jockey	Wt.	Second	Wt.	Third	Wt.	Win Value	Time	Beyer
1979	Danielle B.	3	R. Hernandez	113	Distinct Honor	114	Seascape	118	33,000	1:45.40	
1980	Mitey Lively	3	J. Velasquez	113	Rose of Morn	112	Paintbrush	112	33,480	1:36.40	
1981	Banner Gala	3	A. Cordero Jr	113	Expressive Dance	112	In True Form	118	33,900	1:35.60	
1982	Nafees	3	J. Velasquez	112	Middle Stage	112	Beau Cougar	112	33,120	1:38.40	
1983	Pretty Sensible	3	A. Smith	112	High Schemes	112	Lovin Touch	115	33,600	1:37.80	
1984	Given	3	M.J. Vigliotti	118	Maharadoon	112	Recharged	118	42,960	1:43.40	
1985	Kamikaze Rick	3	A. Cordero Jr	118	Wising Up	115	Videogenic	118	50,490	1:36.00	
1986	Life At the Top	3	C.J. McCarron	118	Lotka	118	Funistrada	115	51,210	1:34.40	
1987	Personal Ensign	3	R.P. Romero	115	One From Heaven	118	Key Bid	118	82,140	1:36.60	
1988	Topicount	3	A. Cordero Jr	115	Toll Fee	112	Fara's Team	115	82,260	1:38.00	
1989	Highest Glory	3	J.A. Santos	115	Warfie	118	Tremolos	113	70,440	1:37.20	
1990	Aishah	3	J.A. Santos	115	Screen Prospect	115	Vitola	112	57,690	1:35.40	103
1991	Dazzle Me Jolie	3	J.A. Santos	115	Grand Girlfriend	112	Wide Country	124	72,000	1:35.60	102
1992	November Snow	3	C.W. Antley	124	Vivano	112	Easy Now	124	66,480	1:35.80	100
1993	Sky Beauty	3	M.E. Smith	124	Fadetta	112	For All Seasons	114	68,400	1:35.60	100
1994	Jade Flush	3	R.G. Davis	111	Lady Affirmed	117	Saxuality	117	67,140	1:46.79	101
1995	Perfect Arc	3	J.R. Velazquez	123	Bail Out Becky	121	Christmas Gift	118	101,070	1:42.20	105
1996	True Flare	3	G.L. Stevens	121	Henlopen	113	Zephyr	114	128,460	1:42.40	96
1997	Auntie Mame	3	J.D. Bailey	122	Parade Queen	115	Swearingen	117	128,040	1:48.40	97
1998	Pharatta	3	C.S. Nakatani	120	Tenski	122	Pratella	115	129,720	1:47.00	107
1999	Perfect Sting	3	P. Day	120	Nordican Inch	116	Ronda	121	129,900	1:49.41	101
2000	Gaviola	3	J.D. Bailey	123	Flawly	115	Millie's Quest	116	150,000	1:48.89	98
2001	Voodoo Dancer	3	C.S. Nakatani	120	Shooting Party	113	Wander Mom	116	150,000	1:47.69	101
2002	Wonder Again	3	E.S. Prado	119	Riskaverse	119	Pertuisane	115	150,000	1:47.33	96
2003	Indy Five Hundred	3	P. Day	113	Dimitrova	122	Campsie Fells	116	150,000	1:48.44	107
2004	Lucifer's Stone	3	J.A. Santos	118	Barancella	116	Noahs Ark	116	180,000	1:48.88	100

Beyer Index: 100.93

Run on main course prior to 1994. Distance 1 1/16 miles in 1979; 1 mile 70 yards, 1984; 1 mile, 1980–83, 1985–93; 1 1/16 miles on turf, 1994–96; Run as Rare Perfume prior to 1998

GARDENIA HANDICAP (G3), 1 1/8 Miles, Fillies and Mares, 3-Year-Olds and Up, Ellis Park, 2004 Purse: $200,000

Year	Winner	Age	Jockey	Wt.	Second	Wt.	Third	Wt.	Win Value	Time	Beyer
1982	Sweetest Chant	4	E. Fires	121	Muriesk	111	Run Tulle Run	112	43,778	1:49.80	
1983	Migola	3	G. Patterson	115	Kitchen	117	Run Tulle Run	113	42,315	1:51.60	
1984	Rambling Rhythm	3	L. Martinez	114	Run Tulle Run	114	Queen of Song	122	39,325	1:50.20	
1985	Crimson Orchid	3	S.E. Miller	114	Electric Fanny	114	Dusty Gloves	116	41,535	1:49.80	
1986	Queen Alexandra	4	D.E. Foster	123	Fleet Secretariat	119	Sherizar	113	63,000	1:49.20	
1987	No Choice	4	C.R. Woods Jr	113	Layovernite	112	Firgie's Jule	112	94,500	1:49.20	
1988	Lt. Lao	4	D. Brumfield	123	Saucy Deb	118	Silk's Lady	112	90,000	1:47.60	
1989	Lawyer Talk	5	M.E. Doser	114	Gallant Ryder	120	Miss Barbour	112	90,000	1:50.00	
1990	Evangelical	4	L. Melancon	113	Degenerate Gal	117	Anitas Surprise	113	90,000	1:49.80	91
1991	Summer Matinee	4	C.A. Black	113	Blissful Union	113	Beth Believes	113	90,000	1:50.40	97
1992	Bungalow	5	F.C. Torres	118	Forever Fond	113	Fappies Cosy Miss	112	120,000	1:48.60	101
1993	Erica's Dream	5	W. Martinez	113	Fappies Cosy Miss	111	Hitch	114	120,000	1:49.80	94
1994	Alphabulous	5	Thorwalth JO	112	Added Asset	115	Hey Hazel	116	120,000	1:50.00	95
1995	Laura's Pistolette	4	Martin EM Jr	115	Sadie's Dream	112	Cat Appeal	116	120,000	1:50.80	102
1996	Country Cat	4	D.M. Barton	115	Bedroom Blues	111	Alcovy	116	120,000	1:49.60	99
1997	Three Fanfares	4	F.A. Arguello Jr	113	Gold N Delicious	119	Birr	116	120,000	1:49.00	96
1998	Meter Maid	4	P.A. Johnson	119	Proper Banner	114	ThreeFanfares	113	120,000	1:51.00	106
1999	Lines of Beauty	4	F.C. Torres	112	Roza Robata	113	Castle Blaze	109	120,000	1:49.60	102
2000	Silent Eskimo	5	J. Lopez	116	Roza Robata	119	Tap to Music	120	120,000	1:50.56	101
2001	Asher	4	M. Guidry	115	Zenith	112	Royal Fair	116	120,000	1:50.16	97
2002	Minister's Baby	4	C. Perret	117	Lakenheath	115	Softly	114	120,000	1:49.73	109
2003	Bare Necessities	4	R.R. Douglas	119	Desert Gold	114	So Much More	115	120,000	1:50.09	106
2004	Angela's Love	4	M. Guidry	115	Miss Fortunate	116	Bare Necessities	119	120,000	1:49.54	98

Beyer Index: 99.60

GAZELLE HANDICAP (G1), 1 1/8 Miles, 3-Year-Old Fillies, Belmont Park, 2004 Purse: $250,000

Year	Winner	Age	Jockey	Wt.	Second	Wt.	Third	Wt.	Win Value	Time	Beyer
1887	Firenze	3	Hamilton	113	Flageoletta	103	Mag. Mitchell	103	1,860	1:56.20	
1888	Winona	3	Martin	108	Blythesome	113	Bella B.	108	1,775	2:03.00	
1889	Gipsy Queen	3	Fitzpatrick	116	Holiday	113	Miss Cody	113	2,510	2:00.20	
1890	Amazon	3	Hamilton	113	Golden Horn	113	Starlight	113	3,510	1:58.20	
1891	Ambulance	3	F. Littlefield	117	Reckon	117	Origeuse	117	3,540	1:59.60	
1892	Yorkville Belle	3	I. Murphy	117	Madrid	117	Ragna	117	2,840	2:04.00	
1893	Naptha	3	Simms	117	Miss Maude	117	Grace Brown	117	2,540	1:59.20	
1894	Nahma	3	Littlefield	117	Jersey Belle	117	Baroness	117	3,590	2:03.00	
1895	The Butterflies	3	Griffin	117	California	117	Roundelay	117	2,570	1:59.20	
1896	Intermission	3	Taral	117	Woodvine	117	Bes Browning	117	2,400	1:58.20	
1897	Casseopia	3	Littlefield	117	Miss Prim	117	Leonore	117	2,400	1:59.20	
1898	Geisha	3	T. Sloan	112	Kitefoot	112	Miss Miriam	112	2,400	1:56.60	
1899	The Rose	3	Maher	114	Bettie Gray	114	Marmarica	114	2,400	1:57.20	
1900	Indian Fairy	3	O'Connor	106	Oneck Queen	114	Motley	106	2,300	1:50.00	
1901	Trigger	3	Odom	106	Janice	114	Morningside	106	2,300	1:48.20	
1902	Blue Girl	3	T. Burns	124	Par Excellance	113	Hanover Queen	113	2,300	1:49.40	
1903	Stolen Moments	3	Gannon	113	Gloriosa	113	Love Note	113	3,250	1:49.60	
1904	Beldame	3	F. O'Neill	124	Graceful	121	Little Em	113	3,590	1:52.60	
1905	Tradition	3	W. Davis	113	Coy Maid	113	Klamesha	113	2,915	1:51.40	
1906	Flip Flap	3	W. Miller	121	Perverse	124	Meddling Daisy	113	3,390	1:48.00	
1907	Court Dress	3	J. Martin	121	Yankee Girl	121	Estimate	111	4,495	1:47.20	
1908	Stamina	3	E. Dugan	121	Anonyma	111	Laughing Eyes	111	4,940	1:48.00	
1909	Maskette	3	Scoville	121	Petticoat	111	Lady Bedford	111	4,045	1:48.00	
1910	Ocean Bound	3	C.H. Shilling	121	Infatuation	106	Ethel D.	106	1,900	1:52.00	
1917	Regret	5	J. Loftus	129	Bayberry Candle	123	Wistful	105	2,600	1:45.40	
1918	Fairy Wand	4	C. Fairbrother	115	Priscilla Mullens	122	Hanovia	122	2,625	1:45.00	
1919	Milkmaid	3	A. Schuttinger	119	Columbine	120	Rose d'Or	107	2,450	1:45.00	
1920	Pen Rose	4	L. Fator	113	Milkmaid	130	Lunetta	113	2,850	1:46.00	
1921	Banksia	3	B. Kennedy	118	Last Straw	109	Chat. Thierry	109	3,000	1:47.60	
1922	Lady Baltimore	3	C. Lang	118	Many Smiles	118	Nancy Shanks	110	2,975	1:45.20	
1923	Untidy	3	E. Sande	124	Sun Quest	109	J'line Julian	109	3,100	1:45.80	
1924	Priscilla Ruley	3	J. Maiben	109	Whetstone	109	Sunayr	109	3,225	1:44.40	
	Lady Belle finished third but was disqualified										
1925	Nedana	3	L. Fator	118	Primrose	109	Beatrice	121	2,975	1:44.80	
1926	Corvette	3	L. Fator	109	Edith Cavell	124	Gavotte	109	2,875	1:44.80	
1927	Flambino	3	D. McAuliffe	110	Frilette	121	Candy May	109	3,325	1:45.00	
1928	Bateau	3	L. McAtee	123	Bradley's Peggy	109	Twitter	121	3,200	1:45.20	
1929	March Hare	3	J.H. Burke	118	Electra	109	Atlantis	121	3,175	1:47.60	
1930	Erin	3	J.H. Burke	118	The Spare	121	Flimsy	118	3,875	1:46.00	
1931	Avenger	3	R. Workman	112	Tambour	121	Lillie D.	105	3,150	1:46.00	
1932	Playfole	3	B. Hanford	111	Argosie	111	Parry	115	2,500	1:45.40	

Year	Winner	Age	Jockey	Wt.	Second	Wt.	Third	Wt.	Win Value	Time	Beyer
1936	Gold Seeker	3	W.D. Wright	121	High Fleet	121	Little Miracle	112	3,875	1:44.60	
1937	Regal Lily	3	J. Stout	109	Drawbridge	112	Rosenna	109	5,125	1:44.00	
1938	Invoke	3	J. Stout	109	Creole Maid	121	Bransome	109	4,550	1:45.40	
1939	Red Eye	3	B. James	109	Hostility	121	Ciencia	121	4,400	1:43.20	
1940	Fairy Chant	3	B. James	121	Raise Up	109	Rosetown	112	5,225	1:46.00	
1941	Tangled	3	E. Arcaro	124	Nasca	121	St'nge Device	118	4,825	1:45.80	
1942	Vagrancy	3	J. Stout	121	Smiles	112	Mackerel	112	4,800	1:45.00	
1943	Anthemion	3	J. Longden	121	Stefanita	118	Legend Bearer	112	4,775	1:48.20	
1944	Whirlabout	3	J. Longden	121	Good Thing	112	Leaving	115	8,245	1:43.60	
1945	Ace Card	3	E. Arcaro	121	Bellicose	112	Elpis	124	7,540	1:45.60	
1946	Bridal Flower	3	A. DeLara	111	Hypnotic	121	Bonnie Beryl	116	16,950	1:46.40	
1947	Cosmic Missile	3	H. Pratt	116	Harmonica	121	Mother	116	20,600	1:46.00	
1948	Sweet Dream	3	R. Permane	111	Scattered	121	Compliance	111	19,350	1:45.20	
1949	Nell K.	3	D. Dodson	121	Jazz Baby	111	Adile	111	16,450	1:47.80	
1950	Next Move	3	E. Guerin	121	Bed o' Roses	116	Renew	112	15,250	1:43.60	
1951	Kiss Me Kate	3	W. Mehrtens	121	Boot All	112	Spanish Cream	112	19,450	1:46.00	
1952	Hushaby Baby	3	R. York	113	Aesthete	115	Hadassah	113	19,325	1:45.60	
1953	Grecian Queen	3	E. Guerin	121	Canadiana	121	Sabette	113	20,950	1:45.80	
1954	On Your Own	3	W. Boland	113	Evening Out	113	Fascinator	121	21,000	1:46.60	
1955	Manotick	3	A. Valenzuela	113	Two Stars	113	High Voltage	121	21,400	1:45.60	
1956	Scampering	3	A. Valenzuela	111	Cosmah	116	Dotted Line	124	21,600	1:43.80	
1957	Bayou	3	E. Arcaro	120	Evening Time	118	Pink Velvet	116	21,550	1:43.20	
1958	Idun	3	W. Hartack	124	Munch	122	Tempted	116	18,680	1:43.20	
1959	Sunset Glow	3	W. Shoemaker	108	Royal Native	121	High Bid	118	14,130	1:36.80	
1959	Cee Zee	3	H. Moreno	111	Aesthetic	112	Toluene	115	13,967	1:36.00	
1960	Berlo	3	E. Guerin	122	Sister Antoine	113	Funny Bone	109	14,569	1:35.80	
1960	Sarcastic	3	H. Moreno	115	Twinkle Twinkle	119	Undulation	112	14,569	1:35.40	
1961	Shimmy Dancer	3	M. Ycaza	112	My Portrait	120	Funloving	122	18,752	1:49.00	
1962	Bramalea	3	B. Baeza	122	Cyclopavia	117	Lincoln Center	113	18,687	1:50.00	
1963	Lamb Chop	3	B. Baeza	125	Delhi Maid	119	Smart Deb	123	19,337	1:50.00	
1964	Face the Facts	3	L. Adams	121	Silwall	113	Castle Forbes	121	18,005	1:51.60	
1965	What a Treat	3	J.L. Rotz	123	Terentia	118	Discipline	118	38,675	1:51.40	
1966	Prides Profile	3	M. Ycaza	113	Lady Pitt	124	Swinging Mood	120	36,270	1:52.40	
1967	Sweet Folly	3	H. Gustines	112	Treacherous	116	Swiss Cheese	115	37,415	1:50.20	
1968	Another Nell	3	C. Perret	122	Gay Matelda	123	Pattee Canyon	116	36,400	1:50.80	
1969	Gallant Bloom	3	J.L. Rotz	127	Pit Bunny	116	Shuvee	127	34,970	1:49.00	
1970	Missile Belle	3	P. Anderson	120	Predictable	114	Fanfreluche	122	37,830	1:50.80	
1971	Forward Gal	3	M. Hole	122	Our Cheri Amour	118	Alma North	123	33,720	1:48.60	
1972	Susan's Girl	3	L. Pincay Jr	124	Honestous	112	Light Hearted	121	33,390	1:48.00	
1973	Desert Vixen	3	J. Velasquez	126	Bag of Tunes	117	Poker Night	120	33,780	1:47.40	
1974	Maud Muller	3	A. Cordero Jr	120	Raisela	115	Stage Door Betty	115	33,900	1:46.80	
1975	Land Girl	3	J. Vasquez	114	Hooray Hooray	109	Let Me Linger	119	33,690	1:49.40	
1976	Revidere	3	A. Cordero Jr	124	Pacific Princess	112	Ancient Fables	112	31,950	1:47.80	
1977	Pearl Necklace	3	S. Cauthen	111	Sensational	120	Road Princess	118	31,770	1:48.00	
1978	Tempest Queen	3	J. Velasquez	117	Lulubo	116	Terpsichorist	113	31,710	1:49.80	
1979	Himalayan	3	E. Maple	113	Croquis	113	Fourdrinier	112	32,580	1:48.40	
1980	Love Sign	3	R. Hernandez	121	Sugar and Spice	117	Kelley's Day	112	32,580	1:49.20	
1981	Discorama	3	R. Hernandez	117	Secrettame	114	Tina Tina Too	114	33,300	1:48.20	
1982	Broom Dance	3	G. McCarron	121	Number	113	Mademoiselle Forli	114	33,360	1:47.60	
1983	High Schemes	3	J.L. Samyn	121	Lass Trump	120	Lady Norcliffe	115	66,720	1:48.20	
1984	Miss Oceana	3	E. Maple	121	Sintra	117	Life's Magic	122	66,840	1:47.60	
1985	Kamikaze Rick	3	A. Cordero Jr	113	Overwhelming	112	Fran's Valentine	121	68,880	1:48.60	
1986	Classy Cathy	3	E. Fires	121	Life at theTop	118	Dynamic Star	116	66,480	1:48.40	
1987	Single Blade	3	C.W. Antley	113	Without Feathers	121	Silent Turn	114	80,100	1:48.20	
1988	Classic Crown	3	R.P. Romero	117	Willa on the Move	120	Make Change	118	69,360	1:49.80	
1989	Tactile	3	R. Migliore	114	Dream Deal	117	Fantastic Find	114	67,440	1:48.40	
1990	Highland Talk	3	J.L. Samyn	111	Dance Colony	116	She Can	116	69,960	1:50.80	97
1991	Versailles Treaty	3	A. Cordero Jr	123	Grand Girlfriend	115	Immerse	112	105,840	1:47.40	95
1992	Saratoga Dew	3	W.H. McCauley	120	Vivano	114	Tiney Toast	113	103,140	1:47.60	101
1993	Dispute	3	J.D. Bailey	120	Silky Feather	117	In Her Glory	112	90,000	1:47.20	102
1994	Heavenly Prize	3	M.E. Smith	123	Cinnamon Sugar	118	Sovereign Kitty	118	90,000	1:47.20	106
1995	Serena's Song	3	G.L. Stevens	124	Miss Golden Circle	113	Golden Bri	121	90,000	1:47.20	105
1996	My Flag	3	J.D. Bailey	121	Escena	121	Top Secret	117	120,000	1:48.00	98
1997	Royal Indy	3	P. Day	113	Starry Dreamer	114	Pearl City	117	120,000	1:49.00	96
1998	Tap to Music	3	P. Day	112	Keeper Hill	122	French Braids	115	120,000	1:49.72	96
1999	Silverbulletday	3	J.D. Bailey	124	Queen's Word	113	Awful Smart	115	120,000	1:47.71	100
2000	Critical Eye	3	M.E. Smith	115	Plenty of Light	116	Resort	116	120,000	1:48.54	104
2001	Exogenous	3	J.J. Castellano	118	Two Item Limit	118	Fleet Renee	122	150,000	1:47.68	110
2002	Imperial Gesture	3	J. Santos	117	Take Charge Lady	121	Bella Bellucci	118	150,000	1:47.12	112
2003	Buy the Sport	3	P. Day	113	Lady Tak	121	Spoken Fur	121	150,000	1:48.57	95
2004	Stellar Jayne	3	R.J. Albarado	122	Daydreaming	115	He Loves Me	117	150,000	1:48.25	97

Beyer Index: 100.93

Distance 1 1/16 miles from 1900-58; 1 mile, 1959-60. Run at Gravesend from 1887-1916; at Aqueduct from 1917-55, 1960, 1962-68

GENERAL GEORGE HANDICAP (G2), 7 Furlongs, 3-Year-Olds and Up, Laurel Park 2004 Purse: $200,000

Year	Winner	Age	Jockey	Wt.	Second	Wt.	Third	Wt.	Win Value	Time	Beyer
1973	Ecole Etage	3	G. Cusimano	113	Bid Red L	113	S'ect Perf'nce	110	18,265	1:44.60	
1974	Sharp Gary	3	C. Barrera	122	Jolly Johu	119	Ground Breaker	110	19,045	1:46.60	
1975	Pendulum Sam	3	L. Gino	110	King of Fools	113	Broadway Reviewer	110	18,005	1:48.20	
1976	Princely Game	3	A. Agnello	119	On the Sly	110	Troll By	116	17,940	1:44.60	
1977	Do the Bump	3	C.J. McCarron	122	John U to Berry	115	Steel Bandit	113	17,778	1:47.20	
1978	Ten Ten	3	W.J. Passmore	122	Game Prince	113	Gala Forecast	113	18,200	1:45.80	
1980	Galaxy Road	3	G. McCarron	122	Leader of the Pack	113	Ashanti Gold	110	36,660	1:24.60	
1981	Classic Go Go	3	W.J. Passmore	122	Thirty Eight Paces	122	Aztec Crown	115	37,115	1:23.20	
1984	Judge McGuire	3	C.H. Mendoza	122	American Artist	110	S.S. Hot Sauce	122	55,543	1:46.60	
1985	Roo Art	3	D.A. Miller Jr	122	Joyfull John	112	I Am the Game	119	55,380	1:37.60	
1986	Broad Brush	3	V. Bracciale Jr	122	Fast Step	113	Swallow	116	54,373	1:44.20	
1986	Lil Tyler	3	M.T. Hunter	122	Fobby Forbes	116	Fork Union Cadet	110	53,723	1:45.60	
1987	Templar Hill	3	G.W. Hutton	116	Hay Halo	122	Win Dusty Win	114	74,620	1:44.00	
1988	Private Terms	3	K.J. Desormeaux	116	Dynaformer	122	Delightful Doctor	122	74,328	1:38.80	
1989	Little Bold John	7	D.A. Miller Jr	122	Oraibi	119	Finder's Choice	117	120,000	1:22.80	
1990	King's Nest	5	M.T. Hunter	119	Wind Splitter	117	Notation	119	120,000	1:22.00	109
1991	Star Touch	5	M.J. Luzzi	118	Profit Key	118	Fire Plug	118	120,000	1:22.80	......
1992	Senor Speedy	5	J.F. Chavez	126	Sunny Sunrise	123	Formal Dinner	123	120,000	1:21.80	108
1993	Majesty's Turn	4	A. Delgado	118	Senor Speedy	118	Ameri Valay	123	120,000	1:22.60	105
1994	Blushing Julian	4	R.E. Colton	118	Chief Desire	123	Who Wouldn't	118	120,000	1:22.80	111
1995	Who Wouldn't	6	J. Rocco	119	Storm Tower	116	Powis Castle	118	120,000	1:22.00	110
1996	Meadow Monster	5	R. Wilson	120	Splendid Sprinter	113	Cat Be Nimble	114	120,000	1:22.00	118
1997	Why Change	4	M. Guidry	113	Appealing Skier	118	Le Grand Pos	111	120,000	1:22.40	108
1998	Royal Haven	6	R. Migliore	122	Purple Passion	116	Wire Me Collect	117	150,000	1:23.00	111
1999	Esteemed Friend	5	M.J. Luzzi	116	Star of Valor	114	Purple Passion	117	150,000	1:22.40	106
2000	Affirmed Success	6	J.F. Chavez	121	Young At Heart	114	Badge	117	120,000	1:22.02	114
2001	Peeping Tom	4	S.X. Bridgmohan	114	Delaware Township	120	Disco Rico	117	120,000	1:22.00	113
2002	Wrangler	4	A.T. Gryder	115	Rusty Spur	111	Affirmed Success	121	120,000	1:22.53	107
2003	My Cousin Matt	4	R.A. Dominguez	113	Peeping Tom	114	Disturbingthepeace	118	120,000	1:22.12	114
2004	Well Fancied	6	E.S. Prado	115	Unforgettable Max	114	Gators n Bears	116	120,000	1:22.49	109

Beyer Index: 110.21

GENEROUS (G3), 1 Mile (Turf), 2-Year-Olds, Hollywood Park, 2004 Purse: $100,000

Year	Winner	Age	Jockey	Wt.	Second	Wt.	Third	Wt.	Win Value	Time	Beyer
1982	Fifth Division	2	L. Pincay Jr	117	Dominating Dooley	114	Mezzo	116	33,450	1:35.60	
1983	Artichoke	2	W. Shoemaker	120	Nagurski	114	Fortune's Kingdom	115	50,100	1:38.40	
1983	Precisionist	2	C.J. McCarron	116	Fali Time	120	Tights	115	50,100	1:37.40	
1984	Overtrump	2	C.J. McCarron	120	Right Con	120	Herat	120	123,350	1:41.80	
1985	Darby Fair	2	A.L. Castanon	120	Snow Chief	120	Acks Lika Ruler	114	119,400	1:37.00	
1986	Persevered	2	G.L. Stevens	120	Wilderness Bound	120	Quietly Bold	115	86,050	1:41.80	
1986	Sweettuc	2	G.L. Stevens	113	Savona Tower	116	Lord Duckworth	114	68,050	1:41.60	
1987	Purdue King	2	C.J. McCarron	121	Chinese Gold	121	Blade of the Ball	115	47,500	1:36.00	
1987	White Mischief	2	J.A. Santos	115	King Alobar	115	Texas Typhoon	115	68,750	1:35.40	
1988	Music Merci	2	G.L. Stevens	121	Double Quick	121	Crown Collection	115	58,220	1:36.40	
1988	Shipping Time	2	C.A. Black	114	Super May	115	Past Ages	116	58,220	1:37.20	
1989	Single Dawn	2	A. Solis	114	Pleasant Tap	118	Doyouseewhatisee	121	69,600	1:35.60	
1990	Satis	2	C.A. Black	115	What a Spell	114	Ev for Shir	114	67,800	1:35.20	86
1991	Silver Ray	2	M.A. Pedroza	114	Thinkernot	115	African Colony	117	74,775	1:35.00	78
1992	Earl of Barking	2	A. Solis	114	Devil's Rock	115	Corby	118	137,500	1:34.40	95
1993	Delineator	2	R. Baze	118	Devon Port	116	Ferrara	114	137,500	1:34.60	86
1994	Native Regent	2	Penna D	121	Dangerous Scenario	116	Claudius	121	137,500	1:37.00	91
1995	Old Chapel	2	Stevens GL	121	Ayrton S	116	Heza Gone West	117	137,500	1:35.00	88
1996	Hello	2	McCarron C. J.	121	Steel Ruhlr	114	Divine Insight	114	150,000	1:34.60	90
1997	Mantles Star	2	McCarron C. J.	114	F J's Pace	116	Commitisize	121	150,000	1:36.60	96
1998	Incurable Optimist	2	Velazquez J. R.	121	Company Approval	114	Brave Gun	117	150,000	1:37.60	101
1999	Jokerman	2	P. Day	118	Purey Cozzene	121	Kleofus	121	120,000	1:35.20	92
2000	Startac	2	A. Solis	118	Broadway Moon	116	Deeliteful Irving	114	120,000	1:34.76	89
2001	Mountain Rage	2	D.R. Flores	116	Miesque's Approval	121	National Park	117	120,000	1:40.31	88
2002	Peace Rules	2	V. Espinoza	118	Lismore Knight	121	Outta Here	115	120,000	1:35.49	92
2003	Castledale	2	J.A. Krone	116	Dealer Choice	116	Lucky Pulpit	116	60,000	1:35.43	92
2004	Dubleo	2	C.S. Nakatani	121	Littlebitofzip	116	Sunny Sky	116	60,000	1:37.21	92

Beyer Index: 90.40

GENUINE RISK HANDICAP (G2), 6 Furlongs, Fillies and Mares, 3-Year-Olds and Up, Belmont Park, 2004 Purse: $147,000

Year	Winner	Age	Jockey	Wt.	Second	Wt.	Third	Wt.	Win Value	Time	Beyer
1984	On the Bench	4	J. Cruguet	115	Nany	117	Grateful Friend	119	33,060	1:09.60	
1985	Alabama Nana	4	J. Velasquez	117	Hare Brain	119	Two Ours	119	49,260	1:10.60	
1986	Clocks Secret	4	W. Shoemaker	122	Le Slew	119	Liz Taylor	109	48,900	1:10.00	
1987	Pine Tree Lane	5	A. Cordero Jr	122	Silent Account	117	Royal Tali	117	47,970	1:10.20	
1988	Tappiano	4	J. Vasquez	122	Cagey Exuberance	122	Hedgeabout	117	50,040	1:09.00	
1989	Safely Kept	3	A. Cordero Jr	114	Aptostar	122	Cagey Exuberance	122	49,410	1:09.40	
1990	Safely Kept	4	C. Perret	122	Diva's Debut	117	Levitation	117	49,140	1:10.20	
1991	Safely Kept	5	C. Perret	122	Missy's Mirage	109	Token Dance	117	68,400	1:10.00	104
1992	Parisian Flight	4	J.A. Santos	117	Serape	117	Devil's Orchid	119	70,680	1:09.00	105
1993	Apelia	4	L. Attard	119	Santa Catalina	117	Reach for Clever	117	69,600	1:10.00	103
1994	Apelia	5	L. Attard	119	Spinning Round	119	Ann Dear	114	64,680	1:09.00	106
1995	Classy Mirage	5	J.A. Krone	122	Through the Door	111	Lottsa Talc	117	64,080	1:11.20	93
1996	Exotic Wood	4	M.E. Smith	119	Lottsa Talc	118	Miss Golden Circle	113	65,100	1:08.40	111
1997	Miss Golden Circle	5	R. Migliore	120	Start At Once	111	Nappelon	110	65,040	1:09.40	102
1998	J J'sdream	5	L.C. Reynolds	118	Tate	112	Capote Belle	118	83,310	1:10.20	93
1999	Foil	4	J.L. Samyn	114	Harpia	118	Gold Princess	115	90,000	1:10.43	101
2000	Imperfect World	4	R.G. Davis	113	Gold Princess	113	Tropical Punch	115	90,000	1:10.00	99
2001	Katz Me If You Can	4	J. Bravo	113	Lucky Livi	114	Shine Again	115	90,000	1:09.55	100
2002	Xtra Heat	4	H. Vega	126	Shine Again	117	La Galerie	114	90,000	1:10.24	108
2003	Shine Again	6	J.L. Samyn	119	Carson Hollow	122	Harmony Lodge	116	90,000	1:09.19	104
2004	Bear Fan	5	J.R. Velazquez	117	Harmony Lodge	120	Kitty Knight	114	90,000	1:08.85	107

Beyer Index: 102.57

GLENS FALLS HANDICAP (G3), 1 3/8 Miles (Turf), Fillies and Mares, 3-Year-Olds and Up, Saratoga Race Course, 2004 Purse: $110,400 (Div 1), $109,300 (Div 2)

Year	Winner	Age	Jockey	Wt.	Second	Wt.	Third	Wt.	Win Value	Time	Beyer
1996	Ampulla	5	S.J. Sellers	113	Look Daggers	118	Electric Society	120	67,500	2:16.40	102
1997	Shemozzle	6	J.D. Bailey	115	Picture Hat	113	Last Aproach	113	64,740	2:12.80	98
1998	Auntie Mame	4	J.R. Velazquez	120	Yvecrique	115	Makethemostofit	111	66,000	2:13.00	106
1999	Idle Rich	4	J.D. Bailey	115	Adrian	114	Bundling	114	65,760	2:12.81	99
2000	I'm Indy Mood	5	H. Castillo Jr	116	Idle Rich	114	Cybil	114	66,120	2:07.41	87
2001	Irving's Baby	4	J.D. Bailey	126	New Assmebly	113	Caveat's Shot	114	65,995	2:07.56	91
2002	Owsley	4	E.S. Prado	116	Mot Juste	116	Sunstone	114	68,100	2:15.99	96
2003	Sixty Seconds	5	J.A. Santos	115	Primetimevalentine	113	Alternate	116	67,860	2:13.96	97
2004	Humaita	4	C. Velasquez	114	Where We Left Off	116	Savedbythelight	115	66,240	2:15.25	94
2004	Arvada	4	J.R. Velazquez	112	Spice Island	118	Film Maker	121	65,580	2:14.12	103

Beyer Index: 97.30

Run at 1 1/4 miles on main track in 2000, 2001

GO FOR WAND HANDICAP (G1), 1 1/8 Miles, Fillies and Mares, 3-Year-Olds and Up, Saratoga Race Course, 2004 Purse: $245,000

Year	Winner	Age	Jockey	Wt.	Second	Wt.	Third	Wt.	Win Value	Time	Beyer
1954	Ballerina	4	S. Small	106	Grecian Queen	113	Gay Grecque	112	18,950	1:37.60	
1955	Oil Painting	4	H. Woodhouse	119	Miss Weesie	104	Clear Dawn	116	18,000	1:36.60	
1956	Searching	4	C. McCreary	123	Happy Princess	107	Pucker Up	112	20,100	1:37.00	
1957	Bayou	3	R. Ussery	118	Rare Treat	116	Pink Velvet	113	20,200	1:37.00	
1958	Tempted	3	R. Ussery	113	Alanesian	123	Annie-Lu-San	111	19,070	1:36.40	
1959	Idun	4	E. Guerin	119	Tempted	126	Bornstar	119	18,875	1:36.00	
1960	Tempted	5	E. Nelson	126	Make Sail	118	Craftiness	108	19,200	1:35.60	
1961	teacation	4	R. Broussard	116	Shimmy Dancer	106	Craftiness	120	18,720	1:36.20	
1962	Shirley Jones	6	D. Pierce	122	Linita	122	Waltz Song	115	19,467	1:36.00	
1963	Waltz Song	5	S. Mellon	120	Linita	121	Doll Ina	114	18,882	1:37.20	
1964	Tosmah	3	S. Boulmetis	123	Old Hat	117	Snow Scene II	113	19,630	1:36.60	
1965	Tosmah	4	S. Boulmetis	128	Affectionately	128	Straight Deal	113	18,720	1:35.20	
1966	Summer Scandal	4	W. Blum	123	Straight Deal	119	Treachery	111	18,687	1:37.80	
1967	Politely	4	A. Cordero Jr	115	Triple Brook	117	Lady Pitt	115	18,687	1:35.60	
1968	Amerigo Lady	4	J. Velasquez	120	Serene Queen	114	Green Glade	112	19,077	1:36.40	
1969	Singing Rain	4	B. Baeza	118	Helen Jennings	107	Show Off	110	18,395	1:38.00	
1970	Native Partner	4	A. Cordero Jr	111	Taken Aback	112	Hasty Hitter	107	18,720	1:36.20	
1971	Double Delta	5	K. Knapp	126	Blessing Angelica	107	Lucky Traveler	112	19,830	1:36.20	
1972	Numbered Account	3	A. Cordero Jr	115	Manta	112	Aladancer	114	16,620	1:35.60	
1973	Light Hearted	4	E. Nelson	126	Convenience	121	Krislin	111	17,040	1:34.80	
1974	Ponte Vecchio	4	J. Vasquez	118	Poker Night	116	Twixt	124	35,850	1:34.60	
	Desert Vixen finished first but was disqualified from purse money										
1975	Let Me Linger	3	L. Pincay Jr	117	Honorable Miss	121	Susan's Girl	128	34,590	1:35.20	
1976	Artfully	4	P. Day	108	Snooze	108	Land Girl	109	25,920	1:34.00	
1976	Sugar Plum Time	4	J. Imparato	111	Pacific Princess	110	Fleet Victress	115	26,220	1:34.00	

Year	Winner	Age	Jockey	Wt.	Second	Wt.	Third	Wt.	Win Value	Time	Beyer
1977	What a Summer	4	J. Vasquez	126	Crab Grass	114	Harvest Girl	111	32,280	1:37.40	
1978	Pearl Necklace	4	R. Hernandez	123	Ida Delia	113	Sensational	117	48,195	1:33.80	
1979	Blitey	3	A. Cordero Jr	112	It's in the Air	122	Pearl Necklace	125	48,015	1:34.80	
1980	Bold n' Determined	3	E. Delahoussaye	122	Genuine Risk	118	Love Sign	120	49,140	1:35.40	
1981	Jameela	5	J. Vasquez	123	Love Sign	123	Island Charm	116	65,280	1:35.00	
1982	Too Chic	3	R. Hernandez	110	Ambassador of Luck	111	Anti Lib	116	67,920	1:34.80	
1983	Ambassador of Luck	4	A. Graell	116	A Kiss for Luck	120	Am Capable	109	67,560	1:36.40	
1984	Miss Oceana	3	E. Maple	120	Paradies	114	Nany	120	70,560	1:35.20	
1985	Lady's Secret	3	J. Velasquez	111	Dowery	117	Mrs. Revere	117	85,020	1:34.80	
1986	Lady's Secret	4	P. Day	125	Steal a Kiss	109	Endear	120	81,060	1:33.40	
1987	North Sider	5	A. Cordero Jr	123	Wisla	116	Funistrada	116	65,500	1:35.00	
1988	Personal Ensign	4	R.P. Romero	123	Winning Colors	118	Sham Say	115	67,080	1:34.20	
1989	Miss Brio	5	J.D. Bailey	116	Proper Evidence	116	Aptostar	123	67,080	1:35.60	
1990	Go for Wand	3	R.P. Romero	118	Feel the Beat	123	Mistaurian	116	68,760	1:35.60	106
1991	Queena	5	A. Cordero Jr	123	Fit to Scout	123	Screen Prospect	116	120,000	1:34.80	104
1992	Easy Now	3	J.D. Bailey	111	Train Robbery	118	Wide Country	116	120,000	1:36.00	95
	Nannerl finished second but was disqualified and placed last										
1993	Turnback the Alarm	4	C.W. Antley	123	Nannerl	116	November Snow	116	120,000	1:36.00	96
1994	Sky Beauty	4	M.E. Smith	123	Link River	123	Life Is Delicious	123	90,000	1:49.40	105
1995	Heavenly Prize	4	P. Day	123	Forcing Bid	108	Little Buckles	111	105,000	1:49.80	97
1996	Exotic Wood	4	C. McCarron	115	Shoop	118	Frolic	113	105,000	1:49.40	107
1997	Hidden Lake	4	R. Migliore	123	Flat Fleet Feet	120	Clear Mandate	113	150,000	1:49.60	105
1998	Aldiza	4	M.E. Smith	114	Escena	124	Tomisue's Delight	116	150,000	1:49.88	102
1999	Banshee Breeze	4	J.D. Bailey	124	Beautiful Pleasure	113	Heritage of Gold	117	150,000	1:49.95	109
2000	Heritage of Gold	5	S.J. Sellers	123	Beautiful Pleasure	125	Roza Robata	114	150,000	1:49.84	107
2001	Serra Lake	4	E.S. Prado	113	Pompeii	114	March Magic	114	150,000	1:49.62	102
2002	Dancethruthedawn	4	J.D. Bailey	118	Transcendental	113	Too Scarlet	112	150,000	1:50.21	100
2003	Sightseek	4	J.D. Bailey	121	She's Got the Beat	112	Nonsuch Bay	113	150,000	1:50.92	115
2004	Azeri	6	P. Day	120	Sightseek	122	Storm Flag Flying	117	150,000	1:47.86	106

Beyer Index: 103.73

Run as Maskette Stakes prior to 1992. Run at Aqueduct in 1959-60, 1962-68

GOLDEN GATE BREEDERS' CUP HANDICAP (G3), 1 1/8 Miles (Turf), 3-Year-Olds and Up, Golden Gate Fields, 2004 Purse: $90,000

Year	Winner	Age	Jockey	Wt.	Second	Wt.	Third	Wt.	Win Value	Time	Beyer
1947	Triplicate	6	J. Longden	115	Bymeabond	112	Autocrat	112	52,450	2:05.20	
1948	Shannon II	7	J. Westrope	124	See-tee-See	116	Stepfather	111	61,000	1:59.80	
1949	Solidarity	4	R. Neves	119	Stepfather	119	Roman In	112	38,200	2:00.00	
1950	Noor	5	J. Longden	127	Citation	126	On Trust	103	32,950	1:58.20	
1951	Palestinian	5	W. Shoemaker	124	Simonsez	107	Moonrush	119	15,250	1:48.00	
1952	Lights Up	5	R. Neves	123	Intent	126	Conversion	104	34,800	1:59.80	
1953	Fleet Bird	4	J. Longden	123	High Scud	112	Goose Khal	124	32,700	1:52.60	
1954	Determine	3	R. York	125	Poona II	104	Blue Trump't'r	106	15,150	1:50.60	
1955	Alidon	4	J. Longden	112	Determine	129	Novarullah	111	29,325	1:59.40	
1956	Battle Dance	4	J. Ruggeri	106	Ole Travis	110	Count Chic	115	12,750	1:49.60	
1957	Barouche	3	M. Volzke	112	Tall Chief II	113	Golden Notes	122	12,750	1:47.60	
1958	Ekaba	4	P. Moreno	116	Social Climber	122	Eddie Schmidt	117	25,500	1:47.40	
1959	Sisters Prince	4	J. Longden	112	Sweet Revenge	109	Mr. Eiffel	121	15,350	2:00.60	
1960	Prince Cohen	4	J. Longden	113	Honk	113	Whiz Bam	110	13,150	2:00.60	
1961	Gem Town	4	J. Longden	119	Fighting Hodge	115	Sea Rover	113	12,650	2:01.40	
1962	Mandate	4	J. Longden	114	Sea Orbit	126	Nite Shift	114	12,950	1:42.00	
1963	Native Diver	4	W. Shoemaker	130	Friendly Fred	112	Ol' Bleu	104	12,200	1:44.80	
1964	Real Good Deal	3	J. Longden	124	Carang	116	Second Honeymoon	104	13,200	1:42.00	
1965	Real Luck	5	D. Ross	118	Carang	116	Mangayte	122	15,875	1:47.40	
1966	Ask Father	5	M. Valenzuela	112	Sheldrake	117	Whit's Pride	117	18,500	1:47.20	
1967	Carang	6	M. Volzke	119	Lucky P.J.	110	Ask Father	114	18,650	1:47.80	
1968	Lucky P.J.	5	B. Jennings	120	Most Host	124	Mainsheet	117	18,700	1:41.40	
1969	Diego Security	4	D. Tierney	118	Most Host	118	Dizzy Babe	115	19,400	1:42.20	
1970	Governors Party	4	J. Leonard	119	Diego Security	118	Figonero	126	18,050	1:41.20	
1971	Imaginative	4	M. Volzke	112	Most Host	115	Inverness Drive	122	23,300	1:41.40	
1972	Panzer Chief	5	H. Grant	122	On the Track	123	Fair Test	119	36,600	1:42.60	
1973	Wing Out	5	R. Schacht	124	Fair Test	116	Yvetot	116	30,800	1:43.80	
1974	Acclimatization	6	S. Valdez	119	Yvetot	118	Wild World	111	46,350	2:27.80	
1975	Pass the Glass	4	F. Olivares	115	Confederate Yankee	116	Ga Hai	118	33,150	1:41.80	
1976	Pass the Glass	5	F. Olivares	119	Willie Pleasant	111	Barrydown	117	31,250	1:41.40	
1977	Announcer	5	M. Castaneda	115	The Fop	114	Sir Jason	116	71,700	1:40.40	
1978	Bad 'n Big	4	A. Diaz	120	Effervescing	123	Jumping Hill	124	65,500	1:44.80	
1979	As de Copas	6	H.E. Moreno	120	True Statement	117	Bywayofchicago	123	62,600	1:43.40	
1980	Eagle Toast	6	P.A. Valenzuela	113	Daranstone	108	Saboulard	116	63,200	1:41.00	
1981	Caterman	5	M. Castaneda	123	Opus Dei	121	His Honor	118	77,000	1:41.40	
1982	Regal Bearing	6	R.A. Baze	117	Visible Pole	110	Score Twenty Four	121	73,900	1:46.00	

Year	Winner	Age	Jockey	Wt.	Second	Wt.	Third	Wt.	Win Value	Time	Beyer
1983	Silveyville	5	D. Winick	115	Ask Me	115	Majesty's Prince	122	165,800	2:16.40	
1984	John Henry	9	C.J. McCarron	125	Silveyville	117	Lucence	116	184,200	2:13.00	
1985	Fatih	5	T. Lipham	119	Fact Finder	115	Semillero	114	171,770	2:15.40	
							Nak Ack	115			
1986	Val Danseur	5	G.L. Stevens	117			Complice II	115	100,375	2:15.40	
	Le Solaret	4	M. Castaneda	113							
1987	Rivlia	5	C.J. McCarron	116	Air Display	115	Reco	113	165,000	2:14.20	
1988	Great Communicator	5	R. Sibille	120	Putting	117	Rivlia	120	165,000	2:15.40	
1989	Frankly Perfect	4	E. Delahoussaye	122	Pleasant Variety	114	Brown Bess	114	165,000	2:15.00	
1990	Petite Ile	4	C.A. Black	113	Valdali	114	Pleasant Variety	116	220,000	2:15.60	107
1991	Forty Niner Days	4	R.Q. Meza	115	Aksar	115	Missionary Ridge	114	220,000	2:17.20	
1992	Algenib	5	L. Pincay Jr	120	Missionary Ridge	114	Never Black	113	220,000	2:13.80	106
1993	Val des Bois	7	P.A. Valenzuela	119	Norwich	116	Never Black	116	165,000	1:48.20	108
1994	Alex the Great	5	P.A. Valenzuela	118	Fanmore	117	Emerald Jig	113	165,000	2:15.00	105
1995	Special Price	6	E. Delahoussaye	122	Bluegrass Prince	122	Sans Ecocide	122	110,000	2:15.00	110
1996	Time Star	5	C.A. Black	116	Sand Reef	116	Bon Point	117	120,000	2:16.20	105
1997	Irish Wings	5	D. Carr	114	Savinio	117	Mufattish	114	120,000	1:49.60	102
1998	Dushyantor	5	C.S. Nakatani	118	Eternity Range	114	Star Performance	116	150,000	2:15.20	103
1999	Sayarshan	4	B. Blanc	124	Alvo Certo	117	Plicck	115	120,000	2:15.56	106
2000	Deploy Venture	4	R.A. Baze	115	Single Empire	121	Bonapartiste	119	120,000	2:19.12	102
2001	Northern Quest	6	V. Espinoza	118	Eagleton	114	Entorchado	115	137,500	1:58.58	102
2002	No Slip	4	K.J. Desormeaux	117	Kerrygold	116	Sumitas	119	82,500	1:49.41	103
2003	Ninebanks	5	R.J. Warren Jr	116	Surprise Halo	115	Royal Gem	118	82,500	1:50.07	97
2004	Tronare	6	R.M. Gonzalez	115	Soud	118	Aly Bubba	116	41,250	1:48.48	101

Beyer Index: 104.07

GOLDEN GATE DERBY (G3), 1 1/16 Miles, 3-Year-Olds, Golden Gate Fields, 2004 Purse: $100,000

Year	Winner	Age	Jockey	Wt.	Second	Wt.	Third	Wt.	Win Value	Time	Beyer
1947	Cutty Hunk	3	F. Zufelt	114	Pretty Mggie	111	Triskelion	117	16,450	1:54.80	
1948	Henpecker	3	J. Longden	117	Smoke Tree	114	Grandpere	123	16,650	1:47.80	
1949	Pedigree	3	J. Westrope	120	Blue Dart	114	Smart Count	114	17,950	1:49.00	
1950	Sir Butch	3	G. Glisson	113	Great Circle	122	War Poppy	113	15,520	1:48.00	
1952	Maracador	3	R.L. Baird	117	Steel	110	Alate		15,900	1:48.40	
1955	Golden Land	3	R. York	126	Beau Busher	126	Bequeath	126	29,325	1:48.60	
1958	Furyvan	3	A. Maese	121	Brief Interlude	110	Harcall	118	25,700	1:42.60	
1959	Mr. Eiffel	3	G. Taniguchi	122	Cellyar	116	Trumpet	112	15,950	1:42.20	
1997	Pacificbounty	3	KJ. Desormeaux	118	Dancer's Kolo	118	Esteemed Friend	118	120,000	1:43.00	91
1998	Clover Hunter	3	R. Baze	120	Mantles Star	120	Allen's Oop	120	120,000	1:43.33	98
1999	Epic Honor	3	L.J. Meche	120	Blue Tune	120	Brave Gun	120	90,000	1:43.58	96
2000	New Advantage	3	A.D. Lopez	120	Nurdlinger	120	Shake Loose	120	90,000	1:42.66	81
2001	Hoovergetthekeys	3	R. Warren Jr	120	High Cascade	120	Media Mogul	120	90,000	1:42.88	90
2002	Danthebluegrassman	3	J.J. Steiner	120	Cappuchino	120	U S S Tinosa	120	68,750	1:43.87	91
2003	Standard Setter	3	R.M. Gonzalez	120	Ozzie Cat	120	Pine for Java	120	55,000	1:43.76	84
2004	Skipaslew	3	E. Saint-Martin	120	O.K. Mikie	120	Bensquito	120	55,000	1:41.84	91

Beyer Index: 90.25

GOLDEN ROD (G2), 1 1/16 Miles, Fillies, 2-Year-Olds, Churchill Downs, 2004 Purse: $215,400

Year	Winner	Age	Jockey	Wt.	Second	Wt.	Third	Wt.	Win Value	Time	Beyer
1910	Helen Barbee	2	Nolan	93	Helene	96	The Hague	102	1,050	1:13.80	
1911	Kaiser	2	Skirvin	98	Island Queen	104	Azylade	102	1,270	1:12.80	
1912	Gowell	2	Loftus	107	Nobby	105	Donerail	103	1,470	1:13.40	
1913	Edith W.	2	J. McCabe	102	Brig's Brother	108	Old Ben	107	1,480	1:12.40	
1914	Vogue	2	J. Metcalf	102	Grecian	98	Aunt Josie	101	1,290	1:13.80	
1915	Milestone	2	A. Mott	104	Checks	103	Pockichoo	105	1,260	1:16.00	
1916	Fan G.	2	M. Buxton	106	Milbrey	98	Opportunity	100	1,400	1:14.80	
1917	Fern Handley	2	O. Willis	100	Sweet Alyssum	100	Hamilton A.	107	1,040	1:15.00	
1918	Legal	2	J. Howard	103	Madge F.	104	Sam Reh	113	1,395	1:14.20	
1919	Busy Signal	2	L. Lyke	110	Prince Pal	112	Orlova	100	5,705	1:40.00	
1920	Rangoon	2	L. Lyke	116	White Star	105	Sir Thos. Kean	106	6,120	1:26.60	
1921	Jeanne Bowdre	2	F. Weiner	105	Rockminister	117	John Finn	117	5,980	1:24.40	
1922	Great Luck	2	E. Pool	109	Alice Blue Gown	105	Donges	119	5,960	1:25.60	
1923	Glide	2	W. Fronk	110	Lord Martin	104	Chilhowee	113	6,480	1:25.00	
1924	Captain Hal	2	J. Heupel	127	King Nadi	110	Blue Ridge	113	5,880	1:26.00	
1925	Rhinock	2	E. Scobie	118	My Colonel	109	Great Sport	103	6,440	1:28.60	
1926	Rolled Stocking	2	W. Crump	111	Ethel Dear	112	Lovely Mannersr	112	6,020	1:25.80	
1927	Easter Stockings	2	R. Russell	107	Mickey D.	110	General Grant	110	5,800	1:27.00	
1962	Sequent	2	F. Callico	114	Golden Sage	113	Power to Strike	114	11,375	1:25.20	
1963	Ivalinda	2	R. Gallimore	114	Cadabra	111	Grecian Princess	114	7,678	1:24.40	
1963	Royal Bund	2	D. Brumfield	119	Valeene	116	Intentorpoise	108	7,776	1:24.40	
1964	Wild Song	2	K. Church	114	Wild Note	111	May's Guide	115	7,654	1:23.80	

Year	Winner	Age	Jockey	Wt.	Second	Wt.	Third	Wt.	Win Value	Time	Beyer
1964	Torrid Miss	2	R. Gallimore	114	Kalispell	114	Gallizzie	119	7,654	1:24.20	
1965	Chalina	2	L. Kunitake	113	Trade Mark	112	Holiday Wish	115	25,990	1:25.40	
1966	Woozem	2	K. Knapp	113	Scottish Heath	110	Thong	116	27,979	1:23.40	
1967	Shenow	2	L. Pincay Jr	119	Moss	113	Lady Tramp	116	40,703	1:23.80	
1968	Spring Sunshine	2	D. Brumfield	116	Double Delta	113	Pink Stocking	113	40,310	1:24.00	
1969	Goddess Special	2	H. Viera	116	Mito Sal	116	Native Tumbler	116	36,166	1:27.00	
1970	Levee Night	2	E. Snell	113	Secret Retreat	116	Magnabid	113	43,186	1:23.60	
1971	Barely Even	2	T. Barrow	119	Apple Jackie	113	La Brisa	116	32,194	1:25.80	
1972	Cam Axe	2	E. Fires	113	Bold Memory	113	Patsy's Girl	116	36,569	1:24.00	
1973	Chris Evert	2	L. Pincay Jr	116	Bundler	119	Kiss Me Darlin	116	38,200	1:25.20	
1974	Mirthful Flirt	2	W.J. Passmore	113	Sun and Snow	119	Yale Coed	116	38,597	1:26.60	
1975	Old Goat	2	M. Hole	119	Co'fort Zone	113	Silent Bidder	114	37,940	1:24.80	
1976	Bring out the Band	2	D. Brumfield	114	Shady Lou	116	Ciao	113	38,688	1:25.20	
1977	Bold Rendezvous	2	P. Nicolo	113	Rainy Princess	116	Silver Spook	113	46,449	1:27.00	
1978	Angel Island	2	E. Delahoussaye	119	Safe	113	Too Many Sweets	119	36,325	1:24.20	
1979	Remote Ruler	2	S. Maple	116	Forever Cordial	116	Peachblow	116	43,095	1:25.00	
1980	Mamzelle	2	M.S. Sellers	116	Switch Point	116	Brent's Star	119	83,236	1:46.20	
1981	Betty Money	2	D. Brumfield	119	Hoist Emy's Flag	116	Subdeb	119	91,669	1:45.80	
1982	Weekend Surprise	2	P. Day	119	National Banner	116	Quarrel Over	116	77,701	1:47.00	
1983	Flippers	2	P. Day	119	Robin's Rob	116	Mallorca	116	86,158	1:47.60	
1984	Kamikaze Rick	2	R. Migliore	118	Boldly Dared	114	Gallant Libby	118	101,156	1:47.80	
1985	Slippin n' Slyding	2	C.R. Woods	116	Turn and Dance	110	Bonded Miss	113	95,693	1:46.20	
1986	Stargrass	2	K.K. Allen	118	Zero Minus	121	Laserette	113	98,358	1:46.60	
1987	Darien Miss	2	P.A. Johnson	118	Tap Your Toes	118	Most Likely	118	83,814	1:48.20	
1988	Born Famous	2	E. Fires	120	Coax Chelsie	120	Darby Shuffle	120	97,500	1:48.20	
1989	De la Devil	2	J.A. Krone	117	Crowned	120	Flew by Em	117	97,500	1:44.60	
1990	Fancy Ribbons	2	J.E. Bruin	114	Nice Assay	115	Til Forbid	113	97,500	1:45.40	88
1991	Vivid Imagination	2	J.M. Johnson	115	Met Her Dream	113	Pennant Fever	113	97,500	1:46.20	85
1992	Boots 'n Jackie	2	M.A. Lee	120	Mollie Creek	115	Dance Account	113	97,500	1:47.20	79
1993	At the Half	2	P. Day	122	Spiritofpocahontas	115	Mystic Union	111	97,500	1:46.80	88
1994	Lilly Capote	2	D.M. Barton	113	Morris Code	113	Cat Appeal	119	97,500	1:46.60	88
1995	Gold Sunrise	2	Martinez W	113	Birr	119	Solana	113	111,150	1:45.40	82
1996	City Band	2	S.J. Sellers	122	Glitter Woman	113	Water Street	122	139,996	1:46.80	95
1997	Love Lock	2	R.J. Albarado	119	Barefoot Dyana	119	Grechelle	111	139,996	1:44.40	90
1998	Silverbulletday	2	G.L. Stevens	122	Here I Go	113	Lefty's Dollbaby	113	134,292	1:43.80	104
1999	Humble Clerk	2	J.K Court	119	Cash Run	122	Secret Status	111	138,880	1:45.26	84
2000	Miss Pickums	2	J.J. Vitek	122	Nasty Storm	112	My White Corvette	119	138,384	1:48.84	81
2001	Belterra	2	J.K. Court	117	Take Charge Lady	122	Lotta Rhythm	122	133,424	1:43.82	88
2002	My Boston Gal	2	C.H. Borel	117	Holiday Lady	115	My Trusty Cat	115	136,152	1:45.00	91
2003	Be Gentle	2	J. McKee	122	Lotta Kim	116	Dynaville	116	142,600	1:45.91	91
2004	Runway Model	2	E.M. Martin Jr	122	Kota	118	Summerly	116	133,548	1:45.97	82

Beyer Index: 87.73

GOODWOOD BREEDERS' CUP HANDICAP (G2), 1 1/8 Miles, 3-Year-Olds and Up, Santa Anita, 2004 Purse: $480,000

Year	Winner	Age	Jockey	Wt.	Second	Wt.	Third	Wt.	Win Value	Time	Beyer
1982	Cajun Prince	5	W.A. Guerra	115	Caterman	122	Rock Softly	116	46,350	1:40.20	
1983	Pettrax	5	K. Black	117	Konewah	115	Stancharry	117	46,650	1:42.60	
1984	Lord at War	4	W. Shoemaker	117	Video Kid	118	Menswear	117	60,150	1:42.00	
1985	Lord at War	5	W. Shoemaker	125	Matafao	106	Last Command	115	62,800	1:50.20	
1986	Super Diamond	6	L. Pincay Jr	122	Epidaurus	115	Prince Don B.	115	65,500	1:41.20	
1987	Ferdinand	4	W. Shoemaker	127	Candi's Gold	117	Skywalker	123	102,500	1:50.80	
1988	Cutlass Reality	6	G.L. Stevens	124	Lively One	116	Stylish Winner	113	130,400	1:47.20	
1989	Present Value	5	E. Delahoussaye	119	Rahy	121	Happy Toss	116	128,800	1:47.20	
1990	Lively One	5	A. Solis	120	Miserden	112	Festin	116	126,800	1:48.00	105
1991	The Prime Minister	4	C.J. McCarron	115	Marquetry	119	Pleasant Tap	117	152,300	1:47.80	108
1992	Reign Road	4	K.J. Desormeaux	116	Sir Beaufort	116	Marquetry	120	125,200	1:48.20	109
1993	Lottery Winner	4	K.J. Desormeaux	114	Region	116	Pleeant Tango	115	127,200	1:47.00	105
1994	Bertrando	5	G.L. Stevens	120	Dramatic Gold	115	Tossofthecoin	115	124,400	1:46.60	113
1995	Soul of the Matter	4	K.J. Desormeaux	121	Tinners Way	121	Alphabet Soup	116	144,450	1:47.40	106
1996	Savinio	6	C.S. Nakatani	117	Dare And Go	122	Alphabet Soup	120	189,300	1:47.80	110
	Alphabet Soup finished first but was disqualified and placed third										
1997	Benchmark	6	E. Delahoussaye	118	Score Quick	114	Hesabull	117	158,700	1:47.60	108
1998	Silver Charm	4	G.L. Stevens	124	Free House	124	Score Quick	115	262,800	1:47.20	111
1999	Budroyale	6	G.K. Gomez	119	General Challenge	120	Old Trieste	120	300,000	1:48.20	118
2000	Tiznow	3	C.J. McCarron	116	Captain Steve	117	Euchre	115	300,000	1:47.38	119
2001	Freedom Crest	5	K.J. Desormeaux	116	Skimming	123	Tiznow	124	300,000	1:48.86	108
2002	Pleasantly Perfect	4	A. Solis	115	Momentum	119	Reba's Gold	116	300,000	1:46.80	116
2003	Pleasantly Perfect	5	A. Solis	116	Fleetstreet Dancer	113	Star Cross	110	300,000	1:48.37	105
2004	Lundy's Liability	4	D.R. Flores	118	Total Impact	119	Supah Blitz	117	300,000	1:48.39	108

Beyer Index: 109.93

GOTHAM (G3), 1 Mile,
3-Year-Olds, Aqueduct, 2004 Purse: $200,000

Year	Winner	Age	Jockey	Wt.	Second	Wt.	Third	Wt.	Win Value	Time	Beyer
1953	Native Dancer	3	E. Guerin	120	Magic Lamp	120	Sickle's Sound	120	24,500	1:44.20	
1953	Laffango	3	N. Shuk	120	Invigorator	120	Fly Wheel	120	24,500	1:44.00	
1954	Fisherman	3	H. Woodhouse	120	Galdar	120	Mel Leavitt	120	27,150	1:46.20	
1955	Go Lightly	3	J. Culmone	120	Mr. Al L.	120	Bangborough	120	21,250	1:46.60	
1956	Career Boy	3	E. Guerin	122	Jean Baptiste	122	Nail	126	20,200	1:45.60	
1957	Mister Jive	3	H. Woodhouse	118	Promised Land	122	Clem	122	21,400	1:45.60	
1958	Oh Johnny	5	W. Boland	114	Paper Tiger	114	Tick Tock	112	18,257	1:43.60	
1959	Atoll	3	E. Arcaro	122	Intentionally	122	Open View	114	18,290	1:43.00	
1960	John William	3	S. Boulmetis	118	New Commander	115	Count Amber	114	18,257	1:36.40	
1961	Ambiopoise	3	R. Ussery	114	Globemaster	114	Merry Ruler	114	37,895	1:35.80	
1962	Jaipur	3	W. Shoemaker	122	Sunrise County	118	Sidluck	114	38,025	1:37.00	
1963	Debbysman	3	L. Adams	114	Bonjour	122	Crewman	122	37,375	1:34.60	
1964	Mr. Moonlight	3	J. Combest	114	Traffic	122	Mr. Brick	122	37,895	1:37.20	
1965	Flag Raiser	3	R. Ussery	118	Dapper Dan	114	Dependability	118	37,310	1:36.60	
1966	Stupendous	3	P. Anderson	114	Impressive	118	Handsome Boy	118	38,480	1:34.60	
1967	Dr. Fager	3	M. Ycaza	122	Damascus	122	Reason to Hail	114	37,570	1:35.20	
1968	Verbatim	3	J.L. Rotz	118	Wise Exchange	126	What a Pleasure	122	39,000	1:34.00	
1969	Dike	3	J. Velasquez	122	Rooney's Shield	114			37,700	1:34.80	
					Reviewer	122					
1970	Native Royalty	3	A. Cordero Jr	114	Delaware Chief	114	Silent Screen	126	37,765	1:36.20	
1971	Good Behaving	3	R. Turcotte	118	Droll Role	114	Sound Off	114	34,080	1:36.00	
1972	Freetex	3	C. Baltazar	126	Eager Exchange	122	Upper Case	126	36,750	1:36.40	
1973	Secretariat	3	R. Turcotte	126	Champagne Charlie	117	Flush	117	33,330	1:33.40	
1974	Stonewalk	3	M.A. Rivera	116	L'Amour Rullah	116	Wing South	119	27,570	1:36.00	
1974	Rube the Great	3	M.A. Rivera	119	Hosiery	116	Cumulo Nimbus	116	27,420	1:35.20	
1975	Laramie Trail	3	M. Venezia	121	Lefty	121	Kalong	116	27,180	1:38.00	
1975	Singh	3	A. Cordero Jr	121	Round Stake	116	Mr. Duds	116	27,630	1:37.00	
1976	Zen	3	J. Vasquez	116	Cojak	124	Play the Red	114	34,740	1:35.60	
1977	Cormorant	3	D. Wright	123	Fratello Ed	121	Papelote	114	22,065	1:43.60	
1978	Slap Jack	3	J. Velasquez	114	Quadratic	123	Shelter Half	121	33,210	1:38.60	
1979	General Assembly	3	J. Velasquez	123	Belle's Gold	123	Screen King	123	49,680	1:43.60	
1980	Colonel Moran	3	J. Velasquez	123	Dunham's Gift	114	Bucksplasher	115	53,370	1:37.00	
1981	Proud Appeal	3	J. Fell	123	Cure the Blues	126	Noble Nashua	123	50,040	1:33.60	
1982	Air Forbes Won	3	M. Venezia	114	Shimatoree	123	Big Brave Rock	114	50,760	1:35.60	
1983	Assault Landing	3	V. Bracciale Jr	114	Bounding Basque	123	Jacque's Tip	123	50,895	1:35.80	
1983	Chas Connerly	3	J. Fell	123	Elegant Life	123	Law Talk	114	50,535	1:36.60	
1984	Bear Hunt	3	D. MacBeth	114	Lt. Flag	123	On the Sauce	114	136,440	1:40.40	
1985	Eternal Prince	3	R. Migliore	114	Pancho Villa	121	El Basco	114	147,840	1:34.40	
1986	Mogambo	3	J. Vasquez	121	Tasso	123	Zabaleta	121	214,200	1:34.40	
1987	Gone West	3	R.G. Davis	114	Shawklit Won	114	Gulch	123	190,200	1:34.60	
1988	Private Terms	3	C.W. Antley	126	Seeking the Gold	114	Perfect Spy	121	181,500	1:34.80	
1989	Easy Goer	3	P. Day	123	Diamond Donnie	114	Expensive Decision	118	168,300	1:32.40	
1990	Thirty Six Red	3	M.E. Smith	114	Senor Pete	121	Burnt Hills	114	182,400	1:33.80	
1991	Kyle's Our Man	3	A. Cordero Jr	121	King Mutesa	118	Another Review	118	150,000	1:34.60	106
1992	Lure	3	M.E. Smith	114			Best Decorated	114	102,500	1:35.60	100
	Devil His Due	3	W.H. McCauley	114							
1993	As Indicated	3	C.V. Bisono	114	Itaka	114	Strolling Along	121	120,000	1:36.20	100
1994	Irgun	3	J.D. Bailey	114	Bit of Puddin	117	Jesse F	114	150,000	1:36.20	105
1995	Talkin Man	3	M.E. Smith	122	Da Hoss	117	Devious Course	117	150,000	1:36.80	110
1996	Romano Gucci	3	J.A. Krone	119	Tiger Talk	117	Feather Box	114	120,000	1:34.40	103
1997	Smokin Mel	3	J.R. Velazquez	112	Ordway	122	Wild Wonder	119	120,000	1:34.20	101
1998	Wasatch	3	J.D. Bailey	117	Dr J	119	Late Edition	114	150,000	1:36.40	97
1999	Badge	3	S.X. Bridgmohan	120	Apremont	120	Robin Goodfellow	113	90,000	1:34.72	104
2000	Red Bullet	3	A. Solis	113	Aptitude	113	Performing Magic	114	120,000	1:34.27	100
2001	Richly Blended	3	R. Wilson	116	Mr. John	116	Voodoo	116	120,000	1:35.14	100
2002	Mayakovsky	3	E.S. Prado	116	Saarland	120	Parade of Music	116	120,000	1:34.90	102
2003	Alysweep	3	R. Migliore	120	Grey Comet	120	Spite the Devil	116	120,000	1:40.60	103
2004	Saratoga County	3	J.J. Castellano	116	Pomeroy	116	Eddington	116	120,000	1:35.53	96

Beyer Index: 101.93

GRAVESEND HANDICAP (G3), 6 Furlongs,
3-Year-Olds and Up, Aqueduct, 2004 Purse: $109,400

Year	Winner	Age	Jockey	Wt.	Second	Wt.	Third	Wt.	Win Value	Time	Beyer
1959	Silver Ship	4	E. Arcaro	126	Discard	115	Besomer	114	17,380	1:10.20	
1960	Brush Fire	3	R. Ussery	118	Vendetta	116	Rick City	126	17,867	1:09.60	

Year	Winner	Age	Jockey	Wt.	Second	Wt.	Third	Wt.	Win Value	Time	Beyer
1961	Bolinas Boy	3	J.L. Rotz	115	Four Lane	122	Chief of Chiefs	126	14,072	1:09.40	
1962	Merry Ruler	4	J. Sellers	123	Rullah Red	115	Hellenic Hero	113	18,200	1:21.40	
1963	Ahoy	3	H. Grant	123	For the Road	120	Merry Ruler	121	14,755	1:08.80	
1964	Delta Judge	4	D. Pierce	122	Valentine	110	Rainy Lake	117	18,167	1:09.40	
1965	Determined Man	4	M. Venezia	109	Kilmoray	113	Dark King	116	18,167	1:10.40	
1966	Winnie	4	E. Belmonte	113	Malicious	124	Understudy	111	17,647	1:09.80	
1967	Tumiga	3	B. Feliciano	120	Beaupy	116	Smooth Seas	109	17,745	1:09.00	
1968	Jim J.	4	A. Cordero Jr	124	Our Michael	114	Royal Exchange	111	18,167	1:10.20	
1969	Royal Exchange	4	A. Cordero Jr	119	Grey Slacks	116	Godspeed	110	1,742	1:09.80	
1970	Distinctive	4	W. Blum	114	Ta Wee	134	Tyrant	121	18,395	1:08.80	
1971	Summer Air	4	A. Cordero Jr	118	Silver Mallet	106	Eastern Fleet	117	20,010	1:10.00	
1972	Silver Mallet	4	B. Baeza	115	Close Decision	111	Rollicking	121	16,425	1:09.20	
1973	Petrograd	4	A. Cordero Jr	120	Full Pocket	120	Delta Oil	111	16,635	1:08.60	
1974	Mr. Prospector	4	J. Vasquez	124	Infuriator	112	Lonetree	119	22,830	1:09.00	
1975	Honorable Miss	5	J. Vasquez	123	Queen City Lad	111	Piamem	118	16,485	1:10.00	
1976	Christopher R.	5	W.J. Passmore	131	Mac Corkle	115	Gallant Bob	120	26,940	1:09.80	
1977	Full Out	4	A. Cordero Jr	116	Great Above	114	Jackson Square	114	22,065	1:10.20	
1978	Half High	5	A. Santiago	113	Intercontinent	114	B'ld and Stormy	107	25,755	1:09.60	
1979	Shelter Half	4	S.A. Boulmetis	116	Double Zeus	114	Tanthem	125	26,220	1:11.00	
1980	Clever Trick	4	J. Velasquez	117	Rise Jim	119	Dr. Blum	114	32,460	1:09.00	
1981	Lines of Power	4	D. MacBeth	116	Stiff Sentence	112	Bayou Black	115	32,760	1:09.60	
1982	Chan Balum	3	J.L. Samyn	108	Maudlin	126	In From Dixie	120	34,320	1:11.20	
1983	Main Stem	5	V. Lopez	109	Havagreatdate	119	In From Dixie	113	34,440	1:14.00	
1984	Elegant Life	4	J. Velasquez	115	Tarantara	120	Top Avenger	126	42,180	1:09.40	
1985	Love That Mac	3	J. Velasquez	111	Raja's Shark	126	Aggressive Bid	110	40,860	1:11.00	
1986	Comic Blush	3	A. Graell	106	King's Swan	122	Cutlass Reality	117	41,100	1:09.40	
1987	Vinnie the Viper	4	J.A. Krone	116	King's Swan	122	Best by Test	117	54,360	1:09.60	
1988	High Brite	4	A. Cordero Jr	122	King's Swan	119	Matter of Hon'r	111	48,540	1:10.60	
1989	Never Forgotten	5	A. Madrid Jr	117	Proud and Valid	111	Garemma	113	40,980	1:12.60	
1990	Mr. Nasty	3	J.D. Bailey	113	Senor Speedy	114	Dargai	113	41,220	1:09.80	
1991	Shuttleman	5	A. Cordero Jr	113	Senor Speedy	120	Gallant Step	112	52,830	1:10.20	113
1992	Hidden Tomahawk	4	J.F. Chavez	111	Smart Alec	113	Miner's Dream	114	52,920	1:08.60	105
1993	Astudillo	3	F.A. Arguello Jr	112	Fabersham	113	Ferociously	113	51,300	1:11.80	94
1994	Mining Burrah	4	Velazquez JR	111	Golden Pro	115	Won Song	113	51,270	1:10.80	101
1995	Cold Execution	4	Pezua JM	116	Crafty Alfel	117	Golden Tent	114	50,820	1:09.40	103
1996	Victor Avenue	3	J.F. Chavez	119	Royal Haven	117	Stalwart Member	114	50,325	1:09.20	109
1997	Royal Haven	5	R. Migliore	122			Laredo	115	32,670	1:10.00	112
	Stalwart Member	4	A. T. Gryder	118					32,670	1:10.00	
1998	Say Florida Sandy	4	S.X. Bridgmohan	117	Esteemed Friend	114	Home On the Ridge	117	50,220	1:11.00	100
1999	Cowboy Cop	5	A. T. Gryder	115	Brushed On	112	Unreal Madness	116	50,370	1:09.40	109
2000	Say Florida Sandy	5	J. Bravo	116	Liberty Gold	115	Lake Pontchartrain	116	51,450	1:09.80	104
2001	Here's Zealous	4	E.S. Prado	114	Peeping Tom	120	Say Florida Sandy	120	64,740	1:10.37	108
2002	Multiple Choice	4	V. Carrero	118	Sing Me Back Home	114	Gold I.D.	113	65,520	1:09.26	107
2003	Shake You Down	5	M.J. Luzzi	124	Way to the Top	114	Gators n Bears	115	65,400	1:09.55	110
2004	Don Six	4	M.J. Luzzi	114	Mr. Whitestone	114	Papua	114	65,640	1:08.97	108

Beyer Index: 105.93

GULFSTREAM PARK BREEDERS' CUP HANDICAP (G1), 1 3/8 Miles (Turf), 3-Year-Olds and Up, Gulfstream Park, 2004 Purse: $190,000

Year	Winner	Age	Jockey	Wt.	Second	Wt.	Third	Wt.	Win Value	Time	Beyer
1986	Sondrio	5	J.A. Santos	113	Chief Run Run	113	Ends Well	115	74,772	1:40.60	
1987	Bolshoi Boy	4	R. Romero	116	Arctic Honeymoon	114	Little Bold John	115	80,286	1:44.60	
1988	Salem Drive	6	G. St. Leon	116	Equalize	112	King's River II	113	94,530	1:40.60	
1989	Equalize	3	J.A. Santos	124	Posen	115	Nisswa	111	93,210	1:41.00	
1990	Youmadeyourpoint	4	D. Valiente	112	Blazing Bart	118	Iron Courage	116	94,560	1:39.60	110
1991	Shy Tom	5	C. Perret	115	Dr. Root	112	Runaway Raja	112	94,800	2:14.60	99
1992	Passagere du Soir	5	J.D. Bailey	114	Colchis Island	111	Crystal Moment	116	95,130	2:15.60	99
1993	Stagecraft	6	J.D. Bailey	115	Social Retiree	116	Futurist	116	93,600	2:13.20	106
1994	Strolling Along	4	J.D. Bailey	117	Conveyor	119	Awad	112	93,150	2:05.00	101
1995	Misil	7	J.A. Santos	119	Myrmidon	113	Star of Manila	118	94,200	2:12.40	104
1996	Celtic Arms	5	M.E. Smith	114	Broadway Flyer	117	Flag Down	118	101,880	2:13.80	106
1997	Lassigny	6	J.D. Bailey	116	Flag Down	117	Awad	119	102,840	2:11.20	107
1998	Flag Down	8	J.A. Santos	120	Buck's Boy	115	Copy Editor	116	120,000	2:12.40	109
1999	Yagli	6	J.D. Bailey	121	Wild Event	117	Unite's Big Red	115	120,000	2:10.60	110
2000	Royal Anthem	5	J.D. Bailey	121	Thesaurus	112	Band Is Passing	116	116,400	2:11.34	110
2001	Subtle Power	4	P. Day	113	Whata Brainstorm	114	Stokofsky	114	60,000	2:13.50	103
2002	Cetewayo	8	C. Velasquez	115	Band Is Passing	117	Profit Option	115	120,000	2:17.44	107
2003	Man From Wicklow	6	J.D. Bailey	119	Just Listen	113	Sardaukar	114	120,000	2:11.62	108
2004	Hard Buck	5	E.S. Prado	117	Balto Star	122	Kicken Kris	118	90,000	2:11.56	104

Beyer Index: 105.53

Distance 1 1/16 miles 1986-90

GULFSTREAM PARK HANDICAP (G2), 1 1/4 Miles, 3-Year-Olds and Up, Gulfstream Park, 2004 Purse: $300,000

Year	Winner	Age	Jockey	Wt.	Second	Wt.	Third	Wt.	Win Value	Time	Beyer
1946	Do-Reigh-Mi	5	B. Strange	112	Reply Paid	120	Cat Bridge	108	11,000	2:07.60	
1947	Armed	6	D. Dodson	129	Pot o' Luck	117	Concordian	116	23,000	2:01.40	
1948	Rampart	6	M. Basile	108	Armed	130	Incline	110	20,050	2:02.00	
1949	Coaltown	4	O. Scurlock	128	Three Rings	118	Armed	116	13,000	1:59.80	
1950	Chicle II	5	H. Woodhouse	125	Count-A-Bit	114	Gangway	106	9,750	2:03.00	
1951	Ennobled	5	J. Stout	113	Mount Marcy	120	Lambent	112	9,500	2:01.60	
1952	Crafty Admiral	4	C. Errico	114	Alerted	114	Why Not Now	113	19,850	2:01.00	
1953	Crafty Admiral	5	K. Church	128	Battlefield	125	Dulat	114	37,400	2:00.80	
1954	Wise Margin	4	K. Stuart	106	Ruhe	114	Intencion	103	43,500	2:02.80	
1955	Mister Black	6	J. Adams	113	Wise Margin	116	Maharajah	112	42,100	2:01.80	
1956	Sailor	4	W. Hartack	119	Mielleux	110	Find	116	83,300	2:00.60	
1957	Bardstown	5	W. Hartack	130	Fabius	123	Needles	126	76,400	2:00.40	
1958	Round Table	4	W. Shoemaker	130	Meeting	111	Oligarchy	111	69,800	1:59.80	
1959	Vertex	5	S. Boulmetis	125	Amerigo	114	Air Pilot	110	80,700	2:01.60	
1960	Bald Eagle	5	M. Ycaza	126	Amerigo	123	On-and-On	121	71,400	2:01.20	
1961	Tudor Way	5	W. Hartack	124	Derrick	112	Don Poggio	122	74,000	2:01.60	
1962	Jay Fox	4	L. Gilligan	112	Yorky	121	Carry Back	126	72,800	2:01.60	
	Yorky finished first but was disqualified and placed second										
1963	Kelso	6	I. Valenzuela	130	Sensitivo	112	Jay Fox	113	70,500	2:03.20	
1964	Gun Bow	4	W. Shoemaker	125	Garwol	113	Admiral Vic	124	76,600	2:01.80	
	Admiral Vic finished second but was disqualified and placed third										
1965	Ampose	4	K. Knapp	112	Tronado	112	Gun Bow	130	71,900	2:04.40	
1966	First Family	4	E. Fires	112	Selari	113	Tie Viejo	113	74,200	2:03.00	
1967	Pretense	4	J. Sellers	126	Amberoid	116	Quinta	117	97,600	2:01.80	
1968	Gentleman James	4	R. Grubb	110	Sacramento	110	Sette Bello	114	86,000	2:02.20	
	Rixdal finished second but was disqualified and placed sixth										
1969	Court Recess	4	M. Miceli	108	Nodouble	125	Tropic King II	116	86,400	2:01.40	
1970	Snow Sporting	4	A. Pineda	118	Twogundian	115	Al Hattab	114	83,600	2:04.00	
1971	Fast Hilarious	5	C. Perret	116	The Pruner	113	Snow Sporting	119	77,040	1:59.40	
1972	Executioner	4	C. Barrera	122	Urgent Message	110	Panicum Repens	110	80,880	2:04.00	
1973	West Coast Scout	5	L. Adams	116	Super Sail	110	Freetex	113	80,880	2:01.00	
1974	Forego	4	H. Gustines	127	True Knight	123	Golden Don	118	72,360	1:59.80	
1975	Gold and Myrhh	4	W. Blum	114	Proud and Bold	120	Buffalo Lark	117	74,520	2:01.80	
1976	Hail the Pirates	6	B. Baeza	116	Legion	113	Packer Captain	113	73,560	2:01.80	
1977	Strike Me Lucky	5	J.D. Bailey	109	Legion	115	Yamanin	122	88,200	2:00.80	
1978	Bowl Game	4	J. Velasquez	112	True Statement	108	Silver Series	126	100,000	2:00.60	
1979	Sensitive Prince	4	J. Vasquez	120	Jumping Hill	126	Silent Cal	119	100,000	1:59.20	
1980	Private Account	4	J. Fell	119	Lot o' Gold	120	Silent Cal	118	100,000	2:01.40	
1981	Hurry Up Blue	4	C. Lopez	119	Yosi Boy	111	Imperial Dilemma	113	114,888	2:03.20	
1982	Lord Darnley	4	M.L. Russ	113	Joanie's Chief	113	Double Sonic	111	91,200	2:01.80	
1983	Christmas Past	4	J. Velasquez	117	Crafty Prospector	115	Rivalero	120	111,630	2:02.60	
1984	Mat Boy	5	J. Valdivieso	118	Lord Darnley	109	Courteous Majesty	114	87,700	1:59.00	
1985	Dr. Carter	4	J. Velasquez	119	Key to the Moon	120	Pine Circle	116	171,480	2:02.00	
1986	Skip Trial	4	R.P. Romero	121	Proud Truth	125	Important Business	113	180,000	2:03.20	
1987	Skip Trial	5	R.P. Romero	118	Creme Fraiche	120	Snow Chief	124	150,000	2:02.80	
1988	Jade Hunter	4	J.D. Bailey	113	Cryptoclearance	122	Creme Fraiche	122	180,000	2:01.60	
1989	Slew City Slew	5	A. Cordero Jr	117	Bold Midway	113	Cryptoclearance	123	180,000	2:03.20	
1990	Mi Selecto	5	J.D. Bailey	114	Tour d'Or	118	Lay Down	113	180,000	2:03.60	109
1991	Jolie's Halo	4	R. Platts	119	Primal	117	Chief Honcho	118	180,000	2:01.00	117
1992	Sea Cadet	4	A. Solis	119	Strike the Gold	115	Sunny Sunrise	114	180,000	2:01.60	120
1993	Devil His Due	4	W.H. McCauley	114	Offbeat	112	Pistols and Roses	114	300,000	2:01.20	114
1994	Scuffleburg	5	C. Perret	113	Migrating Moon	114	Wallenda	117	300,000	2:00.40	109
1995	Cigar	5	J.D. Bailey	118	Pride of Burkaan	114	Mahogany Hall	113	300,000	2:02.80	116
1996	Wekiva Springs	5	J.D. Bailey	117	Star Standard	112	Powerful Punch	113	300,000	2:03.00	110
1997	Mt. Sassafras	5	J.D. Bailey	113	Skip Away	122	Tejano Run	114	300,000	2:02.20	118
1998	Skip Away	5	J.D. Bailey	127	Unruled	112	Behrens	114	300,000	2:03.21	114
1999	Behrens	5	J.F. Chavez	114	Archers Bay	114	Sir Bear	118	210,000	2:01.91	111
2000	Behrens	6	J.F. Chavez	120	Adonis	115	With Anticipation	113	210,000	2:01.79	111
2001	Sir Bear	8	E. Coa	116	Pleasant Breeze	115	Broken Vow	114	120,000	2:02.96	110
2002	Hal's Hope	5	R. Velez	113	Mongoose	115	Sir Bear	117	180,000	2:02.91	109
2003	Hero's Tribute	5	E.S. Prado	115	Aeneas	115	Puzzlement	114	180,000	2:04.24	110
2004	Jackpot	6	J. Bravo	113	Newfoundland	116	The Lady's Groom	113	180,000	2:02.80	107

Beyer Index: 112.33

For 4-year-olds and up in 1946

HAL'S HOPE HANDICAP (G3), 1 1/16 Miles, 3-Year-Olds and Up, Gulfstream Park, 2004 Purse: $100,000

Year	Winner	Age	Jockey	Wt.	Second	Wt.	Third	Wt.	Win Value	Time	Beyer
1990	Big Sal	5	E. Fires	119	Twice Too Many		Groomstick		20,340	1:24.80	
1991	New York Swell	8	J. Alferez	111	Rhythm		Mercedes Won		45,000	1:42.40	
1992	Peanut Butter Onit	6	J.A. Santos	114	Sunny Sunrise		Honest Ensign		45,000	1:43.40	

Year	Winner	Age	Jockey	Wt.	Second	Wt.	Third	Wt.	Win Value	Time	Beyer
1993	Classic Seven	5	C. Lopez	116	Devil on Ice		Keratoid		60,000	1:43.40	
1994	Forever Whirl	4	W.H. McCauley	113	Northern Trend	113	Royal n Gold	113	45,000	1:41.80	106
1995	Warm Wayne	4	J.D. Bailey	112	Meadow Monster	113	Silent Lake	113	45,000	1:43.00	100
1996	Geri	4	J.D. Bailey	114	Halo's Image	120	Second Childhood	113	45,000	1:41.40	113
1997	Louis Quatorze	4	P. Day	121	Strawberry Wine	113	Exalto	108	45,000	1:43.40	110
1998	K.J.'s Appeal	4	J.R. Velazquez	114	Powerful Goer	112	Tour's Big Red	114	45,000	1:42.20	114
1999	Jazz Club	4	P. Day	114	Rock and Roll	113	Hanarsaan	113	45,000	1:42.76	114
2000	Dancing Guy	5	J.D. Bailey	120	Yankee Victor	113	Midway Magistrate	117	45,000	1:44.94	106
2002	Hal's Hope	5	R.I. Velez	112	American Halo	113	Windsor Castle	112	60,000	1:42.40	108
2003	Windsor Castle	5	E.M. Coa	115	Saint Verre	114	Najran	114	60,000	1:42.33	109
2004	Puzzlement	5	J.F. Chavez	116	Bowman's Band	118	Stockholder	114	60,000	1:42.39	110

Beyer Index: 109.00

Run as Creme Fraiche Handicap prior to 2003

HANSHIN CUP HANDICAP (G3), 1 Mile, 3-Year-Olds and Up, Arlington Park, 2004 Purse: $100,000

Year	Winner	Age	Jockey	Wt.	Second	Wt.	Third	Wt.	Win Value	Time	Beyer
1941	Equifox	4	A. Craig	112	Technician	110	Dog House	103	4,190	1:38.20	
1942	Best Seller	4	H. Litzenberger	118	Woof Woof	118	Heartman	109	7,265	1:36.00	
1943	Best Seller	5	F.A. Smith	113	Thumbs Up	113	Some Chance	109	9,800	1:37.00	
1944	Sun Again	5	C. McCreary	127	Georgie Drum	113	Anticlimax	104	9,350	1:36.20	
1945	Equifox	8	A. Bodiou	119	St. Jock	107	Vald'a Lamar	106	18,550	1:38.00	
1945	Daily Trouble	7	F.A. Smith	109	Take Wing	110	Signator	115	18,550	1:37.20	
1946	Witch Sir	4	R. Campbell	110	Old Kentuck	106	Armed	132	24,200	1:37.20	
1947	With Pleasure	4	W. Garner	116	Armed	130	Mighty Story	114	23,150	1:35.00	
1948	Fervent	4	N.L. Pierson	124	Mighty Story	109	Loujac	105	23,000	1:35.20	
1949	Star Reward	5	R.L. Baird	116	Coaltown	132	Carrara Marble	112	18,800	1:35.00	
1950	Oil Capitol	3	K. Church	111	Shy Guy	123	Prop	113	19,700	1:35.00	
1951	Curandero	5	J. Westrope	114	Prop	108	Inseparable	118	18,745	1:40.20	
1952	Woodchuck	4	E. Arcaro	122	Ruhe	112	Andy B.W.	114	22,300	1:37.20	
1953	Ruhe	5	J. Adams	113	Sub Fleet	116	Hill Gail	128	35,500	1:35.40	
1954	Smoke Screen	5	D. Scurlock	116	First Aid	113	Spur On	115	36,000	1:38.60	
1955	Platan	5	J. Adams	111	Smoke Screen	112	Jet Action	120	38,500	1:35.00	
1956	Bardstown	4	W. Hartack	114	Skipper Bill	122	Sir Tribal	124	37,300	1:35.60	
1957	Swoon's Son	4	D. Erb	132	Call Me Lucky	108	Fabius	123	34,900	1:36.80	
1958	Swoon's Son	5	D. Erb	129	Bardstown	122	Indian Creek	107	87,675	1:34.80	
1959	Better Bee	5	J. Choquette	115	Belleau Chief	114	Round Table	132	33,450	1:37.00	
1960	Intentionally	4	W. Hartack	126	Dunce	121	Little Tytus	113	32,200	1:34.40	
1961	Run for Nurse	4	K. Church	115	Pied d'Or	120	John William	114	20,425	1:36.80	
1962	Intervener	5	B. Sorenson	111	Oink	116	Natego	108	19,625	1:37.80	
1963	Wa-Wa Cy	4	W.M. Cook	111	Editorialist	124	B'nding Main	113	19,875	1:38.60	
1964	Tamao	6	R. Broussard	124	Spanish Fort	117	Wa-Wa Cy	114	27,700	1:36.20	
1965	Pia Star	4	J. Sellers	112	Quita Dude	118	Troy Our Boy	112	28,750	1:33.20	
1966	Hedevar	4	W. Blum	116	Tosmah	119	Bold Bidder	124	32,550	1:33.20	
1967	Renewed Vigor	4	M. Heath	111	Estreno II	111	Errante II	114	25,300	1:37.00	
1968	R. Thomas	7	J. Nichols	119	Info	118	Out the Window	114	26,900	1:35.00	
1969	Promise	4	R. Ussery	118	Info	120	Renewed Vigor	113	32,700	1:35.00	
1979	Bask	5	M.R. Morgan	112	Bold Standard	111	Hold Your Tricks	120	22,605	1:33.20	
1980	Prince Majestic	6	G. Patterson	113	Sea Ride	114	Braze and Bold	118	69,300	1:39.20	
1981	J. Burns	6	J.D. Bailey	115	Summer Advocate	115	Brent's Trans Am	114	68,340	1:35.80	
1982	Summer Advocate	5	R.P. Romero	117	Prince Freddie	109	Fabulous Find	110	49,860	1:36.40	
1983	Hale Herk	4	R.D. Evans	113	Thumbsucker	116	Spoonf'l of H'n'y	115	52,560	1:36.00	
1984	Win Stat	7	D. Pettinger	117	Le Cou Cou	116	Harham's Sizzler	111	49,860	1:37.80	
1985	Timeless Native	5	J. Tejeira	122	Par Flite	115	Harham's Sizzler	115	49,275	1:33.80	
1986	Smile	4	J. Vasquez	121	Taylor's Special	124	Red Attack	114	69,180	1:34.00	
1987	Red Attack	5	M.E. Smith	116	Taylor's Special	127	Come Summer	114	48,570	1:34.20	
1989	Present Value	5	P. Olivares	114	Paramount Jet	114	Sutter's Prospect	110	50,310	1:34.40	
1990	Black Tie Affair	4	J. Velasquez	119	Bio	112	New Plymouth	110	47,923	1:36.00	
1991	Bright Again	4	P. Day	112	Secret Hello	115	Irish Swap	112	45,000	1:35.20	
1992	Katahaula County	4	C.C. Bourque	114	The Great Carl	113	Stalwars	116	45,000	1:37.20	103
1993	Split Run	5	E. Fires	114	Gee Can He Dance	114	Danc'n Jake	114	60,000	1:34.80	111
1994	Slerp	5	Fires E	117	Seattle Morn	116	Dancing Jon	113	60,000	1:35.40	99
1995	Tarzans Blade	4	P. Day	115	Swank	114	Come on Flip	113	45,000	1:35.60	103
1996	Golden Gear	5	M. Guidry	122	Exclusive Garth	113	Prospect for Love	113	105,000	1:36.00	107
1997	Announce	5	C.C. Borque	116	Victor Cooley	117	Hunk of Class	116	60,000	1:36.80	106
2000	Yankee Victor	4	H. Castillo Jr	122	Bright Valour	114	Desert Demon	113	60,000	1:34.97	105
	Yankee Victor finished first but was subsequently disqualified from the purse (Battle Mountain placed third)										
2001	Bright Valour	5	R.J. Albarado	115	Apt to Be	114	Castlewood	115	60,000	1:36.21	100
2002	Bonapaw	6	G. Melancon	121	Slider	115	Discreet Hero	116	60,000	1:34.00	109
2003	Apt to Be	6	E. Razo Jr	117	There's Zealous	116	San Pedro	116	60,000	1:34.40	110
2004	Crafty Shaw	6	C. Perret	119	Apt to Be	119	Kodema	116	60,000	1:35.36	111

Beyer Index: 105.82

HASKELL INVITATIONAL HANDICAP (G1), 1 1/8 Miles, 3-Year-Olds, Monmouth Park, 2004 Purse: $1,000,000

Year	Winner	Age	Jockey	Wt.	Second	Wt.	Third	Wt.	Win Value	Time	Beyer
1968	Balustrade	3	E. Walsh	115	Chompion	113	Funny Fellow	116	50,000	1:50.00	
1969	Al Hattab	3	R. Broussard	126	Dot Ed's Bluesky	111	Hydrologist	115	65,000	1:50.20	
1970	Twice Worthy	3	J. Ruane	117	Roman Scout	113	Dust Commander	122	65,000	1:48.40	
1971	West Coast Scout	3	L. Adams	112	Northfields	114	Alma North	111	65,000	1:48.00	
1972	Freetex	3	M. Hole	117	King's Bishop	115	Cloudy Dawn	117	65,000	1:48.40	
1973	Our Native	3	M.A. Rivera	123	Annihilate 'Em	118	Aljamin	118	65,000	1:48.60	
1974	Holding Pattern	3	M. Miceli	117	Little Current	127	Better Arbitor	119	65,000	1:49.80	
1975	Wajima	3	B. Baeza	118	Intrepid Hero	115	My Friend Gus	116	65,000	1:49.60	
1976	Majestic Light	3	S. Hawley	122	Apassionato	113	Honest Pleasure	126	65,000	1:47.00	
1977	Affiliate	3	M.A. Rivera	117	Don Sebastian	112	Iron Constitution	118	65,000	1:50.60	
1978	Delta Flag	3	D. Nied	112	Dave's Friend	120	Special Honor	118	65,000	1:53.20	
1979	Coastal	3	R. Hernandez	127	Steady Growth	120	Worthy Piper	112	65,000	1:48.80	
1980	Thanks to Tony	3	C. Lopez	111	Superbity	124	Amber Pass	121	90,000	1:49.40	
1981	Five Star Flight	3	C. Perret	119	Lord Avie	126	Ornery Odis	112	120,000	1:48.40	
1982	Wavering Monarch	3	R.P. Romero	117	Aloma's Ruler	126	Lejoli	112	120,000	1:47.80	
1983	Deputed Testamony	3	W.H. McCauley	124	Bet Big	116	Parfaitement	116	120,000	1:49.20	
1984	Big Pistol	3	G. Patterson	119	Birdie's Legend	115	Locust Bayou	115	120,000	1:47.80	
1985	Skip Trial	3	J.L. Samyn	116	Spend a Buck	127	Creme Fraiche	126	180,000	1:48.60	
1986	Wise Times	3	C.P. DeCarlo	114	Personal Flag	114	Danzig Connection	123	180,000	1:48.60	
1987	Bet Twice	3	C. Perret	126	Alysheba	126	Lost Code	124	300,000	1:47.00	
1988	Forty Niner	3	C. Perret	126	Seeking the Gold	125	Primal	117	300,000	1:47.60	
1989	King Glorious	3	C.J. McCarron	123	Music Merci	120	Shy Tom	116	300,000	1:49.80	
1990	Restless Con	3	T.T. Doocy	118	Baron de Vaux	117	Rhythm	121	300,000	1:49.20	
1991	Lost Mountain	3	C. Perret	118	Corporate Report	120	Hansel	126	300,000	1:48.00	107
1992	Technology	3	J.D. Bailey	120	Nines Wild	112	Scudan	113	300,000	1:48.60	108
1993	Kissin Kris	3	J.A. Santos	118	Storm Tower	119	Dry Bean	113	300,000	1:49.40	108
1994	Holy Bull	3	M.E. Smith	126	Meadow Flight	118	Concern	118	300,000	1:48.20	115
1995	Serena's Song	3	G.L. Stevens	118	Pyramid Peak	120	Citadeed	118	300,000	1:48.80	110
1996	Skip Away	3	J.A. Santos	124	Dr. Caton	115	Victory Speech	121	450,000	1:47.60	113
1997	Touch Gold	3	C.J. McCarron	125	Anet	120	Free House	125	850,000	1:47.60	114
1998	Coronado's Quest	3	M.E. Smith	124	Victory Gallop	125	Grand Slam	118	600,000	1:48.60	110
1999	Menifee	3	P. Day	124	Cat Thief	123	Forestry	118	600,000	1:48.06	110
2000	Dixie Union	3	A. Solis	117	Captain Steve	118	Milwaukee Brew	117	600,000	1:50.00	111
2001	Point Given	3	G.L. Stevens	124	Touch Tone	115	Burning Roma	119	900,000	1:49.77	106
2002	War Emblem	3	V. Espinoza	124	Magic Weisner	118	Like a Hero	117	600,000	1:48.21	112
2003	Peace Rules	3	E.S. Prado	121	Sky Mesa	118	Funny Cide	123	600,000	1:49.32	109
2004	Lion Heart	3	J. Bravo	121	My Snookie's Boy	116	Pies Prospect	116	600,000	1:48.95	109

Beyer Index: 110.14

Run as Monmouth Invitational Handicap from 1968–80.

HAWTHORNE DERBY (G3), 1 1/8 Miles (Turf) 3-Year-Olds, Hawthorne, 2004 Purse: $250,000

Year	Winner	Age	Jockey	Wt.	Second	Wt.	Third	Wt.	Win Value	Time	Beyer
1965	Bold Bidder	3	E. Nelson	115	Gummo	118	Slystitch	117	37,100	1:43.40	
1966	Handsome Boy	3	L. Moyers	115	Francis U.	116	Whisper Jet	119	37,750	1:41.60	
1967	Gentleman James	3	R. Nono	114	Royal Speed	113	High Tribute	117	36,650	1:48.60	
1968	Te Vega	3	L. Pincay Jr	120	Foreign Comet	117	Francsull	113	34,300	1:41.80	
1969	Oil Power	3	J. Cruguet	113	Fast Hilarious	120	North Flight	124	30,950	1:40.60	
1970	Well Mannered	3	F. Verardi	120	Sarasota Bay	111	Coaltown Cat	118	54,450	1:41.80	
1971	Northfields	3	M. Ycaza	122	New Round	115	Saltwell	111	42,100	1:40.80	
1972	Feloniously	3	E. Fires	118	Sensitive Music	116	Suspected	114	28,750	1:42.40	
1973	Golden Don	3	M. Manganello	116	Impecunious	123	Cades Cove	114	40,600	1:41.20	
1974	Stonewalk	3	R. Turcotte	123	Tytus Casella	116	Mr. Door	114	63,150	1:40.60	
1975	Winter Fox	3	B. Fann	109	Intrepid Hero	125	American History	117	93,800	1:49.20	
1976	Wardlaw	3	J. Tejeira	117	Practitioner	112	Hurricane Ed	117	82,200	1:42.80	
1977	Silver Series	3	L. Snyder	114	Courtly Haste	114	Affiliate	112	100,800	1:41.20	
1978	Sensitive Prince	3	J. Vasquez	118	Gordie H.	112	Esops Foibles	124	73,680	1:39.60	
1979	Architect	3	S.A. Spencer	115	Incredible Ease	112	Door King	112	48,360	1:44.60	
1980	Jaklin Klugman	3	C.J. McCarron	121	Summer Advocate	115	Hurry Up Blue	121	64,440	1:40.80	
1981	Jeremy Jet	3	C. Silva	112	Loose Thoughts	112	Recusant	112	67,200	1:45.60	
1982	Drop Your Drawers	3	P. Day	118	Harham's Sizzler	118	Northern Majesty	118	64,830	1:42.80	
1983	St. Forbes	3	E. Fires	117	His Flower	117	Saverton	117	67,200	1:44.40	
1984	Pass the Line	3	C. Marquez	117	Mr. Japan	117	Bet Blind	115	66,750	1:57.60	
1985	Derby Wish	3	R.P. Romero	123	Day Shift	115	Explosive Darling	123	64,320	2:00.20	
1986	Autobot	3	E. Fires	120	Spellbound	117	Son of the Desert	115	96,360	2:00.40	
1987	Zaizoom	3	E. Fires	119	Sir Bask	114	Rio's Lark	116	89,280	2:09.80	
1988	Pappa's Swing	3	E.S. Prado	119	Djedar	115	Foolish Intent	117	94,200	1:55.80	
1989	Broto	3	S.J. Sellers	115	Joey Jr.	117	Chenin Blanc	115	94,350	1:53.00	

Year	Winner	Age	Jockey	Wt.	Second	Wt.	Third	Wt.	Win Value	Time	Beyer
1990	Tutu Tobago	3	P.A. Johnson	113	Take That Step	122	Seti I.	115	64,710	1:53.60	
1991	Rainbows for Life	3	D. Penna	122	Drummer Boy	117	Kiltartan Cross	115	65,370	1:44.60	101
1992	Bantan	3	C.C. Bourque	117	Words of War	114	Gee Can He Dance	117	60,000	1:48.00	99
1993	Snake Eyes	3	G.K. Gomez	122	Lt. Pinkerton	117	Ft. Bent	115	90,000	1:50.20	102
1994	Chrysalis House	3	Guidry M	115	Unfinished Symph	122	Marvin's Faith	122	90,000	1:51.80	99
1995	Cuzzin Jeb	3	Lopez CC	117	Hawk Attack	122	Seven n Seven	114	90,000	1:48.80	93
1996	Jaunatxo	3	Diaz J. L.	122	Trail City	122	Canyon Run	122	120,000	1:47.00	101
1997	River Squall	3	C. Perret	119	Honor Glide	122	Blazing Sword	115	120,000	1:48.20	107
1998	Stay Sound	3	D' Amico A. J.	115	El Mirasol	111	Yankee Brass	114	150,000	1:47.40	99
1999	Minor Wisdom	3	Zimmerman R.	115	Air Rocket	119	Fred of Gold	113	150,000	1:49.00	102
2000	Hymn	3	L. Pincay Jr	115			Lonely Place	113	100,000	1:53.79	95
	Rumsontheontheriver	3	A.J. Juarez Jr	115							
2001	Kalu	3	J.A. Santos	119	Proud Man	119	Rahy's Secret	115	150,000	1:50.49	93
2002	Flying Dash	3	V. Espinoza	119	Scooter Roach	115	Quest Star	115	150,000	1:58.88	90
2003	False Promises	3	C.H. Marquez Jr	115	Megoman	115	Beau Classic	113	150,000	1:48.48	91
2004	Cool Conductor	3	J.A. Santos	115	Bankruptcy Court	115	Crown Prince	113	150,000	1:47.89	92

Beyer Index: 97.43

HAWTHORNE GOLD CUP HANDICAP (G2), 1 1/4 Miles, 3-Year-Olds and Up, Hawthorne, 2004 Purse: $750,000

Year	Winner	Age	Jockey	Wt.	Second	Wt.	Third	Wt.	Win Value	Time	Beyer
1928	Display	5	J. Maiben	126	Mike Hall	126	Crusader	126	20,200	2:03.00	
1929	Sun Beau	4	F. Coltiletti	126	Misstep	126	Diavolo	126	21,900	2:01.60	
1930	Sun Beau	5	F. Coltiletti	126	Pigeon Hole	126	Alcibiades	117	23,800	2:04.60	
1931	Sun Beau	6	J. Maiben	126	Mate	120	Plucky Play	126	20,700	2:05.00	
1932	Plucky Play	5	G. Woolf	126	Faireno	117	Mate	126	21,450	2:04.20	
1933	Equipoise	5	R. Workman	126	Fal'ant Sir	126	Mr. Khayyam	117	17,250	2:02.80	
1935	Discovery	4	J. Bejshak	126	Top Dog	120	Spanish Babe	117	11,125	2:04.40	
1937	Sahri II	6	F.A. Smith	110	Infantry	116	Dellor	114	11,125	2:04.40	
1938	Espo'se	6	N. Wall	120	Cardinalis	110	Mucho Gusto	118	10,825	2:13.80	
1939	Challedon	3	H. Richards	120	Gridiron	106	Chief On'w'y	108	10,900	2:03.20	
1946	Jack's Jill	4	J. Higley	111	Spy Song	114	Eternal Reward	118	19,450	2:03.00	
1947	Be Faithful	5	W. Garner	116	Letmenow	103	Stud Poker	100	38,500	2:03.20	
1948	Billings	3	M. Peterson	122	Sun Herod	124	Scotch Secret	103	39,700	2:06.00	
1949	Volcanic	4	A.D. Rivera	125	Sun Herod	115	Vulcan's Forge	126	38,100	2:02.80	
1950	Dr. Ole Nelson	4	G. Porch	110	Curandero	112	Volcanic	125	19,750	2:01.40	
1951	Seaward	6	A. Gomez	113	Picador	105	Ruhe	110	27,250	2:04.20	
1952	To Market	4	W. Boland	123	Dr. Ole Nelson	111	Abbe Sting	107	39,800	2:01.40	
1953	Sub Fleet	4	S. Brooks	115	Smoke Screen	114	Indian Hemp	109	67,350	2:00.60	
1954	Rejected	4	E. Guerin	123	Mister Black	114	Hasseyampa	109	61,550	2:11.60	
1955	Hasseyampa	4	B. Fisk	111	Mister Black	117	Sea o Erin	118	55,200	2:04.80	
1956	Dedicate	4	W. Boland	120	Summer Tan	119	Find	119	80,750	2:02.40	
1957	Round Table	3	W. Harmatz	121	Swoon's Son	128	Find	119	75,950	2:00.20	
1958	Round Table	4	W. Shoemaker	126	Swoon's Son	123	Ekaba	113	73,250	1:59.80	
1959	Day Court	4	H. Moreno	113	Easy Spur	115	Tudor Era	116	71,300	1:59.20	
1960	Kelso	3	E. Arcaro	117	Heroshogala	119	On-and-On	122	88,900	2:02.00	
1961	T.V. Lark	4	J. Longden	113	Heroshogala	109	Run for Nurse	119	78,250	2:02.60	
1962	Beau Purple	5	W. Boland	123	Bass Clef	117	Sensitivo	118	82,250	2:04.20	
1963	Admiral's Vic	3	M. Solomone	122	Donut King	115	Piper's Son	110	78,500	2:03.80	
1964	Going Abroad	4	R. Broussard	120	Intercepted	118	Olden Times	123	71,100	2:01.60	
1965	Moss Vale	4	R. Baldwin	116	Lemon Twist	113	Peter P'kin	112	79,600	2:07.80	
1966	Bold Bidder	4	P. Anderson	121	Tronado	118	Come On II	113	75,200	2:02.60	
1967	Dr. Fager	3	B. Baeza	123	Whisper Jet	114	Pointmenow	108	72,360	2:01.20	
1968	Nodouble	3	M. Heath	117	Cabildo	120	Irish Dude	112	83,680	1:59.20	
1969	Nodouble	4	E. Belmonte	125	Vif	111	Verbatim	124	74,280	1:59.80	
1970	Gladwin	4	R. Turcotte	115	Red Reality	117	Etony	114	81,320	1:58.80	
1971	Twice Worthy	4	L. Pincay Jr	119	Royal Harmony	115	Wing Out	105	73,880	1:59.40	
1972	Droll Role	4	E. Maple	113	Good Counsel	118	Hitchcock	117	69,780	2:00.40	
1973	Tri Jet	4	B. Baeza	117	Golden Don	113	Cloudy Dawn	114	75,720	2:01.40	
1974	Group Plan	4	J. Velasquez	115	Buffalo Lark	117	Billy Come Lately	119	66,120	1:58.80	
1975	Royal Glint	5	J. Tejeira	124	Buffalo Lark	123	Group Plan	126	74,480	2:02.20	
1976	Almost Grown	4	M. Morgan	110	Teddy's Courage	113	Romeo	113	86,720	2:01.60	
1977	On the Sly	4	G. McCarron	121	Milwaukee Avenue	114	Romeo	111	75,072	2:01.60	
1979	Young Bob	4	R.L Turcotte	114	All the More	113	Architect	121	62,310	1:51.00	
1980	Tunerup	4	J. Vasquez	125	Pole Position	120	The Trader Man	112	82,590	2:00.60	
1981	Spruce Bouquet	4	K. Clark	119	Lord Gallant	114	Bill Monroe	119	101,760	2:04.20	
1982	Recusant	4	R.J Hirdes Jr	122	Harham's Sizzler	116	Irish Heart	115	98,760	2:01.80	
1983	Water Bank	4	C. Lamance	114	Cad	116	Gallant Gentlem'n	111	130,050	2:01.40	
1984	Proof	4	E. Delahoussaye	118	Jack Slade	119	Bounding Basque	117	160,170	2:01.20	
1985	Garthorn	5	R. Meza	116	Magic North	115	Leroy S.	114	158,220	2:01.80	
1986	Ends Well	5	R.P. Romero	121	Harham's Sizzler	115	Inevitable Leader	113	182,340	2:00.60	

Year	Winner	Age	Jockey	Wt.	Second	Wt.	Third	Wt.	Win Value	Time	Beyer
1987	Nostalgia's Star	5	F. Toro	117	Savings	114	Minneapple	117	277,440	2:02.00	
1988	Cryptoclearance	4	J.A. Santos	117	Cutlass Reality	124	Nostalgia's Star	113	303,690	2:00.20	
1989	Cryptoclearance	5	J.A. Santos	122	Proper Reality	120	Classic Account	112	305,730	2:00.40	
1990	Black Tie Affair	4	J.L. Diaz	116	Mi Selecto	115	Silver Tower	112	307,800	2:03.40	116
1991	Sunny Sunrise	4	C.W. Antley	114	Sports View	116	Discover	114	309,840	2:04.00	111
1992	Irish Swap	5	B.E. Poyadou	115	Sea Cadet	121	Evanescent	112	240,000	2:01.80	115
1993	Evanescent	6	A.T. Gryder	115	Marquetry	123	Valley Crossing	117	240,000	2:02.00	109
1994	Recoup the Cash	4	J.L. Diaz	117	Run Softly	114	Kissin Kris	118	240,000	2:01.80	109
1995	Yourmissinthepoint	4	M. Guidry	113	Basqueian	114	Sky Carr	112	150,000	2:01.00	108
1996	Come On Flip	5	C.A. Emigh	113	Michael's Star	114	Mt. Sassafras	120	180,000	2:03.40	107
1997	Buck's Boy	4	M. Guidry	114	Cairo Express	115	Beboppin Baby	115	180,000	2:00.40	108
1998	Awesome Again	4	P. Day	123	Unruled	114	Muchacho Fino	114	240,000	2:02.60	104
1999	Supreme Sound	5	R. Meier	112	Golden Missile	115	Beboppin Baby	113	300,000	2:01.19	105
2000	Dust on the Bottle	5	T.T. Doocy	114	Guided Tour	114	Maysville Slew	113	300,000	2:03.00	107
2001	Duckhorn	4	R. Meier	112	Lido Palace	114	Guided Tour	116	300,000	2:01.61	116
2002	Hail the Chief	5	J.F. Chavez	114	Dollar Bill	114	Parade Leader	115	300,000	2:02.80	113
2003	Perfect Drift	4	P. Day	122	Tenpins	119	Aeneas	114	450,000	2:03.63	109
2004	Freefourinternet	6	G. Kuntzweiler	112	Perfect Drift	121	Sonic West	115	450,000	2:03.34	104

Beyer Index: 109.40

HAWTHORNE HANDICAP (G3), 1 1/16 Miles, Fillies and Mares, 3-Year-Olds and Up, Hollywood Park, 2004 Purse: $108,600

Year	Winner	Age	Jockey	Wt.	Second	Wt.	Third	Wt.	Win Value	Time	Beyer
1974	Tallahto	4	L. Pincay Jr	119	Sister Fleet	116	Lt.'s Joy	119	23,200	1:20.60	
1975	Tizna	6	J. Lambert	122	Modus Vivendi	121	Lucky Spell	121	22,600	1:20.60	
1976	Swingtime	4	W. Shoemaker	118	Call Me Proper	116	Tuscarora	113	19,150	1:41.80	
1976	Mia Amore	4	F. Toro	116	Bastonera II	118	Sometime Promise	119	19,950	1:41.80	
1977	Cascapedia	4	S. Hawley	123	Bastonera II	124	Star Ball	121	26,850	1:40.80	
1978	Sensational	4	L. Pincay Jr	119	Up to Juliet	114	Grand Luxe	117	27,300	1:41.80	
1979	Country Queen	4	L. Pincay Jr	118	Grande Brisa	113	Sisterhood	120	26,600	1:41.20	
1980	Country Queen	5	L. Pincay Jr	122	Devon Ditty	117	Wishing Well	112	30,800	1:40.60	
1981	Save Wild Life	4	C.J. McCarron	113	Princess Karenda	122	Spiffy Laree	113	37,400	1:42.80	
1982	Weber City Miss	5	S. Hawley	122	Miss Huntington	117	Aduana	115	31,750	1:42.40	
1983	Marisma	5	K. Black	115	Sierva	115	Matching	121	30,700	1:44.80	
1984	Adored	4	F. Toro	117	Holiday Dancer	116	Princess Rooney	123	36,200	1:41.80	
1985	Adored	5	L. Pincay Jr	124	Mitterand	124	Her Royalty	118	45,350	1:34.80	
1986	Dontstop Themusic	6	L. Pincay Jr	121	Till You	115	Fran's Valentine	122	46,950	1:35.40	
1987	Seldom Seen Sue	4	C.J. McCarron	114	Clabber Girl	116	Tiffany Lass	123	59,900	1:33.60	
1988	Integra	4	G.L. Stevens	120	Invited Guest	118	Behind the Scenes	117	59,400	1:36.00	
1989	Bayakoa	5	L. Pincay Jr	122	Goodbye Halo	123	Behind the Scenes	114	61,400	1:32.80	
1990	Bayakoa	6	L. Pincay Jr	125	Stormy but Valid	119	Fantastic Look	115	61,400	1:34.00	100
1991	Brought to Mind	4	P.A. Valenzuela	116	Fantastic Look	118	Fit to Scout	118	62,300	1:41.40	
1992	Sacramentada	6	K.J. Desormeaux	117	Brought to Mind	120	Re Toss	116	61,600	1:43.00	97
1993	Freedom Cry	5	A. Solis	117	Vieille Vigne	114	Miss High Blade	114	67,600	1:41.00	110
1994	Golden Klair	4	K.J. Desormeaux	118	Likeable Style	119	Andestine	117	60,000	1:41.40	100
1995	Paseana	8	C.J. McCarron	122	Pirate's Revenge	117	Top Rung	117	63,300	1:42.40	98
1996	Borodislew	6	C.S. Nakatani	119	Jewel Princess	120	Urbane	118	64,200	1:41.20	104
1997	Twice The Vice	6	C.J. McCarron	120	Chile Chatte	115	Listening	117	64,860	1:42.60	101
1998	I Ain't Bluffing	4	C.J. McCarron	114	Fun in Excess	117	Tomorrows Sunshine	115	63,720	1:41.40	106
1999	Victory Stripes	5	C.J. McCarron	115	Magical Allure	118	Housa Dancer	115	90,000	1:41.60	105
2000	Riboletta	5	C.J. McCarron	117	Excellent Meeting	122	Speaking of Time	111	90,000	1:42.33	105
2001	Printemps	4	C.J. McCarron	116	Feverish	119	Brianda	109	90,000	1:43.21	97
2002	Queen of Wilshire	6	P.A. Valenzuela	115	Alexine	119	Verruma	116	63,660	1:43.16	98
2003	Keys to the Heart	4	J. Valdivia Jr	115	Rhiana	116	Alexine	117	63,240	1:42.97	94
	Se Me Acabo finished third but was disqualified and placed fourth										
2004	Summer Wind Dancer	4	V. Espinoza	116	Pesci	115	Miss Loren	116	65,160	1:41.56	104

Beyer Index: 101.36

HERECOMESTHEBRIDE (G3), 1 1/8 Miles (Turf), 3-Year-Old Fillies, Gulfstream Park, 2004 Purse: $100,000

Year	Winner	Age	Jockey	Wt.	Second	Wt.	Third	Wt.	Win Value	Time	Beyer
1984	Delta Mary	3	F. Pennisi	112	Vast Domain		Ingot Way		14,955	1:42.00	
1984	Oakbrook Lady	3	J. Velez Jr	112	Illaka		Rain Devil		14,655	1:42.80	
1985	Debutante Dancer	3	G. Gallitano	113	One Fine Lady		Affirmance		38,640	1:42.80	
1986	Judy's Red Shoes	3	G. St. Leon	114	Tea for Top		Minstress		35,740	1:43.00	
1987	Sum	3	R. Woodhouse	121	Easter Mary		Dawandeh		25,410	1:43.20	
1988	Topicount	3	J.L. Samyn	112	Aquaba		Above Special		40,350	1:43.20	
1989	Darby Shuffle	3	C. Perret	121	Seattle Meteor		Imago		36,510	1:42.80	
1992	Morriston Belle	3	D. Penna	118	Snazzle Dazzle		Miss Jealski		30,000	1:42.20	87
1993	Sigrun	3	R. Douglas	116	So Say All of Us		Supah Gem		30,000	1:45.60	85

Year	Winner	Age	Jockey	Wt.	Second	Wt.	Third	Wt.	Win Value	Time	Beyer
1994	Cut the Charm	3	W. Ramos	116	Mynameispanama		Tambien Me Voy		30,000	1:43.60	87
1995	Clever Thing	3	C. Perret	114	Transient Trend		Palliser Bay		30,000	1:53.00	73
1996	Lulu's Ransom	3	J.D. Bailey	116	Cymbala		Vashon		30,000	1:47.40	92
1997	Auntie Mame	3	J.Bailey	114	Witchful Thinking	116	Classic Approval	114	45,000	1:46.40	97
1998	Rashas Warning	3	M.E. Smith	118	Quick Lap	116	Runnaway Dream	116	45,000	1:51.40	87
1999	Pico Teneriffe	3	J.D. Bailey	118	European Rose	112	Wild Heart Dancing	114	45,000	1:48.80	89
2000	Gaviola	3	J.D. Bailey	114	Solvig	121	Are You Up	114	45,000	1:47.28	93
2001	Mystic Lady	3	J.D. Bailey	116	Open Minded	114	Ruff	118	60,000	1:46.73	80
2002	Cellars Shiraz	3	C. Velasquez	117	August Storm	121	She's Vested	115	60,000	1:43.21	89
2003	Gal O Gal	3	C.P. DeCarlo	117	Formal Miss	117	Devil at the Wire	117	60,000	1:42.38	87
2004	Lucifer's Stone	3	J.A. Santos	117	Dynamia	115	Honey Ryder	117	60,000	1:52.78	87

Beyer Index: 87.15

Run on main track in 2001

HILL PRINCE (G3), 1 1/8 Miles (Turf), 3-Year-Olds, Belmont Park, 2004 Purse: $110,000

Year	Winner	Age	Jockey	Wt.	Second	Wt.	Third	Wt.	Win Value	Time	Beyer
1975	Don Jack	3	G. Martens	110	Annie's Brat	115	Rapid Invader	113	34,650	2:23.20	
1976	Fifth Marine	3	R. Turcotte	126	Quick Card	120	Drover's Dawn	112	27,405	1:41.20	
1977	Forward Charger	3	J. Vasquez	115	Stir the Embers	112	Winter Wind	112	22,575	1:34.40	
1978	Darby Creek Road	3	A. Cordero Jr	121	John Henry	111	Scythian Gold	111	22,605	1:35.20	
1979	Bends Me Mind	3	J. Velasquez	114	Crown Thy Good	115	T.V. Series	110	34,470	1:46.00	
1980	Ben Fab	3	J. Cruguet	126	Vatzka	113	Don Daniello	117	34,800	1:43.40	
1981	Summing	3	A. Cordero Jr	114	Stage Door Key	114	Sportin' Life	114	35,700	1:42.40	
1982	Majesty's Prince	3	R. Hernandez	114	A Real Leader	115	Honed Edge	109	33,180	1:43.40	
1982	Larida	3	E. Maple	112	Dew Line	117	John's Gold	114	33,180	1:42.60	
1983	Domynsky	3	J.D. Bailey	114	White Birch	114	Macho Duck	114	36,660	1:48.80	
1984	A Gift	3	D. MacBeth	114	Is Your Pleasure	126	Jesse's Hope	117	43,680	1:48.40	
1985	Danger's Hour	3	D. MacBeth	119	Foundation Plan	119	Exclusive Partner	114	59,310	1:40.60	
1986	Double Feint	3	J.A. Santos	121	Glow	121	Jack of Clubs	114	53,190	1:41.40	
1987	Forest Fair	3	J.A. Santos	119	Kindly Court	117	First Patriot	121	86,220	1:42.80	
1988	Sunshine Forever	3	A. Cordero Jr	114	Posen	121	Kris Green	114	85,620	1:41.20	
1989	Slew the Knight	3	C.W. Antley	121	Orange Sunshine	117	Expensive Decision	121	56,520	1:41.00	
1990	Solar Splendor	3	E. Maple	114	Divine Warning	119	Bismarck Hills	114	57,870	1:41.20	
1991	Young Daniel	3	A. Cordero Jr	114	Share the Glory	119	Lech	114	58,050	1:39.80	102
1992	Free at Last	3	J.D. Bailey	126	Casino Magistrate	123	Kiri's Clown	114	53,190	1:41.00	95
1993	Hallsee	3	J.A. Krone	121	Proud Shot	117	Logroller	114	52,020	1:40.80	95
1994	Pennine Ridge	3	J.D. Bailey	112	Check Ride	119	Add the Gold	114	50,925	1:39.80	100
1995	Green Means Go	3	J.D. Bailey	117	Smells and Bells	114	Debonair Dan	119	68,160	1:40.20	101
1996	Optic Nerve	3	Santos J. A.	114	Fortitude	117	Allied Forces	119	66,420	1:39.60	103
1997	Subordination	3	Velazquez J. R.	113	Rob 'n Gin	119	Tekken	119	67,200	1:45.60	101
1998	Recommended List	3	J.F. Chavez	119	Daniel My Brother	119	Availability	119	68,100	1:49.20	94
1999	Time Off	3	Samyn J. L.	113	Hoyle	113	Lenny's Ransom	113	66,720	1:47.40	91
2000	Promontory Gold	3	E.S. Prado	119	Rob's Spirit	113	Avezzano	115	66,540	1:49.15	100
2001	Proud Man	3	R.R. Douglas	122	Package Store	114	Navesink	118	68,760	1:48.25	95
2002	Van Minister	3	M.J. Luzzi	114	Miesque's Approval	120	Westcliffe	114	65,580	1:54.42	92
2003	Happy Trails	3	S.X. Bridgmohan	120	Traffic Chief	114	Chilly Rooster	114	67,860	1:50.13	91
2004	Artie Schiller	3	R. Migliore	120	Timo	122	Big Booster	114	66,000	1:50.06	97

Beyer Index: 96.93

Off the turf in 2003.

HILLSBOROUGH (G3), Abt 1 1/8 Miles (Turf), Fillies and Mares, 4-Year-Olds and Up, Tampa Bay Downs, 2004 Purse: $100,000

Year	Winner	Age	Jockey	Wt.	Second	Wt.	Third	Wt.	Win Value	Time	Beyer
1999	Pleasant Temper	5	P. Day	117	Sandy Gator	115	Scatter Buy	115	34,800	1:42.62	96
2000	St Clair Ridge	4	P. Day	117	Office Miss	122	Royal Bloomer	115	45,000	1:41.17	96
2001	Song for Annie	5	L. Melancon	116	Megans Bluff	116	Inside Affair	122	60,000	1:41.23	99
2002	Platinum Tiara	4	M.R. Cruz	116	Step With Style	116	Ioya Two	116	60,000	1:41.34	95
2003	Strait From Texas	4	J.L. Castanon	118	Dedication	118	Stylish	118	60,000	1:41.14	94
2004	Coney Kitty	6	J.A. Santos	116	Madeira Mist	122	Alternate	116	60,000	1:48.83	92

Beyer Index: 95.33

Distance 1 1/6 miles 1999-2003.

CLEMENT L. HIRSCH HANDICAP (G2), 1 1/16 Miles, Fillies and Mares, 3-Year-Olds and Up, Del Mar, 2004 Purse: $300,000

Year	Winner	Age	Jockey	Wt.	Second	Wt.	Third	Wt.	Win Value	Time	Beyer
1967	Daystar II	5	W. Hartack	118	Nevada Marga	121	Maintain	119	9,050	1:35.20	
1973	Grotonian	4	W. Shoemaker	117	Expediter	115	China Silk	114	12,600	1:50.60	

Year	Winner	Age	Jockey	Wt.	Second	Wt.	Third	Wt.	Win Value	Time	Beyer
1974	Bahia Key	4	A. Pineda	120	Trotteur	117	Soft Victory	122	13,650	1:34.20	
1975	Bahia Key	5	W. Harris	119	Fair Test	119	Top Command	117	12,750	1:34.00	
1976	Uniformity	4	R. Campas	115	White Fir	118	Royal Derby II	119	16,900	1:28.20	
1977	Notably Different	4	C. Baltazar	113	Key Account	114	Pikehall	109	13,375	1:29.40	
1977	Authorization	5	D.G. McHargue	113	Cherry River	117	Mister Dan	114	13,175	1:29.20	
1978	Nantequos	5	D.G. McHargue	120	Lunar Probe	118	Crew of Ocala	114	20,250	1:29.40	
							Around We Go	117			
1979	He's Dewan	4	D.G. McHargue	119	Caro Bambino	119	No No	115	23,950	1:29.00	
1980	Wayside Station	5	P.A. Valenzuela	113	Concussion	117	Mike Fogarty	115	19,775	1:28.80	
1980	Galaxy Libra	4	W. Shoemaker	118	Wickerr	117	T. Be or Not	116	19,375	1:29.00	
1981	Save Wild Life	4	C.J. McCarron	118	Princess Karenda	120	Track Robbery	125	47,650	1:41.60	
1982	Matching	4	R. Sibille	116	Miss Huntington	116	Cat Girl	117	45,850	1:40.00	
1983	Sangue	5	W. Shoemaker	121	Avigaition	122	Skillful Joy	117	46,600	1:42.20	
1984	Princess Rooney	4	P.A. Valenzuela	123	Flag de Lune	115	Moment to Buy	116	60,100	1:40.40	
1985	Dontstop the Music	5	D.G. McHargue	122	Golden Screen	112	Lovlier Linda	119	45,650	1:41.80	
1986	Fran's Valentine	4	W. Shoemaker	119	Cenyak's Star	116	Dontstop the Music	123	59,500	1:41.40	
1987	Infinidad	5	C.A. Black	118	Margaret Booth	117	Le L'Argent	117	63,540	1:41.40	
1988	Clabber Girl	5	C.J. McCarron	120	Annoconnor	118	Integra	119	75,100	1:41.60	
1989	Goodbye Halo	4	C.A. Black	120	Flying Julia	112	Kool Arrival	115	77,450	1:41.80	
1990	Bayakoa	6	L. Pincay Jr	127	Fantastic Look	113	Formidable Lady	112	88,500	1:40.60	100
1991	Vieille Vigne	4	M.A. Pedroza	116	Formidable Lady	113	Lite Light	121	120,300	1:42.60	99
1992	Exchange	4	L. Pincay Jr	120	Fowda	120	Brought to Mind	119	122,100	1:42.00	109
1993	Magical Maiden	4	G.L. Stevens	120	Vieille Vigne	111	Party Cited	117	123,600	1:42.60	92
1994	Paseana	7	C.J. McCarron	123	Exchange	120	Magical Maiden	118	117,100	1:40.40	108
1995	Borodislew	5	C.J. McCarron	118	Lakeway	121	Golden Klair	118	178,100	1:41.80	98
1996	Different	4	C.J. McCarron	120	Top Rung	116	Borodislew	117	189,200	1:42.40	99
1997	Radu Cool	5	C.J. McCarron	117	Supercilious	113	Swoon River	110	180,000	1:42.60	102
1998	Sharp Cat	4	C.S. Nakatani	124	Supercilious	115	Numero Uno	116	180,000	1:42.00	101
1999	A Lady From Dixie	4	C.W. Antley	116	Manistique	124	Yolo Lady	116	180,000	1:43.40	98
2000	Riboletta	5	C.J. McCarron	125	Bordelaise	115	Gourmet Girl	115	180,000	1:42.06	107
2001	Tranquility Lake	6	E. Delahoussaye	120	Gourmet Girl	122	Nany's Sweep	116	180,000	1:41.78	104
2002	Azeri	4	M.E. Smith	126	Angel Gift	114	Se Me Acabo	114	180,000	1:42.66	105
2003	Azeri	5	M.E. Smith	127	Got Koko	118	Tropical Blossom	108	180,000	1:42.12	100
2004	Miss Loren	6	J.K. Court	114	House of Fortune	113	Royally Chosen	116	180,000	1:42.93	102

Beyer Index: 101.60

Run as Chula Vista prior to 2000

CLEMENT L. HIRSCH MEMORIAL TURF CHAMPIONSHIP (G1), 1 1/4 Miles (Turf), 3-Year-Olds and Up, Santa Anita, 2004 Purse: $250,000

Year	Winner	Age	Jockey	Wt.	Second	Wt.	Third	Wt.	Win Value	Time	Beyer
1969	Czar Alexander	4	A. Cordero Jr	126	Pink Pigeon	123	Pink Pigeon	126	68,900	2:23.40	
1970	Daryl's Joy	4	J. Sellers	126	Fiddle Isle	126	Cougar II	126	63,600	2:26.20	
1971	Cougar II	5	W. Shoemaker	126	Vegas Vic	121	Manta	123	60,000	2:24.60	
1972	Cougar II	6	W. Shoemaker	126	Queen's Hustler	122	Bicker	122	60,000	2:27.20	
1973	Portentous	3	J. Ramirez	122	Groshawk	122	Kentuckian	126	60,000	2:25.60	
							Kirrary	122			
1974	Tallahto	4	L. Pincay Jr	123	Within Hail	122	Montmartre	126	60,000	2:25.80	
1975	Top Command	4	W. Shoemaker	126	Top Crowd	126	Buffalo Lark	126	60,000	2:26.00	
1976	King Pellinore	4	W. Shoemaker	126	Royal Derby II	126	L'Heureux	121	60,000	2:31.40	
1977	Crystal Water	4	W. Shoemaker	126	Vigors	126	Ancient Title	126	60,000	2:26.40	
1978	Exceller	5	W. Shoemaker	126	Star of Erin	126	Good Lord	126	90,000	2:24.60	
							As de Copas	126			
1979	Balzac	4	C.J. McCarron	126	Trillion	123	Silver Eagle	126	90,000	2:25.40	
1980	John Henry	5	L. Pincay Jr	126	Balzac	126	Bold Tropic	126	120,000	2:23.40	
1981	John Henry	6	W. Shoemaker	126	Spence Bay	126	The Bart	126	180,000	2:23.40	
1982	John Henry	7	W. Shoemaker	126	Craelius	122	Regalberto	126	180,000	2:24.00	
1983	Zalataia	4	F. Head	123	John Henry	126	Load the Cannons	122	240,000	2:29.20	
1984	Both Ends Burning	4	R.A. Baze	126	Gato Del Sol	126	Raami	121	240,000	2:25.40	
1985	Yashgan	4	C.J. McCarron	126	Both Ends Burning	126	Cariellor	126	240,000	2:27.20	
1986	Estrapade	6	F. Toro	123	Theatrical	126	Uptown Swell	126	240,000	2:26.00	
1987	Allez Milord	4	C.J. McCarron	126	Louis Le Grand	126	Rivlia	126	240,000	2:36.20	
1988	Nasr El Arab	3	G.L. Stevens	121	Great Communicator	126	Circus Prince	126	240,000	2:25.20	
1989	Hawkster	3	R.A. Baze	121	Pay the Butler	126	Saratoga Passage	126	300,000	2:22.80	
1990	Rial	5	R. Meza	126	Eradicate	126	Saratoga Passage	126	300,000	2:23.80	105
1991	Filago	4	P.A. Valenzuela	126	Missionary Ridge	126	Kartajana	123	300,000	2:23.62	109
1992	Navarone	4	P.A. Valenzuela	126	Defensive Play	126	Daros	121	240,000	2:24.29	108
1993	Kotashaan	5	K.J. Desormeaux	124	Luazur	124	Let's Elope	121	180,000	2:25.06	111
1994	Sandpit	5	C.S. Nakatani	124	Grand Flotilla	124	Approach the Bench	124	180,000	2:25.12	112
1995	Northern Spur	4	C.J. McCarron	124	Sandpit	124	Royal Chariot	124	180,000	2:02.37	110
1996	Admise	4	K.J. Desormeaux	121	Khoraz	124	Golden Post	124	180,000	1:58.48	103
	Bon Point (104 Beyer) finished first but was disqualified and placed fifth										
1997	Rainbow Dancer	6	A. Solis	124	Lord Jain	124	Sandpit	124	180,000	2:01.94	108
1998	Military	4	C.S. Nakatani	124	Bonapartiste	124	River Bay	124	180,000	2:02.04	107
	Marlin finished second but was disqualified and placed fourth										

Year	Winner	Age	Jockey	Wt.	Second	Wt.	Third	Wt.	Win Value	Time	Beyer
1999	Mash One	5	D.R. Flores	124	Lazy Lode	124	Bonapartiste	124	180,000	1:59.07	108
2000	Mash One	6	D.R. Flores	124	Boatman	124	Asideo	124	180,000	2:00.67	107
2001	Senure	5	A. Solis	124	White Heart	124	Cagney	124	180,000	1:59.47	107
2002	The Tin Man	4	M.E. Smith	124	Sarafan	124	Blue Steller	124	180,000	1:58.93	109
2003	Storming Home	5	G.L. Stevens	124	Johar	124	Irish Warrior	124	150,000	2:01.64	104
2004	Star Over the Bay	6	T.C. Baze	124	Sarafan	124	Vangelis	124	150,000	1:58.70	105

Beyer Index: 107.53

Distance 1 1/2 miles prior to 1996; Run as Oak Tree Turf Championship prior to 2000; Run as Oak Tree Invitational 1971–1995; Run as Oak Tree Stakes, 1969–1970

JOE HIRSCH TURF CLASSIC INVITATIONAL (G1), 1 1/2 Miles (Turf), 3-Year-Olds and Up, Belmont Park, 2004 Purse: $750,000

Year	Winner	Age	Jockey	Wt.	Second	Wt.	Third	Wt.	Win Value	Time	Beyer
1977	Johnny D.	3	S. Cauthen	122	Majestic Light	126	Crow	126	130,000	2:33.20	
1978	Waya	4	A. Cordero Jr	123	Tiller	126	Trillion	123	130,000	2:26.80	
1979	Bowl Game	5	J. Velasquez	126	Trillion	123	Native Courier	126	150,000	2:28.20	
1980	Anifa	4	A. Gibert	123	Golden Act	126	John Henry	126	180,000	2:39.60	
1981	April Run	3	P. Paquet	118	Galaxy Libra	126	The Very One	123	180,000	2:31.20	
1982	April Run	4	C.B. Asmussen	123	Naskra's Breeze	126	Bottled Water	126	286,080	2:29.80	
1983	All Along	4	W.R. Swinburn	123	Thunder Puddles	126	Erins Isle	126	351,420	2:34.00	
1984	John Henry	9	C.J. McCarron	126	Win	126	Majesty's Prince	126	375,150	2:25.20	
1985	Noble Fighter	3	A. Lequeux	119	Win	126	Strawberry Road II	126	431,100	2:25.40	
1986	Manila	3	J.A. Santos	119	Damister	126	Danger's Hour	126	428,150	2:27.80	
1987	Theatrical	5	P. Day	126	River Memories	116	Talakeno	126	360,000	2:29.20	
1988	Sunshine Forever	3	A. Cordero Jr	121	My Big Boy	126	Most Welcome	126	360,000	2:33.80	
1989	Yankee Affair	7	J.A. Santos	126	El Senor	126	My Big Boy	126	392,550	2:27.20	
1990	Cacoethes	4	R. Cochrane	126	Alwuhush	126	With Approval	126	360,000	2:25.00	111
1991	Solar Splendor	4	W.H. McCauley	126	Dear Doctor	126	Fortune's Wheel	121	300,000	2:27.80	112
	Spinning finished third but was disqualified and placed fourth										
1992	Sky Classic	5	P. Day	126	Fraise	126	Solar Splendor	126	300,000	2:24.40	110
1993	Apple Tree	4	M.E. Smith	126	Solar Splendor	126	George Augustus	126	300,000	2:28.20	111
1994	Tikkanen	3	C.B. Asmussen	121	Vaudeville	121	Yenda	118	300,000	2:25.80	113
1995	Turk Passer	5	J.R. Velazquez	126	Hernando	126	Celtic Arms	126	300,000	2:36.60	109
1996	Diplomatic Jet	4	J.F. Chavez	126	Awad	126	Marlin	121	300,000	2:27.40	111
1997	Val's Prince	5	M.E. Smith	126	Flag Down	126	Ops Smile	126	300,000	2:28.80	109
1998	Buck's Boy	5	S.J. Sellers	126	Cetewayo	126	Lazy Lode	126	300,000	2:33.25	111
1999	Val's Prince	7	J.F. Chavez	126	Dream Well	126	Fahris	126	360,000	2:28.63	108
2000	John's Call	9	J.L. Samyn	126	Craigsteel	126	Ela Athena	123	450,000	2:28.58	109
2001	Timboroa	5	E.S. Prado	126	King Cugat	126	Cetewayo	126	450,000	2:29.43	109
2002	Denon	4	E.S. Prado	126	Blazing Fury	126	Delta Form	126	450,000	2:28.47	108
2003	Sulamani	4	J.D. Bailey	126	Deeliteful Irving	126	Balto Star	126	450,000	2:27.51	110
2004	Kitten's Joy	3	J.R. Velazquez	121	Magistretti	126	Tycoon	121	450,000	2:29.97	114

Beyer Index: 110.33

Run at Aqueduct 1975 and 1976, and 1981 – 1983

HOLLYWOOD BREEDERS' CUP OAKS (G2), 1 1/16 Miles, 3-Year-Old Fillies, Hollywood Park, 2004 Purse: $182,875

Year	Winner	Age	Jockey	Wt.	Second	Wt.	Third	Wt.	Win Value	Time	Beyer
1946	Honyemoon	3	J. Westrope	126	Aptos Honey	112	Good Excuse	106	16,500	1:38.20	
1947	U Time	3	L. Balaski	118	Cold Roll	109	Hemet Squaw	115	18,750	1:23.40	
1948	Flying Rhythm	3	J.W. Martin	110	Belle Jolie	116	Boswell Lady	120	19,050	1:39.60	
1949	June Bride	3	J. Longden	112	Just Why	112	Cosmopolite	113	18,750	1:37.40	
1950	Mrs. Fuddy	3	W. Shoemaker	109	Sea Garden	113	Foxie Green	109	11,750	1:37.20	
1951	Ruth Lily	3	R. Neves	121	Mrs. Traffic	112	Royal Mink	109	15,350	1:44.20	
1952	A Gleam	3	H. Moreno	118	Princess Lygia	118	Tonga	115	16,650	1:42.60	
1953	Fleet Khal	3	J. Burton	117	Smart Barbara	110	Perfection	109	15,000	1:42.80	
1954	Miz Clementine	3	I. Valenzuela	124	Frosty Dawn	115	Free Country	112	14,600	1:50.00	
1955	Baby Alice	3	R. York	112	Auntie Bell	112	Week-End	112	15,050	1:49.20	
1956	Candy Dish	3	W. Shoemaker	112	Triple Jay	121	Tumbling	112	15,800	1:49.60	
1957	Market Basket	3	R. York	121	Pamper Me	115	Molly Maid	109	16,550	1:49.60	
1958	Midnight Date	3	L. Leon	112	Sally Lee	118	Nushie	115	16,050	1:51.00	
1959	Sybil Brand	3	W. Boland	112	Tender Size	112	Ruwenzori	115	15,650	1:49.80	
1960	Paris Pike	3	I. Valenzuela	113	Nathleen	112	Linita	115	16,800	1:48.60	
1961	Rose O'Neill	3	I. Valenzuela	112	Bushel-n-Peck	121	Oil Royalty	118	15,300	1:48.60	
1962	Dingle Bay	3	J. Longden	113	Wish n Wait	112	Table Mate	112	33,650	1:49.80	
1963	Delhi Maid	3	W. Shoemaker	118	Hi Rated	112	Curious Clover	113	34,850	1:49.20	
1964	Loukahl	3	E. Burns	115	Fran La Femme	121	Duchess Khaled	121	34,150	1:49.60	
1965	Straight Deal	3	J. Sellers	112	Sea Eagle	112	Gala Host	118	33,650	1:49.80	
1966	Spearfish	3	D. Pierce	121	Windy Kate	112	Ali's Theme	112	35,950	1:50.20	
1967	Amerigo Lady	3	A.R. Valenzuela	112	Gamely	121	Princessnesian	113	33,300	1:49.20	
1968	Hooplah	3	A. Pineda	112	Morgaise	115	Too Angri	113	32,750	1:48.60	
1969	Tipping Time	3	D. Pierce	121	Commissary	118	Ynez Queen	114	32,100	1:47.40	

Year	Winner	Age	Jockey	Wt.	Second	Wt.	Third	Wt.	Win Value	Time	Beyer
1970	Last of the Line	3	J. Lambert	114	Beja	112	Loved	112	32,650	1:48.00	
1971	Turkish Trousers	3	W. Shoemaker	124	Convenience	115	Balcony's Babe	115	37,650	1:47.80	
1972	Pallisima	3	W. Shoemaker	112	Bert's Tryst	112	Susan's Girl	124	37,350	1:48.60	
1973	Sandy Blue	3	D. Pierce	121	Cellist	121	Jungle Princess	112	50,550	1:48.00	
1974	Miss Musket	3	L. Pincay Jr	124	Lucky Spell	121	Modus Vivendi	121	49,550	1:47.80	
1975	Nicosia	3	W. Shoemaker	121	Snap Apple	112	Mia Amore	112	49,400	1:48.40	
1976	Answer	3	D.G. McHargue	121	Franmari	116	I Going	115	49,200	1:48.40	
1977	Glenaris	3	W. Shoemaker	116	One Sum	116	Taisez Vous	121	68,100	1:48.80	
1978	B. Thoughtful	3	D. Pierce	121	Country Queen	121	Grenzen	121	65,400	1:47.60	
1979	Prize Spot	3	S. Hawley	121	It's in the Air	121	Variety Queen	124	63,300	1:48.20	
1980	Princess Karenda	3	D. Pierce	121	Secretarial Queen	121	Disconiz	121	67,400	1:48.20	
1981	Past Forgetting	3	C.J. McCarron	121	Balletomane	121	Glitter Hitter	121	64,100	1:50.00	
1982	Tango Dancer	3	L. Pincay Jr	121	Faneuil Lass	121	Royal Donna	121	66,100	1:49.00	
1983	Heartlight No. One	3	L. Pincay Jr	121	Preceptress	121	Ready for Luck	121	63,900	1:49.80	
1984	Moment to Buy	3	T.M. Chapman	121	Mitterand	121	Lucky Lucky Lucky	121	97,150	1:49.20	
1985	Fran's Valentine	3	C.J. McCarron	121	Magnificent Lindy	121	Deal Price	121	120,300	1:47.40	
1986	Hidden Light	3	W. Shoemaker	121	An Empress	121	Family Style	121	116,600	1:47.80	
1987	Perchance to Dream	3	R. Sibille	121	Sacahuista	121	Pen Bal Lady	121	93,200	1:48.60	
1988	Pattern Step	3	C.J. McCarron	121	Super Avie	121	Comedy Court	121	94,700	1:48.60	
1989	Gorgeous	3	E. Delahoussaye	121	Kelly	121	Lea Lucinda	121	92,700	1:47.80	
1990	Patches	3	G.L. Stevens	121	Jefforee	121	Pampered Star	121	96,100	1:49.80	102
1991	Fowda	3	E. Delahoussaye	121	Grand Girlfriend	121	Masake	121	94,400	1:49.60	91
1992	Pacific Squall	3	K.J. Desormeaux	121	Race the Wild Wind	121	Alysbelle	121	127,200	1:48.00	109
1993	Hollywood Wildcat	3	E. Delahoussaye	121	Fit to Lead	121	Adorydar	121	130,400	1:48.40	107
1994	Lakeway	3	K.J. Desormeaux	121	Sardula	121	Fancy 'n Fabulous	121	120,000	1:46.80	117
1995	Sleep Easy	3	C.S. Nakatani	121	Predicted Glory	121	Bello Cielo	121	122,400	1:50.20	91
1996	Listening	3	C.J. McCarron	121	Antespend	121	Ocean View	121	110,640	1:48.60	102
1997	Sharp Cat	3	A. Solis	121	Freeport Flight	121	Really Happy	121	120,000	1:49.60	98
1998	Manistique	3	G.L. Stevens	115	Sweet and Ready	119	Yolo Lady	116	120,000	1:48.40	110
1999	Smooth Player	3	E. Delahoussaye	117	Excellent Meeting	121	Nany's Sweep	116	90,000	1:48.00	102
2000	Kumari Continent	3	K.J. Desormeaux	117	Queenie Belle	119	Saudi Poetry	115	90,000	1:49.13	91
2001	Affluent	3	E. Delahoussaye	116	Collect Call	115	Secret of Mecca	116	90,000	1:49.20	97
2002	Adoration	3	G.K. Gomez	115	Sister Girl Blues	114	Saint Bernadette	115	160,080	1:43.73	94
2003	Santa Catarina	3	G.L. Stevens	116	Buffythecenterfold	113	Princess V.	114	127,320	1:41.62	106
2004	House of Fortune	3	A. Solis	119	Elusive Diva	115	Hollywood Story	119	109,725	1:41.55	104

Beyer Index: 101.40

HOLLYWOOD DERBY (G1), 1 1/4 Miles (Turf), 3-Year-Olds, Hollywood Park, 2004 Purse: $500,000

Year	Winner	Age	Jockey	Wt.	Second	Wt.	Third	Wt.	Win Value	Time	Beyer
1938	Specify	3	J. Adams	118	High Strike	118	Fire Marshal	114	11,900	2:04.40	
1939	Shining One	3	J. Westrope	114	Wedding Call	114	Counterpoise	114	18,275	2:03.80	
1940	Big Flash	3	E. Rodriguez	114	Weight Anchor	114	Sweepida	122	18,750	2:03.60	
1941	Staretor	3	G. Woolf	115	Porter's Cap	122	Paperboy	114	19,675	2:03.20	
1945	Busher	3	J. Longden	123	Man o'Glory	112	Quick Reward	121	40,470	1:50.20	
1946	Honeymoon	3	J. Westrope	117	Pere Time	118	Eiffel Tower	118	39,300	2:02.00	
1947	Yankee Valor	3	N. Richardson	118	On Trust	126	Stepfather	118	36,000	2:01.80	
1948	Solidarity	3	J. Longden	119	Drumbeat	122	The Web II	118	33,300	2:02.60	
1949	Pedigree	3	J. Longden	126	Just Why	106	Rhodes Bull	112	42,900	2:03.00	
1950	Valquest	3	J. Westrope	111	Great Circle	126	Sun State	110	17,200	1:49.00	
1951	Grantor	3	W. Shoemaker	110	Australian Ace	111	Gold Note	118	33,600	2:01.80	
1952	A Gleam	3	H. Moreno	118	Arroz	111	Stranglehold	111	36,550	2:01.20	
1953	Rejected	3	R. Neves	110	Fleet Khal	117	Imbros	126	64,500	2:01.40	
1954	Fault Free	3	R. Neves	114	Allied	117	Determine	126	32,850	2:00.80	
1955	Swaps	3	W. Shoemaker	126	Fabulous Vegas	117	Jean's Joe	120	34,700	2:00.60	
1956	Count of Honor	3	E. Arcaro	117	Social Climber	123	Terrang	126	48,950	1:59.40	
1957	Round Table	3	W. Shoemaker	129	Irisher	110	Joe Price	118	69,300	2:00.60	
1958	Strong Bay	3	M. Ycaza	112	The Shoe	122	Hillsdale	118	70,800	2:02.60	
	Hillsdale finished second but was disqualified and placed third										
1959	Bagdad	3	W. Shoemaker	114	Worshiper	111	King O'Turf	110	65,900	1:59.60	
1960	Tempestuous	3	P. Moreno	110	T.V. Lark	122	Blank Check	111	68,700	2:01.40	
1961	Four-and-Twenty	3	J. Longden	126	We're Hoping	110	Bushel-n-Peck	117	77,900	2:00.60	
1962	Drill Site	3	R. Neves	110	Admiral's Voyage	126	Joc Jocoy	122	68,900	2:00.00	
1963	Y Flash	3	E. Burns	123	Get Around	123	Olympiad King	120	79,100	2:00.60	
1964	Real Good Deal	3	J. Longden	123	Close By	123	Performing Art	114	71,000	2:00.80	
1965	Terry's Secret	3	A. Maese	123	Arksoni	123	Easy Lime	114	80,200	2:00.80	
1966	Fleet Host	3	J. Lambert	114	Drin	123	Rehabilitate	114	75,500	2:00.40	
1967	Tumble Wind	3	J. Sellers	117	Duncan Junction	114	Ruken	126	72,900	2:00.20	
1968	Poleax	3	W. Hartack	123	Dewan	123	American Tiger	114	82,000	1:59.80	
1969	Tell	3	D. Pierce	123	Jay Ray	126	Court Road	112	76,600	2:00.00	
1970	Hanalei Bay	3	M. Volzke	114	Corn off the Cob	126	Western Welcome	123	73,200	2:01.20	
1971	Bold Reason	3	L. Pincay Jr	113	Jim French	126	Triple Bend	114	61,200	2:01.00	
1972	Riva Ridge	3	R. Turcotte	129	Bicker	114	Finalista	120	59,900	1:59.60	
1973	Amen II	3	E. Belmonte	126	Groshawk	126	Kirrary	126	90,000	2:27.80	

Year	Winner	Age	Jockey	Wt.	Second	Wt.	Third	Wt.	Win Value	Time	Beyer
1974	Agitate	3	W. Shoemaker	126	Stardust Mel	126	Top Crowd	126	90,000	2:28.20	
1975	Intrepid Hero	3	D. Pierce	126	Terete	126	Sibirri	126	90,000	2:29.00	
1976	Crystal Water	3	W. Shoemaker	122	Life's Hope	122	Double Discount	122	157,750	1:48.40	
1977	Steve's Friend	3	R. Hernandez	122	Affiliate	122	Habitony	122	140,000	1:47.80	
1978	Affirmed	3	S. Cauthen	122	Think Snow	122	Radar Ahead	122	174,750	1:48.20	
1979	Flying Paster	3	D. Pierce	122	Switch Partners	122	Shamgo	122	166,750	1:47.60	
1980	Codex	3	E. Delahoussaye	122	Rumbo	122	Cactus Road	122	195,250	1:47.40	
1981	De La Rose	3	E. Maple	119	High Counsel	122	Lord Trendy	122	68,700	1:47.60	
1981	Silveyville	3	D. Winick	122	French Sassafras	122	Waterway Drive	122	68,700	1:47.60	
1982	Racing is Fun	3	W. Shoemaker	122	Prince Spellbound	122	Uncle Jeff	122	67,150	1:47.20	
1982	Victory Zone	3	E. Delahoussaye	122	The Hague	122	Ask Me	122	70,150	1:47.80	
1983	Royal Heroine	3	F. Toro	119	Interco	122	Pac Mania	122	87,400	1:48.20	
1983	Ginger Brink	3	F. Toro	122	Fifth Division	122	Hur Power	122	86,400	1:49.20	
1984	Procida	3	C.B. Asmussen	122	Executive Pride	122	Reine Mathilde	119	139,250	1:48.40	
1984	Foscarini	3	D.G. McHargue	122	Roving Minstrel	122	Bean Bag	122	140,750	1:47.40	
1985	Charming Duke	3	Y. Saint-Martin	122	Herat	122	La Koumia	119	171,225	1:46.80	
1985	Slew the Dragon	3	J. Velasquez	122	Savannah Dancer	119	Catane	122	168,725	1:46.40	
1986	Thrill Show	3	W. Shoemaker	122	Air Display	122	Bold Arrangement	122	146,000	1:46.80	
1986	Spellbound	3	R. Sibille	122	Double Feint	122	Bruiser	122	147,500	1:46.80	
1987	Political Ambition	3	E. Delahoussaye	122	The Medic	122	Light Sabre	122	101,600	1:48.20	
1987	Stately Don	3	J. Vasquez	122	Lockton	122	Noble Minstrel	122	104,600	1:47.40	
1988	Silver Circus	3	G.L. Stevens	122	Raykour	122	Dr. Death	122	110,000	1:48.40	
1989	Live the Dream	3	A. Solis	122	Charlie Barley	122	River Master	122	110,000	1:47.00	
1990	Itsallgreektome	3	C.S. Nakatani	122	Septieme Ciel	122	Anshan	122	110,000	1:46.60	
1991	Eternity Star	3	E. Delahoussaye	122	Native Boundary	122	Perfectly Proud	122	110,000	1:47.20	103
1991	Olympio	3	E. Delahoussaye	122	Bistro Garden	122	River Traffic	122	110,000	1:47.00	105
1992	Paradise Creek	3	P. Day	122	Bien Bien	122	Kitwood	122	220,000	1:47.20	102
1993	Explosive Red	3	C.S. Nakatani	122	Jeune Homme	122	Earl of Barking	122	220,000	1:46.80	103
1994	River Flyer	3	C.W. Antley	122	Dare and Go	122	Fadeyev	122	220,000	1:47.40	107
1995	Labeeb	3	E. Delahoussaye	122	Helmsman	122	Da Hoss	122	220,000	1:46.40	108
1996	Marlin	3	J.R. Velazquez	122	Rainbow Blues	122	Devil's Cup	122	300,000	1:46.00	105
1997	Subordination	3	J.D. Bailey	122	Lasting Approval	122	Blazing Sword	122	300,000	1:50.00	105
1998	Vergennes	3	J.R. Velazquez	122	Dixie Dot Com	122	Lone Bid	122	300,000	1:49.44	109
1999	Super Quercus	3	A. Solis	122	Manndar	122	Fighting Falcon	122	300,000	1:45.82	111
2000	Brahms	3	P. Day	122	David Copperfield	122	Zentsov Street	122	300,000	1:46.73	104
	Designed For Luck finished first but was disqualified and placed fifth										
2001	Denon	3	C.J. McCarron	122	Sligo Bay	122	Aldebaran	122	300,000	1:49.28	109
2002	Johar	3	A. Solis	122	Mananan McLir	122	Royal Gem	122	300,000	1:48.70	100
2003	Sweet Return	3	J.A. Krone	122	Fairly Ransom	122	Kicken Kris	122	360,000	2:04.27	98
2004	Good Reward	3	J.D. Bailey	122	Fast and Furious	122	Imperialism	122	300,000	2:01.53	104

Beyer Index: 104.87

Run at 1 1/8 miles in 1945, 1950, 1976-2002. Run at 1 1/2 miles 1973-1975. Run on main track 1938-72, 1976-80. Run as Westerner Stakes 1948-58. Run at Santa Anita in 1949.

HOLLYWOOD FUTURITY (G1), 1 1/16 Miles, 2-Year-Olds, Hollywood Park, 2004 Purse: $446,500

Year	Winner	Age	Jockey	Wt.	Second	Wt.	Third	Wt.	Win Value	Time	Beyer
1981	Stalwart	2	C.J. McCarron	121	Cassaleria	121	Header Card	118	365,805	1:47.80	
1982	Roving Boy	2	E. Delahoussaye	121	Desert Wine	121	Fifth Division	121	418,770	1:41.80	
1983	Fali Time	2	S. Hawley	121	Bold T. Jay	121	Life's Magic	118	549,485	1:41.60	
1984	Stephan's Odyssey	2	E. Maple	121	First Norman	121	Right Con	121	627,000	1:43.40	
1985	Snow Chief	2	A. Solis	121	Electric Blue	121	Ferdinand	121	589,600	1:34.20	
1986	Temperate Sil	2	W. Shoemaker	121	Alysheba	121	Masterful Advocate	121	495,000	1:36.20	
1987	Tejano	2	L. Pincay Jr	121	Purdue King	121	Regal Classic	121	495,000	1:34.60	
1988	King Glorious	2	C.J. McCarron	121	Music Merci	121	Hawkster	121	495,000	1:35.60	
1989	Grand Canyon	2	A. Cordero Jr	121	Farma Way	121	Silver Ending	121	495,000	1:33.00	
1990	Best Pal	2	J.A. Santos	121	General Meeting	121	Reign Road	121	495,000	1:35.40	
1991	A.P. Indy	2	E. Delahoussaye	121	Dance Floor	121	Casual Lies	121	329,780	1:42.80	
1992	River Special	2	L. Pincay Jr	121	Stuka	121	Earl of Barking	121	275,000	1:43.20	96
1993	Valiant Nature	2	L. Pincay Jr	121	Brocco	121	Flying Sensation	121	275,000	1:40.60	106
1994	Afternoon Deelites	2	K.J. Desormeaux	121	Thunder Gulch	121	A.J. Jett	121	275,000	1:40.60	111
1995	Matty G	2	A. Solis	121	Odyle	121	Ayrton S	121	275,000	1:41.60	104
1996	Swiss Yodeler	2	A. Solis	121	Stolen Gold	121	In Excessive Bull	121	348,510	1:42.60	92
1997	Real Quiet	2	K.J. Desormeaux	121	Artax	121	Nationalore	121	282,120	1:41.20	102
1998	Tactical Cat	2	L. Pincay Jr	121	Prime Timber	121	Premier Property	121	235,800	1:42.63	93
1999	Captain Steve	2	R.J. Albarado	121	High Yield	121	Cosine	121	245,400	1:43.27	101
2000	Point Given	2	G.L. Stevens	121	Millennium Wind	121	Golden Ticket	121	204,300	1:42.21	101
2001	Siphonic	2	J.D. Bailey	121	The Fonz's	121	Officer	121	274,050	1:42.09	103
2002	Toccet	2	J.F. Chavez	121	Domestic Dispute	121	Coax Kid	121	243,900	1:41.26	102
2003	Lion Heart	2	M.E. Smith	121	St Averil	121	That's an Outrage	121	225,600	1:42.80	99
2004	Declan's Moon	2	V. Espinoza	121	Giacomo	121	Wilko	121	267,900	1:41.63	96

Beyer Index: 100.46

Distance 1 mile 1985-90

HOLLYWOOD GOLD CUP (G1), 1 1/4 Miles, 3-Year-Olds and Up, Hollywood Park, 2004 Purse: $750,000

Year	Winner	Age	Jockey	Wt.	Second	Wt.	Third	Wt.	Win Value	Time	Beyer
1938	Seabiscuit	5	G. Woolf	133	Specifiy	109	Whichcee	114	37,150	2:03.80	
1939	Kayak II	4	G. Woolf	125	Cravat	126	Specify	118	35,075	2:02.60	
1940	Challedon	4	G. Woolf	133	Specify	117	Can't Wait	115	36,200	2:02.00	
1941	Big Pebble	5	J. Westrope	119	Paperboy	98	Mioland	130	62,475	2:02.60	
1944	Happy Issue	4	H. Woodhouse	119	Bull Reigh	122	Okana	126	60,600	2:01.60	
1945	Challenge Me	4	A. Skoronski	108	Bull Reigh	122	Sirde	111	48,230	2:00.40	
1946	Triplicate	5	B. James	113	Honeymoon	113	Historian	117	79,900	2:00.40	
1947	Cover Up	4	R. Permane	117	Burning Dream	117	Honeymoon	114	73,500	2:00.00	
1948	Shannon II	7	J. Adams	116	On Trust	128	Olhaverry	113	67,600	2:01.60	
1949	Solidarity	4	R. Neves	115	Ace Admiral	115	Pretal	112	100,000	2:01.20	
1950	Noor	5	J. Longden	130	Palestinian	122	Hill Prince	130	100,000	1:59.80	
1951	Citation	6	S. Brooks	120	Bewitch	108	Be Fleet	122	100,000	2:01.00	
1952	Two Lea	6	H. Moreno	113	Cyclotron	100	Sturdy One	108	100,000	2:00.20	
1953	Royal Serenade	5	J. Longden	113	Fleet Bird	122	A Gleam	119	100,000	2:00.80	
1954	Correspondent	4	J. Longden	110	Rejected	126	Trusting	107	100,000	2:00.80	
1955	Rejected	5	G. Glisson	118	Alidon	116	Determine	126	100,000	1:59.60	
1956	Swaps	4	W. Shoemaker	130	Mister Gus	117	Porterhouse	119	102,100	1:58.60	
1957	Round Table	3	W. Shoemaker	109	Porterhouse	119	Find	118	102,100	1:58.60	
1958	Gallant Man	4	W. Shoemaker	130	Eddie Schmidt	110	Seaneen	118	102,100	2:01.60	
1959	Hillsdale	4	T. Barrow	124	Find	112	Terrang	120	102,100	1:59.20	
1960	Dotted Swiss	4	E. Burns	107	Bagdad	122	Eddie Schmidt	112	102,100	1:59.40	
							Prized Host	109			
1961	Prince Blessed	4	J. Longden	114	Grey Eagle	111	Whodunit	113	102,100	1:59.80	
1962	Prove It	5	H. Moreno	125	Windy Sands	111	Cadiz	117	102,100	2:00.00	
1963	Cadiz	7	E. Burns	111	Aldershot	110	Olympiad King	111	102,100	1:59.60	
1964	Colorado King	5	R. York	118	Mustard Plaster	119	Native Diver	117	102,100	2:00.40	
1965	Native Diver	6	J. Lambert	124	Babington	114	Hill Rise	121	102,100	2:00.20	
1966	Native Diver	7	J. Lambert	126	O'Hara	112	Travel Orb	118	102,100	2:00.00	
1967	Native Diver	8	J. Lambert	123	Pretense	131	Biggs	117	102,100	1:58.80	
1968	Princessnesian	4	D. Pierce	117	Racing Room	112	Quicken Tree	119	102,100	1:59.80	
1969	Figonero	4	A. Pineda	115	Nodouble	129	Poleax	118	102,100	1:58.80	
1970	Pleasure Seeker	4	L. Pincay Jr	114	Neurologo	109	T.V. Commercial	112	102,100	1:59.40	
1971	Ack Ack	5	W. Shoemaker	134	Comtal	111	Manta	117	100,000	1:59.80	
1972	Quack	3	D. Pierce	115	Droll Role	119	War Heim	112	100,000	1:58.20	
1973	Kennedy Road	5	W. Shoemaker	120	Quack	127	Cougar II	128	90,000	1:59.40	
1974	Tree of Knowledge	4	W. Shoemaker	115	Ancient Title	125	War Heim	114	90,000	1:59.80	
1975	Ancient Title	5	L. Pincay Jr	125	Big Band	115	E. Tarta	115	90,000	1:59.20	
1976	Pay Tribute	4	M. Castaneda	117	Avatar	123	Riot in Paris	123	150,000	1:58.80	
1977	Crystal Water	4	L. Pincay Jr	129	Cascapedia	116	Caucasus	124	210,000	2:00.00	
1978	Exceller	5	W. Shoemaker	128	Text	118	Vigors	129	192,500	1:59.20	
1979	Affirmed	4	L. Pincay Jr	132	Sirlad	120	Text	119	275,000	1:58.40	
1980	Go West Young Man	5	E. Delahoussaye	116	Balzac	120	Caro Bambino	116	220,000	1:58.80	
1981	Eleven Stitches	4	S. Hawley	122	Caterman	120	Super Moment	117	275,000	2:00.40	
	Caterman finished first but was disqualified and placed second										
1982	Perrault	5	L. Pincay Jr	127	Erins Isle	118	It's the One	125	275,000	1:59.20	
1983	Island Whirl	5	E. Delahoussaye	120	Poley	116	Prince Spellbound	120	275,000	1:59.40	
1984	Desert Wine	4	E. Delahoussaye	122	John Henry	125	Sari's Dreamer	114	275,000	2:00.40	
1985	Greinton	4	L. Pincay Jr	120	Precisionist	125	Kings Island	112	275,000	1:58.40	
1986	Super Diamond	6	L. Pincay Jr	118	Alphabatim	120	Precisionist	127	275,000	2:00.40	
1987	Ferdinand	4	W. Shoemaker	124	Judge Angelucci	118			275,000	2:00.60	
					Tasso	118					
1988	Cutlass Reality	6	G.L. Stevens	116	Alysheba	126	Ferdinand	125	275,000	1:59.40	
1989	Blushing John	4	P. Day	122	Sabona	116	Payant	116	275,000	2:00.40	
1990	Criminal Type	5	J.A. Santos	121	Sunday Silence	126	Opening Verse	119	550,000	1:59.80	121
1991	Marquetry	4	D. Flores	110	Farma Way	122	Itsallgreektome	119	550,000	1:59.40	119
1992	Sultry Song	4	J. Bailey	113	Marquetry	118	Another Review	120	550,000	2:00.20	113
1993	Best Pal	5	C.A. Black	121	Bertrando	118	Major Impact	114	412,500	2:00.00	117
1994	Slew of Damascus	6	G.L. Stevens	117	Fanmore	116	Del Mar Dennis	116	412,500	2:00.60	110
1995	Cigar	5	J.D. Bailey	126	Tinners Way	118	Tossofthecoin	118	550,000	1:59.40	118
1996	Siphon	5	D.R. Flores	117	Geri	118	Helmsman	120	600,000	2:00.40	117
1997	Gentlemen	5	G.L. Stevens	124	Siphon	124	Sandpit	124	600,000	1:59.20	121
1998	Skip Away	5	J.D. Bailey	124	Puerto Madero	124	Gentlemen	124	600,000	2:00.16	117
1999	Real Quiet	4	J.D. Bailey	124	Budroyale	124	Malek	124	600,000	1:59.67	115
2000	Early Pioneer	5	V. Espinoza	124	General Challenge	124	David	124	600,000	2:02.40	112
2001	Aptitude	4	L. Pincay Jr	124	Skimming	124	dq-Futural	124	450,000	2:01.79	107
	Futural (Beyer: 109) finished first but was disqualified and placed third										
2002	Sky Jack	6	L. Pincay Jr	124	Momentum	124	Milwaukee Brew	124	450,000	2:01.73	115
2003	Congaree	5	J.D. Bailey	124	Harlan's Holiday	124	Kudos	124	450,000	2:00.48	116
2004	Total Impact	6	M.E. Smith	124	Olmodavor	124	Even the Score	124	450,000	2:00.72	109

Beyer Index: 115.13

Run at Santa Anita in 1949

HOLLYWOOD JUVENILE CHAMPIONSHIP (G3), 6 Furlongs, 2-Year-Olds, Hollywood Park, 2004 Purse: $104,272

Year	Winner	Age	Jockey	Wt.	Second	Wt.	Third	Wt.	Win Value	Time	Beyer
1938	Unerring	2	J. Adams	119	Kenty Miss	113	Valley Lass	116	2,015	1:06.00	
1939	Polymelior	2	R. Neves	118	Loreby	115	Ted's Clover	118	8,320	1:13.00	
1940	Flying Choice	2	J. Longden	115	Lady Bos'n	115	Tin Pan Alley	122	7,600	1:11.60	
1941	Madie Greenock	2	P. Martinez	119			Zaca Rosa	119	6,200	1:12.40	
	Phar Rong	2	G. Woolf	122							
1944	Post Graduate	2	H. Woodhouse	115	Sea Swallow	115	Gold Bolt	115	15,650	1:23.20	
1944	Realization	2	R. Neves	115	War Allies	115	Bismark Sea	115	17,750	1:24.20	
1945	Favorito	2	J. Craigmyle	114	Widow's Peak	115	Please Me	114	21,540	1:24.20	
1946	U Time	2	L. Balaski	114	Stepfather	117	Hemet Squaw	114	21,900	1:10.20	
1947	Zenoda	2	R. Neves	111	Grandpere	118	Solidarity	114	16,800	1:10.00	
1948	Star Fiddle	2	H. Trent	118	Audacious Man	118	Top Turrett	118	21,050	1:12.60	
1949	Thanks Again	2	F. Chojnacki	116	Great Circle	113	Sturdy One	119	31,100	1:11.00	
1950	Gold Capitol	2	R. Neves	113	Frendswood	113	Good Loser	114	28,600	1:43.80	
1951	Prudy's Boy	2	G. Lasswell	114	Alate	114	Big Noise	114	24,900	1:10.80	
1952	Little Request	2	J. Longden	122	Decorated	112	Chanlea	112	20,350	1:10.60	
1953	Arrogate	2	E. LeBlanc	116	Larks Music	116	James Session	119	44,500	1:10.80	
1954	Blue Ruler	2	S. Brooks	113	Colonel Mack	119	Modern World	113	45,700	1:10.80	
1955	Bold Bazooka	2	R. York	116	Blen Host	119	Fortuneway	116	47,200	1:09.80	
1956	Lucky Mel	2	J. Longden	122	Nashville	116	Joe Price	116	61,450	1:09.40	
1957	Old Pueblo	2	E. Arcaro	116	Fleet Nasrullah	119	Strong Ruler	113	49,900	1:10.20	
1958	Tomy Lee	2	W. Shoemaker	122	Finnegan	118	Monk's Hood	122	52,500	1:10.40	
1959	Noble Noor	2	D. Pierce	113	Tompion	116	Warfare	112	118,850	1:10.00	
1960	Pappa's All	2	G. Taniguchi	122	Sullivan's Bud	116	Big Smoky	116	98,200	1:10.00	
1961	Rattle Dancer	2	R. Yanez	116	Doc Jocoy	116	Indian Blood	122	102,800	1:09.80	
1962	Y Flash	2	R. Campas	116	Slipped Disc	116	Court Tower	116	69,100	1:10.40	
1962	Noti	2	E. Burns	116	Copper Student	116	Honey Bunny	116	69,100	1:10.20	
1963	Malicious	2	I. Valenzuela	119	Wil Rad	119	Close BY	119	65,150	1:09.60	
1963	Nevada Bin	2	R. York	116	Nevada P.J.	119	Leisurely Kin	116	66,150	1:10.60	
1964	Charger's Kin	2	P. Moreno	122	Azure Te	116	Gummo	116	86,075	1:09.80	
1964	Neke	2	L. Gilligan	116	Donson	116	Old Mose	116	86,075	1:09.80	
1965	Port Wine	2	W. Shoemaker	122	Ri Tux	122	Flame Tree	122	111,500	1:10.20	
1966	Forgotten Dreams	2	A. Maese	122	Tumble Wind	122	Wilbur Clark	122	101,300	1:09.40	
1967	Jim White	2	W. Hartack	122	Poleax	122	Broad Shadows	122	120,050	1:09.80	
1968	Fleet Kirsch	2	A. Pineda	122	One More Chorus	122	Fleet Allied	122	125,850	1:09.20	
1969	Insubordination	2	L. Pincay Jr	122	With Evidence	122	Windy Tide	122	101,850	1:09.20	
1970	Fast Fellow	2	D. Tierney	122	Kfar Tov	122	Moonsplash	122	106,400	1:10.00	
1971	Royal Owl	2	W. Shoemaker	122	MacArthur Park	122	Wind'n Sand	122	101,000	1:09.20	
1972	Bold Liz	2	J. Tejeira	119	Doc Marcus	122	Bottle Brush	122	83,000	1:09.40	
1973	Century's Envoy	2	J. Lambert	122	Such a Rush	122	Tinsley's Image	122	78,550	1:09.00	
1974	Dimaggio	2	L. PIncay Jr	122	The Bagel Prince	122	George Navonod	122	74,500	1:08.60	
1975	Restless Restless	2	S. Hawley	122	Imacornishprince	122	Telly's Pop	122	79,350	1:09.80	
1976	Fleet Dragoon	2	F. Olivares	122	Grey Moon Runner	122	Red Sensation	117	103,250	1:09.60	
1977	Affirmed	2	L. Pincay Jr	122	He's Dewan	122	Esops Foibles	122	60,975	1:09.20	
1978	Terlingua	2	D. McHargue	119	Flying Paster	122	Exuberant	122	77,000	1:08.80	
1978	Noble Bronze	2	S. Hawley	117	Little Reb	122	Tally Ho the Fox	122	62,225	1:09.80	
1979	Parsec	2	W. Shoemaker	122	Doonesbury	122	Encino	122	89,350	1:10.00	
1980	Loma Malad	2	L. Pincay Jr	122	Motivity	122	Bold Ego	122	101,150	1:10.00	
1981	The Captain	2	L. Pincay Jr	117	Rember John	115	Helen's Beau	120	64,000	1:10.40	
1982	Desert Wine	2	F. Olivares	117	Ft. Davis	117	Full Choke	120	57,900	1:09.60	
1983	Althea	2	L. Pincay Jr	117	Rejected Suitor	117	Auto Commander	117	66,200	1:09.40	
1984	Saratoga Six	2	A. Cordero Jr	117	Ten Grand	117	Spectacular Love	117	90,500	1:10.20	
1985	Hilco Scamper	2	G. Stevens	120	Little Red Cloud	117	Exuberant's Image	117	64,400	1:09.80	
1986	Captain Valid	2	C. McCarron	117	Qualify	117	Jazzing Around	117	73,600	1:11.60	
1987	Mi Preferido	2	A. Solis	117	Mixed Pleasure	120	Purdue King	117	75,900	1:10.00	
1988	King Glorious	2	C. McCarron	120	Bruho	117	Mountain Ghost	117	64,200	1:08.80	
1989	Magical Mile	2	E. Delahoussaye	117	Forty Niner Days	117	Willing Worker	117	61,200	1:10.00	
1990	Deposit Ticket	2	G. Stevens	117	Avenue of Flags	117	Stone God	117	56,500	1:09.00	
1991	Scherando	2	F. Mena	117	Prince Wild	117	Burnished Bronze	120	56,400	1:09.60	101
1992	Altazarr	2	E. Delahoussaye	117	Tatum Canyon	117	Just Sid	117	58,700	1:10.00	90
1993	Ramblin Guy	2	E. Delahoussaye	117	Swift Walker	117	Individual Style	117	57,600	1:10.00	86
1994	Mr Pruple	2	C.J. McCarron	117	Serena's Song	117	Cyrano	117	57,600	1:10.00	86
1995	Hennessy	2	G.L. Stevens	117	Reef Reef	117	Desert Native	117	57,400	1:09.80	91
1996	Swiss Yodeler	2	A. Solis	120	Red	117	Vermillion	117	61,470	1:09.60	94
1997	K. O. Punch	2	Stevens G. L.	120	Old Topper	117	Majorbigtimesheet	120	66,120	1:09.80	86
1998	Yes It's True	2	J.D. Bailey	120	O' Rey Fantasma	117	Worldly Manner	117	61,620	1:09.40	97
1999	Dixie Union	2	A. Solis	117	Exchange Rate	117	High Yield	115	63,780	1:09.80	88
2000	Squirtle Squirt	2	L. Pincay Jr	120	Legendary Weave	117	Drumcliff	117	63,540	1:09.98	93
2001	Came Home	2	C.J. McCarron	117	Metatron	117	A Major Pleasure	117	64,440	1:09.20	105
2002	Crowned Dancer	2	A. Solis	120	Outta Here	117	Chief Planner	117	64,980	1:10.10	92
2003	Perfect Moon	2	P.A. Valenzuela	117	Blairs Roarin Star	117	Ruler's Court	117	61,500	1:10.39	82
2004	Chandtrue	2	V. Espinoza	120	Actxecutive	117	Commandant	115	63,840	1:10.88	80

Beyer Index: 90.79

HOLLYWOOD PREVUE (G3), 7 Furlongs, 2-Year-Olds, Hollywood Park, 2004 Purse: $100,000

Year	Winner	Age	Jockey	Wt.	Second	Wt.	Third	Wt.	Win Value	Time	Beyer
1981	Sepulveda	2	C.J. McCarron	112	Gato del Sol	122	Desert Envoy	112	44,625	1:22.00	
1982	Copelan	2	J.D. Bailey	122	R. Awacs	115	Desert Wine	122	62,850	1:21.40	
1983	So Vague	2	P.J. Cooksey	115	Country Manor	115	French Legionaire	115	76,300	1:22.20	
1984	First Norman	2	W. Shoemaker	112	Teddy Naturally	122	Dan's Diablo	122	63,700	1:22.20	
1985	Judge Smells	2	C.J. McCarron	117	Raised on Stage	112	Old Bid	115	46,850	1:23.00	
1986	Exclusive Enough	2	W. Shoemaker	112	Persevered	122	Gold on Green	116	45,900	1:23.00	
1988	King Glorious	2	C.J. McCarron	122	Past Ages	116	Shipping Time	115	47,150	1:21.20	
1989	Individual'st I	2	R.G. Davis	115	Top Cash	122	Tarascon	115	46,600	1:22.20	
1990	Olympio	2	E. Delahoussaye	116	Barrage	115	General Meeting	114	62,600	1:21.80	
1991	Star of the Crop	2	G.L. Stevens	114	Seahawk Gold	121	Salt Lake	121	57,700	1:22.20	94
1992	Stuka	2	P.A. Valenzuela	118	Codified	114	Altazarr	121	62,350	1:21.80	99
1993	Individual Style	2	C.W. Antley	121	Egayant	117	Soul of the Matter	115	46,100	1:21.00	89
1994	Afternoon Deelites	2	Desormeaux KJ	115	Valid Wager	114	Hunt for Missouri	114	57,500	1:20.80	94
1995	Cobra King	2	C.J. McCarron	121	Hennessy	121	Exetera	116	58,800	1:21.20	103
1996	In Excessive Bull	2	Nakatani C. S.	115	Thisnearlywasmine	118	Constant Demand	116	61,120	1:21.40	106
1997	Commitisize	2	Flores D. R.	116	Buttons N Moes	119	Search Me	117	60,000	1:21.60	94
1998	Premier Property	2	Flores D. R.	119	Select Few	114	American Spirit	115	60,000	1:23.20	89
1999	Grey Memo	2	Garcia M. S.	115	Magical Dragon	115	Cameron Pass	116	60,000	1:24.40	86
2000	Proud Tower	2	V. Espinoza	122	Chinook Cat	116	Yonaguska	122	60,000	1:23.01	95
2001	Fonz's	2	L. Pincay Jr	117	Popular	113	Labamta Babe	113	60,000	1:22.03	97
2002	Roll Hennessy Roll	2	A. Solis	119	Red Apache	115	Hell Cat	114	75,000	1:22.68	95
2003	Lion Heart	2	M.E. Smith	114	Cooperation	116	Voladero	113	60,000	1:20.63	103
2004	Declan's Moon	2	V. Espinoza	122	Bushwacker	114	Seize the Day	117	60,000	1:21.74	98

Beyer Index: 95.86

HOLLYWOOD STARLET (G1), 1 1/16 Miles, 2-Year-Old Fillies, Hollywood Park, 2004 Purse: $389,000

Year	Winner	Age	Jockey	Wt.	Second	Wt.	Third	Wt.	Win Value	Time	Beyer
1981	Skillful Joy	2	C.J. McCarron	120	Header Card	120	Flying Partner	120	220,900	1:43.20	
1982	Fabulous Notion	2	D. Pierce	120	O'Happy Day	120	Stephanie Bryn	120	271,618	1:42.40	
1983	Althea	2	L. Pincay Jr	120	Life's Magic	120	Spring Loose	120	261,250	1:43.00	
1984	Outstandingly	2	W.A. Guerra	120	Fran's Valentine	120	Wising Up	120	386,403	1:44.00	
1985	I'm Splendid	2	C.J. McCarron	120	Trim Colony	120	Twilight Ridge	120	344,217	1:36.00	
1986	Very Subtle	2	P.A. Valenzuela	120	Sacahuista	120	Infringe	120	267,025	1:37.00	
1987	Goodbye Halo	2	J. Velasquez	120	Variety Baby	120	Jeanne Jones	120	274,505	1:36.20	
1988	Stocks Up	2	A. Solis	120	Fantastic Look	120	One of a Klein	120	292,325	1:35.00	
1989	Cheval Volant	2	A. Solis	120	Annual Reunion	120	Special Happening	120	247,500	1:35.60	
1990	Cuddles	2	G.L. Stevens	120	Lite Light	120	Garden Gal	120	247,500	1:36.20	
1991	Magical Maiden	2	G.L. Stevens	120	Looie Capote	120	Soviet Sojourn	120	138,105	1:42.60	94
1992	Creaking Board	2	C.S. Nakatani	120	Passing Vice	120	Madame L'Enjoleur	120	139,425	1:43.60	83
1993	Sardula	2	E. Delahoussaye	120	Princess Mitterand	120	Viz	120	139,095	1:42.20	98
1994	Serena's Song	2	C.S. Nakatani	120	Urbane	120	Ski Dancer	120	137,500	1:41.80	103
1995	Cara Rafaela	2	C.S. Nakatani	120	Advancing Star	120	Chile Chatte	120	137,500	1:43.00	104
1996	Sharp Cat	2	C.S. Nakatani	120	City Band	120	High Heeled Hope	120	165,600	1:44.60	92
1997	Love Lock	2	K.J. Desormeaux	120	Career Collection	120	Snowberg	120	168,600	1:42.00	98
1998	Excellent Meeting	2	K.J. Desormeaux	120	Lacquaria	120	Perfect Six	120	240,000	1:42.14	101
1999	Surfside	2	P. Day	120	She's Classy	120	Abby Girl	120	228,150	1:43.51	100
2000	I Believe in You	2	A. Solis	120	Jetin Excess	120	Whoopddoo	120	205,050	1:43.57	90
2001	Habibti	2	V. Espinoza	120	You	120	Tali'sluckybusride	120	214,800	1:43.12	103
2002	Elloluv	2	P.A. Valenzuela	120	Composure	120	Summer Wind Dancer	120	213,900	1:42.88	94
2003	Hollywood Story	2	P.A. Valenzuela	120	Rahy Dolly	120	House of Fortune	120	209,700	1:42.87	95
2004	Splendid Blended	2	K.J. Desormeaux	120	Sharp Lisa	120	Northern Mischief	120	233,400	1:41.82	92

Beyer Index: 96.21

Distance 1 mile 1985–90

HOLLYWOOD TURF CUP (G1), 1 1/2 Miles (Turf), 3-Year-Olds and Up, Hollywood Park, 2004 Purse: $250,000

Year	Winner	Age	Jockey	Wt.	Second	Wt.	Third	Wt.	Win Value	Time	Beyer
1981	Providential II	4	A. Lequeux	126	Queen to Conquer	123	Goldliko	126	325,500	2:26.80	
1982	Prince Spellbound	3	M. Castaneda	122	Majesty's Prince	122	Lithan	126	220,000	2:14.00	
1982	The Hague	3	F. Toro	122	Caterman	126	It's the One	126	220,000	2:13.40	
1983	John Henry	8	C.J. McCarron	126	Zalataia	123	Palikaraki	126	275,000	2:16.60	
1984	Alphabatim	3	C.J. McCarron	122	Raami	122	Both Ends Burning	126	275,000	2:15.80	
							Scruples	126			
1985	Zoffany	5	E. Delahoussaye	126	Win	126	Vanlandingham	126	275,000	2:28.40	
1986	Alphabatim	5	W. Shoemaker	126	Dahar	126	Theatrical	126	275,000	2:25.80	

Year	Winner	Age	Jockey	Wt.	Second	Wt.	Third	Wt.	Win Value	Time	Beyer
1987	Vilzak	4	P. Day	126	Forlitano	126	Political Ambition	122	275,000	2:27.00	
1988	Great Communicator	5	R. Sibille	126	Putting	126	Nasr El Arab	122	275,000	2:34.40	
1989	Frankly Perfect	4	C.J. McCarron	126	Yankee Affair	126	Pleasant Variety	126	275,000	2:26.60	
1990	Itsallgreektome	3	C.S. Nakatani	122	Mashkour	126	Live the Dream	126	275,000	2:24.80	
1991	Miss Alleged	4	C.J. McCarron	123	Itsallgreektome	126	Quest for Fame	126	275,000	2:30.00	110
1992	Bien Bien	3	C.J. McCarron	122	Fraise	124	Trishyde	119	275,000	2:31.20	105
	Fraise finished first but was disqualified and placed second										
1993	Fraise	5	C.J. McCarron	126	Know Heights	126	Explosive Red	122	275,000	2:32.20	111
1994	Frenchpark	4	C.A. Black	126	Dare and Go	122	Regency	126	275,000	2:25.60	108
1995	Royal Chariot	5	A. Solis	126	Talloires	126	Earl of Barking	126	275,000	2:25.00	105
1996	Running Flame	4	C.J. McCarron	126	Marlin	126	Talloires	126	300,000	2:28.40	109
1997	River Bay	4	A. Solis	126	Awad	126	Flag Down	126	300,000	2:26.40	109
1998	Lazy Lode	4	C.S. Nakatani	126	Yagli	126	Ferrari	126	300,000	2:28.36	109
1999	Lazy Lode	4	L. Pincay Jr	126	Public Purse	126	Single Empire	126	240,000	2:25.85	110
2000	Bienamado	4	C.J. McCarron	126	Northern Quest	126	Lazy Lode	126	240,000	2:25.98	108
2001	Super Quercus	5	A. Solis	126	Bonapartiste	126	Blazing Fury	126	150,000	2:29.86	105
2002	Sligo Bay	4	L. Pincay Jr	126	Grammarian	126	Delta Form	126	150,000	2:27.22	105
2003	Continuously	4	A. Solis	126	Bowman Mill	126	Epicentre	126	150,000	2:29.01	102
	Epicentre finished first but was disqualified and placed third										
2004	Pellegrino	5	G.L. Stevens	126	Megahertz	123	License to Run	126	150,000	2:29.73	101

Beyer Index: 106.93

Distance 1 3/8 miles 1982-84

HOLLYWOOD TURF EXPRESS HANDICAP (G3), 5 1/2 Furlongs (Turf), 3-Year-Olds and Up, Hollywood Park, 2004 Purse: $150,000

Year	Winner	Age	Jockey	Wt.	Second	Wt.	Third	Wt.	Win Value	Time	Beyer
1987	Lord Ruckus	4	L. Pincay Jr	117	Bundle of Iron	114	Faro	115	49,600	1:08.20	
1988	On the Line	4	G.L. Stevens	121	Little Red Cloud	115	Faro	118	47,650	1:09.20	
1989	Summer Sale	3	B.A. Hernandez	114	Ofanto	117	Oraibi	120	51,000	1:07.80	
1990	Answer Do	4	R.A. Baze	115	Waterscape	115	Yes I'm Blue	118	51,200	1:07.00	
1991	Gundaghia	4	C.S. Nakatani	114	Club Champ	116	Sun Brandy	115	61,875	1:01.40	103
1991	Answer Do	5	E. Delahoussaye	120	Apollo	115	Cardmania	116	61,875	1:01.40	103
1992	Answer Do	6	E. Delahoussaye	121	Repriced	118	Gundaghia	117	110,000	1:02.00	104
1993	Wild Harmony	4	C.J. McCarron	117	Robin des Pins	119	Monde Bleu	119	110,000	1:01.80	104
1994	Rotsaluck	3	F.H. Valenzuela	118	Marina Park	116	D'Hallevant	117	82,500	1:02.20	106
1995	Cyrano Storme	5	R.R. Douglas	116	Lakota Brave	115	Pembroke	121	110,000	1:01.60	106
1996	Sandtrap	3	A. Solis	114	Cyrano Storme	118	Suggest	114	120,000	1:01.40	102
1997	Advancing Star	4	K.J. Desormeaux	119	Latin Dancer	116	Surachai	117	240,000	1:02.60	109
1998	Soldier Field	3	R. Wilson.	117	Surachai	118	Bodyguard	115	120,000	1:02.00	99
1999	Mr. Doubledown	5	V. Espinoza	115	Howbaddouwantit	120	Champ's Star	115	120,000	1:01.80	101
2000	El Cielo	6	C.S. Nakatani	122	Texas Glitter	117	Full Moon Madness	121	120,000	1:01.73	107
2001	Swept Overboard	4	E. Delahoussaye	122	Speak In Passing	117	Blu Air Force	118	120,000	1:01.86	111
2002	Texas Glitter	6	J.R. Velazquez	119	Rocky Bar	114	Malabar Gold	118	120,000	1:01.52	106
2003	King Robyn	3	T. Baze	120	Geronimo	116	Golden Arrow	115	90,000	1:02.08	102
2004	Cajun Beat	4	R.A. Dominguez	122	Geronimo	117	Mighty Beau	117	90,000	1:02.08	107

Beyer Index: 104.67

HOLY BULL (G3), 1 1/16 Miles, 3-Year-Olds, Gulfstream Park, 2004 Purse: $100,000

Year	Winner	Age	Jockey	Wt.	Second	Wt.	Third	Wt.	Win Value	Time	Beyer
1990	Home at Last	3	J.D. Bailey	118	Run Turn	122	Sound of Cannons	118	140,160	1:53.20	
1991	Shoot to Kill	3	W.S. Ramos	112	Shotgun Harry J.	114	Cahill Road	114	120,000	1:43.40	99
1992	Waki Warrior	3	E. Fires	114	Scream Machine	112	Careful Gesture	113	78,258	1:44.20	92
1993	Pride of Burkaan	3	J.D. Bailey	112	Kassec	112	Jetting Along	114	45,000	1:44.60	88
1994	Go for Gin	3	J.D. Bailey	119	Halo's Image	114	Senor Conquistador	112	45,000	1:41.60	100
1995	Suave Prospect	3	J.D. Bailey	119	Bullet Trained	114	Rush Dancer	112	45,000	1:44.00	100
1996	Cobra King	3	C.J. McCarron	117	Editor's Note	119	Tilden	114	45,000	1:43.40	107
1997	Arthur L.	3	J.R.Velazquez	122	Acceptable	114	Captain Bodgit	119	60,000	1:42.80	107
1998	Cape Town	3	J.D. Bailey	119	Comic Strip	114	Sweetsouthernsaint	119	60,000	1:44.00	101
1999	Grits'n Hard Toast	3	R.G. Davis	114	Doneraille Court	119	Mountain Range	119	60,000	1:45.20	100
2000	Hal's Hope	3	R.I. Velez	112	Personal First	117	Megacles	113	60,000	1:44.52	100
2001	Radical Riley	3	E. Nunez	119	Buckle Down Ben	119	Cee Dee	117	60,000	1:46.06	90
2002	Booklet	3	E.M. Coa	122	Harlan's Holiday	122	Thiscannonsloaded	116	60,000	1:46.16	101
2003	Offlee Wild	3	M. Guidry	116	Powerful Touch	116	Bham	118	60,000	1:43.00	99
2004	Second of June	3	C.H. Velasquez	122	Silver Wagon	120	Friends Lake	122	60,000	1:43.00	111

Beyer Index: 99.64

Run as Preview Stakes, 1990-95

HONEY FOX HANDICAP (G3), 1 1/16 Miles (Turf), Fillies and Mares, 3-Year-Olds and Up, Gulfstream Park, 2004 Purse: $100,000

Year	Winner	Age	Jockey	Wt.	Second	Wt.	Third	Wt.	Win Value	Time	Beyer
1985	One Fine Lady	3	V. Molina	116	Foxy Deen		Boldly Dared		19,257	1:34.60	
1985	Affirmance	3	E. Maple	116	Miss Delice		Deceit Dancer		19,617	1:35.60	
1986	One Fine Lady	4	J. Velez	112	Shocker T.		Donna's Dolly		29,655	1:22.00	
1986	Gypsy Prayer	5	R. Lester	116	Four Flings		Isayso		29,985	1:21.00	
1987	Small Virtue	4	J. Vasquez	114	Thirty Zip		Chaldea		27,915	1:37.00	
1987	Top Socialite	5	C. Perret	119	Give a Toast		Judy's Red Shoes		27,615	1:37.40	
1988	Allegedum	5	A. Cordero Jr	114	Autumn Glitter		Fama		31,515	1:35.20	
1988	Shaughnessy Road	4	J. Velez	112	Rally for Justice		Fieldy		31,215	1:36.00	
1989	Fieldy	6	C. Perret	114	Miss Unnameable		Aquaba		30,135	1:35.80	
1989	Vana Turns	4	R.P. Romero	113	For Kicks		Stolie		30,435	1:36.00	
1990	Fieldy	7	J.D. Bailey	120	Betty Lobelia		Leave It Be		30,000	1:37.60	100
1991	Vigorous Lady	5	M. Lee	116	Joyce Azalene		Stacie's Toy		30,000	1:40.20	
1992	Explosive Kate	5	D. Penna	113	Indian Fashion		Belleofbasinstreet		30,000	1:43.20	97
1993	Hero's Love	5	E. Fires	114	Quilma		Lady Blessington		30,000	1:42.80	99
1994	Sambacarioca	5	J.D. Bailey	121	Tiney Toast	114	Marshua's River	114	36,000	1:43.40	90
1995	Regal Joy	4	D. Penna	113	Sambacarioca	119	Sovereign Kitty	119	36,000	1:44.60	96
1996	Apolda	5	J.D. Bailey	116	Class Kris	116	Alice Springs	121	45,000	1:41.40	102
1997	Rare Blend	4	J.D. Bailey	118	Queen Tutta	114	Hurricane Viv	121	45,000	1:44.20	103
1998	Parade Queen	4	P. Day	118	Dispersion	113	Dance Clear	114	45,000	1:42.00	99
1999	Colcon	6	J.D. Bailey	119	Lovers Knot	115	Tampico	114	45,000	1:41.60	104
2000	Dominique's Joy	5	J.D. Bailey	113	Circus Charmer	114	Pico Teneriffe	117	45,000	1:39.91	99
2001	Spook Express	7	M.E. Smith	115	Please Sign In	116	Lady Dora	115	60,000	1:35.60	87
2002	Batique	6	J.F. Chavez	117	My Sweet Westly	115	Silver Bandana	114	60,000	1:49.32	100
2003	San Dare	5	M. Guidry	115	Calista	118	Laurica	114	60,000	1:46.19	99
2004	Delmonico Cat	5	J.D. Bailey	116	Coney Kitty	115	Madeira Mist	117	60,000	1:41.30	90

Beyer Index: 97.50

Run at 7 furlongs on main track, 1986; at 1 1/16 miles 1991-2000. Run as Joe Namath Handicap prior to 2001.

HONEYMOON BREEDERS' CUP HANDICAP (G2), 1 1/8 Miles (Turf), 3-Year-Old Fillies, Hollywood Park, 2004 Purse: $184,925

Year	Winner	Age	Jockey	Wt.	Second	Wt.	Third	Wt.	Win Value	Time	Beyer
1956	Triple Jay	3	A. Maese	115	Shes Quick	115	Candy Dish	112	13,500	1:36.40	
1957	Great Pride	3	W. Shoemaker	109	Tourbillonte	109	Inquisitive	110	12,450	1:36.60	
1957	Fanciful Miss	3	J. Longden	109	Royal Rasher	112	Pamper Me	118	12,450	1:36.00	
1958	Foreverett	3	J. Longden	113	Well Away	115	Midnight Date	112	13,600	1:37.60	
1959	Cellyar	3	A. Maese	112	Sybil Brand	112	Just Chargit	112	15,150	1:36.60	
1960	Solid Thought	3	D. Pierce	118	Paris Pike	113	Cherokee Miss	112	13,640	1:36.20	
1961	Bushel-n-Peck	3	W. Shoemaker	112	Rose O'Neill	112	Oil Royalty	118	12,800	1:34.80	
1962	Refanute	3	R. Campas	112	Savaii	112	Sweet Cee Cee	112	16,900	1:36.60	
1963	Molly O'Malley	3	R. York	112	Delhi Maid	118	Hi Rated	112	16,800	1:37.40	
1964	Gim Mah	3	E. Burns	112	Fran La Femme	121	Lil's Nite Out	112	15,500	1:37.20	
1965	Rullahline	3	D. Gorman	112	Bubble Bath	113	Madoo	112	18,825	1:35.80	
1965	Mine Lovely	3	I. Valenzuela	118	Istria	112	Queen Hostess	112	19,325	1:35.40	
1966	April Dawn	3	D. Hall	112	Miss Breakage	112	Fleet Treat	121	20,300	1:36.40	
1967	Spinning Around	3	M. Valenzuela	112	Amerigo Lady	114	Native Honey	118	16,550	1:36.60	
1968	Miss Ribot	3	J. Sellers	118	Time to Leave	121	Saipan	113	15,950	1:42.20	
1969	Marjorie's Theme	3	J. Lambert	114	Commissary	121	Dumpty's Lady	121	16,800	1:41.60	
1970	Street Dancer	3	R. Rosales	112	Opening Bid	121	Hail the Grey	114	16,550	1:34.60	
1971	Turkish Trousers	3	W. Shoemaker	121	Convenience	115	Mia Mood	114	19,850	1:42.40	
1972	Le Cle	3	L. Pincay Jr	115	Pallisima	112	Cautious Bidder	118	20,200	1:42.00	
1973	Meilleur	3	D. Pierce	118	Sphere	118	Goddess Roman	116	20,350	1:42.40	
1974	Bedknob	3	A. Pineda	115	Bold Tullah	118	Bold Ballet	116	20,750	1:42.20	
1975	Katonka	3	L. Pincay Jr	123	Nicosia	125	Just a Kick	118	33,150	1:42.40	
1976	Cascapedia	3	W. Shoemaker	121	Go March	117	Dream of Spring	118	26,750	1:42.20	
1977	Joyous Ways	3	L. Pincay Jr	116	Penny Pueblo	113	Glenaris	119	26,150	1:43.00	
1978	Country Queen	3	M. Castaneda	114	Collect Call	116	Equanimity	121	33,700	1:43.20	
1979	Variety Queen	3	M. Castaneda	114	Prize Spot	117	Whydidju	121	32,550	1:41.60	
1980	Lady Roberta	3	S. Hawley	116	Finance Charge	112	Street Ballet	123	60,050	1:41.80	
1981	Amber Ever	3	C.J. McCarron	114	Verbalize	117	Bee a Scout	115	50,950	1:41.60	
1982	Castilla	3	R. Sibille	116	Tango Dancer	117	Skillful Joy	121	61,400	1:40.60	
1983	Stagedoor C'nt'n	3	C.J. McCarron	118	Saucy Bobbie	117	Hot n Pearly	115	65,200	1:42.00	
1984	Vagabond Gal	3	E. Delahoussaye	118	Heartlight	119	Allusion	115	65,100	1:41.40	
1985	Sharp Ascent	3	E. Delahoussaye	115	Rose Cream	117	Akamini	119	79,400	1:41.40	
1986	An Empress	3	P.A. Valenzuela	115	Top Corsage	118	Miraculous	118	66,900	1:41.80	
1987	Pen Bal Lady	3	E. Delahoussaye	119	Some Sensation	117	Davie's Lamb	115	80,300	1:41.20	
1988	Do So	3	A. Solis	118	Pattern Step	119	Jeanne Jones	120	75,400	1:41.80	
1989	Hot Option	3	E. Delahoussaye	116	Formidable Lady	118	Black Stockings	113	62,600	1:40.20	
1990	Materco	3	E. Delahoussaye	117	Annual Reunion	119	Slew of Pearls	117	65,800	1:41.40	90

Year	Winner	Age	Jockey	Wt.	Second	Wt.	Third	Wt.	Win Value	Time	Beyer
1991	Masake	3	M.A. Pedroza	115	Haunting	114	Now Showing	116	60,400	1:42.00	96
1992	Pacific Squall	3	K.J. Desormeaux	115	Miss Turkana	119	Morriston Belle	118	67,100	1:41.00	90
1993	Likeable Style	3	E. Delahoussaye	122	Adorydor	114	Vinista	113	61,200	1:46.20	95
1994	Work the Crowd	3	McCarron CJ	117	Malli Star	117	Fancy 'n Fabulous	118	64,700	1:39.60	103
1995	Auriette	3	Delahoussaye E	117	Artica	119	Top Shape	118	62,100	1:41.60	94
1996	Antespend	3	C.W. Antley	122	Clamorosa	116	Najecam	113	82,410	1:47.40	100
1997	Famous Digger	3	B. Blanc	116	Freeport Flight	115	Kentucky Kaper	117	65,460	1:47.60	94
1998	Country Garden	3	K.J. Desormeaux	120	Janine Rose	113	Chenille	114	64,080	1:48.60	92
1999	Sweet Ludy	3	G.L. Stevens	116	Tout Charmant	118	Aviate	118	65,160	1:48.05	99
2000	Classy Cara	3	I.L. Puglisi	122	Kumari Continent	119	Minor Details	117	90,000	1:48.05	91
2001	Innit	3	C. McCarron	117	Live Your Dreams	116	Beefeater Baby	115	120,000	2:01.28	93
2002	Megahertz	3	P.A. Valenzuela	120	Arabic Song	117	High Society	116	97,830	1:51.97	91
2003	Quero Quero	3	T.C. Baze	113	Atlantic Ocean	121	Sharpbill	113	130,170	1:49.34	88
2004	Lovely Rafaela	3	V. Espinoza	114	Western Hemisphere	114	Sagitta Ra	116	113,355	1:49.96	93

Beyer Index: 93.93

HONORABLE MISS HANDICAP (G2), 6 Furlongs, Fillies and Mares, 3-Year-Olds and Up, Saratoga Race Course, 2004 Purse: $150,000

Year	Winner	Age	Jockey	Wt.	Second	Wt.	Third	Wt.	Win Value	Time	Beyer
1993	Nannerl	6	J.D. Bailey	117	Vivano	117	Via Dei Portici	117	29,040	1:15.00	93
1994	Classy Mirage	4	J.A. Krone	122	Spinning Round	119	For All Seasons	117	48,675	1:09.60	104
1995	Low Key Affair	5	P. Day	115	Classy Mirage	123	Twist Afleet	120	48,195	1:09.60	102
1996	Twist Afleet	5	M.E. Smith	119	Broad Smile	119	In Conference	113	49,455	1:09.80	101
1997	Dancin Renee	5	R. Migliore	116	Ashboro	116	Vivace	113	48,465	1:09.00	107
1998	Furlough	4	M.E. Smith	113	Angel's Tearlet	114	Dixie Flag	119	48,765	1:11.20	90
1999	Bourbon Belle	4	Johnson P. A.	116	Gold Princess	116	License Fee	114	67,560	1:09.40	106
2000	Debby d'Or	5	S.J. Sellers	114	Tropical Punch	115	Katz Me If You Can	113	66,450	1:10.11	101
2000	Bourbon Belle	5	W. Martinez	116	Cassidy	114	Go to the Ink	114	65,850	1:08.93	115
2001	Big Bambu	4	J.D. Bailey	118	Country Hideaway	118	Dat You Miz Blue	120	63,708	1:09.64	104
2002	Mandy's Gold	4	E.S. Prado	116	Shine Again	116	Dat You Miz Blue	114	65,100	1:09.24	108
2003	Willa on the Move	4	E.S. Prado	114	Shine Again	120	Smok'n Frolic	117	64,560	1:09.92	105
2004	My Trusty Cat	4	P. Day	115	Ebony Breeze	115	Smok'n Frolic	116	90,000	1:10.37	96

Beyer Index: 102.46

FRED W. HOOPER HANDICAP (G3), 1 1/8 Miles, 3-Year-Olds and Up, Calder Race Course, 2004 Purse: $100,000

Year	Winner	Age	Jockey	Wt.	Second	Wt.	Third	Wt.	Win Value	Time	Beyer
1994	Take Me Out	6	M.E. Smith	115	Migrating Moon	119	Meena	114	60,000	1:51.80	104
1994	Halo's Image	3	G. Boulanger	117	Fight For Love	114	Migrating Moon	120	60,000	1:51.40	109
1995	Bound by Honor	4	J.A. Krone	112	Bay Street Star	113	Halo's Image	121	60,000	1:51.80	105
1996	Cimarron Secret	5	Velez J.A.. Jr	115	Laughing Dan	114	Wicapi	116	60,000	1:52.60	101
1997	Shrike	5	J.D. Bailey	113	Wicapi	112	Sir Bear	113	60,000	1:38.60	105
1998	Wicapi	4	J. Bravo	113	Smuggler's Prize	111	Best of the Rest	115	60,000	1:52.00	99
1999	Dancing Guy	4	J.C. Ferrer	120	Wicapi	118	Loon	112	60,000	1:50.83	100
2000	American Halo	4	C. Hunt	111	General Grant	112	Sir Bear	118	60,000	1:51.68	108
2001	Kiss a Native	4	C. Velasquez	116	Hal's Hope	115	Groomstick Stock's	113	60,000	1:51.05	106
2002	The Judge Sez Who	3	C. Velasquez	116	Best of the Rest	121	Dancing Guy	112	60,000	1:50.53	106
2003	Predawn Raid	4	J.F. Chavez	112	Best of the Rest	122	Deeliteful Guy	112	60,000	1:52.47	102
2004	Pies Prospect	3	E.S. Prado	114	Twilight Road	115	Hear No Evil	112	60,000	1:50.74	110

Beyer Index: 104.58

Run as Tropical Park Handicap prior to 1997. For previous runnings, refer to 1994 Manual.

HOPEFUL (G1), 7 Furlongs, 2-Year-Olds, Saratoga Race Course, 2004 Purse: $250,000

Year	Winner	Age	Jockey	Wt.	Second	Wt.	Third	Wt.	Win Value	Time	Beyer
1903	Delhi	2	C. Gannon	112	Highball	112	Palmbearer	112	22,275	1:13.20	
1904	Tanya	2	E. Hildebrand	127	Rose of Dawn	112	Hot Shot	115	29,790	1:13.40	
1905	Mohawk II	2	A. Redfern	130	Athlete	115	Juggler	112	16,490	1:13.40	
1906	Peter Pan	2	W. Knapp	130	McCarter	122	Jope Joan	112	17,640	1:12.20	
1907	Jim Gaffney	2	D. Nicol	115	Fair Play	125	Bar None	115	17,500	1:15.00	
1908	Helmet	2	J. Notter	115	Perseus	115	Fayette	130	10,990	1:12.20	
1909	Rocky O'Brien	2	V. Powers	122	Sweep	130	Barleythorpe	115	17,160	1:13.20	
1910	Novelty	2	A. Thomas	130	Iron Mask	125	Naushon	125	19,140	1:14.00	
1913	Bringhurst	2	J. Loftus	113	Little Nephew	113	Black Broom	107	4,100	1:12.40	
1914	Regret	2	J. Notter	127	Andrew M.	114	Pebbles	127	9,590	1:16.40	
1915	Dominant	2	J. Notter	130	Big Smoke	107	Primero	107	9,150	1:13.80	
1916	Campfire	2	J. McTaggart	130	Omar Khayyam	110	Star Master	110	18,850	1:14.60	
1917	Sun Briar	2	W. Knapp	130	Papp	130	Sycamour	115	30,600	1:15.60	
1918	Eternal	2	A. Schuttinger	115	Daydue	115	War Marvel	115	30,150	1:13.60	

Year	Winner	Age	Jockey	Wt.	Second	Wt.	Third	Wt.	Win Value	Time	Beyer
1919	Man o' War	2	J. Loftus	130	Cleopatra	112	Constancy	124	24,600	1:13.00	
1920	Leonardo II	2	A. Schuttinger	115	Prudery	127	Oriole	115	33,850	1:12.40	
1921	Morvich	2	A. Johnson	130	Kai-Sang	130	Whiskaway	115	34,900	1:12.60	
1922	Dunlin	2	C. Kummer	115	Goshawk	130	Zev	130	38,950	1:12.40	
1923	Diogenes	2	C. Ponce	115	Bracadale	115	Sunspero	122	46,800	1:12.60	
1924	Master Charlie	2	G. Babin	130	Pas Seul	127	K't'y Cardinal	115	48,700	1:13.00	
1925	Pompey	2	L. Fator	127	Flight of Time	125	Chance Play	122	42,850	1:17.80	
1926	Lord Chaucer	2	F. Coltiletti	115	Termahant	112	Scapa Flow	125	48,850	1:19.80	
1927	Brooms	2	J. Maiben	115	Victorian	115	Nassak	127	55,750	1:20.00	
1928	Jack High	2	G. Ellis	127	Blue Larkspur	130	Chestnut Oak	122	54,100	1:18.40	
1929	Boojum	2	R. Workman	117	Whichone	125	Caruso	127	54,750	1:17.00	
1930	Epithet	2	W. Kelsay	117	Jamestown	130	Novelist	117	56,000	1:17.60	
1931	Tick On	2	P. Walls	117	Sweeping Light	117	Polonaise	122	45,950	1:20.40	
1932	Ladysman	2	R. Jones	130	Sun Archer	122	Happy Gal	127	41,400	1:19.40	
1933	Bazaar	2	D. Meade	119	High Quest	117	Discovery	117	35,550	1:19.00	
1934	Psychic Bid	2	M. Garner	122	Rosemont	117	Esposa	114	38,400	1:19.80	
1935	Red Rain	2	R. Workman	124	Bien Joli	122	Sun Teddy	117	38,400	1:19.80	
1936	Maedic	2	E. Litzenberger	122	Billionaire	119	Tedious	116	32,600	1:20.20	
1937	Sky Larking	2	A. Robertson	119	Bull Lea	116	Fighting Fox	122	31,450	1:20.80	
1938	El Chico	2	N. Wall	126	Ariel Toy	116	Johnstown	116	42,550	1:18.40	
1939	Bimelech	2	F.A. Smith	122	Andy K.	126	Boy Angler	119	33,750	1:18.80	
1940	Whirlaway	2	J. Longden	118	Attention	126	Hy-Cop	116	37,850	1:18.00	
1941	Devil Diver	2	J. Skelly	119	Shut Out	122	Amphitheatre	122	35,950	1:18.60	
1942	Devil's Thumb	2	C. McCreary	122	True Blue	116	Bourmont	116	31,750	1:18.40	
1943	Bee Mac	2	S. Young	119	Boy Knight	122	By Jimminy	122	33,300	1:18.40	
1944	Pavot	2	G. Woolf	126	Esteem	122	Great Power	114	51,775	1:18.80	
1945	Star Pilot	2	A. Kirkland	112	Inroc	112	Revoked	126	55,195	1:16.60	
1946	Blue Border	2	A. DeLara	122	Grand Admiral	126	Johnny Dimick	113	46,450	1:17.00	
	Cosmic Bomb finished second but was disqualified										
1947	Relic	2	J. Adams	114	Whirling Fox	109	My Request	126	48,200	1:17.40	
1948	Blue Peter	2	E. Guerin	126	Sport Page	114	Curandero	114	47,750	1:19.20	
1949	Middleground	2	D. Gorman	114	Navy Chief	118	Mr. Trouble	114	44,050	1:18.40	
1950	Battlefield	2	E. Guerin	122	Battle Morn	122	Big Stretch	122	47,550	1:18.00	
1951	Cousin	2	E. Guerin	122	Tom Fool	122	Hannibal	122	51,700	1:19.20	
1952	Native Dancer	2	E. Guerin	122	Tiger Skin	122	Platan	122	51,450	1:18.80	
1953	Artismo	2	D. Gorman	122	War Piper	122	Turn-to	122	58,900	1:18.00	
1954	Nashua	2	E. Arcaro	122	Summer Tan	122	Pyrenees	122	57,050	1:17.80	
1955	Needles	2	J. Choquette	122	Career Boy	122	Jean Baptiste	122	50,000	1:18.20	
1956	King Hairan	2	E. Arcaro	122	Gannet	122	Cohoes	122	48,400	1:18.40	
1957	Rose Trellis	2	F. Lovato	122	Louis d'Or	122	Jimmer	122	40,075	1:18.40	
1958	First Landing	2	E. Arcaro	122	First Minister	122	That Lucky Day	122	36,700	1:17.80	
1959	Tompion	2	W. Shoemaker	122	Vital Force	122	Bourbon Prince	122	73,434	1:17.40	
1960	Hail to Reason	2	R. Ussery	122	Bronzerullah	122	Chinchilla	122	76,602	1:16.00	
1961	Jaipur	2	E. Arcaro	122	Su Ka Wa	122	Sir Gaylord	122	76,229	1:16.40	
1962	Outing Class	2	D. Pierce	122	Alabama Bound	122	Final Ruling	122	76,407	1:17.00	
1963	Traffic	2	M. Ycaza	122	Amastar	122	Count Bud	122	72,394	1:18.60	
1964	Bold Lad	2	B. Baeza	122	Native Charger	122	Time Tested	122	72,231	1:15.60	
1965	Buckpasser	2	B. Baeza	122	Impressive	122	Indulto	122	71,614	1:16.00	
1966	Bold Hour	2	J.L. Rotz	122	Great Power	122	Top Bid	122	70,005	1:17.20	
1967	What a Pleasure	2	B. Baeza	122	Royal Trace	122	Exclusive Native	122	74,084	1:16.40	
1968	Top Knight	2	M. Ycaza	122	Reviewer	122	Bushido	122	80,145	1:16.00	
1969	Irish Castle	2	B. Baeza	122	Hagley	122	Pontifex	122	73,044	1:17.20	
1970	Proudest Roman	2	J.L. Rotz	122	Pass Catcher	122	Cool Morn	122	85,117	1:18.60	
1971	Rest Your Case	2	J. Vasquez	122	Governor Max	122	Loquacious Dan	122	77,355	1:17.40	
1972	Secretariat	2	R. Turcotte	121	Flight to Glory	121	Stop the Music	121	51,930	1:16.20	
1973	Gusty O'Shay	2	P. Kotenko	121	Take by Storm	121	Prince of Reason	121	50,400	1:16.40	
1974	The Bagel Prince	2	A. Cordero Jr	121	Knightly Sport	121	Cardinal George	121	40,995	1:16.80	
1974	Foolish Pleasure	2	B. Baeza	121	Greek Answer	121	Our Talisman	121	41,445	1:16.00	
1975	Jackknife	2	J. Cruguet	121	Ferrous	121	Whatsyourpleasure	121	41,625	1:16.60	
1975	Eustache	2	J. Nichols	121	Iron Bit	121	Gentle King	121	41,850	1:16.40	
1976	Banquet Table	2	J. Cruguet	122	Turn of Coin	122	P. R. Man	122	51,345	1:16.20	
1977	Affirmed	2	S. Cauthen	122	Alydar	122	Regal and Royal	122	48,105	1:15.40	
1978	General Assembly	2	D.G. McHargue	122	Exuberant	122	Fuzzbuster	122	48,600	1:16.40	
1979	J.P. Brother	2	J. Imparato	122	Gold Stage	122	Googolplex	122	50,490	1:16.20	
	Rockhill Native finished first but was disqualified and placed sixth										
1980	Tap Shoes	2	R. Hernandez	122	Lord Avie	122	Well Decorated	122	51,750	1:17.00	
1981	Timely Writer	2	R. Danjean	122	Out of Hock	122	Lejoli	122	51,390	1:16.20	
1982	Copelan	2	J.D. Bailey	122	Victorious	122	Aloha Hawaii	122	69,000	1:16.60	
1983	Capitol South	2	J.D. Bailey	122	Don Rickles	122	Swale	122	72,720	1:17.40	
1984	Chief's Crown	2	D. MacBeth	122	Tiffany Ice	122	Mugzy's Rullah	122	100,440	1:16.00	
1985	Papal Power	2	D. MacBeth	122	Danny's Keys	122	Bullet Blade	122	103,320	1:18.40	
1986	Gulch	2	A. Cordero Jr	122	Persevered	122	Flying Granville	122	126,720	1:16.40	
1987	Crusader Sword	2	R.P. Romero	122	Bill E. Shears	122	Success Express	122	104,850	1:18.60	

Year	Winner	Age	Jockey	Wt.	Second	Wt.	Third	Wt.	Win Value	Time	Beyer
1988	Mercedes Won	2	R.G. Davis	122	Fast Play	122	Leading Prospect	122	142,320	1:16.60	
1989	Summer Squall	2	P. Day	122	Sir Richard Lewis	122	Eternal Flight	122	140,000	1:16.80	
1990	Deposit Ticket	2	G.L. Stevens	122	Hansel	122	Link	122	139,680	1:16.20	98
1991	Salt Lake	2	M.E. Smith	122	Slew's Ghost	122	Caller I.D.	122	120,000	1:17.60	
1992	Great Navigator	2	A.T. Gryder	122	Strolling Along	122	England Expects	122	120,000	1:15.60	98
1993	Dehere	2	C.J. McCarron	122	Slew Gin Fizz	122	Whitney Tower	122	120,000	1:15.80	97
1994	Wild Escapade	2	J.F. Chavez	122	Montreal Red	122	Law of the Sea	122	120,000	1:23.20	89
1995	Hennessy	2	G.L. Stevens	122	Louis Quatorze	122	Maria's Mon	122	120,000	1:23.40	100
1996	Smoke Glacken	2	C. Perret	122	Ordway	122	Gunfight	122	120,000	1:23.60	93
1997	Favorite Trick	2	P. Day	122	K.O. Punch	122	Jesse M	122	120,000	1:23.80	91
1998	Lucky Roberto	2	R.G. Davis	122	Tactical Cat	122	Time Bandit	122	120,000	1:23.81	85
1999	High Yield	2	J.D. Bailey	122	Settlement	122	Exciting Story	122	120,000	1:22.85	94
2000	City Zip	2	J.A. Santos	122			Macho Uno	122	80.000	1:24.52	86
	Yonaguska	2	J.D. Bailey	122							
2001	Came Home	2	C.J. McCarron	122	Mayakovsky	122	Thunder Days	122	120,000	1:21.94	108
2002	Sky Mesa	2	E.S. Prado	122	Pretty Wild	122	ZavatA	122	120,000	1:23.08	103
2003	Silver Wagon	2	J.D. Bailey	122	Chapel Royal	122	Notorious Rogue	122	120,000	1:23.47	92
2004	Afleet Alex	2	J. Rose	122	Devils Disciple	122	Flamenco	122	150,000	1:23.58	90

Beyer Index: 94.57

Distance 6 furlongs before 1925; 6 1/2 furlongs, 1925-93. Run over Widener Course, 1943-45

HUMANA DISTAFF HANDICAP (G1), 7 Furlongs, Fillies and Mares, 4-Year-Olds and Up, Churchill Downs, 2004 Purse: $272,813

Year	Winner	Age	Jockey	Wt.	Second	Wt.	Third	Wt.	Win Value	Time	Beyer
1987	Lazer Show	4	P. Day	120	Weekend Delight		Ten Thousand Stars			1:22.80	
1988	Le L'Argent	6	P. Day	119	Lady Gretchen		Intently			1:22.80	
1989	Sunshine Always	5	P. Day	113	Littlebitapleasure		Lt. Lao			1:24.40	
1990	Medicine Woman	5	P. Day	114	Lost Lode	114	Gallant Ryder	111	36,693	1:23.40	96
1991	Illeria	4	P. Day	112	Nurse Dopey	117	Tipsy Girl	115	37,603	1:23.20	
1992	Ifyoucouldseemenow	4	C. Perret	120	Madam Bear	114	Magal	113	56,599	1:22.22	104
1993	Court Hostess	5	C.J. McCarron	115	Santa Catalina	115	Ifyoucouldseemenow	116	56,550	1:23.18	94
1994	Roamin Rachel	4	M.E. Smith	118	Arches of Gold	121	Glory's Ghost	113	72,345	1:23.83	103
1995	Laura's Pistolette	4	Nakatani CS	114	Morning Meadow	113	Traverse City	114	74,425	1:22.24	97
1996	In Conference	4	M.E. Smith	113	Supah Jess	113	Morris Code	116	72,930	1:23.30	93
1997	Capote Belle	4	J.R. Velazquez	118	Hidden Lake	115	J J'sdream	117	70,060	1:22.38	107
1998	Colonial Minstreal	4	J.R. Velazquez	115	Stop Traffic	114	Meter Maid	114	71,300	1:22.12	105
1999	Zuppardo Ardo	5	S.J. Sellers	114	French Braids	114	Prospector's Song	114	105,183	1:23.40	98
2000	Ruby Surprise	5	J.C. Judice	114	Honest Lady	119	Cassidy	113	102,951	1:21.25	106
2001	Dream Supreme	4	P. Day	120	Le Feminn	115	Nany's Sweep	117	102,300	1:20.70	110
2002	Celtic Melody	4	M. Guidry	114	Gold Mover	115	Hattiesburg	115	141,360	1:22.98	96
	Gold Mover (Beyer: 96) finished first but was disqualified and placed second										
2003	Sightseek	4	J.D. Bailey	116	Gold Mover	119	Miss Lodi	114	137,888	1:22.12	107
2004	Mayo on the Side	5	P. Day	114	Azeri	125	Randaroo	121	174,375	1:22.78	99

Beyer Index: 101.07

HUTCHESON (G2), 7 Furlongs, 3-Year-Olds, Gulfstream Park, 2004 Purse: $150,000

Year	Winner	Age	Jockey	Wt.	Second	Wt.	Third	Wt.	Win Value	Time	Beyer
1954	Buttevant	3	K. Church	113	Jilted Gob	108	Brachs Admiral	111	4,875	1:10.80	
1955	Nance's LAd	3	J. Choquette	113	First Cabin	111	Rouge Falcon	113	9,400	1:16.40	
1956	Decathlon	3	G.R. Martin	122	Busher Fantasy	122	Getthere Jack	122	8,000	1:16.00	
1957	Jet Colonel	3	R. Ussery	119	Barbizon	122	We Trust	144	8,000	1:16.00	
1958	Yemen	3	R. Ussery	114	Belleau Chief	114	Lincoln Road	112	7,425	1:15.80	
1959	Easy Spur	3	L. Batchellor	122	Pointer	114	Octopus	122	7,750	1:16.00	
1960	Will Ye	3	S. Boulmetis	112	Vox Pop	114	Run for Nurse	118	7,825	1:16.20	
1961	Nashua Blue	3	R. Ussery	116	Beau Prince	116	Intensive	122	7,750	1:23.00	
1962	Eidolon	3	L. Adams	112	Sharp Count	115	Two Block Fox	116	8,425	1:24.80	
1963	Sky Wonder	3	R. Ussery	122	Bold Commander	112	Nashver	114	8,375	1:23.40	
1964	Ky Pioneer	3	L. Adams	114	Kentucky Jug	114	Buz On	113	10,900	1:24.00	
1965	Gallant Lad	3	B. Baeza	114	Prime Minister	112	Good Trouble	116	10,700	1:23.80	
1966	Bold and Brave	3	K. Knapp	112	Kauai King	114	All Love	116	11,625	1:22.80	
1967	Glengary	3	J. Giovanni	110	Sir Winzalot	114	Sun Seeker	110	15,025	1:23.20	
1968	Pappa Steve	3	R. Ussery	119	Addy Boy	114	Intentdamless	112	15,175	1:22.80	
1969	Al Hattab	3	R. Broussard	122	I Found Gold	112	Sail Ahoy	112	15,000	1:22.60	
1970	Cassie Red	3	W. Blum	112	Ring for Nurse	122	Native Royalty	113	22,950	1:22.60	
1971	Landing More	3	R. Woodhouse	119	Son Ange	114	Raja Baba	119	20,910	1:21.80	
1972	Spanish Riddle	3	F.Iannelli	114	Gentle Smoke	114	Delta Oil	114	29,820	1:22.80	
1973	Shecky Greene	3	B. Baeza	122	Forego	116	Leo's Pisces	112	17,170	1:20.80	
1974	Frankie Adams	3	R. Turcotte	114	Judger	110			31,845	1:22.40	
					Training Table	113					

Year	Winner	Age	Jockey	Wt.	Second	Wt.	Third	Wt.	Win Value	Time	Beyer
1975	Greek Answer	3	M. Castaneda	122	Fashion Sale	113	Rich Sun	122	20,370	1:21.60	
1976	Sonkisser	3	B. Baeza	116	Gay Jitterbug	116	Star of the Sea	122	19,350	1:21.00	
1977	Silver Series	3	L. Snyder	112	Medieval Man	114	One in a Million	114	20,610	1:22.80	
1978	Sensitive Prince	3	M. Solomone	114	Kissing U.	114	Pipe Major	114	19,890	1:20.80	
1979	Spectacular Bid	3	R.J. Franklin	122	Lot o' Gold	114	Northern Prospect	114	17,766	1:21.40	
1980	Plugged Nickle	3	B. Thornburg	122	Execution's Reason	122	One Son	114	17,640	1:22.60	
1981	Lord Avie	3	C.J. McCarron	122	Spirited Boy	114	Linnleur	114	34,080	1:23.40	
1982	Distinctive Pro	3	J. Velasquez	117	Center Cut	114	Real Twister	114	34,650	1:22.40	
1983	Current Hope	3	A. Solis	114	Highland Park	122	Country Pine	112	39,330	1:22.80	
1984	Swale	3	E. Maple	122	For Halo	114	Darn That Alarm	112	38,790	1:22.20	
1985	Banner Bob	3	K.K. Allen	114	Creme Fraiche	114	Do It Again Dan	114	45,720	1:21.60	
1986	Papal Power	3	D. MacBeth	122	Raja's Revenge	122	Mr. Classic	112	55,440	1:23.80	
1987	Well Selected	3	J. Vasquez	113	Gone West	114	Faster Than Sound	119	53,376	1:23.00	
1988	Perfect Spy	3	J.L. Samyn	114	Forty Niner	122	Notebook	122	52,335	1:23.00	
1989	Dixieland Brass	3	R.P. Romero	114	Western Playboy	112	Tricky Creek	122	58,320	1:22.80	
1990	Housebuster	3	R.P. Romero	119	Yonder	122	Stalker	114	56,787	1:24.40	
1991	Fly So Free	3	J.A. Santos	122	To Freedom	119	Sunny and Pleasant	114	55,527	1:23.20	
1992	My Luck Runs North	3	R.D. Lopez	113	Sneaky Solicitor	117	Frosted Spy	117	55,008	1:24.80	86
1993	Hidden Trick	3	R.P. Romero	114	Great Navigator	119	Forever Whirl	112	54,108	1:23.60	91
1994	Holy Bull	3	M.E. Smith	122	Patton	113	You and I	119	45,000	1:21.20	108
1995	Valid Wager	3	M.A. Pedroza	119	Mr. Greeley	117	Don Juan A	114	45,000	1:23.40	97
1996	Appealing Skier	3	R. Wilson	119	Unbridled's Song	119	Gold Fever	117	45,000	1:24.60	104
1997	Frisk Me Now	3	E. L. King Jr	112	Confide	117	Crown Ambassador	117	60,000	1:22.40	96
1998	Time Limit	3	J.D. Bailey	119	Coronado's Quest	122	Zippy Zeal	114	60,000	1:22.40	107
1999	Bet Me Best	3	J.D. Bailey	122	Texas Glitter	119	Cat Thief	119	90,000	1:22.20	101
2000	More Than Ready	3	J.R. Velazquez	122			American Bullet	113	60,000	1:21.76	102
	Summer Note	3	S.J. Sellers	113							
2001	Yonaguska	3	J.D. Bailey	119	City Zip	122	Sparkling Sabre	112	90,000	1:22.63	95
2002	Showmeitall	3	J.F. Chavez	118	Monthir	116	Royal Lad	116	90,000	1:26.07	96
2003	Lion Tamer	3	J.R. Velazquez	118	Strength Within	116	Crafty Guy	122	90,000	1:22.60	98
2004	Limehouse	3	J.R. Velazquez	122	Deputy Storm	118	Saratoga County	116	90,000	1:22.23	99

Beyer Index: 98.46

ILLINOIS DERBY (G2), 1 1/8 Miles, 3-Year-Olds, Hawthorne, 2004 Purse: $500,000

Year	Winner	Age	Jockey	Wt.	Second	Wt.	Third	Wt.	Win Value	Time	Beyer
1923	In Memoriam	3	N. Barrett	118	General Thatcher	118	Prince K.	115	9,250	2:04.20	
1933	Sweeprush	3	W. Moran	115	Fair Rochester	115	Col. Hatfield	118	3,455	2:00.00	
1934	Mata Hari	3	L. Humphries	117	New Deal	119	Plight	122	8,230	1:49.20	
1935	Sun Portland	3	C. Kurtsinger	114	Roman Soldier	122	Tearout	116	7,570	1:50.00	
1936	Rushaway	3	J. Longden	120	Count Morse	114	Reelon	113	9,660	1:50.80	
1937	Case Ace	3	A. Robertson	126	Grey Count	120	Heelfly	120	9,590	1:51.80	
1938	Gov. Chandler	3	W. Garner	118	Xavier	116	Dolly Val	113	9,560	1:58.00	
1963	Lemon Twist	3	S. LeJeune	119	Finklehoffe	114	Cosmic Tip	124	18,167	1:52.60	
1964	Nushka	3	R. Lawless	114	Climax II	114	Goff's Gay	122	26,211	1:53.60	
1965	Terra Hi	3	L. Spraker	119	Aria	109	Bust Him In	116	20,804	1:51.60	
1965	Turn to Reason	3	T. Powell	116	Asdum	116	Travel Agent	113	20,735	1:52.00	
1966	Michigan Avenue	3	M. Ycaza	119	Abe's Hope	124	B. Golden	121	29,466	1:51.40	
1967	Royal Malabar	3	C. Stone	119	Pointmenow	121	Gentleman James	126	37,922	1:51.20	
1968	Bold Favorite	3	R. Nono	114	Three Carrswold	116	Jet's Kingdom	114	43,629	1:50.20	
1969	King of the Castle	3	B. Baeza	126	Rush Date	119	Happy Intellectual	116	43,697	1:51.40	
1972	Fame and Power	3	A. Rini	119	Gun Tune	119	Beau Julian	124	43,986	1:49.40	
1973	Big Whippendeal	3	L. Adams	119	What Will Be	121	Golden Don	126	43,491	1:50.20	
1974	Sharp Gary	3	G. Gallitano	124	Sr. Diplomat	114	Sports Editor	119	63,060	1:50.00	
1975	Colonel Power	3	P. Rubbicco	124	Ruggles Ferry	124	Methdioxya	124	63,360	1:50.20	
1976	Life's Hope	3	S. Hawley	124	Wardlaw	124	New Collection	116	77,295	1:51.40	
1977	Flag Officer	3	L. Ahrens	124	Time Call	116	Cisk	116	62,955	1:52.20	
1978	Batonnier	3	R.J. Hirdes Jr	124	Raymond Earl	121	Silver Nitrate	124	62,280	1:51.60	
1979	Smarten	3	S. Maple	124	Clever Trick	124	Julie's Dancer	116	91,710	1:49.40	
1980	Ray's Word	3	R. DePass	124	Mighty Return	114	Stutz Blackhawk	121	92,970	1:52.00	
1981	Paristo	3	D.C. Ashcroft	126	Pass the Tab	126	Bitterrook	114	93,300	1:49.60	
1982	Star Gallant	3	R. Sibille	126	Drop Your Drawers	122	Soy Emperor	119	126,420	1:52.60	
1983	Gen'l Practitioner	3	J.A. Santiago	126	Passing Base	114	Aztec Red	124	127,200	1:50.40	
1984	Delta Trace	3	K.K. Allen	124	Wind Flyer	122	Birdie's Legend	124	127,530	1:51.80	
1985	Important Business	3	J.L. Diaz	116	Nostalgia's Star	122	Another Reef	124	192,786	1:51.60	
1986	Bolshoi Boy	3	R. Migliore	118	Speedy Shannon	118	Blue Buckaroo	116	189,432	1:52.20	
1987	Lost Code	3	G. St. Leon	124	Blanco	119	Valid Prospect	112	188,130	1:49.60	
1988	Proper Reality	3	J.D. Bailey	124	Jim's Orbit	122	Classic Account	112	321,000	1:50.20	
1989	Music Merci	3	G.L. Stevens	124	Notation	119	Endow	124	310,150	1:50.20	
1990	Dotsero	3	A.T. Gryder	117	Sound of Cannons	112	Hofre	112	190,290	1:50.60	
1991	Richman	3	J.D. Bailey	124	Doc of the Day	119	Nowork All Play	114	319,200	1:49.20	109

Year	Winner	Age	Jockey	Wt.	Second	Wt.	Third	Wt.	Win Value	Time	Beyer
1992	Dignitas	3	J.D. Bailey	117	American Chance	112	Straight to Bed	114	320,100	1:49.00	104
1993	Antrim Rd.	3	A.T. Gryder	114	Seattle Morn	114	Secret Negotiator	114	300,000	1:48.60	93
1994	Rustic Light	3	E. Fires	117	Amathos	103	Seminole Wind	113	300,000	1:51.80	98
1995	Peaks and Valleys	3	J.A. Krone	124	Da Hoss	117	Western Echo	117	300,000	1:48.80	108
1996	Natural Selection	3	R P Romero	114	El Amante	124	Irish Conquest	114	300,000	1:48.60	108
1997	Wild Rush	3	K.J. Desormeaux	117	Anet	124	Saratoga Sunrise	119	300,000	1:47.40	114
1998	Yarrow Brae	3	W. Martinez	114	One Bold Stroke	117	Orville N Wilbur's	124	300,000	1:51.20	107
1999	Vision and Verse	3	H. Castillo Jr	114	Prime Timber	117	Pineaff	122	300,000	1:48.40	103
2000	Performing Magic	3	S.J. Sellers	119	Country Only	117	Country Coast	114	300,000	1:50.86	101
2001	Distilled	3	M.E. Smith	114	Saint Damien	119	Dream Run	114	300,000	1:51.37	94
2002	War Emblem	3	L.J. Sterling Jr	114	Repent	124	Fonz's	117	300,000	1:49.92	112
2003	Ten Most Wanted	3	P. Day	114	Fund of Funds	114	Foufa's Warrior	118	300,000	1:51.47	110
2004	Pollard's Vision	3	E.M. Coa	114	Song of the Sword	116	Suave	114	300,000	1:50.80	107

Beyer Index: 104.86

INDIANA BREEDERS' CUP OAKS (G3), 1 1/16 Miles, 3-Year-Old Fillies, Hoosier Park, 2004 Purse: $406,300

Year	Winner	Age	Jockey	Wt.	Second	Wt.	Third	Wt.	Win Value	Time	Beyer
1998	French Braids	3	W. Martinez	116	Remember Ike	121	Barefoot Dyana	118	124,080	1:43.00	97
1999	Brushed Halory	3	E.M. Martin Jr	121	The Happy Hopper	116	Chelsea's House	116	124,140	1:44.64	89
2000	Humble Clerk	3	L. Melancon	114	Megans Bluff	121	Miss Seffens	116	92,580	1:42.40	101
2001	Scoop	3	R.J. Albarado	122	Gold Huntress	115	Caressing	121	123,480	1:44.06	93
2002	Bare Necessities	3	J. Valdivia Jr	118	Erica's Smile	121	Tarnished Lady	118	183,840	1:45.83	94
2003	Awesome Humor	3	R. Albarado	116	Cloakof Vagueness	114	Shot Gun Favorite	118	184,140	1:45.75	96
2004	Daydreaming	3	J.R. Velazquez	118	Capeside Lady	121	Stellar Jayne	121	243,780	1:43.65	108

Beyer Index: 96.86

INDIANA DERBY (G2), 1 1/16 Miles, 3-Year-Olds, Hoosier Park, 2004 Purse: $511,300

Year	Winner	Age	Jockey	Wt.	Second	Wt.	Third	Wt.	Win Value	Time	Beyer
1995	Peruvian	3	D. Kutz	117	I Still Believe	117	Mine Inspector	119	66,900	1:43.00	99
1996	Canyon Run	3	F.C. Torres	115	Broadway Bit	113	Hunk of Class	117	64,560	1:41.40	94
1997	Dubai Dust	3	S.P. LeJeune Jr	113	Frisk Me Now	122	Tansit	119	127,440	1:44.00	97
1998	One Bold Stroke	3	R.J. Albarado	122	Dixie Dot Com	117	Da Devil	122	188,700	1:43.00	110
1999	Forty One Carats	3	J.F. Chavez	115	Zanetti	111	First American	122	188,100	1:42.24	105
2000	Mister Deville	3	L.S. Quinonez	119	Performing Magic	122	One Call Close	119	184,500	1:41.80	99
2001	Orientate	3	R.J. Albarado	115	Saratoga Games	121	Trion Georgia	124	188,460	1:42.22	105
2002	Perfect Drift	3	J.K. Court	124	Easyfromthegitgo	124	Premeditation	121	248,820	1:43.50	106
2003	Excessivepleasure	3	J.K. Court	124	Grand Hombre	124	Wando	124	247,080	1:43.48	103
2004	Brass Hat	3	W. Martinez	124	Suave	124	Hasslefree	115	306,780	1:44.04	106

Beyer Index: 102.40

INGLEWOOD HANDICAP (G3), 1 1/16 Miles (Turf), 3-Year-Olds and Up, Hollywood Park, 2004 Purse: $110,900

Year	Winner	Age	Jockey	Wt.	Second	Wt.	Third	Wt.	Win Value	Time	Beyer
1938	Ligaroti	6	N. Richardson	119	No Dice	106	Sweepalot	115	4,250	1:38.80	
1939	Specify	4	C. Corbett	118	Main Man	118	Flying Wild	102	6,975	1:36.40	
1940	Hysterical	4	L. Balaski	116	Specify	122	Wed'g Call	113	7,475	1:43.40	
1941	Sir Jeffrey	4	J. Westrope	113	Woof Woof	120	Mr. Grundy	109	7,975	1:42.40	
1945	High Resolve	4	C. Corbett	126	Prince Ernest	111	Challenge Me	110	11,600	1:22.00	
1946	Quick Reward	4	A. Skoronski	122	Canina	116	Vanslam	109	20,200	1:23.60	
1947	Artillery	4	H. Lindberg	112	Texas Sandman	115	See-tee-see	117	18,900	1:22.00	
1948	With Pleasure	5	J. Westrope	125	Mafosta	126	Fair Truckle	123	18,900	1:11.20	
1949	Ace Admiral	4	F. Zufelt	124	Pretal	110	Amble In	112	18,400	1:42.80	
1950	Miche	5	J. Westrope	122	Dharan	110	Frankly	112	17,550	1:49.00	
1951	Sturdy One	4	R. Neves	109	All Blue	111	Be Fleet	123	17,950	1:42.20	
1952	Sturdy One	5	R. Neves	111	Stormy Cloud	105	Admiral Drake	116	15,700	1:42.20	
1953	Pet Bully	5	R. Neves	123	Royal Serenade	116	Fleet Bird	122	16,250	1:42.00	
1954	High Scud	5	R. Trejos	113	Curragh King	113	Fleet Bird	118	14,900	1:42.00	
1955	Determine	4	R. York	124	Mister Gus	114	Alidon	117	15,250	1:40.80	
1956	Swaps	4	W. Shoemaker	130	Mister Gus	115	Bobby Brocato	121	29,450	1:39.00	
1957	Find	7	R. Neves	118	Eddie Schmidt	112	Pit Boss	109	30,200	1:40.80	
1958	Eddie Schmidt	5	A. Maese	117	How Now	122	Social Climber	117	31,650	1:41.60	
1959	Bug Brush	4	A. Valenzuela	123	Amerigo	110	How Now	112	31,000	1:40.80	
1960	Bagdad	4	W. Shoemaker	121	Sea Orbit	118	Prize Host	110	31,300	1:40.80	
1961	Sea Orbit	5	A. Valenzuela	120	Dress Up	112	First Balcony	124	32,350	1:41.00	
1962	Prove It	5	H. Moreno	122	Sea Orbit	112	Rablero	109	33,450	1:41.00	
1963	Native Diver	4	R. Neves	121	Pirate Cove	115	Aldershot	114	32,450	1:42.20	

Year	Winner	Age	Jockey	Wt.	Second	Wt.	Third	Wt.	Win Value	Time	Beyer
1964	Native Diver	5	J. Lambert	116	Mustard Plaster	118	Mr. Consistency	124	32,700	1:41.60	
1965	Tronado	5	J. Baze	113	Hill Rise	120	Quadrangle	124	32,800	1:40.40	
1966	Native Diver	7	J. Lambert	125	Sledge	115	Tronado	113	35,650	1:41.60	
1967	Quicken Tree	4	F. Alvarez	113	Hill Clown	112	Niarkos	124	26,750	1:41.60	
1967	Pretense	4	J. Sellers	128	Biggs	117	Aurelius II	111	26,250	1:39.80	
1968	Gamely	4	W. Harris	119	Rising Market	120	Hill Shine	118	34,550	1:47.20	
1969	Rising Market	5	L. Pincay Jr	120	Dewan	114	Rivet	114	32,850	1:46.60	
1970	Baffle	5	J. Lambert	122	Pleasure Seeker	111	T.V. Com'l	111	31,650	1:47.20	
1971	Advance Guard	5	W. Shoemaker	118	Manta	119	Far to Reach	111	44,850	1:48.00	
1972	War Heim	5	V. Tejada	112	Kennedy Road	119	Figonero	113	46,600	1:47.40	
1973	Ancient Title	3	F. Toro	122	Groshawk	122	Pontoise	114	32,550	1:21.00	
1974	Shirley's Champion	3	H. Grant	118	Rocket Review	117	Such a Rush	121	20,100	1:14.80	
1975	El Botija	5	J. Tejeira	116	Kirrary	115	Against the Snow	117	25,475	1:41.60	
1975	Gay Style	5	W. Shoemaker	120	Out of the East	116	June's Love	116	26,475	1:41.40	
1976	Riot in Paris	5	J. Lambert	121	Absent Minded	114	Pa's'ate Pi'te	113	25,750	1:41.60	
1976	King Pellinore	4	W. Shoemaker	118	Antique	114	Big Band	117	26,250	1:42.00	
1977	Today 'n Tomorrow	4	S. Hawley	117	Anne's Pretender	122	Sir Jason	118	32,300	1:41.00	
1978	Star Spangled	4	A. Cordero Jr	116	Bad 'n Big	122	No Turning	116	26,800	1:39.80	
1978	Star of Erin II	4	W. Shoemaker	117	Landscaper	113	Life's Hope	117	26,300	1:40.60	
1979	Johnny's Image	4	C.J. McCarron	117	Rich Cream	117	Smoggy	112	26,875	1:40.60	
1979	Star Spangled	5	L. Pincay Jr	119	Bywayofchicago	122	As de Copas	121	25,875	1:40.00	
1980	Red Crescent	4	C.J. McCarron	112	Henschel	118	Numa Pompilius	115	31,300	1:40.60	
1981	Bold Tropic	6	W. Shoemaker	124	The Bart	117	Adraan	117	52,250	1:40.00	
1982	Maipon	5	D.G. McHargue	115	Spence Bay	122	Wickerr	116	68,900	1:40.20	
1983	Bold Style	4	P. Day	115	Noalto	115	Western	118	65,400	1:41.40	
1984	Royal Heroine	4	F. Toro	116	Bel Bolide	120	Vin St. Benet	118	71,500	1:40.20	
1985	Al Mamoon	4	E. Delahoussaye	116	The Noble Player	118	Swoon	114	62,900	1:40.20	
1986	Zoffany	6	E. Delahoussaye	121	Palace Music	124	Truce Maker	112	63,300	1:45.60	
1987	Le Belvedere	4	W. Shoemaker	113	Sharrood	118	Barberty	114	65,100	1:40.40	
1988	Steinlen	5	G.L. Stevens	119	Deputy Governor	120	Galunpe	115	66,200	1:40.40	
1989	Steinlen	6	G.L. Stevens	120	Pasakos	115	Mi Preferido	117	63,400	1:39.60	
1990	Mohamed Abdu	6	G.L. Stevens	117	Peace	117	Classic Fame	117	64,800	1:39.40	107
1991	Tight Spot	4	L. Pincay Jr	121	Somethingdifferent	116	Razeen	114	63,400	1:40.20	110
1992	Golden Pheasant	6	G.L. Stevens	121	Blaze O'Brien	114	Native Boundary	116	64,900	1:39.80	102
1993	The Tender Track	6	E. Delahoussaye	116	Journalism	118	Johann Quatz	117	62,500	1:40.00	106
1994	Gothland	5	C.S. Nakatani	117	Rapan Boy	117	Johann Quatz	117	60,700	1:39.60	110
1995	Blaze O'Brien	8	C.A. Black	116	Savinio	118	Stoller	117	79,800	1:39.40	109
1996	Fastness	6	C.S. Nakatani	122	Helmsman	120	Tyconic	120	79,470	1:39.40	112
1997	El Angelo	5	C.S. Nakatani	115	Irish Wings	114	Tyconic	118	63,900	1:40.20	102
1998	Fantastic Fellow	4	C.S. Nakatani	118	Via Lombardia	116	Sharekann	113	64,740	1:38.60	112
1999	Brave Act	5	G.F. Almeida	120	Lord Smith	119	Expressionist	116	66,420	1:39.00	113
2000	Montemiro	6	V. Espinoza	113	Bonapartiste	118	Takarian	118	66,300	1:40.71	104
2001	Fateful Dream	4	D.R. Flores	114	National Anthem	115	Casino King	115	64,260	1:41.65	99
2002	Night Patrol	6	V. Espinoza	113	Redattore	120	Seinne	117	65,820	1:39.35	107
2003	Gondolieri	4	F.T. Alvarado	116	Truly a Judge	114	Freefourinternet	116	63,540	1:40.32	108
2004	Leroidesanimaux	4	J.K. Court	114	Designed for Luck	118	Devious Boy	115	66,540	1:38.45	111

Beyer Index: 107.47

Off the turf in 2003.

IOWA OAKS (G3), 1 1/16 Miles, 3-Year-Old Fillies, Prairie Meadows, 2004 Purse: $125,000

Year	Winner	Age	Jockey	Wt.	Second	Wt.	Third	Wt.	Win Value	Time	Beyer
1989	Clickety Click	3	K.M. Murray	119	She's Due Black	117	Hurry Home	115	15,450	1:38.80	
1990	Sixmo	3	V.L. Warhol	115	Dance for the Gold	115	Pay Her in Gold	116	11,069	1:46.60	
1991	Chocolate Tuesday	3	C.G. Lowrance	121	Proudest Royal	121	Amdors Love	115	8,266	1:43.10	
1992	Giggles Up	3	G.A. Schaefer	120	Chelle Rae	120	Cobilion	120	10,120	1:46.02	58
1993	Medical History	3	V.L. Warhol	114	Millie's Key	118	Fashioncense	119	8,950	1:42.40	65
1994	Punkerdoo	3	D.G. Schroeck	121	Maria Badria	118	Chateau Queen	114	9,555	1:44.00	68
1995	Our Gaggy	3	D.R. Bickel	118	Don't Tary Stalker	121	Melinda Jo	114	17,184	1:41.80	63
1996	Vaguely Who	3	V.L. Warhol	121	Swiss Saphire	118	Dee's Anny	117	24,439	1:43.63	57
1997	Bon Ami	3	G.W. Corbett	116	Windy City Raja	114	Quick n Steady	121	37,317	1:44.73	44
1998	Shardona	3	K.A. Shino	114	Danzig Foxxy Woman	118	Lady Tamworth	121	43,305	1:46.94	65
1999	Golden Temper	3	S.J. Sellers	121	Undermine	118	Sweeping Story	121	75,000	1:42.95	96
2000	Trip	3	W. Martinez	121	Lady Melesi	118	Fiesty Countess	118	90,000	1:43.56	99
2001	Unbridled Elaine	3	P. Day	115	Supreme Song	115	Sharky's Review	118	90,000	1:43.88	100
2002	Lost at Sea	3	T.J. Thompson	115	See How She Runs	121	Don't Ruffle Me	115	90,000	1:42.27	102
2003	Wildwood Royal	3	D.G. Sukie	121	Golden Reputashn	112	Tulupai	112	75,000	1:41.64	101
2004	He Loves Me	3	J.Z. Santana	118	Prospective Saint	115	Home Court	115	75,000	1:42.80	95

Beyer Index: 77.92

Distance 1 mile in 1989; 1 mile 70 yards in 1990–1998 Run at Canterbury in 1992.

IROQUOIS (G3), 1 Mile, 2-Year-Olds, Churchill Downs, 2004 Purse: $109,600

Year	Winner	Age	Jockey	Wt.	Second	Wt.	Third	Wt.	Win Value	Time	Beyer
1990	Richman	2	P. Day	121	Speedy Cure	114	Honor Grades	116	36,628	1:36.60	
1991	Portroe	2	M.E. Smith	114	Walkie Talker	121	Richard of England	121	76,570	1:37.80	85
1992	Shoal Creek	2	B.E. Bartram	114	Saw Mill	116	Demaloot Demashoot	116	76,375	1:37.40	89
1993	Tarzans Blade	2	B.E. Bartram	121	Dove Hunt	121	Amathos	114	74,945	1:37.00	91
1994	Peruvian	2	J.A. Santos	121	Our Gatsby	116	Super Jeblar	116	77,025	1:36.60	84
1995	Ide	2	C. Perret	121	El Amante	116	City by Night	114	73,645	1:36.80	89
1996	Global View	2	K. Borque	112	Partner's Hero	112	Haint	121	68,200	1:36.40	96
1997	Keene Dancer	2	P. Day	121	Yarrow Brae	113	Dawn Exodus	113	68,882	1:37.80	93
1998	Exploit	2	C.J. McCarron	114	Crowning Storm	114	Olympic Journey	114	71,114	1:36.20	98
1999	Mighty	2	M. St. Julien.	112	Ifitstobeitsuptome	113	Nature	114	68,758	1:35.80	94
2000	Meetyouathebrig	2	G.L. Stevens	118	Hero's Tribute	114	Keats	112	77,066	1:35.24	91
2001	Harlan's Holiday	2	A.J. D'Amico	121	Request for Parole	121	Gold Dollar	116	70,184	1:35.01	97
2002	Champali	2	P. Day	118	Alke	116	What a Bad Day	118	70,804	1:37.06	82
2003	The Cliff's Edge	2	S.J. Sellers	117	Korbyn Gold	121	Grand Score	117	70,494	1:35.57	101
2004	Straight Line	2	B. Blanc	122	Social Probation	120	Greater Good	122	67,952	1:36.62	98

Beyer Index: 92.00

PHILIP H. ISELIN BREEDERS' CUP HANDICAP (G3), 1 1/8 Miles, 3-Year-Olds and Up, Monmouth Park, 2004 Purse: $194,000

Year	Winner	Age	Jockey	Wt.	Second	Wt.	Third	Wt.	Win Value	Time	Beyer
1884	Drake Carter	4	Hayward	120	Heel-and-Toe	108	Kinglike	120	3,460	2:37.60	
1885	Richmond	3	J. McLaughlin	110	Louisette	116	War Eagle	102	4,025	2:38.20	
1886	Hidalgo	4	Spellman	123	Bonanza	114	Maumee	104	3,570	2:39.20	
1887	Kaloolah	4	Church	107	Rupert	103	Eurus	112	3,570	2:42.20	
1888	Firenzi	4	Garrison	123	Exile	118	Belvidere	121	5,385	2:36.00	
1889	Eurus	6	Hayward	124	Senorita	104	Firenzi	124	4,715	2:50.00	
1890	Tea Tray	5	Moore	110	Rhono	118	Lavinia Belle	110	5,335	2:34.00	
1891	Banquet	4	Lamley	113	Peter	101	English Lady	103	5,055	2:40.00	
1892	Reckon	4	Penn	100	Lamplighter	115	Banquet	124	3,770	2:33.20	
1893	Gloaming	6	A. Clayton	100	The Pepper	114	Picknicker	106	3,955	2:33.00	
1946	Lucky Draw	5	C. McCreary	111	Stymie	126	Aonbarr	100	22,970	2:01.80	
1947	Round View	4	L. Hildebrandt	112	Talon	112	Gallorette	119	19,700	2:01.20	
1948	Tide Rips	4	P. Roberts	108	Vertigo II	109	Bug Juice	108	19,850	2:03.20	
1949	Three Rings	4	H. Woodhouse	110	Round View	112	Splash	104	20,200	2:03.60	
1950	Greek Ship	3	J. Culmone	107	Hypocrite II	108	Three Rings	121	21,250	2:02.40	
1951	Arise	5	S. Boulmetis	122	Post Card	117	Why Not Now	106	19,200	2:04.80	
1952	One Hitter	6	T. Atkinson	114	Combat Boots	108	County Delight	124	18,750	2:04.20	
1953	My Celeste	7	L. Batchellor	110	Again II	104	Devilkin	111	23,500	2:05.20	
1954	Bassanio	4	S. Cole	109	Closed Door	115	Level Lea	118	40,700	2:02.20	
1955	Helioscope	4	S. Boulmetis	131	High Gun	135	Punkin Vine	111	56,400	2:02.20	
1956	Nashua	4	E. Arcaro	129	Mr. First	110	Mielleux	107	78,200	2:02.80	
1957	Dedicate	5	E. Arcaro	124	Third Brother	119	Rockcastle	109	72,625	2:01.80	
1958	Bold Ruler	4	E. Arcaro	134	Sharpsburg	113	Bill's Sky Boy	105	70,772	2:01.60	
1959	Sword Dancer	3	W. Shoemaker	120	Amerigo	116	Talent Show	124	72,787	2:05.00	
1960	First Landing	4	E. Arcaro	123	Manassa Mauler	117	Talent Show	117	71,650	2:02.80	
1961	Don Poggio	5	S. Boulmetis	122	Our Hope	117	Black Thumper	108	72,995	2:02.40	
1962	Carry Back	4	J.L. Rotz	124	Kelso	130	Beau Purple	117	70,947	2:00.40	
1963	Decidedly	4	M. Ycaza	120	Mongo	126	Guadalcanal	113	72,345	2:02.00	
1964	Mongo	5	W. Chambers	127	Kelso	130	Gun Bow	124	69,875	2:01.80	
1965	Repeating	4	H. Woodhouse	110	Tenacle	114	Ampose	119	70,395	2:04.20	
1966	Bold Bidder	4	P. Anderson	122	Paoluccio	107	Pluck	114	74,392	2:03.60	
1967	Handsome Boy	4	J. Vasquez	115	Amberoid	118	Good Knight	113	73,060	2:02.00	
1968	Bold Hour	4	W. Boland	116	Mr. Right	114	Damascus	131	72,150	2:03.00	
1969	Verbatim	4	P. Anderson	116	San Roque	113	Chompion	111	73,970	2:02.20	
1970	Gladwin	4	H. Gustines	110	Charles Elliott	112	My Dad George	116	75,660	2:02.60	
1971	Jontilla	4	J. Giovanni	115	Never Bow	122	Pass Catcher	113	75,140	2:01.00	
1972	West Coast Scout	4	J.L. Rotz	113	Hitchcock	114	Eastern Fleet	117	73,775	2:02.20	
1973	West Coast Scout	5	L. Adams	114	Tentam	118	Windtex	113	74,295	2:01.20	
1974	True Knight	5	M.A. Rivera	124	Ecole Etage	112	Hey Rube	111	72,215	2:02.00	
1975	Royal Glint	5	C. Perret	121	Proper Bostonian	118	Stonewalk	121	70,947	2:00.60	
1976	Hatchet Man	5	V. Bracciale Jr	112	Intrepid Hero	119	Forego	136	71,792	2:00.60	
1977	Majestic Light	4	S. Hawley	124	Capital Idea	108	Peppy Addy	116	71,143	2:00.40	
1978	Life's Hope	5	C. Perret	115	Wise Philip	114	Father Hogan	115	72,183	2:03.20	
1979	Text	5	W. Shoemaker	118	Cox's Ridge	120	Silent Cal	115	70,948	1:47.40	
1980	Spectacular Bid	4	W. Shoemaker	132	Glorious Song	117	The Cool Virginian	112	158,160	1:48.00	
1981	Amber Pass	4	C.B. Asmussen	117	Joanie's Chief	108	Ring of Light	114	170,580	1:47.40	
1982	Mehmet	4	E. Delahoussaye	115	Pukka Princess	108	Summer Advoate	117	174,240	1:48.20	
1983	Bates Motel	4	T. Lipham	124	Island Whirl	124	Linkage	115	167,520	1:47.20	
1984	Believe the Queen	4	D.A. Miller Jr	120	World Appeal	121	Bet Big	117	194,040	1:48.20	

Year	Winner	Age	Jockey	Wt.	Second	Wt.	Third	Wt.	Win Value	Time	Beyer
1985	Spend a Buck	3	L. Pincay Jr	118	Carr de Naskra	120	Valiant Lark	115	162,180	1:46.80	
1986	Roo Art	4	W. Shoemaker	117	Precisionist	125	Lady's Secret	120	188,280	1:48.60	
1987	Bordeaux Bob	4	C.W. Antley	115	Silver Comet	114	Lost Code	117	163,920	1:48.20	
1988	Alysheba	4	C.J. McCarron	124	Bet Twice	123	Gulch	122	300,000	1:47.80	
1989	Proper Reality	4	J.D. Bailey	119	Bill E. Shears	112	Mi Selecto	114	150,000	1:48.00	
1990	Beau Genius	5	R.D. Lopez	122	Tricky Creek	112	De Roche	115	150,000	1:48.20	114
1991	Black Tie Affair	5	P. Day	119	Farma Way	122	Chief Honcho	115	300,000	1:47.80	112
1992	Jolie's Halo	5	E.S. Prado	116	Out of Place	113	Valley Crossing	111	300,000	1:46.80	106
1993	Valley Crossing	5	C.W. Antley	113	Devil His Due	123	Bertrando	119	300,000	1:49.20	113
1994	Taking Risks	4	M.T. Johnston	115	Valley Crossing	117	Proud Shot	112	150,000	1:48.20	113
1995	Schossberg	5	D. Penna	118	Poor But Honest	115	Mickeray	114	180,000	1:49.20	111
1996	Smart Strike	4	C. Perret	115	Eltish	116	Serena's Song	115	180,000	1:41.40	115
1997	Formal Gold	4	K.J. Desormeaux	121	Skip Away	124	Distorted Humor	115	250,000	1:40.20	124
1998	Skip Away	5	J.D. Bailey	131	Stormin Fever	113	Testafly	114	300,000	1:47.20	114
1999	Frisk Me Now	5	E.L.King Jr	117	Call Me Mr. Vain	110	Black Cash	112	210,000	1:49.00	109
2000	Rize	4	J.C. Ferrer	112	Sir Bear	118	Talk's Cheap	114	210,000	1:48.42	111
2001	Broken Vow	4	R.A. Dominguez	119	First Lieutenant	115	Sir Bear	117	210,000	1:49.55	108
2002	Cat's at Home	5	J.A. Velez Jr	116	Bowman's Band	117	Runspastum	114	210,000	1:49.10	107
2003	Tenpins	5	R.J. Albarado	119	Aeneas	114	Jersey Giant	115	120,000	1:50.35	110
2004	Ghostzapper	4	J.J. Castellano	120	Presidentialaffair	117	Zoffinger	115	120,000	1:47.66	128

Beyer Index: 113.00

JAIPUR HANDICAP (G3), 7 Furlongs (Turf), 3-Year-Olds and Up, Belmont Park, 2004 Purse: $112,200

Year	Winner	Age	Jockey	Wt.	Second	Wt.	Third	Wt.	Win Value	Time	Beyer
1984	Cannon Shell	5	D.J. Murphy	115	Chan Balum	115	Believe the Queen	115	35,280	1:09.20	
1985	Mt. Livermore	4	J. Velasquez	119	Main Top	117	Cozzene	117	49,020	1:09.20	
1986	Red Wing Dream	5	J.D. Bailey	117	Creme Fraiche	122	Roy	109	48,510	1:23.60	
1986	Basket Weave	5	R. Migliore	117	Alev	117	Judge Costa	117	48,330	1:22.80	
1987	Raja's Revenge	4	M. Venezia	117	Trubulare	117	Give a Toast	114	52,200	1:25.20	
1988	Real Courage	5	J. Vasquez	117	Tinchen's Prince	117	Spectacularphantom	117	60,570	1:22.00	
1989	Harp Inlet	4	C. Perret	117	Fourstardave	119	Down Again	114	57,150	1:27.00	
1990	Fourstardave	5	M.E. Smith	122	Harperstown	117	Wanderkin	119	57,240	1:21.00	
1991	Kanatiyr	5	J.D. Bailey	117	Senor Speedy	117	Fourstardave	122	54,630	1:23.80	103
1992	To Freedom	4	J.A. Krone	117	Fourstardave	122	Smart Alec	117	55,710	1:22.80	102
1993	Home of the Free	5	J.D. Bailey	117	Wind Symbol	117	Fourstardave	117	55,080	1:20.60	106
1994	Nijinsky's Gold	5	Santos JA	114	Dominant Prospect	114	Home of the Free	122	34,905	1:20.00	109
1994	A in Sociology	4	Maple E	119	Roman Envoy	114	Halissee	119	34,905	1:20.20	106
1995	Inside the Beltway	4	Chavez JF	114	Gabr	117	Golden Cloud	114	49,245	1:21.20	99
1995	Mighty Forum	4	Stevens GL	117	Dominant Prospect	117	City Nights	114	49,995	1:21.00	102
1996	Grand Continental	5	R. Migliore	114	Inside The Beltway	115	Goldmine	111	51,720	1:23.60	107
1997	Atraf	4	Velazquez J. R.	114	Mighty Forum	114	Play Smart	113	49,635	1:23.60	90
1998	Elusive Quality	5	J.D. Bailey	115	Bristling	111	Optic Nerve	115	51,750	1:20.80	103
1999	Notoriety	6	Espinoza J. L.	115	Optic Nerve	116	Cryptic Rascal	117	52,335	1:21.20	98
2000	Gone Fishin	4	J.R. Velazquez	114	Weatherbird	113	French Envoy	113	52,290	1:21.73	103
2001	Affirmed Success	7	J.D. Bailey	123	Texas Glitter	116	Bought in Dixie	114	66,475	1:21.69	107
2002	Shibboleth	5	J.D. Bailey	121	Malabar Gold	121	Cozzy Corner	111	67,140	1:20.08	107
2003	Garnered	5	V. Carrero	116	Speightstown	121	Whitewaterspritzer	115	67,260	1:23.49	85
2004	Multiple Choice	6	J.J. Castellano	113	Dedication	114	Geronimo	118	67,320	1:22.32	101

Beyer Index: 101.75

Run at 6 furlongs on dirt, 1984, 1985. Off the turf in 2001, 2003

JAMAICA HANDICAP (G2), 1 1/8 Miles (Turf), 3-Year-Olds, Belmont Park, 2004 Purse: $200,000

Year	Winner	Age	Jockey	Wt.	Second	Wt.	Third	Wt.	Win Value	Time	Beyer
1975	Funalon	3	V. Bracciale Jr	113	Busy Saxon	114	Precious Elaine	113	34,140	1:35.80	
1976	Dance Spell	3	R. Hernandez	119	Cojak	119	Quiet Little Table	114	33,330	1:34.00	
1977	Affiliate	3	A. Cordero Jr	124	Buckfinder	113	Proud Arion	115	33,660	1:35.20	
1978	Regal and Royal	3	J. Fell	116	Squire Ambler	111	Roman Reasoning	112	32,460	1:35.00	
1979	Belle's Gold	3	L. Pincay Jr	118	Lean Lad	108	Gallant Best	113	33,180	1:33.60	
1980	Far Out East	3	C.B. Asmussen	113	Dunham's Gift	112	Settlement Day	111	35,100	1:34.00	
1981	Pass the Tab	3	J. Velasquez	112	Spirited Boy	117	Counter Espionage	112	33,300	1:35.20	
1982	John's Gold	3	A. Cordero Jr	113	Lord Lister	111	Estoril	114	33,180	1:37.00	
1983	Bounding Basque	3	G. McCarron	115	A Phenomenon	120	Bet Big	115	51,480	1:34.00	
1984	Raja's Shark	3	R. Migliore	112	Is Your Pleasure	116	Leroy S.	117	52,560	1:36.60	
1985	Don's Choice	3	D. MacBeth	114	I Enrich	110	Easton	109	53,010	1:36.00	
1986	Waquoit	3	R. Migliore	111	Mogambo	119	Moment of Hope	111	53,280	1:34.20	
1987	Stacked Pack	3	R.P. Romero	110	Gulch	123	Homebuilder	112	67,770	1:34.80	
1988	Ruhlmann	3	G.L. Stevens	113	Teddy Drone	112	Din's Dancer	112	84,540	1:35.40	

Year	Winner	Age	Jockey	Wt.	Second	Wt.	Third	Wt.	Win Value	Time	Beyer
1989	Domasca Dan	3	S. Hawley	116	Garemma	114	Is It True	120	70,920	1:35.40	
1990	Confidential Talk	3	J.F. Chavez	111	Rubiano	112	Sunshine Jimmy	114	52,470	1:35.60	106
1991	Sultry Song	3	C.W. Antley	113	Honest Ensign	110	Take Me Out	116	70,320	1:34.40	108
1992	West by West	3	J.L. Samyn	112	Offbeat	111	Portroe	111	70,320	1:34.20	103
1993	Mi Cielo	3	M.E. Smith	116	Prospector's Flag	113	Cherokee Run	120	70,440	1:35.20	106
1994	Pennine Ridge	3	J.R. Velazquez	118	Holy Mountain	116	I'm Very Irish	113	66,540	1:35.00	101
1996	Allied Forces	3	R. Migliore	119	Cliptomania	116	Lite Approval	114	86,325	1:40.80	111
1997	Subordination	3	J.F. Chavez	120	Premier Krischief	113	Skybound	121	90,000	1:49.00	98
1998	Vergennes	3	J.R. Velazquez	115	Tanghazi	114	Middlesex Drive	114	90,000	1:50.40	104
1999	Monarch's Maze	3	J. Bravo	117	Killer Joe	112	Monkey Puzzle	118	90,000	1:51.60	98
2000	King Cugat	3	J.D. Bailey	123	Mandarin Marsh	114	Parade Leader	115	120,000	1:49.63	95
2001	Navesink	3	E.S. Prado	118	Strategic Partner	118	Baptize	123	120,000	1:51.53	105
2002	Finality	3	J.R. Velazquez	116	Union Place	115	Chiselling	121	120,000	1:46.66	104
2003	Stroll	3	J.D. Bailey	121	Kicken Kris	121	Joe Bear	117	120,000	1:46.02	105
2004	Artie Schiller	3	R. Migliore	123	Rousing Victory	113	Icy Atlantic	120	120,000	1:45.50	105

Beyer Index: 103.50

JEFFERSON CUP (G3), 1 1/8 Miles (Turf), 3-Year-Olds, Churchill Downs, 2004 Purse: $226,200

Year	Winner	Age	Jockey	Wt.	Second	Wt.	Third	Wt.	Win Value	Time	Beyer
1977	Old Jake	3	J. Espinoza	122	Boldero's Orphan	122	Set in My Ways	122	14,219	1:04.80	
1978	Future Hope	3	A. Rini	125	Backstabber	125	Amber White	117	14,073	1:05.20	
1979	Rockhill Native	3	J. Oldham	122	Earl of Odessa	122	Egg's Dynamite	122	19,581	1:05.20	
1980	Golden Derby	3	J. Espinoza	125	Plain Speaking	119	Bold Tyson	125	19,257	1:04.20	
1981	Talent Town	3	B. Sayler	122	Helen's Tip	122	Ken's Revenge	122	19,858	1:05.40	
1982	Wavering Monarch	3	R.P. Romero	111	Forli's Jet	117	Noted	111	23,026	1:44.20	
1983	Pron Regard	3	C. Woods Jr	116	Le Cou Cou	125	Whitesburg Lark	112	36,303	1:51.60	
1984	Coax Me Chad	3	W.H. McCauley	119	Fairly Straight	114	Last Command	110	48,958	1:50.60	
1985	Avey's Brother	3	D. Montoya	110	La Marseillaise	110	Hollywood Hackett	113	50,420	1:50.00	
1986	Buffalo Beau	3	J. McKnight	110	Clear Choice	124	Sumptious	113	53,040	1:52.80	
1987	Fast Forward	3	R. Frazier	120	Unleavened	118	Gretna Green	112	63,109	1:50.00	
1988	Stop the Stage	3	M. McDowell	115	Cold Cathode	114	Bates Fay	115	62,310	1:51.60	
1989	Shy Tom	3	E. Fires	120	Captain Savy	116	Ruszhinka	112	52,114	1:49.20	
1990	Divine Warning	3	J. Deegan	117	Super Abound	115	Bioblast	110	36,238	1:52.20	
1991	Hanging Curve	3	J. Johnson	119	Wall Street Dancer	119	Air Force	112	36,360	1:50.80	94
1992	Senor Tomas	3	P. Day	122	Coaxing Matt	113	Black Question	122	35,945	1:49.80	95
1993	Lt. Pinkerton	3	T. Hebert	115	Snake Eyes		Mi Cielo		35,555	1:48.27	90
1994	Milt's Overture	3	P. Day	112	Jaggery John		Camptown Dancer		53,527	1:48.21	97
1995	Ago	3	S. Sellers	115	Michael's Star		Lemon Drop		56,550	1:49.48	94
1996	Unruled	3	C. Perret	119	Broadway Beau		Trail City		54,201	1:50.07	101
1997	Greed Is Good	3	W. Martinez	115	Royal Strand		Crimson Classic		69,068	1:49.47	98
1998	Buff	3	C. Borel	122	Keene Dancer		Ladies Din		175,770	1:50.80	104
1999	Special Coach	3	C. Velasquez	122	Silver Chadra		Air Rocket		180,110	1:49.82	98
2000	King Cugat	3	R.J. Albarado	122	Four on the Floor	122	Field Cat	122	177,940	1:47.27	106
2001	Indygo Shiner	3	L.J. Meche	113	Strategic Partner	119	Fast City	114	175,150	1:48.81	97
2002	Orchard Park	3	M. Guidry	119	Mr. Mellon	112	Quest Star	113	172,050	1:48.53	93
2003	Senor Swinger	3	R.J. Albarado	120	Remind	116	Rapid Proof	120	136,772	1:47.54	103
2004	Prince Arch	3	B. Blanc	120	Kitten's Joy	122	Cool Conductor	116	140,244	1:50.61	101

Beyer Index: 97.93

JENNY WILEY (G3), 1 1/16 Miles (Turf), Fillies and Mares, 4-Year-Olds and Up, Keeneland Race Course, 2004 Purse: $110,300

Year	Winner	Age	Jockey	Wt.	Second	Wt.	Third	Wt.	Win Value	Time	Beyer
1989	Native Mommy	6	C. Perret	121	Blossoming Beauty	113	Here's Your Silver	115		1:43.60	
1990	Regal Wonder	6	R. Lopez	121	Majestic Legend	121	Phoenix Sunshine	115	36,040	1:46.20	92
1991	Foresta	5	A. Cordero Jr	121	Dance for Lucy	121	The Caretaker	115	37,110	1:43.80	100
1992	Indian Fashion	5	J.A. Santos	115	Spanish Parade	121	Radiant Ring	121	39,760	1:41.20	100
1993	Lady Blessington	5	P. Day	118	Radiant Ring	118	Super Fan	118	34,844	1:42.40	95
1994	Misspitch	4	M.E. Smith	118	Park Dream	112	Sh Band	118	34,658	1:43.80	96
1995	Romy	4	FC Torres	118	Weekend Madness	121	Bold Ruritana	121	52,173	1:43.20	100
1996	Apolda	5	J.D. Bailey	121	Mediation	118	Luzette-BR	121	69,006	1:40.60	104
1997	Thrilling Day	4	W. Martinez	115	Romy	121	Gastronomical	115	68,634	1:41.00	102
1998	Maxzene	5	J. A. Santos	114	Parade Queen	121	Rumpipumpy	114	69,192	1:42.80	104
1999	Pleasant Temper	5	J.D. Bailey	117	Mingling Glances	114	Red Cat	117	70,246	1:40.80	103
2000	Astra	4	C.S. Nakatani	118	Pratella	118	Ronda	116	69,688	1:42.48	101
2001	Penny's Gold	4	J.A. Santos	116	License Fee	118	Solvig	116	70,618	1:40.93	101
2002	Tates Creek	4	K.J. Desormeaux	116	Snow Dance	123	Step With Style	116	70,432	1:42.27	95
2003	Sea of Showers	4	J.D. Bailey	116	Magic Mission	116	Snow Dance	116	70,246	1:41.89	101
2004	Intercontinental	4	J.D. Bailey	116	Ocean Drive	116	Madeira Mist	118	68,386	1:41.41	99

Beyer Index: 99.53

JEROME HANDICAP (G2), 1 Mile, 3-Year-Olds, Belmont Park, 2004 Purse: $150,000

Year	Winner	Age	Jockey	Wt.	Second	Wt.	Third	Wt.	Win Value	Time	Beyer
1866	Watson	3	Abe	110	Ulrica	107	Local	110	2,850	1:48.75	
1867	Metairie	3	Hennessey	110	Fanny Cheatham	107	Morrissey	110	2,100	1:49.50	
1868	Bayonet	3	C. Miller	110	Australia	107	Fanny Ludlow	107	2,900	1:45.25	
1869	Glenelg	3	C. Miller	110	Inverness	107	Onyx	110	3,300	1:48.50	
1870	Kingfisher	3	Burns	110	Haric	110	Midday	107	3,950	1:49.00	
1871	Harry Bassettt	3	J. Rowe	110	Monarchist	110	Alroy	110	5,450	3:54.75	
1872	Joe Daniels	3	J. Rowe	110	Mate	110	Meteor	110	4,450	3:49.25	
1873	Tom Bowling	3	Swim	110	Springbok	110	Fellowcraft	110	4,950		
1874	Acrobat	3	Sparling	110	Madge	107	Bannerette	107	4,150	2:37.75	
1875	Aristides	3	Swim	110	Calvin	110	Joe Cerns	110	3,900	3:43.00	
1876	Charley Howard	3	W. Lakeland	110	Sunburst	110	Red Coat	110	3,550	3:47.75	
1877	Basil	3	Evans	110	Susquehana	107	Bombast	110	4,400	3:43.00	
1878	Duke of Magenta	3	Hughes	118	Spartan	118	Albert	118	3,450	3:11.50	
1879	Monitor	3	Hughes	118	Spendthrift	118	Report	118	4,100	3:12.00	
1880	Grenada	3	Hughes	118	Ferncliff	118	Oden	118	3,200	3:12.75	
1881	Barrett	3	Feakes	118	Priam	118			2,800	3:13.00	
1882	Carley B.	3	J. McLaughlin	115	Elkhorn Lass	115	Duplex	115	2,900	3:21.50	
1883	George Kinney	3	Fitzpatrick	125	Euclid	115	Clonmel	118	3,220	3:19.00	
1884	Water Lily	3	Feakes	115	Bull's Head	118	Thackeray	121	3,920	3:16.00	
1885	Longview	3	Fitzpatrick	118	Tecumseh	118	Saltpetre	118	2,580	3:20.00	
1886	The Bard	3	W. Hayward	125	Elkwood	121	Mollie McCarty's L	115	2,900		
1887	Firenze	3	Garrison	122	Hanover	125			2,403	3:09.75	
1888	Prince Royal	3	Garrison	128	Tea Tray	115	Larchmont	118	3,870	3:10.25	
1889	Longstreet	3	I. Murphy	121	Philosophy	104			3,990	3:11.00	
1890	Tournament	3	Hayward	125	Banquet	118	Masterlode	104	6,100	2:16.00	
1891	Picknicker	3	Clayton	125	Hoodlum	115	Rey del Rey	129	6,250	2:22.75	
1892	Tammany	3	Garrison	129	Yorkville Belle	122	Azra	129	18,415	2:36.25	
1893	Young Arion	3	J. Lamley	93	Don Alonzo	130	Roche	110	3,190	2:08.75	
1894	Rubicon	3	Midgely	122	Declare	107	Harrington	110	5,260	2:09.75	
1895	Counter Tenor	3	Simms	121	Brandywine	105	Maurice	98	1,412	1:54.00	
1896	Souffle	3	J. Hill	112	The Winner	120	Rondo	108	1,950	2:09.25	
1897	Rensselaer	3	Howitt	116	Don d'Oro	115	Tillo	124	1,900	2:07.00	
1898	Handball	3	N. Turner	110	Whistling Con	104	Sailor King	106	2,185	2:06.00	
1899	King Barleycorn	3	Odom	114	Maid of Harlem	100	Sir Hubert	95	2,155	2:09.00	
1900	Alcedo	3	McCue	110	Gonfalon	106	McMeekin	121	2,030	2:07.00	
1901	Blues	3	Shaw	126	Baron Pepper	107	Hernando	111	1,995	2:05.75	
1902	Hermis	3	Rice	126	Hunter Raine	100	Oom Paul	110	2,240	2:06.20	
1903	Eugenia Burch	3	Fuller	116	Grey Friar	111			1,950	2:15.00	
1904	Ostrich	3	Crimmius	93	The Southerner	102	Outcome	106	2,325	2:13.00	
1905	Bedouin	3	Shaw	111	St. Bellane	102	Von Tromp	112	2,415	2:10.60	
1906	Ironsides	3	Radtke	107	Good Luck	114	Running Water	122	2,770	2:10.60	
1907	Perseverance	3	R. McDaniel	102	McCarter	114	Gretna Green	105	3,275	2:13.80	
1908	Fair Play	3	Gilbert	125	Master Robert	106	Gowan	95	2,940	2:10.40	
1909	Fitz Herbert	3	E. Dugan	130	Olambala	120	Mary Davis	99	1,060	2:11.00	
1914	Stromboli	3	C. Turner	117	Gainer	109	Figinny	108	1,060	2:36.60	
1915	Trial by Jury	3	T. McTaggart	127	The Finn	126	Hauberk	105	1,100	1:38.40	
1916	Spur	3	J. Loftus	130	Crimper	120	Air Man	105	2,350	1:39.00	
1917	Bally	3	L. Lyke	107	Straight Forward	114	Liberty Loan	126	2,175	1:38.00	
1918	Sunny Slope	3	J. Callahan	120	Motor Cop	123	Lady Gertrude	108	1,925	1:38.40	
1919	Thunderclap	3	L. Fator	117	Over There	115	Tetley	95	2,575	1:39.40	
1920	Busy Signal	3	C. Kummer	115	Pilgrim	96	On Watch	120	2,625	1:37.60	
1921	Tryster	3	F. Coltiletti	124	Knobbie	118	Frigate	102	2,375	1:38.20	
1922	Kai-Sang	3	L. Fator	133	Athelstan	100	Brainstorm	114	2,850	1:37.00	
1923	Cherry Pie	3	F. Coltiletti	113	Prince of Umbria	106	Flagstaff	120	2,975	1:35.40	
1924	Priscilla Ruley	3	J. Maiben	111	Mad Play	122	Initiate	107	3,400	1:37.80	
1925	Primrose	3	J. Maiben	106	Maid at Arms	114	Bright Steel	104	2,975	1:38.60	
1926	Croyden	3	L. McAtee	120	Edith Cavell	114	Bumpkin	109	3,275	1:38.00	
1927	Osmand	3	E. Sande	122	Jock	115	Candy Hog	100	3,250	1:38.00	
1928	Sun Edwin	3	L. McAtee	118	Royal Stranger	122	Sublevado	105	3,600	1:36.80	
1929	Soul of Honor	3	G. Fields	106	Chicatie	108	Comstockery	110	3,525	1:36.20	
1930	Mr. Sponge	3	M. Garner	117	Caruso	106	Questionnaire	126	3,200	1:37.40	
1931	Ironclad	3	L. Pinchon	102	Mountain Elk	111	Halcyon	109	3,050	1:37.00	
1932	Larranaga	3	R. Workman	117	Dark Secret	115	Sweeping Light	110	2,725	1:37.60	
1933	Golden Way	3	M. Garner	114	Sun Archer	114	Caesars Ghost	116	1,535	1:38.60	
1934	Kievex	3	W.D. Wright	115	Roustabout	111	Somebody	110	4,090	1:37.00	
1935	Good Harvest	3	S. Renick	107	Whopper	114	Psychic Bid	116	5,410	1:36.20	
1936	Goldeneye	3	I. Hanford	105	Maeriel	110	Tatterdemalion	107	5,290	1:36.60	
1937	Pasha	3	L. Balaski	117	Regal Lily	119	Rudie	122	4,920	1:38.20	

Year	Winner	Age	Jockey	Wt.	Second	Wt.	Third	Wt.	Win Value	Time	Beyer
1938	Cravat	3	A. Robertson	115	Can't Wait	116	The Chief	119	5,050	1:36.40	
1939	Easy Mon	3	L. Haas	110	Third Degree	120	Golden Voyage	116	7,225	1:35.80	
1940	Roman	3	W.D. Wright	121	Weigh Anchor	112	Tola Rose	116	6,425	1:37.20	
1941	Stimady	3	P. Roberts	110	Misty Isle	118	Minnelusa	110	6,825	1:37.20	
1942	King's Abbey	3	C. Bierman	112	Bless Me	122	Devil Diver	126	6,325	1:36.40	
1943	Slide Rule	3	J. Westrope	122	Eurasian	119	Famous Victory	115	7,075	1:37.00	
1944	Occupy	3	O. Grohs	110	Bounding Home	120	Free Lance	112	8,050	1:37.20	
1945	Buzfuz	3	T. Luther	115	Greek Warrior	114	Pavot	125	13,010	1:37.20	
1946	Mahout	3	E. Arcaro	114	Rippey	117	Athenia	112	14,000	1:37.00	
							Kitchen Police	108			
1947	Donor	3	J.D. Jessop	115	Cosmic Bomb	126	Cornish Knight	113	21,550	1:37.40	
1948	Coaltown	3	N.L. Pierson	126	Mount Marcy	115	Free America	126	21,450	1:36.00	
1949	Capot	3	T. Atkinson	126	Arise	116	Double Brandy	109	17,400	1:36.80	
1950	Hill Prince	3	E. Arcaro	129	Greek Ship	122	Navy Chief	108	17,150	1:35.80	
1951	Alerted	3	O. Scurlock	115	Mandingo	102	Hall of Fame	128	17,650	1:36.20	
1952	Tom Fool	3	T. Atkinson	120	Marcador	111	Mark-Ye-Well	130	17,100	1:37.00	
1953	Navy Page	3	N. Shuk	114	Scent	106	Landlocked	125	18,800	1:37.00	
							First Aid	118			
1954	Martyr	3	S. Small	110	Fisherman	126	Full Flight	118	18,000	1:35.80	
1955	Traffic Judge	3	E. Arcaro	126	Star Rover	121	Impromptu	118	21,750	1:35.20	
1956	Reneged	3	A. Valenzuela	117	Tick Tock	121	Countermand	115	21,550	1:35.40	
1957	Bold Ruler	3	E. Arcaro	130	Bureaucracy	113	Winged Mercury	106	19,950	1:35.00	
1958	Warhead	3	E. Arcaro	118	Piano Jim	121	Jester	118	19,362	1:37.20	
1959	Intentionally	3	M. Ycaza	126	Atoll	120	Seven Corners	110	35,995	1:35.40	
1960	Kelso	3	E. Arcaro	121	Careless John	116	Four Lane	119	37,945	1:34.80	
1961	Carry Back	3	J. Sellers	128	Garwol	111	Beau Prince	126	37,505	1:36.00	
1962	Black Beard	3	B. Baeza	114	Fauve	109	Dedimoud	116	38,285	1:34.60	
1963	Chateugay	3	B. Baeza	128	Accordant	117	Outing Class	123	37,245	1:36.00	
1964	Irvkup	3	J.L. Rotz	113	Lt. Stevens	114	Quadrangle	109	36,140	1:35.00	
1965	Bold Bidder	3	E. Nelson	110	Cornish Prince	123	Slystitch	114	38,870	1:36.00	
1966	Bold and Brave	3	B. Baeza	115	Understanding	107	Our Michael	116	37,765	1:38.00	
1967	High Tribute	3	L. Pincay Jr	113	In Reality	126	Jim J.	116	37,440	1:34.80	
1968	Iron Ruler	3	J. Velasquez	120	Captain's Gig	122	Dewan	119	38,220	1:35.20	
1969	Mr. Leader	3	J. Velasquez	113	Oil Power	110	Hydrologist	111	37,635	1:36.00	
1970	Great Mystery	3	P.I. Grimm	117	Knight of the Road	112	Estimator Dave	107	37,895	1:34.80	
1971	Tinajero	3	E. Belmonte	116	Twin Time	117	Sic Em Judge	117	34,200	1:35.80	
1972	True Knight	3	A. Cordero Jr	114	Tentam	116	Great Bear Lake	109	35,100	1:36.60	
1973	Step Nicely	3	A. Cordero Jr	118	Forego	124	Linda's Chief	126	34,800	1:34.00	
1974	Stonewalk	3	A. Cordero Jr	126	Best of It	117	Heir to the Line	113	34,470	1:34.00	
1975	Guards Up	3	C. Lopez	114	Valid Appeal	119	Great Above	114	33,720	1:34.20	
1976	Dance Spell	3	R. Hernandez	117	Soy Numero Uno	117	Clean Bill	112	66,600	1:35.00	
1977	Broadway Forli	3	P. Day	111	To the Quick	112	Affiliate	120	66,360	1:36.20	
1978	Sensitive Prince	3	J. Vasquez	118	Darby Creek Road	122	Sorry Lookin	112	62,940	1:36.00	
1979	Czaravich	3	J. Cruguet	122	Valdez	122	Gallant Best	112	65,580	1:35.20	
1980	Jaklin Klugman	3	C.J. McCarron	122	Fappiano	114	Plugged Nickle	124	67,320	1:34.20	
1981	Noble Nashua	3	C.B. Asmussen	120	Maudlin	112	Sing Sing	109	69,000	1:33.20	
1982	Fit to Fight	3	J.D. Bailey	112	John's Gold	115	Lord Lister	107	101,880	1:35.40	
1983	A Phenomenon	3	A. Cordero Jr	116	Desert Wine	124	Copelan	118	104,940	1:35.00	
1984	Is Your Pleasure	3	D. MacBeth	114	Track Barron	124	Concorde Bound	115	109,080	1:35.20	
1985	Creme Fraiche	3	E. Maple	124	Pancho Villa	119	El Basco	114	109,260	1:34.60	
1986	Ogygian	3	W.A. Guerra	126	Mogambo	119	Moment of Hope	111	127,620	1:34.00	
1987	Afleet	3	G. Stahlbaum	115	Stacked Pack	109	Templar Hill	117	107,640	1:33.80	
1988	Evening Kris	3	J.D. Bailey	119	Parlay Me	113	Din's Dancer	113	176,400	1:37.80	
1989	De Roche	3	D. Carr	108	Fast Play	116	I'm Influential	111	134,880	1:34.40	
1990	Housebuster	3	C. Perret	126	Citidancer	114	D'Parrot	112	102,060	1:34.00	118
1991	Scan	3	J.A. Santos	117	Excellent Tipper	113	King Mutesa	113	120,000	1:34.00	112
1992	Furiously	3	J.D. Bailey	113	Colony Light	111	Dixie Brass	122	120,000	1:34.20	107
1993	Schossberg	3	J.D. Bailey	118	Williamstown	118	Mi Cielo	116	120,000	1:35.40	104
1994	Prenup	3	J.D. Bailey	113	Ulises	112	End Sweep	118	120,000	1:34.40	108
1995	French Deputy	3	G.L Stevens	113	Mr. Greeley	117	Top Account	115	120,000	1:33.40	119
1996	Why Change	3	C.C. Lopez	112	Distorted Humor	115	Diligence	117	90,000	1:34.20	108
1997	Richter Scale	3	S.J. Sellers	118	Trafalger	117	Smokin Mel	115	90,000	1:35.80	111
1998	Limit Out	3	J.L. Samyn	117	Grand Slam	120	Scatmandu	115	90,000	1:36.20	105
1999	Doneraile Court	3	C.W. Antley	117	Vicar	120	Badger Gold	115	150,000	1:35.60	100
2000	Fusaichi Pegasus	3	K.J. Desormeaux	124	El Corredor	117	Albert The Great	120	90,000	1:34.07	115
2001	Express Tour	3	J.R. Velazquez	117	Illusioned	117	Burning Roma	120	90,000	1:34.57	104
2002	Boston Common	3	J.F. Chavez	118	Vinemeister	115	No Parole	115	90,000	1:36.12	107
2003	During	3	J.A. Santos	118	Tafaseel	114	Pretty Wild	116	90,000	1:36.32	99
2004	Teton Forest	3	S.X. Bridgmohan	116	Ice Wynnd Fire	116	Mahzouz	112	90,000	1:35.74	110

Beyer Index: 108.47

JERSEY DERBY (G3), 1 1/16 Miles (Turf), 3-Year-Olds, Monmouth Park, 2004 Purse: $100,000

Year	Winner	Age	Jockey	Wt.	Second	Wt.	Third	Wt.	Win Value	Time	Beyer
1942	Salto	3	W. Mehrtens	106	Trierarch	111	Air Current	110	8,450	1:49.80	
1943	Eurasian	3	F. Zehr	116	Royal Nap	110	Water Pearl	118	8,900	1:50.40	
1944	Lucky Draw	3	W.D. Wright	121	Megogo	103	Tex Martin	111	25,300	1:50.40	
1945	Trymenow	3	H. Linberg	118	Buzfuz	115	Turbine	114	25,850	1:51.80	
1946	Mahout	3	W.D. Wright	114	Assault	126	Blue Yonder	113	24,200	1:49.20	
1947	Double Jay	3	J. Gilbert	114	Fervent	125	Lighthouse	109	24,550	1:49.60	
1948	Citation	3	E. Arcaro	126	Macbeth	114	Faraway	111	43,300	2:03.00	
1949	Palestinian	3	H. Woodhouse	114	Olympia	126	Colonel Mike	111	40,700	2:01.80	
1950	Ferd	3	C. McCreary	118	Greek Song	114	Passemson	111	21,850	2:02.80	
1951	Steadfast	3	H. Woodhouse	110	Alerted	119	Joey Boy	112	23,900	2:04.40	
1952	King Jolie	3	J. Stout	111	Primate	118	Topside	111	25,850	2:03.60	
1953	Royal Bay Gem	3	J. Combest	118	Park Dandy	111	Better Goods	112	25,450	1:53.20	
1954	War of Roses	3	J. Westrope	111	Red Hannigan	111	High Gun	111	46,800	1:51.60	
1955	Dedicate	3	S. Boulmetis	118	Saratoga	118	Simmy	113	44,700	1:48.20	
1956	Fabius	3	W. Hartack	126	Kingmaker	111	Career Boy	118	44,700	1:48.80	
1957	Iron Liege	3	W. Hartack	126	Clem	118	We Trust	111	44,300	1:48.00	
1958	Lincoln Road	3	C. Rogers	111	Talent Show	118	Li'l Fella	118	37,865	1:49.00	
1959	Waltz	3	L. Gilligan	111	Scotland	114	Lake Erie	111	37,670	1:49.60	
1960	Bally Ache	3	R. Ussery	126	Tompion	126	Celtic Ash	126	77,995	1:49.00	
1961	Ambiopoise	3	R. Ussery	126	Crozier	126	Globemaster	126	80,600	1:49.20	
1962	Jaipur	3	L. Adams	126	Admiral's Voyage	126	Crimson Satan	126	84,955	1:49.00	
1963	Candy Spots	3	W. Shoemaker	126	Get Around	126	Sky Wonder	126	78,715	1:50.00	
1964	Roman Brother	3	F. Alvarez	126	Mr. Brick	126	National	126	81,445	1:49.60	
1965	Hail to All	3	J. Sellers	126	Reverse	126	Selari	128	86,905	1:48.60	
1966	Creme Dela Creme	3	D. Brumfield	126	Indulto	126	Fathers Image	126	89,635	1:49.60	
1967	In Reality	3	E. Fires	126	Air Rights	126	Gallant Moment	126	77,480	1:48.00	
1968	Out of the Way	3	E. Belmonte	126	Captain's Gig	126	Iron Ruler	126	87,555	1:49.00	
1969	Al Hattab	3	M. Hole	126	Ack Ack	126	Rooney's Shield	126	89,115	1:48.00	
1970	Personality	3	E. Belmonte	126	Corn off the Cob	126	Silent Screen	126	83,460	1:48.20	
1971	Bold Reasoning	3	J. Vasquez	126	Pass Catcher	126	Twist the Axe	126	87,360	1:49.60	
1972	Smiling Jack	3	F. Iannelli	126	Second Bar	126	Halo	126	89,180	1:50.60	
1973	Knightly Dawn	3	J. Arellano	122	Pvt. Smiles	122	Step Nicely	122	85,280	1:53.20	
1974	Better Arbitor	3	C. Barrerra	122	Stonewalk	122	Christoforo	122	104,000	1:50.40	
1975	Singh	3	A. Cordero Jr	122	Honey Mark	122	Bombay Duck	122	88,140	1:50.80	
1976	Life's Hope	3	M.A. Rivera	122	Cojak	122	Strawberry L'd'g	122	86,905	1:52.60	
1977	Cormorant	3	D.R. Wright	122	Iron Constitution	122	Hey Hey J.P.	122	80,730	1:50.40	
1981	Five Star Flight	3	C. Perret	118	Tap Shoes	126	Silver Express	118	107,775	1:50.00	
1982	Aloma's Ruler	3	A. Cordero Jr	126	Star Choice	126	Spanish Drums	126	90,000	1:49.60	
1983	World Appeal	3	J. Vasquez	118	Parfaitement	121	Princilian	121	60,000	1:46.60	
1984	Birdie's Legend	3	W.A. Guerra	118	Key to the Moon	126	Light Spirits	123	60,000	1:49.00	
1985	Spend a Buck	3	L. Pincay Jr	126	Creme Fraiche	126	El Basco	126	2,600,000	2:02.60	
1986	Snow Chief	3	A. Solis	126	Mogambo	126	Tasso	126	600,000	2:03.00	
1987	Avie's Copy	3	M. Solomone	126	Proudest Duke	126	Templar Hill	126	300,000	2:03.40	
1988	Dynaformer	3	C. Perret	126	Tsarbaby	126	Cefis	126	300,000	2:02.80	
1989	Awe Inspiring	3	C. Perret	126	Halo Hansom	126	Faultless Ensign	126	300,000	2:03.00	
1990	Yonder	3	J.D. Bailey	126	Video Ranger	126	Real Cash	126	300,000	2:04.40	
1991	Greek Costume	3	M.E. Smith	126	Subordinated Debt	126	Private Man	126	180,000	1:51.40	93
1992	American Chance	3	P. Day	126	Majestic Sweep	126	Palace Line	126	180,000	1:50.80	100
1993	Llandaff	3	J.A. Krone	116	Logroller	116	Forest Wins	116	90,000	1:42.40	98
1994	Zuno Star	3	M.E. Smith	116	Seattle Rob	116	Mr. Angel	126	90,000	1:43.80	91
							Warn Me	116			
1995	Da Hoss	3	J.A. Krone	119	Claudius	119	Crimson Guard	123	90,000	1:43.00	95
1996	More Royal	3	J.A. Krone	123	Optic Nerve	116	Value Investor	116	90,000	1:42.40	103
1997	Rob 'N Gin	3	J.D. Bailey	119	Tekken	123	Keep It Strait	121	90,000	1:40.80	96
1998	Who Did It and Run	3	F.L Ortiz	116	Essential	116	Cryptic Rascal	126	90,000	1:41.20	107
1999	Swamp	3	R. Migliore	124	Crash Course	117	Good Skate	117	90,000	1:40.80	100
2000	Lendell Ray	3	A.T. Gryder	114	Powerful Appeal	114	Cogburn	113	60,000	1:42.96	96
2001	Mystic Lady	3	F. Leon	114	Sir Brian's Sword	117	What's Your Wish	117	60,000	1:44.31	88
2002	Emergency Status	3	R. Alvarado Jr	122	Kris's Prayer	114	Rapadash	114	60,000	1:42.26	87
2003	Happy Trails	3	A.R. Toribio	114	Stone Canyon	114	Angelic Aura	115	60,000	1:45.40	89
2004	Icy Atlantic	3	C.C. Lopez	115	Commendation	122	Grand Heritage	117	60,000	1:44.51	93

Beyer Index: 95.43

Run on dirt prior to 1991. Run at 1 1/8 miles, 1942–47, 1953–84; at 1 1/4 miles, 1948–52, 1985–90. Off the turf, in 2001, 2003.

JERSEY SHORE BREEDERS' CUP (G3), 6 Furlongs, 3-Year-Olds, Monmouth Park, 2004 Purse: $95,000

Year	Winner	Age	Jockey	Wt.	Second	Wt.	Third	Wt.	Win Value	Time	Beyer
1992	Surely Six	3	R. Wilson	112	Superstrike	122	Salt Lake	119	64,230	1:21.80	103
1993	Montbrook	3	C.J. Ladmer III	122	Evil Bear	114	Shu Fellow	114	63,420	1:21.00	102
1994	End Sweep	3	M.E. Smith	115	Meadow Flight	122	Foxie G	115	63,300	1:21.20	95

Year	Winner	Age	Jockey	Wt.	Second	Wt.	Third	Wt.	Win Value	Time	Beyer
1995	Ft. Stockton	3	J. Bravo	115	Jealous Crusader	115	Gala Knockout	115	64,050	1:22.60	89
1996	Swing and Miss	3	T.G. Turner	112	Seacliff	119	Dixie Connection	115	60,000	1:10.00	96
1997	Smoke Glacken	4	C. Perret	122	Partner's Hero	115	King Buck	115	30,000	1:08.40	117
1998	Good and Tough	3	W.H. McCauley	115	Klabin's Gold	117	El Mirasol	112	45,000	1:10.00	94
1999	Yes It's True	3	J.D. Bailey	122	Erlton	122	Flying Griffoni	112	60,000	1:08.40	106
2000	Disco Rico	3	J. Bravo	115	Max's Pal	122	Stormin Oedy	117	60,000	1:09.05	99
2001	City Zip	3	J.C. Ferrer	119	Sea of Green	117	Songandaprayer	122	60,000	1:09.02	102
2002	Boston Common	3	E.M. Martin Jr	117	Listen Here	117	It's a Monster	115	60,000	1:09.35	103
2003	Gators n Bears	3	C.C. Lopez	115	Mt. Carson	122	Don Six	115	60,000	1:09.80	106
2004	Pomeroy	3	J. Bravo	113	Gotaghostofachance	115	Midnight Express	113	60,000	1:09.07	100

Beyer Index: 100.92

JIM DANDY (G2), 1 1/8 Miles,
3-Year-Olds, Saratoga Race Course, 2004 Purse: $500,000

Year	Winner	Age	Jockey	Wt.	Second	Wt.	Third	Wt.	Win Value	Time	Beyer
1964	Malicious	3	J.L. Rotz	119	Quadrangle	126	Knightly Manner	117	18,265	1:35.60	
1965	Cornish Prince	3	R. Turcotte	114	Pass the Word	114	Beaupy	114	18,655	1:35.60	
1966	Indulto	3	J.L. Rotz	119	Imam	114	Federalist Boy	114	18,427	1:37.00	
1967	Gala Performances	3	E. Belmonte	114	Great Power	119	Tumiga	119	19,565	1:36.20	
1968	Captain's Gig	3	M. Ycaza	119	Dewan	117	Pamir	114	18,817	1:35.80	
1969	Arts and Letters	3	B. Baeza	126	Gleaming Light	119	Mr. Mag	114	18,102	1:36.00	
1970	Personality	3	L. Pincay Jr	126	Loud	114	Plymouth	114	19,532	1:35.80	
1971	Brazen Brother	3	M. Hole	114	Marshua's Dancer	114	Silver Mallet	114	20,820	1:22.80	
1972	Tentam	3	J. Velasquez	114	True Knight	115	Halo	114	17,430	1:49.60	
1973	Cheriepe	3	E. Belmonte	117	Arbees Boy	120	Bemo	123	17,310	1:50.20	
1974	Sea Songster	3	A. Cordero Jr	114	Hatchet Man	120	Bobby Murcer	114	22,860	1:50.60	
1975	Forceten	3	D. Pierce	126			Northerly	114	25,725	1:48.40	
1976	Father Hogan	3	M. Venezia	114	Dance Spell	121	El Portugues	114	22,410	1:48.80	
1977	Music of Time	3	M. Venezia	114	Sanhedrin	114	Super Joy	114	22,830	1:50.40	
1978	Affirmed	3	S. Cauthen	128	Sensitive Prince	119	Addison	114	22,155	1:47.80	
1979	Private Account	3	J. Fell	114	Instrument Landing	126	Pianist	114	25,500	1:48.40	
1980	Plugged Nickle	3	J. Fell	128	Current Legend	121	Herb Water	114	34,140	1:49.40	
1981	Willow Hour	3	E. Maple	117	Lemhi Gold	117	Silver Supreme	114	34,200	1:49.20	
1982	Conquistador Cielo	3	E. Maple	126	Lejoli	114	No Home Run	114	32,700	1:48.60	
1983	A Phenomenon	3	A. Cordero Jr	114	Timeless Native	126	Head of the House	114	33,900	1:49.40	
1984	Carr de Naskra	3	E. Maple	114	Slew the Coup	114	Raja's Shark	114	75,720	1:47.40	
1985	Stephan's Odyssey	3	L. Pincay Jr	123	Don's Choice	114	Government Corner	121	73,080	1:48.80	
1986	Lac Ouimet	3	E. Maple	114	Moment of Hope	114	Wayar	114	69,360	1:48.00	
1987	Polish Navy	3	P. Day	117	Pledge Card	117	Cryptoclearance	126	106,740	1:48.40	
1988	Brian's Time	3	A. Cordero Jr	126	Evening Kris	121	Din's Dancer	114	109,980	1:48.20	
1989	Is It True	3	J.A. Santos	121	Fast Play	114	Roi Danzig	126	99,180	1:48.40	
1990	Chief Honcho	3	M.E. Smith	114	Senator to Be	114	Paradise Found	114	67,680	1:51.60	
1991	Fly So Free	3	J.A. Santos	126	Upon My Soul	114	Strike the Gold	128	107,820	1:48.80	106
1992	Thunder Rumble	3	W.H. McCauley	117	Dixie Brass	126	Devil His Due	126	108,000	1:47.40	110
1993	Miner's Mark	3	C.J. McCarron	117	Virginia Rapids	121	Colonial Affair	126	90,000	1:49.00	105
1994	Unaccounted For	3	J.A. Santos	114	Tabasco Cat	103	Ulises	114	80,820	1:49.60	108
1995	Composer	3	J.D. Bailey	112	Malthus	112	Pat n Jac	112	82,575	1:51.00	106
1996	Louis Quatorze	3	P. Day	124	Will's Way	114	Secreto de Estado	114	90,000	1:47.20	119
1997	Awesome Again	3	M.E. Smith	116	Glitman	114	Affirmed Success	114	150,000	1:51.00	107
1998	Favorite Trick	3	P. Day	119	Deputy Diamond	114	Raffie's Majesty	114	150,000	1:50.00	103
1999	Ecton Park	3	A. Solis	116	Lemon Drop Kid	124	Badger Gold	114	180,000	1:49.40	112
2000	Graeme Hall	3	J.D. Bailey	120	Curule	114	Unshaded	120	240,000	1:48.95	106
2001	Scorpion	3	J.D. Bailey	114	Free Of Love	114	Congaree	123	360,000	1:48.90	105
2002	Medaglia d'Oro	3	J.D. Bailey	121	Gold Dollar	115	Essence of Dubai	115	300,000	1:47.82	120
	Quest finished second but was disqualified and placed eighth										
2003	Strong Hope	3	J.R. Velazquez	121	Empire Maker	123	Congrats	115	300,000	1:48.10	110
2004	Purge	3	J.R. Velazquez	121	The Cliff's Edge	123	Niigon	117	300,000	1:47.56	109
	Eddington finished third but was disqualified and placed fourth										

Beyer Index: 109.00

JOCKEY CLUB GOLD CUP (G1), 1 1/4 Miles,
3-Year-Olds and Up, Belmont Park, 2004 Purse: $1,000,000

Year	Winner	Age	Jockey	Wt.	Second	Wt.	Third	Wt.	Win Value	Time	Beyer
1919	Purchase	3	C. Kummer	118					5,350	2:41.60	
1920	Man o' War	3	C. Kummer	118	Damask	118			5,850	2:28.80	
1921	Mad Hatter	5	E. Sande	125	Grey Lad	114	T. Me Not	114	12,100	3:22.40	
1922	Mad Hatter	6	E. Sande	125	Bit of White	122	Pillory	114	12,700	3:22.60	
1923	Homestretch	3	C. Lang	114	Vigil	114	Pettifogger	114	11,300	3:24.20	
1924	My Play	5	A. Schuttinger	125	King Solomon's Seal	125	My Own	125	14,150	3:25.60	
1925	Altawood	4	E. Sande	120	Aga Khan	125	Swope	114	13,050	3:24.60	
1926	Crusader	3	J. Maiben	114	Espino	114	Altawood	125	13,300	3:26.00	
1927	Chance Play	4	E. Sande	125	Display	125	F'er and Ever	125	12,000	3:23.00	
	Brown Bud finished first but was disqualified										

Year	Winner	Age	Jockey	Wt.	Second	Wt.	Third	Wt.	Win Value	Time	Beyer
1928	Reigh Count	3	C. Lang	114	Chance Shot	125	Display	125	10,850	3:23.00	
1929	Diavolo	4	J. Maiben	125	Double Pay	125	The Nut	114	10,900	3:24.00	
1930	Gallant Fox	3	E. Sande	118	Yarn	114	Frisius	125	10,300	3:24.40	
1931	Twenty Grand	3	C. Kurtsinger	114	Blenheim	114	Barometer	114	10,400	3:23.40	
1932	Gusto	3	B. Hanford	114	Blenheim	125	Masked Knight	118	9,950	3:25.20	
1933	Dark Secret	4	H. Mills	125	Gusto	125	Equipoise	125	6,400	3:25.20	
1934	Dark Secret	5	C. Kurtsinger	125	Faireno	125	Inlander	125	6,200	3:24.60	
1935	Firethorn	3	E. Arcaro	117	Judy o' Grady	114	Gallant Prince	117	6,550	3:24.20	
1936	Count Arthur	4	J. Stout	124	Memory Book	117	Giant Killer	117	6,750	3:24.40	
1937	Firethorn	5	H. Richards	124	Count Arthur	124	Moonton	117	6,050	3:26.00	
1938	War Admiral	4	W.D. Wright	124	Magic Hour	117	Jolly Tar	117	5,500	3:24.80	
1939	Cravat	4	B. James	124	Isolater	124	Shangay Lily	121	5,550	3:23.00	
1940	Fenelon	3	J. Stout	114	Iron Shot	114	Olympus	125	6,700	3:24.40	
1941	Market Wise	3	B. James	114	Whirlaway	114	Fenelon	125	7,325	3:20.80	
1942	Whirlaway	4	G. Woolf	124	Alsab	117	Bolingbroke	124	18,350	3:21.60	
1943	Princequillo	3	C. McCreary	117	Fairy Manhurst	117	Bolingbroke	117	18,350	3:21.60	
1944	Bolingbroke	7	R. Permane	125	Strategic	125	Devil Diver	125	17,645	3:27.20	
1945	Pot o' Luck	3	D. Dodson	114	Eurasian	125	Stymie	125	18,335	3:27.40	
1946	Pavot	4	E. Arcaro	124	Stymie	124	Rico Monte	124	18,250	3:22.60	
1947	Phalanx	3	R. Donoso	117	Talon	124	Stymie	124	17,850	3:21.60	
1948	Citation	3	E. Arcaro	117	Phalanx	124	Beauchef	124	72,700	3:21.60	
1949	Ponder	3	S. Brooks	117	Flying Missel	124	Miss Request	121	36,300	3:22.80	
1950	Hill Prince	3	E. Arcaro	117	Noor	124	Adile	121	36,000	3:23.40	
1951	Counterpoint	3	D. Gorman	117	Hill Prince	124	Kiss Me Kate	114	35,600	3:21.60	
1952	One Count	3	D. Gorman	117	Mark-Ye-Well	117	Crafty Admiral	124	52,100	3:24.20	
1953	Level Lea	3	W. Boland	117	Alerted	124	Platan	117	55,100	3:27.00	
1954	High Gun	3	E. Arcaro	119	Fisherman	119	Bicarb	124	55,150	3:25.80	
1955	Nashua	3	E. Arcaro	119	Thinking Cap	119	Mark's Puzzle	119	52,850	3:24.80	
1956	Nashua	4	E. Arcaro	124	Riley	119	Third Brother	119	36,600	3:20.40	
1957	Gallant Man	3	W. Shoemaker	119	Third Brother	124	Reneged	124	53,850	3:23.00	
1958	Inside Tract	4	C. McCreary	124	Dotted Line	121	Civet	124	52,417	3:23.40	
1959	Sword Dancer	3	E. Arcaro	119	Round Table	124	Tudor Era	124	70,790	3:22.20	
1960	Kelso	3	E. Arcaro	119	Don Poggio	124	Bald Eagle	124	70,205	3:19.40	
1961	Kelso	4	E. Arcaro	124	Hillsborough	124	Peace Isle	124	68,770	3:25.80	
1962	Kelso	5	I. Valenzuela	124	Guadalcanal	124	Nickel Boy	124	70,785	3:19.80	
1963	Kelso	6	I. Valenzuela	124	Guadalcanal	124	Garwol	124	70,785	3:22.00	
1964	Kelso	7	I. Valenzuela	124	Roman Brother	119	Quadrangle	119	70,785	3:19.20	
1965	Roman Brother	4	B. Baeza	124	Berenjenal	124	Brave Lad	124	71,500	3:22.60	
1966	Buckpasser	3	B. Baeza	119	Niarkos	124	O'Hara	124	71,825	3:26.20	
1967	Damascus	3	W. Shoemaker	119	Handsome Boy	124	Successor	119	69,290	3:20.20	
1968	Quicken Tree	5	W. Hartack	124	Funny Fellow	119	Chompion	119	71,370	3:22.80	
1969	Arts and Letters	3	B. Baeza	119	Nodouble	124	Harem Lady	121	69,030	3:22.40	
1970	Shuvee	4	R. Turcotte	121	Loud	119	Hydrologist	124	70,785	3:21.60	
1971	Shuvee	5	J. Velasquez	121	Paraje	124	Loud	124	66,900	3:20.40	
1972	Autobiography	4	A. Cordero Jr	124	Key to the Mint	119	Riva Ridge	119	68,220	3:21.60	
1973	Prove Out	4	J. Velasquez	124	Loud	124	Twice a Prince	119	66,060	3:20.00	
1974	Forego	4	H. Gustines	124	Copte	124	Group Plan	124	67,140	3:21.20	
1975	Group Plan	5	J. Velasquez	124	Wajima	119	Outdoors	124	95,850	3:23.20	
1976	Great Contractor	3	P. Day	121	Appassopmayp	121	Revidere	118	201,360	2:28.80	
1977	On the Sly	4	G. McCarron	126	Great Contractor	126	Cox's Ridge	121	208,080	2:28.20	
1978	Exceller	5	W. Shoemaker	126	Seattle Slew	126	Great Contractor	126	193,080	2:27.20	
1979	Affirmed	4	L. Pincay Jr	126	Spectacular Bid	121	Coastal	121	225,000	2:27.40	
1980	Temperence Hill	3	E. Maple	121	John Henry	126	Ivory Hunter	126	329,400	2:30.20	
1981	John Henry	6	W. Shoemaker	126	Peat Moss	126	Relaxing	123	340,800	2:28.40	
1982	Lemhi Gold	4	C.J. McCarron	126	Silver Supreme	126	Christmas Past	118	337,800	2:31.20	
1983	Slew o' Gold	3	A. Cordero Jr	121	Highland Blade	126	Bounding Basque	126	342,000	2:26.20	
1984	Slew o' Gold	4	A. Cordero Jr	126	Hail Bold King	121	Bounding Basque	126	1,350,400	2:28.80	
1985	Vanlandingham	4	P. Day	126	Gate Dancer	126	Creme Fraiche	121	516,600	2:27.00	
1986	Creme Fraiche	4	R.P. Romero	126	Turkoman	126	Danzig Connection	121	510,300	2:28.00	
1987	Creme Fraiche	5	L. Pincay Jr	126	Java Gold	121	Easy n Dirty	126	650,400	2:30.80	
1988	Waquoit	5	J.A. Santos	126	Personal Flag	126	Easy n Dirty	126	637,800	2:27.60	
1989	Easy Goer	3	P. Day	121	Cryptoclearance	126	Forever Silver	126	659,400	2:29.20	
1990	Flying Continental	4	C.A. Black	126	De Roche	126	Izvestia	121	503,100	2:00.60	117
1991	Festin	5	E. Delahoussaye	126	Chief Honcho	126	Strike the Gold	121	510,000	2:00.60	114
1992	Pleasant Tap	5	G.L. Stevens	126	Strike the Gold	126	A.P. Indy	121	510,000	1:58.80	117
1993	Miner's Mark	3	C.J. McCarron	121	Colonial Affair	121	Brunswick	126	510,000	2:02.60	106
1994	Colonial Affair	4	J.A. Santos	126	Devil His Due	126	Flag Down	126	450,000	2:02.00	113
1995	Cigar	5	J.D. Bailey	126	Unaccounted For	126	Star Standard	121	450,000	2:01.20	111
1996	Skip Away	3	S.J. Sellers	121	Cigar	126	Louis Quatorze	121	600,000	2:00.60	115
1997	Skip Away	4	J.D. Bailey	126	Instant Friendship	126	Wagon Limit	121	600,000	1:58.80	116
1998	Wagon Limit	4	R.G. Davis	126	Gentlemen	126	Skip Away	126	600,000	2:00.62	115
1999	River Keen	7	C.W. Antley	126	Behrens	126	Almutawakel	126	600,000	2:01.40	117
2000	Albert the Great	3	J.F. Chavez	122	Gander	126	Vision and Verse	126	600,000	1:59.24	119

Year	Winner	Age	Jockey	Wt.	Second	Wt.	Third	Wt.	Win Value	Time	Beyer
2001	Aptitude	4	J.D. Bailey	126	Generous Rosi	126	Country Be Gold	126	600,000	2:01.49	123
2002	Evening Attire	4	S.X. Bridgmohan	126	Lido Palace	126	Harlan's Holiday	122	600,000	1:59.58	114
2003	Mineshaft	4	R. Albarado	126	Quest	126	Evening Attire	126	600,000	2:00.25	114
2004	Funny Cide	4	J.A. Santos	126	Newfoundland	126	The Cliff's Edge	122	600,000	2:02.44	112

Beyer Index: 114.87

Distance 2 miles 1921–75; 1 1/2 miles, 1919 and 1920, 1976–89. Run at Aqueduct 1958–61, 1963–67, 1969–74. Slew o' Gold won a $1 million bonus in 1984 for winning the Woodward, Marlboro Cup, and Jockey Club Gold Cup.

JUST A GAME BREEDERS' CUP HANDICAP (G2), 1 Mile (Turf), Fillies and Mares, 3-Year-Olds and Up, Belmont Park, 2004 Purse: $226,333

Year	Winner	Age	Jockey	Wt.	Second	Wt.	Third	Wt.	Win Value	Time	Beyer
1995	Caress	5	R.Davis	119	Coronation Cup	119	Grafin	117	49,320	1:32.40	108
1996	Caress	6	R.Davis	117	Class Kris	122	Upper Noosh	112	94,890	1:33.20	106
	Class Kris finished first but was disqualified and placed second										
1997	Memories of Silver	4	J.Bailey	120	Dynasty	113	Elusive	115	95,370	1:33.33	104
1998	Witchful Thinking	4	McCarron C. J.	118	Sopran Mariduff	117	Dixie Ghost	111	95,745	1:33.40	101
1999	Cozy Blues	5	J.F. Chavez	112	U R Unforgetable	114	Mysterious Moll	115	94,620	1:33.20	101
2000	Peerfect Sting	4	J.D. Bailey	121	Ronda	116	Snow Polina	116	111,800	1:34.48	101
2001	License Fee	6	P. Day	118	Shopping for Love	114	Veil of Avalon	115	114,780	1:32.62	105
2002	Babae	6	J.F. Chavez	115	Tates Creek	117	Stylish	116	67,920	1:34.57	102
2003	Mariensky	4	J.A. Santos	116	Riskaverse	119	Wonder Again	119	128,700	1:43.28	108
2004	Intercontinental	4	J.D. Bailey	118	Vanguardia	113	Etoile Montante	121	150,000	1:33.33	103

Beyer Index: 103.90

KELSO BREEDERS' CUP HANDICAP (G2), 1 Mile (Turf), 3-Year-Olds and Up, Belmont Park, 2004 Purse: $270,000

Year	Winner	Age	Jockey	Wt.	Second	Wt.	Third	Wt.	Win Value	Time	Beyer
1980	Peat Moss	5	F. Lovato Jr	108	Ivory Hunter	114	Ring of Light	117	68,160	3:24.60	
1981	Peat Moss	6	F. Lovato Jr	126	Field Cat	114	Birthday List	114	66,240	3:20.80	
1982	Worthy Too	4	J.L. Samyn	109	Nice Pirate	112	J'd'sa T'k'r	113	69,840	3:24.40	
1984	Who's for Dinner	5	W.A. Guerra	115	Pin Puller	112	Norwick	109	71,100	2:01.20	
1985	Mourjane	5	R. Migliore	117	Cool	116	Palace Panther	116	70,560	2:02.00	
1986	I'm a Banker	4	A. Graell	111	Duluth	113	Premier Mister	113	54,720	2:03.20	
1987	I'm a Banker	5	A. Graell	107	Tertiary Zone	113	Island Sun	112	76,920	2:10.80	
1988	Sans the Shadow	4	C.W. Antley	116	Posen	117	Tinchens Prince	114	72,240	1:42.00	
1989	I Rejoice	6	J.D. Bailey	114	Quick Call	113	Wanderkin	118	75,360	1:36.40	
1990	Expensive Decision	4	J.L. Samyn	112	Who's to Pay	115	Great Commot'n	113	57,420	1:32.40	112
1991	Star of Cozzene	3	J.A. Santos	113	Known Ranger	113	Fourstardave	117	69,720	1:33.20	106
1992	Roman Envoy	4	C. Perret	117	Lure	111	Val des Bois	118	120,000	1:36.20	108
1993	Lure	4	M.E. Smith	125	Paradise Creek	120	Daarik	112	120,000	1:35.80	111
1994	Nijinsky's Gold	5	Santos JA	114	Lure	128	A in Sociology	117	120,000	1:34.00	110
1995	Mighty Forum	4	E. Delahoussaye	115	Fastness	119	Dowty	112	120,000	1:39.40	105
1996	Same Old Wish	6	S.J. Sellers	113	Da Hoss	120	Volochine	116	105,000	1:34.60	106
1997	Lucky Coin	4	R.G. Davis	119	Hawksley Hill	115	Colcon	112	120,000	1:33.60	112
1998	Dixie Bayou	5	J.F. Chavez	112	Sahm	115	Let Goodtimes Roll	112	120,000	1:36.20	103
1999	Middlesex Drive	4	S.J. Sellers	117	Divide and Conquer	114	Wised Up	113	150,000	1:35.40	110
2000	Forbidden Apple	5	J.L. Samyn	116	Affirmed Success	120	Johnny Dollar	113	150,000	1:34.39	109
2001	Forbidden Apple	6	J.A. Santos	118	Sarafan	114	City Zip	112	150,000	1:36.77	104
2002	Green Fee	6	J.R. Velazquez	113	Forbidden Apple	121	Moon Solitaire	117	210,000	1:33.83	110
2003	Freefourinternet	5	J.L. Espinoza	113	Proud Man	114	Rouvres	115	210,000	1:34.73	105
2004	Mr O'Brien	5	E.M. Coa	119	Millennium Dragon	119	Gulch Approval	114	150,000	1:32.69	108

Beyer Index: 107.93

KENT BREEDERS' CUP (G3), 1 1/8 Miles (Turf), 3-Year-Olds, Delaware Park, 2004 Purse: $250,900

Year	Winner	Age	Jockey	Wt.	Second	Wt.	Third	Wt.	Win Value	Time	Beyer
1982	Cagey Cougar	3	V. Bracciale Jr	113	King's Dusty		Big Shot		14,600	1:44.20	
1996	Sir Cat	3	J.Bailey	113	Optic Nerve	122	Fortitude	116	60,000	1:52.80	108
1997	Royal Strand	3	P. Day	122	Subordination	122	Broad Choice	113	90,000	1:48.00	94
1998	Keene Dancer	3	P. Day	117	Red Reef		Danielle's Gray		120,000	1:50.60	97
1999	North East Bound	3	J.A. Velez Jr	114	Courtside	113	Swamp	119	150,000	1:51.80	96
2000	Three Wonders	3	P. Day	115	Field Cat	117	Dawn of the Condor	115	150,000	1:48.95	98
2001	Navesink	3	R.A. Dominguez	115	Bowman Mill	115	Harrisand	115	151,000	1:49.98	95
2002	Miesque's Approval	3	J.D. Bailey	115	Regal Sanction	115	Quest Star	115	150,000	1:48.81	99
							Coco's Madness	115			
2003	Foufa's Warrior	3	R.A. Dominguez	115	Remind	115	Lismore Knight	119	150,000	1:47.44	95
2004	Timo	3	R. Migliore	117	Icy Atlantic	117	Commendation	115	150,000	1:55.75	90

Beyer Index: 96.89

For previous runnings, refer to 1980 Manual.

KENTUCKY BREEDERS' CUP (G3), 5 1/2 Furlongs, 2-Year-Olds, Churchill Downs, 2004 Purse: $132,088

Year	Winner	Age	Jockey	Wt.	Second	Wt.	Third	Wt.	Win Value	Time	Beyer
1988	Island Esccape	2	C. Woods Jr	115	One That Got Away		Papa Leonard			1:04.60	
1989	Summer Squall	2	C. Woods Jr	118	Dr. Bobby A.		Wink Road			1:05.00	
1990	To Freedom	2	J. Espinoza	118	St. Alegis		Maxwell Street			1:05.00	
1991	Hippomenes	2	P. Day	112	Cold Gate		It's Chemistry			1:06.20	
1992	Tempered Halo	2	P. Johnson	121	Mountain Cat		Secret Bundle		50,320	1:05.39	73
	Exclusive Zone finished second but was disqualified and placed fourth										
1993	Asta's Foxy Lady	2	T. Hebert	118	Dish It Out		Riverinn		68,737	1:05.51	77
1994	My My	2	S.J. Sellers	116	Wise Affair		Hyroglyphic		37,310	1:05.96	69
1995	Miraloma	2	D.M. Barton	112	Great Southern		A.V. Eight		68,932	1:04.04	82
1996	Move	2	S.J. Sellers	113	Prairie Junction	115	Live Your Best	112	71,175	1:05.74	91
1997	Favorite Trick	2	P. Day	121	Jess M	115	Cutie Luttie	112	68,882	1:04.80	91
1998	Yes It's True	2	S.J. Sellers	121	Tactical Cat	115	Alannan	115	85,948	1:03.61	97
1999	Chilukki	2	R.J. Albarado	112	Barrier	115	Sky Dweller	115	106,485	1:04.01	93
2000	Gold Mover	2	C. Perret	113	City Zip	115	Unbridled Time	121	101,091	1:03.67	94
2001	Leelanau	2	J.K. Court	115	Gygistar	115	Lakeside Cup	112	100,812	1:03.11	89
2002	Posse	2	D.J. Meche	115	Del Diablo	115	Blackjack Boy	115	102,300	1:03.73	85
2003	Cuvee	2	L.J. Meche	117	First Money	117	Exploit Lad	117	109,554	1:04.45	93
2004	Lunarpal	2	S.J. Sellers	121	Consolidator	115	Smoke Warning	117	86,025	1:04.07	84

Beyer Index: 86.00

KENTUCKY CUP CLASSIC HANDICAP (G2), 1 1/8 Miles, 3-Year-Olds and Up, Turfway Park, 2004 Purse: $350,000

Year	Winner	Age	Jockey	Wt.	Second	Wt.	Third	Wt.	Win Value	Time	Beyer
1994	Tabasco Cat	3	P. Day	120	Mighty Avanti	115	Best Pal	115	260,000	1:50.20	103
1995	Thunder Gulch	3	G.L. Stevens	121	Judge TC	112	Bound by Honor	113	260,000	1:49.40	108
1996	Atticus	4	C.S. Nakatani	115	Judge TC	116	Isitingood	114	325,000	1:47.40	109
1997	Semoran	4	K.J. Desormeaux	116	Distorted Humor	116	Coup d'Argent	114	217,000	1:48.00	107
1998	Silver Charm	4	G.L. Stevens	123			Acceptable	117	207,250	1:47.40	123
	Wild Rush	4	P. Day	117							
1999	Da Devil	4	C.H. Borel	112	Social Charter	115	Cat Thief	117	314,500	1:50.40	108
2000	Captain Steve	3	S.J. Sellers	115	Golden Missile	121	Early Pioneer	120	314,500	1:49.95	116
2001	Guided Tour	5	L. Melancon	118	Balto Star	114	A Fleets Dancer	115	254,000	1:47.90	113
2002	Pure Prize	4	M.E. Smith	115	Dollar Bill	117	Hero's Tribute	113	254,000	1:51.24	108
2003	Perfect Drift	4	P. Day	120	Congaree	124	Crafty Shaw	115	221,500	1:50.43	112
2004	Roses in May	4	J.R. Velazquez	118	Pie n Burger	117	Sonic West	113	221,500	1:49.13	105

Beyer Index: 110.18

KENTUCKY CUP JUVENILE (G3), 1 1/16 Miles, 2-Year-Olds, Turfway Park, 2004 Purse: $100,000

Year	Winner	Age	Jockey	Wt.	Second	Wt.	Third	Wt.	Win Value	Time	Beyer
1986	Rainbow East	2	O.B. Aviles	120	Alysheba	120	David L.'s Rib	120	78,500	1:37.20	
1987	Jim's Orbit	2	P. Day	120	Kingpost	120	Delightful Doctor	120	81,250	1:37.80	
1988	Light Crude	2	R. Frazier	120	Bravoure	120	Revive	120	81,250	1:44.80	
1989	Fighting Fantasy	2	D.W. Cox	120	Top Snob	120	Hardburly	120	81,250	1:48.40	
1990	Fire in Ice	2	J.A. Garcia	120	Wall Street Dancer	120	Gold Shoulder	120	81,250	1:46.60	
1991	Star Recruit	2	R.D. Lopez	120	Pick up the Phone	120	Battenburg	120	97,500	1:45.60	94
1992	Mountain Cat	2	C.R. Woods Jr	120	Saw Mill	120	Shoal Creek	120	97,500	1:43.40	86
1993	Bibury Court	2	S.T. Saito	120	Moving Van	120	Durham	120	81,250	1:47.60	78
1994	Tejano Run	2	J.D. Bailey	120	Gold Miner	120	Bick	120	65,000	1:46.00	80
1995	Editor's Note	2	G.L. Stevens	115	Devil's Honor	118	Never to Squander	110	65,000	1:45.00	87
1996	Boston Harbor	2	D.M. Barton	120	Play Waki for Me	118	Dr. Spine	112	65,000	1:42.80	90
1997	Laydown	2	M.E. Smith	114	Time Limit	118	Da Devil	114	62,600	1:43.00	92
1998	Aly's Alley	2	P.A. Johnson	118	Time Bandit	120	Mac's Rule	116	62,600	1:45.60	78
1999	Millencolin	2	P. Day	114	Personal First	118	Deputy Warlock	118	62,600	1:47.00	86
2000	Point Given	2	S.J. Sellers	114	Holiday Thunder	114	The Goo	116	62,600	1:47.01	81
2001	Repent	2	A.J. D'Amico	114	French Assault	118	Gold Dollar	114	62,750	1:43.78	90
2002	Vindication	2	M.E. Smith	116	Private Gold	118	Tito's Beau	114	62,750	1:46.70	87
2003	Mr. Jester	2	R. Bejarano	118	The Cliff's Edge	114	Pomeroy	116	62,000	1:46.61	85
	Pomeroy finished first but was disqualified and placed third										
2004	Greater Good	2	J. McKee	114	Magna Graduate	114	Norainonthisparty	114	62,000	1:44.96	81

Beyer Index: 85.36

KENTUCKY CUP SPRINT (G3), 6 Furlongs, 3-Year-Olds, Turfway Park, 2004 Purse: $100,000

Year	Winner	Age	Jockey	Wt.	Second	Wt.	Third	Wt.	Win Value	Time	Beyer
1994	End Sweep	3	C.J. McCarron	120	Exclusive Praline	122	Chimes Band	122	97,500	1:09.80	104
1995	Lord Carson	3	M.E. Smith	116	Ft. Stockton	122	Evansville Slew	116	97,500	1:08.60	119
1996	Appealing Skier	3	M.E. Smith	118	Capote Belle	119	Delay of Game	114	97,500	1:08.20	109

Year	Winner	Age	Jockey	Wt.	Second	Wt.	Third	Wt.	Win Value	Time	Beyer
1997	Partner's Hero	3	P. Day	114	Oro de Mexico	116	Prosong	114	74,400	1:09.00	100
1998	Reraise	3	C.S. Nakatani	116	Copelan Too	114	Mr. Bert	114	93,900	1:08.40	119
1999	Successful Appeal	3	E.S. Prado	122	Five Star Day	114	American Spirit	118	74,400	1:09.40	119
2000	Caller One	3	K.J. Desormeaux	120	Millencolin	116	Kings Command	116	93,750	1:09.46	117
2001	Snow Ridge	3	P. Day	114	City Zip	122	Dream Run	117	94,500	1:09.22	103
2002	Day Trader	3	P. Day	118	Premier Performer	114	Ecstatic	114	94,500	1:10.01	108
2003	Cajun Beat	3	C. Velasquez	122	Clock Stopper	116	Champali	122	62,000	1:09.54	113
2004	Level Playingfield	3	J. McKee	116	Cuvee	116	Swift Attraction	116	62,000	1:09.76	97

Beyer Index: 109.82

KENTUCKY CUP TURF HANDICAP (G3), 1 1/2 Miles (Turf), 3-Year-Olds and Up, Kentucky Downs, 2004 Purse: $200,000

Year	Winner	Age	Jockey	Wt.	Second	Wt.	Third	Wt.	Win Value	Time	Beyer
2000	Down the Aisle	7	R.J. Albarado	102	Crowd Pleaser	113	Royal Strand	115	186,000	2:27.60	102
2001	Chorwon	8	J.K. Court	113	The Knight Sky	114	Man From Wicklow	114	186,000	2:28.68	104
2002	Rochester	6	E.M. Martin Jr	115	Nowrass	112	Continental Red	117	186,000	2:38.28	107
2003	Rochester	7	E.M. Martin Jr	116	Quest Star	116	Art Variety	111	124,000	2:31.39	97
	Art Variety finished first but was disqualified and placed third										
2004	Sabiango	6	B. Blanc	119	Rochester	117	Gottabeachboy	115	124,000	2:33.70	95

Beyer Index: 101.00

KENTUCKY DERBY (G1), 1 1/4 Miles, 3-Year-Olds, Churchill Downs, 2004 Purse: $6,154,800

Year	Winner	Age	Jockey	Wt.	Second	Wt.	Third	Wt.	Win Value	Time	Beyer
1875	Aristides	3	O. Lewis	100	Volcano	100	Verdigris	100	2,850	2:37.60	
1876	Vagrant	3	R. Swim	97	Creedmoor	100	Harry Hill	100	2,950	2:38.20	
1877	Baden Baden	3	W. Walker	100	Leonard	100	King William	100	3,300	2:38.00	
1878	Day Star	3	J. Carter	100	Himyar	100	Leveler	100	4,050	2:37.20	
1879	Lord Murphy	3	C. Schauer	100	Falsetto	100	Strathmore	100	3,550	2:37.00	
1880	Fonso	3	G. Lewis	105	Kimball	105	Bancroft	105	3,800	2:37.20	
1881	Hindoo	3	J. McLaughlin	105	Lelex	102	Alhambra	105	4,410	2:40.00	
1882	Apollo	3	B. Hurd	102	Runnymede	105	Bengal	105	4,560	2:40.20	
1883	Leonatus	3	W. Donohue	110	Drake Carter	107	Lord Raglan	110	3,760	2:43.00	
1884	Buchanan	3	I. Murphy	110	Loftin	110	Audrain	110	3,990	2:40.20	
1885	Joe Cotton	3	E. Henderson	110	Bersan	110	Ten Booker	110	4,630	2:37.00	
1886	Ben Ali	3	P. Duffy	118	Blue Wing	118	Free Knight	118	4,890	2:36.20	
1887	Montrose	3	I. Lewis	118	Jim Gore	118	Jackobin	118	4,200	2:39.20	
1888	MacBeth II	3	G. Covington	118	Gallifet	118	White	118	4,740	2:38.20	
1889	Spokane	3	T.Kiley	118	Proctor Knott	118	Once Again	118	4,880	2:34.20	
1890	Riley	3	I. Murphy	118	Bill Letcher	118	Robespierre	118	5,460	2:45.00	
1891	Kingman	3	I. Murphy	122	Balgowan	122	High Tariff	122	4,550	2:52.20	
1892	Azra	3	A. Clayton	122	Huron	122	Phil Dwyer	122	4,230	2:41.20	
1893	Lookout	3	E. Kunze	122	Plutus	122	Boundless	122	3,840	2:39.20	
1894	Chant	3	F. Goodale	122	Pearl Song	122	Sigurd	122	4,020	2:41.00	
1895	Halma	3	J. Perkins	122	Basso	122	Laureate	122	2,970	2:37.20	
1896	Ben Brush	3	W. Simms	117	Ben Eder	117	Semper Ego	117	4,850	2:07.60	
1897	Typhoon II	3	F. Garner	117	Ornament	117	Dr. Catlett	117	4,850	2:12.20	
1898	Plaudit	3	W. Simms	117	Lieber Karl	122	Isabey	117	4,850	2:09.00	
1899	Manuel	3	F. Taral	117	Corsini	122	Mazo	117	4,850	2:12.00	
1900	Lieut. Gibson	3	J. Boland	117	Florizar	122	Thrive	122	4,850	2:06.20	
1901	His Eminence	3	J. Winkfield	117	Sannazarro	117	Driscoll	117	4,850	2:07.60	
1902	Alan-A-Dale	3	J. Winkfield	117	Inventor	117	The Rival	117	4,850	2:08.60	
1903	Judge Himes	3	H. Booker	117	Early	117	Bourbon	110	4,850	2:09.00	
1904	Elwood	3	F.Prior	117	Ed Tierney	117	Brancas	117	4,850	2:08.20	
1905	Agile	3	J. Martin	122	Ram's Horn	117	Layson	117	4,850	2:10.60	
1906	Sir Huon	3	R. Troxler	117	Lady Navarre	117	James Reddick	117	4,850	2:08.80	
1907	Pink Star	3	A. Minder	117	Zal	117	Ovelando	117	4,850	2:12.60	
1908	Stone Street	3	A. Pickens	117	Sir Cleges	117	Dunvegan	114	4,850	2:15.20	
1909	Wintergreen	3	V. Powers	117	Miami	117	Dr. Barkley	117	4,850	2:08.20	
1910	Donau	3	F. Herbert	117	Joe Morris	117	Fighting Bob	117	4,850	2:06.40	
1911	Meridian	3	G. Archibald	117	Governor Gray	119	Colston	110	4,850	2:05.00	
1912	Worth	3	C.H. Shilling	117	Duval	117	Flamma	117	4,850	2:09.40	
1913	Donerail	3	R. Goose	117	Ten Point	117	Gowell	112	5,475	2:04.80	
1914	Old Rosebud	3	J. McCabe	114	Hodge	114	Bronzewing	112	9,125	2:03.40	
1915	Regret	3	J. Notter	112	Pebbles	117	Sharpshooter	114	11,450	2:05.40	
1916	George Smith	3	J. Loftus	117	Star Hawk	117	Franklin	117	9,750	2:04.00	
1917	Omar Khayyam	3	C. Borel	117	Ticket	117	Midway	117	16,600	2:04.60	
1918	Exterminator	3	W. Knapp	114	Escoba	117	Viva America	113	14,700	2:10.80	
1919	Sir Barton	3	J. Loftus	112	Billy Kelly	119	Under Fire	122	20,825	2:09.80	
1920	Paul Jones	3	T. Rice	126	Upset	126	On Watch	126	30,375	2:09.00	
1921	Behave Yourself	3	C. Thompson	126	Black Servant	126	Prudery	121	38,450	2:04.20	

Year	Winner	Age	Jockey	Wt.	Second	Wt.	Third	Wt.	Win Value	Time	Beyer
1922	Morvich	3	A. Johnson	126	Bet Mosie	126	Joe Finn	126	46,775	2:04.60	
1923	Zev	3	E. Sande	126	Martingale	126	Vigil	126	53,000	2:05.40	
1924	Black Gold	3	J.D. Mooney	126	Chilhowee	126	Beau Butler	126	52,775	2:05.20	
1925	Flying Ebony	3	E. Sande	126	Captain Hal	126	Son of John	126	52,775	2:07.60	
1926	Bubbling Over	3	A. Johnson	126	Bagenbaggage	126	Rock Man	126	50,075	2:03.80	
1927	Whiskery	3	L. McAtee	126	Osmand	126	Jock	126	51,000	2:06.00	
1928	Reigh Count	3	C. Lang	126	Misstep	126	Toro	126	55,375	2:10.60	
1929	Clyde Van Dusen	3	L. McAtee	126	Naishapur	126	Panchio	126	53,950	2:10.80	
1930	Gallant Fox	3	E. Sande	126	Gallant Knight	126	Ned O	126	50,725	2:07.60	
1931	Twenty Grand	3	C. Kurtsinger	126	Sweep All	126	Mate	126	52,350	2:01.80	
1932	Burgoo King	3	E. James	126	Economic	126	Stepenfetchit	126	52,350	2:05.20	
1933	Broker's Tip	3	D. Meade	126	Head Play	126	Charley O	126	48,925	2:06.80	
1934	Cavalcade	3	M. Garner	126	Discovery	126	Agrarian	126	28,175	2:04.00	
1935	Omaha	3	W. Saunders	126	Roman Soldier	126	Whiskolo	126	39,525	2:05.00	
1936	Bold Venture	3	I. Hanford	126	Brevity	126	Indian Broom	126	37,725	2:03.60	
1937	War Admiral	3	C. Kurtsinger	126	Pompoon	126	Reaping Reward	126	52,050	2:03.20	
1938	Lawrin	3	E. Arcaro	126	Dauber	126	Can't Wait	126	47,050	2:04.80	
1939	Johnstown	3	J. Stout	126	Challedon	126	Heather Broom	126	46,350	2:03.40	
1940	Gallahadion	3	C. Bierman	126	Bimelech	126	Dit	126	60,150	2:05.00	
1941	Whirlaway	3	E. Arcaro	126	Staretor	126	Market Wise	126	61,725	2:01.40	
1942	Shut Out	3	W. Wright	126	Alsab	126	Valdina Orphan	126	64,225	2:04.40	
1943	Count Fleet	3	J. Longden	126	Blue Swords	126	Slide Rule	126	60,725	2:04.00	
1944	Pensive	3	C. McCreary	126	Broadcloth	126	Stir Up	126	64,675	2:04.20	
1945	Hoop Jr.	3	E. Arcaro	126	Pot O'Luck	126	Darby Dieppe	126	64,850	2:07.00	
1946	Assault	3	W. Mehrtens	126	Spy Song	126	Hampden	126	96,400	2:06.60	
1947	Jet Pilot	3	E. Guerin	126	Phalanx	126	Faultless	126	92,160	2:06.80	
1948	Citation	3	E. Arcaro	126	Coaltown	126	My Request	126	83,400	2:05.40	
1949	Ponder	3	S. Brooks	126	Capot	126	Palestinian	126	91,600	2:04.80	
1950	Middleground	3	W. Boland	126	Hill Prince	126	Mr. Trouble	126	92,650	2:01.60	
1951	Count Turf	3	C. McCreary	126	Royal Mustang	126	Ruhe	126	98,050	2:02.60	
1952	Hill Gail	3	E. Arcaro	126	Sub Fleet	126	Blue Man	126	96,300	2:01.60	
1953	Dark Star	3	H. Moreno	126	Native Dancer	126	Invigorator	126	90,050	2:02.00	
1954	Determine	3	R. York	126	Hasty Road	126	Hasseyampa	126	102,050	2:03.00	
1955	Swaps	3	W. Shoemaker	126	Nashua	126	Summer Tan	126	108,400	2:01.80	
1956	Needles	3	D. Erb	126	Fabius	126	Come on Red	126	123,450	2:03.40	
1957	Iron Liege	3	W. Hartack	126	Gallant Man	126	Round Table	126	107,950	2:02.20	
1958	Tim Tam	3	I. Valenzuela	126	Lincoln Road	126	Noureddin	126	116,400	2:05.00	
1959	Tomy Lee	3	W. Shoemaker	126	Sword Dancer	126	First Landing	126	119,650	2:02.20	
1960	Venetian Way	3	W. Hartack	126	Bally Ache	126	Victoria Park	126	114,850	2:02.40	
1961	Carry Back	3	J. Sellers	126	Crozier	126	Bass Clef	126	120,500	2:04.00	
1962	Decidedly	3	W. Hartack	126	Roman Line	126	Ridan	126	119,650	2:00.40	
1963	Chateaugay	3	B. Baeza	126	Never Bend	126	Candy Spots	126	108,900	2:01.80	
1964	Northern Dancer	3	W. Hartack	126	Hill Rise	126	The Scoundrel	126	114,300	2:00.00	
1965	Lucky Debonair	3	W. Shoemaker	126	Dapper Dan	126	Tom Rolfe	126	112,000	2:01.20	
1966	Kauai King	3	D. Brumfield	126	Advocator	126	Blue Skyer	126	120,500	2:02.00	
1967	Proud Clarion	3	R. Ussery	126	Barbs Delight	126	Damascus	126	119,700	2:00.60	
1968	Forward Pass	3	I. Valenzuela	126	Francie's Hat	126	T.V. Commercial	126	122,600	2:02.20	
	Dancer's Image finished first but subsequently was disqualified from the purse money										
1969	Majestic Prince	3	W. Hartack	126	Arts and Letters	126	Dike	126	113,200	2:01.80	
1970	Dust Commander	3	M. Manganello	126	My Dad George	126	High Echelon	126	127,800	2:03.40	
1971	Canonero II	3	G. Avila	126	Jim French	126	Bold Reason	126	145,500	2:03.20	
1972	Riva Ridge	3	R. Turcotte	126	No Le Hace	126	Hold Your Peace	126	140,300	2:01.80	
1973	Secretariat	3	R. Turcotte	126	Sham	126	Our Native	126	155,050	1:59.40	
1974	Cannonade	3	A. Cordero Jr	126	Hudson County	126	Agitate	126	274,000	2:04.00	
1975	Foolish Pleasure	3	J. Vasquez	126	Avatar	126	Diabolo	126	209,600	2:02.00	
1976	Bold Forbes	3	A. Cordero Jr	126	Honest Pleasure	126	Elocutionist	126	165,200	2:01.60	
1977	Seattle Slew	3	J. Cruguet	126	Run Dusty Run	126	Sanhedrin	126	214,700	2:02.20	
1978	Affirmed	3	S. Cauthen	126	Alydar	126	Believe It	126	186,900	2:01.20	
1979	Spectacular Bid	3	R.J. Franklin	126	General Assembly	126	Golden Act	126	228,650	2:02.40	
1980	Genuine Risk	3	J. Vasquez	121	Rumbo	126	Jaklin Klugman	126	250,550	2:02.00	
1981	Pleasant Colony	3	J. Velasquez	126	Woodchopper	126	Partez	126	317,200	2:02.00	
1982	Gato Del Sol	3	E. Delahoussaye	126	Laser Light	126	Reinvested	126	428,850	2:02.40	
1983	Sunny's Halo	3	E. Delahoussaye	126	Desert Wine	126	Caveat	126	426,000	2:02.20	
1984	Swale	3	L. Pincay Jr	126	Coax Me Chad	126	At the Threshold	126	537,000	2:02.40	
1985	Spend a Buck	3	A. Cordero Jr	126	Stephan's Odyssey	126	Chief's Crown	126	406,800	2:00.20	
1986	Ferdinand	3	W. Shoemaker	126	Bold Arrangement	126	Broad Brush	126	609,400	2:02.80	
1987	Alysheba	3	C.J. McCarron	126	Bet Twice	126	Avie's Copy	126	618,600	2:03.40	
1988	Winning Colors	3	G.L. Stevens	121	Forty Niner	126	Risen Star	126	611,200	2:02.20	
1989	Sunday Silence	3	P.A. Valenzuela	126	Easy Goer	126	Awe Inspiring	126	574,200	2:05.00	102
1990	Unbridled	3	C. Perret	126	Summer Squall	126	Pleasant Tap	126	581,000	2:02.00	
1991	Strike the Gold	3	C.W. Antley	126	Best Pal	126	Mane Minister	126	655,800	2:03.08	
1992	Lil E. Tee	3	P. Day	126	Casual Lies	126	Dance Floor	126	724,800	2:03.04	107
1993	Sea Hero	3	J.D. Bailey	126	Prairie Bayou	126	Wild Gale	126	735,900	2:02.42	105

Year	Winner	Age	Jockey	Wt.	Second	Wt.	Third	Wt.	Win Value	Time	Beyer
1994	Go for Gin	3	C.J. McCarron	126	Strodes Creek	126	Blumin Affair	126	628,800	2:03.72	112
1995	Thunder Gulch	3	G.L. Stevens	126	Tejano Run	126	Timber Country	126	707,400	2:01.27	108
1996	Grindstone	3	J.D. Bailey	126	Cavonnier	126	Prince of Thieves	126	869,800	2:01.06	112
1997	Silver Charm	3	G.L. Stevens	126	Captain Bodgit	126	Free House	126	700,000	2:02.44	115
1998	Real Quiet	3	K.J. Desormeaux	126	Victory Gallop	126	Indian Charlie	126	738,800	2:02.38	107
1999	Charismatic	3	C.W. Antley	126	Menifee	126	Cat Thief	126	886,200	2:03.29	108
2000	Fusaichi Pegasus	3	K.J. Desormeaux	126	Aptitude	126	Impeachment	126	1,038,400	2:01.12	108
2001	Monarchos	3	J.F. Chavez	126	Invisible Ink	126	Congaree	126	812,000	1:59.88	116
2002	War Emblem	3	V. Espinoza	126	Proud Citizen	126	Perfect Drift	126	1,875,000	2:01.13	114
2003	Funny Cide	3	J.A. Santos	126	Empire Maker	126	Peace Rules	126	800,200	2:01.19	109
2004	Smarty Jones	3	S. Elliott	126	Lion Heart	126	Imperialism	126	5,854,800	2:04.06	107

Beyer Index: 109.29

Distance 1 1/2 miles prior to 1896. In 2000, Fusaichi Pegasus earned a $250,000 bonus for winning the Wood Memorial and Kentucky Derby. In 2002, War Emblem earned a $1 million bonus for winning the Illinois Derby and Kentucky Derby. In 2004, Smarty Jones earned a $5 million bonus for winning the Rebel, Arkansas Derby and Kentucky Derby.

KENTUCKY JOCKEY CLUB (G2), 1 1/16 Miles, 2-Year-Olds, Churchill Downs, 2004 Purse: $223,200

Year	Winner	Age	Jockey	Wt.	Second	Wt.	Third	Wt.	Win Value	Time	Beyer
1920	Tryster	2	F. Coltiletti	122	Grey Lag	122	Behave Yourself	122	23,695	1:38.40	
1921	Startle	2	D. Connell	119	Rocket	122	John Finn	122	22,175	1:38.60	
1922	Enchantment	2	L. McAtee	122	Picketer	122	Dongos	122	25,315	1:38.80	
1923	Wise Counsellor	2	M. Garner	122	Mad Play	122	Chilhowee	122	26,990	1:37.40	
1924	Master Charlie	2	C. Kummer	122	Pas Seul	122	Kentucky Cardinal	122	26,010	1:38.20	
1925	Canter	2	C. Turner	122	Flight of Time	122	Rhinock	122	23,315	1:41.00	
1926	Valorous	2	L. McAtee	122	Bostonian	122	Candy Queen	119	26,785	1:43.60	
1927	Reigh Count	2	C. Lang	122	Vito	122	Algernon	122	28,480	1:40.00	
1928	Clyde Van Dusen	2	C. McCrossen	122	Current	119	Windy City	122	32,800	1:38.80	
1929	Desert Light	2	P. Walls	119	Alcibiades	119	Gallant Knight	122	26,865	1:39.00	
1930	Twenty Grand	2	C. Kurtsinger	122	Equipoise	122	Knight's Call	122	25,030	1:36.00	
1931	Kakapo	2	E. Pool	119	Pompeius	122	Air Pilot	122	24,040	1:43.80	
1932	The Darb	2	A. Robertson	122	Caesar's Ghost	122	Dynastic	122	19,945	1:46.80	
1933	Mata Hari	2	H. Schutte	119	Discovery	122	Collateral	122	16,230	1:39.80	
1934	Nellie Flag	2	E. Arcaro	119	Good Flavor	122	Myrtlewood	119	9,820	1:37.60	
1935	Grand Slam	2	W. Hanka	122	Hollyrood	122	Boston Pal	122	9,835	1:39.60	
1936	Reaping Reward	2	A. Robertson	122	Privileged	122	Dellor	122	10,140	1:40.00	
1937	Mountain Ridge	2	A. Robertson	122	King's Heir	122	Dah He	122	8,510	1:38.60	
1938	T.M. Dorsett	2	L. Haas	122	Steel Heels	122	Lightspur	122	8,450	1:38.60	
1946	Double Jay	2	J. Gilbert	122	Education	122	Patmiboy	116	22,690	1:37.00	
1947	Bold Gallant	2	F.A. Smith	116	Shy Guy	119	Papa Redbird	116	21,180	1:38.80	
1948	Johns Joy	2	J. Combest	119	Fleeting Star	116	Our Request	113	23,545	1:37.00	
1949	Roman Bath	2	D. Scurlock	119	Bolingover	116	Sunglow	116	21,340	1:38.20	
1950	Pur Sang	2	T. Barrow	116	Bernwood	116	Mameluke	116	21,995	1:36.60	
1951	Sub Fleet	2	J. Adams	116	Alladier	122	Smoke Screen	113	38,740	1:40.00	
1952	Straight Face	2	B. Green	122	Spy Defense	116	Berseem	116	36,545	1:37.40	
1953	Hasty Road	2	J. Adams	122	Goyamo	116	Pinetum	113	36,185	1:36.00	
1954	Prince Noor	2	J. Adams	113	Fleet Path	116	Parador	116	36,300	1:38.60	
1955	Royal Sting	2	J. Heckmann	116	Jovial Jove	122	Roman Fan	116	40,635	1:37.60	
1956	Federal Hill	2	W. Carstens	119	Tranquil	116	Jet Colonel	116	40,685	1:37.40	
1957	Hill Country	2	L.C. Cook	116	Can Trust	116	Page Seven	113	34,235	1:38.00	
1958	Winsome Winner	2	S. Brooks	116	Pilot	119	John Bruce	116	32,020	1:36.40	
1959	Oil Wick	2	R. Dever	116	All Hands	116	Run for Nurse	116	30,314	1:39.40	
1960	Crimson Fury	2	W. Carstens	117	Safe Swap	116	Wooden Nickel	116	26,574	1:38.00	
1961	Su Ka Wa	2	H. Clark	119	Times Roman	116	Sharp Count	116	29,341	1:36.80	
1962	Sky Gem	2	B. Baeza	119	Copy Chief	116	Telethon	116	34,343	1:37.40	
1963	Journalist	2	K. Church	116	Duel	122	Bleacherite	116	32,074	1:36.40	
1964	Umbrella Fella	2	J. Nazareth	122	Florida State	116	Black Dad	116	31,037	1:36.60	
1965	War Censor	2	R. York	116	Tinsley	122	Old Bag	122	32,909	1:37.60	
1966	Lightning Orphan	2	R. Broussard	119	Gentleman James	116	Monitor	116	33,790	1:37.60	
1967	Mr. Brogann	2	D. Richard	116	Gin-Rob	122	T.V. Commercial	122	36,832	1:35.00	
1968	Traffic Mark	2	C.H. Marquez	119	Indian Emerald	119	Hawaiian Ruler	116	39,705	1:38.20	
1969	Evasive Action	2	J. Tejeira	116	Hard Work	122	Admiral's Shield	116	35,444	1:33.80	
1970	Line City	2	D. Brumfield	116	Granbid	118	Dothan	116	40,908	1:36.80	
1971	Windjammer	2	L. Pincay Jr	122	Billy Rogell	116	Thurloe Square	116	35,685	1:36.80	
1972	Puntilla	2	B. Baeza	116	Golden Don	116	Annihilate 'Em	122	37,895	1:35.60	
1973	Cannonade	2	P. Anderson	119	Satan's Hills	116	Don't Be Late Jim	116	49,510	1:36.80	
1974	Circle Home	2	M. Hole	116	Master Derby	122	Ruggles Ferry	116	36,748	1:36.00	
1975	Play Boy	2	D. Brumfield	116	Khyber King	119	Please Find John	116	30,491	1:36.80	
1975	Pastry	2	B.R. Feliciano	116	Bold Laddie	119	Bid to Fame	116	30,329	1:36.80	
1976	Run Dusty Run	2	D.G. McHargue	122	Get the Axe	116	Silver Series	116	34,830	1:37.20	
1977	Going Investor	2	R. Depass	119	Jaycean	119	Silver Nitrate	119	36,121	1:38.20	

Year	Winner	Age	Jockey	Wt.	Second	Wt.	Third	Wt.	Win Value	Time	Beyer
1978	Lot o' Gold	2	R. Depass	119	Arctic Action	116	Uncle Fudge	119	37,645	1:37.80	
1979	King Neptune	2	D. Brumfield	116	Royal Sporan	119	Silver Shears	116	37,001	1:37.80	
1980	Television Studio	2	D. Brumfield	119	Linnleur	116	Bear Creek Dam	116	73,226	1:47.00	
1981	El Baba	2	R.P. Romero	119	Crown the King	116	Talent Town	119	85,888	1:45.20	
1982	Highland Park	2	D. Brumfield	122	Coax Me Matt	116	Caveat	122	75,859	1:47.00	
1983	Biloxi Indian	2	G. Patterson	119	Country Manor	119	Taylor's Special	119	71,721	1:46.20	
1984	Fuzzy	2	D. Brumfield	114	Banner Bob	119	Nordic Scandal	113	106,902	1:45.00	
1985	Mustin Lake	2	P. Day	116	Bachelor Beau	116	Regal Dreamer	122	87,432	1:46.80	
1986	Mt. Pleasant	2	K.K. Allen	116	Mondulick	113	Funny Tunes	113	93,561	1:46.40	
1987	Notebook	2	J.A. Santos	122	Buoy	122	Hey Pat	119	74,701	1:47.40	
1988	Tricky Creek	2	L. Melancon	118	Western Playboy	116	Revive	118	106,083	1:45.40	
1989	Grand Canyon	2	A. Cordero Jr	121	Insurrection	121	Dusty's Command	118	95,550	1:44.60	
1990	Richman	2	P. Day	121	Discover	116	Honor Grades	116	107,718	1:45.40	
1991	Dance Floor	2	C.W. Antley	121	Waki Warrior	116	Choctaw Ridge	116	104,891	1:45.20	93
1992	Wild Gale	2	S.J. Sellers	116	Mi Cielo	116	Shoal Creek	121	105,918	1:45.60	87
1993	War Deputy	2	G.K. Gomez	112	Tarzans Blade	122	Rustic Light	119	97,500	1:46.60	90
1994	Jambalaya Jazz	2	Maple S	113	You're the One	112	Peaks and Valleys	119	97,500	1:46.40	90
1995	Ide	2	Perret C	122	Editor's Note	119	El Amante	113	106,373	1:44.20	94
1996	Concerto	2	C.H. Marquez Jr	119	Celtic Warrior	113	Carmen's Baby	122	142,104	1:46.80	95
1997	Cape Town	2	W. Martinez	113	Time Limit	119	Real Quiet	116	142,228	1:43.80	96
1998	Exploit	2	C.J. McCarron	122	Vicar	113	Grits n' Hard Toast	113	140,740	1:44.00	101
1999	Captain Steve	2	R.J. Albarado	122	Mighty	122	Personal First	119	143,840	1:43.00	105
2000	Dollar Bill	2	C.H. Borel	113	Holiday Thunder	113	Gift Of The Eagle	113	136,656	1:47.18	96
2001	Repent	2	A.J. D'Amico	122	Request for Parole	117	High Star	115	134,540	1:44.42	92
2002	Soto	2	L. Melancon	117	Ten Cents a Shine	115	Most Feared	122	143,344	1:44.67	94
2003	The Cliff's Edge	2	S.J. Sellers	122	Gran Prospect	116	Proper Prado	118	137,764	1:45.50	94
2004	Greater Good	2	J. McKee	122	Rush Bay	116	Wild Desert	118	138,384	1:45.14	91

Beyer Index: 94.14

KENTUCKY OAKS (G1), 1 1/8 Miles, 3-Year-Old Fillies, Churchill Downs, 2004 Purse: $572,000

Year	Winner	Age	Jockey	Wt.	Second	Wt.	Third	Wt.	Win Value	Time	Beyer
1875	Vinaigrette	3	J. Houston	97	Gyptis	97	Elemi	97	1,175	2:39.60	
1876	Necy Hale	3	James	97	Plenty	97	Lady Clipper	97	1,900	2:42.20	
1877	Felicia	3	James	97	Bradamante	97	Aunt Betsy	97	2,550	2:39.00	
1878	Belle of Nelson	3	Booth	97	Buena Vista	97	Fortuna	97	2,650	2:39.00	
1879	Liahtunah	3	Hightower	97	Ada Glenn	97	Buckden Lass	97	3,350	2:40.20	
1880	Longitude	3	J. McLaughlin	102	Bye and Bye	102	Ersilla	102	3,250	2:41.60	
1881	Lucy May	3	Wolfe	102	Belle of the Highlan	102	Mrs. Chubbs	102	3,000	2:41.00	
1882	Katie Creel	3	Stoval	102	Pinafore	102	Issie	102	3,240	2:39.00	
1883	Vera	3	Stoval	102	Orange Blossom	102	Billetta	102	3,220	2:39.60	
1884	Modesty	3	I. Murphy	105	Highflight	105	Bluette	105	3,030	2:48.20	
1885	Lizzie Dwyer	3	Fuller	105	Constellation	105	Exile	105	3,800	2:40.60	
1886	Pure Rye	3	Garrison	113	Red Girl	113	Ada D.	113	4,170	2:41.00	
1887	Florimore	3	Johnston	113	Wary	113	Bannail	113	3,330	2:40.60	
1888	Ten Penny	3	A. McCarthy Jr	113	Los Angeles	114	Quindaro Belle	114	3,720	2:42.00	
1889	Jewel Ban	3	Stoval	113	Brandolette	113	Retrieve	113	3,850	2:41.00	
1890	English Lady	3	Hollis	113	Marie K.	113			3,610	2:42.20	
1891	Miss Hawkins	3	Britton	117	Ethel	117	Bonnie Bird	117	3,860	2:18.20	
1892	Miss Dixie	3	Ray	117	Unadilla	117	Greenwich	117	3,470	2:14.20	
1893	Monrovia	3	Reagan	117	Elizabeth L.	117	Joanna	117	2,780	2:16.00	
1894	Selika	3	A. Clayton	117	Charity	117	Shuttle	117	2,600	2:15.00	
1895	Voladora	3	A. Clayton	117	Alabama	117	Kathryn	117	1,830	2:16.60	
1896	Souffe	3	Thorpe	112	Myrtle Harkness	112	La Gascogne	112	2,860	1:54.20	
1897	White Frost	3	T. Burns	112	Rosinante	112	Taluca	112	2,410	1:49.00	
1898	Crocket	3	J. Hill	112	Lennep	112	Alleviate	112	2,860	1:51.20	
1899	Rush	3	J. Hill	112	May Hempstead	117	The L. in Blue	112	2,410	1:52.20	
1900	Etta	3	Overton	112	Scarlet Lily	112	Cleora	112	2,410	1:48.00	
1901	Lady Schorr	3	J. Woods	117	Isobel	112	Edith Q.	112	2,410	1:53.00	
1902	Walnamoinen	3	Coburn	112	Marque	112	Autumn Leaves	112	2,410	1:51.20	
1903	Lemco	3	J. Reiff	112	Mary Lavana	112	The Crisis	112	2,410	1:49.60	
1904	Audience	3	Helgesen	117	Outcome	112	White Plume	112	2,410	1:51.00	
1905	Janeta	3	D. Austin	112	Mum	112	Siss Lee	112	2,410	1:49.60	
1906	King's Daughter	3	E. Robinson	112	Lady Navarre	117	Lady Anne	112	2,410	1:47.80	
1907	Wing Ting	3	J. Lee	112	Altuda	112	Lillie Turner	112	2,410	1:50.20	
1908	Ellen-a-Dale	3	V. Powers	105	Boema	112	Estradia	105	2,410	1:46.60	
1909	Floreal	3	Heidel	112	Pink Wings	105	Cordova	112	2,410	1:49.20	
1910	Samaria	3	Scoville	112	Foxy Mary	112	My Gal	112	1,910	1:50.20	
1911	Bettie Sue	3	T. Rice	112	Ilma	112			1,910	1:48.00	
1912	Flamma	3	Butwell	112	Floral Day	112	Beautiful	105	1,910	1:51.20	
1913	Cream	3	Ganz	112	Floral Park	112	Gowell	117	1,950	1:47.60	
1914	Bronzewing	3	W. Obert	117	Casuarina	112	Brackt'n Belle	112	2,320	1:45.60	
1915	Waterblossom	3	E. Martin	117	One Step	112	Lady Rotha	112	2,530	1:46.60	

Year	Winner	Age	Jockey	Wt.	Second	Wt.	Third	Wt.	Win Value	Time	Beyer
1916	Kathleen	3	R. Goose	112	Mandy Hamiton	117	Lady Always	112	2,410	1:47.40	
1917	Sunbonnet	3	J. Loftus	112	Diamond	112	Battle	112	3,035	1:46.80	
1918	Viva America	3	W. Warrington	112	Fern Handley	112	Mistress Polly	112	2,580	1:46.80	
1919	Lillian Shaw	3	T. Murray	117	Milkmaid	117	Dancing Spray	112	4,190	1:45.00	
1920	Lorraine	3	D. Connelly	116	Truly Rural	116	Dresden	116	5,470	1:58.40	
1921	Nancy Lee	3	L. McAtee	116	Prudery	116	Lady Madcap	116	8,980	1:50.40	
1922	Startle	3	D. Connelly	116	Martha Fallon	116	Precious Lula	116	9,920	1:52.60	
1923	Untidy	3	J. Corcoran	116	Sweetheart	116	Gadfly	121	10,060	1:53.00	
1924	Princess Doreen	3	H. Stutts	116	Nellie Morse	121	Befuddle	116	10,160	1:51.80	
1925	Deeming	3	J. McCoy	116	Buckwheat Cake	116	Little Visitor	121	10,280	1:54.00	
1926	Black Maria	3	A. Mortensen	121	Dark Phantom	116	Helen's Babe	116	10,960	1:55.40	
1927	Mary Jane	3	D. Connelly	121	Handy Mandy	111	Fresco	116	10,900	1:53.40	
1928	Easter Stockings	3	W. Crump	116	Pink Lily	116	Reveries' Gal	121	9,140	1:51.60	
1929	Rose of Sharon	3	W. Crump	121	Lady Broadcast	116	Current	116	10,080	1:51.00	
1930	Alcibiades	3	R. Finnerty	116	Rich Widow	116	Galaday	116	9,760	1:52.60	
1931	Cousin Jo	3	E. James	116	Sunny Lassie	116	Town Limit	116	9,610	1:53.00	
1932	Suntica	3	A. Pascuma	116	I Say	116	Depression	116	4,590	1:52.20	
1933	Barn Swallow	3	D. Meade	116	At Top	116	Bright Bauble	116	4,280	1:51.20	
1934	Fiji	3	G. Elston	116	Far Star	116	Penncote	116	2,230	1:51.60	
1935	Paradisical	3	G. Fowler	116	Mid Victorian	116	Spanish Babe	116	2,310	1:51.20	
1936	Two Bob	3	R. Workman	116	Threadneedle	116	Seventh Heaven	116	4,625	1:52.60	
1937	Mars Shield	3	A. Robertson	121	Shatterproof	116	Alkit	116	4,590	1:53.40	
1938	Flying Lee	3	L. Haas	116	Janice	116	Fantine	116	4,720	1:52.80	
1939	Flying Lill	3	C. Bierman	116	Bala Ormont	116	Rude Awakening	110	4,820	1:51.00	
1940	Inscolassie	3	R.L. Vedder	116	June Bee	116	Shine O'Night	116	4,370	1:54.40	
1941	Valdina Myth	3	G. King	116	Silvestra	116	Mys'y Marvel	116	4,240	1:52.60	
1942	Miss Dogwood	3	J. Adams	116	Questvive	116	Miss Glamour	116	4,810	1:47.00	
	Glide finished first but was disqualified										
1943	Nellie L.	3	W. Eads	116	Valdina Marl	116	Edie Jane	116	4,160	1:48.60	
1944	Canina	3	J. Adams	116	Harriet Sue	121	Paddle	110	4,200	1:48.60	
1945	Come and Go	3	C.L. Martin	121	On-Your-Toes	116	Miss Blindfold	116	3,840	1:49.80	
1946	First Page	3	J.R. Layton	116	Athenia	116	Buzzaround	116	9,175	1:51.40	
1947	Blue Grass	3	J. Longden	116	Cosmic Missile	121	Mother	116	21,680	1:51.60	
1948	Challe Anne	3	W. Garner	116	Reigh Belle	116	Back Talk	116	19,800	1:48.60	
1949	Wistful	3	G. Glisson	116	The Fat Lady	116	Lady Dorimar	116	21,450	1:47.40	
1950	Ari's Mona	3	W. Boland	116	Wondring	121	Diamond Lane	116	21,050	1:43.60	
1951	How	3	E. Arcaro	116	Astro	110	Sickle's Image	121	22,700	1:45.60	
1952	Real Delight	3	E. Arcaro	121	Whirla Lea	116	Big Mo	116	23,100	1:45.40	
1953	Bubbley	3	E. Arcaro	116	Cerise Reine	121	Arab Actress	116	21,750	1:45.60	
1954	Fascinator	3	A. DeSpirito	121	Queen Hopeful	121	Blue Violin	116	22,200	1:45.00	
1955	Lalun	3	H. Moreno	116	Lea Lane	121	Mazza	116	21,350	1:46.00	
1956	Princess Turia	3	W. Hartack	116	Doubledogdare	121	Tournure	116	21,650	1:44.80	
1957	Lori-El	3	L.C. Cook	121	Pillow Talk	121	Dale's Delight	121	29,700	1:44.80	
1958	Bug Brush	3	E. Arcaro	116	Galarullah	116	Hasty Doll	116	26,835	1:44.80	
1959	Wedlock	3	J.L. Rotz	116	Ray's Fairy Gold	116	Aesthetic	110	15,509	1:45.00	
1959	Hidden Talent	3	M. Ycaza	121	Indian Maid	116	Kathy H.	116	15,509	1:44.40	
1960	Make Sail	3	M. Ycaza	116	Quaze	116	Airmans Guide	116	25,957	1:44.20	
1961	My Portrait	3	B. Baeza	116	Play Time	121	Times Two	116	28,275	1:47.00	
1962	Cicada	3	W. Shoemaker	121	Flaming Page	116	Fortunate Isle	116	27,820	1:44.60	
1963	Sally Ship	3	M. Ycaza	121	Bonnie's Girl	116	Power to Strike	116	29,965	1:44.80	
1964	Blue Norther	3	W. Shoemaker	121	Miss Cavandish	116	Road to Romance	116	31,184	1:44.20	
1965	Amerivan	3	R. Turcotte	116	Gold Digger	116	Terentia	121	31,541	1:44.40	
1966	Native Street	3	D. Brumfield	121	Lady Pitt	121	Naidni Diam	121	39,357	1:44.80	
1967	Nancy Jr.	3	J. Sellers	121	Gay Sailorette	121	Furl Sail	121	39,620	1:44.00	
1968	Dark Mirage	3	M. Ycaza	121	Miss Ribot	121	Lady Tramp	121	41,437	1:44.60	
1969	Hail to Patsy	3	D. Kassen	121	Double Delta	121	Mrs. Jo Jo	121	38,902	1:44.40	
1970	Lady Vi-E.	3	D.E. Whited	121	Glenary	121	Artists Proof	121	41,437	1:44.80	
1971	Silent Beauty	3	K. Knapp	121	Graffitti	121	At Arms Length	121	42,152	1:44.20	
1972	Susan's Girl	3	V. Tejada	121	Barely Even	121	Fairway Flyer	121	39,894	1:44.20	
1973	Bag of Tunes	3	D. Gargan	121	La Prevoyante	121	Coraggioso	121	43,647	1:44.20	
1974	Quaze Quilt	3	W. Gavidia	121	Special Team	121	Kaye's Commander	121	43,631	1:46.60	
1975	Sun and Snow	3	G. Patterson	121	Funalon	121	Funny Cat	121	42,315	1:44.60	
1976	Optimistic Gal	3	B. Baeza	121	Comfort Zone	121	Carmelita Gibbs	121	40,186	1:44.60	
1977	Sweet Alliance	3	C.J. McCarron	121	Our Mims	121	Mrs. Warren	121	60,889	1:43.60	
1978	White Star Line	3	E. Maple	121	Grenzen	121	Bold Rendezvous	121	60,498	1:45.20	
1979	Davona Dale	3	J. Velasquez	121	Himalayan	121	Prize Spot	121	83,590	1:47.20	
1980	Bold 'n Determined	3	E. Delahoussaye	121	Mitey Lively	121	Honest and True	121	83,915	1:44.80	
1981	Heavenly Cause	3	L. Pincay Jr	121	De la Rose	121	Wayward Lass	121	79,300	1:43.00	
1982	Blush With Pride	3	W. Shoemaker	121	Before Dawn	121	Flying Partner	121	126,133	1:50.20	
1983	Princess Rooney	3	J. Vasquez	121	Bright Crocus	121	Bemissed	121	116,968	1:50.80	
1984	Lucky Lucky Lucky	3	A. Cordero Jr	121	Miss Oceana	121	My Lucky One	121	112,710	1:51.80	
1985	Fran's Valentine	3	P.A. Valenzuela	121	Foxy Deen	121	Rascal Lass	121	118,365	1:50.00	
1986	Tiffany Lass	3	G.L. Stevens	121	Life at the Top	121	Family Style	121	122,103	1:50.60	

Year	Winner	Age	Jockey	Wt.	Second	Wt.	Third	Wt.	Win Value	Time	Beyer
1987	Buryyourbelief	3	J.A. Santos	121	Hometown Queen	121	Super Cook	121	155,415	1:50.40	
1988	Goodbye Halo	3	P. Day	121	Jeanne Jones	121	Willa on the Move	121	156,715	1:50.40	
1989	Open Mind	3	A. Cordero Jr	121	Imaginary Lady	121	Blondeinamotel	121	150,540	1:50.60	
1990	Seaside Attraction	3	C.J. McCarron	121	Go for Wand	121	Bright Candles	121	156,910	1:52.80	91
1991	Lite Light	3	C.S. Nakatani	121	Withallprobability	121	Til Forbid	121	207,285	1:48.80	106
1992	Luv Me Luv Me Not	3	F.A. Arguello Jr	121	Pleasant Stage	121	Prospectors Delite	121	182,455	1:51.40	90
1993	Dispute	3	J.D. Bailey	121	Eliza	121	Quinpool	121	191,230	1:52.40	93
1994	Sardula	3	E. Delahoussaye	121	Lakeway	121	Dianes Halo	121	184,340	1:51.00	99
1995	Gal in a Ruckus	3	W.H. McCauley	121	Urbane	121	Sneaky Quiet	121	235,040	1:50.00	99
1996	Pike Place Dancer	3	C.S. Nakatani	121	Escena	121	Cara Rafaela	121	325,000	1:49.80	101
1997	Blushing K.D.	3	L.J. Meche	121	Tomisue's Delight	121	Storm Song	121	362,514	1:50.20	104
	Sharp Cat finished third but was disqualified and placed eighth										
1998	Keeper Hill	3	D.R. Flores	121	Banshee Breeze	121	Really Polish	121	375,410	1:52.06	100
1999	Silverbulletday	3	G.L. Stevens	121	Dreams Gallore	121	Sweeping Story	121	341,620	1:49.92	107
2000	Secret Status	3	P. Day	121	Rings a Chime	121	Classy Cara	121	378,696	1:50.30	100
2001	Flute	3	J.D. Bailey	121	Real Cozzy	121	Collect Call	121	377,704	1:48.85	98
2002	Farda Amiga	3	C.J. McCarron	121	Take Charge Lady	121	Habibti	121	348,502	1:50.41	108
2003	Bird Town	3	E.S. Prado	121	Santa Catarina	121	Yell	121	355,756	1:48.64	101
2004	Ashado	3	J.R. Velazquez	121	Island Sand	121	Madcap Escapade	121	354,640	1:50.81	102

Beyer Index: 99.93

Distance 1 1/2 miles from 1875-90; 1 1/4 miles 1891-95; 1 1/16 miles, 1896-1919, 1942-81

FRANK E. KILROE MILE HANDICAP (G2), 1 Mile (Turf), 4-Year-Olds and Up, Santa Anita, 2004 Purse: $350,000

Year	Winner	Age	Jockey	Wt.	Second	Wt.	Third	Wt.	Win Value	Time	Beyer
1960	American Comet	4	T. Barrow	118	Porter	110	Aorangi	112	16,650	2:04.40	
1961	Wolfram	5	J.L. Rotz	122	Balsarroch Boy	111	Geechee Lou	121	17,600	2:01.00	
1962	Art Market	4	I. Valenzuela	120	Oink	124	Grey Eagle	116	17,600	2:01.00	
1963	The Axe II	5	P. Moreno	122	Rablero	120	Hy-Nat	116	18,600	2:04.20	
1964	Mr. Consistency	6	K. Church	124	Marlin Bay	118	Cedar Key	118	18,100	1:58.60	
1965	Cedar Key	5	W. Shoemaker	122	Dusky Damion	114	Brambles	116	18,800	2:00.80	
1966	Tudor Fame	4	J. Lambert	113	Plaque	112	Aurelius II	115	18,200	2:02.80	
1967	Fleet Host	4	A. Pineda	116	The Dancer	108			18,050	1:59.80	
					Biggs	113					
1968	Nashua Pilot	4	J. Sellers	114	Tumble Wind	120	Mr. Right	118	21,250	2:00.00	
1969	Rivet	5	M. Volzke	118	Palestin	116	Easy Mark	115	21,850	2:03.20	
1970	Royal Dynasty	4	L. Pincay Jr	114	Quicken Tree	120	High Tribute	111	19,300	2:06.80	
1971	Daryl's Joy	5	J. Sellers	126	Magic Hope II	115	Obelisco	113	26,000	1:59.60	
1972	Buzkashi	5	W. Shoemaker	117	Mayhedo	115	Perpetual	114	22,350	2:00.80	
1972	Knight in Armor	5	D. Pierce	120	Big Shot II	125	Golden Eagle II	119	21,950	2:01.80	
1973	River Buoy	8	D. Pierce	117	Wing Out	116	Mazus	121	20,875	2:02.80	
1973	Kobuk King	7	J. Lambert	116	Triggairo	114	Presidual	116	20,475	2:02.80	
1974	Court Ruling	4	B. Baeza	114	Scantling	116	Barrydown	116	32,800	2:01.40	
1975	Ga Hai	4	J. Vasquez	114	Indefatigable	115	Gold Standard	111	32,800	2:07.00	
1976	Ga Hai	5	F. Olivares	115	Riot in Paris	120	Copper Mel	117	34,050	2:00.40	
1977	Caucasus	5	F. Toro	124	Exact Duplicate	115			33,900	2:00.00	
					Victorian Prince	116					
1978	Exceller	5	W. Shoemaker	126	Soldier's Lark	113	Tacitus	115	31,750	2:01.20	
1979	Fluorescent Light	5	L. Pincay Jr	121	Waya	123	As de Copas	118	39,650	2:03.60	
1980	Henschel	6	W. Shoemaker	114	Silver Eagle	120	Balzac	122	40,900	1:58.80	
1981	Premier Ministre	5	L. Pincay Jr	117	Galaxy Libra	119	Bold Tropic	126	38,350	2:02.60	
1982	Perrault	5	L. Pincay Jr	124	Silveyville	117	Le Duc de Bar	111	47,700	2:04.60	
1983	Manantial	5	K. Black	115	Bohemian Grove	115	Western	120	46,500	2:03.40	
1984	Sir Pele	5	R.Q. Meza	114	Lucence	117	Ginger Brink	117	49,850	2:01.20	
1985	Fatih	5	W. Shoemaker	116	Tsunami Slew	119	Swoon	113	64,300	1:59.60	
1986	Strawberry Road II	7	G.L. Stevens	125	Hail Bold King	116	Schiller	115	75,800	2:03.40	
1987	Thrill Show	4	W. Shoemaker	121	Skywalker	123	Aventino	115	92,150	1:35.00	
1988	Mohamed Abdu	4	E. Delahoussaye	118	The Medic	118	The Scout	118	95,300	1:37.00	
1989	Bello Horizonte	6	E. Delahoussaye	116	Sarhoob	120	Patchy Groundfog	117	64,700	1:36.20	
1990	Prized	4	E. Delahoussaye	124	Happy Toss	115	On the Menu	112	67,000	1:34.40	107
1991	Madjaristan	5	E. Delahoussaye	114	Trebizond	116	Major Moment	111	105,400	1:33.20	
1992	Fly Till Dawn	6	L. Pincay Jr	120	Itsallgreektome	123	Qathif	115	100,200	1:34.60	110
1993	Leger Cat	7	C.S. Nakatani	114	Luthier Enchanteur	116	The Name's Jimmy	115	70,800	1:34.00	107
1994	Megan's Interco	5	C.A. Black	118	Tinners Way	115	Ibero	118	64,400	1:33.80	108
1995	College Town	4	L. Pincay Jr	117	Romarin	120	Finder's Fortune	114	63,800	1:40.60	99
1996	Tychonic	6	G.L. Stevens	116	Debutant Trick	117	Silver Wizard	117	99,400	1:35.40	108
1997	Atticus	5	C.S. Nakatani	117	Pinfloron	115	Rainbow Blues	121	97,400	1:31.80	115
1998	Hawksley Hill	5	P. Day	115	Via Lombardia	117	A Magicman	120	101,190	1:34.80	106
1999	Lord Smith	4	G.K. Gomez	116	Hawksley Hill	122	Ladies Din	120	90,000	1:34.40	111
2000	Commitisize	5	V. Espinoza	112	Chullo	117	Sultry Substitute	114	120,000	1:36.61	106
2001	Road to Slew	6	L. Pincay Jr	117	Val Royal	118	Hawksley Hill	118	240,000	1:35.96	106
							Exchange Rate	115			

Year	Winner	Age	Jockey	Wt.	Second	Wt.	Third	Wt.	Win Value	Time	Beyer
2002	Decarchy	5	K.J. Desormeaux	119	Sarafan	116	Designed For Luck	117	180,000	1:34.04	104
2003	Redattore	8	A. Solis	120	Good Journey	124	Decarchy	118	240,000	1:34.94	109
2004	Sweet Return	4	G.L. Stevens	119	Singletary	117	Inesperado	116	210,000	1:33.87	108

Beyer Index: 107.43

Run as Arcadia Handicap through 2000; run on main track, 1975, 1976, 1978, 1983, 1995, and 2000; run at 1 1/4 miles prior to 1987

KING'S BISHOP (G1), 7 Furlongs, 3-Year-Olds, Saratoga Race Course, 2004 Purse: $250,000

Year	Winner	Age	Jockey	Wt.	Second	Wt.	Third	Wt.	Win Value	Time	Beyer
1984	Commemorate	3	F. Lovato Jr	119	All Fired Up	122	Raja's Shark	115	33,900	1:22.60	
1985	Pancho Villa	3	D. McHargue	122	El Basco	119	Cullendale	115	33,540	1:22.20	
1987	Templar Hill	3	C.J. McCarron	119	Mister S.M.	119	Homebuilder	115	51,660	1:23.00	
1988	King's Nest	3	C.J. McCarron	115	Tejano	117	Parlay Me	115	53,280	1:21.80	
1989	Houston	3	P. Day	119	Fast Play	117	Fierce Fighter	115	51,930	1:22.00	
1990	Housebuster	3	C. Perret	122	Poppiano	115	Sunshine Jimmy	115	54,090	1:21.80	113
1991	Take Me Out	3	M.E Smith	115	Joey the Student	115	To Freedom	119	74,400	1:21.60	
1992	Salt Lake	3	M.E Smith	117	Binalong	115	Agincourt	122	73,440	1:21.40	105
1993	Mi Cielo	3	M.E Smith	115	Williamstown	122	Schossberg	115	74,280	1:21.60	107
1994	Chimes Band	3	J.D. Bailey	117	End Sweep	122	Halo's Image	117	65,700	1:21.82	110
1995	Top Account	3	P. Day	112	Ft. Stockton	120	Excelerate	113	68,100	1:22.40	107
1996	Honour and Glory	3	J.A. Santos	123	Elusive Quality	112	Distorted Humor	115	64,920	1:21.60	113
1997	Tale of the Cat	3	J.A. Krone	114	Oro de Mexico	116	Trafalger	121	90,000	1:21.60	113
1998	Secret Firm	3	E.S. Prado	121	Mint	121	Scatmandu	116	120,000	1:22.60	107
1999	Forestry	3	C.W. Antley	124	Five Star Day	115	Successful Appeal	124	120,000	1:21.00	116
2000	More Than Ready	3	P. Day	124	Valiant Halory	114	Millencolin	121	120,000	1:22.49	103
2001	Squirtle Squirt	3	J.D. Bailey	121	Illusioned	119	City Zip	124	120,000	1:21.97	107
2002	Gygistar	3	J.R. Velazquez	124	Boston Common	121	Thunder Days	115	120,000	1:22.85	113
2003	Valid Video	3	J. Bravo	121	Great Notion	117	Ghostzapper	117	120,000	1:22.14	107
2004	Pomeroy	3	E.S. Prado	121	Weigelia	121	Ice Wynnd Fire	117	150,000	1:20.99	108

Beyer Index: 109.21

KNICKERBOCKER HANDICAP (G2), 1 1/8 Miles (Turf), 3-Year-Olds and Up, Aqueduct, 2004 Purse: $150,000

Year	Winner	Age	Jockey	Wt.	Second	Wt.	Third	Wt.	Win Value	Time	Beyer
1960	Quiz Star	4	W. Shoemaker	119	Catapult	108	Leix	109	18,712	2:49.40	
1961	T.V. Lark	4	J. Longden	119	Nasomo	113	Wise Ship	120	19,077	2:40.00	
1962	The Axe II	4	W. Shoemaker	120	Mongo	120	Irish Dandy	112	19,532	2:13.20	
1963	Parka	5	W. Shoemaker	110	Cedar Key	112	Thygold	110	14,105	1:55.20	
1963	Hellenic Hero	5	H. Woodhouse	109	Lucky Turn	111	Mr. Consistency	113	14,105	1:54.00	
1964	Third Martini	5	M. Ycaza	115	Grand Applause	108	Will I Rule	116	19,305	1:56.20	
1965	Circus	4	M. Sorrentino	112	Purser	110	C'ry F'ord II	116	18,655	1:55.80	
1966	Rego	3	H. Woodhouse	112	Paoluccio	118	Gallup Poll	112	19,597	1:59.60	
1967	Flag	7	S. Hernandez	112	Niarkos	115	Ruffled Feathers	120	14,771	1:58.00	
1967	Dunderhead	4	E. Cardone	111	Kentucky Kin	113	Jean-Pierre	114	14,934	1:58.20	
1968	Flit-to	5	M. Ycaza	117	Sea Castle	116	Goodwood II	111	19,337	1:56.00	
1969	Vent du Nord	4	R.L. Turcotte	116	Nez Perce	113	B'u of the w't	109	15,031	1:57.60	
1969	Zarco	3	R. Turcotte	112	Red Reality	116	Eagle's Sw'p	112	15,031	1:56.40	
1970	Mongo's Pride	3	C.H. Marquez	115	Barking Steeple	106	Asp'sia III	112	19,110	2:44.00	
1971	Fresh Alibhai	3	J. Ruane	109	Specious	110	Triangular	108	20,970	2:57.40	
1972	Triangular	5	J.L. Rotz	119	Dendron	112	Up II	108	16,665	2:57.20	
1973	Asray	4	C. Baltazar	112	Triangular	114	Yvetot	112	34,710	2:39.80	
1974	Shady Character	3	A. Cordero Jr	115	John Drew	111	Crafty Khale	126	33,690	2:41.40	
1975	Shady Character	4	A. Cordero Jr	113	Blue Times	115	Yvetot	113	33,900	2:16.20	
1976	Javamine	3	J. Velasquez	111	Recupere	112	Banghi	118	26,400	2:20.60	
1976	Oilfield	3	S. Hawley	112	Royal Mission	111	Trumpeter Swan	112	26,100	2:22.60	
1977	Dance D'Espoir	5	J. Cruguet	112	Java Rajah	106	Diagramatic	112	26,010	2:05.00	
1977	Keep the Promise	5	J. Cruguet	110	Soldier's Lark	110	Star Spangled	114	26,460	2:04.40	
1978	Fluorescent Light	4	J. Cruguet	115	Banquet Table	109	Scythian Gold	110	34,560	2:14.20	
1979	French Colonial	4	J. Vasquez	114	T.V. Series	113	Golden Reserve	112	35,880	2:21.40	
1980	Foretake	4	J. Ruane	112	El Barril	113	Ministrel	109	33,450	2:22.20	
1980	Lobsang II	4	M. Venezia	111	Match the Hatch	115	King Crimson	111	33,450	2:23.60	
1981	Euphrosyne	5	R. Migliore	110	Our Captain Willie	115	Naskra's Breeze	115	33,300	2:18.40	
1981	Ghazwan	4	C. Hernandez	110	Wicked Will	108	Hunston	107	33,540	2:20.60	
1982	Half Iced	3	D. MacBeth	114	No Neck	109	Erin's Tiger	113	33,330	2:18.20	
1982	If Winter Comes	4	M. Venezia	108	Ten Below	113	Forkali	112	33,330	2:19.60	
1983	Four Bases	4	R.J. Thibeau	105	Moon Spirit	114	Ask Me	117	34,230	2:17.80	
1983	Piling	5	E. Maple	114	Chem	116	Charging Through	110	34,470	2:19.00	
1984	He's Vivacious	4	R.G. Davis	109	Nassipour	109	Lucky Scott	107	46,440	2:26.00	
1985	Putting Green	5	E. Maple	112	Domynsky	105	Capricorn Son	109	54,405	2:23.80	
1985	Rocanadour II	6	J. Cruguet	112	Sondrio	115	He's Vivacious	111	54,405	2:23.80	

Year	Winner	Age	Jockey	Wt.	Second	Wt.	Third	Wt.	Win Value	Time	Beyer
1986	Duluth	4	J. Cruguet	113	Dance of Life	122	Broadway Tommy	109	55,710	2:20.80	
1987	Laser Lane	4	J.A. Santos	113	Yankee Affair	116	Wanderkin	112	73,260	1:51.60	
1988	Jimmy's Bronco	4	J. Cruguet	112	Coeur de Lion	118	Gai Minois	113	58,590	1:54.80	
1989	Trans Banner	4	J.L. Samyn	112	Soviet Lad	112	Impersonator	114	58,770	1:53.60	
1990	Who's to Pay	4	J.D. Bailey	115	Yankee Affair	120	Gr'n L'ne Express	121	57,240	1:49.20	106
1991	Home of the Free	3	J.R. Velazquez	109	Turkey Point	114	Fourstars Allstar	113	56,070	1:48.60	101
1992	Binary Light	3	J. Cruguet	111	Share the Glory	110	Turkey Point	113	56,160	1:52.60	94
1993	River Majesty	4	M.E. Smith	115	Daarik	114	Home of the Free	118	52,920	1:54.40	98
1994	Kiri's Clown	5	Luzzi MJ	114	River Majesty	117	Red Earth	111	52,335	1:49.20	105
1995	Diplomatic Jet	3	M.E. Smith	113	Flag Down	114	Easy Miner	109	87,870	2:04.80	107
1996	Mr. Bluebird	5	M.E. Smith	113	Devil's Cup	107	Ops Smile	116	69,660	1:49.20	105
1997	Sir Cat	4	M.E. Smith	116	Tahmid	116	Outta My Way Man	115	69,060	1:50.00	96
1998	Sahm	4	J.R. Velazquez	116	Glok	113	Let Goodtimes Roll	112	67,440	1:48.60	104
1999	Charge d'Affaires	4	J.A. Santos	114	Comic Strip	119	Nat's Big Party	113	66,480	1:49.00	100
2000	Charge d'Affaires	5	J.A. Santos	115	Devine Wind	116	Understood	111	90,000	1:49.01	103
2001	Sumitas	5	E.S. Prado	115	Manndar	116	Crash Course	115	90,000	2:02.55	103
2002	Dawn of the Condor	5	J.F. Chavez	114	Serial Bride	114	Polish Miner	114	90,000	1:52.54	98
2003	Better Talk Now	4	E.S. Prado	116	Del Mar Show	116	Millennium Dragon	115	90,000	1:50.53	101
2004	Host	4	C.P. DeCarlo	115	Evening Attire	114	Sailaway	113	90,000	1:49.95	103

Beyer Index: 101.60

LA BREA (G1), 7 Furlongs,
3-Year-Old Fillies, Santa Anita, 2004 Purse: $250,000

Year	Winner	Age	Jockey	Wt.	Second	Wt.	Third	Wt.	Win Value	Time	Beyer
1974	Niner Power	3	S. Valdez	117	First Majesty	117	Handsome Native	117	20,350	1:43.80	
1975	Bobby Murcer	3	E. Belmonte	120	Bold Clarion	120	Roger's Dandy	117	20,800	1:43.40	
	Run in January										
1975	Featherfoot	3	W. Shoemaker	114	Banyan Road	120	Graham Heagney	114	13,025	1:42.20	
1975	Big Destiny	3	S. Hawley	114	Bending Away	120	Mark's Place	120	13,325	1:42.80	
	Run in December										
1976	Kirby Lane	3	L. Pincay Jr	117	Tregillick	116	Missing Marbles	116	23,750	1:45.20	
1978	Taisez Vous	3	D. Pierce	121	Ida Delia	114	Sound of Summer	121	26,700	1:22.80	
1979	Great Lady M.	3	L. Pincay Jr	117	Queen Yasna	114			35,800	1:22.60	
					B. Thoughtful	121					
1980	Terlingua	3	D.G. McHargue	121	Glorious Song	116	Prize Spot	121	31,350	1:20.80	
1981	Dynamite	3	W. Shoemaker	114	Bold 'n Determined	125	Pachena	114	31,750	1:21.40	
1982	Nell's Briquette	3	C.J. McCarron	122	Bannockburn	115	Bee a Scout	117	40,150	1:25.80	
1982	Beautiful Glass	3	C.J. McCarron	114	Skillful Joy	122	Header Card	119	42,450	1:21.00	
1983	Lovlier Linda	3	W. Shoemaker	114	Angel Savage	115	Fabulous Notion	124	40,700	1:22.20	
1985	Mitterand	3	E. Delahoussaye	117	Percipient	119	Lady Trilby	117	39,950	1:21.80	
1985	Savannah Slew	3	W. Shoemaker	119	Lady's Secert	124	Ambra Ridge	117	39,150	1:22.40	
	Run in January and December										
1987	Family Style	3	G.L. Stevens	122	Sari's Heroine	119	Winter Treasure	117	46,700	1:22.60	
1988	Very Subtle	4	P.A. Valenzuela	124	Saros Brig	114	Fold the Flag	117	60,300	1:21.60	
1989	Variety Baby	4	C.A. Black	117	T.V. of Crystal	117	Forewarning	117	49,050	1:21.60	
1990	Akinemod	3	G.L. Stevens	117	Fantastic Look	122	Reluctant Guest	117	62,650	1:21.60	101
1990	Brought to Mind	3	A. Solis	117	A Wild Ride	119	Mama Simba	114	65,000	1:21.60	
1991	D'Or Ruckus	3	C.J. McCarron	115	Good Potential	119	Garden Gal	117	48,800	1:22.05	96
1991	Teresa Mc	3	P.A. Valenzuela	119	Remarkably Easy	119	Suziqcute	119	48,800	1:23.05	87
1992	Arches of Gold	3	E. Delahoussaye	116	Race the Wild Wind	121	Terre Haute	117	64,800	1:21.28	101
1993	Mamselle Bebette	3	C.S. Nakatani	115	Desert Stormer	116	Island Orchid	115	65,900	1:20.45	102
1994	Top Rung	3	G.L. Stevens	115	Klassy Kim	119	Twice the Vice	119	63,700	1:21.84	95
1995	Exotic Wood	3	C.J. McCarron	119	Evil's Pic	119	Jewel Princess	119	80,250	1:21.57	99
1996	Hidden Lake	3	C.J. McCarron	115	Belle's Flag	119	Tiffany Diamond	115	80,900	1:22.00	98
1997	I Ain't Bluffing	3	E. Delahoussaye	119	Minister's Melody	119	Praviana	115	99,540	1:21.23	100
1998	Magical Allure	3	G.L. Stevens	121	Gourmet Girl	117	Tranquility Lake	116	120,000	1:22.06	96
1999	Hookedonthefeelin	3	D.R. Flores	119	Olympic Charmer	119	Kalookan Queen	119	120,000	1:21.84	107
2000	Spain	3	V.L. Espinoza	123	Cover Gal	119	Serenita	115	120,000	1:22.27	96
2001	Affluent	3	E. Delahoussaye	121	Royally Chosen	119	Love At Noon	117	120,000	1:21.29	97
2002	Got Koko	3	A. Solis	117	Spring Meadow	119	Erica's Smile	117	120,000	1:22.57	97
2003	Island Fashion	3	K.J. Desormeaux	123	Randaroo	119	Buffythecenterfold	119	150,000	1:21.79	109
2004	Alphabet Kisses	3	M.E. Smith	117	Bending Strings	121	Elusive Diva	119	150,000	1:21.38	101

Beyer Index: 98.88

Run at 1 1/16 miles, for 3-year-olds, 1974–76

LA CANADA (G2), 1 1/8 Miles,
4-Year-Old Fillies, Santa Anita, 2004 Purse: $200,000

Year	Winner	Age	Jockey	Wt.	Second	Wt.	Third	Wt.	Win Value	Time	Beyer
1975	Chris Evert	4	J. Velasquez	128	Mercy Dee	116	Lucky Spell	119	35,400	1:41.60	
1976	Raise Your Skirts	4	W. Shoemaker	119	Fascinating Girl	117	Our First Delight	117	50,150	1:48.40	

Year	Winner	Age	Jockey	Wt.	Second	Wt.	Third	Wt.	Win Value	Time	Beyer
1977	Lucie Manet	4	W. Shoemaker	115	Hail Hilarious	121	Up to Juliet	116	68,300	1:48.20	
1978	Taisez Vous	4	D. Pierce	120	Drama Critic	116	Table the Rumor	117	65,000	1:49.80	
1979	B. Thoughtful	4	D. Pierce	117	Petron's Love	117	Island Kiss	115	69,900	1:48.80	
1980	Glorious Song	4	C.J. McCarron	118	Prize Spot	119	It's in the Air	125	80,350	1:47.60	
1981	Summer Siren	4	M. Castaneda	117	Miss Huntington	116	Tobin's Rose	118	86,250	1:48.60	
1982	Safe Play	4	D. Brumfield	119	Rainbow Connection	116	Native Plunder	117	100,800	1:47.60	
1983	Avigaition	4	E. Delahoussaye	117	Elusive	115	Etoile du Matin	116	101,900	1:49.80	
1984	Sweet Diane	4	R. Sibille	120	Weekend Surprise	115	Lovlier Linda	120	117,200	1:49.20	
1985	Mitterand	4	E. Delahoussaye	121	Percipient	117	Life's Magic	126	90,700	1:48.80	
1986	Lady's Secret	4	C.J. McCarron	126	Shywing	119	North Sider	118	120,200	1:49.80	
1987	Family Style	4	G.L. Stevens	122	Winter Treasure	117	Sari's Heroine	121	94,800	1:49.60	
1988	Hollywood Glitter	4	L. Pincay Jr	117	By Land By Sea	119	Very Subtle	126	94,200	1:49.20	
1989	Goodbye Halo	4	P. Day	126	Seattle Smooth	117	Savannah's Honor	115	125,300	1:54.40	
1990	Gorgeous	4	E. Delahoussaye	125	Luthier's Launch	117	Kelly	116	122,000	1:50.00	105
1991	Fit to Scout	4	J.A. Garcia	120	Vieille Vigne	116	A Wild Ride	121	126,700	1:48.40	
1992	Exchange	4	L. Pincay Jr	119	Winglet	117	Damewood	116	128,250	1:49.80	95
1993	Alysbelle	4	E. Delahoussaye	116	Pacific Squall	119	Interactive	117	130,850	1:49.80	100
1994	Stalcreek	4	G.L. Stevens	119	Alyshena	115	Hollywood Wildcat	122	120,000	1:48.80	96
1995	Dianes Halo	4	C.S. Nakatani	115	Twice the Vice	119	Klassy Kim	119	123,000	1:49.20	93
1996	Jewel Princess	4	A. Solis	119	Dixie Pearl	116	Privity	117	129,900	1:49.40	98
1997	Belle's Flag	4	C.S. Nakatani	119	Chile Chatte	115	Housa Dancer	115	133,200	1:48.20	105
1998	Fleet Lady	4	G.K. Gomez	119	Minister's Melody	117	I Ain't Bluffing	117	120,000	1:48.40	103
1999	Manistique	4	G.L. Stevens	119	Magical Allure	119	Gourmet Girl	117	120,000	1:48.80	107
2000	Scholars Studio	4	C.S. Nakatani	116	Smooth Player	117	The Seven Seas	116	120,000	1:49.14	104
2001	Spain	4	V. Espinoza	122	Chilukki	119	Letter Of Intent	116	120,000	1:49.74	92
2002	Summer Colony	4	G.L. Stevens	119	Azeri	115	Ask Me No Secrets	115	120,000	1:49.26	105
2003	Got Koko	4	A. Solis	121	Sightseek	118	Bella Bellucci	118	120,000	1:48.41	106
2004	Cat Fighter	4	A. Solis	115	Fencelineneighbor	116	Tangle	116	120,000	1:50.41	91

Beyer Index: 100.00

LADIES HANDICAP (G3), 1 1/4 Miles, Fillies and Mares, 3-Year-Olds and Up, Aqueduct, 2004 Purse: $109,400

Year	Winner	Age	Jockey	Wt.	Second	Wt.	Third	Wt.	Win Value	Time	Beyer
1868	Bonnie Braes	3	Hennessey	107	Australia	107	Fanny Ludlow	107	1,850	3:06.75	
1869	Tasmania	3	Miller	107	Invercauld	107	Rapture	107	2,150	3:07.75	
1870	Annette	3	Wilson	107	Midway	107	Nellie James	107	2,800	3:02.00	
1871	Nellie Gray	3	Swim	107	Mary Clark	107	Mary Louise	107	3,400	3:03.00	
1872	Victoria	3	Gradwell	107	Elsie	107	Experience Oaks	107	2,800	3:11.00	
1873	Katie Pease	3	J. Rowe	107	Sally Watson	107	Annie Hall	107	3,150	2:58.25	
1874	Bonaventure	3	A. Lakeland	107	Lava	107	Countess	107	2,850	2:42.25	
1875	Olitipa	3	Evans	107	Mattie A.	107	Invoice	107	2,850	2:42.75	
1876	Sultana	3	Hayward	107	Merciless	107	Patience	107	2,950	2:46.00	
1877	Idalia	3	G. Barbee	107	Zoo Zoo	107	Oriole	107	3,300	2:41.00	
1878	Invermore	3	Sparling	113	Balance All	113	Favorite	113	3,000	2:46.75	
1879	Ferida	3	Costello	113	Magnetism	113	Bonnie Leaf	113	2,900	2:47.00	
1880	Carita	3	Hayward	113	Edelweiss	113	Queen's Own	113	2,350	2:44.50	
1881	Aella	3	Costello	113	Bliss	113	Spark	113	2,400	2:51.00	
1882	Hiawasse	3	Feakes	113	Rica	113	Olivia	113	2,800	2:44.00	
1883	Miss Woodford	3	J. McLaughlin	113	Carnation	113	Fairview	113	3,040	2:43.50	
1884	Duchess	3	W. Donahue	113	Economy	113	Nonage	113	2,360	2:46.00	
1885	Miss Palmer	3	J. McLaughlin	113	Punka	113	Brita	113	2,120	2:47.50	
1886	Bandala	3	J. McLaughlin	113	Charity	113	Long Stop	113	2,270	2:12.50	
1887	Firenze	3	F. Littlefield	113	Flageoletta	113	Almy	113	2,670	2:14.75	
1888	Bella B.	3	J. McLaughlin	113	Golden Reel	113	Inverwick	113	2,970	2:14.50	
1889	Fides	3	Garrison	115	Auricoma	115			4,040	2:00.50	
					Senorita	113					
1890	Sinaloa II	3	Barnes	103	Gloaming	104	Bibelot	103	5,670	1:19.00	
1891	Castalia	3	Taral	117	Equity	117	Graylock	117	3,420	1:20.50	
1892	Yorkville Belle	3	I. Murphy	117	Madrid	117	Ada Blue	117	3,530	1:56.50	
1893	Naptha	3	Simms	117	Lillian Russell	110	Grace Brown	117	3,445	1:42.20	
1894	Nahma	3	Littlefield	120	Lightfoot	109	Kentigerna	117	4,600	1:49.00	
1896	Intermission	3	Littlefield	109	Cassette	113	St. Agnes	109	1,425	1:43.50	
1897	Divide	3	Taral	114	Lady Mitchell	114	Min. Alphonse	114	2,550	1:44.00	
1898	Geisha	3	T. Sloan	117	Miss Miriam	117	Kenmore Queen	117	2,240	1:43.00	
1899	Prestidigitatrice	3	Littlefield	117	Lady Madge	117	Lady Lindsey	117	2,340	1:43.00	
1900	Oneck Queen	3	Maher	121	Indian Fairy	121	Motley	121	2,600	1:40.75	
1901	Janice	3	Piggott	121	Lady of the Valley	121	La Valliere	121	2,485	1:45.25	
1902	Blue Girl	3	T. Burns	121	Hatasoo	121	Hanover Queen	121	2,395	1:42.00	
1903	Girdle	3	T, Burns	121	Stolen Moment	121	Gravina	121	3,445	1:42.20	
1904	Beldame	3	Hildebrand	121	Audience	121	Marjoram	121	4,870	1:41.20	
1905	Flinders	3	Lyne	121	Gold Ten	121	Coy Maid	121	5,345	1:42.40	

Year	Winner	Age	Jockey	Wt.	Second	Wt.	Third	Wt.	Win Value	Time	Beyer
1906	Perverse	3	Lyne	121			Edna Jackson	121	5,000	1:39.80	
1907	Yankee Girl	3	Radtke	121	Adoration	121	Court Dress	121	5,405	1:40.60	
1908	Stamina	3	E. Dugan	121	Anonyma	121	Laughing Eyes	121	6,385	1:40.80	
1909	Maskette	3	Butwel	121	Lady Bedford	121	Field Mouse	121	6,630	1:39.00	
1910	Ocean Bound	3	G. Garner	121	Indian Maid	121	Mexoana	121	1,520	1:43.00	
1913	Flamma	4	H. Radtke	101	Hedge	108	Flying Fairy	117	1,720	1:39.60	
1914	Flying Fairy	4	T. Davies	126	Cadeau	109	Tarts	112	2,110	1:38.00	
1915	Addie M.	4	G. Byrne	106	Lady Rotha	106	Comely	113	1,450	1:39.20	
1916	Celandria	3	M. Garner	113	Capra	124	Fenmouse	111	1,610	1:41.00	
1917	Rhine Maiden	5	R. Ball	108	Wistful	108	Celandria	111	2,060	1:41.00	
1918	Eyelid	3	M. Rowan	110	Priscilla Mullens	117	Dorcas	112	2,130	1:40.00	
1919	Salvestra	4	E. Taplin	117	Enfilade	125	Lady G'trdue	112	1,955	1:37.60	
1920	Milkmaid	4	E. Sande	126	Cleopatra	115	Banksia	111	3,175	1:38.20	
1921	Pen Rose	5	L. Fator	122	La Rablee	114	Lady G'trude	116	1,745	1:40.60	
1922	Many Smiles	3	C. Fairbrother	113	Chateau Thierry	120	Polly Ann	117	3,475	1:37.20	
1923	Solisa	3	B. Marinelli	104	Careful	123	Story Teller	112	3,325	1:38.80	
1924	Relentless	3	J. Maiben	105	Outline	114	Sunayr	105	3,725	1:38.00	
1925	Whetstone	4	A. Johnson	120	Nellie Morse	122	Extra Dry	112	3,400	1:37.80	
1926	Black Maria	3	L. Fator	120	Extra Dry	119	Rapture	122	3,175	1:38.80	
1927	Black Maria	4	F. Coltiletti	127	Jumbo	110	Corvette	111	3,500	1:39.80	
1928	Twitter	3	R. Workman	114	Nixie	110	Bateau	114	3,275	1:40.40	
1929	Lace	4	L. Fator	114	Bateau	126	B'ldey's P'y	107	3,750	1:38.20	
1930	Snowflake	3	L. Schaefer	116	Dustemall	112	Flimsy	114	4,375	1:40.00	
1931	Valenciennes	4	C. Kurtsinger	116	Risque	126	Polly Play	118	2,725	1:37.40	
1932	Top Flight	3	R. Workman	126	Parry	114	Risque	118	2,275	1:37.80	
1933	White Lies	3	M. Garner	110	Sweet Scent	107	Notebook	107	1,030	1:38.40	
1934	Coequal	3	E. Litzenberger	106	Black Queen	105	Slapdash	114	2,030	1:37.40	
1935	Vicaress	3	E. Arcaro	111	Alberta	116	Kate	114	2,325	1:37.40	
1936	Rust	4	E. Yager	113	Maecloud	102	Fortification	111	2,395	1:38.40	
1937	Genie Palatine	4	C. Kurtsinger	119	Rust	117	Sparta	120	2,405	1:38.00	
1938	Idle Miss	4	A. Robertson	123	Jacola	117	Rust	109	5,400	1:37.60	
1939	Red Eye	3	B. James	116	Bass Wood	115	Savage Beauty	111	5,900	1:36.40	
1940	Salaminia	3	D. Meade	115	Pretty Pet	114	Fairy Chant	123	12,250	2:30.00	
1941	Up the Hill	3	C. McCreary	107	Dark Discovery	102	Pretty Pet	115	11,800	2:30.00	
1942	Vagrancy	3	J. Stout	126	Dark Discovery	108	Loveday	117	11,175	2:31.20	
1943	Stefanita	3	C. McCreary	116	Vagrancy	123	Dark Discovery	106	11,025	2:31.80	
1944	Donitas First	3	T. Atkinson	115	Letmenow	112	Moon M'den	113	11,040	2:31.20	
1945	War Date	3	A. Kirkland	124	Surosa	121	Letmenow	113	11,730	2:34.40	
1946	Athenia	3	T. Atkinson	116	Riskolator	109	Rosa Blanca	107	16,700	2:30.60	
1947	Snow Goose	3	T. Atkinson	113	But Why Not	121	Gallorette	123	42,600	2:29.60	
1948	Miss Request	3	T. Atkinson	114	Gallorette	121	Honeymoon	123	40,600	2:30.00	
1949	Gaffery	3	E. Guerin	114	Miss Request	119	Adile	115	24,800	2:29.80	
1950	Next Move	3	E. Guerin	120	My Celeste	106	Wistful	124	20,700	2:29.40	
1951	Marta	4	C. McCreary	111	Bed o' Roses	126	Kiss Me Kate	120	31,250	2:30.20	
1952	How	4	N. Shuk	112	Marta	122	Enchanted Eve	112	40,900	2:31.40	
1953	La Corredora	4	I. Hanford	118	Nothirdchance	111	How	118	40,900	2:30.40	
1954	Lavender Hill	5	S. Small	122	Ming Yellow	113	Riverina	114	43,400	2:32.20	
1955	Manotick	3	A. Valenzuela	117	Misty Morn	124	Countess Fleet	117	43,900	2:31.40	
1956	Flower Bowl	4	W. Shoemaker	116	Dotted Line	111	Bright't Star	107	40,100	2:29.80	
1957	Rare Treat	5	P.J. Bailey	118	Gay Life	107	Snow White	113	40,800	2:31.60	
1958	Endine	4	E. Nelson	114	Dotted Line	123	An'e-Lu-San	108	37,165	2:30.40	
1959	Tempted	4	E. Nelson	128	High Bid	112	Big Effort	115	36,580	2:09.00	
1960	Berlo	3	E. Guerin	124	Woodlawn	112	Who's Ahead	105	38,205	2:30.60	
1961	Mighty Fair	3	P.J. Bailey	115	Craftiness	120	Tritoma	116	37,050	2:11.80	
1962	Royal Patrice	3	H. Grant	114	Waltz Song	115	Oil Royalty	113	37,245	2:10.60	
1963	Goofed	3	J.L. Rotz	113	Suiti	112	Dupage Lady	110	37,765	2:29.40	
1964	Steeple Jill	3	J. Ruane	109	Dupage Lady	109	Tona	115	38,415	2:29.60	
1965	Straight Deal	3	J. Sellers	114	Steeple Jill	126	Yes Please	109	36,335	2:03.60	
1966	Destro	3	B. Baeza	115	Straight Deal	118	Miss Dickey	113	36,725	2:02.40	
1967	Sweet Folly	3	H. Gustines	114	Harem Lady	108	Muse	106	38,090	2:04.60	
1968	Politely	5	A. Cordero Jr	128	Amerigo Lady	118	Raison d'Etre	110	36,335	2:02.60	
1969	Shuvee	3	J. Davidson	117	Amerigo Lady	121	Obeah	121	37,830	2:03.00	
1970	Cathy Honey	3	A. Cordero Jr	115	Manta	116	Taken Aback	122	36,010	2:02.20	
1971	Sea Saga	3	C.H. Marquez	117	Helen Jennings	110	Aqua Belle	109	34,680	2:02.60	
1972	Graf'itti	4	M. Venezia	109	Sea Saga	112	Hill Circus	116	32,250	2:04.80	
1973	Wakefield Miss	5	A. Cordero Jr	113	Roba Bella	112	Ferly	113	33,180	2:03.80	
1974	Coraggioso	4	E. Maple	118	Poker Night	117	Twixt	124	33,300	2:02.00	
1975	Tizna	6	F. Alvarez	124	Pass a Glance	113	Susan's Girl	126	51,390	2:03.60	
1976	Bastonera II	5	A. Cordero Jr	122	Proud Delta	125	Sugar Plum Time	114	65,220	2:01.40	
1977	Sensational	3	M. Venezia	110	Dottie's Doll	114	Charming Story	116	64,560	2:02.80	
1978	Ida Delia	4	A. Santiago	114	Water Malone	122	Cum Laude Laurie	115	65,820	2:02.40	
1979	Spark of Life	4	J. Cruguet	116	Catherine's Bet	113	Six Crowns	117	64,740	2:02.80	
1980	Plankton	4	C.B. Asmussen	119	Sugar and Spice	114	Weber City Miss	119	65,400	2:03.00	

Year	Winner	Age	Jockey	Wt.	Second	Wt.	Third	Wt.	Win Value	Time	Beyer
1981	Jameela	5	A. Cordero Jr	120	Discorama	115	Tina Tina Too	112	66,240	2:01.80	
1982	Tina Tina Too	4	D. MacBeth	110	Weber City Miss	124	Mademoiselle Forli	114	65,520	2:03.00	
1983	Mademoiselle Forli	4	G. McCarron	113	Quixotic Lady	119	Mochila	113	67,320	2:03.40	
1984	Heatherten	5	R.P. Romero	123	Solar Halo	112	Key Dancer	113	71,400	2:04.00	
1985	Videogenic	3	R.G. Davis	114	Basie	113	Alabama Nana	119	67,800	2:02.00	
1986	Life at the Top	3	R.P. Romero	118	Coup de Fusil	116	Steal a Kiss	114	167,160	2:03.80	
1987	Nastique	3	R.G. Davis	110	Tricky Squaw	117	No Choice	113	146,880	2:04.40	
1988	Banker's Lady	3	A. Cordero Jr	113	Make Change	114	Thirty Eight Go Go	115	138,960	2:02.00	
1989	Dance Teacher	4	J.A. Santos	113	Whose Doubt	110	Warfie	112	141,120	2:05.80	
1990	Colonial Waters	5	J.A. Santos	121	Buy the Firm	118	Jessi Jessi	113	104,400	2:05.80	104
1991	Wortheroatsingold	4	E. Maple	113	Summer Matinee	115	Lady D'Accord	116	150,000	2:02.40	99
1992	Brilliant Brass	5	E.S. Prado	120	Low Tolerance	111	Lady Lear	111	150,000	2:03.40	104
1993	Groovy Feeling	4	W.H. McCauley	111	Turnback the Alarm	121	Avie's Daisy	113	120,000	2:05.80	100
1994	Tara Roma	4	F.T. Alvarado	114	Beloved Bea	113	Dancer's Gate	112	84,300	2:06.60	87
1995	Transient Trend	3	J.L. Samyn	111	Lotta Dancing	117	Manila Lila	114	67,800	2:01.40	96
1996	Miss Slewpy	5	L.C. Reynolds	120	Hooded Dancer	109	Very True	113	66,600	2:03.20	95
1997	Prophet's Warning	4	J.F. Chavez	112	Mil Kilates	117	Biogio's Rose	112	67,620	2:06.20	94
1998	Unbridled Hope	4	R. Migliore	114	Manoa	114	Sazarac Jazz	111	85,250	2:03.44	105
1999	Strolling Belle	3	H. Castillo Jr	116	Maiden Fair	112	Sazarac Jazz	115	65,640	2:04.72	95
2000	Strolling Belle	4	H. Castillo Jr	120	dq-Pentatonic	117	Reine Amandine	114	66,000	2:06.60	93
	Pentatonic finished first but was disqualified and placed second										
2001	Summer Colony	3	J.R. Velazquez	114	Stop for Schnapps	113	Strolling Belle	118	66,600	2:05.80	94
2002	Critical Eye	5	M.J. Luzzi	116	Ellie's Moment	114	With Ability	118	64,440	2:04.19	96
2003	Savedbythelight	3	R. Migliore	115	Queen's Triomphe	113	Retroactive	113	67,260	2:05.99	88
2004	Rare Gift	3	R. Migliore	115	Board Elligible	117	Miss Fortunate	117	65,640	2:05.51	90

Beyer Index: 96.00

LADY'S SECRET BREEDERS' CUP HANDICAP (G2), 1 1/16 Miles, Fillies and Mares, 3-Year-Olds and Up, Santa Anita, 2004 Purse: $235,000

Year	Winner	Age	Jockey	Wt.	Second	Wt.	Third	Wt.	Win Value	Time	Beyer
1993	Hollywood Wildcat	3	E. Delahoussaye	117	Re Toss	117	Wedding Ring	113	61,700	1:41.00	106
1995	Borodislew	5	G.L. Stevens	120	Top Rung	116	Golden Klair	117	74,000	1:41.60	109
1996	Top Rung	5	E. Fires	116	Jewel Princess	122	Sleep Easy	116	109,450	1:41.80	107
1997	Sharp Cat	3	A. Solis	117	Twice The Vice	122	Minister's Melody	115	109,400	1:41.40	111
1998	Magical Allure	3	D.R. Flores	116	Victory Stripes	114	Housa Dancer	117	110,280	1:42.40	103
1999	Manistique	4	C.S. Nakatani	123	Cookin Vickie	111	Kalosca	114	125,100	1:42.20	103
2000	Smooth Player	4	E. Delahoussaye	116	Speaking of Time	109	Bordelaise	116	126,360	1:42.27	99
2001	Queenie Belle	4	B. Blanc	116	Letter of Intent	116	Nany's Sweep	116	126,240	1:43.64	96
2002	Azeri	4	M.E. Smith	127	Starrer	115	Mystic Lady	116	130,500	1:41.10	102
2003	Got Koko	4	A. Solis	118	Azeri	128	Adoration	115	180,000	1:42.92	105
	Elloluv finished second but was disqualified and placed fourth										
2004	Island Fashion	4	K. John	120	Miss Loren	116	Elloluv	118	150,000	1:43.43	96

Beyer Index: 103.36

LAFAYETTE (G3), 7 Furlongs, 3-Year-Olds, Keeneland Race Course, 2004 Purse: $109,500

Year	Winner	Age	Jockey	Wt.	Second	Wt.	Third	Wt.	Win Value	Time	Beyer
1937	Chic Maud	2	I. Anderson	114	Green Bottle	117	Knee Deep	114	4,225	:47.20	
1938	Oddesa Beulah	2	M. Calvert	119	Cherry Jam	117	Batter	117	3,600	:45.00	
1939	Roman	2	W. Yarberry	117	Flying Mary	114	Charitable	114	3,550	:47.60	
1940	Misty Isle	2	K. McCombs	114	Blue Lily	114	Blue Pair	117	3,950	:47.00	
1941	Black Raider	2	A. Craig	122	Fade	119	My Choice	114	4,050	:46.40	
1942	Menex	2	E. Arcaro	122	Ogma	114	Sun Jesting	111	4,450	:46.60	
1943	Ogham	2	J. Longden	117	Whirlabout	112	Sweetest Girl	114	4,700	:54.80	
1944	Poca Mas	2	G. Seabo	117	Best Effort	117	Roi Rouge	117	6,475	:53.80	
1946	Colonel O'F	2	W. Bailey	117	Rhodelin	114	Etnom	117	5,750	:46.40	
1947	Phar Mon	2	A. LoTurco	122	Tiger Flash	117	Pelt	114	13,500	:46.20	
1948	Irish Sun	2	A. LoTurco	117	Acoma	114	Olympia	117	11,950	:46.20	
1949	Black Sambo	2	R.L. Baird	117	Wisconsin Boy	117	Go Jeep Go	122	14,050	:47.40	
1950	Mals Boy	2	J.D. Jessop	117	Dydamic	122	Flyamanita	114	15,150	:45.40	
1951	Recover	2	D. Dodson	114	Free for Me	114	Hudgens	117	13,125	:46.60	
1951	Crownlet	2	R.L. Baird	114	Red Curtice	117	Very Special	114	13,125	:46.60	
1952	Happy Carrier	2	G. Porch	117	Ace Destroyer	117	Orofino	111	10,126	:46.20	
1952	Aerolite	2	D. Dodson	114	Bubbley	114	Fighting Eagle	117	9,964	:45.80	
1953	Everett Jr.	2	A. Popara	122	Terrebonne	117	Beanir	114	13,035	:45.40	
1954	Royal Note	2	H. Moreno	117	Smart Devil	114	Tricky Homer	117	12,417	:49.40	
1955	First Lap	2	J.D. Jessop	117	Tiger Wander	114	Skeptical Kid	122	13,425	:50.00	
1956	Round Table	2	S. Brooks	117	Jet Colonel	117	Chookoss	117	12,677	:49.60	
1957	Bumpy Road	2	W. Hartack	117	Alliance	117	Red Hot Pistol	117	9,955	:48.40	
1958	Grand Wizard	2	V. Guajardo	117	Matisse	117	Goshen	114	8,899	:50.80	

Year	Winner	Age	Jockey	Wt.	Second	Wt.	Third	Wt.	Win Value	Time	Beyer
1958	Bagdad	2	J. Heckmann	117	Severn	117	Subway Strike	114	8,834	:50.60	
1959	Vital Force	2	J. Sellers	117	Neshenun	117	Rock Age	117	10,069	:49.00	
1959	Chuckabuck	2	W. Hartack	117	Careless John	114	Pensive Sun	114	10,069	:49.80	
1960	Bright Silver	2	J.L. Rotz	114	Fading Sky	114	Cyclobob	117	8,355	:49.60	
1960	Sal's Beau	2	B. Baeza	117	He's a Pistol	117	Chinchilla	117	8,160	:48.80	
1961	Crimson Satan	2	W. Carstens	117	Mike G.	117	Jetting Home	117	10,221	:49.00	
1962	Donstopnow	2	M. Duhon	122	Sound Trick	117	Bora Bora	117	10,270	:48.60	
1963	Amastar	2	J. Nichols	117	Delirium	117	Doubly Fare	114	8,726	:48.20	
1964	Loom	2	J. Nichols	117	Mahjubill	117	Ramflow	117	8,840	:48.00	
1965	He Jr.	2	J. Fielselman	117	Highest Alp	117	Fearless Knight	117	9,327	:52.00	
1966	Quick Swoon	2	E. Fires	117	Better Bee's Jr.	114	Nascourt	114	8,937	:51.40	
1967	T.V. Commercial	2	K. Knapp	117	Caribbean Line	117	Rhythmic	117	8,905	:52.00	
1968	Santiago Road	2	K. Knapp	117	Star o' Victory	114	February Fun	117	12,106	:52.00	
1968	Traffic Mark	2	M. McDowell	117	Jay Ray	117	Gage Line	114	12,301	:52.60	
1969	Spotted Line	2	D.E. Whited	117	Dee Dee Tees	117	Irish Loom	117	13,877	:51.80	
1970	Seen Alot	2	M. Manganello	117	Beauty's Son	122	Surya	117	14,690	:53.00	
1971	Busted	2	M. Solomone	117	One Nation	117	Rest Your Case	117	15,210	:51.60	
1972	Cari County	2	P. Rubbicco	117	Entity	117	Slander	117	15,665	:52.00	
1973	Mr. A.Z.	2	R. Ussery	118	Hudson County	115	Best of It	116	12,808	:52.60	
1974	Paris Dust	2	C. Perret	122	Commercial Pilot	119	Master Derby	119	12,379	:51.80	
1975	Inca Roca	2	T. Warner	116	Joseph Daniel	116	Khyber King	119	11,927	:52.80	
1976	United Holme	2	W. Gavidia	119	Marve	119	Golden Gossip	119	11,125	:52.00	
1977	Fiddle Faddle	2	W. Gavidia	116	Old Crony	119	Bye Bye Bud	116	11,356	:52.80	
1978	Spy Charger	2	G. Mahon	122	It's a Rerun	119	Trip Over	116	11,278	:53.20	
1979	Raised Socially	2	M.R. Morgan	119	Native Moment	119	Landing Stripes	119	16,380	:52.20	
1980	Firm Boss	2	M.R. Morgan	122	Bend the Times	116	Silver Dollar Boy	122	14,723	:53.00	
1981	Grey Bucket	2	J. Oldham	119	Talent Town	116	Lady Ann's Key	116	15,356	:53.20	
1982	Jungle Blade	3	W.J. Neagle	115	Talk of the Times	118	Baraco	112	39,794	1:10.20	
1983	Freezing Rain	3	D. Brumfield	118	Harry 'n Bill	118	Hamlet	112	36,546	1:11.20	
1984	Delta Trace	3	K.K. Allen	118	Patch of Sun	112	Soybean Trader	112	37,489	1:10.00	
1985	Proudest Hour	3	R.P. Romero	121	Felter on the Quay	112	Don't Hesitate	121	35,133	1:10.80	
1986	Numero Uno Pass	3	C. Perret	113	Color Me Smart	121	Friendly Blue	122	35,945	1:23.60	
1987	Trick Card	3	D.A. Miller Jr	118	War	118	Contractor's Tune	112	35,084	1:23.80	
1988	Forty Niner	3	P. Day	121	Buoy	121	Aloha Prospector	121	46,306	1:22.00	
1989	Belek	3	S.P. Romero	112	Notation	118	Mr. Sea Sanders	118	35,051	1:23.00	
1990	Housebuster	3	C. Perret	121	Sacra Hoxen	114	Critical Choice	113	52,215	1:22.80	
1991	To Freedom	3	C.W. Antley	121	Romiano	114	Broadway's Top Gun	121	54,958	1:22.80	
1992	American Chance	3	P. Day	115	Capitalimprovement	118	Mon Capitan	114	56,770	1:22.00	104
1993	Cherokee Run	3	P. Day	118	Poverty Slew	112	Williamstown	121	52,328	1:21.20	103
1994	Exclusive Praline	3	J.A. Santos	121	Dynamic Asset	115	End Sweep	113	49,321	1:23.80	99
1995	Mr. Greeley	3	J.A. Krone	121	Peaks and Valleys	118	Tethra	121	51,429	1:21.40	109
1996	Wire Me Collect	3	K.L. Chapman	112	Appealing Skier	121	Irish Conquest	112	69,192	1:21.80	99
1997	Trafalger	3	J.D. Bailey	113	Open Forum	118	Muchacho Fino	113	67,456	1:21.60	101
1998	Dontletthebigonego	3	W. Martinez	114	Flashing Tammany	114	Swear By Dixie	114	67,394	1:23.00	100
1999	Yes It's True	3	J.D. Bailey	123	Trickey Crew	118	Fort La Roca	115	66,340	1:22.00	104
2000	Caller One	3	R.G. Davis	120	Sun Cat	116	Littleexpectations	120	70,370	1:21.73	108
2001	Griffinite	3	J.A. Santos	116	Sam Lord's Castle	118	Yonguska	123	68,820	1:22.61	104
2002	Cashel Castle	3	P. Day	116	Governor Hickel	116	Sky Terrace	116	69,006	1:24.47	93
2003	Posse	3	C.J. Lanerie	118	Roll Hennessy Roll	118	Bossanova	116	66,898	1:23.14	108
2004	Bwana Charlie	3	S.J. Sellers	117	Quick Action	116	Tales of Glory	116	67,890	1:24.73	91

Beyer Index: 101.77

LA JOLLA HANDICAP (G2), 1 1/16 Miles (Turf), 3-Year-Olds, Del Mar, 2004 Purse: $150,000

Year	Winner	Age	Jockey	Wt.	Second	Wt.	Third	Wt.	Win Value	Time	Beyer
1937	Topsy Omar	5	T. Sena	108	Grey Count	118	Distribute	108	1,180	1:45.40	
1938	Dogaway	4	E. Yager	122	Capt. Cal	114	Gray Jack	111	1,660	1:37.20	
1940	Justice M.	3	E. Rodriguez	114	Exarch	120	Bachelor Tom	116	1,625	1:37.20	
1941	Vain Grove	3	F. Zufelt	118	Vegas Justice	107	Brown China	113	1,625	1:37.80	
1945	Gold Boom	4	F. Zehr	114	Inflammable	116	Orion	122	3,730	1:37.60	
1946	First to Fight	5	H. Trent	122	Montanes	109	Nanby Pass	109	5,150	1:37.40	
1947	Handlebars	3	L. Balaski	124	Sparky Cannon	112	Winsir	118	4,675	1:38.20	
1948	Henpecker	3	J. Gilbert	122	Lady Zev	107	Belle Jolie	119	6,375	1:37.80	
1949	Dinner Gong	4	R. Neves	126	Challenging	116	Prevaricator	114	6,625	1:36.00	
1950	Blue Reading	3	B. Pearson	115	Manyunk	122	Mercenary	110	6,925	1:36.00	
1951	Oats	3	G. Glisson	117	Grantor	124	Mucho Hosso	120	6,500	1:37.80	
1952	Arroz	3	W. Shoemaker	116	Stranglehold	114	Horsetrader-Ed	110	6,775	1:37.40	
1953	Threesome	3	J. Phillippi	116	Smart Barbara	109	Six Fifteen	112	6,600	1:36.40	
1954	Leterna	3	W. Harmatz	107	War Tryst	119	Indian Red	112	6,500	1:36.00	
1955	Hillary	3	G. Glisson	110	Damocles	116	Valiant Ace	119	6,725	1:35.40	

Year	Winner	Age	Jockey	Wt.	Second	Wt.	Third	Wt.	Win Value	Time	Beyer
1956	Blen Host	3	R. Neves	119	Pit Boss	120	Lucky G.L.	122	8,900	1:37.00	
1957	No Bumps	3	W. Ferguson	108	Mystic Eye	116	Redi-Reading	112	8,875	1:36.80	
1958	Sir Ruler	3	G. Taniguchi	119	The Shoe	122	Foreverett	111	8,550	1:36.60	
1959	Sir Ara	3	D. Pierce	117	Chevalate	111	Mr. Eiffel	110	8,450	1:35.40	
1960	Our Rulla	3	J. Longden	120	Nagea	119	First Balcony	117	8,925	1:35.00	
1961	Apple	3	E. Ohayon	115	Speak John	117	Songman	118	9,075	1:35.20	
1962	Testum	3	D. Hallman	119	Olympiarco	112	Gallant Host	113	8,525	1:35.60	
1963	Top Light	3	J. Leonard	111	Real Luck	121	Broom II	111	7,360	1:36.20	
1963	Big Raff	3	R. Campas	109	Nevada Battler	119	Ahora	111	7,360	1:35.40	
1964	Royal Eiffel	3	J. Lambert	120	War Helmet	114	Pop's Harmony	111	8,950	1:35.80	
1965	Mr. Payne	3	J. Lambert	114	Parking Ticket	110	Nasharco	119	7,350	1:35.40	
1965	Hoist Bar	3	W. Hartack	116	Tivoli	114	Terry's Secret	126	7,350	1:34.80	
1966	Embassy	3	R. Menell	115	Ri Tux	120	Hill Clown	117	9,125	1:35.40	
1967	Jungle Road	3	J. Robinson	119	Charlie Boots	112	Space Ruler	110	10,900	1:34.60	
1968	Baffle	3	W. Hartack	117	Traffic Beat	107	Bargain Day	106	9,650	1:35.40	
1969	Eagle Fly	3	M. Volzke	115	Juliet's Dream	115	Little Scrib	117	9,825	1:35.20	
1970	Sugar Loaf	3	F. Toro	113	Terra Berry	111	War Heim	114	13,400	1:35.40	
1971	Petes Ruler	3	W. Mahorney	113	Niagara	120	Jeff David	114	9,875	1:35.20	
1971	Great Career	3	J. Lambert	115	My Little Man	113	Struck Out	113	9,875	1:35.60	
1972	Solar Salute	3	W. Mahorney	123	New Prospect	121	Woodland Pines	115	15,400	1:34.40	
1973	Groshawk	3	W. Shoemaker	125	Dancing Papa	115	Expression	123	16,300	1:34.20	
1974	Lightning Mandate	3	A. Pineda	125	Within Hail	120	Sea Aglo	113	15,800	1:34.40	
1975	Larrikin	3	D. Pierce	123	Wood Carver	115	Sibirri	119	16,850	1:35.00	
1976	Today 'n Tomorrow	3	D. Pierce	114	Noble Envoy	114	Wood Green	115	19,400	1:35.20	
1977	Stone Point	3	M. Castaneda	114	Pay the Toll	114	Windy Dancer	114	18,850	1:35.80	
1978	Singular	3	D.G. McHargue	114	Misr'presentation	119	Sea Ride	114	23,150	1:35.80	
1979	Relaunch	3	L. Pincay Jr	117	Hyannis Port	122	Pole Position	124	25,600	1:35.40	
1980	Aristocratical	3	C.J. McCarron	117	Son of a Dodo	117	Exploded	117	32,850	1:36.20	
1981	Minnesota Chief	3	C.J. McCarron	122	High Counsel	117	Stancharry	124	40,950	1:35.20	
1982	Hugabay	3	K. Black	115	Bargain Balcony	118	The Captain	118	33,050	1:35.60	
1982	Take the Floor	3	C.J. McCarron	115	Craelius	116	Sword Blade	115	33,050	1:35.60	
1983	Tanks Brigade	3	E. Delahoussaye	120	Dr. Daly	121	Pair of Aces	116	50,150	1:35.80	
1984	Tights	3	C.J. McCarron	120	Ocean View	113	Refueled II	115	59,150	1:35.60	
1985	Floating Reserve	3	P.A. Valenzuela	117	First Norman	116	Derby Dawning	119	62,750	1:34.60	
1986	Vernon Castle	3	E. Delahoussaye	120	First Norman	116	Derby Dawning	119	64,650	1:35.20	
1987	The Medic	3	C.J. McCarron	116	Something Lucky	120	Savona Tower	117	66,250	1:42.20	
1988	Perfecting	3	G.L. Stevens	116	Roberto's Dancer	115	Prove Splendid	115	64,800	1:41.60	
1989	River Master	3	C.J. McCarron	115	Tokatee	113	Art Work	114	65,100	1:42.60	
1990	Tight Spot	3	E. Delahoussaye	118	Itsallgreektome	119	Music Prospector	118	62,100	1:41.80	100
1991	Track Monarch	3	P.A. Valenzuela	116	Soweto	116	Persianalli	115	61,400	1:41.80	93
1992	Blacksburg	3	K.J. Desormeaux	119	Free at Last	121	Fax News	114	64,700	1:41.60	94
1993	Manny's Prospect	3	C.J. McCarron	115	Golden Slewpy	116	Hawk Spell	116	64,700	1:42.00	93
1994	Marvin's Faith	3	C.W. Antley	114	Unfinished Symph	120	Ocean Crest	114	62,800	1:42.20	97
1995	Petionville	3	Nakatani CS	120	Private Interview	115	Beau Temps	115	74,600	1:44.20	92
1996	Ambivalent	3	Douglas R. R.	116	The Barking Shark	114	Caribbean Pirate	117	82,850	1:43.20	100
1997	Fantastic Fellow	3	Solis A.	118	Worldly Ways	119	Falkenham	115	85,450	1:43.40	105
1998	Ladies Din	3	G.L. Stevens	120	Success And Glory	116	Lucayan Indian	116	81,810	1:41.80	103
1999	Eagleton	3	I.D. Enriquez	119	In Frank's Honor	117	Zanetti	117	90,000	1:41.80	97
2000	Purely Cozzene	3	D.R. Flores	120	Duke of Green	117	Sign of Hope	115	90,000	1:41.50	105
2001	Marine	3	C.S. Nakatani	117	Romanceishope	118	Mister Approval	113	90,000	1:41.72	95
2002	Inesperado	3	E. Delahoussaye	118	Regiment	121	Mountain Rage	119	90,000	1:43.92	98
2003	Singletary	3	P.A. Valenzuela	118	Devious Boy	117	Senor Swinger	120	90,000	1:40.39	99
2004	Blackdoun	3	C.S. Nakatani	120	Semi Lost	116	Bedmar	113	90,000	1:41.03	95

Beyer Index: 97.73

LAKE GEORGE (G3), 1 1/16 Miles (Turf), 3-Year-Old Fillies, Saratoga Race Course, 2004 Purse: $113,900

Year	Winner	Age	Jockey	Wt.	Second	Wt.	Third	Wt.	Win Value	Time	Beyer
1996	Memories Of Silver	3	J.Bailey	112	Clamorosa	118	Captive Number	113	33,780	1:42.80	96
1996	Dynasty	3	J.Bailey	112	River Antoine	113	Vashon	116	33,630	1:42.20	89
1997	Auntie Mame	3	J.Bailey	121	Crab Grass	114	Innovate	116	51,120	1:42.80	90
1998	Tenski	3	R. Migliore	114	Pratella	114	Camella	114	50,070	1:40.80	97
1998	Caveat Competitor	3	J.R. Velazquez	116	Mysterious Moll	114	Recording	121	50,060	1:41.00	94
1999	Nani Rose	3	S.J. Sellers	122	Perfect Sting	122	Intrigued	122	67,680	1:40.00	100
2000	Millie's Quest	3	J.R. Velazquez	114	Shopping for Love	117	Battenkill	114	70,080	1:44.52	90
2001	Light Dancer	3	M. Guidry	117	Owsley	115	Cozzy Corner	115	67,050	1:41.06	94
2001	Voodoo Dancer	3	J.D. Bailey	122	Sadler's Sarah	117	O K to Dance	122	67,350	1:41.45	94
2002	Nunatall	3	J.F. Chavez	115	Guana	117	Mariensky	117	69,000	1:40.71	95
2003	Film Maker	3	E.S. Prado	115	Ocean Drive	119	Gal O Gal	122	68,700	1:41.80	95
2004	Seducer's Song	3	J.D. Bailey	115	Venturi	119	Fortunate Damsel	117	68,340	1:42.01	98

Beyer Index: 94.33

LAKE PLACID HANDICAP (G2), 1 1/8 Miles (Turf), 3-Year-Old Fillies, Saratoga Race Course, 2004 Purse: $150,000

Year	Winner	Age	Jockey	Wt.	Second	Wt.	Third	Wt.	Win Value	Time	Beyer
1986	An Empress	3	J.A. Santos	121	Fama	114	Spring Innocence	114	52,200	1:42.00	
1987	Graceful Darby	3	J.D. Bailey	116	Spectacular Bev	114	Token Gift	114	50,760	1:41.40	
1988	Betty Lobelia	3	J.A. Santos	116	Curlew	114	Tunita	114	66,780	1:41.60	
1988	Love You by Heart	3	R.P. Romero	114	Another Paddock	116	Flashy Runner	114	66,780	1:41.80	
1989	Capades	3	A. Cordero Jr	121	To the Lighthouse	116	Vanities	114	55,620	1:41.00	
1990	Jefforee	3	J.A. Santos	114	Toffeefee	114	Colonial Runner	114	60,030	1:49.00	99
1991	Jinski's World	3	J.A. Santos	121	Belleofbasinstreet	114	Verbasle	114	59,760	1:41.00	91
1991	Grab the Green	3	A. Cordero Jr	114	Shareefa	121	Irish Linnet	114	59,280	1:40.20	99
1992	Shannkara	3	M.E. Smith	114	Tiney Toast	116	Favored Lady	114	73,380	1:41.80	90
1992	Heed	3	M.E. Smith	114	Captive Miss	114	Mystic Hawk	114	72,420	1:40.80	91
1993	Amal Hayati	3	J.D. Bailey	121	Eloquent Silver	114	Irving's Girl	114	56,940	1:40.80	95
1993	Statuette	3	M.E. Smith	114	Icy Warning	114	Dispute	118	55,980	1:41.40	88
1994	Coronation Cup	3	J.D. Bailey	114	Stretch Drive	114	Golden Tajniak	118	65,760	1:43.80	102
1994	Alywow	3	M.E. Smith	121	Irish Forever	121	Knocknock	114	66,660	1:43.80	102
1995	Class Kris	3	P. Day	112	In a Daydream	112	Shocking Pleasure	113	67,380	1:40.80	102
1995	Bail Out Becky	3	Sellers SJ	115	Fashion Star	112	Grand Charmer	120	67,680	1:41.80	96
1996	Memories of Silver	3	J.D. Bailey	115	Unify	113	Henlopen	112	68,640	1:47.80	106
1997	Witchful Thinkin	3	S.J. Sellers	123	Miss Huff n' Puff	114	Majestic Sunlight	114	90,000	1:47.60	96
1998	Tenski	3	R. Migliore	119	Naskra's de Light	117	Caveat Competor	118	90,000	1:46.20	102
1999	Badouizm	3	R.G. Davis	113	Confessional	115	Emanating	115	90,000	1:46.40	93
2000	Gaviola	3	J.D. Bailey	122	Good Game	117	Millie's Quest	117	90,000	1:48.04	96
2001	Snow Dance	3	R. Migliore	116	Wander Mom	116	Mystic Lady	117	90,000	1:47.42	95
2002	Wonder Again	3	E.S. Prado	114	Riskaverse	120	Miss Marcia	114	90,000	1:49.24	97
2003	Sand Springs	3	M. Guidry	121	Indy Five Hundred	114	Film Maker	119	90,000	1:49.03	93
2004	Spotlight	3	J.D. Bailey	116	Mambo Slew	120	Fortunate Damsel	116	90,000	1:50.54	100

Beyer Index: 96.65

Run as Nijana prior to 1998

LANDALUCE (G3), 6 Furlongs, 2-Year-Old Fillies, Hollywood Park, 2004 Purse: $106,800

Year	Winner	Age	Jockey	Wt.	Second	Wt.	Third	Wt.	Win Value	Time	Beyer
1945	Widow's Peak	2	J. Longden	116	Me Again	116	Sweet Arline	112	14,035	1:12.00	
1946	U Time	2	L. Balaski	114	Hemet Squaw	119	Hubble Bubble	114	19,650	1:10.20	
1947	Nursery School	2	J. Longden	115	Star Beauty	115	Song Fest	115	20,200	1:05.20	
1948	Brenton Light	2	J. Longden	119	Cosmopolite	119	Sleepers Jinx	119	19,800	1:06.00	
1949	Fleet Rings	2	J. Westrope	119	Dew of June	115	Imago	119	28,850	1:06.40	
1950	Sickle's Image	2	W. Fisk	112	Ruth Lily	107	Worn Out	108	21,750	1:10.00	
1951	Thataway	2	D. Erb	119	Dugout	119	Princess Rita	119	20,850	1:06.00	
1952	Fleet Khal	2	R. Heather	115	Haunted	119	Speedy Ace	115	15,500	1:04.60	
1953	Chorus Khal	2	L. Leon	116	Lady Cover Up	110	Heather Khal	116	17,400	1:05.20	
1954	Fair Molly	2	R. Tejos	111	Madam Jet	111	First Aid Kit	111	18,450	1:04.60	
1955	Miss Todd	2	R. York	115	Doc Upton	111	Carmel	115	18,000	1:04.60	
1956	Darling Adelle	2	J. Longden	119	Royal Rasher	113	Molly Maid	113	16,500	1:04.20	
1957	Sally Lee	2	J. Longden	119	Camloc	113	Pie Face	116	16,300	1:04.80	
1958	Khalita	2	R. York	115	Tassle Dancer	119	Kiddie Book	111	16,800	1:05.80	
1959	Echoic	2	W. Shoemaker	111	Miss Imbros	111	Linita	119	17,200	1:04.00	
1960	Het's Pet	2	G. Taniguchi	111	Regal Weather	111	Never More	119	16,450	1:04.00	
1961	Sunday Slippers	2	P. Moreno	111	Spark Plug	119	Lady's Matinee	112	15,800	1:03.60	
1962	Honey Bunny	2	W. Shoemaker	119	Lanabu	111	Brev Hostess	111	17,650	1:04.00	
1963	Sari's Song	2	J. Leonard	111	Sweet and Fleet	111	Pretty Bubbles	111	17,500	1:04.00	
1964	Getaway Maid	2	S. Trevino	113	Real Sweet Deal	119	Candyean	119	59,275	1:04.80	
1965	Premise	2	M. Yanez	119	Roman Heiress	119	Prides Profile	119	56,800	1:04.00	
1966	Mira Femme	2	I. Valenzuela	119	Native Honey	119	Indovina	119	50,650	1:03.60	
1967	Morgaise	2	W. Shoemaker	119	Hula Bend	119	Esquimau Pie	119	51,050	1:03.80	
1968	Lynne's Orphan	2	J. Sellers	119	Jan Jessie	119	O'Lucky You	119	46,075	1:03.40	
1969	Consider Me Lucky	2	L. Pincay Jr	119	Emmania	119	Court Gem	119	41,500	1:09.80	
1970	June Darling	2	W. Mahorney	119	Sea Frolic	119	Wicked Fairy	119	38,125	1:10.20	
1971	Cautious Bidder	2	J.L. Rotz	119	Miss Lady Bug	119	Bright Bright	119	54,825	1:09.20	
1972	Windy's Daughter	2	W. Shoemaker	119	Protest	119	Rosalie Mae Wynn	119	35,725	1:09.60	
1972	Bold Liz	2	J. Tejeira	119	Kedesh	119	Lucky Jen	119	35,225	1:09.40	
1973	Special Goddess	2	L. Pincay Jr	119	Calaki	119	Fleet Peach	119	53,125	1:09.60	
1974	Hot n Nasty	2	D.G. McHargue	119	Miss Tokyo	119	Angle	119	55,225	1:09.00	
1975	Walk in the Sun	2	F. Olivares	119	Pet Label	119	Doc Shah's Siren	119	56,025	1:10.40	
1976	Wavy Waves	2	L. Pincay Jr	119	Lullaby	114	Any Time Girl	119	55,225	1:10.20	
1977	B. Thoughtful	2	D. Pierce	119	Sweet Little Lady	119	Ubetido	119	53,475	1:10.20	
1978	Terlingua	2	D.G. McHargue	119	Joi'ski	119	Caline	119	48,725	1:08.80	
1979	Table Hands	2	E. Munoz	119	Open Gate	119	Jet Rating	119	54,475	1:10.40	

Year	Winner	Age	Jockey	Wt.	Second	Wt.	Third	Wt.	Win Value	Time	Beyer
1980	Native Fancy	2	L. Pincay Jr	119	Icy Pop	115	Lead Us	119	54,425	1:10.00	
1981	Ticketed	2	D.G. McHargue	119	Orphan's Art	119	First Advance	116	46,200	1:11.40	
1982	Landaluce	2	L. Pincay Jr	117	Bold Out Line	115	Barzell	119	43,750	1:08.00	
1983	Simple Magic	2	E. Delahoussaye	116	Althea	117	Reb's Gateau	116	46,300	1:10.60	
1984	Window Seat	2	E. Delahoussaye	114	Raise a Prospector	119	Full o Wisdom	114	64,550	1:10.00	
1985	Arewehavingfunyet	2	W. Shoemaker	119	Fashion Dynasty	116	La Codorniz	117	59,700	1:10.00	
1986	Delicate Vine	2	G.L. Stevens	116	Anything for Love	114	Purdue Queen	119	58,850	1:10.00	
1987	Over All	2	G.L. Stevens	116	Blue Jean Baby	116	Tomorrow's Child	116	63,400	1:10.60	
1988	Distinctive Sis	2	A. Solis	116	Lea Lucinda	116	Executive Row	116	62,250	1:10.80	
1989	Dominant Dancer	2	E. Delahoussaye	119	Cheval Volant	116	Autumn Beauty	115	60,100	1:10.40	
1990	Garden Gal	2	M. Pedroza	116	Perky Slew	116	Lite Light	116	60,900	1:10.40	
1991	Fluttery Danseur	2	M. Pedroza	116	Soviet Sojourn	116	Prospector's Dame	117	56,200	1:09.40	100
1992	Zealous Connection	2	M. Pedroza	116	Medici Bells	116	Sweet Mama	117	58,500	1:09.80	89
1993	Rhapsodic	2	E. Delahoussaye	116	Miss Gibson County	119	Becky's Appeal	116	59,800	1:10.40	81
1994	Serena's Song	2	G.L. Stevens	116	Embroidered	116	Cat's Cradle	116	66,800	1:10.00	86
1995	Raw Gold	2	A. Solis	116	Wasmi Song	116	Liberty Nite	117	59,600	1:10.60	74
1996	Starry Ice	2	E. Delahoussaye	119	Trav n' Kris	114	Montecito	116	20,720	1;11.20	85
1997	Career Collection	2	C.S. Nakatani	116	Bent Creek City	119	Unreal Squeal	119	62,820	1:10.40	78
1998	Hookedonthefeelin	2	G.L. Stevens	116	Box Office Girl	116	Excellent Meeting	116	62,760	1:09.60	90
1999	Magicalmysterycat	2	C.W. Antley	119	She's Classy	116	Princess Melissa	116	63,120	1:11.00	73
2000	Notable Career	2	C.S. Nakatani	116	Sea Reel	116	Starrer	115	65,040	1:11.10	83
2001	Georgia's Storm	2	C.J. McCarron	119	Respectful	114	Who Loves Aleyna	116	65,040	1:10.45	85
2002	Buffythecenterfold	2	M.S. Garcia	116	Tricks Her	115	Little Bit a Swiss	116	66,360	1:10.51	90
2003	Wacky Patty	2	J. Valdivia Jr	119	Cherish Destiny	116	Platinum Princess	116	60,180	1:10.28	86
2004	Souvenir Gift	2	M.E. Smith	119	Bella Banissa	117	My Miss Storm Cat	116	64,080	1:09.75	90

Beyer Index: 85.00

LANE'S END (G2), 1 1/8 Miles, 3-Year-Olds, Turfway Park, 2004 Purse: $500,000

Year	Winner	Age	Jockey	Wt.	Second	Wt.	Third	Wt.	Win Value	Time	Beyer
1972	Big Dot	3	J. Murchison	109	Tiz Tiz Lou	111	G'sF'rwr'd Thr'st	114	7,125	1:38.80	
1973	Jacks Chevron	3	B. Phelps	117	Trip Stop	116	Mr. Champ	116	9,785	1:42.00	
1973	Bootlegger's Pet	3	M. Solomone	116	Out Ahead	117	Babington's Image	113	9,720	1:41.00	
1974	King of Rome	3	K. Wirth	112	Consigliori	112	Aroyoport	116	12,204	1:44.60	
1974	Aglorite	3	J. Becch Jr	119	Joint Agreement	114	Robard	112	12,236	1:45.40	
1975	Naughty Jake	3	G. Vasquez	119	Promenade Left	114	Jim Dan Bob	112	15,840	1:40.00	
1975	Ambassador's Image	3	E. Snell	122	Clarence Henry	116	Upper Need	116	15,870	1:38.40	
1976	Inca Rosa	3	W. Nemeti	122	Here Comes Jo	116	Brentwood Prince	116	18,780	1:37.40	
1977	Smiley's Dream	3	W. DeStefano	114	Lighten the Load	111	Vestry's Best	111	12,788	1:39.40	
1977	Bob's Dusty	3	J.C. Espinoza	122	A Letter to Harry	116	John Washington	116	12,818	1:38.80	
1978	Five Star General	3	J.C. Espinoza	113	As in Elbow	113	Doc's Rock	119	12,900	1:37.80	
1978	Raymond Earl	3	J.C. Espinoza	113	Washington County	119	Shake Rattle'n Fly	113	12,960	1:38.80	
1979	Lot o' Gold	3	D. Brumfield	122	Julie's Dancer	113	Will Henry	113	29,030	1:37.60	
1980	Major Run	3	M.S. Sellers	119	Ray's Word	122	Misty Bell	113	18,740	1:37.60	
1980	Spruce Needles	3	J.C. Espinoza	119	Avenger M.	122	Summer Advocate	113	18,441	1:36.20	
1981	Mythical Ruler	3	K.B. Wirth	114	Classic Go Go	122	Iron Gem	115	36,460	1:38.00	
1982	Good n' Dusty	3	M.T. Moran	120	Fast Gold	120	Cupecoy's Joy	115	125,450	1:44.60	
1983	Marfa	3	J. Velasquez	120	Noble Home	120	Hail to Rome	120	151,515	1:42.40	
1984	At the Threshold	3	P. Day	121	Bold Southerner	121	The Wedding Guest	121	195,000	1:42.80	
1985	Banner Bob	3	K.K. Allen	121	Image of Greatness	121	Roo Art	121	227,500	1:42.00	
1986	Broad Brush	3	V. Bracciale Jr	121	Miracle Wood	121	Bachelor Beau	121	210,000	1:44.20	
1987	J.T.'s Pet	3	P. Day	121	Faster Than Sound	121	Homebuilder	121	300,000	1:42.80	
1988	Kingpost	3	E.J. Sipus	121	Stalwars	121	Brian's Time	121	300,000	1:50.80	
1989	Western Playboy	3	P. Day	121	Feather Ridge	121	Mercedes Won	121	300,000	1:49.00	
1990	Summer Squall	3	P. Day	121	Bright Again	121	Yonder	121	300,000	1:49.40	
1991	Hansel	3	J.D. Bailey	121	Ruchman	121	Wilder Than Ever	121	300,000	1:46.60	105
1992	Lil E. Tee	3	P. Day	121	Vying Victor	121	Treekster	121	300,000	1:53.40	95
1993	Prairie Bayou	3	C.J. McCarron	121	Proudest Romeo	121	Miner's Mark	121	360,000	1:50.80	98
1994	Polar Expedition	3	C.C. Bourque	121	Powis Castle	121	Chimes Band	121	360,000	1:49.00	103
1995	Serena's Song	3	C.S. Nakatani	116	Tejano Run	121	Mecke	121	360,000	1:49.60	114
1996	Roar	3	M.E. Smith	121	Ensign Ray	121	Victory Speech	121	360,000	1:49.60	95
1997	Concerto	3	C.H. Marquez Jr	121	Jack Flash	121	Shammy Davis	121	360,000	1:48.20	102
1998	Event of the Year	3	R.A. Baze	121	Yarrow Brae	121	Truluck	121	360,000	1:47.00	114
1999	Stephen Got Even	3	S.J. Sellers	121	K One King	121	Epic Honor	121	450,000	1:49.00	104
2000	Globalize	3	F.C. Torres	121	Elite Mercedes	121	Rollin With Nolan	121	360,000	1:49.16	97
2001	Balto Star	3	M. Guidry	121	Halo's Stride	121	Mongoose	121	360,000	1:47.23	112
2002	Perfect Drift	3	E. Delahoussaye	121	Azillion	121	Request for Parole	121	300,000	1:48.83	102
2003	New York Hero	3	N. Arroyo Jr	121	Eugene's Third Son	121	Champali	121	300,000	1:50.68	96
2004	Sinister G	3	P.R. Toscano	121	Tricky Taboo	121	Little Matth Man	121	300,000	1:50.71	93

Beyer Index: 102.14

LA PREVOYANTE HANDICAP (G2), 1 1/2 Miles (Turf), Fillies and Mares, 3-Year-Olds and Up, Calder Race Course, 2004 Purse: $200,000

Year	Winner	Age	Jockey	Wt.	Second	Wt.	Third	Wt.	Win Value	Time	Beyer
1976	Forty Nine Sunsets	3	C. Marquez	116	Cycylya Zee	121	Satan's Cheer	116	27,510	1:46.00	
1976	Redundancy	5	A. Haldar	117	Katonka	125	Yes Dear Maggy	121	26,040	1:41.60	
1978	Len's Determined	4	A. Smith Jr	114	Regal Gal	120	Carolina Moon	114	38,400	1:48.40	
1979	Unreality	5	J.D. Bailey	119	Excitable	117	Sans Arc	117	37,200	1:48.20	
1980	Impetuous Gal	5	E. Fires	113	Tangerine Doll	118	Highland Gypsy	116	23,775	1:52.20	
1980	Jolie Dutch	4	B. Thornburg	116	Reina del Rulo	116	Behave Taurian	108	23,925	1:54.60	
1981	Mairzy Doates	5	O.B. Aviles	121	Champagne Ginny	118	Knightly Noble	110	41,670	1:47.20	
1981	Deuces Over Seven	4	G. Gallitano	114	Little Bounty	121	Quick as Lightning	119	40,950	1:48.00	
1982	Judgable Gypsy	4	J. O'Driscoll	114	Castle Royale	110	Imayrrahtoo	110	42,165	1:50.20	
1982	Just a Game II	6	A. CorderoJr	123	Sweetest Chant	115	Irish Joy	114	41,655	1:50.40	
1983	London Lil	4	A. Smith Jr	117	Betty Money	116	Dana Calqui	114	54,680	1:47.40	
1983	Fact Finder	4	A. Cordero Jr	115	Sunny Sparkler	122	Seaholme	112	54,380	1:48.00	
1983	Canaille II	5	A. Cordero Jr	118	Castle Royale	115	Genuine Diamond	113	54,380	1:46.60	
1984	Bolt From the Blue	4	J.L. Samyn	113	Bezique	112	Gabfest	110	51,960	2:33.40	
1984	Sabin	4	E. Maple	120	Grunip	113	Pat's Joy	118	52,260	2:32.80	
1985	Persian Tiara	5	J. Terry	120	Dictina	117	Silver in Flight	115	85,335	2:28.80	
1985	Sabin	5	D. Brumfield	126	Key Dancer	118	Burst of Colors	117	72,285	2:27.40	
1986	Powder Break	5	J.A. Santos	116	Shocker T.	119	Devalois	118	120,000	2:30.40	
1987	Lotka	4	E. Maple	121	Bonne Ile	116	After Party	112	120,000	2:36.00	
1988	Singular Bequest	5	E. Fires	115	Autumn Glitter	114	Green Oasis	114	120,000	2:25.20	
1989	Judy's Red Shoes	6	D. Valiente	120	Gaily Gaily	111	Beauty Cream	118	90,000	2:26.40	
1990	Yestday's Kisses	4	W.H. McCauley	113	Black Tulip	115	Coolawin	116	60,000	2:30.80	98
1991	Rigamajig	5	J.F. Chavez	114	Roseate Tern	117	Ahead	112	60,000	2:26.00	
1992	Sardaniya	4	J. Cruguet	113	Flaming Torch	112	Expensiveness	111	90,000	2:29.60	99
1993	Lemhi Go	5	M.A. Gonzalez	112	Indian Chris	112	Silvered	118	60,000	2:37.40	90
1994	Trampoli	5	M.E. Smith	120	Putthepowdertoit	115	Adoryphar	112	90,000	2:28.00	103
1994	Abigailthewife	5	J.A. Santos	114	Trampoli	118	Market Booster	118	90,000	2:28.80	102
1995	Interim	4	C.S. Nakatani	116	Northern Emerald	116	Caromana	114	90,000	2:26.20	100
1996	Ampulla	5	S.J. Sellers	122	Miss Caerleona	115	electric Society	117	90,000	2:27.40	104
1997	Last Approach	5	J. A. Krone	110	Flying Concert	118	Grey Way	110	90,000	2:39.00	88
1998	Coretta	4	J.A. Santos	117	Starry Dreamer	114	(DH) Tedarshana	113	90,000	2:26.60	101
1999	Coretta	5	J.A. Santos	120	Idle Rich	116	St. Bernadette	114	90,000	2:27.20	97
2000	Prospectress	5	J.D. Bailey	114	Innuendo	114	Orange Sunset	114	90,000	2:26.97	99
2001	Krisada	5	P. Day	115	Sweetest Thing	115	Great Fever	113	90,000	2:26.63	99
2002	New Economy	4	R.B. Homeister Jr	113	Jennasietta	112	Tweedside	114	120,000	2:28.55	96
2003	Volga	5	R. Migliore	119	Lady Annaliese	116	Lost Appeal	115	120,000	2:26.13	98
2004	Arvada	4	E.S. Prado	117	Humaita	119	Honey Ryder	113	120,000	2:27.19	97

Beyer Index: 98.07

LAS CIENEGAS HANDICAP (G3), About 6 1/2 Furlongs (Turf), Fillies and Mares, 4-Year-Olds and Up, Santa Anita, 2004 Purse: $112,800

Year	Winner	Age	Jockey	Wt.	Second	Wt.	Third	Wt.	Win Value	Time	Beyer
1974	Woodland Pines	5	D. Pierce	120	Pataha Prince	112	Single Agent	116	18,650	1:13.00	
							Pontoise	116			
1976	Life's Hope	3	L. Pincay Jr	116	Sure Fire	119	Private Signal	114	20,100	1:09.40	
1977	Dancing Femme	4	W. Shoemaker	117	Winter Solstice	123	Katonka	120	24,600	1:13.60	
1978	Drama Critic	4	D.G. McHargue	119	Perils of Pauline	118	Litt'e Happiness	120	27,800	1:14.00	
1979	Pressing Date	5	A. Cordero Jr	114	Country Queen	121	Critic	114	27,500	1:16.40	
1980	Great Lady M.	5	P.A. Valenzuela	116	Wishing Well	120	Billie Bets	115	28,100	1:14.80	
1981	Wishing Well	6	F. Toro	122	Back at Two	114	Peppy's Lucky Girl	113	24,250	1:13.40	
1982	Excitable Lady	4	E. Delahoussaye	119	Peppy's Lucky Girl	117	Glitter Hitter	116	37,450	1:14.40	
1983	Faneuil Lass	4	L. Pincay Jr	120	Queen of Song	115	Waving	117	41,200	1:17.40	
1984	Tangent	4	G. Barrera	120	Irish O'Brien	118	Frieda Frame	118	39,600	1:15.00	
1985	Danzadar	4	D.A. Lozoya	114	Pampas	120	Nat'l Summit	116	37,250	1:14.00	
1986	Shywing	4	L. Pincay Jr	120	Reigning Countess	114	Her Royalty	121	37,550	1:18.00	
1987	Lichi	7	G. Baze	115	An Empress	119	Aromacor	112	38,150	1:14.40	
1988	Hairless Heiress	5	G.L. Stevens	117	Chick or Two	115	Aromacor	113	52,050	1:15.00	
1989	Imperial Star	5	R.G. Davis	115	Down Again	117	Serve n' Volley	115	50,450	1:15.60	
1990	Stylish Star	4	C.J. McCarron	117	Stormy but Valid	120	Hot Novel	118	47,100	1:13.00	104
1991	Flower Girl	4	E. Delahoussaye	116	Mahaska	117	Survive	117	49,650	1:13.20	104
1992	Heart of Joy	5	C.J. McCarron	123	Sheltered View	114	Crystal Gazing	119	63,470	1:12.60	107
1993	Glen Kate	6	C.A. Black	121	Heart of Joy	121	Worldly Possession	115	61,225	1:12.60	102
1994	Mamselle Bebette	4	C.J. McCarron	120	Cool Air	122	Bel's Starlet	122	45,975	1:13.00	103
1995	Marina Park	5	A. Solis	119	Pirate's Revenge	116	Rabiadella	118	63,175	1:13.60	101
1996	Ski Dancer	4	G.L. Stevens	117	Klassy Kim	117	Igotrhythm	117	64,300	1:14.40	102
1997	Advancing Star	4	G.L. Stevens	116	Ski Dancer	118	Grab The Prize	116	96,550	1:12.40	105
1998	Dance Parade	4	K.J. Desormeaux	119	Advancing Star	121	Imroz	116	64,800	1:13.60	100
1999	Desert Lady	4	C.S. Nakatani	118	Hula Queen	112	Bella Chiarra	115	65,640	1:13.60	98
2000	Evening Promis	4	D. Sorenson	114	La Madame	116	Reciclada	113	63,840	1:13.66	99
2001	Go Go	4	E. Delahoussaye	118	Separata	118	Dianehill	116	65,700	1:13.54	105

Year	Winner	Age	Jockey	Wt.	Second	Wt.	Third	Wt.	Win Value	Time	Beyer
2002	Rolly Polly	4	K.J. Desormeaux	119	Penny Marie	119	Twin Set	116	65,100	1:12.55	99
2003	Heat Haze	4	J. Valdivia Jr	114	Icantgoforthat	114	Paga	116	66,000	1:13.11	97
2004	Etoile Montante	4	J. Santiago	121	Dedication	118	Any for Love	115	67,680	1:13.32	93

Beyer Index: 101.27

LAS FLORES HANDICAP (G3), 6 Furlongs, Fillies and Mares, 4-Year-Olds and Up, Santa Anita, 2004 Purse: $107,300

Year	Winner	Age	Jockey	Wt.	Second	Wt.	Third	Wt.	Win Value	Time	Beyer
1951	Next Move	4	E. Guerin	124	Special Touch	122	Sickle's Image	117	12,250	1:09.80	
1952	Spanish Cream	4	E. Guerin	117	Great Dream	112	A Gleam	126	12,900	1:10.60	
1954	Vickie Blue	4	W. Shoemaker	114	Smart Barbara	118	Fleet Khal	122	14,900	1:09.40	
1955	Miz Clementine	4	R. Neves	126	Alibhai Lynn	121	Lap Full	116	13,500	1:10.00	
1956	On the Move	5	D. Lewis	112	Scansion	109	Island Queen	106	15,200	1:10.20	
1957	Miss Todd	4	E. Arcaro	116	Our Betters	119	Mary Machree	120	12,750	1:09.80	
1958	Ballet Khal	4	W. Shoemaker	112	Coverit	121	Betty Rose		13,600	1:10.00	
1959	Bug Brush	4	A. Valenzuela	112	Gleaming Star	111	Nushie	113	15,100	1:09.40	
1960	Linita	3	M. Ycaza	116	My Dear Girl	119	Swiss Roll	119	15,000	1:10.20	
1960	Margaretta	5	I. Valenzuela	117	Khalita	115	Indian Maid	120	13,750	1:09.60	
1961	Bright Holly	3	B. Baeza	118	Linita	120	Oil Royalty	116	14,450	1:09.80	
1962	Oil Royalty	4	W. Shoemaker	117	My Portrait	117	Rose O'Neil	123	14,500	1:10.00	
1963	Chop House	3	B. Baeza	113	Red Belle	120	Savaii	117	10,925	1:09.60	
1963	Shimmering Star	3	R. Campas	112	Hi Rated	115	Pixie Erin	122	10,925	1:09.80	
1964	Affectionately	4	W. Shoemaker	125			Curious Clover	120	9,775	1:10.00	
	Chop House	4	I. Valenzuela	119							
1965	Poona Queen	5	I. Valenzuela	117	Respected Way	116	Fairway Fun	116	17,200	1:10.00	
1966	Natashka	3	W. Shoemaker	122	Admirably	121	Miss Moona	114	16,250	1:09.40	
1967	Sharp Curve	3	W. Harris	114	Nevada Marga	118	Peggy's World	109	15,050	1:09.60	
1968	Time to Leave	3	D. Velasquez	125	Morgaise	121	Francine M.	117	14,700	1:10.20	
1970	Everything Lovely	5	L. Pincay Jr	118	Undercover Miss	114	Dumpty Ann	118	17,800	1:09.20	
1972	Chou Croute	4	J.L. Rotz	126	Generous Portion	116	Minstrel M's	114	22,200	1:09.20	
1972	Crowning Glory	4	J. Lambert	116	Goddess Special	113	Minstrel M's	112	23,500	1:09.00	
1973	Sandy Blue	3	D. Pierce	120	Market Again	112	Impressive Style	122	22,150	1:08.60	
1975	Lucky Spell	4	J. Tejeira	120	Tizna	123	Impressive Style	122	21,700	1:09.60	
1976	Just a Kick	4	E. Munoz	114	Raise Your Skirts	121	Mismoyola	115	21,550	1:09.20	
1977	Winter Solstice	5	D.G. McHargue	120	Squander	114	Don's Music	115	26,100	1:11.80	
1977	My Juliet	5	A.S. Black	128	Just a Kick	121	Juliana F.	115	26,750	1:10.20	
1978	Sweet Little Lady	3	D.G. McHargue	117	Grenzen	122	Great Lady M.	114	33,200	1:09.00	
1979	Terlingua	3	D.G. McHargue	121	Powder Room	113	Ideal Exchange	116	32,800	1:08.40	
1981	Shine High	5	T. Lipham	114	Image of Reality	119	Parsley	117	32,600	1:08.60	
1982	Back at Two	5	C.J. McCarron	117	Abisinia	116	Excitable Lady	120	37,750	1:12.40	
1983	Matching	5	L. Pincay Jr	122	Bara Lass	115	Past Forgetting	122	38,650	1:09.00	
1984	Bara Lass	5	P.A. Valenzuela	122	Champagne Isle	116	Bally Knockan	114	40,100	1:09.40	
1985	Foggy Nation	5	L. Pincay Jr	117	Lovlier Linda	124	Tangent	122	37,250	1:09.60	
1986	Baron's Direct	5	E. Delahoussaye	120	Her Royalty	120	Aerturas	113	38,850	1:08.40	
1987	Pine Tree Lane	5	A. Cordero Jr	124	Rangoon Ruby	117	Her Royalty	120	38,350	1:09.80	
1989	Very Subtle	5	L. Pincay Jr	124	Sadie B. Fast	113	Comical Cat	116	44,350	1:08.60	
1990	Stormy but Valid	4	E. Delahoussaye	117	Survive	117	Warning Zone	119	47,850	1:08.20	106
1991	Classic Value	5	G.L. Stevens	116	Devil's Orchid	116	Hasty Pasty	116	60,325	1:10.20	105
1992	Forest Fealty	5	M.A. Pedroza	116	Middleford Rapids	118	Phil's Illusion	113	49,350	1:08.80	99
1993	Bountiful Native	5	P.A. Valenzuela	121	Freedom Cry	119	Forest Fealty	112	60,325	1:09.40	92
1994	Mamselle Bebette	4	Nakatani CS	118	Arches of Gold	120	Aspasante	114	47,475	1:08.20	105
1995	Desert Stormer	5	Desormeaux KJ	117	Velvet Tulip	114	Flying in the Lane	114	59,725	1:08.40	104
1996	Igotrhythm	4	Nakatani C. S.	115	Miss L Attack	115	Little Blue Sheep	115	81,100	1:08.80	110
1997	Our Summer Bid	5	Silva J. G.	114	Track Gal	120	Advancing Star	116	80,100	1:09.00	105
1998	Funallover	4	Solis A.	112	Advancing Star	122	Zenda's Diablo	109	79,800	1:09.20	97
1999	Enjoy The Moment	4	Pincay L. Jr	117	Tomorrows Sunshine	114	Closed Escrow	116	78,720	1:08.40	111
2000	Show Me the Stage	4	K.J. Desormeaux	118	Theresa's Tizzy	117	Woodman's Dancer	115	79,440	1:08.54	110
2001	Go Go	4	E. Delahoussaye	116	La Feminn	120	Cover Gal	119	80,400	1:08.83	103
2002	Above Perfection	4	C.S. Nakatani	117	Kalookan Queen	122	Enchanted Woods	117	78,642	1:08.65	111
2003	Spring Meadow	4	C.S. Nakatani	117	Brisquette	116	Wild Tickle	117	81,300	1:10.20	94
							September Secret	116			
2004	Ema Bovary	5	R.M. Gonzalez	121	Buffythecenterfold	117	Coconut Girl	113	64,380	1:08.02	105

Beyer Index: 103.80

LAS PALMAS HANDICAP (G2), 1 1/8 Miles (Turf), Fillies and Mares, 3-Year-Olds and Up, Santa Anita, 2004 Purse: $150,000

Year	Winner	Age	Jockey	Wt.	Second	Wt.	Third	Wt.	Win Value	Time	Beyer
1969	Manta	3	R. Rosales	116	Commisary	119	Miss Ribot	122	26,850	1:41.80	
1970	Manta	4	R. Rosales	125	Beja	119	Thoroly Blue	115	19,350	1:46.60	
1971	Typecast	5	W. Shoemaker	126	Hail the Grey	116	Aladancer	119	19,150	1:49.80	
1972	Resoutely	5	J. Lambert	115	Pallisima	123	Cruz de Roble	117	24,550	1:47.80	

Year	Winner	Age	Jockey	Wt.	Second	Wt.	Third	Wt.	Win Value	Time	Beyer
1973	Minstrel Miss	6	D. Pierce	123	Cruz de Roble	113	Veiled Desire	111	27,100	1:47.80	
1974	Lucky Spell	3	J. Tejeira	117	Bold Ballet	117	Fresh Pepper	112	26,750	1:47.40	
1975	Charger's Star	5	W. Shoemaker	116	Tizna	126	Hinterland	116	26,000	1:47.20	
1976	Vagabonda	5	O. Vergara	118	Bastonera II	122	Accra II	115	34,500	1:48.60	
1977	Swingtime	5	F. Toro	119	Theia	113	Summertime Promise	118	25,650	1:47.20	
1978	Grenzen	3	L. Pincay Jr	119	Country Queen	119	Drama Critic	123	39,400	1:48.40	
1979	High Pheasant	4	F. Olivares	114	Prize Spot	119	Axe Me Dear	114	39,700	1:54.00	
1980	Ack's Secret	4	P.A. Valenzuela	114	A Thousand Stars	119	Princess Toby	117	40,400	1:46.00	
1981	Ack's Secret	5	D.G. McHargue	119	Queen to Conquer	123	Berry Bush	118	50,500	1:47.00	
1982	Berry Bush	5	M. Castaneda	115	Satin Ribera	115	Northern Fable	115	70,400	1:47.40	
1983	Castilla	4	C.J. McCarron	121	Night Fire	113	Berry Bush	117	64,300	1:49.20	
1984	Fenny Rough	4	K. Black	117	Comedy Act	117	Pride of Rosewood	115	78,800	1:47.40	
1985	Estrapade	5	W. Shoemaker	124	L'Attrayante	118	Johnica	118	69,100	1:47.20	
1986	Outstandingly	4	G.L. Stevens	118	Shywing	118	Justicara	118	63,400	1:47.60	
1987	Autumn Glitter	4	P. Day	116	Galunpe	119	Festivity	117	91,800	1:50.40	
1988	Annoconnor	4	C.A. Black	120	No Review	114	Goodbye Halo	120	97,800	1:47.00	
1989	Nikishka	4	E. Delahoussaye	116	No Review	117	Agirlfromars	111	96,800	1:46.60	
1990	Little Brianne	5	J.A. Garcia	115	Double Wedge	117	Reluctant Guest	121	93,200	1:46.80	103
1991	Kostroma	5	K.J. Desormeaux	117	Kikala	113	Campagnarde	118	80,750	1:43.80	105
1992	Super Staff	4	K.J. Desormeaux	116	Flawlessly	124	Re Toss	115	77,750	1:46.80	106
1993	Miatuschka	5	C.A. Black	114	Skimble	115	Potridee	115	62,600	1:47.80	99
1994	Aube Indienne	4	K.J. Desormeaux	115	Queens Court Queen	115	Skimble	116	61,300	1:49.60	101
1995	Onceinabluemamoon	4	B. Blanc	116	Yearly Tour	117	Don't Read My Lips	117	76,400	1:50.20	103
1996	Wandesta	5	C.S. Nakatani	120	Real Connection	113	Alpride	120	79,700	1:46.60	106
1997	Real Connection	6	G.F. Almeida	115	Toda Una Dama	114	Luna Wells	119	75,000	1:47.60	104
1998	Sonja's Faith	4	E. Ramsammy	115	See You Soon	116	Idealistic Cause	113	90,000	1:48.80	104
1999	Sapphire Ring	4	G.L. Stevens	118	Cyrillic	117	Country Garden	113	150,000	1:48.20	100
2000	Smooth Player	4	E. Delahoussaye	115	Beautiful Noise	115	Happyanunoit	121	150,000	1:46.99	97
2001	Golden Apples	3	G.K. Gomez	115	Dancingonice	113	Janet	120	150,000	1:46.61	105
2002	Tates Creek	4	J.D. Bailey	120	Voodoo Dancer	121	Magic Mission	113	120,000	1:47.69	102
2004	Theater R.N.	4	R.R. Douglas	114	Lots of Hope	117	Good Student	114	90,000	1:47.81	93

Beyer Index: 102.00

Not run in 2003.

LAS VIRGENES (G1), 1 Mile,
3-Year-Old Fillies, Santa Anita, 2004 Purse: $250,000

Year	Winner	Age	Jockey	Wt.	Second	Wt.	Third	Wt.	Win Value	Time	Beyer
1983	Saucy Bobbie	3	L. Pincay Jr	117	A Lucky Sign	121	Little Hailey	113	50,100	1:36.20	
1984	Althea	3	L. Pincay Jr	124	Vagabond Gal	117	My Darling One	114	50,500	1:37.00	
1985	Fran's Valentine	3	P.A. Valenzuela	117	Rascal Lass	121	Wising Up	121	77,150	1:36.40	
1986	Life at the Top	3	R.Q. Meza	114	Twilight Ridge	121	An Empress	117	77,050	1:36.20	
1987	Timely Assertion	3	G.L. Stevens	114	Very Subtle	121	My Turbulent Beau	114	74,900	1:36.80	
1988	Goodbye Halo	3	J. Velasquez	123	Winning Colors	119	Sadie B. Fast	115	74,750	1:35.80	
1989	Kool Arrival	3	L. Pincay Jr	121	Some Romance	123	Fantastic Look	115	77,200	1:36.20	
1990	Cheval Volant	3	A. Solis	123	Nasers Pride	119	Bright Candles	119	78,150	1:38.00	87
1991	Lite Light	3	C.S. Nakatani	121	Garden Gal	121	Nice Assay	119	93,800	1:35.60	104
1992	Magical Maiden	3	G.L. Stevens	121	Golden Treat	115	Red Bandana	115	96,800	1:36.23	91
1993	Likeable Style	3	G.L. Stevens	117	Incindress	117	Blue Moonlight	119	91,000	1:36.67	92
1994	Lakeway	3	K.J. Desormeaux	117	Fancy 'n Fabulous	114	Princess Mitterand	116	93,600	1:35.14	103
1995	Serena's Song	3	C.S. Nakatani	122	Cat's Cradle	118	Urbane	116	92,700	1:35.46	108
1996	Antespend	3	C.W. Antley	120	Cara Rafaela	122	Hidden Lake	116	96,900	1:36.45	98
1997	Sharp Cat	3	C.S. Nakatani	122	High Heeled Hope	118	Demon Acquire	116	98,800	1:35.52	101
1998	Keeper Hill	3	D.R. Flores	114	Star of Broadway	116	Occhi Verdi	116	120,000	1:36.94	95
1999	Excellent Meeting	3	K.J. Desormeaux	122	Tout Charmant	116	Weekend Squall	115	120,000	1:35.45	108
2000	Surfside	3	P.Day	122	Spain	115	Rings a Chime	116	117,600	1:37.00	93
2001	Golden Ballet	3	C.J. McCarron	122	Two Item Limit	120	Affluent	114	120,000	1:36.89	97
2002	You	3	J. Bailey	122	Habibti	122	Tali'sluckybusride	120	120,000	1:36.84	93
2003	Composure	3	J.D. Bailey	120	Elloluv	122	Watching You	116	120,000	1:36.13	96
2004	A.P. Adventure	3	A. Solis	118	Hollywood Story	120	Friendly Michelle	116	150,000	1:36.50	98

Beyer Index: 97.60

LA TROIENNE (G3), 7 1/2 Furlongs,
3-Year-Old Fillies, Churchill Downs, 2004 Purse: $112,200

Year	Winner	Age	Jockey	Wt.	Second	Wt.	Third	Wt.	Win Value	Time	Beyer
1994	Packet	3	J. Johnson	113	Golden Braids		Miss Ra He Ra		55,770	1:24.14	80
1995	Dixieland Gold	3	D.Penna	121	Daylight Ridge		Ivorilla		55,087	1:22.74	96
1996	Rare Blend	3	P.Day	121	Ruby Baby		Prissy One		55,673	1:23.75	93
1997	Star Of Goshen	3	A.Solis	115	Pearl City	115	Flying Lauren	116	70,370	1:22.75	101
1998	Sister Act	3	C. H. Borel	113	Bourbon Belle	118	Marie J	114	69,874	1:24.40	96
1999	Sapphire n' Silk	3	P. Day	113	English Bay	116	Grand Deed	121	69,936	1:23.80	102

Year	Winner	Age	Jockey	Wt.	Second	Wt.	Third	Wt.	Win Value	Time	Beyer
2000	Roxelana	3	L. Melancon	116	Magicalmysterycat	121	Watchfull	116	70,308	1:21.97	105
2001	Caressing	3	P. Day	121	Sweet Nanette	121	Golly Greeley	116	75,020	1:22.90	90
2002	Cashier's Dream	3	D.J. Meche	121	Shameful	113	Colonial Glitter	121	69,812	1:24.83	91
2003	Final Round	3	J.D. Bailey	116	Lovely Sage	116	Fast Cookie	118	69,316	1:22.13	93
2004	Friendly Michelle	3	A. Solis	118	Ender's Sister	122	Bohemian Lady	122	69,564	1:28.26	98

Beyer Index: 95.00

For previous runnings, refer to 1994 Manual.

LAUREL FUTURITY (G3), 1 1/16 Miles, 2-Year-Olds, Pimlico, 2004 Purse: $100,000

Year	Winner	Age	Jockey	Wt.	Second	Wt.	Third	Wt.	Win Value	Time	Beyer
1921	Morvich	2	A. Johnson	122	Lucky Hour	119	Runantell	122	42,750	1:42.00	
1922	Blossom Time	2	A. Johnson	119	Donges	119	Little Celt	122	41,015	1:39.80	
1922	Sally's Alley	2	A. Johnson	116	Martingale	122	My Own	122	41,015	1:39.20	
1923	Beau Butler	2	G.W. Carroll	122	Rustic	122	Aga Khan	117	54,030	1:39.80	
1924	Stimulus	2	H. Thurber	122	Star Lore	119	Candy Kid	122	49,220	1:39.80	
1925	Canter	2	C. Turner	117	Bubbling Over	122	Display	119	53,350	1:40.80	
1926	Fair Star	2	O. Bourassa	119	Jopagan	122	Whiskery	119	59,660	1:40.60	
1927	Glade	2	L. Morris	114	Petee-Wrack	119	Eugene S.	122	53,310	1:41.80	
1928	High Strung	2	L. McAtee	122	Dr. Freeland	122	Neddie	119	50,750	1:39.00	
1929	Flying Heels	2	W. Kelsay	117	Spinach	119	Galaday	116	55,810	1:47.00	
1930	Equipoise	2	R. Workman	119	Twenty Grand	119	Mate	119	50,360	1:48.60	
1931	Top Flight	2	R. Workman	119	Tick On	119	Burgoo King	119	56,170	1:44.80	
1932	Swivel	2	J. Gilbert	116	Golden Way	122	Repaid	119	62,430	1:46.80	
1935	Hollyrood	2	S. Coucci	122	Grand Slam	122	Ned Reigh	119	45,850	1:46.60	
1936	Matey	2	H. Richards	119	Brooklyn	122	Billionaire	122	25,300	1:46.80	
1937	Nedayr	2	W.D. Wright	122	Jacola	119	Dauber	122	28,140	1:45.20	
1938	Challedon	2	G. Seabo	119	Third Degree	119	Gilded Knight	122	28,770	1:45.80	
1939	Bimelech	2	F.A. Smith	122	Rough Pass	122	Straight Lead	122	33,230	1:45.20	
1940	Bold Irishman	2	J. Gilbert	122	Our Boots	119	Whirlaway	122	33,830	1:49.80	
1941	Contradiction	2	K. McCombs	122	Devil Diver	119	Chiquita Mia	119	33,910	1:47.40	
1942	Count Fleet	2	J. Longden	119	Occupation	122	Vincentive	122	30,820	1:43.40	
1943	Platter	2	C. McCreary	119	By Jimminy	119	Smolensko	122	33,440	1:47.60	
1944	Pot o' Luck	2	D. Dodson	122	Plebiscite	122	Recce	119	35,130	1:46.40	
1945	Star Pilot	2	A. Kirkland	122	Billy Bumps	119	Colony Boy	117	36,365	1:47.80	
1946	Jet Pilot	2	J. Gilbert	122	Fervent	122	Bastogne	119	37,615	1:46.00	
1947	Citation	2	D. Dodson	119	Better Self	119	Ace Admiral	122	36,675	1:48.80	
1948	Capot	2	T. Atkinson	119	Slam Bang	122	Sun Bahram	122	47,325	1:45.80	
1949	Oil Capitol	2	E.J. Knapp	122	Lot o Luck	122	Striking	119	48,755	1:44.20	
1950	Big Stretch	2	T. Atkinson	122	Bold	117	General Staff	122	45,090	1:45.40	
1951	Cajun	2	N. Shuk	122	Lord Priam	119	Inyureye	119	46,450	1:47.60	
1952	Isasmoothie	2	B. Mitchell	119	Count Cain	119	County Clare	122	59,410	1:46.60	
1953	Errard King	2	S. Boulmetis	122	War Doings	122	Nirgal Lad	119	61,450	1:45.20	
1954	Thinking Cap	2	D. Dodson	122	Flying Fury	119	Saratoga	122	53,870	1:46.80	
1955	Nail	2	H. Woodhouse	122	Liberty Sun	122	Countermand	122	67,980	1:47.00	
1956	Missile	2	P. Anderson	122	Cohoes	122	Ambehaving	122	71,235	1:45.00	
1957	Jewel's Reward	2	W. Shoemaker	122	Nala	122	Staysail	122	115,347	1:44.20	
1958	Intentionally	2	W. Shoemaker	122	Rico Tesio	122	Black Hills	122	119,571	1:46.00	
1959	Progessing	2	H. Woodhouse	122	All Hands	122	Catapult	122	71,635	1:45.40	
1960	Garwol	2	I. Valenzuela	122	Bal Musette	122	Sherluck	122	67,046	1:45.80	
1961	Crimson Satan	2	W. Shoemaker	122	Green Ticket	122	Endymion	122	72,585	1:46.40	
1962	Right Proud	2	J. Leonard	122	Delta Judge	122	Master Dennis	122	72,637	1:47.00	
1963	Quadrangle	2	W. Hartack	122	Breakspear	122	Bupers	122	110,012	1:47.20	
1964	Sadair	2	M. Ycaza	122	Hail to All	122	Umbrella Fella	122	110,913	1:43.40	
1965	Spring Double	2	H. Hinojosa	122	Fathers Image	122	Amberoid	122	134,543	1:44.80	
1966	In Reality	2	J.L. Rotz	122	Successor	122	Proviso	122	121,667	1:45.80	
1967	Vitriolic	2	B. Baeza	122	T.V. Commercial	122	Gin-Rob	122	113,015	1:45.20	
1968	King Emperor	2	E. Belmonte	122	Dike	122	Mr. Leader	122	114,380	1:44.00	
1969	High Echelon	2	M. Ycaza	122	Toasted	122	Brave Emperor	122	114,803	1:44.20	
1970	Limit to Reason	2	J. Cruguet	122	New Round	122	Droll Role	122	123,526	1:44.80	
1971	Riva Ridge	2	R. Turcotte	122	Festive Mood	122	Drum Fire	122	90,733	1:43.40	
1972	Secretariat	2	R. Turcotte	122	Stop the Music	122	Angle Light	122	83,395	1:42.80	
1973	Protagonist	2	A. Santiago	122	Hasty Flyer	122	Prince of Reason	122	79,911	1:43.20	
1974	L'Enjoleur	2	S. Hawley	122	Wajima	122	Bombay Duck	122	75,564	1:42.60	
1975	Honest Pleasure	2	B. Baeza	122	Whatsyourpleasure	122	Dance Spell	122	91,662	1:42.80	
1976	Royal Ski	2	J. Kurtz	122	For the Moment	122	Medieval Man	122	86,046	1:44.00	
1977	Affirmed	2	S. Cauthen	122	Alydar	122	Star de Naskra	122	82,290	1:44.20	
1978	Spectacular Bid	2	R.J. Franklin	122	General Assembly	122	Clever Trick	122	84,237	1:41.60	
1979	Plugged Nickle	2	B. Thornburg	122	Gold Stage	122	New Regent	122	108,630	1:43.80	
1980	Cure the Blues	2	R.L. Turcotte	122	Matching Gift	122	Kan Reason	122	91,116	1:44.40	

Year	Winner	Age	Jockey	Wt.	Second	Wt.	Third	Wt.	Win Value	Time	Beyer
1981	Deputy Minister	2	D. MacBeth	122	Laser Light	122	Majesty's Prince	122	110,190	1:44.60	
1982	Cast Party	2	J. Velasquez	122	Pax in Bello	122	Primitive Pleasure	122	145,293	1:45.00	
1983	Devil's Bag	2	E. Maple	122	Hail Bold King	122	Pied a' Tierre	122	138,150	1:42.20	
1984	Mighty Appealing	2	G.P. Smith	122	Cutlass Reality	122	Rhoman Rule	122	169,485	1:43.00	
1985	Southern Appeal	2	J. Davidson	122	Papal Power	122	Miracle Wood	122	130,770	1:44.20	
1986	Bet Twice	2	C. Perret	122	Pledge Card	122	Grand Rol	122	146,145	1:45.00	
1987	Antiqua	2	C.B. Asmussen	122	Mister Modesty	122	Kohen Witha K	122	150,000	1:46.00	
1988	Luge II	2	J.A. Santos	122	Ringerman	122	Downtown Davey	122	150,000	1:45.20	
1989	Go and Go	2	C. Perret	122	Robyn Dancer	122	Super Cholo	122	180,000	1:44.00	
1990	River Traffic	2	C.B. Asmussen	122	Fourstars Allstar	122	Share the Glory	122	180,000	1:44.80	
1991	Smiling and Dancin	2	R. Migliore	122	Free at Last	122	Older but Smarter	122	120,000	1:48.60	
1992	Lord of the Bay	2	R. Wilson	122	Glorieux Dancer	122	Halisee	122	120,000	1:45.40	
1993	Dove Hunt	2	R.G. Davis	122	Lotsa Chile	122	Thrilla in Manila	122	81,000	1:49.00	81
1994	Western Echo	2	Prado ES	122	Old Tascosa	122	Shimmering Prince	122	60,000	1:30.80	85
1995	Appealing Skier	2	Wilson A	122	Liberty Road	122	Pirate Performer	122	60,000	1:30.60	87
1996	Captain Bodgit	2	F.G. Douglas	122	Concerto	122	Carrolls Favorite	122	60,000	1:49.40	101
1997	Fight For M'Lady	2	C.H.Marquez Jr	122	Victory Gallop	122	Essential	122	60,000	1:53.60	93
1998	Millions	2	Prado E. S.	122	Raire Standard	122	More Better	122	60,000	1:51.40	84
1999	Scottish Halo	2	Turner T. G.	122	Un Fino Vino	122	Grundlefoot	122	60,000	1:49.20	96
2000	Buckle Down Ben	2	M.J. McCarthy	122	Gift of the Eagle	122	Niner's Echo	122	60,000	1:51.93	88
2002	Toccet	2	J.F. Chavez	122	Ironton	122	Cherokee's Boy	122	60,000	1:46.10	96
2003	Tapit	2	R.A. Dominguez	122	Polish Rifle	122	Ghost Mountain	122	60,000	1:43.81	98
2004	Defer	2	J.D. Bailey	122	Funk	122	Woody's Apache	122	60,000	1:45.48	78

Beyer Index: 89.73

LAWRENCE REALIZATION (G3), 1 1/2 Miles (Turf), 3-Year-Olds, Belmont Park, 2004 Purse: $110,100

Year	Winner	Age	Jockey	Wt.	Second	Wt.	Third	Wt.	Win Value	Time	Beyer
1889	Salvator	3	J. McLaughlin	122	Tenny	109	Long Dance	112	34,100	2:51.00	
1890	Tournament	3	W. Hayward	113	Her Highness	116	Banquet	119	25,300	2:51.00	
1891	Potomac	3	A. Hamilton	119	Montana	109	Strathmeath	116	30,850	2:51.00	
1892	Tammany	3	E. Garrison	119	The Pepper	115	Patron	119	28,470	2:51.40	
1893	Daily America	3	W. Simms	107	St. Leonards	118	Sir Walter	122	24,150	2:50.60	
1894	Dobbins	3	W. Simms	122	Hornpipe	122	Rey el Santa Anita	119	33,400	2:55.00	
1895	Bright Phoebus	3	L. Reiff	115	Keenan	122	King Arthur II	112	29,700	2:51.40	
1896	Requital	3	A. Clayton	119	Peep o' Day	107	Merry Prince	110	17,365	2:49.40	
1897	The Friar	3	F. Littlefield	115	Rennssalaer	112	Buddha	118	18,125	2:48.40	
1898	Hamburg	3	T. Sloan	122	Plaudit	122	George Boyd	112	13,875	2:51.20	
1899	Ethelbert	3	H. Spencer	118	Lothario	122	Filton d'Or	119	12,890	2:51.40	
1900	Prince of Melbourn	3	H. Spencer	126	Ildrim	126	Kilogram	119	14,325	2:49.80	
1901	The Parader	3	P. McCue	126	Commando	121	Mortallo	116	13,555	2:49.80	
1902	Major Daingerfield	3	G. Odom	123	The Rival	111	Goldsmith	123	12,875	2:47.60	
1903	Africander	3	J. Bullman	126	Golden Maxim	126	Savable	126	18,635	2:45.20	
1904	Ort Wells	3	F. O'Niell	126	Mercury	113	Graziallo	122	20,945	2:47.60	
1905	Sysonby	3	D. Nicol	126	Tanya	121	Migraine	116	17,935	2:47.00	
1906	Accountant	3	J. Martin	126	Entree	119	Bull's Eye	116	16,260	2:48.00	
1907	Dinna Ken	3	G. Mountain	123	Frank Gill	126	Salvidere	123	16,880	2:48.00	
1908	Fair Play	3	E. Dugan	126	King James	126	Dorante	126	17,685	2:46.20	
1909	Fitz Herbert	3	V. Powers	122	Olambala	122	Fayette	126	14,900	2:45.00	
1910	Sweep	3	J. Notter	126	Suffragist	116	Hindoo Star	116	9,755	2:53.00	
1913	Rock View	3	T. McTaggart	127	Monocacy	110	Rock Fish	90	2,475	2:51.00	
1916	Star Hawk	3	H.H. Phillips	117	Spur	126	Crimper	111	2,775	2:32.60	
1917	Omar Khayyam	3	M. Buxton	126	Hourless	126	Buckboard	116	5,950	2:33.40	
1918	Johren	3	F. Robinson	126	Whippoorwill	116			10,725	2:55.20	
1919	Vexatious	3	W. Knapp	123	Dunboyne	126	Thunderstorm	116	20,540	2:47.60	
1920	Man o' War	3	C. Kummer	126	Hoodwink	116			15,040	2:40.80	
1921	Touch Me Not	3	F. Coltiletti	126	Grey Lag	126	Sporting Blood	121	17,850	2:43.20	
1922	Kai-Sang	3	E. Sande	126	Bunting	126	Rockminister	122	21,400	2:42.40	
1923	Zev	3	E. Sande	126	Untidy	123	Rialto	119	24,410	2:44.60	
1924	Aga Khan	3	J. Maiben	116	Transmute	126	Mr. Mutt	126	25,120	2:48.40	
1925	Marconi	3	K. Noe	116	Swope	126	Chantley	116	26,500	2:43.80	
1926	Espino	3	L. Fator	126	Crusader	126	Mars	126	26,100	2:42.60	
1927	Nimba	3	H. Thurber	123	Brown Bud	126	Flippant	119	29,470	2:45.00	
1928	Reigh Count	3	C. Lang	126	Diavolo	126	Sortie	126	28,430	2:44.60	
1929	The Nut	3	M. Garner	119	African	119	Beacon Hill	126	31,760	2:45.60	
1930	Gallant Fox	3	E. Sande	126	Questionnaire	123	Yarn	116	29,610	2:41.20	
1931	Twenty Grand	3	C. Kurtsinger	126	Sun Meadow	123	Sir Ashley	123	29,700	2:41.20	
1932	Faireno	3	T. Malley	126	Over Time	116	War Hero	126	24,985	2:43.60	
1933	War Glory	3	J. Gilbert	123	Pomposity	116	Sarada	123	21,400	2:44.60	
1934	Carry Over	3	T. Malley	116	Observant	126	Good Goods	116	18,110	2:44.00	

Year	Winner	Age	Jockey	Wt.	Second	Wt.	Third	Wt.	Win Value	Time	Beyer
1935	Firethorn	3	E. Arcaro	119	Count Arthur	119	Purple Knight	116	16,780	2:42.20	
1936	Granville	3	J. Stout	126	Giant Killer	116	Memory Book	126	19,550	2:43.60	
1937	Unfailing	3	F. Koepel	112	Privileged	119	Moonton	112	19,590	2:44.20	
1938	Magic Hour	3	J. Longden	112	Roseretter	109	Dan He	112	16,800	2:45.00	
1939	Hash	3	E. Arcaro	119	Chip In	112	Shining One	123	18,750	2:42.60	
1940	Fenelon	3	J. Stout	123	Your Chance	123	Romanov	112	18,070	2:44.80	
1941	Whirlaway	3	A. Robertson	126	Alaking	112	Time Counts	112	23,050	2:44.20	
1942	Alsab	3	G. Woolf	126	Vagrancy	115	Trierarch	110	7,900	2:42.00	
1943	Fairy Manhurst	3	J. Longden	109	Eurasian	122	Famous Victory	111	7,475	2:43.00	
1944	By Jimminy	3	G. Woolf	126	Bounding Home	126			13,805	2:43.20	
1945	Pot o' Luck	3	D. Dodson	126	Chief Barker	108	Michaelo	108	20,060	2:43.60	
1946	School Tie	3	T. Atkinson	110	Alamond	114			18,300	2:43.60	
1947	Cosmic Bomb	3	O. Scurlock	114	Phalanx	126	Snow Goose	115	19,050	2:42.80	
1948	Ace Admiral	3	T. Atkinson	114	Noble Hero	114	Shy Guy	112	20,400	2:44.20	
1949	Ponder	3	S. Brooks	126	Blue Hills	110	Prophets Thumb	116	15,500	2:42.60	
1950	Bed o' Roses	3	N. Combest	107	Greek Ship	118	Theory	110	15,600	2:42.60	
1951	Counterpoint	3	D. Gorman	126	Saxony	110	Alerted	114	15,700	2:43.40	
1952	Mark-Ye-Well	3	E. Arcaro	118	One Count	126	Marcador	114	20,000	2:42.00	
1953	Platan	3	C. McCreary	110	Dictar	118	Level Lea	118	20,150	2:43.40	
1954	Fisherman	3	H. Woodhouse	122	Full Flight	122	Privacy	110	18,900	2:44.60	
1955	Thinking Cap	3	P.J. Bailey	114	Westward Ho	122	Sweet Chariot	110	18,250	2:44.40	
1956	Riley	3	T. Atkinson	120	Third Brother	114	Oh Johnny	120	18,450	2:43.40	
1957	Promised Land	3	H. Woodhouse	114	Assemblyman	117	Jocko's Walk	114	19,800	2:43.20	
1958	Martins Rullah	3	W. Shoemaker	117	Warhead	120	Plion	120	17,900	2:43.00	
1959	Middle Brother	3	E. Arcaro	120	Polylad	114	Nasomo	114	18,225	2:44.40	
1960	Kelso	3	E. Arcaro	120	Tompion	123	Tooth and Nail	116	35,800	2:40.80	
1961	Sherluck	3	B. Baeza	123	Ambiopoise	120	Carry Back	123	35,490	2:43.80	
1962	Battle Joined	3	M. Ycaza	116	Smart	116	Comic	120	37,245	2:42.60	
1963	Dean Carl	3	R. Ussery	120	B. Major	120	Master Dennis	116	36,530	2:42.00	
1964	Quadrangle	3	M. Ycaza	126	Roman Brother	123	Knightly Manner	116	35,165	2:45.00	
1965	Munden Point	3	S. Boulmetis	116	Selari	116	Sammyren	120	35,880	2:43.60	
1966	Buckpasser	3	B. Baeza	126	Ring Twice	116	Poker	116	35,490	2:44.20	
1967	Successor	3	B. Baeza	116	Gentleman James	116	Irish Rebellion	116	35,620	2:44.60	
1968	Funny Fellow	3	B. Baeza	116	Draft Card	116	Chompion	123	36,595	2:41.20	
1969	Oil Power	3	J. Cruguet	116	Red Reality	120	Pollution	116	34,970	2:42.20	
1970	Kling Kling	3	J. Cruguet	114	Loud	123	Naskra	120	37,310	2:27.60	
1971	Specious	3	E. Maple	111	Yellow Zorker	114	Gleaming	120	34,740	2:36.80	
1972	Halo	3	B. Baeza	114	Betsy Be Good	112	Ruritania	114	35,280	2:28.20	
1973	Amen II	3	E. Belmonte	128	Big Whippendeal	117	Expropriate	117	34,590	2:26.80	
1974	Prod	3	J. Velasquez	117	Prince of Reason	117	The Scotsman	117	34,050	2:35.00	
1975	Gab Bag	3	J. Cruguet	117	One on the Aisle	117	Martial Law	117	34,590	2:31.60	
1976	Great Contractor	3	P. Day	117	Teddy's Courage	117	Crackle	117	26,130	2:27.60	
1976	L'Heureux	3	D. Pierce	121	Banghi	117	Chati	117	26,130	2:27.80	
1977	Zinov	3	A. Graell	117	Poor Man's Bluff	117	Johnny D.	117	32,500	2:29.20	
1978	Mac Diarmida	3	J. Cruguet	123	Native Courier	114	Robin's Song	114	32,970	2:27.20	
1979	Golden Act	3	S. Hawley	126	Smarten	126	T.V. Series	114	50,355	2:27.60	
1980	Rumbo	3	W. Shoemaker	114	Proctor	117	Pirate Law	114	50,580	2:26.00	
1981	Our Captain Willie	3	A. Cordero Jr	114	Change the Patch	114	Open Call	114	49,050	2:27.40	
1982	Ten Below	3	J. Miranda	114	Majesty's Prince	123	Khatango	121	51,030	2:26.40	
1983	Moon Spirit	3	A. Cordero Jr	114	Win	114	Tough Mickey	114	53,100	2:28.40	
1984	Roving Minstrel	3	K. Skinner	123	Vision	123	Solidified	114	55,530	2:28.00	
1985	Danger's Hour	3	J.D. Bailey	123	Silent Slander	114	Regal Diplomat	114	66,915	2:30.40	
1985	Noisy When Hot	3	J.A. Santos	114	Broadway Tommy	114	Ctutlass Reality	114	54,135	2:30.60	
1986	The Lone Ranger	3	C.J. McCarron	114	Southjet	123	Dark Flood	114	72,600	2:37.40	
1987	Tertiary Zone	3	S. Hawley	114	Major Beard	114	Sport Royal	114	92,100	2:30.00	
1988	Blew by Em	3	C.W. Antley	114	Colchis Island	114	Face Nord	114	86,100	2:27.20	
1989	Caltech	3	R.R. Douglas	123	Pach to Batan	114	Fast 'n' Gold	114	74,280	2:26.00	
1990	Baylis	3	L. Dettori	114	Cozzene's Prince	114	Libor	114	76,920	2:29.00	102
1991	Jaded Dancer	3	J.L. Samyn	117	Pitch In	114	Silvardara	114	72,240	2:32.00	96
1992	Timber Cat	3	R.G. Davis	114	Tomorrow's Spirit	114	Gainzer	113	76,560	2:28.80	91
1993	Strolling Along	3	C.J. McCarron	114	Scattered Steps	113	Noble Sheba	114	75,480	2:32.60	98
1994	Personal Merit	3	Chavez JF	113	Kristen's Baby	111	Holy Mountain	116	67,260	2:29.20	96
1995	Flitch	3	M.E. Smith	117	Look Daggers	109	Diplomatic Jet	118	69,300	2:34.40	103
1996	Da Dean	3	R. Migliore	113	Senor Senor	113	Value Investor	116	68,880	2:39.00	102
1997	Renewed	3	Leon F.	112	Devonwood	112	Belgravia	113	67,320	2:27.20	93
1998	Parade Ground	3	P. Day	121	Pay Zone	112	Vergennes	115	83,595	2:25.80	99
1999	Gritty Sandie	3	M.E. Smith	114	Monkey Puzzle	116	Just Listen	115	90,000	2:28.60	98
2000	Ciro	3	J.A. Santos	123	Whata Brainstorm	115	Lodge Hill	115	90,000	2:31.48	107
2001	Sharp Performance	3	J.R. Velazquez	120	Tiger Trap	116	Whitmore's Conn	114	90,000	2:27.04	102
2002	Fisher Pond	3	J.R. Velazquez	116	Irish Colonial	116	Extra Check	116	90,000	2:30.34	100
2003	Kicken Kris	3	J. Castellano	121	Rowans Park	115	Fortune Writers	113	90,000	2:27.98	99
2004	Gunning For	3	J. Bravo	119	Rousing Victory	115	Second Performance	119	66,060	2:29.91	95

Beyer Index: 98.73

LECOMTE (G3), 1 Mile, 3-Year-Olds, Fair Grounds, 2004 Purse: $100,000

Year	Winner	Age	Jockey	Wt.	Second	Wt.	Third	Wt.	Win Value	Time	Beyer
1943	Valdina Orphan	4	F. Zufelt	122	Moscow II	109	Yankee Dandy	108	3,330	1:51.00	
1944	First Fiddle	5	J. Westrope	118	Pops Pick	115	Rounders	120	2,315	1:45.60	
1946	King Dorsett	4	C. LeBlanc	120	Bold Salute	110	Pique	113	3,345	1:44.60	
1947	Jack S.L.	7	S. Brooks	111	Earshot	114	Republican	112	6,500	1:45.20	
1948	Jack S.L.	8	R.L. Baird	114	Seven Hearts	125	Noble One	118	6,500	1:49.20	
1949	Caillou Rouge	4	J. West	105			Rabies	115	4,780	1:50.80	
	My Request	4	O. Scurlock	123							
1950	Johns Joy	4	D. Scurlock	121	Blue Thanks	113	Red Camelia	104	8,620	1:45.20	
1951	Thelma Berger	4	K. Stuart	107	Little Flower	110	Riverlane	118	9,350	1:45.80	
1952	False	4	E. Van Hook	107	Light Broom	125	The Gink	110	8,050	1:45.60	
1953	Smoke Screen	4	G. Porch	114	Spur On	123	Shy Guy	113	9,850	1:47.80	
1954	Futuresque	7	E. Jenkins	109	Bugledrums	110	Money Broker	111	9,925	1:45.60	
1955	Spur On	7	P.J. Bailey	118	Bobby Brocato	119	Epic King	120	10,850	1:44.40	
1956	Galdar	5	E. Van Hook	114	Nonnie Jo	113	Ja Ja	115	9,900	1:44.00	
1957	Speed Rouser	5	J. Heckmann	121	Big Sweep	110	Ramrod	116	8,975	1:46.60	
1958	Speed Rouser	6	A. Popara	115	Ezgo	112	Tenacious	120	8,625	1:45.40	
1959	Tenacious	5	R. Broussard	119	Shoerullah	112	Jet Colonel	121	8,450	1:43.00	
1960	Tenacious	6	R. Broussard	120	Sun Better	107	Matinal	111	8,350	1:48.40	
1961	Tenacious	7	C. Meaux	113	Tony Graff	112	Road House	115	8,575	1:45.00	
1962	Treasury Note	3	B. Phelps	113	Touch Bar	111	For the Road	114	9,400	1:46.40	
1963	City Line	3	R.L. Baird	123	Lemon Twist	122	Top Gallant	120	8,950	1:42.40	
1964	Susan's Gent	3	R.L. Baird	123	Whit's Pride	121	Gordon W.	109	9,225	1:45.20	
1965	Dapper Delegate	3	J. Heckmann	123	Saber Dance	112	The Dancer	115	10,175	1:43.40	
1966	Sails Pride	3	L. Moyers	120	Royal Franklin	114	Royal Okie	122	9,825	1:50.60	
1967	Grand Premiere	3	J. Combest	119	Jalo Bond	116	Tom's Favor	115	11,600	1:44.60	
1968	Port Digger	3	M. Heath	111	Judge Kilday	120	Forever	115	11,275	1:46.80	
1969	Foolish Prince	3	D.E. Whited	118	Cangirod	114	Rush Date	114	10,625	1:45.80	
1970	Action Getter	3	M. Venezia	117	Herbalist	116	Tenacious Jr.	115	12,500	1:44.20	
1971	Helio Rise	3	P. Rubbicco	121	Felonious	114	List	116	11,950	1:45.00	
1972	No Le Hace	3	P. Rubbicco	122	Feloniously	119	Breakozone	117	14,900	1:44.40	
1973	Vodika	3	T. Barrow	119	Navajo	120	Rocket Pocket	123	15,825	1:46.00	
1974	Crimson Ruler	3	K. LeBlanc	118	Don't Be Late Jim	116	Heavy Mayonnaise	120	17,650	1:43.80	
1975	Colonel Power	3	P. Rubbicco	123	Davey Dan	113	Rustic Ruler	119	18,625	1:40.60	
1976	Tudor Tambourine	3	D. Copling	117	Glassy Dip	112	Go East Young Man	117	18,000	1:46.20	
1977	Clev Er Tell	3	R. Broussard	119	A Letter to Harry	118	Sea Defier	110	16,725	1:44.80	
1978	Dragon Tamer	3	R. Sibille	118	Batonnier	110	Traffic Warning	114	22,050	1:44.60	
1979	Fuego Seguro	3	M.R. Morgan	116	Bo	114	Will Henry	116	21,175	1:46.60	
1980	Withholding	3	B. Fann	108	Brent's Trans Am	120	Bold Source	107	23,650	1:44.20	
1981	Law Me	3	J. McKnight	113	Brazen Ruler	119	Corsicana	114	24,800	1:46.40	
1982	Linkage	3	G.P. Smith	120	Soy Emperor	113	Mid Yell	109	23,350	1:45.00	
1983	Explosive Wagon	3	C. Mueller	116	Found Pearl Harbor	116	Pronto Forli	120	26,900	1:45.00	
1984	Silent King	3	C. Mueller	115	Taylor's Special	122	Fairly Straight	111	24,150	1:45.20	
1985	Encolure	3	A. Doin	114	Northern Bid	119	Ten Times Ten	116	33,450	1:45.80	
1986	Timely Albert	3	P. Rubbicco	109	Irish Irish	114	New Plymouth	117	34,200	1:43.60	
1987	One Tough Cat	3	K.P. LeBlanc	114	Authentic Hero	118	French 'n Irish	113	17,250	1:48.20	
1988	Pastourelles	3	B.J. Walker Jr	113	Risen Star	122	Run Paul Run	114	16,275	1:46.60	
1989	Majesty's Imp	3	S.R. Rydowski	116	Nooo Problema	119	Esker Island	113	16,455	1:45.60	
1990	Martha's Buck	3	B. Walker	113	Axe It	115	Arrowhead Al	112	16,050	1:47.00	
1991	Big Courage	3	T.L. Fox	116	Near the Limit	118	Slick Groom	111	19,725	1:48.20	
1992	Line in the Sand	3	S.P. Romero	115	Greinton's Dancer	113	Best Boy's Jade	116	19,215	1:39.80	88
1993	Dixieland Heat	3	E.J. Perrodin	116	Apprentice	117	Masters Windfall	112	19,995	1:37.60	85
1994	Fly Cry	3	R. Ardoin	119	Smilin Singin Sam	114	Sweet Wager	115	19,905	1:39.29	100
1995	Moonlight Dancer	3	L. Melancon	112	Beavers Nose	114	Timeless Honor	120	25,725	1:40.13	93
1996	Boomerang	3	E. Martin Jr	116	Commanders Palace	116	Playing to Win	115	25,845	1:39.49	82
1997	Cash Deposit	3	R. Ardoin	120	Stroke	114	Kalispell	113	36,000	1:37.97	96
1998	Western City	3	R. Albarado	112	Captain Maestri	116	Slick Report	112	60,000	1:37.84	89
1999	Some Actor	3	E. Martin Jr	114	Desert Demon	114	Silver Chadra	114	60,000	1:38.59	84
2000	Noble Ruler	3	L. Melancon	114	Mighty	122	Peninsula	114	60,000	1:39.11	96
2001	Sam Lord's Castle	3	R. Albarado	122	Wild Hits	122	McMahon	119	60,000	1:37.98	93
2002	Easyfromthegitgo	3	D. Meche	114	Sky Terrace	119	It'sallinthechase	122	60,000	1:37.98	90
2003	Saintly Look	3	S.J. Sellers	122	Call Me Lefty	122	Winning Fans	114	60,000	1:37.62	95
2004	Fire Slam	3	S.J. Sellers	119	Shadowland	118	Two Down Automatic	117	60,000	1:38.48	92

Beyer Index: 91.00

Run at 1 mile 40 yards in 1975, 1994–1995; 1 mile 70 yards in 1944, 1946; Run at 1 1/16 miles in 1947–1948, 1950–1974, 1976–1991; Run at 1 1/8 miles in 1943, 1949; Not run in 1945.

MERVYN LeROY HANDICAP (G2), 1 1/16 Miles, 3-Year-Olds and Up, Hollywood Park, 2004 Purse: $150,000

Year	Winner	Age	Jockey	Wt.	Second	Wt.	Third	Wt.	Win Value	Time	Beyer
1980	Spectacular Bid	4	W. Shoemaker	132	Peregrinator	119	Beau's Eagle	121	120,400	1:40.40	
1981	Eleven Stitches	4	S. Hawley	115	Glorious Song	121	Summertime Guy	114	97,100	1:36.40	

Year	Winner	Age	Jockey	Wt.	Second	Wt.	Third	Wt.	Win Value	Time	Beyer
1982	Mehmet	4	S. Hawley	116	A Run	112	Major Sport	114	63,100	1:34.60	
1983	Fighting Fit	4	W. Shoemaker	115	Island Whirl	122	Kang'roo Court	116	63,600	1:35.80	
1984	Sari's Dreamer	5	R.Q. Meza	112	Fighting Fit	120	Ancestral	115	95,000	1:34.20	
1985	Precisionist	4	C.J. McCarron	126	Greinton	121	My Habitony	115	118,700	1:32.80	
1986	Skywalker	4	L. Pincay Jr	117	Sabona	113	Al Mamoon	120	123,600	1:34.80	
1987	Zabaleta	4	L. Pincay Jr	117	Nostalgia's Star	116	Sabona	114	127,000	1:34.80	
1988	Judge Angelucci	5	E. Delahoussaye	123	Simply Majestic	118	Mark Chip	117	129,600	1:40.80	
1989	Ruhlmann	4	L. Pincay Jr	121	Sabona	114	Perfec Travel	115	122,800	1:40.20	
1990	Super May	4	R.G. Davis	116	Charlatan III	110	Lively One	122	121,600	1:40.80	
1991	Louis Cyphre	5	J.A. Santos	114	Warcraft	115	Anshan	116	110,600	1:40.80	110
1992	Another Review	4	K.J. Desormeaux	116	Sir Beaufort	116	Marquetry	119	86,300	1:41.20	110
1993	Marquetry	6	K.J. Desormeaux	117	Potrillon	117	Lottery Winner	115	92,800	1:49.00	110
1994	Del Mar Dennis	4	S. Gonzales Jr	115	Tinners Way	114	Hill Pass	115	93,300	1:40.40	108
1995	Tossofthecoin	5	C.S. Nakatani	118	Ferrara	114	Polar Route	116	64,600	1:40.60	107
1996	Siphon	5	D.R. Flores	117	Del Mar Dennis	119	Dramatic Gold	117	61,500	1:40.60	116
1997	Hesabull	4	G. F. Alameida	116	Region	112	Kingdom Found	116	63,720	1:41.20	108
1998	Wild Wonder	4	E. Delahoussaye	116	Budroyale	116	Flick	117	64,320	1:40.80	113
1999	Budroyale	6	G.K. Gomez	118	Moore's Flat	107	Wild Wonder	120	90,000	1:42.00	111
2000	Out of Mind	5	E. Delahoussaye	116	Early Pioneer	116	Skimming	111	90,000	1:41.82	112
2001	Futural	5	C.J. McCarron	117	Skimming	119	Moonlight Charger	114	90,000	1:42.02	108
2002	Sky Jack	6	L. Pincay Jr	117	Bosque Redondo	117	Devine Wind	114	90,000	1:41.36	115
2003	Total Impact	5	M.E. Smith	114	Fleetstreet Dancer	114	Piensa Sonando	115	90,000	1:40.88	110
2004	Even the Score	6	D.R. Flores	116	Ender's Shadow	113	Total Impact	116	90,000	1:40.81	103

Beyer Index: 110.07

DONALD LEVINE MEMORIAL HANDICAP (G3), 6 Furlongs, 3-Year-Olds and Up, Philadelphia Park, 2004 Purse: $100,000

Year	Winner	Age	Jockey	Wt.	Second	Wt.	Third	Wt.	Win Value	Time	Beyer
1986	Lazer Show	3	P. Day	112	I Am the Game	115	Purple Mountain	114	92,610	1:22.20	
1987	High Brite	3	J.L. Kaenel	116	Vinnie the Viper	115	Foligno	115	92,550	1:21.60	
1988	Claramount	4	N. Santagata	117	Quick Call	114	Flourescent Gem	112	93,780	1:21.40	
1989	Flourescent Gem	6	J.F. Chavez	113	Quick Call	116	Whiz Along	107	93,390	1:09.20	
1990	Glitterman	5	W.A. Guerra	119	Mr. Nickerson	121	Quick Call	119	93,120	1:09.40	111
1991	Key Spirit	5	R.E. Colton	118	Hadif	115	Pulverizing	113	92,760	1:09.40	105
1992	Smart Alec	4	M.G. Pino	113	Megas Vukefalos	119	Arrowtown	114	92,820	1:09.60	105
1993	Blushing Julian	3	R.E. Colton	111	Thelastcrusade	114	Bruksbookie	112	92,640	1:09.60	107
1994	King Ruckus	4	Kabel TK	122	Friendly Lover	120	Demaloot Demashoot	117	92,580	1:09.00	107
1995	Friendly Lover	7	Wilson R	122	Buffalo Dan	119	Goldminer's Dream	115	93,420	1:08.40	106
1996	Friendly Lover	8	McCauley W. H.	118	Elajjud	113	Goldminer's Dream	114	90,000	1:09.40	104
1997	Cat Be Nimble	5	Rocco J.	122	Wire Me Collect	114	Score a Birdie	114	90,000	1:09.20	106
1998	Buffalo Dan	7	Elliott S.	117	Western Fame	115	Inajam	113	120,000	1:08.80	100
1999	Loaded Gun	4	Flores J. L.	114	Artax	119	Power by Far	115	60,000	1:08.40	107
2000	Iron Punch	6	C. Cruz	114	Say Florida Sandy	117	Just Call Me Carl	118	60,000	1:07.89	108
2001	Say Florida Sandy	7	A.T. Gryder	118	Wake At Noon	119	Max's Pal	118	120,000	1:08.51	112
2002	True Passion	4	A.S. Black	115	Late Carson	118	Really Irish	114	120,000	1:10.72	104
2004	Peeping Tom	7	A.E. Smith	116	Highway Prospector	117	Richierichierich	113	60,000	1:11.05	100

Beyer Index: 105.86

Not run in 2003. Run as Philadelphia Park Breeders' Cup Handicap prior to 2004.

(COOLMORE) LEXINGTON (G2), 1 1/16 Miles, 3-Year-Olds, Keeneland Race Course, 2004 Purse: $325,000

Year	Winner	Age	Jockey	Wt.	Second	Wt.	Third	Wt.	Win Value	Time	Beyer
1984	He Is a Great Deal	3	J.C. Espinoza	111	Swale	123	Timely Advocate	112	34,450	1:45.40	
1985	Stephan's Odyssey	3	L. Pincay Jr	118	Tajawa	112	Northern Bid	112	34,775	1:42.60	
1986	Wise Times	3	K.K. Allen	112	Country Light	115	Momentus	118	71,793	1:44.80	
1987	Risen Star	3	J. Vasquez	118	Forty Niner	121	Stalwars	118	68,673	1:46.00	
1989	Notation	3	P. Day	115	Bionic Prospect	114	Charlie Barley	118	71,663	1:44.40	
1990	Home at Last	3	J.D. Bailey	118	Pleasant Tap	115	Thirty Slews	116	73,385	1:43.40	104
1991	Hansel	3	J.D. Bailey	121	Shotgun Harry J.	115	Speedy Cure	118	86,743	1:42.60	105
1992	My Luck Runs North	3	R.D. Lopez	115	Lure	118	Agincourt	115	89,083	1:44.00	100
1993	Grand Jewel	3	J.D. Bailey	118	El Bakan	113	Truth of It All	118	87,219	1:43.60	91
1994	Southern Rhythm	3	G.K. Gomez	118	Soul of the Matter	118	Ulises	113	85,095	1:45.60	104
1995	Star Standard	3	P. Day	115	Royal Mitch	118	Guadalcanal	115	99,882	1:45.00	97
1996	City By Night	3	S.J. Sellers	113	Prince of Thieves	118	Roar	118	123,473	1:42.20	99
1997	Touch Gold	3	G.L. Stevens	115	Smoke Glacken	118	Deeds Not Words	112	116,963	1:43.20	106
1998	Classic Cat	3	R.J. Albarado	114	Voyamerican	114	Grand Slam	123	228,300	1:42.80	108
1999	Charismatic	3	J.D. Bailey	115	Yankee Victor	115	Finder's Fee	115	234,794	1:41.00	108
2000	Unshaded	3	S.J. Sellers	116	Globalize	120	Harlan Traveler	116	221,588	1:43.72	99
2001	Keats	3	L. Melancon	116	Griffinite	116	Bay Eagle	116	230,315	1:43.54	110
2002	Proud Citizen	3	M.E. Smith	116	Crimson Hero	116	Easyfromthegitgo	116	226,083	1:44.58	95

Year	Winner	Age	Jockey	Wt.	Second	Wt.	Third	Wt.	Win Value	Time	Beyer
2003	Scrimshaw	3	E.S. Prado	116	Eye of the Tiger	116	Domestic Dispute	116	225,479	1:45.47	101
2004	Quintons Gold Rush	3	J.D. Bailey	116	Fire Slam	116	Song of the Sword	116	201,500	1:43.82	102

Beyer Index: 101.93

LEXINGTON (G3), 1 1/4 Miles (Turf), 3-Year-Olds, Belmont Park, 2004 Purse: $111,100

Year	Winner	Age	Jockey	Wt.	Second	Wt.	Third	Wt.	Win Value	Time	Beyer
1961	Wise Ship	4	H. Gustines	120	Our Jeep	125	Art Market	115	36,335	2:41.80	
1962	Mongo	3	C. Burr	118	Dedimoud	117	In Force	117	18,850	1:34.20	
1963	Marlin Bay	3	J. Sellers	114	Running Bowline	117	Wild Card	115	18,752	1:41.20	
1964	Laugh Aloud	3	R. Turcotte	113	Gun Boat	114	National	124	19,142	1:43.00	
1969	Eaglesham	3	P. Anderson	119	Red Reality	110	Larceny Kid	119	18,720	1:46.60	
1970	Roman Scout	3	J. Vasquez	111	On the Track	113	Flying Brick	111	14,771	1:43.20	
1970	Naskra	3	J. Cruguet	115	Tumble Lark	112	Hubbub	116	15,096	1:43.40	
1971	Bold Reason	3	J.L. Rotz	120	Gleaming	126	Northfields	120	33,840	1:54.80	
1972	Big Spruce	3	R. Cespedes	115	Ruritana	113	Tentam	114	34,740	1:56.80	
1973	London Company	3	L. Pincay Jr	125	Rapid Sage	112	Bold Nix	116	35,760	1:56.00	
1974	Jack Sprat	3	R. Turcotte	112	Kin Run	115	Never Explain	116	28,020	1:56.40	
1974	Hasty Tudor	3	V. Bracciale Jr	112	R. Tom Can	115	Splitting Headache	118	27,870	1:56.80	
1975	Dr. Emil	3	M. Venezia	109	Martial Law	109	Le Cypriote	112	27,270	2:07.00	
1975	Brian Boru	3	B. Baeza	116	Rapid Invader	111	Clout	113	27,270	2:07.60	
1976	Fabled Monarch	3	J. Vasquez	114	Fighting Bill	113	Effervescing	112	27,450	1:50.00	
1976	Modred	3	C. Perret	117	Dream'n Be Lucky	112	Spanish Dagger	110	27,300	1:49.40	
1977	Swoon Swept	3	L. Melancon	112	Stir the Embers	112	Lynn Davis	116	32,400	1:41.20	
1977	Johnny D.	3	A. Cordero Jr	113	Forward Charger	117	Best Person	112	32,100	1:41.00	
1978	Mac Diarmida	3	J. Cruguet	126	John Henry	112	Ashikaga	110	34,110	1:41.00	
1979	Virilify	3	R.I. Velez	108	T.V. Series	113	Crown Thy Good	114	50,895	2:02.40	
1980	Good Bid	3	J.L. Samyn	112	Proctor	116	Don Daniello	122	50,310	2:01.00	
1981	Acaroid	3	C.B. Asmussen	117	De la Rose	121	Wicked Will	117	52,380	2:00.20	
1982	Majesty's Prince	3	E. Maple	126	Lamerok	114	Flamingo Two	114	50,310	2:03.00	
1982	Royal Roberto	3	J. Fell	126	Otter Slide	117	Royal Ring	114	5,031	2:01.80	
1983	Kilauea	3	J. Cruguet	114	Fortnightly	126	Top Competitor	114	34,800	2:00.60	
1984	Onyxly	3	J.D. Bailey	114	Dr. Schwartzman	126	Vision	126	58,770	2:01.20	
1985	Danger's Hour	3	J.D. Bailey	123	Foundation Plan	123	Exclusive Partner	114	71,370	2:00.40	
1986	Manila	3	J.A. Santos	126	Glow	123	Dance Card Filled	114	88,980	2:03.20	
1987	Milesius	3	E. Maple	114	Yucca	117	Rio's Lark	114	89,580	2:03.20	
1988	Sunshine Forever	3	A. Cordero Jr	123	Hodges Bay	114	Ask Not	114	85,500	2:03.00	
1989	Coosaragga	3	R. Migliore	114	Valid Ordinate	114	Orange Sunshine	119	69,720	2:00.80	
1990	Solar Splendor	3	E. Maple	123	Rouse the Louse	123	Apple Current	114	56,640	2:01.80	
1991	Lech	3	A. Cordero Jr	114	Fourstars Allstar	123	Lucky Mathieu	114	71,160	1:59.40	100
1992	Spectacular Tide	3	J.A. Krone	114	Preferences	121	Casino Magistrate	123	69,120	2:02.20	96
1993	Llandaff	3	J.A. Krone	123	Strolling Along	114	Eastern Memories	114	52,380	2:02.80	99
1994	Holy Mountain	3	Velazquez JR	112	Islefaxyou	112	Check Ride	117	50,850	1:59.60	96
1995	Green Means Go	3	J.D. Bailey	119	Nostra	112	Flitch	112	66,960	2:01.60	95
1996	Ok by Me	3	J.F. Chavez	122	Value Investor	117	Alzeus	113	68,160	2:03.40	98
1997	Private Buck Trout	3	J.F. Chavez	119	Red Castle	112	Renewed	112	90,000	2:01.20	90
1998	Parade Ground	3	M.E. Smith	117	Ay Rouge	113	La Reine's Terms	113	84,060	2:00.40	99
1999	Mythical Gem	3	J.F. Chavez	117	Monkey Puzzle	113	Bugatti	114	90,000	2:01.20	95
2000	Rob's Spirit	3	J.D. Bailey	113	Plato	113	Rumsonontheriver	115	90,000	2:02.87	104
2001	Sharp Performance	3	J.R. Velazquez	114	Package Store	114	Whitmore's Conn	114	90,000	1:58.93	101
2002	Chiselling	3	J.D. Bailey	114	Finality	114	Irish Colonial	114	90,000	2:00.42	96
2003	Sharp Impact	3	R. Migliore	114	Hidden Truth	118	Urban King	114	90,000	2:02.62	96
2004	Mustanfar	3	J.A. Santos	114	Icy Atlantic	122	Second Performance	118	66,660	2:01.15	94

Icy Atlantic finished first but was disqualified and placed second

Beyer Index: 97.07

LOCUST GROVE HANDICAP (G3), 1 1/8 Miles (Turf), Fillies and Mares, 3-Year-Olds and Up, Churchill Downs, 2004 Purse: $165,750

Year	Winner	Age	Jockey	Wt.	Second	Wt.	Third	Wt.	Win Value	Time	Beyer
1982	Excitable Lady	4	D. McHargue	120	Dawn's Beginning		Sweetest Fantasy			1:37.20	
1983	Try Something New	4	P. Day	117	Kitchen		Naskra Magic			1:45.20	
1984	Heatherten	5	S. Maple	122	Mickey's Echo		Forest Maiden			1:43.20	
1985	Sintra	4	K. Allen	123	Sweet Missus		Switching Trick			1:43.40	
1986	Glorious View		C. Woods Jr	113	Zenobia Empress		Tide			1:44.20	
1987	Luckiest Girl	4	D. Soto	114	Slipping 'n Slyding		Marianna's Girl			1:51.60	
1988	Chez Chez Chez	4	J. Garcia	111	Lt. Lao		How I Wish			1:45.20	
1989	Jungle Gold	4	C. Woods Jr	111	Here's Your Silver		Heretic			1:43.20	
1990	Dibs	4	A. Gryder	111	City Crowds		Phillipa Rush			1:50.60	
1991	Nice Serve	4	J. Johnson	111	Super Fan		Behaving Dancer		73,840	1:51.20	101
1992	Behaving Dancer	5	D. Howard	117	Firm Stance		Olden Rijn		74,750	1:47.27	101
1993	Lady Blessington	5	C. Black	121	Gone Seeking		Cruise		74,425	1:50.16	94

Year	Winner	Age	Jockey	Wt.	Second	Wt.	Third	Wt.	Win Value	Time	Beyer
1994	Life Is Delicious	4	J. Martinez Jr	113	Eurostorm		Obtain		70,850	1:53.87	83
1995	Memories	4	S.Sellers	114	Market Booster	120	Thread	115	71,760	1:47.48	101
1996	Bail Out Becky	4	C.Perret	121	Ms. Isadora	113	Memories	117	72,850	1:47.80	105
1997	Romy	6	F.Torres	121	Yokama	112	Cymbala	116	68,634	1:48.89	97
1998	Colcon	5	Sellers S. J.	118	Leo's Gypsy Dancer	113	Mingling Glances	112	103,974	1:48.40	102
1999	Shires Ende	4	Martinez W.	117	Formal Tango	116	Uanme	112	107,508	1:49.00	97
2000	Colstar	4	A. Delgado	121	Pricearose	113	Histoire Sainte	113	102,300	1:47.44	102
2001	Colstar	5	J.K. Court	121	Solvig	115	Megans Bluff	119	107,136	1:48.79	100
2002	Voodoo Dancer	4	J.A. Santos	120	Blue Moon	116	Solvig	116	104,718	1:46.91	102
2003	Ipi Tombe	5	P. Day	123	Kiss the Devil	116	Quick Tip	117	101,928	1:47.70	99
2004	Shaconage	4	B. Blanc	116	Halory Leigh	111	Sand Springs	119	102,765	1:46.75	98

Beyer Index: 98.71

LONE STAR DERBY (G3), 1 1/16 Miles, 3-Year-Olds, Lone Star Park, 2004 Purse: $250,000

Year	Winner	Age	Jockey	Wt.	Second	Wt.	Third	Wt.	Win Value	Time	Beyer
1997	Anet	3	D.R. Flores	122	Frisk Me Now	122	Holzmeister	122	140,000	1:40.80	105
1998	Smolderin Heart	3	T.T. Doocy	122	Shot of Gold	122	Troy's Play	122	145,000	1:46.20	89
1999	T. B. Track Star	3	E.M. Martin Jr	122	Desert Demon	122	Congratulate	122	165,000	1:42.92	103
2000	Tahkodha Hills	3	E.M. Coa	122	Jeblar Sez Who	122	Big Number	122	180,000	1:44.05	90
2001	Percy Hope	3	J.K. Court	122	Fifty Stars	122	Gift of the Eagle	122	292,500	1:50.27	93
2002	Wiseman's Ferry	3	J.F. Chavez	122	Tracemark	122	Peekskill	122	277,500	1:49.92	104
2003	Dynever	3	E.S. Prado	122	Most Feared	122	Commander's Affair	122	277,500	1:50.43	90
2004	Pollard's Vision	3	J.R. Velazquez	122	Cryptograph	122	Flamethrowintexan	122	150,000	1:42.10	102

Beyer Index: 98.00

LONE STAR PARK HANDICAP (G3), 1 1/16 Miles, 3-Year-Olds and Up, Lone Star Park, 2004 Purse: $300,000

Year	Winner	Age	Jockey	Wt.	Second	Wt.	Third	Wt.	Win Value	Time	Beyer
1997	Connecting Terms	4	L. Melancon	113	Humble Seven	112	Isitingood	122	120,000	1:41.80	104
1998	Mocha Express	4	M.St. Julien	114	Prince of the Mt.	114	Dickey Rickey	114	123,000	1:42.17	103
1999	Mocha Express	5	M. St. Julien	108	Littlebitlively	116	Nite Dreamer	113	183,300	1:43.20	108
2000	Luftikus	4	D.R. Flores	114	Nite Dreamer	118	Sultry Substitute	114	180,000	1:40.87	109
2001	Dixie Dot Com	6	D.R. Flores	118	Fan the Flame	113	Big Numbers	114	180,000	1:40.53	111
2002	Congaree	4	P. Day	119	Prince Iroquois	115	Mercenary	115	180,000	1:42.96	109
2003	Pie n Burger	5	H.J. Theriot II	117	Bluesthestandard	120			180,000	1:42.03	107
					Maysville Slew	114					
2004	Yessirgeneralsir	4	O. Figueroa	114	Sonic West	117	Spanish Empire	117	180,000	1:41.29	104

Beyer Index: 106.88

LONG BRANCH BREEDERS' CUP (G3), 1 1/16 Miles, 3-Year-Olds, Monmouth Park, 2004 Purse: $100,000

Year	Winner	Age	Jockey	Wt.	Second	Wt.	Third	Wt.	Win Value	Time	Beyer
1994	Meadow Flight	3	J. Bravo	120	Red Tazz	114	Don's Sho	114	47,370	1:43.80	111
1995	Pyramid Peak	3	W.H. McCauley	120	Suave Prospect	120	Mighty Magee	118	47,250	1:44.00	108
1996	Dr. Caton	3	J. Bravo	112	Devil's Honor	122	Clash by Night	114	45,000	1:41.80	102
1997	Jules	3	A. Gryder	114	Leestown	120	Capture the Gold	114	60,000	1:42.40	105
1998	Favorite Trick	3	P. Day	116	Tomorrows Cat	113	Arctic Sweep	114	60,000	1:43.20	101
1999	Ghost Story	3	R.G. Davis	112	Unbridled Jet	114	Clever Gem	114	60,000	1:42.60	100
2000	Thistyranthasclass	3	J.A. Velez Jr	114	Graeme Hall	120	Summinitup	114	60,000	1:43.60	105
2001	Burning Roma	3	R. Wilson	122	This Fleet Is Due	114	Thunder Blitz	122	60,000	1:43.28	99
2002	Puck	3	M. Aguilar	122	Shah Jehan	114	Stephentown	114	60,000	1:44.35	97
2003	Max Forever	3	J.C. Ferrer	113	Christine's Outlaw	115	Chilly Rooster	112	60,000	1:43.56	99
2004	Lion Heart	3	J. Bravo	116	My Snookie's Boy	115	Royal Assault	122	60,000	1:43.51	102

Beyer Index: 102.64

For previous runnings, see 1994 Manual.

LONGACRES MILE HANDICAP (G3), 1 Mile, 3-Year-Olds and Up, Emerald Downs, 2004 Purse: $250,000

Year	Winner	Age	Jockey	Wt.	Second	Wt.	Third	Wt.	Win Value	Time	Beyer
1993	Adventuresome Love		G. Baze	117	Sneakin Jake	118	For the Children	116	48,050	1:34.60	93
1994	Want a Winner		V. Belvoir	119	Sneakin Jake	118	Forgotten Days	114	48,250	1:35.20	87
1995	L.J. Express		M. Allen	119	Funboy	121	Secret Damascus	115	50,350	1:34.60	94
1996	Isitingood	5	D.R. Flores	117	Cleante	121	Humpty's Hoedown	114	110,000	1:35.60	105
1997	Kid Katabatic	4	C. Loseth	113	Hesabull	119	Liberty Road	114	110,000	1:34.20	105
1998	Wild Wonder	4	E. Delahoussaye	121	Mocha Express	115	Hal's Pal	117	110,000	1:33.20	111
1999	Budroyale	6	G.K. Gomez	119	Mike K	117	Kid Katabatic	116	137,500	1:34.60	106
2000	Edneator	4	G.V. Mitchell	111	Big Ten	119	Crafty Boy	114	137,500	1:33.20	104
2001	Irisheyesareflying	5	I.L. Puglisi	117	Handy N Bold	119	Makors Mark	118	137,500	1:35.40	100

Year	Winner	Age	Jockey	Wt.	Second	Wt.	Third	Wt.	Win Value	Time	Beyer
2002	Sabertooth	4	N.J. Chaves	114	Moonlight Meeting	119	San Nicolas	115	137,500	1:34.60	96
2003	Sky Jack	7	R.A. Baze	123	Poker Brad	116	Lord Nelson	116	137,500	1:33.00	105
2004	Adreamisborn	5	R.A. Baze	116	Demon Warlock	114	Mr. Makah	112	137,500	1:34.80	99

Beyer Index: 100.42

For previous runnings, refer to 1992 Manual; Run at Yakima, 1993-1995; Run at Longacres prior to 1993

LONG ISLAND HANDICAP (G2), 1 1/2 Miles (Turf), Fillies and Mares, 3-Year-Olds and Up, Aqueduct, 2004 Purse: $150,000

Year	Winner	Age	Jockey	Wt.	Second	Wt.	Third	Wt.	Win Value	Time	Beyer
1956	Third Brother	3	I. Valenzuela	120	Beau Diable	114	Thinking Cap	123	19,300	2:44.00	
1957	Promethean	3	J. Ruane	106	Cavort	117	Beam Rider	114	20,200	2:44.00	
1958	Beau Diable	5	H. Woodhouse	124	Casual Friend	117	Whatit'dyou	122	18,192	2:43.00	
1959	Tudor Era	6	W. Hartack	126	Sailor's Guide	124	Anisado	114	14,227	1:54.00	
1959	One-Eyed King	5	W. Shoemaker	121	Tharp	120	Find	116	14,227	1:54.40	
1960	El Espectador	5	B. Baeza	117	General Arthur	120	Quiz Star	118	19,135	2:16.60	
1961	Wise Ship	4	H. Gustines	115	Wolfram	126	Eurasia	115	18,525	1:58.80	
1962	The Axe II	4	W. Shoemaker	117	T.V. Lark	124	Shield Bearer	118	14,609	2:15.60	
1962	Irish Dandy	4	J. Ruane	109	Royal Record	117	Djezzar	110	13,959	2:15.80	
1963	David K.	4	W. Shoemaker	113	The Axe II	126	Never Bend	120	19,142	1:54.80	
1964	Parka	6	W. Blum	123	Cedar Key	126	Will I Rule	112	18,492	1:54.80	
1965	Parka	7	W. Blum	125	Or et Argent	116	Polar Sea	120	19,207	1:54.60	
1966	Paoluccio	4	H. Gustines	115	Gallup Poll	110	Mostar	107	14,982	1:58.60	
1966	Rego	3	H. Woodhouse	109	Pluck	113	Dunderhead	104	15,145	1:59.20	
1967	Munden Point	5	R. Ussery	117	Royal Comedian	109	Isokeha	112	15,177	1:54.80	
1967	Assagai	4	B. Baeza	126	Fast Count	109	Kentucky Kin	113	15,177	1:54.80	
1968	Ruth's Rullah	3	A. Cordero Jr	112	Ruffled Feathers	118	Czar Alexander	115	15,242	2:14.80	
1968	Flit-to	5	M. Ycaza	115	Tobin Bronze	118	Advocator	120	15,080	2:15.20	
1969	The University	4	A. Cordero Jr	113	Vent du Nord	113	North Flight	118	14,917	2:17.20	
1969	Red Reality	3	J. Velasquez	113	Rhinelander II	113	Tradesman	112	15,080	2:16.80	
1970	Larceny Kid	4	C. Baltazar	112	Bailer	119	Mongolia	114	14,901	2:02.00	
1970	Mongo's Pride	3	C.H. Marquez	113	Shelter Bay	122	Pl't Harbour	116	14,739	2:01.20	
1971	Rudo Bird	4	J. Velasquez	109	Red Reality	116	Bark'g St'ple	107	21,210	2:03.20	
1972	Primsie	3	L. Pincay Jr	114	Candid Catherine	114	Roba Bella	123	14,040	1:37.80	
1972	Twixt	3	R. Woodhouse	112	Table Flirt	116	Bold Place	114	13,965	1:39.20	
1973	Tuerta	3	J. Vasquez	116	North of Venus	117	Spring in the Air	118	17,850	1:43.80	
1974	D.O. Lady	3	M.A. Rivera	115	Speak Action	113	Gulls Cry	116	28,080	1:43.20	
1974	Lie Low	3	J. Velasquez	114	Victorian Queen	120	Markimoff	115	28,080	1:42.00	
1975	Slip Screen	3	G. Intellisano	115	Fleet Victress	115	Jabot	115	33,930	1:42.80	
1976	Javamine	3	J. Velasquez	113	Nijana	115	Fun Forever	112	33,270	1:41.60	
1977	Pearl Necklace	3	R. Hernandez	123	Javamine	121	Leave Me Alone	113	32,430	1:43.80	
1978	Terpsichorist	3	A. Cordero Jr	116	Leave Me Alone	109	Proud Event	113	48,555	2:34.00	
1979	Flitalong	3	R.I. Encinas	107	Terpsichorist	122	Catherine's Bet	114	52,245	2:31.40	
1980	The Very One	5	J. Velasquez	120	Relaxing	113	Proud Barbara	113	68,400	2:35.20	
1981	Euphrosyne	5	R. Migliore	110	Mairzy Doates	120	Noble Damsel	112	70,440	2:33.00	
1982	Hush Dear	4	E. Beitia	111	Canaille II	112	Mintage	111	71,160	2:31.40	
1983	Hush Dear	5	J.L. Samyn	125	Mintage	111	If Winter Comes	113	70,920	2:34.60	
1984	Heron Cove	4	J. Cruguet	114	Key Dancer	115	Secret Sharer	110	109,650	2:32.80	
1985	Faburola	4	E. Legrix	114	Halloween Queen	107	Easy to Copy	114	105,675	2:29.40	
1985	Videogenic	3	J. Cruguet	116	Duty Dance	114	Mariella	110	92,175	2:29.20	
1986	Dismasted	4	J.L. Samyn	120	Dawn's Curtsey	113	Devalois	114	115,560	2:30.40	
1987	Stardusk	3	J. Cruguet	109	Spruce Fir	121	Videogenic	118	115,740	2:30.40	
1988	Dancing All Night	4	J.J. Vasquez	108	Casey	113	Gaily Gaily	111	112,320	2:34.20	
1989	Warfie	3	W.H. McCauley	111	River Memories	113	Noble Links	111	72,480	2:14.40	
1990	Rigamajig	4	J.F. Chavez	110	Narwala	115	Roberto's Hope	112	72,120	2:29.60	
1990	Peinture Bleue	3	J.A. Santos	115	Franc Argument	113	Roseate Tern	119	72,600	2:29.80	108
1991	Shaima	3	L.F. Dettori	115	Highland Penny	116	Franc Argument	111	73,560	2:31.40	101
1992	Villandry	4	M.E. Smith	115	Ratings	116	Gina Romantica	113	71,160	2:29.00	101
1993	Trampoli	4	M.E. Smith	119	Bright Generation	114	Northern Emerald	108	68,760	2:31.40	105
1994	Market Booster	5	M.J. Lukas	115	Tiffany's Taylor	114	Lady Affirmed	113	87,495	2:31.80	103
1995	Yenda	4	C.S. Nakatani	114	Windsharp	111	Market Booster	118	86,400	2:37.00	110
1996	Ampulla	5	S.J. Sellers	121	Wandering Star	118	Beyrouth	113	87,270	2:30.60	108
1997	Sweetzie	5	J.F. Chavez	115	Sweet Sondra	114	Scenic Point	120	90,000	2:16.60	85
1998	Coretta	4	J.A. Santos	114	Starry Dreamer	115	Dixie Ghost	114	60,000	2:29.60	105
1998	Yokama	5	J.D. Bailey	120	Moments of Magic	113	Bristol Channel	114	60,000	2:31.00	96
1999	Midnight Line	4	J.D. Bailey	120	Win For Us	116	Horatia	112	90,000	2:29.60	95
2000	Moonlady	3	C.P. DeCarlo	114	Playact	114	La Ville Rouge	118	90,000	2:17.94	96
2001	Queue	4	J.L. Espinoza	115	Sweetest Thing	115	Lady Dora	114	90,000	2:29.36	97
2002	Uriah	3	N. Arroyo Jr	112	Sunstone	114	Mot Juste	119	90,000	2:42.48	100
2003	Spice Island	4	V. Carrero	117	Volga	120	Banyu Dewi	114	90,000	2:32.58	99
2004	Eleusis	3	J.A. Santos	115	Literacy	114	Arvada	117	90,000	2:31.51	99

Beyer Index: 100.50

Run on main track in 1997, 2000 at 1 3/8 Miles

LOS ANGELES TIMES HANDICAP (G3), 6 Furlongs, 3-Year-Olds and Up, Hollywood Park, 2004 Purse: $150,000

Year	Winner	Age	Jockey	Wt.	Second	Wt.	Third	Wt.	Win Value	Time	Beyer
1955	Karim	5	G. Glisson	112	History Book	110	The Character	109	15,850	1:09.20	
1956	Colonel Mack	4	R. Neves	119	Stranglehold	103	Poona II	117	15,150	1:09.00	
1957	Porterhouse	6	J. Longden	123	Flight History	110	Corn Husker	119	32,700	1:20.80	
1958	How Now	5	W. Harmatz	114	Golden Notes	113	The Searcher	109	31,150	1:21.60	
1959	Hillsdale	4	T. Barrow	124	Seaneen	117	Amerigo	116	32,300	1:21.00	
1960	Finnegan	4	R. Neves	113	Clandestine	116	Dotted Swiss	108	31,400	1:20.80	
1961	T.V. Lark	4	J. Longden	121	New Policy	117	First Balcony	111	33,100	1:21.20	
1962	Winonly	5	W. Harmatz	118	Crazy Kid	106	Windy Sands	112	33,550	1:21.60	
1963	Doc Jocoy	4	W. Harmatz	117	Crazy Kid	116	Winonly	123	32,850	1:20.80	
1964	Cyrano	5	J.L. Rotz	124	Quita Dude	114	Admiral's Voyage	121	32,900	1:21.40	
1965	Native Diver	6	J. Lambert	126	Viking Spirit	126	Tronado	115	32,800	1:20.00	
1966	Nasharco	4	B. Jennings	113	Pelegrin	116	Aurelius II	111	32,200	1:21.60	
1967	Native Diver	8	J. Lambert	128	Shebason	111	Chiclero	114	32,150	1:21.00	
1968	Rising Market	4	L. Pincay Jr	117	Aurelius II	113	Pedrinho	112	32,050	1:20.60	
1968	Kissin' George	5	W. Mahorney	128	Dr. Roy E.	115	Son Jack	112	32,050	1:21.20	
1969	Indulto	6	D. Pierce	122	Rising Market	124	Dewan	121	33,850	1:20.60	
1970	Ack Ack	4	D. Pierce	126	Right or Wrong	114	Baffle	123	31,250	1:20.60	
1971	Fleet Surprise	5	D. Pierce	114	Inverness Drive	115	Master Hand	111	38,900	1:20.80	
1972	Triple Bend	4	D. Pierce	123	Single Agent	122	Miles Tyson	119	37,600	1:19.80	
1973	Soft Victory	5	D. Pierce	118	Crusading	124	Convenience	117	31,850	1:21.00	
1974	Ancient Title	4	L. Pincay Jr	126	Woodland Pines	118	Soft Victory	118	32,200	1:20.40	
1975	Big Band	5	L. Pincay Jr	117	Century's Envoy	121	Shirley's Ch'n	120	32,300	1:20.60	
1976	Century's Envoy	5	S. Hawley	123	Home Jerome	116	Sport'ng Goods	120	31,950	1:20.80	
1977	Beat Inflation	4	D.G. McHargue	120	Full Out	117	Mark's Place	126	30,500	1:20.20	
1978	J.O. Tobin	4	S. Cauthen	130	Maheras	125	Drapier	121	30,200	1:21.40	
1979	Hawk'ns Special	4	D.G. McHargue	117	White Rammer	117	Whatsyourpleasure	117	31,350	1:08.40	
1980	Beau's Eagle	4	L. Pincay Jr	123	Real Soul	116	Minstrel Grey	114	32,400	1:08.20	
1981	Doonesbury	4	S. Hawley	121	Reb's Golden Ale	115	Summer Time Guy	122	37,900	1:08.80	
1982	T'rr'sto's Singer	5	P.A. Valenzuela	113	Remember John	115	Petro D. Jay	116	47,800	1:09.20	
1983	Mr. Prime Minister	7	M.A. Pedroza	115	Poley	118	Unreal Zeal	107	45,500	1:09.80	
1984	Night Mover	4	E. Delahoussaye	118	Debonaire Junior	113	Croeso	117	47,150	1:08.40	
1985	Charging Falls	4	W. Shoemaker	114	Fifty Six Ina Row	117	Premiership	115	48,650	1:08.80	
1986	Rosie's K.T.	5	P.A. Valenzuela	116	Mane Magic	116	Much Fine Gold	112	47,050	1:10.00	
1987	Bedside Promise	5	G.L. Stevens	126	Bolder Than Bold	117	Lincoln Park	115	46,200	1:08.40	
1988	Olympic Prospect	4	A. Solis	116	Happy in Space	113	Sylvan Express	119	47,700	1:08.80	
1989	Sam Who	4	L. Pincay Jr	118	Prospectors Gamble	114	Mi Preferido	119	46,200	1:09.40	
1990	Timeless Answer	4	R.G. Davis	114	Prospectors Gamble	116	Sam Who	120	64,500	1:08.80	108
1991	Black Jack Road	7	R.A. Baze	117	Sunny Blossom	121	Tanker Port	116	62,000	1:09.00	112
1992	Cardmania	6	E. Delahoussaye	118	Gray Slewpy	119	Robyn Dancer	119	61,200	1:08.60	109
1993	Star of the Crop	4	G.L. Stevens	119	Fabulous Champ	116	Wild Harmony	116	63,200	1:08.60	105
1994	J.F. Williams	5	C.J. McCarron	115	Gundaghia	118	Thirty Slews	120	61,900	1:09.00	108
1995	Forest Gazelle	4	K.J. Desormeaux	116	Lucky Forever	114	Cardmania	119	83,650	1:07.80	113
1996	Abaginone	5	G.L. Stevens	119			Score Quick	115	53,480	1:08.20	111
	Paying Dues	4	C.W. Antley	115							
1997	Men's Exclusive	4	L. Pincay Jr	117	First Intent	117	Gold Land	115	80,970	1:08.80	117
1998	Gold Land	4	K.J. Desormeaux	116	Mr. Doubledown	119	The Exeter Man	114	64,800	1:08.00	114
1999	Son of a Pistol	7	A. Solis	122	Men's Exclusive	118	Ray of Sunshine	118	63,300	1:08.00	109
2000	Highland Gold	5	C.J. McCarron	115	Mellow Fellow	113	Your Halo	114	64,260	1:09.11	106
2001	Caller One	4	C.S. Nakatani	124	Stormy Jack	115	Rapidough	115	64,380	1:08.35	116
2002	Kona Gold	8	A. Solis	125	No Armistice	116	Komax	114	64,500	1:08.72	113
2003	Hombre Rapido	6	J. Valdivia Jr	116	Publication	116	Giovannetti	116	120,000	1:08.49	107
2004	Pohave	6	J.K. Court	114	Marino Marini	119	Summer Service	117	90,000	1:08.12	105

Beyer Index: 110.20

LOUISIANA DERBY (G2), 1 1/16 Miles, 3-Year-Olds, Fair Grounds, 2004 Purse: $600,000

Year	Winner	Age	Jockey	Wt.	Second	Wt.	Third	Wt.	Win Value	Time	Beyer
1920	Damask	3	E. Ambrose	118	Bullet Proof	118	Bred Man	118	4,975	1:51.80	
1923	Amole	3	J.D. Mooney	118	Calcutta	122	Setting Sun	118	9,180	1:57.80	
1924	Black Gold	3	J.D. Mooney	126	Brilliant Cast	117	Rinkey	112	14,750	1:57.60	
1925	Quatrain	3	H. Stutts	126	Benedict Vow	114	Brave Bob	114	17,350	1:56.00	
1926	Baggenbaggage	3	E. Blind	116	Boot to Boot	112	Navigator	122	9,800	1:51.20	
1927	Boo	3	G. Johnson	114	Fred Jr	122	Fly Hawk	122	14,250	1:51.80	
1928	Jack Higgins	3	C.E. Allen	118	Beauregard	118	Time Maker	118	15,450	1:52.00	
1929	Calf Roper	3	F. Coltiletti	117	Panchio	114	McGonigle	117	15,825	1:56.00	
1930	Michigan Boy	3	J. Shelton	117	Bad News Bob	117	Brother Rank	117	9,225	2:00.20	

Year	Winner	Age	Jockey	Wt.	Second	Wt.	Third	Wt.	Win Value	Time	Beyer
1931	Spanish Play	3	C. Landolt	120	Prince d'Amour	120	Anne Arundel	107	7,475	1:51.20	
1932	Lucky Tom	3	A. Pascuma	120	Open Hearth	116	Prince Hotspur	116	9,375	1:53.60	
1933	Col. Hatfield	3	C. Meyer	116	Spicson	113	Gyro	113	4,750	1:56.40	
1934	Hickory Lad	3	J. Westrope	113	Cursor	113	Morning Cry	105	2,870	1:53.40	
1935	McCarthy	3	P. Keester	117	Dark Woman	106	Bulstrode	111	2,150	1:54.00	
1936	Rushaway	3	J. Longden	116	Lolschen	111	Professor Paul	119	3,900	1:50.80	
1937	Grey Count	3	C. Corbett	116	Dead Calm	114	Trina	114	7,730	1:50.80	
1938	Wise Fox	3	J. Longden	114	Bunny Baby	111	Sir Raleigh	116	9,510	1:51.20	
1939	Day Off	3	E. Arcaro	114	Alms	111	Patrol Scout	116	9,510	1:52.60	
1943	Amber Light	3	J. Longden	120	Ocean Wave	126	Pops Pick	116	10,750	1:52.60	
1944	Olympic Zenith	3	N. Jemas	117	Gay Bit	120	Weyanoke	120	11,525	1:54.00	
1946	Pellicle	3	A. LoTurco	117	Earshot	115	Kendor	120	11,675	1:52.80	
1947	Carolyn A.	3	R. Nash	118	Lady's Ace	108	Jobstown	117	15,700	1:57.80	
1948	Bovard	3	W. Saunders	111	Shy Guy	123	Riverlane	114	11,500	1:51.60	
1949	Rookwood	3	J. Delahoussaye	111	Petey Cotter	114	Great Shuffle	111	11,600	1:51.20	
1950	Greek Ship	3	C. Errico	123	Sunglow	111	Yogi	111	12,900	1:51.00	
1951	Whirling Bat	3	P. Anderson	111	Bulverde	111	Running Seas	111	15,900	1:53.40	
1952	Gushing Oil	3	A. Popara	111	Happy Go Lucky	111	Hiram Jr.	111	16,400	1:51.20	
1953	Matagorda	3	P.J. Bailey	111	Money Broker	111	Spy Defense	111	31,875	1:51.80	
1954	Gigantic	3	R. McLaughlin	111	Bobby Brocato	117	Red Hannigan	111	36,325	1:53.20	
1955	Roman Patrol	3	D. Dodson	123	Speed Rouser	111	Portersville	111	34,175	1:49.80	
1956	Reaping Right	3	R.L. Baird	111	Mr. Bob W.	111	Frosty Mr.	112	35,525	1:51.00	
1957	Federal Hill	3	W. Carstens	123	Shan Pac	114	Federal Judge	112	33,275	1:49.60	
1958	Royal Union	3	J. Heckmann	114	Noureddin	111	Ebony Pearl	111	34,850	1:52.00	
1959	Master Palynch	3	R. Broussard	115	Sputnik	114	Festival King	114	35,600	1:49.40	
1960	Tony Graff	3	W. Chambers	111	Yorktown	111	Lurullah	111	35,975	1:52.00	
1961	Bass Clef	3	R. Baldwin	111	Loyal Son	111	King of Kentucky	112	37,700	1:50.20	
1962	Admiral's Voyage	3	R. Broussard	121	Roman Line	125	Green Hornet	119	38,150	1:52.60	
1963	City Line	3	R.L. Baird	119	Lemon Twist	119	All Fool's Day	117	31,750	1:50.20	
1964	Grecian Princess	3	K. Broussard	116	Whit's Pride	117	I Owe	117	33,300	1:50.80	
1965	Dapper Delegate	3	J. Heckmann	121	Doctor Brocato	112	Flash Climber	115	33,900	1:50.20	
1966	Blue Skyer	3	R. Broussard	116	Stupendous	115	Williamston Kid	123	36,000	1:50.60	
1967	Ask the Fare	3	D. Holmes	115	Diplomat Way	126	Grand Premiere	120	36,550	1:50.00	
1968	Kentucky Sherry	3	J. Combest	118	Problem Solver	113	Port Digger	120	37,500	1:50.20	
1969	King of the Castle	3	C.H. Marquez	115	Jay Ray	120	Walking Stick	113	35,700	1:52.40	
1970	Jim's Alibi	3	R. Baldwin	115	Elva's King	115	Herbalist	115	38,850	1:55.60	
1971	Northfields	3	W. Blum	118	List	115	Will Hays	115	38,550	1:50.20	
1972	No Le Hace	3	P. Rubbicco	120	Feloniously	117	Fame and Power	115	36,400	1:52.80	
1973	Leo's Pisces	3	R. Breen	115	Navajo	120	Angle Light	118	50,000	1:51.60	
1974	Sellout	3	M. Castaneda	118	Buck's Bid	115	Beau Groton	120	55,800	1:51.20	
1975	Master Derby	3	D.G. McHargue	123	Colonel Power	120	Honey Mark	118	61,000	1:49.60	
1976	Johnny Appleseed	3	M. Castaneda	118	Glassy Dip	113	Gay Jitterbug	118	61,000	1:49.80	
1977	Clev Er Tell	3	R. Broussard	120	Run Dusty Run	123	A Letter to Harry	115	61,000	1:48.80	
1978	Esops Foibles	3	C.J. McCarron	118	Quadratic	123	Battonier	120	79,750	1:50.80	
1979	Golden Act	3	S. Hawley	123	Rivalero	115	Incredible Ease	120	100,750	1:51.20	
1980	Prince Valiant	3	M.A. Gonzalez	115	Native Uproar	118	Brent's Trans Am	123	97,150	1:50.40	
1981	Woodchopper	3	J. Velasquez	113	A Run	123	Beau Rit	126	125,800	1:50.80	
1982	El Baba	3	D. Brumfield	123	Linkage	120	Spoonful of Honey	113	112,000	1:50.60	
1983	Balboa Native	3	J. Velasquez	118	Found Pearl Harbor	113	Slewpy	123	112,000	1:50.60	
1984	Taylor's Special	3	S. Maple	118	Silent King	120	Fight Over	123	112,000	1:49.60	
1985	Violado	3	J. Vasquez	115	Creme Fraiche	120	Irish Fighter	113	112,000	1:50.20	
1986	Country Light	3	P. Day	123	Bolshoi Boy	118	Lightning Touch	118	112,000	1:50.40	
1987	J.T.'s Pet	3	P. Day	115	Authentic Hero	118	Plumcake	115	70,260	1:51.00	
1988	Risen Star	3	S.P. Romero	120	Word Pirate	118	Pastourelles	118	98,520	1:43.20	
1989	Dispersal	3	J.A. Santos	118	Majesty's Imp	118	Dansil	123	100,560	1:43.80	
1990	Heaven Again	3	C.S. Nakatani	113	Big E.Z.	113	Very Formal	113	100,440	1:43.80	96
1991	Richman	3	P. Day	122	Near the Limit	114	Far Out Wadleigh	122	120,000	1:44.40	99
1992	Line in the Sand	3	P. Day	117	Hill Pass	117	Colony Light	112	120,000	1:43.40	93
1993	Dixieland Heat	3	R.P. Romero	117	Offshore Pirate	117	Tossofthecoin	115	180,000	1:44.80	93
1994	Kandaly	3	Perret C	118	Game Coin	118	Argolid	118	195,750	1:42.80	97
1995	Petionville	3	C.W. Antley	122	In Character	118	Moonlight Dancer	122	210,000	1:42.80	96
1996	Grindstone	3	J.D. Bailey	118	Zarb's Magic	122	Commander's Palace	118	222,000	1:42.60	102
1997	Crypto Star	3	P. Day	118	Stop Watch	118	Smoke Glacken	122	240,000	1:42.60	98
1998	Comic Strip	3	S.J. Sellers	122	Nite Dreamer	122	Captain Maestri	122	300,000	1:43.20	94
1999	Kimberlite Pipe	3	R.J. Albarado	122	Answer Lively	122	Ecton Park	122	384,000	1:43.40	103
2000	Mighty	3	S.J. Sellers	122	More Than Ready	122	Captain Steve	122	450,000	1:43.29	105
2001	Fifty Stars	3	D. Meche	122	Millennium Wind	122	Hero's Tribute	122	450,000	1:44.78	94
2002	Repent	3	J.D. Bailey	122	Easyfromthegitgo	122	It'sallinthechase	120	450,000	1:43.86	95
2003	Peace Rules	3	E.S. Prado	122	Kafwain	122	Funny Cide	122	450,000	1:42.67	105
2004	Wimbledon	3	J. Santiago	122	Borrego	122	Pollard's Vision	122	360,000	1:42.71	101

Beyer Index: 98.07

LOUISVILLE BREEDERS' CUP HANDICAP (G2), 1 1/16 Miles, Fillies and Mares, 3-Year-Olds and Up, Churchill Downs, 2004 Purse: $327,000

Year	Winner	Age	Jockey	Wt.	Second	Wt.	Third	Wt.	Win Value	Time	Beyer
1986	Hopeful Word	5	P. Day	119	Little Missouri	116	Czar Nijinsky	121	99,808	1:49.40	
1987	Queen Alexandra	5	D. Brumfield	117	Infinidad	116	I'm Sweets	116	100,295	1:42.80	
1988	By Land by Sea	4	F. Toro	124	Bound	115	Bestofbothworlds	113	100,198	1:43.20	
1989	Darien Miss	4	P.A. Johnson	115	Savannah's Honor	119	Miss Barbour	109	100,750	1:46.00	
1990	Connie's Gift	4	P. Day	111	Affirmed Classic	115	Barbarika	115	100,425	1:45.80	94
1991	Fit for a Queen	5	J.D. Bailey	113	Crowned	115	Topsa	109	101,530	1:43.00	101
1992	Fowda	4	P.A. Valenzuela	117	Dance Colony	114	Fit for a Queen	120	100,750	1:44.00	97
1993	Quilma	6	J.A. Santos	113	Looie Capote	118	Hitch	113	37,570	1:44.60	103
1994	One Dreamer	6	G.L. Stevens	115	Kalita Melody	117	Added Asset	114	136,630	1:43.60	106
1995	Fit to Lead	5	K.J. Desormeaux	116	Jade Flush	115	Teewinot	109	138,125	1:43.40	99
1996	Jewel Princess	4	C.J. McCarron	118	Serena's Song	123	Naskra Colors	113	143,000	1:42.40	108
1997	Halo America	7	C.H. Borel	120	Escena	116	Rare Blend	116	138,012	1:42.60	110
1998	Escena	5	J.D. Bailey	119	One Rich Lady	113	Three Fanfares	109	178,405	1:44.80	104
1999	Silent Eskimo	4	C.H. Borel	113	Lu Ravi	118	Leo's Gypsy Dancer	112	169,415	1:43.80	102
2000	Heritage of Gold	5	S.J. Sellers	119	Roza Robata	112	Bella Chiarra	116	170,655	1:42.99	106
2001	Saudi Poetry	4	V. Espinoza	112	Royal Fair	113	Dreams Gallore	114	172,980	1:42.53	96
2002	Spain	5	J.D. Bailey	118	Mystic Lady	118	De Bertie	115	207,204	1:43.93	102
2003	You	4	J.D. Bailey	118	Fly Borboleta	111	Seven Four Seven	113	201,810	1:43.21	90
2004	Lead Story	5	C.H. Borel	116	Yell	114	Cat Fighter	116	202,740	1:44.37	99

Beyer Index: 101.13

LOUISVILLE HANDICAP (G3), 1 3/8 Miles (Turf), 3-Year-Olds and Up, Churchill Downs, 2004 Purse: $112,400

Year	Winner	Age	Jockey	Wt.	Second	Wt.	Third	Wt.	Win Value	Time	Beyer
1994	L'Hermine	5	L. Melancon	110	Llandaff	116	Snake Eyes	118	70,525	1:48.36	100
1995	Lindon Lime	5	C. Perret	114	Caesour	116	Snake Eyes	116	72,800	1:48.12	108
1996	Nash Terrace	4	D. Barton	105	Vladivostok	117	Hawkeye Bay	110	71,760	2:18.82	106
1997	Chorwon	4	C.H. Borel	113	Down the Aisle	111	Snake Eyes	116	67,952	2:19.45	100
1998	Chorwon	5	P. Day	114	African Dancer	114	Thesaurus	110	69,812	2:17.10	103
1999	Chorwon	6	C.H. Borel	114	Buff	117	Keats and Yeats	115	67,890	2:14.15	102
2000	Buff	5	F.C. Torres	113	Williams News	116	Royal Strand	115	71,734	2:14.31	105
2001	With Anticipation	6	J.K. Court	112	Profit Option	112	Gritty Sandie	115	68,138	2:16.28	109
2002	Pisces	5	R.J. Albarado	116			Red Mountain	114	47,335	2:15.82	101
	Classic Par	4	D.J. Meche	114							
	Two Point Two Mill finished first but was disqualified and placed eighth										
2003	Kim Loves Bucky	6	S.J. Sellers	117	Rochester	117	Dr. Kashnikow	117	69,440	2:14.09	104
2004	Silverfoot	4	R.J. Albarado	114	Rochester	116	Ballingarry	120	69,688	2:17.63	99

Beyer Index: 103.36

For previous runnings, refer to 1994 Manual.

JOHN C. MABEE HANDICAP (G1), 1 1/8 Miles (Turf), Fillies and Mares, 3-Year-Olds and Up, Del Mar, 2004 Purse: $400,000

Year	Winner	Age	Jockey	Wt.	Second	Wt.	Third	Wt.	Win Value	Time	Beyer
1945	Canina	4	J. Westrope	122	Glory Time	113	Frilure	112	3,640	1:37.00	
1959	Boston Again	4	A. Maese	122	Ruwenzori	110	Pie Queen	112	11,150	1:48.40	
1960	Honeys Gem	5	R. Campas	124	Tritoma	115	Jenny Delieu	114	12,750	1:47.60	
1961	Linita	4	R. Mundorf	121	Wiggle II	119	Amri-An	108	12,900	1:47.80	
	Fun House finished second but was disqualified and placed fourth										
1962	Fun House	4	R. York	121	Edie Belle	116	Seems a Queen	112	15,525	1:47.80	
1963	Powder 'n Paint	3	J. Lambert	111	Savaii	118	Corolla	115	16,525	1:48.20	
1964	Jalousie II	5	R. York	122	Quick Luck	111	Gin Mah	115	15,475	1:49.00	
1965	Rullahline	3	K. Church	112	Hi Rated	113	Poona Queen	115	9,725	1:47.80	
1965	Sea Eagle	3	W. Hartack	116	Lycaste	111	Khai Ireland	116	9,825	1:48.80	
1966	Desert Trial	3	A. Maese	113	April Dawn	114	Gabriela	106	10,075	1:48.00	
1966	Fleet Treat	3	R. Menell	114	Maintain	115	Windy Kate	112	10,175	1:48.20	
1967	Desert Trial	4	A. Maese	127	Aquilegia	106	Talleeta	113	17,900	1:48.80	
							Amerigo's Fancy	119			
1968	Scoop Time	4	L. Gilligan	111	Pombal	114	Sand Creek II	111	16,075	1:48.20	
1969	Luz del Sol	5	I. Valenzuela	118	Schatzi Pie	115	Too Angri	110	11,875	1:48.60	
1969	Greta	4	R. Campas	114	Commissary	115	Scoop Time	113	11,575	1:47.00	
1970	Hi Q.	4	H.K. Wellington	115	Windy Mama	116	Boughs o'Holly	116	13,600	1:49.80	
1971	Street Dancer	4	F. Toro	114	Typecast	116	Manta	130	15,950	1:48.80	
1972	Street Dancer	5	F. Toro	117	Hill Circus	122	Countess Market	114	15,700	1:48.20	
1973	Minstrel Miss	6	D. Pierce	122	Le Cle	123	Pallisima	118	19,750	1:49.40	

Year	Winner	Age	Jockey	Wt.	Second	Wt.	Third	Wt.	Win Value	Time	Beyer
1974	Tizna	5	W. Shoemaker	120	Modus Vivendi	118	La Zanzara	122	29,800	1:49.20	
1975	Dulcia	6	W. Shoemaker	122	Tizna	123	Charger's Star	115	33,550	1:48.80	
1976	Vagabonda	5	S. Hawley	115	Stravina	115	Miss Tokyo	116	34,550	1:51.00	
1977	Dancing Femme	4	D.G. McHargue	122	Up to Juliet	113	Swingtime	121	37,150	1:48.40	
1978	Drama Critic	4	D.G. McHargue	120	Country Queen	113	B. Thoughtful	115	47,500	1:49.20	
1979	Country Queen	4	L. Pincay Jr	121	More So	119	Prize Spot	116	69,500	1:48.60	
1980	Queen to Conquer	5	W. Shoemaker	120	A Thousand Stars	118	Wishing Well	122	74,050	1:49.40	
1981	Queen to Conquer	5	M. Castaneda	120	Amber Ever	112	Track Robbery	113	84,000	1:48.80	
1982	Honey Fox	4	M. Castaneda	122	Sangue	123	French Charmer	115	83,900	1:48.80	
1983	Sangue	5	W. Shoemaker	123	Castilla	121	First Advance	115	80,450	1:48.80	
1984	Flag de Lune	4	F. Olivares	115	Royal Heroine	126	Salt Spring	115	97,200	1:48.40	
1985	Daily Busy	4	W. Shoemaker	115	Eastland	114	Envie de Rire	116	93,500	1:48.20	
1986	Auspiciante	5	G.L. Stevens	114	Justicara	119	Sauna	119	81,600	1:48.40	
1987	Short Sleeves	5	E. Delahoussaye	116	Festivity	117	Auspiciante	120	97,900	1:50.20	
1988	Annoconnor	4	C.A. Black	116	Chapel of Dreams	118	Short Sleeves	121	134,000	1:48.40	
1989	Brown Bess	7	J.L Kaenel	117	Daring Doone	117	Galunpe	118	157,750	1:48.80	
1990	Double Wedge	5	R.G. Davis	114	Reluctant Guest	117	Nikishka	116	158,000	1:49.00	107
1991	Campagnarde	4	J.A. Garcia	115	Bequest	118	Somethingmerry	118	196,250	1:49.40	106
1992	Flawlessly	4	C.J. McCarron	123	Re Toss	115	Polemic	116	187,500	1:50.00	95
1993	Flawlessly	5	C.J. McCarron	125	Heart of Joy	114	Let's Elope	118	186,500	1:48.20	107
1994	Flawlessly	6	C.J. McCarron	124	Hollywood Wildcat	124	Skimble	116	181,000	1:48.20	101
1995	Possibly Perfect	5	C.S. Nakatani	123	Morgana	115	Yearly Tour	116	180,600	1:49.80	104
1996	Matiara	4	C.S. Nakatani	118	Alpride	119	Pourquoi Pas	114	193,500	1:49.20	103
1997	Escena	4	P. Day	115	Real Connection	115	Different	121	180,000	1:49.80	103
1998	See You Soon	4	C.S. Nakatani	114	Sonja's Faith	113	Fiji	125	180,000	1:47.43	104
1999	Tuzla	5	D.R. Flores	121	Happyanunoit	115	Spanish Fern	115	240,000	1:47.66	107
2000	Caffe Latte	4	B.R. Blanc	117	Tout Charmant	120	Alexine	115	240,000	1:47.16	102
2001	Janet	4	D.R. Flores	116	Tranquility Lake	123	Minor Details	112	240,000	1:48.20	100
2002	Affluent	4	E. Delahoussaye	118	Golden Apples	120	Janet	118	240,000	1:48.37	103
2003	Megahertz	4	A. Solis	116	Dublino	121			240,000	1:49.09	104
					Golden Apples	122					
					Tates Creek	123					
2004	Musical Chimes	4	K.J. Desormeaux	116	Moscow Burning	117	Notting Hill	113	240,000	1:47.09	102

Beyer Index: 103.20

Distance 1 Mile in 1945; Run on main course prior to 1970

MAC DIARMIDA HANDICAP (G3), 1 3/8 Miles (Turf), 3-Year-Olds and Up, Gulfstream Park, 2004 Purse: $100,000

Year	Winner	Age	Jockey	Wt.	Second	Wt.	Third	Wt.	Win Value	Time	Beyer
1995	Kings Fiction	3	R.G. Davis	112	Ops Smile	112	Mecke	113	30,000	1:43.00	87
1996	A Real Zipper	3	A.T. Gryder	114	Tour's Big Red	114	Shananie's Finale	114	30,000	1:42.60	91
1997	Mecke	5	J.D. Bailey	122	Fabulous Frolic	114	Spicilege	111	45,000	2:05.80	101
1998	Copy Editor	6	J.D. Bailey	114	Inkatha	114	Lafitte The Pirate	112	60,000	2:16.60	105
1999	Panama City	5	J.D. Bailey	114	The Kaiser	113	Notoriety	111	60,000	2:20.60	105
2000	Unite's Big Red	6	J.F. Chavez	113	Thesaurus	112	Carpenter's Halo	113	60,000	2:12.14	97
2002	Crash Course	6	J.D. Bailey	114	Unite's Big Red	112	Eltawaasul	112	60,000	2:12.67	102
2003	Riddlesdown	6	R.I. Velez	113	Macaw	114	Just Listen	113	60,000	2:14.75	104
2004	Request for Parole	5	J.A. Santos	115	Slew Valley	117	Sir Brian's Sword	113	60,000	2:12.58	103

Beyer Index: 99.44

SENATOR KEN MADDY JR. HANDICAP (G3), About 6 1/2 Furlongs (Turf), Fillies and Mares, 3-Year-Olds and Up, Santa Anita, 2004 Purse: $100,000

Year	Winner	Age	Jockey	Wt.	Second	Wt.	Third	Wt.	Win Value	Time	Beyer
1994	Starolamo	5	K.J. Desormeaux	117	Sophisticatedcielo	114	Beautiful Gem	115	47,475	1:16.07	100
1995	Denim Yenem	3	C.J. McCarron	115	Miss L Attack	116	Jacodra's Devil	116	60,400	1:14.92	105
1996	Dixie Pearl	4	E. Delahoussaye	116	Ski Dancer	119	Cat's Cradle	118	66,400	1:12.33	105
1997	Madame Pandit	4	E. Delahoussaye	118	Advancing Star	120	Highest Dream	116	60,000	1:13.82	105
1998	Dance Parade	4	K.J. Desormeaux	120	Advancing Star	121	Green Jewel	116	60,000	1:13.87	99
1999	Hula Queen	5	A. Solis	116	Desert Lady	121	Ecudienne	117	67,740	1:13.05	100
2000	Evening Promise	4	K.J. Desormeaux	118	Strawberry Way	114	Southern House	114	67,020	1:13.05	95
2001	A La Reine	4	A. Solis	115	Nanogram	111	Global	113	66,240	1:13.27	93
2002	Rolly Polly	4	P.A. Valenzuela	119	I'm the Business	117	Nanogram	113	68,460	1:12.86	99
2003	Belleski	4	V. Espinoza	117	Buffythecenterfold	116	Icantgoforthat	115	67,200	1:12.37	99
2004	Belleski	5	C.S. Nakatani	118	Intercontinental	120	Acago	116	60,000	1:12.86	99

Beyer Index: 99.91

Run as Autumn Days Handicap prior to 1999. For previous runnings, refer to 1994 Manual.

MAKER'S MARK MILE (G2), 1 Mile (Turf), 4-Year-Olds and Up, Keeneland Race Course, 2004 Purse: $200,000

Year	Winner	Age	Jockey	Wt.	Second	Wt.	Third	Wt.	Win Value	Time	Beyer
1997	Influent	6	J.L. Samyn	116	Chief Bearhart	114	Foolish Pole	113	69,936	1:34.40	105
1998	Lasting Approval	4	R.J. Albarado	122	Soviet Line	113	Same Old Wish	122	70,060	1:35.40	105
1999	Soviet Line	9	J.R. Velazquez	115	Trail City	115	Rob 'n Gin	120	68,696	1:35.37	101
2000	Conserve	4	S.J. Sellers	116	Marquette	120	Inkatha	116	105,927	1:35.08	102
2001	North East Bound	5	J.A. Velez Jr	120	Brahms	123	Strategic Mission	116	140,492	1:34.44	108
2002	Touchoftheblues	5	K.J. Desormeaux	116	Pisces	123	Boastful	116	124,000	1:35.02	102
2003	Royal Spy	5	R.J. Albarado	118	Miesque's Approval	118	Touch of the Blues	117	124,000	1:35.82	104
2004	Perfect Soul	6	E.S. Prado	116	Burning Roma	116	Royal Spy	116	124,000	1:33.54	105

Beyer Index: 104.00

MALIBU (G1), 7 Furlongs, 3-Year-Olds, Santa Anita, 2004 Purse: $250,000

Year	Winner	Age	Jockey	Wt.	Second	Wt.	Third	Wt.	Win Value	Time	Beyer
1952	Phil D.	4	R. York	118	Intent	115	Black Douglas	110	18,500	1:23.00	
1953	A Gleam	4	E. Arcaro	113	Stranglehold	115	Big Noise	112	15,800	1:22.80	
1954	Imbros	4	R. York	118	Berseem	114	Joe Jones	115	16,600	1:20.60	
1955	Determine	4	R. York	126	Double Reigh	110	El Drag	110	16,900	1:22.60	
1955	Honeys Alibi	3	B. Boland	120	Hillary	120	Beau Busher	120	19,050	1:23.00	
	Run in January and December										
1956	Blen Host	3	D. Lewis	112	Terrang	124	Count of Honour	120	18,650	1:23.00	
1957	Round Table	3	W. Shoemaker	130	Seaneen	114	Mystic Eye	122	16,550	1:22.00	
1958	Hillsdale	3	T. Barrow	126	Jewel's Reward	126	Swaps Kin	114	18,800	1:22.40	
1960	Ole Fols	4	W. Boland	122	Bagdad	126	American Comet	114	15,700	1:23.00	
1960	Tompion	3	M. Ycaza	128	New Policy	124	First Balcony	114	16,100	1:21.40	
	Run in January and Decembe										
1961	Olden Times	3	W. Shoemaker	120	Spy Flight	114	Four-and-Twenty	128	16,900	1:22.00	
1962	Native Diver	3	R. Neves	117	Grid Iron Hero	121	Humoso	114	18,050	1:21.60	
1963	More Megaton	3	R. York	114	Legation	114	Quilta Dude	117	18,950	1:23.00	
1965	Power of Destiny	4	K. Church	112	Maker's Mark	113	Hill Rise	122	19,050	1:22.00	
1966	Terry's Secret	4	A. Maese	123	Hoist Bar	113	Royal Gunner	117	18,950	1:23.00	
1966	Buckpasser	3	B. Baeza	125	Drin	120	Kings Favor	117	18,300	1:22.00	
	Run in January and December										
1968	Damascus	4	W. Shoemaker	126	Rising Market	120	Ruken	123	27,850	1:21.20	
1969	First Mate	4	J. Lambert	117	Skookum	113	Dignitas	117	34,650	1:22.00	
1971	King of Cricket	4	D. Velasquez	113	Hanalei Bay	123	Swift Savage	114	30,450	1:21.20	
1972	Kfar Tov	4	J. Lambert	115	Autobiography	117	Diplomatic Agent	117	28,250	1:21.00	
1972	Wing Out	4	W. Shoemaker	117	Star of Kuwait	113	Tower East	117	29,500	1:21.20	
1973	Bicker	4	G. Brogan	117	Royal Owl	120	Tri Jet	117	39,300	1:21.40	
1974	Ancient Title	4	F. Toro	120	Linda's Chief	126	Dancing Papa	120	34,800	1:22.80	
1975	Lightning Mandate	4	A. Pineda	120	Rocket Review	117	Country's Envoy	120	28,525	1:20.60	
1975	Princely Native	4	B. Baeza	117	First Back	115	Holding Pattern	123	27,775	1:20.80	
1976	Forceten	4	D. Pierce	123	Messenger of Song	120	My Juliet	115	35,450	1:21.00	
1977	Cojak	4	W. Shoemaker	117	Double Discount	117	Little Riva	114	26,050	1:23.00	
1977	Romantic Lead	4	W. Shoemaker	114	Maheras	120	Life's Hope	123	24,800	1:22.40	
1978	J.O. Tobin	4	S. Cauthen	123	Bad 'n Big	120	Eagle Ki	114	35,050	1:23.00	
1979	Little Reb	4	F. Olivares	120	Radar Ahead	123	Affirmed	126	38,200	1:21.00	
1980	Spectacular Bid	4	W. Shoemaker	126	Flying Paster	123	Rosie's Seville	117	47,800	1:20.00	
1981	Doonesbury	4	S. Hawley	117	Roper	114	Unalakleet	114	44,100	1:20.40	
1981	Raise a Man	4	L. Pincay Jr	120	Just Right Mike	114	Aristocratical	117	44,400	1:20.40	
1982	Island Whirl	4	L. Pincay Jr	123	Shanekite	120	It's the One	120	64,000	1:26.00	
1983	Time to Explode	4	L. Pincay Jr	117	Prince Spellbound	123	Wavering Monarch	123	52,550	1:21.00	
1984	Glacial Stream	4	C.J. McCarron	120	Total Departure	120	Hula Blaze	117	43,150	1:22.20	
1984	Pac Mania	4	P.A. Valenzuela	115	Retsina Run	114	Desert Wine	123	43,150	1:22.60	
	Run in two divisions										
1984	Precisionist	3	C.J. McCarron	126	Bunker	117	Milord	115	66,700	1:21.40	
	Run in January and December										
1985	Banner Bob	3	G. Baze	123	Encolure	120	Carload	114	71,600	1:21.00	
1986	Ferdinand	3	W. Shoemaker	123	Snow Chief	126	Don B. Blue	114	72,300	1:21.60	
1987	On the Line	3	A. Cordero Jr	117	Temperate Sil	126	Candi's Gold	123	66,550	1:21.00	
1988	Oraibi	3	L. Pincay Jr	117	Perceive Arrogance	120	Speedratic	114	70,550	1:21.60	
1989	Music Merci	3	L. Pincay Jr	123	Exemplary Leader	117	Doncareer	114	97,300	1:21.60	
1990	Pleasant Tap	3	A. Solis	117	Bedeviled	120	Due to the King	117	67,600	1:21.60	
1991	Olympio	3	E. Delahoussaye	122	Charmonnier	120	Apollo	118	66,850	1:21.28	112
1992	Star of the Crop	3	G.L. Stevens	118	The Wicked North	116	Bertrando	120	67,850	1:20.67	104
1993	Diazo	3	L. Pincay Jr	120	Concept Win	116	Mister Jolie	116	64,700	1:21.00	104
1994	Powis Castle	3	P.A. Valenzuela	117	Ferrara	116	Numerous	118	64,300	1:20.96	113
1995	Afternoon Deelites	3	K.J. Desormeaux	120	Score Quick	120	High Stakes Player	116	100,000	1:21.73	103
1996	King of the Heap	3	K.J. Desormeaux	116	Hesabull	118	Northern Afleet	116	134,300	1:21.84	96
1997	Lord Grillo	3	E. Delahoussaye	119	Silver Charm	123	Swiss Yodeler	115	120,000	1:21.46	109
1998	Run Man Run	3	M.J. Luzzi	115	Artax	119	Event of the Year	121	120,000	1:21.51	105

Year	Winner	Age	Jockey	Wt.	Second	Wt.	Third	Wt.	Win Value	Time	Beyer
1999	Love That Red	3	G.K. Gomez	115	Straight Man	118	Cat Thief	123	120,000	1:22.06	102
2000	Dixie Union	3	A. Solis	121	Caller One	119	Wooden Phone	116	120,000	1:21.62	103
2001	Mizzen Mast	3	K.J. Desormeaux	117	Giant Gentleman	115	I Love Silver	117	120,000	1:22.13	105
2002	Debonair Joe	3	J.A. Krone	119	Total Limit	117	American System	117	120,000	1:22.40	94
2003	Southern Image	3	V. Espinoza	115	Marino Marini	115	Midas Eyes	119	150,000	1:22.65	106
2004	Rock Hard Ten	3	G.L. Stevens	121	Lava Man	115	Harvard Avenue	115	150,000	1:21.89	100

Beyer Index: 104.00

MAN O' WAR (G1), 1 3/8 Miles (Turf), 3-Year-Olds and Up, Belmont Park, 2004 Purse: $500,000

Year	Winner	Age	Jockey	Wt.	Second	Wt.	Third	Wt.	Win Value	Time	Beyer
1959	Dotted Line	6	W. Boland	111	Amerigo	121	Prince Willy	112	71,732	2:40.80	
1959	Tudor Era	6	W. Hartack	124	Marlow Road	113	Anisado	111	72,382	2:41.00	
1960	Harmonizing	6	J. Ruane	126	Bald Eagle	126	Sword Dancer	126	70,530	2:33.20	
1961	Wise Ship	4	H. Gustines	108	Harmonizing	119	Geechee Lou	116	65,000	2:50.40	
1962	Beau Purple	5	W. Boland	126	Kelso	126	The Axe II	126	74,620	2:28.60	
1963	The Axe II	5	J.L. Rotz	126	Will I Rule	122	Guadalcanal	126	73,905	2:45.60	
1964	Turbo Jet II	4	H. Grant	126	Gun Bow	126	Knightly Manner	121	72,670	2:42.80	
1965	Hill Rise	4	M. Ycaza	126	Knightly Manner	126	Or et Argent	126	73,255	2:42.60	
1966	Assagai	3	L. Adams	121	Gallip Poll	121	Knightly Manner	126	72,865	2:44.60	
1967	Ruffled Feathers	3	D. Hidalgo	121	Fort Marcy	121	Handsome Boy	126	75,465	2:42.80	
1968	Czar Alexander	3	J. Velasquez	121	Fort Marcy	126	Advocator	126	75,530	2:30.80	
1969	Hawaii	5	J. Velasquez	126	North Flight	126	Fort Marcy	126	73,645	2:27.20	
1970	Fort Marcy	6	J. Velasquez	126	Loud	121	Drumtop	123	75,465	2:33.80	
1971	Run the Gantlet	3	R. Woodhouse	121	Gleaming	121	Practicante	126	67,200	2:33.20	
1972	Typecast	6	A. Cordero Jr	123	Ruritana	121	Droll Role	126	70,380	2:31.80	
1973	Secretariat	3	R. Turcotte	121	Tentam	126	Big Spruce	126	68,160	2:24.80	
1974	Dahlia	4	R. Turcotte	123	Crafty Khale	126	London Company	126	71,700	2:26.60	
1975	Snow Knight	4	J. Velasquez	126	One on the Aisle	121	Drollery	126	68,400	2:29.20	
	One on the Aisle finished first but was disqualified and placed second										
1976	Effervescing	3	A. Cordero Jr	121	Banghi	121	Erwin Boy	126	67,500	2:31.20	
							Rouge Sang	126			
	Crackle finished third but was disqualified and placed fifth										
1977	Majestic Light	4	S. Hawley	126	Exceller	126	Johnny D.	121	67,860	2:27.60	
1978	Waya	4	A. Cordero Jr	123	Tiller	126	Mac Diarmida	121	79,725	2:16.20	
1979	Bowl Game	5	J. Velasquez	126	Native Courier	126	Czaravich	121	82,425	2:19.00	
1980	French Colonial	5	J. Vasquez	126	Just a Game II	123	Golden Act	126	84,300	2:15.40	
1981	Galaxy Libra	5	W. Shoemaker	126	Match the Hatch	126	Great Neck	126	99,180	2:14.80	
	Native Courier finished third but was disqualified and placed fourth										
1982	Naskra's Breeze	5	J.L. Samyn	126	Sprink	126	Thunder Puddles	121	103,860	2:13.00	
1983	Majesty's Prince	4	E. Maple	126	Erins Isle	126	L'Emigrant	121	176,700	2:23.60	
1984	Majesty's Prince	5	V. Bracciale Jr	126	Win	126	Cozzene	126	214,200	2:14.60	
1985	Win	5	R. Migliore	126	Bob Back	126	Baillamont	121	183,600	2:15.40	
1986	Dance of Life	3	P. Day	121	Duty Dance	123	Pillaster	121	201,000	2:14.40	
1987	Theatrical	5	P. Day	126	Le Glorieux	121	Midnight Cousins	126	351,000	2:15.40	
1988	Sunshine Forever	3	A. Cordero Jr	120	Pay the Butler	126	My Big Boy	126	357,600	2:14.40	
1989	Yankee Affair	7	J.A. Santos	126	My Big Boy	126	Alwuhush	126	282,240	2:20.80	
1990	Defensive Play	3	P. Eddery	126	Shy Tom	126	Ode	126	284,160	2:17.80	
1991	Solar Splendor	4	W.H. McCauley	126	Dear Doctor	126	Beau Sultan	120	240,000	2:12.00	112
1992	Solar Splendor	5	W.H. McCauley	126	Dear Doctor	126	Spinning	126	240,000	2:12.40	111
1993	Star of Cozzene	5	J.A. Santos	126	Serrant	126	Dr. Kiernan	126	240,000	2:23.00	117
1994	Royal Mountain Inn	5	J.A. Krone	126	Flag Down	126	Fraise	126	240,000	2:11.60	110
1995	Millkom	4	G.L. Stevens	126	Kaldounevees	126	Signal Tap	126	240,000	2:12.80	105
1996	Diplomatic Jet	4	J.F. Chavez	126	Mecke	126	Marlin	126	240,000	2:14.20	111
1997	Influent	6	J.D. Bailey	126	Val's Prince	126	Awad	126	240,000	2:11.60	110
1998	Daylami	4	J.D. Bailey	126	Buck's Boy	126	Indy Vidual	126	240,000	2:13.18	110
1999	Val's Prince	7	J.F. Chavez	126	Single Empire	126	Federal Trial	126	300,000	2:16.69	110
2000	Fantastic Light	4	J.D. Bailey	126	Ela Athena	123	Drama Critic	126	300,000	2:17.44	106
2001	With Anticipation	6	P. Day	126	Silvano	126	Ela Athena	123	300,000	2:25.11	111
2002	With Anticipation	7	P. Day	126	Balto Star	126	Man From Wicklow	126	300,000	2:15.05	108
2003	Lunar Sovereign	4	R. Migliore	126	Slew Valley	126	Denon	126	300,000	2:17.99	110
2004	Magistretti	4	E.S. Prado	126	Epalo	126	King's Drama	126	300,000	2:14.65	111

Beyer Index: 110.14

Distance 1 5/8 miles 1961, 1963–67; 1 1/2 miles, 1959–60, 1962, 1968–77

MANHATTAN HANDICAP (G1), 1 1/4 Miles (Turf), 3-Year-Olds and Up, Belmont Park, 2004 Purse: $400,000

Year	Winner	Age	Jockey	Wt.	Second	Wt.	Third	Wt.	Win Value	Time	Beyer
1896	Belmar	4	T. Sloan	120	Dutch Skater	108	Sir Walter	117	1,450	2:07.20	
1898	Sanders	3	Spencer	107	Swiftmas	112	Irish Reel	124	2,520	1:11.00	
1899	Firearm	4	O'Leary	120	Heliobas	106	Tolulea	102	2,280	1:08.60	
1900	Firearm	5	T. Burns	122	Belle of Lexington	109	Vulcain	112	1,510	1:12.00	

Year	Winner	Age	Jockey	Wt.	Second	Wt.	Third	Wt.	Win Value	Time	Beyer
1901	Musette	4	O. Wonderly	100	Redpath	109	King Pepper	98	1,510	1:12.00	
1902	King Pepper	4	Redfern	120	Belle of Lexington	100	Unmasked	120	2,140	1:12.00	
1903	Castalian	3	T. Burns	103	Lux Casta	112	King Pepper	116	2,090	1:09.00	
1904	Broadcloth	3	Crimmins	98	Race King	93	Castalian	105	2,080	1:10.20	
1905	Roseben	4	O'Niell	147	Aeronaut	105	Race King	104	2,120	1:11.60	
1906	Roseben	5	Shaw	147	Suffrage	111	Handzarra	113	2,530	1:12.20	
1907	Baby Wolf	3	E. Dugan	119	Dreamer	112	Jack Atkin	123	2,500	1:12.20	
1908	Delirium	3	Gilbert	104	Half Sovereign	110	Fashion Plate	98	570	1:11.60	
1914	Stromboli	3	C. Turner	122	Comely	107	Frederick L.	115	1,245	1:24.00	
1915	The Finn	3	T. Davis	118	Purdey	108	Montresor	110	1,195	1:26.00	
1916	The Finn	4	A. Schuttinger	130	Short Grass	128	Jacoba	107	1,430	1:39.40	
1917	Stargazer	3	M. Buxton	106	Chiclet	112	Capra	107	1,420	1:39.20	
1918	Naturalist	4	W. Knapp	116	Sunflash II	115	Fairy Wand	104	2,350	1:37.80	
1919	Lucullite	4	L. Fator	130	Star Master	120	Naturalist	137	2,800	1:36.60	
1920	Naturalist	6	C. Kummer	129	Jack Stuart	107	Audacious	117	2,775	1:36.00	
1921	Yellow Hand	4	C.H. Miller	124	Tryster	118	Mad Hatter	132	2,925	1:36.00	
1922	Little Chief	3	L. Fator	115	Thunderclap	130	Brainstorm	103	3,100	1:38.00	
1923	Little Chief	4	E. Sande	119	Untidy	109	Brainstorm	105	3,425	1:35.80	
1924	Sarazen	3	J. Maiben	122	Cherry Pie	108	Mad Play	116	3,500	1:36.40	
1925	Pepp	4	H. Thurber	108	Blind Play	115	Cherry Pie	106	3,575	1:37.40	
1926	Croydon	3	L. McAtee	109	Bumpkin	98	Dr's Parade	115	3,350	1:38.80	
1927	Valorous	3	G. Fields	114	Kiev	109	Osmand	117	3,975	1:37.40	
1928	Victorian	3	L. Fator	118	Princess Tina	109	Penalo	106	3,800	1:37.60	
1929	Ironsides	4	L. McAtee	114	Clean Play	102	Petee-Wrack	128	6,675	1:36.00	
1930	Flying Heels	3	W. Kelsay	114	Petee-Wrack	122	Caruso	104	3,400	1:37.40	
1931	Mr. Sponge	4	M. Garner	121	Jack High	128	Conclave	99	3,325	1:35.80	
1932	Larranga	3	R. Workman	115	Snap Back	103	Mad Frump	111	2,875	1:36.80	
1933	Dark Secret	4	R. Workman	124	Gusto	114	Mr. Khayyam	114	2,560	2:30.00	
1934	Dark Secret	5	C. Kurtsinger	122	Somebody	108	Lady Reigh	106	4,230	2:29.20	
1935	Count Arthur	3	W.D. Wright	117	Judy O'Grady	100	Good Goods	120	4,430	2:30.00	
1936	Action	7	J. Gilbert	122	Count Arthur	112	Ann O'Ruley	103	4,450	2:31.20	
1937	Count Stone	4	F. Kopel	104	Esposa	118	Firethorn	123	4,230	2:30.40	
1938	Isolater	5	J. Stout	108	Regal Lily	108	Seabiscuit	128	4,300	2:31.00	
1939	Sorteado	4	L. Haas	112	Cravat	120	Isolater	118	6,675	2:28.40	
1940	Bolingbroke	3	S. Hebert	95	Mount Vernon II	103	Sickle T.	107	7,725	2:30.00	
1941	Fenelon	4	J. Stout	120	Corydon	110	Welcome Pass	105	8,175	2:29.00	
1942	Bolingbroke	5	H. Lindberg	115	Whirlaaway	132	King's Abbey	111	8,175	2:27.60	
1943	Bolingbroke	6	S. Brooks	122	The Rhymer	108	King's Abbey	112	7,775	2:30.80	
1944	Devil Diver	5	E. Arcaro	125	Caribou	102	Bolingbroke	126	10,595	2:36.60	
1945	Bankrupt	5	A. Kirkland	116	His Jewel	105	Megogo	117	12,475	2:31.00	
1946	Stymie	5	B. James	126	Pavot	121	Flareback	113	20,050	2:29.40	
							Assault	116			
1947	Rico Monte	5	E. Arcaro	123	Stymie	132	Talon	116	19,250	2:29.80	
1948	Loyal Legion	4	T. Atkinson	123	Donor	113	Tide Rips	110	19,600	2:29.80	
1949	Donor	5	W. Mehrtens	118	My Request	125	Stunts	114	20,400	2:28.00	
1950	One Hitter	4	T. Atkinson	110	Noor	128	Ponder	126	20,800	2:29.20	
1951	County Delight	4	E. Guerin	122	One Hitter	118	Busanda	110	19,550	2:29.60	
1952	Lone Eagle	6	C. Errico	107	Combat Boots	110	One Hitter	117	23,950	2:30.80	
1953	Jampol	4	J. Contreras	110	Alerted	120	Royal Vale	126	23,300	2:30.00	
1954	High Gun	3	E. Arcaro	123	Subahdar	110	Bicarb	116	24,150	2:30.60	
1955	Social Outcast	5	E. Guerin	124	Paper Tiger	111	Icarian	108	22,200	2:30.00	
1956	Flying Fury	4	T. Atkinson	108	Honeys Alibi	117	Paper Tiger	114	37,600	2:30.20	
1957	Reneged	4	R. Ussery	125	Cavort	110	Third Brother	125	37,300	2:29.40	
1958	Warhead	3	E. Arcaro	116	Beau Diable	108	Clem	126	36,515	2:28.60	
1959	Round Table	5	W. Shoemaker	132	Bald Eagle	122	Coloneast	112	37,230	2:42.60	
1960	Don Poggio	4	S. Boulmetis	120	Amber Morn	117	Polylad	118	36,255	2:29.60	
1961	Nickel Boy	6	I. Valenzuela	113	Troubadour II	110	Dress Up	114	36,985	2:10.00	
1962	Tuntankhamen	4	B. Baeza	111	Sensitivo	115	Windy Sands	116	37,765	2:28.40	
1963	Smart	4	E. Nelson	114	Will I Rule	112	Garwol	111	38,220	2:28.00	
1964	Going Abroad	4	R. Broussard	116	Sunrise Flight	117	The Ibex	114	37,635	2:26.20	
1965	Roman Brother	4	B. Baeza	125	Hill Rise	119	Knightly Manner	114	36,790	2:43.20	
1966	Moontrip	5	E. Belmonte	110	O'Hara	116	Niarkos	113	38,545	2:42.40	
1967	Munden Point	5	R. Ussery	126	Dunderhead	113	Moontrip	113	37,180	2:41.60	
1968	Quicken Tree	5	W. Hartack	123	Grace Born	114	Harem Lady	109	37,895	2:28.00	
1969	Harem Lady	5	E. Belmonte	113	Chompion	118	Open Road	112	34,580	2:30.20	
1970	Shelter Bay	4	R. Woodhouse	113	Loud	115	Cougar II	119	40,300	2:14.60	
1971	Happy Way	4	H. Gustines	110	Chompion	116	Elephant Walk	112	27,390	2:16.60	
1971	Big Shot II	6	J. Tejeira	112	Gleaming	116	Red Reality	117	27,990	2:16.40	
1972	Star Envoy	4	J. Velasquez	116	Typecast	122	Exotico	111	28,110	2:13.60	
1972	Ruritania	3	R. Turcotte	111	Droll Role	122	Triangular	110	27,960	2:14.00	
1973	London Company	3	L. Pincay Jr	116	Big Spruce	120	Triangular	110	36,120	2:15.60	
1974	Golden Don	4	J. Cruguet	119	Anono	112	R. Tom Can	114	35,970	2:19.80	
1975	Salt Marsh	5	E. Maple	115	Drollery	109	London Company	118	33,600	2:16.60	

Year	Winner	Age	Jockey	Wt.	Second	Wt.	Third	Wt.	Win Value	Time	Beyer
1975	Snow Knight	4	J. Velasquez	123	Shady Character	113	One On the Aisle	114	33,900	2:16.20	
1976	Caucasus	4	F. Toro	120	Trumpeter Swan	113	Kamaraan II	116	33,930	2:14.40	
1977	Gentle King	4	S. Cauthen	111	Double Quill	105	Keep the Promise	112	32,220	2:28.40	
1977	Gallivantor	5	S. Cauthen	112	Gallapiat	112	Togus	112	32,070	2:28.00	
1978	Fabulous Time	4	A. Cordero Jr	112	Bill Brill	109	Tiller	127	48,690	2:01.40	
1979	Fluorescent Light	5	J. Fell	121	Tiller	124	Native Courier	122	51,615	2:04.80	
1980	Morold	5	E. Maple	113	Match the Hatch	111	Foretake	113	53,910	2:00.20	
1981	Match the Hatch	5	J.L. Samyn	114	Mrs. Penny	117	Native Courier	115	52,470	2:03.00	
1982	Sprink	4	J. Miranda	113	Naskra's Breeze	119	Native Courier	116	51,570	2:01.00	
1983	Acaroid	5	A. Cordero Jr	114	Craelius	120	Half Iced	119	72,240	2:00.00	
1984	Win	4	A. Graell	114	Fortnightly	112	Norwick	110	77,520	2:00.60	
1985	Cool	4	J. Vasquez	110	Win	126	Sondrio	107	77,280	2:02.00	
1986	Danger's Hour	4	J.D. Bailey	117	Premier Mister	111	Exclusive Partner	115	87,300	2:02.60	
1987	Silver Voice	4	J.M. Pezua	109	Talakeno	118	Duluth	113	86,220	2:01.40	
1988	Milesius	4	C.W. Antley	112	My Big Boy	114	Maceo	111	71,760	2:04.40	
1989	Milesius	5	R. Migliore	115	Salem Drive	115	My Big Boy	114	73,440	2:00.00	
1990	Phantom Breeze	4	M.E. Smith	113	Green Barb	111	Milesius	116	52,110	2:02.60	
1991	Academy Award	5	A. Madrid Jr	111	Three Coins Up	110	Tarsho	113	111,600	1:59.60	105
1992	Sky Classic	5	P. Day	123	Roman Envoy	111	Leger Cat	116	172,860	2:02.40	107
1993	Star of Cozzene	5	J.A. Santos	118	Lure	124	Solar Splendor	112	90,000	1:58.80	116
1994	Paradise Creek	5	P. Day	124	Solar Splendor	112	River Majesty	113	90,000	1:57.60	117
1995	Awad	5	E. Maple	121	Blues Traveller	119	Kiri's Clown	115	120,000	1:58.40	108
1996	Diplomatic Jet	4	J.F. Chavez	117	Flag Down	119	Kiri's Clown	121	120,000	2:00.00	111
1997	Ops Smile	5	R.G. Davis	116	Flag Down	118	Always a Classic	121	120,000	1:59.00	107
1998	Chief Bearhart	5	J.A. Santos	122	Devonwood	113	Buck's Boy	117	150,000	1:58.25	110
1999	Yagli	6	J.D. Bailey	122	Federal Trial	116	Middlesex Drive	116	180,000	1:58.48	108
2000	Manndar	4	C.S. Nakatani	117	Boatman	113	Spindrift	113	240,000	1:59.61	107
2001	Forbidden Apple	6	C.S. Nakatani	117	King Cugat	120	Tijiyr	115	240,000	2:00.77	110
2002	Beat Hollow	5	A. Solis	118	Forbidden Apple	118	Strut the Stage	117	240,000	2:01.29	110
2003	Denon	5	J.D. Bailey	122	Requete	116	Dr. Brendler	116	240,000	2:14.16	108
2004	Meteor Storm	5	J. Valdivia Jr	117	Millennium Dragon	116	Mr O'Brien	116	240,000	1:59.34	109

Beyer Index: 109.50

Distance 1 1/4 miles in 1896; 6 furlongs over Eclipse Course, 1898–1908; 7 furlongs, 1914–15; 1 mile; 1916–32; 1 1/2 miles, 1933–58, 1960, 1962–64, 1968–69, and 1977, 1 5/16 miles, 1961, 1 5/8 miles, 1959, 1965–67. Run at Morris Park prior to 1905; at Aqueduct, 1959, 1961, 1963–67. Run on main track 1896–1969, 1977, 1979, and 1988

MARYLAND BREEDERS' CUP HANDICAP (G3), 6 Furlongs, 3-Year-Olds and Up, Pimlico Race Course, 2004 Purse: $186,000

Year	Winner	Age	Jockey	Wt.	Second	Wt.	Third	Wt.	Win Value	Time	Beyer
1987	Purple Mountain	5	E. Ortiz Jr	111	Little Bold John	120	Berngoo	106	100,100	1:24.40	
1988	Fireplug	5	J.F. Hampshire	116	Harriman	117	High Brite	121	35,620	1:10.60	
1989	King's Nest	4	J. Rocco	120	Silano	115	Regal Intention	119	92,760	1:09.60	
1990	Norquestor	4	C. Perret	115	Kechi	115	Amerrico's Bullet	112	93,540	1:09.40	111
1991	Jew'ler's Choice	6	C.J. McCarron	115	Shuttleman	116	Hadif	118	92,610	1:10.20	104
1992	Potentiality	6	P. Day	117	Smart Alec	114	Boom Towner	117	93,300	1:10.20	106
1993	Senor Speedy	6	J.D. Bailey	117	He Is Risen	115	Who Wouldn't	113	93,390	1:09.60	110
1994	Secret Odds	4	E.S. Prado	119	Honor the Hero	117	Linear	119	93,615	1:10.20	109
1995	Commanche Trail	4	M.E. Smith	113	Goldminer's Dream	116	Marry Me Do	114	92,850	1:09.20	109
1996	Forest Wildcat	5	J. Bravo	109	Kayrawan	113	Demaloot Demashoot	115	129,720	1:09.00	109
1997	Cat Be Nimble	5	J. Rocco	118	Political Whit	116	Excelerate	114	127,560	1:10.00	105
1998	Richter Scale	4	J.D. Bailey	117	Trafalger	115	Original Gray	112	120,000	1:09.40	106
1999	Yes It's True	3	J.D. Bailey	113	The Trader's Echo	109	Purple Passion	114	120,000	1:09.20	118
2000	Dr. Max	4	S.J. Sellers	113	Moon Over Prospect	114	Crucible	113	60,000	1:10.91	101
2001	Disco Rico	4	H. Vega	118	Flame Thrower	114	Istintaj	116	120,000	1:10.40	106
2002	Snow Ridge	4	M.E. Smith	120	Smile My Lord	113	Clever Gem	116	120,000	1:10.06	114
2003	Pioneer Boy	5	J. Rose	113	Sassy Hound	113	Highway Prospector	115	60,000	1:10.35	105
							Tasty Caberneigh	114			
2004	Gators n Bears	4	C.C. Lopez	117	Highway Prospector	114	Sassy Hound	115	120,000	1:10.84	105

Beyer Index: 107.87

MASSACHUSETTS HANDICAP (G2), 1 1/8 Miles, 3-Year-Olds and Up, Suffolk Downs, 2004 Purse: $500,000

Year	Winner	Age	Jockey	Wt.	Second	Wt.	Third	Wt.	Win Value	Time	Beyer
1935	Top Row	4	G. Woolf	116	Whopper	108	Discovery	138	18,750	1:49.40	
1936	Time Supply	5	R. Workman	121	Gov. Sholtz	100	Stand Pat	119	23,500	1:49.80	
1937	Seabiscuit	4	J. Pollard	130	Caballero II	108	Fair K'htess	108	51,780	1:49.00	
1938	Menow	3	N. Wall	107	Busy K.	107	War Minstrel	106	40,550	1:52.60	
1939	Fighting Fox	4	J. Stout	113	Pompoon	120	Burning Star	110	49,250	1:52.00	
1940	Eight Thirty	4	H. Richards	126	Hash	115	Challedon	130	46,550	1:49.00	
1941	War Relic	3	T. Atkinson	102	Foxbrough	122	Royal Man	106	48,350	1:48.60	

Year	Winner	Age	Jockey	Wt.	Second	Wt.	Third	Wt.	Win Value	Time	Beyer
1942	Whirlaway	4	G. Woolf	130	Rounders	108	Attention	122	43,850	1:48.20	
1943	Market Wise	5	V. Nodarse	126	Salto	103	Don Bingo	114	39,650	1:52.00	
1944	First Fiddle	6	J. Longden	124	Alex Barth	114	Alquest	115	41,850	1:49.00	
1945	First Fiddle	6	J. Longden	121	Dinner Party	108	Megogo	106	42,750	1:49.40	
1946	Pavot	4	A. Kirkland	120	Dinner Party	113	Gallorette	119	41,150	1:49.80	
1947	Stymie	6	C. McCreary	128	Elpis	111	Blue Yonder	111	47,250	1:50.00	
1948	Beauchef	5	R. Denoso	115	Harmonica	110	Double Jay	123	47,750	2:02.60	
1949	First Nighter	4	J. Renick	104	Going Away	103	Michigan III	117	39,200	2:04.60	
1950	Cochise	4	E. Arcaro	120	My Request	119	Loser Weeper	118	21,400	2:01.80	
1951	One Hitter	5	T. Atkinson	113	Lights Up	121	Outland	101	22,000	2:02.20	
1952	To Market	4	W. Boland	110	Tio Ciro	105	One Hitter	116	32,600	2:01.40	
1953	Royal Vale	5	J. Westrope	125	Larry Ellis	113	Count Turf	107	43,300	2:02.20	
1954	Wise Margin	4	K. Stuart	111	Find	121	Royal Vale	126	43,100	2:01.60	
1955	Helioscope	4	S. Boulmetis	126	Social Outcast	126	Wise Margin	114	36,000	2:01.00	
1956	Midafternoon	4	W. Boland	110	Find	118	Miellux	109	38,200	2:04.00	
1957	Greek Spy	4	E. Guerin	118	Illusionist	109	Tick Tock	123	39,100	2:03.20	
1958	Promised Land	4	P. Anderson	119	One-Eyed King	111	Clem	114	36,255	2:01.80	
1959	Air Pilot	5	J. Leonard	116	Day Court	115	Bald Eagle	112	53,880	2:02.40	
1960	Talent Show	5	R. Broussard	117	Polylad	116	Battle Neck	107	35,865	2:03.60	
1961	Polylad	5	E. Arcaro	112	Our Hope	114	Nickel Boy	113	37,505	2:01.80	
1962	Air Pilot	8	L. Moyers	105	Polylad	116	Ambiopoise	118	37,115	2:01.40	
1963	Crimson Satan	4	H. Hinojosa	124	Admiral's Voyage	125	Sunrise County	120	38,545	2:01.20	
1964	Smart	5	E. Nelson	115	Sunrise County	114	Steel Viking	106	35,880	2:03.20	
1965	Smart	6	E. Nelson	117	Gun Bow	131	Tenacle	117	36,205	2:01.60	
1966	Fast Count	3	M. Venezia	108	Pluck	113	Baitman	113	53,430	2:01.20	
1967	Good Knight	5	K. Korte	113	Understanding	114	Heronslea	112	40,154	2:02.40	
1968	Out of the Way	3	J.L. Rotz	112	Big Rock Candy	114	King's Place	114	39,682	2:02.80	
1969	Beau Marker	4	L. Moyers	109	Spring Double	122	Chompion	113	36,741	2:04.60	
1970	Semillant	5	J. Cruguet	113	Drumtop	119	Jungle Cove	115	54,730	2:37.20	
1971	Chompion	6	J. Velasquez	116	The Pruner	113	Close Attention	108	54,421	2:34.40	
1972	Droll Role	4	E. Maple	115	Hitchcock	115	Native Royalty	114	75,920	1:49.20	
1973	Riva Ridge	4	R. Turcotte	125	Crafty Khale	112	Loud	113	36,432	1:48.20	
1974	Billy Come Lately	4	D. MacBeth	109	Forage	114	North Sea	111	45,000	1:48.60	
1975	Stonewalk	4	R. Turcotte	117	Group Plan	118	Mongongo	115	60,000	1:48.60	
1976	Dancing Champ	4	C.J. McCarron	118	Rushing Man	114	El Pitirre	117	60,000	1:49.20	
1977	Blue Times	6	A. Cordero Jr	113	Pension Plan	109	Nearly On Time	106	42,930	1:49.40	
1977	Swinging Hal	4	S.R. Pagano	110	El Pitirre	113	Gentle King	108	43,410	1:49.20	
1978	Big John Taylor	4	J. Vasquez	112	Giboulee	114	Buckfinder	114	67,200	1:48.60	
1979	Island Sultan	4	J. Ruane	110	Western Front	113	Quiet Jay	116	70,140	1:48.60	
1980	Ring of Light	5	F. Lovato Jr	121	Crow's Nest	114	Niteange	110	68,400	1:50.40	
1981	Soldier Boy	5	R. Danjean	114	Niteange	108	Driving Home	114	97,200	1:49.40	
1982	Silver Supreme	4	E. Beitia.	111	Reef Searcher	117	Frost King	127	100,740	1:48.80	
1983	Let Burn	4	J.C. Penney	115	Space Mountain	110	Bemedalled	112	98,220	1:48.80	
1984	Dixieland Band	4	D.J. Murphy	115	Ward Off Trouble	113	Vigumand	107	126,300	1:52.00	
1985	Bounding Basque	5	A. Graell	110	Dr. Carter	122	Hail Bold King	120	124,560	1:47.60	
1986	Skip Trial	4	J.L. Samyn	123	Creme Fraiche	121	El Basco	118	128,040	1:49.80	
1987	Waquoit	4	C.J. McCarron	117	Broad Brush	126	Tour d'Or	114	124,560	1:49.00	
1988	Lost Code	4	C. Perret	127	Waquoit	122	Afleet	123	154,108	1:50.20	
1989	Private Terms	4	K.J. Desormeaux	119	Granacus	113	Simply Majestic	120	180,000	1:49.40	
1995	Cigar	5	J.D. Bailey	124	Poor But Honest	107	Double Calvados	113	450,000	1:48.60	117
1996	Cigar	6	J.D. Bailey	130	Personal Merit	111	Prolanizer	110	300,000	1:49.60	112
1997	Skip Away	4	S.J. Sellers	119	Formal Gold	114	Will's Way	114	500.000	1:47.80	122
1998	Skip Away	5	J.D. Bailey	130	Puerto Madero	116	K.J.'s Appeal	113	500,000	1:47.20	121
1999	Behrens	5	J.F. Chavez	118	Running Stag	113	Real Quiet	121	400,000	1:49.00	117
2000	Running Stag	6	J.R. Velazquez	116	Out Of Mind	116	David	113	400,000	1:49.45	117
2001	Inlcude	4	J.D. Bailey	118	Sir Bear	117	Broken Vow	116	300,000	1:48.61	117
2002	Macho Uno	4	G.L. Stevens	117	Evening Attire	114	Include	120	300,000	1:50.52	110
2004	Offlee Wild	4	E.S. Prado	111	Funny Cide	117	The Lady's Groom	116	300,000	1:49.14	110

Beyer Index: 115.89

Not run 1990-94, 2003

MATCHMAKER (G3), 1 1/8 Miles (Turf), Fillies and Mares, 3-Year-Olds and Up, Monmouth Park, 2004 Purse: $100,000

Year	Winner	Age	Jockey	Wt.	Second	Wt.	Third	Wt.	Win Value	Time	Beyer
1967	Politely	4	R. Broussard	118	Straight Deal	123	Gamely	114	30,000	1:55.20	
1968	Politely	5	A. Cordero Jr	123	Green Glade	115	Amerigo Lady	118	30,000	1:55.20	
1969	Gallant Bloom	3	J.L. Rotz	117	Gamely	123	Singing Rain	118	30,000	1:55.40	
1970	Dedicated to Sue	4	M. Hole	113	Cold Comfort	108	Office Queen	121	30,000	1:56.40	
1971	Deceit	3	J.L. Rotz	113	Sea Saga	114	Double Delta	125	30,000	1:56.80	
1972	Numbered Account	3	L. Pincay Jr	115	Honestous	110	Alma North	115	30,000	1:57.60	
1973	Alma North	5	F. Lovato	118	Light Hearted	121	Susan's Girl	125	30,000	1:55.20	
1974	Desert Vixen	4	L. Pincay Jr	123	Coraggioso	115	Twixt	123	3,000	1:55.20	

Year	Winner	Age	Jockey	Wt.	Second	Wt.	Third	Wt.	Win Value	Time	Beyer
1975	Susan's Girl	6	R. Broussard	121	Aunt Jin	114	Pink Tights	114	20,000	1:54.20	
1976	Dancers Countess	4	C.J. McCarron	119	Vodka Time	114	Garden Verse	119	20,000	1:56.00	
1977	Mississippi Mud	4	J. Tejeira	119	Vodka Time	114	Lucie Manet	124	30,000	1:54.20	
1978	Queen Lib	3	D.MacBeth	112	Debby's Turn	114	Dottie's Doll	117	25,000	1:56.40	
1979	Warfever	4	J.L. Samyn	113	Smooth Journey	106	La Soufriere	118	25,000	2:03.20	
1980	Just a Game II	4	D. Brumfield	120	La Soufriere	115	Record Acclaim	115	25,000	1:57.60	
1981	Mairzy Doates	5	C.B. Asmussen	120	Honey Fox	120	Little Bonny	120	35,000	1:56.00	
1982	Hunston	4	J.L. Samyn	113	Trevita	118	Kuja Happa	115	35,000	1:58.60	
1983	Luminaire	4	B. Thornburg	113	Vestris	113	Lonely Balladier	113	25,000	1:56.80	
1984	Sabin	4	E. Maple	123	Doblique	113	Virgin Bride	113	30,000	1:53.80	
1985	Key Dancer	4	J.D. Bailey	118	Forest Maiden	118	Dictina	115	30,000	2:02.40	
1986	Lake Country	5	V. Bracciale Jr	118	Capo di Monte	120	Top Socialite	120	60,000	1:54.60	
1987	Carotene	4	D.J. Seymour	118	Spruce Fir	115	Cadabra Abra	120	73,500	1:56.60	
1988	Magdelaine	5	E. Maple	120	Spruce Fir	115	Carotene	120	60,000	1:56.20	
1989	Spruce Fir	6	D.B. Thomas	113	Ravinella	120	Native Mommy	120	90,000	1:53.40	
1990	Capades	4	A. Cordero Jr	120	Gaily Gaily	115	Summer Secretary	118	90,000	1:53.60	105
1991	Miss Josh	5	L. Pincay Jr	123	Whip Cream	113	Le Famo	113	90,000	1:54.00	104
1992	Radiant Ring	4	R.E. Colton	115	Highland Crystal	118	La Gueriere	118	60,000	1:55.80	100
1993	Fairy Garden	5	M.E. Smith	120	Saratoga Source	118	Logan's Mist	118	60,000	1:47.80	91
1994	Alice Springs	4	J.A. Krone	118	Hero's Love	118	Cox Orange	118	60,000	1:55.20	105
1995	Avie's Fancy	4	W.H. McCauley	113	Plenty of Sugar	118	Northern Emerald	113	60,000	1:54.00	100
1996	Powder Bowl	4	D.S. Rice	113	Class Kris	120	Turkish Tryst	114	60,000	1:54.60	102
1998	Bursting Forth	4	M.E. Verge	116	French Buster	116	Gastronomical	113	60,000	1:48.40	97
1999	Natalie Too	5	J. Bravo	116	Saralea	116	U R Unforgetable	120	60,000	1:46.81	103
2000	Horatia	4	J.A. Santos	114	Camella	120	Champagne Royal	114	60,000	1:47.52	95
2001	Batique	5	J.C. Ferrer	113	Melody Queen	114	Lucky Lune	114	60,000	1:46.19	99
2002	Clearly	5	E.M. Coa	115	Siringas	116	Platinum Tiara	115	60,000	1:47.76	95
2003	Volga	5	J. Bravo	116	Something Ventured	117	Cocktailsandreams	115	60,000	1:48.22	97
2004	Where We Left Off	4	C.S. Nakatani	118	Mrs. M	118	Spin Control	116	60,000	1:48.80	96

Beyer Index: 99.21

MATRIARCH (G1), 1 Mile (Turf), Fillies and Mares, 3-Year-Olds and Up, Hollywood Park, 2004 Purse: $500,000

Year	Winner	Age	Jockey	Wt.	Second	Wt.	Third	Wt.	Win Value	Time	Beyer
1981	Kilijaro	5	L. Pincay Jr	123	Glorious Song	123	Bersid	120	131,600	1:47.00	
1982	Pale Purple	4	R. Sibille	123	Berry Bush	123	Ticketed	120	104,600	1:48.60	
1982	Castilla	3	R. Sibille	120	Sangue	123	Star Pastures	123	104,600	1:47.40	
1983	Sangue	5	W. Shoemaker	123	Castilla	123	Geraldine's Store	123	110,000	1:49.40	
1984	Royal Heroine	4	F. Toro	123	Reine Mathilde	120	Sabin	123	164,000	1:49.40	
1985	Fact Finder	6	S. Hawley	123	Tamarinda	123	Possible Mate	123	137,000	1:48.20	
1986	Auspiciante	5	C.B. Asmussen	123	Aberuschka	123	Reloy	120	110,000	1:48.00	
1987	Asteroid Field	4	A.T. Gryder	123	Nashmeel	120	Any Song	123	110,000	1:51.00	
1988	Nastique	4	W. Shoemaker	123	Annoconnor	123	White Mischief II	123	110,000	1:47.00	
1989	Claire Marine	4	C.J. McCarron	123	General Charge	120	Royal Touch	123	110,000	1:47.40	
1990	Countus In	5	C.S. Nakatani	123	Taffeta and Tulle	123	Little Brianne	123	110,000	1:46.20	100
1991	Flawlessly	3	C.J. McCarron	120	Fire the Groom	123	Free at Last	123	110,000	1:46.60	106
1992	Flawlessly	4	C.J. McCarron	120	Super Staff	123	Kostroma	123	220,000	1:46.00	108
1993	Flawlessly	5	C.J. McCarron	123	Toussaud	123	Skimble	123	220,000	1:46.60	102
1994	Exchange	6	L. Pincay Jr	123	Aube Indienne	123	Wandesta	120	220,000	1:49.40	105
1995	Duda	4	J.D. Bailey	123	Angel in My Heart	120	Wandesta	123	385,000	2:00.20	105
1996	Wandesta	5	C.S. Nakatani	123	Windsharp	123	Memories of Silver	120	420,000	2:00.00	107
1997	Ryafan	3	A. Solis	120	Maxzene	123	Yokama	123	420,000	2:05.80	106
1998	Squeak	4	A.Solis	123	Real Connection	123	Green Jewel	123	420,000	2:05.08	102
1999	Happyanunoit	4	B. Blanc	123	Tuzla	123	Spanish Fern	123	300,000	1:46.30	107
2000	Tout Charmant	4	C.J. McCarron	123	Tranquility Lake	123	Happyanunoit	123	300,000	1:46.06	109
2001	Starine	4	J.R. Velazquez	123	Lethals Lady	120	Golden Apples	120	300,000	1:50.16	101
2002	Dress to Thrill	3	P.J. Smullen	120	Golden Apples	123	Magic Mission	123	300,000	1:48.31	105
2003	Heat Haze	4	J.R. Velazquez	123	Musical Chimes	120	Dedication	123	300,000	1:34.43	103
2004	Intercontinental	4	J.D. Bailey	123	Etoile Montante	123	Ticker Tape	120	300,000	1:35.87	101

Beyer Index: 104.47

Distance 1 1/4 miles 1995–98; 1 1/8 miles in 1981–1994,1999–2002

MATRON (G1), 1 Mile, 2-Year-Old Fillies, Belmont Park, 2004 Purse: $300,000

Year	Winner	Age	Jockey	Wt.	Second	Wt.	Third	Wt.	Win Value	Time	Beyer
1892	Sir Francis	2	Garrison	118	Miss Maude	112	Roche	105	36,770	1:19.00	
1893	Domino	2	Taral	128	Peacemaker	110	Jack of Spades	121	24,560	1:09.00	
1894	Agitator	2	Taral	111	Handspun	109	Salvation	111	31,310	1:11.00	
1899	Indian Fairy	2	J. Slack	111	Redpath	108	Runaway	113	16,697	1:10.20	
1900	Beau Gallant	2	Bullman	125	Commando	124	The Parader	117	16,297	1:01.20	
1901	Heno	2	Odom	122	Yankee	129	Whiskey King	125	17,593	1:11.20	
1902	Grey Friar	2	N. Turner	124	Surbiton	109	Acefull	122	12,180	1:11.20	

Year	Winner	Age	Jockey	Wt.	Second	Wt.	Third	Wt.	Win Value	Time	Beyer
1902	Eugenia Burch	2	Odom	122	Merry Reel	104	Stolen Moments	109	6,790	1:12.20	
1903	The Minute Man	2	F. O'Neill	117	Hippocrates	111	Collec'r Jessop	112	8,035	1:09.60	
1903	Armenia	2	W. Hicks	112	For Luck	109	Beldame	123	5,525	1:10.20	
1904	Bedouin	2	Shaw	114	Glorifier	125	Dandelion	114	12,725	1:09.00	
1904	Sandria	2	Hildebrand	104	Rose of Dawn	109	Belle Strome	114	13,345	1:08.20	
1905	Burgomaster	2	L. Lyne	124	Penrhyn	119	Battleaxe	122	10,405	1:12.20	
1905	Perverse	2	L. Lyne	109	Early and Often	111	Duenna	109	10,485	1:11.20	
1906	Ballot	2	Radtke	122	Okenite	116	Hickory	112	10,250	1:12.00	
1906	Adoration	2	W. Miller	116	Fantastic	111	Pope Joan	111	9,030	1:11.80	
1907	Colin	2	W. Miller	129	Fair Play	122	Royal Tourist	119	9,340	1:12.00	
1907	Stamina	2	W. Knapp	119	Masquerade	111	Half Sovereign	119	8,940	1:11.80	
1908	Helmet	2	Notter	124	Joe Madden	122	Practical	112	9,625	1:12.60	
1908	Maskette	2	Notter	124	Affliction	106		0	5,895	1:20.80	
1909	Radium Star	2	Creevy	114	Candleberry	112	Rocky O'Brien	129	8,995	1:14.80	
1909	Greenvale	2	Gilbert	111	Fair Louise	111	Indian Maid	114	8,535	1:15.00	
1910	Naushon	2	J. Glass	125	Zeus	119	Footprint	122	9,485	1:12.80	
1910	Bashti	2	C.H. Shilling	117	Love-Not	106	Horizon	106	8,655	1:13.00	
1914	Pebbles	2	J. Butwell	130	Paris	110	Kilkenny Boy	113	1,130	1:15.00	
1914	Charter Maid	2	J. McTaggart	110	Coquette	119	Capra	110	1,045	1:14.00	
1923	Tree Top	2	F. Coltiletti	119	Rosebec	114	Princess Doreen	106	4,150	1:11.60	
1924	Blue Warbler	2	D. Hurn	127	Swinging	114	Martha Martin	109	10,625	1:13.80	
1925	Taps	2	A. Johnson	109	Nellie Morse	122	Asinia	114	15,075	1:13.40	
1926	Pantella	2	L. McAtee	124	Tip Top	119	Bon. Pennant	124	18,275	1:13.40	
1927	Glade	2	G. Ellis	114	One Hour	122	Bateau	119	21,025	1:12.60	
1928	Dreadnaught	2	S. O'Donnell	116	Fly Light	109	Bravery	114	21,725	1:12.00	
1929	Dustemall	2	L. McAtee	115	Murky Cloud	119	Believe Sally	115	25,250	1:11.00	
1930	Baba Kenny	2	J. Smith	115	Buckup	115	Ladana	122	24,650	1:12.00	
1931	Top Flight	2	R. Workman	127	Parry	119	Pintail	115	23,750	1:11.60	
1932	Barn Swallow	2	E. James	115	Iseult	115	Happy Gal	127	20,575	1:11.00	
1933	High Glee	2	J. Gilbert	115	Bazaar	127	Jabot	115	18,800	1:13.60	
1934	Nellie Flag	2	E. Arcaro	115	Judy O'Grady	112	Good Gamble	115	20,550	1:10.80	
1935	Beanie M.	2	D. Meade	119	Victorious Ann	115	Split Second	115	11,900	1:11.80	
1936	Wand	2	H. Richards	115	Dawn Play	115	Talma Dee	115	12,075	1:11.00	
1937	Merry Lassie	2	J. Longden	123	Handcuff	115	Creole Maid	115	10,900	1:11.00	
1938	Dinner Date	2	A. Robertson	119	Ciencia	115	Airacuda	115	16,700	1:13.40	
1939	Miss Ferdinand	2	J. Westrope	115	Piquet	115	Thorn Apple	115	14,825	1:12.00	
1940	Misty Isle	2	W.D. Wright	119	Unquote	115	Silvestra	115	15,710	1:10.40	
1941	Petrify	2	R. Donoso	119	Light Lady	119	Ficklebush	110	17,710	1:11.60	
1942	Good Morning	2	H. Lindberg	109	Askmenow	114	Navigating	114	9,525	1:09.20	
1943	Boojiana	2	T. Atkinson	119	Thread o' Gold	119	Bold Anna	114	7,900	1:09.80	
1944	Busher	2	E. Arcaro	119	Twosy	115	Price Level	123	22,530	1:09.40	
1945	Beaugay	2	A. Kirkland	123	Enfilade	119	Athene	115	23,500	1:09.40	
1946	First Flight	2	E. Arcaro	123	Pipette	123	Quarantaine	115	35,535	1:08.60	
1947	Inheritance	2	J. Jessop	123	Vaudeville	115	Ghost Run	123	36,060	1:10.20	
	Bewitch finished first but was disqualified										
1948	Myrtle Charm	2	T. Atkinson	119	Stole	115	Lithe	115	37,805	1:10.60	
1949	Bed o' Roses	2	E. Guerin	119	Fais Do Do	119	Striking	119	40,210	1:11.20	
1950	Atalanta	2	H. Woodhouse	119	Ruddy	119	Sungari	119	38,690	1:12.00	
1951	Rose Jet	2	H. Woodhouse	119	Knot Hole	119	Landmark	119	44,830	1:11.20	
							A Gleam	119			
1952	Is Proud	2	C. McCreary	119	Aerolite	119	Grecian Queen	119	40,960	1:09.00	
1953	Evening Out	2	O. Scurlock	119	Queen Hopeful	119	Clear Dawn	119	41,345	1:10.40	
1954	High Voltage	2	E. Arcaro	119	Blue Banner	119	Lalun	119	49,330	1:10.00	
1955	Doubledogdare	2	E. Arcaro	119	Glamour	119	Beautillion	119	48,620	1:09.80	
1956	Romanita	2	E. Guerin	119	Jet's Charm	119	Lucky Mistake	119	43,020	1:08.60	
1957	Idun	2	W. Hartack	119	Poly Hi	119	Armorial	119	42,900	1:09.60	
1958	Quill	2	P.J. Bailey	119	Rich Tradition	119	Levelix	119	42,610	1:10.00	
1959	Heavenly Body	2	M. Ycaza	119	Irish Jay	119	Rash Statement	119	58,224	1:10.20	
1960	Rose Bower	2	J.L. Rotz	119	Little Tumbler	119	Good Move	119	58,634	1:10.60	
1961	Cicada	2	W. Shoemaker	119	Jazz Queen	119	Pontivy	119	61,028	1:10.60	
1962	Smart Deb	2	R. Ussery	119	Fashion Verdict	119	Affectionately	119	63,889	1:09.80	
1963	Hasty Matelda	2	J. Combest	119	Baraka	119	Beautiful Day	119	63,596	1:12.00	
1964	Candalita	2	R. Ussery	119	Admiring	119	Gold Digger	119	63,680	1:13.00	
1965	Moccasin	2	J. Adams	119	Lyvette	119	Shimmering Gold	119	67,717	1:11.60	
1966	Swiss Cheese	2	J.L. Rotz	119	Great Era	119	Regal Gleam	119	68,659	1:12.80	
1967	Queen of the Stage	2	B. Baeza	119	Gay Matelda	119	Syrian Sea	119	64,733	1:10.00	
1968	Gallant Bloom	2	E. Belmonte	119	Irradiate	119	Queen's Double	119	62,634	1:10.40	
1969	Cold Comfort	2	J. Velasquez	119	Repoise	119	Grab It	119	68,484	1:11.60	
1970	Bonnie and Gay	2	R. Woodhouse	119	Patelin	119	Make Me Laugh	119	68,009	1:11.00	
1971	Numbered Account	2	B. Baeza	119	Stepping High	119	Informative	119	60,306	1:10.40	
1972	La Prevoyante	2	J. LeBlanc	119	Up Above	119	Corraggioso	119	59,874	1:23.60	
1973	Talking Picture	2	R. Turcotte	119	Dancealot	119	Raisela	119	64,050	1:23.20	

Year	Winner	Age	Jockey	Wt.	Second	Wt.	Third	Wt.	Win Value	Time	Beyer
1974	Alpine Lass	2	A. Cordero Jr	119	Copernica	119	Spring Is Here	119	52,674	1:23.00	
1975	Optimistic Gal	2	B. Baeza	119	Pacific Princess	119	Prowess	119	51,132	1:23.00	
1976	Mrs. Warren	2	E. Maple	119	Negotiator	119	Resolver	119	51,162	1:24.60	
1977	Lakeville Miss	2	R. Hernandez	119	Stub	119	Akita	119	49,335	1:22.80	
1978	Fall Aspen	2	R.I. Velez	119	Fair Advantage	119	Island Kitty	119	58,980	1:23.80	
1979	Smart Angle	2	S. Maple	119	Royal Suite	119	Nuit D'Amour	119	69,075	1:23.80	
1980	Prayers'n Promises	2	A. Cordero Jr	119	Heavenly Cause	119	Sweet Revenge	119	70,725	1:24.60	
1981	Before Dawn	2	J. Velasquez	119	Arabian Dancer	119	Mystical Mood	119	81,210	1:23.20	
1982	Wings of Jove	2	W.H. McCauley	119	Share the Fantasy	119	Weekend Surprise	119	72,600	1:24.00	
1983	Lucky Lucky Lucky	2	A. Cordero Jr	119	Miss Oceana	119	Buzz My Bell	119	76,590	1:23.60	
1984	Fiesta Lady	2	L. Pincay Jr	119	Tiltalating	119	Contredance	119	47,060	1:24.80	
1985	Musical Lark	2	D. MacBeth	119	Family Style	119	I'm Sweets	119	66,240	1:24.00	
1986	Tappiano	2	J. Cruguet	119	Sea Basque	119	Daytime Princess	119	72,000	1:23.40	
1987	Over All	2	A. Cordero Jr	119	Justsayno	119	Flashy Runner	119	82,140	1:24.80	
1988	Some Romance	2	G.L. Stevens	119	Seattle Meteor	119	Dreamy Mimi	119	68,580	1:24.80	
1989	Stella Madrid	2	A. Cordero Jr	119	Golden Reef	119	Miss Cox's Hat	119	72,720	1:24.40	
1990	Meadow Star	2	J.A. Santos	119	Verbasle	119	Clark Cottage	119	93,240	1:22.80	
1991	Anh Duong	2	A. Cordero Jr	119	Miss Iron Smoke	119	Vivano	119	81,300	1:23.40	90
1992	Sky Beauty	2	E. Maple	119	Educated Risk	119	Family Enterprize	119	72,480	1:23.20	92
1993	Strategic Maneuver	2	J.A. Santos	119	Astas Foxy Lady	119	Sovereign Kitty	119	70,680	1:23.80	96
1994	Flanders	2	P. Day	119	Stormy Blues	119	Pretty Discreet	119	64,740	1:35.00	101
	Flanders was subsequently disqualified for medication violation										
1995	Golden Attraction	2	G.L. Stevens	119	Cara Rafaela	119	My Flag	119	90,000	1:36.20	89
1996	Sharp Cat	2	J.D. Bailey	119	Storm Song	119	Fabulously Fast	119	90,000	1:36.00	90
1997	Beautiful Pleasure	2	J.D. Bailey	119	Diamond on the Run	119	Carrielle	119	90,000	1:35.60	98
1998	Oh What a Windfall	2	S.J. Sellers	119	Arrested Dreams	119	Marley Vale	119	90,000	1:39.29	74
1999	Finder's Fee	2	H. Castillo Jr	119	Darling My Darling	119	Circle of Life	119	90,000	1:36.68	94
2000	Raging Fever	2	J.D. Bailey	120	Dancinginmydreams	120	Ilusoria	120	120,000	1:38.20	87
2002	Storm Flag Flying	2	J.R. Velazquez	119	Wild Snitch	119	Fircroft	119	120,000	1:38.52	93
2003	Marylebone	2	E.S. Prado	119	Lokoya	119	Eye Dazzler	119	120,000	1:38.02	78
2004	Sense of Style	2	E.S. Prado	119	Balletto	119	Play With Fire	119	180,000	1:37.67	91

Beyer Index: 90.23

Distance 6 furlongs prior to 1972; 7 furlongs from 1972-93. Run at Morris Park prior to 1905. Run at Pimlico in 1910. Run at Aqueduct 1960, 1962-68. Run over the old straight course 1905-09, 1914, 1923-25. Run on the Widener Course 1926-40, 1942-58. For colts and fillies prior to . 1902. Run in divisions, one for colts and one fillies, 1902-14. Not run in 2001

W.L. McKNIGHT HANDICAP (G2), 1 1/2 Miles (Turf), 3-Year-Olds and Up, Calder Race Course, 2004 Purse: $200,000

Year	Winner	Age	Jockey	Wt.	Second	Wt.	Third	Wt.	Win Value	Time	Beyer
1973	Getajetholme	4	J. Imparato	121	Daring Young Man	120	Outdoors	116	38,700	1:47.20	
1974	Shane's Prince	4	E. Maple	116	Star Envoy	125	Return to Reality	119	35,700	1:46.00	
1975	Snurb	5	G. St. Leon	119	Buffalo Lark	121	Lord Rebeau	116	37,800	1:46.00	
1976	Toonerville	5	G. St. Leon	119	Ameri Flyer	117	Emperor Rex	115	55,800	1:44.60	
1977	H'll of Reason	4	M. Solomone	119	Visier	120	Lightning Thr'st	116	52,200	1:47.20	
1978	Practitioner	5	J.S. Rodriguez	118	Fort Prevel	111	Bob's Dusty	118	56,250	1:48.80	
1979	Bob's Dusty	5	R. Depass	119	Prince Misko	116	Bridewell	112	55,800	1:48.00	
1980	Old Crony	5	D. Brumfield	117	Once Over Lightly	114	Houdini	125	35,565	1:48.40	
1980	Drum's Captain	5	J. Fell	118	Lot O' Gold	125	Scythian Gold	116	34,875	1:48.00	
1981	El Barril	5	J. Vasquez	118	Lord Bawimer	115	Lobsang II	117	51,630	2:28.40	
1981	Buckpoint	5	J.D. Bailey	122	Scythian Gold	116	Proud Manner	112	52,230	2:28.00	
1982	Ghazwan	5	C. Hernandez	120	Gleaming Channel	116	Beyond Recall	110	61,920	2:28.80	
1982	Russian George	6	M.A. Rivera	114	Euphrosyne	117	Nar		61,320	2:29.80	
1983	Current Blade	5	J.D. Bailey	114	Half Iced	122	Leader Jet	113	70,020	2:29.20	
1984	Open Call	6	J. Velasquez	120	Dom Cimarosa	114	Bold Frond	113	63,075	2:30.20	
1984	Nijinsky's Secret	6	J.A. Velez Jr	124	Dom Menotti	112	Four Bases	114	63,675	2:31.20	
1985	Jack Slade	5	G. Gallitano	120	Rake	116	Rilial	120	69,900	2:26.20	
1985	Flying Pidgeon	4	J.A. Santos	114	Pass the Line	114	Selous Scout	110	70,800	2:25.80	
1986	Flying Pidgeon	5	J.A. Santos	117	Creme Fraiche	115	Amerilad	112	120,000	2:39.60	
1987	Creme Fraiche	5	E. Maple	115	Flying Pidgeon	120	Akabir	113	120,000	2:27.00	
1988	All Sincerity	6	C. Hernandez	111	Blazing Bart	118	Creme Fraiche	118	120,000	2:25.40	
1989	Mataji	5	D. Valiente	113	Mi Selecto	118	Creme Fraiche	118	90,000	2:25.60	
1990	Drum Taps	4	J.A. Santos	114	Black Tulip	112	Turfah	115	60,000	2:29.80	99
1991	Stolen Rolls	5	P.A. Rodriguez	115	Runaway Raja	112	Gallant Mel	110	60,000	2:27.00	105
1992	Bye Union Ave.	6	R.R. Douglas	113	Crockadore	113	Skate on Thin Ice	111	90,000	2:27.20	102
1993	Antartic Wings	5	R.R. Douglas	113	Cigar Toss	112	Luv U. Jodi	110	60,000	2:33.40	102
1994	Cobblestone Road	5	J.C. Ferrer	113	Daarik	113	Fraise	126	90,000	2:27.80	104
1995	Flag Down	5	J.A. Santos	116	Mecke	118	Green Means Go	115	90,000	2:24.00	106
1996	Diplomatic Jet	4	J.F. Chavez	123	Marcie's Ensign	123	(DH) Identity	114	90,000	2:24.20	106
1997	Panama City	3	P. Day	117	Slicious	114	Skillington	113	90,000	2:27.00	103
1998	Wild Event	5	S.J. Sellers	116	N B Forrest	114	Glok	114	90,000	2:26.80	104
1999	Wicapi	7	C. Velasquez	114	Special Coach	114	King's Jewel	112	90,000	2:26.20	95

Year	Winner	Age	Jockey	Wt.	Second	Wt.	Third	Wt.	Win Value	Time	Beyer
2000	A Little Luck	6	M.E. Smith	114	Stokosky	115	Whata Brainstorm	113	90,000	2:29.01	100
2001	Profit Option	6	M. Guidry	115	Deeliteful Irving	113	Eltawaasul	114	90,000	2:27.95	96
2002	Man From Wicklow	5	J.D. Bailey	118	Serial Bride	114	Rochester	117	120,000	2:28.05	102
2003	Balto Star	5	J.R. Velazquez	121	Continuously	116	Rowans Park	114	120,000	2:24.87	105
2004	Dreadnaught	4	J.L. Samyn	116	Demeteor	112	Scooter Roach	115	120,000	2:26.60	101

Beyer Index: 102.00

MEADOWLANDS BREEDERS' CUP (G2), 1 1/8 Miles, 3-Year-Olds and Up, The Meadowlands, 2004 Purse: $500,000

Year	Winner	Age	Jockey	Wt.	Second	Wt.	Third	Wt.	Win Value	Time	Beyer
1977	Pay Tribute	5	A. Cordero Jr	117	Father Hogan	112	Super Boy	110	114,920	2:02.60	
1978	Dr. Patches	4	A. Cordero Jr	119	Do Tell George	114	Niteange	115	104,878	2:01.60	
1979	Spectacular Bid	3	W. Shoemaker	126	Smarten	120	Valdez	121	234,650	2:01.20	
1980	Tunerup	4	J. Vasquez	117	Dr. Patches	116	Dewan Keys	115	196,500	2:00.40	
1981	Princelet	3	W. Nemeti	110	Niteange	114	Peat Moss	121	202,080	2:02.40	
1982	Mehmet	4	E. Delahoussaye	118	Thirty Eight Paces	113	John Henry	129	240,000	2:01.40	
1983	Slewpy	3	A. Cordero Jr	116	Deputy Minister	118	Water Bank	117	240,000	2:02.40	
1984	Wild Again	4	R. Migliore	115	Canadian Factor	114	Inevitable Leader	116	300,000	2:00.60	
1985	Bounding Basque	5	R.G. Davis	113	Wild Again	120	Al Mamoon	115	300,000	2:00.40	
1986	Broad Brush	3	J.L. Samyn	117	Skip Trial	122	Little Missouri	116	300,000	2:01.60	
1987	Creme Fraiche	5	L. Pincay Jr	123	Afleet	118	Cryptoclearance	120	300,000	2:01.80	
1988	Alysheba	4	C.J. McCarron	127	Slew City Slew	116	Pleasant Virginian	123	360,000	1:50.00	
1989	Mi Selecto	4	J.A. Santos	115	Make the Most	110	Master Speaker	114	300,000	2:00.20	
1990	Great Normand	5	C. Lopez	113	Norquestor	116	Beau Genius	122	300,000	1:47.20	117
1991	Twilight Agenda	5	C.J. McCarron	121	Scan	116	Sea Cadet	115	300,000	1:46.60	116
1992	Sea Cadet	4	A. Solis	120	Valley Crossing	111	American Chance	109	300,000	1:48.00	108
1993	Marquetry	6	K.J. Desormeaux	120	Michelle Can Pass	110	Northern Trend	112	300,000	1:47.20	115
1994	Conveyor	6	M.E. Smith	113	Personal Merit	109	Bruce's Mill	114	300,000	1:47.80	105
1995	Peaks and Valleys	3	J.A. Krone	116	Poor but Honest	116	Concern	122	300,000	1:48.00	108
1996	Dramatic Gold	5	K.J. Desormeaux	119	Formal Gold	112	Mt. Sassafras	114	450,000	1:48.00	111
1998	K.J.'s Appeal	4	J.R. Velazquez	112	Hal's Pal	116	Sir Bear	119	300,000	1:46.00	107
1999	Pleasant Breeze	4	J.F. Chavez	110	Jazz Club	118	Vision and Verse	112	300,000	1:47.00	110
2000	North East Bound	4	J.A. Velez Jr	116	Lord Sterling	115	Where's Taylor	113	240,000	1:48.84	106
2001	Gander	5	J.R. Velazquez	114	Broken Vow	120	Include	121	300,000	1:47.11	104
2002	Burning Roma	4	E.M. Coa	115	Volponi	116	Windsor Castle	112	240,000	1:48.95	107
2003	Bowman's Band	5	R.A. Dominguez	119	Dynever	120	Volponi	123	240,000	1:46.84	109
	Unforgettable Max finished third but was disqualified and placed fourth										
2004	Balto Star	6	J.R. Velazquez	123	Dynever	119	Gygistar	119	300,000	1:48.68	107

Beyer Index: 109.29

MEMORIAL DAY HANDICAP (G3), 1 1/16 Miles, 3-Year-Olds and Up, Calder Race Course, 2004 Purse: $100,000

Year	Winner	Age	Jockey	Wt.	Second	Wt.	Third	Wt.	Win Value	Time	Beyer
1971	Anchorage	4	J. Moseley	108	Caw King	113	Black Pipe	119	6,600	1:39.00	
1972	Willmar	4	K. Knapp	121	Tall Fellow	117	Asher	111	9,600	1:45.20	
1973	Correbtoso	6	R. Danjean	116	Great Divide	121	Asher	104	10,620	1:47.80	
1974	Snurb	4	G. St. Leon	121	Stariway to Stars	113	Somewhat Striking	113	14,040	1:46.20	
1975	Plagiarize	4	G. St. Leon	118	Rimsky II	115	Trusted	115	13,800	1:45.80	
1976	Freepet	6	R. Broussard	117	Chiliean Chief	119	Rastaferian	112	20,700	1:53.80	
1977	Lightning Thrust	4	G. St. Leon	121	Jatski	110	What a Threat	116	21,780	1:45.80	
1978	One Moment	5	J. Giovanni	114	Out Door Johnny	115	Haverty	112	21,240	1:52.20	
1979	Great Sound	5	W. Guerra	115	Raymond Earl	123	Prince Misko	116	20,835	1:45.40	
1980	Poverty Boy	5	M. Fromin	119	J. Rodney G	115	Irish Swords	117	20,565	1:45.60	
1982	Two's a Plenty	5	A. Smith Jr	122	Catch That Pass	114	Poking	117	19,470	1:45.40	
1983	Bolivar	6	S. Soto	116	Dallas Express	114	Gray Adorn	115	23,700	1:46.00	
1985	Rexson's Hope	4	G. Bain	113	Brother Liam	121	Amerilad	115	33,660	1:43.60	
1988	Billie Osage	4	G. St. Leon	116	Fabulous Devotion	110	Engrupido II	114	33,150	1:46.20	
1989	Hotting Star	4	J. Velez Hr.	116	Val D'enchere	116	Bright Baloon	111	33,300	1:41.20	
1990	Primal	5	H. Castillo Jr	122	Eagle Watch	114	Public Account	113	33,180	1:47.40	
1991	S.W. Wildcard	5	P. Rodriguez	110	So Dashing	119	Bold Circle	113	34,110	1:46.80	
1992	Jodi's Sweetie	4	J. Duarte	114	Scottish Ice	114	Bidding Proud	113	30,000	1:44.20	96
1993	Boots 'n Buck	4	M. Russ	116	Yankee Axe	119	Darian's Reason	112	30,000	1:53.80	95
1994	Final Sunrise	4	P. Rodriguez	113	Crucial Trial	114	Bill Mooney	112	30,000	1:51.80	94
1995	Mr. Light Tres	6	K. Chapman	113	Fabulous Frolic	112	Flying American	116	30,000	1:47.00	92
1996	Marcie's Ensign	4	E.M. Coa	115	Derivative	114	Halo Bird	110	30,000	1:50.00	108
1997	Vilhelm	5	J.C. Ferrer	114	Sir Bear	113	Donthelumbertrader	118	30,000	1:40.80	100
1998	Born Mighty	4	J.A. Rivera II	114	Hard Rock Ridge	114	Auroral	114	30,000	1:40.80	94
1999	Wicapi	7	E.M. Coa	116	Dancing Guy	114	Golf Game	112	30,000	1:46.60	98
2000	Dancing Guy	5	J.C. Ferrer	121	Reporter	111	Groomstick Stock's	111	45,000	1:46.28	108
2001	Hal's Hope	4	R.I. Velez	115	American Halo	115	Tahkodha Hills	118	45,000	1:45.81	107

Year	Winner	Age	Jockey	Wt.	Second	Wt.	Third	Wt.	Win Value	Time	Beyer
2002	Best of the Rest	7	C. Velasquez	123	High Ideal	112	Hal's Hope	117	60,000	1:44.75	109
2003	Dancing Guy	8	R.I. Velez	113	Shotgun Fire	110	High Ideal	113	60,000	1:45.56	92
2004	Twilight Road	7	P.A. Teator	111	Hear No Evil	115	Gold Dollar	112	60,000	1:45.79	104

Beyer Index: 99.77

METROPOLITAN HANDICAP (G1), 1 Mile, 3-Year-Olds and Up, Belmont Park, 2004 Purse: $750,000

Year	Winner	Age	Jockey	Wt.	Second	Wt.	Third	Wt.	Win Value	Time	Beyer
1891	Tristan	6	Taylor	114	Tenny	129	Clarendon	107	7,300	1:51.20	
1892	Pessara	4	Taral	117	Locohatchee	105	Sleipner	107	12,200	1:54.00	
1893	Charade	4	Doggett	108	His Highness	125	Illume	98	13,740	1:52.20	
1894	Ramapo	4	Taral	117	Roche	105	Henry of Navarre	106	6,145	1:52.20	
1896	Counter Tenor	4	Hamilton	115	St. Maxim	109	Sir Walter	112	3,850	1:53.00	
1897	Voter	3	Lamley	99	The Winner	115	Casseopia	99	3,850	1:40.20	
1898	Bowling Brook	3	P. Clay	102	George Keene	102	Octagon	116	4,280	1:44.00	
1899	Filigrane	3	Clawson	102	Ethelbert	106	Sanders	110	6,750	1:39.60	
1900	Ethelbert	4	Maher	126	Box	121	Imp	127	6,250	1:41.20	
1901	Banastar	6	Odom	123	Contestor	112	All Green	102	6,810	1:42.00	
1902	Arsenal	3	J. Daly	90	Herbert	119	Carbuncle	103	8,920	1:42.00	
1903	Gunfire	4	T. Burns	109	Old England	118	Lux Casta	102	11,080	1:38.60	
1904	Irish Lad	4	Shaw	123	Toboggan	103	Beldame	98	10,880	1:40.00	
1905	Sysonby	3	Shaw	107			Colonial Girl	111	5,655	1:41.60	
	Race King	4	L. Smith	97							
1906	Grapple	4	Garner	97	Okenite	99	Roseben	124	10,850	1:39.00	
1908	Jack Atkin	4	C.H. Shilling	128	Restigouche	98	Don Creole	95	10,650	1:40.80	
1909	King James	4	G. Burns	125	Fayette	108	Juggler	112	3,785	1:40.00	
1910	Fashion Plate	4	M. McGee	105	Prince Imperial	97	Jack Atkin	129	3,800	1:37.80	
1913	Whisk Broom II	6	Notter	126	G.M. Miller	100	Meridian	120	3,500	1:39.00	
1914	Buskin	4	C. Fairbrother	114	Figinny	97	Rock View	127	4,200	1:37.80	
1915	Stromboli	4	C. Turner	118	Sharpshooter	103	Fly Fairy	115	2,325	1:39.80	
1916	The Finn	4	A. Schuttinger	120	Stromboli	122	Spur	100	3,350	1:38.00	
1917	Ormesdale	4	J. McTaggart	111	Spur	117	Borrow	117	3,850	1:39.20	
1918	Trompe La Mort	3	L. McAtee	102	Old Koenig	118	Priscilla Mullens	104	3,865	1:38.40	
1919	Lanius	4	J. Loftus	116	Flags	119	Star Master	116	3,865	1:45.40	
1920	Wildair	3	E. Ambrose	107	Thunderclap	114	On Watch	112	3,865	1:38.80	
1921	Mad Hatter	5	E. Sande	127	Audacious	117	Yellow Hand	110	8,150	1:37.40	
1922	Mad Hatter	6	E. Sande	129	Careful	112	Sennings Park	127	8,550	1:36.60	
1923	Grey Lag	5	E. Sande	133	Dinna Care	107	Exodus	110	7,600	1:38.00	
1924	Laurano	3	H. Thurber	101	Bracadale	110	Rialto	119	9,150	1:38.20	
1925	Sting	4	B. Breuning	114	Shuffle Along	112	Serenader	106	8,625	1:37.00	
1926	Sarazen	5	F. Weiner	129	Senaldo	116	Rock Star	105	9,125	1:38.00	
1927	Black Maria	4	F. Coltiletti	116	Osmand	112	Valorous	108	8,225	1:37.40	
1928	Nimba	4	H. Thurber	114	Chance Shot	118	Scapa Flow	125	8,575	1:40.00	
1929	Petee-Wrack	4	S. O'Donnell	120	Buddy Bauer	117	Bateau	114	8,600	1:40.00	
1930	Jack High	4	L. McAtee	110	Balko	120	Questionnaire	103	8,275	1:35.00	
1931	Questionnaire	4	R. Workman	122	Mokatam	122	Aegis	105	7,575	1:38.60	
1932	Equipoise	4	R. Workman	127	Sun Meadow	118	Mate	128	7,525	1:37.00	
1933	Equipoise	5	R. Workman	128	Okapi	102	Scotch Gold	106	4,725	1:37.40	
1934	Mr. Khayyam	4	R. Jones	119	Sun Archer	106	Ladysman	118	3,480	1:37.00	
	Equipoise finished first but was disqualified										
1935	King Saxon	4	C. Rainey	118	Singing Wood	114	Only One	113	7,225	1:38.20	
1936	Good Harvest	4	S. Renick	107	Whopper	123	Singing Wood	120	6,650	1:36.40	
1937	Snark	4	J. Longden	112	Memory Book	115	Whopper	122	6,675	1:37.80	
1938	Danger Point	4	E. Arcaro	112	Snark	124	Caballero II	122	8,450	1:38.00	
1939	Knickerbocker	3	F.A. Smith	100	Heelfly	116	Jacola	115	7,500	1:37.20	
1940	Third Degree	4	E. Arcaro	123	Can't Wait	109	War Dog	108	10,400	1:35.40	
1941	Eight Thirty	5	H. Richards	132	Bold and Bad	102	Hash	123	10,250	1:37.20	
1942	Attention	4	D. Meade	124	Pictor	120	Market Wise	125	11,300	1:36.40	
1943	Devil Diver	4	G. Woolf	117	Marriage	116	Thumbs Up	117	10,900	1:36.80	
1944	Devil Diver	5	T. Atkinson	134	Alquest	109	Boysy	108	10,080	1:35.80	
1945	Devil Diver	6	T. Atkinson	129	Alex Barth	123	Boy Knight	112	18,280	1:36.40	
1946	Gallorette	4	J.D. Jessop	110	Sirde	124	First Fiddle	126	22,050	1:37.00	
1947	Stymie	6	B. James	124	Brown Mogul	113	Gallorette	116	21,650	1:37.40	
1948	Stymie	7	C. McCreary	126	Colosal	117	Rippey	124	21,200	1:36.80	
1949	Loser Weeper	4	H. Woodhouse	105	Vulcan's Forge	126	But Why Not	119	21,400	1:36.40	
1950	Greek Ship	3	H. Woodhouse	106	Piet	121	Cochise	121	22,450	1:36.00	
1951	Casemate	4	D. Gorman	115	Piet	123	Lights Up	122	26,000	1:35.40	
1952	Mameluke	4	G. Porch	112	Battlefield	125	One Hitter	113	25,200	1:36.40	
1953	Tom Fool	4	T. Atkinson	130	Royal Vale	127	Intent	125	25,800	1:35.80	
1954	Native Dancer	4	E. Guerin	130	Straight Face	117	Jamie K.	110	28,300	1:35.20	
1955	High Gun	4	A. DeSpirito	130	Artismo	115	Joe Jones	119	25,500	1:35.60	
1956	Midafternoon	4	W. Boland	111	Switch On	113	Find	116	37,700	1:35.00	
1957	Traffic Judge	5	E. Arcaro	118	Dedicate	126	Greek Spy	114	44,600	1:36.00	

Year	Winner	Age	Jockey	Wt.	Second	Wt.	Third	Wt.	Win Value	Time	Beyer
1958	Gallant Man	4	W. Shoemaker	130	Bold Ruler	135	Clem	114	37,620	1:35.60	
1959	Sword Dancer	3	W. Shoemaker	114	Jimmer	112	Talent Show	115	74,235	1:35.20	
1960	Bald Eagle	5	M. Ycaza	128	First Landing	123	Talent Show	118	73,130	1:33.60	
1961	Kelso	4	E. Arcaro	130	All Hands	117	Sweet William	108	74,100	1:35.60	
1962	Carry Back	4	J.L. Rotz	123	Merry Ruler	120	Rullah Red	111	72,735	1:33.60	
1963	Cyrano	4	R. Ussery	113	George Barton	114	Sunrise County	121	74,815	1:35.00	
1964	Olden Times	6	H. Moreno	119	Quadrangle	113	Saidam	118	75,010	1:34.40	
1965	Gun Bow	5	W. Blum	130	Chieftain	117	Affectionately	121	72,540	1:34.40	
1966	Bold Lad	4	B. Baeza	132	Hedevar	113	Tio Viejo	115	75,140	1:34.20	
1967	Buckpasser	4	B. Baeza	130	Yonder	108	Impressive	113	70,980	1:34.60	
1968	In Reality	4	J.L. Rotz	124	Advocator	117	Full of Fun	110	70,135	1:35.00	
1969	Arts and Letters	3	J. Cruguet	111	Nodouble	129	Promise	119	75,725	1:34.00	
1970	Nodouble	5	J. Tejeira	126	Reviewer	123	Dewan	122	74,490	1:34.60	
1971	Tunex	5	J. Ruane	113	Protanto	112	Knight in Armor	114	72,960	1:35.80	
1972	Executioner	4	E. Belmonte	119	Bold Reasoning	123	Peace Corps	113	70,290	1:35.40	
1973	Tentam	4	J. Velasquez	116	Key to the Mint	127	King's Bishop	118	68,580	1:35.00	
1974	Arbees Boy	4	E. Maple	112	Forego	134	Timeless Moment	109	67,200	1:34.40	
1975	Gold and Myrrh	4	W. Blum	121	Stop the Music	124	Forego	136	66,840	1:33.60	
1976	Forego	6	H. Gustines	130	Master Derby	126	Lord Rebeau	119	66,660	1:34.80	
1977	Forego	7	W. Shoemaker	133	Co Host	111	Full Out	115	68,640	1:34.80	
1978	Cox's Ridge	4	E. Maple	130	Buckfinder	112	Quiet Little Table	118	66,180	1:34.60	
1979	State Dinner	4	C.J. McCarron	115	Dr. Patches	118	Sorry Lookin	113	64,980	1:34.00	
1980	Czaravich	4	L. Pincay Jr	126	State Dinner	117	Silent Cal	120	83,850	1:35.80	
1981	Fappiano	4	A. Cordero Jr	115	Irish Tower	127	Amber Pass	115	85,650	1:33.80	
1982	Conquistador Cielo	3	E. Maple	111	Silver Buck	111	Star Gallant	111	91,800	1:33.00	
1983	Star Choice	4	J. Velasquez	113	Tough Critic	110	John's Gold	111	145,200	1:33.80	
1984	Fit to Fight	5	J.D. Bailey	124	A Phenomenon	126	Moro	116	209,100	1:34.00	
1985	Forzando II	4	D. MacBeth	118	Mo Exception	113	Track Barron	125	207,600	1:34.40	
1986	Garthorn	4	R.Q. Meza	124	Love That Mac	117	Lady's Secret	120	179,700	1:33.60	
1987	Gulch	3	P. Day	110	King's Swan	121	Broad Brush	128	360,900	1:34.80	
1988	Gulch	4	J.A. Santos	125	Afleet	124	Stacked Pack	110	351,600	1:34.60	
1989	Proper Reality	4	J.D. Bailey	117	Seeking the Gold	126	Dancing Spree	113	353,400	1:34.00	
1990	Criminal Type	5	J.A. Santos	120	Housebuster	113	Easy Goer	127	357,000	1:34.40	117
1991	In Excess	4	P.A. Valenzuela	117	Rubiano	111	Gervazy	114	300,000	1:35.40	117
1992	Dixie Brass	3	J.M. Pezua	107	Pleasant Tap	119	In Excess	121	300,000	1:33.60	111
1993	Ibero	6	L. Pincay Jr	119	Bertrando	121	Alydeed	124	300,000	1:34.20	113
1994	Holy Bull	3	M.E. Smith	112	Cherokee Run	118	Devil His Due	122	300,000	1:33.80	122
1995	You and I	4	J.F. Chavez	112	Lite the Fuse	113	Our Emblem	114	300,000	1:34.60	114
1996	Honour and Glory	3	J.R.Velazquez	110	Lite the Fuse	122			240,000	1:32.80	111
					Afternoon Deelites	123					
1997	Langfuhr	5	J.F. Chavez	122	Western Winter	115	Northern Afleet	117	240,000	1:33.00	112
1998	Wild Rush	4	J.D. Bailey	119	Banker's Gold	115	Accelerator	113	300,000	1:33.50	118
1999	Sir Bear	6	J.R.Velazquez	117	Crafty Friend	114	Liberty Gold	114	300,000	1:34.55	114
2000	Yankee Victor	4	H. Castillo Jr	117	Honest Lady	112	Sir Bear	117	450,000	1:34.64	115
2001	Exciting Story	4	P. Husbands	115	Peeping Tom	119	Alannan	118	450,000	1:37.14	108
2002	Swept Overboard	5	J. Chavez	117	Aldebaran	115	Crafty C.T.	116	450,000	1:33.34	122
2003	Aldebaran	5	J.D. Bailey	119	Saarland	114	Peeping Tom	114	450,000	1:34.15	110
2004	Pico Central	5	A. Solis	119	Bowman's Band	114	Strong Hope	119	450,000	1:35.47	116

Beyer Index: 114.67

Distance 1 1/8 miles prior to 1897. Run at Morris Park prior to 1905; at Aqueduct from 1960-67, 1969, 1975

MIAMI MILE BREEDERS' CUP HANDICAP (G3), 1 Mile (Turf), 3-Year-Olds and Up, Calder Race Course, 2004 Purse: $150,000

Year	Winner	Age	Jockey	Wt.	Second	Wt.	Third	Wt.	Win Value	Time	Beyer
1987	Blazing Bart	3	J.A. Santos	117	Silver Voice	115	New Colony	114	93,630	1:44.20	
1988	Simply Majestic	4	J.D. Bailey	117	Sal d'Enchere	116	Racing Star	115	93,900	1:43.60	
1989	Simply Majestic	5	H. Castillo Jr	117	Maceo	113	Bold Circle	110	93,510	1:48.60	
1990	Public Account	5	P. Rodriguez	115	Bold Circle	112	Primal	126	93,300	1:52.00	107
1991	Run Turn	4	G. St. Leon	120	Scottish Ice	116	Hidden Tomahawk	112	93,150	1:52.80	98
1992	Jodi's Sweetie	4	J.D. Bailey	115	Walkie Talker	114	Futurist	117	94,140	1:43.80	104
1993	Carterista	4	M. Lee	117	Wild Forest	112	Mr. Explosive	112	95,610	1:47.40	96
1994	The Vid	4	R.R. Douglas	114	Mr. Angel	118	Carterista	116	94,350	1:48.20	104
1995	Elite Jeblar	5	E. Fires	113	Myrmidon	117	Fabulous Frolic	114	94,200	1:47.60	96
1996	Satellite Nealski	3	J.C. Ferrer	112	Marcie's Ensign	115	Copy Editor	117	95,805	1:47.60	94
1997	Vilhelm	5	J.C. Ferrer	114	Marcie's Ensign	114	Elite Jeblar	113	120,000	1:36.60	103
1998	Unite's Big Red	4	E. Nunez	115	Fig Fest	113	Ensign Ray	113	120,000	1:36.60	100
							Copy Editor	117			
1999	Sharp Appeal	6	J.J. Castellano	114	Shamrock City	114	Hurrahy	115	135,000	1:35.60	102
2000	Band Is Passing	4	E.M. Coa	120	Hurrahy	115	Tiger Shark	112	90,000	1:37.28	100
2001	Mr. Livingston	4	A. Castellano Jr	115	Honorable Pic	114	Pisces	112	90,000	1:33.75	100
2002	Band Is Passing	6	C.H. Velasquez	117	Pisces	116	Doowaley	113	90,000	1:37.78	105

Year	Winner	Age	Jockey	Wt.	Second	Wt.	Third	Wt.	Win Value	Time	Beyer
2003	Tour of the Cat	5	A. Cabassa Jr	115	Last Stand	113	Lavender's Lad	114	90,000	1:38.65	102
2004	Twilight Road	7	P.A. Teator	114	Gold Dollar	114	Paradise Dancer	115	90,000	1:39.56	95

Beyer Index: 100.40

Run at 1 1/8 miles on turf, 1987-89, 1992-96; Run at 1 1/8 miles on main track, 1990-91; Off the turf in 2003.

MIESQUE (G3), 1 Mile (Turf), 2-Year-Old Fillies, Hollywood Park, 2004 Purse: $75,000 (Div 1); $75,000 (Div 2)

Year	Winner	Age	Jockey	Wt.	Second	Wt.	Third	Wt.	Win Value	Time	Beyer
1991	More Than Willing	2	E. Delahoussaye	118	Stormagain	115	Looie Capote	114	61,875	1:35.40	93
1991	Hopeful Amber	2	D.R. Flores	114	Storm Ring	115	Crownette	114	61,875	1:36.60	81
1992	Creaking Board	2	K.J. Desormeaux	115	Ask Anita	117	Zoonaqua	121	137,500	1:32.80	82
1993	Tricky Code	2	C.S. Nakatani	116	Irish Forever	121	Roget's Fact	114	137,500	1:35.00	83
1994	Bail out Becky	2	K.J. Desormeaux	121	Miss Union Avenue	121	Makin Whopee	117	110,000	1:37.20	89
1995	Antespend	2	C.W. Antley	121	Wheatly Special	121	Platinum Blonde	121	110,000	1:34.20	90
1996	Ascutney	2	E. Delahoussaye	116	Wealthy	116	Clever Plot	118	120,000	1:35.00	80
1997	Star's Proud Penny	2	G.K. Gomez	116	Superlative	121	Ransom the Dreamer	121	120,000	1:37.40	87
1998	Here's To You	2	E. Delahoussaye	116	Sweet Lady	118	Nausicaa	116	120,000	1:36.40	88
1999	Prairie Princess	2	Solis A.	116	She's Classy	118	Mary Kies	121	120,000	1:37.20	85
2000	Fantastic Filly	2	G.K. Gomez	116	Smart Timing	115	Eminent	118	120,000	1:35.11	98
2001	Forty On Line	2	C.S. Nakatani	117	Riskaverse	121	Daisyago	118	120,000	1:36.38	85
2002	Atlantic Ocean	2	D.R. Flores	121	Tangle	114	Major Idea	121	120,000	1:34.63	89
2003	Mambo Slew	2	M.E. Smith	116	Ticker Tape	116	Winendynme	116	60,000	1:36.17	81
2004	Louvain	2	R.A. Dominguez	115	Royal Copenhagen	114	La Maitresse	114	45,000	1:37.19	84
2004	Paddy's Daisy	2	C.S. Nakatani	121	Conveyor's Angel	118	Kenza	116	45,000	1:36.92	87

Beyer Index: 86.38

MILADY BREEDERS' CUP HANDICAP (G1), 1 1/16 Miles, Fillies and Mares, 3-Year-Olds and Up, Hollywood Park, 2004 Purse: $228,450

Year	Winner	Age	Jockey	Wt.	Second	Wt.	Third	Wt.	Win Value	Time	Beyer
1952	A Gleam	3	P. Moreno	112	Two Lea	117	Spanish Cream	124	16,600	1:21.60	
1953	A Gleam	4	E. LeBlanc	122	Fortune Teller	119	Spanish Cream	115	13,300	1:22.80	
1954	Flitting Past	5	R. Lunn	104	Bubbley	110	Is Proud	115	13,150	1:36.60	
1955	Countess Fleet	4	J. Longden	121	Jet Lady	109	Alibhai Lynn	123	15,050	1:09.20	
1956	Speedy Edie	4	R. Neves	113	Solid Miss	115	Island Queen	110	17,450	1:10.00	
1957	Coverit	4	R. Neves	118	Pucker Up	120	Myrtle	107	12,850	1:09.20	
1958	Born Rich	5	R. York	115	Annie-Lu-San	111	Mateka	115	12,800	1:37.40	
1959	Honeys Gem	4	W. Shoemaker	126	La Plume	111	Penumbra	115	12,950	1:35.40	
1960	Silver Spoon	4	W. Shoemaker	126	Honeys Gem	120	La Plume	110	13,200	1:34.80	
1961	Mountain Glory	5	P. Moreno	113	Tritoma	119	Wiggle II	120	13,800	1:34.60	
1962	Linita	5	J. Longden	120	Bushel-n-Peck	119	Fun House	117	16,250	1:35.20	
1963	Fortunate Isle	4	J. Leonard	111	Savaii	112	Table Mate	122	15,550	1:35.80	
1964	Jalousie II	5	R. York	120	Savaii	117	Star Maggie	115	16,600	1:35.60	
1965	Savaii	6	W. Harmatz	118	Yes Please	113	Curious Clover	121	19,400	1:35.20	
1966	Fleet Treat	3	R. Menell	110	Ormea	114	Hi Hessie	107	20,700	1:36.00	
1967	Desert Trial	4	A. Maese	125	Natashka	123	April Dawn	118	15,700	1:42.40	
1968	Princessnesian	4	L. Pincay Jr	125	Desert Law	114	Courageously	107	18,850	1:42.40	
1969	Desert Law	5	L. Pincay Jr	118	Peggy's World	111	Luz del Sol	112	19,750	1:40.80	
1970	Everything Lovely	5	F. Alvarez	111	Opening Bid	114	Shake a Shadow	114	15,850	1:35.40	
1971	Street Dancer	4	R. Rosales	110			Manta	131	17,250	1:35.80	
	Opening Bid	4	J. Lambert	114							
1972	Typecast	6	V. Tejada	123	Balcony's Babe	114	Convenience	122	26,400	1:34.20	
1973	Minstrel Miss	6	D. Pierce	118	Susan's Girl	128	Pallisima	115	38,000	1:41.80	
1974	Twixt	5	W. Passmore	123	Tallahto	121	La Zanzara	121	33,900	1:41.00	
1975	Modus Vivendi	4	D. Pierce	121	Tizna	124	Mercy Dee	111	32,100	1:42.00	
1976	Bastonera II	5	L. Pincay Jr	117	Swingtime	120	Just a Kick	121	31,600	1:42.00	
1977	Cascapedia	4	S. Hawley	126	Rocky Trip	115	Just a Kick	118	31,250	1:40.80	
1978	Taisez Vous	4	D. Pierce	127	Drama Critic	118	Sensational	121	32,150	1:41.80	
1979	Innuendo	5	D. Pierce	115	It's in the Air	112	Country Queen	121	32,700	1:41.20	
1980	Image of Reality	4	D.G. McHargue	117	It's in the Air	122	Fondre	113	36,050	1:40.20	
1981	Save Wild Life	4	C.J. McCarron	115	Princess Karenda	120	Swift Bird	115	65,700	1:42.80	
1982	Cat Girl	4	C.J. McCarron	114	Track Robbery	124	Ack's Secret	123	62,500	1:41.60	
1983	Marisma	5	K. Black	118	A Kiss for Luck	113	Sangue	123	63,100	1:42.20	
1984	Adored	4	L. Pincay Jr	119	Princess Rooney	122	Lass Trump	117	63,800	1:41.00	
1985	Adored	5	L. Pincay Jr	125	Lovlier Linda	120	Mitterand	120	73,500	1:33.60	
1986	Dontstop Themusic	6	D.G. McHargue	122	Magnificent Lindy	117	Truffles	110	63,500	1:48.80	
1987	Seldom Seen Sue	4	C.J. McCarron	117	Tiffany Lass	120	Frau Altiva	115	95,000	1:48.20	
1988	By Land By Sea	4	F. Toro	124	Invited Guest	114	Integra	121	89,200	1:43.60	
1989	Bayakoa	5	L. Pincay Jr	124	Flying Julia	113	Carita Tostada	115	91,500	1:42.00	
1990	Bayakoa	6	L. Pincay Jr	127	Fantastic Look	113	Kelly	110	89,700	1:41.20	

Year	Winner	Age	Jockey	Wt.	Second	Wt.	Third	Wt.	Win Value	Time	Beyer
1991	Brought to Mind	4	P.A. Valenzuela	118	Luna Elegante	114	Vieille Vigne	117	95,800	1:41.60	
1992	Paseana	5	C.J. McCarron	125	Re Toss	115	Fowda	119	94,200	1:41.40	102
1993	Paseana	6	C.J. McCarron	125	Bold Windy	114	Re Toss	116	94,500	1:41.60	107
1994	Andestine	4	C.J. McCarron	116	Golden Klair	119	Zarani Sidi Anna	116	94,900	1:41.40	105
1995	Pirate's Revenge	4	C.W. Antley	116	Paseana	123	Private Persuasion	116	91,000	1:41.40	106
1996	Twice the Vice	5	C.J. McCarron	120	Jewel Princess	120	Urbane	117	110,100	1:40.80	113
1997	Listening	4	A. Solis	116	Chile Chatte	114	Exotic Wood	118	95,220	1:41.20	101
1998	I Ain't Bluffing	4	C.J. McCarron	120	Fleet Lady	119	Real Connection	112	158,640	1:42.16	102
1999	Gourmet Girl	4	E. Delahoussaye	115	Yolo Lady	115	Victory Stripes	117	112,440	1:40.97	109
2000	Riboletta	5	C.J. McCarron	120	Bordelaise	117	Excellent Meeting	121	121,860	1:42.01	110
2001	Lazy Slusan	6	V. Espinoza	119	Lady Melesi	116	Feverish	118	157,980	1:42.25	103
2002	Azeri	4	M. Smith	122	Affluent	119	Collect Call	115	126,840	1:42.02	109
2003	Azeri	5	M.E. Smith	125	Enjoy	114	Tropical Blossom	111	127,080	1:41.87	109
2004	Star Parade	5	V. Espinoza	116	Quero Quero	115	Pesci	114	125,670	1:41.83	98

Beyer Index: 105.69

Distance 7 furlongs in 1952-53; 1 1/8 miles, 1986-87; 6 furlongs, 1955-57; 1 mile, 1954,1958-66, 1970-72, 1985

(EARLY TIMES) MINT JULEP HANDICAP (G3), 1 1/16 Miles (Turf), Fillies and Mares, 4-Year-Olds and Up, Churchill Downs, 2004 Purse: $168,300

Year	Winner	Age	Jockey	Wt.	Second	Wt.	Third	Wt.	Win Value	Time	Beyer
1977	Satan's Cheer	5	M. Maganello	115	Comfort Zone	117	Decided Lady	115	14,300	1:24.00	
1978	Time for Pleasure	4	T. Barrow	120	Don't Cry Barbi	119	Dear Irish	119	14,609	1:23.40	
1979	Bold Rendezvous	4	A. Fernandez	115	Likely Exchange	116	Popped Corn	116	17,908	1:25.00	
1980	Likely Exchange	6	D.E. Whited	118	Nauti Lass	119	Dearyouloveme	117	19,728	1:24.40	
1981	Lillian Russell	4	R. Hirdes Jr	118	Run Ky. Run	121	Salud	114	19,468	1:23.20	
1982	Kate's Cabin	4	E. Snell	115	Mean Martha	112	Forever Cordial	114	23,855	1:25.20	
1983	Naskra Magic	4	P. Rubbicco	114	Excitable Lady	120	Charge My Account	112	23,433	1:36.60	
1984	Lass Trump	4	G. Patterson	111	Lady Hawthorn	114	Delhousie	111	26,267	1:37.00	
1985	Stave	4	C. Woods Jr	112	Gerrie Singer	120	Switching Trick	117	21,694	1:35.00	
1986	Zenobia Empress	5	E. Fires	120	Donuts Pride	120	Ante	117	28,418	1:35.80	
1987	Thunderdome	4	S. Bass	119	Acquire	119	No Choice	119	26,247	1:37.80	
1987	Innsbruck	4	S. Hawley	114	Fantasy Lover	114	Marianna's Girl	122	21,470	1:38.00	
1988	How I Wish	4	E. Fires	113	Gaily Gaily	113	No Choice	114	36,660	1:51.00	
1989	Here's Your Silver	4	M. McDowell	115	Lt. Lao	117	Danzig's Bride	114	37,115	1:50.40	
1990	Tunita	5	R. Thibeau	114	Port St. Mary	113	Flags Waving	112	25,821	1:43.80	89
1990	Phoenix Sunshine	5	J. Deegan	116	Vanna Turns	111	Carousel Baby	111	31,476	1:43.20	
1991	Dance for Lucy	5	L. Melancon	116	Welsh Muffin	113	Super Fan	118	37,148	1:43.00	102
1992	Lady Shirl	5	P. Johnson	123	Topsa	112	Behaving Dancer	119	37,083	1:41.41	104
1993	Classic Reign	4	F.A. Arguello Jr	115	Tap Routine	113	Liz Cee	114	37,538	1:42.84	94
1994	Words of War	5	C. Marquez	117	Freewheel	116	Eurostorm	112	55,672	1:40.98	99
1995	Romy	4	J. Diaz	118	Olden Lek	114	Memories	113	54,941	1:42.69	102
1996	Bail Out Becky	4	C. Perret	118	Country Cat	117	Fluffkins	115	54,698	1:41.86	102
1997	Valor Lady	5	R.J. Albarado	114	My Secret	114	Everhope	114	71,238	1:41.20	96
	Romy (Beyer: 96) finished first but was disqualified and placed fourth										
1998	B.A. Valentine	5	F. Torres	116	Lordy Lordy	113	Mingling Glances	112	70,804	1:41.42	96
1999	Mingling Glances	5	L. Melancon	113	Formal Tango	115	Red Cat	116	70,928	1:42.59	101
2000	Pratella	5	L. Melancon	118	Silver Comic	115	Histoire Sainte	113	69,378	1:43.08	99
2001	Megans Bluff	4	C. Perret	118	Sitka	109	Good Game	116	70,432	1:42.88	97
2002	Megans Bluff	5	C. Perret	118	Cozy Island	112	Solvig	117	69,998	1:42.87	98
2003	Kiss the Devil	5	L.J. Meche	115	Quick Tip	119	Cellars Shiraz	120	104,346	1:41.73	93
2004	Stay Forever	7	E. Castro	116	Sand Springs	120	Eternal Melody	115	104,346	1:42.66	96

Beyer Index: 97.87

(ADENA STALLIONS) MISS PREAKNESS (G3), 6 Furlongs, 3-Year-Old Fillies, Pimlico Race Course, 2004 Purse: $100,000

Year	Winner	Age	Jockey	Wt.	Second	Wt.	Third	Wt.	Win Value	Time	Beyer
1986	Marion's Madel	3	C.J. McCarron	115	Zigbelle		Babbling Brook		21,060	1:12.80	
1987	Cutlasee	3	C.J. McCarron	116	I'm Out		Pelcian Bay		21,158	1:12.60	
1988	Caromine	3	C.J. McCarron	115	Light Beat		Saved by Gracer		24,911	1:13.00	
1989	Montoya	3	L. Pincay Jr	118	Another Boom				22,470	1:10.60	
					Cojinx						
1990	Love Me a Lot	3	C.J. McCarron	115	Dixie Landera		Tabs		19,170	1:11.40	
1991	Missy's Music	3	M. Pino	114	Dixie Rouge		Accent Knightly		15,975	1:11.40	
1992	Toots La Mae	3	J. Bravo	113	Missy White Oak	118	Jazzy One	121	26,505	1:11.80	75
1993	My Rosa	3	E.S. Prado	113	Fighting Jet	121	Cole Blum	121	32,175	1:11.20	89
1994	Foolish Kisses	3	E.S. Prado	113	Aly's Conquest	114	Platinum Punch	113	32,730	1:12.40	93
1995	Lilly Capote	3	G.L. Stevens	122	Broad Smile	122	Norstep	122	32,640	1:10.80	88
1996	Nic's Halo	3	R. Wilson	115	Palette Knife	115	Crafty but Sweet	122	32,655	1:11.60	86
1997	Weather Vane	3	M. Pino	122	Move	122	Cayman Sunset	122	64,740	1:11.80	84

Year	Winner	Age	Jockey	Wt.	Second	Wt.	Third	Wt.	Win Value	Time	Beyer
1998	Storm Beauty	3	C.R. Woods Jr	119	Brac Drifter	115	Hair Spray	122	45,000	1:10.80	93
1999	Hookedonthefeelin	3	G.L. Stevens	122	Silent Valay	122	Paula's Girl	122	60,000	1:11.20	90
2000	Lucky Livi	3	R. Wilson	119	Big Bambu	117	Swept Away	119	60,000	1:10.00	96
2001	Kimbralata	3	T. Dunkelberger	117	Carafe	117	Stormy Pick	122	60,000	1:11.20	93
2002	Vesta	3	M. Pino	117	Willa on the Move	117	Shameful	119	60,000	1:10.25	99
2003	Belong to Sea	3	J.J. Castellano	117	Chimichurri	122	Forever Partners	119	60,000	1:11.10	88
2004	Forest Music	3	R.A. Dominguez	115	Stephan's Angel	119	Fall Fashion	119	60,000	1:10.97	100

Beyer Index: 90.31

MODESTY HANDICAP (G3), 1 3/16 Miles (Turf), Fillies and Mares, 3-Year-Old and Up, Arlington Park 2004 Purse: $150,000

Year	Winner	Age	Jockey	Wt.	Second	Wt.	Third	Wt.	Win Value	Time	Beyer
1942	Lotopoise	3	S. Brooks	113	Questvive	113	Waygal	113	2,910	1:37.80	
1943	Burgoo Maid	3	G. Burns	111	Mar-Kell	125	Jerry Lee	109	4,475	1:27.40	
1944	Gold Princess	5	J. Higley	110	Night Shadow	112	Happy Issue	112	10,850	1:39.40	
1945	War Date	3	J. Adams	110	Night Shadow	114	Durazna	120	15,225	1:38.80	
1946	Athene	3	W. Mehrtens	111	Jack's Jill	112	Twosy	121	19,400	1:36.00	
1947	Sea Snack	4	M.N. Gonzalez	117	Miss Kimo	109	Blue Grass	115	19,600	1:11.60	
1948	Bewitch	3	H. Woodhouse	107	Tre Vit	113	Bogle	109	20,850	1:10.20	
1949	No Strings	3	F.A. Smith	101	Two Lea	111	Dandilly	108	19,150	1:10.00	
1950	Myrtle Charm	4	G. Laswell	121	Alsab's Day	121	Fabulous Shake	102	14,400	1:10.00	
1951	Sickle's Image	3	C. Swain	120	Asphalt	105	Two Rainbows	104	16,900	1:10.80	
1952	Real Delight	3	E. Arcaro	126	Sickle's Image	117	Dickie Sue	111	29,600	1:35.60	
1953	Belle Figura	4	D. Wagner	117	Gala Fete	116	Night-Phara	110	10,450	1:10.20	
1954	Sickle's Image	6	D. Dodson	118	Mimi Mine	112	Vixen Fixit	103	13,950	1:10.00	
1955	Insouciant	3	B. Fisk	111	Cajole	110	Queen Hopeful	120	13,850	1:43.40	
1956	Queen Hopeful	5	J. Adams	116	Blue Hawaii	109	Amoret	112	13,450	1:44.80	
1957	Grecian Ayr	4	L. Gilligan	109	Tremor	111	Estacion	116	13,475	1:43.60	
1958	Melody Mine	3	R.L. Barnett	108	Beautillion	118	Market Basket	122	13,500	1:10.80	
1959	A Glitter	4	C. Rogers	118	Tinkalero	120	Wayward Bird	107	9,925	1:10.00	
1960	Indian Maid	4	J.L. Rotz	123	Equifun	112	Judy Jump-Up	113	8,900	1:09.60	
1961	Indian Maid	5	J. Sellers	126	Equifun	111	Our Special Jet	109	9,325	1:09.80	
1962	Goldflower	4	H. Hinojosa	120	Gerts Image	114	Cherry Laurel	112	10,375	1:10.40	
1963	Hushaby	4	W. Hartack	117	Lucky Viola	112	Road Maid	112	9,925	1:23.00	
1964	Alecee	5	W. Blum	118	Abrogate	120	Hushaby	112	9,450	1:23.00	
1965	Isaduchess	4	K. Knapp	119	Tuzana	112	Abrogate	120	24,000	1:23.20	
1966	Margarethen	4	J. Nichols	118	Miss Rincon	114	Bea Hasty	114	12,525	1:37.40	
1966	Treasure Chest	3	J. Beebe	112	Lady Amigo	108	May's Guide	118	12,525	1:37.20	
1967	Amerivan	5	R. Turcotte	119	Ice Water	113	Turn to Talent	113	16,850	1:46.20	
1968	Ludham	4	J. Vasquez	117	Gabby Abbey	123	Doc Nan	113	13,800	1:44.40	
1981	Innocent Victim	3	R. Cox	108	Passolyn	113	Touch of Glamour	112	35,040	1:59.00	
1982	Office Wife	5	E. Fires	113	Sprite Flight	112	Touch of Glamour	117	33,750	1:58.20	
1983	Dana Calqui	5	F. Lovato Jr	114	Unknown Lady	113	Sar'h's Beauty	115	34,470	2:01.40	
1984	Jay's Sue	5	P. Day	123	Dictina	109	Pretty Perfect	113	43,719	2:01.20	
1985	Kapalua Butterfly	4	R.P. Romero	115	Trinado	116	Another Penny	111	44,265	1:55.00	
1986	Zenobia Empress	5	E. Fires	118	Navarchus	112	Flying Girl	118	53,580	1:44.00	
1987	Spruce Luck	6	D. Brumfield	114	Dancing on a Cloud	120	Autumn Glitter	114	34,080	1:51.60	
1989	Gaily Gaily	6	J.A. Krone	123	Baba Cool	117	Coolawin	115	52,740	1:58.20	
1990	Gaily Gaily	7	M.E. Smith	114	Coolawin	123	M'rsha's Dancer	114	51,405	1:55.40	98
1991	Lady Shirl	4	S.J. Sellers	120	Lyphover	114	Country Casual	114	45,000	1:56.40	97
1992	Tango Charlie	3	A.G. Sorrows Jr	114	Alcando	114	Hero's Love	117	45,000	1:58.60	95
1993	Hero's Love	5	E. Fires	120	Villandry	114	Silvered	120	60,000	1:55.20	93
1994	Assert Oneself	4	F.H. Valenzuela	115	One Dreamer	117	Seventies	115	60,000	1:56.00	98
1996	Belle Of Cozzene	4	D.R. Pettinger	114	Trick Attack	112	Naskra Colors	114	60,000	1:58.20	105
1997	War Thief	5	S.J. Sellers	116	My Secret	114	Bog Wild	117	60,000	1:57.40	101
2000	Wade for Me	5	C.A. Emigh	116	Candleinthedark	113	Wild Heart Dancing	115	60,000	1:57.06	97
2001	Ioya Two	6	M. Guidry	115	Megans Bluff	118	Solvig	116	90,000	1:55.47	98
2002	England's Legend	5	R.R. Douglas	121	Quick Tip	114	Innit	116	90,000	1:55.69	101
2003	Owsley	5	R.R. Douglas	120	Bien Nicole	119	Beret	115	90,000	1:55.06	100
2004	Bedanken	5	D.R. Pettinger	119	Aud	116	Shaconage	118	90,000	1:57.00	96

Beyer Index: 98.25

MONMOUTH BREEDERS' CUP OAKS (G2), 1 1/16 Miles, 3-Year-Old Fillies, Monmouth Park 2004 Purse: $200,000

Year	Winner	Age	Jockey	Wt.	Second	Wt.	Third	Wt.	Win Value	Time	Beyer
1871	Salina	3	Swim	107	Mary Clark	107	Mary Louise	107	1,900	2:43.50	
1872	Woodbine	3	Floyd	107	Victoria	107	Elsie	107	2,450	2:42.00	
1873	Lizzie Lucas	3	Barbee	107	Alice Mitchell	107	Sunrise	107	2,850	2:45.00	

Year	Winner	Age	Jockey	Wt.	Second	Wt.	Third	Wt.	Win Value	Time	Beyer
1874	Regardless	3	Sparling	107	Bonaventure	107	Bannarette	107	2,800	2:45.00	
1875	Ascension	3	Lakeland	107	Finework	107	Gyptis	107	2,250	2:46.25	
1876	Patience	3	Feakes	107	Explosion	107	Love Chase	107	2,700	2:48.25	
1877	Zoo-Zoo	3	Barrett	107	Aunt Betsy	107	Miss Bassett	107	2,500	2:44.25	
1879	Ferida	3	Hughes	113	Bonnie Leaf	113	Scotilla	113	2,100	2:16.00	
1880	Nancy	3	Hughes	113	Glidelia	113	Bye-and-Bye	113	2,700	2:19.25	
1881	Thora	3	Donohue	113	Aella	113	Spark	113	2,200	2:14.50	
1882	Hiawasse	3	Feakes	113	Amazon	113	Bonella	113	2,790	2:23.00	
1883	Miss Woodford	3	McLaughlin	113	Carnation	113	Caramel	113	3,100	2:20.50	
1884	Duchess	3	Donohue	113	Water Lilly	113	Tolu	113	2,890	2:14.00	
1885	Wanda	3	Onley	113	Maumee	113			2,690	2:14.25	
1886	Dew Drop	3	McLaughlin	113	Charity	113			2,890	2:10.75	
1887	Firenze	3	Garrison	114	Almy	113	Lady Primrose	113	3,540	2:12.50	
1888	Los Angeles	3	Hayward	113	Belle d'Or	108	Bella B.	114	4,300	2:15.25	
1889	Senorita	3	Hamilton	108	Fides	113	Meriden	109	3,900	2:16.50	
1890	Her Highness	3	Hamiton	113	Gloaming	114	Flora Ban	103	5,040	2:15.00	
1891	Nellie Bly	3	Taral	114	Kildeer	112	Reckon	117	4,620	2:16.25	
1892	Yorkville Belle	3	Murphy	117	Anna B.	110	Alliquipa	110	3,710	2:08.25	
1893	Augusta Belle	3	Lamley	110	Lady Violet	110	Afternoon	117	3,040	2:10.60	
1946	Dorothy Brown	3	E. Guerin	113	Hypnotic	121	Easy Reeling	113	8,660	1:45.20	
1947	First Flight	3	E. Arcaro	117	Frantie's Bid	113	Whipsaw	113	9,000	1:46.00	
1948	Compliance	3	J. Stout	113	Paddleduck	113	Watermill	121	8,050	1:45.00	
1949	Adile	3	E. Arcaro	114	Delta Queen	113	Red Camelia	113	8,500	1:46.00	
1950	Siama	3	E. Arcaro	121	Ouija	113	Honey's Gal	113	8,900	1:45.20	
1951	Ruddy	3	T. Atkinson	121	Pretty Pattern	113	Shy Bim	113	13,750	1:48.00	
1952	La Corredora	3	I. Hanford	117	No Score	117	Devilkin	113	18,950	1:46.00	
1953	Grecian Queen	3	N. Shuk	121	Sabette	113	Arab Actress	121	41,200	1:51.20	
1954	Evening Out	3	E. Arcaro	117	Clear Dawn	121	June Fete	113	44,900	1:50.20	
1955	Misty Morn	3	E. Arcaro	121	Blue Sparkler	121	Manotick	121	43,700	1:50.60	
1956	Levee	3	H. Woodhouse	121	Triple Jay	121	Dotted Line	121	38,500	1:48.80	
1957	Romanita	3	J. Skelly	117	Evening Time	121	Market Basket	121	38,205	1:50.20	
1958	A Glitter	3	I. Valenzuela	121	Spar Maid	113	Craftiness	113	36,190	1:52.40	
1959	Royal Native	3	J. Culmone	113	Indian Maid	117	Silver Spoon	121	35,150	1:50.60	
1960	Teacation	3	W. Blum	113	Refute	117	Rash Statement	121	37,035	1:49.40	
1961	My Portrait	3	R. Broussard	121	Primonetta	121	Funloving	121	36,920	1:48.80	
1962	Firm Policy	3	J. Sellers	113	Royal Patrice	113	Fortunate Isle	113	37,180	1:49.80	
1963	Lamb Chop	3	H. Grant	118	Spicy Living	121	Smart Deb	118	36,465	1:51.60	
1964	Miss Cavandish	3	H. Grant	118	Castle Forbes	118	Silwall	114	36,562	1:50.80	
1965	Summer Scandal	3	G. Patterson	112	Terentia	116	Marshua	118	37,277	1:50.60	
1966	Natashka	3	W. Shoemaker	116	Indian Sunlight	118	Justakiss	118	37,472	1:51.40	
1967	Quillo Queen	3	E. Cardone	121	Secret Promise	112	Swiss Cheese	121	37,797	1:52.20	
1968	Dark Mirage	3	M. Ycaza	121	Singing Rain	118	Guest Room	116	35,522	1:51.40	
1969	Gallant Bloom	3	B. Baeza	121	Hail to Patsy	118	Around the Horn	111	35,197	1:50.80	
1970	Kilts n Kapers	3	G. Patterson	116	Sweet Mist	114	Office Queen	121	37,342	1:50.40	
1971	Forward Gal	3	M. Hole	119	Alma North	114	For No Reason	112	37,505	1:49.20	
1972	Summer Guest	3	R. Turcotte	121	Mindy Malone	114	Wanda	121	36,725	1:50.20	
1973	Desert Vixen	3	M. Hole	114	Ladies Agreement	111	Lady Love	111	37,472	1:49.00	
1974	Honky Star	3	W. Blum	117	Kudara	117	Raisela	117	38,642	1:49.40	
1975	Aunt Jin	3	C.H. Marquez	119	Let Me Linger	112	Sarsar	121	35,295	1:49.20	
1976	Revidere	3	J. Vasquez	121	Javamine	112	Quacker	114	36,237	1:50.60	
1977	Small Raja	3	M. Solomone	121	Herecomesthebride	117	Suede Shoe	114	35,978	1:49.60	
1978	Sharp Belle	3	D.B. Thomas	119	Mucchina	119	Jevalin	117	35,783	1:52.40	
1979	Burn's Return	3	J. Vasquez	117	Heavenly Ade	114	Dominant Dream	114	35,718	1:48.80	
1980	Rose of Morn	3	D. Brumfield	114	Weber City Miss	121	Sami Sutton	117	33,030	1:50.40	
1981	Prismatical	3	D. Brumfield	117	Stunning Native	112	Privacy	117	49,500	1:49.80	
1982	Christmas Past	3	J. Vasquez	121	Milingo	119	Mademoiselle Forli	112	67,050	1:49.40	
1983	Quixotic Lady	3	E. Maple	116	Am Capable	114	Pop Rock	116	64,770	1:50.40	
1984	Life's Magic	3	J. Velasquez	121	Flippers	118	Cassowary	112	94,050	1:50.00	
1985	Golden Horde	3	W.H. McCauley	116	Koluctoo's Jill	121	Tabayour	118	94,380	1:48.00	
1986	Fighter Fox	3	W.H. McCauley	114	Toes Knows	114	Dynamic Star	118	97,170	1:49.60	
1987	Without Feathers	3	C.W. Antley	116	Single Blade	121	Grecian Flight	121	66,240	1:48.00	
1988	Maplejinsky	3	C.W. Antley	113	Make Change	114	Mother of Eight	114	102,000	1:53.60	
1989	Dream Deal	3	C. Perret	114	Some Romance	121	Top of My Life	121	90,000	1:49.20	
1990	Pampered Star	3	J.C. Ferrer	121	Valay Maid	121	Jefforee	112	90,000	1:52.40	
1991	Fowda	3	R. Migliore	121	Shared Interest	114	Nalees Pin	116	90,000	1:50.40	93
1992	Diamond Duo	3	T.G. Turner	121	Secretly	122			90,000	1:51.40	91
					C.C.'s Return	114					
1993	Jacody	3	T.G. Turner	121	Deputy Jane West	121	Sheila's Revenge	114	90,000	1:50.60	104
1994	Two Altazano	3	C. Perret	121	Stellarina	118	Cavada	121	90,000	1:52.00	98
1995	Kathie's Colleen	3	J.S. McAleney	112	Gal in a Ruckus	121	Country Cat	121	90,000	1:51.40	96
1996	Top Secret	3	J. Bravo	114	Yanks Music	121	Mesabi Maiden	121	120,000	1:42.20	101
1997	Blushing K. D.	3	L.J. Meche	121	Holiday Ball	116	Snowy Apparition	121	120,000	1:41.80	107
1998	Kirby's Song	3	T.K. Kabel	121	Santaria	114	Brave Deed	112	120,000	1:43.20	103

Year	Winner	Age	Jockey	Wt.	Second	Wt.	Third	Wt.	Win Value	Time	Beyer
1999	Silverbulletday	3	J.D. Bailey	121	Boom Town Girl	121	Bag Lady Jane	116	150,000	1:43.00	102
2000	Spain	3	J.A. Velez Jr	114	North Lake Jane	116	Prized Stamp	114	150,000	1:42.78	97
2001	Unbridled Elaine	3	E.M. Coa	121	Unrestrained	112	Indy Glory	114	150,000	1:51.02	103
2002	Magic Storm	3	E.L. King Jr	112	Alternate	114	Bronze Aututmn	114	150,000	1:51.17	93
2004	Capeside Lady	3	C.P. DeCarlo	115	Hopelessly Devoted	118	Habiboo	115	120,000	1:42.18	106

Beyer Index: 99.54

Not run in 2003.

MONROVIA HANDICAP (Not graded for 2004), 6 1/2 Furlongs (Off the Turf), Fillies and Mares, 3-Year-Olds and Up, Santa Anita, 2004 Purse: $113,550

Year	Winner	Age	Jockey	Wt.	Second	Wt.	Third	Wt.	Win Value	Time	Beyer
1968	Mellow Marsh	5	M. Vanenzuela	113	Pink Pigeon	115	Telepathy	112	16,900	1:13.40	
1969	Morgaise	4	D. Pierce	121	Desert Law	118	Grey Cricket	110	13,500	1:22.20	
1970	Beautiful Dream	5	J. Lambert	118	Pacific Cross	114	Lovers Quarrel	120	14,750	1:16.20	
1971	Atomic Wings	4	R. Kilborn	112	Formal Marriage	116	Sh'ke a Sh'd'w	114	17,850	1:13.40	
1972	Mia Mood	4	V. Tejada	113	Crowning Glory	119	Generous Portion	118	20,350	1:13.00	
1973	Tizna	4	F. Toro	119	Generous Portion	120	Soul Mate	120	22,700	1:13.80	
1974	Viva la Vivi	4	D. Pierce	118	Impressive Style	120	Charger's Star	113	17,800	1:15.00	
1975	Special Goddess	4	S. Hawley	116	Charger's Star	115	Miss Musket	124	20,700	1:13.80	
1976	Winter Solstice	4	J. Lambert	117	Miss Tokyo	121	Exotic Age	115	20,300	1:17.60	
1977	Winter Solstice	5	M. Sellers	119	Nana Lee	116	Olive Wreath	113	27,600	1:13.60	
1978	Little Happiness	4	L. Pincay Jr	116	Perils of Pauline	115	Harvest Girl	119	26,200	1:16.00	
1979	Camarado	4	W. Shoemaker	119	Pet Label	115	Sister Julie	115	22,900	1:15.40	
1979	Palmistry	4	C.J. McCarron	114	Sing Back	113	Pressing Date	114	22,500	1:15.20	
1980	Fondre	5	F. Olivares	113	Powder Room	117	Celine	118	27,500	1:15.20	
1981	Kilijaro	5	M. Castaneda	127	Love You Dear	115	She Can't Miss	119	34,950	1:12.40	
1982	Cat Girl	4	C.J. McCarron	117	Excitable Lady	122	Chateau Dancer	117	41,250	1:14.60	
1983	Matching	5	R. Sibille	123	Irish O'Brien	115	Night Fire	115	40,600	1:13.20	
1984	Tangent	4	J.A. Garcia	117	Irish O'Brien	115	Frieda Frame	119	41,750	1:14.60	
1985	Lina Cav'leri	5	E. Delahoussaye	121	Air Distingue	117	Tangent	121	39,650	1:14.00	
1986	Water Crystals	5	G.L. Stevens	116	Baroness Direct	120	Solva	116	40,100	1:15.60	
1987	Sari's Heroine	4	P.A. Valenzuela	117	Lichi	116	Aberuschka	124	38,400	1:15.00	
1988	Aberuschka	6	G.L. Stevens	121	Pen Bal Lady	118	Acromacor	114	50,050	1:14.60	
1989	Daloma	5	F.H. Valenzuela	117	Valdemosa	116	Sadie B. Fast	116	49,550	1:16.20	
1990	Down Again	6	C.A. Black	117	Sexy Slew	111	Hot Novel	116	50,520	1:13.00	101
1991	Wedding B'quet	4	K.J. Desormeaux	115	Linda Card	118	Flower Girl	116	51,875	1:13.80	
1992	Middlef'rk Rapids	4	P.A. Valenzuela	116	Remarkably Easy	115	Crystal Gazing	121	51,150	1:12.40	100
1993	Glen Kate	6	C.A. Black	118	Bel's Starlet	122	Heart of Joy	121	48,650	1:12.80	103
1994	Mamselle Bebette	4	C.S. Nakatani	117	Shuggleswon	114	Kalita Melody	117	49,650	1:15.20	95
1995	Rabiadella	4	P.A. Valenzuela	117	Dezibelle's Star	114	Las Meninas	120	47,450	1:14.80	99
1996	Klassy Kim	5	G.F. Almeida	116	Ski Dancer	116	Baby Diamonds	114	65,650	1:14.40	97
1997	Grab The Prize	5	A. Solis	116	Finite E. F.	111	Evil's Pic	116	66,900	1:16.80	95
1998	Madame Pandit	5	E. Delahoussaye	118	Ski Dancer	115	Dixie Pearl	117	65,700	1:15.80	101
1999	Desert Lady	4	C.S. Nakatani	116	Sweet Mazarine	118	Supercilious	119	65,100	1:14.40	89
1999	Show Me The Stage	3	K.J. Desormeaux	117	Chinchim	116	Honest Lady	114	64,140	1:15.00	100
2000	Evening Promise	4	K.J. Desormeaux	120	Squall Linda	113	New Heaven	119	68,640	1:12.62	99
2001	Paga	4	M.E. Smith	117	Twin Set	115	Impeachable	115	70,890	1:15.09	97
2002	Lil Sister Stich	5	L. Pincay Jr	115	Pina Colada	115	I'm the Business	116	68,820	1:13.81	94
2003	Icantgoforthat	4	T. Baze	114	Polygreen	116	Spring Star	119	65,580	1:13.07	97
2004	Resplendency	3	C. Fusilier	112	Puxa Saco	115	Market Garden	115	68,130	1:15.34	99

Beyer Index: 97.73

Off the turf in 2004.

MORVICH HANDICAP (G3), About 6 1/2 Furlongs (Turf), 3-Year-Olds and Up, Santa Anita, 2004 Purse: $100,000

Year	Winner	Age	Jockey	Wt.	Second	Wt.	Third	Wt.	Win Value	Time	Beyer
1994	Rotsaluck	3	F. Valenzuela	115	D'Hallevant	118	Didyme	115	47,925	1:13.66	115
1995	Score Quick	4	G. Almeida	113	Dramatic Gold	120	Fu Man Slew	114	60,700	1:14.60	111
1996	Comininalittlehot	5	K. Desormeaux	117	Wild Zone	116	Wavy Run	116	65,100	1:11.57	107
1997	Reality Road	5	C. Nakatani	115	Latin Dancer	116	Torch Rouge	115	60,000	1:13.60	107
1998	Musafi	4	G. Gomez	117	Fabulous Guy	114	Expelled	119	60,000	1:14.54	104
1999	Riviera	5	E. Ramsammy	118	Kahal	114	Howmaddouwantit	121	66,840	1:12.80	98
2000	El Cielo	6	J. Valdivia Jr	119	Kahal	119	Montemiro	116	67,020	1:12.00	107
2001	El Cielo	7	J. Valdivia Jr	123	Speak in Passing	116	Islander	115	64,680	1:11.46	111
2002	Master Belt	4	T.C. Baze	114	I Love Silver	116	Kachamandi	117	67,020	1:12.26	104
2003	King Robyn	3	A. Solis	117	Medicis	116	Geronimo	115	66,480	1:13.22	102
2004	Leroidesanimaux	4	J.K. Court	117	De Valmont	115	Cayoke	116	60,000	1:11.76	111

Beyer Index: 107.00

For previous runnings, refer to 1994 Manual.

MOTHER GOOSE (G1), 1 1/8 Miles, 3-Year-Old Fillies, Belmont Park, 2004 Purse: $300,000

Year	Winner	Age	Jockey	Wt.	Second	Wt.	Third	Wt.	Win Value	Time	Beyer
1957	Outer Space	3	W. Lester	112	Ambulance	112	Gold Finery	112	20,450	1:42.60	
1958	Idun	3	W. Hartack	118	Lopar	112	Lea Moon	113	18,420	1:43.60	
1959	Quill	3	P.J. Bailey	124	Toluene	118	Geechee Lou	112	18,127	1:49.40	
1960	Berlo	3	E. Guerin	114	Chalvedele	111	Make Sail	121	56,794	1:50.60	
1962	Cicada	3	W. Shoemaker	121	Firm Policy	121	Royal Patrice	121	56,014	1:50.00	
1963	Spicy Living	3	J. Combest	121	Smart Deb	121	Lamb Chop	121	59,621	1:50.40	
1964	Sceree	3	L. Adams	121	Face the Facts	121	Just Fancy That	121	58,646	1:50.80	
1965	Cordially	3	B. Baeza	121	What a Treat	121	Up Oars	121	63,180	1:51.60	
1966	Lady Pitt	3	W. Blum	121	Marking Time	121	Prides Profile	121	56,989	1:50.40	
1967	Furl Sail	3	J. Vasquez	121	Quillo Queen	121	Muse	121	63,570	1:49.60	
1968	Dark Mirage	3	M. Ycaza	121	Guest Room	121	Parida	121	55,672	1:49.40	
1969	Shuvee	3	J. Davidson	121	Hail to Patsy	121	Restless Tornado	121	56,599	1:50.20	
1970	Office Queen	3	C.H. Marquez	121	Cathy Honey	121	Missile Belle	121	77,756	1:49.80	
1971	Deceit	3	J.L. Rotz	121	Graffitti	121	Forward Gal	121	53,955	1:50.20	
1972	Wanda	3	J. Velasquez	121	Susan's Girl	121	Summer Guest	121	50,760	1:48.40	
1973	Windy's Daughter	3	E. Belmonte	121	Lady Love	121	North Broadway	121	52,965	1:48.40	
1974	Chris Evert	3	J. Velasquez	121	Maud Muller	121	Quaze Quilt	121	53,775	1:48.60	
1975	Ruffian	3	J. Vasquez	121	Sweet Old Girl	121	Sun and Snow	121	50,220	1:47.80	
1976	Girl in Love	3	J. Cruguet	121	Optimistic Gal	121	Ancient Fables	121	48,510	1:48.80	
1977	Road Princess	3	J. Cruguet	121	Mrs. Warren	121	Cum Laude Laurie	121	51,480	1:48.80	
1978	Caesar's Wish	3	D.R. Wright	121	Lakeville Miss	121	Tempest Queen	121	48,600	1:47.60	
1979	Davona Dale	3	J. Velasquez	121	Eloquent	121	Plankton	121	63,960	1:48.80	
1980	Sugar and Spice	3	J. Fell	121	Bold 'n Determined	121	Erin's Word	121	68,040	1:49.60	
1981	Wayward Lass	3	C.B. Asmussen	121	Heavenly Cause	121	Banner Gala	121	66,720	1:48.80	
1982	Cupecoy's Joy	3	A. Santiago	121	Christmas Past	121	Blush With Pride	121	69,120	1:48.40	
1983	Able Money	3	A. Graell	121	High Schemes	121	Far Flying	121	84,150	1:49.20	
1984	Life's Magic	3	J. Velasquez	121	Miss Oceana	121	Wild Applause	121	127,620	1:48.80	
1985	Mom's Command	3	A. Fuller	121	Le L'Argent	121	Willowy Mood	121	109,800	1:49.60	
1986	Life at the Top	3	J.A. Santos	121	Dynamic Star	121	Family Style	121	132,300	1:49.60	
1987	Fiesta Gal	3	A. Cordero Jr	121	Grecian Flight	121	Chic Shirine	121	150,240	1:50.20	
1988	Goodbye Halo	3	J. Velasquez	121	Make Change	121	Aptostar	121	142,320	1:49.80	
1989	Open Mind	3	A. Cordero Jr	121	Gorgeous	121	Nite of Fun	121	136,320	1:47.40	
1990	Go for Wand	3	R.P. Romero	121	Charon	121	Stella Madrid	121	136,500	1:48.80	104
1991	Meadow Star	3	J.D. Bailey	121	Lite Light	121	Nalees Pin	121	120,000	1:48.80	100
1992	Turnback the Alarm	3	C.W. Antley	121	Easy Now	121	Queen of Triumph	121	120,000	1:48.80	95
1993	Sky Beauty	3	M.E. Smith	121	Dispute	121	Silky Feather	121	120,000	1:49.60	102
1994	Lakeway	3	K.J. Desormeaux	121	Cinnamon Sugar	121	Inside Information	121	120,000	1:46.40	106
1995	Serena's Song	3	G.L. Stevens	121	Golden Bri	121	Forested	121	120,000	1:50.20	101
1996	Yanks Music	3	J.R. Velazquez	121	Escena	121	Cara Rafaela	121	120,000	1:47.80	100
1997	Ajina	3	M.E. Smith	121	Sharp Cat	121	Tomisue's Delight	121	120,000	1:48.40	101
1998	Jersey Girl	3	M.E. Smith	121	Keeper Hill	121	Banshee Breeze	121	120,000	1:47.77	103
1999	Dreams Gallore	3	R.J. Albarado	121	Oh What a Windfall	121	Better Than Honour	121	150,000	1:48.69	101
2000	Secret Status	3	P. Day	121	Jostle	121	Finder's Fee	121	150,000	1:48.03	102
2001	Fleet Renee	3	J.R. Velazquez	121	Real Cozzy	121	Exogenous	121	150,000	1:47.19	105
2002	Nonsuch Bay	3	J. Bailey	121	Chamrousse	121	Seba	121	150,000	1:49.09	93
2003	Spoken Fur	3	J.D. Bailey	121	Yell	121	Final Round	121	180,000	1:50.41	104
2004	Stellar Jayne	3	R.J. Albarado	121	Ashado	121	Island Sand	121	180,000	1:48.13	100

Beyer Index: 101.13

Distance 1 1/16 miles prior to 1959. Run at Aqueduct 1963-67, 1969, 1975

MR. PROSPECTOR HANDICAP (G3), 6 Furlongs, 3-Year-Olds and Up, Gulfstream Park 2004 Purse: $100,000

Year	Winner	Age	Jockey	Wt.	Second	Wt.	Third	Wt.	Win Value	Time	Beyer
1994	Binalong	5	J.D. Bailey	116	I Can't Believe		Golden Pro		30,000	1:09.60	108
1995	Sweet Beast	5	M.Smith	118	Exclusive Praline		Sweet Reality		30,000	1:09.20	110
1996	Meadow Monster	5	R.Wilson	114	Lord Carson	119	Ponche	118	30,000	1:09.40	117
1997	Punch Line	7	P.Day	116	Appealling Skier	122	Western Warrior	113	45,000	1:08.40	114
1998	Rare Rock	5	P.Day	116	Heckofaralph	115	Banjo	114	45,000	1:08.60	112
1999	Cowboy Cop	5	P. Day	114	Good and Tough	115	Mint	115	45,000	1:08.80	113
2000	Mountain Top	5	J.A. Santos	115	Lifeisawhirl	112	Silver Season	115	45,000	1:10.80	96
2001	Instintaj	5	J.D. Bailey	116	Miners Gamble	115	Smokin Pete	115	60,000	1:09.63	105
2002	Hook and Ladder	5	J.R. Velazquez	116	Kipperscope	114	Red's Honor	114	60,000	1:09.69	111
2003	Baileys Edge	6	G. Boulanger	114	Friendly Frolic	114	Out of Fashion	115	60,000	1:09.95	99
2004	Cajun Beat	4	C.H. Velasquez	121	Gygistar	118	Deer Lake	115	60,000	1:09.06	105

Beyer Index: 108.18

Run as Hallandale Handicap, 1946–2000. For previous runnings, refer to 1994 Manual.

MRS. REVERE (G2), 1 1/16 Miles (Turf), 3-Year-Old Fillies, Churchill Downs, 2004 Purse: $171,150

Year	Winner	Age	Jockey	Wt.	Second	Wt.	Third	Wt.	Win Value	Time	Beyer
1991	Spanish Parade	3	P. Day	117	Liz Cee		Savethelastdance		37,400	1:46.00	97
1992	Mckaymackenna	3	J. Velasquez	119	Spinning Round	122	Aquilegia	117	56,200	1:45.04	95
1993	Weekend Madness	3	C. Woods Jr	117	Flower Circle	117	Amal Hyati	122	74,685	1:46.32	94
1994	Mariah's Storm	3	R. Lester	122	Avie's Fancy	119	Bear Truth	119	75,400	1:43.99	96
1995	Petrouchka	3	D. Penna	122	Christmas Gift	122	Ms. Isadora	117	75,725	1:44.20	96
1996	Maxzene	3	J.A. Krone	117	Fasta	117	Turkappeal	119	72,354	1:43.78	92
1997	Parade Queen	3	P. Day	122	Mystery Code	117	Starry Dreamer	122	108,624	1:45.46	98
1998	Anguilla	3	P. Day	119	Darling Alice	119	White Beauty	119	107,601	1:45.60	93
1999	Silver Comic	3	L. Melancon	115	St. Clair Ridge	119	Circle of Gold	119	108,345	1:45.00	95
2000	Megans Bluff	3	M. Guidry	122	Uncharted Haven	119	Impending Bear	119	107,973	1:43.37	97
2001	Snow Dance	3	C. Perret	122	Stylish	115	Cozy Island	111	106,950	1:42.86	93
2002	Caught in the Rain	3	E.L. King Jr	119	Glia	119	Bedanken	122	107,694	1:46.25	95
2003	Hoh Buzzard	3	R. Fogelsonger	120	Aud	120	Gamble to Victory	116	108,903	1:45.01	95
2004	River Belle	3	K. Fallon	120	Lenatareese	120	Cape Town Lass	114	106,113	1:44.59	92

Beyer Index: 94.86

MERVYN H. MUNIZ JR MEMORIAL HANDICAP (G2), About 1 1/8 Miles (Turf), 4-Year-Olds and Up, Fair Grounds, 2004 Purse: $500,000

Year	Winner	Age	Jockey	Wt.	Second	Wt.	Third	Wt.	Win Value	Time	Beyer
1992	Slick Groom		K. Leblanc	112	Little Bro Lantis	113	Brownsboro	117	31,590	1:52.60	90
1993	Coaxing Matt		E. Martin Jr	114	Dixie Poker Ace	120	Spending Record	115	47,010	1:50.80	97
1994	Pride of Summer		R. King Jr		Alpine Choice	114	Empire Pool	116	76,425	1:49.40	97
1994	Snake Eyes		B. Bartram	115	Yukon Robbery	115	Cozzene's Prince	122	76,305	1:49.40	97
							Dipotamos	111			
1995	Earl Of Barking		G.Almeida	115	Kazabaiyn	114	Coaxing Matt	113	93,375	1:52.00	103
1996	Kazabaiyn	6	K.Desormeaux	113	Party Season	116	Coaxing Matt	112	93,195	1:51.51	102
1997	Always A Classic	4	Martin E. M. Jr	114	Rainbow Blues	120	Snake Eyes	118	131,970	1:54.80	107
1998	Joyeux Danseur	5	Albarado R. J.	121	Martiniquais	118	Hollie's Chief	113	223,980	1:49.20	112
1999	Lord Smith	4	Gomez G. K.	117	Hawksley Hill	122	Chorwon	116	398,160	1:51.20	106
2000	Brave Act	6	C.B. Asmussen	121	Where's Taylot	113	Chester House	114	360,000	1:48.98	107
2001	Tijiyr	5	R.J. Albarado	110	Northcote Road	115	King Cugat	121	360,000	1:50.72	108
2002	Sarafan	5	C.S. Nakatani	116	Beat Hollow	115	Even the Score	116	420,000	1:48.88	105
2003	Candid Glen	6	E.J. Perrodin	114	Rouvres	115	Freefourinternet	115	390,000	1:51.15	101
2004	Mystery Giver	6	R.J. Albarado	120	Herculated	116	Skate Away	117	300,000	1:48.29	105

Beyer Index: 102.64

Run as Explosive Bid Handicap prior to 2004

MY CHARMER HANDICAP (G3), 1 1/8 Miles (Turf), Fillies and Mares, 3-Year-Olds and Up, Calder Race Course, 2004 Purse: $100,000

Year	Winner	Age	Jockey	Wt.	Second	Wt.	Third	Wt.	Win Value	Time	Beyer
1984	Our Reverie	3	G. St. Leon	114	Id Am Fac	114	Break In	110	13,927	1:47.20	
1984	Burst of Colors	4	J.A. Santos	116	Ava Romance	111	Cosmic Sea Queen	115	13,928	1:47.60	
1985	Power Break	4	J.A. Santos	116	Duty Dance	117	Dictina	117	20,555	1:47.50	
1985	Shocker T.	3	G. St. Leon	119	Erin's Dunlop	117	Spruce Luck	112	20,675	1:48.80	
1986	Donna's Dolly	4	M. Lee	112	Fritzie Bay	114	Thirty Zip	113	31,010	1:55.00	
1988	Princely Proof	5	R. Breen	113	Travelin Lieber	112	Judy's Red Shoes	114	33,870	1:46.20	
1988	Fama	5	J. Pezua	111	Singular Bequest	116	Ladanum	115	24,570	1:44.50	
1989	Sunny Issues	3	W. Guerra	109	Beauty Cream	119	Miss Unameable		28,830	1:45.40	
1989	Judy's Red Shoes	5	D. Valiente	117	Orange Motif	113	Chores at Dawn	113	29,130	1:45.60	
1990	Princess Mora	3	M. Gonzalez	111	Coolawin	118	Yestday's Kisses	115	36,000	1:47.60	
1991	Homeland	4	H. Castillo Jr	111	Seaquay	112	Calm Dancer	114	27,975	1:45.40	
1991	Primetime North	3	W. Ramos	112	Igmaar	112	Be Exclusive	113	27,825	1:45.60	
1992	Lady Shirl	5	E. Fires	120	Ratings	115	Seaquay	111	51,150	1:44.60	97
1993	Explosive Kate	5	D. Penna	118	Mia Bird Too	113	Kiwi Mint	114	30,000	1:46.40	93
1993	Julie La Rousse	4	J.D. Bailey	120	Marshua's River	114	Highland Crystal	115	30,000	1:45.60	98
1994	Chickasha	4	R. Lopez	115	Marshua's River	113	Always Nettie	114	30,000	1:47.20	94
1994	Caress	3	R.G. Davis	114	Putthepowdertoit	114	Cox Orange	116	60,000	1:50.60	101
1995	Danish	4	J.Santos	116	Cox Orange	119	Alice Springs	123	60,000	1:46.40	96
1996	Romy	5	F.Torres	114	Delta Love	114	Ms. mostly	115	60,000	1:45.60	96
1997	Overcharger	5	J.Rivera II	116	Dance Clear	113	Hero's Pride	116	60,000	1:48.00	99
1998	Colcon	5	J.Bailey	118	Cuando	117	Winfama	117	60,000	1:50.51	101
1999	Crystal Symphony	3	C. Velazquez	114	Winfama	114	Khumba Mela	120	60,000	1:47.60	90
2000	Wild Heart Dancing	4	J.F. Chavez	116	Megans Bluff	116	Orange Sunset	114	60,000	1:47.58	98
	Megans Bluff finished first but was disqualified and placed second										
2001	Batique	5	J.F. Chavez	116	Please Sign In	114	Wander Man	114	60,000	1:49.85	95
2002	Wander Mom	4	E.M. Coa	114	Strawberry Blonde	114	Babae	121	60,000	1:48.43	96
2003	New Economy	5	R.B. Homeister Jr	115	Something Ventured	116	Ivanavinalot	113	60,000	1:46.97	96
2004	Something Ventured	5	J.R. Velazquez	115	Snowdrops	115	Changing World	117	60,000	1:46.79	98

Beyer Index: 96.53

NASHUA (G3), 1 Mile, 2-Year-Olds, Aqueduct, 2004 Purse: $109,500

Year	Winner	Age	Jockey	Wt.	Second	Wt.	Third	Wt.	Win Value	Time	Beyer
1975	Lord Henribee	2	E. Maple	115	Cojak	120	Expletive Deleted	115	33,030	1:35.80	
1976	Nearly on Time	2	J. Vasquez	114	Ruthie's Native	114	Upper Nile	114	22,005	1:35.60	
1977	Quadratic	2	E. Maple	119	No Sir	114	Quip	114	21,975	1:35.40	
1978	Instrument Landing	2	J. Fell	114	Miroman	114	Bold Ruckus	117	26,520	1:37.00	
1979	Googolplex	2	L. Pincay Jr	117	Thanks to Tony	114	Comptroller	114	32,550	1:36.40	
1980	A Run	2	C.J. McCarron	114	Copper Mine	114	Triocala	114	35,460	1:37.20	
1981	Our Escapade	2	D. MacBeth	114	John's Gold	114	Hostage	114	35,460	1:37.60	
1982	I Enclose	2	R. Hernandez	114	Loose Cannon	114	Moment of Joy	114	35,280	1:36.80	
1983	Don Rickles	2	A. Cordero Jr	114	Arabian Gift	114	Raja's Shark	114	34,800	1:38.40	
1984	Stone White	2	R.G. Davis	119	Banner Bob	117	Old Main	114	71,550	1:38.20	
1985	Raja's Revenge	2	R.G. Davis	117	Royal Doulton	117	Bordeaux Bob	114	56,610	1:44.40	
1986	Bold Summit	2	C.W. Antley	114	Drachma	114	Perdition's Son	114	72,360	1:12.40	
1987	Cougarized	2	J.A. Santos	117	Blew By Em	119	Chicot County	117	104,160	1:46.00	
1988	Traskwood	2	A. Cordero Jr	117	Doc's Leader	119	Triple Buck	117	63,240	1:45.20	
1989	Champagneforashley	2	J. Vasquez	119	Armed for Peace	114	Flathorn	114	66,480	1:45.20	
1990	Kyle's Our Man	2	J.D. Bailey	114	Oregon	114	Vouch for Me	117	55,980	1:45.40	93
1991	Pine Bluff	2	C. Perret	124	Speakerphone	114	Best Decorated	114	75,960	1:46.00	98
1992	Dalhart	2	M.E. Smith	114	Rohwer	114	Peace Baby	114	74,640	1:44.60	99
1993	Popol's Gold	2	W.H. McCauley	114	Personal Merit	117	Sonny's Bruno	114	74,880	1:46.60	84
1994	Devious Course	2	F.T. Alvarado	114	Mighty Magee	112	Old Tascosa	122	65,580	1:37.40	88
1996	Jules	2	J. A.Santos	114	Shammy Davis	114	Sal's Drifter	114	68,340	1:36.80	95
1997	Coronado's Quest	2	M.E. Smith	122	Not Tricky	117	Dice Dancer	119	65,100	1:37.00	89
1998	Doneraile Court	2	J.D. Bailey	115	Successful Appeal	122	Exiled Groom	113	66,600	1:36.00	97
1999	Mass Market	2	M.E. Smith	117	Polish Miner	114	Parade Leader	117	67,020	1:38.60	88
2000	Ommadon	2	A.T. Gryder	115	Windsor Castle	115	Griffinite	115	67,920	1:36.74	99
2001	Listen Here	2	J.D. Bailey	117	Monthir	115	Thunder Days	115	65,680	1:37.61	95
2002	Added Edge	2	P. Husbands	122	Outer Reef	116	Boston Bull	122	65,820	1:36.77	98
2003	Read the Footnotes	2	J.D. Bailey	118	Paddington	120	Who Is Chris G.	116	67,860	1:36.48	92
2004	Rockport Harbor	2	S. Elliott	118	Defer	116	Better Than Bonds	116	65,700	1:36.67	84

Beyer Index: 92.79

NASSAU COUNTY BREEDERS' CUP (G2), 7 Furlongs, 3-Year-Old Fillies, Belmont Park 2004 Purse: $195,000

Year	Winner	Age	Jockey	Wt.	Second	Wt.	Third	Wt.	Win Value	Time	Beyer
1996	Star de Lady Ann	3	J.F. Chavez	114	Stop Traffic	114	JJ'sdream	121	49,590	1:22.00	89
1997	Alyssum	3	J.A. Santos	116	Screamer	121	Sinclara	112	49,515	1:22.80	98
1998	Jersey Girl	3	M.E. Smith	121	Countess Diana	118	Foil	114	48,832	1:22.60	97
1999	Oh What a Windfall	3	M.E. Smith	118	Paved in Gold	118	Things Change	118	66,480	1:23.59	83
2000	C'est L'Amour	3	E.S. Prado	115	Tugger	114	Miss Inquistive	119	90,000	1:23.46	97
2001	Cat Chat	3	J.R. Velazquez	114	Xtra Heat	122	Shooting Party	114	90,000	1:23.02	95
2002	Nonsuch Bay	3	J.J. Castellano	116	Wopping	116	Wilzada	116	120,000	1:23.90	91
2003	House Party	3	J.A. Santos	122	Cyber Secret	122	City Sister	116	120,000	1:23.28	93
2004	Bending Strings	3	J.D. Bailey	116	Grey Traffic	116	A Lulu Ofa Menifee	116	120,000	1:22.70	94

Beyer Index: 93.00

NATIONAL JOCKEY CLUB HANDICAP (G3), 1 1/8 Miles, 3-Year-Olds and Up, Hawthorne, 2004 Purse: $250,000

Year	Winner	Age	Jockey	Wt.	Second	Wt.	Third	Wt.	Win Value	Time	Beyer
1956	Better Goods	6	H. Viera	115	Jimmy the One	115	Key Biscayne	110	20,500	1:45.00	
1957	Point of Order	4	J. Fiesel,am	114	Bernburgoo	116	River Gate	109	20,050	1:52.20	
1958	Racetracker	5	J. Fieselman	114	Pete's Folly	118	Estacion	116	20,750	1:45.00	
1959	Easy Spur	3	J. Nichols	126	Redbird Wish	118	Pete's F'lly	117	18,650	1:49.40	
1960	American Comet	4	B. Walt	115	Rose's Gem	118	Redbird Wish	111	19,900	1:45.60	
1961	Currock	4	L. Spraker	118	Get Lucky	113	Santiago	113	21,250	1:51.60	
1962	Hoop Bound	5	L.C. Cook	109	K'rri San	112	Santiago	113	19,300	1:49.00	
1963	Tollway	5	L. Spraker	120	Kur'i San	117	Sonny Fleet	120	19,500	1:44.60	
1964	Grand Stand	4	E. Coffman	113	Quita Dude	115	Barbaron	117	18,395	1:43.60	
1965	Ramblin Road	4	E. Coffman	119	Take Over	122	Untested	113	15,565	1:45.20	
1966	Sammyren	4	E. Fires	120	Eladio	115	Wild Card	111	20,900	1:45.00	
1967	Royal Course	4	J.R. Lopez	128	Hy Frost	116	Casing Tools	113	21,230	1:46.00	
1968	Hy Frost	5	T. Barrow	115	Road to Rock	116	Abe's Hope	114	18,425	1:46.20	
1969	Bold Favorite	4	D. Richard	115	Happy Intellectual	111	Mr. Swinger	113	17,985	1:48.00	
1970	High Rover	5	J. Lively	115	Terrible Tiger	120	Royal Harmony	133	14,685	1:46.00	
1971	Terrible Tiger	6	D.W. Whited	117	Royal Harmony	128	Elegant Heir	114	15,180	1:45.00	
1972	Full Pocket	3	J.R. Anderson	119	Moonsplash	121	Insubordination	116	21,120	1:16.40	

Year	Winner	Age	Jockey	Wt.	Second	Wt.	Third	Wt.	Win Value	Time	Beyer
1973	Fame and Power	4	A. Rini	118	Full Pocket	122	Chateauvira	113	21,285	1:37.80	
1974	Tom Tulle	4	L. Snyder	120	Smooth Dancer	111	Chateauvira	117	37,800	1:43.40	
1975	Zografos	7	H. Arroyo	120	Sr. Diplomat	116	Sharp Gary	118	34,410	1:44.20	
1976	Honey Mark	4	R. Sibille	124	Heathen Ways	114	Chateauvira	111	46,680	1:46.80	
1977	Yallah Native	4	J. Powell	112	Dare to Command	119	Brown Cabildo	111	31,860	1:37.80	
1978	Auberge	5	O. Sanchez	112	Bill Bonbright	121	Brown Cabildo	116	19,305	1:41.00	
1979	Once Over Lightly	6	S.A. Spencer	113	Batonnier	114	Hold Your Tricks	114	46,800	1:45.60	
1980	All the More	7	L. Snyder	119	Hold Your Tricks	114	Young Bob	117	46,890	1:46.20	
1981	Dusky Duke	5	G.E. Louviere	118	Boyne Valley	117	Good and Early	120	46,350	1:49.00	
1982	Frost King	4	R. Platts	127	Dusky Duke	114	Recusant	115	66,150	1:49.80	
1983	Determined Bidder	4	C.H. Silva	114	Thumbsucker	117	John's Gold	115	64,710	1:52.00	
1984	Price Forli	4	R. Meier	118	Full Flame	119	Spare Card	117	64,080	1:52.60	
1985	Norwick	6	K. Skinner	117	Harham's Sizzler	121	Badwagon Harry	115	81,696	1:51.20	
1986	Magic North	4	J.L. Diaz	117	Rocky Knave	121	Tuner Jr.	113	85,220	1:50.00	
1987	Honor Medal	6	L.E. Ortega	118	Blue Buckaroo	115	Coffer Dam	113	95,490	1:49.80	
1988	Lost Code	4	C. Perret	129	Honor Medal	122	Outlaws Sham	114	125,640	1:49.60	
1989	Present Value	5	W. Shoemaker	112	Super Roberto	113	Honor Medal	121	126,510	1:49.20	
1990	Dual Elements	4	J.L. Diaz	118	Tricky Creek	120	Blue Buckaroo	115	143,730	1:49.60	
1991	Allijeba	5	S.J. Sellers	116	Whiz Along	110	Sound of Cannons	115	157,680	1:50.40	
1992	Stalwars	7	M. Guidry	115	Richman	122	Sunny Prince	113	156,300	1:48.00	105
1993	Stalwars	8	J.L. Diaz	118	Count the Time	115	Richman	119	150,000	1:49.40	99
1994	Recoup the Cash	4	J.L. Diaz	113	Dread Me Not	114	Danc'n Jake	112	150,000	1:49.00	106
1995	Dusty Screen	7	E. Maple	116	Come on Flip	114	Adhocracy	113	150,000	1:51.40	106
1996	Prory	4	C.H. Silva	113	Polar Expedition	116	Shed Some Light	114	150,000	1:50.80	102
	Bucks Nephew finished first but was disqualified and placed fourth										
1997	Bucks Nephew	7	G.K. Gomez	118	Natural Selection	114	Gotha	112	120,000	1:49.80	103
1998	Polar Expedition	7	M. Guidry.	117	Bucks Nephew	115	Shed Some Light	114	120,000	1:49.80	106
1999	Baytown	5	M. Guidry	114	Precocity	120	Fred Bear Claw	116	120,000	1:47.60	106
2000	Take Note of Me	6	R.J. Albarado	120	Glacial	113	Nite Dreamer	118	120,000	1:49.91	106
2001	Chicago Six	6	A.J. Juarez Jr	117	Guided Tour	118	Glacial	114	120,000	1:48.28	106
2002	Hail the Chief	5	J.F. Chavez	114	E Z Glory	115	Ubiquity	115	120,000	1:51.72	110
2003	Fight for Ally	6	E. Razo Jr	116	Colonial Colony	114	Parrott Bay	115	150,000	1:53.46	97
2004	Ten Most Wanted	4	D.R. Flores	121	Colonial Colony	113	New York Hero	113	150,000	1:49.54	110

Beyer Index: 104.77

NATIONAL MUSEUM OF RACING HALL OF FAME HANDICAP (G2), 1 1/8 Miles (Turf), 3-Year-Olds, Saratoga, 2004 Purse: $150,000

Year	Winner	Age	Jockey	Wt.	Second	Wt.	Third	Wt.	Win Value	Time	Beyer
1987	Drachma	3	R.G. Davis	115	Crown the Leader	115	Major Beard	115	51,480	1:49.80	
1988	Posen	3	J.D. Bailey	122	Blew by Em	119	Harp Islet	115	55,710	1:47.00	
1989	Orange Sunshine	3	J. Cruguet	117	Past 'n' Gold	115	Expensive Decision	122	55,980	1:49.00	
1990	Social Retiree	3	M.E. Smith	115	Go Dutch	115	Divine Warning	119	54,720	1:48.20	99
1991	Lech	3	A. Cordero Jr	122	Sultry Song	117	Fourstars Allstar	122	73,920	1:49.00	100
1992	Paradise Creek	3	M.E. Smith	115	Smiling and Dancin	119	Spectacular Tide	122	72,600	1:46.60	100
1993	A in Sociology	3	C.W. Antley	115	Strolling Along	117	Palashall	117	73,080	1:48.80	97
1994	Islefaxyou	3	E. Maple	113	Jaggery John	122	Lahint	115	70,200	1:48.60	99
							Mr. Impatience	119			
1995	Flitch	3	M.E. Smith	113	Diplomatic Jet	120	Nostra	112	83,700	1:48.00	102
1996	Sir Cat	3	J.D. Bailey	113	Fortitude	113	Optic Nerve	120	68,340	1:40.40	101
1997	Rob 'N Gin	3	J. D. Bailley	120	River Squall	114	Subordination	120	66,000	1:42.00	99
1998	Parade Ground	3	S.J. Sellers	120	Vergennes	115	Stay Sound	115	90,000	1:47.80	104
1999	Marquette	3	J.D. Bailey	119	Phi Beta Doc	118	Good Night	118	90,000	1:49.20	99
2000	Turnofthecentury	3	A.T. Gryder	118	Aldo	118	Polish Miner	123	90,000	1:52.35	88
2001	Baptize	3	J.D. Bailey	122	Strategic Partner	120	Saint Verre	113	90,000	1:47.94	101
2002	Quest Star	3	P. Day	117	Union Place	115	Patrol	120	90,000	1:49.66	95
2003	Stroll	3	J.D. Bailey	117	Urban King	115	Saint Stephen	115	90,000	1:49.34	102
2004	Artie Schiller	3	R. Migliore	122	Mustanfar	122	Good Reward	115	90,000	1:47.71	103

Beyer Index: 99.27

NATIVE DIVER HANDICAP (G3), 1 1/8 Miles, 3-Year-Olds and Up, Hollywood Park, 2004 Purse: $100,000

Year	Winner	Age	Jockey	Wt.	Second	Wt.	Third	Wt.	Win Value	Time	Beyer
1979	Life's Hope	6	L. Pincay Jr	117	Hawkin's Special	117	White Rammer	116	31,500	1:35.00	
1980	Replant	6	W. Shoemaker	111	Relaunch	120	Flying Paster	124	63,000	1:34.20	
1981	Syncopate	6	C.J. McCarron	117	King Go Go	115	Wickerr	121	63,500	1:38.80	
1982	Native Tactics	4	E. Delahoussaye	116	Belfort	116	Rock Softly	115	67,000	1:41.60	
1983	Menswear	5	F. Toro	115	Fighting Fit	117	Major Sport	115	63,200	1:42.40	
1984	Lord at War	4	W. Shoemaker	120	Fighting Fit	118	Video Kid	118	62,700	1:35.40	

Year	Winner	Age	Jockey	Wt.	Second	Wt.	Third	Wt.	Win Value	Time	Beyer
1985	Innamorato	4	S. Hawley	107	Beldale Lear	116	Lord at War	125	87,900	1:33.40	
1986	Hopeful Word	5	L. Pincay Jr	117	Epidaurus	115	Nostalgia's Star	118	90,800	1:47.80	
1987	Epidaurus	5	P.A. Valenzuela	116	Midwest King	116	He's a Saros	116	91,200	1:47.60	
1988	Cutlass Reality	6	G.L. Stevens	124	Precisionist	123	Payant	116	63,700	1:48.60	
1989	Ruhlmann	4	C.J. McCarron	121	Lively One	122	Stylish Winner	116	63,100	1:48.00	
1990	Warcraft	3	C.J. McCarron	117	Pleasant Tap	115	Go and Go	115	63,500	1:47.40	104
1991	Twilight Agenda	5	C.J. McCarron	124	Ibero	117	Cobra Classic	114	60,600	1:49.00	109
1992	Sir Beaufort	5	C.J. McCarron	119	Memo	115	Berillon	115	61,700	1:47.80	109
1993	Slew of Damascus	5	C.S. Nakatani	118	Lottery Winner	117	L'Express	115	63,300	1:47.40	107
1994	Best Pal	6	C.J. McCarron	121	Tossofthecoin	117	Royal Chariot	114	109,000	1:48.40	110
1995	Alphabet Soup	4	C.W. Antley	117	El Florista	118	Regal Rowdy	116	61,400	1:47.00	116
1996	Gentlemen	4	G.L. Stevens	121	Dramatic Gold	122	Don't Blame Rio	112	63,840	1:45.20	118
1997	Refinado Tom	4	G.L. Stevens	119	Steel Ruhlr	112	Boggle	114	60,000	1:47.80	104
1998	Puerto Madero	4	K.J. Desormeaux	121	Musical Gambler	117	River Keen	114	60,000	1:48.40	112
1999	General Challenge	3	C.J. McCarron	123	Moore's Flat	117	Koslanin-AR	113	60,000	1:49.00	109
2000	Sky Jack	4	L. Pincay Jr	118	Lethal Instrument	116	Grey Memo	113	60,000	1:46.81	122
2001	Momentum	3	C.S. Nakatani	117	Euchre	121	Last Parade	117	60,000	1:48.24	107
2002	Piensa Sonando	4	L. Pincay Jr	117	Fleetstreet Dancer	112	Nose the Trade	116	60,000	1:48.43	104
2003	Olmodavor	4	A. Solis	117	Nose the Trade	115	Chinkapin	118	60,000	1:49.16	102
2004	Truly a Judge	6	M.A. Pedroza	115	Dynever	119	Calkins Road	116	60,000	1:47.06	111

Beyer Index: 109.60

NEW ORLEANS HANDICAP (G2), 1 1/8 Miles, 4-Year-Olds and Up, Fair Grounds, 2004 Purse: $500,000

Year	Winner	Age	Jockey	Wt.	Second	Wt.	Third	Wt.	Win Value	Time	Beyer
1925	Quatrain	3	E. Legere	105	Prince James	110	President	106	22,100	1:44.60	
1926	Nurmi	3	J. Thomas	101	Scratch	111	Dazzler	112	32,000	1:47.00	
1927	Cotlogomor	5	C. Allen	107	Shark	104	Banton	112	5,000	1:50.20	
1928	Justice F.	4	A. Pascuma	123	Jock	126	Sea Rocket	114	48,975	1:45.80	
1929	Vermajo	3	A. Pascuma	104	Solace	122	Wellet	104	35,537	1:46.40	
1930	Donnay	4	E. Steffen	112	Uncommon Gold	108	Star o' Morn	101	12,225	1:45.40	
1931	Jimmy Moran	4	E. James	105	Rocket Glare	98	Playtime	111	10,775	1:45.80	
1932	Spanish Play	4	C. Landolt	123	Glastonbury	105	Prince Ath'ng	107	1,530	1:54.80	
1933	Rocky News	5	J. Kacala	108	El Puma	100	War Plane	110	1,680	1:52.60	
1934	Slapped	4	B. Haas	107	Uncle Donald	105	War Plane	114	1,655	1:53.60	
1935	Jesting	5	S. Young	111	Learoyd	111	D'ntless Miss	102	435	1:39.40	
1936	Julia Grant	4	H. Spears	100	Palm Island	107	Cristate	109	750	1:47.40	
1937	Skeeter	3	F. Ritz	106	Magnolia Cash	104	Sir Midas	115	1,180	1:41.80	
1938	Novelette	3	V. Nodarse	103	Bunny Baby	110	Robber Bold	105	1,485	1:47.00	
1939	Chance Sweet	4	J.E. Oros	109	Hope Eternal	102	Whipowill	103	1,000	1:46.80	
1940	Rough Diamond	8	A. Sorsen	107	Endy	98	Spillway	108	850	1:49.20	
1943	Marriage	7	A. Craig	115	Rounders	124	Moscow II	108	18,575	1:43.80	
1944	Marriage	8	J. Higley	124	Rounders	122	First Fiddle	120	18,775	1:45.00	
1946	Hillyer Court	4	W.L. Johnson	118	Pique	115	King Dorsett	124	19,650	1:45.00	
1947	Earshot	4	F. Moon	112	Jack S.L.	112	Brown Mogul	115	19,150	1:44.80	
1948	Star Reward	4	S. Brooks	115	Jack S.L.	117	Carolyn A.	111	19,800	1:48.80	
1949	My Request	4	S. Brooks	115	Isigny	106	Miss Request	113	20,150	1:44.40	
1950	Red Camelia	4	P. Milligan	104	Blue Thanks	113	Dart By	122	21,600	1:49.40	
1951	Mount Marcy	6	K. Church	119	Lotowhite	124	Thwarted	116	21,150	1:44.80	
1952	Oil Capitol	5	K. Church	111	Greek Ship	120	Light Broom	118	20,700	1:44.00	
1953	Smoke Screen	4	G. Porch	120	Happy Go Lucky	121	Oil Capitol	123	45,100	1:44.00	
1954	Grover B.	5	P.J. Bailey	114	Smoke Screen	117	Capeador	121	46,700	1:52.00	
1955	Sea O Erin	4	K. Church	114	Wise Margin	115	Spur On	121	44,300	1:50.20	
1956	Find	6	E. Guerin	119	Happy Go Lucky	110	Sea O Erin	119	45,300	1:52.40	
1957	Kingmaker	4	S. Boulmetis	115	Full Flight	111	Speed Rouser	122	42,000	1:50.20	
1958	Tenacious	4	R. Broussard	120	Ezgo	109	Oh Johnny	125	43,400	1:51.00	
1959	Tenacious	5	R. Broussard	120	Pete's Folly	112	Hare Raising	110	43,900	1:50.20	
1960	Tudor Era	7	R.L. Stevenson	123	Noble Sel	112	Day Court	117	40,300	1:50.80	
1961	Greek Star	6	R. Broussard	122	Road House	110	All Hands	121	40,650	1:49.80	
1962	Yorktown	5	J. Nichols	113	Hillsborough	113	Carry Back	129	47,000	1:50.60	
1963	Endymion	4	J. Nichols	115	Loyal Son	118	Hoop Bound	123	45,100	1:51.40	
1964	Green Hornet	5	R. Broussard	115	Bold Commander	119	Tollway	113	44,000	1:50.20	
1965	Valiant Man	5	R. Ussery	116	Tenacle	108	Suspicious	121	46,500	1:49.20	
1966	Just About	4	L. Moyers	115	R. Thomas	120	Benetero	119	50,200	1:48.80	
1967	Cabildo	4	J. Combest	118	I Owe	114	Mike's Red	115	46,600	1:49.60	
1968	Diplomat Way	4	L. Moyers	124	Cabildo	123	High Tribute	115	41,300	1:49.20	
1969	Miracle Hill	5	D.E. Whited	123	San Roque	113	Spring Double	114	45,700	1:51.80	
1970	Etony	5	P. Rubbicco	118	Vif	119	Otomano II	113	50,000	1:49.20	
1971	Rio Bravo	5	F. Valdizan	113	Joe Frazier	114	Herbalist	113	50,000	1:48.80	
1972	Urgent Message	4	G. St. Leon	119	Helio Rise	112	No No Billy	117	50,000	1:49.80	

Year	Winner	Age	Jockey	Wt.	Second	Wt.	Third	Wt.	Win Value	Time	Beyer
1973	Combat Ready	4	L. Moyers	111	Hustlin Greek	111	Guitar Player	114	50,000	1:51.00	
1974	Smooth Dancer	4	L. Adams	116	Trupan	108	Rastaferian	115	56,300	1:50.60	
1975	Lord Rebeau	4	C.H. Marquez	116	Warbucks	113	Diam'nd Bl'ck	110	61,000	1:50.60	
1976	Master Derby	4	D.G. McHargue	127	Hatchet Man	118	Promised City	116	61,000	1:50.00	
1977	T'd'r Tambourine	4	A.J. Trosclair	112	Inca Roca	113	Soy Numero Uno	127	65,000	1:49.80	
1978	Life's Hope	5	C.J. McCarron	112	Silver Series	125	Inca Roca	111	77,550	2:02.20	
1979	A Letter to Harry	5	E. Delahoussaye	126	Prince Majestic	117	Johnny's Image	112	84,050	2:02.60	
1980	Pool Court	5	R. Ardoin	111	Five Star General	112	Book of Kings	113	84,500	2:04.60	
1981	Sun Catcher	4	A. Guajardo	123	Prince Majestic	118	Yosi Boy	112	103,550	2:03.40	
1982	It's the One	4	W.A. Guerra	124	Boys Nite Out	116	Aspro	113	112,000	2:01.80	
1983	Listcapade	4	E.J. Perrodin	121	Bold Style	113	Aspro	114	112,000	2:03.20	
1984	Wild Again	4	P. Day	112	Explosive Bid	112	Crazy Moon	110	112,000	2:02.00	
1985	Westheimer	4	L. Snyder	112	Inevitable Leader	116	Vornorco	108	112,000	2:01.80	
1986	Herat	4	R.Q. Meza	116	Hopeful Word	120	Kamakura	108	112,000	2:01.80	
1987	Honor Medal	6	R.A. Baze	116	Dramatic Desire	117	Inevitable Leader	116	71,040	1:52.20	
1988	Honor Medal	7	P. Day	121	New York Swell	114	Manzotti	115	60,000	1:50.00	
1989	Galba	5	A.L. Castanon	115	Honor Medal	123	Position Leader	116	60,000	1:51.20	
1990	Festive	5	B.J. Walker Jr	117	Majesty's Imp	116	De Roche	116	60,000	1:50.40	
1991	Silver Survivor	5	L. Melancon	120	El Zorzal	110	Sangria Time	115	60,000	1:50.00	
1992	Jarraar	5	B.J. Walker Jr	113	Irish Swap	120	Bayou Reality	113	60,000	1:48.80	107
1993	Latin American	5	G.K. Gomez	112	Delafield	115	West by West	119	90,000	1:49.20	104
1994	Brother Brown	4	P. Day	118	Far Out Wadleigh	112	Eequalsmcsquared	116	120,000	1:48.80	108
1995	Concern	4	M.E. Smith	125	Fly Cry	118	Tossofthecoin	117	120,000	1:49.40	108
1996	Scott's Scoundrel	4	Ardoin R.	116	Knockadoon	113	Patio de Naranjos	114	162,540	1:49.80	106
1997	Isitingood	6	Flores D. R.	121	Western Trader	114	Scott's Scoundrel	113	180,000	1:48.40	107
1998	Phantom On Tour	4	Melancon L.	114	Precocity	114	Lord Cromby	110	300,000	1:48.00	111
1999	Precocity	5	Martin E. M. Jr	118	Real Quiet	122	Allen's Oop	108	320,640	1:49.00	103
2000	Allen's Oop	5	W. Martinez	112	Take Note of Me	116	Ecton Park	117	300,000	1:48.80	112
2001	Include	4	J.D. Bailey	114	Nite Dreamer	112	Valhol	116	300,000	1:49.18	112
2002	Parade Leader	5	C.J. Lanerie	115	Graeme Hall	116	Keats	113	300,000	1:50.44	114
2003	Mineshaft	4	R.J. Albarado	115	Olmodavor	117	Strive	114	300,000	1:48.92	116
2004	Peace Rules	4	J.D. Bailey	119	Saint Liam	114	Funny Cide	118	300,000	1:48.61	113

Beyer Index: 109.31

NEW YORK HANDICAP (G2), 1 1/4 Miles (Turf), Fillies and Mares, 3-Year-Olds and Up, Belmont Park, 2004 Purse: $250,000

Year	Winner	Age	Jockey	Wt.	Second	Wt.	Third	Wt.	Win Value	Time	Beyer
1940	Shot Put	4	W. Garner	106	Equitable	94	High Fidelity	97	42,400	3:48.80	
1941	Fenelon	4	J. Stout	119	Market Wise	118	Corydon	109	93,500	3:47.00	
1942	Alsab	3	C. Bierman	121	Obash	106	Whirlaway	130	21,450	3:47.20	
1943	Bolingbroke	6	S. Brooks	124	Fairy Manhurst	116	Vagrancy	112	19,400	3:52.20	
1944	Caribou	5	T. Atkinson	104	Bolingbroke	126	Great Rush	110	18,485	3:53.00	
1945	Reply Paid	3	W. Mehrtens	105	Pot o' Luck	119	Momo Flag	117	21,055	3:53.80	
1946	Stymie	5	B. James	128	Rico Monte	121	Athenia	109	41,200	3:51.20	
1947	Rico Monte	5	E. Arcaro	126	Talon	122	Phalanx	116	73,700	3:48.40	
1948	Miss Grillo	6	C. McCreary	120	Donor	119	Fire Point	104	19,600	3:53.60	
1949	Donor	5	W. Mehrtens	126	Stymie	122	Chains	110	20,450	3:51.20	
1950	Pilaster	6	R.J. Martin	112	Going Away	115	First Nighter	109	19,250	3:52.60	
1951	Hill Prince	4	E. Arcaro	128	One Hitter	117	Sudan	105	20,700	1:49.00	
1952	Battlefield	4	E. Arcaro	118	General Staff	113	Combat Boots	109	20,250	1:48.40	
1953	Crafty Admiral	5	E. Arcaro	125	Flaunt	105	Jampol	113	20,500	1:48.80	
1954	Bicarb	4	T. Atkinson	111	Trusting	110	Cold Command	118	20,400	1:48.60	
1955	Chevation	4	E. Guerin	116	Queens Beeches	113	Guardian II	106	17,100	2:24.80	
1956	Nearque II	7	I. Valenzuela	118	Prince Morvi	126	Jabneh	115	19,450	2:18.80	
1958	Anxious Moment	4	W. Shoemaker	114	One-Eyed King	117	Mystic II	114	18,745	2:17.20	
1959	Amerigo	4	W. Hartack	112	One-Eyed King	116	Marlow Road	104	19,687	1:47.00	
1960	Nickel Boy	5	I. Valenzuela	118	Sheild Bearer	119	Four Fathoms	113	13,691	1:51.00	
1960	Wolfram	4	E. Nelson	116	King Grail	119	Ambergris	113	13,691	1:50.40	
1961	Wise Ship	4	H. Gustines	113	Art Market	116	Nasomo	113	19,435	2:14.00	
1962	Honey Dear	4	J. Sellers	112	Barnesville Miss	114	Cat Call	113	19,305	2:03.80	
1963	Goofed	3	J. Vasquez	112	Doll Ina	120	Lady Provost	108	14,381	1:56.80	
1963	Blue Thor	3	E. Monacelli	110	Jazz Queen	109	Prodana Neviesta	110	14,381	1:57.00	
1964	Batteur	4	L. Adams	112	Intervene	117	Gay Serenade	113	19,760	1:55.60	
1965	Blue Thor	5	W. Blum	115	Margarethen	113	Monivea	109	15,291	1:42.40	
1965	Batteur	5	M. Ycaza	123	Good Jane	110	Straight Deal	116	15,129	1:42.60	
1966	Indian Sunlite	3	L. Adams	115	Native Street	119	Mount Regina	120	15,080	1:43.40	
1966	Swinging Mood	3	E. Fires	119	Short Fall	112	What a Treat	121	15,080	1:44.00	
1967	Politely	4	R. Broussard	122	Swinging Mood	128	Princessnesian	113	19,272	1:43.20	
1968	Ludham	4	J. Vasquez	123	Mount Regina	117	Who Cabled	113	19,142	1:57.20	
1969	Drumtop	3	L. Adams	114	Helen Jennings	108	Ludham	116	15,080	1:54.40	
1969	Klassy Poppy	4	M. Hole	113	Desert Law	118	Sarita	111	15,242	1:55.40	

Year	Winner	Age	Jockey	Wt.	Second	Wt.	Third	Wt.	Win Value	Time	Beyer
1970	Marchandeuse	4	H. Gustines	114	Turn 'n Turn About	113	A.T's Olie	109	15,096	1:58.00	
1970	Last of the Line	3	L. Pincay Jr	115	Arachne	112	Tudor M'lle	109	14,609	1:57.40	
1971	Telly	3	J.E. Arellano	109	Dee Dee Luxe	113	Careerist	108	16,920	1:55.20	
1971	Princess Pout	5	J. Cruguet	127	Specious	114	Street Dancer	116	16,920	1:56.00	
1972	Barely Even	3	R. Broussard	127	Bold Bikini	108	Mindy Malone	112	17,940	1:23.40	
1976	Sugar Plum Time	4	A. Cordero Jr	113	Desee du Val	120	Dos a Dos	111	33,780	2:03.20	
1977	Fleet Victress	5	R. Hernandez	115	Lady Singer	113	Welsh Pearl	119	33,330	1:39.20	
1978	Pearl Necklace	4	R. Hernandez	122	Waya	116	Dottie's Doll	118	33,360	1:40.00	
1978	Late Bloomer	4	J. Velasquez	115	Island Kiss	108	Fia	113	33,810	1:41.20	
1979	La Soufriere	4	J. Cruguet	111	Navajo Princess	118	Emerald Hill	120	33,600	1:41.20	
1980	Just a Game II	4	D. Brumfield	121	Poppycock	112	Please Try Hard	113	33,720	2:00.40	
1981	Mairzy Doates	5	A. Cordero Jr	120	Love Sign	114	Wayward Lassie	107	33,960	2:04.00	
1982	Noble Damsel	4	J. Velasquez	114	Office Wife	113	Castle Royale	111	34,620	2:07.00	
1983	Sabin	3	E. Maple	111	If Winter Comes	113	Doodle	115	53,010	2:01.00	
1984	Annie Edge	4	J. Velasquez	112	Thirty Flags	114	Geraldine's Store	121	58,950	2:02.20	
1985	Powder Break	4	J.D. Bailey	115	Annie Edge	112	Pull the Wool	107	53,280	2:03.60	
1986	Possible Mate	5	J.L. Samyn	123	Lucky Touch	110	Perfect Point	113	51,750	2:02.40	
1987	Anka Germania	5	C. Perret	117	Videogenic	117	Lead Kindly Light	109	83,580	2:01.00	
1988	Beauty Cream	5	P. Day	119	Antique Mystique	109	Key to the Bridge	114	70,200	2:03.00	
1989	Miss Unnameable	5	R.I. Rojas	108	Love You by Heart	119	Gaily Gaily	113	72,000	2:05.80	
1990	Capades	4	A. Cordero Jr	119	Laugh and Be Merry	114	Key Flyer	109	71,640	1:58.40	105
1991	Foresta	5	A. Cordero Jr	121	Crockadore	112	Flaming Torch	110	72,360	1:59.20	102
1992	Plenty of Grace	5	J.A. Krone	111	Dancing Devilette	111	Flaming Torch	115	72,720	2:00.60	98
1993	Aquilegia	4	J.A. Krone	114	Via Borghese	117	Ginny Dare	108	74,760	1:59.00	101
1994	You'd Be Surprised	5	J.D. Bailey	118	Dahlia's Dreamer	112	Aquilegia	115	65,340	1:59.60	101
1995	Irish Linnet	7	J.R. Velazquez	118	Danish	116	Market Booster	119	65,520	1:59.80	105
1996	Electric Society	5	J.F. Chavez	115	Danish	115	Chelsey Flower	116	90,000	2:03.60	102
1997	Maxzene	4	M.E. Smith	120	Memories Of Silver	122	Shemozzle	114	120,000	1:59.80	106
1998	Auntie Mame	4	J.R. Velazquez	118	Tresoriere	115	Cuando	113	120,000	1:59.40	103
1999	Soaring Softly	4	M.E. Smith	117	Tampico	116	Anguilla	119	150,000	2:02.20	102
2000	Perfect Sting	4	J.D. Bailey	122	Snow Polina	116	Pico Teneriffe	115	150,000	2:05.36	101
2001	England's Legend	4	C.S. Nakatani	115	Gaviola	119	Spook Express	117	150,000	1:59.63	102
2002	Owsley	4	E.S. Prado	114	Volga	116	Janet	119	150,000	1:59.81	98
2003	Snow Dance	5	R. Migliore	116	Pertuisane	115	Riskaverse	119	150,000	1:59.63	104
2004	Wonder Again	5	E.S. Prado	115	Stay Forever	115	Spice Island	118	150,000	2:05.60	103

Beyer Index: 102.20

NEXT MOVE HANDICAP (G3), 1 1/8 Miles, Fillies and Mares, 3-Year-Olds and Up, Aqueduct, 2004 Purse: $108,400

Year	Winner	Age	Jockey	Wt.	Second	Wt.	Third	Wt.	Win Value	Time	Beyer
1975	My Juliet	3	D.G. McHargue	125	Channelette	117	Spring Is Here	113	33,660	1:35.60	
1976	Yes Dear Maggie	4	R. Hernandez	119	Pass a Glance	115	Mary Queenofscots	110	48,360	1:49.40	
1977	Forty Nine Sunsets	4	J. Vasquez	116	Double Quester	115	Shark's Jaws	116	48,915	1:51.00	
1978	One Sum	4	R. Hernandez	121	Crab Grass	121	Sweet Bernice	114	48,690	1:52.80	
1979	One Sum	5	R. Hernandez	116	Kit's Double	111	Municipal Bond	111	48,105	1:53.00	
1980	Water Lily	4	M. Castaneda	113	Plankton	121	Propitiate	116	49,410	1:51.00	
1981	Plankton	5	R. Hernandez	123	Nalee's Fantasy	107	Ms. Balding	109	50,130	1:53.40	
1982	Andover Way	4	J. Velasquez	122	Autumn Glory	112	Who's to Answer	109	50,940	1:50.20	
1983	Chieft'n's Command	4	A. Smith Jr	116	Noble Damsel	115	Pert	113	32,880	1:53.20	
1984	Adept	5	M. Venezia	109	Far Flying	120	Ch'ft'n's Command	123	67,860	1:57.80	
1985	Flip's Pleasure	5	J.L. Samyn	112	Sintrillium	121	Emphatic	104	52,380	1:58.20	
1986	Cherry Jubilee	4	C.H. Marquez Jr	110	Madame Called	109	Lady on the Run	121	68,220	1:56.00	
1987	Tricky Squaw	4	C.W. Antley	110	Ms. Eloise	115	Videogenic	121	70,440	1:58.40	
1988	Triple Wow	5	R. Migliore	116	With a Twist	112	Cuantalamera	104	66,120	1:57.60	
1989	Rose's Cantina	5	E. Maple	118	To the Hunt	111	No Butter	108	49,950	1:59.80	
1990	Bold Wench	5	J. Velasquez	117	Buy the Firm	112	Dactique	113	53,280	1:58.40	
1991	Buy the Firm	5	W.H. McCauley	119	Overturned	115	Won Scent	112	68,850	1:56.40	100
1992	Spy Leader Lady	4	M.E. Smith	112	Haunting	117	Grecian Pass	115	67,560	2:00.20	100
1993	Low Tolerance	4	M.E. Smith	114	Hilbys Brite Flite	112	Lady Lear	114	67,470	1:55.80	102
1994	Groovy Feeling	5	M.J. Luzzi	123	Broad Gains	116	Megaroux	112	63,735	1:59.60	95
1995	Restored Hope	4	M.J. Luzzi	118	Cherokee Wonder	114	Sterling Pound	114	48,975	1:52.20	94
1996	Madame Adolphe	4	F. Leon.	110	Shoop	114	Lotta Dancing	122	49,080	1:51.20	95
1997	Full And Fancy	5	R. Migliore	115	Shoop	117	Prophet's Warning	117	49,500	1:51.20	97
1998	Panama Canal	4	S.X. Bridgmohan	113	Endowment	110	Dewars Rocks	116	40,455	1:51.20	90
1999	Diggins	5	Espinoza J. L.	113	Biogio's Rose	116	Powerful Nation	114	48,915	1:48.80	96
2000	Biogio's Rose	6	N. Arroyo Jr	117	Up We Go	115	Perlinda	114	49,875	1:51.32	96
2001	Atelier	4	E.S. Prado	117	Pompeii	117	Tax Affair	114	64,264	1:50.65	98
2002	With Ability	4	J.J. Castellano	113	Irving's Baby	117	Diversa	113	65,160	1:49.88	105
2003	Smok'n Frolic	4	J.R. Velazquez	120	Ellie's Moment	116	Pupil	113	64,800	1:49.11	95
2004	Smok'n Frolic	5	R. Migliore	119	Stake	112	U K Trick	110	65,040	1:51.55	91

Beyer Index: 96.71

NOBLE DAMSEL HANDICAP (G3), 1 Mile (Turf), Fillies and Mares, 3-Year-Olds and Up, Belmont Park, 2004 Purse: $150,000

Year	Winner	Age	Jockey	Wt.	Second	Wt.	Third	Wt.	Win Value	Time	Beyer
1996	Perfect Arc	4	Velazquez J. R.	125	Fashion Star	112	Tough Broad	112	60,160	1:42.40	103
1997	Colcon	4	J.D. Bailey	113	Antespend	118	Tiffany's Taylor	113	69,360	1:32.80	104
1998	Oh Nellie	4	Velazquez J. R.	116	Heaven's Command	116	Irish Daisy	114	50,400	1:32.80	105
1999	Khumba Mela	4	Santos J. A.	118	Uanme	114	Cyrillic	116	67,740	1:34.40	102
2000	Gino's Spirits	4	E.S. Prado	114	La Ville Rouge	115	Solar Bound	114	66,720	1:36.61	105
2001	Tugger	4	J.D. Bailey	119	Shine Again	123	Tippity Witch	113	68,280	1:35.18	98
2002	Tates Creek	4	J.D. Bailey	119	Amonita	117	Dat You Miz Blue	114	68,640	1:32.79	105
2003	Wonder Again	4	E.S. Prado	117	Dancal	114	Something Ventured	115	90,000	1:33.07	102
2004	Ocean Drive	4	J.R. Velazquez	120	High Court	115	Hour of Justice	116	90,000	1:34.71	104

Beyer Index: 103.11

NORFOLK (G2), 1 1/16 Miles, 2-Year-Olds, Santa Anita, 2004 Purse: $196,000

Year	Winner	Age	Jockey	Wt.	Second	Wt.	Third	Wt.	Win Value	Time	Beyer
1970	June Darling	2	W. Mahorney	115	Jeanenes Lark	118	American Girl	118	45,765	1:43.00	
1971	MacArthur Park	2	W. Shoemaker	118	D.B. Carm	118	Solar Salute	118	59,445	1:41.80	
1972	Groshawk	2	W. Shoemaker	118	Autry	118	Bottle Brush	118	59,025	1:42.20	
1973	Money Lender	2	J. Lambert	118	Merry Fellow	118	Holding Pattern	118	58,050	1:42.60	
1974	George Navonod	2	D. Pierce	118	Diabolo	118	Fleet Velvet	118	77,370	1:42.20	
1975	Telly's Pop	2	F. Mena	118	Imacornishprince	118	Thermal Energy	118	74,295	1:43.60	
1976	Habitony	2	W. Shoemaker	118	Replant	118	Hey Hey J.P.	118	79,290	1:42.00	
1977	Balzac	2	W. Shoemaker	118	Misrepresentation	118	Noble Bronze	118	157,230	1:45.40	
1978	Flying Paster	2	D. Pierce	118	Golden Act	118	Knights Choice	118	118,860	1:42.20	
1979	The Carpenter	2	C.J. McCarron	118	Rumbo	118	Idyll	118	119,280	1:41.60	
1980	Sir Dancer	2	F. Olivares	118	Chiaroscuro	118	Partez	118	100,980	1:43.80	
1980	High Counsel	2	L. Gilligan	118	Regalberto	118	Cogency	118	99,780	1:42.80	
1981	Stalwart	2	C.J. McCarron	118	Racing is Fun	118	Gato del Sol	118	140,900	1:42.20	
1982	Roving Boy	2	E. Delahoussaye	118	Desert Wine	118	Aguila	118	181,110	1:41.60	
1983	Fali Time	2	S. Hawley	118	Life's Magic	117	Artichoke	118	168,930	1:44.20	
1984	Chief's Crown	2	D. MacBeth	118	Matthew T. Parker	118	Viva Maxi	118	201,960	1:42.40	
1985	Snow Chief	2	A. Solis	118	Lord Allison	118	Darby Fair	118	167,340	1:44.60	
1986	Capote	2	L. Pincay Jr	118	Gulch	118	Gold on Green	118	193,680	1:45.20	
1987	Saratoga Passage	2	J.J. Steiner	118	Purdue King	118	Bold Second	118	181,140	1:45.00	
1988	Hawkster	2	P.A. Valenzuela	118	Bold Bryn	118	Double Quick	118	187,740	1:43.40	
1989	Grand Canyon	2	C.J. McCarron	118	Single Dawn	118	Due to the King	118	166,440	1:43.20	
1990	Best Pal	2	P.A. Valenzuela	118	Pillaring	118	Formal Dinner	118	178,620	1:42.80	
1991	Bertrando	2	A. Solis	118	Zurich	118	Bag	118	164,820	1:42.80	95
1992	River Special	2	K.J. Desormeaux	118	Imperial Ridge	118	Devil Diamond	118	120,000	1:43.40	93
1993	Shepherd's Field	2	C.J. McCarron	118	Ramblin Guy	118	Ferrara	118	120,000	1:43.00	87
1994	Supremo	2	G.L. Stevens	118	Desert Mirage	118	Strong Ally	118	120,000	1:43.40	87
1995	Future Quest	2	K.J. Desormeaux	118	Odyle	118	Exetera	118	120,000	1:43.20	94
1996	Free House	2	K.J. Desormeaux	118	Zippersup	118	Swiss Yodeler	118	120,000	1:43.60	92
1997	Souvenir Copy	2	G.L. Stevens	118	Old Trieste	118	Double Honor	118	120,000	1:36.00	100
1998	Buck Trout	2	E. Delahoussaye	118	Eagleton	118	Daring General	118	120,000	1:37.40	87
1999	Dixie Union	2	A. Solis	118	Forest Camp	118	Anees	118	120,000	1:35.60	104
2000	Flame Thrower	2	V. Espinoza	118	Street Cry	118	Mr Freckles	118	120,000	1:34.86	105
2001	Essence of Dubai	2	A. Solis	118	Ibn Al Haitham	118	Ecstatic	118	150,000	1:37.16	93
	Roman Dancer finished third but was disqualified and placed fourth										
2002	Kafwain	2	V. Espinoza	120	Bull Market	120	Listen Indy	120	120,000	1:42.75	92
2003	Ruler's Court	2	A. Solis	120	Capitano	120	Perfect Moon	120	150,000	1:41.27	102
2004	Roman Ruler	2	C.S. Nakatani	120	Boston Glory	120	Littlebitofzip	120	120,000	1:44.27	87

Beyer Index: 94.14

NORTHERN DANCER (G3), 1 1/16 Miles, 3-Year-Olds, Churchill Downs, 2004 Purse: $232,400

Year	Winner	Age	Jockey	Wt.	Second	Wt.	Third	Wt.	Win Value	Time	Beyer
1998	Shot of Gold	3	S.J. Sellers	119	Souvenir Copy	122	Golden Missile	112	46,500	1:35.66	106
1999	Forestry	3	J.D. Bailey	116	Grits'n Hard Toast	117	Fly Forever	110	62,600	1:42.88	97
2000	Exchange Rate	3	C.H. Borel	119	Jimie Son	113	Ultimate Warrior	118	62,750	1:23.39	103
2001	Compendium	3	D.J. Meche	114	Meetyouatthebrig	122	Horrible Evening	113	62,000	1:34.78	104
2002	Danthebluegrassman	3	J.D. Bailey	119	Stephentown	113	Sky Terrace	119	67,890	1:35.04	104
2003	Champali	3	P. Day	122	Lone Star Sky	120	During	114	68,882	1:34.69	104
2004	Suave	3	R. Bejarano	114	J Town	114	Ecclesiastic	114	144,088	1:44.50	103

Beyer Index: 103.00

Run at 1 mile in 1998, 2001-2003. Run at 7 furlongs in 2000.

OAKLAWN BREEDERS' CUP (G3), 1 1/16 Miles, Fillies and Mares, 3-Year-Olds and Up, Oaklawn Park, 2004 Purse: $200,000

Year	Winner	Age	Jockey	Wt.	Second	Wt.	Third	Wt.	Win Value	Time	Beyer
1994	Morning Meadow	4	S.Romero	116	Gravette	113	Her Valentine	113	94,650	1:44.60	96
1995	Halo America	5	C.H. Borel	115	Heavenly Prize	121	Biolage	111	90,000	1:42.40	108
1996	Belle of Cozzene	4	D.R. Pettinger	113	Hamo America	120	Little May	115	90,000	1:43.20	95
1997	Halo America	7	C.H. Borel	109	Gold N Delicious	112	Capote Belle	117	90,000	1:42.00	109
1998	Turn to the Queen	5	T.T. Doocy	112	Danzalert	112	Leo's Gypsy Dancer	118	90,000	1:44.60	92
1999	Sister Act	4	C.H. Borel	113	Glitter Woman	114	Mil Kilates	114	120,000	1:42.00	112
2000	Heritage of Gold	5	S.J. Sellers	112	Lu Ravi	112	Light Line	112	120,000	1:44.15	103
2001	Heritage of Gold	6	R.J. Albarado	116	Lu Ravi	118	Ive Gota Bad Liver	114	120,000	1:44.30	95
2002	Ask Me No Secrets	4	M.E. Smith	116	Red n'Gold	116	Descapate	118	120,000	1:44.56	100
2003	Bien Nicole	5	D.R. Pettinger	122	Red n'Gold	117	Mandy's Gold	117	120,000	1:44.19	94
2004	Golden Sonata	5	C.H. Marquez Jr	117	Keys to the Heart	117	Mayo on the Side	113	120,000	1:44.32	92

Beyer Index: 99.64

For previous runnings refer to 1994 Manual.

OAKLAWN HANDICAP (G2), 1 1/8 Miles, 4-Year-Olds and Up, Oaklawn Park, 2004 Purse: $500,000

Year	Winner	Age	Jockey	Wt.	Second	Wt.	Third	Wt.	Win Value	Time	Beyer
1946	Lights Abeam	5	D. Adams	117	Baruna	112	Rockwood Lou	110	3,720	1:45.00	
1947	Sugar Beet	4	H. Feathston	113	Bymeabond	120	Late Thread	112	3,685	1:43.20	
1948	Dinner Hour	4	R. Camp	108	Cid Play	105	Boden's Pal	118	3,570	1:44.40	
1949	Fancy Flyer	4	P. Milligan	116	Mr. Tuck	103	Cacomo	109	3,520	1:44.60	
1950	Tharted	7	C. Beasy	119	Provocative	126	Bullish	122	3,455	1:43.60	
1951	Boo Boo Shoo	5	A. Skoronski	111	Kings Hope	106	Virtue	102	3,250	1:43.40	
1952	Spur On	4	J. Adams	112	Ruhe	117	Gloriette	105	3,125	1:46.40	
1953	Our Challenge	4	F. Kaelin	118	Joe Graves	113	Old Mason	113	3,125	1:43.60	
1954	Andros	4	H. Trent	105	Peu-a-Peu	112	Phil D.	120	3,125	1:43.60	
1963	Wa-Wa-Cy	4	E. Van Hook	117	Loyal Son	126	Gay Revoke	114	14,820	1:43.00	
1964	Gay Revoke	6	R.J. Campbell	110	Country Squire	119	Rob Roy III	112	19,321	1:43.80	
1965	Gay Revoke	7	C. Stone	117	Prince Reaper	109	El Bora	116	25,050	1:43.60	
1967	Mike's Red	5	J. Lopez	119	Actor II	113	BF's Own	114	35,460	1:42.00	
1968	Diplomat Way	4	L. Moyers	126	Barbs Delight	125	Hy Frost	118	34,050	1:42.80	
1969	Listado	5	R.L. Baird	116	Missouri Gent	110	Old Dudley	110	35,400	1:45.00	
1970	Charlie Jr.	4	L. Snyder	112	Vif	119	Traffic Mark	118	35,160	1:43.60	
1971	Rio Bravo	5	F. Valdizian	117	Sado	116	Great Mystery	121	33,990	1:42.20	
1972	Gage Line	6	L. Spindler	117	Errullah	110	Elegant Heir	122	34,320	1:44.60	
1973	Prince Astro	4	D.W. Whited	116	Herbalist	116	Gage Line	118	34,470	1:43.60	
1974	Royal Knight	4	I. Valenzuela	123	Crimson Falcon	122	Visualizer	121	38,070	1:43.40	
1975	Warbucks	5	D. Gargan	121	Hey Rube	112	Eastern Pageant	115	37,380	1:42.80	
1976	Master Derby	4	D.G. McHargue	125	Royal Glint	128	Dragset	113	70,890	1:41.60	
1977	Soy Numero Uno	4	R. Broussard	123	Romeo	119	Dragset	114	80,610	1:42.40	
1978	Cox's Ridge	4	E. Maple	128	Prince Majestic	115	All the More	120	80,190	1:43.20	
1979	San Juan Hill	4	D. Brumfield	114	Alydar	127	A Letter to Harry	125	101,730	1:43.40	
1980	Unccol	5	J. Velasquez	116	Hold Your Tricks	111	Braze and Bold	118	103,110	1:44.40	
1981	Temperence Hill	4	E. Maple	126	Suncatcher	123	Uncool	114	128,310	1:43.40	
1982	Eminency	4	P. Day	116	Reef Searcher	117	Thirty Eight Paces	120	166,740	1:44.00	
1983	Bold Style	4	P. Day	113	Eminency	123	Listcapade	123	165,180	1:43.00	
1984	Wild Again	4	P. Day	115	Win Stat	114	Dew Line	118	173,940	1:46.80	
1985	Imp Society	4	P. Day	125	Strength in Unity	109	Pine Circle	118	168,540	1:48.40	
1986	Turkoman	4	C.J. McCarron	123	Gate Dancer	123	Red Attack	114	159,180	1:47.40	
1987	Snow Chief	4	A. Solis	123	Red Attack	112	Vilzak	108	163,020	1:46.60	
1988	Lost Code	4	C. Perret	126	Cryptoclearance	122	Gulch	120	300,000	1:47.00	
1989	Slew City Slew	5	A. Cordero Jr	118	Stalwars	113	Homebuilder	115	240,000	1:49.00	
1990	Opening Verse	4	C.J. McCarron	118	De Roche	114	Silver Survivor	116	300,000	1:47.20	
1991	Festin	5	E. Delahoussaye	115	Primal	115	Jolie's Halo	120	300,000	1:48.00	108
1992	Best Pal	4	K.J. Desormeaux	125	Sea Cadet	120	Twilight Agenda	123	300,000	1:48.00	121
1993	Jovial	6	E. Delahoussaye	117	Lil E. Tee	123	Best Pal	123	450,000	1:48.60	111
1994	The Wicked North	5	K.J. Desormeaux	119	Devil His Due	120	Brother Brown	116	450,000	1:47.80	111
1995	Cigar	5	J.D. Bailey	120	Silver Goblin	119	Concern	122	450,000	1:47.20	121
1996	Geri	4	J.D. Bailey	115	Wekiva Springs	119	Scott's Scoundrel	113	450,000	1:47.40	116
1997	Atticus	5	S.J. Sellers	114	Isitingood	120	Tejano Run	115	450,000	1:48.20	114
1998	Precocity	4	C.V. Gonzalez	114	Frisk Me Now	117	Phantom on Tour	117	450,000	1:48.28	114
1999	Behrens	5	J.F. Chavez	116	Littlebitlively	112	Precocity	119	450,000	1:47.77	117
2000	K One King	4	C.H. Borel	113	Almutawakel	117	Cat Thief	118	360,000	1:48.02	115
2001	Traditonally	4	P. Day	112	Mr Ross	117	Wooden Phone	118	360,000	1:48.15	116
2002	Kudos	5	E. Delahoussaye	117	Bowman's Band	114	Dollar Bill	114	300,000	1:48.34	113
2003	Medaglia d'Oro	4	J.D. Bailey	122	Slider	112	Kudos	117	300,000	1:47.66	111
2004	Peace Rules	4	J.D. Bailey	120	Ole Faunty	116	Saint Liam	114	300,000	1:48.26	112

Beyer Index: 114.29

For 3-year-olds and up prior to 1980. Distance 1 1/16 miles prior to 1984

OAK LEAF (G2), 1 1/16 Miles, 2-Year-Old Fillies, Santa Anita, 2004 Purse: $200,000

Year	Winner	Age	Jockey	Wt.	Second	Wt.	Third	Wt.	Win Value	Time	Beyer
1969	Opening Bid	2	R. Rosales	115	Sailors Mate	115	Loved	115	69,855	1:43.60	
1970	June Darling	2	W. Mahorney	115	Sapose Speed	115	Our Madam Lucky	115	44,520	1:43.20	
1971	Sporting Lass	2	F. Alvarez	115	Goldian	115	Miss Lady Bug	115	60,645	1:44.00	
1972	Fresh Pepper	2	J. Lambert	115	Sphere	115	Sleek and Fleet	115	60,045	1:43.80	
1973	Divine Grace	2	S. Valdez	115	Chalk Face	115	Round Rose	115	59,940	1:43.60	
1974	Cut Class	2	F. Toro	115	Double You Lou	115	Sweet Old Girl	115	84,300	1:42.80	
1975	Answer	2	M. Hole	115	Queen to Be	115	Awaken	115	84,720	1:44.20	
1976	Any Time Girl	2	R. Schacht	115	Lady T.V.	115	Glenaris	115	73,140	1:44.00	
1977	B. Thoughtful	2	D.G. McHargue	115	Grenzen	115	High Pheasant	115	73,530	1:43.80	
1978	It's in the Air	2	E. Delahoussaye	115	Caline	115	Spiffy Laree	115	75,570	1:41.20	
1979	Bold 'n Determined	2	A. Cordero Jr	115	Hazel R.	115	Arcades Ambro	115	82,440	1:46.20	
1980	Astrious	2	T. Lipham	115	Irish Arrival	115	Bee a Scout	115	90,180	1:43.80	
1981	Header Card	2	D.G. McHargue	115	A Kiss for Luck	117	Model Ten	115	144,390	1:43.00	
1982	Landaluce	2	L. Pincay Jr	117	Sophisticated Girl	115	Granja Reina	115	155,610	1:41.80	
1983	Life's Magic	2	C.J. McCarron	115	Althea	117	Persistent	115	164,310	1:44.40	
1984	Folk Art	2	L. Pincay Jr	117	Pirate's Glow	115	Wayward Pirate	115	183,540	1:42.60	
1985	Arewehavingfunyet	2	P.A. Valenzuela	115	Trim Colony	115	Laz's Joy	115	192,420	1:44.60	
1986	Sacahuista	2	C.J. McCarron	115	Silk's Lady	115	Delicate Vine	115	187,050	1:44.60	
1987	Dream Team	2	C.J. McCarron	115	Lost Kitty	117	Tomorrow's Child	115	158,910	1:44.40	
1988	One of a Klein	2	C.J. McCarron	115	Stocks Up	115	Lady Lister	115	168,090	1:44.00	
1989	Dominant Dancer	2	E. Delahoussaye	116	Bel's Starlet	115	Materco	115	153,870	1:44.60	
1990	Lite Light	2	R.A. Baze	115	Garden Gal	115	Beyond Perfection	115	148,320	1:42.80	
1991	Pleasant Stage	2	E. Delahoussaye	116	Soviet Sojourn	116	La Spia	115	156,540	1:43.53	89
1992	Zoonaqua	2	C.J. McCarron	115	Turkstand	115	Madame L'Enjoleur	115	120,000	1:43.91	83
1993	Phone Chatter	2	L. Pincay Jr	117	Sardula	116	Tricky Code	115	120,000	1:41.78	98
1994	Serena's Song	2	C.S. Nakatani	115	Call Now	115	Mama Mucci	115	120,000	1:41.83	90
1995	Tipically Irish	2	L. Pincay Jr	117	Ocean View	115	Gastronomical	117	120,000	1:42.60	85
1996	City Band	2	J.A. Garcia	115	Clever Pilot	115	Wealthy	115	120,000	1:44.57	80
1997	Vivid Angel	2	E. Delahoussaye	116	Love Lock	116	Balisian Beauty	115	120,000	1:37.33	90
1998	Excellent Meeting	2	K.J. Desormeaux	115	Antahkarana	115	Stylish Talent	115	120,000	1:37.71	84
1999	Chilukki	2	D.R. Flores	118	Abby Girl	118	Spain	118	120,000	1:36.12	94
2000	Notable Career	2	D.R. Flores	118	Euro Empire	118	Cindy's Hero	118	120,000	1:36.34	90
2001	Tali'sluckybusride	2	J. Valdivia Jr.	117	Imperial Gesture	117	Ms Louisett	117	150,000	1:37.77	85
2002	Composure	2	M.E. Smith	119	Buffythcenterfold	119	Sea Jewel	119	120,000	1:42.65	93
2003	Halfbridled	2	J.A. Krone	119	Tarlow	119	Hollywood Story	119	150,000	1:43.72	98
2004	Sweet Catomine	2	C.S. Nakatani	119	Splendid Blended	119	Memorette	119	120,000	1:42.98	91

Beyer Index: 89.29

Distance 1 mile 1997–2001

OAK TREE BREEDERS' CUP MILE (G2), 1 Mile (Turf), 3-Year-Olds and Up, Santa Anita, 2004 Purse: $246,000

Year	Winner	Age	Jockey	Wt.	Second	Wt.	Third	Wt.	Win Value	Time	Beyer
1986	Palace Music	5	G.L. Stevens	122	Skywalker	122	Mangaki	116	59,350	1:35.00	
1987	Double Feint	4	F. Toro	117	Deputy Governor	118	Vilzak	115	64,810	1:37.00	
1988	Mohammed Abdu	4	G.L. Stevens	120	Mazilier	116	Deputy Governor	121	65,550	1:34.40	
1989	Political Ambition	5	E. Delahoussaye	122	Mister Wonderful I	118	Sabona	117	67,800	1:33.40	
1990	Notorious Pleasure	4	L. Pincay Jr	117	Kanatiyr	114	Fly Till Dawn	114	68,700	1:33.00	107
1991	Ibero	4	A. Solis	115	Val des Bois	118	Tokatee	116	67,000	1:33.60	105
1992	Twilight Agenda	6	C.J. McCarron	120	Luthier Enchanteur	117	Bourgogne	115	65,300	1:33.36	104
1993	Johann Quatz	4	E. Delahoussaye	119	Myrakalu	114	The Tender Track	117	62,350	1:36.28	103
1994	Bon Point	4	E. Delahoussaye	116	Journalism	120	Johann Quatz	117	62,050	1:33.86	109
1995	Ventiquattrofogli	5	G.F. Almeida	116	Megan's Interco	119	Debutant Trick	115	76,850	1:35.30	108
1996	Urgent Request	6	C.J. McCarron	115	Megan's Interco	119	Felon	116	110,300	1:32.44	106
1997	Fantastic Fellow	3	A. Solis	115	Magellan	119	Taiki Blizzard	119	165,000	1:36.23	112
1998	Hawksley Hill	5	A. Solis	123	Mr. Lightfoot	119	Magellan	119	166,200	1:36.72	106
1999	Silic	4	C.S. Nakatani	121	Bouccaneer	119	Brave Act	119	150,000	1:33.76	109
2000	War Chant	3	G.L. Stevens	117	Road to Slew	119	Sharan	119	150,000	1:33.75	107
2001	Val Royal	5	J. Valdivia Jr.	119	Thady Quill	119	I've Decided	119	120,000	1:33.21	111
2002	Night Patrol	6	J. Valdivia Jr.	119	Kachamandi	119	Nicobar	119	150,000	1:32.93	103
2003	Designed for Luck	6	P.A. Valenzuela	119	Sarafan	119	Century City	119	180,000	1:32.61	107
2004	Musical Chimes	4	K.J. Desormeaux	118	Buckland Manor	119	Singletary	119	150,000	1:33.29	106

Beyer Index: 106.87

OAK TREE DERBY (G2), 1 1/8 Miles (Turf), 3-Year-Olds, Santa Anita, 2004 Purse: $150,000

Year	Winner	Age	Jockey	Wt.	Second	Wt.	Third	Wt.	Win Value	Time	Beyer
1969	Tell	3	W. Shoemaker	130	Noholme Jr.	118	Neutral	113	35,000	1:46.80	
1970	Mickey McGuire	3	W. Shoemaker	124	Woodie Can	117	Mayhedo	120	17,200	1:47.40	

Year	Winner	Age	Jockey	Wt.	Second	Wt.	Third	Wt.	Win Value	Time	Beyer
1971	Vegas Vic	3	H. Grant	122	Struck Out	114	Artaxerxes	115	20,050	1:48.20	
1972	Bicker	3	G. Brogan	120	Woodland Pines	116	Queen's Hustler	115	19,650	1:48.20	
1974	Within Hail	3	W. Shoemaker	124	Orders	117	Chief Pronto	113	27,250	1:48.40	
1975	Messenger of Song	3	J. Lambert	119	Larrikin	123	Forceten	125	25,450	1:46.80	
1976	Today 'n Tomorrow	3	L. Pincay Jr	121	Pocket Park	115	Kings Cliffe	115	19,450	1:46.80	
1977	Kulak	3	W. Shoemaker	123	Hill Fox	114	Kaskee	110	19,800	1:46.80	
1978	Wayside Station	3	L. Pincay Jr	117	April Axe	122	John Henry	122	34,600	1:47.80	
1979	Hyannis Port	3	W. Shoemaker	118	Red Crescent	115	Relaunch	126	32,300	1:47.60	
1980	Pocketful of Vail	3	F. Toro	115	Son of a Dodo	118	Always Best	117	39,400	1:47.80	
1981	Seafood	3	M. Castaneda	118			High Counsel	117	33,350	1:49.00	
	Waterway Drive	3	J.D. Bailey	120							
1982	Lamerok	3	L. Pincay Jr	117	Craelius	118	Sari's Dreamer	113	66,300	1:46.20	
1983	Mamaison	3	C.J. McCarron	117	Sunny's Halo	126	Fifth Division	118	63,900	1:49.80	
1984	Tights	3	C.J. McCarron	121	Tsunami Slew	120	Blind Spot	115	65,500	1:46.60	
1985	Justoneoftheboys	3	A. Solis	115	Floating Reserve	118	Schiller	113	65,000	1:47.60	
1986	Air Display	3	G.L. Stevens	114	Armada	117	Vernon Castle	124	64,700	1:48.00	
1987	The Medic	3	S. Hawley	119	Temperate Sil	122	Hot and Smoggy	115	63,800	1:47.80	
1988	Coax Me Clyde	3	P.A. Valenzuela	116	Bel Air Dancer	117	Undercut	120	81,500	1:48.40	
1989	Seven Rivers	3	R.G. Davis	115	Bruho	117	Raise a Stanza	121	66,100	1:45.80	
1990	In Excess	3	G.L. Stevens	117	Warcraft	118	Barton Dene	113	65,300	1:46.60	
1991	General Meeting	3	K.J. Desormeaux	116	Dominion Gold	115	Eternity Star	120	69,500	1:46.60	98
1992	Blacksburg	3	A. Solis	118	Siberian Summer	117	Star Recruit	115	67,700	1:48.00	95
1993	Eastern Memories	3	J.D. Bailey	113	Cigar	118	Snake Eyes	120	66,800	1:48.00	102
1994	Run Softly	3	L. Pincay Jr	117	Alphabet Soup	114	Powis Castle	118	64,800	1:49.80	101
1995	Helmsman	3	C.J. McCarron	115	Virginia Carnival	118	Mr Purple	121	75,650	1:48.80	103
1996	Odyle	3	C.J. McCarron	118	Lago	111	Rainbow Blues	120	80,250	1:46.80	101
1997	Lasting Approval	3	A. Solis	118	Voyagers Quest	118	Early Colony	118	150,000	1:50.80	96
1998	Ladies Din	3	G.L. Stevens	120	Dr Fong	120	Bouccaneer	118	150,000	1:50.20	104
1999	Mula Gula	3	G.L. Stevens	118	Eagleton	118	Super Quercus	118	150,000	1:46.60	100
2000	Sign of Hope	3	A. Solis	118	David Copperfield	118	El Gran Papa	118	150,000	1:47.71	100
2001	No Slip	3	K.J. Desormeaux	118	Sligo Bay	118	Romanceishope	122	90,000	1:46.56	94
2002	Johar	3	A. Solis	118	Rock Opera	118	Mananan McLir	120	90,000	1:46.00	100
2003	Devious Boy	3	J.A. Krone	118	Sweet Return	118	Urban King	118	90,000	1:48.82	94
2004	Greek Sun	3	E.S. Prado	118	Laura's Lucky Boy	118	Hendrix	118	90,000	1:48.08	105

Beyer Index: 99.50

PAT O'BRIEN BREEDERS' CUP HANDICAP (G2), 7 Furlongs, 3-Year-Olds and Up, Del Mar, 2004 Purse: $194,000

Year	Winner	Age	Jockey	Wt.	Second	Wt.	Third	Wt.	Win Value	Time	Beyer
1990	Sensational Star	6	R.Q. Meza	116	Frost Free	116	Earn Your Stripes	116	49,275	1:20.60	113
1991	Bruho	5	C.S. Nakatani	118	Burn Annie	115	Due to the King	116	46,350	1:21.40	105
1992	Light of Morn	6	E. Delahoussaye	116	Three Peat	116	Slerp	114	66,025	1:20.60	110
1993	Slerp	4	A.D. Lopez	117	Porto Ferraio	114	Cardmania	116	47,850	1:21.20	104
1994	D'Hallevant	4	Nakatani CS	115	Minjinsky	117	J.F. Williams	115	59,725	1:20.20	112
1995	Lit de Justice	5	Nakatani CS	118	D'Hallevant	117	Pembroke	119	60,400	1:20.00	113
1996	Alphabet Soup	5	C.W. Antley	118	Boundless Moment	116	Lit de Justice	123	65,450	1:20.60	114
1997	Tres Paraiso	5	G.L. Stevens	115	High Stakes Player	119	Gold Land	114	68,200	1:21.40	108
1998	Old Topper	3	E. Delahoussaye	116	Son of a Pistol	123	Uncaged Fury	115	95,220	1:21.40	108
1999	Regal Thunder	5	C.W. Antley	116	Christmas Boy	118	Bet On Sunshine	116	90,000	1:21.13	117
2000	Love That Red	4	C.S. Nakatani	118	Cliquot	117	Son of a Pistol	117	90,000	1:21.89	105
2001	El Corredor	4	V. Espinoza	119	Swept Overboard	117	Ceeband	114	90,000	1:20.42	119
2002	Disturbingthepeace	4	V. Espinoza	119	Hot Market	115	I Love Silver	117	90,000	1:21.89	105
2003	Disturbingthepeace	5	V. Espinoza	116	Rushin' to Altar	117	Full Moon Madness	119	90,000	1:21.53	106
2004	Kela	6	T.C. Baze	116	Domestic Dispute	116	Pico Central	122	120,000	1:21.17	116

Beyer Index: 110.33

OCEANPORT HANDICAP (G3), 1 1/16 Miles (Turf), 3-Year-Olds and Up, Monmouth Park, 2004 Purse: $100,000

Year	Winner	Age	Jockey	Wt.	Second	Wt.	Third	Wt.	Win Value	Time	Beyer
1947	Polynesian	5	W.D. Wright	134	Misleader	105	Gallant Bull	104	8,195	1:10.40	
1948	Yankee Hill	4	W.J. Passmore	109	Mangohick	116	Brown Mogul	114	8,900	1:12.40	
1949	Rippey	6	J. Gilbert	125	Cacique	104	Mangohick	125	7,875	1:11.40	
1950	Imacomin	4	M. Basile	113	Cacique	109	Noble Impulse	116	8,575	1:11.20	
1951	Tuscany	3	S. Boulmetis	107	War King	113	Call Over	119	7,925	1:10.20	
1952	General Staff	4	W.J. Passmore	112	Hi Billee	112	Northern Star	113	12,100	1:11.40	
1953	Cinda	4	J. Stout	113	Indian Land	118	Squared Away	127	13,700	1:12.00	
1954	Master Ace	5	J. Renick	106	White Skies	136	Eatontown	113	13,000	1:09.00	
1955	Dark Peter	7	S. Boulmetis	118	I Geegee	112	Bobby Brocato	122	13,050	1:10.00	
1956	Decathlon	3	G.R. Martin	116	I Appeal	113	Royal Briar	108	12,250	1:09.40	
1957	Decathlon	4	W. Hartack	130	Itobe	116	Nahodah	122	10,517	1:08.40	

Year	Winner	Age	Jockey	Wt.	Second	Wt.	Third	Wt.	Win Value	Time	Beyer
1958	True Verdict	4	H. Grant	115	Sand Boy	112	Beau Pilot	115	11,151	1:10.60	
1959	Itobe	6	S. Boulmetis	117	Isendu	122	Li'l Fella	117	11,281	1:09.60	
1960	Besomer	7	H. Woodhouse	115	Itobe	121	Seven Corners	112	11,005	1:09.80	
1961	Careless John	4	W. Boland	116	Winonly	120	Watch Your Step	118	11,277	1:09.00	
1962	Jets Pat	4	S. Boulmetis	116	Beau Admiral	117	Will Ye	115	10,936	1:09.60	
1963	Accordant	3	P. Kallai	110	Bull Story	114	Merry Ruler	120	10,920	1:09.20	
1964	Turbo Jet II	4	S. Brooks	111	Thanks Doc	110	Uncle Percy	115	11,619	:59.20	
1965	Uncle Percy	7	E. McIvor	119	Isaduchess	115	Lucky Turn	114	11,391	:58.20	
1966	Canal	5	W. Mayorga	119	Deutron	114	Finance King	111	10,977	:57.40	
1966	Country Friend	4	J. Velasquez	115	Meistersinger	112	Welshwyn	112	10,847	:57.80	
1967	Canal	6	W. Mayorga	121	Valiant Bull	113	Caligerro	113	14,397	:58.00	
1967	County Monaghan	6	J. Leonard	112	Chicot	122	Country Friend	119	14,430	:57.80	
1968	Country Friend	6	J. Vasquez	116	Burning Bridges	111	Vis-a-Vis	109	18,046	1:36.60	
1968	Quite an Accent	5	B. Thornburg	113	More Scents	117	Tornum	112	18,046	1:36.40	
1969	Mara Lark	4	F. Toro	112	Kentucky Kin	112	A Latin Spin	110	15,210	1:37.00	
1969	Swoonland	6	R. Turcotte	113	Palace Ruler	117	Monitor	117	15,145	1:36.20	
1970	Mr. Leader	4	C. Baltazar	114	Good Manners	112	A Latin Spin	110	19,419	1:39.40	
1971	Red Reality	5	F. Ianelli	114	Mister Diz	118	Well Mannered	117	15,080	1:36.60	
1971	Tudor Reward	4	C.H. Marquez	117	Charney	114	Double Gee	113	15,047	1:37.60	
1972	Native Heir	6	V. Bracciale Jr	111	Real Note	115	Red Reality	119	19,354	1:36.20	
1973	Lexington Park	6	J. Imparato	118	Prince of Truth	116	Halo	117	15,056	1:45.20	
1973	Dartsum	4	M. Cedeno	110	Dundee Marmalade	114	Return to Reality	111	14,893	1:46.20	
1974	Mo Bay	5	W. Tichenor	118	Shane's Prince	118	Barbiz'n Streak	116	18,541	1:42.40	
1975	R. Tom Can	4	D. Brumfield	115	Prod	117	Royal Glint	119	15,291	1:49.80	
1975	Haraka	5	J. Velasquez	113	London Company	124	East Sea	115	15,096	1:49.80	
1976	Toujours Pret	7	J.W. Edwards	114	Hat Full	114	Our Hermis	113	15,072	1:43.00	
1976	Break up the G'me	5	E. Delahoussaye	114	Expropriate	120	L'roft'e Bid	118	14,682	1:44.20	
1977	Quick Card	4	M. Solomone	115	Bemo	115	Star of the Sea	115	19,516	1:42.60	
1978	Mr. Red Wing	4	W.H. McCauley	110	Chati	118	Dan Horn	116	23,514	1:43.20	
1979	Revivalist	5	W. Nemeti	117	Horatius	117	Gristle	112	18,866	1:38.00	
1979	Alias Smith	6	M. Solomone	114	Qui Native	114	Fed Funds	114	18,671	1:38.00	
1980	North Course	5	B. Thornburg	114	Horatius	119	Lucy's Axe	116	24,210	1:44.00	
1981	Winds of Winter	4	G. McCarron	113	Foretake	116	No Bend	115	24,225	1:43.40	
1982	McCann	4	J. Fell	114	Sprink	108	Lord Carn'von	111	27,555	1:43.60	
1982	Erin's Tiger	4	K. Skinner	114	Dom Menotti	111	War of Words	114	27,555	1:43.00	
1983	Fray Star	5	O. Vergara	114	Domynsky	112	And More	117	35,190	1:43.40	
1984	World Appeal	4	C. Perret	120	Rocco Reale	109	Castle Guard	120	34,950	1:42.80	
1985	Cozzene	5	W.A. Guerra	121	Stay the Course	119	Roving Minstrel	118	34,470	1:42.40	
1986	Salem Drive	4	D.B. Thomas	115	Exclusive Partner	120	Spellbound	117	34,650	1:42.60	
1987	Sovereign Song	5	J.A. Krone	106	Feeling Gallant	120	Spellbound	117	35,100	1:41.60	
1988	Feeling Gallant	6	C.W. Antley	119	Copper Cup	111	Sovereign Song	107	41,820	1:45.20	
1989	Yankee Affair	7	P. Day	121	River of Sin	116	Primino	110	51,870	1:43.40	
1990	Bill E. Shears	5	R. Wilson	118	Pete the Chief	115	Timely Warning	113	53,910	1:42.80	97
1991	Fiftysevenvette	4	J.C. Ferrer	113	Great Normand	118	Thunder Regent	112	45,000	1:44.80	
1992	Maxigroom	4	R.G. Davis	113	Rocket Fuel	112	Go Dutch	112	45,000	1:41.60	98
1993	Furiously	4	J.D. Bailey	119	Adam Smith	120	Rocket Fuel	114	45,000	1:39.60	106
1994	Nijinsky's Gold	5	Davis RG	120	Winnetou	116	Marco Bay	116	45,000	1:41.60	106
1995	Boyce	4	Black AS	113	Myrmidon	117	Rocket City	112	45,000	1:40.80	102
1997	Boyce	6	J.A. Krone	118	Foolish Pole	113	Jambalaya Jazz	116	60,000	1:40.20	101
1998	Daylight Savings	4	H. Castillo Jr.	115	Mi Narrow	121	Rob 'n Gin	120	60,000	1:42.20	102
1999	Mi Narrow	5	J. Bravo	113	Hurrahy	114	Forbidden Apple	111	60,000	1:39.40	106
2000	North East Bound	4	J.A. Velez Jr.	114	Rize	112	Selective	114	60,000	1:44.60	98
2001	Key Lory	7	C.C. Lopez	111	North East Bound	121	Crash Course	115	60,000	1:40.39	100
2002	Tempest Fugit	5	J.A. Velez Jr.	115	Runspastum	112	One Eyed Joker	114	60,000	1:42.72	110
2003	Runspastum	6	J. Pimentel	113	Balto Star	119	Saint Verre	118	60,000	1:42.31	101
2004	Gulch Approval	4	P. Day	117	Kathir	116	Stormy Roman	115	60,000	1:42.31	96

Beyer Index: 101.77

Off the turf in 2002, 2003

OHIO DERBY (G2), 1 1/8 Miles, 3-Year-Olds, Thistledown, 2004 Purse: $350,000

Year	Winner	Age	Jockey	Wt.	Second	Wt.	Third	Wt.	Win Value	Time	Beyer
1876	Bombay	3	Walker	100	Harry Hill		Preston		1,000	2:46.00	
1877	McWhirter	3	James	100	Oddfellow		Commodore Parisot		975	2:40.00	
1878	Harper	3	McClellan	105	J.R. Swiney		Stella		1,025	2:40.50	
1879	Ben Hill	3	Shauer	105	Cash Clay		Enterprise		750	2:54.50	
1880	Mary Anderson	3		102	Brooklyn	105	Pat Farrell	105	600	2:51.75	
1881	Bootjack	3	Allen	105	Windrush		King Nero		550	2:41.00	
1882	Babcock	3	Kelso	110	Katie Creel	105	Effie H.	105	950	2:45.50	
1883	Pilot	3	Watkins	107	Orange Blossom	105	Standiford Keller	110	1,100	2:55.00	
1924	Black Gold	3	J.D. Mooney	126	Payman	112	Dunoon	108	4,000	1:57.40	

Year	Winner	Age	Jockey	Wt.	Second	Wt.	Third	Wt.	Win Value	Time	Beyer
1925	Millwick	3	K. Noe	111	Almadel	115	Kentucky Cardinal	120	7,320	1:50.80	
1926	Boot to Boot	3	A. Johnson	122	Bolton	114	Brazen	114	7,320	1:57.00	
1928	Sunfire	3	R. Leonard	121	Easter Stockings	119	Golden Racket	115	7,320	1:57.00	
1929	Thistle Fyrn	3	V. Smith	113	Dinah Did Upset	113	Voltear	121	11,880	1:51.60	
1930	Culloden	3	P. Gross	118	Tonto Rock	118	Dark Entry	121	10,480	1:51.60	
1931	A La Carte	3	F. Catrone	118	Spanish Play	121	Up	121	11,580	1:58.00	
1932	Economic	3	F. Horn	118	Springsteel	118	Our Fancy	118	7,760	1:51.60	
1935	Paradisical	3	L. Hardy	114	Clang	116	Whopper	116	4,250	1:51.20	
1952	Carter's Pride	3	S. Bielen	113	Scrub	118	Dr. Noddy	118	3,733	1:54.40	
1953	Find	3	E. Guerin	118	Buck 'n Gee	118	Dictar	126	18,989	1:48.00	
1954	Timely Tip	3	P.A. Ward	122	Rustic Billy	118	Sea o Erin	122	18,704	1:49.80	
1955	Traffic Judge	3	E. Arcaro	126	Selinsgrove	118	Honeys Alibi	126	29,939	1:50.20	
1956	Born Mighty	3	J. Choquette	116	Fabius	124	Toby R.	124	29,041	1:55.80	
1957	Manteau	3	K. Church	120	Shan Pac	116	Air Wonder	112	18,980	1:49.00	
1958	Terra Firma	3	L.C. Cook	118	A Dragon Killer	118	Plion	122	19,710	1:54.20	
1959	On-and-On	3	S. Brooks	120	Sir Hawley	116	Marless	112	19,730	1:49.40	
1960	Playgoer	3	C. Meaux	111	Dress Blue	111	Money Now	117	11,757	1:47.80	
1961	Gay's Pal	3	G. Smithson	115	First Monday	111	Up Scope	111	12,477	1:43.60	
1962	Gushing Wind	3	R.L. Baird	114	Times Roman	110	Submerge	110	15,616	1:42.80	
1963	Lemon Twist	3	S. LeJeune	120	The Baron	110	Grand Stand	113	20,572	1:44.40	
1964	National	3	P. Anderson	115	Morning Cast	111	Roseberry	108	19,435	1:44.60	
1965	Terri Hi	3	R.J. Campbell	120	Victorian Era	116	Little Gray Pet	113	21,020	1:50.00	
1966	War Censor	3	D. Kassen	120	Eladio	120	Squadron E.	113	22,320	1:52.20	
1967	Out the Window	3	B. Wall	113	English Muffin	112	Royal Malabar	124	21,000	1:52.00	
1968	Te Vega	3	M. Manganello	116	Funny Fellow	116	Campion Kid	120	19,075	1:51.00	
1969	Berkley Prince	3	J. Giovanni	124	Mr. Clinch	116	Polar Traffic	116	22,450	1:50.60	
1970	Climber	3	H. Gustines	116	Son Excellence	112	High Quotient	112	25,641	1:50.60	
1971	Twist the Axe	3	R. Woodhouse	122	Spotted Kid	118	Eastern Fleet	122	36,256	1:52.40	
1972	Freetex	3	J. Moseley	122	True Knight	115	Ladiga	115	64,134	1:50.40	
1973	Our Native	3	A. Rini	122	Hearts of Lettuce	112	Arbees Boy	115	63,882	1:50.20	
1974	Stonewalk	3	M.A. Rivera	120	Better Arbitor	122	Sharp Gary	122	63,000	1:53.20	
1975	Brent's Prince	3	B.R. Felciano	115	Sylvan Place	112	Canvasser	115	66,780	1:49.40	
1976	Return of a Native	3	G. Patterson	115	Cojak	122	Dream'n Be Lucky	115	75,000	1:49.80	
1977	Silver Series	3	L. Snyder	122	Cormorant	122	Pruneplum	115	90,000	1:49.20	
1978	Special Honor	3	R. Breen	115	Batonnier	122	Star de Naskra	120	90,000	1:47.80	
1979	Smarten	3	S. Maple	124	Bold Ruckus	115	Picturesque	122	90,000	1:47.40	
1980	Stone Manor	3	P. Day	123	Colonel Moran	123	Hilbizon	114	90,000	1:52.00	
1981	Pass the Tab	3	A. Graell	120	Paristo	123	Classic Go Go	123	90,000	1:49.20	
1982	Spanish Drums	3	J. Vasquez	123	Air Forbes Won	126	Lejoli	114	90,000	1:49.60	
1983	Pax Nobiscum	3	R. Platts	120	Bet Big	114	Fightin Hill	114	90,000	1:50.20	
1984	At the Threshold	3	G. Patterson	123	Biloxi Indian	123	Perfect Player	120	120,000	1:49.60	
1985	Skip Trial	3	J.L. Samyn	114	Encolure	123	Jacque l'Heureux	114	120,000	1:49.00	
1986	Broad Brush	3	G.L. Stevens	126	Bolshoi Boy	123	Forty Kings	114	150,000	1:51.20	
1987	Lost Code	3	G. St. Leon	126	Proudest Duke	117	Homebuilder	114	150,000	1:50.60	
1988	Jim's Orbit	3	S.P. Romero	123	Primal	114	Intensive Command	114	150,000	1:50.60	
1989	King Glorious	3	C.J. McCarron	120	Roi Danzig	114	Caesar	114	180,000	1:50.40	
1990	Private School	3	J. Vasquez	120	Restless Con	123	Real Cash	123	180,000	1:51.20	
1991	Private Man	3	J.R. Velazquez	114	Richman	126	Shudanz	114	180,000	1:50.20	104
1992	Majestic Sweep	3	E. Fires	117	Technology	126	Always Silver	117	180,000	1:50.00	105
1993	Forever Whirl	3	A.R. Toribio	122	Boundlessly	120	Mighty Avanti	114	180,000	1:49.40	101
1994	Exclusive Praline	3	W. Martinez	118	Concern	122	Smilin Singin Sam	122	180,000	1:48.40	104
1995	Petionville	3	P. Day	122	Dazzling Falls	124	Is Sveikatas	116	180,000	1:48.80	97
1996	Skip Away	3	J.A. Santos	122	Victory Speech	118	Clash By Night	118	180,000	1:47.80	110
1997	Frisk Me Now	3	E. L. King Jr.	122	Anet	122	Mr. Groush	118	180,000	1:48.20	111
1998	Classic Cat	3	S.J. Sellers	122	Old Bold Stroke	118	Hot Wells	118	180,000	1:49.80	100
1999	Stellar Blush	3	M.J. McCarthy	119	Ecton Park	116	Valhol	114	180,000	1:49.20	103
2000	Milwaukee Brew	3	M.J. McCarthy	116	Brave Quest	113	Kiss a Native	116	180,000	1:50.40	104
2001	Western Pride	3	D.G. Whitney	119	Woodmoon	113	Macho Uno	119	180,000	1:50.71	105
2002	Magic Weisner	3	R.Migliore	116	Wiseman's Ferry	120	The Judge Sez Who	114	180,000	1:49.96	106
2003	Wild and Wicked	3	S.J. Sellers	114	Hackendiffy	112	Midway Road	114	180,000	1:50.08	101
2004	Brass Hat	3	W. Martinez	115	Pollard's Vision	121	Trieste's Honor	115	210,000	1:49.50	103

Beyer Index: 103.86

OKLAHOMA DERBY (G3), 1 1/8 Miles, 3-Year-Olds, Remington Park, 2004 Purse: $167,250

Year	Winner	Age	Jockey	Wt.	Second	Wt.	Third	Wt.	Win Value	Time	Beyer
1989	Clever Trevor	3	D.R. Pettinger	122	Gauntlett Boy	122	Launch a Ruler	118	152,500	1:43.00	
1990	Wicked Destiny	3	J. Lively	122	Seasabb	118	Penthouse E.	118	150,000	1:43.00	
1991	Queen's Gray Bee	3	P.W. Steinberg	118	Lanyons Star	122	Near the Limit	118	150,000	1:44.20	
1992	Vying Victor	3	R.D. Hansen	122	Ecstatic Ride	122	Capitalimprovement	122	150,000	1:43.60	
1993	Marked Tree	3	G.K. Gomez	122	Brother Brown	122	Ragtime Rebel	122	180,000	1:43.80	

Year	Winner	Age	Jockey	Wt.	Second	Wt.	Third	Wt.	Win Value	Time	Beyer
1994	Smilin Singin Sam	3	L. Melancon	122	Blumin Affair	118	Silver Goblin	122	180,000	1:43.20	112
1995	Dazzling Falls	3	G.Gomez	122	Our Gatsby	122	Capote's Promise	118	180,000	1:42.80	104
1996	Semoran	3	R.Baze	122	Connecting Terms	118	Devil's Honor	122	180,000	1:46.60	95
1997	Wild Rush	3	G.Stevens	121	Blazing Sword	119	Precocity	117	180,000	1:53.60	100
1998	Classic Cat	3	S.Sellers	124	Leave A Legacy	121	Sir Tiff	117	180,000	1:48.00	100
1999	Temperence Time	3	T.Doocy	119	Answer Lively	115	Stellar Brush	124	180,000	1:49.40	102
2000	Performing Magic	3	S.Sellers	124	Mister Deville	124	Del Mar Denny	124	180,000	1:50.20	96
2001	Top Hit	3	G.K. Comez	114	Unbridled Time	118	Compendium	118	180,000	1:49.79	102
2002	The Judge Sez Who	3	C. Velasquez	115	Easyfromthegitgo	121	A.P. Five Hundred	115	177,000	1:49.34	101
2003	Comic Truth	3	M. Berry	115	Excessivepleasure	124	Morning Merry	112		1:49.59	111
2004	Wally's Choice	3	L.S Quinonez	115	Golden Glen	112	Cryptograph	118	100,350	1:50.26	104

Beyer Index: 102.45

ORCHID HANDICAP (G2), 1 1/2 Miles (Turf), Fillies and Mares, 3-Year-Olds and Up, Gulfstream Park, 2004 Purse: $200,000

Year	Winner	Age	Jockey	Wt.	Second	Wt.	Third	Wt.	Win Value	Time	Beyer
1954	Queen Hopeful	3	J. Adams	121	Garb	106	Trisong	110	6,700	1:12.00	
1965	Vassar Grad	3	K Knapp	112	Money to Burn	116	Special T.	112	10,050	1:46.20	
1966	Chalina	3	K. Knapp	114	Lady Pitt	114	Native Street	118	9,700	1:43.40	
1967	Indian Sunlite	4	H. Grant	117	Turn to Talent	113	Shim'g G'd	113	1,317	1:34.60	
1967	Straight Deal	5	J. Velasquez	122	Cologne	111	Pollen	117	13,387	1:35.20	
1968	Chriscinca	4	E. Fires	109	Ring Francis	109	Forest Nan	113	14,725	1:35.80	
1969	Spire	5	R. Broussard	118	Crystal Palace	116	Ludham	123	23,950	1:43.00	
1970	Pattee Canyon	5	E. Fires	119	Klassy Poppy	120	Blue Rage	115	36,950	1:43.00	
1971	Swoon's Flower	4	C. Marquez	115	Stolen Base	115	Toter Back	112	27,915	1:41.60	
1972	Evending Bag	7	W. Gavidia	111	Aladancer	119	Painted Pony	116	29,760	1:41.60	
1972	Toter Back	5	J. Tejeira	114	Gem Wood Betty	113	Flor de S'bra	114	29,760	1:41.60	
1973	Deb Marion	3	F. Ianelli	106	Tico's Donna	113	Barely Even	125	27,240	1:42.60	
1974	Dogtooth Violet	4	D. Brumfield	113	Dove Creek Lady	124	Shearwater	115	38,420	1:41.00	
1975	Protectora	6	H. Gustines	114	Zippy Do	118	Lorraine Edna	116	26,100	1:41.20	
1976	Deessee du Val	5	C. Marquez	116	Redundancy	120	K D Princess	110	28,785	1:41.80	
1977	Copano	5	M. Solomone	122	Jabot	117	Carolina Moon	114	43,400	1:41.40	
1978	Time for Pleasure	4	T. Barrow	115	Late Bloomer	113	Rich Soil	116	37,800	1:41.00	
1979	Sans Arc	5	E. Fires	116	Terpsichorist	122	Time for Pleasure	119	86,093	1:41.40	
1980	Just a Game II	4	D. Brumfield	119	La Soufriere	115	La Rouquine II	114	80,340	1:40.40	
1981	Honey Fox	4	J. Vasquez	115	The Very One	125	Solo Haina	114	88,530	1:41.20	
1982	Blush	4	J. Vasquez	112	Pine Flower	114	Honey Fox	125	76,500	1:41.00	
1983	Sweetest Chant	5	E. Fires	116	Betty Money	114	Norsan	115	53,040	1:43.60	
1983	Larida	4	E. Maple	118	Syrianna	116	Promising Native	115	53,640	1:44.80	
1984	Sabin	4	E. Maple	125	Jubilous	114	Sulemeif	115	70,680	1:41.40	
1985	Pretty Perfect	5	G. Gallitano	120	Early Lunch	113	Trinado	112	61,980	1:41.60	
1985	Aspen Rose	5	J. Velasquez	116	Over Your Shoulder	114	Dictina	117	63,180	1:42.00	
1986	Videogenic	4	R.G. Davis	121	Powder Break	118	Devalois	117	118,440	2:27.20	
1987	Anka Germania	5	C. Perret	117	Singular Bequest	116	Ivor's Image	119	90,000	2:31.40	
1988	Beauty Cream	5	P. Day	115	Ladanum	112	Green Oasis	112	120,000	2:28.40	
1989	Gaily Gaily	6	J.A. Krone	110	Anka Germania	120	Laugh and Be Merry	110	120,000	2:26.80	
1990	Coolawin	4	J.D. Bailey	112	Laugh and Be Merry	113	Gaily Gaily	121	120,000	2:24.20	
1991	Star Standing	4	C.W. Antley	114	Coolawin	118	Peinture Bleue	119	120,000	2:25.00	105
1992	Crockadore	5	M.E. Smith	112	Indian Fashion	112	Sardaniya	114	120,000	2:28.20	100
1993	Fairy Garden	5	W.S. Ramos	115	Rougeur	115	Trampoli	115	120,000	2:25.60	104
1994	Trampoli	5	M.E. Smith	121	Good Morning Smile	110	Northern Emerald	112	120,000	2:25.40	103
1995	Exchange	7	L. Pincay Jr	120	Market Booster	116	Northern Emerald	115	120,000	2:29.00	102
1996	Memories	5	J.A. Santos	114	Caromana	112	Curtain Raiser	113	120,000	2:31.40	98
1997	Golden Pond	4	W.H. McCauley	116	Tocopilla	115	Miss Caerleona	114	120,000	2:26.80	104
1998	Colonial Play	4	R.G. Davis	113	Almost Skint	114	Gastronomical	113	120,000	2:24.60	96
1999	Coretta	5	J.A. Santos	118	Delilah	117	Almost Skint	113	120,000	2:23.80	103
2000	Lisieux Rose	5	J.A. Santos	114	Chamapgne Royal	114	Fly for Avie	114	120,000	2:25.64	97
2001	Innuendo	6	J.D. Bailey	116	Windsong	113	Aiglonne	114	120,000	2:25.24	104
2002	Julie Jalouse	4	J.A. Santos	114	Sweetest Thing	115	Refugee	110	120,000	2:25.89	96
2003	Tweedside	5	R.R. Douglas	116	San Dare	119	Hi Tech Honeycomb	115	120,000	2:32.36	91
2004	Meridiana	4	E.S. Prado	114	Savedbythelight	114	Miss Hellie	114	120,000	2:26.99	95

Beyer Index: 99.86

Off the turf in 2003.

PACIFIC CLASSIC (G1), 1 1/4 Miles, 3-Year-Olds and Up, Del Mar, 2004 Purse: $1,000,000

Year	Winner	Age	Jockey	Wt.	Second	Wt.	Third	Wt.	Win Value	Time	Beyer
1991	Best Pal	3	P.A. Valenzuela	116	Twilight Agenda	124	Unbridled	124	550,000	1:59.80	118
1992	Missionary Ridge	5	K.J. Desormeaux	124	Defensive Play	124	Claret	124	550,000	2:00.80	110
1993	Bertrando	4	G.L. Stevens	124	Missionary Ridge	124	Best Pal	124	550,000	1:59.40	117
1994	Tinners Way	4	E. Delahoussaye	124	Best Pal	124	Dramatic Gold	117	550,000	1:59.40	111

Year	Winner	Age	Jockey	Wt.	Second	Wt.	Third	Wt.	Win Value	Time	Beyer
1995	Tinners Way	5	E. Delahoussaye	124	Soul of the Matter	124	Blumin Affair	124	550,000	1:59.60	112
1996	Dare and Go	5	A. Solis	124	Cigar	124	Siphon	124	600,000	1:59.80	116
1997	Gentlemen	5	G.L. Stevens	124	Siphon	124	Crafty Friend	124	600,000	2:00.40	121
1998	Free House	4	C.J. McCarron	124	Gentlemen	124	Pacificbounty	124	600,000	2:00.29	117
1999	General Challenge	3	D.R. Flores	117	River Keen	124	Barter Town	124	600,000	2:00.57	119
2000	Skimming	4	G.K. Gomez	124	Tiznow	117	Ecton Park	124	600,000	2:01.22	117
2001	Skimming	5	G.K. Gomez	124	Dixie Dot Com	124	Dig For It	124	600,000	1:59.96	119
2002	Came Home	3	M.E. Smith	117	Momentum	124	Milwaukee Brew	124	600,000	2:01.45	116
2003	Candy Ride	4	J.A. Krone	124	Medaglia d'Oro	124	Fleetstreet Dancer	124	600,000	1:59.11	123
2004	Pleasantly Perfect	6	J.D. Bailey	124	Perfect Drift	124	Total Impact	124	600,000	2:01.17	112

Beyer Index: 116.29

PALM BEACH (G3), 1 1/8 Miles (Turf), 3-Year-Olds, Gulfstream Park, 2004 Purse: $100,000

Year	Winner	Age	Jockey	Wt.	Second	Wt.	Third	Wt.	Win Value	Time	Beyer
1990	Dawn Quixote	3	C. Perret	119	Rowdy Regal	119	Always Running	115	30,000	1:23.40	94
1991	Magic Interlude	3	C.W. Antley	114	Island Delay	117	Explosive Jeff	114	38,310	1:43.00	90
1992	Preferences	3	J.C. Duarte	114	Doo You	112	Stress Buster	114	38,940	1:42.60	95
1993	Kissin Kris	3	D. Penna	113	Pride Prevails	112	Awad	119	38,760	1:46.40	87
1994	Mr. Angel	3	W.H. McCauley	112	Clint Essential	114	Fabulous Frolic	119	30,000	1:44.40	91
1995	Admiralty	3	J.A. Krone	114	Nostra	112	Smells and Bells	114	30,000	1:51.00	94
1996	Harrowman	3	M.E. Smith	114	A Real Zipper	117	Ok by Me	119	45,000	1:49.20	90
1997	Unite's Big Red	3	Hernandez R.	117	Trample	112	Tekken	117	45,000	1:47.20	92
1998	Cryptic Rascal	3	M.E. Smith	119	The Kaiser	113	American Odyssey	114	45,000	1:55.00	93
1999	Swamp	3	R. Migliore	114	Marquette	114	Valid Reprized	119	45,000	1:48.20	96
2000	Mr. Livingston	3	S.J. Sellers	114	Powerful Appeal	114	Gateman	117	45,000	1:48.04	96
2001	Proud Man	3	R.R. Douglas	119	One Eyed Joker	114	Strategic Partner	112	60,000	1:48.32	91
2002	Orchard Park	3	J.D. Bailey	118	Lord Juban	118	Red's Top Gun	116	60,000	1:49.80	90
2003	Nothing to Lose	3	J.D. Bailey	122	White Cat	118	Imitation	118	60,000	1:48.28	93
2004	Kitten's Joy	3	J.D. Bailey	122	Prince Arch	118	Pa Pa Da	118	60,000	1:48.76	91

Beyer Index: 92.20

PALOMAR BREEDERS' CUP HANDICAP (G2), 1 1/16 Miles (Turf), Fillies and Mares, 3-Year-Olds and Up, Del Mar, 2004 Purse: $180,000

Year	Winner	Age	Jockey	Wt.	Second	Wt.	Third	Wt.	Win Value	Time	Beyer
1955	Robinar	3	J. Longden	115	Royal Grace	110	Madam Jet	114	6,550	1:09.00	
1956	In Reserve	4	J. Longden	122	Baby Alice	112	Chargers Gal	110	8,375	1:09.40	
1957	Myrtle	4	I. Valenzuela	115	Bettyanbull	110	Mateka	104	8,375	1:09.40	
1958	Camloc	3	P. Moreno	115	Ballet Khal	122	Sweet Land	113	8,375	1:09.80	
1959	Sweet June	3	R. York	110	Boston Again	125	Peeress	108	9,200	1:09.20	
1960	Perizade	4	R. Campas	107	Sweet June	122	Boston Again	121	9,025	1:09.20	
1961	Nascania	4	E. Ohayon	116	Cherokee Miss	112	Ypres	112	9,075	1:09.00	
1962	Sunday Slippers	3	J. Leonard	116	Spark Plug	121	Edie Belle	117	8,875	1:09.20	
1963	Sabina Louise	3	J. Lambert	113	Corolla	114	Kea	115	8,725	1:12.20	
1964	Soldier Girl	3	J. Longden	126	Jam n Jellie	121	C'li's'm h'n'y	113	8,675	1:09.40	
1965	Jam n Jellie	5	W. Hartack	116	Sari's Song	119	Pretty Bubbles	111	8,850	1:08.80	
1966	Fleet Treat	3	F. Alvarez	115	Admirably	127	Maintain	115	9,050	1:08.80	
1967	Admirably	5	J. Lambert	130	Roman Heiress	113	Francine M.	111	10,225	1:08.60	
1968	Pacific Cross	4	J. Sellers	115	Mira Femme	125	Peggy's World	118	8,725	1:09.00	
1969	Time to Leave	4	D. Velasquez	129	Talking Barb	114	Fast Dish	122	20,900	1:08.20	
1970	Lynn's Orphan	4	D. Tierney	117	Hi Q.	116	Poona Downs	116	7,925	1:29.60	
1970	La Sevillana	4	A. Pineda	114	Windy Mama	116	Everything Lovely	117	7,925	1:29.20	
							Boughs o' Holly	117			
1971	Street Dancer	4	W. Shoemaker	118	Shelf Talker	114	Ancient Silk	112	8,500	1:29.20	
1971	Opening Bid	4	J. Lambert	118	Dumpty's Lady	112	Hi Q.	121	8,400	1:29.80	
1972	Minstrel Miss	5	D. Pierce	118	Street Dancer	121	Balcony's Babe	118	10,175	1:28.40	
1973	Meilleur	3	D. Pierce	114	Lady Debbie	116	Probation	113	10,775	1:28.80	
1973	Belle Marie	3	W. Shoemaker	114	Best Go	115	Chargerette	116	9,975	1:28.80	
1974	Sphere	4	S. Valdez	114	Lt.'s Joy	121	Modus Vivendi	122	14,050	1:28.40	
1975	Modus Vivendi	4	F. Toro	122	Move Abroad	113	Tizna	124	14,100	1:28.80	
1976	Just a Kick	4	L. Pincay Jr	120	Our First Delight	114	Effusive	113	15,900	1:29.40	
1977	Dancing Femme	4	D. Pierce	120	Swingtime	121	Dacani	115	17,250	1:35.60	
1978	Drama Critic	4	D. Pierce	118	Afifa	119	Fact	115	26,550	1:36.40	
1979	More So	4	W. Shoemaker	115	Giggling Girl	119	Wishing Well	118	34,150	1:35.40	
1980	A Thousand Stars	5	E. Delahoussaye	115	Wishing Well	121	Devon Ditty	120	34,150	1:34.80	
1981	Kilijaro	5	M. Castaneda	129	Lisawan	115	Satin Ribera	118	40,700	1:35.40	
1982	Northern Fable	4	S. Hawley	114	Sangue	124	Princess Gayle	116	33,500	1:35.20	
1982	Star Pastures	4	W. Shoemaker	117	Honey Fox	122	Cannon Boy	114	34,000	1:35.40	
1983	Triple Tipple	4	C.J. McCarron	118	Castilla	121	First Advance	115	52,050	1:35.60	
1984	Moment to Buy	3	T.M. Chapman	115	L'Attrayante	120	Royal Heroine	125	50,550	1:35.20	

Year	Winner	Age	Jockey	Wt.	Second	Wt.	Third	Wt.	Win Value	Time	Beyer
1985	Capici	5	R.A. Baze	116	L'Attrayante	119	Gala Event	115	50,150	1:35.20	
1986	Aberuschka	4	P.A. Valenzuela	118	Sauna	118	Fran's Valentine	119	62,750	1:34.40	
1987	Festivity	4	A. Solis	115	Adorable Micol	117	Secuencia	117	64,850	1:35.80	
1988	Chapel of Dreams	4	E. Delahoussaye	117	Short Sleeves	121	Davie's Lamb	117	78,000	1:42.60	
1989	Claire Marine	4	R.G. Davis	122	Galunpe	118	Daring Doone	116	64,800	1:43.20	
1990	Jabalina Brown	5	J.A. Garcia	112	Stylish Star	116	Nikishka	117	64,200	1:42.60	
1991	Guiza	4	G.L. Stevens	114	Agirlfromars	114	Run to Jenny	113	49,300	1:42.00	
1991	Somethingmerry	4	L. Pincay Jr	117	Countus In	117	Sweet Roberta	115	48,800	1:41.80	103
1992	Super Staff	4	C.J. McCarron	114	Odalea	114	Only Yours	115	64,900	1:42.40	101
1993	Heart of Joy	6	D.R. Flores	119	Kalita Melody	114	Amal Hayati	114	63,000	1:42.00	104
1994	Shir Dar	4	C.S. Nakatani	114	Baby Diamonds	110	Prying	117	63,600	1:42.80	95
1995	Morgana	4	G.L. Stevens	118	Yearly Tour	118	Lady Affirmed	117	74,450	1:42.40	103
1996	Yearly Tour	5	C.J. McCarron	116	Slewvera	115	Real Connection	114	81,350	1:42.40	101
1997	Blushing Heiress	5	C.J. McCarron	117	Traces of Gold	115	Listening	120	83,200	1:43.20	96
1998	Tuzla	4	C.S. Nakatani	117	Ecoute	114	Call Me	116	80,970	1:42.20	98
1999	Happyanunoit	4	B. Blanc	113	Tuzla	123	Ile de France	118	80,520	1:41.28	101
2000	Tranquility Lake	5	E. Delahoussaye	121	Tout Charmant	121	Miss Of Wales	114	82,170	1:41.01	104
2001	Tranquility Lake	6	E. Delahoussaye	123	La Ronge	116	Al Desima	113	90,000	1:41.94	101
2002	Voodoo Dancer	4	K.J. Desormeaux	120	I'm the Business	114	Skywriting	114	90,000	1:41.56	102
2003	Spring Star	4	A. Solis	116	Magic Mission	117	Garden in the Rain	114	120,000	1:40.78	101
2004	Etoile Montante	4	J. Valdivia Jr	120	Katdogawn	117	Tangle	117	120,000	1:40.59	98

Beyer Index: 100.57

PALOS VERDES HANDICAP (G2), 6 Furlongs, 4-Year-Olds and Up, Santa Anita, 2004 Purse: $150,000

Year	Winner	Age	Jockey	Wt.	Second	Wt.	Third	Wt.	Win Value	Time	Beyer
1951	Northern Star	3	T. Atkinson	118	Admiral Drake	113	Phil D.	113	14,150	1:10.40	
1952	First Glance	5	E. Guerin	119	Reighs Bull	121	Stranglehold	112	13,300	1:10.20	
1953	Heliowise	5	P. Moreno	107	Cyclotron	122	Phil D.	113	14,950	1:09.40	
1954	Imbros	4	J. Longden	128	Berseem	124	Hour Regards	110	14,650	1:09.00	
1955	History Book	5	R. Neves	113	Karim	115	Hour Regards	111	14,050	1:10.80	
1956	Porterhouse	6	E. Arcaro	125	Johnie Mike	119	Scent	119	13,300	1:10.20	
1957	Nashville	3	W. Shoemaker	119	El Khobar	118	Noredski	112	14,100	1:09.60	
1958	Golden Notes	4	E. Arcaro	115	Seaneen	119	The Searcher	113	13,350	1:09.60	
1959	Clandestine	4	W. Shoemaker	113	Fleet Nasrullah	126	Caronat	112	12,750	1:09.20	
1960	Ole Fols	4	W. Shoemaker	117	Henrijan	114	Finnegan	118	14,700	1:09.40	
1961	Revel	5	A. Maese	127	Ole Fols	119	Windy Sands	113	14,250	1:09.80	
1962	Crozier	4	I. Valenzuela	122	Olden Times	126	Songman	110	14,150	1:09.20	
1963	Cyrano	4	M. Ycaza	122	Sledge	118	Olden Times	126	13,450	1:08.40	
1964	Native Diver	5	J. Lambert	125	Viking Spirit	120	Sledge	125	14,350	1:10.20	
1965	Native Diver	6	J. Lambert	129	Isle of Greece	114	Sledge	121	13,800	1:09.00	
1966	Pretense	3	W. Shoemaker	114	Hoist Bar	116	Aurelius II	115	17,950	1:09.20	
1967	Kissin' George	4	W. Mahorney	126	Hoist Bar	114	Suteki	114	16,950	1:09.20	
1968	Rising Market	4	L. Pincay Jr	124	Tumiga	123	Baffle	117	17,650	1:10.40	
1971	King of Cricket	4	H. Grant	120	Brazen Brother	122	Tower East	112	19,900	1:11.00	
1971	Jungle Savage	5	J. Lambert	117	Ack Ack	129	King of Cricket	119	19,350	1:08.60	
1972	Crusading	4	F. Toro	117	Single Agent	122	Grey Papa	115	21,900	1:08.60	
1973	Woodland Pines	4	D. Pierce	115	Tragic Isle	117	Ancient Title	122	20,800	1:09.00	
1974	Ancient Title	4	L. Pincay Jr	126	Princely Native	116	King o't'Bl's	113	20,900	1:08.80	
1975	Messenger of Song	3	J. Lambert	125	Wilmar	115	Rise High	118	19,800	1:08.60	
1976	Maheras	3	L. Pincay Jr	119	Sure Fire	116	Ancient Title	126	29,400	1:08.60	
1977	Impressive Luck	4	S. Hawley	119	Maheras	120	Curr'nt Concept	117	26,000	1:10.40	
1978	Little Reb	3	F. Olivares	116	Crash Program	112	Bad 'n Big	125	33,900	1:08.60	
1979	Beau's Eagle	3	S. Hawley	122	Always Gallant	124	Charley Sutton	115	32,750	1:10.00	
1980	To B. or Not	4	M. Castaneda	121	Unalakleet	115	Syncopate	123	34,000	1:08.20	
1981	I'm Smokin'	5	P.A. Valenzuela	119	To B. or Not	121	Solo Guy	119	39,200	1:08.00	
1982	Chinook Pass	3	L. Pincay Jr	120	General Jimmy	112	Unpredictable	122	40,050	1:07.60	
1983	Fighting Fit	4	E. Delahoussaye	122	Expressman	115	Gemini Dreamer	117	38,150	1:09.00	
1984	Debonaire Junior	3	C.J. McCarron	120	Charging Falls	112	Premiership	117	51,700	1:10.20	
1985	Phone Trick	3	L. Pincay Jr	121	Five North	112	Debonaire Junior	123	50,100	1:08.00	
1986	Bedside Promise	4	G.L. Stevens	123	Bolder Than Bold	116	Rocky Marriage	115	60,000	1:08.40	
1987	High Brite	3	G.L. Stevens	116	Hilco Scamper	117	Zany Tactics	123	62,500	1:09.00	
1988	On the Line	4	G.L. Stevens	124	Claim	118	Basic Rate	115	62,700	1:07.60	
1989	Sunny Blossom	4	G.L. Stevens	115	Olympic Prospect	123	Sam Who	122	62,400	1:07.20	
1990	Frost Free	5	C.J. McCarron	119	Valiant Pete	117	Kipper Kelly	112	61,400	1:08.60	
1992	Individualist	5	L. Pincay Jr	117	High Energy	114	Rushmore	114	65,600	1:08.60	111
1993	Music Merci	7	D.R. Flores	114	Star of the Crop	119	Cardmania	117	63,700	1:08.80	104
1994	Concept Win	4	Stevens GL	115	J.F. Williams	117	Scherando	116	62,100	1:07.60	112
1995	D'Hallevant	5	Nakatani CS	117	Cardmania	120	Subtle Trouble	115	94,400	1:08.40	107
1996	Lit De Justice	6	E. Delahoussaye	122	Siphon	119	Lakota Brave	115	135,100	1:08.80	112
1997	High Stakes Player	5	C.S. Nakatani	114	Rotsaluck	114	Larry the Legend	116	131,600	1;08.40	109

Year	Winner	Age	Jockey	Wt.	Second	Wt.	Third	Wt.	Win Value	Time	Beyer
1998	Funontherun	4	G.F. Almeida	113	Red	116	Elmhurst	119	120,000	1:08.80	107
1999	Big Jag	6	J. Valdivia Jr.	116	Kona Gold	121	Swiss Yodeler	114	120,000	1:08.00	115
2000	Kona Gold	6	A. Solis	121	Big Jag	121	Freespool	115	120,000	1:08.55	112
2001	Men's Exclusive	8	L. Pincay Jr.	116	Big Jag	120	Freespool	116	120,000	1:08.33	112
2002	Snow Ridge	4	M.E. Smith	116	Squirtle Squirt	122	Ceeband	117	90,000	1:07.70	117
2003	Avanzado	6	T.C. Baze	116	Mellow Fellow	117	Disturbingthepeace	120	90,000	1:07.85	117
2004	Bluesthestandard	7	M.E. Smith	117	Marino Marini	115	Our New Recruit	114	90,000	1:08.13	114

Beyer Index: 111.46

PAN AMERICAN HANDICAP (G2), 1 1/2 Miles (Turf), 3-Year-Olds and Up, Gulfstream Park, 2004 Purse: $200,000

Year	Winner	Age	Jockey	Wt.	Second	Wt.	Third	Wt.	Win Value	Time	Beyer
1962	Shirley Jones	6	L. Gilligan	121	Aeroflint	118	Deton	109	11,800	1:51.20	
1963	Sensitivo	6	H. Grant	120	Valetine	118	Tin God	114	11,800	1:50.00	
1964	Babington	5	R. Broussard	117	Totem II	113	Flying Johnnie	114	14,500	1:51.60	
1965	Cool Prince	5	W. Hartack	114	Babington	117	Barbaron	115	45,200	2:26.40	
1966	Pillanlebun	5	F. Toro	117	Cedar Key	122	Rob't's Fl'g	111	40,600	2:26.40	
1967	War Censor	4	E. Fires	120	Voluntario III	113	Ginger Fizz	118	46,500	2:26.00	
1968	Irish Rebellion	4	A. Cordero Jr	114			Pillan'ebun	114	28,850	2:26.40	
	Estreno II	7	D. Hidalgo	109							
1969	Hibernian	4	P. Anderson	114	Irish Rebellion	112	N'dles Stitch	112	42,600	2:28.60	
1970	One for All	4	C. Perret	114	Snow Sporting	122	Eaglesham	113	67,600	2:26.80	
1971	Chompion	6	M. Hole	116	Snow Sporting	119	One for All	114	63,600	2:25.60	
1972	Unanime	5	H. Gustines	110	Double Entry	112	Gleaming	124	74,360	2:26.60	
1973	Lord Vancouver	5	W. Blum	112	Life Cycle	118	Windtex	116	43,520	2:26.60	
1974	London Company	4	A. Cordero Jr	119	Outdoors	112	Bush Fleet	113	84,720	2:26.40	
1975	Buffalo Lark	5	L. Snyder	120	London Company	123	Duke Tom	115	84,120	2:27.60	
1976	Improviser	4	J. Cruguet	114	Green Room	109	P'p'r'd j'bn'h	113	86,880	2:26.60	
1977	Gravelines	5	J.D. Bailey	124	Le Cypriote	110	Gay Jitterbug	124	80,400	2:24.80	
1978	Bowl Game	4	J. Velasquez	117	That's a Nice	116	Court Open	112	100,000	2:30.20	
1979	Noble Dancer II	7	J. Vasquez	129	Fleet Gar	116	Warfever	113	100,000	2:25.20	
1980	Flitalong	4	R.I. Encinas	110	Morning Frolic	119	Novel Notion	117	100,000	2:28.40	
1981	Little Bonny	4	E. Maple	114	Lobsang II	115	Buckpoint	124	121,030	2:32.40	
1982	Robsphere	5	J. Velasquez	117	Come Rain or Shine	110	The Bart	124	102,150	2:26.00	
1983	Highland Blade	5	J. Vasquez	121	Tonzarun	108	Dhausli	113	80,295	2:29.20	
1983	Field Cat	6	J.L. Samyn	110	Pin Puller	112	Santo's Joe	109	82,095	2:29.60	
1984	Tonzarun	6	W.H. McCauley	112	Ayman	114	Nassipour	110	109,275	2:26.80	
1985	Selous Scout	4	R. Platts	112	Norclin	111	Nassipour	115	185,280	2:25.20	
1986	Powder Break	5	S.B. Soto	112	Uptown Swell	116	Flying Pidgeon	118	180,000	2:25.00	
1987	Iroko	5	E. Fires	112	Akabir	113	Glaros	112	150,000	2:26.40	
1988	Carotene	6	D.J. Seymour	115	Ladanum	110	Salem Drive	117	180,000	2:25.00	
1989	Mi Selecto	4	J.A. Santos	114	Pay the Butler	121	Fabulous Indian	112	180,000	2:01.60	
1990	My Big Boy	7	H. Castillo Jr	112	Marksmanship	113	Turfah	115	180,000	2:29.20	101
1991	Phantom Breeze	5	J.A. Krone	116	Dr. Root	114	Runaway Raja	110	180,000	2:29.40	
1992	Wall Street Dancer	4	J. Velasquez	114	Passagere du Soir	116	Missionary Ridge	115	210,000	2:25.40	100
1993	Fraise	5	P.A. Valenzuela	124	Stagecraft	117	Futurist	115	180,000	2:32.80	107
1994	Fraise	6	M.E. Smith	124	Summer Ensign	113	Fairy Garden	115	180,000	2:24.60	104
1995	Awad	5	E. Maple	114	Misil	120	Frenchpark	117	180,000	2:29.40	110
1996	Celtic Arms	5	M.E. Smith	115	Broadway Flyer	116	Flag Down	117	180,000	2:25.60	109
1997	Flag Down	7	J. A. Santos	117	Lassigny	117	Awad	117	180,000	2:27.00	108
1998	Buck's Boy	5	E. Fires	115	African Dancer	115	Royal Strand	114	150,000	2:23.40	108
1999	Unite's Big Red	5	M.E. Smith	114	African Dancer	116	Panama City	116	150,000	2:23.00	106
2000	Buck's Boy	7	E.S. Prado	120	Thesaurus	113	Epistolaire	114	150,000	2:24.80	101
	Beautiful Dancer finished third but was disqualified and placed sixth										
2001	Whata Brainstorm	4	J.R. Velazquez	114	Subtle Power	115	Craigsteel	114	150,000	2:23.75	106
2002	Deeliteful Irving	4	C.P. DeCarlo	113	Cetewayo	118	Mr. Livingston	114	120,000	2:24.14	105
2003	Quest Star	4	E.S. Prado	113	Man From Wicklow	122	Reduit	114	120,000	2:28.45	104
2004	Quest Star	5	P. Day	114	Request for Parole	115	Megantic	112	120,000	2:26.46	101

Beyer Index: 105.00

PEBBLES (G3), 1 1/8 Miles (Turf), 3-Year-Old Fillies, Belmont Park, 2004 Purse: $112,300

Year	Winner	Age	Jockey	Wt.	Second	Wt.	Third	Wt.	Win Value	Time	Beyer
1993	Statuette	3	M.E. Smith	121	Tricky Princess	114	Belle Nuit	115	45,060	1:40.60	86
1994	Saxuality	3	J.A. Krone	114	Lady Affirmed	118	Tensie's Pro	118	41,580	1:34.00	95
1995	Queen Tutta	3	G.Stevens	115	Transient Trend	114	Nappelon	118	53,820	1:43.20	90
1996	Rare Blend	3	G.Stevens	115	Polish Spring	114	Inner Circle	114	52,110	1:44.40	90
1997	Heaven's Command	3	J.Santos	116	Wollastina	110	Colonial Minstrel	110	51,375	1:42.80	95
1998	Sophie My Love	3	J.R.Velazquez	118	Appealing Kris	111	Proud Owner	116	51,150	1:52.20	91
1999	Eze	3	Davis R. G.	113	Colstar	115	Jazz	114	49,950	1:52.80	94

Year	Winner	Age	Jockey	Wt.	Second	Wt.	Third	Wt.	Win Value	Time	Beyer
2000	Lady Dora	3	J.R. Velazquez	114	De Aar	114	Tippity Witch	117	52,245	1:48.76	94
2001	Heads Will Roll	3	E.S. Prado	115	New Economy	114	Salty You	115	66,060	1:47.75	88
2001	Love N' Kiss S.	3	J.A. Santos	114	Calista	118	Shooting Part	115	66,360	1:47.50	90
2002	Glia	3	J.J. Castellano	113	Nonsuch Bay	123	Delta Princess	113	68,580	1:49.68	91
2003	Betty's Wish	3	J.R. Velazquez	116	Mystery Itself	112	Andover Lady	114	66,180	1:51.00	97
2004	Fortunate Damsel	3	J.J. Castellano	119	Venturi	121	Delta Sensation	119	67,380	1:48.80	94

Beyer Index: 91.92

PEGASUS HANDICAP (G3), 1 1/8 Miles, 3-Year-Olds, The Meadowlands, 2004 Purse: $300,000

Year	Winner	Age	Jockey	Wt.	Second	Wt.	Third	Wt.	Win Value	Time	Beyer
1980	Dr. Blum	3	R. Hernandez	115	Bill Wheeler	115	Peace for Peace	115	15,150	1:11.00	
1981	Summing	3	G. Martens	122	Johnny Dance	114	Maudlin	112	133,620	1:51.00	
1982	Fast Gold	3	J.L. Samyn	110	Muttering	120	Exclusive One	116	131,160	1:49.00	
1983	World Appeal	3	A. Graell	114	Hyperborean	118	Bounding Basque	115	135,360	1:46.60	
1984	Hail Bold King	3	J. Velasquez	115	Carr de Naskra	122	Jyp	115	131,040	1:49.20	
							Morning Bob	119			
1985	Skip Trial	3	J.L. Samyn	123	Stephan's Odyssey	123	Violado	117	200,040	1:51.00	
1986	Danzig Connection	3	P. Day	122	Broad Brush	122	Ogygian	124	180,000	1:49.00	
1987	Cryptoclearance	3	J.A. Santos	122	Lost Code	122	Templar Hill	118	180,000	1:48.60	
1988	Brian's Time	3	A. Cordero Jr	121	Festive	110	Congeleur	112	180,000	1:47.00	
1989	Norquestor	3	J.A. Krone	114	Rampart Road	113	Fast Play	116	180,000	1:49.60	
1990	Silver Ending	3	E. Delahoussaye	119	Music Prospector	116	Runaway Stream	113	180,000	1:47.20	
1991	Scan	3	J.A. Santos	119	Sea Cadet	119	Sultry Song	114	180,000	1:46.40	116
1992	Scuffleburg	3	J.A. Krone	111	Nines Wild	113	Agincourt	115	300,000	1:49.00	104
1993	Diazo	3	L. Pincay Jr	117	Press Card	116	Schossberg	116	150,000	1:47.00	109
1994	Brass Scale	3	E.S Prado	114	Hello Chicago	114	Serious Spender	111	120,000	1:49.20	100
1995	Flying Chevron	3	R.G. Davis	112	Da Hoss	122	Ghostly Moves	113	120,000	1:40.80	117
1996	Allied Forces	3	R. Migliore	116	Lite Approval	112	Defacto	116	120,000	1:47.00	108
1997	Behrens	3	J.D. Bailey	117	Anet	120	Frisk Me Now	119	600,000	1:46.60	118
1998	Tomorrows Cat	3	J. Bravo	113	Limit Out	115	Comic Strip	119	300,000	1:46.80	110
1999	Forty One Carats	3	J.F. Chavez	120	Unbridled Jet	116	Talk's Cheap	118	240,000	1:45.40	109
2000	Kiss a Native	3	M.K. Walls	119	Cool N Collective	115	Pine Dance	121	150,000	1:48.33	107
2001	Volponi	3	S.X. Bridgmohan	114	Burning Roma	119	Giant gentlemen	116	150,000	1:46.55	113
2002	Regal Sanction	3	J.A. Santos	115	No Parole	117	This Guns for Hire	115	210,000	1:49.87	94
2004	Pies Prospect	3	E.S. Prado	118	Eddington	118	Zakocity	118	180,000	1:48.57	101

Beyer Index: 108.15

Not run in 2003

PENNSYLVANIA DERBY (G2), 1 1/8 Miles, 3-Year-Olds, Philadelphia Park, 2004 Purse: $750,000

Year	Winner	Age	Jockey	Wt.	Second	Wt.	Third	Wt.	Win Value	Time	Beyer
1979	Smarten	3	S. Maple	122	Incredible Ease	122	Incubator	122	68,880	1:49.20	
1980	Lively King	3	C.J. Baker	122	Mutineer	122	Stutz Blackhawk	122	99,480	1:48.80	
1981	Summing	3	G. Martens	122	Sportin' Life	122	Classic Go Go	122	100,380	1:49.00	
1982	Spanish Drums	3	J. Vasquez	122	Air Forbes Won	122	A Magic Spray	122	101,460	1:49.00	
1983	Dixieland Band	3	W.J. Passmore	122	Jacques Tip	122	Intention	122	136,500	1:49.40	
1984	Morning Bob	3	G. McCarron	122	At the Threshold	122	Biloxi Indian	122	132,240	1:49.40	
							Raja's Shark	122			
1985	Skip Trial	3	J.L. Samyn	122	El Basco	122	Jacque L'Heureux	119	180,000	1:50.20	
1986	Broad Brush	3	A. Cordero Jr	122	Sumptious	122	Glow	122	180,000	1:50.80	
1987	Afleet	3	G. Stahlbaum	122	Lost Code	122	Homebuilder	119	180,000	1:48.20	
1988	Cefis	3	L. Saumell	122	Congeleur	119	Ballindaggin	119	180,000	1:49.60	
1989	Western Playboy	3	K. Clark	122	Roi Danzig	122	Tricky Creek	122	180,000	1:47.60	
1990	Summer Squall	3	P. Day	122	Challenge My Duty	122	Sports View	122	180,000	1:48.20	
1991	Valley Crossing	3	A.J. Seefeldt	119	Gala Spinaway	122	Riflery	117	90,000	1:50.00	
1992	Thelastcrusade	3	V.H. Molina	114	Ecstatic Ride	114	Nines Wild	117	90,000	1:49.40	107
1993	Wallenda	3	W.H. McCauley	114	Press Card	117	Saintly Prospector	122	120,000	1:49.20	100
1994	Meadow Flight	3	J. Bravo	122	Red Tazz	117	Kandaly	122	120,000	1:49.00	106
1995	Pineing Patty	3	L. Melancon	122	Royal Haven	117	Tenants Harbor	117	120,000	1:48.00	108
1996	Devil's Honor	3	A.S. Black	122	Formal Gold	117	Clash by Night	119	120,000	1:48.40	114
1997	Frisk Me Now	3	E. L. King Jr.	122	Envy of the Crown	114	Christian Soldier	114	120,000	1:48.00	114
1998	Rock and Roll	3	H. Castillo Jr	114	Tomorrows Cat	114	Black Blade	119	150,000	1:47.60	110
1999	Smart Guy	3	R. E. Colton	119	Ghost Ring	114	Pineaff	122	180,000	1:49.40	109
2000	Pine Dance	3	M.J. McCarthy	122	Mass Market	122	Cherokeeinthehills	114	180,000	1:49.03	105
2001	Macho Uno	3	G.L. Stevens	116	Unbridled Elaine	119	Touch Tone	122	300,000	1:49.69	104
2002	Harlan's Holiday	3	E.S. Prado	122	Essence of Dubai	122	Make the Bend	119	300,000	1:51.10	96
2003	Grand Hombre	3	J. Bravo	114	Gimmeawink	122	Ashmore	114	450,000	1:49.03	108
2004	Love of Money	3	R.J. Albarado	116	Pollard's Vision	122	Swingforthefences	119	450,000	1:48.42	112

Beyer Index: 107.15

PERSONAL ENSIGN HANDICAP (G1), 1 1/4 Miles, Fillies and Mares, 3-Year-Olds and Up, Saratoga Race Course, 2004 Purse: $392,000

Year	Winner	Age	Jockey	Wt.	Second	Wt.	Third	Wt.	Win Value	Time	Beyer
1948	Carolyn A.	4	C. LeBlanc	114	Gallorette	126	Red Shoes	107	19,450	1:46.80	
1949	But Why Not	5	D. Gorman	116	Allie's Pal	111	Conniver	126	19,600	1:44.80	
1950	Red Camelia	4	P. Milligan	110	Roman Candle	113	Nell K.	123	20,250	1:45.40	
1951	Renew	4	B. Green	112	Thelma Burger	109	Next Move	126	23,750	1:50.60	
1952	Next Move	5	E. Guerin	126	Thelma Burger	110	Kiss Me Kate	123	22,900	1:51.20	
1953	Kiss Me Kate	5	D. Gorman	126	Parading Lady	123	La Corredora	123	24,350	1:50.80	
1954	Parlo	3	T. Atkinson	125	Riverina	115	Spinning Top	110	24,700	1:53.40	
1955	Rare Treat	3	R. Mikkonen	112	Searching	118	White Cross	108	24,900	1:50.80	
1956	Blue Banner	4	W. Boland	115	Happy Princess	109	Manotick	119	19,400	1:49.40	
1957	Gay Life	4	J. Ruane	108	Dotted Line	113	Little Pache	111	20,300	1:50.40	
1958	Hoosier Honey	4	J. Ruane	111	Lopar	112	Mlle. Dianne	113	18,290	1:45.40	
1959	Polamby	4	P. Anderson	116	Merry Hill	111	Starlet Miss	112	17,445	1:50.80	
1960	Clear Road	3	R. York	111	Soladesca	118	Big Effort	114	18,160	1:36.40	
1961	Oil Royalty	3	H. Woodhouse	109	Frimanaha	113	Seven Thirty	116	18,525	1:36.60	
1962	Pocosaba	5	W. Boland	114	Lincoln Center	113	Oil Royalty	113	18,265	1:52.00	
1963	Lamb Chop	3	M. Ycaza	126	Waltz Song	123	Dupage Lady	108	18,167	1:49.80	
1964	Steeple Jill	3	J. Ruane	113	Gold Frame	112	Treachery	110	19,305	1:51.80	
1965	Sailor Princess	3	G. Mineau	111	Straight Deal	118	Petticoat	114	35,880	1:52.20	
1966	Straight Deal	4	R. Ussery	118	Mac's Sparkler	113	Belle de Nuit	112	36,595	1:49.60	
1967	Politely	4	B. Baeza	121	Green Glade	114	Princessnesian	111	37,375	1:53.00	
1968	Politely	5	A. Cordero Jr	131	Obeah	112	Serene Queen	114	37,700	1:49.60	
1969	Amerigo Lady	5	J. Velasquez	121	Shuvee	122	Obeah	120	36,790	1:50.00	
1970	Obeah	5	J.L. Rotz	117	Taken Aback	123	Lunation	114	33,960	1:51.20	
1971	Kittiwake	3	H. Gustines	117	Blessing Angelica	112	Sea Saga	118	34,080	1:50.20	
1972	Manta	6	A. Cordero Jr	115	Society Column	110	Kittiwake	122	37,660	1:50.00	
1972	Aladancer	4	A. Cordero Jr	114	Summit Joy	108	Sea Saga	111	27,660	1:50.80	
1973	Aglimmer	4	M. Venezia	115	Garland of Roses	111	Cathy Baby	120	36,150	1:49.40	
1974	Lie Low	3	J. Velasquez	116	Aglimmer	116	D. O. Lady	115	27,840	1:49.00	
1974	Twixt	5	W.J. Passmore	121	Garland of Roses	114	Fairway Flyer	124	28,290	1:49.80	
1975	Lie Low	4	J. Velasquez	115	Princesse Grey	114	Carolerno	112	35,910	2:15.20	
1976	Sugar Plum Time	4	A. Cordero Jr	113	Ten Cents a Dance	110	Quacker	111	32,610	1:51.00	
1977	Water Malone	3	J.L. Samyn	121	Northernette	120	Sweet Bernice	113	32,280	1:50.40	
1978	Mrs. Warren	4	J. Velasquez	113	Water Malone	121	One Sum	121	32,190	1:51.40	
1979	Catherine's Bet	4	D. Montoya	113	Water Malone	117	Miss Baja	114	32,340	1:50.20	
1980	Relaxing	4	J. Velasquez	118	Sugar and Spice	115	Plankton	121	33,540	1:49.20	
1981	Tina Tina Too	3	D. MacBeth	114	Explorare	114	Office Wife	113	33,060	1:51.00	
1982	Number	3	E. Maple	114	Sintrillium	112	Norsan	112	32,340	1:51.40	
1983	Chieftain's Command	4	A. Cordero Jr	117	Adept	110	Sintrillium	116	34,440	1:51.60	
1984	Solar Halo	3	R.G. Davis	110	It's Fine	109	Quixotic Lady	115	53,640	1:49.20	
1985	Lady on the Run	3	A. Cordero Jr	115	Verbality	112	Halloween Queen	112	51,210	1:52.00	
1986	Shocker T.	4	G. St. Leon	124	Bharal	115	Natania	115	66,840	1:50.00	
1987	Coup de Fusil	5	A. Cordero Jr	116	Clabber Girl	113	I'm Sweets	118	83,700	1:49.20	
1988	Rose's Cantina	4	J.A. Santos	111	Ms. Eloise	115	Clabber Girl	120	67,080	1:49.80	
1989	Colonial Water	4	A. Cordero Jr	116	Topicount	116	Rose's Cantina	119	67,080	1:50.00	
1990	Personal Business	4	C.W. Antley	111	Buy the Firm	112	Lady Hoolihan	110	70,200	1:51.20	88
1991	Fit to Scout	4	C.W. Antley	114	Train Robbery	112	Her She Shawklit	111	120,000	1:50.20	96
1992	Quick Mischief	6	C. Perret	113	Versailles Treaty	122	Sahred Interest	111	120,000	1:47.80	106
1993	You'd Be Surprised	4	J.D. Bailey	115	Avian Assembly	111	Gray Cashmere	114	90,000	1:48.40	105
1994	Link River	4	J.A. Krone	114	You'd Be Surprised	120	Dispute	119	120,000	1:50.40	109
1995	Heavenly Prize	4	P. Day	127	Forced Bid	108	Cinnamon Sugar	114	120,000	2:04.00	106
1996	Urbane	4	A. Solis	119	Shoop	114	Frolic	113	180,000	2:03.00	107
1997	Clear Mandate	5	M.E. Smith	115	Shoop	111	Power Play	117	210,000	2:03.60	105
1998	Tomisue's Delight	4	P. Day	115	Tuzla	114	Once Rich Lady	114	240,000	2:04.08	104
1999	Beautiful Pleasure	4	J.F. Chavez	113	Banshee Breeze	124	Keeper Hill	118	240,000	2:02.57	112
2000	Beautiful Pleasure	5	J.F. Chavez	124	Heritage of Gold	124	Pentatonic	113	240,000	2:03.77	103
	Back in Shape finished second but was disqualified and placed fourth										
2001	Pompeii	4	R. Migliore	117	Beautiful Pleasure	117	Irving's Baby	117	240,000	2:04.60	106
2002	Summer Colony	4	J.R. Velazquez	120	Transcendental	114	Dancethruthedawn	120	240,000	2:03.15	107
2003	Passing Shot	4	J.A. Santos	114	Wild Spirit	122	Miss Linda	114	240,000	2:03.33	92
2004	Storm Flag Flying	4	J.R. Velazquez	116	Azeri	122	Nevermore	114	240,000	2:03.63	99

Beyer Index: 103.00

Distance 1 mile, 1960-61; 1 1/16 miles, 1948-51, 1958; 1 1/8 miles, 1952-57, 1959, 1962-74, 1976-94; 1 3/8 miles, 1975. Run as Firenze Handicap prior to 1987; as John A. Morris Handicap, 1987-98

PETER PAN (G2), 1 1/8 Miles, 3-Year-Olds, Belmont Park, 2004 Purse: $200,000

Year	Winner	Age	Jockey	Wt.	Second	Wt.	Third	Wt.	Win Value	Time	Beyer
1975	Singh	3	E. Maple	114	Majestic One	114	Sir Paulus	115	33,420	1:35.20	
1976	Sir Lister	3	J. Velasquez	114	Jamming	117	El Portugues	114	34,620	1:36.00	

Year	Winner	Age	Jockey	Wt.	Second	Wt.	Third	Wt.	Win Value	Time	Beyer
1977	Spirit Level	3	A. Graell	114	Sanhedrin	114	Lynn Davis	114	32,910	1:49.20	
1978	Buckaroo	3	J. Velasquez	114	Darby Creek Road	117	Star de Naskra	123	32,520	1:48.00	
1979	Coastal	3	R. Hernandez	120	Lucy's Axe	123	Pianist	117	32,820	1:47.00	
1980	Comptroller	3	R.I. Encinas	114	Bar Dexter	117	Suzanne's Star	114	34,080	1:49.20	
1981	Tap Shoes	3	R. Hernandez	126	Willow Hour	117	West on Broad	120	34,080	1:48.40	
1982	Wolfie's Rascal	3	A. Cordero Jr	120	John's Gold	114	Illuminate	117	34,020	1:48.80	
1983	Slew o' Gold	3	A. Cordero Jr	126	I Enclose	123	Foyt	117	34,380	1:46.80	
1984	Back Bay Barrister	3	D. MacBeth	117	Gallant Hour	114	Romantic Tradition	114	57,330	1:50.00	
1985	Proud Truth	3	J. Velasquez	126	Cutlass Reality	114	Salem Drive	114	67,050	1:47.60	
1986	Danzig Connection	3	P. Day	117	Clear Choice	123	Parade Marshal	117	85,380	1:48.40	
1987	Leo Castelli	3	J.A. Santos	114	Gone West	126	Shawklit Won	114	132,360	1:48.00	
1988	Seeking the Gold	3	P. Day	120	Tejano	125	Gay Rights	117	140,880	1:47.60	
1989	Imbibe	3	A. Cordero Jr	117	Irish Actor	126	Pro Style	117	110,160	1:48.60	
1990	Profit Key	3	J.A. Santos	117	Country Day	114	Paradise Found	114	106,560	1:47.20	
1991	Lost Mountain	3	C. Perret	114	Man Alright	114	Scan	126	106,380	1:49.40	104
1992	A.P. Indy	3	E. Delahoussaye	126	Colony Light	114	Berkley Fitz	114	106,380	1:47.40	108
1993	Virginia Rapids	3	E. Maple	114	Colonial Affair	117	Itaka	114	90,000	1:48.40	109
1994	Twining	3	J.A. Santos	122	Lahint	112	Gash	119	90,000	1:49.00	103
1995	Citadeed	3	E. Maple	112	Pat n Jac	113	Treasurer	115	90,000	1:50.00	99
1996	Jamies First Punch	3	J.R. Velazquez	118	Unbridled's Song	123	Diligence	118	90,000	1:47.20	110
1997	Banker's Gold	3	E. Maple	113	Zede	120	Prince Guistino	114	90,000	1:48.60	101
1998	Grand Slam	3	J.D. Bailey	120	Rubiyat	113	Parade Ground	120	90,000	1:49.00	100
1999	Best of Luck	3	J.L. Samyn	113	Treasure Island	114	Lemon Drop Kid	120	90,000	1:47.94	107
2000	Postponed	3	E.S. Prado	113	Unshaded	123	Globalize	123	120,000	1:49.71	99
2001	Hero's Tribute	3	J.F. Chavez	117	E Dubai	123	Dayton Flyer	115	120,000	1:47.47	112
2002	Sunday Break	3	G.L. Stevens	121	Puzzlement	115	Deputy Dash	115	120,000	1:48.10	99
2003	Go Rockin' Robin	3	S.X. Bridgmohan	117	Alysweep	123	Supervisor	115	120,000	1:48.47	93
2004	Purge	3	J.R. Velazquez	115	Swingforthefences	115	Master David	115	120,000	1:47.98	108

Beyer Index: 103.71

OGDEN PHIPPS HANDICAP (G1), 1 1/16 Miles, Fillies and Mares, 3-Year-Olds and Up, Belmont Park, 2004 Purse: $285,000

Year	Winner	Age	Jockey	Wt.	Second	Wt.	Third	Wt.	Win Value	Time	Beyer
1961	Disperse	4	W. Boland	111	Don Poggio	125	Air Medal	111	17,712	2:28.40	
1970	Ta Wee	4	J.L. Rotz	132	Process Shot	127	Grey Slacks	111	18,297	1:10.00	
1971	Cold Comfort	4	M. Venezia	118	Process Shot	124	Dorothy Joan	114	19,920	1:11.60	
1972	Summer Guest	3	J. Vasquez	111	Grafitti	115	Judith	110	17,415	1:47.80	
1973	Light Hearted	4	E. Nelson	123	Inca Queen	116	Blessing Angelica	117	32,880	1:48.80	
1974	Poker Night	4	J. Velasquez	114	Krislin	115	Fairway Flyer	117	33,300	1:48.60	
1975	Raisela	4	E. Maple	114	Pass a Glance	114	Sarsar	115	33,510	1:49.20	
1976	Proud Delta	4	J. Velasquez	124	Garden Verse	111	Let Me Linger	114	33,690	1:48.40	
1977	Pacific Princess	4	E. Maple	112	Mississippi Mud	114	Fleet Victress	113	32,700	1:49.20	
1978	Dottie's Doll	5	J. Vasquez	115	One Sum	123	Water Malone	119	32,040	1:47.60	
1979	Pearl Necklace	5	J. Fell	122	Miss Baja	115	Sweet Woodruff	108	31,470	1:48.60	
1980	Misty Gallore	4	D. MacBeth	125	Blitey	115	What'll I Do	110	32,760	1:48.80	
1981	Wistful	4	D. Brumfield	119	Chain Bracelet	119	Love Sign	115	64,200	1:49.80	
1982	Love Sign	5	R. Hernandez	123	Anti Lib	116	Jameela	122	65,280	1:48.00	
1983	Number	4	E. Maple	117	Dance Number	114	Broom Dance	121	65,880	1:48.40	
1984	Heatherten	5	S. Maple	118	Quixotic Lady	118	Thirty Flags	114	92,400	1:49.20	
1985	Heatherten	6	R. Romero	124	Life's Magic	122	Sefa's Beauty	120	84,300	1:48.80	
1986	Endear	4	E. Maple	115	Lady's Secret	128	Ride Sally	124	97,650	1:48.60	
1987	Catatonic	5	D.A. Miller Jr	116	Ms. Eloise	118	Steal a Kiss	111	137,520	1:50.00	
1988	Personal Ensign	4	R.P. Romero	123	Hometown Queen	109	Clabber Girl	118	131,760	1:47.60	
1989	Rose's Cantina	5	J. Cruguet	117	Make Change	111	Colonial Waters	114	135,120	1:48.60	
1990	Fantastic Find	4	C. Perret	113	Mistaurian	113	Dreamy Mimi	113	139,680	1:50.00	102
1991	A Wild Ride	4	M.E. Smith	120	Fit to Scout	115	Buy the Firm	121	120,000	1:49.00	102
1992	Missy's Mirage	4	E. Maple	118	Harbour Club	110	Versailles Treaty	119	120,000	1:47.00	109
1993	Turnback the Alarm	4	C.W. Antley	119	Deputation	117	You'd Be Surprised	112	90,000	1:48.00	100
1994	Sky Beauty	4	M.E. Smith	128	You'd Be Surprised	118	Schway Baby Sway	109	90,000	1:47.40	107
1995	Heavenly Prize	4	P. Day	122	Little Buckles	111	Sky Beauty	124	90,000	1:43.20	111
1996	Serena's Song	4	J.D. Bailey	125	Shoop	115	Restored Hope	114	120,000	1:41.60	104
1997	Hidden Lake	4	R. Migliore	117	Twice the Vice	121	Jewel Princess	124	150,000	1:40.80	119
1998	Mossflower	4	R.G. Davis	114	Glitter Woman	120	Colonial Minstrel	118	150,000	1:39.90	118
1999	Sister Act	4	P. Day	117	Beautiful Pleasure	117	Catinca	122	150,000	1:40.79	112
2000	Beautiful Pleasure	5	J.F. Chavez	124	Pentatonic	112	Roza Robata	115	150,000	1:41.54	109
2001	Critical Eye	4	M.J. Luzzi	115	Jostle	117	Apple of Kent	117	150,000	1:42.18	104
2002	Raging Fever	4	J. R. Velazquez	120	Transcendental	113	Two Item Limit	117	180,000	1:41.75	102
2003	Sightseek	4	J.D. Bailey	118	Take Charge Lady	119	Mandy's Gold	118	180,000	1:40.89	110
2004	Sightseek	5	J.D. Bailey	120	Storm Flag Flying	117	Passing Shot	116	180,000	1:41.46	99

Beyer Index: 107.20

Run as the Hempstead Handicap until 2002. Distance 1 1/2 miles (for both sexes) in 1961; 6 furlongs in 1970–71

PHOENIX BREEDERS' CUP (G3), 6 Furlongs, 3-Year-Olds and Up, Keeneland Race Course, 2004 Purse: $271,250

Year	Winner	Age	Jockey	Wt.	Second	Wt.	Third	Wt.	Win Value	Time	Beyer
1994	Lost Pan	4	D. Barton	114	Pacific West	116	Fort Chaffe	119	33,728	1:09.40	108
1995	Golden Gear	5	C.Perret	124	Hello Paradise	115	Mississippi Chat	113	67,456	1:08.80	109
1996	Forest Wildcat	5	J.Bravo	121	Valid Expectations	119	Bet On Sunshine	115	101,246	1:09.40	114
1997	Bet On Sunshine	5	F.Torres	122	Receiver	117	Valid Expectations	117	97,464	1:08.60	111
1998	Partner's Hero	4	C.Borel	117	Pyramid Peak	123	High Stakes Player	123	100,533	1:09.20	109
1999	Richter Scale	5	K.J. Desormeaux	117	Bet On Sunshine	117	Vicar	121	166,780	1:08.40	102
2000	Five Star Day	4	G.K. Gomez	119	Istintaj	119	Bet On Sunshine	123	167,245	1:07.90	116
2001	Bet On Sunshine	9	C.H. Borek	123	Robin De Nest	121	Erlton	119	166,470	1:09.65	104
2002	Xtra Heat	4	H. Vega	123	Day Trader	120	Touch Tone	119	155,000	1:10.13	107
2003	Najran	4	J. Castellano	122	Ethan Man	118	Take Achance on Me	118	169,880	1:08.32	111
2004	Champali	4	R. Bejarano	122	Gold Storm	118	Clock Stopper	118	168,175	1:08.72	113

Beyer Index: 109.45

For previous runnings, refer to 1994 Manual.

PIMLICO BREEDERS' CUP DISTAFF HANDICAP (G3), 1 1/16 Miles, Fillies and Mares, 3-Year-Olds and Up, Pimlico Race Course, 2004 Purse: $150,000

Year	Winner	Age	Jockey	Wt.	Second	Wt.	Third	Wt.	Win Value	Time	Beyer
1992	Wilderness Song	4	C. Perret	121	Harbour Club	110	Brilliant Brass	117	150,000	1:49.00	103
1993	Deputation	4	C.W. Antley	114	D. Theatrical Gal	112	Low Tolerance	115	120,000	1:49.00	97
1994	Double Sixes	4	Prado ES	112	Broad Gains	118	Mz. Zill Bear	118	120,000	1:51.00	94
1995	Pennyhill Park	5	M.E. Smith	115	Halo America	117	Calipha	121	120,000	1:49.20	98
1996	Serena's Song	4	Stevens G. L.	123	Shoop	116	Churchbell Chimes	114	120,000	1:49.60	103
1997	Rare Blend	4	J.D. Bailey	114	Scenic Point	114	Aileen's Countess	114	120,000	1:51.40	92
1998	Ajina	4	J.D. Bailey	120	Naskra Colors	112	Pocho's Dream Girl	113	120,000	1:48.60	106
1999	Mil Kilates	6	Sellers S. J.	113	Merengue	121	Unbridled Hope	116	120,000	1:49.00	103
2000	Roza Robata	5	P. Day	114	Bella Chiarra	118	On a Soapbox	116	120,000	1:49.82	105
2001	Serra Lake	4	P. Day	112	Jostle	119	Prized Stamp	114	120,000	1:50,22	99
2002	Summer Colony	4	J.R. Velazquez	119	Dancethruthedawn	119	Happily Unbridled	115	90,000	1:42.90	110
2003	Mandy's Gold	5	J.D. Bailey	117	Summer Colony	121	Stormy Frolic	114	90,000	1:46.32	86
2004	Friel's for Real	4	A. Castellano Jr	115	Saintly Action	114	Nonsuch Bay	116	90,000	1:45.03	95

Beyer Index: 99.31

PIMLICO SPECIAL HANDICAP (G1), 1 3/16 Miles, 4-Year-Olds and Up, Pimlico Race Course, 2004 Purse: $500,000

Year	Winner	Age	Jockey	Wt.	Second	Wt.	Third	Wt.	Win Value	Time	Beyer
1937	War Admiral	3	C. Kurtsinger	128	Masked Admiral	100	War Minstrel	109	5,680	1:58.80	
1938	Seabiscuit	5	G. Woolf	120	War Admiral	120			15,000	1:56.60	
1939	Challedon	3	E. Arcaro	120	Kayak II	126	Cravat	126	10,000	1:59.00	
1940	Challedon	4	G. Woolf	126	Can't Wait	126			10,000	2:03.20	
1941	Market Wise	3	W. Eads	120	Haltal	126			10,000	1:58.80	
1942	Whirlaway	4	G. Woolf	126					10,000	2:05.40	
1943	Shut Out	4	E. Arcaro	126	Slide Rule	120	Fairy Manhurst	120	25,000	2:00.20	
1944	Twilight Tear	3	D. Dodson	117	Devil Diver	126	Megogo	120	25,000	1:56.60	
1945	Armed	4	D. Dodson	126	First Fiddle	126	Stymie	126	25,000	1:58.80	
1946	Assault	3	E. Arcaro	120	Stymie	126	Bridal Flower	117	25,000	1:57.00	
1947	Fervent	3	A. Snider	120	Cosmic Bomb	120	Armed	126	25,000	1:58.40	
1948	Citation	3	E. Arcaro	120					10,000	1:59.80	
1949	Capot	3	T. Atkinson	120	Coaltown	126			15,000	1:56.80	
1950	One Hitter	4	T. Atkinson	126	Chicle II	126	Abstract	126	15,000	1:58.60	
1951	Bryan G.	4	O. Scurlock	126	County Delight	126	Call Over	126	15,000	1:57.40	
1952	General Staff	4	G. Lasswell	126	One Hitter	126			25,000	1:57.40	
1953	Tom Fool	4	T. Atkinson	126	Navy Page	120	Alerted	126	30,000	1:55.80	
1954	Helioscope	3	S. Boulmetis	122	Hasseyampa	122	Fisherman	122	35,000	1:59.00	
1955	Sailor	3	H. Woodhouse	123	Mister Gus	126	Social Outcast	126	40,000	1:57.60	
1956	Summer Tan	4	D. Erb	126	Midafternoon	126	Find	126	35,000	1:56.60	
1957	Promised Land	3	W. Hartack	123	Tick Tock	126	Third Brother	126	35,000	1:57.40	
1958	Vertex	4	S. Boulmetis	126	Sharpsburg	126	Better Bee	126	35,000	2:00.60	
1988	Bet Twice	4	C. Perret	124	Lost Code	126	Cryptoclearance	121	425,000	1:54.20	
1989	Blushing John	4	P. Day	117	Proper Reality	118	Granacus	113	420,000	1:53.20	
1990	Criminal Type	5	J.A. Santos	117	Ruhlmann	124	De Roche	114	600,000	1:53.00	117
1991	Farma Way	4	G.L. Stevens	119	Summer Squall	120	Jolie's Halo	119	450,000	1:52.40	123
1992	Strike the Gold	4	C. Perret	114	Fly So Free	116	Twilight Agenda	122	420,000	1:54.80	111
1993	Devil His Due	4	W.H. McCauley	120	Valley Crossing	112	Pistols and Roses	114	360,000	1:55.40	108
1994	As Indicated	4	R.G. Davis	120	Devil His Due	121	Valley Crossing	113	360,000	1:55.00	115
1995	Cigar	5	J.D. Bailey	122	Devil His Due	121	Concern	121	360,000	1:53.60	114
1996	Star Standard	4	P. Day	111	Key of Luck	120	Geri	118	360,000	1:54.40	111
1997	Gentlemen	5	G.L. Stevens	122	Skip Away	119	Tejano Run	114	360,000	1:53.00	126
1998	Skip Away	5	J.D. Bailey	128	Precocity	115	Hot Brush	113	450,000	1:54.26	118

Year	Winner	Age	Jockey	Wt.	Second	Wt.	Third	Wt.	Win Value	Time	Beyer
1999	Real Quiet	4	G.L. Stevens	120	Free House	124	Fred Bear Claw	113	300,000	1:54.31	113
2000	Golden Missile	5	K.J. Desormeaux	116	Pleasant Breeze	113	Lemon Drop Kid	120	450,000	1:54.65	115
2001	Include	4	J.D. Bailey	114	Albert the Great	121	Pleasant Breeze	114	450,000	1:55.61	117
2003	Mineshaft	4	R.J. Albarado	121	Western Pride	116	Judge's Case	113	400,000	1:56.16	118
2004	Southern Image	4	V. Espinoza	120	Midway Road	116	Bowman's Band	114	300,000	1:55.89	118

Beyer Index: 116.00

For 3-year-olds in 1937, 1954; for 4-year-olds and up, 1988-97; Not run1959-1987, 2002

MOLLY PITCHER BREEDERS' CUP HANDICAP (G2), 1 1/8 Miles, Fillies and Mares, 3-Year-Olds and Up, Monmouth Park, 2004 Purse: $300,000

Year	Winner	Age	Jockey	Wt.	Second	Wt.	Third	Wt.	Win Value	Time	Beyer
1946	Mahmoudess	4	M.A. Buxton	113	Fair Ann	100	Elpis	116	13,500	1:46.60	
1947	Elpis	5	F. Moon	113	Proverb	112	Lawless Miss	108	13,250	1:45.00	
1948	Camargo	4	C. Kirk	115	Imprudence II	113	Halsgal	107	11,900	1:45.40	
1949	Allie's Pal	4	J. Gilbert	116	My Emma	114	Irisen	109	12,300	1:46.20	
1950	Danger Ahead	4	H. Lindberg	111	My Celeste	110	Allie's Pal	112	12,750	1:46.20	
1951	Marta	4	C. McCreary	108	My Celeste	108	Leading Home	111	12,650	1:46.20	
1952	Dixie Flyer	5	P. Roberts	116	My Celeste	112	Valadium	117	17,000	1:45.40	
1953	My Celeste	7	L. Batchellor	110	Atalanta	117	Grandma Josie	106	19,550	1:47.60	
1954	Shady Tune	4	W. Blum	106	Miss Joanne	110	Winning Stride	111	19,900	1:44.00	
1955	Misty Morn	3	S. Boulmetis	112	Clear Dawn	120	Manotick	111	21,650	1:45.40	
1956	Blue Sparkler	4	O. Scurlock	120	Rico Reto	117	Another World	110	18,450	1:44.60	
1957	Manotick	5	J. Choquette	118	Rare Treat	120	Stolen Hour	108	17,835	1:42.80	
1958	Searching	6	H. Keene	120	Rare Treat	112	Pardala	117	18,452	1:44.20	
1959	Miss Orestes	4	L. Gilligan	110	Mlle. Dianne	117	Polamby	114	18,712	1:45.60	
1960	Royal Native	4	W. Hartack	127	Quill	122	Miss Orestes	114	18,517	1:43.80	
1961	Shirley Jones	5	H. Grant	121	Secret Honor	114	Chalvedele	104	20,020	1:43.20	
1962	Primonetta	4	B.Baeza	126	Shirley Jones	123	Dreamflower	112	18,070	1:42.40	
1963	Patrol Woman	4	S. Brooks	113	Frimanaha	118	Decline and Fall	110	14,446	1:44.40	
1964	Spicy Living	4	M. Ycaza	124	Snow Scene II	112	Old Hat	119	19,110	1:43.20	
1965	Miss Cavandish	4	H. Grant	121	Beautiful Day	112	Snow Scene II	116	18,752	1:44.60	
1966	Discipline	4	R. Broussard	117	Straight Deal	120	Lovejoy	112	25,187	1:43.60	
1967	Politely	4	W. Boland	115	Straight Deal	126	Indian Sunlite	117	25,041	1:44.20	
1968	Politely	5	A. Cordero Jr	122	Mac's Sparkler	123	Green Glade	114	25,350	1:45.00	
1969	Singing Rain	4	R. Broussard	119	Gay Sailorette	114	C'ms F'ry G'd	117	25,480	1:43.80	
1970	Double Ripple	5	E. Nelson	112	What a Dream	115	Deb's Darling	114	29,087	1:44.00	
1971	Double Delta	5	K. Knapp	121	Cathy Honey	118	Peaceful Union	113	30,144	1:42.80	
1972	Out in Space	5	C. Barrera	113	Chou Croute	124	Secret Retreat	112	29,429	1:43.80	
1973	Light Hearted	4	E. Nelson	120	Wanda	118	Alma North	121	28,259	1:41.40	
1974	Lady Love	4	M. Hole	117	Ponte Vecchio	116	Belle Marie	117	28,908	1:43.80	
1975	Honky Star	4	J. Tejeira	123	Twixt	126	Bundler	119	36,156	1:43.00	
1976	Garden Verse	4	F. Lovato	112	Spring Is Here	111	Vodka Time	112	26,432	1:46.00	
1977	Dotties Doll	4	C. Perret	113	Proud Delta	123	Mississippi Mud	115	37,180	1:41.80	
1978	Creme Wave	4	D. MacBeth	114	Pearl Necklace	123	Flame Lily	110	36,530	1:45.20	
1979	Navajo Princess	5	C. Perret	120	Frosty Skater	121	Water Malone	116	36,335	1:43.40	
1980	Plankton	4	V. Bracciale Jr	120	Doing It My Way	114	Whose Bid	113	34,950	1:44.20	
1981	Weber City Miss	4	R. Hernandez	119	Jameela	118	Wistful	121	49,455	1:44.00	
1982	Jameela	6	J.L. Kaenel	120	Pukka Princess	114	Prismatical	117	67,620	1:42.60	
1983	Ambassador of Luck	4	A. Graell	117	Kattegat's Pride	122	Dance Number	115	67,830	1:41.20	
1984	Sultry Sun	4	M. Solomone	116	Quixotic Lady	118	Nany	114	68,640	1:41.60	
1985	Sefa's Beauty	6	P. Day	119	Mitterand	119	Dowery	115	69,090	1:42.60	
1986	Lady's Secret	4	P. Day	126	Chaldea	110	Key Witness	112	95,610	1:41.20	
1987	Reel Easy	4	W.H. McCauley	112	Lady's Secret	125	Catatonic	117	99,300	1:42.00	
1988	Personal Ensign	4	R.P. Romero	125	Grecian Flight	119	Le L'Argent	117	90,000	1:41.80	
1989	Bodacious Tatas	4	R. Wilson	111	Make Change	112	Grecian Flight	122	90,000	1:42.40	
1990	A Penny Is a Penny	5	A.T. Gryder	120	Leave It Be	116	Bodacious Tatas	117	90,000	1:43.40	97
1991	Valay Maid	4	M. Castaneda	116	Train Robbery	112	Toffeefee	116	90,000	1:43.80	91
1992	Versaillles Treaty	4	M.E. Smith	120	Quick Mischief	120	Cozzene's Wish	113	90,000	1:43.00	105
1993	Wilderness Song	5	D. Clark	119	Quilma	117	Looie Capote	116	90,000	1:44.60	102
1994	Hey Hazel	4	R.C. Landry	114	Ann Dear	113	Future of Gold	110	120,000	1:46.40	92
1995	Inside Information	4	M.E. Smith	124	Jade Flush	115	Halo America	118	90,000	1:43.80	106
1996	Halo America	6	P. Day	117	Rogues Walk	116	Why Be Normal	112	120,000	1:41.60	112
1997	Rare Blend	4	M.E. Smith	116	Top Secret	116	Chip	115	120,000	1:43.60	102
1998	Relaxing Rhythm	4	P. Day	116	Minister's Melody	117	Glitter Woman	120	120,000	1:42.20	107
1999	Heritage of Gold	5	C.T. Lambert	114	Harpia	116	Tap to Music	116	180,000	1:41.76	111
2000	Lu Ravi	5	P. Day	116	Silverbulletday	118	Bella Chiarra	116	180,000	1:43.17	110
2001	March Magic	4	M.J. Luzzi	113	Vivid Sunset	112	Shine Again	113	180,000	1:43.79	100
2002	Atelier	5	E.M. Coa	115	Summer Colony	119	Spain	122	180,000	1:48.63	105
2003	Summer Colony	5	G.L. Stevens	120	She's Got the Beat	112	Call an Audible	110	180,000	1:51.83	93
2004	La Reason	4	C.C. Lopez	111	Yell	114	Bare Necessities	119	180,000	1:51.10	91

Beyer Index: 101.60

POKER HANDICAP (G3), 1 Mile (Turf), 3-Year-Olds and Up, Belmont Park, 2004 Purse: $112,600

Year	Winner	Age	Jockey	Wt.	Second	Wt.	Third	Wt.	Win Value	Time	Beyer
1988	Wanderkin	5	J.A. Santos	122	Kings River	122	My Prince Charming	117	54,720	1:35.60	
							Silver Voice	117			
1989	Fourstardave	4	J.A. Santos	117	Feeling Gallant	117	Valid Fund	117	56,610	1:33.20	
1990	Scottish Monk	7	A. Cordero Jr	117	Quick Call	117	Yankee Affair	122	52,110	1:33.40	
1991	Who's to Pay	5	J.D. Bailey	117	Scott the Great	117	Senor Speedy	117	56,160	1:33.40	103
1992	Scott the Great	6	J.L. Samyn	117	Kate's Valentine	117	Cigar Toss	117	54,810	1:33.40	101
1993	Fourstardave	8	R. Migliore	117	Adam Smith	122	Lech	117	53,190	1:33.00	107
1994	Dominant Prospect	4	Chavez JF	114	Fourstardave	114	Nijinsky's Gold	114	49,905	1:32.60	109
1995	Caress	4	Davis RG	117	Fourstars Allstar	119	Pennine Ridge	119	51,030	1:34.20	110
1996	Smooth Runner	5	Krone J. A.	113	Mighty Forum	116	Da Hoss	119	51,600	1:33.60	111
1997	Draw Shot	4	Antley C. W.	118	Val's Prince	114	Fortitude	112	51,345	1:33.00	105
1998	Elusive Quality	5	J.D. Bailey	117	Za-Im	114	Fortitude	114	51,240	1:31.60	112
1999	Rob 'n Gin	5	J.F. Chavez	118	Bomfim	115	Wised Up	115	69,120	1:32.80	108
2000	Affirmed Success	6	J.F. Chavez	117	Rabi	114	Weatherbird	113	68,280	1:34.06	108
2001	Affirmed Success	7	J.D. Bailey	121	In Frank's Honor	114	Union One	114	66,240	1:34.60	109
2002	Volponi	4	S.X. Bridgmohan	115	Saint Verre	112	Navesink	117	66,720	1:32.24	109
2003	War Zone	4	J.J. Castellano	117	Trademark	114	Saint Verre	112	69,720	1:32.81	100
2004	Christine's Outlaw	4	S.X. Bridgmohan	113	Millennium Dragon	120	Silver Tree	117	67,560	1:32.46	108

Beyer Index: 107.14

POTRERO GRANDE BREEDERS' CUP HANDICAP (G2), 6 1/2 Furlongs, 4-Year-Olds and Up, Santa Anita, 2004 Purse: $122,488

Year	Winner	Age	Jockey	Wt.	Second	Wt.	Third	Wt.	Win Value	Time	Beyer
1983	Chinook Pass	4	L. Pincay Jr	123	Haughty but Nice	115	The Captain	114	37,050	1:14.60	
1984	Honeyland	5	W. Shoemaker	117	American Legion	113	Shecky Blue	116	40,450	1:15.40	
1985	Fifty Six Ina Row	4	L. Pincay Jr	117	Hula Blaze	120	Coyotero	114	44,650	1:15.40	
1986	Halo Folks	5	C.J. McCarron	124	Bozina	111	American Legion	112	43,050	1:15.60	
1987	Zabaleta	4	L. Pincay Jr	117	Zany Tactics	120	Bedside Promise	125	44,850	1:15.00	
1988	Gulch	4	E. Delahoussaye	123	Very Subtle	120	Gallant Sailor	112	44,050	1:15.00	
1989	On the Line	5	G.L. Stevens	125	Ron Bon	116	Jamoke	114	66,500	1:14.00	
1990	Olympic Prospect	6	P.A. Valenzuela	121	Raise a Stanza	118	Doncareer	114	60,400	1:14.20	121
1991	Jacodra	4	C.S. Nakatani	111	Answer Do	118	Bruho	117	62,300	1:15.00	109
1992	Cardmania	6	E. Delahoussaye	117	Frost Free	117	Answer Do	123	60,200	1:17.16	101
1993	Gray Slewpy	5	K.J. Desormeaux	118	Cardmania	117	Star of the Crop	119	64,700	1:14.91	118
1994	Sir Hutch	4	Valenzuela PA	117	Concept Win	117	Furiously	117	61,100	1:14.48	104
1995	Lit de Justice	5	Nakatani CS	115	Cardmania	119	Phone Roberto	116	63,000	1:14.65	104
1996	Abaginone	5	G.L. Stevens	115	Dramatic Gold	117	Kingdom Found	118	124,400	1:14.59	116
1997	First Intent	8	R.R. Douglas	114	Hesabull	117	Northern Afleet	118	64,250	1:14.75	108
1998	Son Of A Pistol	6	G.K. Gomez	114	White Bronco	114	Gold Land	115	66,420	1:13.71	116
1999	Big Jag	6	K.J. Desormeaux	119	Gold Land	111	Son Of A Pistol	120	123,720	1:15.09	112
2000	Kona Gold	6	A. Solis	122	Old Topper	116	Your Halo	116	123,060	1:14.75	119
2001	Kona Gold	7	A. Solis	126	Hollycombe	114			123,000	1:15.03	112
					Explicit	116					
2002	Kalookan Queen	6	A. Solis	116	Ceeband	116	Elaborate	115	130,620	1:15.31	108
2003	Bluesthestandard	6	M.E. Smith	115	Joey Franco	116	Kona Gold	121	72,000	1:14.86	105
2004	McCann's Mojave	4	J. Valdivia Jr	116	Unfurl the Flag	114	Bluesthestandard	118	66,840	1:15.60	104

Beyer Index: 110.47

PRAIRIE MEADOWS CORNHUSKER BREEDERS' CUP HANDICAP (G3), 1 1/8 Miles, 3-Year-Olds and Up, Prairie Meadows, 2004 Purse: $300,000

Year	Winner	Age	Jockey	Wt.	Second	Wt.	Third	Wt.	Win Value	Time	Beyer
1966	Royal Gunner	4	W. Hartack	121	Sammyren	118	Just About	122	31,075	1:43.00	
1967	Single Needle	4	L.J. Durousseau	110	Tenzing II	112			30,772	1:46.80	
					Lucky Hour	110					
1968	Ninfalo	5	C. Stone	114	Air Boat	111	BF's Own	112	24,764	1:41.80	
1968	Vale of Tears	5	L.J. Durousseau	117	R. Thomas	124	Romanullah	110	24,764	1:41.20	
1969	Vale of Tears	6	L.J. Durousseau	124	Romanullah	109	Zorba II	117	30,827	1:42.20	
1970	Blazing Silk	6	L.J. Durousseau	116	Zorba II	117	Two Bobbs	107	31,432	1:42.60	
1971	Action Getter	4	K. Jones	114	Tripsville	123	Prince Hemp	113	31,034	1:44.00	
1972	Joey Bob	4	L. Moyers	115	Royal Harmony	124	Road Man	117	31,212	1:42.60	
1973	Joey Bob	5	L. Moyers	118	Haveago	121	Prince Astro	114	30,827	1:42.80	
1974	Blazing Gypsey	5	S. Burgos	114	Tom Tulle	122	Super Sail	117	57,963	1:49.60	
1975	Stonewalk	4	R. Turcotte	120	Sharp Gary	115	Rooter	114	59,290	1:48.40	
1976	Dragset	5	S. Maple	112	Sharp Gary	113	Methdioxya	114	60,500	1:49.00	
1977	Private Thoughts	4	R. Perez	118	Latimer	114	Dragset	113	62,783	1:48.00	
1978	True Statement	4	B. Fann	118	Big John Taylor	115	Giboulee	116	60,912	1:48.20	
1979	Star de Naskra	4	J. Fell	125	Prince Majestic	119	Quiet Jay	117	90,613	1:48.40	

Year	Winner	Age	Jockey	Wt.	Second	Wt.	Third	Wt.	Win Value	Time	Beyer
1980	Hold Your Tricks	5	D. Pettinger	116	Overskate	126	Daring Damascus	117	88,688	1:49.20	
1981	Summer Advocate	4	K. Jones	118	Sun Catcher	121	Brent's Trans Am	116	93,143	1:48.20	
1982	Recusant	4	R.J. Hirdes Sr	118	Plaza Star	121	Vodika Collins	118	92,895	1:51.60	
1983	Win Stat	6	D. Pettinger	111	Bersid	116	Aspro	121	92,978	1:53.20	
1984	Timeless Native	4	D. Brumfield	122	Inevitable Leader	120	Wild Again	121	90,000	1:49.40	
1985	Gate Dancer	4	C.J. McCarron	126	Badwagon Harry	114	Eminency	119	100,800	1:48.60	
1986	Gourami	4	T.T. Doocy	116	Honor Medal	114	Smile	120	150,000	1:49.40	
1987	Bolshoi Boy	4	C.W. Antley	117	Forkintheroad	112	Honor Medal	119	120,000	1:48.40	
1988	Palace March	4	J.A. Krone	118	Outlaws Sham	114	Galba	112	120,000	1:49.00	
1989	Blue Buckaroo	6	S.J. Sellers	115	Henbane	115	Advancing Ensign	112	120,000	1:49.40	
1990	Dispersal	4	J. Velasquez	122	No More Cash	114	Protect Yourself	113	90,000	1:50.00	97
1991	Black Tie Affair	5	P. Day	124	Bedeviled	117	Whodam	113	75,000	1:48.60	110
1992	Irish Swap	5	B.E. Poyadou	117	Zeeruler	115	Stalwars	116	75,000	1:47.80	106
1993	Link	5	R. Ardoin	114	Rapid World	115	Flying Continental	117	75,000	1:50.40	98
1994	Zeeruler	6	Lester RN	116	Powerful Punch	118	Dancing Jon	114	75,000	1:50.20	104
1995	Powerful Punch	6	Bourque CC	115	All Gone	115	Glaring	116	90,000	1:49.80	98
1997	Semoran	4	D.R. Flores	117	Mister Fire Eyes	115	Come On Flip	114	120,000	1:48.40	108
1998	Beboppin Baby	5	J.M. Campbell	114	Acceptable	116	Pacificbounty	113	150,000	1:46.60	109
1999	Nite Dreamer	4	R.J. Albarado	113	Mocha Express	117	Worldly Ways	116	231,000	1:48.85	110
2000	Sir Bear	7	E.M. Coa	116	Skimming	111	Ecton Park	117	240,000	1:48.49	111
2001	Euchre	5	G.K. Gomez	116	Dixie Dot Com	119	Sure Shot Biscuit	115	240,000	1:47.72	118
2002	Mr. John	4	M. Guidry	114	Unshaded	115	Fajardo	113	240,000	1:47.97	110
2003	Tenpins	5	R.J. Albarado	118	Bowman's Band	116	Woodmoon	116	210,000	1:48.39	111
2004	Roses in May	4	M. Guidry	115	Perfect Drift	119	Crafty Shaw	117	180,000	1:46.63	113

Beyer Index: 107.36

PREAKNESS (G1), 1 3/16 Miles, 3-Year-Olds, Pimlico Race Course, 2004 Purse: $1,000,000

Year	Winner	Age	Jockey	Wt.	Second	Wt.	Third	Wt.	Win Value	Time	Beyer
1873	Survivor	3	G. Barbee	110	John Boulger	110	Artist	110	1,850	2:43.00	
1874	Culpepper	3	W. Donohue	110	King Amadeus	110	Scratch	110	1,900	2:56.20	
1875	Tom Ochiltree	3	L. Hughes	110	Viator	110	Bay Final	110	1,900	2:43.20	
1876	Shirley	3	G. Barbee	110	Rappahannock	110	Algerine	110	1,950	2:44.60	
1877	Cloverbrook	3	C. Holloway	110	Bombast	110	Lucifer	110	1,650	2:45.20	
1878	Duke of Magenta	3	C. Holloway	110	Bayard	110	Albert	110	2,150	2:41.60	
1879	Harold	3	L. Hughes	110	Jericho	110	Rochester	110	2,550	2:40.20	
1880	Grenada	3	L. Hughes	110	Oden	110	Emily F.	110	2,000	2:40.20	
1881	Saunterer	3	W. Costello	110	Compensation	107	Baltic	110	1,950	2:40.20	
1882	Vanguard	3	W. Costello	110	Heck	110	Col. Watson	107	1,250	2:44.20	
1883	Jacobus	3	G. Barbee	110	Parnell	110			1,635	2:42.20	
1884	Knight of Ellerslie	3	S.H. Fisher	110	Welcher	110			1,905	2:39.20	
1885	Tecumseh	3	J. McLaughlin	118	Wickham	118	John C.	118	2,160	2:49.00	
1886	The Bard	3	S.H. Fisher	118	Eurus	118	Elkwood	118	2,050	2:45.00	
1887	Dubine	3	W. Donohue	118	Mahoney	115	Raymond	118	1,675	2:39.20	
1888	Refund	3	F. Littlefield	118	Colt by Ten Broeck	118	Glendale	118	1,185	2:49.00	
1889	Buddhist	3	H. Anderson	118	Japhet	115			1,130	2:17.20	
1890	Montague	5	W. Martin	103	Philosophy	105	Barrister	104	1,215	2:36.60	
1894	Assignee	3	F. Taral	122	Potentate	117	Ed kearney	117	1,830	1:49.20	
1895	Belmar	3	F. Taral	115	April Fool	105	Sue Kittie	110	1,350	1:50.20	
1896	Margrave	3	H. Griffin	115	Hamilton II	107	Intermission	110	1,350	1:51.00	
1897	Paul Kauvar	3	Thorpe	108	Elkins	103	On Deck	108	1,500	1:51.20	
1898	Sly Fox	3	W. Simms	120	The Huguenot	120	Nuto	120	1,500	1:49.60	
1899	Half Time	3	R. Clawson	104	Filigrane	120	Lackland	107	1,580	1:47.00	
1900	Hindus	3	H. Spencer	110	Sarmatian	106	Ten Candies	106	1,900	1:48.40	
1901	The Parader	3	Landry	118	Sadie S.	103	Dr. Barlow	118	1,605	1:47.20	
1902	Old England	3	L. Jackson	115	Maj. Daingerfield	108	Namtor	118	2,240	1:45.80	
1903	Flocarline	3	W. Gannon	113	Mackey Dwyer	108	Rightful	118	1,875	1:44.80	
1904	Bryn Mawr	3	Hildebrand	108	Wotan	108	Dolly Spanker	115	2,355	1:44.20	
1905	Cairngorm	3	W. Davis	114	Kiamesha	104	Coy Maid	109	2,145	1:45.80	
1906	Whimsical	3	W. Miller	108	Content	103	Larable	103	2,355	1:45.00	
1907	Don Enrique	3	G. Mountain	107	Ethon	115	Zambesi	110	2,260	1:45.40	
1908	Royal Tourist	3	E. Dugan	112	Live Wire	108	Robert Cooper	101	2,455	1:46.40	
1909	Effendi	3	W. Doyle	116	Fashion Plate	111	Hill Top	111	2,725	1:39.00	
1910	Layminster	3	Estep	84	Dalhousie	110	Sager	116	2,800	1:40.20	
1911	Watervale	3	E. Dugan	112	Zeus	118	The Nigger	107	2,700	1:51.00	
1912	Col. Holloway	3	C. Turner	107	Bwana Tumbo	120	Tipsand	110	1,450	1:56.60	
1913	Buskin	3	Butwell	117	Kleburne	111	Barnegat	104	1,670	1:53.40	
1914	Holiday	3	A. Schuttinger	108	Brave Cunarder	112	Defendum	106	1,355	1:53.80	
1915	Rhine Maiden	3	D. Hoffman	104	Half Rock	100	Runes	116	1,275	1:58.00	
1916	Damrosch	3	L. McAtee	115	Greenwood	107	Achievement	126	1,380	1:54.80	
1917	Kalitan	3	E. Haynes	116	Al M. Dick	116	Kentucky Boy	116	4,800	1:54.40	
1918	War Cloud	3	J. Loftus	117	Sunny Slope	107	Lanius	110	12,250	1:53.60	
1918	Jack Hare Jr.	3	C. Peak	115	The Porter	107	Kate Bright	105	11,250	1:53.40	

Year	Winner	Age	Jockey	Wt.	Second	Wt.	Third	Wt.	Win Value	Time	Beyer
1919	Sir Barton	3	J. Loftus	126	Eternal	126	Sweep On	126	24,500	1:53.00	
1920	Man o' War	3	C. Kummer	126	Upset	122	Wildair	114	2,300	1:51.60	
1921	Broomspun	3	F. Coltiletti	114	Polly Ann	110	Jeg	114	43,000	1:54.20	
1922	Pillory	3	L. Morris	114	Hea	114	June Grass	114	51,003	1:51.60	
1923	Vigil	3	B. Marinelli	114	Gen. Thatcher	114	Rialto	114	52,000	1:53.60	
1924	Nellie Morse	3	J. Merimee	121	Transmute	126	Mad Play	126	54,000	1:57.20	
1925	Coventry	3	C. Kummer	126	Backbone	126	Almadel	126	52,700	1:59.00	
1926	Display	3	J. Maiben	126	Blondin	126	Mars	126	53,625	1:59.80	
1927	Bostonian	3	A. Abel	126	Sir Harry	126	Whiskery	126	53,100	2:01.60	
1928	Victorian	3	R. Workman	126	Toro	126	Solace	126	60,000	2:00.20	
1929	Dr. Freeland	3	L. Schaefer	126	Minotaur	126	African	126	52,325	2:01.60	
1930	Gallant Fox	3	E. Sande	126	Crack Brigade	126	Snowflake	121	51,925	2:00.60	
1931	Mate	3	G. Ellis	126	Twenty Grand	126	Ladder	126	48,225	1:59.00	
1932	Burgoo King	3	E. James	126	Tick On	126	Boatswain	126	50,375	1:59.80	
1933	Head Play	3	C. Kurtsinger	126	Ladysman	126	Utopia	126	26,850	2:00.40	
1934	High Quest	3	R. Jones	126	Cavalcade	126	Discovery	126	25,175	1:58.20	
1935	Omaha	3	W. Saunders	126	Firethorn	126	Psychic Bid	126	25,325	1:58.40	
1936	Bold Venture	3	G. Woolf	126	Granville	126	Jean Bart	126	27,325	1:59.00	
1937	War Admiral	3	C. Kurtsinger	126	Pompoon	126	Flying Scot	126	45,600	1:58.40	
1938	Dauber	3	M. Peters	126	Cravat	126	Menow	126	51,875	1:59.80	
1939	Challedon	3	G. Seabo	126	Gilded Knight	126	Volitant	126	53,710	1:59.80	
1940	Bimelech	3	F.A. Smith	126	Mioland	126	Gallahadion	126	53,230	1:58.60	
1941	Whirlaway	3	E. Arcaro	126	King Cole	126	Our Boots	126	49,365	1:58.80	
1942	Alsab	3	B. James	126	Requested	126			58,175	1:57.00	
					Sun Again	126					
1943	Count Fleet	3	J. Longden	126	Blue Swords	126	Vincentive	126	43,190	1:57.40	
1944	Pensive	3	C. McCreary	126	Platter	126	Stir Up	126	60,075	1:59.20	
1945	Polynesian	3	W.D. Wright	126	Hoop Jr.	126	Darby Dieppe	126	66,170	1:58.80	
1946	Assault	3	W. Mehrtens	126	Lord Boswell	126	Hampden	126	96,620	2:01.40	
1947	Faultless	3	D. Dodson	126	On Trust	126	Phalanx	126	98,005	1:59.00	
1948	Citation	3	E. Arcaro	126	Vulcan's Forge	126	Bovard	126	91,870	2:02.40	
1949	Capot	3	T. Atkinson	126	Palestinian	126	Noble Impulse	126	79,985	1:56.00	
1950	Hill Prince	3	E. Arcaro	126	Middleground	126	Dooly	126	56,115	1:59.20	
1951	Bold	3	E. Arcaro	126	Counterpoint	126	Alerted	126	83,110	1:56.40	
1952	Blue Man	3	C. McCreary	126	Jampol	126	One Count	126	86,135	1:57.40	
1953	Native Dancer	3	E. Guerin	126	Jamie K.	126	Royal Bay Gem	126	65,200	1:57.80	
1954	Hasty Road	3	J. Adams	126	Correlation	126	Hasseyampa	126	91,600	1:57.40	
1955	Nashua	3	E. Arcaro	126	Saratoga	126	Traffic Judge	126	67,550	1:54.60	
1956	Fabius	3	W. Hartack	126	Needles	126	No Regrets	126	84,250	1:58.40	
1957	Bold Ruler	3	E. Arcaro	126	Iron Liege	126	Inside Tract	126	66,300	1:56.20	
1958	Tim Tam	3	I. Valenzuela	126	Lincoln Road	126	Gone Fishin'	126	98,950	1:57.20	
1959	Royal Orbit	3	W. Harmatz	126	Sword Dancer	126	Dunce	126	137,800	1:57.00	
1960	Bally Ache	3	R. Ussery	126	Victoria Park	126	Celtic Ash	126	122,600	1:57.60	
1961	Carry Back	3	J. Sellers	126	Globemaster	126	Crozier	126	126,200	1:57.60	
1962	Greek Money	3	J.L. Rotz	126	Ridan	126	Roman Line	126	135,800	1:56.20	
1963	Candy Spots	3	W. Shoemaker	126	Chateaugay	126	Never Bend	126	127,500	1:56.20	
1964	Northern Dancer	3	W. Hartack	126	The Scoundrel	126	Hill Rise	126	124,200	1:56.80	
1965	Tom Rolfe	3	R. Turcotte	126	Dapper Dan	126	Hail to All	126	128,100	1:56.20	
1966	Kauai King	3	D. Brumfield	126	Stupendous	126	Amberoid	126	129,000	1:55.40	
1967	Damascus	3	W. Shoemaker	126	In Reality	126	Proud Clarion	126	151,500	1:55.20	
1968	Forward Pass	3	I. Valenzuela	126	Out of the Way	126	Nodouble	126	142,700	1:56.80	
	Dancer's Image finished third but was disqualified										
1969	Majestic Prince	3	W. Hartack	126	Arts and Letters	126	Jay Ray	126	129,500	1:55.60	
1970	Personality	3	E. Belmonte	126	My Dad George	126	Silent Screen	126	151,300	1:56.20	
1971	Canonero II	3	G. Avila	126	Eastern Fleet	126	Jim French	126	137,400	1:54.00	
1972	Bee Bee Bee	3	E. Nelsom	126	No Le Hace	126	Key to the Mint	126	135,300	1:55.60	
1973	Secretariat	3	R. Turcotte	126	Sham	126	Our Native	126	129,900	1:55.00	
1974	Little Current	3	M.A. Rivera	126	Neapolitan Way	126	Cannonade	126	156,500	1:54.60	
1975	Master Derby	3	D.G. McHargue	126	Foolish Pleasure	126	Diabolo	126	158,100	1:56.40	
1976	Elocutionist	3	J. Lively	126	Play the Red	126	Bold Forbes	126	129,700	1:55.00	
1977	Seattle Slew	3	J. Cruguet	126	Iron Constitution	126	Run Dusty Run	126	138,600	1:54.40	
1978	Affirmed	3	S. Cauthen	126	Alydar	126	Believe It	126	136,200	1:54.40	
1979	Spectacular Bid	3	R.J. Franklin	126	Golden Act	126	Screen King	126	165,300	1:54.20	
1980	Codex	3	A. Cordero Jr	126	Genuine Risk	121	Colonel Moran	126	180,600	1:54.20	
1981	Pleasant Colony	3	J. Velasquez	126	Bold Ego	126	Paristo	126	200,800	1:54.60	
1982	Aloma's Ruler	3	J.L. Kaenel	126	Linkage	126	Cut Away	126	209,900	1:55.40	
1983	Deputed Testamony	3	D.A. Miller Jr	126	Desert Wine	126	High Honors	126	251,200	1:55.40	
1984	Gate Dancer	3	A. Cordero Jr	126	Play On	126	Fight Over	126	243,600	1:53.60	
1985	Tank's Prospect	3	P. Day	126	Chief's Crown	126	Eternal Prince	126	423,200	1:53.40	
1986	Snow Chief	3	A. Solis	126	Ferdinand	126	Broad Brush	126	411,900	1:54.80	
1987	Alysheba	3	C.J. McCarron	126	Bet Twice	126	Cryptoclearance	126	421,100	1:55.80	
1988	Risen Star	3	E. Delahoussaye	126	Brian's Time	126	Winning Colors	121	413,700	1:56.20	
1989	Sunday Silence	3	P.A. Valenzuela	126	Easy Goer	126	Rock Point	126	438,230	1:53.80	

Year	Winner	Age	Jockey	Wt.	Second	Wt.	Third	Wt.	Win Value	Time	Beyer
1990	Summer Squall	3	P. Day	126	Unbridled	126	Mister Frisky	126	445,900	1:53.60	
1991	Hansel	3	J.D. Bailey	126	Corporate Report	126	Mane Minister	126	432,770	1:54.00	117
1992	Pine Bluff	3	C.J. McCarron	126	Alydeed	126	Casual Lies	126	484,120	1:55.60	104
1993	Prairie Bayou	3	M.E. Smith	126	Cherokee Run	126	El Bakan	126	471,835	1:56.60	98
1994	Tabasco Cat	3	P. Day	126	Go for Gin	126	Concern	126	447,720	1:56.40	112
1995	Timber Country	3	P. Day	126	Oliver's Twist	126	Thunder Gulch	126	446,810	1:54.40	106
1996	Louis Quatorze	3	P. Day	126	Skip Away	126	Editor's Note	126	458,120	1:53.40	112
1997	Silver Charm	3	G.L. Stevens	126	Free House	126	Captain Bodgit	126	488,150	1:54.80	118
1998	Real Quiet	3	K.J. Desormeaux	126	Victory Gallop	126	Classic Cat	126	650,000	1:54.75	111
1999	Charismatic	3	C.W. Antley	126	Menifee	126	Badge	126	650,000	1:55.32	107
2000	Red Bullet	3	J.D. Bailey	126	Fusiachi Pegasus	126	Impeachment	126	650,000	1:56.04	109
2001	Point Given	3	G.L. Stevens	126	A P Valentine	126	Congaree	126	650,000	1:55.51	111
2002	War Emblem	3	V. Espinoza	126	Magic Weisner	126	Proud Citizen	126	650,000	1:56.36	109
2003	Funny Cide	3	J.A. Santos	126	Midway Road	126	Scrimshaw	126	650,000	1:55.61	114
2004	Smarty Jones	3	S. Elliott	126	Rock Hard Ten	126	Eddington	126	650,000	1:55.59	118

Beyer Index: 110.43

Distance 1 1/2 miles prior to 1894; 1 1/4 miles in 1889; 1 1/16 miles from 1894–1900, 1908; 1 mile 70 yards, 1901–07; 1 mile, 1909–10; 1 1/8 miles, 1911–24. For 3-year-olds and up in 1890. Run at Morris Park in 1890; at Gravesend, NY, 1894–1908

PRINCESS ROONEY HANDICAP (G2), 6 Furlongs, Fillies and Mares, 3-Year-Olds and Up, Calder Race Course, 2004 Purse: $500,000

Year	Winner	Age	Jockey	Wt.	Second	Wt.	Third	Wt.	Win Value	Time	Beyer
1985	Birdie Belle	4	J. Santiag	121	Private Secretary	119	T.V. Snow	118	32,240	1:24.40	
1986	Classy Tricks	3	R. Lester	112	Fleur de Soleil	113	Southern Velvet	113	28,130	1:25.00	
1987	Classy Tricks	4	M. Suckie	115	Sheer Ice	117	Spirit of Fighter	123	32,040	1:25.00	
1988	Spirit of Fighter	5	O. Londono	121	Stanleys Run	111	Sheer Ice	117	32,550	1:24.60	
1989	Ana T.	4	R. Lester	113	Ells Once Again	111	My Sweet Replica	112	48,990	1:24.80	
1990	Sweet Proud Polly	3	P. Rodriguez	112	Legend One	110	Love's Exchange	117	32,040	1:25.00	
1991	Magal	4	R. Hernandez	112	Joyce Azalene	110	We Ride Run	112	32,550	1:24.60	90
1992	Magal	5	R. Hernandez	117	Fortune Forty Four	111	My Own True Love	116	30,000	1:23.60	95
1993	Lady Sonata	4	M. Lee	115	Fortune Forty Four	112	Treasured	116	30,000	1:23.00	96
1994	Roamin Rachel	4	W. Ramos	119	Sigrun	113	Goldarama	110	60,000	1:24.00	96
1995	Miss Gibson County	4	G.Boulanger	115	Goldarama	113	Sigrun	116	60,000	1:23.00	103
1996	Chaposa Springs	4	L.Pincay, Jr.	126	Reign Dancer	113	Supah Jess	113	60,000	1:23.40	94
1997	Vivace	4	R.Romero	117	Ashboro	119	Special Request	115	150,000	1:10.80	108
1998	U Can Do It	5	E.Coa	118	Closed Escrow	117	Colonial Minstrel	118	150,000	1:10.00	111
1999	Princess Pietrina	5	Homeister R. B.	114	Hurricane Bertie	118	U Can Do It	119	180,000	1:10.40	96
2000	Hurricane Bertie	5	P. Day	117	Bourbon Belle	116	Cassidy	116	240,000	1:11.43	104
2001	Dream Supreme	4	P. Day	122	Hidden Assets	114	Sugar N spice	114	240,000	1:10.48	111
2002	Gold Mover	4	J.D. Bailey	115	Xtra Heat	127	Fly Me Crazy	112	240,000	1:10.21	112
2003	Gold Mover	5	J.D. Bailey	118	Vision in Flight	113	Harmony Lodge	116	294,000	1:11.31	103
2004	Ema Bovary	5	R.M. Gonzalez	119	Bear Fan	122	Lady Tak	119	294,000	1:10.81	107

Beyer Index: 101.86

PRIORESS (G1), 6 Furlongs, 3-Year-Old Fillies, Belmont Park, 2004 Purse: $250,000

Year	Winner	Age	Jockey	Wt.	Second	Wt.	Third	Wt.	Win Value	Time	Beyer
1948	Itsabet	3	R. Permane	116	Picnic Lunch	116	Alablue	113	17,150	1:13.40	
1949	Nell K.	3	D. Dodson	116	Imacomin	116	Sunny Vale	112	12,100	1:13.40	
1950	Next Move	3	E. Guerin	115	Honey's Gal	116	Miss Degree	112	12,525	1:12.20	
1951	Ruddy	3	T. Atkinson	112	Who Dini	112	Fair Self	112	11,387	1:12.60	
1951	Tilly Rose	3	W. Boland	112	Sweet Talk	115	Miss Meggy	112	11,237	1:11.40	
1952	Landmark	3	D. Gorman	121	Jubling	121	Parading Lady	121	12,250	1:12.20	
1953	Grecian Queen	3	E. Guerin	121	Tritium	121	Flitatious	121	17,300	1:13.40	
1954	Trisong	3	H. Woodhouse	121	Open Sesame	121	Incidentally	121	16,150	1:12.40	
1955	Sometime Thing	3	E. Guerin	121	Minnie Moocher	121	Two Stars	121	17,000	1:12.20	
1956	Royal Lark	3	W. Blum	121	Aiming High	121	Levee	121	16,050	1:12.40	
1957	I Offbeat	3	H. Woodhouse	121	Therapy	121	Mlle. Dianne	121	16,250	1:12.00	
1958	Milady Dares	3	A. Chambers	121	Two Cent Stamp	121	Countess Marcy	121	10,946	1:12.80	
1958	Dixie Miss	3	J. Ruane	121	Locust Time	121	Shy Dancer	121	11,076	1:13.40	
1959	Miss Royal	3	R. Ussery	121	Hope Is Eternal	121	Cobul	121	18,355	1:11.80	
1960	Salt Lake	3	R. Yaka	121	Irish Jay	121	Improve	121	19,362	1:11.80	
1961	Primonetta	3	W. Hartack	121	Apatontheback	121	Mighty Fair	121	15,600	1:10.60	
1962	Some Song	3	J. Sellers	121	Leapfrog	121	Annie O.	121	15,080	1:11.00	
1963	Speedwell	3	W. Shoemaker	121	Fashion Verdict	121	Pams Ego	121	15,405	1:10.60	
1964	Nilene Wonder	3	D. Pierce	121	Enchanting	121	Miss Cavandish	121	18,590	1:12.20	
1965	What a Treat	3	J.L. Rotz	121	Admiring	121	Adorable	121	17,907	1:10.40	
1966	My Boss Lady	3	W. Shoemaker	121	Squeeze	121	Spearfish	121	17,875	1:10.60	
1967	Just Kidding	3	E. Belmonte	121	Great Era	121	Lake Chelan	121	17,907	1:10.40	
1968	Dark Mirage	3	A. Cordero Jr	121	Guest Room	121	Pleasantness	121	18,037	1:10.80	

Year	Winner	Age	Jockey	Wt.	Second	Wt.	Third	Wt.	Win Value	Time	Beyer
1969	Ta Wee	3	J.L. Rotz	121	Francis Flower	121	Juliet	121	18,525	1:09.40	
1970	Exclusive Dancer	3	C. Baltazar	121	Restless Life	121	Petunia	121	18,005	1:11.20	
1971	Miss Plumage	3	R. Woodhouse	121	Sea Saga	121	Emperors Desire	121	20,250	1:11.60	
1972	Numbered Account	3	B. Baeza	121	Mindy Malone	121	I Move	121	16,470	1:10.00	
1973	Windy's Daughter	3	B. Baeza	121	Voler	115	Waltz Fan	115	17,355	1:10.20	
1974	Clear Copy	3	D. Montoya	115	Heartful	118	Talking Picture	115	17,745	1:10.20	
1975	Sarsar	3	W. Shoemaker	118	Stulcer	114	Gallant Trial	114	17,070	1:10.80	
1976	Dearly Precious	3	B. Baeza	121	Old Goat	118	Answer	118	22,110	1:09.80	
1977	Ring O'Bells	3	A. Cordero Jr	116	Road Princess	118	Pearl Necklace	116	22,410	1:10.40	
1978	Tempest Queen	3	J. Velasquez	118	Sweet Joyce	112	Silver Ice	115	25,320	1:11.40	
1979	Fall Aspen	3	R.I. Velez	121	Spanish Fake	118	Too Many Sweets	115	25,740	1:11.40	
1980	Lien	3	E. Maple	115	Cybele	112	Nuit D'Amour	115	27,390	1:11.00	
1981	Tina Tina Too	3	C.B. Asmussen	118	Sweet Revenge	121	Ruler's Dancer	112	33,420	1:11.20	
1982	Trove	3	M. Venezia	118	Larida	114	Dearly Too	112	34,380	1:10.00	
1983	Able Money	3	A. Graell	112	Quixotic Lady	118	Captivating Grace	118	34,440	1:11.00	
1984	Proud Clarioness	3	J.L. Samyn	115	Dumdedumdedum	113	Suavite	112	41,400	1:10.40	
1985	Clocks Secret	3	J. Nied Jr	115	Lady's Secret	118	Ride Sally	112	53,010	1:10.00	
1986	Religiosity	3	J.A. Santos	112	Fighter Fox	112	Tromphe de Naskra	114	54,450	1:11.00	
1987	Firey Challenge	3	R. MIgliore	114	Up the Apalachee	118	Monogram	114	69,300	1:10.60	
1988	Fara's Team	3	J.D. Bailey	114	Lake Valley	112	Raging Lady	114	65,700	1:10.20	
1989	Safely Kept	3	A. Cordero Jr	118	Cojinx	114	The Way It's Binn	114	49,770	1:11.60	
1990	Token Dance	3	E. Maple	114	Stella Madrid	121	Charging Fire	114	49,770	1:09.40	
1991	Zama Hummer	3	G.L. Stevens	114	Missy'sirage	114	Devilish Touch	118	74,760	1:09.80	99
1992	American Royale	3	J.A. Santos	118	Debra's Victory	121	Preach	118	68,280	1:09.20	99
1993	Classy Mirage	3	J.A. Krone	114	Missed the Storm	118	Educated Risk	118	67,680	1:08.80	105
1994	Penny's Reshoot	3	J.R. Velazquez	116	Heavenly Prize	121	Beckys Shirt	114	64,500	1:09.00	101
1995	Scotzanna	3	R. Platts	121	Culver City	116	Miss Golden Circle	118	66,840	1:10.60	102
1996	Capote Belle	3	J.R. Velazquez	112	Flat Fleet Feet	118	Miss Maggie	116	67,200	1:08.80	114
1997	Pearl City	3	J.D. Bailey	118	Alyssum	121	Vegas Prospector	121	64,680	1:09.40	100
1998	Hurricane Bertie	3	P. Day	121	Catinca	114	Foil	114	68,220	1:08.80	99
1999	Sapphire n' Silk	3	P. Day	121	Marley Vale	112	Confessional	118	90,000	1:09.40	94
2000	I'm Brassy	3	J.A. Santos	113	Dat You Miz Blue	114	Lucky Livi	121	90,000	1:09.53	104
2001	Xtra Heat	3	R. Wilson	121	Above Perfection	116	Harmony Lodge	116	120,000	1:08.30	112
2002	Carson Hollow	3	J. Velazquez	114	Spring Meadow	121	Proper Gamble	121	120,000	1:08.79	103
2003	House Party	3	J.A. Santos	121	Chimichurri	119	Princess V.	115	120,000	1:09.45	99
2004	Friendly Michelle	3	C.S. Nakatani	119	Feline Story	121	Forest Music	119	150,000	1:09.09	98

Beyer Index: 102.07

PUCKER UP (G3), 1 1/8 Miles (Turf),
3-Year-Old Fillies, Arlington Park, 2004 Purse: $200,000

Year	Winner	Age	Jockey	Wt.	Second	Wt.	Third	Wt.	Win Value	Time	Beyer
1961	Kootenai	3	A. Skoronski	119	My Portrait	122	Play Time	119	13,800	1:38.80	
1962	Royal Patrice	3	I. Valenzuela	112	Polylady	114	Dinner Partner	115	39,300	1:48.80	
1963	Vitamin Shot	3	R. Nono	110	Delhi Maid	119	Solabar	114	33,600	1:49.80	
1964	Sceree	3	W. Hartack	119	Donamus	121	Sabemar	117	33,600	1:49.40	
1965	Mine Lovely	3	W. Shoemaker	118	Nellie D.	110	Amerivan	116	33,250	1:49.40	
1966	Swinging Mood	3	E. Fires	110	Cologne	110	Aunt Tilt	112	33,800	1:35.20	
1967	Gay Sailorette	3	G. Overton	112	Court Circuit	112	Grand Coulee	113	34,500	1:35.40	
1968	Another Nell	3	C. Perret	119	Foggy Note	117	Miss Ribot	121	34,700	1:34.00	
1969	Double Delta	3	C. Perret	120	Nutty Donut	118	Mrs. Jo Jo	114	34,900	1:35.20	
1970	New Leaf	3	H. Arroyo	110	Princess Roycraft	123	Predictable	118	35,300	1:35.20	
1971	Main Pan	3	G. McCarron	122	Sonny Says Quick	121	Gray's Little Girl	119	21,700	1:36.60	
1972	Barely Even	3	R. Broussard	128	Knightly Belle	115	Bridget o' Brick	118	20,000	1:35.40	
1973	Eleven Pleasures	3	H. Arroyo	112	Princess Doubleday	121	Guided Missile	112	16,150	1:37.60	
1974	Tappahannock	3	W. Gavidia	113	Pot Roast Billie	112	Miss Indian Chief	115	22,350	1:47.60	
1975	Kissapotanmus	3	D. Stover	118	Miami Game	118	Be Victorious	113	21,400	1:45.60	
1976	T.V. Vixen	3	M. Manganello	122	Three Colors	119	True Reality	113	36,600	1:48.40	
1977	Rich Soil	3	M.A. Rivera	122	New Scent	114	Ivory Castle	122	34,530	1:50.40	
1978	Key to the Saga	3	J.L. Samyn	119	Pretty Delight	119	Xandu	122	34,650	1:51.40	
1979	Allison's Girl	3	M.R. Morgan	112	Safe	121	Cup of Honey	116	34,500	2:00.40	
1980	Ribbon	3	P. Day	114	Satin Ribera	121	Cannon Boy	113	35,550	1:52.20	
1981	Melanie Frances	3	R. Sibille	116	Safe Play	121	Touch of Glamour	116	33,660	1:51.80	
1982	Rose Bouquet	3	R.P. Romero	121	Stay a Leader	116	Smart Heiress	121	34,710	1:53.60	
1983	Decision	3	E. Fires	121	Narrate	118	W'n'ty'c'meh'me	116	35,310	1:51.20	
1984	Witwatersrand	3	E. Fires	112	Madam Flutterby	118	Mr. T's Tune	112	48,885	1:52.40	
1984	Dictina	3	J.L. Diaz	112	Nettie Cometti	121	Princess Moran	116	48,285	1:51.40	
1985	Itsagem	3	K.K. Allen	118	Miss Ultimo	121	Tide	112	35,520	1:57.60	
1986	Top Corsage	3	S. Hawley	120	Marianna's Girl	115	Innsbruck	114	34,620	1:44.20	
1987	Sum	3	E. Fires	118	Spectacular Bev	118	Lucie's Bower	113	47,790	1:51.80	
1989	Oczy Czarnie	3	C.A. Black	112	Adira	112	Vanities	115	67,680	1:55.00	
1990	Southern Tradition	3	E. Fires	116	Virgin Michael	116	Slew of Pearls	116	71,040	1:49.20	

Year	Winner	Age	Jockey	Wt.	Second	Wt.	Third	Wt.	Win Value	Time	Beyer
1991	Jinski's World	3	A. Madrid Jr	111	Ms. Aerosmith	116	Radiant Ring	121	60,000	1:47.40	101
1992	Ziggy's Act	3	G. Boulanger	116	Bernique	111	Luv Me Luv Me Not	121	60,000	1:48.60	96
1993	Amal Hayati	3	W.S. Ramos	113	Warside	113	Future Starlet	111	60,000	1:53.20	91
1994	Work the Crowd	3	A.T. Gryder	118	Irish Forever	116	Looking for Heaven	116	60,000	1:49.20	96
1995	Grand Charmer	3	P. Day	116	Upper Noosh	116	Set Me Straight	114	60,000	1:49.40	89
1996	Ms. Mostly	3	R P Romero	114	Mountain Affair	116	Clamorosa	121	90,000	1:51.00	87
1997	Witchful Thinking	3	G.K. Gomez	121	Swearingen	116	Cozy Blues	116	75,000	1:48.80	94
2000	Solvig	3	P. Day	121	Zoftig	118	Impending Bear	118	90,000	1:52.40	91
2001	Snow Dance	3	C. Perret	122	Kiss the Devil	116	Twilite Tryst	116	90,000	1:47.93	90
2002	Little Treasure	3	R.R. Douglas	122	Cellars Shiraz	122	Kathy K D	116	90,000	1:49.92	93
2003	Aud	3	B.D. Peck	118	Hail Hillary	116	Julie's Prize	120	105,000	1:49.16	93
2004	Ticker Tape	3	K.J. Desormeaux	122	Spotlight	122	Sister Swank	116	120,000	1:48.63	93

Beyer Index: 92.83

QUEEN ELIZABETH II CHALLENGE CUP (G1), 1 1/8 Miles (Turf), 3-Year-Old Fillies, Keeneland Race Course, 2004 Purse: $500,000

Year	Winner	Age	Jockey	Wt.	Second	Wt.	Third	Wt.	Win Value	Time	Beyer
1984	Sintra	3	K.K. Allen	112	Solar Halo	112	Mr. T's Tune	112	69,644	1:43.40	
1985	Contredance	3	E. Maple	112	Debutante Dancer	116	Folk Art	120	55,608	1:47.00	
1986	Lotka	3	W.A. Guerra	121	Minstress	121	Top Corsage	121	65,000	1:50.00	
1987	Graceful Darby	3	J.D. Bailey	121	Shot Gun Bonnie	121	Sum	121	65,000	1:47.20	
1988	Love You by Heart	3	R.P. Romero	121	Siggebo	121	Glowing Honor	121	65,000	1:44.80	
1989	Coolawin	3	J.A. Velez Jr	121	To the Lighthouse	121	Songlines	121	65,000	1:43.20	
1990	Plenty of Grace	3	J.D. Bailey	121	Christiecat	121	My Girl Jeannie	121	65,000	1:51.40	
1991	La Gueriere	3	B.D. Peck	121	Satin Flower	121	Radiant Ring	121	130,000	1:49.80	101
1992	Captive Miss	3	J.A. Krone	121	Suivi	121	Trampoli	121	124,000	1:48.80	98
1993	Tribulation	3	J.L. Samyn	121	Miami Sands	121	Possibly Perfect	121	124,000	1:53.60	99
1994	Danish	3	J.A. Krone	121	Eternal Reve	121	Avie's Fancy	121	124,000	1:48.80	107
1995	Perfect Arc	3	J.R. Velazquez	121	Auriette	121	Country Cat	121	155,000	1:49.80	106
1996	Memories of Silver	3	R.G. Davis	121	Shake the Yoke	121	Antespend	121	248,000	1:45.80	110
1997	Ryafan	3	A. Solis	121	Auntie Mame	121	Golden Arches	121	248,000	1:46.60	101
1998	Tenski	3	R. Migliore	121	Shires Ende	121	Sierra Virgen	121	248,000	1:48.54	104
1999	Perfect Sting	3	P. Day	121	Tout Charmant	121	Wannabe Grand	121	310,000	1:50.66	103
2000	Collect the Cash	3	S.J. Sellers	121	Blue Moon	121	Theoretically	121	310,000	1:47.94	95
2001	Affluent	3	E. Delahoussaye	121	Golden Apples	121	Snow Dance	121	310,000	1:50.03	99
2002	Riskaverse	3	M. Guidry	121	Zenda	121	Lush Soldier	121	310,000	1:49.84	103
2003	Film Maker	3	E.S. Prado	121	Maiden Tower	121	Casual Look	121	310,000	1:47.82	100
2004	Ticker Tape	3	K.J. Desormeaux	121	Barancella	121	River Belle	121	310,000	1:51.35	96

Beyer Index: 101.57

QUEENS COUNTY HANDICAP (G3), 1 3/16 Miles, 3-Year-Olds and Up, Aqueduct, 2004 Purse: $112,100

Year	Winner	Age	Jockey	Wt.	Second	Wt.	Third	Wt.	Win Value	Time	Beyer
1902	Margraviate	4	O. Wonderly	112	Colonel Padden	119	Oom Paul	120	1,050	1:46.00	
1903	Yellow Tail	6	W. Shaw	108	Dr. Saylor	101	Injunction	101	1,725	1:45.20	
1904	Rosetint	4	T. Burns	105	Colonsay	101	Ostrich	100	1,855	1:39.20	
1905	St. Valentine	4	M. Crimmins	112	Rapid Water	125	Sinister	104	1,715	1:39.20	
1906	Ram's Horn	4	Perrine	118	Batts	90	Race King	101	1,710	1:39.40	
1907	W.H. Carey	4	Mountain	115	Pretension	112	Good Luck	115	1,795	1:40.00	
1908	Jack Atkin	4	P. Musgrave	124	Rifleman	104	Spooner	98	1,555	1:39.00	
1910	Arasee	5	J. Glass	109	Prince Ahmed	118	Magazine	109	1,050	1:39.80	
1914	Flying Fairy	4	T. Davies	120	Meridian	120	Leo Skolny	107	1,190	1:42.80	
1915	Roamer	4	J. Butwell	127	Stromboli	125	Harmonicon	121	2,300	1:39.40	
1916	Short Grass	8	F. Keogh	114	Roamer	129	Gainer	108	0	1:36.40	
1917	Old Rosebud	6	F. Robinson	125	Roamer	129	Chiclet	110	3,825	1:37.60	
1918	Roamer	7	L. Lyke	123	Tom McTaggart	109	H'd Grenade	105	3,775	1:36.60	
1919	Star Master	5	M. Buxton	116	Naturalist	130	Crimper	104	3,825	1:37.40	
1920	Cirrus	4	L. Ensor	120	Wildair	116	Lion d'Or	124	4,050	1:38.00	
1921	John P. Grier	4	F. Keogh	127	Audacious	126	Yellow Hand	112	6,555	1:36.00	
1922	Grey Lag	4	L. Fator	127	Sennings Park	120	Capt. Alcock	112	6,450	1:38.00	
1923	Zev	3	E. Sande	117	Dunlin	107	Nedna	103	7,100	1:37.00	
1924	Mad Hatter	8	E. Sande	127	Rialto	111	Dunlin	111	6,900	1:36.40	
1925	Mad Play	4	L. Fator	128	Shuffle Along	116	Whetstone	111	7,700	1:36.60	
1926	Macaw	3	L. McAtee	110	Navigator	100	Nedana	114	8,150	1:37.00	
1927	Light Carbine	4	J. McCoy	103	Chance Play	123	Mars	128	7,650	1:36.80	
1928	Kentucky II	4	G. Schreiner	115	Black Panther	107	Tantivy	100	8,650	1:38.80	
1929	Comstockery	3	S. Hebert	97	Sortie	117	Mi Vida	108	8,850	1:39.60	
1930	Kildare	4	J. Passero	95	Kai Feng	109	Balko	123	7,350	1:38.60	
1931	Halcyon	3	G. Rose	100	St. Brideaux	100	Mr. Sponge	114	7,500	1:38.60	
1932	Halcyon	4	H. Mills	108	Pompeius	109	Ormesby	108	5,800	1:38.00	
1933	Kerry Patch	3	R. Wholey	108	Okapi	108	Dark Secret	114	2,980	1:38.00	

Year	Winner	Age	Jockey	Wt.	Second	Wt.	Third	Wt.	Win Value	Time	Beyer
1934	Singing Wood	3	R. Jones	114	War Glory	118	Burgoo King	115	22,000	1:38.60	
1935	King Saxon	4	C. Rainey	118	Only One	110	Singing Wood	113	3,700	1:37.20	
1936	Good Gamble	4	S. Renick	112	Clang	110	Good Harvest	113	4,050	1:37.20	
1937	Snark	4	J. Longden	116	Memory Book	117	Scotch Bun	105	4,225	1:37.40	
1938	War Admiral	4	C. Kurtsinger	132	Snark	126	D'ger Point	112	4,425	1:36.80	
1939	Lovely Night	3	J. Longden	106	Heelfly	113	Fighting Fox	121	4,725	1:36.40	
1940	He Did	7	E. Arcaro	118	War Dog	112	The Chief	114	4,600	1:43.20	
1941	Salford II	5	D. Meade	116	Can't Wait	120	Corydon	112	4,270	1:44.40	
1942	Waller	4	B. Thompson	112	Dit	117	Can't Wait	118	4,675	1:44.00	
1943	The Rhymer	5	C. McCreary	112	Kingfisher	105	Boysy	114	4,425	1:45.00	
1944	First Fiddle	5	J. Longden	126	Tola Rose	106	Alex Barth	117	7,780	1:44.20	
1945	Olympic Zenith	4	C. McCreary	108	Stymie	120	Haile	106	7,630	1:45.60	
1946	Helioptic	4	P. Miller	111	Lets Dance	112	Alison Peters	108	7,750	1:43.20	
1947	Gallorette	5	J. Jessop	119	Stymie	129	Mangoneo	104	14,950	1:45.40	
1948	Knockdown	5	F. Zufelt	113	Stymie	132	Gasparilla	107	15,025	1:44.60	
1949	Three Rings	4	T. Atkinson	110	Conniver	114	Bug Juice	107	15,700	1:47.40	
1950	Three Rings	5	H. Woodhouse	126	Mount Marcy	119	Piet	121	15,200	1:44.60	
1951	Sheilas Reward	4	O. Scurlock	113	Lights Up	121	Piet	121	15,000	1:44.60	
1952	County Delight	5	D. Gorman	121	Quiet Step	104	Auditing	113	14,975	1:43.60	
1953	Flaunt	4	S. Cole	105	Indian Land	114	Count Turf	110	20,300	1:44.20	
1954	Find	4	E. Guerin	122	Invigorator	114	Cold Command	118	21,300	1:44.00	
1955	Fabulist	4	T. Atkinson	111	Red Hannigan	111	First Aid	114	20,400	1:43.60	
1956	Blessbull	5	W. Lester	118	Midafternoon	122	Joe Jones	121	20,300	1:42.00	
1957	Bold Ruler	3	E. Arcaro	133	Promised Land	111	Greek Spy	114	19,350	1:42.80	
1958	Oh Johnny	5	W. Boland	120	Whititoldyou	112	Eddie Schmidt	123	18,127	1:43.40	
1959	Whitley	4	E. Guerin	115	Rick City	125	Promised Land	117	18,095	1:36.40	
1960	Cranberry Sauce	3	H. Gustines	110	Promised Land	117	Talent Show	124	19,232	1:36.20	
1961	Manassa Mauler	5	B. Baeza	113	Mail Order	115	Black Th'per	117	19,955	1:36.20	
1962	Grid Iron Hero	3	M. Ycaza	117	Misty Day	120	Nimmer	114	18,980	1:34.00	
1963	Uppercut	4	M. Ycaza	114	Tropical Breeze	111	Get Around	121	19,370	1:35.40	
1964	Third Martini	5	W. Boland	116	Smart	112	Fan Jet	108	36,335	1:50.60	
1965	Prairie Schooner	4	E. Belmonte	112	Tibaldo	112	Just About	113	38,350	1:50.20	
1966	Amberoid	3	W. Blum	121	Exhibitionist	113	Flag Raiser	122	38,025	1:50.60	
1967	Mr. Right	4	H. Gustines	115	Proud Clarion	125	Successor	116	36,140	1:49.60	
1968	Irish Dude	4	S. Hernandez	112	Chompion	113	Ribereno	111	38,025	1:49.60	
1969	Vif	4	L. Adams	113	Misty Run	113	Mr. Right	124	37,505	1:49.20	
1970	Best Turn	4	L. Adams	118	Irurzun	112	Judgable	119	39,130	1:50.00	
1971	Red Reality	5	J. Velasquez	114	Peace Corps	117	Tunex	116	35,880	1:49.60	
1972	Sunny and Mild	3	M. Venezia	109	Chartered Course	111	Rule by Reason	112	35,490	1:54.40	
1973	True Knight	4	A. Cordero Jr	126	Triangular	110	North Sea	117	35,070	1:55.00	
1974	Free Hand	4	J. Amy	109	Arbees Boy	121	Group Plan	123	33,780	1:55.00	
1975	Hail the Pirates	5	R. Turcotte	111	Sharp Gary	110	Herculean	111	34,560	1:55.60	
1976	It's Freezing	4	J. Vasquez	113	Distant Land	111	Nalees Rialto	108	32,640	1:56.60	
1977	Cox's Ridge	3	E. Maple	126	Father Hogan	111	Popular Victory	115	32,670	1:55.80	
1978	Cum Laude Laurie	4	A. Cordero Jr	114	Wise Philip	112	Do Tell George	112	32,580	1:55.80	
1979	Dewan Keys	4	E. Maple	112	Mr. International	108	Gallant Best	116	32,940	1:56.80	
1980	Fool's Prayer	5	J. Velasquez	112	Ring of Light	115	Picturesque	114	33,360	1:56.00	
1981	French Cut	4	D. MacBeth	112	Bar Dexter	110	Alla Breva	109	35,040	1:56.40	
1982	Bar Dexter	5	J. Fell	112	Castle Knight	111	Nice Pirate	110	32,880	1:58.20	
1983	Country Pine	3	J.D. Bailey	118	Count Normandy	108	Megaturn	113	33,240	1:58.00	
1984	Puntivo	4	R.G. Davis	114	High Honors	114	Moro	121	44,640	1:58.00	
1985	Late Act	6	E. Maple	118	Lightning Leap	110	Morning Bob	113	52,380	1:55.40	
1986	Pine Belt	4	E. Maple	111	Scrimshaw	108	Cost Conscious	111	55,260	1:57.20	
1987	Personal Flag	4	R.P. Romero	116	Easy n Dirty	113	Gold Alert	114	64,170	1:59.00	
1988	Lay Down	4	J.L. Samyn	109	Nostalgia's Star	113	Pleasant Virginian	113	64,980	1:57.20	
1989	Its Acedemic	5	J.D. Bailey	115	Homebuilder	113	Ole Atocha	113	52,290	1:58.00	
1990	Sports View	3	C. Perret	114	I'm Sky High	115	Killer Diller	115	53,550	1:57.00	
							Lost Opportunity	112			
1991	Nome	5	E. Maple	112	Runaway Stream	116	Challenge My Duty	114	51,390	1:56.00	109
1992	Shots Are Ringing	5	J.R. Velazquez	117	A Call to Rise	111	Jacksonport	111	51,120	1:54.80	100
1993	Repletion	4	M.E. Smith	111	Dibbs n' Dubbs	111	Primitive Hall	113	53,010	1:44.20	96
1994	Federal Funds	5	D. Carr	111	Jacksonport	110	Contract Court	116	49,665	1:56.40	101
1995	Aztec Empire	5	J.L. Samyn	113	Mighty Magee	115	More to Tell	115	50,340	1:55.40	109
1996	Topsy Robsy	4	P. Keim-Bruno	111	More To Tell	114	Colonial Secretary	116	48,705	1:55.20	103
1997	Mr. Sinatra	3	R. Migliore	115	Delay of Game	118	Draw	113	49,725	1:55.60	105
1998	Fire King	5	F. .Lovato Jr.	113	Las Vegas Ernie	112	Mr. Sinatra	119	49,140	1:56.80	103
1999	Early Warning	4	J.F. Chavez	116	Doc Martin	112	Yankee Victor	114	49,230	1:55.00	105
2000	Boston Party	4	N. Arroyo Jr.	115	Talk's Cheap	115	Turnofthecentury	116	50,340	1:56.32	103
2001	Evening Attire	3	S.X. Bridgmohan	113	Balto Star	118	Top Official	113	67,140	1:55.08	105
2002	Snake Mountain	4	J.A. Santos	117	Docent	115	Cat's at Home	115	66,000	1:56.84	106
2003	Thunder Blitz	5	J.F. Chavez	114	Evening Attire	123	Seattle Fitz	115	64,980	1:55.90	110
2004	Classic Endeavor	6	A.T. Gryder	117	Evening Attire	123	Colita	115	67,260	1:57.13	104

Beyer Index: 104.21

RAILBIRD (G3), 7 Furlongs, 3-Year-Old Fillies, Hollywood Park, 2004 Purse: $109,600

Year	Winner	Age	Jockey	Wt.	Second	Wt.	Third	Wt.	Win Value	Time	Beyer
1963	Well Ordered	3	A. Maese	113	Bre'r Rabbit	123	Sheereen's Porter	120	14,600	1:22.20	
1964	Fran La Femme	3	M. Yanez	112	Lil's Nite Out	112	Roman Goddess	114	13,800	1:22.00	
1965	Mine Lovely	3	J. Baze	113	Cut It Up	112	Quick Win	112	15,625	1:22.60	
1965	Gala Host	3	M. Valenzuela	112	Ardell C.	121	Bubble Bath	113	15,875	1:21.60	
1966	Fleet Treat	3	A. Pineda	112	Mellow Marsh	112	What a Charmer	118	16,000	1:22.00	
1967	Forgiving	3	J. Lambert	118	Gamely	113	Francine M.	113	17,500	1:22.20	
1968	Morgaise	3	J. Lambert	118	Time to Leave	118	Toe Shoes	112	13,250	1:21.20	
1969	Tipping Time	3	M. Valenzuela	114	Marjorie's Girl	115	Dumpty's Lady	121	13,350	1:21.40	
1970	Bold Jil	3	W, Shoemaker	118	Opening Bid	121	Amber Light	115	12,750	1:21.40	
1971	Turkish Trousers	3	W. Shoemaker	121	Convenience	115	Countess Market	115	17,200	1:21.80	
1972	Impressive Style	3	L. Pincay Jr	121	Cautious Bidder	118	Crimson Saint	118	16,600	1:21.00	
1973	Sandy Blue	3	D. Pierce	118	Sphere	113	Goddess Roman	113	20,250	1:21.80	
1974	Modus Vivendi	3	D. Pierce	121	Fleet Peach	118	Fresno Star	118	19,800	1:21.60	
1975	Raise Your Skirts	3	W. Mahorney	118	Miss Tokyo	117	Fascinating Girl	119	19,350	1:20.80	
1976	Hail Hilarious	3	D. Pierce	114	Doc Shah's Siren	119	I Going	115	20,550	1:21.40	
1977	Taisez Vous	3	F. Toro	114	Wavy Waves	122	Silent Wisdom	114	22,650	1:22.60	
1978	Eximious	3	W. Shoemaker	119	B. Thoughtful	122	Joe's Bee	114	25,550	1:22.20	
1979	Eloquent	3	D. Pierce	122	Celine	122	Joy's Jewel	114	26,800	1:20.60	
1980	Cinegita	3	T. Lipham	114	Thundertee	122	Back at Two	119	31,450	1:20.80	
1981	Cherokee Frolic	3	G. Cohen	119	Strangeways	119	Terra Miss	115	32,400	1:22.20	
1982	Faneuil Lass	3	T. Lipham	117	Jones Time Machine	119	Hasty Hannah	119	32,400	1:23.20	
1983	Ski Goggle	3	C.J. McCarron	122	Madam Forbes	115	Gatita	117	33,150	1:23.40	
1984	Mitterand	3	E. Delahoussaye	115	Gene's Lady	122	Lucky Lucky Lucky	122	40,000	1:22.20	
1985	Reigning Countess	3	G.L. Stevens	122	Window Seat	122	Charming Susan	115	38,300	1:22.40	
1986	Melair	3	P.A. Valenzuela	115	Comparability	119	Silent Arrival	122	48,600	1:22.40	
1987	Very Subtle	3	W. Shoemaker	122	Joey the Trip	117	Sacahuista	122	45,750	1:22.60	
1988	Sheesham	3	L. Pincay Jr	122	Affordable Price	114	Super Avie	116	49,700	1:22.60	
1989	Imaginary Lady	3	G.L. Stevens	122	Kiwi	114	Stormy but Valid	122	47,800	1:21.40	
1990	Forest Fealty	3	J.A. Garcia	114	Patches	122	Golden Reef	122	48,950	1:21.60	
1991	Suziqcute	3	C.J. McCarron	119	Zama Hummer	117	Ifyoucouldseemenow	122	62,800	1:21.80	100
1992	She's Tops	3	K.J. Desormeaux	114	Race the Wild Wind	121	Magical Maiden	121	66,500	1:22.60	94
1993	Afto	3	P. Atkinson	114	Fit to Lead	121	Nijivision	113	64,500	1:22.40	93
1994	Sportful Snob	3	P.A. Valenzuela	118	Pirate's Revenge	121	Accountable Lady	116	61,400	1:21.80	96
1995	Sleep Easy	3	C.S. Nakatani	113	Texinadress	118	Laguna Seca	115	64,600	1:22.40	94
1996	Supercilious	3	C.S. Nakatani	121	Tiffany Diamond	118	Raw Gold	121	64,260	1:22.60	91
1997	I Ain't Bluffing	3	E. Delahoussaye	118	Really Happy	121	Montecito	114	65,100	1:22.60	95
1998	Brulay	3	G.L. Stevens	115	Gourmet Girl	119	Unreal Squeal	116	64,260	1:20.80	104
1999	Olympic Charmer	3	C.J. McCarron	115	Dianehill	115	Fee Fi Foe	116	90,000	1:21.00	106
2000	Abby Girl	3	C.S. Nakatani	119	Cover Gal	122	Wired to Fly	122	90,000	1:22.57	96
2001	Golden Ballet	3	C.J. McCarron	123	Starrer	115	Pretty 'n Smart	115	90,000	1:21.57	101
2002	Spetember Secret	3	P.A. Valenzuela	118	Affairs of State	118	Fun House	118	63,780	1:22.95	95
2003	Buffythecenterfold	3	V. Espinoza	123	Honest Answer	117	Dash for Money	115	64,320	1:22.54	88
2004	Elusive Diva	3	P.A. Valenzuela	118	M.A. Fox	116	Speedy Falcon	123	65,760	1:21.36	88

Beyer Index: 95.79

RAMPART HANDICAP (G2), 1 1/8 Miles, Fillies and Mares, 3-Year-Olds and Up, Gulfstream Park, 2004 Purse: $194,000

Year	Winner	Age	Jockey	Wt.	Second	Wt.	Third	Wt.	Win Value	Time	Beyer
1976	Moon Glitter	4	E. Fires	110	Regal Quillo	112	K D Princess	111	9,960	1:22.20	
1981	Wistful	4	D. Brumfield	117	Lillian Russell	109	Deby's Willing	112	54,180	1:44.60	
1982	Sweetest Chant	4	E. Fires	117	Deby's Willing	115	Pretorienne	114	25,662	1:43.40	
1983	Flag Waver	4	A. Solis	108	Prime Prospect	118	Our Darling	112	57,960	1:44.00	
1984	Thinghatab	4	C. Perret	118	National Banner	117	Vestris	112	36,870	1:43.80	
1985	Isayso	6	E. Maple	113	Pretty perfect	122	Basie	114	70,080	1:44.20	
1986	Endear	4	E. Maple	113	Isayso	118	Natania	112	103,080	1:45.80	
1987	Life at the Top	4	R.P. Romero	122	I'm Sweets	119	Natania	113	97,440	1:44.00	
1988	By Land By Sea	4	F. Toro	118	Queen Alexandra	120	Bound	113	120,000	1:43.80	
1989	Colonial Waters	4	W.H. McCauley	112	Savannah's Honor	113	Haiati	112	120,000	1:44.80	
1990	Barbarika	5	C. Perret	113	Fit for a Queen	112	Natala	112	120,000	1:44.20	100
1991	Charon	4	C. Perret	121	Wortheroatsingold	112	Train Robbery	113	120,000	1:43.00	102
1992	Fit for a Queen	6	J.D. Bailey	119	Firm Stance	111	Nannerl	113	120,000	1:43.60	108
1993	Girl on a Mission	4	J.D. Bailey	112	Luv Me Luv Me Not	116	Haunting	114	120,000	1:45.40	92
1994	Nine Keys	4	M.E. Smith	113	Educated Risk	120	Traverse City	113	120,000	1:42.00	97
1995	Educated Risk	5	M.E. Smith	126	Recognizable	117	Jade Flush	113	120,000	1:43.00	105
1996	Investalot	5	S.J. Sellers	114	Queen Tutta	113	Alcovy	117	120,000	1:43.80	99
1997	Chip	4	J. Bravo	114	Rare Blend	122	Hurricane Viv	116	120,000	1:42.40	96
1998	Dance for Thee	4	J. Bravo	113	Escena	119	Glitter Woman	121	120,000	1:44.60	106
1999	Banshee Breeze	4	J.D. Bailey	122	Glitter Woman	119	Timely Broad	114	120,000	1:42.80	108
2000	Bella Chiarra	5	S.J. Sellers	116	Lines of Beauty	114	Up We Go	113	120,000	1:43.27	106

Year	Winner	Age	Jockey	Wt.	Second	Wt.	Third	Wt.	Win Value	Time	Beyer
2001	De Bertie	4	J.F. Chavez	116	Apple of Kent	114	Scratch Pad	116	120,000	1:50.48	103
2002	Forest Secrets	4	P. Day	117	Summer Colony	118	Happily Unbridled	114	120,000	1:49.83	103
2003	Allamerican Bertie	4	J.R. Velazquez	122	Smok'n Frolic	118	Softly	115	120,000	1:47.92	104
2004	Sightseek	5	J.D. Bailey	121	Redoubled Miss	113	Lead Story	117	120,000	1:51.07	101

Beyer Index: 102.00

RANCHO BERNARDO HANDICAP (G3), 6 1/2 Furlongs, Fillies and Mares, 3-Year-Olds and Up, Del Mar, 2004 Purse: $150,000

Year	Winner	Age	Jockey	Wt.	Second	Wt.	Third	Wt.	Win Value	Time	Beyer
1967	Sharp Decline	5	R. Bianco	114	Bern Book	116	Gueenie	116	7,475	1:33.80	
1967	Quicken Tree	4	W. Hartack	116	Blazing Silk	112	Het's Cadet	115	7,475	1:34.80	
1973	Fairly Certain	4	S. Valdez	121	Tannyhill	117	Norm'ndy Glory	115	10,400	1:42.80	
1973	Dollar Discount	4	S. Valdez	119			Dr. Kerlan	118	6,400	1:43.20	
	D.B. Carm	4	F. Toro	119							
1974	Impressive Style	5	R. Rosales	117	Fleet Peach	115	Lt's Joy	120	16,300	1:08.60	
1975	Mama Kali	4	J. Lambert	120	Hooley Ruler	117	Modus Vivendi	124	17,050	1:08.40	
1976	Mama Kali	5	L. Pincay Jr	117	Mismoyola	120	Vol au Vent	120	16,400	1:09.20	
1977	Lullaby Song	4	L. Pincay Jr	120	Miss Rising Market	113	Honeyhugger	117	16,550	1:09.00	
1978	Happy Holme	4	C.J. McCarron	120	Telferner	117	Dallas Deb	113	18,200	1:13.00	
1979	Fantastic Girl	3	W. Shoemaker	112	Happy Holme	120	Delice	122	22,850	1:09.20	
1980	Great Lady M.	5	L. Pincay Jr	121	Sal's High	118	Western Hand	110	25,800	1:08.60	
1981	Forluvofiv	4	E. Delahoussaye	118	Untamed Spirit	122	Ack's Secret	118	31,400	1:09.40	
1982	Lucky Lady Ellen	3	L. Pincay Jr	117	Glitter Hitter	118	Excitable Lady	125	31,850	1:08.60	
1983	Bara Lass	4	C.J. McCarron	120	Excitable Lady	124	Milingo	113	31,800	1:09.40	
1984	Pleasure Cay	4	L. Pincay Jr	121	Lovlier Linda	120	Pride of Rosewood	115	32,250	1:08.60	
1985	Take My Picture	3	F. Olivares	114	Sales Bulletin	118	Mimi Baker	112	33,200	1:09.20	
1986	Bold n Special	3	C.J. McCarron	115	Rangoon Ruby	116	Eloquack	117	30,850	1:14.60	
1987	Julie the Flapper	3	C.J. McCarron	114	Clabber Girl	117	Sari's Heroine	119	33,200	1:15.00	
1988	Clabber Girl	5	L. Pincay Jr	120	Queen Forbes	113	Behind the Scenes	117	38,750	1:14.60	
1989	Kool Arrival	3	L. Pincay Jr	117	Super Avie	117	Survive	116	47,625	1:15.20	
1990	Hot Novel	4	K.J. Desormeaux	118	Sexy Slew	116	Down Again	115	62,875	1:14.60	106
1991	Cascading Gold	5	L. Pincay Jr	117	Survive	120	Suziqcute	114	60,100	1:15.40	103
1992	Bountiful Native	4	P.A. Valenzuela	117	Devil's Orchid	120	She's Tops	114	63,400	1:15.20	100
1993	Knight Prospector	4	K.J. Desormeaux	119	Interactive	119	Bountiful Native	120	45,675	1:16.40	96
1994	Desert Stormer	4	Delahoussaye E	116	Magical Maiden	120	Booklore	117	62,800	1:14.80	103
1995	Track Gal	4	C.J. McCarron	118	Desert Stormer	119	Lakeway	122	58,650	1:14.20	107
1996	Track Gal	5	McCarron C. J.	122	Tricky Code	116	Evil's Pic	117	63,550	1:14.60	110
1997	Track Gal	6	Stevens G. L.	120	Madame Pandit	118	Advancing Star	116	69,125	1:15.60	107
1998	Advancing Star	5	McCarron C. J.	120	Closed Escrow	115	Tiffany Diamond	116	64,140	1:14.60	110
1999	Enjoy The Moment	4	Flores D. R.	119	Snowberg	117	Stop Traffic	121	90,000	1:15.80	100
2000	Theresa's Tizzy	6	L. Pincay Jr.	117	Nany's Sweep	117	Hookedonthefeelin	119	90,000	1:16.23	103
2001	Kalookan Queen	5	A. Solis	119	Go Go	125	Warren's Whistle	111	90,000	1:15.52	103
2002	Kalookan Queen	6	A. Solis	123	Warren's Whistle	116	Fancee Bargain	112	90,000	1:16.40	98
2003	Secret Liaison	5	C.S. Nakatani	116	Lacie Girl	116	Spring Meadow	117	90,000	1:15.53	102
2004	Dream of Summer	5	M.E. Smith	118	Barbara Orr	113	Cyber Slew	117	90,000	1:15.85	100

Beyer Index: 103.20

RAVEN RUN (G2), 7 Furlongs, 3-Year-Old Fillies, Keeneland Race Course, 2004 Purse: $224,200

Year	Winner	Age	Jockey	Wt.	Second	Wt.	Third	Wt.	Win Value	Time	Beyer
1999	Dreamy Maiden	3	P. Day	117	Golden Illusion	117	Cosmic Wing	117	37,706	1:22.64	91
2000	Darling My Darling	3	M.E. Smith	117	Surfside	123	Cat Cay	117	51,104	1:20.88	105
2001	Nasty Storm	3	P. Day	123	Hattiesburg	123	Forest Secrets	123	68,138	1:23.30	100
2002	Sightseek	3	J.D. Bailey	117	Miss Lodi	123	Respectful	117	106,578	1:23.98	98
2003	Yell	3	P. Day	123	Ebony Breeze	123	Tina Bull	117	108,159	1:21.75	102
2004	Josh's Madelyn	3	J. Shepherd	118	Vision of Beauty	116	Feline Story	118	139,004	1:22.86	98

Beyer Index: 99.00

RAZORBACK HANDICAP (G3), 1 1/16 Miles, 4-Year-Olds and Up, Oaklawn Park, 2004 Purse: $100,000

Year	Winner	Age	Jockey	Wt.	Second	Wt.	Third	Wt.	Win Value	Time	Beyer
1976	Royal Glint	6	J. Tejeira	126	Marauding	114	Heaven Forbid	112	35,550	1:42.40	
1977	Dragset	4	J. Kunitake	120	Romeo	120	Last Buzz	115	35,910	1:44.40	
1978	Cox's Ridge	4	E. Maple	125	Dr. Riddick	116	Mark's Place	124	37,110	1:43.00	
1979	Cisk	5	G. Patterson	120	Droll's Reason	113	Prince Majestic	121	53,700	1:45.40	
1980	All the More	7	L. Snyder	114	Prince Majestic	116	Br'ker Br'ker	117	56,400	1:45.40	
1981	Temperence Hill	4	E. Maple	124	Blue Ensign	113	Belle's Ruler	112	11,110	1:44.20	

Year	Winner	Age	Jockey	Wt.	Second	Wt.	Third	Wt.	Win Value	Time	Beyer
1982	Eminency	4	P. Day	111	Reef Searcher	119	Tally Ho the Fox	115	76,200	1:45.20	
1983	Eminency	5	P. Day	120	Cassaleria	115	Bold Style	113	70,740	1:43.60	
1984	Dew Line	5	S. Maple	116	Passing Base	112	Win Stat	115	74,520	1:41.60	
1985	Imp Society	4	P. Day	126	Introspective	113	Strength in Unity	109	97,740	1:42.60	
1986	Red Attack	4	L. Snyder	111	Vanlandingham	125	Inevitable Leader	111	96,900	1:42.00	
1987	Bolshoi Boy	4	R.P. Romero	119	Lyphard's Ridge	110	Sun Master	119	86,520	1:40.80	
1988	Lost Code	4	C. Perret	123	Red Attack	112	Demons Begone	121	73,500	1:40.40	
1989	Blushing John	4	P. Day	117	Lyphard's Ridge	111	Proper Reality	123	60,000	1:43.00	
1990	Opening Verse	4	P. Day	116	Primal	121	Silver Survivor	118	90,000	1:41.40	
1991	Bedeviled	4	D.L. Howard	115	Din's Dancer	117	Black Tie Affair	118	90,000	1:42.40	
1992	Tokatee	6	G.K. Gomez	115	On the Edge	112	Total Assets	110	90,000	1:42.80	
1993	Lil E. Tee	4	P. Day	123	Zeeruler	115	Senor Tomas	114	90,000	1:41.40	116
1994	Prize Fight	5	P.A. Johnson	113	Brother Brown	120	Country Store	113	90,000	1:43.60	111
1995	Silver Goblin	4	D.W. Cordova	124	Joseph's Robe	111	Wooden Ticket	115	120,000	1:42.60	113
1996	Juliannus	7	R.J. Albarado	113	Judge TC	121	Dazzling Falls	118	90,000	1:43.20	98
1997	No Spend No Glow	5	R.N. Lester	115	Illesam	114	Come On Flip	115	90,000	1:43.20	102
1998	Brush With Pride	6	T.T. Doocy	115	Littlebitlively	112	Krigeorj's Gold	115	75,000	1:43.40	105
1999	Desert Air	4	C.J. Lanerie	113	Magnify	113	Black Tie Dinner	112	75,000	1:44.75	101
2000	Well Noted	5	T.T. Doocy	112	Crimson Classic	115	Mr Ross	115	75,000	1:43.21	105
2001	Mr Ross	6	D. Pettinger	119	Graeme Hall	120	Maysville Slew	117	75,000	1:42.60	109
2002	Mr. Ross	7	D. Pettinger	120	Remington Rock	115	Big Numbers	116	60,000	1:44.13	105
2003	Colorful Tour	4	L.S. Quinonez	118	Crafty Shaw	119	Windward Passage	118	60,000	1:43.53	98
2004	Sonic West	5	W. Martinez	113	Crafty Shaw	117	Pie n Burger	119	60,000	1:43.56	104

Beyer Index: 105.58

EDDIE READ HANDICAP (G1), 1 1/8 Miles (Turf), 3-Year-Olds and Up, Del Mar, 2004 Purse: $400,000

Year	Winner	Age	Jockey	Wt.	Second	Wt.	Third	Wt.	Win Value	Time	Beyer
1974	My Old Friend	5	A.L. Diaz	115	Montmartre	116	War Heim	121	22,100	1:49.20	
1975	Blue Times	4	J. Lambert	115	Portentous	112	Confederate Yankee	115	28,200	1:49.20	
1976	Branford Court	6	R. Campas	116	Diode	114	Austin Mittler	115	26,150	1:48.40	
1977	No Turning	4	F. Toro	115	Today 'n Tomorrow	119	Star Ball	111	32,400	1:48.80	
1978	Effervescing	5	L. Pincay Jr	124	Text	123	Bywayofchicago	117	33,050	1:48.60	
1979	Good Lord	8	W. Shoemaker	115	Shagbark	114	True Statement	115	42,450	1:49.20	
1980	Go West Young Man	5	E. Delahoussaye	120	The Bart	118	Bold Tropic	124	64,250	1:47.60	
1981	Wickerr	6	C.J. McCarron	115	Super Moment	117	Mike Fogarty	114	80,750	1:49.80	
1982	Wickerr	7	E. Delahoussaye	119	Spence Bay	122	Perrault	129	95,300	1:48.40	
1983	Prince Spellbound	4	C. Lamance	121	Bel Bolide	117	Ask Me	115	108,000	1:48.80	
1984	Ten Below	5	L. Pincay Jr	117	Silveyville	117	Desert Wine	124	96,200	1:48.20	
1985	Tsunami Slew	4	G.L. Stevens	119	Al Mamoon	118	Both Ends Burning	123	112,300	1:46.80	
1986	Al Mamoon	5	P.A. Valenzuela	121	Zoffany	123	Truce Maker	115	113,400	1:46.60	
1987	Sharrood	4	L. Pincay Jr	120	Santella Mac	115	Skip Out Front	115	133,200	1:48.00	
1988	Deputy Governor	4	E. Delahoussaye	120	Santella Mac	114	Simply Majestic	115	176,500	1:48.80	
1989	Saratoga Passage	4	E. Delahoussaye	116	Skip Out Front	116	Pasakos	116	162,750	1:49.00	
1990	Fly Till Dawn	4	R.Q. Meza	112	Classic Fame	119	Golden Pheasant	122	157,750	1:48.20	
1991	Tight Spot	4	L. Pincay Jr	125	Val des Bois	115	Madjaristan	116	188,500	1:47.20	110
1992	Marquetry	5	D.R. Flores	118	Luthier Enchanteur	116	Leger Cat	115	187,250	1:47.20	112
1993	Kotashaan	5	K.J. Desormeaux	122	Leger Cat	116	Rainbow Corner	114	183,750	1:48.40	109
1994	Approach the Bench	6	C.S. Nakatani	113	Fastness	114	Johann Quatz	116	187,250	1:48.80	104
1995	Fastness	5	G.L. Stevens	115	Romarin	119	Northern Spur	118	182,600	1:48.20	110
1996	Fastness	6	C.S. Nakatani	124	Smooth Runner	114	Gold And Steel	118	193,000	1:47.00	118
1997	Expelled	5	J.A. Garcia	113	El Angelo	119	Marlin	122	180,000	1:48.60	106
1998	Subordination	4	D.R. Flores	117	Bonapartiste	115	Hawksley Hill	120	180,000	1:47.49	107
1999	Joe Who	6	C.W. Antley	116	Ladies Din	119	Bouccaneer	115	240,000	1:48.75	108
2000	Ladies Din	5	K.J. Desormeaux	120	Chester House	114	Gold Nugget	115	240,000	1:48.64	109
2001	Redattore	6	A. Solis	115	Native Desert	116	Super Quercus	115	240,000	1:47.16	106
2002	Sarafan	5	C.S. Nakatani	117	Beat Hollow	122	Redattore	118	240,000	1:46.77	109
2003	Special Ring	6	D.R. Flores	117	Decarchy	117	Irish Warrior	114	240,000	1:45.87	111
2004	Special Ring	7	V. Espinoza	118	Bayamo	119	Sweet Return	119	240,000	1:45.90	110

Beyer Index: 109.21

RED BANK HANDICAP (G3), 1 Mile (Turf), 3-Year-Olds and Up, Monmouth Park, 2004 Purse: $100,000

Year	Winner	Age	Jockey	Wt.	Second	Wt.	Third	Wt.	Win Value	Time	Beyer
1974	Mystery Mood	2	J. Tejeira	115	Molly Ballantine	121	Lucky Leslie	117	18,672	1:45.20	
1975	Kudara	4	D. MacBeth	118	Enchanted Native	111	Twixt	121	18,850	1:42.20	
1976	Collegiate	4	J.W. Edwards	116	Shoe Me How	110	Four Bells	114	25,919	1:40.20	
1977	Playin' Footsie	4	R. Ardoin	110	Desiree	110	Artfully	112	29,510	1:44.40	
1978	Love Jenny	4	M.A. Gomez	108	Table Hopper	111	Chanctonbury	114	28,308	1:46.20	
1979	Navajo Princess	5	J. Vasquez	122	La Soufriere	116	Sans Arc	115	22,441	1:43.20	
1980	Horatius	5	D. MacBeth	117	Pipedreamer	116	North Course	114	24,495	1:35.00	
1981	Colonel Moran	4	G.W. Donohue	116	Dan Horn	115	Contare	108	24,570	1:35.20	

Year	Winner	Age	Jockey	Wt.	Second	Wt.	Third	Wt.	Win Value	Time	Beyer
1982	Alhambra Joe	5	W. Nemeti	111	Pepper's Segundo	117	Timely Counsel	112	23,265	1:38.60	
1983	Sun and Shine	4	J. Terry	115	St. Brendan	116	Mr. Dreamer	113	24,480	1:36.60	
1984	Tough Mickey	4	K. Skinner	118	Fortnightly	117	Roman Bend	108	28,470	1:36.40	
1984	Castle Guard	5	J.C. Ferrer	118	Super Sunrise	123	Fray Star	117	28,530	1:35.80	
1985	Castelets	6	V. Bracciale Jr	115	Evzone	117	Gothic Revival	112	27,885	1:37.00	
1985	Ends Well	4	M.R. Morgan	116	Domynsky	117	Bold Southerner	115	26,065	1:35.40	
1986	Mazatleca	6	C.W. Antley	112	Feeling Gallant	114	Hi Ideal	113	34,800	1:35.80	
1987	Feeling Gallant	5	C.W. Antley	117	Hi Ideal	114	Racing Star	117	35,610	1:37.20	
1988	Iron Courage	4	W.H. McCauley	118	Spellbound	112	Ioskeha	113	42,210	1:35.40	
1989	Arlene's Valentine	4	J.C. Ferrer	115	Yankee Affair	121	Alwasmi	114	52,290	1:40.20	
1990	Norquestor	4	J.L. Samyn	118	Master Speaker	120	Grande Jette	111	52,980	1:36.00	109
1991	Double Booked	6	J.C. Ferrer	122	Great Normand	118	Now Listen	112	45,000	1:33.20	110
1992	Daarik	5	L. Saumell	114	Leger Cat	116	Kate's Valentine	114	45,000	1:34.00	98
1993	Adam Smith	5	J.L. Samyn	116	Fourstars Allstar	116	Rinka Das	115	45,000	1:34.20	103
1994	Adam Smith	6	J.A. Krone	120	Discernment	113	Fourstardave	118	45,000	1:34.40	110
1995	Dove Hunt	4	W.H. McCauley	118	Rare Reason	115	Winnetou	113	45,000	1:33.80	104
1996	Joker	4	Velez A. J. Jr	113	Rare Reason	118	Diplomatic Jet	116	60,000	1:35.80	106
1997	Basqueian	4	Wilson R.	118	Wild Night Out	111	Jambalaya Jazz	117	60,000	1:35.80	103
1998	Statesmanship	4	Santos J. A.	117	Rob 'n Gin	120	Bomfim	114	60,000	1:35.00	104
1999	Inkatha	5	Castillo H. Jr.	114	Rob 'n Gin	119	Soviet Line	118	90,000	1:33.80	104
2000	Mi Narrow	6	C. Velasquez	114	Deep Gold	114	Inkatha	117	90,000	1:34.84	105
2001	Pavillon	7	J. Bravo	112	Western Summer	114	Runspastum	114	90,000	1:36.38	96
2002	Key Lory	8	H. Vega	117	Sardaukar	113	Spruce Run	113	60,000	1:35.92	100
2003	Just le Facts	4	J. Bravo	111	Saint Verre	118	Runspastum	114	60,000	1:37.73	93
2004	Burning Roma	6	J.L. Castanon	120	Remind	117	American Freedom	115	60,000	1:34.73	102

Beyer Index: 103.13

Off the turf in 2003.

REGRET (G3), 1 1/8 Miles (Turf), 3-Year-Old Fillies, Churchill Downs, 2004 Purse: $221,800

Year	Winner	Age	Jockey	Wt.	Second	Wt.	Third	Wt.	Win Value	Time	Beyer
1994	Packet	3	J.Johnson	117	Thread	122	Slew Kitty Slew	112	54,551	1:42.14	90
1995	Christmas Gift	3	C.Woods	122	Bail Our Becky	122	Grand Charmer	117	54,210	1:45.00	94
1996	Daylight Come	3	C.Bourque	117	Fleur de Nuit	112	Esquive	115	55,526	1:45.72	89
1997	Starry Dreamer	3	W.Martinez	122	Cozy Blues	115	Swearingen	122	69,378	1:42.77	94
1998	Formal Tango	3	C.Woods	115	Adel	122	Pratella	112	105,927	1:43.73	90
1999	Nani Rose	3	S.J. Sellers	115	Solar Bound	122	Suffragette	115	104,439	1:42.40	102
2000	Solvig	3	P. Day	122	Trip	117	Miss Chief	115	104,439	1:42.95	89
2001	Casual Feat	3	L. Melancon	115	Amaretta	117	La Vida Loca	119	103,695	1:42.75	95
2002	Distant Valley	3	J.D. Bailey	119	Peace River Lady	115	Styleistick	122	104,811	1:42.71	92
2003	Sand Springs	3	M. Guidry	118	Personal Legend	116	Achnasheen	116	143,220	1:48.78	92
2004	Sister Star	3	B. Blanc	116	Western Ransom	120	Jinny's Gold	118	137,516	1:51.40	93

Beyer Index: 92.73

For previous runnings, refer to 1994 Manual.

REMSEN (G2), 1 1/8 Miles, 2-Year-Olds, Aqueduct, 2004 Purse: $200,000

Year	Winner	Age	Jockey	Wt.	Second	Wt.	Third	Wt.	Win Value	Time	Beyer
1904	Dandelion	2	W. Davis	103	Gamara	110	Pasadena	117	1,535	1:06.80	
1905	Jacobite	2	J. Jones	126	Hermitage	95	Yalagal	100	1,810	1:07.40	
1906	Frank Gill	2	J. Notter	107	Oraculum	115	Killaloe	114	1,635	1:08.00	
1907	King Cobalt	2	E. Dugan	99	Arasee	104	Bellwether	95	1,525	1:07.40	
1909	The Turk	2	C.H. Shilling	108	Grasmere	120	Cherryola	114	1,050	1:08.20	
1918	War Pennant	2	J. Loftus	122	Lord Brighton	119	Sweep On	120	1,925	1:13.20	
1919	Pilgrim	2	C. Fairbrother	110	St. Allan	111	Head Over Heels	117	2,675	1:12.80	
1920	Grey Lag	2	L. Ensor	123	Knobbie	122	Care Free	109	3,625	1:13.00	
1921	Missionary	2	A. Schuttinger	108	Mustard Seed	112	Surf Rider	120	4,450	1:13.60	
1922	Tall Timber	2	J. Butwell	109	Aladdin	106	Blanc Seing	110	4,125	1:12.00	
1923	Ladkin	2	H. Thurber	118	Bracadale	122	Sun Pal	119	4,075	1:12.00	
1924	Master Charlie	2	G. Babin	130	Swope	122	Faddist	106	4,675	1:11.60	
1925	Timmara	2	H. Thurber	109	Sarmaticus	122	Flat Iron	109	4,175	1:13.40	
1926	Sweepster	2	L. Fator	124	Saxon	118	Cheops	114	4,500	1:12.60	
1927	Excalibur	2	G. Ellis	114	Ariel	124	Leonard B.	101	4,950	1:12.00	
1928	Chatford	2	C. Watters	102	Comstockery	112	African	106	4,250	1:12.80	
1929	Flying Heels	2	W. Kelsay	125	Dunsany	108	Polygamous	123	4,350	1:12.80	
1930	Vander Pool	2	A. Abel	124	Rollin In	115	Timely	114	5,100	1:13.80	
1931	Cambal	2	E. Ambrose	114	Regula Baddun	108	Lucky Tom	125	2,895	1:13.00	
1932	Quel Jeu	2	J. Long	122	Balios	118	Kerry Patch	126	1,425	1:11.80	
1933	Sgt. Byrne	2	A. Robertson	120	Peace Chance	117	Slapdash	119	1,690	1:12.60	
1934	Esposa	2	E. Porter	107	Mantagna	109	Below Zero	112	3,660	1:13.40	
1935	The Fighter	2	E. Arcaro	122	Teufel	112	Postage Due	124	3,885	1:12.00	

Year	Winner	Age	Jockey	Wt.	Second	Wt.	Third	Wt.	Win Value	Time	Beyer
1936	Clodion	2	J. Gilbert	110	Night Bud	110	Dogaway	119	3,065	1:12.60	
1937	Bourbon King	2	C. Kurtsinger	117	Mountain Ridge	119	The Chief	118	7,500	1:12.40	
1938	Johnstown	2	J. Stout	126	Lovely Night	122	Beau James	120	7,100	1:11.00	
1939	Camp Verde	2	D. Meade	118	Fenelon	112	Jacomar	119	6,600	1:11.80	
1940	Harvard Square	2	L. Haas	112			Signator	110	6,425	1:11.20	
	Mettlesome	2	A. Robertson	115							
1941	Apache	2	J. Stout	110	Devil Diver	124	Contradiction	119	8,950	1:12.80	
1942	Blue Swords	2	C. Bierman	123	Ocean Wave	117	Joe Burger	110	8,250	1:12.80	
1943	Bellwether	2	J. Longden	112	Dance Team	122	Tropea	114	7,912	1:13.20	
1943	Black Badge	2	W.D. Wright	118	Lucky Draw	126	Sweeping Time	112	8,112	1:11.40	
1944	War Jeep	2	A. Snider	121			Plebiscite	116	5,395	1:12.40	
	Great Power	2	E. Arcaro	116							
1945	Lord Boswell	2	E. Guerin	119	They Say	108	Marine Victory	122	8,595	1:11.20	
1946	Phalanx	2	R. Donoso	117	Tavistock	116	Donor	126	18,000	1:45.80	
1947	Big If	2	C. Givens	117	Escadru	122	My Request	126	17,450	1:47.00	
1948	Eternal World	2	T. Atkinson	122	Eternal Dream	117	Transfluent	117	14,300	1:00.60	
1949	Lights Up	2	O. Scurlock	114	Cornwall	115	Selector	112	8,875	1:13.40	
1950	Repetoire	2	K. Church	112	Rough'n Tumble	120	Pictus	118	8,575	1:11.20	
1953	Galdar	2	J. Nichols	115	By Jeepers	119	Swift Sword	114	19,550	1:46.60	
1954	Roman Patrol	2	D. Dodson	122	Grandpaw	112	Ever Best	122	37,250	1:48.00	
1955	Nail	2	H. Woodhouse	122	Prince John	122	Noorsaga	122	64,425	1:45.20	
1956	Ambehaving	2	L. Batcheller	122	Missile	122	Finlandia	112	64,975	1:45.60	
1957	Misty Flight	2	E. Arcaro	113	Whitley	112	Rose Trellis	120	20,100	1:45.00	
1958	Atoll	2	J. Ruane	117	Rico Tesio	114	Derrick	114	18,322	1:44.60	
1959	Victoria Park	2	E. Guerin	124	Progressing	111	Fleet Greek	114	23,050	1:37.20	
1960	Carry Back	2	J. Sellers	120	Vapor Whirl	111	Ambiopoise	113	22,822	1:36.40	
1961	Figaro Bob	2	J.L. Rotz	113	Daddy R.	111	Melanion	115	19,240	1:36.80	
1962	Rocky Link	2	J.L. Rotz	114	Duc de Thor	113	Ornamento	120	19,305	1:36.40	
1963	Northern Dancer	2	M. Ycaza	124	Lord Date	112	Repeating	117	18,330	1:35.60	
1964	Sum Up	2	D. Pierce	113	Sparkling Johnny	112	Flag Raiser	111	18,427	1:33.80	
1965	Gary G.	2	B. Baeza	119	Amberoid	117	Native Pitt	117	18,460	1:36.00	
1966	Damascus	2	W. Shoemaker	117	Native Guile	117	Reflected Glory	119	19,695	1:37.00	
1967	Salerno	2	M. Ycaza	119	Verbatim	115	Mr. Hasty	119	19,890	1:38.00	
1968	Palauli	2	L. Adams	119	Distinctive	117	I Found Gold	117	18,980	1:36.40	
1969	Protanto	2	J. Velasquez	117	Needles n Pens	115	Fried Eggs Over	117	19,792	1:35.60	
1970	Jim French	2	A. Cordero Jr	119	Win Desmond	119	Misty Moon	115	18,360	1:36.80	
1971	Key to the Mint	2	B. Baeza	119	Determined Cosmic	119	Traffic Cop	117	21,570	1:36.60	
1972	Kinsman Hope	2	E. Maple	115	Restless Jet	115	Imperator	119	18,045	1:37.00	
1973	Heavy Mayonnaise	2	C. Baltazar	112	Hegemony	112	Flip Sal	112	17,925	1:51.40	
1974	El Pitirre	2	M. Venezia	112	Bombay Duck	118	Circle Home	115	34,380	1:49.40	
1975	Hang Ten	2	L. Pincay Jr	116	Dance Spell	113	Play the Red	113	52,290	1:49.20	
1976	Royal Ski	2	J. Kurtz	122	Nostalgia	122	Hey Hey J.P.	116	49,545	1:50.40	
1977	Believe It	2	E. Maple	122	Alydar	122	Quadratic	116	48,015	1:47.80	
1978	Instrument Landing	2	J. Fell	119	Lucy's Axe	117	Picturesque	117	48,375	1:50.20	
1979	Plugged Nickle	2	B. Thornburg	122	Googolplex	117	Proctor	113	64,560	1:50.40	
1980	Pleasant Colony	2	V. Bracciale Jr	116	Foolish Tanner	113	Akureyri	117	67,920	1:50.20	
	Akureyri finished first but was disqualified and placed third										
1981	Laser Light	2	E. Maple	113	Real Twister	115	Wolfie's Rascal	113	103,500	1:50.80	
1982	Pax in Bello	2	J. Fell	113	Chumming	115	Primitive Pleasure	113	141,300	1:50.20	
1983	Dr. Carter	2	J. Velasquez	113	Secret Prince	117	Hail Bold King	113	134,700	1:49.00	
1984	Mighty Appealing	2	G. Smith	122	Hot Debate	117	Bolting Holme	115	178,680	1:53.20	
	Stone White finished first but was subsequently disqualified from the purse money										
1985	Pillaster	2	A. Cordero Jr	119	Mr. Classic	113	Dance of Life	113	175,800	1:49.00	
1986	Java Gold	2	P. Day	114	Talinum	115	Drachma	113	172,680	1:49.60	
1987	Batty	2	J.A. Santos	113	Old Stories	114	Three Engines	113	176,400	1:52.40	
1988	Fast Play	2	A. Cordero Jr	122	Fire Maker	115	Silver Sunsets	122	197,400	1:50.60	
1989	Yonder	2	E. Maple	115	Roanoke	122	Armed for Peace	113	145,680	1:51.20	
1990	Scan	2	J.D. Bailey	119	Subordinated Debt	115	Kyle's Our Man	113	106,560	1:52.40	
1991	Pine Bluff	2	C. Perret	113	Offbeat	113	Cheap Shades	122	120,000	1:50.80	93
1992	Silver of Silver	2	J. Vasquez	122	Dalhart	115	Wild Gale	115	120,000	1:50.20	96
1993	Go for Gin	2	J.D. Bailey	117	Arrovente	113	Linkatariat	113	120,000	1:52.60	95
1994	Thunder Gulch	2	G.L. Stevens	115	Western Echo	119	Mighty Magee	114	120,000	1:53.80	89
1995	Tropicool	2	J.F. Chavez	112	Skip Away	112	Crafty Friend	113	170,000	1:50.20	94
1996	The Silver Move	2	R. Migliore	114	Jules	122	Accelerator	122	120,000	1:53.40	91
1997	Coronado's Quest	2	M.E. Smith	122	Halory Hunter	115	Brooklyn Nick	115	120,000	1:52.20	91
1998	Comeonmom	2	J. Bravo	113	Millions	122	Wondertross	113	120,000	1:49.80	94
1999	Greenwood Lake	2	J.L. Samyn	122	Un Fino Vino	113	Polish Miner	113	120,000	1:50.60	91
2000	Windsor Castle	2	R.G. Davis	116	Ommadon	122	Buckle DownBen	122	120,000	1:51.92	92
2001	Saarland	2	J.R. Velazquez	116	Nokoma	116	Silent Fred	116	120,000	1:51.28	87
2002	Toccet	2	J.F. Chavez	122	Bham	116	Empire Maker	116	120,000	1:50.40	101
2003	Read the Footnotes	2	J.D. Bailey	122	Master David	116	West Virginia	116	120,000	1:50.62	105
2004	Rockport Harbor	2	S. Elliott	120	Galloping Grocer	120	Killenaule	120	120,000	1:48.88	102

Beyer Index: 94.36

LEONARD RICHARDS (G3), 1 1/16 Miles, 3-Year-Olds, Delaware Park, 2004 Purse: $250,600

Year	Winner	Age	Jockey	Wt.	Second	Wt.	Third	Wt.	Win Value	Time	Beyer
1997	Leestown	3	J. Velez Jr.	116	Universe		Bleu Madura		90,000	1:43.40	
1998	Scatmandu	3	R. Migliore	114	Hot Wells		True Silver		90,000	1:42.40	
1999	Stellar Brush	3	M. McCarthy	114	Smart Guy		Successful Appeal		120,000	1:42.78	
2000	Grundlefoot	3	T. Dunkelberger	113	Perfect Cat		Mercaldo		120,000	1:44.04	96
2001	Burning Roma	3	R. Wilson	122	Marciano		Bay Eagle		120,000	1:42.41	114
2002	Running Tide	3	R.A. Dominguez	115	Nothing Flat	115	The Sewickley Kind	115	150,000	1:45.10	97
2003	Awesome Time	3	A.S. Black	115	Christine's Outlaw	115	Cherokee's Boy	122	150,000	1:43.26	95
2004	Pollard's Vision	3	J.D. Bailey	122	Britt's Jules	116	Pies Prospect	115	150,000	1:43.85	105

Beyer Index: 101.40

For previous runnings, refer to 1983 Manual.

RICHTER SCALE BREEDERS' CUP SPRINT CHAMPIONSHIP HCP (G2), 7 Furlongs, 3-Year-Olds and Up, Gulfstream Park, 2004 Purse: $200,000

Year	Winner	Age	Jockey	Wt.	Second	Wt.	Third	Wt.	Win Value	Time	Beyer
1972	Close Decision	4	M. Castaneda	110	Insubordination	118	Intensitivo	115	27,240	1:22.60	
1974	Cheriepe	4	J. Velasquez	115	Shecky Greene	127	Gay Pierre	112	25,236	1:22.40	
1977	Yamanin	5	W. Gavidia	122	Full Out	119	Rexson	114	37,860	1:22.80	
1981	King's Fashion	6	J.L. Samyn	122	Jaklin Klugman	124	Joanie's Chief	108	34,920	1:22.60	
1983	Deputy Minister	4	D. MacBeth	122	Wipe 'Em Out	109	Center Cut	118	38,040	1:22.80	
1984	Number One Special	4	E. Fires	116	Ward Off Trouble	116	El Perico	114	23,793	1:21.80	
1985	Key to the Moon	4	R. Platts	122	For Halo	123	Northern Ocean	112	42,552	1:22.60	
1986	Hot Cop	4	J.L. Samyn	115	Dwight D.	114	Opening Lead	115	45,324	1:22.80	
1987	Dwight D.	5	R.N. Lester	116	Splendid Catch	113	Uncle Ho	112	27,816	1:10.80	
1988	Royal Pennant	5	J.A. Santos	113	Grantley	112			45,612	1:23.20	
					Real Forest	113					
1989	Claim	4	C. Perret	115	Position Leader	117	Prospector's Halo	115	41,904	1:23.40	
1990	Dancing Spree	5	A. Cordero Jr	126	Pentelicus	114	Shuttleman	111	30,000	1:10.00	106
1991	Gervazy	4	W.S. Ramos	115	Shuttleman	114	Swedaus	110	60,000	1:21.40	117
1992	Groomstick	6	W.S. Ramos	112	Ocala Flame	111	Cold Digger	113	60,000	1:23.80	107
1993	Binalong	4	J.D. Bailey	112	Loach	114	Richman	113	60,000	1:21.20	109
1994	I Can't Believe	6	Maple E	113	American Chance	114	British Banker	114	60,000	1:22.40	108
1995	Cherokee Run	5	M.E. Smith	122	Waldoboro	113	Evil Bear	116	60,000	1:21.60	114
1996	Patton	5	R.G. Davis	113	Forty Won	115	Our Emblem	115	100,140	1:21.80	107
1997	Frisco View	4	J.D. Bailey	116	El Amante	114	Templado	114	98,160	1:23.00	113
1998	Rare Rock	5	P. Day	117	Irish Conquest	114	Frisco View	118	120,000	1:22.00	111
1999	Frisk Me Now	5	E.L.King Jr	117	Young At Heart	113	Good and Tough	115	60,000	1:22.80	104
2000	Richter Scale	6	R. Migliore	118	Forty One Carats	116	Kelly Kip	120	120,000	1:23.30	111
2001	Hook and Ladder	4	R. Migliore	115	Trippi	120	Rollin With Nolan	116	120,000	1:21.85	109
2002	Dream Run	4	P. Day	113	Binthebest	114	Burning Roma	118	120,000	1:22.30	104
2003	Tour of the Cat	5	A. Cabassa Jr	116	Burning Roma	116	Highway Prospector	114	120,000	1:21.15	107
2004	Lion Tamer	4	J.R. Velazquez	116	Coach Jimi Lee	115	Wacky for Love	114	120,000	1:21.52	105

Beyer Index: 108.80

Run as Gulfstream Park Sprint Championship Handicap prior to 2003.

RISEN STAR (G3), 1 1/16 Miles, 3-Year-Olds, Fair Grounds, 2004 Purse: $150,000

Year	Winner	Age	Jockey	Wt.	Second	Wt.	Third	Wt.	Win Value	Time	Beyer
1988	Risen Star	3	S. Romero	120	Pastourelles	115	Jim's Orbit	122	12,000	1:40.00	
1989	Nooo Problema	3	S. Romero	117	Alota Strawberry	114	Majesty's Imp	119	12,000	1:42.40	
1989	Dispersal	3	B.J. Walker	114	Island Alibi	114	Major Prospect	114	12,000	1:42.20	
1990	Genuine Meaning	3	R.J. Hirdes	122	Very Formal	114	Diamond Prospector	114	15,000	1:40.80	
1991	Big Courage	3	T.L. Fox	119	Slick Groom	114	Denizen	115	18,000	1:46.60	
1992	Line in the Sand	3	S. Romero	119	Hill Pass	119	Sheik to Sheik	114	19,210	1:45.00	88
1993	Dixieland Heat	3	R.P. Romero	119	O'Star	114	Gold Angle	114	19,995	1:43.20	85
1993	Dry Bean	3	A. Gryder	117	Apprentice	119	Grand Jewel	114	16,020	1:43.80	87
1994	Fly Cry	3	R. Ardoin	122	Smilin Singin Sam	122	Little Jazz Boy	122	31,155	1:43.00	100
1995	Knockadoon	3	W. Martinez	114	Key to Milagra	114	Scott's Scoundrel	122	31,882	1:45.40	90
1995	Beavers Nose	3	K. Bourque	117	Moonlight Dancer	122	Fuzzy Me	114	31,792	1:45.20	92
1996	Zarb's Magic	3	E.J. Perrodin	122	Imminent First	114	Palikar	122	37,950	1:42.80	100
1997	Open Forum	3	D.M. Barton	117	Crypto Star	117	Cash Deposit	122	60,000	1:44.20	91
1998	Comic Strip	3	S.J. Sellers	119	Captain Maestri	122	Time Limit	122	75,000	1:44.20	91
1999	Ecton Park	3	S.J. Sellers	114	Answer Lively	122	Kimberlite Pipe	122	75,000	1:44.80	95
2000	Exchange Rate	3	C.S. Nakatani	119	Mighty	122	Ifitstobeitsuptome	114	75,000	1:44.20	97
2001	Dollar Bill	3	C.J. McCarron	122	Gracie's Dancer	114	Rahy's Secret	122	75,000	1:43.40	102
2002	Repent	3	A.J. D'Amico	122	Bob's Image	115	Easyfromthegitgo	122	90,000	1:43.17	102
2003	Badge of Silver	3	R.J. Albarado	116	Lone Star Sky	122	Defrere's Vixen	114	90,000	1:42.99	108
2004	Gradepoint	3	R.J. Albarado	116	Mr. Jester	122	Nightlifeatbigblue	118	90,000	1:45.36	96

Beyer Index: 94.93

RIVA RIDGE BREEDERS' CUP (G2), 7 Furlongs, 3-Year-Olds, Belmont Park, 2004 Purse: $200,000

Year	Winner	Age	Jockey	Wt.	Second	Wt.	Third	Wt.	Win Value	Time	Beyer
1988	Evening Kris	3	L. Pincay Jr	117	Perfect Spy	122	King's Nest	115	69,120	1:22.80	
1989	Is It True	3	C.W. Antley	122	Mr. Nickerson	115	Fierce Fighter	115	70,200	1:22.20	
1990	Adjudicating	3	J. Vasquez	122	Silent Generation	115	Bayou Blurr	115	68,040	1:23.80	99
1991	Fly So Free	3	J.D. Bailey	122	Formal Dinner	122	Dodge	122	74,040	1:23.00	98
1992	Superstrike	3	J.A. Santos	115	Three Peat	122	Windundermywings	115	70,560	1:22.40	103
1993	Montbrook	3	C.J. Ladner III	117	As Indicated	122	Forever Whirl	122	74,160	1:23.20	99
1994	You and I	3	McCarron CJ	122	End Sweep	114	Slew Gin Fizz	122	67,080	1:20.20	108
1995	Western Larla	3	Stevens GL	119	Mr. Greeley	122	Blu Tusmani	122	66,960	1:24.20	101
1996	Gold Fever	3	M.E. Smith	118	Gameel	114	Bright Launch	120	67,620	1:23.20	94
1997	Smoke Glacken	3	C. Perret	123	Trafalger	123	Wild Wonder	120	66,060	1:20.80	114
1998	Coronado's Quest	3	M.E. Smith	123	Mellow Roll	113	Flashing Tammany	120	82,050	1:22.40	111
1999	Yes It's True	3	J.D. Bailey	123	Lion Hearted	114	Silver Season	113	90,000	1:22.20	103
2000	Trippi	3	J.D. Bailey	123	Bevo	120	Sun Cat	116	90,000	1:23.68	101
2001	Put It Back	3	N.A. Wynter	120	Flame Thrower	120	Touch Tone	123	90,000	1:21.76	106
2002	Gygistar	3	P. Day	119	Draw Play	115	True Direction	119	120,000	1:22.61	105
2003	Posse	3	C.J. Lanerie	123	Midas Eyes	123	Halo Homewrecker	123	120,000	1:22.03	111
2004	Fire Slam	3	P. Day	123	Teton Forest	115	Abbondanza	123	120,000	1:20.94	109

Beyer Index: 104.13

RIVER CITY HANDICAP (G3), 1 1/8 Miles (Turf), 3-Year-Olds and Up, Churchill Downs, 2004 Purse: $174,300

Year	Winner	Age	Jockey	Wt.	Second	Wt.	Third	Wt.	Win Value	Time	Beyer
1978	Inca Roca	5	J.C. Espinoza	118	Perplext	114	Raymond Earl	115	17,859	1:10.40	
1979	Go With the Times	3	G. Gallitano	120	Cossett Charlie	112	Bask	117	19,435	1:10.20	
1980	Tinsley's Hope	6	J.C. Espinoza	114	Go With the Times	122	Withholding	114	19,208	1:11.00	
1981	Suliman	4	L. Snyder	113	Tiger Lure	121	Senate Chairman	113	20,199	1:10.60	
1982	Pleasing Times	3	P. Day	110	Hechizado	115	Rackensack	118	20,719	1:38.20	
1983	Northern Majesty	4	S. Maple	120	Shot n' Missed	123	Straight Flow	115	18,249	1:37.00	
1984	Eminency	6	P. Day	115	Thumbsucker	123	Boyou Hebert	116	18,103	1:38.40	
1985	Banner Bob	3	K.K. Allen	118	Rapid Gray	123	Cullendale	116	29,348	1:36.60	
1986	Taylor's Special	5	P. Day	123	Doonesbear	116	Sumptious	121	30,007	1:36.20	
1987	King's River II	5	M.E. Smith	114	Lord Grundy	119	Boulder Run	117	37,148	1:45.40	
1988	Ile de Jinsky	4	E.J. Sipus Jr	113	Stop the Stage	114	Herakles	117	44,618	1:53.20	
1989	Spark O'Dan	4	J.M. Johnston	113	Exclusive Greer	115	Air Worthy	118	55,429	1:50.80	
1990	Silver Medallion	4	C. Perret	118	Blair's Cove	114	Rushing Raj	114	56,550	1:50.80	
1991	Spending Record	4	P. Day	114	Stage Colony	113	Silver Medallion	118	75,075	1:50.20	105
1992	Cozzene's Prince	5	D. Penna	117	Lotus Pool	118	Stagecraft	114	73,060	1:49.20	103
1993	Secreto's Hideaway	4	W. Martinez	110	Little Bro Lantis	115	Ganges	113	72,670	1:53.80	99
1994	Lindon Lime	4	Sellers SJ	113	Torch Rouge	114	Jaggery John	115	75,660	1:49.20	106
1995	Homing Pigeon		Romero RP	114	Hawk Attack	115	Dusty Asher	111	73,320	1:51.00	99
1996	Same Old Wish	6	Sellers S. J.	119	Jet Freighter	113	Franchise Player	112	70,122	1:49.20	105
1997	Same Old Wish	7	Sellers S. J.	117	Aboriginal Apex	113	Joyeux Danseur	114	106,578	1:50.80	103
1998	Wild Event	5	Sellers S. J.	116	Buff	113	Floriselli	114	116,436	1:49.00	109
1999	Comic Strip	4	P. Day	119	Keats and Yeats	112	Aboriginal Apex	114	106,113	1:50.60	105
2000	Brahms	3	P. Day	112	Vergennes	115	Super Quercus	116	111,879	1:48.09	107
2001	Dr. Kashnikow	4	R.J. Albarado	116	Tijiyr	117	Strategic Mission	115	109,926	1:47.90	104
2002	Dr. Kashnikow	5	R.J. Albarado	116	Foster's Landing	109	Roxinho	115	108,903	1:51.44	100
2003	Hard Buck	4	B. Blanc	118	Warleigh	117	Rowans Park	114	107,136	1:51.60	103
2004	G P Fleet	4	J.R. Martinez Jr	115	Cloudy's Knight	115	Ay Caramba	115	108,066	1:51.26	105

Beyer Index: 103.79

WILL ROGERS (G3), 1 Mile (Turf), 3-Year-Olds, Hollywood Park, 2004 Purse: $109,400

Year	Winner	Age	Jockey	Wt.	Second	Wt.	Third	Wt.	Win Value	Time	Beyer
1938	Dogaway	4	A. Gray	121	Speed to Spare	122	Faithful Maud	114	2,025	1:23.80	
1939	Time Alone	3	E. Tucker	122	Roman Hero	116	Teddy Kerry	115	5,400	1:23.80	
1940	Sweepida	3	R. Neves	122	Weigh Anchor	119	Last Gold	115	7,625	1:23.80	
1941	Battle Colors	3	G. Woolf	124	Strong Arm	113	Painted Veil	114	7,925	1:23.60	
1944	Phar Rong	5	O. Grohs	114	Appleknocker	119	Happy Issue	120	11,200	1:24.20	
1945	Quick Reward	3	A. Skoronski	112	Busher	123	War Allies	110	19,750	1:37.60	
1946	Burra Sahib	3	C. Corbett	115	Enfilade	116	Going With Me	108	20,100	1:24.40	
1947	On Trust	3	J. Longden	126	Handlebars	108	Sullivan	115	20,100	1:22.60	
1948	Speculation	3	F. Chojnacki	115	Stage Glitter	120	Solidarity	124	19,050	1:11.00	
1949	Blue Dart	3	J. Westrope	112	Terry's Man	114	Spotted Bull	111	19,250	1:10.20	
1951	Gold Note	3	W. Shoemaker	114	Ruth Lily	116	Gold Capitol	125	15,650	1:10.20	
1952	Forelock	3	R.L. Baird	110	Alate	110	Warcos	118	17,250	1:09.80	
1953	Imbros	3	R. York	110	Atomic Speed	110	Karim	110	16,450	1:10.00	
1954	Don McCoy	3	I. Valenzuela	110	Rolyat	112	Arrogate	122	16,550	1:09.60	

Year	Winner	Age	Jockey	Wt.	Second	Wt.	Third	Wt.	Win Value	Time	Beyer
1955	Swaps	3	W. Shoemaker	126	Bequeath	122	Mr. Sullivan	118	14,850	1:35.00	
1956	Terrang	3	W. Shoemaker	126	Tecolotito	114	Social Climber	118	17,400	1:35.20	
1957	Round Table	3	R. Neves	122	Joe Price	118	Miquelet	111	16,150	1:34.40	
1958	Hillsdale	3	R. York	110	Prize Host	114	Sir Ruler	110	15,600	1:36.20	
1959	Ole Fols	3	I. Valenzuela	118	Frair Roach	110	Tramore II	110	15,000	1:35.20	
1960	Flow Line	3	J. Longden	123	Natego	114	First Balcony	114	16,000	1:34.80	
1961	Four-and-Twenty	3	J. Longden	126	Olden Times	123	Sonofagun	114	16,000	1:34.40	
1962	Wallet Lifter	3	A. Maese	114	Pirate Cove	114	Drill Site	114	15,425	1:35.00	
1962	Prince of Liberty	3	A. Valenzuela	114	Royal Attack	126	Doc Jocoy	123	15,675	1:34.60	
1963	Viking Spirit	3	J. Longden	114	Y Flash	120	Beekeeper	114	16,675	1:36.60	
1963	Bre'r Rabbit	3	R. York	114	Doolin Point	114	On My Honor	123	16,375	1:36.00	
1964	Count Charles	3	M. Yanez	120	Royal Eiffel	114	Pelegrin	114	20,700	1:36.00	
1965	Terry's Secret	3	A. Maese	120	Easy Lime	114	Arksroni	114	35,000	1:35.20	
1966	Ri Tux	3	I. Valenzuela	113	Drin	114	Galanomad	112	23,925	1:35.80	
1966	Aqua Vite	3	D. Ross	112	Vague Image	116	Postage	112	24,425	1:35.60	
1967	Jungle Road	3	J. Lambert	113	Pagan Gem	113	Tumiga	120	35,450	1:36.40	
1968	Poleax	3	L. Pincay Jr	113	Right or Wrong	116	Glory Hallelujah	114	20,450	1:34.40	
1969	Tell	3	W. Shoemaker	115	Modern Spirit	114	Greek Static	115	19,250	1:35.20	
1970	Lime	3	L. Gilligan	113	Sugar Loaf	112	Sir Wiggle	115	26,200	1:35.80	
1970	Whittingham	3	D. Pierce	114	Colorado King Jr.	115	Rancho Lejos	115	26,200	1:36.00	
1971	Dr. Knighton	3	I. Valenzuela	115	Smooth It	112	Restless Runner	115	32,675	1:35.80	
1971	Fast Fellow	3	L. Pincay Jr	118	Authorize	115	Triple Bend	115	33,175	1:34.80	
1972	Quack	3	W. Shoemaker	112	Finalista	115	Royal Owl	121	32,450	1:34.60	
1973	Groshawk	3	W. Shoemaker	123	Ancient Title	124	Mug Punter	113	33,600	1:35.60	
							Out of the East	118			
1974	Stardust Mel	3	F. Toro	120	Agitate	122	El Seetu	114	32,800	1:40.80	
1975	Uniformity	3	W. Shoemaker	115	Dusty County	117	Exact Duplicate	114	32,150	1:42.00	
1976	Madera Sun	3	L. Pincay Jr	116	An Act	126	Today 'n Tomorrow	115	32,100	1:42.00	
1977	Nordic Prince	3	S. Hawley	117	Sonny Collins	119	Bad 'n Big	123	33,950	1:41.40	
1978	April Axe	3	C.J. McCarron	115	Poppy Popwich	115	He's Dewan	117	33,100	1:41.60	
1979	Ibacache	3	D.G. McHargue	118	Beau's Eagle	121	David's Gotcha	111	32,350	1:40.80	
1980	Stiff Diamond	3	T. Lipham	113	Naked Sky	117	Big Doug	115	34,300	1:41.40	
1981	Splendid Spruce	3	D.G. McHargue	123	Seafood	119	Surprise George	115	38,900	1:41.40	
1982	Give Me Strength	3	D.G. McHargue	123	Ask Me	115	Accoustical	113	26,550	1:40.00	
1982	Sword Blade	3	D.G. McHargue	115	Art Director	114	Lucky Ship	114	26,050	1:41.80	
1983	Barberstown	3	F. Toro	116	Lover Boy Leslie	117	Tanks Brigade	120	35,200	1:41.40	
1984	Tsunami Slew	3	L. Pincay Jr	119	Swinging Scobie	115	Tights	122	37,550	1:39.80	
1985	Pine Belt	3	R.Q. Meza	113	Rich Earth	119	Academy Road	116	40,700	1:41.00	
1986	Mazaad	3	W. Shoemaker	120	Autobot	119	He;s a Saros	115	48,800	1:42.40	
1987	Something Lucky	3	L. Pincay Jr	117	The Medic	115	Persevered	119	49,600	1:43.00	
1988	Word Pirate	3	E. Delahoussaye	119	Perfecting	115	Roberto's Dancer	116	50,400	1:40.20	
1989	Notorious Pleasure	3	L. Pincay Jr	117	Advocate Training	115	First Play	116	66,900	1:40.20	
1990	Itsallgreektome	3	C.S. Nakatani	114	Warcraft	120	Balla Cove	116	66,500	1:40.20	
1991	Compelling Sound	3	P.A. Valenzuela	119	Stark South	116	Persianelli	117	66,100	1:40.60	96
1992	The Name's Jimmy	3	D. Sorenson	116	Bold Assert	117	Prospect for Four	114	63,600	1:40.80	88
1993	Future Storm	3	K.J. Desormeaux	116	Lykatill Hil	119	Earl of Barking	122	68,900	1:40.00	94
1994	Unfinished Symph	3	G. Baze	116	Silver Music	118	Valiant Nature	122	64,600	1:40.60	99
1995	Via Lombardia	3	E. Delahoussaye	117	Mr Purple	119	Bee El Tee	117	63,650	1:34.00	99
1996	Let Bob Do It	3	K.J. Desormeaux	118	Nightcapper	114	Dr. Sardonica	116	67,140	1:34.00	102
1997	Brave Act	3	C.J. McCarron	117	P.T. Indy	118	Without Doubt	116	68,520	1:34.00	96
1998	Magical	3	R.R.Douglas	114	Commitisize	119	Son's Corona	114	65,820	1:33.80	102
1999	Eagleton	3	C.A. Black	118	Hidden Magic	115	Mr. Reignmaker	115	67,800	1:34.20	97
2000	Purely Cozzene	3	V. Espinoza	120	Duke of Green	116	Silver Axe	115	66,000	1:34.67	98
2001	Media Mogul	3	A. Solis	116			Learing at Kathy	116	43,920	1:35.10	91
	Dr. Park	3	T.C. Baze	117							
2002	Doc Holiday	3	D.R. Flores	116	Johar	119	Golden Arrow	115	63,900	1:34.64	99
2003	Private Chef	3	V. Espinoza	115	Banshee King	115	Singletary	117	67,560	1:35.57	94
2004	Laura's Lucky Boy	3	P.A. Valenzuela	119	Toasted	121	Street Theatre	117	65,640	1:33.45	100

Beyer Index: 96.79

ROYAL HEROINE (G3), 1 Mile (Turf), Fillies and Mares, 3-Year-Olds and Up, Hollywood Park, 2004 Purse: $109,700

Year	Winner	Age	Jockey	Wt.	Second	Wt.	Third	Wt.	Win Value	Time	Beyer
1986	Mircaulous	3	G.L. Stevens	118	Seldom Seen Sue	115	Miss Alto	115	22,000	1:41.80	
1998	Tuzla	4	C.S. Nakatani	115	Sonja's Faith	119	Plus	115	42,990	1:34.20	99
1999	Tuzla	5	C.S. Nakatani	123	Isle de France	119	Chime After Chime	113	42,240	1:34.20	103
2000	Tranquility Lake	5	E. Delahoussaye	121	Dianehill	119	Reciclada	119	46,590	1:33.98	104
2001	Kalatiara	4	C.J. McCarron	114	Dianehill	119	Al Desima	116	65,940	1:34.41	94
2002	Surya	4	K.J. Desormeaux	117	Angel Gift	117	Reine de Romance	121	68,880	1:34.73	97
2003	Magic Mission	5	C.S. Nakatani	115	Little Treasure	121	Belleski	115	67,320	1:34.25	100
2004	Janeian	6	K.J. Desormeaux	121	Katdogawn	123	Makeup Artist	121	65,820	1:34.79	95

Beyer Index: 98.86

RUFFIAN HANDICAP (G1), 1 1/16 Miles, Fillies and Mares, 3-Year-Olds and Up, Belmont Park, 2004 Purse: $294,000

Year	Winner	Age	Jockey	Wt.	Second	Wt.	Third	Wt.	Win Value	Time	Beyer
1976	Revidere	3	J. Vasquez	118	Bastonera II	123	Optimistic Gal	118	79,425	2:01.00	
1977	Cum Laude Laurie	3	A. Cordero Jr	114	Mississippi Mud	123	Cascapedia	128	66,480	1:52.20	
1978	Late Bloomer	4	J. Velasquez	122	Pearl Necklace	124	Tempest Queen	117	64,860	1:47.00	
1979	It's in the Air	3	L. Pincay Jr	122	Blitey	113	Waya	126	79,875	1:47.40	
1980	Genuine Risk	3	J. Vasquez	118	Misty Gallore	124	It's in the Air	118	81,900	1:49.20	
1981	Relaxing	5	A. Cordero Jr	123	Love Sign	120	Jameela	122	97,020	1:47.60	
1982	Christmas Past	3	J. Vasquez	117	Mademoiselle Forli	112	Love Sign	123	100,080	1:48.60	
1983	Heartlight No. One	3	L. Pincay Jr	117	Mochila	113	Try Something New	116	103,140	1:47.20	
1984	Heatherten	5	R.P. Romero	118	Miss Oceana	119	Adored	123	103,320	1:48.20	
1985	Lady's Secret	3	J. Velasquez	116	Isayso	115	Sintrillium	118	128,880	1:47.40	
1986	Lady's Secret	4	P. Day	129	Steal a Kiss	109	Endear	119	165,240	1:46.80	
1987	Coup de Fusil	5	A. Cordero Jr	117	Clabber Girl	112	Sacahuista	114	149,760	1:48.60	
	Sacahuista finished first but was disqualified and placed third										
1988	Sham Say	3	J. Vasquez	113	Classic Crown	115	Make Change	114	146,400	1:48.00	
1989	Bayakoa	5	L. Pincay Jr	125	Colonial Waters	118	Open Mind	120	135,840	1:48.40	
1990	Quick Mischief	4	R.I. Rojas	111	Personal Business	113	Mistaurian	115	144,480	1:42.80	96
1991	Queena	5	A. Cordero Jr	120	Sharp Dance	111	Lady D'Accord	113	120,000	1:41.60	104
1992	Versailles Treaty	4	M.E. Smith	120	Quick Mischief	116	Nannerl	119	120,000	1:41.40	106
1993	Shared Interest	5	R.G. Davis	114	Dispute	115	Turnback the Alarm	123	120,000	1:41.80	107
1994	Sky Beauty	4	M.E. Smith	130	Dispute	117	Educated Risk	114	120,000	1:41.60	106
1995	Inside Information	4	M.E. Smith	125	Unlawful Behavior	110	Incincerate	112	120,000	1:40.80	112
1996	Yanks Music	3	J.R. Velazquez	116	Serena's Song	126	Head East	108	150,000	1:41.80	107
1997	Tomisue's Delight	3	J.D. Bailey	113	Clear Mandate	119	Mil Kilates	114	150,000	1:44.40	95
1998	Sharp Cat	4	C.S. Nakatani	124	Furlough	115	Stop Traffic	119	150,000	1:42.48	112
1999	Catinca	4	R. Migliore	119	Furlough	116	Keeper Hill	118	150,000	1:41.94	102
2000	Riboletta	5	C.J. McCarron	125	Gorumet Girl	114	Country Hideaway	114	150,000	1:40.35	115
2002	Mandy's Gold	4	J.A. Santos	116	You	117	Shine Again	117	180,000	1:42.57	107
2003	Wild Spirit	4	J.D. Bailey	121	You	118	Passing Shot	115	180,000	1:41.23	109
2004	Sightseek	5	J.R. Velazquez	122	Pocus Hocus	114	Miss Loren	117	180,000	1:41.51	112

Beyer Index: 106.43

Distance 1 1/4 miles in 1976; 1 1/8 miles, 1977–89. Not run in 2001.

SABIN HANDICAP (G3), 1 1/16 Miles, Fillies and Mares, 3-Year-Olds and Up, Gulfstream Park, 2004 Purse: $100,000

Year	Winner	Age	Jockey	Wt.	Second	Wt.	Third	Wt.	Win Value	Time	Beyer
1991	Fit for a Queen	5	J.D. Bailey	114	Trumpet's Blare		Express Star		46,020	1:42.40	
1992	Lemhi Go	4	R. Lester	113	Trumpet's Blare		Tappanzee		45,000	1:44.60	99
1993	Now Dance	4	M. Guidry	113	Spinning Round		Luv Me Luv Me Not		30,000	1:41.60	98
1994	Hunzinga	5	Felix JE	113	Nine Keys	114	Pleasant Jolie	112	45,000	1:39.40	95
1995	Recognizable	4	M.E. Smith	115	Jade Flush	113	Sambacarioca	118	45,000	1:42.40	101
1996	Lindsay Frolic	4	P. Day	117	Investalot	114	Queen Tutta	113	45,000	1:43.60	91
1997	Rare Blend	4	J.D. Bailey	120	Golden Gale	113	Termly	112	45,000	1:41.20	101
1998	Radiant Megan	5	J.A. Krone	113	Escena	119	Biding Time	113	45,000	1:41.60	95
1999	Timely Broad	5	N.J. Petro	115	Highfalutin	116	Mudslinger	116	45,000	1:42.40	101
2000	Brushed Halory	4	M.E. Smith	115	Roza Robata	115	Mop Squeezer	113	45,000	1:41.84	104
2001	De Bertie	4	J.F. Chavez	115	Royal Fair	113	Frankly My Dear	116	60,000	1:44.74	91
2002	Miss Linda	5	R. Migliore	119	Forest Secrets	117	Tap Dance	113	60,000	1:42.61	108
2003	Allamerican Bertie	4	J.D. Bailey	120	Small Promises	112	Redoubled Miss	114	60,000	1:42.49	105
2004	Roar Emotion	4	J.R. Velazquez	116	Nonsuch Bay	115	Lead Story	119	60,000	1:43.32	100

Beyer Index: 99.15

SAFELY KEPT BREEDERS' CUP (G3), 6 Furlongs, 3-Year-Old Fillies, Pimlico, 2004 Purse: $143,000

Year	Winner	Age	Jockey	Wt.	Second	Wt.	Third	Wt.	Win Value	Time	Beyer
1986	Debtor's Prison	3	D. Byrnes	108	Night Above		Bea Quaility		28,178	1:11.40	
1987	Endless Surprise	3	K.J. Desormeaux	118	Bea Quality		Miracle Wood		28,340	1:17.40	
1988	Clever Power	3	J.A. Krone	120	Lake Valley		Ready Jet Go		65,000	1:16.40	
1989	Safely Kept	3	C. Perret	122	Cojinx		Kathleen the Queen		60,000	1:11.20	
1990	Voodoo Lily	3	K.J. Desormeaux	117	Miss Spentyouth		Catchamenot		60,000	1:10.60	
1991	Missy's Mirage	3	W.H. McCauley	119	Withallprobability		Corporate Fund		60,000	1:10.40	
1992	Meafara	3	B. Swatuk	119	Squirm		Super Doer		60,000	1:10.40	
1993	Miss Indy Anna	3	D. Thomas	113	Ann Dear		Lily of the North		60,000	1:10.00	
1994	Twist Afleet	3	D.Carr	117	Penny's Reshoot	117	Our Royal Blue	113	60,000	1:10.80	97
1995	Broad Smile	3	J.Brown	117	Scotzanna	122	Shebatim's Trick	115	60,000	1:10.20	91
1996	J J's Dream	3	Pino M. G.	122	Flat Fleet Feet	119	Rare Blend	119	60,000	1:09.40	103
1997	Weather Vane	3	Pino M. G.	119	Vegas Prospector	117	Requesting More	115	64,800	1:10.20	90
1998	Hair Spray	3	Velez J. A. Jr.	117	Expensive Issue	115	Ninth Inning	119	66,390	1:10.60	91
1999	Godmother	3	Pino M. G.	117	Superduper Miss	117	Rills	113	60,000	1:09.20	102

Year	Winner	Age	Jockey	Wt.	Second	Wt.	Third	Wt.	Win Value	Time	Beyer
2000	Swept Away	3	J.A Beasley	122	Another	115	Cat Cay	117	60,000	1:09.51	102
2002	Miss Lodi	3	R. Fogelsonger	117	For Rubies	117	Wilzada	117	60,000	1:11.20	99
2003	Randaroo	3	H. Castillo Jr.	119	Follow Me Home	117	Awesome Charm	115	90,000	1:10.54	95
2004	Bending Strings	3	H. Karamanos	119	Smokey Glacken	119	Then She Laughs	117	90,000	1:10.11	95

Beyer Index: 96.50

Run as Columbia Stakes prior to 1996. Run at 6 1/2 furlongs in 1987 and 1988.

SALVATOR MILE HANDICAP (G3), 1 Mile, 3-Year-Olds and Up, Monmouth Park, 2004 Purse: $100,000

Year	Winner	Age	Jockey	Wt.	Second	Wt.	Third	Wt.	Win Value	Time	Beyer
1948	Vertigo II	7	A. Kirklan	112	Coincidence	115	Bright Sword	115	9,425	1:39.00	
1949	Istan	4	H. Mora	114	High Trend	112	Royal Governor	119	9,375	1:37.60	
1950	Noble Impulse	4	W. Downs	114	Faraway	112	Curt'n Time	112	8,600	1:39.00	
1951	Call Over	4	M. Peterson	118	Overexposed	112	Ferd	122	8,225	1:38.80	
1952	General Staff	4	J. Stout	122	Senator Joe	118	Joey Boy	122	18,000	1:39.20	
1953	Tuscany	5	J. Stout	122	Larry Ellis	114	Scobeyville	114	13,950	1:37.40	
1954	Closed Door	5	W. Hartack	114	Resilient	114	Kaster	118	14,200	1:37.00	
1955	Helioscope	4	S. Boulmetis	126	Ifabody	118			12,200	1:36.80	
1956	Skipper Bill	6	J.A. Regalbuto	123	Cedar Hill	113	Sol-Hi	104	14,550	1:37.00	
1957	Nahodah	4	J. Culmone	118	Skipper Bill	115	Tudor Era	111	10,729	1:34.60	
1958	Sonny Dan	4	W. Blum	112	Hicks Error	111	True Verdict	112	10,989	1:37.20	
1959	Li'l Fella	4	W. Hartack	114	Cohoes	114	Talent Show	126	10,810	1:37.20	
1960	Im Willing	4	W. Hartack	114	Open View	114	Pen Bolero	114	10,875	1:37.00	
1961	Careless John	4	W. Boland	122	Black Thumper	113	Francis S.	114	11,294	1:35.00	
1962	Towson	4	D. French	111	Invigor	114	Narokan	111	11,066	1:40.20	
1963	Dedimoud	4	J. Culmone	118	Mongo	126	Narokan	114	11,066	1:36.80	
1964	Inbalance	6	J. Culmone	118	Cool Prince	113	City Line	118	18,557	1:37.00	
1965	Twice As Gay	4	P.I. Grimm	114	Why Lie	114	Prairie Sch'r	120	18,606	1:38.80	
1966	Tom Rolfe	4	W. Shoemaker	126	Steel Pike	113	Twin Teddy	112	17,842	1:37.00	
1967	Swoonaway	6	J. Vasquez	113	Steel Pike	115	Spring Double	116	18,606	1:37.80	
1968	R. Thomas	7	J. Nichols	123	Spring Double	119	Besieger	113	18,557	1:37.00	
1969	Addy Boy	4	M. Hole	116	Irish Dude	115	Iron Ruler	120	18,232	1:37.40	
1970	Tyrant	4	W. Hartack	119	Royal Comedian	114	Futura Bold	115	18,362	1:37.40	
1971	Well Mannered	4	M. Solomone	122	Royal Comedian	114	Tyrant	121	18,330	1:38.80	
1972	Red Reality	6	B. Baeza	116	Towzie Tyke	116	Twin Time	115	21,970	1:37.00	
1973	Prince of Truth	5	W. Blum	117	Windtex	116	New Alibhai	115	17,761	1:35.80	
1974	Okavango	4	W. Blum	112	Hey Rube	114	Escaped	113	18,265	1:35.80	
1975	Proper Bostonian	5	M. Miceli	117	Rastaferian	113	Orbit Round	110	14,576	1:36.20	
1975	Mongogo	6	B. Thornburg	119	Good John	114	Silver Hope	116	14,576	1:36.20	
1976	Royal Glint	6	J. Tejeira	126	Talc	113	Peppy Addy	118	18,395	1:35.20	
1977	Peppy Addy	5	B. Phelps	120	Resound	115	Break up the Game	117	18,168	1:36.00	
1978	Do Tell George	5	W.E. Mize	113	Buckfinder	118	Get Permission	114	17,664	1:36.40	
1979	Revivalist	5	D. MacBeth	122	Horatius	120	Nice Catch	120	25,578	1:35.40	
1980	Convenient	4	V. Bracciale Jr	114	Tunerup	113	Foretake	113	26,640	1:36.60	
1981	Colonel Moran	4	C. Perret	117	Sun Catcher	120	Pikotazo	117	35,190	1:35.60	
1982	Count His Fleet	4	W. Nemeti	116	Explosive Bid	117	Accipiter's Hope	116	35,070	1:35.40	
1983	Naughty Jimmy	6	L. Saumell	114	Castle Guard	115	Star Gallant	120	33,510	1:37.00	
1984	Rumptious	4	W.H. McCauley	115	English Master	111	World Appeal	122	34,260	1:34.60	
1985	Valiant Lark	5	V. Bracciale Jr	116	Pat's Addition	115	Rumptious	116	33,990	1:36.00	
1986	Jyp	5	J. Rocco	115	Minneapple	119	Valiant Lark	117	33,300	1:35.80	
1987	Moment of Hope	4	M. Venezia	118	Owens Troupe	117	Entitled To	116	33,270	1:34.60	
1988	Slew City Slew	4	M. Castaneda	116	Bet Twice	125	Matthews Keep	116	38,880	1:35.00	
1989	Bill E. Shears	4	R. Hernandez	112	Festive	110	Mi Selecto	117	49,890	1:35.40	
1990	Shy Tom	4	J.A. Krone	115	Bill E. Shears	121	Pete the Chief	115	49,020	1:36.00	
1991	Peanut Butter Onit	5	W.S. Ramos	115	Private School	114	Run'way Stream	116	45,000	1:34.40	
1992	Peanut Butter Onit	6	A.T. Gryder	120	Root Boy	114	He Is Risen	118	45,000	1:36.20	107
1993	Dusty Screen	5	E.L. King Jr	117	Count New York	112	Root Boy	118	45,000	1:35.80	113
1994	Storm Tower	4	R. Wilson	119	Cold Digger	113	Koluctoo Jimmy Al	114	45,000	1:36.20	109
1995	Schossberg	5	D. Penna	116	Cast Iron	110	Relentless Star	111	45,000	1:35.80	109
1996	Smart Strike	4	S. Hawley	113	Cozy Drive	113	November Sunset	115	60,000	1:36.20	108
1997	Distorted Humor	4	J.A. Krone	114	Wild Deputy	114	Smooth the Loot	113	60,000	1:36.00	112
1998	El Amante	5	J.A. Krone	119	Stormin Fever	117	Gold Token	114	60,000	1:34.80	116
1999	Truluck	4	J. Bravo	115	Rock and Roll	119	Siftaway	114	90,000	1:35.00	104
2000	Leave It to Beezer	7	R. Alvarado Jr.	120	Delaware Township	112	Prime Directive	114	90,000	1:37.29	106
2001	Sea of Tranquility	5	J.C. Ferrer	115	Knock Again	112	Hal's Hope	117	90,000	1:36.74	100
2002	Sea of Tranquility	6	J.C. Ferrer	120	Free of Love	117	First Lieutenant	114	60,000	1:36.12	99
	First Lieutenant finished first but was disqualified and placed third										
2003	Vinemeister	4	J.A. Velez Jr.	114	Jersey Giant	117	Highway Prospector	113	60,000	1:35.89	98
2004	Presidentialaffair	5	S. Elliott	117	Unforgettable Max	117	Roaring Fever	115	60,000	1:35.27	110

Beyer Index: 107.00

SAN ANTONIO HANDICAP (G2), 1 1/8 Miles, 4-Year-Olds and Up, Santa Anita, 2004 Purse: $245,000

Year	Winner	Age	Jockey	Wt.	Second	Wt.	Third	Wt.	Win Value	Time	Beyer
1935	Head Play	5	C. Kurtsinger	128	Fleam	121	Azucar	128	5,950	1:52.40	
1936	Time Supply	5	T. Luther	116	Pompeys Pillar	105	Ariel Cross	106	6,000	1:49.40	
1937	Rosemont	5	H. Richards	122	Star Shadow	106	Special Agent	117	6,825	1:50.20	
1938	Aneroid	5	C. Rosengarten	118	Seabiscuit	130	Indian Broom	108	7,125	1:50.00	
1939	Whichcee	5	B. James	109	Today	112	Congressman	105	10,950	1:49.40	
1940	Seabiscuit	7	J. Pollard	124	Kayak II	128	Viscounty	110	10,000	1:42.40	
1941	Mioland	4	L. Haas	128	Hysterical	111	Bay View	105	9,460	1:45.40	
1946	First Fiddle	7	J. Longden	123	Autocrat	112	Paperboy	115	44,710	1:50.00	
1947	El Lobo	6	W. Bailey	111	Hank H.	116	Pere Time	108	42,450	1:49.20	
1948	Talon	6	E. Arcaro	122	Double Jay	118	On Trust	126	47,300	1:49.40	
1949	Dinner Gong	4	J. Westrope	114	Autocrat	112	Paperboy	115	36,700	1:49.60	
1950	Ponder	4	S. Brooks	128	Citation	130	Noor	114	37,800	1:50.20	
1951	All Blue	4	W. Shoemaker	111	Sudan	109	Next Move	119	44,850	1:49.40	
1952	Phil D.	4	R. York	117	Intent	118	Bed o' Roses	120	17,450	1:49.80	
1953	Trusting	5	W. Shoemaker	118	Don Rebelde	112	First Glance	120	16,250	1:49.20	
1954	Mark-Ye-Well	5	E. Arcaro	130	Rejected	116	Decorated	114	36,300	1:52.00	
1955	Gigantic	4	R. Lumm	109	Imbros	124	Correspondent	112	36,900	1:48.40	
1956	Mister Gus	5	W. Boland	120	Honeys Alibi	116	Bobby Brocato	124	36,200	1:49.00	
1957	Terrang	4	I. Valenzuela	118	Honeys Alibi	121	Social Climber	121	34,700	1:47.40	
1958	Round Table	4	W. Shoemaker	130	Mystic Eye	108	Promised Land	116	33,300	1:46.80	
1959	Bug Brush	4	A. Valenzuela	113	Hillsdale	120	Terrang	116	3,500	1:46.40	
1960	Bagdad	4	W. Shoemaker	123	First Landing	124	How Now	118	34,400	1:48.20	
1961	American Comet	5	W. Harmatz	113	How Now	116	Grey Eagle	113	35,300	1:48.60	
1962	Olden Times	4	A. Maese	113	Juanro	105	British Roman	110	37,550	1:53.60	
1963	Physician	6	D. Pierce	117	Crimson Satan	127	Game	107	35,500	1:51.00	
1964	Gun Bow	4	W. Shoemaker	125	Cyrano	124	Quita Dude	114	36,200	1:47.40	
1965	Gun Bow	5	M. Ycaza	129	Candy Spots	127	George Royal	113	35,000	1:47.80	
1966	Hill Rise	5	M. Ycaza	125	Teddy's Secret	122	Bold Bidder	125	34,000	1:47.00	
1967	Pretense	4	W. Shoemaker	121	Drin	119	Native Diver	128	35,000	1:48.60	
1968	Rising Market	4	L. Pincay Jr	115	Quicken Tree	117	Suteki	115	54,250	1:48.40	
1969	Praise Jay	5	M. Yanez	113	Racing Room	116	Estambul II	114	53,800	1:49.60	
1970	Dewan	5	L. Pincay Jr	117	Rising Market	123	Comtal	112	50,600	1:47.60	
1971	Ack Ack	5	W. Shoemaker	124	Good Manners	115	Hanalei Bay	117	54,450	1:47.00	
1972	Unconscious	4	A. Cordero Jr	123	Triple Bend	117	Cougar II	128	52,300	1:47.40	
1973	Kennedy Road	5	D. Pierce	119	Crusading	119	Big Spruce	117	49,400	1:47.60	
1974	Prince Dantan	4	L. Pincay Jr	116	Forage	119	Dancing Papa	116	51,550	1:47.60	
1975	Cheriepe	5	A. Santiago	120	First Back	117	Ancient Title	128	52,850	1:46.80	
1976	Lightning Mandate	5	A. Cordero Jr	118	Dancing Papa	117	Messenger of Song	122	54,350	1:48.20	
1977	Ancient Title	7	S. Hawley	119	Double Discount	115	Properantes	114	72,500	1:47.80	
1978	Vigors	5	D.G. McHargue	121	Ancient Title	120	Double Discount	114	67,100	1:46.20	
1979	Tiller	5	A. Cordero Jr	121	Painted Wagon	114	Life's Hope	120	65,800	1:47.00	
1980	Beau's Eagle	4	D. Pierce	121	Relaunch	117	Double Discount	114	79,650	1:48.40	
1981	Flying Paster	5	C.J. McCarron	126	Doonesbury	121	King Go Go	119	91,700	1:46.60	
1982	Score Twenty Four	5	P.A. Valenzuela	115	Super Moment	124	High Counsel	114	124,200	1:47.80	
1983	Bates Motel	4	T. Lipham	114	Time to Explode	121	It's the One	124	132,200	1:47.00	
1984	Poley	5	C.J. McCarron	120	Water Bank	117	Danebo	122	156,900	1:48.00	
1985	Lord at War	5	W. Shoemaker	122	Al Mamoon	114	Hail Bold King	122	125,200	1:48.20	
1986	Hatim	5	L. Pincay Jr	117	Right Con	117	Nostalgia's Star	118	128,700	1:47.40	
1987	Bedside Promise	5	G.L. Stevens	121	Hopeful Word	118	Bruiser	114	129,600	1:47.20	
1988	Judge Angelucci	5	E. Delahoussaye	122	Ferdinand	128	Crimson Slew	115	156,700	1:48.60	
1989	Super Diamond	9	L. Pincay Jr	121	Frankly Perfect	116	Cherokee Colony	120	159,600	1:48.80	
1990	Criminal Type	5	A. Solis	117	Stylish Winner	113	Ruhlmann	122	190,500	1:49.00	
1991	Farma Way	4	G.L. Stevens	118	Anshan	116	Louis Cyphre	111	196,750	1:47.20	113
							Festin	116			
1992	Ibero	5	A. Solis	115	In Excess	123	Cobra Classic	114	189,750	1:47.00	117
1993	Marquetry	6	E. Delahoussaye	117	Sir Beaufort	120	Reign Road	116	155,500	1:48.80	101
1994	The Wicked North	5	K.J. Desormeaux	116	Region	117	Hill Pass	116	155,500	1:47.40	115
1995	Best Pal	7	C.J. McCarron	121	Slew of Damascus	119	Tossofthecoin	117	148,500	1:47.40	111
1996	Alphabet Soup	5	C.W. Antley	119	Soul of the Matter	121	Dare and Go	119	184,900	1:49.80	108
1997	Gentlemen	5	G.L. Stevens	122	Alphabet Soup	122	Kingdom Found	116	180,300	1:47.20	116
1998	Gentlemen	6	G.L. Stevens	124	Da Bull	115	Refinado Tom	120	180,000	1:47.60	109
1999	Free House	5	C.J. McCarron	119	Malek	119	Dramatic Gold	116	180,000	1:48.40	110
2000	Budroyale	7	G.K. Gomez	121	Cat Thief	120	Elaborate	116	180,000	1:48.70	108
2001	Guided Tour	5	L. Melancon	115	Lethal Instrument	116	Moonlight Charger	113	180,000	1:48.26	107
2002	Reddatore	7	A. Solis	116	Euchre	119	Irisheyesareflying	119	150,000	1:48.66	106
2003	Congaree	5	J.D. Bailey	123	Milwaukee Brew	120	Pleasantly Perfect	117	150,000	1:47.60	118
2004	Pleasantly Perfect	6	A. Solis	121	Star Cross	114	Fleetstreet Dancer	116	150,000	1:47.25	109

Beyer Index: 110.57

SAN BERNARDINO HANDICAP (G3), 1 1/8 Miles, 4-Year-Olds and Up, Santa Anita, 2004 Purse: $110,600

Year	Winner	Age	Jockey	Wt.	Second	Wt.	Third	Wt.	Win Value	Time	Beyer
1957	Lightning Jack	3	M. Peterson	112	Mystic Eye	111	Royal Heir	115	16,500	1:49.20	
1958	Terrang	5	W. Boland	125	Porterhouse	123	Seaneen	115	16,550	1:42.00	
1959	Terrang	6	W. Boland	126	How Now	117	Bug Brush	123	29,550	1:42.00	
1960	Restless Wind	4	E. Arcaro	118	Seaneen	117	Top Charger	111	16,650	1:42.20	
1961	New Policy	4	W. Shoemaker	122	Finnegan	118	Resolved	121	16,600	1:42.00	
1962	Four-and-Twenty	4	J. Longden	127	Macdan	112	Juanro	107	17,350	1:48.20	
1963	Crozier	5	B. Baeza	128	Pirate Cove	114	Mr. Consistency	113	30,900	1:41.60	
1964	Cyrano	5	M. Ycaza	126	Drill Site	111	Colorado King	118	16,700	1:42.20	
1965	Real Good Deal	4	D. Pierce	118	Pelegrin	114	Calgary Br'k	113	16,500	1:41.80	
1966	Native Diver	7	J. Lambert	130	Real Good Deal	116	Prairie Schooner	114	15,750	1:40.60	
1967	Sermon	4	L. Pincay Jr	114	Biggs	117	Hill Clown	114	18,450	1:47.40	
1968	Tiltable	4	L. Pincay Jr	113	Model Fool	119	Gamely	118	16,750	1:49.00	
1969	Pinjara	4	W. Shoemaker	121	Laughing Gull	113	Poleax	119	17,850	1:46.40	
1970	Governors Party	4	W. Harris	118	Pinjara	122	Figonero	125	17,050	1:49.60	
1971	Bargain Day	6	L. Pincay Jr	115	Efa	114	Lonny's Secret	117	24,975	1:46.60	
1971	Dendron	4	J. Lambert	114	Batitu	112	Society II	115	24,725	1:47.20	
1972	Golden Eagle II	7	J. Lambert	118	Panzer Chief	118	Dendron	112	38,500	1:46.80	
1973	Quack	4	D. Pierce	125	River Buoy	119	Curious C'se	112	36,500	1:49.00	
1974	Court Ruling	4	B. Baeza	117	Captain Cee Jay	119	Accl'tization	115	25,900	1:48.40	
1974	Wichita Oil	6	L. Pincay Jr	116	Madison Palace	117	Woodland Pines	118	25,800	1:47.60	
1975	Royal Glint	5	W. Shoemaker	120	Against the Snow	115	June's Love	115	34,800	1:45.80	
1976	Zanthe	7	S. Hawley	118	Riot in Paris	121	Mateor	114	34,300	1:45.80	
1977	Today 'n Tomorrow	4	S. Hawley	112	Exact Duplicate	115	Rajab	114	35,300	1:46.40	
1978	J.O. Tobin	4	S. Cauthen	123	Henschel	115	Riot in Paris	119	31,950	1:47.80	
1979	Star Spangled	5	L. Pincay Jr	117	Farnesio	118	State Dinner	118	46,650	1:45.80	
1980	Peregrinator	5	C.J. McCarron	115	Lunar Probe	116	Henschel	120	65,300	1:47.80	
1981	Borzoi	5	W. Shoemaker	118	Shamgo	117	King Go Go	122	64,700	1:46.20	
1982	Super Moment	5	C.J. McCarron	124	Mehmet	116	It's the One	126	75,450	1:48.60	
1983	The Wonder	5	W. Shoemaker	122	Konewah	112	Swing Till Dawn	119	62,500	1:49.20	
1984	Journey at Sea	5	W.A. Guerra	122	My Habitony	118	Fighting Fit	121	102,050	1:48.00	
1985	Greinton	4	L. Pincay Jr	120	Precisionist	127	Al Mamoon	115	117,300	1:47.00	
1986	Precisionist	5	C.J. McCarron	126	Greinton	126	Encolure	116	148,200	1:47.60	
1987	Judge Angelucci	4	W. Shoemaker	115	Iron Eyes	116	Grecian Wonder	113	129,400	1:48.40	
1988	Alysheba	4	C.J. McCarron	127	Ferdinand	127	Good Taste	113	350,000	1:47.20	
1989	Ruhlmann	4	L. Pincay Jr	119	Lively One	120	Saratoga Passage	116	185,600	1:47.20	
1990	Ruhlmann	5	G.L. Stevens	123	Criminal Type	119	Stylish Winner	113	240,800	1:47.20	119
1991	Anshan	4	C.S. Nakatani	115	Louis Cyphre	112	Pleasant Tap	116	158,900	1:47.00	113
1992	Another Review	4	K.J. Desormeaux	114	Defensive Play	115	Loach	116	163,100	1:47.20	114
1993	Memo	6	P. Atkinson	114	Charmonnier	117	Marquetry	118	125,800	1:47.40	113
1994	Del Mar Dennis	4	S. Gonzalez Jr	112	Hill Pass	115	Tinners Way	115	129,400	1:48.20	105
1995	Del Mar Dennis	5	C.W. Antley	117	Wharf	113	Stoller	115	130,000	1:47.20	114
1996	Del Mar Dennis	6	K.J. Desormeaux	118	Just Java	116	Regal Rowdy	115	96,650	1:48.20	108
1997	Benchmark	6	C.J. McCarron	114	Kingdom Found	115	Private Song	122	97,650	1:48.20	105
1998	Budroyale	5	M.S. Garcia	112	Don't Blame Rio	114	Bagshot	116	100,530	1:48.40	108
1999	Classic Cat	4	G.L. Stevens	122	Budroyale	119	Klinsman	115	90,000	1:47.77	112
2000	Early Pioneer	5	M.S. Garcia	113	David	113	General Challenge	123	95,490	1:49.08	112
2001	Futural	5	G.K. Gomez	115	Irisheyesareflying	117	Tribunal	117	90,000	1:47.87	109
2002	Bosque Redondo	5	C.J. McCarron	114	Mysterious Cat	111	Freedom Crest	116	90,000	1:49.11	104
2003	Western Pride	5	P.A. Valenzuela	116	Total Impact	113	Fleetstreet Dancer	112	90,000	1:48.56	112
2004	Dynever	4	C.S. Nakatani	117	Total Impact	116	Even the Score	116	66,360	1:48.07	113

Beyer Index: 110.73

SAN CARLOS HANDICAP (G2), 7 Furlongs, 4-Year-Olds and Up, Santa Anita, 2004 Purse: $150,000

Year	Winner	Age	Jockey	Wt.	Second	Wt.	Third	Wt.	Win Value	Time	Beyer
1935	Jabot	4	A. Robertson	109	Riskulus	109	Top Row	103	5,225	1:42.80	
1936	Discovery	5	J. Bejshak	130	Ariel Cross	106	Beefsteak	104	4,025	1:45.40	
1937	Chanceview	5	J. Pollard	110	Indian Broom	116	Boxthorn	117	4,625	1:45.60	
1938	Pompoon	4	J. Gilbert	124	Star Shadow	107	He Did	114	4,600	1:45.00	
1939	Kayak II	4	J. Adams	110	Specify	119	Whichcee	112	10,050	1:42.40	
1940	Specify	5	C. Bierman	115	Lassator	105	Viscounty	109	9,350	1:23.40	
1941	Gen'l Manager	4	R. Neves	110	Viscounty	116	Hysterical	116	10,000	1:24.40	
1946	Sirde	5	J. Gilbert	117	First Fiddle	126	Lou-Bre	109	20,380	1:23.00	
1947	Texas Sandman	6	M. Peterson	114	El Lobo	112	Fighting Frank	121	45,150	1:22.80	
1948	Autocrat	7	A. Skoronski	108	Rippey	115	Prevaricator	114	42,500	1:22.40	
1949	Manyunk	4	E. Guerin	114	Star Reward	120	Miche	116	42,050	1:23.40	
1949	Autocrat	8	J. Nichols	117	Dinner Gong	115	Rippey	124	41,550	1:25.80	
1951	Bolero	5	E. Arcaro	121	Your Host	126	Blue Reading	109	41,300	1:21.00	
1952	To Market	4	E. Arcaro	116	Bryan G.	126	Gold Note	110	17,100	1:24.00	

Year	Winner	Age	Jockey	Wt.	Second	Wt.	Third	Wt.	Win Value	Time	Beyer
1953	Blue Reading	6	B. Pearson	121	Ruth Lily	104	Big Noise	112	14,350	1:23.40	
1954	Find	4	E. Guerin	123	Hill Gail	117	Heliowise	116	14,300	1:25.20	
1955	Porterhouse	4	E. Arcaro	115	Imbros	130	Encono	114	14,200	1:22.40	
1956	Porterhouse	5	E. Arcaro	119	Karim	110	Hickory Stick	109	14,650	1:22.80	
1957	Duc de Fer	6	R. Neves	118	Mister Gus	128	Lassabatt	114	13,000	1:23.40	
1958	Seaneen	4	W. Harmatz	114	Porterhouse	126	Ole Fols	120	36,100	1:22.20	
1959	Hillsdale	4	T. Barrow	115	Round Table	132	Micarlo	113	38,750	1:22.20	
1960	Clandestine	5	M. Ycaza	112	Ole Fols	120	Mystic Eye	114	37,000	1:22.20	
1961	First Balcony	4	M. Ycaza	111	T.V. Lark	125	Eddie Schmidt	112	33,300	1:21.80	
1962	Four-and-Twenty	4	J. Longden	124	Ole Fols	117	Finnegan	115	31,300	1:21.80	
1963	Crozier	5	B. Baeza	124	OldenTimes	125	Native Diver	125	38,600	1:21.20	
1964	Admiral's Voyage	5	B. Baeza	124	Cyrano	126	Native Diver	125	36,600	1:22.00	
1965	Native Diver	6	J. Lambert	126	Candy Spots	125	Bonjour	114	36,150	1:21.40	
1966	Cupid	5	R. Ussery	115	Hill Rise	126	Quita Dude	115	38,600	1:22.00	
1967	Native Diver	8	J. Lambert	128	Hoist Bar	115	Pretense	118	39,550	1:22.00	
1968	Suteki	4	W. Blum	113	Postage	106	Quicken Tree	116	34,150	1:22.00	
1969	Rising Market	5	L. Pincay Jr	126	Title Game	115	Tumiga	123	34,350	1:22.60	
1970	Rising Market	6	L. Pincay Jr	121	Tell	125	Fleet Wing	118	24,700	1:21.00	
1971	Ack Ack	5	W. Shoemaker	126	Jungle Savage	120	King of Cricket	119	34,150	1:21.00	
1972	KfarTov	4	J. Lambert	120	Riot	113	Long Position	114	35,450	1:21.40	
1973	Crusading	5	F. Toro	119	Kennedy Road	117	Figonero	118	33,850	1:20.80	
1974	Royal Owl	5	L. Pincay Jr	117	Soft Victory	116	Against the Snow	112	35,600	1:23.40	
1975	Ancient Title	5	L. Pincay Jr	128	Hudson County	116			37,750	1:21.20	
					Bahia Key	117					
1976	No Bias	6	L. Pincay Jr	120	Century's Envoy	126	Bahia Key	120	32,200	1:21.80	
1977	Uniformity	5	F. Toro	115	My Juliet	123	Messenger of Song	121	34,050	1:21.60	
1978	Double Discount	5	F. Mena	117	Impressive Luck	120	Romantic Lead	117	32,650	1:22.00	
1979	O Big Al	4	D.G. McHargue	120	Maheras	122	Bad 'n Big	124	40,800	1:22.00	
1980	Handsomeness	4	L. Pincay Jr	118	Relaunch	121	Beau's Eagle	125	49,100	1:24.00	
1981	Flying Paster	5	J. McCarron	124	To B. or Not	123	Double Discount	115	51,550	1:20.20	
1982	Solo Guy	4	W. Shoemaker	118	Smokite	116	King Go Go	119	60,700	1:20.80	
1983	Kangroo Court	6	J.J Steiner	118	Dave's Friend	117	Shanekite	118	40,550	1:21.00	
1984	Danebo	5	L. Pincay Jr	117	Pac Mania	118	Poley	119	54,900	1:21.00	
1985	Debonaire Junior	4	C.J. McCarron	125	Tennessee Rite	112	Fifty Six Ina Row	116	64,300	1:21.60	
1986	Phone Trick	4	L. Pincay Jr	125	Temerity Prince	122	My Habitony	117	78,200	1:20.80	
1987	Zany Tactics	6	J.L. Kaenel	118	Bolder Than Bold	116	Epidaurus	115	65,600	1:22.40	
1988	Epidaurus	6	P.A. Valenzuela	117	Super Diamond	125	Lord Ruckus	118	63,500	1:22.00	
1989	Cherokee Colony	4	R.Q. Meza	119	On the Line	126	Happy in Space	116	62,800	1:20.60	
1990	Raise a Stanza	4	R.A. Baze	117	Oraibi	119	Tanker Port	117	64,500	1:21.60	102
1991	Farma Way	4	G.L. Stevens	115	Yes I'm Blue	117	Tanker Port	117	63,500	1:21.40	113
1992	Answer Do	6	G.L. Stevens	120	Individualist	115	Media Plan	116	63,700	1:21.20	107
1993	Sir Beaufort	6	C.J. McCarron	120	Cardmania	117	Excavate	114	62,900	1:22.20	109
1994	Cardmania	8	E. Delahoussaye	122	The Wicked North	117	Portoferraio	115	63,900	1:21.20	106
1995	Softshoe Sure Shot	9	A. Solis	114	Ferrara	115	Subtle Trouble	115	91,600	1:21.40	103
1996	Kingdom Found	6	C.J. McCarron	116	Lakota Brave	114	Lit de Justice	123	98,850	1:22.20	103
1997	Northern Afleet	4	C.J. McCarron	117	Hesabull	117	High Stakes Player	117	97,700	1:21.40	109
1998	Reality Road	6	C.J. McCarron	116	Gold Land	116	Son Of A Pistol	114	100,530	1:21.60	112
1999	Big Jag	6	J. Valdivia Jr.	118	Kona Gold	120	Dramatic Gold	117	90,000	1:21.00	116
2000	Son of a Pistol	8	G.K. Gomez	117	Kona Gold	122	Old Topper	116	96,930	1:22.11	109
2001	Kona Gold	7	A. Solis	125	Blade Prospector	113	Grey Memo	115	90,000	1:21.35	112
2002	Snow Ridge	4	M.E. Smith	118	Alyzig	112	Grey Memo	114	90,000	1:22.02	106
2003	Aldebaran	5	J. Valdivia Jr	116	Crafty C.T.	116	Grey Memo	116	120,000	1:21.53	110
2004	Pico Central	5	D.R. Flores	116	Publication	116	Pohave	112	90,000	1:21.16	113

Beyer Index: 108.67

SAN CLEMENTE HANDICAP (G2), 1 Mile (Turf), 3-Year-Old Fillies, Del Mar, 2004 Purse: $150,000

Year	Winner	Age	Jockey	Wt.	Second	Wt.	Third	Wt.	Win Value	Time	Beyer
1970	Loved	3	J. Lambert	114	Likely Lark	113	Beja	115	9,775	1:43.80	
1971	Gowran Green	3	R. Rosales	117	At Twillight	117	Fleetaglo	117	9,350	1:43.80	
1972	Bert's Tryst	3	R. Rosales	112	Homespun	115	Ground Song	117	9,600	1:43.00	
1973	Button Top	3	S. Valdez	112	Merry Madeleine	120	Gourmet Lark	117	12,750	1:43.80	
1974	Bold Ballet	3	F. Toro	121	Shah's Envoy	121	Sweet Ramblin Rose	116	13,350	1:44.00	
1975	Miss Francesca	3	D.G. McHargue	113	Summer Evening	115	Bradley's Pago	113	10,275	1:43.80	
1975	Princess Papulee	3	F. Toro	121	Mia Amore	121	Miracolo	113	10,275	1:43.80	
1976	Go March	3	D. Pierce	114	Granja Sueno	112	I Going	115	13,150	1:42.80	
1977	Teisen Lap	3	D.G. McHargue	113	Goldfilled	112	Lullaby	120	12,850	1:44.80	
1978	Miss Magnetic	3	M. Castaneda	117	Secala	112	Agree	114	13,550	1:44.20	
1978	Joe's Bee	3	L. Pincay Jr	120	Fairy Dance	117	Carrie's Angel	115	13,150	1:44.40	
1979	Ancient Art	3	F. Toro	121	Our Suiti Pie	116	Double Deceit	117	23,550	1:44.20	
1980	Plenty O'Toole	3	T. Lipham	116	Potter	115	Swift Bird	113	27,050	1:44.20	

Year	Winner	Age	Jockey	Wt.	Second	Wt.	Third	Wt.	Win Value	Time	Beyer
1981	French Charmer	3	D.G. McHargue	118	Tap Dancer II	113	I Got Speed	121	26,850	1:44.20	
1982	Northern Style	3	M. Castaneda	114	Mama Tia	116	Marl Lee Ann	115	32,100	1:43.40	
1983	Eastern Bettor	3	L. Pincay Jr	113	Nice n Proper	117	Olympic Bronze	116	25,875	1:44.00	
1983	Lituya Bay	3	L. Pincay Jr	121	Corselette	116	Capitalization	115	25,375	1:43.80	
1984	Fashionably Late	3	C.J. McCarron	114	Auntie Betty	117	Patricia James	114	32,800	1:43.20	
1985	Mint Leaf	3	C.J. McCarron	122	Queen of Bronze	115	Stakes to Win	117	33,650	1:42.60	
1986	Our Sweet Sham	3	S.B. Soto	114	Mille et Une	115	T.V. Residual	115	33,450	1:43.20	
1987	Davie's Lamb	3	F. Toro	115	Develop	114	Wild Manor	116	25,500	1:42.80	
1987	Future Bright	3	P.A. Valenzuela	114	Chapel of Dreams	114	Down Again	116	25,300	1:44.60	
1988	Do So	3	A. Solis	121	Affordable Price	115	Variety Baby	117	50,650	1:35.80	
1989	Darby's Daughter	3	G.L. Stevens	120	Sticky Wile	117	Bel Darling	116	66,000	1:36.60	
1990	Nijinsky's Lover	3	G.L. Stevens	118	Bimbo II	113	Slew of Pearls	116	50,300	1:36.40	
1990	Lonely Girl	3	P.A. Valenzuela	116	Bel's Starlet	114	Bidder Cream	113	50,300	1:36.20	91
1991	Flawlessly	3	C.J. McCarron	120	Gold Fleece	114	Miss High Blade	117	64,600	1:34.80	96
1992	Golden Treat	3	K.J. Desormeaux	121	Morriston Belle	118	Alysbelle	118	49,350	1:35.20	91
1993	Hollywood Wildcat	3	E. Delahoussaye	120	Miami Sands	116	Beal Street Blues	117	49,950	1:34.80	107
1994	Work the Crowd	3	CJ. McCarron	120	Pharma	116	Dancing Mirage	115	48,550	1:36.00	99
1995	Jewel Princess	3	C.J. McCarron	115	Auriette	119	Scratch Paper	119	59,650	1:36.00	97
1996	True Flare	3	C.S. Nakatani	116	Gastronomical	119	Najecam	114	67,200	1:35.40	100
1997	Famous Digger	3	B. Blanc	120	Cozy Blues	116	Really Happy	119	71,725	1:36.00	95
1998	Sicy D'Alsace	3	C.S. Nakatani	115	Miss Hot Salsa	117	Tranquility Lake	114	67,500	1:34.80	92
1999	Sweet Ludy	3	C.S. Nakatani	118	Caffe Latte	115	Sweet Life	117	90,000	1:35.00	99
2000	Uncharted Haven	3	A. Solis	116	Automated	117	Islay Mist	118	90,000	1:35.13	96
2001	Reine de Romance	3	E. Delahoussaye	116	Gabriellina Giof	116	La Vida Loca	116	90,000	1:34.88	91
2002	Little Treasure	3	K.J. Desormeaux	117	Pina Colada	115	Arabic Song	118	90,000	1:33.97	93
2003	Katdogawn	3	J.A. Krone	116	Atlantic Ocean	120	Buffythecenterfold	118	90,000	1:33.62	92
2004	Sweet Win	3	V. Espinoza	114	Miss Vegas	121	Victory U.S.A.	119	90,000	1:34.11	94

Beyer Index: 95.53

SAN DIEGO HANDICAP (G2), 1 1/16 Miles, 3-Year-Olds and Up, Del Mar, 2004 Purse: $250,000

Year	Winner	Age	Jockey	Wt.	Second	Wt.	Third	Wt.	Win Value	Time	Beyer
1937	Clean Out	5	D. Smith	107	Illeanna	105	Bollermaker	115	750	1:12.00	
1938	King Saxon	7	J. Adams	110	Count Atlas	116	Advocator	111	2,005	1:45.20	
1945	High Resolve	4	W. Bailey	123	Ended	124	Deer	111	5,245	1:10.00	
1946	Lovonsite	3	N. Wall	106	Pride of Hygro	120	Ended	112	5,150	1:10.40	
1947	Ended	8	J. Nichols	118	Be Fearless	126	Darby D-Day	107	4,700	1:11.00	
1948	Prevaricator	5	A. Gray	122	Iron Maiden	110	Coast Invasion	104	6,475	1:42.60	
1949	Prevaricator	6	M. Caffarella	111	Moonrush	108	Top's Boy	120	6,600	1:42.00	
1950	Manyunk	5	G. Moore	119	Amarillo Kid	118	Frankly	122	6,775	1:42.40	
1951	Blue Reading	4	B. Pearson	120	Home Free	107	Pete Silver	105	6,575	1:41.60	
1952	Moonrush	6	R. Neves	112	Blue Reading	124	Stormy C'd	109	6,275	1:42.20	
1953	Goose Khal	4	W. Shoemaker	107	Chanlea	112	Bernwood	108	6,375	1:42.80	
1954	Stranglehold	5	B. Pearson	122	Golden Abbey	118	Blue Trumpeter	106	6,275	1:41.80	
1955	Trigonometry	4	R. Trejos	111	Arrogate	110	Karim	115	12,500	1:41.20	
1956	Honeys Alibi	4	R. York	115	Poona II	122	Beau Busher	110	12,700	1:41.40	
1957	Eddie Schmidt	4	I. Valenzuela	122	Gigantic	113	Pirnie	109	12,600	1:42.00	
1958	How Now	5	W. Harmatz	125	Swirling Abbey	118	Noredski	111	12,100	1:42.00	
1959	Twentyone Guns	4	G. Taniguchi	115	Find	121	Solid Fleet	113	12,000	1:42.00	
1960	Eddie Schmidt	7	A. Maese	118	King's Marshall	109	Honeys Gem	113	13,050	1:41.20	
1961	New Policy	4	R. Mundorf	119	Nagea	113	First Balcony	122	12,400	1:41.00	
1962	Windy Sands	5	R. York	122	Typhoon II	118	Cadiz	121	13,350	1:40.00	
1963	Native Diver	4	R. Neves	123	Rob Roy II	118	Cadiz	121	12,400	1:40.60	
1964	Native Diver	5	J. Lambert	122	Final Command	109	Drill Site	117	12,550	1:41.80	
1965	Native Diver	6	J. Lambert	131	Nearco Blue	110	Carang	111	12,500	1:40.00	
1966	Old Mose	4	D. Pierce	115	Whit's Pride	114	Silk Hat	114	12,650	1:41.40	
1967	French Fox	5	D.C. Hall	110	Sharp Decline	103	Bern Book	112	15,450	1:41.60	
1968	Rivet	4	M. Yanez	116	Vale of Tears	122	Title Game	113	12,300	1:40.80	
1969	Kissin' George	6	W. Mahorney	122	Rivet	118	Fiddle Isle	117	11,825	1:41.40	
1970	T.V. Commercial	5	D. Pierce	118	Imaginative	118	Quicken Tree	124	12,950	1:41.40	
1971	Advance Guard	5	W. Shoemaker	124	Far to Reach	114	The Field	113	13,400	1:41.00	
1972	Figonero	7	F. Alvarez	114	War Heim	120	Jeff David	117	13,600	1:40.80	
1973	Kennedy Road	5	W. Shoemaker	126	Imaginative	117	New Pr'pect	120	15,700	1:41.40	
1974	Matun	5	W. Shoemaker	121	Chesapeake	113	Imaginative	115	16,150	1:41.00	
1975	Chesapeake	6	F. Olivares	116	Top Command	116	Against the Snow	123	16,800	1:40.60	
1976	Good Report	6	L. Pincay Jr	116	Austin Mittler	117	Holding Pattern	115	19,000	1:42.40	
1977	Mark's Place	5	W. Shoemaker	124	Austin Mittler	113	C'nf. Yankee	114	18,450	1:40.60	
1978	Vic's Magic	5	F. Toro	116	Mr. Redoy	119	Clout	117	25,300	1:40.20	
1979	Always Gallant	5	D.G. McHargue	118	Bad 'n Big	120	Bl'die's Dancer	117	32,050	1:41.00	
1980	Island Sultan	5	M. Castaneda	114	Summer Time Guy	116	Borzoi	120	38,000	1:41.80	
1981	Summer Time Guy	5	S. Hawley	115	Shamgo	117	Exploded	115	48,550	1:41.00	

Year	Winner	Age	Jockey	Wt.	Second	Wt.	Third	Wt.	Win Value	Time	Beyer
1982	Wickerr	7	E. Delahoussaye	117	Cajun Prince	117	Drouilly	114	50,350	1:41.40	
1983	Bates Motel	4	T. Lipham	122	The Wonder	123	Runaway G'm	117	47,650	1:41.00	
1984	Ancestral	4	E. Delahoussaye	116	Retsina Run	117	Slew's Royalty	117	60,550	1:41.20	
1985	Super Diamond	5	R.Q. Meza	115	M. Double M.	119	French Leg'naire	115	48,550	1:41.40	
1986	Skywalker	4	L. Pincay Jr	121	Nostalgia's Star	118	Epidaurus	113	65,350	1:40.80	
1987	Super Diamond	7	L. Pincay Jr	123	Nostalgia's Star	116	Good Command	114	48,050	1:40.80	
1988	Cutlass Reality	6	G.L. Stevens	123	Simply Majestic	115	Nostalgia's Star	116	63,700	1:41.40	
1989	Lively One	4	R.G. Davis	120	Mi Preferido	115	Hot Operator	114	76,200	1:40.80	
1990	Quiet American	4	K.J. Desormeaux	115	Bayakoa	122	Bosphorus	112	89,800	1:40.40	109
1991	Twilight Agenda	5	C.S. Nakatani	118	Roanoke	118	Louis Cyphre	118	90,900	1:47.60	
1992	Another Review	4	L. Pincay Jr	120	Claret	116	Quintana	114	76,050	1:47.00	105
1993	Fanatic Boy	6	C.J. McCarron	114	Memo	116	Missionary Ridge	116	74,450	1:48.40	107
1994	Kingdom Found	4	C.J. McCarron	116	Tossofthecoin	117	Rapan Boy	115	75,850	1:41.20	107
1995	Blumin Affair	4	C.J. McCarron	116	Rapan Boy	116	Luthier Fever	115	87,200	1:41.20	101
1996	Savinio	6	Antley C. W.	116	Misnomer	118	Nonproductiveasset	118	95,350	1:40.80	105
1997	Northern Afleet	4	McCarron C. J.	118	Benchmark	117	New Century	114	100,300	1:41.80	106
1998	Mud Route	4	McCarron C. J.	117	Hal's Pal	113	Benchmark	117	150,300	1:41.20	111
1999	Mazel Trick	4	McCarron C. J.	117	River Keen	116	Tibado	116	150,000	1:40.60	118
2000	Skimming	4	G.K. Gomez	112	Prime Timber	116	National Saint	117	150,000	1:41.06	113
2001	Skimming	5	G.K. Gomez	120	Futural	120	Captain Steve	122	150,000	1:41.62	116
2002	Grey Memo	5	E. Delahoussaye	116	Euchre	116	Congaree	120	150,000	1:43.48	107
2003	Taste of Paradise	4	V. Espinoza	113	Gondolieri	117	Reba's Gold	116	150,000	1:42.62	102
2004	Choctaw Nation	4	V. Espinoza	114	Pleasantly Perfect	124	During	118	150,000	1:42.32	103

Beyer Index: 107.86

SAN FELIPE (G2), 1 1/16 Miles, 3-Year-Olds, Santa Anita, 2004 Purse: $250,000

Year	Winner	Age	Jockey	Wt.	Second	Wt.	Third	Wt.	Win Value	Time	Beyer
1935	Ted Clark	5	C. Turk	104	Jabot	111	Wacoche	94	2,060	1:37.60	
1936	Azucar	8	A. Robertson	115	Ariel Cross	115	Scotch Bun	107	2,100	1:36.00	
1937	Boxthorn	5	G. Woolf	115	Accolade	117	Stand Pat	120	3,425	1:23.60	
1938	Speed to Spare	5	R. Workman	114	Mr. Blaze	106	Woodberry	114	4,525	1:12.40	
1939	Specify	4	J. Adams	118	Main Man	117	Airflame	120	10,000	1:10.20	
1940	Our Mat	4	R. Neves	106	Lassator	104	Sun Egret	117	10,050	1:10.40	
1941	Bull Reigh	3	B. James	117	After Dawn	117	Porter's Cap	126	10,600	1:24.00	
1945	Sir Bim	3	J. Longden	119	Quick Reward	119	Gold Bolt	119	19,235	1:11.80	
1946	Galla Damion	3	R. Neves	116	Hampden	116	Darby D-Day	116	17,505	1:10.20	
1947	Owners Choice	3	J. Longden	118	Yankee Valor	118	On Trust	118	37,950	1:23.60	
1948	May Reward	3	E. Arcaro	123	Solidarity	120	Salmagundi	120	41,400	1:23.60	
1949	Olympia	3	W. Garner	126	Hayseed	120	Admiral Lee	120	51,950	1:22.80	
1950	Your Host	3	J. Longden	126	Great Circle	120	Blue Reading	123	45,000	1:23.40	
1951	Phil D.	3	R. York	122	Gold Note	114	Rough'n Tumble	118	40,700	1:22.80	
1952	Windy City II	3	E. Arcaro	126	Indian Land	118	Marcador	114	18,000	1:44.00	
1953	Decorated	3	J. Longden	120	Chanlea	122	Social Outcast	115	16,950	1:44.20	
1954	Determine	3	R. York	120	Travertine	113			17,800	1:42.40	
					Mr. Mustard	113					
1955	Jean's Joe	3	W. Boland	115	Beau Busher	112	Trentonian	123	17,800	1:43.00	
1956	Social Climber	3	L. Gilligan	108	Count Chic	120	Terrang	124	18,200	1:44.40	
1957	Joe Price	3	G. Glisson	115	Sir William	118	Blue Spruce	111	18,500	1:43.40	
1958	Carrier X.	3	G. Taniguchi	108	Aliwar	119	Furyvan	113	16,350	1:45.60	
1959	Finnegan	3	W. Harmatz	115	Tomy Lee	124	Royal Orbit	118	32,900	1:43.40	
1960	Flow Line	3	W. Boland	118	T.V. Lark	120	John William	121	35,200	1:42.40	
1961	Flutterby	3	J. Longden	122	Olden Times	124	Wire Us	111	36,700	1:42.20	
1962	Doc Jocoy	3	W. Harmatz	113	Royal Attack	119	Admiral's Voyage	122	40,400	1:44.20	
1963	Denodado	3	R. Campas	110	Might and Main	114	Doolin Point	112	42,750	1:45.00	
1964	Hill Rise	3	D. Pierce	124	Wil Rad	124	Real Good Deal	120	38,950	1:41.40	
1965	Jacinto	3	M. Ycaza	126	Lucky Debonair	120	Isle of Greece	118	35,400	1:41.80	
1966	Saber Mountain	3	W. Shoemaker	124	Exhibitionist	119	Hill Clown	112	40,400	1:42.40	
1967	Rising Market	3	L. Pincay Jr	118	Ruken	117	Field Master	113	40,050	1:42.80	
1968	Prince Pablo	3	J. Sellers	118	Aley Fighter	114	Poleax	112	23,900	1:42.40	
1968	Dewan	3	J. Lambert	119	Don B.	122	Proper Proof	115	24,400	1:42.40	
1969	Elect the Ruler	3	E. Belmonte	116	Lonny's Secret	117	Mr. Joe F.	122	36,050	1:44.20	
1970	Cool Hand	3	J. Lambert	115	Plenty Old	117	Sir Wiggle	117	30,050	1:41.80	
1970	Terlago	3	W. Shoemaker	118	George Lewis	122	Willowick	114	29,550	1:41.80	
1971	Unconscious	3	L. Pincay Jr	122	Steal a Dance	114	Fast Fellow	118	36,150	1:42.60	
1972	Solar Salute	3	L. Pincay Jr	121	Quack	117	Indian	114	41,800	1:41.80	
1973	Linda's Chief	3	B. Baeza	126	Ancient Title	120	Out of the East	115	42,700	1:41.80	
1974	Aloha Mood	3	D. Pierce	118	Money Lender	124	Triple Crown	124	43,700	1:42.40	
1975	Fleet Velvet	3	F. Toro	120	George Navonod	122	Diabolo	124	33,200	1:42.40	
1976	Crystal Water	3	W. Shoemaker	117	Beau Talent	117	Double Discount	113	34,000	1:42.60	

Year	Winner	Age	Jockey	Wt.	Second	Wt.	Third	Wt.	Win Value	Time	Beyer
1977	Smasher	3	S. Hawley	115	Habitony	122	Miami Sun	115	32,850	1:42.60	
1978	Affirmed	3	S. Cauthen	126	Chance Dancer	117	Tampoy	118	38,100	1:42.60	
1979	Pole Position	3	S. Hawley	119	Switch Partners	114	Flying Paster	127	48,500	1:41.20	
1980	Raise a Man	3	W. Shoemaker	119	The Carpenter	123	Rumbo	119	64,300	1:41.60	
1981	Stancharry	3	F. Toro	118	Splendid Spruce	116	Flying Nashua	121	69,500	1:42.00	
1982	Advance Man	3	C.J. McCarron	117	Gato del Sol	118	Cassaleria	123	77,550	1:42.20	
1983	Desert Wine	3	W. Shoemaker	124	Naevus	117	Fifth Division	120	62,900	1:41.60	
1984	Fali Time	3	S. Hawley	122	Gate Dancer	117	Commemorate	117	103,450	1:42.60	
1985	Image of Greatness	3	L. Pincay Jr	120	Skywalker	120	Nostalgia's Star	117	106,350	1:43.20	
1986	Variety Road	3	C.J. McCarron	120	Big Play	114	Dancing Pirate	116	7,535	1:45.40	
1987	Chart the Stars	3	E. Delahoussaye	116	Alysheba	120	Temperate Sil	122	107,450	1:43.00	
1988	Mi Preferido	3	C.J. McCarron	119	Purdue King	119	Tejano	122	96,300	1:42.20	
1989	Sunday Silence	3	P.A. Valenzuela	119	Flying Continental	118	Music Merci	124	91,800	1:42.60	
1990	Real Cash	3	A. Solis	113	Warcraft	117	Music Prospector	117	102,600	1:42.00	
1991	Sea Cadet	3	C.J. McCarron	119	Scan	119	Compelling Sound	116	124,200	1:41.80	
1992	Bertrando	3	A. Solis	122	Arp	116	Hickman Creek	116	120,800	1:42.60	97
1993	Corby	3	C.J. McCarron	116	Personal Hope	116	Devoted Brass	122	121,100	1:42.00	100
1994	Soul of the Matter	3	K.J. Desormeaux	116	Brocco	119	Valiant Nature	119	118,500	1:44.60	106
1995	Afternoon Deelites	3	K.J. Desormeaux	119	Timber Country	122	Lake George	116	117,200	1:42.00	99
1996	Odyle	3	C.S. Nakatani	116	Smithfield	116	Cavonnier	122	152,400	1:42.40	101
1997	Free House	3	D.R. Flores	119	Silver Charm	122	King Crimson	116	152,400	1:42.40	103
1998	Artax	3	C.J. McCarron	122	Real Quiet	119	Prosperous Bid	116	150,000	1:41.60	108
1999	Prime Timber	3	D.R. Flores	116	Exploit	122	High Wire Act	116	150,000	1:42.00	106
2000	Fusaichi Pegasus	3	K.J. Desormeaux	116	The Deputy	122	Anees	119	150,000	1:42.66	106
2001	Point Given	3	G.L. Stevens	122	I Love Silver	116	Jamaican Rum	119	150,000	1:41.94	105
2002	Medaglia d'Oro	3	L. Pincay Jr.	116	U S S Tinosa	116	Siphonic	122	150,000	1:41.95	107
2003	Buddy Gil	3	G.L. Stevens	119	Atswhatimtalknbout	116	Brancusi	116	150,000	1:43.64	102
2004	Preachinatthebar	3	J. Santiago	116	St Averil	122	Harvard Avenue	116	150,000	1:42.87	101

Beyer Index: 103.15

SAN FERNANDO BREEDERS' CUP (G2), 1 1/16 Miles, 4-Year-Olds, Santa Anita, 2004 Purse: $221,800

Year	Winner	Age	Jockey	Wt.	Second	Wt.	Third	Wt.	Win Value	Time	Beyer
1952	Counterpoint	4	D. Gorman	118	Phil D.	115	Intent	114	14,300	1:45.20	
1953	Mark-Ye-Well	4	E. Arcaro	122	Stranglehold	112	Southarlington	109	15,550	1:44.20	
1954	By Zeus	4	J. Westrope	112	Resistance	112	Joe Jones	114	16,350	1:49.40	
1955	Poona II	4	W. Shoemaker	112	Miz Clementine	113	Duke's Lea	112	16,550	1:40.80	
1956	Beau Busher	4	J. Westrope	118	Traffic Judge	122	Honeys Alibi	122	17,400	1:43.60	
1957	Holandes II	4	W. Shoemaker	115	Family Album	112	More Glory	112	17,400	1:43.20	
1958	Round Table	4	W. Shoemaker	130	The Searcher	114	Seaneen	124	15,750	1:42.20	
1959	Hillsdale	4	T. Barrow	124	Jewel's Reward	120	Gleeman	114	16,700	1:42.40	
1960	King o' Turf	4	A. Valenzuela	113	First Landing	117	Civic Pride	113	32,100	1:50.00	
1961	Prove It	4	W. Shoemaker	113	Tompion	123	Prince Blessed	113	31,900	1:47.60	
1962	Four-and-Twenty	4	J. Longden	126	Olden Times	120	Obsession	114	31,900	1:48.80	
1963	Crimson Satan	4	H. Hinojosa	117	Native Diver	120	Pirate Cove	114	36,300	1:47.20	
1964	Nevada Battler	4	M. Ycaza	114	B. Major	120	Big Raff	114	26,125	1:48.80	
1964	Gun Bow	4	W. Shoemaker	114	Lamb Chop	115	Win-Em-All	111	26,125	1:47.80	
1965	Hill Rise	4	D. Pierce	123	Pelegrin	114	Canadian B.	113	39,050	1:48.40	
1966	Isle of Greece	4	W. Blum	121	Terry's Secret	121	Bold Bidder	121	36,000	1:48.60	
1967	Buckpasser	4	B. Baeza	124	Fleet Host	121	Pretense	118	34,050	1:48.20	
1968	Damascus	4	W. Shoemaker	126	Most Host	113	Ruken	120	34,450	1:48.80	
1969	Cavamore	4	E. Belmonte	113	Dignitas	117	Dewan	120	36,950	1:49.00	
1971	Willowick	4	E. Belmonte	113	Hanalei Bay	120	War Heim	114	40,600	1:48.80	
1972	Autobiography	4	E. Belmonte	113			Good Counsel	117	35,300	1:47.20	
	Triple Bend	4	D. Pierce	117							
1973	Bicker	4	G. Brogan	120	Royal Owl	120	Commoner	114	56,350	1:48.20	
1974	Ancient Title	4	L. Pincay Jr	120	Linda's Chief	123	Mariache II	114	50,250	1:47.60	
1975	Stardust Mel	4	W. Shoemaker	120	Century's Envoy	120	Princely Native	120	36,700	1:48.60	
1975	First Back	4	J. Vasquez	114	Lightning Mandate	120	Confederate Yankee	117	37,700	1:46.80	
1976	Messenger of Song	4	J. Lambert	120	Avatar	123	Larrikin	120	54,350	1:48.20	
1977	Kirby Lane	4	L. Pincay Jr	120	Double Discount	117	Rajab	114	39,000	1:47.60	
1977	Pocket Park	4	S. Cauthen	114	Properantes	114	Crystal Water	123	38,500	1:48.60	
1978	Text	4	F. Toro	120	J.O. Tobin	123	Centennial Pride	114	65,500	1:49.40	
1979	Radar Ahead	4	D.G. McHargue	123	Affirmed	126	Little Reb	120	69,200	1:48.00	
1980	Spectacular Bid	4	W. Shoemaker	126	Flying Paster	126	Relaunch	120	63,300	1:48.00	
1981	Doonesbury	4	S. Hawley	120	Raise a Man	120	Idyll	117	74,300	1:47.00	
1982	It's the One	4	W.A. Guerra	120	Princelet	123	Rock Softly	114	84,650	1:47.60	
1983	Wavering Monarch	4	E. Delahoussaye	123	Water Bank	120	Prince Spellbound	126	88,400	1:50.00	
1984	Interco	4	P.A. Valenzuela	123	Desert Wine	123	Paris Prince	120	92,850	1:48.60	
1985	Precisionist	4	C.J. McCarron	126	Greinton	120	Gate Dancer	126	123,350	1:47.40	
1986	Right Con	4	R.Q. Meza	117	Nostalgia's Star	120	Fast Account	114	101,800	1:48.40	

Year	Winner	Age	Jockey	Wt.	Second	Wt.	Third	Wt.	Win Value	Time	Beyer
1987	Variety Road	4	L. Pincay Jr	123	Broad Brush	126	Snow Chief	126	96,300	1:49.00	
1988	On the Line	4	J. Santos	120	Candi's Gold	123	Grand Vizier	114	122,400	1:49.00	
1989	Mi Preferido	4	C.J. McCarron	123	Speedratic	120	Perceive Arrogance	120	138,200	1:47.40	
1990	Flying Continental	4	C.A. Black	120	Splurger	114	Secret Slew	114	128,600	1:47.20	
1991	In Excess	4	G.L. Stevens	126	Warcraft	120	Go and Go	123	128,800	1:46.60	
1992	Best Pal	4	K.J. Desormeaux	122	Olympio	122	Dinard	122	130,000	1:48.20	121
1993	Bertrando	4	C.J. McCarron	120	Star Recruit	120	The Wicked North	116	127,800	1:51.20	109
1994	Zignew	4	C.J. McCarron	116	Nonproductiveasset	116	Pleasant Tango	116	135,400	1:47.80	107
1995	Wekiva Springs	4	K.J. Desormeaux	118	Dramatic Gold	120	Dare and Go	116	126,800	1:48.40	105
1996	Helmsman	4	C.J. McCarron	118	Gold and Steel	120	The Key Rainbow	116	134,500	1:48.80	103
1997	Northern Afleet	4	C.J. McCarron	116	Ambivalent	116	Ready to Order	116	194,400	1:48.40	96
1998	Silver Charm	4	G. L. Stevens	122	Mud Route	116	Lord Grillo	120	125,520	1:41.80	112
1999	Dixie Dot Com	4	D. R. Flores	116	Event of the Year	122	Old Topper	118	190,800	1:41.00	114
2000	Saint's Honor	4	K.J. Desormeaux	117	Cat Thief	122	Mr. Broad Blade	118	190,200	1:41.94	105
2001	Tiznow	4	C.J. McCarron	122	Walkslikeaduck	120	Wooden Phone	116	98,880	1:42.05	107
2002	Western Pride	4	G.K. Gomez	122	Orientate	120	Fancy As	120	134,640	1:41.30	110
2003	Pass Rush	4	C.S. Nakatani	116	Tracemark	116	Tizbud	116	131,760	1:42.37	106
2004	During	4	D.R. Flores	120	Toccet	116	Touch the Wire	117	134,280	1:41.63	106

Beyer Index: 107.77

SAN FRANCISCO BREEDERS' CUP MILE HANDICAP (G2), 1 Mile (Turf), 3-Year-Olds and Up, Bay Meadows, 2004 Purse: $148,750

Year	Winner	Age	Jockey	Wt.	Second	Wt.	Third	Wt.	Win Value	Time	Beyer
1948	Prevaricator	5	J. Longden	118	Hemet Squaw	109	Shannon II	122	12,390	1:34.40	
1949	Dinner Gong	4	J. Westrope	124	Miche	109	Cover Up	117	12,690	1:36.00	
1950	Citation	5	S. Brooks	128	Bolero	123	On Trust	116	14,550	1:33.60	
1951	Pension Plan	4	R. York	111	Star Fiddle	114	Bullreigh Jr	110	6,800	1:38.20	
1952	Lights Up	5	R. Neves	120	Phil D.	124	Boomerang Boy	109	17,150	1:35.60	
1953	Goose Khal	4	W. Shoemaker	125	High Scud	113	Fleet Bird	122	15,800	1:36.40	
1954	Golden Abbey	4	J. Westrope	119	Strangehold	120	Imbros	128	9,625	1:35.00	
1955	Determine	4	R. York	128	Poona II	123			29,325	1:38.00	
1956	Arrogate	5	R. Neves	126	Grey Tower	116	Battle Dance	107	12,750	1:34.80	
1957	Battle Dance	5	H. Moreno	125	North End	112	Hi Pardner	111	8,400	1:35.20	
1958	Battle Dance	6	H. Moreno	117	Social Climber	121	Bailarin	113	12,850	1:37.40	
1959	The Searcher	5	G. Lanoway	116	ShahJehan II	116	Battle Dance	120	8,725	1:35.20	
1961	Sea Orbit	5	A. Valenzuela	122	Roman Incense	112	Sparrow C'stle	115	6,100	1:36.60	
1962	Chase Eddie	5	J. Longden	114	Woodhaven	111	Novalook	115	6,250	1:36.40	
1963	Native Diver	4	W. Shoemaker	125	More Megaton	118	Aeroflint	115	9,200	1:35.20	
1964	Switchback	4	R. Neves	110	More Megaton	114	Slegde	116	6,875	1:35.80	
1964	Mustard Plaster	5	D. Hall	115	Upper Half	110	Native Diver	123	6,875	1:34.80	
1965	Viking Spirit	5	K. Church	119	Native Diver	128	Honored Sir	113	8,875	1:36.80	
1966	Lush Life	4	E. Medina	113	Travel Orb	114	Sir Bolco	117	6,350	1:34.20	
1966	Gamin	6	A. Pineda	116	Zulu Lad	113	Sen'r Grande	120	6,350	1:34.40	
1967	Native Diver	8	J. Lambert	133	Perris	113	Triple Tux	113	9,125	1:35.20	
1968	Bi G.	6	R. Peniche	108	Lucky P.J.	116	Little Matador	112	15,850	1:37.00	
1969	Wingover	6	R. Cespedes	114	Glory Hallelujah	120	Fiddler's Gr'n	112	15,950	1:36.80	
1970	Field Master	6	M. Valenzuela	119	Lonny's Secret	115	Baffle	122	16,700	1:37.80	
1971	Figonero	6	A. Pineda	123	Fighting	110	Long Position	111	19,100	1:34.60	
1972	Imaginative	6	W. Mahorney	115	Long Position	116	Quiet Star	116	12,850	1:34.60	
1972	Panzer Chief	5	V. Tejada	119	Against the Wind	117	Du Call	115	12,725	1:36.20	
1973	New Prospect	4	J. Sellers	118	Masked	116	Rock Bath	113	22,150	1:43.20	
1974	Visualizer	4	F. Mena	114	Roka Zaca	117	Larkal II	110	21,900	1:38.00	
1975	Whoa Boy	4	G. Baze	113	Ocala Boy	113	Star of Kuwait	116	18,100	1:39.00	
1977	Crafty Native	4	M. James	112	Cojak	122	Money Lender	119	26,350	1:38.40	
1978	Jumping Hill	6	J. Lambert	121	Boy Tike	115	Dr. Henry K.	109	32,500	1:38.40	
1979	Struttin' Geo	5	T.M. Chapman	117	Crafty Native	111	Foreign Power	115	32,950	1:37.40	
1980	Don Alberto	5	R.M. Gonzalez	114	Saboulard	116	Capt. Don	121	33,300	1:33.40	
1981	Opus Dei	6	F. Olivares	119	Drouilly	116	His Honor	117	41,850	1:34.80	
1982	Silveyville	4	D. Winick	121	Visible Pole	110	A Sure Hit	113	51,050	1:36.80	
1983	King's County	4	E. Munoz	112	Police Inspector	118	Silveyville	121	48,950	1:37.60	
1984	Drumalis	4	E. Delahoussaye	117	Silveyville	117	Ten Below	115	43,275	1:35.60	
1984	Ice Hot	4	M. Castaneda	115	Major Sport	117	Otter Slide	114	34,275	1:35.40	
1985	Truce Maker	7	J.A. Garcia	112	Lina Cavalieri	115	Baron O'Dublin	116	69,500	1:35.20	
1986	Hail Bold King	5	M. Castaneda	117	Right Con	119	Lucky n Green	114	69,900	1:36.40	
1987	Dormello	6	A.L. Diaz	113	Air Display	116	Barbery	115	82,500	1:36.20	
1988	Ifrad	6	T.M. Chapman	115	The Medic	118	Blanco	117	82,500	1:36.20	
1989	Patchy Groundfog	6	F. Olivares	116	No Commitment	113	Mazilier	115	82,500	1:38.20	
1990	Colway Rally	6	C.A. Black	116	River Master	115	Miswaki Tern	117	110,000	1:35.80	
1991	Forty Niner Days	4	T.T. Doocy	113	Exbourne	116	Blaze O'Brien	116	110,000	1:38.80	
1992	Tight Spot	5	L. Pincay Jr	125	Notorious Pleasure	116	Forty Niner Days	116	110,000	1:35.40	108
1993	The Wicked North	4	A. Solis	114	The Tender Track	117	Slew of Damascus	115	55,000	1:41.80	104

Year	Winner	Age	Jockey	Wt.	Second	Wt.	Third	Wt.	Win Value	Time	Beyer
1994	Gothland	5	C.S. Nakatani	116	Emerald Jig	113	The Tender Track	116	110,000	1:35.40	105
1995	Unfinished Symph	4	C.W. Antley	118	Vaudeville	119	Torch Rouge	114	110,000	1:34.00	110
1996	Gold And Steel	4	A. Solis	114	Savinio	115	Debutant Trick	117	120,000	1:35.00	105
1997	Wavy Run	6	B. Blanc	116	Savinio	118	Romarin	118	120,000	1:32.00	106
1998	Hawksley Hill	5	G.L. Stevens	119	Fantastic Fellow	121	Uncaged Fury	117	120,000	1:34.20	109
1999	Tuzla	5	B. Blanc	112	Poteen	116	Rob 'n Gin	117	180,000	1:35.40	104
2000	Ladies Din	5	K.J. Desormeaux	120	Fighting Falcon	116	Self Feeder	116	150,000	1:35.46	107
2001	Redattore	6	J. Lumpkins	115	Hawksley Hill	119	Kerrygold	116	137,500	1:35.14	106
2002	Suances	5	D.R. Flores	116	Decarchy	121	The Tin Man	116	110,000	1:35.19	106
2003	Ninebanks	5	R.J. Warren Jr	117	Nicobar	116	National Anthem	116	110,000	1:37.20	103
2004	Singletary	4	J. Valdivia Jr	119	Captain Squire	116	Gold Ruckus	116	82,500	1:35.16	99

Beyer Index: 105.54

SAN GABRIEL HANDICAP (G2), 1 1/8 Miles (Turf), 3-Year-Olds and Up, Santa Anita, 2003 Purse:$150,000

Year	Winner	Age	Jockey	Wt.	Second	Wt.	Third	Wt.	Win Value	Time	Beyer
1938	Morning Breeze	2	N. Merritt	119	Montecito	119	Alex the Great	122	5,920	:33.40	
1945	Vain Prince	6	G. Woolf	117	Orion	114	Phar Song	117	19,890	1:11.40	
1946	Sun Lady	4	H. Trent	107	High Resolve	122	Jean Miracle	118	17,890	1:10.40	
1952	Windy City II	3	E. Arcaro	114	A Gleam	108	Hill Gail	119	13,350	1:22.40	
1953	Decorated	3	J. Longden	114	Chanlea	122	Boo Who	111	13,100	1:23.00	
1954	Determine	3	R. York	118	Mr. Mustard	114	Brighter Days	118	14,050	1:24.40	
1955	St. Vincent	4	J. Longden	116	Star of the Forest	122	Novarullah	119	19,750	2:00.00	
1956	Star of Ross	4	R. Trejos	110	Mintaka	114	Dictar	111	16,500	2:01.20	
1957	Corn Husker	4	G. Taniguchi	107	High Button	115	Posadas	117	17,450	2:00.20	
1958	Tall Chief II	6	W. Harmatz	117	Ekaba	119	Whatitoldyou	116	17,650	1:59.80	
1959	MacBern	4	H. Moreno	113	Andrew Alan	116	Hakuchikara	119	16,500	2:00.40	
1960	Eddie Schmidt	7	A. Maese	120	Sisters Prince	113	Greek Star	120	16,900	1:49.60	
1961	Geechee Lou	5	J. Longden	112	How Now	125	Sundown II	113	18,050	1:46.60	
1962	Art Market	4	I. Valenzuela	120	Grey Eagle	117	The Axe II	115	17,000	1:48.40	
1963	Dusky Damion	6	I. Valenzuela	117	Rablero	114	Pardao	120	16,300	1:48.40	
1964	Marlin Bay	4	M. Ycaza	116	Gay Challenger II	122	Mr. Consistency	120	17,550	1:48.40	
1965	Biggs	5	W. Harmatz	113	Polizonte	115	Colorado King	125	17,000	1:49.00	
1966	Perfect Sky	4	A. Pineda	111	Or et Argent	118	Cedar Key	123	17,100	1:55.00	
1967	Flag	7	W. Blum	117	Quicken Tree	111	Ultimate	116	18,370	1:47.60	
1968	Rivet	4	M. Volzke	113	Most Host	113	Moontrip	113	18,050	1:50.60	
1969	Easy Mark	4	E. Belmonte	113	Deck Hand	117	Biggs	118	16,800	1:49.00	
1971	Cougar II	5	W. Shoemaker	120	Suerte al Cobre	111	Try Sheep	112	20,500	1:52.60	
1972	Big Shot II	7	E. Belmonte	117	Vegas Vic	120	Far to Reach	118	27,050	1:48.60	
1973	Astray	4	J. Vasquez	115	Golden Doc Ray	115	Kirrary	117	26,250	1:48.20	
1973	Kentuckian	4	D. Pierce	114	Artaxerxes	113	Harkville	112	26,950	1:47.60	
1974	Fair Test	6	A. Santiago	113	Indefatigable	118	Montmartre	118	25,750	1:50.20	
1975	Zanthe	6	S. Hawley	117	Copper Mel	115	Riot in Paris	124	26,550	1:47.40	
1977	Riot in Paris	6	W. Shoemaker	125	Distant Land	115	Ribot Grande	113	34,000	1:50.00	
1978	Mr. Redoy	4	S. Hawley	110	Dr. Krohn	116	Papelote	113	33,100	1:48.40	
1979	Fluorescent Light	5	A. Cordero Jr	118	As de Copas	118	Tiller	127	32,200	1:47.60	
1980	Premiere Ministre	4	L. Pincay Jr	118	Galaxy Libra	117	Fast	118	28,250	1:48.20	
1980	John Henry	5	D.G. McHargue	123	Smasher	111	As de Copas	117	39,300	1:49.80	
1981	The Bart	5	E. Delahoussaye	125	Irish Heart	115	Forlion	114	48,040	1:48.00	
1983	Greenwood Star	8	D. Pierce	119	Tell Again	118	Western	115	51,500	1:47.20	
1984	Prince Fl'r'm'nd	6	P.A. Valenzuela	118	Ten Below	113	Ginger Brink	118	40,225	1:48.20	
1984	Beldale Lustre	5	L. Pincay Jr	118	I'll See You	112	Color Bearer	111	39,425	1:48.80	
1985	Dahar	4	F. Toro	120	Paris Prince	116	Massera	116	50,750	1:47.60	
1986	Yashgan	5	C.J. McCarron	124	Tights	118	Rivlia	116	51,800	1:49.60	
1987	Nostalgia's Star	5	L. Pincay Jr	118	Inevitable Leader	112	Spellbound	116	61,550	1:51.20	
1988	Simply Majestic	4	J.D. Bailey	120	Payant	118	Dr. Death	115	66,150	1:47.40	
1988	Conquering Hero	5	G.L. Stevens	115	Hot and Smoggy	117	Ten Key	116	66,500	1:50.60	
1989	Wretham	4	L. Pincay Jr	117	Patchy Groundfog	117	In Extremis	117	67,700	1:46.20	
1990	In Excess	3	G.L. Stevens	117	Rouvignac	113	Kanatiyr	115	68,100	1:47.20	
1992	Classic Fame	6	E. Delahoussaye	118	Super May	119	Defensive Play	116	64,300	1:46.60	108
1993	Star of Cozzene	5	G.L. Stevens	118	Bistro Garden	114	Leger Cat	115	66,100	1:48.20	107
1994	Earl of Barking	4	C.J. McCarron	118	Fanmore	116	Navarone	119	65,300	1:48.60	104
1995	Romarin	5	C.S. Nakatani	119	Inner City	116	Ianomami	116	62,900	1:49.20	104
1996	Romarin	6	C.S. Nakatani	119	Virginia Carnival	116	Silver Wizard	117	82,050	1:49.60	104
1997	Rainbow Blues	6	G. L. Stevens	119	River Deep	116	Via Lombardia	116	81,500	1:46.80	104
1997	Martiniquais	4	C.S. Nakatani	116	Bienvenido	115	Da Bull	115	99,180	1:48.40	100
1998	Brave Act	4	G.F. Alemeida	118	Mash One	116	Fabulous Guy	113	90,000	1:46.60	108
2000	Brave Act	6	A. Solis	120	Native Desert	116	Manndar	116	97,470	1:49.25	109
2001	Irish Prize	5	K.J. Desormeaux	117	Manndar	121	Here Comes Big C	110	90,000	1:47.88	102
2002	Grammarian	4	J. Valdivia Jr.	117	David Copperfield	117	Decarchy	119	90,000	1:48.12	106
2003	Redattore	8	A. Solis	122	Continental Red	116	Denied	116	90,000	1:48.17	107

Beyer Index: 105.25

SAN GORGONIO HANDICAP (G2), 1 1/8 Miles (Turf), Fillies and Mares, 4-year-Olds and Up, Santa Anita, 2004 Purse: $147,000

Year	Winner	Age	Jockey	Wt.	Second	Wt.	Third	Wt.	Win Value	Time	Beyer
1968	Tumble Wind	4	J. Sellers	122	Sky Gipsy II	118	Poona Khan	113	14,150	1:13.60	
1969	Jimmy Peanuts	4	W. Blum	118	Security Check	119	Royal Come'n	122	15,900	1:52.00	
1971	Never Confuse	5	L. Pincay Jr	120	Pleasant Harbour	122	Gallant Policy	114	18,300	1:51.60	
1972	Tradesman	8	E. Belmonte	114	Delaware Chief	119	Quiet Star	115	23,600	1:49.20	
1973	Extra Hand	7	L. Pincay Jr	118	Timoteo	122	Dundee Marmalade	115	23,200	1:49.00	
1974	Margum	5	W. Shoemaker	115	Harbor Point	117	Expediter	115	22,500	1:50.60	
1975	Madison Place	7	D. Pierce	119	Grotonian	115	At the D'ne	115	21,400	1:48.40	
1976	Tizna	7	F. Alvarez	132	Miss Tokyo	120	Charger's Star	121	25,800	1:47.20	
1977	Lucie Manet	4	W. Shoemaker	121	Theia	116	Claire Valentine	115	32,250	1:54.00	
1977	Merry Lady III	5	L. Pincay Jr	119	Our First Delight	117	Pacara	114	36,200	1:50.80	
1979	Via Maris	4	A. Cordero Jr	113	Drama Critic	122	Donna Inez	114	33,500	1:52.60	
1980	Miss Magnetic	5	L.E. Ortega	111	Maytide	112	Persona	113	39,700	1:50.00	
1981	Kilijaro	5	W. Shoemaker	128	Queen to Conquer	122	Refinish	117	36,300	1:49.20	
1982	Track Robbery	6	E. Delahoussaye	123	Rainbow Connection	117	Targa	114	45,700	1:52.60	
1983	Castilla	4	C.J. McCarron	122	Star Pastures	119	Cat Girl	115	50,800	1:46.40	
1984	First Advance	5	M. Castaneda	115	Avigaition	120	L'Attrayante	121	53,950	1:48.80	
1985	Fact Finder	6	F. Toro	118	Capichi	118	Comedy Act	119	62,500	1:48.20	
1986	Mount'n Bear	5	E. Delahoussaye	118	Royal Regatta	115	Justicara	117	67,150	1:48.40	
1987	Frau Altiva	5	L. Pincay Jr	117	Auspiciante	122	Solva	119	63,100	1:50.20	
1988	Miss Alto	5	E. Delahoussaye	116	Top Corsage	119	My Virginia Reel	115	63,200	1:49.20	
1989	No Review	4	R.Q. Meza	117	Annoconnor	122	White Mischief II	116	79,950	1:48.80	
1990	Invited Guest	6	R.A. Baze	117	White Mischief II	115	Oeilladine	115	83,750	1:46.40	102
1991	Royal Touch	6	C.J. McCarron	118	Countus In	119	Marshua's Dancer	113	83,850	1:47.80	101
1992	Paseana	5	C.J. McCarron	118	Laura Ly	112	Reluctant Guest	117	77,250	1:53.80	97
1993	Southern Truce	5	C.S. Nakatani	114	Laura Ly	114	Lite Light	115	67,100	1:51.20	104
1994	Hero's Love	6	L. Pincay Jr	119	Skimble	118	Miss Turkana	118	66,800	1:47.60	101
1995	Queens Court Queen	6	C.S. Nakatani	117	Wende	117	Vinista	115	62,000	1:48.60	103
1996	Wandesta	5	C.S. Nakatani	119	Matiara	118	Yearly Tour	117	80,550	1:49.00	106
1997	Sixieme Sens	5	C.S. Nakatani	116	Alpride	120	Grafin	116	82,950	1:47.00	106
1998	Golden Arches	4	C.J. McCarron	120	Ecoute	115	Real Connection	116	96,870	1:49.40	103
1999	See You Soon	5	K.J. Desormeaux	118	Sonja's Faith	118	Verinha	115	90,000	1:49.00	105
2000	Lady at Peace	4	G.K. Gomez	115	Spanish Fern	119	Riboletta	116	90,000	1:48.75	101
2001	Uncharted Haven	4	A. Solis	115	Brianda	110	Beautiful Noise	116	90,000	1:50.02	98
2002	Tout Charmant	6	C.J. McCarron	120	Janet	119	Vencera	115	90,000	1:47.22	104
2003	Tates Creek	5	P.A. Valenzuela	121	Megahertz	117	Double Cat	114	90,000	1:46.91	103
2004	Megahertz	5	A. Solis	119	Garden in the Rain	116	Firth of Lorne	116	90,000	1:49.51	98

Beyer Index: 102.13

SAN JUAN CAPISTRANO INVITATIONAL HANDICAP (G2), About 1 3/4 Miles (Turf), 4-Year-Olds and Up, Santa Anita, 2004 Purse: $250,000

Year	Winner	Age	Jockey	Wt.	Second	Wt.	Third	Wt.	Win Value	Time	Beyer
1935	Head Play	5	C. Kurtsinger	115	Top Row	109	Ladysman	122	9,100	1:51.40	
1936	Whopper	4	W. Saunders	112	Tick On	106	Ariel Cross	103	10,950	1:50.00	
1937	Seabiscuit	4	J. Pollard	120	Grand Manitou	108	Special Agent	116	9,200	1:48.80	
1938	Indian Broom	5	H. Richards	110	Star Shadow	110	Amor Brujo	112	8,700	1:51.40	
1939	Cravat	4	J. Westrope	117	Today	111	Jacola	116	25,200	2:30.40	
1940	Mioland	3	J. Adams	117	Weigh Anchor	115	Sweepida	122	10,250	1:45.20	
1941	Mioland	4	L. Haas	130	Gen'l Manager	107	Best Effort	110	36,840	2:30.80	
1945	Bric-A-Bac	4	C. McCreary	122	Wing and Wing	112	Barrancosa	106	44,310	2:29.20	
1946	Triplicate	5	J.D. Jessop	111	War Valor	109	Old English	110	40,030	2:28.40	
1949	Miss Grillo	7	J. Adams	117	Dinner Gong	118	Rose Beam	109	38,100	2:29.00	
1950	Noor	5	J. Longden	117	Citation	130	Mocopo	107	40,400	2:52.80	
1951	Be Fleet	4	J. Longden	114	Repeluz	116	Mocopo	106	37,800	2:56.00	
1952	Intent	4	E. Guerin	122	Be Fleet	116	Bryan G.	117	33,200	2:55.00	
1953	Intent	5	E. Arcaro	126	Don Rebelde	113	Trusting	121	65,100	2:55.60	
1954	By Zeus	4	R. York	110	Rejected	126	Lucrative	110	73,100	2:26.00	
1955	St. Vincent	4	J. Longden	123	Determine	126	Gigantic	110	69,800	2:46.80	
1956	Bobby Brocato	5	G. Taniguchi	124	Manotick	109	Honeys Alibi	119	68,900	2:49.40	
1957	Corn Husker	4	E. Arcaro	116	Spinney	114	Infantry	111	69,400	2:55.00	
1958	Promised Land	4	I. Valenzuela	121	Tall Chief II	120	Eddie Schmidt	115	70,000	2:52.00	
							Solid Sun	113			
1959	Royal Living	4	R. Neves	117	Tall Chief II	114	Infantry	112	70,700	2:45.40	
1960	Amerigo	5	W. Hartack	122	King o' Turf	115	Aorangi	109	73,800	2:47.80	
1961	Don't Alibi	5	W. Shoemaker	118	Prince Blessed	116	Notable II	106	68,100	2:48.00	
1962	Olden Times	4	W. Shoemaker	119	Juanro	109	The Axe II	122	73,000	2:53.00	
1963	Pardao	5	I. Valenzuela	119	Juanro	114	Rablero	119	70,600	2:48.20	
1964	Cedar Key	4	M. Ycaza	115	Follow Thru	112	Desert Chief II	113	53,100	2:48.00	
1964	Mr. Consistency	6	K. Church	125	Puyallup	109	Dusky Damion	119	54,100	2:49.00	
1965	George Royal	4	J. Longden	116	Duel	115	Hill Rise	124	75,000	2:46.80	

Year	Winner	Age	Jockey	Wt.	Second	Wt.	Third	Wt.	Win Value	Time	Beyer
1966	George Royal	5	J. Longden	118	Plaque	115	Tom Cat	114	75,000	2:48.80	
1967	Niarkos	7	A. Pineda	120	Biggs	113	Pretense	126	75,000	2:50.20	
1968	Niarkos	8	A. Pineda	121	Jungle Road	115	Rivet	115	75,000	2:47.80	
1969	Petrone	5	J. Sellers	122	Fort Marcy	124	Rivet	115	75,000	2:47.40	
1970	Fiddle Isle	5	W. Shoemaker	125			Fort Marcy	124	50,000	2:46.40	
	Quicken Tree	7	F. Alvarez	124							
1971	Cougar II	5	W. Shoemaker	126	Try Sheep	114	Hill Run	120	75,000	2:46.20	
	Fort Marcy finished second but was disqualified and sixth										
1972	Practicante	6	L. Pincay Jr	118	Cougar II	127	Nor II	120	75,000	2:45.60	
1973	Queen's Hustler	4	R. Rosales	115	Big Spruce	119	Cougar II	127	75,000	2:46.40	
1974	Astray	5	J. Vasquez	126	El Rey	113	Big Spruce	125	75,000	2:45.40	
1975	La Zanzara	5	D. Pierce	114	Astray	125	Stardust Mel	126	75,000	2:52.20	
1976	One on the Aisle	4	S. Hawley	119	Elaborado	113	Top Crowd	121	75,000	2:50.00	
1977	Properantes	4	D.G. McHargue	120	Top Crowd	118	Caucasus	128	85,000	2:47.60	
1978	Exceller	5	W. Shoemaker	126	Noble Dancer	125	Xmas Box	115	120,000	2:51.00	
1979	Tiller	5	A. Cordero Jr	126	Exceller	127	Noble Dancer	128	120,000	2:48.00	
1980	John Henry	5	D.G. McHargue	126	Fiestero	115	The Very One	113	120,000	2:46.80	
1981	Obraztsovy	6	P.A. Valenzuela	121	Exploded	115	Singularity	115	120,000	2:50.40	
1982	Lemhi Gold	4	W. Guerra	121	Exploded	118	Perrault	129	180,000	2:45.60	
1983	Erins Isle	5	L. Pincay Jr	125	Wolver Heights	118	Victory Zone	115	180,000	2:48.60	
1984	Load the Cannons	4	L. Pincay Jr	119	Jenkins Ferry	114	Norwick	115	180,000	2:48.00	
1985	Prince True	4	C.J. McCarron	124	Estrapade	120	Swoon	117	180,000	2:47.80	
1986	Dahar	5	A. Solis	124	Mountain Bear	115	Jupiter Island	123	220,000	2:47.80	
1987	Rosedale	4	L. Pincay Jr	117	Wylfa	115	Rivlia	115	220,000	2:49.00	
1988	Great Communicator	5	R. Sibille	119	Fiction	116	Carotene	115	220,000	2:51.60	
1989	Nasr El Arab	4	P.A. Valenzuela	123	Pleasant Variety	117	Academic	113	220,000	2:51.40	
1990	Delegant	6	K.J. Desormeaux	115	Valdali	114	Hawkster	123	275,000	2:46.60	108
1991	Mashkour	8	C.J. McCarron	115	River Warden	115	Aksar	116	275,000	2:47.60	104
1992	Fly Till Dawn	6	P.A. Valenzuela	121	Miss Alleged	118	Wall Street Dancer	114	275,000	2:46.53	110
1993	Kotashaan	5	K.J. Desormeaux	121	Bien Bien	119	Fraise	123	220,000	2:45.00	108
1994	Bien Bien	5	C.J. McCarron	122	Grand Flotilla	116	Alex the Great	114	220,000	2:46.69	107
1995	Red Bishop	7	M.E. Smith	119	Special Price	116	Liyoun	112	220,000	2:48.02	107
1996	Raintrap	6	A. Solis	115	Windsharp	116	Awad	120	240,000	2:46.40	107
1997	Marlin	4	E. Delahoussaye	119	Sunshack	118			240,000	2:44.56	107
					African Dancer	114					
1998	Amerique	4	E. Delahoussaye	116	Star Performance	116	Kessem Power	116	240,000	2:47.08	104
1999	Single Empire	5	K.J. Desormeaux	118	Le Paillard	115	Lacayan Indian	113	240,000	2:45.93	105
2000	Sunshine Street	5	J.D. Bailey	115	Single Empire	118	Chelsea Barracks	109	240,000	2:49.06	104
2001	Bienamado	5	C.J. McCarron	122	Persianlux	114	Blueprint	116	240,000	2:42.96	108
2002	Ringaskiddy	6	E. Delahoussaye	116	Staging Post	115	Continental Red	117	240,000	2:44.49	106
2003	Passinetti	7	B. Blanc	111	All the Boys	115	Champion Lodge	117	240,000	2:46.97	104
2004	Meteor Storm	5	J. Valdivia Jr	116	Rhythm Mad	115	Runaway Dancer	115	150,000	2:45.98	102

Beyer Index: 106.07

Distance (main course 1 1/8 miles prior to 1938; 1 1/16 miles in 1940; 1 1/2 miles, 1939, 1941, 1945-49; 1 3/4 miles, 1950-53; (turf course) 1 1/2 miles, 1954. For 3-year-olds in 1940; for 3-year-olds and up in all other years prior to 1968

SAN LUIS OBISPO HANDICAP (G2), 1 1/2 Miles (Turf), 4-Year-Olds and Up, Santa Anita, 2004 Purse: $200,000

Year	Winner	Age	Jockey	Wt.	Second	Wt.	Third	Wt.	Win Value	Time	Beyer
1968	Dr. Isby	4	W. Blum	113	Biggs	118	Deck Hand	115	25,825	2:27.80	
1968	Tumble Wind	4	J. Sellers	120	Model Fool	118	Jungle Road	117	25,825	2:27.00	
1969	Quicken Tree	6	W. Hartack	124	Red Vandal	105	Rivet	120	36,800	2:37.60	
1970	Quilche	6	J. Lambert	115	Royal Dynasty	116	Society II	115	35,600	1:58.00	
1971	Daryl's Joy	5	J. Sellers	128	Cougar II	127	Onandaga	110	38,300	2:29.20	
1972	Practicante	6	W. Shoemaker	118	Golden Eagle II	118	Y'low Zorker	114	35,050	2:26.40	
1972	Lord Derby	5	W. Shoemaker	112	Dendron	115	Moomba Fox	112	35,050	2:27.40	
1973	Queen's Hustler	4	R. Rosales	112	China Silk	115	River Buoy	117	40,800	2:27.20	
1974	Captain Cee Jay	4	F. Alvarez	113	Court Ruling	112	El Rey	112	28,150	2:23.80	
1974	Astray	5	J. Vasquez	118	Scantling	112	Wichita Oil	115	28,150	2:24.40	
1975	Madison Palace	7	L. Pincay Jr	120	Toujours Pret	121	Barclay Joy	118	40,100	2:30.20	
1976	Announcer	4	F. Toro	118	Top Crowd	123	Zanthe	121	38,200	2:30.80	
1977	Royal Derby II	8	W. Shoemaker	126	Gallivantor	115	Anne's Pretender	123	41,700	2:24.80	
1978	Copper Mel	6	S. Hawley	115	Avodire	110	Tacitus	115	42,300	2:28.00	
1979	Fluorescent Light	5	L. Pincay Jr	124	As de Copas	118	Alpha Boy	112	48,950	2:28.20	
							Nostalgia	113			
1980	Silver Eagle	6	W. Shoemaker	120	Balzac	123	Friuli	114	65,100	2:30.20	
1981	John Henry	6	L. Pincay Jr	127	Galaxy Libra	119	Zor	115	62,800	2:24.00	
1982	Regal Bearing	6	J.J. Steiner	114	Le Duc de Bar	114	Goldiko	119	80,450	2:27.20	
1983	Pelerin	6	W. Shoemaker	116	Western	118	Massera	118	67,200	2:24.60	
1984	Sir Pele	5	R.Q. Meza	118	Lucence	118	Debonair Herc	114	79,375	2:27.40	

Year	Winner	Age	Jockey	Wt.	Second	Wt.	Third	Wt.	Win Value	Time	Beyer
1985	Western	7	G.L. Stevens	114	Scrupules	121	Strong Dollar	117	89,250	2:26.00	
1986	Talakeno	6	P.A. Valenzuela	115	Foscarini	117	Strawberry Road II	126	123,750	2:33.20	
1987	Louis le Grand	5	W. Shoemaker	118	Zoffany	125	Schiller	115	96,600	2:28.40	
1988	Great Communicator	5	R. Sibille	117	Trokhos	116	Ivor's Image	114	133,800	2:27.60	
1989	Great Communicator	6	R. Sibille	124	Vallotton	117	Roberto's Dancer	114	122,800	2:30.20	
1990	Frankly Perfect	5	C.J. McCarron	124	Delegant	116	Just as Lucky	114	171,100	2:28.00	101
1991	Rial	6	J. Velasquez	118	Intelligently	113	Royal Reach	113	163,400	2:24.00	107
1992	Quest for Fame	5	G.L. Stevens	121	Cool Gold Mood	114	Miss Alleged	121	158,500	2:28.60	111
1993	Kotashaan	5	K.J. Desormeaux	114	Carnival Baby	113	The Name's Jimmy	115	129,600	2:27.60	108
1994	Fanmore	6	K.J. Desormeaux	116	Bien Bien	124	Navire	114	131,400	2:27.00	108
1995	Square Cut	6	C.W. Antley	114	Ianomami	115	River Rhythm	111	133,200	2:26.00	103
1996	Windsharp	5	E. Delahoussaye	115	Wandesta	114	Virginia Carnival	115	130,800	2:30.20	108
1997	Shanawi	5	B. Blanc	111	Rainbow Dancer	117	Bon Point	117	132,100	2:24.40	101
1998	Bienvenido	5	C.J. McCarron	115	Prize Giving	116	Callisthene	115	120,000	2:29.20	104
1999	Kessem Power	7	G.L. Stevens	115	Brave Act	121	Lazy Lode	120	120,000	2:28.00	106
2000	Dark Moondancer	5	C.J. McCarron	120	The Fly	115	Casino King	116	120,000	2:39.61	106
2001	Persianlux	5	T. Baze	113	Devon Deputy	114	Falcon Flight	116	120,000	2:27.70	105
2002	Nazirali	5	B. Blanc	112	Continental Red	116	Bonapartiste	114	120,000	2:26.09	103
2003	The Tin Man	5	M.E. Smith	121	Special Matter	113	Harrisand	116	120,000	2:31.22	111
2004	Puerto Banus	5	V. Espinoza	115	Continuously	116	Continental Red	117	120,000	2:28.00	102

Beyer Index: 105.60

SAN LUIS REY HANDICAP (G2), 1 1/2 Miles (Turf), 4-Year-Olds and Up, Santa Anita, 2004 Purse: $200,000

Year	Winner	Age	Jockey	Wt.	Second	Wt.	Third	Wt.	Win Value	Time	Beyer
1952	Dark Count	3	G. Glisson	114	Stranglehold	114	Grey Tower	114	11,200	1:24.20	
1953	Tee Dee Gee	3	J. Longden	118	Hour Regards	118	Book Circle	111	10,750	1:11.20	
1954	Allied	3	R. York	109	Fault Free	115	El Drag	109	13,150	1:35.60	
1955	Alidon	4	R. Lumm	106	Ole Travis	113	Salmon Peter	104	17,950	2:26.40	
1956	Blue Volt	7	W. Shoemaker	113	Lychnus	113	Allied	108	17,500	2:28.00	
1957	Posadas	6	W. Shoemaker	113	Infantry	114	Prince of Greine	110	17,300	2:27.60	
1958	Solid Son	5	R. York	120	Roscoe Maney	118	Whatitoldyou	115	17,350	2:30.60	
1959	Infantry	6	G. Taniguchi	113	Lookout Point	112	Whatitoldyou	118	17,200	2:31.80	
1960	Lookout Point	7	D. Pierce	113	Nickel Boy	126	Turin	114	18,250	2:33.40	
1961	Don't Alibi	5	W. Shoemaker	118	Odd Fellow	111	Prince Blessed	119	17,350	2:26.20	
1962	Vinci	4	R. Campas	108	Mr. Erdley	114	Chimorro	111	17,550	2:36.60	
1963	The Axe II	5	P. Moreno	124	Rablero	120	Dr. Kacy	114	33,100	2:34.60	
1964	Inclusive	4	R. Campas	104	Mr. Consistency	127	Dusky Damion	120	36,800	2:25.20	
1965	Cedar Key	5	M. Ycaza	125	Polizonte	116	Or et Argent	117	35,000	2:24.20	
1966	Polar Sea	6	W. Hartack	115	Tudor Fame	116	Ask Father	110	26,525	2:26.40	
1966	Cedar Key	6	W. Shoemaker	122	Plaque	113	O'Hara	116	27,025	2:25.20	
1967	Niarkos	7	W. Shoemaker	120	Poker	113	Moontrip	118	26,175	2:26.00	
1967	Fleet Host	4	J. Lambert	117	Flit-To	114	Hill Clown	114	27,675	2:23.80	
1968	Biggs	8	J. Lambert	117	Tobin Bronze	123	Ole Bob Bowers	113	21,250	2:26.00	
1968	Quicken Tree	5	J. Lambert	119	Rivet	114	Finance World	114	22,250	2:24.60	
1969	Taneb	6	W. Shoemaker	124	Petrone	121	Quicken Tree	125	35,200	2:29.40	
1970	Fiddle Isle	5	W. Shoemaker	124	Hitchcock	118	Noholme Atoll	115	32,650	2:23.00	
1970	Quilche	6	J. Lambert	116	Quicken Tree	124	Royal Dynasty	116	32,650	2:25.40	
1971	Try Sheep	5	F. Alvarez	118	Tampa Trouble	118	Bacuco	124	48,250	2:26.00	
1972	Nor II	5	D. Velasquez	118	Hill Run	118	Rinconcito	114	50,900	2:25.80	
1973	Big Spuce	4	D. Pierce	126	Cicero's Court	126	Cougar II	126	66,800	2:27.60	
1974	Astray	5	J. Tejeira	126	Big Spruce	126	Quack	126	67,000	2:24.40	
1975	Trojan Bronze	4	J. Tejeira	126	Okavango	126	Montmartre	126	63,500	2:29.60	
1976	Avatar	4	L. Pincay Jr	126	Top Crowd	126	Top Command	126	64,300	2:24.80	
1977	Caucasus	5	F. Toro	126	King Pellinore	126	Top Crowd	126	64,400	2:25.60	
1978	Noble Dancer	6	S. Cauthen	126	Properantes	126	Text	126	64,400	2:24.00	
1979	Noble Dancer	7	J. Vasquez	126	Tiller	126	Good Lord	126	95,300	2:34.60	
1980	John Henry	5	D.G. McHargue	126	Relaunch	126	Silver Eagle	126	94,800	2:23.00	
1981	John Henry	6	L. Pincay Jr	126	Obraztsovy	126	Fiestero	126	93,900	2:25.20	
1982	Perrault	5	L. Pincay Jr	126	Exploded	126	John Henry	126	116,200	2:24.00	
1983	Erins Isle	5	L. Pincay Jr	126	Prince Spellbound	126	Majesty's Prince	126	120,900	2:26.20	
1984	Interco	4	P.A. Valenzuela	126	Gato Del Sol	126	John Henry	126	127,200	2:26.80	
1985	Prince True	4	C.J. McCarron	126	Western	126	Dahar	126	147,300	2:25.40	
1986	Dahar	5	A. Solis	126	Strawberry Road II	126	Alphabatim	126	148,600	2:26.40	
1987	Zoffany	7	E. Delahoussaye	126	Louis Le Grand	126	Long Mick	126	121,200	2:27.20	
1988	Rivlia	6	C.J. McCarron	126	Great Communicator	126	Swink	126	158,400	2:27.20	
1989	Frankly Perfect	4	E. Delahoussaye	126	Great Communicator	126	Payant	126	152,400	2:32.80	
1990	Prized	4	E. Delahoussaye	126	Hawkster	126	Frankly Perfect	126	180,000	2:25.20	109
1991	Pleasant Variety	7	G.L. Stevens	126	Royal Reach	126	Mashkour	126	188,250	2:24.40	105
1992	Fly Till Dawn	6	L. Pincay Jr	124	Provins	124	Quest for Fame	124	179,000	2:27.26	110
1993	Kotashaan	5	K.J. Desormeaux	124	Bien Bien	124	Fast Cure	124	148,250	2:23.91	108

Year	Winner	Age	Jockey	Wt.	Second	Wt.	Third	Wt.	Win Value	Time	Beyer
1994	Bien Bien	5	C.J. McCarron	124	Navire	124	Grand Flotilla	124	149,500	2:26.65	111
1995	Sandpit	6	C.S. Nakatani	124	River Rhythm	124	Square Cut	124	155,000	2:27.15	107
1996	Windsharp	5	E. Delahoussaye	117	Wandesta	117	Silver Wizard	122	161,900	2:27.91	108
1997	Marlin	4	C.J. McCarron	122	Sunshack	122	Peckinpah's Soul	122	166,600	2:28.14	107
1998	Kessem Power	6	L. Dettori	122	Storm Trooper	122	Star Performance	122	150,000	2:28.40	103
1999	Single Empire	5	K.J. Desormeaux	122	Kessem Power	122	Alvo Certo	122	150,000	2:27.97	105
2000	Dark Moondancer	5	C.J. McCarron	122	Single Empire	122	Bonapartiste	122	150,000	2:26.00	105
2001	Blueprint	6	G.L. Stevens	116	Devon Deputy	114	Kerryold	116	150,000	2:28.57	103
2002	Continental Red	6	P.A. Valenzuela	116	Keemoon	115	Speedy Pick	112	150,000	2:26.81	103
2003	Champion Lodge	6	A. Solis	116	Special Matter	113	Adminniestrator	116	150,000	2:33.48	108
2004	Meteor Storm	5	J. Valdivia Jr	115	Labirinto	114	Gene de Campeo	114	120,000	2:26.03	102

Beyer Index: 106.27

SAN MARCOS (G2), 1 1/4 Miles (Turf), 4-Year-Olds and Up, Santa Anita, 2004 Purse: $150,000

Year	Winner	Age	Jockey	Wt.	Second	Wt.	Third	Wt.	Win Value	Time	Beyer
1952	Hill Prince	5	E. Arcaro	126	Bryan G.	122	Be Fleet	117	14,750	1:35.80	
1953	Grover B.	4	E. Arcaro	122	Trusting	120	First Glance	126	13,350	1:36.80	
1954	Mark-Ye-Well	5	E. Arcaro	126	Thirteen of Diamon	120	Nothirdchance	112	18,200	2:00.20	
1955	Great Captain	6	W. Boland	110	Poona II	124	High Scud	115	17,700	2:03.80	
1956	Bobby Brocato	5	G. Taniguchi	124	Turk's Delight	117	Jet Stream	111	16,450	2:03.60	
1957	Alidon	6	J. Longden	114	Battle Dance	116	Corn Husker	114	17,200	2:05.80	
1958	Ekaba	4	W. Shoemaker	121	Solid Son	109	Promised Land	125	16,750	2:01.20	
1959	Round Table	5	W. Shoemaker	132	Eddie Schmidt	116	Andrew Alan	115	16,700	1:58.40	
1960	Whodunit	5	R. Neves	114	Anisado	113	Twentyone Guns	109	16,950	2:01.40	
1961	Anisado	7	I. Valenzuela	113	Scotland	116	How Now	120	18,000	1:59.60	
1962	The Axe II	4	R. Yanez	113	Oink	124	Dress Up	114	16,700	2:03.00	
1963	Rablero	5	J. Longden	115	Hy-Nat	115	The Axe II	123	18,150	2:00.40	
1964	Mr. Consistency	6	K. Church	119	Dusky Damion	119	Marlin Bay	120	17,200	2:02.40	
1965	Desert Chief III	9	D. Ross	116	Polizonte	114	Cadiz	114	17,450	2:01.00	
1966	Or et Argent	5	W. Blum	119	Switchback	114	Cedar Key	124	17,250	2:01.60	
1967	Rehabilitate	4	W. Shoemaker	113	Flag	120	Attention III	114	18,350	1:59.80	
1968	Biggs	8	J. Lambert	114	French Fox	109	Deck Hand	114	21,150	2:04.40	
1969	Deck Hand	6	D. Pierce	118	Rivet	118	Noble House	113	19,800	2:05.80	
1971	Cougar II	5	W. Shoemaker	124	Staunch Eagle	115	S'te al C'bre	114	25,100	2:02.00	
1972	Aggressively	5	D. Pierce	114	Lord Derby	114	Bold Inquiry	115	20,725	2:00.60	
1972	Big Shot II	7	E. Belmonte	122	Golden Eagle II	118	The Pruner	116	20,325	1:59.80	
1973	Tuqui II	6	L. Pincay Jr	114	Soudard	115	Aggressively	114	27,000	2:02.20	
1974	Triangular	7	D. Pierce	118	Big Spruce	124	Kentuckian	118	33,000	2:04.80	
1975	Trojan Bronze	4	W. Shoemaker	117	Indefatigable	115	El Botija	114	34,550	1:59.80	
1976	Announcer	4	F. Toro	115	Zanthe	122	Top Crowd	123	32,800	1:58.40	
1977	Royal Derby II	8	W. Shoemaker	124	Anne's Pretender	123	Teddy's Courage	116	34,150	1:58.20	
1978	Vigors	5	D.G. McHargue	121	Pay Tribute	122	Jumping Hill	123	33,350	1:46.60	
1979	Tiller	5	A. Cordero Jr	126	Palton	121	How Curious	112	37,700	1:58.80	
1980	John Henry	5	D.G. McHargue	124	El Fantastico	113	Commemorativo	110	37,350	2:01.60	
1981	Galaxy Libra	5	A. Cordero Jr	116	Bold Tropic	127	Mike Fogarty	116	40,300	2:00.20	
1982	Super Moment	5	L. Pincay Jr	125	Forlion	114	Le Duc de Bar	111	45,900	2:00.60	
1983	Western	5	C.J. McCarron	116	Handsome One	116	Tell Again	117	47,950	2:04.00	
1984	Lucene	5	P.A. Valenzuela	114	Ginger Brink	117	Sir Pele	114	54,200	2:01.80	
1985	Dahar	4	F. Toro	121	Scrupules	122	Alphabatim	124	61,900	2:01.20	
1986	Silveyville	8	C.J. McCarron	120	Strawberry Road II	125	Nasib	115	63,200	2:00.80	
1987	Zoffany	7	E. Delahoussaye	123	Louis le Grand	117	Strawberry Road II	122	64,100	2:00.80	
1988	Great Communicator	5	R. Sibille	115	Schiller	113	Bello Horizonte	113	100,400	2:02.60	
1989	Trokhos	6	L. Pincay Jr.	117	Vallotton	117	Roberto's Dancer	113	97,200	2:02.00	
1990	Putting	7	C.A. Black	114	Colway Rally	115	Live the Dream	119	105,600	1:58.20	
1991	Fly Till Dawn	5	L. Pincay Jr	120	Vaguely Hidden	115	The Medic	115	97,350	1:58.60	108
1992	Classic Fame	6	E. Delahoussaye	120	Fly Till Dawn	120	French Seventyfive	115	90,600	1:58.00	109
1993	Star of Cozzene	5	G.L. Stevens	120	Kotashaan	116	Carnival Baby	112	77,650	2:01.60	107
1994	Bien Bien	5	L. Pincay Jr	122	Explosive Red	116	Myrakalu	113	75,850	2:00.40	107
1995	River Flyer	4	C.W. Antley	118	Silver Wizard	117	Savinio	116	92,200	2:05.60	110
1996	Urgent Request	6	C.W. Antley	115	Bon Point	114	Virginia Carnival	116	97,000	2:02.20	113
1997	Sandpit	8	C.S. Nakatani	123	River Deep	116	Shanawi	112	99,000	2:00.60	108
1998	Prize Giving	5	A. Solis	114	Bienvenido	115	Martiniquais	118	97,380	2:04.40	101
1999	Brave Act	5	G.F. Alemeida	120	Ferrari	117	Native Desert	117	90,000	2:04.20	108
2000	Public Purse	6	A. Solis	119	Dark Moondancer	120	The Fly	114	98,280	1:59.58	108
2001	Bienamado	5	C.J. McCarron	122	Kerrygold	116	Northern Quest	122	90,000	2:02.75	107
2002	Irish Prize	6	G.L. Stevens	122	Continental Red	116	Cagney	119	90,000	2:01.27	105
2003	Johar	4	A. Solis	120	The Tin Man	122	Grammarian	122	90,000	1:57.92	106
2004	Sweet Return	4	G.L. Stevens	121	Nothing to Lose	116	Blue Steller	116	90,000	1:58.82	100

Beyer Index: 106.93

SAN MIGUEL (G3), 6 Furlongs, 3-Year-Olds, Santa Anita, 2004 Purse: $108,100

Year	Winner	Age	Jockey	Wt.	Second	Wt.	Third	Wt.	Win Value	Time	Beyer
1994	Mr. Cooperative	3	M.A. Pedroza	114	Subtle Trouble	118	Rambling Guy	121	48,300	1:09.53	92
1995	Petionville	3	C.W. Antley	114	Regal Fighter	114	Cold N Calculating	116	45,225	1:09.16	98
1996	Honour and Glory	3	G.L. Stevens	121	Afleetaffair	118	Valid Expectations	118	64,350	1:08.93	102
1997	Thisnearlywasmine	3	C.J. McCarron	118	Smokin Mel	114	Renteria	116	64,350	1:08.55	106
1998	Rio Oro	3	D. Lozoya	118	Iron Cat	114	Cat Doctor	114	66,180	1:08.60	105
1999	Cape Canaveral	3	D.R. Flores	118	Aristotle	114	Actin Time	116	62,760	1:09.00	100
2000	Swept Overboard	3	E. Delahoussaye	116	Forest Camp	121	Joopy Doopy	118	64,320	1:08.99	106
2001	Lasersport	3	C.S. Nakatani	116	Early Flyer	114	Bills Paid	114	64,500	1:08.60	104
2002	Popular	3	V. Espinoza	114	Roman Dancer	118	Royal Moro	114	64,740	1:09.00	105
2003	Omega Code	3	M.A. Pedroza	121	Only the Best	121	Jimmy O	118	64,680	1:08.65	103
2004	Hosco	3	T. Baze	118	Roi Charmant	117	Gethsemani	116	64,860	1:09.36	94

Beyer Index: 101.36

For previous runnings, refer to 1994 Manual.

SAN PASQUAL HANDICAP (G2), 1 1/16 Miles, 4-Year-Olds and Up, Santa Anita, 2004 Purse: $150,000

Year	Winner	Age	Jockey	Wt.	Second	Wt.	Third	Wt.	Win Value	Time	Beyer
1935	Bluebeard	3	H. Richards	114	Polish Beau	120	Moonson	122	2,190	1:12.80	
1936	Proclivity	3	T. Luther	112	Indian Broom	110	Jubilee Jim	106	2,370	1:12.00	
1937	Special Agent	5	B. James	114	Chanceview	111	Sangreal	110	3,325	1:42.80	
1938	Sun Egret	3	J. Adams	104	Clingendaal	118	Speed to Spare	110	5,050	1:23.40	
1939	Gosum	5	A. Gray	110	No Dice	108	Quick Devil	108	10,100	1:50.00	
1940	Don Mike	6	L. Balaski	112	Can't Wait	106	Woodberry	100	8,650	1:59.00	
1941	Mioland	4	L. Haas	130	Gen'l Manager	112	V'na Groom	100	8,900	1:51.60	
1945	Thumbs Up	6	J. Longden	125	Bizerte	109	Texas Sandman	119	19,065	1:44.60	
1946	Lou-Bre	5	R. Permane	108	Sirde	123	Bull Reigh	120	41,930	1:42.40	
1947	Lets Dance	5	J. Gilbert	117	Olhaverry	116	Texas Sandman	122	40,900	1:43.60	
1948	Olhaverry	9	M. Peterson	116	Autocrat	117	V-Boy	112	45,000	1:44.00	
1949	Shim Malone	5	R. Neves	110	On Trust	124	Autocrat	122	37,450	1:45.60	
1950	Solidarity	5	R. Neves	121	Noor	112	Ponder	125	44,100	1:43.80	
1951	Moonrush	5	F.A. Smith	103	Manyunk	105	Repeluz	106	38,550	1:42.40	
1952	Be Fleet	5	J. Longden	113	Bryan G.	124	Stormy Cloud	109	15,150	1:44.00	
1953	Moonrush	7	R. Neves	122	Trusting	113	Horsetr'r-Ed	112	15,550	1:43.40	
1954	Phil D.	6	M. Volzke	112	Indian Hemp	117	High Scud	113	16,700	1:41.60	
1955	Rejected	5	W. Shoemaker	128	Tordito	105	Great Captain	114	16,300	2:04.60	
1956	Bobby Brocato	5	G. Taniguchi	123	Nagpuni	116	Prince Hill	112	16,250	1:42.60	
1957	Battle Dance	4	G. Taniguchi	110	Honeys Alibi	120	Porterhouse	126	16,150	1:42.20	
1958	Terrang	5	W. Boland	122	Find	121	Porterhouse	125	16,400	1:41.40	
1959	Tempest II	5	W. Shoemaker	120	The Searcher	111	Eddie Schmidt	120	16,250	1:42.60	
1960	Fleet Nasrullah	5	J. Longden	117	Linmold	110	Crasher	115	16,450	1:41.40	
1961	New Policy	4	I. Valenzuela	120	Free Copy	112	Oink	115	17,300	1:41.60	
1962	Micarlo	6	A. Valenzuela	116	Free Copy	111	Nagea	113	16,800	1:47.80	
1963	Olden Times	5	W. Shoemaker	125	Native Diver	125	Physician	117	16,250	1:42.20	
1964	Olden Times	6	W. Shoemaker	120	Doc Jocoy	118	Donut King	113	17,250	1:44.40	
1965	Candy Spots	5	W. Shoemaker	124	Viking Spirit	118	Bonjour	114	16,300	1:42.20	
1966	Native Diver	7	J. Lambert	128	Cupid	118	Isle of Greece	119	17,250	1:41.00	
1967	Pretense	4	W. Shoemaker	118	Aurelius II	114	Native Diver	132	15,800	1:43.00	
1968	Kings Favor	5	J. Sellers	116	Mr. Right	118	Suteki	119	29,550	1:44.20	
1969	Kings Favor	6	J. Leonard	116	Most Host	118	Jimmy P'nuts	112	28,500	1:45.60	
1970	Nodouble	5	J. Tejeira	128	Field Master	116	Dewan	120	28,650	1:40.40	
1971	Ack Ack	5	W. Shoemaker	129	Delaware Chief	118	Figonero	121	33,300	1:41.40	
1972	Western Wagon	5	L. Pincay Jr	115	Cougar II	128	Star of Kuwait	114	35,100	1:41.20	
1973	Single Agent	5	J. Lamber	119	Kennedy Road	119	Autobiography	125	33,850	1:41.80	
1974	Tri Jet	5	W. Shoemaker	121	Forage	121	Susan's Girl	119	36,550	1:41.40	
1975	Okavango	5	F. Toro	114	Tallahto	118	Cheriepe	114	38,400	1:41.40	
1976	Lightning Mandate	5	S. Hawley	118	Guards Up	113	Ga Hai	116	32,250	1:48.40	
1977	Uniformity	5	F. Toro	117	Distant Land	116	Pisistrato	117	35,500	1:41.00	
1978	Ancient Title	8	D.G. McHargue	124	Mark's Place	120	Double Discount	120	30,250	1:40.20	
1979	Mr. Redoy	5	A. Cordero Jr	117	Life's Hope	116	Big John Taylor	115	38,900	1:42.20	
1980	Valdez	4	L. Pincay Jr	125	Prenotion	111	Balzac	122	46,350	1:40.20	
1981	Flying Paster	5	C.J. McCarron	127	King Go Go	117	Fiestero	113	47,150	1:41.20	
1982	Five Star Flight	4	L. Pincay Jr	120	Tahitian King	122	King Go Go	119	65,000	1:40.80	
1983	Regal Falcon	5	E. Delahoussaye	115	Time to Explode	121	West on Broad	113	53,900	1:43.20	
1984	Danebo	5	L. Pincay Jr	120	Water Bank	118	Honeyland	116	91,900	1:41.80	
1985	Hula Blaze	5	P.A. Valenzuela	115	Video Kid	117	Tennessee Rite	112	95,300	1:42.00	
1986	Precisionist	5	C.J. McCarron	126	Bare Minimum	113	My Habitony	116	90,000	1:41.20	
1987	Epidaurus	5	G. Baze	116	Ascension	114	Nostalgia's Star	120	90,800	1:42.40	

Year	Winner	Age	Jockey	Wt.	Second	Wt.	Third	Wt.	Win Value	Time	Beyer
1988	Super Diamond	8	L. Pincay Jr	125	Judge Angelucci	122	He's a Saros	114	92,300	1:43.00	
1989	On the Line	5	G.L. Stevens	123	Mark Chip	114	Stylish Winner	113	93,300	1:41.00	
1990	Criminal Type	5	C.J. McCarron	114	Lively One	122	Present Value	121	96,300	1:42.40	111
1991	Farma Way	4	G.L. Stevens	116	Flying Continental	122	Stylish Stud	114	93,100	1:40.80	115
1992	Twilight Agenda	6	K.J. Desormeaux	125	Ibero	116	Answer Do	118	22,500	1:42.20	110
1993	Jovial	6	M.K. Walls	115	Marquetry	118	Provins	115	91,400	1:41.80	107
1994	Hill Pass	5	C.J. McCarron	115	Best Pal	122	Lottery Winner	116	87,800	1:41.00	105
1995	Del Mar Dennis	5	A. Solis	118	Slew of Damascus	120	Tossofthecoin	117	116,100	1:41.20	108
1996	Alphabet Soup	5	C.W. Antley	118	Luthier Fever	115	Cezind	114	130,100	1:41.60	108
1997	Kingdom Found	7	G.L. Stevens	115	Savinio	117	Eltish	114	122,200	1:40.60	108
1998	Hal's Pal	5	B. Blanc	112	Malek	116	Flick	116	120,000	1:41.80	103
1999	Silver Charm	5	G.L. Stevens	125	Malek	119	Crafty Friend	118	120,000	1:41.60	109
2000	Dixie Dot Com	5	P.A. Valenzuela	118	Budroyale	122	Six Below	116	120,000	1:40.95	116
2001	Freedom Crest	5	G.L. Stevens	116	Bosque Redondo	114	Sultry Substitute	114	120,000	1:41.94	107
2002	Wooden Phone	5	D.R. Flores	119	Euchre	120	Red Eye	112	120,000	1:41.83	104
2003	Congaree	5	J.D. Bailey	121	Kudos	119	Hot Market	116	90,000	1:41.04	115
2004	Star Cross	7	V. Espinoza	113	Nose the Trade	115	Olmodavor	118	90,000	1:42.22	100

Beyer Index: 108.40

SAN RAFAEL (G2), 1 Mile, 3-Year-Olds, Santa Anita, 2004 Purse: $200,000

Year	Winner	Age	Jockey	Wt.	Second	Wt.	Third	Wt.	Win Value	Time	Beyer
1975	Donna B Quick	4	W. Shoemaker	114	In Prosperity	115	Take Powder	122	11,300	1:09.60	
1976	Vagabonda	5	W. Shoemaker	114	Bastonera II	122	Mia Amore	117	16,825	1:48.20	
1978	Little Happiness	4	S. Cauthen	116			Up to Juliet	110	16,975	1:35.40	
1981	Johnlee n' Harold	3	M. Castaneda	119	Minnesota Chief	115	A Run	119	51,500	1:36.00	
1982	Prince Spellbound	3	M. Castaneda	119	Muttering	121	Unpredictable	119	68,200	1:34.40	
1983	Desert Wine	3	C.J. McCarron	119	Naevus	114	Balboa Native	116	65,900	1:35.60	
1984	Precisionist	3	C.J. McCarron	120	Fali Time	122	Commemorate	118	91,600	1:35.00	
1985	Smarten Up	3	R.Q. Meza	122	Fast Account	122	Stan's Bower	118	94,500	1:36.20	
1986	Variety Road	3	C.J. McCarron	116	Ferdinand	116	Dancing Pirate	116	68,300	1:35.60	
1987	Masterful Advocate	3	L. Pincay Jr	122	Chart the Stars	116	Hot and Smoggy	116	90,500	1:35.80	
1988	What a Diplomat	3	G.L. Stevens	115	Flying Victor	121	Success Express	121	79,350	1:38.00	
1989	Music Merci	3	G.L. Stevens	121	Manastash Ridge	118	Past Ages	118	76,300	1:34.80	
1990	Mister Frisky	3	G.L. Stevens	115	Tight Spot	115	Land Rush	115	80,300	1:36.60	107
1991	Dinard	3	C.J. McCarron	118	Apollo	118	Best Pal	121	91,900	1:35.80	110
1992	A.P. Indy	3	E. Delahoussaye	121	Treekster	116	Prince Wild	118	90,300	1:35.41	100
1993	Devoted Brass	3	K.J. Desormeaux	115	Union City	115	Stuka	118	90,000	1:35.13	106
1994	Tabasco Cat	3	P. Day	121	Powis Castle	115	Shepherd's Field	121	89,700	1:36.39	102
1995	Larry the Legend	3	K.J. Desormeaux	118	Fandarel Dancer	118	Timber Country	121	88,600	1:37.61	100
1996	Honour and Glory	3	G.L. Stevens	121	Halo Sunshine	115	Matty G	121	122,000	1:36.45	103
1997	Funontherun	3	G. F. Alameida	115	Inexcessivelygood	115	Hello	121	121,800	1:36.01	101
1998	Orville N Wilbur's	3	C.S. Nakatani	115	Souvenir Copy	121	Futuristic	115	120,000	1:35.96	108
1999	Desert Hero	3	C.S. Nakatani	116	Prime Timber	115	Capsized	115	120,000	1:36.45	95
2000	War Chant	3	K.J. Desormeaux	116	Archer City Slew	118	Cocky	115	120,000	1:36.45	103
2001	Crafty C.T.	3	E. Delahoussaye	116	Palmeiro	117	Early Flyer	118	120,000	1:35.79	111
2002	Came Home	3	C.J. McCarron	118	Easy Grades	116	Werblin	115	120,000	1:36.24	106
2003	Rojo Toro	3	J.D. Bailey	115	Spensive	118	Crowned Dancer	118	120,000	1:35.89	94
2004	Imperialism	3	V. Espinoza	118	Lion Heart	121	Consecrate	115	120,000	1:36.11	104

Beyer Index: 103.33

SAN SIMEON HANDICAP (G3), About 6 1/2 Furlongs (Turf), 4-Year-Olds and Up, Santa Anita, 2004 Purse: $107,300

Year	Winner	Age	Jockey	Wt.	Second	Wt.	Third	Wt.	Win Value	Time	Beyer
1968	Poona Khan	7	M. Yanez	114	Dr. Roy E.	118	Dizzy Babe	113	14,000	1:22.00	
1969	Ottawa Hills	6	L. Pincay Jr.	117	First Mate	120	Indulto	120	14,850	1:22.20	
1970	Right Cross	4	L. Pincay Jr	116	First Mate	120	Canterbury Road	118	14,050	1:21.40	
1971	Long Position	5	J. Sellers	114	Earl of Milldale	116	Page	118	16,400	1:21.80	
1972	Single Agent	4	H. Grant	122	Long Position	114	Indulto	114	21,200	1:21.00	
1973	Soft Victory	5	D. Pierce	115	Selecting	115	Andrew F'ney	116	23,050	1:21.40	
1974	Matun	5	S. Valdez	118	Selecting	115	Forage	123	21,200	1:21.20	
1975	Century's Envoy	4	J. Tejeira	121	First Back	121	Rocket Rev'ew	120	19,700	1:22.40	
1976	Pay Tribute	4	L. Pincay Jr	118	Against the Snow	118	King Pellinore	122	25,650	1:35.20	
1977	Mark's Place	5	S. Hawley	122	Maheras	118	Painted Wagon	114	26,250	1:21.00	
1978	Maheras	5	L. Pincay Jr	122	Yu Wipi	114	Bad 'n Big	119	25,650	1:22.80	
1979	Bywayofchicago	5	D.G. McHargue	120	Maheras	118	Whatsyourpleasure	117	33,850	1:21.80	

Year	Winner	Age	Jockey	Wt.	Second	Wt.	Third	Wt.	Win Value	Time	Beyer
1980	Dragon Comm'd	6	E. Delahoussaye	115	Numa Pompilius	115	Bywayofchicago	115	29,050	1:12.60	
1981	Syncopate	6	D. Pierce	119	Parsec	117	Matsad'ns Honey	115	31,450	1:16.40	
1982	Shagbark	7	L. Pincay Jr	122	Shanekite	118	Belfort	116	39,850	1:13.00	
1983	Chinook Pass	4	L. Pincay Jr	124	Shanekite	118	Earthquack	121	39,100	1:15.40	
1984	Champagne Bid	5	R. Sibille	121	Retsina Run	115	Famous Star	115	53,350	1:14.40	
1985	Champagne Bid	6	R. Sibille	121	Forzando II	122	Smart and Sharp	118	52,150	1:13.60	
1986	Estate	7	A.L. Castanon	114	Will Dancer	118	Exclusive Partner	116	52,150	1:13.80	
1987	Bolder Than Bold	5	G. Baze	117	Prince Bobby B.	122	Lichi	112	49,800	1:13.60	
1988	Caballo de Oro	4	R.Q. Meza	112	Gallant Sailor	112	Sylvan Express	121	46,700	1:15.40	
1989	Mazilier	5	P.A. Valenzuela	116	Imperial Star	112	Caballo de Oro	116	48,750	1:15.80	
1990	Coastal Voyage	6	A. Solis	118	Patchy Groundfog	117	Raise a Stanza	119	60,000	1:12.20	107
1991	Forest Glow	4	J.A. Garcia	116	Answer Do	119	Shirkee	117	63,900	1:12.40	111
1992	Heart of Joy	5	C.J. McCarron	119	Regal Groom	115	Time Gentlemen	117	69,600	1:12.80	105
1993	Exemplary Leader	7	M.A. Pedroza	113	Prince Ferdinand	119	Wild Harmony	117	64,300	1:13.80	102
1994	Rapan Boy	6	G.L. Stevens	114	The Berkeley Man	115	Artistic Reef	116	63,100	1:13.00	103
1995	Finder's Fortune	6	P.A. Valenzuela	117	Rotsaluck	117	Pembroke	117	64,550	1:13.60	107
1996	Ski Dancer	4	G.L. Stevens	114	Daggett Peak	115	Boulderdash Bay	118	64,200	1:13.80	104
1997	Sandtrap	4	A. Solis	117	Daggett Peak	113	Tyconic	120	96,850	1:12.40	104
1998	Labeeb	6	K.J. Desormeaux	120	Surachai	118	Captain Collins	115	67,860	1:12.80	103
1999	Naninja	6	C.J. McCarron	115	Expressionist	116	Indian Rocket	119	65,220	1:13.20	104
2000	El Cielo	6	J. Valdivia Jr.	117	King Slayer	116	Scooter Brown	117	79,440	1:12.66	104
2001	Lake William	5	V. Espinoza	114	Macward	117	Touchofthe Blues	116	80,175	1:12.34	106
2002	Malabar Gold	5	C.J. McCarron	117	Astonished	117	Nuclear Debate	118	82,825	1:11.73	106
2003	Speak in Passing	6	D.R. Flores	118	Spinelessjellyfish	115	Rocky Bar	116	82,500	1:12.87	100
2004	Glick	8	A. Solis	117	Cayoke	116	Summer Service	117	64,380	1:11.46	110

Beyer Index: 105.07

SAN VICENTE (G2), 7 Furlongs, 3-Year-Olds, Santa Anita, 2004 Purse: $150,000

Year	Winner	Age	Jockey	Wt.	Second	Wt.	Third	Wt.	Win Value	Time	Beyer
1935	Trumpery	4	R. Workman	112	Marooned	106	Rock X.	101	4,800	1:10.00	
1936	Time Supply	5	T. Luther	120	Rosemont	118	Singing Wood	126	4,475	1:10.20	
1937	Merry Maker	3	J. Longden	108	Coramine	112	Upper Birth	108	3,915	1:27.40	
1938	Sun Egret	3	A. Shelhamer	125	Legal Light	118	Sir Raleigh	118	5,125	1:25.40	
1939	Impound	3	S. Coucci	112	Our Mat	118	Porter's Mite	126	10,300	1:23.00	
1940	Gallahadion	3	B. James	113	Sweepida	107	Exarch	113	11,650	1:38.80	
1941	Good Turn	3	C. Bierman	118	Porter's Cap	126	Valdina Groom	114	12,950	1:38.20	
1945	Busher	3	J. Longden	121	Sea Sovereign	121	Bismarck Sea	121	19,300	1:36.60	
1946	Air Rate	3	H. Pratt	122	Favorito	113	Darby D-Day	111	18,550	1:37.80	
1947	Hubble Bubble	3	B. Layton	113	Hormone	109	On Trust	122	38,050	1:43.40	
1948	Salmagundi	3	J. Longden	117	Call Bell	122	Solidarity	120	37,600	1:44.20	
1952	Hill Gail	3	S. Brooks	122	Haltafire	122	Tiger Sir	122	15,950	1:10.00	
1953	Chanlea	3	E. Arcaro	119	Hour Regards	122	Silverado	119	10,600	1:10.60	
1954	James Session	3	J. Phillippi	120	Determine	116	Larks Music	116	13,900	1:09.40	
1955	Swaps	3	W. Shoemaker	116	Trentonian	120	Jean's Joe	114	13,650	1:24.00	
1956	Terrang	3	W. Shoemaker	122	Fathers Risk	122	Bold Bazooka	124	15,500	1:22.80	
1957	Buford	3	I. Valenzuela	116	Seaneen	110	Golden One	117	13,350	1:22.00	
1958	Old Pueblo	3	R. Neves	124	Disdainful	117	Strong Bay	115	13,250	1:22.60	
1959	Ole Fols	3	M. Ycaza	118	Tomy Lee	126	Finnegan	118	13,550	1:22.40	
1960	John William	3	I. Valenzuela	114	New Policy	120	T.V. Lark	120	13,850	1:22.00	
1961	Captain Fair	3	D. Pierce	120	Olden Times	122	Wire Us	114	13,850	1:22.40	
1962	Black Sheep	3	R. Campas	109	Rattle Dancer	118	Killoqua	112	13,900	1:23.60	
1963	Mr. Thong	3	A. Maese	112	Olympiad King	116	Viking Spirit	112	13,700	1:23.80	
1964	Wil Rad	3	W. Shoemaker	120	Perris	120	Real Good Deal	121	15,000	1:22.60	
1965	Lucky Debonair	3	W. Shoemaker	118	Isle of Greece	120	Gummo	122	14,900	1:22.00	
1966	Saber Mountain	3	W. Shoemaker	115	Ri Tux	113	Wingover	121	21,000	1:22.40	
1967	Tumble Wind	3	W. Shoemaker	114	Don B.	124	Disciplarian	118	16,950	1:22.20	
1968	Dignitas	3	M. Ycaza	115	Rising Market	112	Proper Proof	112	18,350	1:22.00	
1969	Majestic Prince	3	W. Hartack	121	Elect the Ruler	115	Inverness Drive	113	17,400	1:25.60	
1971	Diplomatic Agent	3	L. Pincay Jr	114	Steal a Dance	112	Tower East	121	20,100	1:21.60	
							Crimson Clem	121			
1972	Solar Salute	3	L. Pincay Jr	118	D.B. Carm	121	Andrew Feeney	115	25,250	1:21.20	
1973	Ancient Title	3	F. Toro	122	Linda's Chief	122	Out of the East	114	28,150	1:21.00	
1974	Triple Crown	3	B. Baeza	114	El Espanoleto	114	Destroyer	114	28,000	1:22.60	
1975	Boomie S.	3	S. Hawley	114	George Navonod	122	Udonegood	114	21,350	1:22.00	
1976	Thermal Energy	3	W. Shoemaker	117	Stained Glass	122	Bold Forbes	119	20,200	1:21.80	
1977	Replant	3	D.G. McHargue	117	Current Concept	122	Smasher	122	27,750	1:21.20	
1978	Chance Dancer	3	R. Culberson	122	O Big Al	122	Reb's Golden Ale	114	25,600	1:22.20	
1979	Flyting Paster	3	D. Pierce	124	Oats and Corn	119	Infusive	122	37,300	1:21.20	

Year	Winner	Age	Jockey	Wt.	Second	Wt.	Third	Wt.	Win Value	Time	Beyer
1980	Raise a Man	3	W. Shoemaker	114	Super Moment	115	Bold 'n Rulling	117	39,550	1:21.40	
1981	Flying Nashua	3	A. Cordero Jr	114	Minnesota Chief	117	Torso	117	40,450	1:23.40	
1982	Unpredictable	3	E. Delahoussaye	122	Prince Spellbound	122	Sepulveda	119	50,700	1:21.20	
1983	Shecky Blue	3	S. Hawley	114	Full Choke	119	Naevus	115	48,200	1:22.40	
1984	Fortunate Prospect	3	D. Haire	119	Precisionist	122	Tights	117	49,700	1:22.80	
1985	The Rogers Four	3	C.J. McCarron	122	Teddy Naturally	119	Michadilla	122	49,400	1:22.80	
1986	Grand Allegiance	3	R. Hernandez	114	Royal Treasure	114	Dancing Pirate	119	51,050	1:23.20	
1987	Stylish Winner	3	G.L. Stevens	119	Prince Sassafras	116	Mount Laguna	116	46,750	1:23.80	
1988	Mi Preferido	3	A. Solis	120	No Commitment	120	Success Express	123	45,900	1:22.60	
1989	Gum	3	L. Pincay Jr	117	Yes I'm Blue	120	Roman Avie	114	47,600	1:22.40	
1990	Mister Frisky	3	G.L. Stevens	118	Tarascon	120	Top Cash	120	47,250	1:22.60	108
1991	Olympio	3	E. Delahoussaye	120	Dinard	118	Scan	123	61,075	1:21.40	
1992	Mineral Wells	3	P.A. Valenzuela	116	Star of the Crop	116	Prince Wild	118	61,450	1:21.28	104
1993	Yappy	3	P.A. Valenzuela	116	Denmars Dream	118	Devoted Brass	116	63,100	1:22.33	94
1994	Fly'n J. Bryan	3	C.A. Black	114	Gracious Ghost	114	Cois Na Tine	116	60,700	1:22.32	95
1995	Afternoon Deelites	3	K.J. Desormeaux	120	Mr Purple	116	Fandarel Dancer	117	59,725	1:21.35	103
1996	Afleetaffair	3	C.S. Nakatani	116	Honour and Glory	123	Ready to Order	120	63,850	1:22.28	103
1997	Silver Charm	3	C. J. McCarron	120	Free House	120	Funontherun	114	66,400	1:21.07	110
1998	Sea of Secrets	3	K.J. Desormeaux	116	Late Edition	115	Pleasant Drive	116	64,080	1:22.00	93
1999	Exploit	3	C.J. McCarron	123	Aristotle	116	Yes It's True	123	90,000	1:22.00	104
2000	Archer City Slew	3	K.J. Desormeaux	117	Joopy Doopy	116	Gibson County	120	90,000	1:22.18	103
2001	Early Flyer	3	C.J. McCarron	114	Lasersport	120	D'wildcat	117	90,000	1:21.51	108
2002	Came Home	3	C.J. McCarron	123	Jack's Silver	116	Werblin	116	90,000	1:21.92	109
2003	Kafwain	3	V. Espinoza	123	Sum Trick	120	Southern Image	117	90,000	1:21.12	115
2004	Imperialism	3	V. Espinoza	116	Hosco	120	Consecrate	116	90,000	1:22.34	101

Beyer Index: 103.57

SANDS POINT (G3), 1 1/8 Miles (Turf), 3-Year-Old Fillies, Belmont Park, 2004 Purse: $114,800

Year	Winner	Age	Jockey	Wt.	Second	Wt.	Third	Wt.	Win Value	Time	Beyer
1995	Perfect Arc	3	J.R.Velazquez	117	Miss Union Avenue	123	Transient Trend	110	49,395	1:43.00	106
1996	Merit Wings	3	R.Davis	120	Unify	113	Turkappeal	117	51,945	1:45.80	86
1997	Auntie Mame	3	J.Bailey	121	Hoochie Coochie	114	Sagacious	113	66,720	1:46.60	94
1998	Recording	3	J.F. Chavez	113	Royal Ransom	114	Naskra's de Light	116	69,600	1:48.80	89
1999	Perfect Sting	3	P. Day	118	Pico Teneriffe	121	Illiquidity	113	65,160	1:46.80	95
2000	Gaviola	3	J.D. Bailey	121	Shopping for Love	121	Millie's Quest	113	66.780	1:47.77	100
2001	Tweedside	3	R. Migliore	119	Owsley	114	Platinum Tiara	122	66,674	1:50.43	82
2002	Riskaverse	3	R.G. Davis	119	Cyclorama	115	She's Vested	115	69,660	1:51.63	91
2003	Savedbythelight	3	R. Migliore	115	Virgin Voyage	117	Little Bonnet	115	68,760	1:49.18	94
2004	Mambo Slew	3	E.S. Prado	122	Lucifer's Stone	122	Vous	119	68,880	1:47.24	93

Beyer Index: 93.00

Off the turf in 2003.

SANFORD (G2), 6 Furlongs, 2-Year-Olds, Saratoga Race Course, 2004 Purse: $150,000

Year	Winner	Age	Jockey	Wt.	Second	Wt.	Third	Wt.	Win Value	Time	Beyer
1913	Little Nephew	2	T. Killingworth	116	Undaunted	110	Trumps	116	2,650	1:14.80	
1914	Regret	2	J. Notter	127	Solly	113	Dinah Do	107	2,675	1:13.40	
1915	Bulse	2	C. Ganz	127	Marse Henry	110	Jacoba	119	2,675	1:16.80	
1916	Campfire	2	J. McTaggart	125	Rickety	108	The Knocker	107	2,850	1:13.40	
1917	Papp	2	L. Allen	130	Kashmir	118	Escoba	127	3,825	1:15.60	
1918	Billy Kelly	2	E. Sande	130	Lion d'Or	115	Col. Livingston	122	3,925	1:14.60	
1919	Upset	2	W. Knapp	115	Man o' War	130	Golden Broom	130	3,925	1:11.20	
1920	Pluribus	2	J. Rodriguez	127	Serapis	115	Gen. J.G. G'z	112	4,425	1:15.20	
1921	Sir High	2	M. Garner	115	Bigheart	115	Column	130	3,925	1:13.00	
1922	Bo McMillan	2	F. Smith	115	Dan E. O'Sullivan	115	Tall Timber	118	4,425	1:18.00	
1923	Parasol	2	E. Sande	114	Elvina	112	Big Blaze	110	5,425	1:12.80	
1924	Nicholas	2	L. McAtee	123	Crumple	115	Marcellus	110	4,100	1:15.60	
1925	Canter	2	C. Turner	122	Powhatan	115	Fiddlesticks	115	4,925	1:12.60	
1926	Northland	2	J. Maiben	115	Lord Chaucer	115	Bostonian	115	5,175	1:13.00	
1927	Nassak	2	L. Fator	130	Finite	115	Peter Simple	112	4,875	1:12.40	
1928	Chestnut Oak	2	J.H. Burke	115	Holiday	112	Bargello	115	4,275	1:13.00	
1929	Hi-jack	2	L. McAtee	115	Polygamous	115	Grattan	125	5,100	1:12.00	
1930	Sun Meadow	2	E. Watters	118	Surf Board	125	Condescend	118	5,800	1:12.60	
1931	Mad Pursuit	2	T. Malley	118	Ha Ha	112	Lucky Tom	118	5,025	1:12.20	
1932	Sun Archer	2	R. Workman	118	Grand Time	122	Sarada	112	4,025	1:12.80	
1933	First Minstrel	2	R. Jones	113	Cavalcade	123	Soon Over	116	2,675	1:15.00	

Year	Winner	Age	Jockey	Wt.	Second	Wt.	Third	Wt.	Win Value	Time	Beyer
1934	Psychic Bid	2	M. Garner	113	Omaha	113	Boxthorn	122	2,525	1:12.20	
1935	Crossbow II	2	E. Arcaro	113	Bow to Me	113	Sangreal	113	3,600	1:12.40	
1936	Maedic	2	E. Liztenberger	117	Third Count	110	Privileged	110	2,750	1:13.00	
1937	Spillway	2	D. Dubois	113	Maetall	119	Quick Devil	110	2,650	1:14.00	
1938	Birch Rod	2	W.D. Wright	112	Trailer	115	Get Off	107	4,725	1:14.20	
1939	Boy Angler	2	F.A. Smith	113	Epatant	117	Corydon	112	5,125	1:12.20	
1940	Good Turn	2	B. James	110	Grand Party	109	Omission	122	4,300	1:13.20	
1941	Devil Diver	2	D. Meade	114	Ramillies	110	Colchis	117	5,375	1:12.80	
1942	Devil's Thumb	2	C. McCreary	122	Noonday Sun	114	Tip-Toe	110	4,575	1:12.80	
1943	Rodney Stone	2	T. Atkinson	114	Ravenala	117	Free Lance	114	5,700	1:11.20	
1944	The Doge	2	F. Zufelt	114	War Jeep	122	Maransart	116	8,245	1:10.40	
1945	Pellicle	2	C. McCreary	108	Diri	108	Chevalier	108	7,830	1:10.80	
1946	Donor	2	J. Jessop	126	Cornish Knight	116	Lucky Reward	114	8,375	1:11.60	
1947	Inseparable	2	J. Jessop	120	Energetic	113	Faraway	113	8,475	1:11.80	
1948	Slam Bang	2	W. Mehrtens	108	Blue Counselor	113	Swords Town	114	8,250	1:12.00	
1949	Detective	2	T. Atkinson	120	Keep Right	113	Endurable	115	7,450	1:12.80	
1950	Big Stretch	2	E. Arcaro	114	Nullify	126	Silver Wings	120	7,900	1:11.60	
1951	Tom Fool	2	T. Atkinson	113	First Refusal	116	Secant	108	8,800	1:12.60	
1952	Bradley	2	J. Nichols	122	Belfaster	114	Fighting Cock	114	7,975	1:14.60	
1953	Bobby Brocato	2	O. Scurlock	114	War Piper	114	Way Thorn	114	10,200	1:13.20	
1954	Brother Tex	2	C. McCreary	122	Dark Ruler	122	Feast	118	10,325	1:12.80	
1955	Head Man	2	P.J. Bailey	113	Prince John	118	Nan's MInk	118	10,500	1:11.80	
1956	Thin Ice	2	T. Atkinson	116	Clem	116	Bora	116	12,500	1:12.60	
1957	Louis d'Or	2	R. Sterling	116	Deadeye Dick	119	Wing Jet	119	12,600	1:13.20	
1958	Pilot	2	E. Arcaro	119	Royal Anthem	126	Lake Erie	111	11,720	1:13.40	
1959	Weatherwise	2	J. Ruane	114	Tompion	115	Persian Spy	114	24,132	1:12.40	
1960	Hail to Reason	2	R. Ussery	124	Busher's Beauty	114	Apple	114	23,157	1:11.00	
1962	Rash Prince	2	I. Valenzuela	114	Ornamento	114	Valiant Skoal	120	25,301	1:04.60	
1963	Delirium	2	B. Baeza	114	Traffic	114	Golden Louis	114	23,010	1:05.40	
1964	Cornish Prince	2	D. Pierce	114	New Act	120	Tanistair	114	22,685	1:04.60	
1965	Flame Tree	2	R. Ussery	120	Spring Double	115	Impressive	115	23,969	1:04.60	
1966	Yorkville	2	J.L. Rotz	115	Sir Winzalot	115	Top Bid	115	22,490	1:05.00	
1967	Exclusive Native	2	A. Cordero Jr	115	Vitriolic	116	Forward Pass	120	22,474	1:03.60	
1968	King Emperor	2	B. Baeza	115	Hey Good Lookin	115	Winnies Choice	113	23,514	1:03.40	
1969	Walker's	2	A. Cordero Jr	115	High Echelon	115	Very High	124	23,579	1:10.40	
1970	Executioner	2	J. Vasquez	115	Raise Your Glass	120	Dundee Marmalade	115	27,430	1:09.40	
1971	Cohasset Tribe	2	M. Ycaza	120	Tarboosh	124	Buck the System	115	25,500	1:10.60	
1972	Secretariat	2	R. Turcotte	121	Linda's Chief	121	Northstar Dancer	121	16,650	1:10.00	
1973	Az Igazi	2	M. Venezia	121	Prince of Reason	121	Totheend	121	16,680	1:10.60	
1974	Ramahorn	2	C. Baltazar	121	Prop Man	121	Knightly Sport	121	17,205	1:11.00	
1975	Turn to Turia	2	E. Maple	121	Iron Bit	121	Gentle King	121	22,575	1:10.80	
1976	Turn of Coin	2	A. Cordero Jr	122	Hey Hey J.P.	115	Super Joy	115	22,395	1:10.20	
1977	Affirmed	2	S. Cauthen	124	Tilt Up	122	Jet Diplomacy	124	22,290	1:09.60	
1978	Fuzzbuster	2	J. Velasquez	115	Make a Mess	115	Turn Buckle	115	22,230	1:10.80	
1979	I Speedup	2	J. Fell	122	Muckraker	122	My Pal Jeff	117	26,175	1:10.40	
1980	Tap Shoes	2	R. Hernandez	115	Triocala	115	Painted Shield	117	34,260	1:10.00	
1981	Mayanesian	2	J. Vasquez	115	Shipping Magnate	115	Lejoli	115	35,280	1:11.20	
1982	Copelan	2	J.D. Bailey	115	Smart Style	115	Safe Ground	117	33,660	1:10.40	
1983	Big Walt	2	J. Fell	115	Fill Ron's Pockets	122	Agile Jet	115	34,260	1:11.00	
1984	Tiffany Ice	2	G. McCarron	115	Vindaloo	115	Fortunate Dancer	113	51,300	1:10.80	
1985	Sovereign Don	2	J. Velasquez	122	Roy	115	Cause for Pause	119	54,000	1:10.60	
1986	Persevered	2	A. Cordero Jr	115	Perdition's Son	115	Bucks Best	115	51,120	1:10.60	
1987	Forty Niner	2	E. Maple	115	Once Wild	115	Velvet Fog	115	65,340	1:10.00	
1988	Mercedes Won	2	R.G. Davis	119	Leading Prospect	115	Fire Maker	115	55,440	1:10.00	
1989	Bite the Bullet	2	J.A. Santos	115	Graf	115	For Really	113	54,720	1:09.80	
1990	Formal Dinner	2	J.A. Santos	115	Beadaspic	115	Link	117	55,260	1:10.20	
1991	Caller I.D.	2	J.D. Sellers	122	Pick up the Phone	119	Money Run	115	69,000	1:10.80	98
1992	Mountain Cat	2	P. Day	119	Satellite Signal	115	Rule Sixteen	115	73,440	1:10.60	84
1993	Dehere	2	C.J. McCarron	122	Prenup	115	Distinct Reality	122	68,520	1:10.40	90
1994	Montreal Red	2	Santos JA	115	Boone's Mill	115	De Niro	122	64,620	1:10.40	93
1995	Maria's Mon	2	Davis RG	115	Seeker's Reward	115	Frozen Ice	112	68,340	1:10.80	90
1996	Kelly Kip	2	J.L. Samyn	118	Boston Harbor	118	Say Florida Sandy	115	66,840	1:10.20	107
1997	Polished Brass	2	P. Day	116	Double Honor	116	Jigadee	116	65,520	1:10.20	92
1998	Time Bandit	2	P. Day	119	Prime Directive	117	Texas Glitter	117	66,480	1:11.40	89
1999	More Than Ready	2	J.R. Velazquez	122	Mighty	114	Bulling	114	64,560	1:09.60	105
2000	City Zip	2	J.A. Santos	119	Yonaguska	119	Scorpion	114	65,220	1:10.69	90
2001	Buster's Daydream	2	J.R. Velazquez	122	Seeking the Money	117	Heavyweight Champ	117	64,680	1:10.55	96
2002	Whywhywhy	2	E.S. Prado	122	Wildcat Heir	118	Spite the Devil	118	90,000	1:10.40	93
2003	Chapel Royal	2	J.R. Velazquez	122	Blushing Indian	118	Flushing Meadows	118	90,000	1:10.74	100
2004	Afleet Alex	2	J. Rose	120	Flamenco	122	Consolidator	118	90,000	1:09.32	102

Beyer Index: 94.93

SANTA ANA HANDICAP (G2), 1 1/8 Miles (Turf), Fillies and Mares, 4-Year-Olds and Up, Santa Anita, 2004 Purse: $150,000

Year	Winner	Age	Jockey	Wt.	Second	Wt.	Third	Wt.	Win Value	Time	Beyer
1968	Gabby Abby	5	J. Lambert	118	Pink Pigeon	120	Luz Del Sol	115	17,250	1:47.60	
1969	Miss Ribot	4	D. Pierce	122	Desert Law	119	Third Market	111	16,450	1:48.60	
1970	Boughs o'Holly	5	J. Lambert	115	Luz Del Sol	122	Gay Year	115	19,550	1:47.20	
1971	Mizzle	5	J. Lambert	114	Tipping Times	120	Sight to See	110	19,300	1:48.20	
1972	Street Dancer	5	W. Shoemaker	124	Minstrel Miss	115	Balcony's Babe	117	20,100	1:47.00	
1973	Bird Boots	4	E. Belmonte	115	Best Go	119	Resolutely	115	15,600	1:47.00	
1973	Minstrel Miss	6	D. Pierce	119	Rich Return II	118	Hill Circus	124	15,300	1:46.80	
1974	Belle Marie	4	W. Shoemaker	118	Grasping	114	Flying Fur	115	26,800	1:46.60	
1975	Move Abroad	4	S. Hawley	115	Joli Vert	114	Bold Ballet	122	19,500	1:51.40	
1976	Sun Festival	7	D. Pierce	116	Quaze Quilt	122	Cut Class	117	25,450	1:48.40	
1977	Up to Juliet	4	L. Pincay Jr	120	Quintas Fannie	114	Belle o' Reason	115	27,550	1:48.00	
1978	Kittyluck	5	F. Toro	115	Innuendo	111	Belle o' Reason	120	26,750	1:53.00	
1979	Waya	5	A. Cordero Jr	127	Amazer	123	Shua	115	38,450	1:48.20	
1980	The Very One	5	C. Cooke	117	Sisterhood	118	Mairzy Doates	116	37,300	1:48.40	
1981	Queen to Conquer	5	L. Pincay Jr	121	Track Robbery	119	Ack's Secret	123	46,900	1:48.00	
1982	Track Robbery	6	E. Delahoussaye	123	Manzanera	117	Ack's Secret	123	65,100	1:47.20	
1983	Happy Bride	5	C.J. McCarron	116	Avigaition	121	Miss Huntington	115	63,400	1:47.80	
1984	Avigaition	5	W. Shoemaker	118	Pride of Rosewood	116	L'Attrayante	122	93,600	1:48.40	
1985	Estrapade	5	F. Toro	123	Fact Finder	119	Air Distingue	116	67,100	1:47.00	
1986	Videogenic	4	R.G. Davis	120	Capichi	118	Water Crystals	114	62,800	1:48.40	
1987	Reloy	4	W. Shoemaker	116	Northern Aspen	119	North Sider	120	91,300	1:48.00	
1988	Pen Bal Lady	4	E. Delahoussaye	118	Fitzwilliam Place	119	Galunpe	119	94,900	1:47.20	
1989	Maria Jesse	4	G.L. Stevens	116	Fieldy	117	Claire Marine	115	97,100	1:47.20	
1990	Annoconnor	6	C.A. Black	119	Royal Touch	121	Brown Bess	123	94,500	1:47.80	103
1991	Noble and Nice	5	K.J. Desormeaux	113							
	Annual Reunion	4	G.L. Stevens	116			Bequest	117	63,400	1:46.60	103
1992	Gravieres	4	G.L. Stevens	116	Appealing Missy	117	Explosive Ele	115	94,900	1:47.60	104
1993	Exchange	5	L. Pincay Jr	120	Party Cited	116	Villandry	116	89,700	1:46.20	103
1994	Possibly Perfect	4	K.J. Desormeaux	119	Hero's Love	120	Lady Blessington	120	91,000	1:51.00	103
1995	Wandesta	4	C.S. Nakatani	115	Yearly Tour	116	Aube Indienne	120	90,700	1:50.00	104
1996	Pharma	5	C.J. McCarron	116	Angel in My Heart	120	Matiara	120	95,650	1:49.00	105
1997	Windsharp	6	E. Delahoussaye	121	Wheatly Special	114	Donna Viola	120	97,750	1:49.40	100
1998	Fiji	4	K.J. Desormeaux	115	Shake The Yoke	116	Golden Arches	120	96,480	1:49.80	106
1999	See You Soon	5	K.J. Desormeaux	119	Blending Element	116	La Madame	116	90,000	1:49.40	103
2000	Spanish Fern	5	V. Espinoza	119	Virginie	120	Country Garden	116	97,830	1:49.30	98
2001	Beautiful Noise	5	C.J. McCarron	115	High Walden	114	Matiere Grise	113	90,000	1:47.27	100
2002	Golden Apples	4	G.K. Gomez	119	Starine	122	Astra	122	90,000	1:47.05	105
2003	Noches de Rosa	5	M.E. Smith	115	Garden in the Rain	116	Megahertz	117	90,000	1:48.31	100
2004	Katdogawn	4	M.E. Smith	117	Fun House	118	Arabic Song	117	90,000	1:47.36	98

Megahertz finished first but was disqualified and placed seventh

Beyer Index: 102.33

SANTA ANITA DERBY (G1), 1 1/8 Miles, 3-Year-Olds, Santa Anita, 2004 Purse: $750,000

Year	Winner	Age	Jockey	Wt.	Second	Wt.	Third	Wt.	Win Value	Time	Beyer
1935	Gillie	3	S. Coucci	126	Whiskolo	126	Demonstration	126	19,650	1:44.60	
1936	He Did	3	W.D. Wright	126	Valiant Fox	126	Gold Seeker	121	26,000	1:49.40	
1937	Fairy Hill	3	M. Peters	121	Military	121	Ptolemy	121	45,425	1:45.80	
1938	Stagehand	3	J. Westrope	118	Dauber	118	Sun Egret	118	42,350	1:50.40	
1939	Ciencia	3	C. Bierman	115	Xalapa Clown	120	Impound	120	41,850	1:50.60	
1940	Sweepida	3	R. Neves	120	Royal Crusader	120	Weigh Anchor	120	43,850	1:51.60	
1941	Porter's Cap	3	L. Haas	120	Bull Reigh	120	Copperman	120	44,975	1:54.40	
1945	Bymeabond	3	G. Woolf	119	Busher	121	Best Effort	126	37,250	1:50.00	
1946	Knockdown	3	R. Permane	122	Star Pilot	122	Honeymoon	117	74,680	1:50.60	
1947	On Trust	3	J. Longden	118	W.L. Sickle	118	Tropical Sea	118	81,750	2:03.20	
1948	Salmagundi	3	J. Longden	118	Call Bell	118	Drum Beat	118	79,850	1:51.20	
1949	Old Rockport	3	G. Glisson	118	Olympia	118	Admiral Lea	118	94,700	1:50.20	
1950	Your Host	3	J. Longden	118	Sturdy One	118	Great Circle	118	89,800	1:48.80	
1951	Rough 'n Tumble	3	E. Arcaro	118	Interpretation	118	Aegean	118	81,500	1:50.40	
1952	Hill Gail	3	T. Atkinson	118	Windy City II	118	Arroz	118	92,900	1:50.00	
1953	Chanlea	3	E. Arcaro	118	Merryman	118	Correspondent	118	84,500	1:49.80	
1954	Determine	3	R. York	118	Duke's Lea	118	Travertine	118	84,800	1:48.80	
1955	Swaps	3	J. Longden	118	Jean's Joe	118	Blue Ruler	118	90,400	1:50.00	
1956	Terrang	3	W. Shoemaker	118	Social Climber	118	More Glory	118	111,700	1:51.00	
1957	Sir William	3	H. Moreno	118	Swirling Abbey	118	Round Table	118	9,500	1:54.20	
1958	Silky Sullivan	3	W. Shoemaker	118	Harcall	118	Aliwar	118	83,400	1:49.40	
1959	Silver Spoon	3	R. York	113	Royal Orbit	118	Fightin Indian	118	95,300	1:49.00	
1960	Tompion	3	W. Shoemaker	118	John William	118	Eagle Admiral	118	83,300	1:47.80	
1961	Four-and-Twenty	3	J. Longden	118	Ronnie's Ace	118	Flutterby	118	100,100	1:48.00	

Year	Winner	Age	Jockey	Wt.	Second	Wt.	Third	Wt.	Win Value	Time	Beyer
1962	Royal Attack	3	E. Burns	118	Admiral's Voyage	118	Sir Ribot	118	107,100	1:49.60	
1963	Candy Spots	3	W. Shoemaker	118	Sky Gem	118	Round Rock	118	98,300	1:50.20	
1964	Hill Rise	3	D. Pierce	118	Knightly Manner	118	Wil Rad	118	87,400	1:47.40	
1965	Lucky Debonair	3	W. Shoemaker	118	Jacinto	118	Charger's Kin	118	89,300	1:47.00	
1966	Boldnesian	3	W. Blum	118	Saber Mountain	118	Exhibitionist	118	96,900	1:48.40	
1967	Ruken	3	F. Alvarez	118	Tumble Wind	118	Sand Devil	118	94,900	1:49.80	
1968	Alley Fighter	3	L. Pincay Jr	120	Don B.	120	Dewan	120	102,100	1:49.00	
1969	Majestic Prince	3	W. Hartack	120	Mr. Joe F.	120	Lonny's Secret	120	87,200	1:49.20	
1970	Terlago	3	W. Shoemaker	120	George Lewis	120	Aggressively	120	96,400	1:48.40	
1971	Jim French	3	A. Cordero Jr	120	Unconscious	120	Vegas Vic	120	88,400	1:48.20	
1972	Solar Salute	3	L. Pincay Jr	120	Quack	120	Royal Owl	120	88,000	1:47.60	
1973	Sham	3	L. Pincay Jr	120	Linda's Chief	120	Out of the East	120	79,400	1:47.00	
1974	Destroyer	3	I. Valenzuela	120	Aloha Mood	120	Agitate	120	85,200	1:48.80	
1975	Avatar	3	J. Tejeira	120	Rock of Ages	120	Diabolo	120	82,900	1:47.60	
1976	An Act	3	L. Pincay Jr	120	Double Discount	120	Life's Hope	120	97,700	1:48.00	
1977	Habitony	3	W. Shoemaker	120	For the Moment	120	Steve's Friend	120	131,000	1:48.20	
1978	Affirmed	3	L. PIncay Jr	120	Balzac	120	Think Snow	120	127,300	1:48.00	
1979	Flying Paster	3	D. Pierce	120	Beau's Eagle	120	Switch Partners	120	124,900	1:48.00	
1980	Codex	3	P.A. Valenzuela	120	Rumbo	120	Vic's Gold	120	117,200	1:47.60	
1981	Splendid Spruce	3	D.G. McHargue	120	Johnlee n' Harold	120	Hoedown's Day	120	180,600	1:49.00	
1982	Muttering	3	L. Pincay Jr	120	Prince Spellbound	120	Journey at Sea	120	188,300	1:47.60	
1983	Marfa	3	J. Velasquez	120	My Habitony	120	Naevus	120	198,000	1:49.40	
1984	Mighty Adversary	3	E. Delahoussaye	120	Precisionist	120	Prince True	120	189,700	1:49.00	
1985	Skywalker	3	L. Pincay Jr	122	Fast Account	122	Nostalgia's Star	122	219,500	1:48.40	
1986	Snow Chief	3	A. Solis	122	Icy Groom	122	Ferdinand	122	275,000	1:48.60	
1987	Temperate Sil	3	W. Shoemaker	122	Masterful Advocate	122	Something Lucky	122	278,250	1:49.00	
1988	Winning Colors	3	G.L. Stevens	117	Lively One	122	Mi Preferido	122	275,000	1:47.80	
1989	Sunday Silence	3	P.A. Valenzuela	122	Flying Continental	122	Music Merci	122	275,000	1:47.60	
1990	Mister Frisky	3	G.L. Stevens	122	Video Ranger	122	Warcraft	122	275,000	1:49.00	109
1991	Dinard	3	C.J. McCarron	122	Best Pal	122	Sea Cadet	122	275,000	1:48.00	108
1992	A.P. Indy	3	E. Delahoussaye	122	Bertrando	122	Casual Lies	122	275,000	1:49.25	95
1993	Personal Hope	3	G.L. Stevens	122	Union City	122	Eliza	117	275,000	1:49.03	98
1994	Brocco	3	G.L. Stevens	122	Tabasco Cat	122	Strodes Creek	122	275,000	1:48.33	105
1995	Larry the Legend	3	G.L. Stevens	122	Afternoon Deelites	122	Jumron	122	385,000	1:47.99	106
1996	Cavonnier	3	C.J. McCarron	122	Honour and Glory	122	Corker	122	600,000	1:48.91	104
	Alyrob finished second but was disqualified and placed eighth										
1997	Free House	3	K.J. Desormeaux	122	Silver Charm	122	Hello	122	450,000	1:47.60	110
1998	Indian Charlie	3	G.L. Stevens	122	Real Quiet	122	Artax	122	450,000	1:47.00	111
1999	General Challenge	3	G.L. Stevens	122	Prime Timber	122	Desert Hero	122	450,000	1:48.92	108
2000	The Deputy	3	C.J. McCarron	122	War Chant	122	Captain Steve	122	600,000	1:49.08	109
2001	Point Given	3	G.L. Stevens	122	Crafty C.T.	122	I Love Silver	122	450,000	1:47.77	110
2002	Came Home	3	C. McCarron	122	Easy Grades	122	Lusty Latin	122	450,000	1:50.02	96
2003	Buddy Gil	3	G.L. Stevens	122	Indian Express	122	Kafwain	122	450,000	1:49.36	104
2004	Castledale	3	J. Valdivia Jr	122	Imperialism	122	Rock Hard Ten	122	450,000	1:49.24	103
	Rock Hard Ten finished second but was disqualified and placed third										

Beyer Index: 105.07

Distance 1 1/16 miles prior to 1938; 1 1/4 miles, 1947

SANTA ANITA HANDICAP (G1), 1 1/4 Miles, 4-Year-Olds and Up, Santa Anita, 2004 Purse: $1,000,000

Year	Winner	Age	Jockey	Wt.	Second	Wt.	Third	Wt.	Win Value	Time	Beyer
1935	Azucar	7	G. Woolf	117	Ladysman	117	Time Supply	118	108,400	2:02.20	
1936	Top Row	5	W.D. Wright	116	Time Supply	114	Rosemont	116	104,600	2:04.20	
1937	Rosemont	5	H. Richards	124	Seabiscuit	114	Indian Broom	116	90,700	2:02.80	
1938	Stagehand	3	N. Wall	100	Seabiscuit	130	Pompoon	120	91,450	2:01.60	
1939	Kayak II	4	J. Adams	110	Whichcee	112	Main Man	117	91,100	2:01.40	
1940	Seabiscuit	7	J. Pollard	130	Kayak II	129	Whichcee	114	86,650	2:01.80	
1941	Bay View	4	N. Wall	108	Mioland	124	Bolingbroke	106	89,360	2:05.40	
1945	Thumbs Up	6	J. Longden	130	Texas Sandman	116	Gay Dalton	126	82,925	2:01.20	
1946	War Knight	6	J. Adams	115	First Fiddle	126	Snow Boots	112	101,220	2:01.60	
1947	Olhaverry	8	M. Petersen	116	Stitch Again	112	Pere Time	108	98,900	2:01.80	
1948	Talon	6	E. Arcaro	122	On Trust	121	Double Jay	118	102,500	2:03.40	
1949	Vulcan's Forge	4	D. Gorman	119	Dinner Gong	116	Miss Grillo	116	102,000	2:02.80	
1950	Noor	5	J. Longden	114	Citation	132	Two Lea	113	97,900	2:00.00	
1951	Moonrush	5	J. Longden	114	Next Move	116	Sudan	111	97,900	2:02.60	
1952	Miche	7	E. Arcaro	130	Intent	111	Be Fleet	114	104,100	2:01.00	
	Intent finished first but was disqualified and placed second										
1953	Mark-Ye-Well	4	E. Arcaro	130	Trusting	112	First Glance	113	97,900	2:01.20	
1954	Rejected	4	W. Shoemaker	118	Imbros	120	Cyclotron	116	105,900	2:00.60	
1955	Poona II	4	J. Longden	118	Joe Jones	117	Porterhouse	112	103,200	2:03.00	
1956	Bobby Brocato	4	W. Shoemaker	113	Turk's Delight	107	Honeys Alibi	114	97,900	2:04.60	

Year	Winner	Age	Jockey	Wt.	Second	Wt.	Third	Wt.	Win Value	Time	Beyer
1957	Corn Husker	4	R. Neves	105	Holandes II	121	Spinney	108	103,600	2:01.80	
1958	Round Table	4	W. Shoemaker	130	Terrang	119	Porterhouse	120	97,900	1:59.80	
1959	Terrang	6	W. Boland	116	Hillsdale	113	Royal Living	111	97,900	2:00.00	
1960	Linmold	4	D. Pierce	110	Fleet Nasrullah	113	Amerigo	120	97,900	2:00.60	
1961	Prove It	4	W. Shoemaker	115	Oink	110	Grey Eagle	108	100,000	2:00.00	
1962	Physician	5	D. Pierce	114	Olden Times	113	Four-and-Twenty	129	100,000	2:02.60	
1963	Crozier	5	B. Baeza	122	Crimson Satan	125			100,000	2:00.80	
					Game	108					
1964	Mr. Consistency	6	K. Church	120	Doc Jocoy	117	Cyrano	125	102,100	2:01.00	
1965	Hill Rise	4	D. Pierce	120	Candy Spots	127	George Royal	114	100,000	2:00.60	
1966	Lucky Debonair	4	W. Shoemaker	124	Cupid	117	Native Diver	126	100,000	2:00.20	
1967	Pretense	4	W. Shoemaker	118	Native Diver	125	O'Hara	113	100,000	2:00.80	
1968	Mr. Right	5	M. Yanez	115	Jungle Road	117	Ala Ram	111	100,000	2:04.60	
1969	Nodouble	4	E. Belmonte	122	Gamely	122	Quicken Tree	126	100,000	2:01.80	
1970	Quicken Tree	7	F. Alvarez	118	Fiddle Isle	119	Field Master	114	100,000	1:59.60	
1971	Ack Ack	5	W. Shoemaker	130	Cougar II	125	The Field	109	100,000	2:03.00	
1972	Triple Bend	4	D. Pierce	119	Cougar II	126	Unconscious	127	105,000	2:00.00	
1973	Cougar II	7	L. Pincay Jr	126	Kennedy Road	119	Cabin	110	105,000	2:00.00	
1974	Prince Dantan	4	R. Turcotte	119	Ancient Title	125	Big Spruce	122	105,000	2:03.60	
1975	Stardust Mel	4	W. Shoemaker	123	Out of the East	112	Okavango	116	105,500	2:06.40	
1976	Royal Glint	6	J. Tejeira	124	Ancient Title	124	Lightning Mandate	120	155,900	2:00.40	
1977	Crystal Water	4	L. Pincay Jr	122	Faliraki	114	King Pellinore	130	173,550	1:59.20	
1978	Vigors	5	D.G. McHargue	127	Mr. Redoy	120	Jumping Hill	115	100,000	2:01.20	
1979	Affirmed	4	L. Pincay Jr	128	Tiller	127	Painted Wagon	115	192,800	1:58.60	
							Exceller	127			
1980	Spectacular Bid	4	W. Shoemaker	130	Flying Paster	123	Beau's Eagle	122	190,000	2:00.60	
1981	John Henry	6	L. Pincay Jr	128	King Go Go	117	Exploded	115	238,150	1:59.40	
1982	John Henry	7	W. Shoemaker	130	Perrault	126	It's the One	123	310,000	1:59.00	
	Perrault finished first but was disqualified and placed second										
1983	Bates Motel	4	T. Lipham	118	It's the One	123	Wavering Monarch	121	317,350	1:59.60	
1984	Interco	4	P.A. Valenzuela	121	Journey at Sea	117	Gato Del Sol	117	298,650	2:00.60	
1985	Lord at War	5	W. Shoemaker	125	Greinton	120	Gate Dancer	125	275,600	2:00.60	
1986	Greinton	5	L. Pincay Jr	122	Herat	112	Hatim	118	689,500	2:00.00	
1987	Broad Brush	4	A. Cordero Jr	122	Ferdinand	125	Hopeful Word	117	550,000	2:00.60	
1988	Alysheba	4	C.J. McCarron	126	Ferdinand	127	Super Diamond	124	550,000	1:59.80	
1989	Martial Law	4	M. Pedroza	113	Triteamtri	116	Stylish Winner	113	550,000	1:58.80	
1990	Ruhlmann	5	G.L. Stevens	121	Criminal Type	119	Flying Continental	121	550,000	2:01.20	118
1991	Farma Way	4	G.L. Stevens	120	Festin	115	Pleasant Tap	115	550,000	2:00.20	118
1992	Best Pal	4	K.J. Desormeaux	124	Twilight Agenda	124	Defensive Play	115	550,000	1:59.00	123
1993	Sir Beaufort	3	P.A. Valenzuela	119	Star Recruit	117	Major Impact	114	550,000	2:00.55	112
1994	Stuka	4	C.W. Antley	115	Bien Bien	120	Myrakalu	114	550,000	2:00.17	111
	The Wicked North finished first but was disqualified and placed fourth										
1995	Urgent Request	5	G.L. Stevens	116	Best Pal	122	Dare and Go	120	550,000	1:59.25	113
1996	Mr Purple	4	E. Delahoussaye	116	Luthier Fever	114	Just Java	114	600,000	2:02.04	112
1997	Siphon	6	D.R. Flores	120	Sandpit	121	Gentlemen	123	600,000	2:00.23	120
1998	Malek	5	A. Solis	115	Bagshot	113	Don't Blame Rio	117	600,000	2:02.26	108
1999	Free House	5	C.J. McCarron	123	Event of the Year	119	Silver Charm	124	600,000	2:00.67	119
2000	General Challenge	4	C.S. Nakatani	121	Budroyale	122	Puerto Madero	118	600,000	2:01.49	117
2001	Tiznow	4	C.J.McCarron	122	Wooden Phone	117	Tribunal	116	600,000	2:01.55	117
2002	Milwaukee Brew	5	K.J. Desormeaux	115	Western Pride	116	Kudos	116	600,000	2:01.02	116
2003	Milwaukee Brew	6	E.S. Prado	119	Congaree	124	Kudos	117	600,000	1:59.80	116
2004	Southern Image	4	V. Espinoza	118	Island Fashion	115	Saint Buddy	111	600,000	2:01.64	113

Beyer Index: 115.53

SANTA ANITA OAKS (G1), 1 1/16 Miles, 3-Year-Old Fillies, Santa Anita, 2004 Purse: $300,000

Year	Winner	Age	Jockey	Wt.	Second	Wt.	Third	Wt.	Win Value	Time	Beyer
1935	Dunlin Lady	2	W. Saunders	119	Rattlebrain	119	Reelon	118	2,375	:34.00	
1937	Patty Cake	3	A. Gray	113	Alice G.	113	Coramine	116	3,305	1:12.20	
1938	Minulus	3	C. Corbett	109	First Kiss	111	Midwick	112	4,775	1:11.80	
1939	Sweet Nancy	3	J. Longden	112	Ciencia	112	Morning Breeze	118	10,050	1:25.60	
1940	Augury	3	L. Knapp	121	Less Time	112	Wanna Hygro	112	9,450	1:25.20	
1941	Cute Trick	3	B. James	112	Appeasement	112	Transient	112	9,800	1:23.60	
1945	Busher	3	J. Longden	121	Mist	115	Glory Time	115	18,605	1:23.60	
1946	Enfilade	3	A. Kirkland	117	Honeymoon	121	Lovonsite	111	19,440	1:11.00	
1947	Hubble Bubble	3	B. Layton	113	Maharetta	113	Judy-Rae	117	36,500	1:23.80	
1948	Mrs. Rabbit	3	R. Permane	115	Itsabet	118	Candy Kane	118	41,000	1:24.00	
1949	Gaffery	3	W. Litzenberg	118	June Bride	115	Patmigal	115	45,400	1:24.60	
1950	Special Touch	3	E. Arcaro	115	Talking Point	115	Sea Garden	115	46,000	1:23.80	
1951	Ruth Lily	3	J. Adams	115	Sickle's Image	121	Sweet Talk	115	41,700	1:23.40	
	Sweet Talk finished first but was disqualified and placed third										

Year	Winner	Age	Jockey	Wt.	Second	Wt.	Third	Wt.	Win Value	Time	Beyer
1952	Season's Best	3	A. Kolonics	114	Hadassah	108	Your Hostess	117	13,400	1:45.20	
1953	Femme Fatale	3	R. York	111	Schatzi	108	Ramasari	112	13,150	1:45.00	
1954	Quillo Maid	3	J. Phillippi	114	Frosty Dawn	121	Love Factor	119	13,400	1:36.60	
1956	Dupatta	3	R. Trejos	112	Chargers Girl	116	Mrs. Muriel L.	116	11,250	1:24.60	
1957	Market Basket	3	I. Valenzuela	118	Royal Rasher	114	Tourbillonte	116	13,700	1:37.40	
1958	Penumbra	3	W. Boland	112	Well Away	110	Nushie	112	14,100	1:44.80	
1959	Silver Spoon	3	R. York	117	Miss Uppity	117	Bitter Feud	110	13,250	1:41.80	
1960	Darling June	3	D. Pierce	117	Angel Flight	111	Salt Lake	112	13,950	1:44.00	
1961	Fun House	3	G. Taniguchi	111	Oil Royalty	111	Amri-An	117	13,900	1:43.00	
1962	Pixie Erin	3	J. Longden	114	Lincoln Center	112	Dors	112	17,150	1:46.00	
1963	Lamb Chop	3	M. Ycaza	115	Nalee	115	Curious Clover	115	16,150	1:46.40	
1964	Blue Norther	3	W. Shoemaker	115	Face the Facts	115	Roman Goddess	115	26,300	1:41.80	
1965	Desert Love	3	D. Pierce	115	Ardell C.	115	Admiring	115	27,750	1:42.60	
1966	Spearfish	3	D. Pierce	115	Ego Twist	115	Will Hall	115	2,900	1:43.00	
1967	Fish House	3	W. Shoemaker	115	Mira Femme	115			27,800	1:44.20	
					Spinning Around	115					
1968	Allie's Serenade	3	L. Pincay Jr	115	Fish Net	115	Miss Ribot	115	26,550	1:43.20	
1969	Dumpty's Lady	3	W. Shoemaker	115	Hasty Hitter	115	Lover's Quarrel	115	25,900	1:46.00	
1970	Opening Bid	3	D. Pierce	115	Cathy Honey	115	Turn 'n Turn About	115	27,300	1:42.20	
1971	Turkish Trousers	3	W. Shoemaker	115	Generous Portion	115	Sapose Speed	115	31,650	1:42.80	
1972	Susan's Girl	3	V. Teiada	115	Dumpty's Dream	115	Chargerette	115	32,300	1:43.00	
1973	Belle Marie	3	L. Pincay Jr	115	Tallahto	115	Waltz Fan	115	31,800	1:41.80	
1974	Miss Musket	3	W. Shoemaker	115	Out to Lunch	115	Special Team	115	32,800	1:47.00	
1975	Sarsar	3	W. Shoemaker	115	Double You Lou	115	Fascinating Girl	115	33,100	1:42.80	
1976	Girl in Love	3	F. Toro	115	I'm a Charmer	115	Queen to be	115	32,700	1:43.20	
1977	Sound of Summer	3	F. Toro	115	Wavy Waves	115	Lady T.V.	115	33,200	1:42.20	
1978	Grenzen	3	D.G. McHargue	115	Equanimity	115	Mashteen	115	47,800	1:43.80	
1979	Caline	3	W. Shoemaker	115	Terlingua	115	It's in the Air	115	69,000	1:41.60	
1980	Bold 'n Determined	3	E. Delahoussaye	115	Street Ballet	115	Table Hands	115	67,100	1:41.20	
1981	Nell's Briquette	3	W. Shoemaker	115	Bee a Scout	115	Ice Princess	115	82,550	1:42.80	
1982	Blush With Pride	3	W. Shoemaker	115	Skillful Joy	115	Carry a Tune	115	100,400	1:45.80	
1983	Fabulous Notion	3	D. Pierce	115	Capichi	115	O'Happy Day	115	93,900	1:43.60	
1984	Althea	3	L. Pincay Jr	117	Personable Lady	117	Life's Magic	117	118,500	1:43.60	
1985	Fran's Valentine	3	P.A. Valenzuela	117	Rascal Lass	117	Wising Up	117	122,100	1:42.40	
1986	Hidden Light	3	W. Shoemaker	117	Twilight Ridge	117	An Empress	117	120,200	1:42.40	
1987	Timely Assertion	3	G.L. Stevens	117	Buryyourbelief	117	Very Subtle	117	95,100	1:43.60	
1988	Winning Colors	3	G.L. Stevens	117	Jeanne Jones	117	Goodbye Halo	117	89,900	1:42.00	
1989	Imaginary Lady	3	G.L. Stevens	117	Some Romance	117	Kool Arrival	117	125,400	1:43.40	
1990	Hail Atlantis	3	G.L. Stevens	117	Bright Candles	117	Fit to Scout	117	122,800	1:43.00	97
1991	Lite Light	3	C.S. Nakatani	117	Garden Gal	117	Ifyoucouldseemenow	117	122,100	1:42.40	100
1992	Golden Treat	3	K.J. Desormeaux	117	Magical Maiden	117	Queens Court Queen	117	129,300	1:43.37	90
1993	Eliza	3	P.A. Valenzuela	117	Stalcreek	117	Dance for Vanny	117	129,200	1:42.97	99
1994	Lakeway	3	K.J. Desormeaux	117	Dianes Halo	117	Flying in the Lane	117	122,800	1:41.66	101
1995	Serena's Song	3	C.S. Nakatani	117	Urbane	117	Mari's Sheba	117	121,600	1:42.71	106
1996	Antespend	3	C.W. Antley	117	Cara Rafaela	117	Hidden Lake	117	128,600	1:43.04	99
1997	Sharp Cat	3	C.S. Nakatani	117	Queen of Money	117	Double Park	117	128,800	1:42.22	101
1998	Hedonist	3	K.J. Desormeaux	117	Keeper Hill	117	Nijinsky's Passion	117	150,000	1:44.14	91
1999	Excellent Meeting	3	K.J. Desormeaux	117	Tout Charmant	117	Gleefully	117	150,000	1:43.26	96
2000	Surfside	3	P. Day	117	Kumari Continent	117	Classy Cara	117	180,000	1:44.03	93
2001	Golden Ballet	3	C.J. McCarron	117	Flute	117	Affluent	117	180,000	1:41.83	101
2002	You	3	J.D. Bailey	117	Habibti	117	Ile de France	117	180,000	1:42.70	99
2003	Composure	3	J.D. Bailey	117	Elloluv	117	Go for Glamour	117	180,000	1:43.34	102
2004	Silent Sighs	3	D.R. Flores	117	Halfbridled	117	A.P. Adventure	117	180,000	1:42.84	96

Beyer Index: 98.07

Distance 3 furlongs (for 2-year-olds) in 1935; 6 furlongs, 1937-38, 1946; 7 furlongs, 1939-51, 1956; 1 mile in 1954, 1957. Run as Santa Susana Stakes, 1935-51, 1959-85

SANTA BARBARA HANDICAP (G2), 1 1/4 Miles (Turf), Fillies and Mares, 4-Year-Olds and Up, Santa Anita, 2004 Purse: $200,000

Year	Winner	Age	Jockey	Wt.	Second	Wt.	Third	Wt.	Win Value	Time	Beyer
1937	Balking	2	L. Knapp	119	Mainstay	122	Inhale	119	3,580	:33.20	
							Roy T.	122			
1938	Galley Slave	2	R. Workman	119	Batter	122	Likely Lad	122	5,450	:34.40	
1941	Chiquita Mia	2	L. Haas	119	Bold Lucy	119	Doctor Reder	122	6,795	:33.80	
1941	Black Raider	2	L. Balaski	117	Thumbs Up	122	Hooks	122	6,345	:33.60	
1946	Whirlabout	5	T. Atkinson	118	Blue Alibi	112	Canina	112	18,200	1:23.00	
1952	Last Greetings	3	E. Arcaro	119	Season's Best	110	Wild Glory	110	10,900	1:24.60	
1953	De Anza	3	R. Neves	122	Hour Regards	119	Singan	117	12,350	1:10.40	
1954	Frosty Dawn	3	E. Arcaro	116	Sweet as Honey	110	Heather Khal	119	9,350	1:09.60	

Year	Winner	Age	Jockey	Wt.	Second	Wt.	Third	Wt.	Win Value	Time	Beyer
1955	Berseem	5	J. Longden	120	Joe Jones	117	Dawn Lark	107	16,700	1:42.00	
1956	Porterhouse	5	E. Arcaro	116	Colonel Mack	113	Cycoltron	109	15,700	1:43.00	
1957	Pylades	4	R. Sterling	107	Terrang	124	Duc de Fer	120	16,500	1:42.00	
1958	Golden Notes	4	H. Moreno	117	Vino Supremo	112	How Now	117	13,300	1:13.60	
1962	Cat Call	5	B. Baeza	110	Tritoma	116	Barnesville Miss	119	17,350	2:03.00	
1963	Chicha	5	M. Ycaza	115	Barnesville Miss	116	Errcountess	114	17,150	2:02.60	
1964	Oil Royalty	6	J. Longden	121	Glory Hill	117	Curious Clover	121	18,400	2:00.60	
1965	Batteur	5	M. Ycaza	121	Curious Clover	121	Kisco Gal	110	21,200	1:58.40	
1966	Straight Deal	4	W. Shoemaker	122	Miss Rincon	107	Petticoat	113	28,350	1:58.80	
1967	April Dawn	4	W. Shoemaker	114	Pixy Gal II	113	Check Bye	114	20,750	2:01.20	
1967	Ormea	6	I. Valenzuela	114	Maintain	116	Miss Rincon	110	25,800	2:00.80	
1968	Amerigo's Fancy	6	J. Lambert	118	Gamely	128	Lady Pitt	115	25,800	2:02.40	
1968	Princessnesian	4	L. Pincay Jr	124	Amerigo Lady	122	Courageously	114	25,800	2:00.80	
1969	Pink Pigeon	5	D. Pierce	123	Desert Law	117	Gamely	129	34,550	1:58.20	
1970	Sallarina	4	W. Mahorney	112	Drumtop	121	Luz Del Sol	117	33,500	1:59.20	
1971	Manta	5	L. Pincay Jr	128	Hi Q.	113	TippingTime	117	38,700	2:00.20	
1972	Hail the Grey	5	E. Fires	112	Manta	125	Street Dancer	118	38,500	1:58.60	
1973	Susan's Girl	4	L. Pincay Jr	129	Veiled Desire	110	Gray Mirage	112	37,600	2:03.60	
1974	Tallahto	4	L. Pincay Jr	118	La Zanzara	120	Tizna	127	39,600	1:59.20	
1975	Gay Style	5	W. Shoemaker	125	Move Abroad	113	La Zanzara	117	316,000	2:01.40	
1976	Stravina	5	W. Shoemaker	109	Katonka	122	Tizna	127	38,600	1:59.60	
1977	Desiree	4	V. Centeno	110	Swingtime	120	Charger's Star	113	38,100	2:02.60	
1978	Kittyluck	5	L. Pincay Jr	116	Countess Fager	117	Sensational	120	40,100	2:00.60	
1979	Waya	5	A. Cordero Jr	131	Petron's Love	117	Island Kiss	112	49,100	2:01.00	
1980	Sisterhoos	5	L. Pincay Jr	118	Petron's Love	114	Relaxing	118	67,600	2:00.40	
1981	The Very One	6	J. Velasquez	122	Mairzy Doates	117	Ack's Secret	121	65,900	2:01.20	
1982	Ack's Secret	6	L. Pincay Jr	122	Landresse	116	Plenty O'Toole	114	78,550	2:00.60	
1983	Avigaition	4	E. Delahoussaye	121	Happy Bride	120	Comedy Act	116	78,650	1:59.80	
1984	Comedy Act	5	C.J. McCarron	116	L'Attrayante	122	Lido Isle	114	121,200	2:00.40	
1985	Fact Finder	6	G.L. Stevens	118	Love Smitten	117	Salt Spring	114	116,600	2:01.60	
1986	Mountain Bear	5	C.J. McCarron	119	Estrapade	124	Royal Regatta	116	119,300	2:01.00	
1987	Reloy	4	W. Shoemaker	120	Northern Aspen	119	Ivor's Image	119	97,600	2:00.00	
1988	Pen Bal Lady	4	E. Delahoussaye	119	Carotene	121	Galunpe	119	95,800	1:59.60	
1989	No Review	4	E. Delahoussaye	116	Galunpe	117	Annoconnor	121	128,800	2:02.60	
1990	Brown Bess	8	J.L. Kaenel	123	Royal Touch	121	Double Wedge	111	122,000	1:58.40	103
1991	Bequest	5	E. Delahoussaye	117	Noble and Nice	114	Annual Reunion	117	126,400	1:57.40	103
1992	Kostroma	6	K.J. Desormeaux	124	Miss Alleged	124	Free at Last	117	152,700	1:59.60	106
1993	Exchange	5	L. Pincay Jr	121	Trishyde	120	Revasser	114	120,400	2:02.20	105
1994	Possibly Perfect	4	K.J. Desormeaux	121	Pracer	115	Waitryst	114	122,800	2:00.40	103
1995	Wandesta	4	C.S. Nakatani	118	Yearly Tour	116	Morgana	116	126,400	2:01.60	104
1996	Auriette	4	K.J. Desormeaux	116	Angel In My Hart	119	Wandesta	121	190,900	2:02.00	107
1997	Donna Viola	5	G.L. Stevens	120	Fanjica	114	Windsharp	122	197,200	1:59.80	105
1998	Fiji	4	K.J. Desormeaux	119	Pomona	115	Ecoute	114	150,000	2:00.20	107
1999	Tranquility Lake	5	E. Delahoussaye	116	Virginie	118	Midnight Line	118	150,000	2:01.00	102
2000	Caffe Latte	4	C.S. Nakatani	116	Happyanunoit	121	Country Garden	116	150,000	2:00.51	107
2001	Astra	5	K.J. Desormeaux	118	Beautiful Noise	116	Uncharted Haven	116	150,000	2:01.33	106
2002	Astra	6	K.J. Desormeaux	121	Golden Apples	121	Polaire	115	150,000	2:01.40	100
2003	Megahertz	4	A. Solis	117	Trekking	111	Noches de Rosa	117	150,000	2:00.08	102
2004	Megahertz	5	A. Solis	121	Noches de Rosa	116	Mandela	111	120,000	2:00.71	100

Beyer Index: **104.00**

SANTA CATALINA (G2), 1 1/16 Miles, 3-Year-Olds, Santa Anita, 2004 Purse: $150,000

Year	Winner	Age	Jockey	Wt.	Second	Wt.	Third	Wt.	Win Value	Time	Beyer
1990	Music Prospector	3	F. Olivares	114	Senegalaise	114	Tsu's Dawning	120	46,950	1:43.60	
1991	Mane Minister	3	D.R. Flores	114	Conveyor	114	Famed Devil	114	48,375	1:42.60	93
1992	Vying Victor	3	C.A. Black	115	Turbulent Kris	114	Al Sabin	117	51,000	1:43.33	92
1993	Art of Living	3	G.L. Stevens	115	Tossofthecoin	115	Glowing Crown	115	45,900	1:43.48	91
1994	Wekiva Springs	3	K.J. Desormeaux	121	Gracious Ghost	116	Dream Trapp	117	45,900	1:41.94	97
1995	Larry the Legend	3	K.J. Desormeaux	118	In Character	115	Awesome Thoughts	119	45,975	1:42.93	95
1996	Prince of Thieves	3	G.L. Stevens	114	Smithfield	116	Matty G	124	64,250	1:42.94	103
1997	Hello	3	C.J. McCarron	120	Bagshot	116	Carmen's Baby	120	65,950	1:42.60	97
1998	Artax	3	C.J. McCarron	114	Souvenir Copy	120	Allen's Oop	117	64,320	1:42.32	109
1999	General Challenge	3	G.L. Stevens	117	Buck Trout	120	Brilliantly	115	63,900	1:42.93	95
2000	The Deputy	3	C.J. McCarron	115	High Yield	117	Captain Steve	123	64,380	1:43.04	103
2001	Millennium Wind	3	C.J. McCarron	114	Palmeiro	117	Denied	116	64,620	1:42.38	98
2002	Labamta Babe	3	K.J. Desormeaux	115	Siphonic	123	Cottonwood Cowboy	115	90,000	1:42.50	104
2003	Domestic Dispute	3	D.R. Flores	113	Our Bobby V.	113	Scrimshaw	115	90,000	1:42.20	103
2004	St Averil	3	T. Baze	113	Lucky Pulpit	115	Master David	113	90,000	1:41.62	102

Beyer Index: **98.71**

For prior runnings, refer to 1990 Manual.

SANTA MARGARITA INVITATIONAL HANDICAP (G1), 1 1/8 Miles, Fillies and Mares, 4-Year-Olds and Up, Santa Anita, 2004 Purse: $300,000

Year	Winner	Age	Jockey	Wt.	Second	Wt.	Third	Wt.	Win Value	Time	Beyer
1935	Ted Clark	5	C. Turk	101	Pitter Pat	104	Rock X.	104	2,150	1:26.40	
1936	Singing Wood	5	R. Jones	122	Tick On	113	Sound Advice	111	2,130	1:23.00	
1937	Stand Pat	6	W. Saunders	118	Party Spirit	110	Speed to Spare	105	3,145	1:13.00	
1938	Primulus	5	L. Balaski	112	Mars Shield	117	Watersplash	113	4,275	1:49.00	
1939	Flying Lee	4	S. Renick	106	Sweet Nancy	106	Genie Palatine	105	9,500	1:47.20	
1940	Fairy Chant	3	D. Dodson	103	Omelet	110	Sweet Nancy	108	9,000	1:46.80	
1941	Omelet	5	J. Westrope	116	Augury	120	Barrancosa	113	7,100	1:47.20	
1945	Busher	3	J. Longden	126	Whirlabout	123	Canina	117	36,490	1:43.00	
1946	Canina	5	J. Longden	121	Happy Issue	113	Be Faithful	115	39,300	1:43.40	
1947	Monsoon	5	R. Neves	114	Double F.F.	112	Be Faithful	122	3,800	1:43.00	
1948	Miss Doreen	6	J. Longden	116	Elpis	122	Miss Grillo	124	38,400	1:46.00	
1949	Lurline B.	4	W. Litzenberg	108	Danada Gift	112	Alablue	115	38,800	1:53.00	
1950	Two Lea	4	S. Brooks	126	Gaffery	118	But Why Not	116	35,700	1:52.80	
1951	Special Touch	4	W. Shoemaker	114	Bewitch	122	Bed o' Roses	125	36,400	1:48.60	
1952	Bed o' Roses	5	W. Shoemaker	129	Next Move	130	Toto	105	39,550	1:51.40	
1953	Spanish Cream	5	E. Guerin	128	Ruth Lily	112	A Gleam	130	36,800	1:44.80	
1954	Cerise Reine	4	W. Shoemaker	121	Last Wave	112	Wandering Ways	113	38,100	1:47.00	
1955	Blue Butterfly	6	J. Longden	121	Miz Clementine	130	Tessa	112	33,400	1:48.60	
1956	Our Betters	4	E. Arcaro	120	Island Queen	111	Solid Rae	113	34,500	1:49.20	
1957	Our Betters	5	J. Longden	118	Nooran	111	Miss Todd	116	35,600	1:49.00	
1958	Born Rich	5	M. Ycaza	113	Market Basket	123	Nooran	118	34,200	1:50.60	
1959	Bug Brush	4	A. Valenzuela	126	Milly K.	115	Penumbra	110	36,600	1:48.20	
1960	Silver Spoon	4	E. Arcaro	130	Indian Maid	116	Narva	113	34,800	1:48.80	
1961	Sister Antoine	4	W. Harmatz	113	Paris Pike	113	Geechee Lou	118	37,900	1:49.60	
1962	Queen America	6	G. Taniguchi	113	Oil Royalty	117	Tritoma	116	39,600	1:49.40	
1963	Pixie Erin	4	P. Moreno	116	Table Mate	119	Frimannaha	115	36,600	1:54.20	
1964	Curious Clover	4	K. Church	118	Hi Rated	116	Sintesis	118	29,075	1:48.80	
1964	Batteur	4	M. Ycaza	116	Jalousie II	119	Jazz Queen	116	29,075	1:49.00	
1965	Curious Clover	5	K. Church	118	Treachery	117	Petticoat	114	37,850	1:49.60	
1966	Straight Deal	4	W. Shoemaker	121	Pollen	119	Batteur	124	39,300	1:48.60	
1967	Miss Moona	4	L. Pincay Jr	118	Maintain	112	Streamer	114	39,800	1:50.20	
							Lost Message	112			
1968	Gamely	4	M. Ycaza	125	Princessnesian	120	Amerigo Lady	123	60,000	1:49.00	
1969	Princessnesian	5	D. Pierce	125	Guest Room	116	Sinking Spring	113	60,000	1:53.00	
1970	Gallant Bloom	4	J.L. Rotz	129	Commissary	117	Tipping Time	117	60,000	1:50.60	
1971	Manta	5	L. Pincay Jr	126	Beja	118	Last of the Line	123	60,000	1:48.80	
1972	Turkish Trousers	4	W. Shoemaker	125	Convenience	118	Typecast	124	60,000	1:47.80	
1973	Susan's Girl	4	L. Pincay Jr	125	Convenience	123	Minstrel Miss	115	60,000	1:47.80	
1974	Tizna	5	F. Toro	117	Penny Flight	113	Tallahto	119	60,000	1:50.80	
1975	Tizna	6	D. Pierce	120	Susan's Girl	123	Gay Style	125	60,000	1:48.60	
1976	Fascinating Girl	4	F. Toro	115	Summertime Promise	114	Charger's Star	114	60,000	1:49.40	
1977	Lucie Manet	4	D.G. McHargue	119	Bastonera II	126	Hope of Glory	114	60,000	1:48.40	
1978	Taisez Vous	4	D. Pierce	125	Sensational	118	Merry Lady III	114	60,000	1:49.00	
1979	Sanedki	5	W. Shoemaker	124	Surera	115	Ida Delia	117	75,000	1:47.80	
	Queen Yasna finished second but was disqualified and placed seventh										
1980	Glorious Song	4	C.J. McCarron	120	The Very One	116	Kankam	125	82,500	1:48.40	
1981	Princess Karenda	4	L. Pincay Jr	118	Glorious Song	130	Ack's Secret	122	120,000	1:47.20	
1982	Ack's Secret	6	L. Pincay Jr	118	Track Robbery	123	Past Forgetting	122	150,000	1:47.60	
1983	Marimbula	5	S. Hawley	119	Avigaition	120	Sintrillium	114	150,000	1:48.20	
1984	Adored	4	F. Toro	114	High Haven	118	Weekend Surprise	114	150,000	1:48.60	
1985	Lovlier Linda	5	C.J. McCarron	119	Mitterand	123	Percipient	115	180,000	1:48.00	
1986	Lady's Secret	4	J. Velasquez	125	Johnica	120	Dontstop Themusic	122	180,000	1:47.00	
1987	North Sider	5	A. Cordero Jr	117	Winter Treasure	115	Frau Altiva	117	180,000	1:48.80	
1988	Flying Julia	5	F. Olivares	114	Hollywood Glitter	118	Clabber Girl	118	180,000	1:50.40	
989	Bayakoa	5	L. Pincay Jr	118	Goodbye Halo	125	No Review	117	180,000	1:48.40	
1990	Bayakoa	6	C.J. McCarron	127	Gorgeous	125	Luthier's Launch	113	180,000	1:48.40	110
1991	Little Brianne	6	J.A. Garcia	119	Bayakoa	126	A Wild Ride	119	180,000	1:48.40	110
1992	Paseana	5	C.J. McCarron	122	Laramie Moon	116	Colour Chart	118	180,000	1:47.48	110
1993	Southern Truce	5	C.S. Nakatani	115	Paseana	125	Guiza	114	180,000	1:49.46	100
1994	Paseana	7	C.J. McCarron	123	Kalita Melody	117	Stalcreek	119	180,000	1:49.12	104
1995	Queens Court Queen	6	C.S. Nakatani	120	Paseana	123	Klassy Kim	116	180,000	1:48.81	99
1996	Twice the Vice	5	C.J. McCarron	117	Sleep Easy	115	Jewel Princess	119	180,000	1:49.53	101
1997	Jewel Princess	5	C.S. Nakatani	125	Top Rung	116	Hidden Lake	114	180,000	1:49.30	102
1998	Toda Una Dama	5	G.F. Almeida	114	Exotic Wood	123	Praviana	114	180,000	1:48.87	108
1999	Manistique	4	G.L Stevens	122	Magical Allure	118	India Divina	116	180,000	1:48.31	109
2000	Riboletta	5	C.S. Nakatani	115	Bordelaise	114	Snowberg	114	180,000	1:50.40	98
2001	Lazy Slusan	6	D.R. Flores	116	Spain	122	Critikola	116	180,000	1:48.59	99
2002	Azeri	4	M.E. Smith	115	Spain	118	Printemps	116	180,000	1:49.01	110
2003	Starrer	5	P.A. Valenzuela	121	Sightseek	116	Bella Bellucci	116	180,000	1:48.20	111
2004	Adoration	5	M.E. Smith	118	Star Parade	115	Bare Necessities	118	180,000	1:48.85	107

Beyer Index: 105.20

Distance 7 furlongs, 1935-36; 6 furlongs, 1937; 1 1/16 miles, 1938-48, 1953-54. For 3-year-olds and up, prior to 1941, 1942-60. Open to both sexes prior to 1938

SANTA MARIA HANDICAP (G1), 1 1/16 Miles, Fillies and Mares, 4-Year-Olds and Up, Santa Anita, 2004 Purse: $250,000

Year	Winner	Age	Jockey	Wt.	Second	Wt.	Third	Wt.	Win Value	Time	Beyer
1934	Wise Daughter	3	J. Westrope	104	Rock X,	104	Wacoche	101	2,180	1:12.40	
1935	Soon Over	4	S. Coucci	109	Sound Advice	112	Beefsteak	110	2,310	1:11.00	
1936	Papenie	3	L. Haas	110	Half Time	118	Grey Count	109	3,575	1:12.80	
1938	Sun Egret	3	A. Shelhamer	114	Short Notice	116	Specify	116	4,900	1:12.00	
1939	Porter's Mite	3	B. James	123	Sweet Patrice	109	Time Alone	120	9,500	1:12.40	
1940	Augury	3	L. Knapp	105	Camp Verde	120	Liberty Franc	111	10,250	1:14.40	
1941	Phar Rong	2	L. Haas	117	Pan Time	117	Fillibeg	114	8,130	:34.40	
1946	Honeymoon	3	T. Atkinson	118	Ariel Belle	115	Going WIth Me	115	17,205	1:37.40	
1947	On Trust	3	R. Neves	117	Stepfather	117	Owners Choice	122	36,800	1:37.40	
1952	Special Touch	5	E. Arcaro	121	Next Move	128	Blue Cloth	108	13,800	1:39.20	
1953	Spanish Cream	5	E. Guerin	124	Mab's Choice	115	Ruth Lily	113	13,200	1:38.20	
1954	Smart Barbara	4	G. Glisson	119	Auntie	116	Cerise Reine	119	15,300	1:25.60	
1955	Blue Butterfly	6	J. Westrope	118	Mab's Choice	115	Alibhai Lynn	122	14,000	1:22.00	
1956	In Reserve	4	J. Longden	120	Manotick	119	Mary Machree	115	15,100	1:23.20	
1957	King's Mistake	7	W. Shoemaker	115	Triple Jay	119	Noors Queen	109	16,900	1:46.00	
1958	Nooran	6	W. Boland	115	Myrtle	111	Ballet Khal	117	17,500	1:42.80	
1959	Two Cent Stamp	4	G. Taniguchi	111	Milly K.	115	Gleaming Star	114	17,400	1:43.60	
1960	Silver Spoon	4	E. Arcaro	127	La Plume	111	Indian Maid	116	17,250	1:42.60	
1961	Tritoma	5	J. Leonard	113	Perizade	109	Swiss Roll	124	18,600	1:43.20	
1962	Rose O'Neill	4	I. Valenzuela	118	Oil Royalty	117	Teacation	118	17,800	1:44.40	
1963	Linita	6	M. Ycaza	121	Pixie Erin	115	Rose O'Neill	121	17,300	1:42.60	
1964	Curious Clover	4	K. Church	113	Jazz Queen	115	Batteur	116	19,050	1:43.20	
1965	Batteur	5	F. Alvarez	119	Affectionately	122	Curious Clover	118	18,650	1:42.80	
1966	Poona Queen	6	M. Ycaza	119	Straight Deal	121	Gallarush	112	20,650	1:42.40	
1967	Natashka	4	W. Shoemaker	123	Miss Moona	118	Streamer	115	20,300	1:42.40	
1968	Gamely	4	M. Ycaza	122	Princessnesian	117	Moog	110	23,400	1:43.80	
1969	Dark Mirage	4	E. Belmonte	126	Desert Law	115	Sinking Spring	112	20,450	1:43.00	
1970	Gallant Bloom	4	J.L. Rotz	126	Commissary	116	Luz Del Sol	114	21,050	1:42.20	
1971	Last of the Line	4	J. Lambert	120	Night Stalker	111	Manta	127	26,850	1:41.60	
1972	Turkish Trousers	4	W. Shoemaker	123	Typecast	126	Street Dancer	123	34,500	1:41.20	
1973	Susan's Girl	4	L. Pincay Jr	125	Convenience	123	Hill Circus	119	32,900	1:42.00	
1974	Convenience	6	L. Pincay Jr	121	Tizna	117	Tallahto	119	34,750	1:42.80	
1975	Gay Style	5	W. Shoemaker	122	Tizna	120	Susan's Girl	124	34,650	1:42.00	
1976	Gay Style	6	D. Pierce	127	Raise Your Skirts	120	Tizna	127	35,100	1:41.40	
1977	Hail Hilarious	4	D. Pierce	122	Swingtime	120	Bastonera II	126	36,050	1:42.00	
1978	Swingtime	6	F. Toro	122	Winter Solstice	124	Granja Sueno	113	37,500	1:41.40	
1979	Grenzen	4	L. Pincay Jr	124	Ida Delia	118	Drama Critic	122	37,650	1:47.20	
1980	Kankam	5	E. Delahoussaye	123	Flaming Leaves	123	Miss Magnetic	117	47,400	1:41.80	
1981	Glorious Song	5	C.J. McCarron	127	Track Robbery	117	Miss Huntington	113	45,450	1:43.20	
1982	Targa	5	F. Olivares	114	Jameela	124	Track Robbery	124	65,100	1:42.00	
1983	Star Pastures	5	W. Shoemaker	119	Sintrillium	116	Viga	112	49,650	1:42.60	
1983	Sangue	5	L. Pincay Jr	124	Cat Girl	115	Happy Bride	116	50,650	1:41.00	
1984	Marisma	6	L. Pincay Jr	117	Brindy Brindy	114	Sierva	118	69,850	1:44.20	
1984	High Haven	5	R. Sibille	116	Castilla	122	Avigaition	120	50,600	1:42.40	
1985	Adored	5	L. Pincay Jr	124	Dontstop Themusic	121	Lovlier Linda	122	88,800	1:42.40	
1986	Love Smitten	5	C.J. McCarron	120	Johnica	121	North Sider	118	65,600	1:44.60	
1987	Fran's Valentine	5	P.A. Valenzuela	121	North Sider	118	Infinidad	113	91,700	1:42.60	
1988	Mausie	6	G.L. Stevens	114	Miss Alto	118	Novel Sprite	115	63,800	1:43.60	
1989	Miss Brio	5	E. Delahoussaye	119	Bayakoa	118	Annoconnor	122	79,000	1:41.00	
1990	Bayakoa	6	C.J. McCarron	126	Nikishka	117	Carita Tostada	112	90,200	1:43.00	
1991	Little Brianne	6	J. Garcia	117	Luna Elegante	114	Somethingmerry	114	89,700	1:41.60	106
1992	Paseana	5	C.J. McCarron	120	Colour Chart	118	Campagnarde	117	89,100	1:41.94	104
1993	Race the Wild Wind	4	K.J. Desormeaux	117	Paseana	126	Southern Truce	116	90,500	1:41.27	112
1994	Supah Gem	4	C.S. Nakatani	116	Paseana	124	Alysbelle	116	90,700	1:48.83	104
1995	Queens Court Queen	6	C.S. Nakatani	118	Paseana	123	Key Phrase	117	89,300	1:41.61	103
1996	Serena's Song	4	G.L. Stevens	124	Twice the Vice	118	Real Connection	114	95,800	1:42.22	105
1997	Jewel Princess	5	C.S. Nakatani	123	Cat's Cradle	118	Top Rung	117	97,900	1:41.72	114
1998	Exotic Wood	6	C.J. McCarron	121	Toda Una Dama	115	Tuxedo Junction	115	120,000	1:40.95	114
1999	India Divina	5	G.K. Gomez	114	Victory Stripes	115	Belle's Flag	117	120,000	1:42.71	101
2000	Manistique	5	C.S. Nakatani	125	Snowberg	114	Gourmet Girl	115	120,000	1:42.60	105
2001	Lovellon	5	G.L. Stevens	116	Feverish	119	Critikola	115	120,000	1:43.37	99
2002	Favorite Funtime	5	G.L. Stevens	116	Verruma	114	Printemps	116	120,000	1:44.15	101
2003	Starrer	5	P.A. Valenzuela	119	You	118	Rhiana	112	120,000	1:42.75	103
2004	Star Parade	5	V. Espinoza	114	Bare Necessities	118	La Tour	115	150,000	1:43.87	99

Beyer Index: 105.00

SANTA MONICA HANDICAP (G1), 7 Furlongs, Fillies and Mares, 4-Year-Olds and Up, Santa Anita, 2004 Purse: $250,000

Year	Winner	Age	Jockey	Wt.	Second	Wt.	Third	Wt.	Win Value	Time	Beyer
1957	Mary Machree	6	G. Taniguchi	122	Triple Jay	120	Our Betters	121	13,950	1:22.00	
1958	Market Basket	4	R. York	122	Ballet Khal	117	Cold Hands	109	13,750	1:22.80	

Year	Winner	Age	Jockey	Wt.	Second	Wt.	Third	Wt.	Win Value	Time	Beyer
1959	Bug Brush	4	A. Valenzuela	124	Well Away	118	Gleaming Star	114	14,800	1:23.00	
1960	Silver Spoon	4	E. Arcaro	124	Margaretta	121	Indian Maid	120	13,700	1:23.00	
1961	Taboo	4	W. Shoemaker	110	Sue III	117	Paris Pike	113	11,125	1:23.00	
1961	Swiss Roll	4	W. Shoemaker	117	Wiggle II	122	Tritoma	112	10,925	1:22.20	
1962	Perizade	6	R. Campas	115	Queen America	115	Linita	120	14,950	1:22.40	
1963	Table Mate	4	W. Shoemaker	114	Linita	121	My Portrait	118	14,550	1:22.00	
1964	Chop House	4	B. Baeza	116	Sunday Doll	111	Jazz Queen	112	15,650	1:22.80	
1965	Face the Facts	4	M. Ycaza	122	Hi Rated	116	Coliseum Honey	111	12,375	1:22.00	
1965	Chop House	5	I. Valenzuela	120	Affectionately	126	Batteur	118	12,725	1:22.40	
1966	Batteur	6	E. Belmonte	123	Terentia	119	Jalousie II	117	17,450	1:22.40	
1967	Miss Moona	4	L. Pincay Jr	115	Streamer	115	Countess Candy	113	16,650	1:22.40	
1968	Amerigo Lady	4	D. Pierce	118	Amerigo's Fancy	117	Gamely	122	16,450	1:03.00	
1969	Gamely	5	W. Harris	127	Time to Leave	124	Guest Room	115	13,450	1:23.60	
1971	Manta	5	L. Pincay Jr	125	Beja	119	Night Stalker	112	21,900	1:22.20	
1972	Typecast	6	L. Pincay Jr	123	Turkish Trousers	126	Goddess Special	114	29,300	1:21.40	
1973	Chou Croute	5	J.L. Rotz	128	Generous Portion	114	Minstrel Miss	115	27,800	1:23.60	
1974	Tizna	5	F. Toro	116	Susan's Girl	127	Impressive Style	118	28,050	1:24.00	
1975	Sister Fleet	5	F. Toro	115	Susan's Girl	125	Modus Vivendi	123	31,250	1:21.40	
1976	Gay Style	6	D. Pierce	125	Raise Your Skirts	123	Tizna	129	26,650	1:22.00	
1977	Hail Hilarious	4	D. Pierce	119	Bastonera II	125	Modus Vivendi	121	28,150	1:22.60	
1978	Winter Solstice	6	D.G. McHargue	123	Little Happiness	115	Splendid Size	117	27,200	1:21.20	
1979	Grenzen	4	L. Pincay Jr	122	Dottie's Doll	116	Bidding Bold	116	40,600	1:21.60	
1980	Flack Flack	5	W. Shoemaker	117	Shine High	115	Flaming Leaves	123	39,100	1:23.80	
1981	Parsley	5	A. Cordero Jr	116	Ack's Secret	125	Splendid Girl	118	40,050	1:23.40	
1982	Past Forgetting	4	W. Shoemaker	122	Nell's Briquette	118	In True Form	117	49,250	1:20.60	
	Marimbula finished second but was disqualified and placed sixth										
1983	Past Forgetting	5	C.J. McCarron	123	Sierva	119	Bara Lass	115	49,850	1:23.40	
1984	Bara Lass	5	W. Guerra	124	Holiday Dancer	117	Bally Knockan	113	52,250	1:22.00	
1985	Lovlier Linda	5	W. Shoemaker	123	Dontstop Themusic	123	Foggy Nation	119	48,900	1:22.80	
1986	Her Royalty	5	C.J. McCarron	120	North Sider	119	Take My Picture	117	51,300	1:21.60	
1987	Pine Tree Lane	5	A. Cordero Jr	125	Balladry	116	Her Royalty	119	58,140	1:21.80	
1988	Pine Tree Lane	6	G.L. Stevens	121	Fairly Old	115	Le l'Argent	120	73,500	1:23.00	
1989	Miss Brio	5	E. Delahoussaye	117	Valdemosa	116	Josette	115	64,800	1:21.60	
1990	Stormy but Valid	4	G.L. Stevens	119	Survive	118	Hot Novel	117	61,300	1:22.40	108
1991	Devil's Orchid	4	R.A. Baze	116	Stormy but Valid	121	Classic Value	118	90,800	1:21.80	103
	Classic Value finished second but was disqualified and placed third										
1992	Laramie Moon	5	E. Delahoussaye	116	D'Or Ruckus	114	Ifyoucouldseemenow	118	94,700	1:22.66	99
1993	Freedom Cry	5	A. Solis	114	Devil's Orchid	119	Mama Simba	114	91,200	1:21.78	106
1994	Southern Truce	6	G.L. Stevens	116	Arches of Gold	119	Mamselle Bebette	115	93,100	1:21.44	97
1995	Key Phrase	4	C.W. Antley	116	Flying In the Lane	114	Desert Stormer	117	93,100	1:22.82	107
1996	Serena's Song	4	G.L. Stevens	123	Exotic Wood	118	Klassy Kim	116	96,800	1:21.56	108
1997	Toga Toga Toga	5	J.A. Garcia	114	Ski Dancer	117	Grab the Prize	116	96,750	1:23.27	102
1998	Exotic Wood	6	C.J. McCarron	121	Madame Pandit	119	Advancing Star	121	120,000	1:21.07	105
1999	Stop Traffic	6	C.A. Black	120	Belle's Flag	118	Closed Escrow	116	120,000	1:22.17	105
2000	Honest Lady	4	C.S. Nakatani	114	Kalookan Queen	116	Enjoy the Moment	118	132,840	1:21.40	106
2001	Nany's Sweep	5	K.J. Desormeaux	117	Serenita	115	Surfside	121	120,000	1:22.50	100
2002	Kalookan Queen	6	A. Solis	119	Leading Light	115	Spain	120	120,000	1:22.37	106
2003	Affluent	5	A. Solis	119	Sightseek	115	Secret of Mecca	110	120,000	1:22.17	102
2004	Island Fashion	4	K.J. Desormeaux	120	Buffythecenterfold	114	Got Koko	119	150,000	1:21.37	104

Beyer Index: 103.87

For 3-year-olds and up prior to 1960

SANTA YNEZ (G2), 7 Furlongs, 3-Year-Old Fillies, Santa Anita, 2004 Purse: $150,000

Year	Winner	Age	Jockey	Wt.	Second	Wt.	Third	Wt.	Win Value	Time	Beyer
1952	Lap Full	2	E. Arcaro	119	Hug-Me-Tight	115	Khalati	119	10,900	1:11.60	
1952	Last Greetings	3	E. Arcaro	119	A Gleam	119	Season's Best	119	14,700	1:11.20	
1954	Sweet as Honey	3	J. Longden	119	Frosty Dawn	113	Quillo Maid	111	10,550	1:23.00	
1955	In Reserve	3	J. Longden	113	Miss Arlette	119	Solid Rae	116	13,300	1:22.40	
1956	Neva T.	3	G. Taniguchi	116	Mrs. Muriel L.	116	Yutta	116	10,350	1:11.00	
1957	Sully's Trail	3	G. Taniguchi	116	Market Basket	116	Tourbillonte	116	10,400	1:10.20	
1958	Zevs Joy	3	G. Taniguchi	113	Well Away	116	Winking Louise	116	11,550	1:17.40	
1959	Silver Spoon	3	R. York	116	Gun Box	116	Pardal Lassie	113	11,000	1:17.00	
1960	Solid Thought	3	W. Shoemaker	116	Miss Imbros	112	Julie Kate	116	11,200	1:18.00	
1961	Het's Pet	3	W. Shoemaker	119	Bully's Lady	116	Kantankerous K'ty	111	10,550	1:16.80	
1962	Don't Linger	3	W. Shoemaker	115	Jet Parade	115	Pixie Erin	114	10,300	1:17.60	
1963	Nalee	3	K. Church	117	Lamb Chop	117	Delhi Maid	111	13,850	1:16.40	
1964	Face the Facts	3	M. Ycaza	117	Leisurely Kin	120	Roman Goddess	113	13,900	1:15.40	

Year	Winner	Age	Jockey	Wt.	Second	Wt.	Third	Wt.	Win Value	Time	Beyer
1965	Respected	3	M. Ycaza	113	Ardell C.	117	Hock Me Not	113	21,200	1:16.20	
1966	Spearfish	3	D. Pierce	117	Be Suspicious	113	Premise	120	17,750	1:16.20	
1967	Mira Femme	3	W. Blum	121	Forgiving	114	Ellen Gruder	114	16,300	1:24.20	
1968	Allie's Serenade	3	L. Pincay Jr	115	Miss Ribot	118	Fish Net	118	17,600	1:22.60	
1969	Poona Downs	3	W. Shoemaker	112	Dumptys Lady	113	Lover's Quarrel	118	18,300	1:24.00	
1970	Opening Bid	3	D. Pierce	121	Loved	113	Top Frolic	112	20,400	1:22.20	
1971	Turkish Trousers	3	W. Shoemaker	112	Ulla Britta	115	Sapose Speed	114	20,300	1:23.60	
1972	Susan's Girl	3	V. Tejada	118	Foreseer	115	Impressive Style	118	29,200	1:21.80	
1973	Tallahto	3	J. Tejeira	117	Waltz Fan	117	Windy's Daughter	121	25,800	1:21.40	
1974	Modus Vivendi	3	D. Pierce	119	Donna Chere	114	Special Team	121	28,500	1:22.40	
1975	Raise Your Skirts	3	W. Mahorney	117	Fascinating Girl	115	Miss Francesca	117	23,350	1:22.40	
1976	Daisy Do	3	S. Hawley	114	Girl in Love	115	Windy Welcome	117	20,300	1:22.40	
1977	Wavy Waves	3	L. Pincay Jr	121	Don's Music	119	Any Time Girl	121	29,550	1:22.80	
1978	Grenzen	3	D.G. McHargue	119	Extravagant	121	Happy Kin	114	27,600	1:22.20	
1979	Terlingua	3	L. Pincay Jr	121	Caline	119	It's in the Air	121	37,900	1:21.20	
1980	Table Hands	3	W. Shoemaker	124	Street Ballet	119	Hazel R.	119	38,700	1:22.40	
1981	Past Forgetting	3	S. Hawley	119	Rosie Doon	119	Nell's Briquette	121	41,800	1:22.40	
1982	Flying Partner	3	R. Sibille	115	Skillful Joy	124	Carry a Tune	114	49,300	1:22.80	
1983	A Lucky Sign	3	C.J. McCarron	121	Sophisticated Girl	116	Fabulous Notion	124	49,050	1:23.40	
1984	Gene's Lady	3	L. Pincay Jr	117	Kennedy Express	115	Natural Summit	117	41,600	1:23.80	
1984	Boo La Boo	3	L. Pincay Jr	122	Personable Lady	122	Costly Array	117	39,900	1:23.20	
1985	Wising Up	3	E. Delahoussaye	119	Rascal Lass	122	Reigning Countess	119	52,700	1:23.40	
1986	Sari's Heroine	3	A. Solis	119	An Empress	117	Life at the Top	115	52,000	1:23.40	
1987	Very Subtle	3	W. Shoemaker	122	Chic Shirine	119	Young Flyer	122	46,200	1:22.60	
1988	Goodbye Halo	3	J. Velasquez	123	Bolchina	116	Floral Magic	114	46,950	1:22.80	
1989	Hot Novel	3	E. Delahoussaye	121	Fantastic Look	114	Agotaras	121	46,950	1:22.80	
1990	Fit to Scout	3	C.J. McCarron	118	Bright Candles	118	Heaven for Bid	116	60,625	1:23.80	
1991	Brazen	3	C.J. McCarron	121	Fowda	116	Ifyoucouldseemenow	121	46,050	1:23.60	91
1992	Looie Capote	3	K.J. Desormeaux	114	Icy Eyes	118	Soviet Sojourn	121	61,450	1:23.42	97
1993	Fit to Lead	3	C.S. Nakatani	116	Nijivision	114	Booklore	114	62,500	1:22.55	93
1994	Tricky Code	3	Nakatani CS	121	Fancy 'n Fabulous	114	Sophisticatedcielo	116	59,575	1:22.16	89
1995	Serena's Song	3	Nakatani CS	123	Cat's Cradle	121	Call Now	121	59,800	1:21.45	102
1996	Raw Gold	3	C.W. Antley	121	Pareja	121	Hidden Lake	116	64,550	1:22.66	90
1997	Queen Of Money	3	D.R. Flores	116	Goodnight Irene	116	High Heeled Hope	121	65,650	1:22.55	89
1998	Nijinsky's Passion	3	C.A. Black	121	Well Chosen	115	Vivid Angel	123	64,980	1:23.15	87
1999	Honest Lady	3	K.J. Desormeaux	115	Rayelle	118	Controlled	123	63,240	1:21.67	105
2000	Penny Blues	3	E. Delahoussaye	118	Classic Olympio	121	Mean Imogene	117	63,600	1:23.38	89
2001	Golden Ballet	3	C.J. McCarron	123	Affluent	114	Warren's Whistle	116	90,000	1:22.30	99
2002	Dancing	3	G.L. Stevens	116	Respectful	116	Lady George	123	90,000	1:23.07	84
2003	Elloluv	3	P.A. Valenzuela	121	Watching You	116	Himalayan	116	90,000	1:23.03	94
2004	Yearly Report	3	J.D. Bailey	114	House of Fortune	121	Papa to Kinzie	115	90,000	1:21.11	107

Beyer Index: 94.00

SANTA YSABEL (G3), 1 1/16 Miles, 3-Year-Old Fillies, Santa Anita, 2004 Purse: $106,800

Year	Winner	Age	Jockey	Wt.	Second	Wt.	Third	Wt.	Win Value	Time	Beyer
1994	Princess Mitterand	3	C.J. McCarron	119	Dianes Halo	115	Jacodra's Devil	115	44,925	1:43.25	90
1995	Ski Dancer	3	K.J. Desormeaux	115	Dixie Pearl	117	Wilga	115	45,750	1:44.24	83
1996	Antespend	3	C.W. Antley	120	Dancing Prism	114	Rumpipumpy	116	64,950	1:43.87	85
1997	Sharp Cat	3	C.S. Nakatani	120	Clever Pilot	115	Guthrie	116	64,300	1:41.34	94
1998	Love Lock	3	K.J. Desormeaux	120	Nonies Dancer Ali	114	Mamaison Miss	116	63,660	1:44.14	83
	Love Lock was subsequently disqualified for post-race positive; Continental Lea, 4th, placed third										
1999	Holywood Picture	3	O. Vergara	115	Exbourne Free	115	Gleefully	116	64,860	1:43.48	90
2000	Surfside	3	P. Day	123	Rings a Chime	115	She's Classy	118	62,882	1:43.53	103
2001	Collect Call	3	A. Solis	115	Irguns Angel	115	Eminent	115	65,580	1:44.69	85
2002	Bella Bella Bella	3	C.J. McCarron	115	Tamarack Bay	116	No Turbulence	116	64,550	1:44.14	85
2003	Atlantic Ocean	3	D.R. Flores	120	Sea Jewel	115	SummerWindDancer	120	66,540	1:43.25	90
2004	A.P. Adventure	3	A. Solis	115	Salty Romance	120	Wildwood Flower	115	64,080	1:44.27	94

Beyer Index: 89.27

For previous runnngs, refer to 1994 Manual.

SAPLING (G3), 6 Furlongs, 2-Year-Olds, Monmouth Park, 2004 Purse: $100,000

Year	Winner	Age	Jockey	Wt.	Second	Wt.	Third	Wt.	Win Value	Time	Beyer
1883	Duchess	2	W. Donohue	107	Blossom	100	Thackery	110	3,255	1:18.75	
1884	Brookwood	2	Feakes	110	Goano	103	Cholula	110	3,905	1:15.50	

Year	Winner	Age	Jockey	Wt.	Second	Wt.	Third	Wt.	Win Value	Time	Beyer
1885	Savanac	2	Onley	108	Quito	115	Salisbury	105	4,120	1:17.00	
1886	Hanover	2	McLaughlin	115	Spendthrift-Kapang	108	Austriana	105	5,500	1:17.50	
1887	Fitz James	2	Garrison	109	Now or Never	105	Fordham	110	5,825	1:16.50	
1888	Tipstaff	2	Eilke	105	Sensation-Faverdal	115	Tom Ochiltree-Cade	108	6,350	1:15.25	
1889	Devotee	2	Hayward	115	Cayuga	129	Grammercy	105	6,850	1:15.25	
1890	Sorcerer	2	Reagan	113	Russell	123	Foxford	109	6,450	1:16.25	
1891	Air Plant	2	Hamilton	118	Fremont	118	Falsetto	111	5,990	1:12.75	
1892	Don Alonzo	2	Taral	118	Hammie	118	Tom Watson	115	4,640	1:13.75	
1893	Senator Daly	2	Midgley	111	Hyder Abad	118	Henry of Navarre	111	7,510	1:05.00	
1946	Donor	2	J. Jessop	115	Lookout Son	111	Milk Pact	111	11,890	1:12.20	
1947	Task	2	R.J. Martin	111	Itsabet	116	Picture Card	111	10,825	1:11.60	
1948	Blue Peter	2	E. Guerin	122	Harbourton	111	Razzmatazz	111	10,325	1:12.80	
1949	Casemate	2	J. Gilbert	122	Hill Prince	115	Thorn	113	9,900	1:11.60	
1950	Battlefield	2	E. Arcaro	122	Uncle Miltie	115	Lord Putnam	125	10,400	1:10.80	
1951	Landseair	2	J. Stout	111	War Age	111	Master Fiddle	115	11,300	1:12.60	
1952	Landlocked	2	F. Fernandez	113	Game Gene	122	Jamie K.	113	21,275	1:13.00	
1952	Laffango	2	F. Pannell	122	Sun Warrior	113	Chief Fanelli	113	21,525	1:12.80	
1953	Artismo	2	J. Stout	113	Permian	116	Passembud	116	30,200	1:11.00	
1954	Royal Coinage	2	J. Skelly	122	Royal Note	124	Impromptu	113	28,050	1:11.00	
1955	Needles	2	J. Choquette	116	Decathlon	124	Polly's Jet	124	27,000	1:10.60	
1956	King Hairan	2	E. Arcaro	124	Ben Lomond	113	Burma Charm	113	44,700	1:10.80	
1957	Plion	2	N. Shuk	119	Li'l Fella	124	A Dragon Killer	119	37,945	1:11.40	
1958	Watch Your Step	2	E. Guerin	114	Intentionally	124	Restless Wind	124	37,685	1:10.60	
1959	Sky Clipper	2	W. Harmatz	122	Bally Ache	122	Big Biz	122	82,617	1:11.40	
1960	Hail to Reason	2	R. Ussery	122	He's a Pistol	122	Carry Back	122	80,925	1:10.40	
1961	Sir Gaylord	2	I. Valenzuela	122	Battle Joined	122	Green Ticket	122	74,046	1:10.60	
1962	Delta Judge	2	R. Broussard	122	Bonjour	122	Never Bend	122	64,833	1:10.60	
1963	Mr. Brick	2	L. Adams	122	Big Pete	122	Bold Sultan	122	62,976	1:10.60	
1964	Bold Lad	2	B. Baeza	122	Native Charger	122	Sadair	122	61,545	1:09.40	
1965	Buckpasser	2	B. Baeza	122	Quinta	122	Our Michael	122	67,311	1:10.60	
1966	Great Power	2	W. Shoemaker	122	In Reality	122	Disciplinarian	122	62,691	1:09.40	
1967	Subpet	2	R. Broussard	122	What a Pleasure	122	Iron Ruler	122	72,423	1:10.40	
1968	Reviewer	2	B. Baeza	122	Night Invader	122	Al Hattab	122	68,835	1:10.40	
1969	Ring for Nurse	2	M. Miceli	122	Rollicking	122	Hard Work	122	67,548	1:11.80	
1970	Staunch Avenger	2	D.E. Whited	122	Pass Catcher	122	Raise Your Glass	122	81,522	1:11.40	
1971	Chevron Flight	2	M. Fromin	122	Chauffeur	122	King of Cornish	122	70,530	1:11.80	
1972	Assagai Jr.	2	J. Imparato	122	Little Big Chief	122	Swift Courier	122	66,804	1:10.80	
1973	Tisab	2	W. Blum	122	Wedge Shot	122	Go for Love	122	77,721	1:10.20	
1974	Foolish Pleasure	2	J. Vasquez	122	The Bagel Prince	122	Bombay Duck	122	86,997	1:10.40	
1975	Full Out	2	B. Thornburg	122	Riverside Sam	122	Eustace	122	82,227	1:11.60	
1976	Ali Oop	2	L. Saumell	122	Ahoy Mate	122	First Ambassador	122	84,636	1:09.80	
1977	Alydar	2	E. Maple	122	Noon Time Spender	122	Dominant Ruler	122	65,829	1:10.60	
1978	Tim the Tiger	2	J. Fell	122	Groton High	122	Spartan Emperor	122	86,682	1:11.80	
1979	Rockhill Native	2	J. Oldham	122	Antique Gold	122	Gold Stage	122	75,366	1:08.80	
1980	Travelling Music	2	C. Perret	122	Lord Avie	122	Timeless Event	122	78,438	1:11.00	
1981	Out of Hock	2	D. Brumfield	122	T. Dykes	122	What a Wabbit	122	90,591	1:10.20	
1982	O.K. by You	2	C. Perret	122	Willow Drive	122	Love to Laugh	122	79,032	1:10.80	
1983	Smart n Slick	2	D.A. Miller Jr	122	Tonto	122	Triple Sec	122	120,615	1:10.80	
1984	Doubly Clear	2	J.R. Garcia	122	Tiltalating	122	Do It Again Dan	122	120,150	1:10.40	
1985	Hilco Scamper	2	G.L. Stevens	122	Danny's Keys	122	Mr. Spiffy	122	114,555	1:10.80	
1986	Bet Twice	2	C.W. Antley	122	Faster Than Sound	122	Homebuilder	122	120,000	1:10.20	
1987	Tejano	2	J. Vasquez	122	Unzipped	122	Jim's Orbit	122	111,600	1:09.00	
1988	Bio	2	P.A. Johnson	122	Truely Colorful	122	Light My Fuse	122	111,600	1:10.40	
1989	Carson City	2	J.A. Krone	122	Mr. Nasty	122	Adjudicating	122	120,000	1:10.40	96
1990	Deposit Ticket	2	G.L. Stevens	122	Alaskan Frost	122	Hansel	122	120,000	1:11.00	
1991	Big Sur	2	R. Migliore	122	Never Wavering	122	Dr. Fountainstein	122	120,000	1:10.80	102
1992	Gilded Time	2	C.J. McCarron	122	Wild Zone	122	Great Navigator	122	120,000	1:07.80	85
1993	Sacred Honour	2	C. Lopez Sr.	122	Meadow Flight	122	Solly's Honor	117	120,000	1:11.00	85
1994	Boone's Mill	2	P. Day	122	Enlighten	122	Western Echo	122	120,000	1:10.40	92
1995	Hennessy	2	D.M. Barton	122	Built for Pleasure	122	Cashier Coyote	122	120,000	1:10.80	77
1996	Smoke Glacken	2	C. Perret	122	Harley Tune	122	Country Rainbow	122	120,000	1:10.20	86
1997	Double Honor	2	J. Bravo	122	Jigadee	122	E Z Line	122	120,000	1:09.60	95
1998	Yes It's True	2	S.J. Sellers	122	Eriton	122	Heroofthegame	122	120,000	1:10.00	90
1999	Dont Tell the Kids	2	J. Tejeira	122	Outrigger	122	House Burner	122	120,000	1:10.18	80
2000	Shooter	2	J. Bravo	119	Snow Ridge	119	T P Louie	119	120,000	1:10.63	88
2001	Pure Precision	2	E.M. Coa	120	Truman's Raider	120	Wild Navigator	120	90,000	1:10.82	89
2002	Valid Video	2	C.C. Lopez	120	Farno	120	Boston Park	120	60,000	1:09.88	95
2003	Dashboard Drummer	2	J.C. Ferrer	120	Deputy Storm	120	Charming Jim	120	60,000	1:10.84	85
2004	Evil Minister	2	J. Pimentel	120	Park Avenue Ball	120	Upscaled	120	60,000	1:11.21	78

Beyer Index: 88.20

SARANAC HANDICAP (G3), 1 3/16 Miles (Turf), 3-Year-Olds, Saratoga Race Course, 2004 Purse: $108,200

Year	Winner	Age	Jockey	Wt.	Second	Wt.	Third	Wt.	Win Value	Time	Beyer
1901	Dublin	3	Shaw	113	Baron Pepper	104	Choctanunda	109	3,850	1:52.60	
1902	Hermis	3	Rice	122	Whiskey King	104	Cunard	115	5,150	1:51.40	
1903	Molly Brant	3	J. Martin	100	Shorthose	120	Grey Friar	112	5,675	1:55.20	
1904	Dolly Spanker	3	Shaw	115	St. Valentine	112	Fort Hunter	126	3,850	1:53.20	
1905	Dandelion	3	O'Niell	110	Merry Lark	112	Bedouin	118	3,850	1:53.80	
1906	Gallavant	3	Miller	119	Tiptoe	118			3,850	1:56.60	
1907	Vails	3	Miller	113	Rio Grande	90	Don Enrique	102	3,850	1:53.40	
1908	Golconda	3	D. McCarthy	97	Thomas Calhoun	100	Crack Shot	94	350	1:57.40	
1909	Field Mouse	3	E. Dugan	111	Wintergreen	112	Gliding Belle	102	1,410	1:37.60	
1910	Martinez	3	S. Davis	112	Lovetie	107	Starbottle	105	2,315	1:52.20	
1913	Ten Point	3	Loftus	124	Nightstick	106	Leochares	116	1,855	1:39.00	
1914	Stromboli	3	A. Neylon	113	Punch Bowl	114	Gainer	119	1,495	1:38.60	
1915	Regret	3	J. Notter	123	Trial by Jury	114	Lady Rotha	106	1,050	1:42.00	
1916	Dodge	3	F. Murphy	125	Spur	127	Tea Caddy	107	1,500	1:38.00	
1917	Midway	3	J. Butwell	118	Corn Tassel	118	Hollister	116	2,650	1:39.40	
1918	Motor Cop	3	W. Knapp	119	The Porter	118	Tippity Witchet	115	2,575	1:36.80	
1919	Purchase	3	W. Knapp	133	Passing Shower	107	The Trump	105	2,325	1:42.20	
1920	Dinna Care	3	C. Kummer	110	Dr. Clark	120	Busy Signal	112	6,400	1:38.60	
1921	Crocus	3	L. Fator	120	Bit of White	119	Idle Dell	110	5,225	1:37.80	
1922	Little Chief	3	L. Fator	114	Kai-Sang	133	Horologe	111	5,900	1:37.80	
1923	Cherry Pie	3	J. Corcoran	110	Untidy	114	The Clown	116	8,250	1:38.00	
1924	Sarazen	3	J. Maiben	120	Klondyke	114	Wise Counsellor	122	8,250	1:37.60	
1925	Peanuts	3	F. Coltiletti	110	Silver Fox	128	Senalado	110	8,250	1:39.00	
1926	Mars	3	C. Turner	120	Rock Star	120	Croydon	108	9,300	1:39.00	
1927	Osmand	3	E. Sande	123	Valorous	123	Cheops	120	9,400	1:39.60	
1928	Sun Edwin	3	H. Thurber	117	Sunfire	110	Bobashela	117	8,450	1:41.60	
1929	Hard Tack	3	J.H. Burke	114	Vermajo	106	Dr. Freeland	117	10,100	1:37.40	
1931	Danour	3	S. Renick	103	A la Carte	110	Surf Board	111	8,500	1:40.20	
1932	Morfair	3	R. Workman	124	Pompeius	112	Sunmelus	114	7,050	1:41.40	
1933	War Glory	3	J. Gilbert	125	Kerry Patch	120	Okapi	119	3,900	1:38.60	
1934	Kievex	3	W.D. Wright	110	Bazaar	116	Observant	112	3,850	1:37.20	
1935	Good Gamble	3	S. Renick	118	Black Gift	110	Esposa	103	4,675	1:38.40	
1936	Sun Teddy	3	E. Arcaro	112	Pullman	112	Sangreal	112	5,250	1:40.20	
1937	Burning Star	3	H. Richards	117	Forty Winks	114	Rex Flag	113	5,175	1:39.40	
1938	Thanksgiving	3	L. Dupps	113	Encore	106	Lucky Omen	110	3,725	1:38.80	
1939	Heather Broom	3	B. James	113	Golden Voyage	112	Nitro	112	4,025	1:38.80	
1940	Parasang	3	B. James	118	Call to Colors	105	The Finest	110	4,200	1:38.20	
1941	Whirlaway	3	A. Robertson	130	War Relic	117	Omission	112	3,800	1:38.00	
1942	Bless Me	3	S. Young	116	Star Beacon	107	Lochinvar	115	4,100	1:37.20	
1948	Mount Marcy	3	E. Arcaro	116	Better Self	126	Ace Admiral	111	16,000	1:44.80	
1949	Sun Bahram	3	E. Arcaro	120	Eatontown	112	Arise	114	11,950	1:45.00	
1950	Sunglow	3	E. Arcaro	115	Lights Up	126	Bit o' Fate	105	10,825	1:43.60	
1951	Bold	3	E. Arcaro	125	Loridale	111	Mandingo	105	10,950	1:43.60	
1952	Golden Gloves	3	N. Wall	116	Hitex	120	Count Flame	113	16,600	1:45.40	
1953	First Aid	3	A. Catalano	106	Beachcomber	121	Fly Wheel	113	16,450	1:43.80	
1954	Full Flight	3	J. Higley	114	Paper Tiger	111	Red Hannigan	114	21,700	1:44.80	
1955	Saratoga	3	N. Shuk	126	Misty Morn	112	Nance's Lad	123	20,000	1:44.00	
1956	Ricci Tavi	3	P.J. Bailey	122	Bill's Sky Boy	114	Pertshire	115	18,500	1:43.40	
1957	Cohoes	3	T. Atkinson	120	Bureaucracy	113	St. Amour II	116	21,350	1:42.20	
1958	Nasco	3	R. Broussard	113	Nisht Amool	113	Isendu	114	18,225	1:44.40	
1959	Mail Order	3	P.J. Bailey	113	The Irishman	122	Seven Corners	113	18,095	1:41.80	
1960	Divine Comedy	3	M. Sorrentino	113	John William	121	Brush Fire	120	17,867	1:34.60	
1961	Globemaster	3	J.L. Rotz	125	Dr. Miller	118	Hi Greco	110	18,687	1:36.60	
1962	David K.	3	R. Ussery	119	Rainy Lake	114	Subtle	110	18,427	1:35.80	
1963	Outing Class	3	B. Baeza	120	Choker	113	Ahoy	122	18,557	1:36.80	
1964	Lt. Stevens	3	T. Barrow	114	Bupers	116	Lord Date	116	19,045	1:36.40	
1965	La Cima	3	R. Ussery	114	Eurasian	111	Hail to All	127	38,660	1:34.40	
1966	Alexville	3	M. Ycaza	113	Flame Tree	116	Sense of Rhythm	111	37,570	1:36.40	
1967	Bold Hour	3	J.L. Rotz	123	Tumiga	123	Reason to Hail	119	36,530	1:36.00	
1968	Stage Door Johnny	3	H. Gustines	126	Out of the Way	124	Iron Ruler	122	36,205	1:35.40	
1969	Best Turn	3	E. Belmonte	112	Prevailing	118	Buck Run	112	37,830	1:35.60	
1970	Silent Screen	3	J.L. Rotz	123	Aggressively	112	Naskra	117	36,985	1:36.00	
1971	Salem	3	J. Vasquez	121	Farewell Party	117	Highbinder	114	33,960	1:34.80	
1972	Icecapade	3	E. Maple	117	Tentam	114	Traffic Cop	114	34,290	1:33.60	
1973	Linda's Chief	3	B. Baeza	126	Step Nicely	123	Illberightback	117	33,150	1:34.00	
1974	Accipiter	3	A. Santiago	123	Best of It	117	Hosiery	117	34,980	1:36.40	
1975	Bravest Roman	3	E. Maple	114	Wajima	114	Valid Appeal	114	34,380	1:34.80	
1976	Dance Spell	3	A. Cordero Jr	114	Zen	123	Quiet Little Table	114	33,030	1:34.20	
1977	Bailjumper	3	A. Cordero Jr	114	Lynn Davis	114	Gift of Kings	114	39,910	1:35.20	
1978	Buckaroo	3	J. Velasquez	123	Junction	123	Quadratic	123	31,950	1:35.00	

Year	Winner	Age	Jockey	Wt.	Second	Wt.	Third	Wt.	Win Value	Time	Beyer
1979	Told	3	J. Cruguet	114	Crown Thy Good	114	Quiet Crossing	123	35,250	1:34.40	
1980	Key to Content	3	G. Martens	114	Current Legend	114	Ben Fab	123	36,300	1:33.80	
1981	De la Rose	3	E. Maple	112	Stage Door Key	114	Color Bearer	112	35,400	1:34.40	
1982	Prince Westport	3	J.D. Bailey	114	Four Bases	114	A Real Leader	114	35,040	1:39.00	
1983	Sabin	3	E. Maple	113	Fortnightly	117	Domynsky	123	36,600	1:39.40	
1984	Is Your Pleasure	3	A. Cordero Jr	114	Onyxly	114	Loft	123	61,470	1:35.20	
1985	Equalize	3	R.G. Davis	114	Verification	114	Danger's Hour	114	71,820	1:39.00	
1986	Glow	3	E. Maple	114	Manila	114	Pillaster	120	72,270	1:34.60	
1987	Lights and Music	3	E. Maple	114	Forest Fair	114	First Patriot	117	73,560	1:34.80	
1988	Posen	3	D. Brumfield	123	Sunshine Forever	114	Blew by Em	117	73,560	1:38.40	
1989	Expensive Decision	3	J.L. Samyn	114	Ninety Years Young	114	Valid Ordinate	114	55,140	1:36.00	
1989	Slew the Knight	3	J.L. Samyn	114	Verbatree	114	Luge II	123	55,620	1:36.00	
1990	Rouse the Louse	3	J.D. Bailey	114	My Girl Jeannie	118	V.J.'s Honor	114	78,600	1:37.00	
1991	Club Champ	3	A. Cordero Jr	114	Share the Glory	117	Young Daniel	114	81,480	1:34.20	92
1992	Casino Magistrate	3	E. Maple	120	Restless Doctor	114	Smiling and Dancin	117	76,440	1:39.20	
1993	Halisee	3	J.A. Krone	114	Forest Wind	117	Compadre	114	74,280	1:34.20	95
1994	Casa Eire	3	Bravo J	114	Warn Me	114	Presently	117	66,480	1:34.60	93
1995	Debonair Dan	3	Chavez JF	112	Crimson Guard	122	Treasurer	114	50,400	1:33.60	109
1996	Harghar	3	P. Day	113	Sir Cat	123	Defacto	115	68,880	1:48.40	105
1997	River Squall	3	C. Perret	114	Daylight Savings	114	Inkatha	114	68,460	1:52.80	106
1998	Crowd Pleaser	3	Samyn J. L.	115	Parade Ground	122	Reformer Rally	115	66,060	1:53.40	98
1999	Phi Beta Doc	3	Dominguez R. A.	118	Monarch's Maze	114	Big Rascal	113	67,020	1:51.60	105
2000	Rob's Spirit	3	J.D. Bailey	120	Whata Brainstorm	117	Dawn of the Condor	117	68,280	1:55.47	99
2001	Blazing Fury	3	J.J. Castellano	113	Fast City	114	Rapid Ryan	114	67,500	1:54.88	102
2002	Ibn Al Haitham	3	R. Migliore	114	Finality	116	Irish Colonial	115	66,900	1:55.30	97
2003	Shoal Water	3	J.R. Velazquez	116	Urban King	115	Sharp Impact	116	65,280	1:55.43	99
2004	Prince Arch	3	J.J. Castellano	123	Mustanfar	121	Catch the Glory	115	64,920	1:53.89	97

Beyer Index: 99.77

SARATOGA BREEDERS' CUP HANDICAP (G2), 1 1/4 Miles, 3-Year-Olds and Up, Saratoga Race Course, 2004 Purse: $250,000

Year	Winner	Age	Jockey	Wt.	Second	Wt.	Third	Wt.	Win Value	Time	Beyer
1865	Kentucky	4	Gilpatrick	104	Captain Moore	104	Rhinodyne	114	1,850	4:01.00	
1866	Kentucky	5	C. Littlefield	114	Beacon	114	Delaware	114	2,250	4:04.00	
1867	Muggins	4	Clark	118	Onward	114	Delaware	114	1,850	4:03.00	
1868	Lancaster	5	Hayward	114	J.A. Connolly	108	F. Cheath'm	105	1,960	4:14.00	
1869	Bayonet	4	Miller	108	Nellie McDonald	105	Vauxhall	108	2,250	4:10.00	
1870	Helmbold	4	Robinson	108	Hamburg	90	Glenelg	108	1,850	4:03.75	
1871	Longfellow	4	Swim	108	Kingfisher	108			1,550	4:02.75	
1872	Harry Bassett	4	J. Rowe	108	Longfellow	114	Defender	114	1,550	3:59.00	
1873	Joe Daniels	4	McCabe	108	Harry Bassett	114	True Blue	108	1,700	4:10.75	
1874	Springbok	4	Barbee	108	Preakness	114	Katie Pease	105	2,450	4:11.75	
1875	Springbok	5	W. Clark				Grinstead	108	2,250	2:56.25	
	Preakness	6	Hayward	114							
1876	Tom Ochiltree	4	Barbee	118	Parole	97	Big Sandy	118	1,850	4:06.50	
1877	Parole	4	Barrett	115	Tom Ochiltree	124	Athlene	115	2,150	4:04.50	
1878	Parole	5	Barrett	121	Joe	118	Gen. Phillips	118	1,700	4:08.50	
1879	Bramble	4	J. McLaughlin	118	Wilful	100	Lou Lanier	115	1,500	4:11.75	
1880	Long Taw	5	Wolfe	125	Franklin	121			1,300	4:08.00	
1881	Checkmate	6	I. Murphy	120	Monitor	119	Irish King	122	1,800	4:09.75	
1882	Thora	4	Brophy	113	Carley B.	101	Alta B.	96	1,850	4:05.50	
1883	Gen. Monroe	5	Fitzpatrick	122	Boatman	115			1,950	4:21.50	
1884	Gen. Monroe	6	Blaylock	123	Compensation	120	L. Stanhope	118	1,650	4:05.00	
1885	Bob Miles	4	Fitzpatrick	118	Boatman	120	Powh'n III	118	2,150	4:02.00	
1886	Volante	4	I. Murphy	118	Aretino	118			1,700	4:25.00	
1891	Los Angeles	6	I. Lewis	121	Vallera	111	Ind. Rubber	107	2,900	3:43.50	
1901	Blues	3	Shaw	113	Bayou Pepper	113	Imp	122	3,350	2:52.40	
1902	Advance Guard	5	McCue	127	Wyeth	113	A. Williams	113	3,350	3:01.80	
1903	Africander	3	Fuller	113	Heno	126	Waterboy	126	3,350	2:58.00	
1904	Beldame	3	F. O'Neill	108	Africander	126	The Picket	126	8,100	3:03.80	
1905	Caughnawaga	6	Redfern	127	Beldame	121	Cairngorm	113	5,800	3:00.80	
1906	Go Between	5	Shaw	127	Sir Huon	113	Samson	113	6,050	3:05.40	
1907	Running Water	4	W. Miller	121	Nealon	126	Frank Gill	113	6,050	3:06.20	
1909	Olambala	3	Butwell	113	Wintergreen	113	P. and Needl's	122	2,175	2:58.00	
1910	Countless	3	V. Powers	113	Olambala	126	Am' Jenks	108	4,100	2:58.60	
1913	Sam Jackson	5	Loftus	124	Ringling	108	Lahore	124	1,650	3:08.40	
1914	Star Gaze	4	J. McCahey	126	San Vega	113	Flying Fairy	121	2,175	3:10.00	
1915	Roamer	4	J. Butwell	123	Virile	124	Star Gaze	127	2,225	3:01.80	
1916	Friar Rock	3	J. McTaggart	113	Roamer	127	The Finn	126	3,375	3:03.00	

Year	Winner	Age	Jockey	Wt.	Second	Wt.	Third	Wt.	Win Value	Time	Beyer
1917	Omar Khayyam	3	J. Butwell	113	Spur	126	Fair Mac	127	5,050	3:07.80	
1918	Johren	3	F. Robinson	113	Roamer	127			5,250	3:02.20	
1919	Exterminator	4	A. Schuttinger	126	Purchase	126	The Trump	116	5,600	2:58.00	
1920	Exterminator	5	C. Fairbrother	126	Cleopatra	111			4,950	2:56.40	
1921	Exterminator	6	W. Kelsay	126					4,750	3:04.60	
1922	Exterminator	7	A. Johnson	126	Mad Hatter	126	Bon Homme	126	6,800	3:00.40	
1923	My Own	3	E. Sande	116	Bunting	126	Prince James	126	6,850	2:57.20	
1924	Mr. Mutt	3	H. Thurber	116	My Play	126	Aga Khan	116	8,550	3:00.80	
1925	Mad Play	4	L. Fator	126	Swope	116	Flames	126	7,150	2:59.40	
1926	Espino	3	L. Fator	116	Display	116	Princess Doreen	121	7,650	3:00.40	
1927	Chance Play	4	J. Maiben	126	Forever and Ever	126	Espino	126	7,100	3:03.60	
1928	Reigh Count	3	C. Lang	118	Display	126			6,500	2:55.00	
1929	Diavolo	4	J. Maiben	126	Double Play	126	African	116	7,350	2:58.00	
1930	Gallant Fox	3	E. Sande	118	Frisius	126	Gone Away	116	9,275	2:56.00	
1931	Twenty Grand	3	L. McAtee	118	Sun Beau	126	Sir Ashley	118	8,250	3:01.20	
1932	War Hero	3	J. Gilbert	118	Blenheim	126	Dark Secret	118	7,825	2:59.20	
1933	Equipoise	5	R. Workman	126	Gusto	126	Keep Out	118	6,050	3:00.00	
1934	Dark Secret	5	C. Kurtsinger	126	Faireno	126	Cleves	118	5,525	2:59.20	
1935	Count Arthur	3	W.D. Wright	116	Esposa	111	Faireno	126	7,145	2:58.40	
1936	Granville	3	J. Stout	116	Discovery	126			6,520	3:00.80	
1937	Count Arthur	5	L. Balaski	126	Matey	116	Esposa	121	6,425	3:02.20	
1938	War Admiral	4	M. Peters	126	Esposa	121	Anaflame	111	6,600	2:55.80	
1939	Isolater	6	J. Stout	126	Cravat	126			6,400	2:56.20	
1940	Fenelon	3	J. Longden	116					4,650	3:02.00	
	Isolater	7	J. Stout	126							
1941	Dorimar	4	C. McCreary	121	Welcome Pass	116	Fairymant	116	9,850	2:58.40	
1942	Bolingboke	5	H. Lindberg	126	Trierarch	116	Buckskin	116	9,550	2:58.20	
1943	Princequillo	3	S. Brooks	116	Bolingbroke	126	Dark Discovery	121	18,200	2:56.60	
1944	Bolingbroke	7	R. Permane	126	Bounding Home	118	Eurasian	126	17,950	2:57.60	
1945	Stymie	4	J. Longden	126	Olympic Zenith	126	Bankrupt	126	18,645	2:58.00	
1946	Stymie	5	B. James	126					5,975	3:07.40	
1947	Talon	5	J. Adams	126	Hachazo	126	Eb	126	12,300	2:58.40	
1948	Snow Goose	4	J. Jessop	121	Miss Grillo	121	Word of Honor	116	11,000	2:57.80	
1949	Doubtless II	5	T. Atkinson	126	Shackleton	116	Quemadito	126	11,650	2:57.40	
1950	Cochise	4	E. Arcaro	126	Double Brandy	126	Escador	126	11,900	2:57.60	
1951	Busanda	4	E. Guerin	121	Lone Eagle	126	Bit o' Fate	126	10,950	2:59.00	
1952	Busanda	5	T. Atkinson	121	Lone Eage	126	Kiss Me Kate	121	11,325	2:59.80	
1953	Alerted	5	C. McCreary	126	Bit o' Fate	126	Great Captain	126	10,875	3:01.20	
1954	Great Captain	5	E. Arcaro	126	Impulsivo	126	Kazmaier	117	11,075	3:02.40	
1955	Chevation	4	E. Guerin	126	Mark's Puzzle	117	Let's Fly II	126	10,525	3:02.60	
1963	Will I Rule	3	H. Woodhouse	107	Quick Pitch	110	David K.	119	18,622	2:39.80	
1994	Thunder Rumble	5	Migliore R	112	West by West	113	Wallenda	117	150,000	1:48.40	116
1995	L'Carriere	4	J.D. Bailey	113	Yourmissinthepoint	108	Unaccounted For	120	120,000	2:02.80	116
1996	L'Carriere	5	J.F. Chavez	114	Peaks and Valleys	121	Mahogany Hall	116	130,000	2:01.60	116
1997	Cairo Express	5	J.L. Samyn	111	Golden Larch	111	Instant Friendship	108	180,000	2:03.80	106
1998	Awesome Again	4	P. Day	120	Concerto	114	Early Warning	110	180,000	2:03.00	110
1999	Running Stag	5	S.J. Sellers	122	Catienus	115	Golden Missile	115	180,000	2:01.00	116
2000	Pleasant Breeze	5	J.F. Chavez	116	Catienus	114	Gander	114	180,000	2:02.17	109
2001	Aptitude	4	J.D. Bailey	122	Perfect Cat	115	A Fleets Dancer	115	180,000	2:01.55	116
2002	Evening Attire	4	S.X. Bridgmohan	115	Abreeze	113	Dollar Bill	117	180,000	2:02.95	113
2003	Puzzlement	4	J.F. Chavez	113	Volponi	122	Iron Deputy	115	180,000	2:03.54	113
2004	Evening Attire	6	C. Velasquez	115	Funny Cide	118	Bowman's Band	116	150,000	2:00.83	114

Beyer Index: 113.18

SARATOGA SPECIAL (G2), 6 1/2 Furlongs, 2-Year-Olds, Saratoga Race Course, 2003 Purse: $150,000

Year	Winner	Age	Jockey	Wt.	Second	Wt.	Third	Wt.	Win Value	Time	Beyer
1901	Goldsmith	2	N. Turner	122	Blue Girl	119	Masterman	122	14,500	1:08.20	
1902	Irish Lad	2	N. Turner	122	Dazzling	119	Blue Ribbon	122	18,000	1:08.20	
1903	Aristocracy	2	F. O'Neill	122	Broomstick	122	Stalwart	122	21,500	1:11.80	
1904	Sysonby	2	Redfern	122	Hot Shot	122	Britisher	122	14,000	1:07.00	
1905	Mohawk II	2	Redfern	122	Voorhees	122	Tangle	119	16,500	1:07.00	
1906	Salvidere	2	Sewell	119	McCarter	122	Peter Pan	122	15,000	1:12.40	
1907	Colin	2	W. Miller	122	Uncle	122			13,000	1:12.00	
1908	Sir Martin	2	C.H. Shilling	122	Wedding Bells	119	Mediant	119	9,250	1:18.80	
1909	Waldo	2	Nicol	122	Sweep	122	Herkimer	122	4,875	1:15.80	
1910	Novelty	2	C.H. Shilling	122	Iron Mask	122	Naushon	122	6,500	1:13.00	
1913	Roamer	2	Byrne	119	Gainer	122	Black Toney	122	6,500	1:13.00	

Year	Winner	Age	Jockey	Wt.	Second	Wt.	Third	Wt.	Win Value	Time	Beyer
1914	Regret	2	J. Notter	119	Pebbles	122	Paris	122	5,125	1:11.60	
1915	Dominant	2	T. McTaggart	122	Puss in Boots	119	Friar Rock	122	5,125	1:16.00	
1916	Campfire	2	J. McTaggart	122	Tom McTaggart	122	Hourless	116	5,625	1:13.20	
1917	Sun Briar	2	W. Knapp	122	Rosie O'Grady	119	Papp	122	11,750	1:15.00	
1918	Hannibal	2	L. Ensor	122	Terentia	119	Yurucari	122	11,000	1:16.20	
1919	Golden Broom	2	E. Ambrose	122	Wildair	122	King Thrush	122	8,500	1:12.80	
1920	Tryster	2	J. Rodriguez	122	Prudery	122	Dimmesdale	122	9,500	1:12.60	
1921	Morvich	2	F. Keogh	122	Kal-Sang	122	Whiskaway	122	10,500	1:12.20	
1922	Goshawk	2	L. McAtee	122	McKee	122	Bud Lerner	122	12,750	1:12.20	
1923	St. James	2	E. Sande	122	Sun Flag	122	Diogenes	122	12,750	1:11.60	
1924	Sunny Man	2	L. Fator	122	Voltaic	122	Cloudland	112	13,000	1:12.40	
1925	Haste	2	E. Sande	122	Pompey	122	Flight of Time	122	12,000	1:12.40	
1926	Chance Shot	2	E. Sande	122	Scapa Flow	122	Osmand	122	15,750	1:13.00	
1927	Ariel	2	L. Fator	122	Sun Edwin	122	Distraction	122	18,000	1:12.60	
1928	Blue Larkspur	2	A. Pascuma	122	Jack High	122	Too High	119	16,750	1:13.60	
1929	Whichone	2	L. McAtee	122	Pansy Walker	119	Sarazen II	122	16,500	1:13.80	
1930	Jamestown	2	L. McAtee	122	Equipoise	122	Sun Meadow	122	14,050	1:11.40	
1931	Top Flight	2	R. Workman	119	Indian Runner	122	Curacao	122	11,000	1:12.00	
1932	Happy Gal	2	T. Malley	119	Ladysman	122	Caterwaul	122	9,250	1:13.00	
1933	Wise Daughter	2	J. Gilbert	119	Singing Wood	119	Hadagal	122	8,500	1:12.60	
1934	Boxthorn	2	D. Meade	122	Plat Eye	122	Today	122	6,750	1:12.20	
1935	Red Rain	2	R. Workman	122			Bien Joli	122	3,500	1:13.00	
	Coldstream	2	E. Arcaro	122							
1936	Forty Winks	2	R. Workman	122	Flying Scot	122	Galsun	122	7,000	1:13.80	
1937	Pumpkin	2	J. Gilbert	122	Maetall	122	Bull Lea	122	8,000	1:12.60	
1938	El Chico	2	N. Wall	122	Eight Thirty	122	Third Degree	122	8,000	1:10.40	
1939	Bimelech	2	F.A. Smith	122	Briar Sharp	122	Andy K.	122	9,000	1:10.80	
1940	Whirlaway	2	J. Longden	122	New World	122	Good Turn	122	9,750	1:11.20	
1941	Amphitheatre	2	A. Robertson	122	Shut Out	122	Black Raider	122	11,250	1:11.60	
1942	Halberd	2	G. Woolf	122	Collect Call	122	Bourmont	122	8,000	1:13.00	
1943	Cocopet	2	C. McCreary	119	Mrs. Ames	119	Dustman	122	5,500	1:10.60	
1944	Pavot	2	G. Woolf	122	Plebiscite	122	Jeep	122	4,945	1:09.60	
1945	Mist o' Gold	2	W.D. Wright	122	Our Bully	122	Condiment	122	6,435	1:10.20	
1946	Grand Admiral	2	J. Jessop	122	Loyal Legion	122	Khyber Pass	122	6,500	1:13.40	
1947	Better Self	2	E. Arcaro	122	Relic	122	Star Bout	122	14,250	1:12.80	
1948	Blue Peter	2	E. Guerin	122	Sport Page	122	Entrust	122	10,500	1:13.00	
1949	More Sun	2	G. Glisson	122	Suleiman	122	Navy Chief	122	12,750	1:13.80	
1950	Battlefield	2	E. Arcaro	122	Northern Star	122	Battle Morn	122	11,500	1:11.20	
1951	Cousin	2	E. Guerin	122	Old Ironsides	122	Mr. Turf	122	13,000	1:12.00	
1952	Native Dancer	2	E. Guerin	122	Doc Walker	122	South Point	122	17,500	1:13.20	
1953	Turn-to	2	H. Moreno	122	Permian	122	Sir Boss	122	17,250	1:12.80	
1954	Royal Coinage	2	E. Arcaro	122	Pyrenees	122	Summer Tan	122	15,000	1:12.20	
1955	Polly's Jet	2	E. Arcaro	122	Reneged	122	Noorsaga	122	15,250	1:11.40	
1956	Nearctic	2	G. Walker	122	Clem	122	Amarullah	122	13,800	1:13.00	
1957	Grey Monarch	2	J. Nichols	122	Jester	122	Turpitude	122	13,800	1:13.60	
1958	First Landing	2	E. Arcaro	122	Pilot	122	Don't Alibi	122	13,800	1:12.80	
1959	Irish Lancer	2	E. Arcaro	116	Tompion	122	Udaipur	122	38,725	1:12.00	
1960	Bronzerullah	2	R. York	116	Ambiopoise	116	Chinchilla	119	22,822	1:11.60	
1961	Battle Joined	2	M. Ycaza	114	Jaipur	120	Cavalanche	114	24,814	1:10.00	
1962	Mr. Cold Storage	2	J. Sellers	114	Aim n Fire	114	Bold Tim	114	25,837	1:12.60	
1963	Duel	2	B. Baeza	114	Count Bud	114	Traffic	114	21,417	1:10.80	
1964	Sadair	2	M. Ycaza	120	Cornish Prince	124	O'Hara	114	20,995	1:10.60	
1965	Impressive	2	B. Baeza	114	Flame Tree	124	Irish Ruler	114	22,945	1:10.20	
1966	Favorable Turn	2	R. Ussery	116	Bold Hour	120	Top Bid	114	21,547	1:10.60	
1967	Vitriolic	2	B. Baeza	114	Exclusive Native	122	Pappa Steve	114	22,977	1:10.40	
1968	Reviewer	2	B. Baeza	122	Hey Good Lookin	114	Buck Run	122	21,710	1:10.40	
1969	Pontifex	2	P. Anderson	120	Foggy Road	114	High Echelon	114	21,045	1:11.60	
1970	Three Martinis	2	A. Cordero Jr	120	Raise Your Glass	120	Tamtent	120	22,945	1:10.80	
1971	Tarboosh	2	E. Maple	120	Loquacious Don	114	Rest Your Case	122	2,064	1:10.40	
1972	Stop the Music	2	J. Vasquez	117	Step Nicely	117	Macadamion	117	17,145	1:11.20	
1973	Az Igazi	2	M. Venezia	117	Gusty O'Shay	117	Lakeville	117	17,025	1:11.00	
1974	Our Talisman	2	M. Venezia	117	Valid Appeal	117	Knightly Sport	120	17,430	1:10.40	
1975	Bold Forbes	2	J. Velasquez	120	Family Doctor	117	Gentle King	120	22,680	1:09.80	
1976	Banquet Table	2	J. Vasquez	122	Turn of Coin	122	May I Rule	117	22,455	1:11.60	
1977	Darby Creek Road	2	A. Cordero Jr	117	Jet Diplomacy	122	Quadratic	117	22,470	1:10.00	
1978	General Assembly	2	D.G. McHargue	117	Smarten	117	Turn Buckle	117	22,350	1:09.00	
1979	J.P. Brother	2	E. Maple	122	Native Moment	117	Muckraker	122	25,365	1:12.00	
1980	Well Decorated	2	M. Venezia	117	Tap Shoes	117	Motivity	119	34,320	1:10.20	
1981	Conquistador Cielo	2	E. Maple	117	Herschelwalker	117	Timely Writer	122	33,900	1:10.60	
1982	Victorious	2	A. Cordero Jr	122	Pappa Riccio	124	Safe Ground	119	33,960	1:10.60	

Year	Winner	Age	Jockey	Wt.	Second	Wt.	Third	Wt.	Win Value	Time	Beyer
1983	Swale	2	E. Maple	117	Shuttle Jet	117	Big Walt	117	33,720	1:12.60	
1984	Chief's Crown	2	D. MacBeth	117	Do It Again Dan	117	Sky Command	122	42,060	1:10.20	
1985	Soveriegn Don	2	J. Velasquez	122	Hagley Mill	117	Bullet Blade	117	43,200	1:11.40	
1986	Gulch	2	A. Cordero Jr	122	Jazzing Around	117	Java Gold	117	54,990	1:10.00	
1987	Crusader Sword	2	R.G. Davis	117	Tejano	117	Endurance	119	66,420	1:10.20	
1988	Trapp Mountain	2	J.D. Bailey	117	Bio	122	Leading Prospect	117	66,240	1:10.80	
1989	Summer Squall	2	P. Day	124	Dr. Bobby A.	117	Graf	117	53,370	1:09.80	
1990	To Freedom	2	A. Cordero Jr	124	Fighting Affair	117	Eugene Eugene	117	52,710	1:11.40	
1991	Caller I.D.	2	J.D. Bailey	117	Pick Up the Phone	122	Coin Collector	122	71,040	1:09.40	103
1992	Tactical Advantage	2	J.A. Krone	117	Strolling Along	117	Mi Cielo	117	72,600	1:10.40	87
1993	Dehere	2	E. Maple	117	Slew Gin Fizz	117	Whitney Tower	117	71,760	1:09.80	89
1994	Montreal Red	2	J.A. Santos	122	Flitch	115	Law of the Sea	115	64,800	1:17.80	87
1995	Bright Launch	2	J.A. Santos	112	Devil's Honor	114	Severe Clear	113	66,540	1:17.80	79
1996	All Chatter	2	J. F. Chavez	113	Gray Raider	114	Just a Cat	113	84,375	1:16.20	90
1997	Favorite Trick	2	P. Day	122	Case Dismissed	114	K.O. Punch	119	90,000	1:17.00	97
1998	Prime Directive	2	J.F. Chavez	114	Silk Broker	114	Tactical Cat	114	90,000	1:17.00	100
1999	Bevo	2	E.S. Prado	117	Afternoon Affair	114	Settlement	114	90,000	1:17.60	85
2000	City Zip	2	J.A. Santos	122	Scorpion	114	Standard Speed	117	90,000	1:16.88	91
2001	Jump Start	2	P. Day	115	Heavyweight Champ	115	Booklet	117	90,000	1:17.35	86
2002	Zavata	2	J.D. Bailey	122	Lone Star Sky	122	Spite the Devil	116	90,000	1:17.65	101
2003	Cuvee	2	J.D. Bailey	122	Pomeroy	118	Limehouse	122	90,000	1:15.97	103

Beyer Index: 92.15

WILLIAM DONALD SCHAEFER HANDICAP (G3), 1 1/8 Miles, 3-Year-Olds and Up, Pimlico, 2004 Purse: $100,000

Year	Winner	Age	Jockey	Wt.	Second	Wt.	Third	Wt.	Win Value	Time	Beyer
1987	Brilliant Stepper	5	A. Stacy	108	Bagetelle		Fobby Forbes		36,335	1:58.20	
1988	Little Bold John	6	D.A. Miller Jr.	124	Along Came Jones		Entertain		35,571	1:50.40	
1989	Private Terms	4	K.J. Desormeaux	122	Instensive Command		New York Swell		32,025	1:47.20	
1990	Flaming Emperor	4	C.J. Ladner III	112	Loyel Pal		Jet Stream		32,730	1:49.60	
1991	Senator to Be	4	P. Day	112	Flaming Emperor		Challenge My Duty		33,540	1:42.20	
1992	Senator to Be	5	P. Day	114	Fiftysevenette	119	Medium Cool	113	34,260	1:42.60	
1993	Root Boy	5	W.H. McCauley	114	Late Guest	109	Forry Cow How	114	45,000	1:42.60	102
1994	Taking Risks	4	M. Johnston	117	Frottage	115	Super Memory	112	45,000	1:49.40	101
1995	Tidal Surge	5	J.D. Carle	112	Mary's Buckaroo	113	Ameri Valay	119	60,000	1:48.00	110
1996	Canaveral	5	S.J. Sellers	115	Michael's Star	114	Rugged Bugger	114	45,000	1:49.00	108
1997	Western Echo	5	E.S. Prado	116	Suave Dancer	114	Mary's Buckaroo	120	60,000	1:49.40	108
1998	Acceptable	4	J.D. Bailey	118	Littlebitlively	118	Testafly	114	63,000	1:48.60	106
1999	Perfect to a Tee	7	A.C. Cortez	112	Allen's Oop	113	Smile Again	114	60,000	1:49.20	102
2000	Ecton Park	4	P. Day	116	The Groom Is Red	111	Crosspatch	116	60,000	1:49.21	110
2001	Perfect Cat	4	J.D. Bailey	115	Rize	115	Judge's Case	115	60,000	1:49.55	105
2002	Tenpins	4	R.J. Albarado	114	Bowman's Band	117	Tactical Side	113	60,000	1:50.20	104
2003	Windsor Castle	5	J.A. Santos	117	Changeintheweather	113	Tempest Fugit	116	60,000	1:50.08	104
2004	Seattle Fitz	5	R. Migliore	116	The Lady's Groom	115	Roaring Fever	114	60,000	1:49.43	111

Beyer Index: 105.92

SCHUYLERVILLE (G2), 6 Furlongs, 2-Year-Old Fillies, Saratoga Race Course, 2004 Purse: $150,000

Year	Winner	Age	Jockey	Wt.	Second	Wt.	Third	Wt.	Win Value	Time	Beyer
1918	Tuscaloosa	2	G. Walls	107	Herodias	104	Terentia	124	3,300	1:04.60	
1919	Homely	2	W. Kelsay	107	Constancy	127	Miss Jemima	127	2,325	1:06.40	
1920	Careful	2	W. Kelsay	127	Nancy Lee	122	Charity	106	2,950	1:05.60	
1921	Miss Joy	2	M. Garner	127	Second Thoughts	124	Nancy Shanks	106	3,175	1:05.60	
1922	Edict	2	L. Fator	107	Miss Smith	110	Great Luck	104	3,400	1:08.80	
1923	Befuddle	2	L. Lyke	112	Sunny Sal	107	Fluvanna	126	3,925	1:05.80	
1924	Royalite	2	L. Fator	112	Blue Warbler	112	Extra Dry	114	3,925	1:08.40	
1925	Taps	2	A. Johnson	114	Ruthenia	112	Martha Washington	119	3,925	1:07.00	
1926	Aromagne	2	E. Ambrose	107	Bonnie Pennant	112	Candy Star	112	3,925	1:07.40	
1927	Pennant Queen	2	J. Maiben	112	Bateau	122	Anita Peabody	124	4,175	1:07.00	
1928	Atlantis	2	L. McAtee	112	Pennant Lass	111	Brown Elf	115	3,925	1:07.40	
1929	Flying Gal	2	D. McAuliffe	111	Conclave	115	Erin	119	4,925	1:05.40	
1930	Pansette	2	R. Workman	115	Blind Lane	115	Ladana	122	6,075	1:06.00	
1931	Polonaise	2	M. Garner	122	Dinner Time	111	Parry	119	3,925	1:08.00	
1932	Volette	2	R. Workman	115	Notebook	111	Cutie Face	113	3,350	1:07.60	
1933	Slapdash	2	H. Mills	122	Rhythmic	115	Proud Girl	112	2,900	1:06.00	
1934	Uppermost	2	L. Humphries	112	Vicaress	115	Bird Flower	112	2,550	1:05.60	
1935	Parade Girl	2	L. Fallon	112	Beanie M.	112	High Fleet	112	2,475	1:06.20	

Year	Winner	Age	Jockey	Wt.	Second	Wt.	Third	Wt.	Win Value	Time	Beyer
1936	Maecloud	2	E. Litzenberger	110	Magic Circle	110	Pepium	110	2,725	1:07.60	
1937	Creole Maid	2	H. Richards	111	Jacola	113	Merry Lassie	120	2,900	1:05.80	
1938	Soldierette	2	L. Dupps	110	Grey Nurse	110	Dinner Date	110	4,600	1:05.60	
1939	Teacher	2	J. Westrope	120	War Beauty	110	Little Risque	110	4,625	1:05.60	
1940	Nasca	2	R. Donoso	110	Tangled	120	Traffic Court	110	3,725	1:05.20	
1941	Romping Home	2	J. Skelly	113	Mar-Kell	113	Pony Ballet	119	4,800	1:06.40	
1942	Brittany	2	C. McCreary	113	High Bit	113	Flight	113	4,400	1:06.80	
1943	Boojiana	2	T. Atkinson	116	Thread o' Gold	116	Everget	116	5,075	1:04.40	
1944	Ace Card	2	G. Woolf	119	Silver Smoke	112	Leslie Grey	119	7,315	1:04.60	
1945	Red Shoes	2	H. Lindberg	112	Bonnie Beryl	112	Boojie	112	7,385	1:04.40	
1946	Bright Song	2	P. Miller	112	Pipette	122	Maid of Harlem	112	9,250	1:07.40	
1947	Spats	2	E. Guerin	114	Bellesoeur	113	Red Risque	112	9,325	1:04.80	
1948	Gaffery	2	A. Kirklan	112	Greek Blond	115	Gay Mood	112	7,900	1:07.00	
1949	Striking	2	E. Arcaro	115	Sunday Evening	112	Nazma	115	8,000	1:05.40	
1950	Atalanta	2	H. Woodhouse	112	Rose Fern	115	Ruddy	115	8,025	1:06.00	
1951	Rose Jet	2	E. Guerin	115	Star-Enfin	122	Landmark	113	8,375	1:06.20	
1952	Grecian Queen	2	R. York	111	Cold Heart	114	Piedmont Lass	114	9,525	1:07.40	
1953	Evening Out	2	O. Scurlock	123	Riant	119	Incidentally	123	9,400	1:05.40	
1954	Two Stars	2	W. Lester	111	Misty	111	Bless Pat	114	10,150	1:05.80	
1955	Dark Charger	2	A. DeSpirito	119	Pet Child	111	Recherche	111	9,800	1:05.60	
1956	Miss Blue Jay	2	E. Guerin	122	Snow White	119	Tourbillonte	115	11,525	1:06.40	
1957	Pocahontas	2	E. Arcaro	116	Bridgework	119	Gleaming Star	112	12,775	1:07.40	
1958	Rich Tradition	2	W. Boland	116	Lady Be Good	122	Quill	116	11,639	1:07.60	
1959	Irish Jay	2	E. Arcaro	119	Heavenly Body	116	Roving Mary	116	14,065	1:06.00	
1959	Make Sail	2	M. Ycaza	116	Undulation	116	Affection	116	14,390	1:06.20	
1960	Shuette	2	S. Boulmetis	116	Little Tumbler	122	Really Sumthin	116	19,655	1:11.80	
1961	Cicada	2	L. Adams	119	Batter Up	122	Bramalea	116	19,402	1:11.00	
1962	Bold Princess	2	H. Woodhouse	116	Barbwolf	116	Majesta	112	19,012	1:06.00	
1963	Gallatia	2	E. Guerin	116	Hasty Matelda	112	Mechanicville	116	18,980	1:06.80	
1964	Marshua	2	R. Ussery	116	Candalita	116	What a Treat	112	19,890	1:04.80	
1965	Prides Profile	2	D. Pierce	116	Lady Pitt	116	Never in Paris	119	15,177	1:05.00	
1965	Amerala	2	W. Blum	116	Thirty Lima	116	Hula Girl	116	15,502	1:05.40	
1966	Vanilla	2	L. Loughry	116	Northeast Trades	119	Great Era	116	19,532	1:05.00	
1967	Idealistic	2	R. Ussery	116	Copper Canyon	116	Ave Valeque	116	20,150	1:04.60	
1968	Golden Or	2	J.L. Rotz	116	Repercussion	116	Shoo Fly	116	19,272	1:05.60	
1969	Bright Sun	2	E. Belmonte	116	Stolen Base	116	Meritus	116	18,460	1:12.00	
1970	Patelin	2	B. Baeza	116	Bid High	116	Caroline G.	116	19,955	1:10.80	
1971	Numbered Account	2	B. Baeza	119	Bendara	114	Vichy	114	20,220	1:12.60	
1972	La Prevoyante	2	J. LeBlanc	119	Sparkalark	116	Sweet Sop	116	17,850	1:11.40	
1973	Talking Picture	2	B. Baeza	116	Imajoy	116	Celestial Lights	119	17,760	1:10.80	
1974	Our Dancing Girl	2	V. Bracciale Jr	116	Secret's Out	119	But Exclusive	116	16,575	1:11.20	
1974	Laughing Bridge	2	B. Baeza	117	Molly Ballantine	116	Fair Wind	119	16,500	1:09.80	
1975	Nijana	2	J. Velasquez	112	Future Tense	116	Crown Treasure	116	22,680	1:12.20	
1976	Mrs. Warren	2	E. Maple	114	Tickle My Toes	116	Spy Flag	112	22,980	1:11.80	
1977	L'Alezane	2	R. Turcotte	121	Akita	121	Lakeville Miss	114	22,350	1:11.80	
1978	Palm Hut	2	R.I. Velez	114	Hermanville	114	Please Try Hard	114	22,215	1:10.40	
1979	Damask Fan	2	E. Maple	114	Jet Rating	114	Lovin' Lass	112	25,860	1:10.20	
1980	Sweet Revenge	2	J. Velasquez	114	Companionship	114	Heavenly Cause	114	34,980	1:10.40	
1981	Mystical Mood	2	J. Vasquez	114	Aga Pantha	114	Trove	116	34,320	1:11.80	
1982	Weekend Surprise	2	J. Velasquez	114	Share the Fantasy	116	Flying Lassie	114	34,620	1:11.00	
1983	Bottle Top	2	D. Brumfield	114	Officer's Ball	114	Ark	114	34,020	1:11.40	
1984	Weekend Delight	2	C.R. Wood Jr.	119	Resembling	114	Winter's Love	114	4,240	1:11.60	
1985	I'm Splendid	2	A. Cordero Jr.	114	Musical Lark	114	Famous Speech	114	41,820	1:10.80	
1986	Sacahuista	2	C.J. McCarron	115	Our Little Margie	114	Collins	114	54,540	1:10.60	
1987	Over All	2	A. Cordero Jr.	119	Joe's Tammie	119	Flashy Runner	119	68,850	1:10.60	
1988	Wonders Delight	2	J.A. Santos	114	Coax Chelsie	114	Attu	112	67,680	1:09.80	
1989	Golden Reef	2	J.A. Santos	114	Lucy's Glory	119	Miss Cox's Hat	114	54,360	1:10.40	
1990	Meadow Star	2	C.W. Antley	119	Garden Gal	119	Prayerful Miss	114	52,590	1:11.20	
1991	Turnback the Alarm	2	D. Carr	114	Speed Dialer	119	Teddy's Top Ten	114	7,200	1:12.00	
1992	Distinct Habit	2	J.D. Bailey	119	Tourney	114	Lily La Belle	114	72,480	1:11.00	80
1993	Strategic Maneuver	2	J.A. Santos	114	Astas Foxy Lady	119	She Rides Tonite	114	73,560	1:11.00	79
1994	Changing Ways	2	M.E. Smith	114	Unacceptable	119	Artic Experience	114	67,980	1:12.60	73
1995	Golden Attraction	2	D.M. Barton	121	Daylight Come	112	Westerm Dreamer	121	65,940	1:10.80	90
1996	How About Now	2	R. Migliore	115	Exclusive Hold	115	City College	115	68,280	1:12.20	79
1997	Countess Diana	2	S.J. Sellers	116	Love Lock	119	Sequence	116	64,800	1:10.20	99
1998	Call Me Up	2	J.F. Chavez	117	Brittons Hill	117	Fantasy Lake	117	66,060	1:12.80	82
1999	Magicalmysterycat	2	P. Day	122	Circle Of Life	114	Regally Appealing	114	65,700	1:10.80	87
2000	Gold Mover	2	C. Perret	122	Seeking It All	114	Miss Doolittle	114	64,920	1:10.33	93
2001	Touch Love	2	J.F. Chavez	119	Lakeside Cup	117	Lost Expectations	117	65,460	1:11.12	74
2002	Freedom's Daughter	2	J.R. Velazquez	118	Miss Mary Apples	118	Mymich	116	90,000	1:12.14	84
2003	Ashado	2	E.S. Prado	118	Maple Syrple	122	Hermione's Magic	118	90,000	1:12.12	81
2004	Classic Elegance	2	P. Day	122	Angel Trumpet	118	Wild Chick	118	90,000	1:12.48	79

Beyer Index: 83.08

SEABISCUIT BREEDERS' CUP HANDICAP (G3), 1 1/16 Miles, 3-Year-Olds and Up, Bay Meadows, 2004 Purse: $86,250

Year	Winner	Age	Jockey	Wt.	Second	Wt.	Third	Wt.	Win Value	Time	Beyer
1968	Lucky P.J.	5	B. Jennings	122	Speedy King	114	Nasharco	114	12,700	1:09.00	
1969	Royal Fols	4	W. Mahorney	120	Damage Control	115	Speedy King	117	12,950	1:09.80	
1970	Royal Fols	5	W. Mahorney	119	Snappy Nashville	111	Tanfo Gold	119	12,250	1:08.80	
1971	Dizzy Babe	7	J.T. Gonzalez	116	Little Scrib	114	Court Clown	117	12,000	1:09.80	
1972	Long Position	6	J. Sellers	118	Galea Pass	116	Indulto	122	15,050	1:09.20	
1973	Selecting	4	R. Yaka	112	I'm Ed	111	Goalie	120	15,150	1:09.00	
1974	Tragic Isle	5	F. Mena	124	Prince Rameses	113	Times Rush	113	15,000	1:08.80	
1975	Cherry River	5	W. Mahorney	126	El Potrero	115	Black Tornado	116	16,200	:56.80	
1976	Shirley's Champion	5	F. Olivares	114	King Charly	113	Oriental Magic	114	15,800	:56.80	
1977	L'Natural	4	R. Cabellero	114	Maheras	126	Sporting Goods	122	15,800	:56.00	
1978	Maheras	5	W. Mahorney	132	Charley Sutton	115	Oriental Magic	113	15,550	:56.20	
1979	Str'ttn Geo	5	T.M. Chapman	122	Don Alberto	119	Charley Sutton	114	13,100	1:28.00	
1980	California Express	5	J. Aragon	113	Kamehameha	121	Miami Sun	120	19,000	1:29.60	
1981	Borrego Sun	4	R.A. Baze	114	Prenotion	116	Kane County	113	25,550	1:29.60	
1982	Crews Hill	6	R.A. Baze	118	Shagbark	122	Hallowed Envoy	116	64,800	1:29.40	
1983	Major Sport	6	T.M. Chapman	115	Aristocratical	114	Take the Floor	115	50,300	1:29.40	
							Famous Star	115			
1984	Ancestral	4	R. Sibille	115	Otter Slide	116	Silveyville	124	49,750	1:29.20	
1985	Hegemony	4	D.G. McHargue	121	Champion Pilot	121	Nack Ack	117	71,740	1:28.60	
1986	Clever Song	4	F. Toro	122	Truce Maker	114	Ocean View	117	63,000	1:28.00	
1987	Mangaki	6	T.T. Doocy	115	Barbery	116	Santella Mac	115	79,550	1:34.40	
1988	Ifrad	6	T.M. Chapman	117	Stop the Fighting	115	Nickle Band	113	5,500	1:43.40	
1989	Simply Majestic	5	R.D. Hansen	121	Ongoing Mister	113	Astronaut Pr'nce	115	5,500	1:42.40	
1990	River Master	4	R.G. Davis	116	Miswaki Tern	116	Exclusive Partner	117	55,000	1:43.20	101
1991	Forty Niner Days	4	T.T. Doocy	115	Neptuno	116	Trebizond	115	55,000	1:43.60	
1992	Gum	6	G. Boulanger	112	Forty Niner Days	116	Prudent Manner	115	55,000	1:41.60	108
1993	Never Black	6	C.S. Nakatani	115	Stark South	115	Daros	114	55,000	1:42.40	107
1994	Slew of Damascus	6	T.M. Chapman	122	Fast Cure	114	The Tender Track	116	55,000	1:43.60	106
1995	Bluegrass Prince	4	T.M. Chapman	114	Lord Shirldor	116	Kinema Red	113	68,750	1:49.00	101
1996	Tzar Rodney	4	T.M. Chapman	114	Joy of Glory	115	Opera Score	115	60,000	1:49.60	102
1997	Mister Fire Eyes	5	R.J. Warren Jr.	115	Region	115	Tolomeo	113	60,000	1:41.20	99
1998	Wild Wonder	4	Baze R. A.	121	Crypto Star	118	General Royal	115	60,000	1:41.20	99
1999	Worldly Ways	5	Baze R. A.	116	Barter Town	112	Highland Gold	115	60,000	1:40.60	104
							Scooter Brown	114			
2000	Peach Flat	6	J. Valdivia Jr.	114	Boss Ego	115	Casey Girffin	115	75,000	1:42.48	105
2001	Euchre	5	J. Lumpkins	118	Irisheyesareflying	118	Moonlight Charger	115	82,500	1:41.69	103
2002	Palmeiro	4	J. Lumpkins	115	Moonlight Meeting	116	Prodigious	116	82,500	1:42.31	97
2003	Reba's Gold	6	C.J. Rollins	118	Free Corona	116	Truly a Judge	117	55,000	1:41.63	100
2004	Yougottawanna	5	R.A. Baze	116	Gold Ruckus	115	Snorter	118	41,250	1:40.08	103

Beyer Index: 102.50

Run as the All-American Handicap prior to 2003.

SECRETARIAT (G1), 1 1/4 Miles (Turf), 3-Year-Olds, Arlington Park, 2004 Purse: $400,000

Year	Winner	Age	Jockey	Wt.	Second	Wt.	Third	Wt.	Win Value	Time	Beyer
1974	Glossary	3	A. Santiago	114	Stonewalk	123	Talkative Turn	114	96,400	1:42.80	
1975	Intrepid Hero	3	A. Cordero Jr	123	Gab Bag	117	Larrikin	117	94,000	1:49.80	
1976	Joachim	3	S. Maple	123	Romeo	112	L'Heureux	117	88,400	1:50.80	
1977	Text	3	M. Castaneda	120	Run Dusty Run	126	Flag Officer	123	73,140	1:42.00	
1978	Mac Diarmida	3	J. Cruguet	120	April Axe	120	The Liberal Member	114	99,600	2:29.80	
1979	Golden Act	3	S. Hawley	126	Smarten	120	Flying Dad	120	91,080	2:32.80	
1980	Spruce Needles	3	J.C. Espinoza	123	Proctor	120	The Messenger	123	99,960	2:40.80	
1981	Sing Sing	3	M. Venezia	114	Television Studio	117	Jungle Tough	114	96,240	2:53.60	
1982	Half Iced	3	D. MacBeth	114	Dew Line	114	Continuing	114	90,000	2:31.20	
1983	Fortnightly	3	P. Day	117	Jack Slade	114	Reap	114	102,360	2:32.40	
1984	Vision	3	G. McCarron	114	Mr. Japan	114	Pine Circle	114	117,240	2:38.40	
1985	Derby Wish	3	R.P. Romero	114	Day Shift	114	Duluth	123	146,880	2:01.00	
	Racing Star finished second but was disqualified and placed fourth										
1986	Southjet	3	J.A. Santos	113	Glow	120	Tripoli Shores	115	102,510	2:02.00	
1987	Stately Don	3	J. Vasquez	113	The Medic	120	Zaizoom	120	103,590	2:04.60	
1989	Hawkster	3	P.A. Valenzuela	123	Chenin Blanc	114	Ninety Years Young	114	150,000	2:04.00	
1990	Super Abound	3	R.P. Romero	114	Unbridled	126	Super Fan	117	150,000	2:01.60	
1991	Jackie Wackie	3	P. Day	123	Olympio	126	Sultry Song	114	180,000	2:01.20	100
1992	Ghazi	3	R.G. Davis	114	Paradise Creek	123	Tango Charlie	117	180,000	2:01.00	98
1993	Awad	3	J. Velasquez	120	Explosive Red	123	Brazany	114	240,000	2:08.60	106
1994	Vaudeville	3	G.L. Stevens	123	Dare and Go	114	Jaggery John	120	240,000	2:01.00	100
1995	Hawk Attack	3	P. Day	120	Mecke	117	Petit Poucet	114	240,000	2:00.00	101
1996	Marlin	3	S.J. Sellers	114	Trail City	126	Dancing Fred	114	300,000	2:01.00	106
1997	Honor Glide	3	G.K. Gomez	123	Casey Tibbs	116	Glok	114	240,000	2:02.60	105

Year	Winner	Age	Jockey	Wt.	Second	Wt.	Third	Wt.	Win Value	Time	Beyer
2000	Ciro	3	M.J. Kinane	120	King Cugat	123	Guillamou City	117	240,000	2:01.64	108
2001	Startac	3	A. Solis	121	Strut The Stage	123	Sharp Performance	120	240,000	2:04.91	99
2002	Chiselling	3	K.J. Desormeaux	121	Jazz Beat	117	Extra Check	116	240,000	2:04.16	97
2003	Kicken Kris	3	J.J. Castellano	116	Joe Bear	116	Lismore Knight	121	240,000	2:02.53	106
2004	Kitten's Joy	3	J.D. Bailey	123	Greek Sun	121	Moscow Ballet	119	240,000	1:59.65	113

Beyer Index: 103.25

Distance 1 1/16 miles, 1974,1977; 1 1/8 miles, 1975-76, 1 1/2 miles 1978-84. Run on main track in 1977. Run at Hawthorne in 1985. Not run in 1998-99

SENORITA (G3), 1 Mile (Turf), 3-Year-Old Fillies, Hollywood Park, 2004 Purse: $108,900

Year	Winner	Age	Jockey	Wt.	Second	Wt.	Third	Wt.	Win Value	Time	Beyer
1968	Time to Leave	3	D. Velasquez	118	Toe Shoes	112	Saipan	114	14,300	1:36.00	
1969	Prove It Girl	3	W. Mahorney	112	Ynez Queen	114	Sallarina	112	12,850	1:36.40	
1969	Commissary	3	A. Pineda	114	Marjorie's Theme	112	Fourth Round	115	13,050	1:36.40	
1970	Night Staker	3	J. Sellers	115	Tanta Bella	114	Shoosh	112	16,800	1:36.40	
1971	Shelf Talker	3	J. Lambert	114	Lady Debbie	112	Mariways	115	19,400	1:36.00	
1971	Turkish Trousers	3	W. Shoemaker	118	Aladancer	118	Lady of Rome	112	18,800	1:35.80	
1972	Impressive Style	3	L. Pincay Jr	118	Pallisima	112	Logistic	112	20,400	1:35.80	
1973	Cellist	3	J.L. Rotz	119	Jungle Princess	120	Meilleur	119	20,250	1:42.20	
1975	Raise Your Skirts	3	W. Mahorney	119	Fresno Flyer	117	Vol Au Vent	117	19,050	1:36.40	
1976	Raise Pending	3	D. Pierce	117	Cascapedia	115	Queen to Be	119	20,650	1:35.80	
1977	Glenaris	3	W. Shoemaker	114	Countess Fager	119	Shop Windows	114	19,300	1:36.00	
1978	Blue Blood	3	D. Pierce	117	Equanimity	122	Eximious	119	25,000	1:37.00	
1979	Variety Queen	3	R. Rosales	117	Top Soil	119	Whydidju	122	25,850	1:37.00	
1980	Ballare	3	P.A. Valenzuela	114	Street Ballet	122	Cinegita	114	31,600	1:35.00	
1981	Shimmy	3	P.A. Valenzuela	114	Queen of Prussia	117	Bee a Scout	114	37,450	1:36.20	
1982	Skillful Joy	3	C.J. McCarron	119	Phaedra	122	Faneuil Lass	122	31,050	1:34.00	
1983	Stage Door C'n'n	3	C.J. McCarron	114	I'm Prestigious	116	O'Happy Day	115	25,675	1:35.60	
1983	Preceptress	3	M. Castaneda	115	Madam Forbes	114	Toga	116	25,675	1:36.60	
1984	Heartlight	3	L. Pincay Jr	117	Table Ten	115	Dear Carrie	115	38,900	1:35.60	
1985	Akamini	3	F. Toro	117	Charming Susan	115	Sharp Ascent	114	32,250	1:36.60	
1985	Shywing	3	T. Lipham	117	Delaware Ginny	117	Savannah Dancer	119	33,450	1:35.60	
1986	Nature's Way	3	C.J. McCarron	117	An Empress	115	Miraculous	119	39,200	1:42.60	
1987	Pen Bal Lady	3	E. Delahoussaye	117	Sweettuc	119	Dave's Lamb	115	61,350	1:35.40	
1988	Do So	3	A. Solis	117	Pattern Step	119	Sheesham	117	45,950	1:34.20	
1989	Reluctant Guest	3	C.J. McCarron	114	Formidable Lady	119	General Charge	117	50,200	1:34.00	
1990	Brought to Mind	3	A. Solis	114	Tasteful T.V.	119	She's a V.P.	117	62,600	1:34.40	
1991	Paula Revere	3	J.A. Santos	117	Shy Trick	114	Island Shuffle	119	61,850	1:35.40	93
1992	Charm a Gendarme	3	R.Q. Meza	116	Moonlight Elegance	116	Morriston Belle	118	67,250	1:33.60	89
1993	Likeable Style	3	K.J. Desormeaux	121	Adorydar	113	Icy Warning	118	61,250	1:34.40	97
1994	Rabiadella	3	L. Pincay Jr.	118	Magical Avie	116	Fancy 'n Fabulous	118	60,800	1:34.80	98
1995	Top Shape	3	C.S. Nakatani	114	Artica	118	Auriette	116	63,900	1:34.60	92
1996	To B. Super	3	C.W. Antley	118	Gastronomical	118	Ribot's Secret	116	68,940	1:34.80	96
1997	Kentucky Kaper	3	R.R. Douglas	114	Ascutney	120	Ava Knowsthecode	115	66,780	1:34.20	90
1998	Dancing Rhythm	3	K.J. Desormeaux	118	Phone Alex	115	Star's Proud Penny	122	64,920	1:35.20	83
1999	Coracle	3	K.J.Desormeaux	116	Aviate	116	Dianehill	115	67,740	1:34.00	93
2000	Islay Mist	3	D.R. Flores	116	Fire Sale Queen	118	Miss Pixie	114	67,080	1:34.16	88
2001	Fantastic Filly	3	G.K. Gomez	123	Innit	115	Blushing Bride	115	65,880	1:35.13	97
2002	Adoration	3	G.K. Gomez	117	High Society	115	Nunatall	115	64,380	1:34.91	92
2003	Makeup Artist	3	V. Espinoza	117	Rutters Renegade	117	Shapes and Shadows	117	68,100	1:36.54	90
2004	Miss Vegas	3	A. Solis	115	Ticker Tape	121	Amorama	116	65,340	1:34.25	94

Beyer Index: 92.29

SHADWELL TURF MILE (G1), 1 Mile (Turf), 3-Year-Olds and Up, Keeneland Race Course, 2004 Purse: $600,000

Year	Winner	Age	Jockey	Wt.	Second	Wt.	Third	Wt.	Win Value	Time	Beyer
1986	Leprechaun's Wish	4	J.D. Bailey	126	Ingot's Ruler	126	Wop Wop	126	100,848	1:51.80	
1987	Storm on the L'se	4	J.C. Espinoza	126	Uptown Swell	126	Vilzak	126	101,855	1:52.60	
1988	Niccolo Polo	5	D. Brumfield	126	Pollenate	126	Eve's Error	126	101,823	1:53.00	
1989	Steinlen	6	J.A. Santos	116	Crystal Moment	126	Posen	126	122,103	1:52.40	
1990	Itsallgreektome	4	J. Velasquez	126	Opening Verse	126	Super Abound	126	121,973	1:52.20	
1991	Itsallgreektome	4	J. Velasquez	126	Opening Verse	126	Super Abound	126	119,600	1:48.40	109
1992	Lotus Pool	5	C.R. Woods Jr	126	Thunder Regent	126	Chenin Blanc	113	113,646	1:48.20	105
1993	Coaxing Matt	4	E.M. Martin Jr	122	Adam Smith	126	Mr. Light Tres	126	116,420	1:53.00	102
1994	Weekend Madness	4	Sellers SJ	123	Words of War	123	Pennine Ridge	123	116,327	1:38.60	105
1995	Dumaani	4	Krone JA	126	Holy Mountain	126	Mr Purple	123	116,514	1:38.60	99
1996	Dumaani	5	J.A. Krone	126	Desert Waves	126	Dove Hunt	126	133,842	1:35.40	102

Year	Winner	Age	Jockey	Wt.	Second	Wt.	Third	Wt.	Win Value	Time	Beyer
1997	Wild Event	4	M. Guidry	126	Trail City	126	Soviet Line	126	134,075	1:34.60	101
1998	Favorite Trick	3	P. Day	123	Soviet Line	126	Wild Event	126	168,795	1:35.00	109
1999	Kirkwall	5	V. Espinoza	126	Delay of Game	126	Ladies Din	126	281,232	1:37.80	103
2000	Altibr	5	R. Migliore	126	Strategic Mission	126	Quiet Resolve	126	279,744	1:33.72	106
2001	Hap	5	J.D. Bailey	126	Where's Taylor	126	Aly's Alley	126	346,270	1:35.98	110
2002	Landseer	3	E.S. Prado	123	Touch of the Blues	126	Beat Hollow	126	372,000	1:35.55	104
2003	Perfect Soul	5	E.S. Prado	126	Honor in War	126	Touch of the Blues	126	372,000	1:36.01	107
2004	Nothing to Lose	4	R.J. Albarado	126	Honor in War	126	Silver Tree	126	372,000	1:35.55	111

Beyer Index: 105.21

SHAKERTOWN (G3), 5 1/2 Furlongs (Turf), 3-Year-Olds and Up, Keeneland, 2004 Purse: $115,100

Year	Winner	Age	Jockey	Wt.	Second	Wt.	Third	Wt.	Win Value	Time	Beyer
1997	G.H.'s Pleasure	5	J.A. Santos	114	Louie the Lucky	114	Parklo	117	34,410	1:03.00	97
1998	Sesaro	6	S.J. Sellers	123	Brave Pancho	114	Claire's Honor	114	43,850	1:02.35	99
1999	Prankster	6	S.J. Sellers	115	Tyaskin	120	Howbaddouwantit	123	43,850	1:02.43	99
2000	Bold Fact	5	R. Migliore	115	Howbaddouwantit	118	Claire's Honor	115	46,800	1:02.61	101
2001	Airbourne Command	6	J.F. Chavez	118	Final Row	118	Grangeville	118	52,824	1:02.71	100
2002	Morluc	6	R. Albarado	118	Mighty Beau	116	Grangeville	118	52,731	1:02.35	103
2003	No Jacket Required	6	B. Blanc	118	Testify	120	Abderian	120	70,494	1:03.25	100
2004	Soaring Free	5	S.J. Sellers	120	Chosen Chief	118	Banned in Boston	118	71,362	1:01.78	101

Beyer Index: 100.00

SHEEPSHEAD BAY HANDICAP (G2), 1 3/8 Miles (Turf), Fillies and Mares, 3-Year-Olds and Up, Belmont Park, 2004 Purse: $150,000

Year	Winner	Age	Jockey	Wt.	Second	Wt.	Third	Wt.	Win Value	Time	Beyer
1959	Greek Star	4	H. Woodhouse	110	Whitley	115	Oh Johnny	119	17,867	1:42.20	
1960	Tharp	5	R. York	116	Misty Flight	117	Shield Bearer	117	18,907	1:49.00	
1961	Wolfram	5	I. Valenzuela	130	Wise Ship	109	Shield Bearer	120	18,330	1:50.60	
1962	Rose O'Neill	4	M. Ycaza	124	Seven Thirty	123	Play Time	117	18,655	1:34.20	
1963	Cicada	4	L. Adams	128	Nubile	109	Doll Ina	117	18,232	1:42.40	
1964	Intervene	4	M. Ycaza	116	Nubile	112	Princess Arle	114	19,435	1:46.40	
1965	Snow Scene II	5	B. Baeza	115	Treachery	115	Steeple Jill	126	37,765	1:56.80	
1966	Straight Deal	4	W. Blum	122	Mount Regina	120	Treachery	111	37,115	1:55.40	
1967	Indian Sunlite	4	H. Gustines	118	Mount Regina	117	Amerivan	119	37,440	1:54.80	
1968	Ludham	4	J. Vasquez	119	Hail the Queen	117	Lady Diplomat	113	30,420	1:54.80	
1968	Politely	5	A. Cordero	125	Mount Regina	115	Treacherous	114	30,095	1:55.40	
1969	Symona II	3	J. Velasquez	109	Harem Lady	116	Swiss Cheese	108	38,480	1:55.80	
1970	Princess Pout	4	J. Cruguet	108	A.T.;s Olie	109	Klassy Poppy	116	29,640	1:56.40	
1970	Pattee Canyon	5	J.L. Rotz	132	Top Round	115	Jungle Fire II	109	29,640	1:57.40	
1971	Princess Pout	5	J. Cruguet	124	Tanagra	113	Joans Paris	113	35,340	1:56.60	
1972	Sydneys Nurse	4	J. Vasquez	113	Ziba Blue	109	Flor de S'bra	112	27,510	1:57.00	
1972	Inca Queen	4	G. Patterson	122	Kittiwake	118	Society Column	109	27,810	1:56.40	
1973	Shearwater	4	A. Cordero Jr	122	Inca Queen	118	Aglimmer	115	35,610	1:59.80	
1974	North Broadway	4	A. Cordero Jr	116	Lorraine Edna	117	Gnome Home	109	35,190	1:56.20	
1975	Gems and Roses	5	M. Venezia	112	Hinterland	113	Carolerno	110	34,740	2:01.60	
1976	Glowing Tribute	4	J. Velasquez	118	Bubbling	119	Carmelize	109	50,700	1:49.20	
1976	Fleet Victress	4	P. Day	115	Redundancy	123	Summertime Promise	119	51,600	1:49.00	
1977	Glowing Tribute	3	J. Velasquez	118	Fleet Victress	119	Dottie's Doll	116	65,700	1:59.60	
1978	Late Bloomer	4	J. Velasquez	118	Waya	115	Pearl Necklace	124	68,880	2:01.00	
1979	Terpsichorist	4	E. Maple	117	Late Bloomer	123	Warfever	110	67,200	2:01.60	
1980	The Very One	5	C. Cooke	116	Euphrosyne	114	Baby Sister	115	71,520	2:13.00	
1981	Love Sign	4	R. Hernandez	114	Rokeby Rose	115	Mairzy Doates	122	67,680	2:13.00	
1982	Dana Calqui	4	A. Cordero Jr	110	If Winter Comes	110	Noble Damsel	115	66,060	2:14.20	
1983	Sabin	3	E. Maple	112	First Approach	118	Mintage	114	67,920	2:13.80	
1984	Sabin	4	E. Maple	125	Thirty Flags	114	Double Jeux	111	71,880	2:12.80	
1985	Persian Tiara	5	J. Velasquez	116	Key Dancer	118	Dictina	112	86,820	2:16.00	
1986	Possible Mate	5	J.L. Samyn	124	Tremulous	112	Dawn's Curtsey	112	75,480	2:14.00	
1987	Steal a Kiss	4	E. Maple	111	Videogenic	117	Graceful Darby	112	87,180	2:23.80	
1988	Nastique	4	R.G. Davis	111	Princely Proof	115	Anka Germania	124	71,040	2:16.40	
1989	Love You by Heart	4	J. Cruguet	118	Nastique	117	Laugh and Be Merry	112	72,480	2:12.60	
1990	Destiny Dance	4	J.A. Santos	111	Key Flyer	108	Yestday's Kisses	112	55,080	2:19.20	93
1991	Crockadore	4	M.E. Smith	112	Rigamajig	114	Star Standing	114	71,760	2:14.80	104
1992	Ratings	4	J. Cruguet	112	Ristna	110	Dancing Devilette	113	75,000	2:15.00	97
1993	Trampoli	4	M.E. Smith	116	Aquilegia	116	Revasser	114	67,680	2:14.00	98
1994	Market Booster	5	J.A. Santos	114	Irish Linnet	115	Fairy Garden	120	66,960	2:11.60	103
1995	Duda	4	J.D. Bailey	112	Danish	116	Chelsey Flower	112	65,700	2:13.60	105
1996	Chelsey Flower	5	R.G. Davis	114	Look Daggers	114	Transient Trend	113	67,320	2:12.60	101

Year	Winner	Age	Jockey	Wt.	Second	Wt.	Third	Wt.	Win Value	Time	Beyer
1997	Maxzene	4	M.E. Smith	117	Fanjica	117	Future Act	112	90,000	2:11.40	106
1998	Maxzene	5	J.A. Santos	121	Sweetzie	111	Colonial Play	115	90,000	2:14.00	101
1999	Soaring Softly	4	M.E. Smith	114	Starry Dreamer	114	Pinafore Park	113	90,000	2:15.00	101
2000	Lisieux Rose	5	J.A. Santos	116	Melody Queen	113	La Ville Rouge	113	90,000	2:14.16	98
2001	Critical Eye	4	M.J. Luzzi	122	Playact	115	Janet	116	90,000	2:18.18	100
2002	Tweedside	4	J.R. Velazquez	114	Sweetest Thing	119	Golden Corona	114	90,000	2:13.63	95
2003	Mariensky	4	J.R. Velazquez	114	Owsley	119	Silent Crystal	112	90,000	2:28.19	106
2004	Moscow Burning	4	M.E. Smith	114	Spice Island	119	Meridiana	119	90,000	2:18.24	102

Beyer Index: 100.67

SHIRLEY JONES HANDICAP (G3), 7 Furlongs, Fillies and Mares, 3-Year-Olds and Up, Gulfstream Park, 2004 Purse: $100,000

Year	Winner	Age	Jockey	Wt.	Second	Wt.	Third	Wt.	Win Value	Time	Beyer
1976	Regal Quillo		C. Baltazar	114	Forty Nine Sunsets	112	Tristana	112	10,200	1:42.20	
1979	Candy Eclair		A.S. Black	122	Davona Dale	122	Drop Me a Note	114	17,766	1:08.60	
1981	Sober Jig	4	J.P. Souter	112	Likely Exchange	116	Island Charm	115	27,153	1:23.20	
1982	Bushmaid	4	J.D. Bailey	112	Expressive Dance	124	Sweetest Chant	117	19,470	1:23.20	
1983	Meringue Pie	5	J. Velasquez	115	Cherokee Frolic	118	Mara Mia	109	24,717	1:24.20	
1983	Secrettame	5	J. Vasquez	116	Prime Prospect	120	Miss Hitch	114	25,158	1:23.60	
1984	Chic Belle	4	C. Perret	114	Promising Native	114	First Flurry	115	25,578	1:22.40	
1985	Mickey's Echo	6	W.A. Guerra	117	Sugar's Image	117	Nany	122	37,110	1:23.60	
1986	Soli	4	J.D. Bailey	113	Bessarabian	123	Nany	117	39,390	1:23.80	
1987	Life at the Top	4	R.P. Romero	121	I'm Sweets	120	Jose's Bomb	112	35,640	1:22.80	
1988	Tappiano	4	J. Cruguet	115	Cadillacing	111	Bound	115	52,110	1:23.00	
1989	Social Pro	4	J.F. Chavez	110	Haiati	113	Costly Shoes	114	35,640	1:23.60	
1990	Love's Exchange	4	E. Fires	112	Fantastic Find	113	Fit for a Queen	114	36,720	1:23.60	
1991	Love's Exchange	5	H. Castillo Jr	126	Peach of It	116	Tipsy Girl	114	35,820	1:23.20	104
1992	Nannerl	5	J.A. Krone	111	Withallprobability	120	Fit for a Queen	119	36,600	1:23.20	97
1993	Jeano	5	S.J. Sellers	113	Santa Catalina	115	Miss Jealski	111	39,060	1:23.40	94
1994	Santa Catalina	6	P. Day	115	Jeano	113	Traverse City	113	60,000	1:21.80	98
1995	Educated Risk	5	M.E. Smith	125	Elizabeth Bay	115	Clever Act	114	60,000	1:22.80	112
1996	Dust Bucket	5	R.G. Davis	112	Russian Flight	110	Culver City	115	60,000	1:25.80	90
1997	Chip	4	Bravo J.	114	Steady Cat	113	Flat Fleet Feet	117	60,000	1:22.20	101
1998	U Can Do It	5	Sellers S. J.	116	Glitter Woman	123	Flashy n Smart	118	60,000	1:23.20	110
1999	Harpia	5	R. Migliore	118	Scotzanna	115	Memories of Gold	113	60,000	1:22.00	102
2000	Marley Vale	4	J.R. Velazquez	118	Cassidy	113	Class on Class	113	60,000	1:22.24	103
2001	Hidden Assets	4	J.D. Bailey	114	Another	115	Dream Supreme	120	60,000	1:22.40	95
2002	Cat Cay	5	P. Day	118	Raging Fever	120	Vague Memory	112	60,000	1:22.31	102
2003	Harmony Lodge	5	J.R. Velazquez	114	Gold Mover	117	Nonsuch Bay	117	60,000	1:22.35	104
2004	Randaroo	4	J.R. Velazquez	118	Harmony Lodge	121	Halory Leigh	114	60,000	1:21.42	108

Beyer Index: 101.43

SHOEMAKER BREEDERS' CUP MILE (G1), 1 Mile (Turf), 3-Year-Olds and Up, Hollywood Park, 2004 Purse: $456,000

Year	Winner	Age	Jockey	Wt.	Second	Wt.	Third	Wt.	Win Value	Time	Beyer
1938	Air Chute	4	B. James	119	Faithful Maud	107	Speed to Spare	119	2,055	1:11.40	
1939	Don Mike	5	L. Balaski	111	Whichcee	117	Speed to Spare	113	5,325	1:10.80	
1940	Capt. Cal	7	J. Longden	113	Son of War	108	Lassator	117	7,525	1:10.80	
1941	Hysterical	5	E. Rodriguez	123	Exemplify	108	Big Ben	123	8,550	1:11.20	
1944	Civil Code	4	J. Adams	123	Ended	122	Appleknocker	121	7,940	1:12.00	
1945	High Resolve	4	C. Corbett	116	Black Badge	117	stronghold	111	12,472	1:10.80	
1946	Happy Issue	6	H. Trent	108	Quick Reward	120	Enfilade	116	18,550	1:10.40	
1947	El Lobo	6	W. Bailey	119	Be Sure Now	114	Texas Sandman	117	21,850	1:10.00	
1949	The Shaker	6	J. Adams	110	Star Fiddle	111	Bymeabond	118	19,900	1:10.20	
1950	Star Fiddle	4	H. Trent	108	Your Host	125	Bewitch	114	21,700	1:22.20	
1951	Special Touch	4	W. Shoemaker	122	Manyunk	114	Bullreigh Jr.	110	11,450	1:10.00	
1952	Warcos	3	R. Neves	112	Reighs Bull	119	Mohammedan	114	17,300	1:09.80	
1953	Pet Bully	5	W. Shoemaker	120	Big Noise	111	Blue Trumpeter	110	16,100	1:10.20	
1954	Stranglehold	5	W. Shoemaker	115	Imbros	132	Big Noise	110	15,400	1:09.20	
1955	El Drag	4	J. Longden	112	Berseem	128	Porterhouse	119	15,700	1:09.00	
1956	Cyclotron	8	G. Glisson	112	Porterhouse	118	One Ton Tony	112	16,500	1:09.20	
1957	Find	7	R. York	123	Social Climber	118	Porterhouse	124	15,850	1:09.00	
1958	The Searcher	4	W. Ferguson	107	How Now	115	Sw'ng Abbey	115	13,150	1:09.80	
1959	Fleet Nasrullah	4	I. Valenzuela	116	Terrang	124	Seaneen	118	13,500	1:09.00	
1960	Fleet Nasrullah	5	J. Longden	126	Clandestine	120	Ole Fols	122	12,900	1:08.20	
1961	Revel	5	A. Valenzuela	126	Finnegan	118	Henrijan	117	13,950	1:08.80	
1962	Winonly	5	W. Harmatz	115	Double Lea	117	Prove It	123	14,450	1:08.80	
1963	Winonly	6	I. Valenzuela	121	Kisco Kid	112	Double Lea	115	13,550	1:09.40	
1964	Sledge	5	I. Valenzuela	118	Mustard Plaster	117	Double Lea	117	13,850	1:09.00	

Year	Winner	Age	Jockey	Wt.	Second	Wt.	Third	Wt.	Win Value	Time	Beyer
1965	Viking Spirit	5	K. Church	123	Perris	113	Native Diver	127	15,900	1:08.40	
1966	Sledge	7	I. Valenzuela	115	Chiclero	110	Real Good Deal	116	16,200	1:10.20	
1967	Fleet Discovery	4	W. Shoemaker	110	Chiclero	115	Native Diver	131	15,500	1:09.20	
1968	Kissin' George	5	W. Mahorney	126	Rising Market	117	Chiclero	114	15,850	1:08.60	
1969	Indulto	6	D. Pierce	120	Title Game	116	Rising Market	125	16,900	1:08.40	
1970	First Mate	5	J. Lambert	118	Right or Wrong	114	Baffle	124	19,500	1:08.80	
1971	Earl of Milldale	5	J. Lambert	115	King of Cricket	120	Once Over	114	24,750	1:10.40	
1972	Miles Tyson	4	R. Ussery	117	Single Agent	123	Long Position	113	26,900	1:08.00	
1973	Diplomatic Agent	5	R. Rosales	115	Rough Night	111	Selecting	116	20,150	1:09.00	
1974	Beira	5	W. Mahorney	115	Woodland Pines	119	Linda's Chief	124	19,700	1:07.80	
1975	Rise High	5	S. Hawley	116	Selecting	117	Money Lender	115	18,900	1:09.00	
	Shirley's Champion finished second but was disqualified and placed fourth										
1976	Sporting Goods	6	F. Toro	115	Century's Envoy	124	Money Lender	115	20,500	1:08.20	
1977	Barrera	4	L. Pincay Jr	119	Beat Inflation	120	Maheras	124	24,650	1:07.40	
1978	J.O. Tobin	4	S. Cauthen	125	Mr. Redoy	121	Miami Sun	115	30,600	1:41.40	
1979	Farnesio	5	W. Shoemaker	119	Harry's Love	114	Star Spangled	120	31,100	1:41.60	
1980	Peregrinator	5	C.J. McCarron	119	Dragon Command	117	Life's Hope	117	31,850	1:41.60	
1984	Massera	4	E. Delahoussaye	115	Sari's Dreamer	112	Barberstown	119	33,350	1:34.20	
1984	Drumalis	6	E. Delahoussaye	119	Bel Bolide	122	Hula Blaze	114	33,950	1:33.80	
1985	Retsina Run	5	E. Delahoussaye	116			Val Danseur	113	26,500	1:33.40	
	Capture Him	4	C.J. McCarron	120							
1985	Native Charmer II	4	S. Hawley	113	Gato Del Sol	120	Both Ends Burning	123	41,000	1:33.60	
1986	Clever Song	4	F. Toro	116	Poly Test	115	Both Ends Burning	124	49,400	1:38.80	
1987	Clever Song	5	F. Toro	119	Al Mamoon	122	Le Belvedere	114	61,900	1:41.20	
1988	Steinlen	5	G.L. Stevens	119	Siyah Kalem	115	Neshad	115	80,200	1:33.20	
1989	Peace	4	W. Shoemaker	115	Steinlen	121	Political Ambition	122	65,700	1:33.00	
1990	Shining Steel	4	C.J. McCarron	114	Super May	117	Brave Capade	111	63,000	1:34.00	103
1991	Exbourne	5	G.L. Stevens	118	Super May	117	Dansil	111	65,300	1:33.40	106
1993	Journalism	5	A. Solis	114	Lomitas	118	Brief Truce	122	63,800	1:32.80	102
1994	Megan's Interco	5	C.A. Black	119	Furiously	116	Rapan Boy	115	63,200	1:32.60	117
1995	Unfinished Symph	4	C.W. Antley	121	Rapan Boy	118	Journalism	117	98,400	1:33.00	111
1996	Fastness	6	C.S. Nakatani	124	Romarin	124	Atticus	124	420,000	1:32.60	111
1997	Pinfloron	5	D. Flores	124	Surachai	124	Helmsman	124	353,400	1:34.40	108
1998	Labeeb	6	K. Desorneaux	124	Fantastic Fellow	124	Hawksley Hill	124	319,200	1:33.20	111
1999	Silic	4	C.S. Nakatani	124	Ladies Din	124	Hawksley Hill	124	280,200	1:32.95	109
2000	Silic	5	K.J. Desormeaux	124	Ladies Din	124	Sharan	124	292,800	1:33.36	109
2001	Irish Prize	5	G.L. Stevens	120	Touch of the Blues	124	Brahms	124	285,000	1:33.68	107
2002	Ladies Din	7	P.A. Valenzuela	124	Redattore	124	Spinelessjellyfish	124	240,000	1:33.39	110
2003	Redattore	8	A. Solis	124	Special Ring	124	Touch of the Blues	124	225,000	1:33.37	111
2004	Designed for Luck	7	P.A. Valenzuela	124	Singletary	124	Tsigane	124	282,000	1:32.81	109

Beyer Index: 108.86

Run as Premiere Handicap or Hollywood Premier Handicap prior to 1990. For all ages in 1944. Run at Santa Anita in 1949. Distance 6 furlongs, 1938-49, 1951-57; 7 furlongs, 1950; 1 1/16 miles, 1978-80, 1986-87. Ron main track prior to 1984

SHUVEE HANDICAP (G2), 1 Mile, Fillies and Mares, 3-Year-Olds and Up, Belmont Park, 2004 Purse: $200,000

Year	Winner	Age	Jockey	Wt.	Second	Wt.	Third	Wt.	Win Value	Time	Beyer
1976	Proud Delta	4	J. Velasquez	122	Snooze	108	Let Me Linger	115	33,810	1:35.00	
1977	Mississippi Mud	4	J. Vasquez	113	Sweet Bernice	109	Secret Lanvin	111	32,760	1:43.60	
1978	One Sum	4	R. Hernandez	121	Sparkling Topaz	107	Charming Story	113	31,830	1:44.00	
1979	Pearl Necklace	5	J. Fell	121	Tingle Stone	120	Kit's Double	109	32,280	1:41.40	
1980	Alada	4	J. Fell	115	Lady Lonsdale	115	Blitey	116	32,460	1:43.00	
1981	Chain Bracelet	4	R. Hernandez	117	Weber City Miss	118	Wistful	120	32,700	1:42.80	
1982	Anti Lib	4	J. Vasquez	113	Tina Tina Too	112	Funny Bone	108	33,420	1:41.60	
1983	Dance Number	4	A. Cordero Jr	113	Number	117	May Day Eighty	113	49,500	1:40.40	
1984	Queen of Song	5	S. Maple	117	Try Something New	121	Narrate	116	86,340	1:43.00	
1985	Life's Magic	4	J. Velasquez	121	Heatherten	126	Some for All	109	83,820	1:42.40	
1986	Lady's Secret	4	P. Day	126	Endear	115	Ride Sally	125	81,780	1:41.80	
1987	Ms. Eloise	4	R.G. Davis	117	North Sider	120	Clemanna's Rose	114	107,820	1:41.80	
1988	Personal Ensign	4	R.P. Romero	121	Clabber Girl	118	Bishop's Delight	111	102,060	1:41.60	
1989	Banker's Lady	4	A. Cordero Jr	122	Rose's Cantina	117	Grecian Flight	117	104,580	1:40.80	
1990	Tis Juliet	4	R. Migliore	113	Survive	119	Dreamy Mimi	114	102,780	1:43.00	102
1991	A Wild Ride	4	M.E. Smith	119	Buy the Firm	122	Degenerate Gal	117	103,140	1:42.40	101
1992	Missy's Mirage	4	E. Maple	116	Harbour Club	110	Versailles Treaty	119	102,960	1:40.60	100
1993	Turnback the Alarm	4	C.W. Antley	117	Shared Interest	113	Vivano	112	90,000	1:43.00	93
1994	Sky Beauty	4	M.E. Smith	125	For All Seasons	113	Looie Capote	112	90,000	1:40.60	111
1995	Inside Information	4	J.A. Santos	119	Sky Beauty	126	Restored Hope	115	80,220	1:35.00	111
1996	Clear Mandate	4	J.A. Krone	111	Smooth Charmer	111	Restored Hope	115	90,000	1:35.00	97
1997	Hidden Lake	4	R. Migliore	115	Flat Fleet Feet	120	Escena	116	90,000	1:35.20	107
1998	Colonial Minstrel	4	J.R. Velazquez	117	Dixie Flag	120	Hidden Reserve	113	90,000	1:36.20	109

Year	Winner	Age	Jockey	Wt.	Second	Wt.	Third	Wt.	Win Value	Time	Beyer
1999	Catinca	4	R. Migliore	121	Sister Act	117	Tap to Music	115	90,000	1:34.20	110
2000	Beautiful Pleasure	5	J.F. Chavez	122	Biogio's Rose	115	Up We Go	114	120,000	1:35.65	113
2001	Apple of Kent	5	R. Migliore	114	March Magic	113	Country Hideaway	118	120,000	1:35.16	102
2002	Shiny Band	4	R.G. Davis	113	Raging Fever	121	Victory Ride	118	120,000	1:34.95	106
2003	Wild Spirit	4	J.J. Castellano	115	Smok'n Frolic	119	You	120	120,000	1:34.51	106
2004	Storm Flag Flying	4	J.R. Velazquez	116	Passing Shot	117	Roar Emotion	117	120,000	1:36.10	103

Beyer Index: 104.73

SILVERBULLETDAY (G2), 1 1/16 Miles, 3-Year-Old Fillies, Fair Grounds, 2004 Purse: $150,000

Year	Winner	Age	Jockey	Wt.	Second	Wt.	Third	Wt.	Win Value	Time	Beyer
1982	Linda North	3	R. Franklin		Mickey's Echo		Rose Bouquet			1:42.80	
1983	Duped	3	J. Espinoza		Shamivor		Juliet's Pet			1:43.00	
1984	Texas Cowgirl Nite	3	K. Borque		Only Bid		Runny Nose			1:42.00	
1985	Marshua's Echelon	3	R. Franklin		Turn to Wilma		Not Again Debbie			1:45.20	
1986	Tiffany Lass	3	R. Frazier		Super Set		Port of Departure			1:46.00	
1987	Out of the Bid	3	K. Borque		Trapped		Quick Closing			1:47.20	
1988	False Glitter	3	S. Romero		Part Native		Quite a Gem			1:47.40	
1989	Exquisite Mistress	3	C.H. Borel	114	Jewel Bid	117	Lunar Princess	112		1:46.80	
1990	Windansea	3	R. Romero	119	Everlasting Lady	119	A Hula	114		1:46.40	
1991	Nalees Pin	3	K. Borque	122	Oxford Screen	112	Lady Blockbuster	119		1:46.40	80
1992	Prospector's Delite	3	B. Walker Jr.	117	Royal Med	112	Glitzi Bj	119		1:43.80	
1993	Bright Penny	3	R. Ardoin	114	She's A Little Shy	122	Wakerup	112	19,095	1:44.80	85
1994	Playcaller	3	R. Ardoin	119	Two Altazano	112	Briar Road	112	30,000	1:44.20	85
1995	Legendary Princess	3	C.Emigh	113	Broad Smile	122	Hero's Valor	114	25,875	1:44.80	87
1996	Up Dip	3	C.Bourque	114	Brush With Tequila	113	Not Likely	122	37,635	1:44.60	84
1997	Blushing KD	3	L.Meche	122	Tomisue's Delight	114	Morelia	122	60,000	1:42.40	103
1998	Cool Dixie	3	R.Ardoin	122	Lu Ravi	114	Silent Eskimo	112	75,000	1:43.20	102
1999	Silverbulletday	3	G.Stevens	122	Brushed Halory	114	On a Soapbox	119	75,000	1:44.36	100
2000	Shawnee Country	3	D.Meche	122	Chilukki	122	Humble Clerk	122	75,000	1:45.11	91
2001	Lakenheath	3	C. Lanerie	119	Morning Sun	112	Beloved by All	114	75,000	1:46.09	83
2002	Take Charge Lady	3	A.J. D'Amico	122	Charmed Gift	119	Chamrousse	115	90,000	1:42.09	109
2003	Belle of Perintown	3	C.H. Borel	122	Afternoon Dreams	112	Rebridled Dreams	117	90,000	1:44.48	99
2004	Shadow Cast	3	R.J. Albarado	116	Quick Temper	113	Sister Swank	117	90,000	1:46.82	89

Beyer Index: 92.08

Run as the Davona Dale through 2000.

SIXTY SAILS HANDICAP (G3), 1 1/8 Miles, Fillies and Mares, 3-Year-Olds and Up, Hawthorne, 2004 Purse: $250,000

Year	Winner	Age	Jockey	Wt.	Second	Wt.	Third	Wt.	Win Value	Time	Beyer
1976	Enchanted Native	5	L. Snyder	115	Honky Star	121	Regal Rumor	118	31,650	1:40.00	
1977	Kissapotamus	5	G. Baze	115	Kittyluck	116	Lady B Gay	116	22,470	1:38.80	
1978	Drop the Pigeon	4	J.L. Diaz	118	Evelyn's Time	113	Creation	119	16,320	1:39.40	
1979	Strate Sunshine	5	R. Lindsay	113	Timeforaturn	114	Century Type	112	46,830	1:40.80	
1980	Doing It My Way	4	R.J. Hirdes Jr	115	Powerless	118	Cookie Puddin	116	40,335	1:40.20	
1980	Conga Miss	4	G. Gallitano	118	Century Type	120	Royal Villa	115	40,215	1:40.20	
1981	Karla's Enough	4	E. Fires	120	Favorite Prospect	117	Romantic Mood	113	46,890	1:37.60	
1981	Gold Treasure	4	J.L. Diaz	118	Sissy's Time	120	Satin Ribera	120	47,040	1:38.00	
1982	Targa	5	R.D. Evans	116	Really Royal	115	Knights Beauty	115	98,040	1:45.00	
1983	Queen of Song	4	R.J. Hirdes Jr	115	Bersid	121	Sefa's Beauty	120	96,630	1:43.80	
1984	Queen of Song	5	R.J. Hirdes Jr	122	Frosty Tail	120	Herb Wine	118	97,710	1:46.60	
1985	Sefa's Beauty	6	P. Day	122	Farer Belle Lee	115	Princess Moran	113	113,580	1:52.60	
1986	Sefa's Beauty	7	R.P. Romero	124	Flying Heat	122	Farer Belle Lee	118	112,290	1:50.00	
1987	Queen Alexandra	5	D. Brumfield	123	My Gallant Duchess	116	Happy H'll'w Miss	113	126,330	1:49.60	
1988	Top Corsage	5	P.A. Valenzuela	118	Yukon Dolly	114	Inspiracion II	110	125,010	1:52.00	
1989	Valid Vixen	4	J.L. Diaz	116	Scorned Lass	115	Arcroyal	116	156,480	1:52.60	
1990	Leave It Be	5	H.A. Sanchez	119	Anitas Surprise	114	Degenerate Gal	116	156,510	1:53.40	
1991	Balotra	4	R. Meier	112	Charon	122	Beth Believes	113	157,860	1:50.80	
1992	Peach of It	6	E.T. Baird	114	Bungalow	115	Zend to Aiken	113	162,090	1:51.20	91
1993	Pleasant Baby	4	J.L. Diaz	112	Miss Jealski	113	Steff Graf	115	180,000	1:49.20	95
1994	Princess Polonia	4	W.S. Ramos	113	Eskimo's Angel	115	Joyous Melody	113	180,000	1:51.80	95
1995	Eskimo's Angel	6	M. Guidry	114	Little Buckles	113	Norfolk Lavender	112	180,000	1:51.40	93
1996	Alcovy	6	W. Martinez	118	Shoop	118	Lotta Dancing	120	180,000	1:50.60	100
1997	Top Secret	4	C. Perret	115	Hurricane Viv	119	Gold n Delicious	114	180,000	1:49.60	100
1998	Glitter Woman	4	G. L.Stevens	118	Top Secret	115	I'm Out First	112	180,000	1:50.40	102
							Tuxedo Junction	115			
1999	Crafty Oak	5	R. Sibille	114	Highfalutin	115	Lines Of Beauty	114	180,000	1:46.60	97
2000	Lu Ravi	5	P. Day	116	Tap to Music	120	Batuka	116	180,000	1:49.15	104

Year	Winner	Age	Jockey	Wt.	Second	Wt.	Third	Wt.	Win Value	Time	Beyer
2001	License Fee	6	L. Melancon	116	Lady Melesi	116	Megans Bluff	116	180,000	1:49.11	98
2002	With Ability	4	J.J. Castellano	115	Lakenheath	115	Katy Kat	116	180,000	1:51.37	92
2003	Bare Necessities	4	R.R. Douglas	118	Jaramar Rain	114	Lakenheath	114	150,000	1:52.84	102
2004	Allspice	4	C.A. Emigh	115	Bare Necessities	122	Mavoreen	114	150,000	1:50.66	99

Beyer Index: 97.54

SKIP AWAY HANDICAP (G3), 1 1/16 Miles, 3-Year-Olds and Up, Gulfstream Park, 2004 Purse: $100,000

Year	Winner	Age	Jockey	Wt.	Second	Wt.	Third	Wt.	Win Value	Time	Beyer
1955	Swaps	4	W. Shoemaker	130	Galdar		Our Gob		14,100	1:39.60	
1987	Big Blowup	6	C. Baltazar	115	Micanopy Boy		JIm Bowie		34,290	1:44.40	
1990	Primal	5	E. Fires	120	Ole Atocha	113	Wonderloaf	113	60,000	1:43.40	
1991	Chief Honcho	4	M.E. Smith	116	No Marker	112	Barkada	114	45,000	1:48.00	
1992	Honest Ensign	4	J. Cruguet	109	Peanut Butter Onit	114	Strike the Gold	117	45,000	1:49.40	109
1993	Technology	4	J.D. Bailey	118	Barkerville	117	Bidding Proud	114	45,000	1:42.40	107
1994	Devil His Due	5	M.E. Smith	121	Migrating Moon	116	Northern Trend	111	45,000	1:43.00	103
1995	Fight for Love	5	J.D. Bailey	113	Danville	113	Pride of Burkaan	113	45,000	1:43.80	106
	Northern Trend finished second but was disqualified and placed fifth										
1996	Halo's Image	5	P. Day	119	Wekiva Springs	119	Flying Chevron	116	45,000	1:42.60	114
1997	Crafty Friend	4	M.E. Smith	114	Diligence	116	Ghostly Moves	114	45,000	1:42.20	109
1998	Sir Bear	5	E.M. Jurado	112	Black Forest	113	Kiridashi	110	60,000	1:43.20	106
1999	Sir Bear	6	J.D. Bailey	119	Behrens	113	Hanarsaan	119	60,000	1:43.66	109
2000	Horse Chestnut	5	M.E. Smith	117	Isaypete	116	Rock and Roll	120	60,000	1:42.78	110
2001	American Halo	5	R.G. Davis	114	Vision and Verse	114	Pleasant Breeze	118	60,000	1:42.31	108
2002	Sir Bear	9	E.S. Prado	116	Red Bullet	118	Hal's Hope	114	60,000	1:43.98	109
2003	Best of the Rest	8	E.M. Coa	121	Consistency	111	Roger E	114	60,000	1:42.72	105
2004	Newfoundland	4	J.R. Velazquez	116	Supah Blitz	114	Bowman's Band	117	60,000	1:43.26	105

Beyer Index: 107.69

Run as Broward Handicap through 2000. Run for 3-year-olds at about 1 1/16 miles on turf in 1987; Run at 1 1/8 miles in 1991 and 1992; Run as overnight handicap at 1 mile 70 yards in 1955.

SMILE SPRINT HANDICAP (G3), 6 Furlongs, 3-Year-Olds and Up, Calder Race Course, 2004 Purse: $500,000

Year	Winner	Age	Jockey	Wt.	Second	Wt.	Third	Wt.	Win Value	Time	Beyer
1984	I Really Will	4	G. St. Leon	120	Mo Exception	120	El Kaiser	122	33,984	1:12.00	
1985	Opening Lead	5	J. Pezua	117	Rexson's Hope	121	King of Bridlewood	115	32,760	1:24.00	
1986	Jeblar	4	J. Velez Jr.	123	Power Plan	116	Mugatea	115	32,790	1:24.80	
1987	Princely Lad	4	B. Green	116	Rilial	113	Ward Off Trouble	114	32,580	1:23.80	
1988	Position Leader	3	D. Valiente	112	Medieval Victory	112	Hooting Star	113	49,635	1:24.80	
1989	Glitterman	4	W. Guerra	119	Doodle Bug Mel	112	Proud and Valid	112	32,970	1:10.40	
1990	Groomstick	4	P. Rodriguez	113	Country Isle	113	Medieval Victory	119	49,170	1:24.20	
1991	Greg at Bat	6	J. Vasquez	114	Sunny and Pleasant	113	Perfection	115	51,105	1:24.20	
1992	My Luck Runs North	3	R. Lopez	114	Groomstick	119	Cigar Toss	112	45,000	1:17.40	
1993	Song of Ambition	4	R. Lopez	116	Coolin It	113	Daniel's Boy	117	45,000	1:22.40	
1994	Exclusive Praline	3	W. Ramos	117	Migrating Moon	118	Fortunate Joe	114	60,000	1:22.20	
1995	Request a Star	4	A. Toribio	113	Thats Our Buck	113	Halo's Image	118	60,000	1:23.60	
1996	Constant Escort	4	R. Nunez	114	Honest Colors	114	Excelerate	113	60,000	1:21.80	
1997	Vivace	4	R. Romero	114	Score a Birdie	113	Valid Expectations	117	150,000	1:10.60	
1998	Heckofaralph	5	W. Ramos	115	Thunder Breeze	113	Nicholas Ds	115	180,000	1:11.40	
1999	Silver Season	3	E. Coa	112	Son of a Pistol	119	My Jeff's Mombo	116	180,000	1:10.03	107
2000	Forty One Carats	4	J. Castellano	116	Personal First	114	Alice's Notebook	111	180,000	1:08.95	115
2001	Fappie's Notebook	4	J.F. Chavez	116	Thrlllin Discovery	112	Salty Glance	115	120,000	1:09.89	101
2002	Orientate	4	M.E. Smith	119	Echo Eddie	117	Crafty C. T.	117	240,000	1:09.98	115
2003	Shake You Down	5	M.J. Luzzi	119	Private Horde	113	My Cousin Matt	116	294,000	1:10.03	121
2004	Champali	4	J.D. Bailey	117	Clock Stopper	115	Built Up	114	294,000	1:10.14	111

Beyer Index: 111.67

Run as Miami Beach Handicap 1984-1993; Run as Miami Beach Sprint Handicap 1994-1998; Run at 6 1/2 furlongs in 1992; Run at 7 furlongs in 1985-1988, 1990-1991, 1993-1996

RED SMITH HANDICAP (G2), 1 3/8 Miles (Turf), 3-Year-Olds and Up, Aqueduct, 2004 Purse: $150,000

Year	Winner	Age	Jockey	Wt.	Second	Wt.	Third	Wt.	Win Value	Time	Beyer
1960	North Pole II	4	S. Boulmetis	114	King o' Turf	114	Crasher	112	18,550	2:15.00	
1961	Wolfram	5	I. Valenzuela	128	Our Jeep	115	Disperse	113	18,492	2:15.00	
1962	Wise Ship	5	H. Gustines	122	Shield Bearer	120	Dead Center	111	18,460	2:16.00	

Year	Winner	Age	Jockey	Wt.	Second	Wt.	Third	Wt.	Win Value	Time	Beyer
1963	Vimy Ridge	4	S. Boulmetis	118	Prego	110	Shield Bearer	120	18,395	1:59.40	
1964	Will I Rule	5	B. Baeza	116	Marlin Bay	122	Irish Dandy	110	18,557	1:59.40	
1965	Tenacle	5	R. Ussery	115	Hot Dust	119	Purser	114	19,337	1:55.80	
1966	Spoon Bait	4	J.L. Rotz	113	Paoluccio	112	Knightly Manner	116	18,557	1:54.40	
1967	Ginger Fizz	5	F. Toro	117	Chinatower	114	Handsome Boy	111	19,825	1:55.00	
1968	High Hat	4	E. Belmonte	126	Ruffled Feathers	120	Primo Richard	106	18,330	2:20.20	
1969	Majetta	5	A. Cordero Jr	114	Liaison	114	Fort Marcy	126	18,915	2:19.00	
1970	Drumtop	4	A. Cordero Jr	121	Tradesman	113	Chompion	113	19,110	2:20.40	
1971	Drumtop	5	C. Baltazar	124	Kling Kling	113	Practicante	116	19,560	2:16.60	
1972	New Alibhai	4	F. Ianelli	113	Kling Kling	115	Golden Eagle II	120	16,935	2:02.40	
1973	Red Reality	7	J. Velasquez	122	Malwak	114	New Hope	113	16,890	2:13.20	
1974	Take Off	5	R. Turcotte	117	Jogging	112	Red Reality	112	23,070	2:00.40	
1975	Telefonico	4	C. Perret	120	Drollery	114	Barcas	114	17,400	2:03.00	
1976	Erwin Boy	5	R. Turcotte	116	Clout	111	Quick Card	110	28,110	2:01.20	
1977	Clout	5	G. Martens	114	Chati	117	Gay Jitterbug	122	25,928	1:40.00	
1977	Quick Card	4	A. Cordero Jr	112	Bemo	115	Noble Dancer II	119	25,688	1:39.60	
1978	Tiller	4	J. Fell	114	True Colors	116	Tacitus	113	33,960	2:00.20	
1980	Marquee Universal	4	H. Pilar	121	Match the Hatch	114	Lyphard's Wish	122	67,680	1:58.80	
1981	Match the Hatch	5	K. Skinner	114	Passing Zone	108	Great Neck	114	68,160	1:59.60	
1982	Highland Blade	4	J. Vasquez	124	Dom Menotti	109	Open Call	124	69,000	2:06.40	
1983	Super Sunrise	4	C. Perret	114	Mariacho	116	Field Cat	111	67,200	2:06.80	
1983	Thunder Puddles	4	J.L. Samyn	117	John's Gold	112	Open Call	124	67,200	2:06.40	
1984	Hero's Honor	4	J.D. Bailey	117	Win	114	Eskimo	112	102,900	2:02.20	
1985	Sharannpour	5	A. Cordero Jr	112	Inevitable Leader	116	Cold Feet II	110	114,600	2:04.20	
1986	Divulge	4	J. Cruguet	116	Tri for Size	113	Island Sun	118	88,950	1:59.00	
1986	Equalize	4	W.A. Guerra	114	Palace Panther	116	Entitled To	112	103,650	2:02.20	
1987	Theatrical	5	P. Day	122	Dance of Life	122	Equalize	122	116,460	2:00.80	
1988	Pay the Butler	4	R.G. Davis	108	Equalize	116	Yankee Affair	120	118,620	2:01.40	
1989	Rambo Dancer	5	J.A. Santos	113	El Senor	113	Salem Drive	116	72,360	2:01.00	
1990	Yankee Affair	8	J.A. Santos	122	Hodges Bay	116	Phantom Breeze	112	70,560	2:00.20	102
1991	Who's to Pay	5	J.D. Bailey	117	Simili	114	Solar Splendor	114	71,160	1:58.00	108
1992	Montserrat	4	J.A. Krone	118	Preferences	110	First Rate	111	70,920	2:00.20	101
1993	Royal Mountain Inn	4	J.A. Krone	110	Spectacular Tide	113	Share the Glory	111	71,760	1:59.80	106
1994	Franchise Player	5	D.V. Beckner	109	Red Bishop	119	Same Old Wish	112	72,120	2:20.40	105
1995	Flag Down	5	J.A. Santos	114	Party Season	116	Proceeded	110	69,900	2:22.00	103
1996	Mr. Bluebird	5	M.E. Smith	116	Ops Smile	116	Raintrap	117	87,750	2:15.20	106
1997	Instant Friendship	4	J.R. Velazquez	123	Demi's Bret	117	Trample	112	90,000	2:17.00	107
1998	Musical Ghost	6	J.R. Velazquez	115	Rice	115	Plato's Love	109	90,000	2:15.40	105
1999	Monarch's Maze	3	J. Bravo	113	Williams News	114	Gritty Sandie	114	90,000	2:14.40	103
2000	Cetewayo	6	R. Migliore	114	Understood	113	Val's Prince	118	90,000	2:17.93	104
2001	Mr. Pleasentfar	4	J.A. Santos	115	Eltawaasul	114	Regal Dynasty	113	90,000	2:16.94	100
2002	Evening Attire	4	S.X. Bridgmohan	126	Fisher Pond	116	Pleasant Breeze	120	90,000	2:14.81	109
2003	Balto Star	5	J.R. Velazquez	120	Macaw	118	Cetewayo	116	90,000	2:18.86	105
2004	Dreadnaught	4	J.L Samyn	115	Certifiably Crazy	112	Alost	116	90,000	2:18.87	101

Beyer Index: 104.33

Run on main track in 2002

SORRENTO (G3), 6 1/2 Furlongs, 2-Year-Old Fillies, Del Mar, 2004 Purse: $150,000

Year	Winner	Age	Jockey	Wt.	Second	Wt.	Third	Wt.	Win Value	Time	Beyer
1967	Windsor Honey	2	J. Sellers	112	Y. So	114	Free Sample	112	13,125	1:30.60	
1970	June Darling	2	W. Mahorney	119	Ulla Britta	113	Sapose Speed	114	7,737	1:10.80	
1970	Countess Market	2	A. Pineda	113	Balcony's Babe	115	Tried Wings	114	7,837	1:10.40	
1971	Chargerette	2	F. Olivares	113	Miss Lady Bug	116	Impressive Style	113	9,750	1:09.20	
1972	Windy's Daughter	2	W. Shoemaker	119	Bold Liz	119	Sleek and Fleet	114	9,125	1:09.00	
1973	Fleet Peach	2	D. Pierce	113	Calaki	116	Poona's Double	116	12,600	1:09.20	
1974	Spout	2	A. Pineda	115	Just a Kick	115	Cut Class	113	14,000	1:36.80	
1975	Queen to Be	2	D.G. McHargue	113	T.V. Terese	114	Pet Label	116	13,350	1:36.80	
1976	Telferner	2	L. Pincay Jr	117	Lullaby	117	Asterisca	115	16,150	1:36.60	
1977	My Little Maggie	2	W. Shoemaker	114	Extravagant	114	Short Stanza	114	16,150	1:36.40	
1978	Beauty Hour	2	M. Castaneda	114	Hand Creme	117	Top Soil	114	19,150	1:37.00	
1979	Hazel R.	2	C.J. McCarron	117	Arcades Ambo	113	Princess Karenda	114	19,100	1:35.80	
1980	Native Fancy	2	L. Pincay Jr	117	Raja's Delight	115	Wedding Reception	114	22,950	1:38.80	
1981	First Advance	2	W. Shoemaker	113	Merry Sport	115	Skillful Joy	113	26,100	1:38.60	
1982	Time for Sale	2	W. Shoemaker	113	Sharili Brown	117	Infantes	115	32,300	1:38.40	
1983	Leading Ladybug	2	P.A. Valenzuela	115	Bright Orphan	118	Lapidist	116	31,150	1:40.20	
1984	Wayward Pirate	2	W. Shoemaker	114	Doon's Baby	120	Trunk	116	31,350	1:37.20	
1985	Arewehavingfunyet	2	P.A. Valenzuela	120	Life at the Top	116	Python	117	34,250	1:37.00	
1986	Brave Raj	2	P.A. Valenzuela	117	Breech	117	Footy	121	33,250	1:22.60	
1987	Hasty Pasty	2	L. Pincay Jr	121	Lost Kitty	121	Torch of the Track	117	37,200	1:23.00	

Year	Winner	Age	Jockey	Wt.	Second	Wt.	Third	Wt.	Win Value	Time	Beyer
1988	Stocks Up	2	G.L. Stevens	117	Approved to Fly	116	Lea Lucinda	117	48,350	1:23.40	
1989	Cheval Volant	2	L. Pincay Jr	117	Breezing Dixie	115	Dancing Jamie	115	46,575	1:23.80	
1990	Lite Light	2	R.A. Baze	115	Beyond Perfection	117	Dragonetta	117	47,100	1:22.00	
1991	Soviet Sojourn	2	C.S. Nakatani	121	La Spia	117	She's Tops	117	44,475	1:22.20	92
1992	Zoonaqua	2	E. Delahoussaye	117	Eliza	117	Medici Bells	117	49,125	1:22.40	88
1993	Phone Chatter	2	L. Pincay Jr	117	Rhapsodic	121	Noassemblyrequired	117	45,900	1:16.20	85
1994	How So Oiseau	2	P.A. Valenzuela	117	Ski Dancer	117	Serena's Song	121	47,100	1:15.80	92
1995	Batroyale	2	G.L. Stevens	119	Cosmic Fire	117	Waycross	117	59,200	1:15.60	90
1996	Desert Digger	2	E. Delahoussaye	116	Silken Magic	117	Montecito	117	65,950	1:16.00	90
1997	Career Collection	2	C.S. Nakatani	121	Griselle	117	Bent Creek City	121	67,825	1:17.80	74
1998	Silverbulletday	2	G.L. Stevens	121	Excellent Meeting	117	Colorado Song	117	64,980	1:17.40	84
1999	Chilukki	2	D.R. Flores	121	November Slew	117	She's Classy	117	90,000	1:16.40	98
2000	Give Praise	2	L. Pincay Jr.	116	Sea Reef	115	Fort Lauderdale	117	90,000	1:17.88	79
2001	Tempera	2	D.R. Flores	117	Respectful	115	Roaring Blaze	117	90,000	1:16.13	95
2002	Buffythecenterfold	2	M.S. Garcia	121	Tricks Her	115	Indy Groove	117	90,000	1:17.39	84
2003	Tizdubai	2	D.R. Flores	118	Dirty Diana	122	Solar Fire	118	90,000	1:17.15	79
2004	Inspiring	2	D.R. Flores	118	Souvenir Gift	122	Hello Lucky	118	90,000	1:18.29	78

Beyer Index: 86.29

SPECTACULAR BID (G3), 6 Furlongs, 3-Year-Olds, Gulfstream Park, 2004 Purse: $100,000

Year	Winner	Age	Jockey	Wt.	Second	Wt.	Third	Wt.	Win Value	Time	Beyer
1981	Jiggs Alarm	3	P. Day	112	Dame Mysterieuse		Spirited Boy		21,600	1:10.40	
1982	Sharp Future	3	E. Fires	113	Marshaller		Broad Minded		19,425	1:46.60	
1983	Freezing Rain	3	D. Brumfield	114	Write Off		Total Departure		22,194	1:10.00	
1984	Klaytone	3	G. St. Leon	114	Amerilad		Marine		25,851	1:42.60	
1985	Cherokee Fast	3	J.A. Santos	112	Vindalee		Secretary General		30,072	1:10.40	
1986	Groovy	3	C. Perret	113	Kenny Lane		Limited Practice		27,792	1:11.80	
1987	Spectacular Phantom	3	J. Velez	112	Micanopy Boy		Superceded		39,840	1:35.60	
1988	Cook's Brown Rice	3	A. Smith Jr	114	Evening Kris		Riff		35,481	1:11.00	
1989	Halrose	3	D. Valiente	117	Jabotinsky		Winners Laugh		34,770	1:12.00	
1990	Housebuster	3	C. Perret	114	Fit Contender		Stalker		30,000	1:11.40	
1991	To Freedom	3	A. Cordero Jr	119	Dark Brew		Here He Goes		32,817	1:10.40	
1992	Return to Quarters	3	W. Ramos	114	Scream Machine		Majestic Sweep		45,100	1:10.00	106
1993	Great Navigator	3	J.A. Santos	119	Demaloot Demashoot		Hidden Trick		45,078	1:09.40	89
1994	Halo's Image	3	J. Vasquez	114	Distinct Reality	119	Senor Conquistador	113	44,811	1:10.20	97
1995	Mr. Greeley	3	J.A. Krone	112	Make Me	112	Sea Emperor	119	44,823	1:10.60	99
1996	Seacliff	3	R.R. Douglas	122	Built for Pleasure	112	Gomtuu	119	45,000	1:11.80	92
1997	Confide	3	M.E. Smith	114	Kelly Kip	119	Crown Ambassador	117	45,000	1:09.80	94
1998	Time Limit	3	J.D. Bailey	117	Sejm Run	114	Governor Hicks	117	45,000	1:10.40	100
1999	Texas Glitter	3	J.R. Velazquez	117	Valid Trefaire	112	Lifeisawhirl	114	45,000	1:09.80	115
2000	B L's Appeal	3	M.E. Smith	114	American Bullet	114	Tour the Hive	112	45,000	1:10.68	82
2001	Icanseetherain	3	J.A. Santos	114	Diablo's Choice	112	American Century	114	60,000	1:11.04	90
2002	Maybry's Boy	3	J.R. Velazquez	116	Showmeitall	118	Harmony Hall	116	60,000	1:12.19	96
2003	First Blush	3	J.F. Chavez	116	Crafty Guy	120	Silver Squire	120	60,000	1:10.97	93
2004	Wynn Dot Comma	3	J. Bravo	120	Saratoga County	116	Ghost Mountain	120	60,000	1:10.60	95

Beyer Index: 96.00

Run at 1 1/16 miles 1982, 1984, 1987

SPEND A BUCK HANDICAP (G3), 1 1/16 Miles, 3-Year-Olds and Up, Calder Race Course, 2004 Purse: $100,000

Year	Winner	Age	Jockey	Wt.	Second	Wt.	Third	Wt.	Win Value	Time	Beyer
1991	Higgler	3	D. Nied	112	Jodie's Sweetie	115	Treblestaff	112	50,505	1:48.20	
1992	Poulain d'Or	3	P. Rodriguez	112	Ponche	112	Sir Stephenmichael	113	14,000	1:42.20	
1994	Daniel's Boy	6	P. Rodriguez	111	It'sali'lknownfact	110	Aggressive Chief	115	60,000	1:52.68	107
1995	Pride of Burkaan	5	R. Douglas	119	Crafty Chris	114	Dauntless Gem	114	60,000	1:51.96	104
1996	King Rex	4	R. Lopez	116	Derivative	113	Leave'm Inthedark	114	48,945	1:52.80	96
1997	Derivative	6	J. Ferrer	116	Shan's Ready	114	Sur Irish's Secret	114	30,000	1:45.65	99
1998	Unruled	5	G. Boulanger	116	Sir Bear	124	Laughing Dan	113	60,000	1:45.68	107
1999	Best of the Rest	4	E. Coa	114	Dancing Guy	113	High Security	114	60,000	1:44.67	107
2000	Groomstick Stock's	4	R. Homeister Jr.	111	Reporter	113	Broadway Tune	113	60,000	1:44.82	101
2001	Best of the Rest	6	E. Coa	116	Dancing Guy	117	Sir Bear	117	60,000	1:42.59	106
2002	Pay the Preacher	4	C. Velasquez	114	Best of the Rest	121	Built Up	112	60,000	1:44.91	105
2003	Tour of the Cat	5	A. Cabassa Jr.	116	Best of the Rest	122	Dancing Guy	116	60,000	1:46.30	99
2004	Built Up	6	E.M. Coa	115	Super Frolic	117	Gold Dollar	115	60,000	1:45.86	102

Beyer Index: 103.00

Run as Spend a Buck Breeders' Cup Handicap in 1996; Run as Spend a Buck Overnight Handicap in 1992; For 3-year-olds in 1992; Run at 1 mile 70 yards in 1992; Run at 1 1/8 miles in 1994–1996; Not run 1993

SPINAWAY (G2), 7 Furlongs, 2-Year-Old Fillies, Saratoga Race Course, 2004 Purse: $250,000

Year	Winner	Age	Jockey	Wt.	Second	Wt.	Third	Wt.	Win Value	Time	Beyer
1881	Memento	2	Costello	107	Night Cap	107	Tuscaloosa	107	2,100	1:06.00	
1882	Miss Woodford	2	Stoval	103	Tarantella	95	Empress	95	1,800	1:03.00	
1883	Tolu	2	J. McLaughlin	103	Tattoo	100	Economy	95	2,200	1:03.00	
1884	Mission Belle	2	Holloway	103	Radha	95	Floria	107	1,500	1:03.00	
1885	Biggonet	2	Maynard	100	Hattie Carlile	100	Georgie II	95	2,625	1:05.00	
1886	Grisette	2	Miller	103	Lizzie Krepps	103	Agnes	103	2,075	1:03.20	
1887	Los Angeles	2	West	107	Blithesome	103	Cokena	95	2,500	1:02.20	
1888	Gypsy Queen	2	Martin	102	Queen of Trumps	98	Daisy Woodruff	93	2,825	1:03.00	
1889	Daisy F.	2	Richcreek	112	Ruperta	98	Estelle	102	3,750	1:06.20	
1890	Sallie McClelland	2	Allen	117	Helen Rose	107	Ayrshire Lass	104	2,805	1:06.00	
1891	Promenade	2	Simms	105	Selina D.	98	Salonica	110	2,585	1:03.00	
1901	Rossignol	2	T. Burns	112	Disadvantage	119	Amicitia	119	2,625	1:10.00	
1902	Duster	2	Shaw	122	Astarita	121	Jud. Campbell	122	6,150	1:10.80	
1903	Raglan	2	J. Hicks	119	Little Em	116	Memories	119	10,430	1:12.40	
1904	Tanya	2	Shaw	122	Schulamite	114	Linda Lee	119	10,750	1:07.60	
1905	Edna Jackson	2	F. O'Neill	119	Running Water	119	Curiosity	119	11,750	1:08.80	
1906	Court Dress	2	Radtke	122	Kenyetto	112	Martha	122	7,750	1:07.00	
1907	Julia Powell	2	W. Knapp	112	Half Sovereign	119	Adriana	112	9,170	1:06.80	
1908	Maskette	2	Notter	112	Wedding Bells	112	Lady Hubbard	112	8,250	1:05.80	
1909	Ocean Bound	2	Scoville	115	School Marm	112	Sticker	112	7,750	1:06.60	
1910	Bashti	2	S.H. Shilling	122	Love-not	109	Sweepaway	112	7,820	1:06.80	
1913	Casuarina	2	B. Steele	113	Early Rose	110	Cutaway	116	2,395	1:07.00	
1914	Lady Barbary	2	A. Neylon	122	Kaskaskia	127	Montrosa	104	2,765	1:06.00	
1915	Jacoby	2	M. Garner	107	Lorac	107	Feminist	107	2,425	1:11.00	
1916	Yankee Witch	2	T. Davies	112	Koh-I-Noor	122	Tragedy	122	2,545	1:07.40	
1917	Olive Wood	2	E. Martin	112	Enfilade	119	Rosie O'Grady	124	6,250	1:07.40	
1918	Passing Shower	2	A. Johnson	112	Lady Rosebud	116	Tuscaloosa	112	6,450	1:05.60	
1919	Constancy	2	T. Nolan	109	Wedding Cake	109	Germa	112	5,850	1:05.60	
1920	Prudery	2	E. Ambrose	127	Step Lightly	112	Nancy Lee	127	5,900	1:05.00	
1921	Miss Joy	2	M. Garner	127	Calamity Jane	112	Roulette	112	6,100	1:05.20	
1922	Edict	2	E. Sande	122	Fly by Day	112	Brocade	112	7,425	1:09.00	
1923	Anna Marrone II	2	R. Carter	112	Nellie Morse	124	Tree Top	112	7,675	1:12.60	
1924	Blue Warbler	2	D. Hurn	112	Malbird	109	Lightship	109	7,775	1:12.00	
1925	Cinema	2	E. Barnes	112	Asinia	112	Ruthenia	113	7,425	1:15.40	
1926	Bonnie Pennant	2	J. Maiben	112	Candy May	112	Pandera	127	9,850	1:14.40	
1927	Twitter	2	R. Workman	112	Jollity	112	Bateau	122	9,675	1:12.00	
1928	Atlantis	2	G. Ellis	122	Pennant Lass	111	Bravery	115	10,050	1:15.00	
1929	Goose Egg	2	G. Ellis	122	The Spare	122	Snowflake	115	10,500	1:12.20	
1930	Risque	2	E. Steffen	122	Baba Kenny	115	Panasette	122	10,000	1:16.60	
1931	Top Flight	2	R. Workman	127	Dinner Time	111	Brocado	115	8,400	1:12.60	
1932	Easy Day	2	S. Coucci	111	Crazy Jane	115	Barn Swallow	115	8,425	1:13.40	
1933	Contessa	2	E. Steffen	114	Slapdash	126	Sun Celtic	114	5,850	1:15.00	
1934	Vicaress	2	L. Humphries	116	Clean Out	116	Corinne Dailey	116	4,450	1:12.80	
1935	Forever Yours	2	W.D. Wright	121	Parade Girl	119	Tony's Wife	116	6,725	1:12.80	
1936	Maecloud	2	E. Litzenberger	116	Juliet W.	114	Bad Dreams	110	6,450	1:14.20	
1937	Merry Lassie	2	J. Stout	119	Evening Shadow	114	Jacola	114	7,975	1:12.20	
1938	Dinner Date	2	A. Robertson	113	So Rare	113	Grey Nurse	113	9,450	1:13.00	
1939	Now What	2	R. Workman	122	Piquet	113	Jeanne d'Arc	113	8,350	1:13.20	
1940	Nasca	2	R. Donoso	116	Tangled	116	Level Best	119	8,450	1:12.00	
1941	Mar-Kell	2	W. Eads	113	Equipet	113	Petrify	122	8,125	1:13.60	
1942	Our Page	2	C. McCreary	113	Askmenow	113	Wuskenin	113	8,825	1:12.60	
1943	Bee Mac	2	S. Young	113	Red Wonder	113	Whirlabout	116	8,550	1:12.40	
1944	Price Level	2	J. Gilbert	115	Ace Card	119	Safeguard	111	15,305	1:12.20	
1945	Sopranist	2	T. May	110	Bridal Flower	109	Red Shoes	114	16,670	1:09.20	
1946	Pipette	2	T. May	119	Bright Song	115	Tea Olive	111	16,875	1:11.00	
1947	Bellesoeur	2	T. May	113	Inheritance	111	Grey Flight	113	15,025	1:11.60	
1948	Myrtle Charm	2	A. Skoronski	111	Lady Dorimar	111	Gaffery	115	15,075	1:11.60	
1949	Sunday Evening	2	T. Atkinson	111	Striking	115	Fais Do Do	111	14,100	1:11.40	
1950	Atalanta	2	H. Woodhouse	115	Les Abeilles	108	Wisteria	114	14,950	1:13.00	
1951	Blue Case	2	W. Mehrtens	119	Rose Jet	119	Recess	115	15,575	1:13.20	
1952	Flirtatious	2	D. Gorman	119	Grecian Queen	119	Lot o'Honey	115	15,775	1:13.20	
1953	Evening Out	2	O. Scurlock	123	Alines Pet	111			41,050	1:13.60	
1954	Gandharva	2	N. Shuk	111	My Blue Sky	111	High Voltage	123	44,650	1:12.80	
1955	Register	2	T. Atkinson	114	Doubledogdare	119	Aiming High	119	36,550	1:13.40	
1956	Alanesian	2	W. Boland	119	Jota Jota	119	Magic Forest	119	36,100	1:12.60	
1957	Sequoia	2	R. Ussery	119	Armorial	119	Bridgework	119	32,560	1:12.80	
1958	Rich Tradition	2	W. Boland	119	Recite	119	Quill	119	27,711	1:12.80	
1959	Irish Jay	2	E. Arcaro	119	Warlike	119	Natalma	119	51,235	1:12.20	
	Natalma finished first but was disqualified and placed third										
1960	Good Move	2	E. Guerin	119	Honey Dear	119	Little Tumbler	119	53,672	1:12.40	
1961	Cicada	2	I. Valenzuela	119	Pontivy	119	Jazz Queen	119	52,455	1:12.00	

Year	Winner	Age	Jockey	Wt.	Second	Wt.	Third	Wt.	Win Value	Time	Beyer
1962	Affectionately	2	I. Valenzuela	119	Nalee	119	Rare Exchange	119	51,821	1:10.40	
1963	Petite Rouge	2	J. Sellers	119	Hasty Matelda	119	Gailatia	119	53,219	1:12.60	
	Crown Silver finished second but was disqualified and placed last										
1964	Candalita	2	B. Baeza	119	Marshua	119	Queen Empress	119	52,682	1:10.80	
1965	Moccasin	2	L. Adams	119	Swift Lady	119	Forefoot	119	49,627	1:11.00	
1966	Silver True	2	J.L. Rotz	119	Great Era	119	Shirley Heights	119	50,960	1:12.00	
1967	Queen of the Stage	2	B. Baeza	119	Dream Path	119	Gay Matelda	119	52,244	1:10.20	
1968	Queen's Double	2	B. Baeza	119	Show Off	119	Fillypasser	119	52,130	1:11.40	
1969	Meritus	2	M. Ycaza	119	Title	119	Bright Sun	119	51,789	1:10.60	
1970	Forward Gal	2	F. Iannelli	119	Patelin	119	Deceit	119	54,990	1:10.80	
1971	Numbered Account	2	C. Baltazar	119	Rondeau	119	Debby Deb	119	52,770	1:09.80	
1972	La Prevoyante	2	J. LeBlanc	120	Princess Doubleday	120	Behram	120	35,040	1:10.80	
1973	Talking Picture	2	R. Turcotte	120	Special Team	120	Raisela	120	35,040	1:10.00	
1974	Ruffian	2	V. Bracciale Jr	120	Laughing Bridge	120	Scottish Melody	120	33,060	1:08.60	
1975	Dearly Precious	2	M. Hole	120	Optimistic Gal	120	Quintas Vicki	120	47,880	1:10.60	
1976	Mrs. Warren	2	E. Maple	119	Exerene	119	Sensational	119	33,060	1:10.40	
1977	Sherry Peppers	2	A. Cordero Jr	119	Akita	119	Stub	119	32,340	1:10.80	
1978	Palm Hut	2	R.I. Velez	119	Himalayan	119	Golferette	119	31,770	1:10.60	
1979	Smart Angle	2	S. Maple	119	Jet Rating	119	Marathon Girl	119	48,510	1:10.60	
1980	Prayers 'n Promises	2	A. Cordero Jr	119	Fancy Naskra	119	Companionship	119	50,850	1:11.00	
1981	Before Dawn	2	G. McCarron	119	Betty Money	119	Take Lady Anne	119	52,920	1:09.40	
1982	Share the Fantasy	2	J. Fell	119	Singing Susan	119	Midnight Rapture	119	50,040	1:09.80	
1983	Buzz My Bell	2	J. Velasquez	119	Demetria	119	Bottle Top	119	52,740	1:13.20	
1984	Tiltalating	2	A. Cordero Jr	119	Sociable Duck	119	Contredance	119	85,380	1:11.00	
1985	Family Style	2	D. MacBeth	119	Musical Lark	119	Nervous Baba	119	97,680	1:12.00	
1986	Tappiano	2	J. Cruguet	119	Our Little Margie	119	Daytime Princess	119	130,680	1:11.40	
1987	Over All	2	A. Cordero Jr	119	Bold Lady Anne	119	Flashy Runner	119	101,340	1:11.00	
1988	Seattle Meteor	2	R.P. Romero	119	Love and Affection	119	Moonlight Martini	119	141,120	1:12.60	
1989	Stella Madrid	2	A. Cordero Jr	119	Golden Reef	119	Saratoga Sizzle	119	141,840	1:10.40	
1990	Meadow Star	2	J.A. Santos	119	Garden Gal	119	Good Potential	119	143,040	1:10.20	
1991	Miss Iron Smoke	2	M.A. Pedroza	119	Turnback the Alarm	119	Preach	119	120,000	1:10.60	84
1992	Family Enterprize	2	P. Day	119	Standard Equipment	119	Sky Beauty	119	120,000	1:09.80	95
	Sky Beauty finished first but was disqualified and placed third										
	Try in the Sky finished third but was disqualified and placed fourth										
1993	Strategic Maneuver	2	J.A. Santos	119	Astas Foxy Lady	119	Delta Lady	119	120,000	1:10.20	84
1994	Flanders	2	P. Day	119	Sea Breezer	119	Stormy Blues	119	120,000	1:23.00	96
1995	Golden Attraction	2	G.L. Stevens	121	Flat Fleet Feet	121	Western Dreamer	121	120,000	1:23.80	93
1996	Oath	2	S.J. Sellers	121	Pearl City	121	Fabulously Fast	121	120,000	1:23.60	88
1997	Countess Diana	2	S.J. Sellers	121	Brac Drifter	121	Aunt Anne	121	120,000	1:24.00	93
1998	Things Change	2	J.A. Santos	121	Extended Applause	121	Miss Jennifer Lynn	121	120,000	1:24.82	87
1999	Circle of Life	2	J.R. Velazquez	121	Surfside	121	Miss Wineshine	121	120,000	1:23.25	91
2000	Stormy Pick	2	J. Ferrer	121	Nasty Storm	121	Seeking It All	121	120,000	1:24.33	82
2001	Cashier's Dream	2	D.J. Meche	121	Smok'n Frolic	121	Magic Storm	121	120,000	1:23.47	99
2002	Awesome Humor	2	P. Day	121	Forever Partners	121	Midnight Cry	121	120,000	1:24.36	95
2003	Ashado	2	E.S. Prado	121	Be Gentle	121	Daydreaming	121	120,000	1:24.08	84
2004	Sense of Style	2	E.S. Prado	121	Miss Matched	121	Play With Fire	121	150,000	1:23.83	88

Beyer Index: 89.93

Distance 5 furlongs prior to 1901; 5 1/2 furlongs, 1901–22; 6 furlongs, 1923–95. Run at Belmont Park, 1943–45. Run on Widener Course, 1945

(OVERBROOK) SPINSTER (G1), 1 1/8 Miles, Fillies and Mares, 3-Year-Olds and Up, Keeneland Race Course, 2004 Purse: $500,000

Year	Winner	Age	Jockey	Wt.	Second	Wt.	Third	Wt.	Win Value	Time	Beyer
1956	Doubledogdare	3	J. Heckmann	119	Queen Hopeful	123	Lady Swords	119	41,140	1:49.20	
1957	Bornastar	4	K. Church	123	Pucker Up	123	Searching	123	44,480	1:49.20	
1958	Bornastar	5	K. Church	123	Moon Glory	119	Woodlawn	123	43,190	1:49.40	
1959	Royal Native	3	W. Hartack	119	Aesthetic	119	Tacking	119	37,975	1:49.40	
1960	Rash Statement	3	J.L. Rotz	119	Indian Maid	123	Royal Native	123	51,475	1:49.60	
1961	Bowl of Flowers	3	E. Arcaro	119	Primonetta	119	Times Two	119	50,640	1:49.20	
1962	Primonetta	4	W. Shoemaker	123	Royal Patrice	119	Firm Policy	119	44,130	1:48.40	
1963	Lamb Chop	3	M. Ycaza	119	Eleven Keys	119	Laughing Breeze	119	40,635	1:48.40	
1964	Old Hat	5	D. Brumfield	123	Miss Cavandish	119	Time for Bed	119	38,220	1:48.40	
1965	Star Maggie	5	W. Hartack	123	Swoonalong	123	Fairway Fun	119	38,187	1:50.20	
1966	Open Fire	5	B. Baeza	123	Old Hat	123	Summer Scandal	123	38,285	1:50.40	
1967	Straight Deal	5	H. Grant	123	Furl Sail	119	Amerigo Lady	119	39,942	1:49.20	
	Amerigo Lady finished second but was disqualified and placed third										
1968	Sale Day	3	E. Guerin	119	Politely	123	Pattee Canyon	119	38,122	1:51.60	
1969	Gallant Bloom	3	J.L. Rotz	119	Miss Ribot	123	Sale Dale	123	37,310	1:48.80	
1970	Taken Aback	4	E. Belmonte	123	Fanfreluche	119	Pattee Canyon	123	40,397	1:51.40	
1971	Chou Croute	3	R. Kotenko	119	Viewpoise	119	Alma North	119	41,015	1:49.00	
1972	Numbered Account	3	L. Pincay Jr	119	Chou Croute	123	Barely Even	119	38,870	1:47.40	
1973	Susan's Girl	4	B. Baeza	123	Light Hearted	119	Coraggioso	119	38,090	1:48.80	

Year	Winner	Age	Jockey	Wt.	Second	Wt.	Third	Wt.	Win Value	Time	Beyer
1974	Summer Guest	4	D. Montoya	123	Desert Vixen	123	Coraggioso	123	36,952	1:49.40	
1975	Susan's Girl	6	L. PIncay Jr	123	Flama Ardiente	119	Costly Dream	123	37,830	1:49.80	
1976	Optimistic Gal	3	C. Perret	119	Ivory Wand	119	Rocky Trip	123	53,007	1:51.60	
1977	Cum Laude Laurie	3	A. Cordero Jr	119	Mississippi Mud	123	Ivory Wand	123	54,974	1:48.40	
1978	Tempest Queen	3	J. Velasquez	119	Northernette	123	Likely Exchange	123	72,865	1:49.00	
1979	Safe	3	E. Fires	119	Spark of Life	123	Miss Baja	123	79,852	1:49.20	
1980	Bold 'n Determined	3	E. Delahoussaye	119	Love Sign	119	Likely Exchange	123	114,660	1:49.20	
1981	Glorious Song	5	R. Platts	123	Truly Bound	119	Safe Play	119	106,568	1:49.20	
1982	Track Robbery	6	P.A. Valenzuela	123	Blush With Pride	119	Our Darling	119	110,516	1:47.80	
1983	Try Something New	4	P. Day	123	Dance Number	123	Miss Huntington	123	107,689	1:49.80	
1984	Princess Rooney	4	E. Delahoussaye	123	Lucky Lucky Lucky	119	Heatherten	123	123,840	1:50.40	
1985	Dontstop Themusic	5	L. Pincay Jr	123	Life's Magic	123	Dowery	123	110,419	1:50.40	
1986	Top Corsage	3	S. Hawley	119	Endear	123	Life at the Top	119	142,610	1:48.20	
1987	Sacahuista	3	R.P. Romero	119	Ms. Margi	119	Tall Poppy	123	148,395	1:48.60	
1988	Hail a Cab	5	J. Vasquez	123	Willa On the Move	119	Integra	123	171,600	1:51.00	
1989	Bayakoa	5	L. Pincay Jr	123	Goodbye Halo	123	Sharp Dance	119	172,413	1:47.80	
1990	Bayakoa	6	L. Pincay Jr	123	Gorgeous	123	Luthier's Launch	123	174,606	1:47.00	113
1991	Wilderness Song	3	P. Day	119	Screen Prospect	123	Til Forbid	119	226,980	1:49.60	103
1992	Fowda	4	P.A. Valenzuela	123	Paseana	123	Meadow Star	123	209,994	1:49.80	106
1993	Paseana	6	C.J. McCarron	123	Gray Cashmere	123	Jacody	119	209,622	1:48.40	102
1994	Dispute	4	P. Day	123	Lets Be Alert	119	Miss Dominique	123	204,414	1:48.80	112
1995	Inside Information	4	M.E. Smith	123	Jade Flush	123	Mariah's Storm	123	198,276	1:50.00	100
1996	Different	4	C.J. McCarron	123	Top Secret	119	Belle of Cozzene	123	336,040	1:49.60	109
1997	Clear Mandate	5	P. Day	123	Feasibility Study	123	Naskra Colors	123	336,350	1:50.40	91
1998	Banshee Breeze	3	R.J. Albarado	119	Runup the Colors	123	Aldiza	123	341,930	1:47.04	115
1999	Keeper Hill	4	K.J. Desormeaux	123	Banshee Breeze	123	A Lady From Dixie	123	344,410	1:47.19	110
2000	Plenty of Light	3	G.K. Gomez	120	Spain	120	Roza Robata	123	336,970	1:48.18	107
2001	Miss Linda	4	R. Migliore	123	Starrer	120	Printemps	123	348,440	1:49.79	109
2002	Take Charge Lady	3	E.S. Prado	120	You	120	Printemps	123	338,520	1:49.90	109
2003	Take Charge Lady	4	E.S. Prado	123	You	123	Miss Linda	123	310,000	1:49.57	99
2004	Azeri	6	P. Day	123	Tamweel	123	Mayo on the Side	123	310,000	1:49.74	108

Beyer Index: 106.20

For 3-, 4-, and 5-year-olds prior to 1964

SPORT PAGE HANDICAP (G3), 7 Furlongs, 3-Year-Olds and Up, Aqueduct, 2004 Purse: $111,200

Year	Winner	Age	Jockey	Wt.	Second	Wt.	Third	Wt.	Win Value	Time	Beyer
1953	White Skies	4	J. Stout	130	Hilarious	114	Joe Jones	107	15,500	1:11.60	
1954	Joe Jones	4	C. McCreary	118	Canadiana	114	Game Chance	122	19,250	1:12.00	
1955	Squared Away	8	E. Arcaro	119	Dark Peter	119	Gandharva	112	20,100	1:11.00	
1956	Jo Jones	6	C. McCreary	125	Decathlon	126	History Book	111	16,900	1:10.80	
1957	Tick Tock	4	R. Ussery	122	St. Amour II	117	Portersville	121	15,950	1:11.00	
1958	Nahodah	5	J. Culmone	118	Bumpy Road	118	Nan's Mink	110	19,135	1:10.20	
1959	Ole Fols	3	W. Boland	125	Nahodah	116	Tick Tock	125	17,770	1:10.80	
1960	April Skies	3	J. Leonard	118	Mail Order	120	Four Lane	124	17,575	1:10.20	
1961	Intentionally	5	M. Ycaza	129	Windy Sands	112	Gyro	119	15,535	1:10.00	
1962	Misty Day	4	W. Boland	115	Nassau Hall	113	Surfer	114	15,600	1:10.80	
1963	Merry Ruler	5	J. Sellers	118	Uppercut	112	Excl'e Nashua	116	14,690	1:10.00	
1964	Affectionately	4	W. Shoemaker	117	Red Gar	113	Macedonia	116	18,655	1:10.40	
1965	Ornamento	5	W. Boland	112	Affectionately	127	R. Thomas	119	18,362	1:10.40	
1966	Impressive	3	R. Turcotte	126	Vitencamps	110	Hoist Bar	113	18,135	1:09.80	
1967	R. Thomas	6	E. Belmonte	121			Flag Raiser	124	11,900	1:09.60	
	Sun Gala	3	L. Pincay Jr	112							
1968	Kissin' George	5	B. Baeza	124	Jim J.	126	Royal Exchange	115	18,362	1:09.20	
1969	King Emperor	3	B. Baeza	119	Coup Landing	122	Jaikyl	112	18,622	1:09.40	
1970	Fresh 'n Foolish	4	J. Velasquez	110	Ocean Bar	112	True North	116	19,305	1:10.00	
1971	Lonesome River	5	R. Woodhouse	112	Brazen Brother	121	Coup Landing	119	20,940	1:11.00	
1972	Petrograd	3	E. Maple	113	North Sea	116	Tap the Tree	117	17,055	1:10.20	
1973	Timeless Moment	3	B. Baeza	116	Tap the Tree	122	North Sea	124	16,350	1:09.20	
1974	Startahemp	4	J. Velasquez	114	Nostrum	114	Fr'nkie A'ms	121	22,950	1:09.60	
1975	Lonetree	5	E. Maple	122	Petrograd	119	Piamem	114	26,805	1:09.40	
1976	Amerrico	4	S. Hawley	111	Honorable Miss	115	Relent	113	32,610	1:09.80	
1977	Affiliate	3	A. Cordero Jr	124	Intercontinent	112	Gitchee Gumee	117	31,560	1:10.00	
1978	Topsider	4	M. Venezia	109	What a Summer	124	Affiliate	118	32,400	1:10.20	
1979	Amadevil	5	W.H. McCauley	113	Tanthem	123	Dave's Friend	119	32,580	1:09.40	
1980	Dave's Friend	5	V. Bracciale Jr	126	Tilt Up	114	Hawkin's Spec'l	114	34,380	1:08.20	
1981	Well Decorated	3	R. Hernandez	117	Engine One	116	Guilty Conscience	126	32,760	1:10.60	
1982	Maudlin	4	J.D. Bailey	115	Top Avenger	115	Duke Mitchell	115	34,200	1:09.40	
1983	Fast As the Breeze	4	M. Toro	110	Maudlin	120	Swelegant	117	33,180	1:10.60	
1984	Tarantara	5	R. Migliore	117	Muskoka Wyck	114	New Connecti'n	113	46,140	1:10.80	

Year	Winner	Age	Jockey	Wt.	Second	Wt.	Third	Wt.	Win Value	Time	Beyer
1985	Raja's Shark	4	A. Cordero Jr	120	Love That Mac	113	Whoop Up	115	51,120	1:09.60	
1986	Best by Test	4	F. Lovato Jr	112	King's Swan	118	Sun Master	117	66,870	1:08.80	
1987	Vinnie the Viper	4	J.A. Krone	115	King's Swan	123	Banker's Jet	118	67,500	1:10.40	
1988	High Brite	4	A. Cordero Jr	120	Proud and Valid	111	Born to Shop	117	64,980	1:09.60	
1989	Garemma	3	J.F. Chavez	111	Proud and Valid	111	Born to Shop	117	51,120	1:10.20	
1990	Senor Speedy	3	A. Santiago	113	Brave Adventure	116	Dargai	115	53,190	1:10.00	
1991	Senor Speedy	4	J.F. Chavez	119	Shuttleman	113	Gallant Step	113	55,080	1:09.20	110
1992	R.D. Wild Whirl	4	R.G. Davis	114	Senor Speedy	122	Burn Fair	114	51,570	1:09.80	103
1993	Boom Towner	5	F. Lovato Jr	117	Raise Heck	115	Fabersham	113	53,730	1:10.60	116
1994	Man's Hero	4	M.J. Luzzi	111	Itaka	117	Storm Tower	118	51,045	1:22.00	113
1995	Siphon	4	K.J. Desormeaux	117	In Case	113	Ft. Stockton	113	74,160	1:22.00	106
1996	Valid Expectations	3	C.B. Asmussen	117	Diligence	116	Blissful State	117	68,040	1:21.80	112
1997	Stalwart Member	4	A.T. Gryder	114	Basqueian	116	Why Change	115	68,640	1:22.00	109
1998	Stormin Fever	4	R. Migliore	120	Olympic Cat	113	Adverse	113	50,115	1:21.40	112
1999	Scatmandu	4	A.T. Gryder	115	Aristotle	114	Watchman's Warning	112	50,250	1:22.60	103
2000	Stalwart Member	7	N. Arroyo Jr.	117	Istintaj	117	Mister Tricky	112	48,690	1:21.97	108
2001	Yonaguska	3	C.J. McCarron	116	Silky Sweep	116	Big E E	114	65,640	1:15.54	107
2002	Multiple Choice	4	V. Carrero	113	Bowman's Band	118	Sing Me Back Home	113	66,840	1:23.28	108
2003	Voodoo	5	J.F. Chavez	114	Bowman's Band	120	Highway Prospector	114	67,620	1:22.18	111
2004	Mass Media	3	J.J. Castellano	113	Lion Tamer	118	Gygistar	120	66,720	1:21.10	115

Beyer Index: 109.50

Run at 6 furlongs 1963-93; at 6 1/2 furlongs, 2001

STARS AND STRIPES BREEDERS' CUP TURF HANDICAP (G3), 1 1/2 Miles (Turf), 3-Year-Olds and Up, Arlington Park, 2004 Purse: $200,000

Year	Winner	Age	Jockey	Wt.	Second	Wt.	Third	Wt.	Win Value	Time	Beyer
1929	Dowagiac	4	A. Pascuma	108	Misstep	125	Sun Beau	120	15,550	1:50.60	
1930	Blue Larkspur	4	J. Smith	121	Misstep	124	Sun Beau	125	26,050	1:49.40	
1931	Plucky Play	4	D. Trivett	105	Mike Hall	116	The Nut	114	24,650	1:50.80	
1932	Equipoise	4	R. Workman	129	Tred Avon	107	Dr. Freeland	110	22,300	1:54.80	
1933	Indian Runner	4	A. Tipton	114	Gallant Sir	124	Watch Him	103	10,440	1:51.40	
1934	Indian Runner	5	A. Tipton	118	Advising Anna	102	Ladysman	120	10,760	1:49.80	
1935	Discovery	4	J. Bejshak	126	Chief Cherokee	106	Riskulus	118	9,000	1:50.80	
1936	Stand Pat	5	C. McTague	116	Corinto	108	Whopper	122	9,520	1:49.60	
1937	Corinto	5	J. Westrope	109	Infantry	116	Sir Jim Ja's	105	9,000	1:50.00	
1938	War Minstrel	4	I. Hanford	107	Seabiscuit	130	Arabs Arrow	111	9,060	1:54.20	
1939	Count d'Or	4	J. Longden	107	Drudgery	116	Taxes	107	8,620	1:50.80	
1940	Advocator	6	J.E. Oros	118	Joe Schenck	114	Yale o' Nine	109	9,260	1:50.00	
1941	Steel Heels	5	A. Snider	110	Equifox	114	Gallahadion	116	9,900	1:49.80	
1942	Take Wing	4	F.A. Smith	103	Marriage	116	Equifox	116	8,600	1:58.60	
1943	Rounders	4	F. Zufelt	116	Thumbs Up	113	Marriage	116	42,050	1:53.60	
1944	Georgie Drum	5	G. Woolf	113	Equifox	107	Rounders	115	41,000	1:49.80	
1945	Devalue	7	S. Brooks	108	Thumbs Up	130	Sirde	115	40,000	1:51.60	
1946	Witch Sir	4	R. Campbell	115	Richmond Jac	109	Old Kentuck	108	40,100	1:49.40	
1947	Armed	6	D. Dodson	130	With Pleasure	117	Mighty Story	114	37,600	1:49.20	
1948	Citation	3	E. Arcaro	119	Eternal Reward	116	Pellicle	106	38,000	1:49.20	
1949	Coaltown	4	S. Brooks	130	Armed	110	Star Reward	121	36,700	1:48.40	
1950	Inseparable	5	K. Church	114	Seaward	118	Colosal	114	20,375	1:52.20	
1951	Royal Governor	7	E. Arcaro	115	Volcanic	124	Miche	116	41,950	1:49.20	
1952	Royal Mustang	4	P.J. Bailey	109	Cuore	112	Going Away	112	18,625	1:49.20	
1953	Abbe Sting	5	R. Baldwin	110	Armageddon	118	Iceberg II	122	16,675	1:48.40	
1954	Sir Mango	4	D. Erb	124	Iceberg II	123	Stan	114	17,300	1:49.40	
1955	Mark-Ye-Well	6	D. Erb	114	Ruhe	111	Blue Choir	117	16,700	1:48.40	
1956	Sir Tribal	5	W. Hartack	121	Mahan	115	Blue Choir	124	16,875	1:49.00	
1957	Manassas	4	C. Burr	115	Bryn	105	Bernburgoo	112	17,150	1:50.60	
1958	Terra Firma		L.C. Cook	118	Lincoln Road	124	Judge	114	54,800	1:50.60	
1959	Round Table	5	W. Shoemaker	132	Noureddin	110	Tudor Era	117	54,700	1:47.20	
1960	Dunce	4	B. Baeza	121	Martini II	109	King Grail	111	32,200	1:57.60	
1961	Oink	4	J. Sellers	126	Noholme II	117	Resolved	120	21,025	1:50.60	
1962	Porvenir II	8	A. Gomez	122	Oink	120	Gung Ho! II	114	26,875	1:51.20	
1963	Hard Rock Man	4	W. Blum	120	Wa-Wa Cy	113	Intercepted	118	20,100	1:48.20	
1964	Spanish Fort	4	D. Brumfield	112	Irish Dandy	110	Rob Roy III	106	28,500	1:48.60	
1965	Marlin Bay	5	H. Hinojosa	114	Or et Argent	117	Hard Rock Man	114	35,550	1:49.40	
1966	Climax II	5	W. Hartack	115	The Dancer	114	Miss Rincon	110	35,400	1:50.20	
1967	Climax II	6	L. Pincay Jr	113	Dominar	114	Toro Charger	110	33,800	1:49.60	
1968	Out the Window	4	H. Moreno	112	War Censor	117	Irish Rebellion	125	26,100	1:50.40	
1968	Fort Marcy	4	C.H. Marquez	119	The Knack II	110	Nashua Pilot	114	26,000	1:50.60	
1969	Hawaii	5	M. Ycaza	118	Great Cohoes	114	Quilche	112	35,100	1:49.80	
1970	Mr. Leader	4	J. Tejeira	116	Kerry's Time	110	Ribofilio	117	34,900	1:47.40	
1971	Knight in Armor	4	M. Venezia	115	Colorado City	115	Red Bayou	118	33,700	1:51.20	
1972	Unanime	5	W. Gavidia	113	Wing Out	125	Kling Kling	115	34,600	1:51.20	

Year	Winner	Age	Jockey	Wt.	Second	Wt.	Third	Wt.	Win Value	Time	Beyer
1973	Triumphant	4	A. Rini	119	Super Sail	116	Vegas Vic	114	36,400	1:34.80	
1974	Zografos	6	W. Gavidia	113	Smooth Dancer	111	Fun Co K.	109	45,600	1:50.80	
1975	Buffalo Lark	5	L. Snyder	121	Kuryakin	111	Zografos	115	40,600	1:43.00	
1976	Passionate Pirate	5	H. Arroyo	114	Improviser	122	Zografos	115	39,500	1:43.00	
1977	Quick Card	4	M. Solomone	118	Proponent	116			35,640	1:43.00	
					Emperor Rex	116					
1978	Old Frankfort	6	R. Turcotte	112	Capt. Stevens	114	That's a Nice	122	34,380	1:50.20	
1979	Overskate	4	R. Platts	125	That's a Nice	119	Bold Standard	111	33,360	1:44.00	
1980	Told	4	J.L. Samyn	114	Rossi Gold	111	Overskate	130	66,960	1:43.00	
1981	Ben Fab	4	G. Stahlbaum	122			Opus Dei	116	48,600	1:43.80	
	Rossi Gold	5	P. Day	123							
1982	Rossi Gold	6	P. Day	124	Johnny Dance	115	Don Roberto	118	70,560	1:46.00	
1983	Rossi Gold	7	P. Day	122	Who's for Dinner	110	Lucence	115	70,860	1:48.80	
1984	Tough Mickey	4	J.L. Samyn	119	Fortnightly	115	Jack Slade	113	80,460	1:41.40	
1985	Drumalis	5	P. Day	118	Best of Both	116	Lofty	117	91,920	1:42.20	
1986	Explosive Darling	4	E. Fires	115	Clever Song	120	Forkintheroad	113	70,560	1:48.40	
1987	Sharrood	4	F. Toro	120	Explosive Darling	121	Santella Mac	115	52,080	1:56.20	
1989	Salem Drive	7	P. Day	116	Green Barb	115	Delegant	115	69,660	1:55.20	
1990	Mistery Sicy	4	C.A. Black	114	Silver Medallion	115	Careafolie	113	69,900	1:54.40	
1991	Blair's Cove	6	G.K. Gomez	115	Opening Verse	118	Cameroon	112	60,000	1:55.80	99
1992	Plate Dancer	7	E. Fires	114	Little Bro Lantis	114	Stark South	114	60,000	1:55.00	102
1993	Little Bro Lantis	5	C.C. Bourque	114	Stark South	119	Coaxing Matt	115	60,000	1:56.80	101
1994	Marastani	4	A.T. Gryder	113	Snake Eyes	117	The Vid	113	60,000	1:54.60	101
1995	Snake Eyes	5	R.J. Alborado	116	Coaxing Matt	115	Bucks Nephew	114	45,000	1:56.40	104
1996	Vladivostok	5	C. Perret	116	Raintrap	118	Special Price	118	138,075	2:30.20	107
1997	Lakeshore Road	4	C. H. Borel	113	Chief Bearhart	119	Awad	119	140,025	2:29.40	105
2000	Williams News	5	R.J. Albarado	115	Profit Option	110	Buff	114	148,425	2:31.22	104
2001	Falcon Flight	5	R.R. Douglas	114	Langston	114	Williams News	116	96,300	2:27.86	101
2002	Cetewayo	8	R.R. Douglas	118	Private Son	115	Pisces	117	137,475	2:27.50	102
2003	Ballingarry	4	R.R. Douglas	121	Dr. Brendler	118	Jack's Own Time	112	131,520	2:28.30	100
2004	Ballingarry	5	R.R. Douglas	120	Grey Beard	117	Art Variety	116	120,000	2:36.30	99

Silverfoot finished second but was disqualified and placed fourth

Beyer Index: 102.08

STRUB (G2), 1 1/8 Miles, 4-Year-Olds, Santa Anita, 2004 Purse: $300,000

Year	Winner	Age	Jockey	Wt.	Second	Wt.	Third	Wt.	Win Value	Time	Beyer
1948	Flashco	4	J. Westrope	113	On Trust	125	Double Jay	118	83,500	2:03.20	
1949	Ace Admiral	4	J. Westrope	113	Rose Beam	112	Dinner Gong	114	85,200	2:02.20	
1950	Ponder	4	S. Brooks	126	Two Lea	116	Mocopo	112	75,200	2:02.40	
1951	Great Circle	4	W. Shoemaker	115	Lotowhite	116	Bed o' Roses	110	144,325	2:00.40	
1952	Intent	4	E. Arcaro	113	Gold Capitol	114	Black Douglas	113	112,750	2:02.80	
1953	Mark-Ye-Well	4	E. Arcaro	126	Fleet Bird	112	Happy Go Lucky	114	85,600	2:03.40	
1954	Apple Valley	4	M. Volzke	113	By Zeus	114	Cerise Reine	115	85,025	2:08.00	
1955	Determine	4	R. York	126	Miz Clementine	117	James Session	113	87,000	2:00.40	
1956	Trackmaster	4	R. Neves	114	Traffic Judge	123	Honeys Alibi	119	79,600	2:04.80	
1957	Spinney	4	W. Harmatz	113	Beam Rider	112	Lucky G.L.	113	93,870	2:04.80	
1958	Round Table	4	W. Harmatz	126	Seaneen	117	Promised Land	125	80,360	2:01.80	
1959	Hillsdale	4	T. Barrow	123	Royal Living	112	Jewel's Reward	116	91,150	2:02.40	
1960	First Landing	4	E. Arcaro	116	Bagdad	118	Linmold	117	80,490	2:00.60	
1961	Prove It	4	W. Shoemaker	116	Prince Blessed	113	Grey Eagle	113	93,370	2:01.00	
1962	Four-and-Twenty	4	J. Longden	126	Garwol	111	Olden Timems	114	79,910	2:01.00	
1963	Crimson Satan	4	H. Hinojosa	118	Pirate Cove	114	Dr. Kacy	112	92,400	2:00.60	
1964	Gun Bow	4	W. Shoemaker	117	Rocky Link	114	Win-em-All	113	87,000	1:59.80	
1965	Duel	4	M. Ycaza	112	Or Et Argent	113	Pelegrin	114	79,600	2:00.60	
1966	Bold Bidder	4	W. Shoemaker	119	Isle of Greece	120	Terry's Secret	125	89,500	1:59.60	
1967	Drin	4	L. Pincay Jr.	117	Quicken Tree	115	Kings Favor	116	84,800	2:02.00	
1968	Most Host	4	W. Harmatz	114	Damascus	126	Ruken	117	73,700	2:04.00	
1969	Dignitas	4	F. Alvarez	115	Nodouble	123	Cavamore	117	81,300	2:02.00	
	Nodouble finished first but was disqualified and placed second										
1970	Snow Sporting	4	L. Pincay Jr.	114	Might	116	Comtal	114	84,500	1:48.80	
1971	War Helm	4	J. Sellers	115	Hanalei Bay	118	Mickey McGuire	117	87,100	2:00.60	
1972	Unconscious	4	W. Shoemaker	121	Triple Bend	118	Good Counsel	116	85,300	2:00.40	
1973	Royal Owl	4	J. Sellers	116	Big Spruce	117	New Prospect	117	82,800	2:04.00	
1974	Ancient Title	4	L. Pincay Jr.	121	Dancing Papa	116	Prince Dantan	115	85,200	2:00.80	
1975	Stardust Mel	4	W. Shoemaker	120	Confederate Yankee	116	Rube the Great	122	86,300	2:04.20	
1976	George Navonod	4	F. Toro	115	Larrikin	118	Dancing Gun	115	76,900	2:12.00	
1977	Kirby Lane	4	S. Hawley	118	Properantes	114	Double Discount	115	90,900	2:00.40	
1978	Mr. Redoy	4	D. McHargue	116	Text	121	J.O. Tobin	122	140,200	2:01.00	
1979	Affirmed	4	L. Pincay Jr.	126	Johnny's Image	115	Quip	115	142,500	2:01.00	

Year	Winner	Age	Jockey	Wt.	Second	Wt.	Third	Wt.	Win Value	Time	Beyer
1980	Spectacular Bid	4	W. Shoemaker	126	Flying Paster	121	Valdez	122	124,500	1:57.80	
1981	Super Moment	4	F. Toro	116	Exploded	116	Doonesbury	118	145,000	2:01.20	
1982	It's the One	4	W.A. Guerra	118	Dorcaro	116	Rock Softly	115	172,700	2:00.40	
1983	Swing Till Dawn	4	P.A. Valenzuela	115	Wavering Monarch	121	Water Bank	117	178,000	2:02.00	
1984	Desert Wine	4	E. Delahoussaye	117	Load the Cannons	115	Silent Fox	114	221,400	2:02.20	
1985	Precisionist	4	C.J. McCarron	125	Greinton	117	Gate Dancer	126	189,300	2:00.20	
1986	Nostalgia's Star	4	F. Toro	116	Roo Art	117	Fast Account	115	314,250	2:03.60	
1987	Snow Chief	4	P.A. Valenzuela	126	Ferdinand	126	Broad Brush	126	291,750	2:00.00	
1988	Alysheba	4	C.J. McCarron	126	Candi's Gold	117	On The Line	119	275,000	2:00.40	
1989	Nasr El Arab	4	P.A. Valenzuela	123	Perceive Arrogance	117	Silver Circus	120	275,000	2:02.20	
1990	Flying Continental	4	C.A. Black	119	Quiet American	114	Hawkster	126	275,000	2:01.40	
1991	Defensive Play	4	J.A. Santos	122	My Boy Adam	117	In Excess	121	275,000	2:00.80	
1992	Best Pal	4	K.J. Desormeaux	124	Dinard	120	Reign Road	118	275,000	1:59.95	119
1993	Siberian Summer	4	C.S. Nakatani	118	Bertrando	122	Major Impact	118	275,000	2:00.78	114
1994	Diazo	4	L. Pincay Jr	120	Nonproductiveasset	118	Stuka	118	275,000	2:00.33	110
1995	Dare and Go	4	A. Solis	118	Dramatic Gold	124	Wekiva Springs	122	275,000	2:00.15	110
1996	Helmsman	4	C.J. McCarron	122	Afternoon Deelites	120	Mr Purple	118	300,000	2:02.76	106
1997	Victory Speech	4	J.D. Bailey	124	The Barking Shark	118	Ambivalent	118	300,000	2:01.50	108
1998	Silver Charm	4	G.L. Stevens	123	Mud Route	117	Bagshot	117	300,000	1:47.27	113
1999	Event of the Year	4	C.S. Nakatani	119	Dr Fong	121	Hanuman Highway	117	300,000	1:47.65	115
2000	General Challenge	4	C.S. Nakatani	123	Luftikus	117	Saint's honor	121	300,000	1:48.81	112
2001	Wooden Phone	4	C.S. Nakatani	117	Tiznow	123	Jimmy Z	117	300,000	1:48.43	107
2002	Mizzen Mast	4	K.J. Desormeaux	121	Giant Gentleman	117	Fancy As	119	240,000	1:47.25	117
2003	Medaglia d'Oro	4	J.D. Bailey	123	Olmodavor	117	Tracemark	117	240,000	1:48.04	119
2004	Domestic Dispute	4	K.J. Desormeaux	117	During	121	Buckland Manor	117	180,000	1:49.08	107

Beyer Index: 112.08

STUYVESANT HANDICAP (G3), 1 1/8 Miles, 3-Year-Olds and Up, Aqueduct, 2004 Purse: $109,900

Year	Winner	Age	Jockey	Wt.	Second	Wt.	Third	Wt.	Win Value	Time	Beyer
1916	Fernrock	3	E. Haynes	107	Mustard	102	Dad's Choice	100	2,350	1:13.00	
1917	Julialeon	3	R. Troxler	113	Woodtrap	114	Straight Forward	117	3,175	1:14.20	
1918	Motor Cop	3	J. Loftus	115	Flags	113	Jack Hare Jr	129	2,825	1:12.20	
1919	Purchase	3	J. Loftus	129	Eternal	125	Ophelia	107	3,850	1:38.80	
1920	Man o' War	3	C. Kummer	135	Yellow Hand	103			3,850	1:41.60	
1921	Sedgefield	3	F. Coltiletti	100	Knobbie	112	Muskallonge	114	4,650	1:39.60	
1922	Snob II	3	E. Sande	117	Galantman	115	Pirate Gold	116	4,650	1:39.60	
1923	Dot	3	E. Sande	110	Moonraker	107	Great Man	117	4,650	1:39.40	
1924	Ordinance	3	E. Legere	108	Laurano	105	Samaritan	105	4,650	1:38.40	
1937	Chicolorado	3	E. Arcaro	115	Vamoose	102	Guy Fawkes	117	4,425	1:13.00	
1938	Merry Lassie	3	J. Stout	116	Steel Knight	100	Nedayr	126	3,700	1:11.00	
1939	T.M. Dorsett	3	L. Haas	116	Star Runner	109	Entracte	114	3,925	1:12.20	
1963	Rocky Link	3	S. Hernandez	112	Sunrise Flight	117	Yorky	110	18,297	1:49.20	
1964	Macedonia	4	H. Gustines	111	Bonjour	112	Piave	114	18,622	1:37.20	
1965	Flag Raiser		R. Ussery	121	Turn to Reason	115	Cupid	112	39,780	1:35.60	
1966	Understanding	3	A. Cordero Jr	110	Mr. Right	116	Advocator	114	37,765	1:36.00	
1967	Sun Gala	3	R. Turcotte	111	Understanding	110	R. Thomas	119	37,180	1:36.80	
1968	Spring Double	5	C. Baltazar	114	Mile's Fancy	113	Principe	107	38,480	1:36.20	
1969	King Emperor	3	C.H. Marquez	116	Dewan	116	Jaikyl	112	39,520	1:34.40	
1970	Never Bow	4	E. Belmonte	114	Gleaming Light	114	Protanto	112	36,420	1:35.80	
1971	Red Reality	5	L. Pincay Jr	116	Silver Mallet	113	Summer Air	117	36,420	1:35.80	
1972	Icecapade	3	E. Maple	119	Sunny and Mild	108	Tentam	114	36,570	1:34.00	
1973	Riva Ridge	4	E. Maple	130	Forage	116	True Knight	122	34,320	1:47.00	
1974	Crafty Khale	5	J. Cruguet	121	Stop the Music	120	True Knight	121	34,890	1:48.00	
1975	Festive Mood	6	H. Hinojosa	115	Step Nicely	124	Stonewalk	122	33,210	1:48.40	
1976	Distant Land	4	H. Gustines	111	Blue Times	114	It's Freezing	115	32,610	1:49.00	
1977	Cox's Ridge	3	E. Maple	124	Wise Philip	114	Gentle King	112	32,760	1:48.40	
1978	Seattle Slew	4	A. Cordero Jr	134	Jumping Hill	115	Wise Phillip	113	62,310	1:47.40	
1979	Music of Time	5	J. Fell	114	What a Gent	111	Dewan Keys	112	65,220	1:50.40	
1980	Plugged Nickle	3	C.B. Asmussen	122	Dr. Patches	115	Ring of Light	116	68,880	1:50.20	
1981	Idyll	4	C.B. Asmussen	114	Spoils of War	113	Silver Buck	112	68,280	1:48.80	
1982	Engine One	4	R. Hernandez	123	Bar Dexter	112	Fit to Fight	118	67,200	1:49.60	
1983	Fit to Fight	4	J.D. Bailey	117	Deputy Minister	119	Sing Sing	115	70,080	1:51.40	
1984	Valiant Lark	4	V. Bracciale Jr	114	Puntivo	112	Bounding Basque	117	70,080	1:51.40	
1985	Garthorn	5	R.Q. Meza	112	Morning Bob	114	Waitlist	118	70,320	1:48.40	
1986	Little Missouri	4	R.G. Davis	116	Waquoit	115	Let's Go Blue	118	125,280	1:50.00	
1987	Moment of Hope	4	M. Venezia	118	Wind Chill	110	I Rejoice	111	109,080	1:49.60	
1988	Talinum	4	M. Castaneda	112	Nostalgia's Star	113	Pleas'nt Virginian	113	111,240	1:51.20	

Year	Winner	Age	Jockey	Wt.	Second	Wt.	Third	Wt.	Win Value	Time	Beyer
1989	Its Acedemic	5	J.D. Bailey	111	Congeleur	115	Homebuilder	114	70,560	1:48.80	
1990	I'm Sky High	4	M.E. Smith	111	Silver Survivor	113	Lost Opportunity	111	71,760	1:48.20	111
1991	Montubio	6	J.M. Pezua	110	Mountain Lore	112	Timely Warning	114	72,480	1:48.20	108
1992	Shots are Ringing	5	J.R. Velazquez	114	Key Contender	111	Timely Warning	115	69,120	1:49.20	104
1993	Michelle Can Pass	5	J.R. Velazquez	115	Key Contender	115	Primitive Hall	113	70,200	1:51.00	103
1994	Wallenda	4	W.H. McCauley	118	Lost Soldier	110	Pistols and Roses	117	64,560	1:50.60	103
1995	Silver Fox	4	M.E. Smith	113	Yourmissinthepoint	111	Earth Colony	114	68,940	1:48.00	100
1996	Poor But Honest	6	J.F. Chavez	116	Flitch	115	Admirality	117	66,480	1:49.40	108
1997	Delay of Game	4	Samyn J. L.	114	Concerto	118	Mr. Sinatra	117	66,060	1:47.60	108
1998	Mr. Sinatra	4	Gryder A. T.	115	Rock and Roll	114	Accelerator	114	65,280	1:48.00	109
1999	Best of Luck	3	M.E. Smith	114	Wild Imagination	115	Durmiente	113	67,200	1:49.60	108
2000	Lager	6	H. Castillo Jr.	116	Top Official	113	Fire King	115	64,860	1:50.03	97
2001	Graeme Hall	4	J.R. Velazquez	119	Country Be Gold	115	Cat's at Home	114	64,620	1:47.95	113
2002	Snake Mountain	4	J.A. Santos	115	Windsor Castle	115	Docent	115	68,040	1:50.56	103
2003	Presidentialaffair	4	R. Migliore	115	Thunder Blitz	114	Gander	115	66,180	1:50.86	106
2004	Classic Endeavor	6	E.S. Prado	114	Colita	115	Snake Mountain	115	65,940	1:49.70	104

Beyer Index: 105.67

SUBURBAN HANDICAP (G1), 1 1/4 Miles, 3-Year-Olds and Up, Belmont Park, 2004 Purse: $500,000

Year	Winner	Age	Jockey	Wt.	Second	Wt.	Third	Wt.	Win Value	Time	Beyer
1884	Gen. Monroe	6	W. Donohue	124	War Eagle	102	J. of Hearts	120	4,945	2:11.60	
1885	Pontiac	4	H. Olney	102	Richmond	110	Rataplan	121	5,855	2:09.20	
1886	Troubadour	4	W. Fitzpatrick	115	Richmond	110	Savanac	100	5,697	2:12.20	
1887	Eurus	4	G. Davis	102	Oriflame	104	Wickham	114	6,065	2:12.00	
1888	Elkwood	5	W. Martin	119	Terra Cotta	122	Firenze	117	6,812	2:07.20	
1889	Raceland	4	E. Garrison	120	Terra Cotta	124	Gorgo	110	6,900	2:09.80	
1890	Salvator	4	I. Murphy	127	Cassius	107	Tenny	126	66,900	2:06.80	
1891	Loantaka	5	M. Bergen	110	Major Domo	108	Cassius	115	9,900	2:07.00	
1892	Montana	4	E. Garrison	115	Major Domo	115	Lamplighter	104	17,750	2:07.40	
1893	Lowlander	5	P. McDermott	105	Terrifier	95	Lamplighter	129	17,750	2:06.60	
1894	Ramopo	4	F. Taral	120	Banquet	119	Sport	114	12,070	2:06.20	
1895	Lazzarone	4	A. Hamilton	115	Sir Walter	126	S'g a Dance	99	4,730	2:07.80	
1896	Henry of Navarre	5	H. Griffin	129	The Commoner	113	Clifford	126	5,850	2:07.00	
1897	Ben Brush	4	W. Simms	123	The Winner	115	Havoc	104	5,850	2:07.20	
1898	Tillo	4	A. Clayton	119	Semper Ego	106	Ogden	109	5,850	2:07.20	
1899	Imp	5	N. Turner	114	Bannockburn	112	Warrenton	114	6,800	2:08.20	
1900	Kinley Mack	4	P. McCue	125	Ethelbert	130	Gulden	100	6,800	2:06.80	
1901	Alcedo	4	H. Spencer	112	Watercure	102	Toddy	100	7,800	2:05.60	
1902	Gold Heels	4	O. Wonderly	124	Pentecost	99	Blues	124	7,800	2:05.20	
1903	Africander	3	G. Fuller	110	Herbert	118	Hunt. Raine	98	16,490	2:10.40	
1904	Hermis	5	A. Redfern	127	The Picket	124	Irish Lad	127	16,800	2:05.00	
1905	Beldame	4	F. O'Neill	123	Proper	109	First Mason	118	16,800	2:05.40	
1906	Go Between	5	W. Shaw	116	Dandelion	107	Colonial Girl	113	16,800	2:05.20	
1907	Nealon	4	W. Dugan	113	Montgomery	104	Beacon Li't	100	16,800	2:06.40	
1908	Ballot	4	J. Notter	127	King James	98	Fair Play	111	19,750	2:03.00	
1909	Fitz Herbert	3	E. Dugan	105	Alfred Noble	104	Fayette	101	3,850	2:03.40	
1910	Olambala	4	G. Archibald	115	Prince Imperial	101	Ballot	129	4,800	2:04.40	
1913	Whisk Broom II	6	J. Notter	139	Lahore	112	Meridian	119	3,000	2:00.00	
1915	Stromboli	4	C. Turner	122	Sam Jackson	100	Sharpshooter	106	3,925	2:05.40	
1916	Friar Rock	3	M. Garner	101	Short Grass	117	Stromboli	123	3,450	2:05.00	
1917	Boots	6	J. Loftus	122	Borrow	115	The Finn	129	4,900	2:05.20	
1918	Johren	3	F. Robinson	110	Hollister	113	Battle	107	5,850	2:06.00	
1919	Corn Tassel	5	L. Ensor	108	Sweep On	108	Boniface	107	5,200	2:02.20	
1920	Paul Jones	3	A. Schuttinger	106	Boniface	115	Exterminator	123	6,350	2:09.60	
1921	Audacious	5	C. Kummer	120	Mad Hatter	130	Sennings Park	110	8,100	2:02.20	
1922	Captain Alcock	5	C. Ponce	108	Flying Cloud	115	Mad Hatter	130	8,200	2:05.40	
1923	Grey Lag	5	E. Sande	135	Snob II	115	Exodus	119	7,800	2:03.00	
1924	Mad Hatter	8	E. Sande	125	Little Celt	114	Aga Khan	102	9,150	2:03.60	
1925	Sting	4	B. Breuning	122	Cherry Pie	108	Mad Play	124	11,300	2:04.20	
1926	Crusader	3	J. Callahan	104	American Flag	124	K. Sol's Seal	107	13,150	2:03.00	
1927	Crusader	4	C. Kummer	127	Black Maria	120	Macaw	120	11,875	2:02.40	
1928	Dolan	4	J. Callahan	105	Chance Shot	120	Scapa Flow	120	13,675	2:06.60	
1929	Bateau	4	E. Ambrose	112	Petee-Wrack	124	Toro	125	14,100	2:03.40	
1930	Petee-Wrack	5	E. Sande	122	Curate	109	Distraction	119	11,850	2:07.40	
1931	Mokatam	4	A. Robertson	123	Questionnaire	128	Her Grace	111	11,200	2:02.40	
1932	White Clover II	6	R. Workman	115	The Nut	110	Sun Meadow	119	11,100	2:03.40	
1933	Equipoise	5	R. Workman	132	Osculator	107	Apprentice	112	7,250	2:02.00	
1934	Ladysman	4	S. Coucci	114	Equipoise	134	War Glory	115	5,750	2:02.60	

Year	Winner	Age	Jockey	Wt.	Second	Wt.	Third	Wt.	Win Value	Time	Beyer
1935	Head Play	5	C. Kurtsinger	114	Discovery	123	Only One	110	12,175	2:02.00	
1936	Firethorn	4	H. Richards	116	Granville	108	Whopper	119	12,125	2:04.60	
1937	Aneroid	4	C. Rosengarten	110	Esposa	106	Memory Book	116	10,950	2:01.60	
1938	Snark	5	J. Longden	120	Pompoon	128	Aneroid	120	17,050	2:01.40	
1939	Cravat	4	J. Westrope	121	Thanksgiving	120	Handcuff	110	17,750	2:02.80	
1940	Eight Thirty	4	H. Richards	127	Can't Wait	109	Third Degree	124	19,850	2:01.60	
1941	Your Chance	4	D. Meade	114	Hash	119	Shot Put	110	25,200	2:02.60	
1942	Market Wise	4	B. James	124	Whirlaway	129	Attention	124	27,800	2:01.80	
1943	Don Bingo	4	J. Renick	104	Attention	121	Lochinvar	105	27,600	2:01.40	
1944	Aletern	5	H. Lindberg	108	Sun Again	128	Alquest	115	39,210	2:01.20	
1945	Devil Diver	6	E. Arcaro	132	Stymie	119	Olympic Zenith	106	34,995	2:04.00	
1946	Armed	5	D. Dodson	130	Reply Paid	110	Stymie	123	43,000	2:02.00	
1947	Assault	4	E. Arcaro	130	Natchez	120	Talon	113	40,100	2:01.80	
1948	Harmonica	4	W. Mehrtens	109	Stymie	128	Colosal	117	39,700	2:03.00	
1949	Vulcan's Forge	4	E. Arcaro	124	But Why Not	117	Flying Missel	108	43,200	2:03.00	
1950	Loser Weeper	5	N. Combest	115	My Request	119	Hill Prince	113	41,400	2:02.00	
1951	Busanda	4	K. Stuart	102	Lone Eagle	110	County Delight	122	42,100	2:02.60	
1952	One Hitter	6	T. Atkinson	112	Crafty Admiral	113	Mameluke	116	41,900	2:02.00	
1953	Tom Fool	4	T. Atkinson	128	Royal Vale	124	Cold Command	114	40,400	2:00.60	
1954	Straight Face	4	T. Atkinson	118	Bassanio	106	Mandingo	106	44,400	2:03.20	
1955	Helioscope	4	S. Boulmetis	128	High Gun	133	Subahdar	119	61,150	2:00.60	
1956	Nashua	4	E. Arcaro	128	Dedicate	111	Subahdar	112	55,900	2:00.80	
1957	Traffic Judge	5	E. Arcaro	124	Lofty Peak	118	Dedicate	126	58,450	2:02.60	
1958	Bold Ruler	4	E. Arcaro	134	Clem	109	Third Brother	110	53,360	2:01.00	
1959	Bald Eagle	4	M. Ycaza	119	Talent Show	125	Plion	119	71,635	2:01.60	
1960	Sword Dancer	4	E. Arcaro	125	First Landing	122	Waltz	115	69,165	2:01.60	
1961	Kelso	4	E. Arcaro	133	Nickel Boy	112	Talent Show	110	72,735	2:02.00	
1962	Beau Purple	5	W. Boland	115	Kelso	132	Garwol	109	68,380	2:00.60	
1963	Kelso	6	I. Valenzuela	133	Saidam	111	Garwol	112	70,525	2:01.80	
1964	Iron Peg	4	M. Ycaza	116	Kelso	131	Olden Times	128	71,500	2:01.80	
1965	Pia Star	4	J. Sellers	117	Smart	119	Tenacle	114	70,720	2:01.00	
1966	Buffle	3	R. Turcotte	110	Pluck	113	Paoluccio	108	72,085	2:02.00	
1967	Buckpasser	4	B. Baeza	133	Ring Twice	111	Yonder	109	71,370	2:02.20	
1968	Dr. Fager	4	B. Baeza	132	Bold Hour	116	Damascus	133	69,615	1:59.60	
1969	Mr. Right	6	A. Cordero Jr	117	Dike	114	Chompion	111	69,550	2:04.80	
1970	Barometer	5	A. Cordero Jr	111	Verbatim	116	Hitchcock	113	71,565	2:01.20	
1971	Twice Worthy	4	J. Ruane	116	Ejemplo	114	Tunex	117	69,240	2:02.20	
1972	Hitchcock	6	C.H. Marquez	113	West Coast Scout	120	Naskra	110	67,980	2:00.00	
1973	Key to the Mint	4	B. Baeza	126	True Knight	118	Cloudy Dawn	113	65,700	2:00.80	
1974	True Knight	5	A. Cordero Jr	127	Plunk	114	Forego	131	68,880	2:01.40	
1975	Forego	5	H. Gustines	134	Arbees Boy	118	Loud	114	66,840	2:27.80	
1976	Foolish Pleasure	4	E. Maple	125	Forego	134	Lord Rebeau	116	65,280	1:55.40	
1977	Quiet Little Table	4	E. Maple	114	Forego	138	Nearly On Time	104	63,840	2:03.00	
1978	Upper Nile	4	J. Velasquez	113	Nearly On Time	109	Great Contractor	114	63,840	2:01.80	
1979	State Dinner	4	J. Velasquez	118	Mister Brea	120	Alydar	126	79,125	2:01.60	
1980	Winter's Tale	4	J. Fell	114	State Dinner	117	Czaravich	127	92,920	2:00.60	
1981	Temperence Hill	4	D. MacBeth	127	Ring of Light	115	Highland Blade	113	100,620	2:02.00	
1982	Silver Buck	4	D. MacBeth	111	It's the One	124	Aloma's Ruler	112	100,620	1:59.60	
1983	Winter's Tale	7	J. Fell	120	Sing Sing	119	Highland Blade	119	168,600	2:01.60	
1984	Fit to Fight	5	J.D. Bailey	126	Canadian Factor	116	Wild Again	116	201,300	2:00.60	
1985	Vanlandingham	4	D. MacBeth	115	Carr de Naskra	120	Dramatic Desire	109	180,600	2:01.00	
1986	Roo Art	4	P. Day	116	Proud Truth	121	Creme Fraiche	121	197,700	2:01.20	
1987	Broad Brush	4	A. Cordero Jr	126	Set Style	112	Bordeaux Bob	112	323,260	2:03.00	
1988	Personal Flag	5	P. Day	117	Waquoit	121	Bet Twice	126	228,060	2:01.40	
1989	Dancing Spree	4	A. Cordero Jr	114	Forever Silver	116	Easy n Dirty	114	258,720	2:02.40	
1990	Easy Goer	4	P. Day	126	De Roche	113	Montubio	113	239,400	2:00.00	119
1991	In Excess	4	G.L. Stevens	119	Chief Honcho	115	Killer Diller	113	300,000	1:58.20	120
1992	Pleasant Tap	5	E. Delahoussaye	119	Strike the Gold	119	Defensive Play	115	300,000	2:00.20	112
1993	Devil His Due	4	W.H. McCauley	121	Pure Rumor	110	West by West	116	180,000	2:01.20	109
1994	Devil His Due	5	M.E. Smith	124	Valley Crossing	113	Federal Funds	110	210,000	2:02.40	110
1995	Key Contender	7	J.D. Bailey	115	Kissin Kris	113	Federal Funds	107	210,000	2:02.20	108
1996	Wekiva Springs	5	M.E. Smith	122	Mahogany Hall	114	L'Carriere	118	300,000	2:02.60	110
1997	Skip Away	4	S.J. Sellers	122	Will's Way	116	Formal Gold	120	210,000	2:02.20	118
1998	Frisk Me Now	4	E.L.King Jr	118	Ordway	110	Sir Bear	117	210,000	2:00.40	112
1999	Behrens	5	J.F. Chavez	121	Catienus	113	Social Charter	113	240,000	2:01.00	110
2000	Lemon Drop Kid	4	E.S. Prado	122	Behrens	122	Lager	113	300,000	1:58.97	117
2001	Albert the Great	4	J.F. Chavez	123	Lido Palace	115	Include	122	300,000	2:00.39	119
2002	E Dubai	4	J.R. Velazquez	116	Lido Palace	119	Macho Uno	119	300,000	2:00.95	114
2003	Mineshaft	4	R.J. Albarado	121	Volponi	121	Dollar Bill	115	300,000	2:01.57	115
2004	Peace Rules	4	J.D. Bailey	120	Newfoundland	114	Funny Cide	117	300,000	1:59.52	111

Beyer Index: 113.60

SUNSET HANDICAP (G2), 1 1/2 Miles (Turf), 3-Year-Olds and Up, Hollywood Park, 2004 Purse: $150,000

Year	Winner	Age	Jockey	Wt.	Second	Wt.	Third	Wt.	Win Value	Time	Beyer
1940	Kayak II	5	J. Adams	131	Specify	116	Big Flash	109	13,750	2:30.20	
1941	King Torch	4	J. Deering	105	Mioland	128	W. and Wing	105	18,950	2:44.40	
1946	Historian	5	O. Scurlock	121	Paperboy	110	Triplicate	122	37,150	2:40.80	
1947	Cover Up	4	R. Permane	122	Burning Dream	117	Lets Dance	113	32,000	2:41.20	
1948	Drumbeat	3	T. Williams	100	On Trust	126	Shannon II	124	33,100	2:41.00	
1949	Ace Admiral	4	J. Longden	122	Natural	102	Dinner Gong	117	34,650	2:39.80	
1950	Hill Prince	3	E. Arcaro	128	Next Move	114	Great Circle	109	35,300	1:48.60	
1951	Alderman	4	J. Westrope	112	Mocopo	106	Stormy Cloud	105	34,400	2:42.00	
1952	Great Circle	5	R. Heather	112	Stormy Cloud	108	Wistful	112	31,700	2:41.80	
1953	Lights Up	6	J. Westrope	114	Endowment	106	Fleet Bird	120	60,400	2:41.20	
1954	Fleet Bird	5	R. Neves	115	Rejected	128	Six Fifteen	107	63,200	2:40.80	
1955	Social Outcast	5	E. Guerin	121	Rejected	122	Alidon	119	64,400	2:40.60	
1956	Swaps	4	W. Shoemaker	130	Honeys Alibi	108	Blue Volt	108	64,400	2:38.20	
1957	Find	7	R. Neves	119	Eddie Schmidt	109	Porterhouse	122	66,000	2:40.00	
1958	Gallant Man	4	W. Shoemaker	132	Eddie Schmidt	110	St. Vincent	111	61,500	2:41.00	
1959	Whodunit	4	R. York	110	Day Court	114	Find	118	63,700	2:40.80	
1960	Dotted Swiss	4	E. Burns	120	Nickel Boy	112	Turin	112	63,100	2:40.20	
1961	Whodunit	6	M. Ycaza	117	Dress Up	113	Prince Blessed	122	52,800	2:39.00	
1962	Prove It	5	W. Shoemaker	129	Windy Sands	112	Notable II	107	55,000	2:39.60	
1963	Arbitrage	5	P. Moreno	110	Mr. Consistency	117	Cadiz	122	50,350	2:41.20	
1964	Colorado King	5	W. Shoemaker	124	Drill Site	113	Viking Spirit	111	50,650	2:40.80	
1965	Terry's Secret	3	A. Maese	116	Ramant	108	Ask Father	110	48,000	2:41.80	
1966	O'Hara	4	D. Pierce	113	Rehabilitate	106	Silk Hat	109	52,650	2:40.40	
1967	Hill Clown	4	W. Shoemaker	109	Pretense	129	Niarkos	121	63,500	2:27.80	
1968	Fort Marcy	4	L. Pincay Jr	122	Quicken Tree	122	Fiddle Isle	108	73,500	2:26.60	
1969	Petrone	5	J. Sellers	124	Society II	112	Off	109	61,450	3:18.00	
1970	One for All	4	L. Pincay Jr	114	Onandaga	113	Over the Counter	111	75,350	3:21.80	
1971	Over the Counter	7	J. Lambert	114	Cougar II	130	Typecast	110	80,650	3:19.20	
1972	Typecast	6	J. Sellers	120	Over the Counter	112	Violonor	114	78,350	3:20.60	
1973	Cougar II	7	W. Shoemaker	128	Life Cycle	120	Rock Bath	114	80,100	2:26.00	
1974	Greco II	5	W. Shoemaker	113	Big Whippendeal	120	Scantling	118	69,600	2:27.00	
1975	Barclay Joy	5	W. Shoemaker	117	Captain Cee Jay	118	Top Crowd	115	50,450	2:26.80	
1975	Cruiser II	6	F. Olivares	114	Pass the Glance	119	Kirrary	116	49,450	2:27.00	
1976	Caucasus	4	F. Toro	121	King Pellinore	124	Riot in Paris	123	81,350	2:26.40	
1977	Today 'n Tomorrow	4	W. Shoemaker	116	Hunza Dancer	122	Copper Mel	117	104,450	2:27.60	
1978	Exceller	5	W. Shoemaker	130	Diagramatic	122	Effervescing	122	96,600	2:27.00	
1979	Sirlad	5	D.G. McHargue	122	Ardiente	115	Inkerman	119	103,000	2:24.00	
1980	Inkerman	5	W. Shoemaker	115	Balzac	120	Obraztsovy	121	94,700	2:24.40	
1981	Galaxy Libra	5	W. Shoemaker	119	Caterman	122	The Bart	117	136,050	2:25.80	
1982	Erins Isle	4	A. Cordero Jr	118	Don Roberto	117	Exploded	119	129,600	2:25.60	
1983	Craelius	4	C.J. McCarron	118	Palikaraki	115	Decadrachm	115	137,600	2:26.40	
1984	John Henry	9	C.J. McCarron	126	Load the Cannons	118	Pair of Deuces	113	129,800	2:24.80	
1985	Kings Island	4	F. Toro	116	Greinton	122	Val Danseur	114	148,800	2:25.80	
1986	Zoffany	6	E. Delahoussaye	122	Dahar	125	Flying Pidgeon	121	161,500	2:24.40	
1987	Swink	4	W. Shoemaker	112	Forlitano	122	Rivlia	122	165,300	2:25.00	
1988	Roi Normand	5	F. Toro	114	Putting	117	Circus Prince	114	170,000	2:24.60	
1989	Pranke	5	P.A. Valenzuela	117	Frankly Perfect	123	Pleasant Variety	117	157,200	2:28.00	
1990	Petite Ile	4	C.A. Black	115	Live the Dream	116	Soft Machine	110	163,600	2:25.60	102
1991	Black Monday	5	C.S. Nakatani	112	Super May	117	Razeen	116	158,400	2:26.00	107
1992	Qathif	5	A. Solis	114	Seven Rivers	114	Stark South	116	153,600	2:26.60	103
1993	Bien Bien	4	C.J. McCarron	122	Emerald Jig	114	Beyton	117	154,300	2:25.40	106
1994	Grand Flotilla	7	G.L. Stevens	119	Semillon	116	Emerald Jig	116	158,000	2:26.20	105
1997	Marlin	4	D.R. Flores	120	Flyway	117	Percutant	118	240,000	2:25.20	107
1998	River Bay	5	A. Solis	121	Lazy Lode	115	Devonwood	114	210,000	2:27.40	106
1999	Plicck	6	D.R. Flores	116	River Bay	121	Lazy Lode	120	150,000	2:26.80	106
2000	Bienamado	4	C.J. McCarron	122	Deploy Venture	115	Single Empire	120	150,000	2:25.06	105
2001	Blueprint	6	G.L. Stevens	116	Kudos	116	Northern Quest	116	120,000	2:26.16	103
2002	Grammarian	4	B. Blanc	112	Continental Red	116	Lord Flasheart	115	150,000	2:26.59	99
2003	Puerto Banus	4	V. Espinoza	113	Cagney	116	Continental Red	116	90,000	2:26.95	101
2004	Star Over the Bay	6	T.C. Baze	113	Continuously	116	Leprechaun Kid	114	90,000	2:26.47	102

Beyer Index: 104.00

SUPER DERBY (G2), 1 1/8 Miles, 3-Year-Olds, Louisiana Downs, 2004 Purse: $500,000

Year	Winner	Age	Jockey	Wt.	Second	Wt.	Third	Wt.	Win Value	Time	Beyer
1980	Temperence Hill	3	E. Maple	126	First Albert	126	Cactus Road	126	300,000	2:06.60	
1981	Island Whirl	3	L. Pincay Jr	126	Summing	126	Willow Hour	126	300,000	2:03.20	
1982	Reinvested	3	J. Velasquez	126	El Baba	126	Drop Your Drawers	126	300,000	2:01.60	
1983	Sunny's Halo	3	L. Pincay Jr	126	Play Fellow	126	My Habitony	126	300,000	2:01.60	

Year	Winner	Age	Jockey	Wt.	Second	Wt.	Third	Wt.	Win Value	Time	Beyer
1984	Gate Dancer	3	L. Pincay Jr	126	Precisionist	126	Big Pistol	126	300,000	2:00.20	
1985	Creme Fraiche	3	E. Maple	126	Encolure	126	Government Corner	126	300,000	2:02.80	
1986	Wise Times	3	E. Maple	126	Cheapskate	126			300,000	2:04.00	
					Southern Halo	126					
1987	Alysheba	3	C.J. McCarron	126	Candi's Gold	126	Parochial	126	600,000	2:03.20	
1988	Seeking the Gold	3	P. Day	126	Happyasalark Tomas	126	Lively One	126	600,000	2:03.80	
1989	Sunday Silence	3	P.A. Valenzuela	126	Big Earl	126	Awe Inspiring	126	600,000	2:03.20	
1990	Home at Last	3	J.D. Bailey	126	Unbridled	126	Cee's Tizzy	126	600,000	2:02.00	
1991	Free Spirit's Joy	3	C.H. Borel	126	Olympio	126	Zeeruler	126	600,000	2:00.80	
1992	Senor Tomas	3	A. Gryder	126	Count the Time	126	Orbit's Revenge	126	450,000	2:04.00	96
1993	Wallenda	3	W.H. McCauley	126	Saintly Prospector	126	Peteski	126	450,000	2:02.60	101
1994	Soul of the Matter	3	K.J. Desormeaux	126	Concern	126	Bay Street Star	126	450,000	2:03.40	101
1995	Mecke	3	J.D. Bailey	126	Pineing Patty	126	Scott's Scoundrel	126	450,000	2:00.20	110
1996	Editor's Note	3	G.L. Stevens	126	The Barking Shark	126	Devil's Honor	126	450,000	2:02.20	106
1997	Deputy Commander	3	C.J. McCarron	126	Precocity	126	Blazing Sword	126	300,000	2:00.80	111
1998	Arch	3	C.S. Nakatani	126	Classic Cat	126	Sir Tiff	126	300,000	2:01.51	103
1999	Ecton Park	3	A. Solis	126	Menifee	126	Pineaff	126	300,000	2:00.59	117
2000	Tiznow	3	C.J. McCarron	126	Commendable	126	Mass Market	126	300,000	1:59.84	114
2001	Outofthebox	3	L.J. Meche	126	E Dubai	126	Quadrophonic Sound	126	300,000	2:06.20	101
2002	Essence of Dubai	3	J.F. Chavez	124	Walk in the Snow	124	A.P. Five Hundred	124	300,000	1:49.43	105
2003	Ten Most Wanted	3	P. Day	124	Soto	124	Crowned King	124	300,000	1:50.77	107
2004	Fantasticat	3	G. Melancon	124	Borrego	124	Britt's Jules	124	300,000	1:51.40	103

Beyer Index: 105.77

Distance 1 1/4 miles prior to 2002

SUWANNEE RIVER HANDICAP (Not graded for 2004), 1 1/8 Miles (Off the Turf), Fillies and Mares, 3-Year-Olds and Up, Gulfstream Park, 2004 Purse: $100,000

Year	Winner	Age	Jockey	Wt.	Second	Wt.	Third	Wt.	Win Value	Time	Beyer
1947	Ariel Song	4	D. Dodson	114	Nance's Ace	120	Kay Gibson	118	4,100	1:24.20	
							Edified	112			
1948	Buzfuz	6	A. Snider	122	Delegate	114	Gestapo	111	8,200	1:11.20	
1950	Theory	3	E. Nelson	106	John's Joy	120	Beau Dandy	118	3,250	1:09.00	
1951	Circus Clown	6	J. Stout	117	Lextown	119	All at Once	120	4,750	1:10.20	
1952	Penson	6	K. Church	118	Woodford Sir		Swamp Son		1,875	1:11.60	
1953	Sunny Dale	5	K. Church	118	Mad Hare	112	Blue Kay	103	10,800	1:44.60	
1954	Atalanta	6	H.B. Wilson	122	Lavender Hill	110	Intencion	107	10,650	1:43.60	
1955	Queen Hopeful	4	J. Adams	118	Clear Dawn	115	Rosemary B.	115	10,950	1:43.60	
1956	Tremor	4	W. Shoemaker	106	Flower Bowl	106	Queen Hopeful	116	10,505	1:43.00	
1957	Estacion	4	W.M. Cook	109	Amoret	121	Pucker Up	114	17,050	1:42.40	
1958	Rosewood	4	C. Burr	108	Pink Velvet	113	Ficha	106	17,425	1:45.80	
1959	Oil Rich	4	J. Sellers	109	Happy Princess	112	Rosewood	120	9,600	1:44.00	
1960	Royal Native	4	W. Hartack	130	Meadow Miss	107	Woodlawn	110	9,075	1:42.00	
1961	Airmans Guide	4	W. Hartack	120	Shirley Jones	119	Indian Maid	119	9,650	1:22.40	
1962	Coup d'Etat	5	W. Hartack	114	Prim Flower	110	Shirley Jones	122	9,625	1:23.40	
1963	Old Hat	4	H. Grant	117	Cicada	126	Coup d'Etat	111	9,350	1:23.20	
1964	Smart Deb	4	W. Blum	123	Lady Karachi	116	Yes Please	111	9,600	1:23.00	
1965	Old Hat	6	D. Brumfield	125	Abrogate	112	Money to Burn	110	12,775	1:23.00	
1966	Wild Note	4	R. Broussard	116	Clown Around	112	Alondra II	115	13,575	1:22.80	
1967	Cologne	4	L. Moyers	112	Kerensa	115	Indian Sunlite	122	22,200	1:47.00	
1968	Ludham	4	K. Knapp	110	Farest Nan	113	Ring Francis	111	23,300	1:41.80	
1969	Spire	5	R. Broussard	115	Crystal Palace	114	Treacherous	114	14,550	1:39.40	
1970	Blue Rage	4	M. Solomone	112	Director	117	Dark Stream	113	22,300	1:43.20	
1970	Starstrand	4	D. MacBeth	110	Klassy Poppy	120	Thai Silk	112	22,800	1:43.60	
1971	Delta Sal	5	W. Blum	113	Dedicated to Sue	117	Evening Bag	112	15,690	1:35.60	
1971	Sign of the Times	4	J. Velasquez	108	Stolen Base	116	S'nd Speculation	110	15,990	1:36.00	
1972	Irish Party	4	R. Woodhouse	114	Ruth's Edition	113	Glenary	114	16,470	1:37.20	
1972	Stay out Front	6	J. Vasquez	112	Aladancer	121	Wilderness	110	16,620	1:37.20	
1973	Ziba Blue	6	M. Miceli	110	Cathy Baby	113	Barely Even	127	21,270	1:35.80	
1974	Dove Creek Lady	4	M.A. Rivera	121	North Broadway	120	North of Venus	119	21,960	1:36.40	
1975	Deesse du Val	4	M. Hole	115	North of Venus	118	Lorraine Edna	118	20,400	1:35.40	
1976	Jabot	4	H. Gustines	112	Redundancy	119	Deesse du Val	117	21,330	1:34.60	
1977	Bronze Point	4	H. Arroyo	120	Funny Peculiar	114	Collegiate	114	21,390	1:24.20	
1978	Len's Determined	4	J. Cruguet	119	What a Summer	122	Late Bloomer	113	19,260	1:35.60	
1979	Navajo Princess	5	C. Perret	124	La Soufriere	119	Unreality	121	19,650	1:35.20	
1979	Calderina	4	J. Fell	117	Terpsichorist	122	She Can Dance	113	19,200	1:36.20	
1980	Ouro Verde	4	R.I. Encinas	112	No Disgrace	110	Anna Yrrah D.	112	18,870	1:37.20	
1980	Just a Game II	4	D. Brumfield	117	La Soufriere	113	La Voyageuse	120	18,870	1:35.20	
1981	Honey Fox	4	J.L. Samyn	111	Racquette	115	Pompoes	110	22,568	1:35.20	
1981	Exactly So	4	J.L. Samyn	109	Draw In	114	Champagne Ginny	118	22,567	1:35.80	
1982	Pine Flower	4	C. Perret	113	Sweetest Chant	116	Fair Davina	110	27,000	1:35.40	

Year	Winner	Age	Jockey	Wt.	Second	Wt.	Third	Wt.	Win Value	Time	Beyer
1982	Teacher's Pet	5	C. Marquez	114	Shark Song	114	Blush	113	27,300	1:35.20	
1983	Norsan	4	J.D. Bailey	113	Dana Calqui	114	Colatina	111	28,890	1:38.20	
1983	Syrianna	4	J. Vasquez	114	Meringue Pie	115	Plenty O'Toole	114	27,390	1:24.20	
1983	Promising Native	4	D. MacBeth	113	Avowal	117	Our Darling	112	27,060	1:23.80	
1984	Sulemeif	4	J.D. Bailey	113	Jubilous	115	M'lanie Francis	113	39,330	1:36.80	
1985	Early Lunch	4	W.A. Guerra	112	Eva G.	114	Maidenhead	111	28,521	1:35.60	
1985	Sherizar	4	J. McKnight	113	Madam Flutterby	114	Melanie Franc's	115	28,820	1:36.40	
1985	Burst of Colors	5	J.A. Santos	117	Queen of Song	121	Silver in Flight	115	28,820	1:35.60	
1986	Cheshire Kitten	4	J.L. Samyn	112	Chaldea	111	Four Flings	113	30,990	1:44.80	
1986	Videogenic	4	R.G. Davis	120	Contredance	117	Verbality	112	30,690	1:44.60	
1987	Fieldy	4	C. Perret	114			Navarchus	114	17,810	1:44.20	
	Fama	4	R.P. Romero	114							
1987	Singular Bequest	4	E. Fires	114	Cadabra Abra	114	Duckweed	112	26,415	1:43.60	
1988	Go Honey	5	J.M. Pezua	110	Princely Proof	115	Fieldy	118	38,490	1:41.80	
1988	Anka Germania	6	C. Perret	122	Sum	114	Fama	112	39,090	1:41.80	
1989	Love You by Heart	4	R.P. Romero	117	Native Mommy	117	Aquaba	115	37,275	1:41.60	
1989	Fieldy	6	C. Perret	116	Summer Secretary	110	Chapel of Dreams	122	36,975	1:41.60	
1990	Princess Mora	4	M.A. Gonzalez	111	Fieldy	121	Northling	113	38,970	1:41.20	100
1991	Vigorous Lady	5	M.A. Lee	119	Yen for Gold	110	Pr'mier Question	114	36,120	1:45.00	
1992	Julie la Rousse	4	J.D. Bailey	115	Christiecat	117	Grab the Green	120	38,670	1:48.40	102
1993	Via Borghese	4	J.D. Bailey	116	Marshua's River	113	Blue Daisy	114	40,230	1:48.20	103
1994	Marshua's River	7	Santos JA	114	Sheila's Revenge	118	Icy Warning	115	45,000	1:46.60	99
1995	Cox Orange	5	J.D. Bailey	116	Irving's Girl	113	Alice Springs	120	45,000	1:47.40	103
1996	Class Kris	4	P. Day	116	Apolda	118	Majestic Dy	113	45,000	1:49.80	101
1997	Golden Pond	4	J.D. Bailey	114	Rumpipumpy	114	Elusive	113	45,000	1:47.80	98
1998	Seebe	4	Rice D. S.	114	Colcon	115	Parade Queen	119	45,000	1:47.40	102
1999	Winfama	6	R. Migliore	114	Circus Charmer	113	Colcon	120	45,000	1:52.20	101
2000	Pico Teneriffe	4	J.F. Chavez	115	Dominique's Joy	114	Crystal Symphony	115	45,000	1:47.83	97
2001	Spook Express	7	M.E. Smith	116	Gaviola	120	Windsong	113	60,000	1:47.28	96
2002	Snow Dance	4	P. Day	119	Step With Style	114	Windsong	113	60,000	1:49.04	97
2003	Amonita	5	J.L. Samyn	117	What a Price	114	Calista	118	60,000	1:47.90	98
2004	Wishful Splendor	5	J.A. Santos	114	May Gator	113	Mymich	113	60,000	1:54.86	78

Beyer Index: 98.21

Off the turf in 2004.

SWALE (G3), 7 Furlongs, 3-Year-Olds, Gulfstream Park, 2004 Purse: $150,000

Year	Winner	Age	Jockey	Wt.	Second	Wt.	Third	Wt.	Win Value	Time	Beyer
1985	Chief's Crown	3	D. MacBeth	122	Creme Fraiche		Cherokee Fast		30,792	1:22.40	
1986	One Magic Moment	3	C. Perret	113	Admiral's Mirage		Two Punch		31,230	1:22.40	
1988	Seeking the Gold	3	R.P. Romero	114	Above Normal		Perfect Spy		35,100	1:21.60	
1989	Easy Goer	3	P. Day	122	Trion		Tricky Creek		34,290	1:22.20	
1990	Housebuster	3	C. Perret	122	Summer Squall	122	Thirty Six Red	113	34,350	1:22.20	
1991	Chihuahua	3	J.D. Alferez	112	To Freedom	119	Greek Costume	114	51,060	1:23.40	97
1992	D.J. Cat	3	J.D. Bailey	114	Binalong	114	Always Silver	112	71,250	1:23.20	115
1993	Premier Explosion	3	D. Penna	114	Demaloot Demashoot	113	Cherokee Run	114	53,520	1:23.20	100
1994	Arrival Time	3	C.J. McCarron	115	Senor Conquistador	113	Meadow Monster	112	45,000	1:22.40	97
1995	Mr. Greeley	3	J.A. Krone	114	Devious Course	119	Pyramid Peak	114	45,000	1:22.00	103
1996	Roar	3	M.E. Smith	113	Gomtuu	119	Dixie Connection	112	45,000	1:22.40	94
1997	Confide	3	M.E. Smith	117	Country Rainbow	112	The Silver Move	119	45,000	1:23.20	107
1998	Favorite Trick	3	P. Day	122	Good and Tough	114	Dice Dancer	113	60,000	1:22.80	104
1999	Yes It's True	3	J.D. Bailey	122	Texas Glitter	117	Lucky Roberto	119	60,000	1:22.20	103
2000	Trippi	3	J.D. Bailey	113	Ultimate Warrior	117	Harlan Traveler	114	60,000	1:23.43	98
2001	D'wildcat	3	C.S. Nakatani	116	Tarek	112	Yonaguska	122	90,000	1:22.25	110
2002	Ethan Man	3	P. Day	116	Listen Here	120	Governor Hickel	116	90,000	1:22.29	98
2003	Midas Eyes	3	J.D. Bailey	116	Posse	120	Whywhywhy	122	90,000	1:21.06	110
2004	Wynn Dot Comma	3	E.S. Prado	120	Eurosilver	120	Dashboard Drummer	120	90,000	1:22.87	96

Beyer Index: 102.29

SWAPS BREEDERS' CUP (G2), 1 1/8 Miles, 3-Year-Olds, Hollywood Park, 2004 Purse: $409,300

Year	Winner	Age	Jockey	Wt.	Second	Wt.	Third	Wt.	Win Value	Time	Beyer
1974	Agitate	3	W. Shoemaker	123	Stardust Mel	120	Master Music	114	66,300	1:59.60	
1975	Forceten	3	D. Pierce	120	Sibirri	114	Diabolo	123	119,800	1:59.80	
1976	Majestic Light	3	S. Hawley	114	Crystal Water	123	Double Discount	115	98,200	1:59.20	
1977	J.O. Tobin	3	W. Shoemaker	120	Affiliate	117	Text	120	194,900	1:58.60	
1978	Radar Ahead	3	D. McHargue	120	Batonnier	123	Poppy Popowich	115	133,300	2:00.00	
1979	Valdez	3	L. Pincay Jr.	120	Shamgo	114	Paint King	114	124,250	1:59.40	
1980	First Albert	3	F. Mena	123	Amber Pass	123	Mr. Mud	114	162,200	2:00.80	
1981	Noble Nashua	3	L. Pincay Jr.	123	Dorcaro	115	Stancharry	123	127,000	2:01.20	

Year	Winner	Age	Jockey	Wt.	Second	Wt.	Third	Wt.	Win Value	Time	Beyer
1982	Journey at Sea	3	C.J. McCarron	120	West Coast Native	114	Casselaria	123	91,300	2:00.20	
1983	Hyperborean	3	F. Toro	115	My Habitony	120	Tanks Brigade	120	97,500	2:01.00	
1984	Precisionist	3	C.J. McCarron	123	Prince True	120	Majestic Shore	114	121,300	1:59,80	
1985	Padua	3	P.A. Valenzuela	115	Turkoman	115	Don't Say Halo	120	123,500	2:01.40	
1986	Clear Choice	3	C.J. McCarron	120	Southern Halo	114	Jota	116	137,000	2:03.60	
1987	Temperate Sil	3	W. Shoemaker	123	Candi's Gold	123	Pledge Card	115	124,400	2:02.20	
1988	Lively One	3	W. Shoemaker	120	Blade of the Ball	114	Iz a Saros	123	13,200	2:01.00	
1989	Prized	3	E. Delahoussaye	120	Sunday Silence	126	Endow	123	232,400	2:01.80	
1990	Jovial	3	G.L. Stevens	120	Silver Ending	126	Stalwart Charger	126	120,000	2:01.20	108
1991	Best Pal	3	P.A. Valenzuela	116	Corporate Report	114	Compelling Sound	123	120,000	2:00.60	111
1992	Bien Bien	3	C.J. McCarron	119	Treekster	123	Sevengreenpairs	119	123,400	2:02.80	102
1993	Devoted Brass	3	L. Pincay Jr.	123	Future Storm	119	Codified	123	124,000	2:00.60	103
1994	Silver Music	3	C.W. Antley	119	Dramatic Gold	119	Valiant Nature	121	123,800	2:00.60	106
1995	Thunder Gulch	3	G.L. Stevens	126	Da Hoss	118	Petionville	120	275,000	1:49.00	101
1996	Victory Speech	3	J.D. Bailey	118	Prince of Thieves	118	Hesabull	118	300,000	1:48.20	104
1997	Free House	3	K. Desormeaux	122	Deputy Commander	118	Wild Rush	122	300,000	1:45.80	115
1998	Old Trieste	3	C.J. McCarron	118	Grand Slam	120	Old Topper	117	300,000	1:47.00	116
1999	Cat Thief	3	P. Day	120	General Challenge	122	Walk That Walk	117	300,000	1:47.87	107
2000	Captain Steve	3	C.S. Nakatani	120	Tiznow	118	Spacelink	118	300,000	1:48.01	111
2001	Congaree	3	G.L. Stevens	122	Until Sundown	118	Jamaican Rum	118	300,000	1:48.61	106
2002	Came Home	3	M.E. Smith	122	Like a Hero	114	Fonz's	116	300,000	1:48.28	108
2003	During	3	J.D. Bailey	115	Ten Most Wanted	122	Eye of the Tiger	118	240,000	1:49.38	96
							Outta Here	120			
2004	Rock Hard Ten	3	C.S. Nakatani	116	Suave	120	Boomzeeboom	118	252,780	1:47.47	109

Beyer Index: 106.87

Distance 1 1/4 miles prior to 1995

SWORD DANCER INVITATIONAL HANDICAP (G1), 1 1/2 Miles (Turf), 3-Year-Olds and Up, Saratoga Race Course, 2004 Purse: $500,000

Year	Winner	Age	Jockey	Wt.	Second	Wt.	Third	Wt.	Win Value	Time	Beyer
1975	Gallant Bob	3	G. Gallitano	126	Our Hero	113	Due Diligence	113	27,630	1:09.60	
1976	Arabian Law	3	J. Vasquez	112	Full Out	118	Half High	111	26,535	1:10.60	
1977	Effervescing	4	A. Cordero Jr	117	Gentle King	110	Cinteelo	116	33,690	1:39.60	
1978	True Colors	4	M. Venezia	114	Bill Brill	107	Blue Baron	114	34,020	1:41.00	
1979	Darby Creek Road	4	A. Cordero Jr	119	John Henry	119	Poison Ivory	119	34,320	1:41.60	
1980	Tiller	6	R. Hernandez	126	John Henry	126	Sten	126	96,660	2:25.20	
1981	John Henry	6	W. Shoemaker	126	Passing Zone	126	Peat Moss	126	97,380	2:26.80	
1982	Lemhi Gold	4	C.J. McCarron	126	Erins Isle	126	Field Cat	126	99,000	2:26.00	
1983	Majesty's Prince	4	E. Maple	120	Thunder Puddles	118	Erins Isle	128	141,600	2:34.40	
	Hush Dear finished second but was disqualified and placed fourth										
1984	Majesty's Prince	5	E. Maple	124	Nassipour	109	Four Bases	112	176,820	2:31.00	
1985	Tri for Size	4	R.J. Thibeau	110	Talakeno	112	Persian Tiara	113	151,320	2:33.20	
1986	Southern Sultan	4	R.G. Davis	109	Talakeno	114	Tri for Size	111	143,460	2:39.40	
1987	Theatrical	5	P. Day	124	Dance of Life	122	Akabir	114	133,080	2:26.00	
	Dance of Life finished first but was disqualified and placed second										
1988	Anka Germania	6	C. Perret	117	Sunshine Forever	114	Carotene	114	141,120	2:32.20	
1989	El Senor	5	W.H. McCauley	118	Nediym	113	My Big Boy	115	139,920	2:27.00	
1990	El Senor	6	A. Cordero Jr	119	With Approval	124	Hodges Bay	114	140,000	2:28.00	
1991	Dr. Root	4	J.L. Samyn	109	Karmani	113	El Senor	116	150,000	2:25.40	102
1992	Fraise	4	J.D. Bailey	113	Wall Street Dancer	116	Montserrat	113	150,000	2:25.80	105
1993	Spectacular Tide	4	J.A. Krone	112	Square Cut	112	Dr. Kiernan	117	120,000	2:30.20	104
1994	Alex the Great	5	P.A. Valenzuela	118	Kiri's Clown	112	L'Hermine	112	150,000	2:28.60	108
1995	Kiri's Clown	6	M.J. Luzzi	114	Awad	121	King's Theatre	113	150,000	2:25.40	109
1996	Broadway Flyer	5	M.E. Smith	118	Kiri's Clown	113	Flag Down	119	150,000	2:32.00	112
1997	Awad	7	P. Day	117	Fahim	110	Val's Prince	112	150,000	2:23.20	108
1998	Cetewayo	4	C.S. Nakatani	115	Val's Prince	113	Dushyantor	119	180,000	2:29.56	107
1999	Honor Glide	5	J.A. Santos	116	Val's Prince	115	Chorwon	114	240,000	2:28.23	109
2000	John's Call	9	J.L. Samyn	114	Aly's Alley	118	Single Empire	119	300,000	2:32.17	112
2001	With Anticipation	6	P. Day	114	King Cugat	120	Slew Valley	114	300,000	2:26.41	109
2002	With Anticipation	7	P. Day	120	Denon	118	Volponi	115	300,000	2:24.06	109
2003	Whitmore's Conn	5	J.L. Samyn	115	Macaw	114	Slew Valley	114	300,000	2:28.14	107
2004	Better Talk Now	5	R.A. Dominguez	118	Request for Parole	123	Balto Star	120	300,000	2:28.49	106

Beyer Index: 107.64

Distance 6 furlongs (main track) for 3-year-olds prior to 1977; 1 1/16 miles, 1977–79. Run at Aqueduct, 1975–76; at Belmont, 1977–91

SYCAMORE BREEDERS' CUP (G3), 1 1/2 Miles (Turf), 3-Year-Olds and Up, Keeneland Race Course, 2004 Purse: $152,300

Year	Winner	Age	Jockey	Wt.	Second	Wt.	Third	Wt.	Win Value	Time	Beyer
1995	Lindon Lime	5	C. Perret	123	Hyper Shu	114	Lordly Prospect	114	39,098	2:42.11	100
1996	Gleaming Key	4	R. Albarado	114	Nash Terrace	120	Hawkeye Bay	114	32,860	2:44.49	99

Year	Winner	Age	Jockey	Wt.	Second	Wt.	Third	Wt.	Win Value	Time	Beyer
1997	Gleaming Key	5	S.J. Sellers	116	Double Leaf	116	Seattle Blossom	116	33,015	2:45.86	96
1998	Royal Strand	4	S.J. Sellers	116	Thesaurus	116	Lakeshore Road	116	33,015	2:41.93	100
1999	Royal Strand	5	P. Day	117	Arizona Storm	117	Magest	117	42,315	2:38.68	103
2000	Crowd Pleaser	5	C. Borel	118	Dixie's Crown	122	Kim Loves Bucky	114	44,439	2:44.00	101
2001	Rochester	5	P. Day	119	Chorwon	125	Regal Dynasty	119	103,044	2:31.29	98
2002	Rochester	6	P. Day	125	Roxinho	120	Lord Flasheart	120	101,928	2:30.48	101
2003	Sharbayan	5	P. Day	120	Cetewayo	122	Deputy Strike	120	73,904	2:29.55	104
2004	Mustanfar	3	J.A. Santos	118	Deputy Strike	120	Rochester	122	100,626	2:30.88	100

Beyer Index: 100.20

TAMPA BAY DERBY (G3), 1 1/16 Miles, 3-Year-Olds, Tampa Bay Downs, 2004 Purse: $250,000

Year	Winner	Age	Jockey	Wt.	Second	Wt.	Third	Wt.	Win Value	Time	Beyer
1981	Paristo	3	D.C. Ashcroft	112	Bravestofall	120	Darby Gillic	122	43,560	1:45.40	
1982	Reinvested	3	R.D. Luhr	114	Stage Reviewer	120	Real Twister	120	40,140	1:45.20	
1983	Morganmorganmorgan	3	W. Rodriguez	118	Slew o' Gold	118	Quick Dip	118	60,000	1:47.20	
1984	Bold Southerner	3	W. Crews	116	Rexson's Hope	122	Stickler	120	95,400	1:44.60	
1985	Regal Remark	3	J. Fell	122	Verification	122	Sport Jet	118	95,400	1:46.80	
1986	My Prince Charming	3	G. Perret	122	Lucky Rebeau	120	Major Moran	116	98,100	1:46.60	
1987	Phantom Jet	3	K.K. Allen	122	Homebuilder	116	You're No Bargain	116	90,000	1:43.80	
1988	Cefis	3	E. Maple	116	Buck Forbes	118	Twice Too Many	118	90,000	1:44.40	
1989	Storm Predictions	3	S. Gaffalione	120	With Approval	120	Mercedes Won	122	90,000	1:43.80	
1990	Champagneforashley	3	J. Vasquez	122	Slew of Angels	120	Always Running	116	90,000	1:44.60	
1991	Speedy Cure	3	R.D. Lopez	118	Link	118	Shudanz	116	90,000	1:46.20	
1992	Careful Gesture	3	R.N. Lester	118	Chief Speaker	116	Clipper Won	116	120,000	1:45.93	89
1993	Marco Bay	3	R. Allen Jr.	120	Thriller Chiller	116	Tunecke Charlie	118	90,000	1:44.40	93
1994	Prix de Crouton	3	M. Walls	120	Able Buck	120	Parental Pressure	122	90,000	1:46.60	82
1995	Gadzook	3	G. Boulanger	116	Composer	116	Bet Your Bucks	116	90,000	1:45.20	87
1996	Thundering Storm	3	J. Guerra	118	El Amante	118	Natural Selection	116	90,000	1:43.80	100
1997	Zede	3	J.D. Bailey	118	Brisco Jack	116	Favorable Regard	118	90,000	1:44.80	91
1998	Parade Ground	3	P. Day	118	Middlesex Drive	118	Rock and Roll	116	90,000	1:44.20	94
1999	Pineaff	3	J.A. Santos	122	Menifee	120	Doneraile Court	122	90,000	1:45.33	102
2000	Wheelaway	3	R. Migliore	116	Impeachment	116	Perfect Cat	116	90,000	1:43.90	94
2001	Burning Roma	3	R. Migliore	123	American Prince	123	Paging	116	120,000	1:44.30	95
2002	Equality	3	R. Dominguez	118	Tails of the Crypt	123	Political Attack	123	120,000	1:43.66	103
2003	Region of Merit	3	E.M. Coa	120	Aristocat	118	Hear No Evil	123	150,000	1:44.61	95
2004	Limehouse	3	P. Day	118	Mustanfar	116	Swingforthefences	116	150,000	1:43.99	100

Beyer Index: 94.23

TEMPTED (G3), 1 Mile, 2-Year-Old Fillies, Aqueduct, 2004 Purse: $104,600

Year	Winner	Age	Jockey	Wt.	Second	Wt.	Third	Wt.	Win Value	Time	Beyer
1975	Secret Lanvin	2	J. Cruguet	113	Free Journey	121	Imaflash	113	33,600	1:35.40	
1976	Pearl Necklace	2	A. Cordero Jr	114	Our Mims	113	Road Princess	113	22,380	1:39.60	
1977	Caesar's Wish	2	G. McCarron	116	Itsamaza	116	Lucinda Lea	114	22,635	1:36.20	
1978	Whisper Fleet	2	A. Cordero Jr	119	Run Cosmic Run	114	Distinct Honor	113	25,665	1:36.20	
1979	Genuine Risk	2	J. Vasquez	114	Street Ballet	117	Tell a Secret	114	33,060	1:36.00	
1980	Tina Tina Too	2	C.B. Asmussen	114	Prayers'n Promises	121	Explosive Kingdom	114	32,580	1:38.40	
1981	Choral Group	2	J. Velasquez	122	Michelle Mon Amour	114	Middle Stage	113	33,000	1:38.00	
1982	Only Queens	2	M.A. Rivera	114	Future Fun	113	Blue Garter	114	33,180	1:37.00	
1983	Surely Georgie's	2	R. Hernandez	113	Baroness Direct	114	Dumdedumdedum	114	34,320	1:39.60	
1984	Willowy Mood	2	J. Velasquez	121	Koluctoo's Jill	114	Easy Step	116	57,330	1:46.20	
1985	Cosmic Tiger	2	E. Maple	121	Tracy's Espoir	114	Roses for Avie	114	68,580	1:46.80	
1986	Silent Turn	2	C.W. Antley	119	Grecian Flight	119	Chase the Dream	119	74,400	1:46.20	
1987	Thirty Eight Go Go	2	K.J. Desormeaux	121	Best Number	114	Dangerous Type	116	100,920	1:44.60	
1988	Box Office Gold	2	J.A. Santos	116	Dreamy Mimi	116	Surging	116	57,600	1:46.20	
1989	Worth Avenue	2	R.P. Romero	113	Crown Quest	119	Voodoo Lily	114	69,480	1:46.80	
1990	Flawlessly	2	J.D. Bailey	121	Debutant's Halo	121	Slept Thru It	114	56,250	1:46.60	
1991	Deputation	2	D.W. Lidberg	114	Turnback the Alarm	121	Bless Our Home	114	72,600	1:46.60	87
1992	True Affair	2	J. Bravo	121	Broad Gains	121	Touch of Love	114	68,520	1:47.40	87
1993	Sovereign Kitty	2	J.R. Velazquez	112	Seeking the Circle	113	Her Temper	112	69,720	1:46.80	81
1994	Special Broad	2	J.A. Krone	114	Carson Creek	114	Golden Bri	114	66,000	1:37.20	88
1996	Ajina	2	J.D. Bailey	112	Glitter Woman	114	Aldiza	114	66,240	1:36.40	86
1997	Dancing With Ruth	2	T.G. Turner	118	Soft Senorita	118	Aunt Anne	116	65,340	1:37.40	84
1998	Oh What a Windfall	2	J.D. Bailey	121	La Ville Rouge	114	Honour a Bull	114	66,120	1:39.80	65
1999	Shawnee Country	2	J.F. Chavez	116	To Marquet	114	Marigalante	116	65,460	1:38.60	88
2000	Two Item Limit	2	R. Migliore	117	Celtic Melody	115	Twining Star	115	65,520	1:38.53	80
2001	Smok'n Frolic	2	J.R. Velazquez	119	Saintly Action	115	Wopping	117	66,900	1:37.77	89
2002	Chimichurri	2	J.R. Velazquez	119	Reheat	115	Bonay	115	66,240	1:37.52	83
2003	La Reina	2	J.R. Velazquez	115	Eye Dazzler	115	Sisti's Pride	115	66,420	1:36.15	90
2004	Summer Raven	2	S. Elliott	115	K.D.'s Shady Lady	115	Salute	115	63,960	1:36.09	90

Beyer Index: 84.46

TEST (G1), 7 Furlongs,
3-Year-Old Fillies, Saratoga Race Course, 2004 Purse: $250,000

Year	Winner	Age	Jockey	Wt.	Second	Wt.	Third	Wt.	Win Value	Time	Beyer
1922	Emotion	3	L. McAtee	115	Nedna	115			2,004	2:11.20	
1926	Ruthenia	3	E. Sande	121	Corvette	118	What I'll Do	114	2,900	1:25.60	
1927	Black Curl	3	L. Fator	118	Bonnie Khayyam	111	Fairness	114	3,375	1:26.60	
1928	Nixie	3	D. McAuliffe	121	Lace	114	Tokio	114	2,950	1:25.80	
1929	Dinah Did Upset	3	N. LeBlanc	114	On Her Toes	118	Electa	114	3,450	1:24.20	
1930	Conclave	3	D. Lyons	114	Goose Egg	121	The Beasel	118	3,475	1:24.40	
1931	Buckup	3	M. Garner	118	Ladana	121	Risque	121	3,050	1:25.80	
1932	Suntica	3	M. Garner	128	Parry	118	Unique	118	2,975	1:26.00	
1933	Speed Boat	3	J. Gilbert	106	Barn Swallow	121	White Lies	108	1,820	1:24.20	
1934	Bazaar	3	D. Meade	115	Slapdash	108	Coequal	105	1,820	1:24.60	
1935	Good Gamble	3	S. Renick	122	Mid Victorian	113	Clean Out	110	3,075	1:24.80	
1936	Fair Stein	3	E. Yager	113	Little Miracle	113	Fair Knightness	113	2,750	1:24.80	
1937	Evening Tide	3	C. Kurtsinger	110	That One	112	Sweet Desire	113	3,025	1:26.00	
1938	Black Wave	3	J. Gilbert	113	Anaflame	113			3,175	1:25.80	
					Creole Maid	126					
1939	Redlin	3	D. Meade	114	Red Eye	123	Despondent	114	2,725	1:24.00	
1940	Piquet	3	E. Arcaro	123	Fairy Chant	126	Inkling	114	3,050	1:24.40	
1941	Imperatrice	3	J. Skelly	113	Pomayya	113	Proud One	117	2,850	1:25.20	
1942	Vagrancy	3	J. Stout	123	Taunt	113	Smiles	113	2,575	1:26.00	
1943	Stefanita	3	C. McCreary	117	Best Risk	108	Good Morning	120	4,800	1:25.20	
1944	Whirlabout	3	H. Lindberg	123	Vienna	108	Boiling Oil	109	6,360	1:24.80	
1945	Safeguard	3	T. Atkinson	111	Monsoon	111	Surosa	106	6,565	1:24.20	
1946	Red Shoes	3	E. Arcaro	123	Upper Level	111	Bridal Flower	121	6,825	1:23.40	
1947	Miss Disco	3	N. Combest	110	Frantie's Bid	112	Ocean Brief	110	7,300	1:24.40	
1948	Alablue	3	E. Guerin	114	Paddleduck	111	Mackinaw	121	7,500	1:25.80	
1949	Lady Dorimar	3	C. McCreary	111	Tall Weeds	116	Gaffery	124	6,975	1:25.20	
1950	Honey's Gal	3	G. Hettinger	111	Faneuil Miss	111	Supersonic	111	6,475	1:24.40	
1951	Vulcania	3	R. Bernhardt	111	Valadium	111	Atalanta	121	6,100	1:26.00	
1952	Gay Grecque	3	R. York	111	Lily White	114	Devilkin	111	5,875	1:26.80	
1953	Canadiana	3	D. Gorman	124	Home-Made	121	Tritium	121	11,700	1:25.60	
1954	Dispute	3	E. Guerin	115	Case Goods	116	Talora	111	13,150	1:25.60	
1955	Blue Banner	3	E. Arcaro	114	Smart Devil	111	Rico Reto	111	12,825	1:24.80	
1956	Glamour	3	S. Cole	121	Medal Play	111	Levee	124	15,750	1:25.80	
1957	Miss Blue Jay	3	T. Atkinson	118	Outer Space	121	Snow White	115	16,600	1:24.40	
1958	Any Morn	3	J. Ruane	115	Dandy Blitzen	115	Armorial	115	16,260	1:25.80	
1959	Shirley Jones	3	P.J. Bailey	115	Mommy Dear	115	Hidden Talent	121	19,785	1:26.00	
1960	Be Cautious	3	R. Ussery	121	Make Sail	121	Clear Road	114	14,617	1:24.00	
1960	Brave Pilot	3	H. Woodhouse	115	Frimanaha	112	Improve	115	14,780	1:23.80	
1962	Polylady	3	B. Baeza	118	Cyclopavia	115	Batter Up	124	11,229	1:23.40	
1962	Firm Policy	3	J. Sellers	121	Look Ma	115	Royal Patrice	115	11,359	1:23.40	
1963	Bold Consort	3	H. Woodhouse	115	Prodana Neviesta	112	Charspiv	115	11,667	1:25.80	
1963	Barbwolf	3	R. Ussery	115	Lamb Chop	124	No Resisting	121	11,537	1:25.00	
1964	Time for Bed	3	J.L. Rotz	112	Royal Tara	115	Face the Facts	121	20,280	1:23.80	
1965	Discipline	3	W. Blum	118	Terentia	121	Valiant Queen	115	15,454	1:23.60	
1965	Cestrum	3	S. Boulmetis	118	Queen Empress	118	Ground Control	121	15,291	1:23.00	
1966	Belle de Nuit	3	J. Ruane	115	Wake Robin	112	Lady Swaps	112	15,795	1:23.60	
1966	Moccasin	3	B. Baeza	118	Native Street	124	Politely	112	15,632	1:23.40	
1967	Gamely	3	E. Belmonte	121	Wageko	115	Just Kidding	121	15,372	1:21.80	
1967	Treacherous	3	M. Sorrentino	115	Silver True	118	Green Glade	113	15,535	1:23.00	
1968	Heartland	3	J.L. Rotz	115	Twice Cited	115	Teddy's True	115	18,622	1:22.40	
1969	Ta Wee	3	E. Belmonte	124	French Bread	115	Bold Tribute	112	17,940	1:23.60	
1970	Princess Roycraft	3	L. Adams	121	Arachne	115	Meritus	118	14,982	1:22.40	
1970	Hunnemannia	3	E. Belmonte	115	Missile Belle	124	Royal Panic	112	15,307	1:23.60	
1971	Lucky Traveler	3	C. Baltazar	115	Tibb	115	Forward Gal	124	21,300	1:23.80	
1972	Numbered Account	3	J. Vasquez	121	Light Hearted	118	Candid Catherine	121	16,515	1:23.80	
1973	Desert Vixen	3	J. Velasquez	121	Full of Hope	118	Clandenita	118	13,470	1:23.00	
1973	Waltz Fan	3	J. Velasquez	118	Gallant Davelle	116	Tuerta	116	13,545	1:23.60	
1974	Quaze Quilt	3	J. Vasquez	121	Maud Muller	113	Clear Copy	121	20,385	1:22.40	
1974	Maybellene	3	D. Meade Jr	116	Raisela	116	Stage Door Betty	121	20,385	1:23.60	
1975	Hot n Nasty	3	J. Tejeira	122	A Charm	113	Alpine Lass	116	19,665	1:22.00	
	Fleet Victress finished third but was disqualified and placed fourth										
1975	My Juliet	3	J. Vasquez	116	Slip Screen	113	Funalon	113	19,590	1:22.00	
1976	Ivory Wand	3	P. Day	114	Doc Shah's Siren	116	Pacific Princess	114	22,500	1:23.00	
1977	Small Raja	3	M. Solomone	124	Pressing Date	114	Pearl Necklace	116	22,275	1:21.80	
1977	Northern Sea	3	J. Velasquez	121	Northernette	121	Flying Above	114	22,200	1:22.40	
1978	White Star Line	3	J. Fell	121	Silken Delight	114	Zerelda	114	22,095	1:21.40	
1978	Tingle Stone	3	R. Hernandez	114	Mucchina	121	Summer Fling	116	22,020	1:22.00	
1979	Blitey	3	A. Cordero Jr	114	Jameela	118	Spanish Fake	121	25,987	1:22.60	
1979	Clef D'Argent	3	R. Hernandez	114	Alada	114	Syncopating Lady	114	25,988	1:22.20	
1980	Love Sign	3	A. Cordero Jr	116	Weber City Miss	124	Andrea F.	114	33,900	1:22.20	
1981	Cherokee Frolic	3	G. Cohen	121	Maddy's Tune	114	Discorama	114	34,140	1:23.20	

Year	Winner	Age	Jockey	Wt.	Second	Wt.	Third	Wt.	Win Value	Time	Beyer
1982	Gold Beauty	3	D. Brumfield	116	Ambassador of Luck	121	Number	114	35,940	1:22.80	
1983	Lass Trump	3	P. Day	114	Medieval Moon	121	Chic Belle	114	34,380	1:22.20	
1984	Sintra	3	K.K. Allen	116	Wild Applause	121	Lucky Lucky Lucky	124	101,040	1:22.60	
1985	Lady's Secret	3	J. Velasquez	121	Mom's Command	124	Majestic Folly	118	99,600	1:21.60	
1986	Storm and Sunshine	3	C. Perret	118	Classy Cathy	121	I'm Sweets	121	103,500	1:22.80	
1987	Very Subtle	3	P.A. Valenzuela	121	Up the Apalachee	121	Silent Turn	121	116,280	1:21.00	
1988	Fara's Team	3	J.D. Bailey	121	Lake Valley	114	Classic Crown	121	109,980	1:22.60	
1989	Safely Kept	3	C. Perret	121	Fantastic Find	114	Cojinx	116	101,520	1:21.40	
1990	Go for Wand	3	R.P. Romero	124	Secret Prospect	118	Token Dance	118	73,440	1:21.00	114
1991	Versailles Treaty	3	A. Cordero Jr	114	Ifyoucouldseemenow	121	Classy Women	116	104,040	1:22.80	101
	Zama Hummer finished third but was disqualified and placed sixth										
1992	November Snow	3	C.W. Antley	116	Meafara	114	Preach	116	105,480	1:21.20	102
1993	Missed the Storm	3	M.E. Smith	114	Miss Indy Anna	114	Educated Risk	114	90,000	1:22.00	98
1994	Twist Afleet	3	J.D. Bailey	114	Penny's Reshoot	118	Heavenly Prize	121	90,000	1:22.00	106
1995	Chaposa Springs	3	J.D. Bailey	120	Miss Golden Circle	114	Daijin	123	90,000	1:21.80	105
1996	Capote Belle	3	J.R. Velazquez	115	Flat Fleet Feet	115	J J'sdream	123	90,000	1:21.00	107
1997	Fabulously Fast	3	J.D. Bailey	114	Aldiza	114	Pearl City	117	90,000	1:21.60	111
1998	Jersey Girl	3	M.E. Smith	123	Brave Deed	114	Catinca	114	120,000	1:23.02	96
1999	Marley Vale	3	J.R. Velazquez	114	Awful Smart	114	Emanating	114	150,000	1:22.77	95
2000	Dream Supreme	3	P. Day	115	Big Bambu	118	Finder's Fee	123	150,000	1:22.66	104
2001	Victory Ride	3	E.S. Prado	116	Xtra Heat	123	Nasty Storm	120	150,000	1:21.72	107
2002	You	3	J.D. Bailey	123	Carson Hollow	123	Spring Meadow	120	150,000	1:22.84	101
2003	Lady Tak	3	J.D. Bailey	122	Bird Town	122	House Party	122	150,000	1:20.83	110
2004	Society Selection	3	E.S. Prado	120	Bending Strings	120	Forest Music	118	150,000	1:23.69	96

Beyer Index: 103.53

Distance 1 1/4 miles in 1922. Run at Belmont Park 1943–45

TEXAS MILE (G3), 1 Mile, 3-Year-Olds and Up, Lone Star Park, 2004 Purse: $300,000

Year	Winner	Age	Jockey	Wt.	Second	Wt.	Third	Wt.	Win Value	Time	Beyer
1997	Isitingood	6	D.R. Flores	123	Spiritbound	116	Skip Away	116	150,000	1:34.40	106
1998	Littlebitlively	4	C.V. Gonzalez	118	Anet	116	Scott's Scoundrel	118	150,000	1:37.07	113
1999	Littlebitlively	5	C.V. Gonzalez	116	Real Quiet	116	Allen's Oop	113	145,000	1:35.60	110
2000	Sir Bear	7	E.M. Coa	116	Lexington Park	118	Luftikus	118	170,000	1:35.98	105
2001	Dixie Dot Com	6	D.R. Flores	116	Mr Ross	120	Five Straight	115	180,000	1:34.72	110
2002	Unrullah Bull	5	A.J. Lovato	116	Reba's Gold	118	Compendium	116	170,000	1:37.78	107
2003	Bluesthestandard	6	M.A. Pedroza	120	Bonapaw	116	Compendium	116	170,000	1:35.68	108
2004	Kela	6	D. Nuesch	119	Supah Blitz	116	Yessirgeneralsir	114	175,000	1:35.64	114

Beyer Index: 109.13

THE VERY ONE HANDICAP (G3), 1 3/8 Miles (Turf), Fillies and Mares, 3-Year-Olds and Up, Gulfstream Park, 2004 Purse: $100,000

Year	Winner	Age	Jockey	Wt.	Second	Wt.	Third	Wt.	Win Value	Time	Beyer
1987	First Prediction	5	J.M. Pezua	114	Thirty Zip		Lady of the North		37,620	1:35.20	
1990	Storm of Glory	6	J.D. Bailey	113	Tukwila		Topicount		30,000	1:25.00	
1991	Rigamajig	5	R.P. Romero	116	Star Standing		Ahead		30,000	2:15.00	
1992	Bungalow	5	S.J. Sellers	114	Raffinerte		Lover's Quest		30,000	2:05.60	92
1993	Fairy Garden	5	W. Ramos	113	Trampoli		Tango Charlie		30,000	2:14.60	99
1994	Russian Tango	4	J.D. Bailey	112	Maxamount		Camiunch		30,000	2:02.40	95
1995	P.J. Floral	6	S.J. Sellers	113	Trampoli		Memories		30,000	2:14.40	100
1996	Electric Society	5	M.E. Smith	113	Northern Emerald	117	Chelsey Flower	114	30,000	2:15.20	97
1997	Tocopilla	7	B. Peck	114	Ampulla	123	Beyrouth	113	45,000	2:14.20	105
1998	Shemozzle	5	J.R. Velazquez	114	Turkappeal	114	Yoakama	119	45,000	2:19.00	100
1999	Delilah	5	J.D. Bailey	116	Starry Dreamer	114	Beyrouth	113	45,000	2:13.45	97
2000	My Sweet Westly	4	P. Day	110	I'm Indy Mood	114	Manoa	114	45,000	2:06.79	86
2001	Innuendo	6	J.D. Bailey	115	Lucky Lune	114	Silver Bandana	114	60,000	2:13.62	104
2002	Moon Queen	4	J.D. Bailey	118	Jennasietta	114	Sweetest Thing	114	60,000	2:18.38	103
2003	San Dare	5	M. Guidry	116	Tweedside	115	Hi Tech Honeycomb	113	60,000	2:13.76	100
2004	Binya	5	J.R. Velazquez	114	Ocean Silk	115	Boana	114	60,000	2:19.65	98

Beyer Index: 98.15

Run at one mile on turf in 1987; at seven furlongs on main track in 1990; at 1 1/4 miles on the main track in 1992, 1994, and 2000.

THOROUGHBRED CLUB OF AMERICA (G3), 6 Furlongs, Fillies and Mares, 3-Year-Olds and Up, Keeneland Race Course, 2004 Purse: $125,000

Year	Winner	Age	Jockey	Wt.	Second	Wt.	Third	Wt.	Win Value	Time	Beyer
1988	Tappiano	4	J. Vasquez	123	Bound	117	Pine Tree Lane	123	48,750	1:10.20	
1989	Plate Queen	4	R.P. Romero	117	Degenerate Gal	114	Social Pro	123	48,750	1:11.20	
1990	Safely Kept	4	C. Perret	123	Volterra	112	Medicine Woman	117	48,750	1:10.40	

Year	Winner	Age	Jockey	Wt.	Second	Wt.	Third	Wt.	Win Value	Time	Beyer
1991	Avie Jane	7	C. Perret	117	Amen	114	Hoga	114	48,750	1:10.20	89
1992	Ifyoucouldseemenow	4	C. Perret	120	Harbour Club	117	Madam Bear	117	48,750	1:09.60	104
1993	Jeano	5	P. Day	120	Apelia	117	Fluttery Danseur	120	46,500	1:09.20	94
1994	Tenacious Tiffany	4	Perret C	113	Roamin Rachel	120	Jeano	120	46,500	1:11.00	98
1995	Cat Appeal	3	D.M. Barton	116	Russian Flight	113	Traverse City	118	46,500	1:10.00	104
1996	Suprising Fact	3	P. Day	110	Morris Code	118	Mama's Pro	113	62,000	1:10.00	104
1997	Sky Blue Pink	3	P. Day	111	Bluffing Girl	114	Mama's Pro	116	62,000	1:10.00	97
1998	Bourbon Belle	3	Martinez W.	111	J J's Dream	121	Meter Maid	121	62,000	1:08.60	107
1999	Cinemine	4	Martin E. M. Jr.	120	Bourbon Belle	122	Lucky Again	114	62,000	1:08.80	96
2000	Katz Me If You Can	3	J.F. Chavez	115	Hurricane Bertie	123	My Alibi	117	67,394	1:09.42	99
2001	Cat Cay	4	P. Day	118	Spanish Glitter	120	Another	124	67,580	1:09.24	111
2002	French Riviera	3	D.J. Meche	116	Don't Countess Out	120	Away	122	77,500	1:09.75	108
2003	Summer Mis	4	R.R. Douglas	122	Don't Countess Out	122	Born to Dance	122	77,500	1:09.77	90
2004	Molto Vita	4	R. Bejarano	122	My Trusty Cat	124	My Boston Gal	118	77,500	1:09.92	105

Beyer Index: 100.43

TOBOGGAN HANDICAP (G3), 7 Furlongs, 3-Year-Olds and Up, Aqueduct, 2004 Purse: $112,200

Year	Winner	Age	Jockey	Wt.	Second	Wt.	Third	Wt.	Win Value	Time	Beyer
1890	Fides	4	Hamilton	116	Geraldine	122	Blue Rock	120	6,900	1:10.20	
1892	Madstone	6	Garrison	124	Tournament	122	Russell	125	2,215	1:13.00	
1893	Prince George	3	Lamley	109	Yemen	122	G.W. Johnson	112	3,900	1:11.40	
1894	Correction	6	Littlefield	117	Roche	107	Stonell	130	3,900	1:10.40	
1896	Hastings	3	Griffin	114	Hanwell	110	Sherlock	102	1,425	1:12.60	
1897	Octagon	3	Hewitt	107	Irish Reel	119	Lithos	111	1,150	1:12.00	
1898	Octagon	4	Simms	125	Irish Reel	119	Cleophus	126	1,425	1:15.20	
1899	Banastar	4	Maher	116	Sanders	121	Octagon	130	1,820	1:09.00	
1900	Voter	6	Spencer	128	Maribert	110	Contestor	105	1,375	1:12.20	
1901	Banastar	6	Odom	130	King Pepper	103	Unmasked	110	1,210	1:13.40	
1902	Old England	3	J. Woods	105	Arsenal	106	Cervera	120	1,700	1:12.60	
1903	Mizzen	3	Bullman	112	Illyria	93	Invincible	97	2,620	1:11.40	
1904	Hurst Park	4	Odom	111	Kohinoor	96	Gay Boy	120	2,790	1:14.00	
1905	Roseben	4	F. O'Neill	112	Sparkling Star	87	Pasadena	105	2,670	1:13.00	
1906	Clark Griffith	3	W. Miller	100	Tiptoe	102	Oxford	107	3,510	1:11.60	
1907	Ben Ban	4	Garner	95	Pantoufle	100	Red River	109	3,990	1:16.40	
1908	Berry Maid	3	Shreve	100	Baby Wolf	118	Restigouche	105	3,940	1:11.60	
1909	De Mund	5	Butwell	125	Field Mouse	103	Harrigan	108	1,010	1:11.00	
1910	Mary Davis	4	J. Glass	114	Dreamer	104	Field Mouse	101	1,150	1:13.00	
1913	Iron Mask	5	Troxler	130	Spring Board	105	Hes Prynne	99	2,065	1:10.00	
1914	Rock View	4	J. Butwell	126	Figinny	100	Ten Point	128	2,610	1:12.40	
1915	High Noon	3	C. Borel	108	Stromboli	127	Y. Notions	114	1,450	1:09.60	
1916	High Noon	4	J. Loftus	124	Benevolent	108	Phosphor	119	1,990	1:10.80	
1917	Campfire	3	J. McTaggart	115	Stromboli	133	Rickety	111	4,275	1:11.20	
1918	Naturalist	4	M. Buxton	107	Motor Cop	113	Old Koenig	120	3,875	1:10.00	
1919	Billy Kelly	3	J. Loftus	116	Lucullite	127	Papp	114	3,450	1:10.80	
1920	Lion d'Or	4	E. Ambrose	107.5	Motor Cop	128	Naturalist	126	3,325	1:09.60	
1921	Gladiator	4	C. Kummer	125	Sennings Park	111	Mad Hatter	135	6,950	1:08.80	
1922	Rocket	3	L. Penman	106	Dunboyne	130	Tryster	127	7,500	1:11.00	
1923	Mad Hatter	7	E. Sande	128	Runantell	104	Cyclops	109	8,150	1:10.60	
1924	Sheridan	3	L. Fator	105.5	Worthmore	110	Mad Hatter	128	8,750	1:11.60	
1925	Worthmore	4	A. Johnson	125	Silver Fox	112	Noah	111	8,700	1:11.00	
1926	Sarmaticus	3	H. Richards	107	Rock Star	105	Sun Pal	106	9,050	1:12.20	
1927	Chance Play	4	E. Sande	128	Sarmaticus	114	Pompey	120	8,200	1:11.00	
1928	Osmand	4	E. Sande	124	Scapa Flow	124	Happy Argo	125	8,650	1:11.40	
1929	Osmand	5	W. Garner	129	Polydor	123	Finite	108	8,250	1:10.60	
1930	Balko	5	J. Bejshak	111	Flying Heels	117	High Strung	124	8,650	1:11.40	
1931	Caruso	4	J.C. Meek	120	Balko	130	Happy Scot	111	8,250	1:14.80	
1932	Equipoise	4	R. Workman	129	Ironclad	108	Helianthus	110	6,550	1:09.60	
1933	Okapi	3	D. Bellizzi	104	Parry	105	Good Advice	103	3,515	1:11.40	
1934	Okapi	4	M. Garner	117	Kawagoe	105	High Glee	104	3,250	1:10.60	
1935	Identify	4	S. Renick	108	Ajaccio	116	Pompeys Pillar	102	4,225	1:11.60	
1936	Singing Wood	5	J. Gilbert	120	Sation	135	Whopper	123	3,875	1:10.80	
1937	Preeminent	5	H. Richards	113	Snark	114	Tintagel	119	3,625	1:11.20	
1938	Deliberator	5	W.D. Wright	124	Parmelee T.	106	Jay Jay	125	5,350	1:11.00	
1939	Entracte	3	N. Wall	103	Fighting Fox	126	He Did	122	5,500	1:11.00	
1940	Eight Thirty	4	H. Richards	127	War Dog	113	Our Matt	109	6,100	1:09.80	
1941	Eight Thirty	5	H. Richards	129	Dr. Whinny	119	Doubt Not	115	5,275	1:11.20	
1942	Omission	4	J. Gilbert	119	Overdrawn	120	Rosetown	115	5,425	1:10.80	
1943	Devil Diver	4	G. Woolf	116	With Regards	118	Thumbs Up	116	5,650	1:10.00	
1944	Devil Diver	5	E. Arcaro	134	Signator	120	Brownie	114	5,030	1:12.60	
1945	Apache	6	J. Stout	129	Devil Diver	135	Mrs. Ames	107	10,995	1:11.00	

Year	Winner	Age	Jockey	Wt.	Second	Wt.	Third	Wt.	Win Value	Time	Beyer
1946	Polynesian	4	W.D. Wright	124	Cassis	113	King Dorsett	117	11,650	1:13.00	
1947	Buzfuz	5	B. James	121	Degage	114	Polynesian	134	17,900	1:11.00	
1948	Rippey	5	O. Scurlock	129	Owners Choice	114	Buzfuz	121	20,650	1:09.60	
1949	Rippey	6	E. Guerin	129	Pipette	108	Up Beat	120	16,850	1:09.40	
1950	Piet	5	J. Nichols	118	Olympia	126	Nell K.	116	17,250	1:10.60	
1951	Hyphasis	4	R. Bernhardt	110	Tea-Maker	123	Casemate	119	17,650	1:09.40	
1952	Dark Peter	4	A. Widman	108	Crafty Admiral	118	Tea-Maker	120	16,150	1:09.20	
1953	Tuscany	5	N Shuk	122	Hyphasis	116	Dark Peter	122	21,450	1:10.00	
1954	White Skies	5	E. Arcaro	132	Caesar Did	109	Hilarious	120	21,600	1:09.20	
1955	Sailor	3	H. Woodhouse	106	Bobby Brocato	116	White Skies	132	18,950	1:08.80	
1956	Nance's Lad	4	J. Choquette	126	Switch On	124	War Command	118	17,350	1:08.40	
1957	Decimal	5	W. Lester	124	Jovial Jove	126	Gay Warrior	115	15,200	1:08.40	
1958	Bold Ruler	4	E. Arcaro	133	Clem	117	Tick Tock	116	18,582	1:09.00	
1959	Tick Tock	6	R. Ussery	122	Cohoes	125	Warhead	122	18,680	1:10.80	
1960	Intentionally	3	W. Hartack	128	Rick City	122	Vendetta	115	17,835	1:10.60	
1961	Chief of Chiefs	4	J. Leonard	113	April Skies	128	Sweet William	113	14,560	1:10.00	
1962	Merry Ruler	4	I. Valenzuela	116	Rullah Red	113	Hitting Away	120	14.885	1:11.20	
1963	Kilmoray	4	J.L. Rotz	116	For the Road	118	Misty Day	115	14,885	1:10.60	
1964	Scythe	4	W. Hartack	116	Third Martini	115	Exclusive Nashua	115	17,842	1:10.20	
1965	Affectionately	5	W. Blum	124	Chieftain	126	Exclusive Nashua	115	18,167	1:09.40	
1966	Time Tested	4	B. Baeza	126	Beaupy	115	Hoist Bar	125	18,070	1:09.80	
1967	Advocator	4	L. Pincay Jr.	118	Bold and Brave	117	Beaupy	112	18,395	1:10.20	
1968	Jim J.	4	A. Cordero Jr.	119	Air King II	115	Mr. Washington	124	18,200	1:09.80	
1969	Beaukins	4	J. Cruguet	111	Gaylord's Feather	118	Pappa Steve	128	17,550	1:09.80	
1970	Duck Dance	3	J. Ruane	110	Master Hand	115	Jaikyl	115	17,615	1:09.60	
1971	Shut Eye	5	L. Adams	113	Tyrant	122	Cut the Comedy	113	19,860	1:10.60	
1972	Leematt	4	E. Nelson	115	Invested Power	117	Highbinder	113	16,185	1:09.40	
1973	Tentam	4	J. Velasquez	122	Spanish Riddle	115	Tap the Tree	118	16,710	1:09.40	
1974	Mike John G.	4	V. Bracciale Jr.	112	Tap the Tree	115	Delta Champ	113	16,575	1:08.60	
1975	Honorable Miss	5	J. Vasquez	117	Frankie Adams	116	Startahemp	121	16,350	1:09.00	
1976	Due Diligence	4	J. Vasquez	111	Pompini	113	Gallant Bob	129	34,740	1:10.20	
1977	Great Above	5	S. Cauthen	112	Full Out	117	Patriot's Dream	126	32,490	1:09.40	
1978	Barrera	5	R. Hernandez	126	Pumpkin Moonshine	106	Fratello Ed	121	31,890	1:08.80	
1979	Vencedor	5	M.A. Rivera	127	Jet Diplomacy	113	Al Battah	125	32,280	1:10.00	
1980	Tilt Up	5	J. Fell	116	Ardaluan	111	Double Zeus	123	33,660	1:11.00	
1981	Dr. Blum	4	R. Hernandez	123	Guilty Conscience	115	Dunham's Gift	118	32,340	1:11.20	
1982	Always Run Lucky	4	J. Miranda	110	Swelegant	113	In From Dixie	125	33,180	1:10.00	
1983	Mouse Corps	5	R. Alvarado Jr.	111	Top Avenger	123	Prince Valid	115	33,000	1:09.40	
1984	Top Avenger	6	A. Graell	120	Main Stem	109	Elegant Life	116	43,080	1:10.40	
1985	Fighting Fit	5	R. Migliore	123	Entropy	123	Shadowmar	107	51,210	1:09.60	
1986	Rexson's Bishop	4	R. Baez	114	Green Shekel	126	Cullendale	116	50,760	1:11.40	
1987	Play the King	4	R. Hernandez	112	Comic Blush	117	Best by Test	124	50,400	1:09.60	
1988	Afleet	4	G. Stahlbaum	123	Pinecutter	115	Vinnie the Viper	122	66,480	1:09.20	
1989	Lord of the Night	6	J. Velasquez	114	Teddy Drone	117	Vinnie the Viper	115	52,290	1:10.40	
1990	Sunny Blossom	5	E. Maple	117	Diamond Donnie	112	Once Wild	123	51,300	1:09.60	
1991	Bravely Bold	5	M.E. Smith	115	True and Blue	116	Proud and Valid	110	52,020	1:10.60	
1992	Boom Towner	4	D. Nelson	115	Real Minx	112	Gallant Step	114	52,740	1:10.03	115
1993	Argyle Lake	7	D. Carr	109	The Great M.B.	111	Regal Conquest	110	55,530	1:10.11	103
1994	Blare of Trumpets	5	D. Carr	112	Preporant	117	Fabersham	115	49,200	1:09.70	105
1995	Boom Towner	7	F. Lovato Jr.	117	Virginia Rapids	113	Won Song	112	49,080	1:23.77	102
1996	Placid Fund	4	J. Chavez	112	Valid Wager	116	Pat n Jac	112	51,480	1:22.92	111
1997	Royal Haven	5	R. Migliore	115	Jamies First Punch	115	Cold Execution	113	48,600	1:22.47	105
1998	Home on the Ridge	4	W.H. McCauley	114	Wire Me Collect	118	King Roller	116	49,650	1:23.01	104
1999	Wouldn't We All	5	R. Migliore	114	Brushed On	115	Esteemed Friend	120	48,900	1:20.95	110
2000	Brutally Frank	6	S.X. Bridgmohan	114	Master o Foxhounds	114	Watchman's Warning	113	49,410	1:20.77	103
2001	Peeping Tom	4	S.X. Bridgmohan	118	Say Florida Sandy	117	Lake Pontchartrain	113	64,380	1:21.25	110
2002	Affirmed Success	8	R. Migliore	119	Vodka	114	Multiple Choice	111	64,920	1:22.87	109
2003	Affirmed Success	9	R. Migliore	118	Peeping Tom	117	Captain Red	115	65,460	1:09.09	110
2004	Well Fancied	6	E.M. Coa	118	Gators n Bears	115	Don Six	113	67,320	1:22.06	110

Beyer Index: 107.46

Run as Toboggan Slide Handicap prior to 1896. Not run in 1891, 1895, 1911 and 1912. Distance 3-4 mile prior to 1995 and in 2003; 3-4 mile over old straight course prior to 1942; 7 furlongs 1995-2002; Widener Course from 1928 to 1940, inclusive, and from 1942 to 1958, inclusive; main course from 1922 to 1927, inclusive, and in 1941, in 1961 the purse was taken away from Chief of Chiefs and awarded to April Skies; second, Sweet William; third, Mito. Run at Belmont Park prior to 1962.

TOM FOOL HANDICAP (G2), 7 Furlongs, 3-Year-Olds and Up, Belmont Park, 2004 Purse: $142,500

Year	Winner	Age	Jockey	Wt.	Second	Wt.	Third	Wt.	Win Value	Time	Beyer
1975	Kinsman Hope	5	J. Ruane	116	Lonetree	125	Right Mind	113	26,925	1:21.40	
1976	El Pitirre	4	A. Cordero Jr	114	Nalees Knight	110	Honorable Miss	118	26,550	1:24.40	
1977	Mexican General	4	C. Perret	115	Full Out	119	Sticky Situation	110	22,605	1:22.00	

Year	Winner	Age	Jockey	Wt.	Second	Wt.	Third	Wt.	Win Value	Time	Beyer
1978	J.O. Tobin	4	J. Fell	129	White Rammer	119	It's Freezing	116	25,950	1:20.80	
1979	Cox's Ridge	5	E. Maple	119	Nice Catch	121	Tilt Up	119	25,500	1:22.20	
1980	Plugged Nickle	3	J. Fell	121	Dr. Patches	119	Isella	119	33,060	1:22.20	
1981	Rise Jim	5	A. Cordero Jr	119	Proud Appeal	121	Rivalero	119	32,820	1:21.20	
1982	Rise Jim	6	A. Cordero Jr	119	Maudlin	119	And More	119	32,940	1:23.80	
1983	Deputy Minister	4	D. MacBeth	126	Fit to Fight	119	Maudlin	126	52,020	1:22.20	
1984	Believe the Queen	4	J. Velasquez	126	A Phenomenon	119	Cannon Shell	121	70,680	1:22.40	
1985	Track Barron	4	A. Cordero Jr	123	Mt. Livermore	126	Cannon Shell	126	82,260	1:22.00	
1986	Groovy	3	J.A. Santos	112	Phone Trick	126	Basket Weave	119	80,460	1:21.60	
1987	Groovy	4	A. Cordero Jr	128	Sun Master	121	Moment of Hope	119	81,900	1:22.40	
1988	King's Swan	8	A. Cordero Jr	128	Gulch	128	Abject	119	100,980	1:22.40	
1989	Sewickley	4	R.P. Romero	119	Houston	114	Crusader Sword	119	67,920	1:24.00	
1990	Quick Call	6	J.F. Chavez	119	Sewickley	123	Traskwood	119	52,680	1:21.40	
1991	Mr. Nasty	4	A. Cordero Jr	119	Rubiano	121	Senor Speedy	119	67,800	1:21.60	
1992	Rubiano	5	J.A. Krone	126	Take Me Out	119	Arrowtown	119	70,920	1:21.60	108
1993	Birdonthewire	4	C. Perret	119	Fly So Free	119	Take Me Out	119	67,680	1:20.80	111
1994	Virginia Rapids	4	J.L. Samyn	124	Cherokee Run	121	Boundary	119	64,380	1:22.20	112
1995	Lite the Fuse	4	J.A. Krone	117	Our Emblem	115	Evil Bear	118	65,220	1:21.60	116
1996	Kayrawan	4	R. Migliore	113	Cold Execution	112	Lite the Fuse	122	64,869	1:22.80	105
1997	Diligence	4	J.A. Santos	116	Royal Haven	118	Elusive Quality	114	90,000	1:22.40	106
1998	Banker's Gold	4	J.F. Chavez	115	Boundless Moment	115	Partner's Hero	114	90,000	1:21.00	113
1999	Crafty Friend	6	R. Migliore	116	Affirmed Success	119	Aratx	117	90,000	1:20.60	114
2000	Trippi	3	J.D. Bailey	112	Cornish Snow	113	Sailor's Warning	111	90,000	1:21.69	106
2001	Exchange Rate	4	J.D. Bailey	114	Say Florida Sandy	117	Here's Zealous	112	90,000	1:21.24	109
2002	Left Bank	5	J.R. Velazquez	121	Affirmed Success	120	Summer Note	113	90,000	1:20.17	121
2003	Aldebaran	5	J.D. Bailey	122	Peeping Tom	117	State City	118	90,000	1:22.54	105
2004	Ghostzapper	4	J.J. Castellano	119	Aggadan	114	Unforgettable Max	114	90,000	1:20.42	120

Beyer Index: 111.23

TOP FLIGHT HANDICAP (G2), 1 Mile, Fillies and Mares, 3-Year-Olds and Up, Aqueduct, 2004 Purse: $150,000

Year	Winner	Age	Jockey	Wt.	Second	Wt.	Third	Wt.	Win Value	Time	Beyer
1940	True Call	3	D. Meade	107	Piquet	106	Dolly Val	120	6,200	1:43.60	
1941	Tangled	3	C. McCreary	110	Misty Isle	112	Dipsy Doodle	114	4,800	1:44.60	
1942	Level Best	4	D. Meade	123	Up the Hill	114	Transient	112	5,325	1:42.80	
1943	Mar-Kell	4	B. Thompson	122	Yarrow Maid	110	Stefanita	106	4,700	1:44.40	
1944	Boojiana	3	T. Atkinson	106	Mar-Kell	126	Silvestra	112	8,165	1:43.40	
1945	Miss Keeneland	4	A. Snider	122	Legend Bearer	122	Bertie S.	109	7,585	1:45.00	
1946	Sicily	4	E. Arcaro	113	Surosa	113	Recce	118	17,400	1:43.20	
1947	Rytina	4	T. Atkinson	104	Miss Grillo	123	Be Faithful	121	18,550	1:43.60	
1948	Honeymoon	5	D. Dodson	124	Red Shoes	108	Gallorette	126	16,950	1:43.00	
1949	But Why Not	5	D. Gorman	126	Paddleduck	119	Allie's Pal	114	11,450	1:43.60	
1950	Nell K.	4	G. Hettinger	126	Lithe	116	Roman Candlee	116	12,200	1:43.80	
1951	Busanda	4	E. Guerin	120	How	113	Leading Home	107	12,650	1:42.40	
1952	Renew	5	W. Boland	115	Valadium	115	Blue Moon	111	16,850	1:43.80	
1953	Marta	6	C. McCreary	119	Sunshine Nell	112	No Score	110	22,350	1:42.80	
1954	Sunshine Nell	6	E. Guerin	125	Spinning Top	112	La Corredora	125	24,750	1:43.40	
1955	Parlo	4	E. Guerin	126	Gainsboro Girl	114	Spinning Top	113	21,700	1:41.80	
1956	Searching	4	C. McCreary	121	Parlo	124	Rico Reto	107	19,400	1:42.60	
1957	Plotter	4	P. Anderson	116	Outer Space	112	Sorceress	104	19,950	1:42.60	
1958	Plucky Roman	4	H. Grant	114	Outer Space	117	Happy Princess	119	17,672	1:43.00	
1959	Big Effort	4	W. Shoemaker	123	Endine	118	Tempted	118	17,575	1:42.80	
1960	Royal Native	4	W. Hartack	126	Quill	123	Bug Brush	120	36,385	1:43.00	
1961	Make Sail	4	M. Ycaza	116	Funny Bone	112	Rash Statement	114	35,945	1:51.00	
1962	Pepper Patch	5	D. Pierce	113	Counter Call	111	Honey Dear	108	37,050	1:50.20	
1963	Firm Policy	4	M. Ycaza	125	Tamarona	111	Cicada	128	35,880	1:48.60	
1964	Oil Royalty	6	H. Grant	122	Tona	114	Smart Deb	122	37,180	1:50.80	
1965	Affectionately	5	W. Blum	120	Steeple Jill	123	Old Hat	127	37,180	1:49.80	
1966	Summer Scandal	4	G. Patterson	117	Malhoa	113	Straight Deal	119	35,945	1:49.40	
1967	Straight Deal	5	A. Cordero Jr	126	Mac's Sparkler	122	Malhoa	112	36,075	1:49.60	
1968	Amerigo Lady	4	J. Velasquez	119	Serene Queen	111	Muse	109	37,830	1:49.00	
1969	Amerigo Lady	5	M. Ycaza	123	Harem Lady	108	Treacherous	113	35,620	1:50.40	
1970	Shuvee	4	B. Baeza	120	Singing Rain	122	Swiss Cheese	110	37,375	1:48.60	
1971	Shuvee	5	R. Turcotte	127	Cathy Honey	118	Office Queen	127	32,340	1:49.60	
1972	Inca Queen	4	G. Patterson	112	Polly Piper	110	Aladancer	117	33,900	1:50.00	
1973	Poker Night	3	R. Woodhouse	110	Summer Guest	123	Roba Bella	113	33,420	1:48.20	
1974	Lady Love	4	E. Maple	114	Krislin	111	Penny Flight	115	33,120	1:48.60	
1975	Twixt	6	W.J. Passmore	125	Heloise	109	Something Super	116	33,240	1:50.60	
1976	Proud Delta	4	J. Velasquez	120	Let Me Linger	116	Spring Is Here	108	49,455	1:49.00	
1977	Shawi	4	M. Venezia	111	Proud Delta	124	Mississippi Mud	114	48,285	1:49.80	
1978	Northernette	4	J. Fell	121	One Sum	121	Dottie's Doll	116	48,330	1:49.40	

Year	Winner	Age	Jockey	Wt.	Second	Wt.	Third	Wt.	Win Value	Time	Beyer
1979	Waya	5	A. Cordero Jr	128	Pearl Necklace	120	Island Kiss	112	64,680	1:50.80	
1980	Glorious Song	4	J. Velasquez	123	Misty Gallore	126	Blitey	117	66,360	1:49.60	
1981	Chain Bracelet	4	R. Hernandez	115	Lady Oakley	115	Weber City Miss	118	64,680	1:49.60	
1982	Andover Way	4	J. Velasquez	121	Anti Lib	113	Discorama	116	66,360	1:50.00	
1983	Adept	4	K.L. Rogers	109	Broom Dance	122	Dance Number	115	65,160	1:50.00	
1984	Sweet Missus	4	R.J. Thibeau	103	Lady Norcliffe	115	Adept	110	104,040	1:50.20	
1985	Flip's Pleasure	5	J.L. Samyn	117	Sintrillium	119	Some for All	110	101,160	1:51.00	
1986	Ride Sally	4	W.A. Guerra	123	Squan Song	124	Leecoo	107	148,140	1:49.20	
1987	Ms. Eloise	4	R.G. Davis	116	Beth's Song	111	Clemenna's Rose	115	138,480	1:50.20	
1988	Clabber Girl	5	J.A. Santos	117	Psyched	112	Cadillacing	112	141,840	1:49.40	
1989	Banker's Lady	4	A. Cordero Jr	121	Colonial Waters	114	Aptostar	117	133,680	1:51.20	
1990	Dreamy Mimi	4	J.D. Bailey	111	She Can	108	Survive	120	136,800	1:50.40	
1991	Buy the Firm	5	J.A. Krone	119	Colonial Waters	118	Sharp Dance	113	120,000	1:52.20	93
1992	Firm Stance	4	P. Day	114	Haunting	112	Lady d'Accord	117	120,000	1:50.40	92
1993	You'd Be Surprised	4	J.D. Bailey	112	Looie Capote	115	Shared Interest	114	90,000	1:48.80	103
1994	Educated Risk	4	M.E. Smith	120	Triumph at Dawn	111	Imah	111	90,000	1:34.80	108
1995	Twist Afleet	4	M.E. Smith	123	Chaposa Springs	118	Lotta Dancing	114	90,000	1:35.20	106
1996	Flat Fleet Feet	3	M.E. Smith	116	Queen Tutta	114	Miss Golden Circle	116	90,000	1:37.00	91
1997	Dixie Flag	3	M.J. Luzzi	117	Aldiza	112	Mil Kilates	117	90,000	1:35.20	104
1998	Catinca	3	R. Migliore	119	Furlough	115	Glitter Woman	120	90,000	1:35.80	106
1999	Belle Cherie	3	J.R. Velazquez	113	Furlough	118			90,000	1:35.40	104
					Harpia	117					
2000	Reciclada	5	J.D. Bailey	116	Country Hideaway	120	Critical Eye	120	90,000	1:35.54	106
2001	Cat Cay	4	J.R. Velazquez	117	Tugger	116	Atelier	120	90,000	1:35.45	101
2002	Sightseek	3	J.D. Bailey	113	Zonk	116	Nasty Storm	116	90,000	1:35.46	101
2003	Randaroo	3	H. Castillo Jr.	116	Beauty Halo	115	Pocus Hocus	116	90,000	1:36.49	102
2004	Daydreaming	3	J.D. Bailey	117	Bending Strings	118	Roar Emotion	116	90,000	1:35.29	98

Beyer Index: 101.07

TRANSYLVANIA (G3), 1 Mile (Turf), 3-Year-Olds, Keeneland Race Course, 2004 Purse: $113,400

Year	Winner	Age	Jockey	Wt.	Second	Wt.	Third	Wt.	Win Value	Time	Beyer
1989	Shy Tom	3	R. Romero	121	Once Over Knightly	118	Ringerman	121	35,133	1:50.00	
1990	Izvestia	3	R. Romero	112	Scattered	115	Divine Warning	112	36,043	1:43.80	
1991	Eastern Dude	3	S.J. Sellers	121	Magic Interlude	121	January Man	112	36,514	1:42.80	
1992	Casino Magistrate	3	R. Lopez	121	Coaxing Matt	112	Trans Caribbean	115	35,636	1:46.62	89
1993	Proud Shot	3	W.H. McCauley	118	Explosive Red	121	Awad	121	34,364	1:44.17	89
1994	Star of Manila	3	S.J. Sellers	121	Prix de Crouton	118	Carpet	118	33,635	1:42.87	96
1995	Crimson Guard	3	M.E. Smith	118	Dixie Dynasty	114	Nostra	118	42,259	1:44.04	93
1996	More Royal	3	J.A. Krone	112	Defacto	121	Rough Opening	121	43,202	1:35.92	103
1997	Near the Bank	3	P. Day	118	Daylight Savings	114	Song for James	114	44,249	1:36.53	88
1998	Dog Watch	3	R. Davis	116	Reformer Rally	118	American Odyssey	114	45,781	1:34.65	92
1999	Good Night	3	S.J. Sellers	114	Air Rocket	114	Make Your Mark	114	70,308	1:35.00	95
2000	Field Cat	3	M.E. Smith	116	Lendell Ray	116	Go Lib Go	123	70,618	1:35.19	96
2001	Baptize	3	J.D. Bailey	120	Dynameaux	116	Act of Reform	116	70,556	1:35.28	92
2002	Flying Dash	3	J.D. Bailey	116	Back Packer	116	Political Attack	120	62,000	1:35.69	103
2003	White Cat	3	S.J. Sellers	116	Deep Shadow	118	Christmas Away	116	62,000	1:34.98	94
2004	Timo	3	E.S. Prado	123	Mr. J.T.L.	116	America Alive	116	70,308	1:36.52	91

Beyer Index: 93.92

TRAVERS (G1), 1 1/4 Miles, 3-Year-Olds, Saratoga Race Course, 2004 Purse: $1,000,000

Year	Winner	Age	Jockey	Wt.	Second	Wt.	Third	Wt.	Win Value	Time	Beyer
1864	Kentucky	3	Gillpatrack	100	Tipperary	100	Th'g's N'ck Jr.	100	2,950	3:18.60	
1865	Maiden	3	Sewell	97	Oleata	97	Sarah K.	97	3,400	3:18.20	
1866	Merrill	3	Abe	100	Utrica	97	Bayswater	100	3,500	3:29.00	
1867	Ruthless	3	Gillpatrick	103	R.B. Connolly	100	De Courcey	100	2,850	3:18.20	
1868	The Banshee	3	Smith	97	Boaster	100	Albuera	100	3,150	3:10.60	
1869	Glenelg	3	C. Miller	110	Onyx	110	Invercauld	107	3,000	3:14.00	
1870	Kingfisher	3	C. Miller	110	Telegram	110	Foster	110	4,950	3:15.20	
1871	Harry Bassett	3	W. Miller	110	Nellie Gray	107	Alroy	110	5,600	3:21.60	
1872	Joe Daniels	3	J. Rowe	110	Silent Friend	110	Wade Hampton	110	5,500	3:08.20	
1873	Tom Bowling	3	R. Swim	110	Waverly	110	Merodac	110	5,400	3:09.60	
1874	Attila	3	Barbee	110	Acrobat	110	Steel Eyes	110	5,050	3:09.20	
	Race resulted in a dead heat; Attila won the run-off in 3:08.75										
1875	D'Artagnan	3	Barbee	110	Milner	110	Aristides	110	4,850	3:06.20	
1876	Sultana	3	Hayward	107	Barricade	110	Fredericktown	110	3,700	3:15.20	
1877	Baden Baden	3	Sayers	110	Bradamante	107	St. James	110	4,550	3:12.20	
1878	Duke of Magenta	3	Hughes	118	Bramble	118	Spartan	118	4,250	3:08.00	
1879	Falsetto	3	I. Murphy	118	Spendthrift	118	Harold	118	4,950	3:09.20	
1880	Grenada	3	Hughes	118	Open	118	Turfman	118	3,750	3:12.20	

Year	Winner	Age	Jockey	Wt.	Second	Wt.	Third	Wt.	Win Value	Time	Beyer
1881	Hindoo	3	J. McLaughlin	118	Catoctin	118	Getaway	118	2,950	3:07.20	
1882	Carley B.	3	Quantrell	115	Tom Plunkett	118	Mandamus	118	3,450	3:28.60	
1883	Barnes	3	J. McLaughlin	118	Tennyson	118			3,400	3:18.00	
1884	Rataplan	3	Fitzpatrick	118	Blast	118	Tecoma	118	4,150	3:07.20	
1885	Bersan	3	Spellman	118	Irish Pat	118	Boot Black	118	4,025	3:08.20	
1886	Inspector B.	3	J. McLaughlin	118	Elkwood	118	Silver Cloud	118	3,825	3:10.20	
1887	Carey	3	Baylock	118	Oarsman	118	Pendennis	118	3,825	3:17.60	
1888	Sir Dixon	3	J. McLaughlin	118	Los Angeles	113	Falcon	118	4,625	3:07.60	
1889	Long Dance	3	Barnes	118	Flood Tide	118			3,700	3:08.60	
1890	Sir John	3	Bergan	118	Frontenac	118	Burlington	118	4,925	2:39.00	
1891	Vallera	3	R. Williams	122	Hoodlum	122	Silver King	115	2,900	2:49.00	
1892	Azra	3	Clayton	122	Ronald	122			2,750	2:43.60	
1893	Stowaway	3	McDermott	107	Mirage	110	Walnut	107	2,450	2:10.60	
1894	Henry of Navarre	3	Taral	125	Joe Ripley	110	Rey el Santa Anita	125	2,350	2:10.20	
1895	Liza	3	Griffin	104	Rey del Caredes	109	Maurice	111	1,125	1:55.20	
1897	Rensselaer	3	Taral	126	Tragedian	114	Don de Oro	131	1,425	2:12.00	
1901	Blues	3	Shaw	126	Dublin	111	The Parader	129	6,750	1:58.60	
1902	Hermist	3	Rice	111	Gold Cure	116	Cunard	111	6,750	1:54.80	
1903	Ada Nay	3	F. O'Neill	106	Reliable	126	Gimcrack	111	8,150	1:57.00	
1904	Broomstick	3	T. Burns	129	Bobadil	116	Auditor	111	5,850	2:06.80	
1905	Dandelion	3	Shaw	111	Merry Lark	126	Glenecho	126	8,350	2:08.00	
1906	Gallavant	3	W. Miller	111	Mohawk II	111	Reidmore	111	5,800	2:08.20	
1907	Frank Gill	3	Notter	129	Golf Ball	116	Cork Hill	111	5,800	2:07.00	
1908	Dorante	3	J. Lee	116	King James	111	Beaucoup	111	5,800	2:09.60	
1909	Hilarious	3	Scoville	129	Practical	108	Fayette	121	5,800	2:06.00	
1910	Dalmatian	3	C.H. Shilling	129	Barleythorpe	111	Hampton Court	111	4,825	2:10.00	
1913	Rock View	3	T. McTaggart	129	Prince Eugene	126	Barnegat	115	2,725	2:06.60	
1914	Roamer	3	J. Butwell	123	Surprising	126	Gainer	121	3,000	2:04.00	
1915	Lady Rotha	3	M. Garner	106	Saratoga	124	Iron Duke	111	2,150	2:11.40	
	Trial by Jury finished first but was disqualified										
1916	Spur	3	J. Loftus	129	Star Hawk	116	Franklin	111	3,125	2:05.00	
1917	Omar Khayyam	3	J. Butwell	129	Rickety	123	Ticket	120	5,350	2:08.80	
1918	Sun Briar	3	W. Knapp	120	Johren	126	War Cloud	126	7,700	2:03.20	
1919	Hannibal	3	L. Ensor	120	War Pennant	120	Thunderclap	115	9,835	2:02.80	
1920	Man o' War	3	A. Schuttinger	129	Upset	123	John P. Grier	115	9,275	2:01.80	
1921	Sporting Blood	3	L. Lyke	116	Prudery	121			10,275	2:05.80	
1922	Little Chief	3	L. Fator	123	Kal-Sang	120	Sweep By	123	11,325	2:13.40	
1923	Wilderness	3	B. Marinelli	120	Flagstaff	120	Rialto	110	13,550	2:04.00	
1924	Sun Flag	3	F. Keogh	115	Aga Khan	115	Mr. Mutt	120	14,675	2:04.40	
1925	Dangerous	3	C. Kummer	115	Swope	120	Silver Fox	129	13,425	2:10.80	
1926	Mars	3	F. Coltiletti	123	Pompey	123	Display	123	15,050	2:04.60	
1927	Brown Bud	3	L. Fator	120	Nimba	121	Valorous	120	29,925	2:05.40	
1928	Petee-Wrack	3	S. O'Donnell	117	Victorian	126	Sun Edwin	123	30,550	2:08.00	
1929	Beacon Hill	3	A. Robertson	117	Marine	123	The Nut	117	31,825	2:04.20	
1930	Jim Dandy	3	F.J. Baker	120	Gallant Fox	126	Whichone	126	27,050	2:08.00	
1931	Twenty Grand	3	L. McAtee	126	St. Brideaux	120	Sun Meadow	120	33,000	2:04.60	
1932	War Hero	3	J. Gilbert	115	Monday	115	Sunmelus	115	23,150	2:05.80	
1933	Inlander	3	R. Jones	126	Golden Way	115	Keep Out	115	21,050	2:08.00	
1934	Observant	3	L. Humphries	112	Collateral	117	Roustabout	117	14,650	2:05.60	
1935	Gold Foam	3	S. Coucci	112	St. Bernard	115	Count Arthur	112	14,675	2:04.60	
1936	Granville	3	J. Stout	127	Sun Teddy	122	Count Morse	122	14,700	2:05.80	
1937	Burning Star	3	W.D. Wright	117	Up and Doing	112	Matey	120	14,550	2:04.80	
1938	Thanksgiving	3	E. Arcaro	117	Jolly Tar	112	Fighting Fox	124	14,400	2:03.60	
1939	Eight Thirty	3	H. Richards	117	Sun Lover	122	Sir Marlboro	122	16,575	2:06.60	
1940	Fenelon	3	J. Stout	122	Your Chance	122	Asp	112	17,425	2:04.40	
1941	Whirlaway	3	A. Robertson	130	Fairymant	112	Lord Kitch'er	112	16,900	2:05.80	
1942	Shut Out	3	E. Arcaro	130	Trierarch	112	Star Beacon	113	17,825	2:04.40	
1943	Eurasian	3	S. Brooks	112	Fairy Manhurst	112	Famous Victory	112	19,850	2:03.80	
1944	By Jimminy	3	E. Arcaro	126	Free Lance	112	Bounding Home	126	25,015	2:03.40	
1945	Adonis	3	C. McCreary	110	Burning Dream	110	Sir Francis	116	28,680	2:02.80	
1946	Natchez	3	T. Atkinson	124	Mahout	122	School Tie	112	24,750	2:08.00	
1947	Young Peter	3	T. May	124	Phalanx	128	Colonel O'F	122	19,375	2:06.20	
1948	Ace Admiral	3	T. Atkinson	108	Better Self	124	Alairne	108	19,650	2:05.00	
1949	Arise	3	C. Errico	108	Daiquiri	108	Sun Bahram	122	16,600	2:06.20	
1950	Lights Up	3	G. Hettinger	110	Bed o' Roses	109	Passenson	110	16,350	2:03.00	
1951	Battlefield	3	E. Arcaro	123	Yildiz	126	Big Stretch	114	15,000	2:06.20	
1952	One Count	3	E. Guerin	126	Armageddon	123	Tom Fool	114	16,450	2:07.40	
1953	Native Dancer	3	E. Guerin	126	Dictar	120	Guardian II	114	18,850	2:05.60	
1954	Fisherman	3	H. Woodhouse	120	Lychnus	114	Chevation	120	19,500	2:06.00	
1955	Thinking Cap	3	J.P. Bailey	120	Traffic Judge	124	Grandpaw	124	19,150	2:06.40	
1956	Oh Johnny	3	H. Woodhouse	116	Tick Tock	112	Bill's Sky Boy	112	33,200	2:06.20	
1957	Gallant Man	3	W. Shoemaker	126	Bureaucracy	116	Field of Honor	112	29,500	2:04.00	
1958	Piano Jim	3	R. Ussery	112	Grey Monarch	112	Warhead	113	29,920	2:05.80	

Year	Winner	Age	Jockey	Wt.	Second	Wt.	Third	Wt.	Win Value	Time	Beyer
1959	Sword Dancer	3	M. Ycaza	126	Middle Brother	112	Nimmer	120	51,962	2:04.20	
1960	Tompion	3	W. Hartack	126	Count Amber	115	Don Rickles	114	53,165	2:03.40	
1961	Beau Prince	3	S. Brooks	126	Guadalcanal	114	Ambiopoise	126	54,210	2:03.00	
1962	Jaipur	3	W. Shoemaker	126	Ridan	126	Military Plume	114	53,722	2:01.60	
1963	Crewman	3	E. Guerin	120	Hot Dust	114	Chateugay	126	52,910	2:02.40	
1964	Quadrangle	3	M. Ycaza	126	Knightly Manner	120	Hill Rise	123	52,032	2:04.40	
1965	Hail to All	3	J. Sellers	123	Pass the Word	114	Cornish Prince	114	56,777	2:02.20	
1966	Buckpasser	3	B. Baeza	126	Amberoid	123	Buffle	120	53,690	2:01.60	
1967	Damascus	3	W. Shoemaker	126	Reason to Hail	120	Tumiga	117	52,065	2:01.60	
1968	Chompion	3	J. Cruguet	114	Forward Pass	126	Funny Fellow	114	55,802	2:04.80	
1969	Arts and Letters	3	B. Baeza	126	Dike	120	Distray	114	69,290	2:01.60	
1970	Loud	3	J. Vasquez	114	Judgable	117	Plymouth	114	73,385	2:01.00	
1971	Bold Reason	3	L. Pincay Jr	120	West Coast Scout	120	Good Counsel	114	66,420	2:02.40	
1972	Key to the Mint	3	B. Baeza	117	Tentam	114	True Knight	114	66,600	2:01.20	
1973	Annihilate 'Em	3	R. Turcotte	120	Stop the Music	122	See the Jaguar	120	68,280	2:01.60	
1974	Holding Pattern	3	M. Miceli	121	Little Current	126	Chris Evert	121	69,660	2:05.20	
1975	Wajima	3	B. Baeza	126	Media	126	Prince Thou Art	126	65,220	2:02.00	
1976	Honest Pleasure	3	C. Perret	126	Romeo	126	Dance Spell	126	65,040	2:00.20	
1977	Jatski	3	S. Maple	126	Run Dusty Run	126	Silver Series	126	68,160	2:01.60	
	Run Dusty Run finished first but was disqualified and placed second										
1978	Alydar	3	J. Velasquez	126	Affirmed	126	Nasty and Bold	126	62,880	2:02.00	
	Affirmed finished first but was disqualified and placed second										
1979	General Assembly	3	J. Vasquez	126	Smarten	126	Private Account	126	80,850	2:00.00	
1980	Temperence Hill	3	E. Maple	126	First Albert	126	Amber Pass	126	100,980	2:02.80	
1981	Willow Hour	3	E. Maple	126	Pleasant Colony	126	Lord Avie	126	135,600	2:03.80	
1982	Runaway Groom	3	J. fell	126	Aloma's Ruler	126	Conquistador Cielo	126	132,900	2:02.60	
1983	Play Fellow	3	P. Day	126	Slew o' Gold	126	Hyperborean	126	135,000	2:01.00	
1984	Carr de Naskra	3	L. Pincay Jr	126	Pine Circle	126	Morning Bob	126	211,500	2:02.60	
1985	Chief's Crown	3	A. Cordero Jr	126	Turkoman	126	Skip Trial	126	202,800	2:01.20	
1986	Wise Times	3	J.D. Bailey	126	Danzig Connection	126	Personal Flag	126	203,700	2:03.40	
	Broad Brush finished second but was disqualified and placed fourth										
1987	Java Gold	3	P. Day	126	Cryptoclearance	126	Polish Navy	126	673,800	2:02.00	
1988	Forty Niner	3	C.J. McCarron	126	Seeking the Gold	126	Brian's Time	126	653,100	2:01.40	
1989	Easy Goer	3	P. Day	126	Clevor Trevor	126	Shy Tom	126	653,100	2:00.80	
1990	Rhythm	3	C. Perret	126	Shot Gun Scott	126	Sir Richard Lewis	126	707,100	2:02.60	104
1991	Corporate Report	3	C.J. McCarron	126	Hansel	126	Fly So Free	126	600,000	2:01.20	109
1992	Thunder Rumble	3	W.H. McCauley	126	Devil His Due	126	Dance Floor	126	600,000	2:00.80	109
1993	Sea Hero	3	J.D. Bailey	126	Kissin Kris	126	Miner's Mark	126	600,000	2:01.80	109
1994	Holy Bull	3	M.E. Smith	126	Concern	126	Tabasco Cat	126	450,000	2:02.00	115
1995	Thunder Gulch	3	G.L. Stevens	126	Pyramid Peak	126	Malthus	126	450,000	2:03.60	110
1996	Will's Way	3	J.F. Chavez	126	Louis Quatorze	126	Skip Away	126	450,000	2:02.40	114
1997	Deputy Commander	3	C.J. McCarron	126	Behrens	126	Awesome Again	126	450,000	2:04.00	110
1998	Coronado's Quest	3	M.E. Smith	126	Victory Gallop	126	Raffie's Majesty	126	450,000	2:03.40	107
1999	Lemon Drop Kid	3	J.A. Santos	126	Vision and Verse	126	Menifee	126	600,000	2:02.19	110
2000	Unshaded	3	S.J. Sellers	126	Albert the Great	126	Commendable	126	600,000	2:02.59	109
2001	Point Given	3	G.L. Stevens	126	E Dubai	126	Dollar Bill	126	600,000	2:01.40	117
2002	Medaglia d'Oro	3	J.D. Bailey	126	Repent	126	Nothing Flat	126	600,000	2:02.53	113
2003	Ten Most Wanted	3	P. Day	126	Peace Rules	126	Strong Hope	126	600,000	2:02.14	112
2004	Birdstone	3	E.S. Prado	126	The Cliff's Edge	126	Eddington	126	600,000	2:02.45	108

Beyer Index: 110.40

Distance 1 3/4 miles prior to 1890; 1 1/2 miles 1890-92; 1 1/8 miles, 1895, 1901-03. Run at Belmont Park, 1943-45

TRIPLE BEND BREEDERS' CUP INVITATIONAL HANDICAP (G1), 7 Furlongs, 3-Year-Olds and Up, Hollywood Park, 2004 Purse: $300,000

Year	Winner	Age	Jockey	Wt.	Second	Wt.	Third	Wt.	Win Value	Time	Beyer
1979	White Rammer	5	W. Shoemaker	120	Arachnoid	124	Bad 'n Big	122	24,650	1:21.20	
1980	Rich Cream	5	W. Shoemaker	118	I'm Smokin	115	Dragon C'mmand	116	32,250	1:19.40	
1981	Summer Time Guy	5	C.J. McCarron	118	Back'n Time	118	Life's Hope	115	37,400	1:20.20	
1982	Never Tabled	5	C.J. McCarron	112	Shanekite	117	Pompeii Court	116	31,750	1:21.00	
1983	Regal Falcon	5	E. Delahoussaye	117	Island Whirl	123	Kang'roo Court	118	30,700	1:23.40	
1984	Debonair Junior	3	C.J. McCarron	114	Croeso	116	Night Mover	120	37,980	1:21.20	
1985	Fifty Six Ina Row	4	L. Pincay Jr	117	Premiership	115	French Legion'aire	117	38,500	1:20.80	
1986	Sabona	4	C.J. McCarron	114	Innamorato	113	Michadilla	115	47,150	1:21.00	
1987	Bedside Promise	5	R.Q. Meza	124	Zabaleta	118	Bolder Than Bold	118	46,500	1:21.00	
1988	Perfec Travel	6	C.A. Black	115	Rec'nntring	115	Dons Irish M'lody	115	49,600	1:22.20	
1989	Sensational Star	5	R.Q. Meza	114	Oraibi	120	Hot Operator	113	49,700	1:21.40	
1990	Prospectors Gamble	5	J.A. Garcia	114	Raise a Stanza	117	Hot Operator	113	64,200	1:21.40	107
1991	Robyn Dancer	4	L. Pincay Jr	118	Bruho	117	Black Jack Road	118	62,700	1:21.00	
1992	Slew the Surgeon	4	M.G. Linares	111	Softshoe Sure Shot	114	Record Boom	114	64,600	1:21.40	100
1993	Now Listen	6	K.J. Desormeaux	116	Cardmania	116	Star of the Crop	120	66,400	1:20.80	110
1994	Memo	7	P. Atkinson	120	Minjinsky	115	Slerp	119	62,400	1:20.40	113

Year	Winner	Age	Jockey	Wt.	Second	Wt.	Third	Wt.	Win Value	Time	Beyer
1995	Concept Win	5	Valenzuela PA	118	Gold Land	116	Lucky Forever	119	63,100	1:21.00	102
1996	Letthebighossroll	8	C.J. McCarron	116	Score Quick	113	Comininalittlehot	116	125,460	1:21.40	105
1997	Score Quick	5	G.F. Almeida	113	Elmhurst	115	First Intent	116	100,980	1:21.00	104
1998	Son Of A Pistol	6	A. Solis	118	The Exeter Man	114	Benchmark	118	120,000	1:20.80	110
1999	Mazel Trick	4	C.J. McCarron	115	Christmas Boy	111	Regal Thunder	115	180,000	1:19.80	118
2000	Elaborate	5	V. Espinoza	114	Cliquot	116	Lexicon	117	180,000	1:21.19	111
2001	Ceeband	4	M.S. Garcia	110	Squirtle Squirt	114	Elaborate	118	180,000	1:21.17	112
2002	Disturbingthepeace	4	V. Espinoza	113	D'wildcat	115	Mellow Fellow	120	180,000	1:21.09	111
2003	Joey Franco	4	P.A. Valenzuela	118	Publication	116	Primerica	113	180,000	1:21.56	105
	Bluesthestandard finished third but was disqualified and placed sixth										
2004	Pohave	6	V. Espinoza	116	Rojo Toro	115	Revello	110	180,000	1:21.06	103

Beyer Index: 107.93

TROPICAL PARK DERBY (G3), 1 1/8 Miles (Turf), 3-Year-Olds, Calder Race Course, 2004 Purse: $100,000

Year	Winner	Age	Jockey	Wt.	Second	Wt.	Third	Wt.	Win Value	Time	Beyer
1976	Star of the Sea	3	C. Perret	115	Controller Ike	114	Great Contractor	121	55,800	1:44.00	
1977	Ruthie's Native	3	L. Saumell	112	Fort Prevel	121	Dreaming of Moe	112	55,800	1:44.40	
1978	Dr. Valeri	3	R. Rieri Jr	116	Quadratic	119	Galimore	119	73,200	1:45.20	
1979	Bishop's Choice	3	D. MacBeth	111	Lot o' Gold	119	Smarten	119	74,400	1:44.20	
1980	Superbity	3	J. Vasquez	121	Ray's Word	121	Irish Tower	121	69,600	1:45.60	
1981	Double Sonic	3	A. Smith Jr	121	Akureyri	121	Might Be Home	121	70,740	1:46.40	
1982	Victorian Line	3	A. Smith Jr	121	North Cat	121	Sandy Bee's Baby	121	68,280	1:45.40	
1983	My Mac	3	D. MacBeth	121	Caveat	121	Blink	121	100,350	1:46.60	
1984	Morning Bob	3	E. Maple	121	Don Rickles	121	Papa Koo	121	89,310	1:46.00	
1985	Irish Sur	3	J.A. Santos	121	Artillerist	121	Banner Bob	121	107,370	1:45.60	
1986	Strong Performance	3	J. Cruguet	117	Dr. Dan Eyes	114	Real Forest	117	143,760	1:54.40	
1987	Baldski's Star	3	C. Perret	117	Manhattan's Woody	112	Schism	117	139,920	1:54.80	
1988	Digress	3	E. Maple	117	Intensive Command	117	Granacus	117	176,460	1:54.60	
1989	Big Stanley	3	J. Vasquez	114	Appealing Pleasure	114	Prized	114	100,170	1:52.40	
1990	Run Turn	3	E. Fires	117	Country Day	112	Shot Gun Scott	119	66,420	1:52.40	
1991	Jackie Wackie	3	H. Castillo Jr	119	Gizmo's Fortune	119	Paulrus	114	69,120	1:51.80	
1992	Technology	3	J.D. Bailey	119	Majestic Sweep	114	Always Silver	114	134,160	1:53.00	105
1993	Summer Set	3	M.A. Gonzalez	112	Duc d'Sligovil	112	Silver of Silver	122	60,000	1:53.80	89
1994	Fabulous Frolic	3	Cruguet J	112	Wake Up Alarm	117	Gator Back	119	60,000	1:46.80	87
1995	Mecke	3	Castillo H Jr	117	Val's Prince	112	Claudius	119	60,000	1:51.00	88
1996	Ok by Me	3	J.D. Bailey	117	Darn That Erica	114	Tour's Big Red	117	60,000	1:47.20	93
1997	Arthur L.	3	Coa E. M.	119	Unite's Big Red	117	Keep It Strait	117	60,000	1:46.80	94
1998	Draw Again	3	Bravo J.	115	Buddha's Delight	115	Daddy's Dream	117	60,000	1:51.20	84
1999	Vaild Reprized	3	Castellano J. J.	115	Mr. Roark	115	Wertz	119	60,000	1:53.40	93
2000	Go Lib Go	3	J.A. Santos	119	Mr. Livingston	115	Granting	115	60,000	1:46.60	91
2001	Proud Man	3	R.R. Douglas	115	Mr Notebook	119	Cee Dee	119	60,000	1:47.95	88
2002	Political Attack	3	M. Guidry	119	The Judge Sez Who	115	Deeliteful Guy	114	60,000	1:51.71	95
2003	Nothing to Lose	3	J.D. Bailey	115	Millennium Storm	119	Supah Blitz	115	60,000	1:50.45	90
2004	Kitten's Joy	3	J.D. Bailey	119	Broadway View	112	Soverign Honor	117	60,000	1:46.95	91

Beyer Index: 91.38

TROPICAL TURF HANDICAP (G3), 1 1/8 Miles, (Turf), 3-Year-Olds and Up, Calder Race Course, 2004 Purse: $100,000

Year	Winner	Age	Jockey	Wt.	Second	Wt.	Third	Wt.	Win Value	Time	Beyer
1935	Golden Rock II	5	W.D. Wright	112	Top Dog	116	Chasar	117	1,100	1:37.40	
1936	Paradisical	4	G. Seabo	112	Jinnee	100	Two Bob	112	1,200	1:42.80	
1937	Mucho Gusto	5	E. Arcaro	114	Paradisical	110	Bulwark	106	1,000	1:44.00	
1938	Sandy Boot	5	I. Hanford	109	Court Scandal	106	Bob's Boys	110	850	1:44.20	
1946	Statesman	4	O. Scurlock	117	Bel Reigh	112	Crack Reward	115	8,600	1:43.40	
1948	Marchons II	4	W. Saunders	119	Bright Sword	112	Bug Juice	116	5,950	1:43.60	
1949	Irisen	5	J. Robertson	119	Bolo Mack	110	Loriot	115	3,250	1:12.20	
1952	Crystal Boot	6	C. Errico	120	Elixir	115	Recline	119	7,900	1:50.60	
1953	Marked Game	4	W.B. Williams	109	Quick Fire	107	Gulf Stream	110	6,375	1:50.20	
1954	Precious Stone	4	W.M. Cook	115	Scimitar	112	French Bleu	110	7,850	1:50.80	
1955	Marked Game	6	L. Parent	106	Shimke	109	Full Flight	112	7,825	1:50.80	
1956	Dru Away	4	R. Ussery	114	Mr. First	114	Fabricator	117	7,775	1:50.20	
1957	Gray Phantom	4	J. Ruane	124	Juamario	106	Rockcastle	114	7,625	1:49.60	
1958	Hoop Band	5	H. Grant	124	Air Pilot	118	Little Porter	106	6,790	1:50.00	
1959	Stratmat	5	G. Gibb	110	Rare Rice	115	M'ners G'de	110	7,350	1:47.40	
1960	Eurasia	5	S. Boulmetis	114	Heroshogala	122	Moony	119	7,610	1:43.00	
1961	Humane Leader	4	B. Baeza	113	Eurasia	120	Level Flight	114	7,589	1:44.00	
1962	Intercepted	3	W. Hartack	116	Rob Roy III	116	Aw'y With You	113	7,832	1:44.40	
1963	Frankie's Nod	3	K. Korte	112	Deton	115	Sky Wonder	119	7,605	1:42.40	
1964	Somali Bird	6	H. Wajda	112	Suspicious	117	Demigod	113	7,288	1:42.60	

Year	Winner	Age	Jockey	Wt.	Second	Wt.	Third	Wt.	Win Value	Time	Beyer
1964	Tronado	4	C. Gonzalez	120	Doctor Hank K.	117	S'alesman Pr'r	119	7,288	1:42.60	
1965	Turn to Reason	3	R. Ussery	118	Abdul	116	First Family	116	11,099	1:42.20	
1966	Naughty Jester	3	N. Mercier	114	Fathers Image	120	Steel Pike	114	10,839	1:41.40	
1967	Crafty Look	3	C.H. Marquez	115	Peace Pipe	115	Tequillo	115	9,214	1:43.00	
1967	Wild Card	7	A. Cordero Jr	115	Sacramento	117	Aczay	115	9,214	1:43.60	
1968	Abe's Hope	5	R. Grubb	116	Valam	117	Subpet	118	10,425	1:41.40	
1969	Dorileo	5	D. Richard	115	Great Cohoes	122	Elegant Heir	114	10,425	1:41.40	
1969	Barely Even	3	G. Gallitano	119	Vif	121	Ocean Bar	115	10,485	1:41.60	
1970	Irurzun	6	C. Marquez	117	Coaltown Cat	120	Lanzerac	118	15,210	1:43.80	
1971	French Corners	5	D. MacBeth	112	Handsome Kid	113	Jet a Bit	114	18,210	1:41.20	
1972	Prince of Truth	4	J. Vasquez	117	Rastaferian	114	Glazed D'nut	114	17,700	1:46.00	
1973	Proud and Bold	3	R. Woodhouse	121	Outatholme	116	Seminole Joe	1120	17,100	1:45.60	
1974	L. Grant Jr.	4	J. Combest	121	Super Sail	118	El Tordillo	115	18,300	1:45.80	
1979	Lot o' Gold	3	D. Brumfield	123	King Celebrity	117	J. Rodney G.	114	33,330	1:52.60	
1980	Yosi Boy	4	A. Smith Jr	111	Two's a Plenty	120	Von Clausewitz	119	33,180	1:51.80	
1981	The Liberal Member	6	J.D. Bailey	115	Jayme G.	116	Recusant	112	35,130	1:51.80	
1982	Rivalero	6	J. Vasquez	120	Current Blade	115	In All Honesty	110	33,270	1:53.60	
1983	Eminency	5	P. Day	122	World Appeal	118	Ready to Prove	110	34,770	1:51.20	
1984	Biloxi Indian	3	B. Fann	114	Key to the Moon	122	Di Roma Feast	114	32,700	1:54.00	
1985	Ban the Blues	6	G. St. Leon	114	Jim Bracken	112	Bold Southerner	112	34,140	1:53.20	
1986	Arctic Honeymoon	3	R.N. Lester	111	Lover's Cross	121	Darn That Alarm	122	32,550	1:54.00	
1988	Equalize	6	J.A. Santos	122	Val d'Enchere	116	Racing Star	114	35,010	1:45.00	
1989	Vaguely Double	4	W.A. Guerra	118	Mr. Adorable	113	Highland Springs	120	35,490	1:48.80	
1990	Stolen Rolls	4	P.A. Rodriguez	112	Gay's Best Boy	111	Seasabb	111	35,700	1:45.20	
1992	Carterista	3	M.A. Lee	112	Rinka Das	114	Pidgeon's Promise	110	30,000	1:46.20	100
1992	Bidding Proud	3	J.A. Santos	115	Buckhar	118	Plate Dancer	116	30,000	1:46.00	102
1993	Carterista	3	W.S. Ramos	121	Rinka Das	113	Daarik	114	45,000	1:44.80	97
1994	The Vid	4	R.R. Douglas	116	Country Coy	113	Gone for Real	113	60,000	1:49.00	104
1995	The Vid	5	W.H. McCauley	120	Elite Jeblar	114	Scannapieco	113	60,000	1:44.80	112
1996	Mecke	4	R.G.Davis	124	Satellite Nealski	113	Elite Jeblar	114	60,000	1:46.40	102
1997	Sir Cat	4	J.A. Rivera II	116	Foolish Pole	115	Written Approval	112	60,000	1:54.00	102
1998	Unite's Big Red	4	E.O. Nunez	115	N B Forrest	115	Glok	115	60,000	1:48.80	103
1999	Hibernian Rhapsody	4	R.R. Douglas	117	Garbu	117	Shamrock City	114	60,000	1:46.00	98
2000	Stokosky	4	C.A. Hernandez	114	Special Coach	114			60,000	1:48.77	100
					Band Is Passing	119					
2001	Band Is Passing	5	C.V. Gonzalez	118	Crash Course	116	Groomstick's Stock	114	60,000	1:46.90	109
2002	Krieger	4	E.M. Coa	113	Stokosky	113	Serial Bride	114	60,000	1:47.02	101
2003	Political Attack	4	R.R. Douglas	116	Millennium Dragon	116	Sforza	115	60,000	1:45.81	103
2004	Host	4	J.R. Velazquez	118	Silver Tree	118	Demeteor	114	60,000	1:45.74	103

Beyer Index: 102.57

TRUE NORTH BREEDERS' CUP HANDICAP (G2), 6 Furlongs, 3-Year-Olds and Up, Belmont Park, 2004 Purse: $210,830

Year	Winner	Age	Jockey	Wt.	Second	Wt.	Third	Wt.	Win Value	Time	Beyer
1979	Moleolus	4	J.L. Samyn	110	Jet Diplomacy	118	Northern Prospect	116	25,335	1:10.40	
1980	Syncopate	5	L. Pincay Jr	120	Isella	117	Double Zeus	116	33,000	1:09.20	
1981	Joanie's Chief	4	J.L. Samyn	109	Proud Appeal	117	Guilty Conscience	113	33,480	1:09.00	
1982	Shimatoree	3	M. Pino	117	Pass the Tab	121	Will of Iron	112	49,590	1:08.60	
1983	Gold Beauty	4	D. Brumfield	121	Singh Tu	111	Fit to Fight	113	50,760	1:10.40	
1984	Believe the Queen	4	J. Velasquez	114	Muskoka Wyck	112	Cannon Shell	115	52,110	1:09.80	
1985	Cannon Shell	6	D.J. Murphy	114	Basket Weave	114	Mt. Livermore	126	52,200	1:10.80	
1986	Phone Trick	4	J. Velasquez	127	Love That Mac	117	Cullendale	111	66,480	1:09.00	
1987	Groovy	4	A. Cordero Jr	123	King's Swan	120	Sun Master	117	78,780	1:07.80	
1988	High Brite	4	A. Cordero Jr	120	Irish Open	115	King's Swan	122	81,300	1:10.00	
1989	Dancing Spree	4	A. Cordero Jr	113	Dr. Carrington	109	Pok Ta Pok	118	68,160	1:09.40	
1990	Mr. Nickerson	4	C.W. Antley	119	Sewickley	117	Dancing Spree	123	51,360	1:10.40	116
1991	Diablo	4	J.A. Krone	112	Sunny Blossom	120	Bravely Bold	119	69,720	1:08.20	117
1992	Shining Bid	4	E. Maple	112	Arrowtown	113	To Freedom	117	71,880	1:08.20	105
1993	Lion Cavern	4	J.A. Krone	116	Arrowtown	115	Lady's Key	111	69,120	1:10.20	105
1994	Friendly Lover	6	R. Wilson	114	Boundary	117	Birdonthewire	119	67,380	1:09.60	106
1995	Waldoboro	4	E. Maple	112	Corma Ray	111	Mining Burrah	117	66,300	1:09.60	108
1996	Not Surprising	6	R.G. Davis	121	Prospect Bay	113	Forest Wildcat	114	66,720	1:09.00	113
1997	Punch Line	7	R.G. Davis	122	Cold Execution	112	Jamies First Punch	116	66,180	1:08.80	107
1998	Richter Scale	4	J.D. Bailey	119	Trafalger	114	Kelly Kip	122	83,160	1:08.80	116
1999	Kashatreya	5	J.L. Samyn	110	Artax	119	The Trader's Echo	111	90,000	1:09.60	105
2000	Intidab	7	R.G. Davis	117	Brutally Frank	119	Oro de Mexico	113	90,000	1:10.22	109
2001	Say Florida Sandy	7	A.T. Gryder	116	Wake At Noon	117	Explicit	115	90,000	1:08.77	111
2002	Explicit	5	L.J. Meche	119	Entepreneur	115	Late Carson	114	150,000	1:09.98	106
2003	Shake You Down	5	M.J. Luzzi	118	Highway Prospector	115	Vodka	114	90,000	1:09.59	108
2004	Speightstown	6	J.R. Velazquez	119	Cat Genius	116	Pohave	117	126,840	1:08.04	115

Beyer Index: 109.80

TURFWAY BREEDERS' CUP (G3), 1 1/16 Miles, Fillies and Mares, 3-Year-Olds and Up, Turfway Park, 2004 Purse: $175,000

Year	Winner	Age	Jockey	Wt.	Second	Wt.	Third	Wt.	Win Value	Time	Beyer
1988	Darien Miss	3	P.A. Johnson	115	Integra	123	Ms. Eloise	120	101,758	1:43.60	
1989	Winning Colors	4	C.J. McCarron	115	Grecian Flight	123	Lawyer Talk	123	101,368	1:44.80	
1990	Barbarika	5	A.T. Gryder	123	Colonial Waters	114	Luthier's Launch	112	119,015	1:44.00	107
1991	Fit for a Queen	5	R.D. Lopez	123	Til Forbid	118	Screen Prospect	114	117,358	1:43.20	108
1992	Fit for a Queen	6	R.D. Lopez	123	Auto Dial	120	Hitch	112	117,975	1:43.20	109
1993	Gray Cashmere	4	D. Kutz	117	Deputation	120	November Snow	113	117,130	1:43.20	105
1994	Pennyhill Park	4	C. McCarron	123	Roamin Rachel	123	Hey Hazel	123	118,072	1:44.20	97
1995	Mariah's Storm	5	R. Lester	117	Serena's Song	119	Alcovy	117	116,415	1:41.60	120
1996	Golden Attraction	3	G.L. Stevens	114	Bedroom Blues	117	Betty Van	119	205,920	1:42.40	94
1997	Feasibility Study	5	M.E. Smith	119	City Band	114	Gold n Delicious	121	160,022	1:42.40	98
1998	Biding Time	4	C.S. Nakatani	117	Meter Maid	121	Dancing Gulch	119	162,266	1:43.00	102
1999	Ruby Surprise	4	Martinez W.	118	Let	118	French Braids	114	162,886	1:44.80	97
2000	Spain	3	P. Day	118	Ruby Surprise	118	Undermine	118	156,500	1:44.85	101
2001	Trip	4	C. Perret	118	Precious Feather	114	Spain	122	125,500	1:42.47	102
2002	Trip	5	P. Day	116	Mystic Lady	118	Red n'Gold	118	125,500	1:43.01	109
2003	Smok'n Frolic	4	E.S. Prado	122	Awesome Humor	112	So Much More	118	108,500	1:44.98	100
2004	Susan's Angel	3	R. Bejarano	116	Mayo on the Side	120	Angela's Love	122	108,500	1:44.21	89

Beyer Index: 102.53

TURFWAY PARK FALL CHAMPIONSHIP (G3), 1 Mile, 3-Year-Olds and Up, Turfway Park, 2004 Purse: $100,000

Year	Winner	Age	Jockey	Wt.	Second	Wt.	Third	Wt.	Win Value	Time	Beyer
1919	Mad Hatter		L. Fator		Sway		Stockwell			3:06.00	
1920	Cleopatra		C. Fairbrother		On Watch		Damask			2:56.80	
1921	Sporting Blood		F. Keogh		Black Servant		Hymphrey			3:05.60	
1922	Rockminster		M. Garner		Lucky Hour		Surf Rider			2:55.60	
1923	In Memoriam		M. Garner		Zev		My Own			3:00.80	
1924	Chilhowee		M. Garner		Mad Play		Aga Khan			2:54.60	
1925	King Nadi		E. Sande		Old Slip		Drowsy Waters			3:06.40	
1926	Display		J. Maiben		Boot to Boot		Helen's Babe			2:58.80	
1927	Rolled Stocking		W. Crump		Wooldridge		Brown Bud			2:55.60	
1928	Sun Beau		J. Craigmyle		Sortie		Lawley			3:00.60	
1929	The Nut		J. Smith		Curate		Ben Machree			3:26.00	
1930	Spinach		G. Ellis		Yarn		Star Lassie			2:59.60	
1931	St. Brideaux		C. Kurtsinger		Rocky News		Dixie King			3:01.40	
1932	Gallant Sir		G. Woolf		Mad Frump		Gusto			3:12.40	
1933	Pomposity		J. Bejshak		Caesars Ghost		Contraband			3:02.00	
1964	Sought After		J. Warner		Godessa		Renepache			1:58.00	
1965	Busking		J. Lynch		Will Dance		Dandy K			1:51.60	
1966	Brochaza		M. Manganello		Grand Central		Big Darby			1:52.20	
1967	Likely Swap		M. Manganello		Hy Frost		Great Chip			1:51.00	
1968	T.V.'s Princess		M. Manganello		Reigning Count		Swift Gem			1:45.40	
1969	DeMito		M. Manganello		Danton II		Larry's Reward			1:46.60	
1970	Tort-Feazor		O. Torres		Mistong		Broadcloth			1:44.20	
1971	Man of Parts		J. McIntosh		Sea O Joe		Jay Lea			1:44.20	
1971	Tesart		M. Manganello		Second Adventure		Gold Flake			1:44.20	
1973	Knight Counter		D. Brumfield		Divorce Trial		On the Money			1:46.80	
1974	Bootlegger's Pet		G. Solomon		Lesters Jester		Babingtons Image			1:47.60	
1975	Eager Wish		C. Bramble		Zografos		Princess Jilo			1:44.40	
1976	Brustigert		A. Herrera		Faneuil Boy		Visier			1:45.40	
1977	Certain Roman		M. McDowell		The Pepe		Payne Street			1:44.80	
1978	Likely Exchange		M. Sellers		Pirogue		Mr. Pitty Pat			1:45.60	
1979	Lotta Honey		J. Espinoza		Penalty Declined		One Lucky Devil			1:42.40	
1980	Silver Shears		R.R. Matias		Penalty Declined		One Lucky Devil			1:43.20	
1981	Exterminate		D. Foster		Kentucky Scout		Withholding			1:44.40	
1982	Leader Jet		C. Woods Jr.		Rock Steady		Diverse Dude			1:44.00	
1983	Cad		D. Brumfield		His Flower		Noted			1:44.00	
1984	Immediate Reaction		M. McDowell		Fairly Straight		Never Company			1:43.80	
1985	Country Hick		J. Espinoza		Turn Here		McShane			1:43.00	
1986	Big Pistol		L. Melancon		Exit Five B.		Something Cool			1:42.80	
1987	Lord Glacier		M. Solomone		Aggie's Best		Ten Times Ten			1:43.60	
1988	Mr. Odie		S. Neff		Boyish Charm		Government Corner			1:52.40	
1989	Currentsville Lane		W.J. Neagle		Air Worthy		Loyal Pal			1:51.60	
1990	Aly Mar		D. Kutz		Cefis		Cantrell Road			1:49.20	
1991	Allijeba		J. Bruin	116	D.C. Tenacious		Discover		41,420	1:49.60	106
1992	Flying Continental		J. Velasquez	122	Alyten		Regal Affair		27,510	1:48.60	105
1993	Powerful Punch		C. Borque	116	Medium Cool		Benburb		41,047	1:50.40	105
1994	Meena		W. Martinez	114	Powerful Punch		It'sal'ilknownfact		27,284	1:52.80	104

Year	Winner	Age	Jockey	Wt.	Second	Wt.	Third	Wt.	Win Value	Time	Beyer
1995	Bound by Honor	5	R.P. Romero	113	Lord Gordon	113	Lordly Prospect	112	42,600	1:51.40	104
1996	Strawberry Wine	4	B. Peck	114	Kiridashi	121	Prospect for Love	114	65,000	1:50.00	111
1997	Tejano Run	5	W. Martinez	122	Short Stay	114	Thesaurus	112	46,950	1:49.40	101
1998	Acceptable	4	C. Perret	116	Magnify	114	Muchacho Fino	112	62,600	1:51.80	108
1999	Phil the Grip	5	R.J. Albarado	112	Part the Waters	111	Metatonia	110	49,600	1:52.15	95
2000	Mount Lemon	6	R.J. Albarado	117	Unloosened	114	Phil the Grip	117	62,600	1:51.14	98
2001	Generous Rosi	6	L.J. Meche	115	Storm Day	117	Jadada	117	46,500	1:49.83	108
2002	Crafty Shaw	4	J. Lopez	117	Rock Slide	117	Deferred Comp	115	62,750	1:52.29	102
2003	Crafty Shaw	5	C. Perret	117	Cat Tracker	117	Cappuchino	119	62,000	1:36.89	103
2004	Cappuchino	5	D.A. Sarvis	115	Crafty Shaw	122	Added Edge	119	62,000	1:37.19	97

Beyer Index: 103.36

TURNBACK THE ALARM HANDICAP (G3), 1 1/8 Miles, Fillies and Mares, 3-Year-Olds and Up, Aqueduct, 2004 Purse: $110,700

Year	Winner	Age	Jockey	Wt.	Second	Wt.	Third	Wt.	Win Value	Time	Beyer
1995	Incinerate	6	F.Leon	115	Lotta Dancing	115	Pretty Discreet	110	49,005	1:48.80	103
1996	Shoop	5	J.Bailey	121	Queen Tutta	116	Madame Adlophe	113	48,940	1:51.20	92
1997	Mil Kilates	4	J.Bravo	116	Radiant Megan	110	Shoop	114	48,380	1:49.40	89
1998	Snit	4	J.R.Velazquez	117	Manoa	112	Shoop	114	49,740	1:51.20	94
1999	Belle Cherie	3	Velazquez J. R.	112	Brushed Halory	114	Sweet Misty	116	66,000	1:50.00	97
2000	Atelier	3	E.S. Prado	113	Tap to Music	119	Pentatonic	115	67,920	1:48.95	106
2001	Rochelle's Terms	4	R.G. Davis	113	Resort	113	Strolling Belle	118	65,100	1:51.19	87
2002	Svea Dahl	5	R. Migliore	114	Mystic Lady	119	Critical Eye	115	64,800	1:50.42	105
2003	Pocus Hocus	5	J.A. Santos	114	Nonsuch Bay	115	Miss Linda	118	64,500	1:50.67	101
2004	Personal Legend	4	J.D. Bailey	115	Roar Emotion	117	Fast Cookie	114	66,420	1:51.27	97

Beyer Index: 97.10

UNITED NATIONS (G1), 1 3/8 Miles (Turf), 3-Year-Olds and Up, Monmouth Park, 2004 Purse: $750,000

Year	Winner	Age	Jockey	Wt.	Second	Wt.	Third	Wt.	Win Value	Time	Beyer
1953	Iceberg II	5	J. Contreras	120	Brush Burn	118	Royal Governor	118	43,050	1:55.80	
1954	Closed Door	5	W. Hartack	117	Royal Vale	120	Kaster	114	50,000	1:57.00	
1955	Blue Choir	4	W. Hartack	126	Chevation	117	Klairon	111	73,600	2:00.00	
1956	Career Boy	3	S. Boulmetis	116	Find	117	Mister Gus	119	65,000	1:56.20	
1957	Round Table	3	W. Shoemaker	118	Tudor Era	112	Find	122	65,000	1:56.20	
1958	Clem	4	W. Shoemaker	113	Round Table	130	Combustion II	115	65,000	1:54.60	
1959	Round Table	5	W. Shoemaker	136	Noureddin	117	Li'l Fella	120	65,000	1:55.20	
1960	T.V. Lark	3	J. Sellers	120	Sword Dancer	127	Bally Ache	122	65,000	1:57.00	
1961	Oink	4	L. Gilligan	119	Tompion	117	Art Market	116	65,000	1:56.00	
1962	Mongo	3	C. Burr	117	T.V. Lark	123	Wise Ship	123	65,000	1:56.60	
1963	Mongo	4	W. Chambers	124	Never Bend	118	Carry Back	127	75,000	1:55.20	
1964	Western Warrior	5	H. Gustines	114	Parka	121	Turbo Jet II	116	75,000	1:57.80	
1965	Parka	7	W. Blum	119	Hill Rise	118	Chieftain	122	75,000	1:57.80	
1966	Assagai	3	L. Adams	118	Ginger Fizz	114	Toulore	118	65,000	1:58.60	
1967	Flit-to	4	H. Woodhouse	110	Assagai	122	Fort Marcy	117	65,000	1:54.00	
	Munden Point finished third but was disqualified and placed fourth										
1968	Dr. Fager	4	B. Baeza	134	Advocator	112	Fort Marcy	118	65,000	1:55.20	
1969	Hawaii	4	J. Velasquez	124	North Flight	117	Fort Marcy	130	75,000	2:00.60	
1970	Fort Marcy	6	J. Velasquez	125	Fiddle Isle	127	Mr. Leader	119	75,000	1:56.00	
1971	Run the Gantlet	3	R. Woodhouse	117	Twice Worthy	118	Chompion	116	65,000	2:02.00	
1972	Acclimatization	4	R. Woodhouse	117	Dubasoff	117	Red Reality	119	65,000	1:54.00	
1973	Tentam	4	J. Velasquez	123	Star Envoy	116	Return to Reality	113	75,000	1:54.60	
1974	Halo	5	J. Velasquez	118	London Company	123	Scantling	115	65,000	1:56.80	
1975	Royal Glint	5	J. Tejeira	120	Stonewalk	120	R. Tom Can	116	65,000	1:57.00	
1976	Intrepid Hero	4	S. Hawley	125	Improviser	116	Break Up the Game	120	65,000	1:53.40	
1977	Bemo	7	D. Brumfield	116	Quick Card	124	Alias Smith	112	65,000	1:54.00	
1978	Noble Dancer II	6	S. Cauthen	127	Upper Nile	118	Dan Horn	117	81,250	1:56.40	
1979	Noble Dancer II	7	J. Vasquez	125	Dom Alaric	120	Overskate	128	75,000	1:56.60	
1980	Lyphard's Wish	4	A. Cordero Jr	118	Match the Hatch	115	Scythian Gold	111	82,500	1:53.80	
1981	Key to Content	4	G. Martens	121	Ben Fab	123	Match the Hatch	115	82,500	1:52.80	
1982	Naskra's Breeze	5	J.L. Samyn	117	Acaroid	115	Don Roberto	116	90,000	1:53.40	
1983	Acaroid	5	A. Cordero Jr	113	Trevita	116	Majesty's Prince	120	106,200	1:54.00	
1984	Hero's Honor	4	J.D. Bailey	123	Cozzene	114	Who's For Dinner	110	106,200	1:54.00	
1985	Ends Well	4	M.R. Morgan	114	Who's For Dinner	116	Cool	111	107,820	1:54.60	
1986	Manila	3	J.A. Santos	114	Uptown Swell	116	Lieutenant's Lark	121	104,040	1:52.60	
1987	Manila	4	J. Vasquez	124	Racing Star	115	Air Display	110	90,000	1:58.80	
1988	Equalize	6	J.A. Santos	116	Wanderkin	115	Bet Twice	124	120,000	1:52.60	
1989	Yankee Affair	7	P. Day	121	Salem Drive	117	Simply Majestic	119	120,000	1:53.20	
1990	Steinlen	7	J.A. Santos	124	Capades	112	Alwuhush	121	300,000	1:52.00	113

Year	Winner	Age	Jockey	Wt.	Second	Wt.	Third	Wt.	Win Value	Time	Beyer
1991	Exbourne	5	C.J. McCarron	122	Forty Niner Days	116	Goofalik	114	300,000	1:52.60	109
1992	Sky Classic	5	P. Day	123	Chenin Blanc	115	Lotus Pool	114	300,000	1:52.20	106
1993	Star of Cozzene	5	J.A. Santos	120	Lure	123	Finder's Choice	114	300,000	1:53.20	117
1994	Lure	5	M.E. Smith	123	Fourstars Allstar	117	Star of Cozzene	121	300,000	1:52.60	107
1995	Sandpit	6	C.S. Nakatani	122	Celtic Arms	118	Alice Springs	115	300,000	1:57.20	107
1996	Sandpit	7	C.S. Nakatani	122	Diplomatic Jet	117	Northern Spur	122	300,000	1:55.60	111
1997	Influent	6	J.L. Samyn	117	Geri	113	Flag Down	118	240,000	1:53.60	111
1999	Yagli	6	J.D. Bailey	124	Supreme Sound	113	Amerique	115	150,000	2:16.02	103
2000	Down the Aisle	7	R.G. Davis	114	Aly's Alley	111	Honor Glide	116	210,000	2:13.63	102
2001	Senure	5	R.G. Davis	116	With Anticipation	113	Gritty Sandie	112	300,000	2:13.56	106
	With Anticipation (Beyer: 106) finished first but was disqualified and placed second										
2002	With Anticipation	7	P. Day	119	Denon	118	Sarafan	117	300,000	2:12.81	110
2003	Balto Star	5	J.A. Velez Jr	117	The Tin Man	121	Lunar Sovereign	121	450,000	2:12.78	110
2004	Request for Parole	5	E.S. Prado	118	Mr O'Brien	120	Nothing to Lose	118	450,000	2:13.37	108

Beyer Index: 108.57

Run at Atlantic City through 1997; Run as Caesars International 1991-97

VERNON O. UNDERWOOD (G3), 6 Furlongs, 3-Year-Olds and Up, Hollywood Park, 2004 Purse: $100,000

Year	Winner	Age	Jockey	Wt.	Second	Wt.	Third	Wt.	Win Value	Time	Beyer
1981	Shanekite	3	S. Hawley	114	Syncopate	122	Big Presentation	114	50,500	1:08.20	
1981	Smokite	5	D.C. Hall	116	I'm Smokin	120	Stand Pat	114	50,500	1:08.60	
1982	Mad Key	5	E. Delahoussaye	116	Shanekite	120	Dave's Friend	114	70,600	1:08.20	
1982	Unpredictable	3	K. Black	120	Remember John	120	Chinook Pass	112	69,100	1:08.60	
1983	Fighting Fit	4	E. Delahoussaye	120	Expressman	112	Matching	119	101,950	1:09.00	
1984	Fifty Six Ina Row	3	S. Hawley	112	Debonaire Junior	120	Charging Falls	112	91,975	1:09.40	
1984	Lovlier Linda	4	W. Shoemaker	121	Sonrie Jorge	116	Fali Time	121	89,475	1:10.00	
1985	Pancho Villa	3	L. Pincay Jr	122	Charging Falls	122	Temerity Prince	122	121,900	1:08.80	
1986	Bedside Promise	4	G.L. Stevens	122	Bolder Than Bold	114	Pine Tree Lane	117	127,200	1:08.80	
1987	Hilco Scamper	4	C.A. Black	114	Reconnoitering	112	Zabaleta	122	62,800	1:09.60	
1988	Gallant Sailor	5	F. Olivares	116	Reconnoitering	116	Very Subtle	117	63,400	1:09.60	
1989	Olympic Prospect	5	A. Solis	120	Sam Who	122	Order	122	60,200	1:08.80	
1990	Frost Free	5	C.J. McCarron	120	Timebank	112	Sam Who	114	65,300	1:08.20	
1991	Individualist	4	K.J. Desormeaux	114	Thirty Slews	117	Cardmania	120	64,500	1:08.80	105
1992	Gundaghia	5	G.L. Stevens	116	Gray Slewpy	124	Cardmania	124	61,300	1:09.20	113
1993	Meafara	4	G.L. Stevens	119	Arches of Gold	121	Davy Be Good	116	60,900	1:10.00	108
1994	Wekiva Springs	3	K.J. Desormeaux	118	Cardmania	120	Gundaghia	120	63,750	1:08.20	107
1995	Powis Castle	4	G.L. Stevens	114	Lucky Forever	122	Plenty Zloty	116	62,300	1:08.40	108
1996	Paying Dues	4	P. Day.	124	Men's Exclusive	114	Kern Ridge	114	64,860	1:08.20	114
1997	Tower Full	5	C.S. Nakatani	118	Trafalger	118	Swiss Yodeler	114	60,000	1:08.00	106
1998	Love That Jazz	4	K.J. Desormeaux	117	Peyrano-AR	116	Swiss Yodeler	120	60,000	1:08.60	103
1999	Five Star Day	3	A. Solis	120	Your Halo	122	Son of a Pistol	122	60,000	1:09.80	109
2000	Men's Exclusive	7	L. Pincay Jr.	116	Love All the Way	117	Lexicon	122	60,000	1:09.02	108
2001	Men's Exclusive	8	L. Pincay Jr.	120	Tavasco	114	Caller One	124	60,000	1:09.04	102
2002	Debonair Joe	3	J.A. Krone	112	F J's Pace	116	American System	116	60,000	1:09.17	96
2003	Watchem Smokey	3	J.A. Krone	112	Our New Recruit	114	Hasty Kris	116	60,000	1:08.93	101
2004	Taste of Paradise	5	J. Valdivia Jr	122	Watchem Smokey	116	My Master	116	60,000	1:08.04	106

Beyer Index: 106.14

VAGRANCY HANDICAP (G2), 6 1/2 Furlongs, Fillies and Mares, 3-Year-Olds and Up, Belmont Park, 2004 Purse: $150,000

Year	Winner	Age	Jockey	Wt.	Second	Wt.	Third	Wt.	Win Value	Time	Beyer
1948	Conniver	4	T. Atkinson	121	Harmonica	120	Casa Camara	105	20,150	1:43.60	
1952	Marta	5	C. McCreary	117	Renew	118	Valadium	115	19,200	1:45.00	
1953	Home-Made	3	E. Guerin	114	Atalanta	123	Aesthete	108	17,100	1:24.60	
1954	Canadiana	4	C. O'Brien	115	Clear Dawn	113	Dispute	112	23,375	1:23.40	
1955	Searching	3	C. McCreary	111	Blue Banner	114	Parlo	129	19,675	1:23.60	
1955	Talora	4	H. Moreno	111	Tremor	107	Smart Devil	108	19,675	1:24.60	
1956	Miz Clementine	5	E. Arcaro	125	Searching	125	Happy Princ's	110	15,950	1:23.40	
1957	Plotter	4	P. Anderson	120	Searching	126	Nasrina	111	16,450	1:24.20	
1958	Outer Space	4	E. Nelson	121	Mlle. Dianne	113	Alanesian	121	18,940	1:23.80	
1959	Dandy Blitzen	4	P.I. Grimm	113	Honeys Gem	118	Idun	112	18,972	1:22.60	
1960	Mommy Dear	4	W. Boland	120	Wiggle II	121	Craftiness	107	18,680	1:22.60	
1961	Sun Glint	4	S. Cole	116	Undulation	116	Refute	113	16,022	1:23.60	
1962	Rose O'Neill	4	M. Ycaza	123	Play Time	114	Funloving	114	15,145	1:23.60	
1963	Cicada	4	L. Adams	127	Bramalea	120	My Portrait	114	14,137	1:22.80	
1964	No Resisting	4	J.L. Rotz	112	Oil Royalty	125	Look Ma	110	18,622	1:23.80	
1965	Affectionately	5	W. Blum	137	Sought After	111	Face the Facts	119	38,285	1:23.00	

Year	Winner	Age	Jockey	Wt.	Second	Wt.	Third	Wt.	Win Value	Time	Beyer
1966	Queen Empress	4	B. Baeza	123	Petite Rouge	113	M'nt Regina	113	17,647	1:23.20	
1967	Triple Brook	5	B. Baeza	116	Mac's Sparkler	121	Cestrum	111	17,940	1:23.80	
1968	Mac's Sparkler	6	W. Boland	121	Plucky Pan	112	Amerigo Lady	121	18,232	1:22.60	
1969	Grey Slacks	4	E. Belmonte	113	Heartland	125	Sarita	113	18,297	1:23.20	
1970	Process Shot	4	C. Baltazar	127	Powder Mountain	104	Native Partner	110	18,232	1:23.80	
1971	Golden Or	5	J.L. Rotz	114	Process Shot	124	Gay Missile	112	19,740	1:23.00	
1972	Chou Croute	4	R. Kotenko	124	Cyanome	114	Wire Chief	113	17,490	1:22.40	
1973	Krislin	4	M. Castaneda	113	Numbered Account	120	Fairway Flyer	115	16,845	1:22.60	
1974	Coraggioso	4	D. Brumfield	119	Ponte Vecchio	114	Lady Love	118	35,940	1:22.40	
1975	Honorable Miss	5	J. Vasquez	120	Viva la Vivi	126	Coraggioso	121	34,020	1:22.20	
1976	My Juliet	4	J. Velasquez	127	Shy Dawn	119	Kudara	116	32,790	1:22.00	
1977	Shy Dawn	6	A. Cordero Jr	119	Reasonable Win	118	Secret Lanvin	111	31,590	1:23.80	
1978	Dainty Dotsie	4	B. Phelps	124	What a Summer	127	Navajo Princess	110	32,160	1:21.80	
1979	Frosty Skater	4	D. MacBeth	119	Hagany	114	Skipat	126	33,240	1:23.20	
1980	Lady Lonsdale	5	L. Saumell	114	Peaceful Banner	108	Worthy Poise	112	32,700	1:24.40	
1981	Island Charm	4	R. Migliore	110	Contrary Rose	112	The Wheel Turns	114	32,520	1:23.60	
1982	Westport Native	4	J. Velasquez	115	Tell a Secret	115	Raise 'n Dance	113	32,580	1:22.60	
1983	Broom Dance	4	G. McCarron	121	Syrianna	114	Sprouted Rye	115	33,480	1:22.80	
1984	Grateful Friend	4	A. Cordero Jr	114	Pleasure Cay	118	Sweet Laughter	108	52,470	1:24.00	
1985	Nany	5	J. Velasquez	121	Sugar's Image	120	Brindy Brindy	113	52,020	1:23.80	
1986	Le Slew	5	J.A. Santos	113	Clocks Secret	121	Willowy Mood	114	54,630	1:23.80	
1987	North Sider	5	A. Cordero Jr	121	Storm and Sunshine	117	Funistrada	114	64,440	1:24.20	
1988	Grecian Flight	4	C. Perret	121	Nasty Affair	114	Tappiano	123	66,240	1:20.80	
1989	Aptostar	4	A. Cordero Jr	118	Toll Fee	110	Lambros	111	51,570	1:22.80	
1990	Mistaurian	4	W.H. McCauley	113	Feel the Beat	118	Fantastic Find	116	50,040	1:25.20	99
1991	Queena	5	M.E. Smith	115	Missy's Mirage	109	Gottagetitdone	111	55,080	1:22.00	99
1992	Nannerl	5	J.A. Santos	116	Serape	115	Makin Faces	112	51,210	1:22.40	96
1993	Spinning Round	4	J.F. Chavez	112	Reach Forever	114	Nannerl	118	52,740	1:24.40	102
1994	Sky Beauty	4	M.E. Smith	122	For All Seasons	114	Pamzig	107	48,855	1:21.60	97
1995	Sky Beauty	5	M.E. Smith	125	Aly's Conquest	111	Through the Door	110	47,865	1:21.40	105
1996	Twist Afleet	5	Krone J. A.	122	Smooth Charmer	111	Lottsa Talc	120	66,300	1:20.80	100
1997	Inquisitive Look	4	Chavez J. F.	111	Flat Fleet Feet	123	Mama Dean	114	64,800	1:22.00	108
1998	Chip	5	Bravo J.	115	Furlough	114	Parlay	115	48,945	1:15.60	97
1999	Gold Princess	4	Velazquez J. R.	114	Hurricane Bertie	114	Delta Music	113	63,840	1:16.40	97
2000	Country Hideaway	4	J.D. Bailey	117	Hurricane Bertie	118	Imperfect World	115	65,640	1:17.05	103
2001	Dat You Miz Blue	4	J.R. Velazquez	116	Dream Supreme	122	Katz Me If You Can	115	64,080	1:15.32	112
2002	Xtra Heat	4	H. Vega	127	Gold Mover	115	Shine Again	117	90,000	1:16.44	107
2003	Shawklit Mint	4	R. Migliore	115	Shine Again	121	Gold Mover	118	90,000	1:15.38	105
2004	Bear Fan	5	J.R. Velazquez	121	Smok'n Frolic	117	Aspen Gal	109	90,000	1:14.46	112

Beyer Index: 102.60

Run at 1 1/6 miles 1948, 1952; at 7 furlongs, 1953-1997

VALLEY STREAM (G3), 6 Furlongs, 2-Year-Old Fillies, Aqueduct, 2004 Purse: $101,500

Year	Winner	Age	Jockey	Wt.	Second	Wt.	Third	Wt.	Win Value	Time	Beyer
1995	Oxford Scholar	2	J.D. Bailey	112	Zee Lady	120	Stormy Krissy	112	32,430	1:12.00	85
1996	Dixie Flag	2	J.L. Samyn	116	Alyssum	114	Nimble Thread	114	32,490	1:10.00	102
1997	Cotton House Bay	2	J.F. Chavez	114	Foil	116	Kate Again	114	33,990	1:10.00	89
1998	Paula's Girl	2	J.R. Velazquez	116	President's Girl	114	Godmother	121	38,700	1:11.80	81
1999	Magicalmysterycat	2	M.E. Smith	121	Sahara Gold	121	Silentlea	121	49,800	1:10.40	86
2000	Astrapi	2	D. Nelson	116	Major Wager	116	Look of the Lynx	118	48,570	1:10.66	88
2001	Forest Heiress	2	R. Migliore	122	A New Twist	116	On Parade	116	48,465	1:08.66	105
2002	Randaroo	2	J.R. Velazquez	116	House Party	116	Fast Cookie	116	66,780	1:09.46	105
2003	Smokey Glacken	2	J.A. Santos	118	Baldomera	118	Stoic	118	67,320	1:11.18	77
2004	Megascape	2	J.R. Velazquez	122	Alfonsina	118	More Moonlight	118	63,900	1:10.38	88

Beyer Index: 90.60

VALLEY VIEW (G3), 1 1/16 Miles (Turf), 3-Year-Old Fillies, Keeneland Race Course, 2004 Purse: $116,300

Year	Winner	Age	Jockey	Wt.	Second	Wt.	Third	Wt.	Win Value	Time	Beyer
1991	La Gueriere	3	B. Peck	121	Dance o' My Life	121	Spanish Parade	121	29,250	1:43.40	97
1992	Spinning Round	3	F. Arguello Jr.	121	Shes Just Super	121	Enticed	121	23,870	1:41.40	89
1993	Weekend Madness	3	C. Woods Jr	121	Life Is Delicious	121	Augusta Springs	121	23,870	1:43.00	91
1994	Pharma	3	C.W. Antley	121	Mariah's Storm	121	Thread	121	50,747	1:42.40	102
1995	Country Cat	3	D.M. Barton	121	Appointed One	121	Petrouchka	121	50,840	1:44.80	101
1996	Turkappeal	3	D.M. Barton	117	Inner Circle	113	Mariuka	117	52,126	1:46.00	96
1997	Mingling Glances	3	J. Bravo	117	Majestic Sunlight	113	Fluid Move	113	52,592	1:44.40	101
1998	White Beauty	3	C. Borel	113	Shires Ende	117	Leaveemlaughing	117	56,591	1:43.00	91

Year	Winner	Age	Jockey	Wt.	Second	Wt.	Third	Wt.	Win Value	Time	Beyer
1999	Gimmeakissee	3	Cooksey P. J.	115	The Happy Hopper	119	Celestialbutterfly	119	70,122	1:42.00	90
2000	Good Game	3	P. Day	119	Impending Bear	119	Soccory	119	71,176	1:45.69	92
2001	Cozzy Corner	3	L.J. Meche	119			Quick Tip	123	46,576	1:42.93	90
	Chausson Poire	3	R.W. Woolsey	119							
2002	Bedanken	3	D.R. Pettinger	119	Mariensky	119	High Maintenance	119	71,734	1:44.24	95
2003	Dyna da Wyna	3	P. Day	119	Mexican Moonlight	116	Derrianne	123	69,998	1:43.54	94
2004	Sister Swank	3	P. Day	116	Jinny's Gold	116	Shadow Cast	119	72,106	1:46.75	90

Beyer Index: 94.21

ALFRED G. VANDERBILT HANDICAP (G2), 6 Furlongs, 3-Year-Olds and Up, Saratoga Race Course, 2004 Purse: $200,000

Year	Winner	Age	Jockey	Wt.	Second	Wt.	Third	Wt.	Win Value	Time	Beyer
1990	Prospectors Gamble	5	J.A. Garcia	122	Sewickley	115	Mr. Nickerson	122	50,400	1:09.20	113
1991	Kid Russell	5	R. Mojica Jr	115	Mr. Nasty	122	To Freedom	117	71,400	1:09.40	
1992	For Really	5	P. Day	115	Burn Fair	115	Drummond Lane	122	71,520	1:08.60	109
1993	Gold Spring	5	P. Day	119	Friendly Lover	122	Detox	115	70,680	1:09.20	108
1994	Boundary	4	J.R. Velazquez	117	Cherokee Run	120	I Can't Believe	113	65,880	1:08.60	113
1995	Not Surprising	5	R.G. Davis	115	Chimes Band	119	Mining Burrah	116	67,140	1:09.60	114
1996	Prospect Bay	4	J.D. Bailey	113	Honour and Glory	119	Lite the Fuse	123	65,760	1:08.20	123
1997	Royal Haven	5	R. Migliore	116	Cold Execution	116	Punch Line	120	65,220	1:09.60	114
1998	Kelly Kip	4	J.L. Samyn	114	Trafalger	114	Receiver	113	82,545	1:09.60	113
1999	Intidab	6	R.G. Davis	113	Artax	117	Yes It's True	117	90,000	1:09.00	120
2000	Successful Appeal	4	E.S. Prado	118	dq-Intidab	120	Chasin' Wimmin	112	120,000	1:09.21	120
	Intidab finished first but was disqualified and placed second										
2001	Five Star Day	5	G.K. Gomez	117	Delaware Township	116	Bonapaw	117	120,000	1:08.57	111
2002	Orientate	4	J.D. Bailey	121	Say Florida Sandy	115	Multiple Choice	112	120,000	1:09.72	112
2003	Private Horde	4	J. Lumpkins	115	Mountain General	118	Mike's Classic	114	120,000	1:09.18	117
2004	Speightstown	6	J.R. Velazquez	120	Clock Stopper	115	Gators n Bears	118	120,000	1:08.04	117

Beyer Index: 114.57

Run as A Phenomenon prior to 2000

VANITY HANDICAP (G1), 1 1/8 Miles, Fillies and Mares, 3-Year-Olds and Up, Hollywood Park, 2004 Purse: $245,000

Year	Winner	Age	Jockey	Wt.	Second	Wt.	Third	Wt.	Win Value	Time	Beyer
1940	Etoila II	6	N. Pariso	112	Flying Wild	122	Augury	114	7,275	1:37.20	
1941	Painted Veil	3	J. Westrope	113	Cute Trick	114	African Queen	109	7,350	1:43.40	
1944	Happy Issue	4	H. Woodhouse	122	Paula's Lulu	112	Regimental	116	17,150	1:44.00	
1945	Busher	3	J. Longden	126	Canina	114	Paula's Lulu	113	17,455	1:43.80	
1946	Be Faithful	4	J. Westrope	119	Lasting Peace	107	Double F.F.	112	17,850	1:42.00	
1947	Honeymoon	4	J. Westrope	119	Good Excuse	112	Nepotism	108	18,350	1:42.00	
1948	Hemet Squaw	4	R. Neves	114	Iron Maiden	108	Canina	112	16,350	1:43.60	
1949	Silver Drift	4	N. Brennan	105	Honeymoon	124	Good Excuse	112	19,300	1:43.60	
1950	Next Move	3	E. Guerin	128	Bewitch	124	Wistful	125	18,250	1:49.40	
1951	Bewitch	6	S. Brooks	125	Fleet Rings	106	Great Dream	108	16,950	1:42.80	
1952	Two Lea	6	H. Moreno	122	Wistful	112	Jennie Lee	117	15,900	1:43.40	
1953	Fleet Khal	3	J. Burton	114	A Gleam	126	Spanish Cream	125	15,500	1:42.40	
1954	Bubbley	4	R. York	116	Is Proud	118	Lap Full	107	15,350	1:49.60	
1955	Countess Fleet	4	J. Longden	126	Quillo Maid	107	Frosty Dawn	112	15,700	1:47.60	
1956	Mary Machree	5	B. Pulido	113	Our Betters	120	Solid Miss	119	22,200	1:48.60	
1957	Annie-Lu-San	4	W. Skuse	108	Miss Todd	115	Beautillion	122	23,400	1:48.80	
1958	Annie-Lu-San	5	W. Skuse	112	Ballet Khal	114	Summer Story	115	22,700	1:50.00	
1959	Zev's Joy	4	W. Shoemaker	115	Honeys Gem	129	Sybil Brand	109	21,550	1:48.20	
1959	Tender Size	3	W. Shoemaker	106	La Plume	112	Cellyar	112	21,050	1:48.00	
1960	Silver Spoon	4	J. Longden	130	Tritoma	107	Honeys Gem	118	22,950	1:49.00	
1961	Perizade	5	A. Maese	112	Mountain Glory	121	Solid Thought	113	26,900	1:48.60	
1962	Linita	5	J. Longden	126	Fun House	116	Kissing Belle	109	33,150	1:48.40	
1963	Table Mate	4	W. Shoemaker	120	Pixie Erin	118	Dingle Bay	108	33,150	1:48.40	
1964	Star Maggie	4	W. Shoemaker	115	Curious Clover	121	Jalousie II	123	34,700	1:48.40	
1965	Jalousie II	6	J. Longden	115	Yes Please	115	Savaii	121	31,550	1:48.40	
1966	Khal Ireland	6	S. Trevino	110	Ormea	114	Pollen	115	33,400	1:49.20	
1967	Desert Love	4	J. Lambert	114	Natashka	122	Ali's Theme	106	35,100	1:48.80	
1968	Gamely	4	W. Harris	131	Princessnesian	128	Desert Law	115	47,150	1:47.60	
1969	Desert Law	5	L. Pincay Jr	119	Gamely	128	Amerigo Lady	125	47,600	1:48.20	
1970	Commissary	4	W. Harris	118	Pattee Canyon	124	Tipping Time	120	46,500	1:47.60	
1971	Hi Q.	5	F. Toro	113	Manta	129	Swoon's Flower	116	57,000	1:48.80	
1972	Convenience	4	J. Lambert	121	Typecast	126	Street Dancer	115	55,900	1:47.40	
1973	Convenience	5	J.L. Rotz	121	Minstrel Miss	121	Susan's Girl	127	64,500	1:47.80	
1974	Tallahto	4	L. Pincay Jr	126	La Zanzara	120	Dogtooth Violet	118	66,500	1:47.00	
1975	Dulcia	6	W. Shoemaker	118	Susan's Girl	123	La Zanzara	120	67,500	1:47.40	
1976	Miss Toshiba	4	F. Toro	120	Bastonera II	120	Bold Baby	115	67,200	1:48.00	

Year	Winner	Age	Jockey	Wt.	Second	Wt.	Third	Wt.	Win Value	Time	Beyer
1977	Cascapedia	4	S. Hawley	129	Bastonera II	122	Swingtime	117	65,500	1:47.60	
1978	Afifa	4	W. Shoemaker	113	Drama Critic	117	Dottie's Doll	117	77,050	1:46.40	
1979	It's in the Air	3	W. Shoemaker	113	Country Queen	121	Innuendo	116	77,950	1:47.40	
1980	It's in the Air	4	L. Pincay Jr	120	Conveniently	111	Image of Reality	119	94,600	1:47.00	
1981	Track Robbery	5	P.A. Valenzuela	120	Princess Karenda	118	Save Wild Life	117	110,000	1:47.00	
1982	Sangue	4	W. Shoemaker	120	Track Robbery	123	Cat Girl	117	110,000	1:48.00	
1983	A Kiss for Luck	4	C.J. McCarron	114	Try Something New	118	Sangue	122	110,000	1:49.20	
1984	Princess Rooney	4	E. Delahoussaye	120	Adored	120	Salt Spring	113	150,500	1:46.20	
1985	Dontstop Themusic	5	A. Cordero Jr	118	Salt Spring	114	Estrapade	119	110,000	1:47.80	
1986	Magnificent Lindy	4	C.J. McCarron	116	Dontstop TheMusic	124	Outstandingly	118	137,000	2:02.00	
1987	Infinidad	5	C. Black	113	North Sider	121	Clabber Girl	115	110,000	2:00.60	
1988	Annoconnor	4	C. Black	114	Pen Bal Lady	119	Abloom II	113	110,000	1:49.20	
1989	Bayakoa	5	L. Pincay Jr	125	Flying Julia	112	Goodbye Halo	122	110,000	1:47.20	
1990	Gorgeous	4	E. Delahoussaye	124	Fantastic Look	112	Kelly	110	110,000	1:48.20	111
1991	Brought to Mind	4	P.A. Valenzuela	120	Fit to Scout	115	Luna Elegante	114	110,000	1:48.40	94
1992	Paseana	5	C.J. McCarron	127	Fowda	118	Re Toss	115	165,000	1:48.00	98
1993	Re Toss	6	E. Delahoussaye	115	Paseana	126	Guiza	114	165,000	1:47.80	104
1994	Potridee	5	A. Solis	114	Exchange	118	Golden Klair	119	165,000	1:48.00	103
1995	Private Persuasion	4	G.L. Stevens	114	Top Rung	116	Wandesta	119	165,000	1:48.20	108
1996	Jewel Princess	4	C.S. Nakatani	120	Serena's Song	125	Top Rung	116	150,000	1:47.00	116
1997	Twice the Vice	6	K.J. Desormeaux	121	Real Connection	114	Jewel Princess	123	240,000	1:46.40	110
1998	Escena	5	J.D. Bailey	124	Housa Dancer	115	Different	119	210,000	1:48.13	114
1999	Manistique	4	C.J. McCarron	122	Yolo Lady	115	Bella Chiarra	116	240,000	1:48.06	103
2000	Riboletta	5	C.J. McCarron	123	Speaking of Time	108	Excellent Meeting	120	180,000	1:48.54	111
2001	Gourmet Girl	6	G.L. Stevens	119	Lazy Slusan	122	Setareh	114	150,000	1:49.21	100
2002	Azeri	4	M. Smith	125	Affluent	119	Starrer	117	150,000	1:48.88	107
							Collect Call	115			
2003	Azeri	5	M.E. Smith	127	Sister Girl Blues	111	Bare Necessities	118	150,000	1:48.48	109
2004	Victory Encounter	4	A. Solis	116	Adoration	122	Star Parade	117	150,000	1:48.28	93

Beyer Index: 105.40

Distance 1 mile in 1940, 1 1/16 miles, 1941-53, 1 1.4 miles, 1986-87. Run at Santa Anita in 1949

VIOLET HANDICAP (G3), 1 1/16 Miles (Turf), Fillies and Mares, 3-Year-Olds and Up, The Meadowlands, 2004 Purse: $200,000

Year	Winner	Age	Jockey	Wt.	Second	Wt.	Third	Wt.	Win Value	Time	Beyer
1977	Lady Singer	4	A. Cordero Jr	113	Sans Arc	111	Jolly Song	112	35,035	1:48.40	
1978	Navajo Princess	4	C. Perret	115	Pressing Date	114	Fun Forever	118	35,360	1:44.00	
1979	Terpsichorist	4	M. Venezia	122	Spark of Life	111	Sisterhood	117	36,010	1:43.20	
1980	Producer	4	J. Fell	119	Champagne Ginny	116	Cannon Boy	113	26,325	1:41.60	
1980	The Very One	5	J. Velasquez	117	Hey Babe	115	Poppycock	113	26,145	1:42.40	
1981	Honey Fox	4	J.L. Samyn	120	Adlibber	117	Hemlock	116	33,690	1:41.40	
1982	Pat's Joy	4	J.D. Bailey	114	Prismatical	115	Kuja Happa	113	26,670	1:42.20	
1982	Dearly Too	3	J.L. Samyn	114	Tableaux	112	Dance Troupe	114	26,670	1:42.20	
1983	Twosome	4	J.D. Bailey	113	Princess Roberta	115	Svarga	112	26,535	1:41.20	
1983	Geraldine's Store	4	J.L. Samyn	117	Maidenhead	110	Mistretta	116	26,355	1:40.60	
1984	Rash but Royal	4	J.L. Kaenel	114	High Schemes	115	Candlelight Affair	110	49,020	1:42.20	
1984	Aspen Rose	4	J. Velasquez	114	It's Fine	112	If Winter Comes	113	49,020	1:42.00	
1985	Possible Mate	4	J.L. Samyn	119	Eastern Dawn	112	Carlypha	116	52,665	1:42.20	
1985	Vers la Caisse	4	R. Migliore	116	Cato Double	117	Forest Maiden	117	63,240	1:43.00	
1986	Lake Country	5	V. Bracciale Jr	118	Buckweed	111	Anka Germania	114	68,310	1:41.20	
1987	Videogenic	5	J. Cruguet	118	Spruce Fir	119	Cadabra Abra	120	45,180	1:42.00	
1987	Dismasted	5	J.L. Samyn	118	Small Virtue	118	Country Recital	113	44,790	1:41.60	
1988	Just Class	4	C.W. Antley	117	Shadowfay	109	Flying Katuna	115	53,400	1:40.20	
1988	Graceful Darby	4	R.P. Romero	115	Mystical Lass	112	Kim Kimmie	111	42,900	1:41.00	
1989	Gather the Clan	4	C. Perret	117	Sweet Blow Pop	119	Summer Secretary	117	55,260	1:39.60	
1990	Miss Josh	4	M.G. Pino	116	Summer Secretary	117	Leave It Be	118	54,750	1:40.00	101
1991	Southern Tradition	4	J.A. Santos	116	Songlines	115	Memories of Pam	113	45,000	1:43.60	98
1992	Highland Crystal	4	E.S Prado	116	Irish Actress	116	Navarra	111	45,000	1:41.20	96
1993	Mz. Zill Bear	4	E.S. Prado	113	Vivano	115	Topsa	113	45,000	1:44.40	97
1994	It's Personal	4	J.R. Velazquez	111	Carezza	115	Artful Pleasure	109	45,000	1:42.60	97
1995	Symphony Lady	5	J. Bravo	116	Kira's Dancer	115	Irish Linnet	122	60,000	1:45.40	95
1996	Plenty Of Sugar	5	R.E. Colton	117	Brushing Gloom	121	Hello Mom	115	60,000	1:48.60	96
1997	Sangria	4	R. Wilson	114	Fasta	113	Shemozzle	117	60,000	1:42.00	91
1998	Heaven's Command	4	R. Migliore	115	Maxzene	123	Oh Nellie	116	60,000	1:40.60	101
1999	Tookin Down	4	E.S. Prado	113	Proud Run	115	Darling Alice	113	90,000	1:42.20	94
2000	Follow the Money	4	C.J. McCarron	116	Melody Queen	116	Fickle Friends	114	90,000	1:42.65	97
2001	Clearly a Queen	4	C.C. Lopez	119	Salina's Gift	119	Smart as Scot	119	90,000	1:36.40	100
2002	Babae	6	J.F. Chavez	119	Platinum Tiara	115	Stylish	119	90,000	1:41.17	105
2003	Dancal	5	J. Castellano	116	Madeira Mist	116	Something Ventured	116	90,000	1:43.69	99
2004	Changing World	4	P. Fragoso	113	High Court	117	Ocean Drive	121	120,000	1:41.53	100

Beyer Index: 97.80

VIRGINIA DERBY (G3), 1 1/4 Miles (Turf),
3-Year-Olds, Colonial Downs, 2004 Purse: $500,000

Year	Winner	Age	Jockey	Wt.	Second	Wt.	Third	Wt.	Win Value	Time	Beyer
1998	Crowd Pleaser	3	J.L. Samyn	117	Distant Mirage	115	Errant Escort	115	150,000	2:00.28	99
1999	Phi Beta Doc	3	R.A. Dominguez	117	Passinetti	115	North East Bound	119	120,000	1:59.97	101
2000	Lightning Paces	3	G.W. Hutton	115	Sunspot	115	Blaze and Blues	115	120,000	2:02.18	92
2001	Potaro	3	B.E. Bartram	115	Bay Eagle	115	Confucius Say	115	120,000	2:02.17	96
2002	Orchard Park	3	E.S. Prado	119	Flying Dash	119	Touring England	115	300,000	2:03.10	99
2003	Silver Tree	3	E.S. Prado	115	Kicken Kris	115	King's Drama	115	300,000	2:01.11	96
2004	Kitten's Joy	3	E.S. Prado	117	Artie Schiller	117	Prince Arch	119	300,000	2:01.22	108

Beyer Index: 98.71

VOSBURGH (G1), 6 Furlongs,
3-Year-Olds and Up, Belmont Park, 2004 Purse: $490,000

Year	Winner	Age	Jockey	Wt.	Second	Wt.	Third	Wt.	Win Value	Time	Beyer
1940	Joe Schenck	5	R.L. Vedder	115	Nitro	108	T.M. Dorsett	120	4,400	1:23.20	
1941	Joe Schenck	6	W. Eads	109	The Chief	114	Roman	132	4,500	1:24.20	
1942	Parasang	5	D. Meade	112	Devil Diver	124	Rosetown	112	6,375	1:23.00	
1943	Wait a Bit	4	C. Givens	115	Sun Again	117	Adulator	110	6,600	1:23.20	
1944	Cassis	5	T. Atkinson	121			Ariel Lad	116	4,792	1:23.40	
	Paperboy	6	W. Mehrtens	115							
1945	Buzfuz	3	T. Luther	120	First Fiddle	130	Coincidence	112	7,765	1:23.20	
1946	Coincidence	4	T. Atkinson	118	Alexis	109	Polynesian	130	13,950	1:23.80	
1947	With Pleasure	4	J. Westrope	132	Bridal Flower	114	Rabies	105	19,900	1:23.40	
1948	Colosal	5	O. Scurlock	118	Spy Song	129	First Flight	124	22,300	1:23.80	
1949	Loser Weeper	4	E. Guerin	116	Lithe	105	Colosal	118	12,750	1:23.00	
1950	Tea-Maker	7	J. Robertson	118	More Sun	106	Piet	124	13,150	1:23.00	
1951	War King	4	C. McCreary	108	Bryan G.	122	General Staff	112	13,125	1:23.20	
	Miche finished first but was disqualified										
1952	Parading Lady	3	J.N. Hard'b'k	105	Tea-Maker	123	Cyclotron	110	16,150	1:23.80	
1953	Indian Land	4	T. Atkinson	111	Navy Page	115	Cold Command	118	17,200	1:23.60	
1954	Joe Jones	4	C. McCreary	116	Pet Bully	134	Hyphasis	111	17,800	1:23.80	
1955	Nance's Lad	3	H. Woodhouse	122	Red Hannigan	119	Bunny's Babe	110	16,650	1:24.00	
1956	Summer Tan	4	E. Guerin	124	Joe Jones	121	Le Beau Prince	121	17,200	1:23.60	
1957	Bold Ruler	3	E. Arcaro	130	TIck Tock	117	St. Amour II	114	16,000	1:21.40	
1958	Tick Tock	5	W. Shoemaker	118	Mister Jive	122	Nashville	116	15,187	1:23.00	
1959	Rick City	3	R.L. Stevenson	115	The Irishman	117	Nahodah	115	18,550	1:22.80	
1960	Mail Order	4	E. Nelson	110	Wiggle II	112	Four Lane	121	19,330	1:22.60	
1961	Gyro	4	B. Baeza	118	Rose Net	111	Humane Leader	110	14,950	1:23.20	
1962	Commend	4	T. Bove	109	Misty Day	119	Surfer	114	15,762	1:22.20	
1963	Ornamento	3	B. Baeza	111	Uppercut	112	Merry Ruler	120	15,275	1:23.80	
1964	Affectionately	4	H. Grant	120	Red Gar	113	Bonjour	114	18,622	1:22.00	
1965	R. Thomas	4	L. Adams	117	Choker	112	Pia Star	126	39,325	1:23.00	
1966	Gallant Romeo	5	K. Knapp	123	Davis II	122	Flag Raiser	121	37,505	1:22.80	
1967	Dr. Fager	3	B. Baeza	128	Jim J.	115	R. Thomas	122	37,310	1:21.60	
1968	Dr. Fager	4	B. Baeza	139	Kissin' George	127	Jim J.	125	37,050	1:20.20	
1969	Ta Wee	3	J.L. Rotz	123	Plucky Lucky	116			38,220	1:21.60	
					Rising Market	120					
1970	Best Turn	4	L. Adams	115	True North	115	Ocean Bar	113	38,545	1:21.40	
1971	Duck Dance	4	J. Ruane	122	Summer Air	120	Coup Landing	118	36,660	1:21.20	
1972	Triple Bend	4	L. Pincay Jr	116	Tunex	112	Favorecidian	117	35,310	1:22.00	
1973	Aljamin	3	A. Cordero Jr	118	Highbinder	115	Timeless Moment	112	33,660	1:21.20	
1974	Forego	4	H. Gustines	131	Stop the Music	118	Prince Dantan	119	35,550	1:21.40	
1975	No Bias	5	A. Santiago	116	Step Nicely	126	Lonetree	117	34,590	1:22.80	
1976	My Juliet	4	A.S. Black	120	It's Freezing	113	Bold Forbes	126	31,980	1:21.80	
	Bold Forbes finished second but was disqualified and placed third										
1977	Affiliate	3	C. Perret	114	Broadway Forli	118	Great Above	112	49,905	1:21.00	
1978	Dr. Patches	4	A. Cordero Jr	117	What a Summer	124	Sorry Lookin	109	48,960	1:21.00	
1979	General Assembly	3	J. Vasquez	123	Dr. Patches	126	Syncopate	126	48,195	1:21.00	
1980	Plugged Nickle	3	C.B. Asmussen	123	Dave's Friend	126		0	67,440	1:21.40	
1981	Guilty Conscience	5	C.B. Asmussen	126	Rise Jim	126	Well Decorated	123	67,921	1:22.00	
1982	Engine One	4	R. Hernandez	126	Gold Beauty	120	Maudlin	126	65,760	1:23.80	
	Mike Mitchell finished second but was disqualified and placed fourth										
1983	A Phenomenon	3	A. Cordero Jr	123	Fit to Fight	126	Deputy Minister	126	69,000	1:21.00	
1984	Track Barron	3	A. Cordero Jr	123	Timeless Native	126	Raja's Shark	123	109,800	1:22.00	
1985	Another Reef	3	N. Santagata	124	Pancho Villa	124	Whoop Up	126	102,420	1:21.80	
1986	King's Swan	6	J.A. Santos	126	Love That Mac	126	Cutlass Reality	126	141,840	1:21.80	
1987	Groovy	4	A. Cordero Jr	126	Moment of Hope	126	Sun Master	126	139,680	1:22.60	
1988	Mining	4	R.P. Romero	126	Gulch	126	High Brite	126	133,920	1:22.40	
1989	Sewickley	4	R.P. Romero	126	Once Wild	126	Mr. Nickerson	123	135,120	1:23.00	
1990	Sewickley	5	A. Cordero Jr	126	Sunshine Jimmy	122	Glitterman	126	142,080	1:21.00	118
1991	Housebuster	4	C. Perret	126	Senator to Be	126	Sunshine Jimmy	126	120,000	1:21.80	115
1992	Rubiano	5	J.A. Krone	126	Sheikh Albadou	126	Salt Lake	123	120,000	1:22.80	113

Year	Winner	Age	Jockey	Wt.	Second	Wt.	Third	Wt.	Win Value	Time	Beyer
1993	Birdonthewire	4	M.E. Smith	126	Take Me Out	126	Lion Cavern	126	120,000	1:22.20	114
1994	Harlan	5	J.D. Bailey	126	American Chance	126	Cherokee Run	126	120,000	1:21.80	107
1995	Not Surprising	5	R.G. Davis	126	You and I	126	Our Emblem	126	120,000	1:22.40	106
1996	Langfuhr	4	J.F. Chavez	126	Honour and Glory	122	Lite the Fuse	126	120,000	1:21.20	113
1997	Victory Cooley	4	J.F. Chavez	126	Score a Bride	126	Tale of the Cat	122	120,000	1:22.00	113
1998	Affirmed Success	4	J.F. Chavez	126	Stormin Fever	126	Tale of the Cat	126	150,000	1:21.99	119
1999	Artax	5	J.F. Chavez	126	Stormin Fever	126	Mountain Top	126	150,000	1:21.65	111
2000	Trippi	3	J.D. Bailey	123	More Than Ready	123	One Way Love	126	180,000	1:21.66	111
2001	Left Bank	4	J.R. Velazquez	126	Squirtle Squirt	123	Big E E	126	180,000	1:20.73	118
2002	Bonapaw	6	G. Melancon	126	Aldebaran	126	Voodoo	126	180,000	1:22.34	112
2003	Ghostzapper	3	J. Castellano	123	Aggadan	126	Posse	123	300,000	1:14.72	116
2004	Pico Central	5	V. Espinoza	124	Voodoo	124	Speightstown	124	300,000	1:09.74	114

Beyer Index: 113.33

For all ages prior to 1958. Run at Aqueduct in 1959, 1961-74, 1976-77, 1979-83, 1985-86. Distance 7 furlongs prior to 2003; at 6 1/2 furlongs in 2003.

MARTHA WASHINGTON BREEDERS' CUP (G3), 1 1/16 Miles (Turf), 3-Year-Old Fillies, Pimlico, 2004 Purse: $148,500

Year	Winner	Age	Jockey	Wt.	Second	Wt.	Third	Wt.	Win Value	Time	Beyer
1982	Smart Heiress	3	M. Venezia	115	Ring Dancer		Zvetlana		14,445	1:41.40	
1982	Party Bonnet	3	J. Walford	110	Susie Cherie		Dancing Secret		15,075	1:43.00	
1984	Berkeley Court	3	J.L. Samyn	113	La Reine Elaine		Tagalog		34,200	1:43.20	
1985	Duty Dance	3	J. Cruguet	114	Jolly Saint		A Joyful Spray		37,765	1:49.20	
1986	Toes Knows	3	D. Wright	124	Spruce Fir		CountryRecital		38,740	1:47.20	
1987	Cutlasee	3	A. Stacy	109	Doubles Partner		Kerygma		37,229	1:45.80	
1988	Timely Business	3	T. Vega	112	Quaff	115	Siggebo	119	62,250	1:43.60	
1989	Yestday's Kisses	3	F. Lovato Jr	114	Whip Cream	110	Tia Juanita	114	45,000	1:46.20	
1990	Southern Tradition	3	E.S. Prado	120	Starfield	113	Secret Advice	119	45,000	1:40.40	
1991	Polish Holiday	3	M.G. Pino	113	Fashion Miss	114	Monica Faye	115	45,000	1:49.20	
1992	Mz. Zill Bear	3	S.D. Hamilton	112	Star Minister	120	Tootsie	112	45,000	1:48.60	
1993	Tennis Lady	3	A.J. Seefeldt	113	Putthepowdertoit	113	Missymooiloveyou	113	45,000	1:42.80	95
1994	Tee Kay	3	Wilson R	115	Avie's Fancy	119	Lady Ellen	115	60,000	1:45.20	97
1995	Strawberry Reason	3	Prado ES	117	Blue Sky Princess	122	Rosebud	117	30,000	2:15.20	85
1996	Silent Greeting	3	Reynolds L. C.	119	Rare Blend	122	Stop That Broad	115	60,000	1:43.40	102
1997	Cotton Carnival	3	Pino M. G.	122	Romantic Notions	115	Bursting Forth	115	60,000	1:46.20	83
1998	Mysterious Moll	3	Wilson R.	118	Wolfer	114	Proud Owner	117	90,000	1:42.20	94
1999	Colstar	3	Delgado A.	119	Polaire	122	Jazz	115	60,000	1:45.60	95
2000	Tippity Witch	3	J.L. Espinoza	115	Senza Paura	117	Windsong	117	60,000	1:42.20	95
2002	Martha's Music	3	H. Vega	115	Bells for Marlin	122	Restraining Order	115	90,000	1:45.62	82
2003	Derrianne	3	B. Blanc	122	Chic Joy	115	Twining and Dining	115	90,000	1:46.53	92
2004	Western Ransom	3	R. Fogelsonger	122	Plenty	115	With Affection	115	90,000	1:43.26	91

Beyer Index: 91.91

WASHINGTON PARK HANDICAP (G2), 1 3/16 Miles, 3-Year-Olds and Up, Arlington Park, 2004 Purse: $350,000

Year	Winner	Age	Jockey	Wt.	Second	Wt.	Third	Wt.	Win Value	Time	Beyer
1926	Smiling Gus	3	L. Edwards	97	Cudgeller	103	Arabian	96	10,710	2:10.60	
1927	Girl Scout	5	S. Cooper	104	Sanola	109	Pr. of Wales	129	6,490	1:15.00	
1929	Misstep	4	C. McCrossen	124	Golden Prince	117	Cayuga	112	5,510	1:12.20	
1930	Misstep	5	E. Shropshire	126	Brown Wisdow	123	My Dandy	120	6,410	1:12.40	
1931	Tannery	4	R. Heigle	112	Don Leon	111	Stock Market	108	6,210	1:13.00	
1932	Gold Step	5	H. Schutte	107	Silverdale	118	Ladder	112	5,290	1:12.00	
1933	No More	5	E. Arcaro	109	Mr. Sponge	122	Isaiah	111	2,295	1:12.60	
1934	Isaiah	4	J. Kacala	110	Some Pomp	102	Advancing Anna	112	2,240	1:12.00	
1935	Late Date	6	A. Robertson	111	Calumet Dick	102	Watch Him	110	4,220	2:06.80	
1936	Where Away	4	C. Corbett	115	Count Arthur	114	Black Gift	110	8,080	2:03.00	
1938	Dora May	5	K. McCombs	108	Mad Money	114	Chance Ray	106	1,650	1:12.00	
1939	Star Border	3	A. Bodiou	105	Viscounty	117	Some Count	112	4,350	1:50.20	
1940	War Plumage	4	N. Wall	110	Viscounty	118	Burning Star	109	24,800	2:04.00	
1941	Big Pebble	5	J. Westrope	120	Bushwhacker	110	Haltal	115	25,500	2:03.20	
1942	Marriage	6	C. Corbett	114	Alsab	121	Thumbs Up	102	25,200	2:02.40	
1943	Thumbs Up	4	O. Grons	120	Royal Nap	107	Marriage	124	25,950	2:05.00	
1944	Equifox	7	A. Bodiou	113	Daily Trouble	105	Some Chance	109	40,700	2:03.00	
1945	Busher	3	J. Longden	115	Armed	120	Take Wing	112	40,200	2:01.80	
1946	Armed	5	D. Dodson	130	Challenge Me	112	Take Wing	110	39,300	2:01.00	
1947	Armed	6	D. Dodson	130	Honeymoon	111	With Pleasure	123	37,500	2:02.00	
1948	Fervent	4	N.L. Pierson	120	Eternal Reward	119	Stud Poker	118	36,000	2:04.80	
1949	Coaltown	4	S. Brooks	130	Armed	110	Lithe	103	34,800	2:03.80	
1950	Inseparable	5	K. Church	110	Fervent	107	Curandero	113	33,000	2:06.20	
1951	Curandero	5	A. Gomez	115	Oil Capitol	116	County Delight	123	113,950	1:34.60	

Year	Winner	Age	Jockey	Wt.	Second	Wt.	Third	Wt.	Win Value	Time	Beyer
1952	Crafty Admiral	4	E. Guerin	128	To Market	123	Sickle's Image	110	119,900	1:36.80	
1953	Sickle's Image	5	W.M. Cook	106	Ruhe	116	Indian Hemp	114	108,500	1:36.80	
1954	Pet Bully	6	W. Hartack	119	Good Call	108	Spur On	115	110,900	1:34.40	
1955	Jet Action	4	W. Shoemaker	120	Duke's Lea	117	Helioscope	130	96,000	1:34.00	
1956	Swaps	4	W. Shoemaker	130	Summer Tan	115	Sea O Erin	112	85,750	1:33.40	
1957	Pucker Up	4	W. Shoemaker	111	Find	122	Swoon's Son	130	80,800	1:34.80	
1958	Clem	4	J. Sellers	110	Round Table	131	Nadir	114	94,175	1:34.00	
1959	Round Table	5	W. Shoemaker	132	Dunce	114	Belleau Chief	112	72,650	1:47.20	
1960	T.V. Lark	3	J. Sellers	116	Dotted Swiss	123	Talent Show	118	68,600	1:34.20	
1961	Chief of Chiefs	4	C. Meaux	112	Talent Show	110	Run for Nurse	112	72,900	1:34.60	
1962	Prove It	5	W. Shoemaker	131	Try Cash	114	Cadiz	115	68,450	1:33.80	
1963	Crimson Satan	4	H. Hinojosa	126	Piper's Son	110	B. Major	117	68,150	1:49.60	
1964	Gun Bow	4	W. Blum	132	Lemon Twist	111	Going Aboad	114	69,750	1:51.00	
1965	Take Over	4	L. Kunitake	110	Chieftain	126	Gallant Romeo	120	68,600	1:35.20	
1966	Bold Bidder	4	P. Anderson	120	Tom Rolfe	128	Tronado	117	64,200	1:32.80	
1967	Handsome Boy	4	E. Belmonte	122	Pretense	128	Bold Tactics	116	68,000	1:37.60	
1968	Dr. Fager	4	B. Baeza	134	Racing Room	116	Info	112	67,700	1:32.20	
1969	Night Invader	3	D.E. Whited	112	Out the Window	112	Rising Market	121	68,050	1:36.20	
1970	Doc's T.V.	4	D.E. Whited	114	Famed Prince	115	Strong Strong	114	33,900	1:36.60	
1972	Well Mannered	4	M. Solomone	120	No No Billy	116	Intensitivo	112	33,500	1:34.60	
1973	Burning On	5	D. Richard	114	New Hope	113	Vegas Vic	109	32,800	2:02.20	
1974	Super Sail	6	W. Gavidia	118	Smooth Dancer	112	J'a D'm Aw'y	111	38,300	2:03.00	
1975	Hasty Flyer	4	H. Arroyo	115	Group Plan	116	Yaki King	113	38,100	1:48.60	
1976	Double Edge Sword	6	H. Arroyo	116	Zografos	113	Proponent	109	70,400	1:48.20	
1977	Majestic Light	4	M. Venezia	120	Fifth Marine	122	Improviser	122	54,180	1:48.00	
1978	That's a Nice	4	D. Richard	116	Court Open	115	Improviser	117	53,100	1:50.60	
1979	That's a Nice	5	I.J. Jimenez	117	Calderina	113	Me Good Man	112	52,320	1:50.00	
1980	Spectacular Bid	4	W. Shoemaker	130	Hold Your Tricks	119	Architect	119	155,000	1:46.20	
1981	Rossi Gold	5	P. Day	119	John's Monster	112	Lord Gallant	114	81,870	1:48.60	
1982	Summer Advocate	5	P. Day	115	Mythical Ruler	112	Law Me	112	64,920	1:49.80	
1983	Harham's Sizzler	4	J.L Diaz	112	Listcapade	122	Stage Reviewer	112	67,620	1:49.80	
1984	Thumbsucker	5	S. Maple	115	Timeless Native	122	Le Cou Cou	122	80,940	1:48.60	
1985	Par Flite	4	E. Fires	112	Big Pistol	122	Timeless Native	122	78,300	1:47.60	
1987	Taylor's Special	6	J. Lively	118	Blue Buckaroo	120	Fuzzy	114	61,965	1:51.60	
1989	Blushing John	4	P. Day	124	Grantley	112	Paramount Jet	113	48,030	1:50.80	
1990	Lay Down	6	W.H. McCauley	115	Sir Wesley	112	Mercedes Won	112	64,680	1:48.40	108
1991	Black Tie Affair	5	S.J. Sellers	120	Summer Squall	119	Secret Hello	114	150,000	1:49.40	117
1992	Irish Swap	5	B.E. Poyadou	118	Clever Trevor	119	Barkerville	113	90,000	1:47.80	114
1993	Powerful Punch	4	C.C. Bourque	114	Memo	115	Northern Trend	113	120,000	1:50.00	105
1994	Brother Brown	4	P. Day	117	Eequalsmcsquared	113	Antrim Rd.	113	120,000	1:49.60	110
1996	Polar Expedition	5	M. Guidry	115	Knockadoon	115	Tejano Run	117	120,000	1:49.80	111
1997	Beboppin Baby	4	G.K. Gomez	112	City By Night	116	Stephanotis	118	90,000	1:49.00	109
2000	Blazing Sword	6	J.A. Rivera II	113	Mula Gula	114	Nite Dreamer	116	150,000	1:50.59	106
2001	Guided Tour	5	L. Melancon	116	A Fleets Dancer	115	Duckhorn	114	240,000	2:00.76	117
2002	Tenpins	4	R.J. Albarado	116	Generous Rosi	115	Bonus Pack	115	240,000	1:55.07	108
2003	Perfect Drift	4	P. Day	120	Aeneas	115	Flatter	114	240,000	1:55.49	112
2004	Eye of the Tiger	4	E. Razo Jr	116	Olmodavor	121	Congrats	116	210,000	1:56.87	102

Beyer Index: 109.92

WEST VIRGINIA DERBY (G3), 1 1/8 Miles, 3-Year-Olds, Mountaineer Park, 2004 Purse: $600,000

Year	Winner	Age	Jockey	Wt.	Second	Wt.	Third	Wt.	Win Value	Time	Beyer
1958	Sea Hymn	3	J. Contreras	117	Dixie Hill	119	Entangler	114	9,750	1:5520	
1959	Redbird Wish	3	W. Chamber	119	Royal Border	111	Idle Time	117	9,500	1:52.80	
1961	Dip and Whirl	3	B. Walt	114	Besteater	114	Royal Case	114	2,410	1:54.60	
1963	Etimota	3	F. Green	116	Count John	105	Dr. Scott	117	3,570	1:52.00	
1964	Peter Le Grand	3	F. Green	124	A.J.'s Winn	114	Navy Rocket	118	3,025	1:53.00	
1965	Pantuity	3	F. Green	115	Cloud Chief	118	Jayell	115	5,559	1:53.00	
1966	Kerensa	3	F. Green	119	Bellofthefleet	113	Dear Mike	118	5,472	1:50.40	
1967	Miracle Hill	3	R.C. Gallimore	121	More of Mort	126	Air Boat	115	5,498	1:53.20	
1968	Chargertown	3	R. Nakama	115	Son I Rob	118	Frosty Hal	115	10,273	1:54.40	
1969	Roman Partner	3	M. Solomone	121	Polar Traffic	124	Silver Alley	121	17,794	1:51.80	
1970	Two Joys	3	J. Imparato	118	Captain Nash	124	Delicate John	118	18,167	1:53.00	
1971	Trico O'Erin	3	T. DePalo	118	Spoiled Kid	126	Comedy Hour	116	18,785	1:52.20	
1972	Family Table	3	M. Solomone	118	Extra Man	121	Rollin Roman	118	13,000	1:50.60	
1972	Bold Nobleman	3	J. Kelly	118	Aerodrome	118	Prince Selari	115	13,325	1:49.40	
1973	Blue Chip Dan	3	M. Solomone	118	Dr. Pantano	121	Double Edge Sword	124	20,930	1:49.20	
1974	Park Guard	3	B.M. Feliciano	124	Sea Songster	126	Sahib Nearco	124	32,500	1:47.40	
1975	At the Front	3	A. Santiago	117	My Friend Gus	117	Packer Captain	117	32,500	1:48.60	
1976	Wardlaw	3	J. Tejeira	121	American Trader	115	Joachim	121	32,500	1:47.60	
1977	Best Person	3	V. Bracciale Jr.	115	Swoon Swept	115	A Letter to Harry	115	32,500	1:48.60	

Year	Winner	Age	Jockey	Wt.	Second	Wt.	Third	Wt.	Win Value	Time	Beyer
1978	Beau Sham	3	P. Day	115	Silent Cal	115	Morning Frolic	115	32,500	1:48.60	
1979	Architect	3	S.A. Spencer	115	Sir Prince P.	115	Lt. Bert	115	32,500	1:51.00	
1980	Summer Advocate	3	W.L. Floyd	115	Lucky Pluck	115	Foolish Move	115	32,500	1:50.80	
1981	Park's Policy	3	J.S. Lloyd	115	Diverse Dude	115	Iron Gem	115	22,750	1:49.60	
1981	Johnny Dance	3	F. Lovato Jr.	115	Master Tommy	115	Amasham	115	22,750	1:47.80	
1988	Old Stories	3	R. Hernandez	114	Viva Deputy	117	Rising Colors	112	60,000	1:52.20	
1989	Doc's Leader	3	W. Fox Jr.	114	Halo Hansom	120	Downtown Davey	117	60,000	1:50.00	
1990	Challenge My Duty	3	L. Ayarza	113	My Other Brother	115	Gay's Best Boy	115	60,000	1:49.60	
1998	Da Devil	3	J. Court	113	One Bold Stroke	122	Jess M	115	120,000	1:48.80	99
1999	Stellar Brush	3	J. Stokes	122	American Spirit	113	Harry's Halo	119	150,000	1:49.02	108
2000	Mass Market	3	R. Wilson	115	Hal's Hope	122	Bet on Red	122	180,000	1:49.94	100
2001	Western Pride	3	D. Whitney	113	Saratoga Games	115	Thunder Blitz	119	300,000	1:47.20	102
2002	Wiseman's Ferry	3	J.F. Chavez	122	The Judge Sez Who	115	Captain Squire	115	360,000	1:49.63	104
2003	Soto	3	R.A. Dominguez	111	Dynever	117	Colita	111	360,000	1:46.29	114
2004	Sir Shackleton	3	R. Bejarano	117	Pollard's Vision	119	Britt's Jules	115	363,000	1:49.16	105

Beyer Index: 104.57

WESTCHESTER HANDICAP (G3), 1 Mile, 3-Year-Olds and Up, Belmont Park, 2004 Purse: $109,500

Year	Winner	Age	Jockey	Wt.	Second	Wt.	Third	Wt.	Win Value	Time	Beyer
1918	George Smith	5	F. Robinson	127	Star Master	118	Corn Tassel	107	2,150	1:51.60	
1919	Star Master	5	C. Kummer	125	Blairgowrie	95	W. Machine	95	2,275	2:09.20	
1920	Mad Hatter	4	E. Sande	126	War Note	95	Cromwell	100	4,550	2:07.40	
1921	Yellow Hand	4	C.H. Miller	132	Bon Homme	110	Thunder Clap	123	4,850	2:05.60	
1922	Prince James	4	E. Taplin	119	Mad Hatter	126	Horologe	99	5,150	1:53.00	
1923	Hephaistos	4	M. Fator	100	Cherry Pie	112	Nedna	103	4,860	1:53.40	
1924	Mad Play	3	L. Fator	124	Horologe	105	Wilkes Br'e	98	5,510	1:51.60	
1925	Aga Khan	4	F. Stevens	129	Catalan	106	Turf Idol	107	4,990	1:51.80	
1926	Cloudland	4	L. Fator	109	Laura Dianti	104	Copiapo	109	4,970	1:53.80	
1927	Light Carbine	4	C. Zoeller	106	Herodian	106	Cloudland	106	5,390	1:53.60	
1928	Arcturus	3	G. Schreiner	100	Excalibur	114	Wee Burn	103	4,970	1:53.00	
1929	Genie	4	W. Kelsay	110	Sud Edwin	124	Low Gear	105	4,930	1:52.00	
1930	Questionnaire	3	C. Kurtsinger	129	Sun Edwin	118	Sun Mission	115	4,650	1:53.60	
1931	Dr. Freeland	5	J. Bethel	120	Reveille Boy	126	Mad Career	118	2,880	1:53.60	
1934	King Saxon	3	T. Mailey	118	Halcyon	103			1,985	1:54.40	
1935	Good Harvest	3	S. Renick	106	Spanish Way	105	Vicares	107	4,550	1:51.80	
1936	Thorson	4	E. Arcaro	112	Piccolo	107	Seabiscuit	119	4,790	1:52.00	
1937	Thorson	5	E. Roberts	116	Busy K.	105	Da'ger Point	107	7,550	1:54.00	
1938	Great Union	3	S. Renick	107	Esposa	124	Idle Miss	115	6,550	1:52.00	
1939	Third Degree	3	E. Arcaro	123	Don Mike	116	Thanksgiving	118	7,250	1:51.40	
1940	Mioland	3	L. Haas	119	Foxbrough	110	Hash	122	15,950	2:00.20	
1941	Gramps	4	H. Lindberg	105	Tola Rose	107	Boysy	113	19,650	1:59.80	
1942	Riverland	4	A. Robertson	114	Tola Rose	108	Alsab	124	19,850	1:56.40	
1943	Slide Rule	3	J. Westrope	119	Boysy	115	First Fiddle	114	22,700	1:57.60	
1944	Seven Hearts	4	P. Keiper	124	Good Morning	109	Stymie	109	23,515	1:58.00	
1945	Stymie	4	R. Permane	125	Buzfuz	116	Olympic Zenith	117	38,765	1:56.80	
1946	Assault	3	E. Arcaro	122	Lucky Draw	128	Lets Dance	104	38,600	1:56.40	
1947	Bridal Flower	4	W. Mehrtens	108	With Pleasure	130	Donor	112	39,700	1:59.20	
1948	Better Self	3	D. Gorman	119	War Trophy	110	Phalanx	126	39,600	1:57.80	
1949	Three Rings	4	H. Woodhouse	116	Delegate	120	Royal Governor	123	20,200	1:56.80	
1950	Palestinian	4	S. Boulmetis	123	Sunglow	113	Chicle II	122	25,100	1:57.20	
1951	Bryan G.	4	O. Scurlock	117	County Delight	124	Bed o' Roses	116	21,100	1:49.20	
1952	Battlefield	4	A. Schmidl	123	Tom Fool	125	Alerted	125	38,350	1:50.20	
1953	Cold Command	4	H. Woodhouse	112	Crafty Admiral	128	Jampol	112	38,150	1:49.60	
1959	Mystic II	5	M. Sorrentino	110	Whitley	110	Slaipner	119	18,452	1:43.60	
1960	Vendetta	4	J. Leonard	112	Big Effort	109	Mystic II	116	19,005	1:35.20	
1961	Mail Order	5	L. Adams	114	Pied d'Or	115	Talent Show	116	18,655	1:34.00	
1962	Globemaster	4	J.L. Rotz	125	Rideabout	113	Merry Ruler	118	18,687	1:34.60	
1963	Sunrise County	4	J.L. Rotz	111	Key Issue	112	Dedimoud	111	18,005	1:34.20	
1964	Rocky Link	4	D. Pierce	113	Bonjour	115	Morry E.	114	18,947	1:35.20	
1965	Tibaldo	5	B. Baeza	116	Quita Dude	113	P'r of Destiny	115	39,130	1:36.60	
1966	R. Thomas	5	L. Adams	116	Cupid	117	Seaman	114	37,375	1:36.20	
1967	Advocator	4	M. Ycaza	114	Our Michael	116	Model Fool	112	35,815	1:35.20	
1968	R. Thomas	7	J. Nichols	118	Peter Piper	117	Grace Born	111	36,335	1:35.40	
1969	Iron Ruler	4	A. Cordero Jr	117	Beaukins	113	Sky Count	114	36,335	1:35.00	
1970	Dewan	5	E. Belmonte	119	Gaelic Dancer	114	Gleaming Light	117	37,440	1:34.20	
1971	Never Bow	5	V. Tejada	124	Knight in Armor	111	Dan Patch	113	35,580	1:36.40	
1972	Autobiography	4	A. Cordero Jr	119	Tunex	119	Native Royalty	118	34,560	1:34.20	
1973	North Sea	4	R.C. Smith	117	Forage	116	Summer Guest	118	33,990	1:33.60	
1974	Dundee Marmalade	6	M. Hole	113	Infuriator	113	Prove Out	126	32,940	1:36.00	
1975	Step Nicely	5	J. Velasquez	126	Tambac	116	Onion	119	33,900	1:34.00	

Year	Winner	Age	Jockey	Wt.	Second	Wt.	Third	Wt.	Win Value	Time	Beyer
1976	Double Edge Sword	6	A. Cordero Jr	114	Dr. Emil	116	Bold and F'y	111	34,170	1:33.40	
1977	Cinteelo	4	E. Maple	113	Turn and Count	124	Cojak	120	33,090	1:43.40	
1978	Pumpkin Moonshine	4	D.A. Borden	105	Lynn Davis	115	Sharpstone	111	32,250	1:44.40	
1979	Vencedor	5	R. Hernandez	126	Don Aronow	108	Coverack	114	33,060	1:44.00	
1980	Nice Catch	6	J. Fell	120	Ardaluan	119	Lark Oscillation	115	34,020	1:36.80	
1981	Dunham's Gift	4	M. Venezia	115	Ring of Light	114	Dr. Blum	124	33,000	1:35.00	
1982	John Casey	5	J. Fell	114	Brasher Doubloon	111	Accipiter's Hope	120	33,090	1:38.00	
1982	Fabulous Find	4	J.O. Cintron	109	In From Dixie	122	Princelet	126	33,330	1:38.00	
1983	Singh Tu	4	J.L. Samyn	109	Master Digby	114	Fabulous Find	114	33,780	1:35.20	
1984	Jacque's Tip	4	A. Cordero Jr	114	Minstrel Glory	111	Havagreatdate	112	55,440	1:41.80	
1985	Verbarctic	5	G. McCarron	114	Moro	122	Fighting Fit	124	53,460	1:36.60	
1986	Garthorn	6	R. Meza	120	Ends Well	115	Grand Rivulet	110	75,240	1:33.80	
1987	King's Swan	7	J.A. Santos	122	Cutlass Reality	114	Landing Plot	115	69,120	1:36.20	
1988	Faster Than Sound	4	J.A. Krone	113	Ron Stevens	109	King's Swan	133	108,000	1:34.40	
1989	Lord of the Night	6	J. Velasquez	115	Dancing Spree	112	Congeleur	112	71,040	1:35.60	
1990	Once Wild	5	A. Cordero Jr	121	Its Acedemic	116			67,800	1:35.00	107
					King's Swan	113					
1991	Rubiano	4	J.D. Bailey	111	Senor Speedy	113	Killer Diller	115	71,520	1:34.80	114
1992	Rubiano	5	J.A. Santos	117	Out of Place	115	Wild Away	111	68,880	1:34.80	107
1993	Bill of Rights	4	J.L. Samyn	110	Fly So Free	118	Loach	113	72,720	1:34.60	107
1994	Virginia Rapids	4		116	Colonial Affair	121	Cherokee Run	119	65,640	1:34.40	107
1995	Mr. Shawklit	4	Luzzi MJ	112	Devil His Due	124	Our Emblem	110	65,760	1:34.60	107
1996	Valid Wager	4	Pezua J. M.	115	Pat N Jac	111	More To Tell	118	66,240	1:34.60	107
1997	Pacific Fleet	5	Alvarado F. T.	114	Circle of Light	110	Stalwart Member	114	65,940	1:33.80	111
1998	Wagon Limit	4	Samyn J. L.	114	Draw	113	Lucayan Prince	116	66,420	1:34.00	118
1999	Mr. Sinatra	5	Lopez C. C.	116	Laredo	114	Brushing Up	113	64,202	1:35.00	105
2000	Yankee Victor	4	H. Castillo Jr.	115	Golden Missile	116	Watchman's Warning	113	66,000	1:34.37	110
2001	Cat's at Home	4	F. Leon	114	Little Hans	113	Milwaukee Brew	117	64,920	1:33.60	106
2002	Free Of Love	4	J.D. Bailey	114	Dayton Flyer	112	Country Be Gold	114	67,500	1:35.56	102
2003	Najran	4	E.S. Prado	113	Saarland	114	Justification	113	65,820	1:32.24	111
2004	Gygistar	5	J. Bravo	115	Saarland	114	Black Silk	113	65,700	1:35.89	110

Beyer Index: 108.60

WHIRLAWAY HANDICAP (G3), 1 1/16 Miles, 4-Year-Olds and Up, Fair Grounds, 2004 Purse: $100,000

Year	Winner	Age	Jockey	Wt.	Second	Wt.	Third	Wt.	Win Value	Time	Beyer
1973	Guitar Player	5	T. Barrow	118	Holy Land	116	Grocery List	114	12,000	1:41.40	
1974	Tom Tulle	4	C. Perret	119	Navajo	115	Native Cadet	108	12,000	1:38.80	
1975	Burglar Alarm		P. Rubbicco		Faneuil Boy		Sr. Diplomat			1:39.20	
1975	Hearts of Lettuce		A. LeBlanc		Fame and Power		Aerodrome			1:38.80	
1976	Master Derby		D.G McHargue		Strictly Business		Native Drone			1:38.80	
1977	Cylinder		R. Sibille		Minnie Bus		Almost Grown			1:39.60	
1981	Occasionally Monday		A. Trosclair	114	Selma's Boy	115	Dr. Riddick	115		1:40.20	
1985	Rapid Gray	6	R. Romero	122	Hopeful Word	113	Silver Diplomat	118	19,250	1:43.00	
1992	Irish Swap	5	B. Poyadou	118	Jarraar	113	Wild and Tingley	113	18,975	1:43.00	100
1993	West by West	4	J.L. Samyn	117	Place Dancer	112	Genuine Meaning	113	18,885	1:43.80	98
1994	Cool Quaker	5	E. Martin Jr.	114	Dixie Poker Ace	121	Dixieland Heat	114	31,005	1:42.55	99
1995	Adhocracy	5	L. Melancon	112	Dynamic Brush	111	Cool Quaker	113	31,530	1:43.10	101
1996	Bucks Nephew	6	C. Perret	116	Prory	114	Vast Joy	114	38,025	1:43.40	101
1997	Byars	4	C. Bourque	114	Bucks Nephew	117	Clash by Night	113	60,000	1:44.47	91
1998	Moonlight Dancer	6	C. Bourque	114	Precocity	117	Hot Brush	113	75,000	1:44.34	109
1999	Precocity	5	E. Martin Jr.	117	Prory	114	Take Note of Me	117	75,000	1:43.42	108
2000	Take Note of Me	6	R. Albarado	118	Crimson Classic	114	Nite Dreamer	116	75,000	1:42.94	105
2001	Include	4	L. Meche	112	Connected	112	Kombat Kat	113	75,000	1:44.01	105
2002	Valhol	6	R. Albarado	115	Parade Leader	115	Fight for Ally	113	75,000	1:42.94	108
2003	Balto Star	5	E.M. Martin Jr.	118	Mineshaft	116	Bonapaw	115	75,000	1:43.74	111
2004	Olmodavor	5	C.J. Lanerie	121	Spanish Empire	118	Almuhathir	114	60,000	1:45.59	107

Beyer Index: 103.31

Run at 1 mile 40 yards in 1973–1981; Not run 1982–1984, 1986–1991

WHITNEY HANDICAP (G1), 1 1/8 Miles, 3-Year-Olds and Up, Saratoga Race Course, 2004 Purse: $750,000

Year	Winner	Age	Jockey	Wt.	Second	Wt.	Third	Wt.	Win Value	Time	Beyer
1928	Black Maria	5	L. Fator	121	Chance Shot	126	Whiskery	126	6,500	2:06.00	
1929	Bateau	4	E. Ambrose	121	Comstockery	117	Display	126	5,850	2:09.40	
1930	Whichone	3	R. Workman	117	Marine	121	Vanity	116	7,100	2:04.00	
1931	St. Brideaux	3	L. McAtee	117	Curate	116	Blenheim	107	6,900	2:05.00	
1932	Equipoise	4	R. Workman	126	Gusto	117	Rocky News	116	5,450	2:05.60	
1933	Caesars Ghost	3	D. Belizzi	107	Sun Archer	107	Golden Way	102	2,425	2:10.80	
1934	Discovery	3	D. Meade	105	Fleam	107	Time Clock	112	2,475	2:07.80	
1935	Discovery	4	J. Bejshak	126	Esposa	100	Good Goods	114	3,125	2:04.60	

Year	Winner	Age	Jockey	Wt.	Second	Wt.	Third	Wt.	Win Value	Time	Beyer
1936	Discovery	5	J. Bejshak	126	Esposa	121	Rust	106	3,250	2:06.80	
1937	Esposa	5	N. Wall	121	Matey	117	Count Arthur	126	3,000	2:05.20	
1938	War Admiral	4	W.D. Wright	126	Esposa	121	Fighting Fox	117	2,725	2:03.80	
1939	Eight Thirty	3	H. Richards	117	Shangay Lily	121	Handcuff	121	2,750	2:06.20	
1940	Challedon	4	G. Woolf	126	Isolater	126	Dusky Fox	117	2,700	2:03.20	
1941	Fenelon	4	J. Stout	120	Big Pebble	130	Welcome Pass	107	5,000	2:06.40	
1942	Swing and Sway	4	D. Meade	117	Corydon	117	Haltal	117	4,975	2:05.40	
1943	Bolingbroke	6	H. Lindberg	117	Princequillo	103	Water Pearl	103	7,900	2:02.00	
1944	Devil Diver	6	E. Arcaro	117	Princequillo	117	Bolingbroke	117	11,495	2:02.00	
1945	Trymenow	3	H. Lindberg	103	Pavot	117	Stymie	126	12,135	2:02.20	
1946	Stymie	5	B. James	120	Mahout	103	Trymenow	112	19,350	2:07.40	
1947	Rico Monte	5	R. Donoso	113	Gallorette	112	Stymie	126	18,550	2:02.60	
1948	Gallorette	6	A. Kirkland	115	Loyal Legion	112	Natchez	114	15,450	2:05.20	
1949	Round View	6	S. Perez	110	Donor	116	My Request	126	15,400	2:03.20	
1950	Piet	5	N. Combest	116	Sun Bahram	116	Adile	115	16,200	2:06.60	
1951	One Hitter	5	T. Atkinson	120	Cochise	126	Lone Eagle	114	15,300	2:05.00	
1952	Counterpoint	4	D. Gorman	123	Mandingo	114	One Hitter	126	15,800	2:05.60	
1953	Tom Fool	4	T. Atkinson	126	Combat Boots	114			18,250	2:05.40	
1954	Social Outcast	4	E. Guerin	115	Fisherman	121	Domquil	108	40,300	2:04.40	
1955	First Aid	5	H. Woodhouse	113	Diving Board	113	Chevation	120	18,100	1:51.60	
1956	Dedicate	4	W. Boland	116	Summer Tan	120	Paper Tiger	112	31,500	1:49.80	
1957	Kingmaker	4	R. Ussery	115	Riley	112	Tick Tock	111	31,400	1:52.80	
1958	Cohoes	4	J. Ruane	114	Admiral Vee	114	Inside Tract	112	29,205	1:51.60	
1959	Plion	4	M. Ycaza	114	Amerigo	112	Village Idiot	112	37,165	1:53.00	
1960	Warhead	5	W. Sorrentino	111	Talent Show	123	Manassa Mauler	121	37,750	1:51.00	
1961	Kelso	4	E. Arcaro	130	Our Hope	111	Rienzi	114	36,400	1:48.00	
	Our Hope finished first but was disqualified and placed second										
1962	Carry Back	4	J. Sellers	130	Crozier	111	Garwol	110	37,310	1:50.00	
1963	Kelso	6	I. Valenzuela	130	Saidam	111	Sunrise County	117	36,270	1:50.40	
1964	Gun Bow	4	W. Blum	130	Mongo	130	Delta Judge	111	35,295	1:49.20	
1965	Kelso	8	I. Valenzuela	130	Malicious	114	Pia Star	127	35,360	1:49.80	
1966	Staunchness	4	E. Cardone	109	Prolijo	113	Malicious	122	36,140	1:50.20	
1967	Stupendous	4	E. Belmonte	114	Ring Twice	114	Straight Deal	116	36,530	1:48.20	
1968	Dr. Fager	4	B. Baeza	132	Spoon Bait	114	Fort Drum	114	34,775	1:48.80	
1969	Verbatim	4	P. Anderson	121	Tropic King II	114	Dewan	117	35,945	1:50.00	
1970	Judgable	3	R. Woodhouse	112	Hydrologist	119	Dewan	121	39,260	1:48.40	
1971	Protanto	4	J. Velasquez	117	Peace Corps	114	Shuvee	116	36,300	1:49.40	
1972	Key to the Mint	3	B. Baeza	113	Tunex	117	Loud	117	34,350	1:49.20	
1973	Onion	4	J. Vasquez	119	Secretariat	119	Rule by Reason	119	32,310	1:49.20	
1974	Tri Jet	5	L. Pincay Jr	123	Infuriator	120	Stop the Music	120	33,390	1:47.00	
1975	Ancient Title	5	S. Hawley	128	Group Plan	115	Arbees Boy	118	50,085	1:48.20	
1976	Dancing Gun	4	R.I. Velez	108	American History	109	Erwin Boy	116	17,902	1:50.00	
1977	Nearly On Time	3	S. Cauthen	103	American History	112	Dancing Gun	112	49,545	1:49.40	
1978	Alydar	3	J. Velasquez	123	Buckaroo	112	Father Hogan	114	49,545	1:47.40	
1979	Star de Naskra	4	J. Fell	120	Cox's Ridge	117	The Liberal Member	120	65,040	1:47.60	
1980	State Dinner	5	R. Hernandez	120	Dr. Patches	114	Czaravich	123	99,540	1:48.20	
1981	Fio Rito	6	L. Hulet	113	Winter's Tale	121	Ring of Light	114	105,300	1:48.00	
1982	Silver Buck	4	D. MacBeth	115	Winter's Tale	119	Tap Shoes	113	99,000	1:47.80	
1983	Island Whirl	5	E. Delahoussaye	123	Bold Style	114	Sunny's Halo	116	103,860	1:48.40	
1984	Slew o' Gold	4	A. Cordero Jr	126	Track Barron	117	Thumbsucker	115	165,744	1:48.60	
1985	Track Barron	4	A. Cordero Jr	124	Carr de Naskra	120	Vanlandingham	124	160,680	1:47.60	
1986	Lady's Secret	4	P. Day	119	Ends Well	116	Fuzzy	112	202,500	1:49.80	
1987	Java Gold	3	P. Day	113	Gulch	117	Broad Brush	127	173,100	1:48.40	
1988	Personal Ensign	4	R.P. Romero	117	Gulch	124	King's Swan	123	162,300	1:47.80	
1989	Easy Goer	3	P. Day	119	Forever Silver	122	Cryptoclearance	122	172,500	1:47.40	
1990	Criminal Type	5	G.L. Stevens	126	Dancing Spree	121	Mi Selecto	117	140,640	1:48.60	115
1991	In Excess	4	G.L. Stevens	121	Chief Honcho	115	Killer Diller	112	150,000	1:48.00	116
1992	Sultry Song	4	J.D. Bailey	115	Out of Place	115	Chief Honcho	116	150,000	1:47.20	112
1993	Brunswick	4	M.E. Smith	112	West by West	115	Devil His Due	122	150,000	1:47.40	115
1994	Colonial Affair	4	J.A. Santos	117	Devil His Due	125	West by West	113	210,000	1:48.60	111
1995	Unaccounted For	4	P. Day	114	L'Carriere	111	Silver F ox	112	210,000	1:49.20	111
1996	Mahogany Hall	5	J.A. Santos	113	Serena's Song	116	Peaks and Valleys	121	210,000	1:48.60	110
1997	Will's Way	5	J.D. Bailey	117	Formal Gold	120	Skip Away	125	210,000	1:48.20	126
1998	Awesome Again	4	P. Day	117	Tale of the Cat	114	Crypto Star	116	240,000	1:49.71	110
1999	Victory Gallop	4	J.D. Bailey	123	Behrens	123	Catienus	113	360,000	1:48.66	116
2000	Lemon Drop Kid	4	E.S. Prado	123	Cat Thief	117	Behrens	122	680,000	1:48.30	118
2001	Lido Palace	4	J.D. Bailey	115	Albert The Great	124	Gander	113	540,000	1:47.94	114
2002	Left Bank	5	J.R. Velazquez	118	Street Cry	123	Lido Palace	119	450,000	1:47.04	121
2003	Medaglia d'Oro	4	J.D. Bailey	123	Volponi	120	Evening Attire	118	450,000	1:47.69	114
2004	Roses in May	4	E.S. Prado	114	Perfect Drift	117	Bowman's Band	114	450,000	1:48.54	114

Beyer Index: 114.87

Closed to geldings prior to 1971. Distance 1 1/4 miles prior to 1955. For 4-year-olds and up from 1957-59. Run at Belmont, 1961-62. Lemon Drop Kid earned a $230,000 bonus in 2000. Lido Palace earned a $90,000 bonus in 2001

CHARLES WHITTINGHAM MEMORIAL HANDICAP (G1), 1 1/4 Miles (Turf), 3-Year-Olds and Up, Hollywood Park, 2004 Purse: $350,000

Year	Winner	Age	Jockey	Wt.	Second	Wt.	Third	Wt.	Win Value	Time	Beyer
1969	Fort Marcy	5	M. Ycaza	124	Poleax	117	Court Fool	115	55,000	2:27.20	
1970	Fiddle Isle	5	W. Shoemaker	128	Fort Marcy	126	Governors Party	112	55,000	2:25.60	
1972	Typecast	6	J. Lambert	117	Violonor	110	Cougar II	129	68,750	2:25.80	
1973	Life Cycle	4	L. Pincay Jr	115	Wing Out	118	Cougar II	130	75,000	2:25.60	
1974	Court Ruling	4	W. Mahorney	117	Outdoors	113	London Company	123	75,000	2:27.60	
1975	Barclay Joy	5	A.L. Diaz	113	Captain Cee Jay	117	Chief Hawk Ear	119	75,000	2:27.00	
1976	Dahlia	6	W. Shoemaker	117	Caucasus	119	Pass the Glass	121	120,000	2:26.80	
1977	Vigors	4	J. Lambert	117	Causasus	126	Anne's Pretender	122	120,000	2:26.80	
1978	Exceller	5	W. Shoemaker	127	Bowl Game	123	Noble Dancer II	126	110,000	2:25.80	
1979	Johnny's Image	4	S. Hawley	123	Star Spangled	122	Dom Alaric	119	137,500	2:25.20	
1980	John Henry	5	D.G. McHargue	128	Balzac	120	Go West Young Man	117	137,500	2:25.40	
1981	John Henry	6	L. Pincay Jr	130	Caterman	122	Galaxy Libra	118	110,000	2:27.80	
1982	Exploded	5	L. Pincay Jr	117	Lemhi Gold	123	The Bart	125	165,000	2:25.20	
1983	Erins Isle	5	L. Pincay Jr	127	Exploded	115	Prince Spellbound	120	165,000	2:25.80	
1984	John Henry	9	C.J. McCarron	126	Galant Vert	116	Load the Cannons	120	165,000	2:25.00	
1985	Both Ends Burning	5	E. Delahoussaye	121	Dahar	123	Swoon	114	165,000	2:25.60	
1986	Flying Pidgeon	5	S. Soto	120	Dahar	126	Both Ends Burning	122	165,000	2:27.00	
1987	Rivlia	5	C.J. McCarron	117	Great Communicator	112	Schiller	116	165,000	2:24.20	
1988	Political Ambition	4	E. Delahoussaye	119	Baba Karam	116	Great Communicator	120	165,000	1:58.60	
							Skip Out Front	115			
1989	Great Communicator	6	R. Sibille	123	Nasr El Arab	124	Equalize	124	275,000	1:59.40	
1990	Steinlen	7	L. Pincay Jr	124	Hawkster	122	Santangelo	110	275,000	2:03.00	109
1991	Exbourne	5	G.L. Stevens	119	Itsallgreektome	123	Prized	123	275,000	2:00.00	108
1992	Quest for Fame	5	G.L. Stevens	122	Classic Fame	120	River Traffic	114	275,000	1:58.80	105
1993	Bien Bien	4	C.J. McCarron	119	Best Pal	122	Leger Cat	116	275,000	1:57.60	108
1994	Grand Flotilla	7	G.L. Stevens	116	Bien Bien	124	Blues Traveller	114	275,000	1:59.20	110
1995	Earl of Barking	5	G.F. Almeida	115	Sandpit	122	Savinio	117	275,000	1:59.60	110
1996	Sandpit	7	C.S. Nakatani	120	Northern Spur	123	Awad	119	300,000	1:59.40	112
1997	Rainbow Dancer	6	A. Solis	116	Sunshack	118	Marlin	120	240,000	2:00.00	106
1998	Storm Trooper	5	K.J. Desormeaux	117	River Bay	121	Prize Giving	116	240,000	2:03.05	104
1999	River Bay	6	A. Solis	119	Majorien	117	Alvo Certo	115	240,000	2:00.66	105
2000	White Heart	5	K.J. Desormeuax	117	Self Feeder	116	Deploy Venture	112	180,000	2:00.83	103
2001	Bienamado	5	C.J. McCarron	124	Senure	117	Timboroa	116	210,000	1:59.34	111
2002	Denon	4	G. Gomez	116	Night Patrol	114	Skipping	117	210,000	2:01.47	108
2003	Storming Home	5	G.L. Stevens	124	Mister Acpen	115	Cagney	114	210,000	2:00.66	103
2004	Sabiango	6	T.C. Baze	116	Bayamo	116	Just Wonder	116	210,000	2:01.52	106

Beyer Index: 107.20

Distance 1 1/2 miles 1969–87. Run as Hollywood Turf Handicap prior to 1999

WILSHIRE HANDICAP (G3), 1 Mile (Turf), Fillies and Mares, 3-Year-Olds and Up, Hollywood Park, 2004 Purse: $110,900

Year	Winner	Age	Jockey	Wt.	Second	Wt.	Third	Wt.	Win Value	Time	Beyer
1953	Ria Rica	3	B. Pearson	110	Laska	108	Mary Be Good	109	9,925	1:37.20	
1963	Edie Belle	6	W. Shoemaker	110	Pixie Erin	119	Mountain Glory	107	13,200	1:26.40	
1964	Researcher	4	P. Moreno	110	Star Maggie	115	Curious Clover	124	13,850	1:26.40	
1965	Jalousie II	6	J. Longden	112	Savaii	117	Gala Host	112	16,550	1:21.00	
1966	Poona Queen	6	W. Shoemaker	117	Jalousie II	113	Gala Host	115	16,500	1:22.20	
1967	Romanticism	5	J. Lambert	119	Admirably	124	Mellow Marsh	110	14,700	1:22.40	
1968	Gamely	4	W. Harris	125	Romanticism	119	Nev'da M'rga	114	14,150	1:21.00	
1969	Gamely	5	W. Harris	128	Time to Leave	123	Ind'n Love C'l	120	13,150	1:21.00	
1970	Tanta Bella	3	J. Lambert	115	Last of the Line	113	Thoroly Blue	113	13,300	1:48.80	
1971	New Leaf	4	D. Tierney	113	Sallarina	121	Thoroly Blue	121	17,700	1:49.00	
1972	Manta	6	F. Toro	113	Tico's Donna	112	Minstrel Miss	118	16,100	1:48.80	
1973	Balcony's Babe	5	J. Lambert	116	Ground Song	118	Dating	111	17,250	1:48.60	
1973	Convenience	5	J.L. Rotz	124	Pallisima	120	Veiled Desire	109	16,900	1:49.00	
1974	Tallahto	4	L. Pincay Jr	121	Ready Wit	113	Dogtooth Violet	119	33,650	1:47.60	
1975	Tizna	6	J. Lambert	123	Susan's Girl	123	Dulcia	120	33,300	1:48.60	
1976	Miss Toshiba	4	F. Toro	117	Charger's Star	116	Swingtime	120	32,300	1:49.20	
1977	Now Pending	4	R. Campas	114	Swingtime	116	Up to Juliet	116	33,550	1:48.80	
1978	Lucie Manet	5	C.J. McCarron	119	Swingtime	119	Drama Critic	119	30,950	1:49.00	
1979	Country Queen	4	L. Pincay Jr	121	Giggling Girl	116	Camarado	119	33,100	1:40.40	
1980	Wishing Well	5	F. Toro	120	Sisterhood	119	Love You Dear	113	38,500	1:41.60	
1981	Track Robbery	5	P.A. Valenzuela	118	Luth Music	115	Save Wild Life	116	47,550	1:40.80	
1982	Miss Huntington	5	P.A. Valenzuela	115	Mi Quimera	117	French Charmer	116	51,250	1:41.40	
1983	Mademoiselle Forli	4	P.A. Valenzuela	118	Night Fire	117	Nan's Charger	115	47,300	1:44.80	
1984	Triple Tipple	5	L. Pincay Jr	117	Comedy Act	122	Nan's Dancer	116	48,900	1:41.20	
1985	Johnica	4	C.J. McCarron	114	Tamarinda	119	Salt Spring	113	63,100	1:40.60	
1986	Outstandingly	4	G.L. Stevens	117	La Koumia	118	Estrapade	124	75,600	1:41.60	
1987	Galunpe	4	F. Toro	118	Top Socialite	119	Perfect Match	116	75,900	1:41.00	

Year	Winner	Age	Jockey	Wt.	Second	Wt.	Third	Wt.	Win Value	Time	Beyer
1988	Chapel of Dreams	4	G.L. Stevens	115	Fitzwilliam Place	119	Invited Guest	116	64,700	1:39.40	
1989	Claire Marine	4	C.J. McCarron	117	Fitzwilliam Place	119	Galunpe	119	62,700	1:39.00	
1990	Reluctant Guest	4	R.G. Davis	114	Beautiful Melody	115	Estrella Fuega	114	62,400	1:39.40	
1991	Fire the Groom	4	G.L. Stevens	118	Odalea	115	Agirlfromars	114	63,000	1:40.00	107
1992	Kostroma	6	K.J. Desormeaux	123	Danzante	114	Appealing Missy	116	62,500	1:41.20	102
1993	Toussaud	4	K.J. Desormeaux	116	Visible Gold	117	Wedding Ring	115	63,500	1:40.00	100
1994	Skimble	5	E. Delahoussaye	118	Bel's Starlet	118	Miami Sands	116	62,800	1:41.20	99
1995	Possibly Perfect	5	K.J. Desormeaux	121	Morgana	116	Aube Indienne	119	76,600	1:40.20	103
1996	Pharma	5	C.S. Nakatani	118	Didina	116	Matiara	120	79,770	1:40.80	107
1997	Blushing Heiress	5	C.J. McCarron	115	Real Connection	115	De Puntillas	117	65,040	1:40.80	100
1998	Shake The Yoke	5	E. Delahoussaye	118	Traces of Gold	116	Cozy Blues	115	66,240	1:34.00	104
1999	Sapphire Ring	4	G.L. Stevens	119	Bella Chiarra	116	Green Jewel	118	65,160	1:33.86	102
2000	Tout Charmant	4	C.J. McCarron	121	Penny Marie	117	Perfect Copy	117	64,740	1:33.86	99
2001	Tranquility Lake	6	E. Delahoussaye	123	Dianehill	116	Out of Reach	117	65,160	1:34.69	97
2002	Eurolink Raindance	5	C.J. McCarron	115	Crazy Ensign	118	Impeachable	115	63,960	1:34.31	97
2003	Dublino	4	K.J. Desormeaux	120	Southern Oasis	116	Final Destination	118	66,600	1:33.62	106
2004	Spring Star	5	A. Solis	117	Quero Quero	115	Dublino	120	66,540	1:33.41	99

Beyer Index: 101.57

WINSTAR DISTAFF HANDICAP (G3), 1 Mile (Turf), Fillies and Mares, 3-Year-Olds and Up, Lone Star Park, 2004 Purse: $200,000

Year	Winner	Age	Jockey	Wt.	Second	Wt.	Third	Wt.	Win Value	Time	Beyer
2000	Mumtaz	4	V. Espinoza	113	Evening Promise	117	Really Polish	114	120,000	1:37.28	100
2001	Voladora	6	M. Berry	114	Dyna Likes Bingo	109	Iftiraas	118	120,000	1:42.23	99
2002	Queen of Wilshire	6	D.R. Flores	117	Pleasant State	115	Blushing Bride	115	120,000	1:38.96	98
2003	Eagle Lake	5	G. Melancon	116	Little Treasure	117	Magic Mission	116	120,000	1:43.02	95
2004	Academic Angel	5	S.J. Sellers	117	Janeian	119	Katdogawn	120	120,000	1:35.98	95

Beyer Index: 97.40

WINSTAR GALAXY (G2), 1 3/16 Miles (Turf), Fillies and Mares, 3-Year-Olds and Up, Keeneland Race Course, 2004 Purse: $500,000

Year	Winner	Age	Jockey	Wt.	Second	Wt.	Third	Wt.	Win Value	Time	Beyer
1998	Witchful Thinking	4	C.J. McCarron	115	Memories of Silver	120	Starry Dreamer	115	169,415	1:54.20	102
1999	Happyanunoit	4	B. Blanc	119	Pleasant Temper	119	Fiji	117	346,270	1:53.80	109
2000	Tout Charmant	4	C.J. McCarron	117	Perfect Sting	121	License Fee	119	343,480	1:54.74	104
2001	Spook Express	7	M.E. Smith	120	Solvig	118	Veil of Avalon	118	349,370	1:54.24	102
2002	Owsley	3	E.S. Prado	122	Snow Dance	120	Surya	118	337,590	1:56.72	100
2003	Bien Nicole	5	D.R. Pettinger	121	Approach	116	New Economy	121	310,000	1:55.87	100
2004	Stay Forever	7	E. Castro	121	Super Brand	119	Shaconage	121	310,000	1:57.08	96

Beyer Index: 101.86

WITHERS (G3), 1 Mile, 3-Year-Olds, Aqueduct, 2004 Purse: $147,000

Year	Winner	Age	Jockey	Wt.	Second	Wt.	Third	Wt.	Win Value	Time	Beyer
1874	Dublin	3	Ponton	110	Vandalite	107	Reform	110	3,200	1:50.00	
1875	Aristides	3	Swim	110	Rhadamanthus	110	Ozark	110	4,150	1:45.75	
1876	Fiddlesticks	3	Feakes	110	Charley Howard	110	Merciless	107	3,500	1:46.50	
1877	Bombast	3	Barrett	110	Cardinal Wolsey	110	Glen Dudley	110	4,200	1:46.00	
1878	Duke of Magenta	3	Hughes	118	Bramble	118	Danicheff	118	3,500	1:48.00	
1879	Dan Sparling	3	Kelly	118	Spendthrift	118	Report	118	5,395	1:48.00	
1880	Ferncliffe	3	Barrett	118	Grenada	118	Oden	118	3,800	1:49.00	
1881	Crickmore	3	Hughes	115	Prism	118	Filette	113	4,275	1:48.00	
1882	Forester	3	J. McLaughlin	118	Marsh Redon	118	Rica	113	4,600	1:46.50	
1883	Geo. Kinney	3	J. McLaughlin	118	Pizarro	118	Trombone	118	2,990	1:45.00	
1884	Panique	3	Fitzpatrick	118	Richmond	118	Pampero	118	3,240	1:48.00	
1885	Tyrant	3	P. Duffy	118	Himalaya	118	Tecumseh	118	3,070	1:45.25	
1886	Biggonet	3	Maynard	113	Repartee	118	Headland	118	3,260	1:48.00	
1887	Hanover	3	J. McLaughlin	118	Stockton	118	Belvidere	118	3,490	1:46.50	
1888	Sir Dixon	3	Fitzpatrick	118	Prince Royal	118	Tea Tray	119	3,620	1:47.00	
1889	Diablo	3	Godfrey	121	Eric	118	Reporter	118	5,380	1:45.00	
1890	King Eric	3	Garrison	110	Magnate	113	Cayuga	113	8,140	1:41.00	
1891	Picknicker	3	F. Littlefield	117	Montana	117	Laurestan	114	4,190	1:40.75	
1892	Tammany	3	Garrison	122	Patron	122	Yorkville Belle	117	7,460	1:40.00	
1893	Dr. Rice	3	Taral	122	Rainbow	122	Sir Walter	122	9,470	1:42.00	
1894	Domino	3	Taral	122	Henry of Navarre	122	Dobbins	122	7,100	1:40.00	

Year	Winner	Age	Jockey	Wt.	Second	Wt.	Third	Wt.	Win Value	Time	Beyer
1895	Lucania	3	Reiff	109	Brandywine	105	Gotham	111	2,700	1:41.75	
1896	Handspring	3	Simms	122	Hastings	122	Sherlock	112	2,550	1:41.00	
1897	Octagon	3	Simms	119	Ogden	122	Regulator	119	2,550	1:43.00	
1898	The Huguenot	3	Spencer	122	Mr. Baiter	122	Handball	122	3,815	1:43.00	
1899	Jean Bereaud	3	Clawson	122	Filon d'Or	119	The Bouncer	122	4,450	1:42.25	
1900	Kilmarnock	3	N. Turner	126	Mesmerist	126	Ildrim	126	5,470	1:41.25	
1901	The Parader	3	Landry	126	Bonnibert	126	Bellario	126	5,020	1:42.50	
1902	Compute	3	Shaw	126	Old England	123	King Hanover	126	4,815	1:42.00	
1903	Shorthose	3	Haack	126	Mexican	126	Injunction	126	6,395	1:41.00	
1904	Delhi	3	Odom	126	Bryn Mawr	126	Conjurer	126	5,750	1:40.00	
1905	Blandy	3	W. Davis	126	Hot Shot	126	Sparkling Star	126	6,220	1:44.60	
1906	Accountant	3	J. Martin	126	Bohemian	126	Clark Griffith	126	6,850	1:38.80	
1907	Frank Gill	3	Notter	126	Peter Pan	126	Saracinesca	123	7,775	1:40.00	
1908	Colin	3	Notter	126	Fair Play	126	King James	126	12,090	1:41.00	
1909	Hilarious	3	Butwell	126	Joe Madden	126	Fayette	126	11,070	1:41.20	
1910	The Turk	3	M. McGee	126	Prince Imperial	126	Grasmere	126	3,000	1:40.00	
1913	Rock View	3	Butwell	118	Prince Eugene	118	Yan'e Notions	118	2,325	1:39.40	
1914	Charlestonian	3	C. Burlingame	115	Gainer	118	Roamer	115	2,900	1:39.80	
1915	The Finn	3	G. Byrne	118	Sharpshooter	115	Half Rock	118	1,425	1:39.40	
1916	Spur	3	J. Loftus	118	Churchill	118	Friar Rock	118	2,900	1:38.40	
1917	Hourless	3	J. Butwell	118	Rickety	118	Skeptic	118	5,475	1:39.00	
1918	Motor Cop	3	E. Taplin	118	Cum Sah	118	Tr. La Mort	118	7,100	1:39.60	
1919	Sir Barton	3	J. Loftus	118	Eternal	118	Pastoral Swain	118	8,075	1:38.80	
1920	Man o' War	3	C. Kummer	118	Wildair	118	David Harum	118	4,825	1:35.80	
1921	Leonardo II	3	A. Schuttinger	118	Sporting Blood	118	Grey Lag	118	5,475	1:37.40	
1922	Snob II	3	C. Kummer	118	Pillory	118	June Grass	118	17,050	1:35.80	
1923	Zev	3	E. Sande	118	Martingale	118	Barbary Bush	118	18,300	1:37.40	
1924	Bracadale	3	E. Sande	118	Sun Pal	118	Sheridan	118	19,000	1:39.00	
1925	American Flag	3	A. Johnson	118	Silver Fox	118	Gold Stick	118	19,600	1:38.20	
1926	Haste	3	E. Sande	118	Crusader	118	Espino	118	22,800	1:37.60	
1927	Chance Shot	3	E. Sande	118	Sweepster	118	Boise de Rose	118	23,250	1:39.80	
1928	Victorian	3	R. Workman	118	Mowlee	118	Polydor	118	22,300	1:39.00	
1929	Blue Larkspur	3	M. Garner	118	Chestnut Oak	118	Jack High	118	28,250	1:36.00	
1930	Whichone	3	R. Workman	118	Swinfield	118	Starpatic	118	26,150	1:38.20	
1931	Jamestown	3	L. McAtee	118	Ladder	118	Clock Tower	118	27,300	1:36.60	
1932	Boatswain	3	A. Robertson	118	Osculator	118	Pairbypair	118	21,600	1:39.80	
1933	The Darb	3	A. Robertson	118	Golden Way	118	Dark Winter	118	20,550	1:39.00	
1934	Singing Wood	3	R. Jones	118	Roustabout	118	Chicstraw	118	16,000	1:37.80	
1935	Rosemont	3	W.D. Wright	118	Omaha	118	Plat Eye	118	11,250	1:36.60	
1936	White Cockade	3	E. Litzenberger	118	Brevity	118	Teufel	118	18,200	1:37.20	
1937	Flying Scot	3	J. Gilbert	118	Charing Cross	118	Mosawtre	118	15,050	1:37.40	
1938	Menow	3	C. Kurtsinger	118	Thanksgiving	118	Redbreast	118	15,000	1:37.40	
1939	Johnstown	3	J. Stout	118	Hash	118	Porter's Mite	118	15,750	1:35.80	
1940	Corydon	3	E. Arcaro	118	Bimelech	118	Roman	118	16,650	1:37.20	
1941	King Cole	3	J. Gilbert	118	Robert Morris	118	Porter's Cap	118	20,300	1:38.20	
1942	Alsab	3	B. James	126	Lochinvar	126	Fairaris	126	15,500	1:36.20	
1943	Count Fleet	3	J. Longden	126	Slide Rule	126	Tip-Toe	126	12,700	1:36.00	
1944	Who Goes There	3	J. Longden	126	By Jimminy	126	Boy Knight	126	16,150	1:38.00	
1945	Polynesian	3	W.D. Wright	126	Pavot	126	King Dorsett	126	19,125	1:39.80	
1946	Hampden	3	E. Arcaro	126	Natchez	126	Perfect Bahram	126	20,320	1:36.00	
1947	Faultless	3	D. Dodson	126	Brabancon	126	Stage Kid	126	20,950	1:38.20	
1948	Vulcan's Forge	3	D. Dodson	126	Coaltown	126	Better Self	126	20,100	1:37.40	
1949	Olympia	3	E. Arcaro	126	Ocean Drive	126	One Hitter	126	21,150	1:36.80	
1950	Hill Prince	3	E. Arcaro	126	Middleground	126	Ferd	126	20,700	1:35.80	
1951	Battlefield	3	E. Arcaro	126	Jumbo	126	Nullify	126	20,600	1:35.80	
1952	Armageddon	3	R. York	126	One Count	126	Primate	126	22,000	1:37.00	
1953	Native Dancer	3	E. Guerin	126	Invigorator	126	Real Brother	126	23,050	1:36.20	
1954	Jet Action	3	R. Contreras	126	Buttevant	126	High Gun	126	26,250	1:36.60	
1955	Traffic Judge	3	E. Arcaro	126	Nance's Lad	126	Portersville	126	21,850	1:36.00	
1956	Oh Johnny	3	H. Woodhouse	126	Eiffel Blue	126	Lawless	126	20,100	1:45.20	
1957	Clem	3	C. McCreary	126	Cohoes	126	Tenacious	126	19,100	1:36.80	
1958	Sir Robby	3	E. Guerin	126	Clandestine	126	Misty Flight	126	19,362	1:36.20	
1959	Intentionally	3	M. Ycaza	126	Manassa Mauler	126	Bagdad	126	58,072	1:35.60	
1960	John William	3	H. Woodhouse	126	Count Amber	126	Francis S.	126	74,950	1:35.40	
1961	Hitting Away	3	H. Woodhouse	126	Up Scope	126	Nashua Blue	126	38,935	1:35.20	
1962	Jaipur	3	W. Shoemaker	126	Green Ticket	126	Cyrano	126	38,090	1:35.60	
1963	Get Around	3	B. Baeza	126	Sky Wonder	126	Top Gallant	126	39,650	1:36.60	
1964	Mr. Brick	3	R. Ussery	126	National	126	Alphabet	126	40,105	1:35.60	
1965	Flag Raiser	3	R. Ussery	126	Gallant Lad	126	Record Dash	126	39,000	1:34.20	
1966	Indulto	3	J.L. Rotz	126	Creme Dela Creme	126	Fathers Image	126	38,935	1:35.00	
1967	Dr. Fager	3	B. Baeza	126	Tumiga	126	Reason to Hail	126	37,895	1:33.80	
1968	Call Me Prince	3	W. Boland	126	Salerno	126	Verbatim	126	38,220	1:35.20	
1969	Ack Ack	3	M. Ycaza	126	Tyrant	126	Rooney's Shield	126	37,765	1:34.80	

Year	Winner	Age	Jockey	Wt.	Second	Wt.	Third	Wt.	Win Value	Time	Beyer
1970	Hagley	3	R. Turcotte	126	Delaware Chief	126	Tatoi	126	38,805	1:34.80	
1971	Bold Reasoning	3	J. Vasquez	126	Highbinder	126	Salem	126	35,100	1:35.80	
1972	Key to the Mint	3	B. Baeza	126	Icecapade	126	Zulu Tom	126	35,400	1:34.80	
1973	Linda's Chief	3	J. Velasquez	126	Stop the Music	126	Forego	126	33,120	1:34.80	
1974	Accipiter	3	A. Santiago	126	Best of It	126	Hosiery	126	36,240	1:35.60	
1975	Sarsar	3	W. Shoemaker	121	Laramie Trail	126	Ramahorn	126	36,360	1:34.60	
1976	Sonkisser	3	B. Baeza	126	El Portugues	126	Full Out	126	32,760	1:35.00	
1977	Iron Constitution	3	J. Velasquez	126	Cormorant	126	Affiliate	126	33,360	1:37.00	
1978	Junction	3	M. Solomone	126	Star de Naskra	126	Buckaroo	126	32,520	1:36.80	
1979	Czaravich	3	J. Cruguet	126	Instrument Landing	126	Strike the Main	126	33,330	1:35.60	
1980	Colonel Moran	3	J. Velasquez	126	Temperence Hill	126	J.P. Brother	126	34,200	1:34.40	
1981	Spirited Boy	3	A. Cordero Jr	126	Willow Hour	126	A Run	126	33,600	1:36.80	
1982	Aloma's Ruler	3	J.L. Kaenel	126	Spanish Drums	126	John's Gold	126	33,300	1:35.40	
1983	Country Pine	3	J.D. Bailey	126	I Enclose	126	Megaturn	126	52,380	1:35.60	
1984	Play On	3	J.L. Samyn	126	Morning Bob	126	Back Bay Barrister	126	69,750	1:36.40	
1985	El Basco	3	J. Vasquez	126	Another Reef	126	Concert	126	72,990	1:36.60	
1986	Clear Choice	3	J. Velasquez	126	Tasso	126	Landing Plot	126	71,550	1:35.60	
1987	Gone West	3	E. Maple	126	High Brite	126	Mr. S.M.	126	82,620	1:36.40	
1988	Once Wild	3	P. Day	126	Tejano	126	Perfect Spy	126	69,360	1:35.20	
1989	Fire Maker	3	J.D. Bailey	126	Imbibe	126	Manastash Ridge	126	73,800	1:36.40	
1990	Housebuster	3	C. Perret	126	Profit Key	126	Sunny Serve	126	71,040	1:34.80	
1991	Subordinated Debt	3	J.A. Krone	126	Scan	126	Kyle's Our Man	126	73,920	1:34.00	102
1992	Dixie Brass	3	J.M. Pezua	126	Big Sur	126	Superstrike	126	73,080	1:33.60	108
1993	Williamstown	3	C. Perret	124	Virginia Rapids	124	Farmonthefreeway	124	76,800	1:32.60	104
1994	Twining	3	J.A. Santos	123	Able Buck	123	Presently	123	67,140	1:34.60	102
1995	Blu Tusmani	3	J.A. Santos	123	Pat n Jac	123	Northern Ensign	123	67,260	1:35.00	91
1996	Appealing Skier	3	R Wilson	123	Jamies First Punch	123	Roar	123	66,120	1:35.00	104
1997	Statesmanship	3	W.H. McCauley	123	Cryp Too	123	Stormin Fever	123	67,140	1:35.20	95
1998	Dice Dancer	3	J.F. Chavez	123	Rubiyat	123	Limit Out	123	90,000	1:34.40	114
1999	Successful Appeal	3	J.L. Espinosa	120	Best of Luck	116	Treasure Island	116	90,000	1:35.00	96
2000	Big E E	3	H. Castillo Jr.	116	Precise End	123	Port Herman	116	90,000	1:35.69	93
2001	Richly Blended	3	R. Wilson	123	Le Grande Dansuer	120	Telescam	116	90,000	1:35.66	97
2002	Fast Decision	3	J.A. Santos	116	Shah Jehan	118	Listen Here	120	90,000	1:36.41	100
2003	Spite the Devil	3	L. Chavez	116	Alysweep	123	Stanislavsky	116	90,000	1:35.89	96
2004	Medallist	3	J.F. Chavez	116	Forest Danger	123	Two Down Automatic	120	90,000	1:34.49	110

Beyer Index: 100.86

WOOD MEMORIAL (G1), 1 1/8 Miles, 3-Year-Olds, Aqueduct, 2004 Purse: $750,000

Year	Winner	Age	Jockey	Wt.	Second	Wt.	Third	Wt.	Win Value	Time	Beyer
1925	Backbone	3	I. Parke	110	Voltaic	117	Swope	120	7,600	1:43.60	
1926	Pompey	3	B. Breuning	120	Navigator	120	Espino	110	8,700	1:42.00	
1927	Saxon	3	G. Ellis	117	Black Panther	110	Bostonian	110	9,050	1:43.60	
1928	Distraction	3	D. McAuliffe	120	Genie	111	Doctor Wilson	123	11,300	1:46.00	
1929	Essare	3	M. Garner	110	Annapolis	110	Upset Lad	123	11,000	1:44.00	
1930	Gallant Fox	3	E. Sande	120	Crack Brigade	120	Desert Light	120	10,150	1:43.60	
1931	Twenty Grand	3	C. Kurtsinger	120	Clock Tower	110	Camper	110	10,200	1:42.60	
1932	Universe	3	L. McAtee	120	Economic	120	Curacao	114	10,400	1:43.00	
1933	Mr. Khayyam	3	P. Walls	122	De Valera	117	Head Play	126	3,760	1:42.60	
1934	High Quest	3	D. Bellizzi	120	Speedmore	112	Spy Hill	112	3,990	1:43.80	
1935	Today	3	R. Workman	112	Plat Eye	122	Omaha	112	11,350	1:42.80	
1936	Teufel	3	E. Litzenberger	112	Granville	117	Delphinium	117	10,775	1:43.20	
1937	Melodist	3	J. Longden	120	Sir Damion	120	Jewell Dorsett	115	19,150	1:42.80	
1938	Fighting Fox	3	J. Stout	120	Can't Wait	120	Opera Hat	120	17,450	1:43.00	
1939	Johnstown	3	J. Stout	120	Voitant	120	Impound	120	17,675	1:42.00	
1940	Dit	3	L. Haas	120	Red Dock	120	Devil's Crag	120	19,225	1:45.80	
1941	Market Wise	3	D. Meade	120	Curious Coin	120	King Cole	120	16,650	1:45.60	
1942	Requested	3	W.D. Wright	120	Bleu d'Or	120	Apache	120	22,900	1:45.20	
1943	Count Fleet	3	J. Longden	126	Blue Swords	126	Twoses	126	20,150	1:43.00	
1944	Stir Up	3	E. Arcaro	126	Stymie	126	Autocrat	126	19,625	1:44.20	
1944	Lucky Draw	3	J. Longden	126	Broad Grin	126	Hoodoo	126	20,115	1:46.20	
1945	Jeep	3	A. Kirkland	126	Gallorette	121	Dockstader	126	18,945	1:45.80	
1945	Hoop Jr.	3	E. Arcaro	126	Alexis	126	Sir Francis	126	18,945	1:45.00	
1946	Assault	3	W. Mehrtens	126	Hampden	126	Marine Victory	126	22,600	1:46.60	
1947	Phalanx	3	E. Arcaro	126	Carolyn A.	121	Owners Choice	126	31,325	1:43.60	
1947	I Will	3	E. Arcaro	126	Stepfather	126	Cornish Knight	126	31,625	1:45.00	
1948	My Request	3	D. Dodson	126	Mount Marcy	126	Better Self	126	34,600	1:46.20	
1949	Olympia	3	E. Arcaro	126	Palestinian	126	Capot	126	31,850	1:45.00	
1950	Hill Prince	3	E. Arcaro	126	Middleground	126	Ferd	126	34,500	1:43.60	
1951	Repetoire	3	P. McLean	126	Battle Morn	126	Intent	126	35,250	1:44.40	

Year	Winner	Age	Jockey	Wt.	Second	Wt.	Third	Wt.	Win Value	Time	Beyer
1952	Master Fiddle	3	D. Gorman	126	Tom Fool	126	Pintor	126	45,200	1:52.40	
1953	Native Dancer	3	E. Guerin	126	Tahitian King	126	Invigorator	126	87,000	1:50.60	
1954	Correlation	3	W. Shoemaker	126	Fisherman	126	High Gun	126	86,000	1:50.00	
1955	Nashua	3	T. Atkinson	126	Summer Tan	126	Simmy	126	75,100	1:50.60	
1956	Head Man	3	E. Arcaro	126	Golf Ace	126	Oh Johnny	126	42,400	1:50.20	
1957	Bold Ruler	3	E. Arcaro	126	Gallant Man	126	Promised Land	126	40,800	1:48.80	
1958	Jewel's Reward	3	E.Arcaro	126	Noureddin	126	Martins Rullah	126	37,575	1:50.20	
1959	Manassa Mauler	3	R. Broussard	126	First Landing	126	Our Dad	126	55,915	1:49.60	
1960	Francis S.	3	W. Shoemaker	126	Never Give In	126	John William	126	60,465	1:50.20	
1961	Globemaster	3	J.L. Rotz	126	Carry Back	126	Ambiopoise	126	56,062	1:50.20	
1962	Admiral's Voyage	3	B. Baeza	126	Sunrise County	126	Donut King	126	59,702	1:49.80	
1963	No Robbery	3	J.L. Rotz	126	Bonjour	126	Top Gallant	126	59,020	1:49.20	
1964	Quadrangle	3	W. Hartack	126	Mr. Brick	126	Roman Brother	126	58,012	1:49.20	
1965	Flag Raiser	3	R. Ussery	126	Hail to All	126	Bold Lad	126	60,222	1:50.20	
1966	Amberoid	3	W. BOland	126	Advocator	126	Buffle	126	74,425	1:49.60	
1967	Damascus	3	W. Shoemaker	126	Gala Performance	126	Dawn Glory	126	73,060	1:49.60	
1968	Dancer's Image	3	R. Ussery	126	Iron Ruler	126	Verbatim	126	73,775	1:49.00	
1969	Dike	3	J. Velasquez	126	Al Hattab	126	Reviewer	126	72,085	1:49.60	
1970	Personality	3	E. Belmonte	126	Silent Screen	126	Delaware Chief	126	76,570	1:49.40	
1971	Good Behaving	3	C. Baltazar	126	Eastern Fleet	126	Executioner	126	67,320	1:49.80	
1972	Upper Case	3	R. Turcotte	126	True Knight	126	Head of the River	126	71,040	1:49.00	
1973	Angle Light	3	J. Vasquez	126	Sham	126	Secretariat	126	68,940	1:49.80	
1974	Flip Sal	3	A. Cordero Jr	126	Triple Crown	126	Sharp Gary	126	69,360	1:51.40	
1974	Rube the Great	3	M.A. Rivera	126	Friendly Bee	126	Hudson County	126	69,660	1:49.60	
1975	Foolish Pleasure	3	J .Vasquez	126	Bombay Duck	126	Media	126	72,840	1:48.80	
1976	Bold Forbes	3	A. Cordero Jr	126	On the Sly	126	Sonkisser	126	67,560	1:47.40	
1977	Seattle Slew	3	J. Cruguet	126	Sanhedrin	126	Catalan	126	66,180	1:49.60	
1978	Believe It	3	E. Maple	126	Darby Creek Road	126	Track Reward	126	65,940	1:49.80	
1979	Instrument Landing	3	A. Cordero Jr	126	Screen King	126	Czaravich	126	85,650	1:49.20	
1980	Plugged Nickle	3	B. Thornburg	126	Colonel Moran	126	Genuine Risk	121	87,300	1:50.80	
1981	Pleasant Colony	3	J. Fell	126	Highland Blade	126	Cure the Blues	126	98,280	1:49.60	
1982	Air Forbes Won	3	A. Cordero Jr.	126	Shimatoree	126	Laser Light	126	105,120	1:51.00	
1983	Bounding Basque	3	G. McCarron	126	Country Pine	126	Aztec Red	126	100,980	1:51.40	
1983	Slew o' Gold	3	E. Maple	126	Parfaitement	126	High Honors	126	101,700	1:51.00	
1984	Leroy S.	3	J. Cruguet	126	Raja's Shark	126	Bear Hunt	126	207,000	1:51.40	
1985	Eternal Prince	3	R. Migliore	126	Proud Truth	126	Rhoman Rule	126	204,900	1:48.80	
1986	Broad Brush	3	V. Bracciale Jr	126	Mogambo	126	Groovy	126	178,500	1:50.60	
1987	Gulch	3	J.A. Santos	126	Gone West	126	Shawklit Won	126	354,300	1:49.00	
1988	Private Terms	3	C.W. Antley	126	Seeking the Gold	126	Cherokee Colony	126	359,400	1:47.20	
1989	Easy Goer	3	P. Day	126	Rock Point	126	Triple Buck	126	340,800	1:50.60	
1990	Thirty Six Red	3	M.E. Smith	126	Burnt Hills	126	Champagneforashley	126	362,400	1:50.40	103
1991	Cahill Road	3	C. Perret	126	Lost Mountain	126	Happy Jazz Band	126	300,000	1:48.40	109
1992	Devil His Due	3	M.E. Smith	126	West by West	126	Rokeby	126	300,000	1:49.20	99
1993	Storm Tower	3	R. Wilson	126	Tossofthecoin	126	Marked Tree	126	300,000	1:48.40	99
1994	Irgun	3	G.L. Stevens	123	Go for Gin	123	Shiprock	123	300,000	1:49.00	109
1995	Talkin Man	3	S.J. Sellers	123	Knockadoon	123	Is Sveikatas	123	300,000	1:49.20	106
1996	Unbridled's Song	3	M.E. Smith	123	In Contention	123	Romano Gucci	123	300,000	1:49.80	103
1997	Captain Bodgit	3	A. Solis	123	Accelerator	123	Smokin Mel	123	300,000	1:48.20	105
1998	Coronado's Quest	3	R.G. Davis	123	Dice Dancer	123	Parade Ground	123	300,000	1:47.40	116
1999	Adonis	3	J.F. Chavez	123	Best of Luck	123	Cliquot	123	360,000	1:47.30	103
2000	Fusaichi Pegasus	3	K.J. Desormeaux	123	Red Bullet	123	Aptitude	123	450,000	1:47.92	111
2001	Congaree	3	V. Espinoza	123	Monarchos	123	Richly Blended	123	450,000	1:47.96	108
2002	Buddha	3	P. Day	123	Medaglia d'Oro	123	Sunday Break	123	450,000	1:48.61	105
2003	Empire Maker	3	J.D. Bailey	123	Funny Cide	123	Kissin Saint	123	450,000	1:48.70	111
2004	Tapit	3	R.A. Dominguez	123	Master David	123	Eddington	123	450,000	1:49.70	98

Beyer Index: 105.67

WOODFORD RESERVE TURF CLASSIC (G1), 1 1/8 Miles (Turf), 3-Year-Olds and Up, Churchill Downs, 2004 Purse: $453,900

Year	Winner	Age	Jockey	Wt.	Second	Wt.	Third	Wt.	Win Value	Time	Beyer
1987	Manila	4	J. Vasquez	120	Vilzak	112	Lieutenant's Lark	120	110,045	1:48.80	
1988	Yankee Affair	6	P. Day	118	Yucca	112	First Patriot	112	121,225	1:50.00	
1989	Equalize	7	J.A. Santos	118	Yankee Affair	116	Gallant Mel	114	114,140	1:51.40	
1990	Ten Keys	6	K.J. Desormeaux	120	Yankee Affair	120	Stellar Rival	113	110,435	1:50.80	105
1991	Opening Verse	5	C.J. McCarron	116	Itsallgreektome	123	Pedro the Cool	112	125,060	1:47.20	106
1992	Cudas	4	P.A. Valenzuela	117	Sky Classic	123	Fourstars Allstar	118	124,703	1:46.40	105
1993	Lure	4	M.E. Smith	123	Star of Cozzene	118	Cleone	116	181,050	1:46.20	112
1994	Paradise Creek	5	P. Day	118	Lure	123	Yukon Robbery	116	152,067	1:48.20	107
1995	Romarin	5	C.S. Nakatani	118	Blues Traveller	120	Hasten to Add	120	169,585	1:46.80	107
1996	Mecke	4	P. Day	123	Petit Poucet	116	Winged Victory	116	154,960	1:49.40	106

Year	Winner	Age	Jockey	Wt.	Second	Wt.	Third	Wt.	Win Value	Time	Beyer
1997	Always a Classic	4	J.D. Bailey	120	Labeeb	118	Down the Aisle	114	145,328	1:49.40	106
1998	Joyeux Danseur	5	R.J. Albarado	123	Lasting Approval	120	Hawksley Hill	120	174,282	1:48.14	111
1999	Wild Event	6	S.J. Sellers	120	Garbu	116	Hawksley Hill	120	206,646	1:47.25	109
2000	Manndar	4	C.S. Nakatani	114	Falcon Flight	118	Yagli	120	217,310	1:47.91	103
2001	White Heart	6	G.L. Stevens	116	King Cugat	120	Brahms	123	216,938	1:48.75	108
2002	Beat Hollow	5	A. Solis	115	With Anticipation	123	Hap	123	280,550	1:47.35	108
2003	Honor in War	4	D.R. Flores	116	Requete	116	Patrol	114	276,086	1:46.67	110
2004	Stroll	4	J.D. Bailey	121	Sweet Return	123	Mystery Giver	123	281,418	1:53.00	107

Beyer Index: 107.33

For 4-year-olds and up prior to 1992. Run as Early Times Turf Classic prior to 2000

WOODWARD (G1), 1 1/8 Miles, 3-Year-Olds and Up, Belmont Park, 2004 Purse: $500,000

Year	Winner	Age	Jockey	Wt.	Second	Wt.	Third	Wt.	Win Value	Time	Beyer
1954	Pet Bully	6	W. Hartack	126	Joe Jones	111	Impasse	113	43,700	1:35.60	
1955	Traffic Judge	3	E. Arcaro	118	Paper Tiger	107	Dedicate	110	40,000	1:48.20	
1956	Mister Gus	5	W. Hartack	126	Nashua	126	Jet Action	126	52,950	2:03.00	
1957	Dedicate	5	W. Hartack	126	Gallant Man	120	Bold Ruler	120	70,500	2:01.00	
1958	Clem	4	W. Shoemaker	126	Nadir	120	Reneged	126	71,080	2:01.00	
1959	Sword Dancer	3	E. Arcaro	120	Hillsdale	126	Round Table	126	70,170	2:04.40	
1960	Sword Dancer	4	E. Arcaro	126	Dotted Swiss	126	Bald Eagle	126	71,730	2:01.20	
1961	Kelso	4	E. Arcaro	126	Divine Comedy	126	Carry Back	120	71,240	2:00.00	
1962	Kelso	5	I. Valenzuela	126	Jaipur	120	Guadalcanal	126	74,880	2:03.20	
1963	Kelso	6	I. Valenzuela	126	Never Bend	120	Crimson Satan	126	70,720	2:00.80	
1964	Gun Bow	4	W. Blum	126	Kelso	126	Quadrangle	121	70,330	2:02.40	
1965	Roman Brother	4	B. Baeza	126	Royal Gunner	121	Malicious	126	71,240	2:01.80	
1966	Buckpasser	3	B. Baeza	121	Royal Gunner	126	Buffle	121	73,190	2:02.80	
1967	Damascus	3	W. Shoemaker	120	Buckpasser	126	Dr. Fager	120	70,070	2:00.60	
1968	Mr. Right	5	H. Gustines	126	Damascus	126	Grace Born	126	69,420	2:03.00	
1969	Arts and Letters	3	B. Baeza	120	Nodouble	126	Verbatim	126	68,900	2:01.00	
1970	Personality	3	E. Belmonte	121	Hydrologist	126			71,435	2:01.80	
					Twogundan	126					
1971	West Coast Scout	3	J.L. Rotz	121	Tinajero	121	Cougar II	126	67,860	2:00.60	
	Cougar II finished first but was disqualified and placed third										
1972	Key to the Mint	3	B. Baeza	119	Autobiography	126	Summer Guest	116	69,300	2:28.40	
	Summer Guest finished second but was disqualified and placed third										
1973	Prove Out	4	J. Velasquez	126	Secretariat	119	Cougar II	126	64,920	2:25.80	
1974	Forego	4	H. Gustines	126	Arbees Boy	126	Group Plan	126	69,240	2:27.60	
1975	Forego	5	H. Gustines	126	Wajima	119	Group Plan	126	64,920	2:27.20	
1976	Forego	6	W. Shoemaker	135	Dance Spell	115	Stumping	108	103,920	1:45.80	
							Honest Pleasure	121			
1977	Forego	7	W. Shoemaker	133	Silver Series	114	Great Contractor	115	105,000	1:48.00	
1978	Seattle Slew	4	A. Cordero Jr	126	Exceller	126	It's Freezing	126	97,800	2:00.00	
1979	Affirmed	4	L. Pincay Jr	126	Coastal	120	Czaravich	120	114,600	2:01.60	
1980	Spectacular Bid	4	W. Shoemaker	126					73,300	2:02.40	
	Walkover										
1981	Pleasant Colony	3	A. Cordero Jr	123	Amber Pass	126	Herb Water	116	137,400	1:47.20	
1982	Island Whirl	4	A. Cordero Jr	123	Silver Buck	126	Silver Supreme	126	136,500	1:46.80	
1983	Slew o' Gold	3	A. Cordero Jr	118	Bates Motel	123	Sing Sing	117	138,900	1:46.60	
1984	Slew o' Gold	4	A. Cordero Jr	126	Shifty Sheik	116	Bet Big	116	175,200	1:47.80	
1985	Track Barron	4	A. Cordero Jr	123	Vanlandingham	123	Chief's Crown	121	200,400	1:46.60	
1986	Precisionist	5	C.J. McCarron	126	Lady's Secret	121	Personal Flag	110	199,200	1:46.00	
1987	Polish Navy	3	R.P. Romero	116	Gulch	118	Creme Fraiche	119	357,000	1:47.00	
1988	Alysheba	4	C.J. McCarron	126	Forty Niner	119	Waquoit	122	498,600	1:59.40	
1989	Easy Goer	3	P. Day	122	Its Acedemic	109	Forever Silver	119	485,400	2:01.00	
1990	Dispersal	4	C.W. Antley	123	Quiet American	117	Rhythm	120	354,000	1:45.80	118
1991	In Excess	4	G.L. Stevens	126	Farma Way	126	Festin	120	300,000	1:46.20	116
1992	Sultry Song	4	J.D. Bailey	126	Pleasant Tap	126	Out of Place	126	300,000	1:47.00	115
1993	Bertrando	4	G.L. Stevens	126	Devil His Due	126	Valley Crossing	126	425,000	1:47.00	125
1994	Holy Bull	3	M.E. Smith	121	Devil His Due	126	Colonial Affair	126	300,000	1:46.80	116
1995	Cigar	5	J.D. Bailey	126	Star Standard	121	Golden Larch	126	300,000	1:47.00	111
1996	Cigar	6	J.D. Bailey	126	L'Carriere	126	Golden Larch	126	300,000	1:47.00	116
1997	Formal Gold	4	K.J. Desormeaux	126	Skip Away	126	Will's Way	126	300,000	1:47.40	125
1998	Skip Away	5	J.D. Bailey	126	Gentlemen	126	Running Stag	126	300,000	1:47.80	119
1999	River Keen	7	C.W. Antley	126	Almutawakel	126	Stephen Got Even	121	300,000	1:46.85	117
2000	Lemon Drop Kid	4	E.S. Prado	126	Behrens	126	Gander	126	300,000	1:50.53	105
2001	Lido Palace	4	J.D. Bailey	126	Albert The Great	126	Tiznow	126	300,000	1:47.42	113
2002	Lido Palace	5	J.F. Chavez	126	Gander	126	Express Tour	126	300,000	1:47.75	105
2003	Mineshaft	4	R.J. Albarado	126	Hold That Tiger	122	Puzzlement	126	300,000	1:46.21	117
2004	Ghostzapper	4	J.J. Castellano	126	Saint Liam	126	Bowman's Band	126	300,000	1:46.38	114

Beyer Index: 115.47

Distance 1 mile in 1954; 1 1/4 miles, 1956-71, 1978-80, 1988-89; 1 1/2 miles, 1972-75. Run at Aqueduct 1959-60, 1962-67

YELLOW RIBBON (G1), 1 1/4 Miles (Turf), Fillies and Mares, 3-Year-Olds and Up, Santa Anita, 2004 Purse: $500,000

Year	Winner	Age	Jockey	Wt.	Second	Wt.	Third	Wt.	Win Value	Time	Beyer
1977	Star Ball	5	H. Grant	123	Swingtime	123	Theia	123	60,000	2:02.60	
1978	Amazer	3	W. Shoemaker	119	Drama Critic	123	Surera	123	90,000	1:59.20	
1979	Country Queen	4	L. Pincay Jr	123	Prize Spot	119	Giggling Girl	123	90,000	2:00.20	
1980	Kilijaro	4	A. Lequeux	123	Ack's Secret	123	Queen to Conquer	123	120,000	1:59.20	
1981	Queen to Conquer	5	M. Castaneda	123	Star Pastures	119	Ack's Secret	123	180,000	1:58.60	
1982	Castilla	3	R. Sibille	119	Avigaition	119	Sangue	123	180,000	1:58.60	
	Avigation finished first but was disqualified and placed second										
1983	Sangue	5	W. Shoemaker	123	L'Attrayante	119	Infinite	119	240,000	2:02.20	
1984	Sabin	4	E. Maple	123	Grise Mine	118	Estrapade	123	240,000	2:00.00	
1985	Estrapade	5	W. Shoemaker	123	Alydar's Best	118	La Koumia	118	240,000	2:00.40	
1986	Bonne Ile	5	F. Toro	123	Top Corsage	118	Carotene	118	240,000	2:01.40	
1987	Carotene	4	J.A. Santos	123	Nashmeel	119	Khariyda	119	240,000	2:03.80	
1988	Delighter	3	C.J. McCarron	119	Nastique	123	No Review	119	240,000	2:02.40	
1989	Brown Bess	7	J.L. Kaenel	123	Darby's Daughter	119	Colorado Dancer	119	240,000	1:57.60	
1990	Plenty of Grace	3	W.H. McCauley	119	Petite Ile	123	Royal Touch	123	240,000	1:58.40	
1991	Kostroma	5	K.J. Desormeaux	123	Flawlessly	119	Fire the Groom	123	240,000	2:01.01	106
1992	Super Staff	4	K.J. Desormeaux	123	Flawlessly	123	Campagnarde	123	240,000	1:59.36	106
1993	Possibly Perfect	3	C.S. Nakatani	118	Tribulation	118	Miatuschka	122	240,000	2:02.91	101
1994	Aube Indienne	4	K.J. Desormeaux	122	Fondly Remembered	122	Zoonaqua	122	240,000	2:02.32	102
1995	Alpride	4	C.J. McCarron	122	Angel in My Heart	118	Bold Ruritana	122	360,000	2:01.68	105
1996	Donna Viola	4	G.L. Stevens	122	Real Connection	122	Dixie Pearl	122	360,000	2:00.62	105
1997	Ryafan	3	A. Solis	118	Fanjica	122	Memories of Silver	122	300,000	2:03.69	105
1998	Fiji	4	K.J. Desormeaux	122	Sonja's Faith	122	Pomona	122	300,000	2:05.23	108
	See You Soon finished second but was disqualified and placed fourth										
1999	Spanish Fern	4	C.J. McCarron	123	Caffe Latte	118	Shabby Chic	118	300,000	1:59.52	104
2000	Tranquility Lake	5	E. Delahoussaye	123	Spanish Fern	123	Polaire	123	300,000	2:02.98	100
2001	Janet	4	D.R. Flores	123	Tranquility Lake	123	Al Desima	123	300,000	1:58.64	104
2002	Golden Apples	4	P.A. Valenzuela	123	Voodoo Dancer	123	Banks Hill	123	300,000	1:59.72	108
2003	Tates Creek	5	P.A. Valenzuela	123	Musical Chimes	118	Crazy Ensign	123	300,000	2:00.77	107
2004	Light Jig	4	R.R. Douglas	123	Tangle	123	Katdogawn	123	300,000	1:59.28	101

Beyer Index: 104.43

YERBA BUENA BREEDERS' CUP HANDICAP (G3), About 1 1/8 Miles (Turf), Fillies and Mares, 3-Year-Olds and Up, Bay Meadows, 2004 Purse: $113,750

Year	Winner	Age	Jockey	Wt.	Second	Wt.	Third	Wt.	Win Value	Time	Beyer
1973	Live Forever	4	J.T. Gonzalez	112	Fleet Ahead	112	Homespun	111	12,050	2:19.60	
1974	Merry Madeleine	4	F. Mena	113	Hurry Countess	110	Hum Dum	111	17,625	2:31.40	
1975	Joli Vert	4	F. Olivares	115	Lucky Spell	122	Gentleweave	106	31,000	2:16.80	
1976	Our First Delight	4	E. Munoz	120	Graceful Banner	112	L'rking Party	113	33,400	2:16.40	
1977	Star Ball	5	J.L. Vargas	121	Bastonera II	124	Up to Juliet	117	48,350	2:14.80	
1978	Star Ball	6	D.G. McHargue	124	Up to Juliet	114	Surera	112	63,800	2:13.60	
1980	Mairzy Doates	4	F. Mena	116	Sisterhood	121	Smaller Bicker	113	66,900	2:15.00	
1981	Mairzy Doates	5	F. Mena	120	Princess Karenda	123	Princess Toby	117	78,550	2:15.80	
1982	Sangue	4	T.M. Chapman	117	Berry Bush	119	Mademoiselle Ivor	112	78,400	2:16.40	
1983	Dilmoun	4	J.J. Steiner	111	Latrone	112	Berry Bush	119	82,350	2:31.60	
1984	Fact Finder	5	M. Castaneda	115	Lido Isle	114	Her Decision	115	107,200	2:30.20	
1985	Salt Spring	6	T.M. Chapman	115	High Spruce	111	L'Attrayante	120	95,800	2:30.20	
1986	Scythe	5	T.M. Chapman	113	Heat Spell	115	Lock's Dream	114	85,000	2:32.20	
1987	Ivor's Image	4	C.J. McCarron	119	Micenas	115	Royal Regatta	114	82,500	2:29.60	
1988	Magdelaine	5	T.T. Doocy	113	Sweet Roberta	115	Top Corsage	118	82,500	2:14.40	
1989	Brown Bess	7	J.L. Kaenel	119	Carmenetta	114	Flattering News	111	82,500	2:15.60	
1990	Petite Ile	4	C.A. Black	118	Double Wedge	112	Brown Bess	124	82,500	2:15.60	
1991	Free at Last	4	R.D. Hansen	120	Noble and Nice	117	Louve Bleue	114	82,500	2:15.00	
1992	Flaming Torch	5	R.A. Baze	114	Indian Chris	116	Silvered	114	82,500	2:16.20	96
1993	Party Cited	4	R.J. Warren Jr	117	Silvered	115	Rougeur	115	55,000	2:15.00	102
1994	Ask Anita	4	Belvoir VT	116	Miami Sands	115	Oxava	115	55,000	2:15.40	100
1995	Work the Crowd	4	Baze RA	123	Late Sailing	116	Ask Anita	117	68,750	1:49.20	95
1996	Fanjica	4	Carr D.	114	Nimble Mind	115	Dynatar	113	60,000	2:17.40	100
1997	De Puntillas	5	Espinoza V.	116	Dynatar	117	Tricky Code	116	60,000	1:46.60	98
1998	Miss Universal	5	Mercado P.	114	Proud Fillie	115	Squeak	118	75,000	2:15.60	99
1999	Blending Element	6	Gomez G. K.	117	Queen Douna	113	Midnight Line	117	120,000	2:17.20	95
2000	Gleefully	4	R.Q. Meza	113	Country Garden	116	Marie de Bayeux	113	110,000	2:15.99	96
2001	Janet	4	D.R. Flores	115	Keemoon	121	Alexine	119	82,500	2:17.09	99
2002	Peu a Peu	4	R.A. Baze	115	Janet	122	Racene	115	55,000	2:16.39	98
2003	Chiming	5	C.S. Nakatani	116	Noches de Rosa	119	Lindsay Jean	118	55,000	1:45.41	108
2004	A B Noodle	5	J.M. Castro	116	Marwood	116	Hooked on Niners	116	68,750	1:46.66	94

Beyer Index: 98.46

Histories of Canadian Graded Stakes Events and Classics

ATTO MILE (G1-C), 1 Mile (Turf), 3-Year-Olds and Up, Woodbine, 2004 Purse: $1,000,000

Year	Winner	Age	Jockey	Wt.	Second	Wt.	Third	Wt.	Win Value	Time	Beyer
1997	Geri	5	C.W. Antley	117	Helmsman	117	Crown Attorney	117	300,000	1:36.20	107
1998	Labeeb	6	K.J. Desormeaux	121	Jim and Tonic	119	Poteen	117	450,000	1:33.00	114
1999	Quiet Resolve	4	R.C. Landry	117	Rob 'n Gin	119	Jim and Tonic	121	630,000	1:33.19	109
	Hawksley Hill finished first but was disqualified and placed fourth										
2000	Riviera	6	J.R. Velazquez	117	Arkadian Hero	119	Affirmed Success	121	600,000	1:33.18	106
2001	Numerous Times	4	P. Husbands	117	Affirmed Success	119	Quiet Resolve	121	600,000	1:32.79	108
2002	Good Journey	6	P. Day	121	Chopinina	114	Nuclear Debate	121	600,000	1:33.27	108
2003	Touch of the Blues	6	K.J. Desormeaux	119	Soaring Free	121	Perfect Soul	121	600,000	1:33.39	106
2004	Soaring Free	5	T.K. Kabel	119	Perfect Soul	121	Royal Regalia	118	600,000	1:32.72	103

Beyer Index: 107.63

Run as Woodbine Mile 1997-1998.

BALLERINA BREEDERS' CUP (G3-C), 1 1/8 Miles, Fillies and Mares, 3-Year-Olds and Up, Hastings, 2004 Purse: $197,150

Year	Winner	Age	Jockey	Wt.	Second	Wt.	Third	Wt.	Win Value	Time	Beyer
1994	Above the Table	4	S.B. Krasner	109	Regal Andi	120	Pilgrims Treasure	113	52,560	1:50.80	84
1995	Sophie J	3	J. Barton	119	Dark Hours	119	Staraway	120	79,950	1:52.20	90
1996	Kims Turn to Star	4	D.H. Wilson	116	Sophie J	127	Tucumcari	116	72,100	1:49.00	89
1997	Ever Lasting	4	C. Loseth	121	Strawberry Morn	124	Ricadonna	112	70,500	1:49.80	92
1998	Magic Code	3	A. Cuthbertson	118	Strawberry Morn	122	Tucumcari	121	96,026	1:52.20	90
1999	Magic Code	4	A. Cuthbertson	120	Lasting Chance	117	Sagacity	114	105,025	1:50.61	100
2000	Magic Code	5	G. Baze	119	Make Contact	118	Fabulous Flight	116	105,052	1:50.69	93
2001	Grey Tobe Free	4	C. Loseth	123	Fabulous Flight	123	Make Contact	123	81,634	1:49.71	99
2002	Grace for You	3	F.A. Serna	120	Full Scream Ahead	123	Castle Mountain	123	82,757	1:52.87	82
2003	Dancewithavixen	3	F. Valdez	121	Secondary School	124	Shelby Madison	124	100,320	1:52.58	85
2004	See Me Through	3	P.V. Alvarado	121	Summer Symphony	121	You and Nelly	124	108,540	1:51.42	81

Beyer Index: 89.55

Run as a handicap 1996-2000. For previous runnings see the 1994 Manual

BESSARABIAN HANDICAP (G3-C), 7 Furlongs, Fillies and Mares, 3-Year-Olds and Up, Woodbine, 2004 Purse: $212,750

Year	Winner	Age	Jockey	Wt.	Second	Wt.	Third	Wt.	Win Value	Time	Beyer
1994	Early Blaze	4	L. Duffy	120	Valiant Jewel	115	Casual Rendezvous	113	40,716	1:23.20	96
1995	Early Blaze	5	L. Duffy	115	Countess Steffi	116	Heavenly Punch	115	49,095	1:23.80	92
1996	Flat Fleet Feet	3	M.E. Smith	120	Dial a Song	115	Flashy n Smart	113	70,020	1:23.20	92
1997	Autumn Slew	4	T.K. Kabel	118	Flashy n Smart	119	Angel's Tearlet	113	56,940	1:23.40	90
1998	Santa Amelia	5	R.C. Landry	122	Scotzanna	116	Copelan's Piano	113	54,996	1:22.40	89
1999	Barlee Mist	4	P. Husbands	118	Woofy	114	Except for Wanda	115	65,670	1:23.50	104
	Cafe Dancer finished third, was disqualified and placed sixth										
2000	Feathers	3	M.K. Walls	118	El Prado Essence	115	Torrid Affair	116	81,375	1:23.93	92
2001	Elektraline	5	G. Boulanger	119	Feathers	121	Ahead by a Century	115	82,725	1:22.38	93
2002	Sheila's Prospect	4	J.S. McAleney	115	Miss Sweep	117	Lightning Pace	114	100,080	1:22.98	80
2003	Winter Garden	3	D. Clark	121	El Prado Essence	120	Mille Feville	115	98,640	1:24.14	84
2004	Miss Grindstone	5	R.B. Sabourin	113	El Prado Essence	118	Surprised Humor	117	97,650	1:23.21	98

Beyer Index: 91.82

Run as Etobicoke Handicap 1994-1995. For previous runnings see the 1994 Manual

BREEDERS', 1 1/2 Miles (Turf), 3-Year-Olds, Foaled in Canada, Woodbine, 2004 Purse: $500,000

Year	Winner	Age	Jockey	Wt.	Second	Wt.	Third	Wt.	Win Value	Time	Beyer
1994	Basqueian	3	J. Lauzon	126	Pagagar	126	Testalino	126	149,739	2:47.80	96
1995	Charlie's Dewan	3	C. Perret	126	Mt. Sassafras	126	Dagda	126	182,700	2:26.40	93
1996	Chief Bearhart	3	M.K. Walls	126	Firm Dancer	126	Sealaunch	126	171,120	2:28.60	107
1997	John the Magician	3	S.R. Bahen	126	One Emotion	121	Heaven to Earth	121	175,860	2:35.60	89
1998	Pinafore Park	3	R.C. Landry	121	Patriot Love	126	Comet Kris	126	180,000	2:30.20	92
1999	Free Vacation	3	L. Gulas	121	John the Drummer	126	American Falcon	126	195,000	2:28.45	88
2000	Lodge Hill	3	M.E. Smith	126	Master Stuart	126	Scatter the Gold	126	300,000	2:28.97	90
2001	Sweetest Thing	3	J.S. McAleney	121	Flaming Sky	126	Asia	121	300,000	2:29.90	91
2002	Portcullis	3	S. Callaghan	126	El Soprano	126	Mountain Beacon	126	300,000	2:29.80	93
2003	Wando	3	P. Husbands	126	Shoal Water	126	Colorful Judgement	126	300,000	2:28.69	100
2004	A Bit O'Gold	3	J.C. Jones	126	Burst of Fire	126	Silver Ticket	126	300,000	2:27.15	93

Beyer Index: 93.82

Run at Fort Erie in 1994. For previous runnings see the 1994 Manual

BRITISH COLUMBIA BREEDERS' CUP OAKS (G3-C), 1 1/8 Miles, Fillies, 3-Year-Olds, Hastings, 2004 Purse: $192,350

Year	Winner	Age	Jockey	Wt.	Second	Wt.	Third	Wt.	Win Value	Time	Beyer
1994	Take Her to Heart	3	B.G. Winnett Jr	121	Richly Romantic	121	Ride on Ice	121	55,080	1:52.20	78
1995	Dark Hours	3	C. Loseth	121	Sophie J	121	Kims Turn to Star	121	75,260	1:50.40	84
1996	Ever Lasting	3	C. Loseth	121	Tucumcari	121	Vigors Destiny	121	74,420	1:52.20	91
1997	Bali Beauty	3	C. Loseth	121	Ricadonna	121	Winning Agenda	121	77,920	1:51.40	79
1998	Ultimate Force	3	F.P. Fuentes	121	Deputy Sue	121	Kriskeri	121	110,740	1:51.40	84
1999	Lasting Chance	3	C. Loseth	121	Spice Girl	121	Blue in Green	121	105,043	1:50.54	85
2000	Grooms Derby	3	B.R. Russell	121	Make Contact	121	Ajmaer	121	75,584	1:51.05	91
2001	Collect Call	3	C. Loseth	121	Inish Glora	121	Withoutapproval	121	105,000	1:50.45	88
2002	Elana d'Amour	3	P.V. Alvarado	121	Sweet Monarch	121	Grace for You	121	83,198	1:51.67	79
2003	Raylene	3	R. Walcott	121	Dancewithavixen	121	Payton's Pride	121	90,000	1:52.16	85
2004	Summer Symphony	3	C. Hoverson	121	Socorro County	121	See Me Through	121	105,660	1:51.08	79

Beyer Index: 83.91

For previous runnings see the 1994 Manual

BRITISH COLUMBIA DERBY (G3-C), 1 1/8 Miles, 3-Year-Olds, Hastings, 2004 Purse: $351,500

Year	Winner	Age	Jockey	Wt.	Second	Wt.	Third	Wt.	Win Value	Time	Beyer
1994	Squire Jones	3	B.G. Winnett Jr	126	Majestic Silence	126	Old Tucson	126	94,950	1:51.80	86
1995	Flying Sauce	3	R. King Jr	126	Destiny's Command	126	Big Mo	126	106,060	1:50.60	90
1996	Newdigs	3	C. Loseth	126	Timely Stitch	126	Strawberry Morn	121	109,110	1:50.20	92
1997	Bobbin for Stars	3	S.B. Krasner	126	You've Got Action	126	Knave	126	109,670	1:49.80	91
1998	Vernon Invader	3	C. Loseth	126	Summer Prince	126	Ryson	126	129,342	1:51.00	85
1999	Wandering	3	S.B. Krasner	126	Yaletown	126	Digital Dan	126	120,000	1:50.96	91
2000	Makors Mark	3	G. Baze	126	King Jeremy	126	Sign of Fire	126	105,000	1:49.53	94
2001	Fancy As	3	R. Hamel	126	I'm Free	126	Diglett	126	120,000	1:50.71	97
2002	Cruising Kat	3	N. Wright	124	Blowin in the Wind	124	Silver Donn	124	133,432	1:50.49	85
2003	Roscoe Pito	3	P.V. Alvarado	126	Steady Smiler	126	Rindanica	126	198,750	1:51.58	86
2004	Flamethrowintexan	3	R.L. Frazier	126	Lord Samarai	126	Strike Em Hard	126	191,400	1:49.58	92

Beyer Index: 89.91

For previous runnings see the 1994 Manual

CANADIAN DERBY (G3-C), 1 3/8 Miles, 3-Year-Olds, Northlands Park, 2004 Purse: $250,000

Year	Winner	Age	Jockey	Wt.	Second	Wt.	Third	Wt.	Win Value	Time	Beyer
1994	Funboy	3	A. Cuthbertson	126	Latshaw	126	Mr. Morris	126	63,000	2:23.20	78
1995	Sovacianto	3	C.H. McGregor	126	Woodman's Kris	126	Bet Once	126	63,000	2:18.40	77
	Sonabove finished first but was disqualified and placed fifth										
1996	Jan Alta	3	M.J. McMullen	126	Northernprospector	126	Letkingo	126	63,000	2:18.00	87
1997	Smoky Cinder	3	T.G. Adkins	126	Chariot Chaser	126	Music Jamboree	126	63,000	2:20.20	79
1998	A Fleets Dancer	3	R.E. Simard	126	Silver Talk	126	Regal Plan	126	94,500	2:19.40	90
1999	Native Brass	3	A.S. Ferris	121	Divinail's Hope	126	Gray Aras	126	94,500	2:19.00	88
2000	Scotman	3	C.H. McGregor	126	Im Five	126	Breaker Breaker	126	94,500	2:19.20	90
2001	Fancy As	3	R. Hamel	126	Stage Classic	126	Thurston	126	94,500	2:18.00	95
2002	Lady Shari	3	C. Montpellier	121	Sweet Monarch	121	No Time Flat	126	94,500	2:19.40	85
2003	Raylene	3	R. Walcott	121	Taiaslew	126	Reb's Drummer	126	94,500	2:21.60	83
2004	Organ Grinder	3	J.S. McAleney	126	Controlled Meeting	126	Bonspiel	126	157,500	2:22.60	77
							Cariboo Prospector	126			

Beyer Index: 84.45

For previous runnings see the 1994 Manual

CANADIAN HANDICAP (G2-C), About 1 1/8 Miles (Turf), Fillies and Mares, 3-Year-Olds and Up, Woodbine, 2004 Purse: $330,500

Year	Winner	Age	Jockey	Wt.	Second	Wt.	Third	Wt.	Win Value	Time	Beyer
1994	Alywow	3	D. Penna	115	Bold Ruritana	116	Myrtle Irene	120	65,805	1:39.80	96
1995	Bold Ruritana	5	R.C. Landry	122	Hey Hazel	114	Timeless Kisses	109	63,915	1:39.60	97
1996	Daylight Come	3	C. Montpellier	112	Bold Ruritana	124	Mountain Affair	115	69,960	1:44.60	94
1997	Woolloomooloo	5	T.K. Kabel	116	Santa Amelia	117	Colorful Vices	119	66,615	1:40.60	98
1998	Skytrial	3	R.C. Landry	113	Griselda	113	Heliotrope	110	51,615	1:42.80	87
1999	Anguilla	4	P. Day	119	Gandria	114	Midnight Line	118	88,875	1:46.87	101
2000	Wild Heart Dancing	4	J.F. Chavez	113	Nordican Inch	115	Skytrial	114	136,800	1:45.07	98
2001	Diadella	4	D. Clark	115	Nymphenburg	117	Cayman Sunset	116	141,000	1:43.76	98
2002	Calista	4	C.S. Nakatani	117	Diadella	118	Lush Soldier	113	168,750	1:45.04	97
2003	Inish Glora	5	T.K. Kabel	116	Volga	118	Diadella	116	197,400	1:44.56	98
2004	Classic Stamp	4	P. Husbands	117	Inish Glora	121	Heyahohowdy	114	198,300	1:43.59	97

Beyer Index: 96.45

Off the turf in 1996. For previous runnings see the 1994 Manual

(PATTISON) CANADIAN INTERNATIONAL (G1-C), 1 1/2 Miles (Turf), 3-Year-Olds and Up, Woodbine, 2004 Purse: $1,500,000

Year	Winner	Age	Jockey	Wt.	Second	Wt.	Third	Wt.	Win Value	Time	Beyer
1994	Raintrap	4	R. Davis	126	Alywow	116	Volochine	119	606,900	2:25.60	106
1995	Lassigny	4	P. Day	126	Mecke	118	Hasten to Add	126	653,250	2:29.80	106
1996	Singspiel	4	G.L. Stevens	126	Chief Bearhart	118	Mecke	126	600,000	2:33.20	115
1997	Chief Bearhart	4	J.A. Santos	126	Down the Aisle	126	Romanov	119	600,000	2:29.00	111
1998	Royal Anthem	3	G.L. Stevens	119	Chief Bearhart	126	Parade Ground	119	630,000	2:29.60	110
1999	Thornfield	5	R.A. Dos Ramos	126	Fruits of Love	126	Courteous	126	936,000	2:32.39	105
2000	Mutafaweq	4	L. Dettori	126	Williams News	126	Daliapour	126	900,000	2:27.62	106
2001	Mutamam	6	R. Hills	126	Paolini	126	Lodge Hill	126	900,000	2:28.46	107
	Zindabad finished third but was disqualified and placed sixth										
2002	Ballingarry	3	M.J. Kinane	118	Falcon Flight	126	Yavana's Pace	126	900,000	2:31.68	111
2003	Phoenix Reach	3	M. Dwyer	119	Macaw	126	Brian Boru	119	900,000	2:33.62	108
2004	Sulamani	5	L. Dettori	126	Simonas	126	Brian Boru	126	900,000	2:28.64	115

Beyer Index: 109.09

Run as Rothmans Ltd International 1994-1995. Run as Canadian International 1996-2002. Run as Pattison Canadian Internation 2003-04. For previous runnings see the 1994 Manual

CHINESE CULTURAL CENTRE (G2-C), 1 3/8 Miles (Turf), 3-Year-Olds and Up, Woodbine, 2004 Purse: $333,300

Year	Winner	Age	Jockey	Wt.	Second	Wt.	Third	Wt.	Win Value	Time	Beyer
1998	Buck's Boy	5	E. Fires	121	Crown Attorney	119	Terremoto	115	131,520	2:15.40	106
1999	Crown Attorney	6	M.K. Walls	117	Incitatus	117	Desert Waves	119	132,360	2:18.53	97
2000	Quiet Resolve	5	R.J. Albarado	119	Casino King	117	Craigsteel	115	169,950	2:13.20	102
2001	Allende	4	N. Somsanith	115	Muntej	119	Quiet Resolve	124	164,100	2:16.98	100
2002	Strike Smartly	5	L.L. Gulas	115	Quiet Resolve	121	Muntej	115	201,780	2:13.16	101
2003	Strut the Stage	5	T.K. Kabel	121	Perfect Soul	119	Angel on the Wing	115	198,540	2:13.85	103
2004	Shoal Water	4	T.K. Kabel	116	Mobil	121	Strut the Stage	121	199,980	2:12.37	103

Beyer Index: 101.71

Run as Hong Kong Jockey Club Trophy 1998-2001.

CONNAUGHT CUP (G3-C), 1 1/16 Miles (Turf), 4-Year-Olds and Up, Woodbine, 2004 Purse: $164,400

Year	Winner	Age	Jockey	Wt.	Second	Wt.	Third	Wt.	Win Value	Time	Beyer
1994	Shiny Key	6	M.G. Larsen	123	Beau Fasa	121	Road of War	115	42,804	1:35.00	93
1995	Jet Freighter	4	T.K. Kabel	119	Roche Rock	115	Strike a Gold Mine	119	52,380	1:39.20	98
1996	Lahint	5	T.K. Kabel	115	Desert Waves	115	Kiridashi	121	68,940	1:40.20	101
1997	Kiridashi	5	M.K. Walls	124	Firm Dancer	115	Terremoto	113	64,740	1:40.00	105
1998	Kiridashi	6	T.K. Kabel	119	Crown Attorney	121	Ok by Me	119	67,800	1:39.80	104
1999	Incitatus	6	S. Callaghan	113	Crown Attorney	119	Cracker's Folly	119	66,360	1:40.57	93
2000	Super Red	4	E. Ramsammy	115	Red Scare	115	Incitatus	119	101,340	1:43.78	100
2001	Red Sea	5	E. Ramsammy	115	River Boat	119	Silver Axe	115	99,090	1:47.49	100
2001	Del Mar Show	4	R.G. Davis	121	Lodge Hill	119	Kimberlite Pipe	115	99,990	1:48.17	95
2002	Quiet Resolve	7	T.K. Kabel	119	No Comprende	117	Gone Fishin	117	107,100	1:40.88	106
2003	Fly Smartly	5	T.K. Kabel	117	Solitary Dancer	117	Mr. Sulu	117	104,130	1:47.71	94
2004	Slew Valley	7	J.S. McAleney	117	Le Cinquieme Essai	117	Shoal Water	117	98,640	1:40.24	98

Beyer Index: 98.92

Run at Fort Erie in 1994. Run at 1 mile in 1994. Run in divisions in 2001. For previous runnings see the 1994 Manual

DANCE SMARTLY HANDICAP (G3-C), 1 1/8 Miles (Turf), Fillies and Mares, 3-Year-Olds and Up, Woodbine, 2004 Purse: $212,450

Year	Winner	Age	Jockey	Wt.	Second	Wt.	Third	Wt.	Win Value	Time	Beyer
1994	Silky Feather	4	S.R. Bahen	112	Bold Ruritana	115	Ballerina Queen	111	99,708	1:50.00	92
1995	Memories	4	S.J. Sellers	116	Bold Ruritana	122	Ballerina Queen	113	125,340	1:47.20	101
1996	Bold Ruritana	6	R.C. Landry	123	La Turka	115	Ballerina Queen	113	67,440	1:46.60	96
1997	Woolloomooloo	5	T.K. Kabel	116	Classic Wonder	117	Ascot Yael	110	50,265	1:46.80	91
	Santa Amelia finished second but was disqualified and placed fourth										
1998	Colorful Vices	5	T.K. Kabel	118	Noir Velours	113	Classic Wonder	117	67,200	1:46.20	94
1999	Ascot Yael	5	P. Husbands	114	Skytrial	115	No Foul Play	115	66,480	1:47.25	94
2000	Except for Wanda	5	J.S. McAleney	114	Only to You	115	Heliotrope	114	131,370	1:46.61	97
2001	Alexis	5	J.C. Jones	116	Badouizm	117	Only to You	118	102,780	1:47.81	92
2002	Sweetest Thing	4	J.S. McAleney	121	Mountain Angel	118	Rosthern	116	129,360	1:45.72	98
2003	Madeira Mist	4	P. Husbands	116	First Quarter	114	Byzantine	117	103,050	1:48.05	94
2004	Mona Rose	4	E.R. Da Silva	112	Inish Glora	122	Classic Stamp	116	133,844	1:48.18	96

Beyer Index: 95.00

Run as Woodbine Budweiser Breeders' Cup Handicap 1994-1995. For previous runnings see the 1994 Manual

DOMINION DAY HANDICAP (G3-C), 1 1/4 Miles, 3-Year-Olds and Up, Woodbine, 2004 Purse: $217,200

Year	Winner	Age	Jockey	Wt.	Second	Wt.	Third	Wt.	Win Value	Time	Beyer
1994	Pomeroon	4	T.K. Kabel	114	Truth of It All	108	Comarctic	112	101,880	2:02.80	101
1995	Alybro	4	D. Penna	115	Comarctic	117	Major Pots	115	103,050	2:04.20	98
1996	Mt. Sassafras	4	M.K. Walls	118	Major Pots	115	Heaven's Wish	114	96,840	2:03.40	103
1997	Firm Dancer	4	T.K. Kabel	115	Northern Sky	112	Regal Discovery	115	80,250	2:01.40	103
1998	Stephanotis	5	M.K. Walls	117	Northern Sky	115	Terremoto	120	83,025	2:03.60	105
1999	Mt. Sassafras	7	R.A. Dos Ramos	113	Brite Adam	116	Ski Maker	112	84,075	2:01.38	110
2000	The Fed	5	N. Somsanith	114	Ghost Story	118	Tarquinius	119	97,740	2:04.41	103
2001	A Fleets Dancer	6	R.A. Dos Ramos	117	Tarquinius	113	Ground Storm	114	100,080	2:05.69	104
2002	Bonus Pack	4	J.L. Castanon	116	Attest	115	Win City	117	131,880	2:03.01	106
2003	Phantom Light	4	T.K. Kabel	115	Changeintheweather	117	Dance to Destiny	115	135,600	2:01.15	108
2004	Mobil	4	T.K. Kabel	122	Mark One	118	The Judge Sez Who	119	130,320	2:03.34	92

Beyer Index: 103.00

For previous runnings see the 1994 Manual

DUCHESS (G3-C), 7 Furlongs, Fillies, 3-Year-Olds, Woodbine, 2004 Purse: $210,650

Year	Winner	Age	Jockey	Wt.	Second	Wt.	Third	Wt.	Win Value	Time	Beyer
1994	Mysteriously	3	T.K. Kabel	120	Kirby Meadow	114	Her Temper	120	39,816	1:23.40	88
1995	Heavenly Punch	3	D. Penna	114	Lynclar	116	Words of Royalty	114	48,960	1:23.80	82
1996	Autumn Slew	3	R.C. Landry	114	Gambling Girl	114	Miners Mirage	118	49,230	1:23.40	90
1997	Cotton Carnival	3	R.C. Landry	120	Little Champ	114	Exclusive Affair	115	39,312	1:24.80	92
1998	Kissedbyacrusader	3	S.R. Bahen	116	Urban Distraction	114	Lucky Paws	117	50,490	1:22.80	95
1999	Gregorian Chance	3	T.K. Kabel	116	Touch Dial	123	St. Noras	115	64,500	1:22.81	101
2000	Heat It Up	3	G.L. Olguin	116	Cedar Knolls	114	Plenty of Light	120	87,000	1:22.50	93
2001	Meadow Gem	3	D. Clark	115	Gold Mover	120	Poetically	118	83,100	1:22.48	101
2002	Mulrainy	3	C. Sutherland	114	For Rubies	114	Spanish Decree	120	133,410	1:23.98	91
2003	Finally Here	3	P. Husbands	117	Miss Crissy	118	Winter Garden	120	100,350	1:24.15	84
	Winter Garden finished second but was disqualified and placed third										
2004	Blonde Executive	3	R.A. Dos Ramos	123	Silver Bird	118	Search the Church	114	126,390	1:23.26	88

Beyer Index: 91.36

For previous runnings see the 1994 Manual

DURHAM CUP HANDICAP (G3-C), 1 1/8 Miles, 3-Year-Olds and Up, Woodbine, 2004 Purse: $159,450

Year	Winner	Age	Jockey	Wt.	Second	Wt.	Third	Wt.	Win Value	Time	Beyer
1994	Basqueian	3	S.J. Sellers	115	Ivory Regent	109	Bronze Basque	113	50,220	1:50.40	102
1995	Basqueian	4	T.K. Kabel	120	Comarctic	117	Holly Regent	114	68,544	1:51.20	96
1996	Basqueian	5	T.K. Kabel	118	Pagagar	111	Comarctic	113	64,980	1:51.60	105
1997	Northern Sky	5	L.L. Gulas	108	For Pete's Sake	112	Love View	112	64,680	1:49.20	90
1998	Northern Sky	6	L.L. Gulas	116	Mt. Sassafras	116	Regal Courser	117	65,040	1:51.80	97
1999	Deputy Inxs	8	N. Somsanith	120	Mt. Sassafras	119	Parental Pressure	112	65,040	1:48.58	103
2000	Kiss a Native	3	M.K. Walls	118	Milwaukee Brew	120	Gandria	115	95,580	1:49.58	106
2001	A Fleets Dancer	6	R.C. Landry	120	Kiss a Native	119	Win City	117	96,570	1:51.71	104
2002	Dream Launcher	4	R.A. Dos Ramos	115	Parose	116	A Fleets Dancer	117	98,910	1:52.45	101
2003	Parose	9	J.C. Jones	117	Barbeau Ruckus	116	Wake at Noon	121	98,280	1:53.16	94
2004	Norfolk Knight	5	J. Scharfstein	116	Mobil	126	Sky Diamond	117	95,670	1:51.56	100

Beyer Index: 99.82

Run as a stakes in 1998. For previous runnings see the 1994 Manual

ECLIPSE HANDICAP (G3-C), 1 1/16 Miles, 4-Year-Olds and Up, Woodbine, 2004 Purse: $163,350

Year	Winner	Age	Jockey	Wt.	Second	Wt.	Third	Wt.	Win Value	Time	Beyer
1994	Brock Street	4	L.L. Gulas	105	Pomeroon	114	British Banker	117	67,740	1:43.80	101
1995	Northern Lance	4	E. Ramsammy	108	Krisanova	109	Wildly Joyous	117	67,680	1:44.00	99
1996	Mt. Sassafras	4	R.C. Landry	117	For Pete's Sake	114	Comarctic	119	65,640	1:44.20	105
1997	Stephanotis	4	M.K. Walls	120	Firm Dancer	114	Open Ice Hit	110	48,240	1:44.40	105
1998	Ocean Squall	5	N. Somsanith	111	Stephanotis	118	Lager	113	65,940	1:44.00	98
1999	Social Charter	4	P. Husbands	113	Victor Cooley	118	Jazz Club	119	68,340	1:43.00	109
2000	Black Cash	5	M.K. Walls	119	The Fed	112	Catahoula Parish	115	84,000	1:45.64	106
2001	Graeme Hall	4	R.C. Landry	120	Black Cash	118	Gandria	114	82,125	1:44.14	110
2002	Lil Personalitee	5	P. Husbands	116	A Fleets Dancer	123	Dream Launcher	117	96,840	1:44.45	96
2003	Phantom Light	4	R.C. Landry	114	No Comprende	113	Anglian Prince	116	103,590	1:43.62	99
2004	Mark One	5	R.C. Landry	115	Open Concert	113	Rock Again	115	98,010	1:46.70	99

Beyer Index: 102.45

Run as a stakes in 1997. For previous runnings see the 1994 Manual

GREY BREEDERS' CUP (G2-C), 1 1/16 Miles, 2-Year-Olds, Woodbine, 2004 Purse: $270,000

Year	Winner	Age	Jockey	Wt.	Second	Wt.	Third	Wt.	Win Value	Time	Beyer
1994	Talkin Man	2	R.C. Landry	117	Raji	113	Celestial Star	113	69,120	1:46.60	81
1995	Gomtuu	2	D. Penna	117	Kingcanrunallday	115	Red Shadow	113	70,080	1:46.60	87
1996	Cash Deposit	2	T.K. Kabel	115	Holzmeister	111	Touch Gold	111	115,605	1:45.00	95
1997	Black Cash	2	R.C. Landry	113	Dawson's Legacy	115	Patriot Love	120	116,760	1:43.20	89
1998	Certainly Classic	2	C. Montpellier	113	Valid n Bold	115	Gallyn's Star	115	117,810	1:46.20	78
1999	Four on the Floor	2	P. Husbands	120	Gallop'n Gold	115	Prime Time Talkin	112	87,120	1:45.12	68
	Exciting Story finished first but was disqualified and placed fifth										
2000	Macho Uno	2	J.D. Bailey	115	Indygo Shiner	111	Stage Classic	113	168,053	1:44.13	94
2001	Changeintheweather	2	M.K. Walls	118	Eye for an Eye	113	Pat's Expectation	117	174,600	1:47.03	77
2002	Wando	2	R. Migliore	115	Gigawatt	116	Grand	113	164,100	1:45.10	87
2003	Smoocher	2	J.S. McAleney	113	Organ Grinder	116	Niigon	114	166,350	1:46.74	90
2004	Dance With Ravens	2	T.K. Kabel	116	Accountforthegold	114	Criminal Mind	113	162,000	1:47.79	72

Beyer Index: 83.45

For previous runnings see the 1994 Manual

GEORGE C. HENDRIE HANDICAP (G3-C), 6 1/2 Furlongs, Fillies and Mares, 4-Year-Olds and Up, Woodbine, 2004 Purse: $211,250

Year	Winner	Age	Jockey	Wt.	Second	Wt.	Third	Wt.	Win Value	Time	Beyer
1994	Deputy Jane West	4	R.C. Landry	122	Miss Importance	111	Franssica D'Amour	113	38,664	1:16.60	99
1995	Countess Steffi	6	R.A. Dos Ramos	113	Mysteriously	122	Early Blaze	121	51,615	1:18.20	91
1996	Klondike Strike	4	R. Griffith	114	Shooting Sherry	109	Fleet Wahine	118	50,220	1:17.80	98
1997	Eseni	4	M.K. Walls	119	Gambling Girl	117	Ashboro	121	48,528	1:15.60	103
1998	Irish Cherry	4	T.K. Kabel	115	Angel's Tearlet	113	Autumn Slew	119	40,824	1:17.00	93
1999	Kirby's Song	4	T.K. Kabel	121	Barlee Mist	119	Secret Ami	113	55,212	1:15.81	106
2000	Saoirse	4	D. Clark	118	Dimontina	113	No Foul Play	117	91,320	1:16.58	97
2001	Mysterious Affair	4	R.A. Dos Ramos	119	Ruby Park	115	El Prado Essence	116	89,880	1:18.17	87
2002	El Prado Essence	5	T.K. Kabel	117	Feathers	118	Quiet	116	97,470	1:16.86	90
2003	El Prado Essence	6	P. Husbands	120	Leading Role	115	Brass in Pocket	120	103,770	1:15.66	97
2004	Winter Garden	4	D. Clark	122	Spanish Decree	115	Handpainted	119	96,750	1:16.76	99

Beyer Index: 99.36

Run as a stakes in 1995-1996. For previous runnings see the 1994 Manual

(SCOTTS) HIGHLANDER HANDICAP (G3-C), 6 Furlongs (Turf), 3-Year-Olds and Up, Woodbine, 2004 Purse: $219,000

Year	Winner	Age	Jockey	Wt.	Second	Wt.	Third	Wt.	Win Value	Time	Beyer
1994	End Sweep	3	C.J. McCarron	120			Carey the Belle	115	44,120	1:09.80	98
	Swamp King	4	R.C. Landry	113							
1995	Le Magister	4	D. Penna	115	Glanmire	113	King Ruckus	124	68,400	1:10.40	100
1996	Love Grows	4	R.C. Landry	111	Jilin	114	King Ruckus	116	68,400	1:09.60	112
1997	Glanmire	7	T.K. Kabel	117	All Firmed Up	112	Jilin	113	69,540	1:09.40	90
1998	Cocney Lass	3	N.E. Poznansky	110	Seismic Report	117	Deputy Inxs	124	66,540	1:09.60	95
1999	Vice n' Friendly	4	M.K. Walls	118	One Way Love	120	Mr. Epperson	115	83,250	1:09.08	103
2000	Wake at Noon	3	D. Clark	117	Silky Sweep	120	Praise From Dixie	113	99,000	1:10.38	95
2001	Mr. Epperson	6	J. McKnight	117	Olympian	115	Tempered Appeal	115	98,910	1:10.65	101
2002	Wake at Noon	5	E. Ramsammy	126	Cheap Talk	116	Krz Ruckus	120	96,480	1:09.72	98
2003	Forever Grand	4	T.K. Kabel	117	Sophia's Prince	116	Mulligan the Great	115	96,750	1:09.53	104
2004	Soaring Free	5	T.K. Kabel	123	Open Concert	115	Take Achance on Me	116	131,400	1:08.72	98

Beyer Index: 99.45

Run as a stakes in 1994. Run as Highlander H. 1995-2003. For previous runnings see the 1994 Manual

KING EDWARD BREEDERS' CUP HANDICAP (G2-C), 1 1/8 Miles (Turf), 3-Year-Olds and Up, Woodbine, 2004 Purse: $324,300

Year	Winner	Age	Jockey	Wt.	Second	Wt.	Third	Wt.	Win Value	Time	Beyer
1994	Road of War	4	C. Montpellier	112	Strike a Gold Mine	115	Beau Fasa	116	84,675	1:40.80	96
1995	Bold Ruritana	5	R.C. Landry	117	Jet Freighter	120	Roche Rock	114	101,250	1:45.20	101
1996	Kiridashi	4	M.K. Walls	117	Desert Waves	115	Jet Freighter	119	162,450	1:46.00	97
1997	Chief Bearhart	4	J.A. Santos	119	Crown Attorney	108	Kiridashi	124	168,600	1:46.20	110
1998	Crown Attorney	5	M.K. Walls	118	Kiridashi	119	Yagli	122	166,050	1:47.20	108
1999	Desert Waves	9	N.E. Poznansky	110	Crown Attorney	116	Down the Aisle	115	165,750	1:46.49	97
2000	Incitatus	7	S. Callaghan	115	Quiet Resolve	121	Ruxsh	112	194,580	1:49.32	102
2001	Quiet Resolve	6	T.K. Kabel	121	Kimberlite Pipe	115	Spindrift	117	204,840	1:47.12	107
	Red Sea finished third but was disqualified and placed fifth										
2002	Moon Solitaire	5	R.C. Landry	114	Quiet Resolve	120	No Comprende	115	201,420	1:50.26	105
2003	Perfect Soul	5	R.C. Landry	119	Strut the Stage	121	Del Mar Show	119	203,760	1:49.60	106
2004	Slew Valley	7	J.S. McAleney	117	Shoal Water	116	Surging River	112	194,580	1:48.42	100

Beyer Index: 102.64

Run as King Edward Gold Cup Handicap 1994-1995. Run at Fort Erie in 1994. Run at 1 1/16 miles in 1994. For previous runnings see the 1994 Manual

LIEUTENANT GOVERNORS' HANDICAP (G3-C), 1 1/8 Miles, 3-Year-Olds and Up, Hastings, 2004 Purse: $110,582

Year	Winner	Age	Jockey	Wt.	Second	Wt.	Third	Wt.	Win Value	Time	Beyer
1994	Thisisthepoint	5	C. Loseth	114	Flashing Pass	113	Overtime Victory	114	33,600	1:53.40	87
1995	Funboy	4	D.H. Wilson	120	Stop the Blues	115	Go for Glory	115	33,570	1:50.40	90
1996	Apieceoftheaction	4	J. Barton	115	Destiny's Command	111	Thisisthepoint	111	44,120	1:48.80	87
1997	Liberty Road	4	S.B. Krasner	116	Apieceoftheaction	115	Artic Son	111	68,120	1:51.20	92
1998	Kid Katabatic	5	C. Loseth	121	Artic Son	115	Mike K	120	55,590	1:48.40	108
1999	Mike K	5	G.L. Olguin	122	Liberty Road	115	Artic Son	119	64,723	1:51.49	103
2000	Mark My Dreams	6	D.L. Brock	118	Koslanin	114	Yaletown	117	48,078	1:49.44	98
2001	Rampaging Alf	4	P.V. Alvarado	119	Lord Nelson	115	King Jeremy	118	48,645	1:49.95	95
2002	Lord Nelson	5	F.P. Fuentes	120	Jazzy Yacht	111	Kid Katabatic	119	48,870	1:50.28	98
2003	Lord Nelson	6	F.P. Fuentes	119	Let's Go Rusty	114	Commodore Craig	116	66,349	1:50.49	98
2004	Royal Place	4	G.L. Olguin	119	Lord Nelson	123	Roscoe Pito	119	60,000	1:49.08	99

Beyer Index: 95.91

Run as a stakes in 1995-1997. For previous runnings see the 1994 Manual

MAPLE LEAF (G3-C), 1 1/4 Miles, Fillies and Mares, 3-Year-Olds and Up, Woodbine, 2004 Purse: $235,850

Year	Winner	Age	Jockey	Wt.	Second	Wt.	Third	Wt.	Win Value	Time	Beyer
1994	Smiles With a Fist	4	D. Penna	119	Myrtle Irene	121	Plenty of Sugar	122	39,024	2:05.80	89
	Plenty of Sugar finished first but was disqualified and placed third										
1995	Wings of Erin	3	K. Willey	115	Stellarina	119	Holly Regent	126	65,940	2:02.60	100
1996	Wings of Erin	4	J.S. McAleney	121	Stellarina	121	Forever Classic	117	65,700	2:09.00	86
1997	Blue and Red	5	T.K. Kabel	119	Foxy Fiddler	113	Santa Amelia	121	53,448	2:04.60	87
							Ascot Yael	117			
1998	No Foul Play	4	S.R. Bahen	115	Santa Amelia	124	Fly for Avie	113	82,020	2:06.20	94
1999	With Flair	3	D. Clark	114	Native Brass	121	Starlight Gazer	113	67,740	2:05.54	93
2000	On a Soapbox	4	G. Boulanger	121	Gandria	121	Strolling Belle	121	119,175	2:05.94	98
2001	Catch the Ring	4	R.C. Landry	119	Mountain Angel	121	Madame Red	116	139,080	2:03.62	101
2002	Lady Shari	3	C. Montpellier	116	Small Promises	119	Silver Nithi	116	118,650	2:06.22	88
2003	One for Rose	4	E. Ramsammy	121	Winning Chance	121	Clouds of Gold	118	117,750	2:03.50	110
2004	One for Rose	5	E. Ramsammy	126	Clouds of Gold	118	Raylene	117	141,510	2:04.87	100

Beyer Index: 95.09

For previous runnings see the 1994 Manual

MARINE (G3-C), 1 1/16 Miles, 3-Year-Olds, Woodbine, 2004 Purse: $164,100

Year	Winner	Age	Jockey	Wt.	Second	Wt.	Third	Wt.	Win Value	Time	Beyer
1994	Trave	3	S. Hawley	115	Tuxedo Landing	115	Nice to Know	117	46,735	1:46.80	83
1995	Tethra	3	D. Penna	121	Freedom Fleet	115	Blazing Knight	119	50,604	1:45.20	93
1996	Victor Cooley	3	E. Ramsammy	117	Firm Dancer	119	Laredo	117	49,500	1:41.80	107
1997	My Imperial Slew	3	S.R. Bahen	115	Monk's Corner	113	Love View	119	49,230	1:45.40	84
1998	Silver Talk	3	R.C. Landry	113	Ragged Kingdom	114	Thunder Bow	117	49,365	1:46.20	86
1999	Mystic Prince	3	R.M. Pimentel	113	Lenny the Lender	116	Hit the Road Beau	117	66,900	1:45.56	89
2000	Milwaukee Brew	3	R.C. Landry	115	Tempered Appeal	115	Wake at Noon	119	85,050	1:45.11	104
2001	Win City	3	C. Montpellier	117	High Commissioner	114	Lunar Secret	117	81,600	1:45.89	97
2002	Anglian Prince	3	J.S. McAleney	115	Tails of the Crypt	119	Ford Every Stream	117	97,650	1:44.03	101
2003	Wando	3	T.K. Kabel	119	El Ruller	117	Arco's Gold	119	98,280	1:42.61	102
2004	Judiths Wild Rush	3	D. Luciani	119	Organ Grinder	117	Honolua Storm	117	98,460	1:45.96	102

Beyer Index: 95.27

For previous runnings see the 1994 Manual

MAZARINE BREEDERS' CUP (G2-C), 1 1/16 Miles, Fillies, 2-Year-Olds, Woodbine, 2004 Purse: $278,750

Year	Winner	Age	Jockey	Wt.	Second	Wt.	Third	Wt.	Win Value	Time	Beyer
1994	Honky Tonk Tune	2	R.C. Landry	121	Search the Sea	114	Khalifa of Kushog	114	65,640	1:46.80	76
1995	Silken Cat	2	T.K. Kabel	114	Miners Mirage	116	Far Away Kisses	112	67,410	1:48.20	71
1996	Barbed Wire	2	E. Ramsammy	112	Diablo's Story	121	Classic Threat	119	115,500	1:46.40	82
1997	Kirby's Song	2	T.K. Kabel	121	Primaly	113	Port Tack	114	123,270	1:47.60	83
1998	Fantasy Lake	2	R.C. Landry	117	Appealing Phylly	117	With Flair	114	114,240	1:44.80	85
1999	Hello Seattle	2	R.C. Landry	113	Cool Ashlee	115	Judith's Concern	113	131,040	1:45.63	89
2000	Salty You	2	T.K. Kabel	114	Caught Out	117	Dancethruthedawn	113	165,750	1:45.37	79
2001	Lady Shari	2	C. Montpellier	114	Jealous Forum	117	Mulrainy	116	169,950	1:46.99	76
2002	Brusque	2	E. Ramsammy	115	Handpainted	120	Mountain Dawn	115	165,900	1:45.33	82
2003	Dream About	2	P. Husbands	117	America America	115	Brush With Destiny	115	160,950	1:47.54	85
2004	Higher World	2	P. Husbands	117	Didycheatamandhowe	115	Dancehall Deelites	116	167,250	1:47.99	79

Beyer Index: 80.64

For previous runnings see the 1994 Manual

NASSAU (G3-C), 1 1/16 Miles (Turf), Fillies and Mares, 3-Year-Olds and Up, Woodbine, 2004 Purse: $322,250

Year	Winner	Age	Jockey	Wt.	Second	Wt.	Third	Wt.	Win Value	Time	Beyer
1994	Strong and Steady	4	T.K. Kabel	119	Bold Ruritana	117	Myrtle Irene	124	40,752	1:41.20	91
1995	Bold Ruritana	5	R.C. Landry	124	Mysteriously	124	Myrtle Irene	119	50,220	1:41.20	98
1996	Bold Ruritana	6	R.C. Landry	124	Camlan	117	Combination	115	49,050	1:39.60	98
1997	Classic Wonder	5	M.K. Walls	116	Wings of Erin	121	Woolloomooloo	117	54,780	1:41.00	91
1998	Colorful Vices	5	T.K. Kabel	115	Silver Taler	119	Cotton Carnival	124	84.420	1:41.80	95
1999	Anguilla	4	R.C. Landry	124	Forge Ahead	115	Ivastar	115	68,520	1:41.52	101
2000	Heliotrope	5	N.E. Poznansky	113	Only to You	115	La Serina	113	123,900	1:40.14	96
2001	Only to You	5	T.K. Kabel	115	Heliotrope	119	Bristol Pistol	121	117,705	1:47.31	94
2002	Siringas	4	J.A. Santos	115	Rosthern	116	Mountain Angel	119	162,960	1:41.01	98
2003	Strait From Texas	4	R.A. Dos Ramos	119	Chopinina	115	Byzantine	117	166,920	1:42.92	94
2004	Inish Glora	6	T.K. Kabel	121	Ocean Drive	117	Classic Stamp	119	193,350	1:40.38	98

Beyer Index: 95.82

Run at Fort Erie in 1994. For previous runnings see the 1994 Manual

NATALMA (G3-C), 1 Mile (Turf), Fillies, 2-Year-Olds, Woodbine, 2004 Purse: $227,300

Year	Winner	Age	Jockey	Wt.	Second	Wt.	Third	Wt.	Win Value	Time	Beyer
1994	Honolulu Gold	2	J.M. Lauzon	114	Khalifa of Kushog	114	Manila Gold	114	32,820	1:35.60	77
1994	With Care	2	R. Platts	116	Royal Vale	116	Search the Sea	114	33,270	1:35.80	75
1995	Platinum Blonde	2	J.D. Bailey	114	Heavenley Lark	114	Speedy Suzy	114	35,152	1:38.20	73
1995	Mountain Affair	2	C.S. Nakatani	115	Fly North	119	Mooncoin	114	35,152	1:37.80	77
1996	Diablo's Story	2	T.K. Kabel	115	Almost Saintly	114	Barbed Wire	114	52,740	1:35.80	81
1997	Joustabout	2	M.J. Luzzi	114	Port Tack	116	All Slew	115	50,332	1:36.40	78
1997	Kirby's Song	2	T.K. Kabel	116	Marvellous Silver	114	Golden Mirage	116	65,332	1:36.60	76
1998	Dance Diane	2	S.R. Bahen	115	Free Vacation	114	Sassy Tallahassee	114	50,063	1:36.60	84
1998	Pico Teneriffe	2	N. Somsanith	114	Providential Miss	114	Madam du Barri	119	50,063	1:36.60	84
1999	Mema's Turning Red	2	J.M. Lauzon	116	Cryptic Response	114	Geronimo's Joy	114	50,265	1:35.82	86
1999	Hoh Dear	2	R.J. Albarado	116	Diadella	115	Judith's Concern	114	50,715	1:37.03	73
2000	Sky Alliance	2	T.K. Kabel	114	Love Kiss	115	Tuff Chick	115	113,850	1:34.64	80
2001	Ginger Gold	2	R.A. Dos Ramos	119	West Madisyn	114	Southey	115	107,550	1:34.66	88
2001	Lush Soldier	2	M.K. Walls	118	Strait From Texas	114	Bala	114	83,550	1:35.44	81
2002	One and Twenty	2	T.K. Kabel	116	Swift of Flight	115	Sand Springs	116	101,520	1:35.03	88
2002	Fortuitous	2	R.C. Landry	116	Sweet Storm Creek	116	Wawota	114	102,420	1:36.54	73
2003	Pink Champagne	2	R.A. Dos Ramos	114	Saree	117	America America	121	106,200	1:36.53	75
2004	Fearless Flyer	2	E. Ramsammy	114	Sweet Solairo	114	Little Hussy	117	106,380	1:34.99	82

Beyer Index: 79.50

Run in divisions in 1994, 1995, 1997, 1998, 1999, 2001, 2002. For previous runnings see the 1994 Manual

NEARCTIC HANDICAP (G2-C), 6 Furlongs (Turf), 3-Year-Olds and Up, Woodbine, 2004 Purse: $282,750

Year	Winner	Age	Jockey	Wt.	Second	Wt.	Third	Wt.	Win Value	Time	Beyer
1994	King Ruckus	4	T.K. Kabel	114	Megas Vukefalos	114	I Can't Believe	120	87,675	1:09.60	103
1995	Wild Zone	5	S.J. Sellers	116	Bold n' Flashy	117	Blitzer	118	84,225	1:08.40	102
1996	Wild Zone	6	R.C. Landry	119	All Firmed Up	114	O'Martin	114	87,525	1:07.60	101
1997	Jilin	5	D. Clark	114	All Firmed Up	116	Kiridashi	123	68,280	1:08.60	101
1998	Rushiscomingup	5	R.A. Dos Ramos	113	Skybound	116	Smoke	114	70,020	1:08.20	99
1999	Clever Response	4	E. Ramsammy	111	Hawk in Sight	107	Alea Iacta Est	114	103,770	1:10.19	99
2000	Kahal	6	B. Blanc	115	Gone Fishin	117	Mr. Epperson	114	135,120	1:11.07	105
2001	Mr. Epperson	6	J. McKnight	115	Airbourne Command	118	Alea Iacta Est	114	134,040	1:08.86	104
2002	Nuclear Debate	7	D.R. Flores	122	Joe's Son Joey	118	Texas Glitter	120	175,350	1:07.86	106
2003	Soaring Free	4	T.K. Kabel	115	Solitary Dancer	117	Nuclear Debate	121	171,900	1:07.73	105
2004	I Thee Wed	4	J.S. McAleney	114	Chris's Bad Boy	118	Hour of Justice	116	169,650	1:09.36	101

Beyer Index: 102.36

Run on main track in 1994. For previous runnings see the 1994 Manual

NIAGARA BREEDERS' CUP HANDICAP (G2-C), 1 1/2 Miles (Turf), 3-Year-Olds and Up, Woodbine, 2004 Purse: $324,000

Year	Winner	Age	Jockey	Wt.	Second	Wt.	Third	Wt.	Win Value	Time	Beyer
1994	River Majesty	5	M.E. Smith	117	Roche Rock	109	Desert Waves	113	68,940	2:03.20	99
1995	Lindon Lime	5	C. Perret	118	Desert Waves	115	Pagagar	112	97,920	2:27.00	98
1996	Desert Waves	6	S. Hawley	114	Jet Freighter	114	Glenbarra	114	163,500	2:27.00	96
1997	Desert Waves	7	S. Hawley	117	Down the Aisle	115	Crown Attorney	117	166,950	2:30.40	103
1998	Chief Bearhart	5	J.A. Santos	123	Green Means Go	113	Crown Attorney	117	162,450	2:30.00	105

Year	Winner	Age	Jockey	Wt.	Second	Wt.	Third	Wt.	Win Value	Time	Beyer
1999	Thornfield	5	R.A. Dos Ramos	113	Tanaasa	115	Williams News	114	165,450	2:29.32	101
2000	River Boat	7	G. Boulanger	112	Craigsteel	113	Quiet Resolve	122	145,560	2:32.16	103
2001	Honor Glide	7	R.G. Davis	117	Royal Strand	117	Strike Smartly	110	201,060	2:26.52	99
2002	Full of Wonder	4	T.K. Kabel	115	Perfect Soul	115	Muntej	115	201,240	2:26.18	105
2003	Strut the Stage	5	T.K. Kabel	123	Revved Up	118	Better Talk Now	115	202,320	2:27.13	104
2004	Strut the Stage	6	T.K. Kabel	121	Colorful Judgement	115	Mark One	115	194,400	2:25.87	104

Beyer Index: 101.55

Run as a stakes in 1997. Run at 1 1/4 miles in 1994. For previous runnings see the 1994 Manual

PLAY THE KING HANDICAP (G3-C), 7 Furlongs (Turf), 3-Year-Olds and Up, Woodbine, 2004 Purse: $173,400

Year	Winner	Age	Jockey	Wt.	Second	Wt.	Third	Wt.	Win Value	Time	Beyer
1994	Premier Angel	5	S. Hawley	111	Carey the Belle	113	Swamp King	113	49,692	1:10.00	99
1995	King Ruckus	5	T.K. Kabel	120	Tuxedo Landing	108	Le Magister	112	63,642	1:09.80	105
1996	Jilin	4	D. Clark	115	All Firmed Up	115	Thunder Regent	112	53,100	1:23.80	96
1997	Randy Regent	3	S. Hawley	111	Seismic Report	116	Jilin	115	49,545	1:23.40	100
1998	Skybound	4	R.C. Landry	115	Kiridashi	120	Wild Jazz	104	50,175	1:21.00	101
1999	Dawson's Legacy	4	C. Montpellier	112	Mr. Epperson	115	Sky Colony	115	68,280	1:21.87	102
2000	Olympian	3	N. Somsanith	111	Gone Fishin	118	Mr. Epperson	114	84,000	1:21.68	98
2000	Solitary Dancer	4	M.K. Walls	116	Free Agent on Ice	112	Karra Kul	115	83,250	1:22.00	94
2001	Mr. Epperson	6	J. McKnight	116	Heliotrope	113	Alea Iacta Est	114	87,600	1:21.84	98
2002	Zone Judge	4	C. Montpellier	115	Waltzin' Storm	117	Gone Fishin	115	103,860	1:20.42	102
2003	Soaring Free	4	T.K. Kabel	121	Jeb's Wild	114	Frank's Selection	113	99,000	1:23.52	105
2004	Soaring Free	5	T.K. Kabel	126	Frank's Selection	115	Dancin Joey	116	104,040	1:20.97	102

Beyer Index: 100.17

Run as Toronto Breeders' Cup Handicap 1994–1995. Run at 6 furlongs 1994–1995. Run on main train 1994–1995. Run in divisions in 2000. For previous runnings see the 1994 Manual

PREMIER'S HANDICAP (G3-C), 1 3/8 Miles, 3-Year-Olds and Up, Hastings, 2004 Purse: $138,600

Year	Winner	Age	Jockey	Wt.	Second	Wt.	Third	Wt.	Win Value	Time	Beyer
1994	Go for Glory	5	G.L. Olguin	115	Whomsoever Proud	118	Twanger	117	78,130	2:20.00	89
1995	Two Ticky	4	B.T. Bochinsky	119	Lucky Son	112	Destiny's Command	110	80,370	2:22.40	94
1996	Second Chance	6	S.B. Krasner	109	Professor Moriarty	113	Military Hawk	115	75,330	2:16.60	98
1997	Boggle	5	D.H. Wilson	111	Funny Tale	120	Timely Stitch	116	74,500	2:19.00	91
1998	Artic Son	5	F.P. Fuentes	121	Victorious Type	115	Kid Katabatic	122	80,692	2:19.40	102
1999	Victorious Type	6	D.H. Wilson	115	American Justice	117	Mike K	126	75,000	2:17.16	94
2000	American Justice	4	C. Loseth	116	Sunday Stroll	115	Code Name Fred	120	60,000	2:18.00	94
2001	Fancy As	3	R. Hamel	121	Lord Nelson	124	Colonial Secretary	124	60,000	2:20.07	97
2002	Shacane	3	P.V. Alvarado	117	Futural	118	Rim Dancer	114	66,677	2:16.92	93
2003	Roscoe Pito	3	P.V. Alvarado	118	Blowin in the Wind	118	Futural	118	79,200	2:19.86	85
2004	Blowin in the Wind	5	R.V. Skelly	114	Illusive Force	119	Royal Place	121	75,360	2:19.64	90

Beyer Index: 93.36

Run as British Columbia Premier's Championship Handicap 1994–1997. Run as a stakes in 2001. For previous runnings see the 1994 Manual

PRINCE OF WALES, 1 3/16 Miles, 3-Year-Olds, Foaled in Canada, Fort Erie, 2004 Purse: $500,000

Year	Winner	Age	Jockey	Wt.	Second	Wt.	Third	Wt.	Win Value	Time	Beyer
1994	Bruce's Mill	3	C. Perret	126	Basqueian	126	Parental Pressure	126	87,296	1:53.80	103
1995	Kiridashi	3	L. Attard	126	Regal Discovery	126	Mt. Sassafras	126	121,800	1:55.00	101
1996	Stephanotis	3	M.K. Walls	126	Firm Dancer	126	Kristy Krunch	126	121,620	1:55.20	99
1997	Cryptocloser	3	W. Martinez	126	C.C. on Ice	126	Rabbit in a Hat	126	117,600	1:56.00	98
1998	Archers Bay	3	R.C. Landry	126	Nite Dreamer	126	One Way Love	126	118,500	1:55.20	106
1999	Gandria	3	C. Montpellier	121	Woodcarver	126	Euchre	126	175,858	1:56.20	98
2000	Scatter the Gold	3	T.K. Kabel	126	For Our Sake	126	Cool n Collective	126	170,280	1:56.01	98
2001	Win City	3	C. Montpellier	126	Dancethruthedawn	121	Brushing Bully	126	210,000	1:56.14	103
2002	Le Cinquieme Essai	3	B.T. Bochinski	126	Bravely	126	Anglian Prince	126	300,000	1:56.53	95
2003	Wando	3	P. Husbands	126	Arco's Gold	126	Shoal Water	126	300,000	1:55.84	99
2004	A Bit O'Gold	3	J.C. Jones	126	Niigon	126	His Smoothness	126	300,000	1:57.69	100

Beyer Index: 100.00

For previous runnings see the 1994 Manual

QUEEN'S PLATE, 1 1/4 Miles,
3-Year-Olds, Foaled in Canada, Woodbine, 2004 Purse: $1,000,000

Year	Winner	Age	Jockey	Wt.	Second	Wt.	Third	Wt.	Win Value	Time	Beyer
1860	Don Juan										
1861	Wild Irishman										
1862	Palermo										
1863	Touchstone										
1864	Brunette										
1865	Lady Norfolk										
1866	Beacon										
1867	Wild Rose										
1868	Nettie										
1869	Bay Jack										
1870	John Bell										
1871	Floss										
1872	Fearnaught										
1873	Mignonette										
1874	Swallow										
1875	Trumpeter										
1876	Norah P.										
1877	Amelia										
1878	King George										
1879	Moss Ross										
1880	Bonnie Bird	4	Leary	107	Fanny Wiser	94	King Tom	110	300	2:47.00	
1881	Vice Chancellor	4	Brown	115	Jessie McCullough	118	Athlete	119	340	2:53.00	
1882	Fanny Wiser	5	A.E. Gates	112	Williams	115	Tullamore	119	400	2:51.00	
1883	Rhody Pringle	3	Smith	97	Williams	120	Princess Louise	95	420	2:52.50	
1884	Williams	6	Martin	121	Marquis	121	Modjeska	118	415	2:50.75	
1885	Willie W.	4	Jamieson	115	Fred Henry	121	Edmonton	120	470	2:58.00	
1886	Wild Rose	4	C. Butler	113	Fred Henry	121	Wild Bruce	97	490	2:48.25	
1887	Bonnie Duke	5	Wise	119	Fred Henry	122	Aunt Alice	117	357	2:19.00	
1888	Henry Cooper	4	C. O'Leary	118	Evangeline	113	Cast Off	117	487	2:18.50	
1889	Colonist	3	R. O'Leary	106	Bonnie Ino	101	Long Shot	126	322	2:16.00	
1890	Kite String	3	Coleman	105	La Blanche	117	Flip Flop	117	327	2:22.00	
1891	Victorious	3	Gorman	106	La Blanche	121	Moyama	101	407	2:14.50	
1892	O'Donohue	3	Horton	106	Queen Mary	101	Heather Bloom	101	422	2:22.00	
1893	Martello	4	Blaylock	119	Athalo	103	Heather Bloom	117	830	2:14.00	
1894	Joe Miller	4	Booker	122	Bel Demonio	126	Maj. General	106	785	2:28.50	
1895	Bonniefield	3	Booker	106	Millbrook	106	Lochinvar	119	995	2:17.50	
1896	Millbrook	4	Lewis	122	Springal	102	Dictator	126	975	2:19.00	
1897	Ferdinand	3	Lewis	106	Bon Ino	101	Wicker	106	1,015	2:13.00	
1898	Bon Ino	4	R. Williams	117	Dalmoor	122	Maritana II	101	1,010	2:15.50	
1899	Butter Scotch	3	Mason	101	Dalmoor	126	Toddy Ladle	103	1,331	2:15.50	
1900	Dalmoor	6	Lewis	126	The Provost	108	Bellcourt	117	1,395	2:14.00	
1901	John Ruskin	3	Vititoe	105	Bellcourt	121	Fernietickle	101	1,570	2:18.75	
1902	Lyddite	3	Wainwright	101	Fly-in-Amber	117	Opuntia	129	1,725	2:15.00	
1903	Thessalon	3	Castro	104	Nesto	103	Gold'n Crest	117	1,960	2:15.50	
1904	Sapper	3	J. Walsh	103	Nimble Dick	106	War Whoop	106	1,975	2:12.00	
1905	Inferno	3	H. Phillips	106	Will King	106	Half Seas Over	106	2,092	2:15.00	
1906	Slaughter	3	Trebel	106	Court Martial	106	Haruko	101	3,395	2:11.60	
1907	Kelvin	3	Foley	106	Half-a-Crown	106	Bilbery	123	3,707	2:12.60	
1908	Seismic	3	Fairbrother	106	Shimonese	101	Half-a-Crown	122	3,650	2:11.00	
1909	Shimonese	4	Gilbert	119	Tollendal	108	For Garry	108	3,250	2:10.40	
1910	Parmer	3	J. Wilson	105	Commola	104	Jane Shore	103	3,332	2:12.40	
1911	St. Bass	3	E. Dugan	108	Powderman	105	Jane Shore	119	3,395	2:08.80	
1912	Heresy	3	Small	108	Amberite	103	Rustling	103	4,535	2:11.00	
1913	Hearts of Oak	3	J. Wilson	113	Maid of Frome	108	Gold Bud	119	4,335	2:09.20	
1914	Beehive	3	G. Burns	113	Dark Rosaleen	108	Sea Lord	105	4,735	2:10.60	
1915	Tartarean	3	H. Watts	108	Fair Montague	108	Pepper Sauce	113	4,310	2:09.20	
1916	Mandarin	3	A. Pickens	113	Gala Water	108	Gala Day	113	4,015	2:12.00	
1917	Belle Mahone	3	F. Robinson	108	Tarahera	108	Gala Dress	108	6,125	2:08.80	
1918	Springside	3	L. Mink	113	Ladder of Light	119	May Bloom	108	2,540	2:08.80	
1919	Ladder of Light	5	L. Lyke	122	Doleful	108	Hong Kong	113	2,750	2:09.40	
1920	St. Paul	3	R. Romanelli	105	Bugle March	121	Prime	108	6,050	2:09.00	
1921	Herendesy	3	J. Butwell	113	Royal Visitor	113	Moll Cutpurse	103	5,070	2:10.00	
1922	South Shore	4	K. Parrington	122	Paddle	113	El Jesmar	113	7,565	2:12.00	
1923	Flowerful	3	T. Wilson	113	Cheechako	124	Trail Blazer	105	7,745	2:11.00	
1924	Maternal Pride	3	G. Walls	110	Thorndyke	109	Maypole	127	7,825	1:57.60	
1925	Fairbank	3	C. Lang	122	Duchess	112	Jean Crest	112	7,835	1:56.40	
1926	Haplite	3	H. Erickson	117	Attack	113	Taurus	112	7,550	1:59.60	

Year	Winner	Age	Jockey	Wt.	Second	Wt.	Third	Wt.	Win Value	Time	Beyer
1927	Troutlet	3	F. Horn	112	Mr. Gaiety	112	Gems to Let	117	10,820	1:55.80	
1928	Young Kitty	3	L. Pichon	112	Bonnington	112	Hanna Deebe	107	10,775	1:57.00	
1929	Shorelint	3	J.D. Mooney	117	Ichitaro	132	Lindsay	108	10,960	1:57.60	
1930	Aymond	3	H. Little	117	Whale Oil	117	Ichitaro	133	10,980	1:57.20	
1931	Froth Blower	3	F. Mann	117	Bronze	112	Skygazer	112	8,100	1:59.20	
1932	Queensway	3	F. Mann	112	King O'Connor	112	Spey Crest	112	5,870	1:55.20	
1933	King O'Connor	4	E. Legere	127	Easter Hatter	132	Syngo	117	6,360	1:56.40	
1934	Horometer	3	F. Mann	117	Speygold	117	Papalico	132	5,650	1:54.20	
1935	Sally Fuller	3	H. Lindberg	107	Chickpen	112	Gay Sympathy	109	4,290	1:55.40	
1936	Monsweep	3	D. Brammer	117	Stormblown	112	Epicurus	132	5,360	1:55.00	
1937	Goldlure	3	S. Young	117	Cease Fire	117	Silver Jubilee	117	6,180	1:55.40	
1938	Bunty Lawless	3	J.W. Bailey	117	Mona Bell	112	Cabin Gal	112	7,030	1:54.40	
1939	Archworth	3	S.D. Birley	117	Sea General	117	Skyrunner	117	8,970	1:54.40	
1940	Willie the Kid	3	R. Nash	112	Curwen	117	Hood	117	6,720	1:55.80	
1941	Budpath	3	R. Watson	117	Undisturbed	117	Attrisius	112	6,670	1:56.80	
1942	Ten to Ace	3	C.W. Smith	117	Cossack Post	117	Depressor	117	6,680	1:57.80	
1943	Paolita	3	P. Remillard	112	Arbor Vita	117	Tulachmore	117	6,640	2:02.60	
1944	Acara	3	R. Watson	117	Ompalo	117	Korafloyd	117	9,350	1:54.80	
1945	Uttermost	3	R. Watson	119	Tarian	119	Ferry Pilot	118	9,695	1:54.60	
1946	Kingarvie	3	J. Dewhurst	119	David T.	119	Bluesweep	119	9,850	1:55.60	
1947	Moldy	3	C. McDonald	119	Burboy	119	Watch Wrack	119	10,335	1:54.20	
1948	Last Mark	3	H.R. Bailey	119	Lord Fairmond	110	Joey Bomber	119	11,260	1:52.00	
1949	Epic	3	C. Rogers	119	Speedy Irish	119	Filsis	114	11,060	1:52.20	
1950	McGill	3	C. Rogers	119	Sir Strome	119	Unionville	119	14,290	1:52.40	
1951	Major Factor	3	A. Bavington	119	Libertine	119	Bear Field	119	16,152	1:53.00	
1952	Epigram	3	G. Robillard	119	Genthorn	114	Latin Lad	119	17,022	1:58.60	
1953	Canadiana	3	E. Arcaro	114	Blue Scooter	119	Lively Action	114	20,592	1:52.20	
1954	Collisteo	3	C. Rogers	119	Queen's Own	119	King Maple	119	22,452	1:52.00	
1955	Ace Marine	3	G. Walker	119	Baffin Bay	114	Senator Jim	119	25,514	1:52.40	
1956	Canadian Champ	3	D. Stevenson	119	Argent	119	London Calling	119	25,430	1:55.00	
1957	Lyford Cay	3	A. Gomez	126	Chopadette	126	Flying Atom	126	26,210	2:02.60	
1958	Caledon Beau	3	A. Coy	126	White Apache	126	Stole the Ring	121	26,151	2:04.20	
1959	New Providence	3	R. Ussery	126	Major Flight	126	Winning Shot	126	51,767	2:04.80	
1960	Victoria Park	3	A. Gomez	126	Quintain	126	Champagne Velvet	126	42,750	2:02.00	
1961	Blue Light	3	H. Dittfach	126	Just Don't Shove	126	Ramblin Wreck	126	46,475	2:05.00	
1962	Flaming Page	3	J. Fitzsimmons	121	Choperion	126	Peter's Chop	126	51,225	2:04.60	
1963	Canebora	3	M. Ycaza	126	Son Blue	126	Warriors Day	126	54,850	2:04.00	
1964	Northern Dancer	3	W. Hartack	126	Langcrest	126	Grand Garcon	126	49,234	2:02.20	
1965	Whistling Sea	3	T. Inouye	126	Flyalong	126	Blue Mel	126	47,852	2:03.80	
1966	Titled Hero	3	A. Gomez	126	Bye and Near	126	Bright Monarch	126	52,274	2:03.60	
1967	Jammed Lovely	3	J. Fitzsimmons	121	Pine Point	126	Come By Chance	126	51,979	2:03.00	
1968	Merger	3	W. Harris	126	Big Blunder	126	Rouletabille	126	53,775	2:05.40	
1969	Jumpin Joseph	3	A. Gomez	126	Fanfaron	126	Fire n Desire	126	55,157	2:04.20	
1970	Almoner	3	S. Hawley	126	Fanfreluche	121	Top Call	126	57,525	2:04.80	
1971	Kennedy Road	3	S. Hawley	126	Fabe Count	126	Great Gabe	126	54,518	2:03.00	
1972	Victoria Song	3	R. Platts	126	Barachois	126	Gentleman Conn	126	56,278	2:03.20	
1973	Royal Chocolate	3	T. Colangelo	126	Sinister Purpose	126	My Archie Bald	126	80,834	2:08.00	
1974	Amber Herod	3	R. Platts	126	Native Aid	126	Rushton's Corsair	126	96,671	2:09.20	
1975	L'Enjoleur	3	S. Hawley	126	Near the High Sea	126	Mystery Time	126	95,465	2:02.60	
1976	Norcliffe	3	J. Fell	126	Military Bearing	126	Confederation	126	89,804	2:05.00	
1977	Sound Reason	3	R. Platts	126	Northernette	121	Giboulee	126	86,538	2:06.60	
1978	Regal Embrace	3	S. Hawley	126	Overskate	126	L'Alezane	121	107,091	2:02.00	
1979	Steady Growth	3	B. Swatuk	126	Bold Agent	126	Ram Good	126	106,542	2:06.60	
1980	Driving Home	3	W. Parsons	126	Someolio Man	126	Allan Blue	126	119,555	2:04.20	
1981	Fiddle Dancer Boy	3	D. Clark	126	Wayover	126	Frost King	126	119,616	2:04.80	
1982	Son of Briartic	3	J.P. Souter	126	Runaway Groom	126	Le Danseur	126	141,504	2:04.60	
1983	Bompago	3	L. Attard	126	Sir Khaled	126	Rockcliffe	126	151,386	2:04.20	
1984	Key to the Moon	3	R. Platts	126	Let's Go Blue	126	Ten Gold Pots	126	164,352	2:03.80	
1985	La Lorgnette	3	D. Clark	121	Imperial Choice	126	Pre Emptive Strike	126	174,504	2:04.60	
1986	Golden Choice	3	V. Bracciale Jr	126	Cool Halo	126	Steady Effort	126	174,465	2:07.20	
1987	Market Control	3	K. Skinner	126	Afleet	126	One From Heaven	121	204,219	2:03.60	
1988	Regal Intention	3	J.M. Lauzon	126	Regal Classic	126	Granacus	126	199,497	2:06.20	
1989	With Approval	3	D.J. Seymour	126	Most Valiant	126	Domasca Dan	126	257,660	2:03.00	
1990	Izvestia	3	D.J. Seymour	126	Very Formal	126	Iskandar Elakbar	126	235,200	2:01.80	
1991	Dance Smartly	3	P. Day	121	Wilderness Song	121	Shudanz	126	234,840	2:03.40	
1992	Alydeed	3	C. Perret	126	Grand Hooley	126	Benburb	126	228,900	2:04.60	
1993	Peteski	3	C. Perret	126	Cheery Knight	126	Janraffole	126	218,600	2:04.20	
1994	Basqueian	3	J.M. Lauzon	126	Bruce's Mill	126	Parental Pressure	126	267,942	2:03.40	103
1995	Regal Discovery	3	T.K. Kabel	126	Freedom Fleet	126	Mt. Sassafras	126	261,660	2:03.80	99

Year	Winner	Age	Jockey	Wt.	Second	Wt.	Third	Wt.	Win Value	Time	Beyer
1996	Victor Cooley	3	E. Ramsammy	126	Stephanotis	126	Kristy Krunch	126	255,480	2:03.80	102
1997	Awesome Again	3	M.E. Smith	126	Cryptocloser	126	Sovereign Storm	126	255,420	2:04.20	100
1998	Archers Bay	3	K.J. Desormeaux	126	Brite Adam	126	Kinkennie	126	300,000	2:02.20	106
1999	Woodcarver	3	M.K. Walls	126	Gandria	121	Euchre	126	300,000	2:03.13	97
2000	Scatter the Gold	3	T.K. Kabel	126	I and I	126	For Our Sake	126	600,000	2:05.53	91
2001	Dancethruthedawn	3	G. Boulanger	121	Win City	126	Brushing Bully	126	600,000	2:03.78	94
2002	T J's Lucky Moon	3	S.R. Bahen	126	Anglian Prince	126	Forever Grand	126	600,000	2:06.88	86
2003	Wando	3	P. Husbands	126	Mobil	126	Rock Again	126	600,000	2:02.48	111
2004	Niigon	3	R.C. Landry	126	A Bit O'Gold	126	Will He Crow	126	600,000	2:04.72	97

Beyer Index: 98.73

Run as King's Plate 1902-1951. Run at old Woodbine prior to 1956. Run in 1-mile heats 1860-1867. Run at 2 miles 1868-1870. Run at 1 3/4 miles in 1871. Run at 1 1/2 miles 1872-1886. Run at 1 1/4 miles 1887-1923. Run at 1 1/8 miles 1924-1956. For 3-year-olds and up 1860-1937. For 3- and 4-year-olds in 1938. Prior to 1959 for horses bred and owned in Canada.

ROYAL NORTH HANDICAP (G3-C), 6 Furlongs (Turf), Fillies and Mares, 3-Year-Olds and Up, Woodbine, 2004 Purse: $217,550

Year	Winner	Age	Jockey	Wt.	Second	Wt.	Third	Wt.	Win Value	Time	Beyer
1994	Early Blaze	4	L. Duffy	116	Apelia	123	Super Doer	111	23,461	1:10.40	97
1995	Bar U Mood	5	T.K. Kabel	121	Countess Steffi	117	Lynclar	112	47,340	1:10.40	94
1996	Special Moves	4	V.H. Molina	117	Shooting Sherry	116	Klondike Strike	119	52,155	1:09.40	90
1997	Domasca Bella	5	D. Clark	115	Lynclar	114	Sports Front Champ	114	55,428	1:09.40	89
1998	Going to Extremes	4	P. Husbands	116	Start at Once	118	Song of Africa	117	49,140	1:09.00	91
1999	Hide the Bride	4	M.K. Walls	118	Prospective Rosie	115	Heavenly Lark	112	50,085	1:10.61	92
2000	Confessional	4	R.A. Dominguez	120	Ahead by a Century	115	Pete's Fancy	115	84,675	1:08.35	96
2001	Confessional	5	R.A. Dominguez	124	Heliotrope	121	Ahead by a Century	112	85,575	1:09.10	96
2002	Quick Blue	4	E. Ramsammy	116	Mysterious Affair	120	Marisa Go	116	128,730	1:09.53	92
2003	Chopinina	5	T.K. Kabel	120	Alpha Heat	117	Leading Role	116	131,430	1:12.19	100
2004	Hour of Justice	4	T.K. Kabel	118	With Patience	118	Boozin' Susan	120	100,530	1:07.83	99

Beyer Index: 94.18

Run on main track 1994-1995. For previous runnings see the 1994 Manual

SEAWAY (G3-C), 7 Furlongs, Fillies and Mares, 3-Year-Olds and Up, Woodbine, 2004 Purse: $186,500

Year	Winner	Age	Jockey	Wt.	Second	Wt.	Third	Wt.	Win Value	Time	Beyer
1994	Prospective Dolly	7	D. Penna	121	Miss Importance	113	A Gal for Gordo	115	39,780	1:22.40	91
1995	Bar U Mood	5	T.K. Kabel	115	Countess Steffi	119	Franssica D'Amour	115	48,600	1:23.40	95
1996	Ashboro	3	S. Hawley	110	Heavenly Punch	115	Blue Basin	114	50,310	1:22.60	99
1997	Santa Amelia	4	R.C. Landry	119	Flashy n Smart	119	Mindy Gayle	115	53,670	1:23.40	99
1998	Urban Distraction	3	R.B. Sabourin	113	Santa Amelia	119	Rare Executive	113	54,960	1:23.00	92
1999	Gregorian Chance	3	M.K. Walls	118	Kirby's Song	121	Sararegal	115	53,376	1:22.95	90
2000	Saoirse	4	D. Clark	121	Dimontina	114	Sararegal	113	90,060	1:24.15	85
2001	El Prado Essence	4	P. Husbands	116	Meadow Gem	116	Ahead by a Century	113	65,640	1:24.24	94
2002	El Prado Essence	5	T.K. Kabel	119	Hattiesburg	116	Feathers	115	81,900	1:24.48	91
2003	Brass in Pocket	4	D. Clark	121	El Prado Essence	119	Whiletheiron'shot	115	114,225	1:24.45	92
2004	Brass in Pocket	5	T.K. Kabel	119	Winter Garden	119	El Prado Essence	117	111,900	1:22.26	98

Beyer Index: 93.27

For previous runnings see the 1994 Manual

SELENE (G2-C), 1 1/16 Miles, Fillies, 3-Year-Olds, Woodbine, 2004 Purse: $275,000

Year	Winner	Age	Jockey	Wt.	Second	Wt.	Third	Wt.	Win Value	Time	Beyer
1994	Holly Regent	3	D.J. Seymour	116	Stellarina	113	Alywow	123	65,760	1:43.20	99
1995	Daijin	3	T.K. Kabel	124	Scattered Dreams	114	Miss Oceanette	112	66,900	1:44.40	96
1996	Briarcliff	3	D. Penna	114	Flashy n Smart	116	Northern Hilite	116	68,940	1:44.40	91
1997	Cotton Carnival	3	R.C. Landry	114	No Foul Play	118	Mordacious	120	50,935	1:44.00	91
1998	Lady Beverly	3	N. Somsanith	118	Primaly	120	Numberonedance	114	65,580	1:44.60	87
1999	Roaring Twenties	3	A.T. Gryder	114	Swingin on Ice	116	With Flair	115	131,520	1:47.84	92
2000	Zoftig	3	M. St. Julien	116	North Lake Jane	116	Inspired Kiss	118	167,550	1:48.59	83
2001	Dark Ending	3	P. Husbands	115	Turner's Hall	114	Royal Fact	114	164,850	1:48.02	80
2002	See How She Runs	3	D.R. Pettinger	123	Ginger Gold	123	Mulrainy	116	168,150	1:45.49	95
2003	Too Late Now	3	R.C. Landry	116	Handpainted	118	Winter Garden	118	166,650	1:44.36	92
2004	Eye of the Sphynx	3	T.K. Kabel	118	Silver Bird	118	Sweet Problem	116	165,000	1:48.28	82

Beyer Index: 89.82

For previous runnings see the 1994 Manual

SKY CLASSIC HANDICAP (G2-C), 1 3/8 Miles (Turf), 3-Year-Olds and Up, Woodbine, 2004 Purse: $275,250

Year	Winner	Age	Jockey	Wt.	Second	Wt.	Third	Wt.	Win Value	Time	Beyer
1994	Shiny Key	6	D. Clark	117	Avid Affection	113	Testalino	111	40,032	1:47.60	94
1994	Ride With Pancho	4	S. Hawley	107	Kissin Kris	119	Roche Rock	106	40,392	1:47.40	96
1995	Jet Freighter	4	T.K. Kabel	118	Alywow	117			68,400	2:13.40	99
					Make'n It Happen	115					
1996	Lassigny	5	J.A. Krone	119	Windsharp	119	Roche Rock	111	67,740	2:18.00	104
1997	Chief Bearhart	4	J.A. Santos	123	Honor Glide	119	Intheblinkofani	111	65,100	2:13.40	112
1998	Chief Bearhart	5	J.A. Santos	125	Green Means Go	114	Desert Waves	112	65,700	2:15.60	104
1999	Dawson's Legacy	4	C. Montpellier	114	Buck's Boy	124	Thornfield	116	64,560	2:13.05	106
2000	Muntej	3	R.C. Landry	113	Free Vacation	114	American Falcon	115	102,060	2:18.83	99
2001	Stage Classic	3	C. Montpellier	113	Strike Smartly	114	Silver Axe	113	101,700	2:21.79	99
2002	Strut the Stage	4	T.K. Kabel	119	Cetewayo	118	Man From Wicklow	119	167,700	2:19.33	103
2003	Bowman Mill	5	B. Blanc	113	Lenny the Lender	110	Mobil	115	163,050	2:23.14	100
2004	Colorful Judgement	4	S. Callaghan	114	Lenny the Lender	110	Longship	107	165,150	2:16.19	94

Beyer Index: 100.83

Run at 1 1/8 miles in 1994. Run as Jockey Club Cup Handicap 1994–1996. Run in divisions in 1994. For previous runnings see the 1994 Manual

SUMMER (G2-C), 1 Mile (Turf), 2-Year-Olds, Woodbine, 2004 Purse: $277,750

Year	Winner	Age	Jockey	Wt.	Second	Wt.	Third	Wt.	Win Value	Time	Beyer
1994	Native Regent	2	D. Penna	122	Always a Rainbow	122	Houston Connection	122	72,540	1:34.40	81
1995	Blazing Hot	2	T.K. Kabel	119	Sealaunch	122	Captivator	122	75,180	1:35.00	89
1996	Synastry Express	2	M.K. Walls	122	Cash Deposit	122	Divine Insight	122	74,520	1:38.00	87
1997	Patriot Love	2	S. Hawley	122	Dawson's Legacy	122	Gudai Might	122	69,840	1:37.40	75
1998	Riddell's Creek	2	J. McKnight	122	Certainly Classic	122	Gallyn's Star	122	78,360	1:37.40	77
1999	Four on the Floor	2	J.S. McAleney	122	King Cugat	122	Precise End	122	89,160	1:35.41	87
2000	Speed Gun	2	E. Ramsammy	122	Waltzin' Storm	122	Strut the Stage	122	102,480	1:34.51	90
2001	El Soprano	2	G.L. Stevens	122	Miesque's Approval	122	North Brooklyn	122	109,050	1:35.14	84
2002	Lismore Knight	2	P. Day	122	Wando	122	Walls of Jericho	122	174,750	1:35.33	86
2003	Bachelor Blues	2	T.K. Kabel	122	Victory Light	122	America America	119	171,300	1:34.95	89
	Commendation finished third, was disqualified and placed 10th										
2004	Dubleo	2	C.S. Nakatani	122	Dance With Ravens	122	Go to the Sun	122	166,650	1:34.69	82

Beyer Index: 84.27

For previous runnings see the 1994 Manual

E.P. TAYLOR (G1-C), 1 1/4 Miles (Turf), Fillies and Mares, 3-Year-Olds and Up, Woodbine, 2004 Purse: $750,000

Year	Winner	Age	Jockey	Wt.	Second	Wt.	Third	Wt.	Win Value	Time	Beyer
1994	Truly a Dream	3	C.J. McCarron	118	Bold Ruritana	123	Hero's Love	123	207,180	2:01.60	95
1995	Timarida	3	L. Dettori	117	Matiara	117	Bold Ruritana	123	213,120	2:03.60	111
1996	Wandering Star	3	W.H. McCauley	118	Flame Valley	118	Carling	123	204,120	2:04.60	109
1997	Kool Kat Katie	3	O. Peslier	118	Mousse Glacee	118	L'Annee Folle	123	206,460	2:02.00	103
1998	Zomaradah	3	G.L. Stevens	118	Tresoriere	123	Griselda	118	273,600	2:02.40	102
1999	Insight	4	M.E. Smith	123	Cerulean Sky	118	Midnight Line	123	300,000	2:05.34	101
2000	Fly For Avie	5	T.K. Kabel	123	Lady Upstage	117	Innuendo	123	300,000	2:02.78	96
2001	Choc Ice	3	J.P. Murtagh	119	Volga	117	Spring Oak	121	300,000	2:03.01	98
2002	Fraulein	3	K. Darley	117	Alasha	117	Volga	123	450,000	2:10.03	100
2003	Volga	5	R. Migliore	123	Tigertail	123	Hi Dubai	118	450,000	2:05.68	96
2004	Commercante	4	J.R. Velazquez	123	Punctilious	118	Classic Stamp	123	450,000	2:04.02	100

Beyer Index: 101.00

For previous runnings see the 1994 Manual

TORONTO CUP HANDICAP (G3-C), 1 1/8 Miles (Turf), 3-Year-Olds, Woodbine, 2004 Purse: $168,600

Year	Winner	Age	Jockey	Wt.	Second	Wt.	Third	Wt.	Win Value	Time	Beyer
1994	St. Clair Winger	3	R. King Jr	115	Dixieland Rhythm	112	Cut and Gun	112	40,500	1:45.20	85
1995	All Firmed Up	3	R.C. Landry	119	Charlie's Dewan	116	Loud Swords	117	51,615	1:49.40	91
1996	Ok by Me	3	C. Velasquez	122	Sealaunch	119	Jubarsky	112	49,995	1:47.40	95
1997	Skybound	3	E. Ramsammy	118	John the Magician	117	Prior Approval	112	39,852	1:47.00	99
1998	Ragged Kingdom	3	D. Clark	118	Ski Maker	113	Patriot Love	118	49,635	1:47.40	92
1999	Zanetti	3	D. Clark	119	Fred of Gold	114	American Falcon	118	49,365	1:47.88	88
1999	Apalachian Chief	3	R.A. Dos Ramos	119	Certainly Classic	119	Double Blue	114	49,365	1:47.22	87
2000	Think Red	3	T.K. Kabel	119	Master Stuart	112	Paco el Prado	115	83,925	1:48.76	95
2001	Strut the Stage	3	T.K. Kabel	122	Stage Classic	115	Legal Heir	113	83,396	1:47.91	98
2002	Portcullis	3	S. Callaghan	120	El Soprano	119	Funny Soldier	118	97,830	1:47.98	90
2003	Mobil	3	T.K. Kabel	122	Strizzi	119	Moonshine Hall	121	98,460	1:49.15	92
2004	Silver Ticket	3	T.K. Kabel	117	Bachelor Blues	118	Burst of Fire	116	101,160	1:47.35	93

Beyer Index: 92.08

Run at Fort Erie in 1994. Run at 1 1/16 miles in 1994. Run in divisions in 1999. For previous runnings see the 1994 Manual

VIGIL HANDICAP (G3-C), 7 Furlongs, 4-Year-Olds and Up, Woodbine, 2004 Purse: $160,800

Year	Winner	Age	Jockey	Wt.	Second	Wt.	Third	Wt.	Win Value	Time	Beyer
1994	Berry Moonolow	5	J. McKnight	113	Blitzer	122	Megas Vukefalos	117	46,578	1:21.80	101
1995	Sea Wall	4	R.A. Dos Ramos	118	Blitzer	118	Rustic Light	122	50,400	1:23.00	102
1996	Kiridashi	4	S. Hawley	119	King Ruckus	120	Glanmire	114	48,645	1:22.80	98
1997	Kiridashi	5	M.K. Walls	124	Langfuhr	124	Mindy Gayle	109	39,060	1:21.80	105
1998	Deputy Inxs	7	N. Somsanith	115	Kiridashi	119	Cache In	117	50,265	1:22.40	101
1999	Deputy Inxs	8	N. Somsanith	122	One Way Love	117	Cache In	118	50,985	1:23.54	99
2000	One Way Love	5	P. Husbands	120	Catahoula Parish	114	Saratoga Prince	117	83,700	1:22.66	109
2001	Exciting Story	4	P. Husbands	116	Wake at Noon	125	Grand End Sweep	113	82,425	1:23.49	111
2002	Wake at Noon	5	E. Ramsammy	123	Exciting Story	120	Geraint	116	99,000	1:23.13	97
2003	Wake at Noon	6	E. Ramsammy	124	Shaws Creek	114	Cheap Talk	120	98,820	1:23.25	100
2004	Mobil	4	T.K. Kabel	120	Chris's Bad Boy	122	Awesome Action	115	96,480	1:21.81	104

For previous runnings see the 1994 Manual

Beyer Index: 102.45

(LABATT) WOODBINE OAKS, 1 1/8 Miles, Fillies, 3-Year-Olds, Foaled in Canada, Woodbine, 2004 Purse: $500,000

Year	Winner	Age	Jockey	Wt.	Second	Wt.	Third	Wt.	Win Value	Time	Beyer
1994	Plenty of Sugar	3	R.A. Dos Ramos	121	Mysteriously	121	Alywow	121	125,991	1:49.60	95
1995	Gal in a Ruckus	3	W.H. McCauley	121	Kathie's Colleen	121	Honky Tonk Tune	121	128,739	1:51.20	100
1996	Silent Fleet	3	S.R. Bahen	121	Autumn Slew	121	Buxton Spice	121	124,062	1:50.20	100
1997	Capdiva	3	R.C. Landry	121	Montgomery Belle	121	Almost Saintly	121	155,478	1:50.80	83
1998	Kirby's Song	3	T.K. Kabel	121	Primaly	121	Pinafore Park	121	180,000	1:50.80	100
1999	Touch Dial	3	M.K. Walls	121	Roaring Twenties	121	Free Vacaction	121	210,000	1:51.33	93
2000	Catch the Ring	3	R.C. Landry	121	Mountain Angel	121	Forest Princess	121	300,000	1:53.16	81
2001	Dancethruthedawn	3	G. Boulanger	121	Dancen in the Sun	121	Quick Blue	121	300,000	1:51.74	97
2002	Ginger Gold	3	R.A. Dos Ramos	121	Silver Nithi	121	Alpha Heat	121	300,000	1:51.56	90
2003	Too Late Now	3	R.C. Landry	121	Seeking the Ring	121	Santerra	121	300,000	1:53.05	81
2004	Eye of the Sphynx	3	T.K. Kabel	121	Touchnow	121	My Vintage Port	121	300,000	1:53.11	89

Beyer Index: 91.73

Run as Canadian Oaks 1994–2000. For previous runnings see the 1994 Manual

WOODBINE SLOTS CUP HANDICAP (G3-C), 1 1/16 Miles, 3-Year-Olds and Up, Woodbine, 2004 Purse: $157,950

Year	Winner	Age	Jockey	Wt.	Second	Wt.	Third	Wt.	Win Value	Time	Beyer
1994	Comarctic	5	J.S. McAleney	115	Brock Street	112	Ivory Regent	113	41,220	1:44.00	101
1995	Freedom Fleet	3	T.K. Kabel	115	Kiridashi	119	Oronero	113	52,110	1:41.80	102
1996	Stephanotis	3	M.K. Walls	115	Suave Prospect	113	For Pete's Sake	114	67,020	1:42.60	106
1997	Terremoto	6	S. Hawley	116	Stephanotis	119	For Pete's Sake	114	40,608	1:42.20	109
1998	Cache In	4	M.K. Walls	117	Regal Courser	117	Deputy Inxs	118	83,775	1:45.00	102
1999	Vice n' Friendly	4	M.K. Walls	118	Deputy Inxs	124	Mt. Sassafras	119	48,600	1:45.63	97
2000	One Way Love	5	P. Husbands	126	A Fleets Dancer	116	Tiltam	114	102,344	1:43.59	103
2001	Win City	3	C. Montpellier	117	Wicklow Highlands	107	Kiss a Native	119	98,280	1:44.83	100
2002	Parose	8	T.K. Kabel	117	Attest	114	Divine Luck	113	100,620	1:45.10	93
2003	No Comprende	5	P. Husbands	117	Mobil	119	Parose	118	99,990	1:43.93	98
2004	Mark One	5	R.C. Landry	119	A Bit O'Gold	120	Norfolk Knight	120	99,508	1:45.00	97

Beyer Index: 100.73

Run as Autumn Handicap 1994–2001. For previous runnings see the 1994 Manual

American Match Races

Match races are scheduled for two horses, usually a winner-take-all, or skewered purse distribution. Two-horse races are those in which three or more were entered, but only two actually ran.

MATCH RACES

Contestants	Location	Date
American Eclipse - Sir Charles	Washington D. C.	November 20, 1822
American Eclipse - Henry	Union Course, Long Island, New York	May 27, 1823
Ariel - Lafayette	Union Course, Long Island, New York	October 6, 1825
Flirtilla - Ariel	Union Course, Long Island, New York	October 31, 1825
Arietta - Ariel	Union Course, Long Island, New York	May 8, 1830
Portsmouth - Boston	Petersburg, Virginia	April, 16, 1839
Black Maria - Brilliant	Union Course, Long Island, New York	October 23, 1839
Boston - Gano	Augusta, Georgia	December 7, 1840
Fashion-Boston	Union Course, Long Island, New York	May 10, 1842
Peytona - Fashion	Union Course, Long Island, New York	May 13, 1845
Fashion - Peytona	Camden, New Jersey	May 27, 1845
Lexington - Sallie Waters	New Orleans, Louisiana	December 2, 1853
Lexington - Le Comte	New Orleans, Louisiana	April 14, 1855
Kentucky - Aldebaran	Paterson, New Jersey	September 17, 1864
Norfolk - Lodi	San Francisco, California	May 23, 1865
Norfolk - Lodi	Sacramento, California	September 18, 1865
Norfolk - Lodi	Sacramento, California	September 23, 1865
Flora - Pele	San Francisco, California	January 6, 1866
Ooltawa - Muggins	Nashville, Tennessee	April 7, 1866
Lewis E. Smith - Maiden	New Orleans, Louisiana	April 20, 1866
Mike Edwards - Red Oak	St. Louis, Mo.	May 15, 1866
Maid of Honor - Redwing	Jerome Park, New York	October 3, 1866
Derringer - Susie B. Moore	San Francisco, California	January, 14, 1867
Tornado - Minnie C.^	New Orleans, Louisiana	January 22, 1867
De Courcy - Maid of Honor	Jerome Park, New York	May 25, 1867
Raquette - Redwing	Jerome Park, New York	November 9, 1867
Maid Of Honor - Trovatore	Jerome Park, New York	November 7, 1868
Nannie McNairy - Le Noir	New Orleans, Louisiana	December 7, 1868
Nannie McNairy - Lewis E. Smith	New Orleans, Louisiana	April 8, 1869
Miss Alice - The Gloamin colt	Jerome Park, New York	June 3, 1869
Glenelg - Rapture	Jerome Park, New York	June 3, 1869
Intrigue - El Dorado	Jerome Park, New York	June 6, 1869
Finesse - Intrigue*	Saratoga Springs, New York	July 31, 1869
Pasta Filly - Miss Alice*	Saratoga Springs, New York	July 31, 1869
Finesse - Intrigue	Jerome Park, New York	October 6, 1869
Nannie McNairy - Sarah McDonald	New Orleans, Louisiana	December 4, 1869
By the Sea - The Gloamin colt*	Jerome Park, New York	October 13, 1870
Vigil - Chalmette	New Orleans, Louisiana	May 20, 1871
Alarm - Inverary	Saratoga Springs, New York	August 16, 1871
Thad Stevens - Nettie Brown	San Francisco, California	February 22, 1873
Thad Stevens - Ben Wade	Oakland, California	June 28, 1873
Nell Flaherty - Abi	Oakland, California	June 28, 1873
Survivor - Aerolite	Monmouth, New Jersey	July 21, 1873
Girl of the Period - Ophelia	Jerome Park, New York	October 4, 1873
Shylock - M. A. B.	Jerome Park, New York	October 4, 1873
Joe Daniels - Nell Flaherty	San Francisco, California	December 25, 1873
Limestone - Revenge**	Charleston, South Carolina	March 9, 1874
Shylock - Vaultress	Monmouth, New Jersey	July 18, 1874
Bullet - Trouble***	Jerome Park, New York	June 10, 1875
Shirley - Resolute	Pimlico, Maryland	October 28, 1876
Basil - Cloverbrook	Jerome Park, New York	June 18, 1877
Rappahannock - Kilburn	Pimlico, Maryland	October 26, 1877
Jake - Madge Duke	San Francisco, California	November 29, 1877
Mollie McCarthy - Jake	Sacramento, California	March 2, 1878
Ten Broeck - Mollie McCarthy	Louisville, Kentucky	July 4, 1878

Contestants	Location	Date
Spartan - Bramble	Monmouth Park, New Jersey	July 6, 1878
Rocco - Fibbertigibbet	Jerome Park, New York	June 10, 1879
Jallop - Kester	Riverside, California	June 22, 1880
Luke Blackburn - Uncas	Sheepshead Bay, Long Island, New York	September 14, 1880
Maggie May - Lilla G.	Dallas, Texas	November 22, 1880
Marathon - Geranium	Jerome Park, New York	June 4, 1881
Geranium - Marathon	Sheepshead Bay, Long Island, New York	June 23 1881
Onondaga - Sachem	Sheepshead Bay, Long Island, New York	June 25, 1881
Eole - Getaway	Saratoga Springs, New York	August 12, 1881
Hiawasse - Memento	Monmouth Park, New Jersey	August 20, 1881
Crickmore - Hindoo	Sheepshead Bay, Long Island, New York	September 17,1881
Sisterly - Clifton Bell	Denver, Colorado	April 29, 1882
Ida - Duke of Montrose	Monmouth Park, New Jersey	May 3, 1882
Pearl Jennings - Cinderella	Denver, Colorado	May 6, 1882
Red Boy - Wildmoor	Salt Lake City, Utah	June, 17, 1882
Wildmoor - Euchre	Salt Lake City, Utah	July 5, 1882
Corsair - Hospodar	Monmouth Park, New Jersey	July 8, 1882
Pearl Jennings - Maria F.	Salt Lake City, Utah	July 17, 1882
Longstride - Belle of the West	Salt Lake City, Utah	July 19, 1882
Pearl Jennings - Red Boy	Salt Lake City, Utah	July 22, 1882
Wildmoor - Red Boy	Salt Lake City, Utah	August 2, 1882
Vampire - Hospodar	Monmouth Park, New Jersey	August 2, 1882
Adams Mare - Jim Douglas	Sacramento, California	May 21, 1883
Premium- Kelpie	Sacramento, California	Sept. 15, 1883
Pitchfork Johnnie - Tom Green	Trinidad, Colorado	June 3, 1884
East Lynne - Cricket	Monmouth Park, New Jersey	July 24, 1884
Wallflower - Eulogy	Saratoga Springs, New York	August 2, 1884
Miss Woodford - Drake Carter	Sheepshead Bay, Long Island, New York	September 18, 1884
Marmosette - Sungleam	Lexington, Kentucky	November 18, 1884
Dundee - Hobson's Choice	Jerome Park, New York	May 28, 1885
General Harding - Shelby Barnes	Brighton Beach, Long Island, New York	June 19, 1885
Miss Woodford - Freeland	Monmouth Park, New Jersey	August 20, 1885
Blue Bird - Lela B	Fort Worth, Texas	November 20, 1885
Billy Johnson - Albemarle	San Francisco, California	January 9, 1886
Boomerang - Red Girl	Denver, Colorado	May 26 1886
Volante - Tyrant*	St. Louis, Mo.	June 17, 1886
Troubadour - Miss Woodford	Coney Island, New York	June 29, 1886
Salvatore - Tenny	Sheepshead Bay, Long Island, New York	June 25, 1890
Long Street - Tenny	Morris Park, New York	August 1, 1891
Kingston - Van Buren	Garfield Park, Chicago, Illinois	August 31, 1891
Domino - Dobbins^^	Sheepshead Bay, Long Island, New York	August 31, 1893
Domino - Henry of Navarre^^	Gravesend, Brooklyn, New York	September 15, 1894
Cleophas - Suisun	Churchill Downs, Louisville, Kentucky	May 14, 1896
Admiration - May Hempstead	Sheepshead Bay, Long Island, New York	July 1, 1899

** Walkover; ** Over Hurdles; *** Steeplechase; ^ Winning owner took loser's horse; ^^ Dead Heat*

MATCH RACES SINCE 1900

Winner	Age	Wt.	Winrs Lead	Second	Age	Wt.	Track	Distance	Date	Net Value	Time
Ethelbert	4	126	10	Jean Bereud	4	126	Gravesend	1 1/4 m	June 2 1900	$6,005	2:08 1/5
End'ce by Right	2	112	1	Heno	2	115	Gravesend	about 6f	Sept. 28 1901	1,775	1:08 3/5
Dick Welles	3	112	1	Grand Opera	4	115	Harlem	1 m	Aug. 14 1903	1,000	1:37 2/5
Novelty	2	122	3	Textile	2	122	Saratoga	6 f	Aug. 17 1910	5,005	1:13 1/5
Iron Mask	6	115	5	Pan Zereta	4	110	Juarez	6 f	Jan. 4 1914	400	1:09 3/5
Hourless	3	126	1	Omar Khayyam	3	126	Laurel	1 1/4 m	Oct. 18 1917	10,200	2:02
Eternal	2	122	head	Billy Kelly	2	122	Laurel	6 f	Oct. 28 1918	20,000	1:12
Man O' War	3	120	7	Sir Barton	4	126	Kenilworth	1 1/4 m	Oct. 12 1920	80,000*	2:03
Zev	3	126	5	Papyrus	3	126	Belmont	1 1/2 m	Oct. 20 1923	85,000*	2:35 2/5
Sarazen	2	118	2	Happy Thoughts	2	115	Laurel	6 f	Oct. 26 1923	15,025	1:14
Zev	3	126	nose	In Memoriam	4	115	Churchill	1 1/4 m	Nov. 17 1923	25,000	2:06 3/5
Marietta	3	105	2 1/2	Liberty	4	114	Smithville, Mo.	1 1/16 m	Sept. 30 1927	500	1:54 3/5
Winooka	5	120	4 1/2	Onrush	3	105	Longacres	6 f	Sept. 16 1933	5,000	1:14

Winner	Age	Wt.	Winrs Lead	Second	Age	Wt.	Track	Distance	Date	Net Value	Time
Dirigible	4	112	4	Suitor	9	117	Agua Caliente	6 f	April 14 1935	400	1:12 3/5
Myrtlewood	3	110	nose	Clang	3	110	Hawthorne	6 f	Sept. 25 1935	2,000	1:10 4/5
Clang	3	110	nose	Myrtlewood	3	110	Coney Island	6 f	Oct. 12 1935	2,000	1:09 1/5
Myrtlewood	4	118	3	Miss Merriment	5	118	Keeneland	6 f	Oct. 24 1936	No Purse	1:11 4/5
Rought Time	3	108	2	Appealing	3	115	Suffolk	6 f	Aug. 14 1937	1,000	1:10 2/5
Seabiscuit	5	130	nose	Ligaroti	6	115	Del Mar	1 1/8 m	Aug. 12 1938	25,000	1:49
Sky Pirate	5	111	1 1/2	Susi Q	3	107	Longacres	6 f	Sept. 18 1938	No Purse	1:10 3/5
Seabiscuit	5	120	4	War Admiral	4	120	Pimlico	1 3/16 m	Nov. 1 1938	15,000	1:56 3/5
Little Cartago	2	122	3	Mar Quick	2	122	Agua Caliente	4 f	May 7 1939	500	:46 4/5
Unerring	3	110	2	Flying Lill	3	110	Wash. Park	1 m	Aug. 31 1939	6,250	1:37 4/5
Beaver Lake	8	112	1 1/2	Miss Monte	5	107	Fairmont	6 f	June 5 1940	Gold Cup	1:13 3/5
Annibal	7	140	1 1/2	Ossabaw	6	140	Belmont	abt 2 m	June 6 1940	3,000	3:41 2/5
Bonnie Sea	5	114	nose	Rushaway	7	114	Agua Caliente	1 1/2 m	June 30 1940	1,000	2:30 3/5
Soup and Fish	4	112	3/4	Betty Main	3	106	Beulah	1 m	Sept. 20 1941	1,000	1:37 4/5
Alsab	2	122	3 1/2	Requested	2	122	Belmont	6 1/2 f	Sept. 23 1941	10,000	1:16
Lee Torch	6	125	nose	Abide	5	125	Agua Caliente	1 m	Oct. 5 1941	700	1:41 2/5
Lee Torch	6	125	7	Abide	5	125	Agua Caliente	1 m	Oct. 12 1941	1,000	1:42
Wise Moss	3	108	2 3/4	Sweet Willow	4	118	Rockingham	6 f	Nov. 2 1941	5,000	1:11 1/5
Wanche	2	110	3	Cabecilla	2	110	Havana	3 f	Feb. 24 1942	2,000	:37 2/5
Sir Winsome	4	115	4	Urge Me	7	115	Agua Caliente	6f	July 19 1942	700	1:12
Lavengro	7	115	2 1/2	Sir Winsome	4	110	Longacres	3 f	Aug. 16 1942	2,005	1:10
Alsab	3	119	nose	Whirlaway	4	126	Narragansett	1 3/16 m	Sept. 19 1942	25,000	1:56 2/5
Grayce P.	2	115	5	Dandy Day	2	118	Mexico City	5 1/2 f	Oct. 12 1944	1,547	1:08
Busher	3	115	3/4	Durazna	4	115	Wash. Park	1 m	Aug. 29 1945	25,000	1:37 4/5
Here's How	2	116	3 1/2	Lady Gunner	2	116	Narragansett	6 f	Sept. 15 1945	7,500	1:12 4/5
Dinner Party	6	120	1	Float Me	5	120	Rockingham	1 1/8 m	Nov. 23 1946	10,000	1:57 3/5
Armed	6	126	8	Assault	4	126	Belmont	1 1/4 m	Sept. 27 1947	100,000	2:02 4/5
Tardado	3	117	4	Pretencioso	3	112	Mexico City	6 f	Feb. 12 1949	No Purse	1:14 1/5
Capot	3	120	12	Coaltown	4	126	Pimlico	1 3/16 m	Oct. 28 1949	15,000	1:56 4/5
Virginia Fair	2	121	1/2	Virden	2	118	Edmonton	abt 5 f	Aug. 15 1952	1,000	1:00 2/5
Coquetona	2	115	1 1/4	Bandara Negra	2	115	Mexico City	4 f	May 15 1954	800	:49
Vicious Vixen	7	113	10	Calolet	8	119	Mexico City	7 1/2 f	May 23 1954	800	1:32 4/5
Manzanero	7	118	3	Katy's Prince	3	112	Mexico City	6 f	Jan. 23 1955	800	1:12 1/5
La Mexicana	2	115	2	Don Nico	2	117	Mexico City	2 f	Feb. 15 1955	650	:22 1/5
Nashua	3	126	6 1/2	Swaps	3	126	Washington	1 1/4 m	Aug. 31 1955	100,000	2:04 1/5
Queen Doris	3	115	12	Molly Darling	4	120	Centennial	5 1/2 f	July 28 1956	2,500	1:05 3/5
Noorahge	4	120	4 1/4	Early Bull	7	120	Wheeling Downs	6 1/2 f	Sept. 14 1957	2,000	1:24
Wildoath	3	108	2 1/4	War Marshal	4	112	Fresno, Calif.	1 1/16 m	Oct. 12 1957	1,200	1:43 3/5
Alumni	3	115	2 1/2	Rogation	5	115	Oriental Park	6 f	Oct. 13 1957	1,000	1:41
Lori Lynn	4	115	1 1/2	Salmon Peter	9	120	Centennial	1 1/4 m	Aug. 22 1959	1,200	2:05
Roman Colonel	4	126	neck	Benedicto	5	115	Detroit	6 f	June 11 1960	12,000	1:10 2/5
Matisse	4	111	1 1/2	Tondi	4	111	Albuquerque	5 1/2 f	Sept. 24 1960	2,000	1:03
Routeen	2	119	8	Modest Step	2	110	Latonia	6 f	Oct. 1 1960	1,000	1:13 3/5
Witchita Maid	4	112	3/4	Gilhooley	5	112	Centennial	5 1/2 f	Aug. 19 1961	1,200	1;04 2/5
Cesca	2	119	5 3/4	Aim n Fire	2	122	Woodbine	5 1/2 f	July 7 1962	15,000	1:04 3/5
Short Nail	2	115	6	Florida Cracker	2	115	Garden State	6 f	Dec. 4 1962	1,500	1:13 2/5
Poplar	3	115	4	Tono	3	115	Mexico City	6 f	March 10 1963	800	1:13 1/5
Try It	8	115	2 3/4	Spinney	10	115	Turf Paradise	1 1/2 m	April 14 1963	2,250	2:30 2/5
Before Sun	2	115	head	Princess Cloud	2	115	Hazel Park	4 f	June 2 1964	No Purse	:47
Over Current	5	115	3 1/2	Golden Briar	5	115	Exhibition	6 f	June 27 1964	1,500	1:11 3/5
Wandering Boy	6	115	2 3/4	Mr. McCoy	5	115	Turf Paradise	2 f	April 11 1965	5,739	:21 2/5
Wandering Boy**	6	118	nose	Air Space	3	118	Turf Paradise	2 f	Dec. 5 1965	4,500	:21 1/5
Nancycee	4	113	1	Nasharco	4	118	Turf Paradise	5 f	Mar. 20 1966	2,500	:56 1/5
Nasharco	4	118	4 3/4	Nancycee	4	113	Turf Paradise	5 1/2 f	April 10 1966	2,500	1:10 1/5
Permano	4	114	7	Frannie	5	114	Exhibition	6 1/2 f	Sept. 7 1966	1,000	1:17
Christopher G.	3	120	neck	Moroni Joe	6	125	Prescott	5 1/2 f	Aug. 27 1967	525	1:06 2/5
Pocomoke	5	120	3	Murata San	6	115	Agua Caliente	6 f	Feb. 2 1969	500	1:11 2/5
Mr. Longwait	6	115	neck	Sunday Cruz	5	115	Thistledown	1 m	Mar. 22 1969	No Purse	1:44
Rowdy Lad	4	115	nose	Tebbad	6	120	Sunland Park	5 f	Mar. 29 1969	No Purse	:59 2/5
Emerald Chief	4	129	5	High Nail	6	140	Shenandoah	3 1/2 f	Nov. 15 1969	1,000	:40
Princess Khal	4	127	1	Off to Market	5	108	Centennial	1 m70 yds	Aug. 16 1970	3,000	1:41 3/4
Convenience	4	120	head	Typecast	6	120	Hollywood	1 1/8 m	June 17 1972	250,000	1:47 3/5
Jovial John	4	115	1	Blunt Man	9	115	Cahokia Downs	5 f	Nov. 16 1972	1,000	1:00 4/5
Ponderosa Jane	5	118	2 1/2	Distant U	6	118	Calder	6 f	Oct. 10 1973	2,000	1:13 2/5
Distant U	6	118	1/2	Ponderosa Jane	5	118	Calder	6 f	Oct. 20 1973	2,000	1:14

Bob Twinklet's**	4	117	1 1/2	Deleterious	4	117	Latonia	1 m	April 4 1974	2,500	1:44 4/5
Chris Evert	3	121	50	Miss Musket	3	121	Hollywood	1 1/4 m	July 20 1974	350,000	2:02
Dennis Beau	5	115	nose	Scottish Time	4	120	Lincoln Downs	1 m	Oct.10 1974	4,000	1:39 3/5
Scottish Time	4	120	1 1/4	Dennis Beau	6	118	Lincoln Downs	1 m	Oct. 17 1974	4,000	1:42 1/5
Foolish Pleasure ^	3	126	1	Ruffian	3	121	Belmont Park	1 1/4 m	July 6 1975	225,000	2:02
Jobim	4	121	1 1/4	Bitache	5	121	Mexico City	4 1/2 f	Mar. 7 1976	4,000	:52 4/5
Fleet and Ready	6	120	1 1/2	Moms Freddy	7	120	Agua Caliente	6 f	Dec. 12 1976	5,000	1:10
Keen Traveler	3	114	neck	Graphic Miss	3	114	Centennial	5 f	June 7 1981	6,000	:57 4/5
Mr. McMoose	4	115	nose	Hail Satan	5	115	Agua Caliente	1 1/4 m	June 19 1982	7,500	2:02 3/5
Baltanas	8	115	5	Skillful Look	4	115	Agua Caliente	1 1/2 m	Nov. 23 1985	2,500	2:33
Who Doctor Who	5	125	3 1/2	Explosive Girl	4	120	Ak-Sar-Ben	1 m70 yds	July 23 1988	40,000	1:42
Slash Adder	5	122	4 1/2	Win Your Heart	4	122	Les Bois Park	4 1/2 f	Sept. 18 1988	2,000	:51 2/5

Winner	Second	Track	Distance	Date	Race	Surf
Soviet Problem	Lazor	Golden Gate	6 f	May 12 1994	6	Dirt
Soviet Problem	Mamselle Bebette	Del Mar	5 f	Aug. 21 1994	10	Turf
Busy Banana	Richard Of England	Santa Anita	1 1/2 m	Mar. 23 1996	11	Dirt
Isthataclaimgirl	Calico Rose	Prairie Meadows	6 f	June 24 1996	8	Dirt
Maybe Jack	Pro On Ice	Suffolk	1 m	Dec. 14 1997	7	Dirt
Rosy Way	Howthewestwaswon	Boise	6 1/2 f	July 21 1999	9	Dirt
Call Me Mr. Vain	Diplomacy	Suffolk Downs	6 f	Oct. 22, 2003	6	Dirt
Chester's Choice	Woke Up Dreamin	Del Mar	1 1/16 m	Sep. 7, 2003	4	Dirt

* Includes 5,000 Gold Cup; ** Three-horse match race; On Dec. 5, 1965 at Turf Paradise, Madabet (3), 118 finished 3rd beaten by 2 1/2 length: on April 4, 1974, at Latonia, Quipid (4) 112 finished 3rd, beaten by 1 1/2 lengths. ^ After completing three and one half furlongs, Ruffian broke down and could not finish.

2-HORSE RACES SINCE 1993

Track	Date	Race	Dis	Surf	Winner	Place
PIM	08/06/93	3	9	D	Sleek N Graceful	Ebonizer
TET	08/28/93	11	7	D	Persuasive Murr	Meritip
FL	11/06/93	1	6	D	Explosive Kiss	Princess Stacy
DEL	07/19/94	5	5	D	Hafef	Don't Blush Doctor
MTH	06/14/95	7	8.5	D	November Sunset	Trucking Baron*
MD	08/20/95	3	6.5	D	Burst Of Autumn	Butterscotchripple
PIM	09/26/95	6	8.5	D	Java Royal	Dr. Chicollini
PRE	08/17/96	2	5.5	D	Quintons Fan Club	Darting Garanda
PHA	09/22/96	7	9	D	Sansue's Castle	Wishful Dream
PHA	09/23/96	8	8.32	D	Manassa Station	Light Crusader
PRE	09/01/97	12	7	D	Tio Saros	Littlefield
DEL	10/25/97	7	8	D	Select Session	Tote Dancer
PRE	09/07/98	5	5.5	D	Real Dancer	Covered Wells
MD	09/13/98	2	8.5	D	Rouge Royale	Glue Stick
CNL	09/26/98	9	9	T	Kerfoot Corner	Poncho Duck
MTH	08/26/99	9	8.5	D	Sunny Stutz	Essential
TAM	12/18/99	1	5	D	Belle Of The South	Doasyouaretold
MNR	02/07/00	9	1M 70Y	D	Bow Legged Honey	War Genie
PHA	05/20/00	5	5 1/2F	D	Dark Tag	Bessie
PHA	05/27/00	5	6F	D	Trastevere	Dr. Marvel
MID	10/08/00	4	Ab.3 miles	Timber	Holzmann	IvorgorianNO
WRD	4/15/01	7	2	D	Avenue of Style	Mr. Debernardo
PHA	3/30/01	2	5 1/2	D	Dashing Patriot	Nicks Hope
ATH	4/14/01	5	2 3/8 M	T	Dalton River (CHI)	Crowned Crane
BOI	5/19/01	5	5	D	Im Ok So Far	Hodson
OXM	5/27/01	5	3 M	T	Fast Steppin Man	De Laurentis (CHI)
TIL	8/11/01	4	5	D	Bubba's T K O	Running Justice
YAV	8/13/01	6	8	D	Spitfire Dancer	Savannah Smiles
SJ	9/16/01	6	5 1/2	D	Cathedral Miss	Huddled
UN	6/8/02	2	5 1/2F	D	Mr Juan Sock	Afta David
PHA	6/15/02	8	1M 70Y	D	Run for Joy	Als Delight
FAX	9/21/02	6	About3M	T	Complete Verdict	Temperence Night
ELP	7/10/03	3	1M	D	Heldinhighesteem	If You Believe
ELK	8/31/03	1	5 1/2F	D	Thats Final	Seanster
DEL	9/23/03	7	6F	D	Boston Common	Sing Me Back Home
KAM	8/29/04	2	A6 1/2F	D	Everyone's N. V.	King of the Yukon
MDA	10/11/04	1	A5 1/2F	D	Knightly Swinger	Spice the Price
MDA	10/11/04	5	A5 1/2F	D	Early Results	Electric Affair

*Trucking Baron was placed 1st due to disqualification

Record of Walkovers

The walkover, one of racing's rarities these days, typically consists of a horse going over the course alone as the only starter in a race. The 1997 Bayakoa Handicap, in which only Sharp Cat ran, was the first walkover in a major event since Horse of the Year Spectacular Bid concluded his career with a solo gallop under Bill Shoemaker in the 1980 Woodward at Belmont Park. Prior to that, the last walkover in a major event came in 1949 when Coaltown faced no rivals in the Edward Burke Handicap at Havre de Grace.

Another kind of walkover is a race in which the horses competing all belong to the same interest or individual. The last known instance of this extreme oddity occurred in 1943 when stablemates Azogue Speed and Clara C. were the only entrants in the Juvenile Debut Stakes at Havana in Cuba.

Walkovers since 1913

Horse	Name of Stakes where applicable	Track	Date
Web Carter	Gracefield Cup Steeplechase	Great Neck, NY	Nov. 8, 1913
Roamer	Autumn Stakes	Belmont Park, NY	Sep. 19, 1914
Napier		Saratoga, NY	Aug. 13, 1915
Purchase	Jockey Club Stakes	Belmont Park, NY	Sep. 13, 1919
Reliance		Belmont Park Term	May 22, 1920
Royce Rools	Gramatan Handicap	Empire City, NY	Jly. 15, 1921
Exterminator	Saratoga Cup	Saratoga, NY	Aug. 31, 1921
Doublet		Belmont Park Term	Sep. 1, 1921
Millwick	Hempstead Highweight Handicap	Belmont Park, NY	May 24, 1927
Saguenay	King's Plate	Blue Bonnets, Que	Aug. 5, 1927
Maelstrom	Waverly Purse	Saratoga, NY	Sep. 2, 1927
Crack Willow	United Hunts Double Event (2nd)	Belmont Park, NY	Nov. 5, 1929
Questionnaire	Mount Kisco Stakes	Empire City, NY	Jly. 23, 1930
Awake *(entrymate of Questionnaire)*			
Little Nap	West Point Claiming Handicap	Empire City, NY	Oct. 29, 1930
Sun Meadow	Sysonby Purse	Belmont Park, NY	Jun. 9, 1931
Pilate	Waterboy Handicap	Saratoga, NY	Aug. 14, 1933
St. Francis	Old Glory Steeplechase Handicap	Aqueduct, NY	Jly. 2, 1936
Isolater	Saratoga Cup	Saratoga, NY	Aug. 31, 1940
Fenelon *(entrymate of Isolater)*			
Whirlaway	Pimlico Special	Pimlico, MD	Oct. 28, 1942
Azogue Speed	Juvenile Debut Stakes	Havana, Cuba	Jan. 31, 1943
Clara C. *(entrymate of Azogue Speed)*			
Star of Padula		Jamaica, NY	Apr. 10, 1944
Stymie	Saratoga Cup	Saratoga, NY	Aug. 31, 1946
Casa Camara	Diamond Ring Stakes	Long Branch, Ont	Oct. 26, 1946
Canada's Teddy	King's Plate Trial	Blue Bonnets, Que	Jly. 21, 1948
Citation	Pimlico Special	Pimlico, MD	Oct. 29, 1948
Coaltown	Edward Burke Handicap	Havre de Grace, MD	Apr. 23, 1949
Foxy Fighter	The Colonel Purse	Oxmoor, KY	Jun. 2, 1956
Appointed Hour	H.P. Stewart Memorial Challenge Cup	Media, PA	Oct. 13, 1962
Spectacular Bid	Woodward Stakes (G1)	Belmont Park, NY	Sep. 20, 1980
Chinese Export		Ligonier, PA	Sep. 18, 1982
Hawa		Middleburg, VA	Oct. 5, 1986
Quico		Middleburg, VA	Oct. 5, 1986
Alylad		Marquis Downs, Sask	Oct. 4, 1992
Impatient You		Atokad Park, NE	Jly. 2, 1995
Sharp Cat	Bayakoa Handicap (G2)	Hollywood Park, CA	Dec. 7, 1997
Young Dubliner		Foxfield, VA	Sep. 27, 1998

Triple Dead–Heats for Win

The most famous triple dead-heat to win in North American racing came in the 1944 running of the Carter Handicap at Aqueduct on June 10, when Brownie, Bossuet and Wait a Bit were deadlocked at the end of the seven-furlong event run over a sloppy track.

Triple dead-heats for win since 1940

Date	Track	Winners		
Sep. 21, 1940	Willows Park	My Debut	Margery Daw	Saucy Maid
Oct. 6, 1942	Detroit Fairgrounds	Sabra	Cutloose	Queen Echo
Jun. 10, 1944	Aqueduct	Brownie	Bossuet	Wait a Bit
Oct. 3, 1945	Wheeling Downs	Second Thought	Idle Knight	Palkin
Oct. 22, 1955	Caliente Race Track	Stormsorno	Beaufair	Chance Speed
Jly. 3, 1957	Hollywood Park	Joe's Pleasure	Challenger Tom	Leaful
Aug. 10, 1963	Arlington Park	Royal Redress	Livingston	Mr. S. Chance
Nov. 18, 1965	Sportsman's Park	Paddy o' Rock	Me Willwin	Miss Brendy
Aug. 27, 1966	Fairmount Park	Noholts Bard	Turn Tattle	Off Short
Sep. 5, 1966	Scarborough Downs	Around the Moon	Gold Bomb	Rebel Cheer
May 2, 1968	Beulah Park	Payola Joy	City Market	Equicharge
Mar. 22, 1974	Latonia	Deleterious	Quipid	Bob Twinkletoes
Feb. 9, 1975	Sunland Park	Flying Envoy	Ronny J.	Reserve Clause
Jun. 11, 1980	Santa Fe Downs	Pantaroni	Prince Kukui	Iron Hulk
Jun. 17, 1980	Northlands Park	Anne Ivers	Slightly Shady	Naughty Cage
Nov. 9, 1980	Sunland Park	Moon Barb	Teddy's Table	Grins Spirit
Oct. 23, 1981	Lincoln (Neb)	I Will Be	One Way	El Lark Rise
Dec. 31, 1981	Suffolk Downs	Great Combination	Dawn's Count	Needachant
May 20, 1990	Arlington	All Worked Up	Marshua's Affair	Survival
Oct. 7, 1991	Belmont Park	Space Appeal	Scorecard Harry	Cafe Lex
May 12, 1996	Yakima Meadows	Terri After Five	Allihavonztheradio	Fly Like a Angel
Dec. 7, 1997	Hollywood Park	Tina Celesta	Chans Pearl	Cool Miss Ann

Steeplechase and Hurdle Racing – 2004

By JOE CLANCY

Born in Ireland and raced in England, the well-traveled Hirapour needed a third country to find true stardom.

Hirapour took down the 2004 Eclipse Award as America's champion steeplechase horse with a late-season victory in the Grade 1 Colonial Cup for Eldon Farm and trainer Doug Fout. Rated off the early pace by Matt McCarron in the 2 3/4-mile classic, Hirapour charged past 2003 champion McDynamo, Sur La Tete and Preemptive Strike in the final furlong to get the win and ice the championship.

The victory capped a stellar season for Hirapour, an 8-year-old son of Kahyasi. In four starts, he compiled a record of two wins and two seconds - all in the highest company. Hirapour finished second to Preemptive Strike in the Grade 3 Carolina Cup March 27 and avenged that defeat with a powerful score in Keeneland's Grade 1 Royal Chase April 16. The bay gelding (the 6-5 favorite) rallied four wide on the final turn to win by 1 3/4 lengths under jockey Clayton Chipperfield, who celebrated the win with a flying backflip dismount in the winner's circle.

Rested on Fout's Virginia farm for the summer, Hirapour returned with two standout efforts in the fall under new jockey Matt McCarron. Hirapour finished a game second to McDynamo in the $175,000 Breeders' Cup (Gr. I) in October, reaching the favorite's neck before the last fence but coming up 1 1/2 lengths short at the wire. As usual, the season-ending Colonial Cup (Nov. 21) stood as a final test for championship contenders with five horses bringing legitimate championship hopes into the race. Hirapour aced the test with a superb effort. Saving ground throughout, McCarron sent Hirapour to the front at the last fence and won by 2 3/4 lengths over Preemptive Strike with Sur La Tete third. McDynamo was fourth.

Tenacity, heart, courage - those are the things that describe Hirapour according to his trainer.

"He got mad after (losing) the Breeders' Cup," said Fout. "I've never seen a horse's attitude change like his did. Every day, he wanted to go out there and out-gallop, out-work, out-school everybody we took him out there with. He's a kind, sweet horse but when he's out on the track he's a bear."

Hirapour sold at England's Tattersalls sales for 150,000 guineas as a 3-year-old and won four flat races before going to Tattersalls again in 2002 and bringing just 12,000 guineas. He quickly proved a bargain with five consecutive English hurdle victories before being sold to Eldon (owned by Atlanta-area resident Ken Luke) and Fout in the summer of 2003. Through 2004, Hirapour had earned $259,625 racing over jumps in the U.S. with three wins in five starts while his career steeplechase record stood at eight wins in 13 starts with more than $320,000 bankrolled.

Hirapour wasn't the only star of 2004 as McDynamo (who missed much of the year recovering from off-season surgery to a hock), Tres Touche, Sur La Tete, Racey Dreamer, Paradise's Boss and Cherokeeinthehills each won at least one Grade 1 hurdle race. Divisional championships went to Paradise's Boss (novice hurdle horse), Bubble Economy (timber horse), Gold Mitten (filly/mare) and Underbidder (3-year-old).

Kinross Farm (the stable of Virginia residents Lisa and Zohar Ben-Dov) won its first National Steeplechase Association owner championship with $383,590 earned thanks in large part to triple stakes winner Sur La Tete. Maryland-based Jack Fisher won 28 races and saddled the winners of $585,051 to take his second consecutive trainer title. Hirapour's jockey McCarron ran away with the riding title, piling up 24 victories and $592,743 in purses won including three Grade 1 scores. Nephew of Hall of Fame flat jockey Chris McCarron, Matt also won the title in 2003.

As usual, there was plenty of crossover between flat racing and jump racing. Eclipse Award-winning owners Ken and Sarah Ramsey continued to support steeplechasing with several horses in training with Tom Voss. Other owners with major connections to both forms of Thoroughbred racing included Martin Cherry, Augustin Stable and Timber Bay Farm among others. The Voss-trained Dreadnaught began 2004 as a jumper, placing second in two maiden races, before switching back to the flat and winning four times including back-to-back Grade 2 turf stakes scores late in the year.

The National Steeplechase Association carded 225 races worth $4.9 million in 2004 with stops at 34 race meets in 11 states plus at least one race at Atlantic City, Belmont Park, Colonial Downs, Keeneland, Monmouth Park, Philadelphia Park and Saratoga racetracks. The race meets raise purse money through corporate sponsorship and gate receipts, with just one meet (Fair Hill in Maryland) having pari-mutuel wagering. The seven racetracks carded 37 steeplechase races complete with full pari-mutuel wagering and hurdles set up on the turf course.

Joe Clancy is the editor and publisher of Steeplechase Times newspaper, and a co-founder of ST Publishing which produces The Saratoga Special newspaper and the Thoroughbred Racing Calendar.

2004 Leaders

Owner – Money Won

Name	Sts	1st	2d	3d	Money Won
Kinross Farm	70	12	11	16	$381,990
Eldon Farm Stable	26	4	3	3	269,678
Mrs. S. K. Johnston Jr.	51	8	5	5	223,229
Augustin Stables	43	7	9	9	195,545
Barracuda Stable	16	3	2	0	178,714
Mrs. Henry F. Stern	12	6	3	1	153,600
Marilyn S. Ketts	8	2	3	0	153,337
EMO Stables	21	6	1	0	142,350
Arcadia Stable	28	4	8	5	135,457
Irvin S. Naylor	45	9	9	4	133,600

Trainer – Money Won

Name	Sts	1st	2d	3d	Money Won
Jack Fisher	153	27	22	24	$575,651
Doug Fout	91	16	10	12	552,393
Jonathan Sheppard	89	18	12	16	445,912
Sanna N. Hendriks	77	19	17	13	445,595
Neil R. Morris	70	12	11	16	381,990
Ricky Hendriks	74	10	8	12	295,414
Katherine Neilson	101	10	15	11	286,641
Thomas H. Voss	68	8	14	9	278,436
F. Bruce Miller	82	9	13	7	236,508
Paul A. Rowland	13	3	4	0	134,888

Rider – Money Won

Name	Sts	1st	2d	3d	Money Won
Matthew McCarron	109	24	13	12	$592,743
David Bentley	85	13	10	13	391,674
Tom Foley	75	16	10	13	375,564
Gus Brown	64	11	17	11	309,371
Robert Massey	85	11	9	8	291,731
Robert Walsh	84	9	19	3	275,911
Danielle Hodsdon	72	13	9	14	243,843
Chip Miller	60	11	7	6	237,848
Blair Waterman	39	6	9	4	199,294
Christopher Read	25	5	2	7	196,810

Horse – Money Won

Name	Sts	1st	2d	3d	Money Won
Sur la Tete	6	3	0	3	$207,060
Hirapour (Ire)	4	2	2	0	199,625
Tres Touche	9	3	2	0	171,510
Cherokeeinthehills	8	2	3	0	153,337
Preemptive Strike	6	3	2	0	130,688
Paradise's Boss	7	4	1	0	116,400
Racey Dreamer	4	4	0	0	112,500
McDynamo	2	1	0	0	101,250
Serazzo	4	1	2	0	71,368
Snowball Flannagan	4	2	1	0	67,250

Leading Steeplechase Earners in North America (through 2004)

Horse	Foaled	Owner	Trainer	Raced	Wins	Earnings
Lonesome Glory	1988	Mrs. Walter Jeffords Jr.	F.B. Miller	1991-99	17	$965,809
Victorian Hill	1985	William C. Lickle	J. Elliot	1988-96	15	748,370
Rowdy Irishman	1989	Vesta Balestiere	B. Haynes	1994-01	9	644,528
*Flat Top	1993	Mrs. Henry A. Gerry	J. Elliot	1996-04	9	592,306
*McDynamo	1997	Michael Moran	S. Hendriks	2001-04	9	567,679
*Tres Touche	1997	Contrarian Stable Barracuda Stable	R. Hendriks	2000-04	10	567,300
*Praise The Prince	1995	Augustin Stables	S. Hendriks	2000-04	9	561,806
Mistico	1986	R.D. Hubbard	J. Sheppard	1991-96	8	517,347
Ninepins	1987	Hudson River Farms	J. Sheppard	1992-00	9	516,179
*Al Skywalker	1993	F.D. Adams/J. Majette	J. Majette	1997-04	13	466,841
Warm Spell	1988	John K. Griggs	J.K. Griggs	1991-94	12	457,964
Highland Bud	1985	Jesse M. Henley, Jr	J. Sheppard	1989-93	4	437,500
All Gong	1994	Calvin Houghland	F.B. Miller	1999-02	3	435,989
Polar Pleasure	1982	William L. Pape	J. Sheppard	1986-90	5	433,222
Saluter	1989	Mrs. Henry Stern	J. Fisher	1993-00	21	429,489
Census	1978	George Chase	J. Elliot	1982-89	14	426,524
Flatterer	1979	William L. Pape	J. Sheppard	1983-87	16	421,146
Double Bill	1983	Frank Loving	J. Sheppard	1987-95	9	417,548
Steve Canyon	1980	John K. Griggs	J.K. Griggs	1983-89	16	388 102
Romantic	1992	Timber Bay Farm	J. Sheppard	1995-01	8	379,102
Pompeyo	1994	Augustin Stables	S. Hendriks	2000-01	7	353,280
It's A Giggle	1994	William L. Pape	J. Sheppard	1997-02	9	347,790
Summer Colony	1983	Augustin Stables	J. Sheppard	1987-90	10	347,422
Yaw	1982	Timber Bay Farm	J. Sheppard	1987-94	11	335,327
Master McGrath	1987	William C. Lickle	J. Elliot	1990-01	6	331,355
Declare Your Wish	1986	Valerie McGonigal Mrs. Jack M. Bass Jr.	A. King J. Elliot	1989-95	5	325,600
Campanile	1994	Gregory Hawkins	J. Elliot	1998-01	5	319,508
Grabel	1983	Patrick Kehoe	P. Mullins	1990	1	312,224
*Darn Tipalarm	1993	Mrs. Henry Stern	J. Fisher	1998-04	9	306,490
Pinkie Swear	1994	Arcadia Stable	C. Fenwick J. Fisher	1998-02	5	296,590
Zaccio	1976	Mrs. Lewis C. Murdock	W.B. Cocks	1979-84	18	286,299
*Sur La Tete	1998	Kinross Farm	N. Morris	2002-04	5	284,560
Uptown Swell	1982	Virginia Kraft Payson	F.B. Miller	1988-90	5	283,860
Double Reefed	1976	Augustin Stables	J. Sheppard	1980-85	11	280,168
Polar Parallel	1981	William L. Pape	J. Sheppard	1985-94	11	279,150
Neji	1950	Mrs. Ogden Phipps	G.H. Bostwick D.M. Smithwick	1954-60	17	271,225
Irish Approach	1989	Augustin Stables	J. Sheppard	1993-96	6	260,180

*Active in 2004. Earnings do not include bonuses or foreign purses.

BREEDERS' CUP STEEPLECHASE. $175,000. Distance: 2 5/8 Miles (Hurdle). Far Hills, New Jersey.

Year	First (Age)	Rider	Wt.	Second (Age)	Wt.	Third (Age)	Wt.	Win Val.	Time
2004	McDynamo (7)	Thornton	156	Hirapour (8)	156	Sur La Tete (6)	156	$96,250	5:06^{4}
2003	McDynamo (6)	Thornton	156	Pelagos (8)	156	Mulahen (8)	146	96,250	5:24
2002	Flat Top (9)	Massey	156	Tres Touche (5)	156	All Gong (8)	156	137,500	5:19^{2}
2001	Quel Senor (6)	Murphy	156	Lord Zada (8)	156	Praise The Prince (6)	156	137,500	4:54^{1}
2000	All Gong (6)	B. Miller	156	Popular Gigalo (6)	156	Allgrit (5)	156	137,500	4:53^{4}
1993	Lonesome Glory (5)	B. Miller	156	Highland Bud (8)	156	Mistico (7)	156	125,000	4:53^{2}
1992	Highland Bud (7)	Dunwoody	156	Mistico (6)	156	Sassello (5)	156	125,000	4:56^{2}
1991	Morley Street (7)	Frost	156	Declare Your Wish (5)	156	Cheering News (4)	146	125,000	5:10^{3}
1990	Morley Street (6)	Frost	156	Summer Colony (7)	156	Moonstruck (7)	156	125,000	4:53^{1}
1989	Highland Bud (4)	Dunwoody	146	Polar Pleasure (7)	156	Victorian Hill (4)	146	125,000	4:58^{4}
1988	Jimmy Lorenzo (6)	McCourt	156	Kalankoe (7)	153	Polar Pleasure (6)	156	125,000	5:12^{2}
1987	Gacko (6)	Duchene	156	Inlander (6)	156	Gateshead (8)	156	125,000	5:15^{1}
1986	Census (8)	Teter	156	Kesslin (6)	156	Pont du Loup (6)	156	125,000	4:27^{3}

First run in 1986. Distance 2 3/8 miles in 1986. Run at Fair Hill, Md. 1986–88 and 1991; Far Hills, N.J. 1989 and 2000; Belmont Park 1990, 1992 and 1993. Not run 1994–99.

COLONIAL CUP. $100,000. Distance: 2 3/4 Miles (Hurdle). Springdale Race Course. Camden, South Carolina.

Year	First (Age)	Rider	Wt.	Second (Age)	Wt.	Third (Age)	Wt.	Win Val.	Time
2004	Hirapour (8)	McCarron	156	Preemptive Strike (6)	156	Sur La Tete (6)	156	$60,000	5:04^{3}
2003	McDynamo (6)	Thornton	156	Lord Zada (10)	156	Pelagos (8)	156	60,000	5:05^{2}
2002	Flat Top (9)	Massey	156	Tres Touche (5)	156	All Gong (8)	156	60,000	5:25^{1}
2001	Lord Zada (8)	Brown	156	All Gong (7)	156	Al Skywalker (8)	156	60,000	5:05^{3}
2000	Romantic (8)	Kingsley	156	Campanile (6)	156	All Gong (6)	156	60,000	5:19^{1}
1999	Ninepins (12)	Kingsley	156	Muscle Car (5)	156	Campanile (5)	156	60,000	5:07
1998	Flat Top (5)	Ryan	156	Romantic (6)	156	Dictador (8)	156	60,000	5:11^{2}
1997	Lonesome Glory (9)	B. Miller	156	Rowdy Irishman (8)	156	Master McGrath (10)	156	69,540	5:11^{2}
1996	Correggio (5)	Teter	160	Stop and Listen (6)	162	Mr. Yankee (9)	162	60,000	5:09^{2}
1995	Lonesome Glory (7)	B. Miller	162	Rowdy Irishman (6)	162	Mistico (9)	162	60,000	5:20^{1}
1994	Lonesome Glory (6)	B. Miller	162	Mistico (8)	162	Victorian Hill (9)	162	60,000	5:08^{1}
1993	Declare Your Wish (7)	Smith-Eccles	162	Simonov (4)	151	Lonesome Glory (5)	160	60,000	5:07^{4}
1992	Mistico (6)	S. Neilson	162	Victorian Hill (7)	162	Chief Of The Clan (9)	162	36,000	5:12
1991	Moonstruck (8)	Beggan	162	Made Noble (5)	160	Double Bill (8)	162	36,000	5:14
1990	Victorian Hill (5)	Hendriks	160	Sarh (4)	148	Moonstruck (7)	162	36,000	5:09^{3}
1989	Highland Bud (4)	Dunwoody	151	Opacity (5)	160	Dawson (5)	160	36,000	5:17^{4}
1988	Jimmy Lorenzo (6)	Smart	162	Le Sauvage (4)	151	Polar Pleasure (6)	151	36,000	5:15^{4}
1987	Inlander (6)	Morris	162	Ormus (10)	162	Statesmanship (7)	162	36,000	5:21^{1}
1986	Flatterer (7)	Fishback	162	Turtle Head (8)	162	Jean Rapier (9)	162	36,000	5:12^{4}
1985	Flatterer (6)	Fishback	162	Salute (7)	162	Gateshead (6)	162	36,000	5:14^{1}
1984	Flatterer (5)	Fishback	160	Census (6)	162	Eremite (4)	151	30,000	5:09
1983	Flatterer (4)	Francome	151	Twas Ever Thus (4)	151	Census (5)	160	30,000	5:18
1982	Zaccio (6)	Hendriks	162	Sailor's Clue (6)	162	Double Wrapped (6)	159	30,000	5:11
1981	Zaccio (5)	Morris	160	Al Arof (4)	151	Sailor's Clue (5)	160	30,000	5:14^{3}
1980	Sailor's Clue (4)	Fout	151	Corrib Chieftain (6)	162	Martie's Anger (5)	160	30,000	5:32^{2}
1979	Martie's Anger (4)	Quanbeck	151	Leaping Frog (6)	162	Quixotic (4)	151	30,000	5:21^{4}
1978	Grand Canyon (8)	Barry	162	Deux Coup (6)	155	Cafe Prince (8)	162	60,000	5:10^{2}
1977	Cafe Prince (7)	Fishback	162	Bel Iman (4)	151	Leaping Frog (4)	146	60,000	5:22^{3}
1976	Grand Canyon (6)	Barry	162	Fire Control (8)	162	Crag's Corner (5)	160	60,000	5:12^{2}
1975	Cafe Prince (5)	Washer	160	Augustus Bay (9)	162	Soothsayer (8)	162	30,000	5:30^{1}
1974	Augustus Bay (8)	Skiffington	142	Tarrantine (5)	143	John U. (7)	153	30,000	5:24
1973	Lucky Boy III (6)	Brittle	149	Soothsayer (6)	162	Dream Magic (6)	153	30,000	5:21^{4}
1972	Soothsayer (5)	Aitcheson	158	Inkslinger (5)	158	Shadow Brook (8)	160	60,000	5:23^{4}
1971	Inkslinger (4)	Carberry	149	Soothsayer (4)	149	Top Bid (7)	160	63,000	5:17
1970	Top Bid (6)	Aitcheson	160	Shadow Brook (6)	160	Jaunty (5)	158	63,000	5:20

First run in 1970. Distance 2 miles, 6 1/2 furlongs 1970–75. Run as a handicap 1973–74.

IROQUOIS. $100,000. Distance: 3 Miles (Hurdle). Iroquois Steeplechase. Nashville, Tennessee.

Year	First (Age)	Rider	Wt.	Second (Age)	Wt.	Third (Age)	Wt.	Win Val.	Time
2004	Tres Touche (7)	Bentley	158	Snowball Flannagan (9)	158	Duke Of Earl (5)	158	$60,000	5:38^{3}
2003	Pelagos (8)	Foley	158	Praise The Prince (8)	158	Storm Touch (7)	158	60,000	5:46^{3}
2002	All Gong (8)	B. Miller	158	Praise The Prince (7)	158	Flat Top (9)	158	60,000	5:32^{2}
2001	Rand (7)	Lamb	158	All Gong (7)	158	Electron (8)	158	60,000	5:35^{3}
2000	Pinkie Swear (6)	Clancy	154	All Gong (6)	154	Greek Hero (7)	154	60,000	5:50
1999	Rowdy Irishman (10)	Marzullo	156	Avanico (8)	156	High Card (8)	156	60,000	5:50^{3}
1998	Rowdy Irishman (9)	Marzullo	156	Confidente (9)	156	Correggio (7)	156	60,000	5:51^{4}
1997	Correggio (6)	Kingsley	156	Lonesome Glory (9)	156	Confidente (8)	156	66,240	5:30^{2}

Year	First (Age)	Rider	Wt.	Second (Age)	Wt.	Third (Age)	Wt.	Win Val.	Time
1996	To Ridley (6)	Clancy	156	Rowdy Irishman (7)	156	Mistico (10)	156	50,000	5:41^{4}
1995	Lonesome Glory (7)	B. Miller	156	Confidente (6)	156	Victorian Hill (10)	156	50,000	5:32^{4}
1994	Mistico (8)	Thornton	168	Warm Spell (6)	168	Victorian Hill (9)	168	50,000	5:28^{3}
1993	Mistico (7)	S. Neilson	168	Warm Spell (5)	163	Darby Sky (6)	168	50,000	5:43
1992	Victorian Hill (7)	B. Miller	168	Mistico (6)	168	Warm Spell (4)	158	50,000	5:31^{4}
1991	Victorian Hill (6)	B. Miller	168	Highland Bud (6)	168	Declare Your Wish (5)	163	50,000	5:59^{2}
1990	Pacific Spy (6)	Bosley	168	Shamrock Keys (7)	168	Jamaica Bay (5)	163	50,000	5:51^{4}
1989	Kesslin (9)	C. Fenwick	168	Steve Canyon (9)	168	Polar Pleasure (7)	168	50,000	5:40
1988	Steve Canyon (8)	Griggs	168	Mountain Brook II (7)	168	Reagan (8)	168	50,000	5:35
1987	Flatterer (8)	Thomson-Jones	168	Same Echelon (6)	168	Eremite (7)	168	50,000	5:27^{3}
1986	Uncle Edwin (9)	Smithwick	168	Census (8)	168	Eremite (6)	168	60,000	5:25^{4}
1985	Uncle Edwin (8)	Smithwick	168	Boniperti (7)	168	Quixotic (10)	168	20,000	5:24^{1}
1984	Census (6)	C. Fenwick	168	Uncle Edwin (7)	168	The Hall of Famer (6)	168	12,000	5:32^{4}
1983	Census (5)	Wood	163	Double Reefed (7)	168	The Hall of Famer (5)	163	12,000	5:38^{1}
1982	Uncle Edwin (5)	Smithwick	163	Owhata Chief (13)	168	Carrig Willy (7)	168	7,500	5:51^{3}
1980	Ready Perk (5)	Griggs	158	Quixotic (5)	163	Tall Award (10)	168	7,500	5:35^{3}
1979	Owhata Chief (10)	Strawbridge	168	Bay Ridge Bill (7)	168	El Viento II (11)	168	7,500	5:46^{1}
1978	Owhata Chief (9)	Strawbridge	168	Crag's Corner (7)	168	Blue Nearco (7)	168	6,000	5:57^{4}
1977	Alvaro II (7)	Hall	168	Happy Intellectual (11)	168	Conserje (8)	168	6,000	5:33^{2}
1976	Hes Trouble (8)	G. Sloan	168	Celtic Song III (9)	168	Alvaro II (6)	168	6,000	5:31^{4}
1975	Conserje (6)	Wood	168	Alvaro II (5)	163	Breaking Dawn (7)	168	4,000	5:44^{3}

First run in 1941. Run over natural brush fences and restricted to amateur jockeys prior to 1993.

NEW YORK TURF WRITERS CUP. $100,000 Added. 2 3/8 Miles (Hurdle).
Saratoga. Saratoga Springs, New York.

Year	First (Age)	Rider	Wt.	Second (Age)	Wt.	Third (Age)	Wt.	Win Val.	Time
2004	Tres Touche (7)	Bentley	152	Cherokeeinthehills (7)	138	Barzulu (7)	144	$63,030	4:19^{2}
2003	Praise The Prince (8)	Brown	150	Tres Touche (6)	148	Indispensable (9)	142	68,280	4:13^{3}
2002	Zabenz (5)	Thornton	146	Double Leaf (9)	140	Flat Top (9)	150	65,760	4:28
2001	It's A Giggle (7)	B. Miller	142	Canta Ke Brave (5)	152	Praise The Prince (6)	160	64,620	4:12
2000	Ninepins (13)	Kingsley	150	Campanile (6)	160	Allgrit (5)	138	65,520	4:21
1999	Campanile (5)	B. Miller	148	Willstown (6)	138	Romantic (7)	152	67,260	4:22
1998	Hokan (5)	Clancy	142	Romantic (6)	143	Sundin (7)	142	65,100	4:12
1997	Bisbalense (8)	Kingsley	142	Confidente (8)	140	Lonesome Glory (9)	156	64,620	4:31
1996	Petroski (6)	K. O'Brien	160	T.V. Gold (6)	140	Prime Legacy (7)	138	66,300	4:14
1995	Lonesome Glory (7)	B. Miller	166	Mistico (9)	160	Rowdy Irishman (6)	142	64,600	4:12^{4}
1994	Mistico (8)	Thornton	168	Cheering News (7)	142	Lonesome Glory (6)	168	65,460	4:30
1993	Warm Spell (5)	Lawrence	161	Castleworth (7)	142	Darby Sky (6)	145	70,800	4:15^{2}
1992	Yaw (10)	Smart	146	Three Bells For Me (5)	140	Make Azilian (8)	142	69,840	4:23
1991	Yaw (9)	Smart	145	Moonstruck (8)	148	Double Bill (8)	149	70,920	4:26^{4}
1990	Double Bill (7)	Guessford	146	French Hill (5)	154	Peer Prince (5)	134	52,380	4:19^{4}
1989	Double Bill (6)	Guessford	142	Uptown Swell (7)	152	Polar Pleasure (7)	149	69,240	4:18^{1}
1988	Rio Claro (5)	Morris	152	Steve Canyon (8)	162	Jive With Five (4)	146	32,100	4:15^{2}
1987	Chief Of The Clan (4)	Lawrence	148	Gateshead (8)	154	Chammsky (8)	152	33,180	4:20^{2}
1986	Le Sauteur (7)	Houghton	157	Twas Ever Thus (7)	150	Eremite (6)	146	32,460	4:16^{2}
1984	Flatterer (5)	Fishback	164	Census (6)	155	Double Reefed (8)	158	25,950	4:22
1983	Double Reefed (7)	Cushman	161	Sugar Bee (5)	135	Census (5)	148	25,995	4:27^{4}
1982	Zaccio (6)	Hendriks	161	Give a Whirl (5)	146	Running Comment (8)	145	26,145	4:19
1981	Running Comment (7)	McWade	143	Codicioso (6)	144	Red Invader (8)	142	26,715	4:16
1980	Zaccio (4)	McWade	157	Running Comment (6)	142	Leaping Frog (7)	152	26,190	4:14^{1}
1979	Leaping Frog (6)	Christison	159	Tan Jay (7)	150	Canadian Regent (5)	143	12,855	4:17^{4}
1978	Happy Intellectual (12)	Martin	152	Popular Hero (5)	138	Leaping Frog (5)	157	13,020	4:19
1977	Happy Intellectual (11)	Aitcheson	152	Naval Person (5)	143	Cassamayor (7)	150	12,960	4:18^{4}
1976	Happy Intellectual (10)	Elser	152	Life's Illusion (5)	160	Straight and True (6)	155	13,290	4:19^{2}
1975	Life's Illusion (4)	Quanbeck	145	Soothsayer (8)	160	Arctic Joe (8)	148	13,680	4:20^{1}
1971	Soothsayer (4)	Fishback	153	Predominio (7)	141	Wustenchef (6)	162	20,088	4:55^{4}
1970	El Martirio (6)	Plain	138	Wustenchef (5)	151	Shadow Brook (6)	155	15,925	4:49^{1}

First run in 1938. Distance 2 1/2 miles in 1970; 2 5/8 miles in 1971. Run at Belmont Park 1970-71. Not run 1972-74, or 1985.

ROYAL CHASE. $150,000 Added. 2 1/2 Miles (Hurdle).
Keeneland. Lexington, Kentucky.

Year	First (Age)	Rider	Wt.	Second (Age)	Wt.	Third (Age)	Wt.	Win Val.	Time
2004	Hirapour (8)	Chipperfield	148	Preemptive Strike (6)	150	Dancewel (7)	142	$95,625	4:41^{2}
2003	McDynamo (6)	Thornton	158	Shamrock Isle (8)	158	Praise The Prince (8)	158	95,775	4:44^{1}
2002	It's A Giggle (8)	B. Miller	158	Al Skywalker (9)	158	Flat Top (9)	158	109,650	4:39^{2}
2001	Pompeyo (7)	Brown	158	All Gong (7)	158	Rand (7)	158	111,525	4:34^{2}
2000	Flat Top (7)	B. Miller	154	Campanile (6)	154	Pinkie Swear (6)	154	111,525	4:42^{1}
1999	Lonesome Glory (11)	B. Miller	154	Dalton River (11)	154	Master McGrath (12)	154	112,800	4:36
1998	Clearance Code (6)	Petty	154	Master McGrath (11)	154	Confidente (9)	154	103,540	4:04^{3}

First run in 1998. Distance 2 1/4 miles in 1998.

FOREIGN RACING

YEAR IN REVIEW

TIMEFORM RATINGS

INTERNATIONAL CLASSIFICATIONS

STAKES HISTORIES

2004 STAKES RESULTS

2004 LEADERS

MAJOR EUROPEAN TRACK PROFILES

Racing in Europe – 2004

By Alan Shuback

Future historians may not be remiss in overlooking the achievements of the European racehorse in the year 2004. While there were a handful of sparkling highlights turned in, most of them by fillies, a depleted roster of older horses and a disappointing crop of 3-year-old colts combined to make a mixed bag out of proceedings across the Atlantic.

Matters got off to slow start before 2003 had even ended when the Aga Khan announced that his champion 3-year-old, the Arc and French Derby winner Dalakhani, was being retired. At the same time, His Highness sold his Irish Derby and King George winner Alamshar to stand at stud in Japan. Thus were the two highest-rated sophomores of the previous year lost to racing.

Hopes for the new 3-year-old crop were dashed early on with the failure of One Cool Cat to recapture the form that had earned him winter-book favoritism for the 2000 Guineas. The Aidan O'Brien trainee finished tailed off in the Newmarket classic, complaints of an abnormal heartbeat repeated when he produced a similar performance in the Group 3 International Stakes at the Curragh the following month. O'Brien suffered an even greater disappointment when his highly promising Epsom Derby favorite Yeats was sidelined with hind leg and back muscle problems after he had scored victories in Group 2 and Group 3 events to remain undefeated through three starts. And when Europe's 2003 juvenile champion, Bago, suffered a series of setbacks early in the season, forcing him to miss the springtime classics, questions were raised about the overall value of Europe's classic form.

Haafhd burst out of the gate looking very much like a champion with impressive scores in both the Group 3 Craven Stakes and the 2000 Guineas. Barry Hills had his Alhaarth colt ready early as he took that pair of Newmarket miles in such convincing fashion that he maintained leadership atop the standings of European milers throughout the year. That achievement, however, had at least as much to do with the subsequent failure of any of Europe's older horses to make an impression at that distance. When Haafhd flopped in the St. James's Palace Stakes, the Royal Ascot mile that virtually serves as Europe's 3-year-old mile championship for colts, the value of his Guineas triumph looked suspect. That race fell to Azamour by a neck from French 2000 Guineas runner-up Diamond Green with Haafhd fourth and Irish 2000 champ Bachelor Duke only seventh. The 3-year-old milers' season cut up after this as both Azamour and Haafhd raised their sights to 1 1/4 miles for the remainder of the season.

Meanwhile, the milers in France were distinguishing themselves by their mediocrity. American Post had looked a pale imitation of Haafhd when taking the Group 3 Prix de Fontainebleau, a course and distance prep for the Poule d'Essai des Poulains, or French 2000 Guineas. He was then handed the latter race on a silver platter when the unpredictable Antonius Pius slammed into the rail after taking a seemingly invincible lead near the line. American Post's season unravelled thereafter. Criquette Head sent him to Epsom where he was a non-staying sixth in the Derby. Following a three-month layoff he returned to a mile in the Prix du Moulin de Longchamp in which he finished a dull 10th. Two months later he was retired with problems in a hind leg.

But while coltish form at a mile may have been questionable, that among 3-year-old fillies was not. In the shape of Attraction, Mark Johnston produced a filly who captured the hearts of racegoers with her courage as well as her front-running style. Rather modestly bred - she is by Efisio out of a Pursuit of Love mare - Attraction had caught the eye at 2 with a stunning five-length runaway in the six-furlong Group 2 Cherry Hinton Stakes in July. A series of injuries, capped by a cracked pedal bone in her left hind leg in September, forced her to miss all of her late season juvenile engagements.

Johnston persevered, however, and had her ready for the 1000 Guineas at Newmarket on May 2. There she led 15 rivals a merry dance to score by half a length over Sundrop. Three weeks later it was the same again at the Curragh where her one-length victory over subsequent late season Hong Kong Cup winner Alexander Goldrun made Attraction the first filly in history to pull off the 1000 Guineas/Irish 1000 Guineas double. If there were any doubts that Attraction was the best 3-year-old filly miler on the planet, they were erased on June 18 when she led throughout again to defeat the talented Majestic Desert by 2-1/2 lengths in the Coronation Stakes, the Group 1 Royal Ascot mile that has the same cachet for 3-year-old fillies as the St. James's Palace has for 3-year-old colts.

Crooked in front and with an ungainly action that hardly stamps her as a champion, Attraction's brave front-running tactics were seen to best advantage on firm ground. But whereas Haafhd and Azamour didn't bother with entering Europe's best weight-for-age miles, Attraction pitched right in against older fillies and mares. But without success. She found the redoubtable Soviet Song too strong in both the Falmouth Stakes in July, going down by 2-1/2 lengths, and the Matron Stakes in September, when she just failed to last by half a length. In between she failed in her lone try on soft ground when 10th and last behind Whipper in the Prix Jacques le Marois at Deauville. Back against fillies and mares, but not Soviet Song, in the Sun Chariot Stakes at Newmarket on Oct. 2, Attraction dazzled again when holding off Chic by half a length. Attraction looked like a perfect fit for the Breeders' Cup Mile around the tight turns of Lone Star Park, where firm ground was a near certainty. She was, however, not nominated to the Cup, and her owner the Duke of Roxburghe declined the honor of coughing up $120,000 to make her eligible.

The 3-year-old picture at 1 1/2 miles mirrored that of the mile scene. The Ed Dunlop-trained filly Ouija Board, the only horse owned by Lord Derby, swept the English and Irish Oaks in impressive fashion, while the English, Irish and French Derbys produced no clear leader amongst the clots. In providing Michael Stoute with his second Epsom Derby winner in a row (and fourth overall), North Light was a solid if unspectacular Blue Riband winner. By the all-conquering sire Danehill out of the excellent staying mare Sought Out, North Light had beaten the Derby runner-up and subsequent St. Leger winner Rule of Law three weeks earlier in the Group 2 Dante Stakes at 1 1/4 miles, 88 yards at York. He was somewhat exposed when failing to run down Irish 2000 Guineas third Grey Swallow in the Irish Derby next time. He was then forced into a three-month absence due to nagging injuries prior to his run in the Arc, in which he weakened late to finish fifth. Ouija Board herself was given an 11-week rest between her Irish Oaks heroics and her own Arc run, in which she was a little unlucky to finish a fast-closing third after experiencing trouble at the head of the stretch. Her Arc, however, set her up perfectly for a bloodless score in the Breeders' Cup Filly & Mare Turf, in which her 11 rivals were severely outclassed, the sporting Lord Derby having put up a $90,000 supplementary nomination fee to get her into the race.

In France, Voix du Nord was taking advantage of Bago's absence to whip future Arc runner-up Cherry Mix by three lengths in the Group 2 Prix Noailles. He prepped for his date in the Prix du Jockey-Club (French Derby) with a hard-fought nose victory over Millemix in the Group 1 Prix Lupin and was barely 24 hours from stepping into the gate as favorite for the French classic at Chantilly when disaster struck. A leisurely pre-race gallop resulted in a fractured right-fore pastern and Voix du Nord's season was finished. That left it to the unprepossessing Blue Canari to take French Derby laurels at 33-1 from Prospect Park. The winner ran closer to form in the autumn when fifth in Valixir's Prix Niel and 12th in Bago's Arc.

Latice proved herself to be the best of a moderate bunch of French fillies with her three-quarter-length tally over Millionaia in the Prix de Diane (French Oaks). She looked exposed when eighth in Sweet Stream's Prix Vermeille, on the rebound when seventh in Bago's Arc, but outclassed when 10th in Alexander Goldrun's Hong Kong Cup. She will race at 4 in the United States.

Meanwhile, the best older male milers were exposed early on when Russian Rhythm gave them a beating in the Lockinge Stakes at Newbury on May 15. Sadly, the Michael Stoute-trained daughter of Kingmambo never raced again. That left it to another filly, Soviet Song, to pick up where she left off. In addition to her two Group 1 victories over Attraction, the James Fanshawe-trained daughter of Marju claimed a subpar Sussex Stakes against colts but failed to maintain her season-long form in her finale when sixth behind Rakti in the Queen Elizabeth II Stakes at Ascot on Sept. 25.

Rakti himself had appeared to pick up at Royal Ascot where he had left off in 2003, i.e., as one of the world's best 10-furlong performers. Winner of the Champion Stakes the previous October, he ran the race of his life when chasing home Falbrav two months later in the Hong Kong Cup. However, the promise of his two-length victory over Powerscourt in the Prince of Wales's Stakes in June fizzled when he was just eighth behind Refuse To Bend in the Eclipse Stakes on July 3. The Irish Champion Stakes on Sept. 11 would be next on the agenda for Rakti. In it, he would renew rivalry with the since disqualified winner of the Arlington Million, Powerscourt, as well as meeting King George VI and Queen Elizabeth Diamond Stakes winner Doyen, and Irish Derby champ Grey Swallow. With winners like High Chaparral, Fantastic Light, Giant's Causeway and Daylami, and runners-up like Galileo and Falbrav, the Irish Champion Stakes may rank as the best race in the world at any distance since 1999. This time it lost a little luster in going to the 3-year-old upstart Azamour, who improved on his St. James's Palace victory to beat his older rivals half a length, the gallant Norse Dance adding to his string of overachieveing seconds in top-class company. Rakti would bounce back when dropped down in distance in the Queen Elizabeth II, just as Haafhd would relish the step up to 10 furlongs in the Champion Stakes at Newmarket. But with so many horses taking turns beating each other, it was becoming difficult to find a clear overall division leader anywhere.

Doyen had seemed to fit that bill. A record-setting performance when a six-length winner of the 1 1/2-mile Group 2 Hardwicke Stakes at Royal Ascot was followed by an apparently definitive three-length tally over the Ken McPeek-trained American invader Hard Buck in the King George VI and Queen Elizabeth Diamond Stakes, in which his Saeed bin Suroor-trained stablemate, subsequent Juddmonte International and Canadian International winner Sulamani, was third. In Doyen, Godolphin had what looked like world champion material. After his King George win the Sadler's Wells 4-year-old was promptly installed as favorite for the Arc, but everything soon went haywire. The Godolphin brain trust made an uncustomary error when it decided to drop Doyen back to 1 1/4 miles for the Irish Champion. Since his 1 1/8-mile juvenile debut on Oct. 2, 2002, at Maisons-Laffitte, Doyen had run eight straight times at 1 1/2 miles. In against proven 10-furlong types at Leopardstown,

Doyen was outpaced in the Irish Champion, finishing seventh of eight, beaten five and a quarter lengths behind the ex-miler Azamour. Fearing soft ground at Longchamp for the Arc, Godolphin then ruled Doyen out of the Arc. A minor injury then appeared to end his season. He was ruled out of the Breeders' Cup Turf but somehow found his way into the Champion Stakes at Newmarket on Oct. 16, over an inadequate 1 1/4 miles and on soft ground no less! It was a recipe for failure. He was seventh again, this time finishing 11-1/2 lengths behind another ex-miler, Haafhd.

It was ultimately left to Bago, Europe's 2003 juvenile champion, to provide some fireworks. Denied his chance at a Guineas or a Derby, he reappeared at Chantilly after a seven-month absence on June 6, Prix du Jockey-Club day, by upstaging French Derby winner Blue Canari with a stunning three-length rout of Cacique in the 1 1/8-mile Prix Jean Prat. He followed three weeks later with a half-length score over the same horse in the 1 1/4-mile Grand Prix de Paris. That ran the record of the Jonathan Pease-trained, Niarchos Family-owned Nashwan colt to six-for-six. It was time to try older horses, and English ones at that. York was the site of the Juddmonte International Stakes, a Group 1 contest at 1 1/4 miles, 88 yards in which Bago would meet failure for the first time at the hands of Sulamani with the game Norse Dancer second. Bago was never catching the first two and his hopes for a championship season seemed to go down the drain next time when he finished a length third behind Valixir and Prospect Park in the 3-year-old colts' Arc prep, the Prix Niel. That was Bago's first stab at a mile and a half and, once again, he appeared one-paced in the late stages.

His prospects for the Arc didn't look promising, even though the great race was shaping up for its weakest renewal in many years. Sent off as the fifth choice in a field of 19 at 7.70-1, Bago defied doubts about his ability to stay, coming late to defeat Cherry Mix by a half-length with Ouija Board closing fastest of all to take third a length behind the runner-up. With North Light fifth, Blue Canari 12th and Grey Swallow 19th, Bago had snatched European 3-year-old honors at the latest possible moment. A trip to Lone Star Park for the Breeders' Cup Classic was mooted by the winning connections but ultimately scrapped, the better to prepare him for a 4-year-old campaign that could include a BC Classic try at Belmont Park.

With victories in the 6-1/2-furlong Group 1 Prix Maurice de Gheest and the seven-furlong Group 1 Prix de la Foret, Somnus rated as the best sprinter in Europe. Var, formerly trained by Bill Mott, took the five-furlong Group 1 Prix de l'Abbaye de Longchamp for new trainer Clive Brittain from Group 2 King's Stand Stakes winner The Tatling, but the lackluster form of European sprinters in general was sadly exposed when those two finished unplaced behind the undefeated Silent Witness in the Hong Kong Sprint on Dec. 12.

While Godolphin may have gone off the rails with Doyen, the Maktoum juggernaut had a propserous year nonetheless. They had nine winners of 11 different Group 1 races in Britain, Ireland, Italy, the U.S., Canada and Hong Kong with horses bred in Britain, Ireland, the U.S. and South Africa. Among them were Papineau, their Ascot Gold Cup winner who edged out Westerner for the second straight year as champion European stayer.

If 2004's leading 2-year-olds can maintain their form in 2005, Godolphin should be playing some very strong hands during the classic season. Dubawi, a member of Dubai Millennium's lone, abbreviated crop, is from the family of Epsom Derby winner High-Rise and Breeders' Cup Turf winner In The Wings. Still undefeated, Dubawi is the winter-book favorite for the Epsom Derby by dint of his victory in the seven-furlong Group 1 National Stakes at the Curragh in September.

He may not, however, be the best 3-year-old in Saeed bin Suroor's barn. That honor could go to Shamardal. A member of Giant's Causeway's successful first crop, Shamardal topped his perfect juvenile campaign with a 2-1/2-length score over Aidan O'Brien's Group 1 Prix Jean-Luc Lagardere winner Oratorio in the seven-furlong Group 1 Dewhurst Stakes. Previously he had beaten subsequent Breeders' Cup Juvenile winner Wilko by the same margin in the Group 2 Vintage Stakes. Those two victories came under the tutelage of Mark Johnston, but Shamardal has since been taken over by Godolphin, who plucked him away from their Dubai business associate Abdullah Bulhaleeba after the latter had become involved in some shenanigans of which the Maktoums disapproved. Shamardal is being considered for the Kentucky Derby, a not illogical target for the son of a horse who narrowly missed in the Breeders' Cup Classic, and one who already holds a decisive decision over Wilko, who slammed most of America's best 2-year-olds at Lone Star Park.

In Divine Proportions, the Niarchos Family and Pascal Bary had themselves one of Europe's more accomplished juvenile fillies in recent years. By Kingmambo, she is a Kentucky-bred half-sister to Prix Jacques le Marois winner Whipper. In a season that stretched from May 26 to Oct. 3, Divine Proportions ran off four successive wins against colts, the last three in the Group 3 Prix du Bois, the Group 2 Prix Robert Papin and the Group 1 Prix Morny. Stepped up to a mile for her first try against her own sex in the Group 1 Prix Marcel Boussac, she responded with a handsome two-length victory. Divine Proportions should make up for the disappointing year her connections had with 2003 Breeders' Cup Mile winner Six Perfections who, winless in four starts, was emblematic of the difficulties experienced by Europe's older horses throughout the year.

Richest Stakes Races in the World in 2004

Race Rank/Name	Track	Conditions	Purse
1-Dubai World Cup (G1)	Nad Al Sheba (UAE)	1 1/4m(D) 4yo+	$6,000,000
2-Japan Cup (G1)	Tokyo (Jpn)	1 1/2m(T) 3yo+	4,674,818
3-Breeders' Cup Classic (G1)	**Lone Star Park (USA)**	**1 1/4m(D) 3yo+**	**3,668,000**
4-Melbourne Cup Hcp (G1)	Flemington (Aus)	2m(T) 3yo+	3,363,300
5-Arima Kinen (G1)	Nakayama (Jpn)	1 9/16m(T) 3yo+	3,303,107
6-Tokyo Yushun (Japanese Derby) (G1)	Tokyo (Jpn)	1 1/2m(T) 3yo c&f	3,092,900
7-Kikuka Sho (Japanese St Leger) (G1)	Kyoto (Jpn)	1 7/8m(T) 3yo	2,560,570
8-Epsom Derby (G1)	Epsom (GB)	1 1/2m(T) 3yo c&f	2,537,269
9-Spring Tenno Sho (G1)	Kyoto (Jpn)	2m(T) 4yo+ c&f	2,527,166
10-Japan Cup Dirt (G1)	Tokyo (Jpn)	1 5/16m(D) 3yo+	2,460,891
11-Autumn Tenno Sho (G1)	Tokyo (Jpn)	1 1/4m(T) 3yo+ c&f	2,408,553
12-Takarazuka Kinen (G1)	Hanshin (Jpn)	1 3/8m(T) 3yo+	2,372,608
13-Hong Kong Cup (G1)	Sha Tin (HK)	1 1/4m(T) 3yo+	2,314,800
14-Golden Slipper Stakes (G1)	Rosehill (Aus)	6f(T) 2yo	2,260,500
15-Cox Plate (G1)	Moonee Valley (Aus)	1 1/4m,44y(T) 3yo+	2,218,500
16-Satsuki Sho (Japanese 2000 Guineas) (G1)	Nakayama (Jpn)	1 1/4m(T) 3yo c&f	2,174,352
17-Yushun Himba (Japanese Oaks) (G1)	Tokyo (Jpn)	1 1/2m(T) 3yo f	2,042,680
18-Dubai Duty Free (G1)	Nad Al Sheba (UAE)	1 1/8m(T) 4yo+	2,000,000
18-Dubai Golden Shaheen (G1)	Nad Al Sheba (UAE)	6f(D) 3yo+	2,000,000
18-Dubai Sheema Classic (G1)	Nad Al Sheba (UAE)	1 1/2m(T) 4yo+	2,000,000
18-UAE Derby (G2)	Nad Al Sheba (UAE)	1 1/8m(D) 3yo	2,000,000
22-Pr de l'Arc de Triomphe (G1)	Longchamp (Fr)	1 1/2m(T) 3yo+ c&f	1,985,920
23-Oka Sho (Japanese 1000 Guineas) (G1)	Hanshin (Jpn)	1m(T) 3yo f	1,981,644
24-Queen Elizabeth II Commemorative Cup (G1)	Kyoto (Jpn)	1 3/8m(T) 3yo+ f&m	1,856,658
25-Breeders' Cup Distaff (G1)	**Lone Star Park (USA)**	**1 1/8m(D) 3yo+ f&m**	**1,834,000**
25-Breeders' Cup Turf (G1)	**Lone Star Park (USA)**	**1 1/2m(T) 3yo+**	**1,834,000**
27-Hong Kong Mile (G1)	Sha Tin (HK)	1m(T) 3yo+	1,800,400
27-Hong Kong Vase (G1)	Sha Tin (HK)	1 1/2m(T) 3yo+	1,800,400
29-Hong Kong Derby (G1)	Sha Tin (HK)	1 1/4m(T) 4yo	1,796,200
30-Queen Elizabeth II Cup (G1)	Sha Tin (HK)	1 1/4m(T) 4yo+	1,794,800
31-Doncaster Handicap (G1)	Randwick (Aus)	1m(T) 3yo+	1,789,200
32-Mile Championship (G1)	Kyoto (Jpn)	1m(T) 3yo+	1,788,201
33-Takamatsunimiya Kinen (G1)	Chukyo (Jpn)	6f(T) 4yo+	1,753,610
34-February Stakes (G1)	Tokyo (Jpn)	1m(D) 4yo+	1,690,743
35-Yasuda Kinen (G1)	Tokyo (Jpn)	1m(T) 3yo+	1,674,427
36-Sprinters Stakes (G1)	Nakayama (Jpn)	6f(T) 3yo+	1,667,931
37-Singapore Airlines International Cup (G1)	Kranji (Sin)	1 1/4m(T) 3yo+	1,646,284
38-JBC Classic (G1)	Ohi (Jpn)	1 1/4m(D) 3yo+	1,600,040
39-Shuka Sho (G1)	Kyoto (Jpn)	1 1/4m(T) 3yo f	1,596,291
40-Irish Derby (G1)	Curragh (Ire)	1 1/2m(T) 3yo c&f	1,584,180
41-Caulfield Cup Handicap (G1)	Caulfield (Aus)	1 1/2m(T) 3yo+	1,571,650
42-Breeders' Cup Mile (G1)	**Lone Star Park (USA)**	**1m(T) 3yo+**	**1,540,560**
43-BMW Classic (G1)	Rosehill (Aus)	1 1/2m(T) 3yo+	1,516,000
44-AJC Australian Derby (G1)	Randwick (Aus)	1 1/2m(T) 3yo	1,416,450
45-King George VI and Queen Elizabeth Diamond Stks (G1)	Ascot (GB)	1 1/2m(T) 3yo+	1,381,125
46-Breeders' Cup Juvenile (G1)	**Lone Star Park (USA)**	**1 1/16m(D) 2yo**	**1,375,500**
47-Prix du Jockey Club (French Derby) (G1)	Chantilly (Fr)	1 1/2m(T) 3yo c&f	1,325,060
48-Breeders' Cup Filly & Mare Turf (G1)	**Lone Star Park (USA)**	**1 3/8m(T) 3yo+ f&m**	**1,292,970**
49-Hong Kong Sprint (G1)	Sha Tin (HK)	5f(T) 3yo+	1,286,000
50-JBC Sprint (G1)	Ohi (Jpn)	6f(D) 3yo+	1,280,032

Race Rank/Name	Track	Conditions	Purse
51-Teio Sho (G1)	Ohi (Jpn)	1 1/4m(D) 4yo+	1,249,704
52-Canadian International (G1)	**Woodbine (Can)**	**1 1/2m(T) 3yo+**	**1,228,350**
53-Irish Champion Stakes (G1)	Leopardstown (Ire)	1 1/4m(T) 3yo+	1,226,600
54-Derby Italiano (G1)	Capannelle (Ity)	1 1/2m(T) 3yo c&f	1,209,186
55-Kentucky Derby (G1)	**Churchill Downs (USA)**	**1 1/4m(D) 3yo**	**1,184,000**
56-CBC Sho (G2)	Chukyo (Jpn)	6f(T) 3yo+	1,181,031
57-Sankei Osaka Hai (G2)	Hanshin (Jpn)	1 1/4m(T) 4yo+	1,173,099
58-Nikkei Sho (G2)	Nakayama (Jpn)	1 9/16m(T) 4yo+	1,170,969
59-Nikkei Shinshun Hai (G2)	Kyoto (Jpn)	1 1/2m(T) 4yo+	1,162,376
60-American Jockey Club Cup (G2)	Nakayama (Jpn)	1 3/8m(T) 4yo+	1,157,755
61-Hanshin Daishoten (G2)	Hanshin (Jpn)	1 7/8m(T) 4yo+	1,151,397
62-Kyoto Kinen (G2)	Kyoto (Jpn)	1 3/8m(T) 4yo+	1,139,595
63-Nakayama Kinen (G2)	Nakayama (Jpn)	1 1/8m(T) 4yo+	1,134,951
64-Mainichi Okan (G2)	Tokyo (Jpn)	1 1/8m(T) 3yo+	1,125,869
65-Kyoto Daishoten (G2)	Kyoto (Jpn)	1 1/2m(T) 3yo+	1,125,137
66-Hanshin Juvenile Fillies (G1)	Hanshin (Jpn)	1m(T) 2yo f	1,122,567
67-Sapporo Kinen (G2)	Sapporo (Jpn)	1 1/4m(T) 3yo+	1,121,371
68-Sankei Sho All-Comers (G2)	Nakayama (Jpn)	1 3/8m(T) 3yo+	1,120,967
68-Victoria Derby (G1)	Flemington (Aus)	1 9/16m(T) 3yo	1,120,200
70-Futurity Stakes (G1)	Nakayama (Jpn)	1m(T) 2yo c&f	1,096,752
71-Swan Stakes (G2)	Kyoto (Jpn)	7f(T) 3yo+	1,088,460
72-Copa Repub Argentina (G2)	Tokyo (Jpn)	1 9/16m(T) 3yo+	1,060,786
73-Yomiuri Milers Cup (G2)	Hanshin (Jpn)	1m(T) 4yo+	1,060,115
74-Stewards Cup (G1)	Sha Tin (HK)	1m(T) 4yo+	1,030,400
75-Hong Kong Classic Mile (G1)	Sha Tin (HK)	1m(T) 4yo+	1,029,600
76-Hong Kong Gold Cup (G1)	Sha Tin (HK)	1 1/4m(T) 4yo+	1,028,800
77-Hong Kong Champions & Chater Cup (G1)	Sha Tin (HK)	1 1/2m(T) 4yo+	1,025,600
78-Keio Hai Spring Cup (G2)	Tokyo (Jpn)	7f(T) 4yo+	1,014,125
79-Hanshin Himba Stakes (G2)	Hanshin (Jpn)	1m(T) 3yo+ f&m	1,103,899
80-Arkansas Derby (G2)	**Oaklawn Park (USA)**	**1 1/8m(D) 3yo**	**1,000,000**
80-Arlington Million (G1)	**Arlington Park (USA)**	**1 1/4m(T) 3yo+**	**1,000,000**
80-Barretts/CTBA Classic	**Santa Anita (USA)**	**1 1/8m(D) 4yo+**	**1,000,000**
80-Belmont Stakes (G1)	**Belmont Park (USA)**	**1 1/2m(D) 3yo**	**1,000,000**
80-Delta Jackpot	**Delta Downs (USA)**	**1 1/16m(D) 2yo**	**1,000,000**
80-Florida Derby (G1)	**Gulfstream Park (USA)**	**1 1/8m(D) 3yo**	**1,000,000**
80-Godolphin Mile (G2)	Nad Al Sheba (UAE)	1m(D) 3yo+	1,000,000
80-Jockey Club Gold Cup (G1)	**Belmont Park (USA)**	**1 1/4m(D) 3yo+**	**1,000,000**
80-Pacific Classic (G1)	**Del Mar (USA)**	**1 1/4m(D) 3yo+**	**1,000,000**
80-Preakness Stakes (G1)	**Pimlico (USA)**	**1 3/16m(D) 3yo**	**1,000,000**
80-Santa Anita Handicap (G1)	**Santa Anita (USA)**	**1 1/4m(D) 4yo+**	**1,000,000**
80-Travers Stakes (G1)	**Saratoga (USA)**	**1 1/4m(D) 3yo**	**1,000,000**
92-Tokai Stakes (G2)	Chukyo (Jpn)	1 7/16m(D) 3yo+	999,609
93-New Zealand Trophy (G2)	Nakayama (Jpn)	1m(T) 3yo c&f	998,558
94-Breeders' Cup Sprint (G1)	**Lone Star Park (USA)**	**6f(D) 3yo+**	**972,000**
95-Kawasaki Kinen (G1)	Kawasaki (Jpn)	1 5/16m(D) 4yo+	967,164
96-Spring Stakes (G2)	Nakayama (Jpn)	1 1/8m(T) 3yo c&f	965,654
97-Grosser Prs von Baden (G1)	Baden-Baden (Ger)	1 1/2m(T) 3yo+	965,280
98-St Lite Kinen (G2)	Nakayama (Jpn)	1 3/8m(T) 3yo	956,984
99-Aoba Sho (G2)	Tokyo (Jpn)	1 1/2m(T) 3yo	954,407
100-Kobe Shimbun Hai (G2)	Hanshin (Jpn)	1 1/4m(T) 3yo c&f	951,554

Bold-faced type indicates races in North America.

2004 Timeform Ratings

2-YEAR-OLDS

Horse	Rating	Horse	Rating	Horse	Rating
Shamardal	126p	Iceman	117	Walk In The Park	114
Dubawi	123p	Layman	117	Albert Hall	113p
Motivator	122p	Cupid's Glory	116	f-Playful Act	113p
Ad Valorem	121p	Manduro	115p	f-Damson	113
f-Divine Proportions	119	Berenson	114p	Merger	112p
Etlaala	119	Footstepsinthesand	114p	Caesar Beware	112
Oratorio	119	Henrik	114p	f-Centifolia	112
Early March	118	Librettist	114p	f-Dubai Surprise	112
Helios Quercus	118	Andronikos	114	Perfectperformance	112
Montgomery's Arch	118	Musketier	114	Russian Blue	112
Rebuttal	118	Satchem	114	Galeota	111
Wilko	118	Southern Africa	114	f-Maids Causeway	111

3-YEAR-OLDS

Horse	Rating	Horse	Rating	Horse	Rating
Smarty Jones	134	Shirocco	125	Let The Lion Roar	122
Bago	130	Whipper	125	f-Alexander Goldrun	121
Cherry Mix	129	Snow Ridge	124	American Post	121
Haafhd	129	Acropolis	124	Diamond Green	121
Azamour	128	Egerton	124	Latice	121
Lucky Story	128	f-Quiff	124	Maraahel	121
Grey Swallow	127	Mister Monet	123	Mikado	121
North Light	126	One Cool Cat	123	Percussionist	121
f-Attraction	125	Pastoral Pursuits	123	Crocodile Dundee	120
Electrocutionist	125	Tycoon	123	f-Grey Lilas	120
f-Ouija Board	125	Antonius Pius	123	Intendant	120
Rule Of Law	125	Bachelor Duke	122		

4-YEAR-OLDS & UP

Horse	Rating	Horse	Rating	Horse	Rating
Ghostzapper	137	Somnus	126	Powerscourt	124
Doyen	132	f-Soviet Song	126	Var	124
Roses In May	131	f-Tante Rose	126	Salselon	124
Pleasantly Perfect	130	Zenno Rob Roy	126	Arakan	123
Rakti	129	Firebreak	125	f-Chic	123
Refuse To Bend	128	f-Makybe Diva	125	Ikhtyar	123
Silent Witness	128	Tap Dance City	125	Patavellian	123
Sulamani	128	Norse Dancer	125	Royal Millennium	123
Vinnie Roe	128	Bandari	124	The Tatling	123
Hard Buck	127	Gamut	124	The Trader	123
Warrsan	127	Magistretti	124	Westerner	123
Exceed And Excel	126	National Currency	124		
Nayyir	126	Papineau	124		

Timeform Codes
f-Filly or mare
p-Likely to improve

2004 World Thoroughbred Racehorse Rankings

The International Federation of Horseracing Authorities (IFHA) World Thoroughbred Racehorse Rankings were first compiled in December 2004 with input from delegates from Argentina, Australia, France, Germany, Great Britain, Hong Kong, Ireland, Italy, Japan, Macau, New Zealand, North America (United States and Canada), Singapore, South Africa and the United Arab Emirates. The ratings will be compiled twice a year: in December, to rate horses who raced or trained in countries with a racing season from Jan. 1 through Dec. 31, and in August, to rate horses who raced or trained in countries with a racing season from Aug. 1 through July 31. The 2-year-old ratings only include horses trained in Europe.

2-YEAR-OLDS (European-trained horses only.)

Horse	Rating
Shamardal	123
Ad Valorem	122
Dubawi	122
Rebuttal	122
Wilko	119
f-Divine Proportions	117
Motivator	117
Oratorio	117
Berenson	116
Early March	116
Iceman	116
Layman	116
Montgomery's Arch	116
f-Damson	114
Etlaala	114
Librettist	114
Satchem	114
f-Fraloga	113
Galeota	113
Helios Quercus	113
Perfectperformance	113
f-Playful Act	113
Russian Blue	113
f-Soar	113
f-Titian Time	113

3-YEAR-OLDS

Horse	Cat	Rating
Smarty Jones	I	128
Bago	L	126
Cherry Mix	L	125
Haafhd	I	124
Azamour	I	123
Grey Swallow	L	123
Haafhd	M	122
Kitten's Joy	L	122
Lucky Story	M	122
North Light	L	122
Acropolis	L	120
Birdstone	I-L	120
f-Ouija Board	L	120
Rule Of Law	E	120
Tycoon	L	120
Shirocco	L	119
f-Attraction	M	118
Bachelor Duke	M	118
Electrocutionist	L	118
Let The Lion Roar	L	118
Smarty Jones	M	118
Snow Ridge	M	118
Whipper	M	118
Antonius Pius	M	117
f-Ashado	M	117
Cosmo Bulk	L	117
Diamond Green	M	117
Egerton	L	117
King Kamekameha	M-L	117
f-Latice	I	117
Lion Heart	I	117
f-Quiff	L	117
Voix du Nord	I	117
f-Alexander Goldrun	I	116
Blue Canari	L	116
Delta Blues	L	116
f-Grey Lilas	M	116
Intendant	I	116
Millemix	I	116
Mister Monet	I	116
f-Quiff	E	116
Valixir	I-L	116
American Post	M	115
Artie Schiller	M-I	115
f-Ashado	I	115
Cacique	I	115
Groom Tesse	L	115
f-Lune d'Or	I	115
Maraahel	E	115
Mikado	E	115
f-Millionaia	I	115
Percussionist	L	115
Prospect Park	L	115
Purge	M	115
Read The Footnotes	M	115
f-Society Selection	I	115
The Cliff's Edge	M-I	115

4-YEAR-OLDS & Up

Horse	Cat	Rating
Ghostzapper	I	130
Doyen	L	127
Pleasantly Perfect	I	126
Medaglia d'Oro	I	124
Ghostzapper	M	123
Pico Central	S	123
Rakti	M	123
Roses In May	I	123
Silent Witness	S	123
Sulamani	I	123
Southern Image	M-I	122
Speightstown	S	122
Zenno Rob Roy	L	122
Better Talk Now	L	121
Norse Dancer	I	121
Refuse To Bend	M-I	121
Durandal	M	120
Hard Buck	L	120
Powerscourt	I	120
Tap Dance City	L	120
Warrsan	I	120
Papineau	E	119
Peace Rules	M-I	119
Perfect Drift	M-I	119
Saint Liam	M	119
f-Soviet Song	M	119
Vinnie Roe	E	119
f-Azeri	M	118
Bandari	L	118
Gamut	L	118
Kela	S	118
Midas Eyes	S	118
Nayyir	M	118
f-Sightseek	M	118
Singletary	M	118
Somnus	M	118
Westerner	E	118
Ancient World	M	117
f-Azeri	I	117
f-Chic	M	117
f-Chorist	I	117
Epalo	I	117
Kicken Kris	I	117
Magistretti	L	117
Millenary	E	117
Mr Dinos	E	117
Mubtaker	L	117
f-Russian Rhythm	M	117
Simonas	L	117
Special Ring	M	117
Total Impact	I	117
Touch of Land	I	117
Var	S	117

f-filly or mare **Italics-Rating earned on dirt**
S-Sprints **M-Mile** **I-Intermediate** **L-Long distance** **E-Stayers**

Foreign Stakes Histories

Australia

MELBOURNE CUP HANDICAP. 2 Miles. 3-year-olds and upward.

(Flemington, Melbourne, Victoria)

FIRST RUN IN 1851

Year	First	Age	Jockey	Wt	Second	Age	Wt	Third	Age	Wt	Time	Win Value
1955	Taparoa	7	N Sellwood	106	Rising Fast	6	140	Sir William	5	108	3:28 1/4	$22,625
1956	Evening Peal	4	G Podmore	112	Red Craze	6	143	Caranna	4	124	3:19 1/2	33,600
1957	StraighT Draw	5	N McGrowdie	117	Prince Darius	3	104	Pansie Sun	5	119	3:24 1/2	49,550
1958	Baystone	6	M Schumaker	121	Monte Carlo	5	132	Red Pine	4	102	3:21 1/4	30,000
1959	Mac Dougal	6	P Glennon	123	Nether Gold	7	104	white Hills	6	112	3:23	33,600
1960	Hi Jinx	5	W Smith	108	Howsie	5	118	Illumquh	5	118	3:23 4/5	56,000
1961	Lord Fury	4	R Selkrig	105	Grand Print	4	110	Dhaulagiri	5	131	3:19	46,480
1962	Even Stevens	5	L G. Coles	117	Comicquita	5	108	Aquanita	5	130	3:21 2/5	31,500
1963	Gatum Gatum	5	J Johnson	110	Illumquh	8	124	Grand Print	6	128	3:21.1	43,120
1964	Polo Prince	6	R Taylor	115	Elkayah	6	119	Welltown	4	105	3:19 3/5	43,023
1965	Light Fingers	4	R Higgins	116	Ziema	4	118	Midlander	3	95	3:21.1	46,652
1966	Galilee	4	J Miller	125	Light Fingers	5	127	Duo	5	113	3:21.9	41,300
1967	Red Handed	7	R Higgins	121	Red Crest	7	118	Floodbird	5	105	3:20 1/5	46,251
1968	Rain Lover	4	J Johnson	114	Fileur	4	119	Fans	6	118	3:19.1	41,300
1969	Rain Lover	5	J Johnson	133	Alsop	4	104	Ben Lomond	5	129	3:21 1/2	51,100
1970	Bagdad Note	5	E J Disham	119	Vanisittart	4	112	Clear Prince	3	96	3:19.7	51,100
1971	Silver Knight	4	R B Marsh	121	Igloo	4	115	Tails	6	126	3:19 1/2	69,900
1972	Piping Lane	6	J Letts	106	Maginfique	4	115	Gunsynd	5	133	3:19.3	72,900
1973	Gala Supreme	4	F Reys	108	Glengowan	6	125	Daneson	5	106	3:19 1/2	67,900
1974	Think Big	4	H White	117	Leilani	4	122	Captain Peri	6	115	3:23 1/5	108,900
1975	Think Big	5	H White	129	Holiday Waggon	4	110	Medici	7	101	3:23 3/5	110,000
1976	Van Der Hum	5	R J Skelton	120	Gold and Black	4	110	Kythera	6	112	3:34.1	129,097
1977	Gold and Black	5	J Duggan	126	Reckless	7	125	Hyperno	4	115	3:18 2/5	126,779
1978	Arwon	5	H White	111	Dandeleith	6	111	Karu	7	107	3:24.3	149,890
1979	Hyperno	6	H White	123	Salamander	6	122	Red Nose	4	113	3:21.8	214,012
1980	Beldale Ball	5	J Letts	109	My Blue Denim	5	118	Love Bandit	6	112	3:19.8	228,481
1981	Just A Dash	4	P Cook	118	El Laurena	5	115	Flashing Light	4	108	3:21.2	223,080
1982	Gurner's Lane	4	L Dittman	123	Kingston Town	6	130	Noble Comment	5	109	3:21	182,247
1983	Kiwi	6	J Cassidy	115	Noble Comment	6	111	Mr. Jazz	4	110	3:18.9	178,249
1984	Black Knight	5	P Cook	110	Chagemar	5	120	Mapperley Heights	4	112	3:18.9	280,475
1985	What A Nuisance	7	P Hyland	116	Koiro Corrie May	6	113	Tripsacum	4	108	3:23	435,175
1986	At Talaq	5	M Clarke	120	Rising Fear	4	117	Sea Ledgend	4	108	3:21.7	417,105
1987	Kensei	5	L Olsen	113	Empire Rose	5	110	Rosedale	5	123	3:22	551,687
1988	Empire Rose	6	T Allan	118	Natski	5	121	Na Botto	4	112	3:19.9	879,986
1989	Tawrrific	5	R S Dye	119	Super Impose	5	123	Kudz	6	116	3:17.1	925,160
1990	Kingston Rule	5	D Breadman	117	The Phantom	5	120	Mr. Brooker	5	117	3:16.3	1,024,400
1991	Let's Elope	4	S King	112	Shiva's Revenge	4	118	Magnolia Hall	5	116	3:18.9	1,043,970
1992	Subzero	4	G Hall	120	Veandercross	3	120	Casteltown	7	126	3:243/5	904,670
1993	Vintage Crop	7	M J Kinane	122	Te Akau Nick	5	123	Mercator	7	119	3:252/5	870,408
1994	Jeune	6	W Harris	125	Paris Lane	4	122	Oompala	6	116	3:19.80	962,780
1995	Doriemus	5	D M Oliver	120	Nothin' Leica Dane	3	105	Vintage Crop	9	130	3:27.60	1,015,001
1996	Saintly	4	D Beadman	122	Count Chivas	5	126	Skybeau	4	110	3:18.8	1,152,955
1997	Might and Power	4	J Cassidy	123	Doriemus	7	127	Markham	4	116	3:18.33	1,030,774
1998	Jezabeel	6	C J Munce	112	Champagne	4	112	Persian Punch	6	125	3:18.59	1,070,503
1999	Rogan Josh	7	J Marshall	110	Central Park	5	127	Zazabelle	4	108	3:19.64	1,175,318
2000	Brew	6	K McEvoy	108	Yippyio	5	115	Second Coming	6	116	3:18.68	1,077,940
2001	Ethereal	3	S Seamer	114	Give The Slip	4	121	Persian Punch	8	126	3:21.08	944,656
2002	Media Puzzle	6	D M Oliver	116	Mr Prudent	8	115	Beekeeper	4	117	3:16.97	1,139,439
2003	Makybe Diva	6	G Boss	112	She's Archie	4	110	Jardines Lookout	6	122	3:19.90	1,655,844
2004	Makybe Diva	7	G Boss	123	Vinnie Roe	6	128	Zazzman	6	116	3:28.55	2,092,720

Britain

ASCOT GOLD CUP-G1

2-1/2 miles, 4-year-olds & up, Royal Ascot

FIRST RUN IN 1807.

Year	1st (Age)	Jockey	Trainer	Owner	2nd	3rd	Time
1970	Precipice Wood (4)	J. Lindley	Mrs R. Lomax	R. McAlpine	Blakeney	Clairon	4:27.4
1971	Random Shot (4)	G. Lewis	A. Budgett	Mrs G. Benskin	Orosio	Charlton	4:41.4*
1972	Erimo Hawk (4)	Pat Eddery	G. Barling	Y. Yamamoto	Rock Roi	Irvine	4:28.6
1973	Lassalle (4)	J. Lindley	R. Carver	Z Yoshida	Celtic Cone	The Admiral	4:33.4
1974	Ragstone (4)	R. Hutchinson	J. Dunlop	Duke of Norfolk	Proverb	Lassalle	4:35
1975	Sagaro (4)	L. Piggott	F Boutin	G. Oldham	Le Bavard	Kambalda	4:48

Year	1st (Age)	Jockey	Trainer	Owner	2nd	3rd	Time
1976	Sagaro (5)	L. Piggott	F Boutin	G. Oldham	Crash Course	Sea Anchor	4:26
1977	Sagaro (6)	L. Piggott	F Boutin	G. Oldham	Buckskin	Citoyen	4:28.4
1978	Shangamuzo (5)	G. Starkey	M. Stoute	Mrs E Charles	Royal Hive	Hawkberry	4:27.4
1979	Le Moss (4)	L. Piggott	H Cecil	C. d'Alessio	Buckskin	Arapahos	4:25.2
1980	Le Moss (5)	J. Mercer	H Cecil	C. d'Alessio	Ardross	Vincent	4:27.6
1981	Ardross (5)	L. Piggott	H Cecil	C. St George	Shoot A Line	Ayyabaan	4:51.2
1982	Ardross (6)	L. Piggott	H Cecil	C. St George	Tipperary Fixer	El Badr	4:35.2
1983	Little Wolf (5)	W. Carson	W. R. Hern	Lord Portchester	Khairpour	Indian Prince	4:24.2
1984	Gildoran (4)	S. Cauthen	B. Hills	R. Sangster	Ore	Condeil	4:18.8
1985	Gildoran (5)	B. Thomson	B. Hills	R. Sangster	Longboat	Destroyer	4:25.2
1986	Longboat (5)	W. Carson	W. R. Hern	R. D. Hollingsworth	Eastern Mystic	Spicey Story	4:22
1987	Paean (4)	S. Cauthen	H Cecil	H de Walden	Sadeem	Saronicos	4:33.2
1988+	Sadeem (5)	G. Starkey	G. Harwood	Sheikh Mohammed	Sergeyevich	Chauve Souris	4:15.6
1989	Sadeem (6)	W. Carson	G. Harwood	Sheikh Mohammed	Mazzacano	Lauries Crusader	4:22.6
1990	Ashal (4)	R. Hills	H T Jones	H Al Maktoum	Tyrone Bridge	Thethingaboutitis	4:28.4
1991	Indian Queen (6f)	W. R. Swinburn	Lord Huntingdon	G. Brunton	Arazanni	Warm Feeling	4:23.8
1992	Drum Taps (6)	L. Dettori	Lord Huntingdon	Y. Asakawa	Arcadian Heights	Turgeon	4:18.2
1993	Drum Taps (7)	L. Dettori	Lord Huntingdon	Y. Asakawa	Assessor	Turgeon	4:32.57
1994	Arcadian Heights (6)	M. Hills	G. Wragg	J. Pearce	Vintage Crop	Sonus	4:27.67
1995	Double Trigger (4)	J. Weaver	M. Johnston	R. Huggins	Moonax	Admiral's Well	4:20.25
1996	Classic Cliche (4)	M. J. Kinane	S. bin Suroor	Godolphin	Double Trigger	Nononito	4:23.2
1997	Celeric (5)	Pat Eddery	D. Morley	C. Spence	Classic Cliche	Election Day	4:26.19
1998	Kayf Tara (4)	L. Dettori	S. bin Suroor	Godolphin	Double Trigger	Three Cheers	4:32.36
1999	Enzeli (4)	J. P Murtagh	J. Oxx	Aga Khan	Invermark	Kayf Tara	4:18.85
2000	Kayf Tara (6)	M J Kinane	S bin Suroor	Godolphin	Far Cry	Compton Ace	4:24.53
2001	Royal Rebel (5)	J P Murtagh	M Johnston	P D Savill	Persian Punch	Jardines Lookout	4:18.92
2002	Royal Rebel (6)	J P Murtagh	M Johnston	P D Savill	Vinnie Roe	Wareed	4:25.64
2003	Mr Dinos (4)	K Fallon	P Cole	C Shiacolas	Persian Punch	Pole Star	4:20.15
2004	Papineau (4)	L Dettori	S bin Suroor	Godolphin	Westerner	Darasim	4:20.90

*Rock Roi finished first but was disqualified from purse money.
+Royal Gait finished first but was disqualified and placed last.

CHAMPION STAKES-G1

1-1/4 miles, 3-year-olds & up, Newmarket (Rowley Mile Course)

FIRST RUN IN 1877

Year	1st (age)	Jockey	Trainer	Owner	2nd	3rd	Time
1970	Lorrenzaccio (5)	G Lewis	N Murless	C St George	Nijinsky II	Hotfoot	2:05.8
1971	Brigadier Gerard(3)	J Mercer	W R Hern	Mrs J Hislop	Rarity	Welsh Pageant	2:17.8
1972	Brigadier Gerard(4)	J Mercer	W R Hern	Mrs J Hislop	Riverman	Lord David	2:07.4
1973	Hurry Harriet (3f)	J Cruguet	P Mullins	M Thorp	Allez France	Sharp Edge	2:08.4
1974	Giacometti (3)	L Piggott	H Price	C St George	Northern Gem	Pitcairn	2:09.4
1975	Rose Bowl (3f)	W Carson	R J Houghton	Mrs C Engelhard	Allez France	Ramirez	2:05.2
1976	Vitiges (3)	Pat Eddery	P Walwyn	Mme M Laloun	Rose Bowl	Northern Treasure	2:09.6
1977	Flying Water (3)	Y Saint-Martin	A Penna	D Wildenstein	Relkino	North Stoke	2:06.8
1978	Swiss Maid (3f)	G Starkey	P Kelleway	M Fine	Hawaiian Sound	Gunner B	2:03.8
1979	Northern Baby (3)	P Paquet	F Boutin	Mme A d'Estainville	Town And Country	Haul Knight	2:03.8
1980	Cairn Rouge (3f)	A Murray	M Cunningham	D Brady	Master Willie	Nadjar	2:05.6
1981	Vayraan (3)	Y Saint-Martin	F Mathet	H H Aga Khan	Cairn Rouge	Amyndas	2:08
1982	Time Charter (3f)	W Newnes	H Candy	R Barnett	Prima Voce	Noalto	2:10.6
1983	Cormorant Wood(3f)	S Cauthen	B Hills	R McAlpine	Flame Of Tara	Miramar Reef	
1984	Palace Music (3)	Y Saint-Martin	P-L Biancone	N B Hunt	Pebbles	Raft	2:01
1985	Pebbles (4f)	Pat Eddery	C Brittain	Sheikh Mohammed	Slip Anchor	Palace Music	2:04.6
1986	Triptych (4f)	A Cruz	P-L Biancone	A Clore	Celestial Storm	Park Express	2:09.4
1987	Triptych (5f)	A Cruz	P-L Biancone	A Clore	Most Welcome	Saint Andrews	2:10.8
1988	Indian Skimmer(4f)	M Roberts	H Cecil	Sheikh Mohammed	Persian Heights	Doyoun	2:10.4
1989	Legal Case (3)	W R Swinburn	L Cumani	G White	Dolpour	Ile de Chypre	2:02.8
1990	In The Groove (3f)	S Cauthen	D Elsworth	B Cooper	Linamix	Legal Case	2:05.6
1991	Tel Quel (3)	T Jarnet	A Fabre	Sheikh Mohammed	Cruachan	In The Groove	2:01.8
1992	Rodrigo de Triano(3)	L Piggott	P Chapple-Hyam	R Sangster	Lahib	Environment Friend	2:02.4
1993	Hatoof (4f)	W R Swinburn	C Head	M Al Maktoum	Ezzoud	Dernier Empereur	2:06.8
1994	Dernier Empereur(4)	S Guillot	A Fabre	G Tanaka	Grand Lodge	Muhtarram	2:05.65
1995	Spectrum (3)	J Reid	P Chapple-Hyam	Lord Weinstock	Riyadian	Montjoy	2:02.55
1996	Bosra Sham (3f)	Pat Eddery	H Cecil	W Said	Halling	Timarida	2:03.71
1997	Pilsudski (5)	M J Kinane	M Stoute	Lord Weinstock	Loup Sauvage	Bahhare	2:05.46
1998	Alborada (3f)	G Duffield	M Prescott	K Rausing	Insatiable	Daylami	2:03.69
1999*	Alborada (4f)	G Duffield	M Prescott	K Rausing	Shiva	Kabool	2:05.57
2000	Kalanisi (4)	J P Murtagh	J Oxx	HH Aga Khan	Montjeu	Distant Music	2:05.59
2001	Nayef (3)	R Hills	M Tregoning	H Al Maktoum	Tobougg	Indian Creek	2:07.72
2002	Storming Home (4)	M Hills	B Hills	M Al Maktoum	Moon Ballad	Noverre	2:01.42
2003	Rakti (4)	P Robinson	M Jarvis	G A Tanaka	Carnival Dancer	Indian Creek	2:03.34
2004	Haafhd (3)	R Hills	B Hills	H Al Maktoum	Chorist	Azamour	2:06.90

*Run on the July Course.

CHEVELEY PARK STAKES-G1

6 furlongs, 2-year-old fillies, Newmarket (Rowley Mile Course)

FIRST RUN IN 1899.

Year	1st	Jockey	Trainer	Owner	2nd	3rd	Time
1970	Magic Flute	A Barclay	N Murless	H de Walden	Ballet	Francais Melodina	1:12.63
1971	Waterloo	E Hide	J Watts	Mrs R Stanley	Marisela	Miss Paris	1:13.6
1972	Jacinth	J Gorton	B Hobbs	Lady Butt	Caspian	Marble Arch	1:12.6
1973	Gentle Thoughts	W Pyers	T Curtin	N B Hunt	Red Berry	Lady Tan	1:15
1974	Cry Of Truth	J Gorton	B Hobbs	P Johnston	Delmora	Rose Bowl	1:15.2
1975	Patsy	Pat Eddery	P Walwyn	G Williams	Dame Foolish	Solar	1:15
1976	Durtal	L Piggott	B Hills	R Sangster	Be Easy	Rings	1:14.4
1977	Sookera	W Swinburn	D K Weld	R Sangster	Fair Salinia	Smarten Up	1:11.4
1978	Devon Ditty	G Starkey	H T Jones	E McAlpine	Kilijaro	Do Be Darling	1:12
1979	Mrs Penny	J Matthias	I Balding	E Kronfeld	Millingdale Lillie	Abeer	1:13.4
1980	Marwell	L Piggott	M Stoute	E Loder	Welshwyn	Pushy	1:12.6
1981	Woodstream	Pat Eddery	M V O'Brien	R Sangster	On The House	Admiral's Princess	1:14.2
1982	Ma Biche	F Head	C Head	Mme A Head	Favoridge	Super Entente	1:14.6
1983	Desirable	S Cauthen	B Hills	Mrs J Corbett	Pebbles	Prickle	1:14.8
1984	Park Appeal	D Gillespie	J Bolger	P Burns	Polly Daniels	Al Bahathri	1:13.8
1985	Embla	A Cordero Jr	L Cumani	C St George	Kingscote	Rose Of The Sea	1:12.4
1986	Minstrella	J Reid	C Nelson	E P Evans	Canadian Mill	Shaikiya	1:12.4
1987	Ravinella	G Moore	C Head	Ecurie Aland	First Waltz	Ela Romara	1:14.2
1988	Pass The Peace	T R Quinn	P Cole	B Bell	Dancing Tribute	Jaljuli	1:11.8
1989	Dead Certain	C Asmussen	D Elsworth	G Marten	Line Of Thunder	Chimes Of Freedom	1:14.8
1990	Capricciosa	J Reid	M V O'Brien	R Sangster	Imperfect Circle	Divine Danse	1:12.2
1991	Marling	W R Swinburn	G Wragg	E Loder	Absurde	Basma	1:11.6
1992	Sayyedati	W R Swinburn	C Brittain	M Obaida	Lyric Fantasy	Poker Chip	1:11.8
1993	Prophecy	Pat Eddery	J Gosden	K Abdullah	Risky	Lemon Souffle	1:14.68
1994	Gay Gallanta	Pat Eddery	M Stoute	Cheveley Park Stud	Tanami	Harayir	1:11.08
1995	Blue Duster	M J Kinane	D Loder	Sheikh Mohammed	My Branch	Najiya	1:12.78
1996	Pas de Reponse	F Head	C Head	Wertheimer & Frere	Moonlight Paradise	Ocean Ridge	1:11.16
1997	Embassy	K Fallon	D Loder	Sheikh Mohammed	Crazee Mental	Royal Shyness	1:12.26
1998	Wannabe Grand	Pat Eddery	J Noseda	B McAllister	Imperial Beauty	Subeen	1:12.4
1999*	Seazun	T R Quinn	M Channon	J Breslin	Torgau	Crimplene	1:12.92
2000	Regal Rose	L Dettori	M Stoute	Cheveley Park Stud	Toroca	Mala Mala	1:13.75
2001	Queen's Logic	S Drowne	M Channon	Jaber Abdullah	Sophisticat	Good Girl	1:12.34
2002	Airwave	C Rutter	H Candy	H Candy & Partners	Russian Rhythm	Danaskaya	1:10.72
2003	Carry On Katie	L Dettori	J Noseda	Mohammed Rashid	Majestic Desert	Badminton	1:13.03
2004	Magical Romance	R Winston	B Meehan	F C T Wilson	Suez	Damson	1:12.61

*Run on the July Course.

CORONATION CUP-G1

1-1/2 miles, 4-year-olds & up, Epsom

FIRST RUN IN 1902

Year	1st (Age)	Jockey	Trainer	Owner	2nd	3rd	Time
1970	Caliban (4)	A. Barclay	N. Murless	S. Joel	Park Top	Shoemaker	2:49.2
1971	Lupe (4f)	G. Lewis	N. Murless	Mrs S. Joel	Stintino	Quayside	2:37.6
1972	Mill Reef (4)	G. Lewis	I Balding	P Mellon	Homeric	Wenceslas	2:34.8
1973	Roberto (4)	L. Piggott	M. V O'Brien	J. Galbreath	Attica Meli	Baragoi	2:34.4
1974	Buoy (4)	J. Mercer	W. R. Hern	R. Hollingsworth	Tennyson	Dahlia	2:36.4
1975	Bustino (4)	J. Mercer	W. R. Hern	Lady Beaverbrook	Ashmore	Mil's Bomb	2:33.4
1976	Quiet Fling (4)	L Piggott	J. Tree	J. H Whitney	Libra's Rib	Major Green	2:38
1977	Exceller (4)	G. Dubroeucq	F Mathet	N. B. Hunt	Quiet Fling	Smuggler	2:36.8
1978	Crow (5)	P. Eddery	P Walwyn	D. Wildenstein	Balmerino	Smuggler	2:34.4
1979	Ile de Bourbon (4)	J. Reid	R. J. Houghton	P Oppenheimer	Frere Basile	Gay Mecene	2:43.4
1980	Sea Chimes (4)	L Piggott	J.. Dunlop	J. Thursby	Niniski	Soleil Noir	2:35.8
1981	Master Willie (4)	P. Waldron	H Candy	R. Barnett	Prince Bee	Vielle	2:44.4
1982	Easter Sun (5)	B. Raymond	M.. Jarvis	Lady Beaverbrook	Glint Of Gold	Critique	2:35
1983	Be My Native (4)	L. Piggott	R. Armstrong	K. Hsu	Electric	Old Country	2:45.2
1984	Time Charter (5f)	S. Cauthen	H Candy	R. Barnett	Sun Princess	Lovely Dancer	2:40.6
1985	Rainbow Quest (4)	P. Eddery	J. Tree	K. Abdullah	Old Country	Long Pond	2:35.8
1986	Saint Estephe (4)	P. Eddery	A. Fabre	Y. Houyvet	Triptych	Petoski	2:34.8
1987	Triptych (5f)	A. Cruz	P-L Biancone	A. Clore	Rakaposhi King	Acatenango	2:35.8
1988	Triptych (6f)	S. Cauthen	P-L Biancone	P Brant	Infamy	Moon Madness	2:34.8
1989	Sheriff's Star (4)	R. Cochrane	Lady Herries	Duchess of Norfolk	Ile de Chypre	Green Adventure	2:35.4
1990	In the Wings (4)	C. Asmussen	A. Fabre	Sheikh Mohammed	Observation Post	Ibn Bey	2:36.4
1991	In The Groove (4f)	S. Cauthen	D. Elsworth	B. Cooper	Terimon	Rock Hopper	2:36.2
1992	Saddlers' Hall (4)	W. R. Swinburn	M. Stoute	Lord Weinstock	Rock Hopper	Terimon	2:35.6
1993	Opera House (4)	M. Roberts	M. Stoute	Sheikh Mohammed	Environment Friend	Apple Tree	2:35.13
1994	Apple Tree (5)	T Jarnet	A. Fabre	Sultan Al Kabeer	Environment Friend	Blush Rambler	2:35.43
1995	Sunshack (4)	Pat Eddery	A. Fabre	K. Abdullah	Only Royale	Time Star	2:35.85
1996	Swain (4)	L Dettori	A. Fabre	Sheikh Mohammed	Singspiel	De Quest	2:40.27
1997	Singspiel (5)	L Dettori	M. Stoute	Sheikh Mohammed	Dushyantor	Le Destin	2:37.72

Year	1st (Age)	Jockey	Trainer	Owner	2nd	3rd	Time
1998	Silver Patriarch (4)	P. Eddery	J. Dunlop	P Winfield	Swain	Ebadiyla	2:37.6
1999	Daylami (5)	L Dettori	S. bin Suroor	Godolphin	Royal Anthem	Dream Well	2:40.26
2000	Daliapour (4)	K Fallon	M Stoute	HH Aga Khan	Fantastic Light	Border Arrow	2:41.63
2001	Mutafaweq (5)	L Dettori	S bin Suroor	Godolphin	Wellbeing	Millenary	2:36.70
2002	Boreal (4)	K Fallon	P Schiergen	Gestut Amerland	Storming Home	Zindabad	2:45.01
2003	Warrsan (5)	P Robinson	C E Brittain	S Manana	Highest	Black San Bellamy	2:35.68
2004	Warrsan (6)	D Holland	C E Brittain	S Manana	Doyen	Vallee Enchantee	2:35.96

CORONATION STAKES-G1

1 mile, 3-year-old fillies, Ascot

FIRST RUN IN 1840

Year	1st	Jockey	Trainer	Owner	2nd	3rd	Time
1970	Humble Duty	D Keith	P WAlwyn	Jean Lady Ashcombe	Black Satin	Spotty Bebe	
1971	Magic Flute	G Lewis	N Murless	Lord Howard de Walden	Seaswan	Favoletta	
1972	Calve	L Piggott	P J Prendergast	Lord Granard	Waterloo	Miss Paris	
1973	Jacinth	J Gorton	B Hobbs	Lady Butt	Silver Birch	Melodramatic	
1974	Lisadell	L Piggott	M V O'Brien	John A Mulcahy	Himawari	Matuno God	
1975	Roussalka	L Piggott	H Cecil	N Phillips	Tender Camilla	Highest Trump	
1976	Kesar Queen	Y Saint-Martint	A Breasley	Ravi N Tikkoo	Guichet	Clover Princess	
1977	Orchestration	Pat Eddery	A Maxwell	Major V McCalmont	Lady Capulet	No Cards	
1978	Sutton Place	W Swinburn	D K Weld	Mrs T Donahue	Ridaness	Baccalaureate	
1979	One In A Million	J Mercer	H Cecil	Helena Springfield Ltd	Topsy	Yanuka	
1980	Cairn Rouge	A Murray	M Cunningham	D Brady	Quick As Lightning	Our Home	
1981	Tolmi	E Hide	B Hobbs	G Cambanis	Happy Bride	Nasseem	
1982	Chalon	L Piggott	H Cecil	M Riordan	Grease	Dancing Rocks	
1983	Flame Of Tara	D Gillespie	J Bolger	Miss P O'Kelly	Favoridge	Magdalena	
1984	Katies	P Robinson	M J Ryan	T P Ramsden	Pebbles	So Fine	
1985	Al Bahathri	A Murray	H Thomson Jones	H Al Maktoum	Top Socialite	Soprano	
1986	Sonic Lady	W R Swinburn	M R Stoute	Sheikh Mohammed	Embla	Someone Special	
1987	Milligram	W R Swinburn	M R Stoute	Helena Springfield Ltd	Shaikiya	Martha Stevens	
1988	Magic Of Life	Pat Eddery	J Tree	S Niarchos	Inchmurrin	Ravinella	
1989	Golden Opinion	C B Asmussen	A Fabre	Sheikh Mohammed	Magic Gleam	Guest Artiste	
1990	Chimes Of Freedom	S Cauthen	H Cecil	S Niarchos	Hasbah	Heart Of Joy	1:41.29
1991	Kooyonga	W J O'Connor	M Kauntze	M Haga	Shadayid	Gussy Marlowe	1:42.54
1992	Marling	W R Swinburn	G Wragg	E J Loder	Culture Vulture	Katakana	1:39.01
1993	Gold Splash	G Mosse	C Head	J Wertheimer	Elizabeth Bay	Zarani Sidi Anna	1:47.68
1994	Kissing Cousin	M J Kinane	H Cecil	Sheikh Mohammed	Eternal Reve	Mehthaaf	1:39.96
1995	Ridgewood Pearl	J P Murtagh	J Oxx	Anne Coughlan	Smolensk	Harayir	1:38.58
1996	Shake The Yoke	O Peslier	E Lellouche	S Brunswick	Last Second	Dance Design	1:40.45
1997	Rebecca Sharp	M Hills	G Wragg	A E Oppenheimer	Ocean Ridge	Sleepytime	1:42.04
1998	Exclusive	W R Swinburn	M R Stoute	Cheveley Park Stud	Zalaiyka	Winona	1:43.98
1999	Balisada	M Roberts	G Wragg	A E Oppenheimer	Golden Silca	*Valentime Waltz	1:41.43
2000	Crimplene	P Robinson	C E Brittain	Marwan Al Maktoum	Princess Ellen	Bluemamba	1:41.55
2001	Banks Hill	O Peslier	A Fabre	K Abdullah	Crystal Music	Tempting Fate	1:39.61
2002	Sophisticat	M J Kinane	A P O'Brien	Tabor & Magnier	Zenda	Dolores	1:41.69
2003	Russian Rhythm	K Fallon	M R Stoute	Cheveley Park Stud	Soviet Song	Mail The Desert	1:38.51
2004	Attraction	K Darley	M Johnston	Duke of Roxburghe	Majestic Desert	Red Bloom	1:38.54

*In 1999 Valentine's Waltz finished in a deadheat for 3rd with Wannabe Grand.

DEWHURST STAKES-G1

7 furlongs, 2-year-old colts & fillies, Newmarket (Rowley Mile Course)

FIRST RUN IN 1875

Year	1st	Jockey	Trainer	Owner	2nd	3rd	Time
1974	Grundy	Pat Eddery	P Walwyn	C Vittadini	Steel Heart	Baldur	1:33.6
1975	Wollow	G Dettori	H Cecil	C d'Alessio	Malinowski	All Hope	1:25.8
1976	The Minstrel	L Piggott	M V O'Brien	R Sangster	Saros	Crown Bowler	1:28.2
1977	Try My Best	L Piggott	M V O'Brien	R Sangster	Sexton Blake	Camden Town	1:28.6
1978	Tromos	J Lynch	B Hobbs	G Cambanis	More Light	Warmington	1:24.6
1979	Monteverdi	L Piggott	M V O'Brien	R Sangster	Tyrnavos	Romeo Romani	1:26
1980	Storm Bird	Pat Eddery	M V O'Brien	R Sangster	To-Agori-Mou	Miswaki	1:29
1981	Wind And Wuthering	P Waldron	H Candy	R Cyzer	Be My Native	Tender King	1:26.6
1982	Diesis	L Piggott	H Cecil	H de Walden	Gordian Tough	Commander	1:27.4
1983	El Gran Senor	Pat Eddery	M V O'Brien	R Sangster	Rainbow Quest	Siberian Express	1:24.8
1984	Kala Dancer	G Baxter	B Hanbury	R Tikkoo	Law Society	Local Suitor	1:27.6
1985	Huntingdale	M Hills	J Hindley	Mrs P Threlfall	Bakharoff	Sure Blade	1:26.2
1986	Ajdal	W R Swinburn	M Stoute	Sheikh Mohammed	Genghiz	Mister Majestic	1:28.8
1987	RACE NOT RUN						
1988	Prince Of Dance*	W Carson	N Graham	M Sobell			
1988	Scenic *	M Hills	B Hills	Sheikh Mohammed	-	Saratogan	1:27.6

Year	1st	Jockey	Trainer	Owner	2nd	3rd	Time
1989	Dashing Blade	J Matthias	I Balding	J C Smith	Call To Arms	Anshan	1:25.4
1990	Generous	T R Quinn	P Cole	Prince F Salman	Bog Trotter	Surrealist	1:28.4
1991	Dr Devious	W Carson	P Chapple-Hyam	L Gaucci	Great Palm	Thourios	1:23.4
1992	Zafonic	Pat Eddery	A Fabre	K Abdullah	Inchinor	Firm Pledge	1:23.6
1993	Grand Lodge	Pat Eddery	W Jarvis	H de Walden	Stonehatch	Nicolotte	1:28.27
1994	Pennekamp	T Jarnet	A Fabre	Sheikh Mohammed	Green Perfume	Eltish	1:25.41
1995	Alhaarth	W Carson	W R Hern	H Al Maktoum	Danehill Dancer	Tagula	1:24.64
1996	In Command	M Hills	B Hills	M Al Maktoum	Musical Pursuit	Air Express	1:25.93
1997	Xaar	O Peslier	A Fabre	K Abdullah	Tamarisk	Impressionist	1:24.81
1998	Mujahid	R Hills	J Dunlop	H Al Maktoum	Auction House	Stravinsky	1:25.31
1999+	Distant Music	M Hills	B Hills	K Abdullah	Brahms	Zentsov Street	1:26.84
2000	Tobougg	C Williams	M Channon	Ahmed Al Maktoum	Noverre	Tempest	1:27.93
2001	Rock Of Gibraltar	M J Kinane	A P O'Brien	Ferguson & Magnier	Landseer	Tendulkar	1:28.70
2002	Tout Seul	S Carson	R JhnsnHoughton	Eden Racing	Tomahawk	Trade Fair	1:23.99
2003	Milk It Mick	D Holland	J Osborne	P J Dixon	Three Valleys	Haafhd	1:25.22
2004	Shamardal	K Darley	M Johnston	Gainsborough Stud	Oratorio	Montgomery's Arch	1:27.16

*Prince Of Dance and Scenic finished in a deadheat in 1988.
+Run on the July Course.

ECLIPSE STAKES-G1

1-1/4 miles, 3-year-olds & up, Sandown Park

FIRST RUN IN 1886. RUN AT KEMPTON PARK IN 1973.

Year	1st (Age)	Jockey	Trainer	Owner	2nd	3rd	Time
1970	Connaught (5)	A Barclay	N Murless	H Joel	Karabas	Nor	2:06
1971	Mill Reef (3)	G Lewis	I Balding	P Mellon	Caro	Welsh Pageant	2:05.4
1972	Brigadier Gerard (4)	J Mercer	W R Hern	Mrs J Hislop	Gold Rod	Home Guard	2:20.2
1973	Scottish Rifle (4)	R Hutchison	J Dunlop	A Struthers	Moulton	Sun Prince	2:12.4
1974	Coup de Feu (5)	Pat Eddery	D Sasse	F Sasse	Ksar	Mount Hagen	2:08.8
1975	Star Appeal (5)	G Starkey	T Grieper	W Zeitelhack	Taros	Royal Manacle	2:06
1976*	Wollow (3)	G Dettori	H Cecil	C d'Alessio	Radetzky	Ann's Pretendre	2:05.4
1977	Artaius (3)	L Piggott	M V O'Brien	Mrs G Getty II	Lucky Wednesday	Arctic Tern	2:05.4
1978	Gunner B (5)	J Mercer	H Cecil	Mrs P Barratt	Balmerino	Radetzky	2:05
1979	Dickens Hill (3)	A Murray	M O'Toole	Mme J Binet	Crimson Beau	Northern Baby	2:06,2
1980	Ela-Mana-Mou (4)	W Carson	W R Hern	S Weinstock	Hello Gorgeous	Gregorian	2:10
1981	Master Willie (4)	P Waldron	H Candy	R Barnett	Vielle	Fingal's Cave	2:07.4
1982	Kalaglow (4)	G Starkey	G Harwood	A Ward	Lobkowiez	Rocamadour	2:08.8
1983	Solford (3)	Pat Eddery	M V O'Brien	R Sangster	Muscatite	Tolomeo	2:06.2
1984	Sadler's Wells (3)	Pat Eddery	M V O'Brien	R Sangster	Time Charter	Morcon	2:04.4
1985	Pebbles (4f)	S Cauthen	C Brittain	Sheikh Mohammed	Rainbow Quest	Bob Back	2:07.21
1986	Dancing Brave (3)	G Starkey	G Harwood	K Abdullah	Triptych	Teleprompter	2:06
1987	Mtoto (4)	M Roberts	A Stewart	Al Maktoum	Reference Point	Triptych	2:04.2
1988	Mtoto (5)	M Roberts	A Stewart	A Al Maktoum	Shady Heights	Triptych	2:06
1989	Nashwan (3)	W Carson	W R Hern	H Al Maktoum	Opening Verse	Indian Skimmer	2:07.2
1990	Elmaamul (3)	W Carson	W R Hern	H Al Maktoum	Terimon	Ile de Chypre	2:04.
1991	Environment Friend(3)	G Duffield	J Fanshawe	W Gredley	Stagecraft	Sanglamore	2:07.6
1992	Kooyonga (4f)	W O'Connor	M Kauntze	M Haga	Opera House	Sapience	2:10.8
1993	Opera House (5)	M J Kinane	M Stoute	Sheikh Mohammed	Misil	Tenby	2:06.25
1994	Ezzoud (5)	W R Swinburn	M Stoute	M Al Maktoum	Bob's Return	Erhaab	2:04.7
1995	Halling (4)	W R Swinburn	S bin Suroor	Godolphin	Singspiel	Red Bishop	2:05.32
1996	Halling (5)	J Reid	S bin Suroor	Godolphin	Bijou d'Inde	Pentire	2:08.05
1997	Pilsudski (5)	M J Kinane	M Stoute	Lord Weinstock	Benny the Dip	Bosra Sham	2:12.51
1998	Daylami (4)	L Dettori	S bin Suroor	Godolphin	Faithful Son	Central Park	2:06.82
1999	Compton Admiral(3)	D Holland	G Butler	E Penser	Xaar	Fantastic Light	2:06.42
2000	Giant's Causeway (3)	G Duffield	A P O'Brien	Mrs J Magnier/M Tabor	Kalanisi	Shiva	2:05.32
2001	Medicean (4)	K Fallon	M Stoute	Cheveley Park Stud	Grandera	Bach	2:04.65
2002	Hawk Wing (3)	M J Kinane	A P O'Brien	Mrs J Magnier	Sholokhov	Equerry	2:13.34
2003	Falbrav (5)	D Holland	L Cumani	Scuderia Rencati	Nayef	Kaieteur	2:05.59
2004	Refuse To Bend (4)	L Dettori	S bin Suroor	Godolphin	Warrsan	Kalaman	2:08.31

*Trepon finished first but was disqualified from purse money.

ENGLISH OAKS-G1

1-1/2 miles, 3-year-old fillies, Epsom

FIRST RUN IN 1779

Year	1st	Jockey	Trainer	Owner	2nd	3rd	Time
1970	Lupe	A. Barclay	N. Murless	Mrs S Joel	State Pension	Arctic Wave	2:41.4
1971	Altesse Royale	G. Lewis	N. Murless	F Hue-Williams	Maina	La Manille	2:36.8

Year	1st	Jockey	Trainer	Owner	2nd	3rd	Time
1972	Ginerva	A Murray	H Price	C St George	Regal Exception	Arkadina	2:39.4
1973	Mysterious	G. Lewis	N. Murless	G Pope Jr	Where You Lead	Aureoletta	2:36.4
1974	Polygamy	P. Eddery	P Walwyn	L Freedman	Furioso	Matuta	2:39.4
1975	Juliette Marny	L Piggott	J. Tree	J Morrison	Val's Girl	Moonlight Night	2:39
1976	Pawneese	Y. Saint-Martin	A. Penna	D Wildenstein	Roses For The Star	African Dancer	2:35.2
1977	Dunfermline	W. Carson	W. R. Hern	The Queen	Freeze The Secret	Vaguely Deb	2:36.4
1978	Fair Salinia	G. Starkey	M. Stoute	S Hanson	Dancing Maid	Suni	2:36.8
1979	Scintillate	Pat Eddery	J. Tree	J Morrison	Bonnie Isle	Britannia's Rule	2:43.6
1980	Bireme	W. Carson	W. R. Hern	R D Hollingsworth	Vielle	The Dancer	2:34.2
1981	Blue Wind	L Piggott	D. K. Weld	Mrs B Firestone	Madam Gay	Leap Liveley	2:40.8
1982	Time Charter	W. Newnes	H Candy	R Barnett	Slightly Dangerous	Last Feather	2:34.2
1983	Sun Princess	W. Carson	W. R. Hern	M Sobell	Acclimatise	New Coins	2:40.8
1984	Circus Plume	L Piggott	J. Dunlop	R McAlpine	Media Luna	Poquito Queen	2:38.8
1985	Oh So Sharp	S. Cauthen	H Cecil	Sheikh Mohammed	Triptych	Dubian	2:41.2
1986	Midway Lady	R. Cochrane	B. Hanbury	H Ranier	Untold	Maysoon	2:35.6
1987	Unite	W. R. Swinburn	M. Stoute	Sheikh Mohammed	Bourbon Girl	Three Tails	2:38
1988	Diminuendo	S. Cauthen	H Cecil	Sheikh Mohammed	Sudden Love	Animatrice	2:35
1989	Snow Bride	S. Cauthen	H Cecil	M Al Maktoum	Roseate Tern	Mamaluna	2:34.2*
1990	Salsabil	W. Carson	J. Dunlop	H Al Maktoum	Game Plan	Knight's Baroness	2:38.6
1991	Jet Ski Lady	C. Roche	J. Bolger	M Al Maktoum	Shamshir	Shadayid	2:37.2
1992	User Friendly	G. Duffield	C. Brittain	W Gredley	All At Sea	Pearl Angel	2:39.6
1993	Intrepidity	M. Roberts	A. Fabre	Sheikh Mohammed	Royal Ballerina	Oakmead	2:34.19
1994	Balanchine	L Dettori	H Ibrahim	Godolphin	Wind In Her Hair	Hawajiss	2:40.37
1995	Moonshell	L Dettori	S. bin Suroor	Godolphin	Dance A Dream	Pure Grain	2:35.44
1996	Lady Carla	Pat Eddery	H Cecil	W. Said	Pricket	Mezzogiorno	2:35.55
1997	Reams Of Verse	K. Fallon	H Cecil	K. Abdullah	Gazelle Royale	Crown Of Light	2:35.59
1998	Shahtoush	M. J. Kinane	A P O'Brien	Nagle & Magnier	Bahr	Midnight Line	2:38.23
1999	Ramruma	K. Fallon	H Cecil	Prince F Salman	Noushkey	Zahrat Dubai	2:38.72
2000	Love Divine	T R Quinn	H Cecil	Lordship Stud	Kalypso Katie	Melikah	2:43.11
2001	Imagine	M J Kinane	A P O'Brien	Magnier & Nagle	Flight Of Fancy	RelishTheThought	2:36.70
2002	Kazzia	L Dettori	S bin Suroor	Godolphin	Quarter Moon	Shadow Dancing	2:44.52
2003	Casual Look	M Dwyer	A Balding	W S Farish III	Yesterday	Summitville	2:38.07
2004	Ouija Board	K Fallon	E Dunlop	Lord Derby	All Too Beautiful	Punctilious	2:35.41

*Aliysa finished first but was disqualified from purse money.

DERBY STAKES (EPSOM DERBY)-G1

1-1/2 miles, 3-year-old colts & fillies, Epsom

FIRST RUN IN 1780. RUN AT 1 MILE 1780-1784.

Run at Newmarket (July Course) as the New Derby 1915-1918 and 1940-1945.

Year	1st	Jockey	Trainer	Owner	2nd	3rd	Time
1780	Diomed	S Arnull	R Teasel	Sir C Bunbury	Boudrow	Spitfire	
1781	Young Eclipse	C Hindley	D O'Kelly		Crop	Prince Of Orange	
1782	Assassin	S Arnull	F Neale	Earl of Egremont	Sweet Robin	Fortunio	
1783	Saltram	C Hindley	F Neale	J Parker	Dungannon	Parlington	
1784	Serjeant	J Arnull	D O Kelly	Carlo Khan	Dancer	-	
1785	Aimwell	C Hindley	J Pratt	Earl of Clermont	Grantham	Verjuice	
1786	Noble	J White	F Neale	T Panton	Meteor	Claret	
1787	Sir Peter Teazle	S Arnull	Saunders	Earl of Derby	Gunpowder	Bustler	
1788	Sir Thomas	W South	F Neale	Prince of Wales	Aurelius	Feenow	
1789	Skyscraper	S Chifney Sr	M Stephenson	Duke of Bedford	Sir George	Skylark	
1790	Rhadamanthus	J Arnull	J Pratt	Lord Grosvenor	Asparagus	Lee Boo	
1791	Eager	M Stephenson	M Stephenson	Duke of Bedford	Vermin	Proteus	
1792	John Bull	F Buckle	J Pratt	Lord Grosvenor	Speculator	Bustard	
1793	Waxy	W Clift	R Robson	Sir F Poole	Gohanna	Triptolemus	
1794	Daedalus	F Buckle	J Pratt	Lord Grosvenor	Ragged Jack	Leon	
1795	Spread Eagle	A Wheatley	R Prince	Sir F Standish	Caustic	Pelter	
1796	Didelot	J Arnull	R Prince	Sir F Standish	Stickler	Leviathan	
1797	c by Fidget	J Singleton Jr	M Stephenson	Duke of Bedford	Esculus	Plaistow	
1798	Sir Harry	S Arnull	F Neale	J Cookson	Telegraph	Young Spear	
1799	Archduke	J Arnull	R Prince	Sir F Standish	Gislebert	Eagle	
1800	Champion	W Clift	T Perren	C Wilson	Tag	Mystery	
1801	Eleanor (f)	J Saunders	J Frost	Sir C Bunbury	by Fidget	Remnant	
1802	Tyrant	F Buckle	R Robson	Duke of Grafton	by Young Eclipse	Orlando	
1803	Ditto	W Clift	J Lonsdale	Sir H Williamson	Sir Oliver	c by Sir Peter Teazle	
1804	Hannibal	W Arnull	F Neale	Earl of Egremont	Pavilion	Hippocampus	
1805	Cardinal Beaufort	D Fitzpatrick	D Boyce	Earl of Egremont	Plantagenet	Goth	
1806	Paris	J Shepherd	R Prince	Baron Foley	Trafalgar	Hector	
1807	Election	J Arnull	D Boyce	Earl of Egremont	Giles Scroggins	Coriolanus	
1808	Pan	F Collinson	J Lonsdale	Sir H Williamson	Vandyke	Chester	
1809	Pope	T Goodisson	R Robson	Duke of Grafton	Wizard	Salvator	

Year	1st	Jockey	Trainer	Owner	2nd	3rd	Time
1810	Whalebone	W Clift	R Robson	Duke of Grafton	The Dandy	Eccleston	
1811*	Phantom	F Buckle	J Edwards	Sir J Shelley	Magic	-	
1812	Octavius	W Arnull	D Boyce	R Ladbroke	Sweep	Comus	
1813	Smolensko	T Goodisson	Crouch	Sir C Bunbury	Caterpillar	Illusion	
1814*	Blucher	W Arnull	D Boyce	Baron Stawell	Perchance	-	
1815	Whisker	T Goodisson	R Robson	Duke of Grafton	Raphael	Busto	
1816	Prince Leopold	W Wheatley	W Butler	Duke of York	Nectar	Pandour	
1817*	Azor	J Robinson	R Robson	J Payne Young	Wizard	-	
1818	Sam	S Chifney Jr	T Perren	T Thornhill	Raby	Prince Paul	
1819*	Tiresias	W Clift	R Prince	Duke of Portland	Sultan	-	
1820	Sailor	S Chifney Jr	W Chifney	T Thornhill	Abjer	Tiger	
1821	Gustavus	S Day	Crouch	J Hunter	Reginald	Sir Huldibrand	
1822	Moses	T Goodisson	W Butler	Duke of York	Figaro	Hampden	
1823*	Emilius	F Buckle	R Robson	J Udney	Tancred	-	
1824*	Cedric	J Robinson	J Edwards	Sir J Shelley	Osmond	-	
1825	Middleton	J Robinson	J Edwards	Earl of Jersey	Rufus	Hogarth	
1826*	Lap-Dog	G Dockeray	Bird	Earl of Egremont	Shakspeare	-	
1827	Mameluke	J Robinson	J Edwards	Earl of Jersey	Glenartney	Edmund	
1828*	Cadland	J Robinson	D Boyce	Duke of Rutland	The Colonel	-	
1829*	Frederick	J Forth	J Forth	G Gratwicke	The Exquisite	-	
1830	Priam	S Day	W Chifney	W Chifney	Little Red Rover	Mahmoud	
1831	Spaniel	W Wheatley	J Rogers	Viscount Lowther	Riddlesworth	Incubus	
1832	St Giles	W Scott	J Webb	R Ridsdale	Perion	Trustee	
1833	Dangerous	J Chapple	I Sadler	I Sadler	Connoisseur	Revenge	
1834	Plenipotentiary	P Conolly	G Payne	S Batson	Shilelagh	Glencoe	
1835*	Mundig	W Scott	J Scott	J Bowes	Ascot	-	
1836*	Bay Middleton	J Robinson	J Edwards	Earl of Jersey	Galdiator	-	
1837*	Phosphorus	G Edwards	J Doe	Baron Berner	Caravan	-	
1838	Amato	J Chapple	R Sherwood	Sir G Heathcote	Ion	Grey Momus	
1839*	Bloomsbury	S Templeman	W Ridsdale	W Ridsdale	Deception	-	
1840	Little Wonder	W Macdonald	J Forth	D Robertson	Launcelot	Discord	
1841*	Coronation	P Conolly	Painter	A Rawlinson	Van Amburgh	-	
1842*	Attila	W Scott	J Scott	G Anson	Robert De Gorham	-	
1843*	Cotherstone	W Scott	J Scott	J Bowes	Gorhambury	-	
1844	Orlando	N Flatman	W Cooper	J Peel	Ionian	Bay Momus	
1845	The Merry Monarch	F Bell	J Forth	G Gratwicke	Annandale	Old England	
1846	Pyrrhus The First	S Day	J Day	J Gully	Sir Tatton Sykes	Brocardo	2:55
1847	Cossack	S Templeman	J Day Jr	T H Pedley	War Eagle	Van Tromp	2:52
1848	Surplice	S Templeman	J Kent	Viscount Clifden	Springy Jack	Shylock	2:48
1849	The Flying Dutchman	C Marlow	J Fobert	Earl of Eglinton	Hotspur	Tadmor	3:00
1850	Voltigeur	J Marson	R Hill	Earl of Zetland	Pitsford	Clincher	2:50
1851	Teddington	J Marson	A Taylor Sr	Sir J Hawley	Marlborough Buck	Neasham	2:51
1852	Daniel O'Rourke	F Butler	J Scott	J Bowes	Barbarian Chief	Baron Nicholson	3:02
1853	West Australian	F Butler	J Scott	J Bowes	Sittingbourne	Cineas	2:55
1854	Andover	A Day	J Day Jr	J Gully	King Tom	The Hermit	2:52
1855	Wild Dayrell	R Sherwood	J Rickaby	F Popham	Kingstown	Lord Of The Isles	2:54
1856	Ellington	T Aldcroft	T Dawson	O Harcourt	Yellow Jack	Cannobie	3:04
1857	Blink Bonny (f)	J Charlton	W I'Anson	W I'Anson	Black Tommy	Adamas	2:45
1858	Beadsman	J Wells	G Manning	Sir J Hawley	Toxophilite	The Hadji	2:54
1859	Musjid	J Wells	G Manning	Sir J Hawley	Marionette	Trumpeter	2:59
1860	Thormanby	H Custance	M Dawson	J Merry	The Wizard	Horror	2:55
1861	Kettledrum	R Bullock	G Oates	C Towneley	Dundee	Diophantus	2:45
1862	Caractacus	J Parsons	R Smith	C Snewing	The Marquis	Buckstone	2:45.5
1863	Macaroni	T Chaloner	J Godding	R Naylor	Lord Clifden	Rapid Rhone	2:50.5
1864	Blair Athol	J Snowden	W I'Anson	W I'Anson	General Peel	Scottish Chief	2:43
1865	Galdiateur	H Grimshaw	T Jennings	Comte Fde Lagrange	Christmas Carol	Eltham	2:56
1866	Lord Lyon	H Custance	J Dover	R Sutton	Savernake	Rustic	2:50
1867	Hermit	J Daley	G Bloss	H Chaplin	Marksman	Vauban	2:52
1868	Blue Gown	J Wells	J Porter	Sir J Hawley	King Alfred	Speculum	2:43.5
1869	Pretender	J Osborne	T Dawson	J Johnstone	Pero Gomez	The Drummer	2:52.5
1870	Kingcraft	T French	M Dawson	Viscount Falmouth	Palmerston	Muster	2:45
1871	Favonius	T French	J Hayhoe	M de Rothschild	Albert Victor	King Of The Forest	2:50
1872	Cremorne	C Maidment	W Gilbert	H Savile	Pell Mell	Queens Messenger	2:45.5
1873	Doncaster	F Webb	R Peck	J Merry	Gang Forward	Kaiser	2:50
1874	George Frederick	H Custance	T Leader	W Cartwright	Couronne de Fer	Atlantic	2:46
1875	Galopin	J Morris	J Dawson	Prince G Batthyany	Claremont	Remorse	2:48
1876	Kisber	C Maidment	J Hayhoe	A Baltazzi	Forerunner	Julius Caesar	2:44
1877	Silvio	F Archer	M Dawson	Viscount Falmouth	Glen Arthur	Rob Roy	2:50
1878	Sefton	H Constable	A Taylor Sr	W S Crawfurd	Insulaire	Childeric	2:56
1879	Sir Bevys	G Fordham	J Hayhoe	L N de Rothschild	Palmbearer	Visconti	3:02
1880	Bend Or	F Archer	R Peck	Duke of Westminster	Robert The Devil	Mask	2:46
1881	Iroquois	F Archer	J Pincus	P Lorillard	Peregrine	Town Moor	2:50
1882	Shotover (f)	T Cannon	J Porter	Duke of Westminster	Quicklime	Sachem	2:45.6

Year	1st	Jockey	Trainer	Owner	2nd	3rd	Time
1883	St Blaise	C Wood	J Porter	Sir F Johnstone	Highland Chief	Galliard	2:48.4
1884^	Harvester	S Loates	J Jewitt	Sir J Willoughby			
1884^	St Gatien	C Wood	R Sherwood	J Hammond	–	Queen	2:46.2
1885	Melton	F Archer	M Dawson	Baron Hastings	Paradox	Royal Hampton	2:44.2
1886	Ormonde	F Archer	J Porter	Duke of Westminster	The Bard	St Mirin	2:45.6
1887	Merry Hampton	J Watts	M Gurry	G Baird	The Baron	Martley	2:43
1888	Ayrshire	F Barrett	G Dawson	Duke of Portland	Crowberry	Van Dieman's Land	2:43
1889	Donovan	T Loates	G Dawson	Duke of Portland	Miguel	El Dorado	2:44.4
1890	Sainfoin	J Watts	J Porter	Sir J Miller	Le Nord Orwell	Sir J Miller	2:49.8
1891	Common	G Barrett	J Porter	Sir F Johnstone	Gouverneur	Martenhurst	2:56.8
1892	Sir Hugo	F Allsopp	T Wadlow	Earl of Bradford	La Fleche	Bucentaure	2:44
1893	Isinglass	T Loates	J Jewitt	H McCalmont	Ravensbury	Raeburn	2:43
1894	Ladas	J Watts	M Dawson	Earl of Roseberry	Matchbox	Reminder	2:45.8
1895	Sir Visto	S Loates	M Dawson	Earl of Roseberry	Curzon	Kirkconnel	2:43.4
1896	Persimmon	J Watts	R Marsh	Prince of Wales	St Frusquin	Earwig	2:42
1897	Galtee More	C Wood	S Darling	J Gubbins	Velasquez	History	2:44
1898	Jeddah	O Madden	R Marsh	J Larnach	Batt	Dunlop	2:47
1899	Flying Fox	M Cannon	J Porter	Duke of Westminster	Damocles	Innocence	2:42.8
1900	Diamond Jubilee	H Jones	R Marsh	Prince of Wales	Simon Dale	Disguise	2:42
1901	Volodyovski	L Reiff	J Huggins	W C Whitney	William The Third	Veronese	2:40.8
1902	Ard Patrick	S Martin	S Darling	J Gubbins	Rising Glass	Friar Tuck	2:42.2
1903	Rock Sand	D Maher	G Blackwell	Sir J Miller	Vinicius	Flotsam	2:42.8
1904	St Amant	K Cannon	A Hayhoe	L de Rothschild	John O'Gaunt	St Denis	2:45.4
1905	Cicero	D Maher	P Peck	Earl of Roseberry	Jardy	Signorino	2:39.6
1906	Spearmint	D Maher	P Gilpin	E Loder	Picton	Troutbeck	2:36.8
1907	Orby	J Reiff	F MacCabe	R Croker	Wool Winder	Slieve Gallion	2:44
1908	Signorinetta (f)	B Bullock	O Ginistrelli	O Ginistrelli	Prime	Llangwm	2:39.8
1909	Minoru	H Jones	R Marsh	King Edward VII	Louviers	William The Fourth	2:42.4
1910	Lemberg	B Dillon	A Taylor	A Cox	Greenback	Charles O'Malley	2:35.2
1911	Sunstar	G Stern	C Morton	J B Joel	Stedfast	Royal Tender	2:36.8
1912	Tagalie (f)	J Reiff	D Waugh	W Raphael	Jaeger	Tracery	2:38.8
1913+	Aboyeur	E Piper	T Lewis	A Cunliffe	Louvois	Great Sport	2:37.6
1914	Durbar	M MacGee	T Murphy	H Duryea	Hapsburg	Peter The Hermit	2:38.4
1915	Pommern	S Donoghue	C Peck	S B Joel	Let Fly	Rossendale	2:32.6
1916	Fifinella (f)	J Childs	D Dawson	Sir E Hulton	Kwang-Su	Nassovian	2:36.6
1917	Gay Crusader	S Donoghue	A Taylor	A Cox	Dansellon	Dark Legend	2:40.6
1918	Gainsborough	J Childs	A Taylor	Lady J Douglas	Blink	Treclare	2:33.2
1919	Grand Parade	F Templeman	F Barling	Baron Glanely	Buchan	Paper Money	2:35.8
1920	Spion Kop	F O'Neill	P Gilpin	G Loder	Archaic	Orpheus	2:34.8
1921	Humorist	S Donoghue	C Morton	J B Joel	Craig An Eran	Lemonora	2:36.2
1922	Captain Cuttle	S Donoghue	F Darling	Baron Woolavington	Tamar	Craigangower	2:34.6
1923	Papyrus	S Donoghue	B Jarvis	B Irish	Pharos	Parth	2:38
1924	Sansovino	T Weston	G Lambton	Earl of Derby	St Germans	Hurstwood	2:46.6
1925	Manna	S Donoghue	J Maher	H Morriss	Zionist	The Sirdar	2:40.6
1926	Coronach	J Childs	F Darling	Baron Woolavington	Lancegaye	Colorado	2:47.8
1927	Call Boy	C Elliott	J Watts	F Curzon	Hot Night	Shian Mor	2:34.4
1928	Felstead	H Wragg	O Bell	Sir H Cunliffe-Owen	Flamingo	Black Watch	2:34.4
1929	Trigo	J Marshall	D Dawson	W Barnett	Walter Gay	Brienz	2:36.4
1930	Blenheim	H Wragg	D Dawson	Aga Khan	Iliad	Diolite	2:38.2
1931	Cameronian	F Fox	F Darling	J A Dewar	Orpen	Sandwich	2:36.6
1932	April The Fifth	F Lane	G Whitelaw	T Walls	Dastur	Miracle	2:43
1933	Hyperion	T Weston	G Lambton	Earl of Derby	King Salmon	Statesman	2:34
1934	Windsor Lad	C Smirke	M Marsh	Maharaja of Rajpipla	Easton	Colombo	2:34
1935	Bahram	F Fox	F Butters	Aga Khan	Robin Goodfellow	Field Trial	2:36
1936	Mahmoud	C Smirke	F Butters	Aga Khan	Taj Akbar	Thankerton	2:33.8
1937	Mid-Day Sun	M Beary	F Butters	L Miller	Sandsprite	Le Grand Duc	2:37.6
1938	Bois Roussel	C Elliott	F Darling	P Beatty	Scottish Union	Pasch	2:39.2
1939	Blue Peter	E Smith	J Jarvis	Earl of Roseberry	Fox Cub	Heliopolis	2:36.8
1940	Pont I Eveque	S Wragg	F Darling	F Darling	Turkhan	Lighthouse	2:30.8
1941	Owen Tudor	B Nevett	F Darling	C Macdonald-Buchanan	Morogoro	Firoze Din	2:32
1942	Watling Street	H Wragg	W Earl	Earl of Derby	Hyperides	Ujiji	2:29.6
1943	Straight Deal	T Carey	W Nightingall	D Paget	Umiddad	Nasrullah	2:30.4
1944	Ocean Swell	B Nevett	J Jarvis	Earl of Roseberry	Tehran	Happy Landing	2:31
1945	Dante	B Nevett	M Peacock	Sir E Ohlson	Midas	Court Martial	2:26.6
1946	Airborne	T Lowrey	D Perryman	J Ferguson	Gulf Stream	Radiotherapy	2:44.6
1947	Pearl Diver	G Bridgland	P Carter	Baron G de Waldner	Migoli	Sayajirao	2:38.4
1948	My Love	R Johnstone	R Carver	Aga Khan	Royal Drake	Noor	2:40
1949	Nimbus	C Elliott	G Colling	M Glenister	Amour Drake	Swallow Tail	2:42
1950	Galcador	R Johnstone	C Semblat	M Boussac	Prince Simon	Double Eclipse	2:36.8
1951	Arctic Prince	C Spares	W Stephenson	J McGrath	Sybil s Nephew	Signal Box	2:39.4
1952	Tulyar	C Smirke	M Marsh	Aga Khan	Gay Time	Faubourg	2:36.4
1953	Pinza	G Richards	N Bertie	Sir V Sassoon	Aureole	Pink Horse	2:35.6
1954	Never Say Die	L Piggott	J Lawson	R S Clarke	Arabian Night	Darius	2:35.8
1955	Phil Drake	F Palmer	F Mathet	S Volterra	Panaslipper	Acropolis	2:39.8

Year	1st	Jockey	Trainer	Owner	2nd	3rd	Time
1956	Lavandin	R Johnstone	A Head	P Wertheimer	Montaval	Roistar	2:36.4
1957	Crepello	L Piggott	N Murless	Sir V Sassoon	Ballymoss	Pipe Of Peace	2:35.4
1958	Hard Ridden	C Smirke	J M Rogers	Sir V Sassoon	Paddy's Point	Nagani	2:41.2
1959	Parthia	H Carr	C Boyd-Rochfort	Sir H de Trafford	Fidalgo	Shantung	2:36
1960	St Paddy	L Piggott	N Murless	Sir V Sassoon	Alcaeus	Kythnos	2:35.6
1961	Psidium	R Poincelet	H Wragg	E Plesch	Dicta Drake	Pardao	2:36.4
1962	Larkspur	N Sellwood	M V O'Brien	R Guest	Arcor	Le Cantilien	2:37.6
1963	Relko	Y Saint-Martin	F Mathet	F Dupre	Merchant Venturer	Ragusa	2:39.4
1964	Santa Claus	A Breasley	J M Rogers	J Ismay	Indiana	Dilettante	2:41.98
1965	Sea-Bird	P Glennon	E Pollet	J Ternynck	Meadow Court	I Say	2:38.41
1966	Charlottown	A Breasley	G Smyth	Lady Z Wernher	Pretendre	Black Prince	2:37.63
1967	Royal Palace	G Moore	N Murless	J Joel	Ribocco	Dart Board	2:38.36
1968	Sir Ivor	L Piggott	M V O'Brien	R Guest	Connaught	Mount Athos	2:38.73
1969	Blakeney	E Johnson	A Budgett	A Budgett	Shoemaker	Prince Regent	2:40.3
1970	Nijinsky II	L Piggott	M V O'Brien	C Engelhard	Gyr	Stintino	2:34.68
1971	Mill Reef	G Lewis	I Balding	P Mellon	LInden Tree	Irish Ball	2:37.14
1972	Roberto	L Piggott	M V O'Brien	J Galbreath	Rheingold	Pentland Firth	2:36.09
1973	Morston	E Hide	A Budgett	A Budgett	Cavo Doro	Freefoot	2:35.92
1974	Snow Knight	B Taylor	P Nelson	S Phillips	Imperial Prince	Giacometti	2:35.04
1975	Grundy	Pat Eddery	P Walwyn	C Vittadini	Nobiliary	Hunza Dancer	2:35.34
1976	Empery	L Piggott	M Zilber	N B Hunt	Relkino	Oats	2:35.69
1977	The Minstrel	L Piggott	M V O'Brien	R Sangster	Hot Grove	Blushing Groom	2:36.44
1978	Shirley Heights	G Starkey	J Dunlop	Earl of Halifax	Hawaiian Sound	Remainder Man	2:35.3
1979	Troy	W Carson	W R Hern	M Sobell	Dickens Hill	Northern Baby	2:36.59
1980	Henbit	W Carson	W R Hern	E Plesch	Master Willie	Rankin	2:34.77
1981	Shergar	W R Swinburn	M Stoute	Aga Khan	Glint Of Gold	Scintillating Air	2:44.21
1982	Golden Fleece	Pat Eddery	M V O'Brien	R Sangster	Touching Wood	Silver Hawk	2:34.27
1983	Teenoso	L Piggott	G Wragg	E Moller	Carlingford Castle	Shearwalk	2:49.07
1984	Secreto	C Roche	D V O'Brien	L Miglietti	El Gran Senor	Mighty Flutter	2:39.12
1985	Slip Anchor	S Cauthen	H Cecil	H de Walden	Law Society	Damister	2:36.23
1986	Shahrastani	W R Swinburn	M Stoute	Aga Khan	Dancing Brave	Mashkour	2:37.13
1987	Reference Point	S Cauthen	H Cecil	L Freedman	Most Welcome	Bellotto	2:33.9
1988	Kahyasi	R Cochrane	L Cumani	Aga Khan	Glacial Storm	Doyoun	2:33.84
1989	Nashwan	W Carson	W R Hern	H Al Maktoum	Terimon	Cacoethes	2:34.9
1990	Quest For Fame	Pat Eddery	R Charlton	K Abdullah	Blue Stag	Elmaamul	2:37.26
1991	Generous	A Munro	P Cole	Prince F Salman	Marju	Star Of Gdansk	2:34
1992	Dr Devious	J Reid	P Chapple-Hyam	S Craig	St. Jovite	Silver Wisp	2:36.19
1993	Commander In Chief	M J Kinane	H Cecil	K Abdullah	Blue Judge	Blues Traveller	2:34.51
1994	Erhaab	W Carson	J Dunlop	H Al Maktoum	King's Theatre	Colonel Collins	2:34.16
1995	Lammtarra	W R Swinburn	S bin Suroor	S M Al Maktoum	Tamure	Presenting	2:32.31
1996	Shaamit	M Hills	W Haggas	K A Dasman	Dushyantor	Shantou	2:35.05
1997	Benny The Dip	W Ryan	J Gosden	L Knight	Silver Patriarch	Romanov	2:35.77
1998	High-Rise	O Peslier	L Cumani	M O Al Maktoum	City Honours	Border Arrow	2:33.88
1999	Oath	K Fallon	H Cecil	The Thoroughbred Corp	Daliapour	Beat All	2:37.43
2000	Sinndar	J P Murtagh	J Oxx	HH Aga Khan	Sakhee	Beat Hollow	2:36.75
2001	Galileo	M J Kinane	A P O'Brien	Magnier & Tabor	Golan	Tobougg	2:33.27
2002	High Chaparral	J P Murtagh	A P O'Brien	Tabor & Magnier	Hawk Wing	Moon Ballad	2:39.45
2003	Kris Kin	K Fallon	M R Stoute	S Suhail	The Great Gatsby	Alamshar	2:33.35
2004	North Light	K Fallon	M R Stoute	Ballymacoll Stud	Rule Of Law	Let The Lion Roar	2:33.72

*No horse was officially placed third.

^Harvester and St Gatien finished in a deadheat in 1884.

+Craganour finished first but was disqualified and placed last.

FILLIES' MILE-G1

1m, 2-year-old fillies, Ascot

FIRST RUN IN 1973.

Run as the Green Shield Stakes in 1973. Run as the Argos Stakes 1975–1977.

Year	1st	Jockey	Trainer	Owner	2nd	3rd	Time
1973	Escorial	L Piggott	I Balding	The Queen	Evening Venture	Gaily	1:51.37
1974	RACE NOT RUN						
1975	Icing	C Roche	P Prendergast	Lady Iveagh	Bedfellow	Gliding	1:46.6
1976	Miss Pinkie	L Piggott	N Murless	H J Joel	Dunfermline	Triple First	1:45.31
1977	Cherry Hinton	L Piggott	H Wragg	R B Moller	Tartan Pimpernel	Watch Out	1:42.52
1978	Formulate	J Mercer	H Cecil	Mrs D Butler	Odoon	Rimosa's Pet	1:43.61
1979	Quick As Lightning	W Carson	J Dunlop	O M Phipps	Viollo	Sharp Castan	1:43.17
1980	Leap Lively	J Matthias	I Balding	P Mellon	Exclusively Raised	Fiesta Fun	1:41.80
1981	Height Of Fashion	J Mercer	W R Hern	The Queen	Stratospheric	Zinzara	1:44.72
1982	Acclimatise	A Murray	B Hobbs	J Hembro	Dancing Meg	Alligatrix	1:47.28
1983	Nepula	B Crossley	G Huffer	A Al Qemias	Nonesuch Bay	Circus Plume	1:44.68
1984	Oh So Sharp	L Piggott	H Cecil	Shaikh Mohammed	Helen Street	Morning Devotion	1:42.44
1985	Untold	W R Swinburn	M Stoute	R H Cowell	Moonlight Lady	Sue Grundy	1:40.92

Year	1st	Jockey	Trainer	Owner	2nd	3rd	Time
1986	Invited Guest	S Cauthen	R Armstrong	Kinderhill Corp	Mountain Memory	Shining Water	1:43.47
1987	Diminuendo	S Cauthen	H Cecil	Sheikh Mohammed	Haiati	Ashayor	1:43.10
1988	Tessla	Pat Eddery	H Cecil	C St George	Pick Of The Pops	Rain Burst	1:43.96
1989	Silk Slippers	M Hills	B Hills	R Sangster	Moon Cactus	Fujaiyrah	1:42.49
1990	Shamshir	L Dettori	L Cumani	Shaikh Mohammed	Safa	Atlantic Flyer	1:43.27
1991	Midnight Air	Pat Eddery	P Cole	C Wright	Culture Vulture	Mystery Play	1:46.11
1992	Ivanka	M Roberts	C Brittain	A Saeed	Ajfan	Iviza	1:46.65
1993	Fairy Heights	C Asmussen	N Callaghan	F Golding	Dance To The Top	Kissing Cousin	1:44.44
1994	Aqaarid	W Carson	J Dunlop	H Al Maktoum	Jural	Snowtown	1:44.70
1995	Bosra Sham	Pat Eddery	H Cecil	W Said	Bint Shadayid	Matiya	1:43.13
1996	Reams Of Verse	M J Kinane	H Cecil	K Abdullah	Khassah	Sleepytime	1:44.32
1997	Glorosia	L Dettori	L Cumani	R H Smith	Jibe	Exclusive	1:42.31
1998	Sunspangled	M J Kinane	A O'Brien	Tabor & Magnier	Calando	Edabiya	1:44.79
1999	Teggiano	L Dettori	C Brittain	A S Bul Hab	Britannia	My Hansel	1:49.69
2000	Crystal Music	L Dettori	J Gosden	A Lloyd-Webber	Summer Symphony	Hotelgenie Dot Com	1:44.44
2001	Gossamer	J P Spencer	L Cumani	G W Leigh	Maryinsky	Esloob	1:46.40
2002	Soviet Song	O Urbina	J Fanshawe	Elite Racing Club	Casual Look	ReachForTheMoon	1:42.32
2003	Red Bloom	K Fallon	M R Stoute	Cheveley Park Stud	Sundrop	Punctilious	1:40.81
2004	Playful Act	J Fortune	J Gosden	Sangster Family	Maids Causeway	Dash To The Top	1:42.22

JUDDMONTE INTERNATIONAL STAKES-G1

1 mile, 2 furlongs, 85 yards, 3-year-olds & up, York

FIRST RUN IN 1972.

Run as the Benson & Hedges Gold Cup through 1985.
Matchmaker International 1986-7. International Stakes in 1988.

Year	1st (age)	Jockey	Trainer	Owner	2nd	3rd	Time
1972	Roberto (3)	B Baeza	M V O'Brien	J Galbreath	Brigadier Gerard	Gold Rod	2:07.0
1973	Moulton (4)	G Lewis	H Wragg	R Moller	Scottish Rifle	Rheingold	2:20.4
1974	Dahlia (4f)	L Piggott	M Zilber	N B Hunt	Imperial Prince	Snow Knight	2:09.6
1975	Dahlia (5f)	L Piggott	M Zilber	N B Hunt	Card King	Star Appeal	2:10.8
1976	Wollow (3)	G Dettori	H Cecil	C d'Alessio	Crow	Patch	2:11.6
1977	Relkino (4)	W Carson	W R Hern	Lady Beaverbrook	Artaius	Orange Bay	2:09.2
1978	Hawaiian Sound (3)	L Piggott	B Hills	R Sangster	Gunner B	Jellaby	2:09.8
1979	Troy (3)	W Carson	W R Hern	M Sobell	Crimson Beau	Lyphard's Wish	2:13.4
1980	Master Willie (3)	P Waldron	H Candy	W Barnett	Cairn Rouge	Cracaval	2:13.2
1981	Beldale Flutter (3)	Pat Eddery	M Jarvis	M Kelly	Kirtling	Master Willie	2:13.2
1982	Assert (3)	Pat Eddery	D V O'Brien	R Sangster	Norwick	Amyndas	2:09.0
1983	Caerleon (3)	Pat Eddery	M V O'Brien	R Sangster	Hot Touch	John French	2:16.2
1984	Cormorant Wood(4)	S Cauthen	B Hills	R McAlpine	Tolomeo	Chief Singer	2:09.8
1985	Commanche Run (4)	L Piggott	L Cumani	I Allan	Oh So Sharp	Triptych	2:18.6
1986	Shardari (4)	W R Swinburn	M Stoute	Aga Khan	Triptych	Damister	2:08.2
1987	Triptych (5f)	S Cauthen	P-L Biancone	A Clore	Ascot Knight	Sir Harry Lewis	2:15.4
1988	Shady Heights (4)	W Carson	R Armstrong	G Tong	Indian Skimmer	Persian Heights	2:06.2
1989	Ile de Chypre (4)	A Clark	G Harwood	G Christodoulou	Cacoethes	Shady Heights	2:06.8
1990	In The Groove (3f)	S Cauthen	D Elsworth	B Cooper	Elmaamul	Batshoof	2:08.6
1991	Terimon (5)	M Roberts	C Brittain	Lady Beaverbrook	Quest For Fame	Stagecraft	2:16
1992	Rodrigo de Triano(3)	L Piggott	P Chapple-Hyam	R Sangster	All At Sea	Seattle Rhyme	2:07
1993	Ezzoud (4)	W R Swinburn	M Stoute	M Al Maktoum	Sabrehill	Spartan Shareef	2:12.16
1994	Ezzoud (5)	W R Swinburn	M Stoute	M Al Maktoum	Muhtarram	King's Theatre	2:08.85
1995	Halling (4)	W R Swinburn	S bin Suroor	Godolphin	Bahri	Annus Mirabilis	2:06.42
1996	Halling (5)	L Dettori	S bin Suroor	Godolphin	First Island	Bijou d'Inde	2:06.88
1997	Singspiel (5)	L Dettori	M Stoute	Sheikh Mohammed	Desert King	Benny the Dip	2:12.1
1998	One So Wonderful(4)	Pat Eddery	L Cumani	Helena Springfield Ltd	Faithful Son	Chester House	2:06.46
1999	Royal Anthem (4)	G Stevens	H Cecil	Thoroughbred Corp	Greek Dance	Chester House	2:06.91
2000	Giant's Causeway (3)	M J Kinane	A P O'Brien	Mrs J Magnier/M Tabor	Kalanisi	Lear Spear	2:09.13
2001	Sakhee (4)	L Dettori	S bin Suroor	Godolphin	Grandera	Medicean	2:08.27
2002	Nayef (4)	R Hills	M Tregoning	H Al Maktoum	Golan	Noverre	2:08.74
2003	Falbrav (5)	D Holland	L Cumani	Scuderia Rencati	Magistretti	Nayef	2:06.84
2004	Sulamani (5)	L Dettori	S bin Suroor	Godolphin	Norse Dancer	Bago	2:11.81

KING GEORGE VI AND QUEEN ELIZABETH DIAMOND STAKES-G1

1-1/2 miles, 3-year-olds & up, Ascot

First run in 1951.

Year	1st (Age)	Jockey	Trainer	Owner	2nd	3rd	Time
1954	Aureole (4)	E Smith	C Boyd-Rochfort	The Queen	Vamos	Darius	2:44
1955	Vimy (3)	R Poincelet	A Head	P Wertheimer	Acropolis	Elopement	2:33.6
1956	Ribot (4)	E Camici	U Penco	Marchese Incisa	High Veldt	Todrai	2:40.24
1957	Montaval (4)	F Palmer	G Bridgland	R Strassburger	Al Mabsoot	Tribord	2:41.02
1958	Ballymoss (4)	A Breasley	M V O'Brien	J McShain	Almeria	Doutelle	2:36.33

Year	1st (Age)	Jockey	Trainer	Owner	2nd	3rd	Time
1959	Alcide (4)	W Carr	C Boyd-Rochfort	H de Trafford	Gladness	Balbo	2:31.39
1960	Aggressor (5)	J Lindley	J Gosden	H Wernher	Petite Etoile	Kythnos	2:35.21
1961	Right Royal (3)	R Poincelet	E Pollet	Mme E Couturie	St Paddy	Rockavon	2:40.34
1962	Match (4)	Y Saint-Martin	F Mathet	F Dupre	Aurelius	Arctic Storm	2:32.02
1963	Ragusa (3)	G Bougoure	P Prendergast	J Mullion	Miralgo	Tarqogan	2:33.8
1964	Nasram (4)	W Pyers	E Fellows	Mrs H Jackson	Santa Claus	Royal Avenue	2:33.15
1965	Meadow Court (3f)	L Piggott	P Prendergast	G Bell	Soderini	Oncidium	2:33.27
1966	Aunt Edith (4f)	L Piggott	N Murless	J Hornung	Sodium	Prominer	2:35.06
1967	Busted (4)	G Moore	N Murless	S Joel	Salvo	Ribocco	2:33.64
1968	Royal Palace (4)	A Barclay	N Murless	H Joel	Felicio	Topyo	2:33.22
1969	Park Top (5f)	L Piggott	B van Cutsem	Duke of Devonshire	Crozier	Hogarth	2:32.46
1970	Nijinsky II (3)	L Piggott	M V O'Brien	C Engelhard	Blakeney	Crepellana	2:36.16
1971	Mill Reef (3)	G Lewis	I Balding	P Mellon	Ortis	Acclimitization	2:32.56
1972	Brigadier Gerard (4)	J Mercer	W R Hern	Mrs J Hislop	Parnell	Riverman	2:32.91
1973	Dahlia (3f)	W Pyers	M Zilber	N B Hunt	Rheingold	Our Mirage	2:30.43
1974	Dahlia (4f)	L Piggott	M Zilber	N B Hunt	Highclere	Dankaro	2:33.03
1975	Grundy (3)	Pat Eddery	P Walwyn	C Vittadini	Bustino	Dahlia	2:26.98
1976	Pawneese (3f)	Y Saint-Martin	A Penna	D Wildenstein	Bruni	Orange Bay	2:29.36
1977	The Minstrel (3)	L Piggott	M V O'Brien	R Sangster	Orange Bay	Exceller	2:30.48
1978	Ile de Bourbon (3)	J Reid	J F Houghton	D McCall	Hawaiian Sound	Montcontour	2:30.53
1979	Troy (3)	W Carson	W R Hern	M Sobell	Gay Mecene	Ela-Mana-Mou	2:33.75
1980	Ela-Mana-Mou (4)	W Carson	W R Hern	S Weinstock	Mrs Penny	Gregorian	2:35.39
1981	Shergar (3)	W R Swinburn	M Stoute	Aga Khan	Madam Gay	Fingals Cave	2:35.4
1982	Kalaglow (4)	G Starkey	G Harwood	A Ward	Assert	Glint Of Gold	2:31.58
1983	Time Charter (4f)	J Mercer	H Candy	R Barnett	Diamond Shoal	Sun Princess	2:30.78
1984	Teenoso (4)	L Piggott	G Wragg	E Moller	Sadler's Wells	Tolomeo	2:27.95
1985	Petoski (3)	W Carson	W R Hern	Lady Beaverbrook	Oh So Sharp	Rainbow Quest	2:27.61
1986	Dancing Brave (3)	Pat Eddery	G Harwood	K Abdullah	Shardari	Triptych	2:29.49
1987	Reference Point (3)	S Cauthen	H Cecil	L Freedman	Celestial Storm	Triptych	2:34.63
1988	Mtoto (5)	M Roberts	A Stewart	A Al Maktoum	Unfuwain	Tony Bin	2:37.33
1989	Nashwan (3)	W Carson	W R Hern	H Al Maktoum	Cacoethes	Top Class	2:32.27
1990	Belmez (3)	M J Kinane	H Cecil	Sheikh Mohammed	Old Vic	Assatis	2:30.76
1991	Generous (3)	A Munro	P Cole	Prince F Salman	Sanglamore	Rock Hopper	2:28.99
1992	St. Jovite (3)	S Craine	J Bolger	V K Payson	Saddlers' Hall	Opera House	2:30.85
1993	Opera House (5)	M Roberts	M Stoute	Sheikh Mohammed	White Muzzle	Commander In Chief	2:33.94
1994	King's Theatre (3)	M J Kinane	H Cecil	Sheikh Mohammed	White Muzzle	Wagon Master	2:28.92
1995	Lammtarra (3)	L Dettori	S bin Suroor	S M Al Maktoum	Pentire	Strategic Choice	2:31.01
1996	Pentire (4)	M Hills	G Wragg	Mollers Racing	Classic Cliche	Shaamit	2:28.11
1997	Swain (5)	J Reid	S bin Suroor	Godolphin	Pilsudski	Helissio	2:36.45
1998	Swain (6)	L Dettori	S bin Suroor	Godolphin	High-Rise	Royal Anthem	2:29.06
1999	Daylami (5)	L Dettori	S bin Suroor	Godolphin	Nedawi	Fruits Of Love	2:29.35
2000	Montjeu (4)	M J Kinane	J Hammond	M Tabor	Fantastic Light	Daliapour	2:29.98
2001	Galileo (3)	M J Kinane	A P O'Brien	Magnier & Tabor	Fantastic Light	Hightori	2:27.71
2002	Golan (4)	K Fallon	M Stoute	Est of Lord Weinstock	Nayef	Zindabad	2:29.70
2003	Alamshar (3)	J P Murtagh	J Oxx	H H Aga Khan	Sulamani	Kris Kin	2:33.26
2004	Doyen (4)	L Dettori	S bin Suroor	Godolphin	Hard Buck	Sulamani	2:33.18

MIDDLE PARK STAKES-G1

6 furlongs, 2-year-old colts, Newmarket (Rowley Mile Course)

FIRST RUN IN 1866

Year	1st	Jockey	Trainer	Owner	2nd	3rd	Time
1970	Brigadier Gerard	J Mercer	W R Hern	Mrs J Hislop	Mummy's Pet	Swing Easy	1:15.1
1971	Sharpen Up	W Carson	B van Cutsem	Mrs B van Cutsem	Philip Of Spain	Sun Prince	1:13.4
1972	Tudenham	J Lindley	D Smith	L Holliday	Quentillian	Wohurst	1:15.6
1973	Habat	Pat Eddery	P Walwyn	C Vittadini	Pitcairn	Boots Green	1:13.7
1974	Steel Heart	L Piggott	D K Weld	R Tikkoo	Royal Manacle	Auction Ring	1:15.7
1975	Hittite Glory	F Durr	A Breasley	R Tikkoo	Duke Ellington	Patris	1:17.4
1976	Tachypous	G Lewis	B Hobbs	G Cambanis	Nebbiolo	Mandrake Major	1:16.3
1977	Formidable	Pat Eddery	P Walwyn	P Goulandris	Persian Bold	Labienus	1:11.2
1978	Junius	L Piggott	M V O'Brien	S Fraser	Young Generation	Lightning Label	1:11
1979	Known Fact	W Carson	J Tree	K Abdullah	Sonnen Gold	Lord Seymour	1:13.2
1980	Mattaboy	L Piggott	R Armstrong	R Tikkoo	Bel Bolide	Poldhu	1:11.4
1981	Cajun	L Piggott	H Cecil	J Stone	Lucky Hunter	Wattlefield	1:16.4
1982	Diesis	L Piggott	H Cecil	H de Walden	Orixo	Krayyan	1:13.2
1983	Creag-An-Sgor	S Cauthen	C Nelson	Mrs W Tulloch	Superlative	Vacarme	1:13.2
1984	Bassenthwaite	Pat Eddery	J Tree	S Niarchos	Doulab	Primo Dominie	1:13.4
1985	Stalker	J Mercer	P Walwyn	P Fetherston Godley	Silvino	Laird o' Montrose	1:12
1986	Mister Majestic	R Cochrane	R Williams	D A Johnson	Risk Me	Genghiz	1:13.6
1987	Gallic League	S Cauthen	B Hills	R Sangster	Rahy	Persian Heights	1:13.8
1988	Mon Tresor	M Roberts	R Boss	Mrs P Fitsall	Pure Genius	Northern Tryst	1:12.2
1989	Balla Cove	S Cauthen	R Boss	H Cohen	Rock City	Cordoba	1:11

Year	1st	Jockey	Trainer	Owner	2nd	3rd	Time
1990	Lycius	C Asmussen	A Fabre	Sheikh Mohammed	Distinctly North	Majlood	1:10
1991	Rodrigo de Triano	W Carson	P Chapple-Hyam	R Sangster	Lion Cavern	River Falls	1:11
1992	Zieten	S Cauthen	A Fabre	Sheikh Mohammed	Pips Pride	Factual	1:11.2
1993	First Trump	M Hills	G Wragg	Mollers Racing	Owington	Redoubtable	1:13.74
1994	Fard	W Carson	D Morley	H Al Maktoum	Green Perfume	Fallow	1:11.36
1995	Royal Applause	W R Swinburn	B Hills	M Al Maktoum	Woodborough	Kahir Almaydan	1:11.4
1996	Bahamian Bounty	L Dettori	D Loder	M Al Maktoum	Muchea	In Command	1:11.95
1997	Hayil	R Hills	D Morley	H Al Maktoum	Carrowkeel	Designer	1:12.39
1998	Lujain	L Dettori	D Loder	Sheikh Mohammed	Bertolini	Vision Of Night	1:14.74
1999*	Primo Valentino	Pat Eddery	P Harris	Primo Donnas	Fath	Brahms	1:12.83
2000	Minardi	M J Kinane	A P O'Brien	Magnier & Tabor	Endless Summer	Red Carpet	1:12.75
2001	Johannesburg	M J Kinane	A P O'Brien	Tabor & Magnier	Zipping	Doc Holiday	1:11.73
2002	Oasis Dream	J Fortune	J Gosden	K Abdullah	Tomahawk	Elusive City	1:09.61
2003+	Balmont	Pat Eddery	J Noseda	S R Robertson	Holborn	Auditorium	1:10.68
2004	Ad Valorem	J P Spencer	A P O'Brien	Mrs John Magnier	Rebuttal	Iceman	1:12.19

*Run on the July Course
+Three Valleys finished first but was disqualified form purse money.

NUNTHORPE STAKES-G1
5 furlongs, 2-year-olds & up, York
FIRST RUN IN 1903

Year	1st (age)	Jockey	Trainer	Owner	2nd	3rd	Time
1970	Huntercombe (3)	A Barclay	A Budgett	H Renshaw	The Brianston	Raffingora	1:04
1971	*Swing Easy (3)	L Piggott	J Tree	J H Whitney	Green God	Native Bazaar	1:00.8
1972	Deep Diver (3)	W Williamson	P Davey	D Robinson	Stilvi	Parsimony	:57.7
1973	Sandford Lad (3)	A Murray	H Price	C Olley	Balliol	The Go-Between	1:00.6
1974	Blue Cashmere (4)	E Hide	M Stoute	R Clifford-Turner	Rapid River	Saritamer	:59.21
1975	Bay Express (4)	W Carson	P Nelson	P Cooper	Willy Willy	Polly Poachum	:58.99
1976	Lochnager (4)	E Hide	M Easterby	C Spence	Faliraki	Polly Poachum	:58.92
1977	Haverold (3)	E Hide	N Adam	T Newton	Godswalk	Lady Constance	1:01.47
1978	Solinus (3)	L Piggott	M V O'Brien	D Schwartz	Smarten Up	Epsom Imp	:59.23
1979	Ahonoora (4)	G Starkey	F Durr	E Alkhalifa	Abdu	Double Form	1:00.58
1980	Sharpo (4f)	Pat Eddery	J Tree	Miss M Sheriffe	Valariga	Abdu	1:01.2
1981	Sharpo (4f)	Pat Eddery	J Tree	Miss M Sheriffe	Marwell	Moorestyle	1:00.86
1982	Sharpo (5f)	S Cauthen	J Tree	Miss M Sheriffe	Chellaston Park	Kind Music	:58.68
1983	Habibti (3f)+	W Carson	J Dunlop	M Mutawa	Fine Edge	Chellaston Park	:57.99
1984	Committed (4f)	B Thomson	D K Weld	R Sangster	Jonacris	Habibti	:57.24
1985	Never So Bold (5)	S Cauthen	R Armstrong	K Kessly	Primo Dominie	Storm Warning	:59.81
1986	Last Tycoon (3)	Y Saint-Martin	R Collet	R Strauss	Double Schwartz	Green Desert	:57.47
1987	Ajdal (3)	W R Swinburn	M Stoute	Sheikh Mohammed	Sizzling Melody	Perion	:58.48
1988	Handsome Sailor (5)	M Hills	B Hills	R Sangster	Silver Fling	Perion	:58.73
1989	Cadeaux Genereux (4)	Pat Eddery	A Scott	M Al Maktoum	Silver Fling	Statoblest	:57.67
1990	Dayjur (3)	W Carson	W R Hern	H Al Maktoum	Statoblest	Pharaoh's Delight	:56.16
1991	Sheikh Albadou (3)	Pat Eddery	A Scott	H Salem	Paris House	Blyton Lad	:58.21
1992	Lyric Fantasy (2f)	M Roberts	R Hannon	Lord Carnarvon	Mr Brooks	Diamonds Galore	:57.39
1993	Lochsong (5f)	L Dettori	I Balding	J C Smith	Paris House	College Chapel	:58.12
1994	Blue Siren (3)	M Hills	M Channon	J Mitchell	Piccolo	Mistertopogigo	:57.61
1995	So Factual (5)	L Dettori	S bin Suroor	Godolphin	Ya Malak	Hever Golf Rose	:57.47
1996	Pivotal (3)	G Duffield	M Prescott	Cheveley Park Stud	Eveningperformance	Hever Golf Rose	:56.53
1997	Coastal Bluff (5)	K Darley	T Barron	Mrs D Sharp	Ya Malak	Averti	:59.58
1998	Lochangel (4f)	L Dettori	I Balding	J C Smith	Sainte Marine	Dashing Blue	:56.83
1999	Stravinsky (3)	M J Kinane	A P O'Brien	Tabor & Magnier	Sainte Marine	Proud Native	:59.33
2000	Nuclear Debate (5)	G Mosse	J Hammond	J R Chester	Bertolini	Pipalong	:57.83
2001	Mozart (3)	M J Kinane	A P O'Brien	Tabor & Magnier	Nuclear Debate	Bishops Court	:57.27
2002	Kyllachy (4)	J P Spencer	H Candy	Thurloe Thrghbrds	Malhub	Indian Prince	:58.10
2003	Oasis Dream (3)	R Hughes	J Gosden	K Abdullah	The Tatling	Acclamation	:56.20
2004	Bahamian Pirate (9)	S Sanders	D Nicholls	Lucayan Stud	The Tatling	One Cool Cat	:58.89

*In 1971 Green God finished first but was disqualified and placed second.
+In 1983 Soba finished first but was disqualified and placed last.

1000 GUINEAS STAKES-G1
1 mile, 3-year-old fillies, Newmarket (Rowley Mile Course)
FIRST RUN IN 1814.

Year	1st	Jockey	Trainer	Owner	2nd	3rd	Time
1970	Humble Duty	L Piggott	P Walwyn	Lady Ashcombe	Gleam	Black Satin	1:42.13
1971	Altesse Royale	Y Saint-Martin	N Murless	F Hue-Williams	Super Honey	Catherine Wheel	1:40.90
1972	Waterloo	E Hide	J Watts	Mrs R Stanley	Marisela	Rose Dubarry	1:39.49
1973	Mysterious	G Lewis	N Murless	G Pope	Jacinth	Shellshock	1:42.12
1974	Highclere	J Mercer	W Hern	The Queen	Polygamy	Mrs Twiggywinkle	1:40.32

Year	1st	Jockey	Trainer	Owner	2nd	3rd	Time
1975	Nocturnal Spree	J Roe	S Murless	Mrs D O'Kelly	Girl Friend	Joking Apart	1:41.65
1976	Flying Water	Y Saint-Martin	A Penna	D Wildenstein	Konafa	Kesar Queen	1:37.83
1977	Mrs McArdy	E Hide	M Easterby	Mrs E Kettlewell	Freeze The Secret	Sanedtki	1:40.07
1978	Enstone Spark	E Johnson	B Hills	R Bonnycastle	Fair Salinia	Seraphima	1:41.56
1979	One In A Million	J Mercer	H Cecil	Helena Springfield Ltd	Abbeydale	Yanuka	1:43.06
1980	Quick As Lightning	B Rouse	J Dunlop	O Phipps	Our Home	Mrs Penny	1:41.89
1981	Fairy Footsteps	L Piggott	H Cecil	H Joel	Tolmi	Go Leasing	1:40.43
1982	On The House	J Reid	H Wragg	P Oppenheimer	Time Charter	Dione	1:40.45
1983	Ma Biche	F Head	C Head	M Al Maktoum	Favoridge	Habibti	1:41.71
1984	Pebbles	P Robinson	C Brittain	M Lemos	Meis El-Reem	Desirable	1:38.18
1985	Oh So Sharp	S Cauthen	H Cecil	Sheikh Mohammed	Al Bahathri	Bella Colora	1:36.85
1986	Midway Lady	R Cochrane	B Hanbury	H Ranier	Maysoon	Sonic Lady	1:41.54
1987	Miesque	F Head	F Boutin	S Niarchos	Milligram	Interval	1:38.48
1988	Ravinella	G Moore	C Head	Ecurie Aland	Dabaweyaa	Diminuendo	1:40.88
1989	Musical Bliss	W R Swinburn	M Stoute	Sheikh Mohammed	Kerrera	Aldbourne	1:42.69
1990	Salsabil	W Carson	J Dunlop	H Al Maktoum	Heart Of Joy	Negligent	1:38.06
1991	Shadayid	W Carson	J Dunlop	H Al Maktoum	Kooyonga	Crystal Gazing	1:38.18
1992	Hatoof	W R Swinburn	C Head	M Al Maktoum	Marling	Kenbu	1:39.45
1993	Sayyedati	W R Swinburn	C Brittain	M Obaida	Niche	Ajfan	1:37.34
1994	Las Meninas	J Reid	T Stack	R Sangster	Balanchine	Coup de Genie	1:36.71
1995	Harayir	R Hills	W R Hern	H Al Maktoum	Aqaarid	Moonshell	1:36.72
1996	Bosra Sham	Pat Eddery	H Cecil	W Said	Matiya	Bint Shadayid	1:37.75
1997	Sleepytime	K Fallon	H Cecil	Greenbay Stables Ltd	Oh Nellie	Dazzle	1:37.66
1998	Cape Verdi	L Dettori	S bin Suroor	Godolphin	Shahtoush	Exclusive	1:37.86
1999*	Wince	K Fallon	H Cecil	K Abdullah	Wannabe Grand	Valentine Waltz	1:37.91
2000	Lahan	R Hills	J Gosden	Hamdan Al Maktoum	Princess Ellen	Petrushka	1:36.38
2001	Ameerat	P Robinson	M Jarvis	A Al Maktoum	Muwakleh	Toroca	1:38.36
2002	Kazzia	L Dettori	S bin Suroor	Godolphin	Snowfire	Alasha	1:37.85
2003	Russian Rhythm	K Fallon	M R Stoute	Cheveley Park Stud	Six Perfections	Intercontinental	1:38.43
2004	Attraction	K Darley	M Johnston	Duke of Roxburghe	Sundrop	Hathrah	1:36.78

*Run on the July Course.

QUEEN ELIZABETH II STAKES-G1

1 mile, 3-year-olds & up, Ascot

First run in 1955.

Year	1st	Jockey	Trainer	Owner	2nd	3rd	Time
1970	Welsh Pageant (4)	A Barclay	N Murless	H J Joel	Gold Rod	Prince de Gellos	1:42.08
1971	Brigadier Gerard (3)	J Mercer	W R Hern	Mrs J Hislop	Dictus	Ashleigh	1:41.39
1972	Brigadier Gerard (4	J Mercer	W R Hern	Mrs J Hislop	Sparkler	Redundent	1:39.96
1973	Jan Ekels (4)	J Lindley	G Harwood	A E Bodie	Pompous	Loyal Manzer	1:47.20
1974	RACE NOT RUN						
1975	Rose Bowl (3)	W Carson	R Houghton	Mrs C Engelhard	Gay Fandango	Anne's Pretender	1:48.97
1976	Rose Bowl (4)	W Carson	R Houghton	Mrs C Engelhard	Ricco Boy	Dominion	1:43.49
1977	Trusted (4)	W Carson	J Dunlop	Duchess of Norfolk	Air Trooper	Radetzky	1:41.40
1978	Homing (3)	W Carson	W R Hern	Lord Rotherwick	Stradavinsky	Caro Bambino	1:40.39
1979	Kris (3)	J Mercer	H Cecil	H de Walden	Fovoros	Jellaby	1:40.69
1980	Known Fact (3)	W Carson	J Tree	K Abdullah	Kris	Gift Wrapped	1:40.02
1981	To-Agori-Mou (3)	L Piggott	G Harwood	Mrs A Muinos	Kittyhawk	Cracaval	1:48.76
1982	Buzzards Bay (4)	W R Swinburn	H Collingridge	Mrs B McKinney	Noalcoholic	Achieved	1:44.98
1983	Sackford (3)	G Starkey	G Harwood	A E Bodie	Adonijah	Montekin	1:39.85
1984	Teleprompter (4)	W Carson	J Watts	Lord Derby	Katies	Sackford	1:42.96
1985	Shadeed (3)	W R Swinburn	M Stoute	M Al Maktoum	Teleprompter	Zaizafon	1:38.80
1986	Sure Blade (3)	B Thomson	B Hills	Sheikh Mohammed	Teleprompter	Efisio	1:41.71
1987	Milligram (3f)	Pat Eddery	M Stoute	Helena Springfield Ltd	Miesque	Sonic Lady	1:40.04
1988	Warning (3)	Pat Eddery	G Harwood	K Abdullah	Salse	Persian Heights	1:40.51
1989	Zilzal (3)	W R Swinburn	M Stoute	M Al Maktoum	Polish Precedent	Distant Relative	1:40.57
1990	Markofdistinction(4)	L Dettori	L Cumani	G Leigh	Distant Relative	Green Line Express	1:39.7
1991	Selkirk (3)	R Cochrane	I Balding	G Strawbridge	Kooyonga	Shadayid	1:44.34
1992	Lahib (4)	W Carson	J Dunlop	H Al Maktoum	Brief Truce	Selkirk	1:44.50
1993	Bigstone (3)	Pat Eddery	E Lellouche	D Wildenstein	Barathea	Kingmambo	1:42.89
1994	Maroof (3)	R Hills	R Armstrong	H Al Maktoum	Barathea	Bigstone	1:42.75
1995	Bahri (3)	W Carson	J Dunlop	H Al Maktoum	Ridgewood Pearl	Soviet Line	1:40.54
1996	Mark Of Esteem (3)	L Dettori	S bin Suroor	Godolphin	Bosra Sham	First Island	1:40.95
1997	Air Express (3)	O Peslier	C Brittain	M Obaida	Rebecca Sharp	Faithful Son	1:40.61
1998	Desert Prince (3)	O Peslier	D Loder	Lucayan Stud	Dr Fong	Second Empire	1:39.63
1999	Dubai Millennium (3	L Dettori	S bin Suroor	Godolphin	Almushtarak	Gold Academy	1:46.24
2000	Observatory (3)	K Darley	J Gosden	K Abdullah	Giant's Causeway	Best Of The Bests	1:41.40
2001	Summoner (4)	R Hills	S bin Suroor	Godolphin	Noverre	Hawkeye	1:44.54
2002	Where Or When (3)	K Darley	T G Mills	John Humphreys Ltd	Hawk Wing	Tillerman	1:41.37
2003	Falbrav (5)	D Holland	L Cumani	Scuderia Rencati	Russian Rhythm	Tillerman	1:38.99
2004	Rakti (5)	P Robinson	M Jarvis	G A Tanaka	Lucky Story	Refuse To Bend	1:39.82

RACING POST TROPHY-G1

1 mile, 2-year-old colts & fillies, Doncaster

FIRST RUN IN 1961.

Run as the Timeform Gold Cup 1961-1964. Run as the Observor Gold Cup 1965-1975.
Run as the William Hill Futurity 1976-1988. Run at Newcastle in 1989.

Year	1st	Jockey	Trainer	Owner	2nd	3rd	Time
1970	Linden Tree	D Keith	P Walwyn	Mrs D McCalmont	Minsky	Fine Blade	1:39.4
1971	High Top	W Carson	B Van Cutsem	Sir J Thorn	Steel Pulse	Pentland Firth	1:40.8
1972	Noble Decree	L Piggott	B van Cutsem	N B Hunt	Ksar	Stanleyville	1:42.8
1973	Apalachee	L Piggott	M V O'Brien	J Mulcahy	Mississipian	Alpine Nephew	1:43.6
1974	Green Dancer	F Head	A Head	Mme P Wertheimer	Dea Break	No Alimony	1:45.2
1975	Take Your Place	G Dettori	H Cecil	C d'Alessio	Earth Spirit	Gallapiat	1:40.00
1976	Sporting Yankee	Pat Eddery	P Walwyn	William Hill Racing	Sultan's Ruby	Orchestra	1:45.6
1977	Dactylographer	Pat Eddery	P Walwyn	S Niarchos	Julio Mariner	Home Run	1:43.8
1978	Sandy Creek	C Roche	C Collins	A McClean	Warmington	Lyphard's Wish	1:38.4
1979	Hello Gorgeous	J Mercer	H Cecil	D Wildenstein	Choucri Moomba	Masquerade	1:42.4
1980	Beldale Flutter	Pat Eddery	M Jarvis	A Kelly	Shergar	Sheer Gift	1:43.4
1981	Count Pahlen	G Baxter	B Hobbs	Mrs A Villar	Paradis Terrestre	Jalmood	1:42.4
1982	Dunbeath	L Piggott	H Cecil	M Riordan	Cock Robin	Lyphard's Special	1:44.00
1983	Alphabatim	G Starkey	G Harwood	K Abdullah	Mendez	Ilium	1:41.2
1984	Lanfranco	L Piggott	H Cecil	C St George	Damister	Brave Bambino	1:43.8
1985	Bakharoff	G Starkey	G Harwood	K Abdullah	Nomrood	Water Cay	1:41.2
1986	Reference Point	Pat Eddery	H Cecil	L Freedman	Bengal Fire	Love The Groom	1:45.00
1987	Emmson	W Carson	W R Hern	M Sobell	Sheriff's Star	Salse	1:42.6
1988	Al Hareb	W Carson	N Graham	H Al Maktoum	Zalazi	Frequent Flyer	1:40.6
1989	Be My Chief	S Cauthen	H Cecil	P Burrell	Baligh	Qathil	1:42.99
1990	Peter Davies	S Cauthen	H Cecil	C St George	Mukaddamah	Marcham	1:46.00
1991	Seattle Rhyme	C Asmussen	D Elsworth	H J Senn	Mack The Knife	Assessor	1:39.58
1992	Armiger	Pat Eddery	H Cecil	K Abdullah	Ivanka	Zind	1:39.70
1993	King's Theatre	W Ryan	H Cecil	M Poland	Fairy Heights	Bude	1:41.04
1994	Celtic Swing	K Darley	Lady Herries	P Savill	Annus Mirabilis	Juyush	1:40.04
1995	Beauchamp King	J Reid	J Dunlop	E Penser	Even Top	Mons	1:38.89
1996	Medaaly	G Hind	S bin Suroor	Godolphin	Poteen	Benny The Dip	1:41.12
1997	Saratoga Springs	M J Kinane	A P O'Brien	Tabor & Magnier	Mudeer	Mutamam	1:40.36
1998	Commander Collins	J Fortune	P Chapple-Hyam	Sangster & Collins	Magno	Housemaster	1:47.80
1999	Aristotle	G Duffield	A P O'Brien	Mrs J Magnier	Lermontov	Ekraar	1:45.60
2000	Dilshaan	J P Murtagh	M Stoute	S Suhail	Tamburlaine	Bonnard	1:45.87
2001	High Chaparral	K Darley	A P O'Brien	Tabor & Magnier	Castle Gandolfo	Redback	1:45.39
2002	Brian Boru	K Darley	A P O'Brien	Mrs J Magnier	Powerscourt	Illustrator	1:46.01
2003	American Post	C Soumillon	C Head-Maarek	K Abdullah	Fantastic View	Magritte	1:39.57
2004	Motivator	K Fallon	M Bell	RylAscotRacingClub	Albert Hall	Henrik	1:42.62

ST. JAMES'S PALACE STAKES-G1

1 mile, 3-year-old colts, Royal Ascot

FIRST RUN IN 1833.

Year	1st	Jockey	Trainer	Owner	2nd	3rd	Time
1970	Saintly Song	A Barclay	N Murless	J Stanhope	Gold Rod	Pithiviers	
1971	Brigadier Gerard	J Mercer	W R Hern	Mrs J Hislop	Sparkler	Good Bond	
1972	Sun Prince	J Lindley	W R Hern	Sir Michael Sobell	Home Guard	Grey Mirage	1:44.02
1973	Thatch	L Piggott	M V O'Brien	J Mulcahy	Owen Dudley	*	1:40.52
1974	Averof	B Taylor	C E Brittain	Captain M Lemos	Cellini	Hard Fighter	1:41.53
1975	Bolkonski	G Dettori	H Cecil	C d'Alessio	Royal Manacle	Nurabad	1:42.50
1976	Radetzky	Pat Eddery	C E Brittain	C Elliot	Earth Spirit	Patris	1:40.44
1977	Don	E Hide	W Elsey	E Ryan	Marinsky	Tachypous	1:46.67
1978	Jaazeiro	L Piggott	M V O'Brien	R E Sangster	Persian Bold	Formidable	1:40.81
1979	Kris	J Mercer	H Cecil	Lord H de Walden	Young Generation	Alert	1:41.72
1980	Posse	Pat Eddery	J Dunlop	O M Phipps	Final Straw	Last Fandango	1:44.74
1981	To-Agori-Mou	G Starkey	G Harwood	Mrs A Muinos	Kings Lake	Bel Bolide	1:39.90
1982	Dara Monarch	M J Kinane	L Browne	Mrs L Browne	Tender King	Ivano	1:41.09
1983	Horage	S Cauthen	M McCormack	A Rachid	Tolomeo	Dunbeath	1:40.08
1984	Chief Singer	R Cochrane	R Sheather	J C Smith	Keen	Kalim	1:38.90
1985	Bairn	L Piggott	L Cumani	Sheikh Mohammed	Scottish Reel	Vin de France	1:41.05
1986	Sure Blade	B Thomson	B Hills	Sheikh Mohammed	Green Desert	Sharrood	1:41.50
1987	Half A Year	R Cochrane	L Cumani	J C Mabee	Soviet Star	Risk Me	1:43.42
1988	Persian Heights	Pat Eddery	G A Huffer	HH Prince Yazid Saud	Raykour	Caerwent	1:39.57
1989	Shaadi	W R Swinburn	M R Stoute	Sheikh Mohammed	Greensmith	Scenic	1:39.33
1990	Shavian	S Cauthen	H Cecil	Lord H de Walden	Rock City	Lord Florey	1:41.52
1991	Marju	W Carson	J Dunlop	H Al Maktoum	Second Set	Hokusai	1:41.97
1992	Brief Truce	M J Kinane	D K Weld	Moyglare Stud Farms	Zaadi	Ezzoud	1:39.32
1993	Kingmambo	C B Asmussen	F Boutin	S Niarchos	Needle Gun	Ventiquattrofogli	1:44.05

Year	1st	Jockey	Trainer	Owner	2nd	3rd	Time
1994	Grand Lodge	M J Kinane	W Jarvis	Lord H de Walden	Distant View	Turtle Island	1:38.83
1995	Bahri	W Carson	J Dunlop	H Al Maktoum	Charnwood Forest	Vettori	1:40.15
1996	Bijou d'Inde	J Weaver	M Johnston	J S Morrison	Ashkalani	Sorbie Tower	1:39.70
1997	Starborough	L Dettori	D Loder	Sheikh Mohammed	Air Express	Daylami	1:39.18
1998	Dr Fong	K Fallon	H Cecil	The ThoroughbredCorp	Desert Prince	Duck Row	1:41.33
1999	Sendawar	G Mosse	A de Royer-Dupre	HH Aga Khan	Aljabr	Gold Academy	1:39.99
2000	Giant's Causeway	M J Kinane	A P O'Brien	Magnier & Tabor	Valentino	Medicean	1:42.61
2001	Black Minnaloushe	J P Murtagh	A P O'Brien	Magnier & Tabor	Noverre	Olden Times	1:41.37
2002	Rock Of Gibraltar	M J Kinane	A P O'Brien	Ferguson & Magnier	Landseer	Aramram	1:40.91
2003	Zafeen	D Holland	M Channon	J Abdullah	Kalaman	Martillo	1:39.91
2004	Azamour	M J Kinane	J Oxx	HH Aga Khan	Diamond Green	Antonius Pius	1:39.02

*In 1973 only 2 ran.

ST LEGER STAKES-G1

1 mile, 6 furlongs, 132 yards, 3-year-old colts & fillies, Doncaster

FIRST RUN IN 1776.

Run at Ayr in 1989.

Year	1st	Jockey	Trainer	Owner	2nd	3rd	Time
1970	Nijinsky	L Piggott	M V O'Brien	C Engelhard	Meadowville	Politico	3:06.4
1971	Athens Wood	L Piggott	H T Jones	Mrs J Rogerson	Homeric	Falkland	3:14.9
1972	Boucher	L Piggott	M V O'Brien	O Phipps	Our Mirage	Ginerva	3:28.71
1973	Peleid	F Durr	W Elsey	W Behrens	Buoy	Duke Of Ragusa	3:08.21
1974	Bustino	J Mercer	W R Hern	Lady Beaverbrook	Giacometti	Riboson	3:09.02
1975	Bruni	A Murray	R Price	C St George	King Pellinore	Libra's Rib	3:09.02
1976	Crow	Y Saint-Martin	A Penna	D Wildenstein	Secret Man	Scallywag	3:13.17
1977	Dunfermline (f)	W Carson	W R Hern	The Queen	Alleged	Classic Example	3:05.17
1978	Julio Mariner	E Hide	C Brittain	M Lemos	Le Moss	M-Lolshan	3:04.94
1979	Son of Love	A Lequeux	R Collet	A Rolland	Soleil Noir	Niniski	3:09.02
1980	Light Cavalry	J Mercer	H Cecil	H Joel	Water Mill	World Leader	3:11.48
1981	Cut Above	J Mercer	W R Hern	J Astor	Glint Of Gold	Bustomi	3:11.60
1982	Touching Wood	P Cook	H T Jones	M Al Maktoum	Zilos	Diamond Shoal	3:03.53
1983	Sun Princess (f)	W Carson	W R Hern	M Sobell	Esprit du Nord	Carlingford Castle	3:16.65
1984	Commanche Run	L Piggott	L Cumani	I Allan	Baynoun	Alphabatim	3:09.93
1985	Oh So Sharp (f)	S Cauthen	H Cecil	Sheikh Mohammed	Phardante	Lanfranco	3:07.13
1986	Moon Madness	Pat Eddery	J Dunlop	Duchess of Norfolk	Celestial Storm	Untold	3:05.03
1987	Reference Point	S Cauthen	H Cecil	L Freedman	Mountain Kingdom	Dry Dock	3:05.91
1988	Minster Son	W Carson	N Graham	Lady Beaverbrook	Diminuendo	Sheriff's Star	3:06.80
1989	Michelozzo	S Cauthen	H Cecil	C St George	Sapience	Roseate Tern	3:20.72
1990	Snurge	T R Quinn	P Cole	M Arbib	Hellenic	River God	3:08.78
1991	Toulon	Pat Eddery	A Fabre	K Abdullah	Saddlers' Hall	Micheletti	3:03.12
1992	User Friendly (f)	G Duffield	C Brittain	W Gredley	Sonus	Bonny Scot	3:05.48
1993	Bob's Return	P Robinson	M Tompkins	Mrs G Smith	Armiger	Edbaysaan	3:07.85
1994	Moonax	Pat Eddery	B Hills	Sheikh Mohammed	Broadway Flyer	Double Trigger	3:04.19
1995	Classic Cliche	L Dettori	S bin Suroor	Godolphin	Minds Music	Istidaad	3:09.74
1996	Shantou	L Dettori	J Gosden	Sheikh Mohammed	Dushyantor	Samraan	3:05.10
1997	Silver Patriarch	Pat Eddery	J Dunlop	P Winfield	Vertical Speed	The Fly	3:06.92
1998	Nedawi	J Reid	S bin Suroor	Godolphin	High And Low	Sunshine Street	3:05.61
1999	Mutafaweq	R Hills	S bin Suroor	Godolphin	Ramruma	Adair	3:02.75
2000	Millenary	T R Quinn	J Dunlop	L N Jones	Air Marshall	Chimes At Midnight	3:02.58
2001	Milan	M J Kinane	A P O'Brien	Tabor & Magnier	Demophilos	Mr Combustible	3:05.16
2002	Bollin Eric	K Darley	T Easterby	N Westbrook	Highest	Bandari	3:02.92
2003	Brian Boru	J P Spencer	A P O'Brien	Mrs J Magnier	High Accolade	Phoenix Reach	3:04.64
2004	Rule Of Law	K McEvoy	S bin Suroor	Godolphin	Quiff	Tycoon	3:06.29

SUSSEX STAKES-G1

1 mile, 3-year-olds & up, Goodwood

FIRST RUN IN 1878.

Year	1st	Jockey	Trainer	Owner	2nd	3rd	Time
1970	Humble Duty (3f)	D Keith	P Walwyn	Lady Ashcombe	Gold Rod	Joshua	1:40.6
1971	Brigadier Gerard (3)	J Mercer	W R Hern	Mrs J Hislop	Faraway Son	Joshua	1:41.8
1972	Sallust (3)	J Mercer	W R Hern	M Sobell	High Top	Sparkler	1:37.4
1973	Thatch (3)	L Piggott	M V O'Brien	J Mulcahy	Jacinth	Sun Prince	1:39.4
1974	Ace of Aces (4)	J Lindley	M Zilber	N B Hunt	Habat	Mount Hagen	1:41.2
1975	Bolkonski (3)	G Dettori	H Cecil	C d'Alessio	Rose Bowl	Lianga	1:39.4

Year	1st (Age)	Jockey	Trainer	Owner	2nd	3rd	Time
1976	Wollow (3)	G Dettori	H Cecil	C d'Alessio	Free State	Poacher's Moon	1:39.6
1977	Artaius (3)	L Piggott	M V O'Brien	Mrs G Getty II	Free State	Relkino	1:39.4
1978	Jaazeiro (3)	L Piggott	M V O'Brien	R Sangster	Radetzky	Formidable	1:40.4
1979	Kris (3)	J Mercer	H Cecil	H de Walden	Swiss Maid	Alert	1:41.6
1980	Posse (3)	Pat Eddery	J Dunlop	O Phipps	Final Straw	Star Way	1:41.6
1981	King's Lake (3)	Pat Eddery	M V O'Brien	Mme J Binet	To-Agori-Mou	Noalto	1:39.4
1982	On The House (3)	J Reid	H Wragg	P Oppenheimer	Sandhurst Prince	Achieved	1:37.6
1983	Noalcoholic (6)	G Duffield	G Pritchard-Gordon	W du Pont III	Tolomeo	Wassl	1:37.4
1984	Chief Singer (3)	R Cochrane	R Sheather	J C Smith	Creag-An-Sgor	Wassl	1:38.2
1985	Rousillon (4)	G Starkey	G Harwood	K Abdullah	Bairn	King Of Clubs	1:41.0
1986	Sonic Lady (3f)	W R Swinburn	M Stoute	Sheikh Mohammed	Scottish Reel	Pennine Walk	1:39.6
1987	Soviet Star (3)	G Starkey	A Fabre	Sheikh Mohammed	Star Cutter	Hadeer	1:38.8
1988	Warning (3)	Pat Eddery	G Harwood	K Abdullah	Then Again	Most Welcome	1:39.8
1989	Markofdistinction	R Cochrane	L Cumani	Mana Al Maktoum	Most Welcome	Opening Verse	1:36.77
1990	Distant Relative (4)	W Carson	B Hills	W Said	Green Line Express	Shavian	1:36.0
1991	Second Set (3)	L Dettori	L Cumani	R Duchossois	Shadayid	Priolo	1:40.4
1992	Marling (3f)	Pat Eddery	G Wragg	E Loder	Selkirk	Second Set	1:36.6
1993	Bigstone (3)	D Boeuf	E Lellouche	D Wildenstein	Sayyedati	Inchinor	1:40.19
1994	Distant View (3)	Pat Eddery	H Cecil	K Abdullah	Barathea	Grand Lodge	1:35.71
1995	Sayyedati (5f)	B Doyle	C Brittain	M Obaida	Bahri	Darnay	1:36.17
1996	First Island (4)	M Hills	G Wragg	Mollers Racing	Charnwood Forest	Alhaarth	1:37.75
1997	Ali-Royal (4)	K Fallon	H Cecil	Greenbay Stables Ltd	Starborough	Allied Forces	1:37.98
1998	Among Men (4)	M J Kinane	M Stoute	Tabor & Magnier	Almushtarak	Lend A Hand	1:40.23
1999	Aljabr (3)	L Dettori	S bin Suroor	Godolphin	Docksider	Almushtarak	1:35.66
2000	Giant's Causeway (3)	M J Kinane	A P O'Brien	Mrs J Magnier/M Tabor	Dansili	Medicean	1:38.65
2001	Noverre (3)	L Dettori	S bin Suroor	Godolphin	No Excuse Needed	Black Minnaloushe	1:37.12
2002	Rock Of Gibraltar (3)	M J Kinane	A P O'Brien	Ferguson & Magnier	Noverre	Reel Buddy	1:38.29
2003	Reel Buddy (5)	Pat Eddery	R Hannon	Speedlith Group	Statue Of Liberty	Norse Dancer	1:40.00
2004	Soviet Song (4f)	J P Murtagh	J Fanshawe	Elite Racing Club	Nayyir	Le Vie dei Colori	1:36.98

2000 GUINEAS STAKES-G1

1 mile, 3-year-old colts & fillies, Newmarket (Rowley Mile Course)

FIRST RUN IN 1809

Year	1st	Jockey	Trainer	Owner	2nd	3rd	Time
1970	Nijinsky II	L Piggott	M V O'Brien	C Engelhard	Yellow God	Roi Soleil	1:41.54
1971	Brigadier Gerard	J Mercer	W Hern	Mrs J Hislop	Mill Reef	My Swallow	1:39.2
1972	High Top	W Carson	B van Cutsem	J Thorn	Roberto	Sun Prince	1:40.82
1973	Mon Fils	F Durr	R Hannon	Mrs B Davis	Noble Decree	Sharp Edge	1:42.97
1974	Nonoalco	Y Saint-Martin	F Boutin	Mme M Berger	Giacometti	Apalachee	1:39.53
1975	Bolkonski	G Dettori	H Cecil	C d'Alessio	Grundy	Dominion	1:39.53
1976	Wollow	G Dettori	H Cecil	C d'Alessio	Vitiges	Thieving Demon	1:38.09
1977	Nebbiolo	G Curran	K Prendergast	N Schibbye	Tachypous	The Minstrel	1:38.54
1978	Roland Gardens	F Durr	D Sasse	J Hayter	Remainder Man	Weth Nan	1:47.33
1979	Tap On Wood	S Cauthen	B Hills	A Shead	Kris	Young Generation	1:43.6
1980	Known Fact+	W Carson	J Tree	K Abdullah	Posse	Alert	1:40.46
1981	To-Agori-Mou	G Starkey	G Harwood	Mrs A Muinos	Mattaboy	Bel Bolide	1:41.43
1982	Zino	F Head	F Boutin	G Oldham	Wind And Wuthering	Tender King	1:37.13
1983	Lomond	Pat Eddery	M V O'Brien	R Sangster	Tolomeo	Muscatite	1:43.87
1984	El Gran Senor	Pat Eddery	M V O'Brien	R Sangster	Chief Singer	Lear Fan	1:37.41
1985	Shadeed	L Piggott	M Stoute	M Al Maktoum	Bairn	Supreme Leader	1:37.41
1986	Dancing Brave	G Starkey	G Harwood	K Abdullah	Green Desert	Huntingdale	1:40
1987	Don't Forget Me	W Carson	R Hannon	J Horgan	Bellotto	Midyan	1:36.74
1988	Doyoun	W R Swinburn	M Stoute	Aga Khan	Charmer	Bellefella	1:41.73
1989	Nashwan	W Carson	W R Hern	H Al Maktoum	Exbourne	Danehill	1:36.44
1990	Tirol	M J Kinane	R Hannon	J Horgan	Machiavellian	Anshan	1:35.84
1991	Mystiko	M Roberts	C Brittain	Lady Beaverbrook	Lycius	Ganges	1:37.83
1992	Rodrigo de Triano	L Piggott	P Chapple-Hyam	R Sangster	Lucky Lindy	Pursuit Of Love	1:38.37
1993	Zafonic	Pat Eddery	A Fabre	K Abdullah	Barathea	Bin Ajwaad	1:35.32
1994	Mister Baileys	J Weaver	M Johnston	G R Bailey Ltd	Grand Lodge	Colonel Collins	1:35.08
1995	Pennekamp	T Jarnet	A Fabre	Sheikh Mohammed	Celtic Swing	Bahri	1:35.16
1996	Mark Of Esteem	L Dettori	S bin Suroor	Godolphin	Even Top	Bijou d'Inde	1:37.59
1997	Entrepreneur	M J Kinane	M Stoute	Tabor & Magnier	Revoque	Poteen	1:35.64
1998	King Of Kings	M J Kinane	A O'Brien	Tabor & Magnier	Lend A Hand	Border Arrow	1:39.25
1999*	Island Sands	L Dettori	S bin Suroor	Godolphin	Enrique	Mujahid	1:37.14
2000	King's Best	K Fallon	M Stoute	S Suhail	Giant's Causeway	Barathea Guest	1:37.77
2001	Golan	K Fallon	M Stoute	Lord Weinstock	Tamburlaine	Frenchmans Bay	1:37.48
2002	Rock Of Gibraltar	J P Murtagh	A P O'Brien	Ferguson & Magnier	Hawk Wing	Redback	1:36.50
2003	Refuse To Bend	P J Smullen	D K Weld	Moyglare Stud Farm	Zafeen	Norse Dancer	1:37.98
2004	Haafhd	R Hills	B Hills	H Al Maktoum	Snow Ridge	Azamour	1:36.64

+Nureyev finished first but was disqualified and placed last.

*Run on the July Course

FRANCE

CRITERIUM DE SAINT-CLOUD-G1

2000 meters (1-1/4 miles), 2-year-old colts & fillies, Saint-Cloud

Year	1st	Jockey	Trainer	Owner	2nd	3rd	Time
1970	Rheffic	Y Saint-Martin	F Mathet	Mme F Dupre	Toulon	Sigisbee	2:11.7
1971	Gay Saint	A Barclay	F Boutin	Mrs A Manning	Pardner	Lassalle	2:12.7
1972	Simbir	W Pyers	F Mathet	A Plesch	Robertino	Ben Trovato	2:14.4
1973	Ribecourt	Y Saint-Martin	F Boutin	Mme J Couterie	La Tulipe	Exceptionnel	2:19.6
1974	Easy Regent	W Pyers	G Delloye	Mme P de Moussac	Olmeto	Roses Market	2:23.8
1975	Kano	G Rivases	R Poincelet	M Boussac	Loredo	La Girouette	2:17.4
1976	Conglomerat	P Paquet	F Boutin	J Ternynck	Seguro	Istre	2:17.5
1977	Tarek	Y Saint-Martin	A Hawa	M Fustok	Orange Marmelade	Kutuzov	2:16.3
1978	Callio	A Badel	J Sens	J Bossuyt	Echion	Lord Zara	2:10.8
1979	Providential	F Head	F Boutin	B R Firestone	Belgio	Karellaan	2:22.7
1980	The Wonder	A Gibert	J de Chevigny	Mme A du Breil	Mont Pelion	Brinkbero	2:18.7
1981	Bon Sang	A Gibert	M Saliba	M Fustok	Marcao	Coussika	2:17.6
1982	Escaline (f)	M Philipperon	J Fellows	Mme J Fellows	White Spade	Pietru	2:26.9
1983	Darshaan	Y Saint-Martin	A de Royer-Dupre	Aga Khan	Grand Orient	Real Gold	2:07.4
1984	Mouktar	Y Saint-Martin	A de Royer-Dupre	Aga Khan	Hello Bill	Siberian Hero	2:25
1985	Fast Topaze	A Badel	G Mikhalides	M Fustok	Flying Trio	Manetho	2:15.5
1986	Magistros	E Legrix	G Bonnaventure	P Coudert	Sir David	Groom Dancer	2:23.9
1987	Waki River	A Lequeux	B Secly	J Clerico	Hours After	Blushing John	2:20.6
1988	Miserden	Pat Eddery	A Fabre	K Abdullah	Louis Cyphre	Plein d'Esprit	2:16.4
1989	*Intimiste	G Mosse	F Boutin	I della Rochetta	Snurge	Guiza	2:19.3
1990	Pistolet Bleu	D Boeuf	E Lellouche	D Wildenstein	Pigeon Voyageur	Fortune's Wheel	2:17.8
1991	Glaieul	D Boeuf	E Lellouche	D Wildenstein	Calling Collect	Contested Bid	2:20.3
1992	Marchand de Sable	D Boeuf	E Lellouche	L De Angeli	Infrasonic	Arinthod	2:19.4
1993	Sunshack	T Jarnet	A Fabre	K Abdullah	Zindari	Tikkanen	2:15.2
1994	Poliglote	F Head	C Head	J Wertheimer	Solar One	Highest Cafe	2:19.4
1995	Polaris Flight	J Reid	P Chapple-Hyam	R Kaster	Ragmar	Oliviero	2:13.7
1996	Shaka	J-R Dubosc	J-C Rouget	R Bousquet	Daylami	Sendoro	2:15.8
1997	Special Quest	O Doleuze	C Head	Wertheimer & Frere	Asakir	Daymarti	2:11.9
1998	Spadoun	D Boeuf	C Laffon-Parias	J Gonzalez	Bienamado	Cupid	2:21.5
1999	Goldamix (f)	D Boeuf	C Laffon-Parias	Wertheimer & Frere	Petroselli	Cosmographe	2:15.7
2000	Sagacity	O Peslier	A Fabre	J-L Lagardere	Reduit	Sligo Bay	2:17.80
2001	Ballingarry	J P Spencer	A P O'Brien	Magnier & Tabor	Castle Gandolfo	Black Sam Bellamy	2:24.60
2002	Alberto Giacometti	M J Kinane	A P O'Brien	Mrs J Magnier	Summerland	Marshall	2:25.90
2003	Voix du Nord	D Boeuf	D Smaga	Zuylen de Nyevelt	Simplez	Day or Night	2:16.00
2004	Paita (f)	A Suborics	Mario Hofer	Manfred Hofer	Yehudi	Laverock	2:19.00

*Snurge finished first but was disqualified and placed second.

PRIX JEAN-LUC LAGARDERE-G1

1400 meters (7 furlongs), 2-year-old colts & fillies, Longchamp

Run at 1600 meters (1 mile) through 2000

Run as the Grand Criterium through 2002

Year	1st	Jockey	Trainer	Owner	2nd	3rd	Time
1970	My Swallow	L Piggott	P Davey	D Robinson	Bonami	Marche Persan	1:43.2
1971	Hard to Beat	W Pyers	R Carver	S Sokolow	Steel Pulse	Prodice	1:41.1
1972	Satingo	H Samani	A Head	Mme Wertheimer	Ben Trovato	Thyratron	1:44.6
1973	Mississippian	W Pyers	M Zilber	N B Hunt	Nonoalco	Mount Hagen	1:39.7
1974	Mariacci	G Rivases	J-M de Choubersky	G de Rothschild	Val de l'Orne	Free Round	1:46.2
1975	Manado	P Paquet	F Boutin	Mme S Vanian	Comeram	French Swandee	1:40.4
1976	Blushing Groom	H Samani	F Mathet	Aga Khan	Amyntor	J.O. Tobin	1:44.7
1977	Super Concorde	P Paquet	F Boutin	W Haefner	Pyjama Hunt	Acamas	1:43.93
1978	Irish River	M Phillipperon	J Cunnington Jr	Mme R Ades	Inshalla	Boitron	1:39
1979	Dragon	A Goldsztejn	M Saliba	M Fustok	Nice Havrais	Princesse Lida	1:41.3
1980	Recitation	G Starkey	G Harwood	A Bodie	Critique	Dunphy	1:44.2
1981	Green Forest	A Gibert	M Saliba	M Fustok	Norwick	Rollins	1:46.2
1982	Saint Cyrien	F Head	C Head	Mme A Head	L'Emigrant	The Noble Player	1:46.5
1983	Treizieme (f)	G Dubroeucq	M Zilber	T Tatham	Truculent	Mendez	1:38.8
1984	Alydar's Best (f)	C Roche	D V O'Brien	A Clore	River Drummer	No Pass No Sale	1:49
1985	Femme Elite (f)	A Lequeux	M Zilber	S Fradkoff	Bold Arrangement	Kadrou	1:40
1986	Danishkada (f)	Y Saint-Martin	A de Royer-Dupre	Aga Khan	Lockton	Fotitieng	1:40.7
1987	Fijar Tango	A Gibert	G Mikhalides	M Fustok	Pasakos	Most Precious	1:45.2
1988	Kendor	M Phillipperon	R Touflan	A Bader	Along All	Ecossais	1:40.8
1989	Jade Robbery	C Asmussen	A Fabre	Z Yoshida	Linamix	Honor Rajana	1:40.6
1990	Hector Protector	F Head	F Boutin	S Niarchos	Masterclass	Beau Sultan	1:41.1
1991	Arazi	G Mosse	F Boutin	A E Paulson	Rainbow Corner	Seattle Rhyme	1:41.4
1992	Tenby	Pat Eddery	H Cecil	K Abdullah	Blush Rambler	Basim	1:46.9
1993	Lost World	O Peslier	E Lellouche	D Wildenstein	Signe Divin	Psychobabble	1:45.9

Year	1st	Jockey	Trainer	Owner	2nd	3rd	Time
1994	Goldmark	S Guillot	A Fabre	Sheikh Mohammed	Walk on Mix	Montjoy	1:43.4
1995	Loup Solitaire	O Peslier	A Fabre	D Wildenstein	Manninamix	Eternity Range	1:37.6
1996	Revoque	J Reid	P Chapple-Hyam	R Sangster	Majorien	King Sound	1:37.7
1997	Second Empire	M J Kinane	A P O'Brien	Tabor & Magnier	Charge d'Affaires	Alboostan	1:47.76
1998	Way of Light	C Asmussen	P Bary	Niarchos Family	Red Sea	Glamis	1:52.5
1999	Ciro*	M J Kinane	A P O'Brien	Tabor & Magnier	Barathea Guest	Ocean of Wisdom	1:50.5
2000	Okawango	O Doleuze	C Head	Wertheimer & Frere	King's County	Honours List	1:41.80
2001	Rock Of Gibraltar	M J Kinane	A P O'Brien	Ferguson & Magnier	Bernebeau	Dobby Road	1:22.98
2002	Hold That Tiger	K Fallon	A P O'Brien	Tabor & Magnier	Le Vie dei Colori	Intercontinental	1:20.40
2003	American Post	R Hughes	C Head-Maarek	K Abdullah	Charming Prince	Ximb	1:24.50
2004	Oratorio	J P Spencer	A P O'Brien	Magnier & Tabor	Early March	Layman	1:19.30

*Barathea Guest finished first but was disqualified and placed second.

GRAND PRIX DE PARIS-G1

2000 meters (1-1/4 miles), 3-year-old colts & fillies, Longchamp

FIRST RUN IN 1863

Run at 3000 meters (1-7/8 miles) until 1987

Year	1st	Jockey	Trainer	Owner	2nd	3rd	Time
1970	Roll of Honour	L Piggott	R Carver	E Scheib	Fontarabal	High Moon	3:23.9
1971	Rheffic	W Pyers	F Mathet	Mme F Dupre	Point de Rhiz	Valdrague	3:27.5
1972	Pleben	M Depalmas	G Watson	Baron de Rede	Sukawa	Talleyrand	3:23.6
1973	Tennyson	A Gibert	P Head	F Burmann	Authi	Rasgavor	3:17.7
1974	Sagaro	L Piggott	F Boutin	G Oldham	Bustino	Kamaraan	3:27.6
1975	Matahawk	R Jallu	H Van de Poele	Mme E Stern	Citoyen	Avance	3:17.9
1976	Exceller	Y Saint-Martin	F Mathet	N B Hunt	Secret Man	Caron	3:20.5
1977	Funny Hobby	P Paquet	J de Chevigny	Mme T Caralli	Valinsky	Midshipman	3:21.7
1978	Galiani	A Lequeux	M Zilber	A Ben Lassim	Roi de Mai	Whitstead	3:18.2
1979	Soleil Noir	H Samani	F Mathet	G de Rothschild	Son of Love	Stout Fellow	3:21.7
1980	Valiant Heart	A Gibert	B Secly	A Michel	What a Joy	Water Mill	3:25.1
1981	Glint Of Gold	J Matthias	I Balding	P Mellon	Tipperary Fixer	Vayrann	3:25.5
1982	Le Nain Jaune	H Samani	F Mathet	G de Rothschild	Chem	Rhoecus	3:18.4
1983	Yawa	P Waldron	G Lewis	Elisha Holdings	Fubymam du Tenu	Jasper	3:24
1984	At Talaq	A Murray	H T Jones	H Al Maktoum	Woolskin	Spicy Story	3:14
1985	Sumayr	Y Saint-Martin	Aga Khan	A de Royer-Dupre	Exactly Right	Montecito	3:20
1986	Swink	W Swinburn	J Pease	N B Hunt	War Hero	Silver Word	3:19.3
1987	Risk Me	S Cauthen	P Kelleway	L Norris	Seattle Dancer	Trempolino	2:08.3
1988	Fijar Tango	A Cruz	G Mikhalides	M Fustok	Pasakos	Welkin	2:05.8
1989	Dancehall	C Asmussen	A Fabre	T Wada	Norberto	Creator	2:03.6
1990	Saumarez	S Cauthen	N Clement	B McNall	Priolo	Tirol	2:07.5
1991	Subotica	T Jarnet	A Fabre	O Lecerf	Sillery	Kotashaan	2:05.2
1992	Homme de Loi	T Jarnet	A Fabre	P de Moussac	Kitwood	Guislaine	2:03.9
1993	Fort Wood	S Guillot	A Fabre	Sheikh Mohammed	Bigstone	Siam	2:01.6
1994	Millkom	J-R Dubosc	J-C Rouget	J-C Gour	Solid Illusion	Celtic Arms	2:04.4
1995	Valanour	G Mosse	A de Royer-Dupre	Aga Khan	Singspiel	Diamond Mix	2:02.2
1996	Grape Tree Road	T Jarnet	A Fabre	M Tabor	Glory of Dancer	Android	2:02.3
1997	Peintre Celebre	O Peslier	A Fabre	D Wildenstein	Ithaki	Shaka	2:08.4
1998	Limpid	O Peslier	A Fabre	Sheikh Mohammed	Almutawakel	Croco Rouge	2:03.2
1999	Slickly	T Jarnet	A Fabre	J-L Lagardere	Indian Danehill	Sardaukar	2:03.9
2000	Beat Hollow	T R Quinn	H Cecil	K Abdullah	Premier Pas	Rhenium	2:03.70
2001	Chichicastenango	A Junk	P Demercastel	Mme B Brunet	Mizzen Mast	Bonnard	2:01.00
2002	Khalkevi	C Soumillon	A de Royer-Dupre	HH Aga Khan	Shaanmer	WithoutConnexion	2:02.40
2003	Vespone	C-P Lemaire	N Clement	Ecurie Mister Ess A S	Magistretti	Look Honey	2:01.10
2004	Bago	T Gillet	J Pease	Niarchos Family	Cacique	Alnitak	2:05.60

GRAND PRIX DE SAINT-CLOUD-G1

2400 meters (1-1/2 miles), 3-year-olds & up, colts & fillies, Saint-Cloud

FIRST RUN IN 1903

Year	1st (age)	Jockey	Trainer	Owner	2nd	3rd	Time
1970	Gyr (3)	W Williamson	E Pollet	W Guest	Grandier	Hallez	2:36.8
1971	Ramin (4)	H Samani	G Watson	Baron de Zuylen	Hokkaio	Tarbes	2:43.7
1972	Rheingold (3)	Y Saint-Martin	B Hills	H Zeizel	Arlequino	Hard to Beat	2:41.9
1973	Rheingold (4)	Y Saint-Martin	B Hills	H Zeizel	Direct Flight	Roybet	2:35.6
1974	Dahlia (4f)	Y Saint-Martin	M Zilber	N B Hunt	On My Way	Direct Flight	2:39.4
1975	Un Kopeck (4)	M Philipperon	J Cunnington Jr	J Marx	Ashmore	On My Way	2:38
1976	Riverqueen (3f)	F Head	C Datessen	Mme A Head	Ashmore	Tip Moss	2:34.9
1977	Exceller (4)	F Head	F Mathet	N B Hunt	Riboboy	Iron Duke	2:32.8
1978	Guadanini (4)	H Samani	R Carver	J Kaida	Trillion	Noir et Or	2:41.7
1979	Gay Mecene (4)	F Head	A Head	J Wertheimer	Ela-Mana-Mou	Gain	2:33.4
1980*	Dunette (4f)	G Doleuze	E Chevalier du Fau	Mme Love			
1980*	Shakapour (4)	Y Saint-Martin	F Mathet	Aga Khan	-	Policeman	2:39.8

Year	1st (age)	Jockey	Trainer	Owner	2nd	3rd	Time
1981	Akarad (3)	Y Saint-Martin	F Mathet	Aga Khan	Bikala	Lancastrian	2:38.9
1982	Glint Of Gold (4)	Pat Eddery	I Balding	P Mellon	Lancastrian	Real Shadai	2:41.4
1983	Diamond Shoal (4)	S Cauthen	I Balding	P Mellon	Lancastrian	Zalataia	2:34.9
1984	Teenoso (4)	L Piggott	G Wragg	E Moller	Fly Me	Esprit du Nord	2:34.5
1985	Strawberry Road (6)	Y Saint-Martin	P-L Biancone	D Wildenstein	Seismic Wave	Treizieme	2:34.5
1986	Acatenango (4)	S Cauthen	H Jentzsch	Haras Fahrhof	Saint Estephe	Noble Fighter	2:37.2
1987	Moon Madness (4)	Pat Eddery	J Dunlop	Duchess of Norfolk	Tony Bin	Grand Pavois	2:26.5
1988	Village Star (5)	C Asmussen	A Fabre	A J Richards	Saint Andrews	Frankly Perfect	2:36.3
1989	Sheriff's Star (4)	T Ives	Lady Herries	Duchess of Norfolk	Golden Pheasant	Boyatino	2:35.8
1990	In the Wings (4)	C Asmussen	A Fabre	Sheikh Mohammed	Ode	Zartota	2:29.6
1991	Epervier Bleu (4)	D Boeuf	E Lellouche	D Wildenstein	Rock Hopper	Passing Sale	2:28.1
1992	Pistolet Bleu (4)	D Boeuf	E Lellouche	D Wildenstein	Magic Night	Subotica	2:30.3
1993	User Friendly (4f)	G Duffield	C Brittain	W Gredley	Apple Tree	Modhish	2:28.5
1994	Apple Tree (5)	T Jarnet	A Fabre	Sultan Al Kabeer	Muhtarram	Zimzalabim	2:30
1995	Carnegie (4)	T Jarnet	A Fabre	Sheikh Mohammed	Luso	Only Royale	2:35.2
1996	Helissio (3)	O Peslier	E Lellouche	E Sarasola	Swain	Poliglote	2:27.4
1997	Helissio (4)	C Asmussen	E Lellouche	E Sarasola	Magellano	Riyadian	2:29.5
1998	Fragrant Mix (4)	O Peslier	A Fabre	J-L Lagardere	Romanov	Gazelle Royale	2:31.3
1999	El Condor Pasa (4)	M Ebina	Y Ninomiya	T Watanabe	Tiger Hill	Dream Well	2:28.8
2000	Montjeu (4)	C Asmussen	J Hammond	M Tabor	Daring Miss	Sagamix	2:31.40
2001	Mirio (4)	C Soumillon	J de Choubersky	E Soderberg	Perfect Sunday	Egyptband	2:29.30
2002	Ange Gabriel (4)	T Jarnet	E Libaud	Mme H Devin	Polish Summer	Aquarelliste	2:28.60
2003	Ange Gabriel (5)	T Jarnet	E Libaud	Mme H Devin	Polish Summer	Loxias	2:30.90
2004	Gamut (5)	K Fallon	M R Stoute	Mrs G Smith	Policy Maker	Visorama	2:36.10

*Dunette and Shakapour finished in a deadheat in 1980.

POULE D'ESSAI DES POULAINS (French 1000 Guineas)-G1
1600 meters (1 mile), 3-year-old colts, Longchamp
FIRST RUN IN 1883

Year	1st	Jockey	Trainer	Owner	2nd	3rd	Time
1970	Caro	W Williamson	A Klimscha	Comtesse Batthyany	Breton	Faraway Son	1:41.3
1971	Zug	J-C Desaint	J Cunnington	W Hawn	Tarbes	Breeders Dream	1:37.6
1972	Riverman	J-C Desaint	A Head	Mme Wertheimer	Gift Card	Daring Display	1:38.6
1973	Kalamoun	H Samani	F Mathet	Aga Khan	Bally Game	Satingo	1:41.8
1974	Moulines	M Philipperon	R Carver	J Kashiyama	Mississippian	Contraband	1:43.9
1975	Green Dancer	F Head	A Head	J Wertheimer	Condorcet	Dandy Lute	1:39.3
1976	Red Lord	F Head	A Head	J Wertheimer	Roan Star	Comeram	1:42.3
1977	Blushing Groom	H Samani	F Mathet	Aga Khan	Pharly	Hasty Reply	1:41.8
1978	Nishapour	H Samani	F Mathet	Aga Khan	Rusticaro	Pyjama Hunt	1:46.1
1979	Irish River	M Philipperon	J Cunnington Jr	Mme Ades	Sharpman	Nadjar	1:39.8
1980	In Fijar	G Doleuze	M Saliba	M Fustok	Moorestyle	Argument	1:38.4
1981	Recitation	G Starkey	G Harwood	A Bodie	Redoutable	Cresta Rider	1:40.7
1982	Melyno	Y Saint-Martin	F Mathet	S Niarchos	Tampero	Day is Done	1:38.6
1983	L'Emigrant	C Asmussen	F Boutin	S Niarchos	Crystal Glitters	Margouzed	1:46.3
1984	Siberian Express	A Gibert	A Fabre	M Fustok	Green Paradise	Mendez	1:35.8
1985	No Pass No Sale	Y Saint-Martin	R Collet	R C Strauss	Candy Stripes	Synefos	1:38.1
1986	Fast Topaze	C Asmussen	G Mikhalides	M Fustok	Highest Honor	Art Francais	1:48.3
1987	Soviet Star	G Starkey	A Fabre	Sheikh Mohammed	Noble Minstrel	Glory Forever	1:36.2
1988	Blushing John	F Head	F Boutin	A E Paulson	French Stress	Tay Wharf	1:37.2
1989	Kendor	M Philipperon	R Touflan	A Bader	Goldneyev	Ocean Falls	1:36.1
1990	Linamix	F Head	F Boutin	J-L Lagardere	Zoman	Funambule	1:35.9
1991	Hector Protector	F Head	F Boutin	S Niarchos	Acteur	Francais Sapieha	1:37.6
1992	Shanghai	F Head	F Boutin	S Niarchos	Rainbow Corner	Lion Cavern	1:38.2
1993	Kingmambo	C Asmussen	F Boutin	S Niarchos	Bin Ajwaad	Hudo	1:39.1
1994	Green Tune	O Doleuze	C Head	J Wertheimer	Turtle Island	Psychobabble	1:37.4
1995	Vettori	L Dettori	S bin Suroor	Godolphin	Atticus	Petit Poucet	1:40.4
1996	Ashkalani	G Mosse	A de Royer-Dupre	Aga Khan	Spinning World	Tagula	1:37.6
1997	Daylami	G Mosse	A de Royer-Dupre	Aga Khan	Loup Sauvage	Visionary	1:42.6
1998	Victory Note	J Reid	P Chapple-Hyam	Magnier & Sangster	Muhtathir	Desert Prince	1:34.5
1999	Sendawar	G Mosse	A de Royer-Dupre	Aga Khan	Dansili	Kingsalsa	1:36.2
2000	Bachir	L Dettori	S bin Suroor	Godolphin	Berine's Son	Valentino	1:39.40
2001*	Vahorimix	C Soumillon	A Fabre	J-L Lagardere	Clearing	Denon	1:35.40
2002	Landseer	M J Kinane	A P O'Brien	Tabor & Magnier	Medecis	Bowman	1:36.80
2003	Clodovil	C Soumillon	A Fabre	Famille Lagardere	Catcher In The Rye	Krataios	1:36.40
2004	American Post	R Hughes	C Head-Maarek	K Abdullah	Diamond Green	Byron	1:36.50

*Noverre finished first but was disqualified from purse money.

POULE D'ESSAI DES POULICHES (French 1000 Guineas)-G1
1600 meters (1 mile), 3-year-old fillies, Longchamp
FIRST RUN IN 1883

Year	1st (age)	Jockey	Trainer	Owner	2nd	3rd	Time
1970	Pampered Miss	M Philipperon	J Cunnington Jr	N B Hunt	Prudent Miss	Popkins	1:40.6
1971	Bold Fascinator	W Williamson	J Fellows	W Rosso	Malva	Tawny Owl	1:39.7

Year	1st (age)	Jockey	Trainer	Owner	2nd	3rd	Time
1972	Mata Hari	J Cruguet	A Penna	Comtesse Batthyany	Bisaltis	If	1:44.7
1973	Allez France	Y Saint-Martin	A Klimscha	D Wildenstein	Princess Arjumand	Dahlia	1:44.6
1974	Dumka	A Lequeux	J de Chevigny	C Bauer	Hippodamia	Curtain Row	1:47.5
1975	Ivanjica	F Head	A Head	J Wertheimer	Nobiliary	Broadway Dancer	1:38.4
1976	Riverqueen	F Head	C Datessen	Mme A Head	Suvannee	Sky's Sunny	1:38.6
1977	Madelia	Y Saint-Martin	A Penna	D Wildenstein	Beaune	Durtal	1:39.9
1978	Dancing Maid	F Head	A Head	J Wertheimer	Fruhlingstag	A Thousand Stars	1:45.3
1979	Three Troikas	F Head	C Head	Mme A Head	Nonoalca	Waterway	1:46.00
1980	Aryenne	M Philipperon	J Fellows	D Volkert	Safita	Princesse Lida	1:43.6
1981	Ukraine Girl	Pat Eddery	R Collet	Mme J Mullion	Star Pastures	Ionian Raja	1:41.00
1982	River Lady	L Piggott	F Boutin	R Sangster	Typhoon Polly	Vidor	1:39.6
1983	L'Attrayante	A Badel	O Douieb	Mme Theriot	Mysterieuse Etoile	Maximova	1:42.5
1984	Masarika	Y Saint-Martin	A de Royer-Dupre	Aga Khan	Boreale	Speedy Girl	1:39.3
1985	Silvermine	F Head	C Head	Mme A Head	Top Socialite	New Bruce	1:40.7
1986	Baiser Vole	G Guignard	C Head	R Sangster	Secret Form	River Dancer	1:39.9
1987	Miesque	F Head	F Boutin	S Niarchos	Sakura Reiko	Libertine	1:38.1
1988	Ravinella	G Moore	C Head	Ecurie Aland	Duckling Park	Sacre Look	1:38.3
1989	Pearl Bracelet	A Gibert	R Wojtowiez	Ecurie Fustok	Pass the Peace	Golden Opinion	1:37.1
1990	Houseproud	Pat Eddery	A Fabre	K Abdullah	Pont Aven	Gharam	1:38.5
1991	Danseuse du Soir	D Boeuf	E Lellouche	D Wildenstein	Sha-Tha	Caerlina	1:38.6
1992	Culture Vulture	T R Quinn	P Cole	C Wright	Hydro Calido	Guislaine	1:37.00
1993	Madeleine's Dream	C Asmussen	F Boutin	A E Paulson	Ski Paradise	Gold Splash	1:36.4
1994	East of the Moon	C Asmussen	F Boutin	S Niarchos	Agathe	Bella Argentine	1:37.1
1995	Matiara	F Head	C Head	Ecurie Aland	Carling	Shaanxi	1:42.4
1996	Ta Rib	W Carson	E Dunlop	H Al Maktoum	Shake the Yoke	Sagar Pride	1:38.7
1997	Always Loyal	F Head	C Head	M Al Maktoum	Seebe	Red Camellia	1:40.2
1998	Zalaiyka	G Mosse	A de Royer-Dupre	Aga Khan	Cortona	La Nuit Rose	1:35.7
1999	Valentine Waltz	R Cochrane	J Gosden	Kirby Maher Synd	Karmifira	Calando	1:36.00
2000	Bluemamba	S Guillot	P Bary	Ecurie Skymarc Farm	Peony	Alshakr	1:40.20
2001	Rose Gypsy	M J Kinane	A P O'Brien	Magnier & Tabor	Banks Hill	Lethals Lady	1:36.70
2002	Zenda	R Hughes	J Gosden	K Abdullah	Firth of Lorne	Sophisticat	1:37.00
2003	Musical Chimes	C Soumillon	A Fabre	M Al Maktoum	Maiden Tower	Etoile Montante	1:36.00
2004	Torrestrella	O Peslier	F Rohaut	B Bargues	Grey Lilas	Miss Mambo	1:35.70

PRIX DE DIANE (French Oaks)-G1
2100 meters (1-5/16 miles), 3-year-old fillies, Chantilly
FIRST RUN IN 1843

Year	1st	Jockey	Trainer	Owner	2nd	3rd	Time
1970	Sweet Mimosa	W Williamson	S McGrath	S McGrath	Highest Hopes	Pampered Miss	2:11
1971	Pistol Packer	F Head	A Head	Mme A Head	Cambrizzia	Dixie	2:12.2
1972	Rescousse	Y Saint-Martin	G Watson	Baron de Rede	Prodice	Paysanne	2:10.3
1973	Allez France	Y Saint-Martin	A Klimscha	D Wildenstein	Dahlia	Virunga	2:07.5
1974	Highclere	J Mercer	W R Hern	The Queen	Comtesse de Loir	Odisea	2:07.7
1975	RACE NOT RUN						
1976	Pawneese	Y Saint-Martin	A Penna	D Wildenstein	Riverqueen	Lagunette	2:09
1977	Madelia	Y Saint-Martin	A Penna	D Wildenstein	Trillion	Fabuleux Jane	2:10.3
1978	Reine de Saba	F Head	A Head	J Wertheimer	Cistus	Calderina	2:09.4
1979	Dunette	G Doleuze	E Chevalier de Fau	Mme H Love	Three Troikas	Producer	2:08.6
1980	Mrs Penny	L Piggott	I Balding	E Kronfeld	Aryenne	Paranete	2:10.1
1981	Madam Gay	L Piggott	P Kelleway	G Kaye	Val d'Erica	April Run	2:06.5
1982	Harbour	F Head	C Head	Ecurie Aland	Akiyda	Paradise	2:16.8
1983	Escaline	G Moore	J Fellows	Mme J Fellows	Smuggly	Air Distingue	2:07.8
1984	Northern Trick	C Asmussen	F Boutin	S Niarchos	Grise Mine	Pampa Bella	2:11.6
1985	Lypharita	L Piggott	A Fabre	L T Al Swaidi	Fitnah	Persona	2:05.90
1986	Lacovia	F Head	F Boutin	G Oldham	Secret Form	Galunpe	2:07.00
1987	Indian Skimmer	S Cauthen	H Cecil	Sheikh Mohammed	Miesque	Masmouda	2:11.4
1988	Resless Kara	G Mosse	F Boutin	J-L Lagardere	Riviere d'Or	Raintree Renegade	2:07.5
1989	Lady in Silver	A Cruz	R Wojtowiez	A Karim	Louveterie	Premier Amour	2:10.6
1990	Rafha	W Carson	H Cecil	Prince A Faisal	Moon Cactus	Air de Rien	2:11.7
1991	Caerlina	E Legrix	J de Roualle	K Nitta	Magic Night	Louve Romaine	2:10.5
1992	Jolypha	Pat Eddery	A Fabre	K Abdullah	Sheba Dancer	Verveine	2:09.5
1993	Shemaka	G Mosse	A de Royer-Dupre	Aga Khan	Baya	Dancienne	2:16.00
1994	East of the Moon	C Asmussen	F Boutin	S Niarchos	Her Ladyship	Agathe	2:07.9
1995	Carling	T Thulliez	C Barbe	Ecurie Delbart	Matiara	Tryphosa	2:07.7
1996	Sil Sila	C Asmussen	B Smart	L Alvarez-Cervera	Miss Tahiti	Matiya	2:07.3
1997	Vereva	G Mosse	A de Royer-Dupre	Aga Khan	Mousse Glace	Brilliance	2:08.2
1998	Zainta	G Mosse	A de Royer-Dupre	Aga Khan	Abbatiale	Insight	2:11.2
1999	Daryaba	G Mosse	A de Royer-Dupre	Aga Khan	Star of Akkar	Visionnaire	2:16.1
2000	Egyptband	O Doleuze	C Head	Wertheimer & Frere	Volvoreta	Goldamix	2:08.50
2001	Aquarelliste	D Boeuf	E Lellouche	D Wildenstein	Nadia	Time Away	2:09.50
2002	Bright Sky	D Boeuf	E Lellouche	Ecurie Wildenstein	Dance Routine	Ana Marie	2:07.60
2003	Nebraska Tornado	R Hughes	A Fabre	K Abdullah	Time Ahead	Musical Chimes	2:08.10
2004	Latice	C Soumillon	J-M Beguigne	E Ciampi	Millionaia	Grey Lilas	2:07.00

PRIX DE L'ABBAYE DE LONGCHAMP-G1

1000 meters (5 furlongs), 2-year-old & up, colts & fillies, Longchamp

Year	1st (age)	Jockey	Trainer	Owner	2nd	3rd	Time
1970	Balidar (4)	L Piggott	J Winter	D Prenn	Huntercombe	Raffingora	:58.40
1971	Sweet Revenge 4)	G Lewis	T Corbett	Mrs Attenborough	Swing Easy	Calahorra	1:02.00
1972	Deep River (3)	W Williamson	P Davey	D Robinson	Home Guard	Primaticcio	:57.00
1973	Sandford Lad (3)	A Murray	H Price	C Olley	Abergwaun	Supreme Gift	:59.20
1974	Moubariz (3)	H Samani	F Mathet	Aga Khan	Ace of Aces	La Poesie	:59.70
1975	Lianga (4f)	Y Saint-Martin	A Penna	D Wildenstein	Primo Rico	Mendip Man	:59.20
*1976	Mendip Man (4)	A Gibert	A Paus	Mme J Davis			
*1976	Gentilhombre (3)	T McKeown	N Adam	T Robson	-	Raga Navarro	1:00.30
1977	Gentilhombre (4)	P Cook	N Adam	J Morrell	Madang	Haverold	:58.00
1978	Sigy (2f)	F Head	C Head	Mme A Head	Solinus	Double Form	:59.00
1979	Double Form	J Reid	R J Houghton	Baronne	Thyssen Kilijaro	Greenland Park	:56.70
1980	Moorestyle (4)	L Piggott	R Armstrong	M J Furman Ltd	Sharpo	Valeriga	:56.30
1981	Marwell (3f)	W R Swinburn	M Stoute	E Loder	Sharpo	Rabdan	:58.70
1982	Sharpo (5)	Pat Eddery	J Tree	Mlle Sheriffe	Fearless Lad	King Music	1:00.20
1983	Habibti (3f)	W Carson	J Dunlop	M Mutawa	Soba	Sicyos	:54.30
1984	Committed (4f)	S Cauthen	D K Weld	R Sangster	Habibti	Anita's Prince	:59.80
1985	Committed (5f)	M J Kinane	D K Weld	A E Paulson	Vilikaia	Parioli	:55.20
1986	Double Schwartz (5)	Pat Eddery	C Nelson	R Sangster	Parioli	Hallgate	:56.80
1987	Polonia (3f)	C Roche	J Bolger	H deKwiatkowski	La Grande Epoque	Tenue de Soiree	:56.70
1988	Handsome Sailor (5)	M Hills	B Hills	R Sangster	Caerwent	Silver Fling	:57.00
1989	Silver Fling (4f)	J Matthias	I Balding	G Strawbridge	Zadracarta	Nabeel Dancer	:59.90
1990	Dayjur (3)	W Carson	W R Hern	H Al Maktoum	Lugana Beach	Pharaoh's Delight	:58.70
1991	Keen Hunter (4)	S Cauthen	J Gosden	Sheikh Mohammed	Sheikh Albadou	Magic Ring	:59.40
1992	Mr Brooks (5)	L Piggott	R Hannon	P C Greem	Keen Hunter	Elbio	1:02.30
1993	Lochsong (5f)	L Dettori	I Balding	J C Smith	Stack Rock	Monde Bleu	:59.70
1994	Lochsong (6f)	L Dettori	I Balding	J C Smith	Mister Lopogigio	Spain Lane	:57.20
1995	Hever Golf Rose (4f)	J Weaver	T J Naughton	M Hanson	Cherokee Rose	Eveningperformance	:57.70
1996	Kistena (3f)	O Doleuze	C Head	Wertheimer & Frere	Anabaa	Hever Golf Rose	:59.30
1997	Carmine Lake (3f)	J Reid	P Chapple-Hyam	R Sangster	Pas de Reponse	Royal Applause	:56.90
1998	My Best Valentine (8)	R Cochrane	V Soane	The Valentines	Averti	Sainte Marine	:58.90
1999	Agnes World (4)	Y Take	H Mori	T Watanabe	Imperial Beauty	Keos	1:01.40
2000	Namid (4)	J P Murtagh	J Oxx	Lady Clague	Superstar Leo	Pipalong	:55.10
2001	Imperial Beauty (5f)	Y Take	J Hammond	Mrs J Magnier	Bahamian Pirate	Pipalong	:58.88
2002	Continent (5)	D Holland	D Nicholls	Lucayan Stud	Slap Shot	Zipping	:57.20
2003	Patavellian (5)	S Drowne	R Charlton	D J Deer	The Trader	The Tatling	:59.30
2004	Var (5)	L Dettori	C E Brittain	M Rashid	The Tatling	Royal Millennium	:55.00

*Mendip Man and Gentilhombre finished in a deadheat in 1976.

PRIX DE L'ARC DE TRIOMPHE-G1

2400 meters (1-1/2 miles), 3-year-olds & up colts & fillies, Longchamp

FIRST RUN IN 1920

Year	1st (age)	Jockey	Trainer	Owner	2nd	3rd	Time
1950	Tantieme (3)	J Doysabere	F Mathet	F Dupre	Alizier	L'Amiral	2:34.22
1951	Tantieme (4)	J Doysabere	F Mathet	F Dupre	Nuccio	Le Tyrol	2:32.84
1952	Nuccio (4)	R Poincelet	A Head	Aga Khan	La Mirambule	Dynamiter	2:39.8
1953	La Sorellina (3f)	M Larraun	E Pollet	P Duboscq	Sinet	Worden	2:31.9
1954	Sica Boy (3)	W Johnstone	P Pelat	Mme J Cochery	Banassa	Philante	2:36.4
1955	Ribot (3)	E Camici	U Penco	Marchese Incisa	Beau Prince	Picounda	2:35.6
1956	Ribot (4)	E Camici	U Penco	Marchese Incisa	Talgo	Tanerko	2:34.8
1957	Oroso (4)	S Boullenger	D Lescalle	R Meyer	Denisy	Balbo	2:33.4
1958	Ballymoss (4)	A Breasley	M V O'Brien	J McShain	Fric	Cherasco	2:37.9
1959	Saint Crespin (3)	G Moore	A Head	Prince Aly Khan	Midnight Sun	Le Loup Garou	2:33.3
1960	Puissant Chief (3)	M Garcia	C Bartholomew	H Aubert	Hautain	Point d'Amour	2:43.9
1961	Molvedo (3)	E Camici	A Maggi	E Verga	Right Royal	Misti	2:38.4
1962	Soltikoff (3)	M Depalmas	R Pelat	Mme C Del Duca	Monade	Val de Loir	2:30.9
1963	Exbury (4)	J Deforge	G Watson	G de Rothschild	Le Mesnil	Misti	2:34.9
1964	Prince Royal II (3)	R Poincelet	G Bridgland	R Ellsworth	Santa Claus	La Bamba	2:35.5
1965	Sea-Bird (3)	P Glennon	E Pollet	J Ternynck	Reliance	Diatome	2:35.5
1966	Bon Mot (3)	F Head	W Head	F Burmann	Sigebert	Lionel	2:39.8
1967	Topyo (3)	W Pyers	M Bartholomew	Mme L Volterra	Salvo	Ribocco	2:38.2
1968	Vaguely Noble (3)	W Williamson	E Pollet	Mrs R Franklyn	Sir Ivor	Carmarthen	2:35.2
1969	Levmoss (4)	W Williamson	S McGrath	C McGrath	Park Top	Grandier	2:29.00
1970	Sassafras (3)	Y Saint-Martin	F Mathet	A Plesch	Nijinsky II	Miss Dan	2:29.7
1971	Mill Reef (3)	G Lewis	I Balding	P Mellon	Pistol Packer	Cambrizzia	2:30.3
1972	San San (3f)	F Head	A Penna	Comtesse Batthyany	Rescousse	Homeric	2:28.3
1973	Rheingold (4)	L Piggott	B Hills	H Zeizel	Allez France	Hard to Beat	2:35.8

Year	1st (age)	Jockey	Trainer	Owner	2nd	3rd	Time
1974	Allez France (4f)	Y Saint-Martin	A Penna	D Wildenstein	Comtesse de Loir	Margouillat	2:36.9
1975	Star Appeal (5)	G Starkey	T Grieper	W Zeitelhack	On My Way	Comtesse de Loir	2:33.6
1976	Ivanjica (4f)	F Head	A Head	J Wertheimer	Crow	Youth	2:39.4
1977	Alleged (3)	L Piggott	M V O'Brien	R Sangster	Balmerino	Crystal Palace	2:30.6
1978	Alleged (4)	L Piggott	M V O'Brien	R Sangster	Trillion	Dancing Maid	2:36.1
1979	Three Troikas (3f)	F Head	C Head	Mme A Head	Le Marmot	Troy	2:28.9
1980	Detroit (3f)	Pat Eddery	O Douieb	R Sangster	Argument	Ela-Mana-Mou	2:28.00
1981	Gold River (4f)	G Moore	A Head	J Wertheimer	Bikala	April Run	2:35.2
1982	Akiyda (3f)	Y Saint-Martin	F Mathet	Aga Khan	Ardross	Awaasif	2:37.00
1983	All Along (4f)	W R Swinburn	P-L Biancone	D Wildenstein	Sun Princess	Luth Enchantee	2:28.1
1984	Sagace (4)	Y Saint-Martin	P-L Biancone	D Wildenstein	Northern Trick	All Along	2:39.1
1985*	Rainbow Quest (4)	Pat Eddery	J Tree	K Abdullah	Sagace	Kozana	2:29.5
1986	Dancing Brave (3)	Pat Eddery	G Harwood	K Abdullah	Bering	Triptych	2:27.7
1987	Trempolino (3)	Pat Eddery	A Fabre	P de Moussac	Tony Bin	Triptych	2:26.3
1988	Tony Bin (5)	J Reid	L Camici	Mme V Gaucci del Bono	Mtoto	Boyatino	2:27.3
1989	Carroll House (4)	M J Kinane	M Jarvis	A Balzarini	Behera	Saint Andrews	2:30.8
1990	Saumarez (3)	G Mosse	N Clement	B McNall	Epervier Bleu	Snurge	2:29.8
1991	Suave Dancer (3)	C Asmussen	J Hammond	H Chalhoub	Magic Night	Pistolet Bleu	2:31.4
1992	Subotica (4)	T Jarnet	A Fabre	O Lecerf	User Friendly	Vert Amande	2:39.00
1993	Urban Sea (4f)	E Saint-Martin	J Lesbordes	D Tsui	White Muzzle	Opera House	2:37.9
1994	Carnegie (3)	T Jarnet	A Fabre	Sheikh Mohammed	Hernando	Apple Tree	2:31.1
1995	Lammtarra (3)	L Dettori	S bin Suroor	S M Al Maktoum	Freedom Cry	Swain	2:31.8
1996	Helissio (3)	O Peslier	E Lellouche	E Sarasola	Pilsudski	Oscar Schindler	2:29.9
1997	Peintre Celebre (3)	O Peslier	D Wildenstein	A Fabre	Pilsudski	Borgia	2:24.6
1998	Sagamix (3)	O Peslier	A Fabre	J-L Lagardere	Leggera	Tiger Hill	2:34.5
1999	Montjeu (3)	M J Kinane	J Hammond	M Tabor	El Condor Pasa	Croco Rouge	2:38.5
2000	Sinndar (3)	J P Murtagh	J Oxx	HH Aga Khan	Egyptband	Volvoreta	2:25.80
2001	Sakhee (4)	L Dettori	S bin Suroor	Godolphin	Aquarelliste	Sagacity	2:35.87
2002	Marienbard (5)	L Dettori	S bin Suroor	Godolphin	Sulamani	High Chaparral	2:26.70
2003	Dalakhani (3)	C Soumillon	A de Royer-Dupre	HH Aga Khan	Mubtaker	High Chaparral	2:32.30
2004	Bago (3)	T Gillet	J Pease	Niarchos Family	Cherry Mix	Ouija Board	2:25.00

*Sagace finished first in 1985 but was disqualified and placed second.

CRITERIUM INTERNATIONAL-G1

1600 meters (1 mile), 2-year-old colts & fillies, Saint-Cloud

Replaced the Prix de la Salamandre (7 furlongs, Longchamp) in 2001

Year	1st	Jockey	Trainer	Owner	2nd	3rd	Time
1970	My Swallow	L Piggott	P Davey	D Robinson	La Mie au Roy	Swing Easy	1:22.2
1971	Our Mirage	L Piggott	B Hills	Mrs S Enfield	Trait d'Union	Citheron	1:26
1972	Zapoteco	A Barclay	F Boutin	Mme M-F Berger	Thyratron	Ruling	1:24.8
1973	Nonoalco	L Piggott	F Boutin	Mme M-F Berger	Lion du Nord	Moulines	1:26.8
1974	Delmora (f)	F Head	F Boutin	G Oldham	Free Round	Sky Commander	1:20.7
1975	Manado	P Paquet	F Boutin	Mme S Vanian	Vitiges	Comeran	1:22.9
1976	Blushing Groom	H Samani	F Mathet	Aga Khan	Assez Cuite	Alpherat	1:24.8
1977	John de Coombe	G Baxter	P Cole	H Warren	Bilal	Kenmare	1:22.5
1978	Irish River	M Philipperon	J Cunnington Jr	Mme R Ades	Boitron	Nadjar	1:22.3
1979	Princesse Lida (f)	F Head	A Head	J Wertheimer	Choucri	Koboko	1:21.8
1980	Miswaki	P Paquet	F Boutin	Mme A Plesch	Prince Mab	Silver Express	1:22.7
1981	Green Forest	A Gibert	M Saliba	M Fustok	Zino	Star Princess	1:24.3
1982*	Deep Roots	W Carson	P Bary	C Barbe			
1982*	Maximova (f)	F Head	C Head	Haras d'Etreham	–	Crystal	1:23.2
1983	Seattle Song	C Asmussen	F Boutin	S Niarchos	Siberian Express	Blushing Scribe	1:24.3
1984	Noblequest	Y Saint-Martin	R Collet	Prince Al Kabir	Northern Walker	No Pass No Sale	1:29.2
1985	Baiser Vole (f)	F Head	C Head	R Sangster	Regal State	Bold Arrangement	1:22.1
1986	Miesque (f)	F Head	F Boutin	S Niarchos	Sakura Reiko	Whakilyric	1:25.5
1987	Common Grounds	F Head	F Boutin	S Niarchos	Most Precious	Miss Boniface	1:21.8
1988	Oczy Czarnie (f)	G Moore	J-M Beguigne	G de Rothschild	Kendor	Star Touch	1:25
1989	Machiavellian	F Head	F Boutin	S Niarchos	Qirmazi	Ernani	1:24.8
1990	Hector Protector	F Head	F Boutin	S Niarchos	Lycius	Booming	1:20.8
1991	Arazi	G Mosse	F Boutin	A E Paulson	Made of Gold	Silver Kite	1:20.9
1992	Zafonic	Pat Eddery	A Fabre	K Abdullah	Kingmambo	Splendent	1:23.3
1993	Coup de Genie (f)	C Asmussen	F Boutin	S Niarchos	Majestic Role	Volochine	1:23.1
1994	Pennekamp	T Jarnet	A Fabre	Sheikh Mohammed	Montjoy	Bin Nashwan	1:22.9
1995	Lord Of Men	L Dettori	J Gosden	Sheikh Mohammed	With Fascination	Woodborough	1:27
1996	Revoque	J Reid	P Chapple-Hyam	R Sangster	The West	Zamindar	1:20.9
1997	Xaar	O Peslier	A Fabre	K Abdullah	Charge d'Affaires	Speedfit Too	1:21.6
1998	Aljabr	L Dettori	S bin Suroor	Godolphin	Kingsalsa	Zirconi	1:24
1999	Giant's Causeway	M J Kinane	A O'Brien	Tabor & Magnier	Race Leader	Bachir	1:22.9
2000	Tobougg	C Williams	M Channon	Ahmed Al Maktoum	Honours List	Wooden Doll	1:22.20
2001	Act One	T Gillet	J Pease	G W Leigh	Landseer	Guys And Dolls	1:47.10

Year	1st	Jockey	Trainer	Owner	2nd	3rd	Time
2002	Dalakhani	C Soumillon	A de Royer-Dupre	HH Aga Khan	Chevalier	Governor Brown	1:52.00
2003	Bago	T Gillet	J Pease	Niarchos Family	Top Seed	Acropolis	1:47.00
2004	Helios Quercus	A Roussel	C Diard	T Maudet	Dubai Surprise	Walk in the Park	1:45.30

*Deep Roots and Maximova finished in deadheat for first in 1982.

PRIX DU JOCKEY-CLUB (French Derby)-G1

2400 meters (1-1/2 miles), 3-year-old colts & fillies, Chantilly

FIRST RUN IN 1836

Year	1st	Jockey	Trainer	Owner	2nd	3rd	Time
1952	Auriban	W Johnstone	C Semblat	M Boussac	Corindon	Silnet	2:29.4
1953	Chamant	M Garcia	C Bartholomew	H Letellier	Sephiros	Marly Known	2:29.8
1954	Le Petit Prince	R Bertiglia	C Semblat	L Lawrence	Antares	Sica Boy	2:43.6
1955	Rapace	F Palmer	R Wallon	Comte de Ganay	Vimy	Beignet	2:37.8
1956	Philius	S Boullenger	C Elliot	M Boussac	Saint-Raphael	Tanerko	2:45.2
1957	Amber	M Garcia	R Carver	Mme A Mariotti	Guard's Tie	Le Haar	2:34
1958	Tamanar	J Deforge	J Cunnington	R Beaumonte	Bella Paola	Pepin le Bref	2:34.8
1959	Herbager	G Chancelier	P Pelat	Mme Del Duca	Dan Cupid	Midnight Sun	2:34
1960	Charlottesville	G Moore	A Head	Aga Khan	Night and Day	Bonjour	2:34.8
1961	Right Royal	R Poincelet	E Pollet	Mme J Couturie	Match	My Prince	2:31.6
1962	Val de Loir	F Palmer	M Bonaventure	Marquise du Vivier	Picfort	Exbury	2:29.4
1963	Sanctus	M Larraun	E Pollet	J Ternynck	Nycros	Duc de Gueldre	2:33.4
1964	Le Fabuleux	J Massard	W Head	Mme Weisweiller	Trenel	Djel	2:32.4
1965	Reliance	Y Saint-Martin	F Mathet	F Dupre	Diatome	Carvin	2:36.2
1966	Nelcius	Y Saint-Martin	M Clement	P Duboscq	Bon Mot	Behistoun	2:36.8
1967	Astec	A Jezequel	A Lieux	Baron de la Rochette	Minamote	Taj Dewan	2:29.8
1968	Tapalque	Y Saint-Martin	F Mathet	A Plesch	Timmy My Boy	Val d'Aoste	2:32.2
1969	Goodly	F Head	W Head	M Lehmann	Beaugency	Djakao	2:30.4
1970	Sassafras	Y Saint-Martin	F Mathet	A Plesch	Roll of Honour	Caro	2:31.1
1971	Rheffic	W Pyers	F Mathet	Mme F Dupre	Nymbio	Tarbes	2:32
1972	Hard to Beat	L Piggott	R Carver	J Kashiyama	Sancy	Flair Path	2:27.1
1973	Roi Lear	F Head	A Head	Mme Wertheimer	Tennyson	Gunter	2:34.2
1974	Caracolero	P Paquet	F Boutin	Mme M Berger	Dankaro	Kamaraan	2:32.1
1975	Val de l'Orne	F Head	A Head	J Wertheimer	Patch	Marriacci	2:35.2
1976	Youth	F Head	M Zilber	N B Hunt	Twig Moss	Malacate	2:27.4
1977	Crystal Palace	G Dubroeucq	F Mathet	G de Rothschild	Artaius	Concertino	2:29.6
1978	Acamas	Y Saint-Martin	G Bonnaventure	M Boussac	Frere Basile	Turville	2:32.3
1979	Top Ville	Y Saint-Martin	F Mathet	Aga Khan	Le Marmot	Sharpman	2:25.3
1980	Policeman	W Carson	C Milbank	F Tinsley	Shakapour	Providential	2:27.3
1981	Bikala	S Gorli	P-L Biancone	J Ouaki	Akarad	Gap of Dunloe	2:29.5
1982	Assert	C Roche	D V O'Brien	R Sangster	Real Shadai	Bois de Grace	2:29.5
1983	Caerleon	Pat Eddery	M V O'Brien	R Sangster	L'Emigrant	Esprit du Nord	2:27.3
1984	Darshaan	Y Saint-Martin	A de Royer-Dupre	Aga Khan	Sadler's Wells	Rainbow Quest	2:32.2
1985	Mouktar	Y Saint-Martin	A de Royer-Dupre	Aga Khan	Air de Cour	Premier Role	2:34
1986	Bering	G Moore	C Head	Mme A Head	Altayan	Bakharoff	2:24.1
1987	Natroun	Y Saint-Martin	A de Royer-Dupre	Aga Khan	Trempolino	Naheez	2:30.8
1988	Hours After	Pat Eddery	P-L Biancone	Marquise de Moratall	Ghost Buster's	Emmson	2:33.4
1989	Old Vic	S Cauthen	H Cecil	Shaikh Mohammed	Dancehall	Galetto	2:28.7
1990	Sanglamore	Pat Eddery	R Charlton	K Abdullah	Epervier Bleu	Erdelistan	2:24.6
1991	Suave Dancer	C Asmussen	J Hammond	H Chalhoub	Subotica	Cudas	2:27.4
1992	Polytain	L Dettori	A Spanu	Mme Houillion	Marignan	Contested Bid	2:30.3
1993	Hernando	C Asmussen	F Boutin	S Niarchos	Dernier Empereur	Hunting Hawk	2:27.2
1994	Celtic Arms	G Mosse	P Bary	J-L Bouchard	Solid Illusion	Alriffa	2:31.3
1995	Celtic Swing	K Darley	Lady Herries	P Savill	Poliglote	Winged Love	2:32.8
1996	Ragmar	G Mosse	P Bary	J-L Bouchard	Polaris Flight	Le Destin	2:27.2
1997	Peintre Celebre	O Peslier	A Fabre	D Wildenstein	Oscar	Astarabad	2:29.6
1998	Dream Well	C Asmussen	P Bary	Niarchos Family	Croco Rouge	Sestino	2:39.3
1999	Montjeu	C Asmussen	J Hammond	M Tabor	Nowhere to Exit	Rhagaas	2:33.5
2000	Holding Court	P Robinson	M Jarvis	J R Good	Lord Flasheart	Circus Dance	2:31.80
2001	Anabaa Blue	C Soumillon	C Lerner	C Mimouni	Chichicastenango	Grandera	2:27.90
2002	Sulamani	T Thulliez	P Bary	Niarchos Family	Act One	Simeon	2:25.00
2003	Dalakhani	C Soumillon	A de Royer-Dupre	HH Aga Khan	Super Celebre	Coroner	2:26.70
2004	Blue Canari	T Thulliez	P Bary	Jean-Louis Bouchard	Prospect Park	Valixir	2:25.20

PRIX DU MOULIN DE LONGCHAMP-G1

1600 meters (1 mile), 3-year-olds & up, colts & fillies, Longchamp

Year	1st (age)	Jockey	Trainer	Owner	2nd	3rd	Time
1970	Gold Rod (3)	L Piggott	R Ackekure	Mrs C Dick	Faraway Son	Prudent Miss	1:37.8
1971	Faraway Son (4)	Y Saint-Martin	M Zilber	D Wildenstein	Gold Rod	Blinis	1:38.3
1972	Sallust (3)	J Mercer	W R Hern	M Sobell	Lyphard	Daring Display	1:35.7
1973	Sparkler (5)	L Piggott	R Armstrong	Mme Mehl-Mulhens	Kalamoun	Princess Arjumand	1:41.7
1974	Mount Hagen (3)	P Paquet	A Penna	D Wildenstein	Northern State	Liunga	1:48.5
1975	Delmora (3f)	P Paquet	F Boutin	G Oldham	Son of Silver	Riot in Paris	1:41
1976	Gravelines (4)	Y Saint-Martin	A Penna	D Wildenstein	Dona Barod	Manado	1:42
1977	Pharly (3)	M Philipperon	J Cunnington Jr	A Blasco	Monseigneur	Sanedtki	1:40.6

Year	1st (age)	Jockey	Trainer	Owner	2nd	3rd	Time
1978	Sanedtki (4f)	A Lequeux	O Douieb	S Fradkoff	Homin	Nishapour	1:37.9
1979	Irish River (3)	M Philipperon	J Cunnington Jr	Mme R Ades	Lyphard's Wish	Boitron	1:38.8
1980	Kilijaro (4f)	F Head	O Douieb	S Fradkoff	Nadjar	Katowice	1:36.9
1981	North Jet (4)	F Head	O Douieb	S Fradkoff	Hilal	The Wonder	1:35.2
1982	Green Forest (3)	A Gibert	M Saliba	M Fustok	The Wonder	Sandhurst Prince	1:34.9
1983	Luth Enchantee (3f)	M Philipperon	J Cunnington Jr	P de Moussac	L'Emigrant	Wassl	1:38.9
1984	Mendez (3f)	C Asmussen	F Boutin	S Niarchos	Lear Fan	Meis El Reem	1:43.4
1985	Rousillon (4)	G Starkey	G Harwood	K Abdullah	Kozana	Procida	1:39
1986	Sonic Lady (3f)	W Swinburn	M Stoute	Sheikh Mohammed	Thrill Show	Lirung	1:35.8
1987	Miesque (3f)	F Head	F Boutin	S Niarchos	Soviet Star	Grecian Urn	1:37.5
1988	Soviet Star (4)	C Asmussen	A Fabre	Sheikh Mohammed	Miesque	Gabina	1:40.3
1989	Polish Precedent (3)	C Asmussen	A Fabre	Sheikh Mohammed	Squill	Cadeaux Genereux	1:38.5
1990	Distant Relative (4)	Pat Eddery	W Said	B Hills	Linamix	Priolo	1:38.38
1991	Priolo (4)	G Mosse	F Boutin	Ecurie Skymarc Farm	Mukaddamah	Lycius	1:38.4
1992	All At Sea (3f)	Pat Eddery	H Cecil	K Abdullah	Brief Truce	Hatoof	1:40.7
1993	Kingmambo (3)	C Asmussen	S Niarchos	F Boutin	Ski Paradise	Bigstone	1:37.6
1994	Ski Paradise (4f)	Y Take	A Fabre	T Yoshida	East of the Moon	Green Tune	1:37.8
1995	Ridgewood Pearl (3f)	J P Murtagh	J Oxx	A Coughlan	Shaanxi	Missed Flight	1:36.9
1996	Ashkalani (3)	G Mosse	A de Royer-Dupre	Aga Khan	Spinning World	Shake the Yoke	1:37.2
1997	Spinning World (4)	C Asmussen	J Pease	Niarchos Family	Helissio	Daylami	1:37.1
1998	Desert Prince (3)	O Peslier	D Loder	Lucayan Stud	Gold Away	Second Empire	1:40.9
1999	Sendawar (3)	G Mosse	A de Royer-Dupre	Aga Khan	Gold Away	Dansili	1:35.2
2000	Indian Lodge (4)	C Asmussen	A Perrett	S Cohn & E Parker	Kingsalsa	Diktat	1:40.80
2001	Slickly (5)	L Dettori	S bin Suroor	Godolphin	Banks Hill	Hawkeye	1:39.00
2002	Rock Of Gibraltar (3)	M J Kinane	A P O'Brien	Ferguson & Magnier	Banks Hill	Gossamer	1:39.30
2003	Nebraska Tornado (3f)	R Hughes	A Fabre	K Abdullah	Lohengrin	Bright Sky	1:38.70
2004	Grey Lilas (3f)	E Legrix	A Fabre	Gestut Amerland	Diamond Green	Antonius Pius	1:37.50

PRIX GANAY-G1

2100 meters (1-5/16 miles), 4-year-olds & up, colts & fillies, Longchamp

Year	1st	Jockey	Trainer	Owner	2nd	3rd	Time
1970	Grandier (6)	M Philipperon	J Cunnington Jr	Mme P Ribes	Yelapa	Prince Regent	2:14.2
1971	Caro (4)	M Philipperon	A Klimscha	Comtesse Batthyany	Amadou	Stintino	2:08.6
1972	Mill Reef (4)	G Lewis	I Balding	P Mellon	Amadou	El Toro	2:16.2
1973	Rheingold (4)	Y Saint-Martin	B Hills	H Zeisel	Bog Road	Citheron	2:17.2
1974	Allez France (4f)	Y Saint-Martin	A Penna	D Wildenstein	Tennyson	Gombos	2:23.2
1975	Allez France (5f)	Y Saint-Martin	A Penna	D Wildenstein	Card King	Comtesse de Loir	2:12
1976	Infra Green (4f)	J Taillard	E Bartholomew	Mme Pochna	Kasteel	Ivanjica	2:14.8
1977	Arctic Tern (4)	M Philipperon	J Fellows	Mrs J Knight	Exceller	Infra Green	2:11.6
1978	Trillion (4f)	L Piggott	M Zilber	E Stephenson	Monseigneur	Sirlad	2:18.2
1979	Frere Basile (4)	J-L Kessas	B Secly	J-P Binet	Trillion	Pevero	2:17.2
1980	Le Marmot (4)	P Paquet	F Boutin	R Schafer	Three Troikas	Northern Baby	2:15
1981	Argument (5)	A Lequeux	M Zilber	B McNall	Armistice Day	In Fijar	2:12.2
1982	Bikala (4)	S Gorli	P-L Biancone	J Ouaki	Lancastrian	Al Nasr	2:09.7
1983	Lancastrian (6)	A Lequeux	D Smaga	M Sobell	Cadoudal	Welsh Tern	2:16.9
1984	Romildo (4)	C Asmussen	F Boutin	G Oldham	Sagace	Adonijah	2:12
1985	Sagace (5)	Y Saint-Martin	P-L Biancone	D Wildenstein	Romildo	Careillor	2:10.3
1986	Baillamont (4)	F Head	F Boutin	S Niarchos	Mersey	Saint Estephe	2:11.7
1987	Triptych (5f)	A Cruz	P-L Biancone	A Clore	Takfa Yahmed	Highest Honor	2:15.1
1988	Saint Andrews (4)	A Badel	J-M Beguigne	Mme Volterra	Grand Fleuve	Triptych	
1989	Saint Andrews (5)	A Badel	J-M Beguigne	Mme Volterra	Star Lift	Mansonnien	2:20.8
1990	Creator (4)	C Asmussen	A Fabre	Sheikh Mohammed	In the Wings	Ibn Bey	2:13
1991	Kartajana (4f)	W Mongil	A de Royer-Dupre	Aga Khan	Passing Sale	Dear Doctor	2:18.4
1992	Subotica (4)	T Jarnet	A Fabre	O Lecerf	Pistolet Bleu	Suave Dancer	2:09.3
1993	Vert Amande (5)	D Boeuf	E Lellouche	E Sarasola	Opera House	Misil	2:02.1
1994	Marildo (7)	G Guignard	D Smaga	D Smaga	Intrepidity	Urban Sea	2:11.9
1995	Pelder (5)	L Dettori	P Kelleway	O Pedroni	Alderbrook	Richard of York	2:20.7
1996	Valanour (4)	G Mosse	A de Royer-Dupre	Aga Khan	Luso	Swain	2:10.9
1997	Helissio (4)	O Peslier	E Lellouche	E Sarasola	Le Destin	Pilsudski	2:12.1
1998	Astarabad (4)	G Mosse	A de Royer-Dupre	Aga Khan	Que Belle	Taipan	2:21.5
1999	Dark Moondancer (4)	G Mosse	A de Royer-Dupre	B Arbib	Dream Well	Croco Rouge	2:11.3
2000	Indian Danehill (4)	O Peslier	A Fabre	Baron E de Rothschild	Greek Dance	Chelsea Manor	2:27.20
2001	Golden Snake (5)	Pat Eddery	J Dunlop	The National Stud	Egyptband	With the Flow	2:16.70
2002	Aquarelliste (4f)	D Boeuf	E Lellouche	Ecurie Wildenstein	Execute	Sensible	2:11.40
2003	Fair Mix (5)	O Peslier	M Rolland	Ecurie Week-End	Execute	Falbrav	2:13.00
2004	Execute (7)	T Gillet	J Hammond	Ecurie Chalhoub	Vespone	Fair Mix	2:14.60

PRIX JACQUES LE MAROIS-G1

1600 meters (1 mile), 3-year-olds & up, colts & fillies, Deauville

Year	1st (age)	Jockey	Trainer	Owner	2nd	3rd	Time
1970	Priamos (6)	A Gibert	H Jentzsch	V Oppenheimer	Faster	Yellow God	1:41.3
1971	Dictus (4)	Y Saint-Martin	R de Mony-Pajol	J-M Soriano	Sparkler	Roi Soleil	1:37.4
1972	Lyphard (3)	F Head	A Head	Mme P Wertheimer	High Top	Jan Ekels	1:38.2

Year	1st (age)	Jockey	Trainer	Owner	2nd	3rd	Time
1973	Kalamoum (3)	H Samani	F Mathet	Aga Khan	Rose Laurel	Sparkler	1:36
1974	Nonoalco (3)	L Piggott	F Boutin	Mme M-F Berger	El Toro	Coup de Feu	1:37.2
1975	Lianga (4)	Y Saint-Martin	A Penna	D Wildenstein	Sky Commander	Delmora	1:34.6
1976	Gravelines (4)	G Moore	A Penna	D Wildenstein	Radetzky*	Vitiges*	1:35.1
1977	Flying Water (4)	Y Saint-Martin	A Penna	D Wildenstein	Blushing Groom	Trepan	1:44.2
1978	Kenmare (3)	A Badel	F Mathet	G de Rothschild	Sanedtki	Faraway Times	1:38.6
1979	Irish River (3)	M Philipperon	J Cunnington Jr	Mme R Ades	Bellypha	A Thousand Stars	1:35.5
1980	Nadjar (4)	A Lequeux	A Paus	A D Rogers	Final Straw	Manjam	1:38.4
1981	Northjet (4)	F Head	O Douieb	S Fradkoff	To-Agori-Mou	King's Lake	1:34.5
1982	The Wonder (4)	Pat Eddery	J de Chevigny	Marquise de Moratalla	Green Forest	Zino	1:35.5
1983	Luth Enchantee (3f)	M Philipperon	J Cunnington Jr	P de Moussac	L'Emigrant	Montekin	1:35.9
1984	Lear Fan (3)	Pat Eddery	G Harwood	A Salman	Palace Music	Siberian Express	1:34.9
1985	Vin de France (3)	E Legrix	P-L Biancone	D Wildenstein	Vertige	River Mist	1:38.2
1986	Lirung (4)	S Cauthen	H Jentzsch	Haras Fahrhof	Regal State	Efisio	1:36.4
1987	Miesque (3f)	F Head	F Boutin	S Niarchos	Nashmeel	Hadeer	1:35
1988	Miesque (4f)	F Head	F Boutin	S Niarchos	Warning	Gabina	1:38.6
1989	Polish Precedent (3	C Asmussen	A Fabre	Sheikh Mohammed	French Stress	Magic Gleam	1:37.3
1990	Priolo (3)	A Lequeux	F Boutin	Ecurie Skymarc Farm	Linamix	Distant Relative	1:38.2
1991	Hector Protector (3)	F Head	F Boutin	S Niarchos	Lycius	Danseuse du Soir	1:39.4
1992	Exit to Nowhere (4)	C Asmussen	F Boutin	S Niarchos	Lahib	Cardoun	1:40.8
1993	Sayyedati (3f)	W Swinburn	C Brittain	M Obaida	Ski Paradise	Kingmambo	1:39.8
1994	East of the Moon(3f)	C Asmussen	F Boutin	S Niarchos	Sayyedati	Mehthaaf	1:35.7
1995	Miss Satamixa (3f)	S Guillot	A Fabre	J-L Lagardere	Sayyedati	Shaanxi	1:35.7
1996	Spinning World (3)	C Asmussen	J Pease	Niarchos Family	Vetheuil	Shaanxi	1:39.1
1997	Spinning World (4)	C Asmussen	J Pease	Niarchos Family	Daylami	Neuilly	1:34.4
1998	Taiki Shuttle (4)	Y Okabe	K Fujisawa	Taiki Farm Inc	Among Men	Cape Cross	1:37.4
1999	Dubai Millennium(3)	L Dettori	S bin Suroor	Godolphin	Slickly	Dansili	1:44.3
2000	Muhtathir (5)	L Dettori	S bin Suroor	Godolphin	Sendawar	Kingsalsa	1:34.60
2001+	Vahorimix (3)	O Peslier	A Fabre	J-L Lagardere	Banks Hill	Noverre	1:38.80
2002	Banks Hill (4f)	O Peslier	A Fabre	K Abdullah	Domedriver	Best Of The Bests	1:35.19
2003	Six Perfections (3f)	T Thulliez	P Bary	Niarchos Family	Domedriver	Telegnosis	1:38.30
2004	Whipper (3)	C Soumillon	Robert Collet	R C Strauss	Six Perfections	My Risk	1:38.40

*Radetzky and Vitiges finished in a deadheat for second in 1976.
+Proudwings finished first but was disqualified and placed last.

PRIX MARCEL BOUSSAC-G1

1600 meters (1 mile), 2-year-old fillies, Longchamp

Year	1st	Jockey	Trainer	Owner	2nd	3rd	Time
1970	Two to Paris	J-C Desaint	J Cunnington	L Doherty	Tawny Owl	Bold Fascinator	1:42.1
1971	Dark Baby	G Doleuze	J Laumain	M Fournier	Paysanne	Rose de Saron	1:39.5
1972	Allez France	Y Saint-Martin	A Klimscha	D Wildenstein	Kerlande	Fiery Diplomate	1:38
1973	Hippodamia	W Pyers	M Zilber	N B Hunt	Comtesse de Loir	La Tulipe	1:43
1974	Oak Hill	Y Josse	G Bridgland	Mme S Houyvet	Margravine	Harmonise	1:47.8
1975	Theia	Y Saint-Martin	R Touflan	Baronne Lopez-Tarrag	Suvanee	Luna Real	1:44.3
1976	Kamicia	F Flachi	J Laumain	Mme H Rabatel	Doha	Orchid Miss	1:49.7
1977	Tarona	P Paquet	F Boutin	G Oldham	Cistus	Praise	1:41.9
1978	Pitasia	A Gibert	A Paus	D Clague	Minstrel Girl	Cheerfully	1:48.3
1979	Aryenne	Y Saint-Martin	J Fellows	D Volkert	Pompoes	Teacher's Pet	1:41.3
1980	Tropicaro	A Lequeux	M Zilber	B Coates	Coral Dance	Salmana	1:43.4
1981	Play It Safe	L Piggott	F Boutin	Mrs B Firestone	River Lady	Perlee	1:46.9
1982	Goodbye Shelley	J Lowe	S Norton	Mrs S Brook	Mysterieuse Etoile	L'Attrayante	1:47.4
1983	Almeira	D Vincent	J-C Cunnington	Comtesse Batthyany	Masarika	Feerie Boreale	1:38.8
1984	Triptych	A Lequeux	D Smaga	A Clore	Silvermine	Coup de Folie	1:46.7
1985	Midway Lady	L Piggott	B Hanbury	H Ranier	Fieldy	Riverbride	1:37.9
1986	Miesque	F Head	F Boutin	S Niarchos	Milligram	Sakura Reiko	1:37.5
1987	Ashayer	W Carson	J Dunlop	H Al Maktoum	Riviere d'Or	Harmless Albatross	1:37.4
1988	Mary Linoa	A Lequeux	D Smaga	D Smaga	Rose de Crystal	Reine du Ciel	1:41.2
1989	Salsabil	W Carson	J Dunlop	H Al Maktoum	Houseproud	Alchi	1:40.3
1990	Shadayid	W Carson	J Dunlop	H Al Maktoum	Caerlina	Sha-Tha	1:40.7
1991	Culture Vulture	T R Quinn	P Cole	C Wright	Hatoof	Verveine	1:40.6
1992	Gold Splash	G Mosse	C Head	J Wertheimer	Kindergarten	Love of Silver	1:44.9
1993	Sierra Madre	G Mosse	P Bary	J-L Bouchard	Flagbird	Mehthaaf	1:45.4
1994	Macoumba	F Head	C Head	Haras d'Etreham	Piquetnol	Chrysalu	1:43.8
1995	Miss Tahiti	O Peslier	A Fabre	D Wildenstein	Shake the Yoke	Solar Crystal	1:40.2
1996	Ryafan	L Dettori	J Gosden	K Abdullah	Yashmak	Family Tradition	1:39.8
1997	Loving Claim	O Doleuze	C Head	M Al Maktoum	Isle de France	Plaisir des Yeux	1:37.6
1998	Juvenia	O Doleuze	C Head	Wertheimer & Frere	Crystal Downs	Blue Cloud	1:43.0
1999	Lady of Chad	O Peslier	R Gibson	J D Martin	New Story	Lady Vettori	1:44.9
2000	Amonita	T Jarnet	P Bary	Mme P de Moussac	Karasta	Choc Ice	1:36.30
2001	Sulk	L Dettori	J Gosden	J Wigan	Danseuse d'Etoile	Kournakova	1:41.95
2002	Six Perfections	T Thulliez	P Bary	Niarchos Family	Etoile Montante	Luminata	1:37.90
2003	Denebola	C-P Lemaire	P Bary	Niarchos Family	Green Noon	Tulipe Royale	1:40.90
2004	Divine Proportions	C-P Lemaire	P Bary	Niarchos Family	Titian Time	Fraloga	1:36.70

PRIX MORNY-G1

1200 meters (6 furlongs), 2-year-old colts & fillies, Deauville

Year	1st	Jockey	Trainer	Owner	2nd	3rd	Time
1970	My Swallow	L Piggott	P Davey	D Robinson	Impertinent	Tarbes	1:17.7
1971	Daring Display	F Head	W Head	Lady Granard	Rose de Saron	Pompous	1:13.7
1972	Filiberto	J Cruguet	A Penna	Comtesse Batthyany	Zapoteco	El Rastro	1:10.8
1973	Nonoalco	L Piggott	F Boutin	Mme M-F Berger	Insistance	Cake	1:10.8
1974	Broadway Dancer (f)	Y Saint-Martin	A Penna	D Wildenstein	Janthina	Princesse Lee	1:11.7
1975	Vitiges	G Rivases	G Philippeau	Mme Laloum	Imogene	Wood Green	1:11.4
1976	Blushing Groom	H Samani	F Mathet	Aga Khan	Water Boy	Alpherat	1:12.4
1977	Super Concorde	P Paquet	F Boutin	W Haefner	Little Love	El Muleta	1:12.0
1978	Irish River	M Philipperon	J Cunnington Jr	Mme R Ades	Pitasia	Young Generation	1:12.7
1979	Princesse Lida (f)	F Head	A Head	J Wertheimer	Varingo	Firyal	1:11.7
1980	Ancient Regime (f)	M Philipperon	J Fellows	R Scully	Miswaki	Prince Mab	1:10.1
1981	Green Forest	A Gibert	M Saliba	M Fustok	Maelstrom Lake	River Lady	1:11.9
1982	Deep Roots	W Carson	P Bary	C Barbe	On Stage	Ma Biche	1:11.1
1983	Siberian Express	A Gibert	M Saliba	M Fustok	Ti King	Masarika	1:10.1
1984	Seven Springs (f)	G Moore	J Fellows	R Scully	Gallanta	Noblequest	1:09.9
1985	Regal State (f)	D Beadman	J Fellows	R Scully	River Dancer	Baiser Vole	1:12.6
1986	Sakura Reiko (f)	E Legrix	P-L Biancone	E Zen	Shy Princess	Miesque	1:14.5
1987	First Waltz (f)	M Philipperon	E Bartholomew	R McAlpine	Common Grounds	Balawaki	1:12.8
1988	Tersa (f)	G Mosse	F Boutin	Ecossais	A E Paulson	Money Movers	1:15.6
1989	Machiavellian	F Head	F Boutin	S Niarchos	Qirmazi	Mill Lady	1:12.8
1990	Hector Protector	F Head	F Boutin	S Niarchos	Divine Danse	Acteur Francais	1:14.4
1991	Arazi	G Mosse	F Boutin	A E Paulson	Kenbu	Lion Cavern	1:13.3
1992	Zafonic	Pat Eddery	A Fabre	K Abdullah	Secrage	Marina Park	1:14.8
1993	Coup de Genie (f)	C Asmussen	F Boutin	S Niarchos	Psychobabble	Spain Lane	1:13.1
1994	Hoh Magic (f)	M Hills	M Bell	D Allport	Bruttina	Tereshkova	1:11.7
1995	Tagula	W R Swinburn	I Balding	Mr & Mrs R Hitchens	With Fascination	Barricade	1:11.6
1996	Bahamian Bounty	L Dettori	D Loder	Lucayan Stud Ltd	Zamindar	Pas de Reponse	1:11.0
1997	Charge d'Affaires	G Mosse	A de Royer-Dupre	Marquise de Moratalla	Xaar	Heeremandi	1:12.7
1998	Orpen	M J Kinane	A P O'Brien	Tabor & Magnier	Exeat	Golden Silca	1:10.5
1999	Fasliyev	M J Kinane	A P O'Brien	Tabor & Magnier	Warm Heart	Bachir	1:11.00
2000	Bad As I Wanna Be	G Mosse	B Meehan	J Allbritton	Endless Summer	Noverre	1:10.30
2001	Johannesburg	M J Kinane	A P O'Brien	Tabor & Magnier	Zipping	Meshaheer	1:10.40
2002	Elusive City	K Fallon	G Butler	Thoroughbred Corp	Zafeen	Loving Kindness	1:10.40
2003	Whipper	S Maillot	Robert Collet	E Zaccour	Much Faster	Denebola	1:14.00
2004	Divine Proportions(f)	C-P Lemaire	P Bary	Niarchos Family	Layman	Russian Blue	1:12.80

PRIX VERMEILLE-G1

2400 meters (1-1/2 miles), 3 &4-year-old fillies, Longchamp

(3-year-old fillies only through 2003)

Year	1st	Jockey	Trainer	Owner	2nd	3rd	Time
1970	Highest Hopes	J Mercer	W R Hern	L Holliday	Miss Dan	Parmelia	2:29.2
1971	Pistol Packer	F Head	A Head	Mme A Head	Cambrizzia	Pink Pearl	2:34.7
1972	San San*	J Cruguet	A Penna	D Wildenstein			
1972	Paysanne*	H Samani	G Watson	G de Rothschild -	–	Decigale	2:35.6
1973	Allez France	Y Saint-Martin	A Klimscha	D Wildenstein	Hurry Harriet	Fi Mina	2:43.4
1974	Paulista	Y Saint-Martin	A Penna	D Wildenstein	Comtesse de Loir	Gaily	2:33.6
1975	Ivanjica	G Moore	A Head	J Wertheimer	Nobiliary	May Hill	2:34.7
1976	Lagunette	P Paquet	F Boutin	M Berghgracht	Sarah Siddons	Floressa	2:40.2
1977	Kamicia	A Badel	J Laumain	Mme H Robatel	Royal Hive	Fabuleux Jane	2:30.5
1978	Dancing Maid	F Head	A Head	J Wertheimer	Relfo	Amazer	2:34.0
1979	Three Troikas	F Head	C Head	Mme A Head	Salpinx	Pitasia	2:30.3
1980	Mrs Penny	J Matthias	I Balding	E Kronfeld	Little Bonny	Detroit	2:34.9
1981	April Run	P Paquet	F Boutin	Mrs B Firestone	Leandra	Madam Gay	2:32.9
1982	All Along	G Starkey	P-L Biancone	D Wildenstein	Akiyda	Grease	2:29.9
1983	Sharaya	Y Saint-Martin	A de Royer-Dupre	Aga Khan	Estrapade	Vosges	2:42.1
1984	Northern Trick	C Asmussen	F Boutin	S Niarchos	Circus Plume	Treizieme	2:40.9
1985	Walensee	E Legrix	P-L Biancone	D Wildenstein	Fitnah	Galla Placidia	2:32.7
1986	Darara	Y Saint-Martin	A de Royer-Dupre	Aga Khan	Reloy	Lacovia	2:38.7
1987	Bint Pasha	Pat Eddery	P Cole	Prince F Salman	Three Tails	Something True	2:31.7
1988	Indian Rose	A Cruz	J-M Beguigne	G de Rothschild	Sudden Love	Light the Lights	2:28.8
1989	Young Mother	A Badel	J-M Beguigne	J-M Beguigne	Sierra Roberta	Colorado Dancer	2:33.1
1990	Salsabil	W Carson	J Dunlop	H Al Maktoum	Miss Alleged	In The Groove	2:29.6
1991	Magic Night	A Badel	P Demercastel	Mme P Demercastel	Pink Turtle	Crnagora	2:27.8
1992	Jolypha	Pat Eddery	A Fabre	K Abdullah	Cunning	Urban Sea	2:32.8
1993	Intrepidity	T Jarnet	A Fabre	Sheikh Mohammed	Wemyss Bight	Bright Moon	2:36.8
1994	Sierra Madre	G Mosse	P Bary	J-L Bouchard	Yenda	State Crystal	2:35.3
1995	Carling	T Thulliez	C Barbe	Ecurie Delbart	Valley of Gold	Larrocha	2:32.8
1996	My Emma	C Asmussen	R Guest	Matthews Breeding&Racng	Papering	Miss Tahiti	2:31.3
1997	Queen Maud	O Peslier	J de Roualle	G Tanaka	Gazelle Royale	Brilliance	2:28.2
1998	Leggera	T R Quinn	J Dunlop	Mrs A Focke	Cloud Castle	Zainta	2:41.4
1999	Daryaba	G Mosse	A de Royer-Dupre	Aga Khan	Etizaaz	Cerulean Sky	2:30.6

Year	1st	Jockey	Trainer	Owner	2nd	3rd	Time
2000	Volvoreta	M J Kinane	C Lerner	Mme M S Vidal	Reve d'Oscar	Egyptband	2:26.30
2001	Aquarelliste	D Boeuf	E Lellouche	D Wildenstein	Diamilina	Mare Nostrum	2:27.95
2002	Pearly Shells	C Soumillon	F Rohaut	6C Racing Ltd	Ana Marie	Bright Sky	2:26.00
2003	Mezzo Soprano	L Dettori	S bin Suroor	Godolphin	Yesterday	Fidelite	2:26.10
2004	Sweet Stream (4)	T Gillet	J Hammond	Team Valor	Royal Fantasy	Pride	2:29.50

*San San and Paysanne finished in a deadheat in 1972.

IRELAND

IRISH CHAMPION STAKES-G1

1-1/4 miles, 3-year-olds & up, Leopardstown

FIRST RUN IN 1984

Run as the Phoenix Champion Stakes at Phoenix Park prior to 1991.

Year	1st	Jockey	Trainer	Owner	2nd	3rd	Time
1984	Sadler's Wells	Pat Eddery	M V O'Brien	R Sangster	Seattle Song	Princess Pati	2:00.9
1985	Commanche Run	L Piggott	L Cumani	I Allan	Bob Back	Damister	2:09.2
1986	Baillamont	F Head	J Bolger	P H Burns	Sharrood	Supreme Leader	2:02.5
1987	Triptych	A S Cruz	P-L Biancone	A Clore	Entitled	Cockney Lass	2:06.7
1988	Indian Skimmer (4f)	M Roberts	H Cecil	Sheikh Mohammed	Shady Heights	Triptych	2:06.5
1989	Carroll House (4)	M J Kinane	M Jarvis	A Balzarini	Citidancer	Petrullo	2:04.0
1990	Elmaamul (3)	W Carson	W R Hern	H Al Maktoum	Sikeston	Kostroma	2:02.9
1991	Suave Dancer (3)	C Asmussen	J Hammond	H Chalhoub	Environment Friend	Stagecraft	2:06.8
1992	Dr Devious (3)	J Reid	P Chapple-Hyam	S Craig	St. Jovite	Alflora	2:10
1993	Muhtarram (4)	W Carson	J Gosden	H Al Maktoum	Opera House	Lord Of The Field	2:06.1
1994	Cezanne (5)	M J Kinane	M Stoute	Godolphin	Del Deya	Grand Lodge	2:07.9
1995	Pentire (3)	M Hills	G Wragg	Mollers Racing	Freedom Cry	Flagbird	2:04.4
1996	Timarida (4f)	J P Murtagh	J Oxx	Aga Khan	Dance Design	Glory Of Dancer	2:06.2
1997	Pilsudski (5)	M J Kinane	M Stoute	Lord Weinstock	Desert King	Alhaarth	2:04.7
1998	Swain (6)	L Dettori	S bin Suroor	Godolphin	Alborada	Xaar	2:10.2
1999	Daylami (5)	L Dettori	S bin Suroor	Godolphin	Dazzling Park	Dream Well	2:08.4
2000	Giant's Causeway (3)	M J Kinane	A P O'Brien	Mrs J Magnier/M Tabor	Greek Dance	Best Of The Bests	2:03.10
2001	Fantastic Light (5)	L Dettori	S bin Suroor	Godolphin	Galileo	Bach	2:01.80
2002	Grandera (4)	L Dettori	S bin Suroor	Godolphin	Hawk Wing	Best Of The Bests	2:04.70
2003	High Chaparral (4)	M J Kinane	A P O'Brien	M Tabor/Mrs J Magnier	Falbrav	Islington	2:03.30
2004	Azamour (3)	M J Kinane	J Oxx	H H Aga Khan	Norse Dancer	Powerscourt	2:01.97

IRISH DERBY-G1

1-1/2 miles, 3-year-old colts & fillies, The Curragh

FIRST RUN IN 1866

Year	1st	Jockey	Trainer	Owner	2nd	3rd	Time
1950	Dark Warrior	J Thompson	P Prendergast	F M O'Ferrall	Eclat	Pardal	2:37.6
1951	Fraise du Bois II	C Smirke	H Wragg Begum	Aga Khan	Signal Box	Bolivar	2:33
1952	Thirteen Of Diamonds	J Mullane	P Prendergast	A. Hawkins	Prince Of Fairfield	D.C.M.	2:31.67
1953	Chaumier*	W Rickaby	M V O'Brien	Mrs F Vickerman	Sea Charger	Clonleason	2:34.6
1954	Zarathustra	P Powell Jr	M Hurley	T Gray	Hidalgo	Tale Of Two Cities	2:34.8
1955	Panaslipper	J Eddery	S McGrath	J McGrath	Hugh Lupus	Ann s Kuda	2:37.84
1956	Talgo	E Mercer	H Wragg	G Oldham	Roistar	No Comment	2:30.92
1957	Ballymoss	T Burns	M V O'Brien	J McShain	Hindu Festival	Valentine Slipper	2:39.12
1958	Sindon	L Ward	M Dawson	Mrs A Biddle	Paddy's Point	Royal Highway	2:58.9
1959	Fidalgo	J Mercer	H Wragg	G Oldham	Bois Belleau	Anthony	2:33.5
1960	Chamour	G Bougoure	A S O'Brien	F Burmann	Alcaeus	Prince Chamier	2:37.5
1961	Your Highness	H Holmes	H Cottrill	G Bell	Soysambu	Haven	2:33.5
1962	Tambourine	R Poincelet	E Pollet	Mrs H Jackson	Arctic Storm	Sebring	2:28.8
1963	Ragusa	G Bougoure	P Prendergast	J Mullion	Vic Mo Chroi	Tiger	2:45.6
1964	Santa Claus	W Burke	J M Rogers	J Ismay	Lionhearted	Sunseeker	2:35.6
1965	Meadow Court	L Piggott	P Prendergast	G Bell	Convamore	Wedding Present	2:46.8
1966	Sodium	F Durr	G Todd	R Sigtia	Charlottown	Paveh	2:31.5
1967	Ribocco	L Piggott	R J Houghton	C Engelhard	Sucaryl	Dart Board	2:32.4
1968	Ribero	L Piggott	R J Houghton	C Engelhard	Sir Ivor	Val d Aoste	2:33.9
1969	Prince Regent	G Lewis	E Pollet	Comtesse de la Valdene	Ribofilio	Reindeer	2:36.1
1970	Nijinsky II	J Ward	M V O'Brien	C Engelhard	Meadowville	Master Guy	2:33.6
1971	Irish Ball	A Gibert	P Lallei	F Littler	Lombardo	Guillemot	2:36.6
1972	Steel Pulse	W Williamson	A Breasley	R Tikkoo	Scottish Rifle	Ballymore	2:39.8
1973	Weavers' Hall	G McGrath	S McGrath	S McGrath	Ragapan	Buoy	2:32.0
1974	English Prince	Y Saint-Martin	P Walwyn	Mrs V Hue-Williams	Imperial Prince	Sir Penfro	2:33.4
1975	Grundy	Pat Eddery	P Walwyn	C Vittadini	King Pellinore	Anne's Pretender	2:31.1

Year	1st	Jockey	Trainer	Owner	2nd	3rd	Time
1976	Malacate	P Paquet	F Boutin	Mme M-F Berger	Empery	Northern Treasure	2:31.2
1977	The Minstrel	L Piggott	M V O'Brien	R Sangster	Lucky Sovereign	Classic Example	2:31.9
1978	Shirley Heights	G Starkey	J Dunlop	Lord Halifax	Exdirectroy	Hawaiian Sound	2:32.3
1979	Troy	W Carson	W R Hern	M Sobell	Dickens Hill	Bohemian Grove	2:30.6
1980	Tyrnavos	A Murray	B Hobbs	G Cambanis	Prince Bee	Ramian	2:34.8
1981	Shergar	L Piggott	M Stoute	Aga Khan	Cut Above	Dance Bid	2:32.6
1982	Assert	C Roche	D V O'Brien	R Sangster	Silver Hawk	Patcher	2:33.2
1983	Shareef Dancer	W R Swinburn	M Stoute	M Al Maktoum	Caerleon	Teenoso	2:29.4
1984	El Gran Senor	Pat Eddery	M V O'Brien	R Sangster	Rainbow Quest	Dahar	2:31.4
1985	Law Society	Pat Eddery	M V O'Brien	S Niarchos	Theatrical	Damister	2:29.8
1986	Shahrastani	W R Swinburn	M Stoute	Aga Khan	Bonhomie	Bakharoff	2:32.0
1987	Sir Harry Lewis	J Reid	B Hills	H Kaskel	Naheez	Entitled	2:40.2
1988	Kahyasi	R Cochrane	L Cumani	Aga Khan	Insan	Glacial Storm	2:32.4
1989	Old Vic	S Cauthen	H Cecil	Sheikh Mohammed	Observation Post	Ile de Nisky	2:29.8
1990	Salsabil (f)	W Carson	J Dunlop	H Al Maktoum	Deploy	Belmez	2:33.0
1991	Generous	A Munro	P Cole	Prince Fahd Salman	Suave Dancer	Star Of Gdansk	2:33.3
1992	St. Jovite	C Roche	J Bolger	V K Payson	Dr Devious	Contested Bid	2:25.6
1993	Commander In Chief	Pat Eddery	H Cecil	K Abdullah	Hernando	Foresee	2:31.2
1994	Balanchine (f)	L Dettori	H Ibrahim	Godolphin	King's Theatre	Colonel Collins	2:32.7
1995	Winged Love	O Peslier	A Fabre	Sheikh Mohammed	Definite Article	Annus Mirabilis	2:30.1
1996	Zagreb	P Shanahan	D K Weld	A E Paulson	Polaris Flight	His Excellence	2:30.6
1997	Desert King	C Roche	A O'Brien	Tabor & Magnier	Dr Johnson	Loup Sauvage	2:32.5
1998	Dream Well	C Asmussen	P Bary	Niarchos Family	City Honours	Desert Fox	2:44.3
1999	Montjeu	C Asmussen	J Hammond	M Tabor	Daliapour	Tchaikovsky	2:30.1
2000	Sinndar	J P Murtagh	J Oxx	HH Aga Khan	Glyndebourne	Ciro	2:33.90
2001	Galileo	M J Kinane	A P O'Brien	Magnier & Tabor	Morshdi	Golan	2:27.10
2002	High Chaparral	M J Kinane	A P O'Brien	Tabor & Magnier	Sholokhov	Ballingarry	2:32.20
2003	Alamshar	J P Murtagh	J Oxx	HH Aga Khan	Dalakhani	Roosevelt	2:28.20
2004	Grey Swallow	P J Smullen	D K Weld	Rochelle Quinn	North Light	Tycoon	2:28.70

*Premonition finished first but was disqualified and placed last.

IRISH OAKS-G1

1-1/2 miles, 3-year-old fillies, The Curragh

FIRST RUN IN 1895

Year	1st	Jockey	Trainer	Owner	2nd	3rd	Time
1970	Santa Tina	L Piggott	C Milbanks	S O'Flaherty	Parmella	Sweet Mimosa	2:34.9
1971	Altesse Royale	G Lewis	N Murless	F Hue-Williams	Vincennes	Lavendula Rose	2:32
1972	Regal Exception	M Philipperon	J Fellows	R Scully	Arkadina	Pidget	2:32
1973	Dahlia	W Pyers	M Zilber	N B Hunt	Mysterious	Hurry Harriet	2:43.8
1974	Dibidale	W Carson	B Hills	N Robinson	Gaily	Polygamy	2:35.2
1975	Juliette Marny	L Piggott	J Tree	J Morrison	Tuscarora	Nobiliary	2:29.8
1976	Lagunette	P Paquet	F Boutin	M Berghgarcht	Sarah SiddonsI've A	Bee	2:33
1977	Olwyn	J Lynch	R Boss	S Vanian	Sassabunda	Nanticious	2:35
1978	Fair Salinia	G Starkey	M Stoute	S Hanson	Sorbus	Relfo	2:35.2
1979	Godetia	L Piggott	M V O'Brien	R Sangster	Producer	Queen To Conquer	2:33.6
1980	Shoot A Line	W Carson	W R Hern	A Budgett	Little Bonny	Racquette	2:39.4
1981	Blue Wind	W R Swinburn	D K Weld	B R Firestone	Condessa	Stracomer Queen	2:35.8
1982	Swiftfoot	W Carson	W R Hern	Lord Rotherwick	Prince's Polly	Rosananti	2:33.8
1983	Give Thanks	D Gillespie	J Bolger	Mrs O White	High Hawk	Green Lucia	2:32.2
1984	Princess Pati	P Shanahan	C Collins	Mrs J Mullion	Circus Plume	Marble Run	2:28.6
1985	Helen Street	W Carson	W R Hern	M Sobell	Alydar's Best	Dubian	2:39.8
1986	Colorspin	Pat Eddery	M Stoute	Helena Springfield Ltd	Fleur Royale	Untold	2:40.8
1987	Unite	W R Swinburn	M Stoute	Sheikh Mohammed	Bourbon Girl	Eurobird	2:34.8
1988	Diminuendo*	S Cauthen	H Cecil	Sheikh Mohammed			
1988	Melodist*	W R Swinburn	M Stoute	Sheikh Mohammed	-	Silver Lane	2:36.4
1989	Alydaress	M J Kinane	H Cecil	Sheikh Mohammed	Aliysa	Petite Ile	2:31..0
1990	Knight's Baroness	T R Quinn	P Cole	Prince F Salman	Atoll	Assertion	2:31.6
1991	Possessive Dancer	S Cauthen	A Scott	A Al Maktoum	Jet Ski Lady	Eileen Jenny	2:31.0
1992	User Friendly	G Duffield	C Brittain	W Gredley	Market Booster	Arrikala	2:33.7
1993	Wemyss Bight	Pat Eddery	A Fabre	K Abdullah	Royal Ballerina	Oakmead	2:35.8
1994	Bolas	Pat Eddery	B Hills	K Abdullah	Hawajiss	Gothic Dream	2:37.6
1995	Pure Grain	J Reid	M Stoute	R Barnett	Russian Snows	Valley Of Gold	2:33.6
1996	Dance Design	M J Kinane	D K Weld	Moyglare Stud Farm	Shamadara	Key Change	2:29.7
1997	Ebadiyla	J P Murtagh	J Oxx	HH Aga Khan	Yashmak	Brilliance	2:33.7
1998	Winona	J P Murtagh	J Oxx	Lady Clague	Kitza	Bahr	2:39.8
1999	Ramruma	K Fallon	H Cecil	Prince F Salman	Sunspangled	Sister Bella	2:33.00
2000	Petrushka	J P Murtagh	M Stoute	Highclere Thor. Racing	Melikah	Inforapenny	2:31.20
2001	Lailani	L Dettori	E Dunlop	M Al Maktoum	Mot Juste	Karsavina	2:30.50
2002	Margarula	K J Manning	J Bolger	Mrs J Bolger	Quarter Moon	Lady's Secret	2:37.40
2003	Vintage Tipple	L Dettori	P Mullins	P J O'Donovan	L'Ancresse	Casual Look	2:28.30
2004	Ouija Board	K Fallon	E Dunlop	Lord Derby	Punctilious	Hazarista	2:28.20

*Diminuendo and Melodist finished in a deadheat in 1988.

IRISH 1000 GUINEAS-G1

1 mile, 3-year-old fillies, The Curragh

FIRST RUN IN 1922

Year	1st	Jockey	Trainer	Owner	2nd	3rd	Time
1970	Black Satin	R Hutchinson	J Dunlop	W Reynolds	Lovely Kat	Miralife	
1971	Favoletta	L Piggott	H Wragg	R Moller	Mariel	Spring Garden	
1972	Pidget	W Swinburn	K Prendergast	N Butler	Arkadina	Klairlone	
1973	Cloonagh	G Starkey	H Cecil	A Boyd-Rochfort	Annerbelle	Desert Nymph	
1974	Gaily	R Hutchinson	W R Hern	M Sobell	Northern Gem	Pepi Image	
1975	Miralla	R Parnell	F Nugent	Lady Lister-Kaye	Silky	Highest Trump	
1976	Sarah Siddons	C Roche	P Prendergast	Mrs J Mullion	Clover Princess	Lady Singer	
1977	Lady Capulet	T Murphy	M V O'Brien	R Sangster	Bold Fantasy	Lady Mere	
1978	More So	C Roche	P Prendergast	L Gelb	Sorbus	Ridaness	
1979	Godetia	L Piggott	M V O'Brien	R Sangster	La Samanna	Fair Davina	
1980	Cairn Rouge	A Murray	M Cunningham	D Brady	Millingdale Lillie	Mrs Penny	
1981	Arctique Royale	G Curran	K Prendergast	J Binet	Blue Wind	Martinova	
1982	Princess Polly	W R Swinburn	D K Weld	T Nicholson	Woodstream	On The House	1:40.4
1983	L'Attrayante	A Badel	O Douieb	Mme C Theriot	Maximova	Annie Edge	1:49.2
1984	Katies	P Robinson	M Ryan	T Ramsden	Alianna	So Fine	1:38.6
1985	Al Bahathri	A Murray	H T Jones	H Al Maktoum	Vilikaia	Top Socialite	1:41.2
1986	Sonic Lady	W R Swinburn	M Stoute	Sheikh Mohammed	Lake Champlain	Asteroid Field	1:44.8
1987	Forest Flower	T Ives	I Balding	P Mellon	Milligram	Taking Steps	1:43.6
1988	Trusted Partner	M J Kinane	D K Weld	Moyglare Stud	Dancing Goddess	Jingle Gold	1:39.8
1989	Ensconse	R Cochrane	L Cumani	Sheikh Mohammed	d Aldbourne	Run To Jenny	1:38.4
1990	In The Groove	S Cauthen	D Elsworth	B Cooper	Heart Of Joy	Performing Arts	1:41.2
1991	Kooyonga	W O'Connor	M Kauntze	M Haga	Julie La Rousse	Umniyatee	1:37.2
1992	Marling	W R Swinburn	G Wragg	E Loder	Market Booster	Tarwiya	1:41.4
1993	Nicer	M Hills	B Hills	Mrs J Corbett	Goodnight Kiss	Danse Royale	1:44.2
1994	Mehthaaf	W Carson	J Dunlop	H Al Maktoum	Las Meninas	Relatively Special	1:49
1995	Ridgewood Pearl	C Roche	J Oxx	A Coughlan	Warning Shadows	Khaytada	1:43.9
1996	Matiya	W Carson	B Hanbury	H Al Maktoum	Dance Design	My Branch	1:39.8
1997	Classic Park	S Craine	A O'Brien	S Burns	Strawberry Roan	Caiseal Ros	1:42.2
1998	Tarascon	J P Spencer	T Stack	Mrs J Rowlinson	Kitza	La Nuit Rose	1:38.4
1999	Hula Angel	M Hills	B Hills	J R Fleming	Golden Silca	Dazzling Park	1:38.8
2000	Crimplene	P Robinson	C E Brittain	Marwan Al Maktoum	Amethyst	Storm Dream	1:39.80
2001	Imagine	J A Heffernan	A P O'Brien	Magnier & Nagle	Crystal Music	Toroca	1:41.10
2002	Gossamer	J P Spencer	L Cumani	G Leigh-Cancerbacup	Quarter Moon	Starbourne	1:45.50
2003	Yesterday	M J Kinane	A P O'Brien	Mrs J Magnier	Six Perfections	Dimitrova	1:40.80
2004	Attraction	K Darley	M Johnston	Duke of Roxburghe	Alexander Goldrun	Illustrious Miss	1:37.60

IRISH 2000 GUINEAS-G1

1 mile, 3-year-old colts & fillies, The Curragh

FIRST RUN IN 1921

Year	1st	Jockey	Trainer	Owner	2nd	3rd	Time
1970	Decies	L Piggott	B van Cutsem	N B Hunt	Great Heron	Mon Plaisir	
1971	King's Company	F Head	G Robinson	B R Firestone	Sparkler	King's View	
1972	Ballymore	C Roche	P Prendergast	Mrs J Mullion	Martinmas	Flair Path	
1973	Sharp Edge	J Mercer	W R Hern	J Astor	Midsummer Star	Dapper	
1974	Furry Glen	G McGrath	S McGrath	P McGrath	Pitcairn	Cellini	
1975	Grundy	Pat Eddery	P Walwyn	C Vittadini	Monsanto	Mark Anthony	
1976	Northern Treasure	G Curran	K Prendergast	A Brennan	Comeran	Lucky Wednesday	
1977	Pampapaul	G Dettori	H Murless	H Paul	The Minstrel	Nebbiolo	
1978	Jaazeiro	L Piggott	M V O'Brien	R Sangster	Strong Gale	Columbanus	
1979	Dickens Hill	A Murray	A O'Toole	Mme J Binet	Brother Philips	Mister Niall	
1980	Nikoli	C Roche	P Prendergast	Lord Iveagh	Last Fandango	Final Straw	
1981	Kings Lake	Pat Eddery	M V O'Brien	Mme J Binet	To-Agori-Mou	Prince Echo	
1982	Dara Monarch	M J Kinane	L Browne	Mrs L Browne	Tender King	Red Sunset	1:41.8
1983	Wassl	A Murray	J Dunlop	A Al Maktoum	Lomond	Parliament	
1984	Sadler's Wells	G McGrath	M V O'Brien	R Sangster	Procida	Secreto	1:38.2
1985	Triptych (f)	C Roche	D V O'Brien	A Clore	Celestial Bounty	Sun Valley	1:42.8
1986	Flash Of Steel	M J Kinane	D K Weld	B R Firestone	Mr John	Sharrood	1:53.4
1987	Don't Forget Me	W Carson	R Hannon	Jim Horgan	Entitled	Stately Don	1:38
1988	Prince Of Birds	D Gillespie	M V O'Brien	R Sangster	Caerwent	Intimidate	1:39.0
1989	Shaadi	W R Swinburn	M Stoute	Sheikh Mohammed	Great Commotion	Distant Relative	1:37.4
1990	Tirol	Pat Eddery	R Hannon	John Horgan	Royal Academy	Lotus Pool	1:39.2
1991	Fourstars Allstar	M E Smith	L O'Brien	R Bomze	Star Of Gdansk	Lycius	1:38.6
1992	Rodrigo de Triano	L Piggott	P Chapple-Hyam	R Sangster	Ezzoud	Brief Truce	1:41.6
1993	Barathea	M Roberts	L Cumani	Sheikh Mohammed	Fatherland	Massyar	1:43

Year	1st	Jockey	Trainer	Owner	2nd	3rd	Time
1994	Turtle Island	J Reid	P Chapple-Hyam	R Sangster	Guided Tour	Ridgewood Ben	1:50.1
1995	Spectrum	J Reid	P Chapple-Hyam	Lord Weinstock	Adjareli	Bahri	1:40.3
1996	Spinning World	C Asmussen	J Pease	Niarchos Family	Rainbow Blues	Beauchamp King	1:38.8
1997	Desert King	C Roche	A P O'Brien	M Tabor	Verglas	Romanov	1:38.3
1998	Desert Prince	O Peslier	D Loder	Lucayan Stud	Fa-Eq	Second Empire	1:36.25
1999	Saffron Walden	O Peslier	A P O'Brien	Tabor & Magnier	Enrique	Orpen	1:38.1
2000	Bachir	L Dettori	S bin Suroor	Godolphin	Giant's Causeway	Cape Town	1:39.80
2001	Black Minnaloushe	J P Murtagh	A P O'Brien	Magnier & Tabor	Mozart	Minardi	1:41.40
2002	Rock Of Gibraltar	M J Kinane	A P O'Brien	Ferguson & Magnier	Century	Della Frnacesca	1:47.20
2003	Indian Haven	J F Egan	P D'Arcy	Gleeson/Smith/Conway	France	Tout Seul	1:41.50
2004	Bachelor Duke	S Sanders	J Toller	Est/Duke of Devonshire	Azamour	Grey Swallow	1:40.00

GERMANY

GROSSER PREIS VON BADEN-G1

1-1/2 miles, 3-year-olds & up, Baden-Baden (Ger)

Year	1st	Jockey	Trainer	Owner	2nd	3rd	Time
1970	Alpenkonig (3)	F Dreschler	H Jentzsch	Gestut Schlenderhan	Cortez	Snraceno	2:34
1971	Cortez (6)	O Langner	S von Mitzlaff	Gestut Zoppenbroich	Segnes	Spirit	2:32.2
1972	Caracol (3)	O Langner	S von Mitzlaff	Gestut Fahrhof	Experte	Arratos	2:30.5
1973	Athenagoras (3)	H Remmert	S von Mitzlaff	Gestut Zoppenbroich	Arratos	Telemach	2:32
*1974	Meautry (4)	E Sauvaget	G Pezerll	F Baral	Bakuba	Recupere	2:34.6
*1974	Marduk (3)	P Remmert	H Bollow	Comtesse Batthyany	Card King	Athenagoras	2:34.8
1975	Marduk (4)	P Remmert	H Bollow	Comtesse Batthyany	Lord Udo	Card King	2:41
1976	Sharper (3)	W Carson	A Hecker	A van Kaick	Windwurf	Tutlinger	2:38
1977	Windwurf (5)	G Lewis	H Gummelt	Gestut Ravensberg	Stuyvesant	Casaque	2:32.4
1978	Valour (3)	J Reid	R J Houghton	G Ward	Tip Moss	Marzvogel	2:38.4
1979	M-Loishan (4)	B Taylor	R Price	E Alkhalifa	Konigsstuhl	Perougos	2:30.9
1980	Nebos (4)	L Mader	H Bollow	Comtesse Batthyany	Cherubin	Marraci	2:37.6
1981	Pelerin (4)	G Starkey	H Wragg	Sir P Oppenheimer	Hohritt	Maivogel	2:27.6
1982	Glint Of Gold (4)	Pat Eddery	I Balding	P Mellon	Orofino	Ti amo	2:29.1
1983	Diamond Shoal (4)	S Cauthen	I Balding	P Mellon	Abary	Prima Voce	2:28
1984	Strawberry Road (5)	B Thomson	J Nicholls	R F Stehr	Esprit du Nord	Abary	2:29.6
1985	Gold And Ivory (4)	S Cauthen	I Balding	P Mellon	Daun	Crazy	2:37.8
1986	Acatenango (4)	G Bocskai	H Jentzsch	Gestut Fahrhof	St Hilarion	Daun	2:28.3
1987	Acatenango (5)	G Bocskai	H Jentzsch	Gestut Fahrhof	Moon Madness	Winwood	2:34.7
1988	Carroll House (3)	B Raymond	M Jarvis	A Balzarini	Helikon	Boyatino	2:52.7
1989	Mondrian (3)	K Woodburn	U Stoltefuss	Stall Hanse	Per Quod	Summer Trip	2:29.6
1990	Mondrian (4)	M Hofer	U Stoltefuss	Stall Hanse	Ibn Bey	Per Quod	2:34.6
1991	Lomitas (3)	P Schiergen	A Wohler	Gestut Fahrhof	Temporal	Wajd	2:28.8
1992	Mashaallah (4)	J Reid	J Gosden	A Al MAktoum	Platini	Sapience	2:37.8
1993	Lando (3)	A Tylicki	H Jentzsch	Gestut Haus Ittlingen	Platini	George Augustus	2:28.2
1994	Lando (4)	P Schiergen	H Jentzsch	Gestut Haus Ittlingen	Monsun	Kornado	2:27.3
1995	Germany (4)	L Dettori	B Schutz	J Abdullah	Lecroix	Right Win	2:37.7
1996	Pilsudski (4)	W R Swinburn	M Stoute	Lord Weinstock	Germany	Sunshack	2:26.7
1997	Borgia (3f)	K Fallon	B Schutz	Gestut Ammerland	Luso	Predappio	2:28.5
1998	Tiger Hill (3)	A Suborics	P Schiergen	Baron G von Ullmann	Caitano	Public Purse	2:40.1
1999	Tiger Hill (4)	T Hellier	P Schiergen	Baron G von Ullmann	Flamingo Road	Belenus	2:29.9
2000	Samum (3)	A Starke	A Schutz	Stall Balnkenese	Catella	Fruits Of Love	2:38.95
2001	Morshdi (3)	P Robinson	M Jarvis	Darley Stud Mngmnt	Boreal	Sabiango	2:31.27
2002	Marienbard (5)	L Dettori	S bin Suroor	Godolphin	Salve Regina	Noroit	2:34.93
2003	Mamool (4)	L Dettori	S bin Suroor	Godolphin	Black Sam Bellamy	Dano-Mast	2:32.75
2004	Warrsan (6)	K McEvoy	C E Brittain	S Manana	Egerton	Shirocco	2:32.79

*Run in two divisions in 1974.

PREMIER ASIAN STAKES

DUBAI WORLD CUP-G1

2000 meters (1-1/4 miles) (Dirt), 4-year-olds & up, Nad Al Sheba

FIRST RUN IN 1996

Year	1st	Jockey	Trainer	Owner	2nd	3rd	Time
1996	Cigar (6)	J D Bailey	W I Mott	A E Paulson	Soul of the Matter	L'Carriere	2:03.84
1997	Singspiel (5)	J D Bailey	M Stoute	Sheikh Mohammed	Siphon	Sandpit	2:01.91
1998	Silver Charm (4)	G Stevens	B Baffert	R & B Lewis	Swain	Loup Sauvage	2:04.29
1999	Almutawakel (4)	R Hills	S bin Suroor	H Al Maktoum	Malek	Victory Gallop	2:00.65
2000	Dubai Millennium (4)	L Dettori	S bin Suroor	Godolphin	Behrens	Public Purse	1:59.50
2001	Captain Steve (4)	J D Bailey	B Baffert	M E Pegram	To The Victory	Hightori	2:00.40
2002	Street Cry (4)	J D Bailey	S bin Suroor	Godolphin	Sei Mi	Sahkee	2:01.18
2003	Moon Ballad (4)	L Dettori	S bin Suroor	Godolphin	Harlan's Holiday	Nayef	2:00.48
2004	PleasantlyPerfect(6)	A Solis	R Mandella	Diamond A Racing Corp	Medaglia d'Oro	Victory Moon	2:00.24

HONG KONG CUP-G1

2000 meters (1-1/4 miles), 3-year-olds & up, Sha Tin

FIRST RUN IN 1990

Run twice in 1993, in April and December.

Run as Hong Kong International Cup at 1800 meters (1-1/8 miles) 1990-1998.

Year	1st (age)	Jockey	Trainer	Owner	2nd	3rd	Time
1990	Kessem (5)	K Moses	B J Smith	Durcan & Smith	Livistona Lane	Colonial Chief	1:48.4
1991	River Verdon (4)	G Mosse	D Hill	O Cheung	Prudent Manner	Majestic Boy	1:49.8
1992	RACE NOT RUN						
1993	Romanee Conti (4)	G Childs	L K Laxson	P J & P M Vela	Fraar	Charmonnier	1:48.2
1993	Motivation (5)	J Marshall	J Moore	S Hui	Verveine	Stark South	1:49.2
1994	State Taj (5)	D Oliver	J Riley	H & Mrs L Croll	River Majesty	Volochine	1:48.4
1995	Fujiyama Kenzan (7)	M Ebina	H Mori	T Fujimoto	Ventquattrofogli	Jade Age	1:47.0
1996	First Island (4)	M Hills	G Wragg	Mollers Racing	Seascay	Kingston Bay	1:48.2
1997	Val's Prince (5)	C J Asmussen	J Picou	Martin & Weiner	Oriental Express	Wixim	1:47.2
1998	Midnight Bet (4)	H Kawachi	H Nagahama	Shadai Racehorse Co	Johan Cruyff	Almushtarak	1:46.9
1999	Jim and Tonic (5)	G Mosse	F Doumen	J D Martin	Running Stag	Lear Spear	2:01.4
2000	Fantastic Light (4)	L Dettori	S bin Suroor	Godolphin	Greek Dance	Jim and Tonic	2:02.20
2001	Agnes Digital (4)	H Shii	T Shirai	T Watanabe	Tobougg	Terre a Terre	2:02.80
2002	Precision (4)	M J Kinane	D Oughton	Wu Sai Wing	Paolini	Dano-Mast	2:07.10
2003	Falbrav (5)	L Dettori	L Cumani	Scuderia Rencati	Rakti	Elegant Fashion	2:00.90
2004	AlexanderGoldrun(3f)	K J Manning	J Bolger	Mrs N O'Callaghan	Bullish Luck	Touch of Land	2:03.30

JAPAN CUP-G1

2400 meters (1-1/2 miles), 3-year-olds & up, Tokyo

FIRST RUN IN 1981

Year	1st (age)	Jockey	Trainer	Owner	2nd	3rd	Time
1981	Mairzy Doates (5f)	C Asmussen	J Fulton	A Schefler	Frost King	The Very One	2:25.3
1982	Half Iced (3)	D MacBeth	S Hough	B R Firestone	All Along	April Run	2:27.1
1983	Stanerra (5f)	B Rouse	F Dunne	F Dunne	Kyoei Promise	Esprit du Nord	2:27.6
1984	Katsuragi Ace (4)	K Nishiura	K Domon	I Node	Bedtime	Symboli Rudolf	2:26.3
1985	Symboli Rudolf (4)	Y Okabe	Y Nohira	Symboli Bokujo	Rocky Tiger	The Filbert	2:28.8
1986	Jupiter Island (7)	Pat Eddery	C Brittain	Marquess of Tavistock	Allez Milord	Miho Shinzan	2:25
1987	Le Glorieux (3)	A Lequeux	R Collet	Mme S Wolf	Southjet	Dyna Actress	2:24.9
1988	Pay the Butler (4)	C McCarron	R Frankel	E Gann	Tamamo Cross	Oguri Cap	2:25.5
1989	Horlicks (6f)	L O'Sullivan	D O'Sullivan	G de Gruchy	Oguri Cap	Pay the Butler	2:22.2
1990	Better Loosen Up (5)	M Clarke	D Hayes	G Farrah	Ode	Cacoethes	2:23.2
1991	Golden Pheasant (5)	G Stevens	C Whittingham	B McNall	Magic Night	Shaftesbury Avenue	2:24.7
1992	Tokai Teio (4)	Y Okabe	S Matsumoto	M Uchimura	Naturalism	Dear Doctor	2:24.6
1993	Legacy World (4)	H Kawachi	H Mori	Y Souma	Kotashaan	Winning Ticket	2:24.4
1994	Marvelous Crown(4)	K Minai	M Osawa	S Sasahara	Paradise Creek	Royce And Royce	2:23.6
1995	Lando (5)	M Roberts	H Jentzsch	Gestut Ittlingen	Hishi Amazon	Hernando	2:24.6
1996	Singspiel (4)	L Dettori	M Stoute	Sheikh Mohammed	Fabulous la Fouine	Strategic Choice	2:23.8
1997	Pilsudski (5)	M J Kinane	M Stoute	Lord Weinstock	Air Groove	Bubble Gum Fellow	2:25.8
1998	El Condor Pasa (3)	M Ebina	Y Ninomiya	T Watanabe	Air Groove	Special Week	2:25.9
1999	Special Week (4)	Y Take	T Shirai	H Usuda	Indigenous	High-Rise	2:25.5
2000	T.M. Opera O (4)	R Wada	I Iwamoto	M Takezono	Meisho Doto	Fantastic Light	2:26.10
2001	Jungle Pocket (3)	O Peslier	S Watanabe	Y Saito	T.M. Opera O	Narita Top Road	2:23.80
*2002	Falbrav (4)	L Dettori	L Brogi	Scuderia Rencati	Sarafan	Symboli Kris S	2:12.20
2003	Tap Dance City (6)	T Sato	S Sasaki	Yushun Horse	That's The Plenty	Symboli Kris S	2:28.70
2004	Zenno Rob Roy (4)	O Peslier	K Fujisawa	S Oosako	Cosmo Bulk	Delta Blues	2:24.20

*Run at Nakayama at 1 3/8 miles.

MAJOR JUMP RACES

CHAMPION HURDLE-G1

2-1/16 miles (8 hurdles), 5-year-old & up, Cheltenham (GB)

FIRST RUN IN 1927

Year	1st (age)	Jockey	Trainer	Owner	2nd	3rd	Time
1968	Persian War (5)	J Uttley	C Davies	H Alper	Chorus	Black Justice	4:03.8
1969	Persian War (6)	J Uttley	C Davies	H Alper	Drumikill	Privy Seal	4:41.8
1970	Persian War (7)	J Uttley	C Davies	H Alper	Major Rose	Escalus	4:13.8
1971	Bula (6)	P Kelleway	F Winter	E Edwards	Persian Rose	Major Rose	4:22.2
1972	Bula (7)	P Kelleway	F Winter	E Edwards	Boxer	Lyford Cay	4:25.2
1973	Comedy Of Errors (6)	W Smith	F Rimell	E Wheatley	Easby Abbey	Captain Christy	4:07.8
1974	Lanzarote (6)	R Pitman	F Winter	H de Walden	Comedy Of Errors	Yenisei	4:17.7

Year	1st (age)	Jockey	Trainer	Owner	2nd	3rd	Time
1975	Comedy Of Errors (8)	K White	F Rimell	E Wheatley	Flash Imp	Tree Tangle	4:28.5
1976	Night Nurse (5)	P Broderick	M Easterby	R Spencer	Birds Nest	Flash Imp	4:05.9
1977	Night Nurse (6)	P Broderick	M Easterby	R Spencer	Monksfield	Dramatist	4:24.0
1978	Monksfield (6)	T Kinane	D McDonogh	M Mangan	Sea Pigeon	Night Nurse	4:12.7
1979	Monksfield (7)	D T Hughes	D McDonogh	M Mangan	Sea Pigeon	Beacon Light	4:27.0
1980	Sea Pigeon (10)	J J O'Neill	M Easterby	P Muldoon	Monksfield	Birds Nest	4:06.9
1981	Sea Pigeon (11)	J Francome	M Easterby	P Muldoon	Pollardstown	Daring Run	4:11.4
1982	For Auction (6)	C Magnier	M Cunningham	P Heaslip	Broadsword	Ekbalco	4:12.4
1983	Gaye Brief (6)	R Linley	M Rimell	A Abu Khamsin	Boreen Prince	For Auction	3:57.08
1984	Dawn Run (6f)	J J O'Neill	P Mullins	Mrs C D Hill	Cima	Very Promising	3:52.6
1985	See You Then (5)	S Smith Eccles	N Henderson	Stype Wood Stud	Robin Wonder	Stans Pride	3:51.7
1986	See You Then (6)	S Smith Eccles	N Henderson	Stype Wood Stud	Gaye Brief	Nohalmdun	3:53.3
1987	See You Then (7)	S Smith Eccles	N Henderson	Stype Wood Stud	Flatterer	Barnbrook Again	3:57.3
1988	Celtic Shot (6)	P Scudamore	F Winter	D Horton	Classical Charm	Celtic Chief	4:14.4
1989	Beech Road (7)	R Guest	G Balding	A Geake	Celtic Chief	Celtic Shot	4:02.1
1990	Kribensis (6)	R Dunwoody	M Stoute	Sheikh Mohammed	Nomadic Way	Past Glories	3:50.7
1991	Morley Street (7)	J Frost	G Balding	M Jackson	Nomadic Way	Ruling	3:54.6
1992	Royal Gait (9)	G McCourt	J Fanshawe	Sheikh Mohammed	Oh So Risky	Ruling	3:57.2
1993	Granville Again (7)	P Scudamore	M Pipe	E Scarth	Royal Derbi	Halkopous	3:51.6
1994	Flakey Dove (8)	M Dwyer	R Price	J Price	Oh So Risky	Large Action	4:02.0
1995	Alderbrook (6)	N Williamson	K Bailey	E Pick	Large Action	Danoli	4:03.0
1996	Collier Bay (6)	G Bradley	J Old	W Stuart	Alderbrook	Pridwell	3:59.0
1997	Make A Stand (6)	A P McCoy	M Pipe	P A Deal	Theatreworld	Space Trucker	3:48.4
1998	Istabraq (6)	C Swan	A P O'Brien	J P McManus	Theatreworld	I'm Supposin	3:49.1
1999	Istabraq (7)	C Swan	A P O'Brien	J P McManus	Theatreworld	French Holly	3:56.8
2000	Istabraq (8)	C Swan	A P O'Brien	J P McManus	Hors La Loi III	Blue Royal	3:48.10
2001	RACE NOT RUN						
2002	Hors La Loi III (7)	D Gallagher	J Fanshawe	P Green	Marble Arch	Bilboa	3:53.80
2003	Rooster Booster (9)	R Johnson	P J Hobbs	T Warner	Westender	RhinestoneCowboy	3:54.70
2004	Hardy Eustace (7)	C O'Dwyer	D Hughes	L Byrne	Rooster Booster	Intersky Falcon	

CHELTENHAM GOLD CUP STEEPLECHASE-G1

3-1/4 miles (22 fences), 6-year-olds & up, Cheltenham (GB)

FIRST RUN IN 1924

Year	1st (age)	Jockey	Trainer	Owner	2nd	3rd	Time
1970	L'Escargot (7)	T Carberry	D Moore	R Guest	French Tan	Spanish Steps	6:47.4
1971	L'Escargot (8)	T Carberry	D Moore	R Guest	Leap Frog	The Dikler	8:00.6
1972	Glencaraig Lady (8f)	F Berry	F Flood	P Doyle	Royal Toss	The Dikler	7:17.8
1973	The Dikler (10)	R Barry	F Walwyn	Mrs D August	Pendil	Charlie Potheen	6:37.2
1974	Captain Christy (7)	H Beasley	P Taafe	Mrs J Samuel	The Dikler	Game Spirit	7:05.5
1975	Ten Up (8)	T Carberry	J Dreaper	Dchss of Westminster	Soothsayer	Bula	7:51.4
1976	Royal Frolic (7)	J Burke	F Rimell	E Hanmer	Brown Lad	Colebridge	6:40.1
1977	Davy Lad (7)	D Hughes	M O'Toole	Mrs J McGowan	Tied Cottage	Summerville	7:13.8
1978	Midnight Court (7)	J Francome	F Winter	Mrs O Jackson	Brown Lad	Master H	6:57.3
1979	Alverton (9)	J J O'Neill	M Easterby	Snailwell Stud	Royal Mail	Aldaniti	7:01
*1980	Master Smudge (8)	R Hoare	A Barrow	A Barrow	Mac Vidi	Approaching	7:14.2
1981	Little Owl (7)	Mr A Wilson	M Easterby	R Wilson	Night Nurse	Silver Buck	7:09.9
1982	Silver Buck (10)	R Earnshaw	M Dickinson	Mrs C Feather	Bregawn	Sunset Cristo	7:11.3
1983	Bregawn (9)	G Bradley	M Dickinson	J Kennelly	Captain John	Wayward Lad	6:57.6
1984	Burrough Hill Lad (8)	P Tuck	J Pitman	R Riley	Brown Chamberlain	Drumlargan	6:41.4
1985	Forgive 'N' Forget (8)	M Dwyer	J FitzGerald	T Kilroe & Sons	Righthand Man	Earls Brig	6:48.3
1986	Dawn Run (8f)	J J O'Neill	P Mullins	Mrs C D Hill	Wayward Lad	Forgive'N' Forget	6:35.3
1987	The Thinker (9)	R Lamb	W Stephenson	T McDonagh Ltd	ybrandian	Door Latch	6:56.1
1988	Charter Party (10)	R Dunwoody	D Nicholson	Mrs C Smith	Cavvies Clown	Beau Ranger	6:58.9
1989	Desert Orchid (10)	S Sherwood	D Elsworth	R Burridge	Yahoo	Charter Party	7:17.6
1990	Norton's Coin (9)	G McCourt	S Griffiths	S Griffiths	Toby Tobias	Desert Orchid	6:30.9
1991	Garrison Savannah (8)	M Pitman	J Pitman		The Fellow	Desert Orchid	6:49.8
1992	Cool Ground (10)	A Maguire	G Balding	Whitcombe Manor	The Fellow	Docklands Express	6:47.5
1993	Jodami (8)	M Dwyer	P Beaumont	J Yeardon	Rushing Wild	Royal Athlete	6:34.4
1994	The Fellow (9)	A Kondrat	F Doumen	Marquise de Moratalla	Jodami	Young Hustler	6:40.6
1995	Master Oats (9)	N Williamson	K Bailey	P Matthews	Dubacilla	Minnehoma	6:56.1
1996	Imperial Call (7)	C O'Dwyer	F Sutherland	Lisselan Farm	Rough Quest	Couldnt Be Better	6:42.5
1997	Mr Mulligan (9)	A P McCoy	N Chance	M & G Worcester	Barton Bank	Dorans Pride	6:35.5
1998	Cool Dawn (10)	A Thornton	R Alner	Miss D Harding	Strong Promise	Dorans Pride	6:39.5
1999	See More Business (9)	M FitzGerald	P Nicholls	Barber & Keighley	Go Ballistic	Florida Pearl	6:41.9
2000	Looks Like Trouble	R Johnson	N Chance	T Collins	Florida Pearl	Strong Promise	6:30.30
2001	RACE NOT RUN						
2002	Best Mate (7)	J Culloty	H C Knight	J Lewis	Commanche Court	See More Business	6:50.10
2003	Best Mate (8)	J Culloty	H C Knight	J Lewis	Truckers Tavern	Harbour Pilot	6:39.00
2004	Best Mate (9)	J Culloty	H C Knight	J Lewis	Sir Rembrandt	Harbour Pilot	6:42.60

*Tied Cottage finished first in 1980 but was disqualified from purse money.

GRAND NATIONAL STEEPLECHASE HANDICAP-G3

4-1/2miles (30 fences), 7-year-olds & up, Aintree (GB)

FIRST RUN IN 1839

Year	1st (age)	Jockey	Trainer	Owner	2nd	3rd	Time
1950	Freebooter (9)	J Power	R Renton	Mrs L Brotherton	Wot No Sun	Acthon Major	9:24.2
1951	Nickel Coin (9)	J Bullock	J O'Donaghue	J Royle	Royal Tan	Derrinstown	9:48.8
1952	Teal (10)	A Thompson	N Crump	H Lane	legal Joy	Wot No Sun	9:21.5
1953	Early Mist (8)	B Marshall	M V O'Brien	J Griffin	Mont Tremblant	Irish Lizard	9:22.8
1954	Royal Tan (10)	B Marshall	M V O'Brien	J Griffin	Tudor Line	Irish Lizard	9:32.8
1955	Quare Times (9)	P Taafe	M V O'Brien	Mrs W Welman	Tudor Line	Carey's Cottage	10:19.2
1956	E.S.B. (10)	D Dick	F Rimell	Mrs L Carver	Gentle Moya	Royal Tan	9:21.4
1957	Sundew (11)	F Winter	F Hudson	Mrs G Kohn	Wyndburgh	Tiberetta	9:42.4
1958	Mr What (8)	A Freeman	T Taafe	D J Coughlan	Tiberetta	Green Drill	9:59.8
1959	Oxo (8)	M Scudamore	W Stephenson	J Bigg	Wyndburgh	Mr What	9:37.8
1960	Merryman II (9)	G Scott	N Crump	Miss W Wallace	Badanloch	Clear Profit	9:26.2
1961	Nicolaus Silver (9)	H Beasley	F Rimell	C Vaughan	Merryman II	O'Malley Point	9:22.6
1962	Kilmore (12)	F Winter	R Price	N Cohen	Wyndburgh	Mr What	9:50
1963	Ayala (9)	P Buckley	K Piggott	P Raymond	Carrickbeg	Hawa s Song	9:35.8
1964	Team Spirit (12)	G Robinson	F Walwyn	J Goodman	Purple Silk	Peacetown	9:46.8
1965	Jay Trump (8)	Mr T C Smith	F Winter	Mrs M Stephenson	Freddie	Mr Jones	9:30.6
1966	Anglo (8)	T Norman	F Winter	S Levy	Freddie	Forest Prince	9:52.8
1967	Foinavon (9)	J Buckingham	J Kempton	C Watkins	Honey End	Red Alligator	9:49.6
1968	Red Alligator (9)	B Fletcher	D Smith	J Manners	Moidore's Token	Different Class	9:28.8
1969	Highland Wedding (12)	E P Harty	G Balding	T McCoy Jr	Steel Bridge	Rondetto	9:30.8
1970	Gay Trip (8)	P Taafe	F Rimell	A J Chambers	Vulture	Miss Hunter	9:38
1971	Specify (9)	J Cook	J Sutcliffe	F Pontin	Black Secret	Astbury	9:34.2
1972	Well To Do (9)	G Thorner	T Forster	T Forster	Gay Trip	Black Secret	10:08.4
1973	Red Rum (8)	B Fletcher	D McCain	N Le Mare	Crisp	L'Escargot	9:01.9
1974	Red Rum (9)	B Fletcher	D McCain	N Le Mare	L'Escargot	Charles Dickens	9:20.3
1975	L'Escargot (12)	T Carberry	D Moore		Red Rum	Spanish Steps	9:31.1
1976	Rag Trade (10)	J Burke	F Rimell	P Raymond	Red Rum	Eyecatcher	9:20.9
1977	Red Rum (12)	T Stack	D McCain	N Le Mare	Churchtown Boy	Eyecatcher	9:30.3
1978	Lucius (9)	B Davies	G W Richards	Mrs D Whitaker	Sebastian V	Drumroan	9:33.9
1979	Rubstic (10)	M Barnes	J Leadbetter	J Douglas	Zongalero	Rough And Tumble	9:52.9
1980	Ben Nevis (12)	Mr C Fenwick	T Forster	R Stewart Jr	Rough And Tumble	The Pilgarlic	10:17.4
1981	Aldaniti (11)	R Champion	J Gifford	S Embiricos	Spartan Missile	Royal Mail	9:47.2
1982	Grittar (9)	Mr C Saunders	F Gilman	F Gilman	Hard Outlook	Loving Words	9:12.6
1983	Corbiere (8)	B De Haan	J Pitman	B Burrough	Greasepaint	Yer Man	9:47.4
1984	Hallo Dandy (10)	N Doughty	G W Richards	R Shaw	Greasepaint	Corbiere	9:21.4
1985	Late Suspect (11)	H Davies	T Forster	Dchss of Westminster	Mr Snugfit	Corbiere	9:42.7
1986	West Tip (9)	R Dunwoody	M Oliver	P Luff	Young Driver	Classified	9:33.0
1987	Maori Venture (11)	S Knight	A Turnell	H Joel	The Tsarevich	Lean Ar Aghaidh	9:19.3
1988	Rhyme N' Reason (9)	B Powell	D Elsworth	Miss J Reed	Durham Edition	Monanore	9:53.5
1989	Little Polveir (12)	J Frost	G Balding	E Harvey	West Tip	The Thinker	10:06.8
1990	Mr Frisk (11)	Mr M Armytage	K Bailey	Mrs H Duffey	Durham Edition	Rinus	8:47.8
1991	Seagram (11)	N Hawke	D Barons	E Parker	Garrison Savannah	Auntie Dot	9:29.9
1992	Party Politics (8)	C Llewellyn	N Gaselee	Mrs D Thompson	Romany King	Laura's Beau	9:06.3
1993	RACE VOID						
1994	Minnehoma (11)	R Dunwoody	M Pipe	F Starr	Just So	Moorcroft Boy	10:18.8
1995	Royal Athlete (12)	J F Titley	J Pitman	G & L Johnson	Party Politics	Over the Deel	9:04.1
1996	Rough Quest (10)	M Fitzgerald	T Casey	A Wates	Encore Un Peu	Superior Finish	9:00.8
1997	Lord Gyllene (9)	A Dobbin	S Brookshaw	S Clarke	Suny Bay	Camelot Knight	9:05.9
1998	Earth Summit (10)	C Llewellyn	N Twiston-Davies	Summit Prtnrshp	Suny Bay	Samlee	10:51.4
1999	Bobby Jo (9)	P Carberry	T Carberry	R Burke	Blue Charm	Call It A Day	9:14.1
2000	Papillon	R Walsh	T M Walsh	Mrs B Moran	Mely Moss	Niki Dee	9:09.70
2001	Red Marauder (11)	R Guest	N B Mason	N B Mason	Smarty	Blowing Wind	11:00.1
2002	Bindaree (8)	J Culloty	N Twiston-Davies	H R Mould	What's Up Boys	Blowing Wind	9:08.60
2003	Monty's Pass (10)	B J Geraghty	J J Mangan	Dee Racing Syndicate	Supreme Glory	Amberleigh House	9:21.70
2004	AmberleighHouse (12)	G Lee	D McCain	Halewood Intl Ltd	Clan Royal	Lord Atterbury	9:20.30

GRAND STEEPLECHASE DE PARIS-G1

5800 meters (3-5/8 miles) (23 obstacles), 6-year-olds & up, Auteuil (Fr)

Year	1st (age)	Jockey	Trainer	Owner	2nd	3rd	Time
1970	Huron (6)	C Drieu	A Adele	B Larrouse	Haroue	Karcimont	8:02.00
1971	Pot d'Or (5	J-J Declercq	M Wallon	R Weill	Haroue	Morgex	8:09.00
1972	Morgex (6)	J-P Ciravegna	J Sens	Mme M Marie	Vaillance	Tirizano	8:12.00
1973	Giquin (6)	J-P Creveuil	A Adele	Mme M-F Berger	Silvery Moon	Spoleto	8:18.00
1974	Chic Type (7)	J-P Renard	J-J Beaume	G Murray	hasty Love	Lucky Boy	8:28.00
1975	Air Landais (5)	P Beyer	G Pelat	Mme C Frolich	Captain Christy	Hasty Love	8:58.00
1976	Piomares (5)	G Negrel	D Perea	J Kalda	Air Landais	Royal Exile	8:39.00
1977	Corps a Corps (5)	A Fabre	A Adele	Baron T de Zuylen	Le Pompier	Mentocha	8:41.00

Year	1st (age)	Jockey	Trainer	Owner	2nd	3rd	Time
1978	Mon Filleul (5)	J-L Llorens	B Secly	J-C Weill	Piomares	Chinco	8:43.00
1979	Chinco (7)	P Brame	J-P Gallorini	G Campanella	Mon Filleul	Fiasquito	8:20.00
1980	Fondeur (7)	M Legrand	A Fabre	A Bezard	Tanlas	Lapo d'Or	8:28.00
1981	Isopani (7)	A Chelet	A Fabre	P David	Carmont	Ardiera	7:02.00
1982	Metatero (9)	B Jollivet	A Fabre	G Margogne	Azmi	Lord Gag	7:02.00
1983	Jasmin II (8)	M Chirol	A Fabre	M Thibault	Altimetre	Brodi Dancer	7:03.00
1984	Brodi Dancer (6)	D Leblond	P-L Biancone	Mme C Diallo	V'a Parame	Le Pontif	7:18.00
1985	Sir Gain (6)	S Berard	L Gaumondy	Mme L Belotti	Le Pontif	Lamie Bleue	7:38.00
1986	Otage du Perche (6)	S Berard	P Lamotte d'Argy	P Lamotte d'Argy	Nupsala	Le Pontif	7:33.00
1987	Oteuil (7)	B Jollivet	R Cherruau	Mme R Soulais	Otage du Perche	Mister Sy	7:51.00
1988	Katko (5)	D Vincent	B Secly	Comte de Montesson	Nupsala	Cyborg	7:09.00
1989	Katko (6)	J-Y Beaurain	B Secly	Comte de Montesson	Oteuil	Ouragan Collonges	7:09.00
1990	Katko (7)	J-Y Beaurain	B Secly	Comte de Montesson	Sabre d'Estruval	The Fellow	7:15.00
1991	The Fellow (6)	D Vincent	F Doumen	Marquise de Moratalla	Sabre d'Estruval	Oteuil	7:14.00
1992	El Triunfo (6)	D Vincent	F Rohaut	Mme M Montauban	Ucello II	Ubu III	7:20.00
1993	Ucello II (7)	C Aubert	F Doumen	Marquise de Moratalla	Al Capone II	Vorentin	7:16.00
1994	Ucello II (8)	C Aubert	F Doumen	Marquise de Moratalla	Venus de Mirande	Arenice	7:07.00
1995	Ubu III (9)	P Chevalier	F Doumen	Marquise de Moratalla	Val d'Alene	Bannkipour	7:20.00
1996	Arenice (8)	P Sourzac	G Macaire	Mme M Montauban	Al Capone II	Bannkipour	7:07.00
1997	Al Capone II (9)	J-Y Beaurain	B Secly	R Fougedoire	Cand'Or	Gracky	7:42.00
1998	First Gold (5)	T Doumen	F Doumen	Marquise de Moratalla	Saint-Quenin	Chamberko	7:10.00
1999	Mandarino (6)	P Chevalier	M Rolland	Mme D Ricard	Al Capone II	Chant Royal	7:43.00
2000	Vieux Beaufai (7)	P Bigot	F Danloux	Ecurie Siklos	Or Jack	First Gold	7:19.00
2001	Kotkijet (6)	T Majorcryk	J-P Gallorini	D Wildenstein	Ilare	El Paso III	7:13.00
2002	Double Car (6)	C Cheminaud	B de Watrigant	J Biraben	El Paso III	Batman Senora	7:31.00
2003	Line Marine (6f)	C Pieux	C Aubert	Mme G Vuillard	Batman Senora	Urga	7:37.00
2004	Kotkijet (9)	T Majorcryk	J-P Gallorini	Ecurie Wildenstein	Kamillo	Majadal	7:21.00

GRANDE COURSE DE HAIES D'AUTEUIL (French Champion Hurdle)-G1
5100 meters (3-3/16 miles) (16 obstacles), 5-year-olds & up, Auteuil (Fr)

Year	1st (age)	Jockey	Trainer	Owner	2nd	3rd	Time
1970	Samour (5)	C Mabe	J Laumain	Mme H Seutet	Saboulo	Francois Saubaber	
1971	Le Pontet (6)	F Bonni	G Philippeau	Mlle J Rossi	Depou	Next Time	
1972	Hardatit (6)	C Fornaroli	R Pelat	C Sweeny	Marco Polo	Next Time	
1973	Hardatit (7)	P Costes	R Pelat	C Sweeny	Boniface	Yaxilio	
1974	Baby Taine (5)	R Dupon	A Adele	G Blizniansky	Porto Rafti	Boniface	
1975	Mazel Tov (5)	S Roux	A Adele	Mme J Decrion	Dom Helion	Itau	
1976	Les Roseaux (7)	D Merle	G Boeuf	Mlle N Sarmant	Acreon	Endless	
1977	Top Gear (5)	D Costard	G Pelat	D Wildenstein	Sampietro	Schoeller	
1978	Roselier (5)	S Berard	L Gaumondy	Mme L Gaumondy	Great Mist	Holm Oak	
1979	Paiute (6)	M Blackshaw	G Pelat	D Wildenstein	El Condor	Rosator	
1980	Paiute (7)	D Costard	J-H Barbe	D Wildenstein	Carmont	Nellio	
1981	Bison Fute (5)	D Costard	J de Chevigny	Mme J Couturie	Paiute	Val d'Ajol	
1982	World Citizen (5)	N Peguy	P Rago	D Wildenstein	Tell Harmall	Gaye Chance	
1983	Melinoir (5)	D Bailliez	J-H Barbe	F Wintz	World Citizen	For Auction	
1984	Dawn Run (6f)	A Mullins	P Mullins	Mrs C D Hill	Mister Jack	Salute	
1985	Le Rheusois (5)	R Duchene	P Rago	C Ouyoucef	Video Tape	Point Vernal	
1986	Le Rheusois (6)	D Leblond	P Rago	C Ouyoucef	Flatterer	Gacko	
1987	Claude le Lorrain (8)	P-A Sauvat	L Audon	A Bergalet	Gacko	Petite Fortune	
1988	Goodea (8)	B Marie	J-P Gallorini	P Elmoznino	Marly River	Rocarvin	
1989	Sire Rochelais (5)	L Manceau	G Cherel	J-C Evain	Frappeuse	Afkal	
1990	Tongan (7)	D Vincent	G Collet	W Nikolic	Isabey	Ma Puce	
1991	Rose Or No (7)	V Sartori	P Demercastel	Ecurie Ouaki	Ubu III	March On	
1992	Ubu III (6)	A Kondrat	F Doumen	Marquise de Moratalla	Roi d'Ecajeul	Crystal Spirit	
1993	Ubu III (7)	A Kondrat	F Doumen	Marquise de Moratalla	True Brave	Gabarret	
1994	Le Roi Thibault (5)	Y Fouin	G Doleuze	Haras du Reuilly	Ubu III	Bog Frog	
1995	Matchou (6)	D Mescam	J Lesbordes	Mlle Montauban	Royal Chance	Chinese Gordon	
1996	Earl Grant (7)	J-Y Beaurain	B Secly	L Gautier	Mysilv	Montperle	
1997	Bog Frog (8)	J-Y Beaurain	B Secly	Mme Scarisbrick	Alpha Tauri	Royal Chance	
1998	Mantovo (6)	F Benech	M Rolland	F A McNulty	Earl Grant	Nononito	
1999	Vaporetto (6)	T Majorcryk	J-P Gallorini	D Wildenstein	Mon Romain	Asolo	6:25.00
2000	Le Sauvignon (6)	T Majorcryk	J Bertran de Balanda	D J Jackson	Full of Ambition	Vaporetto	6:09.00
2001	Le Sauvignon (7)	D Bressou	J Bertran de Balanda	D J Jackson	Gilder	Bounce Back	6:19.00
2002	Laveron (7	T Doumen	F Doumen	D Grauert	Vic Toto	Galant Moss	6:19.00
2003	Nobody Told Me (5f)	D J Casey	W Mullins	Amber Syndicate	Karly Flight	Katiki	6:25.00
2004	Rule Supreme (8)	D J Casey	W Mullins	J Fallon	Great Love	Kotkijet	6:20.00

Results of 2004 Group Races in Europe and Asia

BRITAIN

DATE	TRACK	RACE	CONDITIONS	1st	2nd	3rd
Apr14	Newmarket	Nell Gwyn S-G3	7f 3yo f	Silca's Gift	Incheni	Roseanna
Apr14	Newmarket	Earl of Sefton S-G3	1 1/8m 4yo+	Gateman	Kalaman	Hurricane Alan
Apr15	Newmarket	Craven S-G3	1m 3yo c&g	Haafhd	Three Valleys	Peak To Creek
Apr17	Newbury	John Porter S-G3	1 1/2m 4yo+	Dubai Success	Gamut	Imperial Dancer
Apr17	Newbury	Greenham S-G3	7f 3yo c&g	Salford City	Fokine	So Will I
Apr17	Newbury	Fred Darling S-G3	7f 3yo f	Majestic Desert	Nyramba	Nataliya
Apr23	Sandown	Classic Trial-G3	1 1/4m 3yo	African Dream	Privy Seal	Gold History
Apr24	Sandown	Sandown Mile-G2	1m 4yo+	Hurricane Alan	Gateman	Soviet Song
Apr24	Sandown	Gordon Richards S-G3	1 1/4m 4yo+	Chancellor	Nysaean	Sunstrach
Apr28	Ascot	Sagaro S-G3	2m,45y 4yo+	Risk Seeker	Dusky Warbler	Millenary
May1	Newmarket	2000 Gunieas S-G1	1m 3yo c&f	Haafhd	Snow Ridge	Azamour
May1	Newmarket	Palace House S-G3	5f 3yo+	Frizzante	Avonbridge	Boogie Street
May2	Newmarket	1000 Guineas S-G1	1m 3yo f	Attraqction	Sundrop	Hathrah
May2	Newmarket	Jockey Club S-G2	1 1/2m 4yo+	Gamut	Systematic	Warrsan
May2	Newmarket	Dahlia S-G3	1 1/8m 4yo+ f&m	Beneventa	Silence Is Golden	Special Delivery
May6	Chester	Chester Vase-G3	a1 9/16m 3yo c/g	Red Lancer	Privy Seal	Temple Place
May7	Chester	Ormonde S-G3	a1 5/8m 4yo+	Systematic	The Whistling Teal	Compton Bolter
May7	Chester	Dees S-G3	a1 1/4m 3yo c&g	African Dream	Putra Sas	Mutawassel
May8	Lingfield	Derby Trial-G3	1 7/16m 3yo c&g	Percussionist	Hazyview	Five Dynasties
May8	Lingfield	Chartwell S-G3	7f 3yo+ f&m	Illustrious Miss	Gonfilia	Golden Nun
May11	York	Duke of York S-G2	6f 3yo+	Monsieur Bond	Steenberg	Arakan
May11	York	Musidora S-G3	a1-5/16m 3yo f	Punctilious	Glen Innes	Bay Tree
May12	York	Dante S-G2	a1 5/16m 3yo	North Light	Rule Of Law	Let The Lion Roar
May12	York	Middleton S-G3	1 5/16m 4yo+ f&m	Crimson Palace	Beneventa	Summitville
May13	York	Yorkshire Cup-G2	1 3/4m 4yo+	Millenary	Alcazar	Jelani
May15	Newbury	Lockinge S-G1	1m 4yo+	Russian Rhythm	Salselon	Norse Dancer
May31	Sandown	Henry II S-G2	2m78y 4yo+	Papineau	Mr Dinos	New South Wales
Jun1	Sandown	Brigadier Gerard S-G3	1 1/4m 4yo+	Bandari	Ikhtyar	Sunstrach
Jun4	Epsom	English Oaks-G1	1 1/2m 3yo f	Ouija Board	All Too Beautiful	Punctilious
Jun4	Epsom	Coronation Cup-G1	1 1/2m 4yo+	Warrsan	Doyen	Vallee Enchantee
Jun4	Epsom	Temple S-G2	5f 3yo+	Night Prospector	Autumn Pearl	Bishops Court
Jun6	Epsom	Epsom Derby-G1	1 1/2m 3yo c&f	North Light	Rule Of Law	Let The Lion Roar
Jun6	Epsom	Diomed S-G3	1 1/16m 3yo+	Passing Glance	Dutch Gold	Gateman
Jun15	Royal Ascot	St James's Palace S-G1	1m 3yo c	Azamour	Diamond Green	Antonius Pius
Jun15	Royal Ascot	Queen Anne S-G1	1m 3yo+	Refuse To Bend	Soviet Song	Salselon
Jun15	Royal Ascot	King's Stand S-G2	5f 3yo+	The Tatling	Cape of Good Hope	Frizzante
Jun15	Royal Ascot	Coventry S-G2	6f 2yo	Iceman	Council Member	Capable Guest
Jun16	Royal Ascot	Prince of Wales'sS-G1	1 1/4m 4yo+	Rakti	Powerscourt	Ikhtyar
Jun16	Royal Ascot	Windsor Forest S-G2	1m 4yo+ f&m	Favourable Terms	Monturani	Soldera
Jun16	Royal Ascot	Jersey S-G3	7f 3yo	Kheleyf	Fokine	Cartography
Jun16	Royal Ascot	Queen Mary S-G3	5f 2yo f	Damson	Soar	Sharplaw Star
Jun17	Royal Ascot	Ascot Gold Cup-G1	2 1/2m 4yo+	Papineau	Westerner	Darasim
Jun17	Royal Ascot	Ribblesdale S-G2	1 1/2m 3yo f	Punctilious	Sahool	Quiff
Jun17	Royal Ascot	Norfolk S-G3	5f 2yo	Blue Dakota	Mystical Land	Skywards
Jun18	Royal Ascot	Coronation S-G1	1m 3yo f	Attraction	Majestic Desert	Red Bloom
Jun18	Royal Ascot	King Edward VII S-G2	1 1/2m 3yo c&g	Five Dynasties	Elshadi	Barati
Jun18	Royal Ascot	Queen's Vase-G3	2m,45y 3yo	Duke Of Venice	Two Miles West	Top Seed
Jun19	Royal Ascot	Golden Jubilee S-G1	6f 3yo+	Fayr Jag	Crystal Castle	Cape of Good Hope
Jun19	Royal Ascot	Hardwicke S-G2	1 1/2m 4yo+	Doyen	High Accolade	Persian Majesty
Jun26	Newcastle	Chipchase S-G3	6f 3yo+	Royal Millennium	Somnus	Ruby Pocket
Jun26	Newmarket	Criterion S-G3	7f 3yo+	Arakan	Desert Destiny	Trade Fair
Jly3	Sandown	Eclipse S-G1	1 1/4m 3yo+	Refuse To Bend	Warrsan	Kalaman
Jly3	Sandown	Champagne Sprint S-G3	5f 3yo+	Orientor	Ringmoor Down	Colonel Cotton
Jly3	Haydock	Lancashire Oaks-G2	1 1/2m 3yo+f&m	Pongee	Sahool	Danelissima
Jly6	Newmarket	Falmouth S-G1	1m 3yo+ f&m	Soviet Song	Attraction	Baqah
Jly6	Newmarket	Cherry Hinton S-G2	6f 2yo f	Jewel In The Sand	Salsa Brava	Extreme Beauty
Jly7	Newmarket	Princess of Wales's S-G2	1 1/2m 3yo+	Bandari	Sulamani	High Accolade
Jly7	Newmarket	July S-G2	6f 2yo c&g	Captain Hurricane	Council Member	Mystical Land
Jly9	Newmarket	July Cup-G1	6f 3yo+	Frizzante	Ashdown Express	Balmont
Jly9	Newmarket	Superlative S-G3	7f 2yo	Dubawi	Henrik	Wilko
Jly10	York	Summer S-G3	6f 3yo+ f&m	Tante Rose	Ruby Rocket	Lochridge
Jly10	Chepstow	Golden Daffodil S-G3	1 1/4m 3yo+ f&m	Felicity	Kinnaird	Tidal
Jly10	Ascot	Silver Trophy-G3	1m 4yo+	Shot To Fame	Gateman	Hurricane Alan
Jly19	Ayr	Scottish Derby-G2	1 1/4m 3yo+	Kalaman	Gateman	Ikhtyar
Jly24	Ascot	King Geo/Queen. Eliz S-G1	1 1/2m 3yo+	Doyen	Hard Buck	Sulamani
Jly24	Ascot	Princess Margaret S-G3	6f 2yo f	Soar	Valentin	Kissing Lights
Jly27	Goodwood	Lennox S-G2	7f 3yo+	Byron	Suggestive	Kheleyf
Jly27	Goodwood	Gordon S-G3	1 1/2m 3yo	Maraahel	Go For Gold	Remaadd
Jly27	Goodwood	Molecomb S-G3	5f 2yo	Tournedos	Mary Read	Safari Sunset
Jly28	Goodwood	Sussex S-G1	1m 3yo+	Soviet Song	Nayyir	Le Vie dei Colori
Jly28	Goodwood	Vintage S-G2	7f 2yo	Shamardal	Wilko	Fox
Jly29	Goodwood	Goodwood Cup-G2	2m 3yo+	Darasim	Royal Rebel	Misternando
Jly29	Goodwood	King George S-G3	5f 3yo+	Ringmoor Down	Boogie Street	The Tatling
Jly30	Goodwood	Richmond S-G2	6f 2yo	Montgomery's Arch	Mystical Land	Silver Wraith
Jly30	Goodwood	Oak Tree S-G3	7f 3yo + f&m	Phantom Wind	Nyramba	Chic
Jly31	Goodwood	Nassau S-G1	1 1/4m 3yo+f&m	Favourable Terms	Silence Is Golden	Chorist
Jly31	Goodwood	Lillie Langtry S-G3	1 3/4m 3yo+ f&m	Astrocharm	Pongee	Summitville
Aug7	Haydock	Rose of Lancaster S-G3	1 5/16m 3yo+	Mister Monet	Muqbil	Checkit

DATE	TRACK	RACE	CONDITIONS	1st	2nd	3rd
Aug7	Newmarket	Sweet Solera S-G3	7f 2yo f	Maids Causeway	Slip Dance	Park Romance
Aug12	Salisbury	Sovereign S-G3	1m 3yo c&g	Norse Dancer	Lucky Story	Hurricane Alan
Aug14	Newbury	Geoffrey Freer S-G2	a1 5/8m	Mutaker	Dubai Success	Compton Bolter
Aug14	Newbury	Hungerford S-G3	7f 3yo+	Chic	Suggestive	Rum Shot
Aug17	York	Juddmonte Intl S-G1	a1 5/16m	Sulamani	Norse Dancer	Bago
Aug17	York	Great Voltigeur S-G2	1 1/2m 3yo c&g	Rule Of Law	Let The Lion Roar	Go For Gold
Aug17	York	Lonsdale Cup-G2	2m 3yo+	First Charter	Dancing Bay	Millenary
Aug18	York	Yorkshire Oaks-G1	1 1/2m 3yo+ f/m	Quiff	Pongee	Hazarista
Aug18	York	Gimcrack S-G2	6f 2yo c&g	Tony James	Andronikos	Abraxas Antelope
Aug19	York	Nunthorpe S-G1	5f 2yo+	Bahamian Pirate	The Tatling	One Cool Cat
Aug19	York	Lowther S-G2	6f 2yo f	Soar	Salsa Brava	Spirit Of Chester
Aug21	Sandown	Solario S-G3	7f 2yo	Windsor Knot	Embossed	Propinquity
Aug28	Goodwood	Celebration Mile-G2	1m 3yo+	Chic	Nayyir	Hurricane Alan
Aug28	Windsor	Winter Hill S-G3	1 1/4m 3yo+	Ancient World	Gateman	Fruhlingssturm
Aug29	Goodwood	Prestige S-G3	7f 2yo f	Dubai Surprise	Nanabanana	Red Peony
Sep1	York	Strensall S-G3	1 1/8m 3yo+	Red Bloom	Salselon	Imperial Dancer
Sep4	Haydock	HaydockPkSprintCup-G	6f 3yo+	Tante Rose	Somnus	Patavellian
Sep4	Kempton	September S-G3	1 1/2m 3yo+	Mamool	Alkaased	Bandari
Sep4	Kempton	Sirenia S-G3	6f 2yo	Satchem	Council Member	Visionist
Sep8	Doncaster	Park Hill S-G2	1 13/16m3yo+ f&m	Echoes In Eternity	Mazuna	Bowstring
Sep9	Doncaster	Doncaster Cup-G2	2 1/4m 3yo+	Millenary	Kasthari	Dancing Bay
Sep9	Doncaster	May Hill S-G2	1m 2yo f	Playful Act	Queen Of Poland	Maids Causeway
Sep9	Doncaster	Park S-G2	7f 3yo+	Pastoral Pursuits	Firebreak	Court Masterpiece
Sep10	Doncaster	Champagne S-G2	7f 2yo c&g	Etlaala	Iceman	Oude
Sep11	Doncaster	St Leger S-G1	a1 13/16m 3yo c&f	Rule Of Law	Quiff	Tycoon
Sep11	Doncaster	Flying Childers S-G2	5f 2yo	Chateau Istana	Tournedos	Kissing Lights
Sep12	Goodwood	Select S-G3	1 1/4m 3yo+	Alkaadhem	Battle Chan	Salselon
Sep17	Newbury	Arc Trial-G3	1 3/8m 3yo+	Sights On Gold	Imperial Dancer	Compton Bolter
Sep18	Newbury	Mill Reef S-G2	6f 2yo	Galeota	Mystical Land	Rebuttal
Sep18	Newbury	Dubai Airport Trophy-G3	5f,34y 3yo+	The Tatling	Var	Airwave
Sep18	Ayr	Firth of Clyde S-G3	6f 2yo f	Golden Legacy	Nufoos	Castelletto
Sep24	Ascot	Princess Royal S-G3	1 1/2m 3yo+ f&m	Mazuna	My Renee	Hidden Hope
Sep25	Ascot	Queen Elizabeth II S-G1	1m 3yo+	Rakti	Lucky Story	Refuse To Bend
Sep25	Ascot	Fillies Mile-G1	1m 2yo f	Playful Act	Maids Causeway	Dash To The Top
Sep25	Ascot	Royal Lodge S-G2	1m 2yo c&g	Perfectperformance	Scandinavia	Wilko
Sep25	Ascot	Diadem S-G2	6f 3yo+	Pivotal Point	Airwave	The Tatling
Sep26	Ascot	Cumberland Lodge-G3	1 1/2m 3yo+	High Accolade	Self Defense	Bandari
Sep30	Goodwood	Supreme S-G3	7f 3yo+	Mac Love	Vanderlin	Polar Way
Sep30	Newmarket	Cheveley Park S-G1	6f 2yo f	Magical Romance	Suez	Damson
Sep30	Newmarket	Somerville Tattersalls-G3	7f 2yo c&g	Diktatorial	Crimson Sun	Mister Genepi
Oct1	Newmarket	Middle Park S-G1	6f 2yo c	Ad Valorem	Rebuttal	Iceman
Oct1	Newmarket	Joel S-G3	1m 3yo+	Polar Ben	Salselon	Funfair
Oct2	Newmarket	Sun Chariot S-G1	1m 3yo+f&m	Attraction	Chic	Nebraska Tornado
Oct8	Salisbury	Autumn S-G3	1m 2yo	RACE NOT RUN		
Oct15	Newmarket	Bentinck S-G3	6f 3yo+	Royal Millennium	Moss Vale	Quito
Oct16	Newmarket	Champion S-G1	1 1/4m 3yo+	Haafhd	Chorist	Azamour
Oct16	Newmarket	Dewhurst S-G1	7f 2yo c&f	Shamardal	Oratorio	Montgomery's Arch
Oct16	Newmarket	Challenge S-G2	7f 3yo+	Firebreak	Keltos	Polar Bear
Oct16	Newmarket	Rockfel S-G2	7f 2yo f	Maids Causeway	PenekennaPrincess	Favourita
Oct16	Newmarket	Jockey Club Cup-G3	2m 3yo+	Millenary	Franklins Gardens	True Lover
Oct16	Newmarket	Darley S-G3	1 1/8m 3yo+	Autumn Glory	Sights On Gold	Babodana
Oct16	Newmarket	Cornwallis S-G3	5f 2yo	Castelletto	Cornus	Kay Two
Oct22	Newbury	Horris Hill S-G3	7f 2yo c&g	Cupid's Glory	Johnny Jumpup	King Marju
Oct23	Newbury	St Simon S-G3	1-1/2m 3yo+	Orcadian	Frank Sonata	Self Defense
Oct23	Doncaster	Racing Post Trophy-G1	1m 2yo c&f	Motivator	Albert Hall	Henrik

FRANCE

DATE	TRACK	RACE	CONDITIONS	1st	2nd	3rd
Mar6	Saint-Cloud	Prix Exbury-G3	1 1/4m 4yo+	Polish Summer	Bright Sky	Samando
Mar27	Saint-Cloud	Prix Edmond Blanc-G3	1m 4yo+	My Risk	Art Moderne	Sarre
Mar30	Longchamp	Prix d'Harcourt-G2	1-1/4m 4yo+	Vangelis	Execute	Short Pause
Apr9	Saint-Cloud	Prix Penelope-G3	1 5/16m 3yo f	Ask for the Moon	Super Lina	Miss France
Apr11	Longchamp	Prix Noailles-G2	1 3/8m 3yo c&f	Voix du Nord	Cherry Mix	Fast and Furious
Apr22	Longchamp	Prix de Barbeville-G3	1 15/16m 4yo+	Westerner	Forestier	Idaho Quest
Apr25	Longchamp	Prix Greffulhe-G2	1 5/16m 3yo c&f	Millemix	Day or Night	Vassilievsky
Apr25	Longchamp	Prix de Fontainebleau-G3	1m 3yo c	American Post	Blackdoun	Diamond Green
Apr25	Longchamp	Prix de la Grotte-G3	1m 3yo f	Grey Lilas	Petit Calva	Denebola
May1	Saint-Cloud	Prix du Muguet-G2	1m 4yo+	Martillo	Sarre	Maxwell
May2	Longchamp	Prix Ganay-G1	1 5/16m 4yo+	Execute	Vespone	Fair Mix
May2	Longchamp	Prix Vanteaux-G3	1 1/8m 3yo f	Latice	Asti	Green Swallow
May5	Saint-Cloud	Prix La Force-G3	1 1/4m 3yo	Delfos	Young Tiger	Kurm
May6	Longchamp	Prix d'Hedouville-G3	1 1/2m 4yo+	Short Pause	Kindjhal	Maredsous
May7	Chantilly	Prix Allez France-G3	1 1/2m 4yo+ f&m	Pride	Russian Hill	Samando
May11	Saint-Cloud	Prix Cleopatre-G3	1 5/16m 3yo f	Steel Princess	Love and Bubbles	Barancella
May13	Longchamp	Prix Hocquart-G2	1-1/2m 3yo c&f	Lord du Sud	Prospect Park	Cherry Mix
May13	Longchamp	Prix de Guiche-G3	a1 1/8m 3yo c	Mister Sacha	Red Tune	Charmo
May16	Longchamp	Poule d'Essai P'lains-G1	1m 3yo c	American Post	Diamond Green	Byron
May16	Longchamp	Poule d'Essai P'liches-G1	1m 3yo f	Torrestrella	Grey Lilas	Miss Mambo
May16	Longchamp	Prix Lupin-G1	1 5/16m 3yo c&f	Voix du Nord	Millemix	Valixir
May16	Longchamp	Prix de Saint-Georges-G3	5f 3yo+	The Trader	The Tatling	Patavellian

DATE	TRACK	RACE	CONDITIONS	1st	2nd	3rd
May23	Longchamp	Prix d'Ispahan-G1	a1 1/8m 4yo+	Prince Kirk	Six Perfections	Checkit
May23	Longchamp	Prix Saint-Alary-G1	1 1/4m 3yo f	Ask for the Moon	Asti	Agata
May23	Longchamp	Pr Vicomtesse Vigier-G2	1 15/16m 4yo+	Forestier	Westerner	Clear Thinking
May27	Longchamp	Prix du Palais-Royal-G3	7f 3yo+	Puppeteer	Saratan	Crystal Castle
May31	Saint-Cloud	Prix Corrida-G2	1 5/16m 4yo+ f&m	Actrice	Visorama	Pride
Jun5	Chantilly	Prix de Royaumont-G3	1-1/2m 3yo f	Silverskaya	Kalatuna	Reverie Solitaire
Jun6	Chantilly	Prix du Jockey-Club-G1	1-1/2m 3yo c&f	Blue Canari	Prospect Park	Valixir
Jun6	Chantilly	Prix Jean Prat-G1	1-1/8m 3yo c&f	Bago	Cacique	Ershaad
Jun6	Chantilly	Prix de Sandringham-G2	1m 3yo f	Baqah	Miss Mambo	Dolma
Jun6	Chantilly	Prix du Gros-Chene-G2	5f 3yo+	Avonbridge	Porlezza	The Trader
Jun13	Chantilly	Prix de Diane-G1	1 5/16m 3yo f	Latice	Millionaia	Grey Lilas
Jun13	Chantilly	Grand Prix de Chantilly-G2	1 1/2m 4yo+	Policy Maker	Fair Mix	Short Pause
Jun13	Chantilly	Pr Chemin de Fer Nord-G3	1m 4yo+	My Risk	Charming Groom	Star Valley
Jun17	Longchamp	La Coupe-G3	1 1/4m 4yo+	Aubonne	Soldier Hollow	Look Honey
Jun21	Chantilly	Prix de la Jonchere-G3	1m 3yo c&g	Art Master	Joursanvault	Charmo
Jun24	Chantilly	Prix Chloe-G3	1 1/8m 3yo f	Love and Bubbles	Cattiva Generosa	Cloon
Jun27	Longchamp	Grand Prix de Paris-G1	1 1/4m 3yo c&f	Bago	Cacique	Alnitak
Jun27	Longchamp	Prix du Lys-G3	1 1/2m 3yo c&g	Prospect Park	Lord Darnley	Lyonels Glory
Jun27	Longchamp	Pr de la Porte Maillot-G3	7f 3yo+	Charming Groom	Millennium Force	Sunday Doubt
Jun28	Chantilly	Prix du Bois-G3	5f 2yo	Divine Proportions	Great Blood	Salut Thomas
Jly4	Saint-Cloud	Grand Prix de St-Cloud	1 1/2m 3yo+	Gamut	Policy Maker	Visorama
Jly4	Saint-Cloud	Prix de Malleret-G2	1 1/2m 3yo f	Lune d'Or	Buoyant	Dream Play
Jly10	Deauville	Prix de Ris-Orangis-G3	6f 3yo+	The Trader	Swedish Shave	Vasywait
Jly11	Deauville	Prix Messidor-G3	1m 3yo+	Ryono	Diamond Green	Special Kladoun
Jly14	M-Laffitte	Prix Eugene Adam-G2	1 1/4m 3yo	Valixir	Delfos	Hazyview
Jly17	M-Laffitte	Prix Maurice de Nieuil-G2	1 7/8m 4yo+	Forestier	Royal Fantasy	Clear Thinking
Jly21	Vichy	Grand Prix de Vichy-G3	1 1/4m 3yo+	Bailador	Demon Dancer	Mister Farmer
Jly29	M-Laffitte	Prix Daphnis-G3	1 1/8m 3yo c&g	Cacique	Ershaad	High Flash
Jly29	M-Laffitte	Prix Robert Papin-G2	5 1/2f 2yo c&f	Divine Proportionsr	Shifting Place	Portrayal
Aug1	Deauville	Prix de Cabourg-G3	6f 2yo	Layman	Inhabitant	Salut Thomas
Aug1	Deauville	Prix d'Astarte-G2	1m 3yo+ f&m	Marbye	Majestic Deser	Nebraska Tornado
Aug3	Deauville	Prix de Psyche-G3	1 1/4m 3yo f	Quilanga	Kinnaird	Cloon
Aug7	Deauville	Prix de Pomone-G2	1 9/16m 3yo+ f&m	Lune d'Or	Hidden Hope	Sweet Stream
Aug8	Deauville	Prix Maurice de Gheest-G1	6-1/2f 3yo+	Somnus	Whipper	Dolma
Aug15	Deauville	Prix Jacques le Marois-G1	1m 3yo+ c&f	Whipper	Six Perfections	My Risk
Aug21	Deauville	Prix Guillaume d'Ornano-G2	1 1/4m 3yo	Mister Monet	Delfos	Islero Noir
Aug14	Deauville	Prix Gontaut-Biron-G3	1 1/4m 4yo+	Special Kaldoun	Demon Dancer	Mamool
Aug21	Deauville	Prix du Calvados-G3	7f 2yo f	Cours de la Reine	Royal Copenhagen	Gorella
Aug22	Deauville	Prix Morny-G1	6f 2yo c&f	Divine Proportions	Layman	Russian Blue
Aug22	Deauville	Prix Kergorlay-G2	1 7/8m 3yo+	Gold Medallist	Brian Boru	Cut Quartz
Aug22	Deauville	Prix Jean Romanet-G2	1 1/4m 4yo+ f&m	Whortleberry	Pride	Chorist
Aug24	Deauville	Prix de la Nonette-G3	1 1/4m 3yo f	Grey Lilas	Trinity Joy	Polyfirst
Aug24	Deauville	Prix Minerve-G3	1 9/16m 3yo f	Silverskaya	Reverie Solitaire	Anabaa Republic
Aug29	Deauville	Grand Prix de Deauville-G2	1 9/16m 3yo+	Cherry Mix	Martaline	Bailador
Aug29	Deauville	Prix Quincey-G3	1m 3yo+	Autumn Glory	Keltos	Mister Sacha
Aug29	Deauville	Prix de Meautry-G3	6f 3yo+	Star Valley	Swedish Shave	Striking Ambition
Sep5	Longchamp	Prix du Moulin-G1	1m 3yo+	Grey Lilas	Diamond Green	Antonius Pius
Sep5	Longchamp	Prix du Petit Couvert-G3	5f 3yo+	Pivotal Point	The Tatling	Chineur
Sep8	Chantilly	Prix d'Arenberg-G3	5-1/2f 2yo	Toupie	Crossover	Salut Thomas
Sep9	Longchamp	Prix de Lutece-G3	1 7/8m 3yo	Etendard Indien	Reefscape	Double Green
Sep9	Longchamp	Prix La Rochette-G3	7f 2yo	Early March	Stop making Sense	Osidy
Sep12	Longchamp	Prix Vermeille-G1	1 1/2m 3&4yo f	Sweet Stream	Royal Fantasy	Pride
Sep12	Longchamp	Prix Niel-G2	1 1/2m 3yo c&f	Valixir	Prospect Park	Bago
Sep12	Longchamp	Prix Foy-G2	1 1/2m 4yo+ c&f	Policy Maker	Short Pause	Nysaean
Sep12	Longchamp	Prix Gladiateur-G3	1 15/16m 4yo+	Westerner	Cut Quartz	Clear Thinking
Sep13	Chantilly	Prix d'Aumale-G3	1m 2yo f	Birthstone	Portrayal	Faint Heart
Sep18	Longchamp	Pr du Prince d'Orange-G3	1 1/4m 3yo	Delfos	Apsis	Lyonels Glory
Sep18	Longchamp	Prix des Chenes-G3	1m 2yo c&g	Helios Quercus	Musketier	Vatori
Sep18	Longchamp	Prix du Pin-G3	7f 3yo+	Comete	Puppeteer	Keltos
Sep21	M-Laffitte	La Coupe de M-Laffitte-G3	1 1/4m 3yo+	Fair Mix	Marshall	Special Kaldoun
Oct1	Chantilly	Prix Eclipse-G3	6f 2yo	Tremar	Crossover	Nipping
Oct2	Longchamp	Pr Daniel Wildenstein-G2	1m 3yo+	Cacique	Hurricane Alan	Mister Sacha
Oct2	Longchamp	Prix Dollar-G2	1 3/16m,55y 3yo+	Touch Of Land	Gateman	Special Kaldoun
Oct2	Longchamp	Prix de Royallieu-G2	1 9/16m 3yo+ f/m	Samando	Russian Hill	Behkara
Oct2	Longchamp	Prix Hubert de Chaudenay-G2	1 7/8m 3yo	Reefscape	Lord du Sud	Percussionist
Oct3	Longchamp	Prix de l'Arc de Triomphe-G1	1 1/2m 3yo+ c&f	Bago	Cherry Mix	Ouija Board
Oct3	Longchamp	Prix de l'Opera-G1	1 1/4m 3yo+ f&m	Alexander Goldrun	Grey Lilas	Walkamia
Oct3	Longchamp	Prix de l'Abbaye-G1	5f 2yo+	Var	The Tatling	Royal Millennium
Oct3	Longchamp	Prix Marcel Boussac-G1	1m 2yo f	Divine Proportions	Titian Time	Fraloga
Oct3	Longchamp	Pr JeanLuc Lagardere-G1	7f 2yo c&f	Oratorio	Early March	Layman
Oct3	Longchamp	Prix du Cadran-G1	2 1/2m 4yo+	Westerner	Cut Quartz	Le Carre
Oct7	Saint-Cloud	Prix Thomas Bryon-G3	1m 2yo	Vatori	Guillaume Tell	Stop Making Sense
Oct9	Longchamp	Prix de la Foret-G1	7f 3yo+	Somnus	Denebola	Le Vie dei Colori
Oct13	Le Bouscat	Prix Andre Baboin-G3	1-1/4m 3yo+	Valentino	Marshall	Tunduru
Oct17	Longchamp	Prix du Conseil de Paris-G2	1 1/2m 3yo+	Pride	Simplex	Geordieland
Oct17	Longchamp	Prix de Conde-G3	1 1/8m 2yo	Musketier	Doctor Dino	Wingman
Oct19	Deauville	Prix des Reservoirs-G3	1m 2yo f	Songerie	Soignee	Ysoldina
Oct24	Longchamp	Prix Royal-Oak-G1	1 15/16m 3yo+	Westerner	Behkara	Alcazar
Oct26	Saint-Cloud	Prix de Flore-G3	1-5/16m 3+ f&m	Australie	Elopa	Dream Play
Oct29	M-Laffitte	Criterium de M-Laffitte-G2	6f 2yo	Centifolia	Salut Thomas	Campo Bueno

Oct29	M-Laffitte	Prix de Seine-et-Oise-G3	6f 3yo+	Miss Emma	Striking Ambition	Patavellian
Oct31	Saint-Cloud	Criterium International-G1	1m 2yo c&f	Helios Quercus	Dubai Surprise	Walk in the Park
Oct31	Saint-Cloud	Prix Perth-G3	1m 3yo+	Valentino	Svedov	Keltos
Nov2	M-Laffitte	Prix Miesque-G3	7f 2yo f	Stella Blue	Mirabilis	Arabian Spell
Nov 6	Saint-Cloud	Criterium de St-Cloud-G1	1-1/4m 2yo c&f	Paita	Yehudi	Laverock
Nov11	Toulouse	Prix Fille de l'Air-G3	1-5/16m 3+ f&m	Linda Regina	Delightful Sofie	Tocopilla

IRELAND

DATE	TRACK	RACE	CONDITIONS	1st	2nd	3rd
Apr4	Curragh	Gladness S-G3	7f 3yo+	Monsieur Bond	Steenberg	Rockets N'Rollers
Apr18	Leopardstown	Ballysax S-G3	1 1/4m 3yo	Yeats	Dabiroun	Lord Admiral
April25	Curragh	Athasi S-G3	7f 3yo+up f&m	Lucky	Golden Nun	Megec Blis
May1	Curragh	Mooresbridge S-G3	1 1/4m 4yo+	Nysaean	Latino Magic	Akshar
May3	Curragh	Tetrarch S-G3	7f 3yo c&g	Leitrim House	Grand Reward	Mokabra
May9	Leopardstown	Derrinst'n Stud Derby Tr.-G2	1 1/4m 3yo	Yeats	Relaxed Gesture	Medicinal
May9	Leopardstown	1000 Guineas Trial-G3	7f 3yo f	Alexander Goldrun	Misty Heights	Miss Childrey
May14	Cork	Blue Wind S-G3	a1 1/4m 3yo+ f&m	Hazarista	Cache Creek	Felicity (Ire)
May22	Curragh	Irish 2000 Guineas-G1	1m 3yo c&f	Bachelor Duke	Azamour	Grey Swallow
May22	Curragh	Ridgewood Pearl S-G2	1m 4yo+ f&m	Soviet Song	Livadiya	Hanami
May22	Curragh	Greenlands S-G3	6f 3yo+	The Kiddykid	Arakan	Ringmoor Down
May23	Curragh	Irish 1000 Guineas	1m 3yo f	Attraction	Alexander Goldrun	Illustrious Miss
May23	Curragh	Tattersalls Gold Cup-G1	1 5/16m 4yo+	Powerscourt	Livadiya	Nysaean
May23	Curragh	Gallinule S-G3	1 1/4m 3yo	Meath	Cairdeas	Barati
Jun9	Leopardstown	Ballycorus S-G3	7f 3yo+	Naahy	Hamairi	Latino Magic
Jun12	Cork	Ballyogan S-G3	5f 3yo+ f&m	Golden Nun	Simianna	Topkamp
Jun16	Naas	Noblesse S-G3	1 1/2m 3yo+ f&m	Danelissima	Summitville	Tarakala
Jun26	Curragh	Pretty Polly S-G1	1 1/4m 3yo+ f&m	Chorist	Alexander Goldrun	Ivowen
Jun26	Curragh	Curragh Cup-G3	1 3/4m 3yo+	Mkuzi	Dubai Success	Cruzspiel
Jun27	Curragh	Irish Derby-G1	1 1/2m 3yo c&f	Grey Swallow	North Light	Tycoon
Jun27	Curragh	Railway S-G3	6f 2yo	Democratic Deficit	Russian Blue	L'Altro Mondo
Jly3	Leopardstown	Brownstown S-G3	7f 3yo+ f&m	Tropical Lady	Majestic Desert	Red Feather
Jly17	Curragh	International S-G3	1m 3yo	Red Feather	Trefflich	Wathab
Jly18	Curragh	Irish Oaks-G1	1 1/2m 3yo f	Ouija Board	Punctilious	Hazarista
Jly18	Curragh	Anglesey S-G3	6f,63y 2yo	Oratorio	Cougar Cat	Indesatchel
Jly18	Curragh	Minstrel S-G3	7f 4yo+	Trade Fair	One More Round	Millennium Force
Jly24	Leopardstown	Meld S-G3	1 1/4m 3yo+	Latino Magic	Solskjaer	Cache Creek
Aug8	Curragh	Phoenix S-G1	6f 2yo c&f	Damson	Oratorio	Russian Blue
Aug8	Curragh	Phoenix Sprint S-G3	6f 3yo+	One Cool Cat	The Kiddykid	Nights Cross
Aug8	Curragh	Royal Whip S-G2	1 1/4m 3yo+	Solskjaer	Tropical Lady	Medicinal
Aug8	Curragh	Debutante S-G2	7f 2yo f	Silk And Scarlet	Luas Line	Chelsea Rose
Aug15	Leopardstown	Desmond S-G3	1m 3yo+	Ace	Hamairi	Grand Passion
Aug21	Curragh	Futurity S-G2	7f 2yo	Oratorio	Democratic Deficit	Elusive Double
Sep5	Curragh	Moyglare Stud S-G1	7f 2yo f	Chelsea Rose	Pictavia	Saoire
Sep5	Curragh	Flying Five-G3	5f 3yo+	Ringmoor Down	Benbaun	Osterhase
Sep5	Curragh	Round Tower S-G3	6f 2yo	Cherokee	Lock And Key	Indesatchel
Sep11	Leopardstown	Irish Champion S-G1	1 1/4m 3yo+	Azamour	Norse Dancer	Powerscourt
Sep11	Leopardstown	Matron S-G1	1m 3yo+ f&m	Soviet Song	Attraction	Phantom Wind
Sep18	Curragh	Irish St Leger-G1	1 3/4m 3yo+	Vinnie Roe	Brian Boru	First Charter
Sep18	Curragh	Renaissance S-G3	6f 3yo+	Royal Millennium	Moss Vale	Grand Reward
Sep19	Curragh	National S-G1	7f2yo c&f	Dubawi	Berenson	Russian Blue
Sep19	Curragh	Blandford S-G2	1 1/4m 3yo+ f&m	Monturani	Kinnaird	All Too Beautiful
Oct2	Curragh	Park S-G3	7f 2yo f	Jazz Princess	Saoire	Virginia Waters
Oct3	Tipperary	Concorde S-G3	7-1/2f 3yo+	Hamairi	Fearn Royal	Poetical
Oct10	Curragh	Beresford S-G2	1m 2yo	Albert Hall	Merger	Sant Jordi
Oct25	Leopardstown	Killavullan S-G3	7f 2yo	Footstepsinthesand	Gaff	Clash Of The Ash

GERMANY

DATE	TRACK	RACE	CONDITIONS	1st	2nd	3rd
Apr4	Cologne	GP der Bremer Wirtschaft-G3	1 5/16m 4yo+	Olaso	Flambo	Winning Dash
Apr18	Krefeld	Dr Busch-Memorial-G3	1 1/16m 3yo	Assiun	Tarlac	Delsun
Apr25	Frankfurt	Fruhjhars Dreijahrigen-G3	1 1/4m 3yo	Apeiron	Mensatiger	Siberion
May2	Cologne	Gerling-Preis-G2	1 1/2m 4yo+	Olaso	Well Made	Senex
May9	Dusseldorf	Henkel-Rennen-G2	1m 3yo f	Shapira	La Ina	Coqueteria
May16	Cologne	Mehl-Mulhens-Rennen-G2	1m 3yo c&f	Brunel	Lazio	Assiun
May16	Cologne	Diana-Trial-G3	1 3/8m 3yo f	Amarette	Saldentigerin	Vallera
May22	Baden-Baden	Betty Barclay-Rennen-G3	2m 4yo+	Darasim	Bailamos	King of Boxmeer
May23	Baden-Baden	Badener-Meile-G3	1m 3yo+	Bear King	Horeion Directa	Madresal
May28	Baden-Baden	Benazet-Rennen-G3	6f 3yo+	Lucky Strike	Topkamp	Sacho
May30	Baden-Baden	Grosser Mercedes-Benz-G2	1 3/8m 4yo+	Touch of Land	Rotteck	Scott's View
May31	Munich	Bavarian Classic-G3	1 1/4m 3yo	Fight Club	Egerton	Gentle Tiger
Jun6	Mulheim	Preis der Diana-G1	1 3/8m 3yo f	Amarette	La Ina	Saldentigerin
Jun13	Cologne	Oppenheim-Union-Rennen-G2	1 3/8m 3yo	Malinas	Omikron	Shirocco
Jun20	Dortmund	GP der Wirtschaft-G3	1m,165y 3yo+	Tahreeb	Anolitas	Morbidezza
Jun26	Hamburg	Deutscher Herold-Preis-G3	1m 3yo+	Sambaprinz	Pepperstorm	Eagle Rise
Jun27	Hamburg	Idee Hansa-Preis-G2	1 3/8m 3yo+	Rotteck	Storm Trooper	Aolus
Jun30	Hamburg	Fahrhofer Stutenpreis-G3	1m 3yo+ f&m	Eyeq	Nightdance Forest	Arlecchina
Jly2	Hamburg	Pr Jnghnrch Gblstplr-G3	1 3/8m 3yo+ f&m	Vallera	Next Gina	Give Me Five
Jly3	Hamburg	Holsten-Trophy-G3	6f 3yo+	Lucky Strike	Fiepes Shuffle	Areias
Jly4	Hamburg	Deutsches Derby-G1	1 1/2m 3yo c&f	Shirocco	Malinas	Omikron
Jly11	Hoppegarten	Berlin-Brndnburg Trphy-G2	1m 3yo+	Martillo	Assiun	Checkit
Jly18	Frankfurt	Hessen-Pokal-G3	1-1/4m 3yo+	Soldier Hollow	Anolitas	Winning Dash
Jly25	Dusseldorf	Deutschlandpreis-G1	1-1/2m 3yo+	Albanova	Dayano	Rotteck

Aug1	Cologne	Kolner-Meile-G3	1m 3yo+	Pepperstorm	Eagle Rise	Tahreeb
Aug1	Munich	Bayerisches Zuchtrennen-G1	1 1/4m 3yo+	Intendant	Powerscourt	Imperial Dancer
Aug8	Hoppegarten	GP von Berlin-G3	6-1/2f 3yo+	Felicity (Ger)	Key To Pleasure	Gold Type
Aug15	Cologne	Rheinland-Pokal-G1	1 1/2m 3yo+	Albanova	High Accolade	Malinas
Aug22	Bremen	GrssrStutenprsBremen-G3	1 3/8m 3yo+ f&m	Vallera	Daytona	Mity Dancer
Aug27	Baden-Baden	Spreti-Rennen-G3	1 1/4m 4yo+	Soldier Hollow	Longridge	Morbidezza
Aug29	Baden-Baden	Furstenberg-Rennen-G3	1 1/4m 3yo	Lyonels Glory	Saldentigerin	Quilanga
Aug31	Baden-Baden	Oettingen-Rennen-G2	1m 3yo+	Pepperstorm	Checkit	Assiun
Sep1	Baden-Baden	Golden Peitsche-G2	6f 3yo+	Raffelberger	Key To Pleasure	Lucky Strike
Sep3	Baden-Baden	Maurice Lacroix-Trophy-G2	6f 2yo	Daring Love	Beirut	Tournedos
Sep5	Baden-Baden	Grosser Preis von Baden-G1	1 1/2m 3yo+	Warrsan	Egerton	Shirocco
Sep19	Frankfurt	Euro-Cup-G2	1-1/4m 3yo+	Soldier Hollow	Fight Club	Morbidezza
Sep25	Cologne	Grosse Europa-Meile-G2	1m 3yo+	Eagle Rise	Putra Pekan	Assiun
Sep26	Cologne	Preis von Europa-G1	1 1/2m 3yo+	Albanova	Saldentigerin	Darsalam
Sep26	Cologne	OppenheinStutenMeile-G3	1m 3yo+ f&m	Secret Melody	Snow Goose	Kitcat
Oct3	Hoppegarten	Prs Deutschen Einheit-G3	1 1/4m 3yo+	Omikron	Anna Victoria	Salonhonor
Oct3	Dortmund	Deutsches St Leger-G2	1 3/4m 3yo c&f	Darsalam	Sword Roche	Fiepes Winged
Oct10	Frankfurt	Frnkfrtr Stutenpreis-G3	1 5/16m 3yo+ f&m	Give Me Five	Mity Dancer	Golden Rose
Oct10	Dusseldorf	GP von Dusseldorf-G3	1 1/16m 3yo+	Peppercorn	Glad Lion	Putra Pekan
Oct17	Cologne	Pr des Winterfavoriten-G3	1m 2yo	Manduro	Kahn	Early Wings
Oct24	Baden-Baden	Preis der Winterkonigin-G3	1m 2yo f	Sorrent	Gonbarda	Kahlua
Oct24	Baden-Baden	Baden-Wrttmbrg-Trphy-G3	1 3/8m 3yo+	Deva	Champion's Day	Mity Dancer
Oct24	Baden-Baden	Baden Sprint-Cop-G3	7f 3yo+	Areias	Ket To Pleasure	Lindholm
Oct31	Bremen	GP von Bremen-G3	1m 3yo+	Tiberius Caesar	Madresal	So Royal

ITALY

DATE	TRACK	RACE	CONDITIONS	1st	2nd	3rd
May1	Capannelle	Premio Parioli-G2	1m 3yo c	Spirit of Desert	Bravo Tazio	Ceprin
May1	Capannelle	Premio Regina Elena-G2	1m 3yo f	Rumba Loca	Super Bobbina	Dorr
May1	Capannelle	Premio Carlo Chiesa-G3	1m 4yo+ f&m	Miss Nashwan	Sayuri	Arlecchina
May15	San Siro	Pr Paolo Mezzanotte-G3	1 1/4m 4yo+ f&m	Deva	Jacira	Vale Mantovani
May16	Capannelle	Pr Pres Della Repubblica-G1	1 1/4m 4yo+ c&f	Altieri	Vespone	Nonno Carlo
May23	San Siro	Oaks d'Italia-G1	1 3/8m 3yo f	Menhoubah	Step Dancer	Loriana
May30	Capannelle	Derby Italiano-G1	1 1/2m 3yo c&f	Groom Tesse	Dayano	Privy Seal
May30	Capannelle	Premio Carlo d'Alessio-G2	1 3/4m 4yo+	Simonas	Darrel	Vale Mantovani
May30	Capannelle	Premio Tudini-G3	6f 3yo+	St Paul House	Krisman	Glad To Be Fast
Jun2	San Siro	Premio Emilio Turati-G2	1m 3yo+	Marbye	Honey Bunny	Lindholm
Jun20	San Siro	Gran Premio di Milano-G1	1 1/2m 3yo+ c&f	Senex	Maktub	The Great Gatsby
Jun20	San Siro	Premio Primi Passi-G3	6f 2yo	Shifting Place	Obe Gold	Tenderlit
Jun20	San Siro	Premio Mario Incisa-G3	1 1/2m 3yo+ f&m	Vale Mantovani	Deva	Landinium
Jly11	Naples	GP Citta di Napoli-G3	5f 3yo+	T E Lawrence	Regina Saura	Benbaun
Oct2	San Siro	Premio Federico Tesio-G3	1-3/8m 4yo+	Without Connexion	Serenus	One Little David
Oct10	San Siro	Pr Vittorio di Capua-G1	1m 3yo+ c&f	Ancient World	Majestic Desert	Hurricane Alan
Oct10	San Siro	Premio Dormello-G3	1m 2yo f	Nouvelle Noblesse	Gold Marie	Umniya
Oct17	San Siro	GP del Jockey Club-G1	1 1/2m 3yo+ c&f	Shirocco	Electrocutionist	Sweet Stream
Oct17	San Siro	Gran Criterium-G1	1m 2yo c&f	Konigstiger	Idealist	Hearthstead Wings
Oct17	San Siro	Premio Sergio Cumani-G3	1m 3yo+ f&m	Snow Goose	Kitcat	Secret Melody
Oct17	San Siro	Premio Omenoni-G3	5f 2yo+	Raffelberger	Krisman	Regina Saura
Oct24	Capannelle	Pr Guido Berardelli-G3	1 1/8m 2yo	Le Giare	Tedo	Bernard
Oct24	Capannelle	Premio Lydia Tesio-G1	1 1/4m 3yo+f&m	Lune d'Or	Walkamia	Super Bobbina
Oct31	San Siro	Premio Chiusura-G3	7f 2yo+	Horeion Directa	Arc Bleu	Glad To Be Fast
Nov7	Capannelle	Premio Roma-G1	1 1/4m 3yo+ c&f	Soldier Hollow	Imperial Dancer	Gateman
Nov7	Capannelle	Premio Ribot-G2	1m 3yo+	Eagle Rise	Martillo	Salselon
Nov7	Capannelle	Premio Umbria-G3	6f 2yo+	St Paul House	Stoxx	Key To Pleasure

UNITED ARAB EMIRATES

DATE	TRACK	RACE	CONDITIONS	1st	2nd	3rd
Mar27	Nad Al Sheba	Dubai World Cup-G1	1 1/4m 4yo+	Pleasantly Perfect	Medaglia d'Oro	Victory Moon
Mar27	Nad Al Sheba	Dubai Duty Free-G1	a1 1/8m 4yo+	dh-Paolini dh-Right Approach		
Mar27	Nad Al Sheba	Dubai Sheema Classic-G1	1 1/2m 4yo+	Polish Summer	Hard Buck	Scott's View
Mar27	Nad Al Sheba	Dubai Golden Shaheen-G1	6f 3yo+	Our New Recruit	Alke	Conroy
Mar27	Nad Al Sheba	UAE Derby-G2	1 1/8m 3yo	Lundy's Liability	Petit Paris	Little Jim
Mar27	Nad Al Sheba	Godolphin Mile-G2	1m 3yo+	Firebreak	Tropical Star	Excessivepleasure

JAPAN

DATE	TRACK	RACE	CONDITIONS	1st	2nd	3rd
Nov28	Tokyo	Japan Cup Dirt-G1	1 1/8m 3yo+	Time Paradox	Admire Don	Gene Crisis
Nov28	Tokyo	Japan Cup-G1	1 3/8m 3yo+	Zenno Rob Roy	Cosmo Bulk	Delta Blues

HONG KONG

DATE	TRACK	RACE	CONDITIONS	1st	2nd	3rd
Apr25	Sha Tin	Queen Eliz II Cup-G1	1-1/4m 3yo+	River Dancer	Elegant Fashion	Scott's View
Dec12	Sha Tin	Hong Kong Cup-G1	1 1/4m 3yo+	Alexander Goldrun	Bullish Luck	Touch of Land
Dec12	Sha Tin	Hong Kong Vase-G1	1 1/2m 3yo+	Phoenix Reach	Sights On Gold	Vallee Enchantee
Dec12	Sha Tin	Hong Kong Mile-G1	1m 3yo+	Firebreak	Perfect Partner	The Duke
Dec12	Sha Tin	Hong Kong Sprint-G1	5f 3yo+	Silent Witness	Cape Of Good Hope	Natural Blitz

SINGAPORE

DATE	TRACK	RACE	CONDITIONS	1st	2nd	3rd
May16	Kranji	Singapore Air Intl Cup-G1	1-1/4m 3yo+	Epalo	Surveyor	Bowman's Crossing

European Leaders in 2004

LEADING JOCKEYS IN BRITAIN-2004

Jockey	Mts	1st	2nd	3rd	W%	Earnings
Fallon K	1109	200	166	125	.180	$8,949,053
Dettori L	850	193	133	89	.227	8,411,853
Sanders S	1002	165	119	87	.165	3,330,828
Holland D	1178	152	137	137	.129	4,325,993
Moore R L	1008	132	125	107	.131	2,712,323
Callan N	1030	126	117	103	.122	1,813,815
Winston R	1008	114	105	113	.113	2,135,673
Ahern E	1016	111	99	108	.109	2,158,833
Culhane A	1048	111	104	108	.106	1,680,421
Hanagan P	829	101	70	100	.122	1,932,987
Other notables						
Drowne S	1115	99	93	103	.089	2,339,055
Darley K	822	85	97	89	.103	3,229,303
Murtagh J P	574	78	57	60	.136	3,496,133
Quinn T R	689	76	79	75	.110	2,374,086
Hughes R	661	73	76	70	.110	1,942,072
Fortune J	615	72	87	76	.117	2,389,292
Robinson P	552	67	58	67	.121	2,655,295
Hills R	454	66	49	65	.145	3,020,020
Hills M	510	66	60	42	.129	1,787,651
McEvoy K	322	42	30	32	.130	2,454,414
Kinane M J	90	9	10	17	.100	1,682,080
Mosse G	8	2	1	1	.250	159,065
Smullen P J	27	2	3	0	.074	140,636
Stevens G L	16	0	3	2	.000	539,577
Peslier O	9	0	1	0	.000	96,094
Soumillon C	3	0	0	0	.000	13,598
Gillet T	2	0	0	1	.000	91,743

LEADING OWNERS IN BRITAIN-2004

Owner	Sts	1st	2nd	3rd	W%	Earning
Godolphin	455	115	75	42	.253	$7,840,028
Al Maktoum H	464	73	46	66	.157	3,179,243
Cheveley Pk Stud	218	58	29	29	.266	2,074,580
Ballymacoll Stud	28	8	3	2	.286	1,691,237
Abdullah K	328	54	45	38	.165	1,675,145
Al Maktoum M	235	33	32	29	.140	1,406,491
Sheikh Mohammed	311	52	42	38	.167	1,206,514
Elite Racing Club	64	16	7	6	.250	1,016,942
Duke of Roxburghe	5	3	1	0	.600	883,013
H H Aga Khan	42	11	6	6	.262	842,199
Al Maktoum A	266	36	49	26	.159	840,635
Other notables						
Tanaka G A	12	3	0	1	.250	667,732
Manana Saeed	87	8	12	6	.092	661,262
Smith J C	109	6	11	16	.055	656,437
Magnier & Tabor	22	2	3	4	.091	596,217
Sangster Family	30	8	8	1	.267	584,406
Lucayan Stud	164	20	21	14	.122	557,855
Magnier Mrs J	14	1	1	1	.071	504,696
Lord Derby	2	2	0	0	1.000	399,607
The Queen	82	15	18	11	.183	384,708
Tabor & Magnier	19	2	3	2	.105	336,393
Gainsborough Stud	9	1	0	3	.111	280,119
Ecurie Wildenstein	7	1	1	2	.143	265,191
Tabor M	61	9	4	10	.148	264,973
Niarchos Family	37	5	1	5	.135	255,974
Strawbridge G	48	6	7	3	.125	162,989

LEADING TRAINERS IN BRITAIN-2004

Trainer	Sts	1st	2nd	3rd	W%	Earnings
Suroor S bin	455	115	75	42	.253	$7,840,028
Stoute M R	400	87	49	46	.218	5,334,549
Johnston M	799	119	111	77	.149	4,419,726
Channon M R	1039	98	124	100	.094	3,150,675
Hills B W	636	82	76	61	.129	2,822,568
Hannon R	1201	113	123	127	.094	2,654,606
Jarvis M A	371	65	49	44	.175	2,376,370
Gosden J H M	458	65	65	59	.142	2,291,661
Fanshawe J	294	44	39	33	.150	2,148,581
Dunlop J L	513	55	51	63	.107	2,124,847
Other notables						
Cumani L M	293	42	45	35	.143	1,919,017
Meehan B J	506	60	47	54	.119	1,554,276
Dunlop E A L	393	49	45	47	.125	1,478,474
O'Brien A P	60	4	8	7	.067	1,458,543
Brittain C E	315	28	32	20	089	1,290,761
Balding A M	542	48	59	57	.089	1,233,958
Cole P F I	366	41	37	37	112	1,168,762
Tregoning M	190	26	27	23	.137	1,117,172
Prescott M	234	66	30	15	.282	960,071
Noseda J	215	34	34	29	158	901,203
Loder D R	342	45	36	36	.132	833,252
Oxx J M	11	3	0	4	.273	524,675
Cecil H R A	150	21	14	27	.140	427,836
McPeek K	1	0	1	0	.000	302,346
Lellouche E	7	1	1	2	143	265,191
Fabre A	6	0	1	1	.000	204,996

LEADING JOCKEYS IN IRELAND-2004

Jockey	Mts	1st	2nd	3rd	W%	Earnings
Spencer J P	361	93	59	42	.258	$3,786,688
Berry F M	476	66	42	34	.139	1,557,973
Smullen P J	545	65	83	66	.119	3,349,267
McDonogh D P	399	54	39	45	.135	1,423,792
Kinane M J	433	49	69	53	.113	2,907,993
McCullagh N G	466	38	39	41	.082	1,054,877
Manning K J	357	34	42	35	,095	1,605,142
O'Shea T P	477	33	41	37	.069	910,160
Gannon Catherine	369	32	26	35	.087	736,753
Cleary R P	336	29	15	32	.086	694,051
Other notables						
Heffernan J A	522	28	43	43	.054	1,064,083
Cosgrave P	355	18	17	26	.051	368,064
O'Donoghue C	240	18	19	15	.075	551,212
Murtagh J P	55	10	3	5	.182	664,758
Supple W J	31	5	1	2	161	173,306
Fallon K	20	2	2	6	.100	999,127
Winston R	1	1	0	0	1.000	66,395
Holland D	2	1	0	0	.500	200,207
Hughes R	5	1	1	0	.200	96,274
McEvoy K	5	1	0	0	.200	19,944
Darley K	6	1	3	0	.167	409,224
Dettori L	6	1	1	0	.167	383,177
Sanders S	7	1	0	1	.143	316,016
Ahern E	12	1	1	1	.083	37,763

Trainer	Sts	1st	Plc	W%	Earnings

LEADING TRAINERS IN IRELAND-2004

Trainer	Sts	1st	2nd	3rd	W%	Earnings
O'Brien A P	252	77	40	33	.306	$3,708,527
Weld D K	540	61	67	60	.113	3,262,874
Oxx J M	383	51	48	44	.133	2,374,600
Prendergast K	334	51	34	35	.153	1,647,019
Bolger J S	337	34	43	31	.101	1,640,505
Wachman D	160	19	16	14	.119	849,712
Halford M	351	28	32	30	.080	647,136
Collins C	125	20	17	9	.160	617,134
Lynam E	188	20	22	14	.106	575,472
Grassick M J	221	18	20	28	.081	472,532
Other notables						
Suroor S bin	7	1	1	0	.143	388,412
Stoute M R	4	0	2	1	.000	380,240
Johnston M	3	1	1	0	.333	353,938
Stack T	100	10	7	15	.100	350,772
Fanshawe J R	3	2	0	0	.667	330,316
Dunlop E A L	2	1	0	0	.500	306,312
Channon M R	22	3	2	4	.136	297,380
Wragg G	5	2	1	1	.400	213,295
Haggas W J	1	1	0	0	1.000	199,186
Johnson Houghton R	2	1	0	0	.500	107,694
Hannon R	8	1	0	2	.125	126,023
Charlton R	2	2	0	0	1.000	112,112
Meehan B	5	1	0	1	.200	109,029

LEADING OWNERS IN IRELAND-2004

Owner	Sts	1st	2nd	3rd	W%	Earnings
Magnier Mrs J	170	56	24	23	.329	$2,916,870
H H Aga Khan	140	25	22	18	.179	1,650,323
Quinn Rochelle	5	2	0	1	.400	1,066,601
Lady O'Reilly	196	27	31	18	.138	802,596
Al Maktoum H	103	20	10	8	.194	693,178
Tabor M	77	18	11	8	.234	589,151
MoyglareStudFarm	100	19	16	17	.190	506,152
Dobson D H W	92	9	10	11	.098	392,901
Godolphin	7	1	1	0	.143	388,412
O'Brien Mrs A M	81	9	13	13	.111	380,537
Other notables						
Duke of Roxburghe	2	1	1	0	.500	350,618
Ballymacoll Stud	2	0	1	0	.000	320,612
Elite Racing Club	3	2	1	0	.667	320,357
Lord Derby	1	1	0	0	1.000	295,290
Sheikh Mohammed	44	5	4	10	.114	279,267
Bolger Mrs J S	93	5	10	10	.054	271,515
Smurfit M W J	74	7	15	10	.095	259,653
Smith J C	1	0	1	0	.000	241,321
Al Maktoum M	25	4	5	2	.160	207,616
Sangster Family	11	3	3	2	.273	206,040
Cheveley Park Stud	3	1	0	0	.333	204,931
Abdullah K	2	1	0	1	.500	96,273
Firestone B R	21	3	0	2	.143	56,894
O'Brien M V	46	0	6	4	.000	55,928
Niarchos Family	2	0	1	1	.000	25,798
Tanaka G A	1	0	0	0	.000	23,759
Tabor & Magnier	3	0	1	1	.000	20,618

Owner	Sts	1st	Plc	W%	Earnings

LEADING JOCKEYS IN FRANCE-2004

Jockey	Mts	1st	*Plc	W%	Earnings
Mendizabal I	969	220	414	.227	$4,778,982
Soumillon C	1020	165	475	.162	6,771,002
Peslier O	823	123	307	.149	4,664,398
Pasquier S	970	100	430	.103	3,478,533
Boeuf D	849	95	360	.112	3,335,944
Jarnet T	732	85	320	.116	3,245,086
Blondel F	642	79	275	.123	1,606,980
Thulliez T	846	73	330	.086	3,708,959
Lemaire C-P	799	71	300	.089	3,506,856
Sogorb P	479	70	229	.146	1,043,414
Other notables					
Gillet T	536	62	189	.116	4,154,901
Bonilla D	664	62	247	.093	2,255,513
Stevens G L	246	51	125	.207	2,612,719
Blancpain M	555	50	195	.090	1,693,914
Legrix E	738	46	246	062	2,324,587
Spanu F	610	40	175	.066	1,204,491
Dubosc J-R	199	34	82	.171	540,855
Placais O	410	28	128	.068	667,415
Maillot S	486	27	149	.056	866,768
Hughes R	13	4	5	.308	459,763
Fallon K	8	2	2	.250	387,747
Spencer J P	18	2	11	.111	593,479
Dettori L	22	2	7	.091	317,290
Kinane M J	3	1	0	.333	139,776

*Plc-2nd thu 5th, i.e.., all horses that earned money.

LEADING TRAINERS IN FRANCE-2004

Trainer	Sts	1st	*Plc	W%	Earnings
Fabre A	515	103	268	.200	$5,411,325
Rouget J-C	643	215	300	.334	3,845,799
Collet Robert	1025	76	346	.074	2,831,874
Lellouche E	487	54	216	.111	2,795,102
Laffon-Parias C	482	75	207	.156	2,567,122
Bary P	219	42	115	.192	2,525,665
Pease J	177	37	68	.209	2,454,646
Head-Maarek C	450	66	197	.147	2,371,138
Royer-Dupre A de	342	51	160	.149	1,963,057
Pantall H-A	774	100	360	.129	1,911,834
Other notables					
Gibson R	289	44	141	.152	1,708,090
Rohaut F	385	49	175	.127	1,388,472
Libaud E	285	63	153	.221	1,330,898
Beguigne J-M	183	32	80	.175	1,169,467
Smaga D	213	31	94	.146	1,105,285
Hammond J	144	25	62	.174	1,068,256
Sepulchre D	371	51	149	.137	1,041,843
Head F	208	21	91	.101	884,754
Clement N	202	23	85	.114	774,956
Doumen F	300	24	98	.080	683,970
Demercastel P	197	18	75	091	576,637
O'Brien A P	16	1	10	.063	574,508
Stoute M R	3	1	1	.333	300,577
Gosden J H M	14	0	9	.000	243,874
Suroor S bin	10	0	3	.000	118,243

*Plc-2nd thru 5th, i.e., all horses that earned money.

Trainer	Sts	1st	Plc	W%	Earnings

LEADING OWNERS IN FRANCE-2004

Owner	Sts	1st	*Plc	W%	Earnings
Niarchos Family	104	22	51	.212	$2,794,147
SNCLagardereElevage	194	55	101	284	2,455,593
Abdullah K	244	51	115	.209	2,301,299
Ecurie Wildenstein	318	56	140	.176	2,221,333
Wertheimer & Frere	350	55	153	157	1,929,795
Marquise de Moratalla	413	69	210	.167	1,303,103
Sheikh Mohammed	249	41	130	.165	1,292,676
Ecurie J-L Bouchard	55	11	27	.200	1,061,999
Seroul J-C	324	51	153	.157	919,233
Strauss R C	107	14	51	.131	812,420
Marinopoulos L	149	19	64	.128	698,023
Other notables					
Gestut Ammerland	26	6	13	.231	618,234
H H Aga Khan	141	20	74	.142	605,740
Zuylen de Nyevelt T de	114	13	48	.114	568,032
Head A	92	14	33	.152	562,742
Rothschild Baron E de	100	15	48	.150	476,856
Al Maktoum H	56	11	25	.196	432,011
Al Maktoum M	112	16	53	.143	420,386
Ecurie Chalhoub	66	6	29	.111	414,490
Collet Robert	278	16	62	.058	373,682
Strawbridge G	73	13	31	.178	329,625
Ecurie Bader	90	7	34	.078	292,706
Head Mme A	79	12	31	152	292,566
Magnier & Tabor	4	1	0	250	244,608
Lord Derby	1	0	1	.000	226,991
Ecurie Fabien Ouaki	79	12	23	.152	203,781
Lady O'Reilly	49	8	25	.163	191,171
Devin Mme H	46	10	28	.217	187,795
Team Valor	3	1	1	.333	188,205
Gestut Ittlingen	38	8	23	.211	182,633
Tanaka G A	29	6	12	.207	169,889
Godolphin	10	0	3	.000	118,243

*Plc-2nd thru 5th, i.e., all horses that earned money.

European Track Diagrams

ASCOT, ENGLAND

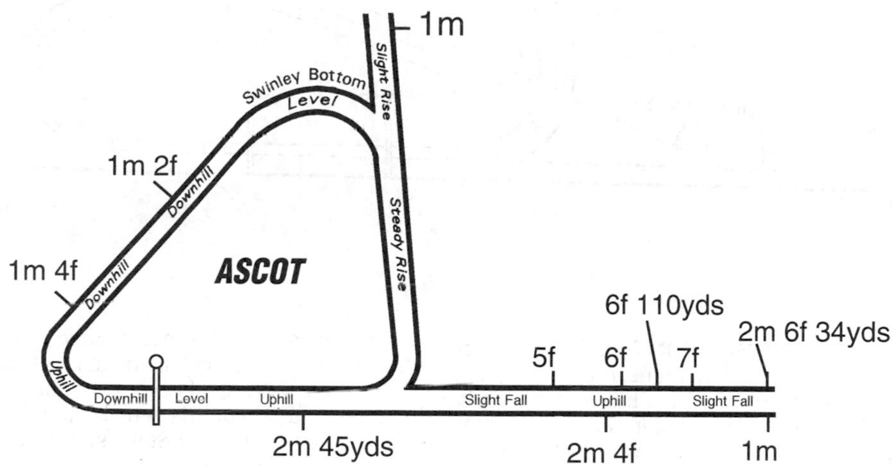

Course Discription Ascot is a right-handed, triangular course, 1 3/4 miles around with a stretch of 2-1/2 furlongs. There is also a one-mile straight course which joins the triangular course at the head of the stretch.

Races at 1 1/2 miles, e.g., the King George VI and Queen Elizabeth Diamond Stakes, begin with a downhill run of half a mile to Swinley Bottom, a right-hand bend at the lowest point in the track. From the mile pole it is almost entirely uphill past the 90-degree turn into the stretch. The final furlong is level. The straight course is mildly undulating throughout.

One-mile races are run from two different starting points. Those on the Old Mile, e.g., Queen Elizabeth II Stakes, St. James's Palace Stakes, Coronation Satkes, start from a chute near Swinley Bottom and are almost entirely uphill until the final furlong. Other mile races, e.g., the Queen Anne Stakes and big handicpas like the Royal Hunt Cup Handicap, are run on the straight course. All races shorter than a mile are run on the straight course.

Ascot places a premium on stamina and is ideal for long-striding gallopers. The Old Mile, over which the Queen Elizabeth II Stakes is run in late September, is hardly an ideal prep for the Breeders' Cup Mile as its uphill nature makes it a stayers mile as opposed to the near sprint that is the BC Mile. No winner of the QEII has ever won the BC Mile. The ground at Ascot can be very testing when soft or heavy, especially in the lower regions at Swinley Bottom.

History: Ascot was founded in 1711 by Queen Anne after she bought the property following a stag hunt. It has been in the hands of the Royal Family ever since. That first meeting, held on August 13, was the premier Royal Meeting. It would develop into the four-day Royal Ascot festival held annually during the third week of June. Outside of those four days of Royal Ascot, the track is referred to simply as Ascot. The racecourse conducts 22 days of racing annually, 13 on the flat and nine over jumps.

CHANTILLY, FRANCE

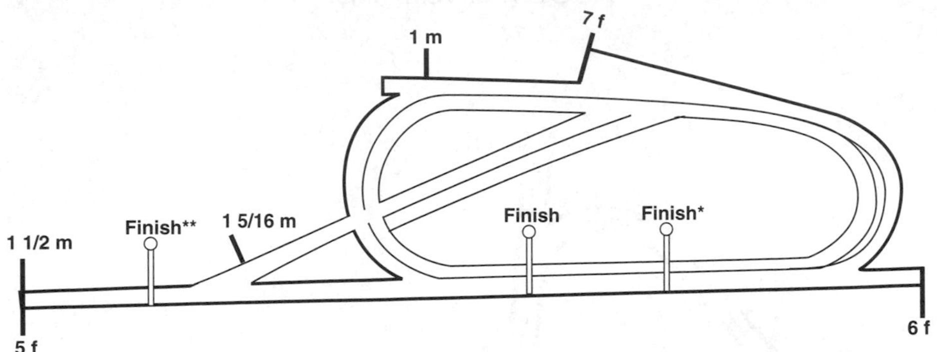

Course Description: Chantilly is a right-handed track with a number of configurations. The Piste du Jockey-Club, over which is run the Prix du Jockey-Club (French Derby), is 1 1/2 miles in length. After the first furlong, there is a mild left-handed bend onto the backstretch. On the turn for home there is a decline followed by a rise midway through the right-handed turn which lasts until the horses reach the stretch, three frulongs from the line.

The Prix de Diane (French Oaks) is run over the same course, but starts 1 1/2 furlongs later on the backstretch. Five-furlong races start in the same place as the French Derby and are run past the stands on the level straight course. Six-furlong races are also run on the straight course in front of the grandstand, but in the opposite direction.

There is also a right-handed inner course, or petite piste.

History: The first races at Chantilly were run under the auspices of the Duc d'Orleans. The first Prix du Jockey-Club was was organized by the Englishman Lord Seymour in 1836, with the premier Prix de Diane following in 1843. The current racecourse was founded by the Duc d'Aumale in 1886 on property owned by the Duc de Conde.

Racing at Chantilly is provided with perhaps the most beautiful backdrop of any course in the world. On what we in America would call the far turn there sits the Chateau de Conde, ancestral home of the Ducs de Conde. One such 18th century duke was convinced he would be reincarnated as a Thoroughbred. So that he would be able to live in suitable digs upon his return, he built the Grandes Ecuries (Grand Stables), the palatial barn on the Chantilly backstretch. Both the chateau and the ecuries are now museums, open to the public on racedays and dark days.

Chantilly holds much the same place in French racing that Newmarket does in England. The town and nearby Lamorlaye contain the yards of most of France's leading trainers. This year there were 2,558 horses-in-training at Chantilly, accounting for 70 percent of all the runners on the Parisian circuit: Chantilly, Longchamp, Saint-Cloud, Maisons-Laffitte and Deauville. This high concentration of top class Thoroughbred bloodstock is the reason why racing on the Parisian circuit possesses the highest concentration of class in the world. The gallops, or training tracks, cut through the local forest, and are perhaps the world's most beautiful, topped by the unparalled Les Aigles.

Until eight years ago, Chantilly held just six days of racing per year, all of them in June around the running of the Prix du Jockey-Club on the first Sunday in June and the Prix de Diane on the second Sunday of that month. There were 14 days of racing this season, which was curtailed after June for the refurbishment of the outdated fin-de-siecle grandstand. Next year Chantilly will return to its full complement of 26 days.

THE CURRAGH, IRELAND

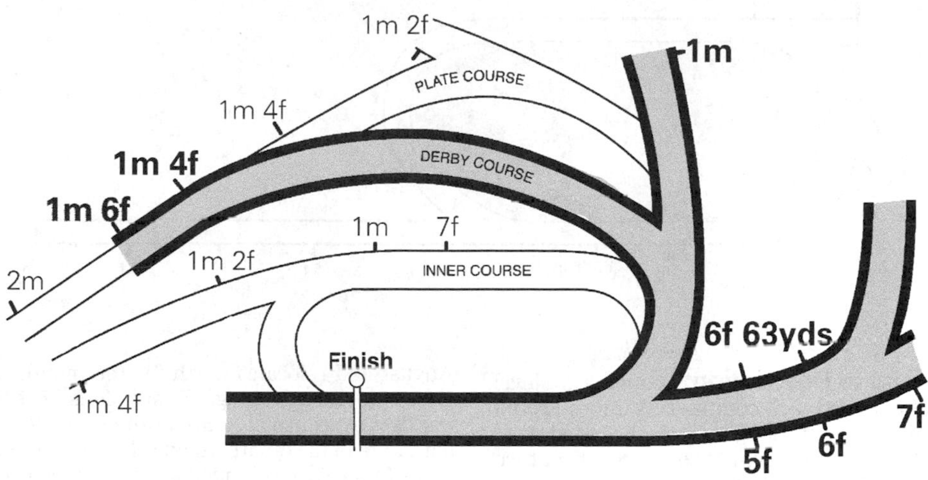

Course Description: The Curragh is an undulating, right-handed track. The round course is horseshoe-shaped and 1 3/4 miles in length, the last 1 1/2 miles of which is the Irish Derby course, the first two furlongs of which are straight, followed by a mild right-hand bend. Then comes another two-furlong straight followed by a sweeping right-hand turn into the uphill three-furlong stretch. There is also a one-mile track that is virtually straight but includes a mild righ-hand bend after 2-1/2 furlongs. It meets the round course at the head of the stretch, three furlongs from the line and is the track over which both the Irish 1000 and 2000 Guineas is run.

As Ireland receives considerably more rain than even England, the ground at the Curragh is more likely to be yielding, soft or heavy than good or firm. Stamina is at a premium here and it is essential that horses possess the ability to see out the trip, especially given the uphill finish. A preponderance of the country's best group races are run at the Curragh, so a horse that does well in good company here can be expected to acquit himself well in America, but only if he finds the same ground in the U.S. that he is used to running on in Ireland. It must also be noted that two trainers, Aidan O'Brien and Dermot Weld, have a majority of the best horses in Ireland, with Jim Bolger and Kevin Prendergast the only others who can compete with them on anything approaching a regular basis.

History: Curragh is the Gaelic word for course, or racecourse. Racing has been conducted there in one form or another since the 12th century. The first recorded match was run in 1679, with organized races becaming commonplace in the early 18th century. From time to time racing was abandoned due to the ìtroublesî. The Irish Turf Club was founded at the Curragh in 1790 and has ben in charge of the sport ever since.

By that time the Curragh had become the unquestioned center of Irish racing, in much the same way that Newmarket serves English racing. Many of Ireland's leading trainers have their stables nearby.

All five of Ireland's classic races are run at the Curragh. The first Irish Derby was run in 1866, the first Irish Oaks in 1895, and the first Irish St. Leger in 1915. The two Guineas both had their inaugural runnings in 1921.

The Curragh conducts 15 days of racing a year, all on the flat.

DEAUVILLE, FRANCE

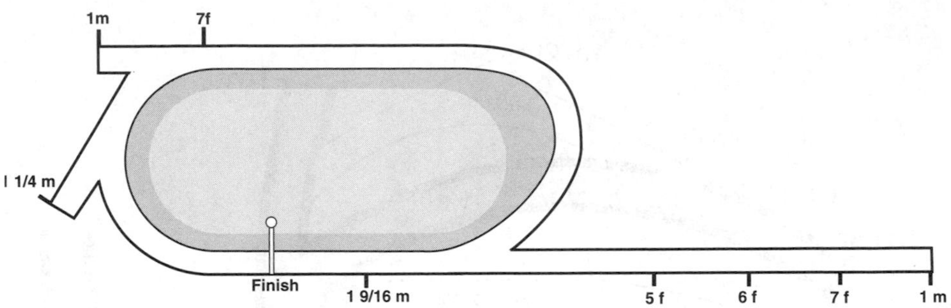

Course Description: Deauville is a level, right-handed oval course, 1 3/8 miles around with a three-furlong stretch. Races at 1 1/4 miles start from a chute beyond the first turn. The turns are very mild. Indeed, they are so mild that they make those on Belmont's main track seem tight by comparison. There is a one-mile straight course which is very mildly undulating until it joins the oval course three furlongs from the finish. There is also a less frequently used course inside the main track called the petite piste.

Deauville is a very wide as well as a very fair course that does not confer an advantage on any particular type of horse. It always yields a number of 3-year-olds who later run with success at Del Mar and at the Hollywood Turf Festival.

History: The racecourse at Deauville was founded by the Duc de Morny in 1864, the same year that Saratoga opened, but the two tracks share more than a founding date.

Deauville serves the same purpose vis-a-vis Parisian racing that Saratoga does for racing in New York. That is to say, the entire racing community in Paris, including the bulk of the training centers at Chantilly and Maisons-Laffitte, pull up stakes on or about the first of August and relocates north for the month to Deauville. Like Saratoga, Deauville is host to the first exposure of many of the best 2-year-olds. Late in the month, Agence Francaise conducts France's most important yearling sale in the town.

As a diversion, there is a second racecourse about two miles up the road from Deauville at Clairefontaine. On days in August when Deauville is dark, Calirefontaine is likely to be open. In addition to flat racing of a slightly lower standard, Clairefontaine, a 1 1/4-mile right-handed oval with a 3-furlong stretch, offers hurdle and steeplechase racing on a course inside its flat track, thus bringing similarities to Saratoga full circle.

The charms of Deauville are many. Before racing there are the attractions of one of the world's most fashionable beaches. Apres piste, for those who have any money left, there are the temptations of the famous beachfront casino.

Deauville conducts 24 days of racing annually, sixteen during its prestigious August meeting, five days in July, and three days in late October. During the August meeting, Clairefontaine runs eight mixed meetings (flat and jumps).

EPSOM, ENGLAND

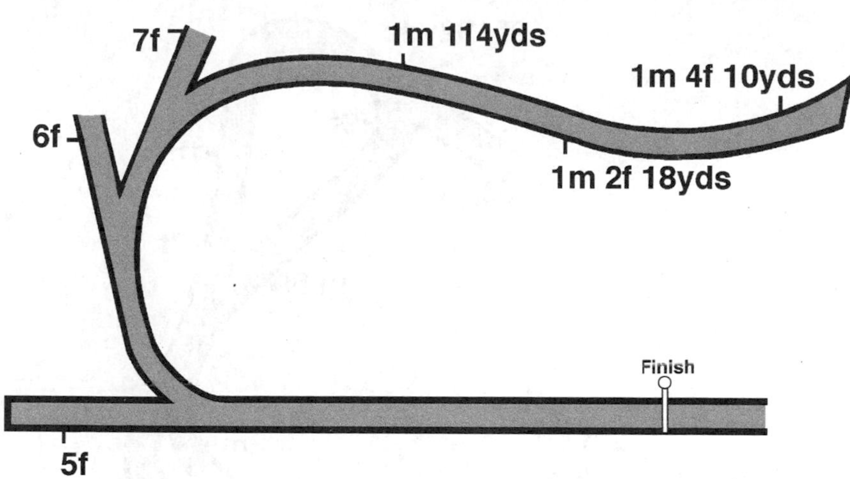

Course Description: Epsom is a left-handed, horseshoe-shaped track, its 1 1/2-mile circumference being the distance of the Derby and the Oaks The Derby course is stiffly uphill for the first six furlongs with a very mild right-hand bend 1-1/2 furlongs after the start. The course levels off at the top of the hill at halfway, or six furlongs from the line, after which there is a descent around an unbanked left-handed turn. That descent is at its steepest half a mile from home at Tattenham Corner, where the horses turn into the 3-1/2-furlong stretch which, while continuing downhill, is banked towards the inner rail. The final 110 yards is a slight rise to the finish.

Races at six and seven furlongs start from chutes at the top of the hill. There is also a five-furlong straight course that joins the Derby course at the head of the stretch. It is entirely and steeply downhill until the final sixteenth.

It takes an athletic type to successfully manouver Epsom's hills, unbanked turns and the infamous switchback, the term used to describe what happens when speeding horses being constrained to keep a straight line through Tattenham Corner suddenly meet the stretch with its ground cambered towards the inner rail. Horses with a high action or big, long striding gallopers frequently have trouble at Epsom.

History: It would be difficult to overestimate the importance of Epsom's 1 1/2-mile course in the history of racing. From the inception of the Derby in 1780 until the middle of the 20th century, it was the testing ground over which the best of the Thoroughbred breed was determined in both the Derby and the Oaks. During that period Derby winners routinely sired Derby winners and winners of other major races in England and the rest of the world. While the great race was challenged in mid-century by the Kentucky Derby and the French Derby, and while it suffered a decline in the 1990's, it still ranks as one of the world's most important Thoroughbred contests, especially from a breeder's point of view.

Epsom conducts eight days of racing a year, all on the flat.

GOODWOOD, ENGLAND

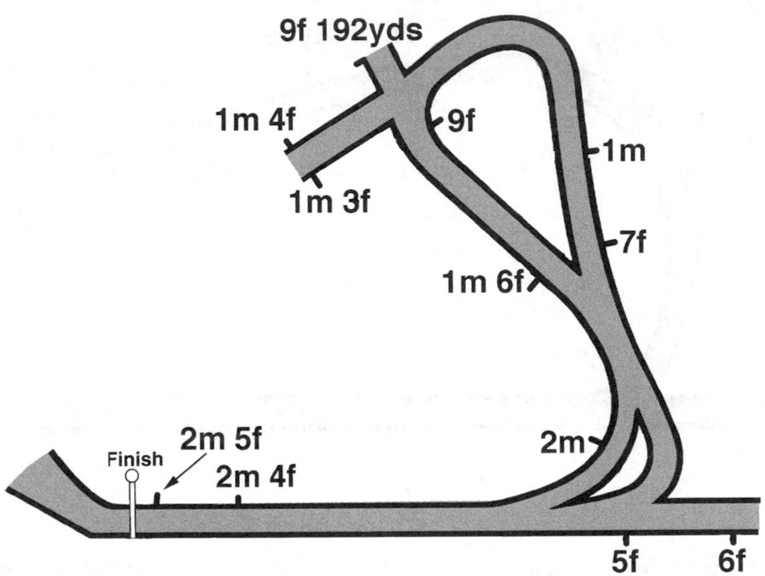

Course Description: No racecourse in the world differs more from America's standardized ovals than Goodwood. There is a six-furlong straight course which is slightly uphill at the start, then generally downhill until the final sixteenth, which is level. What separates Goodwood from all other tracks is its triangular right-handed loop built on the edge of a ridge. Races at 1 1/2 miles start from a chute with the horses running away from the finish line. They go uphill for 2-1/2 furlongs before turning right. The remainder of the course is undulating.

Races between two and 2 1/2 miles start in the stretch with the horses running away from the finish towards the loop. To complicate matters, there are two spurs used for entry into the stretch. Races at 1 1/8 miles and 1 1/4 miles, which go uphill in the opposite direction used in two-mile races, take the outer spur onto a 4-furlong stretch. All other races of seven furlongs or longer use the inner spur into a 3-furlong stretch.

Goodwood favors handy types who can manouver its undulations and rather sharp turns, although at races of nine furlongs or longer, there is no advantage to any given type. As a ìsharpî track where speed is at a premium, Goodwood should generally produce runners able to adapt to American tracks with their tight turns, this in spite of the vast differences in configuration between it an places like Hollywood or Keeneland. A singular example would be Tolomeo, who used the Sussex Stakes to vault to victory in the Arlington Million.

History: Goodwood was founded by the third Duke of Richmond in 1801. In 1839 it became the first racecourse to incorporate post position draws. The great undefeated (54-for-54) Hungarian mare Kincsem won the Goodwood Cup there in 1878, by which time the track's five-day late July, early August meeting, now dubbed Glorious Goodwood, had become part of the English social season along with Royal Ascot, the Henley Regatta, Wimbledon and the British Open.

Goodwood conducts thirteen days of racing a year, all on the flat.

LEOPARDSTOWN, IRELAND

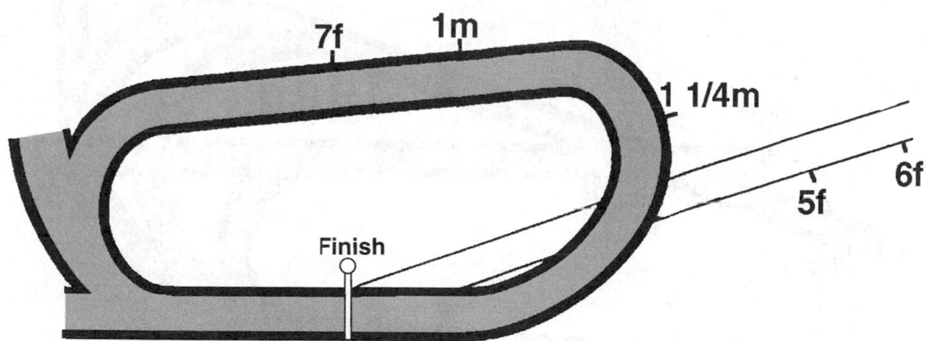

Course Description: Leopardstown is a left-handed oval, 1 3/4 miles in length and is virtually level except for an uphill finish. The turns are mild and the stretch is slightly longer than two furlongs. There is also a six-furlong straight course that dissects the oval course in much the same fashion as the old Widener Chute did at Belmont Park. Leopardstown is a very wide track that seems to suit gallopers a bit more than close-actioned types. The track is also used for jump racing from November through March.

History: Leopardstown is patterned after England's Sandown Park, which was the first enclosed track in Europe. It was opened on August 27, 1888, its name derived from its medieval title, Lepers Town, as the area had become known due to the lepers' hospital that had long been situated there. With the demise of Phoenix Park in central Dublin after the 1990 season, Leopardstown became the capital area's only racecourse.

At that time the 1 1/4-mile Irish Champion Stakes was moved to Leopardstown. The stakes record of 2:01.80 was set by Fantastic Light in his tremendous duel with Galileo in 2001.

While the quality of the flat racing is undoubtedly high- the same horses that run at the Curragh can always be seen at Leopardstown- the jump racing there takes precedence in a country that is first and foremost in love with the jumpers. The 4-day jump race meeting held at Leopardstown between Christmas and New Year's is one of the world's best.

Leopardstown conducts 30 days of racing a year, 15 on the flat and 15 over jumps.

LONGCHAMP, FRANCE

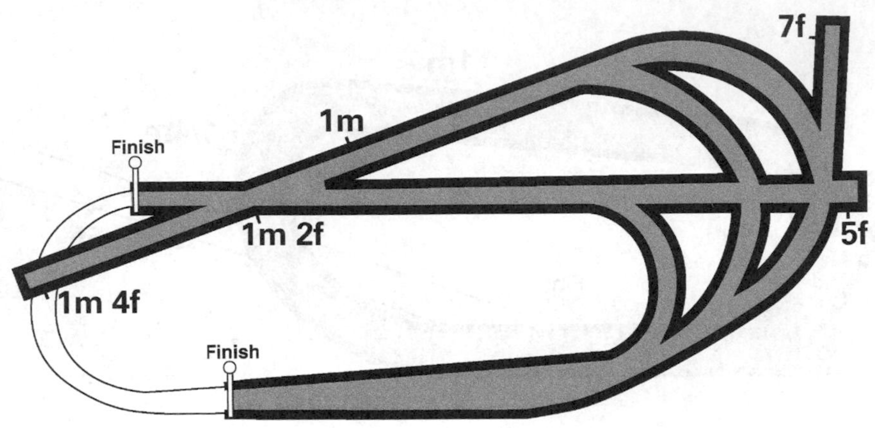

Course Description: Longchamp is a right-handed track with five separate courses, some of which share parts of others.

The grande piste is 1 5/8 miles, 55 yards around. It is on this course that the 1 1/2-mile Prix de l'Arc de Triomphe is run. That race starts from a short chute at the head of the backstretch. It is steadily uphill for the first six furlongs where the long right-handed, downhill turn begins. The course levels off after a mild bend into the one-furlong ìfalse straightî, so called because many an inexperienced rider has mistaken it for the actual straight, which follows after another mild right-hand bend and is 2-1/2 furlongs in length.

The 1 9/16-mile moyenne piste, or middle course, occupies the same ground as the grande piste until breaking off a furlong earlier for a downhill descent of its own to midway on the false straight.

The nouveau piste, or new course, starts behind the far turn. It is used primarily for seven-furlong races and is slightly downhill for the first two furlongs before joining the grande piste. Seven-furlong races at Longchamp finish at the deuxieme poteau, or second finish line, 100 meters past the premier poteau, or first finish line, which is used for a majority of races, including the Arc. Even with its downhill start, the nouveau piste produces unusually fast times for seven furlongs. The course is perhaps 20 meters short of its officially listed 1400 meters, a distance that is already seven yards short of seven furlongs.

The rarely used 1 5/16-mile, 55-yard petite piste lies inside the moyenne piste but shares the stretch with the two larger courses. Five-furlong races are run right to left on the ligne droite, or straight course.

Longchamp is an eminently fair course with what is, at 2-1/2 furlongs, a stretch that is short by most European standards. As in most French races, the early pace can be painfully slow, with the field bunching up on the approach to the final turn, after which horses fan out in their search for running room. The racing at Longchamp is high class. Horses that succeed there at any level- allowance, handicap, listed or group race- not infrequently find success at least one level higher in America.

History: The first races were run at Longchamp in 1857 with Emperor Napoleon III present as master of ceremonies. From the mid 1860's until the start of World War II, the Grand Prix de Paris routinely attracted up to 100,000 Parisians on the last Sunday in June. On April 4, 1943, the track was bombed by American reconaissance planes after they were fired upon by a jittery German artillery gunner who was manning one of the occupying forces' defense weapons deployed on the racecourse infield. Seven racegoers perished in the bombing.

The first Prix de l'Arc de Triomphe was run in 1920 in celebration of France's victory in World War I. Since 1955, the year of Ribot's first Arc triumph, it has reigned supreme as Europe's championship event.

Longchamp conducts 30 days of racing annually, all on the flat.

NEWMARKET, ENGLAND

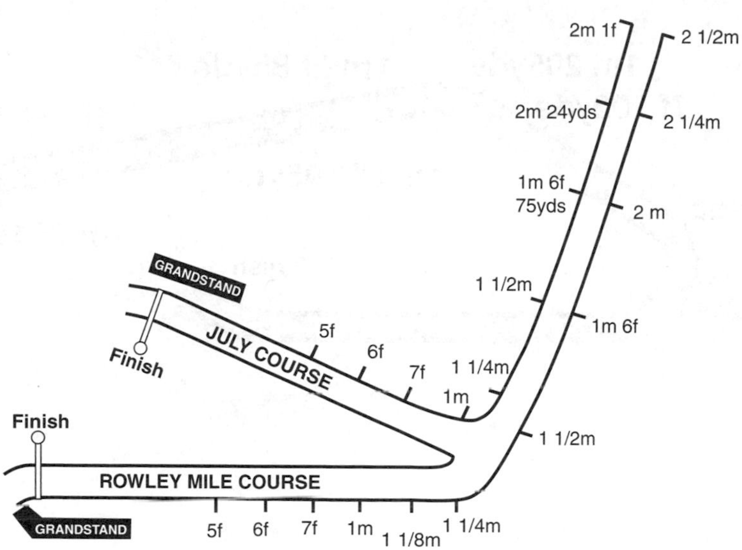

Course Description: Newmarket is, in reality, two courses in one. The Rowley Mile Course, used in April, May, September, October and November, shares a one-mile spur with the July Course, which is used in June, July and August.

That spur creates a 2 1/2-mile course used in the spring and fall. The spur is generally downhill until meeting a sharp rise about furlong before the right-handed turn into the Rowley Mile Course, which is a straight 1 1/4 miles, the last mile of which is used for both the 1000 and 2000 Guineas. It is undulating throughout with the penultimate furlong a pronounced downhill prior to The Dip, which is followed by an uphill run to the finish.

Including the spur it shares with the Rowley Mile Course, the July Course is 2 1/8 miles in length with a straight one-mile stretch known as the Bunbury Mile, which is similar to the proportions of the Rowley Mile.

The two tracks with their separate grandstands are separated by Devil's Dyke, a prehistoric manmade embankment. Both courses are very wide and ideal for long striding gallopers with the stamina necessary to see out every inch of the trip. Like the Guineas, the 1 1/4-mile Champion Stakes is run entirely on the straight, placing a premium on stamina and an ability to change leads when required without the signposts built into American ovals.

With so many trainers nearby, Newmarket attracts large fields and runs some of the most important maiden races in the world. A horse that wins a Newmarket maiden first time out usually possesses a touch of class which can translate into a certain success in America.

History: Racing on the broad, windswept plains of Newmarket has been conducted since the reign of James I in the early 17th century, but the first officially recorded race there was run on March 8, 1622. When Charles II was restored to the throne in 1660, Newmarket became a racing and social center, as all and sundry flocked to imitate the king, who, before and after racing, would dally in the town with his mistress Nell Gwyn, after whom a key April prep for the 1000 Guineas is named.

For nearly 300 years Newmarket has been the headquarters of British racing. In addition to its two tracks, it is home to at least 50 trainers' yards and numerous training tracks, or gallops. Tattersalls, the leading British sales company, is based in Newmarket, as is the British Racing Museum, the headqurters of the Jockey Club, and various other offical racing bodies.

Newmarket holds 33 days of racing per year, all on the flat. Eighteen of those are run on the Rowley Mile Course, eight in the spring and ten in the autumn. The other fifteen days are held on the July Course.

YORK, ENGLAND

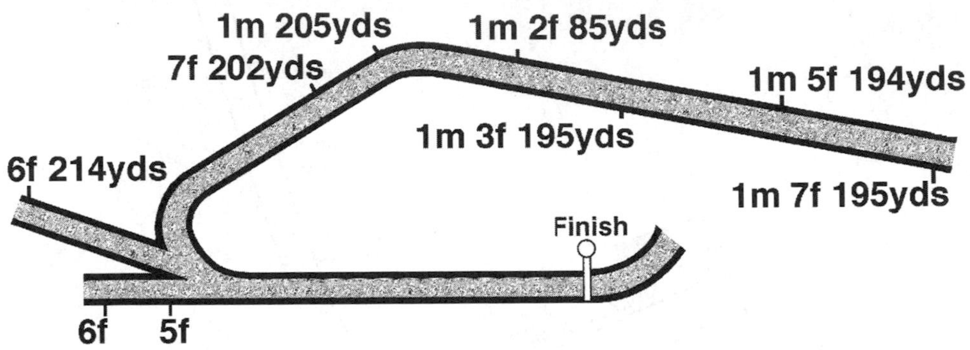

Course Description: York is a left-handed, perfectly level, horseshoe shaped course, two miles in length. Five and six-furlong races are run on a straight course that meets the left-handed course at the top of its 4-1/2-furlong stretch. Seven furlong races start from a chute, after which there is a mild left-handed bend at the head of the stretch.

Long striding gallopers will take to the long straights and mild turns of York, but in fact, the track really does not confer advantages to any particular type of horse. It is considered one of the fairest tracks in England, unlike a track like Chester, with its almost continual left-handed bends and realtively short two-furlong stretch.

But although York is left-handed and level, that does not translate into automatic success in America for winners there, especially as many of York winners have been given plenty of time to find room and crank up through the long stretch. By comparison, even the longest stretches in America are less than half the length of York's.

History: The earliest recorded race in York was run in 1530, although the course as we know it today did not see competition until 1709. The track is built on an ancient mudheap near the banks of the River Ouse known as the Knavesmire, so-called as it was so adept at slowing the progress of escaped criminals. As one of England's oldest racecourses, York now drains well and the track dries out rather quickly after rain.

York was the site of one of the most famous match races in history on May 13, 1851 when 1850 Derby and St. Leger winner The Flying Dutchman defeated the 1849 Derby and St. Leger winner Voltigeur. In the inaugural Benson & Hedges Gold Cup (now the Juddmonte International) in 1972, Braulio Baeza gave British jockeys a lesson in pace when he guided John Galbreath's Roberto to a pillar-to-post victory over the undefeated Brigadier Gerard. Roberto set a course record for 1 1/4 miles, 85 yards that stood for sixteen years.

The most important track in the north of England, York conducts fifteen days of racing a year, all on the flat. Its two best meetings are the three-day May Meeting, when key preps for the Derby and Oaks are run.

Top Money-Winning European Runners in 2004

Horse	Age	Sex	Starts	1st	2d	3d	Earn. US $
North Light (IRE)	3	C	4	2	1	0	$1,961,555
Bago (FR)	3	C	5	3	0	2	1,729,227
Rule of Law	3	C	5	2	2	0	1,233,320
Attraction (GB)	3	F	7	4	2	0	1,210,348
Azamour (IRE)	3	C	5	2	1	2	1,191,232
Warrsan (IRE)	6	H	6	2	1	1	1,054,442
Doyen (IRE)	4	C	5	2	1	0	1,047,627
Grey Swallow (IRE)	3	C	6	2	0	1	1,041,518
Soviet Song (IRE)	4	F	8	4	2	1	973,999
Ouija Board (GB)	3	F	4	3	0	1	926,758
Blue Canari (FR)	3	C	6	1	0	2	802,195
Haafhd (GB)	3	C	5	3	0	0	772,558
Refuse To Bend (IRE)	4	C	6	2	0	1	766,803
Sulamani (IRE)	5	H	4	1	1	1	711,523
Cyrlight (FR)	4	G	8	7	1	0	708,125
Shirocco (GER)	3	C	6	3	1	2	699,292
Rakti (GB)	5	H	4	2	0	0	655,822
Cherry Mix (FR)	3	C	7	2	3	2	626,464
Norse Dancer (IRE)	4	C	10	1	2	1	626,062
Oratorio (IRE)	2	C	7	4	2	0	599,157
Groom Tesse (GB)	3	C	4	2	1	0	589,106
Grey Lilas (IRE)	3	F	7	4	2	1	547,572
Azertyuiop (FR)	7	G	6	3	2	1	537,452
Kicking King (IRE)	6	G	9	5	3	0	535,528
Maia Eria (FR)	4	F	12	5	2	2	516,283
Kotkijet (FR)	9	G	6	3	1	1	505,824
Powerscourt (GB)	4	C	5	1	2	1	505,237
Westerner (GB)	5	H	7	4	2	0	500,063
Alexander Goldrun (IRE)	3	F	6	3	2	0	490,001
Hardy Eustace (IRE)	7	G	6	2	3	1	487,257
Best Mate (IRE)	9	G	3	2	1	0	481,076
Divine Proportions	2	F	5	5	0	0	481,006
Quiff (GB)	3	F	4	2	1	1	465,753
Moscow Flyer (IRE)	10	G	5	4	0	0	457,888
Prospect Park (GB)	3	C	7	3	3	0	451,901
Gamut (IRE)	5	H	5	2	1	0	450,073
Chorist (GB)	5	M	5	2	1	2	427,797
The Tatling (IRE)	7	G	11	2	4	3	417,987
Caesar Beware (IRE)	2	G	4	3	1	0	416,954
Damson (IRE)	2	F	5	4	0	1	413,988
Beef Or Salmon (IRE)	8	G	6	3	0	1	412,391
Let The Lion Roar (GB)	3	C	6	1	1	2	409,828
Somnus (GB)	4	G	6	2	2	0	401,733
Rule Supreme (IRE)	8	G	12	3	1	4	396,437
Papineau (GB)	4	C	3	3	0	0	390,292
Whipper	3	C	5	2	1	0	389,850
Cacique (IRE)	3	C	7	4	2	0	388,323
Latice (IRE)	3	F	4	2	0	0	387,142
Altieri (GB)	6	H	5	3	0	0	386,428
Punctilious (GB)	3	F	5	2	1	1	384,199
Turgot (FR)	7	G	10	2	1	4	371,301
Rooster Booster (GB)	10	G	8	1	5	0	368,373
Favourable Terms (GB)	4	F	3	2	0	0	365,145
Ancient World	4	C	6	3	2	0	362,850
Lune d'Or (FR)	3	F	6	4	0	1	359,744
Frizzante (GB)	5	M	6	2	1	1	359,743
Shamardal	2	C	3	3	0	0	359,680
Valixir (IRE)	3	C	6	3	0	2	359,411
Obe Gold (GB)	2	C	12	3	2	3	356,600
Majestic Desert (GB)	3	F	9	1	4	0	355,248
Monkerhostin (FR)	7	G	9	4	2	2	350,757
Soldier Hollow (GB)	4	C	8	4	2	0	350,376
American Post (GB)	3	C	5	3	0	0	346,005
Albanova (GB)	5	M	3	3	0	0	342,950
Dayano (GER)	3	C	5	2	2	0	337,796
Mephisto (IRE)	5	G	6	4	0	0	336,729
Menhoubah	3	F	6	1	1	0	325,035
Tante Rose (IRE)	4	F	3	3	0	0	317,589
Helios Quercus (FR)	2	C	8	6	0	0	315,949
Millenary (GB)	7	H	5	3	0	2	309,835
Gateman (GB)	7	G	11	2	6	2	307,362
Diamond Green (FR)	3	C	6	0	4	1	306,046
Pivotal Point (GB)	4	G	8	4	1	0	304,544
Hard Buck (BRZ)	5	H	1	0	1	0	302,346
Well Chief (GER)	5	G	5	3	1	1	299,822
Balko (FR)	3	C	9	4	2	1	298,117
Playful Act (IRE)	2	F	4	3	1	0	297,320
Rhinestone Cowboy (IRE)	8	G	4	3	0	1	295,795
Northerntown	8	G	6	4	1	0	295,081
Macs Joy (IRE)	5	G	8	4	2	2	293,598
Celestial Gold (IRE)	6	G	4	3	1	0	290,283
Brave Inca (IRE)	6	G	6	3	3	0	284,850
Torrestrella (IRE)	3	F	4	3	0	0	281,928
Great Love (FR)	6	G	7	1	2	2	280,278
Bachelor Duke	3	C	3	1	0	0	279,700
Salamanca (GB)	2	F	3	2	0	0	273,260
Harchibald (FR)	5	G	7	4	0	1	272,867
Tropical Lady (IRE)	4	F	9	5	1	0	272,758
Ceprin (IRE)	3	C	9	5	2	1	272,733
Bahamian Pirate	9	G	15	4	1	0	272,020
Pongee (GB)	4	F	5	2	2	1	270,990
Fayr Jag (IRE)	5	G	5	1	0	0	266,655
Grande Haya (FR)	5	G	10	3	1	2	265,836
Ad Valorem	2	C	3	3	0	0	258,357
Grey Abbey (IRE)	10	G	5	4	0	0	258,106
Marbye (IRE)	4	F	7	3	0	0	257,233
Kalaman (IRE)	4	C	5	2	1	1	255,573
Privy Seal (IRE)	3	G	7	1	3	1	255,533
Amarette (GER)	3	F	2	2	0	0	255,183
Senex (GER)	4	C	5	1	0	2	252,886
Policy Maker (IRE)	4	C	5	2	1	0	251,887
Tycoon (GB)	3	C	4	0	0	2	250,494
River Charm (FR)	4	G	10	1	3	1	250,141

Earnings for races in England, France, Germany, Ireland and Italy only.

Top Money–Winning Runners in England in 2004

Horse	Age	Sex	Starts	1st	2d	3d	Earn. US $
North Light (IRE)	3	C	2	2	0	0	$1,599,446
Rule of Law	3	C	4	2	2	0	1,180,915
Doyen (IRE)	4	C	4	2	1	0	1,047,627
Attraction (GB)	3	F	4	3	1	0	879,649
Haafhd (GB)	3	C	5	3	0	0	772,558
Refuse To Bend (IRE)	4	C	6	2	0	1	766,803
Sulamani (IRE)	5	H	4	1	1	1	711,523
Soviet Song (IRE)	4	F	6	2	2	1	670,032
Rakti (GB)	5	H	3	2	0	0	632,517
Azertyuiop (FR)	7	G	6	3	2	1	537,452
Quiff (GB)	3	F	4	2	1	1	465,753
Warrsan (IRE)	6	H	4	1	1	1	451,342
Best Mate (IRE)	9	G	2	2	0	0	442,293
Caesar Beware (IRE)	2	G	4	3	1	0	416,954
Ouija Board (GB)	3	F	2	2	0	0	404,477
Norse Dancer (IRE)	4	C	9	1	1	1	394,235
Papineau (GB)	4	C	3	3	0	0	390,292
Azamour (IRE)	3	C	3	1	0	2	388,437
Let The Lion Roar (GB)	3	C	5	1	1	2	373,229
Favourable Terms (GB)	4	F	3	2	0	0	365,145
Frizzante (GB)	5	M	5	2	1	1	359,743
Shamardal	2	C	3	3	0	0	359,680
Monkerhostin (FR)	7	G	9	4	2	2	350,757
Mephisto (IRE)	5	G	6	4	0	0	336,729
Hardy Eustace (IRE)	7	G	2	1	1	0	335,212
Rooster Booster (GB)	10	G	7	1	4	0	330,705
Obe Gold (GB)	2	C	10	3	1	3	324,014
Tante Rose (IRE)	4	F	3	3	0	0	317,589
The Tatling (IRE)	7	G	7	2	1	3	317,249
Millenary (GB)	7	H	5	3	0	2	309,835
Moscow Flyer (IRE)	10	G	3	2	0	0	304,341
Hard Buck (BRZ)	5	H	1	0	1	0	302,346
Well Chief (GER)	5	G	5	3	1	1	299,822
Playful Act (IRE)	2	F	4	3	1	0	297,320
Celestial Gold (IRE)	6	G	4	3	1	0	290,283
Punctilious (GB)	3	F	4	2	0	1	288,093
Kicking King (IRE)	6	G	2	1	1	0	278,917
Salamanca (GB)	2	F	3	2	0	0	273,260
Bahamian Pirate	9	G	14	4	1	0	272,020
Pongee (GB)	4	F	5	2	2	1	270,990
Fayr Jag (IRE)	5	G	4	1	0	0	266,655
Pivotal Point (GB)	4	G	7	3	1	0	260,518
Grey Abbey (IRE)	10	G	5	4	0	0	258,106
Kalaman (IRE)	4	C	5	2	1	1	255,573
Baracouda (FR)	9	G	4	3	1	0	249,064
Chic (GB)	4	F	6	2	1	1	247,186
Royal Auclair (FR)	7	G	12	1	4	2	245,605
Gatwick (IRE)	3	C	11	4	0	1	241,311
Bandari (IRE)	5	H	9	4	0	2	238,846
Maids Causeway (IRE)	2	F	7	3	3	1	234,174

Top Money–Winning Runners in France in 2004

Horse	Age	Sex	Starts	1st	2d	3d	Earn. US $
Bago (FR)	3	C	4	3	0	1	$1,636,755
Blue Canari (FR)	3	C	6	1	0	2	802,195
Cyrlight (FR)	4	G	8	7	1	0	708,125
Cherry Mix (FR)	3	C	7	2	3	2	626,464
Grey Lilas (IRE)	3	F	7	4	2	1	547,572
Maia Eria (FR)	4	F	12	5	2	2	516,283
Kotkijet (FR)	9	G	6	3	1	1	505,824
Divine Proportions	2	F	5	5	0	0	481,006
Prospect Park (GB)	3	C	7	3	3	0	451,901
Westerner (GB)	5	H	6	4	1	0	402,616
Latice (IRE)	3	F	4	2	0	0	387,142
Whipper	3	C	4	2	1	0	376,515
Turgot (FR)	7	G	10	2	1	4	371,301
Valixir (IRE)	3	C	6	3	0	2	359,411
Cacique (IRE)	3	C	6	4	2	0	346,290
Helios Quercus (FR)	2	C	8	6	0	0	315,949
American Post (GB)	3	C	4	3	0	0	308,495
Balko (FR)	3	C	9	4	2	1	298,117
Northerntown	8	G	6	4	1	0	295,081
Somnus (GB)	4	G	2	2	0	0	282,226
Torrestrella (IRE)	3	F	4	3	0	0	281,928
Great Love (FR)	6	G	7	1	2	2	280,278
Grande Haya (FR)	5	G	10	3	1	2	265,836
Policy Maker (IRE)	4	C	5	2	1	0	251,887
River Charm (FR)	4	G	10	1	3	1	250,141
Oratorio (IRE)	2	C	1	1	0	0	248,228
Gamut (IRE)	5	H	1	1	0	0	246,408
Mesange Royale (FR)	4	F	11	3	2	1	241,026
Ouija Board (GB)	3	F	1	0	0	1	226,991
Nickname (FR)	5	H	4	2	1	0	217,576
Kiko (FR)	3	G	6	4	0	0	214,448
Ask for the Moon (FR)	3	F	5	4	0	0	212,315
Alexander Goldrun (IRE)	3	F	2	1	0	0	211,622
King's Daughter (FR)	3	F	16	4	1	3	211,348
Pride (FR)	4	F	8	2	1	2	209,697
Ennemi d'Etat (FR)	5	G	8	0	3	3	209,696
Diamond Green (FR)	3	C	4	0	3	1	208,865
Voix Du Nord (FR)	3	C	2	2	0	0	208,171
Delfos (IRE)	3	C	8	4	3	0	197,365
Centifolia (FR)	2	F	5	4	0	0	196,969
Grand Cyborg (FR)	6	G	10	2	0	4	192,680
Psychee Du Berlais (FR)	4	F	13	1	1	4	192,080
Don't Be Shy (FR)	3	G	9	1	4	2	191,582
Ma Royale (FR)	4	F	7	2	2	0	188,932
Sweet Stream (ITY)	4	F	3	1	0	1	188,769
Willdance (FR)	3	F	13	2	3	5	186,621
Forestier (FR)	4	C	4	3	1	0	181,564
Salut Thomas (FR)	2	C	15	2	3	4	175,090
Layman	2	C	4	2	1	1	175,082
Rule Supreme (IRE)	8	G	2	1	0	1	174,050

Top Money-Winning Runners in Germany in 2004

Horse	Age	Sex	Starts	1st	2d	3d	Earn. US $
Warrsan (IRE)	6	H	1	1	0	0	$603,100
Shirocco (GER)	3	C	5	2	1	2	512,167
Albanova (GB)	5	M	3	3	0	0	342,950
Amarette (GER)	3	F	2	2	0	0	255,183
Malinas (GER)	3	C	7	2	2	2	248,846
Egerton (GER)	3	C	7	0	3	0	209,349
Saldentigerin (GER)	3	F	6	1	3	1	170,820
Omikron (IRE)	3	C	7	1	1	1	160,179
La Ina (GER)	3	F	4	1	2	0	154,865
Rotteck (GER)	4	C	5	2	1	1	154,400
Lucky Strike (GB)	6	G	4	3	0	1	151,757
Soldier Hollow (GB)	4	C	6	3	1	0	138,284
Shapira (GER)	3	F	2	1	1	0	138,284
Furstenberg (IRE)	2	C	3	2	0	0	135,253
Pepperstorm (GER)	3	C	5	2	1	1	128,703
Intendant (GER)	3	C	5	2	0	1	121,830
Brunel (IRE)	3	C	1	1	0	0	118,810
Assiun (GER)	3	C	6	2	1	3	110,232
Manduro (GER)	2	C	2	2	0	0	109,166
Key to Pleasure (GER)	4	C	5	2	3	0	102,295
Touch of Land (FR)	4	C	1	1	0	0	100,155
Vallera (GER)	3	F	5	2	0	2	98,221
Darsalam (IRE)	3	C	2	1	0	1	97,799
Olaso (GER)	5	G	3	2	0	0	97,746
Felicity (GER)	3	F	7	3	0	1	95,375
Areias (GER)	6	H	9	2	1	2	90,061
Daring Love (GER)	2	F	3	3	0	0	85,602
Eagle Rise (IRE)	4	C	5	2	1	1	84,749
Sorrent (GER)	2	F	2	2	0	0	79,492
Fight Club (GER)	3	C	6	2	1	0	79,473
Raffelberger (GER)	3	G	2	1	0	0	79,216
Martillo (GER)	4	C	1	1	0	0	78,196
Auengunst (GER)	2	F	3	2	1	0	77,933
Kahn (GER)	2	C	3	2	1	0	75,503
Kahlua (GER)	2	F	4	2	1	1	75,278
Soterio (GER)	4	C	7	4	0	1	72,342
Lazio (GER)	3	C	7	1	2	1	64,927
Fiepes Shuffle (GER)	4	C	10	3	2	1	61,173
Azzuri (GER)	2	F	5	2	0	1	60,515
Nightdance Forest (IRE)	3	F	5	2	3	0	58,759
Bear King (GER)	7	H	6	1	1	0	57,301
Freedom (GER)	3	F	8	3	0	0	55,146
Give me Five (GER)	3	F	7	2	1	2	54,814
Apeiron (GER)	3	C	4	1	0	0	54,450
Matrix (GER)	3	C	7	1	1	1	53,508
Fiepes Winged (GER)	3	C	9	2	2	2	53,497
Tiberius Caesar (FR)	4	C	5	3	0	0	52,927
Mity Dancer (GER)	4	F	6	1	1	3	52,443
Bailamos (GER)	4	C	6	1	1	2	51,964
Imola (GER)	2	C	3	0	2	1	51,512

Top Money-Winning Runners in Ireland in 2004

Horse	Age	Sex	Starts	1st	2d	3d	Earn. US $
Horse	Age	Sex	Starts	1st	2d	3d	Earn. US$
Grey Swallow (IRE)	3	C	4	2	0	1	$1,014,848
Azamour (IRE)	3	C	2	1	1	0	802,795
Beef Or Salmon (IRE)	8	G	5	3	0	1	380,299
Attraction (GB)	3	F	2	1	1	0	330,699
North Light (IRE)	3	C	1	0	1	0	305,312
Soviet Song (IRE)	4	F	2	2	0	0	303,967
Powerscourt (GB)	4	C	2	1	0	1	302,510
Damson (IRE)	2	F	3	3	0	0	301,792
Ouija Board (GB)	3	F	1	1	0	0	295,290
Bachelor Duke	3	C	1	1	0	0	279,700
Alexander Goldrun (IRE)	3	F	4	2	2	0	278,379
Tropical Lady (IRE)	4	F	9	5	1	0	272,758
Kicking King (IRE)	6	G	7	4	2	0	256,611
Oratorio (IRE)	2	C	4	3	1	0	246,426
Chelsea Rose (IRE)	2	F	3	2	0	1	233,427
Norse Dancer (IRE)	4	C	1	0	1	0	231,827
Vinnie Roe (IRE)	6	H	3	1	2	0	228,765
Macs Joy (IRE)	5	G	7	3	2	2	221,411
Rathgar Beau (IRE)	8	G	12	3	4	1	213,508
Osterhase (IRE)	5	G	7	3	0	1	204,965
Chorist (GB)	5	M	1	1	0	0	189,680
Cloone River (IRE)	8	G	5	3	1	1	183,575
Russian Blue (IRE)	2	C	6	3	1	2	181,917
Beaver Patrol (IRE)	2	C	1	1	0	0	181,001
Brave Inca (IRE)	6	G	5	2	3	0	179,812
Ulfah	3	F	9	3	0	0	162,564
Palace Star (IRE)	3	F	10	3	0	2	158,420
Yeats (IRE)	3	C	2	2	0	0	156,875
Cloudy Bays (IRE)	7	G	10	2	2	1	154,259
Solskjaer (IRE)	4	C	4	2	2	0	153,614
Moscow Flyer (IRE)	10	G	2	2	0	0	153,547
Kestrel Cross (IRE)	2	G	6	3	1	1	152,889
Democratic Deficit (IRE)	2	C	4	2	1	0	152,182
Hardy Eustace (IRE)	7	G	4	1	2	1	152,045
Slip Dance (IRE)	2	F	6	2	0	1	149,808
Silk And Scarlet (GB)	2	F	4	2	1	0	149,488
Keepatem (GB)	8	G	6	2	0	1	147,987
Tycoon (GB)	3	C	1	0	0	1	147,245
Florida Pearl (IRE)	12	G	2	2	0	0	146,796
Forget The Past (GB)	6	G	7	3	2	1	146,330
Hi Cloy (IRE)	7	G	6	3	1	2	144,397
Dubawi (IRE)	2	C	1	1	0	0	143,017
Addario (IRE)	4	F	11	5	2	0	137,776
Cache Creek (IRE)	6	M	11	3	1	1	135,603
Crystal View (IRE)	2	F	9	4	1	0	133,482
Hazarista (IRE)	3	F	5	2	0	1	130,638
Rosaker	7	H	8	3	1	3	129,281
Stashedaway (IRE)	7	M	7	3	1	2	128,281
Colca Canyon (IRE)	7	G	7	2	1	1	127,396

Top Money-Winning Runners in Italy in 2004

Horse	Age	Sex	Starts	1st	2d	3d	Earn. US $
Groom Tesse (GB)	3	C	4	2	1	0	$589,106
Altieri (GB)	6	H	5	3	0	0	386,428
Menhoubah	3	F	1	1	0	0	299,850
Dayano (GER)	3	C	3	2	1	0	295,435
Ceprin (IRE)	3	C	9	5	2	1	272,733
Senex (GER)	4	C	1	1	0	0	242,800
Distant Way	3	C	8	3	3	0	232,133
Electrocutionist	3	C	4	3	1	0	219,259
Step Danzer (IRE)	3	F	7	1	2	2	208,970
Rumba Loca (IRE)	3	F	6	1	2	0	202,043
Spirit of Desert (IRE)	3	C	3	2	1	0	201,181
Soldier Hollow (GB)	4	C	1	1	0	0	194,490
Lune d'Or (FR)	3	F	1	1	0	0	190,110
Shirocco (GER)	3	C	1	1	0	0	187,125
Konigstiger (GER)	2	C	1	1	0	0	187,125
Ancient World	4	C	1	1	0	0	186,105
St Paul House (GB)	6	H	7	5	1	0	183,287
Bravo Tazio (IRE)	3	C	3	1	1	0	173,948
Golden Stravinsky	2	C	10	5	3	1	173,249
Patapan	2	C	9	6	0	2	170,724
Le Giare (IRE)	2	C	10	5	3	1	170,535
Super Bobbina (IRE)	3	F	4	2	1	1	168,955
Rose Shift (IRE)	4	F	9	5	1	0	155,436
Loriana (IRE)	3	F	8	2	0	2	146,236
Scabiun (IRE)	6	H	10	4	1	1	144,788
Simonas (IRE)	5	G	4	3	0	0	133,555
Sfilzatore (ITY)	3	C	15	4	3	3	132,215
Privy Seal (IRE)	3	G	1	0	0	1	131,911
Vespone (IRE)	4	C	1	0	1	0	130,691
Krisman (IRE)	5	H	11	2	2	2	127,561
Principe Di Galles (GB)	3	G	14	2	5	3	123,470
Honey Bunny (GB)	4	C	10	3	3	0	121,446
Absolut Taft (IRE)	3	C	14	3	4	2	121,444
Tedo (GER)	2	C	6	4	1	0	119,790
Golden Wild (GB)	3	C	15	3	3	2	119,473
Tenderlit	2	F	9	4	0	2	117,321
Gun Power (IRE)	4	C	8	3	1	1	114,463
Marbye (IRE)	4	F	5	2	0	0	113,428
Nordhal (GB)	5	G	10	3	1	2	112,326
Jalys (IRE)	3	F	9	3	2	1	109,560
Gasat (IRE)	3	C	11	5	3	1	109,446
Maktub (ITY)	5	H	1	0	1	0	106,832
Gold Marie (IRE)	2	F	7	2	3	1	106,391
Blu for Life (IRE)	7	H	10	4	2	0	104,417
Cocktail (GB)	3	F	7	4	0	1	104,304
Vale Mantovani (GB)	4	F	4	1	1	2	103,429
Guglielmo Tell (IRE)	3	C	11	5	0	3	103,377
Without Connexion (IRE)	5	H	4	2	0	0	103,213
Arrears	4	C	17	2	4	4	101,432

Top Money-Winning Runners in Japan in 2004

Horse	Age	Sex	Starts	1st	2d	3d	Earn. US $
Zenno Rob Roy (JPN)	4	C	7	3	3	0	$6,681,748
King Kamehameha (JPN)	3	C	6	5	0	1	3,743,956
Time Paradox (JPN)	6	H	12	5	1	2	3,408,062
Admire Don (JPN)	5	H	6	3	2	0	3,251,772
Dance in the Mood (JPN)	3	F	7	3	2	0	2,716,978
Cosmo Bulk (JPN)	3	C	8	3	2	0	2,626,305
Tap Dance City	7	H	3	2	1	0	2,548,869
Delta Blues (JPN)	3	C	11	4	1	1	2,525,023
Silk Famous (JPN)	5	H	6	2	1	2	2,449,025
Daiwa el Cielo (JPN)	3	F	7	3	1	1	2,157,825
Sweep Tosho (JPN)	3	F	7	3	1	1	2,118,418
Admire Groove (JPN)	4	F	6	2	0	1	1,837,708
Adjudi Mitsuo (JPN)	3	C	6	2	2	1	1,777,628
Sunningdale (JPN)	5	H	9	2	0	3	1,680,778
Durandal (JPN)	5	H	3	1	2	0	1,668,992
Heart's Cry (JPN)	3	C	10	3	1	2	1,617,370
Lord Prevail	6	H	10	6	0	0	1,609,743
Meiner Select (JPN)	5	H	4	3	0	0	1,541,061
Blandices (JPN)	7	G	2	2	0	0	1,503,453
Ingrandire (JPN)	5	H	3	1	2	0	1,485,928
Calstone Light O (JPN)	6	H	4	2	1	1	1,470,483
Daitaku Bertram (JPN)	6	H	8	2	0	0	1,460,156
Meisho Battler (JPN)	4	F	10	2	4	1	1,451,985
Daiwa Major (JPN)	3	C	7	2	0	1	1,421,605
Narita Century (JPN)	5	H	8	3	1	0	1,419,924
Seeking the Dia	3	C	6	4	0	1	1,407,809
Telegnosis (JPN)	5	H	5	1	2	1	1,395,504
En Dehors (JPN)	5	H	8	4	0	0	1,332,602
Merci Taka O (JPN)	5	G	6	1	1	2	1,304,707
Osumi Haruka (JPN)	4	F	6	2	2	0	1,252,860
Le Mars Girl	4	F	10	3	2	0	1,224,177
Win Radius (JPN)	6	H	6	2	0	1	1,221,894
Hishi Atlas (JPN)	4	C	10	3	3	2	1,188,500
Utopia (JPN)	4	C	9	1	1	1	1,182,225
Personal Rush	3	C	8	4	0	1	1,165,761
Higher Game (JPN)	3	C	8	2	0	1	1,154,282
Agnes Wing	4	C	9	5	2	1	1,136,535
My Sole Sound (JPN)	5	H	8	2	0	0	1,123,516
Meiner Recolte (JPN)	2	C	5	4	0	0	1,122,495
Divine Silver	6	H	11	3	1	0	1,121,192
Win Duel (JPN)	5	H	7	6	1	0	1,114,536
Heavenly Romance (JPN)	4	F	10	3	1	1	1,109,499
Super Gene (JPN)	6	H	7	2	1	2	1,099,722
Precious Cafe (JPN)	5	H	5	4	0	0	1,079,555
Hikari Zirconia (JPN)	5	H	11	5	3	0	1,077,989
Nike a Delight (JPN)	4	C	8	2	1	2	1,071,104
Tsurumaru Boy (JPN)	6	H	5	1	0	0	1,071,080
Koolinger (JPN)	5	H	9	2	2	2	1,068,057
Hookipa Wave (JPN)	3	C	7	1	3	1	1,058,933
Win Generale (JPN)	4	C	5	1	1	1	1,049,017

Top Money–Winning Runners in Puerto Rico in 2004

Horse	Age	Sex	Starts	1st	2d	3d	Earn. US $
Omar Alejandro	3	C	11	5	4	1	$234,440
Spago (PAN)	3	C	1	1	0	0	168,200
Hispanica	4	F	12	8	1	3	157,720
Triano	2	C	11	8	2	1	146,640
Coordinadora	3	F	6	4	0	1	144,534
El Tio Mingo	3	C	7	5	0	0	136,176
Special Concerto	3	F	11	7	2	2	135,700
Dusty's Lil Book	5	M	12	8	1	2	135,118
Concerto's Crown	3	F	14	3	4	3	128,108
Mueca	2	F	8	5	1	0	127,900
Divac	3	C	9	7	0	1	127,812
Chilenito	3	C	6	3	1	0	121,944
Portentoso	3	C	8	5	1	0	119,151
Outstanding Lady	3	F	12	6	4	0	116,592
Despreciado	4	C	11	5	1	2	106,440
El Truckero	2	C	12	4	1	3	101,788
Roble Temible	3	C	15	1	6	5	97,140
Launch Sequence	2	F	5	4	0	1	97,020
Mi Pradera	6	M	8	4	2	0	90,136
Master Quality	4	C	7	3	1	0	88,920
Little Franky Boy	3	C	17	4	5	4	82,522
Might Bea Princess	2	F	7	2	5	0	77,320
El Delegado	3	C	16	4	4	3	77,202
La Corozalena	2	F	15	4	7	1	76,900
Malcadi	3	F	8	4	3	1	75,740
La Via Apia	2	F	7	3	1	1	69,904
Guerrillera	2	F	10	5	2	1	69,732
Dona Ingrid	5	M	12	2	1	7	69,410
Flamanteguille	3	C	22	10	5	2	66,558
Libertador	5	G	17	2	5	3	65,488
Archiduquesa	3	F	12	3	4	1	65,133
Monoestrellado	4	C	5	3	0	1	64,740
Gran Rojo	6	H	19	11	2	0	63,384
Bancada	4	F	13	3	2	1	62,434
Triangulo	4	G	20	10	4	1	62,078
Tantalizing Tease	5	H	9	3	4	1	60,328
Lightning Al Boy	2	C	9	2	2	1	59,480
Indio Caribe	2	C	3	2	1	0	58,360
Casty (MEX)	3	F	1	0	1	0	58,000
Miss Pioneer	3	F	14	3	4	4	57,898
Super Cherokee	3	C	15	6	1	5	57,883
Stormin Irish	2	C	8	4	0	0	57,852
Arroz Con Leche	3	C	10	4	1	2	57,298
Eltish Thunder	2	C	7	3	1	0	55,330
Roxana Milagros	5	M	19	8	6	2	55,232
Barrio Palmas	2	C	6	2	3	1	55,040
Kylemore Abbey	5	H	6	2	1	0	53,200
Express Bandid	5	M	14	3	6	2	53,152
Arzak (VEN)	4	C	1	1	0	0	52,200
Runaway Boy	4	C	22	9	4	3	50,686

Top Money–Winning Runners in United Arab Emirates in 2004

Horse	Age	Sex	Starts	1st	2d	3d	Earn. US $
Pleasantly Perfect	6	H	1	1	0	0	$3,600,000
Lundy's Liability (BRZ)	4	C	3	1	1	0	1,242,500
Polish Summer (GB)	7	H	1	1	0	0	1,200,000
Our New Recruit	5	H	1	1	0	0	1,200,000
Medaglia d'Oro	5	H	1	0	1	0	1,200,000
Victory Moon (SAF)	5	H	4	2	0	2	940,000
Right Approach (GB)	5	H	2	2	0	0	891,000
Paolini (GER)	7	H	1	1	0	0	800,000
Firebreak (GB)	5	H	1	1	0	0	600,000
Petit Paris (CHI)	4	C	3	1	1	0	497,500
Hard Buck (BRZ)	5	H	1	0	1	0	400,000
Alke	4	C	1	0	1	0	400,000
Little Jim (ARG)	4	C	3	1	0	2	377,500
Scott's View (GB)	5	G	5	2	0	1	367,500
Conroy	6	G	2	1	0	1	330,000
Grand Hombre	4	G	1	0	0	0	300,000
Tropical Star (IRE)	4	G	5	1	3	1	284,847
Tamarillo (GB)	3	F	5	1	1	0	207,500
Nayyir (GB)	6	G	1	0	0	1	200,000
Conceal (GB)	6	G	12	4	0	1	194,128
King's Boy (GER)	7	H	1	0	0	0	180,000
Razkalla	6	H	3	1	0	0	175,000
Surveyor (SAF)	5	G	4	1	1	1	173,000
Fair Mix (IRE)	6	H	2	1	0	0	170,000
Catstar	3	F	1	1	0	0	162,500
Festive Style (SAF)	4	F	5	1	1	1	160,317
Jack Sullivan	3	C	2	0	1	0	150,000
Winisk River (IRE)	4	C	2	2	0	0	146,250
Walmooh (GB)	8	H	9	2	2	1	142,465
Cat Belling (IRE)	4	F	11	2	0	0	136,500
Crimson Palace (SAF)	5	M	2	1	0	0	132,500
Prince Of War (AUS)	6	G	4	1	2	1	128,500
San Salvador	7	G	6	2	1	2	121,222
Domestic Dispute	4	C	1	0	0	0	120,000
Mubeen (IRE)	4	C	5	1	2	0	118,222
State Shinto	8	H	8	1	1	0	117,378
Burnt Ember	5	H	6	2	1	0	114,878
Conflict (FR)	8	H	5	2	0	0	114,345
Feet So Fast (GB)	5	G	5	1	0	1	103,134
Cajun Beat	4	G	1	0	0	0	100,000
Excessivepleasure	4	G	1	0	0	1	100,000
D'Anjou (GB)	7	G	3	1	0	0	97,500
Cherry Pickings	7	G	3	2	0	0	96,890
Sleeping Weapon	5	H	9	2	4	0	94,482
National Currency (SAF)	5	H	1	1	0	0	91,000
Deodatus	6	H	5	2	0	2	89,847
Gonfilia (GER)	4	F	2	1	0	0	84,500
Checkit (IRE)	4	C	4	0	0	2	82,000
Hazelhatch (GB)	4	G	16	2	2	1	80,356
Menhoubah	3	F	3	0	1	1	75,000

2004

RECORDS OF HORSES

The record of each thoroughbred who raced in the United States and Canada during 2004 appears in this section, showing the sex, age, number of starts, firsts, seconds and thirds, as well as the total amount of money earned.
If any record shows either first, second or third placings but no money earned, trophies were awarded instead.

Horse	Age	Sex	Sts	1st	2d	3d	Won
A B C Cat	3	F	14	0	1	1	6,026
A B C Order	3	C	13	0	2	4	23,405
A B History	3	G	4	1	0	0	7,350
A B Noodle	5	M	8	3	1	3	161,550
A Bag a Day	3	G	6	0	1	0	2,345
A Bag of Gold	3	G	8	1	0	3	22,225
A Bag of Porpourie	5	M	13	0	0	0	4,162
A Bag On Top	3	F	2	1	0	0	24,772
A Barry Good Act	6	M	6	0	0	1	5,140
A Barry Good Actor	5	G	13	2	2	2	16,485
A Barry Good Girl	4	F	13	2	1	1	17,830
A Beautiful Heart	4	G	18	4	5	2	35,900
A Bet of Honey	3	F	17	3	3	2	16,399
A Bid for Courage	3	F	2	0	0	0	250
A Big Tip	3	G	7	0	0	1	2,460
A Bit Foolish	4	F	7	2	0	0	12,363
A Bit of Luck	3	G	6	0	4	2	10,790
A Bit O'Gold	3	G	7	4	3	0	1,060,790
A Bit Spellbound	2	F	2	0	0	0	155
A Blaze of Fury	5	H	3	0	0	1	770
A Boy Name Sue	8	G	4	0	0	0	477
A Brush With Luck	2	C	1	0	0	0	0
A Buccaneer's Life	3	F	2	0	0	1	1,567
A Buck for Kimbell	5	M	2	0	0	1	900
A Buck Forty Nine	4	G	10	1	1	2	17,550
A C Junior	3	G	6	1	1	1	8,335
A Call for Gertie	3	F	5	1	0	2	21,455
A Call to Post	8	G	2	0	0	0	44
A Cartier Girl	2	F	2	0	0	0	635
A Case of Class	3	F	9	3	2	1	57,800
A Certain Smile	3	F	6	1	0	0	6,125
A Champ for Sara	3	G	9	3	1	1	27,682
A Chance to Harbor	4	F	4	1	1	0	18,930
A Classic	4	F	13	0	5	1	13,809
A Classic Life	2	F	3	3	0	0	42,983
A Coady Moment	4	F	3	0	0	0	0
A Colt Named Sue	2	G	4	0	2	0	10,981
A Cool Starfish	2	F	5	0	0	1	2,360
A C's Nurse	5	M	10	1	1	1	12,723
A Darling Orchid	2	F	3	0	1	1	3,153
A Dash of Grey	2	C	1	0	0	0	135
A Dashi Affair	2	C	7	0	0	0	3,762
A Date With Ruby	3	F	2	0	0	0	0
A Day for Florence	4	F	4	0	0	0	231
A Delightful Day	5	M	15	2	1	2	7,992
A Demi	3	G	9	0	3	2	6,451
A Diligent Ruckus	4	C	14	5	4	1	33,437
A Diller a Dollar	6	M	10	2	3	0	39,789
A Diplomat Manor	5	G	3	0	0	0	0
A Dream of Mine	5	G	9	1	3	1	7,935
A F Repson	5	G	9	0	2	1	5,075
A Familiar Face	3	F	6	2	1	0	46,618
A Far Out Igloo	2	F	6	0	2	1	10,492
A Few Good Friends	2	C	3	1	0	0	4,465
A Few Z's	3	F	11	1	1	1	6,505
A Fiesta Champ	2	G	3	0	0	0	610
A Fine Cat	5	H	7	0	0	1	734
A Fine Irish Son	4	C	4	0	0	1	724
A Fine One	3	F	15	4	2	4	42,200
A Firm Bridge	3	G	8	1	1	2	20,040
A Firm Prospect	3	F	1	0	0	0	0
A Flash of Green	3	G	18	1	1	1	6,427
A Fool for Gin	2	F	1	0	0	0	250
A Gallant Discover	3	G	7	2	0	2	46,565
A Galloping Ghost	2	F	7	1	1	2	30,735
A Genius for Place	4	G	3	2	0	1	32,700
A Gentle Man	4	G	15	2	1	4	27,215
A Gentlemans Joy	3	F	5	0	0	0	0
A Girl Named Phil	3	F	10	1	2	1	13,036
A Gold Star for Me	2	F	2	0	0	0	405
A Golden Time	3	G	2	1	1	0	19,500
A Good Day to Run	5	G	8	2	1	3	22,666
A Grade Above	5	G	9	1	0	0	9,400
A Grand Smile	2	C	2	0	0	0	330
A Great Hunt	3	G	8	2	1	2	46,880
A Groom With Class	3	F	2	0	0	0	0
A Hero Like Me	4	G	5	0	0	0	86
A Huevo	8	G	4	1	0	0	136,250
A J and George	3	G	6	3	0	0	17,400
A J Dustdevil	6	H	16	2	3	3	7,571
A J Meadow	2	C	3	0	2	0	11,150
A J's Gone	3	G	5	0	0	1	1,145
A J's Lady Slew	5	M	8	1	1	0	4,320
A J's Prospect	4	G	3	0	0	0	0
A J's Ticket	3	G	14	0	3	2	10,351
A J's Wild Man	4	C	2	0	0	0	0
A King's Smile	3	G	4	0	1	1	5,140
A Knight Mission	6	G	6	0	2	1	2,198
A Known Feu	9	M	8	1	1	2	2,620
A K's Barron	5	G	10	1	0	0	4,539
A K's Quest	3	G	13	2	2	4	18,636
A La Carte Only	2	F	2	0	1	1	7,280
A Lady's Caress	4	F	14	1	1	2	29,839
A Lady's Treasure	3	F	6	0	0	3	2,700
A Lil' Alimony	2	F	2	1	0	0	9,375
A Li'l Tejada	3	G	2	0	0	0	0
A Little Bit Iffy	3	G	2	0	0	0	0
A Little Bit Royal	4	F	7	0	1	0	4,399
A Little Evil	3	F	2	0	0	0	1,230
A Little Gold	4	F	8	1	0	1	25,508
A Little Insane	3	G	5	0	0	0	0
A Little Nervous	3	C	2	0	0	0	70
A Little Respect	8	M	2	0	0	0	423
A Little Smooch	5	M	5	0	0	0	570
A Little Syn	7	M	4	0	0	0	511
A Little Western	5	M	4	1	0	0	2,920
A Loose Kisser	5	M	18	3	0	0	17,680
A Lot of Diamond	4	F	5	1	2	0	22,400
A Lotta Lad	3	C	5	0	1	1	4,610
A Lotta Leo	3	C	6	0	0	0	675
A Lovely Pickle	3	F	1	0	0	0	180
A Lulu Ofa Menifee	3	F	10	3	1	2	144,996
A M Queen	3	F	3	0	0	0	150
A Man	2	G	8	0	4	0	12,386
A Mandolin	4	F	17	3	2	2	27,721
A Match to Dy For	3	F	10	0	0	2	15,550
A May Zing Devil	5	G	16	2	1	3	15,396
A Memo for Avie	4	G	3	0	1	0	5,000
A Million Foricos	3	G	3	0	0	0	0
A Name to Remember	3	F	8	1	2	1	5,867
A New Leaf	5	M	7	0	1	2	8,660
A Newlove	3	F	13	3	1	3	38,185
A Nice Splash	4	G	9	4	0	0	112,620
A Nicer Fleet	3	F	5	0	0	0	2,472
A Nifty Trick	2	F	4	0	2	1	16,867
A Nip of Vodka	4	F	5	0	0	0	238
A One Rocket	5	G	8	3	3	0	82,155
A Pachee Girl	5	M	14	4	2	0	37,193
A Passing Motion	2	F	9	1	3	1	16,180
A Patch of Jade	7	G	8	0	1	0	3,023
A Penny At a Time	4	F	1	0	0	1	2,640
A Perfect Dream	3	C	1	0	0	1	2,280
A Perfect Wood	3	C	11	0	0	1	12,773
A Pisa Work	2	F	5	0	2	1	7,285
A Pitch From Bklyn	5	H	8	0	1	1	6,909
A Pizza for Nick	4	G	13	2	1	3	12,815
A Plus Plus	3	F	5	0	2	0	7,700
A Precious Memory	3	F	3	1	0	1	32,280
A Prize for Luck	2	G	3	0	0	0	100
A Proven Fact	5	H	8	1	0	2	4,428
A P's Belek	3	G	11	0	2	1	8,948
A P's Rebel	5	G	8	1	1	2	7,509
A Ps Special Jet	2	F	2	1	0	0	9,480
A Queen's Smile	4	F	4	1	0	0	30,540
A Quiet Beauty	2	F	1	0	0	0	400
A R Crackers	3	C	13	3	2	4	38,936
A R Spun	5	G	19	5	4	1	38,989
A Rack of Bengies	5	G	8	1	1	0	2,389
A Rainbow Princess	3	F	8	0	2	1	11,204
A Ram Sam Sam	3	C	1	1	0	0	2,880
A Rare Book	6	G	4	1	0	0	10,815
A Rare Brunswick	6	M	8	1	1	1	7,324
A Rash Inski	4	G	10	0	0	3	7,650
A Ray of Magic	6	M	11	1	2	2	33,014
A Real Good Man	2	C	6	0	0	0	4,980
A Real King	5	G	6	0	2	0	4,355

Horse	Age	Sex	Sts	1st	2d	3d	Won
A Real Knockout	6	M	6	0	1	0	1,232
A Real Lady	3	F	2	0	0	0	190
A Real Nor'easter	7	M	3	1	1	0	13,234
A Real Runaround	4	F	10	1	0	0	1,407
A Real Trip	3	F	2	0	0	0	0
A Red Rainbow	3	F	2	0	0	0	600
A Reel Tizzy	4	F	10	3	0	1	75,160
A Regal Reflection	4	F	11	0	1	0	3,848
A River Ran Slewit	5	H	3	0	0	0	300
A Rizzi Rueben	3	C	14	0	1	1	5,830
A Rose an Excluse	4	G	6	1	0	0	1,585
A Rose for Chris	2	F	4	0	1	1	17,643
A Royal Scam	3	G	14	1	0	3	9,180
A Royale Tizzy	8	G	5	0	0	0	311
A Ruff Way to Go	5	G	13	0	1	2	6,217
A Run for My Money	4	F	3	0	0	0	86
A Run On Broadway	3	F	3	1	0	0	13,308
A Runyon Story	5	G	7	0	0	0	535
A Second Try	6	G	2	1	1	0	6,620
A Secret No More	3	G	5	1	1	1	33,044
A Secret Scoop	5	G	11	3	0	1	25,350
A Shaky Start	4	F	9	4	2	2	154,356
A Shortt Tour	4	F	14	3	2	0	32,727
A Silent Greek	3	G	12	2	1	0	9,330
A Sleeve for Eve	3	G	1	0	0	0	0
A Slew of Eagles	5	G	9	1	0	0	7,204
A Slew of Scotts	6	G	12	1	1	2	2,545
A Smart Punch	5	M	7	4	2	0	66,625
A Smashing Bull	4	C	7	1	1	0	5,856
A Smile Per Mile	6	M	3	0	1	0	14,560
A Song in A Minor	3	F	3	2	0	0	62,200
A Spectacular Fact	4	G	1	0	0	0	0
A Spire a Dream	3	F	14	1	3	0	15,715
A Splash of That	2	G	1	1	0	0	17,880
A Spot of Greatnes	3	C	7	2	1	3	48,920
A Spunky's Crow	3	G	5	0	2	0	4,029
A Stand Out Storm	7	H	1	0	0	0	0
A Star Above	6	M	6	1	2	0	40,011
A Star in Time	4	F	11	3	1	1	24,465
A Step Beyond	6	M	8	2	3	0	5,645
A Storm Is Brewing	7	G	4	0	0	0	450
A Stormy Rose	2	F	2	0	0	1	1,400
A T Secondairborne	4	C	5	0	2	1	12,265
A Table for Three	5	H	11	0	1	2	4,203
A Tad Early	5	M	5	1	0	0	9,782
A Taste for Gold	2	F	2	0	0	0	157
A Team Leader	3	G	12	3	2	2	45,720
A Tempting Light	7	M	6	0	1	0	1,604
A Thrilling Trick	4	F	1	1	0	0	5,460
A Timeless Lady	3	F	2	0	0	0	0
A to the Z	4	G	10	3	3	1	312,612
A Toast to Life	3	C	5	1	1	0	38,671
A Touch of Thunder	3	G	7	0	0	2	2,720
A Trick for Sarah	4	F	10	2	1	0	10,377
A Trick for You	3	F	5	2	1	0	14,656
A Tru Queen	3	F	5	0	0	0	960
A True Star	2	F	5	0	0	1	11,250
A Tune for Bud	2	G	1	0	0	0	540
A Twist of Sherree	4	F	8	0	2	3	14,748
A Very Young Jet	2	G	5	1	3	0	50,430
A Vision in Gray	4	F	11	3	1	2	108,305
A Walk With Class	3	F	13	1	0	2	12,600
A Wheaties Girl	7	M	7	0	1	0	878
A Wild Elegance	2	G	1	0	0	0	0
A Wild Minute	2	G	2	0	0	0	286
A Wild Tour	4	F	10	1	1	1	4,146
A Wish for Travis	4	F	7	1	1	1	15,672
A Zest for Lace	2	C	1	0	0	0	0
A. B. Mutah	6	G	2	0	0	0	762
A. C. Danzer	4	C	5	0	0	0	362
A. Caterina	4	F	8	1	2	1	38,958
A. F. Annsel	4	F	10	0	2	1	6,120
A. J. Cat	3	C	8	1	0	1	7,883
A. J. Groom	2	G	9	1	0	0	10,820
A. J. Melini	3	C	8	1	0	2	28,370
A. J. the Great	3	C	2	0	0	0	0
A. J.'s Express	3	G	11	3	0	2	13,654
A. J.'s Luck	8	G	2	0	0	0	109
A. J's Cafe	4	G	11	4	2	2	60,920
A. K. A. Diamond	3	F	2	0	0	0	0
A. K. A. Market	5	G	6	0	1	3	6,300
A. K. A. Quasimodo	2	C	2	0	1	1	4,700
A. M.'s Spirit	3	C	12	1	4	2	20,930
A. P Brit	3	G	2	0	0	0	387
A. P. Adventure	3	F	5	2	0	2	268,080
A. P. Agenda	6	G	7	0	1	3	4,790
A. P. Andretti	2	G	3	0	0	0	0
A. P. Aspen	5	G	4	0	0	0	0
A. P. Bird	2	C	3	0	0	1	756
A. P. Brownie	3	G	14	2	0	0	18,060
A. P. Carson	3	G	6	1	1	1	16,880
A. P. Dixie	2	C	1	0	1	0	5,300
A. P. Jetta	4	F	5	0	0	0	970
A. P. Lax	3	C	6	0	2	0	13,910
A. P. Shadow	4	G	10	1	1	1	6,103
A. P. Sheauxgirl	2	F	11	1	0	2	11,644
A. P. Slew	5	H	7	0	1	1	16,010
A. P. Topper	6	G	5	0	1	0	5,775
A. P. Trapp	6	H	6	0	1	0	1,000
A. P. Tyrone	2	C	3	0	0	2	12,150
A. Peezing Gina	4	F	5	2	2	0	10,739
A. V. Eight Queen	3	F	8	1	0	2	8,455
A. V. Eight Tee	3	G	10	2	1	2	14,234
A. V. Seven	3	G	5	0	1	1	3,460
Aaannd Loving It	3	F	9	1	3	3	59,232
Aaronasher	3	C	5	1	0	1	29,000
Aaron's Carr	3	F	4	1	0	0	2,769
Aaron's Favorite	7	G	6	0	0	0	1,685
Aarons Last Dance	2	G	7	0	2	0	6,210
Aaron's Magic	7	G	16	1	1	1	6,485
Aaron's to Run	7	G	3	0	1	0	2,886
Aaron's Trick	4	G	4	0	1	1	1,835
Aaron's Tug	2	G	4	1	1	0	12,000
Aba Daba Doo	4	G	12	2	1	1	29,036
Abadbaddude	6	G	2	1	0	0	1,640
Abagintwo	5	H	5	2	0	1	10,425
Abandon Ship	3	C	3	0	0	0	300
Abarouge	5	G	15	0	2	2	3,410
Aba's Joy	2	C	4	0	0	0	660
Abatares	4	G	14	3	2	3	58,130
Abatement	5	G	6	1	0	0	5,392
Abba Do	5	G	9	3	1	1	32,686
Abba Gooba Gail	4	F	4	0	0	0	0
Abbadance	5	M	13	1	1	2	7,135
Abbagione	2	F	4	0	1	0	9,712
Abbey Bridge	6	M	4	1	0	1	49,800
Abbeys Runner	3	F	9	2	1	0	50,555
Abbeywood	5	M	1	0	0	0	36
Abbie's Gale	3	F	10	1	1	3	8,762
Abbi's Choice	6	G	14	6	1	0	113,642
Abbondanza	3	C	11	4	2	1	223,305
Abbott	3	C	7	1	1	0	8,400
Abbott N Costelli	3	G	5	0	0	0	586
Abby Coole	7	M	3	0	0	0	0
Abby Zone	2	F	2	0	0	0	0
Abby's Legend	3	F	5	0	0	0	4,865
Abby's Not Normal	4	F	2	0	1	0	11,620
Abby's Sister	4	F	14	1	2	1	15,960
Abderian (IRE)	7	G	9	1	1	1	84,794
Abdication	3	G	12	1	2	2	16,041
Abe	5	G	3	0	0	0	130
Abeam	5	G	20	1	4	6	17,886
Abernathy's Deed	4	G	7	0	0	0	1,596
Abesi	4	F	4	0	0	1	1,200
Ability Springs	3	G	8	0	1	3	7,965
Abit Eratic	9	G	9	2	0	0	16,270
Abitofadandy	6	M	9	1	3	2	20,052
Able Ally	6	M	2	0	0	0	0
Able Hero (AUS)	7	G	10	2	2	2	11,460
Ablebuzz	3	G	9	0	0	2	4,565
Ablo	2	C	4	2	0	0	191,040
Abnegate	3	G	6	0	1	2	9,240
Abo Cat	3	F	10	0	0	1	1,365
Abo Halo	3	G	5	1	1	0	5,241
Abobe	6	M	5	2	0	0	6,435
Abottleinfrontofme	5	G	8	0	0	1	1,966
Abounding Love	5	M	1	0	1	0	950
Abounding Truth	4	F	3	1	0	0	23,400

Horse	Age	Sex	Sts	1st	2d	3d	Won
About Face Ace	2	G	1	0	0	0	0
About Love	5	M	2	0	0	0	0
About Respect	6	M	6	0	1	1	5,275
About Time to Win	9	G	7	0	0	0	345
Above All Others	3	F	11	2	4	2	31,918
Above Average	2	F	2	0	0	0	370
Above Cause	9	G	3	0	0	0	581
Above the Clouds	3	C	7	2	0	4	25,693
Above the Devil	3	F	14	3	1	1	54,179
Above the Harbor	6	M	8	0	3	1	21,660
Above the Sky	4	G	3	0	0	0	0
Above the Storm	5	G	10	2	1	2	22,185
Above the Wind	7	G	9	3	0	1	75,598
Abovo	5	M	1	0	0	0	192
Aboynamedguinevere	5	G	2	0	0	0	0
Abradan of April	4	G	15	0	2	2	14,163
Abraham	3	C	5	1	1	0	22,720
Abrasive Stone	5	G	6	1	1	0	21,588
Abreeze	9	G	13	5	0	2	78,820
Abrigail	8	M	1	0	0	0	0
Abroad	3	C	5	2	1	2	36,260
Absconder	2	G	4	0	0	0	1,465
Absealutely Daring	5	G	3	0	0	0	0
Absent Friend	4	G	9	3	0	1	75,510
Absent Lover	4	G	12	5	1	3	38,630
Absolute	2	C	2	1	0	0	13,980
Absolute Ability	3	C	13	1	1	0	9,895
Absolute Advantage	6	G	2	0	0	0	500
Absolute Attitude	4	F	11	2	2	1	13,204
Absolute Charmer (IRE)	5	M	2	0	0	0	0
Absolute Glory	2	C	2	0	1	0	7,400
Absolute Harmony	8	H	1	0	0	0	268
Absolute Jack	4	C	5	1	1	0	5,695
Absolute Jo	4	F	7	1	0	0	10,080
Absolute Kris	4	G	20	1	3	2	10,301
Absolute Nectar	3	F	8	1	1	2	47,750
Absolute Pleasure	4	G	10	0	0	1	2,300
Absolute Rocks	3	F	8	0	1	0	8,035
Absolutely Citron	4	F	12	0	0	0	2,015
Absolutely Gifted	6	M	10	5	1	0	25,587
Absolutely Joe	3	C	6	1	0	2	50,370
Absolutely Lovely	5	M	6	2	0	0	32,770
Absolutely True	4	G	9	3	0	0	52,950
Absolutly Orange	5	M	6	0	0	2	3,042
Abstract Forces	6	G	1	0	0	0	0
Abstract Image	6	M	11	1	0	1	5,231
Abstract Motion	2	C	2	0	0	0	356
Absurd	2	G	4	1	0	1	6,396
Abtastic	2	G	3	1	0	1	9,320
Abu Leil	8	G	20	3	4	4	21,825
Abullwithapurpose	2	C	3	1	1	1	16,496
Abulous	3	G	1	0	0	0	0
Aburn Angel	4	F	3	0	2	0	2,980
Abyss	5	M	3	0	0	0	1,514
Abyssal Storm	5	G	7	0	0	1	1,155
Abyssinian	4	G	5	0	0	0	2,140
Acacian Express	6	G	2	0	0	1	1,030
Acacian Song	8	M	2	0	0	0	146
Academic	7	G	8	1	1	4	21,210
Academic Angel	5	M	7	3	0	2	210,520
Academic Lass	3	F	6	0	2	0	11,205
Academic Queen	3	F	12	3	0	1	60,790
Academically Right	10	G	8	0	1	2	6,106
Academy Bay	5	G	4	1	0	0	4,095
Academy Brass	2	F	2	1	0	0	26,850
Academy Dancer	2	C	3	0	0	0	210
Academy Girl	2	F	2	1	1	0	9,400
Academy Lass	3	F	1	0	0	0	0
Academy Road	8	M	3	0	0	1	507
Academy Spy	5	G	7	2	2	0	85,380
Acago	4	F	2	0	0	1	15,000
Acalady	5	M	12	2	4	1	23,748
Acalgroom	3	F	15	2	6	1	21,295
Acanthus	3	F	5	1	1	1	30,054
Acaroids Jewel	3	G	3	0	0	0	0
Acatatlast	4	G	5	0	0	0	3,160
Acca	6	G	5	0	0	0	1,102
Accelerando	3	G	3	0	0	0	0
Accent Mark	3	G	4	2	0	2	22,475

Horse	Age	Sex	Sts	1st	2d	3d	Won
Accent of Gold	6	M	15	0	6	1	16,634
Accept	6	H	3	1	0	0	18,150
Accept Domra	4	F	17	2	6	2	22,587
Accept for Ryan	3	G	3	0	0	1	3,120
Acceptable Bid	3	F	8	2	2	0	74,755
Acceptable Choice	3	G	3	0	0	0	210
Acceptable Venture	4	C	2	0	0	0	2,438
Acceptaburl	4	F	10	2	1	0	12,886
Acceptance	2	F	8	0	0	0	3,353
Accepting	3	F	2	0	0	0	0
Acceptor	5	G	7	0	1	0	2,620
Acceptwithpleasure	3	F	9	1	1	1	27,070
Access Agenda	6	G	6	2	0	1	38,320
Access Approved	5	G	11	3	0	2	63,071
Access Success	2	F	5	0	0	1	3,604
Accessible	3	F	4	0	0	0	77
Accidental Magic	3	G	3	1	1	1	20,874
Acclimate	3	C	6	0	1	1	18,389
Accomack	3	F	3	0	0	0	0
Accomplish	3	C	18	0	7	3	16,215
Accord	5	H	8	0	1	4	26,020
Accordian Man	3	C	3	0	0	0	503
According to Hoyle	2	C	3	0	1	0	2,398
Account	3	C	4	0	0	0	302
Account Executive	4	G	7	0	1	0	4,620
Account for Me	6	G	13	2	6	2	92,226
Account Renewed	5	G	7	0	0	2	2,900
Accountable Boy	8	G	1	0	0	0	0
Accountable Guy	5	G	16	3	3	4	17,474
Accountabold	3	G	1	0	0	0	0
Accountant's Dream	3	F	1	0	1	0	2,730
Accounted	2	F	1	0	0	0	0
Accounted For	7	G	5	2	0	0	32,165
Accountforthegold	2	C	3	1	1	1	103,325
Accra	5	G	11	3	0	2	25,180
Accretion	2	F	4	2	0	1	62,820
Accurate	2	C	6	2	0	1	115,688
Ace Blue (BRZ)	4	C	1	0	0	0	740
Ace Connection	6	G	6	1	0	0	2,532
Ace in Place	4	F	6	1	2	2	17,510
Ace In the Hole	2	F	7	0	0	2	4,334
Ace of Club	4	G	7	0	0	1	986
Ace On the River	2	C	2	0	0	0	491
Ace the Experts	4	F	12	1	0	0	8,607
Aceface	3	G	2	1	1	0	6,400
Aceinthebag	4	G	8	1	1	0	8,541
Aces and Eights (PER)	5	H	11	3	0	2	13,500
Ace's Cappella	3	F	11	4	1	1	84,357
Aces Full	4	G	6	3	1	0	13,800
Ace's High	3	F	2	0	0	0	300
Aces of Gold	4	G	8	1	0	5	23,290
Aces Up	5	G	9	0	0	0	586
Ace's Valentine	6	M	11	1	2	2	19,515
Acey Deucey	2	F	3	1	1	1	37,100
Achancetoshine	3	F	8	3	0	1	34,172
Achari	6	M	10	3	1	0	74,396
Aches N Pains	2	C	1	1	0	0	9,600
Achill	5	G	8	0	1	0	2,037
Achilles	4	G	7	0	0	0	445
Achilles Trick	3	G	2	1	0	0	4,680
Achoo	6	G	6	1	0	1	1,578
Acid Rain	8	G	10	1	0	2	6,257
Ack Attack	2	C	2	0	0	0	180
Ack of Congress	3	G	12	3	0	4	12,262
Acklen	3	F	5	0	0	2	3,245
Ack's Best	4	F	9	1	1	0	9,645
Acks Like Dusty	6	G	3	0	0	0	0
Ack's of War	3	F	11	0	1	1	5,153
Ackybacky	7	M	16	1	0	3	8,451
Aclare	7	G	14	3	1	1	10,065
Aclassysassylassy	2	F	7	5	2	0	498,800
Aclevershadeofjade	4	F	8	2	1	0	75,804
Aconarkbuilder	6	G	3	0	0	0	0
Aconcagua	4	C	7	1	1	0	4,745
Aconfirmedtornado	6	H	5	0	1	1	1,831
Acquiescent	4	F	8	1	0	2	8,141
Acraduck	4	F	1	0	1	0	840
Acreditado (BRZ)	3	C	3	0	1	0	3,446
Acres	7	G	7	1	0	2	20,160

RECORDS OF HORSES

Horse	Age	Sex	Sts	1st	2d	3d	Won
Acrobatic Champ	2	G	1	1	0	0	7,950
Across the Miles	4	G	2	1	0	0	6,600
Across the Sky	2	G	2	0	0	0	0
Acrostic	5	G	7	0	2	1	24,460
Ac's Blackcat	4	F	8	2	0	1	15,470
Act Classy	3	G	10	1	1	0	7,667
Act First	3	F	9	0	0	3	2,449
Act Foolish	5	M	5	2	0	1	43,080
Act Glittery	2	C	3	0	1	1	2,770
Act Like Fappiano	2	C	3	0	0	0	378
Act Natural	2	F	6	0	2	0	7,540
Act Nice	4	G	12	2	0	3	12,226
Act of Glory	3	F	1	0	0	0	460
Act of Reform	6	H	9	1	2	1	43,418
Act of War	6	H	7	0	0	1	21,596
Act Special	5	M	2	0	0	0	218
Act the Part	2	C	1	0	1	0	1,600
Act With Pride	6	G	5	0	0	0	927
Actaeon	3	C	5	0	1	1	14,368
Actalittle	3	F	10	3	1	2	29,535
Actalot	7	G	7	1	0	0	3,798
Actceed	5	H	3	0	1	0	828
Actcelerate	3	G	19	1	4	2	21,549
Actcellent	4	F	5	1	0	3	38,621
Actcentric	3	F	10	2	1	3	23,245
Actin Time	8	G	2	0	0	0	0
Acting Class	5	G	1	0	0	0	80
Acting Decision	3	C	2	0	0	0	0
Acting Deputy	5	M	1	0	0	0	500
Acting Maudlin	5	M	5	0	0	1	2,550
Acting Report	3	G	9	1	1	1	9,117
Acting Tips	9	G	14	2	1	2	11,978
Acting Tricky	4	F	14	1	2	5	16,424
Acting Up	6	G	9	0	1	1	5,262
Action Attraction	5	M	17	4	7	2	83,750
Action Cat	3	C	5	0	0	0	911
Action for Real	9	G	11	1	0	1	4,972
Action Forthe Year	7	M	3	0	0	0	292
Action Girl	3	F	3	1	0	1	40,778
Action Hero	2	G	3	1	0	0	7,390
Action Request	6	H	14	2	4	2	68,575
Action This Day	3	C	5	0	0	0	5,284
Action Tonight	4	G	21	4	2	2	31,698
Actionable	3	F	2	0	0	0	640
Activado's Image	4	G	10	2	0	2	3,860
Activate	6	G	4	0	0	0	522
Active Angel	7	M	5	0	0	1	168
Active Radium	6	G	8	0	0	0	364
Active Zone	3	C	4	0	0	1	690
Actress E.	2	F	3	2	0	0	28,200
Acts Like Reign	2	F	2	0	0	0	1,230
Actsclamation	6	M	14	3	1	0	18,388
Actscuse	4	G	5	1	1	0	9,627
Actslikechamp	4	G	10	0	2	3	5,021
Actsposure	6	M	5	0	0	0	1,111
Actstatic	2	F	7	1	1	1	19,935
Acttractive	4	F	9	0	0	4	3,481
Actual	2	C	1	0	0	0	1,080
Actual Illusion	5	G	13	2	3	1	36,370
Actuary's Son	6	G	14	6	2	2	106,222
Actxecutive	2	C	4	1	2	0	74,692
Actxotic	7	M	13	1	4	3	17,403
Actxpedite	3	C	6	0	1	1	9,240
Actxpressive	4	G	21	1	0	8	24,940
Actxpresso	3	F	2	1	0	0	10,740
Actxtravagant	4	F	6	1	0	1	7,720
Acumen	7	G	11	2	0	0	21,690
Acupuncture	3	G	12	1	3	1	41,320
Acure for Geri	5	M	2	0	0	0	0
Adage	3	C	3	0	0	0	816
Adagio Twinkles	8	G	8	0	1	0	3,632
Adalgisa	5	M	2	0	0	0	1,530
Adam Lets Share	9	M	1	0	0	0	0
Adam Man	4	G	9	0	0	2	4,040
Adam T	7	G	1	0	0	0	0
Adamant Victor	4	C	8	0	0	1	1,740
Adamexpress	3	G	5	0	0	0	1,129
Adamic	4	G	8	2	1	0	10,933
Adam's Able	6	G	17	2	3	4	23,937

Horse	Age	Sex	Sts	1st	2d	3d	Won
Adam's Gold	3	C	8	1	1	0	10,537
Adam's Jag	4	C	1	0	1	0	8,184
Adam's Lucky Star	3	G	8	1	0	1	27,722
Adams Peak	5	G	3	0	1	0	2,610
Adam's Pullet	6	M	7	0	0	1	6,386
Adam's R Pic	4	G	1	0	0	0	480
Adam's Reality	8	G	2	0	0	0	0
Adams Tribe	5	H	10	0	0	1	28,581
Adam's Way	4	G	3	0	0	1	927
Adamsawherfirst	4	F	3	0	0	0	0
Adanac	7	G	12	1	2	1	15,068
Adance for Corinne	4	F	3	0	0	0	0
Adancingscore	4	F	6	0	1	0	2,496
Adaptation	3	G	14	2	2	1	49,446
Adapted	3	G	2	0	0	0	280
Add a Moment	4	G	9	1	3	1	7,407
Add It Up	5	H	8	1	2	0	24,520
Add the Numbers	6	G	6	0	0	1	4,930
Adda Devil	4	F	10	3	0	0	8,723
Addakiss	6	H	16	2	3	2	20,225
Added Annuity	4	F	12	1	2	3	37,363
Added Edge	4	C	8	3	1	2	170,075
Addicks	5	G	14	1	0	2	15,520
Addie Go	3	F	17	1	4	2	12,539
Addie's Adventure	4	C	1	0	0	0	300
Addie's Native	5	G	10	1	2	2	6,979
Addieville	4	G	3	0	0	0	0
Addington	2	G	4	0	0	3	3,855
Addinson	8	G	1	0	0	1	0
Addler Creek	3	G	9	1	2	3	6,619
Adealforyou	3	G	2	0	0	0	0
Adele Lucille	3	F	13	3	1	0	34,360
Adele's Wild Storm	3	C	1	0	1	0	1,700
Adella	5	M	12	1	2	0	17,567
Adevilslight	3	G	8	0	0	2	8,135
Adham (CHI)	6	G	16	5	3	3	52,235
Adhesive	5	G	2	0	0	0	218
Adieu and Farewell	4	F	11	4	3	1	82,390
Adif	7	M	10	1	1	0	9,500
Adima	3	F	1	0	0	0	0
Adimaride	5	M	10	1	0	4	9,975
Adina's Star	8	M	3	1	0	0	4,542
Adinatha	4	F	2	1	0	0	17,040
Adine	3	F	8	3	1	1	26,255
Adios Baby	3	G	1	0	0	0	400
Adios Birdie	5	M	8	0	0	0	1,844
Adios Bobby	2	C	2	0	0	0	137
Adios Meadowlake	4	F	3	0	0	1	5,320
Adios Nonino (URU)	6	G	11	2	1	2	9,597
Adios Reality	2	F	3	0	3	0	6,615
Adiostra	3	C	14	0	3	1	8,687
Adirondack Counsel	4	G	12	0	1	2	4,164
Adjalah	5	H	7	1	0	1	57,571
Adjust	8	G	7	2	1	2	49,430
Adjutant	8	G	5	0	1	0	1,429
Adjutant (GB)	9	G	8	2	1	1	16,282
Adlib	6	M	6	1	0	0	5,560
Administration	4	C	5	0	1	1	2,330
Adminniestrator	7	G	7	0	1	1	21,960
Admirable Promise	4	C	6	1	1	0	4,118
Admiral Albert	5	G	4	0	2	1	16,580
Admiral Bo	11	G	8	1	0	2	7,425
Admiral Canaris	4	G	12	0	3	4	13,349
Admiral Dewey	7	G	11	0	1	0	4,250
Admiral Fox	4	G	9	1	1	1	4,400
Admiral Lance	4	G	10	1	1	1	25,288
Admiral Roxbury	10	G	7	3	0	1	5,220
Admiral Slew	5	H	6	0	1	0	10,360
Admiral West	2	C	2	1	0	0	7,935
Admiralinthenavy	3	C	7	1	1	0	39,246
Admirality Drive	5	M	1	0	0	0	0
Admiral's Cup (IRE)	7	G	14	1	3	5	13,341
Admiral's Pride	9	M	2	0	0	0	1,035
Admirals Royalty	5	G	2	0	0	0	270
Admiralty Arch	4	C	8	3	2	0	106,040
Admiration	5	H	16	1	1	2	16,505
Admirelle	2	F	3	0	0	0	393
Admo Jr.	5	G	4	1	0	0	4,164
Ado	4	G	13	2	1	3	20,313

Horse	Age	Sex	Sts	1st	2d	3d	Won
Adobe Canyon	6	M	2	0	0	0	304
Adobe Gold	3	F	12	4	3	0	130,288
Adopted Daughter	4	F	5	1	3	1	66,805
Adopting Habit	4	G	11	0	4	0	17,900
Adoption	4	G	13	0	2	0	4,182
Adorable	4	F	11	2	0	0	19,338
Adorable Audrey	5	M	6	1	1	1	21,085
Adoration	5	M	5	3	1	0	607,304
Adore Me	2	F	4	0	0	2	5,480
Adoring	5	M	5	0	0	0	275
Adreality	4	F	5	1	2	1	21,030
Adreamisborn	5	G	10	5	2	2	257,740
Adreamsicklepitch	5	M	2	0	0	0	600
Adrenalin Running	3	F	8	1	4	0	35,010
Adriad's Cape	2	F	3	0	2	0	20,630
Adrian's Way	5	G	6	0	1	1	2,152
Adriatic Sea	3	F	12	2	0	2	58,342
Adrienne K	4	F	8	0	0	0	2,070
Adroitly Superb	6	G	12	2	3	3	71,720
Advance to Go	3	G	9	1	1	0	15,025
Advanced Notice	4	F	14	0	2	1	7,514
Advancewithcaution	6	M	11	0	2	1	7,200
Advancing Victory	2	G	1	0	0	0	66
Advantage (CHI)	7	H	3	0	0	0	143
Advantage Plus	8	M	2	0	0	0	224
Advantageoverbrook	7	G	7	0	0	0	0
Adventura	2	C	5	0	0	1	5,090
Adventure	3	F	6	2	0	1	57,370
Adventure Cat	4	F	5	0	0	1	5,040
Adventurous	10	G	4	0	1	0	510
Adversary	5	G	9	1	1	2	12,880
Adversative	4	F	2	0	0	0	840
Advocate Annie	5	M	9	0	2	1	4,916
Advocate General	4	G	14	2	2	4	12,152
Advocate's Legacy	3	G	13	2	1	0	7,800
Aegean Green	4	G	9	1	1	4	11,210
Aeneas	5	H	3	0	1	2	14,960
Aer Afrik	6	G	11	2	0	2	9,174
Aeras	5	G	8	1	3	0	25,445
Aerial Command	4	G	5	1	1	1	40,715
Aerialist	5	M	5	0	0	1	1,279
Aerie Bayadere	7	M	6	0	0	1	614
Aerodrew	4	G	6	1	2	0	11,698
Aerojack	3	C	12	3	2	2	58,900
Aerolass	4	F	8	1	0	0	5,322
Aeropeter	3	C	12	2	1	0	20,920
Aeropostale	5	H	1	0	0	0	125
Aetha	6	M	2	0	1	0	3,640
Afar	3	C	4	0	0	0	1,280
Afastfact	4	C	7	1	1	0	14,380
Afeher	2	C	5	0	0	0	700
Afeica	2	F	3	0	0	0	294
Aferds Finale	3	F	4	1	0	0	1,700
Aferds Key	3	G	9	3	2	0	35,716
Aferds Legacy	3	G	3	1	1	0	7,713
Affable	4	G	5	1	0	0	7,850
Affair Day	7	M	2	0	0	0	548
Affair in the Air	6	G	12	0	3	2	37,512
Affair Lady	3	F	9	0	0	1	1,683
Affair Play	5	G	8	0	1	1	9,316
Affair to Be	8	G	12	0	3	3	4,685
Affairoftherose	4	F	3	0	0	0	340
Affair's Over	2	C	1	0	0	0	300
Affectation	3	F	8	3	0	1	24,130
Affectionate Girl	3	F	1	0	0	0	110
Affidavit	3	C	2	1	0	0	11,400
Affirm Cat	5	G	4	0	0	1	878
Affirm Challenge	7	G	8	1	2	1	5,875
Affirm Strategy	4	G	1	0	0	0	0
Affirm the Light	3	F	6	0	0	0	1,116
Affirm the Vow	2	F	1	0	0	0	205
Affirmative	5	H	3	0	1	0	9,400
Affirmative Vote	3	C	3	0	0	0	0
Affirmed Admiral	6	H	1	0	0	1	270
Affirmed Angel	4	G	10	1	1	0	3,802
Affirmed Destiny	3	G	13	0	1	0	4,553
Affirmed Emotion	3	G	4	0	1	0	3,850
Affirmed Fever	3	G	6	1	0	0	14,000
Affirmed Gold	3	C	1	0	0	0	70
Affirmed Honor	2	C	2	0	0	0	158
Affirmed Illusion	4	F	6	0	2	0	13,796
Affirmed Manner	3	F	13	2	0	4	26,630
Affirmed Miesque	3	F	5	0	0	0	507
Affirmed Perfect	5	G	6	0	1	0	4,510
Affirmed Pleasure	5	G	5	0	1	0	9,470
Affirmed Reality	6	G	8	1	1	0	6,585
Affirmed Rizzi	3	G	5	1	0	2	21,340
Affirmed Royalty	3	F	1	0	0	0	2,100
Affirming Rush	2	G	7	1	0	0	10,550
Affirming Storm	5	G	9	1	1	0	4,819
Affirmlode	3	G	15	3	5	2	39,682
Affixed	5	G	11	1	1	2	7,838
Afflict	3	F	5	0	0	0	0
Affluent Appeal	2	F	3	0	2	0	8,628
Afforce of Course	4	F	2	0	2	0	7,860
Affordability	4	F	3	1	1	0	20,526
Affordable	6	G	4	0	0	0	750
Affordable Advice	3	C	6	0	0	0	1,260
Affordable Fun	6	G	10	1	1	2	11,426
Afieromeno	4	G	8	1	0	0	7,300
Afikomen	5	M	3	0	0	0	322
A'fire	7	G	12	3	0	2	29,737
Afleet Alex	2	C	6	4	2	0	680,800
Afleet Angel	4	F	8	1	1	2	29,545
Afleet Buck	5	G	8	1	2	0	43,380
Afleet Canadian	4	F	1	0	0	0	0
Afleet Cat	3	F	14	1	3	2	19,390
Afleet Command	3	G	10	2	3	2	51,480
Afleet Diablo	4	F	3	1	0	0	5,340
Afleet Loyd	5	H	7	1	1	0	9,921
Afleet Nice	2	G	5	1	3	0	18,640
Afleet Shawklit	3	C	4	1	1	0	15,490
Afleetilation	4	F	10	1	3	1	10,208
Afleetkitty	4	F	11	0	4	1	16,115
Afoolandhismoney	5	G	1	0	0	1	713
Afortunado	4	G	18	3	3	4	45,004
Africa Hot	3	G	7	2	1	1	28,600
African Nights	4	F	6	0	0	2	3,029
African Princess	5	M	9	2	1	3	51,320
African Skyline	5	M	8	2	1	1	39,300
African Wildfire	4	G	12	3	2	0	10,800
African Wind	3	F	4	0	0	0	0
Afta David	7	G	1	0	0	0	0
After Ben	2	G	4	0	0	0	944
After Clouds	3	F	2	0	0	0	1,150
After Five Shorty	3	G	2	0	0	0	480
After the Goldrush	3	C	9	2	0	1	18,600
After the Knight	2	F	4	1	1	1	33,033
After the Run	7	G	13	1	2	5	53,567
After the Tone	3	F	12	2	4	4	112,507
Afterdinnerdrink	4	G	6	0	0	1	1,205
Afterdinnerthunder	3	G	15	1	4	1	11,162
Afterguard	2	C	2	0	1	0	1,730
Afternoon Charlie	3	C	4	0	2	0	14,180
Afternoon Clinic	3	G	12	3	1	2	46,140
Afternoon Dreams	4	F	5	0	0	1	4,094
Afternoon Edition	4	C	9	2	1	0	11,300
Afternoon in Rio	3	G	5	1	1	1	28,120
Afternoon Krystal	3	F	5	0	0	0	0
Afternoon Magick	5	M	14	1	1	2	12,745
Afternoon Martini	3	G	8	3	3	0	35,400
Afternoon Pleasure	6	G	10	2	2	4	29,815
Afternoon Punch	2	G	2	1	0	0	6,670
Afternoon Reward	4	G	10	0	1	0	2,673
Afternoon Siesta	3	F	4	0	0	1	3,010
Afterthreemartinis	6	G	7	0	0	1	660
Aftica	4	F	8	2	0	1	61,898
Agadir	2	C	2	0	1	1	18,228
Again Kitty	3	G	4	0	0	1	1,460
Against My Will	2	F	1	0	0	0	180
Agame	4	G	16	2	2	4	38,640
Agana Harbor	3	G	5	0	1	0	300
Agapanther	4	G	2	0	0	0	45
Agata (FR)	3	F	6	0	1	2	64,745
Agate Basin	3	C	7	0	1	0	2,929
Agate's Saint	6	H	9	0	0	0	546
Agave	4	F	5	1	1	1	13,675
Agbayani	5	M	12	0	3	1	11,332

Horse	Age	Sex	Sts	1st	2d	3d	Won
Agenda Girl	3	F	2	0	0	0	37
Agenda's Trouble	4	G	1	0	0	0	100
Agent Danseur	3	C	6	1	0	2	34,843
Agent Grey	2	C	4	0	0	3	1,410
Agent Q	2	G	3	0	1	0	2,444
Agent Talk	4	G	17	2	3	1	14,904
Agent Won	2	G	10	2	3	0	31,532
Aggadan	5	H	10	4	3	1	263,371
Aggie Grit	3	C	12	2	1	3	47,810
Aggie Lawyer	2	G	6	0	0	1	1,014
Aggie Minister	5	M	6	0	0	0	78
Aggie Miss Tree	2	F	1	0	0	0	810
Aggie Peach	4	F	14	0	0	1	2,393
Aggie Roo	5	M	5	0	2	0	1,953
Aggie Socks	4	F	3	1	1	0	3,512
Aggieblitz	5	M	11	0	0	0	2,496
Aggieinfront	3	F	8	0	2	1	3,516
Aggies Hideaway	7	M	8	0	0	1	3,168
Aggies Style	5	M	14	1	2	2	10,112
Aggies Wild	2	C	1	0	0	0	0
Aggravating Annie	3	F	10	1	4	2	39,925
Aggressive	7	G	12	1	5	1	30,740
Aggressive Action	7	G	5	1	0	0	3,542
Aggressive Dixie	5	M	7	1	1	3	9,614
Aggressive Edge	6	M	6	0	1	1	2,789
Aggressive Man	4	G	9	2	0	1	6,633
Aggressive Miss	2	F	4	1	0	0	9,546
Aggressive Nanny	5	G	15	1	5	1	19,152
Agile Aly	6	M	4	1	1	1	9,700
Agile Lover	5	H	3	0	0	0	490
Agilena	3	F	10	2	1	3	15,250
Agincourt	5	M	14	1	0	2	14,308
Agitato	3	F	4	0	0	0	406
Ago Ruhles	4	F	5	0	0	0	499
Agone	4	G	5	0	0	0	2,065
Agoody Too	2	F	3	0	0	0	900
Agree to Disagree	4	F	12	3	5	1	69,600
Agree With Me	2	F	1	0	0	0	216
Agreeable Enough	3	F	1	0	0	0	0
Agretta Darling	3	F	16	1	1	4	13,080
Agrivating General	5	G	4	3	0	0	76,200
Agro	3	G	15	2	4	0	33,900
Agua Frio	7	G	16	1	0	2	5,470
Aguara	4	F	12	2	2	5	38,831
Ah Boo	4	G	13	3	2	3	65,460
Ah Salute	2	C	3	0	0	0	1,380
Ah Still Suits Me	5	M	1	0	0	0	88
Ah Wilderness	4	G	7	0	0	0	2,355
Ahead of the Pack	3	F	5	2	1	1	10,562
Ahmee's Best	5	M	11	0	1	2	5,272
Ahnee Dios	2	F	4	0	1	0	9,183
Ahnold	2	G	4	1	2	0	3,800
Aho Acre	3	C	13	2	2	1	29,280
Ahoy	3	F	12	1	1	1	7,867
Ahoy El Paso	3	G	14	2	0	0	10,476
Ahpo Here	7	G	5	2	1	0	50,680
Ahsogroovy	4	F	7	1	0	1	5,945
Ahtee	3	G	6	3	0	0	8,812
Ahumado	2	C	1	0	0	0	96
Ahuriri Hikawai (NZ)	5	M	4	1	0	0	35,807
Aibrean	5	G	7	2	4	0	22,100
Aidan's Turn	4	G	5	1	2	0	35,765
Aileen's Derby	4	G	11	2	1	1	13,605
Aileen's Pride	2	C	1	0	0	0	205
Aileen's Valay	6	M	3	0	0	0	552
Aim for the Wire	2	F	3	1	0	1	17,893
Aim of the Game	9	M	8	0	1	3	2,987
Aim Straight	2	F	5	1	0	0	37,298
Aim to Win	6	G	9	1	3	1	17,290
Aima (IRE)	7	G	13	2	0	3	9,288
Aime Moi Toujour	4	F	14	1	1	3	9,815
Aimees Pride	4	G	3	0	0	1	1,567
Aimer	3	F	4	0	0	1	7,800
Aimless Breeze	9	G	2	0	0	0	80
Aint	4	G	8	1	0	1	8,617
Aint Dat Right Ted	3	F	6	2	2	0	12,564
Ain't I Kool	4	F	11	0	4	0	9,178
Aint Misbehavin	2	G	1	0	0	0	0
Ain't No Big Deal	9	M	3	0	0	0	672
Ain't No Bullzip	4	G	12	1	2	1	9,933
Aint No Connection	6	H	11	2	3	1	26,473
Ain't No Sunshine	4	G	5	0	1	1	2,415
Ain't No Yank	10	G	1	0	0	0	0
Ain't Paintin Buck	3	F	1	0	0	0	0
Ain't She a Beauty	3	F	13	1	4	3	18,740
Ain't She Special	4	F	1	0	0	0	0
Ain't Tellin'	4	F	7	1	0	2	1,857
Ainthatrighthoney	4	G	11	1	2	1	34,795
Air Academy	3	C	14	3	4	3	87,020
Air Adair	4	F	6	2	0	1	51,260
Air Alibi	6	M	1	0	0	0	52
Air American	3	C	3	0	1	1	6,658
Air Annie	7	M	12	1	3	3	16,373
Air Base	5	G	10	2	1	0	26,610
Air Brush	3	G	11	0	2	3	25,750
Air Cactus Lil	3	F	7	0	1	3	2,790
Air Command	3	C	10	1	1	0	11,462
Air Cool	10	H	8	3	2	0	19,376
Air Driver	4	F	6	1	0	2	20,460
Air Forbes	5	G	13	4	5	2	19,910
Air Forbes Too	7	H	6	4	0	1	5,750
Air Hadif	3	C	15	2	2	2	15,311
Air Janalex	6	M	3	0	0	0	0
Air Jones	3	C	2	0	1	0	7,400
Air Julie	2	F	9	2	1	2	37,161
Air Kaper	3	F	4	0	1	0	1,755
Air Karakorum	6	M	10	1	3	1	25,612
Air King	4	G	3	0	0	0	391
Air Kiss	5	G	15	1	0	2	9,665
Air Lordan	4	C	2	0	1	0	2,766
Air Marshall	4	F	9	1	3	3	62,830
Air Med	3	G	1	0	0	0	0
Air Rail	5	G	7	0	1	0	3,770
Air Security	3	C	5	0	1	1	2,635
Air Tech	6	G	13	1	1	3	8,943
Air Travel	3	F	1	0	0	0	780
Air Turbulence	5	G	12	1	0	2	4,883
Airborne Shuttle	11	G	13	1	2	3	13,540
Airbourne Command	9	G	5	1	0	0	25,416
Aircobra (ARG)	4	F	8	1	4	1	28,140
Aireslew	3	G	10	1	1	2	15,001
Airialissue	4	F	9	1	1	0	23,034
Airiasaffair	7	G	7	0	0	1	4,591
Airizon	2	F	1	0	0	0	205
Airlineinthesand	2	G	4	0	2	1	7,503
Airman	3	G	5	1	0	0	9,320
Airness	3	F	6	0	1	1	8,320
Air'nsea	8	G	12	4	3	0	22,315
Airolo (FR)	6	G	4	0	1	0	6,000
Airport Kate	4	F	8	3	0	0	57,540
Airship	6	G	3	1	0	0	3,330
Airspeed Alive	3	C	5	1	0	0	7,562
Airtight Alibi	9	G	4	0	0	0	1,153
Airtiteanni	3	F	14	6	1	2	48,800
Airtogroundcontrol	2	C	2	0	0	0	1,398
Airtune	7	G	1	0	0	0	66
Airzone	3	G	9	2	1	1	15,780
Aislamiento	5	M	11	0	1	0	2,573
Aisle Light	4	F	2	2	0	0	40,398
Aisle Model	2	F	2	0	0	0	125
Aizarunner	2	R	12	1	1	3	31,960
Aj Cielo	5	G	9	1	3	1	15,345
Aja	3	F	8	1	0	0	10,309
Ajax Jet	4	F	16	2	4	1	11,282
Ajedrez (ARG)	5	H	11	1	1	3	44,130
Ajergabead	5	G	13	0	0	1	5,060
Aj's Dancin Emblem	2	F	1	0	0	0	0
Aj's Here to Win	4	G	11	1	3	1	11,987
Aj's Honor	5	G	13	2	1	1	14,860
Aka Skoshee	3	G	6	0	0	1	645
Akamai	4	G	2	0	0	1	2,360
Akana	4	F	6	3	1	1	68,880
Akanti (IRE)	4	G	11	5	1	1	102,300
Akatsakat	4	G	4	0	1	1	7,302
Akdah	5	H	3	1	1	0	14,050
Akimboalogo	4	G	10	3	2	1	19,546
Akissifyouwin	4	F	1	0	0	0	63
Akka Brava (IRE)	4	F	2	0	0	0	0

Horse	Age	Sex	Sts	1st	2d	3d	Won
Akram's Rudy	5	G	14	2	1	5	22,270
Akram's Weehee	6	M	6	0	1	3	11,170
Akron Blue	5	M	13	0	1	0	842
Aksarben Aly	2	F	3	0	1	1	2,877
Akvatinta's Trick	3	G	8	0	0	2	7,247
Akvavit	3	C	3	0	0	0	1,330
Al Anoosh	3	C	2	0	0	0	0
Al Cory Lucas	7	G	13	0	4	0	6,081
Al Dente	5	H	10	1	1	0	12,440
Al Farris	3	G	12	1	4	1	14,820
Al Geel	3	F	5	0	0	0	1,780
Al Hajji	8	G	11	0	0	0	1,172
Al Johnstan	2	C	2	0	0	1	4,613
Al Khaaser	6	H	4	0	0	0	2,070
Al Mukhtar	3	C	3	0	1	1	11,710
Al Prospector	7	G	14	0	2	4	10,155
Al Rock	6	G	14	1	4	1	15,695
Al Saqaar	4	C	15	2	0	0	25,337
Al Skywalker	11	G	3	1	0	1	37,000
Al Tomatoes	3	C	23	2	1	4	18,091
Al Tony O's Babe	4	G	2	0	0	1	1,912
Al Turf (IRE)	4	C	2	0	0	0	1,500
Al Yafil (AUS)	4	F	3	0	0	0	1,620
Ala Freeda	3	G	11	2	0	2	13,539
Alabama Clay	3	C	2	0	1	0	6,760
Alabama Princess	5	M	2	0	0	0	0
Alabama Rain	2	G	6	3	2	1	136,784
Alabama Rose	8	M	1	0	0	0	0
Alabastrino	4	C	11	1	4	1	6,646
Aladdin's Lamp	3	C	1	0	0	0	123
Aladin Sane	5	G	12	4	3	0	23,225
Alafair	3	F	1	0	0	0	0
Alakayfa	6	M	10	1	0	0	5,250
Alaki's Jet	4	C	5	3	0	0	35,920
Alalila	4	F	17	1	3	3	32,670
Alameda Duke	7	G	16	1	1	1	11,373
Alamo Rose	5	M	1	0	0	0	0
Alamomiss	4	F	10	0	0	1	2,370
Alamos Star	3	G	5	0	0	0	329
Alamoshirman	3	G	9	0	0	0	1,540
Alan Bandler	3	C	2	0	0	0	100
Alandem	6	G	2	0	0	0	89
Alannadontstop	4	F	8	0	0	1	2,380
Alan's Plum Frozen	3	G	5	0	0	0	0
Alar	5	G	14	1	1	2	9,639
Alarkandadove	3	F	6	1	2	0	38,850
Alarm Code	8	G	18	0	2	8	10,525
Alarm On the Farm	3	C	14	2	2	2	48,980
Alarm System	3	G	11	1	1	0	4,671
Alarm the C. E. O.	5	G	10	2	1	3	44,745
Alarmed	2	C	2	0	0	1	1,000
Alarming Fantasy	3	F	12	2	1	0	23,627
Alarming Leader	10	G	13	0	3	0	5,925
Alarming Velocity	3	G	6	0	0	0	0
Alarmingly Charmin	2	G	3	1	1	0	11,361
Alas Elak	3	G	3	0	0	0	1,077
Alashan	3	C	2	0	0	1	934
Alaska Ash	3	F	7	3	0	0	79,842
Alaskan Beau	4	G	16	2	1	2	28,858
Alaskan Buck	13	G	1	0	0	0	104
Alaskan Glory	7	M	14	0	1	0	3,428
Alaskan Gold	5	G	14	0	1	0	9,886
Alaskan Hill	7	G	8	1	0	0	3,404
Alaskan Idabel	4	C	5	0	0	0	225
Alaskan Jinx	3	G	3	0	0	1	2,860
Alaskan Lights	10	G	11	4	1	2	17,195
Alaskan Moon	3	G	3	0	0	0	780
Alaskan Nights	7	G	10	2	1	2	9,378
Alaskan Vodka	9	G	9	0	0	1	1,212
Alaskana	3	F	8	2	1	0	12,296
Alaskee	8	G	3	0	0	0	0
Alathry	3	G	3	0	0	0	600
Alaya	3	F	5	0	1	1	20,587
Alayna's Louski	7	M	1	0	0	0	0
Albaaz	4	C	3	0	0	0	2,520
Albadar	9	G	11	2	0	5	7,399
Albany Boy	6	G	14	2	2	2	8,482
Albany County	2	F	3	1	0	0	28,050
Albarino	3	G	9	1	2	1	72,108
Albatros (ARG)	7	H	6	0	3	2	31,140
Albert and Baby	4	G	11	1	0	1	9,146
Albert E.	4	G	14	3	2	3	88,115
Albert Slewsky	4	G	13	1	3	2	17,378
Albert the Joker	2	F	6	1	1	0	11,635
Albert Walk	2	C	2	0	0	1	2,400
Alberta Brass	4	F	5	1	2	0	10,476
Alberta Clipper	3	G	9	1	1	1	10,420
Alberta Devil	3	G	10	1	1	1	8,379
Alberta Energy	4	G	10	0	1	1	4,765
Alberta Oak	6	G	5	0	0	0	2,352
Albertmyman	6	G	15	2	1	2	3,621
Alberto Giacometti (IRE)	4	C	1	0	0	0	1,200
Albert's Crossing	4	G	11	5	3	0	43,180
Albrannon	9	G	10	1	2	1	7,941
Alcantare	2	C	1	0	0	0	205
Alchema	3	F	3	0	0	0	3,600
Alchemist	4	F	11	1	4	1	95,488
Alcina	2	F	3	0	0	1	4,270
Alcohol	4	C	1	0	1	0	6,080
Alcohol Flats	5	G	2	0	0	0	174
Alcohol Related	4	G	5	0	0	0	309
Alcres George	3	G	8	0	2	0	13,980
Alden's Card	6	H	6	3	1	0	36,825
Alden's Malibu	3	G	9	2	1	1	21,665
Aldina From Medina	6	M	1	0	0	0	46
Aldoc	6	H	4	0	3	0	7,594
Alecks	5	M	7	0	0	0	700
Alec's Lil Angel	3	F	7	0	0	1	2,879
Aledo Affair	4	F	21	2	6	2	22,435
Aledo Cougar	4	C	5	0	0	0	978
Aledo Magic	2	F	2	0	1	0	2,800
Aledo Pass	4	G	12	2	4	1	62,380
Alegorico (ARG)	6	G	10	3	1	3	30,130
Alegrita	4	F	4	0	0	0	0
Aleke	4	G	8	0	0	0	1,282
Alena's Boy	3	C	8	1	1	0	23,105
Alena's Tornado	7	G	6	1	2	1	19,898
Alencino	4	G	14	2	1	3	8,618
Alert Cat	4	C	6	0	0	1	475
Alert Dancer	2	G	8	0	0	0	5,535
Alert David	10	G	1	0	0	0	0
Alerting	4	F	9	1	0	0	7,540
Alertly	4	G	8	0	0	0	1,156
Alesia Gold Boy	6	G	16	0	1	3	3,796
Alesias Affair	5	G	12	1	2	1	23,018
A'leuring Star	6	G	15	3	3	1	25,663
Aleutian Frost	5	G	17	2	2	4	23,915
Alex Darlin	2	F	3	0	1	0	2,760
Alex the Mad Dog	5	H	1	0	0	0	300
Alexa Grace	4	F	14	0	2	2	4,195
Alexa M J	3	F	2	0	0	0	300
Alexander Charlote (IRE)	3	F	5	1	0	1	31,368
Alexander Looker	7	M	9	0	0	0	514
Alexander's Belle	3	F	15	3	4	2	24,275
Alexander's Bid	3	C	2	0	0	0	626
Alexanders Charm	7	G	10	4	0	0	28,190
Alexander's Sword	6	G	19	0	3	4	21,972
Alexandersrun	2	C	6	0	3	1	78,933
Alexandra's Hope	3	F	5	2	0	0	26,280
Alexandria	4	F	5	1	0	0	13,110
Alexis Pony	5	G	19	4	1	5	33,363
Alexisourdestiny	3	F	6	0	0	0	960
Alex's Allure	2	F	2	0	0	0	0
Alex's Dream	5	G	2	0	0	0	0
Alex's Hot Fudge	4	F	7	1	3	1	37,300
Alex's Love	6	G	13	1	2	0	10,464
Alex's Pal	5	H	4	1	0	2	37,290
Alex's Sister	4	F	1	0	1	0	1,500
Aleyeska	4	G	8	1	0	0	5,716
Alfaari Queen	4	F	1	0	0	0	340
Alfaari's Lass	5	M	1	0	0	0	120
Alfaari's Magic	4	G	5	2	0	2	25,030
Alfaari's Solo	5	G	12	3	1	0	34,244
Alferrari	5	G	14	3	2	3	33,164
Alfi Sez	2	G	3	0	0	1	1,036
Alfie	6	M	8	2	1	1	10,673
Alfir's Ace	4	F	2	1	0	0	10,640
Alfonsina	2	F	3	2	1	0	76,630

Horse	Age	Sex	Sts	1st	2d	3d	Won
Alfredo	4	G	8	0	1	2	3,713
Alfred's Bluff	10	G	7	1	1	0	3,200
Alfurune	6	G	8	1	0	1	31,397
Algerias Queen	3	F	14	4	4	0	43,338
Alghero	4	G	13	3	2	3	22,119
Algonquin	6	H	3	0	0	0	299
Algonquin Farewell	5	G	10	0	1	2	4,444
Algonquin Flag	3	G	14	0	2	1	17,851
Algorhythm	5	G	8	0	1	0	2,945
Alhambra Circle	3	F	5	1	2	0	11,180
Alhorsesgotoheaven	6	G	10	0	2	3	12,787
Ali Be Contender	5	G	1	0	0	0	90
Ali G.	8	M	7	0	0	0	324
Ali Kan	3	F	1	0	0	0	160
Ali Master	2	G	3	0	0	0	306
Ali Mingeaux	3	F	10	2	1	0	29,813
Ali Olah	4	F	6	1	0	0	7,255
Ali On the Sly	4	F	1	0	0	0	0
Ali Online	4	F	1	0	1	0	2,400
Ali P Slick	3	F	16	2	1	2	21,400
Ali the Cat	3	F	8	0	0	0	1,060
Ali Won	3	G	9	1	2	0	16,005
Aliado	2	F	1	0	0	0	795
Alias Blackout	5	G	13	1	0	1	5,491
Alibi Expert	7	M	5	0	0	1	1,811
Alibob	4	F	7	2	2	2	56,158
Alic From Dallas	3	F	4	0	0	0	225
Alice From Marigny	6	G	11	2	3	0	63,968
Alice Nevada	7	M	14	4	1	3	46,476
Alice's Blue Gown	5	M	5	0	0	0	1,662
Alice's Notebook	8	G	8	0	1	2	7,380
Alices Silver Lady	5	M	8	1	2	0	58,860
Alice's Thunder	2	F	3	0	0	0	400
Alicia N.	2	F	1	0	0	0	184
Alicia's Buck	3	G	3	0	0	0	1,812
Alicias Quick Draw	5	G	6	1	0	0	5,970
Alicia's Song	3	F	8	0	0	2	6,698
Alicita My Love	4	F	9	2	1	3	59,024
Alicnator	4	G	6	1	1	1	2,810
Alienated	5	M	2	0	0	0	1,500
Alienist	6	G	11	1	1	3	11,081
Alie's Del Prado	3	C	2	0	1	1	11,920
Alie's Mink	2	C	1	0	1	0	3,600
Alii Kai	3	F	8	0	2	1	19,653
Alii Kat Al	3	F	6	0	2	0	2,494
Alina Alina	5	M	10	2	1	0	46,630
Alipalooza	4	F	11	2	2	0	11,575
Ali's Best Chance	4	F	5	0	0	0	404
Ali's Charger	3	F	4	0	0	0	1,620
Ali's Glori	5	M	7	2	1	3	10,951
Ali's Gold	4	G	8	1	2	0	14,633
Ali's Honor	3	C	4	0	0	0	0
Ali's Little Toy	4	F	3	0	0	0	114
Ali's Merhaba	3	F	2	0	0	0	530
Ali's Miss Leader	4	F	11	2	0	0	15,246
Ali's Pride	4	C	3	0	0	0	1,302
Alisa's Hope	2	F	13	1	0	1	27,490
Alise's Fighter	2	C	3	0	0	0	322
Alishowest	4	G	8	0	0	0	1,006
Alison Kate	7	M	17	2	1	0	27,320
Alison's Winner	7	M	1	0	0	1	1,500
Alisos Park	3	F	4	1	0	1	6,610
Alissa's Atm	2	F	3	1	0	1	9,725
Alitabithot	3	F	7	1	1	0	7,147
Alittlebitbrassy	6	M	6	1	2	1	35,015
Alittlebitextra	2	F	6	1	0	0	13,625
Alittlebitgrumpy	4	F	5	1	2	1	46,811
Alittlebitofheaven	4	F	1	0	0	0	0
Alittlebitofsleet	3	G	3	0	0	2	5,500
Alittlehardtohold	5	M	12	3	1	2	10,660
Alivento	3	C	1	0	0	0	0
Alix M	4	F	9	5	3	1	166,620
Aliyoyo	3	F	1	0	0	0	77
Alize	3	F	5	1	0	2	29,385
Alkaban	4	C	1	0	0	0	0
Alkali Ike	6	G	5	2	0	2	30,500
Alkarnak	7	G	18	2	4	3	31,030
Alkatraz Island	3	G	11	2	1	0	6,474
Alke	4	C	3	2	1	0	482,800
Alki Run	7	G	4	0	0	1	2,216
Alkris Baby	3	F	18	1	3	4	14,429
All a Blur	6	M	5	0	0	2	2,237
All Ablaze	4	F	12	1	1	2	20,361
All About Color	3	F	12	3	1	2	89,762
All About Conner	5	G	12	2	1	2	18,383
All About Dave	2	G	2	0	1	0	2,280
All About Elsie	4	F	12	4	1	1	30,628
All About Mary	3	F	11	0	1	1	1,889
All About Me	5	H	16	2	3	1	25,459
All About Speed	5	M	12	3	1	5	25,280
All About You Bob	5	G	14	2	2	0	24,100
All Academic	4	C	12	1	0	2	16,420
All Aces	3	C	2	0	0	0	560
All Aglow	3	F	5	1	1	2	32,200
All American Blond	3	F	7	1	0	2	16,480
All American Blue	4	G	11	0	1	2	15,677
All American Chris	5	G	12	2	1	2	16,808
All American Coach	2	C	1	0	0	0	205
All American Ernie	3	G	19	2	2	3	19,522
All American Girl	5	M	2	0	0	1	802
All American Pride	3	F	15	1	5	1	12,736
All and All	4	G	10	0	4	2	11,987
All Apologies	6	M	3	0	2	0	9,840
All Around Town	4	C	11	1	3	1	26,640
All Ashore	3	C	1	0	0	0	140
All At Once	4	F	6	1	1	0	40,599
All Bluff	3	G	5	0	0	0	750
All by Chance	4	F	10	1	1	0	12,473
All Canadian	2	G	4	0	0	1	2,523
All Cat	4	G	5	2	0	0	22,660
All Chance	4	C	5	0	1	1	5,600
All Circuits Go	3	F	5	1	0	2	19,600
All Dash	6	M	3	0	0	0	91
All Day Long	6	G	12	0	1	1	2,538
All Disco	3	C	1	0	0	0	2,400
All Dolled Up	3	F	4	1	0	0	16,350
All Ears	5	M	4	0	0	0	0
All Electric	3	F	6	1	1	0	28,000
All Flags Flying	3	F	4	1	1	1	19,920
All for Joann	3	F	3	0	0	1	1,575
All for Love	3	G	9	1	1	2	28,870
All for Mandy	2	F	5	1	1	0	7,020
All for Me	7	M	7	0	0	0	551
All for Now	3	G	6	0	0	0	470
All for One	6	M	16	1	1	0	4,330
All for Sunny	6	M	10	0	0	1	1,421
All for the Game	4	F	9	1	2	1	7,990
All Four Chads	5	M	1	0	0	0	80
All Geared Up	5	G	10	3	3	0	12,288
All Glory	5	M	3	0	0	0	2,900
All Gone Cat	5	G	9	0	1	2	5,528
All Gone John	3	G	18	0	2	2	6,170
All Hail Stormy	3	C	13	5	1	4	168,081
All I Do for You	3	F	7	1	2	1	23,964
All I Got	6	G	4	1	1	0	6,849
All in Favor	5	G	13	4	2	0	25,910
All in the Gate	9	G	8	0	2	0	3,146
All Inclusive	4	F	3	0	0	1	779
All Inspired	4	G	19	0	0	2	6,290
All Intoxicated	3	G	2	0	0	0	0
All Irish	3	G	9	1	3	1	37,965
All Is Bright	6	M	3	0	0	0	828
All Is Calm	3	G	11	2	2	3	22,665
All Kidding Aside	3	F	5	1	0	1	11,550
All Knight Music	4	G	25	2	3	3	18,074
All Line	5	G	15	1	1	1	25,713
All Lucky Fab	3	F	6	0	0	0	1,185
All My Money	3	F	4	0	0	0	396
All N the Game	4	G	1	0	1	0	2,180
All New Terms	3	F	8	1	0	0	6,600
All Night Party	4	C	13	0	1	2	2,750
All Night Rebel	2	F	5	0	2	1	6,320
All of Me	5	M	2	1	0	0	27,150
All of Roanoke	3	G	3	0	0	0	585
All Okie	6	G	10	1	1	0	4,294
All Out Springs	5	G	2	0	0	0	110
All Over the Citi	7	G	8	0	0	1	962
All Pent Up	6	G	3	0	0	0	192

Horse	Age	Sex	Sts	1st	2d	3d	Won
All Power	3	G	13	0	3	0	5,649
All Prayers	4	F	15	1	1	2	20,631
All Pride	5	M	4	0	0	0	325
All Purpose	5	G	12	2	4	2	28,136
All Right Kathy	3	F	12	0	0	1	1,634
All Rise	3	G	8	1	3	1	26,336
All Round Cowgirl	2	F	3	0	1	2	18,861
All Seymoura	4	F	16	1	2	2	16,992
All Souped Up	3	G	13	2	2	3	37,775
All Star Frank	4	G	10	1	3	3	45,290
All Star Girl	4	F	15	1	2	0	19,674
All Star Lover	5	G	9	0	1	0	29,277
All Star Prospect	4	G	6	3	1	0	46,200
All Talk	4	G	4	1	2	0	28,400
All Teed Up	4	G	9	1	3	1	25,570
All Terrain	4	G	1	0	0	0	690
All That Chatter	3	F	1	0	0	0	1,260
All That Glitters	10	M	6	0	1	0	12,148
All That Magic	5	G	3	0	0	0	106
All That Sass	4	F	9	0	0	3	4,955
All That's Nice	2	C	1	0	0	0	0
All the Boys	7	G	7	2	0	2	71,580
All the Colors	2	F	1	0	0	0	0
All the Difference	4	F	4	1	0	0	20,550
All the Doe	3	G	4	0	1	1	8,528
All the Girls	7	M	1	0	0	0	0
All the Honor	4	F	4	2	0	0	57,600
All the Numbers	4	C	11	0	0	1	10,170
All the Way Nick	2	C	1	0	0	0	410
All the Wile	2	G	7	1	1	1	43,670
All the Words	2	F	4	0	2	2	15,360
All Thee B	3	F	9	3	1	1	23,578
All Things French	5	G	9	2	0	2	43,888
All This 'n Change	2	F	4	1	0	0	20,851
All to True	3	G	14	1	3	0	13,960
All too Groovy	5	M	3	0	0	0	0
All True	3	C	10	1	1	0	17,630
All Trumps	2	C	3	1	0	0	31,682
All Tuned Up	3	F	1	0	0	0	0
All We Have	4	F	9	1	3	3	18,154
All Weekend Long	4	F	3	0	1	1	11,770
All Wheel Drive	3	C	1	0	0	0	0
All Winner (ARG)	5	G	5	0	1	0	4,607
All Wired Up	2	C	1	0	0	1	2,227
All Y'all	5	G	11	4	1	0	13,370
All Zoomed Up	3	F	2	0	0	0	0
Alla Breve	4	G	9	0	0	1	3,155
Alla Tigger	7	G	9	0	0	1	1,878
Allahvi	4	G	1	0	0	0	0
Allai	6	G	3	0	1	0	1,111
Allamerican Beauty	3	F	2	0	0	1	4,910
Allamystique	3	C	9	1	0	1	3,425
Allan G.	4	G	13	2	5	0	10,648
Allans Money	6	G	11	0	0	1	1,481
Allbow	3	F	5	0	2	1	4,660
Alldafax	3	G	16	3	3	1	22,629
Alldiablo	2	C	1	1	0	0	6,000
Alleged Bells	3	G	1	0	0	0	0
Alleged Feu	9	G	14	4	2	3	7,333
Alleged Hug	2	C	1	0	0	0	0
Alleged Light	4	F	10	1	5	2	39,970
Alleged Master	2	C	5	1	0	2	5,830
Alleged Ruler	3	C	11	3	2	1	140,594
Alleged Storm	7	G	8	0	2	1	2,080
Alleged Whisper	4	F	10	2	2	1	36,070
Allegedly (IRE)	3	F	4	0	0	0	1,193
Allegedly an Angel	6	M	1	0	0	0	0
Allegra's Affair	3	F	10	2	1	2	24,755
Allegro Lady	3	F	1	0	0	0	434
Alleluia Anthem	2	C	4	0	0	0	925
Allens Blessing	4	F	11	2	2	3	47,030
Allen's Dream	2	C	2	1	0	0	13,240
Allen's Goldgorian	7	G	6	1	0	0	3,480
Allen's Heiress	4	F	16	0	0	0	1,560
Allen's Jet	4	F	2	0	0	0	174
Allen's Kat	2	G	12	1	4	2	64,805
Allen's Protege	6	G	2	0	0	0	0
Allen's Sphinx	7	H	4	0	1	0	4,375
Allen's Treasure	2	G	12	0	5	1	19,685
Allensky	4	C	9	3	2	1	72,210
Allenswood	4	G	7	0	0	0	1,440
Allentown	3	G	2	0	0	0	540
Aller Baby	4	G	3	0	0	0	631
Allerap	4	G	1	0	0	0	126
Alley Cat Jack	6	G	1	0	0	0	0
Alley Creek	3	F	9	1	0	0	10,335
Alley Door	2	G	2	0	0	0	800
Alley's Account	3	F	2	0	0	0	126
Alley's Derby	5	G	7	0	0	0	315
Alley's Lady	2	F	1	0	0	1	1,910
Alley's Rainbow	4	F	5	0	1	1	7,000
Allie Boy	5	G	5	2	0	0	26,230
Allie McBeast	3	F	4	1	0	0	4,599
Allie McGoof	3	F	3	0	0	0	352
Allie Ohlee	5	M	9	0	0	0	1,272
Allied Commander	2	C	3	0	0	0	0
Allied Dancer	2	F	4	0	0	1	2,300
Allied Prospector	2	G	2	0	0	0	515
Allied Wonder	4	F	7	1	0	0	9,695
Allie's Excavator	6	G	5	0	0	1	3,730
Allie's Hope	5	M	2	0	0	0	1,001
Allies Love	6	M	3	0	0	0	504
Allie's Prospect	2	C	5	0	0	1	3,980
Allieslildiamond	4	F	8	1	0	0	4,802
Alliesunrun	7	M	11	2	2	1	20,656
Alligator Pattie	6	M	5	0	0	1	560
Alligator Tears	3	G	8	2	0	2	22,492
Allimac (IRE)	7	G	3	1	1	0	7,800
Alli's Dream	3	F	12	1	4	1	25,240
Allison Elise	8	M	3	0	0	0	0
Allison Rose	3	F	8	2	0	0	32,400
Allison's Cat	4	F	14	0	0	2	2,389
Allison's Hope	3	F	1	0	0	0	0
Allison's Princess	2	F	1	0	0	0	2,050
Allisons Smile	5	G	14	1	1	1	40,900
Allknightwithyou	3	F	6	2	2	0	6,373
Allnall	4	G	6	0	1	1	5,382
Allofeverything	3	F	4	0	0	0	335
Allondra	7	M	15	0	0	3	7,072
Allou	4	F	2	0	0	0	160
Allourwishes	3	F	8	1	2	1	6,650
Allovertheplace	6	G	16	1	1	3	5,729
Allpower No Outage	3	F	3	0	0	0	705
Allready	5	G	7	3	2	0	21,549
Allright	2	G	2	0	0	0	800
Allrightea	4	G	11	0	5	0	5,920
Allspice	4	F	8	2	2	0	191,394
Allstar Michael	3	G	2	0	0	0	300
Allstate Performer	5	G	8	0	0	0	210
Allswellendswell	4	F	11	0	2	2	8,458
Allswellthatnswell	3	F	6	2	1	1	96,464
Alltappedout	5	M	16	3	5	1	63,431
Allthatcatcanbe	3	F	6	0	0	0	330
Allthatwhite	4	G	9	1	0	0	5,360
Allthechips	4	C	4	0	2	0	3,500
Allthewayalydeed	4	C	3	0	0	0	891
Alltheway gone	4	G	11	1	1	0	5,751
Alltime Blues	6	G	4	2	0	0	2,136
Alltroienne	5	M	6	2	2	0	43,880
Alluded	5	G	1	0	0	0	0
Allure l'Amour	6	M	2	0	0	0	450
Alluring	5	M	3	0	0	0	3,860
Alluring Trapp	5	M	6	0	0	0	866
Allwood	4	C	3	0	0	0	1,085
Allwreckdup	4	C	1	0	0	0	320
Ally McSqueal	4	F	10	3	0	2	26,395
Ally Scats	5	M	8	4	0	0	29,500
Allynn's Deal	3	G	5	0	0	0	1,980
Allys Big Boy	3	C	3	0	0	0	0
Allys Golden Smile	2	F	3	1	0	1	20,080
Allys Thunder	4	G	10	1	2	1	8,755
Ally's Valentine	6	M	5	0	1	0	1,676
Alma Dancer	10	G	12	4	4	1	21,474
Almaz	5	H	5	0	0	0	353
Almenora	7	M	6	0	0	2	1,409
Almiddina (IRE)	7	M	5	1	0	0	16,250
Almighty Above	5	G	15	2	3	1	8,919
Almighty Cochise	5	G	14	1	4	2	8,951

Horse	Age	Sex	Sts	1st	2d	3d	Won
Almitra	5	M	4	0	0	0	204
Almond Blossom	4	F	12	3	4	1	107,965
Almond Eyes	4	G	1	0	0	0	275
Almost a Scandal	7	M	4	0	0	0	230
Almost a Valentine	6	M	5	0	1	0	1,632
Almost Allegend	3	G	2	1	0	0	9,954
Almost Amos	3	G	11	1	0	3	5,815
Almost Dissuaded	4	F	20	0	2	5	7,498
Almost Doris	3	G	10	1	0	1	13,896
Almost Fooled	4	F	2	1	0	0	24,270
Almost Golden	10	G	6	1	0	3	11,370
Almost Holy	4	C	12	2	2	3	29,000
Almost Kentucky	3	G	2	0	0	0	348
Almost Legal	2	G	2	0	0	0	289
Almost President	3	F	6	1	1	1	32,925
Almost There	8	M	6	1	1	2	24,300
Almostagentleman	3	G	4	1	0	0	3,900
Almudin	5	G	10	1	1	4	28,753
Almuhathir	6	H	6	1	1	1	58,818
Almungid	5	H	13	1	4	2	15,851
Alnaab the Gold	6	G	12	0	1	2	7,851
Alnaabadancer	7	G	6	0	0	2	2,882
Alnahaam (IRE)	6	H	5	3	0	0	52,767
Alnaskra	6	G	11	2	0	4	14,762
Alnbill	5	G	11	1	1	1	5,359
Alnwick Castle	3	G	5	0	0	0	562
Alocadito (ARG)	5	H	5	1	0	2	39,660
Aloe Cat	4	F	3	0	0	0	498
Aloha Bold	6	H	11	2	1	5	111,200
Aloha Bound	4	G	14	1	2	1	8,270
Aloha Braedon	3	G	5	1	1	0	21,800
Aloha Class	4	F	12	2	0	0	7,896
Aloha Evening	2	C	1	0	0	0	140
Aloha Hayley	2	F	7	1	0	2	17,500
Aloha Lola	4	F	9	2	1	3	8,176
Aloha Mya	3	C	7	0	1	1	6,915
Aloha Pirate	3	C	9	2	1	1	36,920
Aloha Rosa	4	F	15	1	0	1	18,505
Aloha Siberia	4	G	2	0	0	0	800
Aloha's Girl	7	M	11	2	4	1	25,092
Aloma's Cobra	5	H	14	2	1	1	12,114
Aloma's Daisey	3	F	4	0	0	0	222
Aloma's Rose	3	F	6	0	1	1	8,815
Alone Again	3	G	6	1	1	0	3,912
Alone At Home	6	G	9	1	1	1	8,559
Alone At Last	3	C	5	1	2	0	15,980
Along Came George	7	G	9	3	1	1	8,441
Along Came Tones	2	G	1	0	0	0	235
Along Comes Jones	2	F	2	0	0	0	0
Alongcameachance	3	F	4	2	0	0	3,460
Alongcameaspider	4	F	1	0	0	0	125
Alost (FR)	4	G	9	1	1	2	64,173
Alota Green	4	G	9	0	1	1	2,367
Alotaboo	5	M	4	1	0	1	13,971
Alotacherokee	3	F	6	1	2	1	14,520
Alotawanna	5	G	12	1	2	1	21,160
Alotazip	2	F	1	0	0	0	0
Alotta Numbers	6	G	12	3	3	1	51,070
Alotta Spirit	4	F	9	1	2	1	10,096
Alotta Threshold	4	G	14	3	0	1	16,127
Alotta Tomfoolery	3	C	9	2	2	0	9,554
Alottadar	3	C	5	1	0	1	28,885
Alottafunfortherun	5	M	6	0	2	0	4,920
Aloween	8	G	8	2	1	1	9,847
Alowmdah	6	G	15	0	6	2	12,110
Alozaina (IRE)	5	M	2	1	0	1	40,320
Alpena Magic	14	G	17	1	2	2	12,950
Alpenglow	2	F	1	1	0	0	9,600
Alpenwald	3	F	7	2	0	2	34,460
Alpha Capo	3	G	11	4	2	0	108,476
Alpha Heat	5	M	3	0	0	1	7,469
Alpha King	4	G	4	0	0	0	1,986
Alpha Lady	4	F	3	0	1	0	765
Alpha Light	4	F	2	0	0	0	640
Alpha Mama	5	M	1	0	0	0	2,940
Alpha Ray	5	M	4	0	0	1	1,902
Alpha Saphire	4	F	3	1	0	0	45,200
Alpha Star Omega	3	C	11	1	2	0	5,225
Alpha Strike	6	G	2	0	0	0	1,200
Alpha to Omega	3	C	6	2	0	2	45,280
Alphabet City	2	C	2	0	1	0	5,040
Alphabet Gold	4	F	3	1	0	0	7,800
Alphabet Kisses	3	F	9	5	2	1	326,910
Alphabet Scout	3	C	3	1	0	1	29,087
Alphabet Song	5	M	1	0	0	0	0
Alphabet Storm	3	G	13	3	1	2	37,975
Alphabetic	4	G	7	1	0	1	13,125
Alphabetical	5	H	12	2	2	2	52,780
Alphabetical Lady	3	F	1	0	0	0	114
Alphabetizing	5	H	16	2	3	0	20,400
Alphabetty	5	M	7	1	1	0	8,460
Alphagirl	4	F	10	0	3	1	7,227
Alpha's Target	5	H	12	0	1	3	3,083
Alpine Angel	3	F	2	0	0	0	360
Alpine Cat	4	F	1	0	0	0	480
Alpine Creek	3	F	8	2	0	3	13,850
Alpine Mountain	4	G	3	0	0	0	0
Alpine Silver	6	M	17	0	2	2	8,343
Alpine Singer	4	F	11	2	0	1	44,430
Alpine Sport	2	C	3	1	0	2	16,800
Alpine Walk	5	M	2	0	0	0	320
Alpler	4	G	4	0	0	0	252
Already Taken	3	G	9	0	0	2	3,075
Alright With Me	2	G	7	0	1	2	6,937
Alroyed	5	G	2	0	0	0	0
Al's Bad Boy Will	3	G	6	1	1	1	6,875
Al's Boy	4	G	4	2	0	1	29,844
Al's Dearly Bred	7	G	10	2	4	0	70,840
Als Dream Boy	6	G	3	0	0	0	0
Al's Miss Zee	2	F	2	0	0	0	149
Al's Music	7	G	8	1	2	2	2,692
Al's Odds	6	G	7	0	3	2	15,289
Al's Rose	2	F	2	0	0	0	0
Al's Silver Ghost	3	C	5	0	1	1	3,385
Al's Swan	8	M	1	0	0	0	0
Alsace	4	G	3	0	0	0	213
Alsalsa	4	G	13	2	0	0	54,290
Alsoknownas Bubba	3	C	2	0	0	0	1,500
Alstott	4	G	16	1	1	1	5,989
Alsu (IRE)	2	F	9	1	0	3	10,365
Alsystemsgohouston	4	F	10	0	0	0	2,860
Alszette	4	F	4	1	1	1	11,630
Alta Aire	3	F	6	0	2	0	17,962
Alta Clocker	5	M	15	0	0	3	5,121
Altar Girl	2	F	1	0	0	1	1,350
Altar Offering	2	C	2	0	0	0	2,500
Alter Ego	7	H	15	2	4	1	53,200
Alternate	5	M	7	1	1	2	133,092
Alternative	4	G	10	1	0	3	14,544
Alternative Energy	3	F	1	0	0	0	61
Altiro	3	G	17	1	0	2	6,926
Altitune	5	G	1	0	0	0	125
Alto Maestro (FR)	6	G	10	1	3	1	14,000
Alton Bay	4	C	5	0	1	1	7,504
Altruistic	4	F	1	0	0	0	0
Altura	8	G	9	1	0	1	12,301
Aluckyperk	4	G	4	0	0	0	2,500
Aluga Island	4	F	12	0	1	2	6,205
Alumni	7	G	12	2	1	0	26,370
Alumni Hall	5	H	10	4	2	1	191,045
Alumni News	4	C	2	0	0	0	900
Aluringact	2	G	3	0	1	1	3,060
Alvaro Al	4	G	5	0	0	0	414
Alvin P	5	G	5	0	1	1	2,056
Alvinia	4	F	5	1	2	2	29,150
Alwajd	3	G	7	2	2	1	16,770
Always a Fox	5	M	15	1	0	1	9,609
Always a Gamble	5	M	6	0	1	0	1,030
Always a Gem	3	F	10	2	1	2	41,785
Always a Hero	3	G	9	1	1	2	45,666
Always a Houston	4	C	13	2	0	1	14,342
Always a Player	5	G	11	1	0	1	5,971
Always a Sailor	2	G	4	0	2	0	8,640
Always A. E.	8	G	3	0	0	0	150
Always Alert	3	G	9	1	1	0	7,218
Always Annie's	4	F	10	2	1	1	25,611
Always Awesome	4	F	5	2	0	1	95,000
Always Clever	7	M	4	0	0	0	315

Horse	Age	Sex	Sts	1st	2d	3d	Won
Always Close	2	C	4	1	0	1	7,245
Always Daring	4	F	12	2	3	1	18,825
Always Devilish	4	F	10	1	0	4	14,179
Always Dreaming	4	F	10	3	2	2	62,914
Always Fame	5	M	3	0	1	0	1,560
Always Fire	5	M	1	0	0	0	80
Always First	5	G	5	2	0	0	8,781
Always Gamble	2	F	5	0	0	1	1,425
Always Half Moon	10	M	1	0	0	0	61
Always Honorable	4	C	5	0	2	0	2,157
Always Hope	3	F	3	0	1	0	12,540
Always in Action	5	H	7	2	1	0	15,395
Always in Front	5	M	10	0	2	1	6,390
Always in the Red	4	G	11	1	1	3	12,650
Always Indy Mood	4	G	12	1	5	2	16,912
Always Jim	2	C	7	0	0	0	1,145
Always Liability	2	F	4	0	0	0	325
Always Lisa	6	M	6	3	0	0	5,388
Always Loaded	2	F	3	0	0	0	0
Always My Lady	4	F	20	0	2	6	6,335
Always Noble	3	C	4	2	1	0	28,210
Always Original	3	G	14	2	2	1	45,171
Always Picked On	2	G	10	3	3	0	43,090
Always Playfair	3	G	6	0	1	0	940
Always Possible	2	F	4	0	0	1	870
Always Precious	5	M	5	0	0	0	237
Always Present	3	C	8	1	0	1	9,370
Always Remember	4	G	7	2	1	0	34,650
Always Saturday	3	F	3	0	1	1	2,620
Always Take Cash	5	G	11	4	1	0	21,766
Always Tomorrow	3	F	11	1	2	0	11,224
Always Tool Time	6	G	11	2	1	1	12,402
Always Twining	6	M	5	0	0	0	735
Always Valiant	4	G	9	2	1	1	21,185
Always Welcome	3	C	5	1	2	0	19,420
Always Yours	3	F	7	1	1	1	35,906
Alwaysacontender	7	G	12	2	2	2	32,825
Alwaysonmymind	3	F	6	0	1	1	2,322
Alwayswantmore	3	G	5	1	1	0	35,260
Aly Aly Aly	5	M	3	0	0	0	114
Aly Aly O	7	G	3	0	0	0	600
Aly Bubba	5	G	5	0	1	1	37,125
Aly Champ	6	M	1	0	0	0	0
Aly Etbauer	3	F	4	1	0	1	18,160
Aly Magee	2	F	1	0	0	0	120
Aly Mania	7	H	5	0	0	0	556
Aly Order	6	G	14	2	3	0	14,112
Aly Queen	5	M	21	1	6	3	28,574
Aly Rally	5	G	14	2	2	1	17,795
Aly Ron	6	G	8	1	1	0	11,135
Aly Troll	7	H	6	0	0	0	240
Aly Victory	5	G	10	2	1	1	20,159
Aly Vita	6	G	6	1	2	2	4,900
Alyazuli	3	C	7	1	0	0	10,394
Alybea	6	M	1	0	0	0	0
Alyblues	5	G	1	0	0	0	0
Alybri	8	G	8	1	4	1	4,425
Alybye	4	F	8	1	0	1	10,610
Alycaly	3	F	7	1	1	0	8,049
Alydarling	5	G	2	1	0	0	6,612
Alyde	2	C	6	1	1	0	20,511
Alydeed a Charmer	3	G	7	0	0	0	2,154
Alydeed's Leader	5	G	9	0	0	0	1,981
Alydelta	6	G	3	0	1	1	5,800
Alyhouston	2	C	2	1	0	0	4,355
Alyjam	2	C	4	0	2	0	1,150
Alyjeb	8	G	1	0	0	0	208
Alykris	3	C	6	1	0	0	4,800
Alylouis	5	G	6	1	0	1	3,692
Alymir	9	G	6	0	0	1	1,336
Alyou	6	H	6	0	0	0	613
Alyplace	5	G	7	0	3	1	2,984
Alyrida's Storm	3	F	11	4	1	1	21,605
Alyround the Flag	5	M	1	0	0	0	0
Aly's Act	3	G	1	0	0	0	2,340
Aly's Alpha Boy	3	G	14	4	1	0	58,243
Alys' Charmer	2	G	4	0	1	1	2,653
Aly's Event	3	F	4	1	0	1	6,800
Aly's Fever	6	G	19	5	2	2	28,956
Aly's Flyer	2	F	3	0	0	0	1,044
Aly's Friends	4	C	1	0	0	0	50
Alys Good Deed	6	M	14	2	4	5	15,854
Aly's Leader	7	M	13	8	4	1	86,115
Aly's Little Star	4	F	14	1	1	2	7,800
Aly's Martini	4	C	3	1	1	0	18,351
Aly's Open	3	F	3	0	0	0	197
Aly's Rita	2	F	3	1	0	0	17,160
Aly's War Lady	4	F	6	0	0	3	3,644
Alys Wildcat	4	G	12	2	4	2	26,360
Alysage	8	M	6	1	1	0	5,034
Alyshar	5	G	2	0	0	0	1,427
Alysheba Storm	4	G	10	0	0	1	1,927
Alyshebegood	5	M	4	0	0	0	450
Alyswell	9	G	17	1	0	2	13,364
Alytress	6	M	4	0	0	0	329
Alytrompc	6	G	10	1	1	3	19,955
Alyvia	4	F	3	0	0	0	1,834
Am a Dancer	8	G	4	0	0	0	186
Am a Ranch	4	C	5	1	1	1	19,996
Am All Jazzed Up	5	G	6	0	0	0	768
Ama Missprint	3	F	5	0	1	2	5,878
Ama No Peak	3	G	4	0	0	1	2,170
Ama Ray	4	F	14	1	4	3	53,155
Amador	3	C	11	2	1	3	68,562
Amadora	2	F	3	1	1	0	16,730
Amafastbaby	5	G	10	0	4	0	5,873
Amamia	3	F	7	1	1	1	16,044
Amanda Louise (IRE)	4	F	1	0	0	0	262
Amanda Lynn	3	F	11	2	0	2	19,874
Amanda Marie	3	F	11	3	2	3	32,705
Amandancer	4	F	6	0	3	1	23,770
Amanda's Bold One	4	F	3	0	0	0	0
Amanda's Deelite	5	M	1	0	0	0	0
Amanda's Fancy	3	G	4	0	0	1	3,300
Amanda's Mon	4	G	5	1	1	0	8,340
Amanda's Run	4	F	10	1	1	1	4,715
Amanda's World	2	F	7	0	1	2	7,211
Amandine	2	F	1	0	0	0	1,025
Amanjena	2	F	1	0	0	1	2,460
Amankila	3	F	2	0	0	0	125
Amante Amichevole	3	F	1	0	0	0	140
Amanuensis	3	F	9	2	1	2	65,895
Amanzi	2	F	1	0	0	0	65
Amapola's Wish	5	M	8	0	1	0	6,520
Amara J	2	F	3	0	0	0	100
Amaral A. B. C.	4	G	16	2	2	1	11,835
Amaranthine	2	F	3	1	0	0	19,380
Amaras	3	F	3	0	0	0	325
Amarelle	5	M	1	0	0	0	1,560
Amaretto	4	F	24	3	1	2	29,023
Amarillo Rose	3	F	4	0	0	1	5,275
Amarillo Star	7	G	11	1	0	3	12,121
Amarukontherocks	3	F	6	1	0	0	7,322
Amasoldier	4	G	1	0	0	0	1,200
Amateur Hour	3	G	4	1	0	1	5,780
Amazel Me	2	F	2	0	0	0	281
Amazem Grace	3	F	14	4	1	2	79,905
Amazer	3	F	2	0	1	0	6,110
Amazing Again	3	C	2	0	0	1	5,000
Amazing Ben	7	G	6	1	1	1	2,676
Amazing Buy	2	F	1	0	0	1	4,100
Amazing Capt. Mike	6	G	2	0	0	0	0
Amazing Fast Eddie	3	G	2	0	0	0	166
Amazing G	3	G	10	1	2	0	13,890
Amazing Girl	2	F	2	2	0	0	20,600
Amazing Lady	5	M	1	0	0	0	3,000
Amazing Max	5	G	8	1	1	3	7,278
Amazing Maz	2	C	1	0	0	0	510
Amazing Philly	4	F	3	0	0	1	2,110
Amazing Slew	6	H	10	0	0	0	139
Amazing Spin	3	F	7	0	2	0	10,780
Amazing Stone	7	G	6	1	2	1	1,904
Amazing Sue	5	M	5	2	1	1	13,235
Amazing Thunder	4	F	8	1	1	0	10,130
Amazing Truth	9	M	2	0	1	0	5,400
Amazinglygraced	5	M	16	1	0	4	4,610
Amazon Ace	7	G	7	0	2	1	8,055
Amazon Court	6	H	7	2	0	0	29,700

Horse	Age	Sex	Sts	1st	2d	3d	Won
Amazon River	6	G	9	0	0	1	9,925
Amazonian Drummer	3	C	1	0	0	0	1,710
Amazonian River	3	F	3	0	0	0	0
Amazonian Stalker	4	F	16	3	2	4	29,725
Amazonian Wish	5	G	11	1	1	1	13,916
Ambe	9	H	3	0	0	1	1,502
Ambe Two	5	G	12	1	1	2	5,012
Ambenay	6	G	9	0	0	1	4,690
Amber Ale	6	G	12	0	4	0	14,438
Amber Chalice	3	G	9	0	1	0	7,080
Amber Comet	7	M	3	1	0	0	6,060
Amber Dawn	2	F	4	1	0	0	1,650
Amber Forces	3	F	6	0	0	0	1,695
Amber Hills	4	F	3	0	1	0	30,913
Amber Jule	4	F	15	3	2	2	56,370
Amber Myth	4	F	1	0	0	0	145
Amber Note	4	F	5	1	1	1	8,778
Amber Song	5	M	5	0	0	0	0
Amber Token	5	M	3	0	0	0	360
Amber Twilight	4	F	8	1	1	1	19,786
Amber Two	3	F	8	2	1	0	5,840
Amber Waves	3	F	15	0	0	2	3,148
Amberall	4	F	9	0	0	0	1,020
Amberprospect	2	C	3	0	1	0	3,460
Amber's County	6	M	9	3	1	2	21,462
Amber's Girl	3	F	8	2	1	2	18,475
Amber's Glow	7	M	7	0	0	0	2,764
Amber's Last Hope	2	F	5	0	0	0	510
Amber's Picture	3	F	6	0	0	0	0
Ambers Smile	5	M	5	0	0	0	790
Ambi's Bro	8	G	1	0	0	0	300
Ambition Unbridled	3	F	9	4	1	2	140,286
Ambition's End	7	G	2	0	0	0	0
Ambitious	3	G	12	1	1	0	7,982
Ambitious Buster	5	G	12	3	1	1	23,512
Ambitious Cat	3	F	4	1	2	0	61,425
Ambitious Choice	8	M	2	0	0	0	682
Ambitious Dancer	8	G	2	0	0	0	80
Ambitious Gulch	3	F	14	1	3	1	18,600
Ambitious One	3	G	1	0	0	1	2,400
Ambsah	3	G	12	1	2	2	16,830
Ambulance Chaser	2	C	1	0	0	0	0
Ambusher	9	G	15	2	3	1	13,123
Amdor's Nick	8	G	11	1	0	2	4,535
Amedeo	3	F	1	0	1	0	5,200
Amelia E.	3	F	6	1	1	0	9,135
Amelia True Heart	2	F	5	1	0	1	6,963
Amell	2	F	5	1	1	0	9,210
Amen Brother	3	G	9	2	0	0	5,649
Amenable	3	C	2	1	0	0	20,770
Amere	6	G	11	0	1	1	3,968
Amerethreethousand	3	F	23	1	1	6	12,127
Ameri Brilliance	5	G	7	2	3	1	112,560
Ameri Dream	4	C	7	3	0	0	58,930
Ameri Holly	6	M	9	1	2	3	16,075
Ameri Lady	3	F	10	2	3	0	57,300
Ameri Princess	5	M	11	1	0	0	9,831
Ameribrill	4	G	9	2	3	0	34,340
America Alive	3	C	6	2	2	1	106,141
America America	3	F	10	1	1	1	104,410
America the Brave	4	G	5	1	2	0	12,790
America West	4	G	12	3	2	2	30,906
American All Star	4	G	10	2	0	3	62,740
American Amber	3	F	8	1	2	2	11,289
American Anthem	4	F	7	0	2	0	20,608
American Approval	3	G	3	0	1	0	2,600
American Avenger	3	F	1	0	0	0	0
American Baby	2	F	2	0	0	0	600
American Band	5	H	4	0	0	0	222
American Boundary	4	G	10	3	3	0	40,170
American Boy	4	C	15	1	0	2	7,594
American Bull	4	G	14	0	3	1	10,124
American Byline	3	G	15	0	2	2	30,043
American Candidate	3	G	10	1	0	1	5,941
American Car	9	G	19	1	3	1	12,645
American Cat	4	G	9	1	2	3	10,695
American Century	6	H	8	3	1	2	70,925
American Challenge	4	F	4	1	1	1	22,640
American Champion	3	G	11	2	1	5	10,553
American Charmer	6	G	2	0	0	0	490
American Cherokee	3	C	13	1	0	0	18,840
American Choice	3	G	5	0	1	3	3,560
American Class	7	H	8	0	2	1	7,606
American Colony	3	F	4	0	0	0	436
American Comedy	3	C	11	2	1	2	65,854
American Del Siglo	3	F	2	0	0	0	0
American Deputy	5	H	7	0	0	1	12,269
American Diamond	3	F	7	3	2	0	49,500
American Doc	3	F	2	0	0	0	2,255
American Dreams	3	F	5	1	0	0	6,775
American Fable	3	G	3	0	0	0	0
American Flame	5	M	14	0	1	2	7,078
American Forum	5	G	9	2	1	1	21,844
American Freedom	6	G	7	1	0	3	90,779
American Fury	4	C	9	1	4	0	99,730
American Grace	4	F	1	0	0	0	40
American Guy	4	G	12	4	3	1	31,998
American Hero	8	G	18	1	3	2	12,617
American Hooter	3	G	3	0	0	0	444
American Hope	3	G	12	2	1	1	17,287
American in Paris	7	M	3	0	1	0	6,484
American Ingot	4	F	14	1	3	1	9,674
American Jade	3	G	15	2	3	3	36,745
American Jet	3	G	2	0	0	0	0
American Jewel (NZ)	6	M	10	3	1	1	25,493
American Joe	2	C	5	0	1	1	7,540
American Liberty	4	C	6	2	2	0	76,640
American Link	3	C	19	3	4	2	71,854
American Llave	5	M	14	2	0	2	17,419
American Man	2	C	2	0	0	0	1,310
American Miner	3	G	5	0	0	0	2,235
American Miss	3	F	10	2	1	2	63,140
American Moud	3	F	10	1	0	1	9,516
American Moxie	4	G	18	2	1	3	14,476
American Mud	2	G	6	0	1	3	2,908
American Music	4	G	14	1	2	1	32,030
American Outlaw	4	G	1	0	0	0	70
American Pasha	3	F	4	0	0	0	486
American Pastime	6	G	8	0	0	1	6,674
American Pioneer	3	C	1	0	0	0	0
American Poet	2	G	7	1	1	2	5,284
American Power	3	G	15	1	5	1	20,160
American Pride	2	C	2	0	0	0	55
American Prince	6	G	9	1	2	2	28,630
American Profit	5	M	3	0	0	0	260
American Proud	4	G	13	4	5	1	125,080
American Quest	4	C	9	0	2	0	20,895
American Racer	3	G	6	1	1	0	49,686
American Red	4	C	1	1	0	0	5,940
American Resolve	4	G	7	1	0	1	3,366
American Ruler	2	G	4	2	0	0	13,145
American Saga	4	F	1	0	0	0	880
American Scene	3	G	10	1	0	1	14,465
American Secret	2	F	1	0	0	0	0
American Senorita	3	F	10	0	0	2	2,981
American Son	4	C	5	0	2	1	28,420
American Song	4	G	5	1	1	1	30,360
American Splendor	3	F	5	0	0	0	0
American Star	3	G	13	2	0	3	29,480
American Strike	5	M	5	0	1	0	2,943
American Style	5	H	8	0	2	0	30,545
American Sweets	3	F	2	0	0	0	0
American Thunder	3	G	11	0	3	1	33,037
American Toast	3	F	7	1	0	1	5,580
American Toga	3	G	12	2	2	1	26,920
American Token	3	G	14	2	0	1	30,044
American Up There	8	G	10	3	1	0	15,185
American View	2	F	2	0	0	0	2,370
American Vision	4	C	5	0	0	1	852
American Will	3	F	16	1	0	0	5,651
American Winner	4	G	8	1	0	1	3,137
American Writer	5	G	7	3	1	2	17,153
Americana Miss	3	F	5	0	0	0	420
Americani	2	G	3	0	0	0	1,575
Americanize	2	C	3	1	0	0	5,665
Americansweetheart	2	F	4	0	0	0	960
Americas Amazing	7	H	19	0	0	4	3,361
Americas Cat	3	F	9	0	3	3	35,120

Horse	Age	Sex	Sts	1st	2d	3d	Won
America's Dream	4	G	2	0	0	0	285
America's Gal	4	F	1	0	0	0	0
America's Girl	2	F	2	1	0	0	7,673
Americas Hope	3	G	8	1	0	2	9,285
Americas Pride	3	F	11	2	2	1	20,006
America's Punch	3	F	15	2	3	0	45,900
America's Roar	4	G	7	1	0	0	4,692
Americelebration	5	M	5	0	0	1	3,750
Amerifly	3	G	6	2	1	0	33,180
Amerika's Future	2	F	1	0	0	0	360
Ameriken Coin	3	G	11	2	1	4	37,148
Amerikiss	3	F	8	0	1	0	2,900
Amerinda	3	F	2	0	0	0	0
Amerindio (ARG)	7	H	2	1	1	0	44,400
Amerrico's Card	4	G	14	2	3	0	20,280
Amersham	7	G	1	0	0	0	0
Amescua	6	G	9	0	0	2	640
Amherst Wildcat	5	G	2	0	0	0	202
Ami Queeny	3	F	1	0	0	1	1,485
Amiable Amy	4	F	4	2	0	0	73,164
Amico and Paesano	3	C	1	0	0	0	0
Amidst Storm	4	F	12	3	0	2	18,392
Amien	4	F	7	1	1	2	22,700
Amiga	4	F	4	0	0	0	0
Amigo	3	G	3	0	0	0	4,893
Amigo Rojo	2	G	3	2	1	0	16,105
Amigos Hermano	3	C	7	1	1	1	2,350
Amir Elumara (PER)	5	G	1	0	0	0	0
Amiriya	2	F	1	0	0	0	0
Amjaad	6	H	1	0	0	0	0
Ammalu	4	F	2	0	1	0	7,380
Ammann	3	C	19	4	0	4	75,360
Amme Star	4	F	12	0	1	3	3,261
Ammo Bag	7	H	2	0	0	0	291
Ammodio	5	G	10	0	0	0	1,380
Ammoexcavate	4	F	4	0	2	0	7,862
Ammogator	3	G	1	0	0	0	0
Amo a Mi Papa'	4	F	8	1	1	0	9,095
Amo Ebaci	4	G	11	2	1	2	37,536
Amodeed	4	F	11	4	1	0	48,320
Amok	6	H	10	0	3	2	5,920
Amon	4	C	3	0	0	0	1,840
Among My Souvenirs	3	F	3	2	0	0	72,855
Among the Stars	3	G	8	0	2	1	5,909
Amongtheprivileged	5	M	12	4	2	0	80,080
Amorama (FR)	3	F	8	1	1	2	257,683
Amoramente	2	F	2	0	1	0	7,450
Amore Dulce	2	F	7	2	1	0	21,125
Amoreena	3	F	10	2	1	1	14,722
Amores Peregrinos	3	F	16	0	3	5	8,645
Amores Perros	2	C	1	0	0	0	330
Amorini	4	F	9	0	0	1	500
Amos's Savage	4	F	15	5	3	3	37,322
Amoureux	2	F	4	0	2	1	22,800
Amphorae	5	M	1	0	0	0	192
Amplitude	4	G	13	2	4	2	29,381
Amstel River	4	F	8	0	1	2	4,251
Amsterdam Ave	3	C	10	1	0	1	16,760
Amtodd	3	C	1	0	1	0	1,620
Amuffintogo	3	F	7	2	0	1	26,224
Amuse	3	G	8	0	0	2	2,115
Amusingly	4	F	11	2	0	0	39,454
Amy Ruckus	3	F	2	0	0	0	894
Amygotherway	4	F	3	0	0	0	318
Amy's Boy	2	G	4	0	1	2	24,567
Amy's Eclipse	3	F	3	0	0	0	992
Amy's Fourbidden	7	G	11	0	0	0	621
Amy's Hannah	4	F	9	1	0	1	10,215
Amys Love	3	G	1	0	0	0	125
Amy's Miss	3	F	1	0	0	0	0
Amy's Pearl	5	M	2	0	0	0	0
Amys Punch	5	G	1	0	0	0	0
Amy's Runaway	2	F	3	0	0	0	370
Amy's Three	7	M	1	0	0	0	95
Amzac	4	G	13	1	2	1	9,373
An American Idol	3	G	2	1	0	0	13,680
An Annika Moment	3	F	11	1	5	1	74,660
An Even Mark	2	C	1	0	0	0	173
An Grianan	3	G	1	0	0	0	0
An Naabi	8	G	8	1	2	2	5,165
An Open Account	2	C	1	0	0	0	0
An Oscar for Bert	7	G	15	3	2	3	57,560
Ana	7	M	7	0	0	0	472
Ana Babe	2	F	5	1	0	0	11,780
Anabatic	4	F	6	0	1	1	6,019
Anabeltaylor	4	F	9	1	1	3	47,918
Anacosta	4	F	2	0	1	0	2,210
Anacot Steal	2	G	5	1	1	1	15,920
Anaf	3	C	8	2	2	1	67,960
Analytically	3	G	6	0	0	0	930
Analyze	5	M	2	0	1	0	2,295
Analyze It	2	G	2	0	0	0	0
Anamericanbid	3	G	9	3	0	0	36,190
Anand	6	G	5	0	1	1	3,915
Ananda Paradisa	3	F	3	0	0	1	6,500
Anandalou Is Here	3	F	12	1	1	2	10,255
Anangelnameddawn	2	F	2	0	0	0	170
Anapest	3	F	6	1	0	0	20,520
Anariel	2	F	1	0	0	0	400
Ana's Lady Bird	3	F	2	0	0	1	6,640
Anasham	3	F	7	1	0	0	18,088
Anasheed	4	C	4	0	0	0	1,959
Anat	3	F	8	0	1	0	11,287
Anatolo's Last Hope	4	G	2	0	0	0	0
Anaturalbluff	5	G	6	2	1	0	16,218
Anbar	6	G	17	3	6	2	35,650
Ancestral Mine	2	C	9	0	1	2	6,560
Ancestry	4	F	9	2	1	0	36,520
Anchor Alert	5	G	3	0	0	1	1,490
Ancient Beauty	5	M	11	1	3	3	15,131
Ancient Boundary	2	F	2	0	0	1	950
Ancient City	7	G	12	2	2	4	13,845
Ancient Hill	4	G	5	0	1	1	3,646
Ancient Kite	3	F	3	0	1	1	4,808
Ancient Myth	3	C	5	1	2	0	27,360
Ancient Remedy	4	G	6	2	1	0	25,321
Ancient Ruins	4	G	7	1	1	3	7,920
Ancient Ruler	4	G	19	2	1	4	13,896
Ancient Traveler	7	G	4	1	0	3	1,380
Ancient Treasures	4	G	8	0	3	3	16,820
Ancient Ways	5	G	5	0	0	0	422
Ancram	2	F	2	0	0	0	2,255
And Herecumdejudge	5	G	8	1	1	1	1,600
And Heres to You	4	G	10	0	1	1	2,976
And I	6	G	7	4	0	0	46,064
And Nobody Knows	4	F	18	2	1	4	49,625
And One for Me	3	F	2	0	0	0	0
And So It Goes	3	G	11	2	2	2	29,142
And That's It	3	F	10	0	1	1	1,902
And Thats My Story	5	M	13	1	2	1	24,185
And the Eagle Flys	2	C	4	1	0	1	18,500
And What	3	G	4	1	0	1	10,340
Andalusian	2	C	2	0	0	0	3,762
Andanight	2	C	1	0	0	1	1,100
Andean Orchid	5	M	5	0	0	0	214
Andele	6	G	10	1	2	3	14,439
Andelegend	5	H	12	3	3	1	51,190
Andes Pride	6	M	3	0	0	0	0
Andial	6	G	1	1	0	0	9,000
Andiamo	3	G	7	3	1	0	65,460
Andimon	9	H	3	0	0	0	1,665
Andlikethathesgone	2	C	1	1	0	0	11,400
Andoras Attitude	3	F	15	1	1	6	13,558
Andover Boy	3	G	12	1	4	3	41,130
Andover Forest	4	C	2	0	0	0	410
Andover Lady	4	F	6	1	1	1	54,196
Andoverend	7	M	1	0	0	0	0
Andrea	3	F	1	0	0	0	190
Andrea Allstar	6	M	3	0	0	0	310
Andrea Jeanne	5	M	5	0	1	0	1,496
Andrea Star	6	M	9	0	3	0	5,183
Andreana Gail	3	F	12	0	1	0	1,490
Andrea's Angel	3	F	15	4	3	2	49,000
Andrea's Jet	4	F	14	1	2	2	6,089
Andrea's Mustang	4	G	13	1	1	3	6,036
Andrea's Wish	2	F	4	1	2	0	19,700
Andrew C.	4	G	7	1	2	0	4,728
Andrew J	4	C	11	1	1	0	4,705

Horse	Age	Sex	Sts	1st	2d	3d	Won
Andrew Now	3	G	8	0	0	1	1,212
Andrew the Man	7	G	11	2	0	2	20,942
Andrews Ace	5	H	2	0	0	0	0
Andrews Advantage	2	G	4	0	0	1	2,515
Andrews Joy	3	C	8	0	0	0	615
Andriana	3	F	4	1	0	0	28,003
Andromeda's Hero	2	C	2	1	0	1	17,300
Andro's (PER)	5	G	13	2	1	1	37,030
Andtheliviniseasy	2	F	2	0	0	0	700
Andwho'syourdaddy	2	F	3	0	0	0	0
Andy Can Run	3	G	6	1	0	1	3,901
Andy Man	3	G	9	1	1	1	11,696
Andy Nest	4	G	7	0	4	0	7,195
Andyardo	3	C	1	0	0	0	0
Andy's Gray Lady	4	F	7	2	3	1	12,318
Andy's Jet	9	G	15	1	3	1	7,807
Andy's Lilly	3	F	9	2	1	1	20,756
Andy'struleymissed	5	G	4	0	0	0	199
Anearlyfil	3	F	3	0	0	1	5,000
Aneat Amaani	3	F	4	0	1	0	2,370
Anefew	2	C	1	0	0	0	0
Anegada	3	F	8	2	2	2	72,845
Anel de Bamba (BRZ)	4	C	1	0	0	0	0
Anets Enuff	3	C	1	0	0	1	1,540
Anet's Moment	2	F	6	0	0	1	3,037
Angalexica	3	F	2	0	0	0	210
Angel Aglo	3	G	10	3	3	0	40,388
Angel Approval	5	G	4	0	0	0	865
Angel Baby	2	F	4	2	0	0	19,439
Angel Bayou	2	F	4	1	1	1	16,785
Angel Be Great	5	M	14	1	4	2	17,459
Angel by Day	4	G	19	2	3	2	14,422
Angel by Night	3	F	7	1	3	2	28,358
Angel Claire	4	F	2	0	0	0	0
Angel Connection	5	M	6	3	1	0	23,340
Angel D Tour	2	F	6	1	1	1	11,870
Angel Dancer	3	F	3	0	0	0	2,357
Angel Days	3	F	7	0	0	1	3,380
Angel Deelite	3	F	9	1	2	1	18,392
Angel for a Judge	4	F	5	1	0	0	2,900
Angel Gift	6	M	2	0	1	0	15,210
Angel I'm Not	4	F	8	0	0	0	664
Angel in Harlem	4	F	12	2	5	2	105,376
Angel in Seattle	2	G	2	0	0	0	894
Angel in Style	4	F	8	0	0	3	1,890
Angel in the Cloud	5	M	5	2	1	1	6,830
Angel in Tights	4	F	7	2	1	2	71,877
Angel Layne	4	F	5	0	0	0	800
Angel Luck	4	F	4	1	0	1	2,230
Angel of Goliad	4	F	11	1	2	1	7,103
Angel of Justice	4	G	9	1	0	1	6,413
Angel of Sharacco	7	M	3	0	0	1	486
Angel of War	3	F	2	1	0	0	6,920
Angel On the Wing	5	G	1	0	0	0	0
Angel On Track	4	F	5	0	0	0	1,240
Angel Punch	4	F	5	0	0	2	9,580
Angel Royale	3	F	7	0	0	1	1,562
Angel Saint Claire	6	M	1	0	0	0	0
Angel Shark	3	F	2	0	2	0	5,740
Angel Slipper	6	M	12	1	1	0	10,077
Angel Springs	6	G	3	1	0	0	4,875
Angel Tree	3	F	9	1	0	2	4,483
Angel Trumpet	2	F	8	3	3	1	146,456
Angel Wine	5	M	8	3	0	2	24,627
Angela Marjorie	2	F	3	1	0	1	9,880
Angela's Angel	2	F	7	0	2	0	5,669
Angelas Butterfly	5	M	9	1	0	1	3,430
Angela's Diary	6	M	16	3	5	1	19,748
Angela's Express	3	F	2	0	0	0	0
Angela's Love	4	F	9	3	0	2	224,795
Angela's Pride	3	F	9	1	1	3	30,440
Angela'stoughwater	5	G	1	0	0	0	0
Angelcatcher	3	F	3	1	0	0	7,305
Angelic	3	F	2	0	0	0	1,000
Angelic Aura	4	G	5	3	0	1	138,100
Angelic Gal	4	F	17	2	0	2	15,368
Angelic Halo	5	M	13	3	2	1	21,660
Angelic Hero	5	G	13	2	2	4	17,040
Angelic Hope	3	F	8	2	0	1	18,977
Angelic Jewel	5	M	10	1	2	0	36,997
Angelic Light	3	F	11	1	2	2	31,038
Angelic Look	2	F	1	0	0	0	540
Angelic Mood	4	G	7	0	0	1	809
Angelic Morgan L.	3	G	10	5	2	1	61,409
Angelic Star	3	F	4	0	0	0	435
Angelica Slew	3	F	8	4	2	2	92,820
Angelina J	3	F	9	0	2	0	19,196
Angelina Rose	4	F	3	0	0	1	1,119
Angelinas Nik	6	G	3	0	0	1	1,870
Angeline	6	M	1	1	0	0	6,000
Angeline W	4	F	5	0	0	0	0
Angelona's Girl	4	F	1	0	0	0	0
Angelo'sport	5	G	7	0	1	0	2,275
Angelrose	5	M	9	2	0	3	4,976
Angels and Saints	3	F	14	3	2	3	26,665
Angel's Bull	5	G	13	1	1	4	18,316
Angels Cut	5	M	3	0	0	1	362
Angel's Dowry	4	F	5	1	0	0	3,890
Angels Dream	8	M	17	0	1	2	4,152
Angel's Gone	3	G	8	0	0	2	1,930
Angel's Lovesong	4	G	2	0	0	0	275
Angels Playboy	8	G	3	0	0	0	0
Angels Ruse	8	G	9	2	1	1	10,155
Angel's Sing	7	M	8	1	0	1	3,486
Angel's Victor E	6	G	7	0	0	1	2,705
Angel's Wisdom	4	G	13	2	3	2	83,302
Angelswatchnoverme	3	C	6	1	2	0	9,965
Anger	3	G	10	2	2	3	37,670
Angie and Pam	3	F	9	2	1	0	16,357
Angies Emperor	3	G	3	0	0	0	408
Angies First Shot	4	G	10	1	1	0	4,349
Angie's Legacy	4	F	10	1	3	1	15,088
Angie's Marquee	2	F	1	0	0	0	968
Angie's Picture	6	H	1	0	0	0	0
Angie's Reason	6	G	8	0	0	0	1,486
Angies Storm Creek	4	F	12	3	2	3	33,871
Anglian Prince	5	G	9	0	0	1	19,407
Angliana	2	C	2	1	0	0	27,450
Angliana Dancer	4	F	10	2	2	2	40,610
Anglo Saxon	4	C	6	1	0	1	22,168
Angora	3	C	6	2	2	0	38,555
Angry Angel	2	F	5	1	1	0	9,400
Angryarguingalex	4	G	12	1	0	1	5,165
Anguished Thespian	5	H	3	0	0	0	117
Angus Halo	5	G	4	1	0	0	3,489
Angus Maximus	3	C	3	0	0	0	183
Angus Reef	3	F	4	1	0	0	2,080
Anh's Magic Prince	2	C	1	0	0	0	0
Anice's Finale	3	C	7	2	0	0	22,050
Anima Mundi (IRE)	5	M	10	0	3	1	22,403
Animperial Win	3	C	18	0	2	3	18,619
Anise's Wild Girl	2	F	4	0	1	1	3,603
Anissina	3	F	6	1	0	0	18,195
Anita Champ	2	G	2	0	0	0	255
Anita Cocktail	6	M	2	0	0	0	1,030
Anita Doreen	5	M	6	1	2	0	3,150
Anita Garibaldi	4	F	4	1	0	1	24,220
Anita K. B.	3	F	3	0	0	0	200
Anita Lynn	2	F	3	0	0	1	1,729
Anita Rocket	3	G	12	1	2	2	4,718
Anita Xanax	3	F	7	2	0	0	19,260
Anita's Charm	3	F	9	1	1	2	23,010
Anita's Golden Boy	3	G	18	2	3	2	20,775
Anita's Niner	4	F	5	0	0	0	288
Anita's Slew	5	M	9	1	0	1	7,970
Anja	4	F	6	1	1	0	14,934
Anja (IRE)	4	F	1	0	0	0	0
Anjiz Dream	7	M	2	0	0	0	81
Anjiz Prince	2	G	8	3	0	1	29,435
Anjiz's Prospect	8	G	15	1	0	1	9,399
Anjolie	3	F	1	0	1	0	7,280
Anjo's Legend	3	G	12	4	2	0	24,736
Ann Dear	4	F	2	0	0	0	342
Ann Frances	5	M	6	1	1	0	3,746
Ann Michelle	5	M	1	0	0	0	0
Ann Summers Two	3	F	5	1	1	1	36,980
Anna Allen	4	F	5	1	0	2	14,460
Anna Austin	3	F	3	0	0	0	0

Horse	Age	Sex	Sts	1st	2d	3d	Won
Anna Em	3	F	11	5	2	0	175,286
Anna Grabo	3	F	6	3	0	1	25,030
Anna K.	4	F	10	1	2	0	9,605
Anna Lee Anno	3	F	4	0	0	0	1,198
Anna Rose	3	F	19	0	1	5	16,725
Anna Vee	3	F	12	2	1	0	16,524
Annabarr	2	F	3	1	0	1	12,027
Annabelles Missile	2	F	1	0	0	0	112
Annabelle's Song	3	F	7	1	1	1	29,614
Annabelly	4	F	2	1	1	0	47,000
Annabel's Answer	5	M	4	0	0	0	1,613
Annacoco	3	F	9	0	2	1	6,855
Annamae'swillpower	5	H	9	0	0	1	1,715
Annapolis Sandy	3	F	4	0	0	0	0
Anna's Cat	4	F	10	2	0	0	16,670
Anna's Code	6	M	14	0	1	2	6,178
Anna's Good Heart	2	F	2	0	0	0	400
Anna's Hannah	4	F	6	1	1	0	6,000
Annas Love	3	F	3	0	0	0	372
Anna's Pro	4	F	5	1	3	0	15,765
Anna's Prospect	3	C	6	0	0	1	620
Annas Royal Prince	4	G	1	0	0	0	69
Annasterian	5	M	11	2	1	1	7,357
Annettos Prize	5	M	4	0	0	0	3,900
Annexcel	3	G	3	0	0	0	225
Anney's Trick	7	G	3	0	0	0	151
Annie B	2	F	3	1	1	0	9,462
Annie Bee Magic	3	F	4	0	0	0	225
Annie Fitch	4	F	16	2	4	3	52,137
Annie Flo	7	M	6	2	1	1	11,400
Annie Go	5	M	7	1	0	1	5,335
Annie Houston	3	F	5	0	0	1	4,220
Annie Lee	3	F	2	0	0	1	885
Annie Mans Dream	2	F	1	0	0	0	0
Annie N Me	4	F	8	1	1	0	7,418
Annie Oakleaf	2	F	2	1	0	1	1,584
Annie Pannie	4	F	4	0	0	0	0
Annie Pok	3	F	2	0	0	0	0
Annie Pokely	4	F	9	0	0	0	174
Annie Potcake	5	M	3	0	0	0	0
Annie Siren	3	F	2	0	0	0	35
Annie T	5	M	4	0	0	1	3,901
Annie Up	6	M	5	0	0	1	1,771
Annie's Award	2	F	5	1	1	1	13,950
Annie's Boot	2	C	4	0	0	1	2,245
Annie's Deelite	4	F	3	0	1	0	4,700
Annie's Honor	7	M	9	1	1	3	24,495
Annie's No Orphan	8	M	9	0	2	1	3,429
Annie's Pal	5	G	10	1	0	0	7,625
Annies Pistol	7	G	2	0	0	0	102
Annies Prospect	4	F	5	0	4	0	26,310
Annie's Runaway	4	F	16	2	1	3	21,905
Annies Shadow	6	M	1	0	0	0	840
Annie's Sister Ida	5	M	4	0	0	0	675
Annie's Tuff	3	F	1	1	0	0	5,580
Anniesatlanticgold	2	F	1	0	1	0	2,945
Annieville	2	F	2	1	0	0	7,150
Annika Belle	3	F	3	0	1	1	8,160
Annika Lass	3	F	6	3	1	0	63,176
Annika Rules	3	F	1	0	0	0	320
Anniversary Bonus	3	C	4	0	0	1	6,538
Anniversary Man	2	C	2	0	0	0	800
Anniversary Mint	2	G	5	0	0	1	1,925
Announce of Charm	3	F	13	2	1	5	18,075
Announce of Gold	3	G	3	0	0	2	3,325
Announcier	3	G	4	1	0	0	8,257
Ann's Emblem	6	M	17	5	3	3	39,918
Ann's Glory	5	G	5	1	0	0	4,354
Anns Got Rythym	2	F	2	0	0	0	165
Ann's Quality	3	F	5	0	0	1	3,258
Ann's Tax	2	F	1	0	0	0	110
Annslee	4	F	1	0	0	0	1,710
Annual Challenge	4	G	10	3	0	1	14,461
Annuit Coeptis	2	F	4	0	0	1	2,472
Anoiden Time	5	M	5	1	0	1	6,709
Anointed One	5	M	7	3	0	0	20,820
Anonymous	2	F	4	0	2	0	12,740
Another Alphabet	3	C	7	1	1	0	22,770
Another Altitude	6	M	3	0	1	0	649
Another Angelica	5	M	1	0	0	0	0
Another Angie	4	F	4	1	1	0	7,800
Another Award	2	C	1	0	0	0	45
Another Birdie	4	F	9	1	3	1	9,528
Another Brianna	3	F	17	2	1	1	24,280
Another Cafe	5	M	1	0	0	0	105
Another Career	5	M	4	0	2	2	7,780
Another Carson	3	G	7	0	0	0	2,130
Another Chaka	6	G	3	0	0	0	442
Another Chance	4	F	4	0	0	0	570
Another Chapter	4	F	10	1	3	0	27,320
Another Cyclone	2	G	1	0	0	0	0
Another Deputy	3	C	5	0	1	0	7,160
Another Devil	2	G	2	0	0	0	0
Another Diamond	2	G	4	1	0	1	9,000
Another Dilemma	2	C	7	2	2	0	38,690
Another Direct	2	F	3	2	1	0	27,900
Another Dream	5	H	3	0	0	0	316
Another Elusive	4	C	8	1	1	0	14,038
Another Fast Frog	2	C	1	0	0	0	140
Another Flavor	4	F	12	1	2	2	18,025
Another Freddy	3	C	9	1	1	0	20,389
Another Freebie	2	G	4	0	0	0	600
Another Gear	6	G	12	2	3	2	36,922
Another Gem	4	G	2	0	0	0	399
Another George	4	G	7	0	2	1	5,385
Another Hi	6	G	4	0	0	0	429
Another Ivory	6	M	1	0	0	0	891
Another Joy	2	F	6	0	0	0	1,102
Another Laugh	3	F	1	0	0	0	0
Another Lovelysong	3	F	9	2	1	1	20,501
Another Marcus	4	G	10	0	3	0	12,079
Another Mimi	3	F	7	1	0	3	4,661
Another Minstrel	4	G	3	0	0	0	0
Another Misty Morn	7	M	7	0	0	0	225
Another Monarch	2	C	1	0	0	0	2,150
Another Moochie	3	F	5	0	2	1	16,260
Another Moon	2	G	12	1	2	3	13,730
Another One	4	G	5	0	0	0	280
Another Pleasure	6	M	2	0	0	0	125
Another Quest	6	M	13	3	1	2	24,638
Another Red Wind	8	M	1	0	0	0	0
Another Rocket	4	G	11	1	0	1	8,605
Another Show	4	G	6	0	0	1	8,660
Another Sis	3	F	12	1	4	0	14,098
Another Story	3	C	7	2	1	1	6,590
Another Sunset	2	C	1	0	0	0	115
Another True Manor	3	F	4	0	0	0	478
Another Tsu Tsu	3	F	9	2	0	4	17,760
Another Variety	4	F	11	0	6	3	24,350
Another Whirl	5	H	2	0	0	0	175
Anotherbagman	5	G	6	2	0	0	3,500
Anotherbusride	2	F	3	0	1	0	4,901
Anothershotatfame	2	F	3	0	0	0	0
Anouncing Fresno	4	G	15	1	3	2	19,236
Ansar (IRE)	8	G	4	1	0	0	134,548
Ansky	7	G	5	0	2	1	5,650
Anstar (GB)	7	G	4	0	2	0	12,780
Answer Me Al	9	G	13	1	3	0	8,197
Answer On	2	G	7	0	0	0	1,870
Answer the Storm	4	F	12	3	2	1	34,575
Answer This	6	G	12	0	3	2	7,578
Answerback	6	M	5	0	1	1	2,011
Answertoeverything	5	H	3	0	0	0	309
Ant Cara	5	M	4	0	0	0	0
Antaeus (NZ)	6	G	3	0	0	0	1,040
Antartida (ARG)	6	M	5	1	0	2	25,504
Ante Mia	3	F	10	0	1	3	15,211
Ante Oaklee	4	F	15	1	1	2	17,811
Ante Up Eva	4	F	10	0	2	0	7,198
Ante Up Pete	3	G	2	1	0	0	8,100
Ante Up Red	2	F	2	0	0	0	181
Anthem Hill	5	G	12	2	3	1	18,994
Anthonia	4	F	12	1	3	2	75,928
Anthony B.	8	G	16	0	5	2	12,194
Anthony Eats	3	G	4	0	0	2	5,340
Anthony J.	2	R	5	1	1	1	213,630
Anthony Ruhls	5	G	10	1	3	1	12,275
Anthony Soprano	5	G	10	3	2	2	93,633

Horse	Age	Sex	Sts	1st	2d	3d	Won
Anthony's Gem	4	F	20	1	3	3	16,772
Anthony's Legacy	3	G	4	0	0	0	236
Anthony's Nockover	3	G	5	0	2	1	3,710
Anthony's Only Way	3	F	8	3	2	1	18,540
Anticipate Magic	6	G	13	3	2	0	9,786
Anties Boy	7	G	17	1	0	0	33,811
Antietam	5	H	7	0	0	1	2,192
Antifreezette	2	F	4	0	0	0	2,360
Antigravity	4	F	6	0	0	0	96
Anting Anting	4	C	5	3	0	2	4,920
Antique Crystal	3	F	10	2	1	0	19,074
Antique Dealer	2	C	2	0	0	1	2,625
Antique Freak	6	M	12	0	0	2	3,068
Antonio Francisco	2	G	4	0	0	0	1,762
Antonio Star	8	H	1	0	0	0	0
Antonio Stradivari (IRE)	2	C	5	0	0	1	2,675
Antonius Pius	3	C	9	0	1	2	460,158
Antranig	3	C	8	0	1	1	4,785
Antsy	4	G	10	0	2	1	17,172
Anuska	2	F	4	2	1	0	25,095
Anvil Dancer	4	F	14	1	1	4	6,161
Anwar	3	C	5	0	0	1	1,730
Anxious Alex	5	M	6	0	0	1	1,492
Anxiously Awaiting	2	C	2	0	0	0	2,500
Any Doodle Do	2	F	1	0	0	1	1,764
Any for Love (ARG)	6	M	6	3	0	1	120,747
Any Lie's Better	4	F	1	0	0	0	0
Any Old Disk	4	G	10	1	1	3	18,611
Any Old Port	3	F	9	1	2	1	38,262
Any One Wish	4	G	2	1	1	0	3,680
Any Questions	3	G	9	2	2	3	44,580
Any Reason	5	M	1	0	0	0	150
Any Way At All	5	H	5	0	0	2	12,936
Any Wonder	5	M	2	0	0	0	100
Anybuddee	5	M	5	0	0	0	0
Anyone Anywhere	3	F	10	1	1	1	5,282
Anyplace Anytime	4	F	15	2	2	1	58,090
Anything But That	2	C	9	1	1	0	23,791
Anything Gold	2	C	6	0	1	1	5,770
Anytime Eddie	4	G	7	0	2	2	6,344
Anywhere Anytime	6	M	5	2	2	1	6,880
Anza	4	G	14	0	2	3	16,287
Anzari (IRE)	7	G	4	0	1	0	15,700
Anziy Time	3	G	1	0	0	0	0
Anziyan Holiday	2	C	1	0	0	0	300
Anziyan Royalty	4	C	7	2	1	1	139,940
Ap to Be a Lady	3	F	12	0	2	2	3,719
Ap to Be Duff	5	G	2	0	1	0	325
Ap to Cash	11	G	10	0	0	2	926
Apache Babe	2	F	3	0	0	1	3,130
Apache Bee	4	F	10	0	2	1	5,989
Apache Brave	3	G	14	2	1	2	13,540
Apache Connection	3	G	7	1	1	0	5,509
Apache Corner	4	F	11	4	4	0	37,400
Apache Dance	4	G	11	0	0	2	4,124
Apache Dispatch	5	G	5	0	0	1	1,590
Apache Flyer	3	C	3	2	0	0	12,985
Apache General	2	G	1	0	1	0	1,800
Apache Gunship	2	C	3	0	0	3	9,530
Apache Lee	2	C	4	0	0	1	2,780
Apache Lord	3	C	4	0	1	1	7,535
Apache Point	2	C	1	1	0	0	15,600
Apache Surprise	4	G	10	2	3	2	65,605
Apache Thunder	5	G	2	0	0	0	150
Apache Tribe	4	G	6	2	0	1	11,645
Apache Wings	6	G	3	0	0	2	16,962
Apache's Belle	4	F	4	0	0	0	778
Apak	11	G	2	0	0	0	375
Apalachee Cola	3	C	2	0	1	0	16,016
Apalachee Island	7	G	3	0	1	0	1,573
Apalachee Prince	2	C	1	0	0	0	56
Apalachee Road	2	C	9	0	0	1	3,040
Apalachee Special	9	G	12	1	1	0	23,980
Apalachee Tiger	2	C	2	0	1	0	10,200
Apalachee's Native	7	G	16	2	3	1	28,480
Apalachian Thunder	4	C	3	1	1	0	37,970
Aparecida	3	F	3	0	1	0	13,250
Apartfromanna	3	F	6	0	0	0	424
Apassinglimerick	2	F	4	0	0	0	1,950
Apeak	9	G	4	1	0	0	1,382
Apenitas	3	G	12	1	1	1	14,451
Aperfectladydoctor	6	M	6	0	1	1	1,766
Apex Predator	7	H	4	0	0	0	680
Aphonic	4	G	13	3	1	1	32,038
Aphrodites	4	F	4	0	0	0	262
Aphrotheetee	2	F	2	0	0	0	1,032
Apian Way	9	G	3	0	0	0	264
Apico	8	G	4	0	1	0	460
Aplomado	11	G	6	0	0	0	348
Aplusnick	4	C	3	0	0	0	184
Apolla Eleven	3	F	2	0	0	0	196
Apollo Jack	3	G	12	1	3	2	13,605
Apollo Jones	2	C	6	1	1	1	44,240
Apollo King	3	G	12	1	3	1	43,932
Apollo Miss	2	F	2	0	0	0	0
Apollo Mission	2	C	1	1	0	0	11,100
Apollo Pirate	2	C	1	0	0	0	0
Apollo Treasure	5	M	18	2	7	4	29,028
Apollo Willfool'ya	6	M	10	2	2	3	39,360
Apollo Won	4	F	3	0	0	1	3,080
Apollon	5	G	3	0	1	1	2,520
Apollonea	4	F	7	2	1	0	20,993
Apollonesian	3	F	6	2	0	2	59,205
Apollonian	4	G	4	0	0	1	6,645
Apollo's Lady	2	F	2	0	0	0	131
Apollo's Magic	4	G	6	0	0	1	4,700
Apollo's Ray	4	F	7	1	3	1	5,240
Apollo's Rooks	3	G	23	3	4	4	43,438
Apollo's Valentine	8	G	9	2	1	0	5,100
Apolo Leah	2	G	2	1	0	1	1,991
Apologize	4	F	3	0	0	1	250
Apology Accepted	2	F	4	1	0	1	13,760
Apoptotic	2	G	4	0	2	0	5,100
Apostrophe Pete	3	C	2	0	1	0	4,250
App App	3	G	3	0	0	1	2,017
Appalachee Bay	2	F	2	0	0	1	6,270
Appas Tappas	4	G	5	0	1	2	23,618
Appawling	10	G	1	0	0	0	0
Appeal	7	H	3	0	0	1	1,045
Appeal Denied	3	F	1	0	0	0	400
Appeal to Heaven	2	F	2	1	0	0	3,660
Appealing Air	2	C	1	0	0	0	0
Appealing Borders	2	F	2	0	1	0	2,960
Appealing Bride	2	F	3	2	0	1	19,035
Appealing Class	3	F	3	1	0	0	8,545
Appealing Future	3	G	7	1	3	1	16,684
Appealing Grades	4	G	14	0	0	2	5,402
Appealing Greeley	5	M	8	1	2	2	10,500
Appealing Janeen	3	F	11	0	1	0	1,079
Appealing Jet	6	M	6	1	0	0	9,600
Appealing Lauren	4	F	9	1	1	2	19,734
Appealing Liaison	3	C	10	0	2	1	17,403
Appealing Okie	2	F	3	1	0	0	12,000
Appealing Pinky	4	F	1	0	0	0	0
Appealing Pond	3	F	8	2	2	1	46,340
Appealing Promise	7	G	10	1	4	1	2,705
Appealing Reality	4	G	10	2	0	1	8,733
Appealing Ruckus	3	F	5	1	1	0	9,005
Appealing Saint	2	G	3	0	0	0	5,280
Appealing Secret	3	C	12	2	2	2	27,391
Appealing Space	4	F	3	2	0	0	10,671
Appealing Wayz	4	G	1	0	0	0	0
Appealing Wolf	4	G	13	1	2	0	7,610
Appealingfire	3	F	15	3	1	1	26,485
Appealingly Bold	7	M	2	0	1	0	2,583
Appelative	3	F	7	1	1	0	14,140
Append	4	F	1	0	0	0	0
Apple Appeal	4	F	9	1	0	0	3,906
Apple Bloome (HUN)	6	M	3	0	0	0	870
Apple Butter Annie	5	M	4	0	0	1	1,434
Apple Cart	4	G	8	2	3	1	57,600
Apple Creek	3	F	1	0	0	0	320
Apple Deelish	2	F	5	0	0	0	850
Apple Juice Tea	4	F	8	0	2	2	34,400
Apple Krisp	3	C	6	1	2	1	36,763
Apple o' Dale	5	H	3	0	0	0	3,620
Apple Queen	4	F	1	0	0	0	42
Apple Rose	3	F	10	0	0	0	2,100

Horse	Age	Sex	Sts	1st	2d	3d	Won
Apple Waites	2	C	2	0	1	0	2,300
Appleby Gardens	4	F	4	0	0	1	18,155
Applejackie	3	F	9	0	1	0	1,715
Apple's Delight	6	M	16	3	2	2	18,247
Apples Hoss	6	M	6	0	0	2	3,000
Appleton (MEX)	6	G	14	4	4	0	29,405
Appleturnover Mike	7	G	4	0	1	0	2,300
Appoint Victory	2	C	2	0	1	0	5,600
Appointed	5	G	2	0	0	0	840
Apprentice	2	C	2	1	0	1	32,100
Appro	4	F	8	2	1	3	31,960
Approach	6	G	14	0	1	1	2,425
Approach (GB)	4	F	1	1	0	0	21,600
Approval Pending	5	M	9	0	1	2	7,945
Approximate Odds	5	G	3	0	0	0	630
Appygolucky	7	G	14	2	3	2	10,299
Apres Minuit	6	M	8	4	1	1	32,189
Apricot Wine	3	F	7	0	0	0	372
April Afternoon	4	F	11	4	0	1	24,810
April Baby	6	G	10	1	2	1	28,225
April Bay	3	F	10	2	1	2	21,590
April Blues	5	G	15	1	2	3	13,536
April Brown	3	F	4	0	1	0	1,300
April Cap	3	C	1	0	0	0	75
April Castelli	4	F	8	2	0	2	19,300
April Deer	3	F	16	0	2	1	6,430
April Eyes	4	F	12	3	3	3	74,101
April Fool Girl	9	M	7	0	1	0	1,240
April Foolish	4	F	9	3	2	1	59,253
April in Texas	3	F	4	0	0	0	660
April Morning	7	M	11	0	1	3	6,490
April Neige	2	F	4	0	0	0	950
April On Time	4	F	6	1	2	0	10,314
April Serenade	3	F	12	1	2	1	10,684
April Seven	5	M	10	0	0	2	2,194
April Spirit	2	F	3	0	0	0	252
April Spring	2	F	2	0	0	0	184
April Springs	3	F	7	1	1	2	7,479
April Steel (FR)	6	G	7	0	1	1	5,060
April Sunshine	7	G	3	0	0	0	222
April Talent	5	M	7	0	2	1	4,960
April Trick	3	F	11	1	0	0	8,190
April Trust	4	F	5	0	0	0	3,069
April's Bluff	3	F	7	0	1	1	9,500
April's Here	2	F	3	0	0	0	0
April's Lucky Boy	5	G	10	1	3	2	43,520
April's Miss Thing	3	F	5	0	0	0	409
April's Prince	3	G	14	4	1	5	44,625
April's Project	7	G	4	0	0	0	166
April's Shawklit	2	G	3	0	0	0	2,750
April's Summer	3	F	2	0	0	0	0
April's Whirlwind	3	F	4	0	2	1	6,440
Aprizedslew	7	G	2	0	0	0	312
Apsara	2	F	1	0	0	0	700
Apt	3	F	1	0	0	0	2,250
Apt to Be	7	G	6	1	3	0	67,475
Apt to Please	4	F	7	1	0	0	6,174
Aptlyput	4	C	4	0	0	0	360
Apto Fire	3	G	10	1	0	3	10,338
Aqua Kitty	4	F	4	0	0	0	164
Aqua Pierra	2	F	1	0	0	0	0
Aquaduck	5	M	7	2	2	3	20,255
Aquaduct Charlie	5	G	3	0	0	0	0
Aquamarine	2	F	1	0	0	0	2,580
Aquarian Girl	3	F	4	1	0	0	5,155
Aqueentium	3	C	6	0	0	0	1,900
Aquiess	4	G	13	1	1	4	28,926
Aquina's Rose	4	F	8	0	0	1	1,995
Aquitted	5	G	3	0	0	0	150
Arab Angel	3	G	7	0	0	0	1,969
Arab Bride	3	F	8	3	1	1	43,610
Arab Influence	3	F	7	0	2	0	3,495
Arab Miss	4	F	9	2	1	1	44,800
Arab Verse	3	F	4	0	0	0	780
Arab Warning	7	G	11	1	0	1	5,067
Arabian Gem	2	F	4	1	0	0	6,505
Arabian Navy	4	G	8	0	0	1	2,024
Arabian Nights	3	F	2	1	0	0	8,400
Arabic Song (IRE)	5	M	3	0	0	1	28,125
Arabica's Boy	7	G	9	0	0	1	1,328
Aragone's	4	G	7	0	2	1	9,280
Arama Gold	5	G	2	0	0	0	420
Aran Island	10	G	8	3	1	1	8,359
Aran Narayan	5	G	11	2	1	2	10,290
Arana Capulina	2	F	1	0	0	0	400
Aranjuez Amor	7	G	2	0	0	0	445
Aranmore	5	G	14	0	2	0	2,872
Aran's Lad	5	G	2	0	1	0	3,150
Arbiter	7	G	14	1	2	3	55,480
Arbitrageuse	3	F	9	0	2	0	7,724
Arbitrary Andrew	5	G	18	1	0	2	7,682
Arbitrate	4	C	12	2	3	0	67,285
Arbitration	3	G	2	0	0	0	150
Arbor Day	7	G	3	0	1	0	1,426
Arborway Dream	2	F	1	0	0	0	225
Arbroath	5	G	3	1	0	0	4,845
Arbun (IRE)	4	F	4	0	1	0	7,700
Arcadia Light	5	G	7	0	1	1	4,400
Arcana	3	F	12	3	1	1	25,010
Arcatec	3	G	8	2	1	1	23,104
Arch Ability	4	F	6	1	0	0	14,340
Arch Angel Gabriel	5	G	5	0	0	0	669
Arch Hall	3	C	8	3	2	1	187,342
Arch Lady	4	F	10	4	2	2	68,570
Arch Madness	2	C	5	0	0	0	2,275
Arch Stanton	2	G	7	1	0	1	26,315
Archabella	3	F	6	0	0	1	3,488
Archer County	9	G	5	0	0	0	0
Archer Fleet	3	C	7	1	1	2	62,392
Archers Bow	3	C	9	3	1	2	198,145
Archers Buckfinder	3	F	6	0	0	0	1,758
Archers Dolly	3	F	9	1	0	0	50,532
Archers Dream	3	F	6	2	0	1	68,736
Archer's Dreamer	2	F	4	1	0	1	44,813
Archers Gal	6	M	3	0	0	0	1,410
Archers Image	2	F	1	0	0	0	0
Archeval	4	G	13	5	2	2	131,720
Archie B	3	C	6	0	0	1	12,125
Archie Chinook	5	G	9	0	0	1	832
Archiehitthegold	3	G	6	0	0	0	0
Archie's Dream	3	G	13	0	0	3	12,100
Archie's Gal	2	F	5	1	1	0	77,489
Archimedes	4	G	12	2	3	0	20,570
Architecture	4	G	14	3	4	3	29,175
Archivist	3	F	2	0	0	0	100
Archmon	3	C	7	1	0	0	3,660
Archness	3	G	11	1	4	1	37,660
Archos	3	G	6	1	0	1	15,510
Archy	6	H	13	0	0	4	9,484
Arco Iris	3	F	7	4	0	0	45,421
Arcola Lane	5	H	5	1	1	0	7,196
Arcola Playboy	5	G	8	1	0	0	6,640
Arctic Annie	3	F	10	1	2	3	19,156
Arctic Catcher	3	F	10	1	1	2	8,002
Arctic Dove	4	F	5	0	0	2	4,740
Arctic Eyre	2	C	1	0	0	0	0
Arctic Heat B B	4	G	6	0	0	0	724
Arctic Horizon	8	G	7	0	3	3	7,320
Arctic Irish	3	G	7	1	0	0	3,188
Arctic Lightning	6	H	6	1	1	0	2,168
Arctic Mint	3	F	2	1	0	0	8,400
Arctic Prize	9	G	8	1	0	1	2,068
Arctic Prospector	3	C	1	0	0	0	0
Arctic Quiet	2	F	3	0	0	1	4,635
Arctic River	7	G	9	0	3	0	13,345
Arctic Roar	4	G	18	0	6	5	17,428
Arctic Rumble	4	C	12	2	2	4	46,680
Arctic Sand	5	G	15	1	2	4	15,275
Arctic Sea	4	F	1	0	0	0	0
Arctic Sleigh	5	H	6	2	0	3	17,879
Arctic Sweep	9	G	13	2	2	1	14,643
Arctic Taliyah	2	F	2	0	1	0	2,000
Arctic Tap	3	G	4	0	0	1	5,500
Arctic Trail	5	M	2	1	0	0	9,660
Arctic Voyageur	3	G	4	0	0	0	0
Arctic Warning	4	G	3	0	0	0	0
Arctic Warrior	2	C	5	1	1	1	17,800
Arcturus	2	C	4	2	0	1	64,600

Horse	Age	Sex	Sts	1st	2d	3d	Won
Arcus	3	G	8	1	0	1	58,750
Ardennes	4	F	9	1	1	1	13,872
Ardent Admirer	4	G	3	0	0	0	0
Ardent Eddy	4	G	12	0	3	4	34,191
Ardent Sister	3	F	10	1	0	1	35,284
Ardmayle	3	G	9	0	0	1	5,117
Ardsley	4	G	15	2	2	1	15,450
Ardum Relaunch	5	M	5	1	0	0	40,660
Ardum Rose	3	F	8	0	2	1	11,908
Are N Are	2	G	2	0	0	1	1,148
Are We Rich	6	M	1	0	0	0	0
Are You Blue	6	G	4	1	0	1	8,425
Are You Dale	3	G	1	0	0	0	77
Are You Down	5	G	7	0	2	1	16,760
Are You Home	4	F	10	0	2	2	26,940
Are You Irish	4	F	2	1	0	0	9,831
Are You Lookn	4	G	2	0	1	0	4,580
Are You Saved	4	G	13	2	1	1	9,211
Are You Serious	2	G	2	0	0	1	6,270
Are You There	3	F	14	3	5	1	48,380
Area Code	2	C	4	0	1	0	11,739
Area Limits	2	C	3	0	0	1	35,000
Areallyniceguy	7	G	11	3	1	1	4,698
Areasonforfreedom	5	H	3	0	0	0	900
Areek	3	F	9	2	2	1	71,080
Arel	3	G	4	0	0	0	314
Areyouamused	4	C	7	2	0	1	12,070
Areyoukidding Me	6	G	2	0	0	0	130
Areyoutalkintome	3	G	11	4	5	1	268,352
Arezzo	3	C	1	0	0	0	0
Argent Francais (FR)	4	F	3	0	0	0	1,692
Argentine Dancer	3	G	5	0	0	1	922
Argentinisima (ARG)	5	M	10	0	2	4	45,520
Argento	2	C	2	0	0	0	258
Argentum	5	M	1	0	0	0	0
Argosy North	6	G	11	1	3	0	5,238
Argufy	3	G	4	0	0	0	423
Arguing Aggie	3	F	4	0	0	0	0
Argyl Rose	4	F	6	4	1	1	11,320
Arianna's Song	7	M	13	1	2	0	11,628
Arianne	4	F	21	1	2	1	4,629
Aria's Diva	7	M	3	0	1	0	2,668
Arielle Crown	3	G	8	0	1	1	19,750
Ariel's Melody	5	M	8	0	2	0	29,908
Aries Rising	2	G	4	0	0	2	6,450
Ariesdotcom	6	G	18	1	2	0	13,166
Arikara	4	F	1	0	0	0	1,764
Arion Sands	3	G	14	1	4	3	12,458
Arion's Creek	6	M	6	1	0	0	8,850
Arions Gal	5	M	2	0	0	0	107
Arisen Angel	4	F	1	0	0	0	330
Arisin Horizon	3	C	2	0	0	0	164
Aristide the Great	5	G	1	0	0	0	0
Aristocat	4	C	2	0	0	1	4,680
Aristocat O'Malley	2	G	4	0	1	1	7,509
Aristocracy	3	G	7	0	0	0	1,250
Aristocrat	2	C	1	0	0	0	2,250
Aristocrat Cat	3	G	12	1	1	3	13,291
Aristoi	3	G	10	2	0	2	18,065
Aritelli	7	G	4	0	0	0	465
Arizona Academy	3	G	6	2	2	0	23,600
Arizona Bay Cat	4	G	16	1	1	3	8,857
Arizona Creek	5	M	6	1	2	1	5,267
Arizona Express	5	G	6	1	2	1	2,714
Arizona Gold	9	G	8	0	0	1	852
Arizona Lightning	5	M	1	1	0	0	2,880
Arizona Nocturne	3	F	10	3	2	0	15,246
Arizona Rose	2	F	7	1	2	0	44,410
Arizona Sky	3	G	12	4	2	1	31,470
Arizona Slew	5	M	6	0	0	0	245
Arizona Superstar	7	G	12	0	3	3	13,725
Arjay's Flag	4	C	8	0	1	1	5,166
Arjumad	4	F	4	1	1	1	5,780
Ark Mo	6	H	4	1	0	1	3,257
Arkansas Dee Lite	2	F	3	0	0	0	264
Arkansas Swinger	3	F	7	0	1	0	960
Arkansasprospector	3	G	10	1	3	1	13,505
Arkie's Nozetta	4	F	10	0	1	1	4,100
Arkoudi	3	F	16	0	3	5	33,810
Arky Holler	9	G	5	0	1	0	3,080
Arlean's Pirate	3	F	6	0	0	1	852
Arlene's Wildevent	2	F	4	2	0	0	40,840
Arlie Carlie	5	G	2	0	0	0	135
Arlington Hall	3	G	7	1	1	1	13,235
Arlington Pond	3	F	8	2	0	1	8,440
Arlo	8	G	1	0	0	0	0
Arma Springs	3	G	9	2	1	1	10,097
Armada Missy	5	M	6	0	0	2	800
Arman	5	G	2	0	0	0	1,260
Armed Angel	2	F	1	0	0	0	0
Armed 'n Crafty	6	G	10	2	1	1	11,688
Armedwith Patience	7	M	3	0	0	1	847
Armenian Summer	2	C	1	0	0	0	700
Arminto	3	G	2	0	0	0	374
Arms in Action	3	G	4	0	0	0	624
Arms Wide Open	5	G	7	1	1	1	9,450
Armsofanangel	6	M	7	0	0	1	4,355
Army Blue	2	C	6	1	1	0	21,538
Army Boots	3	C	3	0	0	0	540
Army Cat	5	H	4	1	1	0	9,645
Army Discharge	3	F	8	3	1	1	41,168
Army Games	4	F	9	1	1	2	4,922
Army General	5	G	6	1	1	1	5,279
Army Hero	4	G	19	6	2	3	40,162
Army Man	4	G	9	2	2	0	12,900
Arnchew Gorgeous	5	M	8	1	1	1	7,265
Arnie	3	C	1	0	0	0	0
Arnie Starlet	8	G	3	0	0	0	0
Arnold's Candle	6	G	12	0	2	0	6,745
Aroarable	3	F	4	1	0	1	20,730
Arogos	5	G	4	0	0	0	243
Around the Cape	2	C	2	0	1	1	8,400
Arpeggio	9	M	1	0	0	0	106
Arpent	4	C	16	3	2	2	28,247
Arrabell Rose	4	F	3	1	0	0	18,125
Arrangement	4	F	8	3	2	0	25,560
Arrest Me Red	5	M	10	1	0	1	2,737
Arrestare	7	G	2	0	0	0	750
Arrive	3	G	8	0	0	0	225
Arrogance	4	F	11	5	3	0	115,506
Arrow Angel (NZ)	7	M	2	0	0	0	654
Arroway	2	G	2	0	0	1	1,540
Arrowhead Cruiser	3	C	1	0	0	0	0
Arroyo Bay	5	M	4	0	1	1	1,000
Arsen	5	G	7	1	2	2	63,680
Arsen Annie	4	F	11	1	5	1	87,656
Art Fair	5	M	4	0	1	2	7,764
Art Fan	3	F	7	1	1	1	147,105
Art Form	4	F	4	1	0	0	10,940
Art Major	2	G	2	0	0	1	4,080
Art N Guile	3	F	1	0	0	0	750
Art of War	5	H	13	1	2	2	13,711
Art to Rain	9	G	10	2	2	2	14,245
Art Variety (BRZ)	6	H	8	2	0	2	89,761
Artabee	4	G	11	0	0	0	2,609
Artabegood	2	F	7	1	3	0	27,760
Artax Dancer	3	F	10	2	0	0	54,000
Artax Too	5	H	1	0	0	0	0
Artaxes At Work	3	C	1	0	0	0	300
Artech	3	C	4	2	1	0	32,975
Artema's Style	2	C	1	0	0	0	0
Artemio	8	G	5	0	0	0	1,000
Artemus Eagle	4	G	5	0	0	1	1,820
Artemus Paperboy	3	C	6	0	1	1	17,784
Artemus Sunrise	3	C	12	4	3	0	124,620
Artesia	3	F	2	0	0	0	210
Artesian	3	C	1	1	0	0	9,420
Arteur	3	C	3	1	0	1	26,870
Artful Act	3	G	7	0	0	0	1,531
Artful Way	4	G	7	1	0	0	3,762
Arthel	4	F	13	3	5	1	36,665
Arthrojet	2	C	3	0	0	0	770
Arthur	6	G	4	0	0	0	650
Arthur Roy	7	G	13	3	2	0	16,160
Arthuron	4	C	3	0	0	0	700
Arthur's Dream	6	G	3	0	1	0	3,540
Arthur's Ring	4	C	1	0	0	1	1,000
Artic Art (BRZ)	5	G	1	0	0	0	400

Horse	Age	Sex	Sts	1st	2d	3d	Won
Artic Blast	5	G	1	0	0	0	130
Artic Dream	3	G	7	0	2	2	29,866
Artic Fox	5	M	12	2	4	1	6,838
Artic Gamble	4	G	12	3	2	0	17,214
Artic Ghost	3	F	6	1	0	3	11,265
Artic Ice	5	G	11	1	0	1	14,864
Artic Jazz	3	F	11	2	2	1	15,938
Artic Kiss	3	F	3	0	1	1	6,500
Artic Sonnet	6	M	9	1	1	3	13,362
Artic Squire	8	G	4	0	0	0	2,676
Artic Stage	4	G	11	2	2	3	7,583
Artie Schiller	3	C	8	5	1	0	467,578
Artie Takes Two	3	G	8	0	0	0	1,240
Artien	3	C	2	0	1	0	1,412
Arties Lady	7	M	6	3	1	1	31,364
Artillery Man	4	C	9	2	0	1	42,240
Artist Johanna (ARG)	6	M	8	0	1	0	20,380
Artistic Concerto	2	C	5	0	0	0	1,010
Artistic Design	5	G	10	0	2	4	9,727
Artistic Dreamer	4	F	13	1	2	2	9,828
Artistic License	6	G	5	1	0	0	7,574
Artist's Meeting	4	G	8	2	1	0	13,873
Artist's Studio	4	F	4	0	0	0	3,180
Artoo Run	5	M	13	0	3	2	2,705
Arts	5	M	6	0	1	0	1,680
Art's Prospect	3	G	12	1	3	4	17,349
Art'scooking	4	G	2	0	0	0	434
Artsy	3	F	2	0	0	0	260
Arturo	4	C	3	1	0	1	26,740
Artwork	6	G	9	1	1	1	15,380
Arty	3	G	7	0	0	1	3,770
Arunjs Spring Slew	3	G	1	0	0	0	0
Arvada (GB)	4	F	7	3	2	1	251,700
Arvalany	5	M	11	0	0	0	1,366
Arvilla Priscilla	3	F	10	0	2	4	33,710
Arwa	3	F	4	1	0	0	16,630
Arwen's Fate	2	F	2	0	0	0	640
As Advertised	3	C	1	0	0	0	0
As Always Mimi	2	F	2	0	0	0	0
A's an B's	6	G	12	4	0	1	14,027
A's Anchorman	5	G	10	1	2	1	10,435
A's Chilla Lilla	5	M	3	0	0	0	75
As de Oro	9	H	2	2	0	0	7,530
As Devils Fury	2	F	1	0	0	0	0
As Expected	5	G	10	2	2	0	104,526
As If I Care	7	G	5	0	0	0	696
As the Crow Flies	3	G	7	0	0	0	596
As We Play	4	F	3	0	0	1	2,062
As Wicked	6	G	12	0	1	3	15,315
As You Like It	3	G	1	0	0	0	400
Asa Diamonds	5	G	12	3	3	2	11,740
Asa Un Fuegos	5	H	3	0	0	1	770
Asailortorember	4	G	9	2	1	0	37,250
Asaja	3	F	11	0	0	0	3,469
Asari	2	F	6	0	4	1	15,659
Asbury Lane	5	G	14	2	0	5	19,719
Ascertain (IRE)	3	G	7	2	1	0	101,079
Ascertain Groom	6	G	10	1	1	0	4,407
Asclepius	3	G	8	2	0	2	12,721
Ascorbicus	3	G	9	0	0	0	3,525
Ascot Devil	3	G	1	0	0	0	0
Ascot Doll	10	G	9	1	0	0	5,810
Ascot Gavotte	2	F	2	0	0	0	0
Ascot Girl	3	F	14	1	1	0	12,470
Ascot in the Gate	3	F	12	2	1	2	38,607
Ascot Sparkle	4	F	10	2	2	2	101,006
Ascribe	3	C	5	0	1	0	2,671
Asesina	2	F	1	0	0	0	400
Asfastasshecannow	3	F	4	0	1	0	6,600
Asgoodas	3	F	5	0	0	0	0
Ash Grove	4	G	15	2	2	1	11,591
Ash the Flash	5	M	3	0	0	0	137
Ashado	3	F	8	5	2	1	2,259,640
Ashagio	6	G	16	2	3	0	68,727
Ashar	9	G	5	0	0	0	3,725
Ashary (GER)	4	F	2	0	0	0	400
Ashby Hill	2	C	2	0	0	1	3,064
Ashdown's Dream	6	M	5	0	0	1	731
Ashe Ole'	4	G	12	3	3	1	30,121

Horse	Age	Sex	Sts	1st	2d	3d	Won
Ashes of Angels	3	F	2	0	0	2	1,380
Ashford Seven	5	G	13	1	6	4	12,946
Ashlar	4	F	11	3	3	1	23,248
Ashlee's Bella	3	F	8	1	3	2	102,770
Ashleigh Riehl	3	G	5	0	0	0	825
Ashley and I	2	F	5	2	2	0	27,348
Ashley Brook	5	G	3	0	0	0	0
Ashley County	3	F	5	1	0	0	8,220
Ashley Kate	6	M	7	1	1	2	3,637
Ashley 'n Robert	3	F	1	0	0	0	495
Ashley Williams	3	F	6	0	1	1	3,880
Ashleys Account	3	F	1	0	0	1	1,500
Ashley's Affair	5	M	12	4	0	1	30,444
Ashleys Art	3	F	11	1	4	0	38,870
Ashleys Attitude	5	M	11	3	6	1	10,458
Ashleys Bon Bon	3	F	8	4	0	0	9,350
Ashley's Clan	4	F	4	1	0	1	8,320
Ashley's Fear	3	F	2	0	0	0	0
Ashley's Joy	5	M	7	0	0	2	2,810
Ashley's Luck	4	F	12	1	2	2	10,898
Ashleys' Pride	6	M	2	0	0	0	86
Ashley's Response	3	G	7	1	0	0	5,575
Ashleys Sparkle	3	F	6	1	1	2	8,855
Ashley's Summer	6	G	1	0	0	0	550
Ashley'sbabyboy	3	G	3	0	0	0	0
Ashley'ssummergold	4	F	5	0	1	0	2,000
Ashmont	3	G	5	0	0	0	1,191
Ashoka	4	C	2	1	0	0	31,200
Ashore Play	2	F	5	1	2	1	27,960
Ashtons Dreams	4	G	9	4	2	0	21,655
Ashwin	2	F	2	0	0	0	630
Ashwood C C	6	M	8	1	3	2	58,656
Asian Knight	3	G	1	0	0	0	119
Asian Native	5	M	14	3	2	0	14,238
Asian Son	4	G	9	2	0	1	13,026
Asia's Class	4	F	2	0	0	0	0
Asiceit	5	G	11	1	1	0	10,149
Ask Abby	3	F	7	2	1	1	16,415
Ask Alie to Dance	2	G	6	0	0	1	8,030
Ask Dorothy	5	M	1	0	0	0	825
Ask Dr. Dave	3	G	6	1	0	0	5,369
Ask for Ashley	3	F	8	0	0	1	1,254
Ask for the Bucks	4	G	6	0	0	0	613
Ask Linda	4	F	12	0	0	1	4,341
Ask Molly	2	F	6	0	1	1	9,525
Ask Nancy	6	G	1	0	0	0	46
Ask Nicely	2	F	8	1	1	0	21,113
Ask Not	5	M	11	2	3	2	72,980
Ask Queenie	3	F	8	2	3	3	75,600
Ask Sidney	3	C	3	0	0	0	210
Ask Skip's Tigress	7	M	11	0	1	1	774
Ask Stitches	2	C	2	0	0	0	0
Ask the Lord	7	G	13	4	2	1	192,030
Aska Ba Ba	6	G	7	0	0	3	3,194
Askforaraise	4	F	6	1	0	3	57,940
Askham	6	H	4	0	1	0	7,860
Askim (NZ)	8	G	2	1	0	0	17,000
Asking for Luck	10	G	6	0	0	2	2,931
Asmokeafterdinner	4	F	14	1	1	2	21,484
Asong for Billy	5	G	4	1	0	0	28,000
Asp	4	C	4	0	1	0	1,993
Aspen Creek	2	F	5	0	1	0	2,370
Aspen Dancer	4	F	2	0	0	0	50
Aspen Edge	2	G	4	0	1	1	14,468
Aspen Falls	3	F	2	1	0	0	4,045
Aspen Flower	5	M	11	3	4	1	95,270
Aspen Gal	3	F	5	1	1	1	75,096
Aspen Hill	5	M	6	2	1	0	43,200
Aspen Leaf	3	F	8	1	2	0	6,523
Aspen Moon	3	G	11	1	4	3	31,495
Aspen Ridge	5	H	10	1	3	1	19,927
Aspen Slopes	9	H	2	0	0	0	600
Aspen Tree	2	F	3	1	2	0	47,061
Aspirin	6	G	6	2	0	2	13,007
Aspiring Gold	2	F	6	1	1	0	16,825
Aspiring Gulch	3	F	1	0	0	0	0
Asplashtoremember	2	F	3	0	0	1	945
Aspurr Luck	3	G	2	0	0	0	410
Assaggini	5	M	11	7	1	1	83,975

Horse	Age	Sex	Sts	1st	2d	3d	Won
Assault Commander	3	C	11	1	0	0	15,960
Assault Storm	3	G	2	1	0	0	7,980
Assaulting Ride (BRZ)	9	G	17	3	0	2	15,347
Assembly	8	H	1	0	0	0	0
Assemblyman	2	C	4	1	0	1	15,530
Assert N Advantage	4	G	8	1	2	1	31,240
Asserted	4	C	11	1	1	0	9,459
Assertive One	4	F	5	0	1	0	1,095
Assertive Stuff	3	G	13	3	4	2	67,574
Assertive Winner	6	M	12	1	2	1	27,195
Assessor's Dream	3	G	10	0	0	1	5,075
Asset Allocation	10	G	1	0	0	0	375
Asset of Choice	2	G	1	0	0	0	0
Assets 'n Action	2	G	2	0	0	0	515
Assets of Gold	4	F	20	2	5	2	41,580
Assets of Luck	3	G	14	2	3	3	16,181
Assignment	5	M	11	2	2	3	15,134
Assinippi	2	F	5	1	1	1	18,670
Assistant	4	G	3	1	0	0	16,370
Assmar	6	H	5	0	1	0	6,690
Assumed Risk	6	G	9	4	0	1	41,499
Assumption	6	G	6	0	0	0	1,019
Assured	3	F	14	2	2	4	10,270
Assuring Touch	5	M	12	1	0	1	6,536
Astaire Danseur	3	F	18	3	3	7	26,053
Astana	4	F	10	3	4	0	66,317
Astapay	3	C	7	2	0	5	7,790
Astarak (IRE)	5	G	7	1	0	1	30,160
Asti (IRE)	3	F	8	1	3	0	109,678
Asti Casino	6	M	5	0	0	0	250
Aston Magna	3	C	1	0	0	0	0
Astonish	5	G	4	0	0	0	270
Astonished (GB)	8	G	5	2	1	0	55,980
Astonishingmemory	4	C	2	0	0	0	0
Astor Bar	4	C	2	0	0	0	115
Astor Street	4	G	18	2	1	1	23,739
Astorbilt	5	M	17	1	3	1	28,070
Astra Athena	3	F	2	0	0	0	1,000
Astra D	6	G	5	0	0	1	385
Astra Ridge	9	H	2	0	0	0	460
Astral	3	C	9	0	0	0	2,440
Astral Plane	4	C	12	3	1	2	28,769
Astral Victor	3	G	13	1	1	2	9,074
Astralled	4	G	9	1	1	1	26,248
Astra's Sister	3	F	6	3	0	1	18,110
Astrel Angel	4	F	12	2	0	1	10,005
Astrickyas	5	M	8	1	1	0	4,328
Astro Flight	6	G	6	0	0	0	391
Astro Rex (ARG)	7	H	1	0	0	0	713
Astrologist	6	H	6	1	1	1	35,830
Astromaticat	2	F	3	0	1	1	13,525
Astronian Sound	5	G	12	0	0	0	255
Astronic	3	F	5	1	0	0	15,900
Astronn	2	G	6	0	1	1	3,760
Astros Choice	4	F	1	0	1	0	2,100
Astuta	4	F	9	1	0	3	9,635
Astutely	3	F	5	0	0	0	1,400
Astuto	3	G	20	3	4	1	39,066
Asummerforwindy	7	M	9	1	2	4	16,585
Asun	5	M	14	3	1	1	29,129
Aswift Kip	3	C	2	0	0	0	223
At a Boy Harry	3	G	7	1	0	0	18,840
At a Boy Luther	5	G	8	1	2	0	49,643
At a Country	3	F	6	0	0	1	6,801
At a Glance	4	F	5	2	1	0	41,894
At a Premium	6	M	6	0	0	0	528
At Dawn	4	G	3	0	0	1	3,920
At Ease Diablo	5	M	6	0	1	1	3,395
At First Sight	2	F	3	0	0	0	0
At Jimmy D's	4	G	10	2	0	1	6,342
At Presidents Day	4	G	6	0	0	1	1,001
At Sunrise	2	G	5	1	0	2	5,383
At the Ball	5	M	5	1	1	1	3,180
At the Bar	2	G	1	0	0	0	400
At the Copa	5	M	1	0	1	0	1,900
At the Dock	6	G	14	2	0	1	9,478
At the Hop	3	G	7	0	1	0	3,795
At the Moment	4	G	10	1	4	1	14,058
At the Office	3	F	1	0	0	0	0

Horse	Age	Sex	Sts	1st	2d	3d	Won
At the Top	3	C	3	0	0	0	351
At the Wheel	5	G	17	0	4	2	13,741
Ata Olympio	3	G	4	4	0	0	83,280
Ata Rahy	4	G	7	1	0	0	10,860
Ata Slew	5	G	5	2	0	0	8,150
Atagirl Genius	2	F	5	0	0	1	4,098
Atahualpa	10	G	8	1	2	1	8,437
Ataka Cue	5	G	4	0	0	0	109
Ataka Go Go	6	G	16	0	0	1	2,263
Ataka Ridge	6	H	2	1	0	0	2,400
Atanarjuat	4	F	11	0	2	0	3,033
Atanas	2	C	1	0	1	0	11,400
Atascaderan	4	G	3	1	1	0	7,037
Atchafalaya	4	G	6	1	0	1	11,485
Atempt Snooker	7	G	7	0	0	1	580
Atfirst Blush	4	C	10	1	0	2	36,209
Athena Girl	3	F	14	3	0	5	22,523
Athlete	4	C	5	0	0	2	13,280
Atiba	11	G	8	0	0	0	1,695
Atid	3	G	2	0	0	0	250
Atitudeofgratitude (IRE)	3	F	8	2	2	3	37,490
Atlanta Rose	4	F	17	3	2	0	26,392
Atlantic Affair	3	F	3	0	0	0	0
Atlantic Ave	4	C	5	0	0	0	2,781
Atlantic Blueblood	3	G	4	0	0	0	935
Atlantic Coast	2	C	2	1	0	0	4,575
Atlantic Frost	3	F	9	3	0	5	60,500
Atlantic Hero	3	F	3	1	1	0	6,060
Atlantic Ocean	4	F	2	0	0	0	0
Atlantic Patrol	3	F	9	3	1	2	30,980
Atlantic Romance	3	F	8	1	1	1	21,884
Atlantic Snow	3	F	10	1	0	0	5,044
Atlantic Squall	3	C	2	0	0	0	0
Atlantic Sweep	2	F	3	0	0	0	655
Atlantic Wedding	2	F	2	0	0	0	365
Atlantic Zone	3	C	10	1	1	0	7,390
Atlantica	3	F	6	0	0	0	1,000
Atlantis Crusader	5	G	6	2	1	1	21,070
Atlantis Dream	5	H	15	1	5	4	33,271
Atlas Peak	3	C	5	1	2	0	15,945
Atlas Valley	2	F	2	0	2	0	19,400
Atlas's Johnny	3	C	2	0	0	0	708
Atm Angie's Rodeo	3	F	5	0	0	0	811
Atom Skier	4	G	16	4	2	4	54,821
Atomic	6	H	2	0	1	0	4,235
Atomic Energy	4	G	6	1	0	0	7,210
Atomic Sub	5	G	10	0	3	1	16,140
Atouratoura	4	G	10	0	0	2	14,534
Atria	3	F	4	1	0	0	22,590
Atsena Otie	3	F	6	0	0	0	1,470
Atstheway	3	F	3	0	0	0	250
Atta Boy Bo	10	G	4	1	0	1	4,070
Attaboy Eskimo	8	H	11	1	1	2	7,736
Attaboyvic	3	G	1	0	0	0	114
Attabrook	5	G	2	0	0	0	0
Attacat's Right	3	G	5	1	0	0	1,797
Attack Alert	3	C	4	2	0	0	69,540
Attack Force	4	G	15	3	8	2	119,665
Attack the Books	5	H	7	2	1	1	66,978
Attack Zak	5	M	7	1	0	0	8,933
Attacksum	6	G	11	1	0	4	15,011
Attackux	5	G	10	0	2	0	4,418
Attagirl Bailey	2	F	2	0	0	0	0
Attainable	4	G	6	1	0	1	21,490
Attakapa	6	G	12	0	2	3	10,476
Attalid	4	G	9	0	0	1	4,640
Attasta	6	M	7	0	1	0	1,273
Attaway Jones	3	F	1	0	0	0	0
Attawayo	4	G	1	0	1	0	6,600
Attempt	4	G	4	2	0	1	16,675
Atten Hut	3	C	8	4	0	0	114,020
Attend to Me	4	F	9	2	1	0	10,499
Atterbury	5	G	5	2	1	2	36,720
Atteridge Road	3	G	2	0	0	0	600
Attest	8	G	9	3	1	1	84,288
Atti Girl Fergie	3	F	2	0	0	1	4,985
Attic	4	C	10	4	2	2	97,070
Attic Sale	5	G	2	0	0	0	222
Atticus Forever	5	G	5	0	0	1	952

Horse	Age	Sex	Sts	1st	2d	3d	Won
Atticus' Goddess	4	F	9	2	3	0	24,554
Atticus Kristy	3	G	7	3	1	2	56,260
Atticus Lady	3	F	5	1	0	0	9,000
Atticus River	3	C	2	0	0	0	280
Atticus Star	4	G	2	1	0	0	27,784
Attiki	5	M	8	0	2	0	32,584
Attila's Storm	2	C	1	0	0	1	5,280
Attitana	5	H	5	0	0	2	646
Attitudal	4	F	1	0	0	0	0
Attitude City	4	F	4	0	1	0	2,820
Attitude Dude	4	G	3	0	0	0	186
Attitude E. Ree	4	G	15	0	4	2	11,582
Attitude Princess	3	F	6	0	0	0	581
Attobigboy	6	G	2	0	0	0	436
Attonotauto	5	G	16	3	2	2	53,384
Attorney At Law	3	G	15	1	1	4	26,800
Attracta Dancer	3	F	10	0	3	4	3,307
Attractive Brass	4	G	6	0	1	0	1,752
Atwaar	7	H	1	0	0	0	0
Atwater	6	H	13	2	0	4	9,658
Atylia	3	F	4	0	0	1	1,680
Atys Pistol	5	M	4	0	0	0	198
Au Fever	6	G	6	0	0	2	3,095
Auat	6	G	7	0	0	0	456
Aubee's Prospect	4	G	7	1	2	2	16,770
Aubonne (GER)	4	F	6	2	0	0	107,549
Aubrianna	6	M	6	1	0	0	2,826
Auburn Forever	3	F	11	2	3	4	63,675
Aud	4	F	9	2	3	0	257,578
Audacious Alice	6	M	7	0	2	2	1,840
Audacious Chime	2	F	3	0	2	0	10,200
Audacious Explorer	8	G	3	0	0	1	1,580
Audacious Jane	3	F	7	0	0	0	0
Audio Express	4	F	10	0	2	1	5,720
Audioslave	3	C	6	0	1	1	3,663
Audit Exception	5	M	1	0	0	0	110
Audrey Hep	4	F	7	1	0	3	50,865
Audreys Dream	5	M	1	0	0	0	95
Aufluential	10	M	3	2	0	0	18,222
Augment (UAE)	2	C	1	0	1	0	8,400
August Game	4	F	12	0	0	0	650
Augustan	5	H	8	0	0	1	3,146
Augustness	4	F	3	0	0	0	1,125
Augusttown Maxi	5	H	13	1	0	0	29,421
Augustus Gold	3	C	9	1	0	2	5,187
Aukbar	4	G	10	0	4	1	19,801
Auke Bay	4	G	11	1	0	0	5,505
Aunt Connie	4	F	12	3	1	2	37,817
Aunt Dot Dot	2	F	4	1	1	1	43,100
Aunt Franny	3	F	4	0	0	0	812
Aunt Gemma	3	F	4	0	0	1	1,100
Aunt Ike	4	F	9	1	4	0	12,361
Aunt Jewell	7	M	4	0	1	0	763
Aunt Kay	2	F	4	1	0	0	14,160
Aunt Lynn	3	F	2	0	0	1	2,170
Aunt Lynnie	6	M	4	0	1	0	1,550
Aunt Minerva	4	F	4	0	0	0	122
Aunt Pansy	5	M	13	1	1	1	7,225
Aunt Sandy	2	F	1	0	0	0	80
Aunt Shee Shee	5	M	11	0	0	2	1,560
Aunt Sophie	6	M	7	3	1	2	108,250
Auntie Inda Attic	3	F	5	3	1	1	35,500
Auntie's Affair	2	F	1	0	0	0	0
Auntie's Bag	4	F	7	1	1	3	45,005
Auntie's Echo	2	C	1	0	0	0	100
Auratax	3	F	8	0	1	2	10,632
Aurelia	3	F	2	0	1	0	10,320
Aureliano	2	C	5	0	0	1	5,660
Auriferous	5	G	7	0	1	0	3,569
Aurify	3	F	6	0	0	3	10,170
Aurora G.	4	F	5	0	1	0	675
Aurora Gold	4	F	11	1	1	3	8,661
Aurora Guadalupe	4	F	4	0	0	0	1,298
Aurora Regina	7	M	3	0	0	0	0
Aurora Too	3	F	4	1	0	1	30,413
Aurora's Charm	3	F	1	0	0	0	0
Aurora's Delight	3	F	1	0	0	0	57
Auser Blue	5	M	10	2	0	2	9,575
Auspiciously	6	G	4	0	2	0	4,714

Horse	Age	Sex	Sts	1st	2d	3d	Won
Aussie Girl	7	M	7	1	2	0	16,140
Aussie Sweet	2	F	2	0	0	0	0
Austere	3	F	8	1	1	0	3,528
Austin Barber	3	G	9	1	1	1	38,349
Austin L.	3	C	6	0	0	3	7,278
Austin Richard	7	G	7	0	0	0	300
Austin W	3	C	6	0	3	1	4,777
Austin's Ace	4	F	12	0	1	1	4,037
Austin's Assassin	4	G	9	3	0	3	29,524
Austin's Awesome	5	G	11	2	2	1	17,583
Austin's Belle	4	F	8	2	1	0	63,720
Austin's Charm	7	G	7	1	0	0	5,658
Austin's Mom	4	F	3	2	1	0	116,831
Austin's Prospect	2	C	1	0	0	0	410
Australis	5	M	5	1	1	0	22,932
Austrian Devil	6	G	9	1	1	2	14,130
Austyn's Rose	6	M	2	0	0	1	696
Authentic Tour	3	G	3	0	0	2	6,046
Authenticated	4	F	14	0	2	1	3,798
Autistic Girl	4	F	2	0	0	0	630
Auto Be a Chuto	3	G	13	1	2	2	19,493
Auto Be Del	3	F	1	0	0	0	0
Auto City	4	C	6	0	1	1	17,750
Auto Focus	2	F	2	0	0	0	0
Auto Pilot	3	C	6	1	0	0	31,580
Autobesarah	6	M	12	1	1	0	50,367
Autocrat	3	C	6	0	1	0	4,247
Autocry	5	H	1	0	0	0	0
Automatic Deposit	3	G	9	0	2	2	7,351
Automatic O. D.	7	H	9	0	0	1	900
Automatic Teller	6	G	5	0	0	0	365
Automatic Tie	5	M	1	0	0	0	61
Automatic Weapon	3	C	12	0	1	1	10,910
Autonomy (IRE)	7	H	8	0	0	2	10,400
Autopro	3	F	3	0	1	1	6,922
Autopscot	4	G	18	3	4	2	67,800
Autowin	3	C	4	1	0	0	10,540
Autum Pie	3	F	6	1	1	0	11,610
Autum Proof	4	F	6	0	0	0	1,095
Autumn Accent	3	F	10	1	0	2	45,894
Autumn Account	3	C	4	0	0	1	632
Autumn Bliss	3	F	8	2	1	1	59,241
Autumn Clevermagic	3	G	1	0	0	0	0
Autumn Colors	4	F	7	1	2	0	25,445
Autumn Due	5	G	6	0	0	0	2,658
Autumn Express	3	G	2	0	0	0	640
Autumn Glow	5	M	10	0	0	1	4,821
Autumn Highlights	4	F	6	0	0	0	309
Autumn in May	5	M	10	0	0	1	10,390
Autumn Legacy	3	F	8	1	1	0	9,051
Autumn Miss	4	F	4	0	1	0	3,008
Autumn Prospect	4	F	6	2	1	1	43,387
Autumn Runner	7	G	1	0	0	0	0
Autumn Snow	2	C	3	0	0	1	6,270
Autumn Squall	3	G	4	1	0	0	9,180
Autumn Trick	3	F	3	0	0	0	0
Autumn's Molly	3	F	3	0	1	1	2,710
Ava and Ashley	3	F	5	0	0	1	1,380
Ava Anne	4	F	3	1	0	1	31,240
Ava Darling	4	F	6	0	0	0	12,520
Ava Jayne	5	M	1	0	0	0	0
Ava Marisa	5	M	15	1	2	4	22,802
Avail	5	G	2	0	0	0	514
Available	6	G	5	1	1	0	7,856
Available Jones	2	C	1	0	0	0	105
Available Katie	4	F	5	0	0	1	1,729
Avalanche Alert	3	G	10	1	1	0	11,785
Avalanche Bay	3	F	15	4	3	4	90,353
Avalanche Express	3	F	3	0	0	0	201
Avalanche Lily	4	F	5	1	1	0	15,296
Avalancher	12	G	11	1	0	1	5,580
Avalino	3	G	12	5	1	1	63,460
Avalon Prep	3	G	3	0	0	0	1,400
Avalon's Racer	2	F	3	0	0	1	1,372
Avalueforever	5	G	9	2	3	1	6,445
Avaricity	3	F	12	2	1	1	49,744
Avary too Step	5	M	3	0	2	1	8,700
Ava's Future	3	F	12	1	0	1	4,504
Avast	6	M	3	0	0	0	282

Horse	Age	Sex	Sts	1st	2d	3d	Won
Avatar Moon	3	G	9	1	1	0	10,417
Ave de Rapina	8	G	6	0	0	0	730
Avellino	6	H	1	0	0	0	0
Avengence	2	F	3	0	0	0	1,200
Avenging Buck	5	H	2	0	0	0	0
Avenging Bullet	4	G	15	3	3	3	24,950
Avenging Eagle	9	G	2	0	0	0	110
Avenging Hill	9	G	3	0	0	0	120
Avenging Kat	2	F	2	2	0	0	73,786
Avenging Lady	3	F	8	0	0	1	1,488
Avenging Passion	7	M	8	3	0	1	50,930
Avenging Tree	3	G	8	0	0	1	1,000
Avenida Del Cielo	5	M	1	0	0	0	127
Avenida Lady	5	M	3	0	1	0	3,386
Aventura Place	4	C	5	2	0	2	67,360
Aventurous Sword	4	G	8	0	1	1	6,344
Avenue of Charm	2	F	4	0	0	0	2,124
Avenue of Magic	4	G	8	2	1	2	9,128
Avenue of Royalty	5	G	4	0	0	1	1,443
Avenue of Siam	5	G	9	3	0	1	18,767
Avenue Spectical	5	G	6	0	0	1	788
Avenueofknowledge	5	G	4	0	0	1	3,620
Avenue's Lady	3	F	1	1	0	0	4,785
Average Forum	3	F	10	2	1	2	38,210
Average Star	3	F	9	3	1	2	27,854
Averill Park	4	F	4	0	0	0	632
Averinsky	2	F	2	0	0	0	432
Avert	3	G	5	0	0	0	0
Avery Grace	2	F	1	0	0	0	0
Avery Hall	2	F	2	1	1	0	52,000
Avery S	2	F	1	0	0	0	375
Ave's Princessa	4	F	14	2	1	2	17,785
Avian	7	M	1	0	0	0	0
Aviation Dare	2	F	5	1	1	1	14,946
Aviation Vacation	6	M	13	1	3	3	10,210
Avid Achiever	5	G	10	3	1	1	11,802
Avid David	5	G	19	2	2	0	12,086
Avid Skier	3	C	14	4	1	0	124,203
Avid Spell	3	C	10	0	0	1	1,464
Avie Street	5	G	2	0	0	0	457
Avie's d'Light	2	C	3	1	0	1	15,510
Avies Overdrive	2	F	4	0	1	1	3,419
Avies Perfect Copy	4	F	14	1	0	1	6,093
Avie's Princess	5	M	1	0	0	0	0
Avimora	4	F	6	0	1	1	14,040
Avirat	2	G	2	0	0	1	2,779
Avoid Mark	3	C	1	0	0	0	0
Avon Grove	2	F	1	0	0	0	0
Avril	3	F	1	0	0	1	1,550
Awad of Bills	4	G	11	1	2	0	25,910
Awad of Money	4	G	4	0	0	0	0
Awadawin	4	G	5	0	0	1	6,240
Awadist	4	F	1	0	0	0	0
Awad's Jackie	4	F	9	0	0	0	0
Awad's Quest	3	F	5	0	1	1	15,210
Awaiting Good News	4	F	9	0	1	0	3,576
Awake America	5	M	4	0	0	0	300
Awaken the Dragon	4	C	2	0	0	2	9,000
Awanda	4	F	11	0	2	2	22,385
Award	3	F	1	0	0	0	400
Award Winning	3	F	5	0	1	1	8,540
Award Winning Team	4	G	14	3	1	1	47,880
Award Yu	3	F	12	3	6	1	33,930
Away Ahead	2	F	2	1	0	0	23,486
Away to Boston	3	C	7	0	1	0	8,827
Away to Go	4	F	5	0	1	1	3,950
Away to Impress	2	C	1	0	0	0	0
Awayne	4	G	2	0	0	0	288
Awayo	5	M	11	0	0	0	1,795
Awe	4	G	14	2	2	4	60,710
Awesome Action	4	G	7	2	1	2	142,238
Awesome Adam	4	G	16	3	2	2	20,118
Awesome Alarm	3	G	3	0	1	1	5,630
Awesome Alec	5	G	6	3	2	0	11,709
Awesome Allen	3	C	17	2	3	3	34,065
Awesome American	6	G	9	0	0	0	1,294
Awesome Anew	3	F	14	1	3	3	29,240
Awesome Attorney	3	G	10	0	1	2	20,192
Awesome Beginning	3	F	8	0	2	2	30,605
Awesome Blossom	6	M	1	0	0	0	0
Awesome Cannonball	4	C	4	1	0	0	25,610
Awesome Charm	4	F	8	0	1	1	17,490
Awesome Charmer	4	F	9	0	0	2	3,517
Awesome Commander	3	G	8	0	2	0	8,975
Awesome Dancer	6	G	11	2	1	0	4,164
Awesome Dancing	4	G	1	1	0	0	14,750
Awesome Deduction	3	F	9	1	2	2	38,005
Awesome Devil	3	G	8	3	2	0	54,039
Awesome Dividend	4	C	5	3	1	0	63,520
Awesome Doe	2	F	9	1	1	1	17,550
Awesome Echo	4	C	5	0	0	0	0
Awesome Feu	4	C	6	1	2	0	20,271
Awesome for Sure	4	F	5	2	1	0	22,423
Awesome Form	4	G	12	0	1	2	5,470
Awesome Fox	5	M	6	0	2	1	1,840
Awesome Frances	4	F	4	1	1	1	22,860
Awesome George	2	G	3	0	0	0	1,200
Awesome Glory	3	F	6	2	1	1	41,010
Awesome Honeymoon	8	M	3	0	0	0	276
Awesome Jason	3	G	7	0	0	0	0
Awesome Knight	9	G	3	0	0	0	0
Awesome Lad	3	G	4	1	2	0	11,200
Awesome Lady	3	F	14	3	2	0	105,685
Awesome Look	3	C	5	1	0	1	3,022
Awesome Memories	3	G	2	0	0	0	0
Awesome Out West	6	H	2	0	1	0	945
Awesome Potential	3	G	9	1	0	0	3,187
Awesome Powers	4	F	13	3	3	2	72,430
Awesome Pro	2	C	1	0	0	0	205
Awesome Prospect	3	G	8	1	0	3	7,896
Awesome Punch	4	F	4	0	0	0	0
Awesome Reef	4	F	7	3	2	0	31,120
Awesome Royale	4	G	2	1	1	0	5,644
Awesome Rush	4	G	3	0	2	0	25,120
Awesome Sign	2	C	1	0	0	0	400
Awesome Song	4	F	5	0	1	0	6,110
Awesome Takeover	3	F	3	0	0	0	660
Awesome Time	4	C	1	0	0	0	240
Awesome Touch	4	F	4	1	1	1	28,620
Awesome Venture	2	C	2	0	0	0	4,500
Awesome Victory	2	F	2	0	0	0	720
Awesome Weapon	4	G	3	0	0	0	258
Awesomebabyawesome	3	G	10	1	0	1	7,160
Awesomely	3	F	2	0	0	0	431
Awesomeness	3	F	7	2	0	0	58,171
Awesomewithbroads	3	G	8	1	1	4	35,400
Awestruck	3	G	4	0	0	0	306
Awful Tricky	3	C	5	0	0	2	2,725
Awfullee Bold	2	C	3	0	0	0	0
Awhimaway	3	F	2	0	1	0	800
Awholelotanothin	3	F	14	1	2	2	20,315
Awholelotofmalarky	6	H	6	4	0	0	53,660
Awininthepipeline	3	C	9	0	0	0	3,906
Awishandaprayer	3	F	8	2	1	0	9,300
Awitchinourtown	10	M	2	0	0	0	176
Awol	5	M	1	0	0	0	146
Awol Honey	8	G	3	0	0	0	188
Awol Soldier	5	G	12	5	1	2	61,451
Awsom Light	3	C	2	0	0	1	2,253
Awsome Cause	5	M	3	1	0	0	7,380
Awtair	4	G	12	3	2	2	22,215
Axe's Fancy Blaze	4	F	2	0	0	0	0
Axident	2	G	2	0	1	0	2,280
Axis	5	G	10	0	0	0	4,555
Axle	4	C	1	0	0	0	0
Axle Powder	5	G	1	0	0	0	0
Axtell G R	5	G	9	1	1	2	4,705
Ay Caramba (BRZ)	4	C	5	1	1	1	86,030
Ay Dee Dee	3	F	8	2	0	2	46,265
Aye a Hot Shot	4	C	2	0	0	0	0
Aye Aye Captain	7	H	6	1	0	0	3,035
Aye Begor	3	G	5	0	1	1	3,100
Aye Chihuahua	4	G	13	2	2	1	18,092
Aye Glide Along	7	G	10	0	2	3	11,190
Ayita	4	F	6	0	0	1	1,976
Ayita Page	4	F	6	1	0	0	6,470
Ayla	3	F	2	1	0	0	15,600
Ayla Bella	2	F	3	0	0	0	2,136

Horse	Age	Sex	Sts	1st	2d	3d	Won
Ayr Three Miles	6	G	13	2	1	1	11,536
Aza	3	G	13	5	3	1	88,020
Azal	6	H	4	0	0	0	0
Azalean	5	M	13	2	0	1	19,990
Azazel	6	G	1	0	0	0	400
Azdeck	3	F	10	2	1	1	40,727
Aze Gold	3	G	4	2	1	0	7,540
Azer	3	C	13	1	3	0	17,360
Azeri	6	M	8	3	2	0	1,035,000
Azichill	4	F	4	0	0	0	1,221
Azidiscount	3	F	9	2	0	3	41,041
Azininer	2	F	1	0	0	0	55
Aziorder	4	G	10	1	2	3	7,985
Aziyan	4	G	8	3	1	1	67,706
Aziza	2	F	4	0	0	0	1,680
Azle	6	G	8	0	0	2	3,041
Azna	4	F	4	0	0	0	322
Aztec	3	F	2	0	0	0	1,760
Aztec Pearl	5	M	5	0	2	2	38,080
Azteco de Oro	4	G	4	1	0	1	8,075
Aztek Sky	6	G	6	1	2	1	10,635
Azucaa	3	F	5	0	0	1	3,715
Azure	6	M	8	2	0	2	23,726
Azure Ciel	8	G	15	4	4	0	43,125
Azure Spring	4	F	4	0	1	0	11,760
B a Diamond	2	F	1	0	0	0	0
B an R Money	3	M	6	0	0	0	1,590
B B Approval	3	G	7	0	0	0	1,087
B B Bobbin	3	C	2	0	1	0	4,244
B B Brite	4	G	8	0	1	0	2,291
B B Cat	3	F	5	0	0	0	339
B B Choice	3	F	10	2	3	3	38,620
B B Dancer	6	G	6	0	0	1	2,161
B B Max	7	G	9	1	3	2	3,712
B B Saunter	3	C	11	1	2	2	8,975
B Bop Aloopa	6	M	8	0	1	0	2,164
B B's Account	4	C	2	0	0	0	1,020
B B's Pleasure	5	M	10	1	2	1	12,889
B C Charmer	4	G	12	1	2	1	21,195
B Emilys Enjoyment	5	M	3	2	0	0	12,670
B Flat Major	9	G	8	1	1	2	10,317
B G Drums	5	G	1	0	0	0	42
B Great Today	4	F	10	2	5	1	13,994
B G's Best Chance	3	G	15	2	1	1	9,510
B G's Suzy Q	3	F	6	1	1	1	13,710
B Illuminated	3	C	4	0	0	0	228
B J Bullet	4	F	2	0	0	0	924
B J Grace	5	M	2	0	0	0	122
B J Valentine	4	G	8	0	1	1	3,799
B J's Bandit	6	G	2	0	0	0	0
B J's Black Gold	5	M	11	5	0	1	13,912
B J's Mon	6	G	6	0	0	0	675
B J's Mr Gold	8	G	6	0	0	1	835
B J's Pistol	5	G	10	4	4	1	53,070
B J's Smile	5	G	7	0	0	0	785
B J's Star Budget	3	G	6	0	0	1	978
B K Stubby	5	G	3	1	0	0	4,471
B K's On the Park	3	C	13	1	4	1	25,955
B L Cool	3	G	16	3	0	6	22,353
B L T to Go	4	G	13	0	0	3	2,268
B L's Banker	3	C	6	1	1	0	9,965
B L's Love	2	F	2	0	1	0	2,700
B L's Sancho	2	C	2	0	0	1	2,585
B Mark	5	G	2	0	0	0	129
B My Slew	3	F	1	0	0	0	570
B n' Bay	4	F	12	0	2	0	2,637
B N One	3	G	14	1	1	2	7,236
B Onefifty	3	C	21	1	2	3	12,770
B R Lady	3	F	14	2	2	2	37,753
B R Sweetie	4	F	1	0	0	0	0
B Rock	5	G	9	0	0	0	698
B Rules	5	H	10	3	3	1	57,870
B Silver Girl	2	F	3	0	0	0	236
B T Cruiser	3	G	6	0	1	0	1,298
B Trick	2	C	8	0	5	1	45,942
B T's Birthday	5	M	7	0	0	0	138
B V Dubya	4	F	5	0	0	0	1,165
B Van	2	G	1	0	0	0	78
B. a. Tabbie	3	G	3	0	0	0	675

Horse	Age	Sex	Sts	1st	2d	3d	Won
B. A. Way	4	C	10	5	1	1	273,561
B. B. Best	2	C	7	4	0	1	360,710
B. B. Ruckus	3	F	8	4	0	1	24,165
B. B.'s Finest	3	C	2	0	0	0	0
B. B.'s Johnny	3	C	1	0	0	0	486
B. B.'s Pride	4	G	2	0	0	0	0
B. C. Road	3	C	2	0	0	0	300
B. C. West	6	G	11	0	0	4	16,027
B. C.'s Hero	3	G	12	3	4	1	16,671
B. Carson	4	G	6	0	0	0	640
B. D. Victor	7	G	6	1	0	0	9,717
B. E. Tex Mex	3	G	6	1	0	1	5,185
B. Extreme	9	G	14	2	2	1	8,140
B. Fabulous	6	M	11	3	1	1	15,578
B. G. Tiger	5	H	11	2	4	1	63,217
B. G.'s Choice	3	F	9	4	3	0	24,126
B. G.'s Dream	3	F	1	0	0	1	2,860
B. G.'s Trix	3	F	7	1	0	1	6,600
B. Geri	5	G	4	0	1	0	3,211
B. Good Hero	4	C	2	0	0	0	795
B. H. Dream	4	F	11	0	0	0	516
B. J. Bear	5	M	6	0	1	0	3,960
B. J. Beau Kiz	3	F	1	0	0	0	0
B. J. Star	4	G	14	0	0	2	2,776
B. J.'s Baby	5	M	11	1	1	0	3,988
B. J.'s Secret	3	C	15	1	0	1	13,702
B. J.'s Toy	10	H	1	0	0	0	0
B. K. Stronghold	2	C	2	0	0	0	500
B. Linda L.	4	F	2	0	0	0	0
B. Mr. Lucky	10	G	1	0	0	0	225
B. Murray	2	C	3	0	0	1	5,100
B. Nile	8	G	12	3	0	0	51,620
B. Nimble Jak	9	G	10	3	0	1	16,447
B. R. Prospector	7	G	6	0	0	0	440
B. S. Smoked Duck	7	G	5	2	2	0	3,135
B. Seger	7	G	8	2	2	0	7,200
B. Soft Hoedown	2	F	1	1	0	0	17,160
B. T. Hudson	6	G	10	0	4	4	11,408
B. T.'s Pirate	2	C	2	0	0	0	288
B. V. Express	3	F	1	0	0	0	400
B. W. Bihm	5	G	1	0	0	0	0
B. Z. Jones	5	G	11	4	1	2	50,525
Ba Ba Boom	4	C	9	3	3	1	71,180
Ba Ma Mama	5	M	7	0	0	0	2,059
Baba Blue	4	F	9	0	2	1	9,563
Baba Gonzo	3	F	12	3	1	1	48,810
Bababing	4	F	1	0	0	0	65
Babaganush	2	F	4	1	1	1	104,900
Babai Blues	3	F	12	1	1	1	12,029
Babalu (PER)	5	M	3	1	1	0	10,740
Babarocke	3	G	17	1	3	3	9,854
Baba's Best	4	G	3	0	0	0	308
Babay Julep	3	F	4	0	0	0	177
Babble On	4	F	8	0	1	0	8,749
Babbler	5	M	6	1	1	1	7,057
Babbling Girl	2	F	5	1	0	2	11,790
Babe Ruthie	5	M	6	1	0	1	4,560
Babee Punch	3	C	8	0	1	0	3,196
Babel	3	C	7	2	1	1	60,780
Babe's a Babe	2	F	2	1	0	0	8,380
Babe's Baby	3	F	6	0	0	0	504
Babe's Bet	4	G	13	1	3	2	32,583
Babe's Boy	3	C	2	0	1	0	2,370
Babe's Dream	7	G	1	0	0	0	0
Babes Glory	3	G	10	1	0	0	5,325
Babe's Match	5	G	11	0	0	0	702
Babes Wont Tell	5	H	9	1	1	3	12,994
Babeth (BRZ)	5	M	6	1	0	1	29,608
Babilicious Bride	3	F	1	0	0	1	1,430
Babinsky	5	G	12	2	2	2	24,738
Babson	5	G	1	1	0	0	7,500
Baby Angel	4	F	13	1	1	0	13,532
Baby Ankles	4	F	9	1	1	1	7,800
Baby Be Good	2	F	2	0	0	0	980
Baby Be True	3	F	5	0	0	0	210
Baby Bea	5	M	2	0	0	0	0
Baby Bear's Soup	4	C	10	2	1	1	15,707
Baby Bird C C	4	F	11	0	1	0	11,331
Baby Book	5	M	14	7	5	1	43,634

Horse	Age	Sex	Sts	1st	2d	3d	Won
Baby Bubbles	5	M	4	0	0	0	354
Baby Butz	10	G	2	0	0	0	160
Baby Concerto	4	F	17	5	3	2	52,677
Baby Corn	5	M	8	0	0	1	1,348
Baby Ego	6	M	2	0	0	0	321
Baby Gap	2	F	3	0	1	0	2,500
Baby Genius	3	F	15	0	0	2	5,241
Baby Girl Malia	3	F	11	2	0	0	10,947
Baby Girl Paula	3	F	10	1	2	1	13,447
Baby Gotta Go	3	F	5	0	0	0	1,340
Baby Hailey	4	F	4	1	0	0	17,976
Baby Hold On	3	F	5	1	0	0	2,325
Baby I'm Bad	3	G	3	0	0	1	1,325
Baby I'm Gone	4	G	4	0	0	1	593
Baby I'm the One	3	C	7	1	0	2	17,420
Baby I'm Wild	4	F	1	0	0	0	210
Baby J	6	M	1	0	0	0	149
Baby Jewel	3	F	9	1	1	0	6,013
Baby Leena	4	F	11	2	1	0	13,005
Baby Let's Groove	3	F	7	1	0	1	11,143
Baby Let's Roll	4	F	2	1	0	0	9,480
Baby Milo	5	G	8	0	1	3	2,028
Baby Needs Shoes	2	F	3	0	0	1	6,170
Baby Niner	3	F	3	0	0	0	241
Baby Poppy	8	G	5	0	1	1	4,375
Baby Roy	4	F	3	0	0	0	744
Baby Run	3	G	3	0	2	0	1,737
Baby Shaq	7	G	15	0	2	2	8,740
Baby Skates	3	F	10	1	1	4	19,200
Baby Supreme	3	F	9	2	0	2	9,484
Baby Trend	7	G	18	3	3	5	20,762
Baby Van	2	F	5	1	1	3	8,590
Baby Wallys Joy	4	F	6	1	1	0	4,360
Baby Wave	8	G	3	1	0	0	1,540
Baby Winalot	6	M	9	2	0	1	7,011
Baby Zone	2	F	2	0	0	0	1,320
Babygotdablues	3	F	3	0	0	0	120
Babyimastar	3	F	21	0	2	4	16,274
Babypaws	5	G	12	1	0	0	6,003
Baby's Babycakes	3	F	8	0	0	0	1,628
Babys Gold Record	2	F	2	1	0	0	9,292
Baby'sfirstdeposit	3	F	4	0	0	0	675
Baca	7	M	14	3	1	2	51,446
Bacardi Boys	8	G	4	0	0	0	545
Baccalaureate	5	G	2	0	0	0	1,985
Baccarat Babe	2	F	1	0	0	0	184
Bachelor Blues	3	C	8	0	2	1	61,293
Bachelor Forever	5	G	5	0	2	1	3,728
Bachelor Girl	3	F	8	0	0	0	291
Bachelor of Arts (GB)	3	C	8	0	0	2	9,790
Bachelorette	5	M	12	0	1	2	3,363
Bachelor's Delight	4	F	13	5	4	2	73,050
Bachelor's Gold	4	G	13	2	2	3	16,990
Bachelor's Gulch	2	C	5	0	2	0	20,930
Back Again Ben	3	G	11	5	1	0	73,420
Back Bay Bea	3	F	6	1	1	0	16,550
Back Bay Lady	4	F	8	1	1	0	12,881
Back Booth	4	G	17	1	2	2	10,675
Back Door Man	5	G	1	0	0	0	135
Back in the Saddle	3	C	2	0	0	0	615
Back in Town	3	G	8	1	0	2	16,353
Back It Up	2	F	7	0	2	2	9,315
Back of the Pack	9	H	9	0	1	0	3,708
Back Peddle	7	G	2	0	0	1	1,400
Back Stage Harlot	7	M	12	0	1	1	1,776
Back Street Gal	4	F	6	2	0	0	6,460
Back to Bernie	2	C	3	0	0	1	2,195
Back to Capetown	4	F	5	1	1	1	15,740
Back to Win	2	G	1	0	0	0	135
Back to Work	4	G	14	3	0	3	37,930
Back Twacking	6	M	8	1	1	2	7,258
Back With Hope	4	F	5	1	2	1	2,900
Backbone	4	C	10	2	0	0	18,345
Backfield N Motion	3	F	4	2	1	0	83,880
Backhaul	7	G	6	1	1	1	7,287
Backinthebusiness	4	F	5	0	0	1	5,324
Backoffboyz	4	F	14	0	3	6	5,917
Backonbabyside	4	G	7	2	2	2	6,064
Backroad Lullaby	2	G	1	0	0	0	662
Backseat Becka	2	F	5	3	1	0	102,599
Backseat Lingo	4	C	2	0	0	0	0
Backseat Memories	3	G	8	0	1	1	2,042
Backseat Romance	5	M	14	3	2	2	46,691
Backside Bully	4	G	7	1	2	2	9,230
Backstage	3	F	12	3	1	1	47,760
Backstreet Music	5	G	7	2	0	0	3,430
Backstretch Gossip	4	F	3	0	0	0	390
Backus	2	G	5	0	0	0	7,540
Backwater Hope	4	F	5	1	0	0	6,675
Backwater Nikki	7	M	16	1	1	2	5,452
Backwoodsmoking	3	C	7	0	2	1	17,940
Backyard Case	4	G	1	0	0	0	0
Bad	3	F	3	0	0	0	0
Bad Angel	3	F	3	0	1	1	3,280
Bad Baby Bubbie	2	C	1	0	0	0	230
Bad Bad Brenda	7	M	17	3	1	1	20,122
Bad Bad Dancer	6	G	4	0	0	0	0
Bad Bad Deal	4	G	1	0	0	0	86
Bad Bad Girl	3	F	2	0	1	0	2,380
Bad Bad Lady	5	M	1	0	0	0	40
Bad Becky	3	F	2	0	0	0	0
Bad Betsy	3	F	10	2	1	3	32,772
Bad Big Wolf	2	F	3	0	0	2	4,250
Bad Blood	2	C	3	0	0	0	1,000
Bad Boy Bill	3	G	4	0	0	2	1,570
Bad Boy Bobby	8	G	3	1	0	0	7,064
Bad Boy Yankee	7	H	1	0	0	1	1,147
Bad Case	3	C	3	0	1	0	1,480
Bad Cattitude	4	F	3	0	0	0	232
Bad Cop	3	G	3	2	0	0	9,265
Bad Cop Good Cop	5	G	14	3	1	2	20,578
Bad Credit	2	C	4	0	1	0	4,090
Bad Dog	8	G	10	1	1	3	7,390
Bad Dog Press	6	H	2	0	0	0	450
Bad Dream	3	F	4	0	2	1	4,178
Bad Gambler	4	G	13	3	1	2	30,160
Bad Hock Rock	4	G	12	1	0	1	13,988
Bad Ice	2	G	7	0	0	0	645
Bad Irish Gal	3	F	10	0	2	3	13,425
Bad Kitty	3	F	5	0	1	1	19,480
Bad Ladd	4	C	10	0	1	0	3,633
Bad Little Bernie	2	F	4	1	3	0	34,226
Bad Little Fellow	5	G	9	1	1	2	21,088
Bad Machine	5	M	9	0	1	1	3,242
Bad Man's Bride	3	F	9	1	1	1	7,530
Bad Penny	2	G	1	0	0	0	460
Bad to the Bone	6	G	2	0	0	0	535
Bad Toda Bone	12	G	7	1	0	0	2,522
Bad White	6	G	6	0	0	0	750
Bada Bam Bada Boom	6	G	11	2	1	2	86,978
Bada in Nevada	3	C	7	1	1	1	22,060
Badaboom	5	M	9	0	1	0	5,362
Badasbill	4	C	5	1	1	0	3,673
Badasiwantabe	9	G	6	0	0	0	124
Badcopnodonut	5	G	1	1	0	0	2,778
Badfish	3	G	8	0	0	0	1,010
Badge of Glory	3	C	5	0	1	1	2,847
Badge of Silver	4	C	4	1	2	0	108,000
Badger Bob	4	G	12	1	0	7	25,721
Badger Don	9	G	3	0	1	0	760
Badger Gold	8	G	8	0	2	2	8,540
Badger K. Eli	5	G	8	2	0	0	15,579
Badger Ridge	5	G	8	1	1	2	6,465
Badger's Lass	5	M	9	1	1	2	12,560
Badgerup	4	C	2	0	1	0	4,420
Badgett At Night	3	F	11	0	1	4	11,401
Badgett Beach	2	F	4	0	0	1	3,301
Badgett of Honor	4	G	8	0	0	2	10,282
Badgett's Mandate	3	C	2	0	0	1	18,380
Badgett's Mango	5	M	3	0	0	0	0
Badgett's Native	3	G	3	0	0	0	0
Badgett's Teeza	3	G	3	0	0	0	0
Badinage	4	F	8	2	2	0	66,450
Badlands Bronco	4	G	7	0	2	0	960
Badolstory	4	G	6	0	0	0	152
Badshot	4	G	13	3	3	1	26,497
Badtotheboneandrew	2	C	8	1	0	0	20,021
Baena	2	F	4	1	0	0	19,460

Horse	Age	Sex	Sts	1st	2d	3d	Won
Baendaz	8	G	7	0	0	0	470
Bag a Bit	7	G	16	2	3	4	25,720
Bag a Buckie	4	C	2	0	0	1	1,013
Bag 'Em	4	G	12	0	1	0	3,920
Bag It Sister	3	F	1	0	0	0	0
Bag It Up	5	G	10	1	0	0	7,974
Bag Me One	5	M	4	0	0	0	0
Bag Me Up	5	H	5	0	0	0	690
Bag of Gems	4	G	12	1	2	2	20,949
Bag of Jules	4	G	8	0	1	1	8,219
Bag of Miracles	3	F	1	0	0	0	0
Bag of Mischief	5	H	1	1	0	0	6,600
Bag of Quarters	2	F	4	1	0	0	4,805
Bag of Snow	6	G	11	0	1	1	5,393
Bag of Stars	6	M	11	2	2	2	35,880
Bag of Wings	4	F	1	0	0	0	0
Bag the Gold	4	G	12	1	2	3	13,844
Bag to the Bone	3	G	3	1	0	1	21,350
Bagalicious	3	C	11	2	1	1	25,059
Bagapooh	2	C	2	0	0	0	0
Bagdad Gambler	4	G	10	0	0	0	3,005
Bagdad Sands	5	M	3	0	0	0	0
Bagesy's First	3	C	5	0	0	0	293
Baggage	4	G	3	0	0	0	0
Baggerina	4	F	5	0	0	1	1,292
Baghran	3	G	12	1	1	2	29,701
Bagitdon'tchargeit	3	F	10	3	1	1	43,390
Bagless	6	G	3	0	0	0	0
Bagnil	5	G	7	0	2	0	1,685
Bagobucks	5	G	10	1	0	0	23,153
Bagofwhispers	4	F	1	0	0	0	0
Bags and Baggage	2	G	7	0	0	1	810
Bag's Soul	9	G	1	0	0	0	0
Baguette Diamond	2	F	1	0	0	0	0
Bah Humbug	3	C	4	0	0	0	594
Baha Bailey	4	G	6	0	0	0	412
Bahama Bank	3	G	4	0	0	0	1,930
Bahama Beau	2	C	2	0	0	1	1,300
Bahama Buz	3	C	3	0	0	0	100
Bahama John	4	C	6	2	1	1	65,760
Bahroba	6	G	5	0	0	1	4,690
Baie (FR)	4	F	1	0	0	0	0
Baie Dankie	3	G	3	1	0	0	4,150
Bail Bond	7	M	1	0	0	0	570
Bail Me Out Again	3	F	8	0	1	2	2,695
Bail N Out	4	G	6	1	1	0	5,400
Bail Out	3	F	3	0	0	0	2,355
Bailamos	5	G	13	1	1	3	21,710
Bailar	5	M	8	1	1	0	18,940
Bailarina	4	F	4	1	1	1	11,955
Bailee's Clue	7	M	11	1	0	1	5,664
Bailer Twine	2	C	11	1	1	1	17,530
Bailero (ARG)	5	H	10	2	2	2	81,830
Bailey Gail	4	F	3	0	0	0	174
Bailey Jazz	3	F	2	0	1	0	1,640
Bailey Marie	5	M	3	0	0	0	0
Baileys Affair	4	F	12	3	3	2	87,610
Baileys Attire	3	G	18	1	1	2	20,640
Bailey's Best	5	G	3	0	0	0	921
Bailey's Chance	4	F	5	1	0	0	6,000
Baileys Eagle	5	M	8	0	1	0	10,121
Baileys Edge	7	G	6	0	0	1	5,099
Baileys Ire	3	F	1	0	0	0	0
Baileys Queen	4	F	11	2	1	2	11,233
Bailey's Reprized	3	F	18	3	4	5	54,135
Bailey's Toy	4	F	4	0	0	0	0
Bailey's Yodeler	3	G	13	6	4	2	74,150
Baileyspet	6	G	15	3	2	5	23,250
Bailie's Band	5	G	9	1	2	1	42,780
Baillie's Beauty	4	F	11	1	0	0	6,326
Bailout With Style	3	C	1	0	0	0	0
Bails Only Miracle	3	F	1	0	0	0	0
Baine Brook	3	C	3	0	0	0	105
Baiser d'Amour	5	M	11	3	2	2	92,599
Baited Field	3	C	13	1	5	1	25,280
Baits 'Em	6	G	10	1	0	1	7,823
Baja Babe	3	F	7	0	0	1	4,185
Baja Dancer	4	F	8	1	0	2	15,060
Baja Harri	8	G	2	0	0	0	0
Baja Rosa	4	F	14	2	3	2	14,373
Baked Alaskan	3	G	3	0	0	0	0
Baker Road	7	H	11	1	1	2	49,038
Baker Road Joe	5	G	13	1	1	2	7,000
Baker Sign	4	G	3	0	0	0	510
Baker's Cake	3	F	3	0	0	0	291
Bakers Dozen	3	F	7	0	1	1	1,795
Baker's Gold Won	3	F	13	1	1	2	16,810
Baker's Lil Babe	3	F	2	0	0	0	0
Bakewell Tart (IRE)	4	F	1	0	0	0	416
Bal Bay	8	H	1	0	0	0	140
Bal Harbour	9	G	15	3	0	1	22,661
Baladi	5	G	20	2	1	3	14,778
Balance Sheet	4	G	15	2	1	1	12,292
Balance the Books	4	C	7	1	1	0	14,993
Balanced Bodgit	5	G	3	0	0	0	0
Balanced Flight	4	C	9	3	0	3	27,888
Balancetheaccount	8	M	1	0	0	1	130
Balancethebudget	11	G	11	2	1	0	10,533
Balancethecurtain	4	G	5	2	0	1	5,260
Balandra	3	C	3	0	0	1	9,483
Balantrae	6	M	12	3	0	1	38,540
Balanza	3	F	11	3	3	1	74,639
Balarat	7	G	5	1	0	0	15,240
Balarney's Magic	3	F	1	0	0	0	0
Balazo	2	G	1	0	0	0	0
Balboa Native Jr.	6	G	10	0	0	0	705
Balcarres	7	M	6	0	0	0	1,246
Bald Hill Native	8	G	3	0	0	0	0
Bald N Blue	3	F	1	0	0	0	320
Baldachino	5	M	11	2	1	5	80,706
Balderdash	6	G	12	0	2	1	6,885
Baldjim	8	G	15	6	3	2	11,290
Baldomera	3	F	9	3	0	2	120,548
Baldski's Image	4	C	3	0	0	1	1,275
Baldski's Lassie	2	F	7	0	0	0	855
Baldski's Line	3	F	19	2	1	3	17,278
Baldstyle	5	G	7	1	0	0	6,412
Baldwin County	6	G	8	2	3	0	62,820
Baldy	2	C	3	1	0	1	6,680
Baldy Brook	4	F	6	1	2	0	7,615
Baldy's Cup	4	G	4	0	0	0	186
Baldy's Darlin	4	F	11	2	1	1	13,446
Baleful	3	F	6	1	0	0	1,321
Balenos (BRZ)	6	G	9	3	1	1	18,158
Balestrini (IRE)	4	C	7	0	3	1	57,450
Bali Cruise	3	F	3	0	0	0	2,870
Balineas Lastdance	4	F	2	0	0	0	0
Balin's Sword (IRE)	4	G	7	0	0	0	5,180
Balint	2	C	2	0	0	1	3,450
Balkan	5	H	14	1	2	2	9,099
Balko Bay	8	G	5	0	1	1	2,620
Ball Four	3	G	9	2	0	3	76,270
Ball Girl	2	F	2	1	1	0	36,600
Ball N Swain	3	G	4	0	0	1	3,234
Balla Twine	6	M	9	2	1	2	48,800
Balladeer	6	H	14	1	4	1	16,137
Ballade's Joy	3	F	4	0	0	0	810
Ballado	2	C	1	0	0	0	140
Ballado Breeze	3	C	4	0	0	1	6,950
Ballado Hill	4	F	2	0	0	0	509
Ballado Melody	5	M	4	0	0	1	2,657
Ballado On Tour	3	F	1	0	0	0	0
Ballado's Baby	6	M	5	0	1	0	8,570
Ballado's Cat	3	F	3	0	1	0	9,040
Ballado's Devil	6	H	3	0	0	1	1,262
Ballado's Halo	5	M	1	0	0	1	5,000
Ballalaika	2	F	1	0	0	0	400
Ballari	2	F	6	0	0	1	2,332
Ballen Isle	4	C	7	0	0	2	17,554
Ballence	4	F	7	0	0	1	3,750
Ballerina Cat	2	F	7	0	2	0	8,600
Ballerina Prima	3	F	2	0	0	0	0
Ballerina's Halo	4	G	5	0	0	0	3,067
Ballet Babe	2	F	2	0	0	0	780
Ballet Critic	6	H	3	0	0	0	1,270
Ballet King	3	G	7	1	0	1	19,556
Balletto (UAE)	2	F	5	3	2	0	614,000
Ballingarry (IRE)	5	H	7	1	0	2	197,074

RECORDS OF HORSES

Horse	Age	Sex	Sts	1st	2d	3d	Won
Ballistic	8	G	14	2	1	0	16,044
Ballistic Angel	4	F	20	2	5	4	111,870
Ballistic Babe	5	M	11	2	1	2	25,010
Ballistic Missile	4	C	7	0	2	1	17,810
Ballonenostrikes	4	G	7	0	1	1	16,880
Ballotade	4	F	8	1	1	1	13,585
Ballroom Blitz	3	G	8	1	0	2	4,271
Ballroom Champ	4	G	5	1	1	3	10,800
Ballroom Deputy	3	F	8	2	1	1	99,720
Bally Boy	3	C	1	0	0	0	0
Bally Cat	6	M	11	3	4	0	15,064
Ballygawley Lad	2	C	2	0	0	1	4,170
Ballygulch	3	F	2	0	0	0	0
Ballymaloe	3	F	14	1	1	3	22,583
Ballymena (GB)	2	F	1	0	0	0	1,380
Bally's Fun Guy	4	G	13	2	4	1	14,949
Ballyvalogue (IRE)	9	G	1	1	0	0	6,000
Balmy	5	M	5	0	1	2	35,288
Balmy Night	2	C	2	0	0	0	375
Balsora	3	G	6	0	0	0	105
Balthazar	3	G	4	0	0	1	7,930
Baltic City	4	F	14	0	1	4	16,746
Baltic Hydra	3	F	5	0	0	2	4,590
Baltic Maria	4	F	11	0	3	2	19,295
Baltic Marque	7	H	8	1	0	2	2,986
Baltic Prince	4	G	11	2	3	2	59,880
Baltic Sun	2	C	4	0	0	1	2,504
Balto Star	6	G	5	1	1	1	410,834
Baltusrol	3	G	3	0	0	0	894
Balustrade	4	C	8	1	1	0	52,503
Balvanera	5	M	11	2	1	0	10,949
Balzell	7	H	10	0	1	2	12,452
Bam Attack	3	F	2	0	0	0	171
Bam Bam Nelson	4	G	11	0	1	3	6,149
Bam That Martini	4	G	16	1	1	0	7,905
Bama Belle	7	M	9	3	1	3	27,898
Bama Brae	3	F	6	0	3	1	6,463
Bama Jack	3	G	7	0	0	0	2,424
Bama Point	3	F	9	0	0	0	672
Bama Red	6	G	4	1	0	0	3,402
Bama Royal	5	G	3	0	1	2	4,970
Bamam	4	F	3	0	0	0	210
Bamba	4	F	2	0	1	0	15,600
Bamber	5	M	2	0	0	0	0
Bamboo Belle	4	F	9	1	2	4	16,690
Bamboo Orient	3	F	4	0	1	1	9,388
Bamboo Royal	2	F	1	0	0	0	0
Bamboozled	2	C	1	0	0	0	840
Bamboozler	4	G	8	2	1	1	44,720
Bambotto	4	G	7	0	0	1	1,156
Bambury	4	F	7	0	4	1	11,730
Bampton Place	3	G	9	0	1	2	8,144
Ban Tom Six	5	G	19	0	2	2	4,787
Banana B.	3	G	12	1	4	2	7,521
Banana Mama	3	F	3	0	0	0	161
Banana Wind	9	G	2	0	0	0	54
Banannie Boy	3	C	2	0	1	0	2,400
Banche	2	C	2	0	0	1	935
Banco de Datos	5	M	9	1	1	1	6,615
Banco de Oro	3	C	5	1	0	1	21,540
Band Aight	4	C	4	1	2	0	10,710
Band Director	2	G	5	0	3	1	11,220
Band Dixie	3	C	5	0	0	5	12,760
Band Leader	7	H	3	0	0	0	0
Band of Gold	6	M	7	1	1	1	11,585
Band of Reflection	6	M	8	0	1	0	1,415
Band Performance	12	G	6	2	2	1	10,646
Bandaid Boy	2	C	1	0	0	0	70
Bandana	7	G	12	3	0	2	29,567
Bandeau	3	F	1	0	0	0	150
Banded One	4	G	12	0	2	0	9,504
Bandera County	3	G	7	0	2	0	9,300
Bandera Dude	4	C	10	2	3	1	17,662
Banderas	5	H	5	0	0	2	3,710
Banderberg	4	C	6	2	2	0	31,740
Banderole	3	C	14	3	2	3	26,787
Bandidazo (ARG)	8	G	10	1	0	1	7,114
Bandido Leyenda	5	G	1	0	0	0	107
Bandido Lode	3	G	5	2	1	0	28,454
Bandido Rial	5	G	14	0	3	2	5,235
Bandini	2	C	1	0	0	0	180
Bandi's Big Red	4	C	5	0	0	1	3,128
Bandit Nailhead	3	C	17	1	4	2	68,125
Bandit Time	2	F	1	0	0	0	160
Bandito	4	G	2	0	0	0	342
Banditsmexicanwinr	2	G	1	0	0	0	155
Banditti	4	G	5	2	1	1	7,186
Bandura	3	C	6	1	1	1	21,194
Bandy	7	M	20	0	0	6	8,785
Baneful	3	F	2	0	0	0	0
Banff Springs	5	G	11	0	0	0	2,069
Bang	4	G	4	3	0	0	81,924
Bang It Out	3	F	2	0	0	0	350
Bangbangonthedoor	3	F	12	3	2	3	81,462
Bangin' On Bongos	3	G	13	0	0	1	2,591
Bangkok by Night	3	G	16	1	2	2	13,594
Bangle	6	M	4	1	1	0	4,000
Bangzoom Birdie	6	M	11	2	0	3	10,498
Banish Misfortune	3	G	1	0	0	0	140
Banished Lover	6	M	12	6	2	0	164,753
Banjo Babe	3	F	12	2	5	0	43,142
Banjo Gal	3	F	8	2	2	0	13,130
Banjo Picker	4	G	7	2	2	2	38,174
Bank Audit	3	F	12	5	1	3	136,210
Bank Bag	4	G	6	0	0	0	375
Bank Balance	3	G	1	0	0	0	0
Bank Draft	5	G	5	0	0	0	1,230
Bank Me	4	G	6	0	0	0	1,310
Bank of Kanata	6	G	8	0	0	0	458
Bank On a Scholar	3	F	4	0	0	0	115
Bank On Batonnier	3	F	8	1	3	0	5,892
Bank On Della	3	F	8	1	0	0	4,470
Bank On Frank	4	G	2	1	0	0	8,550
Bank On Greida	4	F	7	0	0	1	4,303
Bank On Henry	4	C	3	0	0	0	225
Bank On Line	3	G	3	0	0	0	400
Bank On the Champ	2	G	6	1	2	2	48,830
Bank On Victor	2	F	1	0	0	0	400
Bank President	2	G	2	0	0	1	4,637
Bank Roll	3	G	11	1	1	5	30,230
Bank Task	3	F	17	3	4	4	34,835
Bank Ticket	6	G	1	0	0	0	0
Banker Badgett	3	G	4	1	0	0	10,635
Banker Boy	4	G	9	1	0	1	19,500
Banker Jason	5	G	11	0	1	2	2,973
Banker Wallace	4	C	7	0	0	2	1,405
Bankerette	4	F	6	0	1	1	5,809
Bankers Creek	3	F	5	0	1	1	3,448
Banker's Dinner	2	G	5	1	0	1	15,220
Banker's Heiress	3	F	13	3	2	0	49,777
Banker's Hill	3	C	3	0	0	1	1,685
Banker's Holiday	2	C	10	1	0	0	5,794
Banker's Note	3	G	5	0	1	1	5,600
Banker's R. N.	4	F	14	1	2	3	6,880
Banker's Touch	7	H	1	0	0	0	102
Banker's Trapp	3	G	3	0	0	0	0
Banker's Wife	3	F	15	3	3	2	27,808
Bankers Wish	10	G	1	0	0	0	0
Bankin On Blossom	3	F	1	0	0	0	0
Bankin On Slew	2	G	1	0	0	0	0
Banking	2	G	7	2	1	0	16,680
Bankitbaby	2	F	5	1	0	2	8,375
Bankrupe	4	F	13	2	1	2	16,064
Bankruptcy Bound	10	G	3	0	0	0	0
Bankruptcy Court	3	C	8	3	3	2	139,450
Bank's Hand	3	C	5	1	0	0	14,610
Bannack	4	C	7	0	0	1	8,854
Banned in Boston	4	C	8	0	0	4	53,315
Banner Boy	10	G	7	0	0	0	4,925
Banner Elk	3	F	6	1	0	2	14,330
Banner Key	7	M	3	1	1	1	9,670
Banner Queen	4	F	1	0	0	0	215
Banners Flying	5	G	10	1	4	0	5,245
Banners Wave	5	M	4	0	1	1	3,855
Bannerstone	5	M	17	2	4	4	21,309
Bannister	7	H	11	1	1	0	1,737
Bannock	2	C	1	0	0	0	140
Bannock Burner	4	G	6	1	0	0	21,093

Horse	Age	Sex	Sts	1st	2d	3d	Won
Bannon	2	G	1	0	0	0	0
Bannon's Pick	5	M	3	0	2	0	4,020
Bano's Adil	4	C	11	0	0	0	640
Banquero	6	G	9	0	1	0	1,541
Banshee Boy	4	G	12	2	4	1	25,355
Banshee Brad	6	G	15	4	2	2	75,994
Banshee Bridesmaid	3	F	14	4	1	1	18,711
Banshee Connection	6	G	10	1	0	2	25,209
Banshee King	4	G	2	0	0	0	480
Bantamweight	4	G	16	3	4	4	16,205
Baphomet	3	C	5	0	2	1	16,710
Baptistry	3	C	2	0	1	0	2,100
Baquera	3	F	7	1	0	1	4,827
Baquero's Chick	2	F	9	0	3	1	4,492
Bar B Drew	9	G	9	0	0	0	510
Bar B John	9	G	2	0	0	0	0
Bar Bailey	4	F	9	4	1	3	51,345
Bar Buddy	5	H	8	0	3	0	2,859
Bar Code	5	G	2	0	1	0	2,580
Bar Dance	5	H	5	2	0	2	20,038
Bar Fly	5	M	10	5	2	1	67,490
Bar Girl	4	F	9	1	0	1	11,262
Bar Leah	2	F	5	0	0	0	4,476
Bar Lite	2	F	2	1	0	1	15,840
Bar Room Brawler	5	G	4	0	2	0	2,420
Bar Shoe	7	G	6	0	0	0	750
Bar the Hatch	5	M	4	0	0	0	0
Bar U Anio	4	G	11	3	0	1	22,228
Barabara	5	G	5	0	0	0	630
Baramundi Jan	3	G	2	0	0	0	0
Barancella (FR)	3	F	6	1	2	1	174,379
Barath	5	G	9	5	1	1	140,461
Baravus	8	H	1	0	0	0	0
Barb	3	F	1	0	0	0	0
Barb the Vet	3	F	2	0	0	0	0
Barbaloona	3	F	9	1	3	1	8,586
Barbara O'Brien	5	M	1	0	0	0	15,000
Barbara Orr	4	F	4	1	1	0	59,140
Barbaralynnehogan	3	F	15	1	0	0	5,244
Barbara's Jewel	4	G	10	0	1	2	9,480
Barbara's Lastlove	7	G	10	2	0	1	18,025
Barbara's Song	5	M	1	0	0	0	0
Barbaray's Claim	5	M	8	1	1	2	10,076
Barbarian	3	G	2	0	0	0	0
Barbary Coast	3	C	1	0	0	0	2,623
Barbeau Ruckus	5	G	4	1	1	1	123,243
Barbecue Bob	3	C	1	0	0	0	234
Barber Talk	4	C	10	0	0	1	2,567
Barber's Magic	3	G	10	2	1	1	21,798
Barbers Mariah Two	3	G	4	1	0	0	3,984
Barbers Pride	4	F	2	0	0	0	0
Barbie Jo Jo	4	F	10	0	1	3	10,418
Barbs and Bows	4	F	14	0	5	1	25,928
Barb's Bid	3	C	1	0	0	0	0
Barb's Ghazi	3	F	9	1	0	2	4,256
Barb's Lucky Lady	5	M	5	0	0	1	1,363
Barb's Promise	4	F	7	0	0	0	1,084
Barb's Speed Dial	3	F	1	0	0	0	0
Barb's Valentine	3	F	4	0	0	0	353
Barb's Word	4	F	8	1	2	2	8,817
Barbsasmilin	2	F	1	1	0	0	12,480
Barbski	6	M	2	0	0	0	0
Barbwire and Roses	4	F	11	0	1	0	3,648
Barby's Shamrock	3	F	5	2	0	1	18,845
Barcelona Beauty	2	F	1	0	0	1	2,500
Barcelona Cat	2	F	1	0	1	0	3,528
Barcllona Boy	3	G	8	0	0	0	660
Bardic	8	G	3	0	0	0	0
Bardstale	4	C	4	0	1	0	2,750
Bardstown	2	C	5	0	0	0	6,100
Bardy Woman	3	F	5	0	0	2	11,620
Bare Beware	4	F	19	4	3	3	25,047
Bare Legs	7	M	14	2	2	1	27,757
Bare Necessities	5	M	9	1	3	3	328,970
Barefoot Hugh	5	G	7	2	0	0	7,940
Barefoot Jerry	5	G	5	1	1	1	10,552
Barefoot Lady	2	F	4	0	0	0	1,170
Barely Sovereign	5	M	10	1	0	2	8,275
Barelyinourbodgit	3	G	4	0	1	1	15,795

Horse	Age	Sex	Sts	1st	2d	3d	Won
Barfly Babe	4	F	6	1	1	0	3,116
Bargain	8	G	15	3	3	2	18,872
Bargain Belle	5	M	3	0	1	0	8,160
Bargain Betty	5	M	1	0	0	0	73
Bargain Dancer	5	M	11	0	2	1	4,346
Bargette	4	F	10	0	0	0	720
Bargin Man	5	G	1	0	0	0	0
Bariloche	2	G	1	0	0	0	300
Bark Alley	2	F	7	0	0	1	1,471
Bark for Mercy	4	C	11	1	0	4	11,490
Barken	2	G	2	1	1	0	20,800
Barkenlor Cat	9	G	2	0	0	0	50
Barkerman	3	G	7	1	0	0	15,470
Barley Charlie	2	G	4	1	1	0	9,400
Barley Creek	9	G	11	1	2	2	14,367
Barlow Road	9	G	2	0	0	0	938
Barn Bug	3	G	3	1	1	0	22,000
Barn Dance	3	F	9	1	0	2	29,891
Barn Door	2	F	5	0	0	1	1,470
Barnabus	6	G	4	0	1	1	7,300
Barnacle Steve	5	G	9	0	0	4	23,810
Barnard Man	5	G	8	0	3	1	24,020
Barney B	4	G	11	2	3	1	14,907
Barney Rumble	4	G	4	0	0	0	675
Barney Smith	5	G	16	2	1	2	63,181
Barnsy	3	F	8	3	0	1	88,650
Barnwell	8	G	3	0	0	0	160
Barnyard Bunny	3	F	4	0	0	0	0
Barometer Rising	2	C	1	0	0	0	400
Barometric	5	H	3	0	0	1	10,800
Baron Balmoral	2	C	1	0	0	0	0
Baron Et All	4	G	8	2	1	1	23,516
Baron the Big Red	4	G	10	0	2	2	5,692
Baron Von Ruckus	5	G	11	0	1	0	4,053
Baron Von Tap	3	C	8	1	2	2	55,775
Baron Von Tom	11	G	11	3	4	2	15,916
Baronage	3	C	5	1	0	2	61,350
Baroness Silvia	3	F	8	2	1	1	26,190
Barongin	3	G	14	1	0	2	12,027
Baron's Diamond	3	C	2	0	0	0	0
Barons Hoolic	5	H	1	0	0	0	149
Baron's Prodigy	7	G	3	0	0	0	0
Baron's Rank	4	G	9	1	0	0	6,102
Barqaa	3	F	3	0	0	0	0
Barquest	3	G	10	1	0	0	10,340
Barra Steel	3	F	15	1	5	2	33,117
Barraza	5	G	5	1	0	0	2,400
Barrel Racer	3	F	7	1	1	2	53,179
Barren Creek	4	G	9	1	1	0	23,040
Barretodo	10	G	12	0	0	0	3,246
Barrett Kathryn	5	M	21	1	4	4	26,180
Barricade Point	4	G	16	3	6	1	15,540
Barricaded	3	G	8	3	1	0	30,500
Barricade's Missy	2	F	10	1	0	2	7,506
Barrington Lady	3	F	13	1	6	2	21,605
Barron Dan	7	G	13	0	1	2	5,459
Barron H	6	G	7	2	2	1	45,245
Barroom Ballet	3	F	2	1	1	0	3,000
Barry County	6	G	5	2	0	0	4,554
Barry Line	7	G	2	0	0	0	684
Barry the Law	2	C	3	1	0	0	14,000
Bars Thunder	4	F	15	1	2	2	9,067
Barsafire	4	F	9	0	1	0	1,449
Barsnit	3	F	5	0	0	0	0
Bartax	3	C	10	0	1	3	11,975
Bartee Pride	6	G	3	0	1	0	1,444
Bartella's Way	4	F	1	0	0	0	0
Bartender	6	G	6	2	0	1	14,230
Bartending Mike	4	G	11	2	1	2	22,309
Bartendress	6	M	5	1	0	0	3,831
Barth	2	G	2	1	1	0	7,753
Bartholemew	4	G	12	1	2	1	8,172
Bartko	5	G	9	1	0	2	9,662
Bartlett Run	3	F	2	0	0	0	166
Bartley	6	M	6	0	1	1	4,890
Bartok Lady	2	F	2	1	0	0	21,000
Bartok's Ballet	2	G	5	0	0	0	1,470
Bartok's Beau	4	F	1	0	0	0	0
Bartok's Blithe	4	F	11	0	1	3	119,778

RECORDS OF HORSES

Horse	Age	Sex	Sts	1st	2d	3d	Won
Bartolo	2	C	3	0	1	1	10,700
Bartons Barndance	3	G	8	0	0	0	475
Barton's Breeze	4	G	12	3	2	1	12,520
Bart's Galaxy	6	G	3	0	0	0	216
Bartus Christian	3	G	7	0	2	3	13,661
Baryshnikov's Song	7	G	14	5	1	3	51,012
Barzulu (NZ)	7	G	5	0	0	2	27,715
Bas Giant	3	G	4	2	0	0	19,972
Bas Image	2	F	2	0	0	0	1,451
Base Hit	3	G	4	0	1	1	2,149
Base Stealer	4	F	9	1	0	1	34,089
Baseball	7	G	8	3	1	0	35,322
Basedonreality	3	F	1	1	0	0	4,785
Baseline Road	7	G	9	1	1	1	4,816
Baseport	3	C	12	1	2	1	5,366
Basha's Charm	3	F	23	3	2	8	40,759
Basha's Queen	2	F	3	0	1	0	5,970
Bashful Blue	5	M	2	0	0	0	212
Bashful Bob	4	G	5	0	0	1	816
Bashful Bull	3	C	3	0	1	0	4,940
Bashful Terror	3	C	2	0	0	0	0
Bashfull Bo	2	G	3	0	0	0	210
Basic Bug	4	G	10	1	2	1	8,134
Basic Concern	7	G	6	0	2	0	5,643
Basic Credit	3	F	2	0	0	1	650
Basic D	3	G	4	0	0	0	339
Basically Noble	5	G	6	0	1	0	1,815
Basically Radical	4	G	3	1	0	0	4,372
Basically Sexy	3	F	6	2	1	1	12,456
Basier Ma Ack	5	G	6	1	0	0	5,828
Basil Wolf	3	G	9	1	1	1	8,536
Basilides	3	G	3	0	0	1	1,040
Basilio	3	C	1	0	0	0	400
Basilisk	5	G	9	4	1	1	29,496
Basil's Rhythm	6	H	10	1	1	0	28,620
Basin of Beauty	6	M	2	0	0	0	110
Basinbob	7	G	10	4	1	1	26,383
Basket of Dreams	3	F	10	1	3	2	33,614
Basketball Court	3	C	3	2	1	0	47,390
Basketfullofposies	4	F	1	0	0	0	310
Baskket	5	M	5	0	0	0	1,150
Basque of Love	3	F	15	1	1	1	11,872
Bass Creek	10	G	1	0	0	0	60
Bass Lake	3	F	7	1	2	0	10,469
Bassam	6	G	15	3	1	1	24,428
Bassant	6	G	10	0	1	0	10,075
Bassett Hall	4	C	5	1	0	0	3,060
Bassmaster	3	G	12	1	0	0	7,292
Bass's Chance	3	G	3	0	0	0	540
Bastante	5	M	1	0	0	0	0
Bastante Grande	4	G	10	1	0	0	7,971
Bastaya	4	G	14	2	5	0	42,680
Bastille	2	C	2	0	0	1	4,729
Bastione	4	G	4	1	1	1	11,340
Bat Lady	4	F	1	0	0	0	217
Bat Mobile	4	C	5	0	3	0	34,000
Bat Runner	6	G	5	0	1	2	5,285
Batabano	3	G	7	0	0	2	5,200
Batafurai	2	G	4	0	0	1	836
Batai Warrior	3	G	6	0	0	2	5,010
Bates	6	G	9	1	0	1	20,610
Bates Castle	4	G	17	2	4	1	12,405
Bates City	4	C	11	3	1	2	28,987
Bates Honor	7	M	13	1	1	2	11,341
Bath House Bet	4	F	6	3	1	0	18,570
Bathing Expressive	8	G	3	0	1	0	612
Bathurst St Blues	7	M	1	0	0	0	91
Batman Robin	3	C	1	0	0	0	250
Batonnier's Way	4	G	5	0	0	0	228
Batson Challenge	2	C	3	1	0	0	15,965
Battante	5	M	6	0	0	1	2,928
Battar	5	G	8	0	1	0	1,988
Battin' Ghosts	6	G	6	0	0	0	550
Battle	6	H	3	0	0	1	1,680
Battle Babe	2	F	5	0	2	0	5,034
Battle Boots	4	G	6	0	1	0	705
Battle Bunker	3	F	12	0	1	2	9,781
Battle Ghost	7	G	4	0	0	0	244
Battle Hero	3	C	6	1	1	0	24,080
Battle of Trenton	2	C	4	0	0	0	630
Battle Op	4	G	1	0	1	0	2,700
Battle Prince	3	G	13	1	4	2	32,320
Battle Prospect	4	C	5	1	0	0	8,484
Battle Red	3	C	2	0	0	1	3,120
Battle Roar	7	G	3	0	0	0	263
Battle Tank	4	G	5	0	2	0	15,200
Battle Tap	5	G	3	0	0	0	250
Battle Tested	4	C	3	0	0	0	0
Battle Tough	5	G	20	1	3	0	7,914
Battle Won	4	G	9	3	2	2	192,829
Battledar	6	G	12	2	1	2	31,296
Battledress	3	F	8	0	2	1	22,960
Battleing Tigress	8	M	8	1	1	1	3,998
Battlements	4	G	8	0	0	2	23,546
Battleship Louis	4	G	6	0	0	1	4,060
Battlin Billy	7	G	3	0	0	0	0
Battlin Syke	4	G	13	1	0	1	5,362
Battling Buzz	3	C	9	1	0	4	15,110
Battling Miss	7	M	4	0	0	0	172
Batture Boy	3	G	4	0	0	0	0
Bavarian Baron	2	C	3	0	0	1	7,410
Bavarian Prince	3	G	7	0	2	3	17,740
Bavario	11	G	2	0	0	0	0
Baviera (GB)	4	F	3	1	0	0	18,600
Bawl	5	M	12	0	2	0	9,098
Baxter Creek	2	G	7	0	0	0	6,555
Baxter Hall	3	F	9	2	2	1	78,642
Bay Angus	3	G	8	0	0	0	940
Bay Be Rocker	5	M	8	2	1	1	5,180
Bay Blaze	3	F	5	0	1	0	810
Bay Breezer	4	F	12	2	3	1	30,705
Bay Citi Girl	3	F	10	2	2	1	57,076
Bay Com Three	2	G	3	1	0	0	8,688
Bay Commander	5	G	2	0	0	1	975
Bay Dancer	2	F	4	1	0	2	13,700
Bay Dawn	2	C	7	0	0	2	2,061
Bay Day	3	F	16	1	0	4	8,417
Bay Dock	2	G	4	2	0	0	22,460
Bay Dragon	7	M	12	1	1	1	25,861
Bay Eagle	6	G	8	1	0	1	33,845
Bay Ghost	4	G	9	1	1	1	6,227
Bay Guard	3	C	4	1	0	0	10,377
Bay Kisses	3	F	9	0	0	1	5,105
Bay Marvel	5	G	6	4	1	0	84,040
Bay Minette	3	F	5	0	0	1	5,100
Bay Minister	3	G	2	0	0	0	170
Bay Not Gray	5	M	3	0	0	0	204
Bay of Bulls	3	F	13	2	1	2	47,278
Bay of Love	5	G	12	2	3	1	63,330
Bay Raider	4	G	5	0	3	1	8,520
Bay Resort	2	C	3	1	0	0	6,240
Bay Scout	3	C	2	0	0	0	67
Bay Shark	5	G	5	0	3	0	3,783
Bay Smoker	3	F	4	0	0	0	180
Bay Street Belle	7	M	8	2	0	0	9,665
Bay Street Blues	9	G	11	1	0	2	2,355
Bay Street Boy	3	G	16	1	2	3	15,546
Bay Sweetie Babe	3	F	8	3	2	0	194,153
Bay Town Boy	6	G	3	0	0	1	5,040
Bay Tree (IRE)	3	F	6	0	0	1	14,961
Bay View Sue	2	F	4	2	2	0	42,431
Bay West	3	F	9	1	1	2	8,720
Bay Wide Total	4	G	10	1	1	2	8,640
Bay Window	3	F	9	0	1	2	5,686
Bay Wolf	2	C	4	0	1	0	2,400
Bayakoa Slew	5	G	3	0	0	0	111
Bayakoa's Image	5	M	2	0	0	0	125
Bayamo (IRE)	5	G	5	2	2	0	272,400
Bayani	4	F	9	1	2	1	40,589
Baybandit	2	C	8	0	0	1	2,233
Baybe Paces	6	H	5	0	0	0	810
Baycliff	2	G	1	0	0	0	0
Baycourt	2	F	2	0	0	0	700
Bayfront	3	F	5	2	0	1	41,920
Bayjur	4	F	6	1	2	2	22,550
Baylaura	3	F	6	1	0	1	8,928
Bayley Bopp	7	G	11	3	1	2	20,133
Baylor B.	2	F	6	1	0	0	12,375

Horse	Age	Sex	Sts	1st	2d	3d	Won
Baymont	3	F	14	3	3	5	107,020
Bayou Accacia	5	G	9	1	1	1	11,863
Bayou Bank	3	G	12	0	0	1	7,149
Bayou Beauty	3	F	16	1	3	1	16,300
Bayou Bend	2	F	8	1	1	2	20,283
Bayou Breeze	2	F	1	0	0	0	118
Bayou Buster	5	G	8	1	0	2	27,302
Bayou D' Indre	8	G	13	0	0	1	1,894
Bayou Deroche	4	G	13	2	0	3	8,408
Bayou Flower	3	F	9	2	3	1	41,650
Bayou Hopper	3	F	5	0	1	2	5,105
Bayou Jaguar	6	G	10	2	2	2	16,149
Bayou Jessie	2	F	1	0	0	0	55
Bayou Lawyer	4	G	13	0	1	1	4,792
Bayou Moon	4	G	7	0	0	0	243
Bayou Queen	5	M	2	0	0	0	128
Bayou Star	2	F	2	0	0	1	1,595
Bayou the Moon	6	H	2	0	1	0	6,087
Bayowolf	3	G	10	2	1	2	10,698
Baystreet Pleasure	3	F	6	1	0	2	21,418
Bayswater	2	G	8	0	0	2	15,450
Bayville	5	M	9	2	0	1	8,428
Baywood Drive	2	F	2	0	0	1	2,631
Bazooka Blaze	4	C	5	1	2	1	7,360
Bazooka Joe	4	G	6	3	0	0	4,246
Bc's Music	3	G	16	2	4	2	44,015
Be a Halo	2	G	2	0	1	1	7,580
Be a Honey	3	F	1	0	1	0	1,905
Be a Hunter	5	G	1	0	0	0	189
Be a Leah Mackee	4	F	5	1	0	0	1,294
Be Able	3	G	10	2	2	2	23,870
Be Ambitious	2	F	2	1	1	0	12,100
Be Berry Quiet	3	F	3	0	1	0	2,700
Be Better	5	G	9	2	1	5	16,210
Be Blessed	6	M	14	4	0	2	20,087
Be Clever Evelyn	3	F	10	1	0	2	3,468
Be Cool Fool	3	G	9	1	1	1	15,985
Be Do Have	4	C	9	1	1	2	17,325
Be Factual	5	M	3	1	1	0	43,840
Be Free	3	G	4	0	0	1	3,380
Be Fuhr Real	4	F	2	0	0	0	0
Be Grateful	2	G	4	0	0	0	3,655
Be Like Mike	5	H	3	0	1	1	17,740
Be Magnificent	3	F	15	2	2	2	34,023
Be Mine Sunshine	7	M	12	0	0	0	2,009
Be My Buddy	3	C	8	2	1	0	37,330
Be My Friend	7	M	8	2	0	1	45,680
Be My Molly	4	F	12	2	2	2	12,982
Be My Prince	3	C	6	1	2	2	52,500
Be My Sun	7	G	6	1	1	0	2,720
Be My Valentine	5	M	6	4	0	0	87,996
Be Not Afraid	4	C	3	0	0	0	0
Be Oh Be	2	C	3	1	1	0	6,670
Be On the Look Out	4	F	5	0	1	0	920
Be Positive	3	F	1	0	0	0	180
Be Quiet	3	F	9	1	3	1	15,673
Be Still My Heart	5	M	10	4	1	0	13,165
Be That Way	5	G	5	0	2	2	5,360
Be the Bunny	8	G	14	2	1	3	12,843
Be True Rene	4	F	5	0	0	0	435
Be Valiant	8	H	10	0	2	1	7,084
Bea Careless	4	G	3	0	0	0	229
Bea Princess	4	F	7	0	2	1	8,046
Bea Slick	3	G	8	0	0	1	1,813
Beabasque	5	H	12	4	4	1	69,770
Beach Bertie	4	F	6	0	1	1	4,411
Beach Bound	4	G	12	1	0	2	11,898
Beach Club	4	G	4	1	1	2	18,980
Beach Fit	4	G	9	0	0	0	112
Beach of Bali	4	F	11	2	3	2	31,159
Beach Pizza	3	F	5	2	0	1	46,000
Beach Plum	4	F	5	1	0	1	7,740
Beach Side	3	F	15	2	1	1	19,080
Beach Walker	5	G	14	1	3	3	13,147
Beachblanket Bingo	2	F	4	1	0	0	4,719
Beached	5	M	7	2	3	2	35,930
Beachhouse	3	F	6	0	0	3	5,815
Beachstreet Boogie	5	M	10	1	1	2	15,771
Beachy Head	5	M	7	0	0	1	2,470

Horse	Age	Sex	Sts	1st	2d	3d	Won
Beacon Brite	2	G	1	1	0	0	6,325
Beacon of Hope	2	F	2	0	0	2	3,500
Beacontree	3	F	13	1	0	3	10,052
Beaded Butterfly	2	F	2	0	0	0	1,162
Beam Queen	2	F	3	0	1	0	11,350
Beamer One	3	G	7	0	1	2	11,700
Beamer'n Glick	3	C	12	1	2	2	44,756
Beaming Heat	3	F	10	2	3	3	28,600
Beaming Star	5	G	3	0	0	1	2,678
Bean Burrito	4	G	1	0	0	0	300
Beanie Genie	6	M	1	0	0	0	0
Beaniegirl	4	F	4	0	0	1	340
Beanie's Bad Boy	4	G	11	2	1	1	43,685
Beans in the Teens	6	G	7	0	0	0	174
Beans On Toast	3	G	12	0	2	1	5,797
Bear Boot's	2	G	3	0	2	0	7,535
Bear Champ	2	G	1	0	0	0	0
Bear Country	4	G	1	0	0	0	64
Bear Cut	7	G	2	0	0	0	0
Bear Fan	5	M	6	4	1	1	496,180
Bear Force Won	5	G	15	0	4	1	28,556
Bear Hug Slew	4	F	4	0	0	0	262
Bear in the House	5	M	12	2	3	1	43,159
Bear in the Woods	3	C	5	2	0	0	65,600
Bear King	3	G	11	0	1	1	2,416
Bear Knows	2	F	2	0	0	0	294
Bear On My Mind	4	C	1	0	0	1	1,560
Bear On Tour	4	C	12	0	0	1	2,650
Bear Picasso	2	G	5	0	0	4	14,570
Bear Press	3	G	13	1	2	1	13,765
Bear Sign	2	C	2	0	0	0	720
Bear Trick	3	G	6	1	0	2	19,898
Bearacer	5	G	2	0	0	0	750
Bearcat Brawl	3	C	1	0	0	0	110
Bearcat Drive	4	G	9	3	2	1	17,595
Bearcat Jett	8	G	4	0	0	0	810
Bearcat Kenyon	4	C	12	1	3	1	12,773
Bearhouse	8	G	1	0	0	0	0
Bearlee Naked	3	F	2	0	0	0	1,770
Bears Mo Red	2	G	4	1	0	0	6,325
Bearspaw	6	G	6	1	0	1	1,750
Beartrack Cove	3	F	10	2	2	3	54,820
Beary	5	G	3	0	0	0	0
Bea's Big Man	3	G	1	0	0	0	0
Bea's Bionda	2	F	5	1	1	0	21,860
Bea's Gal	3	F	2	0	1	0	2,700
Beat Army	3	C	7	0	1	0	2,236
Beat the Chalk	2	G	5	2	1	0	88,630
Beat the Storm	4	F	3	0	0	0	140
Beat the Traffic	3	C	5	3	0	1	37,000
Beat You There	8	H	1	0	0	0	195
Beater	6	M	5	0	1	0	3,653
Beating Heart	5	M	5	0	0	2	720
Beating Michigan	3	F	10	3	0	0	18,959
Beatlestix	3	G	3	1	0	0	6,300
Beatnik	7	G	7	0	0	1	1,144
Beatrix	5	M	9	1	3	1	14,885
Beau	2	G	11	0	3	3	40,180
Beau Alaric	5	G	5	1	1	0	13,677
Beau Allure	3	G	20	1	4	3	18,034
Beau an Airo	7	G	1	0	0	0	37
Beau Bailey	4	G	12	2	3	0	17,733
Beau Brass	4	G	8	3	0	1	130,236
Beau Buddy	6	G	2	0	0	0	0
Beau Bunny	3	F	5	1	1	0	10,750
Beau C Fuss	2	G	3	0	0	0	1,222
Beau Classic	4	C	3	1	1	0	12,060
Beau Devious	3	G	13	1	3	0	6,859
Beau Emperor	5	H	2	0	0	0	186
Beau Filou (NZ)	5	G	4	0	0	1	3,750
Beau Happy	3	F	5	1	2	0	32,000
Beau Jackson	4	C	4	0	2	0	4,986
Beau Jake	5	G	1	0	0	0	305
Beau Joey	6	G	3	1	0	1	7,221
Beau Kent	3	G	2	0	0	0	0
Beau Maggie	2	G	6	2	0	1	24,292
Beau Manners	5	G	11	2	0	1	19,438
Beau Matt	6	G	1	0	0	0	0
Beau On Tour	4	G	6	0	0	0	1,670

Horse	Age	Sex	Sts	1st	2d	3d	Won
Beau Pip	5	G	1	0	0	0	0
Beau Ring	7	G	9	1	2	1	7,310
Beau Rivage	3	C	3	0	0	0	2,530
Beau Ryder	4	G	9	1	1	2	16,524
Beau Selecto	2	G	1	0	0	0	105
Beau Slew	2	C	3	0	0	0	300
Beau Soleil	4	C	4	3	1	0	191,920
Beau Tanner	5	G	1	0	0	0	85
Beau Tie	7	G	15	0	4	2	50,476
Beau Watch	3	F	8	3	1	1	65,888
Beau Willie	7	G	8	0	1	0	4,169
Beauallis	6	M	14	4	3	0	34,926
Beaucatcher	3	F	1	0	0	0	100
Beaucette	4	F	8	3	1	0	103,600
Beaucoup Trois	6	M	3	0	1	1	3,375
Beaudazzler	8	G	13	6	1	1	37,200
Beaudelair Jones	7	H	9	3	0	1	10,300
Beaudiggity	6	G	4	0	0	0	1,740
Beaufighter (NZ)	6	G	5	0	0	0	0
Beauford T.	2	C	1	0	0	1	2,035
Beaugar	4	G	11	3	2	1	48,610
Beaugeste	2	F	7	1	1	1	37,546
Beaugie	8	G	4	0	0	0	44
Beaujestic	3	F	9	2	1	1	15,215
Beaujolie	3	G	6	0	0	0	1,416
Beaulena	4	F	6	0	1	2	13,675
Beaulieu	4	G	13	1	2	1	8,847
Beaumaris	11	H	2	0	0	0	195
Beaunaskra	7	M	5	0	0	0	280
Beau's Ace	4	F	5	0	0	0	1,256
Beau's City	3	F	2	0	0	0	0
Beau's County	3	C	4	1	0	0	3,900
Beau's Diva	3	F	10	2	2	1	31,005
Beau's Fantasy	6	G	12	1	0	1	12,108
Beau's Gem	5	M	12	3	0	1	18,418
Beau's Laura	2	F	1	0	0	0	0
Beau's Party Date	2	F	3	0	0	1	2,025
Beau's Regal Gal	5	M	4	0	0	1	1,925
Beau's Surprise	6	G	3	0	0	0	0
Beau's Town	6	G	6	2	1	1	112,530
Beau's Trip	2	F	4	1	0	0	21,930
Beau's Wager	6	G	4	3	0	0	23,400
Beausox	5	M	9	1	1	1	18,150
Beaut	3	F	1	0	0	0	400
Beautiful America	4	F	8	1	2	3	98,161
Beautiful Angel	3	G	15	1	2	1	25,395
Beautiful Balance	7	G	3	1	2	0	45,680
Beautiful Baroness	4	F	8	1	2	2	62,151
Beautiful Bay	3	F	1	1	0	0	26,400
Beautiful Becke	5	M	7	1	1	1	9,185
Beautiful Bets	4	F	8	2	0	1	44,752
Beautiful Call	4	F	4	0	1	2	4,000
Beautiful Chant	3	F	3	0	0	0	314
Beautiful Charm	2	F	1	0	0	0	0
Beautiful Crazy	4	F	2	1	0	0	21,100
Beautiful Dreamer	3	F	7	2	2	0	13,505
Beautiful East	3	F	10	2	0	2	51,345
Beautiful Eyes	5	M	2	0	0	0	545
Beautiful Honor	4	F	5	1	1	0	17,500
Beautiful Joyce	2	F	3	0	0	0	0
Beautiful Lady	5	M	2	0	0	1	1,650
Beautiful Lassie	5	M	12	5	3	1	30,146
Beautiful Love	5	M	5	1	2	2	11,435
Beautiful Mistress	2	F	6	1	1	1	12,240
Beautiful Prize	4	F	4	0	0	0	455
Beautiful Spy	4	F	5	0	2	2	18,435
Beautiful Starlet	5	M	10	2	1	2	29,077
Beautiful Stella	3	F	3	0	0	1	1,456
Beautiful Sunrise	3	F	6	0	0	1	1,400
Beautiful Treasure	4	F	2	0	0	0	1,040
Beautiful Vision	2	F	1	0	0	0	0
Beautifulbutbored	3	F	7	1	2	0	18,722
Beautify	2	F	3	0	0	0	1,394
Beautify Life	3	G	6	1	1	1	17,698
Beauty and Glory	3	F	4	2	1	0	23,645
Beauty Charm	4	F	12	0	2	3	26,738
Beauty Go Leor (IRE)	8	G	3	0	0	0	0
Beauty Halo (ARG)	5	M	1	0	0	0	750
Beauty in Paradise	3	F	6	0	1	1	2,097
Beauty Nina	6	M	4	3	0	0	4,724
Beauty of Bath	2	F	1	0	0	0	0
Beauty On Duty	4	F	9	0	2	2	19,835
Beauty Pagent	3	F	5	1	0	0	4,531
Beauty to a T	3	F	10	0	1	0	7,970
Beauty to Boot	4	F	7	0	2	0	5,520
Beautybeyondbasics	3	F	15	1	0	2	18,875
Beautybyaday	4	F	5	0	0	0	3,845
Beautycanfly	4	G	1	0	0	0	0
Beauty's Dream	6	M	2	0	0	0	124
Beauty's Kitty	3	F	9	3	0	1	26,330
Beauty's Outlaw	6	G	15	1	1	4	7,305
Beauty's Pride	3	F	4	0	0	0	4,686
Beauty's Protected	7	M	2	0	0	0	500
Beauvalay	5	G	1	0	0	0	0
Beaux Artes	5	M	9	0	1	2	9,045
Beauzak	4	G	9	1	0	1	15,298
Beaver Cat	5	G	1	0	0	0	138
Beaver Tales	4	G	8	1	0	0	5,099
Beaverton	3	G	10	3	0	2	14,203
Beback	3	G	1	1	0	0	5,850
Bebe Betz	4	F	1	0	0	0	450
Bebe Garcon	4	G	10	2	2	1	84,733
Beboppin Baby	11	G	1	0	0	0	0
Bebopping Gold	4	F	12	3	1	4	11,455
Becalmed	7	G	4	0	0	1	1,432
Because of Barbie	5	G	1	0	0	0	98
Because Youre Mine	6	M	12	1	2	2	18,893
Becca's Salut	4	C	11	2	2	0	36,013
Beccas' Shoulder	2	C	5	1	0	2	8,214
Becham	3	C	5	0	3	2	13,340
Beckabase	2	G	4	0	1	1	1,875
Beckelman	7	G	19	1	7	4	30,980
Beckeys Benz	3	G	7	0	0	0	920
Beckon the King	8	G	8	4	2	0	39,418
Beckson	3	G	2	1	0	0	5,143
Becky B Mine	5	M	11	1	4	5	29,834
Becky Bain	3	F	2	0	0	0	270
Becky Beth	4	F	1	0	0	0	0
Becky in Pink	3	F	8	4	0	0	106,674
Becky Sharp	2	F	2	0	1	1	17,670
Becky Special	3	F	2	0	0	1	1,537
Becky's Cat	2	F	4	0	0	0	1,850
Becky's Rock	5	M	4	0	0	0	855
Becky's Skirt	2	F	2	1	0	0	1,630
Becloud	4	F	13	1	0	1	4,150
Bed Pro	4	F	11	2	0	1	13,209
Bedanken	5	M	8	3	0	1	222,555
Bedazzle 'Em	4	F	10	1	4	0	60,932
Bedevil	3	F	9	1	3	2	11,767
Bedford Road	4	G	6	0	0	1	740
Bedford's Comet	5	M	8	1	0	3	6,936
Bedillion	5	G	7	3	0	2	27,157
Bedline	3	C	12	0	1	0	1,437
Bedmar (GB)	3	G	9	0	0	4	43,897
Bedoobee	2	F	3	0	0	1	327
Bedouina	5	M	11	2	0	1	24,182
Bedroom Kisser	6	G	13	2	1	3	30,300
Bedtime Lullaby	5	M	3	0	0	0	169
Bee a Gold Mine	6	G	3	2	0	0	9,270
Bee a Lion	2	F	3	0	1	0	11,408
Bee Bee Doubleyou	4	F	15	2	1	3	13,361
Bee Bee Gun	3	G	9	1	0	1	10,468
Bee Faster	2	F	6	1	1	0	10,073
Bee Flat	3	F	10	0	2	2	5,854
Bee Fly	5	G	7	1	0	4	12,721
Bee Honey	6	G	12	1	2	0	4,597
Bee Line Genius	5	M	14	3	1	3	26,492
Bee Mountain	5	G	3	3	0	0	43,800
Bee My Selecto	5	M	7	2	0	1	9,273
Bee On Track	5	M	10	1	3	0	10,051
Bee Zee Carson	2	F	1	0	0	0	390
Beebe Lake	4	F	7	2	1	0	70,995
Beebe's Famoose	3	G	2	0	0	0	975
Beeboppin Cousin	3	G	11	2	0	2	24,158
Beecher	6	G	9	0	0	2	1,480
Beeda	3	F	16	3	3	1	39,638
Beef'n Brew	5	G	7	0	1	0	5,011
Beeline	3	F	1	1	0	0	7,800

Horse	Age	Sex	Sts	1st	2d	3d	Won
Beeline Express	6	G	1	0	0	0	38
Beelzebubba	4	G	12	3	0	1	16,250
Beem's Boots	2	G	1	0	0	0	250
Been Broke	3	C	12	1	0	1	4,591
Been Done Dat Dare	3	C	8	0	0	2	2,385
Been Smokin	3	G	9	1	1	2	13,700
Been Wavering	5	G	10	5	2	1	71,470
Beenonabender	4	G	10	0	2	2	5,835
Beep and Go	5	G	5	0	0	0	922
Beep Bandit	3	F	3	0	0	0	289
Beep Beep Beep	4	G	16	0	0	1	10,850
Beep Me	10	G	17	0	7	3	11,580
Beep Zone	3	F	12	1	2	1	8,535
Beep's Starwalker	4	G	4	0	0	0	1,590
Beer for Breakfast	4	G	2	0	1	0	775
Beer Goggles	6	G	10	1	1	0	5,838
Beer Me	5	G	12	1	1	0	11,629
Beer On Tap	2	F	5	0	0	1	510
Beer Run	4	G	5	1	0	1	3,420
Beer Stien	2	G	7	1	0	1	18,776
Beermeathebit	5	G	9	0	0	0	36
Bee's Cat	3	F	5	1	1	0	12,200
Beetrap	4	G	9	0	0	0	1,728
Beeville	4	F	10	0	2	6	21,680
Beezer	3	F	13	3	3	3	76,300
Before Midnight	2	F	1	0	0	0	0
Before the Court	4	G	4	0	0	1	1,020
Begborrowanddeal	3	G	2	0	0	0	5,837
Begone Quick	4	G	7	0	2	0	1,076
Begonebydaylight	3	F	4	0	2	0	2,017
Begoodatit	7	G	15	1	1	0	7,450
Begotten Son	3	G	4	1	0	0	5,425
Behaving Badly	3	F	1	1	0	0	29,400
Behind Bars	5	M	4	0	0	0	235
Behind Enemy Lines	5	G	10	2	1	2	54,420
Behind On Points	4	G	10	1	3	1	27,140
Behind the Plate	4	G	4	1	0	1	14,260
Behind the Screen	2	G	1	1	0	0	24,600
Behkat	4	G	2	0	0	0	650
Behler's Beauty	4	F	5	0	0	1	5,645
Behrnik	4	F	10	1	1	3	56,311
Behrometer	2	G	1	0	0	0	480
Bein	6	M	3	0	0	0	440
Bein' Friendly	3	G	3	0	0	0	550
Being Green	7	G	10	1	1	1	6,303
Being Native	7	M	6	1	0	1	6,994
Being With You	4	F	13	2	5	3	33,177
Bejoyfulandrejoyce	7	M	1	0	0	0	2,220
Beknown to Me	8	G	13	2	0	1	78,018
Bel Baie	5	M	1	0	0	1	2,970
Bel Chateau	4	F	15	3	2	0	27,180
Bela Bartok	2	F	5	1	0	1	3,468
Bela Carol	3	F	2	1	0	0	12,836
Bela Kiani	3	F	5	0	0	1	1,800
Belal	9	G	9	1	1	0	3,963
Belanso	4	G	6	0	1	1	2,231
Belarion	2	C	6	1	2	2	55,873
Belazar	4	F	6	0	0	0	626
Belbart	2	C	7	3	2	1	51,280
Belding	3	F	3	1	1	0	6,020
Beleive a Caper	3	G	7	0	1	0	6,360
Belek's Court	3	F	3	1	0	0	6,930
Belek's Princess	3	F	7	1	0	1	9,473
Belen Bullet	3	G	7	1	0	1	4,795
Belfast Drive	8	G	16	1	1	0	4,133
Belibhai	7	G	9	0	0	2	2,863
Belichick	4	C	9	0	2	2	29,790
Belie	5	M	13	1	1	1	15,040
Believable Copy	3	G	11	1	0	0	6,772
Believable Dolly	3	F	6	0	1	0	2,797
Believable Host	4	G	4	1	0	1	14,793
Believable Nemo	2	G	1	0	0	0	0
Believable Shirley	4	F	9	0	0	1	3,160
Believable Trick	4	F	12	0	2	2	3,491
Believe a Countess	4	F	14	1	3	2	18,820
Believe I Can Fly	5	H	11	0	1	0	22,132
Believe I'm Gold	2	C	5	0	0	0	2,355
Believe Im Special	5	G	11	3	1	4	95,808
Believe in Angels	3	F	1	0	0	0	0
Believe in Missy	3	F	11	4	0	2	107,602
Believe It Is So	4	F	1	0	0	0	0
Believe Its Brooke	3	F	12	2	0	0	12,196
Believe Its Mojo	3	C	2	0	0	0	0
Believe My Reality	2	F	1	0	0	0	1,020
Believe She Can	6	M	5	0	0	0	1,473
Believe the D J	12	G	5	0	0	0	237
Believe the Devil	6	G	8	0	0	0	1,074
Believe the Doctor	4	F	5	0	0	0	293
Believe You Me	8	G	9	0	0	1	2,745
Believein Mud Bugs	4	G	9	2	1	1	24,927
Believeinkarakorum	2	F	4	0	0	0	560
Believeitohko	4	G	6	0	0	0	0
Believeits a Cat	3	G	9	1	0	2	5,883
Believemewenitellu	4	C	14	2	3	1	15,580
Believen It	4	F	12	3	0	1	58,456
Believer in Me	2	F	1	0	0	0	0
Believer's Dolly	5	M	13	0	1	2	10,001
Believer's Lucky	5	G	9	2	1	2	45,473
Believer's Ruckus	3	G	5	0	0	0	2,276
Belittlenot	3	F	2	0	0	0	753
Beliveau	3	G	2	0	0	0	0
Belknap County	2	C	8	0	1	1	13,348
Bell Boy	5	G	7	0	0	0	1,117
Bell Brass	3	F	2	0	0	0	1,800
Bell Court	2	C	1	0	0	0	184
Bell Express	5	G	8	0	0	1	817
Bell of the Year	3	F	9	1	2	1	26,990
Bell Power	5	H	8	3	2	0	35,480
Bell Sara	3	F	17	3	2	5	40,020
Bella and Whistles	3	F	9	2	0	1	18,471
Bella Babe	3	F	2	1	0	0	6,670
Bella Baloosa	4	F	11	1	1	2	20,424
Bella Bandit	3	F	2	0	0	0	2,520
Bella Banissa	2	F	3	0	2	0	37,630
Bella Bella Bailey	5	M	12	1	0	4	28,833
Bella Belle	7	M	5	0	1	1	795
Bella Bianca	3	F	7	1	1	1	48,705
Bella Boo	3	F	9	0	2	2	2,580
Bella Bourie	3	F	13	2	1	3	63,722
Bella Cantu	2	F	5	0	1	1	11,836
Bella Cat	5	M	6	0	0	0	699
Bella Cobra	3	F	17	4	6	4	81,410
Bella Coola Bebe	5	M	3	0	1	0	2,034
Bella Corona	3	F	10	1	1	1	21,591
Bella de Fattoria	4	F	13	0	2	1	11,115
Bella Favola	5	M	9	1	2	1	9,215
Bella Fumatori	4	F	16	3	0	4	31,520
Bella Giorno	4	F	13	2	4	1	69,890
Bella Girl	5	M	8	1	2	0	39,750
Bella Isabella	3	F	6	0	1	0	3,950
Bella Katrina	4	F	5	2	0	0	22,487
Bella La Ghosi	3	F	9	1	0	2	10,944
Bella Luchia	2	F	5	0	0	0	4,040
Bella Luna Baby	3	F	1	0	0	0	0
Bella Magic	3	F	1	0	1	0	3,800
Bella Mama	2	F	2	0	0	1	5,491
Bella Mosella	2	F	2	0	0	0	0
Bella Noelle	3	F	2	0	1	1	6,700
Bella Nunzi	4	F	12	4	1	3	71,900
Bella Queen	3	F	3	0	0	0	1,200
Bella Rouge	6	M	4	0	4	0	25,200
Bella Rubia	3	F	6	2	0	1	13,361
Bella Savella	4	F	15	4	2	3	56,775
Bella Siena	4	F	4	0	0	0	1,620
Bella Sierra	4	F	3	1	0	0	5,490
Bella Sophia	2	F	1	0	0	0	400
Bella Stella	2	F	5	0	0	0	3,425
Bella Tizzy	6	M	6	1	0	2	9,520
Bella Trieste	2	F	1	0	0	0	860
Bellacuzin	3	F	3	1	0	1	8,315
Belladumaani	3	C	6	0	0	0	8,728
Bellagio Bob	3	C	3	2	0	0	32,230
Bellamente	3	F	10	1	2	2	10,608
Bellamy Road	2	C	3	2	0	1	140,400
Bellanique	3	F	8	2	2	1	79,280
Bellanova	4	F	8	2	1	1	33,180
Bellaral	4	F	14	2	3	2	17,046
Bellarama	3	F	5	0	1	1	4,710

RECORDS OF HORSES

Horse	Age	Sex	Sts	1st	2d	3d	Won
Bellaroma	5	M	3	0	1	1	2,221
Bella's Ballet	2	F	2	0	0	1	1,848
Bellatia	3	F	3	0	0	0	1,398
Bellator	2	G	5	0	1	0	3,880
Bellavena	4	F	11	2	2	2	12,063
Belle Ange (FR)	3	F	13	4	1	3	115,828
Belle Angel	4	F	6	2	1	0	39,205
Belle Armour	3	F	2	0	0	0	1,220
Belle Arti	4	G	4	2	0	0	10,800
Belle Artiste	6	M	1	0	0	0	3,000
Belle City Baby	4	F	6	0	0	0	1,200
Belle City Boy	3	C	7	1	1	0	19,970
Belle Dame	2	F	5	1	0	2	7,730
Belle de Naskra	5	M	10	2	2	4	29,656
Belle de Neuville	3	F	12	0	2	2	18,696
Belle de Sand	4	F	8	1	0	0	3,602
Belle Dreamer	3	F	1	0	0	0	0
Belle Flamme	5	M	6	0	0	0	388
Belle Fourche	3	F	4	0	0	0	1,330
Belle Gully	3	C	3	0	0	1	7,117
Belle Isle	4	F	3	0	0	0	486
Belle of Broadway	4	F	3	0	0	0	512
Belle of Claxton	2	F	10	2	2	3	21,110
Belle of Indiana	3	F	5	1	0	1	12,502
Belle of Orleans	2	F	3	0	0	0	1,662
Belle of the Ball	8	M	2	0	0	0	0
Belle of the Mt.	2	F	5	1	0	0	4,200
Belle Rebelle	4	F	9	0	2	1	3,585
Belle Riviere	8	M	6	0	1	1	3,702
Belle Rosia	4	F	1	0	0	0	0
Belle Sherri	5	M	11	1	0	1	4,993
Belle Toujours	4	F	11	2	1	0	13,530
Bellefontaine	6	M	9	0	2	0	3,291
Bellefonte Charlie	3	G	2	0	0	0	402
Belleloise	3	F	7	0	0	0	3,868
Belle's Applause	4	G	4	1	1	0	5,500
Belle's Beast	3	G	8	0	0	0	1,386
Belle's Best Baby	3	F	10	1	1	2	16,330
Belle's Blaze	4	F	12	0	4	0	28,430
Belle's Deed	5	M	1	0	0	0	0
Belle's Eryn	3	F	13	1	1	3	10,908
Belle's Halo	5	M	3	0	0	0	122
Belles Lettres	5	M	10	1	0	3	49,768
Belleski	5	M	4	3	0	0	136,567
Belleview Lady	4	F	5	1	0	1	9,210
Bellgallo	4	F	1	0	0	1	420
Bellicose Papa	8	G	1	0	0	0	58
Bellini Gal	4	F	6	1	0	0	4,695
Bellini Martini	3	F	10	0	0	1	9,891
Bellisa	8	M	7	1	0	3	2,552
Bellissimo Magic	2	G	4	0	0	0	1,875
Belljar	4	C	17	0	0	3	5,317
Bellow	3	F	11	2	2	0	27,829
Bells Fool	4	G	7	4	1	0	28,905
Bell's Lass	3	F	7	1	1	2	64,395
Bells 'o Joy	4	F	3	0	0	0	0
Bells of Thunder	6	G	7	0	0	3	9,022
Bells On Her Toes	4	F	5	0	0	0	899
Bellville Bookie	3	G	2	0	0	0	0
Belmont Babe	3	F	11	2	1	2	29,991
Belmont Groovy	3	G	4	0	0	1	1,330
Belmont Harbor	3	F	3	1	1	1	8,640
Belmont Mac	2	C	2	0	0	0	780
Belong to Sea	4	F	5	1	2	0	48,700
Belongs Fast	7	M	2	0	0	0	790
Belong's to Three	4	G	20	3	6	4	62,710
Belongstospeed	5	M	2	0	0	0	0
Beloved Invader	3	C	1	0	0	0	420
Below Freezing	6	M	8	2	0	0	13,875
Below Zero	2	F	1	0	0	1	3,975
Belt	5	G	4	1	1	1	9,830
Beltaire	2	C	1	0	0	0	230
Belted Dawn	4	F	4	0	0	1	490
Beltway	3	G	7	2	1	0	23,534
Belusko's Babe	3	F	15	2	1	2	29,240
Belva Casey	4	F	18	3	3	3	22,859
Belvedere Belle	3	F	2	0	0	1	4,900
Bemuse	2	F	1	0	0	0	400
Bemybabytonite	3	F	3	0	0	0	220
Ben a Lover	4	G	12	0	2	3	9,060
Ben H	4	G	4	2	1	0	17,905
Ben Speedin	7	H	2	0	1	0	1,544
Ben the Bookie	5	G	1	0	0	0	0
Ben the Cat	3	G	8	2	3	1	25,837
Ben the Man	7	G	4	0	0	0	4,395
Ben Told	10	G	2	0	0	0	566
Bench Atara	4	F	7	1	0	3	9,978
Bench Maker	4	C	7	2	1	0	50,185
Bench Mench	4	G	12	4	2	3	28,034
Bench Press	3	C	5	0	1	1	11,380
Benchly	3	C	7	1	1	1	21,540
Benchmark Bargain	4	F	15	2	5	3	24,188
Benchrun	3	F	10	2	4	3	17,382
Bend	3	F	2	0	0	0	2,100
Bend a Little	3	F	5	1	0	3	19,133
Bend the Track	6	H	10	1	0	0	6,353
Bendalee	5	M	9	3	1	2	24,946
Benden Weyr	9	G	7	0	0	1	3,355
Bending Strings	3	F	13	3	5	0	495,150
Bendito	4	C	10	1	0	1	2,573
Benedict A. Kite	6	G	11	0	0	0	3,219
Beneficial Bartok	3	F	7	1	0	2	49,238
Beneficio	3	G	4	2	1	0	41,696
Benefit M	3	F	1	0	0	0	0
Benefit Party	5	M	1	0	1	0	2,080
Beneteau	7	G	3	0	0	0	157
Benevolento	2	G	1	0	0	0	0
Benewin	3	G	10	3	2	2	34,118
Bengalesa (ARG)	6	M	5	0	0	1	3,320
Benge B	6	G	3	1	0	1	5,183
Bengoa	4	G	1	0	0	0	400
Beniamino	4	C	13	1	2	2	14,484
Benicio (IRE)	4	G	2	0	0	0	0
Beniflower	3	F	12	0	3	1	7,095
Benita	3	F	6	1	0	0	14,050
Benjamin Baby	2	C	6	1	2	2	55,430
Benjamin Bag	6	G	9	0	0	1	1,770
Benjamin Swanson	4	G	3	0	1	0	2,070
Benjamin's Foxy	7	M	7	1	0	0	7,800
Benji'special Blue	4	G	6	0	0	0	540
Bennie Ben Benny	4	G	6	1	0	0	33,935
Bennington	3	F	18	2	3	5	29,109
Benny G	3	G	5	1	2	0	12,705
Benny the Hawk	5	G	7	0	0	0	2,736
Benny the Lip	5	G	6	0	0	1	2,010
Benny's Atlas	3	G	2	0	0	0	77
Benny's Boy	4	G	6	0	0	0	819
Benny's Gem	4	F	3	0	0	0	395
Bennys Lady	4	F	1	0	0	0	0
Bennys Tune	5	G	14	5	2	4	44,783
Benoit	4	G	8	2	0	0	18,072
Benray's Flash	7	M	2	0	0	0	770
Bens Babe	3	F	7	0	0	0	962
Ben's Choice	5	G	5	0	2	0	6,455
Ben's Courage	3	G	5	1	0	0	17,400
Ben's Hammer	4	G	13	0	1	2	6,703
Ben's Lady	4	F	9	3	3	0	10,403
Ben's Reflection	4	G	9	6	0	3	109,880
Bensquito	3	C	1	0	0	1	15,000
Bent for Glory	4	G	7	1	0	0	7,880
Bent On Bodacious	3	F	4	0	1	0	1,764
Bent On Speed	4	G	16	5	4	3	22,674
Bent Suze	3	F	11	3	2	2	18,271
Bent Tree Miracle	5	M	6	1	0	2	17,725
Benthams	5	G	6	0	0	0	952
Benton	4	G	5	1	0	1	2,635
Bentucky	4	G	5	0	0	0	460
Benz Boy	3	C	4	0	0	2	16,068
Benza Winner	11	G	1	0	0	1	180
Beppe	4	G	8	2	0	1	10,610
Bequia Tequila	6	M	18	1	4	5	13,973
Bequick Or Bedazed	9	G	6	0	0	0	395
Bequoit	6	G	8	1	0	0	7,994
Berani	4	G	4	1	0	0	1,346
Beranjiz	4	F	10	0	0	0	1,550
Berbatim	2	F	4	2	1	0	56,120
Berdelia	2	F	8	2	1	2	173,248
Beret	5	M	7	3	0	0	138,086

Horse	Age	Sex	Sts	1st	2d	3d	Won
Berfy	4	G	14	1	1	4	10,631
Berg	4	G	5	0	0	0	355
Bergen	2	F	3	0	0	0	875
Beringly	3	F	4	1	0	0	2,805
Bering's Crest	2	G	1	0	0	0	105
Beriskaio (IRE)	7	G	1	0	0	0	0
Berkelhammer	3	C	6	1	0	1	15,570
Berkley's Gold	5	M	6	1	2	2	4,846
Berkshire Eagle	4	C	14	3	1	2	27,680
Berkshire Princess	3	F	9	0	2	2	15,684
Berlanga	4	G	6	1	1	1	8,745
Berlin (IRE)	6	G	1	0	0	0	0
Bermuda Blizzard	3	G	15	1	3	3	23,794
Bermuda Isle	3	F	2	1	0	0	9,120
Bermuda Triangle	3	C	6	2	2	0	24,226
Bernadine	3	F	10	1	0	0	8,934
Bernardo	3	G	5	1	1	0	7,055
Bernard's Candy	5	G	6	1	0	1	22,330
Bernice	2	F	1	0	0	0	164
Bernie Blue	2	G	2	2	0	0	16,320
Bernie's Baby	2	F	4	1	1	1	13,620
Bernstein's Babe	2	F	5	0	3	0	38,521
Bernt Out	2	C	4	2	0	0	15,468
Berrigo Creek	3	F	8	0	0	1	829
Berry Berry	3	F	1	0	0	0	1,320
Berry Brick	3	F	1	0	0	0	0
Berry Good	3	F	7	1	0	1	8,659
Berry Southern	4	F	5	0	0	0	2,000
Berry Viva	3	F	8	4	0	1	29,904
Berry's a Smoking	6	G	10	0	0	4	8,490
Berrythegold	3	G	7	1	2	0	41,014
Bert Allen	2	G	4	0	3	0	14,180
Bert Frankie	3	G	2	0	0	0	274
Bert n' Aly	3	C	4	0	2	1	4,716
Bertelli (NZ)	6	M	9	2	0	1	33,640
Bertha Jo	2	F	6	1	0	2	44,496
Bertha's Bikini	8	M	8	1	0	0	2,055
Berthon (BRZ)	8	G	9	1	0	2	7,835
Bertie's Dream	3	G	13	1	3	2	9,668
Bertie's Halo	5	M	4	0	1	0	3,572
Bertolucci (GB)	3	G	6	0	0	1	770
Bertrando Russell	4	G	5	2	0	1	9,560
Bertrando's Babe	2	F	5	2	0	0	31,920
Bertrando's Choice	2	C	8	1	3	1	17,932
Bertrando's Model	5	M	6	0	0	2	9,620
Bertrandos Natural	3	F	1	0	0	0	400
Bertrando's Return	3	C	3	0	0	0	400
Bert's Babe	2	F	1	0	0	0	0
Bert's Bar	4	C	4	0	0	0	802
Bert's Best	3	G	12	2	1	1	18,348
Bert's Ghost	3	G	8	1	0	1	8,867
Bert's House	3	G	17	1	2	1	10,255
Bert's Nicky	5	G	11	1	0	5	7,316
Bertshero	5	H	5	1	2	1	5,765
Beryl Bear	4	F	1	0	0	0	0
Beryl's Quest	4	F	5	0	0	1	1,349
Besheft	4	G	12	0	0	3	6,165
Besige	5	M	9	2	1	1	21,825
Beso Del Sol	6	M	3	0	0	2	2,090
Bessiesfinesthour	2	F	3	0	0	0	323
Bessiesimage	3	F	3	0	0	0	0
Best Advantage	5	M	15	4	3	0	28,496
Best All Around	3	G	2	0	0	1	2,570
Best At Law	2	G	7	0	1	0	3,553
Best Attack	3	G	7	1	1	0	21,830
Best Bet	6	M	5	0	0	0	202
Best Bird	3	G	24	1	5	0	37,814
Best Bluff	2	G	5	0	0	0	1,348
Best Call	3	G	13	2	0	0	13,962
Best Caper	3	C	7	0	1	1	3,291
Best Card	5	M	7	0	1	2	3,123
Best Cat	5	G	4	0	0	0	226
Best Choice	2	C	2	0	0	0	1,200
Best Chum	3	C	8	0	5	0	24,090
Best Echo	4	G	2	0	0	0	0
Best Epic	6	G	3	0	1	0	1,160
Best Foot Forward	5	M	13	1	3	2	31,801
Best Friend	5	M	1	0	0	0	360
Best Friend Gracie	2	F	1	0	1	0	9,800
Best From the West	8	G	5	0	0	0	662
Best Gamble	3	G	13	1	0	3	19,634
Best Game in Town	3	G	7	1	2	1	14,833
Best Girl Yet	6	M	4	0	0	0	170
Best Hope	5	H	1	0	0	0	0
Best in the Storm	3	F	12	1	1	1	24,300
Best Interview	4	F	5	1	1	0	34,110
Best Issue	4	F	3	1	0	1	18,393
Best Jest B a Lady	6	M	1	0	0	0	70
Best Kept Secret	5	M	5	1	0	0	6,668
Best Knight Ever	2	G	7	2	0	1	18,370
Best Marked Tree	7	H	1	0	0	0	0
Best Minister	4	C	6	2	1	0	109,270
Best Minister Yet	2	C	3	2	0	0	18,750
Best of Change	3	G	9	1	1	1	7,868
Best of Class	4	C	8	0	0	2	3,515
Best of Glory	4	G	6	0	0	0	251
Best of Honor	3	G	5	1	1	0	9,214
Best of K C	7	G	7	1	3	1	33,570
Best of Show	2	C	1	0	0	0	115
Best of the Duck	8	G	13	1	4	0	25,592
Best of the East	5	M	3	0	0	1	930
Best Offer	2	F	3	0	1	0	3,018
Best On Tap	4	G	10	3	3	1	46,830
Best One	2	F	1	1	0	0	30,145
Best Pal Louie	2	C	6	0	2	0	5,553
Best Pick	3	G	5	0	0	3	6,355
Best Pine Yet	6	G	15	2	1	4	10,979
Best Practices	4	F	13	2	2	2	17,326
Best Quality	4	G	15	2	2	2	37,000
Best Reflection	2	C	1	0	0	0	155
Best Return	5	G	10	0	1	4	6,620
Best Shod	3	F	6	0	0	3	3,595
Best Surprise	4	G	7	0	1	1	2,990
Best Take	2	F	1	0	0	0	100
Best to Be Elusive	3	C	7	0	1	2	6,740
Best to Be King	3	C	3	0	1	0	2,335
Best to Best	5	G	5	0	2	0	1,978
Best Tribute	2	F	6	1	0	0	3,620
Best World	5	G	14	0	0	0	1,066
Bestofmoose	2	G	8	1	3	2	29,605
Bestow the Crown	4	G	8	2	0	1	6,072
Bestrongspeaktrue	3	C	12	2	1	0	19,045
Besttobeabachelor	9	G	11	1	3	2	8,004
Bet a Bargann	6	G	5	0	1	0	2,025
Bet a Bunch	3	G	8	2	1	2	18,216
Bet a Heather	4	F	5	1	1	1	4,133
Bet a Whirl	9	G	5	0	0	1	934
Bet Brick	8	G	10	1	1	1	4,120
Bet Gold	4	G	13	0	0	0	522
Bet Hez Trouble	3	C	2	0	0	0	100
Bet Judge	3	C	2	0	0	0	120
Bet Mar	3	F	2	0	0	0	0
Bet Me Best	8	G	2	0	0	1	5,500
Bet Me Jack	6	G	7	0	1	0	1,886
Bet Me Now	3	F	3	0	0	0	0
Bet On a Star	3	C	7	0	1	2	3,835
Bet On a Vision	4	F	5	0	1	0	1,302
Bet On Boston	4	G	7	2	0	0	30,644
Bet On Brad	5	G	5	1	2	1	2,680
Bet On Grace	2	F	6	0	0	2	5,304
Bet On Joe	6	H	4	0	0	0	3,060
Bet On Lori	6	M	3	0	0	0	144
Bet On the Rainbow	4	F	11	0	2	2	36,727
Bet Once	12	G	8	1	1	1	1,572
Bet Seventeen	2	C	1	0	0	0	0
Bet Star Yet	3	G	4	1	0	1	12,350
Bet the Bay	3	G	2	0	0	0	0
Bet the Breeze	4	G	8	2	1	0	23,960
Bet the Farm	4	F	8	0	1	1	2,179
Bet the Line	11	G	5	1	1	1	6,557
Bet the Ranch	4	C	7	3	2	1	44,983
Bet the Reality	5	G	10	1	0	2	7,160
Bet the Rock	5	G	3	0	1	0	1,012
Bet Whom	7	M	5	0	0	0	620
Bet Your Stars	6	G	12	1	3	3	11,618
Betabet On Betty	4	F	6	0	0	0	459
Betcha's Brat	4	G	16	4	3	1	26,660
Beth Byars	3	F	1	0	1	0	3,000

Horse	Age	Sex	Sts	1st	2d	3d	Won
Bethel Heights	3	G	6	2	2	1	14,593
Bethel Road	6	G	9	0	0	1	2,554
Bethestar	5	G	10	0	0	0	1,487
Bethlehem Morn	4	C	3	0	0	0	416
Beths Baby	5	G	6	1	0	1	11,981
Beth's Choice	6	H	9	0	1	0	1,560
Beth's Expectation	5	M	2	0	0	0	1,763
Betido	4	F	3	0	1	0	3,595
Betimfantastique	6	G	18	0	1	0	1,851
Betkatjo	4	F	2	0	0	0	575
Betnow	2	C	2	0	1	1	15,107
Betondegray	3	G	10	1	3	0	7,930
Betphone	3	C	16	1	3	3	31,600
Betray	6	M	2	0	0	0	390
Betstushelly	2	F	1	0	0	0	235
Betsy Boo	6	M	9	0	1	4	9,294
Betsy N	4	F	10	2	1	2	33,253
Betsy's Forum	7	G	8	0	0	0	447
Betta Bing	4	G	10	1	1	4	6,365
Bette	7	M	5	2	1	0	9,626
Better	7	M	4	0	0	1	2,460
Better Butter	3	F	11	0	0	4	5,665
Better Choice	10	G	8	2	0	2	11,367
Better Dancer	2	C	4	0	0	1	1,100
Better Daze	4	F	12	3	5	1	57,965
Better Get Busy	2	C	2	0	0	2	6,270
Better Guess Again	5	M	3	0	0	0	332
Better Idol	5	G	14	1	0	1	12,685
Better Place	4	F	10	2	2	1	11,960
Better Plan	5	G	1	0	0	0	0
Better Quality	3	C	2	0	1	0	2,950
Better Road	7	G	7	2	1	1	13,940
Better Senorita	5	M	6	0	1	0	3,260
Better Talk Now	5	G	8	2	2	0	1,407,000
Better Than Best	3	G	5	0	0	0	675
Better Than Bonds	2	C	5	2	1	1	114,370
Better Than Ever	2	C	6	1	1	0	22,790
Better Than That	7	G	12	1	2	1	6,567
Better Zbetter	4	C	7	1	1	1	19,118
Betterbegoodtome	7	G	11	0	0	2	2,322
Betterhitanother	5	M	1	0	0	0	375
Bettermaid	5	M	15	3	2	5	19,063
Betterthanexpected	5	G	9	1	1	1	6,530
Bette's Half Dozen	5	M	1	0	0	0	0
Bettheredwild	2	C	1	0	0	0	420
Bettie G. Mac	2	F	1	0	0	0	0
Bettie's Dancer	6	M	1	0	0	0	300
Bettin On M J	2	G	2	0	0	0	1,029
Bettor Best	2	C	5	0	0	0	828
Bettor Cote	8	G	2	0	0	0	0
Bettor Knot	3	F	13	3	5	1	63,567
Bettor Royalty	6	G	7	2	0	3	31,950
Bettorbeleveawoman	4	F	7	1	2	2	12,590
Betty	2	F	1	0	0	1	720
Betty B	5	M	1	0	0	0	110
Betty Booper	2	F	4	0	0	0	255
Betty C	7	M	1	0	0	0	0
Betty Jo	2	F	8	0	1	4	9,230
Betty Lee	4	F	3	0	0	0	226
Betty Mae A.	8	M	3	0	0	0	116
Betty Rae	2	F	3	0	0	0	625
Betty Shea Miller	3	F	2	0	0	0	840
Betty Spaghetti	4	F	7	2	1	1	21,223
Betty Sue	5	M	7	2	0	1	9,974
Bettylou's Badboy	4	G	4	0	0	0	0
Betty's Boop	4	F	4	1	0	0	6,804
Betty's Little Bit	4	F	7	0	0	3	8,255
Betty's Solutions	4	F	1	0	0	0	798
Bettys Tribute (GB)	3	F	6	0	0	2	14,480
Betty's Wish	4	F	1	0	0	1	6,000
Betwineyouandme	5	M	8	1	2	1	27,021
Betyourluckystars	3	G	5	1	0	1	21,113
Beupydae	3	F	2	0	0	0	364
Beurocracy	2	G	2	0	0	0	215
Beverley Minster	4	F	2	0	0	0	80
Beverly Greedy	9	G	9	1	0	3	29,483
Beverly Kay	5	M	3	0	0	0	0
Beverly Tricks	4	F	11	0	2	3	12,526
Beverly's Best	4	F	11	0	2	2	5,412
Beverlys Joy	2	F	1	0	0	0	300
Bevie's Dare	5	G	12	2	0	1	21,450
Bevys Affair	4	F	2	0	0	0	0
Bevys Boy	3	G	10	1	2	2	18,253
Beware Avalanche	8	G	16	2	2	1	42,650
Beware of Jules	3	G	11	1	1	1	8,035
Beware the Heir	2	G	4	1	1	1	7,530
Beware the Ides	9	G	12	1	0	1	3,912
Bewareoftheredhead	2	F	6	0	1	3	9,085
Bewitching Bartok	3	G	6	0	0	1	8,340
Bewitching Blonde	3	F	8	0	0	0	630
Bewitching Eyes	10	M	17	3	5	1	27,677
Bewitching Hour	3	F	10	4	0	2	43,222
Bewitchury	5	M	11	2	2	1	12,300
Bexley	3	F	16	3	2	0	32,127
Bexley Heath	2	G	3	0	0	0	0
Beyers	2	C	3	0	0	0	1,480
Beyers Real Deal	6	G	2	0	0	0	0
Beyond Brilliant	6	G	12	6	2	0	149,828
Beyond Chance	5	H	10	4	1	2	50,653
Beyond Great	3	F	6	1	0	1	2,218
Beyond Infinity (FR)	4	G	11	0	0	0	6,855
Beyond Joy	5	M	4	0	0	0	305
Beyond Our Wildest	5	G	5	2	0	1	36,760
Beyond Reach	5	M	9	2	3	2	4,599
Beyond Reasoning	4	F	10	0	1	1	3,372
Beyond the Blue	2	F	2	0	0	1	6,897
Beyond the Horizon	3	F	10	1	2	1	90,124
Beyond the Light	4	G	5	0	0	0	1,160
Beyond Thunder	2	F	2	0	1	0	2,040
Beyond Time	5	H	3	0	1	0	1,905
Beyond Winnie	6	M	13	2	4	2	19,196
Bfifty Two	3	G	2	0	0	0	780
Bh Whata Challenge	6	G	2	0	0	0	105
Bhaskar	10	G	11	1	0	2	4,240
Bia Valentine	3	F	7	2	0	1	40,391
Biagio	5	G	11	0	1	3	8,667
Bianarma	3	F	4	1	1	1	7,574
Bianca	3	F	8	1	1	1	7,135
Bianca's Beauty	3	F	8	2	0	3	11,071
Biancerie	3	C	3	0	0	0	200
Bianco Appeal	6	G	18	2	2	2	23,123
Bianconi Baby	3	F	4	2	0	1	65,657
Bianconi's Boy	2	C	6	1	0	0	29,350
Biancool	3	F	4	0	1	1	11,160
Bianfast	3	F	3	0	0	0	390
Biangood	3	F	14	1	1	1	10,820
Biaplayer	3	C	13	1	3	1	10,025
Bibda Love	3	F	8	0	0	0	1,557
Bibelot	4	F	1	0	0	0	0
Bibi	4	F	4	0	0	0	200
Biblical	6	G	14	1	2	1	14,494
Biblical Scholar	3	C	11	1	3	1	57,137
Bibye	6	G	17	1	3	3	35,600
Bicentennial	6	H	2	0	0	0	460
Bicho de Luz (ARG)	7	G	4	0	0	0	1,860
Bid	2	C	2	0	0	0	1,325
Bid Day	2	F	3	0	0	0	2,670
Bid for Silver	2	F	1	0	0	0	274
Bid From Bourtai	2	G	3	0	0	1	2,880
Bid Her Sweet	5	M	7	1	1	1	12,055
Bid Made	2	F	2	0	0	0	1,200
Bid N Battle	4	G	7	1	0	1	5,981
Bid On a Dancer	2	F	1	0	0	0	360
Bid On My Basket	6	M	27	2	1	1	4,292
Bid the Moon	2	F	4	0	1	0	2,380
Bid the Zeal	10	G	14	1	2	2	8,600
Bid Zup	4	G	4	0	0	0	288
Bidderlucknexttime	4	G	1	0	0	0	88
Bidders Champ	8	H	9	0	0	0	644
Bidders Out	6	G	13	0	0	1	1,649
Bidder's Prospect	2	C	7	0	3	1	21,820
Bidding Pro	4	F	5	0	0	1	8,040
Biddy Biddy	10	G	8	0	1	1	2,410
Biddy's Lad	4	G	9	0	1	2	27,895
Bideflyck	4	G	6	0	1	3	1,542
Bidless	3	C	6	1	0	2	31,820
Bid's for Gold	5	G	9	2	2	2	5,160
Biedermeier	3	G	7	1	1	1	8,333

Horse	Age	Sex	Sts	1st	2d	3d	Won
Bieganow	3	C	2	0	0	0	523
Bien Amie	5	M	2	0	0	0	135
Bien Blushing	6	G	16	1	1	2	23,110
Bien Brooke	3	F	6	1	0	2	7,490
Bien Dancing	7	G	10	0	3	1	6,658
Bien's Trick	3	G	9	1	2	1	14,400
Bienvenue	5	H	1	0	0	0	0
Bierstadt	4	C	6	0	0	0	4,440
Biff	5	G	9	0	1	3	9,250
Biff America	4	C	11	0	0	0	360
Big Al T	7	G	10	5	1	1	11,620
Big Alley Cat	3	G	3	0	0	0	0
Big American Force	4	C	9	4	0	2	80,132
Big and Classy	3	G	13	0	1	0	6,095
Big Ankle Ben	3	G	13	0	3	3	6,923
Big Apple Daddy	2	C	6	1	3	0	100,394
Big Aristotle	6	G	8	0	4	0	3,360
Big Arthur's Joy	3	G	3	0	0	0	522
Big B in the Lead	2	G	1	0	0	0	1,680
Big Bad Bagdad	4	C	8	1	1	0	2,226
Big Bad Bert	3	C	2	1	0	0	22,878
Big Bad Bill	3	G	13	1	3	2	37,390
Big Bad Bue	5	G	9	2	1	1	16,470
Big Bad Bull	5	H	1	1	0	0	3,900
Big Bad George	7	H	8	3	1	1	54,245
Big Bad Girl	4	F	7	2	0	0	3,860
Big Bad Joe	2	G	4	0	0	0	720
Big Bad Juan	6	G	1	0	0	0	0
Big Bad Louie	3	G	10	2	3	2	35,860
Big Bad Norm	7	G	4	0	0	0	0
Big Bad Sally	5	M	14	1	5	2	50,205
Big Banker	4	G	11	0	1	1	7,248
Big Baqa	3	F	9	0	1	0	1,430
Big Bay Brite	7	G	2	0	0	1	1,640
Big Becker	9	G	8	1	2	1	18,613
Big Bid	10	G	2	1	0	0	3,990
Big Big Bert	4	C	1	0	0	0	0
Big Big Stanley	5	G	1	0	0	0	150
Big Bill	5	G	1	0	1	0	800
Big Bing	9	G	4	0	0	0	314
Big Black Sky	3	G	5	1	0	0	5,865
Big Blackie Blue	3	G	2	2	0	0	32,700
Big Bloke	5	H	5	1	2	1	17,810
Big Blue Adventure	4	C	3	0	0	0	132
Big Blue Cat	2	C	3	0	0	0	525
Big Blue Lens	4	C	1	0	0	0	67
Big Bluff	10	G	2	0	0	0	186
Big Bobastar	3	G	2	0	0	0	225
Big Bobby Joe	4	F	12	1	5	1	10,514
Big Bold Place	2	C	5	0	0	1	7,110
Big Bold Rush	3	G	1	0	0	0	840
Big Bold Sweep	4	G	10	2	2	1	84,899
Big Bold Wil	3	C	2	0	0	0	0
Big Bonus	5	G	15	3	1	1	15,460
Big Booster	3	C	10	1	1	2	53,865
Big Bossy	2	C	5	0	0	0	0
Big Boy Blaze	3	G	2	0	0	0	0
Big Boy Jesse	8	G	11	1	0	2	6,636
Big Boy Slew	3	G	2	0	0	0	261
Big Bragger	4	G	4	0	0	0	219
Big Brassy Bill	5	G	6	2	0	2	2,686
Big Broken Straw	6	G	11	2	1	2	23,307
Big Brother Don	4	G	7	0	0	0	871
Big Brown Bear	6	G	5	0	1	0	5,826
Big Brown Cat	3	G	9	0	1	0	4,743
Big B's Prospect	2	C	2	1	0	0	15,780
Big Buckle Winner	4	G	9	0	0	0	6,179
Big Bud	2	C	4	1	0	0	10,290
Big Buddy	2	C	3	1	1	0	20,558
Big Burnt	2	G	4	0	0	0	1,750
Big Cajun Cat	3	G	6	0	0	0	555
Big Cam	4	G	8	2	0	1	13,875
Big Cheque	4	F	8	0	3	1	73,494
Big Chestnut	3	C	7	0	0	0	1,513
Big City	5	G	1	0	0	0	340
Big City Boy	6	G	7	0	3	1	4,251
Big City Bull	4	C	3	0	0	0	936
Big City Danse	2	F	6	1	3	0	58,278
Big City Lover	4	F	3	0	0	0	127
Big City Money	4	C	2	0	0	0	0
Big City Spender	3	C	7	3	1	2	117,343
Big Colony	2	C	4	0	2	1	7,560
Big Concern	3	G	3	1	1	0	15,700
Big Country	4	C	4	0	0	0	1,108
Big Creek	5	G	10	2	3	0	34,527
Big Daddy Dave	7	G	14	3	1	2	22,735
Big Daddy G	5	H	2	0	0	0	920
Big Daddy Longlegs	7	G	3	0	0	0	1,680
Big Daddy Salomone	3	G	5	0	1	0	1,725
Big Daddy Tee	6	G	3	0	0	0	0
Big Decision	4	G	9	1	2	3	14,330
Big Deed	5	G	7	0	1	0	3,943
Big Dividend	6	G	13	2	0	2	23,610
Big Doc	2	C	2	0	0	0	360
Big Dreamer	2	G	2	0	1	0	2,111
Big E E	7	H	2	0	0	0	5,400
Big Easy Blues	4	G	13	2	3	0	21,500
Big Ern	3	G	2	0	0	0	600
Big Ez	2	C	3	0	0	0	300
Big Feathers	3	C	8	1	1	2	46,204
Big Feeler	4	G	2	1	0	0	6,050
Big Fish Marlin	5	G	13	0	1	2	4,841
Big Future (GB)	7	H	6	1	0	3	33,473
Big Glori	4	G	11	1	3	2	37,960
Big Gold Martini	7	G	2	0	0	0	106
Big Gun	4	C	3	0	1	0	3,920
Big Gun Annie	6	M	9	0	1	2	2,992
Big Guru	3	C	2	0	0	0	0
Big Guy's Prospect	3	C	8	2	1	1	13,305
Big Harry Smacker	4	C	1	0	0	0	0
Big Head Phil	5	G	7	2	1	0	8,588
Big Hearted Man	4	G	3	0	1	0	2,040
Big Hearted Wayne	5	G	6	0	0	0	2,630
Big Hero	3	G	9	0	1	1	7,813
Big Hope	6	G	1	0	0	0	500
Big Horn Tom	3	G	3	0	1	0	3,760
Big Hunter	3	F	1	0	0	0	0
Big Ide	5	M	5	2	0	1	18,030
Big Impact	6	G	10	0	1	1	2,490
Big in the Game	3	C	9	2	0	2	32,406
Big Irish	3	G	6	1	0	1	6,091
Big Jax	2	G	4	1	0	1	4,216
Big Jer	3	G	4	0	1	0	9,786
Big Joe Little Joe	3	G	5	1	1	0	13,000
Big Joe Zee	3	G	5	0	4	0	22,910
Big Joes Girl	4	F	1	0	0	0	0
Big John Dempsey	3	C	7	0	1	2	12,337
Big John Henry	3	G	12	0	3	2	6,823
Big Johnny	5	G	6	0	0	0	328
Big K	2	G	5	1	1	0	12,595
Big Kahuna	4	G	10	1	2	1	19,195
Big Komotion	3	F	4	1	1	0	15,163
Big L. L. B.	4	C	4	0	0	1	671
Big League	6	H	4	0	0	1	2,414
Big Lonesome Train	4	G	11	0	1	2	15,034
Big Lord Nelson	4	G	9	1	1	1	7,261
Big Luck (PER)	6	G	2	0	0	0	280
Big Lucky	4	G	11	1	4	3	7,436
Big Ma Moo	2	F	3	1	1	0	20,750
Big Mac Mtn.	6	G	6	0	0	1	944
Big Mag	5	M	11	0	1	0	3,784
Big Mama Pearl	4	F	11	2	0	4	19,177
Big Man	5	G	3	0	0	1	840
Big Matt	3	G	6	2	0	1	8,919
Big Meadow	3	F	13	3	4	1	39,944
Big Meany	6	G	10	2	3	2	37,530
Big Mic	3	G	13	0	0	1	3,377
Big Mike	3	C	4	0	1	0	6,480
Big Momma B	4	F	4	1	0	0	4,725
Big Mountain	5	G	7	2	1	2	24,795
Big Nana's Boy	3	C	10	1	2	0	43,023
Big Numbers	7	H	8	0	1	2	16,260
Big Odds	2	C	1	0	0	0	300
Big O'l Boy	3	G	4	0	0	0	780
Big Orrdeal	4	G	1	0	0	0	240
Big Out	4	G	6	2	0	0	29,660
Big Oxx	8	G	2	0	0	0	89
Big Pain	5	H	9	1	2	0	10,038

Horse	Age	Sex	Sts	1st	2d	3d	Won
Big Papa	6	G	4	0	1	0	949
Big Pappa Stopper	5	H	2	0	0	0	0
Big Pa's Girl	4	F	2	0	0	0	0
Big Pete	5	G	3	0	0	1	825
Big Pete's Rib	4	G	11	0	2	1	3,171
Big Profit	2	C	1	0	1	0	2,700
Big Promise	2	F	7	0	2	0	6,150
Big Queen	5	M	28	2	4	7	20,790
Big Quest	7	H	5	0	2	0	6,200
Big Quiet	2	C	2	0	0	0	435
Big Ransom	3	F	3	0	1	0	6,475
Big Rascal	8	G	6	1	0	1	8,910
Big Red Chunk	5	H	1	0	0	0	105
Big Red Fan	8	G	8	0	0	1	1,007
Big Red Fantasy	2	G	3	1	1	0	11,670
Big Red Irishman	12	G	7	1	2	0	9,030
Big Red Mercedes	3	G	3	0	0	0	195
Big Red Robyn	6	G	14	1	2	0	32,910
Big Red Ruler	3	G	4	0	2	0	3,679
Big Red Storm	3	G	5	1	2	0	5,620
Big Reds Back	3	G	8	2	1	1	26,491
Big Ruby K	5	G	15	1	0	2	43,380
Big Sancho	3	G	9	0	1	1	4,425
Big Sand	5	G	4	0	0	2	8,675
Big Sand River	4	F	7	0	0	1	990
Big Sandy	6	G	9	2	2	0	24,220
Big Scale	3	G	4	1	1	1	5,400
Big Score	4	F	8	2	0	3	90,246
Big Shaker	3	C	5	0	0	0	383
Big Shakespeare	6	G	8	1	4	2	9,090
Big Shoulders	3	G	9	0	0	1	1,068
Big Sid's Party	6	G	8	2	2	2	96,365
Big Sky Bevie	2	F	7	0	3	0	5,438
Big Sky Blue	3	G	11	1	1	2	11,449
Big Sky River	4	G	4	0	0	1	2,249
Big Slew	2	C	3	0	0	1	3,765
Big Smoothy	3	G	4	1	0	0	9,240
Big Squeeze	3	G	8	1	1	0	43,820
Big Stone Gap	4	G	12	1	0	1	9,916
Big Sugar	3	F	10	0	1	0	2,176
Big Swed	4	G	8	0	3	1	10,518
Big Talkin Man	6	G	13	5	2	2	148,785
Big Team Spirit	7	G	3	1	2	0	10,875
Big Tease	4	F	15	3	1	2	129,650
Big Terrel	4	G	9	0	1	1	2,205
Big Tex	3	C	9	0	4	0	18,500
Big Thunder	7	H	8	2	0	1	18,956
Big Ticker	5	G	10	1	3	0	15,288
Big Ticket	3	G	5	0	0	1	1,856
Big Time Bonus	3	G	2	0	0	0	0
Big Time Cat	2	F	1	1	0	0	6,000
Big Time Flyer	8	G	16	2	1	3	14,438
Big Time Hope	5	G	6	0	2	0	2,602
Big Time Luck	8	M	1	0	0	0	531
Big Time Spender	6	G	15	0	1	1	4,497
Big Tom	4	G	5	0	0	1	1,068
Big Tom Rhat	3	G	18	1	0	0	5,513
Big Top Cat	2	C	2	0	0	0	225
Big Town	5	G	12	1	2	1	16,785
Big Wagner	3	G	11	2	3	0	17,024
Big Wells	9	G	9	1	2	3	10,997
Big Whinnyings	6	G	17	3	3	4	21,295
Big Whiskey	4	G	17	2	3	2	24,705
Big Will	6	G	14	0	2	3	34,130
Big Wolf	4	F	13	2	4	4	57,870
Big Yankee Fan	4	G	9	2	1	2	8,574
Bigado	9	H	1	0	0	0	0
Bigamo (URU)	6	G	13	1	1	2	12,312
Bigbadbubba	3	C	9	4	1	1	37,470
Bigboybdancing	2	C	5	1	2	0	32,750
Bigbucksnowhammies	4	G	11	1	2	1	11,136
Bigcuz	6	M	4	0	0	0	248
Bigdayinthemarquet	2	C	3	1	0	0	6,175
Bigeyelittleyou	2	G	3	1	1	1	25,740
Biggems	3	G	11	0	1	1	3,609
Biggen	9	G	6	1	0	0	1,310
Bigger Wagner	3	G	9	1	3	1	15,038
Biggest Wagner	2	G	1	0	0	0	0
Biggieandbellboy	6	H	3	0	0	0	0
Biggiejune	2	C	1	0	0	0	840
Biggin Won	4	F	1	0	0	0	125
Biggly Slew	4	C	5	0	0	0	1,115
Biggly Star	5	H	3	0	0	0	510
Biggs	4	G	11	1	0	3	3,385
Bigmike Littlemike	3	G	11	0	0	0	1,201
Bigmixes Boy	5	G	1	0	0	0	0
Big'n'jazzy	2	G	3	0	1	0	1,788
Bignose	2	F	8	2	1	1	25,200
Bigolcountryboy	6	G	7	1	0	1	6,185
Bigoneontheend	5	G	7	0	0	0	1,585
Bigredcoup	4	G	7	1	3	1	5,430
Bigrockcandymountn	3	G	4	0	1	1	5,575
Bigshotangie	3	F	9	0	0	0	1,148
Bigtimeaffair	3	F	5	0	1	1	4,240
Bijou	5	M	11	1	0	1	40,503
Bijou Belle	5	M	3	0	0	0	2,390
Bikini Beach	4	F	8	1	1	0	4,173
Bikini Model	3	F	1	0	0	0	0
Bikini Moon	3	F	2	1	1	0	21,560
Bikini Ransom	2	F	5	0	0	1	2,170
Bikini Wiggle	3	F	12	1	2	1	53,173
Bikinisandmartinis	4	F	2	0	0	0	52
Biko	3	G	2	0	0	0	0
Bilateral	3	G	10	2	0	2	14,530
Bilbo Baggins	4	G	7	0	0	0	1,605
Bilbo Had the Ring	3	G	3	0	0	0	0
Bilini North	9	G	1	0	0	0	0
Bill and Jim	4	C	14	3	2	2	21,919
Bill Bp Casey	3	C	3	0	0	0	0
Bill Dandy	2	G	5	1	0	2	23,926
Bill Heinz	3	G	8	0	1	0	5,935
Bill Is in Love	4	G	13	2	4	3	22,400
Bill the Banker	6	G	6	2	1	0	30,216
Bill the Great	4	G	8	2	2	0	77,884
Billanetta	4	F	16	1	3	3	10,847
Billanksphonetrick	5	G	5	0	0	0	294
Billet Doux	4	F	13	0	3	1	7,682
Billiard (GB)	3	F	4	0	0	0	6,340
Billie P. Beads	3	F	3	0	0	0	260
Billnlou's Deemell	2	G	5	0	0	0	2,332
Bills Bull	3	G	6	1	1	0	5,580
Bill's Lady	4	F	17	2	3	4	18,720
Bill's Lil Fappi	5	M	7	0	0	0	3,175
Bill's No Trouble	3	C	2	1	0	0	10,460
Bills Paid	6	G	1	0	0	0	680
Bills Proud Mary	4	F	9	2	4	1	6,084
Bills Royal Honey	4	F	12	0	1	1	2,734
Bill's Shadow	6	M	2	0	0	0	75
Billstown	8	G	6	1	0	1	6,200
Billy Angel	4	C	11	1	2	2	14,257
Billy B. Esquire	2	C	2	1	0	1	6,075
Billy Be Normal	5	G	6	0	0	0	527
Billy Bell	3	G	6	0	0	1	3,360
Billy Big Rigger	6	G	3	1	0	0	8,745
Billy Bigelow	3	G	3	0	0	0	0
Billy Bill Flash	5	G	9	2	2	3	17,955
Billy Bird	4	G	9	1	3	2	7,061
Billy Boo Boo	2	G	4	0	0	0	2,138
Billy Bowlegs	5	G	16	5	1	4	31,486
Billy D. Kid	4	G	7	1	3	1	21,148
Billy Dixon	3	G	5	1	3	1	32,950
Billy Etbauer	3	C	15	2	2	2	15,300
Billy Flynn	2	G	2	0	0	0	950
Billy Gilman	4	G	9	1	2	1	20,724
Billy Gumbo	5	H	2	0	0	0	0
Billy Ho Jo	2	G	6	0	3	1	22,541
Billy Idel	4	G	14	2	0	2	30,883
Billy Jeans Bag	7	M	3	0	0	0	201
Billy McKeever	4	G	4	0	0	0	427
Billy Stark	2	G	4	1	0	1	14,919
Billy White Shoes	4	G	9	0	4	2	3,395
Billy Wright	4	G	11	1	0	0	13,153
Billyball	6	G	12	2	1	2	17,873
Billybeck	2	C	6	2	1	0	37,337
Billybob Bly	3	C	10	0	2	4	11,140
Billybob Bobaloo	3	G	2	0	0	0	0
Billyhyde	3	G	6	0	1	0	4,812
Billyjack	3	G	4	1	0	2	6,385

Horse	Age	Sex	Sts	1st	2d	3d	Won
Billy's Ace	3	G	13	1	1	1	12,575
Billy's Echo	6	G	8	2	2	0	86,860
Billy's Plan	3	G	6	0	2	0	2,509
Billysberry	5	M	4	1	0	1	1,023
Bilo	4	G	6	3	2	1	110,636
Bilori	4	F	1	0	0	0	310
Biloxi Breeze	2	C	4	0	1	0	6,410
Biloxi Palace	2	C	4	2	1	0	45,150
Biloxi Pride	3	G	11	4	1	2	73,330
Biloxi Prospect	4	F	3	0	0	1	5,060
Biloxi Purple Haze	4	G	11	2	0	1	20,027
Bimbo's Kiss	9	M	1	0	0	0	0
Bimini Breeze	2	F	4	1	0	0	35,994
Bim's Baby Bun	4	C	2	0	0	0	0
Bin Dere Did Dat	6	G	7	1	2	0	14,400
Bin Rejoicing	5	M	4	0	0	0	638
Bin Rockin'	7	H	9	2	2	2	24,555
Bin Sneakin Around	2	G	2	0	0	0	848
Bin to Miami	6	M	1	0	0	0	0
Bin to War	3	G	9	2	0	0	12,540
Bin Working	4	C	5	0	1	1	5,970
Bin Zin	3	F	3	0	0	0	450
Binahoni	5	M	9	2	0	1	8,206
Binalady	5	M	5	1	0	0	5,363
Binalong Summer	4	F	6	0	0	0	443
Binalonglongday	3	G	10	1	1	1	7,345
Binalongtimecom'en	5	M	8	1	0	1	20,499
Binandgone	4	F	13	0	0	0	1,635
Binary	6	G	2	0	0	0	192
Binbo	5	H	4	0	0	0	2,790
Binder	5	G	12	3	3	1	46,260
Bing an a Prayer	4	G	3	0	0	0	240
Bingo Caller	3	F	7	2	0	2	10,222
Bingo Card	6	G	2	0	0	0	840
Bingo Liz	4	F	12	0	1	1	2,949
Bingo McGruder	5	M	6	0	0	0	432
Bingo Susie	3	F	6	1	1	2	25,930
Bingobear	3	G	11	2	3	1	47,654
Bingo's Orphan	4	G	13	4	5	0	21,218
Bings Fine Silk	2	F	3	1	1	1	17,739
Binks'belle	3	F	9	0	0	0	189
Binlookingforyou	2	G	3	0	0	0	746
Binn Here	2	F	4	0	1	1	7,360
Binn Tin Tin (FR)	8	G	10	1	0	1	15,730
Binnaroundtheblock	2	G	3	0	0	1	1,760
Binny's Trick	4	G	5	0	0	2	13,020
Bint Jumeriah	5	M	5	0	2	0	1,522
Bint Tell	4	F	1	0	0	0	0
Binya (GER)	5	M	5	2	0	1	101,640
Biogio's Beauty	4	F	3	0	0	2	13,567
Biogio's Dream	4	F	13	2	3	1	79,829
Biometal	4	G	9	1	2	0	6,330
Bionic Bold	7	M	8	0	0	0	1,825
Bionic Brine	2	C	5	1	0	2	8,545
Bionic Galt	3	G	4	0	1	0	1,097
Bionic Lad	4	G	6	1	0	2	9,460
Bionic Streak	11	M	3	0	0	0	287
Biorhythm	5	H	2	1	0	1	9,450
Bippy d'Or	4	F	11	1	0	1	13,221
Birch Bay	3	G	5	1	0	0	6,258
Bird Call	4	C	13	1	4	1	25,272
Bird Chatter	3	F	7	3	2	0	35,600
Bird Dog Bill	4	G	13	1	1	1	30,660
Bird Harbor	2	F	1	1	0	0	29,395
Bird Hunt	2	F	1	0	0	0	0
Bird in Flight	3	G	21	3	0	1	17,215
Bird in the Tunnel	2	C	5	0	0	0	1,164
Bird Key	4	F	13	6	0	3	65,794
Bird of Courage	6	M	9	0	4	0	20,346
Bird of Paradise	2	C	5	1	1	0	20,477
Birdcee	5	M	7	1	0	1	11,840
Birdie Barrage	3	F	6	1	0	0	9,535
Birdie in the Dark	5	M	1	0	0	0	50
Birdie Putt	6	M	10	2	0	1	21,784
Birdie Shooter	4	F	12	1	3	2	12,614
Birdieonthewire	6	G	10	0	0	0	1,441
Birdies Secret	3	F	11	4	1	2	32,440
Birdie's Spirit	3	G	2	0	0	0	1,110
Birdie's World	5	M	14	0	1	1	2,489
Birdland	4	G	14	2	1	2	18,380
Birdonthehighwire	6	G	4	0	1	1	2,287
Birdontheridge	3	G	1	0	0	0	3,420
Bird's Advantage	5	M	4	0	0	0	0
Bird's Valentine	4	F	5	0	0	0	235
Birdseed	3	F	4	1	0	1	24,176
Birdstone	3	C	6	3	0	0	1,236,600
Birth Sign	6	G	6	0	0	2	5,350
Birthday Bash	2	G	2	0	0	1	825
Birthday Boy Louie	3	C	12	2	1	0	20,860
Birthday Dancer	4	G	7	0	0	0	560
Birthday Lover	2	F	1	0	0	0	1,250
Birthday Song	3	F	13	3	1	3	69,070
Birthday Suit	2	F	3	0	0	0	250
Bis Repetitas	4	C	4	0	1	0	18,300
Biscay Appeal	5	G	9	3	0	1	20,888
Biscuit Bun	3	F	3	0	0	0	0
Biscuits With Ham	2	F	2	0	0	0	925
Bishoftu	6	H	8	0	1	1	10,540
Bishop Court Hill	4	C	6	1	0	1	48,410
Bishop to King	4	G	10	0	0	0	1,260
Bishop Wins	5	G	6	1	0	2	1,984
Bishop's Gate	4	F	2	0	0	0	154
Bishops Tree	4	G	1	0	0	1	770
Bishop's Vine	5	M	3	0	0	1	795
Bisquik	2	G	4	1	0	2	16,382
Bisti Badlands	4	G	7	0	2	2	11,041
Bistro Mathematics	4	G	8	5	1	0	41,210
Bit a Country	2	G	1	1	0	0	5,720
Bit Moody	3	F	8	0	0	0	1,396
Bit o' Mortlock	3	G	6	0	0	0	0
Bit of a Chap	2	C	3	0	1	0	5,980
Bit of a Snit	3	F	8	0	0	3	3,867
Bit of Dixie	3	F	6	0	0	1	3,640
Bit of Folly	3	F	11	2	2	1	61,480
Bit Shee Believer	4	F	8	0	0	0	878
Bite My Bumpers	4	F	4	0	0	0	1,078
Bite N Red	4	F	5	3	0	0	3,825
Biterman	3	G	2	0	0	1	2,926
Biting Feather	3	F	6	1	0	0	17,520
Biting Warrior	4	G	9	0	2	1	3,919
Bitingly Cold	7	M	1	0	0	1	2,520
Bitsnspurs	4	C	4	0	0	0	603
Bitsy's Double Z	3	F	7	2	3	0	29,595
Bitter Luck	4	C	5	0	0	0	0
Bitter Truth	4	G	8	2	0	1	8,646
Bitterroot	3	C	2	0	1	1	5,048
Bitterroot Range	3	G	7	0	0	0	2,055
Bitterroot River	4	F	7	2	2	1	66,530
Bittersweet Bonnie	3	F	5	1	0	0	8,588
Bittersweet Rain	4	F	2	0	0	0	6,276
Bitterweed	2	F	1	0	0	0	420
Bitting Boy	3	G	7	1	0	1	8,320
Bity Rose	5	M	7	1	1	1	8,205
Bix	4	G	10	2	0	2	2,552
Bixby Knolls	5	H	13	1	0	2	6,756
Bizzy Bee	3	F	12	3	2	3	28,820
Bizzy Trick	2	C	8	2	1	0	49,730
Bizzyweekend	3	G	13	4	2	1	19,711
Bj's Brave	5	G	6	1	0	1	7,062
Bk's Dippybroad	4	F	2	1	0	0	8,235
Bk's Tricky Native	7	G	7	2	1	3	14,919
Blaazan Dyer	2	G	3	1	0	0	17,940
Black Ace	4	G	1	0	0	0	98
Black Banana	4	F	11	0	1	3	1,816
Black Barry Velvet	5	M	12	3	1	1	5,432
Black Bart	5	G	13	6	1	1	254,720
Black Beard	5	G	7	0	0	0	160
Black Beauty Cutie	3	F	3	0	0	0	1,035
Black Betty	2	F	3	0	1	0	4,040
Black Bird Creek	2	G	7	0	0	2	5,850
Black Bullet	7	H	1	0	0	0	0
Black Butler	4	G	3	0	0	0	550
Black Butte	3	G	11	1	1	3	23,850
Black Caddie	3	G	13	1	1	0	6,155
Black Cadillac	3	G	9	2	0	1	27,760
Black Canyon	5	H	12	1	0	1	1,720
Black Canyon Bart	4	G	10	2	2	2	4,739
Black Canyon City	3	G	8	0	2	1	6,705

Horse	Age	Sex	Sts	1st	2d	3d	Won
Black Card	2	C	4	0	0	0	1,480
Black Cat Mountain	3	C	9	1	0	2	19,170
Black Cloud	6	H	1	0	0	0	0
Black Clouds Above	3	G	5	0	1	0	4,570
Black Cougar	6	G	10	1	1	0	6,504
Black Cove	8	G	12	2	4	1	12,697
Black Deed	3	G	7	0	0	0	636
Black Diva	5	M	4	0	1	1	1,650
Black Elk	3	G	12	1	3	2	8,703
Black Escort	3	F	7	1	3	1	56,535
Black Eyed Girl	4	F	2	0	0	0	750
Black Eyed Susie	2	F	2	1	0	1	13,700
Black Flash	2	F	7	1	2	0	9,852
Black Forest	10	G	5	0	1	0	4,931
Black Fox	3	G	4	0	0	0	184
Black Gem	2	F	1	0	0	0	0
Black Glitter	3	G	8	3	1	0	27,495
Black Heart	4	F	2	1	0	1	12,650
Black Hole	7	G	5	2	1	0	12,800
Black Horse Money	3	G	10	1	3	0	39,640
Black Horse Silver	3	C	4	0	0	0	790
Black Hummer	3	G	1	0	0	0	0
Black Hurricane	3	G	9	3	0	0	11,416
Black It Out	7	M	1	0	0	0	130
Black Jack Attack	3	G	4	0	0	1	3,950
Black Jet	4	G	12	0	1	1	3,967
Black Joe	4	C	2	1	0	0	10,200
Black Label	4	G	3	0	0	0	178
Black Lace	5	M	1	0	0	0	360
Black Lace Sam	3	F	12	1	3	3	18,680
Black Lagoon	5	G	13	2	5	3	32,555
Black Licorice	5	H	6	0	0	0	218
Black Lightning	5	M	10	1	0	1	6,446
Black Lilly	4	F	6	1	0	2	10,222
Black Mac's Maniac	3	C	1	0	0	0	0
Black Magic Damsel	5	M	4	0	0	0	0
Black Magic Lady	3	F	5	2	1	1	57,920
Black Mambo	5	H	11	2	1	1	46,990
Black Mariah	3	F	13	3	2	7	85,880
Black Market	5	G	9	5	0	2	55,932
Black Phantom	3	C	1	0	0	0	78
Black Powder Smoke	3	G	5	0	0	0	321
Black Rainbow	6	G	15	1	1	3	18,462
Black Ransom	3	G	8	1	1	0	5,225
Black Raptor	3	C	4	0	0	1	4,570
Black Raven	3	F	5	0	0	0	0
Black Rock Road	3	F	4	3	0	0	173,040
Black Silk (GB)	8	G	8	4	1	1	142,642
Black Springs	2	C	2	0	0	0	0
Black Street	3	G	4	0	0	0	120
Black Tast	5	M	4	0	0	0	816
Black Team	6	G	10	3	2	0	10,495
Black Teddie	2	F	1	0	0	0	0
Black Tejano	4	F	17	2	4	6	20,793
Black Tie	2	G	3	1	2	0	35,260
Black Tie Classic	3	G	4	0	0	1	810
Black Tie Joe	3	G	4	1	0	0	5,700
Black Tie Justice	6	G	9	1	0	2	20,334
Black Tie Trick	6	G	13	1	2	2	11,110
Black Ties Ferrari	8	G	4	0	0	0	186
Black Topper	4	F	9	1	2	2	16,968
Black Tornado	7	M	5	1	1	0	7,200
Black Twenty Nine	3	G	10	1	0	0	8,156
Black Wagner	2	C	5	1	1	0	18,870
Blackberry	5	M	12	2	2	3	27,270
Blackberry Beau	2	C	6	0	0	1	3,282
Blackberry Rain	4	G	4	0	0	0	375
Blackberry Sizzle	2	F	8	1	1	1	8,760
Blackberry Springs	4	C	6	3	0	1	48,100
Blackbird	3	G	3	0	0	0	1,200
Blackcatsnladyluck	5	M	8	0	0	0	1,255
Blackchesters (GB)	11	G	3	0	1	0	3,950
Blackdoun (FR)	3	C	9	4	2	1	440,864
Blackeye	2	G	3	0	0	2	2,124
Blackeyed Special	3	F	8	0	0	2	2,165
Blackfeet	2	G	2	1	0	0	7,270
Blackfoot Maiden	4	F	8	2	1	0	19,623
Blackhawk's Double	5	M	3	0	0	0	0
Blackhearted	7	G	3	0	0	0	0
Blackie Baby	4	F	5	0	0	0	193
Blackinton	4	G	11	2	4	0	66,800
Blackjack Again	2	C	2	0	1	0	2,000
Blackjack Boy	4	C	6	0	1	1	5,181
Blackjack Canyon	3	C	9	3	1	1	32,770
Blackjack Gambler	2	C	4	0	1	0	5,600
Blackjack Jones	3	G	2	0	0	0	535
Blackjack Queen	2	F	3	0	0	0	1,405
Blackjack Willy	2	G	2	1	0	0	12,852
Blackjackledo	3	G	5	0	0	0	115
Blackjacks Rollin	4	G	3	0	0	0	0
Blacklacestockings	2	F	1	0	0	1	600
Blackmagicdiamond	3	G	9	0	1	4	14,081
Blackmailer	3	C	3	1	0	2	23,180
Blacksher	9	M	11	2	1	0	10,862
Blacksmith Girl	3	F	3	0	0	0	690
Blackton	2	G	4	0	1	1	3,515
Blackwater Angel	4	F	2	0	0	0	680
Blackwell's Way	2	C	2	0	0	0	800
Blackwood Chief	6	G	7	0	1	0	2,475
Blade Ae	10	G	2	1	0	0	1,761
Blade Danzer	2	C	1	0	0	0	104
Blades of Silver	2	C	1	0	0	0	205
Blahodatny	5	M	1	0	0	0	0
Blaine County High	6	G	4	1	0	0	2,976
Blaine Inspired	2	F	7	0	0	0	2,225
Blaine's Secret	3	F	10	0	0	2	7,690
Blaine's Storm	3	C	9	2	3	2	42,490
Blairs General	4	G	7	2	0	0	73,180
Blairs Roarin Star	3	G	11	3	2	3	110,571
Blairsden Bound	3	F	2	0	0	0	600
Blaise Pascale	4	G	5	0	1	1	17,910
Blake B.	2	G	9	1	1	2	13,605
Blakelock	4	C	7	2	1	1	69,000
Blakes Jewel	2	G	4	1	0	1	9,178
Blake's Tricky	4	G	3	0	0	0	934
Blakesmyboy	5	G	7	1	1	0	11,520
Blakestone	6	G	3	0	0	0	420
Blame It On Beau	5	G	13	2	0	0	12,975
Blame the Malt	2	G	3	0	0	0	0
Blameitonblake	4	G	3	0	1	0	2,715
Blameitontherain	5	G	1	1	0	0	2,640
Blameitonthewine	4	G	2	1	1	0	4,700
Blamethebossanova	2	C	4	0	1	0	11,250
Blanc	6	G	11	0	0	0	1,500
Blanchetta	3	F	10	2	3	4	30,129
Blantyre	8	G	8	1	1	1	16,200
Blarney Boy	4	G	3	1	0	0	7,325
Blarney Stream	5	G	8	1	0	0	9,550
Blasphemous	6	G	3	0	0	0	1,500
Blast Away	3	F	3	1	0	0	3,460
Blast of Class	4	G	14	1	2	2	4,712
Blast Off	3	C	8	3	1	1	34,723
Blasten Run	4	C	1	0	0	0	0
Blather Skite	4	G	13	3	2	2	33,134
Blaze of Gold	3	F	1	0	0	0	0
Blaze of Honor	6	M	2	0	1	0	4,500
Blaze On Ice	8	G	2	0	0	0	0
Blaze to Glory	4	G	10	1	1	1	7,106
Blaze Too	4	F	4	1	0	0	7,860
Blaze'n Light	4	G	18	1	5	5	10,249
Blazen Right Cross	2	G	2	1	0	0	10,250
Blazer Mania	4	F	4	2	0	1	3,725
Blazikin Red Heat	2	F	3	0	0	0	0
Blazin Dar	3	G	6	1	0	0	3,480
Blazin Sunrise	5	G	10	1	0	0	5,553
Blazing Bartok	3	F	8	2	1	0	36,745
Blazing Birdie	5	G	1	0	0	0	37
Blazing Boo Kay	4	F	3	0	0	0	300
Blazing Cat	4	F	7	1	0	2	28,520
Blazing Chaak	3	G	2	0	0	0	0
Blazing Ciara	2	F	2	1	1	0	14,250
Blazing Colors	8	G	3	0	0	0	225
Blazing Count	7	H	8	2	1	1	77,061
Blazing Countess	4	F	14	6	0	3	80,176
Blazing Deputy	5	M	1	0	0	0	0
Blazing Devil	9	G	5	0	0	1	893
Blazing Element	4	G	9	1	3	1	42,020
Blazing Exploit	2	C	5	3	1	0	61,947

Horse	Age	Sex	Sts	1st	2d	3d	Won
Blazing Flame	2	F	1	0	0	0	0
Blazing Forest	5	G	12	1	0	2	23,276
Blazing Freedom	4	C	6	2	0	0	30,090
Blazing Fury	6	G	5	0	0	0	3,385
Blazing Genius	8	G	8	3	2	1	6,193
Blazing Halo	5	M	5	0	0	0	206
Blazing Heatrix	2	G	3	0	0	0	800
Blazing Mama	3	F	1	0	0	0	0
Blazing Maple	3	F	6	0	0	1	3,790
Blazing Miss Fufu	3	F	10	3	0	1	31,728
Blazing Prince	3	C	2	0	0	0	0
Blazing Purrsuit	3	C	3	1	0	2	35,200
Blazing Reign	2	G	1	0	0	0	164
Blazing Road	6	G	5	0	0	2	12,364
Blazing Rocket	4	F	6	0	1	0	2,172
Blazing Ruby	3	F	5	1	1	0	15,774
Blazing Seven	6	G	8	0	0	2	1,961
Blazing Silver	3	F	1	0	0	0	195
Blazing Song	4	C	16	1	6	1	80,173
Blazing Star	4	F	4	1	1	0	21,766
Blazing Tune	4	F	9	1	0	2	30,410
Blazing Wind	7	G	15	0	2	1	5,604
Blazing Wings	2	F	5	1	2	1	11,431
Blazinmint's Lady	5	M	7	2	2	0	12,353
Blaz'n Penny	5	M	16	1	3	0	8,122
Blazshotthebutler	2	G	5	0	1	0	2,132
Bleached	4	G	17	1	1	6	10,824
Bleacher Creature	2	C	2	1	0	0	16,230
Blennerhassett	5	M	3	1	1	0	6,750
Bless Her Heart	3	F	6	2	1	2	33,600
Bless Him	6	G	12	0	0	0	1,215
Bless Me	4	C	12	2	3	1	15,640
Bless My Soles	5	M	6	3	2	0	20,135
Bless My Stars	3	F	8	0	1	3	9,450
Bless the Tide	2	C	2	0	0	0	280
Bless Thismess	4	F	4	0	0	0	1,038
Blessed Conquista	4	G	10	0	0	1	1,337
Blessed Fager	3	G	10	1	0	1	2,199
Blessed Peace	4	F	2	0	0	0	136
Blessed Sun	5	G	3	0	0	0	0
Blessing Angelica	3	F	14	0	0	1	3,059
Blessings	5	M	6	0	0	1	4,840
Bleu Glace	5	M	6	0	1	0	2,080
Bleu Royale	2	G	2	1	1	0	15,140
Bleuesville	3	F	1	0	0	0	105
Bleu's Apparition	3	F	6	1	2	1	35,506
Blind Canyon	3	F	20	4	7	3	106,550
Blind Reality	6	M	12	1	1	2	5,305
Blind River Fox	2	G	5	0	1	1	11,499
Blindfold	3	F	3	0	0	0	225
Blinding Prospect	3	G	15	3	3	2	50,865
Bling Bling	3	F	5	0	1	0	2,082
Blink and Go	3	F	4	1	0	1	12,600
Blink His Gone	4	G	5	1	0	0	4,938
Blink N Miss Me	4	F	18	1	3	2	11,670
Blink of an Eye	5	G	14	1	2	0	7,124
Blink Twice	4	F	2	0	0	0	387
Blinkanhesgone	2	G	5	1	1	1	44,056
Blinkit	3	F	13	3	4	1	16,034
Bliss Landing	4	G	15	6	2	1	29,558
Blissful Ignorance	2	F	2	0	0	0	330
Blissful Morning	7	M	10	0	1	1	5,020
Blisteringfraction	6	G	5	0	0	0	265
Blitz Away	4	C	6	2	1	1	9,720
Blitz the Star	8	G	4	0	0	0	0
Blitzen	2	F	1	0	0	1	4,300
Blitzen Tucker	4	C	8	0	1	1	6,440
Blitzy	3	C	10	1	2	0	2,538
Blizzard Bliss	3	C	1	0	0	0	240
Blizzard Mountain	3	G	13	1	1	3	22,318
Blizzard of Oz	4	G	12	2	1	1	17,258
Blkice	6	G	12	3	2	2	20,003
Blockade Runner	6	G	8	0	1	0	2,880
Blockbuster (ARG)	5	H	5	0	0	0	2,288
Blocked Call	4	C	16	1	3	0	14,741
Blofeld (GB)	3	G	9	1	1	0	26,886
Blond Dancer	6	M	2	0	0	2	13,920
Blondage	6	M	3	0	0	0	485
Blonde Dynamite	5	M	12	2	1	0	24,118
Blonde Executive	3	F	6	5	0	0	414,263
Blonde Okie	6	M	8	2	1	0	15,110
Blonde Wisdom	2	F	5	1	2	0	44,165
Blondel de Nesle	5	G	2	0	0	1	3,171
Blondes	2	F	3	0	0	0	300
Blondie's Tune	2	F	2	0	0	0	0
Blondz Away	3	F	12	1	2	2	30,895
Blood	4	C	7	0	2	1	3,916
Blood Red Bay	3	F	1	0	1	0	1,485
Bloodshot	4	F	6	0	1	1	9,711
Bloody Baron	5	H	3	0	0	0	240
Bloody Bonnet	3	F	1	0	1	0	420
Bloody Liz	5	M	9	2	1	2	40,810
Bloomin Justice	3	F	9	1	1	0	6,840
Bloomination	2	F	7	0	0	0	2,500
Blooming Grove	5	G	1	0	0	0	600
Blossom Belle	4	F	4	2	1	0	12,561
Blossom Hill	5	M	10	2	1	3	16,370
Blossom Point	3	F	6	0	1	0	6,510
Blossum	5	M	1	0	0	0	0
Blow Em Away	5	G	1	0	0	0	0
Blowin in the Wind	5	G	9	3	2	0	121,410
Blowin the Gold	3	G	5	0	1	0	1,960
Blowing Bartok	3	F	2	0	0	0	800
Blown Audit	2	C	3	0	0	0	300
Blown Away	4	F	8	3	0	1	15,387
Blown Overboard	4	G	4	0	0	0	785
Blown Surprise	4	F	10	1	1	1	25,680
Blown to Sea	5	M	5	0	0	0	841
Blu Barry Buckle	3	G	3	1	0	0	3,720
Blu Spur	5	M	2	0	1	0	7,300
Blu Starr Lady	4	F	11	5	0	2	39,732
Blue Afleet	4	C	4	2	1	1	96,620
Blue Angel's Echo	6	G	12	1	2	1	25,090
Blue Atlantis	4	F	10	2	1	3	7,756
Blue Barrett	4	F	7	0	2	2	5,801
Blue Blitzen	2	F	2	0	0	0	257
Blue Blood Boot	4	G	7	0	0	1	7,020
Blue Blood Bullet	3	G	6	1	0	0	10,452
Blue Blood Warrior	2	C	4	0	0	1	6,125
Blue Blue Sea	5	G	3	0	0	1	1,470
Blue Blueyes	4	F	8	3	1	0	25,395
Blue Boar Ten	4	G	3	1	0	0	5,553
Blue Boat	5	H	2	0	0	0	4,300
Blue Bodgit	5	M	7	1	0	1	3,456
Blue Bug	9	G	4	0	0	0	263
Blue Burn	5	H	3	1	0	0	11,175
Blue by Slew	3	G	10	1	1	1	7,706
Blue Cay	3	F	7	1	2	1	23,400
Blue Chapeau	5	M	11	2	4	0	13,629
Blue Chip Gal	5	M	15	2	1	4	8,275
Blue Chip Girl	2	F	8	1	0	1	6,435
Blue Chips Rule	3	G	9	0	0	1	2,240
Blue Copy	4	F	11	0	0	1	985
Blue Corner	2	C	1	0	0	0	400
Blue Craft	4	G	8	0	1	2	2,041
Blue Crane	2	C	3	0	0	0	500
Blue Creek Bart	5	G	1	0	0	0	0
Blue Creeker	5	M	6	1	0	0	14,006
Blue Crush	2	F	2	0	0	0	1,860
Blue Dancer	5	G	12	4	1	2	37,571
Blue Daze	5	M	4	0	2	0	5,148
Blue Electra	6	M	6	2	1	0	9,047
Blue Escapade	2	C	2	0	1	1	2,620
Blue Explosion	7	G	15	4	4	1	32,775
Blue Eyed Annie	3	F	10	1	1	0	26,466
Blue Eyed Blond	2	C	3	1	0	0	15,110
Blue Eyed Buck	6	G	6	0	1	1	2,159
Blue Eyed Tiger	5	G	8	2	0	0	9,350
Blue Eyes Princess	3	F	1	0	0	1	2,520
Blue Finally	4	C	7	1	1	1	38,120
Blue Forest	2	F	1	0	0	0	975
Blue Frosty Mug	9	M	6	0	1	1	3,630
Blue Game	3	G	4	1	1	1	4,366
Blue Gem	3	F	10	0	1	0	1,931
Blue Grass Angel	4	F	12	1	2	1	11,303
Blue Grass Blues	11	G	9	0	0	0	657
Blue Grass Boy	2	G	1	0	0	0	115
Blue Grass Dancer	3	F	12	3	1	1	55,700

Horse	Age	Sex	Sts	1st	2d	3d	Won
Blue Green Dancer	4	G	11	0	3	0	4,471
Blue Grey	8	G	6	0	0	1	4,210
Blue Guru	6	M	13	1	0	5	55,690
Blue Harbor	4	G	16	4	2	2	32,262
Blue Heaven	2	G	7	0	1	1	6,788
Blue Hill Ave	6	G	5	0	0	0	122
Blue Hills	6	M	2	0	1	0	7,350
Blue Imp	4	F	13	4	4	0	66,118
Blue Jean Racer	8	G	7	1	1	1	10,920
Blue Julie	2	F	5	3	0	1	24,076
Blue Kentucky	3	G	5	0	0	0	464
Blue Krismas	8	G	1	0	0	0	40
Blue Label	4	G	8	0	0	2	3,763
Blue Lace	3	F	5	0	0	0	555
Blue Lake	3	F	8	2	0	0	40,050
Blue Launch	7	G	2	0	0	0	110
Blue Lou	4	C	4	0	0	2	1,676
Blue Lupin	3	F	4	1	1	0	9,320
Blue Magnolia	5	M	7	0	0	0	650
Blue Mambo	5	G	15	1	1	1	12,300
Blue Marque	2	C	1	0	0	0	205
Blue Martinis	4	F	3	0	0	0	610
Blue Max	3	G	1	0	0	0	400
Blue Mill	4	G	5	0	3	0	1,471
Blue Mingo	3	G	6	0	1	1	3,260
Blue Moon Bay	4	F	4	1	1	0	7,445
Blue Moon Night	6	M	10	0	0	0	668
Blue Moon Rising	5	M	7	3	1	1	64,900
Blue Moonray	6	M	15	2	6	3	31,955
Blue N Beyond	8	M	4	0	0	0	465
Blue Nose	3	F	4	3	0	1	20,057
Blue On The Rocks (NZ)	5	G	7	1	0	0	10,540
Blue Pepsi Lodge	2	C	2	1	0	0	20,950
Blue Puffette	4	F	5	0	0	0	1,038
Blue Reality	6	M	14	2	3	1	12,900
Blue Red Bullet	4	G	3	1	1	0	15,309
Blue Rhapsody	2	F	1	0	1	0	6,000
Blue Ribbon Time	4	F	12	0	0	1	2,398
Blue Ridge Linda	3	F	12	4	4	1	64,523
Blue Ridge Robbery	5	H	10	1	1	0	13,540
Blue Rob	4	C	4	0	0	0	236
Blue Rodeo	2	C	1	0	0	0	795
Blue Russian	8	G	2	0	0	0	0
Blue Saffire	2	F	3	1	0	1	12,621
Blue Scarf	3	F	8	0	0	4	6,419
Blue Seti	4	G	1	0	0	0	0
Blue Silver Dollar	6	G	5	0	0	0	364
Blue Skies Ahead	4	G	12	3	2	2	93,130
Blue Sky Baby	6	M	5	1	0	1	34,706
Blue Sky's Coyota	4	F	1	0	0	0	59
Blue Slew	4	G	10	1	1	1	2,376
Blue Slew's Shoes	5	H	5	1	0	2	23,950
Blue Song	3	F	10	2	2	1	29,773
Blue Spade	4	C	3	0	0	0	0
Blue Stardust	8	G	1	0	0	0	0
Blue Starlite	3	F	1	0	0	0	87
Blue Steel High	10	G	1	0	0	0	0
Blue Steller (IRE)	6	H	1	0	0	1	18,000
Blue Submarine	4	G	6	0	1	0	5,482
Blue Sunday	2	C	1	1	0	0	24,600
Blue Tejano	10	G	4	2	1	0	12,408
Blue Tiffany Ice	2	C	3	1	0	0	5,929
Blue Tomorrow	2	F	3	0	0	0	420
Blue Tower	9	G	2	0	0	0	1,025
Blue Tricon	4	C	4	0	0	1	1,234
Blue Two	4	F	15	1	2	1	8,382
Blue Voyage	5	G	2	0	0	0	0
Blue Warbler	2	F	10	0	3	5	52,935
Blue Warrior	5	G	22	4	3	1	18,629
Blue White	3	F	6	0	0	1	2,846
Blue Zephyr	5	M	11	0	2	2	2,770
Blueberry Pie	3	F	7	1	0	1	6,136
Bluebird's Song	4	F	16	3	2	3	32,039
Bluefinger	3	G	10	1	4	1	41,590
Bluefish	3	G	3	0	1	1	3,745
Bluegrass Belle	4	F	1	0	0	0	2,250
Bluegrass Fever	2	C	9	0	3	1	16,815
Bluegrass Madam	2	F	2	0	1	0	2,200
Bluegrass Sara	3	F	5	0	0	2	12,400
Bluegrass Ted	5	G	15	1	4	3	20,690
Bluegrayday	7	H	2	2	0	0	8,640
Blueknob	5	G	11	2	1	1	22,949
Blues Are Fast	2	G	4	0	0	0	411
Blues At Sunrise	4	F	3	0	0	1	2,150
Blues Away	10	G	14	3	2	1	36,589
Blue's Diamond	3	F	14	2	1	1	34,640
Blue's First Baby	3	F	15	1	1	0	21,500
Blues Highway	4	G	4	1	0	0	28,584
Blues in Advance	4	F	11	3	0	1	3,577
Blues Mountain	3	C	2	0	2	0	7,690
Blues Night Out	3	G	14	1	0	3	12,319
Blue's Secret	3	C	12	0	2	1	4,650
Blues Traveler	3	C	5	0	0	0	715
Bluesbdancing	2	F	4	3	1	0	104,140
Blueseeker	3	G	4	0	0	0	335
Blueskiesfromnowon	5	M	13	0	0	1	1,630
Bluesman	3	G	6	1	1	0	11,980
Bluesmaster	2	G	1	0	1	0	8,200
Bluesnclues	4	C	1	0	0	0	0
Bluesnorthernlight	2	F	5	0	1	0	1,800
Bluespeedwhitelite	3	F	10	1	1	2	24,910
Bluesthestandard	7	G	6	1	2	1	132,633
Bluewaters	3	G	11	1	3	0	9,345
Bluff	2	C	2	0	2	0	11,890
Bluffen Go	2	C	5	1	0	3	28,393
Bluffie Slew	4	F	14	3	1	3	107,810
Bluffin Monarch	2	G	1	0	0	0	62
Bluffin Rail	4	F	6	2	1	0	20,030
Bluffing	3	F	2	0	0	0	0
Blufflette	4	F	13	1	2	2	21,770
Bluffthepass	3	F	6	0	0	0	625
Blumin Crafty	2	C	3	0	0	0	315
Blumin Exuberant	6	M	13	2	3	2	33,092
Blumin Gold	3	F	8	1	0	1	11,350
Blumin Henry	4	G	8	0	0	0	165
Blumurr	5	M	12	1	2	1	5,263
Blurrs Got a Halo	5	G	5	1	1	0	2,254
Blurry Dawn	9	G	13	3	0	1	16,631
Blush	3	F	3	1	0	1	18,430
Blush Boldly	2	F	3	0	0	0	1,450
Blush Brush	2	F	2	0	0	1	4,420
Blushes Beauty	4	F	4	0	0	0	530
Blushing Barbie	4	F	13	1	1	2	15,789
Blushing Ciel	4	G	18	2	2	4	45,300
Blushing Factor	3	F	2	0	0	0	143
Blushing Frisco	4	G	16	4	1	8	28,410
Blushing Indian	3	C	2	1	0	0	20,400
Blushing Judith	5	G	9	1	1	3	19,111
Blushing Megastar	2	F	3	0	0	0	1,560
Blushing Melissa	2	F	7	0	0	0	9,670
Blushing Quakey	3	C	3	0	1	0	705
Blushing Rainbow	5	M	5	0	0	0	1,893
Blushing Starlite	3	F	4	0	0	0	495
Blushing Wildly	3	F	7	1	1	0	7,633
Blushing Witness	6	M	6	1	2	0	11,122
Blushingkittentale	3	F	7	2	2	0	28,190
Blush'n Frolic	5	M	8	0	0	4	6,853
Bluvalley Tiger	3	G	14	5	1	3	104,876
Bluwillow	4	F	8	0	2	0	2,264
Blythewood	4	F	17	4	2	3	45,000
Bo Barley	8	G	15	3	2	4	42,900
Bo Bo the Great	3	G	7	1	3	1	10,006
Bo Bo's Hunter	3	F	3	1	0	0	25,670
Bo Bo's Thunder	5	M	5	0	2	2	9,100
Bo Bo's Vice	4	G	8	0	1	1	13,950
Bo Dippity	4	F	9	0	0	2	452
Bo Knows	4	C	4	0	0	0	0
Bo n' Aero	5	G	2	0	0	0	150
Bo Simpson	11	G	6	1	0	0	15,738
Bo Wonder Can Run	3	G	10	0	1	4	5,322
Boalex Party	6	H	10	2	1	1	18,543
Boana (GER)	6	M	7	1	0	1	45,800
Board Elligible	4	F	15	5	4	0	302,921
Board to Run	4	G	6	1	1	1	1,733
Boarded Hall	4	C	2	0	1	0	4,400
Boardroom Banter	6	G	5	1	0	0	1,610
Boardroom Drama	5	G	18	2	4	3	24,665
Boardroom Scandal	2	F	1	0	0	0	118

Horse	Age	Sex	Sts	1st	2d	3d	Won
Boardwalk Babe	2	F	1	0	1	0	8,600
Boardwalk City	2	C	1	0	0	0	0
Boa's Lemon Drop	3	F	6	0	1	0	1,352
Boast	3	F	10	2	3	0	41,715
Boasting	3	F	3	2	1	0	64,600
Boat Ride	4	F	4	1	0	0	5,100
Boathouse Symphony	6	G	3	0	0	0	201
Boatswain	3	G	16	1	0	0	5,253
Bob and a Half	2	G	4	0	0	0	470
Bob Jo	6	M	9	3	1	1	23,203
Bob 'n Velma	3	G	7	2	1	1	17,991
Bob Roy	7	G	12	2	1	0	14,093
Bob Stories	8	G	10	3	3	1	18,830
Bobandrob	3	C	7	2	1	0	33,294
Bobaway	5	H	11	2	2	2	12,077
Bobbiblue Bayou	7	H	1	0	0	0	84
Bobbie Blue	5	M	8	0	0	0	266
Bobbie Gene	4	F	5	1	2	0	22,387
Bobbie Use	3	F	4	1	0	0	60,429
Bobbie Wagner	3	F	11	2	0	1	12,002
Bobbie's Beauty	4	F	9	1	4	3	36,981
Bobbie's Brat	2	F	4	0	0	0	824
Bobbie's Concerta	3	F	3	0	1	1	4,120
Bobbie's Crown	4	F	1	0	0	0	0
Bobbies Sunrise	5	M	4	0	0	0	594
Bobbie's the Best	2	F	3	0	0	1	6,064
Bobbin' for Loot	2	G	1	1	0	0	6,240
Bobbinjean	4	F	10	3	1	1	20,088
Bobbi's Girls	3	F	4	1	0	0	18,840
Bobb's Rizzi	2	C	5	1	1	0	13,460
Bobby Blurr	8	H	4	1	0	1	5,496
Bobby E. Lee	4	G	10	0	1	3	38,372
Bobby Luvs P. R.	4	C	9	0	0	1	3,545
Bobby M C Q	5	G	1	0	0	0	175
Bobby McGee	4	G	2	0	0	0	550
Bobby Naz	6	G	14	2	1	4	12,868
Bobby the Bagger	2	C	1	1	0	0	25,800
Bobby Twice	11	G	2	0	0	0	105
Bobby Z.	6	H	6	1	1	0	1,759
Bobby's Buckaroo	8	G	3	1	0	1	13,430
Bobbys Day	3	G	9	1	0	0	7,209
Bobby's Red Jet	5	H	9	0	3	4	7,514
Bobcat Greeley	2	F	1	0	0	0	205
Bobi Cat	3	F	5	0	2	0	6,520
Bobjinski	4	G	2	0	0	0	0
Boboman	3	C	1	0	0	0	0
Bobonnier	4	C	2	0	0	0	0
Bobplicity	3	C	8	1	2	0	11,225
Bob's Barb	2	F	4	0	0	0	1,195
Bobs Beauty	2	F	4	2	0	0	29,253
Bobs Big Idea	7	G	7	0	0	0	969
Bob's Boomer	3	G	9	0	1	0	3,385
Bob's Buck	3	C	9	0	1	1	4,650
Bobs Gray	2	G	2	0	0	1	2,550
Bob's Hat Trick	6	M	6	0	0	0	380
Bobs Last Hope	3	C	5	0	0	0	400
Bob's Lit'l Miss	2	F	5	1	1	1	16,450
Bob's Luck	7	G	14	4	1	5	9,370
Bob's Proud Moment	3	C	16	3	4	2	140,290
Bob's Retired	5	G	14	0	0	3	3,913
Bob's Rockn'	5	H	6	1	2	1	2,240
Bob's Shadow	4	G	6	1	0	1	6,474
Bob's Silverbullet	4	F	2	0	0	0	84
Bobs Spunky Girl	3	F	7	0	3	3	6,460
Bob's Toy	5	M	4	0	1	0	2,270
Bob's Valentine	3	F	12	3	1	1	27,660
Bobski	3	C	2	0	0	0	653
Bobsthebigdog	4	G	19	1	3	3	12,361
Bobsway	5	G	1	0	0	0	0
Boca Beacon	3	F	1	0	0	0	600
Boca Bound	4	G	12	2	2	2	28,490
Boca Rose	5	M	5	0	0	0	1,175
Bocage	3	G	14	2	4	3	29,543
Bocca Al Lupo	4	C	4	0	1	2	20,260
Bocce Girl	2	F	4	0	0	1	2,325
Bocciolo	5	G	11	4	1	1	23,119
Bocelli	4	G	11	1	0	1	5,479
Bocelli (IRE)	7	G	11	4	4	1	24,185
Boco Trick	3	C	5	0	0	0	341
Bodacious Beauty	2	F	3	0	0	0	1,840
Bodacious Bubba	10	G	5	0	0	0	1,185
Bodacious Cat	4	F	3	0	0	2	2,805
Bodacious Dream	6	G	9	0	0	5	4,049
Bodacious Justin	4	G	5	0	0	0	1,167
Bodacious Nathan	3	G	4	0	0	0	0
Bodacious Stuart	3	C	5	0	0	0	0
Bodes Well	3	G	10	2	2	0	25,640
Bodgit Be Tru	3	G	2	0	0	0	0
Bodgit Bucks	2	C	1	0	0	0	80
Bodgiteer	4	G	7	4	1	0	88,060
Bodi's Buddy	6	G	3	0	0	0	0
Body Building	6	G	3	0	0	0	0
Body by Katrina	2	F	4	1	1	1	14,130
Body Image	5	M	3	0	0	0	200
Bodyguard (GB)	9	G	2	0	0	0	0
Boeing (CHI)	8	G	8	2	2	0	14,978
Boeotia	3	F	11	0	0	2	2,390
Bog Hunter	5	G	7	1	3	1	25,035
Bogangles	3	G	7	0	1	1	22,870
Bogart	7	G	21	1	4	4	27,304
Bogart's Cat	2	C	4	2	0	0	19,083
Bogey Free	5	G	15	1	2	4	11,696
Boggy Creek	2	C	5	3	0	0	120,111
Boggy Creek Dancer	2	G	5	0	0	1	4,902
Bogner Regis	6	G	4	1	0	0	2,241
Bogota Bill	3	G	9	3	1	1	88,460
Bohemia Slew	7	G	12	3	3	1	34,094
Bohemian Lady	3	F	6	2	1	1	121,682
Bohemian Rain	2	F	4	0	1	0	6,720
Bohica	2	F	1	0	0	0	95
Bohunk	4	G	14	0	3	1	16,750
Boiling Point	4	G	6	0	1	0	4,728
Boink	5	G	5	0	2	1	2,095
Bois D' Arc	7	G	10	1	0	1	3,492
Boji Breeze	4	F	20	4	5	5	39,549
Boji's At Six	3	G	9	1	2	2	23,380
Bokonon	4	G	10	2	1	2	24,225
Bola Soup	3	G	5	2	1	0	64,320
Bolaro	4	F	11	0	0	3	11,556
Bold Action	3	C	4	0	0	0	566
Bold Al	3	G	11	0	1	1	8,707
Bold Alliance	2	C	3	0	0	0	1,500
Bold America	4	C	5	0	0	0	3,750
Bold and Brassy	8	H	8	0	1	0	3,430
Bold and Classy	2	F	7	0	0	0	2,646
Bold and Lively	11	G	11	0	1	0	800
Bold and Royal	3	C	10	1	3	2	11,412
Bold Armageddon	6	G	10	0	0	0	640
Bold Artic Ice	4	F	4	2	0	1	119,184
Bold B	6	G	9	3	0	3	5,455
Bold Bailey	5	G	2	0	0	0	378
Bold Banker	4	C	3	0	0	0	2,520
Bold Baron	4	C	1	0	0	0	0
Bold Bayou Baby	3	F	7	3	0	0	47,100
Bold Beat	3	G	14	2	1	3	23,430
Bold Becky	3	F	5	0	1	1	10,898
Bold Betsy	7	M	4	0	0	2	1,530
Bold Blush	6	M	11	0	0	1	1,084
Bold Bobo	3	G	9	0	1	0	5,012
Bold Boo	3	G	2	0	0	0	0
Bold Brigade	4	C	6	1	2	0	10,517
Bold Buster	8	G	9	1	0	0	6,066
Bold Caleb	8	G	6	0	0	0	300
Bold Caller	5	G	12	2	0	1	31,004
Bold Caper	2	C	4	0	0	0	780
Bold Cesar	4	G	11	4	3	1	14,314
Bold Charge	2	G	4	0	1	2	5,270
Bold Charm	3	C	3	0	1	1	3,045
Bold Civette	4	F	1	0	0	0	1,500
Bold Classic	4	F	10	2	2	1	20,758
Bold Clover	2	F	4	1	1	0	28,037
Bold Clu	3	G	4	0	0	0	0
Bold Connection	4	G	18	2	1	3	15,322
Bold Contender	9	H	10	1	0	4	3,400
Bold Corsair	4	G	9	1	1	1	5,272
Bold Cover	2	C	4	0	1	0	6,929
Bold Creek	4	G	10	2	0	2	17,679
Bold Crypto	4	G	9	1	1	3	14,844

Horse	Age	Sex	Sts	1st	2d	3d	Won
Bold Dare	7	H	4	0	1	0	582
Bold Days	5	G	9	3	2	4	90,770
Bold Decision	2	C	1	1	0	0	24,600
Bold Demarche	4	F	6	0	0	1	649
Bold Demi	6	G	1	0	0	0	0
Bold Emancipator	3	G	5	0	0	2	3,570
Bold Emblem	3	G	5	1	0	0	5,945
Bold Encounter	2	F	1	0	0	0	0
Bold Executress	4	F	16	0	1	2	30,535
Bold Expectations	3	F	14	4	1	3	32,143
Bold Explorer	3	C	7	1	1	1	11,590
Bold Feather	3	F	1	0	0	1	6,270
Bold Finish	2	C	1	0	0	0	0
Bold Force	3	G	1	0	0	0	0
Bold Frenchy	3	F	10	2	0	0	18,207
Bold Gale	6	M	3	0	0	0	546
Bold General	2	C	1	1	0	0	4,758
Bold Glare	5	G	6	1	0	1	8,687
Bold Glo	3	G	1	0	0	0	155
Bold Green	3	F	11	2	2	0	42,037
Bold Grenadier	2	C	1	1	0	0	34,200
Bold Grill	3	G	6	0	0	1	3,600
Bold Groom	5	H	10	0	3	3	8,760
Bold Groton	4	G	9	1	0	4	7,877
Bold Gypsy	4	F	2	0	0	0	0
Bold Honor	8	G	1	0	0	0	150
Bold Honoree	4	F	7	0	3	0	14,815
Bold Hush	3	G	7	1	0	2	11,340
Bold in a Storm	3	G	11	1	1	2	24,486
Bold in Deed	4	F	3	0	0	0	194
Bold Intruder	3	G	5	0	0	0	590
Bold Irishman	4	G	13	0	1	0	4,920
Bold Jet	8	G	4	0	0	0	384
Bold Joi'ski	2	F	2	0	0	0	328
Bold Josh Sally	7	M	10	0	0	2	3,730
Bold Jubilation	3	F	9	2	0	2	27,874
Bold Kissin Kris	2	C	3	0	0	0	240
Bold Kris	5	G	14	1	0	0	44,748
Bold Leadership	2	C	2	1	0	0	27,210
Bold Legacy	4	C	5	1	1	0	26,361
Bold Line	7	M	9	0	0	1	3,250
Bold Lion	2	G	2	1	0	0	15,600
Bold Lisa	4	F	3	0	0	0	0
Bold Little Lass	3	F	11	0	4	4	80,390
Bold Lover	4	G	6	2	1	0	12,290
Bold Mango	5	G	16	0	0	6	20,080
Bold Mark	6	M	4	2	1	0	12,976
Bold Marty	2	F	8	2	1	0	16,683
Bold Match	7	G	3	0	0	0	385
Bold Meadow	4	G	3	0	0	0	220
Bold Meghan	8	M	5	0	0	0	595
Bold Merit	3	G	3	2	0	0	54,868
Bold Mind	5	G	2	0	1	0	900
Bold Minister	3	G	3	1	1	0	27,500
Bold Missionary	2	C	1	0	0	0	0
Bold Missy	4	F	16	2	4	2	16,313
Bold Money	3	F	4	0	0	0	280
Bold Moro	4	G	14	1	0	1	9,538
Bold Move	4	G	13	3	5	0	32,985
Bold Mystique	4	F	6	1	1	0	28,967
Bold N Alert	4	F	7	0	1	1	2,170
Bold 'n Bashful	6	M	5	0	0	0	200
Bold N Dark	3	F	11	1	1	3	10,474
Bold n' Elegant	3	F	6	0	2	1	9,016
Bold n' Fancy	7	G	5	0	0	0	1,854
Bold 'n Keen	5	H	9	1	0	3	36,966
Bold N Love	2	F	5	1	1	0	22,000
Bold N Old	6	G	1	0	0	0	0
Bold n' Perfect	5	G	13	2	2	2	25,541
Bold n' Pretty	6	M	6	1	0	1	8,348
Bold N True	3	F	2	0	0	0	440
Bold Northern	5	G	5	0	0	0	603
Bold Nxs	3	G	8	0	1	2	8,843
Bold Offer	4	G	8	2	1	1	8,076
Bold Outlook	2	F	4	2	1	1	68,400
Bold Parisian	7	G	9	1	2	1	13,576
Bold Passage	2	F	7	2	0	3	53,978
Bold Passer	7	G	9	6	0	0	19,965
Bold Patches	5	M	7	1	2	1	5,866
Bold Performer	4	F	4	1	2	1	5,180
Bold Pete	6	G	9	0	0	0	568
Bold Philosopher	6	M	6	0	0	0	236
Bold Pilot	9	G	7	1	0	0	14,100
Bold Pistol	5	G	3	0	0	0	177
Bold Pleasure	3	G	1	0	0	0	225
Bold Position	2	G	1	0	0	0	0
Bold Prospect	5	G	9	0	3	0	10,313
Bold Raffie	3	G	2	0	0	0	0
Bold Reality	3	C	5	1	0	2	8,850
Bold Reply	7	H	15	2	2	5	43,584
Bold Rhapsody	6	M	11	0	2	2	4,337
Bold Rhythm	4	G	13	1	2	1	26,280
Bold Riot	3	C	6	0	0	2	12,298
Bold Rita	4	F	7	1	2	2	17,618
Bold Roberta	6	M	9	0	2	1	91,036
Bold Runaway	3	G	5	0	0	1	723
Bold Rush	4	G	5	0	0	0	564
Bold Shadante	3	F	7	0	1	0	1,263
Bold Shakopee	2	F	4	0	0	1	2,688
Bold Shamrock	6	M	4	0	0	1	400
Bold Sheik	5	H	8	0	0	2	6,740
Bold Snow Dancer	3	F	7	2	1	1	16,605
Bold Sparkle	5	G	6	0	0	3	906
Bold Speculator	7	G	11	0	0	0	2,366
Bold Squall	3	G	16	1	3	2	13,050
Bold Starlet	3	F	8	1	1	0	41,844
Bold Sterling	3	G	11	3	2	1	42,880
Bold Stock	3	C	6	0	2	0	19,860
Bold Stroke	3	G	9	2	4	0	19,656
Bold Tactician	5	G	4	0	0	0	279
Bold Taz	3	G	1	1	0	0	9,075
Bold Temptress	2	F	2	0	0	1	1,965
Bold Tena	3	F	6	0	0	0	600
Bold Texas	4	G	5	1	2	0	33,280
Bold Thing	2	C	5	0	0	0	3,420
Bold Times	3	G	8	0	0	0	1,322
Bold Tizzy	4	F	3	0	0	0	576
Bold to Gold	7	M	13	0	2	0	7,325
Bold Trader	3	G	9	2	1	1	41,534
Bold Trick	4	G	15	2	4	3	72,945
Bold Truth	5	H	3	0	0	0	615
Bold Turn	3	G	4	1	0	0	9,005
Bold Twister	2	F	3	0	0	2	5,980
Bold Victoress	7	M	2	0	0	0	0
Bold Wind	4	G	6	2	0	0	25,194
Bold Witch	2	F	1	0	0	0	0
Bold Won	2	C	1	0	0	0	0
Boldandahalf	4	G	13	2	0	5	20,693
Boldandsizzling	3	F	2	0	0	0	0
Boldanzar	6	G	7	3	3	1	56,347
Boldest Angel	3	G	14	2	3	2	33,450
Boldest Heart	5	G	7	1	1	2	14,971
Boldest of All	4	F	9	1	0	2	63,526
Boldfalcon	5	G	10	0	1	2	830
Boldirish	5	G	2	0	0	0	166
Boldly Certain	7	M	6	0	0	0	1,030
Boldly Clever	6	G	15	3	5	1	39,829
Boldly Inspired	7	G	19	0	0	2	5,967
Bold'n Courageous	3	G	3	0	0	1	2,350
Boldness	4	F	9	2	3	1	14,505
Boldsea	5	M	13	0	0	1	11,057
Bolele's Billy	3	C	12	2	1	3	14,845
Bolero Type	10	G	13	2	4	1	6,259
Bolido	2	G	4	1	2	0	15,650
Bolivar	7	G	10	0	0	2	5,559
Bolshoi Ballet	3	F	13	3	3	0	56,907
Bolshoi Dancer	3	F	3	1	1	0	4,600
Bolshoi Girl	3	F	3	0	0	1	540
Bolt Action	3	G	5	1	0	0	3,480
Bolted Heart	3	C	6	2	1	1	29,260
Bolted Prince	2	C	1	0	1	0	1,500
Boltin' Brian	3	G	6	1	0	2	19,270
Bolton Landing	3	F	13	3	0	0	27,940
Bolywood	5	G	8	1	0	0	2,913
Bom Luna (ARG)	7	M	18	0	2	3	19,110
Bomar Key	8	G	9	0	0	0	1,920
Bomartini	4	G	7	0	1	1	4,460
Bomb Squad	5	G	9	1	3	1	9,592

Horse	Age	Sex	Sts	1st	2d	3d	Won
Bomb Threat	4	F	4	1	1	1	6,820
Bombay Blues	5	M	12	1	0	3	19,830
Bombay Dreams	2	F	1	0	0	0	840
Bombay Lad	4	G	1	1	0	0	20,400
Bombay Lady	2	F	1	0	0	0	130
Bombay Slew	3	G	4	0	1	0	6,250
Bombazine	3	G	3	0	0	1	7,820
Bomber Ace	4	G	10	1	2	1	7,207
Bomber Beau	4	G	14	1	2	0	8,389
Bombofalooker	3	G	9	2	2	1	21,726
Bombs Away Nickie	4	G	10	0	1	1	5,150
Bombshell Baby	3	F	8	4	0	1	23,232
Bomby	5	G	1	0	0	0	0
Bomer's Gold	3	G	4	0	1	0	2,780
Bompa's Briana	3	F	6	0	1	3	6,118
Bon Affair	3	G	1	0	0	0	0
Bon Amigo	7	H	8	0	0	0	2,502
Bon Appeal	4	F	3	0	0	0	1,010
Bon Bon Bonnie	2	F	2	0	1	0	4,800
Bon Caddo	3	G	2	0	0	0	1,020
Bon Candy	4	F	1	0	1	0	2,000
Bon Echo Babe	4	F	3	1	1	1	11,020
Bon Fleur	4	G	8	2	0	1	34,860
Bon Geo T Ka	4	F	4	0	0	0	0
Bon Giorno	4	F	10	0	1	0	1,754
Bon Jour Paris	4	F	8	0	1	1	12,290
Bon Marie	3	C	1	0	0	0	1,650
Bon Place	6	M	5	1	0	1	11,535
Bon Temps Pette	3	F	1	0	0	0	0
Bon to Run	12	G	22	5	4	2	13,419
Bona Fide Rebel	4	G	4	0	0	0	504
Bonabrooke	2	F	2	0	0	0	0
Bonafide Lady	9	M	3	0	0	0	284
Bonafide Rock	2	C	1	0	0	0	145
Bonaguil	7	G	11	1	1	2	42,100
Bonaire (GB)	3	F	6	0	0	3	31,029
Bonanza Jellybean	3	F	8	2	0	1	58,430
Bonaparte	4	G	5	0	2	0	14,399
Bonapaw	8	G	2	0	0	0	0
Bonay	4	F	3	0	0	0	2,160
Bonbelle	3	F	14	0	2	1	10,007
Bonberry	4	F	11	1	2	1	16,226
Bonche	4	G	3	0	0	0	0
Bond Arbitrage	3	C	4	0	0	0	1,085
Bond King	2	C	3	0	1	0	4,305
Bond Midnight (IRE)	4	F	6	1	0	0	10,115
Bonded	6	G	8	0	0	2	1,984
Bondi Beach	7	G	1	0	0	0	0
Bondsman	4	G	15	1	2	2	18,225
Bone Collector	4	G	9	0	0	1	2,158
Bone Daddy	3	G	4	0	1	0	1,080
Bonefide Reason	6	M	2	0	0	0	3,302
Bonehead	3	G	4	0	1	0	4,180
Bones Ferrone	2	C	1	0	0	0	1,230
Bonfante	3	C	7	3	1	0	84,856
Bonfo	4	G	10	0	3	3	34,050
Bongee	4	F	2	2	0	0	9,120
Bongo Kitty	3	F	6	2	1	2	17,510
Bongsilver	6	G	8	0	0	1	1,545
Bonilla	5	G	10	3	2	1	68,758
Bonita Gata	4	F	2	0	0	0	80
Bonita Lady	4	F	6	1	1	0	5,916
Bonita Mexicana	5	M	10	1	0	1	6,727
Bonita Rose	6	M	11	1	0	2	17,820
Bonita Spell	4	F	1	0	0	0	0
Bonita Tyger	4	F	2	0	1	0	2,640
Bonita's Reinbeau	3	F	4	0	1	1	8,810
Bonjour	6	M	8	2	0	0	4,733
Bonjourno My Lady	3	F	6	1	0	1	2,785
Bonne Idee	4	F	1	0	0	0	0
Bonnechere	6	M	7	0	1	0	7,560
Bonney Lake	4	F	14	1	4	1	18,820
Bonnie Ballew	3	F	3	0	0	0	0
Bonnie Be Quick	4	F	7	1	1	1	10,840
Bonnie Belle	8	M	9	1	0	0	5,477
Bonnie Bo	7	M	4	1	0	0	1,900
Bonnie Brighton	4	F	6	0	1	0	9,700
Bonnie Clyde	5	M	8	0	0	2	670
Bonnie J.	4	F	9	2	0	2	50,405
Bonnie o' Mine	3	F	5	1	0	1	18,820
Bonnie Pancho	6	M	10	2	3	2	12,208
Bonnie Rose	3	F	4	1	0	1	17,140
Bonnie's Angel	2	F	5	0	2	0	3,319
Bonnie's Bag	10	G	4	0	1	0	3,230
Bonnie's Dancer	5	M	12	1	0	2	5,040
Bonnies Kaper	3	F	1	0	0	0	265
Bonnies Knight	4	F	4	0	0	0	353
Bonny Danzer	2	F	5	1	0	0	10,086
Bonny Go Lightly	3	F	7	1	1	0	26,550
Bonny Johnny	5	G	4	0	0	1	1,076
Bono Striker	6	G	15	3	2	0	14,930
Bonobo	8	H	4	0	0	0	235
Bonquelo	2	F	1	0	0	0	0
Bonspiel	3	G	13	5	3	1	71,636
Bontrando	5	H	2	0	0	0	0
Bonus Baby	3	F	3	0	0	1	1,090
Bonus Bea	3	F	3	0	0	0	116
Bonus Bid	5	M	15	3	2	3	74,000
Bonus Bouquet	3	F	1	0	0	0	0
Bonus Dessert	3	G	5	0	0	0	0
Bonus Extra	4	F	4	0	1	0	10,690
Bonus Honor	3	G	4	0	0	0	407
Bonus Move	4	F	4	0	1	0	2,373
Bonus Pack	6	G	5	1	0	0	35,370
Bonus Parlay	3	F	9	1	0	1	3,747
Bonus Pay Day	6	G	1	0	0	0	2,340
Bonus Return	3	F	2	0	0	0	112
Bonus Royal	3	F	15	2	1	0	36,010
Bonyev	3	C	1	0	0	0	400
Bon'zer	3	F	10	1	2	0	15,135
Boo Aahhhh	4	G	9	1	2	1	11,795
Boo Boo	3	G	5	0	0	0	795
Boo Boo Honey	4	F	8	1	2	0	11,520
Boo Cat	3	F	3	0	0	0	470
Boo Roo	7	G	5	1	0	0	988
Boo Yeah	5	G	3	0	0	0	0
Boocfuss	3	C	2	0	1	0	11,200
Boogaylynn	5	M	9	0	0	2	1,507
Booggie Cat	3	G	15	1	2	0	13,929
Boogie After Dark	2	G	7	1	0	2	26,749
Boogie Board	5	H	3	0	2	0	2,700
Boogie City	3	F	4	1	0	0	3,920
Boogie Girl	3	F	16	1	3	2	4,560
Boogie Lill	4	F	13	1	2	0	7,305
Boogie On	4	C	3	1	0	0	9,000
Boogie Piano	4	F	11	1	1	2	27,160
Boogie Power	4	F	13	2	0	2	13,588
Boogie Pro	2	C	1	0	0	0	0
Boogie Rhythmn	3	G	4	0	1	0	1,665
Boogie Woogie Man	4	G	8	5	1	0	31,755
Boogie Woogie Type	6	G	4	0	1	0	4,540
Boogieboogieboy	5	G	11	0	0	4	3,361
Boogieboom	5	M	6	0	1	0	6,284
Boogieforjoy	4	G	4	1	0	0	7,962
Book Club	4	C	16	2	2	1	12,755
Book of the Year	4	C	7	0	0	0	2,880
Book Seven	5	G	13	2	3	1	43,842
Book Smart	7	M	3	0	1	0	1,250
Book the Bet	4	C	1	0	0	0	0
Book the Bullet	2	F	5	1	0	0	21,260
Book the Cat	5	M	15	3	2	2	37,030
Booked Home	3	C	2	0	0	0	82
Bookem Carl	5	G	5	0	0	0	0
Booker D	9	G	1	0	0	0	152
Booker D J	6	G	1	0	0	0	0
Bookle Bo	8	G	13	3	2	0	35,892
Bookmaker	2	C	4	0	1	0	3,749
Bookmaster	4	C	4	1	1	1	38,790
Boom a Cat a Boom	3	C	10	2	2	0	50,440
Boom Baby	3	F	14	5	1	2	54,961
Boom Bah Yay	4	F	7	1	0	1	9,698
Boom Boom Cha Cha	6	M	9	0	3	0	10,602
Boom Chicka Boom	4	F	3	0	1	1	582
Boom City	5	H	13	2	3	0	24,525
Boom Day	2	F	1	0	0	0	300
Boom Shakalaka	3	F	11	0	0	0	1,680
Boomanji	2	F	2	0	0	0	4,860
Boomboomgirl	5	M	9	1	3	1	38,958

Horse	Age	Sex	Sts	1st	2d	3d	Won
Boomer Creek	4	G	12	1	0	0	8,385
Boomerang Billilea	5	M	15	0	0	1	1,137
Boomeray	5	G	1	0	0	0	61
Boomer's Boot	4	G	12	1	4	3	9,065
Boomer's Express	4	C	9	1	0	2	8,460
Boomers in Town	4	G	17	0	0	1	3,339
Boomika	3	F	2	0	0	0	0
Boomin	5	G	5	0	0	0	326
Booming Along	2	G	5	1	3	1	41,023
Booming Buckaroo	2	C	1	0	0	1	1,550
Booming Echo	5	M	6	0	0	0	1,210
Booming Economy	2	G	2	0	1	1	5,045
Booming Sound	3	G	19	3	1	5	18,904
Boomslang	5	G	9	0	0	1	6,817
Boomtown Red	4	G	9	1	2	1	26,399
Boomtown Thief	3	G	9	0	1	1	4,458
Boomzeeboom	3	C	6	3	0	1	162,276
Boondock	5	G	8	0	0	1	911
Boone Avie	7	G	10	2	0	1	5,100
Boone Town Lady	5	M	16	1	0	2	5,288
Booneomatic	4	C	1	0	0	0	40
Boone's Big Boy	5	G	5	0	0	2	3,640
Boone's Creek	7	G	6	0	0	0	377
Boone's Dad	4	F	7	1	1	3	10,565
Boone's Diamond	5	M	11	2	4	1	61,450
Boone's Gold	6	M	9	0	3	0	18,466
Boone's Silent	4	C	11	0	3	2	5,726
Boonesboro Beach	5	M	11	1	3	2	16,555
Booneslittledancer	4	F	11	1	1	0	7,694
Boone'ssimplydbest	4	G	17	1	2	3	13,084
Boonesville	7	G	17	3	4	3	18,398
Booneton	6	M	3	0	0	0	0
Booney B	4	G	9	0	0	0	330
Boortz	3	C	3	1	0	1	18,470
Boo's Boy	8	G	9	1	2	2	12,726
Boo's Shayna Punim	2	F	2	0	0	0	870
Booster	4	G	11	1	1	3	27,698
Boot Hill	7	G	12	1	3	1	19,033
Boot Scoot Boogie	3	G	4	0	0	0	100
Boot Scooter	3	F	13	3	4	1	26,420
Boot Scootn Austin	6	G	2	0	0	0	0
Boot Special	4	F	8	2	0	1	8,228
Boot Strap	3	F	6	1	1	1	22,950
Booties	5	M	3	0	0	0	120
Bootleg and Susy	5	M	17	4	2	3	31,073
Bootleg'n Baby	3	F	1	0	0	0	0
Boots a Flyin'	3	F	12	1	2	1	5,858
Boots Are Walking	3	G	10	1	2	6	39,855
Boots Malone	8	G	1	0	0	0	200
Boots Prospect	5	M	2	0	1	0	1,600
Boozen Blues	2	G	6	0	1	1	4,938
Boozin Blonde	3	F	14	2	1	4	97,905
Boozin' Susan	5	M	6	0	1	2	44,096
Bop She Bop	3	F	4	0	0	1	1,035
Bora Bora	4	F	2	0	0	0	960
Borasca	5	M	4	2	1	1	60,680
Borboleta	4	F	9	0	1	1	3,121
Border Beat	9	G	12	1	2	3	9,585
Border Blues	4	F	12	2	4	2	96,597
Border Bound	4	F	9	2	1	2	79,424
Border Jones	3	C	7	0	2	3	5,200
Border Raider	4	G	7	0	0	0	0
Border Reiver	4	G	12	0	1	0	4,958
Border Runner	4	G	12	1	2	1	12,367
Border War	2	C	6	0	1	1	5,623
Borderline Crazy	3	F	6	1	0	2	9,628
Borders Edge	4	C	7	1	1	1	12,020
Bordgonmagnificent	3	F	17	3	0	4	15,983
Boreal	3	C	4	1	1	0	8,140
Boreas	8	G	2	0	0	0	300
Boricua Kid	2	G	9	0	1	1	3,576
Boring Blues	3	F	6	0	2	2	1,601
Boris Jordan	3	C	9	0	1	0	13,592
Boris the Blade	4	G	6	0	0	1	4,232
Born	2	G	3	0	0	0	570
Born a Charmer	3	G	6	0	0	0	1,335
Born a Roman	3	G	6	2	1	1	27,420
Born Blonde	3	F	5	1	1	1	14,880
Born Dusty	3	G	20	3	3	3	19,055
Born Gifted	4	F	5	1	0	1	7,875
Born On Fire	3	F	1	0	0	0	56
Born Something (IRE)	6	M	1	0	1	0	8,740
Born Survivor	3	G	5	0	0	1	1,235
Born to Be Classy	4	F	12	1	5	1	7,708
Born to Bop	7	M	7	0	0	2	2,803
Born to Dance	5	M	2	0	1	0	2,400
Born to Pic	7	G	5	2	0	0	29,950
Born to Run Fast	6	G	8	0	1	0	1,959
Born Wild Again	4	G	9	0	0	1	1,673
Borntobealeader	5	G	10	1	2	2	6,773
Borntobeloved	5	M	9	1	2	2	20,458
Borntobelucky	4	G	17	0	0	2	2,981
Borntoberegal	7	G	15	0	3	1	11,830
Bornwithit	3	G	13	3	1	2	102,455
Borrego	3	C	8	0	5	0	452,190
Borrow the Gold	3	G	5	0	0	1	2,079
Borrowed Money	3	C	1	0	0	0	31
Borstal Boy	6	G	11	0	2	0	9,376
Borzov	4	G	1	0	0	0	0
Bo's a Ten	4	F	8	1	0	1	7,365
Bo's Bursting Star	8	H	5	1	1	0	1,470
Bo's Miss	2	F	4	1	0	2	8,570
Bo's Sand Tunnel	3	C	19	1	2	5	23,625
Bo's Sister	5	M	5	1	1	0	23,530
Bo's Typhoon	2	F	3	1	0	0	5,015
Boschee	5	G	4	0	1	0	1,210
Boscobelle	3	F	4	0	0	1	3,464
Bosefa	3	G	9	1	4	2	39,564
Boshonto	11	G	10	0	0	0	284
Bosia	4	F	5	1	0	0	1,448
Bosko's Crown	4	C	14	2	0	0	9,977
Bosox Babe	3	F	2	0	0	1	1,370
Boss Cat	2	C	1	0	0	0	300
Boss Chenin	5	M	3	0	3	0	10,600
Boss Ego	8	H	11	1	5	0	57,580
Boss Gable	4	G	2	0	0	0	150
Boss Jim	2	G	6	0	2	0	2,400
Boss Nass	3	C	3	1	1	0	45,080
Bossa Rio	3	C	2	0	1	1	7,275
Bossanova	4	C	1	0	0	0	0
Bossem	3	C	2	1	0	0	4,200
Bossie D J	7	M	9	0	2	1	5,109
Bosskiri	2	F	2	2	0	0	114,330
Boston Bar	3	G	11	1	4	1	23,619
Boston Bay	6	G	8	0	0	4	7,905
Boston Bean	3	G	11	1	1	2	15,985
Boston Belga	2	F	3	2	0	0	14,685
Boston Blitz	2	C	2	0	0	0	0
Boston Brahmin	3	C	9	1	2	0	26,600
Boston Bull	4	C	8	2	0	0	27,107
Boston Common	5	G	6	3	1	0	141,960
Boston Express	3	F	8	3	1	2	115,219
Boston Flyer	2	F	5	1	1	0	24,505
Boston Fox	4	G	1	0	0	0	0
Boston Garden	3	G	8	1	0	0	18,736
Boston Glory	2	C	4	1	1	1	67,850
Boston Gold	4	F	2	0	1	0	9,000
Boston Heat	2	F	1	0	0	0	400
Boston Lass	4	F	6	0	0	0	1,809
Boston Maggie	3	F	6	0	1	1	7,700
Boston Navigator	3	C	1	0	0	1	3,250
Boston Park	4	C	3	0	0	0	4,555
Boston Post Road	3	F	15	3	0	3	28,505
Boston Raider	2	G	5	2	0	0	51,306
Boston Shuttle	4	G	11	2	2	2	38,320
Boston Song	3	F	2	0	0	0	1,690
Boston Storm	4	F	17	5	1	2	29,389
Boston Symphony	3	F	2	0	0	0	110
Bostwick	6	G	4	1	0	0	3,635
Botella	3	F	5	0	0	0	660
Both Guns Poppin	5	G	6	1	0	1	2,584
Botime	3	F	9	4	0	0	11,816
Bottle Cap	2	C	2	0	0	0	1,360
Bottle Fever	2	G	2	0	0	0	1,998
Bottled Excitement	6	M	13	1	0	0	7,650
Bottom Bay	3	G	6	1	1	0	55,124
Bottom Close	2	F	1	0	0	0	600
Boty's Topper	3	G	3	0	0	0	0

Horse	Age	Sex	Sts	1st	2d	3d	Won
Botzworth	4	G	12	0	1	1	5,275
Boublitchky	3	F	13	3	3	1	45,046
Bought in Dixie	8	H	2	0	0	0	710
Boula Boula	3	F	9	0	3	0	6,759
Boulder Chip	3	F	2	0	0	0	192
Boulder Tiger	2	C	1	0	0	0	55
Boule	4	G	3	0	1	2	3,655
Boulevardier	3	C	1	0	0	0	0
Boulevardofdreams (NZ)	4	F	1	0	0	0	0
Bounce	3	F	5	0	0	1	4,340
Bounce Forever	2	G	2	0	0	0	969
Bound Along	3	C	10	1	2	3	28,691
Bound by a Legacy	5	G	1	0	0	0	0
Bound by Honour	6	G	6	1	1	0	7,191
Bound by the Heart	6	G	6	0	2	2	3,070
Bound for Fame	3	C	5	1	0	1	35,870
Bound for Freedom	4	G	3	0	0	0	1,500
Bound for Victory	3	C	3	2	0	0	27,930
Bound On Bi	7	M	10	1	2	2	57,839
Bound to B Fast	3	F	1	0	0	0	75
Bound to Be Great	6	H	1	0	0	0	0
Bound to Be Lucky	4	F	9	1	2	4	11,036
Bound to Be Sunny	3	G	1	1	0	0	3,060
Bound to Impress	4	G	7	1	1	0	18,747
Bound to Thaw	3	F	3	0	0	0	580
Bound With Honour	5	H	1	0	0	0	135
Boundary Bay	3	C	8	2	0	1	62,548
Boundary Stone	4	G	3	1	1	0	26,410
Boundforthetop	4	G	8	1	1	1	4,729
Bounding Buck	2	C	2	0	0	0	410
Bounding Cat	4	G	5	0	1	0	3,400
Bounding Charm	4	F	8	4	1	0	134,500
Bounding Leap	3	G	1	0	0	0	0
Bounding Two	6	G	2	0	1	0	792
Bounding Zeal	3	F	10	2	3	2	27,235
Boundry Layer	3	G	8	0	0	0	1,200
Bounty Bill	4	G	12	3	0	4	20,595
Bounty Miss	4	F	6	0	0	0	0
Bounty of Spring	4	F	4	1	1	1	3,760
Bounty's Beauty	3	F	2	0	0	0	0
Bountywood	3	G	10	1	0	0	3,711
Bounzuz	4	F	2	0	0	1	2,282
Bourbon	7	G	11	1	3	2	9,751
Bourbon Ambassador	4	F	4	0	0	2	2,259
Bourbon Ball	3	F	2	1	0	1	26,200
Bourbon Borderline	2	G	5	1	0	0	5,675
Bourbon Brownie	5	M	10	1	2	2	12,330
Bourbon Chaser	2	C	1	0	0	1	219
Bourbon County	5	H	4	0	0	0	25,000
Bourbon Cowboy	3	G	4	1	1	0	20,763
Bourbon Creek	4	G	9	3	0	2	28,134
Bourbon Jack	4	G	10	1	1	0	4,803
Bourbon Lane	5	G	2	1	0	0	4,834
Bourbon N Blues	3	C	6	1	1	1	40,230
Bourbon N Coke	6	H	12	2	3	1	20,440
Bourbon Party	4	G	19	3	3	3	41,710
Bourbon Ridge	4	G	4	0	0	0	344
Bourbon St. Hussy	3	F	6	0	0	2	5,275
Bourbonnais (IRE)	4	C	5	1	0	0	26,640
Bourn a Cowboy	9	G	5	0	0	0	222
Bourne Ruler	8	G	6	1	0	0	7,103
Bouvet	2	F	3	0	0	0	2,160
Bow Confide	3	C	1	0	0	0	80
Bow Out	4	G	8	1	0	0	15,070
Bow Spray	6	G	4	1	2	0	9,020
Bow Time	2	F	6	1	0	0	6,300
Bowditch	6	H	1	0	0	0	0
Bowen Hill	4	G	15	3	4	4	40,920
Bowen's Dream	3	C	3	0	0	1	4,800
Bowerman Road	4	G	11	0	0	1	1,377
Bowery Care	3	F	4	0	0	0	2,006
Bowkeen	6	M	5	1	1	0	30,221
Bowl of Fire	5	M	4	0	1	0	2,884
Bowler	2	G	2	0	0	0	250
Bowman Mill	6	H	3	0	0	0	2,100
Bowman Too	4	G	12	0	0	0	2,534
Bowman's Band	6	H	12	0	3	5	439,334
Bowman's Crossing	11	H	2	0	0	0	0
Bowmans Legend	3	C	1	0	0	0	0
Box Cutter	3	F	16	5	2	2	63,360
Box of Chocolates	3	F	1	0	0	0	0
Box of Moonlight	4	F	3	0	0	0	0
Box Office	5	H	3	0	0	1	1,080
Box Office Smash	4	F	13	2	0	1	6,725
Box Seat Lover	10	G	5	0	0	0	317
Box Turtle	3	F	5	0	0	0	270
Boxcar Bertha	3	F	4	0	0	0	384
Boxed In	3	G	10	0	2	2	9,328
Boxer	2	G	5	1	1	0	25,360
Boxley	3	G	10	2	2	0	15,560
Box's Girl	5	M	3	0	0	0	0
Boy Cor	6	G	16	1	1	0	4,533
Boy Genius	10	G	9	2	1	1	34,137
Boy Scout Alan	3	G	11	0	3	2	11,980
Boy Willy	7	G	10	1	1	1	8,065
Boy Zee	3	G	7	0	0	0	986
Boyfriend	4	G	10	0	1	2	5,115
Boyisdue	10	G	18	3	1	3	8,313
Boyle Heights Kid	6	G	2	0	1	0	3,800
Boys Night Out	6	G	1	0	0	0	220
Boys Revenge	13	G	1	0	0	0	0
Boyum	7	G	13	2	4	3	30,450
Boywhataboy	3	G	7	1	0	0	3,679
Braak's Biz	8	G	1	0	0	0	0
Braak's Bizzy Boy	6	G	9	0	1	1	2,061
Braaks Love	9	G	2	0	0	0	80
Braak's Plain	4	F	4	0	1	0	1,086
Braak's Special	8	H	4	0	0	0	214
Bracey's Prospect	5	M	10	4	1	1	37,840
Bracing Beauty	5	M	2	0	1	0	6,260
Brackenber	3	F	9	0	0	1	12,045
Brackenberry	2	F	2	0	0	1	1,238
Brackets	5	M	11	1	0	1	7,909
Brad Man	5	G	2	0	0	0	600
Brad Z	6	G	7	0	0	0	308
Brademi	3	C	15	2	2	3	25,155
Braden's Best	3	C	2	0	0	1	935
Braden's Hope	4	F	11	2	0	0	9,748
Bradford	3	G	9	0	3	2	45,142
Bradleys Son	4	G	10	2	0	1	4,185
Brad's Brat	6	G	10	4	0	1	42,483
Brad's On Patrol	4	G	10	0	2	0	6,860
Brady	6	H	16	3	3	1	22,529
Brae Prospect	2	C	1	0	0	0	0
Braetta	5	M	8	4	1	1	77,007
Brag Bag	3	F	7	1	1	0	35,436
Bragg Power	9	G	17	1	1	2	7,067
Braggadoojo	3	G	13	0	2	2	5,175
Bragger	2	C	6	1	1	1	5,610
Braggin On Braydon	5	M	3	0	0	0	138
Braggnificent	3	C	1	0	0	0	50
Braggs Little Mag	9	G	8	1	0	1	3,440
Brahma	3	C	2	0	0	0	1,260
Brahma Bull	4	C	3	0	2	0	20,200
Brains and Beauty	2	F	7	1	1	0	18,200
Brake Check	4	G	3	0	0	0	207
Bramble Bush	4	G	7	1	1	0	32,120
Brancaster	8	G	2	0	0	0	225
Branch Chief	7	G	6	0	0	1	1,037
Branch Office	4	G	12	1	1	1	8,784
Brand Me Evil	2	G	5	0	1	2	3,145
Brand Name	3	C	4	1	0	2	45,700
Brand New Address	3	G	11	0	1	1	4,667
Brandala	6	M	8	1	0	0	57,416
Branded in Gold	2	F	6	2	1	1	40,400
Brandenburg Gate	3	G	6	0	0	1	1,020
Brandie Bee	2	F	3	0	0	2	2,315
Brandi's Charm	5	G	2	0	0	0	153
Brandish	9	G	17	0	1	4	3,818
Brandmeararefool	2	F	2	0	0	0	390
Brando	4	G	6	0	0	1	4,010
Brandon Blaine	4	G	11	0	2	1	5,110
Brandon's Attitude	3	G	3	0	0	0	600
Brandon's Babydoll	5	M	13	4	2	2	28,385
Brandon's Brother	3	G	6	0	0	0	795
Brandons Colors	5	G	12	0	1	0	9,517
Brandon's Luck	3	F	15	0	3	3	5,479
Brandon's Marfa	3	G	7	0	4	2	60,300

Horse	Age	Sex	Sts	1st	2d	3d	Won
Brandon's Secret	2	C	2	0	0	0	450
Brandons Sister	2	F	2	0	0	0	0
Brandons Wild Cat	3	F	6	0	0	2	2,689
Brandrews Choice	6	G	15	4	1	3	36,032
Brands Hatch	3	C	7	1	0	0	41,556
Brandy Blaze	3	G	9	3	0	0	19,255
Brandy Creek	4	F	12	0	4	2	5,508
Brandy Doll	5	M	4	0	0	1	621
Brandy Gulch	3	F	3	2	0	0	12,213
Brandy o' Nite	3	F	5	0	0	2	2,411
Brandy Vee	5	M	18	0	3	2	3,257
Brandys Goal	7	M	4	0	0	0	542
Brandy's Irish	2	C	1	0	0	0	155
Branford	5	G	14	0	1	1	7,266
Branjolisa	4	F	8	0	2	2	6,518
Brankman	14	G	3	1	1	1	6,600
Brant Point	3	F	14	1	4	0	21,365
Branton's Breeze	4	F	6	1	1	0	7,460
Brant's Pride	7	G	2	0	0	1	1,067
Brash Attitude	3	G	6	0	1	0	2,243
Brass Act	5	G	1	0	0	0	205
Brass Arrow	5	G	14	2	3	1	56,715
Brass Boots	4	G	13	5	2	0	51,986
Brass Bucket	4	F	13	0	0	0	1,306
Brass Bull	3	G	2	0	0	0	195
Brass Bunny	3	F	10	0	2	1	4,143
Brass Courage	3	G	1	0	0	0	0
Brass Dixie	7	G	13	1	4	4	17,936
Brass Flash	3	G	5	0	1	1	4,909
Brass Halo	5	G	1	0	0	0	0
Brass Hat	3	G	9	3	4	0	624,430
Brass in Pocket	5	M	9	4	2	0	371,038
Brass Jazz Band	4	C	1	0	0	0	0
Brass Kat	3	F	11	1	1	1	5,704
Brass Key	8	G	8	1	2	1	10,718
Brass Letters	2	G	3	1	0	1	6,965
Brass 'n Braid	3	G	3	0	0	0	0
Brass Pendant	4	F	10	0	1	0	10,033
Brass Punch	4	G	11	3	0	1	34,473
Brass Rail	3	F	11	1	1	2	6,742
Brass Robin	5	G	6	1	1	0	2,865
Brass Ruckus	5	G	4	0	0	0	104
Brass Ruhler	6	G	9	2	2	2	18,082
Brass Support	8	M	2	0	0	1	3,750
Brass Tacks	2	G	1	0	1	0	1,560
Brass Tango	5	G	2	0	0	0	0
Brass Tiger	3	G	9	1	0	0	4,166
Brass Wind	2	C	3	0	0	0	225
Brassy B	5	M	7	0	2	1	3,930
Brassy Babe	6	H	4	0	2	1	5,640
Brassy Boots	2	F	8	2	0	4	83,920
Brassy Crystal	2	F	3	0	0	1	2,194
Brassy Fred	10	H	4	0	2	1	11,890
Brassy Karakorum	3	G	17	4	0	3	67,213
Brassy Kid	4	G	11	0	1	1	1,951
Brassy Kitten	3	F	14	0	3	4	48,482
Brassy Light	3	G	10	2	1	0	34,779
Brassy Punch	3	G	3	0	2	0	6,601
Brassy Shirley	3	F	15	2	3	3	40,531
Brat	6	M	2	0	0	0	161
Brat's Secert	5	M	2	0	0	0	0
Bratsy Girl	2	F	2	0	0	0	0
Brattie Mattie	2	F	2	0	0	0	450
Brattothecore	4	F	5	0	0	2	10,362
Bratty Patty	2	F	4	1	1	0	12,000
Brave All the Way	9	G	9	1	0	2	5,500
Brave Boco	3	F	4	0	0	0	4,660
Brave Byars	4	G	3	1	0	0	10,170
Brave Call	4	C	3	0	0	1	6,720
Brave Claim	4	F	3	1	1	0	6,350
Brave Columbus	3	C	5	0	1	1	5,760
Brave Destiny	4	F	5	1	1	0	16,220
Brave From Heaven	2	F	4	0	0	0	1,612
Brave Heartofclass	7	G	7	0	1	0	1,425
Brave Joe	4	G	8	1	3	2	54,400
Brave Miner	10	G	10	1	1	2	8,171
Brave Miss	4	F	7	1	0	0	17,780
Brave 'n Away	4	C	5	1	0	0	8,378
Brave Oath	3	G	17	2	4	1	36,981
Brave Opponent	7	M	11	1	4	1	9,348
Brave Rifle	3	G	3	0	0	0	0
Brave Solution	3	C	2	0	0	0	0
Brave Soviet	4	C	1	0	0	1	500
Brave Star	5	G	3	0	0	0	61
Brave Step	2	C	5	0	0	1	1,633
Brave Tale	2	F	1	0	0	0	400
Brave Vixen	3	F	1	0	0	0	0
Braveandbeautiful	3	F	8	0	2	1	5,565
Bravehearted Lady	7	M	16	1	2	4	35,083
Bravely	5	G	2	0	0	0	3,881
Bravest	5	M	8	1	2	1	6,540
Bravest and Finest	4	C	3	0	0	1	1,630
Bravest Heart	4	G	10	2	1	1	10,277
Bravo Brad	3	G	10	0	0	1	5,291
Bravo Dome Cat	7	G	4	0	0	0	224
Bravo Ragasso (IRE)	4	G	7	0	0	0	300
Bravo Romano	3	G	9	0	1	1	2,017
Bravura	2	F	6	2	0	1	59,035
Brawn	3	C	4	1	1	0	5,575
Brax Lee's Toy	3	G	12	1	2	1	23,572
Braxton's Yum Yum	5	G	6	0	1	0	827
Braytonville	3	F	4	1	0	2	21,980
Brazen Attitude	3	F	6	0	1	1	4,054
Brazen Bomber	4	G	12	3	0	0	15,303
Brazen Brandy	6	G	10	1	1	2	5,956
Brazen Dancer	2	G	5	0	1	1	3,210
Brazen n' Bold	5	G	9	1	1	2	22,744
Brazen Outlaw	4	G	2	0	1	0	1,842
Brazen Prospect	5	G	12	3	3	1	51,340
Brazen Star	3	C	11	1	4	2	32,929
Brazen Virtue	4	F	13	1	4	2	22,687
Brazen Wildcat	3	F	2	0	0	0	0
Brazil Nut	5	G	14	2	3	1	25,935
Brazilian	2	F	3	1	1	0	19,320
Brazilian Baby	4	F	2	0	0	1	4,218
Brazilian Mama	5	M	15	0	3	3	8,125
Brazilian Symphony	3	F	4	0	0	1	5,170
Brazos County	3	C	8	1	0	0	17,340
Brazos Shuttle	5	M	1	0	0	0	61
Bre Ex	4	G	6	3	0	0	18,396
Breach of Promise	5	M	8	3	0	2	46,658
Break Dancer	3	C	5	0	0	1	3,300
Break of the Day	3	C	2	0	1	0	6,100
Break Out	3	G	6	1	1	0	9,515
Break the Barrier	3	C	9	2	0	1	58,968
Break the Clock	5	H	1	0	0	0	0
Breakaway	3	C	8	1	1	1	97,304
Breakaway Brad	3	G	2	0	0	0	237
Breakaway Max	2	G	4	0	0	0	192
Breakaway Quietly	6	G	10	2	4	1	23,726
Breakfast At T's	4	F	1	0	0	0	0
Breakfast in Maui	5	G	9	1	0	1	9,695
Breakin My Heart	3	F	10	3	1	3	20,751
Breaking Contact	3	G	6	0	1	0	3,110
Breaking Ruhls	4	F	2	0	0	0	0
Breakittomeeasily	7	M	7	0	1	0	2,853
Breanna's Smile	4	G	17	5	2	6	76,895
Breathe	4	F	2	1	0	0	6,195
Breathless	7	G	1	0	0	0	50
Breeze Basket	7	M	9	1	3	2	3,925
Breeze Catcher	5	H	5	1	0	2	6,686
Breeze Easy	4	F	5	1	0	0	10,414
Breeze Home Jessie	3	F	5	0	0	1	896
Breeze On	2	C	2	0	0	0	2,168
Breeze the Weasel	8	M	6	0	1	0	6,290
Breeze Through	3	F	12	1	2	0	7,217
Breezeville	7	H	1	0	0	0	0
Breezin Brook	3	F	5	1	0	1	2,425
Breezin On	6	G	3	0	0	0	565
Breezin On By	2	C	2	0	0	0	330
Breezin Tactics	6	H	1	0	1	0	820
Breezing Away	3	G	5	0	1	0	2,762
Breezing Bandit	9	G	13	0	1	3	4,106
Breezing Louise	2	F	6	1	2	0	8,725
Breezy Bray	4	F	7	1	1	0	22,270
Breezy Bri	6	M	10	2	3	2	35,550
Breezy Cat	2	C	3	0	1	1	2,800
Breezy Flats	5	G	5	0	1	1	925

Horse	Age	Sex	Sts	1st	2d	3d	Won
Breezy Ridge	2	G	6	1	0	0	6,510
Breezy Way	2	C	1	0	0	0	205
Bremer Red Rose	3	F	7	0	3	1	9,700
Brenda From Dixie	4	F	11	1	3	3	14,117
Brenda Jayne	3	F	2	0	0	0	0
Brendan Mac	4	G	16	1	1	1	9,832
Brendan's Aunt	4	F	6	1	0	1	21,512
Brenda's Angel	7	G	6	2	1	2	22,808
Brendaswhinybrat	7	M	12	0	1	2	3,784
Brendon's Goal	4	G	15	1	2	2	8,697
Brendynballerina	2	F	2	0	1	0	3,160
Brenna Belle	2	F	6	0	0	0	341
Brennan D	6	M	14	2	1	3	15,776
Brennan the Kid	4	G	11	1	1	1	6,055
Brenta's Prospect	4	F	10	2	2	2	18,050
Brentlin	2	C	7	1	0	0	17,294
Brent's Barrera	3	C	2	0	0	0	104
Brents Burner	4	C	3	0	0	0	120
Brent's Challanger	5	G	11	3	3	2	66,141
Brents Mercer	4	G	11	1	3	0	18,107
Brent's Tune	7	G	10	1	1	0	7,555
Brent's Victory	5	G	9	1	4	0	24,865
Brenzotti	4	F	4	0	0	0	0
Brett 'n Butter	4	F	5	0	0	0	590
Brettitus	2	C	4	0	1	0	5,542
Brett's Cat	3	F	2	0	0	0	0
Brevard	4	F	7	0	0	0	788
Brew a Slew	4	G	5	1	0	1	3,971
Brewing Mischief	3	F	8	0	0	0	2,899
Brewski	3	G	3	0	2	0	2,419
Brewton	4	F	6	2	1	0	15,726
Brian Boru (GB)	4	C	9	1	2	1	331,104
Brian Dude	4	C	6	1	2	0	28,000
Brian Strikes Back	7	G	6	1	1	0	2,246
Briana's Spirit	3	F	6	0	0	1	811
Brianmeister	4	G	5	0	0	1	315
Brian's a Pro	4	G	2	0	0	0	339
Brian's Barbers	3	G	11	2	3	1	23,555
Brian's Buddy	2	G	6	0	0	1	1,622
Brian's Dancer	8	G	9	1	2	2	9,820
Brian's Echo	5	G	8	0	1	0	7,885
Brians Joy	7	G	2	0	0	1	2,246
Brian's Lassie	6	M	8	0	0	2	2,174
Brian's Lil Bud	4	G	7	0	0	0	489
Brians Move	4	F	16	5	4	2	67,255
Brian's Shot	6	G	2	0	0	0	0
Brian's Trust	9	G	7	0	0	2	1,953
Briar Patch Kid	3	G	7	0	0	0	1,250
Briartic Belle	4	F	7	1	0	1	6,797
Briartic Feature	2	F	1	0	0	0	0
Briartic Gold	7	G	7	2	2	1	49,158
Briartic Jade	4	G	4	0	0	0	0
Bric n' Bag	7	G	10	2	1	0	14,884
Brick Cat	5	G	8	0	0	0	409
Brick Salthouse	7	M	16	1	3	3	17,506
Brickabrack	7	G	10	2	3	0	13,465
Brickell	3	C	10	1	4	4	71,240
Brickies Refund	2	F	3	0	0	2	3,235
Brickinthewall	4	C	9	0	1	1	1,862
Brickly Bear	2	F	2	0	0	0	2,340
Brick's	4	G	2	0	0	0	1,456
Bricks Princess	4	F	10	2	3	2	11,620
Bricksaren't Tardy	2	G	1	0	0	1	840
Bricktona	5	M	9	0	2	1	3,686
Bricky	3	C	2	0	0	0	550
Brickys First	4	F	3	0	0	0	430
Bridal Ballad	6	M	5	0	0	0	0
Bridal Buster	3	F	7	0	0	1	1,437
Bridal Creek	4	G	14	2	2	5	17,037
Bridal Gal	4	F	11	3	3	0	51,717
Bridal Path	3	F	12	2	4	1	69,875
Bride N Groom	4	F	7	1	2	1	2,689
Bride's Best Boy	3	C	7	2	0	0	43,225
Bridesman	2	C	4	0	0	1	4,250
Bridestone	4	G	12	1	2	1	9,170
Bridge	4	G	10	0	0	0	1,641
Bridge Builder	4	G	7	1	1	0	4,775
Bridge Creek Bob	5	G	1	0	0	0	0
Bridge Jumper	4	C	8	1	1	1	11,520
Bridge Out Again	4	G	2	0	1	0	6,400
Bridge Place (GB)	2	C	6	1	2	1	13,776
Bridge to Romance	4	G	9	2	0	2	33,648
Bridgeontheriver	3	G	9	0	1	0	5,342
Bridgeport	9	G	1	0	0	0	0
Bridger	10	G	1	0	0	0	390
Bridgespan	4	G	4	0	1	1	766
Bridget Says	4	F	7	3	2	1	53,110
Bridget's Last	4	F	4	0	1	0	2,520
Bridget's Sequel	4	F	9	0	1	0	2,764
Bridget's Wild Cat	2	C	4	0	0	2	6,185
Bridgetspoint	3	G	3	0	0	0	77
Bridgewood	5	M	5	0	0	0	1,022
Bridie's Twist	4	F	19	1	3	7	25,075
Bridle On	3	G	11	1	1	1	35,626
Bridle Registry	3	F	8	1	2	0	15,990
Bridled	3	F	1	0	0	0	0
Bridled Gold	5	G	10	3	2	2	8,759
Bridlespur	5	G	4	0	0	1	896
Bridlestone	4	F	6	0	1	0	10,260
Bridletime	5	R	10	1	0	0	4,842
Brieanna's Boy	4	C	2	1	1	0	40,635
Brief Affair	4	F	5	0	0	0	0
Brief Babe	2	F	3	0	1	0	6,620
Brief Contact	3	F	2	0	0	0	4,958
Brief Indulgence	3	G	11	3	2	1	15,000
Brief Intoxication	4	F	12	0	3	0	21,133
Brief Message	6	G	6	1	0	1	8,660
Brief Statement	6	M	2	0	0	0	0
Brief Time Machine	6	G	5	0	0	0	0
Briefchic	7	M	15	3	3	3	18,574
Briefdiamond	6	M	8	0	0	1	1,581
Briefly	7	M	9	0	1	1	4,433
Briefly Mythical	6	G	6	0	1	0	2,841
Briefton	3	G	9	1	2	0	16,233
Brigade	8	H	5	0	1	0	4,359
Brigader	3	G	11	3	3	0	100,770
Brigadier Brooks	2	C	1	0	0	0	172
Brigadier Jones (IRE)	5	G	2	0	0	0	2,840
Brigadoon	4	F	16	5	4	2	44,209
Brigette's Dream	3	F	11	2	2	4	58,575
Brighid	4	F	3	1	0	0	6,522
Bright Accent	3	G	2	0	0	0	0
Bright Amber	3	F	6	0	2	1	8,550
Bright and Shiny	3	F	8	1	0	1	41,664
Bright Anna	4	F	5	1	0	1	7,887
Bright Appeal	4	F	12	1	1	3	5,313
Bright Big Star	4	G	13	2	3	3	22,495
Bright Blaze	3	G	10	0	1	1	7,662
Bright Briana	4	F	11	4	1	0	21,330
Bright Brush	3	C	3	0	0	0	0
Bright Bullet	3	C	2	0	0	0	0
Bright Don	2	G	4	0	0	0	1,064
Bright Engagement	3	F	5	1	0	0	22,941
Bright Flame	4	F	10	1	1	2	13,570
Bright Galax	3	G	16	1	6	1	10,302
Bright Gold	4	F	15	3	4	3	96,292
Bright Hall	3	C	1	0	0	1	4,700
Bright Harbor	5	H	6	2	0	1	25,082
Bright Lightning	6	G	4	0	1	0	1,458
Bright Little Star	5	M	11	1	1	0	4,107
Bright Mike	3	C	9	1	0	3	35,167
Bright N Foxy	3	F	2	0	0	0	0
Bright N Timely	2	C	6	0	0	0	785
Bright Path	8	M	3	0	0	1	286
Bright Poppy	3	G	4	0	0	0	136
Bright Queen	2	F	1	0	1	0	1,615
Bright Reagent	3	F	13	1	5	2	48,924
Bright Red	2	C	2	0	0	0	669
Bright Sea	5	G	13	2	1	2	28,526
Bright Spirit	3	F	3	0	0	0	602
Bright Spot	2	F	1	0	0	0	460
Bright Star Busted	3	G	12	2	1	1	12,139
Bright Stout	6	G	8	3	0	1	5,018
Bright Village	4	G	12	4	1	2	20,139
Bright Weekend	2	C	4	0	0	0	614
Brighten My Day	5	M	9	0	0	0	2,310
Brighter Blue	7	M	18	3	2	4	51,410
Brightest Gold	3	F	5	0	0	0	460

Horse	Age	Sex	Sts	1st	2d	3d	Won
Brightest Hour	4	G	2	0	0	0	0
Brightest Ice	5	G	11	1	0	3	21,564
Brightest Link	3	F	1	0	0	0	105
Brightest Star	5	M	12	1	3	1	8,214
Brightly Bound	3	G	4	1	1	0	5,470
Brightly Glowing	3	F	4	0	0	0	968
Brightly Victoria	3	F	12	0	0	1	1,233
Brighton Belle	6	M	4	1	0	1	19,084
Brighton Bull	2	G	6	2	1	1	42,230
Brighton Ridge	4	C	4	1	0	0	21,895
Bright's Delight	3	F	5	1	0	0	5,599
Brightside	4	F	6	0	0	0	3,370
Brightstar High	3	F	10	1	2	2	15,230
Brightstone	5	G	13	2	2	3	18,664
Brijetta Light	2	F	10	0	2	3	14,555
Brill	4	G	12	3	2	1	24,410
Brillant Slew	3	C	1	0	0	0	105
Brillant Success	2	F	3	1	1	0	15,332
Brillcase	3	F	2	0	0	0	450
Brilliant Beau	3	C	16	3	6	1	37,750
Brilliant Bluff	6	G	2	0	0	0	206
Brilliant Bride	3	F	12	1	2	3	14,260
Brilliant Buffy	4	F	1	0	0	0	0
Brilliant Deniro	7	H	7	2	4	1	31,620
Brilliant Jewel	4	F	21	1	5	3	33,170
Brilliant Light	3	F	3	0	0	0	0
Brilliant Man	2	C	4	1	1	0	17,070
Brilliant Mistake	3	F	5	0	1	0	1,744
Brilliant Move	4	F	2	0	0	0	3,120
Brilliant Music	7	H	10	0	0	1	3,084
Brilliant Peaks	3	F	8	3	0	3	52,380
Brilliant Sermon	4	G	15	1	2	5	27,074
Brilliant Touch	5	M	5	0	0	0	360
Brim Storm	5	G	2	0	0	0	183
Brimson	4	G	5	0	0	1	3,714
Brimstone	5	G	17	2	3	3	21,431
Brinello	2	C	3	0	0	1	4,004
Bring Him Gold	3	G	6	0	1	0	1,955
Bring Home Thegold	6	G	10	1	1	2	31,595
Bring Me Diamonds	3	F	2	0	0	0	122
Bring Me the Money	4	G	1	0	0	0	0
Bring On the Blues	2	C	1	0	0	0	0
Bring On the Crown	3	F	12	0	1	1	10,060
Bring Out the Best	4	C	14	4	2	1	61,740
Bringem Jung	5	G	4	1	1	0	8,496
Bringhometheloot	5	M	1	0	0	0	183
Bringin It to Ya	3	G	6	1	0	0	21,999
Bringing Up Susan	3	F	3	1	0	0	8,982
Bringmesomemoney	5	G	11	1	0	2	7,463
Bringontherain	4	F	12	2	3	1	10,984
Brink of War	3	G	5	1	0	0	8,627
Brinton Bridge	9	G	8	2	0	2	38,710
Briony	3	F	9	1	0	2	9,640
Bri's Bad Boy	5	G	12	3	2	3	18,388
Brisa	9	M	13	0	5	0	16,517
Brishane	4	G	1	0	0	0	0
Brishlin	7	M	11	1	2	3	16,340
Brisk Report	5	M	2	0	0	1	1,265
Briskie	3	G	3	0	1	0	1,648
Brisote	6	G	15	3	2	3	30,663
Bristol Bomber	3	G	15	1	3	2	23,574
Bristolville	8	G	13	5	4	1	94,893
Brit	4	C	1	0	0	0	400
Brit Kay	6	M	10	0	2	2	10,000
Brite Anne Bonney	3	F	4	0	1	0	960
Brite Betty	4	F	5	1	1	0	49,747
Brite Bounty	6	G	6	1	2	1	19,460
Brite Cloud	2	F	2	0	0	0	600
Brite Colors	4	F	6	2	0	1	47,421
Brite Dancer	6	M	10	1	0	0	5,128
Brite Delite	4	F	4	0	0	0	217
Brite Diamond	3	F	9	2	1	1	43,380
Brite Donna	3	F	7	1	3	1	12,580
Brite F X	5	M	7	3	0	0	15,975
Brite Future	7	G	11	1	3	1	16,782
Brite Hope	6	G	2	0	0	0	763
Brite Horizon	6	M	13	1	2	5	11,798
Brite Lassie	3	F	9	2	4	1	24,700
Brite Lorelei	2	F	2	1	1	0	19,400
Brite Luci	2	F	9	0	3	4	22,757
Brite Memory	3	C	13	4	4	2	101,420
Brite Mon	3	C	2	0	1	0	4,200
Brite Nite	7	G	4	2	0	0	7,467
Brite Red Bloomers	2	F	3	0	1	1	4,200
Brite Road	7	M	6	0	0	0	1,450
Brite Rock Too	3	G	14	4	1	1	55,725
Brite Roxie	3	F	1	0	0	0	747
Brite Steel	4	F	8	2	2	0	5,508
Brite Sunny Day	5	M	3	1	0	0	29,038
Brite Thrill	4	F	11	0	1	2	1,624
Brite Time	3	G	8	4	2	0	20,676
Brite Valentin	6	G	16	1	0	0	4,167
Briteliteinthenite	4	G	17	1	3	4	24,240
Briteman	4	G	2	0	0	0	0
British Attitude	2	C	1	0	0	0	0
British Blue	4	C	4	1	1	0	22,415
British Event	2	F	3	1	0	0	10,930
Britnee's Bouquet	4	F	3	0	0	0	441
Britney B.	3	F	1	0	0	0	250
Britney's Starr	2	F	2	0	0	0	0
Britomartis	3	F	13	2	4	1	39,000
Brittany Bay	3	F	1	0	0	0	50
Brittany River	4	F	2	0	0	0	83
Brittany's Battle	3	F	13	3	1	1	14,045
Brittanys First	3	F	6	1	0	0	11,891
Brittney Dianne	3	F	1	0	0	0	1,350
Brittney's Secret	5	M	3	0	0	0	0
Britt's Babe	5	M	10	2	2	2	8,340
Britt's Jules	3	G	11	3	2	4	272,500
Britts Signal	3	G	8	1	0	1	3,500
Britts Xpress	5	G	2	0	1	0	1,192
Briviesca (GB)	3	F	7	3	0	0	59,525
Bro Raja	7	G	9	2	1	1	12,476
Bro Zeri	2	C	7	0	1	2	8,005
Broad Acres	2	C	6	0	1	1	10,390
Broad Base	3	C	5	1	0	1	37,863
Broad Creek	6	M	15	3	2	2	20,059
Broad Focus	4	F	6	0	0	1	1,045
Broad Gale	4	F	8	0	0	0	5,477
Broad Initiative	6	G	5	0	0	2	2,015
Broad Lane	2	C	2	0	0	0	740
Broad Minded	3	F	7	2	0	0	52,480
Broad Reach	9	M	2	0	0	0	0
Broad Sanctions	4	G	8	1	2	2	30,290
Broad Scheme	4	F	12	2	1	1	22,780
Broad Sojourn	4	F	2	0	0	0	0
Broad Sound	3	F	5	1	1	0	19,830
Broad Spirit	5	H	7	1	1	1	8,866
Broad Sweep	3	G	5	1	1	1	27,140
Broad Vision	6	G	10	1	1	2	11,790
Broadcasting	3	F	7	1	0	1	5,620
Broadside	8	G	3	0	0	1	466
Broadway Bernie	3	G	5	0	0	0	1,710
Broadway Bull	4	G	8	1	0	0	11,349
Broadway Buzz	4	C	18	6	4	3	42,006
Broadway Chief	3	G	5	0	0	0	1,118
Broadway Flash	4	F	2	0	0	0	218
Broadway Gold	2	F	4	2	0	0	107,420
Broadway Idol	2	C	2	1	0	0	30,277
Broadway Jerry	5	G	5	2	0	2	11,040
Broadway Johnny	6	G	14	1	2	0	12,670
Broadway Lady	4	F	8	2	0	0	63,847
Broadway Phill	5	G	13	1	2	0	7,730
Broadway Scarlet	3	F	6	0	0	1	3,720
Broadway Show	7	H	11	1	0	0	7,431
Broadway Snowman	7	G	5	1	1	0	21,601
Broadway Stenz	6	H	7	1	1	0	10,141
Broadway View	3	C	10	3	2	0	200,213
Broadwaybuck	2	G	7	1	1	2	12,190
Brobbel	5	G	1	0	0	1	732
Brocco Baby	6	M	10	0	1	1	3,816
Brocco Bob	6	G	13	3	4	1	38,750
Brocco Bry	7	G	10	0	2	1	11,027
Brocco Gold Strike	6	G	8	3	1	0	11,972
Broccoboy	6	G	8	0	2	2	5,310
Brocco's Magick	8	G	10	1	0	1	4,871
Brochure	4	G	5	0	0	0	0
Brockton Laddie	7	G	8	0	0	0	247

Horse	Age	Sex	Sts	1st	2d	3d	Won
Brocky's Dream (AUS)	6	M	8	1	3	0	60,240
Brodnicki	3	F	10	1	2	1	12,170
Brodrick	8	G	2	0	0	1	1,587
Brogans Shield	4	G	7	1	0	1	14,042
Brogdens Girl	4	F	6	1	0	1	3,482
Brokate	3	C	1	0	0	0	0
Broke Again	4	G	5	2	1	1	11,950
Broke But Stylin	5	G	18	3	3	4	42,927
Broke Egg	6	M	2	0	0	0	156
Broke First	4	G	9	1	1	2	6,700
Broke in Blairsden	6	M	4	0	0	2	8,170
Broke Luck	2	G	2	0	0	0	0
Broke Sharply	2	C	1	0	0	0	145
Broke Spoke	9	G	10	0	0	2	2,028
Broke the Slump	6	M	6	0	2	0	13,691
Broke to Fight	4	G	8	1	1	2	12,420
Broke Trying	3	F	17	5	1	5	43,540
Broke Us	3	G	11	2	0	3	17,849
Broken Aero	4	G	10	0	5	0	5,720
Broken Fuse	2	C	4	1	0	0	4,768
Broken Halter	2	G	3	0	0	0	300
Broken Jaw	7	G	5	0	2	1	3,147
Broken Monarch	4	G	14	1	2	4	21,450
Broken Ring	5	M	8	0	0	0	188
Broken Star	3	C	5	0	0	0	544
Broken Top	3	F	4	1	0	0	4,957
Broken Treaty	2	F	6	1	0	1	9,347
Broker Assault	4	G	4	0	1	0	4,750
Broker Prospect	3	G	8	1	1	1	10,430
Broker Town	2	C	2	0	0	0	55
Brokerage	4	G	9	0	2	0	6,515
Broker's Bonus	3	F	19	3	4	5	43,610
Brollinary	3	C	1	0	0	0	90
Bronc	4	G	7	0	0	0	312
Bronco Buster	4	C	5	0	0	0	550
Bronsonstorm	5	G	16	0	0	0	1,170
Bronwyn	4	F	13	0	2	2	5,374
Bronx	5	G	3	0	0	0	180
Bronx Cheer	4	F	8	3	2	2	34,992
Bronxville Doll	8	M	10	0	0	1	2,024
Bronxville Express	5	M	2	1	0	0	4,530
Bronze Abe	5	M	10	4	1	3	241,900
Bronze Bayou	5	G	11	0	1	3	27,094
Bronze Glow	3	F	1	0	1	0	5,200
Bronze Magic	7	G	3	0	0	0	441
Bronze Olympian	3	G	2	0	0	0	800
Bronze Sword	3	F	9	2	0	1	11,770
Brook by the Sea	6	M	11	1	0	1	8,223
Brook the Wind	5	G	1	0	1	0	1,140
Brookamous	4	F	1	0	0	0	0
Brooker B. Tee	2	F	3	1	1	0	26,149
Brooke's Dancer	3	F	13	4	0	3	36,637
Brooke's Halo	2	F	1	1	0	0	15,800
Brooke's Song	3	F	1	0	0	0	0
Brookes Trick	5	G	16	2	4	4	43,830
Brookevale	2	F	3	0	0	1	1,740
Brooklet	2	C	1	0	0	0	0
Brooklyn Bridge	8	G	11	2	3	2	45,032
Brooklyn Farmer	3	G	3	1	0	0	4,392
Brooklynsangel	3	F	1	0	0	0	0
Brook's Approval	2	F	8	1	0	0	6,068
Brooks Blach	2	G	7	1	3	0	31,320
Brook's Blaze	4	G	12	1	1	1	6,400
Brooks Comeback	2	C	3	0	0	0	0
Brooksbobnbucky	7	G	6	0	0	2	773
Brookside Drive	5	G	8	2	0	0	12,245
Brooksidedancer	3	F	7	1	0	2	20,810
Brooksidehitman	4	F	9	1	0	1	3,773
Brookston	7	G	4	1	1	0	8,816
Brookstreet	4	G	3	0	0	1	1,224
Brooksville	3	C	6	0	1	0	2,700
Brookville	4	G	15	1	0	2	7,854
Broom	5	G	1	0	0	0	750
Broomshot	2	C	4	0	0	0	600
Brosnan	3	C	2	0	0	0	2,100
Brother Andruw	3	G	7	1	1	0	6,167
Brother Baileys	3	G	3	0	0	0	105
Brother Blaise	9	G	6	2	0	2	16,527
Brother Blen	4	G	11	1	1	1	7,422
Brother Butch	5	G	7	0	0	1	2,242
Brother Darcy	8	G	10	2	0	1	26,310
Brother Dude	3	G	10	1	1	2	10,270
Brother Huz	9	G	9	3	0	4	9,744
Brother Indy	5	G	3	0	2	0	800
Brother Julius	6	G	13	1	1	0	12,030
Brother Love	8	G	12	3	2	3	44,330
Brother Moon (ARG)	7	H	1	0	0	0	0
Brother Pat	5	G	5	0	1	0	13,884
Brother Rabbit	8	G	1	0	0	0	0
Brother Roy	3	G	12	1	1	2	34,860
Brother Scott	2	C	3	0	1	1	13,790
Brother Skip	4	C	3	0	0	0	665
Brother Slocum	5	G	1	0	0	0	200
Brother Steve	4	G	13	0	4	5	8,685
Brother Walt	5	G	14	1	1	1	17,390
Brother's Sister	3	F	1	0	1	0	3,180
Broward County	3	G	15	1	2	2	34,486
Brown Beauty	3	F	5	0	0	0	170
Brown Bird	2	F	4	0	1	1	3,024
Brown Chequer	5	G	15	1	3	4	23,715
Brown Eyed Beauty	5	M	1	0	0	1	6,600
Brown Eyed Lady	6	M	6	2	0	0	21,967
Brown Eyed Mini	4	F	11	3	1	3	40,528
Brown Eyed Sugar	4	F	6	2	0	3	9,692
Brown Id Girl	6	M	9	2	0	2	10,850
Brown Jet	4	G	11	2	4	0	9,632
Brown Native	4	G	7	0	0	0	476
Brown Rouge	5	M	11	0	4	3	29,630
Brown Screen	5	G	14	2	0	0	16,431
Brown Spider	3	F	3	0	0	1	2,640
Brown Whiskey	5	H	1	0	0	0	778
Brownbottleflu	8	G	19	1	1	3	10,110
Brownie Deelite	2	C	2	0	0	1	1,230
Brownies Fire	3	G	11	1	1	2	8,036
Brown's Champion	9	G	1	0	0	0	50
Browns Derby Cat	3	G	15	1	0	1	9,670
Browns Velvet	7	M	9	0	0	2	3,956
Brownsmill	3	F	6	1	0	1	3,207
Brownstown	4	G	15	1	1	1	7,419
Browse	2	F	4	0	0	0	1,185
Bru Jak	2	C	1	0	0	0	800
Bruce and T. D.	3	G	2	0	0	0	0
Bruce On the Loose	2	C	4	3	1	0	64,100
Bruce's Way	4	G	7	1	0	0	10,375
Bruceybruceybrucey	3	G	14	1	4	3	43,630
Brucker's Brother	5	G	16	3	1	1	130,465
Bruheria	4	F	1	0	0	0	0
Bruise Control	6	G	3	1	0	1	6,046
Bruiser	5	G	11	1	2	0	20,635
Bruiser's Pride	2	C	2	1	0	0	15,780
Bruja Negra	3	F	9	1	0	0	7,088
Brule River	6	G	1	0	0	0	545
Brumby	2	G	5	1	1	0	32,270
Brummy	6	G	12	1	0	2	15,650
Bruna Slew	2	F	1	0	0	0	0
Bruneau Time	6	M	5	1	0	0	14,640
Brunei's Boy	4	C	6	0	0	2	2,591
Bruney	4	G	18	1	2	4	40,110
Brunfelsia	7	M	2	0	0	0	80
Brunilda (ARG)	4	F	6	2	0	1	55,982
Bruno Castelli	9	H	3	0	0	0	2,250
Bruno the Dog	9	G	13	0	0	2	2,136
Brunswick Belle	6	M	2	0	0	0	124
Brunswick Light	7	G	13	1	4	1	7,340
Brunswick Sue	7	M	2	0	0	0	136
Brunswood	5	G	6	2	1	1	10,659
Brush Ahead	4	G	5	1	1	1	7,125
Brush Country	4	G	2	0	0	0	214
Brush of Fortune	3	F	1	0	0	0	320
Brush the Law Agin	4	G	14	2	3	1	17,273
Brush Up	4	C	16	1	2	2	28,540
Brush With Destiny	3	F	5	0	0	0	5,796
Brush With Fame	3	G	4	1	0	0	13,570
Brush With Glory	10	G	12	1	0	1	5,148
Brush With Gold	4	G	13	3	2	3	58,430
Brushabybaby	3	F	10	1	1	1	7,715
Brushed Aside	4	C	8	0	2	3	8,090
Brushed by the Law	5	M	7	2	0	1	28,825

Horse	Age	Sex	Sts	1st	2d	3d	Won
Brushed Dusty	3	F	12	1	1	1	10,995
Brushed Ice	4	G	11	1	2	3	34,027
Brushed Up	4	G	12	0	4	4	31,300
Brushed With Glory	4	G	10	1	2	1	12,035
Brusher	7	G	5	0	1	2	3,463
Brushher	3	F	7	0	2	0	8,040
Brushme On	2	F	7	1	0	2	38,128
Brushpopper	3	C	5	1	0	0	6,630
Brush's Branch	3	G	8	0	2	0	6,245
Brushy Cartel	2	F	1	0	0	0	105
Brussels Lace	2	F	2	0	0	0	840
Brut's Boomin	4	G	11	1	0	1	4,101
Brutus Maximus	4	G	3	1	0	0	6,712
Brutus O'Tiger	3	C	7	0	2	0	2,364
Bruzer Com Stock	4	G	5	1	0	0	5,047
Bryans Hope	5	G	3	0	0	0	400
Bryan's Love	3	G	3	0	0	0	0
Bryan's Pick	7	G	2	0	0	0	70
Bryanzole'	5	G	4	0	0	0	484
Bryceslittlesecret	2	G	4	1	1	1	30,180
Bryden's Babe	8	M	8	0	0	1	455
Brymic's Treasure	4	G	10	0	0	3	6,289
Brynes Girls	5	M	12	3	3	1	16,169
Brynhild	7	H	3	1	1	0	2,472
Bryns Finale	5	M	7	0	0	0	971
Brysons Bullet	2	G	2	0	0	0	1,350
B's Big Boy	4	G	8	0	0	1	1,487
B's Brat	3	G	8	1	0	1	5,554
B's Buddy	3	G	6	1	0	0	16,058
B's Cat	4	F	10	0	0	0	594
Bs Golden Mop	4	G	1	1	0	0	2,310
B's Lil Champ	4	G	5	1	0	1	2,250
Bub	4	G	10	1	1	1	27,290
Buba's Caper	7	M	10	2	0	3	35,700
Bubba Appeal	6	H	9	0	0	3	2,263
Bubba Be Slick	4	G	1	0	0	0	0
Bubba Bianconi	3	C	1	0	0	1	1,375
Bubba Black	4	G	10	0	1	0	1,350
Bubba Boom Boom	5	G	5	0	0	0	175
Bubba Boy	2	C	1	0	0	0	0
Bubba Dune	4	G	1	0	0	0	220
Bubba Galpin	3	G	6	1	3	0	2,407
Bubba Gum	3	C	11	3	1	1	55,553
Bubba Guy	3	G	8	0	1	2	6,277
Bubba Hyde	4	G	9	1	2	0	22,700
Bubba Ray'n Chris	3	G	1	0	0	0	0
Bubba Sparks	3	C	8	3	0	3	93,514
Bubbah	4	G	17	1	1	1	12,805
Bubbalou	5	G	10	0	2	2	9,790
Bubba's Birthday	3	G	3	0	1	1	2,625
Bubba's Colors	6	G	17	3	4	3	54,341
Bubba's Doll House	3	G	13	5	1	1	48,725
Bubba's Last	2	C	4	0	0	1	1,848
Bubba's Prospect	2	C	3	0	0	0	0
Bubbasgotadance	5	G	15	1	2	2	7,201
Bubbawuzdrinkun	3	F	1	0	0	0	0
Bubbe Bets	4	F	7	2	0	0	15,130
Bubble Dourbon	4	F	7	3	0	2	39,377
Bubble Economy	5	G	7	2	3	1	60,560
Bubble N Squeak	2	F	7	1	3	0	35,530
Bubblegum Kid	6	G	9	2	0	1	56,120
Bubblegum Red	5	M	13	1	3	2	3,818
Bubbleoni	3	F	5	1	2	1	11,998
Bubbles Again	3	F	1	0	0	0	300
Bubbles Cachet	5	M	1	0	1	0	7,220
Bubbles Dujur	3	F	8	2	2	0	4,370
Bubble's Girl	5	M	4	0	1	0	2,711
Bubbles McGruder	5	M	11	0	0	0	2,231
Bubbles N Bliss	4	F	4	0	1	0	7,290
Bubbly	4	F	11	1	2	1	10,094
Bubby's Bag	4	F	3	0	0	0	788
Bub's First Dance	4	G	8	1	2	0	13,097
Bub's Towne Starr	5	M	6	2	1	0	15,300
Bub's Turn	8	G	8	0	2	1	6,348
Bubu Cat	3	C	14	1	0	2	4,066
Bubwiser	3	F	12	2	1	2	25,763
Buc Fan	3	G	9	2	3	2	44,590
Bucanero Gris	4	G	3	0	1	0	14,740
Buccaneer Babe	4	F	1	0	0	0	350

Horse	Age	Sex	Sts	1st	2d	3d	Won
Buccaneer Fever	3	G	14	1	1	3	12,256
Bucharest	2	C	4	1	0	1	36,455
Buck a Shot	4	F	6	2	1	1	14,097
Buck and Wing	2	F	2	0	0	0	275
Buck City	6	G	13	2	3	2	9,672
Buck for Luck	3	C	3	0	1	0	2,030
Buck Grove	7	G	6	0	0	0	0
Buck Henry	4	G	2	0	0	1	1,925
Buck Knight	2	G	7	2	0	0	22,469
Buck Mountain	5	M	6	1	1	0	44,129
Buck One	5	G	16	3	2	3	12,953
Buck Raja	6	G	14	2	1	1	6,987
Buck Snort	4	G	9	1	1	1	3,012
Buck Spice	3	G	2	0	0	0	93
Buck Starts Here	2	C	3	0	0	0	0
Buck Stops Here	6	G	4	0	0	0	866
Buck the Tiger	3	G	13	0	2	1	3,756
Buck Trail	6	G	17	4	3	4	18,592
Buck Trout's Niece	3	F	17	1	2	3	27,581
Buck Tuddy Buck	2	G	1	0	0	0	400
Buck Two	6	G	11	0	1	1	3,661
Buckaroo B M W	3	F	2	0	0	0	60
Buckaroo Boy	4	G	2	0	0	0	675
Buckaroo's Magic	8	G	6	2	0	0	21,093
Buckaroot	4	G	2	0	2	0	780
Buckarules	2	C	1	0	0	0	0
Buckey Boy	5	H	4	0	0	0	590
Buckeye Bates	7	G	7	2	1	2	37,961
Buckeye Bert	6	G	9	1	1	0	20,367
Buckeye Bound	2	F	4	0	0	0	1,383
Buckeye Buckaroo	6	G	10	1	0	0	4,948
Buckeye Buddy	2	C	2	1	0	0	14,955
Buckeye Fever	3	G	6	1	1	0	4,351
Buckeye's Regret	8	G	2	0	0	0	0
Buckflanker	2	C	6	1	0	2	19,820
Buckhari	7	G	8	1	3	1	22,259
Buckhars Tiger	4	C	3	0	0	0	120
Buckie Is a Hoolie	2	G	4	0	0	0	2,060
Buckies Exclusive	5	G	7	0	0	4	1,197
Buckin Bronc	3	G	5	0	3	1	8,090
Buckingham Prince	2	C	2	0	0	0	96
Buckjano	2	C	5	0	0	1	6,180
Buckland Manor	4	G	7	1	1	1	136,000
Buckle Bunny	2	F	6	1	0	1	8,995
Buckle Down Ben	6	H	9	3	4	1	80,820
Buckle Up Cart	3	F	13	4	1	3	38,180
Buckmeister Ryan	2	G	1	0	0	0	0
Buckmier	10	G	9	0	2	0	1,539
Buckmont (ARG)	7	G	9	0	0	1	1,500
Buckmountaincreek	6	G	19	0	2	4	31,136
Buck'n and Duck'n	6	G	4	0	0	0	553
Buckner Bert	4	G	12	1	4	1	14,137
Buck'n'pearl	5	M	9	1	2	0	4,853
Bucko Wins	7	G	5	2	1	1	16,758
Buckrub	4	G	7	2	0	1	15,950
Buck's Appeal	3	G	13	3	3	2	41,220
Bucks Away	4	G	3	2	1	0	10,620
Buck's Banner	3	G	16	1	3	1	11,278
Buck's Best Boy	8	G	6	0	0	0	1,142
Bucks County Fred	5	G	5	0	1	2	8,830
Buck's Double	3	G	8	0	0	0	1,140
Bucks for Gaz	2	C	1	0	0	0	276
Buck's Jack	4	G	1	1	0	0	3,300
Buck's Lad	5	H	7	2	1	1	7,414
Bucks Little Bean	4	G	8	1	0	0	7,511
Buck's Little Imij	4	G	7	0	1	0	2,065
Buck's Lucky Star	4	F	5	0	0	0	345
Buck's Lullaby	3	F	6	0	0	1	2,030
Bucks Our Boy	3	G	8	1	0	0	9,684
Buck's Out Again	10	G	2	0	0	0	0
Buck's Pal	4	G	13	1	1	2	16,576
Buck's Shar	3	F	17	2	2	4	12,830
Bucks Superstar	7	M	7	0	0	0	569
Buck's Wine	2	G	14	0	3	0	18,351
Bucksbrighteststar	5	H	9	0	0	0	3,840
Buckshot John	7	G	14	0	1	2	4,981
Buckshot Rabbit	4	G	1	0	0	0	0
Buckshot Slew	2	F	2	0	1	0	5,750
Buckskin	3	G	5	0	1	1	19,938

Horse	Age	Sex	Sts	1st	2d	3d	Won
Buckskin Baby	5	M	15	2	1	2	21,897
Bucksome Girl	4	F	7	0	1	0	2,707
Bucksweep	5	G	13	2	2	4	10,010
Bucktown Belle	2	F	3	1	0	0	7,500
Buckuphenry	4	G	6	0	0	0	435
Buckwheat	3	C	7	0	0	0	517
Bucky Be Fast	4	G	3	0	0	0	2,100
Bucky Belle	4	F	1	0	0	0	140
Bucky Blue Jeans	4	G	7	0	0	1	3,092
Bucky Moon	2	F	2	0	0	0	0
Buckymikgrif	4	G	16	2	2	1	9,842
Bucky's Son	2	C	7	0	1	2	11,073
Buckystrick	3	G	3	0	0	0	325
Bucquista	7	M	13	5	3	0	68,647
Bucyrus	3	C	11	2	0	2	30,540
Bud Chaffee	4	G	1	0	0	0	320
Bud Crainer	3	G	12	1	0	0	8,790
Bud Draft Please	3	F	6	2	2	1	29,710
Bud Longneck	4	G	8	1	2	0	12,755
Bud Man Bill	4	G	8	1	1	1	5,704
Bud Wyse Blur	7	G	5	1	0	0	4,652
Budds Landing	4	G	12	0	2	2	13,290
Buddstark	8	G	4	1	0	0	7,462
Buddy Baby	5	G	10	1	1	0	8,372
Buddy Baquero	3	G	11	0	0	1	652
Buddy Belle	4	F	1	0	0	0	0
Buddy Cinnamon	2	G	1	0	0	0	690
Buddy Gil	4	G	7	1	2	0	74,612
Buddy of Mine	6	G	4	0	0	2	5,394
Buddy Puddy	5	G	18	0	5	5	13,279
Buddydevon	3	G	3	0	0	1	1,530
Buddys Express	2	F	7	0	0	0	2,925
Buddys Rebel	2	C	3	1	0	0	15,458
Bude 'Em	7	M	13	4	1	1	34,429
Budget Bob	5	G	11	1	2	3	28,279
Budget Breaker	3	G	20	3	5	1	19,938
Budget Surplus	3	G	4	1	1	0	30,470
Budini	2	C	3	0	0	0	1,560
Bud's Bayou	5	G	15	0	1	2	5,760
Buds Boy	4	G	2	0	0	0	0
Buds Life	4	G	3	0	0	0	630
Bud's Magic	6	G	1	0	0	0	0
Bud's Move	4	G	9	0	0	0	165
Bue Moon	4	F	9	2	2	3	36,469
Buellton	7	G	10	1	1	1	9,232
Buenobambino	4	F	3	0	0	0	644
Buff 'n Polish	3	F	8	0	3	1	18,470
Buff Naked	3	G	8	2	3	0	80,313
Buffalo Alice	2	F	3	0	0	1	4,213
Buffalo Bob	7	H	13	5	2	3	42,320
Buffalo Boy	9	G	6	2	1	0	2,806
Buffalo Dance	5	M	1	0	0	0	340
Buffalo River	5	G	12	0	2	4	7,310
Buffalo Run	3	C	6	2	0	2	23,430
Buffs Magic	2	C	2	0	0	0	0
Buffy Babe	2	F	6	0	1	0	3,815
Buffy My Love	3	F	4	1	1	1	41,080
Buffythecenterfold	4	F	3	0	2	0	76,710
Bufon	4	G	9	2	1	2	35,961
Bug Hunter	2	C	6	3	1	1	62,300
Bug in a Bottle	5	H	12	3	2	2	15,662
Bug River	11	H	3	2	0	0	48,000
Bugalu Girl	6	M	6	0	0	0	645
Bugatti Lace	3	F	2	1	0	0	4,650
Bugatti's Booty	3	G	4	0	0	0	375
Buggins	3	F	8	0	0	0	405
Buggy Blew	2	F	2	1	0	0	12,250
Bugsy N Tuff	6	H	8	3	1	0	5,215
Bugwiser	5	M	1	0	0	0	340
Bugzy Boy	4	C	16	0	1	0	1,915
Buhl	8	G	1	0	0	0	34
Buildakiss	2	C	2	0	0	0	0
Buildaparty	3	C	9	1	2	3	25,680
Builders Option	2	C	6	1	1	2	42,653
Built by Apollo	2	G	1	0	1	0	1,800
Built to Last	3	G	14	2	4	1	14,931
Built Up	6	G	13	3	2	2	217,195
Builtforhumanity	3	F	6	0	0	0	495
Buju	4	C	2	1	0	0	23,400
Bukat Timah (GB)	4	F	3	0	0	1	10,120
Bukela	3	F	1	0	1	0	1,200
Bukowski	5	G	12	0	0	1	2,188
Bula	3	F	1	0	0	1	5,880
Bulawayo	3	G	3	0	0	0	2,630
Bulette's Bullet	6	G	1	0	0	0	0
Bulita	2	F	9	1	4	1	65,028
Bull Bat	8	G	3	1	0	1	6,840
Bull Buster	5	M	6	0	0	0	794
Bull Creek	11	G	3	0	0	0	138
Bull Dancer	2	C	2	1	1	0	17,339
Bull Force	3	G	7	0	0	0	1,043
Bull Head	4	C	5	0	0	1	1,605
Bull Headed Harry	4	G	7	1	1	0	8,000
Bull Headed Wynn	3	G	12	3	2	2	49,580
Bull Leave It	6	G	9	3	0	1	8,668
Bull Market	4	C	6	2	1	2	86,341
Bull Moose	3	G	8	1	2	1	27,040
Bull N Bob	3	G	11	1	2	1	11,370
Bull O Indiana	5	G	3	0	0	0	169
Bull of Bush	4	C	2	0	0	1	1,650
Bull Pen	5	H	6	1	1	1	5,643
Bull Power	2	C	4	1	0	0	13,329
Bull Ranch	2	C	1	0	0	0	2,100
Bull Riding Chick	3	F	4	2	1	0	21,800
Bull Shooter	5	G	10	0	1	0	3,190
Bull Tai	6	G	2	0	0	0	186
Bullbank	3	C	2	0	0	0	99
Bulldacious	3	G	2	0	0	0	0
Bulldog George	5	G	3	0	0	0	1,730
Bulldog Mugsy	3	G	9	1	1	2	18,614
Bulldog Zeal	2	C	4	1	0	0	11,679
Bullero	6	G	8	2	2	1	5,810
Bullet Again	6	G	12	2	1	0	10,694
Bullet Crane	2	G	3	0	0	0	330
Bullet Gone West	3	C	8	1	1	1	24,434
Bullet Gulch	3	C	1	0	0	0	126
Bullet Jay Bird	5	H	9	0	0	0	1,795
Bullet Line	2	G	8	0	0	2	3,270
Bullet Proof	10	G	5	0	0	0	257
Bulletin Board	7	G	5	0	0	0	348
Bulletman Jack	5	H	2	0	1	0	3,146
Bullets Blade	5	M	1	0	1	0	1,480
Bulletta Day	2	F	2	0	2	0	3,440
Bulletthebluesky	5	G	11	3	0	2	31,415
Bulling	7	G	11	0	0	2	2,531
Bullinsky	6	G	12	3	4	2	17,461
Bullion	2	C	3	0	0	2	11,500
Bullish	4	G	13	2	1	1	17,489
Bullish Ego	2	C	4	1	0	0	16,606
Bullish Executive	3	G	7	1	1	3	71,318
Bullishdemands	2	F	2	1	1	0	6,180
Bullistic	4	G	3	0	0	2	15,120
Bullistic Flight	5	G	12	1	1	0	15,575
Bull'o the Woods	2	C	2	1	0	1	17,441
Bullringer	4	G	12	3	1	4	34,065
Bulls Companion	5	M	3	0	1	0	2,690
Bull's Ear	3	F	10	1	4	3	29,418
Bull's Eye	7	G	10	0	0	0	320
Bull's Notions (JPN)	3	C	6	0	1	3	24,280
Bull's Revenge	5	G	12	2	1	3	30,265
Bullseye Bess	3	F	13	2	1	3	60,810
Bullseye Bill	4	G	10	2	1	0	20,901
Bullslinger	6	G	2	0	0	0	114
Bullvon	2	C	6	0	2	0	3,680
Bullwhip	4	C	17	2	0	2	17,870
Bully Bodgit	3	F	1	0	0	0	450
Bully Bully	6	G	8	1	0	3	15,210
Bully Creek	8	G	2	1	0	0	2,760
Bully Up	4	C	3	0	0	0	0
Bully's North	6	G	13	3	4	0	42,800
Bully's South	7	H	5	2	0	0	1,957
Bumkin McGruder	5	G	14	1	1	0	12,337
Bump	3	G	8	3	0	1	14,655
Bump in the Road	2	C	4	0	0	0	0
Bump Run	6	G	9	0	1	2	1,458
Bump Shot	5	G	6	1	0	1	2,292
Bumper Doo	3	F	2	1	0	0	3,885
Bumper Jack	4	G	2	0	0	0	230

Horse	Age	Sex	Sts	1st	2d	3d	Won
Bumper to Bumper	5	M	14	1	2	1	30,243
Bumpin Hub	10	G	5	0	0	0	576
Bumpitee	3	G	14	2	2	2	19,113
Bunches of Silver	6	M	6	0	0	2	872
Bundle City	3	G	11	2	3	1	19,175
Bundle of Emotions	6	G	8	0	1	2	5,204
Bundle of Joy	3	G	18	0	6	4	15,515
Bundle of Love	2	F	2	0	0	0	202
Bundle of Roses	3	F	12	3	2	5	123,674
Bundle This	4	G	8	1	0	1	4,518
Bundy Rum	6	G	7	0	0	0	1,232
Bungalow Eight	3	F	17	0	1	2	10,909
Bunigay	4	F	11	1	2	2	19,660
Bunker Buster	3	G	10	1	1	0	3,321
Bunker Jones	3	G	13	1	0	2	11,438
Bunkman	9	G	7	1	0	1	5,770
Bunny Bubble	4	F	8	2	3	0	8,649
Bunny Bugs	5	M	4	0	0	0	330
Bunny Cat	2	F	2	0	0	0	0
Bunny Lake	4	F	4	0	1	0	13,409
Bunny Slope	4	F	9	1	3	2	14,800
Bunnyinthebank	4	F	14	3	1	1	23,727
Bunny's Bingo Lady	3	F	3	0	0	0	1,012
Bunny's Return	3	G	5	2	1	0	14,238
Bunratty Castle	6	G	6	1	3	0	8,205
Bunt	3	G	2	0	0	0	388
Burant Orange	2	F	6	0	1	2	22,198
Burchfield	4	G	3	1	1	0	31,450
Burdakin	5	G	11	3	2	1	48,810
Burgandy Tower	5	G	9	1	0	1	8,734
Burke's Legend	3	G	6	0	1	1	7,220
Burlap	4	G	10	1	0	4	13,936
Burley A	3	G	20	1	1	2	14,645
Burlington Bertie	3	G	10	1	2	1	8,098
Burlington House	10	G	12	3	1	2	12,972
Burlyq Queen	3	F	1	0	0	0	90
Burma Jade	4	C	5	0	1	0	5,600
Burma Road	2	C	1	0	0	0	0
Burmese Cat	2	F	2	0	1	0	5,300
Burn a Spark	4	G	17	1	1	3	15,353
Burn Dixie Burn	4	F	2	1	0	0	4,952
Burnin' Memories	5	M	4	1	0	1	7,035
Burning Affair	2	F	7	1	1	1	30,480
Burning Bridges	2	F	1	0	0	0	132
Burning Brite	5	M	12	2	1	3	65,150
Burning Crown	2	F	2	0	0	0	488
Burning Fever	3	F	2	1	0	1	26,270
Burning Fluid	4	F	16	4	3	2	59,754
Burning Marque	8	H	13	2	1	2	30,177
Burning Memories	6	M	7	3	1	2	60,290
Burning Rambo	3	C	11	1	4	3	46,450
Burning Roma	6	H	8	2	1	2	176,163
Burning Sea	7	M	9	2	1	2	5,183
Burning Sun	5	H	3	1	0	0	86,295
Burningtobefirst	4	F	7	0	3	0	4,286
Burninit	6	G	8	2	0	3	15,938
Burnish	2	F	4	2	1	0	71,807
Burnished	3	G	9	1	1	0	14,050
Burnished Steel (GB)	4	F	6	1	0	1	25,120
Burnrubber	3	C	7	1	4	0	20,692
Burn's Future	5	H	3	0	0	0	354
Burnt Bush	4	F	13	2	3	1	29,401
Burnt Foot Brown	3	G	6	1	1	2	6,696
Burnt Mill Road	10	G	12	2	3	2	48,196
Burnt Sugar	5	G	4	0	0	0	84
Burnt Umber	5	G	11	0	0	2	2,401
Burson	7	G	4	0	0	0	755
Burst First	10	G	5	0	1	2	9,760
Burst of Applause	2	F	3	1	1	0	10,667
Burst of Dawn	5	M	11	2	1	3	28,010
Burst of Diamonds	3	C	2	0	0	0	990
Burst of Fire	3	G	11	4	2	2	290,765
Burst Your Bubble	5	G	11	2	2	1	30,181
Burt	3	G	17	0	1	3	5,454
Burt's Cozzene	8	M	8	1	0	1	16,553
Buryclever Diamond	2	F	1	0	0	0	0
Bus Express	3	G	6	2	1	1	10,322
Bus Man Jack	3	G	6	1	1	1	20,570
Buscando Fortuna	2	G	5	0	1	1	5,084
Bush	5	G	9	2	3	2	29,815
Bush Cabin	5	G	7	0	0	0	2,980
Bush Landslide	3	F	3	0	0	0	130
Bush Time	4	F	4	0	1	1	1,899
Busher's Chad	4	G	17	2	1	2	22,871
Bushes Victory	4	F	5	1	0	0	10,646
Bushmill Girl	2	F	1	0	0	0	0
Bush's Song	3	F	6	0	1	0	14,340
Bushwacked	2	C	1	0	0	1	1,560
Bushwacker	2	C	3	1	1	0	41,000
Bushwick	4	G	5	0	2	1	4,960
Bushy Lady	3	F	3	0	0	0	0
Bushy's Delight	5	M	3	0	0	2	2,144
Bushy's Jay	6	G	2	0	0	0	450
Business Decision	11	G	19	1	3	2	7,974
Busisa	3	F	3	1	1	0	5,345
Busser	4	G	7	1	2	0	3,067
Bust	4	G	18	2	1	6	45,960
Bust the House	9	G	6	1	1	0	4,920
Bust the Must	3	F	11	1	1	1	25,315
Bust Your Bubble	4	G	3	1	1	0	25,160
Bustastar	3	G	4	0	1	0	1,519
Busted Flat	4	G	8	1	2	0	6,008
Busted Trust	4	G	4	2	1	0	57,910
Buster Bailey	6	G	12	1	0	2	13,466
Buster the Cat	4	G	10	0	2	0	13,253
Buster the Vid	4	G	3	0	1	0	1,550
Busterbad Boy	3	G	2	0	0	1	584
Buster's Dream	6	H	5	0	1	1	4,200
Buster's Report	3	F	2	0	0	0	0
Bustheroses	3	G	12	1	0	5	14,985
Bustin by U	8	G	8	2	1	2	3,332
Bustin Thru	8	G	2	0	0	0	126
Bustin'dreams	5	H	13	1	1	3	11,958
Busy	6	M	10	3	4	0	50,150
Busy Bob	3	G	19	2	3	7	21,370
Busy Bonnie	5	M	7	0	2	1	6,810
Busy Ears	4	F	3	0	0	0	2,240
Busy Line	3	F	7	2	0	2	10,901
Busy Mis	3	F	12	2	1	0	29,620
Busy Patsy	3	F	5	0	0	0	70
Busy Prospect	2	C	5	1	0	2	12,490
But I'm Innocent	4	F	4	0	0	0	755
But Mommy	3	F	16	5	4	3	97,670
But of Course	4	G	8	0	1	2	18,015
But Some Girls Doo	4	F	5	1	0	0	3,252
Butch Pistol	5	G	5	0	0	1	405
Butch's Man	4	G	1	0	0	0	0
Buteo	3	G	9	2	2	1	30,220
Butler On Duty	10	G	7	0	0	0	1,190
Butt Out	7	G	1	0	0	0	462
Butte City	5	G	13	5	1	3	61,880
Butter Crunch	3	F	9	2	1	5	55,898
Butter Me Up	5	M	7	0	0	4	3,494
Butter Me Up Tiny	4	F	10	1	1	1	12,886
Butter Money	2	C	2	0	0	0	375
Buttercup Express	4	F	14	0	4	3	12,342
Butterface	6	M	15	0	7	1	67,634
Butterfly Bloom	2	F	3	1	0	2	30,435
Butterfly McGruder	4	F	2	0	0	0	161
Butternut Red	6	G	2	0	1	0	1,342
Butterscotch Dave	9	G	11	1	1	0	14,757
Buttertart	4	F	13	3	2	0	55,045
Button	7	G	3	0	0	0	0
Button Button	4	F	7	0	0	1	1,305
Button My Shoes	3	C	3	0	0	0	2,580
Button Soup	4	F	8	1	0	1	5,143
Buttonwood Angel	4	F	9	0	0	0	300
Buttonwood Ida	5	M	6	2	1	1	26,940
Buttonwood Steve	4	G	1	0	0	1	1,600
Buttonwood Thunder	4	G	10	1	0	0	4,610
Buwee Buwee	4	G	7	2	1	1	25,456
Buy Out Time	4	F	1	1	0	0	18,815
Buy the Four N Ten	7	M	7	0	0	1	1,465
Buy the Sport	4	F	1	0	0	0	560
Buyah	3	G	2	0	0	0	1,860
Buysometime	4	F	6	0	0	1	1,445
Buz Away	4	C	8	0	0	0	736
Buzz Around	10	M	7	0	0	0	540

Horse	Age	Sex	Sts	1st	2d	3d	Won
Buzz Barton	4	G	7	1	0	0	4,615
Buzz Cat	7	G	14	7	3	1	44,015
Buzz' Dixie Chick	4	F	3	0	1	0	1,730
Buzz of the Party	3	F	11	1	0	3	14,913
Buzz Oliver	3	G	10	1	1	2	9,008
Buzz Song	2	F	3	2	0	1	92,100
Buzz Strikes	2	C	1	0	0	0	205
Buzzard Road	9	G	6	0	1	0	1,120
Buzzards Bay	2	C	4	1	1	1	24,440
Buzzaway	2	G	3	0	1	2	4,300
Buzzer Bob	3	G	9	1	3	0	6,825
Buzzin Fly	3	C	5	0	0	0	77
Buzzisa Niner	2	C	7	1	0	0	7,460
Buzzle Ways	4	G	14	1	2	4	46,300
Buzz's Affair	2	C	3	0	0	0	0
Buzzy Bee	3	G	3	1	1	0	6,785
Buzzy O	3	C	6	0	1	0	3,502
Buzzy's a Bad Boy	3	G	3	0	0	0	195
Buzzy's Gold	4	C	8	2	1	2	83,507
Bwana Charlie	3	C	10	4	2	2	349,690
By a County Mile	4	F	4	0	1	1	1,278
By a Nose	5	G	11	2	0	3	11,348
By Cracky	3	F	4	1	0	0	8,280
By Daylight	4	F	5	2	1	0	20,010
By Default	3	G	6	0	0	0	2,551
By Far a Lady	2	F	3	0	0	0	300
By Far the Best	3	C	11	2	2	2	81,398
By Grace	4	F	7	2	1	0	13,475
By Grace Alone	2	F	7	1	3	0	45,050
By Himself	4	G	8	0	0	0	1,722
By Jasper	3	G	11	2	0	3	11,355
By Jove	4	F	6	0	0	0	1,542
By Royal Design	3	F	6	1	2	0	12,341
By the Bay	4	G	13	1	1	5	17,162
By the Grace	2	F	2	1	0	0	7,500
By the Sword	4	G	9	0	1	1	20,192
By U Lane	3	F	2	0	0	0	0
By Yourself Lady	6	M	13	1	4	4	8,191
Bya Banana	5	G	10	1	3	2	6,775
Byandlarge	4	G	7	1	1	1	23,627
Byanosejoe	2	G	2	1	0	0	24,887
Byanoz Rose	3	F	9	2	1	0	6,301
Byarbelle	2	F	3	0	0	0	0
Byars and Keepers	4	G	12	2	0	2	50,752
Byars and Lookers	4	F	17	5	0	1	24,420
Byars Buzz	3	C	1	0	0	0	0
Byars Choice	3	C	2	0	1	0	2,415
Byars of Gold	3	C	13	2	1	1	24,955
Byar's Red	3	G	3	0	0	0	0
Byars Time	3	C	14	0	1	1	3,759
Byasmile	8	G	11	1	1	3	4,463
Byback	5	G	12	2	2	1	36,982
Byby Ike's Cat	4	G	11	2	7	1	6,030
Bybymisamarycanpie	5	M	4	0	0	0	0
Bycarbs Destiny	3	C	8	0	0	1	4,338
Bye Bird	6	G	1	0	0	0	0
Bye Birdie	3	F	2	1	0	0	3,342
Bye Bye Beylen	5	G	15	1	3	6	31,100
Bye Bye Birdie	5	M	10	2	2	2	36,393
Bye Bye Bunny	4	F	5	1	0	0	7,546
Bye Bye Butterfly	4	F	1	0	0	0	0
Bye Bye Crafty	2	C	1	0	0	0	0
Bye Bye Hart	6	M	8	2	3	1	15,835
Bye Bye Jewel	3	G	1	0	0	0	702
Bye Bye Katie Pie	2	F	3	1	0	0	15,945
Bye Lite	3	G	2	0	0	0	0
Bye the Cherokee	4	G	14	3	2	0	16,058
Bye Won	4	G	7	0	0	0	720
Byeairmail	3	F	12	2	3	2	10,704
Byebyebyebabygoodbye	3	G	3	1	1	1	23,250
Byeseeyouchow	2	F	3	0	0	0	1,764
Byestarterhijudge	3	G	8	0	0	0	0
Byllee Jessie Ruby (NZ)	5	M	2	0	0	0	1,230
Byreasonofinsanity	4	G	7	4	0	2	18,075
Byro	5	H	5	1	0	0	4,920
Bythefloor	4	G	9	0	1	1	2,800
Bythepound	3	G	1	0	1	0	6,500
Byway	3	F	5	2	0	0	26,415
Byzantium	2	F	7	0	1	0	24,600
Byzantium (BRZ)	5	G	3	1	0	0	8,965
C B Account	11	H	9	2	2	2	14,471
C B Gold Won	4	G	1	0	0	0	402
C B Stu	10	G	12	1	1	1	10,849
C Baby Go	2	F	2	0	0	1	2,160
C Barney Run	11	H	5	0	0	0	310
C B's Back	10	G	10	1	1	3	6,215
C Bs Deposit	5	G	1	0	0	0	0
C C Cat	5	G	9	2	1	3	11,995
C C Forever	3	F	7	1	1	0	11,645
C C Red	7	M	7	0	0	1	1,515
C C Ryder	2	C	1	0	0	0	126
C C Sera Valay	3	F	7	1	0	1	6,350
C C Sky Dancer	5	M	8	2	1	1	4,854
C C Strider	4	C	3	0	0	0	0
C Crafty Go	4	G	6	0	3	0	2,752
C Crafty Peak	3	G	1	0	0	0	0
C Cs Candyman	4	C	13	0	2	3	13,007
C C's Heart	4	G	8	0	0	0	765
C C's Last Stand	3	C	12	1	1	0	9,702
C C's Prospect	3	F	7	1	3	2	19,615
C C's Ruler	3	F	7	0	0	1	2,825
C Cubed	3	G	2	2	0	0	31,146
C D Cruzer	6	G	4	0	1	0	4,720
C D Player	3	F	10	1	5	1	29,920
C D World	4	G	11	2	1	1	14,392
C Drive	5	M	9	2	1	0	11,518
C D's Amulet	5	M	5	0	0	0	538
C D's Trinket	6	M	2	0	0	0	88
C' est Sea Bun	2	G	1	0	0	0	294
C F Knight Bondage	4	G	3	0	0	1	1,609
C F Slew of Storms	6	G	7	0	0	1	1,659
C Frank	4	G	12	1	2	1	9,963
C Frisky Bizzness	3	C	4	0	0	0	470
C J Best	5	M	8	0	3	2	17,184
C J Come Home	2	G	6	1	0	1	15,004
C J Sirius	3	F	10	1	3	3	36,261
C Joe Blush	11	G	7	1	0	0	3,465
C J's Heat	3	G	4	0	0	0	1,350
C J's Jet	2	G	4	0	0	0	0
C J's Lil'frosty	5	G	2	0	0	0	0
C J's Rolex	6	G	12	2	0	1	7,865
C K Jett	3	C	8	2	0	1	29,446
C L Gray	3	G	7	0	0	0	0
C M Braveheart	4	C	1	0	0	0	0
C M Copycat	2	C	2	0	1	0	420
C M U Slew	3	F	4	0	0	1	1,887
C Major	4	G	4	0	0	2	2,750
C Merrill Run	8	G	1	0	0	0	0
C' mon Camilla	4	F	4	0	0	0	850
C M's Mark	7	G	2	1	1	0	10,700
C P Ridge Angel	2	F	1	0	0	0	60
C R Charm	4	F	7	1	0	1	8,748
C R Diligent Dizz	3	F	5	0	0	0	710
C R Dixie Moon	4	G	2	0	0	0	0
C R Fascination	4	F	5	0	1	0	4,656
C R Paracount	2	G	3	1	0	0	7,925
C R Power	2	G	8	1	1	4	27,440
C R Rheas Freckles	2	F	4	0	2	1	5,525
C Slew C	5	G	5	0	3	0	2,454
C Squared	5	G	6	0	0	0	517
C T King Oftheroad	6	G	19	3	4	4	25,970
C Tallie Run	5	M	12	1	4	1	6,752
C the Minister	4	G	1	0	0	0	0
C T's Rail	4	F	9	1	0	2	13,684
C U inthe Fastlane	5	G	8	0	0	0	650
C U Later Deviator	3	C	6	0	0	0	2,193
C V N Isabel	3	F	3	0	0	0	0
C V N Marysol	3	F	3	0	0	0	2,040
C W It's a Breeze	5	H	11	3	2	1	21,262
C Ya	5	G	8	1	1	0	3,684
C. A. D.'s Combo	5	M	17	3	3	2	31,345
C. C. Charisma	2	F	3	0	0	1	3,060
C. C. Coaler	2	G	4	0	0	1	1,138
C. C. Diamond	5	G	4	0	0	0	228
C. C. Minister	4	G	6	1	1	2	26,260
C. C. Seven	3	F	4	0	0	0	644
C. C. Union	4	G	15	0	2	1	8,222
C. C. Water Back	5	G	14	0	0	1	985

Horse	Age	Sex	Sts	1st	2d	3d	Won
C. C. Williams	5	M	6	0	1	0	7,505
C. C. With Water	3	F	3	0	0	1	2,359
C. C.'s Cash	2	F	2	0	0	0	0
C. C.'s Crane	4	F	5	0	0	2	1,375
C. C.'s Crane Man	3	C	8	4	0	0	7,927
C. C.'s Rocket	3	F	10	0	0	3	3,255
C. D. Haj	7	G	6	0	1	0	2,926
C. F. Power Lane	5	G	6	1	1	3	10,021
C. F. Touch Wood	4	G	3	0	0	0	0
C. Garrett	4	G	8	1	1	1	5,508
C. G's Dollar	2	G	6	1	1	0	17,869
C. J.'s Dream	3	F	9	1	3	1	13,908
C. J.'s Gold Rose	4	F	1	0	0	0	0
C. J.'s Magee	6	G	3	0	0	0	0
C. L. Crimson Tide	4	G	4	0	0	0	520
C. L. Rib	7	G	10	0	1	1	17,650
C. O. Storm	2	G	2	0	0	0	218
C. O. Too	2	G	2	0	0	0	661
C. R. Dancing Fox	2	G	6	0	2	1	8,420
C. R. Flying Star	4	G	5	1	2	0	15,534
C. R. Pace	7	M	17	0	2	0	4,820
C. R. Slolom Fox	3	G	9	1	2	1	19,003
C. Russell Run	3	G	8	1	2	2	17,660
C. S. Wells	4	C	4	0	0	1	848
C. T. Cruiser	5	M	8	1	2	0	8,948
C. T.' S Bay Watch	3	F	11	0	2	4	14,708
C. T.'s Lady	2	F	5	0	2	0	5,000
C. U. for Dinner	2	G	4	1	0	1	8,857
Ca Ching the Green	2	F	5	1	1	0	31,796
Ca d'Zan	3	C	11	0	0	1	1,644
Ca Marche	3	G	6	1	2	1	9,550
Cab Driver	3	C	7	1	2	1	30,070
Cab Renee	3	F	3	0	0	0	799
Caballero Negro	3	C	11	4	1	3	168,440
Caballero's Quest	2	C	3	0	0	0	420
Cabaret Dancer	5	G	5	0	1	1	3,220
Cabaret Star	2	F	4	0	0	0	1,925
Cabell County	3	C	6	0	0	0	0
Cabernet	4	G	10	2	1	0	9,612
Cabernet Lassie	3	F	4	0	1	0	2,880
Cabert	7	G	3	0	0	1	1,274
Cabeza Dura	3	G	3	0	0	0	217
Cabildo Bag	3	F	4	0	1	1	11,140
Cabin Boy	7	G	1	0	0	0	0
Cabin One	5	M	11	0	0	1	1,407
Cabin Stabin	4	G	11	4	1	1	45,412
Cabincreekcassie	3	F	4	0	0	0	424
Cabincreekconnie	3	F	6	1	2	1	12,593
Cabinet Minister	4	G	13	0	0	1	4,134
Cable Ready	5	G	9	1	2	4	7,566
Cable Vision	2	G	3	0	2	0	12,820
Cabo de Noche	3	F	11	0	1	2	25,863
Cabo Sunrise	4	F	2	0	0	2	7,260
Cabo Wabo	4	G	6	1	2	0	42,952
Cabobble	3	G	3	0	0	0	270
Caboret Note	5	M	12	1	0	1	5,679
Cabos	4	C	12	1	2	1	41,956
Cabo's Dawn	2	C	1	0	0	0	400
Cabot Trail	6	G	16	2	1	1	26,735
Cabreo	7	G	17	7	2	5	31,133
Cabriolass	3	G	9	2	4	0	123,293
Cabrita Point	8	G	9	2	0	1	6,030
Cachaca	2	F	1	0	0	0	230
Cache Is King	3	G	8	1	1	0	6,475
Cache Monster	3	G	11	1	2	0	9,441
Cachinnated	2	F	3	0	1	0	4,435
Cachito's Dancer	4	G	3	0	0	0	1,200
Cacht Wells (ARG)	4	C	7	1	2	0	55,620
Cachuma Blu Bye U	3	G	5	0	0	0	1,125
Cachuma's Dancer	4	F	5	0	0	0	846
Cachuma's Ladd	3	G	3	0	0	0	570
Cachuma's Lil Man	4	C	6	1	1	1	20,922
Cachumas Trickster	3	G	7	0	3	0	8,235
Cactus Classic	3	G	12	1	2	0	7,700
Cactus Glacken	5	G	7	0	2	0	3,496
Cadder	5	G	8	0	1	0	2,449
Caddo	4	G	9	0	2	2	6,398
Caddo Red	3	G	14	1	3	1	21,145
Cadeau de Ciel	2	C	1	0	0	0	795

Horse	Age	Sex	Sts	1st	2d	3d	Won
Cadenhead	7	G	10	1	2	3	38,580
Cadet Nurse	2	F	8	1	1	3	24,050
Cadilac Queen	4	F	1	0	0	0	0
Cadillac Bay	6	M	1	0	0	0	0
Cadillac Cruiser	2	C	3	1	0	0	33,940
Cadillac Gold	3	G	2	0	0	0	0
Cadillac Jack	4	G	5	1	0	2	9,320
Cadillac Jackie	4	F	5	0	0	0	245
Cadillac Key	2	C	3	0	0	0	283
Cadillac Pat	2	C	5	0	0	0	1,520
Cadillac Sam	8	G	4	0	0	0	123
Cadillacing Comet	2	F	3	0	0	0	336
Cadiz	5	G	6	0	0	0	1,918
Cadron Creek	7	G	4	1	0	1	5,850
Cady's Cafe (MEX)	5	M	6	0	1	2	4,591
Caelly Nethia	3	F	8	3	1	2	42,950
Caesarion (IRE)	5	H	5	0	1	0	20,784
Caesar's Tribute	3	C	2	0	0	0	0
Cafe Carefree	3	F	13	3	2	0	26,485
Cafe Cat	2	C	1	0	0	0	420
Cafe de France	9	M	3	0	0	1	640
Cafe Espresso	4	F	9	1	1	1	6,439
Cafe Flore	4	F	2	1	1	0	40,850
Cafe Katy	2	F	3	0	1	0	6,500
Cafe Momus	6	G	14	1	4	2	16,450
Cafe Noir	4	C	8	0	0	2	8,493
Cafe Photo	3	G	16	3	2	2	15,957
Cafe's Miracle	3	F	1	0	0	0	0
Caffeine and Booze	4	C	13	1	3	0	25,741
Caged	5	M	14	3	1	1	5,330
Caged Glory	2	F	1	0	0	0	0
Caged Spirit	3	G	3	0	0	0	190
Cagney	2	C	1	0	0	0	230
Cahilina	3	F	3	0	0	0	0
Cahill Gold	8	G	4	0	0	0	163
Cahill Holly	4	F	11	4	1	1	93,520
Cahill in Vogue	3	F	8	2	0	2	9,699
Cahill Kid	7	H	2	0	0	0	2,230
Cahill Mango	3	G	13	3	4	2	89,008
Cahill Royalty	2	F	3	1	1	0	9,085
Cahill Ruler	2	G	4	2	0	0	16,767
Cahill's Catrina	4	F	6	1	0	2	10,296
Cahootin	7	G	14	2	3	2	12,518
Cai Shen	3	C	1	0	0	0	0
Caillech	2	F	3	0	0	1	5,560
Caiman	3	C	16	2	1	1	80,732
Cain's Train	4	C	2	0	0	1	1,203
Cairne	3	G	15	2	6	2	81,710
Cairo Sam	3	C	4	0	0	0	891
Caisson	8	G	5	1	0	1	6,410
Caities Majesty	4	F	19	1	2	6	5,410
Caitlins Dancer	4	F	11	3	3	1	19,458
Caitlin's Idol	4	F	7	1	1	3	56,260
Caitlin's Playboy	3	G	9	2	1	1	42,430
Cajin Eskimo	2	C	7	1	0	3	15,480
Cajole	4	C	10	2	4	2	62,320
Cajulena	3	F	5	2	1	0	27,800
Cajun Addiction	3	G	3	0	0	1	4,497
Cajun Angel	3	C	7	2	1	0	15,060
Cajun Bad Blade	5	H	7	0	0	1	3,607
Cajun Beat	4	G	6	2	1	0	326,800
Cajun Bisque	3	F	3	0	0	0	278
Cajun Bluffer	3	F	9	0	0	0	1,043
Cajun Brogue	4	G	6	1	1	0	9,787
Cajun Concert	7	G	8	1	3	1	15,760
Cajun Countess	4	F	2	0	1	0	1,740
Cajun Crane	9	G	1	0	0	0	0
Cajun Dawn	3	F	2	0	0	0	161
Cajun Emblem	4	G	3	0	0	0	0
Cajun Kelly	4	F	1	0	0	0	215
Cajun Lass	5	M	6	1	0	1	1,455
Cajun Law	4	G	12	1	3	2	4,275
Cajun Memories	4	G	7	0	1	1	7,544
Cajun Miss	4	F	12	0	0	1	5,330
Cajun Music	4	G	8	2	3	0	49,905
Cajun Pepper	2	G	5	5	0	0	112,242
Cajun Princess	5	M	14	3	1	3	38,574
Cajun Purchase	3	F	2	0	0	0	300
Cajun Razor	6	G	11	2	3	0	18,994

Horse	Age	Sex	Sts	1st	2d	3d	Won
Cajun Rullah	4	G	7	1	2	1	22,592
Cajun Slewzy	3	F	2	0	0	0	0
Cajun Soup	4	F	13	1	2	1	17,510
Cajun Star	8	G	7	0	1	1	7,473
Cajun Twang	4	G	6	0	2	0	2,355
Cajun Wager	3	F	6	1	1	0	11,243
Cajuns Crown	4	G	2	0	0	0	1,632
Cake Knife	3	G	2	0	0	0	760
Cal Brite	6	M	4	0	1	0	932
Cal Gal	2	F	2	0	0	0	600
Cal Slew	4	G	4	0	0	0	178
Cala Springs	3	G	17	2	1	1	14,492
Calabar	4	G	4	0	0	0	1,125
Calabres (ARG)	5	G	4	1	0	0	8,113
Calabria Bella	3	C	5	1	2	0	50,155
Caladesi Breeze	2	F	1	0	0	0	0
Calahan's Jet	5	G	4	0	1	0	4,316
Calahoo Maid	2	F	1	0	0	0	0
Calaja	2	C	2	0	0	0	375
Calamander	3	G	2	0	0	0	700
Calamiamine	3	F	7	3	0	0	35,220
Calamity Jane	5	M	11	3	4	1	24,168
Calaverite	3	G	16	1	0	3	4,016
Calce Clunes	5	M	2	0	0	1	1,394
Calcite	3	F	8	1	1	1	11,590
Calculator	3	G	15	2	2	4	95,803
Calculus	3	G	8	0	0	0	1,313
Caldera Peak	2	F	3	1	0	2	25,020
Caldonias Ghost	2	F	3	0	0	0	171
Caleb's Hotdog	5	M	9	0	1	3	2,808
Caleb's Trophy	3	F	12	1	0	0	10,989
Caledon Colleen	6	M	14	0	0	3	6,316
Caledonia Road	3	C	2	0	0	0	1,650
Caledonna	4	F	11	1	3	1	13,632
Calends	5	H	13	4	2	1	71,955
Cale's Surprise	3	G	4	0	0	0	423
Calformecalifornia	5	M	15	3	4	2	27,812
Calhoun Bag	4	G	2	0	0	0	0
Cali Randi	2	F	8	1	1	0	10,183
Caliban	7	G	9	0	0	1	5,382
Calibration	5	M	1	0	0	0	0
Calico Creek	7	M	8	0	1	1	4,042
Calico Sioux	6	H	1	0	0	0	600
Caliente Fuego	5	M	13	2	2	1	22,304
Caliente Light	4	F	1	1	0	0	5,600
Caliente Oro	7	M	1	0	0	0	0
Califo	6	G	7	1	2	3	14,585
California Casual	5	M	2	1	0	0	5,616
California Chick	4	F	4	0	0	0	44
California Choice	2	C	1	1	0	0	14,575
California Concept	3	F	9	0	0	0	5,355
California Dame	3	F	1	0	0	0	0
California Fire	4	F	4	0	0	2	2,745
California Heart	3	C	2	1	0	0	22,200
California Kiss	5	G	10	2	2	2	20,666
California Limited	6	M	1	0	0	0	192
California Power	5	G	12	3	2	1	34,565
California Sage	6	H	1	0	0	0	385
California Star	4	F	2	1	0	1	8,655
California Storm	5	G	6	0	0	0	1,163
California Thunder	2	F	2	0	0	1	6,780
Californian (GB)	4	C	5	0	0	0	11,360
Calista Regent	4	F	4	0	0	0	219
Calista's Star	5	M	4	0	1	0	7,620
Calisthenic	5	G	11	5	3	0	99,550
Caliterra	3	F	10	3	1	0	33,263
Calkins Road	5	H	6	2	0	1	131,385
Call a Judge	4	F	5	1	2	1	54,400
Call an Interview	4	G	10	2	0	0	48,755
Call Anytime	2	G	4	0	0	2	6,475
Call At Night	2	F	5	0	0	2	3,500
Call Back	4	G	1	0	0	0	54
Call Call	4	F	9	1	0	0	4,054
Call Carson	3	F	4	2	1	1	33,256
Call Cielo	3	C	11	1	5	1	12,359
Call Columbo	4	G	8	1	5	0	32,610
Call Denied	3	F	2	0	0	0	1,090
Call Early	3	G	13	2	0	4	43,532
Call Em Lovey	6	G	4	0	0	1	971

Horse	Age	Sex	Sts	1st	2d	3d	Won
Call Fiorello	9	G	1	0	0	0	0
Call for Freedom	3	G	10	1	1	0	8,820
Call Forwarding	4	F	9	0	0	2	1,370
Call From the Bar	3	F	13	2	0	0	22,622
Call Granny	6	M	10	2	1	3	19,030
Call Her Bluff	2	F	3	0	0	0	1,350
Call Her Michele	4	F	2	0	0	0	0
Call Her Starlight	2	F	5	1	1	0	6,488
Call Him Back Man	6	G	12	2	1	1	15,565
Call Him Wildfire	5	H	11	0	2	1	7,995
Call His Bluff	5	G	13	1	1	1	9,293
Call Home Etbauer	3	F	11	2	4	0	23,740
Call in the Note	2	F	1	0	0	0	131
Call It	5	G	5	0	1	1	15,546
Call It in the Air	7	G	6	0	0	0	1,000
Call Late	3	F	2	0	0	0	0
Call Leader	4	G	13	1	0	2	9,390
Call Me a Prince	9	G	10	0	2	1	1,206
Call Me Awesome	3	C	4	0	1	1	14,312
Call Me Back	3	F	8	0	1	0	2,100
Call Me Ben	2	C	1	0	0	0	0
Call Me Bobby	4	G	9	0	0	0	486
Call Me C. J.	7	G	10	0	2	0	6,430
Call Me Charlie	2	F	1	0	0	0	0
Call Me Chief	2	F	5	0	1	0	4,690
Call Me Cobra	6	G	2	0	0	0	220
Call Me Do	4	G	2	0	0	0	1,354
Call Me Dorie	4	F	11	2	4	2	72,980
Call Me Eppi	2	F	2	0	0	0	2,330
Call Me Famous	4	G	10	1	2	4	6,205
Call Me Frosty	4	G	8	1	0	1	11,890
Call Me Glitter	2	F	2	0	1	1	3,850
Call Me Glory	4	G	12	0	1	2	8,953
Call Me Gold	3	G	9	1	1	2	10,588
Call Me Grace	5	M	10	1	3	0	8,070
Call Me Home	6	G	7	0	0	0	1,785
Call Me Honey	3	F	1	0	0	0	0
Call Me Inky	5	M	5	1	0	0	3,984
Call Me Joyce	5	M	7	0	0	0	0
Call Me Kaitlin	3	F	5	0	0	0	336
Call Me Lightning	5	G	8	2	1	1	17,190
Call Me Loverboy	7	H	1	1	0	0	6,900
Call Me Madonna	3	F	4	1	0	1	17,700
Call Me Meg	5	M	10	1	2	1	32,460
Call Me Mike	5	G	1	0	0	0	0
Call Me Mister C	4	G	13	1	2	1	11,115
Call Me Moe	3	G	14	3	3	2	76,801
Call Me Mr. Chad	2	C	1	0	0	0	67
Call Me Mr. Vain	10	G	9	0	2	1	7,380
Call Me Pete	4	G	9	2	1	3	54,920
Call Me Proper	4	G	3	0	1	0	1,217
Call Me Roy	5	G	5	0	1	1	1,457
Call Me Shane	3	C	3	1	0	0	24,995
Call Me Silver	2	F	6	0	1	0	3,534
Call Me Special	5	G	3	0	0	1	365
Call Me Sue	5	M	9	1	2	1	32,201
Call Me Taz	3	G	4	0	0	1	1,380
Call Me Terminator	3	G	4	0	0	0	922
Call Me the Champ	3	G	17	2	3	4	14,488
Call Me West	4	C	13	0	5	1	9,967
Call Me Windy	3	F	7	1	0	0	3,655
Call Mom	2	G	8	0	0	1	3,770
Call My Bluff	2	C	2	0	1	0	7,680
Call My Cellphone	2	G	4	0	0	0	1,720
Call My Girl	2	F	4	0	0	0	2,906
Call My Lawyer	4	F	11	2	1	1	32,775
Call Newport	6	H	7	1	4	1	3,618
Call Roy	3	C	6	2	1	1	32,320
Call Sign	4	G	9	2	1	0	17,790
Call Sign Maverick	2	G	8	0	1	1	9,680
Call Sis	4	F	1	0	0	0	40
Call the Clocker	2	F	5	1	0	0	10,959
Call the Dance	2	C	1	0	0	0	70
Call the Director	3	G	6	1	1	0	13,820
Call the Groom	6	G	5	0	0	0	169
Call the Lark	3	G	4	1	1	0	36,180
Call the Lord	2	C	2	1	0	1	10,005
Call the Marines	2	C	2	0	1	0	7,760
Call the Queen	3	F	4	0	0	0	365

Horse	Age	Sex	Sts	1st	2d	3d	Won
Call the Thunder	2	F	1	0	1	0	9,000
Call the Witness	3	F	6	0	0	0	1,240
Call Time Out	2	F	2	0	0	0	139
Call to Colors	4	G	4	0	0	0	123
Call to Honor	7	H	2	0	0	0	215
Call Trace	7	G	10	0	0	1	1,873
Call Waiting	7	G	7	1	1	2	20,805
Call Works	3	G	2	0	0	0	105
Callabove	3	F	6	0	2	0	8,970
Callarula Gold	3	F	3	0	0	1	795
Callbeforeucome	3	G	10	2	1	3	22,625
Callbright	3	C	4	0	0	0	480
Callcan	3	G	14	3	1	0	32,990
Callcat	3	G	10	1	1	1	40,061
Calldara	4	F	5	0	0	0	2,843
Calldownthelaw	6	M	1	0	0	0	50
Calle	3	F	12	2	4	0	22,973
Caller a Cowgirl	2	F	3	0	0	0	0
Caller an Angel	3	F	2	0	0	0	0
Caller Back	3	F	17	1	3	2	9,825
Caller Blocked	3	G	10	1	2	1	11,741
Caller Dixie	2	F	1	0	0	0	305
Caller Jilly Bean	3	F	8	0	0	0	4,896
Caller Junction	7	G	1	0	0	0	0
Caller Karla	2	F	3	0	0	0	0
Caller One	7	G	1	0	0	1	5,500
Caller Pete	8	G	15	4	3	3	29,118
Caller to Post	3	F	2	0	0	0	140
Caller Up	2	F	4	0	1	0	1,100
Caller's Image	5	M	13	2	2	5	26,190
Callfire	3	G	1	0	1	0	5,300
Callheracitygirl	3	F	3	0	0	0	235
Callherswiss	2	F	4	0	0	0	0
Callie Mae	5	M	19	4	4	4	25,316
Calliehadaprenup	6	G	12	3	1	1	15,204
Callies Remark	4	F	6	0	0	0	492
Callieseacat	2	F	3	0	0	1	605
Calligraphist	2	C	12	1	3	0	12,225
Callin Collect	5	H	6	0	0	0	944
Callin Doctor Fran	6	G	16	1	1	2	18,941
Callin Dr Casey	4	F	8	1	1	1	6,438
Calling	4	F	19	1	0	2	8,535
Calling All Angels	3	F	9	1	0	0	7,608
Calling All Forbes	3	G	15	2	4	0	29,045
Calling Angels	3	F	6	1	0	2	12,710
Calling Home	2	G	7	0	0	4	17,173
Calling Mary Mac	3	F	20	0	0	1	3,050
Calling Nicole	3	F	5	0	1	1	3,150
Calling Randy	4	G	14	5	2	2	32,155
Calling Unity	2	F	7	0	1	3	8,760
Callinthetroops	3	F	8	2	1	1	24,386
Callmebrandy	4	F	16	1	6	4	16,866
Callmefrenchie	7	G	7	0	0	0	2,497
Callmelauryn	3	F	4	3	0	0	44,795
Callmeluckylucy	2	F	1	0	1	0	9,800
Callmetony	3	G	12	1	4	3	32,745
Callnew	3	G	10	2	4	0	41,845
Callone	3	F	7	3	1	0	49,114
Callseven	3	C	3	1	0	0	11,170
Callsports	3	F	10	1	5	0	21,800
Callter	3	F	14	0	1	4	11,510
Callthesheriff	5	G	6	1	0	1	30,525
Callum	3	G	13	2	3	3	23,803
Callvi	3	G	9	1	0	0	3,828
Callya Later	9	G	13	4	0	1	17,091
Callydon'tdally	3	F	3	0	1	0	2,340
Calm Again	3	F	1	0	0	1	1,200
Calm Cool Vonflue	3	C	1	0	0	0	400
Calm in the East	3	F	8	2	1	1	30,942
Calm Waters	6	G	8	1	0	1	8,325
Calmar Norma	3	F	6	0	1	0	1,686
Calmego	3	G	1	0	0	0	0
Calming Effect	6	G	10	3	2	2	33,300
Cal's Baby	6	M	5	1	1	3	16,430
Cal's Choice	5	M	6	0	0	0	1,023
Calsby	3	C	8	1	2	1	17,673
Calster	6	G	6	0	0	1	9,760
Calverstown	5	G	10	2	3	0	46,640
Calvin Clyde	4	G	11	2	2	3	11,700
Calypso Band	2	C	3	1	0	1	31,000
Calzada Kid	5	M	2	1	0	1	36,984
Cam a Retta	6	M	7	0	1	3	11,000
Cama Cat	3	F	8	1	0	2	17,358
Camacho	3	G	10	2	0	0	10,000
Camacho (NZ)	7	G	11	0	1	1	18,425
Camara Gold	4	F	10	1	1	2	7,363
Camaron's Harbor	5	G	9	1	2	0	25,975
Cambaco	3	G	4	1	0	0	24,480
Camberley	4	F	3	0	0	2	3,604
Camber's American	4	F	7	0	1	1	1,350
Cambie Street	2	F	1	0	0	0	636
Cambiocorsa	2	F	1	0	0	0	400
Cambria	2	F	4	0	0	2	4,070
Cambria Rd	2	C	2	0	0	0	192
Camden Pine	6	G	10	3	0	2	12,176
Came From Paris	3	G	5	1	0	2	20,825
Camela Carson	2	F	2	1	0	1	21,500
Camello	3	G	6	0	0	0	1,512
Camelotbay	3	C	2	0	0	0	1,272
Cameo Appearance	4	F	9	1	2	2	11,676
Cameo Castle	3	F	2	0	1	0	3,160
Cameo's Covergirl	6	M	18	1	3	1	15,025
Camera Copy	6	M	4	0	0	0	500
Cameron Be Good	3	F	10	0	1	1	6,995
Camerons Delight	2	G	2	0	0	0	0
Cameron's Way	4	G	3	1	0	0	3,675
Camford	9	G	3	0	0	0	0
Camikaze Cookie	11	G	11	0	0	0	892
Camille's Princess	5	M	1	0	0	0	0
Camino	9	G	11	1	1	3	7,749
Camino Di Oro	7	H	18	0	1	1	2,871
Camisade	3	F	4	0	0	1	11,454
Camjack	4	G	1	0	0	0	0
Cammy Be Kwik	6	M	10	0	2	3	10,675
Cammy's Jet	4	F	3	1	0	0	16,200
Camp Clark	4	G	10	1	0	0	5,300
Camp David	5	H	3	0	0	3	15,050
Camp Del Mar Rules	3	F	10	1	3	3	33,280
Camp Nagawicka	4	G	10	2	2	2	58,220
Camp On Wood	3	F	11	2	2	2	82,059
Camp Randall	5	G	5	0	0	0	799
Camp Takatoka	4	G	10	0	0	0	1,580
Campaign	2	C	8	1	0	2	7,480
Campaign Andover	6	M	15	2	2	5	45,790
Campaigner	5	G	11	2	2	1	22,580
Camperchano	6	G	10	1	0	2	4,335
Campfire Burning	3	G	13	4	4	1	84,100
Campfire Ridge	7	G	3	0	0	0	280
Campiano	4	G	6	1	0	1	10,095
Campinout	5	G	17	5	3	3	83,130
Campionessa	2	F	2	0	0	0	2,760
Campo	2	G	1	1	0	0	15,600
Campo de Maniobras	3	F	8	2	2	1	18,952
Campo Ridge	3	F	6	0	3	2	10,745
Campton Hills	3	G	10	1	2	0	16,280
Camptown King	2	C	2	0	0	1	4,420
Camrynlee	2	F	2	0	0	0	405
Cam's Cat	4	F	10	3	0	1	5,615
Camsdancer	2	G	6	1	2	0	25,140
Can Belong	4	G	17	3	4	1	28,446
Can I	4	F	7	1	0	0	5,475
Can I Call You Dad	4	F	8	2	0	2	53,161
Can I Do It	4	G	5	0	0	2	4,390
Can I Make It	5	M	7	1	0	1	4,409
Can Ihavethisdance	3	F	8	3	2	0	152,568
Can You Hear Me	4	F	3	0	0	0	164
Can You See Me Now	3	F	3	0	2	1	10,200
Cana Creek	4	G	10	1	3	2	18,570
Cana Diesel	4	G	1	0	0	0	190
Canaan Land	4	G	12	1	2	2	38,210
Canaberry	2	F	3	0	0	3	4,870
Canadian Attorney	3	F	1	0	0	0	0
Canadian Cat	3	F	6	0	1	1	25,284
Canadian Clipper	5	M	1	0	0	0	243
Canadian Cowboy	2	C	3	0	0	1	4,430
Canadian Crusader	3	F	7	1	0	0	19,474
Canadian Currency	5	M	9	0	0	0	929
Canadian Deputy	2	G	4	0	1	1	4,228

Horse	Age	Sex	Sts	1st	2d	3d	Won
Canadian Edition	5	G	13	0	0	1	4,307
Canadian Flyer	7	G	10	1	0	2	10,211
Canadian Frontier	5	H	8	5	0	0	214,962
Canadian Fury	5	M	6	0	0	1	2,232
Canadian Gem	2	F	6	2	2	0	125,580
Canadian Music	2	C	6	1	1	1	29,613
Canadian Navy	7	G	10	0	1	1	2,667
Canadian Northern	3	G	9	2	0	3	24,556
Canadian River	3	G	6	4	0	0	80,100
Canadian Scarlett	4	F	1	0	0	0	91
Canadian She Devil	3	F	2	0	0	0	0
Canadian Star	3	F	6	1	0	0	10,521
Canadian Trick	3	G	2	0	0	0	0
Canadian Warrior	3	C	12	2	1	2	54,740
Canadian Way	3	G	13	0	4	4	11,969
Canadian Wrangler	4	G	8	1	1	2	8,321
Canadiana Hopefull	3	F	9	0	2	1	5,283
Canadier	3	F	7	0	2	0	11,680
Canagua	2	F	4	0	0	0	383
Canal Lake	4	G	12	0	2	1	7,665
Canal Town	7	G	12	1	1	3	9,825
Canaletto (GB)	8	G	7	0	2	0	11,622
Canape	2	F	3	0	1	0	11,195
Canapuddlejump	2	F	5	1	1	0	21,920
Canasta	4	G	7	0	0	0	634
Canasto Boy	5	G	8	0	1	1	9,105
Canavati	3	G	16	1	1	3	13,515
Canaveral Affair	2	C	3	0	0	1	3,659
Canaverous	5	G	7	1	1	0	15,300
Canbeanangel	4	F	4	0	0	2	1,700
Canby Dancer	5	M	10	5	2	1	51,370
Cancan Cakewalk	2	C	8	0	0	1	1,634
Cancion Alegre	7	G	11	0	1	4	13,020
Cancovina	3	F	2	0	0	0	483
Cancun's Award	4	F	5	0	0	0	50
Candeelite	4	F	9	3	0	0	35,690
Candelotto	11	G	6	0	4	0	7,586
Candi Colette	3	F	13	1	0	1	2,260
Candi Dancin	5	G	4	0	0	0	156
Candi Fair	3	F	8	1	1	2	5,668
Candi Man Can	8	G	13	1	3	2	5,867
Candi Step	5	M	2	0	0	1	130
Candid Ballerina	7	M	13	2	1	1	11,630
Candid Glen	7	G	2	1	1	0	29,200
Candid Lady	2	F	2	0	0	0	345
Candid Remark	6	G	11	4	3	1	41,996
Candid Reply	3	G	1	0	0	0	0
Candida	4	F	10	4	0	1	23,946
Candi's Avenue	5	G	1	0	0	0	300
Candi's Court	3	F	1	0	0	0	300
Candi's Dandi	5	G	4	0	0	0	1,055
Candi's Golden Cat	6	M	6	0	0	0	1,560
Candi's Soft Touch	3	G	13	3	1	2	35,380
Candi's Treasure	3	F	4	1	1	1	37,390
Candle Snuffer	9	G	6	1	1	0	4,815
Candlebrook	3	F	4	0	0	0	0
Candlelight Only	4	G	2	0	0	0	0
Candlelight Prince	4	G	5	0	1	0	11,791
Candler	7	G	8	3	1	2	9,292
Candles N Scandals	2	F	4	0	0	0	765
Candlestick Darren	2	G	4	0	0	0	536
Candooz	4	F	6	0	0	0	4,303
Canduru	3	F	2	0	0	0	101
Candy Adventure	6	M	12	1	2	1	33,571
Candy Basket	4	F	2	0	0	0	0
Candy Cane C C	4	F	8	2	0	0	20,267
Candy Clouds	4	F	5	2	2	0	35,430
Candy Factor	7	H	6	1	1	0	3,815
Candy Factory	3	F	5	2	0	1	59,920
Candy Flute	4	F	5	0	1	1	4,178
Candy Glide	4	F	10	3	1	0	34,190
Candy Go	4	F	5	2	1	2	11,330
Candy Haze	6	M	6	2	2	0	50,640
Candy Kat	9	G	7	1	0	0	1,750
Candy Kisses	5	M	3	0	0	0	375
Candy Legs	3	F	9	0	2	2	1,311
Candy Motion	9	M	5	0	0	0	395
Candy Runner	4	G	12	2	3	2	24,864
Candy Striper (GB)	2	F	2	0	0	1	4,750
Candy Verse	5	M	8	1	1	4	37,600
Candy Win	3	F	6	3	1	0	12,905
Candyator	3	F	2	0	1	0	2,480
Candybag	6	G	11	0	0	1	2,420
Candybedandy	4	F	11	3	2	3	101,700
Candyman Who	4	G	4	0	1	0	3,800
Candyman's Girl	3	F	3	0	0	0	400
Candyndawn	3	F	8	2	0	0	10,391
Candy's Advantage	5	M	8	0	0	0	2,160
Candys Plan	3	F	2	0	1	0	920
Candy's Prospect	4	G	4	0	0	0	170
Cane Garden	3	C	5	0	0	2	4,390
Cane Garden Boy	3	G	3	0	0	1	3,300
Cane River Wynner	3	C	9	3	1	1	27,475
Cane Vale	5	M	5	1	0	0	18,014
Caner Medley	3	G	2	0	1	0	4,660
Canfield	7	H	3	0	0	0	894
Canigetawhatwhat	2	F	2	0	0	0	280
Canna Belle	5	M	11	0	3	0	2,400
Canna Lac	3	G	11	1	0	1	5,374
Cannacorn	3	G	8	2	0	0	13,825
Canned Heat	4	G	9	1	3	2	10,749
Canned Heat (NZ)	8	G	12	1	2	2	11,612
Cannon in G	4	F	17	1	1	1	20,981
Cannonball Red	5	G	4	0	0	0	1,054
Cannonball Rock	5	G	5	0	1	0	10,990
Cannon's Joker	5	G	15	0	1	1	6,585
Cannot Chase	3	G	13	1	4	4	14,871
Canny Fly (AUS)	7	G	7	3	1	0	72,740
Canoe Princess	2	F	3	0	0	0	735
Canoe Ridge	3	G	7	1	1	0	7,122
Canondale	3	F	17	1	2	2	22,401
Canonicus	5	G	10	0	1	1	888
Canora	4	F	12	2	0	0	17,634
Canought Pass	4	F	3	0	0	0	0
Canrock	8	G	11	1	2	3	13,563
Can't Be an Angel	4	F	6	0	0	2	1,582
Can't Be Denied	3	F	16	2	0	2	55,060
Can't Be Wild	4	G	5	0	1	0	1,498
Can't Buy Class	3	F	11	0	5	2	39,710
Can't Catch	2	G	7	0	0	4	5,922
Can't Escape Me	4	F	18	3	4	3	24,773
Can't Fool Clyde	5	G	3	0	0	0	247
Can't Get Enough	3	F	3	0	0	0	1,440
Can't Get Me	5	G	6	0	3	1	17,740
Can't See Me	2	F	2	1	0	0	12,620
Cant Smoke Me	2	F	6	1	0	1	16,125
Can't Stop	2	G	3	0	0	0	1,190
Can't Stop James	6	G	14	2	2	0	26,170
Can't Stop Kobe	3	G	11	0	5	1	8,985
Can't Trick Jake	2	C	4	1	1	0	36,520
Can't You See	6	M	15	1	1	1	14,500
Canta Bonita (ARG)	5	M	3	0	0	0	0
Cantaloupe	7	M	4	0	2	0	20,942
Can'tcarryatune	2	F	3	0	1	1	2,170
Cantcatcharose	2	F	2	0	0	0	0
Canterra	3	F	2	0	0	0	0
Cantey	3	G	5	1	0	0	15,600
Can'tfindmyglasses	5	G	6	0	0	0	2,105
Cantil	7	H	4	1	0	0	13,225
Cantilator	2	G	4	0	0	1	975
Canton Connection	6	G	1	0	0	0	80
Cantouchis	4	F	8	0	1	0	8,748
Cantresistthiskiss	2	G	8	1	0	0	7,380
Cantus	3	G	3	0	0	0	364
Cantyoukeepasecret	3	F	2	0	0	0	600
Canuck	5	G	1	0	0	0	0
Canuseemenow	3	C	8	1	0	0	6,265
Canuto	5	G	18	1	1	2	16,797
Canvas' Honey	4	F	14	3	1	1	13,110
Canvas Lady	3	F	6	0	0	0	1,337
Canyon Beauty	2	F	3	0	0	0	1,481
Canyon Crook	7	G	14	1	4	1	22,775
Canyon Dan	3	G	2	0	0	0	176
Canyon de Oro	5	H	6	1	1	1	22,560
Canyon Dream	2	F	1	0	0	0	0
Canyon Gold	2	C	1	0	0	1	3,975
Canyon Key	4	G	7	1	1	1	11,034
Canyon Runner	3	C	3	0	0	0	920

Horse	Age	Sex	Sts	1st	2d	3d	Won
Canyon Strategy	3	F	9	2	1	1	24,634
Canyon Turn	4	G	9	1	2	1	41,410
Canyon's First	3	G	2	0	0	1	3,630
Canyon's My Honey	3	G	1	0	0	0	0
Canyon's Way	5	G	13	3	2	2	39,015
Canyon's Wildcat	8	G	11	5	1	0	15,797
Canyouhearmerunnin	3	C	3	0	0	0	0
Canzady	5	M	3	1	1	0	1,960
Canzonetta	4	G	3	0	1	0	3,600
Cap	6	G	11	3	2	3	56,330
Cap d'Antibes	3	F	3	1	0	0	8,645
Cap Ferrat (ARG)	7	H	8	0	1	1	18,717
Cap 'n America	5	G	20	3	3	1	17,788
Capability	3	C	1	1	0	0	16,240
Capable Capers	5	H	12	3	3	2	32,765
Capable Dancer	4	G	4	2	0	0	4,013
Capac	3	C	3	1	0	0	15,450
Capazuri	6	G	12	3	1	2	45,150
Cape Breeze	3	F	9	3	0	1	47,570
Cape Cat	2	F	7	0	0	0	750
Cape Clare	3	C	4	3	0	0	41,700
Cape Cod Gray	4	C	6	0	0	0	1,236
Cape Cod Princess	3	F	8	1	2	1	10,125
Cape Cod Rose	2	F	4	1	2	0	16,470
Cape Colony	6	M	11	0	1	2	6,262
Cape Cosmo	2	F	7	1	3	0	34,250
Cape County	2	F	1	0	0	0	1,230
Cape Crusader	3	G	10	1	2	3	11,203
Cape Elizabeth	7	M	7	3	1	0	15,800
Cape Fear	4	G	1	0	0	0	195
Cape Fear Fury	5	H	8	0	1	0	7,172
Cape Flyaway	3	C	2	1	0	0	34,800
Cape Good Hope	4	C	10	1	3	1	58,314
Cape Hope	2	F	3	1	0	1	21,690
Cape Kendor	3	G	5	0	0	0	1,268
Cape Kennedy	2	C	1	0	0	0	400
Cape Kid	4	G	9	1	2	1	18,610
Cape Love	2	F	2	0	0	0	1,272
Cape Montauk	3	F	9	0	1	2	8,435
Cape of Good Hope	2	F	4	0	2	1	24,550
Cape Peer	4	G	5	0	0	2	1,873
Cape Pogue	4	C	12	0	0	3	19,390
Cape Power	5	G	4	0	0	1	4,200
Cape Town Classic	2	F	1	0	0	0	0
Cape Town Girl	2	F	3	1	0	1	7,980
Cape Town Gold	3	G	8	0	0	1	2,239
Cape Town Lass	3	F	7	2	0	3	63,604
Cape Trafalgar (IRE)	3	F	4	0	1	2	22,737
Capeable Cat	3	F	2	0	0	0	0
Caped Crusade	2	C	1	1	0	0	15,600
Caped Crusader	6	G	7	0	0	0	0
Capehart (JPN)	3	F	7	1	0	0	13,646
Capejinsky	3	C	7	1	1	0	37,996
Capella	2	F	4	0	0	0	490
Caperex	3	G	3	0	0	0	0
Caper's Bel	2	F	4	0	0	0	730
Capers Town	2	C	4	0	0	2	6,100
Caperucita Roja	6	M	11	0	0	2	2,835
Cape's Fury	3	F	11	1	2	2	33,309
Capeside Lady	3	F	7	2	1	2	266,220
Capespringseternal	3	F	8	2	2	1	34,210
Capias	3	C	13	3	1	3	90,507
Capistrano	2	F	2	1	0	1	28,379
Capitaine	3	G	5	2	2	0	14,183
Capital Asset	5	G	19	1	1	1	9,664
Capital Charm	3	G	17	1	3	3	14,245
Capital Dee	3	C	2	0	0	0	0
Capital Dreams	4	F	7	0	1	0	5,162
Capital Excess	3	C	1	0	0	0	788
Capital Honor	3	F	6	1	0	2	6,719
Capital Peak	5	G	7	2	1	2	58,720
Capital Spending	4	C	12	2	4	1	107,515
Capitalina	4	F	2	0	0	0	50
Capitan Cook (CHI)	7	G	10	0	0	1	2,530
Capitan Jess	3	C	6	0	2	1	3,615
Capitano	3	C	7	1	3	1	128,058
Capitan's Cowboy	4	G	9	1	2	1	12,157
Capitol Man	5	G	5	0	0	1	2,100
Capitol Reality	5	G	20	3	3	6	21,585
Capitol Won	3	G	14	0	0	0	1,017
Capitola	3	F	9	4	2	1	96,508
Capitulate	3	G	2	0	0	0	1,260
Capitulation	2	F	1	1	0	0	12,300
Cap'n Cottontail	4	G	7	0	0	1	2,723
Cap'n Jeff	4	G	19	2	3	3	22,626
Cap'n Jerry	6	G	7	0	0	0	330
Cap'n Red	3	G	6	0	1	1	11,115
Capo	3	C	7	2	1	3	87,846
Capo Di Tuti	3	C	7	1	0	1	10,605
Capo Grosso (CHI)	6	G	4	0	1	0	5,810
Capone	3	C	4	0	0	0	1,810
Capote Dancer	4	C	9	1	0	1	5,533
Capote Express	6	G	4	0	0	0	450
Capote's Crystal	3	F	3	0	0	1	1,055
Capote's Frost	2	C	2	0	0	1	1,650
Capote's Storm	3	F	4	0	0	0	0
Capow	3	G	8	2	0	1	31,580
Capped	5	M	2	0	0	1	644
Cappistol	5	G	4	0	0	0	573
Cappuccia	3	F	3	0	1	1	2,270
Cappuchino	5	H	7	1	0	0	71,460
Cappucino Carly	3	F	5	0	0	1	1,931
Cappucino Kid	6	G	7	1	2	2	51,085
Cappy Ricks	3	G	4	1	0	0	8,070
Capreta	3	F	14	1	0	0	5,231
Capri Key	3	F	2	0	0	0	490
Capria	3	F	15	2	1	2	21,874
Capricha	5	M	2	0	0	0	2,040
Capricious Charm	3	F	2	0	0	0	316
Capriva	3	C	3	0	0	0	0
Caprock	3	G	5	1	1	0	14,300
Capsacin	3	F	1	1	0	0	9,600
Capsule	5	G	1	0	0	0	0
Capt. Career	4	C	5	0	0	1	3,355
Capt. Defrere	7	G	2	0	0	1	3,595
Capt. Fly Hook	7	G	1	0	0	0	1,875
Capt. Henry Rhoads	3	G	5	0	0	0	1,210
Capt. Jayger	5	G	10	0	2	0	1,440
Capt. Mc Craiger	2	G	1	1	0	0	21,600
Capt. Morgan Gold	2	G	2	0	0	0	256
Capt. Smooth	3	C	3	0	0	0	0
Captain Aluppa	5	G	5	0	1	0	1,440
Captain Amour	4	R	10	2	2	1	46,088
Captain Anthony	3	G	4	1	1	0	16,400
Captain B Crook	4	G	3	0	1	1	3,390
Captain Backdraft	3	G	2	0	0	1	1,560
Captain Badgett	5	G	10	1	1	2	9,670
Captain Ben	7	G	6	1	1	0	16,759
Captain Bill	3	G	12	2	2	1	13,421
Captain Binge	3	C	9	1	2	0	16,670
Captain Blue	3	G	4	0	0	0	0
Captain Bob	5	G	1	0	0	0	0
Captain Bob Jo Jr.	2	C	4	1	1	0	12,600
Captain Bold	4	C	6	1	0	0	5,033
Captain Boo	4	C	9	1	0	3	5,480
Captain Brad	2	G	4	0	0	0	3,000
Captain Briggs	4	G	7	1	1	3	18,170
Captain Buck	5	G	12	2	1	2	8,150
Captain Burke	2	C	2	0	0	0	322
Captain Cahill	4	G	11	2	0	4	26,885
Captain Carby	8	G	11	1	1	2	10,237
Captain Carter	5	G	8	2	2	0	5,287
Captain Cause	5	H	7	0	0	3	5,195
Captain Chaos	2	G	1	0	0	0	1,350
Captain Chessie	5	G	9	3	2	0	83,905
Captain Chic	3	G	5	0	1	1	3,890
Captain Colors	8	G	2	0	0	0	280
Captain Colton	3	G	6	1	0	0	10,492
Captain Comet	7	G	10	0	0	0	0
Captain Corelli	2	C	6	1	0	2	24,600
Captain Craig	10	H	10	3	0	3	9,819
Captain Creek	7	G	7	1	0	3	24,982
Captain Crossgrain	4	C	2	0	0	0	0
Captain Curt	2	C	3	0	0	0	371
Captain Cyclops	4	G	11	1	0	2	7,400
Captain Dean	5	G	13	3	2	2	19,196
Captain Dennis	3	G	4	0	0	0	4,230
Captain Des	6	G	1	0	0	0	0

Horse	Age	Sex	Sts	1st	2d	3d	Won
Captain Discover	4	G	8	0	0	0	985
Captain Dodge	2	G	2	0	0	0	140
Captain Dudley	2	G	2	0	0	1	1,355
Captain Fancy	3	G	9	1	2	2	15,795
Captain Fantastic	4	C	7	0	2	2	5,535
Captain Fiddle	4	G	7	0	0	1	492
Captain Flash	3	G	5	1	0	0	17,370
Captain George	5	G	11	1	0	4	27,955
Captain Gill	5	G	6	1	2	0	3,735
Captain Greybeard	4	G	2	0	0	1	1,155
Captain Halo	4	C	12	0	7	2	12,310
Captain Holloway	5	G	4	2	1	0	28,340
Captain Jacob	2	G	4	0	0	1	1,200
Captain Jim	7	M	12	0	0	2	3,268
Captain Joe	7	G	9	2	1	2	28,168
Captain Keenan	5	G	12	1	1	3	14,790
Captain Kirby	5	G	5	0	0	0	0
Captain Larkin	5	G	13	2	3	1	17,058
Captain Lindsay	2	C	6	2	0	1	60,350
Captain Listo	3	C	1	0	0	0	310
Captain Lovely	4	C	3	0	1	0	489
Captain Malory	5	G	7	1	2	3	19,255
Captain Mike	4	G	21	1	1	3	9,241
Captain Nepal	2	F	2	0	2	0	8,840
Captain Nicholas	6	G	6	2	1	0	36,020
Captain Niner	2	G	2	0	0	0	192
Captain Paul	3	G	1	0	0	0	400
Captain Phillip	5	G	9	3	1	0	77,018
Captain Prudent	3	C	4	1	0	2	10,759
Captain Red	7	H	3	0	0	0	2,130
Captain Scott	4	G	11	0	1	1	2,665
Captain Sinclair	3	G	9	2	3	0	17,065
Captain Skyhawk	3	G	4	1	1	0	8,575
Captain Slew	2	C	3	0	0	0	3,540
Captain Smith	5	G	11	2	0	1	61,510
Captain Spaulding	3	C	10	0	1	1	8,673
Captain Speed	5	G	16	2	2	5	14,161
Captain Squire	5	G	6	1	2	1	84,040
Captain Stats	6	G	16	0	5	4	16,758
Captain Sventhomas	4	C	1	0	0	0	775
Captain Thunder	4	C	4	0	1	0	11,300
Captain Tommy G	2	G	3	1	2	0	17,250
Captain Twilight	5	H	6	0	0	0	0
Captain Valentine	3	F	5	1	0	1	10,628
Captain Wallstreet	6	H	12	2	3	2	24,765
Captain Wheat	5	G	7	0	2	0	14,736
Captain Zones	3	C	3	0	0	0	1,500
Captainbluegrass	4	G	3	0	0	0	600
Captainofindustry	5	G	3	0	0	3	5,500
Captain's Daughter	4	F	5	1	1	1	26,000
Captain's Kiddo	2	G	3	0	0	1	366
Captain's Maneuver	4	G	2	0	2	0	11,000
Captain's Presto	3	F	2	0	0	1	671
Captain's Song	5	M	1	0	0	0	0
Captain's Surprise	4	F	18	0	0	3	9,900
Captain's Table	6	G	7	1	0	0	8,083
Captian Bell	7	G	1	0	0	0	400
Captian His Due	4	G	12	3	0	2	26,955
Captian Literati	4	G	2	1	0	0	984
Captianmorganbay	2	G	10	0	1	0	3,531
Captilea (IRE)	5	M	13	2	3	3	14,378
Captiva Bay	2	F	2	0	0	0	1,585
Captiva Cat	4	F	1	0	0	0	230
Captivated	3	F	3	0	0	1	7,430
Captivating	2	F	1	0	0	0	0
Captivating Star	3	F	4	0	1	0	5,512
Captive Forcett	4	F	7	0	0	0	240
Captive Lady	2	F	2	0	0	0	505
Captive Sky	5	M	2	0	0	0	150
Capt'nemos	4	C	9	1	1	1	18,426
Capture the Fire	2	F	2	0	0	0	910
Capture the Flight	5	M	4	0	0	0	450
Capture the Purse	2	G	4	0	0	0	960
Capture the Silver	5	H	11	2	0	3	18,730
Capture the Sun	3	F	14	1	3	3	16,695
Capture the Wind	2	G	3	0	0	0	1,575
Capture the Wolf	4	C	9	1	3	1	54,850
Captured	5	G	9	1	1	0	16,185
Capucine	3	F	12	2	1	0	22,301
Capulette (IRE)	4	F	3	0	1	0	7,175
Capwikann	2	C	5	0	0	1	1,525
Car Account	4	G	15	2	1	3	9,700
Car Lady	3	F	1	0	0	0	400
Car Salesman	9	G	5	0	0	0	0
Cara Bella	3	F	3	0	0	0	240
Cara Kitty	3	F	1	0	0	0	164
Cara Veronica	4	F	7	1	2	0	5,634
Carabineer	2	G	5	0	0	2	8,619
Carablanca (COL)	3	C	5	0	0	0	1,940
Caracal Mist	2	G	2	0	0	0	155
Carafar	2	G	4	0	0	0	695
Carah	2	F	1	0	0	0	0
Caramel Prospector	4	F	3	0	0	0	255
Caramel Queen (NZ)	6	M	3	1	1	1	23,850
Caramel's Express	7	G	8	1	0	0	16,185
Caras Lad	4	C	1	0	0	0	160
Cara's Lassie	6	M	5	2	1	0	10,908
Cara's Prince	3	G	4	0	0	0	3,528
Caratofdiamonds	2	C	3	1	0	0	17,340
Carbon Comet	8	G	13	1	3	0	13,217
Carbon Express	2	G	4	0	0	1	2,520
Carbon River	2	F	2	0	0	0	0
Carbonax	5	G	1	0	0	0	0
Carbonera	3	F	8	2	1	0	21,080
Card Game	3	F	8	0	0	1	1,395
Card Sound	6	M	8	3	1	0	29,010
Card Traitor	3	F	15	1	0	1	11,593
Cardanessta	2	F	4	1	0	0	7,707
Carden Road	2	G	5	1	1	1	12,402
Cardhu	2	G	3	0	0	0	3,123
Cardiac Arrest	4	G	1	0	0	0	61
Cardiff Arms	6	G	1	0	0	0	0
Cardiff Beauty	4	F	4	0	0	0	50
Cardinal and Gold	4	G	11	0	4	3	7,302
Cardinal Joe	4	G	15	1	2	3	6,218
Cardinal Rule	3	C	5	0	3	0	25,532
Cardinal Ryan	5	G	5	0	1	0	4,172
Cardinalli	3	F	6	1	1	1	13,630
Cardinal's Echo	4	G	16	1	1	2	8,502
Cardiogenic	11	G	6	1	0	0	4,852
Care Free Lady	8	M	3	0	0	0	531
Careadancer (ARG)	7	G	1	0	0	0	1,050
Career Advantage	7	G	4	1	3	0	9,100
Career Dancer	2	F	1	0	0	0	145
Career Party	5	M	10	2	1	0	7,008
Career Run	4	C	10	3	0	2	41,550
Carefree	7	G	8	1	2	1	9,180
Carefree Jim	5	G	12	3	4	1	46,115
Carefull	5	M	6	0	1	2	4,229
Carefulwhatyouwish	3	F	4	0	0	2	3,660
Careless Candidate	3	G	5	0	1	0	6,800
Careless Dream	4	F	14	1	2	2	12,283
Careless Love	3	F	7	1	1	1	13,802
Careless Navigator	2	G	3	3	0	0	68,520
Careless Ocean	6	M	1	0	0	0	0
Carey's Gold	5	H	16	4	4	1	95,787
Carey's Lil Boy	5	G	13	2	1	6	9,040
Carey's Trouble	4	F	1	0	0	0	0
Carfax Abbey	7	G	8	3	1	1	71,155
Cargi	7	G	7	3	2	0	33,888
Cargo Ship	4	G	9	2	4	1	66,989
Cariano	6	M	3	1	0	0	2,030
Caribbean Code	6	G	3	0	0	0	490
Caribbean Cruiser	2	C	4	3	0	0	228,140
Caribbean Cutie	7	M	6	0	1	1	850
Caribbean Prince	2	C	4	0	0	0	0
Caribbean Storm	4	G	4	0	1	1	3,920
Caribbean Sun	2	F	1	0	0	0	274
Caribben Carnival	8	G	1	0	0	0	0
Caribeno (URU)	5	H	11	1	0	1	8,785
Cariboo Prospector	3	G	10	0	3	3	67,342
Cariel	4	F	2	0	0	0	200
Carillon	3	F	4	0	1	0	3,315
Carina	4	F	7	0	1	2	7,934
Carinoso	5	H	15	2	2	6	9,709
Carisma One	3	G	14	2	2	1	20,582
Carissa's Shine	2	F	3	1	0	0	8,180
Carl	3	G	11	2	0	3	37,667

Horse	Age	Sex	Sts	1st	2d	3d	Won
Carla Mia	2	F	1	0	0	0	0
Carla Rose	4	F	15	4	3	3	85,800
Carla Sparkles	11	M	12	1	0	2	13,611
Carlando	3	G	5	1	0	0	9,360
Carla's Calling	2	F	3	1	0	1	10,600
Carlasrangoruckus	3	F	1	0	0	0	75
Carlea	2	F	2	0	1	0	14,820
Carleana's Secret	3	F	3	0	1	0	5,130
Carley Country	4	G	7	0	0	2	1,165
Carley's Call	4	F	11	3	1	1	14,985
Carleystarlet	5	M	5	1	0	0	15,720
Carline	4	F	5	1	0	1	14,384
Carlingford	6	H	3	0	0	1	200
Carlins Magic Slew	2	F	3	0	0	0	0
Carli's Key	3	G	5	0	1	1	6,670
Carli'silver Prize	4	G	18	2	1	3	9,944
Carlisle	3	F	5	0	0	1	4,941
Carlisle's Tune	2	C	1	0	0	0	405
Carlow	2	F	9	1	0	4	35,105
Carl's Cash	4	G	3	0	0	0	970
Carls Favorite	4	G	12	2	2	0	5,292
Carlson's Queen	2	F	1	0	0	0	118
Carly Pooh	7	M	8	0	1	1	4,300
Carlyn Road	4	F	10	1	1	2	13,310
Carly's a Twin Too	4	F	15	1	2	4	11,236
Carly'ssilvercharm	2	F	8	2	2	1	55,131
Carmaleta Rose	3	F	2	1	0	0	4,560
Carmalley	4	F	6	1	0	1	6,810
Carmandia	2	F	4	1	2	0	44,163
Carmel Swirl	3	F	3	0	1	0	3,500
Carmel Valley Moon	2	F	2	0	0	0	700
Carmelita Kitten	3	F	5	1	1	3	5,740
Carmella	4	F	15	4	3	1	17,740
Carmella Maria	4	F	9	1	1	1	8,950
Carmen Country	6	G	6	1	0	0	2,743
Carmen Rouge	3	F	4	0	0	2	4,750
Carmic Delight	3	F	7	1	0	3	7,205
Carminooch	2	C	5	2	0	1	64,536
Carneros	2	F	6	2	0	1	22,540
Carneros Champ	3	G	2	1	0	0	5,085
Carni Das	4	F	13	4	0	2	40,850
Carnie's Moon	7	M	11	0	3	6	16,388
Carnie's Thunder	5	G	11	2	2	1	16,155
Carnival Hero	3	C	5	0	0	0	0
Carnival Match	6	G	11	0	0	0	690
Carnival Sass	4	F	7	0	0	0	1,883
Carnival Trade	5	G	5	0	0	2	4,170
Carnival World	4	F	2	0	0	0	0
Carno Rebel	2	C	2	0	0	0	555
Carnojosh	2	C	2	0	0	0	1,350
Caro Line Lulu	7	M	2	0	0	0	162
Caroleena	2	F	5	0	0	0	533
Carole's Spirit	5	G	11	5	1	0	25,293
Carolina Act	3	G	8	0	0	0	2,092
Carolina Lily	3	F	2	1	0	0	8,080
Carolina Rose	3	F	8	2	2	1	67,140
Carolina Storm	4	F	12	0	1	4	6,231
Carolina Sunrise	4	F	3	1	0	1	7,017
Carolina Ties	4	F	9	1	1	0	7,770
Carolina's Punch	3	G	10	0	0	2	7,967
Caroline Marie	3	F	3	0	0	0	630
Caroline's Candy	4	F	14	3	2	2	53,180
Caroline's Gold	2	F	4	1	0	2	41,210
Caroline's Morning	5	M	7	0	0	0	1,259
Caroline's Prince	3	G	13	1	2	3	32,937
Carolinia Miner	4	G	8	1	0	0	4,998
Caroller	4	G	20	1	3	2	35,618
Carol's Amore	3	F	1	0	0	0	410
Carol's Choice	6	M	7	1	1	2	9,555
Carol's Country	3	F	2	0	0	0	0
Carol's Hottie	3	G	7	1	0	0	4,101
Carol's Magic	3	C	8	0	0	1	3,960
Carol's Mate	3	C	7	0	1	2	11,339
Carol's Memories	3	F	1	0	0	0	434
Carols Pic	6	G	6	0	0	0	1,220
Carols' Prospect	3	F	8	0	0	0	0
Carolyn Frances	4	F	8	1	2	2	43,740
Carolyn's Birthday	2	F	6	1	0	0	9,511
Carolyns Blazer	3	F	5	0	0	1	1,180
Carolyn's Find	4	F	2	0	0	0	52
Carolyn's Tour	3	G	12	0	0	2	3,274
Carolyns'point	2	F	1	0	0	0	0
Caromon	3	C	2	1	1	0	21,060
Caro's Alley	5	G	7	1	0	0	10,800
Caro's Mark	7	G	5	1	0	0	4,728
Caro's Royalty	11	G	5	0	0	2	4,218
Carouge	3	F	8	0	0	1	1,832
Carouse	5	G	15	3	3	5	36,802
Carpet Slipper	7	M	1	0	0	0	0
Carr de Bon Bon	7	M	1	0	0	0	40
Carr de Dancer	3	F	10	1	5	1	26,064
Carr Fourty Four	6	G	9	0	0	0	1,688
Carr On the Run	4	G	8	1	1	1	5,540
Carr Queen	7	M	10	2	2	1	33,257
Carreau Account	3	C	3	0	0	1	760
Carrforthecourse	8	G	7	0	1	3	1,110
Carribean Gold	4	G	4	0	0	0	847
Carrie Boone	5	M	9	4	1	1	22,751
Carrie Me Back	4	F	21	2	5	1	42,896
Carried Away	9	G	7	3	1	2	45,317
Carried Interest	4	G	8	0	0	0	1,005
Carrie's a Jewel	3	F	6	1	4	0	20,583
Carrie's Luck	3	F	6	1	0	1	3,580
Carrie's Turn	7	M	8	2	0	0	24,783
Carrington	3	G	6	1	0	0	24,608
Carriza Planes	6	M	2	0	0	0	0
Carrizo Springs	5	G	11	1	0	2	5,834
Carrlana	4	F	3	0	0	0	410
Carroll County	3	C	1	1	0	0	18,600
Carrot Gal	6	M	4	0	0	0	270
Carrot Juice	3	G	2	1	0	0	2,970
Carrothers	2	C	5	0	3	2	18,220
Carrots Only	3	G	9	3	1	1	82,660
Carrsonetclaire	3	G	13	2	3	2	24,800
Carrtiff	4	G	3	1	0	1	11,840
Carry Jig	3	G	7	1	0	1	13,515
Carry On Carson	6	H	1	0	0	0	0
Carry the Tune	3	F	3	0	0	0	208
Carson Beach	9	G	6	1	1	0	18,150
Carson City Kid	10	G	17	3	5	2	34,052
Carson City Limits	6	H	3	0	0	0	318
Carson City Star	4	G	6	1	1	0	15,812
Carson Coded	3	G	8	1	1	1	27,755
Carson Cove	4	F	4	1	0	0	24,000
Carson Grove	5	M	1	0	0	0	0
Carson Guy	3	G	9	1	1	1	16,378
Carson Kit	2	F	2	0	0	1	9,690
Carson Unleashed	3	C	14	2	1	4	52,080
Carsonetta	3	F	9	1	1	1	31,436
Carsonic	9	G	3	0	0	0	0
Carson's Angel	2	F	1	0	0	0	363
Carson's Band	2	C	3	0	0	0	734
Carson's Bridge	2	C	2	1	0	0	29,532
Carson's Cat	4	F	4	1	1	0	6,501
Carson's Clover	2	F	3	1	1	0	19,935
Carson's Lady	3	F	3	0	1	0	2,133
Carson's Rumor	3	F	4	0	1	0	1,920
Carson's Star	2	F	5	0	1	1	8,530
Cart Attack	2	G	1	0	0	0	0
Cart Bypass	2	F	5	1	1	0	13,920
Cart San	5	G	8	1	0	2	3,780
Cart Surgin'	2	G	7	0	1	0	7,460
Carta Brava (COL)	4	F	8	0	2	0	6,040
Carta Gold	3	C	1	0	0	0	140
Cartage Agent	3	C	5	0	2	0	18,687
Carte Madera	5	M	9	3	2	0	43,170
Carter and Phillip	3	G	2	0	0	0	0
Carters Boy	5	H	6	2	1	1	16,670
Carters Place	3	G	10	1	0	1	4,610
Carthage	4	G	7	3	1	1	69,570
Cartoon	7	M	11	1	1	1	6,442
Cartoonist	3	C	1	0	0	1	4,600
Cart's Behalf	6	M	3	0	0	0	289
Cart's Big Boy	5	G	8	0	1	2	18,090
Cart's Cash	3	G	12	2	0	2	17,215
Cart's Cutie	3	F	6	0	0	1	825
Carts Forty More	4	G	15	2	1	3	21,299
Cart's Good News	3	F	16	3	2	2	23,883

Horse	Age	Sex	Sts	1st	2d	3d	Won
Cart's Jannie	2	F	4	0	0	1	4,420
Cart's Magic	6	G	3	0	0	0	220
Cart's Main Man	2	G	6	0	0	0	2,460
Cart's Maybe So	3	F	10	4	2	0	58,042
Cart's On Cruise	3	G	8	0	3	0	20,160
Cart's Snappy	6	M	5	1	0	0	8,043
Cart's Turn	2	F	7	2	0	2	48,922
Cart's Upper Crust	5	M	2	0	0	0	138
Carus Is Loose	2	G	3	0	0	0	375
Carwin	3	C	3	0	0	0	690
Cary Creek	4	F	1	0	0	0	88
Cary's Our Man	9	G	13	1	3	1	6,208
Casa Chica	5	G	5	0	1	1	6,410
Casa Libre	3	G	12	1	1	3	52,008
Casa Nekia	3	F	17	4	3	4	63,710
Casadistruggere	3	G	1	0	0	0	400
Casamo	4	G	2	0	1	0	2,575
Casanova Express	2	G	4	0	1	0	5,690
Casanova Red	4	G	2	0	0	0	189
Casanova Slammer	4	G	11	2	1	3	42,450
Casas Caballo	4	C	4	1	0	0	33,600
Cascade Casey	7	G	12	1	1	1	12,467
Cascade Corona	4	F	7	2	1	0	73,510
Cascade County	3	G	2	2	0	0	18,600
Cascade Jack	2	C	1	0	0	0	42
Cascade Lace	4	F	11	3	3	0	7,305
Cascade Range	5	G	8	1	1	3	11,027
Cascadiansasquatch	2	C	4	1	1	0	12,672
Cascanuez (ARG)	4	G	2	0	0	0	800
Cascarina	3	F	6	0	0	1	3,163
Case Charmer	4	G	9	3	2	1	90,761
Case Closer	3	G	2	0	0	0	0
Case Load	6	M	12	4	1	1	38,855
Case Notes	2	C	1	0	0	0	205
Case of Bubbly	3	F	4	0	1	1	14,634
Case of Champagne	5	M	9	0	0	2	2,320
Case of Pride	5	M	11	2	0	2	22,974
Case of Roses	2	C	6	0	0	0	1,120
Case of the Heart	3	F	12	1	3	1	11,100
Case Said	4	F	7	1	0	0	11,465
Case the Ace	3	G	14	2	2	2	24,905
Case Worker	2	G	3	1	1	0	23,840
Cases Surprise	4	F	10	1	1	2	11,175
Casey B	5	G	6	1	1	2	10,847
Casey Belle	3	F	7	2	0	0	12,570
Casey Cobalt	4	G	9	1	1	1	27,695
Casey Darling	3	F	4	0	0	0	910
Casey House	4	C	4	0	0	0	276
Casey Jean	3	F	12	2	0	1	13,470
Casey Jones	3	F	2	1	0	0	14,820
Casey the Cat	3	C	6	1	0	0	2,952
Casey's Bid	5	M	5	0	0	1	1,610
Casey's Biscuit	2	G	5	1	0	2	18,370
Casey's Bluff	4	G	13	0	1	1	3,003
Caseys Case	4	F	7	0	0	0	912
Casey's Castaway	4	C	8	0	1	1	4,600
Casey's Castle	5	G	9	1	0	1	7,625
Casey's Crimson	4	G	12	1	1	0	7,472
Casey's Gold Fever	2	C	4	0	0	1	2,987
Casey's Millie	3	F	14	1	1	2	17,418
Caseys Pride	4	F	5	0	0	0	539
Caseys Storm	3	F	4	0	0	0	0
Cash Attitude	3	C	8	0	1	1	3,270
Cash B. Fast	7	G	9	1	1	0	6,808
Cash Bandit	3	G	6	0	0	1	1,471
Cash Bar	6	G	6	0	0	1	1,485
Cash Broker	3	G	7	0	2	1	8,590
Cash Button	3	C	3	0	0	1	1,170
Cash Career	5	M	13	2	2	1	21,609
Cash Case	4	G	8	3	1	0	40,024
Cash Cheque	3	F	1	0	0	0	0
Cash Collection	2	F	3	0	0	1	450
Cash Commander	3	G	7	1	2	0	22,077
Cash Converter	7	M	9	1	2	2	7,370
Cash Counter	2	F	6	2	0	0	42,555
Cash Creek	4	G	6	1	0	0	3,417
Cash Dancer	3	G	10	2	2	1	35,496
Cash Economy	2	F	2	0	0	0	0
Cash Excess	3	G	5	0	1	1	2,820
Cash Fast	4	F	1	0	0	0	0
Cash Fever	4	F	8	2	2	2	12,325
Cash Forever	3	G	5	1	0	2	3,080
Cash in Hand	5	H	14	0	3	2	9,185
Cash in the Bank	2	G	5	1	2	0	48,620
Cash Instrument	4	F	6	0	1	2	10,301
Cash It Baby	6	M	8	2	2	1	11,740
Cash King	3	C	6	0	0	2	8,205
Cash Marquet	4	G	8	3	0	1	10,185
Cash Me If You Can	2	F	3	0	1	1	1,510
Cash Not Credit	3	G	7	1	0	0	8,985
Cash Performer	3	G	4	0	0	1	3,278
Cash Prospect	6	G	5	2	0	1	10,047
Cash Ransom	4	G	7	3	1	1	18,090
Cash Return	3	G	10	1	0	0	3,022
Cash Reward	7	M	5	1	0	0	7,192
Cash Settlement	2	F	8	2	1	2	31,460
Cash Sweep	3	G	6	0	0	1	4,123
Cash Trap	4	G	8	3	2	0	10,320
Casha Blanca	3	F	3	0	0	0	141
Cashcurestheblues	2	G	2	0	0	0	0
Cashel Calling	3	F	3	0	0	0	720
Cashel Castle	5	H	1	0	0	0	3,600
Cashfromnaevus	6	G	9	0	0	1	1,325
Cashier's Wager	5	M	5	0	1	3	8,640
Cashing Tickets	2	F	4	0	1	1	9,320
Cashisgoodasmoney	3	G	1	0	0	0	400
Cashlan (IRE)	4	C	8	1	0	0	6,330
Cashman	6	H	3	0	0	0	0
Cashmere and Silk	4	F	11	0	2	1	13,190
Cashmere Carly	2	F	2	0	0	0	700
Cashmere Kelly	2	F	4	0	0	2	1,700
Cashmere Lady	3	F	4	1	1	0	4,361
Cashmere Miss	4	F	10	2	1	3	119,057
Cashmula	2	C	4	0	0	3	18,700
Cash's Dynamite	3	F	11	1	3	0	12,025
Casimir (IRE)	8	G	15	4	4	1	18,626
Casing the Raw Bar	3	F	10	0	2	0	4,802
Casino Casey	4	G	6	1	0	0	9,320
Casino Diva	3	F	9	1	2	0	29,090
Casino Knight	4	G	7	1	0	0	9,987
Casino Miss	3	F	2	0	0	0	882
Casino Orton	2	C	1	0	0	1	3,553
Casino Princess	3	F	10	1	1	1	6,200
Casino Raider	6	G	11	4	0	0	50,571
Casino Rebel	3	G	6	0	0	0	942
Casino Red	4	C	7	1	0	3	37,810
Casino Sting	4	F	4	0	0	0	0
Casino Wager	4	C	16	1	1	0	11,456
Casmon	2	C	3	0	1	0	5,750
Casper Peterson	4	C	10	3	3	0	112,430
Casperino	4	G	9	1	2	3	58,872
Casperius See	6	G	9	0	0	2	5,595
Cassa Della	3	F	2	0	0	1	1,245
Cassaforte	5	G	5	0	0	0	1,027
Cassanova Kid	3	G	11	2	6	2	30,276
Cassanova Mitch	5	G	9	0	0	0	485
Cassa's Affair	4	F	6	1	2	1	14,149
Cassas Mark	2	C	7	0	0	1	2,385
Cassette Case	2	F	3	1	0	2	33,100
Cassette Dancer	4	G	4	1	0	2	8,911
Cassidy County	2	F	5	1	0	2	12,682
Cassidy Jean	4	F	3	0	0	0	0
Cassidy Loves You	4	G	11	2	1	0	26,678
Cassidy Princess	4	F	9	2	2	0	23,211
Cassidy's Cat	4	F	10	1	2	0	7,085
Cassie Cat	5	M	9	1	1	0	7,207
Cassie Erin	6	M	5	0	0	0	0
Cassie the Martyr	3	F	12	2	2	0	12,073
Cassie the Slewor	4	F	3	0	0	0	224
Cassie Vanish	4	F	9	0	0	0	240
Cassie's Boy	4	G	2	0	0	0	0
Cassie's Casper	7	G	13	3	1	1	33,727
Cassies Quiet	3	F	9	0	3	1	7,890
Cassique	3	G	6	0	1	1	5,095
Cassirer (IRE)	5	G	5	0	0	0	1,500
Cassopolis	4	F	10	0	2	3	11,480
Cassy's Star	3	G	2	0	0	0	280
Cast No Shadow	2	C	7	1	0	4	18,591

Horse	Age	Sex	Sts	1st	2d	3d	Won
Cast of Gold	5	G	7	2	1	2	9,154
Castelli's Ace	4	F	12	2	2	3	32,918
Castelli's Gypsy	4	F	12	2	2	0	15,600
Castello Bianco	4	C	3	1	0	1	7,130
Castello d'Oro	2	G	1	0	0	1	2,640
Castilian	5	G	1	0	0	0	63
Castillonis	6	G	5	1	1	0	7,273
Casting Sun	4	G	11	0	0	0	768
Castle Back	8	G	17	1	0	3	10,115
Castle Concert	3	C	4	0	0	0	1,940
Castle Crane	9	G	6	0	0	0	467
Castle Dark	4	G	5	0	0	1	1,116
Castle Gandolfo	5	H	1	0	0	0	380
Castle Heights	3	C	9	1	2	3	56,880
Castle Hill	3	G	2	1	0	0	15,900
Castle Knight	3	G	5	0	0	1	450
Castle Prospect	2	C	5	1	1	1	64,213
Castle Rock	6	G	8	1	3	0	7,690
Castlebridge	3	G	10	0	0	0	1,710
Castledale (IRE)	3	C	3	1	0	0	450,000
Castlegate	3	G	2	1	0	0	7,192
Castletown	5	G	8	0	0	0	646
Castlevali	2	C	2	0	0	0	0
Castlewood	7	G	5	1	0	1	7,560
Castner	5	G	10	2	0	0	7,664
Castor Troy (IRE)	4	G	5	1	0	0	30,400
Casu	6	M	4	0	0	0	279
Casual Attitude	4	F	9	3	2	2	100,406
Casual Cash	2	G	4	0	0	1	2,940
Casual Cat	3	G	1	0	0	1	2,860
Casual Country	6	G	4	1	0	2	7,940
Casual Dance	4	F	3	0	0	0	247
Casual Fashion	3	F	8	1	0	3	19,100
Casual Gold	4	C	5	0	0	0	92
Casual Thunder	5	G	4	0	1	2	21,500
Casually Urbane	7	G	16	0	6	1	12,695
Casualy Explosive	4	F	16	1	2	3	9,916
Cat a Cold Eye	2	G	2	0	0	1	2,320
Cat Albert	3	G	2	0	0	0	90
Cat Alert	4	F	6	3	3	0	120,360
Cat Ante	5	G	11	1	2	5	54,265
Cat At Dawn	3	C	5	1	1	0	8,545
Cat Babu	7	G	11	0	0	0	795
Cat Ballew	4	G	6	0	1	2	2,604
Cat Box	3	G	2	0	0	1	1,650
Cat Buster	3	C	6	2	1	1	72,315
Cat Carson	3	F	5	2	0	1	64,040
Cat Choo	4	F	8	1	2	1	16,170
Cat Connection	3	G	15	2	3	3	16,396
Cat Creek	9	M	1	0	0	0	0
Cat Creek Christy	5	M	6	0	1	0	2,205
Cat Crossing	5	M	3	2	1	0	10,260
Cat Crusher	5	H	11	2	1	2	26,950
Cat Express	5	G	9	1	0	0	15,636
Cat Face	3	F	11	3	2	0	19,396
Cat Factor	2	C	2	0	1	0	5,750
Cat Fighter	4	F	5	1	1	3	206,060
Cat Genius	4	C	9	2	3	1	211,280
Cat Girls Love	7	M	9	0	0	2	2,311
Cat Gotcha	4	G	1	0	0	0	0
Cat Gun	3	G	10	0	1	2	5,307
Cat in Deed	4	F	9	2	2	0	15,759
Cat in the Box	2	F	2	0	1	0	5,840
Cat in the Country	4	G	15	0	1	2	5,011
Cat in the Nat	5	M	9	0	1	2	8,515
Cat Jumper	4	F	9	1	1	0	6,200
Cat Leader	2	G	3	0	0	0	405
Cat Line	4	C	2	0	0	0	415
Cat Looker	5	G	7	1	2	0	4,764
Cat Lover	4	F	13	0	1	2	4,140
Cat Man	2	C	5	0	2	1	8,105
Cat Miss	2	F	3	0	0	0	552
Cat Mommy	2	F	6	0	0	0	1,140
Cat Music	3	F	16	1	1	5	22,426
Cat 'n Cadoodle	2	F	9	1	0	0	6,396
Cat N Dolls	2	F	3	0	0	1	1,044
Cat n' Mouse	5	M	4	0	0	0	223
Cat Navigator	3	C	12	3	0	1	22,110
Cat Nippin	3	F	9	0	0	1	3,394
Cat of the Future	3	G	11	1	0	3	18,077
Cat of Tomorrow	3	G	12	2	1	1	22,130
Cat On a Rail	3	C	1	1	0	0	24,600
Cat On a Ridge	2	C	2	1	0	0	17,160
Cat On a Wire	2	C	3	0	0	0	720
Cat On the Grass	4	G	13	2	2	2	40,140
Cat On the Move	3	G	5	1	0	0	3,897
Cat Out of the Bag	2	G	3	0	0	0	845
Cat Pass	3	G	7	1	0	0	4,952
Cat Patrol	4	C	7	0	2	2	25,460
Cat Rig	3	F	1	0	0	0	0
Cat Robber	2	C	2	1	0	0	22,600
Cat Royal	5	M	2	0	0	0	0
Cat Ruckus	4	F	3	1	0	1	7,476
Cat Scratch	3	F	14	1	0	1	10,923
Cat Shaker	2	C	5	1	0	1	19,915
Cat Singer	4	G	9	2	2	2	97,350
Cat Sound	3	C	10	1	1	4	14,119
Cat Story	4	G	5	0	0	0	2,710
Cat Striker	3	G	11	1	3	1	51,751
Cat Tap	4	C	2	0	0	0	557
Cat Tide	2	G	4	0	0	1	2,150
Cat Time	5	G	10	0	0	1	1,328
Cat Tourn	2	C	7	4	0	1	71,028
Cat Toy	5	G	4	0	0	0	2,605
Cat Tracker	6	G	4	1	2	1	39,580
Cat Tracks	6	G	4	0	1	0	921
Cat Trina D.	4	F	11	1	2	2	5,306
Cat Tuesday	2	G	3	0	0	2	4,109
Cat Walkin	6	H	3	0	0	0	0
Cat Woman	5	M	12	2	0	2	20,613
Catabatic Wind	5	G	5	1	2	0	7,590
Catachip	2	F	3	1	0	1	36,120
Catahoula Blue	4	F	13	1	3	2	13,133
Catahoula Hope	4	F	5	1	0	1	21,615
Catahoula Huff	4	G	1	0	0	0	0
Catahoula Mister	3	G	2	0	1	0	6,180
Catahoula Otis	4	G	3	0	0	0	310
Catahoula Rose	6	M	9	0	0	0	11,652
Catahoula Sweetpea	4	F	6	0	0	0	983
Catale Shine	3	F	6	1	2	1	6,016
Catalina Bay	4	F	1	0	0	0	96
Catalina Cat	4	F	8	0	2	0	20,050
Catalinas Spell	3	F	6	0	0	0	491
Catalindy	3	F	3	1	0	0	30,780
Catalissa	4	G	7	2	1	0	63,380
Catalog	7	H	2	0	0	0	450
Catalone	4	G	9	3	2	1	55,303
Catalyze	4	G	5	0	0	0	210
Cataman	3	G	6	1	1	1	16,935
Catamongus	5	M	9	1	2	1	2,146
Catana	2	F	3	1	0	0	17,640
Cataria	3	F	14	1	5	1	66,960
Catarina Dorata	2	F	1	1	0	0	19,860
Catasauqua	5	G	4	0	0	0	525
Catascatcan	3	C	4	0	2	1	17,160
Catastrophe Cat	3	C	3	0	0	0	270
Catawhompus	5	G	8	1	2	2	11,146
Catbird Seat	6	G	1	0	0	0	0
Catbite	5	G	2	1	0	1	5,390
Catblewbyu	2	F	1	0	0	1	2,400
Catboat	3	F	12	6	3	1	184,598
Catcantscratchit	3	C	7	2	1	1	23,018
Catch a Diamond	2	G	2	1	1	0	7,206
Catch a Dream	7	G	11	0	3	3	28,756
Catch a Fire	4	F	5	1	0	1	38,028
Catch a Fox	5	H	4	0	0	0	600
Catch a Hoolie	3	F	2	0	0	0	0
Catch a Leprechaun	5	H	9	1	2	1	17,230
Catch a Parade	3	G	13	3	0	5	15,809
Catch a Wink	2	G	5	0	1	0	2,887
Catch a Winner	4	F	3	0	1	0	4,740
Catch Bullets	5	G	7	1	2	1	8,840
Catch Catch Can	4	F	4	0	1	0	3,573
Catch Confide	3	F	2	0	0	0	210
Catch Crafty	2	C	2	0	0	0	0
Catch Elvis	3	G	3	0	0	0	878
Catch Me	2	C	4	1	0	1	19,755
Catch Me Eye	6	M	9	0	0	1	5,082

Horse	Age	Sex	Sts	1st	2d	3d	Won
Catch Me First	4	G	9	3	1	0	36,630
Catch My Cat	3	G	10	3	0	4	78,096
Catch My Ice	4	G	9	1	2	3	5,389
Catch On	3	G	6	1	1	1	5,298
Catch Shorty	2	G	6	0	0	0	375
Catch Simon	4	C	7	0	1	2	10,550
Catch That Tiger	2	F	1	0	0	0	300
Catch the Bullet	3	F	8	2	0	1	20,868
Catch the Devil	2	F	1	0	0	0	135
Catch the Dew	7	G	11	4	3	0	51,200
Catch the Glory	3	C	8	2	1	1	74,580
Catch the Joy	3	F	1	0	0	0	400
Catch the Storm	3	G	11	2	0	2	14,954
Catch the Sun	6	G	2	0	0	0	89
Catch This Bird	6	M	3	0	1	0	2,652
Catch This Coin	3	F	6	0	1	0	2,174
Catch This Jokar	6	G	1	0	0	0	76
Catchaluckystar	4	F	8	0	0	0	682
Catchaser	6	M	3	0	0	1	1,600
Catchatune	3	G	7	2	1	1	37,140
Catch'em All	6	G	12	0	1	3	5,208
Catcher in the Hay	5	G	2	0	0	0	0
Catchin Some Rays	5	M	11	0	3	1	12,890
Catchin' Z's	4	F	3	0	0	1	2,164
Catching Fire	5	H	6	0	0	0	165
Catching Up	4	G	5	0	1	0	902
Catchula	3	G	1	0	0	0	80
Catchum	4	G	9	1	1	1	9,131
Catchy Expression	2	C	1	0	0	0	274
Catchy Music	4	F	1	0	0	0	0
Catchy Phrase	5	H	1	0	0	0	0
Catchy Word (GB)	7	G	3	0	0	0	180
Catchyounextime	3	F	8	0	5	0	25,935
Catechol	7	H	9	0	0	2	18,888
Category Kat	3	G	16	2	3	2	14,501
Category One	2	F	5	0	2	0	8,665
Cater to Sarah	3	F	1	0	0	0	0
Cateress	5	M	4	1	2	0	21,030
Caterette	3	F	8	1	1	1	13,740
Caterin	3	F	2	0	0	0	289
Caterwal	3	G	5	0	2	2	2,115
Caterwauling On	6	M	2	0	0	0	72
Cate's My Angel	5	M	9	1	0	0	13,430
Catessa	4	F	8	1	0	3	48,230
Catessence	4	F	2	0	0	0	183
Catfish Alley	4	F	7	0	1	2	9,661
Catfish Junction	8	H	9	0	0	1	1,650
Catgia	3	F	4	1	0	1	3,400
Cathay West	3	F	4	0	0	0	0
Cathedral Friend	7	G	6	0	1	3	6,620
Cathedral Knight	3	G	12	1	2	0	28,119
Cathedral Tower	9	G	13	0	1	3	3,715
Catherine Again	2	F	2	0	0	0	192
Cathouse Saint	2	F	5	1	0	1	20,120
Cathrine Marie	4	F	10	4	1	1	14,984
Cathy Dear	5	M	2	0	0	0	0
Cathy the Great	4	F	3	0	0	0	174
Cathy's Bright	2	F	3	0	0	2	6,556
Cathy's Choice	2	F	5	0	1	0	10,948
Cathy's Condo	7	M	9	1	2	2	17,368
Cathy's Dream	5	M	3	0	0	0	465
Cathy's Gold	3	F	9	1	0	1	17,970
Cathy's Luck	3	G	2	0	0	0	0
Cathy's Star	6	M	4	0	0	1	1,920
Catilexus	4	F	1	0	0	0	0
Catillac Style	4	C	6	0	0	1	1,181
Catillacsandlevis	4	F	10	3	0	2	43,137
Cativa	4	F	5	3	1	1	99,500
Catjur	4	F	16	2	1	3	12,343
Catlaan	3	F	10	3	2	4	82,790
Catlaunch	3	C	13	3	2	2	29,988
Catlett Comet	8	G	11	3	1	0	61,735
Catlike Dancer	4	F	7	4	1	0	53,180
Catlike Move	5	G	11	2	3	2	83,540
Catmaker	2	F	1	0	0	0	112
Catmansdream	4	G	16	0	4	2	13,250
Catmeifyoucan	2	C	7	2	2	0	39,820
Catmobile	6	G	4	0	0	0	130
Cat'n Around	4	G	1	0	0	0	75
Catnabout	5	M	15	2	2	3	31,805
Catnamedadam	3	F	12	1	2	1	9,720
Catness	3	C	4	0	0	2	1,968
Catniro	7	H	9	3	0	1	54,047
Catnour	2	G	1	0	0	0	600
Catomize	5	M	3	0	0	0	0
Catonia	2	F	2	1	0	0	15,430
Catonie Time	3	G	5	0	1	2	5,608
Caton's Banner	5	M	10	0	0	0	738
Caton's Crown	5	G	3	0	0	0	29
Caton's Promise	3	F	1	0	0	0	130
Catpasser	5	G	11	2	4	0	13,478
Catquit	2	C	1	0	0	0	720
Catrageous	3	C	5	0	0	1	1,360
Catriona	3	F	1	0	0	0	0
Cat's a Prowler	3	C	9	1	0	1	8,434
Cat's a Rockin	2	C	3	1	0	0	4,500
Cat's Account	3	F	5	1	0	1	29,850
Cat's At Bat	4	C	2	0	0	0	0
Cats Beauty	4	G	7	0	0	0	2,335
Cats Cafe	3	F	4	0	0	0	0
Cat's Cat	4	F	11	0	5	1	78,015
Cat's Child	2	C	1	0	0	0	155
Cats' Claws	4	C	9	1	1	0	5,191
Cats Copy	3	F	9	4	1	0	105,458
Cat's Craft	4	G	15	2	4	0	17,758
Cat's Cyclone	3	G	4	0	0	0	206
Cat's Dorthy	2	F	2	0	0	0	0
Cat's Forty	2	F	3	0	1	0	2,500
Cats Fury	5	G	12	0	2	1	7,095
Cat's Gambol	5	G	15	3	4	1	38,130
Cat's Glow	5	M	1	0	0	0	1,900
Cat's Hot	3	G	15	2	2	1	12,046
Cat's Lad	2	C	1	0	0	0	2,050
Cat's Luck	3	G	5	0	0	0	252
Cat's Mark	3	G	2	0	0	0	188
Cats Menow	3	F	3	0	0	0	164
Cat's Revenge	3	C	4	0	1	1	11,005
Cat's Roar	3	F	8	2	2	3	105,440
Cats Rule	3	F	10	3	1	1	20,957
Cat's Secret	3	F	1	0	0	0	1,200
Cat's Theme	5	M	9	2	1	3	23,364
Cat's Touch	4	G	11	2	3	3	9,160
Cats Tower	4	F	12	1	4	1	50,520
Cats Unlimited	3	G	3	1	0	0	2,722
Cat's Way Home	2	C	1	0	0	0	0
Catscape	4	G	14	3	2	1	19,990
Catsgotninelives	3	G	7	0	3	1	38,000
Cat'sladykaytelyn	2	F	2	0	1	0	1,400
Cat'sshootingstar	3	G	4	3	0	0	14,310
Catsuit	4	F	4	0	1	0	6,380
Catsure	4	C	14	1	0	0	7,460
Cattail Lake	2	G	1	0	0	0	100
Catticus	3	G	15	2	5	1	27,260
Cattle Drive	2	G	5	2	0	1	12,025
Cattleman Prospect	3	G	11	3	5	0	74,109
Cattleya	3	F	9	0	2	3	18,880
Cattolica	3	F	19	0	1	2	5,295
Catty Laddie	4	G	19	2	1	1	13,590
Catvantageous	7	G	1	0	0	0	330
Catwalk Lake	2	G	2	0	0	0	2,705
Catwalker	2	F	1	0	0	0	0
Catwillcatchyou	5	M	7	0	0	2	2,010
Catza	2	F	5	1	1	1	9,230
Catzinga	4	F	10	4	3	0	55,444
Catzzene	6	M	13	0	0	4	10,606
Caublu	10	H	1	0	0	0	0
Caucus	4	F	1	0	0	0	2,215
Caught a Slew	6	M	7	0	0	1	2,122
Caught Heart	2	G	1	0	0	0	400
Caught in the Act	3	F	5	0	0	0	6,030
Caught In The Dark (GB)	4	F	12	1	2	2	24,405
Caught in the Rain	5	M	10	3	0	2	138,820
Caught in Traffic	2	C	1	0	0	0	78
Caught You Running	4	G	8	0	1	0	2,716
Caught'n	5	H	6	1	0	0	1,888
Cause for Concern	4	F	4	1	0	0	8,400
Cause I'm a Rebel	4	G	11	0	3	2	10,004
Cause I'm Fancy	4	F	4	0	0	1	2,525

Horse	Age	Sex	Sts	1st	2d	3d	Won
Cause of Action	3	G	15	1	6	2	44,139
Causeimacajun	6	G	8	0	1	1	4,770
Causetic Fuhr	3	G	5	1	0	0	5,520
Caustic	4	G	9	1	0	0	1,307
Caustic Fusion	2	G	5	0	0	2	7,484
Caution Beware	5	G	8	0	0	2	9,127
Cautions	4	G	11	0	2	0	3,401
Cauy	6	M	2	0	0	0	0
Cauzican	3	G	4	0	0	1	1,815
Cavalia	2	G	4	0	0	0	2,982
Cavalier Billie	5	M	7	1	0	1	39,728
Cavallo Grigio	4	F	10	1	2	1	20,190
Cavallo Nero	4	G	6	1	0	2	3,924
Cavalry Charge	2	C	1	0	0	1	4,680
Cavans Lane	3	G	7	1	1	0	42,780
Cave Creek Chrissy	3	F	1	0	0	0	0
Cave Creek Queen	5	M	9	5	3	1	33,172
Cave Hill	6	G	18	2	3	4	27,539
Cave Man	2	G	4	0	0	0	1,020
Caveats Prospect	5	G	12	2	2	2	30,003
Cavecreek Blitz	5	H	3	0	0	1	695
Caviar Emptor	4	F	7	1	2	0	37,290
Cavista	3	F	9	0	0	1	2,733
Cavort	5	G	1	0	0	0	0
Cayce Lady	2	F	3	1	1	0	19,550
Cayenne Call	5	G	13	0	0	1	10,525
Cayenne Carny	2	F	4	0	0	2	2,180
Cayenne Gold	5	G	2	0	0	0	129
Cayenne Red	3	G	11	7	2	1	113,458
Cayerless and Bold	4	G	13	1	2	3	33,612
Cayerless and Hot	3	F	3	0	0	2	4,555
Cayman Gold	3	F	4	1	0	0	4,800
Caymus	6	G	11	0	0	1	3,335
Cayoke (FR)	7	H	9	3	2	2	186,780
Cayuga's Waters	2	F	2	0	1	0	8,564
Cazadotes	4	G	11	1	1	2	9,440
Ce Fitzrovia	3	F	4	0	0	0	2,420
Cearamic	10	G	9	0	0	1	3,430
Ceara's Gold	2	F	4	0	0	1	1,061
Ceasar's Fate	4	G	6	1	2	0	12,300
Ceasar's Ghost	4	G	12	2	7	2	19,063
Cease Span	5	M	2	1	0	0	13,200
Ceba	3	F	1	1	0	0	7,980
Cebolla Miss	2	F	1	0	0	0	0
Cecelia Rose	4	F	4	2	0	1	54,693
Cecil County	5	G	10	2	0	0	18,070
Cecilia's Girl	5	M	5	0	0	0	3,301
Cedar	3	F	11	0	2	4	19,794
Cedar and Satin	4	F	5	0	0	0	1,140
Cedar Cliff	2	F	1	0	1	0	3,360
Cedar Dream	4	F	2	0	0	0	278
Cedar Key	4	G	10	2	0	2	27,525
Cedar Point	3	G	4	1	0	0	14,600
Cedar River	2	G	8	1	0	5	20,744
Cedar River Bill	5	G	10	3	0	1	13,604
Cedar Runs Case	5	M	4	1	1	0	25,110
Cedar Slew	3	F	9	0	0	2	5,694
Cedar Smiles	2	F	9	1	2	2	31,756
Cedar Summer	3	F	10	1	0	3	39,210
Cedar Top	4	G	6	0	0	0	1,071
Cee Cruiser	4	G	3	0	0	0	492
Cee Dee Riverkamm	3	G	6	0	0	0	1,745
Cee E T Sing	6	G	3	0	0	0	576
Cee El	5	G	13	2	1	3	32,695
Cee Mister B	3	C	7	2	2	0	87,620
Cee Rose	3	F	9	1	2	1	9,930
Cee Senor Cuzzin	3	G	2	0	0	0	142
Cee Tees Comanche	4	F	3	0	0	1	1,630
Cee the Devil	2	C	2	0	0	1	2,727
Cee the Lead	5	M	1	1	0	0	1,540
Cee Till Dawn	5	G	5	1	0	1	7,895
Ceecat	3	F	3	1	0	0	4,875
Ceecee's Wilddance	3	F	4	0	0	1	1,546
Ceecil	4	G	8	1	1	2	10,213
Ceedie Pop	6	G	11	0	0	1	1,869
Ceehawk	6	M	10	1	3	3	18,153
Ceelinctive	5	G	10	1	3	1	12,547
Ceely's Classic	5	M	6	1	1	0	20,766
Cee's a Flirt	3	F	11	2	1	3	15,546

Horse	Age	Sex	Sts	1st	2d	3d	Won
Cee's a Lady	4	F	8	1	3	1	14,285
Cee's a Tart	3	F	3	0	0	0	800
Cee's Assert	3	G	7	1	0	0	3,840
Cee's Bloomer	3	F	3	0	0	0	1,100
Cee's Cheetah	4	G	10	3	4	0	23,917
Cee's Dude	6	G	8	2	1	0	4,820
Cee's Irish	2	F	5	2	2	0	93,960
Cee's Madness	4	G	10	1	2	1	2,706
Cee's Marfa	9	G	6	0	0	1	920
Cee's the Moment	4	F	12	1	1	4	23,721
Cee's the Point	2	C	3	1	2	0	36,200
Ceesharp	6	G	2	0	0	0	0
Ceetart	4	G	9	2	3	2	17,164
Ceetoit	9	G	1	0	0	0	52
Cee'z the Dream	4	F	9	6	0	0	9,460
Ceez the Minute	3	G	9	6	0	1	89,077
Ceiling Zero	2	G	1	0	0	0	235
Celcius Slew	4	C	7	2	1	0	31,142
Celebrate the Sun	4	F	15	2	4	2	17,340
Celebrated Anna	3	F	1	0	0	0	0
Celebrated Danz	3	C	2	0	0	0	139
Celebration Time	3	G	2	0	0	0	225
Celebrity Alert	6	H	6	0	0	1	3,421
Celebrity Girl	3	F	13	1	0	0	6,994
Celebrity Lass	2	F	4	0	0	1	4,000
Celebrity Tip	3	G	4	0	0	0	900
Celebs Boy	5	G	3	0	0	1	2,002
Celera	5	H	12	0	1	3	9,290
Celerity Slew	5	M	5	0	1	1	2,246
Celestia	2	F	1	0	0	0	1,200
Celestial Harmony	4	F	4	0	0	0	255
Celestial Light	5	M	5	1	1	0	6,331
Celestial Moment	5	M	17	1	1	2	10,605
Celestial Prince	4	G	12	0	1	2	2,914
Celestial Sea	6	M	14	2	2	4	17,339
Celestial Star	3	F	8	2	2	2	53,405
Celestialbutterfly	8	M	4	0	0	0	800
Celestine's Swivet	3	F	5	1	0	2	8,949
Celestino D	5	G	3	0	1	0	2,398
Celia Fate	3	F	4	0	2	1	17,540
Celiac	4	F	10	0	0	0	670
Cella Luna	3	F	5	0	1	1	13,489
Cellars Merlot	6	G	11	1	3	1	23,440
Cellars Shiraz	5	M	4	0	0	1	8,000
Cells Bells	5	M	4	0	0	0	2,460
Cellular Call	7	G	1	0	0	0	50
Cellular Joe	8	G	8	0	1	0	4,050
Cellular Sarah	2	F	3	0	0	2	3,454
Celona's Girl	7	M	2	1	1	0	6,000
Celophane Man	3	G	13	3	1	0	25,280
Celosita Mag (ARG)	5	M	19	4	1	1	40,878
Celt	5	G	6	1	0	2	21,705
Celtic Approval	5	G	8	1	1	1	17,030
Celtic County	4	G	4	1	0	0	5,115
Celtic Dance	7	M	11	2	0	0	14,862
Celtic Duchess	3	F	5	0	2	1	13,850
Celtic Eclipse	4	F	12	3	4	2	22,987
Celtic Innis	2	G	3	1	1	1	20,590
Celtic Isle	2	C	6	0	0	1	2,785
Celtic Jet	6	M	5	0	0	0	552
Celtic King	7	G	7	2	0	2	8,936
Celtic Memories	4	G	9	1	4	2	83,560
Celtic Mojo	3	C	4	0	2	2	20,220
Celtic Moon	6	M	5	0	2	0	2,766
Celtic Note	5	H	2	0	0	0	0
Celtic Park	5	H	2	0	1	0	2,500
Celtic Rhapsody	4	F	3	0	0	0	1,470
Celtic Ride	4	F	8	1	1	1	55,670
Celtic Sky	6	H	6	1	0	1	39,243
Celtic Smoke	7	M	11	1	1	1	21,370
Celtic Spirit	4	F	1	0	0	0	40
Celtic Sword (ARG)	5	G	1	0	1	0	9,400
Celtic Tune	4	F	2	0	0	0	0
Cent T Mint	3	F	14	0	4	4	13,067
Centaur Chiron	3	F	2	0	0	0	76
Centauress's Witch	11	G	6	0	0	1	550
Centcom	3	C	7	1	1	2	16,665
Center	5	G	8	1	4	1	24,906
Center Court Jon	3	G	12	1	1	2	9,895

Horse	Age	Sex	Sts	1st	2d	3d	Won
Center Line	4	G	13	2	1	1	34,170
Center Point Blaze	7	M	8	2	1	0	9,730
Center Seven	4	F	9	1	3	1	6,674
Center Stage Honey	2	F	5	1	0	2	18,960
Centerfold Queen	4	F	3	0	0	0	0
Centerofattraction	3	F	3	0	0	0	0
Centerton Miss	4	F	17	0	0	0	3,030
Central	2	F	4	0	0	0	145
Central Market	3	G	11	2	1	0	10,803
Cents Who	2	F	7	1	3	0	22,060
Centsability	5	M	1	0	0	0	274
Centsible Slew	4	G	12	2	2	2	6,197
Centsible Wager	5	M	12	1	0	5	5,176
Centurian Man	7	H	1	0	0	0	65
Centurion	12	G	3	1	0	1	4,310
Century Boulevard	3	G	5	0	0	1	1,804
Century Mark	4	F	3	0	0	1	1,438
Cepharonious	4	G	3	1	0	0	5,302
Cepheus Star	2	C	6	3	0	1	44,100
Cercatore	2	F	2	0	2	0	10,310
Ceremonial	4	F	4	0	1	1	6,376
Ceremony	3	F	11	4	3	1	30,745
Cercse Sunrise	4	F	8	1	3	0	27,480
Certain Act	4	G	11	0	3	1	20,460
Certain Lady	3	F	10	2	1	4	24,260
Certain Party	2	F	4	0	0	0	280
Certainly a Dilly	5	G	11	2	3	1	38,803
Certainly Appealin	3	G	13	1	1	3	11,673
Certainly Can	5	M	11	1	1	0	15,150
Certainly Regal	3	F	4	1	1	1	20,520
Certam Swecp	4	G	7	0	0	0	4,330
Certantee	7	G	1	0	1	0	5,600
Certickie	3	C	1	1	0	0	7,070
Certifiably Crazy	4	G	10	1	6	1	144,729
Certification	4	G	4	0	1	0	2,250
Certified Approval	6	M	6	0	0	0	1,115
Certified Coin	7	G	4	0	2	0	1,790
Certified Fact	3	G	2	1	0	0	2,608
Certify	5	G	11	0	3	2	9,059
Certitude	3	F	13	0	3	1	15,320
Cerulean	5	M	3	1	1	0	4,300
Cerulean Moon	2	G	6	2	0	1	30,580
Cervelo	3	C	12	2	4	0	82,570
Cerveza Lite	2	F	2	0	0	0	750
Cerveza Tom	4	G	10	0	1	3	14,450
Cervoise (ARG)	7	M	3	0	0	0	750
C'Est Lulu	5	M	4	0	1	1	4,960
Cetewayo	10	H	1	0	0	0	0
Ceviche	6	G	16	0	2	3	12,675
Ceyenne Ranchero	3	C	5	0	0	0	955
Cf Sparks a Flying	6	M	2	1	1	0	7,166
Cf Valentine Wins	2	G	1	0	0	0	396
Cha Cha Chaffee	3	F	4	2	0	0	10,764
Cha Cha Hedy	10	M	3	0	0	0	450
Cha Cha Kita	3	F	3	1	1	0	7,380
Chablis	2	F	3	0	0	0	1,370
Chachacharlie	3	C	8	4	0	0	73,896
Chaching Chaching	4	G	1	0	0	0	82
Chaco	4	F	12	0	2	2	4,653
Chad	5	G	3	0	0	0	235
Chad Counted	4	G	13	1	3	3	22,010
Chaddy Jon Jon	5	G	20	1	5	2	12,924
Chad's Best	3	G	13	0	0	2	2,637
Chad's Boy R C T	3	G	16	4	4	2	27,144
Chad's Hope	4	C	4	0	0	0	5,322
Chadwicks Well (IRE)	5	G	10	2	1	0	21,045
Chadychadybangbang	4	G	2	0	0	0	0
Chaffed Lips	3	F	3	0	1	0	2,320
Chaffery	4	G	9	0	0	0	1,227
Chain	5	G	9	2	1	2	32,544
Chain Blue	5	M	1	0	0	0	1,225
Chain Dancer	2	G	2	0	1	0	3,600
Chain Letter	7	M	1	0	0	0	0
Chain Lightning	6	G	5	0	1	0	4,970
Chain of Miracles	3	C	7	1	1	2	20,000
Chain Reprisal	6	G	9	1	3	2	21,546
Chairman Bob	4	G	14	2	1	1	19,323
Chairman Cella	6	G	20	3	3	5	35,996
Chairman of Vice	4	G	3	0	0	0	189
Chairman's Agenda	3	F	3	0	1	0	6,400
Chakalaka Baby	3	F	10	1	0	0	8,300
Chalas Cliper	6	G	3	0	0	0	661
Chalas Hunter	4	G	1	0	0	0	0
Chalet Chanteuse	3	F	10	3	2	0	38,195
Chalifioux	5	M	9	4	1	3	25,540
Chalkaholic	4	G	6	0	0	2	2,349
Chalkalot Hill	3	F	6	0	2	0	1,525
Chalkolotte	3	C	2	0	0	0	800
Challenge Cole	3	G	10	1	0	1	11,270
Challenge Did It	4	G	6	0	3	1	8,405
Challenge Seven	6	G	1	0	0	0	84
Chamaco	5	G	6	1	0	0	18,700
Chambers Creek	4	C	1	0	0	1	190
Chameleon	4	G	12	1	3	5	55,060
Chami Q Too	3	F	4	1	1	0	7,721
Chamine	2	F	2	0	0	0	482
Chamoix	5	M	6	2	0	0	9,091
Champagne Account	4	C	6	1	1	0	25,530
Champagne Billy	4	G	8	0	0	1	6,780
Champagne Brunch	2	C	6	2	0	2	41,810
Champagne Cocktail	3	F	4	1	1	1	59,117
Champagne Day	6	G	12	3	2	0	26,823
Champagne Doll	5	M	8	1	1	1	14,495
Champagne Dream	2	F	3	0	0	1	4,954
Champagne Ending	2	F	3	0	1	0	9,778
Champagne Girl	2	F	8	3	0	0	36,130
Champagne Glade	3	F	2	0	1	1	2,940
Champagne Man	3	G	3	0	0	1	2,040
Champagne Mountain	7	G	11	1	3	4	6,817
Champagne 'n Stars	6	G	7	1	1	1	1,615
Champagne Now	3	F	15	1	3	1	21,211
Champagne Punch	4	F	11	0	3	1	22,849
Champagne Reed	3	G	13	0	0	0	1,252
Champagne Rep	7	M	4	0	0	0	0
Champagne Rose	2	F	3	0	0	0	1,350
Champagne Royale	3	F	2	1	1	0	16,240
Champagne Shimmer	5	M	7	0	0	0	1,045
Champagne Slew	4	C	8	1	1	0	7,038
Champagne Star	3	F	7	1	4	0	16,746
Champagne Summer	4	F	7	1	0	0	17,076
Champagne Toast	3	F	11	0	1	0	2,353
Champagne Velvet	5	M	4	0	1	0	1,337
Champagne Way	5	G	3	0	0	0	0
Champagneandlace	4	F	8	0	0	2	2,387
Champagnecelebrity	4	F	9	0	0	0	0
Champagneforalydar	6	G	4	0	0	1	550
Champagneforcarly	6	M	1	0	0	0	0
Champagneforshelby	7	M	14	3	3	2	20,666
Champagneforwilbur	5	G	3	0	0	0	0
Champagnencashmere	4	F	12	4	0	4	37,724
Champagne's Reddy	3	G	6	1	1	1	17,930
Champagns Holiday	5	G	5	0	0	1	1,775
Champaign Powder	5	M	14	3	3	1	44,570
Champaign Rush	3	C	7	1	2	0	24,350
Champali	4	C	8	4	1	1	634,398
Champange Bottle	2	F	4	1	0	0	7,500
Champchu	2	G	1	0	0	0	118
Champie G	7	G	11	0	0	0	3,097
Champignon Du Bois	5	G	9	1	0	0	9,754
Champion Bones	4	G	7	0	3	3	7,620
Champion Proof	4	F	7	1	2	0	19,796
Champion Ri	4	C	5	1	0	1	32,610
Champ's Amour	6	G	15	2	0	1	9,739
Champ's Ole'	4	F	6	1	0	1	13,680
Champ's Rocket	3	F	12	3	2	4	92,000
Chamrousse	5	M	3	1	1	0	30,020
Chan Chan	5	H	4	0	1	0	9,380
Chance Aire	6	G	8	0	1	0	1,195
Chance America	4	G	7	1	4	1	23,025
Chance Anew	9	G	9	2	0	1	7,129
Chance Arrest	5	M	8	2	1	1	9,966
Chance Dance	4	F	14	7	3	3	303,125
Chance Five	2	C	1	0	0	1	1,622
Chance for Us	2	F	8	2	1	2	56,194
Chance Kyl	7	G	8	4	3	1	16,502
Chance of War	3	G	4	1	0	1	26,360
Chance 'ola	4	C	9	1	3	3	13,330
Chance to Dance	4	G	17	3	2	4	58,112

RECORDS OF HORSES

Horse	Age	Sex	Sts	1st	2d	3d	Won
Chanceamillion	4	C	4	0	0	0	708
Chancefordiamonds	3	F	7	1	1	1	5,912
Chancellor M. H.	7	G	2	0	0	0	0
Chancenalex	2	C	2	0	0	0	525
Chances Chiquitin	4	G	6	0	0	0	208
Chance's Domain	4	F	8	0	0	1	4,745
Chanceux Vous	2	C	4	1	1	1	39,450
Chancey Light	3	F	12	1	3	0	32,835
Chanchala	2	F	4	0	0	0	840
Chancier	3	F	3	0	0	0	378
Chancy Chancy	4	F	5	0	0	3	3,450
Chancy Toss	5	M	4	0	0	0	140
Chandler Brooks	5	G	11	1	1	0	3,654
Chandler Cup (ARG)	6	G	13	0	4	4	36,190
Chandler's Midge	4	G	16	2	2	2	20,686
Chandlersthename	5	M	17	3	3	1	13,898
Chandrika	5	M	14	1	1	2	16,316
Chandtrue	2	C	4	4	0	0	182,970
Chanel Islands	3	F	9	2	1	1	36,060
Chanelly's Dancer	3	F	10	0	1	2	3,999
Chanels Star	3	F	7	1	3	2	8,284
Chanel's Valentine	4	C	2	0	0	1	1,705
Change Course	4	C	8	3	1	1	79,758
Change Me	7	M	5	0	0	0	206
Change of Fortune	3	F	7	0	0	0	1,025
Change of Plans	5	G	5	0	0	1	294
Change the Record	5	G	11	1	3	2	36,630
Change the Tude	4	G	6	0	0	2	4,305
Changer	5	H	6	1	0	2	4,970
Changesinlattitude	4	F	7	4	1	1	9,563
Changing Gears	3	F	3	0	0	0	50
Changing Light	6	G	11	0	4	1	16,890
Changing Times	5	G	4	0	0	0	1,398
Changing World	4	F	4	2	0	1	168,500
Channa's Beau	3	C	2	0	0	0	0
Channel Fire	6	M	3	0	0	0	450
Channel Lock	3	F	1	0	0	0	450
Channing Way	6	M	8	1	1	3	72,857
Chanseydancer	4	F	4	0	0	0	402
Chant for Gold	2	C	3	1	0	1	36,160
Chantilly Creek	2	F	1	0	0	0	0
Chantilly Lad	9	G	3	0	1	0	600
Chantilly Light	3	F	13	2	2	2	32,820
Chantilly Philly	5	M	7	1	0	1	11,700
Chantre	4	F	12	1	2	1	9,756
Chantz	4	G	5	1	0	1	5,085
Chaos	5	M	5	1	3	0	27,018
Chaos Theory	4	F	9	1	2	0	6,396
Chaotic Achiever	3	G	2	2	0	0	12,600
Chaotica	4	G	16	1	2	2	13,343
Chapeau	5	M	5	1	0	1	42,640
Chapel Gold	3	C	9	0	0	1	3,066
Chapel Hill	10	G	5	0	1	0	881
Chapel Lass	2	F	3	1	0	0	8,592
Chapel Lites	5	M	7	1	1	0	6,838
Chapel Ridge	2	G	3	1	0	1	7,062
Chapel Ring	3	G	9	0	1	2	3,702
Chapel Road	5	M	9	2	3	0	33,844
Chapel Royal	3	C	2	0	0	0	10,816
Chapelbelle	3	F	7	0	0	0	1,131
Chaperlaro	4	G	18	1	2	2	8,376
Chapie	10	G	6	0	1	0	3,321
Chapilkim	5	M	13	1	1	1	21,750
Chaposa	3	F	5	1	0	1	12,520
Chapter and Verse	3	G	1	0	0	1	1,575
Char	5	G	15	2	2	4	24,887
Char Beans	3	F	4	0	1	1	5,040
Char Da Valley	6	M	12	2	1	4	8,204
Character Actor	3	G	16	1	2	6	22,737
Character Builder	2	F	2	0	0	0	1,230
Character Witness	4	G	2	0	0	0	1,980
Characterize	2	G	1	0	0	1	2,640
Charade	3	F	8	1	2	1	19,803
Charade Event	2	G	8	0	2	1	13,280
Charannhar	3	C	5	0	1	0	12,820
Charbar	4	G	9	0	1	2	5,805
Charbonnier	3	G	3	0	0	0	4,000
Charcoal Bin	7	G	11	3	1	0	16,269
Charcoal Canyon	5	M	18	0	5	4	13,899
Charcoal Portrait	4	G	6	0	0	0	75
Charcot	3	C	14	1	2	4	35,059
Chard Black	3	G	2	0	0	0	0
Chardonay's Beau	6	G	7	0	0	2	1,050
Charge	4	C	4	1	0	0	35,970
Charge Ahead	3	C	4	0	0	0	540
Charge and Send	5	M	16	5	3	5	38,155
Charge Back	3	G	2	0	0	0	0
Charge n' Reason	5	G	14	2	0	0	9,763
Charged Circuit	5	G	7	2	1	0	2,714
Charged Up	4	G	19	2	2	4	25,136
Charged Up Taco	10	G	11	2	1	3	6,667
Chargeitplease	3	F	2	0	0	2	3,080
Chargeittothegame	3	F	8	1	0	2	10,441
Charger's Diamond	6	H	1	0	0	0	0
Charger's Haymaker	5	H	3	0	0	0	330
Charging	2	F	3	1	1	1	8,100
Charging Current	4	C	6	1	1	0	13,805
Charging Too	2	G	1	0	0	0	140
Chargins On J	2	G	2	1	0	0	7,563
Charian	3	F	4	0	0	1	3,538
Charimount	2	C	6	0	0	1	5,052
Chariot	6	H	5	0	2	0	4,450
Charioteer	5	H	9	0	3	0	13,462
Charisantley	2	C	4	0	0	0	1,036
Charismagic	2	F	2	0	0	0	0
Charismatic Appeal	3	F	11	4	1	1	92,081
Charismatic Caller	3	C	11	1	3	3	33,560
Charismatic Katy	2	F	1	0	0	0	140
Charismatic Kid	3	G	7	1	1	0	18,000
Charismatic Lady	4	F	1	0	0	0	460
Charismatic Rob	3	G	9	0	0	0	7,187
Charismatic Storm	2	F	1	0	0	0	114
Charismatic's Gift	3	G	6	0	0	1	3,080
Charity Gal	5	M	10	0	0	0	2,440
Charity Girl	3	F	2	0	0	1	5,470
Charity Line	7	G	1	1	0	0	6,612
Charity Man	4	G	6	1	0	0	6,135
Charity's Snowball	4	G	9	0	0	2	1,418
Charla Begone	4	F	12	0	0	1	2,064
Charla's Norm	3	F	10	2	0	3	8,005
Charlee Chop Chop	3	F	7	1	0	1	2,235
Charleen's Remark	9	M	12	2	1	1	4,505
Charlenesuperblend	3	F	7	4	1	0	67,600
Charles	5	G	3	0	0	0	2,750
Charles B.	4	G	1	0	0	0	80
Charles County	2	G	1	0	0	0	0
Charles Harbor	4	G	11	2	2	3	44,500
Charleston Cathy	4	F	10	2	2	2	19,258
Charleton	6	G	1	0	0	0	0
Charlevoix	3	G	4	1	0	1	31,345
Charley B	3	F	1	0	0	0	0
Charley's Bailey	3	F	9	2	1	1	14,746
Charley's Ensign	4	C	9	2	0	2	22,676
Charley's Love	4	G	5	0	0	0	315
Charlie Bill	3	C	9	3	2	1	48,405
Charlie Broads	3	C	2	0	1	1	4,050
Charlie Cartwright	2	C	1	0	0	0	600
Charlie Choo Choo	2	G	4	0	0	1	870
Charlie Go Bear	4	G	3	0	0	0	375
Charlie Haan	6	G	11	2	1	1	18,914
Charlie Horst	6	G	12	1	0	1	5,856
Charlie Lambert	8	H	10	1	3	1	6,097
Charlie Man	9	G	3	0	0	0	0
Charlie Moloney	2	G	3	0	0	0	1,690
Charlie My Boy	2	F	11	3	4	0	43,740
Charlie Papa	3	F	13	4	4	1	41,851
Charlie Pit	3	G	10	0	0	4	2,345
Charlie Riddell	5	G	13	1	5	2	27,490
Charlie Waller	6	G	12	0	0	0	794
Charlie Whiskey	4	G	11	1	0	3	32,170
Charlies Bandito	4	G	4	0	0	0	0
Charlie's Beau	7	H	3	0	0	0	294
Charlie's Bullet	3	G	8	2	0	0	14,805
Charlie's Charmer	4	F	11	1	1	4	16,492
Charlies Cook	5	M	6	0	0	1	640
Charlie's Dewan	12	G	1	0	0	0	900
Charlies Good Girl	5	M	10	2	0	2	29,220
Charlies Indian	4	F	8	4	2	2	66,249

Horse	Age	Sex	Sts	1st	2d	3d	Won
Charlie's Meadow	3	F	6	1	3	0	25,995
Charliesfavorite	4	C	2	0	0	0	0
Charlize	3	F	6	1	0	1	18,095
Charlomaine	3	F	14	2	2	2	47,050
Charlotte Bay	3	F	10	2	2	1	23,060
Charlotte Forever	6	M	11	2	4	0	49,820
Charlotte Jones	4	F	3	0	0	0	481
Charlottenburgh	2	F	1	0	0	0	0
Charlotteohara	2	F	4	1	0	0	10,103
Charlottes Find	8	M	8	4	1	0	25,457
Charlottes Website	2	F	3	0	0	1	2,005
Charlston Blue	7	H	3	0	0	0	752
Charm Attack	5	G	10	1	3	1	14,404
Charm Away	3	F	9	1	1	2	15,293
Charm Boy	4	G	3	0	0	0	200
Charm Cat	3	C	4	1	1	0	17,040
Charm City	4	G	2	0	2	0	10,080
Charm My Heart	2	F	8	2	1	2	37,807
Charm My Socks Off	2	F	5	0	0	1	4,870
Charm Seeker	4	C	2	0	0	0	0
Charm the Angels	5	M	12	3	0	2	13,694
Charm the Giant (IRE)	2	F	1	0	0	0	700
Charmane J.	3	F	14	2	2	1	18,375
Charmd N Dangerous	3	F	5	0	0	1	1,272
Charmed Again	3	F	11	0	3	1	18,390
Charmed All Theway	4	C	2	0	0	0	0
Charmed Flight	4	G	5	0	1	0	2,600
Charmed Invader	2	G	3	0	0	0	100
Charmeleon	6	G	16	1	2	4	6,475
Charmer Baron	4	G	1	0	0	0	0
Charmer Jim	3	C	11	2	0	1	17,022
Charmer Mac	3	G	19	2	1	1	13,260
Charmico	6	G	3	0	0	0	0
Charmie	5	M	5	0	0	0	255
Charmie's Secret	4	F	7	2	1	1	17,015
Charmin' Lil	4	F	3	0	0	0	630
Charmin' Middling	4	G	2	0	0	0	195
Charmin Prince	2	C	1	0	0	1	2,915
Charmin' Romeo	3	G	3	0	0	0	1,075
Charmin' Wizard	4	G	3	0	0	0	250
Charming Alex	4	G	9	0	1	1	5,245
Charming Allcome	3	F	5	0	0	1	1,156
Charming Attiude	5	M	15	2	2	2	26,800
Charming Bid	4	F	8	2	1	1	47,080
Charming Boy	3	C	5	0	0	0	1,816
Charming Boy (ARG)	8	G	9	3	1	1	62,720
Charming Charlie	3	C	4	1	0	0	627
Charming Cherokee	4	F	6	0	0	1	2,340
Charming Clover	4	F	11	0	1	0	4,633
Charming Colleen	2	F	5	2	2	0	69,113
Charming Colony	5	G	11	1	2	1	11,181
Charming Eileen	2	F	1	0	0	0	2,100
Charming Eyes	8	G	4	0	1	1	2,468
Charming Hero	6	G	4	0	0	0	478
Charming Home	7	G	9	2	0	3	6,840
Charming Hope	8	G	8	0	1	0	1,925
Charming Humor	3	F	3	2	0	0	46,685
Charming Janie	2	F	2	0	1	0	3,600
Charming Jim	3	G	13	2	3	2	70,630
Charming John	4	G	11	1	4	2	21,218
Charming Jones	2	F	6	1	0	2	11,030
Charming Kelly	8	M	2	0	0	0	188
Charming Knight	5	M	8	1	0	0	5,262
Charming Lass	7	M	1	0	0	0	61
Charming Naskra	8	G	2	0	0	0	812
Charming Pat	3	F	1	0	0	0	0
Charming Playboy	4	C	2	0	0	0	125
Charming Proposal	3	F	9	2	1	1	83,286
Charming Robber	4	C	4	0	1	0	2,116
Charming Royalty	5	M	5	3	0	2	13,430
Charming Ruckus	2	F	4	1	2	0	52,160
Charming Ruler	5	G	4	0	0	0	0
Charming Sammy	4	C	11	1	1	1	10,030
Charming Silver	3	C	4	0	0	1	616
Charming Socialite	3	G	18	6	4	2	152,210
Charming Star	6	G	4	0	0	0	0
Charming Trieste	2	C	1	0	0	0	0
Charmonix	3	G	1	0	0	0	0
Charmopoly	3	C	5	0	1	1	6,120
Charm's Love	3	G	13	0	0	2	4,040
Charm's Lucky Lady	5	M	6	2	0	0	22,104
Charmsil	2	F	1	0	0	0	1,260
Charolais	5	G	2	0	0	1	1,040
Charrua's Hill (ARG)	6	G	8	0	0	0	6,020
Char's Bob'n Robin	5	G	14	6	2	1	74,937
Char's Still Here	3	F	10	2	3	3	47,620
Chartwell	8	G	10	0	0	1	2,974
Chase a Star	6	M	13	1	1	3	21,495
Chase Creek	4	G	13	2	3	0	20,687
Chase Express	5	G	14	1	1	1	5,552
Chase Gap	5	M	9	0	4	0	31,675
Chase the Charmer	4	F	18	3	2	1	26,855
Chase the Sauce	3	F	7	0	0	0	278
Chase to Victory	5	H	3	0	0	0	280
Chaseafallenstar	5	M	8	1	2	2	14,065
Chase'n Cammie	5	M	12	0	0	0	1,966
Chasenclay	2	F	1	0	0	0	0
Chasenthebluesaway	3	F	5	1	0	0	9,400
Chaser	6	H	1	0	0	0	0
Chaserville	9	G	6	1	2	1	2,025
Chases Comet	3	G	9	2	0	0	10,350
Chasestripransom	2	F	1	0	0	0	0
Chasethegold	4	F	5	2	1	0	73,000
Chaseur	3	C	4	0	1	0	8,900
Chasin' Chasan	2	F	2	0	0	1	5,560
Chasin the Wind	2	G	3	1	0	1	8,050
Chasing a Dream	8	M	10	1	1	3	2,461
Chasing Amy	3	F	5	1	1	1	24,455
Chasing September	4	F	2	0	0	0	550
Chasing Shadows	7	G	9	0	0	0	1,082
Chasing Skirts	4	G	9	1	0	0	3,024
Chasing Stanley	5	G	4	1	0	0	17,664
Chasing the Fox	2	G	7	1	2	1	58,166
Chasing the Ghosts	3	G	10	1	1	1	11,840
Chasing Yield	2	F	1	0	0	0	2,050
Chasity's Hurdler	2	F	4	0	0	1	1,914
Chasmo	5	G	11	0	1	3	8,246
Chasnick	6	G	14	2	0	3	8,294
Chasseur's Tresor	8	G	10	2	1	2	15,275
Chassis	4	G	11	1	1	2	19,459
Chaste Fondness	4	F	5	1	0	3	5,446
Chasteen's Reward	7	G	3	0	0	0	1,200
Chaster	8	M	8	1	3	1	15,908
Chat Man	4	G	10	1	2	2	22,760
Chataquos' Chance	4	G	6	2	1	1	19,604
Chateau	2	G	5	1	0	2	26,343
Chateau Haut Brion	3	G	5	1	0	0	16,330
Chateau Lady	4	F	5	0	1	0	797
Chateau Neuf	6	H	5	1	1	0	7,577
Chatelian	3	F	3	2	0	0	19,226
Chateux	2	C	2	0	1	0	4,200
Chatham Strait	2	C	5	0	0	0	1,183
Chattabucktoo	3	G	10	1	4	0	15,031
Chattahoochee War	2	C	2	1	0	0	29,400
Chattanooga Red	5	G	1	0	0	0	340
Chatter Chatter	3	F	3	0	0	0	10,470
Chatter Fox	5	M	5	0	1	1	1,443
Chatterbox Miss	3	F	12	0	0	1	5,061
Chattonugachoochoo	5	G	5	1	1	0	10,710
Chaud	3	F	1	0	0	0	750
Chauffe Au Rouge	8	G	8	1	1	1	12,735
Chaun Michael	5	G	7	0	0	0	75
Chauncey	3	G	6	1	1	1	40,120
Chautaqua Gal	3	F	7	0	0	1	2,677
Chautauqua	5	M	1	0	0	0	865
Chautauqua Native	7	G	7	0	2	2	1,374
Chaya	4	F	4	0	0	2	8,220
Chazmandu	2	C	8	1	3	1	36,010
Che Canela	2	F	1	0	0	0	220
Che Papusa (COL)	3	F	1	0	0	0	0
Cheadles	4	C	1	0	0	0	130
Cheap But Classy	3	F	5	1	0	0	6,480
Cheap Charlie	8	G	2	0	2	0	6,940
Cheap Justice	3	C	9	1	2	0	16,752
Cheap Talk	5	G	2	0	0	0	0
Cheap Talk N Wine	3	G	9	2	2	1	10,584
Cheaperthansandee	4	G	8	1	0	1	11,320
Cheapertokeepher	3	F	6	1	2	0	16,300

Horse	Age	Sex	Sts	1st	2d	3d	Won
Cheat the Sea	3	F	9	2	1	1	13,375
Cheata Passer	2	F	8	1	2	1	26,795
Cheater Lady	3	F	2	0	0	0	1,348
Cheatin Charlie	5	G	6	1	0	0	7,037
Cheatin N Fibbin	4	G	13	0	2	3	2,168
Cheatinsideoftown	2	G	2	1	0	0	28,080
Check and Go	5	G	5	1	0	1	3,420
Check Bouncer	4	G	16	2	2	2	15,995
Check by Check	5	G	12	1	0	1	4,835
Check Her Out	5	M	14	1	4	1	16,046
Check It	4	G	5	0	0	0	103
Check My Luck	4	G	4	0	0	0	1,302
Check Station	3	G	12	1	2	1	17,300
Check the Gate	2	C	5	0	0	0	1,742
Check This Out	6	M	4	0	0	0	200
Check Ya Later	2	F	5	0	1	0	1,995
Checker Flag	3	C	1	0	0	0	0
Checker Sue	4	F	7	0	2	1	14,228
Checking In	4	F	8	0	0	0	601
Checking Out Early	5	M	2	0	0	0	237
Checkmynumber	4	F	12	1	2	2	5,970
Checkthisgroove	4	F	4	0	0	1	5,040
Checotah Cat	10	G	13	1	3	4	12,711
Checotah Cowboy	4	G	9	0	0	1	1,162
Checotah Dee	8	G	4	0	0	0	70
Checotah Move	5	G	6	1	0	0	1,636
Cheddar	4	C	19	1	2	3	21,945
Cheechako	5	G	11	2	0	0	7,764
Cheek Trick	2	F	4	0	1	0	2,378
Cheeky Miss	6	M	2	0	0	0	144
Cheer for Molly	7	M	8	0	3	0	3,300
Cheer Girl	2	F	4	1	0	1	19,500
Cheer the Heroes	2	F	2	0	1	0	3,300
Cheer the Score	4	G	12	3	1	2	19,387
Cheerful	2	F	2	0	1	1	13,500
Cheerful Bag	4	F	15	2	5	4	64,629
Cheerful Cookie	5	H	12	0	0	3	1,452
Cheering Thy Name	2	G	1	0	0	0	0
Cheer's Echo	2	F	6	2	0	1	13,130
Cheers O'Glory	3	G	2	0	0	0	600
Cheersto Glory	4	G	2	0	0	0	0
Cheery Hour	3	G	4	1	0	1	5,367
Cheery One	4	F	4	0	0	0	886
Cheese Puff	4	F	13	1	4	2	8,767
Cheeta Is Coming	3	F	4	0	0	0	0
Cheetah Reta	5	M	4	1	0	0	3,435
Cheetah Speed	3	G	7	1	0	2	36,227
Chef Bear	5	G	3	0	0	0	1,650
Chef Du Jour	3	G	6	0	3	0	18,517
Chef Lauren View	5	G	10	0	1	4	6,945
Chef Vittorina	5	M	11	0	0	1	1,718
Chef's Choice	6	M	10	0	2	0	39,749
Chehalis	6	G	8	4	1	0	6,497
Cheiron	3	C	9	3	1	0	293,822
Cheirourgos	6	G	7	2	2	1	4,895
Chekhov	2	C	1	0	1	0	10,000
Cheko	2	G	2	0	1	0	1,650
Chelcee's Delight	4	F	4	0	0	1	525
Chelea	7	M	1	0	0	0	43
Chelino	3	C	4	0	1	1	3,885
Chelopech	2	F	4	1	0	1	20,297
Chelsea B	10	M	1	0	0	0	0
Chelsea Chick	2	F	1	0	0	0	60
Chelsea Revenge	3	F	3	0	0	1	3,322
Chelsea Rose	3	F	1	1	0	0	11,400
Chelsea's Gold	4	F	7	0	2	3	12,680
Chelsea's Grey Boy	2	G	4	0	0	2	3,740
Chelsea's Pearl	3	F	2	0	0	0	0
Chelsey Charmer	4	F	11	2	2	1	9,727
Chelsey's Bid	3	F	9	4	0	0	51,000
Chelsey's Dyna Sea	4	G	11	0	6	1	23,135
Chelyan	3	G	11	3	2	2	87,200
Chemistry	3	F	11	0	2	1	13,724
Chemistry Class	3	G	11	1	3	1	86,803
Chemold	3	G	6	0	1	4	11,485
Chemstone	4	G	22	0	0	1	4,249
Chene Rouge	3	F	11	2	2	2	56,720
Chenia	3	F	7	3	0	0	58,295
Chenier Tigre	2	C	3	0	0	0	0
Chepa	2	F	2	0	0	0	400
Chephron	11	G	2	0	0	0	68
Chepo Star	6	G	2	0	1	0	1,575
Chepper	3	F	9	5	0	1	45,665
Cheq's a Comin	3	G	10	0	0	2	3,135
Cheque Marqe	3	G	16	5	2	2	70,260
Cheque Out Kristen	4	F	12	1	0	1	3,729
Cheque the Green	3	F	9	0	0	0	544
Chequer Account	4	F	14	1	0	1	4,543
Chequered Love	5	M	8	2	1	0	47,215
Chequer'out	5	M	14	2	1	1	12,757
Chequerticket	3	F	9	0	0	0	80
Cher Chateau	3	F	9	1	1	2	5,494
Cherbourg	3	C	2	1	0	0	4,440
Cherie's Digger	4	G	7	0	4	2	10,690
Cheris' Dancer	6	M	8	3	2	0	33,585
Cheris' Jet	4	F	9	2	1	1	19,552
Cheris' Prospect	7	H	3	0	0	0	375
Cheris' Star	4	G	1	0	0	0	218
Cherish Destiny	3	F	6	2	0	0	66,043
Cherish Me	2	F	3	0	0	0	605
Cherish the Groom	3	F	7	0	1	0	1,428
Cherished Bid	3	F	4	0	1	0	5,860
Cherishing Duke	5	M	1	0	0	0	0
Cheriton	4	F	1	0	0	0	0
Cherniavsky	3	C	2	1	1	0	20,900
Cherokee Act	4	F	8	2	2	1	15,670
Cherokee Ambush	3	G	3	0	0	0	0
Cherokee Babe	5	M	10	4	1	1	16,384
Cherokee Benge	3	C	4	0	0	1	4,840
Cherokee Charge	4	G	8	2	0	0	6,018
Cherokee Charlie	3	G	7	3	0	0	19,250
Cherokee Chase	2	G	9	2	0	3	79,890
Cherokee Chief	2	C	6	1	0	2	35,695
Cherokee Chocktaw	6	G	3	0	0	0	0
Cherokee Dancer	2	C	2	0	0	1	6,270
Cherokee Dash	6	G	9	0	3	2	15,652
Cherokee Eyes	2	F	5	0	1	0	8,205
Cherokee Fighter	5	H	5	0	0	2	9,440
Cherokee Flower	2	F	2	0	0	1	3,220
Cherokee Honor	5	H	9	1	0	1	19,550
Cherokee King	4	G	2	0	0	0	0
Cherokee Lee	4	G	9	1	0	1	11,630
Cherokee Lite	4	F	5	0	0	1	13,191
Cherokee Lover	6	H	1	0	0	1	1,810
Cherokee Magic	3	G	3	0	0	0	1,035
Cherokee Park	4	C	3	1	0	0	2,620
Cherokee Path	2	C	5	2	0	0	98,365
Cherokee Play	3	F	9	0	0	1	3,965
Cherokee Prince	4	G	3	0	0	1	5,690
Cherokee Prospect	7	H	10	4	3	1	57,120
Cherokee Raid	9	G	9	1	2	4	2,618
Cherokee Rap	3	C	10	3	3	1	121,440
Cherokee Sauce	6	G	4	0	1	0	3,555
Cherokee Scout	3	F	10	1	1	1	14,530
Cherokee Secret	3	C	6	0	0	0	180
Cherokee Sky	4	F	15	1	2	4	17,509
Cherokee Spires	2	F	4	2	0	0	37,440
Cherokee Spook	3	C	9	1	3	1	59,422
Cherokee Trail	5	H	1	0	0	0	72
Cherokee Tyger	2	C	2	0	1	0	1,266
Cherokee Warrior	2	C	1	0	0	0	130
Cherokee Wine	5	G	12	0	0	2	2,026
Cherokee Women	3	F	13	3	2	2	38,440
Cherokee World	5	G	5	0	0	0	840
Cherokeeinthehills	7	G	8	2	3	0	155,438
Cherokee's Boy	4	C	13	3	3	3	144,407
Cherokee's Disco	4	F	6	2	0	0	38,700
Cherokee's Moment	3	F	1	0	1	0	1,600
Cheroo	8	M	2	0	0	0	120
Cheroot	3	C	3	0	0	0	880
Cherri Knight	5	M	11	1	3	0	9,800
Cherry Bank	2	F	2	1	0	0	7,673
Cherry Blend	5	M	3	0	0	0	0
Cherry Bomb	3	F	4	2	1	0	65,091
Cherry Bombshell	3	F	3	0	0	0	400
Cherry Chassie	2	F	1	0	0	0	235
Cherry Festival	7	M	9	0	1	1	2,220
Cherry Gold	3	F	1	0	0	0	1,590

Horse	Age	Sex	Sts	1st	2d	3d	Won
Cherry Grove	2	F	1	0	1	0	3,690
Cherry Lifesaver	3	F	5	2	0	1	13,345
Cherry Martini	5	M	1	1	0	0	1,010
Cherry On Top	6	G	12	0	1	0	3,290
Cherry Pickings	7	G	6	2	0	0	103,890
Cherry Pie	5	M	9	1	2	0	15,044
Cherry Point Girl	3	F	2	0	0	1	1,335
Cherry Slerp	4	G	2	0	0	0	0
Cherry Springs	3	F	3	0	0	1	2,250
Cherry Street Gal	7	M	5	1	0	0	3,670
Cherry Tree Hill	6	M	2	0	0	1	5,850
Cherryblossomroad	3	F	4	0	0	0	420
Cherrys Crane	5	G	5	0	0	0	80
Cherry's Hunter	3	F	6	2	1	0	63,924
Cherrywood Lover	2	F	9	1	0	1	7,158
Chervil Centaur	4	F	8	0	1	1	3,084
Cheryl Again Again	4	F	12	1	3	0	10,600
Cheryl's Cookie	3	F	3	0	0	0	750
Cheryl's Myth	4	F	13	0	2	4	32,485
Cherylville Slew	5	M	12	4	4	0	152,000
Chesapeake Charlii	6	G	1	0	0	0	45
Chesney Carolina	5	M	13	2	2	1	17,674
Chess Play	3	F	8	1	1	1	5,282
Chessie's Hero	4	G	5	0	0	1	1,420
Chester Dillion	2	C	4	0	0	0	340
Chester River	3	G	9	1	2	1	20,810
Chester Street	4	G	5	1	1	1	10,536
Chester's Best	2	C	1	0	1	0	5,200
Chester's Chance	3	G	6	1	1	0	30,580
Chester's Choice	4	C	3	0	2	0	20,800
Chestnut Anna	3	F	3	0	0	0	134
Chestnut Lane	3	C	1	0	0	0	0
Chestnut Tree	6	M	2	0	0	0	0
Chet	2	C	6	1	0	0	7,490
Chet Minty	3	G	7	1	0	0	4,118
Chetak (IRE)	4	F	5	0	0	1	6,640
Chev d'Or	2	G	6	1	0	1	14,179
Chev Emblem	4	G	9	2	1	1	13,296
Cheval de Joi	3	F	4	1	0	2	6,380
Chevalier Bay	5	M	1	0	0	0	318
Chevaux	6	M	10	3	1	1	62,726
Chevaux d'Or	4	G	23	1	3	3	27,200
Chevello Creek	4	G	3	0	0	0	476
Cheverly Gold	4	C	5	1	2	0	23,480
Chevis	3	G	8	2	0	0	21,500
Chevron Fleet	5	G	7	2	0	1	3,189
Chex	4	G	13	4	0	2	13,072
Chey	3	F	1	0	0	0	0
Chey Mandolin	3	F	11	0	4	1	7,095
Cheyenne Breeze	5	G	11	6	2	0	134,204
Cheyenne Lil	4	F	5	0	4	0	7,140
Cheyenne Night	6	G	9	0	1	0	1,751
Cheyenne Owl Woman	3	F	7	0	0	0	724
Cheyenne Rocket	2	F	2	0	0	0	140
Cheyenne Sister	3	F	2	0	0	0	105
Cheyenne Spring	4	G	9	1	1	0	37,076
Cheyenne's Big Boy	3	C	4	0	0	1	1,065
Chez Audra	4	F	15	3	1	3	87,790
Chez Black	4	C	8	1	0	0	7,473
Chez Blanc	4	C	3	0	0	0	0
Chi Cat	5	G	11	2	1	0	36,800
Chi O Queen	6	M	10	1	1	1	7,218
Chi Town	3	G	6	1	0	2	12,760
Chi Town Slew	4	F	9	2	1	0	20,280
Chiacchierone	3	F	5	1	1	0	15,790
Chiave	4	G	12	0	4	1	9,678
Chiawa	4	F	2	0	0	0	86
Chic Called Sue	5	M	1	0	0	0	0
Chic Dancer	3	F	6	2	1	0	34,600
Chic Domestique	5	M	4	0	1	1	7,325
Chic Girl	2	F	2	0	0	0	264
Chic Joy	4	F	6	0	2	0	20,090
Chic On the Take	5	M	7	1	0	1	5,619
Chic Princess	6	M	2	0	0	0	0
Chic Thief	2	F	1	0	0	0	145
Chicago Al	3	G	4	0	0	0	0
Chicago Bill	2	C	5	0	0	0	2,850
Chicago Gold	3	G	5	0	1	0	2,775
Chicago Joe	6	G	2	1	0	1	3,375
Chicago Love	4	F	1	0	0	0	60
Chicago Rock	5	G	3	0	1	1	3,594
Chicago Sky	2	C	2	0	0	0	240
Chicago's Girl	4	F	14	6	3	1	77,108
Chicamun Jett	5	G	10	0	0	3	2,988
Chick Fever	5	G	12	1	5	1	24,982
Chicka Hermosa	5	M	6	3	2	0	26,360
Chickadee Creek	6	M	13	1	2	2	10,620
Chickamauga Trail	7	H	10	3	1	1	15,609
Chickamonkey	3	F	5	0	0	0	1,595
Chickaroo	4	G	17	3	2	3	24,220
Chicken Casserole	3	F	2	0	0	0	0
Chicken George	5	H	5	0	1	0	2,400
Chicken Little	4	F	6	1	1	1	10,267
Chicken Soup Kid	4	C	8	1	2	0	31,610
Chicken Tracks	5	M	2	0	0	2	1,795
Chickenpotpie	2	F	2	1	0	0	7,200
Chickie	6	M	6	0	0	1	819
Chick's Frat Boy	5	G	15	1	2	1	21,062
Chick's Hope	7	M	11	2	2	3	9,233
Chickster	3	G	4	1	0	0	13,280
Chicky Poo	4	F	4	2	2	0	18,138
Chicolot	3	F	5	0	0	0	1,416
Chico's Gold	5	G	6	1	1	2	5,072
Chidester Rules	11	G	3	0	0	0	245
Chief Arias	10	G	3	0	0	1	1,612
Chief Beauregard	5	G	5	0	0	1	1,419
Chief Begone	4	G	4	0	0	2	1,290
Chief Black Hawk	5	H	11	0	2	0	4,715
Chief Blue	6	G	6	0	0	0	1,137
Chief Braveheart	6	H	1	1	0	0	1,980
Chief Bright Sun	2	C	7	0	0	1	1,825
Chief Cahill	4	G	14	7	1	3	41,000
Chief Caleb	5	G	4	0	0	1	2,294
Chief Cat	4	C	3	1	0	0	4,762
Chief Commander	2	C	4	1	0	0	37,200
Chief Conquistador	3	C	3	0	0	0	0
Chief Diamond	3	C	1	0	0	0	40
Chief Dragonfly	2	G	2	0	0	0	255
Chief Engineer	8	G	11	0	2	2	3,190
Chief Exchequer	4	G	5	0	0	0	330
Chief Export	2	C	1	0	0	0	161
Chief Four Shoes	4	C	12	1	0	1	6,714
Chief Gray Wolf	7	G	12	0	2	1	3,364
Chief Jake	3	C	1	0	0	0	0
Chief Joseph	5	G	11	2	1	3	11,343
Chief Little Dan	4	F	3	0	1	0	10,400
Chief Logan	3	G	4	0	0	2	2,695
Chief Magistrate	4	G	8	3	3	1	33,315
Chief Mandu	6	G	1	0	0	0	0
Chief Manteo	8	G	2	0	0	1	1,308
Chief Mathias	4	G	7	0	2	0	3,550
Chief Mtn	3	G	8	2	2	0	49,250
Chief Negotiator	4	G	9	1	3	1	47,890
Chief Okie Dokie	8	H	1	0	0	0	510
Chief Omni	3	C	12	0	1	3	9,597
Chief Pawhuska	5	G	16	3	0	2	17,566
Chief Powhatan	5	G	7	1	1	1	8,975
Chief Problem	6	G	4	0	0	0	277
Chief Rainbow	8	G	13	1	2	0	16,008
Chief Rima	3	C	1	0	0	0	0
Chief Runamuck	5	G	17	0	3	3	10,980
Chief Secretary	3	F	1	1	0	0	9,600
Chief Sequoyah	2	G	2	0	0	0	3,680
Chief Swan	7	G	11	2	1	2	12,615
Chief Tamahka	3	G	9	3	0	0	21,465
Chief Truckee	3	G	4	0	1	1	11,054
Chief Tudor	7	G	7	1	1	0	36,853
Chief Two Socks	4	G	7	0	1	3	4,927
Chief Victor	3	G	12	2	1	1	12,441
Chief White Sox	4	G	14	1	0	1	8,193
Chief Yatahay	5	G	1	0	0	0	0
Chief Yukon	5	G	15	1	4	1	9,307
Chief's Avie	3	G	7	1	0	1	3,426
Chief's Brother	6	G	8	0	0	0	1,080
Chief's Fire	7	G	4	0	0	1	1,885
Chief's Hogan	7	G	10	0	1	3	5,965
Chiefs Jet	7	G	2	0	0	0	0
Chief's Spokesman	3	G	4	1	2	1	26,000

Horse	Age	Sex	Sts	1st	2d	3d	Won
Chiefs Tam	4	F	4	0	0	0	0
Chieftaincy	6	G	15	1	1	3	7,734
Chig Car Go Bull	2	G	7	1	0	2	17,020
Chihuly	3	F	1	0	0	0	0
Chikara	6	M	8	0	0	2	2,661
Chikaskia	7	M	12	0	0	0	900
Chikendinnerwinner	3	G	10	1	0	1	19,360
Chilcotin	3	G	1	0	0	0	3,528
Child of Light	3	G	9	0	1	0	10,037
Childhooddream	5	G	18	0	1	0	3,588
Childress	6	M	11	5	3	1	154,150
Chile' File'	4	F	12	2	0	1	15,670
Chilena	2	F	2	0	0	0	0
Chilham Castle	3	F	4	0	2	0	27,402
Chili Bean	3	G	8	0	0	3	870
Chili Dan	3	C	10	1	3	4	13,204
Chili Doggie	8	H	12	1	1	0	7,965
Chili Y Garbo	4	C	2	0	0	1	1,980
Chilipin	6	M	11	2	1	1	17,545
Chilitas	3	F	2	0	0	0	100
Chilitodayhotamale	3	F	2	0	0	0	131
Chilkat	3	G	1	1	0	0	6,441
Chill Master	3	G	8	3	1	1	23,374
Chill Town	3	F	10	0	0	1	2,918
Chill Town Banner	3	F	6	0	3	0	9,277
Chillin' Chester	4	G	1	0	0	0	0
Chilling Effect	5	M	13	2	1	3	66,173
Chilling Sweep	8	H	3	0	0	0	500
Chilly A.	8	G	11	1	1	3	9,886
Chilly Buttons	6	M	12	0	1	1	7,197
Chilly Charlie	7	H	11	2	3	3	10,424
Chilly Flier	5	M	1	0	0	0	0
Chilly Gentilly	8	G	6	1	1	0	6,211
Chilly Got Willy	2	C	4	0	1	0	4,188
Chilly N Slick	9	G	1	0	0	0	381
Chilly Rooster	4	G	9	1	0	1	86,218
Chilly Verde	2	C	3	0	0	0	900
Chilly Wink	4	F	13	2	4	2	13,754
Chiltepin	3	F	4	1	1	1	24,660
Chimborazo	4	G	5	0	1	1	15,952
Chime Choir	6	H	2	0	0	0	0
Chimera	3	F	8	2	0	1	14,621
Chimes Lass	3	F	3	1	1	0	13,388
Chimes Motel	6	H	7	0	0	0	380
Chimes Rebel	6	G	13	1	0	0	13,641
Chiming	9	G	13	5	2	3	27,610
Chimney Slew	4	G	15	1	3	3	30,488
Chimo	5	G	13	4	3	2	50,495
Chin Chin	6	G	4	1	0	0	4,303
Chin Gone	6	G	4	1	1	0	16,680
China Gold	3	C	7	1	1	1	46,485
China Grind	5	H	1	0	0	1	3,600
China Kitten	4	F	10	0	0	0	1,136
China Paint	4	F	11	1	1	0	6,281
China Princess	4	F	7	1	1	2	37,452
Chinagashi	2	G	2	0	0	0	894
Chinati Gal	5	M	2	0	0	0	0
Chinatown Cricket	2	F	5	0	0	0	1,360
Chindi	10	G	10	0	2	6	43,217
Chinese	4	C	9	1	3	2	14,070
Chinese Checkers	2	G	3	2	0	0	32,448
Chinese Tea	4	F	9	1	2	3	38,580
Chinese Whisper	7	G	3	2	0	0	27,750
Chingachamp	3	G	1	0	0	0	0
Chinkapin	8	G	2	2	0	0	28,200
Chino	4	G	5	1	0	0	9,742
Chino Charlie	3	G	3	1	1	0	13,160
Chino Valley	9	G	12	0	2	1	5,270
Chinoe	2	G	3	1	0	0	6,000
Chinoiro	7	H	1	0	0	0	406
Chinoiserie	2	F	1	0	0	1	2,050
Chinook Cat	6	G	11	1	2	2	17,020
Chinook to Knight	9	G	11	1	1	3	5,579
Chinooka	4	F	2	0	0	1	2,360
Chinsegut	6	M	1	0	0	0	0
Chip Hunter	2	C	5	1	0	0	8,700
Chip Shot	5	M	1	0	0	0	0
Chip the Vault	3	G	3	0	0	0	537
Chipaway	2	F	4	0	1	1	3,362
Chipeak	4	C	6	0	1	1	1,132
Chipinge	2	C	1	0	0	0	170
Chipofftheblock	3	G	16	1	1	2	10,237
Chipotle	3	C	6	1	1	0	21,049
Chipper C	5	H	11	0	1	2	11,940
Chipper Skipper	3	C	1	0	0	0	0
Chippewa Day	6	M	8	1	3	0	4,834
Chippewa Trail	3	G	6	1	0	1	51,402
Chippi Creek	4	C	12	2	3	3	27,792
Chips and Beer	2	G	6	0	0	1	2,264
Chips Are Down	2	C	6	2	2	0	74,825
Chips Damascus	5	M	8	0	0	0	339
Chip's Diamond	3	G	6	1	1	1	22,930
Chip's N Dip	4	F	2	0	0	1	1,685
Chips N Salsa	6	M	7	1	0	0	4,320
Chips Pride	9	G	2	0	0	0	0
Chip's Sister	6	M	2	0	0	1	1,302
Chipshantinformony	4	G	2	0	0	0	0
Chiquilina	5	M	5	2	0	0	26,790
Chiquito	4	G	13	2	1	2	8,293
Chiricahua Chief	7	G	1	0	0	0	0
Chirimoya	5	M	10	1	2	2	94,548
Chirinda Forest	2	C	1	0	0	0	145
Chirp Chirp	2	F	3	0	0	1	1,798
Chirundu	5	G	9	0	0	1	1,640
Chis Magic	3	C	3	0	1	0	3,400
Chiseled	3	G	5	1	0	0	5,352
Chisholm	7	G	12	8	0	1	85,886
Chispazo	3	C	13	3	2	1	62,520
Chispiro	4	G	9	2	1	0	18,180
Chispiski	5	M	2	0	0	0	6,900
Chisum	2	C	4	0	0	1	1,430
Chital the Charger	5	G	7	0	0	0	1,345
Chitchat Chitchat	4	F	12	1	2	2	37,680
Chitter Box	4	F	12	0	1	2	5,084
Chivalric	3	C	9	2	1	1	48,289
Chivann	7	G	5	2	1	1	3,960
Chivas	4	G	11	2	0	2	93,998
Chloe Miss	3	F	3	0	0	1	624
Chloe's Cat	2	F	3	0	0	0	950
Chloe's Choice	3	F	9	3	1	3	33,550
Chocawad	4	F	4	0	0	0	0
Chock Full	3	G	4	1	0	0	6,370
Chockablock	2	C	2	0	2	0	7,800
Chocolate Almond	5	G	2	0	0	0	386
Chocolate Brown	2	F	3	2	0	0	76,206
Chocolate Cowgirl	10	M	9	1	2	0	6,027
Chocolate Factory	6	M	12	4	0	0	11,007
Chocolate Fix	4	G	1	0	0	0	75
Chocolate Gal	3	F	9	1	0	1	29,097
Chocolate Gem	6	G	16	0	0	5	11,770
Chocolate Knight	4	G	10	1	3	2	21,292
Chocolate Lover	4	F	7	2	0	1	5,952
Chocolate Mauk	3	F	1	0	0	0	300
Chocolate Miss	3	G	4	0	0	0	255
Chocolate Nut	2	G	2	1	0	0	14,010
Chocolate One	4	G	10	3	0	1	4,460
Chocolate Pie Togo	6	M	2	0	1	0	1,470
Chocolate Prize	3	G	6	0	0	0	0
Chocolate Puffy	3	G	15	1	1	0	3,899
Chocolate Rose	4	F	13	3	2	3	38,749
Chocolate Sip	4	F	6	0	1	0	2,417
Chocolate Sox	3	G	10	1	0	1	8,953
Chocolate Sprinkle	4	F	8	0	1	0	2,370
Chocolate Tale	3	F	5	1	2	0	10,385
Chocolate Warrior	3	G	9	2	2	1	49,940
Chocolateonhisface	5	G	6	0	0	0	870
Chocolateonmymind	3	G	7	0	1	1	1,672
Chocolatevalentine	6	H	4	0	0	0	1,000
Chocolateville	4	F	8	2	2	1	21,725
Chocolatkiss	2	F	1	0	0	0	1,230
Chocoleta'	3	G	3	0	0	1	1,634
Chocomount	5	G	3	0	0	1	2,413
Chocotini	3	F	9	2	1	1	19,272
Choctaw Bid	3	G	5	1	1	0	4,340
Choctaw Charlie	4	G	11	3	7	0	92,780
Choctaw Lady	4	F	16	1	2	7	30,864
Choctaw Nation	4	G	6	5	0	0	301,800
Choctaw Ridge	6	G	8	4	2	1	120,297

Horse	Age	Sex	Sts	1st	2d	3d	Won
Choctaw Sky	5	M	4	0	0	1	950
Choice Forum	5	G	2	0	0	0	105
Choice Paces	4	F	1	0	0	0	192
Choice Rumor	4	C	13	0	0	1	1,862
Choice Slew	5	M	5	2	1	1	9,743
Choice Union	3	G	9	2	1	1	26,603
Choicey Jett	2	F	1	0	0	0	0
Choir Leader	2	C	7	1	0	1	11,790
Choir Master	4	G	4	0	0	1	2,646
Choke a Tune	3	F	1	0	0	0	107
Choke N Go	8	G	3	0	0	0	1,142
Choker	6	G	3	1	0	0	2,700
Choke's Secret	5	G	5	0	0	0	440
Chokettes Pride	5	G	7	1	1	0	5,310
Choktow	5	G	9	1	3	3	7,823
Chola	3	G	9	1	0	1	7,452
Cholly Mon	3	G	3	1	0	0	7,906
Cholo	4	G	1	0	0	0	0
Chomp	6	G	12	0	1	1	2,071
Chonita	3	F	7	4	1	1	69,730
Choo Choo Chad	6	G	10	1	0	2	9,722
Choo Choo Charlie	4	C	5	0	0	1	1,945
Choose	3	C	6	4	0	0	103,610
Choose Faith	8	M	3	0	0	0	201
Choose the Greek	5	G	13	0	0	1	1,690
Choose the Right	3	F	5	0	1	1	11,181
Choose to Play	2	G	7	0	1	2	19,358
Choose Wisely	6	M	16	1	1	3	13,672
Choosing Sides	4	G	9	0	2	4	3,192
Chop Chop Bop	2	F	1	0	0	0	215
Chop Chop George	7	G	19	0	2	3	5,744
Chop House	3	G	14	5	2	2	14,545
Chopard	3	F	3	0	0	0	1,920
Chopin's First	4	F	11	2	0	2	6,998
Choppa Toulouse	5	H	16	1	2	1	13,472
Chopper Won	6	H	2	1	0	0	34,240
Choppers Choice	3	G	11	2	0	0	3,257
Choppy Sea	5	G	9	1	1	2	7,302
Chopt At Dawn	5	G	16	0	1	0	2,519
Chords of Fame	7	M	7	2	0	3	37,894
Choreography	4	G	18	2	8	0	189,430
Chortle	7	G	11	0	1	1	1,740
Chory Four	5	G	13	0	2	0	11,674
Chosen Chief	5	G	7	1	3	2	79,290
Chosen Hero (GB)	3	C	13	0	3	3	44,550
Chosen Honor	5	M	8	2	1	0	56,440
Chotzie	3	C	12	2	1	3	40,644
Chouette Player	7	H	7	0	0	0	480
Chow Down	7	G	10	3	3	0	42,437
Chowder's First	3	C	8	3	0	1	222,328
Chretien's Dawn	8	M	10	1	0	2	6,911
Chris Can Travy	9	G	8	1	0	1	5,160
Chris Cross Cat	3	G	10	1	1	2	5,866
Chris' Facts	5	M	13	4	1	4	28,340
Chris Hunts	4	G	12	3	1	3	20,440
Chris My Man	6	H	2	0	0	0	37
Chris Run	7	G	1	0	0	0	181
Chrisanda	5	H	3	0	0	0	270
Chrismitch	6	M	14	0	1	4	7,839
Chrisn'denise	4	G	3	0	0	0	1,200
Chris's Bad Boy	7	G	7	3	2	0	261,480
Chris's Counter	6	G	2	0	0	0	228
Chris's Salty Dog	3	G	3	0	0	0	305
Chris's Spirit	3	G	2	0	0	0	0
Chris'slittlegirl	3	F	3	1	0	0	16,740
Chrissy de Rio	7	M	6	1	1	0	2,092
Chrissy Jay	3	F	14	2	2	2	38,035
Chrissysshadow	3	F	3	0	1	0	490
Christal's Gift	6	G	2	0	0	0	169
Christavilla	5	M	15	3	5	1	26,010
Christel Flame (GB)	5	M	3	1	0	1	24,440
Christian Anthony	3	G	14	1	0	3	53,704
Christian Gulch	4	G	15	0	1	1	8,170
Christian Ridge	3	G	9	0	0	1	1,745
Christian X.	2	C	3	0	1	0	10,085
Christijeau	6	M	11	2	0	2	11,598
Christina Sanchez	4	F	1	0	0	0	0
Christina's Angel	2	F	8	1	3	2	12,480
Christina's Hope	4	F	6	0	0	0	813
Christina's Image	3	F	1	0	0	0	0
Christina's Office	3	F	2	0	0	0	77
Christine Account	3	F	2	0	0	0	1,590
Christines Dream	2	F	2	0	0	0	2,187
Christine's Outlaw	4	C	9	3	1	0	145,199
Christines Patty	4	F	6	0	0	0	1,644
Christine's Prize	3	F	9	1	0	2	20,189
Christmas At Last	2	C	6	0	0	0	371
Christmas Away	4	C	5	0	0	0	600
Christmas Card	3	F	7	1	2	0	45,667
Christmas Joy	3	F	7	1	1	0	16,820
Christmas Memory	4	F	8	0	0	0	1,500
Christmas Money	3	F	5	0	0	0	571
Christmas Slippers	2	F	2	0	2	0	10,500
Christmas Table	4	F	14	1	1	2	11,353
Christmas Time	4	F	10	3	4	1	134,360
Christo Hallelujah	7	G	10	0	0	1	616
Christo Israel	4	G	10	0	0	3	7,440
Christo Lollipop	6	M	1	0	0	0	0
Christo Rain	6	G	8	0	1	0	2,419
Christo Wings	5	G	14	2	4	5	17,404
Christopher Cat	3	G	3	1	0	0	2,900
Christopher J	4	G	5	1	2	0	12,057
Christopher Lee	6	G	4	1	0	0	1,856
Christopher Robyn	2	C	6	1	0	1	13,070
Christophers Boy	3	G	8	0	0	1	1,100
Christy Brown	3	C	6	2	0	0	17,637
Christy Marie	5	M	2	0	0	0	1,020
Christy T.	4	F	10	3	1	2	69,031
Christy's Miracle	3	F	8	0	0	1	4,000
Christy's Secret	5	M	6	0	0	2	3,597
Chrizzy	2	C	9	1	1	1	20,290
Chromatic Cadence	2	F	1	0	0	0	420
Chrome Castle	3	F	2	0	0	0	613
Chrome Cowboy	2	G	4	2	0	0	16,620
Chrome Soldier	3	C	11	1	2	3	39,590
Chrome Spot	3	G	2	0	0	0	0
Chrome Wheels	3	G	7	1	0	0	2,200
Chronic Iced Tea	4	G	6	2	1	0	11,323
Chronic Tychonic	4	F	17	2	2	4	16,300
Chronicle	2	C	2	0	0	0	1,364
Chronicle S.	9	G	5	2	0	0	9,520
Chrusciki	4	F	12	4	4	2	174,770
Chrysalis Court	5	H	2	0	0	1	1,045
Chrysalis Village	5	M	5	0	0	0	512
Chubaka	3	G	4	0	1	1	5,105
Chubasco Red	3	G	8	1	0	3	35,244
Chubbs Last Call	2	F	6	4	1	0	52,850
Chubby Buddy	5	H	20	2	3	2	17,102
Chubby Is Ready	3	F	4	0	2	1	2,450
Chubby Slic	4	G	7	1	0	1	7,329
Chuck O Luck	4	G	12	1	2	4	6,496
Chuck Yeager	4	G	21	2	6	3	21,307
Chuckalee	3	G	11	0	5	3	9,849
Chuckels	4	C	5	1	3	0	17,450
Chuckieourlaw	4	G	5	0	0	1	5,041
Chuckie's in Love	4	C	13	2	3	0	63,632
Chuckling	2	C	3	0	0	0	2,645
Chuck's Angel	4	F	10	1	1	1	4,460
Chuck's Mobile Bay	3	G	1	0	0	0	0
Chucks Playboy	5	G	7	1	0	0	2,760
Chug a Brew	3	C	4	1	1	0	13,220
Chuky Strode	7	G	7	0	0	0	664
Chul Chul	4	F	2	1	1	0	14,263
Chula	5	M	1	0	0	0	755
Chullo Uno	2	G	1	1	0	0	5,225
Chum	5	G	9	1	2	1	13,564
Chummin	2	C	2	0	1	0	7,800
Chump Change	3	G	4	0	0	0	2,045
Chundoo	4	G	5	0	0	0	895
Chunk Change	4	G	10	2	1	2	10,194
Chunk of Love	3	F	2	1	0	1	10,490
Chunky Cheeks	4	F	2	0	1	0	1,463
Chupacabras	7	G	4	0	1	1	7,610
Chuparosa	5	M	4	0	1	1	2,602
Church Affair	3	F	5	0	0	0	8,620
Church Cart	2	G	5	1	1	0	27,280
Church Cross (IRE)	5	G	1	0	0	0	0
Church Editor	3	F	12	1	3	3	83,120

RECORDS OF HORSES

Horse	Age	Sex	Sts	1st	2d	3d	Won
Church Gal	4	F	2	0	0	0	607
Church Ghost	5	G	6	2	0	2	17,950
Church Goer	4	F	2	0	0	1	660
Church Secretary	5	M	10	0	2	1	4,350
Churchbridge	3	G	9	4	0	2	37,831
Churchhill	4	C	3	1	0	1	9,695
Churchill Chap	2	C	1	0	0	0	155
Church's Out	4	F	7	0	1	0	10,360
Churlee Sweet	8	M	4	0	0	1	640
Chute the Breeze	4	G	11	1	0	0	39,076
Chuzz	2	G	6	0	2	0	5,911
Chynna's Beauty	4	F	2	0	0	0	240
Chystalline	3	F	4	0	0	0	0
Ciano Belle	3	F	11	0	0	1	1,327
Ciano Casino	2	G	3	0	1	0	1,968
Ciano Country	3	G	14	6	1	0	82,272
Ciano Silence	3	F	2	0	0	1	680
Ciano Warrior	3	G	14	0	2	4	6,497
Ciano's First	3	F	9	4	0	0	23,602
Ciano's Prospect	2	G	1	0	0	1	1,764
Ciano's Six Pack	3	F	9	1	1	0	16,825
Ciao Rhoma	4	G	6	1	1	0	14,420
Ciara C	2	F	3	0	0	1	1,634
Ciavoli	3	F	2	0	0	0	146
Cibagof Gold	3	G	16	1	1	0	8,663
Cibo	4	G	14	2	2	0	47,354
Ciccy's Star	3	F	16	1	2	1	12,089
Cicero Grimes	5	G	10	1	3	2	36,032
Cicisbeo	2	C	3	0	0	1	3,400
Cider	6	G	8	1	0	0	4,287
Ciel Avenue	3	G	8	2	1	0	15,015
Ciel Classic	4	F	10	3	1	2	34,470
Ciel Noir	8	G	2	0	0	0	0
Cielavia	2	F	3	0	0	0	510
Cieli	2	F	2	0	1	1	8,350
Cielo Blincoe	3	G	12	3	0	1	64,740
Cielo Canosa	9	G	4	1	0	0	3,400
Cielo City	6	H	8	1	3	1	19,006
Cielo Girl	5	M	4	1	0	1	35,527
Cielo Moon	4	F	13	0	2	4	53,685
Cielo's Bluff	5	G	4	0	0	0	585
Cielo's Cat	3	F	5	1	2	0	9,100
Cielo's Edge	2	C	8	1	2	0	35,500
Cielo's Garden	5	G	8	1	2	0	20,000
Cielo's Honour	6	G	14	0	3	3	16,450
Cielo's Majesty	5	M	5	0	0	0	375
Cielovation	5	G	1	0	0	0	180
Cien Rosebuds	3	F	1	0	0	0	0
Cien Seas	7	G	1	0	0	0	150
Cien Seattle	6	M	20	1	4	3	12,898
Cien Wins	4	G	6	0	0	0	390
Ciens Storm	4	F	10	0	0	0	2,730
Ciento	6	H	3	3	0	0	144,000
Cierra's Junebug	3	F	5	2	1	1	24,360
Cigar Pal	3	C	3	1	0	0	21,880
Cigno d'Oro	5	M	10	0	4	1	65,956
Cilento	4	C	10	2	2	1	12,745
Cimarron City	3	G	12	1	1	1	26,350
Cimarron Hills	3	F	8	2	1	0	23,965
Cimarron Summer	3	F	1	0	0	0	0
Cimarrona	3	F	8	1	3	0	10,414
Cimarron's Jade	3	F	13	0	0	2	2,637
Cimarrons Song	3	F	2	0	0	1	1,724
Cimarron's Time	2	C	5	1	0	1	12,395
Cimmering Kat	3	G	4	0	0	0	0
Cimmy's Simmy	2	F	2	0	0	1	1,717
Cin Cin	2	C	5	3	0	1	157,140
Cin Slew Eve	4	C	7	0	0	1	1,283
Cinbuster	5	G	10	1	0	0	20,520
Cincinnati Jay	3	G	10	1	1	1	14,888
Cincinnati Red	2	C	3	1	1	0	9,940
Cincinnati Reuben	10	G	4	0	0	1	533
Cincodemayocaballo	5	H	1	0	1	0	860
Cindarullah	3	F	12	1	3	1	35,070
Cindee	7	M	2	0	0	0	0
Cinder Cat	8	G	6	0	0	0	689
Cinder Ron	3	C	8	2	2	1	44,060
Cinder Rose	3	F	2	0	0	0	800
Cinderchance	2	G	5	0	0	2	10,206

Horse	Age	Sex	Sts	1st	2d	3d	Won
Cinderdela	7	M	11	1	2	1	10,979
Cinderelarockefela	3	F	1	0	0	0	0
Cinderella's Fella	6	G	11	0	2	3	3,430
Cinderellas Music	4	F	5	0	0	0	3,000
Cinderellaslipper	4	F	5	0	0	0	3,645
Cindy Embers	2	F	3	0	0	1	2,264
Cindy Lou Slew	6	M	1	0	0	0	112
Cindy Lou Two	4	F	9	0	2	0	3,492
Cindy Ridge	3	F	5	0	0	0	0
Cindy Windy	2	F	2	1	0	0	4,350
Cindys Devil	6	G	6	0	0	0	329
Cindy's Doll	8	M	11	2	3	1	12,849
Cindy's Girl	5	M	15	0	0	0	2,446
Cindy's Hobby	7	M	14	1	6	1	23,839
Cindy's Majic	4	F	4	0	1	0	1,695
Cindys Morningstar	4	F	13	2	1	3	13,930
Cinema Magic	4	G	1	0	0	0	0
Cinema Star	3	G	8	2	0	3	40,360
Cinemagic	3	F	7	2	0	1	25,650
Cinematic	3	G	6	1	1	0	41,220
Cinfull Hillary	3	F	3	0	0	0	0
Cinnabar Sky	3	F	4	1	1	0	10,992
Cinnamon Bay	3	C	11	1	1	0	12,954
Cinnamon Brown	2	F	5	2	1	1	36,544
Cinnamon Bull	2	F	5	0	0	0	611
Cinnamon Cat	7	G	9	0	0	3	3,356
Cinnamon Girl	2	F	3	0	0	0	736
Cinnamon Kiss	3	F	1	0	0	0	0
Cinnamon Ridge	4	G	6	0	0	0	3,735
Cinnamon Schnapps	3	C	1	0	0	0	114
Cinnamon Secret	4	F	8	0	2	1	9,630
Cinnamon Silk	4	F	9	1	2	0	28,695
Cinnapie	3	F	6	2	0	1	27,850
Cino	4	C	2	0	0	0	324
Cinquante Cinq	3	G	7	0	1	1	9,164
Circle a Star	6	M	6	0	0	0	0
Circle Danz	3	F	4	1	1	0	6,340
Circle M Lighting	4	F	4	0	0	0	455
Circle M Midnight	6	G	2	0	0	0	92
Circle of Peace	4	F	8	0	2	2	8,775
Circle the Globe	5	M	9	1	4	0	49,668
Circle Z	4	F	6	1	2	0	15,662
Circlethewinner	2	C	5	0	0	0	1,640
Circuit Preacher	2	C	1	0	0	0	104
Circuit Rider	2	C	1	0	0	0	137
Circulating Coin	4	C	2	0	0	0	612
Circulating Sziget	3	F	8	1	1	2	11,986
Circulation	3	C	1	0	0	0	77
Circulator	2	G	2	1	0	1	9,520
Circumstancial	5	M	4	0	0	0	0
Circus Devil	2	F	3	0	0	0	1,200
Circus Du Joy	3	F	9	3	2	1	106,933
Circus Flyer	5	H	9	0	2	1	5,800
Circus Halo	2	F	1	0	0	0	0
Circus Marquee	2	G	4	0	1	1	13,350
Circus Park's Taco	4	F	8	0	0	1	1,448
Circus Peanuts	2	G	2	0	0	1	1,304
Circus Queen	3	F	6	0	0	0	1,815
Circus Star	8	M	1	0	0	0	50
Circus Storm	3	G	4	0	0	0	255
Circus Tricks	3	G	2	0	0	0	210
Circus Vision	4	F	13	1	1	2	9,022
Cirilo	7	H	16	2	6	3	17,994
Cirius	4	G	5	0	0	0	609
Cirque	4	F	9	0	0	1	1,507
Cirrus Minor	3	C	10	1	0	1	10,065
Cisco Kid	5	G	6	0	0	1	1,494
Cisco Moon	6	G	1	0	0	0	0
Cisco 'n' Vic	4	G	13	3	1	1	23,933
Cisco Socks	4	G	10	1	1	0	6,605
Ciscolightly	4	G	6	1	0	1	2,102
Cisco's Kite	6	G	9	0	0	1	4,180
Cisco's Redbone	3	F	7	0	0	1	310
Cissy (ARG)	4	F	1	0	0	0	85
Citadella	3	F	11	2	3	0	19,698
Citation Jet	10	G	1	0	0	0	0
Citi Buster	3	C	2	0	0	0	1,080
Citi Feeling	2	C	1	0	0	0	3,420
Citi Music	3	F	11	1	0	3	23,092

Horse	Age	Sex	Sts	1st	2d	3d	Won
Citi Rhythm	4	C	3	0	0	0	580
Citi State	4	F	16	1	2	3	41,680
Citiblitz Diamond	3	C	5	0	0	0	1,180
Citibrat	3	F	1	0	0	0	400
Citidellino	6	H	11	2	2	3	47,491
Citiflash	5	G	9	0	1	0	2,708
Citikitti	6	M	2	0	0	0	1,000
Citiparrot	3	C	5	1	2	0	11,760
Citiroyal	6	G	12	3	2	1	22,272
Cititime Diamond	3	C	3	0	1	0	2,640
Cititree Diamond	4	G	8	0	1	1	4,510
Citiworld	10	G	2	0	0	0	0
Citizen's Request	2	C	8	2	2	0	23,580
Citizenship	3	C	9	3	3	1	110,372
Citizip Diamond	3	C	9	0	0	3	8,840
City Academy	4	G	5	0	0	0	4,771
City Affair	3	G	6	1	0	0	18,090
City Ambassador	2	F	4	1	0	0	8,980
City and State	2	G	4	1	1	1	13,625
City Ballet	4	C	5	0	0	1	1,210
City Blues	4	G	8	1	2	1	35,530
City Boy	4	G	12	1	4	1	16,078
City Brave	4	G	16	0	4	4	8,988
City Circle	10	G	6	0	1	1	1,585
City Clerk	8	G	4	1	1	0	3,605
City Code	2	C	5	2	0	2	52,040
City Diamond	3	F	10	1	1	3	12,550
City Express	3	C	5	0	1	1	7,000
City Fear	5	G	7	1	0	0	6,682
City Fire	4	F	8	1	1	1	54,835
City Forum	2	F	1	0	0	0	115
City Fox	2	G	3	1	0	1	2,220
City Island	6	G	9	1	1	1	7,783
City Jewel	2	F	1	0	0	0	624
City Jitters	3	F	7	0	0	0	322
City Kid	6	G	11	1	1	1	8,375
City Kitty	4	F	20	5	4	5	32,413
City Lights	3	G	8	0	5	0	17,075
City Lights Sonata	6	M	13	1	1	4	7,529
City Limit	3	F	2	0	0	0	556
City Line Ave	3	C	22	2	5	7	87,746
City Mix	4	G	10	1	0	2	11,591
City Momma	3	F	2	0	0	0	0
City News	4	G	13	2	1	2	38,620
City of Evansville	3	F	4	0	0	0	877
City of Faith	4	G	16	1	1	1	6,011
City of Heroes	3	G	1	0	0	0	42
City of Peace	7	H	1	0	0	0	0
City of Riches	6	G	11	1	3	3	13,158
City Parkway	5	G	16	5	4	4	16,874
City Pilgrim	6	G	13	0	4	0	4,346
City Planner	4	G	2	0	0	0	203
City Prayer	4	F	9	2	1	1	7,230
City Prince	3	G	19	1	2	2	19,980
City Rain	4	F	2	1	1	0	26,200
City Rapid	5	H	1	0	0	0	0
City Ridge	3	F	10	1	0	1	3,440
City Sister	4	F	3	0	0	0	3,160
City Sleeper	4	F	5	0	1	3	22,987
City Sprint	2	C	2	0	0	0	0
City Styling	4	F	1	0	0	0	906
City Trapp	3	G	10	0	1	3	8,555
City Trick	3	C	3	1	1	1	8,320
City Weekend	2	C	1	0	0	0	150
City Zoom	3	F	6	1	2	1	21,510
City's Honey	3	C	12	1	3	0	40,330
Civil Bond (ARG)	5	H	2	0	0	0	800
Civil Revolt	6	G	11	0	3	2	11,986
Civility Cat	4	F	1	0	0	0	0
Civilize	3	C	6	0	2	1	19,530
Civita	3	F	4	0	0	0	990
Cj's Pride	5	G	10	2	2	2	27,278
Claddagh Bay	6	M	2	0	0	0	202
Cladhopper	3	C	4	0	0	0	581
Claim Check	8	G	10	0	2	0	4,884
Claim Form	3	G	8	2	2	0	10,311
Claim My Love	5	M	2	0	0	0	396
Claim to Fame	2	C	1	0	0	0	0
Claims to Be Good	4	F	9	0	0	3	3,009
Claims to Be Lucky	5	G	1	0	0	0	0
Claire	6	M	4	0	0	0	370
Claire City	4	F	6	1	0	2	11,815
Claire's Rockette	3	F	14	0	1	2	3,799
Clairified	2	C	4	1	0	0	12,978
Clairlyn	5	M	5	0	1	0	9,462
Clairvoyant Gipsy	9	M	13	2	3	1	9,845
Clamato	3	F	13	0	1	1	11,457
Clammed Up	2	C	3	0	0	0	875
Clamor	6	G	5	0	0	0	450
Clamps Dream Queen	3	F	3	0	1	1	570
Clandestine	3	F	8	3	0	2	64,090
Clapton	8	G	8	1	0	1	14,402
Clara Allen	5	M	8	1	2	1	9,077
Clara Cee	2	F	4	0	0	0	1,240
Clara Dee	3	F	1	0	0	0	0
Clara James	3	F	6	0	0	0	0
Clara's Boy	4	G	8	1	0	0	4,740
Clara's Choice	2	G	1	0	0	0	653
Clara's Legacy	3	F	4	0	0	0	190
Clara's Tiger	3	F	8	1	0	0	3,886
Clare's Bunny	4	F	8	1	2	0	7,561
Clare's Counting	6	M	1	0	0	0	40
Clare's Mark	4	F	2	0	0	0	0
Clare's Queenie	2	F	4	1	1	0	8,642
Claria's Case	3	G	6	1	0	2	5,235
Claridges	6	M	1	0	0	0	0
Clarins	3	F	3	1	1	0	33,240
Clarion's Star	5	M	12	2	1	0	9,953
Clark Fork	8	G	2	0	0	0	362
Clark K	5	H	1	0	0	0	303
Clark S Man	5	G	12	1	0	2	14,586
Clarks Landing	3	G	3	0	0	0	272
Clarksburg	4	G	13	2	0	1	16,780
Clarksburg Queen	3	F	9	2	2	0	80,478
Clarksdale	6	G	12	3	0	0	13,382
Clarousel Wing	3	F	3	0	0	0	110
Claseybeat	5	G	10	1	0	0	26,370
Clasic Clown	3	G	9	1	2	1	11,265
Clasp	7	G	16	2	3	2	14,874
Class Above	3	F	8	1	0	2	123,358
Class Ack	2	C	2	0	0	1	4,420
Class Adoption	8	G	3	0	0	2	559
Class All Over	7	H	3	0	0	0	233
Class Approval	5	M	1	0	0	0	130
Class Atack	3	C	9	1	3	3	21,110
Class Be Ready	4	G	4	0	0	0	159
Class by Itself	4	F	11	1	5	1	26,812
Class Choice	4	F	1	0	0	0	1,188
Class Concern	3	G	9	2	2	0	92,233
Class Cool	5	G	4	0	0	1	3,496
Class Crimson	4	G	1	0	0	0	300
Class Cutie	4	F	8	0	1	0	1,138
Class Edition	3	F	9	1	4	3	44,040
Class Five	2	C	5	1	0	0	11,146
Class Halo	4	G	8	1	0	0	5,023
Class Honors	2	G	2	0	0	0	120
Class in Action	2	C	1	0	1	0	5,000
Class of Her Own	6	M	1	0	0	0	0
Class of Seventy	5	G	7	2	1	2	57,470
Class of Wheaton	2	F	5	2	1	1	33,640
Class Prospector	2	F	1	0	0	0	0
Class Shall Tell	4	F	13	2	4	0	35,598
Class Sprite	4	C	12	2	0	3	43,193
Class Vigor	3	F	6	0	0	1	2,952
Class Yankee	6	M	2	0	1	0	4,747
Classa Red Wine	3	F	7	1	1	0	29,312
Classalwayshows	4	G	9	0	1	3	6,575
Classi Rum	2	C	2	1	0	0	9,900
Classiano	5	M	7	0	1	2	1,894
Classic Academy	2	G	2	0	0	0	0
Classic Advantage	3	G	4	0	2	0	10,970
Classic and Regal	3	C	21	3	2	2	15,449
Classic Appeal	7	H	2	0	0	0	4,452
Classic Band	4	C	13	1	2	2	16,649
Classic Beech	4	C	13	2	1	2	40,925
Classic Berti	2	C	1	0	0	0	0
Classic Bonnie	5	M	11	1	1	1	14,304
Classic Boom	4	G	10	0	0	1	1,694

Horse	Age	Sex	Sts	1st	2d	3d	Won
Classic Born	4	F	12	2	3	2	35,880
Classic Brush	9	G	1	0	0	0	40
Classic Cal	10	H	1	0	0	0	0
Classic Caller	6	G	9	1	2	0	14,622
Classic Campaign	2	C	2	0	0	0	491
Classic Canvas	3	F	1	0	0	0	1,600
Classic Case	5	G	12	1	1	5	18,785
Classic Casey	5	G	5	1	1	0	3,520
Classic Caton	3	G	9	0	0	0	1,492
Classic Chaps	7	G	13	1	3	5	8,720
Classic Chunt	6	H	1	0	0	1	570
Classic Cielo	3	C	5	0	0	1	12,336
Classic City	4	F	6	0	0	0	0
Classic Coleen	3	F	7	0	0	0	397
Classic Connection	2	F	1	0	0	0	0
Classic Country	2	C	1	0	0	0	0
Classic Deputy	5	G	15	2	1	0	11,040
Classic Destiny	4	F	7	1	2	0	10,780
Classic Devil	4	F	16	5	3	2	25,590
Classic Display	5	M	7	1	0	0	5,943
Classic Dreamer	3	F	1	0	0	0	155
Classic Elegance	2	F	6	3	0	1	204,006
Classic Encore	5	M	16	1	4	0	13,722
Classic Endeavor	6	H	15	5	2	0	248,798
Classic Esteem	8	G	12	1	4	0	9,440
Classic Example	3	F	12	2	3	0	47,756
Classic Falcon	3	G	6	0	0	0	1,120
Classic Fool	5	G	16	0	0	1	10,455
Classic Forli	2	F	6	1	1	1	7,805
Classic Form	6	G	14	2	2	4	34,140
Classic Fran	2	C	2	0	0	0	2,218
Classic Gale	5	M	4	1	1	2	22,400
Classic Hawiian	3	C	7	2	0	0	8,160
Classic Hello	5	H	7	0	1	0	3,616
Classic Henry	3	G	4	1	0	0	17,280
Classic Hit	4	F	9	2	0	0	2,723
Classic Home	3	G	6	1	1	0	3,912
Classic Hour	3	G	7	0	0	1	6,735
Classic Houston	3	G	10	1	0	1	5,355
Classic Jammer	3	C	6	2	0	1	20,720
Classic Jett	3	G	1	0	0	0	300
Classic Jourdan	5	M	7	2	0	0	10,921
Classic Key	3	F	3	0	0	0	210
Classic Kid	4	G	14	3	1	5	43,280
Classic La	5	G	1	0	0	0	54
Classic Lass	6	M	2	0	0	0	186
Classic Leighn	3	C	5	1	0	0	9,010
Classic Lena	2	F	5	0	0	0	636
Classic Lover	5	M	12	0	2	3	7,933
Classic Man	4	C	3	0	0	0	188
Classic Manner	6	G	3	1	1	1	18,570
Classic Marilyn	3	F	9	0	0	3	16,926
Classic Mop	4	F	17	3	5	1	27,235
Classic Motion	4	F	9	0	1	2	5,097
Classic Music	5	M	3	0	0	0	555
Classic Nightmare	5	G	16	0	3	3	8,800
Classic Nix	7	M	4	0	0	0	180
Classic Onyx	6	G	3	0	0	1	760
Classic Pancho	4	F	3	0	0	0	0
Classic Par	6	G	11	1	0	2	53,860
Classic Patton	3	C	4	0	0	0	3,663
Classic Piper	3	G	9	2	1	0	72,162
Classic Place	8	G	3	0	0	0	120
Classic Play	2	G	1	1	0	0	9,000
Classic Pro	3	C	6	0	0	0	776
Classic Rapper	3	F	1	0	0	0	0
Classic Rascal	3	G	6	1	1	1	7,380
Classic Rebel	3	F	1	0	0	0	0
Classic Relative	4	C	7	1	0	1	14,618
Classic Rocknroll	4	G	11	1	1	1	19,115
Classic Royalist	6	G	1	1	0	0	2,700
Classic Run	5	H	8	1	1	1	6,442
Classic Runaway	5	G	15	2	0	3	19,424
Classic Ryder	4	C	9	2	2	2	32,452
Classic Sands	4	F	5	0	0	0	345
Classic Sleigh	5	G	3	0	0	0	4,494
Classic Solo	7	G	10	1	2	0	6,440
Classic Spectrum	3	G	9	1	0	1	20,805
Classic Stag	5	H	4	0	0	1	3,030
Classic Stamp	4	F	8	2	2	3	425,043
Classic Storm	3	F	10	1	0	1	7,315
Classic Testamony	5	G	2	0	0	0	150
Classic Trouble	4	G	10	2	3	3	21,626
Classic Verse	7	G	13	1	2	3	26,520
Classic Visit	4	F	13	1	2	2	13,186
Classic Wheels	5	M	3	0	0	0	0
Classic White Wine	7	M	15	0	0	1	4,530
Classic Wine	3	C	6	0	4	1	29,590
Classic Zone	5	G	15	3	3	2	27,436
Classical Affirm	2	C	2	0	0	0	0
Classical Dancer	5	M	6	0	1	0	500
Classical Della	4	F	10	1	4	1	34,955
Classical Dice	4	F	9	2	1	2	20,195
Classical Guitar	9	H	9	4	3	1	6,571
Classical Gus	3	F	3	0	1	0	2,990
Classical Hunter	5	G	22	2	5	5	19,258
Classical Lady	2	F	1	0	0	0	1,140
Classical Music	3	F	7	0	0	1	4,190
Classical Note	3	G	6	0	1	0	1,925
Classical Pleasure	3	C	1	0	0	0	0
Classical Ruckus	5	M	14	1	2	0	40,462
Classical Rule	3	F	2	1	0	0	3,600
Classical's First	7	M	3	0	0	0	0
Classiccanaveral	5	G	9	2	2	0	27,830
Classicredcabernet	3	G	14	5	1	3	39,635
Classie Cassie	4	F	10	2	3	0	35,962
Classie Drone	6	G	5	1	0	0	3,448
Classie Green	4	F	12	2	4	1	11,957
Classie Smokey	4	G	6	1	1	0	12,000
Classified Secret	4	G	6	2	1	0	79,880
Classified Special	3	F	5	0	0	2	1,516
Classifier	4	G	14	0	1	2	6,142
Classlylilprincess	6	M	2	0	0	0	0
Classmate (ARG)	7	G	5	1	0	0	3,165
Classoffiftyseven	5	G	11	1	3	2	31,326
Classwilltell	6	G	8	2	1	0	9,788
Classy Advance	6	M	7	2	1	2	3,566
Classy Anthony	5	G	9	0	0	0	1,710
Classy Be Gone	3	F	16	2	3	5	19,320
Classy Bid	5	G	7	0	0	0	777
Classy Brass	5	M	9	1	2	0	9,193
Classy Cade	3	G	6	3	3	0	12,615
Classy Camper	5	H	1	0	0	0	0
Classy Charm	2	F	3	1	0	0	31,230
Classy Choice	2	F	6	3	1	1	66,360
Classy Claud	2	G	1	0	0	0	126
Classy Commander	4	F	3	0	1	0	4,660
Classy Connection	5	M	9	1	0	1	10,081
Classy Crane	4	G	9	2	0	0	8,564
Classy Diana	3	F	2	0	0	0	103
Classy E. T.	7	H	15	0	0	1	11,060
Classy Excess	3	F	3	1	0	0	16,200
Classy Fella	5	G	7	1	1	0	18,060
Classy Flower	4	F	12	1	4	0	33,614
Classy Gent	3	C	3	0	0	0	161
Classy Hannah	2	F	4	0	0	0	480
Classy Heroine	4	F	12	2	2	0	28,750
Classy J	2	C	4	1	1	0	21,260
Classy Jack Clark	6	G	9	2	2	4	17,010
Classy Lauren	3	G	4	0	0	0	1,116
Classy Leah	6	M	3	0	0	0	678
Classy Legend	3	G	13	1	2	3	18,604
Classy Lil Chassi	3	F	6	2	0	0	6,739
Classy Li'l Fella	4	G	6	0	1	0	1,128
Classy Lover	2	G	6	1	0	2	13,305
Classy Maid	4	F	6	1	1	2	4,826
Classy Maria	3	F	10	0	2	1	5,045
Classy Migration	3	G	8	2	3	0	117,130
Classy Miss	7	M	4	0	0	0	0
Classy Miss Alley	6	M	3	1	0	0	1,483
Classy Miss M.	4	F	16	2	2	4	13,033
Classy Moves	3	F	1	0	0	0	0
Classy Nickie	3	F	13	0	3	0	6,680
Classy Okie	7	G	3	0	0	0	830
Classy Ole	3	F	3	0	1	0	4,980
Classy Pac	2	F	9	1	1	0	14,965
Classy Payday	4	F	8	1	1	1	9,263
Classy Prince	6	G	8	0	0	3	6,546

Horse	Age	Sex	Sts	1st	2d	3d	Won
Classy Report	5	M	12	1	0	2	14,782
Classy Retsina	3	G	3	0	0	0	329
Classy Road	4	F	2	1	0	0	11,266
Classy Rubiano	2	C	2	0	0	0	400
Classy Serenade	5	M	12	1	0	1	9,227
Classy Sheikh	8	G	8	2	4	0	46,096
Classy So n' So	3	C	10	0	0	2	1,169
Classy Solution	6	M	3	0	0	2	6,765
Classy Spider Girl	4	F	2	0	0	0	0
Classy Splash	2	F	2	0	1	0	2,138
Classy Stella	3	F	3	0	0	0	102
Classy Storm Bird	2	F	2	0	0	0	160
Classy Strike	5	G	9	3	1	0	17,751
Classy Tiger	3	G	6	0	0	0	84
Classy Word	5	M	3	2	0	0	9,931
Classys Half Moon	5	M	2	0	0	0	105
Claudia's Agenda	3	F	7	3	0	0	32,185
Claudia's Type	4	F	2	0	0	0	207
Claudie Rose	3	F	14	1	1	1	5,744
Claudines Kitten	5	M	2	0	1	0	1,205
Claudine's Revenge	4	F	11	0	1	1	9,258
Claudio	4	G	4	0	0	0	250
Claxton Bay	4	C	14	2	4	0	16,790
Clay City	6	G	12	2	1	4	9,414
Clay Time	5	G	3	2	0	0	10,684
Claydif	5	G	5	1	1	1	6,933
Claymore	5	G	4	1	0	0	10,822
Clays Awesome	4	G	1	0	1	0	5,670
Clay's Gamble	4	G	2	0	0	0	260
Clay's Rocket	3	F	1	1	0	0	22,200
Clayton St. Dancer	4	F	3	0	0	0	0
Clayton's Cat	3	F	7	1	1	2	7,960
Clayton's Dream	2	F	1	0	0	0	750
Clayton's Party	2	C	7	0	2	2	18,160
Clayton's Trick	4	C	4	2	1	0	49,440
Clean Living	6	G	4	0	0	0	2,485
Cleaning House	4	C	6	2	0	0	16,650
Clear Action M. D.	5	G	8	0	0	0	479
Clear Advantage	3	G	16	0	1	1	6,517
Clear and Cold	3	F	17	4	1	2	26,652
Clear as Daylight	4	F	6	0	0	0	3,520
Clear Creek Canyon	4	G	8	3	1	2	72,020
Clear Denial	5	M	9	4	0	2	15,265
Clear Design	6	G	11	0	1	0	2,872
Clear Destiny	5	M	3	0	0	1	9,855
Clear for Launch	3	G	6	0	0	0	1,575
Clear for Take Off	5	G	13	0	0	0	706
Clear Forecast	3	C	2	1	0	0	33,022
Clear in the West	4	F	5	2	1	2	73,800
Clear Intent	2	F	3	1	1	1	24,460
Clear Panache	3	F	5	0	0	0	270
Clear Terms	4	C	4	0	0	2	2,750
Clear the Bases	3	C	8	2	2	3	86,970
Clear the Benches	4	G	6	0	0	1	1,260
Clear the Court	3	F	5	0	0	0	2,070
Clear the Runway	5	M	3	1	0	0	4,788
Clear Tips	4	F	6	0	0	0	620
Clear Title	5	G	8	2	0	0	29,955
Clear to Close	2	C	6	1	1	0	20,930
Clear to Land	8	M	1	0	0	0	0
Clear to the Top	2	F	14	1	5	3	19,106
Clear Victory	3	G	11	0	0	3	4,583
Clearance Light	6	M	9	0	2	2	4,276
Clearcreekdelight	3	F	13	1	0	2	6,301
Cleard for Action	3	G	7	0	1	3	5,254
Cleared to Go	5	M	12	1	1	2	16,402
Clearedtofly	3	G	4	0	0	1	3,960
Clearforapproach	2	F	3	1	1	1	9,770
Clearing	3	C	4	0	2	0	12,180
Clearly a King	3	G	11	1	0	2	16,788
Clearly A. K. O.	3	F	10	5	2	3	64,945
Clearly Defined	4	G	5	0	1	1	8,380
Clearly Ideal	2	F	2	1	0	1	14,700
Clearly Irish	6	G	16	2	2	1	11,314
Clearly Kathy	2	F	6	0	0	1	6,195
Clearly Stated	2	F	2	0	0	1	4,560
Clearsoul	3	F	13	1	4	1	15,669
Cleartalker	3	G	2	2	0	0	37,320
Cleat	8	G	10	0	4	1	13,025
Cleata D	2	F	2	0	1	1	3,153
Cleavers Hill	2	C	1	0	0	1	6,270
Clef Note	7	G	15	2	2	2	12,045
Cleft	2	F	2	0	0	0	800
Clegg	4	G	5	0	2	1	6,644
Cleito	3	F	4	0	0	0	827
Clem Da Claimer	3	G	6	0	0	0	1,437
Clem Sky	4	C	10	1	0	0	12,372
Clemency	6	G	7	1	0	0	7,585
Clemente	3	G	6	1	1	0	17,056
Clementia	3	F	2	1	0	1	9,100
Clemson You	2	C	9	1	5	2	63,310
Clerbuent	5	G	10	0	0	0	0
Clergy	5	G	2	0	0	0	0
Clerpark	3	C	2	1	0	0	27,760
Cleven's Prince	3	G	8	0	2	0	8,674
Clever Affair	3	G	8	1	2	1	18,704
Clever and Fancy	5	H	8	0	0	0	1,914
Clever Anet	4	F	10	1	2	2	9,611
Clever Assault	2	C	3	0	1	0	4,324
Clever At Midnight	7	G	12	2	3	0	3,901
Clever Ballad	3	F	9	1	1	2	12,286
Clever Bates	5	M	12	4	2	3	20,094
Clever Blonde	5	M	6	0	0	0	1,675
Clever Bluff	4	G	6	0	1	3	6,711
Clever Book	4	C	14	2	4	3	41,898
Clever Brick	7	G	17	0	2	1	9,660
Clever Bride	3	F	4	1	2	1	13,140
Clever Brute	2	C	3	0	0	0	520
Clever Bull	3	G	13	1	4	0	17,036
Clever Chance	3	G	5	0	2	0	5,095
Clever Charlie	3	G	4	0	0	0	599
Clever Cody	3	C	3	0	0	0	0
Clever Coed	6	M	8	6	1	0	83,085
Clever Colleen	3	F	5	0	0	0	650
Clever Comique	3	F	12	1	1	3	17,860
Clever Concorde	5	M	7	0	1	3	20,990
Clever Connection	3	F	11	0	1	0	3,785
Clever Course	4	C	9	0	0	1	1,800
Clever Cowboy	4	C	4	1	0	0	26,890
Clever Coyote	5	G	7	1	0	0	3,886
Clever Crawford	5	H	8	0	2	1	2,392
Clever Crossing	3	F	7	1	1	1	12,920
Clever Dance	4	G	14	1	4	1	15,675
Clever Deputy	6	G	7	1	1	1	7,383
Clever Edition	4	C	6	1	2	0	10,942
Clever Electrician	5	H	10	5	1	3	220,870
Clever Endeaver	5	G	7	0	0	1	1,150
Clever Fancy	3	F	2	0	0	0	0
Clever Fer Sure	3	F	4	0	0	0	0
Clever Fit	3	C	3	1	0	0	10,930
Clever Friend	2	C	3	1	0	1	7,815
Clever Game	3	F	3	0	0	0	450
Clever Gent	9	G	4	0	0	1	4,465
Clever Greek	3	C	2	2	0	0	22,800
Clever Jack	4	G	6	0	0	2	8,662
Clever Jim	4	G	5	0	0	3	2,101
Clever Jimmy C	4	G	15	5	3	2	44,953
Clever Jove	3	G	2	0	0	1	1,424
Clever Katie	3	F	5	1	0	1	12,755
Clever Keypsake	4	G	9	1	0	1	5,953
Clever Kid	2	F	6	0	0	1	550
Clever Kim	2	F	1	0	0	0	0
Clever Kiss	3	F	11	5	1	1	29,375
Clever Knight	5	H	3	0	0	0	158
Clever Legend	4	G	13	1	4	1	5,361
Clever Lil Girl	4	F	5	0	1	0	2,490
Clever Louis	5	G	11	3	2	2	59,200
Clever M. D.	2	F	5	1	3	0	19,800
Clever Maid	3	F	12	3	2	0	69,758
Clever Melody	3	F	3	1	1	1	21,925
Clever Miss	2	F	5	1	0	2	20,136
Clever Miss Caper	8	M	7	1	3	0	13,095
Clever Miss Trixie	4	F	16	3	0	3	28,645
Clever Moon	4	F	6	1	1	0	39,317
Clever Note	3	F	6	1	2	0	25,435
Clever Nureyev	7	G	8	2	2	0	12,165
Clever Pancho	5	H	7	1	1	0	18,740
Clever Peace	3	F	7	0	0	1	6,230

Horse	Age	Sex	Sts	1st	2d	3d	Won
Clever Play	4	G	6	1	0	0	11,600
Clever Quoit	8	G	5	0	0	0	1,320
Clever Red	4	G	9	2	2	2	12,020
Clever Red Head	3	F	4	0	0	1	1,925
Clever Revolution	6	G	4	0	0	1	543
Clever Roberto	6	G	8	0	1	1	2,037
Clever Rose	4	F	17	0	3	4	9,473
Clever Sis	4	F	1	0	0	0	0
Clever Smile	5	G	3	0	0	0	300
Clever Spy	3	G	6	0	0	2	2,338
Clever Tactics	3	G	2	0	0	0	250
Clever Thorne	6	H	16	2	4	0	12,932
Clever to Me	3	F	7	0	1	0	5,900
Clever Traitor	4	G	6	0	2	1	8,210
Clever Truce	4	G	13	3	1	3	30,320
Clever Truth	2	C	2	1	0	0	13,800
Clever Victor	6	G	9	2	1	1	16,091
Clever Woman	4	F	1	0	0	0	0
Clever Yankee	3	G	5	1	3	1	32,900
Cleverbagatricks	4	G	8	0	1	0	3,345
Cleverita	4	F	6	2	0	0	16,980
Clevermen	5	G	8	0	1	0	2,215
Clevertrickyman	3	C	8	1	1	1	6,770
Cleves Delite	3	C	1	0	0	0	0
Clibrig	5	M	5	0	1	0	22,594
Click Here	3	C	3	0	0	0	690
Click On Sleet	7	M	11	2	1	2	7,719
Clickety Cat	5	M	10	2	2	3	69,090
Clickitorticket	2	G	1	0	0	1	2,640
Client Tension	2	G	2	0	0	0	1,585
Clifden (IRE)	3	C	4	0	0	1	10,077
Clifden Star	6	M	13	1	2	1	17,038
Cliff Notes	6	H	13	4	4	1	89,038
Cliffe Dreamer	3	C	3	0	0	1	771
Cliffs of Dover	3	F	11	2	2	0	26,136
Cliffside	5	H	3	0	0	0	456
Clif's Storm	2	C	3	1	1	1	22,110
Climatic Fever	3	G	13	3	0	2	40,485
Climb	5	M	6	0	0	1	2,780
Climber Doug	3	G	2	0	0	0	2,280
Clinch	3	C	5	0	0	0	3,575
Cling	6	M	7	0	1	1	4,165
Clinker Dagger	10	M	1	0	0	1	1,390
Clinton's Country	3	G	9	1	0	4	15,810
Clint's Nature	4	G	9	2	2	3	29,560
Clints Way	4	G	5	1	1	0	10,200
Clip	9	G	21	2	0	3	16,918
Clip Joint	7	G	14	0	2	2	3,581
Clip N Save	4	F	10	0	1	1	6,813
Clipboard Eddie	8	G	4	0	0	0	244
Clipper Cat	3	F	4	0	0	0	872
Clipping Coins	5	G	10	2	2	0	29,880
Cloak and Suiter	2	C	2	0	0	0	2,255
Cloakof Vagueness	4	F	10	1	4	0	126,691
Clobber	4	C	3	0	1	1	11,980
Clock Me Right	4	G	2	0	0	0	340
Clock Stopper	4	G	8	1	3	2	292,725
Cloda's Joy	2	F	6	0	2	1	8,190
Clod's Crypto	3	G	14	1	2	0	14,270
Cloee Irene	4	F	12	1	3	1	9,113
Clog Dance	3	F	2	0	0	0	550
Clonakilty Rose	3	F	5	0	0	2	2,827
Cloned Colony	3	G	10	1	3	1	11,871
Clonfor	4	F	3	0	1	1	2,325
Clonmany (IRE)	7	G	8	0	1	2	5,920
Clooney	7	G	13	5	2	1	27,045
Cloque and Dagger	5	G	7	0	1	0	2,688
Close Clearance	3	F	16	4	6	0	25,862
Close Copy	2	G	2	0	0	0	215
Close Dance	4	G	11	1	0	1	11,528
Close Dancing	3	F	12	3	2	2	18,158
Close Lover	3	G	12	2	0	0	15,405
Close On Time	6	G	9	0	2	1	4,398
Close Quarters	3	F	6	1	1	1	27,170
Close the Book	9	G	1	0	0	0	0
Close to Perfect	3	F	5	0	2	1	13,965
Close to the Stars	2	G	6	1	0	0	7,970
Closeeyesfantasize	5	M	7	0	1	1	640
Closely Held	3	C	12	3	1	0	6,415
Closing Argument	2	C	5	2	2	1	421,984
Closing Derby	5	G	1	1	0	0	7,620
Closing Remarks	2	F	2	1	0	0	17,880
Closing Stitch	3	C	1	1	0	0	12,586
Cloud Cat	3	F	1	0	0	0	300
Cloud Chief	3	G	16	1	5	1	20,130
Cloud Counting	4	F	14	3	1	4	54,653
Cloud Forty Nine	2	F	4	1	2	0	23,800
Cloud Jumper	5	G	10	0	1	2	36,546
Cloud Monster	3	G	5	2	0	0	20,260
Cloud Surfer	4	F	6	2	1	1	25,453
Cloud Walker	4	C	7	4	0	1	106,844
Cloudier	3	F	2	0	0	0	186
Cloudman	11	G	16	1	1	2	13,340
Clouds Class	10	G	6	0	1	2	2,420
Cloud's Honor	3	F	6	0	0	1	8,580
Clouds of Gold	5	M	10	1	3	2	141,242
Clouds On the Walk	4	C	5	1	1	1	32,446
Cloudsplitter	3	C	8	1	0	1	3,769
Cloudy All Day	2	F	6	1	0	0	17,920
Cloudy Dia	2	F	1	0	0	0	700
Cloudy Gray	3	F	16	4	3	2	51,575
Cloudy Mist	5	G	2	0	0	0	0
Cloudy Money	3	G	13	1	2	3	23,490
Cloudy Morning	3	C	11	1	1	0	12,499
Cloudy Range	3	F	2	0	0	0	3,060
Cloudy's Knight	4	G	10	4	2	1	148,155
Clover Mountain	3	F	1	0	0	0	0
Clover Patch Kid	4	C	6	0	0	0	150
Clover Situation	4	G	14	0	1	4	17,013
Clown N Coke	3	G	10	1	3	1	13,307
Clown Prince	3	G	13	0	4	1	10,170
Clownaround	8	G	10	0	0	0	2,360
Clu Too	4	C	10	1	0	2	13,520
Club Forty One	4	G	7	1	2	1	33,125
Clubay	6	M	6	3	1	0	115,440
Clusivity	3	G	5	0	0	0	655
Cluster Bomb	3	C	6	1	3	1	51,130
Cluster of Gems	2	F	8	0	2	1	22,295
Clydes Agenda	5	H	3	0	0	0	409
Cmego	4	G	15	3	3	2	106,614
C'Mon Cletus	8	H	1	0	0	0	84
C'Mon Hammer	2	C	2	0	0	0	1,090
C'Mon Josie	3	F	2	1	0	0	15,361
C'Mon Kreed	2	G	9	1	1	1	6,372
Cmonbabylitemyfire	3	F	1	0	0	0	0
Co Chief King	4	G	9	0	2	3	13,264
Co Co Heart	5	M	9	1	1	1	43,547
Co Twining Niner	5	G	16	8	0	0	33,484
Coach Connor	2	C	2	0	0	0	175
Coach Gatlin	7	G	12	1	1	4	8,821
Coach Gay's Day	6	G	15	2	4	3	25,862
Coach Jenny	3	F	5	0	0	0	1,087
Coach Jimi Lee	4	G	12	3	4	1	240,618
Coach Lass	2	C	4	0	2	0	3,900
Coach Numero Uno	3	G	8	0	0	0	846
Coach Rags	8	G	5	1	0	0	25,275
Coach Read	7	G	8	0	0	0	1,560
Coach's Corner	5	G	6	1	2	1	11,430
Coahoma	5	H	8	1	2	3	53,788
Coal Black Rose	4	F	16	3	3	2	32,722
Coal Cash	3	G	10	1	1	0	6,964
Coal Creek Slew	6	H	2	0	0	0	270
Coal Inmy Stocking	4	F	10	1	0	0	6,729
Coal Smudge	3	G	8	2	0	0	53,291
Coalbank	3	C	7	1	3	0	6,998
Coalcango	2	F	4	1	0	1	7,250
Coalfield	3	C	5	1	0	0	13,975
Coalition	4	G	10	0	1	2	28,166
Coalition Lad	2	C	1	0	0	1	4,100
Coalpepper	4	G	7	0	0	1	2,394
Coalson	2	C	2	0	0	0	208
Coaly's Odds	3	G	1	0	0	0	116
Coast Line	3	G	3	3	0	0	67,400
Coastal Boundary	3	F	10	1	1	0	8,000
Coastal Candy	3	F	4	0	0	0	555
Coastal Cat	5	G	8	0	2	0	11,025
Coastal Colony	4	G	4	0	0	0	326
Coastal Display	11	G	13	0	1	1	5,444

Horse	Age	Sex	Sts	1st	2d	3d	Won
Coastal Flag	2	F	6	0	0	3	11,600
Coastal Fortress	2	F	6	2	1	1	165,309
Coastal Lady	2	F	1	0	0	0	625
Coastal Strike	2	F	2	2	0	0	89,520
Coastal War	3	G	14	0	0	1	3,961
Coastal Wolf	3	F	10	0	1	1	5,722
Coastalegionaire	3	F	4	0	0	0	416
Coastalota	7	M	4	0	2	0	16,000
Coastin' Bird	3	C	4	1	0	0	6,940
Coasting Barnie	4	G	3	0	0	0	165
Coat of Armor	7	G	13	5	3	1	52,165
Coax a Red Bird	5	G	3	0	2	0	2,320
Coax Kid	4	C	7	2	0	1	20,540
Coax Me a Grand	3	F	9	0	0	0	856
Coax Me Bragg	4	G	12	1	0	1	7,595
Coax Me Cody	5	G	9	0	2	3	7,084
Coax Me Irish	4	F	2	0	0	0	240
Coax Me Katink	3	F	6	1	0	0	6,025
Coax No More	4	G	3	0	0	0	207
Coax On Jodi	4	F	1	0	0	0	49
Coaxed	3	C	4	1	0	0	21,400
Coaxial	3	F	6	0	0	0	1,641
Coaxing Halo	3	F	7	0	2	1	5,569
Coaxingriches	8	M	2	0	0	0	88
Cobalt Casey	3	G	11	0	0	3	10,390
Coban	2	C	2	0	0	0	120
Cobashack	8	G	2	0	0	0	128
Cobb County	6	G	13	3	3	2	16,737
Cobb Road	4	G	3	0	0	0	0
Cobble Street	3	G	2	1	1	0	23,820
Cobbley's Jewel	3	F	14	2	1	3	53,800
Cobbley's Mark	7	H	2	0	1	0	2,921
Cobbley's Pride	3	G	13	2	0	2	39,205
Cobb's Sweetie	3	F	2	1	0	0	4,576
Cobi Ky	3	F	12	3	1	0	39,527
Cobra Devil	6	G	14	2	1	4	9,550
Cobra Lady	4	F	7	3	1	0	81,189
Cobra Lips	4	C	3	0	0	0	0
Cobra Luana	3	F	2	0	0	0	750
Cobra Power	4	G	13	3	2	2	47,445
Cobra Son	5	G	3	0	0	2	2,985
Cobra Squeeze	5	M	7	0	0	1	1,656
Cobra Star	4	G	6	1	1	2	46,442
Cobra Tongue	5	G	6	0	0	0	749
Cobra Torch	4	F	3	0	0	0	100
Cobra's Prince	6	G	3	1	0	1	3,710
Cobra's Princess	4	F	9	3	1	1	15,440
Coby Appeal	8	G	15	1	3	3	19,580
Cocked	4	G	3	0	0	2	1,230
Cocked N Locked	8	G	10	0	0	0	200
Cockle Burr Man	5	G	9	4	1	2	28,840
Cockleburr Kate	3	F	5	0	0	0	292
Cockleshell	3	C	6	3	0	0	68,460
Cocktail Dancer	2	F	3	0	0	0	1,080
Cocktailchicattire	2	F	2	0	0	0	800
Cocktailsandreams	7	M	11	0	2	1	28,750
Cocky'n Sure	4	G	11	0	0	0	1,241
Coco an Creme	3	F	6	0	0	1	2,484
Coco Beware	3	F	12	1	1	1	9,785
Coco de Bentwood	5	M	2	0	0	0	0
Coco Lady	3	F	11	1	1	1	18,090
Coco Mocha	5	M	15	4	5	1	19,867
Coco Rico	5	G	7	0	0	1	833
Cocoa Classic	2	C	2	0	0	0	830
Cocoa Cream	3	F	11	1	1	3	20,700
Cocoa Latte	3	G	11	6	2	1	89,680
Cocoa Mio	3	F	6	0	0	1	2,875
Cocoa On	2	F	1	0	1	0	2,700
Cocoa's Gabriella	5	M	8	1	0	0	3,428
Cocodan	3	G	11	2	1	2	29,280
Cocodrie	5	G	11	5	0	1	20,073
Cocolette	4	F	6	1	1	1	5,299
Coconut Girl	5	M	9	2	1	2	154,686
Coconut Mango	5	G	1	0	0	0	0
Coconut Martini	3	F	6	1	0	0	26,755
Coconut Popsicle	2	F	7	1	0	2	38,795
Coconut Willy	7	G	7	1	4	0	16,318
Coconuts Baby	3	G	14	2	1	1	17,170
Cocorite	4	F	13	0	5	3	12,755

Horse	Age	Sex	Sts	1st	2d	3d	Won
Coco's Clown	4	C	2	0	0	0	120
Coco's for Real	3	F	11	3	2	1	64,280
Coco's Girl	3	F	2	0	0	0	0
Coco's Minister	4	G	18	4	4	0	47,280
Coco's Pal	3	G	2	0	0	0	0
Coco's World	2	F	8	0	0	5	16,543
Codatori	3	C	8	0	1	1	5,977
Coddle Creek	3	F	6	0	5	0	18,800
Code Ack Moment	5	M	9	2	2	1	21,270
Code Blind	3	G	8	1	1	1	7,100
Code Blush	5	G	4	1	0	1	10,730
Code Cracker	3	G	2	1	0	0	20,700
Code Found	9	G	5	0	2	1	3,410
Code Hey	4	F	2	1	0	0	700
Code Lady	4	F	12	0	2	3	3,480
Code Man	5	G	5	0	0	1	946
Code Name Elmer	4	G	15	3	4	2	17,475
Code Name Flirt	4	F	1	1	0	0	7,500
Code Name Fred	8	G	8	0	2	3	28,729
Code Name Louie	7	H	5	2	0	0	9,900
Code Name Romeo	4	C	2	0	0	0	143
Code of Angels	3	G	6	0	0	0	3,160
Code of Ethics	3	F	12	4	2	0	109,070
Code of Justice	3	F	13	5	3	1	84,353
Code Song	3	F	2	0	0	0	2,040
Code Sugar	5	G	9	0	2	3	6,270
Coded Account	5	M	11	2	5	0	14,737
Coded Message	6	G	8	3	0	2	78,220
Coded Princess	2	F	3	1	0	0	13,850
Coded Warning	3	C	10	2	2	2	87,654
Codeofmanycolors	3	C	5	0	0	0	674
Coder Steve	5	G	1	0	0	0	300
Code's Decree	5	M	11	0	1	2	15,447
Codes Miss Doc	3	F	10	0	2	1	5,032
Codes Preshisone	6	M	9	3	1	1	52,714
Codes Spit Fire	5	H	15	2	0	4	13,497
Codex Dancer	3	C	4	0	0	2	3,320
Codexs Heiress	6	M	19	1	0	0	4,306
Codrington (JPN)	4	F	3	0	0	0	2,200
Cody Girl	3	F	2	0	0	0	0
Cody Grove	3	G	2	1	0	0	15,790
Cody H.	4	C	2	1	0	0	16,320
Cody Light	6	G	11	1	5	1	25,120
Cody Man West	7	G	8	0	0	0	1,284
Cody Ody	4	G	8	0	0	5	10,730
Cody Steele	5	G	16	3	3	2	17,988
Cody to Reggie	4	G	9	1	4	2	33,655
Cody Wade	3	G	5	1	0	2	3,200
Codyinthelead	4	F	7	2	3	0	18,906
Cody's Colony	3	G	8	0	0	1	2,781
Cody's Con	4	G	10	2	2	3	16,545
Cody's Encore	2	F	3	1	0	0	4,822
Cody's History	3	C	14	1	4	1	35,423
Cody's Kisses	3	F	5	0	0	1	1,306
Codys Lucky Appeal	4	C	21	3	3	3	51,442
Codys My Boy	3	G	10	3	0	2	34,780
Codys Odds	4	C	1	0	0	0	0
Cody's Vidalia	3	F	2	0	0	0	0
Coed Cutie	4	F	11	1	0	2	8,755
Coercion	4	F	6	2	2	0	12,370
Coeur Di Leone	4	G	1	0	0	0	0
Coeur Joie	3	C	5	0	1	1	9,863
Coeus	3	C	3	1	0	2	35,600
Cofema	5	G	4	0	0	0	0
Coffee and Creme	9	G	7	1	1	1	9,241
Coffee Bubbles	7	G	7	1	1	0	2,400
Coffee Gully	3	C	1	0	0	0	130
Coffee House	2	F	3	0	0	2	5,720
Coffee Street	4	G	6	3	0	0	33,174
Cog	5	H	1	0	0	0	156
Cogar	3	G	1	0	0	0	37
Coggon	6	G	8	1	0	1	22,085
Cognac Supreme	6	G	9	1	2	1	6,758
Cogs My Man	4	C	3	0	0	1	1,806
Cohassett Rocks	3	C	16	4	2	2	24,544
Coherent	4	F	4	1	1	0	30,410
Cohiba Kid	5	G	8	0	0	1	1,032
Cohn Blue (IRE)	3	C	2	0	0	0	710
Coil N Strike	6	G	13	2	2	3	30,032

Horse	Age	Sex	Sts	1st	2d	3d	Won
Coilide	3	G	2	0	0	2	3,430
Coin Charger	5	G	13	2	2	2	7,379
Coin Collection	3	F	1	0	0	0	0
Coin Maker	3	G	13	3	1	3	45,088
Coin Patch	3	G	2	0	0	0	0
Coin Silver	2	C	1	0	0	0	2,150
Coin Toss	3	G	9	2	2	0	10,708
Coin Treasure	4	G	6	0	1	1	3,170
Coin Trick	4	F	2	0	0	2	2,420
Coincide	5	H	7	1	0	1	23,170
Coincidence	3	F	9	0	0	1	4,431
Coined for Success	3	G	13	4	1	1	151,693
Cointreau	4	C	2	0	1	0	11,160
Coja	4	G	11	2	1	2	17,595
Cojet	5	G	7	0	0	4	29,205
Coker Road	3	G	8	0	1	1	5,842
Coke's Melody	3	F	9	1	2	2	63,107
Coke's Tribute	6	G	4	1	0	0	5,310
Col Garrett	3	G	1	0	0	0	0
Colbeer	2	C	4	1	0	0	4,524
Colby Flash	3	F	13	2	0	2	13,426
Colby Jordan	2	G	5	0	0	1	1,650
Colby's Boy	4	C	3	0	0	0	503
Colby's Spirit	2	G	2	0	0	0	800
Colchis	5	H	5	0	0	0	1,165
Cold and Windswept	4	F	16	4	5	4	40,455
Cold Beauty	2	F	1	0	0	1	935
Cold Blow Lane	6	G	7	0	0	2	7,220
Cold Call Cowboy	5	G	4	0	0	0	1,300
Cold Cash Reward	5	H	1	0	0	0	0
Cold Chicken	2	G	1	0	0	0	137
Cold Chill	5	H	2	0	0	0	250
Cold Chillin	5	M	9	3	2	1	21,486
Cold Chisel	10	G	9	1	0	0	2,716
Cold Claim	6	G	3	0	0	0	680
Cold Cocked	2	G	2	0	0	0	425
Cold Cold Facts	6	G	5	0	1	0	1,443
Cold Day in July	2	F	1	0	0	0	110
Cold Express	8	G	17	0	5	2	13,533
Cold Fax of Life	3	F	6	1	2	0	5,704
Cold Front	3	F	4	1	0	0	22,700
Cold Game	3	G	5	1	3	0	11,120
Cold Hard Dash	2	F	5	2	0	1	50,100
Cold Hard Truth	9	G	9	0	1	1	2,958
Cold Hearted Crook	3	G	5	0	0	0	0
Cold Hearted Woman	3	F	7	1	0	3	13,970
Cold Market	5	G	4	0	1	0	5,200
Cold N Evil	4	G	6	0	0	1	1,680
Cold N Tricky	2	G	1	1	0	0	5,225
Cold North Wind	3	G	12	2	1	1	45,218
Cold Play	3	F	13	4	2	1	23,876
Cold Prospect	5	G	1	0	0	0	120
Cold Shower	4	G	1	0	0	0	400
Cold Sky	4	G	4	0	0	0	0
Cold Spring	6	M	13	2	0	1	11,774
Cold Stone Steve	5	H	6	1	1	0	6,500
Cold Suggestion	3	G	12	4	1	2	16,716
Cold Toes	2	F	4	0	0	1	4,310
Cold Trail	3	G	9	0	0	0	2,112
Cold Truth	4	G	11	2	2	1	57,845
Cold Tudor	3	G	19	2	4	3	18,415
Cold Turkey	6	M	3	1	0	2	28,490
Cold War	3	G	13	1	1	4	25,760
Cold Water	3	G	7	3	0	1	60,185
Cold Wynnter	3	F	3	0	1	1	24,680
Coldbeerathebit	3	F	12	1	4	1	29,046
Coldblooded Pirate	4	G	11	1	0	2	3,892
Colder's Belonging	3	G	6	1	0	0	7,770
Coldiron Slew	5	G	1	0	0	0	0
Coldntight	3	R	6	0	0	0	6,060
Coldstream	5	G	9	1	1	1	10,530
Cole	6	G	8	1	1	2	27,798
Cole James	2	G	7	1	4	1	20,896
Cole Younger	5	G	2	0	0	0	0
Colebrook Creek	8	G	12	3	3	0	21,000
Colebrook Crusader	6	G	2	0	0	0	111
Colebrook Fighter	7	M	6	1	1	2	24,452
Colebrook Glory	7	G	8	0	0	3	2,870
Colebrook Red	7	G	7	0	0	0	0
Colebrook Ruckus	6	G	12	1	2	1	38,528
Colebrook Striker	4	G	3	2	0	0	15,371
Coleman Bonner	3	G	4	0	3	1	12,650
Colemans Cheval	7	G	4	0	0	0	1,479
Colero Wildfire	4	F	5	0	0	0	0
Coles a Champ	4	G	7	0	3	2	15,830
Cole's a Warrior	3	C	1	0	0	0	2,250
Colesburg	4	G	9	0	0	2	1,667
Coleslew	4	G	13	1	4	1	22,954
Colihan	8	G	5	0	1	0	1,250
Colin Road	6	G	2	0	0	0	135
Colins Buddy	5	G	3	0	0	0	1,350
Colita	4	C	7	2	3	1	120,330
Collateral Damage	4	G	8	2	2	1	87,415
Collateral Maker	3	G	2	1	0	0	1,650
Collect Deposit	6	H	2	0	0	0	310
Collect the Gold	4	G	8	0	2	0	3,537
Collectdance	3	G	3	0	0	0	245
Collection	5	M	7	0	0	2	3,543
Collector's Club	4	F	3	0	0	0	1,200
Colleen's Jackpot	4	F	18	3	4	0	29,218
Colleen's Mint	4	F	1	0	0	0	75
Colleen's Star	2	G	4	0	0	1	3,860
College Dean	9	G	4	2	0	0	20,940
College Education	3	F	2	0	0	0	400
College Graduate	2	C	3	0	0	0	5,160
Collier Gold	4	C	12	1	0	0	4,493
Collier Slew	3	G	20	1	4	2	42,573
Collier's Pleasure	6	M	1	0	0	0	0
Collingwood	2	G	1	0	0	0	0
Collinstown	4	G	5	0	0	2	3,009
Collymore Hall	4	F	1	0	0	0	250
Cologny	4	F	15	7	4	2	280,408
Colombini	3	G	5	0	1	1	4,800
Colominas	3	F	5	0	1	1	7,280
Colondelivery	5	G	4	0	0	0	3,561
Colonel Beep	2	G	1	0	0	1	935
Colonel Bradshaw	4	C	4	0	0	1	840
Colonel Cleator	3	G	7	1	0	0	22,215
Colonel Courtney	4	G	14	4	1	4	38,780
Colonel Dan	4	G	1	0	0	0	0
Colonel Day	3	G	4	2	0	1	34,500
Colonel Duncan	2	C	7	1	0	1	16,350
Colonel Fordyce	10	G	2	0	1	0	1,700
Colonel Jake	4	G	6	2	0	0	2,721
Colonel Kelly	9	G	1	1	0	0	4,400
Colonel Lyle	5	G	1	0	0	0	123
Colonel Matt	2	C	1	0	0	0	0
Colonel Rib	3	C	4	1	1	1	9,360
Colonel Spike	11	G	8	0	0	1	1,117
Colonel Warden	4	C	4	1	0	0	27,424
Colonel's Letters	4	G	2	0	0	0	265
Colonel's Passion	4	G	3	0	0	0	238
Colonial Bay	5	G	5	1	0	0	34,435
Colonial Billy	4	G	7	2	1	2	30,315
Colonial Cat	3	F	9	0	0	1	3,057
Colonial Colony	6	H	9	1	1	1	607,625
Colonial Fire	5	H	1	0	0	0	67
Colonial Gift	5	H	7	0	1	0	3,575
Colonial Gray	5	G	9	2	1	1	19,310
Colonial Inca	4	C	8	3	0	1	36,259
Colonial Justice	5	G	7	1	0	0	3,342
Colonial Loot	8	H	22	5	3	4	45,740
Colonial Mint	4	F	11	3	0	0	17,058
Colonial Native	6	G	12	0	0	2	2,620
Colonial Policy	8	G	6	0	0	0	731
Colonial Power	10	H	2	0	0	0	0
Colonial Prospect	4	C	12	1	3	0	22,889
Colonial Reign	3	C	6	1	2	1	52,040
Colonial Relay	11	H	1	0	0	0	500
Colonial Run (IRE)	3	G	3	0	0	0	1,461
Colonial Silver	2	C	1	0	0	1	4,100
Colonial Strike	2	F	6	0	0	1	9,790
Colonial Surprise	4	F	7	2	1	0	92,480
Colonial Trust	6	G	12	1	0	1	3,486
Colonials Princess	7	M	3	0	0	0	132
Colony	6	G	3	0	0	0	136
Colony Landing	2	C	3	0	0	0	300
Colony Lane	5	G	4	0	0	1	3,677

Horse	Age	Sex	Sts	1st	2d	3d	Won
Colony Ridge	5	G	6	0	0	1	870
Colony Sands	3	F	2	0	0	0	780
Colony Times	3	F	13	1	0	0	9,329
Color Blind	4	G	12	3	1	2	26,285
Color by d'Or	7	G	5	1	1	0	30,680
Color Me Fast	6	M	9	0	3	1	20,970
Color Me Free	2	C	3	0	1	1	6,720
Color Me Gone	4	C	7	1	1	1	17,669
Color Me Lucky	4	G	10	0	0	0	1,974
Color Me Perfect	3	F	5	1	0	0	4,250
Color My Canvas	3	F	1	0	1	0	2,500
Color My Day	5	M	9	1	1	0	14,363
Color My Rainbow	5	G	21	1	1	0	7,347
Color of Diamonds	2	C	5	0	0	1	4,148
Color Prospector (BRZ)	8	H	2	0	0	0	0
Color Wheel	3	F	8	0	0	3	2,486
Colora	3	F	1	0	0	0	250
Colorado Charmer	3	F	3	0	0	0	0
Colorado Cobra	6	M	5	0	1	0	5,083
Colorado Colleen	2	F	6	0	0	0	1,474
Colorado River	2	C	4	0	0	0	840
Colorado Storm	5	M	2	0	0	0	86
Colorbynumbers	2	F	1	0	0	0	400
Coloreado (CHI)	6	G	14	3	1	5	11,775
Colorful Carol	4	F	10	1	0	3	9,627
Colorful Consomme'	4	F	14	4	1	3	23,519
Colorful Creek	3	F	3	0	0	0	0
Colorful Judgement	4	G	5	2	1	0	277,602
Colorful One	4	G	15	3	2	4	45,484
Colorful Saint	5	G	12	1	1	1	7,075
Colorful Tour	5	H	13	1	2	3	58,070
Colorful Zee	4	C	1	0	0	0	0
Colorfull Banner	4	G	16	1	5	2	32,268
Colormegreen	9	M	3	0	0	0	0
Colors 'n Scents	5	M	4	0	0	0	807
Colors of an Angle	6	M	8	0	1	2	4,381
Colors of the Wind	3	F	5	0	0	1	3,131
Colorswiththewind	8	G	12	0	0	0	1,768
Colstrip	3	G	2	0	0	0	540
Colt Python	4	C	11	2	3	2	94,870
Coltie	7	G	6	0	0	1	436
Colton's Charm	5	H	2	0	0	0	0
Colton's Comet	2	C	9	1	0	0	9,090
Coltrane	3	G	12	1	3	3	63,096
Columba	4	F	10	3	2	0	47,350
Columbia Gorge	9	G	13	1	0	3	4,520
Columbia Moon	3	C	2	2	0	0	29,357
Columbia Road	3	C	2	0	0	0	480
Columbian Cat	7	M	16	1	1	1	7,771
Columbus Hero	2	C	1	0	0	0	0
Colville Beach	3	F	4	1	1	1	7,770
Colville Zeal	2	F	5	0	0	0	3,390
Colway Bobbie	4	F	7	2	0	0	7,246
Comacina	2	F	6	1	0	3	55,902
Comalagold	4	F	8	3	1	2	83,590
Comanche Dancer	7	H	5	0	0	0	174
Comanche Queen	4	F	15	5	4	1	32,160
Comanche Star	3	F	11	1	2	5	72,450
Comanche Station	3	G	7	2	1	2	19,553
Comanchee Uprising	3	G	3	0	0	0	56
Comanchero's Treat	3	F	2	0	0	0	0
Comandante Kyle	4	G	7	0	1	1	2,024
Combat Boots	5	H	4	0	0	0	306
Combat Chief	4	G	15	2	4	0	20,896
Combat Cutie	7	M	7	0	0	0	456
Combat Mission	4	G	2	0	0	0	276
Combat Soldier	4	F	7	0	0	1	3,080
Combat Zone	3	G	5	1	1	0	13,600
Combeau Tuffy	5	G	12	1	2	2	6,635
Combinatorial	4	G	3	0	1	0	1,403
Combine	5	H	4	0	0	0	470
Combustion	4	G	7	0	0	0	0
Come a Stridin	11	G	4	0	0	0	75
Come About	6	G	3	0	0	1	2,415
Come Back Ronnie	9	H	2	0	0	1	2,160
Come Close	2	C	2	0	0	0	1,684
Come Dance	3	F	7	2	3	0	42,894
Come Fly With Me	11	M	10	0	1	0	3,438
Come Follow Me	2	C	2	0	0	0	0
Come for the Gold	4	F	7	1	3	0	7,900
Come From Sonora	3	G	3	1	1	1	14,250
Come Hither Look	5	M	11	1	2	3	23,057
Come Home George	3	G	6	1	0	2	7,850
Come Loded	3	G	4	0	0	0	186
Come On Back	5	G	4	0	0	1	1,045
Come On Chas	2	C	7	0	2	1	18,360
Come On Coyote	10	G	1	0	0	0	0
Come On Cricket	4	F	3	0	0	0	450
Come On Crystal	3	F	6	0	1	0	1,588
Come On Dan	3	C	3	0	0	0	0
Come On Expresso	3	F	1	0	0	0	125
Come On Five	3	F	13	0	2	4	2,707
Come On Helen	2	F	1	0	0	0	110
Come On Jazz	3	C	10	3	3	1	91,145
Come On John	2	F	3	0	0	0	1,177
Come On Nifty	5	G	13	1	1	2	10,647
Come On Precious	3	F	12	3	3	2	26,885
Come On Red	3	C	3	0	0	0	0
Come On Smokey	4	G	10	0	2	1	9,880
Come On Spider	7	G	13	2	1	1	16,447
Come Out Roll	3	C	7	0	0	0	817
Come Out Shining	2	G	2	0	0	0	600
Come Out Smokin'	3	C	11	2	0	1	75,251
Come to Cashel	4	F	4	0	0	2	6,360
Come to Pass	5	G	10	3	1	0	6,376
Come With Thunder	2	F	4	0	2	2	14,030
Comealive	2	G	5	1	1	0	18,937
Comealong	2	C	1	0	0	0	0
Comearocking	3	F	5	1	0	0	4,323
Comeawaywithme	3	F	9	1	2	2	30,515
Comecatchme	3	F	2	0	0	2	2,880
Comedy Cat	3	C	1	0	0	0	287
Comedy Club	7	G	8	0	1	0	3,490
Comedy Event	2	F	2	0	0	0	800
Comedy Flyer	4	F	9	1	1	1	8,671
Comedy Hour	2	C	2	1	0	0	2,280
Comedy Show	4	G	12	1	2	0	9,107
Comeon	5	M	2	0	0	0	700
Comeon and Play	2	C	6	1	1	2	20,750
Comeon Dixie	4	F	2	0	0	0	640
Comeongal	2	F	5	1	0	1	18,580
Comes a Tide	4	G	15	0	1	1	9,923
Comes the Dawn	5	M	5	1	0	1	17,227
Comes Unglued	3	F	5	1	0	0	11,595
Comesmilewithme	5	M	9	0	1	3	2,170
Comet Blue	5	M	12	1	3	3	13,636
Comet Junior	3	C	6	1	2	0	2,948
Comet Kris	9	G	5	0	0	2	2,300
Comet Returns	5	G	17	0	4	2	8,103
Comet Revenge	3	G	12	1	1	1	8,728
Comet Surprise	7	G	5	1	0	0	4,875
Cometary	5	G	18	1	2	1	4,860
Cometeo	7	M	4	0	0	0	600
Cometes	4	G	8	0	1	0	2,983
Comet's Light	3	F	9	1	2	0	8,379
Comets Mystery	7	M	5	1	0	0	8,100
Comfort Me	3	G	8	1	0	0	8,069
Comfortable Win	5	G	5	0	0	0	242
Comic Ack	3	C	9	2	3	1	31,800
Comic Book	4	G	8	1	1	1	8,495
Comic Cat	2	G	4	0	0	1	6,778
Comic Empress	3	F	7	1	1	2	14,025
Comic Express	3	G	7	3	1	1	20,275
Comic Opera	3	F	9	1	0	0	12,076
Comic Pride	3	G	3	0	0	1	1,400
Comic Truth	4	C	3	1	0	1	9,960
Comic Valentine	4	F	11	2	0	2	13,179
Comical Judith	3	F	16	0	1	1	5,275
Comics Dream	2	F	1	0	0	0	2,100
Comin On Thru	3	G	3	0	0	0	196
Coming About	3	G	6	0	0	0	794
Comingdownthelane	2	C	2	0	0	0	216
Comingupforair	4	G	8	1	1	2	11,545
Comkey	3	G	3	0	0	0	1,487
Commanche Feather	2	C	1	0	0	0	0
Commanchero Kid	3	C	10	1	3	1	14,250
Command Center	4	C	14	0	1	4	34,003
Command Frankie (GB)	3	G	2	0	0	0	695

RECORDS OF HORSES

Horse	Age	Sex	Sts	1st	2d	3d	Won
Command Power	8	G	6	1	1	1	7,143
Command Respect	3	C	8	3	1	1	25,275
Command the Best	4	C	10	1	0	3	11,739
Commandant	2	C	7	0	0	2	25,368
Commandeer	5	G	2	0	0	0	0
Commander	5	H	3	0	0	0	0
Commander B C	4	C	1	0	0	0	0
Commander Benno	4	C	3	0	0	0	510
Commander Buck	3	G	3	1	0	0	6,600
Commander Case	4	G	7	0	1	2	980
Commander Hal	4	G	6	2	0	3	45,760
Commander Jag	4	G	6	1	1	0	7,636
Commander Maximus	3	G	11	1	2	2	10,880
Commander Niko (NZ)	6	G	3	0	0	0	1,258
Commander Pat	2	C	3	0	2	0	15,560
Commander Perry	3	G	4	0	1	0	2,601
Commander Robin	3	C	9	2	1	0	15,485
Commander Slew	6	G	2	0	0	0	0
Commander Zack	3	G	2	0	0	0	135
Commander's Affair	4	G	12	3	4	0	26,695
Commander's Flag	5	H	4	1	0	0	48,150
Commander's Lady	4	F	6	0	0	0	6,453
Commanding	4	F	3	0	0	0	1,200
Commanding Creek	4	G	5	0	0	1	3,470
Commanding Force	3	G	12	1	1	2	10,679
Commanding Heights	2	G	8	1	0	0	8,390
Commanding Lady	3	F	10	2	1	2	68,481
Commanding Link	5	G	10	0	1	2	5,721
Commanding Victory	3	G	8	0	0	0	1,590
Commandment	3	C	14	1	2	2	23,788
Commandra	3	F	5	0	0	2	5,504
Commangetit	2	C	1	0	0	0	0
Commemorate's Note	3	F	5	0	0	0	1,000
Commendable Diva	2	F	5	0	1	1	5,260
Commendation	3	C	11	0	3	2	85,836
Commentator	3	G	5	5	0	0	180,692
Commercant Vic	4	C	9	2	1	0	50,093
Commercante (FR)	4	F	4	2	1	0	630,000
Commercial Break	2	F	1	0	0	0	0
Commercial Desirer	4	G	2	0	0	0	0
Commercialize	2	F	4	0	2	1	13,250
Commission	4	C	3	1	0	0	22,140
Commit Me	2	F	8	1	1	2	12,335
Commitisize Me	2	F	5	2	0	1	36,468
Committed Actress	3	F	2	0	0	0	2,940
Commodity	4	C	2	0	1	0	5,040
Commodity Trader	2	C	1	0	0	1	4,100
Commodore Craig	5	G	8	1	3	2	51,153
Commodore's Flag	4	G	9	1	0	1	11,446
Common Friday	6	G	10	0	3	1	4,781
Common Ground	3	G	12	2	0	1	8,979
Community Honors	4	C	6	1	0	0	7,230
Como Candie	4	F	13	1	3	1	10,258
Comondon	4	G	10	0	1	1	5,844
Comp	4	G	8	1	2	2	23,650
Compact's Boy	3	G	2	0	0	0	240
Compadre Dancer	4	G	8	0	1	1	5,683
Compadre Just Ten	3	G	5	0	0	1	2,079
Compadre's Peach	5	M	14	0	2	0	5,994
Companero	3	C	7	0	0	0	2,358
Company Coming	9	M	2	0	0	0	0
Company Ink	2	G	3	1	0	1	7,650
Company Jet	6	H	13	2	2	2	15,763
Company Lawyer	3	F	7	1	0	0	13,020
Company Man	5	G	3	0	0	0	1,900
Company Memo	4	F	2	0	0	0	0
Company of Mary	4	F	2	0	0	0	0
Comparison	3	F	9	2	1	2	31,207
Compassionate Girl	3	F	19	1	1	4	14,099
Compeer's Bequest	6	M	2	0	0	0	0
Compelled	4	G	1	0	0	0	225
Compelling Fantasy	3	F	11	1	0	2	25,145
Compelling Launch	7	G	5	0	0	1	2,185
Compelling Rose	3	F	3	0	0	0	705
Compelling Secret	4	F	3	0	0	0	0
Compelling Story	5	H	2	0	0	0	0
Compelling Wind	3	F	3	0	0	0	385
Compelling World	6	G	3	0	0	1	3,650
Compendium	6	H	1	0	0	0	276
Compensator	3	G	11	1	0	0	10,083
Competitive Dancer	3	C	2	0	0	0	0
Competitive Dude	2	C	3	0	0	0	835
Competitive Edge	4	F	1	1	0	0	4,740
Competitive Nature	5	G	7	0	1	0	3,180
Complements	8	M	6	0	0	0	1,324
Complete Approval	8	M	3	0	0	1	2,730
Complete Coverage	3	G	12	1	1	2	11,570
Complete Edition	6	M	3	1	0	0	4,000
Complete Lady	3	F	4	0	1	0	4,615
Complete Tizzy	3	G	9	1	1	3	5,870
Complete Verdict	8	G	3	0	0	1	1,125
Complete Warrior	3	G	5	0	0	1	3,595
Complete Withdrawl	4	C	5	0	0	0	1,309
Completely Lost	5	M	10	0	1	1	5,500
Completion	3	F	14	5	1	3	59,760
Completo (ARG)	5	H	2	0	0	0	0
Complex Goals	2	C	2	0	0	0	730
Complicated	2	G	1	0	0	0	50
Comply With Di	9	G	4	1	0	1	4,240
Compound	3	C	8	0	1	1	9,314
Comprado	3	G	5	0	0	0	102
Comprador	4	C	8	2	2	0	31,140
Comprehensively	4	G	18	2	2	0	12,418
Comprobante	3	F	6	0	3	0	8,230
Compulsive	2	C	1	1	0	0	29,400
Compute	2	C	2	0	0	0	720
Computer Diana	3	F	16	3	2	2	31,020
Computer Gate	5	G	3	0	1	0	5,325
Comstock Dream	4	F	5	0	0	0	379
Comstock Glory	5	M	8	1	3	0	6,181
Comte Du Rainier	5	G	5	0	1	0	3,735
Con	7	G	7	1	2	2	4,790
Con Air Won	6	M	11	1	2	1	14,830
Con Con Man	2	C	5	0	1	1	14,463
Con Dot Dixie	5	H	15	0	3	1	5,063
Con Quixote	6	G	8	2	2	0	72,561
Con Say One	2	G	1	0	0	0	162
Con Totally	3	F	1	0	0	0	0
Conazz	3	F	7	1	2	0	8,865
Conbest	7	M	13	0	0	3	2,444
Conbird	5	M	4	0	0	3	3,650
Conceal	4	F	5	0	0	0	0
Conceal the Deal	3	F	11	1	1	1	35,250
Concern Buddy	3	G	9	2	3	1	21,602
Concert Bythe Lake	2	F	3	1	0	0	9,140
Concert Classic	5	G	9	1	0	0	5,790
Concert Goer	3	G	5	0	1	0	7,296
Concerta	4	F	15	3	4	3	24,524
Concerto Grosso (CHI)	9	G	4	1	1	0	13,200
Concertoville	4	F	4	0	0	0	820
Concession Speech	4	G	12	3	3	0	28,232
Concetta	3	F	3	1	1	0	7,700
Concho Honcho	6	H	5	0	2	0	701
Conchy Joe	6	H	3	0	0	1	1,247
Concierto De Varsovia (CHI)	3	C	3	0	0	0	1,720
Conciliator	5	G	3	0	0	0	161
Concisely	4	G	18	6	3	1	88,433
Concoction	4	F	8	1	2	2	6,226
Concord Miss	2	F	11	1	2	0	20,889
Concordance	5	M	16	2	4	1	9,957
Concorde Country	3	G	5	0	0	0	1,250
Concorde Illusion	9	G	11	0	0	1	1,476
Concorde Vigil	2	F	2	0	0	0	195
Concorde Wind	2	C	1	0	0	0	150
Concorde's Appeal	5	H	4	1	0	0	7,000
Concorde's Term	4	G	12	1	2	1	14,225
Concrete Block	4	G	1	0	0	0	910
Concurrent	9	G	8	1	0	0	7,110
Condeleezza S.	4	F	2	0	0	0	110
Condesa	3	F	10	1	3	0	19,775
Conditional	3	G	11	4	2	0	26,300
Conditional Love	5	M	3	1	0	1	8,975
Condo Bob	6	G	7	1	1	3	2,362
Condo Prison	5	G	7	1	0	2	20,800
Condor	4	G	15	0	2	1	10,890
Condor Pasa	9	H	1	0	0	1	275
Condotierri	4	G	7	0	0	0	3,068
Conduct	2	F	6	0	0	2	10,101

Horse	Age	Sex	Sts	1st	2d	3d	Won
Cone of Silence	4	G	12	5	1	1	73,210
Cones Pride	5	G	6	1	0	2	4,376
Conestoga	3	G	8	0	3	1	29,250
Coney Island King	3	C	18	1	5	2	25,220
Coney Kitty (IRE)	6	M	9	2	1	2	136,145
Confederate Camp	3	C	1	0	0	0	0
Confederate Jack	5	G	5	1	0	0	6,300
Confederate Symbol	7	G	1	0	0	0	40
Confer	5	G	11	2	0	0	13,256
Conference Called	4	C	1	0	0	0	0
Confess to Me	4	C	9	1	1	0	4,620
Confession	4	G	6	0	2	0	10,717
Confiance Moi	6	H	4	0	0	0	675
Confidability	3	F	6	0	1	1	6,400
Confidare	3	G	4	0	0	0	390
Confide in Tyler	4	G	11	1	1	2	6,928
Confident Cat	3	C	4	2	0	0	54,400
Confident Girl	3	F	1	0	0	0	300
Confident Heart	4	F	9	1	1	1	16,425
Confident Spirit	3	F	2	0	0	0	101
Confident Tyler	2	C	5	1	2	1	24,860
Confidential Ave.	3	C	6	0	3	0	6,670
Confidential Call	2	G	3	0	0	0	3,596
Confidenza	4	F	19	2	3	2	40,533
Confidital	4	F	2	0	0	0	330
Confirmed	3	C	11	3	6	1	154,137
Confirmed Countess	6	M	2	0	0	0	240
Confirmed Playgirl	4	F	6	0	0	2	1,845
Confirmed Temper	3	F	2	0	1	0	1,770
Conflagasion	6	H	7	4	1	0	25,610
Confrontation	5	M	1	0	0	0	0
Confrontational	2	C	2	0	0	0	409
Confused	4	C	5	1	0	0	12,205
Confused Dreamer	4	C	4	0	0	0	710
Confused Genius	5	M	12	2	3	1	13,723
Conga Line	2	F	1	0	0	0	285
Congaree	6	H	2	0	0	0	26,090
Congenial Spot	3	F	5	0	0	0	0
Congi	5	G	17	3	3	0	17,473
Congo Swing	4	G	10	1	0	2	3,971
Congomambo	5	G	14	1	2	2	12,470
Congrats	4	C	6	2	0	1	160,832
Congress Park	5	G	11	3	2	2	31,490
Congressional Run	3	G	13	3	3	1	86,750
Congressionalhonor	3	C	10	2	2	3	99,638
Conguito	2	G	2	0	0	0	720
Coning Eston	6	M	2	0	0	0	0
Conjecture	5	G	2	0	0	1	682
Conjurer	3	C	2	0	1	0	7,280
Conjuring Creek	4	F	8	1	2	0	8,077
Conman Cunningham	6	H	3	1	0	1	35,900
Connected Way	4	G	3	0	0	0	136
Connecticut River	8	G	15	1	1	2	5,032
Connecting	6	G	4	0	0	0	6,350
Connection Cajun	5	G	1	0	0	0	0
Connectivity	3	G	15	1	1	1	48,004
Conned Again	5	G	7	1	1	2	28,830
Connell Town	3	F	2	1	0	1	44,198
Conner's Brittany	2	F	4	1	1	1	17,640
Connie Belle	2	F	2	0	0	0	4,350
Connie Dar Kid	5	G	1	1	0	0	1,980
Connie Gail	10	G	1	0	0	0	40
Connie One	4	F	2	0	0	2	1,280
Connie's Broke	5	M	12	2	4	0	10,175
Connie's Caboose	4	F	17	0	4	5	18,597
Connie's Deputy	5	G	14	2	1	3	19,452
Connie's Devil	3	G	7	0	0	3	7,917
Connie's Hero	3	G	4	2	1	0	41,650
Connies Joy	5	M	2	0	0	1	1,915
Connie's Magic	8	G	15	4	1	3	80,860
Connies Monster	4	F	11	3	3	2	14,002
Connie's Passion	5	M	11	1	1	1	22,887
Connies Travels	5	M	7	1	0	1	11,661
Connie's Wedding	4	F	1	0	0	0	0
Conniescharmclass	5	M	13	2	1	2	25,183
Conniving Bryan	3	G	12	3	1	1	16,319
Connolly	8	G	2	0	0	0	0
Connor's Clay	3	G	6	1	0	0	9,640
Connor's Colleen	2	F	3	0	0	0	1,360
Connor's Glory	5	G	13	2	3	3	22,149
Connor's Trophy	3	G	10	0	0	0	1,156
Connywithay	5	G	15	2	8	2	40,341
Conowingo	3	F	8	0	0	1	2,459
Conquer of Mine	4	F	1	0	0	0	0
Conquer the Day	5	M	9	2	1	4	54,432
Conquer the Devil	4	C	4	0	0	1	6,643
Conquer the Night	2	C	1	0	0	0	1,850
Conquer This	7	G	9	0	0	2	2,892
Conquestor	5	G	2	0	0	0	0
Conquestress	4	F	7	1	2	1	42,445
Conquista Crossing	3	C	1	0	0	0	0
Conquistador Lad	5	G	14	1	4	3	20,336
Conquistador Starr	3	C	1	0	0	0	0
Conquistadordelite	3	F	10	2	0	1	78,472
Conquistador's Cat	3	C	4	2	0	0	16,440
Conquistador's Joy	3	F	13	1	1	4	16,320
Conquistaprofit	3	F	2	0	0	0	215
Conquistar Dinero	4	G	2	0	1	0	3,000
Conroe's Star	2	C	2	0	0	0	330
Cons Affair	3	G	3	1	0	0	7,875
Con's Night Flight	9	M	8	0	5	0	9,481
Con's Perfectlady	4	F	5	1	1	1	8,228
Consabi	5	M	3	0	1	1	3,700
Conscious Contact	4	G	6	0	0	3	11,510
Conscious Thought	4	G	6	1	0	1	6,548
Consecrate	3	G	14	1	4	4	207,904
Consecreek	4	G	15	2	2	1	14,430
Consent	4	G	9	2	0	0	17,430
Consenting	3	F	5	0	0	1	1,611
Consequential	3	G	9	1	2	1	17,520
Conservation	4	G	11	2	1	3	82,046
Conservationist	3	C	7	2	1	0	76,752
Conserve	8	G	2	0	1	1	6,620
Consfirst	3	F	7	1	1	2	18,102
Consider	3	G	6	1	2	1	16,060
Consiglieres Star	3	G	5	2	0	2	9,996
Consigliore	7	G	3	0	0	0	660
Consignada (CHI)	5	M	1	1	0	0	24,000
Consilience	6	M	4	0	0	1	2,284
Consistency	5	G	1	0	1	0	3,135
Consistent	3	C	1	0	0	1	4,200
Consistently	4	F	2	0	0	0	2,655
Consolidated Fact	4	G	12	4	1	1	32,200
Consolidation	3	G	7	0	0	0	0
Consolidator	2	C	7	2	1	1	480,260
Consoling Granny	4	F	7	0	1	2	6,421
Consort Music	5	M	2	0	0	1	15,040
Conspirator	2	G	3	1	0	0	11,800
Conspire	3	G	6	1	1	0	22,880
Conspiring	4	F	7	1	1	2	62,440
Constancy	4	F	7	1	2	1	39,923
Constant Commotion	4	G	7	1	1	2	24,192
Constant Point	3	G	8	1	2	1	8,266
Constant Pressure	3	C	7	2	2	0	33,970
Constant Thunder	5	G	5	0	1	0	9,255
Constant Touch	4	F	6	2	0	1	67,771
Constant Velocity	2	C	4	1	0	2	11,940
Constant Vigil	3	G	6	0	1	0	6,630
Constantine	2	C	4	0	0	1	3,604
Constantly	6	M	1	0	0	0	259
Constantly the Man	2	C	2	0	0	0	700
Constituent	5	G	9	1	2	1	18,685
Constitution	5	H	2	0	0	0	470
Constitutional	4	F	3	0	0	0	910
Constrictor	5	G	12	2	0	3	10,590
Consultant	6	G	17	1	0	4	7,762
Contagious (GB)	3	F	6	0	2	2	24,451
Contante (ARG)	4	C	1	0	0	0	0
Conte Amour	5	G	21	5	1	8	20,200
Conte Di Dinero	7	G	6	1	1	2	7,200
Conte N Me	2	F	3	0	0	0	500
Contearie Jet	3	C	3	0	1	0	5,420
Contemplation	2	F	2	0	0	0	340
Contemptuous	3	F	13	1	1	0	40,020
Contend	3	G	6	0	0	2	2,657
Contenders Emotion	3	F	7	0	1	1	15,638
Content Cot	3	G	1	0	0	0	0
Contentious Red	4	G	5	1	1	0	5,328

Horse	Age	Sex	Sts	1st	2d	3d	Won
Contessa Bella	2	F	5	0	0	0	0
Contessa Del Rem	3	F	1	0	0	0	0
Contessa Kristine	2	F	1	0	0	0	300
Contessa Renee	3	F	3	0	0	0	263
Contessa Slaney	3	F	8	2	1	2	17,478
Contested	5	G	11	0	1	0	3,072
Contexte	7	G	8	0	0	2	9,360
Continental Bishop	6	H	8	0	0	0	548
Continental Boogie	4	G	11	0	1	2	10,283
Continental Breeze	5	G	2	0	0	0	122
Continental Caller	2	F	6	1	0	0	12,785
Continental Diva	2	F	2	0	0	0	280
Continental Drift	4	G	5	0	0	0	276
Continental Event	4	F	11	0	0	1	4,060
Continental Issue	6	M	15	4	2	1	19,768
Continental Lu	6	M	4	0	1	0	20,520
Continental Man	6	G	12	2	0	3	5,429
Continental Miss	7	M	4	0	0	0	2,600
Continental Music	7	H	8	0	5	2	3,089
Continental Peak	8	G	3	0	1	0	505
Continental Red	8	G	8	0	2	2	132,800
Continental Reins	3	G	3	0	0	2	8,520
Continental Trail	6	M	14	3	1	4	20,759
Continental Wine	4	F	2	1	0	0	8,250
Continentalcolonel	5	G	12	1	2	0	6,804
Continentalsuccess	8	G	4	0	0	0	3,108
Continentalvictory	2	G	4	0	0	1	2,525
Continuously	5	H	5	0	2	0	70,000
Continuum	4	G	3	1	0	0	16,560
Conto de Natal	6	G	7	0	1	0	8,042
Contraction	5	G	3	0	0	1	2,090
Contractor (GB)	4	C	2	0	0	0	245
Contradiction	5	G	13	0	2	3	12,760
Contrarian	6	G	5	4	0	0	41,710
Contrary Creek	3	G	10	0	0	0	2,206
Contribute	4	C	9	2	0	1	31,323
Contributor	3	G	3	2	1	0	27,200
Control Alt Delete	4	F	11	0	2	1	6,654
Control Cat	4	G	14	1	1	2	5,842
Control Signal	6	G	13	0	0	2	4,305
Control the Devil	3	C	2	0	0	0	470
Control Tower	5	H	5	0	0	2	55,090
Controlled Chaos	3	G	11	0	1	2	3,184
Controlled Meeting	3	C	7	3	2	0	104,204
Controller	3	G	2	0	0	0	800
Controls Free	6	G	9	2	2	3	15,229
Controversialcomet	3	F	4	1	0	1	1,669
Conventionalwisdom	4	C	3	0	0	0	1,967
Convergence Zone	2	G	10	0	2	0	1,522
Convert N Collect	5	M	10	1	1	2	13,710
Convertible Bond	3	C	9	1	3	1	27,839
Convexity	4	C	16	6	4	1	32,697
Convey a Little	3	G	10	0	1	0	10,660
Convey the Moment	5	G	12	0	0	2	2,410
Convey This	6	G	14	1	1	2	2,975
Convey to Me	5	M	3	1	0	0	8,230
Conveyor's Angel	2	F	6	2	1	0	82,530
Conveyors Girl	4	F	7	2	0	0	8,640
Conviche	2	F	1	0	0	0	0
Conwell	6	G	5	0	0	0	0
Conwiss	5	M	1	0	0	0	240
Coo Cold Bird	4	F	20	2	1	1	15,665
Coogamonga	4	G	14	5	2	4	55,850
Cookie Bight Cove	3	F	7	1	0	2	10,603
Cookie Crumbles	2	F	1	0	0	0	1,238
Cookie Crumbs	3	F	10	5	3	2	130,460
Cookie Cutouts	4	F	6	0	2	0	8,038
Cookie Man	3	C	5	0	0	0	1,180
Cookie Marie	6	M	4	0	0	0	1,493
Cookie's Compadre	3	G	4	0	0	1	846
Cookies N Cream	7	M	3	0	0	0	660
Cookie's Tigeress	8	M	1	0	0	0	120
Cookie's Toy	3	G	12	1	0	0	9,450
Cookin Carol	2	F	2	0	0	0	1,180
Cookin Out West	4	F	4	0	0	1	2,693
Cooking Lil	4	F	12	3	0	3	25,150
Cooking With Gas	2	G	6	1	0	1	7,230
Cookin's Cast	3	F	13	1	0	2	23,920
Cook'n Light	6	M	11	0	5	2	21,117

Horse	Age	Sex	Sts	1st	2d	3d	Won
Cooks Lane	6	M	3	0	0	0	396
Cooky Joe Fletcher	5	G	10	2	1	1	17,191
Cool Alec	7	G	4	1	0	0	3,240
Cool and Calm	4	F	6	2	0	0	7,980
Cool and Collect	5	M	9	0	0	1	1,674
Cool Attitude	4	G	2	0	0	0	591
Cool Autumn	2	F	2	0	0	1	900
Cool Baba	4	G	2	0	1	0	1,187
Cool Batonic	6	G	7	0	0	1	2,452
Cool Bender	4	G	8	1	2	0	25,079
Cool Bid	5	G	2	0	0	1	1,870
Cool Birdy	3	F	7	1	0	0	4,448
Cool Blast	2	F	4	1	1	1	6,810
Cool Boots	5	M	6	0	1	1	1,266
Cool Boy	7	H	7	0	0	1	2,760
Cool Breeze Lil	3	F	9	2	1	0	15,960
Cool Brew	5	G	13	1	1	1	7,336
Cool Brook	6	M	7	1	0	0	9,845
Cool Cactus	3	G	10	1	4	1	35,520
Cool Cafe	4	C	10	1	6	2	37,380
Cool Cart	3	G	6	0	1	0	5,305
Cool Cash	5	H	15	4	0	3	48,983
Cool Cat Interview	3	G	9	0	4	2	46,140
Cool Cat Sam	3	G	6	1	0	1	13,221
Cool Chaos	4	F	6	0	1	1	1,155
Cool Cherri	3	F	8	1	4	0	9,400
Cool Cinder	5	M	8	0	2	2	4,792
Cool Citidiamond	4	C	12	1	3	1	21,041
Cool Competitor	3	G	11	2	4	1	22,797
Cool Composure	6	G	14	2	3	4	14,225
Cool Conductor	3	C	9	2	1	3	298,295
Cool Cool Cool	3	F	2	0	0	0	0
Cool Criminal	3	G	12	0	2	0	12,010
Cool Crown	2	F	1	0	0	0	726
Cool Cucurri	3	F	6	1	0	2	15,660
Cool Dancer	7	G	2	0	0	0	480
Cool Days	2	C	3	1	1	0	33,500
Cool Diggins	2	C	1	0	0	1	6,270
Cool Diva	2	F	1	0	0	0	164
Cool Drink O Water	5	G	3	0	1	0	2,324
Cool Dude Sam	3	G	8	0	0	0	1,037
Cool Falstaff	7	G	8	3	2	1	12,730
Cool Fastness	6	M	1	0	0	0	0
Cool Fellow	4	G	10	0	3	0	7,040
Cool Friday	5	G	3	0	0	0	0
Cool George	6	G	14	3	2	4	24,169
Cool Hal	4	G	3	1	0	0	27,007
Cool Hand Doc	3	F	1	0	0	0	0
Cool Heavy Bull	5	G	4	0	0	0	634
Cool Honor	3	C	19	2	2	3	28,050
Cool Irony	4	C	3	0	0	0	1,848
Cool Kate	5	M	7	1	0	2	4,355
Cool Kitty	5	M	12	0	3	2	14,379
Cool Lad	3	G	10	1	2	3	22,625
Cool Lake	5	G	4	0	1	0	1,202
Cool Lava	5	G	12	1	0	1	9,807
Cool Love	4	G	6	2	1	0	38,650
Cool Luke	6	H	9	0	2	4	22,958
Cool Mission	9	G	1	0	0	0	0
Cool N Cautious	2	G	8	0	0	2	3,052
Cool N Collective	7	G	6	0	1	2	43,415
Cool N Easy	5	M	2	0	0	0	0
Cool N Spunky	4	C	15	0	1	0	1,696
Cool Oasis	3	F	9	1	1	1	4,681
Cool Papa Rick	5	G	16	0	1	2	3,150
Cool Patriot	4	G	2	0	0	1	932
Cool Pidgeon	3	F	1	0	0	0	0
Cool Rain Falling	5	H	17	4	3	0	27,564
Cool Rebel	3	F	1	0	0	0	0
Cool Red	2	G	4	0	0	1	4,055
Cool Remark	4	G	5	0	0	1	710
Cool Rocket	2	C	4	1	0	0	6,000
Cool Ruler	3	C	7	0	1	1	18,201
Cool Runnings	3	C	12	1	2	1	5,340
Cool Rush	3	C	11	0	4	3	27,500
Cool Season	5	G	10	1	0	0	17,709
Cool Selection	5	G	7	2	1	1	66,804
Cool Sir	4	G	7	1	0	0	1,905
Cool Spell	2	F	3	1	0	2	44,050

Horse	Age	Sex	Sts	1st	2d	3d	Won
Cool Spirit	7	M	2	0	0	0	315
Cool Sport	3	C	7	1	1	0	13,625
Cool Springs Saint	2	C	1	0	0	0	205
Cool Sweep	7	G	14	5	5	0	91,090
Cool Toad	3	G	2	0	0	1	675
Cool Track	8	G	9	1	0	0	3,294
Cool Tsunami	5	M	1	0	0	0	43
Cool Tunnel	3	C	6	0	0	2	2,087
Cool Up	4	F	16	1	0	2	15,409
Cool Water	3	G	3	0	0	0	730
Cool Zone	7	G	7	1	0	0	5,040
Coola Hula	6	M	5	1	0	0	8,464
Coolandwild	5	M	5	0	0	0	350
Coolasacat	5	G	8	3	0	3	89,296
Coolenoughtosizzle	3	F	7	0	1	2	2,946
Coolest	3	C	4	1	0	0	9,600
Coolest Guy	3	C	3	0	1	0	5,115
Coolidge	5	G	15	4	4	0	22,706
Coolie's Son	4	G	4	0	0	1	1,296
Coolin' Down	4	F	4	0	0	0	120
Coolkareen	2	F	4	0	1	0	1,260
Coolmars	9	G	7	0	1	1	12,005
Coolridge Cat	2	C	2	1	1	0	8,136
Coolridge Mia	3	F	1	0	0	1	3,140
Coolsteal	6	H	8	1	1	0	11,287
Cooly Ruler	3	F	5	0	0	0	372
Cooper Country	3	G	7	0	0	0	4,140
Cooper's Song	5	M	6	2	0	1	16,263
Cooperstown	3	G	6	1	0	1	7,585
Cooperstown Hero	5	G	8	2	0	0	13,105
Coopman	8	G	10	1	2	2	4,954
Coordinate	3	F	15	2	3	0	28,035
Coordinating Moves	2	F	2	0	0	0	0
Coorsworth	6	G	2	0	0	0	243
Cooter Cat	2	F	4	0	0	1	1,287
Cop Out	9	G	12	0	3	1	1,830
Copa de Oro	3	F	2	0	0	0	800
Copalis	6	M	5	1	0	1	1,680
Copano	6	G	14	1	1	2	8,907
Cope With an Image	5	H	2	1	0	0	2,440
Cope With Dorothy	6	M	2	0	0	0	0
Copelan's Bluff	4	F	1	0	0	0	0
Copelan's Choice	7	G	4	0	0	2	1,120
Copelan's Gold	3	F	5	0	0	2	5,276
Copelan's Number	9	G	18	2	5	3	18,486
Copelan's Pic	5	G	6	0	0	0	895
Copelan's Quack	5	G	6	0	0	1	1,233
Copernica	4	G	4	0	0	0	480
Copewithhoneybrown	6	M	3	0	2	0	2,920
Copewiththegeneral	3	C	4	1	1	1	22,885
Copia	5	G	10	1	2	3	7,401
Coping	5	G	11	1	5	1	66,094
Coping With David	3	G	4	1	1	0	14,200
Copious Chips	4	C	12	1	2	2	8,425
Copper	3	F	4	0	0	0	1,461
Copper Cat	4	G	8	2	1	3	16,691
Copper Chevelle	4	C	3	0	0	0	121
Copper City	7	G	7	0	0	1	433
Copper Classic	4	C	7	1	2	2	4,845
Copper Creek	8	G	3	0	0	0	183
Copper Criminal	3	G	8	2	1	0	6,631
Copper Dollar	5	M	8	1	0	1	10,553
Copper Glow	6	G	7	2	2	1	22,815
Copper Gold	5	G	1	0	0	0	40
Copper Hannah	3	F	6	2	1	0	16,724
Copper Karat	4	C	15	0	2	1	4,640
Copper Kettle	5	G	12	1	0	0	7,779
Copper Kid	3	G	10	2	1	4	11,842
Copper King	3	G	6	1	1	0	18,124
Copper Miner	9	H	2	0	0	0	68
Copper Mist	3	G	15	1	6	3	70,460
Copper Moccasin	3	G	11	3	2	3	39,401
Copper Moon	2	F	2	0	0	0	820
Copper Mountain	6	G	9	1	2	2	3,410
Copper Native	6	M	6	0	0	0	334
Copper Point	2	G	1	0	0	0	0
Copper Ripple	4	G	7	2	2	1	29,884
Copper Sparks	3	G	2	0	0	0	0
Copper Special	4	F	15	2	0	1	8,409
Copper Sword	8	G	11	0	2	4	4,690
Copper Topper	2	C	1	0	0	0	0
Copper Trail	3	G	9	1	1	1	104,274
Coppergoldn'silver	4	F	7	0	1	0	2,078
Coppers 'n' Brass	5	G	11	1	1	1	8,582
Coppertans Lady	3	F	7	0	0	0	653
Copski	3	C	5	0	1	3	10,120
Copy Bien	5	H	4	0	0	0	0
Copy Copy Copy	3	F	2	0	0	0	800
Copy My Notes	2	C	6	2	0	1	77,749
Copy Queen	3	F	10	1	0	2	29,457
Copy Runner	3	G	10	1	2	1	28,330
Copyco	2	C	3	1	0	0	26,350
Coq D' Or	4	F	11	2	0	1	14,215
Coquettish	4	F	2	0	0	0	1,800
Coquinerie	3	F	10	1	2	0	50,523
Coral Bay	2	F	4	0	0	0	75
Coral Creek	3	F	13	2	1	3	14,583
Coral Gold	3	G	6	1	0	1	7,851
Coralann	5	M	4	0	0	0	312
Coral's Colony	3	F	8	1	0	1	9,272
Coralsting	11	G	2	0	0	0	0
Corarrow	4	F	17	1	2	8	5,806
Cora's Rib	6	M	15	1	4	1	7,679
Cora's Saga	5	M	1	1	0	0	3,480
Corazon de Acero	3	F	6	0	1	2	4,500
Corazon de Africa	3	F	4	0	0	0	0
Corazon Del Diablo	2	G	4	0	0	0	774
Corbin Park	5	M	13	3	4	1	21,074
Corcovado	7	G	7	1	0	0	4,880
Cordelia (ARG)	7	M	3	0	0	0	61
Cordell	8	G	3	0	1	0	1,700
Cordes	4	C	2	1	0	0	6,030
Cordial Connie	4	F	1	0	0	0	0
Cordianted Lineage	3	G	3	0	0	0	179
Cordillera Storm	2	F	1	0	0	0	400
Cordon Azul	2	F	6	0	0	0	835
Cords	3	G	8	0	2	2	6,560
Corduroy Road	10	G	7	1	2	2	23,695
Corduroy's Pride	2	G	2	0	1	0	898
Core Idea	10	G	3	0	1	0	1,680
Core Sample	3	C	11	0	2	1	17,520
Corella	5	G	9	1	1	2	9,602
Corenn	4	F	15	3	1	1	45,180
Corey's Girl	3	F	1	0	1	0	2,000
Corey's Luck	3	G	8	0	2	0	4,053
Corey's Special	4	G	8	1	1	1	2,805
Cori Bates	2	G	6	0	1	1	4,050
Cori Supreme	4	F	10	1	2	1	5,819
Corinas Poise	10	M	2	0	0	0	580
Corine's Daddy	3	C	1	0	0	0	0
Corinthian Star	3	F	11	0	1	1	7,543
Coriolanus	5	G	21	4	5	5	38,363
Cork the Barber	2	G	5	2	0	0	12,228
Corkage Fee	4	G	1	0	0	0	400
Corkie's Princess	5	M	2	0	0	0	89
Corking Dancer	2	C	5	0	1	0	4,465
Corky Ridge	8	M	6	0	1	1	2,371
Corn Bread Red	3	C	3	0	0	0	88
Corn Kicker	7	G	2	0	0	0	0
Corn Mash	8	G	4	0	1	0	1,516
Cornbread N Honey	3	F	3	0	1	0	2,940
Corner Man	8	G	13	3	0	2	12,870
Corner Romance	10	G	1	0	0	0	0
Cornicopia	4	G	16	3	2	4	21,278
Corning	5	M	2	0	1	0	960
Cornish Princess	3	F	1	0	0	0	75
Cornish Zeal	8	G	14	1	1	2	6,393
Cornpatch Road	5	G	2	0	0	0	1,553
Cornplanter	2	C	3	0	0	0	2,721
Corona Del Hielo	3	F	10	6	1	1	41,722
Coronado Kid	4	G	16	1	2	4	23,750
Coronado Rose	2	F	5	3	1	1	99,770
Coronado's Cat	3	C	7	1	0	1	18,650
Coronado's Gold	3	C	7	1	1	1	26,796
Coronado's Pride	3	G	12	3	2	3	97,135
Corp Trip	4	G	14	1	5	1	10,930
Corp. Jct	3	G	1	0	0	0	0
Corporal Cat	6	G	4	0	0	0	120

Horse	Age	Sex	Sts	1st	2d	3d	Won
Corporal Cobra	4	G	6	1	0	2	16,487
Corporal Greiner	3	F	13	3	4	1	77,082
Corporal Rules	4	G	6	1	0	1	4,740
Corporate Attitude	6	M	4	1	0	1	3,007
Corporate Cat	10	G	11	2	1	3	7,115
Corporate Class	4	F	4	0	1	1	2,101
Corporate Crusher	2	C	1	0	0	0	330
Corporate Cure	5	G	3	0	1	0	2,568
Corporate Empress	3	F	5	0	0	0	174
Corporate Honey	5	M	6	0	0	0	402
Corporate Intrigue	4	G	5	0	0	1	1,320
Corporate Kitty	4	F	13	1	2	3	15,846
Corporate Ladder	3	C	8	1	2	1	30,691
Corporate Level	2	C	3	0	0	0	1,080
Corporate Missile	7	G	6	0	0	1	1,550
Corporate Player	2	C	2	1	0	1	22,560
Corporate Plum	5	M	6	0	0	0	0
Corporate Quest	3	G	4	0	0	0	850
Corporate Robbery	3	F	2	0	0	0	0
Corporate Scandal	2	F	1	0	0	0	0
Corporate Tea	3	G	1	0	0	0	0
Corpus Sand	2	C	3	0	0	0	0
Corque	5	G	1	0	0	0	0
Corrales Rose	4	F	10	1	1	0	11,745
Corre Native Corre	4	G	2	0	0	0	0
Correjidora	2	F	3	0	2	0	5,200
Correlation	2	F	5	0	0	0	0
Correle	2	F	5	0	0	0	900
Corrian	7	G	4	0	0	1	1,815
Corrider's Choice	5	G	4	0	0	1	974
Corrigan	5	M	2	0	0	1	3,300
Corroboree	6	G	10	2	0	0	19,091
Corruption	6	G	4	2	1	1	31,960
Corsario	5	M	7	0	0	0	750
Corsario Tom (ARG)	6	G	25	1	1	2	6,701
Cort Sport	6	M	11	3	2	2	25,184
Cortina	4	F	20	4	5	3	21,187
Cortney	5	M	3	0	0	0	0
Cortney's Cielo	3	F	1	0	0	0	300
Cort's P. B.	4	G	8	1	3	2	50,543
Coruscant	3	F	11	5	3	2	62,775
Corvallis	4	F	6	0	1	1	963
Corvallis Dee	3	G	2	0	0	0	0
Corvet	7	G	10	0	0	0	2,140
Corwyn Bay Keys	3	C	11	2	2	2	30,792
Corwyn Duchess	7	M	7	0	0	2	4,066
Corwyn Lace	2	F	3	1	1	0	7,382
Corwyns Correction	3	F	1	0	0	0	0
Corwyn's Gold	3	C	14	0	3	0	11,602
Cory S Blurr	2	C	3	2	0	0	18,896
Corydon's Forloon	2	F	7	0	3	2	15,860
Cosa Segura	4	F	10	3	2	1	18,105
Cosbys Bottom	4	F	6	0	0	0	741
Cosmic Account	4	C	3	0	0	0	228
Cosmic Charlie	3	G	6	0	0	2	964
Cosmic Colors	2	F	1	0	0	0	145
Cosmic Comic	2	G	1	0	0	0	1,380
Cosmic Dove	4	G	1	0	0	0	0
Cosmic Forces	2	F	1	0	0	0	230
Cosmic Glitter	3	G	6	1	1	1	38,135
Cosmic Gold	4	F	11	1	0	1	4,888
Cosmic Green	5	M	5	1	0	0	15,060
Cosmic Halo	2	C	3	0	0	0	290
Cosmic High	5	G	16	4	4	3	23,656
Cosmic Illusion	2	G	3	0	0	2	3,895
Cosmic Jet	4	C	7	1	1	0	36,347
Cosmic Kris	2	G	3	0	1	0	6,680
Cosmic Lady	2	F	8	2	2	0	41,425
Cosmic Light	2	F	3	0	2	0	7,335
Cosmic Messenger	5	M	13	1	1	1	6,500
Cosmic Rain	7	M	12	2	0	0	15,116
Cosmic Run	4	G	18	1	1	6	11,096
Cosmic Sea	5	G	14	0	3	3	7,504
Cosmic Snowman	8	H	3	0	0	0	244
Cosmic Train	4	C	4	0	1	0	6,305
Cosmic Verse	4	G	10	3	0	2	42,406
Cosmic Wave	3	F	6	0	3	0	8,270
Cosmic Wish	3	F	1	0	0	0	340
Cosmipolitan	7	G	4	1	0	1	1,980
Cosmo	5	G	4	0	2	0	9,660
Cosmonaut	2	C	1	0	0	0	225
Cosmos Mariner	3	R	9	2	3	3	64,192
Cosmo's Tee	2	G	3	0	0	0	1,595
Cosporosity	2	G	4	0	0	1	2,220
Cossatot Falls	5	G	10	0	0	1	2,191
Cossinade	3	F	4	0	0	0	218
Cost Me Plenty	5	M	6	0	0	1	2,930
Costa Pretty Penny	5	M	3	0	0	0	473
Costly Castle	3	G	4	2	1	0	61,690
Costly Fun	11	H	3	2	1	0	10,350
Costly Traits	4	G	4	0	0	0	322
Costly Whim	3	F	1	0	0	0	0
Costume Designer	3	F	5	2	0	1	64,565
Cot Ty	2	G	2	0	0	1	2,280
Cote des Vents	3	G	11	1	1	2	41,449
Cotinga	2	F	1	0	0	0	0
Cotive	4	G	3	0	0	0	294
Cotta Gold	3	F	6	0	1	3	11,160
Cottage (ARG)	6	G	8	0	2	1	35,290
Cotta's Jewel	2	F	3	0	0	0	745
Cotte	5	G	4	2	1	1	6,870
Cotton Boll	4	F	7	1	0	0	9,717
Cotton Club (CHI)	4	G	4	0	0	1	6,360
Cotton Gin	4	C	6	2	1	1	12,226
Cotton Tail	5	H	3	1	0	0	10,400
Cotton Valley	5	G	12	1	1	0	11,100
Cottonball	3	G	2	0	0	0	75
Cottonuous Peaks	3	F	14	2	1	2	45,840
Couch Man	10	G	3	0	0	0	0
Cougar Ann	2	F	4	0	0	1	5,320
Cougar Bar	3	C	4	0	0	0	5,292
Cougar Divide	2	G	4	1	0	2	5,750
Cougar Slew	5	G	14	1	2	4	3,781
Cougar Streak	4	G	5	0	0	0	0
Cougar Tracks	3	G	2	0	1	0	1,985
Cougar's Den	3	G	12	3	1	2	37,815
Coul Monet	5	M	1	0	0	0	90
Coulda Shoulda	4	C	1	0	1	0	1,404
Couldbmoonshine	5	G	12	2	1	3	14,552
Couldthisbemagic	7	G	9	1	1	2	6,783
Could've Been Mine	2	C	6	0	1	1	5,699
Couleur d'Amour	4	F	1	0	0	0	38
Coulon's Rambo	5	H	1	0	0	0	0
Counsellors Lady	7	M	4	0	1	0	2,608
Counselor Mitchell	7	H	7	0	0	0	185
Counselor Neil	7	H	3	0	1	0	2,950
Counselorette	5	M	10	3	2	2	7,245
Count Again	8	G	6	1	0	1	3,496
Count Armada	2	C	2	0	0	0	0
Count Basic	6	G	10	1	1	1	5,093
Count Bellefonte	4	G	3	0	0	0	0
Count Blue	3	C	2	0	0	0	150
Count Brocco	7	G	15	0	0	0	1,548
Count Caldiero	3	C	5	0	0	0	0
Count Centavos	6	G	12	6	0	3	28,215
Count Commander	2	G	5	1	1	0	9,685
Count Crusader	3	C	6	1	1	0	8,867
Count Custodio	6	G	3	0	0	0	210
Count Endeavorance	2	C	2	0	0	0	1,590
Count Gold	2	F	1	0	0	0	0
Count Greeley	4	C	5	1	1	0	8,570
Count Henry	4	G	15	0	2	2	11,566
Count Higher	3	G	2	0	0	0	48
Count K. C.	3	G	2	0	0	0	0
Count Katahaula	5	G	11	1	2	2	12,253
Count Kaydence	3	C	4	0	0	1	744
Count Kokand	3	G	14	2	1	2	12,924
Count Me Double	7	M	8	0	0	0	562
Count Money	7	G	6	0	0	0	348
Count Montbrook	3	C	7	1	0	2	27,530
Count of Kings	8	G	11	0	1	2	2,662
Count of Macedonia	4	G	14	1	4	1	12,639
Count On Bill	2	C	5	0	2	1	23,191
Count On Cindi	3	F	10	2	2	2	10,235
Count On Count	3	G	7	0	2	1	24,880
Count On Dacat	4	G	10	0	0	2	5,217
Count On Dolly	7	M	14	0	1	3	24,766
Count On Lucy	3	F	1	0	0	0	118

Horse	Age	Sex	Sts	1st	2d	3d	Won
Count On Massimo	3	G	2	1	0	0	18,840
Count On Me	2	C	7	2	0	0	30,930
Count On My Word	5	H	7	1	0	3	29,320
Count On Sam	3	C	13	2	2	3	20,830
Count On the Tuna	3	G	8	2	0	0	50,651
Count Orange	3	G	11	3	4	0	43,803
Count Quick	3	G	10	2	1	0	6,750
Count Quillo	5	H	13	0	0	0	1,363
Count Remains	4	G	5	0	0	0	414
Count Rizzi	3	G	15	3	4	2	21,742
Count Rmil	2	C	6	1	1	1	10,875
Count Rocky	3	G	4	0	0	0	140
Count Rutledge	5	G	13	1	1	0	16,550
Count Sonna's Time	6	M	11	1	1	2	10,040
Count Stymie	3	G	7	2	1	1	32,706
Count Swish	7	G	6	0	2	1	4,008
Count the Bucks	2	G	3	1	1	1	11,885
Count the Dreams	2	C	4	1	0	0	9,824
Count the Rings	3	G	3	0	0	1	1,430
Count the Silver	2	C	5	0	0	0	640
Count the Wins	3	G	8	0	3	1	11,116
Count Them All	7	M	7	0	2	0	1,287
Count to Ten	6	H	1	0	0	0	152
Count Trial	4	C	8	0	1	0	2,685
Count Xanadu	5	G	9	2	2	1	24,460
Count Your Nickles	4	F	13	2	4	1	23,050
Countdown	4	F	12	3	3	0	48,812
Counter Punch	4	C	9	1	1	1	23,550
Counter Score	3	G	6	1	0	3	9,215
Counterfeit Cash	3	G	3	1	0	0	4,694
Countervail	3	F	3	0	1	2	12,840
Countess Bareeq	3	F	2	0	0	0	215
Countess Gigi	3	F	2	0	0	1	1,650
Countess Judith	8	M	4	0	0	0	731
Countess Mondago	3	F	1	0	0	0	0
Countess Rebecca	5	M	8	0	0	1	3,290
Countessa	6	M	1	0	0	0	360
Countforjudgement	5	M	5	0	0	0	659
Countin' Katy	6	M	2	0	0	0	515
Countin On Court	3	G	3	0	0	1	1,067
Counting Visions	6	M	1	0	0	0	109
Countinonamiracle	3	C	1	0	0	0	0
Countless Gold	3	G	13	2	2	0	26,238
Counto	4	G	10	0	2	1	4,667
Countontherun	7	G	13	2	1	4	22,004
Country Angel	5	M	9	0	1	0	3,490
Country Basket	2	F	6	1	0	0	4,993
Country Be Gold	7	H	14	2	1	2	129,474
Country Beauty	6	M	2	0	0	0	452
Country by Nature	5	G	13	0	4	3	11,909
Country Charmer	3	F	1	1	0	0	7,200
Country Chimes	4	F	13	1	3	1	21,780
Country Clover	4	G	12	2	4	3	5,587
Country Cody	3	F	2	0	0	0	225
Country Coursing	6	G	7	0	1	0	521
Country Creek	4	F	8	0	1	0	7,000
Country Deputy	2	G	4	0	0	0	0
Country Dove	4	C	20	2	1	7	21,095
Country Dragon	6	G	3	0	1	1	3,263
Country Fair	7	G	11	0	2	1	3,916
Country Favorite	4	F	5	1	2	0	7,575
Country Fox	3	F	5	1	1	0	4,811
Country General	5	G	6	1	0	0	4,911
Country Jeweler	6	G	4	0	0	0	192
Country Joe	8	G	16	5	2	2	54,595
Country Judge	4	C	12	3	5	3	149,840
Country Kat	2	F	5	1	1	0	46,529
Country Landing	4	C	5	0	0	0	276
Country Lawyer	4	C	14	2	3	3	24,660
Country Legionaire	8	G	11	0	1	1	2,866
Country Lord	5	G	6	1	0	1	6,124
Country Lyric	3	G	3	0	0	0	0
Country Mark	3	F	4	0	0	0	0
Country Meadow	3	F	11	0	0	0	718
Country Miss	3	F	7	0	0	0	0
Country Moonbeam	3	F	10	0	3	2	7,493
Country Music	7	G	6	1	0	0	9,550
Country 'n Western	3	F	1	0	0	0	0
Country Native	3	F	1	0	0	0	109
Country Only	7	H	6	0	0	1	5,096
Country Paradise	3	F	8	1	1	1	4,485
Country Park	11	G	4	0	0	0	206
Country Pie	2	F	4	0	1	2	11,504
Country Prince	4	G	4	0	0	0	420
Country Princess	7	M	7	0	0	1	953
Country Que	6	M	11	1	3	3	10,849
Country Rascal	6	G	3	0	0	0	208
Country Ridge	3	F	6	1	0	0	3,594
Country Slew	3	G	7	1	0	1	7,190
Country Tango	3	F	2	1	0	0	2,225
Country Tune	4	C	5	0	0	0	700
Country Valentine	5	G	7	0	1	0	6,130
Country Warrior	5	G	8	1	1	2	39,257
Country Wild	3	C	3	0	0	1	2,040
Countryfide	4	F	11	6	1	1	93,730
Country's Cool	3	F	4	0	0	0	1,942
Countrys Finale	5	G	14	1	0	0	2,592
Countrywide Flyer (IRE)	3	G	11	3	2	1	85,551
Count's Last Reply	3	F	11	1	1	1	6,411
Counttheblessings	3	F	2	2	0	0	24,300
County	2	G	1	0	0	0	1,020
County Brass	3	F	5	2	0	1	38,985
County Cakewalk	4	F	4	1	2	0	19,470
County Cat	7	G	10	0	0	2	5,027
County Chalk	6	H	1	0	0	0	55
County Chief	7	G	5	0	1	1	3,170
County Court	3	F	1	1	0	0	4,320
County Creek	5	G	1	0	0	0	0
County Doctor	6	G	1	0	0	0	0
County Green	4	G	11	2	1	2	26,140
County Jail	6	G	2	0	0	0	0
County Lineman	4	G	10	0	0	2	3,465
County Recount	5	M	12	1	3	3	12,990
County Road Four	4	G	10	3	0	0	12,914
County Time Kat	4	G	9	0	0	1	1,766
County Trial	4	C	13	3	2	4	47,280
County Watchman	3	G	5	0	0	0	1,195
Coup	9	G	7	3	0	1	22,570
Coup D Etat	2	C	2	0	0	0	2,580
Coup de Grace	3	G	13	4	2	2	69,440
Coupdeville Jack	6	G	8	0	0	1	1,395
Couple Whiles	3	F	6	0	2	1	4,116
Cour de Justice	2	F	2	0	0	0	215
Courageous Act	3	C	11	2	3	3	206,521
Courageous Cici	3	F	4	0	0	1	3,380
Courageous Deputy	6	G	8	0	0	2	1,907
Courageous Journey	3	G	4	1	0	1	9,116
Courageous King	3	C	4	1	0	2	25,500
Courageous Valor	4	F	9	0	1	3	14,826
Courageousbull	2	G	2	0	0	0	600
Courriel	3	F	4	1	0	0	18,846
Court a Native	3	F	4	1	1	0	10,397
Court Action	11	G	12	3	3	2	21,480
Court Angel	5	M	4	0	0	1	1,870
Court Appointed	5	G	1	0	0	0	77
Court Costs	9	H	6	0	1	0	1,152
Court Gold	3	G	4	1	1	1	1,715
Court Key	6	H	1	0	0	0	870
Court Lite Kenny	7	H	4	0	2	1	7,370
Court Notes	5	G	1	0	1	0	4,660
Court of Maximus	4	G	11	1	2	2	13,284
Court Savvy	10	G	11	1	1	1	4,462
Court Seeker	2	F	5	0	1	0	5,000
Court Shenanigans	9	G	12	3	2	2	47,710
Court Verdict	4	C	14	4	0	2	19,421
Courtcase	3	G	19	1	1	3	8,028
Courtenay	6	M	11	2	1	1	11,651
Courtesan Star	3	F	2	0	0	1	450
Courthouse	3	G	12	1	4	6	34,840
Courthouse Junkie	3	G	3	0	0	0	0
Courtier	3	G	11	1	1	1	21,875
Courtin Monica	6	M	6	0	0	0	486
Courting Chance	5	G	7	1	0	0	1,184
Courting Concorde	4	C	9	0	1	2	24,210
Courting Fire	4	G	2	0	0	0	225
Courtingaway	4	C	1	0	0	0	0
Courtly Jazz	3	G	3	1	0	1	32,120
Courtly Love	3	F	3	0	0	0	6,460

Horse	Age	Sex	Sts	1st	2d	3d	Won
Courtly Riches	6	G	11	0	2	0	6,965
Courtnall	3	C	2	1	0	0	25,800
Courtney's Castle	2	F	7	0	0	1	5,660
Courtney's Express	3	F	5	0	1	0	2,886
Courtney's Friend	3	F	7	0	1	2	12,333
Courtneys Keepsake	11	G	4	0	0	0	0
Courtneys Pleasure	7	M	15	0	1	3	9,475
Courtney'sbirthday	3	F	9	1	1	0	12,314
Courtricity	5	G	8	1	1	0	10,995
Courtroom Drama	7	G	6	1	2	0	6,949
Court's in Session	5	G	11	5	0	1	134,485
Courtyard Barbi	5	M	1	0	1	0	1,460
Coushatta	7	G	13	3	0	2	31,628
Cousin Bill	4	G	14	3	2	2	12,343
Cousin Charlotte	5	M	7	2	1	1	33,624
Cousin Maggie	9	M	1	0	0	0	61
Cousin Montineque	4	F	12	2	1	3	15,005
Cousin 'n Company	8	G	3	0	0	0	775
Cousin of Mine	5	M	1	0	0	0	0
Cousin Randy	2	C	4	1	0	0	11,016
Cousin Sally	3	F	1	0	0	1	6,270
Cousin Tommy	3	C	2	0	0	0	320
Cousin Woody	3	G	16	2	2	3	28,045
Cousineau	3	F	3	1	0	0	30,200
Covad	6	G	8	2	1	0	2,835
Covant	2	C	5	0	0	0	900
Cove Creek	3	F	7	0	0	2	8,190
Cove Hill Missle	5	M	13	4	3	2	77,880
Cove Kat	4	F	7	0	0	1	1,560
Cover Guy	3	G	2	0	0	0	800
Cover Keeper	8	G	2	0	0	0	90
Cover Me Lover	3	G	8	0	0	1	3,135
Cover Now	2	G	3	2	0	0	23,840
Cover the Cash	3	G	3	0	0	0	210
Cover the Fire	2	C	2	0	0	0	0
Cover Up	3	F	7	2	2	0	12,692
Covered Treasure	5	G	2	0	0	1	420
Covergirl Blond	2	F	3	0	0	0	420
Covering Ground	4	G	14	1	2	1	30,440
Coverly	4	F	1	0	0	0	320
Coveryourbets	3	G	14	1	1	2	14,387
Covet	3	G	12	2	0	0	10,679
Covey	2	C	4	0	0	0	0
Covey of Dove	4	F	6	0	0	0	920
Covey Roost	6	M	6	2	2	0	22,100
Covincing	6	M	6	0	2	1	18,000
Covington	4	G	11	1	0	3	10,755
Covumel	8	G	10	2	1	4	17,964
Cow Paddy	4	C	7	1	0	1	3,880
Cowboy Auctioneer	4	G	6	1	1	2	4,180
Cowboy Badgett	2	G	5	1	1	1	18,870
Cowboy Ballet	3	G	5	0	0	0	1,418
Cowboy Brown	3	G	7	1	1	0	17,600
Cowboy Buck	2	G	2	0	0	0	1,260
Cowboy Cat	5	G	7	0	0	0	1,122
Cowboy Chili	5	M	5	3	1	1	100,800
Cowboy Classic	3	G	8	1	1	1	7,008
Cowboy Clide	4	C	2	0	0	0	0
Cowboy Cobra	4	G	10	1	2	2	13,900
Cowboy Code	3	G	11	4	2	1	73,730
Cowboy Contender	3	G	6	2	2	1	26,400
Cowboy Court	3	C	9	1	2	0	28,343
Cowboy Cumbia	6	G	7	1	1	0	5,056
Cowboy Drifter	4	C	29	3	1	7	23,110
Cowboy Frolic	2	G	1	0	0	0	750
Cowboy Hardware	2	G	3	0	0	2	6,005
Cowboy Harrison	3	G	1	0	0	0	235
Cowboy Hurricane	4	G	4	2	0	0	12,684
Cowboy Jack T	4	C	6	2	1	2	3,352
Cowboy Junction	5	G	10	2	0	1	11,519
Cowboy Justice	5	G	16	2	1	0	9,342
Cowboy Kyle	9	G	7	1	2	0	13,691
Cowboy Rascal	3	C	4	0	1	0	680
Cowboy Shane	4	G	14	1	3	1	12,135
Cowboy Stuff	5	H	6	2	0	2	60,940
Cowboy Up	2	C	1	0	0	0	0
Cowboy's Limelite	5	G	16	1	2	1	13,340
Cowboys Sissy	4	F	5	0	2	0	1,130
Cowgirl Cumbia	4	F	6	0	0	0	0
Cowgirl in Lace	4	F	5	2	0	0	11,820
Cowgirl Secret	3	F	7	0	0	1	1,224
Cowgirl Stuff	3	F	13	3	4	1	27,902
Cowgirl Tough	2	F	3	1	1	0	8,418
Cowgirl Way	2	F	4	0	0	1	1,340
Cowgirls Account	5	M	5	3	0	0	12,600
Cowgirls Grit	9	M	10	0	0	1	2,571
Cowgirls n Indians	3	F	13	4	2	2	18,548
Cowpet Bay	3	G	8	0	0	1	1,854
Cox's Farrara	6	M	5	1	0	0	2,566
Coyote Bait	3	C	6	1	0	2	9,955
Coyote Cowgirl	4	F	9	1	2	2	10,306
Coyote Face	3	G	3	0	0	0	195
Coyote Fever	3	C	11	1	0	1	9,109
Coyote Hill	2	G	5	2	1	0	24,275
Coyote Joe	2	C	1	0	0	0	0
Coyote Junction	5	G	5	0	0	1	1,240
Coyote Kid	4	G	5	1	1	1	6,835
Coyote Message	4	C	11	1	2	3	10,730
Coyote Point	4	C	12	0	1	2	5,641
Coyote Rose Bud	3	F	2	0	0	0	0
Coyoteshighestcall	2	C	10	1	3	1	36,750
Coys Big Geb	3	C	1	0	0	0	0
Coz He's Mean	5	G	15	4	1	0	19,242
Coz Z. Josey	4	C	1	0	0	0	0
Cozenza	3	C	3	0	0	0	630
Cozforfire	3	G	8	2	0	0	5,801
Cozie Advantage	5	M	6	0	1	1	21,960
Cozy	7	M	6	0	0	2	12,000
Cozy Anna	3	F	2	0	0	0	120
Cozy Cat	5	M	11	0	0	3	5,081
Cozy Cay	4	F	6	1	2	1	49,980
Cozy City	7	M	6	0	0	1	2,470
Cozy Coed	5	M	9	0	1	2	10,460
Cozy Con	5	M	19	2	2	2	33,851
Cozy Dance	6	G	19	3	2	4	22,263
Cozy Dreams	3	C	18	2	3	1	25,485
Cozy Fellow	4	G	9	3	0	0	15,693
Cozy Glow	4	F	12	3	2	1	59,390
Cozy Guy	3	G	10	5	2	1	324,504
Cozy J D	3	F	4	0	1	1	8,330
Cozy Legend	4	F	15	2	3	3	43,655
Cozy Man	7	G	10	3	2	0	39,310
Cozy One	4	F	8	1	3	1	45,559
Cozy Reporter	2	F	2	0	0	2	2,860
Cozy Style	3	G	3	0	1	0	2,350
Cozy Town	4	F	10	2	2	3	8,715
Cozys Jamboree	3	F	2	0	0	0	150
Cozy's Mint Julip	8	M	13	0	1	2	6,257
Cozz Star	4	G	14	2	1	2	16,330
Cozzen Vinny	3	G	8	0	0	1	9,890
Cozzene Appeal	6	G	9	0	0	0	2,115
Cozzene Continued	4	G	11	1	1	4	14,035
Cozzene's Cat	5	G	2	0	0	1	3,120
Cozzene's Devil	5	H	4	1	0	0	4,740
Cozzene's Silver	7	G	13	2	2	3	13,842
Cozzening	5	H	5	1	0	0	13,811
Cozzy Prospects	3	F	2	0	0	1	4,160
Cozzy Temper	4	F	1	0	0	0	435
Cr Proud Count	4	G	12	2	0	1	6,882
Cr Sunny Melba	4	F	4	0	2	1	2,300
Craam Creek Lady	4	F	8	1	1	1	10,230
Crab Creek	4	G	13	0	4	4	10,381
Crab Man	6	G	9	0	1	1	4,519
Crack Corn	3	F	6	0	0	0	507
Crack the Books	5	M	3	0	1	0	2,805
Crack the Latch	3	G	1	0	0	0	120
Crack the Sky	2	C	7	1	0	2	13,785
Crack the Vault	6	G	10	5	3	0	99,733
Crack the Veneer	4	G	15	3	0	1	72,520
Crackajack	5	H	3	0	0	0	690
Cracked Actor	3	G	2	0	0	0	427
Cracked Conch	3	F	10	0	2	0	6,026
Crackenthorpe	3	C	8	1	1	2	37,594
Cracker B	8	G	13	0	1	1	2,448
Cracker Day (NZ)	6	G	2	0	0	0	0
Cracker Jack Man	4	G	15	4	2	1	37,904
Crackerbox Palace	5	G	12	2	1	1	15,262
Cracker's Best	8	M	7	1	2	1	3,926

Horse	Age	Sex	Sts	1st	2d	3d	Won
Cracker's Project	4	G	10	2	1	1	13,910
Cracklin' Ice	7	M	9	0	3	1	2,015
Cracklin Red Rosie	2	F	3	1	1	0	8,432
Crackling	5	G	1	0	0	1	2,860
Crackling Tiger	3	C	3	1	0	0	5,160
Crackmeup	3	G	7	0	1	0	5,735
Crackup	4	G	9	0	1	0	6,260
Craft Brewin	9	G	5	1	1	1	1,770
Crafty Account	5	G	16	3	1	2	15,395
Crafty Affair	2	F	3	0	0	0	180
Crafty Anchor	3	C	6	0	0	0	655
Crafty Angler	5	G	4	0	0	2	2,301
Crafty Answer	3	F	9	1	0	2	29,212
Crafty Babe	3	F	7	2	0	2	32,903
Crafty Beau	5	G	9	1	2	1	24,887
Crafty Boo	3	C	3	0	0	0	324
Crafty Brat	4	F	10	0	1	6	37,020
Crafty Brent	3	C	6	2	2	1	11,636
Crafty Broad	2	F	7	0	4	1	43,290
Crafty Cammack	3	G	9	2	1	2	73,800
Crafty Captain	5	G	18	1	0	2	16,378
Crafty Carni	3	F	13	2	4	2	94,603
Crafty Case	9	G	14	2	3	1	9,032
Crafty Cash Too	2	F	1	0	0	0	0
Crafty Cause	4	F	1	0	0	0	0
Crafty Celt	7	G	1	0	0	0	800
Crafty Chatter	4	F	4	1	0	1	4,690
Crafty Cindy	6	M	1	0	0	0	0
Crafty Closure	3	F	3	0	0	0	302
Crafty Comet	3	F	11	1	4	2	10,610
Crafty Commander	3	G	2	0	0	0	55
Crafty Comment	8	M	6	0	0	0	440
Crafty Company	2	F	3	0	0	0	552
Crafty Connection	4	G	8	0	0	1	4,326
Crafty Cop	3	G	13	1	0	1	9,805
Crafty Course	5	H	9	0	1	1	2,092
Crafty Coyote	4	F	3	0	0	0	670
Crafty Creation	4	G	4	0	0	0	485
Crafty Creek	6	M	3	0	0	1	1,600
Crafty Crypto	4	F	14	2	2	1	25,422
Crafty Dahl	3	F	2	0	1	0	7,100
Crafty Dame	5	M	6	0	1	2	3,615
Crafty Dan	3	G	13	0	1	2	4,752
Crafty Dawn	7	G	12	2	1	1	8,143
Crafty Deed	7	G	8	0	1	2	2,784
Crafty Deer	5	G	9	0	2	0	3,016
Crafty Demon	9	G	7	0	1	1	2,325
Crafty Diamond	2	F	5	2	2	0	22,200
Crafty Diplomat	6	M	3	1	0	0	3,155
Crafty Diva	4	F	15	1	2	3	43,310
Crafty Donna	2	F	2	0	0	0	200
Crafty Dream	5	H	7	2	2	0	7,501
Crafty Dutchman	7	G	11	2	0	0	6,035
Crafty Edition	4	G	4	0	1	0	3,140
Crafty Emily	2	F	3	0	0	0	855
Crafty Flair	5	M	5	0	0	0	0
Crafty Fortune	7	H	6	2	0	1	17,088
Crafty G	2	F	2	0	0	1	1,179
Crafty Gold	3	F	5	1	1	0	7,199
Crafty Guy	4	C	4	2	0	0	39,136
Crafty Hero	4	G	20	2	3	4	17,578
Crafty Hug	3	F	7	1	1	2	4,885
Crafty Ice	2	F	1	0	0	0	70
Crafty Icepick	2	C	4	0	1	1	5,180
Crafty Idol	3	C	8	2	2	0	9,160
Crafty Illusion	7	G	12	0	0	2	1,080
Crafty Jarrett	5	G	7	0	0	1	1,113
Crafty Jay	3	G	11	2	2	3	25,056
Crafty Jazz	2	C	1	0	0	0	0
Crafty Jigg	3	F	2	0	0	0	894
Crafty Joanne	6	M	11	1	2	0	5,720
Crafty Junction	6	H	7	0	3	0	7,355
Crafty Katarina	2	F	5	1	0	0	13,120
Crafty Kid	2	C	2	0	0	0	661
Crafty Kitty	2	F	2	0	0	0	0
Crafty Launch	4	C	1	0	0	0	0
Crafty Lawyer	4	G	4	0	0	0	0
Crafty Leader	3	F	6	0	0	0	440
Crafty Line	4	G	13	2	4	1	42,684

Horse	Age	Sex	Sts	1st	2d	3d	Won
Crafty Loom	5	M	7	1	0	2	5,751
Crafty Lover	5	G	8	0	0	0	349
Crafty Luck	5	M	1	0	0	0	1,475
Crafty Madness	4	F	9	2	0	0	23,180
Crafty Maneuvers	5	M	7	0	0	1	1,544
Crafty Margarita	3	F	2	0	0	0	0
Crafty Match	3	G	12	2	3	1	30,159
Crafty Maverick	4	C	14	2	0	3	7,184
Crafty Meme	2	F	2	0	0	1	1,680
Crafty Michelle	3	F	5	1	0	2	8,754
Crafty Miss	3	F	12	0	0	1	3,015
Crafty Miss G	2	F	2	0	0	0	53
Crafty Mountain	4	F	11	1	1	1	5,512
Crafty Move	4	F	4	0	0	3	13,140
Crafty N Happy	3	F	3	0	0	0	0
Crafty 'n Smooth	5	M	13	0	1	1	7,720
Crafty Nat	4	F	11	1	0	2	16,184
Crafty Notebook	4	F	6	1	0	1	6,100
Crafty Number	8	H	8	0	0	2	2,785
Crafty Paces	7	M	7	1	2	1	9,100
Crafty Pal	4	G	10	2	1	1	13,705
Crafty Pete	5	G	10	1	1	0	12,934
Crafty Player	3	C	13	2	3	2	52,558
Crafty Prince	2	C	2	0	0	0	0
Crafty Purchase	3	G	12	1	4	3	45,312
Crafty Reflection	4	G	12	1	2	0	23,355
Crafty Rhythm	7	G	13	1	0	0	2,400
Crafty Rocket	4	C	4	1	0	1	24,266
Crafty Roo	4	F	7	2	0	1	8,807
Crafty Runner	7	H	10	1	1	1	8,665
Crafty Ruth	2	F	4	0	0	2	2,414
Crafty Saint	4	C	2	0	0	0	550
Crafty Sarah	3	F	11	1	2	0	16,500
Crafty Schemer	5	G	6	1	1	0	27,510
Crafty Shaanshu	6	M	10	1	2	0	14,262
Crafty Shaw	6	H	8	2	3	2	190,000
Crafty Slew	2	C	1	0	0	0	135
Crafty Song	4	C	3	1	0	1	33,915
Crafty Spirit	3	F	5	0	0	0	884
Crafty Stag	2	C	1	0	0	0	0
Crafty Taylor	5	M	9	2	2	2	53,170
Crafty Tears	3	F	3	1	1	0	36,150
Crafty Texan	4	C	4	0	0	2	4,235
Crafty Valentine	3	F	8	3	1	0	18,896
Crafty Value	4	G	11	1	6	1	20,383
Crafty Vixen	2	F	6	1	2	1	47,620
Crafty Wac	4	F	16	6	3	0	26,286
Crafty Wanda	3	F	4	1	0	1	2,907
Crafty Who	3	G	5	0	0	0	838
Crafty Will	3	G	8	1	0	0	8,650
Crafty Woman	2	F	1	0	0	0	1,020
Craftycajunfriend	2	F	6	0	1	2	8,562
Craftyette	3	F	1	0	0	0	0
Craftyrhonda	3	F	6	3	2	0	20,025
Crafty's Go Bo	5	G	7	0	0	3	2,233
Crafty's Love	5	G	7	0	0	1	790
Craigend	3	C	2	0	0	1	1,119
Craigs Hope	4	G	1	0	0	0	0
Craklin' Suzie	3	F	8	1	1	0	5,428
Cramming	5	G	5	0	1	0	4,226
Cranberry Lake	2	F	7	1	0	1	22,538
Cranberry Red	3	F	8	0	2	2	10,960
Crane	5	G	10	0	0	1	1,738
Crane Away	5	G	10	1	1	2	5,195
Crap Shooter	5	H	3	0	1	1	3,645
Crash Course	8	G	5	0	0	1	3,250
Crash McGoon	4	G	6	1	1	2	22,080
Crash the Party	4	G	15	2	0	1	12,669
Crashboat	5	M	1	0	0	0	0
Crashpad	8	G	9	0	2	1	7,819
Crastinator	3	G	8	0	2	2	4,090
Craton (ARG)	7	G	1	0	0	0	0
Crave the Wave	3	G	1	0	0	0	0
Cravens	4	C	5	0	0	0	1,000
Cravingo	3	F	11	1	4	1	41,617
Craw Fish	4	C	2	0	0	0	230
Crawfish Etouffee	4	G	8	0	0	1	2,183
Crawfish King	2	C	2	1	1	0	35,000
Crawling	4	F	3	0	1	0	3,330

Horse	Age	Sex	Sts	1st	2d	3d	Won
Crazed	6	G	15	2	1	0	17,344
Crazy Baby	4	F	4	0	0	0	0
Crazy Caro	2	F	2	2	0	0	28,600
Crazy Crystal	5	M	4	0	1	0	2,315
Crazy Debutante	4	F	7	2	1	0	10,598
Crazy Deputy	5	H	1	0	0	0	0
Crazy Grace	3	F	11	1	1	2	29,752
Crazy Horse Saloon	4	G	9	1	0	0	3,911
Crazy Larrys	6	G	5	0	1	1	3,100
Crazy Old Lady	3	F	4	1	0	1	20,370
Crazy Song	5	G	5	1	0	0	30,293
Crazy Talent	5	H	9	2	3	1	32,812
Crazybrook	2	C	1	0	0	0	205
Crazyluck	3	F	11	0	1	1	16,041
Cream and Sugar	3	F	6	0	0	0	385
Cream Creek	5	M	2	0	0	0	1,290
Cream No Sugar	2	G	1	0	0	0	0
Creame Burlee	7	M	1	0	0	0	73
Creamy	6	M	1	0	0	0	105
Crease Infraction	6	G	9	0	0	2	37,589
Creative Ace	4	C	13	1	1	1	17,524
Creative Dance	3	C	6	1	1	0	36,035
Creative Flight	9	G	8	2	1	2	22,086
Creative Grace	3	F	3	1	0	0	7,920
Creative Iron	4	G	5	0	1	1	4,880
Creative Lady	4	F	2	0	0	0	0
Creative Patsy	4	F	2	0	0	0	270
Creative Touch	2	F	2	1	0	0	8,454
Creative Uga	4	F	1	0	0	0	0
Creative's Dream	4	C	5	0	0	1	4,580
Credentialed	3	F	15	2	3	2	27,115
Credit Balance	5	G	19	0	0	4	2,983
Credit Call	7	G	10	1	0	1	6,334
Credit Gal	6	M	16	6	3	0	93,475
Credit Gold	6	G	14	1	2	1	7,272
Credit Is Due	3	F	9	0	0	1	680
Credit River	3	G	14	4	0	2	78,181
Creditcardpurchase	4	F	9	1	0	3	26,220
Creditforpleasure	4	G	9	0	3	0	7,705
Creditville	4	F	1	0	0	0	0
Cree	4	G	12	3	4	1	56,780
Cree Power	5	G	10	1	3	0	36,722
Creed's Fury	5	M	2	0	0	0	122
Creek	5	G	10	0	0	1	1,760
Creek Bank	5	H	4	0	1	2	5,025
Creek Code	6	H	2	0	0	0	620
Creek Connection	5	M	6	1	0	0	4,426
Creek Executive	3	G	6	2	0	0	22,108
Creek Song	3	F	1	0	0	0	400
Creeker's Surprise	3	F	6	1	1	2	34,610
Creekline	4	G	1	0	0	0	42
Creek's Shore	6	G	7	1	0	2	48,526
Creeky Lane	9	G	9	1	0	1	10,341
Creeky Monster	2	F	3	1	1	0	7,365
Creeky Witness	3	G	5	1	2	0	9,069
Creepy Mousey	3	G	9	0	0	0	2,190
Creeque Alley	5	M	9	0	2	1	10,720
Creme D' Argent	5	G	3	0	0	0	1,950
Creme 'd Lite	5	M	2	0	0	0	167
Creme de La Crop	3	F	14	1	0	1	4,675
Creme of Champagne	4	C	11	1	1	1	43,038
Creole O Gold	5	M	14	2	2	2	24,396
Crescent Chief	5	G	3	0	0	0	765
Crescent Lake	2	F	3	0	2	0	10,450
Crescent Remark	5	G	13	1	1	0	7,250
Crescent Street	4	F	1	0	0	0	0
Cresco Big Train	5	G	12	2	0	0	5,970
Cresco Blaze	6	G	18	1	2	3	7,986
Cresco Chief	7	H	3	0	0	0	0
Cresco Class Act	4	F	7	1	0	0	4,280
Cresco Dan	4	G	11	2	1	3	18,408
Cresco Flyer	3	F	1	0	0	0	0
Cresco Jam Runner	5	M	8	1	1	1	4,168
Cresco Jester	4	F	10	2	1	4	9,224
Cresco Machine	4	F	4	0	0	1	504
Cresco Predominant	3	C	4	0	1	0	1,380
Cresco Real Jammer	3	G	3	0	0	0	195
Cresco Ruler	6	G	9	0	1	0	4,420
Cresent City Cat	3	C	7	2	1	1	37,583
Crest Dancer	7	M	8	0	2	1	2,426
Cresta Red	9	G	4	0	0	0	0
Cresty's Wild One	5	M	7	0	0	0	628
Crete (AUS)	8	G	11	2	3	1	58,420
Crew Cut	6	G	10	1	0	0	4,733
Cribber	3	C	1	0	0	0	42
Cribsheet	6	M	5	2	0	1	9,158
Cricket Wicket	4	F	8	2	1	1	91,498
Crickets Freckle	2	F	2	0	0	0	0
Crikey	2	G	3	0	2	1	14,260
Criminal Brain	5	M	3	0	0	0	144
Criminal Cat	3	G	3	0	0	0	0
Criminal Chucky	4	G	5	0	0	0	2,167
Criminal Intent	2	C	3	0	0	0	720
Criminal Mind	2	C	5	1	2	1	83,010
Crimp	3	G	13	1	0	0	4,783
Crimsanna	5	M	2	0	0	1	1,574
Crimson	3	F	8	1	0	2	21,460
Crimson and Roses	4	F	5	0	1	0	16,880
Crimson Avenger	10	G	3	0	0	1	1,525
Crimson B B	4	F	5	0	0	1	1,762
Crimson Caper	3	G	3	0	0	0	1,260
Crimson Clover	3	F	8	0	0	0	0
Crimson Code	2	F	2	0	0	0	282
Crimson Comet	6	M	15	3	0	1	15,112
Crimson Commando	4	G	13	1	1	1	14,033
Crimson Courtier	6	M	5	0	0	2	15,536
Crimson Dancer	2	F	1	0	0	0	75
Crimson Delight	4	F	7	1	1	2	17,840
Crimson Design	3	G	7	3	0	0	31,090
Crimson Dew	4	C	1	0	0	0	45
Crimson Flame	2	F	5	2	1	1	30,830
Crimson Ide	3	G	13	1	2	3	12,870
Crimson Island	5	H	10	2	0	2	5,431
Crimson Kristine	2	F	7	0	2	0	6,200
Crimson Meadow	2	F	1	0	0	0	0
Crimson Mint	5	G	10	1	0	5	20,136
Crimson Moon	2	F	8	0	1	0	7,155
Crimson N Clover	8	M	3	0	0	0	190
Crimson Oak	5	G	14	1	3	1	16,690
Crimson Palace (SAF)	5	M	5	3	0	0	637,731
Crimson Patriot	6	G	6	0	0	1	1,652
Crimson Prospect	8	G	9	1	0	3	11,761
Crimson Rising	4	F	18	4	5	1	38,580
Crimson Royale	3	F	10	2	3	2	60,020
Crimson Silk (GB)	4	G	9	0	0	2	14,404
Crimson Socks	3	F	14	2	2	5	56,000
Crimson Stag	2	C	6	2	1	1	102,050
Crimson Wave	4	G	3	0	0	0	377
Crimson Wind	3	F	4	0	0	0	232
Crimsonite	3	G	7	0	0	0	2,800
Crippen	4	C	8	0	0	0	347
Cripple Creek	5	G	6	1	1	1	33,590
Crisane	2	F	6	3	2	1	70,120
Crisantemo (CHI)	6	G	5	0	0	1	11,725
Crisis Situation	4	G	17	0	5	7	12,253
Crissy's Cricket	5	M	4	0	0	1	817
Cristal's Native	3	G	3	0	0	0	176
Cristofi	4	G	1	0	1	0	8,800
Critical Battle	6	G	9	3	1	1	50,190
Critical Bull	4	F	9	1	0	1	11,760
Critical Cat	3	F	8	1	0	0	30,610
Critical Chant	2	F	2	0	0	0	2,170
Critical Velocity	3	G	8	0	1	2	1,982
Critically	6	M	14	1	1	4	8,803
Criticism	4	G	1	0	0	0	0
Crittenden	5	G	14	0	5	2	11,690
Cro Cro Cro	2	F	7	0	0	0	1,065
Croc	2	C	1	0	0	1	1,320
Crocker Road	3	C	4	1	2	0	43,792
Crockett	3	G	3	1	0	0	6,683
Crockett's Critter	6	M	12	2	2	1	7,246
Crockett's Way	4	G	3	1	0	1	13,625
Crocogator	4	G	5	0	0	0	275
Crocrock	7	G	8	3	1	0	75,680
Croissant	3	F	13	2	3	1	24,277
Cronenbold	3	C	5	0	1	2	21,760
Cronista	3	F	10	2	2	2	39,247
Crook On the Run	10	G	4	1	0	2	10,912

Horse	Age	Sex	Sts	1st	2d	3d	Won
Crooked Key	5	G	8	2	1	1	29,001
Crooked Sky	4	G	2	1	1	0	1,580
Crooked Tail	4	C	2	0	0	0	210
Crook's Baby	3	F	4	0	0	1	1,320
Crook's Bullet	4	G	2	0	0	0	0
Crook's Cantu	3	G	5	1	0	0	8,400
Crook's Cher	5	M	1	0	0	1	550
Crook's Lad	2	C	2	0	0	0	420
Crook's Miss	2	F	1	0	0	0	0
Crop Angel	5	M	11	0	1	3	14,602
Crop Buster	2	C	1	0	0	0	118
Crosby	2	C	1	0	0	0	0
Cross Buck	6	G	3	0	0	0	440
Cross Canyon	3	C	13	4	0	2	53,945
Cross Checker	2	C	1	0	0	1	6,270
Cross Creek	3	F	5	0	1	1	13,356
Cross Keys	3	G	6	1	0	0	13,460
Cross of Steel	2	G	4	0	0	3	7,535
Cross the Border	4	G	6	0	0	1	4,853
Cross the Infield	5	M	10	0	0	0	744
Cross the Plate	4	G	9	1	1	0	4,126
Crossbar	8	G	4	0	0	0	3,010
Crosscut	3	C	4	0	1	1	12,880
Crossett Light	4	G	12	3	1	1	23,385
Crossfield	4	F	11	1	3	1	41,390
Crossfire Trail	4	F	12	1	1	4	9,123
Crossing	4	F	9	2	1	0	28,110
Crossing Again	2	F	7	1	1	0	9,510
Crossing Borders	2	G	3	1	0	0	21,480
Crossing Creek	5	G	8	0	3	1	21,374
Crossing First	8	G	5	0	0	0	0
Crossing Piney	3	F	14	4	3	2	63,580
Crossing Point	7	G	10	2	2	2	124,615
Crosslander	3	G	5	1	1	0	23,230
Crossledged	8	G	14	2	0	2	10,619
Crosspoint	4	G	10	2	1	1	76,673
Crossroad Willie	2	G	4	0	0	1	1,980
Crossroads Pine	3	G	3	0	1	1	1,463
Crosstown Caper	4	G	13	1	4	0	19,515
Crosswicks Creek	4	F	13	4	2	1	48,055
Crossword Clue	6	G	5	0	1	1	1,676
Crouching Tiger	4	G	13	0	0	2	12,208
Crow Autumn	2	F	6	0	0	0	3,200
Crow Fair	3	G	2	0	0	0	800
Crow Road	4	G	11	1	0	1	12,484
Crowbow	2	C	4	0	1	1	9,476
Crowd Watcher	6	G	8	2	0	0	22,290
Crowded Meadow	6	G	4	1	0	2	13,750
Crowded Room	4	F	6	2	2	1	79,140
Crowd's Delight	2	C	3	0	1	1	9,220
Crown Butte	9	G	10	0	1	3	3,717
Crown Command	3	G	6	0	0	1	1,001
Crown Fever	3	G	6	1	2	0	19,265
Crown Him King	3	G	3	0	0	0	253
Crown Me Augie	7	G	8	0	0	0	780
Crown Me Later	4	F	8	2	1	5	23,935
Crown Myst	3	G	12	4	1	2	45,744
Crown N Seven	3	G	2	0	0	0	140
Crown of Pearls	4	F	22	2	3	4	9,310
Crown of Will	3	G	10	2	0	1	9,234
Crown Pacific	4	G	8	1	0	0	16,830
Crown Parisian	3	G	2	0	0	1	2,310
Crown Point	2	C	7	2	1	0	90,847
Crown Point Summer	6	G	11	2	1	1	23,359
Crown Prince	3	C	6	2	0	1	64,490
Crown Proof	3	F	2	0	1	0	2,800
Crown Prosecutor	3	G	9	0	2	2	7,853
Crown Rhythm	5	G	2	0	1	0	1,600
Crown Rocket	6	G	1	0	0	0	61
Crown Royal King	4	G	8	0	0	2	8,925
Crown the Knight	9	G	8	0	0	1	2,581
Crown the Tiger	7	G	1	1	0	0	1,100
Crown Victoria	3	F	7	0	2	1	7,596
Crowned Dancer	4	C	5	1	1	0	14,320
Crowned King	4	C	15	1	3	0	69,930
Crowned Lover	5	G	4	0	0	0	122
Crowned Savannah	3	G	10	1	1	2	16,410
Crowning Act	3	F	3	0	0	0	795
Crowning Adventure	5	M	3	0	0	1	2,671
Crowning Camilla	2	F	2	1	0	0	17,515
Crowning Event	2	G	1	0	0	0	540
Crowning Moment	4	G	14	0	0	1	3,390
Crowning Quest	4	F	6	0	1	0	1,419
Crowning Sea	4	G	10	0	0	0	305
Crowning Step	4	F	1	0	0	0	291
Crowning the Queen	4	F	11	2	3	1	5,475
Crowning Victory	2	C	1	0	1	0	7,000
Crownroyal Moment	4	G	3	1	0	0	2,880
Crown's Justice	4	G	15	1	4	3	56,176
Crows (ARG)	10	H	8	1	0	0	10,042
Crows Mile	5	H	3	0	0	0	43
Croydons Game	3	F	16	4	1	4	39,715
Crozet	3	F	11	3	1	0	98,925
Crozier Lex	8	G	4	0	0	0	160
Crucial Honor	4	G	19	5	2	3	43,680
Cruciare	2	F	3	0	1	0	1,595
Cruel	3	F	7	2	0	2	16,350
Cruella de Swain	4	F	5	0	0	0	0
Cruguet (ARG)	3	C	5	0	0	0	500
Cruise Along	6	M	2	0	0	0	8,480
Cruisen N Dancin	4	F	8	0	0	0	837
Cruisenrightalong	4	G	8	1	1	3	13,223
Cruiseship	4	G	14	1	4	2	10,912
Cruisin' Carlos	5	G	20	0	3	3	5,896
Cruisin Man	6	G	11	1	0	2	18,998
Cruisin N	4	G	4	0	0	0	0
Cruisin Scooter	8	G	14	1	1	1	8,543
Cruisin Together	3	F	6	0	1	0	11,174
Cruising Bullet	6	G	8	0	0	0	2,590
Cruising Executive	4	F	10	0	0	1	14,500
Cruising for Gold	3	C	2	0	0	0	0
Cruising Kat	5	G	8	2	1	0	17,407
Crumb Bullena	2	F	1	0	0	0	0
Crunch Time	8	G	7	0	2	3	4,685
Crusader Jo	5	G	8	0	0	3	12,990
Crusader's Passage	6	M	8	0	1	3	4,285
Crusader's Quest	3	C	5	0	0	0	1,215
Crusading Kip	4	G	11	1	2	2	8,400
Crusading Time	3	F	8	1	1	1	25,260
Crush This	3	G	9	0	0	0	3,185
Crushing Velvet	3	F	1	0	0	0	0
Crusty Duck	3	F	1	0	0	0	0
Crutcher	4	G	4	2	1	0	21,485
Crux	3	G	7	0	0	1	1,019
Cruzan Midnight	4	F	10	3	1	0	18,654
Cruzcat	3	C	3	1	0	2	17,210
Cruzen's Babydoll	4	F	2	0	0	0	112
Cruzin With Ashley	2	F	3	0	0	0	1,200
Cruzin With Cara	3	F	7	1	0	0	2,800
Cruz'n O. C.	5	M	2	0	0	0	189
Cruz'n Ocala	2	F	8	0	2	2	5,485
Cry a Note	5	M	1	0	0	0	109
Cry Baby Cry	10	M	6	0	0	1	735
Cry Louder Taylor	9	G	8	0	0	1	2,939
Cry Misty	4	F	2	1	0	0	3,918
Cry No More	6	G	1	0	0	0	270
Cry of the Cat	4	F	8	1	2	0	21,047
Cry of the Wild	3	F	6	0	2	0	25,080
Cry the Blues	4	G	12	2	0	0	11,915
Cry Witch	3	F	3	0	0	0	208
Crying Out Wild	4	F	6	0	0	0	190
Crypt	5	G	11	2	1	3	18,055
Crypt de Chine	9	H	2	0	0	0	0
Crypt Keeper	2	F	3	0	0	0	0
Cryptic Attitude	7	G	4	0	0	0	780
Cryptic Code	5	G	4	0	1	1	7,050
Cryptic Devil	6	G	4	2	0	0	39,460
Cryptic John	4	G	7	1	1	0	9,571
Cryptic Lass	4	F	9	0	1	2	4,419
Cryptic Quest	2	R	4	1	0	0	12,450
Cryptic Skier	3	G	5	1	0	1	21,800
Cryptic Smile	4	G	3	0	0	0	378
Cryptic Star	3	F	7	0	0	2	4,464
Cryptic Storm	5	M	12	0	3	2	3,828
Cryptically	3	F	16	2	1	1	10,005
Crypto Bella	4	G	10	0	0	1	1,924
Crypto Cream	5	M	4	1	1	1	10,670
Crypto Cum Laude	11	G	7	3	1	1	3,680

Horse	Age	Sex	Sts	1st	2d	3d	Won
Crypto Devil	5	G	5	0	0	0	378
Crypto Dixie	5	H	11	3	4	0	67,802
Crypto Dynamo	2	C	3	0	1	1	2,340
Crypto Em	3	F	11	3	3	0	77,100
Crypto Gal	4	F	15	2	2	1	22,977
Crypto 'n Cruise	4	F	6	1	2	0	13,596
Crypto Pool	5	G	2	0	0	0	86
Crypto Prince	6	G	5	0	0	1	1,300
Crypto Runs Again	3	C	2	0	0	0	0
Crypto Secret	3	F	10	4	0	0	60,165
Crypto Storm	5	M	1	0	0	0	0
Crypto Willie	3	G	6	1	0	1	11,320
Cryptoanne	4	F	7	1	0	0	6,285
Cryptobeat	5	G	3	0	0	0	254
Cryptobillie	4	F	9	1	1	1	11,230
Cryptocraft	4	G	7	1	0	2	9,500
Cryptocruiser	4	G	14	2	0	4	10,780
Cryptoeskimo	4	G	16	1	2	1	12,429
Cryptofem	4	F	8	1	1	0	41,725
Cryptofire	2	F	2	0	0	0	166
Cryptograph	3	C	10	4	1	2	257,398
Cryptointhestars	5	M	1	0	0	0	183
Cryptologic	6	G	15	1	1	1	6,038
Cryptoman	6	G	18	1	2	2	13,660
Cryptonym	2	C	1	0	0	0	0
Cryptopro	3	G	3	0	0	0	0
Cryptoreport	3	F	12	1	0	0	5,525
Cryptorouge	7	M	3	0	1	0	3,495
Cryptorush	5	M	5	1	1	0	3,995
Cryptos' Best	3	F	7	1	1	1	46,020
Crypto's Cadillac	4	G	4	0	0	1	1,560
Crypto's Friend	4	G	9	0	3	2	9,180
Crypto's Laurel	4	G	10	1	1	2	12,405
Crypto's Pride	3	G	11	0	0	3	3,589
Crypto's Prospect	3	G	9	3	0	1	72,750
Crypto's Silver	4	G	5	0	0	2	2,475
Crypto's Spinks	4	G	9	1	0	0	9,375
Crypto's Trial	3	G	4	1	1	0	20,640
Crypto's Trick	4	F	13	1	2	4	9,800
Crypto's View	4	F	9	1	0	0	6,145
Crypto's Wild	2	F	2	0	0	0	15,408
Cryptoscript	5	M	2	0	0	0	0
Crypto'slittlestar	3	F	7	2	0	0	16,240
Cryptosummer	3	F	14	0	0	1	5,495
Cryptotune	7	H	13	0	0	1	1,974
Cryptovinsky	3	G	3	0	0	0	520
Cry's Sassy Lady	5	M	9	0	0	0	585
Crystal Appeal	6	M	11	3	0	0	13,080
Crystal Appeal M	3	F	3	1	0	0	644
Crystal Archer	3	G	14	2	4	1	27,684
Crystal Beach	3	F	10	1	2	3	31,255
Crystal Billing	5	H	1	0	0	0	0
Crystal Boots	5	M	3	0	0	0	189
Crystal Castle	6	G	6	0	1	2	135,701
Crystal Charm	4	F	13	0	0	1	2,508
Crystal Cinders	10	M	8	1	0	1	2,082
Crystal Clarity	5	M	8	1	2	1	7,417
Crystal Class	4	C	4	1	0	1	5,920
Crystal Clear	4	F	14	1	2	0	5,764
Crystal Clipper	4	F	2	0	0	0	0
Crystal Clout	5	G	4	0	0	0	1,500
Crystal Colony	5	G	8	0	1	2	10,037
Crystal Conquest	5	H	7	0	0	0	735
Crystal Crest	2	F	4	0	1	0	3,543
Crystal Dancer	4	F	15	2	5	2	37,330
Crystal Dawn	7	M	10	3	2	2	39,690
Crystal Dew	9	M	7	0	0	0	1,385
Crystal Gail	4	F	3	0	0	1	750
Crystal Gala	3	F	11	1	1	1	21,602
Crystal Harmony	6	M	6	2	3	0	100,460
Crystal House	2	F	2	0	1	0	7,400
Crystal Lee	6	G	12	1	0	1	15,743
Crystal Magic	3	F	4	1	1	0	18,300
Crystal Marina	3	F	4	0	1	0	6,185
Crystal Mt. Stevie	3	F	7	0	0	0	743
Crystal n' Reign	7	M	2	0	0	2	2,790
Crystal n'Silver	4	F	1	0	0	1	1,575
Crystal On Fire	4	C	1	0	0	0	0
Crystal Pattern	6	M	1	0	0	0	365
Crystal Pond	2	F	1	0	0	1	1,755
Crystal Prediction	9	M	8	0	1	0	2,924
Crystal Sally	7	M	11	1	3	3	8,393
Crystal Season	6	G	1	0	0	0	300
Crystal Sound	5	G	11	1	0	1	1,816
Crystal Souvenir	3	G	4	0	0	2	1,500
Crystal Sweet	4	F	1	0	0	0	260
Crystal Tide	3	F	2	0	0	0	0
Crystal Tiger	2	F	1	0	1	0	8,200
Crystal Vision	4	G	3	0	0	0	223
Crystal Vite	3	F	1	0	0	0	500
Crystalaire	5	G	5	0	0	3	4,185
Crystalen Tiffany	5	M	2	0	0	0	528
Crystallization	4	G	16	2	3	4	35,726
Crystallo	7	G	9	3	1	0	38,900
Crytovictory	3	C	1	0	0	0	1,860
Cryyoulittledevil	8	G	3	0	0	0	0
C's Victory	3	G	3	0	0	1	5,520
Cu At the Bailey	5	G	8	0	2	2	3,975
Cuando Dinero	3	G	1	0	0	1	2,750
Cub n' Rum	3	F	10	2	0	5	32,107
Cuba	3	C	9	2	1	2	78,220
Cuba Road Red	3	C	8	1	1	1	6,801
Cuban Coffee	4	F	12	0	0	0	1,155
Cuban Cutie	4	F	5	0	0	0	0
Cuban Leaf	4	G	9	1	1	0	4,799
Cubanero	4	G	14	2	1	2	24,716
Cubby Bear	4	G	8	0	1	1	3,635
Cube	2	C	1	0	0	0	0
Cube's Kat	6	G	14	2	2	3	12,739
Cubicle	4	F	12	3	3	1	25,209
Cub's Power	2	C	5	1	0	2	9,925
Cubster	3	G	6	0	0	0	2,155
Cuca	4	F	6	1	1	0	17,520
Cuccinella	5	M	1	0	0	0	0
Cuchalian	7	M	5	1	0	1	4,770
Cucuri	8	G	2	0	0	0	247
Cucurri Babe	5	M	7	0	0	1	2,191
Cuddlebrink	3	G	12	2	4	1	22,165
Cudo	8	G	1	0	0	0	50
Cued Up	5	G	12	2	1	1	22,742
Cuerdas	7	M	9	2	1	0	16,993
Cuervo Brown	2	C	3	0	1	0	1,733
Cuervo Kayak	2	C	3	0	1	0	2,042
Cuff the Quote	3	G	6	0	1	1	1,860
Cugini Gold	4	G	3	0	0	0	96
Cukros	6	M	12	1	1	1	8,563
Culet	2	F	6	0	1	0	13,035
Culinary	2	F	3	2	0	0	78,000
Cullen	3	G	9	1	0	1	16,420
Culley	5	M	17	1	3	4	11,583
Cullowhee	4	F	3	0	1	1	7,260
Culmen (ARG)	5	H	7	1	2	2	28,760
Culpeper Moon	3	F	4	1	2	0	13,230
Culturally Current	3	C	8	2	3	1	39,390
Culture Clash	2	F	4	1	0	0	41,400
Cum Laude	5	G	12	4	1	3	26,255
Cumberland Boy	5	G	3	0	0	0	327
Cumberland Gap	12	G	10	0	3	1	7,930
Cumberland River	7	G	9	0	0	1	1,082
Cumberland Road	6	M	4	0	0	1	835
Cumby Texas	4	C	14	7	4	1	127,780
Cummerbund	4	C	2	0	2	0	4,720
Cummings	3	C	3	0	1	1	4,800
Cumulus	5	G	11	2	2	3	19,054
Cunning Cat	3	G	5	1	0	1	20,485
Cunningly	3	F	4	1	0	0	24,720
Cuore d'Oro	4	F	7	0	0	3	2,198
Cup of Coco	4	F	5	0	1	0	13,100
Cupalo	5	G	4	0	0	1	1,190
Cupar	3	F	2	0	0	1	3,840
Cupasoup	5	M	4	0	0	0	3,330
Cupid Season	4	F	12	0	1	1	39,277
Cupids Angel	3	F	3	0	0	0	465
Cupid's Arrow	3	F	10	2	2	2	67,885
Cupid's Dixie	2	F	2	0	0	2	7,840
Cupid's Honour	5	G	15	0	0	3	5,986
Cupid's Power	4	F	7	1	2	1	2,432
Cup's Final Shine	3	C	11	2	0	3	9,350

Horse	Age	Sex	Sts	1st	2d	3d	Won
Curb	4	G	10	2	2	2	58,370
Curbettes	2	F	5	0	0	1	5,500
Curbside Check In	2	G	3	0	0	0	1,938
Cure the Devil	9	H	1	0	0	0	0
Curicular	4	F	5	0	1	1	949
Curio Cat	3	F	9	0	0	0	2,354
Curiosity	4	F	12	1	1	2	81,722
Curious Archer	3	C	1	0	0	0	154
Curious Conundrum	6	M	4	0	0	1	3,500
Curious Critter	3	C	1	0	0	0	0
Curious Gamble	3	G	12	2	2	1	42,474
Curious Indy	3	G	1	0	0	0	420
Curlew Road	2	C	5	0	1	3	19,930
Curli Babi	3	F	7	0	0	0	309
Curls	4	F	3	0	1	0	2,580
Curly Bill	3	G	3	0	0	1	1,355
Curly Carnivalay	9	G	11	0	1	3	2,730
Curly Halo	4	F	17	3	2	4	47,332
Curly Jake	6	G	3	0	0	1	361
Curly Joe	7	G	14	1	1	0	6,972
Curly Wurly	3	F	9	2	1	0	10,510
Curly's Pride	3	F	11	1	1	3	47,556
Curly's Sea Star	2	F	2	0	0	0	318
Curmudgeon	5	H	10	0	1	1	4,121
Curno J. C.	5	G	14	0	0	2	9,411
Currahee	5	G	11	0	2	1	3,311
Currahee Bravo Six	3	G	4	0	0	0	1,600
Currency Trader	2	G	2	0	2	0	19,600
Current Hitter	9	M	9	1	0	0	2,950
Current Miss	3	F	6	0	1	2	4,720
Current Niner	3	C	4	1	0	0	17,820
Current Odds	2	F	3	0	0	0	315
Current Tirade	4	G	3	0	0	0	672
Currituck Springs	4	G	7	0	4	0	14,423
Cursitor	3	G	4	1	0	0	5,522
Curtain Climber	5	G	1	1	0	0	2,120
Curtee	5	G	2	0	0	0	811
Curt's First Bid	5	G	10	5	3	0	84,335
Curve Ball	7	G	10	1	1	2	14,613
Curve Buster	4	F	4	0	1	1	7,290
Cuse	3	G	11	1	2	0	15,480
Cussing Gus	8	G	3	0	0	0	72
Custer's Farewell	4	F	4	0	1	0	1,426
Custers Last	5	M	1	0	0	0	690
Custom Cruiser	2	G	6	0	0	1	1,908
Custom Framing	4	G	2	0	0	1	4,440
Custom Made Jade	3	G	12	1	3	1	30,713
Customary	3	F	3	0	0	0	0
Customize	3	F	9	3	4	1	39,090
Customs	3	F	8	2	1	0	12,777
Cut a Wager	5	M	10	3	1	1	42,884
Cut and Shoot	3	C	6	2	2	0	155,700
Cut Back	3	C	15	4	3	3	76,465
Cut Class	5	G	13	4	3	2	27,992
Cut It Out Rudy	3	G	9	0	2	0	7,765
Cut Me In	6	H	9	0	1	0	8,770
Cut Me Loose	2	C	1	0	0	0	0
Cut Number	4	F	12	2	3	3	43,695
Cut of Music	4	G	16	2	3	3	42,959
Cut Stone	3	G	8	3	0	1	20,365
Cut the Mustard	2	F	5	1	2	0	70,400
Cut the Ribbon	4	G	10	0	1	2	4,719
Cut the Star	2	C	2	0	0	0	0
Cut to the Chase	3	F	6	0	0	0	3,260
Cut to the Hunt	4	G	5	0	0	0	590
Cut Trail	2	G	1	0	0	0	400
Cute as a Bug	2	F	4	0	1	0	5,835
Cute as an Angel	3	F	5	0	1	2	9,600
Cute Cat	3	F	1	1	0	0	8,700
Cute Connie	3	F	15	2	1	4	60,280
Cute Crafty	4	C	3	0	0	0	210
Cute N Noble	4	F	10	0	0	2	31,597
Cute Operator	2	F	4	1	2	0	33,940
Cuteasshecanbee	2	F	1	0	0	0	356
Cutelilblondechick	3	F	1	0	0	0	161
Cutiecantoo	5	M	12	1	1	1	9,169
Cutlass Cutie	3	F	6	2	0	0	25,145
Cutlass Prince	4	G	6	0	1	0	2,603
Cutmeabreak	2	C	2	0	0	0	0
Cutnstyle	5	M	9	1	1	0	12,940
Cutoffs	4	F	5	2	1	0	36,780
Cuts Like a Knife	3	C	2	0	0	0	0
Cutshin	4	G	9	0	1	1	4,436
Cuttin Cash	4	F	11	2	1	1	4,457
Cuttin In	2	F	4	2	1	0	19,203
Cutting a Rug	3	F	5	1	0	0	1,882
Cutting Points	3	G	6	1	0	0	11,482
Cutting the Rug	5	G	8	2	1	3	51,124
Cutty	6	G	5	0	0	1	1,602
Cuvee	3	C	3	0	2	0	41,340
Cuyahoga	3	F	5	3	0	1	97,540
Cuz Your My Baby	7	G	3	0	0	0	0
Cviano	7	G	6	0	1	0	1,814
Cy	3	C	2	0	0	0	0
Cya Baby	3	F	11	1	3	2	48,043
Cya Cahill	2	F	5	0	1	2	2,322
Cya Sal	3	F	5	0	0	2	4,270
Cyalady	2	F	2	0	1	0	5,250
Cyane's Thunder	6	H	8	1	0	0	29,030
Cyanne Slew	6	G	1	0	1	0	320
Cyb Her Speed	2	F	4	0	1	1	3,929
Cyber City Slew	3	G	5	1	0	1	21,975
Cyber Dawn	2	F	2	0	0	0	2,320
Cyber Hacker	3	C	12	3	1	2	32,395
Cyber Move	6	M	16	3	2	2	10,309
Cyber Ruckus	4	G	1	0	0	0	85
Cyber Slew	4	F	14	5	1	3	262,215
Cyber Stock	6	H	1	0	0	0	52
Cyber Trick	2	G	1	0	0	0	0
Cyberchase	3	F	17	1	6	1	32,750
Cyberchic	3	F	3	0	0	0	111
Cyberdevil	4	G	4	0	0	0	1,031
Cyberflash	4	G	13	2	4	0	52,855
Cybergames	3	F	2	0	0	0	183
Cybergate	5	H	4	2	0	1	24,370
Cybers' Image	3	C	5	0	0	0	500
Cybershine	3	F	6	0	0	0	2,436
Cybersimon	4	F	2	1	0	0	6,736
Cyberspace Phone	3	G	5	0	0	0	225
Cyberwiz	4	G	8	0	0	0	881
Cyberzone	6	M	7	0	1	0	1,312
Cycle of Life	4	F	7	0	0	0	1,492
Cyclical	4	F	5	2	1	1	3,192
Cyclone Bar	3	G	2	0	0	0	0
Cyclone Slew	4	F	6	1	1	0	10,925
Cyclone Tower	3	G	4	0	0	0	0
Cyclotron	4	C	1	0	0	0	2,940
Cymbelina's Genie	3	C	3	1	0	0	8,050
Cymbidium	4	F	1	0	0	0	700
Cyndi's Beauty	2	F	5	0	0	1	2,123
Cyndi's Dancer	3	F	3	0	1	1	3,090
Cynical	2	F	1	1	0	0	13,200
Cynics Quest	5	G	14	1	2	3	14,985
Cynthia Hurricane	4	F	3	0	0	0	0
Cynthiana's Song	4	G	15	4	0	4	84,847
Cynthia's Anna	3	F	11	1	1	0	13,122
Cynthia's Field	4	F	19	0	2	3	7,416
Cynthus	4	F	9	0	2	4	8,290
Cypress Cove	4	G	10	2	0	1	67,350
Cypress Hill	4	F	2	0	2	0	5,420
Cypress Trail	5	M	1	0	0	0	0
Cypriata	3	F	7	2	1	2	54,256
Cyratoga	6	G	4	0	1	0	1,950
Cytherea	3	F	7	0	0	2	5,313
Czar	5	G	10	5	0	1	19,135
Czar d'Or	4	G	4	0	0	0	1,840
Czar of Cozzene	3	G	8	2	1	1	26,320
Czardas Dancer	8	G	15	3	1	3	18,650
Czarist	5	G	8	2	1	3	15,705
Czar's Witch	3	F	5	1	0	0	13,317
Czartina	4	F	10	2	3	0	26,829
Czech Mate	4	G	5	1	1	1	17,675
D B Free Bird	3	F	8	0	0	1	4,259
D' Cash	2	G	2	0	0	0	140
D C's Thunder	3	G	7	3	0	0	124,148
D D Dot Comm	7	G	6	4	1	0	16,415
D D Ruby	3	F	3	1	0	1	25,890
D D Stormy	6	G	12	2	1	1	10,407

Horse	Age	Sex	Sts	1st	2d	3d	Won
D Devil	2	G	3	0	0	1	450
D D's Big Hug	3	G	4	0	0	0	688
D E Barron	3	G	6	0	0	0	385
D E Intimidator	4	G	11	0	1	1	2,910
D' Esprit	5	M	9	0	2	2	9,775
D Fine Okie	2	F	4	2	0	0	31,280
D Girl in Blue	2	F	1	1	0	0	12,720
D Gypsy	3	F	4	0	0	0	399
D J North	12	G	5	1	0	1	3,348
D J's Angel	4	F	2	0	0	0	753
D J's Going Places	6	G	12	3	4	0	29,000
D J's Jubilee	12	G	10	3	5	1	20,600
D J's Runnaway	3	F	7	1	0	0	5,674
D J's Sailor	3	G	2	0	0	0	400
D J's Show Time	8	G	14	1	3	2	10,871
D J's Thunderhead	8	G	3	0	0	0	194
D J's Tridon	5	G	1	0	0	0	0
D K Dickens	7	G	10	1	0	1	9,541
D L Scooter	2	G	8	0	1	1	4,401
D' Lady Scarlett	3	F	2	0	1	0	1,595
D Lux Chimes	3	G	1	0	1	0	900
D M Special	4	F	11	3	1	0	27,235
D Misterious Angel	5	M	6	0	0	1	1,483
D M's Awsum Koko	6	M	4	0	0	0	558
D' Nile	4	F	9	1	1	2	36,840
D P Dancer	4	C	14	2	3	5	31,440
D Ranger	3	C	1	0	0	0	170
D Running Devil	5	G	4	0	0	1	1,522
D Silver Bandette	3	F	2	0	0	0	84
D' Special	8	G	6	0	0	0	495
D Style	5	G	4	0	0	0	1,326
D' Wildcat Speed	4	F	4	1	2	0	49,000
D W's Rose Bud	6	G	2	0	0	0	309
D. A. Way	4	G	5	0	0	0	0
D. B. Cooper	3	G	6	0	1	1	1,370
D. C. Lady	3	F	2	0	0	0	232
D. G. Dusty	3	C	6	0	0	1	4,880
D. J. Devil Cat	3	F	3	1	0	0	4,980
D. J. Justice	3	F	3	0	0	0	1,660
D. J. Tyler	5	G	6	1	0	0	19,109
D. J.'s Grades	3	G	10	0	0	0	1,620
D. J.'s Hero	3	C	5	2	2	0	40,700
D. J.'s Hope	7	H	2	0	1	0	7,320
D. J.'s Slew	3	F	11	2	0	3	20,764
D. Jeter	3	G	4	0	0	0	2,244
D. K.'s Navigator	3	G	3	0	0	0	541
D. L. Renzo	3	C	21	5	1	1	88,535
D. W. Song	5	M	3	0	0	0	1,005
Da Beauty	4	F	2	0	0	0	324
Da Birdman	3	C	13	4	1	1	36,515
Da Boxer	3	C	9	1	2	2	33,464
Da Breeze	6	G	8	1	3	0	13,999
Da Cardinal	2	C	3	0	2	1	58,886
Da Da Rumba	4	G	7	1	0	0	6,444
Da Dance	4	F	7	1	1	0	10,500
Da Forty Four	3	G	2	0	0	1	780
Da' Fox	5	G	2	0	0	0	0
Da Gangsta	3	G	13	1	3	3	19,915
Da Great Pretender	3	F	10	1	0	1	8,325
Da Lawyer	4	G	5	0	0	0	495
Da Little Guy	3	G	2	1	1	0	6,000
Da Mamboking	3	C	10	1	1	2	12,527
Da Meister	6	G	3	1	0	0	3,000
Da Noodles	2	F	1	0	0	0	0
Da Pillar	3	G	8	1	2	1	12,560
Da Rodeo Man	4	G	9	2	1	1	14,556
Da Svedonya	4	F	13	1	5	2	34,300
Da Travelin Man	3	C	5	3	0	0	25,944
Da Will Ta Win	4	F	1	0	0	0	0
Daad's Hot	5	G	10	0	0	1	2,465
Dab of Wheelock	4	G	2	0	0	0	0
Dabney	2	F	5	0	1	2	4,519
Dabney Carr	9	G	4	0	0	1	1,645
Dacarly	3	F	2	0	0	0	1,140
Dacota Desert	5	G	1	1	0	0	2,700
Dactique's Quest	4	F	3	0	0	1	6,400
Dad Bell's Baby	3	G	8	1	0	0	8,700
Dad Grands Girl	5	M	9	0	3	0	5,009
Dad Says Yes	3	F	13	4	0	0	25,921
Dad Smoked Cigar	5	M	12	0	1	1	12,310
Dadadafense	3	G	2	0	0	0	161
Daddy Cool	6	G	7	5	1	0	243,358
Daddy Joe	2	C	5	1	1	1	42,600
Daddy Says No	4	G	7	0	0	2	2,463
Daddy Who	3	F	1	0	0	0	93
Daddy's Baby Girl	4	F	7	1	0	1	9,025
Daddys Bright Star	5	H	5	3	1	0	24,205
Daddy's Crane	3	C	10	2	3	1	25,618
Daddy's Destiny	4	F	1	0	0	0	0
Daddy's Petunia	3	F	8	2	2	0	51,676
Daddy's Punkin	4	F	4	1	1	1	11,370
Daddys Shoes	3	G	10	0	1	2	5,200
Daddysangbass	2	C	1	1	0	0	14,400
Dads Destiny	2	G	5	0	0	1	2,633
Dads Destroyer	4	F	2	0	1	0	5,530
Dad's Double	11	G	4	0	0	0	500
Dads Last Won	2	F	2	1	0	0	5,610
Dad's Lessons	3	G	7	0	0	0	8,440
Dad's Love	4	F	4	0	0	1	1,027
Dad's Star	3	F	7	0	1	0	6,880
Daffodil Lil	5	M	11	2	0	3	7,446
Daffodil Princess	4	F	10	3	1	1	28,510
Dafne's Echo	3	F	3	1	0	0	21,800
Dagny Taggert	6	M	8	1	1	3	15,765
Dahlberg (BRZ)	9	G	2	0	0	0	800
Dahlia's Diamond	3	F	4	3	0	0	22,620
Dahlias Trempolino	4	G	8	0	0	1	1,704
Daily Dance	4	F	1	0	0	0	135
Daily Forecast	2	F	4	1	1	0	18,700
Daily Report	5	M	15	3	2	0	28,874
Daily Total	4	G	9	1	0	0	5,758
Dainty Dish	5	M	4	0	0	0	0
Daisy Be Good	5	M	12	1	0	1	5,615
Daisy Cutter	4	F	3	0	0	1	3,310
Daisy Daisy	3	F	6	1	1	0	8,325
Daisy Double	11	M	2	0	0	1	540
Daisy Maid	4	F	2	0	0	1	1,529
Daisy Mountain	2	F	6	1	0	1	19,912
Daisy Slew	3	F	12	2	4	2	14,502
Daisyago	5	M	8	0	1	1	29,090
Daisye Duxster	6	M	3	0	0	0	344
Daisys Don't Tell	4	F	8	2	0	1	8,110
Daisys Genius	3	F	3	0	0	0	0
Daisy's Memory	7	G	13	3	4	1	19,284
Daisy's Our Dream	4	F	11	1	3	0	8,519
Daisy's Secret	2	F	1	0	0	0	1,200
Daivon Jones	5	H	3	0	0	1	4,890
Dajudge	6	G	22	1	1	5	34,615
Dakang	3	C	1	0	0	0	42
Dako Rika	8	G	5	0	0	0	262
Dakota Bells	3	G	5	0	1	0	1,360
Dakota Bullet	5	M	3	0	0	0	592
Dakota Cowboy	4	G	16	0	2	2	10,955
Dakota Danzig	13	G	6	0	0	0	402
Dakota Destiny	4	G	2	0	0	0	100
Dakota Diamond	5	G	9	0	0	2	2,364
Dakota Dixie	3	G	11	2	4	0	32,626
Dakota Duke	2	C	3	0	0	2	8,080
Dakota Gold	8	H	3	0	0	0	0
Dakota Hondo	3	G	5	0	1	1	2,687
Dakota Ice	4	G	9	1	2	4	7,755
Dakota Kid	3	G	7	1	3	1	10,060
Dakota Light	4	F	12	1	1	4	78,730
Dakota Max	2	C	1	0	0	0	135
Dakota North	2	G	8	1	1	3	27,220
Dakota Scout	2	C	1	0	0	0	135
Dakota West	4	G	3	1	0	0	6,100
Dakota Winter Air	4	C	9	0	0	3	1,331
Dakota's Angel	4	F	2	0	0	0	200
Dal Reo Lad	12	G	4	0	0	0	301
Dalavin	3	G	10	3	4	0	196,125
Dalder	7	G	5	0	0	0	1,002
Dale	3	G	5	0	0	0	0
Dale Evans	2	F	2	0	0	0	528
Dale's Boy	3	G	13	1	0	1	3,849
Dale's Deluxe	4	G	9	0	5	0	21,238
Dale's Irishmelody	6	G	14	1	1	1	7,187
Dale's Prospect	3	C	7	3	2	1	71,860

Horse	Age	Sex	Sts	1st	2d	3d	Won
Dalewoods Promise	3	G	9	0	0	0	2,202
Dalia Dolly	5	M	14	2	1	1	30,180
Dalia's Whirl	6	M	7	1	0	1	6,282
Dallas County	3	C	20	2	4	0	14,303
Dallas Express	4	G	13	0	1	2	10,590
Dallas Maverick	2	C	2	0	0	0	0
Dally May	2	F	10	0	2	0	12,940
Dalovaly Linda	3	F	17	3	1	1	45,809
Dalton Town	7	G	5	0	0	0	336
Dalt's Kingpin	5	G	15	2	2	3	56,699
Dalybuck	4	C	1	0	0	0	0
Daly's Corner	3	G	13	1	1	3	14,790
Dam Cat	3	G	9	2	3	1	26,750
Dama de Millon	2	F	3	0	0	0	2,139
Damar Wayne	5	G	8	3	2	0	119,142
Damariscotta	3	F	12	2	3	2	29,775
Damascus Boy	3	C	9	0	0	0	833
Damascus Dancer	3	C	4	0	0	2	1,290
D'amber Dream	2	C	2	0	1	0	4,100
Dame Bertie	4	F	13	2	1	1	8,095
Dame Eliza	2	F	1	0	0	0	0
Dame Fame	4	F	8	0	2	1	12,055
Dame Sterling	3	F	2	0	0	0	0
Dames Best Man	5	H	7	0	1	0	1,693
Damican	5	H	10	3	1	1	17,008
D'amiga	2	F	1	0	0	0	0
Damn the Torpedoes	7	G	7	2	3	0	43,920
Damon T.	4	G	12	0	0	3	3,445
Damspicy	6	G	8	1	1	2	1,975
Damus's Dancer	5	G	11	0	0	2	1,825
Dan D La Kar	9	G	3	0	0	0	150
Dan Is Fast	2	C	5	1	0	0	17,000
Dan of Distinction	3	G	11	0	1	1	2,801
Dan Ray	2	G	2	0	0	0	955
Dana	3	F	5	0	0	1	1,010
Dana Did It	3	F	2	1	0	0	19,390
Dana Dragrace	4	F	5	0	0	0	261
Danadar	6	G	13	3	2	1	17,592
Danaher	3	G	2	0	0	0	0
Danaly Miss	5	M	1	0	0	0	0
Danar	9	G	7	0	1	0	3,526
Dana's Lucky Lady	3	F	11	2	2	1	96,700
Dana's Pet	3	G	7	0	0	0	180
Danas Story	7	M	4	0	0	0	128
Danaslam	2	C	1	0	0	0	370
Dance a Bit	6	G	13	0	2	0	4,168
Dance Act	3	F	8	0	1	2	5,775
Dance Affair	5	G	7	2	1	2	19,045
Dance Again	3	F	4	0	0	0	698
Dance All Night	3	F	4	1	1	1	37,387
Dance Aly Dance	4	G	13	2	2	2	14,089
Dance and Begone	2	F	2	0	1	1	1,310
Dance and Dazzle	6	G	5	1	3	1	48,304
Dance and Whirl	6	M	14	1	2	3	8,917
Dance Apollo	4	C	7	0	0	1	13,974
Dance At Noon	3	C	5	1	0	0	6,223
Dance Away Capote	2	F	5	2	1	0	124,450
Dance Away Home	3	C	11	1	1	1	22,320
Dance Buster	3	G	4	0	0	0	280
Dance Captain	4	C	8	1	0	0	13,640
Dance Commander	3	F	7	0	2	3	7,680
Dance Dance	5	M	8	0	3	1	19,660
Dance Date	3	F	6	0	0	1	1,550
Dance Dime	6	M	1	0	0	0	630
Dance Engagement	4	C	6	1	0	0	55,974
Dance Fee	3	F	13	1	3	4	69,700
Dance for Dash	3	F	4	1	0	0	37,620
Dance for Em	3	G	2	0	0	0	470
Dance for Fun	6	M	1	1	0	0	3,720
Dance for Gold	7	M	11	1	2	3	16,624
Dance for John	6	G	5	0	2	0	6,598
Dance for Nance	2	G	1	0	0	0	1,110
Dance for Olga	7	M	1	0	0	0	0
Dance for Pharos	3	G	11	0	2	1	6,828
Dance for Romeo	4	C	1	0	0	0	0
Dance for Rosel	11	G	2	0	0	0	0
Dance for Sheree	7	M	3	0	0	0	303
Dance Hall Dandy	4	C	12	3	1	2	25,200
Dance Hall Hero	4	C	3	0	0	1	3,400
Dance in Flight	4	F	3	0	0	2	2,040
Dance in the Mood (JPN)	3	F	9	3	3	0	2,866,978
Dance in the Park	6	G	11	0	0	0	2,488
Dance in the Snow	4	G	4	1	0	0	4,760
Dance in the Wind	4	F	13	2	1	0	22,255
Dance Instructor	3	F	2	1	1	0	10,200
Dance Jane	4	F	6	0	0	1	1,408
Dance King	6	G	4	0	0	1	3,504
Dance Kuntakete	4	F	11	2	2	0	35,575
Dance Lessons	5	M	6	0	0	0	795
Dance Lil' Sister	4	F	9	0	2	0	4,803
Dance Lil Zar	6	G	12	1	0	3	9,602
Dance Lover	2	F	1	0	0	0	400
Dance Lovley	4	F	4	0	0	0	0
Dance Man	3	G	4	1	0	0	3,600
Dance Mary Anne	6	M	18	2	3	1	26,225
Dance Mattic	4	F	13	4	2	3	21,824
Dance Me Free	5	G	10	3	0	1	56,696
Dance Molly Dance	3	F	5	0	0	1	2,871
Dance Music (ARG)	7	H	2	1	0	0	9,130
Dance My Lady	7	M	7	1	1	0	4,955
Dance My Number	4	F	5	0	0	0	194
Dance N Kiss	4	G	6	0	0	0	2,985
Dance N the Blues	4	F	9	1	3	4	3,628
Dance No More	3	G	8	0	0	2	4,015
Dance Note	5	G	8	2	0	0	18,875
Dance of Joy	4	F	8	0	2	3	17,550
Dance of the Year	3	F	7	1	1	0	38,260
Dance On Home	4	G	11	2	1	0	43,581
Dance On Slew	2	F	2	0	0	1	1,590
Dance Pepper Dance	3	F	15	2	3	1	26,237
Dance Pro	4	G	13	2	3	2	50,426
Dance Proudly	4	G	10	0	2	1	10,762
Dance Quiet	2	C	2	0	0	0	430
Dance Rhythm	6	M	18	0	2	2	13,520
Dance Season	2	G	2	0	0	0	0
Dance Seeker	4	G	12	3	1	1	16,165
Dance Sister Dance	2	G	8	2	3	1	32,585
Dance Special	3	F	7	0	1	1	12,190
Dance Sweetly	4	F	11	0	3	2	6,365
Dance the Green	4	F	14	3	1	6	69,281
Dance Thief	2	C	5	0	2	2	33,770
Dance to Destiny	5	H	2	0	1	1	11,880
Dance to Dixie	2	F	1	0	1	0	3,640
Dance to Remember	2	G	5	1	0	0	39,160
Dance Tune	3	F	10	2	3	1	108,840
Dance Turn	3	C	1	0	0	0	0
Dance Winner	3	F	20	6	1	5	43,515
Dance With a Fool	7	G	19	4	4	1	17,055
Dance With Bo	4	F	10	2	0	3	14,297
Dance With Delight	4	F	6	1	1	0	9,758
Dance With Genie	4	F	10	0	0	0	1,121
Dance With Kelly	8	H	2	0	0	0	107
Dance With Lance	2	F	1	0	0	0	200
Dance With Legend	2	C	5	1	1	0	33,526
Dance With Lu	2	C	1	0	0	0	0
Dance With Mia	3	G	4	0	1	0	2,950
Dance With Pride	4	G	6	0	2	1	9,045
Dance With Ravens	2	C	3	1	1	1	223,820
Dance With Teddi	4	F	6	0	0	0	548
Danceable	2	F	6	2	0	1	67,464
Danceallthewayhome	3	G	14	3	3	1	19,731
Danceandbefestive	3	G	14	4	2	1	32,511
Dancescore	5	G	3	0	0	0	800
Danceaway Dixie	4	F	7	0	2	1	5,935
Danceaway Girl	3	F	12	2	1	1	20,475
Dancedetide	5	M	2	0	0	1	1,683
Dancefortyniner	3	C	12	2	3	1	59,450
Dancehall Deelites	2	F	7	1	2	3	140,002
Danceing Deano	6	G	3	0	0	1	495
Danceingann	3	F	1	0	0	0	0
Danceinthecircus	4	F	10	0	2	4	9,255
Danceinthemorning	4	F	13	0	0	2	2,720
Danceinthevalley	5	G	14	1	1	0	7,665
Dancelikeasoldier	2	F	3	0	0	1	1,375
Dancemaker	3	G	8	1	2	1	45,890
Dancen in the Sun	6	M	3	1	0	0	29,748
Danceobeahthenight	7	G	11	3	1	2	40,346
Dancer and You	4	G	3	0	1	0	3,309

Horse	Age	Sex	Sts	1st	2d	3d	Won
Dancer C C	5	M	9	0	0	1	3,503
Dancer Cielo	5	G	2	0	0	1	4,060
Dancer Memo	4	F	1	0	0	0	675
Dancer Prancer	2	C	2	0	1	0	4,137
Dancer Sonata	4	G	19	0	2	5	11,834
Dancers Boy	3	G	3	0	0	0	2,247
Dancer's Code	4	F	6	0	1	1	11,070
Dancer's Defense	3	F	10	1	4	0	12,124
Dancer's Flyer	3	G	10	0	0	2	25,246
Dancer's Guest	5	G	11	1	0	0	42,792
Dancer's Honour	3	F	8	2	1	1	16,041
Dancer's Into It	4	F	1	0	1	0	1,500
Dancers Memories	7	G	11	1	0	0	3,068
Dancers Pal	5	M	2	0	0	0	0
Dancer's Prospect	4	F	13	2	1	2	13,976
Dancer's Rage	6	G	12	1	2	1	5,450
Dancer's Wish	7	G	15	1	3	2	35,996
Dances On Clouds	4	F	4	1	0	0	6,715
Dances With Czars	2	C	9	0	0	2	9,770
Dances With Eagles	2	C	5	1	0	1	5,701
Dances With Joy	4	G	7	0	0	1	4,970
Dances With Victor	3	F	2	0	0	0	54
Dancethcontinental	6	G	2	0	0	0	0
Dancetheblues	2	G	2	1	0	1	16,430
Danceville	4	G	1	0	0	0	300
Dancewel	7	G	5	1	2	1	34,287
Dancewithadolly	5	M	18	5	1	3	63,020
Dancewithasoldier	4	F	2	0	2	0	13,320
Dancewithavictor	7	G	8	4	1	0	73,235
Dancewithavixen	4	F	7	3	2	1	108,674
Dancewithmeashley	6	M	8	0	0	0	1,118
Dancewithmercedes	4	F	8	2	1	1	13,222
Dancewithslew	2	G	4	1	0	0	4,755
Danceworth	2	F	1	0	0	0	0
Dancin Atthe Crest	2	F	1	0	0	0	400
Dancin Beauty	5	M	6	0	0	0	123
Dancin Candy	3	G	9	1	1	5	50,749
Dancin Chilly	3	F	2	0	0	0	114
Dancin Christy	4	F	9	0	1	0	2,122
Dancin' Dennis	3	G	3	0	0	0	326
Dancin Doll	4	F	17	3	3	2	16,192
Dancin Dottie	3	F	11	3	4	0	82,159
Dancin Dusty	3	C	12	3	0	2	102,160
Dancin Falcon	6	G	6	0	0	0	2,384
Dancin for Gold	4	F	10	3	1	5	133,179
Dancin Girl	5	M	7	0	1	3	13,540
Dancin Guffey	4	C	6	0	0	0	74
Dancin in the Barn	2	G	4	0	0	0	3,668
Dancin in the Dark	5	M	18	0	0	2	3,168
Dancin Jean	5	M	13	1	3	3	11,242
Dancin Joey	4	G	5	1	1	1	79,114
Dancin Kaity	6	M	10	0	0	0	1,871
Dancin Kelly Z	3	F	5	0	2	2	7,775
Dancin Kristina	3	F	12	2	1	2	16,850
Dancin Lance	4	G	2	0	0	1	1,370
Dancin Little T	2	F	3	1	0	0	4,464
Dancin Mortlock	3	G	18	1	0	1	4,978
Dancin On Broadway	2	F	3	2	1	0	58,600
Dancin On Thin Ice	2	F	3	0	0	0	0
Dancin Rahy	8	H	1	0	0	0	0
Dancin Red Wolf	8	G	4	1	0	0	16,940
Dancin Regiment	8	M	11	0	1	2	2,078
Dancin too Close	4	F	6	1	1	3	3,570
Dancin With Motion	3	F	8	1	0	0	3,570
Dancin With Tori	4	F	6	2	0	2	45,390
Dancinandsingin	3	F	9	2	0	4	60,680
Dancinasfastasican	3	F	8	2	0	1	42,850
Dancing At Midnite	5	G	10	0	0	1	10,217
Dancing Baba	3	C	7	1	1	0	7,864
Dancing Bull	7	G	7	0	0	0	490
Dancing by U	2	F	2	0	1	0	6,348
Dancing Cajun	5	M	8	0	0	0	122
Dancing Capote	6	M	3	0	0	1	4,239
Dancing Chequer	5	M	8	1	0	1	7,623
Dancing Chevron	5	M	12	1	0	1	5,005
Dancing Claire	2	F	2	0	0	1	880
Dancing Coins	3	F	3	1	1	1	28,944
Dancing Colors (IRE)	3	F	3	2	0	1	55,650
Dancing Courtesan	3	F	1	0	0	0	0
Dancing Crisis	5	M	16	0	1	1	3,072
Dancing Dames	3	F	10	1	0	3	12,520
Dancing Debt	3	G	2	0	0	0	122
Dancing Deer	5	M	15	1	2	3	24,446
Dancing Delite	3	G	8	5	0	0	38,250
Dancing Dilemma	5	M	2	0	2	0	3,168
Dancing Doc	5	G	6	0	3	3	4,240
Dancing Edie	2	F	4	0	1	1	15,880
Dancing Emily	2	F	2	0	0	0	840
Dancing Event	3	F	9	1	3	2	43,020
Dancing Fairy	4	F	9	1	1	2	11,730
Dancing Faster	2	G	1	0	0	0	1,140
Dancing Flowers	4	F	8	1	0	0	6,990
Dancing for Dinner	3	F	6	0	1	0	1,886
Dancing Freely	2	F	5	0	0	0	1,065
Dancing Fruition	4	F	2	0	1	0	1,680
Dancing Gate	5	M	1	0	0	0	77
Dancing Gem	4	F	8	5	0	1	28,332
Dancing Guy	9	G	7	1	0	1	34,360
Dancing Halo	6	G	3	0	0	1	2,820
Dancing Heniu	5	G	7	0	1	0	1,902
Dancing Hing	3	F	16	1	2	3	12,258
Dancing in Puddles	6	M	7	1	2	2	27,270
Dancing in the Fog	5	G	10	1	4	0	26,830
Dancing Indiscreet	6	M	4	1	0	0	25,607
Dancing Jet G	4	F	14	2	1	0	8,585
Dancing Jo Jo	4	G	3	0	0	0	336
Dancing Kakie	6	M	4	0	0	0	318
Dancing Lara	4	F	1	0	0	1	110
Dancing Laur	4	F	3	0	0	0	0
Dancing Lehsa	3	F	5	0	0	2	2,238
Dancing Liebling	3	F	13	3	2	3	79,541
Dancing Lillian	2	F	2	0	0	0	450
Dancing Man	3	G	2	0	0	0	1,764
Dancing Manila	8	M	1	0	0	0	0
Dancing Master (IRE)	6	H	1	0	0	0	310
Dancing Meg	3	F	13	1	1	3	47,200
Dancing Miss	3	F	3	0	0	0	216
Dancing Moves	2	C	2	0	0	1	894
Dancing On a Star	3	G	5	0	0	0	0
Dancing On Air	6	M	5	0	0	0	408
Dancing Pioneer	3	G	2	0	0	0	535
Dancing Rain	2	F	1	0	1	0	4,480
Dancing Raptor	3	G	8	1	0	1	16,065
Dancing Rasha	3	F	7	0	0	1	920
Dancing Rebel	8	G	3	1	0	1	15,014
Dancing Recovery	3	F	1	0	0	0	142
Dancing River	3	G	4	0	1	0	1,677
Dancing Romantic	3	F	19	2	0	3	20,739
Dancing Sands (NZ)	6	M	6	0	1	1	16,815
Dancing Savage	3	G	16	1	0	2	8,263
Dancing Spell	7	M	4	1	1	1	10,230
Dancing Spirit	2	F	1	0	0	0	0
Dancing Spray	4	F	6	0	0	2	20,229
Dancing Steal	6	G	4	0	0	0	249
Dancing Stripes	2	F	2	0	0	2	4,950
Dancing Sunshine	3	G	4	0	1	0	1,806
Dancing Target	4	F	4	1	0	0	3,127
Dancing Thief	3	F	2	0	0	0	0
Dancing Thunder	2	F	5	1	1	1	8,768
Dancing Tune	3	G	9	0	0	3	3,185
Dancing Ty	5	G	9	1	0	0	8,241
Dancing Villian	4	F	1	0	0	0	0
Dancing Warren	5	H	6	0	2	1	22,997
Dancing Warrior	4	G	7	1	3	1	65,560
Dancing Western	4	F	5	2	1	0	2,447
Dancing With Me	5	M	10	0	0	3	17,890
Dancinginflorida	4	F	9	1	0	1	6,939
Dancinginocidental	2	G	2	0	1	0	2,200
Dancinginthesky	3	G	6	2	3	0	37,208
Dancinginthewoods	4	G	3	0	0	1	935
Dancinglion	4	G	1	0	0	0	0
Dancingstardiamond	4	F	7	0	2	1	5,920
Dancingvoyage	3	F	1	0	0	0	400
Dancingwithattitud	3	F	3	0	0	0	107
Dancingwithpassion	5	M	15	4	3	3	53,122
Dancinharlan Honey	2	C	1	0	0	0	795
Dancininthenight	4	G	9	0	1	2	3,250
Dancinintheshadows	6	M	10	0	0	0	511

Horse	Age	Sex	Sts	1st	2d	3d	Won
Dancinontheceiling	3	C	13	3	1	1	18,485
Dancinthenightaway	3	G	13	2	2	0	14,200
Dancinwiththunder	4	G	4	0	0	0	950
Danciyan	4	C	4	1	0	0	5,485
Danclare	3	F	5	0	1	0	11,422
Dancret	5	M	1	0	0	0	0
Dandee's Beau	5	G	7	1	1	0	4,264
Dandenong	6	G	15	2	3	5	15,552
Dandi Candi	4	G	16	2	2	4	26,410
Dandione	5	M	14	4	1	1	48,311
Dandoon	3	C	7	2	0	1	56,580
Dand'or	7	G	10	0	1	4	10,342
Dandy Alibhai	7	G	5	1	2	0	27,655
Dandy Belle	3	F	22	1	4	2	19,703
Dandy Breeze	5	M	1	0	0	0	0
Dandy Dane	4	C	4	0	1	0	6,460
Dandy Dulce	6	M	3	1	1	1	7,720
Dandy Gentleman	4	G	21	1	0	1	12,046
Dandy Opportunity	7	G	1	0	0	0	114
Dandy Randy	4	C	13	1	3	0	11,919
Dandy Rose	4	F	10	1	0	1	14,032
Dandy Squall	4	G	12	1	1	0	20,130
Dane Again	9	G	7	0	0	0	458
Danees	2	F	1	0	0	0	420
Daneleta (IRE)	5	M	1	0	0	0	3,600
Danesbury	3	C	4	0	0	0	6,907
Danesville Slew	3	G	6	1	2	1	22,396
Dangel	4	G	9	2	0	3	44,817
Danger Crocodile	10	G	2	0	0	0	120
Danger Pay	2	F	4	1	1	0	34,992
Danger Quest	3	C	9	1	2	1	28,306
Dangerous Girl	6	M	7	0	0	0	154
Dangerous Justice	5	G	6	0	0	0	627
Dangerous Ridge	3	G	6	0	0	2	5,710
Dangerous Summer	2	C	2	0	0	0	1,474
Dangerous Sword	3	C	3	1	1	0	7,240
Dangerous Woman	3	F	12	1	4	1	16,855
Dangerously	3	F	8	2	0	1	47,580
Dangler	7	G	5	1	1	0	9,768
Dangling Prospect	8	H	8	0	0	0	968
Dania Bay	6	M	16	4	3	3	70,460
Daniel Alexander	5	H	11	0	2	1	9,848
Daniel Prayed	3	C	10	0	0	2	4,620
Daniel Striped Cat	7	G	14	0	2	0	2,415
Daniellagram	3	F	6	0	0	0	864
Danielles Magic	5	H	13	1	0	0	11,354
Danielo	3	G	7	0	0	0	540
Daniel's Ace	2	C	8	1	0	1	9,165
Daniel's Boy	5	G	10	2	1	3	10,376
Daniel's Gift	3	C	3	0	0	0	0
Danieltown	3	G	16	7	4	1	279,361
Danier	6	G	4	0	0	0	67
Dani's Bliss	4	G	8	1	0	0	7,410
Dani's Destiny	4	G	12	0	3	1	15,405
Danis Time	4	F	7	1	2	0	15,550
Danish Bonus	4	G	11	0	5	3	11,968
Danish Dancer (ARG)	5	H	9	2	1	0	63,941
Danish Danseur	4	G	9	0	1	2	3,529
Danish Fairytale (DEN)	4	F	10	2	1	0	80,795
Daniz Slavic	4	C	6	0	0	1	1,371
Danjel	3	F	5	1	1	0	17,963
Danjo	6	G	5	0	0	0	1,785
Danjurific	2	F	3	0	1	0	1,855
Danjurous	4	C	1	0	0	0	285
Danjurs Rose Petal	2	F	2	0	0	2	1,740
Danke Schoen	5	G	1	0	0	0	840
Danlee	6	G	5	1	0	1	10,354
Danlins World	10	G	1	0	0	0	310
Danmark (ARG)	6	M	14	1	2	4	19,365
Danner	5	H	10	1	1	2	5,170
Danni Sue	2	F	2	0	0	0	0
Dann's Prospect	3	F	14	2	6	1	16,534
Danny B.	3	G	8	2	1	1	13,210
Danny C.	5	G	19	3	4	3	48,023
Danny Dingle	2	C	4	2	1	1	47,485
Danny Divver	3	G	4	0	0	0	170
Danny Dream Dancer	7	M	5	0	0	1	1,202
Danny Duke	3	G	6	0	0	0	420
Danny E	6	G	1	0	0	0	840
Danny the Blade	4	G	12	3	0	1	37,381
Danny's Alibi	5	H	7	1	0	1	4,416
Danny's Emerald	4	G	11	1	1	3	5,734
Dannys Storey	10	G	12	0	2	1	3,561
Dannys Tiger	7	G	15	3	2	2	14,715
Danny's Way	4	C	12	0	0	2	2,861
Dannysupermarket	3	C	14	5	4	1	64,360
Dan's Advantage	4	C	3	0	0	1	3,410
Dan's Cowboy	3	G	12	1	1	1	7,710
Dan's Groovy	8	G	9	2	2	0	25,410
Dan's Jet	2	G	10	0	3	1	7,744
Dan's Moment	3	G	1	0	0	0	0
Dans Rambler	8	M	5	0	0	0	255
Dan's Rebel	3	G	14	0	0	1	1,432
Dan's Report	8	G	7	1	2	1	12,639
Dan's Soldier	2	G	8	1	3	0	21,710
Danse Du Mort	4	F	4	1	1	0	20,080
Danse Kongo	2	F	2	0	0	0	1,420
Dansetta Light	2	F	9	4	1	0	165,080
Danseur Chaud	2	F	4	0	1	0	4,050
Dansil's Angel	5	M	6	0	3	1	3,460
Danswithalexis	3	F	2	0	0	0	223
Dante's Rocket	5	M	5	1	0	2	19,880
Danthebluegrassman	5	H	3	0	0	0	3,510
Dantor	2	G	1	0	1	0	4,400
Danubio (MEX)	9	G	12	1	0	1	11,590
Danyell Lee	4	F	1	0	0	0	40
Danyelle's Court	8	M	11	2	1	2	12,843
Danyelle's Tabby	5	M	14	1	1	2	16,996
Danyiel's Bull	3	G	4	0	0	0	1,005
Danz	4	G	16	1	2	0	10,975
Danz Gracefully	2	F	3	0	0	0	600
Danz Twelve Pack	3	G	1	0	0	0	172
Danza	7	G	4	1	0	0	2,617
Danza Del Sol	3	C	11	1	1	2	29,480
Danzabar	3	F	2	0	0	0	88
Danzafina	3	C	10	1	0	1	6,082
Danzalnite	3	C	14	3	0	3	18,047
Danzalore	3	F	2	0	0	0	331
Danzaman	7	G	7	0	0	1	3,697
Danzanaskra	4	G	4	0	0	0	310
Danzarina Gaucha	4	F	10	2	0	0	9,154
Danzasouth	4	F	5	0	0	1	980
Danzatames Award	4	F	4	0	0	0	312
Danzatames Reality	4	F	14	1	3	1	24,774
Danzhound	5	G	12	0	3	0	20,349
Danzi Blurr	3	F	5	0	0	0	148
Danziana	3	F	15	3	0	1	38,016
Danzig Ballerina	3	F	5	3	0	0	11,388
Danzig Del Siglo	6	H	2	0	0	0	96
Danzig Good Time	4	G	4	0	1	2	3,440
Danzig in the Dark	3	G	3	2	0	1	21,935
Danzig in the Rain	3	G	3	1	1	0	17,575
Danzigca	7	M	8	1	1	1	9,084
Danzig's Farewell	3	G	7	0	0	2	2,935
Danzig's Gold	5	G	9	1	1	0	3,624
Danzig's Jade	3	G	7	0	0	0	5,880
Danzig's Sword	8	G	7	0	0	0	1,358
Danzilation	6	G	3	0	0	0	840
Danzin Tyson	3	G	9	1	1	0	9,588
Danzing Commander	2	G	1	0	0	0	400
Danzingfree	3	F	2	0	0	0	0
Dapper Dan Man	2	C	1	0	0	0	1,764
Dapper Dandy	3	C	2	0	0	0	240
Dapper Danny	3	C	7	1	1	2	8,593
Dappers Chance	4	G	7	0	1	1	4,877
Dappledan	5	G	9	0	0	2	1,996
Dar Ma Lee	3	F	10	0	3	1	5,285
Darbie D	5	M	2	0	0	0	140
Darby Book	2	F	2	0	0	0	223
Darby Creek Dancer	3	F	8	0	2	1	4,412
Darby Creek Doc	5	H	1	0	0	0	220
Darby Creek Honey	7	M	3	0	0	1	669
Darby Haven	5	M	14	4	3	3	56,595
Darby Lane	5	M	18	4	1	0	29,130
Darby's Boy	5	G	8	0	1	0	3,268
Darby's Charm	5	M	7	2	3	0	60,174
Darby's Price	2	F	4	1	1	0	12,900
Darcys Sister	6	M	9	2	2	1	18,778

Horse	Age	Sex	Sts	1st	2d	3d	Won
Dare Go Jo	3	F	1	0	0	0	0
Dare He Goes	3	C	12	1	2	1	13,624
Dare Me Clearance	3	C	3	0	0	0	0
Dare to Be Great	4	G	14	2	2	4	35,029
Dare to Be Wild	6	G	10	1	1	0	10,538
Dare to Care	3	F	1	0	0	0	0
Dare to Colour	3	G	16	2	1	4	14,869
Dare to Cross	2	F	2	0	0	1	1,740
Dare to Drip	3	C	3	0	0	0	2,860
Dare to Flash	2	C	3	0	0	0	0
Dare to Mambo	4	F	6	0	0	2	10,845
Dare to Rum	4	G	6	1	0	1	7,571
Dare to Run	6	H	13	1	0	3	7,655
Daredevil Adam	5	H	11	4	1	3	61,292
Daredevil Bull	3	G	9	0	1	2	13,650
Dare'n Darren	4	G	1	0	0	0	86
Darentogo	3	G	4	0	0	1	2,056
Daretobebare	3	F	1	0	0	1	2,860
Darewood Park	5	H	9	0	2	2	3,368
Darfromaphar	8	M	16	2	5	3	10,357
Darghan (IRE)	4	G	11	0	1	0	8,867
Darian Skye	2	F	2	1	1	0	23,800
Darien's Approval	3	G	11	2	0	1	21,370
Daring Bid	6	H	4	1	1	1	19,240
Daring Child	3	G	3	1	0	0	6,420
Daring Daygata	3	G	12	2	1	1	13,020
Daring Deeds	8	G	9	2	1	1	8,388
Daring Do	2	C	1	0	0	0	990
Daring Habit	2	G	6	1	2	0	28,080
Daring Julie	3	F	2	0	0	0	555
Daring Mood	3	C	8	3	0	1	44,425
Daring Pegasus	6	G	10	2	0	1	14,900
Daring Six	3	G	9	1	0	2	3,456
Daring Skipper	4	C	1	0	0	0	351
Daring Smile	5	M	8	1	2	2	12,900
Daring Wager	4	G	10	0	1	0	3,814
Daring Wit	4	F	6	0	0	0	571
Darinquest	7	M	2	0	0	0	156
Dariyoun's Command	6	G	7	1	1	1	2,734
Dark Amour	6	G	4	0	0	0	515
Dark Bark	7	M	1	0	0	0	360
Dark Bay	6	M	5	0	1	1	1,918
Dark Beauty	2	F	4	0	0	1	8,776
Dark Brew	3	G	1	0	0	0	475
Dark Cape	4	G	3	0	0	0	0
Dark Chocolate	4	G	2	0	0	0	0
Dark Cloud	3	C	3	0	0	0	322
Dark Command	4	G	1	0	0	0	400
Dark Demon	4	G	10	0	1	4	3,558
Dark Denim	3	F	12	0	1	0	4,420
Dark Energy	3	G	6	0	0	0	905
Dark Equation	3	C	8	2	0	3	77,925
Dark Fool	8	G	12	2	1	1	5,122
Dark Indulgence	2	G	6	1	0	1	25,250
Dark Intent	4	G	7	1	3	0	24,186
Dark Lightning	3	C	4	1	1	1	24,180
Dark Lochnagar	3	F	5	0	0	1	1,848
Dark Magic	6	G	12	6	1	3	24,107
Dark Moonlight	5	H	1	0	0	0	0
Dark Neo	3	G	4	1	0	1	6,678
Dark Obsession	2	F	1	0	0	1	3,080
Dark of the Moon	2	F	1	0	0	0	55
Dark Okie	4	G	6	0	0	0	570
Dark Plot	2	C	6	1	0	2	19,730
Dark Plume	3	F	8	1	0	3	37,770
Dark Prospect	4	G	12	1	2	2	8,663
Dark Rapids	5	M	9	1	2	1	24,520
Dark Sage	4	F	5	0	0	0	437
Dark Sorcerer (GB)	5	G	8	0	6	0	57,700
Dark Starling	4	F	11	1	1	2	5,836
Dark Tigerlily	7	M	8	1	4	1	7,507
Dark Torment	5	M	1	0	0	0	125
Dark Whisper	4	C	1	0	0	1	4,600
Darker Than Gold	6	G	12	0	1	1	2,312
Darkest Mirage	6	M	3	0	0	0	0
Darkest Night	4	G	2	0	0	0	0
Darkinvader	7	G	4	2	0	1	9,838
Darkly Noon	4	G	7	2	1	0	32,257
Dark'n Debonaire	3	F	9	2	0	1	9,235
Darkness	3	F	1	0	0	0	0
Darknessontheedge	5	G	4	1	0	1	11,760
Darkside	2	F	1	0	0	0	135
Darksideofthebull	4	G	8	2	1	1	26,190
Darkus	5	M	5	2	0	0	22,500
Darla Darla	7	M	5	0	0	0	148
Darla Dee	2	F	2	0	0	0	213
Darlanda	7	M	14	0	1	2	7,887
Darlene's Daughter	4	F	10	2	1	1	30,625
Darlin Corey	4	F	13	2	3	0	56,512
Darlin Daisy	5	M	2	0	0	0	700
Darlin Josie	3	F	11	0	0	1	3,870
Darlin Maggie	3	F	1	0	0	0	0
Darlin Queen	3	F	8	3	2	0	29,765
Darlin Tom	4	G	10	1	0	0	7,005
Darlinchil	3	F	12	2	5	0	15,814
Darling Angel	4	F	9	3	1	2	15,570
Darling Bee	3	F	15	3	4	0	22,558
Darling Bobi	8	M	7	1	0	0	5,480
Darling Daphne	5	M	4	0	0	0	268
Darling Demon	4	F	1	1	0	0	10,200
Darling Edna	4	F	10	0	0	2	6,670
Darling Sandy	4	G	10	0	0	0	844
Darling Silver	3	F	14	4	2	1	25,833
Darlington Guard	2	G	5	2	0	0	27,335
Darluna	2	F	3	0	1	0	5,750
Darlyon	4	G	2	0	0	0	0
Darn Crazy	3	F	7	0	0	2	6,335
Darn Right	4	C	3	0	0	0	2,523
Darn That Cat	6	M	6	0	0	1	825
Darn That Cobra	3	G	10	3	1	0	31,767
Darn That Girl	2	F	5	1	1	0	60,234
Darn That Image	10	M	1	0	0	0	60
Darn That Jack	5	H	2	0	0	0	0
Darn That Moon	3	F	10	1	2	0	8,778
Darn Tipalarm	11	G	5	2	2	1	37,200
Darn Tootin	8	G	1	0	0	0	92
Darn Wild	3	F	9	1	3	2	28,698
Darn Yankee	4	G	7	0	1	0	6,180
Darnation	2	F	3	0	1	1	2,784
Darned Alarm	5	G	10	0	4	2	15,630
Darned Bold	5	G	9	0	0	1	2,275
Darned Silly	2	F	2	0	0	0	750
Darned Traitor	3	G	11	1	0	0	6,000
Darnedest Thing	2	G	3	0	0	0	610
Darnell's Dream	7	M	15	0	1	0	3,600
Darnestown	5	M	2	0	0	0	5,400
Darnthefrost	4	G	13	1	1	1	11,061
Darnthemelves	3	G	2	0	0	0	0
D'aroak	5	M	8	0	3	0	12,719
Darsela	5	M	9	0	2	1	5,498
Darshana	4	F	3	0	0	0	0
Dart for Dough	6	G	6	1	0	0	18,560
Dart Parade (ARG)	6	H	2	0	0	0	1,900
D'artagnans'spirit	2	G	1	1	0	0	11,200
Darth	9	G	6	0	1	0	1,027
Darthys Keebler	3	G	1	0	0	0	0
Darting Dot	5	M	5	0	1	2	13,580
Darwood	6	G	1	0	0	0	0
Daryamar (FR)	3	C	6	1	1	0	36,658
Daryl's Birthday	6	G	6	1	0	0	5,226
Das Flask	8	H	2	0	0	0	127
Dash and Dream	3	F	1	0	0	0	189
Dash Baby	2	F	4	0	1	2	4,910
Dash Built	4	G	4	0	0	0	481
Dash Dot	4	F	15	2	0	2	10,592
Dash for Daylight	7	G	9	1	4	1	57,530
Dash Home	4	F	5	0	0	0	1,050
Dash Inside	4	F	10	1	2	3	10,112
Dash Man	3	C	1	0	0	0	822
Dash 'n Dance	6	G	17	1	3	5	61,818
Dash O'Brandy	2	G	5	0	0	0	611
Dash of Blue	6	M	7	0	1	0	825
Dash of Class	2	C	9	0	0	1	5,260
Dash of Fame	3	C	8	1	2	2	8,170
Dash of Humor	4	F	9	3	0	2	60,000
Dash of Love	2	F	3	0	0	0	1,070
Dash Rendar	3	C	1	1	0	0	7,200
Dasha	2	F	5	1	0	1	8,475

Horse	Age	Sex	Sts	1st	2d	3d	Won
Dashanella	4	F	5	0	0	0	320
Dashboard Drummer	3	G	10	1	2	3	98,920
Dasheen	5	M	5	1	0	2	10,029
Dashfortheroses	3	F	10	1	0	1	14,253
Dashhound	4	F	10	0	0	0	846
Dashigoes	4	F	5	0	0	0	714
Dashin' Daniel	3	G	13	1	3	2	16,250
Dashin N Cattin	5	G	20	1	4	2	13,176
Dashincase	4	C	6	0	0	0	0
Dashing Admiral	3	C	8	2	1	3	186,473
Dashing Ariel	4	F	3	0	1	0	4,393
Dashing Billy	2	F	4	0	1	0	9,630
Dashing Cat	3	G	1	0	0	0	0
Dashing Darla	5	M	9	1	3	0	9,709
Dashing Deputy	3	C	9	1	0	3	26,084
Dashing Derby	3	G	9	0	0	1	3,095
Dashing Diva	3	F	4	1	0	0	2,666
Dashing Express	3	F	8	2	0	1	22,030
Dashing Girl	6	M	12	1	2	0	4,837
Dashing Lady	4	F	10	3	1	1	22,814
Dashing Monty	3	G	14	1	1	1	41,444
Dashing Princess	5	M	11	2	2	1	24,539
Dashing Regent	4	G	7	0	0	1	2,229
Dashing Rita	3	F	12	0	0	1	4,326
Dashing Style	6	G	3	0	0	1	1,810
Dash'n Danielle	5	M	7	2	2	1	32,210
Dash'n Krugerand	5	G	15	3	3	0	17,861
Dasl Cammy	3	F	12	1	1	4	28,257
Dastardly Dan	4	C	5	0	0	0	740
Dat Grey Cat	3	F	3	0	0	0	0
Data Stream	3	G	9	1	1	1	19,140
Database	5	M	5	1	0	1	33,990
Date Me	4	F	5	0	0	0	750
Date More Minors	6	H	2	0	0	0	64
Date Night	3	F	3	1	0	1	19,460
Date Tree Bay	4	F	14	1	3	0	30,253
Datebook	3	G	11	1	2	0	21,716
Dateland	5	G	2	0	0	1	480
Dating Prospect	10	G	15	4	3	2	43,342
Datruth	3	C	4	0	0	0	0
Dats All Folks	5	G	14	1	1	3	7,141
Dats Y	8	H	2	0	1	0	463
Datsallme	3	C	2	1	0	0	12,390
Datsyuk	2	C	6	0	2	2	29,980
Datticus	4	G	1	0	0	1	5,880
Dattts Joesrainbow	3	G	8	0	1	0	5,516
Dattt's My Luck	4	G	7	1	3	1	12,415
Datttsdawayilikeit	3	F	7	1	1	1	45,250
Datzig	2	G	3	0	0	2	3,157
Dauger	3	C	10	1	2	0	14,055
Daughter's Promise	2	F	1	0	0	0	0
Daulide (ARG)	4	F	1	0	0	0	400
Daunte	5	G	9	1	1	0	5,894
Daunting	6	G	4	1	0	1	43,065
Daunting Presence	6	G	1	0	0	0	0
Dauntless	2	F	2	0	0	0	360
Dauphin	7	G	9	0	2	1	26,000
Dav Mar One	3	G	5	0	3	0	13,905
Davanti	3	C	2	1	0	0	14,751
Davdaas	2	C	5	1	0	2	12,400
Dave	3	G	4	1	1	2	42,000
Dave Budd	3	G	10	0	0	0	1,560
Dave the Knave	2	G	3	2	1	0	123,575
Davene	5	M	2	0	0	0	338
Daves Baby	5	M	2	0	0	1	440
Dave's Cahill Boy	4	G	4	2	2	0	18,980
Daves Commander	3	G	7	0	1	2	3,025
Daves Mercedes	3	F	3	0	0	0	501
Dave's Pat	3	G	4	1	0	0	12,783
Davesday	7	G	22	3	2	3	25,560
Davey's Cutlass	8	G	15	0	1	0	8,655
David Strike Back	4	G	1	0	0	0	152
Davida's Destiny	4	G	1	0	0	0	235
David's Beauty	2	F	3	0	0	1	2,175
David's Best Bet	3	G	1	0	0	0	158
David's C Biscuit	3	C	15	1	1	3	33,510
David's Destiny	6	M	16	1	2	5	7,411
David's Dignity	4	F	1	0	0	1	1,694
David's Dilemma	4	F	9	2	2	2	57,783

Horse	Age	Sex	Sts	1st	2d	3d	Won
David's Dream	11	G	2	0	0	0	328
Davids Expectation	5	H	4	0	2	0	17,460
David's Goal	4	F	3	1	0	0	6,392
David's Groom	7	G	11	1	3	3	9,848
David's Halo	5	G	12	0	1	4	8,115
David's Islander	3	C	2	0	1	0	2,400
David's Melody	4	F	6	1	0	1	3,508
Davis Mint	3	F	5	1	0	0	6,160
Davis's Punch	4	F	8	4	1	1	52,500
Davonic (GB)	7	G	7	1	0	1	17,651
Davonnier	4	G	1	0	0	0	235
Davvy	8	G	17	1	1	0	5,254
Davy Jones	6	G	12	1	1	0	27,856
Dawaytostorm	2	F	5	0	2	0	5,355
Dawdle	2	C	3	0	0	0	500
Dawg Fan	4	G	4	1	0	0	3,132
Dawn Charger	6	M	12	2	1	1	28,312
Dawn Edition	6	M	5	0	0	0	4,008
Dawn Exodus	9	G	10	1	1	1	14,428
Dawn of the Condor	7	G	13	1	2	1	43,927
Dawn of Time	2	F	4	0	0	0	1,349
Dawn Power	2	F	7	1	0	2	8,375
Dawn Renee	5	M	3	0	0	0	0
Dawn Till Dask	2	F	6	0	0	0	0
Dawn Till Dust	6	M	11	2	1	3	27,029
Dawn Wan	10	G	6	0	0	0	150
Dawn Watcher	6	G	8	3	0	0	83,148
Dawn's Amber Light	3	F	4	1	0	0	1,234
Dawn's Angel	3	F	8	2	1	1	78,540
Dawn's Baby	4	F	7	0	1	0	2,697
Dawns Ben	6	G	10	0	2	3	3,831
Dawn's Contender	3	C	2	0	0	0	42
Dawn's Creek	5	H	8	1	1	4	21,524
Dawn's Delta Belle	3	F	12	2	1	1	19,200
Dawns Early Dancer	3	G	6	0	1	1	2,096
Dawn's Honey	5	M	2	0	0	0	360
Dawn's Magic Bag	4	F	8	1	2	0	12,160
Dawn's Moment	2	F	6	1	0	0	6,030
Dawns My Lady	3	G	10	2	2	1	9,555
Dawn's Project	4	G	5	0	0	1	1,150
Dawn's Prospect	4	F	10	3	3	0	47,165
Dawn's Revenge	3	G	10	1	2	1	28,826
Dawn's Star	6	G	12	2	2	3	11,128
Dawns Tough Girl	3	F	3	0	1	0	625
Dawson Creek	10	M	3	0	0	0	128
Dawson Trail	4	G	1	0	0	0	0
Day Bue	6	G	8	0	0	1	8,031
Day Court	3	F	3	0	0	0	2,610
Day Dream Buster	4	G	1	0	0	0	0
Day Dreamer	2	F	5	0	0	0	517
Day Flyer	4	G	1	0	0	0	0
Day Journey	7	H	3	0	0	0	0
Day Later	5	M	11	1	2	1	13,056
Day Lee Bargain	2	G	4	1	1	1	4,780
Day Long Trip	4	G	16	4	1	3	34,155
Day of Atonement	6	M	10	1	0	3	15,490
Day of Infamy	4	G	2	1	0	0	4,950
Day of Judgement	13	G	2	0	0	0	200
Day of the Hunt	2	G	2	0	0	0	0
Day Planner	5	M	2	0	0	1	1,161
Day Run	3	G	2	0	0	0	0
Day Secret	4	G	7	0	0	0	635
Day to Dash	2	G	2	1	0	0	12,720
Day Trade	8	G	15	2	0	1	12,447
Day Trader	5	H	9	2	0	1	52,606
Day Walker	3	C	3	0	0	0	0
Day Willy	4	F	3	1	1	0	9,875
Dayblue	3	G	1	0	0	0	0
Daydream Deelite	3	G	20	2	0	1	8,039
Daydreaming	3	F	8	5	1	1	483,180
Daydreams	4	F	2	0	0	0	0
Dayglogreen	2	F	4	0	4	0	11,666
Dayjur Can	6	G	4	0	0	0	976
Dayjurette	3	F	3	2	1	0	40,210
Dayjur's Lane	3	F	5	1	0	0	3,566
Daylason	3	G	9	2	0	0	12,615
Daylene Machine	3	F	11	2	0	1	9,906
Daylight	4	F	11	3	1	1	45,647
Daylight Again	5	G	1	0	0	0	285

Horse	Age	Sex	Sts	1st	2d	3d	Won
Daylight Memory	6	M	3	0	0	0	165
Daylight Robbery	4	F	16	1	1	5	8,945
Daylight Run	6	H	5	1	0	0	16,050
Daylightin Dizzy	7	H	4	0	0	0	117
Daylights End	2	F	2	0	1	1	12,300
Daymeon	3	G	1	0	0	0	125
Day's Sunset	4	F	1	0	0	0	0
Daysman	3	F	9	2	2	2	78,765
Daytime Delight	2	F	5	1	1	0	14,885
Daytime Event	3	F	2	0	1	0	9,000
Daytime Girl (IRE)	3	F	6	1	0	1	14,704
Daytime Riches	6	M	10	0	0	2	1,581
Daytime Robbery	8	G	12	1	0	1	8,606
Dayton Flyer	6	H	2	0	0	0	600
Dayton Michael	3	G	7	2	0	0	4,215
Dayton's Bluff	7	G	7	0	3	1	4,603
Daz All Folks	6	M	2	0	0	0	360
Dazu	3	G	11	0	1	2	2,882
Dazzel 'Em Indy	3	G	5	0	1	0	5,854
Dazzle Cat	4	F	3	0	0	1	510
Dazzle Me	3	F	6	4	0	0	266,276
Dazzle Me Darlin	2	F	1	0	1	0	8,200
Dazzle N Daze	6	M	4	0	0	0	360
Dazzle Prince	8	G	11	0	1	1	2,755
Dazzle Some	6	H	2	0	0	0	210
Dazzlelikethis	5	M	10	3	3	3	15,496
Dazzling American	3	C	6	1	0	1	18,998
Dazzling Contrast	3	F	6	1	0	2	20,990
Dazzling Dana	6	M	10	2	4	2	15,969
Dazzling Deb	4	F	6	2	0	1	4,727
Dazzling Deelite	4	F	3	0	0	2	13,750
Dazzling Dimples	2	F	2	0	0	0	2,545
Dazzling Dr. Cevin	2	G	6	2	2	2	38,010
Dazzling Fluff	5	M	2	0	0	0	605
Dazzling Gem	2	F	1	0	0	0	220
Dazzling Gold	3	F	9	1	0	2	12,604
Dazzling J. R.	5	G	14	4	6	1	19,326
Dazzling Jane	5	M	2	0	1	0	4,590
Dazzling Marjorie	2	F	4	0	0	0	995
Dazzling Rubies	5	M	10	1	3	1	51,240
Dazzling Silver	5	M	12	0	1	1	10,864
Dazzling Skies	4	F	13	2	2	3	10,992
Dazzling Spirit	4	G	7	0	0	1	2,077
Dazzling Sunny	5	G	8	3	1	0	24,385
Dazzling Tara	6	M	2	0	0	0	0
Dazzling Twist	5	G	5	1	1	2	3,100
Dazzlingexcellence	4	G	8	0	1	1	4,269
Dazzlinpersonality	5	G	14	2	3	1	16,655
Dazzmataz	5	G	10	0	2	2	6,002
Dazzy	3	F	4	1	0	1	7,037
Dbig Tower	4	F	9	1	0	0	4,570
Dbl Ott	4	G	4	1	0	1	13,080
Dble Diamond Norma	3	F	19	2	8	4	13,481
Dc Carleysprospect	2	F	4	0	1	1	4,010
D'court's Speed	2	C	4	1	2	0	44,800
De Braaks Boy	4	G	10	2	0	1	7,209
De Braak's Proper	4	F	8	0	0	3	3,381
De Bunny	6	G	6	1	1	1	12,082
De Chirrico	3	G	6	2	0	0	19,628
De Coax	6	H	1	0	0	0	61
De Dancer	5	M	2	0	0	0	315
De Free Spirit	2	F	2	0	0	0	450
De Gold Stuff	5	M	5	3	0	0	4,540
De Guerin Rebel	3	C	2	0	0	0	0
De Gus	2	C	3	0	0	1	3,080
De La Costa (AUS)	4	G	4	0	0	0	7,380
De la Cruz	7	H	3	1	0	0	2,745
De la Danzig	5	G	12	0	0	0	3,957
De la Mothe	3	C	5	1	0	0	7,250
De Lamp	5	H	4	0	0	0	230
De Lane Dancer	3	F	7	1	2	0	10,158
De Magic Moment	3	G	12	3	3	3	66,729
De Oro	3	C	4	0	1	1	7,280
De Pollock	4	G	17	0	0	2	3,063
De Qui	3	G	1	0	0	0	0
De Real Deal	5	H	1	0	0	1	1,870
De Ride	4	F	2	0	0	0	0
De Shay	5	M	1	0	0	0	0
De Sis	5	M	7	0	0	2	2,598
De Soto	7	G	14	1	1	2	8,528
De Spike	4	G	9	1	0	0	4,036
De Toby	3	G	2	0	0	0	0
De Troy (ARG)	4	C	7	1	1	1	20,280
De Valmont (AUS)	7	G	4	2	1	0	91,400
De Voodoo Man	5	G	2	0	0	0	0
De Wishbone	2	G	4	0	0	0	0
Deacon Drive	5	G	1	0	0	0	0
Deacon Lake	4	F	4	0	0	0	8,470
Deacon Springs	5	G	9	1	3	2	22,656
Deacons Road	3	F	7	1	0	1	5,518
Dead Broke	4	G	6	1	0	0	12,320
Dead Centre	5	M	2	1	0	0	6,540
Dead Dog Gorgeous	4	F	9	1	0	1	4,330
Dead Level	4	G	7	1	1	2	10,075
Dead of Winter	5	M	18	1	3	4	15,577
Dead Ringer	3	G	13	2	3	1	53,580
Deadline	4	G	2	0	0	0	2,560
Deadline Dude	10	G	13	0	0	3	11,835
Deadly Force	9	G	6	0	0	0	1,000
Deadly Talons	2	G	4	1	1	0	8,102
Deadly Tonic	3	F	9	1	2	2	16,436
Deadly Weapon	4	G	7	0	1	1	7,813
Deadon	5	H	3	0	0	0	0
Deal 'Em Jack	5	G	7	0	2	1	8,360
Deal in Spades	4	G	16	3	1	2	14,827
Deal Me In	3	G	11	2	2	1	28,905
Deal Me the Moon	7	M	8	1	3	0	8,958
Deal N Dollars	3	G	11	1	1	3	15,817
Deal the Cards	2	F	9	1	2	1	33,120
Deal Withthe Devil	4	F	6	1	1	1	15,520
Dealer	9	G	4	0	0	0	227
Dealer Choice (FR)	3	C	2	0	0	1	16,180
Dealer's Delight	5	M	1	0	0	0	567
Dealers Irish Kiss	3	F	4	1	0	0	6,586
Dealer's Secret	3	G	4	0	0	2	5,602
Dealer's Suprise	5	G	5	1	2	1	11,742
Dealin Aces	3	F	9	2	2	1	13,504
Dealin Jo	6	H	7	0	0	0	643
Dealing Shelby	5	G	6	0	0	0	0
Dealing With Daisy	4	F	7	0	2	3	26,794
Dealingwiththeidle	5	G	10	0	0	0	833
Dealinwithinsanity	4	G	6	0	1	1	7,680
Dealmenandmakeabuc	3	G	11	2	0	2	24,555
Deals a Deal	3	G	11	0	4	2	6,146
Deamon's Flight	7	M	9	1	1	2	10,946
Dean the Dude	6	G	10	0	1	0	1,595
Deanies Daydreamer	3	C	4	2	0	1	17,018
Deanna M	6	M	4	1	1	1	4,538
Deannies Express	3	G	4	0	0	0	195
Deans Digger	4	G	5	0	1	0	339
Deans Flier	9	G	7	1	1	0	4,683
Deans Mill	2	F	4	0	2	0	4,081
Dean's Rose	3	G	4	0	0	2	2,231
Dear Alicia	3	F	9	2	1	1	52,325
Dear Bull	3	C	8	0	0	1	4,940
Dear Deputy	4	F	3	1	0	0	9,375
Dear Dixie	3	F	11	1	3	1	27,910
Dear Emerald	3	F	3	0	0	0	450
Dear Gulch	2	F	4	0	0	0	416
Dear Henry	3	C	1	0	0	0	450
Dear Hunter	6	G	8	1	0	1	6,010
Dear John	8	H	15	1	3	1	4,831
Dear Lucy	3	F	1	0	0	0	0
Dear Pappa	5	G	1	0	0	0	0
Dear Pickles (GB)	6	M	6	1	2	0	13,255
Dear Princess	5	M	9	1	2	1	10,251
Dear Prospector	7	M	5	0	0	0	1,176
Dear Shirley	2	F	5	0	0	1	4,300
Dear Silver	3	F	5	2	0	0	25,528
Dear Soldier	2	C	6	1	1	1	21,660
Dear to Me	4	G	1	0	0	1	1,800
Dear to My Heart	5	M	15	1	3	2	15,642
Dearest Enemy	5	M	1	0	0	0	62
Dearest Heart	3	F	7	0	0	1	12,507
Dearest Jack	6	G	8	4	0	1	25,355
Dearest Mon	2	C	2	1	0	0	29,250
Dearly Dearly	3	F	5	0	0	0	353
Dearly Dee	4	F	12	1	1	1	5,750

Horse	Age	Sex	Sts	1st	2d	3d	Won
Deas Island	5	G	2	0	0	0	625
Death Trappe	8	G	9	2	1	0	41,245
Deb Pixum	2	F	5	0	1	2	12,425
Deb Spent Da Bucks	2	F	1	0	0	0	0
Debatable	8	H	3	1	0	1	22,659
Debate	7	M	6	0	0	0	792
Debating	3	G	8	2	1	1	15,362
Debauchery	7	G	4	0	0	0	582
Debbie Dipper	2	F	1	0	0	0	810
Debbie Sue	3	F	8	2	1	2	49,160
Debbiedoodonniedoo	4	F	5	0	0	0	725
Debbie's Assault	2	F	2	1	0	0	9,680
Debbie's Best	3	F	8	0	1	1	7,328
Debbie's Gone	4	F	17	3	3	1	43,840
Debbies Mine	4	F	10	1	5	1	32,325
Debbies Toy	4	F	2	0	0	0	0
Debbie's Turn	3	F	14	1	1	3	32,174
Debby Do	6	M	6	2	2	0	7,670
Debby Lou	3	F	4	0	0	0	3,280
Debere	3	F	6	1	1	0	20,940
Debi's Sportscar	5	M	6	2	0	0	20,923
Debit Or Credit	2	F	1	0	0	0	150
Debonair Joe	5	G	8	0	1	4	57,410
Debonaire	2	F	3	0	0	0	216
Debonaire Gambler	3	C	8	0	2	4	2,219
Debonairo	2	C	1	0	0	0	0
Deborah Welsh	4	F	7	0	0	3	11,670
Deborah's Doings	7	M	1	0	0	0	0
Deb's Charm	3	F	3	0	1	0	12,190
Deb's Dawaytogo	5	G	7	0	1	0	999
Deb's Delight	3	G	4	0	1	1	7,955
Debs Diamond	2	C	6	1	1	2	11,923
Deb's Favoite Gift	3	F	8	2	3	0	60,828
Debs Jett	2	F	2	1	0	0	6,315
Debs Li'l Escapade	5	M	5	0	1	1	2,473
Debt of Honor	5	G	8	2	3	1	16,060
Debt Reduction	3	G	3	0	0	0	77
Debt to Equity	5	G	18	2	2	2	18,380
Debussy	2	C	3	1	0	0	17,825
Decadent Dancer	2	F	3	1	0	1	6,041
Decadent Dash	4	F	17	2	4	4	38,298
Decaf	5	G	6	0	2	1	13,760
Deceitful Darling	4	F	8	0	2	2	11,065
December Fire	2	C	6	0	1	2	19,732
Decencia (ARG)	7	M	2	0	1	0	7,200
Decency	5	G	11	2	0	2	15,755
Decent Sara	4	F	2	0	0	0	240
Deceptive Move	4	F	8	4	0	0	32,888
Decibel	3	C	8	1	1	2	34,710
Decided	3	G	4	0	2	1	3,880
Decided to Be Wild	5	G	7	1	0	2	6,449
Decidedlydifferent	3	F	8	1	0	1	25,810
Deciding Factor	3	C	8	1	2	1	5,458
Decimal	7	G	12	1	1	0	9,210
Decimal Point	5	G	6	0	0	0	1,433
Decimate	5	G	4	1	0	0	7,630
Decision	6	G	2	0	0	0	0
Decision Point	5	G	15	0	1	5	4,377
Decisional	4	C	1	0	0	0	400
Decisive	6	G	3	0	1	0	3,075
Decisive Strike	4	G	10	1	2	1	27,067
Decker	5	G	3	1	0	1	4,550
Decker Chapel	3	F	12	0	0	2	2,485
Declan's Moon	2	G	4	4	0	0	507,300
Declined Amx	7	M	3	0	0	0	810
Deco	2	F	2	0	0	0	1,218
Deco Statls	5	G	3	0	0	0	488
Decoder	4	C	1	1	0	0	21,000
Decoding the Gray	8	G	4	2	0	1	5,515
Decorador (ARG)	5	H	9	0	0	0	3,950
Decorate	4	G	13	1	3	3	13,157
Decorate the Town	6	G	9	2	1	2	7,872
Decorated Angel	5	M	9	1	1	1	4,746
Decorated Breeze	3	G	7	1	4	0	15,805
Decorated Cart	4	G	12	0	6	3	6,446
Decorated Decor	3	C	2	0	0	0	0
Decorated Drums	10	G	7	0	0	0	2,144
Decorated Laabity	3	G	3	0	0	0	0
Decorated Soldier	2	G	2	0	0	1	4,345
Decorated Storm	8	G	14	1	1	0	4,557
Decorated Streak	3	G	13	2	0	2	13,619
Decors Best Deal	3	F	3	0	0	0	630
Deco's Lassie	3	F	7	0	0	0	3,495
Deco's Secret	4	G	13	1	3	0	25,220
Decourcey	2	C	1	0	0	0	410
Dedamo	3	G	3	0	0	0	229
Dede's Surprise	6	M	2	0	0	0	0
Dedicated Caper	4	F	10	3	1	1	8,842
Dedicated Line	9	G	1	0	0	1	1,000
Dedication (FR)	5	M	8	2	2	0	156,660
Deduct Box	5	G	9	2	0	0	22,164
Deductive Reasonin	6	M	5	1	0	0	1,356
Dee Be Better	3	F	8	2	0	2	9,535
Dee Beau Black	4	G	24	1	0	6	10,093
Dee Dee Dancer	5	G	5	1	2	1	20,340
Dee Dee's Angel	3	F	7	0	1	0	5,622
Dee Dee's Cat	3	F	12	1	2	2	5,358
Dee Dee's Diner	4	F	10	3	3	0	108,340
Dee Dee's Dynamite	4	F	9	1	0	3	10,017
Dee Dee's Ruby	3	F	8	0	2	1	4,884
Dee Dee's Spell	3	F	5	1	0	0	14,200
Dee Dee's Wildcat	3	F	6	2	2	0	36,386
Dee Double Ya Dan	5	G	17	2	4	2	34,212
Dee Gray Ghost	4	F	2	0	0	0	0
Dee I Do	5	M	16	1	3	3	21,775
Dee Northern Girl	3	F	17	1	2	4	18,668
Dee Note	4	G	2	0	0	0	145
Dee Ron	4	G	1	0	0	0	63
Deed to the Gate	4	F	7	1	2	0	39,511
Deedarling	4	F	9	1	1	2	14,707
Deedee	4	F	7	1	1	0	4,947
Deedle E Dee	3	F	6	1	3	0	53,092
Deejaycrusader	3	C	3	0	0	0	78
Deelightful Dan	4	G	10	1	1	3	5,168
Deelightfulden	3	C	5	0	0	0	308
Deeliteful Bonus	2	F	2	0	0	1	3,090
Deeliteful Boy	2	G	4	1	0	1	11,515
Deeliteful Dude	2	G	3	1	1	0	10,400
Deeliteful Guy	5	G	10	0	1	0	27,880
Deeliteful Topper	4	F	13	1	3	1	34,175
Deelites Gold	3	C	4	1	1	0	34,294
Deemed Ready	3	G	14	2	3	0	32,333
Deemed Worthy	4	C	10	2	3	0	17,505
Deep Blue Goodbye	4	G	8	1	2	1	17,680
Deep Desire	3	F	4	0	1	0	2,720
Deep Finesse	4	F	11	2	0	1	10,172
Deep Green	2	F	5	1	2	1	26,845
Deep in the Woods	3	F	6	1	1	0	11,817
Deep Mischief	8	M	5	1	2	1	9,085
Deep Purple	3	G	9	1	0	0	16,770
Deep Shadow	4	C	1	0	0	0	0
Deep South	3	F	4	0	1	1	7,110
Deep Steel	3	C	2	0	0	0	125
Deep Sun	3	C	3	2	0	0	20,133
Deep Sweet Reason	3	F	5	2	0	0	6,005
Deep Thunder	5	G	10	1	1	0	7,206
Deep Woods	2	F	1	0	0	0	0
Deepinnegotiations	2	F	6	1	2	1	17,865
Deer Creek Lady	3	F	21	2	2	7	31,828
Deer Danny Boy	4	G	19	2	2	4	27,961
Deer in the Wind	4	F	17	1	2	2	12,838
Deer Lake	5	H	6	0	1	2	29,510
Deer Power	4	G	11	0	4	1	29,560
Deer Run	7	G	7	0	1	0	15,840
Deer Trail	4	G	15	2	1	1	22,954
Deerbrook	2	F	1	0	1	0	4,000
Deerfoot	4	C	1	0	0	0	0
Deering Legend	3	F	8	1	1	1	4,902
Deerview Lady	3	F	6	0	1	2	3,293
Deerwood Lass	8	M	6	0	1	2	8,770
Deerzee	3	F	12	1	0	0	13,160
Dee's Copycat	3	F	4	0	0	0	200
Dee's Dilemma	4	F	2	0	0	0	300
Dee's Echo	4	F	9	2	1	0	8,850
Dee's Justice	3	F	9	1	2	0	22,500
Dee's Little Dee	2	F	2	0	0	0	1,350
Dee's Love	4	F	4	0	0	0	2,681
Dee's Missy	5	M	5	0	0	0	0

Horse	Age	Sex	Sts	1st	2d	3d	Won
Dee's Rebel	7	G	17	2	3	2	24,172
Dee's Trick	2	F	1	0	0	0	0
Dee's Way	3	F	16	3	4	1	17,652
Deesalia	4	F	2	0	0	0	299
Defcon Five	3	G	5	1	0	0	11,040
Defend the Crown	3	G	2	0	0	0	0
Defend Your Honor	3	G	12	0	1	1	4,243
Defense Motion	3	C	10	4	2	3	102,860
Defensive	6	G	13	2	1	1	21,732
Defensive Gem	7	G	5	1	0	0	6,355
Defensive Kat	4	G	6	0	0	0	760
Defer	2	C	3	2	1	0	108,900
Deference	2	C	2	1	0	0	9,450
Deferred Comp	6	H	3	1	0	0	19,500
Defiant Dandy	7	H	8	2	1	2	36,510
Defiant Fighter	6	G	8	0	0	0	0
Defiant Kid	4	C	7	1	1	1	17,061
Defiant Lord	4	C	8	2	2	0	25,967
Defiant Warrior	6	G	25	4	0	4	23,519
Defiantly Bold	4	C	5	0	0	1	4,620
Deficit	4	G	1	0	0	0	300
Defined Borders	3	F	8	2	2	0	47,580
Definitely	8	G	16	0	1	4	4,059
Definitivepleasure	3	G	7	0	0	0	3,160
Definitly Social	6	M	7	0	1	2	5,666
Deflation	3	F	6	1	0	2	37,198
Defrench	4	G	11	2	4	1	65,915
Defrere's Image	5	M	11	0	2	3	24,181
Defrere's Venture	3	F	8	4	1	1	102,145
Defrere's Vixen	4	C	9	4	0	0	81,930
Defrills	3	F	6	3	0	1	20,610
Defrocked	3	G	10	3	0	0	53,210
Defuhr	3	F	9	2	1	2	52,060
Defy Logic	4	C	6	2	2	0	49,700
Defy the Odds	2	C	2	0	0	0	1,720
Defying Angel	7	M	1	0	0	0	0
Defying Odds	2	G	7	1	1	0	9,337
Degas Vu	7	G	11	0	0	2	2,885
Degenerate Gambler	3	G	12	0	2	1	16,165
Dehere Blues	4	G	6	1	0	1	22,274
Dehim	4	G	11	2	1	5	26,009
Deidre Lou	4	F	1	0	1	0	2,000
Deja	4	F	2	0	0	1	7,120
Deja Bouti	3	G	7	1	0	3	6,917
Deja Brew	3	G	13	3	1	2	31,957
Deja Dancer	4	F	8	0	0	0	685
Deja l'Eau	4	G	7	0	1	1	2,944
Deja Voodoo	4	G	1	0	0	0	653
Deja Vu Diva	5	M	14	2	1	5	20,344
Dejavualloveragain	3	G	13	1	3	1	33,692
Dek Dee	2	G	2	0	0	0	696
Dekalb	5	G	11	2	4	0	29,200
Dekay	3	G	5	1	0	0	10,230
Deke's Star	4	G	11	1	0	1	3,021
Del Chiaro	5	G	6	3	0	1	28,308
Del Dancer	5	G	4	0	0	3	2,351
Del Diablo	4	G	5	1	1	0	3,992
Del Mar Breeze	2	G	5	0	1	1	5,010
Del Mar Dancer	9	G	5	0	2	0	5,286
Del Mar Danny	7	G	4	1	0	1	6,550
Del Mar Darling	8	M	1	0	0	1	420
Del Mar Diamond	3	F	10	1	1	2	25,990
Del Mar Dreamin'	3	F	6	0	0	0	0
Del Mar Gray	9	G	4	0	0	0	330
Del Mar Red	3	G	6	0	3	3	14,030
Del Mar Show	7	H	8	1	1	1	54,024
Del Mar Silver	2	C	1	0	0	0	2,100
Del Mar Storm	2	C	2	0	2	0	7,400
Del Mar Ticket	3	F	5	1	0	1	36,836
Del Norte	4	G	10	2	2	1	31,670
Del Rae	4	F	8	0	1	1	20,745
Delacroix	4	G	6	1	1	0	39,723
Delafield	4	G	6	2	1	1	44,620
Delake	2	F	7	0	1	0	9,220
Delane	3	C	6	0	0	2	9,700
Delano's Tricks	4	G	3	1	0	0	4,530
Delante	5	G	9	0	2	0	1,569
Delavallade	6	M	2	1	0	0	26,400
Delaverne Blues	2	G	2	0	1	0	2,565
Delaverne Run	3	F	6	0	0	0	111
Delaware Abbey	3	F	15	2	4	1	9,473
Delaware Brew	5	G	4	1	1	0	4,460
Delaware River	3	G	11	3	2	0	56,690
Delaware Squeeze	3	G	9	1	1	1	6,472
Delay	6	M	3	0	0	1	2,888
Delayed Kiss	4	C	8	2	2	0	20,730
Delayed Vacation	4	G	8	0	1	2	10,214
Delcastle	4	G	15	3	1	2	19,685
Delceda	5	M	6	1	0	0	7,163
Delegancy	4	F	5	0	1	0	4,600
Delfinia	9	M	10	1	0	2	4,767
Delft Buttons	3	F	6	1	0	0	3,510
Delia's Gone	3	F	3	0	1	0	9,594
Deliberate Attack	6	M	5	1	0	1	1,707
Delicate an Demure	5	M	6	0	0	1	1,063
Delicate Dusty	3	F	5	1	0	0	10,620
Delicate Legacy	6	M	3	0	0	0	0
Delicate Prince	4	G	6	2	0	0	13,200
Delicatessa	5	M	8	1	1	1	74,694
Delicious Devil	6	G	3	0	0	0	230
Delicious Dish	3	F	16	2	3	1	16,896
Delicious Gift	5	M	12	2	2	3	16,529
Deliciously	2	F	1	0	0	0	450
Delies Delight	2	F	4	0	1	0	1,558
Delight At Dawn	4	G	8	0	0	0	0
Delight Choice	3	C	7	0	0	0	233
Delight My Fire	6	H	1	0	0	0	0
Delightful Action	3	F	11	1	0	1	3,714
Delightful Change	3	F	2	0	1	0	1,710
Delightful Demi	3	G	14	1	5	1	21,828
Delightful Devil	6	H	4	1	1	0	3,700
Delightful Doris	2	F	4	0	0	2	11,120
Delightful Indy	3	G	1	0	0	0	0
Delightful King	3	G	4	0	0	0	0
Delightful Power	3	G	8	0	0	3	8,950
Delightful Reef	8	G	5	0	1	0	1,240
Delightfully Red	3	G	1	0	0	0	135
Delightster	4	G	10	1	0	1	7,645
Delineator's Dream	6	G	11	3	1	1	8,562
Delinquenator	3	G	7	3	2	0	10,612
Delirious Laughter	5	G	14	2	2	2	16,228
Deliteful Lover	3	F	7	1	0	1	4,539
Delitooabank	8	M	3	0	0	0	84
Deliver Hope	6	G	13	4	2	1	27,300
Deliver Lu	2	F	5	0	0	0	960
Deliver Me Quick	3	F	2	0	2	0	10,600
Deliver the Gold	3	F	6	1	0	2	7,610
Deliver the Roses	4	F	15	2	3	1	20,485
Delivering Speed	3	C	1	0	0	0	940
Delivery	4	C	2	1	0	0	5,020
Delivery Cart	2	F	9	1	0	1	21,926
Delizia	4	F	8	2	0	1	67,231
Dell Place	5	G	9	3	1	2	133,840
Della Francesca	5	H	2	0	0	0	2,750
Della Jhamela	5	M	5	1	0	1	2,170
Della n' Time	3	F	13	3	1	3	32,794
Della Street	3	F	4	0	1	0	5,320
Dellamonte	4	F	2	0	0	0	324
Dellasue	3	F	2	0	0	0	160
Delloyd's Delite	5	M	4	0	0	0	479
Delly Elly	4	F	10	1	0	1	9,765
Delmar Annie	2	F	4	1	0	1	20,060
Delmar Diva	3	F	3	0	0	0	195
Delmar Zeal	3	G	7	1	0	4	27,040
Delmarvelous	5	G	14	1	1	2	20,445
Delmonico Cat	5	M	2	1	0	0	60,000
Delong	5	G	15	3	3	1	18,887
Delphina Bay	3	F	2	0	0	0	1,565
Delphiness	5	M	6	0	0	1	2,414
Delray Dancer	5	G	12	1	3	3	19,590
Delray Darling	6	M	5	0	0	0	450
Del's Delight	7	G	5	1	1	0	9,378
Delta Al	3	C	4	0	0	0	233
Delta Bull	3	F	4	0	0	1	1,700
Delta Captain	2	C	1	0	0	0	75
Delta Charlie	2	C	3	1	1	0	19,439
Delta Command	6	H	10	0	0	3	2,850
Delta Decorum	2	F	1	0	0	0	0

Horse	Age	Sex	Sts	1st	2d	3d	Won
Delta Epsilon	6	G	11	5	2	3	83,073
Delta Express	8	M	9	1	3	3	3,320
Delta Flyer	5	M	2	1	1	0	8,280
Delta Ghost	3	C	7	2	1	1	69,390
Delta Guard	3	C	2	0	0	0	575
Delta Kat	4	F	5	0	0	1	2,474
Delta Lord	4	C	15	4	1	2	31,033
Delta Mirage	4	F	13	2	2	1	5,252
Delta Miss	3	F	12	2	1	2	16,182
Delta Monarch	2	G	4	0	0	2	6,422
Delta Pirate	3	G	15	1	4	2	20,120
Delta Princess	5	M	9	2	1	0	109,312
Delta Rate	4	F	5	0	0	0	1,535
Delta Run	2	F	5	1	0	0	7,890
Delta Sand	2	C	2	0	0	0	1,065
Delta Sea	4	G	8	1	0	0	32,786
Delta Sensation	3	F	11	5	0	1	164,526
Delta Sky	2	C	1	0	1	0	5,300
Delta Storm	3	G	2	1	0	0	19,520
Delta Tango	2	C	1	0	0	0	450
Delta Wheel	6	G	8	0	1	1	6,713
Delta Wing	3	G	10	0	1	0	4,146
Deltaport	5	H	3	0	0	0	120
Delta's Pet	4	C	7	1	2	1	6,121
Delta's Snake Eyes	4	C	5	0	0	0	409
Deltatron	4	G	10	0	0	0	1,638
Deluca	3	G	12	1	0	1	7,092
Delune	3	F	7	0	0	1	3,409
Delusion	2	F	2	1	0	0	16,800
Delusional Lad	4	G	2	0	1	0	1,800
Delux Fantasy	6	H	5	2	0	0	5,120
Deluxe Edition	2	F	1	1	0	0	13,200
Deluxe Kite	3	F	7	1	1	0	4,400
Dem Dancin' Shoes	3	F	2	0	0	0	750
Demabella	3	F	12	1	7	1	24,237
Demagoguery	2	G	6	2	1	2	108,423
Demajake	5	G	17	0	3	4	23,265
Demand	2	F	2	0	0	0	0
Demanding Case	2	F	2	1	0	0	13,005
Demanding Cat	3	G	17	1	3	3	14,000
Demanding Lady	2	F	2	0	0	0	800
Demarcus	3	G	7	1	0	0	12,983
Demarocks	5	M	10	3	1	0	23,869
Demashoot Demawail	4	F	9	4	1	1	53,768
Demeteor	5	G	6	1	1	1	68,560
Demetra's Love	4	F	11	2	0	1	42,840
Demetrias Brother	4	G	1	0	0	0	40
Demi Country	5	M	2	0	0	0	132
Demi Deluxe	3	G	15	1	0	2	10,539
Demi Kat	6	M	10	1	2	0	2,614
Demi Paige	5	M	9	2	2	0	14,165
Demidoff Lilly	4	F	4	1	0	1	4,331
Demidoll	7	M	1	0	0	0	0
Demin Red	2	G	5	0	0	0	416
Demiparfait	5	M	4	0	1	1	10,410
Demi's Secret	3	F	10	1	1	1	24,890
Demizel Tedi	3	F	10	0	2	3	8,920
Demizoe	4	F	19	4	4	2	21,979
Demolition Man	5	G	5	0	0	1	1,439
Demolition Zone	2	C	3	0	0	0	2,132
Demon Dancer	6	G	10	4	2	0	41,820
Demon Fever	3	F	1	0	0	0	100
Demon Jazz	3	G	4	0	0	0	0
Demon Tea	4	F	9	2	2	0	4,643
Demon Warlock	4	C	11	6	2	2	192,990
Demonax	3	G	8	0	1	0	2,637
Demonic Storm	2	F	1	0	0	0	400
Demonigal	3	F	6	1	0	1	13,634
Demons Charmer	5	M	9	1	1	2	5,070
Demons Lad	5	G	5	0	2	1	1,482
Demon's Prince	6	G	15	5	2	2	57,935
Demopolis	4	C	4	0	1	1	2,170
Demson	3	G	4	0	0	0	286
Demus	3	F	11	2	2	2	17,854
Denaejur	2	F	1	0	0	0	0
Denali's Shadow	4	G	1	0	0	0	0
Dendillo	4	G	11	1	4	0	12,350
Denebola	3	F	6	0	2	1	101,503
Denied	6	G	1	0	1	0	14,000
Denim Dancer	2	C	1	0	0	0	230
Denim Debutante	3	F	2	1	0	0	3,480
Denim Genes	4	F	2	0	0	0	124
Denim to Diamonds	7	M	14	4	2	1	15,328
Denim Wildcat	3	F	15	2	4	3	51,920
Denimsanddiamonds	4	F	11	2	1	2	36,600
Deniro's Delight	5	M	11	4	1	1	19,432
Deniro's Lad	6	G	7	0	0	1	1,085
Denium Cowgirl	2	F	9	3	1	1	44,260
Dennis' Demons	5	G	8	1	2	0	49,840
Dennisport	3	C	6	2	0	1	22,934
Denniston	2	C	4	1	0	0	10,673
Denny H	4	G	1	0	0	0	0
Denny's Devil Baby	5	M	10	1	0	2	8,952
Denny's Victory	3	C	8	2	1	0	34,130
Denocandu	2	C	3	0	1	0	3,800
Denominator	3	G	1	0	0	0	37
Denon	6	H	1	0	0	0	4,869
Deno's Connection	3	F	10	3	2	2	75,840
Denoun N Deverb	2	F	8	1	2	0	33,842
Denouncer's Girl	4	F	5	1	0	1	3,560
Densgripinagin	3	G	17	3	0	0	12,575
Dented Chad	4	F	5	1	1	1	7,395
Denton County	6	G	2	1	1	0	6,580
Denton Sings Ruby	4	F	12	4	0	2	14,979
Dentons Ruby	6	M	5	0	0	0	649
Denver Hi	9	G	3	0	0	1	533
Denver Sam	2	G	3	0	0	0	216
Deocat	3	G	14	0	1	0	2,136
Deon	10	M	7	0	0	0	878
Dep	2	F	3	0	0	0	164
Departing Dynamo	7	G	6	0	0	2	1,632
Departing Now	2	G	5	2	0	1	71,106
Departing South (ARG)	6	M	12	2	2	4	20,227
Dependability	2	F	6	2	1	0	37,849
Dependable Herbie	4	C	12	3	0	2	71,030
Dependable Will	8	G	5	1	1	0	7,052
Deploy	3	C	2	0	1	0	6,760
Deploy Venture (GB)	8	G	6	1	0	1	7,364
Depop	3	G	1	0	0	0	0
Deporte	8	H	2	0	0	0	262
Deporte Total (CHI)	7	G	7	2	0	2	16,525
Deposit Dancer	7	H	3	1	0	1	1,280
Deposit Day	3	F	9	1	0	1	7,715
Deposit On Time	4	G	1	0	0	0	0
Deposit Thatticket	6	M	12	0	0	2	1,661
Deposit the Cash	7	M	4	0	0	0	1,077
Deposit the Loot	5	M	2	0	0	0	218
Deposit This	3	G	13	0	4	4	16,545
Deposited	3	F	5	1	1	1	22,750
Depository	4	G	12	3	3	1	35,462
Depurata	4	F	6	1	0	2	6,880
Deputariat Song	2	C	1	0	0	0	0
Deputedlaura	4	F	1	0	0	0	0
Deputies Agent	4	C	2	0	0	0	191
Deputie's Notebook	2	F	3	0	0	1	4,325
Deputized	3	G	7	0	2	0	17,855
Deputy Ambassador	3	G	6	2	0	0	17,328
Deputy Apollo	4	G	3	0	0	0	0
Deputy Badman	4	G	14	1	2	2	11,928
Deputy Brawler	3	G	6	0	1	0	2,472
Deputy Call	8	G	15	2	4	1	34,611
Deputy Champ	6	G	1	0	0	0	340
Deputy Circle	5	H	4	0	1	0	2,046
Deputy Connor	5	G	19	3	2	2	36,356
Deputy Country	6	H	10	6	0	0	171,250
Deputy Cures Blues	4	F	7	0	0	2	23,443
Deputy Danny Boy	7	H	8	0	0	0	2,360
Deputy David K	4	G	12	0	0	2	4,310
Deputy Dee	4	G	3	0	0	0	179
Deputy Defrere	4	G	8	1	3	2	15,725
Deputy Des	2	F	1	0	0	0	213
Deputy Devil	4	F	2	0	1	0	1,140
Deputy Director	4	C	8	1	2	2	47,820
Deputy Dirty Deeds	5	G	6	1	0	0	14,115
Deputy Do Right	5	G	7	1	1	1	3,108
Deputy Doc	4	G	10	0	2	1	13,080
Deputy Doc Renzi	3	G	2	1	1	0	48,020
Deputy Dolly	3	F	5	1	0	1	16,330

Horse	Age	Sex	Sts	1st	2d	3d	Won
Deputy Doo Dah	4	F	14	2	3	0	18,363
Deputy Drone	6	G	9	1	1	2	28,167
Deputy Dude	5	G	10	3	4	0	43,020
Deputy Eagle	5	G	4	0	0	0	0
Deputy Express	3	G	7	1	1	2	8,975
Deputy Festes	2	G	5	0	0	0	1,230
Deputy Fox	5	G	2	0	0	0	126
Deputy French	2	C	4	1	2	0	19,500
Deputy Fudge	4	G	9	2	2	1	34,356
Deputy Gold	3	C	12	2	1	5	48,859
Deputy Halo	4	G	5	0	0	0	435
Deputy Hunter	2	C	1	0	0	0	0
Deputy in Charge	4	G	13	1	2	1	6,295
Deputy Indy	2	C	1	1	0	0	27,000
Deputy Jack	4	G	16	5	2	2	58,940
Deputy Jazz	6	G	12	5	1	2	71,894
Deputy Kate	3	F	9	3	0	2	58,880
Deputy Kris	2	C	1	0	0	0	2,340
Deputy Lad	4	G	11	3	2	2	72,600
Deputy Lee	4	G	4	1	0	0	15,600
Deputy Lou	4	G	3	0	0	1	1,640
Deputy Magic	2	G	1	0	0	0	540
Deputy Mary	5	M	5	0	0	0	724
Deputy Mauk	3	G	16	2	3	2	37,345
Deputy O'Neal	2	C	3	0	0	0	1,590
Deputy Punch	2	G	4	1	0	0	9,630
Deputy Ridge	4	G	9	2	3	1	4,393
Deputy Ruckus	4	G	5	0	0	0	0
Deputy Ruler	6	G	7	3	1	1	33,950
Deputy Rummy	3	C	5	2	1	1	42,500
Deputy Savannah	5	M	6	0	1	1	969
Deputy Seabreeze	4	G	9	1	1	2	4,113
Deputy Sheriff	5	G	9	4	4	0	57,766
Deputy Slerp	3	G	2	0	0	0	0
Deputy Squealie	3	F	6	1	2	1	51,430
Deputy Storm	3	C	3	1	1	0	73,585
Deputy Strike	6	G	5	2	2	0	94,375
Deputy Stripe	6	G	5	0	0	0	712
Deputy Thief	4	G	7	0	0	0	6,396
Deputy Tombe	4	F	6	2	0	1	87,906
Deputy Villa	3	G	4	0	0	1	1,265
Deputy Vita	2	F	6	0	1	2	6,490
Deputy Warrior	4	G	10	1	0	1	8,353
Deputy Wild	4	C	5	2	1	0	9,404
Deputy Wild Child	3	F	8	2	0	1	17,072
Deputy Woman	5	M	5	0	0	0	561
Deputymayormargret	3	F	2	0	0	1	5,620
Deputy's Destiny	3	C	7	2	0	1	36,145
Deputy's Image	3	G	7	1	1	2	13,522
Deputy's Legacy	6	H	11	1	2	3	22,680
Deputy's Reward	5	H	3	1	1	0	5,230
Deputy's Son	4	C	1	0	0	0	0
Der Ali	3	G	7	0	0	0	3,560
Der He Is	5	G	9	2	0	3	10,565
Derby Brass	3	G	6	0	1	0	1,897
Derby Caper	2	G	2	0	0	2	4,730
Derby Charm	3	F	4	0	0	0	176
Derby Clearance	6	G	2	0	0	0	131
Derby Day Baby	3	C	13	2	1	1	17,023
Derby Day Debut	8	M	14	1	1	3	5,850
Derby Day Hope	4	G	9	1	3	1	7,873
Derby Day Rally	3	F	7	3	0	1	26,031
Derby Doll	4	F	12	3	1	2	14,739
Derby Drifter	2	G	5	1	2	1	10,426
Derby Drive	5	H	1	0	0	0	725
Derby Duke	7	G	13	0	3	3	17,687
Derby Fan	4	F	11	2	1	1	10,158
Derby Fever	3	C	5	1	0	1	34,622
Derby for Darby	3	G	3	0	1	0	8,688
Derby Girl	4	F	5	0	2	0	8,680
Derby King Mutesa	6	G	15	1	1	5	3,585
Derby Opportunity	2	G	1	0	1	0	1,410
Derby Rider (ARG)	5	G	6	2	2	1	39,705
Derby Road	3	G	5	1	1	0	6,502
Derby Storm	2	G	2	0	0	0	0
Derby Trefaire	3	G	12	3	2	0	15,925
Derby Tri	2	C	5	0	0	1	3,870
Derby Wish Mist	5	M	5	0	0	0	0
Derby's Buckeye	3	C	12	0	0	0	423
Derby's Hellraiser	3	F	8	2	2	0	49,920
Derbytown	2	F	2	0	0	0	450
Derbywulf	3	C	1	0	0	0	0
Derek's Announced	4	G	1	0	0	0	0
Derek's Cape Town	4	G	1	0	0	0	0
Deriga Bay	6	G	19	2	6	4	13,823
Derman	7	G	3	1	0	1	6,140
Deroleo	5	G	11	2	3	2	13,837
Derrianne	4	F	4	1	0	1	28,056
Derrick	3	G	12	2	3	1	20,016
Derry Connor	6	G	3	0	0	0	1,435
Dervorghilla	6	M	6	1	0	1	4,520
Derwin's Hope	2	C	4	2	0	0	23,070
Des Arc	5	G	11	1	2	0	27,660
De's Boots	3	F	1	0	0	0	255
Des Howl	5	G	1	0	0	0	0
De's Story	10	G	3	0	0	0	200
De's Sweet Dream	2	F	5	0	0	0	2,200
Descout	8	G	4	0	0	1	1,595
Desdemona's Dream	3	F	8	1	2	1	28,720
Deseo	3	G	18	4	1	3	38,855
Desert Amor	3	F	10	2	2	1	8,798
Desert Anger (GB)	3	C	4	1	0	1	30,744
Desert Bloom	4	F	1	0	0	0	558
Desert Bloomer	8	G	8	1	1	0	6,686
Desert Blues	3	G	1	0	0	0	235
Desert Boom	4	G	11	5	0	1	105,890
Desert Boot	4	F	4	0	0	1	1,183
Desert Border	3	G	11	1	1	1	28,510
Desert Bounty	4	G	8	2	0	2	3,893
Desert Brian	2	C	2	0	0	0	195
Desert Cactus	4	G	5	0	0	0	398
Desert Conquest	5	M	15	2	1	4	31,756
Desert Crank	4	F	2	0	0	1	1,500
Desert Crown	3	F	10	0	2	2	13,556
Desert Dancer (ARG)	6	H	3	0	0	0	310
Desert Dancing	3	F	2	0	0	0	0
Desert Darby	7	H	7	1	3	1	72,644
Desert Deed	3	F	5	1	1	1	29,349
Desert Delight	8	H	5	0	1	0	488
Desert Display	5	G	7	1	2	0	8,601
Desert Duty	3	C	4	0	1	2	4,284
Desert Frost	5	M	3	1	0	0	5,100
Desert Gal	4	F	9	3	4	0	72,308
Desert Gambler	3	G	4	1	0	1	7,950
Desert Gem	4	F	16	0	3	3	5,199
Desert Girl	4	F	2	0	0	0	214
Desert Hawk	10	G	4	0	0	0	265
Desert House	2	F	4	0	1	1	2,588
Desert Justice	2	F	5	1	0	1	11,120
Desert King	3	G	15	0	2	2	26,868
Desert Lady	3	F	5	2	1	0	10,414
Desert Launch	6	H	8	4	1	0	6,286
Desert Lew	8	H	7	0	3	0	1,671
Desert Master	4	G	13	6	0	1	16,638
Desert Monarch	4	G	6	1	2	0	20,848
Desert Nova	3	F	3	0	0	0	10,200
Desert Paran	4	G	19	2	4	7	29,990
Desert Pass	6	M	4	0	0	0	1,090
Desert Passion	5	M	12	1	1	4	10,338
Desert Patrol	3	C	9	4	1	0	51,685
Desert Pearls	4	F	5	0	3	0	30,400
Desert Pines	3	C	1	1	0	0	7,920
Desert Place	8	G	12	3	0	2	9,177
Desert Pride	2	F	4	2	0	0	23,515
Desert Prospector	2	C	3	2	0	0	25,716
Desert Qui	3	F	6	1	1	2	11,197
Desert Ranger	2	C	2	1	0	0	9,576
Desert Ruler	4	G	10	2	4	2	11,490
Desert Saker	2	C	9	0	1	0	8,250
Desert Scholar	5	G	5	1	1	2	16,300
Desert Shadow	5	G	6	0	0	0	88
Desert Singer	5	H	2	0	0	0	122
Desert Solitaire	3	F	6	1	0	0	9,274
Desert Spark	3	G	1	0	0	0	0
Desert Spirit (IRE)	4	G	2	0	0	0	400
Desert Star	5	M	11	0	3	2	17,714
Desert Stop In	4	F	13	1	0	1	7,890
Desert Surge	7	G	3	0	1	0	770

Horse	Age	Sex	Sts	1st	2d	3d	Won
Desert Surprise	3	C	1	0	0	0	320
Desert Swing (FR)	4	G	3	0	0	0	9,600
Desert Sword	4	G	10	3	2	1	34,392
Desert Tent	3	F	4	1	1	1	37,560
Desert Thief	3	C	7	2	0	1	8,705
Desert Toi	4	F	9	0	0	0	490
Desert View (GB)	4	F	1	0	0	0	0
Desert War	3	G	1	0	0	0	110
Desert Wolf Girl	5	M	8	2	0	3	14,677
Desiard	11	G	16	1	6	1	24,436
Designated Winner	4	G	6	0	0	4	2,024
Designed for Luck	7	G	4	1	1	0	311,180
Designer Digs	3	C	5	3	0	0	17,665
Designer Genes	6	M	10	0	0	1	1,352
Designer Image	4	F	12	3	1	1	12,447
Designer's Gold	4	F	1	0	0	0	350
Designer's Year	3	C	6	2	0	0	10,043
Designing Miss	2	F	4	0	2	0	10,120
Designs by Vera	5	M	2	1	0	0	5,460
Desilver	5	M	25	2	0	9	15,585
Desirable Moment	5	M	9	4	2	1	100,770
Desirabledancer	4	F	9	0	2	2	19,560
Desirae's Dove	3	G	5	1	0	1	17,336
Desiraes My Candy	6	M	1	0	0	0	0
Desiraes Myhotbaby	4	F	9	2	3	1	21,960
Desirous	3	F	6	1	1	0	5,086
Desktop	9	H	12	2	1	1	11,081
Desnuda	3	F	4	0	0	0	1,580
Desperado Kid	3	C	2	1	0	0	24,270
Desperation	5	G	5	0	1	0	3,704
Despina	2	F	2	0	0	0	255
Despite	4	G	13	2	1	0	24,376
Desputed Western	3	G	4	0	0	0	39
Dessa's Dream	4	G	20	1	3	5	31,662
D'este	3	F	1	1	0	0	22,200
Destello del Cielo (CHI)	7	G	4	1	0	2	10,000
Destin	3	C	1	0	0	0	0
Destination Heaven	2	C	4	1	0	1	14,430
Destined to Star	2	C	1	0	0	0	0
Destined to Win	4	G	7	2	1	1	46,570
Destinedtobeastar	3	F	11	2	2	3	16,236
Destiny and Roses	3	F	5	0	0	0	1,060
Destiny Bay	3	F	2	0	0	1	5,300
Destiny by Chance	3	G	5	1	0	0	6,275
Destiny Calls	4	F	8	6	1	0	271,670
Destiny Red	4	G	2	0	1	0	13,560
Destiny's Design	4	F	8	1	2	2	27,828
Destiny's Doorstep	3	G	11	2	1	1	14,148
Destiny's Dream	4	C	3	0	0	0	120
Destiny's Echo	3	C	1	0	0	0	0
Destinys Island	3	G	5	0	0	0	2,000
Destinys Pleasure	2	F	1	0	0	0	164
Destiny's Ruler	4	G	4	1	0	0	4,813
Detained	5	G	13	0	0	1	1,719
Detective Sipowicz	3	G	2	0	0	0	75
Detector	7	G	5	0	1	0	3,254
Determined	3	G	3	1	1	0	36,015
Determined Lady	3	F	8	0	1	0	3,576
Detramental	5	G	7	0	0	1	1,420
Detroit Tiger	2	C	5	0	0	1	2,517
Deuce's Girl	4	F	9	3	3	1	45,569
Deux Mille	5	G	10	2	2	3	22,680
Devant	4	F	11	4	2	2	58,700
Devdrudan	2	F	4	2	0	0	18,049
Develish Turn	6	M	4	1	0	0	6,102
Deviant Princess	3	F	8	0	0	0	844
Devil A' Doria	3	F	7	0	1	1	2,522
Devil Action	3	G	13	1	4	1	22,694
Devil At Sea	2	C	1	1	0	0	12,300
Devil Badgett	4	G	15	4	1	3	149,756
Devil by Choice	4	F	10	1	1	0	2,810
Devil Chaser	3	C	1	0	0	0	2,300
Devil Cop	3	G	3	0	0	1	644
Devil Dancing	5	M	11	2	2	3	75,415
Devil Dear	4	F	15	0	1	5	11,827
Devil Girl	4	F	14	3	1	2	23,081
Devil Hawk	5	M	7	1	0	2	4,195
Devil Hunter	5	H	1	0	0	0	125
Devil in Excess	2	C	2	0	0	0	359
Devil in Pink	6	M	6	0	1	0	2,532
Devil in Red	6	G	5	0	0	0	0
Devil in the Sky	4	G	3	0	0	0	0
Devil Lace	3	F	3	1	1	1	45,593
Devil Last	5	M	10	2	1	1	13,218
Devil Man	4	G	8	0	2	1	11,939
Devil Me Care	8	H	4	0	1	0	2,705
Devil Me Too	4	F	7	0	0	0	833
Devil of a Time	4	G	3	0	1	0	4,834
Devil of a Trip	4	C	3	0	0	0	1,934
Devil On Deck	5	H	17	0	1	2	4,830
Devil On the Moon	4	G	10	3	1	0	33,315
Devil On the Run	4	F	5	2	1	0	13,515
Devil One	5	G	11	0	0	1	3,255
Devil Over Due	5	M	8	2	2	1	13,268
Devil Ray	8	G	2	0	0	0	391
Devil Shade	2	F	3	0	0	0	181
Devil Time	7	G	4	1	1	0	38,132
Devil to Remember	3	G	13	1	1	0	9,550
Devil Valentine	6	G	17	3	3	2	59,093
Devil You Say	5	G	4	0	0	0	1,090
Devilastro	7	G	8	2	2	1	34,738
Devilbeastranger	3	F	5	0	2	0	6,886
Devildunit	2	C	2	0	0	1	945
Deviled Shrimp	3	F	4	0	0	0	274
Devilin Ruckus	7	G	11	3	3	0	25,850
Devilinaredsuit	2	C	1	0	0	0	1,440
Devilinbluedenim	5	M	4	0	1	1	3,294
Devilindetail	3	G	9	1	2	1	5,965
Devilish Dawn	2	F	3	0	0	1	4,140
Devilish Dove	4	G	19	4	6	3	28,324
Devilish Fact	3	G	5	0	1	3	9,965
Devilish Lady	6	M	2	0	0	0	909
Devilish Niner	3	F	2	0	1	0	3,330
Devilish Prospect	4	G	9	0	2	1	13,117
Devilish Sefa	2	C	5	0	0	0	299
Devilishly Bold	2	F	5	0	1	0	7,660
Devilishly Unique	3	F	11	2	1	1	11,931
Devilite	3	F	12	1	4	1	19,916
Devilment	2	C	2	1	1	0	22,200
Devilnine	4	G	5	1	0	3	28,844
Devilontheborder	3	G	1	0	0	0	0
Devil's Ace	2	C	1	0	0	0	0
Devil's Act	3	C	3	0	0	0	0
Devil's Agent	3	C	1	0	0	0	0
Devils Ago Go	4	F	4	0	0	0	0
Devils Alias	3	F	18	1	3	4	12,015
Devil's Babydoll	3	F	3	0	0	0	70
Devil's Bag Boy	2	C	1	0	0	0	0
Devil's Bandit	6	G	5	0	0	1	5,300
Devil's Barroness	3	F	2	0	0	0	0
Devil's Bay	2	G	4	1	0	1	11,860
Devil's Bid	7	G	11	0	0	1	2,916
Devil's Brigade	4	G	2	0	1	0	500
Devil's Bro	4	G	20	3	2	5	32,146
Devil's Case	3	G	6	0	0	2	3,090
Devil's Cat	4	G	7	1	0	0	3,920
Devil's Chick	3	F	19	2	8	1	14,354
Devil's Classic	4	C	15	4	1	2	28,330
Devil's Command	3	C	5	0	0	2	11,065
Devil's Con	5	G	9	2	2	3	50,740
Devil's Damsel	3	F	12	1	4	0	15,148
Devil's Dandy	6	G	1	0	0	0	73
Devil's Danzer	3	G	1	0	0	0	42
Devil's Dare	5	G	3	0	0	0	293
Devils Day Off	4	G	19	2	1	3	19,298
Devil's Diary	3	G	11	1	2	3	35,620
Devils Disciple	2	G	5	3	2	0	161,800
Devil's Dixie	3	C	3	0	0	1	3,166
Devil's Dynasty	7	G	4	0	1	2	2,148
Devil's Eclipse	3	F	9	3	2	1	49,649
Devil's Flag	2	C	2	0	0	0	560
Devil's Flame	4	G	12	3	0	3	29,107
Devil's Gate	7	G	14	0	1	1	2,814
Devil's Girlfriend	3	F	10	1	0	3	10,771
Devil's Gulch	5	G	12	3	6	1	67,030
Devil's Honey	5	M	2	0	0	2	2,070
Devil's Joyride	3	C	2	0	0	0	90
Devil's Judge	8	G	3	0	0	0	672

RECORDS OF HORSES

Horse	Age	Sex	Sts	1st	2d	3d	Won
Devil's Justice	2	C	5	1	1	2	15,870
Devil's Kitchen	2	G	10	0	1	2	11,250
Devil's Last Dance	3	F	9	1	1	1	41,355
Devil's Lock	4	F	3	2	0	0	14,100
Devils Lyre	7	G	5	0	0	0	0
Devils Madwoman	8	M	2	0	0	0	579
Devil's Magic	2	F	2	0	0	0	739
Devil's Manner	3	G	2	0	0	0	489
Devil's Mark	6	G	20	5	5	2	68,922
Devils Match	5	G	11	0	3	3	7,715
Devil's Money	3	G	4	1	1	0	18,660
Devil's Nugget	3	G	5	1	2	1	4,846
Devils Partner	8	G	24	2	5	5	12,343
Devil's Pik	2	G	2	0	0	0	322
Devils Proposition	3	G	1	0	0	0	69
Devils R Fabulous	2	F	11	0	1	1	5,146
Devil's Ransom	9	G	7	0	0	0	0
Devil's Reflection	4	G	5	0	0	0	229
Devil's Reine	8	H	6	0	0	0	1,259
Devils Right Hand	3	G	14	4	2	1	79,642
Devil's Rightt	4	C	1	0	0	0	3,762
Devil's Scripture	6	G	9	1	0	1	9,581
Devil's Secret Out	4	F	4	1	0	0	8,904
Devil's Serenade	3	F	13	2	3	1	22,137
Devil's Sis	3	F	7	2	1	0	11,977
Devil's Sky	3	F	8	0	1	1	3,930
Devil's Snare	4	G	9	1	0	2	4,725
Devils Snow	2	G	2	0	0	0	410
Devil's Treasure	2	C	5	1	2	0	27,830
Devil's Triangle	4	C	4	0	0	0	327
Devil's Vintage	4	G	10	2	1	1	25,700
Devil's Way	9	G	7	1	0	0	3,898
Devil's Weapon	4	G	2	0	0	0	0
Devils Wild	3	G	8	3	0	1	31,603
Devil's Wing	4	F	9	2	3	2	39,480
Devil'sdime	3	C	3	0	1	0	4,588
Devilsfood Cupcake	4	F	4	0	2	1	5,467
Devilsgonnagetcha	3	F	8	1	2	0	35,500
Devilsh Intentions	5	G	6	2	1	2	18,340
Devilsheis	2	F	4	0	0	0	566
Devilsville Slew	3	C	2	0	0	0	278
Devin Is Due	5	G	4	0	1	2	1,892
Devine Cozzene	2	C	4	1	0	0	15,425
Devine Dining	3	F	1	0	0	0	0
Devine Faith	4	F	1	0	0	1	820
Devine Force	2	F	4	1	0	0	16,500
Devine Lad	3	G	15	2	0	3	26,754
Devine Lightening	2	F	4	1	0	0	12,460
Devine Premonition	3	C	1	0	0	0	0
Devine Valentine	6	M	1	0	0	0	76
Devine Will	2	F	2	0	1	0	11,250
Devine Wind	8	G	6	3	1	0	72,920
Devinedeputy	7	G	15	4	3	1	23,476
Devin's Cash Crop	5	H	6	1	0	2	25,274
Devin's Magic	3	C	1	0	0	0	0
Devious Bebe	5	M	12	1	3	1	8,052
Devious Boy (GB)	4	G	2	0	0	1	13,308
Devious Cat	2	F	4	0	0	1	2,360
Devious Court	2	C	1	0	0	0	0
Devious Dame	4	F	10	1	0	2	11,587
Devious Darren	4	G	16	0	0	4	4,200
Devious Decision	4	F	17	2	1	1	13,575
Devious Deed	5	G	1	0	0	0	0
Devious Devin	3	G	17	0	5	1	21,999
Devious Dezibelle	5	M	11	3	3	1	33,620
Devious Diva	5	M	18	2	0	2	13,137
Devious Impact	4	F	2	0	1	0	12,600
Devious Kyle	5	G	15	2	3	2	7,458
Devious Morn	5	M	11	1	1	1	7,682
Devious Rhome	3	F	5	2	1	1	29,660
Devious Thorne	3	C	6	2	1	0	11,090
Devious Wish	4	C	18	2	2	0	15,590
Devise	3	C	1	0	0	0	42
Devlish	5	M	8	0	2	0	4,980
Devoldidit	4	C	5	2	1	0	8,327
Devon Hunt	5	M	1	0	0	0	83
Devon Ice	4	F	10	3	2	1	35,747
Devon Rules	2	C	4	0	2	1	6,897
Devon Special	3	C	11	3	2	0	25,714
Devon White Dove	4	G	2	0	0	0	0
Devon Zee	3	F	9	1	1	1	8,471
Devonairess	3	F	13	2	2	0	27,130
Devondale	2	G	3	0	0	2	2,378
Devonford	5	G	3	1	1	1	5,720
Devons Bride	4	F	3	0	0	0	718
Devon's Cadillac	4	C	4	1	0	0	5,736
Devon's Diamond	3	C	11	1	3	5	40,698
Devons Gona Roll	3	C	8	1	1	1	5,918
Devon's Lucky Lady	3	F	6	1	1	1	20,677
Devons Set	3	G	4	1	1	0	13,437
Devons Snow	4	F	2	0	0	0	176
Devon's Song	3	F	9	0	1	0	10,752
Devons Storm	4	G	2	0	0	0	1,410
Devote	4	G	14	1	3	1	47,940
Devoted Lover	3	G	11	1	3	2	35,740
Devoted to You	2	F	2	0	1	0	4,200
Devotion Motion	4	F	3	0	0	1	1,805
Devotion Unbridled	4	F	4	0	0	1	11,200
Devout	4	G	2	0	0	0	220
Devout Sinner	6	M	2	0	0	0	0
Dew Too	3	F	7	1	1	1	14,000
Dewar's Dunit	5	G	3	0	0	1	1,686
Dewdledanzigdancer	4	G	1	0	0	0	0
Dewey	4	G	6	0	2	1	8,642
Dewey's Trick	3	F	8	2	1	1	78,980
Dewolf	3	G	3	0	0	0	840
Dewrag	5	H	7	3	1	1	19,445
Dexcavate	5	G	4	0	1	1	3,977
Dexter's Dream	3	F	4	0	0	0	697
Dextro Tempore	6	G	2	0	0	0	750
D'gons Legacy	3	F	6	2	3	0	18,041
Dhaffir (CHI)	8	G	11	1	2	3	33,565
Dhamma	4	F	1	0	0	0	0
Dharma Girl	5	M	6	2	0	0	84,401
Di Grazia Girl	4	F	1	0	0	1	2,040
Dia	3	C	1	0	0	0	570
Dia Alegre (CHI)	5	G	12	3	1	4	79,420
Diablesse	6	M	5	1	1	0	28,695
Diablo Be Gone	2	G	4	0	1	1	4,630
Diablo Contento	4	G	10	0	0	4	7,602
Diablo de Frio	2	F	2	0	0	0	0
Diablo de Tierra	4	C	4	0	0	1	6,635
Diablo de Viernes	3	G	11	1	1	2	8,448
Diablo d'Light	3	C	5	1	1	0	11,747
Diablo for Certain	7	H	4	0	0	0	270
Diablo Mio	2	G	1	0	0	0	272
Diablo Reigns	6	G	2	0	0	0	0
Diablo S Stake	4	C	2	0	0	0	0
Diablo's Aisle	5	G	6	0	2	1	6,315
Diablo's Caper	7	G	4	0	0	1	1,232
Diablo's Crown	7	G	4	0	2	0	2,080
Diablo's Darlin'	3	F	4	0	0	1	749
Diablo's Donna	6	M	6	0	1	0	2,109
Diablo's Fable	6	G	6	0	0	0	0
Diablos Ordination	9	G	1	0	0	0	0
Diablo's Terete	3	C	18	3	0	1	16,322
Diablo's Well	6	H	2	0	0	0	300
Diablosangeleyes	7	M	10	1	0	2	31,604
Diabolic	3	F	7	2	0	1	10,614
Dial a Dancer	4	C	4	0	0	0	304
Dial a Hero	5	H	4	0	0	0	5,195
Dial Anthony	3	C	5	0	1	0	2,223
Dial for Dollars	8	G	14	1	1	2	7,151
Dial for Me	4	F	7	1	1	0	7,278
Dial for Speed	3	G	10	2	1	2	31,530
Dialogue (AUS)	5	M	1	0	0	0	980
Diamant (ARG)	8	H	1	1	0	0	8,800
Diamant Lady	2	F	9	1	1	0	21,755
Diamanta	3	F	4	0	0	0	1,460
Diamente	3	F	2	0	0	0	0
Diamon Su	4	F	12	0	0	1	8,445
Diamond a Day	3	G	14	2	1	1	18,600
Diamond Advantage	3	G	5	0	0	1	2,245
Diamond Amore	3	F	3	0	0	0	948
Diamond and Gem's	3	F	2	0	0	0	434
Diamond Bag	2	C	6	1	1	0	13,420
Diamond Ballroom	5	G	3	0	0	0	0
Diamond Beau	5	G	6	0	0	1	1,870

Horse	Age	Sex	Sts	1st	2d	3d	Won
Diamond Beauty	3	F	1	0	0	0	0
Diamond Betsy	2	F	3	1	1	0	8,400
Diamond Blues	3	C	3	0	0	0	1,680
Diamond Bo Dixie	2	F	2	0	0	0	0
Diamond Broker	3	G	10	1	0	3	7,643
Diamond Bucks	3	C	3	0	0	0	600
Diamond Bullet	4	G	16	4	4	3	59,880
Diamond Clip	2	G	8	1	1	3	58,798
Diamond Creole	2	F	4	1	0	0	6,600
Diamond Crusader	8	G	1	0	0	0	0
Diamond Cruz	5	G	7	2	0	2	13,631
Diamond Cutter	2	C	1	0	0	0	135
Diamond Czar	3	G	10	1	0	1	10,500
Diamond Dale	3	C	13	2	1	0	29,950
Diamond David	3	G	7	2	2	1	44,490
Diamond Dawn	5	G	14	4	1	3	49,775
Diamond Dayjur	4	F	7	1	1	0	6,870
Diamond Deal	3	G	21	2	2	1	24,630
Diamond Demon	5	G	10	0	0	0	1,225
Diamond Derby	4	F	1	0	0	0	52
Diamond Duchess	5	M	9	1	0	0	4,601
Diamond Edition	3	F	6	0	0	1	3,574
Diamond Eyes	3	F	5	0	0	0	395
Diamond Finish	3	F	12	2	1	1	19,106
Diamond Fire	4	F	1	0	0	0	135
Diamond Flight	5	M	4	2	2	0	9,708
Diamond Fury	3	R	7	1	2	0	39,420
Diamond Gal	2	F	3	0	0	0	630
Diamond Girl	5	M	4	1	1	0	6,760
Diamond Green (FR)	3	C	7	0	4	1	306,046
Diamond Hard Cut	2	G	3	0	0	1	3,278
Diamond Heirloom	4	F	10	3	2	0	34,400
Diamond Hondo	3	C	2	0	0	0	0
Diamond Hope	5	G	11	0	1	3	24,210
Diamond Hunter	4	F	6	0	0	1	3,824
Diamond Ice	4	F	4	0	0	0	0
Diamond Ina Bag	2	F	4	1	0	0	12,150
Diamond Indy	3	C	3	1	0	0	31,400
Diamond Isle	2	C	4	1	1	2	122,030
Diamond Jack W.	3	G	5	0	0	0	144
Diamond Jake	4	G	5	0	0	0	795
Diamond Jerry	5	H	2	0	0	0	123
Diamond Joe	5	G	11	1	2	2	13,321
Diamond Judy	4	F	12	1	4	2	2,620
Diamond Kind	3	F	12	0	0	0	1,565
Diamond Kitty	3	F	5	1	0	1	5,702
Diamond Kylie	4	F	13	1	1	1	6,105
Diamond Lane Don	2	G	4	0	0	0	635
Diamond Leap	7	H	12	2	3	1	9,462
Diamond Lilo	2	F	6	0	0	0	900
Diamond Little Bit	4	F	13	1	3	6	8,008
Diamond Luster	3	F	4	0	2	0	1,740
Diamond Machine	6	G	5	0	0	0	250
Diamond Mary	3	F	13	2	2	1	17,300
Diamond Mine	5	M	8	0	0	1	4,100
Diamond Passer	6	G	15	3	1	1	9,971
Diamond Passion	3	F	5	1	0	1	7,221
Diamond Point	5	M	11	1	1	1	14,740
Diamond Possession	3	C	3	0	0	0	870
Diamond Princess	2	F	2	0	0	0	0
Diamond Raiser	6	G	15	1	2	4	19,376
Diamond Reunion	2	F	6	0	2	0	4,946
Diamond Rock Candy	4	F	8	1	0	0	3,448
Diamond Rocket	4	G	12	1	3	2	15,718
Diamond Roo	6	G	7	0	3	3	6,730
Diamond Sammy	4	C	8	0	0	1	4,705
Diamond Sheena	5	M	4	1	0	1	3,398
Diamond Skier	3	F	9	0	1	0	2,986
Diamond Solitaire	2	F	4	0	2	0	12,240
Diamond Sugar Bear	9	G	2	0	0	0	432
Diamond Supreme	6	G	10	3	0	1	23,226
Diamond T	6	G	14	5	2	1	37,991
Diamond Terner	3	G	4	2	0	0	25,234
Diamond Tiara	5	M	5	1	0	2	49,320
Diamond Tip	3	C	2	0	0	0	720
Diamond Trail	6	M	11	4	3	1	44,351
Diamond Treasure	3	F	11	1	0	0	6,329
Diamond Trip	3	C	20	4	2	6	40,025
Diamond Up	3	F	16	5	0	2	43,670
Diamond View	4	G	9	1	2	2	18,243
Diamond Wildcat	2	C	2	1	1	0	33,600
Diamond Wonder	4	F	11	0	0	1	2,504
Diamond Year	7	G	1	0	0	0	0
Diamond Zim	4	G	8	0	1	1	2,518
Diamondinthebluff	4	C	2	1	0	0	8,400
Diamondintherough	6	G	8	0	0	0	873
Diamonds and Curls	3	F	2	0	0	0	0
Diamonds and Fuhr	3	F	14	2	2	3	42,209
Diamonds and Lace	3	F	7	0	0	1	4,457
Diamonds for Alyse	2	F	3	0	0	0	1,740
Diamonds for Dixie	2	G	3	0	0	0	2,720
Diamonds in Style	3	G	7	4	2	0	29,730
Diamonds N Excess	3	G	12	4	0	1	19,265
Diamonds of Luck	2	F	7	0	1	1	8,369
Diamonds Only	4	F	9	0	2	2	22,910
Diamonds Specs	3	F	7	2	0	2	25,725
Diamonds Trump	5	M	3	0	0	0	0
Diamondsareforever	3	F	6	0	0	0	640
Diamondsfor Crissy	4	F	3	0	1	0	1,586
Diamondsfora Lady	3	F	6	1	0	4	50,200
Diamondsnrainbows	3	F	3	0	0	0	145
Diamondsofemblems	3	F	8	0	1	0	1,650
Diamondsonhishoes	3	C	1	0	0	0	0
Diamondsrbueno	3	F	10	3	1	3	25,473
Diamonice	7	G	10	1	2	2	5,457
Diamonique	4	F	1	0	0	0	0
Diana Moseley	6	M	7	1	0	0	8,004
Diana of the Woods	4	F	8	1	2	2	28,207
Diana Rose	3	F	12	1	0	0	33,224
Diana's Dollar	2	F	4	0	0	1	2,100
Diana's Gold	2	F	2	0	0	0	0
Diana's Ready	2	F	6	1	2	0	13,880
Diana's Toll	3	F	1	0	0	0	0
Dianas Welcome	3	G	14	0	4	4	18,222
Diane Again	2	F	5	1	0	1	17,280
Diane's Design	3	F	1	0	0	0	450
Diane's Paranoide	4	G	10	1	1	0	8,193
Dianne's Debut	2	F	4	1	0	2	28,269
Dianthus	3	F	10	1	2	1	17,330
Diatheke	5	G	8	0	1	0	3,730
Diatribe	4	C	10	1	2	0	13,805
Diavla	3	F	14	3	2	1	77,501
Diazo Jo	5	G	9	1	0	1	4,055
Diazo's Diamond	4	F	4	0	1	0	885
Diazo's Duck	3	F	3	0	0	0	123
Dice and Slice	3	C	7	1	1	1	22,570
Dice in a Vice	2	F	3	1	0	0	8,200
Dice On Dice	3	F	12	1	1	2	8,813
Dice Roll	3	F	1	0	0	0	90
Dick Ford	4	C	4	0	0	0	450
Dickey Rickey	11	G	6	0	1	0	4,738
Dick's Chick	5	M	11	0	2	1	34,000
Dick's Hunter	3	G	12	2	1	1	14,216
Dick's Orphan	5	G	4	0	0	0	0
Dicky	5	G	9	0	2	0	3,595
Dicy Choice	4	F	14	0	4	3	7,206
Did He Biteyou	5	G	11	0	2	4	29,820
Did My Time	2	C	5	0	0	0	1,515
Did We Win	4	F	7	0	1	1	5,880
Did You Ring	2	C	2	0	1	0	2,050
Diddly Doolittle	2	C	1	0	0	1	2,400
Diditellyou	4	F	7	0	0	1	3,530
Didsbury	3	F	4	0	1	2	3,384
Didycheatamandhowe	2	F	2	1	1	0	76,330
Dieago	9	G	3	0	1	0	2,640
Diego Garcia	3	G	2	0	0	0	0
Dieppe	2	G	2	0	0	1	7,980
Diero	4	C	5	1	0	2	5,285
Diesec Um	7	H	4	0	0	0	0
Diesel Annie	4	F	3	1	0	0	9,540
Diesel Dog	2	G	4	1	0	0	8,970
Diesel Earl	4	G	8	0	0	0	0
Diesel Electric	7	G	8	0	0	1	774
Different Class	5	G	10	1	3	2	22,001
Different Kind	4	C	4	1	0	0	6,820
Difficult Teenager	3	G	10	1	3	0	15,270
Diffina	4	F	12	1	2	1	13,116
Dig Deeplee	2	G	4	1	0	2	17,316

Horse	Age	Sex	Sts	1st	2d	3d	Won
Dig for Diamonds	3	F	14	1	3	0	20,392
Dig for Dinner	2	F	3	0	0	1	3,450
Dig for It	9	H	11	1	3	1	37,120
Dig That Man	3	G	5	0	0	0	797
Dig That Rhythm	3	G	5	0	1	0	1,130
Dig This Coyote	6	H	5	0	0	1	1,582
Dig This Hoss	5	G	12	2	2	1	13,356
Digenforit	2	C	2	1	0	1	13,600
Digger Ben	4	G	6	0	1	1	7,492
Digger Dorain	3	G	1	0	0	0	61
Digger of Diamonds	3	G	12	0	2	0	13,359
Digger's Pride	2	F	3	1	0	0	6,102
Diggers Rest	5	G	13	0	1	0	2,548
Digger's Ridge	4	G	7	1	0	0	6,113
Digger's Star	5	M	1	0	0	0	660
Diggin After Dark	4	G	10	0	0	1	1,154
Diggin' for Fun	9	G	8	1	0	2	10,886
Diggin On Doug	3	G	8	1	1	0	2,854
Digginginoklahoma	5	G	7	0	0	1	1,037
Diggit (IRE)	8	H	1	0	0	0	400
Diggs	4	G	9	1	0	1	3,510
Diggy Fresh	3	C	5	3	0	1	62,770
Diggy's Dream	3	C	4	2	1	0	35,950
Digimon	4	G	14	1	4	1	19,968
Digit Dancer	5	G	9	2	2	0	30,610
Digital Delight	2	F	8	1	0	2	34,620
Digital Doll	3	F	11	3	1	3	41,540
Digital Dove	3	F	1	0	0	0	0
Digital Man	8	H	10	2	0	1	11,468
Dig'n Summer	3	F	1	0	0	0	0
Dignatario	4	G	5	0	1	1	3,345
Dignified Donovan	5	G	7	1	1	0	44,336
Dignified Pen	4	F	5	0	0	1	1,264
Digniflite	8	G	5	1	1	0	21,475
Dignitas Ball	3	F	3	0	0	0	0
Dignitas Queen	5	M	3	1	0	0	1,140
Dignus	4	G	5	0	1	2	3,880
Digwest	3	G	13	0	4	1	9,976
Dil	4	G	11	1	0	0	6,022
Dileb'sroughgirl	5	M	3	0	0	1	1,914
Dilechance	5	G	11	1	3	1	20,590
Diligent Don	2	C	1	0	0	0	230
Diligent Gambler	3	C	15	9	2	3	196,400
Diligent Manners	6	M	5	2	0	0	28,382
Diligent Prospect	2	C	3	2	0	1	59,760
Diligent Spirit	3	G	1	0	0	0	75
Diligent Won	4	C	14	2	2	2	30,730
Dilistar	3	C	11	1	1	4	50,670
Dillinger	5	G	7	1	2	0	93,060
Dillionaire (GB)	8	G	8	0	2	1	4,229
Dilly Dally	6	M	1	0	0	0	0
Diloot	4	F	8	3	2	1	25,641
Diluvial	5	M	5	0	0	0	0
Dim Sum Gal	2	F	7	1	3	0	16,230
Dimar Moon Lark	5	G	4	0	1	0	1,725
Dimashq	5	H	2	0	0	0	312
Dime Apiece	3	F	4	1	0	1	5,472
Dimilynne	4	F	8	1	0	0	8,146
Dimitrova	4	F	5	0	0	0	95,404
Dimming	6	G	2	0	0	0	0
Dimple Pinch	2	F	2	2	0	0	32,400
Dimpled Ballot	6	G	11	3	3	0	58,953
Dimpled Chad	5	M	2	0	0	0	327
Dina Gold	2	F	3	0	0	1	3,450
Dinadoon	4	F	2	1	0	0	5,425
Dinah's Pearls	4	F	9	0	2	0	29,004
Dinan (ARG)	6	G	10	2	1	2	50,090
Dindi	3	F	3	0	1	0	6,070
Dine At Tiffany	5	M	6	1	0	1	1,456
Dinero	5	G	12	1	0	0	3,371
Ding Dang Outlaw	5	G	9	2	2	2	22,225
Ding Dong Dandy	2	G	5	3	1	1	32,666
Dingle Bay	2	C	1	0	0	0	0
Dingo Ringo	5	G	11	2	2	2	31,851
Dini Dee	7	M	8	0	0	0	1,791
Dinkers Angel	4	F	12	4	3	1	25,313
Dinkers Cheqmate	5	M	13	1	4	0	10,928
Dinkers Diva	2	F	3	0	0	0	739
Dinkers Forever	3	G	13	1	1	1	7,680
Dinkers Good News	4	G	14	1	5	2	13,501
Dinkers Legend	2	G	3	0	0	1	2,240
Dinkers Pride	4	F	15	1	1	5	9,258
Dinner At Ago's	3	G	12	3	0	1	31,041
Dinner At Arlene's	2	F	1	0	0	0	0
Dinner At Lido's	5	M	8	0	1	0	5,812
Dinner Axe	5	G	3	0	0	0	189
Dinner Band	7	G	11	4	4	0	18,553
Dinner Bound	5	G	7	0	0	0	1,474
Dinner by Moonlite	3	F	6	0	0	1	5,400
Dinner Cider	4	G	7	0	0	0	288
Dinner Date	3	F	9	2	0	1	60,766
Dinner Drums	5	G	15	0	1	1	1,936
Dinner Flight	3	C	21	2	1	3	16,066
Dinner for Sure	4	F	8	2	0	0	6,919
Dinner Mint	3	F	12	3	2	2	25,325
Dinner Soon	5	G	3	0	0	0	186
Dinner Sweets	4	F	17	2	5	5	68,520
Dinner With Ivy	3	F	1	0	1	0	1,440
Dinner Withawinner	4	F	13	1	2	2	21,620
Dinnerathepalms	7	G	9	1	0	0	2,680
Dinnerinoccidental	2	G	3	0	0	0	835
Dinner's On Dom	6	M	3	0	0	0	72
Dino Camino	2	C	12	2	2	2	47,717
Dino the Immigrant	3	G	14	1	1	2	23,907
Dinos Dashofsugar	2	F	3	1	0	0	1,650
Dino's Promise	4	F	1	1	0	0	6,150
Dins Delight	2	C	4	0	0	0	1,128
Din's Dynasty	2	G	1	0	0	0	400
Din's Got Game	5	G	15	2	2	2	12,336
Din's Punch	3	C	3	0	0	0	232
Din's Shadow	2	G	2	0	0	0	600
Dionnah	2	F	2	0	0	0	630
Dio's Pleasure	4	G	3	1	0	1	6,133
Diosa Del Sol	5	M	13	2	2	1	12,179
Dip N Chips	3	F	3	1	2	0	12,238
Diplomat	9	G	15	0	6	2	19,024
Diplomate Girl	5	M	3	0	0	0	0
Diplomatic Agent	3	C	3	1	0	0	17,300
Diplomatic Bag	4	C	1	1	0	0	90,000
Diplomatic Lady	4	F	1	0	0	0	139
Diplomatic Quest	3	F	6	0	1	2	5,550
Diplomatic Ties	4	G	4	0	0	0	520
Diplomatic Woman	2	F	1	0	0	0	0
Diplomatical	7	G	4	1	0	1	6,464
Diplomats Money	6	G	8	1	0	0	5,702
Diplomat's Reward	9	G	13	2	1	1	20,280
Dipper Doos Voyage	5	M	5	0	0	0	0
Dippin At Dawn	3	F	5	0	1	0	1,290
Dipsydoodle Dancer	3	F	9	2	0	0	20,252
Dipthehalk	3	C	6	1	0	0	6,644
Dira Lee	3	F	6	0	0	0	660
Dire Pfeynt	3	F	16	3	2	0	10,875
Direct	5	M	7	2	1	2	49,446
Direct Attack	4	F	7	2	0	1	13,595
Direct Bluff	2	F	1	0	0	0	0
Direct Call	2	C	7	1	2	1	15,410
Direct Charge	8	G	7	0	2	0	3,445
Direct Current	9	G	13	1	0	0	4,993
Direct Gold	5	G	11	0	2	2	8,387
Direct Hamer	3	G	11	3	1	0	11,345
Direct Investment	12	G	5	0	0	0	360
Direct Male	4	G	11	2	2	1	77,420
Direct Reflection	4	G	7	0	0	0	626
Direct Shot	2	F	7	1	3	1	33,462
Direct Target	2	G	1	0	0	0	1,590
Direct the Flag	7	H	4	0	0	0	668
Direct Won	3	G	6	0	0	1	1,607
Directaccess	6	G	7	1	0	2	6,525
Directed Verdict	8	G	3	0	0	0	149
Director of Sports	3	G	2	0	0	0	155
Directors Choice	4	G	13	1	2	1	12,340
Directs Unique One	3	C	4	1	1	0	19,866
Dirt Ball	3	G	10	0	2	0	3,300
Dirt Devil Drew	3	G	11	2	0	1	26,854
Dirt Road	5	H	1	0	0	0	0
Dirt Road Devil	5	G	5	0	0	0	825
Dirtdobler	6	G	14	2	1	3	17,931
Dirty Bird	6	G	12	1	1	2	7,563

RECORDS OF HORSES

Horse	Age	Sex	Sts	1st	2d	3d	Won
Dirty Blonde	5	M	8	0	0	3	4,780
Dirty Diana	3	F	2	0	0	0	800
Dirty Doug	8	G	11	1	0	3	11,582
Dirty Duke	8	G	15	4	3	3	48,983
Dirty Gerdy	5	M	2	0	0	0	64
Dirty Harryette	5	M	12	2	2	1	50,185
Dirty Martini	3	G	7	0	1	2	19,525
Dirty Mike	9	G	4	0	0	0	900
Dirty O Harry	3	G	5	0	0	0	0
Dirty Red	7	G	4	0	0	0	2,760
Dirty Secret	4	F	13	0	1	2	3,298
Dirty Tactics	4	G	3	0	0	0	340
Dirtylittlesecrets	2	F	3	0	0	1	1,570
Dirtymoposse	3	C	19	3	3	2	52,870
Di's Delight	4	F	13	0	1	4	37,406
Di's Last Gift	3	C	13	2	3	0	16,883
Di's Little Guy	4	G	8	1	0	1	3,091
Dis Miss	3	F	9	3	3	0	80,851
Disappearance	6	G	10	1	2	1	9,349
Disappearing	4	G	13	2	2	1	16,355
Disappearing Dan	4	G	14	3	1	2	21,149
Disbelief	3	G	1	0	0	0	135
Discern	3	G	3	2	0	1	26,900
Discernment	4	G	11	3	2	0	21,671
Discipline	7	G	7	0	0	0	780
Disco Belle	3	F	11	0	0	2	2,976
Disco Bull	2	F	1	0	0	0	230
Disco Hope	3	F	6	0	1	1	1,750
Disco John	5	G	6	0	1	1	1,563
Disco Lights	4	C	9	1	1	0	13,176
Disco Pie	2	G	2	0	0	0	1,055
Disco Time	2	F	3	0	0	0	0
Disconect	6	H	2	0	0	0	301
Disconnected	3	F	2	0	0	0	0
Discordant	5	H	1	0	0	0	65
Discos Pearl	6	M	7	0	1	1	5,802
Discounted	3	F	11	1	3	0	34,920
Discounted Dame	3	F	6	0	0	2	4,348
Discover My Dream	3	F	2	0	1	0	2,400
Discover the Glory	4	C	5	1	1	0	34,814
Discover the Irish	3	G	3	0	0	0	0
Discover This	4	G	2	0	0	0	0
Discovering Money	6	G	10	0	1	1	1,955
Discovering You	4	G	12	2	2	4	36,411
Discreet Caper	7	G	10	0	2	0	6,040
Discreet Gal	2	F	7	1	1	2	37,808
Discreet Hero	6	G	11	4	1	2	175,427
Discreet River	3	F	1	0	0	0	60
Discreet Ways	2	G	5	1	1	0	6,175
Discreetly Irish	6	M	10	3	1	2	31,640
Discrete	2	F	3	0	1	0	6,837
Discriminator	3	G	4	0	0	0	875
Disearnment	4	G	7	1	0	2	10,495
Disenfranchised	6	M	11	2	1	3	20,876
Disengage	3	G	6	0	0	0	2,090
Disgruntled	5	G	15	4	2	1	26,121
Disirable Danzig	3	F	8	2	2	0	2,542
Dismissedhertouch	3	F	3	0	0	0	1,549
Disorderly Conduct	3	C	13	0	1	0	4,713
Disorientated Al	6	G	13	0	0	0	1,150
Disperse Gold	6	G	14	3	2	0	11,641
Disputed Intent	5	M	6	1	2	2	5,641
Disqueada (ARG)	9	M	8	0	0	3	1,946
Disrupt	4	F	1	0	0	0	0
Disrupter	2	C	1	0	0	0	0
Disruption	5	G	8	1	3	0	21,947
Distance Power	5	G	10	2	0	0	5,795
Distant Beau	3	F	4	0	0	0	0
Distant Daughter	6	M	9	3	1	1	41,060
Distant Fantasy	4	F	10	2	2	0	43,420
Distant Formation	3	G	5	0	0	0	1,165
Distant Kid	6	G	12	0	0	1	3,045
Distant Kin	6	M	14	1	1	9	7,723
Distant Moon	7	G	9	4	2	1	37,360
Distant Mountain	4	C	6	1	2	2	7,196
Distant Venture	9	G	1	0	0	0	0
Distant Wizard	3	G	14	1	2	3	11,461
Distante	5	H	7	2	0	0	12,438
Distinct Advantage	5	G	8	2	1	1	13,902

Horse	Age	Sex	Sts	1st	2d	3d	Won
Distinct Irish Lad	2	C	3	0	0	0	645
Distinct Power	8	G	2	0	0	0	0
Distinct Rainbow	2	C	3	0	0	1	5,478
Distinct View	2	F	1	0	1	0	4,000
Distinct Vision	4	G	8	1	1	1	46,420
Distinction	5	H	1	0	0	0	380
Distinctive Blues	4	G	9	2	1	0	9,096
Distinctive Cal	5	H	5	0	2	1	4,077
Distinctive Code	5	M	3	0	0	0	0
Distinctive Deed	4	F	13	1	0	2	10,435
Distinctive Devil	4	G	15	3	3	2	18,775
Distinctive Ed	4	G	9	1	5	0	14,280
Distinctive Flyer	5	M	10	2	3	0	29,127
Distinctive Kid	2	G	2	0	0	0	2,170
Distinctive Kitten	4	F	15	3	3	3	145,197
Distinctive Livin	3	F	1	0	0	0	164
Distinctive Melody	4	F	9	2	2	1	14,108
Distinctive Mr. B	8	G	1	0	0	0	220
Distinctive One	6	G	12	1	0	0	2,720
Distinctive Pirate	3	C	1	0	0	0	63
Distinctive Trick	2	C	7	1	0	3	50,452
Distinctively R C	3	G	8	0	1	0	2,318
Distinctly	5	M	8	0	1	1	4,697
Distinctly Carotic	9	G	8	1	0	1	3,200
Distinctly Curious	4	C	6	0	1	1	2,865
Distinctly Perfect	3	G	9	4	2	1	28,052
Distinctly Western	3	C	3	0	0	0	0
Distinguish	3	C	7	1	0	2	13,056
Distinguishable	4	C	1	0	0	1	3,520
Distinguished Gent	4	G	14	0	4	1	28,944
Distorted	2	C	1	1	0	0	11,400
Distorted Cat	4	G	10	0	2	0	12,649
Distorted Humor Jr	4	G	1	0	0	0	0
Distorted Power	7	G	12	2	1	4	52,600
Distorted Rumor	3	C	3	1	1	1	23,385
Distorted Trail	2	F	3	1	0	0	8,540
Distorted Truth	3	F	2	0	0	0	570
Distressed Debt	3	G	8	0	1	1	9,438
Distribute	6	G	11	2	0	0	16,011
District	7	H	2	0	0	0	0
Disturbingthepeace	6	G	2	0	0	0	3,240
Disuasivo (ARG)	4	C	8	0	0	1	4,269
Ditch Digger (ARG)	9	G	10	3	4	0	85,620
Ditka	7	G	16	1	2	1	4,590
Ditto Bro	2	C	1	0	0	1	2,300
Ditty	4	F	7	0	3	0	5,204
Diva Bride	2	F	1	1	0	0	4,200
Diva Del Sol	5	M	2	0	0	0	1,140
Diva Lair A	4	F	3	0	0	0	620
Diva Star	3	F	16	0	1	1	5,630
Dive for Gold	5	H	6	0	0	3	2,173
Diversifieddiamond	3	G	6	0	1	1	3,315
Diversionary	3	G	15	3	3	2	31,704
Divide	3	F	2	0	0	0	92
Divided Nation	4	G	7	2	0	1	7,378
Dividendum	5	G	12	1	3	1	6,790
Divine Addition	3	G	5	0	0	0	1,465
Divine Assurance	5	G	13	0	2	2	6,587
Divine Buck	3	C	9	1	2	2	20,920
Divine Climb	4	F	8	1	1	0	6,800
Divine Dancer	3	G	10	0	4	1	11,160
Divine Ending	3	F	3	0	0	0	349
Divine Hammer	6	G	4	0	1	0	3,380
Divine Hope	4	F	5	2	0	1	37,717
Divine Inspiration	3	C	5	1	0	0	8,600
Divine Lady	3	F	2	0	1	1	13,800
Divine Love	4	F	2	0	0	0	680
Divine Luck	7	H	2	0	0	0	716
Divine Madness	5	G	13	1	1	0	12,797
Divine Mark	2	F	3	1	1	0	16,200
Divine Miss N	3	F	6	1	1	2	6,004
Divine Order	8	G	1	0	0	0	61
Divine Quest	3	C	2	1	1	0	11,827
Divine Right	5	G	8	0	0	0	1,631
Divine Silence	3	G	3	1	1	0	38,400
Divine Spirit	6	H	9	2	2	0	16,503
Divine Touch	3	C	7	1	2	0	62,180
Divine Warrior	3	G	3	0	0	0	0
Divino Blanco	3	G	3	0	0	0	240

Horse	Age	Sex	Sts	1st	2d	3d	Won
Divisional Champ	7	G	7	1	1	1	10,761
Divorce Lawyer Jay	4	G	15	2	2	4	28,424
Divot	7	G	1	0	0	0	70
Divy's Charm	3	F	6	1	0	0	6,913
Dixey Bull	4	G	13	2	1	0	8,707
Dixiana Sky	2	F	4	0	0	2	6,055
Dixie Babie	4	F	7	1	2	0	17,200
Dixie Baghdad	4	G	8	0	0	0	5,495
Dixie Bar the Door	3	F	11	1	2	0	3,802
Dixie Beauty	9	M	4	0	1	0	1,566
Dixie Boom	2	F	2	0	1	0	9,180
Dixie Bound	4	F	12	1	1	1	4,916
Dixie Bourbon	4	C	12	1	7	2	99,080
Dixie Boy	3	C	16	2	3	3	72,480
Dixie Can Can	4	F	9	1	2	3	61,724
Dixie Cheer	3	G	1	0	0	0	840
Dixie Chill	2	F	4	1	0	0	8,687
Dixie Chixie	3	F	6	0	1	1	7,255
Dixie Code Red	4	C	9	1	0	0	12,889
Dixie Coffee	3	G	9	0	1	2	4,722
Dixie Colonel	9	G	1	0	0	0	0
Dixie Colony	4	G	15	5	3	4	92,890
Dixie Colors	3	F	12	2	3	3	22,076
Dixie Cup	4	G	9	0	1	2	14,040
Dixie Dan	3	C	2	0	0	0	250
Dixie Dance	3	F	6	0	0	1	4,100
Dixie Dance Band	8	G	8	2	1	0	4,068
Dixie Decor	3	G	4	0	1	0	4,135
Dixie Deputy	3	G	2	0	0	2	1,800
Dixie Digger	3	F	6	0	0	0	915
Dixie Dos	4	F	2	1	0	0	27,380
Dixie Drifter	7	G	6	1	0	1	1,959
Dixie Drummer	6	G	7	3	1	1	54,170
Dixie Emerald	3	F	5	0	0	0	1,956
Dixie Feline	5	M	18	0	2	3	31,339
Dixie G	5	M	2	0	0	0	0
Dixie Gemstone	2	F	2	1	0	1	17,750
Dixie Heart	3	F	5	1	0	0	3,720
Dixie High	3	F	1	0	0	1	30,000
Dixie Jam	2	F	1	0	0	0	118
Dixie Jane	4	F	7	0	1	1	3,616
Dixie Jazz	4	G	5	0	1	0	1,800
Dixie Jig	4	G	10	3	1	1	14,964
Dixie Kiss	2	F	2	1	1	0	14,604
Dixie Law	8	G	5	0	0	2	16,080
Dixie Legs	3	F	8	0	1	0	2,200
Dixie Mama	3	F	2	0	0	0	0
Dixie Meister	2	G	8	1	0	2	50,150
Dixie Melinda	2	F	2	0	0	0	0
Dixie Miracle	3	G	2	0	0	0	900
Dixie Preacher	4	G	4	2	1	0	62,028
Dixie Pro	3	C	1	0	0	0	162
Dixie Pumpkin	5	G	14	1	5	3	12,561
Dixie Punch	3	F	9	2	1	1	18,174
Dixie Rap	4	G	6	2	0	1	24,780
Dixie Ridge	5	M	5	1	0	0	14,160
Dixie Rocker (NZ)	6	M	9	0	2	2	19,415
Dixie Roll	4	F	10	1	1	0	29,374
Dixie Run	7	H	7	2	1	1	20,730
Dixie Setongo	5	M	4	0	0	0	0
Dixie Slew	2	C	5	0	0	1	10,760
Dixie Soup	4	F	9	0	3	2	38,694
Dixie Stripes	5	G	13	2	3	1	16,914
Dixie Sue	3	F	2	0	0	0	418
Dixie Talking	2	F	2	2	0	0	73,680
Dixie Tea Party	2	F	2	0	0	0	2,160
Dixie Thrill	8	G	13	2	0	4	45,645
Dixie Two Thousand	6	H	10	0	3	1	55,035
Dixie Waltz	3	F	1	0	0	0	1,428
Dixie Whistler	6	G	15	1	3	0	7,579
Dixie Wildcat	2	F	2	0	0	0	0
Dixie Witch	5	M	10	1	1	2	15,909
Dixiecrat	3	F	4	1	0	1	10,225
Dixiedouble	3	G	6	0	0	1	2,485
Dixieland Bear	4	C	8	1	0	0	5,180
Dixieland Cash	2	C	4	1	0	0	5,845
Dixieland Chick	3	F	6	1	0	1	13,685
Dixieland Dixie	3	F	10	1	0	1	11,223
Dixieland Gem	2	F	1	0	0	0	0
Dixieland Gulch	4	F	1	0	0	0	1,800
Dixieland Heater	3	G	5	0	1	0	12,540
Dixieland King	4	C	6	0	0	0	1,893
Dixieland Man	3	C	1	0	0	0	0
Dixieland Moon	4	G	8	1	5	1	13,808
Dixieland Native	2	C	5	1	0	0	4,318
Dixieland Rose	4	F	15	1	4	2	18,627
Dixielandvalentine	6	M	4	0	0	1	829
Dixiemore	7	G	18	3	4	8	76,750
Dixie's Band	6	H	19	3	3	4	27,950
Dixies Eskimo	4	G	6	2	0	0	26,580
Dixie's Hero	4	G	11	2	0	2	35,700
Dixie's Irish	4	G	10	2	1	1	8,290
Dixie's Wild Again	4	C	3	1	1	0	21,710
Dixie's Wolf	2	G	3	1	0	0	11,460
Dixietownlady	6	M	12	1	1	4	12,101
Dixton Boy	5	G	2	0	0	0	90
Diz's World	3	G	2	0	0	0	0
Dizzi Mister Rizzi	4	C	13	2	5	1	24,970
Dizzy Diggy	7	H	2	0	0	0	500
Dizzy Kizzy	3	F	11	0	0	0	3,377
Dizzy Miss Lizzy	5	M	5	0	0	0	356
Dizzy Miss Moore	2	F	1	0	0	0	357
Dizzy Spell	4	C	4	0	1	1	11,070
Django	4	C	1	0	0	0	0
Dj's Baby	3	G	4	0	0	1	5,085
Dj's Bucky Buster	4	G	13	2	2	1	12,764
Dj's Choice	2	C	3	1	1	0	30,440
Dk Gold	3	F	2	0	0	0	1,367
Dlassy Dee	5	M	5	1	0	1	2,582
D'lene's Dream	4	F	1	0	0	0	0
Dmitrilynne	3	F	8	2	0	1	51,513
Dm's Dancing Dolly	6	M	4	1	1	0	3,560
Do Da Princess	2	F	5	0	3	1	21,400
Do I Ever	9	G	2	1	0	0	8,550
Do It Again Bragg	5	G	15	2	2	1	9,882
Do It Again Dad	4	G	2	0	0	0	260
Do It Again Honey	8	M	2	0	0	0	114
Do It Deputy	5	G	18	0	1	2	7,607
Do It Girl	8	M	2	0	0	2	946
Do Mark	5	M	11	2	2	1	11,735
Do Me a Favor	2	F	1	0	0	0	125
Do My Thing	3	F	4	0	0	0	760
Do N Time	6	G	15	0	2	0	2,777
Do No Wrong	3	F	14	2	0	2	42,820
Do Not Pass	4	F	12	1	0	2	8,890
Do Run Run	2	C	9	1	1	2	27,510
Do That Again	3	F	11	1	2	2	13,519
Do the Boogie	3	C	2	0	0	0	410
Do the Dance	5	M	1	0	0	0	43
Do the Deal	3	G	13	2	3	1	20,469
Do the Due	3	C	4	0	0	0	0
Do the Impossible	3	G	13	4	1	3	56,458
Do the Wave	2	G	1	0	0	1	2,860
Do This Do That	4	G	10	1	2	1	13,207
Do Tri	4	C	3	0	0	0	1,263
Do Udo Voodoo	3	F	4	1	0	0	7,825
Do You Love It	3	F	1	0	0	0	0
Do You Say	6	G	2	0	0	0	292
Dobbie Joe	9	G	4	0	0	0	522
Dobbins Fuego	2	C	6	0	0	1	605
Dobbins Halo	2	F	10	0	3	3	9,940
Dobies Little Girl	5	M	14	2	3	2	23,483
Doble Aguila (CHI)	7	G	15	3	3	0	13,708
Doc Art	9	G	14	1	2	1	5,354
Doc Baker's Charm	3	G	10	2	0	2	39,203
Doc Benson	3	G	7	2	1	1	14,658
Doc Byar	3	G	3	0	0	0	935
Doc Cain	4	C	12	0	3	0	13,170
Doc Camp	3	C	3	0	0	0	0
Doc Carson	2	G	1	1	0	0	19,380
Doc D	5	G	11	2	5	1	120,880
Doc Fever	2	G	2	0	0	0	410
Doc Holiday (IRE)	5	H	4	0	2	1	26,860
Doc Jamnani	4	C	1	0	0	0	65
Doc Knows Best	5	M	1	0	0	0	450
Doc Malagar	3	G	10	1	0	2	26,392
Doc Murdock	11	G	7	3	0	1	5,368
Doc N Jag	6	G	11	1	2	2	14,323

Horse	Age	Sex	Sts	1st	2d	3d	Won
Doc Pepper	5	G	5	0	0	0	342
Doc Putnam	4	C	7	1	0	0	3,684
Doc Raider	3	G	2	0	0	0	1,215
Doc Robbins	4	C	4	0	0	0	1,020
Doc Ron	7	G	9	1	0	2	5,995
Doc Roshon	4	C	8	2	0	0	5,529
Doc Safari	6	G	16	1	2	2	14,887
Doc Senter	6	G	17	1	2	2	14,030
Doc Shawk	3	G	7	0	1	1	3,200
Doc Tanner	3	G	2	0	0	0	84
Doc Taught Me	3	C	2	0	0	0	0
Doc Torry	3	G	12	2	2	0	15,022
Doc Wallace	5	G	9	0	2	1	5,891
Doc Wild	5	G	10	2	0	2	28,430
Doc Zotti	6	G	4	0	0	0	0
Docalot	3	C	5	2	1	0	17,670
Doce Memoria	3	F	11	5	2	1	25,927
Docent	6	G	8	1	3	0	62,188
Docket	4	F	3	0	1	0	5,168
Doclange	3	C	7	0	0	3	1,360
Doc's Affair	5	H	8	1	2	2	5,360
Doc's Allowance	5	G	5	0	1	0	3,220
Doc's Avenger	3	G	3	0	0	0	300
Doc's Belle	3	F	2	0	0	0	750
Doc's Blaze	4	F	10	2	0	2	12,970
Docs Boy	8	G	2	0	0	0	0
Doc's Bratt	3	F	7	3	1	1	11,189
Doc's Classy Ack	3	F	1	0	0	0	1,000
Doc's Dingo	7	G	3	0	0	0	0
Doc's Doll	4	F	7	2	0	0	51,500
Doc's Fourth Girl	2	F	2	0	0	1	4,145
Doc's Golden Bear	8	H	19	1	3	4	11,940
Doc's Got Game	7	G	3	0	0	0	468
Docs Gotta Wish	7	G	4	0	2	0	1,522
Doc's Honey	5	M	4	1	0	0	11,216
Doc's In	7	G	17	3	2	3	28,707
Doc's Jewel	5	G	13	4	1	1	23,249
Doc's Knot	7	M	2	0	0	0	0
Doc's Last Moment	3	F	6	0	0	0	3,900
Doc's Last Shot	10	G	3	0	0	0	288
Doc's Legacy	3	F	5	0	0	0	310
Doc's Legency	6	M	12	2	3	3	21,057
Doc's Legend	3	C	2	0	0	0	0
Doc's Lil' Angel	5	M	4	0	1	0	5,700
Doc's Lil Secret	6	G	3	0	0	0	0
Doc's Magic Dream	9	G	2	0	0	0	80
Docs Oliver	4	G	9	0	1	1	3,607
Doc's Option	4	G	12	3	4	1	37,070
Docs Plan	9	G	5	0	0	0	453
Docs Puddin	6	M	6	0	0	0	3,294
Doc's Rasheed	7	G	8	1	1	1	2,736
Doc's Redhead	4	F	8	0	0	0	815
Doc's Rock	4	F	2	0	0	0	0
Doc's Treasure	5	M	20	4	5	3	35,333
Docs Tyrant	6	H	11	5	1	2	14,260
Doctor America	4	F	10	3	1	3	37,979
Doctor Attitude	2	C	3	0	0	0	8,932
Doctor Bob D	2	G	1	0	0	0	140
Doctor D. K.	9	G	8	1	0	0	7,638
Doctor Doctor Mrmd	4	C	6	1	0	0	8,217
Doctor Dragon	5	G	11	4	5	0	29,700
Doctor Free	4	F	3	2	1	0	12,495
Doctor Fun	3	G	4	0	0	0	415
Doctor Hilary	4	F	6	0	1	2	6,312
Doctor J. R.	3	G	5	0	0	0	296
Doctor Jalili	4	C	3	0	1	0	9,890
Doctor Jane	3	F	2	0	0	0	290
Doctor Jenkins	2	C	1	0	0	0	480
Doctor John	10	G	9	0	0	0	629
Doctor Kananga (IRE)	2	G	5	1	0	1	14,753
Doctor Mike	7	H	4	0	1	0	9,150
Doctor My Eyes	3	F	6	1	0	1	16,660
Doctor Price	4	G	10	1	0	0	7,294
Doctor Rio	3	G	9	3	1	0	21,549
Doctor Rock	3	C	2	1	0	1	16,560
Doctor Ron	2	C	1	0	0	0	0
Doctor Ted	4	C	2	0	1	0	12,320
Doctor Turko	4	G	16	2	5	3	35,745
Doctor Voodoo	2	C	7	3	1	2	109,745
Doctor Who	4	C	10	1	0	1	28,400
Doctor Wilhelm	3	C	5	2	0	0	9,900
Doctor Woodson	2	G	1	0	0	0	0
Doctor Zaid	4	C	3	0	1	1	1,829
Doctorinthehouse	5	G	5	3	0	0	35,772
Doctorinthenews	2	F	3	0	0	0	762
Document Express	4	G	14	0	2	1	6,330
Documento	9	G	11	1	0	2	5,978
Documoments	4	F	15	1	4	3	13,474
Dodd	3	F	9	2	2	1	26,500
Doddles	2	G	3	1	0	1	19,530
Dodge City Annie	5	M	10	0	1	0	1,864
Dodge City Girl	4	F	9	3	3	0	22,072
Dodge Me Dove	3	C	3	0	2	0	7,715
Dodgers Island	7	H	2	0	0	0	0
Dodgeville	4	C	6	0	0	1	3,710
Dodi N Me	3	F	21	2	0	1	18,720
Doeny	6	H	6	0	1	0	8,272
Doeny's Doe Boy	2	G	4	0	0	0	540
Doeny's Sparkle	2	F	6	1	1	0	20,392
Doesn't Suit	4	F	6	0	0	1	517
Doey Wild	4	F	12	0	3	1	19,455
Dofomi	2	F	1	0	0	0	0
Dog Days	5	G	3	0	0	1	4,840
Dog Gone Lucky	3	G	13	1	3	2	35,750
Dog House	5	G	5	0	0	1	3,914
Dog Red	3	G	7	0	0	1	1,761
Dog Tags	7	H	6	2	0	1	19,631
Doghouse Dave	2	G	2	0	0	1	2,680
Dogleg Left	3	C	10	0	2	0	4,675
Dogonstormy	3	C	3	0	0	0	480
D'ohana (ARG)	6	M	8	1	2	0	41,860
Doin Dixie	4	G	12	0	1	4	8,745
Doin' Wheelies	7	G	2	0	0	0	0
Doing It Our Way	3	F	13	1	1	3	31,990
Doingtime	3	F	4	0	0	0	1,710
Doinit My Way	4	G	2	0	0	0	0
Doinitforpleasure	9	G	10	2	4	1	13,735
Doitdoitdoit	5	M	8	1	1	2	4,240
Dolce Diva	2	F	7	0	2	0	16,055
Dolce Latte	3	F	9	1	0	0	4,308
Dolcetta	4	F	11	1	2	2	14,453
Doll and a Half	2	F	5	1	1	1	25,625
Doll Gift	4	F	2	0	0	0	122
Doll Lure	2	F	2	0	0	0	500
Dollar a Dip	3	C	6	0	0	1	8,945
Dollar a Minute	5	M	2	1	1	0	9,680
Dollar Core	6	G	14	2	3	1	8,242
Dollar Diplomacy	4	G	3	0	0	0	370
Dollar for Dollar	4	G	19	2	1	5	39,468
Dollar Pete	4	G	4	1	0	0	2,520
Dollars and Sense	13	G	6	0	0	0	560
Dollarwatchcrosing	3	G	6	0	1	1	695
Dolliver Park	3	G	3	0	0	0	0
Dolljeta	5	M	9	0	0	2	3,592
Dolly	2	F	4	0	0	0	702
Dolly Dame	4	F	10	0	0	1	1,689
Dolly Does Tricks	2	F	1	0	0	0	140
Dolly M	5	M	4	0	0	0	157
Dolly Wells (ARG)	4	F	5	0	2	2	30,080
Dolly's Castle	3	F	8	1	0	1	3,840
Dolly's Cruiser	3	F	2	0	0	0	1,098
Dollys Renegade	7	G	7	0	0	0	1,027
Dolly's Wager	6	M	15	2	1	4	44,094
Dolpheen	3	F	1	0	0	0	168
Dolphin Band	4	F	4	0	0	3	14,910
Dolphin Star	4	F	3	0	0	0	786
Dolvotto	6	H	3	0	0	0	215
Domandi	2	F	2	0	0	0	200
Domasca Sports	6	M	4	0	0	1	1,903
Domascas Consort	3	G	10	2	0	1	78,873
Domestic Arts	2	F	6	0	1	2	13,467
Domestic Crime	4	G	1	0	0	0	250
Domestic Dispute	4	C	7	1	2	0	413,428
Domestic Security	2	G	1	0	0	0	400
Dominant Diva	3	F	2	0	0	2	4,410
Dominant Package	4	G	1	0	0	1	600
Dominant Punch B B	4	G	9	0	0	0	1,232
Dominant's Man	5	H	8	0	1	1	1,170

Horse	Age	Sex	Sts	1st	2d	3d	Won
Dominate Jolie	3	F	14	1	3	1	11,690
Dominated Day	5	G	13	3	4	3	35,435
Dominated Girl	4	F	4	0	3	1	12,120
Dominating	3	F	7	1	1	0	20,355
Domingo Juan (ARG)	6	G	10	2	1	2	69,300
Dominican Doctor	4	G	3	0	0	1	1,829
Dominican Waltz	5	H	7	1	0	1	10,091
Dominiques Darling	3	F	4	1	0	0	33,835
Dominus	7	G	6	1	1	0	4,208
Domnonia	7	M	9	0	1	1	5,421
Dom's Destiny	3	F	6	0	1	1	2,922
Dom's Little Girl	3	F	16	1	1	0	10,243
Domybadpartnerin	2	C	1	0	0	0	0
Don Agustin	2	C	4	0	1	0	3,200
Don Amin	5	H	4	1	0	0	8,620
Don Corleone	3	C	9	2	1	0	137,848
Don Double D	7	G	22	2	5	3	11,179
Don E Looker	7	G	7	1	0	1	6,584
Don Fernando (MEX)	4	C	9	1	2	1	6,757
Don Golden (MEX)	9	G	9	1	0	1	5,667
Don Hector	4	G	10	3	2	0	26,890
Don Kruse	4	G	11	1	0	1	6,566
Don Luis Felipe	4	G	4	1	0	0	13,308
Don Manuel	3	C	16	1	4	2	51,220
Don Pan	6	G	10	2	4	1	13,326
Don Peppe the Man	3	G	3	1	0	0	5,255
Don Peppino	3	G	7	1	0	2	12,568
Don Peso	2	F	9	0	1	1	10,400
Don Salomon	2	C	4	0	0	1	3,100
Don Six	4	C	11	4	1	2	218,733
Don Taco	3	G	10	1	0	1	3,206
Don the Cookster	6	G	13	1	1	2	16,516
Don Tiger (ARG)	4	C	5	0	0	0	690
Don Veran (ARG)	6	H	7	0	1	1	9,215
Don Wilson	4	G	4	0	1	0	4,036
Dona Bay	2	F	2	1	0	0	9,750
Dona Dance	3	G	4	1	0	0	8,745
Dona Goyita (CHI)	6	M	6	0	0	1	9,880
Dona Ridge	6	M	6	2	0	0	7,538
Donaho Dancer	9	G	5	0	0	0	0
Donald David	4	G	5	0	0	1	3,860
Donald Do Right	5	G	13	2	2	2	23,553
Donald Notrump	7	G	6	0	0	0	1,068
Donald's Creek	2	C	2	0	0	0	645
Donald's Pride	4	C	7	0	3	1	53,880
Donald's Tomorrow	7	G	1	0	0	0	0
Donaren	2	F	2	0	1	0	5,000
Donchalisentoumdun	10	G	5	1	0	1	3,620
Donde Estaras	4	F	16	3	3	4	44,010
Dondi	3	G	4	1	1	0	11,357
Done Deal	2	C	6	0	1	0	2,695
Done Dreaming	10	G	12	1	0	0	3,020
Done Slew's Way	3	C	5	0	0	1	2,870
Done With Class	3	F	7	0	0	1	3,950
Donebroke	5	M	1	0	0	0	498
Donegal Lady	3	F	2	0	0	0	800
Doneit	2	C	4	0	1	0	1,595
Doneraile Gal	2	F	6	1	0	0	24,765
Doniphan	8	G	3	0	0	0	412
Donivan's Trick	4	G	18	3	0	2	16,080
Donizetti	4	G	10	2	1	3	28,957
Donizetti (IRE)	4	C	3	0	0	0	540
Donna C	5	M	13	0	2	4	19,225
Donna Jean	5	M	2	0	0	0	75
Donna Lynn	6	M	3	0	0	0	0
Donna Royalle	5	M	9	2	5	1	41,954
Donnagle Bay	3	C	2	0	0	1	649
Donnalark	5	M	1	0	0	0	97
Donnas Destiny	4	F	7	2	1	1	20,894
Donna's Dream	4	F	2	0	0	0	0
Donna's Fantasy	3	F	1	0	0	0	95
Donna's Gem	3	F	14	3	2	0	20,720
Donna's Golddigger	4	G	11	1	0	0	11,580
Donna's Hope	3	F	7	2	0	1	17,979
Donna's Link	6	M	9	2	0	1	15,170
Donna's Mailbag	5	G	2	0	0	2	8,470
Donnas Trial	3	F	12	0	0	6	21,330
Donna's Vaudeville	3	F	2	0	0	0	0
Donner Pass	3	F	3	1	0	1	10,800
Donner Queen	3	F	10	1	1	1	3,256
Donnies Pick	5	G	7	0	3	3	18,053
Donnies Pride	2	C	1	0	0	0	0
Donny	4	G	10	1	2	2	14,450
Donny Boy	4	G	8	1	1	1	18,055
Donnybrook Joy	2	C	4	0	0	0	286
Donnybrook Pride	2	C	7	1	2	1	56,700
Donnys Dimund Slew	5	H	7	0	1	2	2,881
Donovan Scores	6	G	13	2	4	1	7,357
Don's Dreamcatcher	5	H	4	0	0	0	663
Dons Hope	4	G	1	0	0	0	140
Dons Mobil	2	G	2	0	0	0	210
Don's Nell	5	M	6	0	0	2	3,137
Don's Prospector	6	G	12	2	0	0	16,791
Don's Reggin	4	F	2	0	0	0	0
Don's Revenge	4	G	1	0	1	0	1,500
Don't Agitate	4	G	12	3	4	1	30,705
Don't Back Down	3	G	8	1	0	2	4,318
Don't Be Concerned	2	F	3	0	1	0	6,540
Don't Be Cruel	4	G	7	0	2	0	9,960
Don't Be Late Jake	9	G	3	0	0	0	0
Don't Be Long Z	8	G	4	1	0	0	16,305
Dont Bother Me Now	5	G	6	1	0	1	6,206
Don't Call Me Baby	4	F	12	2	2	1	45,608
Don't Call Mom	2	F	1	0	0	0	306
Don't Catch Me	5	M	10	0	0	0	2,798
Don't Chequer	3	F	5	0	1	0	1,860
Don't Cross Granny	2	G	1	0	0	0	420
Don't Cross Us	2	C	2	0	0	0	880
Don't Cry for Me	5	H	1	0	0	1	3,360
Don't Do It	4	F	11	1	1	0	11,686
Don't Get Mad	2	C	2	2	0	0	60,290
Don't Hang Up	5	G	12	3	4	1	14,603
Don't Hesitate Boy	5	H	2	0	0	0	332
Dont Hold Me Down	5	G	4	0	0	0	0
Don't Holler	5	G	8	2	2	1	16,530
Don't Ignore Her	7	M	7	2	2	0	10,949
Don't Ignore Me	2	F	2	0	0	0	870
Don't Kiss N Tell	5	H	9	0	2	3	15,372
Dont Knock America	3	C	16	3	5	3	147,565
Don't Knock Tap	3	F	4	1	2	0	23,000
Don't Know Diddley	3	G	11	3	1	1	37,485
Dont Know Jack	3	G	2	0	0	0	273
Dont Make Me Blush	3	F	4	1	0	2	9,350
Don't Miss Imie	10	M	1	0	0	0	41
Don't Not	7	G	12	2	2	0	17,305
Don't Pali Me	4	G	1	0	0	0	0
Dont Pay the Bill	3	F	6	0	1	0	3,040
Don't Peek	4	G	4	0	0	0	362
Don't Quit On Me	6	G	11	0	2	2	4,504
Dont Run Back	4	F	5	1	1	1	5,870
Dont Run Getthegun	7	M	12	0	0	1	3,442
Dont Say No Sierra	2	F	5	3	1	0	57,250
Don't Seven Out	8	G	2	0	0	0	568
Don't Step Back	5	M	10	0	3	1	7,852
Don't Stop Now	4	F	5	0	0	1	1,305
Don't Strike Out	4	G	11	4	2	0	42,342
Don't Sugah Me	4	F	9	1	0	2	12,960
Don't Tell Aly	5	M	1	0	0	0	100
Don't Tell Ashlie	3	F	5	1	1	0	40,480
Don't Tell Harry	2	F	3	0	0	0	990
Dont Tell Jac	4	C	6	1	0	0	18,435
Don't Tell Lisa	6	M	6	0	1	2	890
Don't Tell Mom	4	F	14	2	3	1	29,650
Don't Tell Nina	7	M	1	0	0	0	750
Don't Tell Papa	4	F	13	3	1	0	33,220
Dont Tell the Kids	7	G	9	1	1	1	14,520
Don't Tell Tina	2	F	1	1	0	0	7,200
Don't Tell Wendy	4	F	11	0	0	3	6,140
Don't Touch	6	G	2	0	0	0	114
Don't Tread On Me	3	C	10	1	1	2	18,402
Don't Trick Me	9	G	1	0	0	0	61
Don't Walk At Nite	8	H	1	0	0	0	146
Dont Ya Like Dat	4	G	7	0	0	0	535
Don't You Know	4	F	2	0	0	0	293
Don'takememints	3	F	12	1	3	1	14,085
Don'taskdon'ttell	4	G	5	0	1	1	4,220
Dontaskwhy	3	G	12	1	1	1	5,269
Dontbeabully	2	C	5	0	0	0	930

Horse	Age	Sex	Sts	1st	2d	3d	Won
D[illegible]botherknocking	6	C	[illegible]	3	1	0	68,040
Don'tcallmeacowb[illegible]	9	H	7	0	1	0	3,795
D[illegible]ledirt	2	G	5	1	0	1	15,807
Don'tcallmefrisco	3	C	13	1	1	4	37,335
Dontcallmeillcallu	2	F	6	0	2	2	4,005
Dontcloseyoureyes	3	C	7	1	2	1	25,430
Dontcounthimout	7	G	6	1	2	0	9,635
Don'tdropthebacon	3	G	2	0	0	0	0
Don'tforgetthememo	3	G	3	0	1	0	2,280
Dontgethuffy	3	G	5	0	1	2	5,747
Donthatetheplayer	5	G	16	2	0	0	16,097
Dontjazzmearound	4	G	5	1	1	1	4,320
Dontmesswithbill	5	H	6	0	0	1	2,448
Don'tmindifido	5	G	9	0	0	0	659
Don'tplaywithfire	4	G	4	0	0	0	0
Dontsayaword	4	F	10	0	0	0	768
Don'tsellmeshort	3	C	9	0	2	1	107,970
Dontshootthemsngr	2	C	3	2	0	0	19,833
Don'ttrapthemouse	5	G	13	1	1	2	6,029
Don'twritemeoff	2	C	1	0	0	0	440
Donut Beat All	8	G	11	2	1	1	5,147
Donut Dipper	3	F	4	0	0	1	1,529
Donuts Tomorrow	6	M	8	3	0	3	16,325
Donz Jade	2	C	1	0	0	0	0
Donzroar	4	G	23	3	8	3	17,795
Doo Da Do	4	C	4	0	0	0	1,361
Doodle Gal	3	F	5	0	1	1	5,412
Doogielosthismind	6	G	12	1	2	3	13,222
Doolittle Jen	3	F	2	0	0	0	0
Doolittleguinevere	5	M	2	0	0	0	0
Doomsday D.	7	G	7	1	3	2	14,442
Doonboy	2	C	4	0	0	0	0
Door to Houston	3	G	4	1	1	0	20,100
Doorcrasher	3	F	10	2	1	1	14,384
Doots	3	F	2	0	0	2	2,665
Doppio	2	C	2	0	1	1	11,200
Doppler Radar	5	G	9	4	2	2	49,830
Dor V Dor	4	G	2	2	0	0	27,000
Dorado Rules	4	G	11	2	1	3	7,470
Doral Dancer	2	F	3	1	0	0	27,750
Doran	10	H	2	0	0	0	766
Dora's Girl	3	F	3	0	0	1	2,701
Dorcheat Captain	2	C	2	0	0	0	0
Dorchester County	3	G	7	0	3	0	22,200
Dorel	7	M	5	0	0	0	585
Dorella	3	F	6	1	1	1	24,840
Dorisee	4	F	14	1	2	1	11,253
Dormella	3	F	1	0	0	0	0
Doro's Don Juan	2	C	2	0	1	1	4,450
Doro's Pet Cat	3	C	4	0	0	1	990
Dorothy's It	2	F	7	0	0	0	905
Dorsey	4	G	7	1	1	2	4,710
Dorst	3	G	15	6	2	2	116,300
Dorsy Champ	5	G	18	1	1	2	9,856
Dorthys Champ	3	G	8	2	2	0	25,280
Dorus Daymaker	6	M	4	0	1	0	900
Dos Amigos	7	G	5	1	1	1	10,870
Do's Buckshot	6	G	2	0	1	1	5,250
Dos de Mayo	3	G	5	0	0	1	6,425
Dos Deals	6	M	5	2	0	2	18,730
Dos Reyes	4	C	2	0	2	0	2,040
Dossier	3	F	2	1	0	0	14,100
Dot	6	M	3	0	0	1	2,300
Dot Come On	2	F	4	0	0	0	414
Dot the Page	4	F	11	3	2	1	20,925
Dot Your I's	2	F	1	0	0	0	103
Dotabar	9	G	3	0	0	1	1,430
Dotage	6	H	5	1	0	0	7,760
Dotar Sojet	6	G	2	0	0	0	200
Dotcode	5	G	3	0	0	0	143
Dothan	3	C	9	0	0	0	2,409
Dothedevilin	5	G	9	0	1	0	1,262
Dotheminer'sdance	2	C	2	0	0	0	0
Dothewildthing	3	G	12	2	2	3	43,915
Dot's Candyman	7	H	4	0	1	0	546
Dots Cove	8	G	10	0	0	0	2,224
Dots N Dashes	5	M	8	0	1	0	2,841
Dotsie's Choice	5	M	7	0	0	0	242
Dotted Swiss	4	F	13	2	0	0	18,180
Dottheiinpete	3	G	10	2	3	0	10,882
Dottie Booth	2	F	5	0	1	1	16,650
Dottie Mae	2	F	6	2	0	2	15,015
Dottie Poo	3	F	11	3	1	1	24,793
Dottie's Pick	2	F	2	1	0	0	11,150
Dou Temps	3	C	5	2	1	0	15,464
Double Affair	10	G	14	3	2	2	30,953
Double Again	4	C	8	1	1	1	18,655
Double Airs	4	G	13	1	2	2	6,724
Double Banner	2	C	1	0	0	0	1,560
Double Barrell	6	G	10	1	1	0	5,851
Double Bars	4	G	5	0	0	0	138
Double Belvedere	3	G	3	0	0	0	1,825
Double Bid	4	G	10	1	1	1	8,638
Double Bling	3	F	10	0	0	0	938
Double Blue	8	G	12	1	6	1	24,210
Double Brite	4	F	6	1	0	0	3,726
Double Bucks G H S	7	G	1	0	0	0	40
Double Buy Buy	5	H	1	0	0	0	47
Double Candi	4	F	11	1	1	0	9,816
Double Cannon	3	F	7	1	1	0	12,080
Double Checker	2	C	1	0	0	0	0
Double Chocolate	5	H	13	1	4	1	31,130
Double Click	4	G	14	1	3	3	10,042
Double Coast	3	F	2	0	0	0	185
Double Cola	6	G	11	3	0	3	27,880
Double Commotion	3	F	1	0	0	0	0
Double Conquest	8	G	14	0	2	2	5,738
Double Covey	3	F	8	2	4	1	28,715
Double Crossed	4	C	8	0	0	1	3,165
Double Cupcake	4	F	1	0	0	0	0
Double D Appeal	2	F	3	2	0	1	73,530
Double D Glo	2	G	2	0	1	0	7,275
Double D Money	3	G	10	1	4	1	14,570
Double D Rocks	2	G	3	0	0	1	3,899
Double 'd' Special	3	F	7	1	2	1	25,914
Double Dance	3	F	4	0	1	0	5,600
Double Demons	10	G	4	0	0	0	134
Double Diamond Joe	3	G	12	0	0	0	1,213
Double Didgit Baby	3	F	13	2	0	1	15,932
Double Digit	5	M	10	2	0	2	24,057
Double Doc	4	G	8	1	2	0	27,088
Double Dog Dare Ya	5	G	10	1	0	1	7,916
Double Dose	2	F	1	0	0	0	0
Double Down	3	C	9	2	0	0	20,486
Double Down On Red	4	F	6	0	0	0	400
Double Dreamin Deb	7	M	16	1	4	2	13,940
Double Duces	5	G	2	1	1	0	3,120
Double E Double L	4	C	18	2	2	1	15,092
Double Exuberance	11	G	10	2	0	2	11,047
Double Fly Pass	7	G	13	5	2	2	44,497
Double Foreigner	7	G	2	1	1	0	17,700
Double Freeze	4	F	13	0	1	0	3,795
Double Glitter	3	F	3	0	1	0	3,374
Double Gone	7	G	3	0	0	0	0
Double Good Lookin	3	G	14	2	0	0	8,326
Double Grace	4	G	13	1	1	4	11,502
Double Halo	4	F	5	0	0	1	3,970
Double Hat Trick	7	M	15	1	4	1	20,733
Double Haul	3	G	2	0	0	0	310
Double Hi	7	M	6	0	0	1	2,349
Double House	3	C	3	0	0	0	2,400
Double Impact	3	C	12	0	1	0	3,597
Double Intrigue	4	G	3	0	0	0	463
Double It	9	H	8	0	0	3	2,129
Double J Ranch	4	G	15	1	4	1	14,544
Double Jab	13	G	5	0	0	1	538
Double Jack	8	G	8	1	0	1	2,993
Double Jeopardy	3	F	2	0	0	0	1,422
Double Jim	2	G	1	0	0	0	300
Double Justice	3	C	1	0	0	0	94
Double Lee	4	G	11	1	1	1	7,180
Double Legacy	3	F	3	0	0	2	1,855
Double Life	4	G	14	4	1	2	59,722
Double Lock	3	F	8	0	2	1	27,190
Double Luck	3	G	20	2	3	5	44,360
Double Lyph	3	F	4	0	2	0	8,138
Double Matrix	2	C	6	0	0	0	1,260
Double Milion	4	G	6	1	0	0	3,290

Horse	Age	Sex	Sts	1st	2d	3d	Won
Double My Prospect	5	H	10	1	0	0	6,074
Double No	2	C	2	1	0	0	9,420
Double O One	3	G	3	0	1	0	600
Double O Special	4	G	15	0	2	1	3,969
Double Option	5	G	6	1	1	2	20,080
Double Oxygen	4	G	9	0	1	0	2,359
Double Platinum	9	G	10	1	0	1	7,546
Double Play	6	G	9	0	1	1	5,190
Double Portage	3	F	3	0	0	0	275
Double Powder	5	G	12	0	3	0	5,448
Double Quack	5	M	6	1	1	1	26,400
Double Reel Blaze	3	G	12	1	1	1	3,857
Double Reward	4	F	7	0	0	2	1,650
Double Ridge	3	F	3	1	1	0	7,260
Double Scoop	4	F	4	1	0	0	25,500
Double Seeded	4	G	12	2	4	1	20,345
Double Shotgun	3	G	5	1	1	0	23,515
Double Six	7	H	2	0	0	0	0
Double Slam	4	G	10	1	1	1	15,072
Double Snip	6	G	8	0	0	1	1,363
Double Spark	3	G	6	1	1	2	17,601
Double Sweet	3	F	3	0	0	2	2,910
Double Talk	4	G	2	0	0	0	0
Double Talkin	8	M	8	2	1	1	28,115
Double the Bucks	4	G	5	0	0	2	1,927
Double the Day	2	F	1	0	0	0	0
Double the Magic	3	C	7	1	0	0	13,140
Double the Speed	3	G	10	0	1	1	3,640
Double Time	6	G	11	5	1	1	13,100
Double Tower	6	G	11	1	1	3	7,692
Double U Dee	2	C	3	0	0	0	1,512
Double Warrior	4	G	5	0	0	0	689
Double Your Will	7	G	10	0	0	5	2,689
Doubleback	4	G	4	1	1	0	12,100
Doubledar Diamond	9	G	2	0	0	0	1,188
Doubledigitdomedog	5	G	16	1	4	4	8,261
Doubledriven	6	H	1	0	0	0	0
Doublerodeo	3	F	6	1	0	1	31,310
Doubleroni	5	M	1	0	0	0	0
Doubletrouble Bear	4	F	6	0	0	1	1,474
Doubly Appealing	2	F	1	0	0	0	460
Doubly Brite	6	G	4	0	0	0	3,540
Doubly Clever	2	G	2	0	0	0	166
Doubly Fortunate	3	F	4	0	0	0	4,147
Doubly Hard	3	G	6	2	2	0	48,585
Doubly Irish	4	F	4	1	0	1	19,874
Doubt Her Not	5	M	3	0	0	0	610
Doubtful Diva	4	F	13	0	4	1	18,437
Doubtful Escapade	3	F	2	1	0	0	2,562
Douceur	4	G	10	0	1	3	18,109
Doug the Slug	7	G	10	0	1	0	2,870
Dough Girl	5	M	13	0	2	2	6,835
Doughty	5	M	6	2	1	0	20,820
Douglas	5	G	4	0	0	0	813
Doug's Glory	5	M	4	0	0	0	186
Doug's Lad	5	G	12	0	2	2	14,205
Doug's Prospect	3	C	8	2	1	0	13,935
Doug's Shadow	9	G	7	0	1	1	8,057
Doust (FR)	4	G	4	1	0	0	17,562
Doux Slew	5	G	4	0	0	1	5,980
Douxrah	3	F	5	0	1	1	15,100
Dove Above	4	G	6	0	2	2	16,400
Dove Creek	6	M	9	3	0	0	22,069
Dove Field	3	F	7	1	1	1	8,275
Dove in Flight	5	M	11	2	3	1	5,098
Dove Love	3	C	9	0	2	1	11,660
Dove Mountain	3	G	13	2	1	1	16,458
Dovedale	4	F	11	0	2	2	7,565
Doveena	5	M	7	1	1	0	2,060
Dover Dere	2	C	6	2	0	3	88,618
Dover Queen	4	F	6	0	1	1	6,875
Dovesahighnote	4	F	2	0	0	1	1,680
Dovetail	5	M	2	0	0	1	693
Dovishness	3	F	6	4	0	0	38,300
Down and Locked	4	C	1	0	0	0	49
Down and Out	7	G	9	0	1	2	1,702
Down by the Sea	3	F	3	0	0	1	3,740
Down Hill Racer	8	G	2	0	1	0	8,032
Down in the Dirt	5	G	18	1	2	3	16,775
Down Music Lane	2	C	2	0	0	1	770
Down Play	4	G	5	0	0	0	233
Down Right Crafty	3	F	1	0	0	0	0
Down Set Hut	3	C	4	1	0	0	8,700
Down the Canyon	5	G	5	3	0	1	10,270
Down the Creek	3	F	5	0	0	2	1,250
Down the Nile	4	F	1	0	0	0	135
Down the Runway	2	F	4	1	0	1	11,565
Down the Shore	6	G	9	1	1	2	27,681
Down to Dixie	3	F	4	2	1	0	30,806
Down Up	3	G	13	3	3	2	29,383
Downhill Champ	2	F	4	0	1	1	12,560
Downhill Skier	3	F	12	1	0	3	8,673
Downing's Joker	7	G	12	3	3	3	13,824
Downthehill	2	R	9	1	1	1	22,520
Downthelane Ayeeee	2	C	1	0	0	0	0
Downtheroadinstyle	6	M	13	0	0	0	1,016
Downthestretch Doc	4	F	4	0	0	0	0
Downtime	4	G	11	1	2	2	28,740
Downtomylastbuck	4	G	7	2	3	0	27,530
Downtown Event	3	F	12	1	0	2	11,303
Downtown Fresno	2	F	6	0	0	1	4,245
Downtown Girl	4	F	7	0	1	0	1,095
Downtown Golfer	3	G	11	3	1	1	30,530
Downtown Huron	2	F	4	0	0	2	6,315
Downtown Johnny	4	G	6	1	0	0	8,320
Downtown Kid	4	G	3	1	0	0	2,400
Downtown Laddie	6	G	1	0	0	0	50
Downtown Man	4	G	9	2	1	1	10,389
Downtown Suzie	3	F	10	0	0	0	918
Downtown Willy	3	G	13	0	0	1	4,809
Downtownsundown	2	F	2	0	0	1	4,264
Downtownwillybrown	5	G	7	0	0	4	1,357
Downunderthunder (GB)	3	F	4	0	2	0	7,011
Dowry	4	F	4	1	1	0	27,330
Doxologist	3	F	8	2	1	0	17,315
Doyanoyet	3	G	6	2	0	0	3,195
Doyle's Dream	4	F	7	0	1	1	1,935
Doyouhavethetime	4	G	1	0	0	0	0
Doyouhearmenow	3	C	1	0	0	0	0
D'part	7	G	5	0	0	0	1,080
Dr Ante	5	G	10	3	2	0	27,590
Dr Blue Eyes	3	G	7	1	2	4	8,882
Dr Boo Boo Better	5	M	7	0	2	3	31,418
Dr Carson	7	G	2	0	0	0	127
Dr Chequer	4	G	12	2	0	0	10,274
Dr Chiang Mai	4	C	7	0	0	2	4,269
Dr Debbie	2	F	1	0	0	0	0
Dr Detroit	5	G	9	1	3	3	74,510
Dr Devil	5	G	3	0	0	0	0
Dr Dryuit	4	G	14	3	0	2	10,936
Dr F Laparco	7	M	15	2	4	3	17,947
Dr Gold	5	G	3	0	0	1	7,380
Dr Huck	2	C	3	0	0	0	1,440
Dr Jones	3	G	6	0	1	1	1,020
Dr Mehta	5	G	17	2	0	0	20,033
Dr of Love	6	M	8	1	2	0	10,131
Dr Said To	2	F	4	0	0	1	3,980
Dr Sharen G	5	M	4	1	0	1	8,158
Dr Silver Packet	3	C	9	1	0	0	10,480
Dr T's Miracle	5	M	4	0	0	0	348
Dr Turchi	3	G	5	1	1	0	13,406
Dr Vetanze	6	G	8	0	2	0	2,540
Dr Yaru	4	G	12	0	1	1	4,035
Dr. Adoue	4	G	7	0	0	1	3,680
Dr. Albert	4	C	7	1	2	1	38,351
Dr. Alexander	5	G	3	0	0	1	1,215
Dr. Bill	5	H	6	0	0	0	1,100
Dr. Bloomer	3	G	4	1	0	1	16,530
Dr. Bluebird	2	G	3	0	0	1	2,598
Dr. Bombay	4	G	5	0	0	0	585
Dr. Bones	3	G	12	2	1	3	18,323
Dr. Brendler	6	H	3	0	1	0	10,280
Dr. Brick	7	G	12	0	1	4	6,068
Dr. Brooks	3	G	1	0	0	0	0
Dr. Can Do	5	G	8	1	0	0	3,600
Dr. Cann	6	G	12	1	2	1	10,990
Dr. Casola	4	G	13	0	2	1	4,810
Dr. Cassius	2	C	2	0	0	0	920

Horse	Age	Sex	Sts	1st	2d	3d	Won
Dr. Clayton	5	G	8	0	0	0	621
Dr. Cool Beans	6	G	4	1	0	1	6,840
Dr. Coz	4	C	2	0	0	0	0
Dr. Cruse	7	G	11	0	0	2	2,464
Dr. Dazzle	4	G	4	0	2	0	2,200
Dr. Don's Promise	2	F	6	0	0	1	2,520
Dr. Dreamsteamer	5	M	8	1	0	2	4,337
Dr. Dubai	4	C	9	2	0	2	38,380
Dr. E. Claire	4	G	11	1	1	2	20,157
Dr. Exotic	3	G	9	0	2	2	4,340
Dr. Feelgood	2	C	3	0	1	0	2,370
Dr. Foozy	5	G	17	0	2	5	14,120
Dr. Frosty	6	G	1	0	0	0	0
Dr. Gary	7	G	2	0	0	0	0
Dr. Glitter	5	G	10	2	2	2	11,829
Dr. Greeley	5	G	6	1	0	0	8,415
Dr. G's Hot Sauce	3	F	5	1	1	0	35,080
Dr. Guiliani	5	H	6	1	0	1	8,229
Dr. Hager	5	G	4	1	0	0	3,448
Dr. Hawkeye	5	G	1	0	0	0	105
Dr. Hill (BRZ)	7	G	11	1	3	2	30,594
Dr. Hinni	3	C	3	0	0	0	0
Dr. Hocking	2	G	6	1	1	0	24,900
Dr. Hunter	5	G	7	0	1	1	5,630
Dr. J. M. T.	4	C	6	1	1	0	19,420
Dr. John M.	4	G	2	0	0	0	351
Dr. John T.	3	G	4	1	0	0	10,406
Dr. Justy	4	C	4	0	1	1	892
Dr. Kashnikow	7	G	6	1	1	0	132,080
Dr. Kate	2	F	4	0	0	2	3,080
Dr. Kathy	3	F	2	0	0	0	8,800
Dr. Ken	4	G	4	0	0	0	461
Dr. Kitten	10	G	5	1	0	1	1,564
Dr. Kris	3	G	4	0	0	1	6,760
Dr. Liz Syzek	3	F	9	1	1	2	11,135
Dr. Longlegs	4	C	1	0	0	0	0
Dr. Marty	3	C	5	1	0	0	10,910
Dr. Mary Belle	4	F	7	0	0	1	1,425
Dr. Maturin	3	G	14	0	1	5	9,327
Dr. Meatball	2	C	1	1	0	0	34,200
Dr. Miller	4	G	3	0	0	0	1,145
Dr. Mo	5	G	9	1	3	1	31,088
Dr. Morehead	4	G	13	2	4	2	23,866
Dr. Phil	4	C	6	0	0	1	4,420
Dr. Pingo (ARG)	7	G	3	1	0	0	3,344
Dr. Piper	5	M	12	1	0	1	8,190
Dr. Precise	3	F	12	3	1	0	11,612
Dr. Quick	4	F	3	1	1	0	6,210
Dr. Quirk	2	G	5	1	3	0	50,103
Dr. Ramos	3	G	11	1	6	3	29,770
Dr. Ramsey	10	G	6	1	0	0	18,700
Dr. Rand V.	3	G	1	0	0	0	0
Dr. Raymond	6	G	5	0	1	1	1,350
Dr. Ready	11	G	7	0	0	0	0
Dr. Red Man	7	H	4	0	0	0	320
Dr. Robbie	7	G	8	4	2	0	24,814
Dr. Rockett	5	H	15	1	0	4	57,298
Dr. Rodelo M. D.	4	C	1	0	0	0	300
Dr. Sal	8	G	13	2	3	4	16,740
Dr. Scribble	6	G	7	0	1	1	1,890
Dr. Seabird	8	G	2	0	0	0	786
Dr. Slew	6	G	9	1	2	2	13,080
Dr. Socrates	2	C	4	1	2	1	77,260
Dr. Song	2	C	4	0	0	0	0
Dr. Spellbinder	4	G	6	1	0	1	14,370
Dr. Stone	4	G	5	0	1	0	1,165
Dr. Sunshine	4	G	4	0	0	0	0
Dr. Thunder	6	G	4	0	0	1	2,450
Dr. Tom B.	5	G	10	1	3	2	3,288
Dr. Tom Herzog	3	G	5	0	0	2	1,289
Dr. Tony	4	G	13	6	1	2	60,749
Dr. Walsh	4	G	15	2	3	1	60,222
Dr. Wireless	3	F	1	0	0	0	0
Draco City	4	C	7	0	1	1	4,288
Draco's Way	3	G	9	1	3	1	22,110
Dracula	7	G	1	0	0	0	320
Dragon King	3	C	2	0	0	0	800
Dragon the Pot	2	C	12	1	2	0	13,520
Dragonflyer	3	F	1	0	0	0	0

Horse	Age	Sex	Sts	1st	2d	3d	Won
Dragonwood	3	G	11	0	0	0	348
Draiman	2	C	2	1	0	0	6,668
Drakensberg	6	H	9	2	4	0	38,071
Drake's Victory	3	G	7	2	1	2	76,780
Drakesburg	2	G	2	0	0	1	450
Dralion	3	G	1	0	0	0	119
Drama King	3	G	4	1	0	0	18,870
Drama Queen	5	M	7	0	1	3	18,430
Drama's Dandy	5	G	12	1	1	2	6,659
Dramatic Chance	3	F	4	0	1	0	7,250
Dramatic Lion	4	F	4	0	0	0	1,435
Dramatic Run	3	G	13	4	4	0	38,577
Dramatic Vision	3	G	2	0	0	0	1,092
Draol	5	M	1	0	0	0	0
Drastic Demand	2	F	2	0	0	1	4,640
Drastic Measures	3	G	1	0	0	0	115
Draven's Fellow	3	G	11	3	0	3	10,412
Draw a Hardline	2	G	2	0	1	0	8,330
Draw Fire	4	C	10	1	2	2	59,570
Draw Nigh	6	M	6	0	1	1	1,440
Draw Off	3	C	13	3	1	1	72,000
Draw Play	5	G	4	0	1	0	7,360
Draw Your Guns	3	F	6	2	2	0	21,956
Drcouttsoncall	3	G	2	0	0	0	65
Dread That Alarm	6	M	3	0	0	0	110
Dreadnaught	4	G	10	3	4	0	271,243
Dream a Dream	4	F	1	1	0	0	2,580
Dream A Dream (GB)	5	M	12	0	3	2	13,100
Dream About	3	F	2	0	0	0	11,033
Dream Boldly	4	F	8	2	0	2	19,610
Dream Breaker	2	G	10	3	2	4	45,770
Dream by Design	4	G	13	1	2	2	28,703
Dream Chick	6	M	5	0	1	0	1,742
Dream City	5	M	1	0	0	0	110
Dream Counter	9	G	5	1	0	1	12,500
Dream Dancer	6	M	15	1	2	2	12,475
Dream Day	5	M	3	0	0	0	1,220
Dream Deliverer	4	C	11	1	1	2	17,797
Dream Dude	2	G	6	1	2	0	10,740
Dream Dust	5	M	4	0	1	0	1,680
Dream Eternal	5	M	4	0	0	0	180
Dream Fever	3	F	4	1	0	0	18,798
Dream Fleet	3	F	14	1	2	5	27,490
Dream for Gold	4	G	1	0	1	0	2,100
Dream From Above	3	C	9	0	5	0	23,081
Dream Gal	3	F	2	0	1	0	2,340
Dream Lady	2	F	3	1	0	1	34,400
Dream Landing	6	M	14	0	0	4	4,669
Dream Launcher	6	G	7	0	2	3	61,435
Dream Legend	5	M	10	0	3	1	12,030
Dream Machine	2	F	1	1	0	0	6,726
Dream Machine (FR)	5	G	6	1	3	0	56,480
Dream Mount	2	F	2	1	0	0	13,800
Dream of an Act	3	F	1	0	0	0	50
Dream of Dashing	4	G	8	0	0	0	3,500
Dream of Dust	5	M	8	0	1	0	2,232
Dream of Gem	4	C	13	1	3	1	12,375
Dream of Summer	5	M	4	4	0	0	309,000
Dream of Wealth	4	G	11	3	1	3	25,580
Dream On Boys	3	G	4	0	0	0	0
Dream On Doc	3	F	15	1	1	4	6,871
Dream On Dream On	2	C	7	0	1	1	11,095
Dream Out Loud	3	F	2	0	0	0	0
Dream Package	2	F	5	1	1	1	20,550
Dream Performance	3	F	2	0	0	0	186
Dream Place	3	C	4	0	1	3	38,360
Dream Ruler	4	C	1	0	0	0	67
Dream Speaker	3	G	4	0	0	0	0
Dream Spirit	3	F	3	0	0	0	136
Dream Stream	3	C	11	1	2	1	9,259
Dream Time	2	F	1	1	0	0	25,800
Dream Trapper	5	H	11	0	6	1	21,642
Dream Tripper	7	H	1	0	0	0	0
Dream Wedding	5	M	1	0	0	0	0
Dream Weekend	8	H	5	1	2	0	7,570
Dreamadreamforme	3	F	14	4	1	4	90,303
Dreamcatcher	4	G	10	2	1	3	7,555
Dreamer Be There	7	G	2	0	0	0	138
Dreamers Glory	5	M	1	0	0	0	1,400

Horse	Age	Sex	Sts	1st	2d	3d	Won
Dreamer's Lad	9	G	7	0	0	0	1,989
Dreamers Point	7	G	11	0	0	0	3,173
Dreametta	7	M	3	0	0	0	230
Dreamfornatalie	2	F	2	0	0	0	84
Dreamin Demon	5	G	9	1	2	1	12,085
Dreamin of Green	2	C	6	0	1	0	2,190
Dreamin' of Love	3	C	1	0	0	0	0
Dreamin Private	3	C	5	2	1	0	13,581
Dreaming of Gold	3	F	4	0	0	1	1,065
Dreaming of Roses	4	C	3	1	0	0	9,913
Dreaming the Blues	5	H	6	1	1	0	33,609
Dreamingrichard	4	G	6	0	0	0	500
Dreamlin	4	F	2	0	0	0	0
Dreamon Dearest	3	G	10	1	0	0	3,346
Dreamoneir	4	G	7	2	1	2	4,179
Dreampark	4	G	3	0	0	0	0
Dreamport	3	G	3	0	0	0	192
Dreams and Egos	3	F	7	1	0	0	7,300
Dreams Are Forever	5	M	6	0	2	0	3,671
Dreams At Sunset	4	F	6	1	0	2	48,459
Dream's Bestyet	3	G	9	0	2	3	10,259
Dreams Happen	3	C	9	1	0	3	9,044
Dream's Hihope	4	F	5	0	0	0	620
Dreams in the Mist	3	F	12	0	0	1	3,360
Dreams of Ranco	4	F	5	0	2	0	12,125
Dreams to Go	3	F	1	0	0	0	525
Dreamscancometrue	2	F	2	0	0	0	328
Dreamslingeron	5	G	11	1	3	2	17,929
Dreamsville	6	G	5	0	1	1	2,805
Dreamswillcometrue	3	F	7	0	0	5	6,466
Dreamy Desperado	3	G	8	1	0	0	2,070
Dreamy Dream	5	M	6	2	0	0	32,310
Dreamy Temper	6	M	12	1	0	1	10,161
Dreamy Yolanda	3	F	5	0	1	1	1,962
Dress Boot	3	G	11	2	0	1	10,760
Dress for Success	2	C	1	0	0	0	1,560
Dress to Impress	4	F	6	0	0	1	7,145
Dress Up	4	F	6	2	0	1	13,015
Dressed as a Star	2	F	1	0	1	0	1,800
Dressed for Action	4	F	4	1	1	1	75,657
Dressed for Succes	2	F	4	2	0	1	61,900
Dressed in Black	3	C	9	1	2	1	17,912
Dressupforsuccess	2	F	4	0	2	0	4,500
Drew Away	5	M	9	0	1	0	21,510
Drew Lil Slew	2	C	5	0	0	2	7,600
Drew's Delight	4	G	14	1	3	1	36,170
Drew's Super Slat	3	G	5	1	1	0	15,654
Drexel Monorail	5	M	5	1	1	0	48,570
Drez	3	C	1	1	0	0	4,500
Driana	5	M	1	0	0	0	360
Drifa	6	M	1	0	0	0	163
Drift Along	6	M	7	1	0	1	5,503
Drift On Maya	6	M	1	0	0	0	96
Drifter	3	G	11	1	0	1	15,019
Drifting Free	8	G	2	0	0	0	80
Drifting Memory	4	G	1	0	0	0	0
Driftwood Lodge	4	G	6	0	1	1	11,130
Driftwood Promise	3	F	5	0	0	1	1,141
Driftwood Sea	4	G	12	1	1	2	17,113
Drill	4	C	10	1	1	0	5,752
Drill Hall	5	G	4	1	1	0	9,120
Drill Sergeant	4	C	12	4	0	2	31,390
Driller	8	G	6	0	0	0	175
Driller Man	3	G	10	0	5	2	31,510
Drina's Thunder	2	F	1	0	0	0	0
Drink a Toast	5	G	6	0	0	2	16,560
Drinkin Bones	2	C	1	0	0	0	75
Drinkoneforcherie	2	F	4	1	0	0	11,420
Drinksatthegrille	4	F	1	0	0	0	0
Drinksonme	3	F	9	0	3	1	11,326
Drinkwater	2	C	3	1	0	0	25,961
Drip Drop	3	G	13	1	2	4	10,006
Dripdry	3	F	4	0	0	2	3,062
Drippingindiamonds	5	M	1	0	0	0	0
Drislen Jillian	8	H	1	0	0	0	180
Drive	6	G	4	0	1	0	5,418
Drive in the Lane	4	F	8	1	0	0	4,154
Drive My Way	4	F	3	0	0	0	0
Drive the Avenue	10	G	4	1	0	1	5,234
Drive Your Stake	5	G	9	0	1	0	821
Driven Force	8	G	13	3	3	3	8,542
Driven Storm	4	G	2	0	0	0	186
Driven to Gamble	3	G	15	2	2	3	40,850
Drivenbydesire	4	F	5	0	0	0	183
Drivers Seat	5	G	11	2	1	0	8,815
Drivinfordough	10	G	9	0	1	2	2,040
Driving Me Wild	2	F	1	0	0	0	75
Driving Miss Helen	2	F	5	1	0	2	13,155
Driving Miss M	3	F	2	0	1	0	2,237
Driving Mr. Bert	9	G	5	0	0	0	339
Driving Music	4	C	4	0	1	1	3,625
Driving Rosa Wild	3	F	18	1	0	1	4,670
Driving the Alley	3	F	3	0	0	2	5,000
Drivingthelane	3	C	6	0	1	0	15,005
Droll Dancer	8	G	7	0	1	1	4,740
Drop the Buck	8	G	15	3	0	4	14,435
Drop the Gun	10	G	8	0	0	1	2,310
Dropdeaddelicious	2	C	5	0	1	1	2,860
Drosophila	5	M	5	1	1	0	5,931
Drought Breaker	3	F	9	4	3	0	129,720
Drouilly's Devil	4	G	5	0	0	0	340
Drown the Sorrows	4	F	17	6	3	4	42,553
Drum Call	3	F	16	1	1	0	6,393
Drum Dollars	3	G	3	0	0	0	990
Drum Major	2	C	4	1	1	1	46,008
Drum Money	6	M	2	0	0	0	270
Drum Ring	4	G	4	1	0	0	13,860
Drum Roll Please	4	C	15	3	4	0	36,940
Drumcliff	6	G	8	2	0	1	8,847
Drumheller	2	C	3	0	0	1	1,540
Drunken Brawl	2	G	4	0	1	1	2,275
Dry County Girl	3	F	13	4	0	1	34,877
Dry Humor	3	G	10	1	0	2	11,783
Dry Ice	6	G	14	4	2	2	38,605
D's Dessert	2	G	4	1	2	0	13,200
D's Honey	2	F	4	0	0	0	765
D's Magic Man	2	G	3	0	0	0	229
D's Rocky Ridge	4	F	1	0	0	0	125
D's Royal Flush	4	G	12	3	2	3	16,220
D's Valentine	4	G	16	2	4	1	28,343
D'termining	4	G	16	2	1	3	9,502
Dual Axle	4	G	2	0	0	0	620
Dual Doppler	3	F	10	2	1	2	50,994
Dual Fuel	2	C	3	0	1	1	12,110
Dual Wager	3	F	15	1	1	1	11,217
Duanes Litlelizzie	3	F	3	0	0	1	190
Duanesdarlingcupie	5	M	7	0	1	0	2,497
Dubai Cat	5	H	10	3	1	1	52,100
Dubai Dolly	3	F	9	3	0	2	51,280
Dubai Sheikh	5	G	10	1	3	3	73,430
Dubai Special	5	G	4	0	0	0	164
Dubai Surprise	2	F	2	0	0	0	280
Dubaian Duel (GB)	3	F	3	1	0	0	27,330
Dubious Command	5	H	11	4	2	1	36,196
Dubleo	2	C	9	6	1	1	360,899
Dublin Darlin	4	F	13	0	2	0	4,180
Dublin Deb	2	F	2	0	0	0	0
Dublin Grade	3	G	11	2	2	2	18,597
Dublino	5	M	2	0	1	1	26,308
Dublin's Woodwin	5	G	11	1	2	1	21,900
Dubuque	2	C	2	0	0	0	360
Dubya	4	G	6	1	1	0	9,324
Dubya D Forty	3	C	6	1	0	1	7,670
Duc D Fer	2	G	5	0	4	0	7,925
Duc Moriniere (FR)	11	G	1	0	0	0	0
Ducati Demon	4	G	15	3	2	2	49,165
Duce's Image	3	G	14	1	4	2	36,325
Duce's Ready	10	G	3	0	0	0	0
Duchess City	2	F	4	0	0	1	2,150
Duchess County	4	F	11	1	3	1	53,850
Duchess d'Or	2	F	4	0	1	0	2,330
Duchess Ida Clare	3	F	12	1	6	2	30,044
Duchess of Cocoa	5	M	2	0	0	0	720
Duchess of Houston	6	M	2	0	0	0	0
Duchess of Orange	3	F	2	0	0	0	0
Duchwonderman	4	G	4	0	0	0	0
Duck and Frolic	4	G	6	1	0	0	6,008
Duck Blaze	3	F	4	0	0	0	404

Horse	Age	Sex	Sts	1st	2d	3d	Won
Duck Down Under	4	F	3	0	3	0	13,360
Duck Duck Goose	6	H	10	1	5	1	13,422
Duck for Dinner	6	G	15	4	4	2	32,879
Duckberg Flyer	3	G	7	1	1	0	10,780
Ducks and Pizza	2	F	3	0	1	2	5,880
Ducky's Ho Oh	3	F	2	0	0	0	0
Duddly Doo Run	5	G	14	2	4	0	34,638
Dude	6	G	3	0	0	1	583
Dude Anonymous	5	G	4	0	1	0	1,403
Dudeman	5	G	8	0	0	0	454
Dudewithanattitude	4	G	13	2	1	2	15,581
Dudley Dewfein	7	G	11	0	2	0	4,959
Due	3	G	14	3	2	4	51,560
Due Brilliance	3	F	7	0	3	0	5,609
Due Elegance	6	M	6	0	0	1	2,576
Due Now	2	F	2	0	0	0	0
Due Season	5	H	5	0	0	1	120
Due the Empress	7	M	9	0	0	1	2,556
Due to Win	9	M	11	3	2	1	111,400
Due to Win Again	6	M	11	4	2	1	140,880
Duece Trey	3	C	2	0	0	0	0
Dueling Banjo	4	G	4	0	0	0	835
Dueling Edge	7	G	21	2	0	2	9,696
Dueln Lit'l Joe	7	G	9	0	0	1	920
Dues for the Blues	4	G	8	0	3	0	8,916
Duesenberg	5	G	2	1	0	0	5,210
Duet	3	F	5	0	0	0	10,413
Duetherightthing	7	M	5	0	1	2	823
Duffy	4	G	12	1	1	1	29,185
Duffy's Trick	4	C	5	1	1	1	9,004
Dugald	2	C	1	0	0	0	184
Dugout Doug	3	G	19	2	0	3	15,147
Duke Crane	8	G	9	2	0	1	5,460
Duke Doyouseemenow	2	G	3	0	0	1	1,954
Duke of Dazzby	2	G	1	0	0	0	0
Duke of Dutton	5	G	10	1	3	1	9,211
Duke of Earl (IRE)	5	G	3	0	0	1	11,500
Duke of Flatbush	3	G	2	0	1	1	3,176
Duke of Haz	4	G	1	0	0	0	0
Duke of Kent	4	G	14	5	4	0	40,451
Duke of Paoli	6	G	11	4	1	2	22,328
Duke Ora	10	G	10	2	0	1	16,755
Duke Wayne	2	C	3	0	0	0	1,310
Duke Wilson	3	C	5	0	0	0	106
Duke's Clone	5	G	9	2	0	2	4,395
Duke's Crossing	5	G	4	0	0	0	5,014
Dukes Falcon	4	G	4	0	1	0	2,126
Duke's Hi	4	G	11	0	2	1	3,555
Dukes Mixture	4	C	11	1	1	2	32,750
Duke's Phantom	8	G	4	0	0	0	0
Duke's Revenge	4	G	4	0	0	1	4,105
Dukes Shawklit	3	G	6	2	2	0	33,400
Duke's Show Biz	6	M	14	1	0	2	7,645
Duke's Tempo	6	H	4	0	0	0	0
Duke's Wildcat	9	G	14	2	3	0	11,999
Duking in Dixie	8	G	1	0	0	0	0
Dulce de Leche	5	H	14	4	1	2	83,721
Dulcet	4	F	3	1	1	1	27,460
Dulciana	3	F	15	4	2	2	79,032
Dulcinia	4	F	10	1	2	1	8,540
Dumaani Music	4	G	1	0	0	0	38
Dumaani of Course	5	H	8	3	1	2	59,618
Dumaani Star	6	G	9	0	1	1	32,537
Dumaani's Princess	3	F	4	1	1	0	8,205
Dummy	4	G	4	0	0	1	1,139
Dummy Up	4	G	1	0	0	1	693
Dumtell	3	F	11	2	1	1	30,215
Dun	3	G	5	0	0	1	2,820
Dun Ringill	6	G	10	3	0	1	19,256
Dun Roamin Hero	2	G	1	0	0	0	1,200
Dunbar	3	G	6	0	0	0	366
Duncan Hill	5	G	1	0	0	0	0
Duncan Idaho	5	H	12	1	0	0	12,420
Duncan Miss	7	M	13	0	2	0	2,245
Duncan's Dancer	4	F	1	0	0	0	0
Duncan's Gold	4	G	18	4	2	3	26,023
Dungeon	5	G	14	2	3	0	16,099
Dunham's Bag	8	H	3	0	0	0	0
Dunham's Social	8	M	8	1	0	0	4,628
Dunkaman	7	G	3	0	0	0	0
Dunloe Gap	4	G	9	3	1	1	29,213
Dunne Right	5	G	13	2	1	5	12,939
Dunnell Lane	2	C	7	1	0	0	13,445
Dunvegan Ablaze	3	F	9	0	0	2	1,770
Duo de Tango	3	G	4	2	0	0	34,780
Dupers' Double T	4	C	3	0	0	0	0
Dupes Delight	3	G	4	1	0	1	16,260
Duplicate Award	3	F	18	2	2	7	21,190
Duplicate Copy	5	H	9	1	1	0	11,659
Duplicate Ticket	6	G	3	1	1	0	12,200
Dura Ace	4	G	13	2	2	4	35,323
Durable	3	F	2	0	1	1	3,600
Durable Mac	3	C	4	0	0	0	548
Durable Silver	3	F	3	0	1	0	6,050
Duracat	3	G	7	2	0	0	44,409
Durandal	3	C	2	0	0	0	145
Durando	4	C	2	0	0	0	124
Durango	3	G	13	2	0	2	24,617
Durango Invader	3	G	2	0	0	0	400
Duration Bob	4	G	9	0	0	1	938
Durazno Oro	3	F	2	0	0	0	120
During	4	C	9	1	1	3	307,614
Durkin's Call	3	G	7	2	0	1	36,050
Durmiente (CHI)	10	G	6	0	0	0	2,897
Durrymane	3	F	8	0	1	1	7,100
Durvish	7	G	13	0	6	2	8,514
Dusk Till Dawn	4	G	16	1	2	4	10,411
Dusky Devil	7	G	7	0	0	0	376
Duson Minstrel	4	G	6	0	0	0	0
Dust Bag	7	G	15	3	0	1	9,486
Dust Cover (GB)	4	G	4	0	1	1	13,880
Dust in Time	5	G	10	0	3	1	8,740
Dust On the Bottle	9	H	10	0	0	1	12,400
Dust Pebble	5	M	10	2	1	0	14,514
Dust Up	3	G	4	0	0	0	501
Dust'em Justin	4	G	1	0	0	0	400
Dustexpress	2	F	3	0	0	0	1,264
Dusthof	6	G	11	4	3	3	7,116
Dustineer	8	G	18	0	1	0	1,788
Dusting of Powder	5	M	5	1	1	0	10,080
Dustinontherun	3	F	16	3	2	3	29,960
Dustin's Luckylady	5	M	4	0	0	1	1,652
Dustins Mozart	4	G	11	1	0	1	6,636
Dustinsdestiny	4	G	11	0	4	1	3,134
Dusti's Tune	5	M	4	0	0	0	5,832
Dusty Adams	4	C	5	2	1	0	43,880
Dusty Beau	4	G	8	1	4	0	6,319
Dusty Betsy	6	M	2	0	0	0	0
Dusty Boots	2	G	3	0	1	0	905
Dusty Call	4	G	2	0	0	0	114
Dusty Cat	5	M	11	1	0	5	13,684
Dusty Conn	6	G	2	0	0	0	200
Dusty Decision	4	G	2	0	0	0	0
Dusty Evening	4	F	8	2	1	1	57,455
Dusty Gold	4	F	9	1	1	2	10,778
Dusty Guitar	3	G	2	0	0	0	540
Dusty Irish Lass	3	F	12	1	0	1	5,025
Dusty Jug	4	G	8	0	0	0	1,193
Dusty Mexican	4	F	1	0	0	0	130
Dusty Minister	2	C	7	2	1	1	53,930
Dusty Noel	4	F	7	2	1	2	11,171
Dusty Ol' Cognac	4	C	6	0	0	5	6,688
Dusty Pat	3	F	21	1	2	5	11,456
Dusty Quaker	6	G	15	0	0	4	2,787
Dusty Slew	6	G	19	5	3	3	17,115
Dusty Spike	5	G	11	0	2	2	58,490
Dusty Sprinkles	3	F	1	0	0	0	460
Dusty Tunnel	3	C	11	1	3	2	25,360
Dustys Birthday	5	H	7	0	1	1	14,420
Dusty's Express	3	G	8	1	0	1	12,260
Dusty's Gone	4	F	9	0	1	1	4,320
Dustys Unbridled	2	C	1	0	0	0	55
Dustysarollin	7	G	14	3	1	3	21,876
Dutch Apple	3	G	5	2	0	2	2,842
Dutch One's Storm	3	F	1	0	0	0	370
Dutch Uncle	9	G	6	0	0	1	619
Dutch Wind Mill	5	G	3	0	0	1	1,297
Dutches's Crown	5	M	5	0	0	0	3,327

Horse	Age	Sex	Sts	1st	2d	3d	Won
Dutchess Dear	4	F	14	2	1	2	15,017
Dutchess Eben	4	F	7	1	0	0	7,381
Dutchess Gold	4	F	1	0	0	0	150
Dutchie	4	F	10	4	0	0	79,380
Dutrap	4	C	4	0	0	0	0
Duty Yeoman	2	C	4	0	0	0	250
Duvalier	5	G	10	0	1	2	21,660
Dwango	3	C	2	0	0	1	6,720
Dwayo	3	G	8	2	2	0	14,237
Dwellerinthevalley	3	G	2	0	0	0	0
Dwendi	6	M	4	0	0	0	1,641
Dwight Polite	2	C	7	1	1	3	17,780
Dyersburg	4	G	8	0	0	0	988
Dyess	3	C	3	0	0	0	0
Dyf	5	G	17	1	4	0	14,580
Dylan	4	G	8	1	1	1	27,800
Dylan Heritage	2	G	2	0	0	0	0
Dylans Destiny	3	G	7	3	0	0	49,641
Dylan's Girl	5	M	10	1	4	1	8,443
Dylans Rose	3	F	1	0	0	0	77
Dylans Secret	4	G	15	6	0	2	23,511
Dylan's Wish	3	F	3	0	2	1	7,095
Dylon's Public	4	C	2	0	0	0	114
Dyna Da Wyna	4	F	6	4	0	1	171,183
Dyna Del	4	F	10	3	2	3	73,440
Dyna Flair	3	F	12	2	2	0	28,105
Dyna Flyer	4	F	4	0	0	0	2,800
Dyna Girl	3	F	15	3	1	0	47,260
Dyna King	7	G	15	3	2	2	5,006
Dyna Mae	5	M	6	0	0	0	2,366
Dyna Penny	5	M	1	0	0	0	1,920
Dyna Strip	3	G	7	0	0	1	4,420
Dyna Wild	3	F	10	3	2	1	64,585
Dynabid	3	F	4	0	0	0	2,628
Dynabin	2	F	3	0	2	0	14,600
Dynaboy	9	G	6	1	1	0	11,905
Dynacrown	3	G	7	1	0	2	22,370
Dynadevil	2	C	7	0	0	2	9,170
Dynadoll	2	F	1	0	0	0	105
Dynadusty	6	H	6	2	1	0	7,186
Dynafire	3	C	6	0	0	1	6,776
Dynakitten	3	F	1	0	0	0	154
Dynakris	4	F	5	0	0	0	920
Dynalook	3	F	10	2	0	1	76,225
Dynalympic	3	C	5	2	0	1	54,050
Dynamation	3	F	8	1	0	1	21,780
Dynamia	3	F	2	1	1	0	36,800
Dynamic	2	F	1	0	0	0	0
Dynamic Diva	5	M	10	2	2	2	19,047
Dynamic Dixie	3	F	8	2	0	3	10,111
Dynamic Energy	5	M	4	0	0	0	174
Dynamic Investment	2	F	1	0	0	0	0
Dynamic Justice	4	F	9	1	1	3	12,776
Dynamic Lady	5	M	2	0	0	0	2,040
Dynamic Lisa	5	M	5	0	0	0	12,174
Dynamic Lord	5	H	2	0	0	0	600
Dynamic Pic	8	M	2	0	0	0	383
Dynamic Prospect	5	G	8	1	0	2	16,705
Dynamic Red	5	M	3	1	2	0	9,500
Dynamic Ruhler	6	M	2	0	0	0	76
Dynamic Storm	2	C	4	0	1	1	10,420
Dynamic Vision	3	G	13	2	4	1	37,126
Dynamic Wonder	3	F	12	1	0	2	11,112
Dynamic Word	3	F	6	0	0	0	0
Dynamick C B	8	M	3	0	0	0	0
Dynamist	2	F	2	1	1	0	34,140
Dynamite Cocktail	4	F	3	1	0	1	39,378
Dynamite Dani	3	F	4	0	0	0	0
Dynamite Dinner	4	G	1	0	0	0	0
Dynamite Dot	5	M	9	0	0	0	522
Dynamite Duck	3	F	11	2	1	3	26,972
Dynamite Flyer	3	G	4	3	0	0	73,564
Dynamite Ghost	5	G	7	0	1	2	1,864
Dynamite Guy	4	C	7	0	0	2	3,335
Dynamite Kate	2	F	1	0	0	0	140
Dynamite Lass	2	F	2	2	0	0	33,000
Dynamite Wes	4	G	10	1	1	0	4,790
Dynamite Whirlwind	8	G	16	0	0	3	2,068
Dynamite Willie	3	G	11	1	2	1	12,150

Horse	Age	Sex	Sts	1st	2d	3d	Won
Dynamo Don	5	G	4	0	2	1	9,607
Dynamo Gold	2	C	4	0	0	1	2,656
Dynamo Hum	2	F	7	1	2	0	45,804
Dynamo Ridge	3	F	6	0	0	0	586
Dynamometer	4	C	1	0	0	0	160
Dynantonia	2	C	4	1	0	1	26,930
Dynappeal	2	C	3	0	0	0	860
Dynaquoit	3	F	2	0	0	0	2,330
Dynareign	4	C	11	2	2	2	79,295
Dynaruler	4	G	16	0	3	2	34,258
Dyna's Dynamo	3	F	10	1	0	3	36,646
Dyna's Legacy	5	G	4	0	0	0	3,378
Dyna's Wicked Ride	5	M	5	0	1	0	5,709
Dynastar	7	G	4	0	1	1	9,940
Dynastic Power	4	G	10	3	0	1	23,885
Dynastyle	4	C	5	2	1	1	33,920
Dynatron	9	G	13	1	0	0	4,317
Dynaville	3	F	4	1	1	1	89,695
Dynavolt	7	G	4	1	0	0	6,900
Dynawave	5	M	3	0	1	0	2,530
Dynaway	3	G	6	0	0	0	5,899
Dynawhite	2	C	5	0	1	1	12,694
Dynever	4	C	7	1	3	0	254,694
Dyno Don	3	G	10	2	2	1	17,381
Dynomynt	3	G	13	1	1	0	29,623
Dysfunctional Lady	3	F	13	4	1	1	17,930
E and D's Dreams	2	C	3	1	1	0	8,685
E B Express	3	G	19	4	1	3	26,982
E C's Way	4	G	13	2	3	1	9,961
E Freddys Money	3	C	2	0	0	0	600
E J Harley	12	G	1	1	0	0	4,500
E K Power	2	G	7	0	1	2	12,480
E Mail Pat	6	M	12	1	1	3	33,195
E Mail Trail	7	G	10	3	3	2	6,423
E Man	4	G	7	1	0	1	7,740
E N Harrison	3	C	3	0	1	0	6,910
E O's Flash	3	G	10	1	1	3	18,277
E R Britt	2	F	1	0	0	0	135
E T Phone Laura	5	M	15	1	3	3	22,520
E Z Event	2	C	1	0	0	0	0
E Z Glory	7	H	1	0	0	0	1,020
E Z Line	9	G	6	1	0	0	6,930
E Z Smile	3	F	14	1	0	2	14,259
E Z Traveler	3	G	1	0	0	0	0
E. B. Mitchell	5	G	12	0	0	2	2,211
E. B. Striker	2	C	6	0	1	0	6,955
E. C. Cat	4	F	1	0	0	0	115
E. P. Hillary	4	C	2	0	0	0	426
E. R. Nurse	5	M	2	0	0	0	100
E. T.'s Little Sis	6	M	2	0	0	0	0
E. Ticket	3	F	9	2	0	1	58,759
E. Z. Bree Z.	4	F	2	0	0	0	164
Eager Conduction	3	G	3	0	0	0	3,020
Eager Lee	5	G	10	3	0	1	13,187
Eagerness	6	G	6	0	0	0	558
Eagle Cat	5	M	18	2	1	0	13,683
Eagle Charger	7	G	11	1	0	3	22,360
Eagle Eagle	4	G	4	0	0	0	77
Eagle Eyrie	4	G	18	3	2	2	21,480
Eagle Mountain	2	C	10	2	1	1	29,490
Eagle Peak	7	G	10	3	0	1	24,010
Eagle Point	3	G	9	0	0	0	465
Eagle Road	2	G	6	0	2	1	11,724
Eagle Rock	2	G	3	0	0	0	175
Eagle Time	7	H	12	3	3	0	71,224
Eagleiere	2	F	1	0	0	0	100
Eagleinflight	2	G	5	1	1	2	23,940
Eagle's Buddy	4	G	5	1	0	0	7,075
Eagles Cry	6	G	8	1	0	1	4,755
Eagle's Echo	2	C	1	0	0	0	0
Eagles Hill	4	C	5	0	0	0	2,382
Eagle's Luck	4	G	8	0	2	3	7,851
Eagles Nest	3	F	5	1	2	0	24,229
Eaglesandbeavers	3	G	7	1	0	0	6,210
Eaglesfield	7	G	1	0	0	0	0
Eagleton	8	G	5	0	0	0	4,434
Eaglez Crown	4	G	4	1	1	0	10,617
Earhart	2	F	3	1	1	0	33,254
Earl Penny	5	H	5	0	0	0	598

Horse	Age	Sex	Sts	1st	2d	3d	Won
Earl the Pearl	6	G	8	0	0	0	1,101
Earlene	4	F	8	0	0	0	1,484
Earl's Babe	4	F	1	0	0	0	0
Earl's Son (IRE)	4	C	1	0	0	0	0
Early Advantage	3	G	9	0	0	1	1,127
Early Arrival	7	M	12	0	0	1	3,635
Early Class	3	F	2	0	0	0	600
Early Cotton	4	G	16	1	4	2	66,281
Early Esteem	2	G	5	1	1	0	11,950
Early Morning Rain	3	G	5	0	0	0	3,528
Early Primrose	5	M	1	0	0	0	73
Early Results	3	C	2	1	0	0	1,079
Early Ruler	2	F	5	0	2	0	11,250
Early Signal	5	M	9	0	1	2	12,196
Early Snow	4	G	5	1	0	1	39,888
Early Sunday Morn	3	G	8	1	0	0	10,063
Early T Sauce	4	G	6	1	1	0	8,585
Early Term	3	C	8	2	1	0	4,045
Early Tide	3	F	2	0	0	2	4,560
Earmark	8	G	5	1	2	0	18,400
Earn Mia Hardt	3	G	6	1	0	0	48,360
Earned Run	3	F	2	0	0	0	1,378
Earnest Storm	6	G	11	1	2	0	17,606
Ears	3	F	3	0	1	0	1,950
Earsay	2	F	2	0	0	0	1,350
Earth Pleasure	5	G	4	0	0	1	1,767
Earth Power	4	C	8	3	1	2	121,830
Earth Shaker	5	M	9	1	2	1	36,485
Earth Shaking	8	G	9	2	1	0	15,257
Earth to Heaven	7	M	16	5	2	2	17,331
Earth To Siena	9	M	3	0	0	0	243
Earthquake Eddie	4	G	3	1	0	0	1,125
Earthquake Ride	3	F	9	1	0	3	36,312
Ease Your Mind	2	C	5	1	1	0	21,500
Easianna	4	F	13	1	0	0	6,080
Easiersaidthandone	5	G	6	0	0	1	1,814
Easiersgold	4	F	3	0	0	1	1,365
Easily	2	F	4	1	0	1	34,785
Easily Assembled	7	G	13	2	3	5	16,426
East and West	6	G	7	0	1	1	2,320
East Bay	3	F	1	0	0	0	900
East Coker	3	G	7	0	0	1	1,410
East Lorraine	3	F	7	0	1	1	2,464
East Memory	3	G	11	1	3	1	10,257
East of Amwell	3	G	11	0	0	0	1,290
East of Suez	2	C	4	1	0	1	14,004
East River Tatonka	7	G	12	2	1	1	7,071
East Texas Red	3	G	2	0	0	0	315
East Texas Sam	5	G	8	2	2	0	10,342
East Vali	5	G	6	0	0	2	805
East Wing	3	C	2	0	0	0	0
Easter Basket	2	F	3	1	0	0	1,950
Easter Boutinierre	7	M	11	1	0	0	1,865
Easter Buddy	4	F	12	1	1	0	11,263
Easter Bug	7	G	2	0	0	0	125
Easter Dawn	4	F	13	1	3	1	10,481
Easter Guardian	3	G	6	0	0	1	4,869
Easter Halo	5	G	5	0	0	0	385
Easter Ice	3	F	1	0	1	0	560
Easter Jill	4	F	7	1	1	1	7,082
Easter Lady	2	F	4	0	0	0	810
Easter Lillyhopper	4	F	4	0	0	0	549
Easter Melody	3	F	1	0	0	0	0
Easter Prospect	2	F	5	0	0	1	1,317
Easter Saga	5	M	8	1	1	1	9,280
Easter Sunny	5	G	10	3	1	1	13,578
Easter Treasure	5	G	7	2	0	0	5,850
Easter Tryst	3	F	10	2	1	1	17,890
Easter Weekend	3	F	9	1	4	2	15,893
Easterly Breeze	2	F	3	0	1	1	13,650
Eastern Accent	3	G	6	1	0	2	17,408
Eastern All Star	3	G	13	0	0	1	3,350
Eastern Avenue	3	C	2	0	1	0	3,843
Eastern Bay	3	C	12	2	3	2	44,770
Eastern Bid	8	G	8	1	0	0	2,778
Eastern Cat	6	G	9	1	0	1	6,529
Eastern Crown	4	C	7	0	3	2	51,288
Eastern Daydream	9	H	5	1	1	0	8,640
Eastern Gale	4	F	8	2	3	2	105,100

Horse	Age	Sex	Sts	1st	2d	3d	Won
Eastern Halo	2	F	5	0	0	1	1,609
Eastern Lily	2	F	1	0	0	0	230
Eastern Memory	4	F	10	0	0	0	4,980
Eastern Pilot	3	G	10	1	0	0	7,833
Eastern Point	3	C	3	0	1	1	14,280
Eastern Sand	2	G	5	2	1	0	50,520
Eastern Sham	2	C	2	0	0	0	170
Eastern Sky	4	F	11	2	0	0	23,550
Eastern Storm	4	F	9	1	0	2	7,272
Eastern Turk	4	G	4	0	0	0	62
Eastern War Lord	9	G	7	1	1	1	25,378
Eastern Wildcat	3	G	12	1	0	3	12,400
Eastersonitsway	4	G	2	0	0	0	0
Eastland Hope	2	F	1	0	0	0	500
Eastover	9	G	14	1	3	2	16,823
Eastover Express	2	F	2	0	0	0	0
Eastside Ballad	4	F	1	0	0	1	5,880
Eastside McKinley	3	G	2	0	0	0	364
Eastside Park	2	G	2	0	0	0	830
Eastside Ruckus	3	F	4	0	0	2	5,635
Eastwood's Song	4	C	6	1	1	2	13,122
Easy (IRE)	6	G	3	1	0	0	15,000
Easy Approval	3	F	3	1	0	1	7,150
Easy Approval (PER)	4	F	12	3	1	2	32,690
Easy as Abc	3	G	12	1	1	1	6,556
Easy Bar	5	G	4	0	0	0	815
Easy Big Cat	2	C	6	1	1	0	12,880
Easy Change	5	G	13	0	0	0	332
Easy Chase	2	C	4	1	0	0	6,000
Easy Chief	5	G	3	0	0	1	154
Easy Child	3	F	1	0	0	0	0
Easy Cruiser	4	C	7	1	0	5	70,569
Easy Double	2	F	4	0	0	2	10,070
Easy Drifter	2	C	2	0	0	1	2,640
Easy E	5	M	3	0	0	0	272
Easy Earl	2	G	1	0	0	0	300
Easy Edna	4	F	4	0	0	0	0
Easy Elegance	3	F	5	0	0	1	10,360
Easy Ellis	3	G	12	0	1	1	12,249
Easy Enough	5	G	2	0	0	0	0
Easy Entrance	3	C	5	0	1	0	5,140
Easy Fit	2	C	9	1	0	0	4,200
Easy Game	5	G	14	4	1	2	49,280
Easy Going Will	2	C	1	0	0	0	45
Easy Grades	5	G	7	2	1	0	47,695
Easy Grinder	3	F	4	1	1	2	18,900
Easy Ian	5	G	6	1	0	0	4,501
Easy Ice Hole	5	H	5	0	0	0	0
Easy Idea	5	M	5	1	1	0	988
Easy Lassie	4	F	13	2	2	0	43,150
Easy Loot	2	F	3	0	0	0	1,309
Easy Lovin	6	G	7	4	1	1	15,197
Easy Million	4	C	13	2	3	6	69,968
Easy Mission	6	G	14	2	1	0	11,453
Easy Miswaki Gold	3	F	8	0	1	1	2,243
Easy Money	2	G	2	0	0	0	600
Easy N Jazzy	4	G	12	1	2	1	6,605
Easy Operator	3	G	12	0	2	2	4,205
Easy Orders	6	G	3	0	0	0	120
Easy Pickins	3	G	9	2	2	0	8,704
Easy Question	3	F	4	0	0	0	2,100
Easy Red	2	C	1	0	0	0	0
Easy Return	2	F	1	0	0	0	300
Easy Rival	5	G	2	0	0	1	720
Easy Road	4	G	1	0	0	0	0
Easy Rodney	2	C	2	0	0	0	488
Easy Runaway	7	G	7	0	1	0	2,201
Easy Secret	2	F	2	0	0	0	0
Easy Star	3	F	5	1	2	1	17,800
Easy Swinger	3	G	5	0	0	0	1,220
Easy Thunder	6	H	1	0	0	0	0
Easy to Be Me	4	F	12	3	2	1	13,448
Easy to Believe	4	G	19	1	3	5	18,569
Easy too Easy	4	G	12	3	1	1	18,982
Easy Vote	2	F	8	1	2	1	10,948
Easy Way	2	F	1	0	0	0	280
Easyfromthegitgo	5	H	1	0	0	0	276
Easyhar	7	G	11	1	1	0	9,051
Eat a Bug	4	F	12	2	2	1	24,960

Horse	Age	Sex	Sts	1st	2d	3d	Won
Eat My Dust Boys	3	G	3	1	1	0	4,682
Eat My Dust Buster	6	G	8	0	1	0	523
Eatdrinkandbemerry	3	F	3	0	0	0	590
Eaton's Award	3	F	9	1	1	2	18,194
Eatonville Cruiser	4	G	14	1	1	3	13,532
Eavesdropper	4	C	10	2	3	1	118,214
Ebben Estoora	6	G	11	1	2	2	38,260
Ebee's	5	G	16	1	2	6	10,170
Eber	6	G	9	0	0	0	1,041
Ebon Storm	3	F	9	1	1	1	18,523
Ebonoir	6	M	7	0	0	0	1,653
Ebony Angel	6	M	11	1	3	1	7,391
Ebony Boy	6	H	2	0	0	0	618
Ebony Breeze	4	F	9	2	3	1	255,360
Ebony Cat	3	F	6	0	0	1	1,800
Ebony Copy	3	F	8	1	0	1	3,125
Ebony Lady	3	F	7	3	1	0	49,665
Ebony Magic	2	G	1	0	0	1	2,079
Ebony Post	4	F	16	3	4	4	21,116
Ec Lady (GB)	5	M	3	0	0	2	6,990
Eccentric	4	G	2	0	0	0	735
Eccentric Tycoon	8	G	12	2	2	1	13,673
Eccentric Type	6	G	4	0	2	0	5,315
Ecclesiastic	3	C	10	2	2	2	111,670
Ech Leebidee Angel	3	F	1	0	0	0	0
Echelon	6	G	1	0	0	0	0
Echelon Star	9	G	4	1	0	0	2,480
Echeverria	4	C	2	0	0	0	113
Echo Army	3	G	4	0	2	0	880
Echo Canyon	8	G	1	0	0	0	325
Echo Creek	3	G	4	1	1	0	5,595
Echo Freddie	2	C	1	0	0	0	385
Echo Harbor	3	F	3	1	0	0	14,931
Echo Heiress	3	F	2	0	0	0	0
Echo Jo	4	F	8	0	1	0	11,340
Echo Lady	4	F	6	0	0	0	1,410
Echo Land	4	F	7	2	2	0	29,011
Echo Landing	8	G	3	0	0	0	377
Echo Location	4	F	7	2	0	0	6,906
Echo of Freedom	3	G	14	1	3	1	14,615
Echo Prince	3	G	1	0	0	0	0
Echo Proof	2	F	4	0	0	0	570
Echo Rocket	4	G	15	2	2	2	14,779
Echo Spring	4	F	9	4	0	2	59,430
Echo Test	6	H	3	0	1	1	4,123
Echo Weaver	3	F	13	1	1	1	9,349
Echoes in Hilco	3	F	9	0	0	1	5,280
Echoes of Glory	3	F	1	0	0	0	250
Echoes of Heaven	2	C	1	0	0	0	76
Echoing Cheer	3	F	9	2	0	0	12,745
Echoman	4	G	14	1	0	2	9,812
Echos Angel	3	F	14	3	2	0	27,470
Echo's Word	5	G	1	0	0	0	0
Echota	3	G	12	3	1	0	59,810
Eckelson	3	C	2	0	0	1	650
Eckmo	4	G	11	5	2	0	15,569
Eclat	4	G	14	1	3	1	11,468
Eclipse Winner	3	F	9	1	3	0	25,046
Eclipsing	3	F	6	0	1	1	1,635
Eclipsio	5	G	6	0	0	0	504
Ecology	3	F	2	0	0	0	0
Economic Trend	8	H	19	1	2	4	7,584
Economist At Last	3	G	12	3	2	1	66,370
Ecstatic	5	H	1	0	0	0	3,900
Ecstatic Blue	8	G	3	0	0	0	238
Ecstatic Bunny	5	M	2	0	0	0	99
Ecumenical	4	G	3	0	0	0	450
Ed Bowen	2	C	4	0	0	0	123
Ed Gray Sports	2	G	3	1	0	0	10,555
Ed Man Knocking	2	C	1	0	0	0	0
Ed Miracle	2	C	8	0	2	2	8,894
Edawah	3	C	4	1	2	0	6,580
Eddie Boy	4	G	10	3	0	2	22,300
Eddie the Spouse	4	G	7	0	1	0	6,584
Eddie White Sox	5	G	14	2	1	0	13,915
Eddie Wilson	8	G	4	1	0	1	6,512
Eddienojado	4	G	10	1	0	3	5,453
Eddies Bad Boy	5	G	4	1	1	0	8,500
Eddies Girl	3	F	1	0	0	0	174
Eddiesboysings	3	C	10	2	1	1	49,168
Eddington	3	C	11	3	2	4	605,360
Eddy	4	G	15	1	2	1	8,221
Eddy's Wisdom	3	G	10	2	3	0	57,464
Edelweiss Song	3	F	10	1	2	1	12,055
Eden Park	4	F	10	1	0	2	10,610
Edge Creek	4	G	14	2	3	2	17,267
Edge of a Dream	2	G	5	1	1	1	15,878
Edge of a Kiss	4	C	6	0	4	0	7,390
Edge of Destiny	3	F	15	2	0	1	9,800
Edge Out	3	G	3	0	0	1	4,900
Edgefield	8	G	11	1	1	1	14,444
Edgerrin	3	G	12	3	1	1	54,330
Edge's Heat	2	C	4	0	2	2	10,550
Edgestone	8	H	3	0	0	0	0
Edgewater Savior	3	F	15	1	1	2	14,485
Edgie Regina	3	F	2	0	0	0	0
Edicawels	4	G	6	0	1	0	3,710
Edies Memo	5	M	7	1	1	0	10,564
Edie's Rebel	8	M	2	0	0	0	0
Edify	4	G	8	1	0	1	7,085
Ediko	5	G	2	0	0	0	0
Edile's Spirit	6	M	6	0	1	3	4,625
Edison Field	3	G	1	0	0	0	300
Edison Lanes	3	F	11	2	0	1	36,076
Edit It	4	F	13	2	3	2	67,725
Edith Ann	2	F	1	1	0	0	6,850
Edith Prickley	2	F	4	0	1	0	33,780
Editiorial	4	G	9	3	2	0	44,410
Editor's a Natural	4	G	13	2	1	2	14,820
Editor's Cat	4	G	6	0	0	2	8,840
Editors Copy	5	M	7	0	0	3	7,378
Editors Not	3	F	6	1	1	0	9,524
Editor's Page	3	G	15	2	2	2	41,179
Editor's Pride	4	F	2	0	0	0	250
Editors Shake	4	F	3	0	1	0	3,375
Editor's Wild Note	2	F	2	0	0	1	4,220
Editress	4	F	7	0	1	0	2,014
Edna Clouds	3	F	4	0	0	0	0
Edna Violet	3	F	3	0	0	0	498
Edna's Eleven	4	F	5	1	1	0	8,214
Edna's Fancy	5	M	9	0	0	1	1,950
Edna's Girl	2	F	4	0	0	0	150
Edna's Way	3	F	1	0	0	0	135
Eds Brother Fred	3	G	3	0	0	0	315
Ed's Devil	3	C	2	0	0	0	0
Ed's Party Boy	4	G	5	2	1	0	19,660
Eecchhoo	3	C	1	1	0	0	4,500
Eecheero	3	G	5	2	1	0	11,848
Eejay	8	G	6	1	0	2	9,500
Eek Meek	3	G	11	0	0	3	2,431
Effective Icarus	5	G	21	0	4	2	13,271
Efficacious	4	G	15	0	4	1	7,437
Effortless	6	M	2	0	0	0	100
Efforts Reward	5	M	1	0	0	0	0
Effrene	6	M	5	0	0	0	870
Effusive	6	G	2	0	1	0	880
Efrain (ARG)	6	H	2	0	1	0	6,400
Egads	3	F	4	1	1	0	17,122
Egbert Lad	4	G	4	0	0	0	630
Egbert Picture	2	F	5	1	0	2	14,226
Egbert's Spirit	2	C	1	0	0	0	0
Egg Head	2	C	1	0	1	0	8,600
Egg Toss	2	F	1	0	0	0	400
Eggbert	7	G	3	0	0	0	2,550
Eggs Galaxy	7	M	3	0	0	0	80
Ego Me Go	2	F	6	0	0	3	3,058
Ego Sport	4	C	2	0	0	0	443
Egotist	4	G	10	1	1	1	11,381
Egret Miss	3	F	3	0	0	0	0
Egretfully True	5	M	9	0	0	0	441
Egyptian Exile	7	G	1	0	0	0	40
Egyptian Melody	6	M	2	0	0	1	451
Ehbeeceedee Ef Gee	2	C	2	0	0	0	800
Ehorse (AUS)	6	G	5	1	0	0	7,090
Ehorseracing	4	C	11	1	0	3	9,150
Ehukai	3	C	3	0	1	0	3,450
Eiffelegionaire	6	M	11	1	0	3	6,495
Eight a Lot	4	G	3	0	1	0	1,023

Horse	Age	Sex	Sts	1st	2d	3d	Won
Eight and Two	2	F	1	0	0	0	400
Eight Karat	3	F	10	1	3	2	56,284
Eight Madison Road	4	F	12	0	3	1	10,260
Eight O Eight	4	G	10	1	0	0	5,667
Eight Ten Special	2	C	3	0	0	0	618
Eighteen Issues	2	F	7	0	2	4	8,517
Eighteen Jewels	6	H	16	2	2	4	22,519
Eighteen Shots	2	F	1	0	0	0	120
Eighteenkaratgold	11	G	3	0	0	0	330
Eighties	9	G	12	3	1	0	12,561
Eights and Aces	3	G	3	0	0	0	315
Eightsecondstglory	4	C	3	0	0	0	200
Eighty Eighty	2	C	4	1	0	2	7,747
Eighty Nine	3	F	5	0	0	0	0
Eighty Proof	6	M	1	0	0	0	0
Eilunebs Dream	6	M	2	0	0	0	469
Einar	4	G	11	1	3	2	6,433
Eire of Domasca	8	M	7	0	0	1	1,470
Eisenhower	6	G	10	0	1	0	2,945
Eishin Illini Now	4	F	12	0	2	3	5,368
Eisman Stillwater	2	C	2	0	0	0	470
Either Orr	4	G	10	1	4	2	38,755
Ekati	5	G	12	0	1	5	19,015
Ekim Cielo	5	G	10	0	2	1	6,586
El Abigeo	5	H	7	0	1	1	5,930
El Aguilio	10	G	4	0	1	0	2,974
El Alteno	2	C	2	1	0	0	8,400
El Amigaso	2	C	2	0	0	0	0
El Amuleto (ARG)	7	G	9	2	1	1	5,765
El Andaliego	3	G	1	0	0	0	0
El Armstrong	3	C	7	1	0	1	4,927
El Arrabal (ARG)	4	G	3	1	0	0	5,850
El Arrabalero (ARG)	7	H	5	0	0	1	1,490
El Baby Grand	3	C	6	0	1	0	7,310
El Bambino	4	G	11	1	2	1	6,015
El Barranco	4	G	11	1	2	0	18,762
El Basque	7	G	1	0	0	0	0
El Batallon	2	C	7	1	0	3	45,620
El Belajo	3	F	9	1	1	2	10,010
El Bomba	5	G	6	2	1	0	40,402
El Bon	8	G	2	0	0	0	0
El Brette	5	G	8	0	0	1	5,292
El Cap	3	G	3	0	1	0	2,910
El Case	5	G	17	3	2	1	32,720
El Cassique	3	C	5	2	0	1	20,960
El Caurel (ARG)	6	H	10	1	1	3	18,105
El Chaparro	2	C	4	0	0	0	492
El Charro	3	C	2	0	0	0	480
El Chaval	5	G	5	0	0	0	1,056
El Chepo Cosa	5	G	8	1	1	2	14,922
El Chorro	6	H	2	0	0	0	0
El Cisc	4	G	13	1	3	4	52,138
El Citador	6	G	11	1	0	1	6,082
El Cometa	5	H	4	0	0	0	50
El Condor	5	G	10	1	4	1	49,820
El Cordoves	3	C	5	1	3	0	29,360
El Courageous	6	G	7	3	0	0	27,840
El Crusader	5	H	8	1	2	3	14,471
El Curioso	7	G	15	2	3	2	45,065
El Damien	3	F	5	1	0	1	22,030
El Delegado	3	C	17	4	4	3	77,372
El Depressa (BRZ)	6	G	15	3	1	4	30,405
El Diago	8	G	6	2	1	0	29,966
El Divinidoso	3	G	4	0	0	0	610
El Domenico	5	G	3	0	1	1	4,590
El Don	3	G	6	2	0	1	80,442
El Dorado Fair	3	G	3	0	0	0	260
El Dorado Shooter	7	G	6	0	1	0	20,982
El Duque	3	C	8	2	1	0	15,065
El Duro	5	H	3	0	0	0	250
El Elogiado (ARG)	4	C	3	0	1	1	19,080
El Fabio	4	G	9	1	3	1	20,655
El Frio	4	G	14	3	0	2	21,965
El Fumar	5	G	4	0	0	0	2,100
El Galante	3	C	3	0	1	0	7,800
El Gallo	3	G	16	2	1	0	21,355
El General	5	G	3	2	0	1	48,000
El Giuliani	5	G	6	1	1	2	2,295
El Gordo Sam	3	G	7	0	2	2	12,080
El Graduado (CHI)	7	G	11	0	1	1	5,315
El Gran Andre	2	C	4	1	0	1	38,723
El Gran Fran (ARG)	7	H	18	2	3	0	8,538
El Gran Jesse	2	C	6	0	0	0	2,154
El Gran Maestro	4	C	7	0	0	0	17,058
El Gran Marco	4	G	20	3	4	5	63,050
El Gran Patagon	5	G	15	3	5	2	34,960
El Gran Philip	3	G	4	0	0	0	149
El Grand Hank	2	C	9	0	2	1	17,349
El Grande Eloper	4	G	10	0	1	2	3,475
El Grande Seville	2	G	10	1	1	2	23,750
El Guapito (ARG)	7	H	13	2	1	1	20,522
El Guappo	5	G	9	1	0	2	7,480
El Guardaespalda (CHI)	7	G	4	1	1	1	26,700
El Habanero	5	G	5	1	0	2	57,620
El Halcon (ARG)	5	H	5	0	2	1	6,692
El Halito	3	G	12	1	3	3	21,049
El Hielo Hombre	2	C	7	2	0	0	19,860
El Huichol	5	G	19	1	1	0	7,318
El Hustlero	3	G	1	0	0	1	2,400
El Insolente	4	C	1	0	0	0	98
El Jai Ton	5	G	5	2	0	1	7,594
El Keko	3	G	10	2	0	0	15,559
El Machi (ARG)	5	H	4	0	0	0	1,139
El Malicia	5	H	4	1	1	0	5,433
El Maloso	4	G	2	0	0	0	822
El Master	9	G	17	3	2	1	39,925
El Mat	4	G	5	0	0	0	34
El Merlot (ARG)	5	H	9	1	0	1	25,945
El Minuto	2	C	5	2	0	0	22,411
El Monstro	5	G	1	0	0	0	105
El Nil	3	F	3	0	0	0	262
El Nino Caliente	6	G	19	4	2	1	29,862
El Nino Mi Amor	6	G	3	0	0	0	342
El Noel	3	F	10	2	0	3	38,916
El Ojo Diablo	4	F	4	2	0	1	11,550
El Once (URU)	7	G	9	1	0	0	4,792
El Paso Ed	5	G	5	1	1	0	8,910
El Patron Grande	6	G	5	0	0	1	2,452
El Payaso Negro	10	G	1	0	0	0	0
El Pequeno	3	G	2	0	0	0	1,125
El Perfecto	2	G	3	0	1	0	9,000
El Poderoso	5	G	11	0	0	2	2,975
El Prado Diamond	4	F	12	1	2	3	10,627
El Prado Essence	7	M	4	0	3	1	90,035
El Prado in Action	6	G	4	0	0	1	4,520
El Prado Rob	3	C	9	0	0	0	37,714
El Prado's Boy	3	G	4	1	1	1	19,750
El Prado's Gal	3	F	6	1	0	1	33,101
El Prado's Plata	4	F	6	0	0	0	1,600
El Prados Treasure	6	G	10	2	1	0	2,636
El Primo Mayor	3	C	1	0	0	0	0
El Privado	3	G	3	0	0	0	797
El Progreso	6	G	10	0	1	0	16,770
El Puma	3	C	6	0	2	1	13,830
El Raja	3	C	12	0	0	5	4,708
El Rayo (ARG)	4	C	6	0	0	1	2,680
El Remolino	3	C	11	1	0	3	10,540
El Reno de Oro	4	G	8	0	0	3	2,584
El Rey de Oro	5	G	8	1	0	0	3,033
El Rodeo	3	C	6	1	1	0	6,237
El Rojo Grande	2	C	2	0	1	0	5,000
El Ronda	3	F	5	0	0	1	1,403
El Ruller	4	C	4	0	0	2	12,120
El S You	3	G	3	0	2	0	5,558
El Saba	3	G	4	0	0	0	567
El Segundo Joe	3	G	14	2	4	3	60,950
El Siete	3	G	3	0	1	0	1,416
El Siete O Siete	3	C	10	0	1	2	4,093
El Sloridno	2	C	3	0	0	1	6,468
El Soprano	5	H	3	0	0	1	7,700
El Spedito	4	G	11	4	1	2	38,121
El Spotro	3	G	4	0	0	0	0
El Superhombre	5	H	1	1	0	0	5,100
El Tampaino	5	G	6	0	0	3	3,999
El Tara	3	F	6	2	0	1	65,790
El Tazar	8	G	4	0	0	0	132
El Temperamental	8	G	4	0	0	0	774
El Teporocho	8	G	11	3	3	1	5,320

Horse	Age	Sex	Sts	1st	2d	3d	Won
El Tio Luis	4	G	7	0	1	0	2,288
El Tirador	3	C	2	0	0	1	4,050
El Tricko	2	G	1	0	0	0	0
El Trickster	3	F	5	0	0	0	2,751
El Troppo	5	G	1	0	1	0	2,200
El Unica	3	G	2	0	0	0	0
El Veloz	3	G	8	1	1	1	7,703
El Veneno	4	G	7	1	0	0	4,290
El Vigia (MEX)	9	G	2	0	0	0	0
El Waco	5	G	7	3	0	0	10,630
El Yunque	3	C	8	0	1	2	5,643
El Zacatecano	3	G	4	1	0	0	10,400
Ela Ela	4	F	6	0	1	1	17,941
Elaboration	4	F	9	2	2	1	31,510
Elaine Marie	3	F	11	1	1	3	12,295
Elaine's Wolfer	3	C	3	0	1	0	5,425
Elaine's Wolfette	4	F	6	0	0	0	1,796
Elakouklamou	3	F	8	0	0	0	1,223
Elana d'Amour	5	M	6	0	1	1	11,965
Elated Spirit	4	C	4	0	1	0	2,919
Elated Won	3	G	7	0	2	1	11,068
Elbe	5	G	1	0	1	0	1,780
Elberton	7	G	4	0	0	0	1,500
Elberton Ellie	5	M	15	0	1	1	10,830
Elberton Lass	5	G	18	0	1	1	6,029
Elberton Miss	3	F	5	0	0	1	980
Elbow Creek	5	G	8	2	1	0	9,324
Elcoquisound	4	C	4	0	0	0	125
Eldahma	2	F	4	0	0	0	0
Elder	2	C	3	1	0	1	34,350
Elder Statesman	3	C	7	1	1	2	28,841
Eldixie	3	G	8	1	0	1	6,081
Eldo the Cad	6	G	7	2	0	0	2,695
Eldons Dancer	4	G	17	2	4	3	14,175
Eldorado Gold	8	G	5	0	1	1	1,788
Eldorado Ridge	6	G	2	0	0	0	470
Eleanor Rose	3	F	8	2	0	1	25,930
Eleanor's Gift	3	G	11	1	3	1	34,585
Election Night	4	G	17	1	3	1	8,399
Electoral College	5	G	6	1	1	0	14,003
Electric	2	C	2	0	0	0	2,170
Electric Affair	4	F	10	0	2	0	1,118
Electric Chair	4	F	4	2	0	1	54,840
Electric Fuse	3	G	11	2	1	3	21,219
Electric Guitar	4	G	5	0	0	2	2,990
Electric Heat	3	F	5	1	0	1	8,480
Electric Light	2	C	3	1	0	1	34,395
Electric Princess	2	F	2	0	0	0	254
Electric Prospect	3	G	5	0	0	1	1,045
Electric Punch	5	G	15	0	0	0	1,179
Electric Salt	5	G	11	1	0	2	3,974
Electric Star	6	M	7	0	1	0	1,950
Electric Storm	4	F	4	0	0	0	214
Electric Wire	3	F	7	1	0	2	17,519
Electrical Carlita	4	F	17	6	5	0	200,795
Electrification	2	F	1	0	0	0	180
Electrified	2	F	3	0	0	0	414
Electrisicul	4	G	8	1	0	0	5,565
Electrode	5	G	6	2	0	2	43,150
Elegant Alex	2	F	2	0	0	0	204
Elegant Ambassador	4	C	5	0	1	2	3,274
Elegant and Bold	3	F	8	1	0	0	4,961
Elegant Beau	8	G	5	0	0	0	0
Elegant Bobbi	3	F	2	0	0	0	500
Elegant by Design	3	F	5	0	0	1	2,465
Elegant Canyon	4	F	5	0	0	0	552
Elegant Chance	2	F	3	0	0	1	2,550
Elegant Colors	7	M	7	0	2	0	6,100
Elegant de Ledo	4	F	2	0	1	1	1,030
Elegant Designer	4	F	4	0	1	1	23,675
Elegant Edge	4	F	3	2	1	0	35,260
Elegant Era	2	F	3	0	1	0	2,788
Elegant Expo	3	F	2	1	0	0	2,035
Elegant Fame	3	C	9	4	1	3	96,546
Elegant Force	3	G	1	0	0	0	96
Elegant Fox	5	M	7	1	0	1	7,431
Elegant Heiress	3	F	4	1	0	1	7,704
Elegant Hunter	5	H	11	1	1	0	36,119
Elegant Jude	3	G	2	0	0	0	105
Elegant Lass	7	M	2	0	0	0	240
Elegant Legacy	2	C	3	0	1	0	6,440
Elegant Light	4	F	12	3	1	0	17,875
Elegant Luck	4	F	2	0	0	0	252
Elegant Magic	8	M	8	1	2	1	6,528
Elegant Mercedes	4	F	9	3	2	0	109,175
Elegant Miss Match	6	M	6	0	0	1	1,390
Elegant Ore	4	F	2	0	0	0	0
Elegant Paradox	3	F	16	1	2	2	42,469
Elegant Rosey	4	F	15	2	3	3	9,654
Elegant Serenade	5	M	8	0	0	1	2,348
Elegant Sunrise	6	M	8	0	0	1	1,886
Elegant Touch	4	F	4	0	0	0	959
Elegant Trend	6	H	5	0	2	2	12,400
Elegante Senor	6	G	12	2	0	1	6,031
Elegantly Wasted	7	M	11	1	1	3	14,920
Element K.	3	F	3	0	0	0	0
Elena's Fame	4	C	3	0	0	0	288
Eleusis	3	F	7	6	1	0	165,801
Elevado	2	G	1	0	0	0	300
Eleven Oclock Rock	3	G	8	3	1	0	42,730
Eleven Red	3	G	3	0	1	0	4,900
Eleven Roses	2	F	1	0	0	0	0
Eleven Stars	3	C	6	1	0	0	25,490
Eleven Sterling	4	G	6	1	1	1	13,203
Eleven Twentythree	3	G	3	0	0	0	269
Eleven West	6	G	8	3	0	0	7,910
Elevenlittledevils	5	M	4	0	0	0	570
Eleventh Street	2	F	5	0	2	2	31,664
Eleventhirtynews	4	G	10	0	2	1	4,055
Elfin	4	F	10	1	1	1	8,450
Elgatoesmio (ARG)	6	G	7	0	2	4	10,170
Elhew Henderson	4	C	4	0	1	0	4,109
Elhew Midway	4	F	11	1	1	3	31,589
Eli Lilliput	7	H	1	0	0	0	275
Eligance	6	M	4	0	1	1	1,990
Eligant Susan	3	F	3	0	0	0	300
Eligible Bachelor	4	C	10	4	0	0	28,053
Eligible Receiver	5	G	5	1	2	0	15,300
Elijah Hill	10	G	10	1	2	0	6,860
Elijah M.	2	C	4	0	0	0	980
Elijah the Profit	9	G	2	0	0	0	112
Elijah's Buck	4	G	9	2	1	1	20,095
Elijah's Profit	9	G	1	0	0	0	0
Elijah's Song	3	C	1	0	0	0	320
Elijan	7	G	1	0	0	0	69
Eliminate	5	G	18	4	1	5	40,565
Elin	5	M	15	2	1	3	20,065
Elio Monti	9	G	4	0	0	0	430
Elisa Jane	4	F	3	0	1	1	2,410
Elisa's Energy	2	F	1	0	1	0	7,000
Eliseebeau	3	G	2	0	0	0	0
Elisha Joy	4	F	9	0	1	1	4,087
Elite	3	G	13	2	1	0	30,790
Elite Brother	4	G	9	0	1	1	4,396
Elite Cat	6	M	9	0	1	2	4,911
Elite Commander	2	C	3	0	0	0	0
Elite Cove	5	G	8	0	0	0	310
Elite Elion	4	G	1	0	0	0	215
Elite Express	3	F	8	0	1	1	2,520
Elite Guard	5	G	15	4	4	1	16,498
Elite Jet	9	G	1	0	0	0	90
Elite Mercedes	7	G	7	1	1	0	27,920
Elite Nine	4	F	12	0	0	2	860
Elite Service	3	G	13	1	0	3	18,336
Elite Tour	4	F	5	0	2	1	4,321
Elitra Rx	4	F	3	0	0	0	0
Eliza Bella	3	F	4	0	1	1	3,830
Eliza Ra	4	F	6	1	0	0	2,941
Elizabeth Said No	3	F	11	0	1	1	3,815
Eliza's Cat	4	F	1	0	0	0	200
Elke	2	F	7	2	3	1	110,800
Ella Bella	4	F	2	1	0	0	16,955
Ella F.	3	F	8	0	1	2	10,238
Ella Va Wish	4	F	3	0	0	0	304
Ellaroo	4	F	7	1	1	0	4,748
Ella's Forum	5	M	7	0	0	0	1,695
Elle Runaway	2	F	5	1	1	0	31,962
Ellen in Disguise	5	M	14	0	0	0	846

Horse	Age	Sex	Sts	1st	2d	3d	Won
Ellena	4	F	1	0	0	0	425
Ellens Dream	4	F	1	0	0	0	0
Ellen's Epiphany	5	G	6	0	0	0	180
Ellens Kid	3	G	7	1	0	0	2,363
Ellens Lucky Star	5	M	8	4	1	1	95,766
Ellen's Souvenir	4	F	1	0	0	0	80
Ellensburg	7	M	11	2	0	2	21,494
Ellenton Lass	4	F	8	3	0	1	16,898
Ellerbeck Street	2	C	1	0	0	0	0
Elle's Terms	4	F	16	0	0	2	3,844
Ellie E	2	F	1	0	0	0	100
Ellie Gator	3	F	3	0	0	0	0
Ellie Gee	3	F	5	0	1	0	3,899
Ellie Q	4	F	5	0	0	0	1,965
Ellie Sue	5	M	4	0	0	1	481
Ellieburg	7	M	3	1	0	1	2,634
Ellieonthemarch	3	F	5	2	0	0	43,296
Ellie's Choice	6	G	8	3	1	1	24,910
Ellie's Princess	5	M	6	0	1	1	6,974
Ellie's Quest	5	M	8	1	1	1	19,335
Ellie's Rainbow	4	F	1	0	0	0	0
Ellie's Wesh	2	G	1	0	0	0	1,380
Ellie's Wish	6	G	7	1	2	1	7,128
Elliesakeeper	3	F	3	0	0	0	165
Ellingtonian	6	G	4	0	0	0	750
Elliot Bay	3	G	6	0	2	0	3,094
Elliot's Way	2	G	6	0	1	0	2,460
Ellishugh	2	C	4	1	0	2	13,454
Elloluv	4	F	5	1	0	1	75,600
Ells Editor	3	F	18	4	2	2	40,265
Ellston	7	G	3	0	0	0	0
Ellsworth	3	G	18	1	5	2	20,678
Elly On My Mind	3	F	6	1	0	1	6,581
Elm	3	G	11	1	1	2	14,216
Elmer and Harriet	2	G	2	0	0	0	615
Elmo's Boots	3	G	1	0	0	0	90
Elm's Girl	2	F	1	0	0	0	0
Elm's Legacy	9	G	12	0	0	1	3,324
Eloquent Dawn	3	F	8	1	0	1	5,577
Eloquent Ginette	3	F	10	3	1	2	28,460
Eloquent Wager	5	G	15	5	4	0	80,510
Eloquently	2	F	5	0	0	0	1,700
Elora	4	F	11	1	5	0	20,228
Elpeeda	3	F	7	0	0	1	1,650
Elrita (NZ)	6	M	7	0	0	0	1,072
Elrod Petry	4	G	1	0	0	1	1,529
Elron	3	G	10	2	1	0	17,838
Elroy	6	G	7	0	0	1	742
Els Belle	6	M	6	0	0	0	725
El's Big Hit	3	F	1	0	0	0	90
El's Demaloot	3	G	7	0	1	1	6,014
El's Legacy	3	C	8	1	2	3	10,990
El's Red Cat	4	F	6	0	3	0	11,355
El's Well	4	F	5	1	1	1	15,924
El's Wish	4	F	2	0	0	0	120
Elsa's Place	3	F	4	0	0	0	1,881
Elshaan	3	C	1	0	1	0	9,200
Elsie Lucille	2	F	5	0	1	2	11,900
Elsie Rose	3	F	2	0	0	1	2,320
Eltish Lady	3	F	1	1	0	0	16,400
Eltish Ride	2	C	3	0	1	0	4,500
Elton	4	G	16	2	1	3	28,650
Elton D	8	G	6	0	0	0	0
Elttaes Bay	7	G	3	0	1	0	741
Elty	2	F	1	0	0	0	0
Elusion	8	G	3	0	0	1	2,255
Elusive A. C.	4	F	3	2	1	0	64,780
Elusive Angel	3	F	3	0	0	0	900
Elusive Ashlee	5	M	5	1	0	0	13,392
Elusive Aussie	3	C	8	1	0	0	16,560
Elusive Chris	2	C	6	2	3	0	122,570
Elusive City	4	C	1	0	0	0	0
Elusive Dawn	3	F	4	1	1	1	34,785
Elusive Diva	3	F	9	3	1	2	221,470
Elusive Figure	4	G	7	1	1	1	15,220
Elusive Fleet	3	F	1	0	0	0	0
Elusive Gal	3	F	1	1	0	0	10,004
Elusive Gentleman	4	C	2	0	1	0	2,500
Elusive Glory	3	C	5	1	0	1	26,882
Elusive Honey	4	F	8	1	2	2	45,610
Elusive Indian	4	G	15	3	1	1	26,285
Elusive Jo Jo	4	F	2	0	0	0	878
Elusive Jordan	3	C	8	2	1	1	40,208
Elusive Joy	3	F	4	0	1	0	5,191
Elusive King	3	G	8	1	1	2	16,680
Elusive Knight	3	C	9	1	2	1	71,942
Elusive Magic	4	G	8	2	1	0	18,840
Elusive Miss	4	F	1	0	0	0	106
Elusive Princess	4	F	2	0	0	1	4,420
Elusive Project	3	F	7	0	3	0	25,100
Elusive Queen	3	F	4	1	0	0	15,090
Elusive Reply	7	G	4	1	0	0	6,586
Elusive Road	4	F	8	1	1	0	17,750
Elusive Smile	3	F	5	1	2	0	36,100
Elusive Speed	3	F	12	1	3	1	15,153
Elusive Thought	4	F	2	0	0	0	1,115
Elusive Thunder	2	C	7	2	1	0	75,420
Elusive Time	3	G	8	1	1	1	21,360
Elusive Toga	2	F	1	0	0	0	0
Elusive Touch	3	F	10	0	0	3	15,310
Elusive Wolf	6	M	13	3	1	3	19,015
Elusively	3	C	3	1	0	0	9,000
Elvis Impressme	4	G	7	0	0	1	2,149
Elvis On Ice	6	G	15	0	0	0	1,495
Elvis Presto	7	G	9	1	3	1	6,000
Elvisvader	4	C	1	0	0	0	140
Elway Uran	5	M	3	1	1	0	24,400
Elway's Way	5	G	17	3	2	0	22,426
Elwha	4	G	9	3	1	1	28,744
Elwood Blues	10	G	2	0	0	0	0
Elwood's Apple	4	G	6	0	0	2	4,751
Elwood's Wishes	4	C	13	1	0	4	29,807
Ely Hasseen	4	G	7	2	0	0	7,418
Elyon	4	G	14	1	2	4	42,908
Ely's Boy	9	G	2	0	0	0	0
Ely's Shadow	3	G	5	0	1	0	2,940
Elyse Lane	4	F	8	0	2	1	5,595
Elysian Elway	6	G	7	0	1	0	5,908
Elysian Springs	5	M	7	0	0	0	808
Elzabad	6	H	3	1	1	0	10,340
Em B. Aye	3	G	7	2	1	0	41,916
Em Vee	6	M	15	2	4	2	12,538
Ema Bovary (CHI)	5	M	5	4	1	0	521,780
Ema Dancer	4	F	3	1	1	0	14,279
Emagine That	5	M	2	0	0	0	357
Email Eddie	5	G	7	0	0	0	310
Emancipatorempress	3	F	6	0	0	0	0
Embank	3	F	10	1	1	2	37,556
Embarassing Moment	3	F	7	1	0	2	4,741
Embarkation	3	C	2	0	1	0	6,935
Embassey Gardens	2	F	4	1	1	0	18,920
Embassy Storm	2	G	1	0	0	1	900
Embattle	5	G	8	1	1	0	33,381
Embel	3	G	7	1	0	2	12,549
Embers to Ashes	2	F	1	0	0	0	56
Emblem Blues	2	C	3	0	2	1	8,000
Emblematic One	4	G	3	0	0	1	2,200
Emblem's Glory	3	F	8	1	1	2	19,436
Emblitterate	4	F	11	0	0	1	2,941
Embon	5	H	8	0	1	3	14,830
Embrace Reality	2	C	3	0	0	0	2,088
Embraccable Slew	2	F	1	0	0	0	400
Embraceable You	2	F	5	1	0	1	28,060
Embracing Monty	5	H	1	0	0	0	0
Embrasse Moi	4	F	7	4	1	0	73,380
Embullievable	5	G	9	0	1	2	8,939
Emerald Cliff	3	C	2	0	0	0	125
Emerald Drive	7	G	11	4	1	1	25,194
Emerald Earrings	3	F	9	5	4	0	285,406
Emerald Flame	3	F	4	0	0	0	0
Emerald Forest	10	G	5	0	0	1	896
Emerald Green	5	M	6	0	0	0	3,060
Emerald Irish	3	F	10	1	1	3	9,048
Emerald N Pearls	3	F	14	2	1	1	35,095
Emerald Sea	3	F	9	1	0	3	22,818
Emerald Verse	7	M	1	0	0	0	0
Emerald Vie	4	F	13	4	0	2	15,429
Emerald's Pause	4	F	11	2	4	0	27,276

Horse	Age	Sex	Sts	1st	2d	3d	Won
Emeraude	3	F	4	0	0	0	540
Emergency Status	5	G	4	0	0	0	571
Emerging Spirit	4	G	7	0	0	1	8,882
Emeritus	4	C	1	0	0	0	880
Emerson Drive	3	G	10	1	1	6	25,719
Emerson's Go Jo	3	F	7	1	0	0	8,350
Emery	4	G	12	1	5	2	10,794
Eme's Sister	3	F	3	0	0	0	0
Emil Brook	3	G	11	1	3	1	23,950
Emilie	4	F	9	0	0	1	1,735
Emilin	3	G	22	2	2	6	27,980
Emily Blaze	3	F	4	2	0	1	27,875
Emily P.	6	M	11	0	2	2	12,374
Emily Ring	6	M	4	0	1	2	21,000
Emily Spinach	4	F	5	1	0	0	7,329
Emily Wild	3	F	11	3	3	1	38,272
Emily's Attitude	7	M	2	0	0	1	715
Emily's Call	3	F	4	0	1	2	4,095
Emilys Collegefund	5	M	2	0	0	0	78
Emily's Emerald	2	F	8	0	3	1	7,464
Emily's Gal	4	F	14	1	0	2	16,572
Emily's Mark	5	M	5	1	1	2	21,320
Emilys Oyster	3	C	4	0	1	0	3,800
Emily's Partytime	2	F	1	0	0	0	0
Emily's Rare Trick	5	M	14	2	1	5	26,041
Emily's Reprized	5	M	6	0	0	0	478
Emily's Secret	4	F	8	0	0	0	3,050
Emily's Sugarbear	4	C	6	1	1	2	14,630
Eminent Victory	7	H	4	0	1	0	300
Emissary	2	C	1	0	0	0	125
Emjay H.	4	F	13	2	2	1	28,705
Emma Anne	3	F	7	1	1	0	47,354
Emma M.	3	F	5	0	0	0	4,734
Emma Nicole	2	F	6	0	0	2	2,778
Emma Renee	3	F	4	0	0	0	4,911
Emmanellie	2	F	1	0	1	0	4,600
Emma's Acquittal	2	F	2	0	0	0	2,208
Emmas Aunt Amy	2	F	4	0	1	0	6,307
Emma's Cat	3	G	7	0	0	1	748
Emma's Delite	6	M	6	0	0	0	1,435
Emma's Frown	3	F	11	0	2	3	12,973
Emma's Honor	8	M	8	3	0	0	26,230
Emma's R Hope	3	F	6	0	1	0	2,110
Emma's Wish	3	F	15	2	2	4	13,940
Emmet Square	4	G	8	2	3	0	25,108
Emmett Express	3	G	2	0	0	0	124
Emmie's Turn	5	M	11	0	3	1	5,229
Emmitts Black Book	4	G	6	1	1	0	8,981
Emmy Winner	2	F	2	1	0	0	4,600
Emmylou One Too	2	F	1	0	0	1	2,915
Emmy's Storm	2	F	2	1	1	0	25,000
Emo	4	C	15	2	1	1	32,170
Emolument	6	H	6	0	0	0	1,021
Emor	7	G	4	1	0	1	4,531
Emotion in Motion	2	F	2	0	1	0	1,515
Emotion Ontheocean	2	F	1	0	0	0	0
Emotional Belle	4	F	9	0	2	0	1,384
Emotional Bluff	3	F	8	1	2	1	31,053
Emotional Ending	4	G	21	4	0	1	24,236
Emotional Episode	2	F	6	0	2	1	6,980
Emotional Era	4	G	7	0	0	0	791
Emotional Girl	7	M	2	0	0	0	0
Emotional Rosie	4	F	5	0	0	0	1,860
Emotional Storm	4	F	3	1	1	0	15,570
Emotrin	4	G	7	2	1	1	69,127
Emperer Walz	3	C	1	0	0	0	260
Emperor's Holiday	2	G	2	0	0	0	278
Emperor's Victory	7	G	2	0	0	1	888
Emphatic Cayanna	4	F	3	0	0	0	0
Empire Builder	5	G	17	2	0	1	7,363
Empire Knight	8	G	1	0	0	0	196
Empire Man (ARG)	5	G	6	1	0	1	13,860
Empire of Glory (ARG)	6	H	19	2	0	4	13,240
Empire Savannah	7	G	8	0	1	0	2,215
Empire Storm	6	H	2	0	0	0	190
Emporia	6	G	10	2	2	0	23,370
Empowered Shark	3	G	10	1	0	0	5,346
Empowerment	2	C	1	0	0	0	115
Empress Anna	6	M	1	0	0	0	0
Empress of Sheba	4	F	7	2	1	1	71,669
Empress Zita	4	F	6	2	1	1	9,466
Emptor	3	F	11	1	2	4	36,485
Empty Holster	3	G	11	2	1	0	36,025
Empty Portrait	3	F	2	0	0	0	0
Empty Promises	4	G	6	0	0	0	136
Empty Revolver	3	C	9	1	1	3	10,812
Empty the Tank	3	C	4	1	0	0	9,158
Em's Echo	4	C	21	0	3	2	9,719
Emtyazat (GB)	3	F	7	1	1	2	34,052
Emy Sue	4	F	6	1	4	0	15,767
Emyil's Dreamer	3	C	11	1	1	4	13,230
En Avant	3	F	12	1	1	2	7,733
En El Fuego	2	G	6	0	2	2	40,260
En La Zona	3	F	8	0	3	2	8,743
En Safari	9	G	4	0	0	1	2,062
Encantador	4	G	12	1	2	2	19,103
Encanto Oro	3	F	2	0	0	0	150
Enchanted Fan	3	G	6	0	0	0	766
Enchanted Ghost	9	H	1	0	0	0	0
Enchanted Grounds	3	F	5	0	0	0	410
Enchanted Indy	3	G	2	0	0	1	1,600
Enchanted Kitten	4	F	1	0	0	0	60
Enchanted Looker	5	M	6	0	1	0	4,582
Enchanted Magic	3	C	1	1	0	0	7,200
Enchanted Moment	3	F	7	1	1	0	3,852
Enchanted Prospect	3	F	11	1	0	1	6,035
Enchanted Stag	2	F	1	0	0	0	184
Enchanting Gal	3	F	10	0	0	1	4,136
Enchanting Gold	4	F	3	0	0	0	493
Enchanting Lady	2	F	1	0	1	0	7,000
Enchanting Lass	5	M	3	0	0	0	276
Enchanting Thing	3	F	3	0	0	0	142
Encinal	2	C	2	0	0	0	1,680
Encino Cat	7	H	6	0	0	0	257
Encino Ump	5	G	3	2	1	0	7,360
Encompass	3	C	4	0	0	2	1,325
Encore	2	F	1	0	0	0	0
Encore Encore	3	F	3	0	0	0	2,288
Encore Express	9	M	4	0	0	1	921
Encore Prince	6	G	9	0	1	2	7,264
Encrypted	2	C	3	1	1	0	14,310
End All	5	G	2	0	0	0	0
End Leader	7	G	1	0	0	0	735
End of an Era	3	C	7	1	0	1	28,840
End of Love	3	G	17	2	2	1	11,745
End Sweep's Gold	4	G	12	0	4	2	12,515
End the Terror	4	G	9	0	0	0	1,068
End Up	7	G	12	1	6	2	27,275
End Wisely	6	G	14	3	2	1	38,210
Endearings Wish	3	F	4	0	0	0	0
Ended	3	G	10	1	3	3	50,637
Endemaj	4	C	2	0	0	0	0
Ender Wiggin	8	G	1	0	0	0	840
Enderby	3	G	1	0	0	0	0
Ender's Shadow	4	G	5	1	1	0	86,816
Ender's Sister	3	F	7	2	3	1	317,580
Endian Outlaw	5	G	8	0	1	3	3,363
Endigo Prince	5	G	2	0	0	0	0
Endless Dream	2	F	3	0	1	0	13,270
Endless Endeaver	3	G	6	1	0	0	5,291
Endless Fable	4	G	17	1	2	1	8,210
Endless Fanfare	3	C	1	0	0	0	0
Endless Good	4	F	10	1	0	1	6,089
Endless Mountain	2	C	7	0	1	2	10,650
Endless Obsession	7	G	9	0	2	2	7,031
Endless Pleasure	4	F	8	1	2	1	8,660
Endless Posibility	5	M	11	1	2	1	16,551
Endless Quest	3	F	11	0	0	1	6,400
Endless Song	6	G	1	0	0	0	110
Endless Torrential	6	G	1	0	0	0	0
Endofthestorm	5	H	13	2	5	2	31,430
Endorse Here	3	C	4	1	0	2	9,945
Endskip	5	M	12	0	0	0	2,865
Endure	3	F	2	0	0	0	0
Enduring Freedom	4	F	4	0	0	3	4,950
Enduring Grace	3	F	6	0	3	1	28,480
Enduring Light	3	F	10	3	1	3	31,173
Enduring Will	2	F	3	2	1	0	78,800

Horse	Age	Sex	Sts	1st	2d	3d	Won
Enemy Lines	3	F	4	1	0	0	2,668
Enemy Mine	3	F	7	1	2	0	15,205
Enemy Number Two	4	F	3	0	0	0	0
Energetic Music	2	C	2	0	0	1	2,860
Energetic Storm	3	C	9	3	0	1	50,632
Energized	7	G	6	0	0	1	1,750
Energy Berry	4	F	14	1	3	0	10,342
Energy Lass	3	F	22	3	2	4	36,775
Energy Rush	3	F	12	4	2	0	102,040
Enfatyouated	4	G	4	0	0	1	1,549
Engineered	4	C	9	2	2	1	78,025
England Calling	3	G	3	0	0	0	0
English Channel	2	C	1	1	0	0	27,600
English Gentlemen	7	G	13	0	1	0	3,664
English Harbour	4	G	6	2	1	1	43,795
English Princess	3	F	5	0	0	0	251
English Rain	2	C	3	0	0	0	3,690
Engraved	5	G	5	0	1	1	5,517
Engreido	3	G	5	1	1	0	6,860
Engulf	4	G	4	0	0	0	666
Enhanced Edition	3	G	9	1	0	1	25,835
Enjoy Idle Time	5	M	5	0	0	3	1,998
Enjoy the Dance	3	G	6	0	0	0	1,062
Enjoy the Journey	4	F	10	2	1	2	57,368
Enjoy the Wine	4	F	17	0	5	3	13,030
Enjoythe Afternoon	2	F	2	1	0	0	16,150
Enkidu	4	G	15	2	1	2	19,605
Enlightened Lassy	3	F	1	0	0	0	0
Enlist	4	G	4	0	0	1	1,860
Enmienda	2	F	2	1	0	0	7,710
Ennscho	5	G	9	1	1	1	11,180
Enorme	5	G	4	0	0	0	545
Enough Already	7	G	8	1	2	0	12,626
Enough Is Enough	2	C	5	2	1	1	199,410
Enough Music	7	G	5	0	0	1	1,657
Enpointe	2	F	1	0	0	0	0
Ensenada	3	F	8	2	2	1	66,055
Ensign Collins	2	G	9	0	0	0	2,829
Ensign D C	6	G	18	1	3	1	19,336
Ensign Jake	2	G	5	0	0	0	535
Ensign Meg	6	M	4	0	0	0	160
Ensign Slew	4	F	7	1	0	3	20,062
Ensign's Hope	3	F	2	0	0	0	120
Ensigns Spy	4	G	5	0	0	1	3,240
Entangle	7	G	15	2	1	0	9,999
Entanglement	3	F	9	0	0	1	2,042
Entendu	4	F	3	0	1	0	5,460
Enter Stage Left	2	F	3	0	1	0	5,430
Entergalatico	6	G	10	2	0	2	4,261
Enterprise Coast	3	F	1	0	0	0	975
Entertainthedollar	3	G	4	1	0	1	4,200
Entice Me	4	F	8	2	1	2	29,621
Enticing Beauty	4	F	8	0	1	2	5,804
Entitledtowin	6	G	8	1	0	1	5,189
Entitlement	5	H	3	0	0	1	4,800
Entour	4	F	11	2	2	0	11,513
Entrancing	5	M	5	1	2	1	11,712
Entrant	2	F	3	0	0	0	0
Entregada	2	F	3	0	1	0	8,278
Entrepreneurial	8	G	7	2	0	0	14,661
Entry Doon	6	M	5	0	0	0	1,271
Entry Point	3	C	4	1	0	1	28,800
Entushab	4	C	18	2	4	5	35,940
Entwiningars	6	G	2	0	0	1	1,134
Enuffdancin	4	G	4	0	1	1	1,167
Enumclaw Red	3	G	7	1	2	2	7,733
Environmentalist	4	C	2	0	0	0	0
Eolica	4	F	3	0	0	0	570
Eolo (IRE)	6	G	8	0	1	0	1,715
Epalo (GER)	5	H	5	2	2	1	1,141,228
Epaulet	3	G	12	0	3	3	9,425
Epee	6	G	4	1	0	1	8,367
Epic	4	G	4	0	0	1	9,396
Epic Account	3	G	1	0	0	0	90
Epic Commander	2	C	3	0	1	1	10,595
Epic Dish	2	F	3	0	0	0	1,443
Epic Drama	3	F	12	2	2	3	19,085
Epic Fling	3	G	12	1	4	1	18,275
Epic Gold	3	G	17	2	2	2	13,724

Horse	Age	Sex	Sts	1st	2d	3d	Won
Epic Holiday	3	F	12	1	1	2	13,031
Epic Knight	3	G	6	2	0	0	26,072
Epic Power	3	G	14	4	2	3	89,854
Epic Pursuit (IRE)	6	H	1	0	0	0	125
Epic Tale	2	G	6	2	0	2	5,775
Epic Thief	3	F	3	0	0	0	900
Epic Wood	6	G	15	2	5	3	16,310
Epica	3	F	2	0	0	0	640
Epicat	4	G	4	0	0	0	0
Epicentre	5	H	4	2	0	0	134,125
Episode On Tour	3	G	14	2	3	3	38,160
Episodic	2	F	1	0	0	0	0
Epona's Destiny	4	F	5	1	0	2	25,072
Epoxy	4	G	4	2	0	0	57,900
Epsomline	3	G	8	0	0	3	3,110
Equal Chance	8	G	2	0	0	1	1,140
Equal Rights (ARG)	6	G	10	2	1	0	54,240
Equay	3	F	6	1	2	1	9,904
Equestrian Girls	2	F	6	3	2	1	115,820
Equi Power	5	G	3	1	0	0	21,350
Equine Affair	5	M	5	0	0	1	1,372
Equip	6	G	7	0	0	0	588
Equit	3	G	16	1	2	1	8,883
Equivalence	5	M	3	1	0	1	3,558
Equivocate	6	G	2	0	0	0	80
Equus Maximas	5	G	1	0	0	0	0
Era Dynamic	6	M	10	0	0	3	3,330
Eradikate	4	F	7	1	0	1	6,777
Erase	4	F	9	0	1	4	30,859
Erda	5	M	2	1	0	1	25,560
Erewhon	3	C	3	1	2	0	67,070
Erhu	3	F	10	3	3	0	115,165
Eric C	4	G	7	0	0	0	595
Eric Da Bomb	7	G	7	1	1	3	37,475
Erica J	3	F	12	1	2	2	21,869
Erica's Chance	3	F	5	1	0	0	8,448
Erica's Money	5	M	7	1	0	0	7,504
Ericas Native	6	M	2	0	0	0	0
Erica's Num Num	3	G	4	0	0	0	160
Ericasdcllilah	3	F	2	0	0	0	0
Ericka's Eyes	3	F	7	1	1	0	22,207
Ericka's Lass	3	F	7	3	1	2	84,890
Erickson	5	G	1	0	0	0	0
Eric's Comet	7	H	10	0	1	1	4,294
Eric's Goody	3	C	1	0	0	0	0
Eric's Shark	2	F	3	0	0	1	1,745
Erik the Advisor	6	G	2	0	0	0	100
Erika Is a Hotty	3	F	1	0	0	0	39
Erika Miss Amerika	5	M	2	0	0	0	165
Erikas Pride	3	C	7	1	0	2	19,427
Erik's Chance	4	G	12	1	1	2	11,738
Erik's the Charm	3	C	5	1	1	0	35,800
Erimos (IRE)	5	M	11	2	2	2	34,920
Erin	4	F	6	3	2	0	42,814
Erin G.	8	M	1	0	0	0	960
Erin Go Bragh (NZ)	5	G	8	2	3	1	38,500
Erin Heights	4	G	3	0	2	0	2,720
Erindale Wild	2	F	1	1	0	0	6,600
Erin's Behaviour	2	F	2	0	0	0	300
Erin's Hope	4	F	3	0	0	0	0
Erin's J T	4	G	10	1	2	1	5,838
Erins Jewel	6	M	4	1	0	0	4,592
Erin's Parade	3	F	1	0	0	0	130
Erin's Place	2	F	2	1	0	0	17,880
Erin's Silver Star	3	F	1	0	0	0	235
Erin's Storm	4	C	5	0	0	0	4,104
Erinsdesertsunrise	5	G	10	2	2	0	10,529
Erin'smalarky	5	M	15	2	1	1	11,673
Erinsouthernman	4	G	6	2	1	0	37,956
Eris Miss	3	F	2	0	0	0	800
Ernabel	4	F	8	0	2	1	18,547
Ernestgoestorace	4	G	3	0	0	0	567
Ernie Art	7	G	10	2	1	0	12,957
Ernie Bay	4	C	2	0	0	0	0
Ernie Cat	2	G	5	2	1	0	26,690
Ernie's Choice	3	G	1	0	1	0	8,200
Eroberer	3	C	10	2	0	4	50,786
Eros	3	G	16	5	3	1	68,960
Erotic	4	F	6	0	2	0	2,438

Horse	Age	Sex	Sts	1st	2d	3d	Won
Erotico	3	C	12	3	3	3	29,180
Erroneous I D	3	C	2	1	1	0	11,700
Erronous	5	G	1	0	0	0	0
Erudite	4	C	4	0	1	2	18,000
Erv's Creek	5	G	13	1	5	1	19,470
E's Beautiful	4	F	1	0	0	0	0
E's Happy Tune	5	G	16	1	2	1	6,696
Es Mi Sueno	2	F	2	1	0	0	3,625
Es Muy Stormy	4	F	9	1	1	3	9,315
Es Savoie	3	F	6	0	0	1	1,747
Es Special	4	G	10	2	2	0	23,938
E's Special Paddok	6	H	2	0	0	0	128
Escalade	7	G	12	2	4	3	10,457
Escalante	2	C	3	0	2	0	4,380
Escalate	4	C	8	1	1	2	16,473
Escalating	5	G	4	1	0	0	5,184
Escalero	4	G	18	2	2	5	11,772
Escalier	3	G	10	0	0	2	4,443
Escapade	3	F	10	3	1	2	18,064
Escaped Prisoner	3	G	9	0	0	0	3,600
Escaping Glory	2	F	1	0	0	0	0
Escapist	2	C	1	0	0	0	0
Escavating Haillie	3	F	1	0	0	0	0
Eskimo Aly	4	F	12	2	1	0	21,229
Eskimo Baby	5	M	2	0	0	0	275
Eskimo Hunter	5	G	9	0	0	1	1,419
Eskimo Ice	4	F	4	0	0	0	355
Eskimo Passion	8	G	14	2	2	2	30,938
Eskimo Pie Alamode	5	G	5	1	0	0	12,000
Eskimo Princess	4	F	14	1	3	1	17,780
Eskimo Scout	3	G	7	0	2	3	5,055
Eskimobelle	4	F	15	3	3	2	27,430
Eskimo's Deluxe	3	G	15	1	3	1	13,934
Eskimo's Igloo	3	F	4	0	1	0	1,810
Eslan	3	C	1	0	0	0	1,250
Esmay (AUS)	5	M	7	0	2	1	34,440
Esor's Hope	4	G	7	1	0	0	3,477
Espalier	3	G	3	0	0	0	0
Especialista (ARG)	6	G	5	2	1	1	17,373
Especially Honored	5	G	8	2	1	2	15,100
Especially Nice	3	F	21	3	4	3	16,391
Especially Royal	3	F	7	1	1	1	8,085
Especially Wild	5	M	10	2	1	0	13,600
Espee Ess	5	G	11	2	1	1	43,479
Espeedo	6	G	13	0	1	2	6,528
Esperanza Jazz	3	F	1	0	0	0	135
Esperanza Michele	4	F	1	0	0	0	119
Espiga	4	F	13	1	2	2	15,182
Espinoso (ARG)	5	G	9	2	1	1	10,449
Espirito Nocturno	3	C	3	0	0	2	2,090
Esplendida	3	F	6	1	0	1	21,514
Espresso Oro	9	G	9	1	0	1	9,943
Espy	4	F	5	0	3	1	36,300
Essa's Sharp	4	F	4	0	0	1	738
Esse Bee Gee	3	F	9	0	0	1	1,703
Essence	3	F	9	3	1	1	132,272
Essence of Snow	4	F	2	0	0	0	0
Essex Girl	4	F	9	0	0	2	2,472
Essie d'Or	7	M	10	0	0	0	1,773
Essuvee	4	F	4	0	1	0	672
Esta A.	7	M	4	1	0	0	4,405
Establish	6	G	8	1	3	0	25,590
Established Law	5	G	11	2	3	1	18,215
Establishmentcreek	3	F	7	1	1	2	28,810
Estacada	2	F	4	2	1	0	22,820
Estampa	3	F	3	0	0	1	1,375
Esta's Diamond	5	G	11	1	1	0	9,250
Esteban Miguel	3	C	5	1	1	1	18,474
Esteemed	5	G	12	3	1	2	28,015
Estella Corona	2	F	4	1	1	1	5,745
Este's Fiesta	4	F	3	0	0	0	1,218
Estevan	3	C	6	0	1	1	45,779
Esther Egg	9	G	15	2	6	1	32,400
Esther Honey	2	F	2	0	0	0	600
Esthers Ball	3	F	3	0	0	0	0
Esther's Pride	6	M	1	0	0	0	0
Esther's Star	4	F	12	1	2	1	59,776
Estherwood	4	F	4	1	1	0	9,150
Estilo de Cuervo	4	G	6	0	0	0	2,797
Estimated Prophet	4	G	8	1	1	1	11,886
Esto Hunter	3	F	3	0	0	1	2,813
Esto Music	4	G	9	0	1	1	2,370
Estonia	7	G	7	0	0	1	6,796
Estrada	5	M	7	1	0	1	22,487
Estravagario	9	G	7	1	1	0	9,496
Estrela de Roma (BRZ)	4	F	6	0	0	0	2,220
Estrelita D' Cielo	3	F	2	1	0	0	4,410
Estrella Belle	3	F	11	2	0	2	11,016
Estrella Fugas	4	F	13	2	0	2	9,415
Estrella Prisa	8	G	4	1	0	1	3,330
Et Tu Brute	2	C	1	0	0	0	0
Et Tu Brutus	3	C	7	1	0	0	5,123
Etamine	2	F	2	1	0	0	21,400
Etbauer Isle	3	F	5	1	0	0	6,215
Etbauer's Flush	3	F	10	1	1	1	9,940
Etbauer's Gift	3	C	5	1	3	0	9,200
Etbauer's Starlet	3	F	6	1	1	1	15,905
Etch	3	F	5	1	2	2	56,628
Eternal Cup	4	F	5	2	1	0	72,700
Eternal Dawn	3	F	14	4	5	2	40,354
Eternal Echo	6	G	11	0	2	0	3,234
Eternal Force	3	G	9	2	3	0	37,641
Eternal Glitter	3	G	13	1	2	1	19,620
Eternal Glow	4	C	10	2	1	1	18,006
Eternal Joy	2	F	4	1	0	0	9,453
Eternal Leader	9	G	5	0	0	2	1,391
Eternal Look	6	G	10	1	2	3	37,660
Eternal Melody (NZ)	4	F	3	1	0	1	57,630
Eternal Pass	2	G	1	1	0	0	8,100
Eternal Secrecy	7	G	9	0	1	0	8,984
Eternal Secret	5	M	9	0	0	1	1,134
Eternal Son	4	G	9	0	0	0	0
Eternal Sonset	2	C	6	0	0	0	3,450
Eternal Spirit	5	M	4	0	0	0	431
Eternal Summer	3	F	2	0	0	0	81
Eternal Tune	4	G	11	0	0	0	2,892
Eternally Irish	6	G	2	0	0	0	403
Ethan	4	C	2	0	0	0	94
Ethan's Legend	3	G	3	0	0	1	2,235
Ethel	3	F	5	0	0	2	2,975
Ethel On Tour	6	M	15	4	4	1	17,936
Ethical Actions	8	G	2	1	0	0	15,000
Etoile d'Or	3	F	5	0	0	0	2,518
Etoile Montante	4	F	6	2	2	1	340,149
Etoile Petite	2	F	5	1	2	1	41,161
Ett Ouimet	4	G	10	2	2	1	19,177
Etta's Current	10	G	11	2	0	1	11,019
Ettrick (GB)	8	H	2	1	0	1	19,400
Eufala	6	G	10	1	1	2	7,256
Eugapae	4	F	6	2	0	1	23,730
Eugenius Eugene	3	G	11	0	0	0	3,625
Eula Jane	2	F	1	0	0	0	155
Eunever	4	C	5	0	1	1	3,142
Eureka Moment	5	M	17	1	2	0	8,304
Eureka Valentine	4	F	1	0	0	0	140
Eurhrates	5	M	5	0	2	1	3,301
Euro Bond	7	G	5	1	0	1	17,700
Euro Liner	3	C	1	0	0	0	0
Euro Mazing Zarb	2	C	4	0	0	0	1,215
Eurocat	3	C	5	0	2	1	8,905
Euroclydon	9	G	12	1	2	3	17,635
Europe Again	3	F	3	0	1	0	9,250
European (IRE)	4	C	3	1	1	0	40,192
European Defense	7	G	13	2	4	1	16,004
European Flair	5	M	1	0	0	0	310
Eurosilver	3	C	4	1	2	0	90,860
Eusebio	2	G	2	0	1	0	4,672
Eva Mae	3	F	2	0	0	0	511
Evaluation	4	F	6	0	0	0	1,009
Evan N Harrys Miss	4	F	3	0	0	0	0
Evanescent	6	G	14	3	0	2	15,381
Evangelista	3	F	12	2	1	2	24,515
Evangelizer	3	F	3	1	1	0	36,140
Evanglie	4	G	10	0	1	2	4,204
Evans Catbird	3	F	12	0	3	2	9,385
Evan's Diamond	5	G	6	0	0	0	435
Evanwood	4	G	6	1	0	0	4,437
Evas Boy	3	C	2	0	0	0	0

Horse	Age	Sex	Sts	1st	2d	3d	Won
Eva's Pegasus	4	F	13	1	1	3	16,935
Eva's Prospector	4	F	3	0	0	0	411
Eva's Royalty	3	F	6	1	1	0	15,667
Evasive	3	F	3	1	2	0	38,840
Evasive Decision	6	G	1	0	0	0	0
Evasive Justice	3	F	1	0	1	0	2,700
Evasive Vision	4	F	2	0	0	0	490
Eve Harrington	8	M	8	0	0	1	5,274
Eve of Battle	4	F	11	2	1	1	27,180
Evelyn Negri	4	F	5	0	0	2	9,840
Evelyn's Escapades	8	M	6	0	0	0	400
Even Again	2	F	2	0	0	2	9,700
Even At Last	2	G	1	0	0	0	235
Even Flow	4	G	6	0	2	0	12,330
Even the Score	6	H	4	2	0	2	343,272
Eveniano	4	F	8	1	0	0	7,436
Evening After	5	M	2	0	0	0	505
Evening Attire	6	G	11	1	6	0	420,040
Evening Clinic	4	G	11	3	2	1	54,070
Evening Edition	3	F	12	1	3	3	50,378
Evening Encore (GB)	4	F	10	1	0	0	17,930
Evening Ice	3	G	8	1	1	0	9,085
Evening Interlude	3	G	7	0	0	0	1,160
Evening News	8	G	15	2	7	2	30,346
Evening On Rainier	4	F	6	0	0	1	6,790
Evening Pals	2	G	4	0	1	1	5,860
Evening Pleasures	3	C	3	1	0	0	15,180
Evening Proof	3	F	6	0	1	0	10,370
Evening Puzzles	5	G	4	1	0	0	4,581
Evening Shadows	4	F	10	2	0	0	22,690
Evening Show	4	F	1	0	0	0	500
Evening Star Rose	5	M	2	0	0	0	0
Evening Toni	2	F	3	0	0	0	0
Evening Trial	3	C	5	1	1	2	36,600
Evening Trick	3	F	1	0	0	0	118
Evening Winds	6	M	7	0	0	0	243
Evening's Luck	5	M	2	0	0	0	0
Eveningtime	3	F	7	0	1	2	4,690
Evensup	6	G	5	0	1	0	1,473
Event	6	G	16	3	1	2	27,331
Eventual	3	G	15	1	3	2	10,869
Eventually	3	F	4	0	0	0	976
Ever Forever	5	M	19	0	1	4	2,103
Everetts Codey	6	M	12	1	1	2	7,752
Everglades City	3	C	5	0	2	0	9,180
Everglades Drifter	2	G	3	1	0	1	9,320
Everglide	2	F	6	0	2	3	46,505
Everheart	3	F	5	2	1	1	61,300
Everlasting Gold	5	G	6	0	0	0	519
Everlasting Life	6	G	1	0	0	0	0
Everlasting Night	6	G	16	1	5	2	10,389
Everlasting Suave	5	G	8	0	1	0	6,050
Everlight	3	C	6	0	0	0	2,121
Eversmile	3	F	5	0	0	0	1,570
Everviligent	4	G	10	1	3	0	9,338
Everwhat	6	G	7	2	1	3	33,590
Everwood	3	C	3	0	0	2	9,090
Every Advantage	3	G	10	2	2	1	61,100
Every Hope	9	G	10	0	0	1	605
Every Mountain	4	C	6	0	0	1	9,218
Every Other Memory	2	F	6	1	1	1	26,680
Every Trick	3	F	9	1	2	1	51,700
Everybodylovesfuzz	7	G	4	1	1	0	14,761
Everybodywantssome	3	G	12	1	2	1	21,786
Everybottiwins	5	M	11	2	3	2	76,040
Everybuddysbizness	5	M	9	2	0	0	10,060
Everyday Magic	2	G	3	1	0	0	7,524
Everydayissaturday	3	C	10	3	1	0	130,909
Everyone Knows	4	G	7	1	1	0	16,421
Everyone's N. V.	4	C	7	2	2	1	4,080
Everything Is True	4	G	1	0	1	0	2,200
Everything to Gain	5	G	8	3	0	2	122,680
Everything Wild	3	G	9	1	1	1	15,380
Everythings Groovy	2	C	4	1	0	0	25,857
Everything's Jake	3	G	2	0	0	0	700
Everytricknthebook	3	G	8	3	0	3	18,379
Eves Eden	4	F	6	0	0	2	1,494
Eviction Notice	3	G	9	1	1	1	20,861
Evie's Appeal	8	M	10	1	2	2	9,646
Evil Axis	4	C	3	0	0	0	1,944
Evil Empress	2	F	3	0	0	0	2,184
Evil Eye Aly	4	F	8	1	0	1	25,205
Evil Eyes	7	M	6	0	2	0	3,733
Evil Hiss	7	H	10	2	0	0	6,673
Evil Ina	4	F	8	1	1	0	6,399
Evil Ivan	4	G	1	0	0	0	0
Evil Lady	5	M	5	1	1	1	17,345
Evil Minister	2	C	5	2	0	1	120,530
Evil Storm	3	G	11	1	0	3	20,070
Evil Tricks	7	M	15	0	1	2	4,227
Evitan Native	5	M	2	0	0	0	1,350
Evoke	4	C	1	0	0	0	0
Evolution	3	C	5	1	2	0	45,540
Evora	4	F	6	0	0	1	4,315
Evrstrive Evrshine	4	F	12	4	2	0	17,680
Evrybdyluvsdaheat	3	G	6	2	0	2	53,320
Evrybodylvsraymond	4	G	12	1	5	1	19,650
Evvy	7	M	8	0	0	0	2,965
Ex Federali	7	H	5	2	0	0	11,438
Ex Kay E	6	G	5	0	0	0	3,483
Ex Pirate	5	G	2	0	0	0	0
Ex Post Facto	7	G	2	0	0	0	535
Ex Pressed Blade	3	F	2	0	0	0	180
Ex Who	6	G	10	1	2	3	44,053
Ex. Alta	3	G	4	0	0	0	640
Exackary	4	G	16	0	6	4	11,927
Exactafact	2	F	1	0	0	0	555
Exaggerate This	3	G	12	2	4	0	105,794
Exaggeration	5	G	9	2	2	0	7,293
Exallent	3	F	9	3	1	1	32,890
Exalted Cat	2	C	1	0	1	0	8,400
Exanastasis	3	F	11	3	1	0	40,439
Excalate	6	H	8	1	1	0	9,750
Excaper	4	C	5	1	2	0	12,010
Excavadora	4	F	3	1	1	1	10,647
Excavation	5	G	12	1	1	1	16,585
Excavatress	5	M	5	0	0	1	2,492
Exceedinlegallimit	7	M	15	3	3	2	37,673
Excel for Me Marie	4	F	1	0	0	0	0
Excel Please	4	G	8	0	0	0	869
Excel to Accel	3	F	3	0	1	0	1,835
Excell to Fly	5	G	9	0	2	2	7,465
Excell to Indy	3	G	7	0	0	1	2,217
Excell to Victory	3	G	7	0	0	0	240
Excell Why Not	5	G	13	1	5	1	16,655
Excell With Elle	2	F	2	0	1	0	3,550
Excellenceinmotion	5	G	14	2	5	1	15,433
Excellent Advice	5	M	1	0	0	0	0
Excellent Band	3	C	7	0	0	0	8,882
Excellent Blend	3	G	4	0	0	0	995
Excellent Charisma	3	F	6	1	0	1	36,880
Excellent Cut (IRE)	4	C	2	1	0	0	12,300
Excellent Era	6	M	7	0	0	0	132
Excellent Idea	4	F	8	2	0	0	38,450
Excellent Job	3	G	19	5	4	1	48,975
Excellent Mandate	2	C	2	0	0	0	485
Excellent Minute	7	M	14	4	0	0	27,487
Excellent Payback	3	C	9	1	1	0	10,870
Excellent Play	3	F	10	1	1	2	8,405
Excellent Ways	4	F	8	0	0	0	2,206
Excellentcharacter	5	G	6	1	0	0	13,940
Exceller Lip	5	M	3	0	0	0	0
Excellwithluck	5	H	6	1	0	0	7,727
Exceptional Gift	6	G	18	2	3	2	17,740
Exceptional Ride	2	C	8	3	0	2	106,303
Exceptional Sunset	4	G	12	1	5	3	16,535
Exceptional Sway	2	F	5	0	0	0	800
Exceptional Tune	4	F	13	1	0	4	12,033
Exceptional Weave	5	M	7	0	1	1	1,749
Exceptionally	3	F	10	3	0	4	96,621
Exceptionally Fit	3	G	5	0	0	0	300
Exceptionalmiss	2	F	4	1	0	0	6,712
Exceso	3	G	1	0	0	0	74
Excess Caper	2	C	6	0	2	0	3,900
Excess Star	4	F	6	0	1	0	1,408
Excess Summer	4	G	6	1	1	2	228,200
Excess Taxes	3	G	2	0	0	1	5,280
Excess Yes	4	G	3	0	1	0	2,495

Horse	Age	Sex	Sts	1st	2d	3d	Won
Excessed	3	F	10	3	0	2	92,400
Excessive Barb	4	C	5	1	1	1	30,854
Excessive Behavior	5	H	7	3	1	0	49,940
Excessive Contact	3	G	4	1	1	0	23,400
Excessive Couture	2	F	2	0	1	0	1,844
Excessive Ego	4	F	12	0	3	1	16,447
Excessive Gray	2	F	10	0	2	3	13,043
Excessive Hayate	4	G	10	5	2	1	90,560
Excessive Hearts	2	F	2	1	0	1	14,750
Excessive Noise	6	H	4	0	0	0	1,930
Excessive Options	2	C	6	2	1	0	39,610
Excessive Reign	3	F	10	2	0	4	39,349
Excessive Storm	2	F	3	0	1	0	2,900
Excessive Tab	4	G	9	1	0	1	19,631
Excessive Term	4	G	6	1	0	0	4,980
Excessive Witch	2	F	3	0	0	0	129
Excessively Bold	3	G	5	2	0	0	11,200
Excessively Nice	2	F	2	1	0	1	50,220
Excessivelycasual	7	M	7	4	1	0	19,555
Excessiveobsession	2	F	2	0	0	0	2,500
Excessivepleasure	4	G	5	0	1	1	133,588
Exchange Bay	4	F	6	0	1	1	19,470
Exchange for Gold	4	C	3	1	1	0	8,175
Excitable	3	F	13	1	3	4	46,334
Excited At Last	5	G	9	0	0	1	1,233
Exciting Jewel	6	M	5	0	0	0	307
Exciting Metro	3	C	2	1	0	0	30,895
Exciting Prospect	3	F	12	0	1	1	2,525
Exciting Slippers	4	F	2	0	0	0	0
Exciting Times	2	C	8	0	0	0	9,090
Exciting Trick	4	G	12	2	2	1	12,595
Exciting Venture	5	G	5	0	0	1	5,521
Exclamation	3	G	1	0	0	0	400
Exclusive Attitude	5	H	3	0	0	0	482
Exclusive Autumn	3	G	1	0	0	0	0
Exclusive Babe	2	F	2	0	0	0	270
Exclusive Banker	5	G	12	0	1	2	14,285
Exclusive Becky	3	F	1	0	0	0	105
Exclusive Bud	6	G	5	0	0	0	0
Exclusive Charm	3	F	1	0	0	0	235
Exclusive Chief	4	G	12	0	2	1	3,968
Exclusive Dawn	7	G	7	2	3	1	11,572
Exclusive Delight	5	M	3	0	0	0	340
Exclusive Deposit	5	M	8	1	2	0	42,026
Exclusive Firm	3	G	6	1	0	1	14,450
Exclusive Glory	3	F	6	2	0	0	3,102
Exclusive Gold	3	G	11	1	3	2	16,341
Exclusive Honor	4	G	7	1	1	0	6,493
Exclusive Hopper	4	F	12	0	4	1	26,955
Exclusive Image	4	F	3	0	0	0	174
Exclusive Issue	5	M	3	0	0	1	740
Exclusive Kid	5	G	8	0	1	1	2,441
Exclusive Lore	3	C	1	0	0	0	0
Exclusive Molly	6	M	4	2	2	0	34,940
Exclusive Print	3	F	5	0	1	2	10,650
Exclusive Rio	3	G	5	0	0	0	540
Exclusive Run	10	G	7	1	0	3	14,800
Exclusive Slew	4	G	14	2	2	2	17,860
Exclusive Swinger	3	F	4	0	0	0	0
Exclusive Tale	6	G	3	0	0	0	355
Exclusive Talent	5	M	7	0	3	1	3,374
Exclusive Time	5	G	7	1	0	0	4,432
Exclusively High	3	C	3	0	0	0	186
Exclusively Pretty	6	M	3	0	0	0	271
Exclusively Risque	11	G	11	1	1	2	4,712
Exclusively Wild	3	F	5	2	0	0	62,356
Exclusivenjoyment	3	G	9	3	4	1	131,170
Exclusivewishes	2	F	1	0	0	0	300
Excommunicate	2	C	1	0	0	0	0
Excon	7	G	9	0	0	0	730
Excusabull	2	F	4	1	0	0	27,768
Excuse	5	M	8	1	1	1	14,537
Excuse Me Miss	2	F	1	1	0	0	29,395
Excuse My French	6	G	13	3	6	1	42,205
Excuseforthejuice	7	G	11	0	2	2	6,546
Excuses Excuses	3	F	2	0	0	0	0
Execptional Game	3	G	10	3	2	0	28,792
Execuqueen	3	F	2	0	0	0	395
Executioness Fires	3	F	1	1	0	0	4,200
Executive Affair	3	F	3	1	0	0	38,976
Executive Aide	3	G	4	0	0	2	4,930
Executive Air	5	M	2	0	1	0	634
Executive Angel	3	F	1	0	0	0	0
Executive Attitude	3	F	15	1	2	0	39,348
Executive Belle	4	F	2	1	0	0	14,868
Executive Brat	5	G	9	2	2	0	10,178
Executive Celtic	5	G	17	0	0	1	4,787
Executive Charger	3	C	5	0	2	0	3,527
Executive Choice	3	G	2	1	0	0	13,600
Executive Derby	5	G	7	0	0	0	174
Executive Guest	3	G	8	1	0	1	5,893
Executive Jimmy	3	C	8	1	2	0	58,306
Executive Legacy	4	G	7	1	0	1	36,180
Executive Mansion	4	F	1	1	0	0	10,800
Executive Time	3	F	10	1	0	3	21,378
Executive Willie	3	G	10	0	0	1	6,724
Executive Woman	3	F	2	0	0	0	526
Executivesecretary	3	F	1	0	0	0	0
Exemplar	3	F	1	0	0	0	250
Exemplary	6	H	3	1	0	0	8,400
Exempt	2	F	6	0	1	2	11,780
Exercising	2	G	1	0	0	0	230
Exertion	4	C	9	0	0	0	515
Exfirmed	4	G	8	2	0	1	18,212
Exfuseme	4	F	11	2	0	2	12,232
Exhalt	4	G	12	1	2	4	30,460
Exile Lark (BRZ)	7	H	5	1	0	0	6,174
Exist	3	F	17	4	0	0	64,030
Exit Card	3	G	12	1	1	1	15,547
Exit Forty One	5	M	1	0	0	0	0
Exit Laughing	4	F	8	1	1	1	27,526
Exit Sixtysix	5	G	6	1	0	0	4,698
Exmaman	2	C	7	1	2	0	28,360
Exmore	4	G	2	0	0	0	135
Exmut (ARG)	6	H	13	0	1	0	8,297
Exoctic Gold	5	M	3	0	1	0	850
Exofficio	2	C	2	0	0	0	0
Exorbitant	3	F	9	1	2	3	21,140
Exorcized	7	M	4	0	0	0	765
Exotic Bid	3	C	4	0	0	1	3,390
Exotic Cat	2	F	1	0	0	0	0
Exotic Crystal	3	F	5	0	1	0	1,600
Exotic Elegance	3	F	2	0	0	1	6,860
Exotic Gem	6	M	17	4	0	2	30,234
Exotic Hoedown	5	G	8	0	1	0	720
Exotic Michelle	2	F	3	0	0	0	680
Exotic Red	6	G	3	0	0	0	407
Exotic Sheeba	3	F	12	1	4	0	10,828
Expansive	4	G	17	1	4	2	28,640
Expect a Mint	5	M	3	1	0	0	8,060
Expect a Ship	5	G	9	2	3	0	61,928
Expect a Star	3	F	4	2	0	1	24,570
Expect a Surprise	3	F	6	1	0	1	15,054
Expect an Angel	4	F	8	4	0	0	106,230
Expect Justice	3	G	13	2	4	1	21,159
Expect Lace	2	F	1	0	0	1	1,210
Expect Nothing	3	F	14	3	3	1	128,682
Expect Roses	4	F	17	0	3	0	16,952
Expect the Gold	5	H	3	0	0	0	609
Expect Will	2	C	10	6	2	0	251,496
Expect Wings	2	C	4	1	1	1	49,848
Expectacat	3	C	10	2	2	1	34,135
Expectant	4	F	8	1	1	1	23,949
Expectant Diva	3	F	7	1	1	0	17,017
Expectawildrush	4	F	7	1	0	1	4,031
Expected Command	5	G	16	0	3	2	39,844
Expected Flirt	5	G	8	2	2	2	56,508
Expected Hero	3	F	10	1	2	1	8,527
Expected Hour	5	G	9	2	2	2	42,005
Expected Song	4	F	9	3	0	2	149,617
Expected Touch	5	G	9	1	0	2	41,301
Expecting Joy	5	G	7	1	2	1	14,533
Expecting Pat	5	G	10	1	0	3	11,717
Expecting Sugar	4	F	9	1	0	2	16,028
Expecting to Fly	3	G	2	0	0	0	186
Expecting You	5	M	12	2	1	5	15,805
Expedient	3	G	11	2	1	2	15,495
Expedite	3	C	3	2	0	0	9,394

Horse	Age	Sex	Sts	1st	2d	3d	Won
Expedite It	4	F	17	3	5	1	71,340
Expedited	2	F	4	0	0	0	1,500
Expedition Leader	3	F	10	2	2	5	74,830
Expelliarmus	3	F	5	0	0	0	703
Expendable	4	F	10	1	4	0	51,125
Expensive Baby	4	F	17	4	2	1	19,910
Expensive Day	3	F	4	0	0	0	274
Expensive Flower	4	F	5	0	0	0	274
Expensive Lesson	3	F	2	0	1	0	10,500
Expensive Racer	3	F	3	0	0	0	0
Expensive Risk	5	G	11	1	4	2	32,751
Expensive Road	4	C	14	2	1	1	14,397
Expensive Verdict	7	M	19	2	3	5	19,951
Expensivo	7	G	6	0	1	1	4,410
Expert	6	G	3	2	1	0	25,020
Expert Design	3	C	7	1	0	4	16,779
Experts Only	4	F	10	4	1	1	85,303
Expletive	3	C	9	2	1	0	47,953
Explicit Action	4	C	2	0	0	0	680
Explicit Moon	5	G	1	0	0	0	0
Explicitly	3	F	5	0	3	0	17,480
Exploded Silence	3	F	14	1	1	2	11,438
Exploding Affair	3	G	9	2	0	1	18,170
Exploding Star	3	F	2	0	1	0	6,400
Explodo Red	10	G	16	1	0	3	7,189
Exploisive Delight	2	F	4	0	0	0	684
Exploit Choice	3	F	12	1	1	1	15,594
Exploit Echo	3	C	6	1	1	0	17,366
Exploit Exposed	2	C	4	0	0	0	920
Exploit Lad	3	G	14	2	4	3	75,666
Exploitable	2	G	1	0	0	0	184
Exploitation	3	F	6	1	1	0	11,770
Exploited	3	C	8	0	0	0	3,980
Exploited Nites	3	F	9	0	0	0	1,002
Exploited Power	3	C	7	2	1	0	14,305
Exploited Storm	3	C	13	4	1	1	104,466
Exploit'em	3	C	5	0	0	3	15,640
Exploiting	3	C	8	3	1	1	17,390
Exploitive	3	F	3	1	0	1	7,650
Exploit's Ticket	2	F	3	1	0	0	7,200
Explorationist	5	G	4	1	0	1	17,300
Explosive Affair	3	F	3	0	0	1	3,234
Explosive Alliance	5	G	3	0	0	0	0
Explosive Appeal	4	G	4	1	2	1	12,810
Explosive Buck	3	G	6	0	0	0	710
Explosive C. C.	7	G	15	0	0	0	1,768
Explosive Charade	3	F	13	3	1	2	48,850
Explosive Count	6	G	12	4	4	0	88,930
Explosive Coyote	3	C	8	0	0	0	510
Explosive Doon	3	F	9	0	0	3	6,212
Explosive Edition	6	M	5	0	1	1	2,490
Explosive Feeling	5	H	1	0	0	0	615
Explosive Gas	2	C	1	0	0	1	2,210
Explosive Green	4	G	9	1	2	0	34,680
Explosive Halo	5	M	1	0	0	0	75
Explosive Harley	10	G	10	2	2	0	12,789
Explosive Jackie	4	F	2	0	0	1	851
Explosive Jasmine	5	M	17	1	3	3	15,508
Explosive Lad	2	G	3	0	0	0	1,590
Explosive Mac	6	G	12	3	2	2	6,930
Explosive Meagan	3	F	6	2	1	0	57,410
Explosive Play	6	G	3	0	0	0	1,012
Explosive Reply	8	H	12	4	3	0	12,233
Explosive Revival	3	G	12	4	1	5	32,680
Explosive Saint	3	C	1	0	0	0	1,416
Explosive Starlet	5	M	4	0	0	0	1,830
Explosive Talk	5	M	1	0	0	0	0
Explosive Test	5	H	4	1	0	2	5,480
Explosive Times	7	M	12	0	0	0	2,148
Explosive Truth	5	H	1	0	0	0	0
Explosive Vice	4	F	2	0	0	0	338
Explosive Vicky	4	F	1	0	0	0	0
Explosivepresident	3	G	3	0	0	0	0
Expose	3	F	5	0	0	0	2,940
Exposed Film	5	G	5	0	0	0	1,600
Exposer	4	G	7	1	0	0	8,090
Express Caper	5	G	9	1	1	0	11,040
Express Enjoyment	3	G	8	4	1	1	44,260
Express Lover	4	F	10	3	3	2	41,480
Express Post	7	H	4	1	0	0	2,813
Expressionator	4	G	7	2	0	1	23,130
Expressionist	9	H	5	1	1	0	13,900
Expressive Word	8	M	9	1	1	1	8,045
Expressly	3	F	4	0	0	0	105
Expresso Bay	7	G	8	1	2	0	50,965
Expresso Love	5	M	3	0	0	1	3,019
Exquisite Princess	3	F	13	0	2	2	4,425
Exquisite Ruckus	4	F	3	1	0	0	5,817
Exspressway West	3	G	7	1	0	0	2,960
Exstreamly Supreme	4	F	8	4	1	0	71,900
Exsweety	2	F	2	0	0	0	0
Extended Credit	4	G	10	0	0	2	1,465
Extensive Quality	4	G	3	1	0	0	6,155
Extent	2	F	2	1	0	0	28,150
Extra	4	C	6	0	0	0	3,360
Extra Bases	2	F	6	1	1	0	71,097
Extra Bold	9	G	1	0	0	0	0
Extra Check	5	G	8	0	2	2	20,136
Extra Cool	4	G	17	2	1	3	15,320
Extra Deep	6	G	2	0	0	0	0
Extra Dry Martini	4	F	11	0	0	0	1,223
Extra Exclusive	2	C	2	1	1	0	10,100
Extra Fighter (ARG)	5	H	5	0	0	0	1,535
Extra Fit	4	G	15	2	5	1	76,070
Extra Fuse	2	F	2	0	1	0	2,980
Extra Gold	5	G	12	0	2	2	4,349
Extra Holy	3	F	2	0	0	0	2,376
Extra Kick	3	G	5	0	0	0	744
Extra Kipper	3	F	5	0	0	0	0
Extra Lucky	2	F	2	1	0	0	15,900
Extra Pockets	3	G	9	0	1	0	3,448
Extra Postage	3	F	8	2	0	1	14,569
Extra Push	3	C	4	0	0	0	555
Extra Robin	3	F	8	0	0	2	5,825
Extra Secrets	4	G	1	0	0	0	0
Extra Spice	4	G	6	0	0	2	3,350
Extra Sweet	3	F	1	0	0	0	0
Extra Swift	4	F	4	0	0	1	616
Extra Wildcat	3	G	15	0	0	2	5,333
Extradyne	3	G	16	0	1	2	11,520
Extraordinaryevent	3	G	3	0	0	2	2,255
Extravagant Gal	2	F	4	0	0	0	2,580
Extreme Caution	2	C	1	0	0	0	72
Extreme d'Or	2	C	10	1	2	1	21,970
Extreme Fighter	4	C	15	4	4	1	32,650
Extreme Hero	3	C	4	0	1	1	4,275
Extreme Machine	4	C	9	1	2	0	45,150
Extreme Spice	3	F	1	0	0	0	400
Extreme Tide	4	G	1	0	0	0	75
Extreme Zone	5	G	12	1	0	1	3,362
Extremely Majestic	3	G	3	0	0	0	235
Extremely Smart	4	F	10	1	1	0	14,730
Exuberant Husband	2	F	3	0	0	0	170
Exuberant Pride	5	G	10	2	0	0	5,140
Exuberant Rush	3	G	10	0	2	1	4,171
Exuberant Wagon	3	F	1	0	0	0	125
Exude	4	G	6	1	0	2	17,450
Exultant	9	G	7	0	1	0	3,600
Exy	5	M	10	1	1	2	7,455
Exzachary	3	G	10	1	0	4	18,205
Exzottica	8	M	1	0	0	0	65
Eyad (IRE)	4	G	3	0	1	0	13,120
Eye Con	7	G	3	0	0	0	52
Eye Dazzler	3	F	4	2	1	0	81,870
Eye Found It	6	G	10	1	1	2	3,392
Eye Gone	3	F	3	1	0	1	1,490
Eye M Sam	3	G	3	0	0	0	0
Eye O Wa Dancer	4	G	4	1	0	1	18,150
Eye O You	4	G	11	0	0	0	868
Eye of the Artist	3	F	3	0	0	0	0
Eye of the City	3	F	5	1	0	0	4,275
Eye of the Comet	5	G	2	0	0	0	454
Eye of the Hawk	5	M	4	1	0	0	5,040
Eye of the Lion	3	C	1	0	0	0	795
Eye of the Sphynx	3	F	7	4	2	0	688,340
Eye of the Tiger	4	C	8	2	1	1	296,450
Eye of the Wind	3	F	3	0	0	1	2,624
Eye of Z Storm	4	F	2	0	0	0	0

Horse	Age Sex	Sts	1st	2d	3d	Won
Eye Pea Oh	8 G	8	3	1	2	74,280
Eye Spy	7 G	7	0	3	2	3,950
Eye Stopper	3 F	19	0	3	4	38,418
Eye Witness	5 H	12	0	0	2	9,626
Eyeballbillie	3 F	1	0	0	0	250
Eyebrow Raiser	6 G	9	1	0	1	9,060
Eyeforglory	2 C	2	2	0	0	22,940
Eyeful	2 F	7	0	0	2	6,886
Eyena	5 M	8	3	1	0	25,562
Eyeofthehunter	3 C	1	0	0	0	0
Eyeoutofhere	3 C	1	0	0	0	235
Eyes a Fox	4 F	2	0	1	0	6,060
Eyes Are Upon You	3 G	17	2	1	1	23,120
Eyes Cream	3 F	4	1	1	0	16,180
Eyes for Hannah	5 G	10	1	0	1	6,652
Eyes Left	2 C	2	0	0	0	104
Eyes Like Fire	5 G	9	2	0	0	20,400
Eyes of Berthold	5 M	4	0	0	0	636
Eyes of the Critic	4 G	10	0	1	0	2,894
Eyes of the World	4 C	2	0	0	0	161
Eyes On Eddy	2 F	2	1	0	1	21,500
Eyes On Target	2 G	2	0	0	0	1,350
Eyes Sucha Delight	7 M	4	0	1	1	1,735
Eyes the Duchess	5 M	7	0	1	1	15,374
Eyes Wide Open (FR)	6 G	14	1	3	1	17,009
Eyesaderbyfantasy	4 C	3	1	0	0	8,820
Eyeseedocgolightly	4 G	5	0	0	0	744
Eyeshadow	4 F	12	2	1	3	13,480
Ez Money Honey	4 F	8	1	1	2	43,268
Ezee Target	3 G	12	3	3	2	15,608
Ezepart	5 G	11	0	1	0	3,110
Ezio	7 G	13	1	1	2	7,687
Ezman	5 M	2	0	0	0	478
Ezra	5 G	7	0	2	1	30,650
F J's Pace	9 G	10	4	0	3	132,054
F. F. Arada	7 G	2	0	0	0	0
F. J. Girl	3 F	19	2	2	1	15,830
Fa Mulan	2 F	7	0	0	4	4,180
Fa Vid	4 F	16	1	0	3	7,217
Fab Four	2 F	3	0	1	0	3,300
Fabeled War	6 H	12	0	2	0	3,372
Fabio	3 C	1	0	0	0	150
Fabi's Legacy	3 C	1	0	0	0	600
Fabled Fog	8 G	9	2	0	2	8,781
Fabled Wings	4 C	10	1	1	1	4,573
Faborito	2 C	3	1	0	2	7,350
Fabrina (PER)	4 F	2	1	0	0	3,603
Fabuleux Joy	2 F	2	0	2	0	8,600
Fabulist (ARG)	5 H	13	2	3	0	29,641
Fabulosity	3 F	10	2	2	4	89,810
Fabulous Action	2 F	1	0	1	0	1,520
Fabulous Agent	3 G	17	1	3	3	7,694
Fabulous Amy	7 M	5	0	1	2	1,240
Fabulous Breeze	3 F	3	0	0	0	455
Fabulous Brew	3 G	3	0	0	0	1,273
Fabulous Caper	4 F	8	1	1	0	6,728
Fabulous Change	5 G	3	0	0	0	282
Fabulous Charmer	3 F	2	1	0	0	8,400
Fabulous Court	4 C	2	0	0	0	154
Fabulous Faker	3 G	4	2	1	0	71,760
Fabulous Feb	2 F	9	1	3	1	22,330
Fabulous Fey	2 F	3	1	1	0	19,530
Fabulous Fortune	6 G	18	4	4	2	40,125
Fabulous Fox	5 M	15	0	2	1	3,864
Fabulous Fraser	5 G	11	1	1	0	2,490
Fabulous Fun	5 M	15	1	0	2	5,172
Fabulous Fury	5 M	11	3	2	0	45,330
Fabulous Gal	2 F	6	1	1	0	9,065
Fabulous Gin	3 F	4	0	0	0	629
Fabulous Groom (FR)	3 C	1	1	0	0	29,400
Fabulous Irony	2 F	5	0	0	0	645
Fabulous Kiss	3 F	1	0	0	0	0
Fabulous Lady	5 M	9	2	3	3	13,467
Fabulous Laughter	3 G	5	1	0	0	5,931
Fabulous Looker	3 F	10	2	3	2	27,740
Fabulous Lyn R	3 F	6	1	0	0	4,600
Fabulous Maid	5 M	8	0	0	2	6,185
Fabulous Notebook	3 F	7	1	2	0	16,350
Fabulous Numbers	4 C	4	0	1	0	2,915
Fabulous Passion	4 F	7	0	0	3	10,275
Fabulous Peak	5 G	15	5	3	1	81,835
Fabulous Play	4 F	5	0	0	0	477
Fabulous Prince	2 G	1	0	0	1	1,890
Fabulous Rose	2 F	10	2	1	0	19,280
Fabulous Ruler	3 G	6	0	0	2	5,938
Fabulous Satin	2 F	6	0	0	3	9,570
Fabulous Sway	3 F	9	1	0	2	4,261
Fabulous Wealth	4 G	11	3	0	1	11,775
Fabulous West	4 G	6	2	0	1	70,780
Fabulous World	4 G	2	0	0	0	0
Fabulous Wully	2 C	2	0	0	0	420
Fabulously Clever	5 M	1	0	0	0	0
Fabulously Mine	3 F	13	1	1	1	8,800
Fabulus Bell	5 M	1	0	0	0	0
Fabutam	3 F	5	0	1	1	6,395
Faccia Bella	8 M	1	0	0	0	0
Face Down Dave	3 G	9	1	1	0	15,700
Face in the Crowd	3 F	4	1	0	1	12,414
Face It	4 F	6	0	3	0	6,675
Face of Fortune	4 C	13	2	1	5	14,952
Face Paint	3 F	3	0	0	0	0
Face the Band	6 H	11	3	2	0	85,039
Face the Facts	5 G	8	0	0	2	1,534
Face the Nation	6 M	1	0	0	0	0
Facial Wager	4 G	7	0	0	0	1,310
Fact Based	4 G	6	0	1	0	1,402
Fact Not Fiction	8 G	6	0	0	0	278
Factor Fiction	5 M	2	0	2	0	2,000
Factory Mill	5 G	9	1	2	2	7,451
Factory Reject	3 F	12	1	4	2	40,301
Factual Contender	3 F	10	2	2	0	73,342
Factual Lady	3 F	5	5	0	0	76,620
Fad	8 M	2	0	0	0	99
Fade Away	4 F	7	2	0	2	11,711
Fade Oraculo (ARG)	7 H	1	0	0	0	0
Fade Sabihonda (ARG)	6 M	16	1	1	0	14,480
Fade to Blue	8 G	13	4	3	1	143,652
Faded Love	4 F	1	0	0	0	0
Fading Memories	5 M	2	1	0	0	7,076
Fadski	7 G	3	0	1	1	748
Faeton	4 G	18	3	0	3	19,427
Fafnir	6 M	10	1	1	0	26,914
Fager Chic	5 M	10	0	0	0	2,419
Fagers Reward	3 G	3	1	0	0	4,800
Fager's Wager	4 G	17	2	4	2	27,668
Fahana	8 M	2	0	0	0	180
Fail Me Not (ARG)	5 H	7	2	1	1	58,380
Faint Star	2 F	1	0	0	0	0
Fair Amapola	3 F	8	0	0	0	2,315
Fair and Grey	6 M	4	0	0	0	442
Fair and Lucky	4 F	12	1	1	0	19,910
Fair Believer	4 G	12	2	3	0	27,378
Fair Enough	4 C	3	0	1	0	3,680
Fair Goer	4 F	7	0	0	0	948
Fair Juliet	3 F	1	0	0	0	100
Fair Lady Camille	5 M	9	0	1	1	5,506
Fair Lee Quiet	3 F	11	1	1	0	18,129
Fair Magic	5 M	2	0	1	0	1,950
Fair Millielillie	3 F	5	1	1	1	52,460
Fair Minister	3 G	3	0	0	1	975
Fair Model	5 M	4	1	0	0	3,240
Fair of Night	5 M	3	0	0	0	224
Fair Offer (NZ)	6 M	6	0	0	2	4,492
Fair Prospect	3 F	10	4	1	2	45,997
Fair Reward	3 G	6	1	0	0	2,658
Fair Sophia	5 M	4	0	0	1	1,898
Fair Storm	3 C	2	0	0	0	585
Fair Tango	3 G	2	0	0	1	550
Fair Winds	4 G	11	1	0	0	6,140
Fair Woman	5 M	9	1	0	0	4,342
Fairberry Lady	4 F	3	0	0	0	855
Fairest Mims	2 F	1	0	0	0	713
Fairest Warning	2 F	3	1	0	0	4,510
Fairforforest	3 C	6	1	1	1	25,310
Fairly Crafty	4 C	15	3	3	2	142,144
Fairly Fasty	4 G	9	0	2	0	4,199
Fairly Honest	3 G	11	2	2	1	31,085
Fairly Ransom	4 C	4	1	0	0	30,000

Horse	Age	Sex	Sts	1st	2d	3d	Won
Fairly Run (FR)	3	C	8	1	0	0	22,959
Fairly True	3	C	11	1	1	1	10,634
Fairly Valued	4	G	6	3	0	1	13,446
Fairly Well Tuned	6	M	9	1	1	1	10,287
Fairly's Pirate	3	G	1	0	0	0	114
Fairmont Dedo	3	F	2	0	0	0	161
Fairmont Road	3	G	9	0	1	1	5,570
Fairway Fox	4	F	3	0	0	0	215
Fairway Joey	5	G	7	0	1	1	2,642
Fairway Miss	2	F	10	2	3	0	26,600
Fairway to Heaven	9	G	14	1	2	2	13,421
Fairwell Madrid	2	F	2	0	0	0	0
Fairy Dust	7	M	7	1	0	0	3,132
Fairy Gold	4	F	12	3	2	2	33,755
Fairy Image	2	G	8	1	1	1	19,820
Fairy Prince	2	C	1	0	0	0	2,100
Fairy Tale Dream	2	F	7	1	0	2	37,800
Fairy Valley	5	M	3	0	0	1	3,280
Fairytale Romance	5	M	6	0	0	0	1,324
Fait Accompli	3	F	6	2	0	1	80,876
Faith and Glory	4	G	8	0	0	0	1,753
Faith and Honor	2	F	6	2	1	1	23,290
Faith Forever	4	F	8	2	1	2	8,618
Faith Hall	5	M	1	0	0	0	70
Faith Heylin	4	G	5	0	0	0	267
Faith in God	2	C	5	2	1	0	34,330
Faith in You	4	F	1	0	0	0	525
Faith Keeper	4	F	13	2	1	2	43,125
Faith Love N Hope	3	C	4	0	0	0	0
Faith of the West	3	G	12	2	2	1	22,721
Faithful Flyer	2	F	3	1	1	1	10,880
Faithful Girl	4	F	11	0	1	3	3,867
Faithful Lad	3	C	4	0	0	1	1,680
Faithful Star	2	F	1	0	0	0	205
Faithisourhope	3	F	6	0	2	2	5,440
Faiths Hope	5	G	8	0	1	0	4,043
Faiths Wish	6	H	3	0	0	0	500
Faithtrustpixidust	3	F	3	0	1	0	2,800
Fajardo	7	G	4	3	0	1	65,000
Fajita	3	G	11	2	2	1	13,877
Fake I. D.	5	G	4	0	0	0	2,857
Fake It	8	G	3	0	1	0	1,380
Fake Plastic Tree	2	F	7	0	3	0	6,593
Fakeyouout	3	F	5	0	0	1	5,300
Falcon Eagle	3	F	2	0	2	0	3,570
Falcon Eddie	6	G	6	1	2	1	2,848
Falcon Flash	3	G	6	0	0	0	0
Falcon Gentle	4	F	2	1	0	0	3,540
Falcon in Flight	3	G	15	4	2	0	24,812
Falcon Inn	4	F	10	1	1	2	18,040
Falcon Queen	4	F	6	0	0	0	600
Falcon Wood	3	F	3	0	0	0	50
Falconer (IRE)	5	G	8	1	2	1	50,280
Falconinthenight	6	G	2	0	0	1	1,000
Falcon's Peak	2	C	2	0	1	0	4,780
Falcon's Pleasure	3	G	2	0	0	1	5,058
Falcon's Swoop	4	G	6	1	1	2	11,475
Falcon's Wings	8	G	3	0	1	1	1,364
Falconwithahat	4	G	5	1	1	1	10,463
Falhour	9	G	2	0	0	0	76
Falklands Girl	4	F	11	1	0	3	6,565
Fall Affair	6	G	15	0	2	1	13,084
Fall Colors	4	F	7	0	0	2	2,080
Fall Fantasy	3	F	1	0	0	1	3,278
Fall Fashion	3	F	9	2	1	2	84,170
Fall for Me	5	G	12	2	2	2	4,348
Fall in Line	3	C	16	1	1	0	6,157
Fall in Place	4	F	9	3	1	1	19,290
Fall Reign	5	G	7	0	0	1	1,582
Fall Season	2	F	2	0	0	0	0
Fall Term	2	F	2	1	0	0	12,720
Fall Wonder	3	C	1	0	0	0	630
Fallen for Freedom	2	F	6	0	0	1	4,640
Fallfree	2	G	9	3	3	1	146,186
Fallible	3	F	9	1	1	1	9,150
Falling Leaves	2	F	2	0	0	0	1,320
Falling Star	3	F	4	0	0	0	831
Falluja	2	F	7	0	1	1	7,208
False Empire	8	M	1	0	0	0	0

Horse	Age	Sex	Sts	1st	2d	3d	Won
False Evidence	6	H	3	0	0	1	2,002
False Promises	4	G	7	0	1	1	37,346
Falsify	6	M	9	0	0	1	3,171
Falso Testimonio (ARG)	6	H	8	2	2	2	69,184
Falstaffgoldenlady	5	M	5	0	0	0	352
Falstaff's Road	8	G	7	0	1	1	1,470
Falstaffs's Jewel	6	M	2	0	1	0	1,243
Fame and Fortune	3	G	9	1	4	1	14,205
Fame and Frolic	2	C	4	0	0	0	523
Fame and Honour	6	G	7	0	0	0	1,071
Fame Game	3	G	13	1	0	1	29,137
Fame Ina Minute	4	C	5	0	2	0	18,993
Fame Is Fleeting	3	G	3	0	0	0	0
Fames Legs	10	G	1	0	0	0	0
Fame's Pleasure	4	F	8	0	0	0	1,248
Fame's Star	5	M	2	0	0	0	192
Family Appeal	2	G	9	1	0	2	17,090
Family Book	3	G	13	2	1	2	42,560
Family Business	3	F	12	2	4	2	108,645
Family Covenant	7	M	1	0	0	0	315
Family Event	2	F	3	0	0	0	0
Family Facet	2	F	2	0	0	0	300
Family Favorite	3	F	10	1	4	1	53,770
Family Fewd	6	G	15	1	3	4	11,153
Family Fortune	4	C	10	2	3	2	49,381
Family Fun	3	G	1	0	0	0	0
Family Ghost	2	G	5	2	0	2	31,970
Family Locket	3	C	2	1	0	0	4,200
Family Money	3	G	18	5	4	2	40,358
Family Operator	2	C	4	0	1	0	2,000
Family Outing	2	F	2	1	0	0	10,540
Family Prospector	2	G	2	0	0	1	1,540
Family Secret	2	C	3	1	0	0	7,365
Family Tales	3	F	9	0	2	1	3,280
Famous Amos	5	H	4	0	0	0	361
Famous Bid	5	M	4	1	0	0	6,996
Famous Call	4	R	8	0	0	0	2,200
Famous Chef	6	H	5	1	0	0	6,845
Famous Dreamin	6	G	10	3	1	2	32,546
Famous Flame	3	G	5	0	2	0	2,915
Famous Flash	3	G	4	0	0	1	3,640
Famous Forest	3	C	4	0	0	0	1,560
Famous Fury	3	G	8	1	2	1	25,173
Famous Honoree	4	G	4	1	2	0	5,720
Famous Minstrel	6	M	9	1	1	0	4,192
Famous Olympian	4	G	15	3	2	1	36,555
Famous Rich	3	C	5	1	1	0	6,805
Famous Seeker	4	G	1	0	1	0	3,000
Famous Shamus	5	G	7	0	0	1	2,740
Famous Spirit	4	F	9	1	4	1	44,791
Famous Statesman	3	G	23	2	4	4	24,762
Famous Woman	4	F	6	1	0	0	16,020
Famously Free	10	G	5	0	0	1	812
Famula (ARG)	6	M	12	2	1	2	31,585
Fan Attack	3	F	9	1	3	1	14,838
Fan Club's Mister	6	H	1	0	0	0	0
Fan Jet Falcon	5	G	8	1	1	2	8,445
Fan of the Cat	2	C	4	0	1	2	12,240
Fan Tan Allie	4	C	1	0	0	0	0
Fan the Flame	7	H	11	5	2	2	48,283
Fanatic Alachee	4	G	1	0	0	0	372
Fanatic Avenger	3	G	9	2	1	2	29,737
Fanaway	4	G	12	0	0	0	241
Fancatstik	3	C	3	1	0	0	26,922
Fancebel	5	M	8	0	0	0	464
Fancee Bargain	8	M	2	0	0	1	16,650
Fanci Frills	8	M	4	0	0	0	0
Fanciwith	7	M	5	0	0	4	6,050
Fancy As	6	G	5	0	0	1	7,890
Fancy B My Name	6	M	1	0	0	0	0
Fancy Batchler	7	G	10	3	1	4	14,552
Fancy Be Quick	5	M	10	3	3	1	19,914
Fancy Begining	5	M	7	0	0	2	6,333
Fancy Boy	4	C	9	1	1	2	9,041
Fancy Bru	4	G	8	1	3	1	38,965
Fancy Buckles	4	F	7	2	1	2	108,820
Fancy Bull	2	G	6	1	0	1	7,867
Fancy Comanche	3	F	13	1	1	0	1,695
Fancy Crown	6	G	1	0	0	0	0

Horse	Age	Sex	Sts	1st	2d	3d	Won
Fancy Dealer	4	F	13	2	3	5	26,283
Fancy Drinks	4	F	13	0	0	1	16,640
Fancy Empire	3	F	7	2	2	0	24,063
Fancy Firenight	5	H	6	0	0	0	0
Fancy First	5	H	4	1	0	1	5,915
Fancy Flare	3	F	5	0	1	1	1,640
Fancy Flight	4	F	4	0	0	1	1,710
Fancy Fluff	2	F	1	0	0	1	2,880
Fancy Forum	4	F	9	4	3	1	47,890
Fancy Free 'n Such	4	F	8	2	2	2	8,470
Fancy Free Playboy	9	G	2	0	0	0	0
Fancy Friend	3	F	4	0	0	1	1,535
Fancy Injun	6	M	8	0	1	2	6,493
Fancy Irish Dancer	3	F	3	0	0	0	165
Fancy M. D.	5	G	15	6	5	1	62,555
Fancy Mama	2	F	2	0	0	0	179
Fancy Man	3	G	7	2	3	0	54,666
Fancy Me Yours	5	M	16	1	1	6	8,207
Fancy Mocha	3	F	10	0	0	0	1,126
Fancy n' Fit	4	F	7	1	2	1	8,160
Fancy Nanc	3	F	2	0	0	0	0
Fancy Numbers	3	F	8	2	1	1	30,063
Fancy Retsina	3	G	2	0	0	1	2,017
Fancy Rose	3	F	3	0	0	0	475
Fancy Shmancy	4	F	12	0	0	0	808
Fancy Slam	3	F	6	0	0	0	2,810
Fancy Speeding	2	C	1	0	0	0	96
Fancy Tal One	4	G	10	0	1	0	2,433
Fancy Tango	2	F	9	2	2	1	23,045
Fancy Threat	4	G	11	3	1	0	25,228
Fancy Thrill	4	C	1	0	0	0	75
Fancy Trick	5	M	8	3	1	2	17,103
Fancy Ways	3	F	18	2	2	2	14,978
Fancy Zone	3	F	11	1	0	2	4,706
Fancyghost	3	C	6	3	1	1	39,471
Fancyismyname	5	M	4	0	0	1	150
Fancyman Jack	4	G	8	1	3	1	23,377
Fancys Fantasy	2	F	1	0	0	0	0
Fancy's Frosty	4	F	7	0	1	1	2,051
Fanning	2	F	8	0	1	0	8,255
Fantasia Di Dolci	5	M	3	0	0	1	704
Fantastic Allie	6	M	10	0	1	2	29,357
Fantastic Blond	4	F	14	1	1	1	12,043
Fantastic Brew	4	G	6	2	0	1	24,720
Fantastic Career	2	F	4	1	0	1	10,700
Fantastic Caroline	4	F	1	1	0	0	6,000
Fantastic Day	4	G	6	2	1	0	110,671
Fantastic Dream	3	F	6	0	2	2	5,305
Fantastic Ed	3	G	1	0	0	0	0
Fantastic Ego	3	G	8	1	0	0	4,206
Fantastic Finish	8	G	9	1	1	0	11,668
Fantastic Fling	3	F	5	0	2	2	12,900
Fantastic Fredde	3	F	10	0	0	0	743
Fantastic Groom	6	G	5	0	0	0	8,402
Fantastic Journey	5	M	2	0	0	1	2,321
Fantastic Joy	4	F	8	0	0	1	5,334
Fantastic Lover	4	G	9	1	1	0	4,340
Fantastic Reality	7	G	6	0	0	0	462
Fantastic Spain	4	C	3	1	1	0	40,000
Fantastic Tricks	3	C	8	0	0	0	249
Fantastic Voyage	4	G	5	2	0	1	31,140
Fantastic Year	2	F	2	0	1	0	7,400
Fantastica	3	F	4	0	0	0	300
Fantasticat	3	C	14	3	4	2	418,400
Fantasy Boy	8	G	9	0	0	0	360
Fantasy Jet	5	M	13	0	3	1	9,390
Fantasy Life	4	G	17	1	3	4	16,566
Fantasy On Fire	4	F	4	1	2	0	14,750
Fantasy Quest	4	F	2	1	0	0	9,020
Fantasy Tap	6	G	9	1	1	2	8,835
Fantasy Valley	6	G	5	1	1	1	6,239
Fantasy's Champ	4	C	7	0	1	2	1,036
Fantazmic	3	G	3	1	0	1	6,173
Fanteria	3	G	9	3	3	1	18,938
Fantino	3	C	13	1	4	2	72,941
Fantom Fury	8	G	8	2	0	0	10,075
Fanzoca	4	F	5	0	1	0	10,912
Fappa Fire	7	G	6	0	1	1	4,160
Fappadoon	3	F	12	2	5	1	48,325
Fappiano'srjourney	5	G	3	0	0	0	300
Fappilongstockings	5	M	2	0	0	0	190
Fappisured	3	F	1	0	0	0	186
Fappitune	4	G	10	0	1	1	2,905
Fappy's Walker	2	F	1	0	1	0	1,400
Far Afield	3	F	4	2	0	1	64,104
Far and Near	5	M	12	3	3	2	89,557
Far Away Bell	5	G	12	4	2	2	37,120
Far Better Journey	5	G	6	0	1	0	1,276
Far Better Lis	3	F	9	0	2	0	4,184
Far Beyond	2	F	3	1	0	0	4,200
Far East of Eden	7	H	2	0	0	0	135
Far From Frail	4	F	6	0	1	0	16,132
Far From Home	2	F	4	0	0	0	1,272
Far Island	4	C	4	0	0	0	403
Far Out	7	G	2	0	0	1	1,015
Far Out Babe	3	F	5	0	0	0	0
Far Out Chris	4	G	13	0	2	3	16,301
Far Out Slew	11	G	2	0	0	0	252
Far Side	5	G	8	0	0	0	3,816
Far too Sinful	4	F	9	0	1	0	2,007
Farah Love	8	M	2	0	0	0	1,020
Faraway Prospect	7	G	7	2	1	1	16,780
Farber	3	G	8	0	0	0	2,387
Fare Thee Wild	4	F	2	1	0	0	14,910
Fare You Well	3	F	2	0	0	0	0
Farewell Cowboys	3	G	9	0	2	1	8,005
Farewell To Arms (GB)	3	F	9	1	2	2	11,440
Farewell to Charm	3	C	5	0	0	0	510
Farewell Val	6	G	8	0	0	2	3,790
Farfalla	6	G	3	0	0	0	130
Farfalletto	4	G	10	0	0	0	1,019
Farfromreality	3	F	2	0	0	0	0
Fargo Forbes	2	G	4	2	1	0	17,180
Fargo Time	2	G	3	1	1	0	6,149
Fargo's Freind	3	G	14	0	2	1	6,115
Fargo's Secret	3	G	4	0	0	0	324
Farhana	3	F	8	0	3	0	29,253
Farinelli	2	G	2	0	0	0	0
Fariseo	4	G	2	0	0	0	0
Farlo	4	G	6	1	1	2	6,126
Farm Account	3	G	3	0	0	0	42
Farm Fuel	4	G	7	1	1	0	3,664
Farm Saver	9	G	13	1	2	3	9,495
Farma Way Jr.	4	G	6	0	1	0	1,166
Farmall Red	4	G	5	0	0	1	963
Farma's Best	9	H	1	0	0	1	700
Farmer Jake	6	G	3	0	1	0	9,770
Farmer Tan	3	G	5	0	0	0	376
Farnham	3	F	6	1	1	0	13,440
Farno	4	C	1	0	0	0	2,250
Farnum Alley	3	G	6	1	0	0	51,206
Faro	4	G	11	1	1	3	18,130
Farragal	3	F	1	0	0	0	0
Farrar	3	F	12	4	2	0	29,935
Farrelyn's Prize	4	C	11	0	1	1	2,960
Farrus' Smile	4	F	4	0	0	1	1,339
Farsighted	2	F	3	1	0	0	14,910
Fascio (ARG)	8	H	1	0	0	0	130
Fashion At Dawn	3	F	16	1	0	2	5,624
Fashion Award	5	G	12	1	1	0	28,455
Fashion Bolt	3	C	7	0	0	0	0
Fashion Diamond	4	F	11	2	2	3	8,521
Fashion Folder	3	F	2	0	0	0	0
Fashion Girl	3	F	7	0	1	2	25,080
Fashion Hunter	3	F	11	3	0	2	13,020
Fashion Idol	7	M	10	1	1	2	48,599
Fashion Island	5	M	3	0	1	2	7,800
Fashion Line	3	F	9	1	1	1	13,259
Fashion Maker	3	F	5	0	0	0	90
Fashion Police	2	C	4	1	0	0	15,130
Fashion Proof	4	F	1	0	0	0	178
Fashion Sense	4	F	1	0	0	0	340
Fashionable Caton	4	F	13	1	3	1	30,500
Fashionable Kim	4	F	1	0	1	0	6,040
Fashionable Steve	4	G	12	1	4	3	9,810
Fashionably Lite	3	F	10	2	2	2	24,825
Fasnet	2	C	5	0	0	2	3,640
Fasole	5	M	10	1	1	2	8,692

Horse	Age	Sex	Sts	1st	2d	3d	Won
Fast Access	3	F	6	0	0	2	11,706
Fast Activation	4	F	1	0	0	0	63
Fast Advice	6	M	8	3	0	1	20,633
Fast Agin	4	G	7	1	0	1	2,378
Fast and Fluid	3	F	13	0	3	2	25,988
Fast and Free	5	M	10	3	1	3	26,438
Fast and Furious (FR)	3	C	6	2	1	1	169,048
Fast Announcement	4	F	5	0	0	0	231
Fast Baby	2	F	7	2	2	3	34,040
Fast Ball	7	G	9	0	1	3	2,526
Fast Call	3	F	5	0	0	1	5,965
Fast Cookie	4	F	8	2	0	3	110,346
Fast Dan	3	C	6	1	1	1	8,894
Fast Dane	4	G	5	1	0	0	2,670
Fast Decision	5	H	8	1	1	3	46,186
Fast Delighter	5	M	3	0	0	0	405
Fast Deo	3	G	8	0	1	0	4,185
Fast Dish	5	G	12	1	4	1	22,910
Fast Easy 'n Free	5	G	9	1	0	1	7,871
Fast Eddie Charles	2	C	3	1	0	1	7,085
Fast Eddie D.	4	C	3	0	0	0	165
Fast Entry	3	F	5	0	0	0	251
Fast Escape	3	C	18	2	2	2	12,450
Fast Exercise	3	G	12	3	2	2	56,300
Fast Explosion	4	F	11	2	0	0	13,980
Fast Fast Freddie	5	G	2	0	0	0	945
Fast Faster	5	G	6	1	0	0	2,990
Fast Favorite	7	H	7	0	0	1	927
Fast Felix	3	G	2	1	0	0	4,542
Fast Flight	2	G	7	0	1	3	5,915
Fast Focus	2	C	1	1	0	0	1,500
Fast Force	4	G	16	2	0	5	11,885
Fast Forest	4	G	1	0	0	0	87
Fast Fox Trot	8	G	6	1	0	0	9,278
Fast Getaway	6	H	1	0	0	0	202
Fast Going	5	M	7	3	3	0	27,020
Fast Gun	6	G	11	2	2	4	5,396
Fast Hand	2	F	4	2	1	0	43,670
Fast Iz a Turtle	2	G	2	1	0	0	26,650
Fast Jazz	5	G	11	1	0	0	3,525
Fast Jinks	11	G	12	1	0	3	9,781
Fast Knockout	5	M	3	0	0	0	227
Fast Lad	5	G	10	0	2	0	4,574
Fast Lady J	3	F	6	0	1	1	3,550
Fast Lane Neelie	4	F	9	0	2	4	4,396
Fast Laner	3	F	4	1	0	0	18,620
Fast Line	6	G	13	3	2	5	45,685
Fast Lisa	2	F	3	0	0	1	5,060
Fast Lovin Lizzie	4	F	20	1	2	3	26,270
Fast Machine	5	G	8	0	1	0	1,698
Fast Mack	2	G	4	0	0	0	456
Fast Market	2	G	8	2	0	4	38,410
Fast Maybe	6	G	9	1	0	1	12,226
Fast N Fearless	4	C	4	0	1	0	8,010
Fast N Foremost	3	G	5	0	0	0	1,035
Fast N Front	4	G	6	0	0	1	996
Fast Puppy	2	G	2	0	0	0	800
Fast River (CHI)	5	G	3	0	0	0	548
Fast Runaway	2	F	1	0	0	0	510
Fast Secretary	5	M	8	0	0	0	914
Fast Senorita	4	F	13	2	4	2	14,845
Fast Silver	5	G	13	2	3	1	35,905
Fast Skeeter	4	G	2	0	0	0	0
Fast Splash	3	F	7	1	1	2	14,642
Fast Spot	5	G	17	3	1	1	27,846
Fast Steppin Man	8	G	4	0	0	0	750
Fast Summer	4	G	7	1	0	0	13,571
Fast Talker	3	G	7	1	1	1	7,978
Fast Talkin Girl	3	F	3	1	1	0	11,496
Fast Tease	3	G	3	0	0	0	345
Fast Track Bob	4	G	9	1	2	1	10,080
Fast Tracker	5	G	13	5	1	1	78,420
Fast Train	3	C	6	1	0	0	22,812
Fast Trapp	6	G	5	0	0	1	687
Fast Tude	6	G	1	0	0	0	205
Fast Willie	5	G	2	0	0	0	86
Fast Zone	2	F	2	0	0	0	0
Fastbid	4	G	16	1	2	4	7,410
Fastcut	3	G	8	0	2	1	8,625

Horse	Age	Sex	Sts	1st	2d	3d	Won
Faster Prospect	3	C	13	1	1	4	14,365
Faster Than Light	4	C	5	0	0	1	1,787
Faster Than Music	8	G	6	1	1	2	2,312
Fastest	8	G	3	0	0	1	560
Fastest Key	3	C	5	0	0	0	0
Fastest Star	2	F	3	1	1	0	22,548
Fastest Traffic	3	G	3	0	0	0	390
Fastette	4	F	11	3	0	0	32,846
Fastfoot Freddie	9	G	20	4	3	2	7,025
Fastivist	3	G	5	0	0	2	4,016
Fastlight	3	G	6	1	1	0	51,980
Fastman	6	H	4	0	0	0	990
Fastnloose	3	F	5	0	0	0	0
Fastrak Folly	7	G	1	0	0	0	0
Fastridge	3	G	12	0	0	1	412
Fastrip	4	F	4	0	1	0	6,560
Faststeppin Jack	8	G	4	1	1	0	5,760
Fastsweettowngirl	3	F	2	0	1	1	9,355
Faswiga	3	F	10	0	4	0	83,278
Fat Cat	4	C	7	3	1	0	32,810
Fat Farm	5	M	6	1	0	3	12,942
Fat Harry's Girl	3	F	15	1	0	4	14,453
Fat Lear	2	G	1	0	0	0	420
Fatal Binge	4	G	14	1	0	0	4,405
Fatal Caper	4	F	16	7	2	3	110,474
Fatapiano	4	F	11	0	0	1	1,882
Father Bob	4	G	3	0	0	0	1,062
Father Bryan's Gem	5	G	2	0	0	0	760
Father Confessor	5	G	16	3	3	2	42,196
Father Dan	4	G	15	2	2	0	12,456
Father Dooley	3	G	13	0	1	3	4,056
Father James	3	C	6	1	0	0	11,340
Father Joe	2	C	9	1	1	0	8,370
Father Krismas (GB)	9	G	1	0	0	1	1,500
Father Mark	5	G	4	0	0	0	244
Father Mike	4	G	12	0	1	2	4,190
Father of All Wins	7	G	3	0	0	0	850
Father Paul	6	G	6	0	0	1	1,887
Father Thames (GB)	6	H	6	0	0	2	12,950
Father Tom	2	C	1	0	0	0	230
Father Tony	5	H	11	3	1	0	18,690
Father Weist	2	C	6	1	1	1	50,050
Father's Magic	9	G	7	2	0	0	13,460
Fathom	5	G	13	1	1	2	10,668
Fathom Drive	2	G	1	1	0	0	21,600
Fathom Miss	3	F	6	0	2	1	3,747
Fathomsfoxydestiny	3	F	4	1	0	1	5,159
Fatik	4	C	1	0	0	1	2,090
Fatima Dias	2	F	1	0	0	0	85
Fatima's Gold	8	M	10	0	1	0	1,465
Fatima's Princess	5	M	14	2	1	2	24,968
Fatmandu	3	G	3	0	0	0	77
Faultless Cassie	5	M	10	1	3	0	9,914
Faust	5	G	6	0	1	0	2,700
Faux Pas	5	M	2	0	0	0	670
Favalora	2	G	4	2	0	1	52,390
Favorable Decision	7	G	14	1	4	2	20,649
Favorable Terms	4	G	14	3	1	1	25,800
Favored Sweep	8	G	15	1	0	1	4,016
Favorite Affair	7	G	15	4	2	4	25,717
Favorite Angel	4	F	11	1	0	1	13,430
Favorite Birdie	3	G	1	0	0	0	37
Favorite Brat	4	F	7	0	1	1	4,867
Favorite Cat	2	F	1	1	0	0	11,113
Favorite Companion	4	G	17	2	3	0	11,570
Favorite Dispersal	7	G	12	0	0	1	1,895
Favorite Fun	2	C	6	1	2	1	55,230
Favorite Girl	3	F	9	1	2	0	43,330
Favorite Gold	2	F	1	0	0	0	0
Favorite Lady T	3	F	5	0	0	0	1,250
Favorite Lil Devil	5	M	7	1	1	3	12,216
Favorite Minit	2	C	3	2	1	0	57,150
Favorite Miss	7	M	3	0	1	0	5,160
Favorite Moment	3	G	8	1	2	1	26,200
Favorite Numbers	4	F	1	1	0	0	9,000
Favorite One	4	G	5	2	1	0	14,835
Favorite Opening	5	G	13	1	1	4	13,468
Favorite Pastime	2	F	1	0	0	0	220
Favorite Seat	7	G	10	1	1	2	5,745

Horse	Age	Sex	Sts	1st	2d	3d	Won
Favorite Sweep	5	H	14	1	1	4	53,002
Favorite Times	3	F	6	3	3	0	54,930
Favorite Tune	5	M	14	1	5	2	29,812
Favorite Vice	3	F	8	2	0	0	9,198
Favour for Joey	4	G	6	0	1	4	15,219
Favre	2	C	5	1	3	0	57,940
Fax a Freddy	7	G	7	1	1	1	17,108
Fax Dance	4	C	17	3	2	1	16,502
Fax Forward	2	G	7	0	0	0	877
Fax Machine	4	G	7	0	1	2	7,180
Fax Me a Song	2	C	3	0	0	0	1,560
Fax Seven Copies	5	M	1	0	0	0	0
Fax the Paige	5	M	12	1	2	2	15,783
Faxamillion	5	H	7	1	0	0	8,761
Faxappeal	2	F	1	0	0	1	693
Faxed Kisses	3	F	6	1	0	0	7,050
Faxene	3	F	5	1	3	0	31,455
Faxer Than You	4	G	17	1	2	3	12,396
Faxin It Down	6	G	18	0	0	1	10,060
Faxination	2	F	7	1	1	1	14,140
Faxing	6	G	8	0	1	0	4,930
Faxing the Blues	3	G	10	1	1	3	8,217
Faye and Howard	3	G	6	1	1	1	10,900
Faye Kinitt	3	F	17	4	2	5	28,740
Fayette County	6	M	10	0	3	2	13,098
Faygo Dancing Home	3	G	9	1	0	1	25,853
Faygo Rocks	4	F	1	0	0	0	0
Faylagra	3	G	10	0	1	0	5,363
Fazlollah	2	G	4	0	0	0	164
Fe Fe's Spirits	5	M	13	0	2	2	9,960
Fe Trickie Bell	3	F	2	0	0	0	0
Fear de Bay	3	G	7	1	0	1	16,860
Fear Factory	4	C	2	0	1	0	3,105
Fear of Secrets	2	G	5	1	0	2	38,841
Fear the Cape	3	C	3	1	0	0	22,203
Fear the Creek	2	C	2	0	0	0	165
Fearless Anthony	3	G	15	3	1	3	20,343
Fearless Dancer	2	F	5	0	1	1	3,585
Fearless Firl	3	F	4	1	0	1	6,567
Fearless Flyer (IRE)	2	F	6	2	0	2	119,775
Fearless Frolic	3	F	5	1	0	1	5,817
Fearless Legacy	4	C	1	0	0	0	120
Fearless Peer	10	G	11	1	3	0	9,113
Fearless Storm	4	F	17	0	5	2	3,763
Fearless Warrior	4	C	4	0	1	0	1,640
Fearsome	6	G	5	0	0	0	223
Fearsome Eagle	2	C	1	0	1	0	7,030
Fearsome Foursome	5	G	7	2	2	1	25,157
Feather Bed Lane	2	C	4	1	0	1	52,562
Feather Boa	4	F	4	0	2	1	19,678
Feather Fan	6	M	1	0	1	0	1,280
Feather Maraine	4	F	6	1	0	1	53,443
Feather Rose	2	F	3	0	0	0	995
Featherweightchamp	5	G	13	1	2	3	10,010
Feature Story	4	G	13	5	1	2	78,840
Featured Flick	4	C	5	0	0	1	579
Feb Eleven	3	G	12	2	4	0	69,827
February Feb	4	F	15	0	0	1	947
Februarys Lady	3	F	10	0	0	0	2,399
Fed Ex Air Pro	6	G	1	0	0	0	90
Fedelisima	3	F	7	1	1	1	6,493
Federal Agent	3	G	10	3	1	0	14,472
Federal Highway	5	G	10	1	1	2	19,742
Federale	4	C	8	3	1	2	36,800
Feed for Speed	4	F	5	1	1	0	12,878
Feedman's Daughter	3	F	6	0	0	2	12,060
Feel the Charm	2	F	2	0	0	0	800
Feel the Dance	4	F	12	3	1	3	50,445
Feel the Fury	3	G	6	0	0	1	5,000
Feel the Gold	3	G	16	1	3	0	12,219
Feel the Heat	2	F	2	0	0	1	5,860
Feel the Storm	2	F	1	1	0	0	6,283
Feel the Wind	5	G	10	1	2	0	38,865
Feelin Salty	4	C	3	0	0	0	126
Feelin' the Breeze	3	F	8	3	2	1	57,600
Feeling Lucky	4	F	3	1	0	0	6,360
Feeling Maudlin	8	M	9	2	0	0	8,899
Feeling Naughty	3	F	7	0	3	0	11,241
Feeling So Pretty	10	M	7	1	2	1	40,680
Feeling Wicked	4	F	2	0	0	0	180
Feeling Wild	3	C	2	0	0	0	225
Feelingoodisenuf	2	F	6	1	1	0	19,930
Feelinlikeamackee	6	G	4	0	0	2	1,538
Feels Like Thunder	2	G	2	0	0	0	1,013
Feet of Fire	6	G	7	0	0	0	1,403
Feet of Flames	6	G	19	2	3	3	12,146
Fehr	4	C	5	0	1	0	6,900
Feijoada	4	F	11	0	1	0	8,930
Feinster	4	G	15	4	2	1	50,110
Feistee Deer	2	F	2	1	0	0	34,200
Feistier	3	F	1	0	0	0	0
Feisty Bull	4	F	8	1	1	2	46,133
Feisty Cherokee	4	F	1	0	0	0	110
Feisty Fox	3	G	7	1	0	0	19,449
Feisty Fun	4	F	11	3	3	2	46,255
Feisty Princess	4	F	3	0	0	0	0
Feisty Red	3	F	9	1	4	1	15,428
Feisty Snoman	4	G	6	2	2	0	48,190
Feisty Vick	8	G	7	0	1	3	7,060
Felena	9	M	9	2	1	1	6,575
Feline Story	3	F	9	2	4	2	224,985
Felix	4	G	2	0	0	0	480
Felix De La Luna	4	G	5	0	2	2	14,282
Felix Legions	5	M	10	0	2	1	10,330
Felix's Fire	4	C	7	0	0	1	1,945
Feliz Baby	2	F	3	0	2	0	8,104
Felling	3	F	6	0	0	0	3,108
Fellini	4	C	1	0	0	0	0
Fellner	4	G	6	1	0	0	11,660
Fellowship Road	3	F	7	1	3	2	86,110
Felo	4	G	8	0	2	0	4,980
Female Accomplice	4	F	5	1	0	0	4,147
Fence Cat	2	G	7	1	2	0	17,647
Fence Jumper	4	F	3	0	0	0	450
Fencelineneighbor	4	F	8	1	1	1	117,300
Fench	3	F	1	0	0	0	0
Fentastic Pay Day	7	M	8	0	0	0	360
Fenter Ridge	3	C	6	0	0	0	331
Fenter's Queen	3	F	5	0	0	1	1,460
Fentor's Charm	3	F	1	0	0	0	0
Fentrick	2	C	7	1	3	0	24,840
Fenway	4	C	2	2	0	0	9,120
Fenway Flyer	3	G	6	0	0	0	2,295
Ferdinand's Dancer	4	F	3	0	0	0	0
Ferdinand's Quest	4	G	1	0	0	0	0
Ferene	7	H	1	0	0	0	75
Fergie Storm	3	G	3	0	0	0	120
Fergie's Showtime	8	G	4	1	1	1	11,350
Fergiessharkattack	4	G	11	2	2	0	19,563
Fern Valley Lass	3	F	5	0	1	0	2,195
Fernie Honey	2	F	1	0	0	0	66
Ferocious	5	G	10	2	1	2	10,997
Ferrara's Medina	2	F	3	0	0	0	129
Ferras Flyer	3	F	7	2	2	0	20,729
Ferrazzi	6	G	13	2	3	0	34,506
Ferriday	4	F	12	1	2	2	9,348
Ferro's Best Yet	4	G	4	0	0	0	152
Fervid	4	C	1	0	0	0	340
Fe's Groom	4	G	9	3	4	1	32,370
Festina Did It	8	M	2	0	0	0	0
Festival (JPN)	5	M	3	1	0	0	90,000
Festival Chairman	10	G	11	0	1	2	6,526
Festival Lady	4	F	14	0	1	2	6,594
Festival Moon	6	G	2	0	0	0	155
Festival of Fun	3	F	10	0	0	1	4,031
Festive Bidder	9	H	7	0	1	0	1,500
Festive Fellow	6	G	5	1	0	2	4,190
Festive Forever	9	G	7	0	0	0	0
Festive Lady	6	M	2	0	0	1	4,480
Festive Nicholas	4	G	14	4	2	1	27,602
Festive Spirit	6	G	7	0	0	1	7,818
Festooned	5	M	1	0	0	0	0
Festy Eskimo	4	G	9	1	3	0	18,630
Fetch Dinner	8	H	5	0	0	1	6,690
Fetch Me Cap	4	F	15	1	0	1	15,191
Fetch's Fuse	3	F	5	0	0	1	3,510
Fethard	8	G	14	1	1	2	7,490
Fetzer	8	H	1	0	0	0	0

Horse	Age	Sex	Sts	1st	2d	3d	Won
Feu Kan Promise	6	M	6	0	2	1	1,540
Feu On Fire	7	M	12	2	0	4	5,583
Feu R Gold	4	G	9	0	0	1	1,436
Feudal Lady	4	F	7	0	2	1	3,084
Feu's Bebe	5	M	4	0	0	0	0
Fever Fire	3	G	14	1	0	3	12,580
Fever Like	4	C	2	0	0	0	130
Fever N Chills	4	F	12	1	1	2	8,575
Feverinthesouth	5	G	17	3	1	2	20,705
Feverish Affair	2	C	6	1	1	0	37,440
Feverish Devil	3	G	7	0	1	0	1,310
Fi	2	F	2	1	0	0	18,600
Fiber Magee	2	F	2	0	0	0	249
Fiber Optic	3	C	1	0	1	0	4,440
Fickle Factor	4	F	6	1	0	1	18,685
Fiddle Dee Dee	4	F	7	1	0	0	5,583
Fiddle McGee	4	F	3	0	0	0	396
Fiddlebid	4	F	2	0	0	0	240
Fiddlers Angel	2	F	1	0	0	0	215
Fiddlers Cat	3	C	4	1	1	0	35,737
Fiddlers Fancy	3	F	4	0	0	0	704
Fiddlers Lass	3	F	12	1	1	3	19,623
Fiddlers Pride	3	C	12	1	2	4	41,884
Fiddlers Sister	3	F	3	1	0	2	8,066
Fiddlers Star	2	F	3	0	0	0	1,555
Fiddlin Devil	3	C	8	3	0	2	21,455
Fidget	5	M	10	3	2	2	94,480
Fiel	3	C	5	1	1	0	4,960
Field Command	3	F	2	0	0	0	775
Field Day	9	G	2	0	1	1	5,200
Field Judge	4	G	3	0	0	0	456
Field of Honour	7	M	1	0	0	0	0
Field Promotion	3	G	2	0	0	0	270
Field Six	3	C	1	0	0	0	140
Field Surveyor	3	F	4	1	1	0	13,610
Fielding	2	G	7	0	2	1	14,160
Fields Ertel	12	G	2	0	0	0	101
Fields of Flowers	2	F	2	0	0	0	600
Fields of Gail	3	F	12	0	2	6	25,425
Fierce Cat	2	C	9	3	2	0	80,000
Fierce Contender	3	C	7	1	0	1	17,248
Fierce Delight	3	G	4	0	0	0	219
Fierce Flight	3	G	8	0	1	1	2,107
Fierce Heart	8	G	2	0	0	1	1,488
Fierce Knight	3	G	9	1	4	2	62,880
Fierce Princess	3	F	9	1	0	0	23,220
Fierce Resistance	3	F	7	0	1	1	12,021
Fierce Storm	3	C	4	0	0	0	2,567
Fierceinterrogator	2	F	8	1	1	2	24,390
Fiero Bandera	4	G	2	0	0	0	590
Fierro's Choice	2	R	5	2	0	2	54,170
Fiery Catch	3	F	5	1	1	0	9,867
Fiery Colony	5	G	17	3	0	6	12,788
Fiery Diablo	6	G	7	2	3	0	59,400
Fiery Dreamer	2	C	1	0	0	0	0
Fiery Love	4	F	11	3	0	2	21,748
Fiery Salsa	4	F	9	2	1	0	17,395
Fiery Six	9	G	21	1	1	2	6,349
Fiery Start	3	F	2	1	1	0	14,070
Fiesta	4	F	10	1	0	3	31,820
Fiesta Weekend	3	F	17	2	3	2	14,016
Fiesty	3	G	13	2	1	4	20,348
Fiesty Amber	4	F	10	1	2	0	5,399
Fiesty Duke	5	G	15	2	2	3	19,471
Fiesty Fannie	5	M	7	2	2	0	12,373
Fiesty Inez	4	F	9	3	2	1	31,425
Fiesty Jones	3	F	6	6	0	0	52,200
Fiesty Motel	3	F	4	0	0	0	174
Fifteen Dimes	3	F	10	3	4	0	28,360
Fifteen Rounds	4	G	7	3	0	0	67,098
Fifteen Wall	2	G	4	0	0	0	597
Fifteenth East	3	F	7	0	1	2	17,352
Fifth Amendment	3	G	17	1	0	6	17,674
Fifth Avenue Doll	6	M	8	1	2	0	17,799
Fifth Avenue Girl	3	F	10	0	2	2	5,232
Fifth Demension	4	C	5	0	0	0	2,055
Fifth Edition	3	C	5	1	1	0	38,776
Fifth of Hennessy	4	C	7	2	0	1	23,215
Fifth Overture	3	F	10	2	0	2	76,301
Fifth Page	2	G	1	0	0	0	140
Fifth Position	3	F	2	0	0	0	0
Fifth Song	2	G	11	0	0	2	3,281
Fifty Caliber	3	G	7	0	0	0	420
Fifty East	5	G	2	0	0	0	280
Fifty Fifty	6	M	4	0	0	0	252
Fifty Fly	3	C	7	3	1	0	27,840
Fifty Second Place	8	G	6	1	0	2	4,712
Fifty Six Fan	3	G	2	0	0	0	0
Fifty Three Cards	3	G	11	1	0	1	6,327
Fiftycaliber Jones	2	C	2	0	0	0	0
Fight Club (GER)	3	C	7	2	1	0	79,473
Fight Festival	4	C	2	0	0	0	0
Fight for a Crown	3	G	2	0	0	0	0
Fight for a Queen	9	M	12	1	0	2	3,534
Fight for Ally	7	G	1	1	0	0	7,800
Fight for Life	4	G	13	4	2	3	39,810
Fight for Peace	3	F	2	0	1	0	950
Fight Forever	6	M	2	0	1	0	5,634
Fight Like a Pro	2	G	1	0	0	0	118
Fight Over Sea	5	M	3	0	0	1	1,000
Fighten Firgie	4	F	3	0	1	0	9,597
Fighter Del Diablo	5	G	15	1	1	1	7,054
Fighter Jet	2	C	3	0	1	1	14,680
Fighter Ray	4	G	11	0	0	0	1,191
Fightforacure	2	F	2	0	1	1	3,100
Fightin Sixty	3	G	11	3	0	5	28,840
Fighting Bride	2	F	1	0	0	0	155
Fighting Deputy	4	G	1	0	0	0	0
Fighting Duke	4	G	8	0	1	1	6,495
Fighting Empress	3	F	1	1	0	0	14,250
Fighting Fever	4	F	13	1	3	3	85,677
Fighting Frazier	3	G	2	0	0	0	219
Fighting Indians	5	G	9	0	0	1	20,930
Fighting Jerry	3	G	11	2	2	3	27,175
Fighting Justice	4	G	10	1	1	1	19,872
Fighting Phil Furr	2	C	1	0	0	0	0
Fighting Roy Kelly	4	G	7	1	1	0	26,694
Fighting Skinny	4	F	12	5	2	0	53,640
Fighting Song	6	M	5	0	2	0	7,200
Fighting Speedy	2	F	5	1	1	1	21,824
Fighting Spirit	6	H	1	0	0	0	90
Fighting Wolf	4	G	9	3	1	2	35,316
Fightingtosurvive	4	C	9	0	3	1	5,739
Fightingupastorm	5	G	11	2	1	2	12,331
Fightoverhoney	5	G	8	0	0	0	324
Figment	4	G	2	0	0	1	2,636
Figueras	2	F	3	0	0	1	7,440
Fiji Rascal	5	M	2	0	0	0	468
Fiji Times Express	3	F	14	1	3	3	12,812
File Corrupted	7	G	5	0	0	1	1,190
Filipino Wind	7	H	6	0	0	1	510
Filippone	4	G	2	0	0	0	466
Fill the Bucket	3	G	2	1	0	0	1,640
Filles Fance Smile	3	G	3	0	0	0	630
Fille's Won	2	F	3	1	0	1	13,452
Filly Chilly	3	F	17	1	3	3	16,908
Filly Dulce	7	M	7	0	1	0	1,409
Filly Fanatic	3	F	10	2	3	0	21,420
Filly Filly Gumbo	5	M	2	0	0	0	260
Filly of Soul	2	F	7	1	0	1	6,950
Fillypasser	5	M	8	1	2	0	12,200
Filly's Gone Wild	2	F	3	1	0	0	5,825
Filly's Rhul	3	F	3	0	0	0	0
Film Critic	5	M	2	0	0	0	960
Film Maker	4	F	6	1	2	1	470,430
Film Star	6	G	11	0	0	2	5,418
Filmore	6	H	9	1	1	2	12,128
Filmos	4	G	1	0	0	0	0
Filosa	3	F	3	0	0	0	0
Fin Addict	2	G	3	0	0	2	8,920
Fin Entertainment	6	G	12	4	2	1	45,013
Fina	3	F	1	0	0	0	300
Fina Dui	10	G	11	3	1	4	29,246
Fina Payola	2	F	3	0	0	2	5,950
Final Agenda	5	H	9	1	0	1	5,752
Final Assault	3	F	7	2	2	2	96,169
Final Assembly	3	C	10	3	0	1	22,923
Final Attack	4	F	10	3	1	0	23,914

Horse	Age	Sex	Sts	1st	2d	3d	Won
Final Attempt	8	G	6	2	1	1	2,508
Final Bounty	4	G	13	0	4	3	16,155
Final Cheer	3	C	9	0	0	0	355
Final Chorus	5	G	1	0	0	0	80
Final Decision	5	G	11	2	2	2	21,390
Final Delivery	3	C	5	0	0	0	4,050
Final Discount	4	F	6	0	0	2	11,948
Final Dispersal	6	M	1	0	0	0	190
Final Draft	3	C	5	3	0	1	26,290
Final Dream	7	G	4	0	0	0	2,005
Final Edit	5	G	4	0	0	0	3,738
Final Endeavor	5	G	13	1	5	3	31,658
Final Exam	4	F	12	3	2	2	21,809
Final Eyes	8	G	11	0	1	2	3,246
Final Finale	4	G	13	3	4	2	51,909
Final Four Girl	2	F	5	1	0	1	10,170
Final Goal	2	G	2	1	0	0	6,600
Final Hero	6	G	16	3	1	3	22,521
Final Jeopardy	3	F	10	1	0	0	7,302
Final Lover	5	M	2	0	0	1	883
Final Marriage	3	F	4	0	0	0	1,900
Final Movement	4	C	7	1	2	2	13,030
Final Night	3	F	9	0	0	0	1,037
Final Occasion	3	G	4	0	1	1	470
Final Order	3	C	3	1	0	1	5,685
Final Payment	8	G	8	0	1	2	1,400
Final Prince	3	G	3	0	0	0	0
Final Prophecy	5	H	10	3	2	0	147,784
Final Response	2	C	4	1	0	0	7,560
Final Round	4	F	7	2	0	2	102,476
Final Score	5	H	5	1	0	0	8,640
Final Shot	3	F	10	1	1	1	11,373
Final Statement	4	C	7	0	1	3	6,300
Final Step	3	G	9	1	1	0	8,129
Final Story	2	C	3	0	1	1	8,280
Final Success	3	F	12	3	2	1	15,894
Final Sweep	6	M	3	0	0	0	0
Final Table	5	G	6	1	0	2	13,904
Final Thunder	6	G	13	0	2	0	4,076
Final Valentine	2	G	2	0	0	0	1,348
Final Wager	3	F	4	0	0	0	72
Finale Speaks	3	F	9	0	0	2	3,044
Finalgame	5	M	6	2	0	1	4,109
Finally a Boy	3	G	10	2	0	3	16,342
Finally a Prince	2	C	3	0	0	1	1,700
Finally Blonde	3	F	13	1	0	1	34,580
Finallytothebank	6	G	10	3	0	1	5,951
Finaly Affirmed	6	M	3	0	0	0	183
Financial	4	G	11	1	2	2	35,140
Financial Diplomat	6	H	2	0	0	0	310
Financial Flag	4	G	1	0	0	0	0
Financial Line	3	G	11	0	0	0	1,452
Financial Risk	3	F	12	3	3	0	65,815
Financial Security	2	F	4	1	0	0	8,420
Financialstatement	2	G	2	0	0	0	280
Financingavailable	3	F	10	4	2	2	294,151
Fincastle	3	F	3	0	0	0	0
Find Me Time	4	G	10	0	0	0	829
Find My Halter	5	G	11	3	2	3	19,939
Find Our Star	11	G	9	3	1	1	37,181
Find Sara	3	F	12	1	4	4	14,261
Find the Groom	3	F	17	1	0	0	7,566
Find the Mine	9	G	5	0	0	0	1,458
Find the Time	7	G	10	2	2	1	21,834
Findee's Keepee's	3	G	9	2	1	0	59,300
Finders Chance	4	G	7	1	0	0	8,852
Finding Speed	4	F	9	1	0	2	22,440
Findyourniche	3	G	12	3	3	0	19,564
Fine Affair	9	G	1	0	0	0	0
Fine and Dandy	5	H	7	0	0	1	5,491
Fine Answer	4	C	8	1	2	2	12,340
Fine Approval	3	F	3	0	1	0	1,475
Fine by Me	4	F	9	3	4	0	30,221
Fine Dreams	2	F	4	1	2	1	8,702
Fine Fashion Frank	2	C	1	0	0	0	420
Fine Prince	2	C	4	0	0	1	1,540
Fine Quality	3	C	2	0	0	1	2,531
Fine Results	4	G	10	2	4	1	36,343
Fine Ridge	4	F	9	2	1	3	9,679
Fine Shine	2	C	1	0	0	0	2,250
Fine Stormy	5	G	10	3	2	1	126,456
Fine Strike	3	C	9	0	4	1	30,800
Fine Tuner	4	C	8	1	1	4	10,040
Finea	4	F	2	0	0	0	190
Fineonthefarm	4	G	7	1	2	1	25,300
Finery	4	F	7	2	2	0	127,920
Fines Creek	4	G	14	3	2	0	80,274
Finessable	4	F	16	1	3	3	54,796
Finesse	4	F	10	1	1	2	11,768
Finest Gold	2	F	4	1	0	1	21,175
Finest Half Hour	3	G	4	2	0	0	13,650
Finest Jade	3	F	5	0	0	0	1,320
Finest Kreem	3	F	11	2	4	1	26,222
Finest Spell	3	F	12	2	3	3	26,177
Finish	2	C	2	0	1	0	4,780
Finish 'Em Off	6	M	9	1	1	4	16,470
Finish Line	4	G	14	3	3	0	23,196
Finish With Class	3	F	1	0	0	0	860
Finishing Touches	4	G	3	0	0	1	639
Finisterre Rock	8	G	18	1	1	1	13,179
Finleycreek	5	G	1	0	0	0	0
Finn Cantwinatgin	3	G	12	1	1	1	29,239
Finnbar's Promise	2	C	3	0	0	1	2,000
Finnegans in Again	3	G	11	1	2	2	49,374
Finnerty's Frolic	3	F	10	1	0	2	43,647
Finny	3	G	8	2	3	0	25,435
Fino Chino	3	F	3	0	0	0	157
Fintastic Lite	3	G	14	1	1	0	18,050
Fiona Isabella	4	F	11	1	2	0	5,518
Fiona Macintosh	3	F	7	0	1	1	5,535
Fiore Di Napoli	2	F	5	0	1	0	6,000
Fircroft	4	F	7	1	1	1	56,687
Fire Again	5	H	7	0	0	0	0
Fire Aly	4	G	3	0	0	0	173
Fire and Glory	5	G	6	0	0	1	7,840
Fire and Icy	10	G	5	0	1	0	2,750
Fire Ant	2	G	2	1	0	1	11,820
Fire Away	2	G	2	0	0	1	2,680
Fire Ball John	10	H	5	2	1	0	3,257
Fire Captain	3	G	10	1	1	0	13,593
Fire Crackle	2	C	2	0	0	0	4,260
Fire Dance	4	G	13	1	0	2	13,569
Fire Drill	2	F	1	0	0	0	360
Fire Em Up	3	F	2	0	0	0	0
Fire Emblem	3	F	7	1	2	1	32,145
Fire Fox	6	G	6	0	0	2	6,587
Fire Hero	3	C	17	3	3	1	95,315
Fire Hot	3	F	5	0	0	1	4,740
Fire House Slew	3	G	4	0	0	2	4,045
Fire in the Soul	7	G	13	1	2	0	9,931
Fire Inu Wire	5	M	11	0	1	0	2,490
Fire It Up	2	C	2	0	1	0	5,600
Fire Lane	5	G	6	0	0	0	990
Fire Makers Witch	4	F	5	0	1	0	2,216
Fire Me	8	H	9	1	0	1	4,570
Fire Monkey	3	F	3	2	0	0	31,420
Fire Mound	2	C	5	1	0	1	19,820
Fire Outa Control	8	G	13	1	0	0	5,046
Fire Pants	4	F	8	0	1	1	3,212
Fire Path	2	C	4	1	0	0	16,550
Fire Place	4	F	9	0	2	1	4,669
Fire Play	2	G	2	0	0	0	340
Fire Power	2	C	2	1	0	1	20,212
Fire Proof	5	H	7	0	0	0	1,590
Fire Slam	3	C	9	4	2	0	427,381
Fire Steed	4	F	14	3	1	1	46,631
Fire Strike	3	C	11	1	3	0	20,600
Fire the Bum	8	M	10	3	3	1	50,005
Fire the Firm	5	G	15	1	3	1	30,885
Fire the Rockets	8	G	6	0	1	0	2,478
Fire the Vet	4	G	3	0	0	0	735
Fire to the Wire	3	C	7	0	0	2	2,885
Fire Within Fire	4	G	15	1	3	3	11,928
Fire Wood	2	C	2	0	2	0	8,600
Firebaby	2	F	4	0	0	1	6,468
Fireball	2	C	1	0	0	0	145
Fireballer	5	G	1	0	0	0	84
Fireboll	3	F	8	2	0	0	12,213

Horse	Age	Sex	Sts	1st	2d	3d	Won
Firebolt's Colony	3	G	5	0	1	0	4,540
Fireborne	8	M	9	2	1	1	8,266
Fireboy	5	H	1	0	0	0	0
Firecard	6	M	8	2	0	2	58,000
Firedup for Real	3	C	8	1	0	0	6,140
Firedup Trick	2	F	4	0	0	0	1,210
Firefall	8	G	13	5	2	1	20,255
Fireflash	2	G	1	0	0	0	0
Fireflower	3	F	3	0	0	0	300
Firefly	2	F	2	0	0	0	0
Firefly Dancer	5	M	14	1	5	1	11,558
Firefree	5	M	2	0	0	1	1,268
Firehawk	2	G	5	0	0	0	3,776
Firehouse Affair	6	M	2	0	0	0	0
Firehouse Charlie	4	G	11	2	4	0	30,834
Firehouse Quatorze	4	F	5	1	1	1	10,087
Fireinthekitchen	4	G	2	0	0	0	860
Fireman Bert	3	C	8	0	1	2	6,475
Fireman Rahill	4	G	12	1	1	0	9,637
Firenorth	5	M	9	0	1	1	2,291
Fireonthemountain	6	H	3	0	0	0	0
Fires Image	2	G	5	0	0	1	2,155
Firespike	3	C	7	0	0	0	3,242
Firestone Special	6	G	6	0	0	1	200
Firestorm Sammy	2	F	3	0	0	2	3,456
Firetail	3	F	14	1	2	0	10,870
Firey Banker	3	F	5	0	0	0	225
Firey Dinner	6	M	2	0	0	0	0
Firey Fantasy	3	F	2	0	0	0	0
Firey Isle	3	F	6	1	0	1	3,513
Firey Malek	2	F	4	0	1	3	10,120
Firey New Love	3	G	11	4	1	1	25,644
Firey Nina	4	F	17	2	3	3	26,799
Firing Note	5	G	14	1	4	3	26,980
Firm Command	4	G	9	1	1	0	11,700
Firm Halo	5	M	13	2	2	3	16,766
Firm Reality	4	F	11	2	1	1	46,533
Firm Tag	2	F	2	0	0	1	1,880
Firmament	5	M	11	1	1	3	19,967
Firmly Done	6	G	12	3	2	2	29,618
First Affair	6	H	3	0	1	1	900
First Aly Pie	6	M	7	0	1	2	11,379
First Amendment	7	G	7	0	0	0	885
First and Ten	5	G	1	0	0	0	119
First Approval	3	F	11	1	0	2	30,560
First Arrival	8	G	15	3	0	2	59,790
First At Last	3	C	12	3	3	1	44,396
First At War	4	C	3	0	0	0	202
First Away	4	G	12	2	1	1	12,470
First Blast	5	G	11	2	1	3	11,223
First Blush	4	C	8	3	1	2	111,567
First Book	6	G	8	1	2	0	7,524
First Bounce	2	C	4	0	0	0	1,380
First Boy	4	C	9	0	0	1	2,378
First Casting	4	C	4	0	1	0	3,280
First Cause	3	C	7	1	0	2	14,966
First Class Code	7	M	3	0	0	1	1,536
First Class Honors	5	G	6	0	1	0	5,144
First Class Lady	8	M	13	2	0	3	10,241
First Class Trip	4	G	11	1	0	1	25,160
First Clu	4	F	5	1	0	1	12,705
First Comes Love	3	F	7	1	3	1	22,910
First Copy	5	G	11	0	6	2	27,174
First Corinthian	4	G	3	0	0	0	0
First Count	2	G	5	1	0	0	8,568
First Curtain Call	5	M	1	0	0	0	80
First Dark	3	F	4	0	0	0	0
First Dixie	4	G	10	1	1	0	6,340
First Dollar	4	G	7	0	2	1	2,526
First Draft	5	M	9	3	0	2	106,114
First Draw	4	G	7	0	0	2	4,015
First Effort	3	C	3	0	0	0	220
First Encounter	4	F	1	0	0	0	167
First Endevor	2	F	7	1	2	1	14,170
First Escapade	5	G	14	2	2	4	9,905
First Ever Clever	5	M	5	1	0	1	2,094
First Expression	2	G	2	0	0	0	238
First Fantacy	6	M	5	0	1	0	2,001
First Farrier	3	G	1	0	0	0	300
First Glory	2	F	2	0	0	2	9,360
First Gold Bar	3	F	1	0	0	0	0
First Govenor	7	H	9	0	0	2	1,175
First Great Lady	2	F	3	1	0	0	7,236
First Hoedown	6	G	9	3	2	1	10,321
First Honoree	3	C	4	0	0	0	365
First in Port	3	G	11	2	0	1	17,938
First Insight	5	G	1	0	0	0	0
First Interview	3	F	9	2	0	0	38,680
First Knighter	8	G	1	0	0	0	0
First Lady (ARG)	4	F	7	1	0	0	14,714
First Ladys a Pro	2	F	2	0	0	0	750
First Lieutenant	7	H	6	1	1	2	55,870
First Littledancer	4	F	12	0	0	1	4,378
First Magic	2	G	1	0	0	0	189
First Mohican	4	G	13	3	2	1	45,048
First Money	3	C	4	1	1	1	26,953
First Moon	3	F	8	1	1	1	35,875
First Move	3	F	5	0	0	0	2,880
First N Goal	2	F	3	1	1	0	25,320
First Note	3	G	6	0	0	0	1,760
First October	5	M	14	4	3	3	16,706
First Ole	4	G	8	1	4	1	15,223
First Printing	5	M	9	1	2	0	10,128
First Quarter	5	M	7	1	0	2	101,689
First Rate Event	3	C	3	0	0	1	8,612
First Rock	3	F	13	2	1	1	10,360
First Row	4	F	1	0	0	0	333
First Search	5	G	2	0	0	0	0
First Service (GER)	10	G	8	2	0	1	9,280
First Shot	7	G	9	2	3	1	44,000
First Sign of Rain	5	G	1	0	0	0	122
First Sip	5	G	19	4	2	3	9,033
First Soprano	5	M	4	0	1	0	966
First Spear	6	G	5	0	1	1	9,230
First Starella	4	F	1	0	0	0	0
First Storm	3	F	1	0	0	0	78
First Time Luck	5	G	4	0	0	0	0
First Trip	6	G	14	1	3	1	18,395
First Try	7	G	6	0	0	1	901
First Union	2	C	2	0	0	0	290
First Up	5	G	13	1	2	2	14,190
First Waltz	3	F	4	0	1	0	1,860
First War	3	F	2	0	0	0	180
First Whitney	2	G	5	0	0	0	2,315
First Wolf	7	G	19	2	7	0	20,545
First You Dream	4	G	6	1	0	0	12,340
Firstclass Upgrade	4	G	11	1	1	0	9,054
Firstgear	3	G	10	1	2	0	23,199
Firsthere	3	G	13	0	1	3	8,852
Firstimage	6	M	7	0	0	1	494
Firstladypresident	3	F	12	2	2	2	19,239
Firstlinc	2	F	4	1	1	1	23,250
Firstonehome	4	F	9	2	0	1	4,299
Firstoneinthewater	4	F	1	0	0	0	0
Firstonthewire	6	G	1	0	0	1	1,240
Firstround Ko	6	G	1	0	0	1	3,300
Firstship	3	G	4	0	0	1	5,760
Firstsonofmachone	5	G	4	0	0	0	3,290
Firststatedeposit	6	G	11	6	2	1	112,800
Firsttriplexington	2	C	1	0	0	0	0
Firth of Lorne (IRE)	5	M	2	0	0	1	18,000
Fiscal Nobility	10	G	3	0	0	0	128
Fiscal Storm	2	C	1	0	1	0	6,270
Fiscally Speaking	5	G	3	0	1	0	7,200
Fish Guys	3	G	9	0	0	0	2,470
Fisher Pond	5	H	6	1	0	0	42,035
Fisher Station	5	G	6	0	0	1	662
Fisherman's Friend	3	G	12	1	2	2	21,760
Fishes Freak	3	F	5	2	0	0	29,380
Fishie's Boy	4	G	13	0	0	1	2,097
Fishtale	3	C	1	0	0	0	171
Fishy Advice	2	C	2	0	0	0	3,680
Fishy Testimony	2	F	4	0	1	0	7,010
Fision	3	G	11	1	2	2	32,064
Fist Full	5	G	9	0	0	2	4,430
Fistbump	4	G	4	0	0	0	348
Fit and Bushy	8	G	15	3	1	2	9,502
Fit and Tough	2	C	3	1	0	0	9,760

Horse	Age	Sex	Sts	1st	2d	3d	Won
Fit as a Fiddle	7	H	4	0	1	1	1,400
Fit Faze	2	C	10	2	1	0	40,170
Fit for a Lady	2	F	4	0	0	1	2,030
Fit for Flight	3	C	7	0	0	0	255
Fit for Glory	3	F	8	1	0	3	9,275
Fit for Silk	6	M	13	0	0	1	4,928
Fit for the Fight	3	G	7	2	0	2	13,350
Fit Legit	4	G	11	1	0	2	6,622
Fit of Passion	3	C	4	0	0	0	250
Fit Performer	7	M	6	2	1	1	116,809
Fit Por Fast	3	F	2	0	0	0	0
Fit Soldier	3	G	2	0	0	0	840
Fit to Be a Gent	9	G	10	0	1	4	5,302
Fit to Be Annie	2	F	1	0	0	0	0
Fit to Be Royal	7	G	3	0	0	0	615
Fit to Flee	3	F	2	0	0	0	0
Fit to Keep	4	G	15	2	0	0	9,985
Fit to Kill	4	F	2	0	0	0	640
Fit to Skate	4	G	11	1	2	1	13,569
Fitadip	4	G	11	2	0	0	9,539
Fitfull Rage	4	F	4	0	0	0	810
Fitness	3	G	7	1	4	0	52,610
Fitstoatee	7	G	7	1	2	0	7,300
Fitting Tribute	3	G	12	2	2	4	41,430
Fitts Village	4	G	3	0	0	0	231
Fitz Roy	3	C	3	0	0	0	1,200
Fitzbid	4	F	2	0	0	1	1,199
Fitzgerald	4	G	8	0	0	0	895
Fitzroyal	5	G	4	0	0	0	4,890
Five Alarm Flyer	3	F	8	2	3	1	34,099
Five Bells	2	F	6	0	1	1	9,190
Five Bucks	6	G	13	0	1	0	2,194
Five Card Monty	3	C	10	1	3	0	36,920
Five Cousins	6	G	8	3	2	0	13,144
Five Crystals	2	F	2	1	0	0	7,604
Five Elements	3	F	5	1	0	1	25,220
Five Flags	3	C	11	0	1	1	3,473
Five for Five	4	F	13	3	3	0	19,680
Five Nickels	3	F	8	1	2	2	70,520
Five North	4	F	6	1	1	1	3,842
Five O Five	4	C	7	2	2	0	13,773
Five O Two	3	G	7	0	0	0	1,900
Five Partners	5	G	6	0	1	0	1,386
Five Point Star	4	G	5	3	0	0	79,562
Five Rivers	5	M	12	1	1	4	23,020
Five Roads (IRE)	4	G	7	2	0	1	15,030
Five Rubies	2	C	7	2	0	3	44,598
Five Schillings	8	R	1	0	0	0	0
Five Star Account	3	G	12	4	0	2	123,086
Five Star Affair	4	F	9	0	0	2	2,151
Five Star Award	6	G	8	0	3	0	8,074
Five Star Command	3	F	2	0	0	1	1,100
Five Star Fund	2	F	3	1	0	0	31,410
Five Star Gene	6	G	8	1	3	1	10,240
Five Star Gold	3	G	4	0	0	0	3,554
Five Star Meeting	4	F	4	1	2	0	45,851
Five Star Semoran	3	C	7	0	0	0	1,225
Five Steps	3	C	4	1	2	0	29,896
Five Straight	7	G	14	3	2	0	12,948
Five String Banjo	3	G	11	1	0	1	5,602
Five Swings	4	F	2	0	0	0	152
Five Tango Charlie	10	G	13	0	2	3	7,550
Five to Four	6	M	9	0	0	0	780
Five Travoltas	4	G	1	0	0	0	85
Five Wild Cats	3	G	12	3	0	5	46,556
Five Wishes	5	M	6	0	0	0	450
Fiveoclock Charley	4	G	13	0	2	2	5,517
Fiveoclocksumwhere	3	G	7	0	0	0	390
Fiveofour	5	G	18	0	5	2	18,010
Fivestargirl	5	M	10	2	1	1	13,040
Fivexj	3	G	2	0	0	0	93
Fix Bayonets	4	C	2	1	0	0	20,400
Fixcall	3	C	10	0	2	3	29,944
Fixed Amount	2	F	2	1	0	1	28,900
Fixed Image	5	G	7	0	0	0	1,116
Fixin To	4	G	8	2	0	1	10,446
Fixitmiss	4	F	2	0	0	0	0
Fixture's Return	5	G	5	1	0	0	1,441
Fizz	5	G	6	0	2	0	3,540
Fizzicus	2	C	1	0	1	0	2,070
Fjj Slavic	3	G	1	0	0	0	0
Flag Angel	4	F	7	0	0	0	654
Flag Day	4	F	8	0	0	0	707
Flag Em Down	4	G	14	1	2	3	9,390
Flag Girl	4	F	13	2	3	0	13,338
Flag Is Up	4	G	2	0	0	0	260
Flag Lady B	4	F	13	3	2	1	32,350
Flag Minister	3	G	12	2	1	2	24,267
Flag of Orion	3	G	12	1	2	2	39,060
Flag the Groom	4	G	11	0	2	0	4,038
Flag the Mint Down	4	F	6	0	0	0	1,500
Flag to Fly	4	G	9	1	1	1	31,240
Flag Tower	3	G	17	0	2	2	10,353
Flager (ARG)	5	M	7	2	0	0	62,223
Flagg's Crossing	7	H	10	0	2	1	11,467
Flags a Flyin	4	F	4	0	0	0	0
Flags Gold	5	M	9	0	0	0	0
Flag's Magic	2	F	4	1	0	0	12,780
Flags of Courage	3	G	6	0	0	1	450
Flag's Up	3	G	3	1	0	0	9,800
Flagship Mission	2	G	6	0	0	0	2,200
Flagshipenterprise	3	C	2	0	0	0	450
Flagsofourfathers	3	G	7	1	2	1	20,319
Flagstaff	2	C	5	0	2	2	29,600
Flagwave	8	G	17	3	2	8	31,980
Flail	5	M	16	5	2	1	23,275
Flair and Square	5	G	4	0	1	1	8,149
Flair of Justice	3	F	2	0	0	0	0
Flair Play	3	F	2	0	0	0	133
Flair to Spare	4	G	17	4	2	4	46,497
Flake O	6	G	10	1	2	1	13,410
Flame Catcher	4	F	17	2	2	1	32,027
Flame in My Heart	4	F	2	0	1	0	854
Flame of Love	4	F	10	3	3	2	82,612
Flame Song	6	M	4	1	0	0	34,370
Flame Tetra	4	F	12	2	5	1	16,722
Flame Trick	2	F	4	0	0	1	3,055
Flamenco	2	C	6	4	1	1	303,085
Flamethrowintexan	3	G	11	7	1	1	368,813
Flamin Al	4	G	5	0	2	1	10,040
Flamin Creek Dream	3	G	2	0	0	0	350
Flamin' Jolie	7	G	8	2	1	0	18,600
Flaming Bull	4	G	6	0	2	0	3,068
Flaming Cajun	3	G	8	1	3	1	23,113
Flaming Cloud	7	M	7	0	1	1	2,385
Flaming Dixie	3	F	11	2	6	1	75,840
Flaming Fire	4	G	20	1	1	7	20,333
Flaming Moe	4	G	2	0	1	0	11,440
Flaming Money	4	F	6	1	0	1	6,543
Flaming Night	5	M	12	1	0	5	31,728
Flaming Phoenix	3	G	8	1	0	1	2,050
Flaming Prospector	4	G	18	1	0	4	11,659
Flaming Remark	2	F	5	0	1	1	3,644
Flaming Ridge	4	F	10	2	2	2	9,599
Flaming Spare	5	H	19	1	1	2	13,640
Flaming Springs	4	C	12	0	2	2	18,466
Flaming Sunset	5	M	9	0	1	1	1,276
Flaming Villa	5	G	1	0	0	0	92
Flamingo Fan	3	F	6	1	0	0	26,303
Flamingo Flash	5	M	10	1	1	1	12,589
Flamingo Lane	4	F	7	1	1	1	7,180
Flamingo Phil	9	G	2	0	0	0	0
Flamingo Red	4	G	11	2	3	3	24,635
Flamingo's World	5	G	6	0	0	1	2,100
Flaminsun	2	G	2	0	1	1	7,680
Flan for You	3	F	10	1	3	1	23,915
Flandins Cat	4	G	1	0	1	0	2,940
Flange	3	C	3	0	1	0	5,096
Flank Attack	4	C	6	0	1	0	8,570
Flank Drive	4	C	12	3	3	1	18,520
Flank Stake	4	G	11	1	3	1	7,713
Flanker	3	C	2	0	0	0	515
Flannigan	8	H	3	0	0	0	0
Flapper Girl	2	F	2	0	0	0	0
Flaps Lane	3	F	9	1	0	0	13,359
Flare Flyer	4	F	5	0	0	1	689
Flare Up	4	F	8	0	0	0	228
Flaring Moon	9	G	19	1	3	4	8,984

Horse	Age	Sex	Sts	1st	2d	3d	Won
Flarions Flame	4	G	7	1	2	0	11,892
Flash Ante	4	C	13	0	2	4	10,344
Flash Buy	5	H	11	2	1	1	16,654
Flash Can Dance	4	G	13	4	1	2	59,326
Flash Forward	5	G	14	3	1	1	17,873
Flash Frame	4	F	14	2	5	1	18,577
Flash From Heaven	5	H	4	0	0	0	490
Flash King	4	C	6	0	0	0	526
Flash o' Socks	3	F	3	0	0	0	339
Flash of Fashion	3	F	8	0	0	0	6,030
Flash Photo	2	C	1	0	0	0	0
Flash Run Bepop	4	F	15	3	0	1	18,155
Flash the Field	3	F	7	0	0	3	4,430
Flash the Green	3	G	13	1	1	2	16,639
Flash Your Cash	4	G	3	0	0	0	134
Flashavenue	3	G	4	1	0	1	3,090
Flashback Ack	4	G	1	0	0	0	0
Flashback Dancer	3	F	11	1	2	1	21,812
Flashdance Missy	3	F	5	1	0	0	28,498
Flashdance Star	3	F	4	0	1	1	8,840
Flashin Lady	2	F	3	0	1	0	15,288
Flashing Red	4	C	4	2	0	0	25,620
Flashintheknight	2	F	1	0	0	0	181
Flashinthesky	3	G	9	0	2	1	42,130
Flashpoint	5	M	8	0	1	0	4,758
Flashy	3	F	11	2	1	2	70,929
Flashy Anna	3	F	11	4	2	0	210,773
Flashy Boy	2	C	3	0	1	0	4,795
Flashy Brass	3	F	8	0	2	1	4,972
Flashy Dash	4	G	8	1	1	1	35,272
Flashy Gal	4	F	3	0	0	1	5,752
Flashy I. D.	6	M	3	0	0	0	216
Flashy in Black	7	M	8	2	2	1	13,043
Flashy Island Girl	4	F	2	1	0	1	6,745
Flashy Joe	4	C	3	0	0	0	249
Flashy Katherine	5	M	6	0	1	0	5,225
Flashy Lil Sis	5	M	10	1	1	0	6,600
Flashy Lover	5	H	5	0	0	0	624
Flashy Machine	3	F	2	0	0	1	2,310
Flashy Matter	3	C	7	0	1	1	13,041
Flashy Mike	2	C	2	0	0	0	0
Flashy Player	6	M	3	0	0	0	428
Flashy Prospect	7	G	10	1	2	1	5,975
Flashy Rocket	3	C	2	1	0	0	15,900
Flashy Silver	5	M	10	0	0	1	14,894
Flashy Tale	2	F	6	1	0	0	9,070
Flashy Three (GB)	2	F	2	1	1	0	21,680
Flashy Thunder	5	M	6	0	0	3	38,354
Flat Rock	2	C	2	1	0	0	44,802
Flat Top	11	G	1	0	0	0	0
Flatfoot Scotty	4	G	7	0	0	0	3,422
Flatland Flyer	9	G	6	2	1	1	5,786
Flatline	6	M	14	3	0	2	39,650
Flatter Me Not	3	G	3	0	1	0	7,632
Flauntingly	3	F	5	1	0	0	2,770
Flavour Flavour	3	G	9	0	0	3	8,099
Flawless Treasure	2	F	2	0	0	0	2,300
Flaxen Flyer	5	M	3	0	0	1	5,896
Flea Powder	4	F	6	1	0	0	3,780
Fleabiscuit	3	G	14	0	1	1	4,813
Fle'che Rouge	5	M	9	1	1	0	7,867
Fled	3	G	13	2	1	1	19,220
Flee the Blues	5	G	2	0	0	1	3,234
Fleeing Intent	4	F	2	0	0	0	205
Fleet Aint	4	G	15	2	2	1	15,992
Fleet Amyanne	4	F	2	0	0	1	2,543
Fleet and Sweet	4	F	7	1	0	1	6,442
Fleet Ballado	3	F	4	0	1	0	5,031
Fleet Boss	8	G	16	2	2	3	17,206
Fleet Christina	5	M	9	3	1	2	24,043
Fleet Deed	7	M	5	0	0	1	2,445
Fleet Deputy	3	C	7	2	1	2	35,988
Fleet Dust	6	G	5	1	0	1	9,328
Fleet Expense	5	G	13	0	1	2	4,326
Fleet Feet Pete	4	G	13	1	1	0	11,648
Fleet Final	5	G	19	1	3	4	11,156
Fleet Flight	5	M	10	2	0	2	10,638
Fleet Foot Fox	4	C	5	0	1	0	3,288
Fleet Forum	5	G	14	2	2	0	28,057
Fleet Freckles	3	F	15	1	0	0	5,154
Fleet Goeen	4	F	6	0	0	0	957
Fleet Indian	3	F	7	4	0	1	139,350
Fleet Irish Miss	3	F	4	1	0	1	5,610
Fleet Line	5	G	6	2	0	0	7,954
Fleet Man	6	G	3	0	0	0	0
Fleet Music	4	G	7	1	2	0	14,775
Fleet of Honour	3	G	6	0	0	2	5,048
Fleet Pamplona	3	F	11	1	1	1	22,370
Fleet Phillie	3	F	8	0	0	0	1,950
Fleet Ruhlmann	8	G	10	0	0	1	1,272
Fleet Sail	10	G	6	0	3	1	3,000
Fleet Selena	3	F	2	0	0	1	6,270
Fleet Sleet	2	C	3	0	0	0	1,150
Fleet Street	6	G	4	0	0	0	540
Fleet Sweet	3	F	5	0	0	1	3,310
Fleet Valentine	4	F	1	0	0	0	0
Fleet Willy	5	M	11	3	1	1	18,845
Fleet Zepphyr	4	F	5	1	0	0	5,041
Fleeta Dif	5	M	8	3	1	2	100,000
Fleetengly	6	M	10	1	0	2	6,837
Fleetest of All	3	F	4	0	0	0	336
Fleetest of Feet	4	F	3	0	0	0	0
Fleeting	3	F	2	0	0	0	380
Fleeting Alliance	4	G	15	2	3	1	20,096
Fleeting Beauty	4	F	9	0	0	1	1,319
Fleeting Feline	4	F	3	0	0	1	4,810
Fleeting Glance	3	C	13	2	3	1	18,657
Fleeting Riverman	2	G	8	1	0	1	9,899
Fleeting Term	5	G	1	0	0	0	0
Fleetingdream	3	G	3	0	0	0	0
Fleetmaster	7	G	12	1	1	1	13,470
Fleetmoon	3	F	6	2	2	1	28,284
Fleet's Promise	8	G	2	0	1	1	648
Fleetski	5	M	9	0	0	0	1,065
Fleetstreet Dancer	6	G	2	0	0	1	30,000
Fleetway	3	C	7	3	1	0	45,380
Fleety	7	G	11	1	1	1	11,613
Flemish Cap	6	G	10	4	3	1	79,320
Fleur de Frost	2	F	5	0	0	1	4,420
Fleur de Girl	3	F	5	0	0	0	805
Fleur de Lil	5	G	6	0	0	0	258
Fleur de May	4	F	1	0	0	1	1,540
Fleur Savage	4	F	8	2	3	0	34,800
Fleurdebel	6	M	2	0	0	0	308
Flexible Princess	2	F	2	2	0	0	30,550
Flick Creek	6	G	9	0	3	1	9,294
Flick of Justice	2	F	7	0	4	2	24,040
Flicker	2	F	1	0	0	0	55
Flickering Silk	6	M	8	2	0	1	3,550
Flies With Eagles	8	G	6	1	0	0	8,944
Flight	5	G	13	1	1	6	15,679
Flight At Eight	6	G	10	0	0	0	400
Flight Court	5	M	10	3	0	2	16,046
Flight Dancer	4	G	3	0	0	0	150
Flight Design	3	F	6	0	0	0	758
Flight for Life	3	C	2	0	0	0	0
Flight of Fancy	2	F	2	0	0	0	2,436
Flight of Ideas	6	M	8	1	1	2	6,175
Flight of Love	3	F	18	1	1	2	9,663
Flight of Time	4	F	4	0	0	0	764
Flight Ops	3	F	15	1	4	3	51,992
Flight Path	7	H	11	1	2	1	12,410
Flight Pattern	3	F	7	1	1	1	4,808
Flight Ready	2	C	2	0	1	1	12,600
Flight Seven	6	G	15	2	3	3	13,973
Flight to Eden	2	C	1	0	0	0	675
Flight to Justice	3	C	10	1	2	0	24,305
Flight Training	4	G	13	3	1	2	34,876
Flight Wings	3	F	5	0	0	1	4,270
Flight Zone	6	H	11	2	2	3	10,285
Flightofthebuffalo	5	G	10	3	4	0	64,590
Flighttwotwenty	3	G	3	0	0	0	0
Flighty Forty Nine	7	M	15	1	1	2	5,609
Fling	4	F	12	3	2	3	29,515
Flint Ridge	2	F	2	1	1	0	17,260
Flintville	3	G	13	5	4	2	88,916
Flip	4	C	5	3	0	1	56,690
Flip and Stu	4	G	13	2	1	1	13,460

Horse	Age	Sex	Sts	1st	2d	3d	Won
Flip de Lite	3	C	3	0	0	0	2,286
Flip Flop Fly	2	G	4	1	0	1	10,789
Flip Side	2	F	5	1	1	1	9,214
Flip Tour	3	G	14	3	3	1	32,980
Flip's Buddy Bert	3	G	8	1	2	1	10,084
Flipsider	5	M	8	0	1	3	14,493
Flipthescript	3	F	2	0	1	0	1,490
Flirt by Knight	3	F	4	0	0	0	0
Flirt to Music	6	G	21	2	1	3	13,965
Flirt With Danger	9	M	4	3	0	1	29,490
Flirt With Fortune	4	C	2	0	0	1	2,332
Flirtation Card	5	M	2	0	0	1	1,060
Flirtatious Class	5	M	10	1	1	1	11,129
Flirtatious Heart	6	M	1	0	0	0	774
Flirting Ways	4	F	1	0	0	1	4,200
Flirting With Fame	3	F	4	0	0	0	335
Flirting With Fate	3	F	7	1	1	1	26,580
Flirting Wolf	8	G	2	0	0	0	164
Flirtingwithmagic	5	G	4	0	0	0	0
Flirty Girl	3	F	3	0	2	0	15,100
Flitter Bug	6	M	1	0	0	0	290
Flitwick's Charms	3	G	3	0	0	0	1,110
Flo Hope	3	F	2	0	0	0	172
Flo Rose 'n Net	3	F	10	0	3	0	8,595
Float and Sting	5	M	7	1	0	0	22,400
Floater	3	G	9	2	2	2	72,460
Floating Meeting	5	G	14	1	1	0	4,745
Floaway	3	F	15	4	2	3	48,990
Flom's Flyer	6	G	16	0	2	1	3,251
Flood Level	4	G	17	1	2	2	11,658
Flood Watch	2	C	1	0	0	0	1,440
Floor Dancer	3	C	7	3	1	0	37,680
Floor It Man	6	H	11	0	1	1	3,800
Floor Play	9	G	6	2	1	0	19,150
Flopper	5	G	14	1	3	6	50,700
Flor de Durazno	3	G	1	0	0	0	0
Flor de Forestal	3	F	3	1	2	0	8,265
Flor Del Sol	4	F	10	0	2	2	22,021
Flora Mac Flimsey	6	M	7	0	0	3	9,775
Florabama	3	F	9	0	0	2	3,700
Floral Avenue	4	G	4	0	0	2	4,170
Florence	4	F	9	0	0	2	13,604
Florida Chad	4	G	8	0	1	0	2,244
Florida Express	3	G	1	0	0	0	340
Florida Forum	4	F	1	0	0	0	93
Florida Jet	4	C	17	1	0	2	11,580
Florida Kat	4	C	3	0	0	1	1,505
Florida Keys	3	C	5	1	0	1	15,540
Florida Man	2	C	4	2	0	1	21,845
Florida On Fire	6	M	11	1	0	1	12,005
Florida Recount	5	G	2	0	0	0	1,710
Florida Transfer	4	G	8	1	0	0	3,172
Floridacon	2	G	4	0	1	0	2,610
Florik's Baby	3	F	3	0	0	0	690
Flo's Bo	5	G	13	2	0	2	40,600
Flo's Gold	6	G	16	1	6	5	42,680
Flo's Lil Lady	6	M	16	1	0	1	4,257
Flo's Wish	9	G	2	0	0	0	260
Flo'ssweetie	5	M	19	1	4	1	11,955
Flosy Roma (ARG)	4	F	11	0	0	1	5,440
Flota	2	F	7	2	3	1	31,305
Flota Star	6	M	6	0	0	0	56
Flotilla	6	G	7	0	0	2	5,823
Flourishing	3	F	6	1	2	0	13,975
Flower Alley	2	C	1	0	0	1	2,460
Flower Cart	5	M	12	2	1	0	16,455
Flower Dance	2	F	1	1	0	0	6,555
Flower Flag	2	F	4	1	0	2	13,475
Flower Forest	4	F	2	1	0	0	42,396
Flower Hunter	4	F	2	0	0	0	0
Flower Lane	5	G	15	1	0	1	5,228
Flower Mound	4	F	5	1	1	1	7,900
Flower Time	6	M	5	0	0	0	150
Flowers and Fun	4	G	8	1	1	1	6,002
Flowers Isle Bay	5	G	1	0	0	0	0
Flowers My Lady	7	M	18	1	0	1	10,635
Flowers Onthe Wall	5	M	9	0	1	2	16,284
Flowing Southward	5	M	7	0	1	1	2,712
Fluff My Feathers	4	F	5	1	0	0	4,690
Fluffernutter	3	G	6	2	0	1	16,475
Fluffy Feeling	7	M	3	0	0	0	0
Fluid Gold	12	G	1	0	0	0	154
Fluidity	3	F	4	0	0	0	0
Fluidly	3	F	14	1	5	0	25,050
Flu's Last Rumble	4	F	1	0	0	0	0
Flush Draw	4	F	3	0	1	0	1,673
Flush Flush Flush	4	G	6	1	0	1	3,350
Flute Song	5	G	7	0	0	0	191
Flutter Butterfly	2	F	1	1	0	0	10,650
Flutterflies	7	M	3	0	0	0	858
Fly Abby Fly	2	F	6	0	1	1	4,194
Fly Again	4	G	11	0	2	1	4,208
Fly Amelia Fly	2	F	7	0	1	0	6,211
Fly Amery Fly	3	F	15	0	3	4	23,608
Fly and Eagle	5	G	17	2	2	1	48,150
Fly Away Angel	3	F	11	3	3	1	119,530
Fly Badger Fly	4	G	12	1	0	4	8,504
Fly Beside Me	6	G	5	1	0	0	7,615
Fly Big Bird Fly	2	C	6	0	0	0	1,500
Fly Blue Devil	5	G	8	0	1	0	2,470
Fly Borboleta	5	M	1	0	0	0	380
Fly by Em	6	M	4	0	1	0	500
Fly by Moonlight	3	G	6	3	0	0	35,666
Fly By Night (NZ)	5	M	4	0	0	1	6,960
Fly by Peru	3	G	4	0	1	0	1,215
Fly by You	6	M	5	2	1	2	23,000
Fly Bye Dawn	7	M	6	0	0	1	2,415
Fly Eagle Fly	3	F	9	0	0	1	1,037
Fly Esteem	3	G	6	2	0	0	84,388
Fly Fire	8	M	2	0	0	0	0
Fly Fly Away	4	F	6	1	0	0	1,580
Fly Fly Fly	2	F	2	0	0	0	0
Fly Forever	8	G	14	2	2	5	17,283
Fly Foxy Fly	4	F	1	0	0	0	0
Fly Girl	4	F	11	0	0	1	6,325
Fly Harold	8	G	7	1	0	2	5,839
Fly High Red	3	C	1	0	0	0	92
Fly Honor Fly	4	G	6	0	1	1	7,400
Fly Little Totum	2	C	5	0	0	1	1,310
Fly Maggie	8	M	5	1	0	0	13,654
Fly Me Ali	3	F	11	4	0	2	66,320
Fly Me Nina	3	F	15	3	5	1	50,820
Fly On By	8	G	11	1	2	2	5,830
Fly On Home	5	M	5	0	0	1	4,135
Fly Our Flag	4	F	3	0	0	0	144
Fly Over Early	10	M	8	1	3	2	5,875
Fly Seattle	6	G	4	0	0	0	0
Fly Slama Jama	6	G	7	2	2	2	55,160
Fly Smartly	6	G	7	1	0	3	42,008
Fly Socks	3	C	1	1	0	0	15,600
Fly to the Bank	4	G	12	2	1	2	13,747
Fly to the Music	4	F	13	0	1	3	4,263
Fly to the Wire	4	G	1	0	0	0	1,506
Fly Tricky	4	G	12	2	2	2	9,362
Fly With Hope	6	G	10	4	1	1	6,333
Fly With Karakorum	4	F	14	1	3	2	67,999
Flyawaybutterfly	2	F	2	0	0	0	0
Flybykiss	3	F	3	1	0	0	15,588
Flyer Mine	3	G	3	0	1	0	7,900
Flyer's Sister	3	F	3	0	0	0	0
Flyhigher	5	M	2	0	0	1	680
Flyin ' Alfredo	3	C	5	0	0	0	375
Flyin Brian	6	G	7	1	0	1	6,398
Flyin Four Shoes	3	G	13	1	0	4	7,270
Flyin On Bye	2	C	5	1	0	0	9,225
Flyin Slew	2	C	3	0	0	1	2,325
Flyin Y	3	F	8	1	0	1	4,900
Flyindownbaylaurel	4	F	3	0	1	0	1,740
Flying	6	M	13	0	3	0	6,785
Flying Accelerator	3	G	7	1	1	1	11,880
Flying Alibi	8	M	15	3	0	2	39,463
Flying Away	3	G	6	1	2	0	10,135
Flying Baby	10	G	3	0	0	1	460
Flying Bearcat	3	G	5	0	0	2	5,520
Flying Biscuit	3	F	1	1	0	0	11,000
Flying Canuck	4	G	3	1	1	0	19,220
Flying Carpet	5	H	1	0	1	0	2,700
Flying Castelli	5	G	6	1	1	1	8,317

Horse	Age	Sex	Sts	1st	2d	3d	Won
Flying Catman	3	G	13	2	2	3	7,845
Flying Chance	2	C	9	1	3	1	28,640
Flying Chockli	3	F	15	3	1	2	22,359
Flying Circle	2	F	1	0	0	1	2,255
Flying Cisco	4	G	9	0	3	1	1,604
Flying Cobra	4	F	12	2	0	4	13,437
Flying Commander	6	G	5	0	1	0	2,980
Flying Cowboy	3	G	9	0	0	0	973
Flying Danjur	3	G	2	0	0	1	662
Flying Delight	3	C	5	1	1	0	13,710
Flying Devil	3	F	2	0	0	1	3,840
Flying Double Up	3	F	2	0	0	0	866
Flying Dubya	4	C	3	0	0	2	2,387
Flying Eagle	2	G	1	0	0	0	105
Flying Elvis	2	G	5	1	0	0	17,915
Flying Falcon	2	F	4	1	0	1	32,020
Flying Far	4	F	15	0	1	4	10,183
Flying Feathers	4	G	13	1	1	2	33,326
Flying Fire	4	G	4	0	0	1	2,040
Flying Fleet	10	G	17	0	2	3	6,133
Flying Free	5	H	6	0	1	0	10,030
Flying Frisbee	2	C	4	0	0	1	3,165
Flying Fugitive	5	G	12	3	1	3	22,064
Flying Gal	5	M	8	0	0	0	4,980
Flying General	4	G	2	0	0	0	580
Flying Glitter	2	F	2	1	0	0	29,575
Flying Haddi	3	F	6	0	0	1	1,870
Flying Hamer	6	M	4	0	0	0	176
Flying Heart	5	M	2	0	0	0	800
Flying High Again	6	G	6	0	0	0	950
Flying Humor	2	F	3	0	0	0	879
Flying Is Fun	4	C	1	0	0	0	120
Flying Jackie	6	M	12	2	2	1	16,765
Flying Jazz	4	C	3	1	1	0	34,988
Flying Jeb	7	G	4	0	0	1	768
Flying Jessie	3	F	10	1	2	1	10,605
Flying Kegan	4	G	3	0	0	0	0
Flying King	6	G	14	0	4	4	10,875
Flying Kitty	6	M	3	2	1	0	17,000
Flying Lady Cue	4	F	3	1	1	0	5,610
Flying Lea	4	F	6	1	0	1	8,521
Flying Lingo	4	F	16	3	3	4	13,913
Flying Liz	6	M	7	0	0	1	1,552
Flying Llama	4	G	8	0	2	2	12,294
Flying Memo	3	F	3	0	0	2	5,505
Flying Metro	7	G	5	2	1	0	11,580
Flying Moment	3	G	1	0	1	0	1,408
Flying Moon	5	M	2	0	0	0	0
Flying Nuggets	4	G	14	0	3	4	21,475
Flying Oleta	4	F	9	4	1	1	22,000
Flying Passage	4	F	2	0	0	0	680
Flying Past U	5	H	10	3	2	2	6,210
Flying Patriot	2	C	9	0	0	1	2,840
Flying Peace	2	G	2	0	0	1	2,120
Flying Peacock	4	F	3	0	0	2	3,240
Flying Peak	3	G	8	2	0	0	32,499
Flying Pembroke	5	G	1	0	0	0	0
Flying Petra	4	F	10	1	2	1	13,938
Flying Phantom	3	F	2	1	0	0	10,020
Flying Pickle	4	F	11	0	1	3	7,221
Flying Piper	4	F	3	0	0	0	204
Flying Pro	5	G	14	0	3	2	8,370
Flying Promise	4	G	5	0	0	2	1,400
Flying Pulpit	4	F	6	1	0	0	18,680
Flying Retsina Run	9	G	6	0	2	0	5,355
Flying Robert	4	G	2	0	0	0	0
Flying Robinson	2	G	2	0	0	0	0
Flying Rocket	4	G	7	2	1	0	15,600
Flying Ruby	4	F	12	2	0	0	7,171
Flying Rudolph	7	G	3	1	0	0	2,948
Flying Scotsman	4	G	4	0	1	1	8,290
Flying Shaheen	2	F	1	1	0	0	5,166
Flying Sharon	3	F	14	1	0	1	19,203
Flying Shirttail	4	C	7	2	0	0	5,256
Flying Singer	8	H	6	2	3	0	16,720
Flying Skater	2	C	5	1	0	1	19,309
Flying Soldier	5	G	12	0	1	1	5,769
Flying Supercon	5	G	7	0	1	0	9,230
Flying Supremo	4	G	11	2	0	3	10,064
Flying to Fenix	2	G	3	1	0	0	6,960
Flying Tommy D	5	H	4	0	0	0	350
Flying Valor	3	F	10	1	0	1	8,610
Flying Vi	2	F	2	0	0	0	325
Flying Vixie Dust	5	M	8	2	2	2	10,438
Flying With Angels	6	M	1	0	0	0	0
Flying With Class	3	F	8	0	3	4	4,943
Flying Zig	3	G	6	0	0	0	591
Flyingby	4	C	6	0	1	2	2,376
Flyinghawk	3	G	3	0	0	0	1,200
Flyingpaster Power	4	G	13	1	5	2	12,938
Flyingsofine	4	G	7	2	2	1	17,393
Flyininthezone	3	G	5	0	0	0	928
Flylikeadove	2	F	1	0	0	0	348
Flymore	3	F	6	0	1	1	4,545
Fly'n Cody	4	G	13	2	0	0	11,174
Flyn Grey Devil	2	F	3	0	0	1	962
Flynkus	7	M	18	0	2	2	5,138
Flynn's Flash	6	G	3	0	0	0	0
Flyrock	2	C	7	1	2	0	30,871
Fly's to Honey	9	M	2	0	0	0	0
Flyswatter	5	M	3	0	1	0	1,243
Flytodixie	2	C	7	0	0	2	4,660
Foamy Water	2	F	4	0	0	0	5,643
Focal Point	3	G	11	2	2	1	16,561
Focus Factor	3	G	6	0	1	1	3,975
Focus On Marty	8	G	12	1	2	1	10,656
Focused to Win	3	F	4	0	0	0	878
Foe Fives	4	G	16	5	1	2	18,890
Fofie's Pooka	4	F	10	2	3	2	13,578
Fog Bound	5	M	13	1	1	2	6,007
Fog Buster	4	G	5	1	1	1	41,392
Fog City Willy	8	G	4	0	2	1	11,255
Fogged In	3	G	4	0	1	2	11,680
Foggerinthevalley	4	F	9	1	0	0	8,587
Foggia	4	F	11	5	2	1	86,170
Foggyhour	3	C	4	0	0	1	3,258
Foglin	5	M	10	2	1	3	4,095
Foglite Flanker	3	G	11	0	1	1	5,142
Foiled Again	7	G	2	0	0	0	1,040
Foist	3	F	4	0	0	1	8,485
Folderol	5	G	2	0	0	0	340
Foley's Halo	7	H	2	1	0	0	8,006
Foley's Pub	6	G	2	0	0	0	336
Folk Art	3	F	3	1	0	2	30,214
Folkestone Park	5	G	4	0	0	1	6,600
Follow Me Home	4	F	4	0	0	0	1,220
Follow the Cat	3	G	3	1	0	1	34,570
Follow the Clouds	2	F	6	0	1	0	6,873
Follow the Lite	2	F	3	1	0	1	16,390
Follow the Path	3	C	3	0	0	0	0
Follow the Piper	6	G	4	0	1	0	10,640
Follow the Sun	3	C	5	2	1	0	87,428
Follow This Dream	3	G	7	2	1	1	20,489
Following a Notion	6	M	4	0	0	0	369
Followmefools	4	C	1	0	0	0	120
Followmetothewire	2	F	5	0	1	0	4,600
Folton	4	G	14	1	2	2	6,864
Fon Fon	4	F	4	0	0	0	351
Fond	3	F	6	1	0	0	54,411
Fonda Ronda	2	F	5	0	1	0	12,400
Fondly Recommended	2	F	2	0	0	0	1,380
Fontainebleau Cat	3	C	2	0	0	0	440
Fontanero	5	G	2	0	0	0	104
Fonte Di Trieste	2	C	2	0	0	0	800
Fonz's	5	G	9	0	2	2	37,120
Food Chain	4	G	6	0	0	0	546
Food Stamp	3	C	7	0	0	0	0
Foofaraw	2	F	5	1	0	1	46,158
Fool Crazy	5	H	2	0	1	0	4,400
Fool Proof Appeal	4	G	3	0	0	0	280
Fool the Devil	4	G	8	0	2	1	7,790
Fool You	6	H	1	0	0	0	0
Foolah Rullah	4	G	10	3	1	1	26,608
Fooled You Twice	2	G	3	0	1	0	4,012
Fooler	4	G	13	5	3	1	83,580
Foolin Type	4	F	3	0	0	1	736
Foolininthemeadow	2	F	5	4	0	1	155,987
Foolish Act	3	G	3	0	0	0	408

Horse	Age	Sex	Sts	1st	2d	3d	Won
Foolish Behaviour	2	C	1	0	0	0	106
Foolish Colors	4	G	1	0	0	0	0
Foolish Groom	3	G	7	1	1	1	14,170
Foolish Guy	2	C	1	0	0	0	600
Foolish Jones	5	G	10	0	4	0	17,643
Foolish Kat	10	M	5	0	0	0	0
Foolish Kristin	3	F	7	1	1	0	9,204
Foolish Luck	3	F	3	0	0	0	0
Foolish Megan	6	M	10	1	2	0	17,582
Foolish Monarch	2	F	3	0	0	0	1,200
Foolish Moon	3	F	11	1	3	2	24,880
Foolish Paradise	4	G	4	0	0	0	992
Foolish Pride	5	H	1	0	0	0	190
Foolish Raja	7	G	11	2	2	1	16,060
Foolish Tee	2	F	4	1	1	0	12,852
Foolish Wish	3	F	1	0	0	0	0
Foolish Zeal	5	M	1	0	0	0	342
Foolishly	3	F	3	0	0	0	4,750
Foolofit	3	F	3	1	0	0	8,257
Fool's Boy	3	C	3	0	0	0	300
Fools Day	3	C	11	3	3	2	42,753
Fool's Destiny	2	G	2	0	0	0	0
Fool's Detente	4	F	12	2	4	2	13,481
Fool's Game	5	M	7	0	1	1	1,960
Fool's Last Word	6	M	4	1	0	1	3,762
Fool's Mate	5	M	7	2	1	0	21,368
Foolsn Their Money	4	G	18	0	1	4	7,070
Foot On the Floor	4	G	12	2	0	3	24,154
Foot Soldier	3	C	2	0	1	0	2,790
Foot Trick	3	C	12	4	3	0	89,971
Football Passer	2	C	3	0	0	0	355
Football Rusher	3	G	4	0	2	0	3,515
Footbolt	2	G	5	0	1	0	2,644
Footlights	4	F	11	2	2	2	53,290
Foots	7	H	4	1	0	0	13,904
For a Fee	6	G	12	0	4	1	10,665
For a Song	4	F	1	0	1	0	3,600
For and Aft	4	C	2	1	0	0	2,440
For and For	2	C	1	0	0	0	0
For Angel	3	G	17	4	5	3	25,522
For Bailey's Sake	6	M	5	0	1	0	1,883
For Deposit Only	4	G	8	1	0	3	11,659
For Freedom	4	G	5	0	0	0	0
For Fun	4	F	14	1	1	4	27,380
For Getful Andy	2	G	4	0	1	0	3,320
For Gillian	3	F	6	1	3	0	35,590
For Gold	4	C	11	0	1	4	21,940
For Good Measure	3	G	10	2	2	2	97,607
For Laughs	2	F	3	0	1	0	5,000
For Liberty	5	G	6	0	1	1	2,234
For Lili	8	M	13	0	1	2	17,059
For Love and Honor	7	G	10	0	2	0	25,270
For Love and Money	2	F	1	1	0	0	24,600
For Love of Darby	5	M	1	0	0	0	244
For Midge	6	M	7	2	2	0	19,126
For My Angel	4	F	12	1	1	2	37,890
For My Pleasure	6	M	13	0	1	1	5,100
For My Wife	3	F	7	1	1	1	21,510
For Paul's Sake	4	G	6	0	0	1	1,742
For Peter's Sake	3	F	13	1	2	4	20,100
For Rubies	5	M	1	0	0	0	2,000
For the Dream	6	G	5	1	0	0	2,752
For the Fdny Heros	4	C	12	0	1	1	10,654
For the Prize	2	C	1	0	0	0	0
For the Taste	3	F	6	0	1	1	8,460
For Who for What	3	F	1	0	0	0	460
For Your Love	3	F	10	1	1	2	16,720
Forafeubucksmore	4	G	3	0	0	0	492
Forafewdollarsmore	5	H	4	0	1	2	5,695
Foramusementonly	5	M	11	0	2	0	6,000
Foran Gap	4	F	10	1	1	3	8,668
Foray	6	G	4	0	0	0	252
Forbes Creek	4	G	13	1	4	3	31,648
Forbes Flyer	6	G	7	1	0	1	3,080
Forbes Gunner	4	G	8	1	1	0	6,747
Forbes Halo	6	G	14	0	3	1	4,778
Forbettysboyz	6	G	7	2	1	1	28,029
Forbid	12	G	4	0	1	0	630
Forbidden Duel	4	G	4	0	0	1	3,990
Forbidden Fruit	4	F	8	0	0	1	3,037
Forbidden Glory	2	F	2	0	0	0	0
Forbidden Gold	6	G	19	2	4	3	47,670
Forbidden Horizon	8	H	1	0	0	0	0
Forbidden John	3	C	6	2	0	1	10,130
Forbidden Kiss	3	F	1	0	0	0	320
Forbidden Sea	3	F	5	1	1	0	34,453
Forbidden Sin	3	F	8	1	0	3	10,273
Forbidden Star	4	F	6	1	0	0	12,575
Forbidden Zone	4	F	3	1	0	0	7,980
Forbiddenchocolate	3	F	3	1	0	1	11,656
Force Forty Nine	4	G	15	2	4	1	21,298
Force in Excess	6	H	1	0	0	0	70
Force King	5	G	8	0	0	0	310
Force of Power	3	G	7	2	0	0	9,473
Force One	2	C	1	0	0	0	0
Force Recon	2	C	8	1	6	1	21,415
Force the Pace	2	G	1	0	0	0	195
Force the Way	4	F	7	1	0	2	15,720
Forceful Guy	9	G	14	0	0	0	362
Forces Command	3	G	14	2	1	2	24,405
Forcible	3	C	2	0	1	0	5,166
Ford Every Stream	5	H	2	0	0	0	0
Fordestiny	3	C	2	0	0	1	2,720
Fore Payne	5	G	9	2	1	2	10,083
Foreal	5	M	14	4	0	1	24,261
Forecastor	2	C	2	0	1	0	13,279
Foregone	5	H	8	2	0	1	16,979
Foreign Accent (GB)	5	G	4	1	0	0	11,460
Foreign Authority	5	G	12	1	1	1	8,456
Foreign Beux	3	G	6	0	0	1	5,290
Foreign Body	2	F	1	0	0	0	0
Foreign Cash	7	M	8	0	0	2	5,514
Foreign Cat	5	M	3	0	0	0	150
Foreign Flame	8	G	8	1	1	0	18,710
Foreign Frost	3	F	4	0	0	0	975
Foreign Horizon	3	G	6	0	0	0	0
Foreign Image	7	G	7	0	1	0	4,670
Foreign Intrigue	3	G	6	0	1	0	3,015
Foreign Justice	3	G	11	1	3	1	28,107
Foreign Kiss	5	M	6	0	0	0	1,007
Foreign Mamatwo	5	M	4	0	0	0	150
Foreign Melody	4	C	8	1	1	2	12,082
Foreign Office	3	G	3	1	0	0	4,200
Foreign Policy	2	C	1	0	0	0	1,025
Foreign Regret	3	F	1	0	0	0	0
Foreign Robber	5	M	1	0	0	0	0
Foreign Ruckus	3	G	13	2	1	0	44,320
Foreign Secretary	7	G	5	3	2	0	52,200
Foreign Slew	4	F	4	0	0	0	99
Foreign Spike	3	G	1	0	0	0	170
Foreign Trip	3	G	7	0	1	0	2,400
Foreing Banker	6	M	2	0	0	0	0
Foresaw	3	G	8	0	0	2	7,121
Foreseeable	3	F	1	0	0	0	135
Forest Bo K	3	F	5	0	0	1	1,400
Forest City	7	G	15	2	3	3	14,460
Forest Colony	2	C	6	0	3	1	7,770
Forest Cricket	4	G	8	0	1	0	3,863
Forest Dancer	3	F	1	0	0	0	600
Forest Danger	3	C	4	3	1	0	159,600
Forest Dream	3	C	4	0	0	1	3,145
Forest Express	3	C	1	0	0	0	250
Forest Grove	3	C	10	4	1	0	145,060
Forest Heir	6	H	2	0	0	0	850
Forest Hunter	3	C	9	1	1	0	34,316
Forest Kitty	3	F	2	0	1	0	5,520
Forest Landing	4	G	4	0	2	1	14,850
Forest Legend	6	H	4	0	1	0	2,160
Forest Monarch	7	H	3	0	0	0	210
Forest Music	3	F	7	3	0	3	188,590
Forest Native	4	F	10	1	2	1	41,260
Forest Park	3	C	4	3	0	0	57,000
Forest Picnic	4	G	14	1	2	2	31,056
Forest Prospect	4	F	6	1	0	1	9,624
Forest Rain	4	G	10	1	3	1	18,279
Forest Rhythm	3	C	5	0	3	1	33,450
Forest Snitch	5	G	1	0	0	0	940
Forest Waltz	5	G	9	2	0	1	8,026

Horse	Age	Sex	Sts	1st	2d	3d	Won
Forest Way	3	C	4	0	0	0	1,600
Forest Wild Flower	4	F	10	1	0	1	18,828
Forestier	3	F	5	1	2	1	63,200
Forestina	3	F	3	0	0	2	10,220
Forestville	5	G	12	3	2	2	6,881
Forestwood	3	C	4	1	1	0	25,444
Foretell	6	G	10	1	1	3	9,032
Foretold (IRE)	4	G	7	2	1	0	34,250
Forever Amber	5	G	14	5	3	0	34,165
Forever and a Day	3	F	3	0	0	0	1,100
Forever Auburn	5	M	6	0	0	2	5,065
Forever Bad Secret	6	M	2	0	0	0	0
Forever Bertie	2	F	2	0	0	0	2,835
Forever Brilliant	2	F	1	0	0	1	3,850
Forever Daisy	6	M	2	0	0	0	150
Forever Diligent	4	F	11	4	2	2	32,399
Forever Eve	3	F	14	0	2	1	11,344
Forever Flawless	3	F	16	3	3	0	54,471
Forever for You	3	F	1	0	0	0	220
Forever Foxy	2	G	5	3	0	0	73,800
Forever Gold	6	G	5	0	0	0	1,355
Forever Grand	5	G	7	3	2	0	185,343
Forever Hopeful	2	F	2	0	0	0	0
Forever in Love	6	M	1	0	0	0	0
Forever Jan	5	M	4	0	3	0	1,952
Forever Joe	4	C	13	0	0	0	8,296
Forever Joy	3	F	7	3	0	1	34,065
Forever Kath	2	F	4	1	0	0	12,720
Forever Kris	4	F	6	1	0	0	16,148
Forever Loving	4	F	6	1	2	2	10,140
Forever Luck	5	M	19	0	2	5	24,115
Forever Lucky	5	M	8	1	1	1	10,823
Forever Miss Otis	5	M	5	0	1	0	4,415
Forever Monteiro	5	G	15	3	5	3	51,443
Forever Naevus	4	F	18	4	2	0	20,311
Forever Now	4	F	4	1	0	0	21,880
Forever Phyl	4	G	8	1	0	0	4,154
Forever Rascal	2	G	4	2	0	0	43,444
Forever Ready	5	M	11	1	0	2	13,690
Forever Regal	6	M	15	2	1	1	36,860
Forever Rush	3	C	2	2	0	0	70,080
Forever Singing	3	F	1	0	0	0	78
Forever Smart	2	F	3	0	1	1	12,640
Forever Sunshine	5	G	12	0	2	1	4,390
Forever Timeless	6	M	4	0	0	0	407
Forever Wild	2	C	1	0	0	0	135
Forever Zam	2	C	1	0	0	0	205
Forevercharismatic	3	F	4	0	0	0	240
Foreverdo	3	C	2	0	0	1	1,935
Foreverness	5	G	5	1	3	0	76,275
Forevor Due	3	G	7	0	1	2	11,250
Forewarned	4	F	10	1	2	1	13,658
Forge Away	6	G	16	7	2	1	40,590
Forget	4	F	9	0	1	0	12,640
Forget the Judge	5	G	6	0	2	3	26,015
Forget the Punch	3	C	13	3	1	2	46,420
Forgin' Ahead	6	G	7	0	0	1	2,366
Forgiveable Sin	3	G	10	3	0	0	59,257
Forgiving	3	F	1	0	0	0	840
Forgot My Fox	3	F	3	0	0	0	416
Forgotten Bid	5	M	7	1	1	0	7,814
Forgotten Cat	3	C	8	1	1	1	18,385
Forgotten Photo	8	H	7	0	1	0	740
Forgotten Promise	3	F	11	4	0	4	94,854
Forgotten Weekend	2	G	2	0	0	0	0
Foriegn Deputy	7	G	5	1	0	3	4,178
Foritz	4	G	5	2	0	0	10,710
Forjonyaknow	4	G	12	1	1	4	5,281
Forlaan	7	G	5	0	0	1	2,560
Forlec	3	C	1	0	0	0	0
Forli Fedora	4	F	2	0	0	0	76
Forli Fight	3	G	3	0	0	0	276
Forli's Chance	4	F	2	0	0	0	104
Forli's Con Man	3	G	11	1	1	1	22,255
Forli's Match	3	G	13	1	0	2	5,206
Forloveofshirley	3	F	3	0	0	1	9,412
Form	3	G	6	3	1	0	54,210
Formada (ARG)	6	M	8	0	0	2	12,155
Formal and Fancy	4	F	15	6	2	2	116,400

Horse	Age	Sex	Sts	1st	2d	3d	Won
Formal Attire	4	C	6	2	1	1	62,335
Formal Blossom	2	F	3	0	0	0	1,440
Formal Charade	4	C	10	2	2	0	73,810
Formal Commander	3	C	6	1	1	1	36,140
Formal Deal	4	F	5	1	1	3	52,225
Formal Decree	4	G	12	2	1	1	57,570
Formal Diplomacy	4	G	9	0	1	2	2,951
Formal Escape	4	C	9	2	1	0	9,530
Formal Etiquette	2	C	5	1	0	1	10,701
Formal Evening	3	F	10	1	1	0	30,670
Formal Event	4	C	12	5	1	2	46,730
Formal Fanny	3	F	19	3	3	3	63,100
Formal Feast	9	G	11	1	0	2	6,050
Formal Finish	3	C	3	0	0	0	1,920
Formal Fire	2	C	3	0	0	0	550
Formal Flame	4	F	9	1	1	0	23,875
Formal Green	8	G	6	0	1	0	1,755
Formal Hadif	5	H	5	1	1	0	4,032
Formal Jackie	4	F	7	1	0	4	10,063
Formal Lady	3	F	16	4	3	4	67,030
Formal Meeting	8	G	6	0	1	2	2,860
Formal Miss	4	F	14	4	3	0	152,550
Formal Night	4	F	2	0	1	0	2,205
Formal Odyssey	4	F	2	0	0	1	2,040
Formal Pass	3	C	12	2	1	4	50,440
Formal Prince	5	H	4	0	1	1	2,195
Formal Raise	4	G	7	0	0	1	1,328
Formal Regards	7	H	9	2	0	2	10,254
Formal Rush	2	F	1	1	0	0	6,300
Formal Spirit	3	C	4	0	0	1	4,131
Formal Tricks	3	F	3	0	0	0	161
Formal Victory	4	F	12	2	1	0	12,243
Formalities Aside	2	F	5	1	1	1	38,089
Formality	6	G	1	0	0	0	46
Format	3	F	12	3	2	2	77,396
Former Stormer	3	F	8	0	0	1	2,715
Formidable Fox	4	G	2	1	0	0	8,160
Formidable Gold	4	C	11	2	0	3	38,420
Formidable Storm	3	F	11	2	3	0	28,269
Formidibull	3	C	13	2	5	3	41,521
Formoreamour	2	F	8	0	0	2	5,510
Formosa Strait	4	G	2	0	0	0	204
Forpointo	3	F	8	0	0	3	6,140
Forrer Hall	5	G	11	3	0	1	26,334
Forrester Found	3	G	15	2	1	3	15,090
Forrore	4	G	6	0	0	0	446
Forsberg	8	G	8	0	1	1	4,488
Forseeable Future	4	G	11	1	0	1	7,079
Forsureathrill	4	G	3	0	0	0	50
Fort	5	G	10	1	2	0	11,644
Fort Alex	4	G	7	0	0	0	875
Fort Bragg	4	G	11	1	2	2	8,452
Fort Carson	4	G	6	1	0	1	12,610
Fort Chestnut	2	C	9	1	0	1	13,872
Fort Coventry	5	G	3	0	0	0	172
Fort Hancock	7	G	10	2	2	1	13,010
Fort Jessup	9	H	4	0	0	0	0
Fort Jill	4	F	12	2	0	1	21,500
Fort Masada	4	G	14	2	1	4	30,839
Fort Metfield	10	G	12	4	3	1	28,163
Fort Monmouth	5	G	12	1	1	1	13,765
Fort Out East	7	G	4	0	0	1	840
Fort Point	5	G	7	0	0	0	235
Fort Prado	3	C	10	3	2	0	125,692
Fort Providence	4	G	1	0	0	0	0
Fort Rocky	4	G	19	2	2	4	26,677
Fort Ross	8	G	7	0	0	3	2,581
Fort Ruckus	3	G	5	0	0	1	2,475
Fort Seattle	2	G	6	0	0	1	3,825
Fort Smith	4	C	12	4	2	0	84,200
Fort Sully Band	2	G	3	0	0	0	266
Fort Teller	5	H	16	0	2	3	13,365
Forteecarrs	3	C	5	1	1	1	12,735
Forteyounzer	6	G	13	0	0	1	1,857
Forth and Forever	3	G	10	2	2	1	27,250
Forthcoming	3	G	3	0	1	1	9,875
Forthegoodguys	7	M	5	2	0	1	20,065
Fortify	4	G	6	1	0	1	4,729
Fortisima (ARG)	4	F	5	0	0	0	3,150

Horse	Age	Sex	Sts	1st	2d	3d	Won
Fortress Hill	3	F	1	0	0	1	4,420
Fortuna Vena	4	F	5	1	0	0	3,500
Fortunate Angel	3	F	14	0	3	1	7,710
Fortunate Buy	3	G	15	2	2	0	49,850
Fortunate Caitlin	6	M	3	0	0	0	0
Fortunate Caller	3	G	11	0	2	0	4,433
Fortunate Chance	4	F	15	3	3	2	32,778
Fortunate Conquest	4	G	8	0	1	0	2,161
Fortunate Damsel	3	F	12	4	2	2	192,312
Fortunate Event	2	F	5	0	1	1	27,056
Fortunate Honor	4	F	6	1	2	1	7,030
Fortunate Island	3	C	11	1	2	1	21,775
Fortunate Kiss	2	C	4	1	0	0	19,567
Fortunate Match	4	F	10	1	0	2	9,700
Fortunate Mia	5	M	6	1	0	1	3,503
Fortunate One	6	G	14	6	0	0	53,320
Fortunate Prince	2	G	5	1	0	0	9,670
Fortunate Princess	2	F	5	1	0	0	10,020
Fortunate Romeo	8	G	1	0	0	0	303
Fortunate Royal	5	H	10	3	0	3	34,805
Fortunate Son	3	G	18	0	0	1	5,083
Fortunate Storm	2	C	3	0	0	0	2,635
Fortunate Swing	4	F	23	0	8	7	30,202
Fortunate Ticket	3	G	7	3	0	0	10,318
Fortunate Trail	3	G	12	3	4	2	56,808
Fortunate Trip	2	C	3	1	0	0	41,640
Fortunate Vince	3	G	3	0	0	0	250
Fortunate Winds	7	G	11	1	3	0	24,815
Fortunately (GB)	3	F	4	0	0	2	21,402
Fortune Catcher	3	G	16	1	2	1	20,076
Fortune Dane	4	G	16	0	1	2	10,680
Fortune Maker	2	C	1	0	1	0	6,460
Fortune n' Fame	6	G	3	0	0	0	0
Fortune Seeker	3	F	7	1	1	2	10,920
Fortune Writers	4	C	3	1	1	0	39,050
Fortunes' Bounty	4	G	12	2	0	1	17,890
Fortune's Fancy	5	H	6	1	0	3	11,563
Fortune's Fool	3	G	3	1	0	0	21,490
Fortunes of Gold	9	G	9	1	0	4	4,360
Fortunistic	3	F	3	1	1	1	24,830
Fortuoso	10	H	4	3	0	0	7,332
Forty Babes	2	F	6	1	3	0	42,272
Forty Below Zero	4	F	8	3	0	1	9,404
Forty Dolls	4	F	11	3	3	1	73,142
Forty Durango (ARG)	6	H	12	1	1	4	11,453
Forty Ensign (ARG)	5	G	11	1	2	2	20,295
Forty Ensueno (ARG)	5	G	2	2	0	0	13,200
Forty Five	3	C	5	1	2	0	39,780
Forty Fivecalibur	2	C	5	0	1	1	10,420
Forty Floozies	3	F	17	1	1	2	2,563
Forty Forth Anna	4	F	6	0	1	0	2,465
Forty Grand	3	F	14	3	1	0	43,326
Forty Karat Gold	2	F	4	0	1	1	8,188
Forty Karats Jade	8	G	1	0	0	0	40
Forty Languido (ARG)	6	H	5	2	0	0	10,770
Forty Lengths	5	G	12	1	0	1	16,816
Forty Licks	3	F	10	0	0	1	1,097
Forty Marinesca (ARG)	6	M	2	0	0	0	860
Forty Milito (ARG)	6	H	3	1	0	1	28,320
Forty Moves	3	F	9	2	2	1	91,990
Forty Nine Deeds	5	H	13	1	2	1	20,249
Forty Nine Shines	5	M	2	0	0	0	0
Forty Niner Course	5	G	8	3	1	0	20,420
Forty Niner Gold	4	G	8	3	0	2	34,300
Forty One Charms	3	F	5	2	0	0	19,988
Forty Paulina (ARG)	4	F	2	0	0	0	1,240
Forty Pureza (ARG)	6	M	14	3	2	4	34,430
Forty Seasons	3	G	13	1	0	0	7,852
Forty Second St.	4	C	6	0	0	1	1,240
Forty Si (ARG)	6	M	13	3	0	2	19,834
Forty Socks	4	G	14	0	0	0	2,070
Forty Star	4	C	3	0	1	1	4,355
Forty Suertudo (ARG)	5	H	10	1	2	2	72,640
Forty Sweeps	4	C	9	0	0	3	3,347
Forty Times	5	M	12	2	3	1	8,140
Forty Two Slew	4	F	1	0	0	0	0
Forty Would	4	C	1	0	0	0	0
Fortyninejules	4	F	2	0	0	0	135
Forty's Boy	4	G	11	1	1	1	12,483
Fortysunflowers	3	F	14	1	0	1	15,391
Fortythreedays	2	F	4	0	0	2	5,360
Fortywon Thirtysix	4	G	12	2	2	3	47,240
Forum Quorum	4	C	5	1	0	0	17,880
Forum Rules	3	C	6	1	0	0	9,390
Foruteddyb	2	G	5	0	0	0	1,700
Forward Glance	3	F	7	4	0	2	43,912
Forward Impact	4	F	13	0	1	0	4,375
Forward March	7	R	5	2	0	1	30,160
Forwhomthebelcalls	2	C	4	1	0	0	13,510
Foryourearsonly	4	C	1	0	0	0	78
Foryourinfo Nancy	3	F	5	2	1	0	17,002
Forzas Pride	2	G	6	1	1	0	10,725
Forzeen (GB)	2	G	14	4	2	2	48,251
Fo's Lad	6	G	9	3	1	0	9,250
Fossie's Jill	5	M	10	0	0	0	300
Fosston	6	G	1	0	0	0	0
Foster Care	3	C	2	0	0	0	340
Foster Hill	8	G	8	3	0	1	17,210
Foster's Landing	6	H	1	0	0	0	320
Fostress	4	F	12	1	2	2	19,625
Fotogenico (ARG)	6	G	18	3	2	1	37,306
Foufa's Warrior	4	G	8	1	2	2	113,140
Foul Weather	7	G	1	0	0	0	300
Found a Nickle	7	G	12	0	0	1	1,441
Found Her	4	F	1	0	0	0	1,125
Found My Guard	3	F	1	0	0	0	103
Founded On Truth	3	G	10	3	2	0	31,354
Founding Chairman	4	G	9	0	1	1	22,955
Fountain Grove	3	C	11	1	2	3	40,440
Fountain Ridge	3	F	6	1	1	2	5,516
Four Above	2	F	1	0	0	0	140
Four Acres	3	G	12	0	0	0	1,035
Four Alarm Slew	3	G	7	1	0	3	18,644
Four Alarmer	3	G	13	2	1	1	25,367
Four Alert	7	H	11	1	1	3	51,105
Four and Out	8	G	1	0	0	1	825
Four Anne Affair	6	M	7	0	2	0	21,090
Four Bagger	4	G	12	3	4	1	17,093
Four Beers	4	G	14	1	2	1	14,552
Four Card Bob	9	G	5	0	0	1	1,797
Four Cards Too	5	G	10	6	1	1	60,325
Four Checker	5	G	12	1	3	1	38,660
Four Columns	3	C	11	1	1	1	13,056
Four Corners	5	G	9	1	1	2	14,455
Four Dancee	4	F	12	3	1	3	14,798
Four Dollar Limit	2	G	2	0	0	0	576
Four F Regal Bar	7	G	1	0	0	0	0
Four Fifteen	8	G	2	0	0	0	0
Four Girls	5	M	14	3	2	1	54,358
Four Janet	3	F	1	0	0	1	649
Four K's Dream	5	M	1	0	0	0	0
Four O Won	3	C	3	1	1	0	38,180
Four On a Match	5	G	2	0	0	0	142
Four One None	4	G	6	0	3	0	4,801
Four Pennies	5	M	1	0	0	0	0
Four R Approval	4	G	10	2	0	0	35,895
Four Runner	6	G	5	0	0	0	556
Four Seas	5	M	2	0	0	0	144
Four Secrets	4	G	5	0	0	0	225
Four Song Limit	3	G	6	2	0	2	73,902
Four Speed	4	F	6	1	1	1	11,568
Four Star Admiral	5	H	1	0	0	0	0
Four Steps Ahead	2	F	5	0	0	0	3,140
Four Storms	6	G	13	1	0	1	3,393
Four Sweeper	5	G	9	3	2	1	17,215
Four Times a Charm	6	M	7	0	0	3	4,340
Four Twenty Seven	4	F	1	0	0	0	79
Fourcarrotdiamond	8	M	5	1	2	1	9,052
Fourchon	4	G	13	2	0	1	16,945
Fourforty	5	G	9	0	1	1	2,183
Fourjaysstormynite	4	G	11	2	2	0	7,872
Fourlitefeet	4	F	10	0	1	2	2,316
Fourpeppermary	4	F	13	0	0	8	11,030
Fours and Tens	7	G	3	0	0	0	0
Fourstargeorge	5	G	9	1	0	1	7,573
Fourteen Candles	4	F	9	1	0	1	32,756
Fourteen Pieces	2	F	5	0	0	1	3,089
Fourteen Roses	3	F	6	1	1	1	27,663

Horse	Age	Sex	Sts	1st	2d	3d	Won
Fourteen Ten	7	G	5	0	0	0	180
Fourth Amendment	5	G	11	0	0	2	2,285
Fourth and Long	4	G	9	1	1	1	12,680
Fourth and Six	10	G	4	2	1	0	28,290
Fourth Down Gamble	3	G	10	2	2	1	11,229
Fourth Edition	3	G	5	1	0	0	4,508
Fourth Floor	6	H	4	2	1	1	47,300
Fourth of July	3	G	8	0	3	1	14,280
Fourtheboys	4	F	10	0	0	2	5,590
Fourthirteen	3	G	8	2	3	1	99,026
Fourtimesaruler	4	G	12	2	3	3	36,410
Fourty Bucks	6	G	5	0	1	0	1,896
Fourty Four Red	6	G	14	3	1	1	59,191
Fourty Niners Son	3	C	6	1	1	1	39,445
Fourwheeler	2	F	5	0	0	1	1,022
Fowler Creek	3	G	5	1	0	0	8,460
Fox Drive	6	H	5	0	0	0	2,070
Fox H	5	M	2	0	0	0	169
Fox On Tour	6	G	9	0	1	0	1,922
Fox Valley Toots	4	F	10	1	1	0	17,920
Foxay Illusion	3	F	6	0	0	1	596
Foxboat	5	G	13	2	0	5	28,942
Foxey Jeblar	5	H	9	1	1	2	9,420
Foxey Krissie	4	F	3	2	0	0	7,320
Foxeyfortyniner	5	G	2	0	0	0	0
Foxhat	4	F	2	0	0	1	701
Foxhole	6	H	11	0	0	0	1,296
Foxi Attitude	4	F	6	0	1	0	2,459
Foxie Bertie	3	F	10	3	1	2	62,550
Foxie Josie	4	F	9	1	0	0	7,342
Foxie One	3	F	3	0	0	0	0
Foxie's Boy	2	G	5	1	0	1	34,601
Foxlair	4	G	9	1	5	3	81,004
Foxman	5	G	11	1	1	2	5,834
Foxs Bodacious Gal	6	M	9	0	0	0	1,190
Foxs Consort	2	F	1	0	0	0	1,710
Foxs Final Answer	3	F	3	0	0	0	170
Fox's Flyjinsky	10	G	6	2	0	1	10,485
Foxs Gold Digger	4	G	12	1	1	3	28,085
Fox's Legacy	4	G	7	0	1	0	2,717
Foxs Wheaton	2	G	1	0	0	0	230
Foxtracker	2	G	6	0	0	0	230
Foxtrot Oscar	3	G	10	1	2	4	49,060
Foxwood Star	6	H	4	0	0	0	0
Foxx On Fox	4	F	7	0	1	4	2,214
Foxy Allure	4	F	18	1	2	3	20,129
Foxy and Sweet	3	F	1	0	0	0	164
Foxy Bid	4	F	9	2	1	1	15,995
Foxy Blue Trail	4	F	11	1	2	0	7,482
Foxy Boxy	3	F	6	0	0	0	0
Foxy Captain	4	G	3	0	0	0	1,455
Foxy Clout	4	F	11	0	0	3	4,180
Foxy Dude	2	G	3	0	0	0	170
Foxy Elena	3	F	12	0	3	1	7,529
Foxy Email	3	F	10	0	0	0	813
Foxy Endeavor	2	F	9	0	2	1	7,795
Foxy Fantasma	3	F	11	1	2	1	10,253
Foxy Feu	3	F	5	1	1	0	3,640
Foxy Fey	4	F	1	0	0	0	212
Foxy Friend	3	F	1	0	0	0	90
Foxy Fritzy	6	G	7	0	0	0	309
Foxy Gray	3	F	10	1	1	1	9,403
Foxy Graydon	4	F	4	0	0	0	0
Foxy Guy	4	G	3	1	0	0	7,980
Foxy J. R.	7	G	16	0	2	2	14,138
Foxy Jean	3	F	11	1	2	0	64,333
Foxy Jenny	5	M	14	3	4	1	10,137
Foxy Johnny	6	G	2	0	0	0	126
Foxy Julie	5	M	9	0	1	0	2,460
Foxy Kairewich	3	G	17	1	3	3	23,067
Foxy Kinda Guy	3	G	3	0	0	0	136
Foxy Knickers	2	G	1	0	1	0	11,400
Foxy Lover	5	G	1	1	0	0	4,140
Foxy Maid	2	F	2	0	0	1	450
Foxy Meg	2	F	5	2	0	0	23,940
Foxy Old Charger	2	F	5	0	0	0	1,060
Foxy Ole'	5	M	10	2	2	1	11,245
Foxy Power	6	M	5	0	0	0	1,155
Foxy Pro	5	M	12	2	3	1	16,148
Foxy Redfox	3	G	7	1	1	2	10,230
Foxy Roxy	5	M	9	0	1	0	2,544
Foxy Scott	3	C	1	0	0	0	160
Foxy Walker	8	G	8	1	0	0	1,633
Foxy Woman	5	M	12	0	0	2	6,156
Foxyirish	4	G	13	0	1	3	11,505
Foxyvali	2	F	2	0	0	0	0
Foxzy Lady	4	F	12	2	0	1	23,760
Fr. John O	3	G	8	0	1	0	3,036
Frabjous Female	4	F	6	1	0	0	9,129
Fractious Lady	2	F	1	0	0	0	400
Fractious Sue	2	F	3	0	0	1	1,510
Fragile	2	F	1	0	1	0	4,800
Fragrance	3	F	2	0	0	0	1,050
Fragrantly	3	F	4	1	1	0	19,787
Fraidy Cat	3	F	10	2	2	2	27,025
Frajana	6	M	12	3	3	2	26,681
Fran	6	G	3	0	0	0	201
Fran the Man	4	G	4	0	1	0	2,658
Franbulo (CHI)	8	G	5	0	1	0	1,960
Franc Brooks	3	G	3	0	1	1	5,280
France	3	F	8	1	1	1	13,450
France Soir (CHI)	6	M	5	0	1	0	12,460
Frances in Command	3	F	6	1	0	1	9,200
Frances Wren	4	F	4	0	1	1	4,370
Francesca Slew	2	F	1	0	0	0	765
Francescas Lullaby	4	F	13	1	4	1	21,585
Francestina	3	F	1	0	0	0	400
Franchise Player	4	C	8	0	2	0	6,741
Franci Dancer	3	F	8	1	2	2	12,520
Francis Albert	12	G	20	3	1	1	7,391
Francis' Tab	7	G	8	0	1	1	2,436
Franco Dinero	4	G	13	1	1	1	7,436
Franco Lobo	4	G	3	0	0	0	401
Frandy	3	H	4	0	0	0	878
Franie Nannie	6	M	1	0	0	0	70
Frank Fencepost	4	G	15	1	1	0	8,007
Frank Headley	6	G	10	0	0	0	7,454
Frank Houser	4	G	1	0	0	0	600
Frank the Fixer	7	G	8	0	0	0	2,319
Frank the Tank (AUS)	4	C	3	1	1	1	45,770
Frankel	3	G	6	0	1	0	4,000
Frankelstein	3	G	3	1	0	2	37,740
Frankeneddie	3	G	20	3	2	2	24,250
Frankfivethousand	2	G	6	0	1	1	5,100
Frankie and Me	4	F	16	1	1	3	14,392
Frankie B	4	G	6	1	0	0	5,560
Frankie Eyelashes	5	M	10	4	1	0	23,461
Frankie Grande	7	G	5	0	0	0	780
Frankie Peppers	2	G	6	0	1	1	9,985
Frankie R's Winner	5	G	15	2	1	6	92,749
Frankie the Cat	5	H	4	0	0	0	630
Frankiefourfingers	4	G	6	1	0	2	25,502
Frankie's Fire	4	C	12	2	2	3	73,156
Frankie's Image	4	F	4	0	1	1	3,125
Frankie's Star	5	M	9	0	1	1	16,827
Frankies Valentine	4	G	12	0	2	5	11,201
Franklin D.	2	G	3	0	0	1	1,080
Franklin Street	2	C	4	0	0	0	640
Franklin's Tower	2	G	5	1	1	0	16,585
Frankly Foolish	5	G	3	0	0	1	620
Frankly My Scarlet	2	F	4	0	0	0	790
Frank's Approval	8	G	6	0	0	0	389
Franks Boy	4	C	7	1	0	1	4,526
Franks Eldorado	9	G	10	0	2	1	2,926
Frank's Quest	6	G	6	0	0	0	132
Frank's Selection	8	H	7	0	3	2	67,627
Frank'satschanks	2	G	3	1	0	0	10,954
Frankyouverymuch	3	G	7	0	0	1	2,382
Franny Maguire	6	G	1	0	0	0	0
Fran's First	3	F	1	0	0	0	570
Fran's Jet	3	G	12	1	0	0	6,028
Fran's Uncle Al	4	C	5	1	1	1	4,751
Franscat	3	F	9	1	2	1	48,185
Frantanic Panic	3	F	2	0	0	1	1,705
Frantastic	4	G	8	1	2	2	11,898
Frantic Pace	3	C	6	1	1	1	33,750
Franzia	3	F	2	0	0	0	0
Frappay	3	F	2	0	0	0	800

Horse	Age	Sex	Sts	1st	2d	3d	Won
Frasca	3	F	5	0	0	1	3,979
Fraser Canyon	2	C	3	0	0	1	2,691
Fraser Serenade	5	H	3	0	0	0	848
Fraserriversspell	4	G	11	1	1	3	15,489
Fraserview	2	G	1	0	0	0	0
Fraserwood	4	G	4	0	0	0	306
Frat Party	3	G	9	1	2	0	17,855
Fraternity	3	G	11	4	1	0	79,310
Frau Blucher	4	F	10	2	1	2	11,546
Fraulein Helga	2	F	2	0	0	0	600
Fraulien Ruckus	6	M	5	0	0	0	3,420
Frauline Maria	2	F	5	0	0	1	4,430
Frazee's Folly	7	G	11	2	1	0	33,436
Frazzled	6	M	13	1	0	4	9,558
Freakin Streakin	3	F	4	2	0	0	59,898
Freaky Fast	3	C	15	5	2	2	118,857
Freaky Feature	5	M	5	0	0	0	445
Freckle Frick	3	F	5	0	0	2	6,700
Frecuente (CHI)	6	G	4	0	1	1	9,500
Fred and Me	4	G	14	3	1	3	54,760
Fred Bear Claw	10	G	2	0	0	0	0
Fred Bob	2	G	8	0	1	1	8,195
Fred N Annie	4	G	4	0	0	0	795
Fred of Gold	8	H	10	1	0	2	13,749
Fred the Mystic	3	G	7	1	0	0	1,900
Freda Z	4	F	11	2	2	1	12,376
Freda's Diamond	3	F	7	2	0	1	20,145
Freddi the Dancer	5	G	5	0	2	0	3,600
Freddie the Leader	6	G	4	0	0	1	1,300
Freddie's Folly	5	M	14	3	1	2	57,240
Freddie's Memories	5	G	5	0	1	0	1,160
Freddy (ARG)	5	H	3	0	0	1	8,920
Freddy Cat	2	G	4	0	0	0	1,720
Freddy Kruger	4	C	9	0	1	1	2,567
Freddy the Cap	2	C	5	1	2	0	61,426
Freddy Time	4	C	8	0	1	2	19,080
Frederick's Finest	6	G	2	0	0	0	0
Fredericksburg	4	C	10	2	1	1	9,613
Fredericktown	5	H	5	0	0	1	5,493
Fredexpo	6	G	6	2	1	1	8,268
Fredlea	7	G	1	0	0	1	3,020
Fredlyn	5	M	5	0	0	0	6,578
Fred's Notebook	4	G	6	0	0	1	1,575
Fred's Passion	5	G	2	0	0	1	594
Fred's Sister	2	F	4	1	0	3	20,580
Free a Way	2	G	1	0	0	0	0
Free Admission	5	G	6	1	0	2	19,442
Free After Five	3	G	7	0	0	0	324
Free American	2	C	11	1	5	1	37,355
Free and Bold	9	G	7	1	0	0	2,729
Free and Fancy	3	F	11	2	1	0	3,700
Free and Lucky	3	F	7	1	2	2	9,325
Free as the Wind	6	M	5	0	0	0	305
Free At Sea	3	F	2	0	0	0	2,700
Free Bid	3	F	1	0	0	0	400
Free Blast	3	G	7	0	0	2	2,693
Free Bonus	2	F	4	4	0	0	80,100
Free B's Flying	4	F	11	4	2	2	24,560
Free Cat	5	M	7	0	1	2	2,568
Free Cheers (AUS)	5	G	6	0	1	1	15,200
Free Chew	5	G	5	0	0	0	807
Free China	3	F	5	2	1	0	73,060
Free Climb	3	G	11	1	1	0	9,076
Free Cocktails	3	G	7	1	1	1	13,651
Free Destiny	6	M	1	0	0	0	0
Free Dip	3	F	12	2	2	2	63,110
Free Doctor	3	F	13	2	2	2	25,572
Free Dreamin Kelly	3	F	7	1	2	0	7,513
Free Drinks	2	C	1	0	0	0	0
Free Expresso	5	M	8	4	2	1	77,449
Free for the Road	5	G	9	2	1	1	10,080
Free From Pre	2	F	2	0	0	0	649
Free Hit	3	C	6	0	1	0	6,620
Free Home	3	C	3	0	0	0	245
Free Jazz	9	G	6	0	0	0	230
Free Juice	5	M	6	0	1	0	10,464
Free Kin Passion	2	C	1	0	0	0	0
Free Lance Cat	2	G	7	2	0	1	17,225
Free Lance Dancer	6	M	1	0	0	0	46
Free Love	3	F	5	0	0	0	461
Free Miles	3	F	10	1	3	2	13,565
Free Moonshine	4	F	3	1	0	1	18,120
Free My Soul	4	F	10	2	1	1	16,131
Free 'n Foxy	4	F	13	0	2	2	11,988
Free N Wild	3	C	13	4	3	3	21,731
Free of Love	6	H	8	1	1	2	66,000
Free On Ice	4	G	7	0	0	0	610
Free Pass	5	G	3	0	2	0	3,480
Free Play	5	M	8	0	2	1	10,738
Free Pour	4	G	6	0	1	1	6,144
Free Queen	4	F	6	3	0	1	15,705
Free Rent	3	F	10	1	3	3	47,130
Free Rocket	3	C	3	0	0	1	9,780
Free Rox	4	G	7	2	2	1	3,580
Free Rules	3	G	11	1	1	0	4,870
Free Scarlet	4	F	7	1	1	0	18,110
Free Society	2	F	6	0	0	0	1,045
Free Spin	6	M	2	0	0	2	11,880
Free Strategy	4	G	2	0	0	0	0
Free Strike	3	F	14	1	1	1	11,741
Free Stylin'	4	F	11	1	0	1	4,161
Free the Eagle	2	F	3	0	1	0	4,779
Free Thinking	3	C	6	1	0	1	22,586
Free Tide	3	F	18	1	0	0	5,994
Free to Please	3	G	7	0	2	0	7,600
Free to Run	7	G	17	3	5	3	16,565
Free Training	2	C	4	2	0	0	18,934
Free Will	8	G	16	3	2	1	17,110
Free Will E	2	C	3	0	1	1	6,016
Freeable	7	G	9	1	0	0	4,756
Freebird	2	C	1	0	0	0	0
Freedom At Bay	4	G	12	0	1	1	2,769
Freedom Call's	5	M	2	1	0	0	4,581
Freedom Class	4	G	3	0	0	1	2,860
Freedom Counts	3	C	11	1	2	1	29,515
Freedom Crest	8	G	2	0	0	0	1,840
Freedom Fair	3	G	8	2	1	1	6,730
Freedom Forever	4	F	8	3	1	0	13,240
Freedom Fries	3	F	6	0	2	0	11,770
Freedom Highway	5	G	13	3	2	0	16,875
Freedom Hill	4	F	4	0	0	0	0
Freedom in Flight	3	F	2	1	1	0	4,953
Freedom Land (AUS)	6	G	3	0	0	1	1,540
Freedom Lane	4	C	1	0	0	0	151
Freedom March	4	F	9	1	2	2	11,053
Freedom Peaks	3	F	11	1	3	3	20,070
Freedom Rd	7	M	7	0	4	1	6,328
Freedom Rider	4	G	15	2	0	0	12,737
Freedom Ridge	3	F	6	0	0	0	5,130
Freedom Roar	5	G	12	3	1	3	24,180
Freedom Song	4	G	6	0	1	1	3,970
Freedom Stand	3	G	11	1	1	1	10,107
Freedom Storm	2	C	2	0	0	0	459
Freedom Walk	4	G	15	1	1	0	6,379
Freedom Won	8	H	1	0	0	0	0
Freedomdontcomfree	3	F	2	0	0	0	0
Freedom's Forum	3	F	6	0	0	1	7,430
Freedom's Harmony	4	F	2	0	0	0	0
Freedom's Honor	4	G	6	1	1	0	57,470
Freedom's Key	4	C	7	1	1	1	41,960
Freefourinternet	6	H	9	2	1	0	527,693
Freefrom Floyd	3	G	3	0	1	0	580
Freefur	2	F	2	0	0	1	975
Freeholder	2	C	1	0	0	1	3,240
Freei	4	F	8	3	2	0	104,279
Freeland	4	G	2	0	0	0	0
Freely Bend	11	G	9	2	1	1	7,800
Freer	6	G	13	1	5	2	11,362
Freeroll	3	F	10	1	0	4	52,437
Free's Lil Lass	3	F	9	1	5	1	60,680
Freestate Rambler	3	G	10	0	0	4	5,413
Freestone	7	G	13	2	0	3	20,208
Freestyle	2	C	1	0	0	0	400
Freestyle Spirit	5	H	13	4	2	4	20,345
Freetobeme	4	F	7	2	2	0	11,653
Freetouch	3	F	7	1	2	0	15,440
Freeway Freddie	6	G	8	0	0	0	396
Freeway Ticket	6	G	11	2	1	2	38,725

Horse	Age	Sex	Sts	1st	2d	3d	Won
Freewheelin Freddy	7	G	6	0	0	1	1,006
Freeze a Roo	5	G	7	1	2	0	5,253
Freeze Alert	7	G	8	0	1	1	9,810
Freeze Bull	6	G	11	3	2	2	23,595
Freeze Em Out	4	F	2	0	1	0	4,767
Freeze the Win	4	G	15	3	4	4	33,918
Freezin Frolic	3	F	8	0	1	3	5,081
Freeznbtweensheets	3	F	9	0	0	0	732
Freidalicious	4	F	12	1	3	2	7,003
Freiheffer	3	G	2	0	0	0	0
Freire Tail	7	G	8	3	0	3	32,238
French Account	3	F	10	4	0	1	58,319
French Alley	3	C	3	0	0	0	433
French Babe	3	F	1	0	0	0	57
French Brandy	4	G	14	1	1	3	17,190
French Charmer	5	G	2	0	0	0	9,000
French Clu	2	F	1	1	0	0	10,800
French Coach	2	F	8	0	1	3	9,840
French Cognac	7	G	14	2	0	3	12,875
French Dish	3	F	1	0	1	0	8,800
French Dressing	3	C	4	2	0	2	56,470
French Facts	4	F	7	1	0	0	6,950
French Favor	3	C	1	0	0	0	0
French Flag (GB)	4	F	5	0	0	0	4,466
French Flight	3	F	2	0	0	0	1,480
French Flower	8	M	8	0	1	0	2,558
French Gigi	2	F	3	1	0	0	8,459
French Halo	3	G	8	0	0	0	0
French Hideaway	5	M	6	2	1	0	71,480
French Horn	3	C	7	0	1	2	22,297
French Jeannette	4	F	6	4	1	0	82,050
French Jubilee	3	F	7	0	0	1	1,510
French Lady (NZ)	4	F	1	0	0	0	0
French Lieutenant	4	C	8	2	0	0	69,682
French Miss	6	M	3	0	0	0	552
French One	2	F	3	0	0	0	216
French Packet	7	G	8	2	2	0	12,819
French Passion	7	H	2	0	0	0	180
French Peach	2	F	1	0	0	1	570
French Peak	4	F	2	0	0	0	374
French Picture	6	H	3	0	0	0	1,365
French Polo (FR)	4	G	3	1	0	0	22,560
French Prince	4	G	9	0	2	0	3,474
French Rascal	4	G	9	2	0	3	4,739
French Rebel	6	H	13	2	3	4	27,880
French Republic	5	M	10	1	3	2	54,062
French Road	3	G	6	0	0	0	1,560
French Roast	3	C	9	3	0	1	55,813
French Schemer	6	G	2	0	0	0	750
French Season	4	G	12	1	3	3	10,747
French Selection	4	G	16	1	1	4	28,262
French Sham	2	C	7	1	0	0	7,222
French Smile (IRE)	6	H	5	1	0	1	10,290
French Summer	3	F	2	0	0	0	125
French Teacher	8	M	2	0	0	0	1,500
French Toast	4	F	3	0	0	0	0
French Twist	6	M	7	1	0	1	9,316
French Veto	3	G	2	2	0	0	10,260
French Victory	5	G	5	0	0	0	349
French Village	3	F	3	1	0	0	27,200
French Wench	4	F	6	0	0	4	3,982
Frenchburg	3	G	12	4	2	3	59,530
Frenchglen	3	F	7	3	1	1	133,191
Frenchie	4	F	9	0	0	1	1,005
Frenchman's Reef	2	G	1	0	0	0	180
Frenchminer	2	G	2	0	0	0	215
Frenchmore	4	G	2	0	1	0	1,010
Frenchport	4	G	3	0	0	0	400
Frenchys Native	6	H	2	0	0	0	42
Frenetic Peg	4	F	5	0	0	1	391
Frenzy	4	G	2	0	0	0	420
Frere This	3	G	6	1	1	0	7,840
Fresal	4	F	4	0	0	0	6,680
Fresco	4	F	10	2	0	1	18,682
Fresh and Sassy	4	F	9	0	2	1	5,165
Fresh Believer	7	M	2	0	0	0	285
Fresh Hot Buns	3	F	3	1	0	0	12,300
Fresh Slate	2	G	2	0	0	0	425
Fresh Squeezed	3	F	1	0	1	0	2,600
Fresh Thunder	5	G	12	2	1	0	28,552
Fresh Tracks	5	M	2	0	0	0	4,607
Fresh Victor	6	G	4	1	1	0	1,343
Fresh Water Bay	2	G	3	1	0	1	18,119
Fresquita	4	F	8	0	0	0	970
Frew	2	C	1	0	0	1	1,425
Freya's Fire	4	F	9	1	2	3	11,655
Friar Tuck	9	G	6	0	1	0	1,080
Friday's a Comin'	6	G	13	4	0	1	39,929
Fridays Gold	2	G	3	0	0	1	2,902
Friday's Partners	3	F	7	0	1	1	11,680
Friel's for Real	4	F	6	5	1	0	204,450
Friend Atthetrack	3	G	3	0	0	0	700
Friend Laura	3	F	4	0	0	0	350
Friend of a Friend	2	F	3	1	0	0	12,500
Friend of Mine	8	G	5	1	1	0	5,614
Friend Til the End	2	C	4	0	0	2	4,460
Friendly Act	3	G	10	2	0	0	12,182
Friendly Affair	3	G	11	0	0	1	1,550
Friendly Banker	3	G	5	1	0	0	10,480
Friendly Beau	4	G	8	1	0	0	4,380
Friendly Bidder	3	G	7	1	1	1	4,856
Friendly Bye Bye	3	F	4	0	1	1	3,224
Friendly Chad	8	G	1	0	0	0	0
Friendly Cop	9	G	13	2	3	2	15,782
Friendly Departure	5	G	7	2	0	2	14,682
Friendly Expense	3	G	15	0	1	2	6,860
Friendly Frolic	5	G	1	0	1	0	3,400
Friendly Gal	4	F	7	2	0	1	38,160
Friendly Gamble	2	C	7	0	0	0	1,901
Friendly Girl	4	F	6	0	0	0	0
Friendly Hall	3	F	1	0	0	0	1,350
Friendly Heat	4	C	6	0	1	0	5,750
Friendly Houston	3	F	7	0	0	0	434
Friendly Island	3	C	7	5	0	0	172,214
Friendly K J	4	G	2	0	0	0	0
Friendly Lass	5	M	6	0	0	0	0
Friendly Man	5	G	16	3	6	0	20,736
Friendly Michelle	3	F	7	3	0	2	335,754
Friendly Mickey	4	F	18	3	6	1	32,920
Friendly Mike	4	C	2	0	0	1	9,000
Friendly Niner	3	G	10	1	1	0	4,236
Friendly Noble	4	G	2	0	0	0	153
Friendly Party	4	F	4	0	1	0	2,475
Friendly Passage	2	F	2	0	1	0	7,429
Friendly Pioneer	6	M	10	3	2	0	28,079
Friendly Rebel	3	G	10	2	1	1	35,663
Friendly Slew	5	M	7	0	5	0	7,056
Friendly Takeover	3	C	3	0	0	0	0
Friendly Theresa	4	F	12	1	2	1	40,710
Friendofthedevil	4	G	7	0	1	0	4,502
Friendofthefamily	4	F	15	2	2	4	52,762
Friend's Case	2	F	8	0	1	0	2,465
Friends Lake	3	C	4	1	0	1	611,800
Friendship Avenue	6	G	1	0	0	0	220
Friendship Bell	3	F	10	2	0	1	11,840
Friendship Circle	2	F	1	1	0	0	27,000
Friendship Terrace	3	F	13	2	5	1	53,996
Friggero	3	G	5	0	0	1	1,650
Frightful	3	G	6	1	0	0	15,350
Frigidon	5	G	14	0	2	4	2,433
Frillery	3	F	8	1	0	0	8,575
Frills and Thrills	6	M	1	0	0	0	100
Frillsandfurbelows	2	F	3	0	1	0	2,580
Frilly Fun	5	M	8	1	2	1	53,015
Fringe Comment	4	G	7	0	0	1	450
Frio Flag	5	G	8	1	0	2	10,280
Frioguette	2	G	4	0	0	1	2,370
Frisby Flyer	3	F	1	0	0	0	0
Frisco Belle	4	F	8	1	0	3	48,350
Frisco Breeze	5	G	4	0	0	0	329
Frisco Cat	5	G	6	0	0	1	1,077
Frisco Flare	7	H	5	0	0	0	138
Frisco Frisky	8	G	10	0	2	0	3,550
Frisco Johnny	4	G	8	0	0	2	5,083
Frisco Lady	6	M	10	0	0	0	413
Frisco Light	3	C	7	0	0	1	2,100
Frisco Racer	4	C	6	2	0	1	5,163
Frisco Slew	3	F	3	1	0	0	17,820

Horse	Age	Sex	Sts	1st	2d	3d	Won
Frisk for Jade	3	F	2	0	0	1	770
Frisk Me Again	3	F	8	2	3	1	24,129
Frisk Me Later	3	F	5	0	0	0	477
Frisk Me Minnie	3	F	7	1	0	0	11,040
Frisk Meow	3	F	3	0	0	0	345
Frisky Anne	4	F	5	0	0	0	0
Frisky Attitude	9	G	8	1	1	0	3,957
Frisky Devil	5	M	4	1	0	1	10,510
Frisky Mark	3	G	12	1	2	1	27,000
Frisky Money	2	C	6	1	2	1	18,012
Frisky Mood	4	F	11	0	2	0	3,785
Frisky Phoebe	6	M	5	1	1	0	13,719
Frisky Spider	3	C	13	4	0	2	148,600
Friskys Profit	3	G	10	3	2	3	51,442
Frisqued	2	F	2	0	0	0	0
Fritz Blitz	4	G	1	0	0	0	0
Fritzi's Michelle	4	F	21	1	5	3	14,645
Fritzl	6	G	1	0	0	0	64
Fritzli	4	C	4	0	1	1	3,080
Fritz's Fan	3	G	7	1	0	1	4,177
Fritzy Hour	4	F	11	1	1	2	14,680
Frizzi	2	F	1	0	0	0	112
Froehlich	8	G	2	0	0	0	570
Frog Eyes	3	G	6	1	1	2	4,600
Frog Point	4	G	8	0	1	2	5,935
Froggy's Magic Boy	3	G	4	0	2	2	12,322
Froggywentacourtin	11	G	3	1	0	1	5,105
Frogman Henry	3	C	6	1	3	1	42,310
Frolic Away	3	F	2	0	0	0	410
Frolic for Joy	3	C	13	3	3	5	72,250
Frolic in Da Sun	5	G	9	1	1	1	13,866
Frolicking Prince	3	G	10	1	0	1	32,670
Frolly Cart	2	F	3	0	0	0	0
From A to Z	5	H	3	0	0	0	0
From Away	3	F	9	1	3	3	98,500
From B to B	3	F	8	1	0	0	6,952
From Charlie	4	G	10	3	0	1	20,154
From Heaven Sent	4	F	14	1	2	0	5,417
From Mars	5	G	1	0	0	0	0
From Mike's Heart	5	H	5	0	0	0	900
From the Beginning	5	M	1	0	0	0	0
From Your Lips	4	G	1	0	0	0	0
Fromage a Trois	3	G	4	0	0	0	1,275
Fromajack to Aking	3	G	7	0	2	1	35,739
Frome	3	G	8	1	4	0	20,900
Fromheretobrazil	4	F	4	1	1	0	3,475
Fromoutoftheclouds	7	H	8	0	0	0	268
Fromthebackjack	4	F	10	1	1	1	23,467
Front Cover Dreams	8	G	2	1	0	0	6,720
Front Line	3	F	4	0	1	1	14,190
Front Nine	5	G	8	1	0	0	30,000
Front Paige Gal	3	F	11	1	2	3	16,670
Front Tees	2	C	1	0	0	0	0
Frontena Cat	5	G	6	1	1	0	10,520
Frontera Power	4	G	11	0	0	0	675
Frontier Footsteps	2	C	1	0	0	0	250
Frontier Groom	3	G	14	0	1	2	11,125
Frontier Image	3	G	4	0	0	0	189
Frontier Man	3	G	13	0	0	2	3,325
Frontier Rider	9	G	6	0	0	0	483
Frontrera One	7	H	16	0	0	0	1,266
Frost Alert	2	G	6	0	0	1	3,640
Frost Lady	2	F	1	0	1	0	2,415
Frost N Honey	5	G	3	0	0	0	525
Frost Princess	2	F	5	1	0	0	22,200
Frost Warning	4	G	5	2	0	0	42,210
Frosted Face	3	F	13	2	4	2	25,740
Frosteen	5	M	5	0	0	0	492
Frostmark	2	G	1	0	0	0	400
Frostoria	4	F	10	1	0	1	3,018
Frosty Alibhai	8	G	3	1	0	0	4,800
Frosty Astra	2	G	5	0	1	1	6,477
Frosty Avenger	2	G	2	0	0	0	400
Frosty Breeze	6	M	11	1	0	2	12,421
Frosty Coco	6	G	12	0	0	0	908
Frosty Coy	10	G	3	0	0	0	352
Frosty Event	3	G	7	2	1	1	16,860
Frosty Face	3	G	5	0	1	0	8,120
Frosty Halo	2	C	4	0	0	0	408
Frosty Hill	4	C	9	1	2	2	12,297
Frosty King	3	C	1	0	0	0	0
Frosty La	8	M	4	0	0	0	549
Frosty Lady	5	M	17	1	0	1	4,330
Frosty Lass	2	F	5	0	0	0	1,200
Frosty Nails	5	M	10	2	2	2	14,160
Frosty Naylor	10	G	7	0	1	0	2,538
Frosty Note	5	M	4	1	1	0	11,862
Frosty Nugget	3	C	5	0	1	0	4,865
Frosty Paws	4	G	6	1	0	1	5,049
Frosty Play	3	G	5	0	1	0	4,050
Frosty Pop	4	G	9	1	1	1	8,632
Frosty Prince	5	G	13	1	2	1	7,508
Frosty Prospector	6	M	15	2	1	2	13,443
Frosty Quoit	12	G	8	0	0	3	1,430
Frosty Reason	3	G	2	0	0	0	0
Frosty Remark	6	M	9	2	2	2	29,184
Frosty Royalty	2	F	8	1	3	3	74,060
Frosty Starlight	7	G	15	1	0	3	11,160
Frosty Valentine	3	F	10	1	1	2	10,535
Frosty Wayne	3	G	6	0	0	2	1,821
Frosty Weekend	3	F	7	0	0	1	3,665
Frostydaisical	3	F	13	0	2	3	9,692
Frosty's Babe	4	F	2	0	0	0	0
Frosty's Champ	4	G	14	0	0	0	2,892
Frosty's Course	4	C	9	1	1	2	22,108
Frosty's Pleasure	5	M	8	0	1	1	7,360
Frown'n	5	M	3	0	0	0	0
Frozen Dream	6	G	11	0	0	0	568
Frozen Fax	3	G	2	0	0	2	1,870
Frugal	6	G	5	0	2	1	12,410
Fruit Jar	4	C	3	0	0	0	0
Fruit of the Zoom	2	F	1	0	1	0	1,730
Fruit Rapport	7	H	9	3	2	2	12,398
Fruition's First	4	G	1	0	0	0	400
Fruits	5	M	12	2	3	3	71,657
Fruits of Labour	4	F	7	0	0	1	3,963
Fruitsoup Olaf	5	G	5	0	1	2	7,744
Frumeh Labow	4	F	5	0	0	0	0
Frysland	3	F	5	1	1	1	50,040
Ft. Mann	5	M	5	0	0	2	12,467
Fuchsia Gold	2	F	5	2	1	0	40,796
Fuddle Duddle	2	F	4	1	0	0	8,367
Fuddy Buddy	6	G	6	3	1	0	6,478
Fuddy's Dream	3	F	15	1	0	1	5,200
Fudge	5	M	7	1	1	2	4,954
Fudge Fatale	4	F	6	1	0	1	64,510
Fue Follet Gris	4	G	11	1	4	1	30,469
Fuego Dancer	3	F	9	0	0	0	750
Fuego Maximo (ARG)	6	G	2	1	0	0	5,525
Fuego Popular	6	G	7	0	0	0	454
Fuegos Alibhai	3	F	7	0	0	1	1,605
Fuelling	3	C	16	2	2	1	24,860
Fugheddaboutit Sid	5	H	1	0	0	0	76
Fugitives Justice	4	G	7	2	0	1	11,036
Fuhr Elise	4	F	10	0	2	1	7,079
Fuhr Ore	4	G	9	1	1	1	26,150
Fuhr Real	4	F	9	1	2	1	40,474
Fuhrever Dancing	2	G	8	0	2	1	38,056
Fuhrfy	4	G	4	0	0	0	369
Fuhrious Tale	3	C	12	0	1	1	4,783
Fuhrluck	3	G	12	3	5	2	39,950
Fuhry	5	G	8	0	0	1	3,260
Fujiyama Dino	4	G	5	0	0	0	1,224
Fulcrum	2	G	5	0	1	2	7,710
Fulfillment	4	F	1	0	0	0	0
Fulham	5	G	8	0	1	2	2,294
Full Account	5	G	7	0	0	1	1,117
Full Blown Storm	3	F	6	1	0	0	17,236
Full Boat	3	G	3	1	0	1	1,620
Full Brush	9	G	4	0	1	0	4,700
Full Carat	4	F	12	0	1	1	6,460
Full Champ	5	G	1	0	0	0	91
Full Command	9	G	3	1	0	1	5,198
Full Cooler	4	C	2	1	0	0	11,485
Full Dress Parade	7	G	3	0	0	0	0
Full Flow	7	G	10	2	1	3	79,280
Full Force Gale	7	G	7	2	0	4	23,620
Full Keg	3	G	6	1	2	0	43,516

Horse	Age	Sex	Sts	1st	2d	3d	Won
Full Legacy	5	G	3	0	0	0	192
Full Moon Cat	2	C	6	1	0	0	3,300
Full Moon Dancer	5	G	13	2	3	1	8,573
Full Moon Lady	6	M	5	1	0	1	5,755
Full Moon Madness	9	G	7	0	5	2	81,920
Full Moons Arisin	3	C	3	0	0	0	540
Full of Charm	2	G	5	1	1	0	8,374
Full of Fun	2	F	2	1	0	1	20,500
Full of Giggles	6	M	7	1	0	0	4,621
Full of Gratitude	5	H	7	2	2	0	18,906
Full of Joy	3	F	9	1	0	1	9,865
Full of Laughs	2	F	2	0	0	0	570
Full of Luck	5	G	14	2	3	2	53,175
Full of Secrets	3	F	1	0	0	0	220
Full Response	6	G	7	0	0	0	738
Full Speed Ahead	6	G	9	2	1	1	13,386
Full Tank	4	G	12	3	1	2	28,510
Full Term	3	F	4	0	1	0	1,145
Full Throttle Lil	2	F	1	0	0	0	0
Full Tilt	5	M	9	0	1	0	2,175
Full Time Dancer	4	F	9	1	2	2	38,340
Full Time Spirit	7	M	3	0	0	0	700
Full Trick	4	G	11	1	1	1	3,541
Full Value	3	C	3	0	0	1	398
Fulla Vink (NZ)	6	M	4	0	0	0	1,875
Fullaner	2	F	1	0	0	1	1,100
Fullblown Affair	5	G	4	0	0	0	123
Fullbridled	3	C	2	0	1	0	10,040
Fuller	2	C	3	0	0	0	570
Fuller's Delight	4	F	8	0	0	0	225
Fulloblarny	3	F	1	0	0	0	60
Fullpoint	4	G	3	0	0	0	1,635
Fullthrottlerocket	4	G	1	0	0	0	40
Fully Committed	2	C	1	1	0	0	6,102
Fully Confident	3	F	2	0	0	0	640
Fully Engaged	3	C	2	1	0	0	20,232
Fully Packed	5	G	14	4	1	4	77,299
Fully Vested	3	G	13	2	1	2	55,830
Fulmine	3	F	9	2	1	2	45,308
Fulton	4	G	14	3	1	4	23,067
Fumante (BRZ)	5	M	10	0	2	0	8,574
Fumph Around	3	C	16	0	2	2	15,950
Fun Bus	3	G	2	0	0	0	225
Fun Fum First	5	G	12	0	2	3	8,435
Fun House	5	M	10	1	4	2	175,476
Fun in Motion	3	C	1	0	0	0	348
Fun Maggie	3	F	19	2	3	2	17,057
Fun Meeting You	9	G	12	2	0	1	20,225
Fun On Ice	3	G	11	0	1	0	7,163
Fun On the Weekend	2	F	2	0	0	0	460
Fun to Fly	11	G	9	1	0	0	2,725
Fun to Play	2	F	3	0	0	0	352
Fun to Run	11	G	2	0	0	0	280
Fun Town	2	F	6	0	2	2	5,920
Funaroundthetable	5	H	1	0	0	0	0
Fundable	4	G	9	1	0	0	11,415
Fundamental	5	G	8	0	1	0	5,630
Funewgie	3	G	6	0	1	0	2,596
Funga Safari	3	G	5	0	0	0	1,240
Fungee	3	G	7	0	1	0	15,480
Funk	2	C	5	2	1	1	74,960
Funky Cowboy	10	G	8	0	0	0	1,825
Funky Pirate	3	G	3	1	0	0	5,050
Funkytown	2	F	2	0	0	0	0
Fun'ngames Toknite	3	F	6	0	0	2	10,663
Funnin and Runnin	3	C	1	0	0	0	0
Funny Bone	6	M	14	2	1	1	39,255
Funny Cat	3	F	12	0	0	2	2,893
Funny Cide	4	G	10	3	2	3	1,075,100
Funny Colero	5	M	2	0	0	0	0
Funny Copy	3	F	2	0	1	1	8,240
Funny Farm	4	F	6	1	1	0	23,305
Funny Honey	3	F	6	0	1	3	23,077
Funny Mood (ARG)	7	M	4	1	0	0	17,140
Funny Numbers	7	G	4	0	1	0	1,430
Funny Sky	3	F	2	0	0	0	490
Funny Soldier	5	H	9	0	1	0	10,832
Funny Tom (ARG)	9	H	8	1	2	0	9,597
Funny Way (ARG)	4	F	6	0	1	0	9,485
Funny Woman	4	F	5	3	0	1	49,080
Funroe	3	C	10	0	1	0	7,103
Funshine	3	F	2	0	0	0	0
Funtime Freddie	4	G	7	2	0	2	3,826
Funtotouch	5	G	3	0	0	0	388
Funzone	4	F	7	0	2	0	10,915
Fur Elise	2	F	1	0	0	0	0
Fur Gohan	4	C	7	0	0	0	642
Furando	3	G	1	0	0	1	1,305
Fureur France (IRE)	7	G	3	0	0	0	0
Furious Chad	5	G	6	0	0	0	3,504
Furious Fever	3	C	4	0	1	0	8,565
Furious Victory	8	G	9	1	0	4	2,421
Furizi	2	F	3	0	1	0	1,581
Furniture Man	13	G	1	0	0	0	73
Furrari's Image	7	M	3	0	0	0	0
Further	7	G	6	3	0	1	44,340
Furthermore	5	H	3	1	0	0	9,143
Furtive Glance	2	F	3	1	1	0	18,980
Furtivo (ARG)	7	G	5	0	0	1	2,990
Fury's Song	2	G	6	2	2	0	16,385
Fusaichi Donight	3	C	3	0	0	0	300
Fusaichi Heart	2	F	10	1	3	1	34,215
Fusaichi Rock Star	2	C	4	1	0	1	48,366
Fusaichi Samurai	2	C	1	1	0	0	21,000
Fusaichi Towani	3	F	4	1	0	1	19,610
Fusaichi's Dance	3	G	5	0	1	1	3,145
Fusaichi's Wind	3	F	3	0	0	0	870
Fuse It	6	M	14	3	6	2	156,530
Fuse Quick	6	G	14	4	3	1	34,637
Fuselier	4	G	12	2	0	0	5,762
Fusionista	3	F	11	1	4	2	34,490
Fussy Fever	5	M	2	0	0	0	206
Fussy Photo	5	G	5	0	0	0	490
Fussy's Kid	7	G	7	2	0	0	36,682
Fusto	5	H	4	2	1	0	6,340
Fusty	5	G	16	2	2	1	15,963
Futloosanfancyfree	3	F	7	3	1	0	21,435
Futural	8	G	8	0	2	2	16,128
Future Article	5	G	3	0	0	0	390
Future Blessing	6	M	18	5	0	3	18,741
Future Crown	12	G	10	2	0	0	8,892
Future Destiny	4	G	5	0	0	0	141
Future Fantasy	3	G	14	4	2	0	53,960
Future Flash	3	G	10	2	3	0	69,089
Future Flyer	4	C	8	1	0	1	4,386
Future Force	4	G	10	0	0	1	2,860
Future Gold	3	G	10	3	1	2	7,243
Future Grace	3	C	1	0	0	0	400
Future Justice	3	F	12	3	0	1	29,728
Future Launch	3	G	7	1	0	0	3,245
Future Leader	8	H	6	0	0	1	426
Future Rainbow	6	M	6	0	0	3	2,989
Future Running	4	G	14	1	0	2	5,350
Future Saint	2	F	1	1	0	0	15,625
Future Thought	5	M	4	1	0	0	35,520
Future Wealth	4	G	6	1	0	1	10,365
Future With Humor	2	F	3	1	0	1	17,850
Futures Market	3	F	4	0	0	0	4,829
Fuzdaisy	2	F	3	0	0	0	1,263
Fuzz E Delight	4	F	14	1	5	3	29,815
Fuzzette	2	F	1	0	0	0	0
Fuzzie's First	4	F	10	3	1	0	28,614
Fuzzie's Hero	3	C	9	0	3	0	5,480
Fuzzy Abby	6	M	13	2	3	0	21,585
Fuzzy Chai	3	F	6	0	1	0	5,000
Fuzzy Dice	4	F	9	0	0	0	1,048
Fuzzy Eagle	9	H	6	1	1	1	4,275
Fuzzy Ferd	7	G	18	0	1	4	4,757
Fuzzy Star	5	H	3	1	1	0	22,920
Fuzzy Was Affirm	5	G	7	0	0	0	240
Fuzzyheadedlizard	2	G	6	1	0	2	14,505
Fuzzyisasfuzzydoes	2	C	3	0	1	1	1,510
Fynbos	5	M	10	3	1	2	31,938
Fynmarr	3	G	5	1	2	0	9,785
Fyrbreathingdragon	5	G	8	0	1	1	5,356
G All Day	7	G	11	1	0	3	22,896
G Dance	2	G	6	0	0	0	2,100
G G's Millennium	4	F	8	1	1	0	7,413

Horse	Age	Sex	Sts	1st	2d	3d	Won
G I Jayne	4	F	9	0	0	0	1,650
G I Thunder	4	G	5	1	1	1	15,720
G Is for Go	3	C	13	0	2	0	2,740
G J Lost and Found	3	F	4	0	0	0	232
G L Mickey	4	C	4	0	0	1	2,070
G L's Gold Strike	7	G	9	0	1	4	8,351
G M Jake	3	G	16	3	1	5	32,374
G Mans Gal	4	F	7	0	1	1	8,349
G P Fleet	4	G	11	4	3	1	247,786
G P's Black Knight	2	C	7	2	2	1	89,500
G T' S Golden Tap	2	F	1	0	0	0	1,788
G T' S Levendy	3	G	13	1	5	4	45,018
G T'sstillbelievin	5	M	8	0	0	0	1,268
G U Devil	5	M	17	0	1	1	3,799
G. I. Dream	4	F	11	0	1	1	1,748
G. I. Jana	3	F	12	2	6	0	50,965
G. I. Speed	4	G	7	2	1	0	13,812
G. P. Glove	8	G	4	1	1	1	1,950
G. R.'s Dream	9	G	1	0	0	0	0
G. Starr	5	M	7	1	0	3	20,320
G. T. Crusader	3	G	5	1	0	3	9,643
G. T.'s Gone West	4	F	6	0	1	0	4,053
G. W. Sprout	3	C	7	1	1	1	5,262
G. W.'s Deputy	6	G	9	0	2	2	24,670
G. W.'s Skippie	4	C	3	0	0	0	1,680
G. W.'s Squall	3	F	6	0	0	1	5,600
Gab Bag	3	C	13	2	1	3	15,669
Gabby Blue	4	F	7	1	1	2	20,822
Gabby Dancer	5	M	12	1	1	1	13,598
Gabby Glib	4	G	8	1	0	0	3,136
Gabby Jacqui	4	F	1	0	0	0	145
Gabby Lou	5	G	10	0	3	1	34,655
Gabby Wears Gucci	4	F	3	0	0	0	150
Gabe	6	G	3	0	0	0	338
Gabianna	4	F	16	1	4	2	36,370
Gabourel Bank	2	F	2	0	1	0	5,980
Gabrieles Princess	5	M	3	2	0	0	71,250
Gabriel's Call	3	C	4	0	0	1	1,155
Gabriel's Pat	6	G	8	3	0	1	14,115
Gabriel's Prospect	9	G	2	0	0	0	80
Gabriel's Way	3	G	4	0	0	0	0
Gaby G	6	M	5	1	0	1	8,546
Gacky	2	G	1	0	0	1	1,200
Gadace's Khamseh	3	C	8	3	2	1	74,754
Gadarenes	2	G	7	1	1	0	6,195
Gaddingabout	2	G	3	0	0	0	0
Gadget Man	3	G	18	2	6	3	80,730
Gadir	7	G	1	0	0	0	192
Gaebel's Gamble	6	M	18	2	5	5	35,231
Gaelic Chief	4	G	3	0	0	0	280
Gaelic Hope	7	G	4	1	0	0	5,390
Gaelic Issue	3	C	5	1	1	2	47,100
Gaelic Miss	4	F	10	2	2	0	55,920
Gaelic Sunrise	3	C	8	1	0	2	31,650
Gaelic Terms	3	C	2	0	0	0	4,260
Gaelic Thunder	7	G	5	1	1	2	5,110
Gaelic's a King	6	G	7	3	1	2	2,740
Gaellic Warrior	6	G	18	1	3	2	10,454
Gaetano's Way	4	C	14	1	4	1	78,625
Gaff	2	C	3	1	1	0	57,246
Gaffney	5	G	9	0	1	2	7,032
Gai Copper	5	M	5	0	0	0	792
Gailpickedthisone	4	F	12	1	5	0	15,151
Gail's Drive	6	G	9	2	5	0	55,125
Gail's Melody	5	M	6	1	0	1	2,266
Gainango	3	C	8	1	3	2	37,257
Gainey Best Star	4	G	13	2	2	3	32,899
Gaining Talent	4	G	6	0	0	0	455
Gairloch	9	G	2	0	0	0	0
Gaiter Girl	7	M	10	2	1	0	7,647
Gakkel Ridge	4	C	2	0	0	0	454
Gal Friday	3	F	9	2	0	2	13,493
Gal O Gal	4	F	11	0	0	0	13,620
Gal On Skis	4	F	13	3	2	0	24,270
Gala Cause	3	F	8	0	3	0	19,465
Gala Gold County	4	G	1	0	0	0	230
Gala Lady	3	F	7	0	2	2	4,426
Gala Mag (ARG)	5	M	14	3	3	3	34,510
Gala Reckoning	5	M	5	0	0	1	3,190
Gala Regatta	2	F	1	0	0	1	3,080
Galactic Cat	2	F	5	2	1	1	49,400
Galactic Fire	5	G	9	1	2	3	7,641
Galacticus	4	G	9	0	1	0	3,490
Galago	4	G	10	0	0	0	4,545
Galakazoo	2	F	2	0	0	0	696
Galan Fantasma (CHI)	4	G	4	0	1	1	11,940
Galarus	5	G	2	0	0	0	160
Gala's Trick	8	H	2	0	0	0	0
Galatea Cat	5	M	13	1	5	1	64,706
Galatian	5	G	12	1	3	1	7,588
Galavant	9	G	6	1	0	2	4,320
Galaxy	2	C	6	1	3	1	109,504
Galaxy Belle	7	M	7	2	2	1	36,752
Galaxy Lady	2	F	4	0	1	1	7,525
Gale Force	2	C	1	0	0	0	230
Gales of November	3	F	9	1	1	0	12,705
Galette	4	F	12	2	1	3	22,953
Galezeroni	3	F	17	3	0	3	20,443
Galic Boy	9	H	15	4	1	0	64,909
Galica	3	F	7	1	1	1	24,608
Galilee Sea	3	F	1	0	0	0	0
Galileo's Star	4	F	7	1	1	0	14,179
Galimoto	3	G	3	0	0	0	1,120
Galindo	8	G	3	1	0	0	6,491
Galintherain	5	M	6	3	1	1	30,081
Galivantor	5	G	4	0	0	0	990
Gallant (GB)	7	H	9	2	1	2	94,700
Gallant American	4	C	5	0	0	0	0
Gallant and Brave	6	G	11	0	0	0	5,415
Gallant Angel	6	M	7	0	0	3	15,824
Gallant Approval	4	G	4	0	1	0	868
Gallant Bandit	2	C	3	0	1	1	8,740
Gallant Beau	7	G	2	0	0	0	240
Gallant Brave	4	C	6	0	0	1	4,991
Gallant Envoy	3	G	5	0	1	0	1,562
Gallant Gold	2	C	5	0	0	1	9,787
Gallant Honour	3	G	5	0	0	0	200
Gallant Intern	7	M	4	0	0	0	0
Gallant Jon	2	G	5	0	0	1	2,684
Gallant Jules	4	G	7	0	0	0	809
Gallant Lass	2	F	1	1	0	0	6,199
Gallant Leader	5	G	7	1	3	0	11,086
Gallant Manor	7	G	10	1	0	0	4,852
Gallant Princess	2	F	6	1	0	2	27,036
Gallant Search	2	G	7	0	0	2	6,711
Gallant Secret	2	F	6	2	1	2	77,950
Gallant Sioux	6	M	2	0	0	0	252
Gallant Sir	5	G	9	3	2	3	121,180
Gallant Snowman	6	G	12	0	1	0	8,570
Gallant Soldier	4	G	9	1	1	1	10,864
Gallant Tale	4	G	8	2	0	0	17,559
Gallant Talk	4	G	5	0	0	0	1,465
Gallant Turk	8	G	7	2	0	0	21,800
Gallapiat's Fame	7	M	6	0	0	2	2,028
Gallapiat's Ghost	4	F	15	3	1	3	16,363
Gallapiat'smydaddy	6	G	10	0	0	2	4,090
Gallardo	2	R	3	0	0	1	5,240
Gallatin Gateway	6	G	5	0	1	0	760
Gallatin Kid	5	G	7	1	0	1	33,579
Galleria Daze	4	F	6	0	0	0	660
Gallery Place	3	F	6	0	4	1	44,600
Galley Bay	3	F	7	1	2	2	12,945
Galliant	4	G	1	0	0	0	70
Gallo Del Bar (CHI)	4	C	5	1	1	0	32,065
Gallop Fat Boys	4	G	9	0	2	1	18,800
Gallop to Victory	3	C	4	1	0	0	26,104
Galloping Christos	4	G	20	0	3	2	4,991
Galloping Dancer	4	F	2	0	0	0	660
Galloping Gal	3	F	7	1	1	0	124,480
Galloping George	7	G	3	0	0	0	258
Galloping Gourmet	6	G	10	1	0	1	10,320
Galloping Grocer	2	G	4	3	1	0	150,400
Galloping Lu	6	M	1	0	0	0	0
Galloping to Tea	3	F	15	1	3	1	12,146
Gallotin	3	G	5	0	0	0	188
Galopin Charger	3	C	8	3	0	1	21,345
Galpin Joe	3	G	1	0	0	0	84
Galpin's Candi	5	G	12	1	1	1	2,160

Horse	Age	Sex	Sts	1st	2d	3d	Won
Galray	4	G	5	1	1	0	1,434
Gal's Hunter	2	C	4	1	0	3	4,004
Galtee Miss	2	F	3	0	0	0	721
Galvanizer	4	C	15	0	4	2	22,476
Galway Miner	5	G	9	0	0	2	2,884
Gamble	5	G	9	2	0	0	32,360
Gamble Les	8	G	13	1	1	1	9,421
Gamble Monger	3	G	10	2	2	0	52,298
Gamble On Me	5	G	12	1	0	2	10,722
Gamble On Red	3	G	4	1	0	0	10,161
Gamble to Victory	4	F	6	0	4	0	38,880
Gamblen Derek	4	G	14	0	2	1	6,101
Gambler's Edge	5	G	13	1	1	0	6,699
Gambler's Gift	8	M	9	0	0	1	1,736
Gambler's Law	3	G	12	2	2	2	18,162
Gambler's Mark	4	G	10	1	2	1	49,854
Gamblers Passion	4	F	12	5	1	0	66,780
Gambler's Prize	2	G	3	0	0	1	2,040
Gambler's Prospect	5	G	23	1	2	4	28,974
Gambler's Route	2	C	1	0	0	1	2,400
Gambler's Secret	4	G	5	0	0	0	0
Gambler's Share	8	G	10	4	2	0	45,612
Gamblers Slew	2	C	2	1	0	0	35,280
Gamble's Answer	5	M	14	0	4	2	32,425
Gamble's Ghost	4	F	7	1	0	1	19,965
Gamblin	3	C	9	3	0	1	107,450
Gamblin Annie	4	F	11	0	3	3	11,074
Gamblin Caper	4	G	11	0	0	3	6,671
Gamblin Jake	7	G	13	1	1	2	5,268
Gamblin Ruth	6	M	2	0	0	0	0
Gambling Bob	6	G	7	0	0	0	430
Gambling Cherokee	3	F	12	1	1	2	9,864
Gambling Gold	8	G	9	1	0	1	5,980
Gambling Green	3	F	4	0	0	1	7,540
Gambling Hope	3	F	20	1	4	4	14,060
Gambling King	5	G	4	0	0	0	519
Gambling Native	3	G	14	4	0	0	88,919
Gambling Rent	3	G	7	4	1	1	48,270
Gambling Slew	3	G	5	1	0	1	9,247
Gambling Time	3	C	16	4	4	0	21,962
Gambol	3	F	9	1	2	2	14,902
Gambol Goldfish	3	F	6	1	2	0	13,135
Game Bag	4	C	17	1	2	1	10,202
Game Bird	8	H	5	0	2	0	7,760
Game Box	4	C	11	1	0	3	22,770
Game Boy Johnny	2	G	4	1	0	0	20,970
Game Boy Justin	2	C	3	1	0	0	15,840
Game Cadillac	5	G	15	2	7	3	13,810
Game Called	6	G	11	1	1	1	16,659
Game Card	3	F	3	1	1	1	23,920
Game Day	4	G	9	4	2	0	45,890
Game Day Hero	3	G	4	0	0	1	12,114
Game Effort	6	G	12	3	2	2	59,775
Game Fighter	4	G	7	0	0	0	721
Game Girl	4	F	13	2	3	1	17,177
Game in the Wind	3	F	6	1	2	1	21,913
Game Keeper	4	C	1	0	1	0	1,995
Game Lady	3	F	4	1	0	0	25,106
Game Load	3	F	9	1	2	0	26,685
Game Magic	6	G	21	0	2	2	4,391
Game Master	3	C	6	2	2	1	9,482
Game Princess	4	F	9	1	1	1	10,492
Game Prize	3	G	9	1	0	0	5,088
Game Set Match	5	G	11	3	1	2	23,338
Game Ticket	6	G	9	4	1	1	18,382
Game Within a Game	3	G	9	2	0	1	32,077
Gamebri Boy	5	G	12	1	3	2	9,371
Gamely Glittering	5	M	12	1	2	0	8,427
Gamer	5	G	3	0	1	0	2,736
Games of Chance	6	M	14	1	4	3	27,354
Games People Play	3	C	3	0	0	0	190
Gametracker	3	C	9	0	1	1	8,276
Gaming	3	G	16	0	4	1	14,545
Gaminis Cloud	2	C	1	0	0	0	105
Gamini's Secret	3	F	6	0	0	0	394
Gammagoat Kid	5	G	15	2	2	3	6,926
Gammy Dan	3	G	1	0	0	0	0
Gamut	3	C	10	3	0	0	28,350
Ganador	7	G	1	0	0	0	184
Gandalf the Grey	3	G	11	2	0	3	19,592
Gander	8	G	5	1	0	0	62,828
Gandolfini	4	G	4	1	0	0	11,435
Gandy Dancer	2	G	2	0	0	2	1,990
Ganendyl	4	F	1	0	1	0	4,800
Ganeska	2	C	3	1	0	1	8,475
Gangster	3	G	10	4	2	0	160,118
Gangster Whitewals	2	C	1	1	0	0	9,900
Gangtrous	10	M	8	0	4	0	2,038
Ganharva	4	F	17	1	5	6	32,545
Gankster	7	G	2	0	1	0	2,500
Gannett Peak	3	C	2	0	0	1	3,520
Ganny Girl	3	F	7	0	2	2	16,130
Gansta Affair	4	F	5	0	0	0	221
Gap's Alibi	3	G	5	0	0	0	1,046
Garavogue	3	F	4	2	0	0	44,900
Garb	5	G	13	0	1	4	6,225
Garbo's Secret	2	F	1	0	0	0	400
Garces Lady	4	F	10	3	1	2	19,632
Garden Dance	5	M	7	2	0	0	48,440
Garden in the Rain (FR)	7	M	1	0	1	0	30,000
Garden of Avie	4	F	6	0	0	0	1,543
Garden Tracer	6	G	12	0	0	2	2,029
Garden Whimsy	3	F	3	1	0	0	23,214
Garden Wildcat	4	F	2	0	0	0	0
Gardeness's Gem	4	F	10	2	0	0	14,964
Garesche	5	G	10	1	2	1	79,750
Garfield's Bluff	3	C	2	0	0	0	340
Garland County	4	F	2	0	0	0	360
Garland of Love	4	F	3	0	0	0	900
Garlax	3	G	12	1	3	0	7,399
Garrard	4	C	4	1	0	1	19,800
Garret (CHI)	5	G	17	2	2	3	25,397
Garret's Gulch	3	G	13	2	4	4	97,480
Garrett Champ	8	G	12	0	4	1	6,187
Garrett Junior	4	G	8	0	0	1	3,321
Garrett Seven	2	G	5	0	0	1	2,795
Garrett's Girl	3	F	13	6	4	1	128,610
Garrett's Glider	5	G	3	2	0	0	5,340
Garretts Gray	3	G	8	1	0	0	7,299
Garrett's Tiger	3	G	6	2	1	0	11,350
Garrettslilnora	6	M	5	1	0	1	24,312
Garrison Hill	5	G	11	3	1	3	53,498
Garrison's Bonus	3	C	2	0	0	1	1,800
Garrison's Gun	3	F	14	1	0	0	6,375
Garros	4	G	8	2	1	0	38,205
Gar's Mam	5	M	15	3	3	3	34,495
Garson Rouge	10	G	6	0	0	2	1,729
Garth	3	G	5	0	0	0	1,870
Gary Battle Wise	4	G	6	1	1	0	2,175
Gary L	3	C	5	0	0	1	530
Gary the Neighbor	5	G	20	0	1	6	13,385
Garyigordon	5	G	5	1	0	0	4,140
Gary's Agenda	5	G	2	0	0	0	0
Gary's Key	6	G	5	0	0	0	2,130
Gary's Little Lady	2	F	2	0	0	1	1,148
Gary's Sherry	3	F	3	0	0	0	0
Gary's Speedy Miss	9	M	13	1	3	2	8,621
Gary's Stuka	5	G	2	0	0	0	0
Garysrappingranny	5	M	4	0	0	0	660
Garytheman	3	G	3	0	0	0	0
Gas House Mouse	5	M	1	0	0	0	0
Gas Pedal	3	F	12	1	3	2	8,889
Gasparilla Queen	9	M	6	0	0	1	1,627
Gasperillo Daze	7	G	6	0	0	1	4,495
Gassan Honey	4	G	6	0	2	1	10,740
Gassan Rock	3	G	7	3	0	1	52,640
Gassan Royal	4	C	5	2	1	1	118,000
Gassi	4	C	1	0	0	0	0
Gastons Gold	5	G	7	0	0	0	519
Gastown	3	G	11	3	2	0	65,442
Gata Be Patient	4	F	4	0	0	1	7,337
Gata Be Wild	4	F	11	0	2	0	12,628
Gata Bella	3	F	2	0	1	1	8,680
Gata Black Dahlia	2	F	3	0	0	0	225
Gata Veloz	3	F	5	0	0	0	4,696
Gate Card	6	H	12	2	1	1	13,112
Gate Crasher	3	G	4	0	1	2	8,323
Gate Jumper	3	F	1	0	0	0	0

Horse	Age	Sex	Sts	1st	2d	3d	Won
Gate Master	4	G	4	0	0	0	267
Gate Ovation	2	C	1	0	0	0	0
Gatebuster	10	G	12	3	3	1	17,464
Gated Entrance	4	F	8	1	0	1	14,180
Gateman	2	C	3	0	0	1	4,728
Gater Power	5	M	9	2	2	1	13,495
Gates Avenue	3	C	12	4	0	0	104,756
Gate's Goal	5	G	7	0	0	1	1,828
Gate's Sunny Boy	6	G	3	0	0	0	450
Gather No Moss	3	G	7	1	0	2	22,010
Gather the Roses	8	G	14	1	2	3	17,420
Gathering Gold	3	G	5	0	1	0	12,380
Gathering Storm	3	G	10	0	0	2	11,678
Gatita	3	F	1	0	0	0	0
Gatito Fuerte	2	G	7	3	3	0	63,990
Gato Bob	3	C	5	1	0	1	8,600
Gato de Dia	2	G	2	0	0	0	280
Gato Montanes	3	G	13	0	1	4	4,982
Gato Montes	3	C	12	0	4	3	5,870
Gato Negro	4	G	11	0	4	2	8,660
Gato Pichon (ARG)	5	H	1	0	0	0	0
Gato Pirato	3	G	4	0	1	1	2,188
Gato Sol Mitts	4	F	12	1	1	2	5,386
Gatopresson	5	G	10	1	2	0	3,428
Gator Attack	5	M	2	0	0	0	102
Gator Lake	5	G	3	0	0	0	262
Gator Maid	5	M	3	0	0	0	277
Gator the Great	3	G	14	2	1	1	11,165
Gators Get	6	G	16	6	2	2	95,149
Gators N Bears	4	C	8	3	1	2	357,910
Gattina Bella	2	F	9	2	1	2	32,540
Gatto Fortunato	6	G	12	0	4	1	6,701
Gatto Selvaggio	3	F	1	1	0	0	6,600
Gaturro (ARG)	5	H	1	0	0	0	0
Gauche Victory	2	C	1	0	0	0	87
Gaucho Girl	3	F	16	1	2	4	15,543
Gauntlet	7	G	2	0	0	0	0
Gav	3	G	3	0	0	0	0
Gavelock	6	G	8	0	2	3	13,450
Gavins Wish	3	G	15	4	4	2	38,778
Gaviota Pass	7	G	16	1	3	2	6,609
Gavro	4	C	4	1	0	0	40,680
Gavster	5	G	16	1	1	0	2,856
Gay and J Mac	7	M	13	0	0	0	2,994
Gay Mood	4	F	5	2	0	0	10,070
Gay Slewpy	6	G	1	0	0	0	29
Gaylas Kitty	5	M	1	0	0	0	50
Gayla's Storm	3	F	7	0	0	2	5,030
Gayles Lioness	4	F	8	0	0	1	1,184
Gayle's Sabie	3	C	9	1	0	0	19,005
Gazeemo	5	M	10	0	0	0	1,090
Gazillion	5	M	4	0	1	2	52,100
Gear Up	3	F	7	2	0	0	5,810
Gearbox	3	G	3	1	0	0	9,455
Geardown	4	G	16	4	4	3	143,517
Geared	2	F	1	0	0	0	145
Gearupbaby	2	F	5	1	0	2	19,580
Geaux Gabriel	4	G	10	1	3	2	32,150
Gebb's Dixie	5	M	7	1	2	2	55,564
Gebb's Flag	4	G	16	4	2	2	53,395
Gebb's Glory	6	M	12	0	1	3	7,995
Gebb's Prince	8	G	15	3	0	2	16,891
Gebb's Princess	6	M	12	1	0	1	7,519
Gebb's Rodeo	3	G	11	0	3	2	16,955
Gee Cashman	4	G	5	0	0	0	0
Gee Don't You Wish	7	M	14	1	4	3	25,580
Gee Dubya	5	G	7	0	1	1	2,860
Gee Dubya Bee	4	G	12	0	0	2	7,855
Gee Gee's Grand	6	M	1	0	0	0	0
Gee Honey	2	F	2	1	0	0	7,110
Gee Leclair	3	F	3	1	0	0	7,221
Gee Look At Me	5	H	3	0	0	0	140
Gee Louisi	3	G	3	0	0	0	590
Gee Marie	2	F	2	0	0	0	1,290
Gee One	3	F	5	0	0	1	1,343
Gee Queen	3	F	5	0	0	0	300
Gee Tee O	3	G	7	4	0	0	22,895
Geebeekay (IRE)	4	G	4	0	0	0	1,155
Geechee Lou	6	M	3	0	0	0	220
Gee's Bend	2	F	7	1	3	0	23,800
Gee's He's Grand	3	C	19	0	2	1	4,107
Geeser	7	G	5	0	0	0	120
Geestahn	2	F	3	0	1	1	3,700
Gehrig	5	G	8	0	2	1	13,075
Geiger Gold	2	C	3	1	1	0	45,391
Geiger Tiger	4	G	17	3	2	1	26,037
Geist Buster	3	C	7	1	0	0	8,400
Gela	4	G	8	0	3	0	8,830
Geleta	3	F	3	0	0	0	0
Geli's Pie	4	F	8	1	0	0	3,653
Gelli	4	F	8	5	1	0	95,500
Gem Cat	2	F	2	0	0	0	328
Gem Fire	2	F	2	0	0	0	1,590
Gem Gate	6	G	15	1	4	3	8,828
Gem Lea	2	F	8	1	0	2	17,595
Gem of a Day	3	G	2	1	0	0	33,456
Gem of a Guy	6	G	12	2	3	2	30,789
Gem Royale	4	F	1	0	0	0	400
Gem West	4	F	4	0	0	0	300
Gemilli	2	F	3	1	2	0	53,240
Gemini Cruiser	6	G	8	2	1	0	4,504
Gemini Dream	3	C	7	2	1	1	56,138
Gemini Girl	3	F	6	1	0	0	6,855
Gemini's Revenge	2	F	3	1	0	0	19,668
Geminized	2	F	6	1	0	0	9,705
Gemjolie	4	G	5	0	0	0	488
Gemma Kyle	4	F	8	0	2	1	7,048
Gemma Nunz	5	G	5	0	0	0	1,075
Gemmie a Satellite	3	C	9	0	2	0	14,582
Gems and Roses	3	F	10	1	4	0	11,536
Gems Fella	7	G	7	2	1	2	6,430
Gem's Flora	5	M	7	1	0	1	10,200
Gem's Honor	3	G	11	0	4	0	24,873
Gems of Wisdom	4	F	5	2	1	0	42,440
Gem's Wager	5	M	19	2	3	1	32,304
Gen Fall	5	G	5	0	1	1	10,780
Gen Sterling Price	4	G	6	3	0	1	21,329
Genal Syd	5	M	11	1	2	1	9,715
Gender Dance	4	F	2	0	0	0	198
Gene	9	G	6	2	0	0	5,664
Gene de Campeao (BRZ)	5	H	8	0	1	1	51,800
Geneaudrey	9	G	2	0	0	0	81
General Alexander	4	G	4	0	0	0	0
General Appeal	2	G	2	0	0	0	280
General Approval	3	C	9	3	1	0	25,070
General Ascot	4	G	5	0	0	1	1,707
General Athenium	5	G	17	2	1	1	10,805
General Be	4	C	2	0	0	0	1,800
General Benefit	2	F	1	0	0	0	56
General Biltmore	4	G	9	3	2	1	20,968
General Bob	3	C	3	0	0	0	1,940
General Bull	4	G	8	0	1	2	1,550
General Cara Lee	4	F	3	0	0	0	0
General Celmar	4	G	5	0	1	1	5,935
General Charley	2	C	2	0	0	1	5,100
General Code	7	G	3	0	0	0	360
General Commander	4	C	2	0	0	1	1,903
General Congress	3	G	1	0	1	0	8,200
General Creek	3	G	12	1	4	0	11,129
General Danzer	3	G	13	0	1	4	4,240
General Director	2	G	1	0	0	0	300
General Exceptions	4	F	4	0	0	0	0
General Express	9	G	1	0	0	1	1,760
General Expression	3	F	4	1	1	0	40,000
General Fox	3	G	6	2	2	1	59,480
General Genius	2	G	4	0	0	1	1,071
General George S	3	G	11	2	1	1	8,920
General Guidelines	4	C	3	0	0	1	470
General Hector	2	C	3	1	0	0	4,320
General Howze	2	C	2	0	0	0	390
General Insanity	4	G	10	2	1	2	18,625
General Jay	4	G	12	1	2	1	30,440
General John B	2	G	3	2	0	0	35,400
General Jones	2	G	5	1	3	0	13,900
General Josh	4	G	10	1	2	3	10,692
General Kiridashi	3	C	11	1	1	1	63,899
General Lee	4	C	11	2	1	1	21,212
General Martin	3	G	7	0	0	0	1,363

Horse	Age	Sex	Sts	1st	2d	3d	Won
General Mauk	3	G	6	0	0	2	4,569
General Mill	5	G	8	0	0	0	1,091
General Money	3	G	8	1	3	1	8,220
General Moody	3	G	2	0	1	0	9,580
General Naevus	2	G	10	1	2	1	13,160
General Pat	6	G	13	5	3	0	40,945
General Plot	4	G	13	2	1	1	8,696
General Price	3	G	2	0	0	0	1,090
General Principle	2	G	3	1	0	0	19,060
General Reward	4	C	1	0	0	0	0
General Roanoke	5	G	9	0	0	2	5,550
General Sacrifice	2	F	4	0	0	0	1,265
General Schuyler	3	C	2	1	0	0	9,215
General Search	3	C	4	2	0	0	11,100
General Session	2	F	1	0	0	0	70
General Sheba	5	G	1	0	0	0	885
General Sickles	2	C	1	0	0	0	0
General Silverfoot	4	C	6	0	0	0	203
General Slim	3	C	1	0	0	0	176
General Tap	4	G	3	0	0	0	824
General Terms	6	G	10	0	1	3	6,905
General Thomas	2	C	6	1	1	0	14,525
General Tommy	3	C	13	3	1	0	56,440
General Trick	3	G	3	0	0	1	1,980
General Vassili	9	G	12	2	1	1	10,168
General Villa	9	G	7	2	1	2	10,975
General Waki	5	G	12	0	3	3	2,799
General Will	4	G	11	3	2	0	31,700
General World	2	G	4	0	0	0	395
General Year	5	G	8	2	1	0	7,392
General Zapata	8	G	4	0	0	0	173
Generalist	2	C	8	1	2	0	85,839
Generalito	3	G	5	0	0	1	1,800
Generally On	8	G	4	0	1	0	3,535
General's First	7	H	2	0	0	0	0
Generals Passion	4	F	7	1	1	2	15,373
Generals Sword	6	G	7	1	0	0	15,780
Generals Wardancer	5	M	4	0	0	1	8,126
Generalsprettygirl	3	F	3	0	0	0	0
Generations	7	H	1	0	1	0	1,500
Generous One	3	C	6	1	2	1	50,427
Generous Rosi (GB)	9	H	11	2	0	1	36,363
Generously	6	G	20	1	5	4	12,089
Gene's Bid to Win	5	G	6	0	0	0	422
Gene's Dream	5	M	1	0	0	0	0
Gene's Faith	3	G	8	0	2	0	3,332
Geneva Cross	4	G	14	3	3	4	24,254
Geneva Red	2	F	6	0	2	0	6,140
Genevil	4	F	14	2	1	3	50,895
Genie Magic	5	M	22	3	3	5	46,760
Genius Rules	8	M	5	0	1	0	4,030
Geniusatwork	3	C	2	0	0	1	6,260
Geniver	3	F	9	2	2	1	93,112
Genji	5	G	2	0	0	0	0
Gennie's Challenge	5	M	17	2	2	2	43,515
Gennifer Wren	3	F	6	3	1	1	14,417
Genome	4	G	1	0	0	1	1,600
Genska	5	M	4	1	1	0	25,590
Gent	5	H	9	2	1	0	94,740
Gent a Babe	3	G	9	1	4	1	10,021
Gentblos	3	F	4	0	0	0	0
Genteel	5	M	16	1	2	3	9,497
Genteel Lady	6	M	13	3	2	3	35,858
Gentille Alouette	6	M	9	1	0	1	36,310
Gentle Affair	3	F	5	0	0	0	738
Gentle Air	3	F	1	0	0	0	57
Gentle Bien	5	G	12	1	0	0	10,796
Gentle Breeze	2	F	5	1	0	1	30,510
Gentle Charmer	2	F	5	1	0	1	22,545
Gentle Cielo	5	G	8	1	1	1	7,444
Gentle Damascus	4	C	1	0	0	0	135
Gentle Fun	3	F	9	2	2	0	27,540
Gentle Glide	6	M	9	0	1	0	1,694
Gentle John	4	G	11	3	1	2	17,821
Gentle Melody	2	F	1	0	0	0	800
Gentle Nudge	4	G	3	0	0	0	2,700
Gentle R	5	M	9	1	1	3	6,187
Gentle Wind	3	F	2	0	1	1	4,779
Gentleman Count	2	C	4	1	1	1	69,216
Gentleman Jerry	5	G	14	7	3	1	51,700
Gentleman Jones	3	G	5	2	2	1	44,673
Gentleman Player	3	G	3	0	0	0	550
Gentleman's Affair	3	G	7	0	1	2	2,914
Gentleman's Bet	3	G	2	0	0	0	201
Gentleman's Girl	3	F	4	1	1	0	26,625
Gentleman's Honor	4	G	1	0	1	0	4,200
Gentleman's Lady	4	F	1	0	0	0	480
Gentlemen Duel	3	G	9	1	0	0	5,876
Gentlemen J J	4	C	9	0	2	3	59,560
Gentlemen's Club	4	G	3	0	0	0	1,329
Gentlemen's Game	3	G	3	0	0	0	1,700
Gentlemen's Guest	4	F	5	0	0	1	3,640
Gentlestone	4	G	6	1	1	0	30,935
Gentlman Hawk	4	C	6	1	0	2	12,284
Gentree	9	G	12	0	0	1	4,296
Gent's Advantage	4	C	4	0	1	1	5,040
Gents Big Cat	7	G	11	0	0	0	1,390
Genuine Act	4	C	3	0	0	1	2,500
Genuine Blues	6	M	1	0	0	0	0
Genuine Colonel	2	G	3	0	0	1	938
Genuine Count	3	G	2	0	0	0	1,240
Genuine Draft	3	G	15	0	2	2	16,360
Genuine Dream	7	M	11	0	0	1	1,236
Genuine Fire	6	M	7	0	0	1	1,812
Genuine Fox	2	F	3	0	0	0	0
Genuine Glory	4	F	3	0	0	0	175
Genuine Miss	2	F	7	2	2	0	47,708
Genuine Pat	3	F	23	5	4	0	29,166
Genuine Performer	5	M	15	1	0	0	5,871
Genuine Regard	5	G	14	3	6	2	47,750
Genuine Regret	3	F	6	0	0	0	1,750
Genuine Ruler	5	G	13	1	1	5	14,763
Genuity	2	F	3	1	0	0	12,540
Geo Quercus (IRE)	6	H	10	1	0	0	5,051
Geodude	6	G	17	0	2	4	5,240
Geometry	5	G	13	1	1	0	25,888
George Atthe Stick	2	F	8	0	1	1	9,360
George Bailey	5	G	10	1	2	0	12,212
George Double You	4	G	5	0	0	0	0
George Edward	4	G	16	2	1	2	21,180
George L Brown	2	G	4	1	1	0	22,658
George M	7	G	19	5	2	1	21,135
George Taylor	5	G	14	5	3	1	93,883
George's Boy	4	C	2	0	0	0	0
George's Brother	3	C	15	3	1	1	16,376
George's Gain	4	G	9	2	1	1	43,490
George's Girl	3	F	5	1	0	0	16,740
George's Lil Demon	4	G	4	0	0	0	104
George's Stick	4	G	5	0	1	1	2,585
Georgetown Gal	3	F	7	2	0	0	55,224
Georgia B	3	F	7	1	0	0	4,936
Georgia Cracker	3	G	2	0	0	0	2,700
Georgia Crown	8	H	3	1	0	0	6,848
Georgia Gentleman	3	G	5	1	2	0	11,975
Georgia Glory	5	G	11	2	2	1	36,610
Georgia Ok	3	F	4	1	0	0	10,193
Georgia Overdrive	2	F	1	0	0	0	450
Georgian Door	5	G	6	1	0	1	15,209
Georgian Queen	3	F	2	0	0	0	3,528
Georgia's Lady	4	F	7	1	0	0	930
Georgie	4	G	2	0	0	0	282
Georgie Gem	5	M	6	2	0	2	10,831
Georgie Porgee	6	G	10	0	0	0	1,011
Georgio J.	6	G	7	0	0	0	728
Georgios B.	3	G	5	0	0	1	5,061
Geotex	3	G	4	0	1	1	1,190
Gerald's Memory	4	F	4	0	0	0	0
Geri Gold	4	G	13	0	2	2	12,631
Geri Kelly	3	F	5	2	0	1	20,720
Geri Laine	2	F	2	0	0	0	565
Geri Lewis	4	C	4	0	0	1	6,270
Geririg	4	G	9	0	2	0	13,204
Geri's Affair	5	G	7	1	2	1	4,898
Geri's Dancin	4	G	2	0	0	0	0
Germain's Man	8	G	11	1	1	3	7,818
German Angi	4	F	1	0	0	0	0
Germanicus	4	G	9	0	2	1	11,326
Germanna Colonies	4	F	11	3	1	1	61,380

Horse	Age	Sex	Sts	1st	2d	3d	Won
Geronimo	5	G	4	0	0	0	110
Geronimo (CHI)	5	G	10	3	3	1	187,987
Geronimo Joe	3	G	3	1	1	0	8,445
Geronimos Renegade	3	G	12	1	2	2	20,045
Gerri's Rogue	4	G	8	0	2	2	8,390
Gerry Fantasy	3	F	7	1	2	0	4,698
Gerry Gerry Gerry	3	G	9	1	1	3	28,962
Gershowitz	3	F	9	1	0	1	17,796
Gert in Vegas	3	F	11	1	4	3	5,280
Gerts Girl	2	F	2	0	0	1	1,194
Gerty's Loot	2	F	1	0	0	0	114
Geruase	4	G	14	4	4	1	33,962
Get	4	F	10	2	0	1	7,370
Get a Life	2	C	4	0	1	0	3,095
Get Busy	4	F	2	0	0	0	70
Get Control	8	M	3	2	0	0	9,097
Get Crackin	3	F	13	2	1	1	25,680
Get Down	2	C	2	2	0	0	70,080
Get Down Wolfie	6	G	8	1	2	1	42,325
Get Festive	3	C	10	1	1	2	9,515
Get Fiscal	4	C	2	0	0	0	103
Get Going Gracie	3	F	2	0	0	0	1,260
Get Happy	4	F	11	0	1	0	5,684
Get Holme	2	F	5	1	0	0	11,310
Get Home Racso	7	G	3	0	0	0	1,797
Get Inspired	4	F	5	0	2	0	14,672
Get My Drift	6	G	4	0	0	1	1,022
Get My Keys	5	M	6	0	1	0	2,120
Get Off the Phone	10	G	12	0	5	2	2,177
Get On Track	2	F	3	0	0	1	2,905
Get Out Happy	3	C	4	0	0	1	2,640
Get Outta Dodge	3	G	9	0	0	0	1,127
Get Set	3	F	7	2	0	1	53,900
Get Smarter	4	G	1	0	0	0	360
Get the Doc	5	G	1	0	0	0	0
Get the Dough	4	C	11	2	2	5	22,675
Get the Edge	3	G	2	0	0	0	0
Get the Hook	3	F	3	0	0	0	1,830
Get the Picture	8	G	14	0	2	3	16,992
Get Thee Behind Me	2	C	2	0	0	0	0
Get Up and Go	4	G	9	0	0	2	17,956
Get Up Greeley	3	F	9	1	1	0	13,540
Get Wild	2	C	5	2	0	1	62,365
Getaway Candidate	2	C	2	0	0	1	6,897
Getaway Grace	3	F	1	0	0	1	900
Getaway Holme	6	G	8	4	2	2	64,050
Getaway in Style	7	G	8	0	2	2	7,273
Getaway Man	3	C	2	0	0	0	940
Getcozywithkaylee	3	F	16	5	2	2	78,455
Getdapartystarted	3	F	6	0	1	1	6,355
Geteem G. W.	3	G	10	2	2	1	19,024
Getem Frank	5	G	8	0	1	0	5,650
Getenough	2	F	1	0	0	0	130
Gethsemani	3	C	8	0	0	1	19,091
Getitgirl	4	F	1	0	0	0	0
Getjiggywitit	3	F	9	1	2	0	8,366
Getnby	8	G	3	0	0	0	340
Geton	5	M	13	1	0	0	4,200
Getoutofmyvalay	4	F	7	1	1	1	14,640
Getoutoftheway	6	M	5	1	0	1	3,568
Getouttamykitchen	3	F	1	0	0	0	235
Getreadytorumba	3	F	1	0	0	0	0
Getta Klew	3	F	8	1	1	0	1,883
Gettarman	4	G	7	1	0	2	16,103
Getthepartystarted	4	F	5	1	1	0	32,650
Gettin Better	4	F	19	4	3	6	19,328
Gettin' Overtime	12	G	1	0	0	0	0
Getting Grey	3	G	15	1	1	3	13,409
Getting Old	11	G	3	0	0	1	650
Getty Up N Go	3	G	13	1	2	2	13,120
Gettys Luck	6	G	6	1	0	0	7,330
Getum Casey	3	G	4	0	0	0	1,070
Getyourgunsannie	3	F	6	1	2	1	20,700
Geyser Road	2	C	4	1	0	2	33,610
Gezee Wizz	3	G	7	0	1	1	4,500
Ghannam	5	H	6	2	2	0	47,600
Ghazada	3	F	14	3	2	2	35,988
Ghazelle	6	G	4	0	1	2	8,136
Ghazette	5	M	9	2	3	2	10,391
Ghazi Dust	4	F	9	2	1	2	11,691
Ghazi Gazelle	4	F	3	0	0	0	177
Ghazi Osbourne	3	G	5	0	0	0	795
Ghazi Town	3	F	3	1	0	0	6,300
Ghazi War	4	G	3	1	2	0	27,080
Ghazihasit	4	F	4	0	0	0	119
Ghazirella	6	M	6	3	0	0	58,630
Ghazi's Flight	6	M	13	3	1	1	26,326
Ghazi's Ghost	4	C	3	0	0	1	1,507
Ghazi's Gold	3	F	8	1	0	1	5,511
Ghazi's Impala	3	G	13	1	3	1	11,635
Ghazis Majestic	5	H	1	0	0	0	125
Ghazoline	7	H	1	0	0	0	0
Ghen	3	G	3	0	1	1	7,360
Ghent	3	G	4	0	1	1	4,352
Ghetto	3	G	6	0	0	0	540
Ghetto Fabulous	3	G	14	0	2	2	12,230
Gho Sailing	3	F	3	0	1	0	5,751
Ghoastly Prize	6	G	14	1	1	3	18,623
Ghost Actor	3	G	8	3	1	0	28,593
Ghost Chatter	4	F	9	3	2	1	94,850
Ghost Creek	2	G	2	0	0	1	1,680
Ghost Dreams	2	F	3	0	0	0	300
Ghost Employee	2	F	5	0	0	0	875
Ghost Fever	8	G	2	0	0	0	0
Ghost Flyer	3	F	7	0	0	1	2,578
Ghost Harbor	2	F	1	0	0	0	0
Ghost Launcher	3	G	10	1	1	0	8,759
Ghost Leader	2	C	3	0	2	1	10,024
Ghost Mate	4	G	10	3	2	0	26,057
Ghost Memo	4	G	3	0	0	2	6,850
Ghost Mountain	3	C	6	1	1	1	55,870
Ghost Pride	3	C	4	0	1	0	4,619
Ghost Rider in Red	2	C	7	3	0	2	33,590
Ghost to Ghost	3	F	1	0	0	0	0
Ghost to the Post	4	G	6	1	0	0	1,419
Ghost Whisper	3	F	1	0	0	0	76
Ghost Wolf	3	G	5	0	1	1	1,766
Ghosthunter	3	G	20	1	1	1	7,497
Ghostly Concern	3	C	3	1	0	0	10,980
Ghostly Dance	2	C	3	0	0	1	2,656
Ghostly Endeavor	5	H	15	1	0	1	7,070
Ghostly Gal	3	F	12	2	0	3	32,280
Ghostly Gate	3	F	7	3	2	0	69,920
Ghostly Image	4	C	1	0	0	0	505
Ghostly Maneuvers	3	C	4	0	0	1	2,393
Ghostly Moon	5	G	5	0	0	0	1,145
Ghostly Numbers	6	H	7	2	0	2	44,120
Ghostly Pretender	2	F	2	0	0	0	0
Ghostly Smile (NZ)	6	G	10	0	1	0	7,693
Ghostly Victor	4	G	11	1	2	1	5,334
Ghostwriter	3	C	4	1	1	0	13,395
Ghostzapper	4	C	4	4	0	0	2,590,000
Giacobbe	5	G	4	0	1	0	4,500
Giacomo	2	C	4	1	1	1	119,440
Gianna Yulla	2	F	2	0	0	0	936
Giannico	5	M	1	0	0	0	0
Giant Hope	2	C	2	0	1	0	5,010
Giant Slam	4	G	4	2	1	0	15,795
Giant Swordsman	2	C	1	0	0	0	145
Giant Thief	2	C	4	0	1	1	5,090
Giant Wrecker	2	C	1	0	0	0	137
Giant's Song	3	C	5	0	0	1	1,045
Giants Temptation	2	F	5	1	0	0	6,844
Gib Merlin	4	C	7	0	2	0	7,290
Gibbar	3	G	12	3	1	1	18,228
Gibberjabberpitch	5	H	4	1	0	0	10,580
Gibbons Terrace	3	C	16	3	0	3	58,335
Gibbs Beach	4	G	12	1	4	0	12,262
Gibford	3	G	12	0	4	1	20,527
Gib's Pal	4	C	2	0	0	0	0
Gibson City	5	G	1	0	0	0	0
Gibson Station	4	G	8	0	2	1	6,893
Gibson Witch	3	F	12	1	1	2	20,753
Giddy Lilly	4	F	2	0	0	0	250
Giddy Up Lloyd	8	G	11	2	3	1	4,386
Gideon	6	G	10	0	3	2	29,204
Gifford Road	4	C	10	1	2	1	19,930
Gift of April	3	F	13	3	3	2	34,593

Horse	Age	Sex	Sts	1st	2d	3d	Won
Gift of Faith	2	C	2	0	0	0	150
Gift of Music	2	C	3	0	0	0	1,650
Gift of the Eagle	6	H	7	0	0	2	45,036
Gift of the Heart	3	F	2	1	0	0	22,620
Gift Wrap	4	G	3	0	0	0	2,327
Gifted Athlete	7	G	11	2	0	1	8,239
Gifted Dream	3	F	4	1	2	0	10,170
Gifted Speaker	5	G	3	0	0	0	0
Gifted Warrior	4	G	3	2	1	0	3,600
Gifty Dancer	3	G	5	2	0	0	31,020
Gigabyte	8	H	9	0	0	3	7,077
Gigawatt	4	C	10	4	2	0	141,067
Giggandjogg	4	F	9	1	2	1	10,430
Gigger	2	C	1	1	0	0	12,300
Giggle Box	4	G	14	1	5	2	25,753
Giggles and Smiles	4	G	3	0	0	0	0
Gigha	5	G	17	3	6	5	16,744
Gigi From Fiji	3	F	4	0	0	1	1,470
Gigi's Charm	2	F	2	0	0	1	2,870
Gigi's Skyflyer	5	M	2	0	1	0	8,500
Gigiski	4	F	12	1	0	5	28,776
Gigli (BRZ)	6	H	3	0	0	1	15,000
Gigolo Jayson	3	G	7	0	0	1	1,161
Gig's Star	2	F	5	0	1	2	2,811
Gijima	3	F	5	1	3	1	58,130
Gilbertslewogold	6	G	11	1	0	1	3,660
Gilded Bertrando	3	G	3	0	1	0	8,540
Gilded Cove	3	C	7	0	1	2	5,520
Gilded Crown	2	G	2	0	1	0	8,600
Gilded Deputy	4	G	2	0	0	1	686
Gilded Edge (GB)	4	F	2	0	0	0	230
Gilded Edition	6	G	10	2	0	3	4,949
Gilded Emperor	7	G	12	0	3	2	14,450
Gilded Gold	3	F	7	3	1	0	96,238
Gilded Gold Flyer	4	C	6	0	1	0	2,750
Gilded Graces	3	G	2	0	0	0	0
Gilded Honor	3	G	5	0	0	1	4,800
Gilded Nip	5	M	7	0	0	4	25,520
Gilded Oreo	4	C	8	1	1	1	10,963
Gilded Pin	4	C	2	1	0	0	13,670
Gilded Queen	5	M	1	0	0	0	0
Gilded Son	10	G	1	0	0	0	0
Gilded Touch	2	C	1	0	0	0	400
Gilded Venture	8	G	12	0	0	0	1,028
Gilded Way	6	H	5	0	0	0	0
Gilded Wings	5	M	7	1	1	2	34,700
Gildersleeves	3	C	11	2	0	2	12,500
Gildmore	5	G	10	2	0	0	18,660
Gilgal	2	G	1	0	1	0	2,320
Gille Mhor	2	G	3	0	0	0	1,398
Gillespie	3	G	7	1	0	4	21,508
Gillys a Ham	4	G	12	2	2	2	12,310
Gilradden	5	G	7	0	0	2	2,090
Gimeone Stall Ples	4	C	7	0	0	0	1,092
Gimme a Clue	6	M	12	1	3	2	33,275
Gimme a Hint	5	G	8	1	0	0	6,060
Gimme a Vee	3	F	18	1	3	3	11,956
Gimme an A	5	G	4	1	2	0	28,800
Gimme Fever	4	F	11	4	0	2	69,940
Gimme Five	4	F	7	1	0	1	3,105
Gimme Grace	2	F	3	0	1	0	2,255
Gimme Half a Break	5	G	6	0	1	1	3,695
Gimme No Lip	5	G	10	1	1	4	30,364
Gimme Shelter	3	C	2	0	0	0	272
Gimme Some Love	3	F	3	1	0	1	38,771
Gimme the Willys	6	M	11	7	2	1	82,000
Gimmeawink	4	C	4	0	1	2	15,330
Gimmesumoneyhoney	7	H	4	0	4	0	1,262
Gimmesumsugar	3	F	14	4	2	0	22,497
Gin and Sin	4	G	9	4	3	0	210,125
Gin and Tea	2	C	1	0	0	0	120
Gin Dandy	5	G	7	0	1	2	4,360
Gin Fizz Dancer	2	F	8	1	0	1	7,115
Gin Is It	4	F	7	0	1	2	9,000
Gin n' Tychonic	4	F	7	2	2	0	10,858
Gin Real Officer	4	G	8	0	4	2	26,340
Gin Rummy	2	F	5	1	1	0	18,530
Gin Rummy Champ	3	C	13	2	6	0	101,170
Gin Runner	3	F	10	2	2	2	14,501
Gin Star	4	F	19	2	2	2	22,258
Gin Time	5	M	5	0	0	0	1,560
Gina Serena	4	F	2	0	0	0	87
Gina's Actress	6	M	4	0	0	0	80
Gina's Eyes	6	G	22	0	0	2	4,799
Ginas Girl	5	M	13	3	2	2	46,440
Gina's Star	3	C	11	0	1	2	19,432
Gina's Zaroyev	6	M	3	0	0	0	0
Gincessive	2	G	2	0	0	0	1,026
Gindigo	5	G	14	1	1	4	20,190
Ging	6	G	12	1	0	1	1,850
Ginger Ale	5	H	9	2	1	0	79,283
Ginger Bear	2	F	2	0	0	0	1,380
Ginger Creek	3	F	8	1	0	1	12,290
Ginger Daddy	8	G	10	0	0	1	1,503
Ginger Dancer	8	M	2	0	0	0	77
Ginger for Pluck	5	G	8	1	1	2	12,818
Ginger Gold	5	M	7	2	1	0	116,304
Ginger Hoffa	4	F	8	0	1	1	4,866
Ginger Man	3	G	2	0	0	0	320
Ginger Moon	5	M	5	0	0	0	0
Ginger N Sugar	3	F	3	2	1	0	61,400
Ginger Roo	6	M	20	5	4	1	39,767
Ginger Spin	7	M	4	0	0	0	441
Gingerbread Miss	2	F	1	0	0	0	205
Gingerella	4	F	11	3	2	3	39,755
Ginger's Fella	2	C	6	2	0	1	30,620
Ginger's Gnash	4	F	1	0	0	0	0
Ginger's Honor	4	F	1	0	0	0	181
Gingham and Lace	3	F	3	1	1	0	43,740
Gingham Curtains	4	F	2	0	0	0	140
Gingivere	2	F	1	0	1	0	9,200
Gini Quick	5	M	1	0	0	0	92
Ginnie With a G	2	F	5	0	0	0	590
Ginny Fizz	2	F	3	0	0	0	525
Ginny Hooper	4	F	7	0	1	0	5,265
Ginnypoo	3	F	6	2	0	0	19,436
Ginny's Queen	3	F	3	1	0	0	13,780
Gino Massetti	3	G	11	2	1	1	29,798
Ginontherocks	7	H	1	0	0	0	0
Gins Award	4	F	2	0	0	0	80
Gins Majesty	2	F	2	0	0	0	440
Gin's Rebelette	3	F	1	0	0	0	0
Ginseng King	9	G	6	0	0	0	0
Ginstone	3	C	4	1	0	0	6,424
Ginzano	6	G	5	1	2	1	44,120
Gion	5	M	21	0	0	1	8,677
Giorono	3	C	2	1	0	0	6,955
Giovannetti	5	G	8	1	0	0	63,824
Gip Jr.	5	G	1	0	0	0	0
Gipp	5	G	5	0	0	0	3,048
Gipsy Limits	3	F	12	3	0	3	41,470
Gipsy's Noactor	5	G	5	0	0	0	259
Girard	5	G	19	1	1	5	18,261
Girded	6	M	4	0	1	2	1,100
Girl Cat	2	F	4	1	0	1	13,360
Girl Fever	4	G	9	2	0	1	36,940
Girl From Harvard	5	M	4	0	0	0	72
Girl Gone Bye Bye	3	F	1	0	0	0	0
Girl Gone Crazy	3	F	4	0	0	0	315
Girl Gone West	2	F	2	1	0	0	13,940
Girl Gone Wild	4	F	5	0	0	0	380
Girl Hunter	3	G	2	0	0	0	0
Girl in the Grove	2	F	5	0	0	0	1,410
Girl On Go	3	F	12	1	4	3	43,480
Girl Reporter	4	F	10	0	0	2	3,580
Girl Secrets	3	F	15	5	1	4	63,865
Girl Talk	7	M	9	2	1	0	16,460
Girl Warrior	3	F	6	2	0	0	57,320
Girlfriend C.	4	F	3	0	0	0	70
Girlish Giggle	3	F	10	3	1	3	40,453
Girl's At Play	3	F	7	0	1	0	11,462
Girl's Best Friend	3	G	14	2	2	2	48,580
Girls First Love	7	M	8	2	0	2	6,933
Girls' Glory	4	F	13	0	0	0	3,229
Girl's Got Rhythm	3	F	10	1	3	1	12,070
Girls Got Skills	3	F	17	2	3	3	19,200
Girls Rule	3	F	8	0	0	0	686
Girlsintheoffice	3	F	8	3	2	0	61,220

Horse	Age	Sex	Sts	1st	2d	3d	Won
Girly Girl	2	F	2	0	0	0	3,480
Girusol	4	F	13	3	3	3	44,020
Gisellous	3	F	11	2	1	6	59,735
Gist	5	M	1	0	0	0	0
Gist of Art	7	G	16	2	1	1	37,301
Gitalong Jim	3	G	9	0	1	2	3,152
Gitano Dancer (ARG)	10	G	2	0	0	0	450
Gitem Willie	4	F	1	0	0	0	0
Gitgo	3	G	6	1	0	0	8,355
Gitngo Star	9	G	12	0	0	0	940
Giuseppe's Champ	5	G	9	0	1	1	11,170
Giuseppe's Majesty	6	G	11	2	1	0	16,120
Giuseppe's Ole Pal	4	G	10	0	0	0	2,022
Giuseppe's Turn	4	C	3	0	0	0	0
Give and Take	5	M	14	1	0	6	44,580
Give Faith	3	C	5	1	1	0	52,954
Give God the Glory	5	M	2	0	1	0	1,582
Give Me a Double	5	H	10	3	3	0	42,163
Give Me a Lite	2	G	6	0	1	3	7,750
Give Me a Shot	2	G	3	0	0	0	450
Give Me a Smoke	3	C	1	0	0	0	0
Give Me an Inch	2	C	1	0	0	0	3,420
Give Me Luck	3	F	7	1	0	2	7,382
Give Me the Money	7	G	2	0	0	0	122
Give Me Victory	4	G	13	0	2	2	8,385
Give Up the Cash	5	G	12	1	1	1	17,035
Give Ya What I Got	2	F	3	0	0	0	780
Givemeatri	5	M	12	4	0	1	43,067
Givemeawink	3	G	8	0	1	2	4,668
Givememore (BRZ)	3	F	1	1	0	0	24,000
Givemesomegoodnews	3	G	9	0	1	1	17,679
Givemethejackpot	3	C	1	0	0	0	130
Givemethemine	5	M	4	0	0	0	0
Givemethreedimes	6	G	13	6	3	0	74,845
Givemethreesteps	4	F	8	0	0	1	2,018
Givemyregardstotim	4	G	3	0	0	0	127
Given Probation	3	G	8	1	0	0	11,430
Given to Fly	6	H	1	0	0	0	0
Givensilver	4	G	11	2	1	3	40,174
Givetheboyacigar	4	G	13	0	1	2	11,090
Giving	7	M	6	0	0	1	720
Giving Orders	4	G	11	3	3	0	12,543
Giving Tree	4	G	8	2	1	0	39,060
Givonna S	4	F	1	0	0	0	168
Glace	6	M	3	0	0	0	309
Glace Queen (NZ)	5	M	4	0	0	0	0
Glacial Victoire	4	F	3	0	0	1	3,300
Glacier Gal	4	F	7	3	0	0	26,530
Glacier Point	8	G	14	4	1	3	24,675
Glaciers End	5	H	2	1	0	0	26,520
Glacken	4	G	10	2	1	2	36,280
Glacken Bird	2	F	8	0	0	1	5,055
Glad as Knight	3	F	9	1	1	0	18,355
Glad Hunter (GER)	4	G	3	0	0	0	3,740
Glad It's Holly	4	F	9	1	2	0	14,838
Glad Mary	2	F	1	0	0	1	2,915
Glad Tidings	7	G	16	1	3	3	8,783
Glad to Be a Lady	4	F	10	1	5	2	15,353
Glad You Dance	3	C	10	1	0	0	7,350
Glade Hunter	3	G	9	1	0	0	9,689
Gladiator Guy	3	G	18	1	1	0	9,786
Gladiator Queen	3	F	9	2	1	2	114,880
Gladiator's Battle	4	G	3	1	0	0	1,980
Gladiators Consort	3	F	9	1	1	0	13,539
Gladiator's Drift	4	F	7	0	0	1	11,094
Gladiator's Gold	4	C	11	1	2	0	10,311
Gladyougottoseeme	4	F	2	0	0	0	0
Gladys Friday	3	F	5	1	1	0	7,215
Gladys G	3	F	5	0	0	0	482
Gladys Pembroke	4	F	13	1	2	0	9,476
Glamdring	5	G	11	1	3	3	37,431
Glamorama	4	F	2	0	1	1	3,590
Glamorize	4	F	12	3	3	2	31,057
Glamorous Life	5	M	7	0	0	2	7,410
Glamour Cat	3	F	5	0	2	2	26,960
Glamour Puss	4	F	8	1	0	0	9,835
Glamourus Affair	4	F	5	1	0	1	5,112
Glance Remark	7	G	10	2	1	2	40,098
Glance Wink Smile	4	F	11	2	0	1	21,982
Glarenmore	4	G	10	2	3	2	28,859
Glaring Ego	4	F	11	0	1	2	5,723
Glaring for a Win	3	G	4	0	0	0	966
Glaring Invader	3	G	5	0	1	2	6,358
Glaring Keyhole	4	C	5	0	1	0	1,850
Glasgow	2	F	1	0	1	0	6,600
Glass and Glow	4	G	13	1	1	0	8,548
Glass Petal	2	F	10	0	2	2	11,360
Glass Trick	2	C	9	1	2	2	23,846
Glassy	3	F	5	1	2	0	45,800
Glassy Act	2	G	4	1	3	0	37,870
Glastonbury	3	F	9	2	1	0	13,167
Gleam Supreme	5	G	10	0	1	2	4,114
Gleaming Looker	3	F	4	0	0	0	288
Glean	7	G	5	0	1	0	12,100
Gleana	2	F	6	3	0	2	24,840
Glee	4	F	8	1	0	2	23,870
Gleeful King	4	G	6	0	0	1	2,000
Gleeful Kleven	4	F	4	0	0	1	2,130
Gleeful Tyler	4	G	11	0	0	2	1,322
Gleichen Reserve	6	M	6	2	1	1	31,730
Glen Canyon	3	G	6	3	1	0	31,335
Glen Conscience	4	F	9	0	2	0	1,252
Glencairn	4	G	8	0	0	1	5,770
Glencreek	7	G	9	3	2	0	16,075
Glenda Kay	4	F	8	1	0	0	9,136
Glendale Lane	4	G	2	0	1	0	1,995
Glenleary	3	G	10	1	1	3	15,265
Glenmalure	3	C	4	0	0	1	6,930
Glenmars Addiction	4	G	3	0	0	1	1,001
Glenmary	5	M	9	1	2	1	5,709
Glennascaul	3	F	8	1	0	1	13,139
Glenners	3	G	8	1	0	1	12,360
Glennon	3	C	7	0	2	0	16,730
Glenoak	3	G	6	2	0	1	16,515
Glenora	2	F	5	0	2	0	6,016
Glenrothes	2	C	5	0	1	0	4,115
Glens Devil Due	7	G	10	2	0	0	10,368
Glens Friend	2	G	2	1	0	0	11,113
Glen's Love	6	G	8	0	0	1	1,688
Glens Muffin	3	G	8	0	0	1	1,594
Glenville Dottie	6	M	1	0	0	0	0
Glenwood Springs	6	G	13	1	2	1	7,697
Glick	8	H	8	3	2	0	160,960
Glide Path	2	F	7	0	2	0	3,795
Glides Emigrant	8	G	13	0	1	2	13,654
Gliding Dancer	10	G	2	0	1	0	2,640
Glifter	4	F	3	1	0	0	8,940
Glimmer Twin	4	F	6	0	1	1	10,520
Glimmering Cat	4	F	5	0	1	2	4,970
Glimmering Moon	3	G	8	0	2	0	9,565
Glimpse	4	C	9	2	1	1	23,550
Glimpse of Glamour	4	F	5	1	0	2	5,617
Glint	5	H	4	0	1	0	5,317
Glint Eastward	7	G	1	0	0	0	40
Glisten	3	F	2	0	0	0	2,330
Glister Girl	3	F	2	0	0	0	400
Glit	9	G	8	2	2	4	8,820
Glitter Act	4	F	6	1	1	1	41,390
Glitter All Over	5	G	3	0	0	0	285
Glitter Baby	6	M	11	0	2	0	6,118
Glitter Bit	2	C	5	0	0	0	165
Glitter Cat	5	G	13	1	3	4	21,189
Glitter Copy	3	F	10	1	2	2	7,837
Glitter Cove	4	F	10	1	2	5	18,775
Glitter in Blue	4	G	12	1	4	3	41,150
Glitter Jane	3	F	12	0	1	1	1,256
Glitter Lil Star	4	F	8	2	0	0	10,140
Glitter Maid	4	F	10	3	3	0	31,360
Glitter Me	2	F	1	0	0	1	5,160
Glitter Mean	4	G	10	2	2	2	53,792
Glitter n Glimmer	14	G	3	0	0	2	2,500
Glitter of Hope	5	G	11	2	2	1	10,960
Glitter Point	4	G	18	2	3	2	20,984
Glitter Queen	3	F	7	0	1	3	19,710
Glitter Sexy	2	F	8	1	1	2	43,081
Glitter Slinky	3	F	8	0	1	1	8,280
Glitter Star	2	F	1	0	0	1	2,079
Glitter Storm	4	G	3	0	0	0	144

Horse	Age	Sex	Sts	1st	2d	3d	Won
Glitter Time	4	F	1	0	0	0	0
Glitterama	4	G	3	0	0	0	220
Glitterati	3	C	12	3	1	0	50,454
Glitteration	3	F	7	0	3	1	37,380
Glitterbdancing	4	F	11	3	0	0	66,493
Glitterbend	5	G	7	1	0	1	4,910
Glittergem	3	C	8	0	0	2	12,158
Glittergroup	4	G	5	0	0	1	1,005
Glitterin' Gold	5	M	16	4	4	2	26,826
Glittering Betty	4	F	3	0	0	0	75
Glittering Chad	5	M	9	0	3	0	13,532
Glittering Jenna	8	M	13	0	1	4	2,130
Glittering Man	5	G	3	0	0	1	1,100
Glittering Pewter	3	G	15	0	4	0	6,647
Glittering Prize (FR)	3	F	2	0	0	0	123
Glittering Racket	5	M	11	4	0	0	68,470
Glittering Success	4	F	9	0	0	2	3,259
Glittering Tax	2	F	4	1	2	0	17,900
Glitterwan	4	C	2	1	0	0	7,905
Glittery	3	F	5	0	1	0	3,095
Glo and Go	7	G	1	0	0	0	40
Glo Most Hot	4	F	20	1	2	5	7,010
Gloat	6	H	2	0	1	0	3,200
Global Arena	3	G	18	1	4	3	15,718
Global Attraction	4	C	1	0	0	0	104
Global Dancer	4	F	7	2	1	1	14,615
Global Dream	6	G	4	1	1	0	6,663
Global Empire	4	G	10	2	2	1	40,540
Global Games	4	G	6	0	0	2	2,945
Global Image	5	M	11	1	2	1	13,546
Global Link	5	G	9	1	3	0	16,220
Global Quest	5	H	1	0	0	0	380
Global Tour	4	F	10	3	0	0	14,030
Global Trade	3	G	2	0	1	0	3,700
Global Trader	2	C	1	1	0	0	11,800
Global's Outlaw	11	G	4	0	0	1	983
Globe Fish	2	C	3	0	0	0	590
Globel Pine	3	C	8	1	0	2	23,200
Glok	10	G	1	0	0	0	135
Glorado	7	M	11	0	2	0	15,215
Gloria Gold Cross	5	M	5	0	0	1	1,354
Gloria Switch	2	F	7	0	0	0	3,630
Gloriababy	4	F	12	2	0	4	26,515
Gloried Dancer	2	F	11	5	1	1	72,640
Glorieta Pass	2	F	1	0	0	0	0
Gloriosa	5	M	4	1	0	0	21,920
Gloriosity	5	M	1	0	0	0	358
Glorious Again	4	F	9	3	3	2	86,148
Glorious Angel	8	G	6	0	0	0	666
Glorious Belle	11	M	6	0	0	0	280
Glorious Future	2	G	5	2	1	0	13,775
Glorious Jenna	4	F	10	2	0	1	28,280
Glorious Jet	7	M	4	0	0	0	140
Glorious Jo	5	M	6	1	1	0	7,130
Glorious King	5	G	15	1	1	4	21,970
Glorious Miss	4	F	3	2	0	1	57,220
Glorious Morn	3	F	9	2	3	2	21,240
Glorious Prospect	2	F	1	1	0	0	9,000
Glorious Quest	4	F	9	4	2	1	57,558
Glorious Raj	3	F	19	5	4	1	52,545
Glorious Ride	3	F	10	1	1	1	14,220
Glorious Survivor	3	G	3	0	0	0	0
Glorious Thunder	2	F	4	0	0	0	1,484
Glorious West	4	G	17	3	1	2	29,087
Glory and Faith	2	F	3	0	0	0	3,420
Glory and Power	2	F	2	0	1	0	4,400
Glory B Look At Me	2	F	1	0	0	0	70
Glory Ball	2	F	1	0	0	0	145
Glory Be Good	4	F	6	1	0	2	30,160
Glory Be to Winloc	4	G	7	1	0	1	23,852
Glory Brick	3	F	9	1	1	0	24,640
Glory Dance	3	C	2	1	0	0	5,676
Glory Dancer	2	F	4	0	1	0	4,993
Glory d'Or	6	G	14	2	2	5	20,075
Glory Glory Glory	3	F	4	0	0	0	517
Glory Hymn	4	G	6	1	1	0	15,410
Glory Jean	4	F	5	0	1	1	8,140
Glory Lane	3	F	1	1	0	0	13,680
Glory Me	3	F	2	0	0	0	265
Glory Morning	2	F	2	0	1	1	6,900
Glory N Truce	2	G	4	0	1	0	1,602
Glory of Love	5	M	7	1	0	3	35,180
Glory Ride	3	G	4	0	1	1	2,400
Glory Royale	4	F	7	0	0	1	11,455
Glory Run	3	F	5	1	2	1	14,640
Glory Star	2	F	3	0	0	0	210
Glory to God	3	F	1	0	0	0	135
Glory Win	3	F	4	1	0	0	6,545
Glory With Grace	8	G	1	0	0	0	285
Glorycourt	3	C	2	0	0	0	0
Glory's Ace	9	G	10	2	3	0	26,937
Glorys Gotcha	6	M	9	1	0	2	5,954
Glory's Memory	3	G	15	1	2	4	13,359
Glory's Wish	4	G	14	0	2	1	4,719
Glo's Moe	9	G	4	2	0	1	6,731
Glow Brook	5	M	9	1	0	0	9,245
Glow of Love	3	F	4	1	1	0	16,740
Glowbulette	6	M	11	0	2	2	3,464
Glowing Breeze	4	F	4	1	1	1	27,190
Glowing Brite	3	F	11	1	2	1	10,145
Glowing Charm	2	C	5	0	1	0	6,640
Glowing Discovery	3	F	12	2	2	0	8,532
Glowing Glory	2	F	2	0	0	0	750
Glowing Gold	7	G	5	0	0	1	698
Glowing Miss	5	M	10	1	4	0	17,479
Glowing Review	9	G	10	1	1	2	4,508
Glowing West	4	F	10	3	0	1	9,818
Glows Codetoo	6	G	13	0	2	3	4,905
Glynzatore	3	F	13	1	1	1	6,181
Gman Chris	3	G	3	0	0	1	630
Gmork	3	C	8	2	3	0	65,480
Gn. Group Meeting	2	F	2	1	1	0	25,600
Gnarl	12	G	6	0	0	0	560
Gnarler	6	H	6	0	2	0	6,170
Gnarly Charley	5	G	2	0	0	0	74
Gneiss Lady	3	F	14	1	1	1	34,294
Gneiss Limo	3	C	10	0	1	1	9,455
Gneiss Pick	3	F	7	1	0	0	12,420
Gnomes Star	6	G	3	0	1	0	2,580
Go Aloft Randy	6	G	3	0	0	0	205
Go America	3	C	1	0	1	0	4,000
Go Annika	3	F	20	2	2	4	32,440
Go Archie Go	3	C	2	0	0	1	1,092
Go Ask Daisy	3	F	7	0	1	2	33,704
Go Avie Go	4	G	3	2	0	0	7,790
Go Baby Geo	5	G	5	0	0	0	720
Go Baby Ice	4	F	3	1	0	0	31,660
Go Baby Slew	5	M	13	1	0	0	4,795
Go Bama Go	3	C	5	0	0	0	233
Go Bart Go	4	G	3	0	0	0	305
Go Bella Go	3	F	14	3	1	4	23,435
Go Big Blue	6	G	3	0	0	2	2,810
Go Bob (ARG)	4	C	1	0	1	0	9,200
Go Bon	2	C	4	1	0	0	28,230
Go Browns	5	G	11	2	0	2	23,708
Go Bubbles Go	5	M	10	0	1	2	1,760
Go Bux	11	G	7	2	0	0	7,378
Go Bye Bye	3	F	5	1	1	0	26,240
Go Caleb Go	2	G	6	0	0	0	4,750
Go Cassie Jo	5	M	11	3	2	3	26,825
Go Chilean Go	3	G	9	2	2	1	21,060
Go Chloe Go	5	M	1	0	0	0	103
Go Coyote Joe	2	C	1	0	0	0	400
Go Crystal Go	4	F	1	0	0	0	0
Go Derek Go	4	G	1	0	0	0	33
Go Devil Go	3	G	6	2	2	0	22,191
Go Directlyto Jail	3	C	14	2	7	2	65,540
Go Doctor Mo	4	G	8	2	0	1	10,576
Go Fernando Go	2	C	5	0	1	1	18,330
Go Fletch Libby	3	F	7	2	1	2	7,740
Go for Bust	4	G	16	3	4	1	34,623
Go for Diamonds	3	F	3	1	1	0	7,448
Go for Four	4	C	7	0	0	0	590
Go for Glitter	6	G	8	2	3	2	30,281
Go for Gray	2	C	4	1	1	0	12,380
Go for Kash	2	G	3	0	0	0	0
Go for Launch	5	M	12	0	2	3	7,488
Go for Leslie	6	M	13	3	3	1	14,066

Horse	Age	Sex	Sts	1st	2d	3d	Won
Go for Matty	3	F	9	3	2	1	29,834
Go for Now	4	G	11	1	2	2	25,948
Go for Puddin	7	M	5	1	0	0	16,500
Go for the Gals	4	G	16	1	2	1	12,615
Go for Twenty Five	3	C	2	0	0	0	90
Go Four Silver	4	F	2	0	0	0	360
Go Gavin Go	8	G	3	1	1	1	20,846
Go Get Em Harry	5	G	12	5	2	0	11,308
Go Girl Go	5	M	1	0	0	1	1,188
Go Girlfriend Go	3	F	10	2	1	1	23,311
Go Go Baby Go	5	M	5	1	0	0	49,178
Go Go Big Red	4	C	10	1	2	2	18,500
Go Go Get Em	6	G	2	0	0	0	0
Go Go Glory	3	F	3	0	0	1	1,333
Go Go Godzilla	2	F	1	0	0	0	105
Go Go Hasty	7	M	7	1	2	0	10,566
Go Go Leslie	5	M	2	0	1	0	1,625
Go Go Mary Jo	2	F	3	0	0	0	290
Go Go Neigh	2	F	2	0	0	0	1,710
Go Go Pete	5	G	10	0	0	0	670
Go Go Rachael	4	F	16	2	2	2	18,917
Go Go Tommy Joe	5	G	12	2	0	1	13,556
Go Go Wild	3	F	1	0	0	0	154
Go Grace Go	3	F	13	2	3	1	49,185
Go Grant Go	9	G	9	1	1	2	4,946
Go Gretta Go	3	F	1	0	0	0	500
Go Hailey Go	2	F	2	0	0	0	3,310
Go High	5	M	2	0	0	0	208
Go Honey Go	3	F	2	0	0	0	2,200
Go Jambalasa	5	G	8	2	0	1	24,373
Go Jeanaie Go	4	F	14	1	2	2	44,815
Go Jelly Bean Go	5	M	11	1	1	0	17,855
Go Jesse Tyler	5	H	1	0	0	0	420
Go Johnny Go	3	G	2	0	0	1	1,524
Go Joma	6	G	9	0	0	1	2,330
Go Karina	4	F	15	1	4	0	8,471
Go Kathy	2	F	4	0	0	0	3,528
Go Kitty Go	3	C	11	2	3	0	102,602
Go Lauren	3	F	10	0	1	0	3,541
Go Legs Go	5	G	10	3	1	0	62,150
Go Leroy Go	2	C	5	1	0	0	9,970
Go Lexi Go	2	F	3	1	1	0	15,570
Go Lib Go	7	G	2	0	0	0	0
Go Lionel Go	3	C	6	1	2	0	37,650
Go Lite Gold	6	G	13	0	0	0	132
Go Little Joe Go	4	G	9	1	1	3	7,900
Go Lively	10	G	6	2	0	0	2,776
Go Margo	4	F	9	2	1	0	15,050
Go Max Go	4	G	11	1	0	2	5,233
Go Mercy Go	5	H	10	0	1	0	1,825
Go Mike	6	G	3	1	0	0	1,062
Go Minerva Go	5	M	11	2	0	2	11,329
Go Miss Bag	4	F	9	1	0	3	31,830
Go Misty Go	2	F	1	0	0	0	216
Go Mitzie Go	3	F	9	0	1	0	2,153
Go Mr. Manner	3	G	2	0	0	0	0
Go Naz	6	G	4	0	0	0	0
Go Niner	5	M	16	2	1	2	17,580
Go North	4	G	8	1	0	0	32,262
Go Not Whoa	9	G	11	1	3	5	22,561
Go Now	3	C	14	2	5	2	112,543
Go On Baby	6	M	7	0	1	3	32,055
Go On Forever	7	H	6	0	1	1	4,312
Go On Green	5	G	7	1	0	1	14,350
Go On Orange	6	G	8	1	0	1	11,726
Go On Prince	5	G	4	0	0	0	0
Go On Red	5	H	1	0	0	0	80
Go Rail Go	6	G	7	0	0	1	4,952
Go Rene Go	2	F	2	0	0	0	142
Go Rhythm	4	G	2	0	0	0	0
Go Ricky Go	2	C	6	0	3	1	10,460
Go Robert Go	4	C	7	0	2	0	4,928
Go Roberta	5	M	6	0	0	0	0
Go Robin	3	F	8	2	3	1	108,775
Go Rockin' Robin	4	C	6	0	0	1	8,846
Go Rolls Go	6	G	1	0	0	0	73
Go Rose	4	F	8	2	1	1	41,570
Go Salem Go	7	G	1	0	0	0	0
Go Sebastian	4	C	3	0	0	0	0
Go See Michelle	4	F	8	1	0	0	28,153
Go Shefar	5	M	10	1	4	0	8,210
Go Shockers	3	G	5	0	0	0	315
Go Silver	2	F	4	1	1	1	36,270
Go Sis Go	7	M	2	0	1	0	375
Go Slew Go	3	G	14	2	0	1	7,314
Go Smokey Go	5	M	7	0	1	0	1,964
Go Star Buster	4	G	12	2	2	4	32,580
Go Steady	3	F	7	2	3	1	93,955
Go Steph Go	4	F	17	1	2	4	10,098
Go Surfer (IRE)	6	H	1	0	0	0	400
Go Tamer Go	3	F	2	0	0	0	0
Go Tell John	3	G	5	0	1	1	5,162
Go Tiff Go	4	F	9	0	0	0	1,291
Go to Harvard	6	G	12	0	1	1	3,169
Go to the City	2	G	5	1	1	1	23,050
Go to the Jungle	3	F	3	0	0	0	315
Go to the Sun	2	C	5	1	0	1	72,253
Go Tori Go	4	F	13	1	4	3	11,880
Go Went Gone	7	M	6	0	0	1	2,379
Go West Again	3	G	7	0	0	1	4,427
Go West Jenny	4	F	1	0	0	0	86
Go Wild	3	G	7	1	1	2	47,760
Go Wild Willie	2	G	5	1	1	1	5,648
Go Your Own Way	8	M	7	0	2	1	1,629
Go Yoyo	4	F	6	1	1	0	7,460
Go Zede Go	3	C	2	0	0	1	2,475
Goal	4	G	10	1	1	3	16,665
Goal Post	3	C	9	0	1	2	27,070
Goat Pick Runner	3	G	4	0	0	0	0
Goaway Doctor	5	G	1	0	0	0	0
Gobber	5	G	11	3	1	1	14,674
Gobi Dan	5	G	9	0	4	2	26,840
God Bless Slew	2	F	1	0	0	0	161
God of Thunder	2	G	1	0	0	0	105
Godchild	6	G	10	1	0	2	12,316
Goddard	5	G	4	0	1	0	2,252
Goddess Athena	5	M	18	2	2	5	35,515
Goddess of Love	2	F	4	0	2	0	13,468
Godiva'n Champagne	4	F	14	0	3	3	3,128
Godot	3	G	4	0	0	0	0
Gods Ear	4	F	6	0	0	2	14,731
God's Little Girl	4	F	3	0	1	0	1,550
God's Promice	7	H	4	0	0	0	204
Godsandodds	3	F	4	0	0	0	559
Godsend	4	G	8	3	0	1	37,395
Goer Wart	4	C	4	0	2	1	6,685
Goes	2	C	9	1	5	0	58,611
Gofortheroses	2	F	4	0	0	1	3,760
Gogarrettgo	6	G	7	2	1	0	7,144
Gogarty's Way	5	G	10	1	3	1	14,217
Gogo Lilly	4	F	10	0	1	0	3,711
Gogogadget	2	G	5	0	0	3	9,755
Gohalo	4	G	17	2	0	3	22,093
Goin Deep	7	G	17	1	4	2	7,037
Goin' Down Town	3	C	8	1	1	1	15,881
Goin N Style	5	G	6	0	1	0	2,148
Goin On Faith	4	F	1	0	0	0	750
Goin Savin	4	C	5	1	0	0	9,120
Goin' Tap City	3	G	13	2	3	1	32,279
Goin' to Reno	9	M	6	0	0	0	440
Going Again	4	F	14	0	3	0	5,679
Going Away	3	F	3	0	1	2	9,290
Going Boldly	6	G	6	0	0	0	936
Going Commando	4	C	3	0	0	0	1,155
Going for Broke	5	G	3	0	0	0	75
Going for Two	5	G	8	0	0	1	950
Going Going Going	4	F	2	0	0	0	0
Going Going Gone	4	G	1	0	0	0	510
Going Hollywood	3	F	2	0	0	0	254
Going Home	2	F	1	0	0	0	400
Going On Again	2	F	11	2	1	3	44,640
Going Out Playin	3	F	7	1	0	0	7,040
Going Round	5	G	13	2	0	0	7,555
Going Sober	2	C	1	0	0	0	0
Going to Saratoga	4	C	1	0	0	0	35
Going Wild	2	C	4	1	2	1	46,900
Going Zarb	2	C	1	0	0	0	0
Gojaz	3	F	1	0	0	0	0

Horse	Age	Sex	Sts	1st	2d	3d	Won
Gojoetu	4	C	7	1	2	2	12,813
Golani (IRE)	7	H	8	1	0	0	9,000
Golazo	3	C	5	1	0	0	10,825
Golconda	5	G	10	1	1	2	25,460
Gold Accent	3	F	8	1	6	0	44,200
Gold Act	4	G	13	2	1	2	9,584
Gold Adventure	4	G	12	1	3	0	37,115
Gold and Crystal	3	C	9	0	3	2	17,810
Gold and Roses	2	G	4	0	2	0	18,568
Gold Aqua	5	H	13	1	2	1	9,449
Gold At Last	5	M	8	0	1	1	2,280
Gold Attache	5	G	10	1	3	0	47,708
Gold Baby Gold	4	F	1	0	0	0	124
Gold Bag	2	F	1	0	0	0	0
Gold Band	4	F	2	1	0	0	16,300
Gold Bankers Gold	3	G	11	1	1	2	50,173
Gold Bars	5	G	4	3	0	0	15,210
Gold Beat	5	G	4	0	0	1	1,160
Gold Bidder	8	G	12	1	3	1	17,090
Gold Binder	4	F	5	2	1	0	10,929
Gold Blue	5	G	18	2	1	1	22,950
Gold Boot	3	G	5	0	1	1	4,650
Gold Bowl	2	F	4	0	2	0	9,480
Gold Bridle	2	C	2	1	0	0	8,595
Gold Buckle Dreams	3	G	4	1	0	0	2,030
Gold Bug	2	F	2	0	0	0	145
Gold Bull	6	G	1	0	0	0	0
Gold Bunch	3	F	8	1	0	1	4,891
Gold Butter	4	F	14	3	4	2	49,925
Gold by Design	4	F	14	5	0	3	38,627
Gold by Gold	3	G	4	1	1	0	8,424
Gold by Jove	2	F	2	0	0	0	600
Gold Cake	3	G	3	0	0	0	0
Gold Case Motel	2	F	4	1	1	0	13,095
Gold Case Pleasure	4	C	2	0	0	0	0
Gold Casing	2	C	2	0	2	0	10,080
Gold Chance	2	C	2	0	0	0	1,200
Gold Charade	5	G	15	2	1	4	17,238
Gold Circle	7	G	10	2	1	0	10,529
Gold City Slew	5	H	6	1	3	0	13,706
Gold Clara	4	F	14	4	1	0	28,396
Gold Cluster	3	C	14	4	0	1	61,090
Gold Commander One	4	G	14	2	3	4	27,196
Gold Conquest	3	C	5	0	0	2	3,810
Gold Covergirl	5	M	3	0	0	0	1,018
Gold Crazy	4	F	4	0	1	0	2,175
Gold Crewman	3	G	9	1	0	1	10,760
Gold Crusader	7	G	11	1	4	2	8,713
Gold Cuff Links	2	G	3	0	0	0	800
Gold Dancer	3	F	13	2	3	2	92,980
Gold Dealer	6	G	3	0	0	0	0
Gold Desert Wind	10	G	9	2	1	1	2,628
Gold Deville	2	F	5	2	0	0	13,050
Gold Dial	6	G	12	2	1	1	10,660
Gold Digger Gal	4	F	13	2	2	3	21,785
Gold Diggin Darlin	4	F	2	0	0	0	0
Gold Diggin Devil	2	F	7	0	2	0	4,210
Gold Diggin Lova	3	F	4	0	0	1	3,400
Gold Dollar	5	H	12	2	1	4	111,660
Gold Dot Supreme	4	F	17	0	0	2	6,332
Gold Earring	3	F	3	0	0	0	500
Gold Ending	2	G	4	0	2	1	8,450
Gold Envoy	4	G	9	1	1	1	19,557
Gold Expedition	2	C	2	0	2	0	4,590
Gold Explorer	4	G	14	0	1	0	14,344
Gold Fabuleux	5	M	12	0	3	0	6,529
Gold Falstaff	3	G	8	2	0	0	9,495
Gold Felt Blue	4	G	4	1	1	1	43,226
Gold Fevers Gift	6	H	11	5	1	2	9,308
Gold Flinger	3	F	13	3	2	1	63,750
Gold Folley	3	F	6	0	1	0	1,675
Gold Foot	3	F	1	0	0	0	0
Gold for Andrew	3	G	8	2	0	0	20,448
Gold for Canada	4	F	9	2	1	1	24,626
Gold for Ghost	5	G	13	2	1	2	8,591
Gold for Me	5	M	9	2	2	0	22,485
Gold for Nina	2	F	5	0	2	1	12,760
Gold Format	2	G	2	0	0	0	800
Gold Forum	3	G	18	0	1	1	4,050
Gold Fun	3	C	6	2	0	0	13,197
Gold Fuse	3	C	6	2	0	1	35,700
Gold Garters	4	F	5	2	3	0	37,600
Gold Ginny	3	F	11	3	2	0	73,590
Gold Glory Won	4	G	12	1	0	0	11,015
Gold Gold Gold	5	M	5	0	2	2	10,900
Gold Goose	4	C	15	1	4	4	21,825
Gold Gunner	3	C	10	2	0	1	69,686
Gold Harvest	9	G	2	0	0	0	82
Gold Honey	3	F	1	0	0	0	0
Gold Hornet	3	G	7	0	0	4	12,420
Gold Hunt	5	M	9	0	1	2	5,815
Gold Ice	3	F	1	0	0	0	0
Gold in the Bank	2	G	6	1	0	0	7,200
Gold Inside	3	G	15	1	0	1	8,900
Gold Irish	5	M	7	0	1	1	3,771
Gold Jigger	2	G	3	0	1	0	2,900
Gold Joy	2	C	6	2	1	1	110,002
Gold Justice	4	G	9	0	0	1	2,151
Gold Kat	7	M	3	0	0	0	255
Gold Khalifa	3	F	5	1	0	0	41,376
Gold Kingdom	3	G	12	0	2	1	6,300
Gold Lace	3	F	6	0	0	2	3,878
Gold Lad	3	G	4	1	0	1	9,250
Gold Lady	4	F	2	0	0	0	0
Gold Lane	2	C	5	0	2	0	3,470
Gold Like U	3	F	6	2	0	3	66,540
Gold Limericks	9	G	2	0	0	0	0
Gold Linkage	5	M	2	0	0	0	288
Gold Lode	2	F	3	0	0	0	1,574
Gold Luck Go Baby	2	C	6	1	0	0	10,350
Gold Lure	3	F	3	1	1	0	23,920
Gold Mace	4	G	1	0	0	0	140
Gold Magic	3	C	2	0	0	0	640
Gold Margarita	3	F	8	2	1	2	54,190
Gold Medal Winner	2	C	4	0	1	0	5,250
Gold Meister	2	C	4	0	0	1	3,455
Gold Melody	3	F	5	1	1	0	29,870
Gold Meteor	4	G	4	1	1	0	36,188
Gold Mind	6	M	17	1	1	3	12,391
Gold Mine	5	H	2	0	0	0	0
Gold Mine Ops	2	G	5	0	0	3	3,455
Gold Minister	2	C	2	0	1	0	9,313
Gold Mint	2	C	1	0	0	0	460
Gold Miss	4	F	7	0	0	0	120
Gold Mitten	4	F	6	2	2	0	45,000
Gold Moon	3	F	2	0	1	0	1,674
Gold N Fancy	5	M	12	2	1	0	28,495
Gold 'n Harvest	3	F	11	1	0	2	18,395
Gold N Hollywood	5	M	1	0	0	0	0
Gold N Jade	4	G	10	2	2	1	6,285
Gold N Leeroyal	8	G	9	1	1	2	11,380
Gold N Nickle	2	G	8	1	1	1	8,180
Gold N Silver Wind	4	G	7	0	2	0	7,595
Gold Not Diamonds	5	M	13	2	1	0	10,368
Gold Notebook	3	F	3	0	1	1	5,430
Gold Opera	4	G	4	0	1	1	9,270
Gold Options	8	G	7	3	1	1	13,170
Gold Panic	3	G	13	2	1	0	13,283
Gold Panning Annie	3	F	8	0	0	0	0
Gold Patrol	3	G	1	0	0	0	405
Gold Pearl	6	G	7	0	1	1	3,100
Gold Pence	3	F	2	0	0	0	0
Gold Penny	6	M	9	0	1	3	2,542
Gold Pentelicus	3	G	1	0	0	0	130
Gold Performer	2	F	5	0	0	1	4,830
Gold Play	5	G	13	2	0	0	7,272
Gold Player	4	F	9	1	1	2	52,890
Gold Prize	2	G	2	0	0	1	1,205
Gold Pursuit	4	G	9	1	1	0	5,285
Gold Pyrite	4	C	9	0	0	0	264
Gold Quill	2	F	2	2	0	0	38,700
Gold Ray	4	C	8	1	0	1	3,798
Gold Regal	3	G	3	0	0	1	3,560
Gold Relaunch	2	C	3	0	0	1	1,192
Gold Reserve	3	G	12	2	1	5	57,310
Gold Rhapsody	2	F	5	0	1	1	5,303
Gold Ringer	3	F	3	0	1	0	8,245
Gold Rocket	8	G	3	0	0	0	144

Horse	Age	Sex	Sts	1st	2d	3d	Won
Gold Ruckus	6	G	12	1	2	4	139,920
Gold Run Type	4	F	12	3	3	1	46,970
Gold Rush Banker	2	G	3	0	1	0	2,613
Gold Rush Jones	3	C	6	2	1	1	30,487
Gold Scammer	5	M	12	2	2	2	28,756
Gold Scepter	5	M	12	4	2	1	38,626
Gold Search	4	C	2	0	2	0	8,680
Gold Secret	4	F	6	0	0	1	3,554
Gold Seize	4	G	6	1	0	0	2,760
Gold Sensation	7	G	3	0	0	0	130
Gold Sequence (PER)	5	H	2	0	0	0	0
Gold Shadeed	5	H	23	3	4	2	46,978
Gold Shaker	2	F	1	0	0	0	0
Gold Shield	3	C	11	2	1	2	48,150
Gold Shoes	3	G	11	3	3	2	61,326
Gold Sign	4	F	9	0	2	3	4,538
Gold Silks	2	C	1	1	0	0	9,000
Gold Slew	3	G	6	1	1	2	14,415
Gold Sneaker	4	C	13	2	1	0	9,236
Gold Song	4	G	10	1	1	3	15,840
Gold Spike	3	F	7	2	0	3	39,340
Gold Spot	3	F	12	2	3	3	16,430
Gold Squall	3	G	21	0	2	5	5,594
Gold Star Gal	2	F	4	0	0	0	150
Gold Star Gum	4	F	12	0	0	4	2,526
Gold Storm	4	C	8	3	1	2	207,300
Gold Stormy	3	G	5	1	1	1	4,550
Gold Strike	2	F	3	2	1	0	51,592
Gold Sunset	4	G	9	1	1	1	13,462
Gold Taker	5	G	2	1	0	0	7,200
Gold Tango	5	H	4	2	0	1	42,925
Gold Trick	7	H	6	0	0	0	627
Gold Twine	5	G	8	1	1	1	9,610
Gold Vault	4	F	7	3	2	1	104,400
Gold Vision	4	G	6	2	0	1	13,760
Gold Wager	3	F	3	0	0	1	896
Gold Way West	3	G	11	2	2	3	41,560
Gold Will	3	F	10	2	0	6	37,230
Gold Winger	3	C	4	0	0	0	176
Gold Wings	6	H	9	2	0	3	36,865
Gold With Honor	2	F	1	0	0	0	355
Gold Zapper	3	G	12	1	4	0	87,871
Goldalmighty	3	G	6	1	0	0	8,075
Goldberg	6	H	11	0	1	2	1,414
Goldberger	3	F	8	2	1	2	40,040
Goldbrook	2	F	8	0	1	0	6,230
Goldbuster	9	G	3	0	0	0	0
Goldcappedtooth	4	G	3	0	0	0	113
Goldcardmember	3	G	8	0	3	4	8,334
Goldchild	8	G	5	0	0	0	770
Golddigger Beware	4	F	10	5	2	1	111,795
Golden Acorn	4	C	8	1	2	1	18,600
Golden Affirmation	4	G	12	0	2	2	6,577
Golden Agenda	2	C	1	0	0	1	1,430
Golden Alabama	2	G	3	0	2	0	4,335
Golden Amigo	2	G	4	0	1	0	4,200
Golden Appeal	4	F	12	2	1	1	10,550
Golden Approval	7	G	9	1	1	0	15,869
Golden Archer	2	C	3	0	0	0	1,580
Golden Arm	6	G	3	1	0	0	5,700
Golden Arrow	5	H	7	1	2	1	75,659
Golden Aura	3	F	11	1	2	0	19,180
Golden Authority	4	F	12	1	0	2	11,713
Golden Bag	5	G	5	1	1	1	10,257
Golden Ballerina	3	F	3	0	0	0	1,710
Golden Barbi	4	F	4	0	0	0	72
Golden Barroness	3	F	6	1	0	0	4,693
Golden Bee	3	F	10	0	4	3	22,155
Golden Bid	6	M	8	4	2	2	22,950
Golden Blaise	4	G	4	1	1	1	38,140
Golden Blue Chip	3	G	8	0	1	2	3,319
Golden Bonus	6	G	9	2	1	1	68,900
Golden Brass	3	F	9	1	0	1	7,526
Golden Brook	5	G	3	1	0	0	3,711
Golden Butte	4	F	8	1	1	1	16,555
Golden Buzz	3	G	13	1	0	2	15,980
Golden Cab	5	M	2	0	0	0	0
Golden Carousel	6	M	10	0	0	3	5,974
Golden Ciara	4	F	1	0	0	0	0
Golden Coin	4	F	15	4	4	1	38,990
Golden Commander	4	G	8	2	1	3	133,149
Golden Concern	6	M	3	0	0	0	253
Golden Contender	6	G	4	1	0	2	34,850
Golden Corner	5	M	4	0	0	0	72
Golden Corsage	4	F	9	1	2	1	57,212
Golden Count	7	G	15	1	1	0	9,415
Golden Courtney	3	F	7	1	0	2	11,977
Golden Damsel	4	F	4	0	1	0	25,451
Golden Decree	6	G	5	0	0	1	2,552
Golden Defense	2	C	1	0	0	0	0
Golden Demand	2	F	4	1	0	0	12,435
Golden Derek	3	G	9	1	3	0	54,864
Golden Dewdrop	3	F	4	1	1	0	12,360
Golden Diamond	3	C	15	3	3	3	72,832
Golden Dinner	7	G	14	2	2	1	12,930
Golden Diva	3	F	9	2	2	0	39,292
Golden Doc	3	G	4	0	0	0	315
Golden Dollar	6	M	4	0	0	0	513
Golden Donn	3	C	6	0	0	1	5,275
Golden Door	5	G	9	1	2	1	11,600
Golden Dragon (FR)	4	F	1	0	0	0	0
Golden Dragon (GB)	6	G	5	1	1	0	51,440
Golden Drive	3	G	6	1	0	1	8,634
Golden Eclipse	3	F	1	0	0	0	0
Golden Ellen	4	F	9	0	0	1	6,560
Golden Embers	4	G	4	0	0	0	3,034
Golden Empress	5	M	2	0	0	0	0
Golden Eyes	7	M	3	0	0	0	186
Golden Fable	6	G	6	2	0	1	17,910
Golden Fifty	4	C	8	0	0	0	688
Golden Foil	7	H	9	1	0	1	9,947
Golden Gatita	3	F	5	1	0	2	18,190
Golden Gator	3	C	9	2	2	3	77,090
Golden Genes	8	M	3	1	2	0	8,945
Golden Glacken	5	G	9	2	1	1	30,250
Golden Glen	3	C	10	3	2	1	112,301
Golden Glint	4	F	11	1	4	0	6,042
Golden Gloves	5	M	10	0	1	0	4,740
Golden Glow Two	4	F	15	2	0	1	27,981
Golden Goddess	2	F	1	0	0	0	370
Golden Grace	4	F	3	0	0	0	0
Golden Grail	3	C	1	1	0	0	8,100
Golden Griffin	4	G	4	1	1	0	972
Golden Gump	3	G	1	0	0	1	220
Golden Hair	3	F	6	1	2	0	10,880
Golden Halo	6	M	12	2	2	2	43,707
Golden Hare	5	H	6	0	1	1	14,240
Golden Heiress	2	F	2	0	0	0	0
Golden Heritage	3	G	2	0	0	0	0
Golden Hex	2	C	4	0	0	0	420
Golden Hit	6	G	5	0	0	0	225
Golden Hunt	2	C	4	1	2	0	28,761
Golden Idol	3	G	11	2	2	2	41,234
Golden Intelect	4	F	8	1	0	4	15,432
Golden Irish Belle	2	F	3	0	0	0	840
Golden Izzy	3	F	11	1	4	1	10,881
Golden Jackie	5	M	5	0	0	0	317
Golden Jet Eye	5	G	12	1	2	0	8,109
Golden Jewel	3	F	12	0	5	2	49,308
Golden Judith	2	F	2	0	0	0	165
Golden K K	4	F	11	0	2	2	39,974
Golden Karats	8	M	13	3	1	2	7,040
Golden Laces	2	C	5	1	0	1	16,700
Golden Lark	6	M	3	0	0	0	423
Golden Legacy	5	M	8	3	2	2	14,823
Golden Lies	4	G	7	0	0	0	693
Golden Lightning	6	G	7	0	2	1	6,065
Golden Lion	3	F	5	0	0	0	3,120
Golden Locket	2	F	1	0	0	0	205
Golden Look	3	C	7	2	1	0	84,900
Golden Loom	4	F	4	1	0	1	3,150
Golden Loretta	3	F	6	1	1	0	5,331
Golden Lou	4	F	2	0	0	0	682
Golden Louisia	4	F	6	2	0	0	11,010
Golden Malibu	2	F	5	3	0	1	87,610
Golden Man	2	G	8	2	1	1	21,020
Golden Mark	3	C	6	2	1	0	27,922
Golden Marlin	4	F	9	1	4	3	115,302

Horse	Age	Sex	Sts	1st	2d	3d	Won
Golden Matter	3	C	6	0	0	0	110
Golden Mercy	5	G	1	0	0	0	0
Golden Mira	4	F	11	1	1	0	6,307
Golden Mirror	2	F	4	1	0	0	14,100
Golden Moon	6	M	10	0	3	0	11,729
Golden Motion	3	F	2	0	0	1	820
Golden Move	2	C	2	0	0	0	2,435
Golden Myrrh	3	F	8	1	1	0	4,800
Golden Niblet	4	G	11	2	3	3	26,171
Golden Nicolas	8	G	17	3	3	1	32,288
Golden Niner	2	F	1	0	0	1	2,300
Golden Nugget	5	G	7	0	0	1	1,093
Golden O Boy	4	G	4	0	0	0	268
Golden Oak	5	G	14	2	1	1	23,789
Golden Oldie	8	H	7	0	1	0	9,054
Golden Opal	3	F	1	0	0	0	0
Golden O's	7	G	11	2	0	0	10,189
Golden Palate	3	F	4	0	1	2	6,045
Golden Parachute	3	G	9	1	0	2	40,395
Golden Park	3	F	2	0	0	0	0
Golden Pass	7	G	3	0	1	0	5,160
Golden Passion	5	G	4	0	0	0	351
Golden Patriot	2	F	2	0	0	0	409
Golden Paul	7	G	15	0	1	2	2,085
Golden Penny	4	F	8	2	2	1	44,374
Golden Peppen	3	F	15	1	3	1	12,210
Golden Pet	5	C	21	3	0	3	11,520
Golden Po	3	F	20	1	5	6	31,580
Golden Prestige	4	F	7	0	1	0	4,109
Golden Profile	3	F	2	1	1	0	21,800
Golden Promises	3	G	5	0	0	0	240
Golden Prophecy	9	G	14	1	3	3	13,547
Golden Proposition	3	F	2	0	0	0	567
Golden Prospect	4	F	1	0	0	0	1,600
Golden Prune	5	H	2	1	0	1	14,980
Golden Pursuit	3	G	9	3	3	1	44,229
Golden Quest	3	F	1	0	0	0	0
Golden Rail	3	F	7	3	0	1	21,325
Golden Rainbow	2	G	6	1	4	1	47,790
Golden Raja	5	G	12	2	0	0	9,700
Golden Ram	5	G	6	0	0	0	183
Golden Reaction	3	G	10	4	1	0	19,287
Golden Reputashn	4	F	12	1	0	3	27,360
Golden Retablo	2	G	3	0	0	0	690
Golden Returns	8	H	6	1	2	0	16,374
Golden Robb	2	C	2	0	0	0	504
Golden Romance	4	F	3	0	0	1	1,755
Golden Romani	6	M	4	0	1	1	2,892
Golden Rula	3	F	7	0	2	4	4,920
Golden Rule (GB)	9	G	2	0	0	0	1,250
Golden Sands	3	C	3	0	0	0	458
Golden Scrambler	5	M	9	2	1	2	29,052
Golden Secret	2	F	1	0	0	0	100
Golden Seductress	3	F	4	0	0	0	5,380
Golden Serpent	5	M	10	3	1	1	9,540
Golden Sheriff	5	G	18	1	2	1	9,311
Golden Shine	2	C	2	1	0	0	28,380
Golden Slinkee	6	G	3	0	1	0	2,130
Golden Sludog	3	G	2	0	0	0	0
Golden Sonata	5	M	4	2	0	0	166,000
Golden Soup	4	G	1	0	0	0	400
Golden Souvenir	3	G	7	1	4	1	72,220
Golden Spats	5	G	10	3	1	0	11,775
Golden Spear	2	C	2	0	1	0	10,740
Golden Spur	4	C	11	2	1	2	44,760
Golden Starlight	4	G	4	2	0	0	24,978
Golden Sunshine	4	F	4	2	1	0	23,538
Golden Surge	5	G	7	0	0	2	1,080
Golden Swinger	3	F	10	1	2	1	13,525
Golden Symphony	4	F	2	0	0	0	0
Golden Taj	3	G	9	0	2	1	10,237
Golden Tangle	6	G	1	0	0	0	146
Golden Tango	3	F	6	2	0	0	28,980
Golden Tax	2	F	2	0	0	0	0
Golden Toast	3	F	3	0	0	1	3,707
Golden Tomorrow	4	F	11	0	0	2	2,914
Golden Tour	4	F	3	2	0	0	40,650
Golden Trail	4	G	11	2	2	0	6,745
Golden Trevally	5	M	8	0	1	1	26,115
Golden Tribute	2	F	1	0	0	0	300
Golden Trieste	2	C	4	0	1	0	3,449
Golden True	4	G	5	0	0	1	3,255
Golden Trumpet	3	F	5	1	0	1	10,960
Golden Trust	2	F	1	1	0	0	6,000
Golden Turquoise	8	G	12	4	1	3	17,842
Golden Twining	3	F	6	2	1	1	4,710
Golden Unbridled	4	G	4	0	1	0	5,140
Golden Union	2	C	7	1	1	1	29,753
Golden Value	3	F	2	0	0	0	0
Golden Verse	3	G	12	3	1	2	28,355
Golden Victory	6	H	5	1	1	2	13,420
Golden Victress	3	F	7	0	2	0	16,230
Golden Vintage	4	F	5	0	0	0	3,880
Golden Walk	6	M	6	0	5	0	23,986
Golden Wave	4	C	9	3	0	1	17,790
Golden Way	6	G	8	0	1	0	3,922
Golden Well	2	F	3	0	1	1	7,285
Golden Witness	2	F	1	0	0	0	135
Golden Works	4	F	7	2	3	0	14,520
Goldenalden's Card	5	G	8	4	0	0	22,825
Goldenberg's Gift	3	C	7	3	1	1	16,324
Goldendoon	4	F	1	0	0	0	0
Goldenmiranda's	2	C	12	2	2	4	35,519
Golder Than Gold	2	C	5	1	1	1	31,820
Goldfellow	5	G	9	1	1	3	11,405
Goldfingerstouch	2	C	2	1	0	0	17,074
Goldgivespleasure	5	G	11	0	1	3	4,084
Goldglovekid	4	G	14	3	2	0	40,945
Goldharbor Express	4	C	14	4	2	3	20,227
Goldhearted Kris	4	F	1	0	0	1	1,567
Goldiana	3	F	4	0	1	0	2,495
Goldian's Derby	7	G	1	0	0	0	0
Goldie Dancer	3	G	7	1	0	0	6,102
Goldie Joy	5	M	7	0	0	0	645
Goldie Rio	4	F	7	1	4	1	34,242
Goldie Tunes	3	F	4	0	0	1	839
Goldie's Baby	3	F	6	2	1	0	41,080
Goldie's Cat	3	F	12	2	3	3	73,405
Goldie's Gal	3	F	11	1	2	0	4,783
Goldies Legacy	4	C	1	0	0	0	400
Goldies Meeting	2	F	3	0	0	1	3,080
Goldie's Road	4	F	4	1	1	0	16,632
Goldilocks N Bear	4	F	7	0	1	1	7,270
Goldin Ocala	3	G	18	1	5	0	11,525
Goldin Pawn	4	G	9	1	1	0	21,168
Goldini	2	G	6	1	2	1	21,298
Goldinthevalley	3	G	10	1	0	0	7,250
Goldiscold	2	F	5	2	0	0	32,794
Goldleafed Mirror	4	F	12	4	2	1	73,746
Goldminers Gin	2	F	1	0	0	0	0
Gold'n Grandeur	7	G	12	1	1	4	10,530
Gold'n'regant	4	C	5	0	0	0	405
Goldon	4	C	4	1	1	1	13,147
Goldpricesrising	3	F	9	2	0	1	20,900
Goldrush Destiny	3	F	3	1	0	0	6,102
Goldrush Lady	2	F	5	1	0	1	13,445
Gold's First	5	G	3	0	0	0	130
Gold's General	5	G	1	0	0	0	0
Goldsatalking	5	M	7	2	1	2	11,030
Goldsboro	2	G	2	0	1	0	1,280
Goldscheider	2	C	2	1	0	0	6,510
Goldshy	3	G	7	1	0	0	2,267
Goldstar Night	5	M	7	0	0	3	2,918
Goldswhereyafindit	6	G	16	2	4	3	17,156
Goldtariat	3	G	2	0	0	0	0
Goldtogowith	4	F	2	0	0	0	990
Goldtoken Tristan	3	G	12	1	1	0	8,832
Goldust Wishes	2	G	3	0	0	0	2,158
Goldville Miss	5	M	3	0	0	0	150
Goldy Gulch	5	M	10	1	2	0	9,093
Goldy Rock	4	F	7	1	2	3	57,790
Goldzilla	3	C	1	0	0	0	0
Goldzinger	3	G	2	1	0	0	2,503
Golf Game	9	G	3	0	0	1	600
Golf Pro	4	G	6	0	1	1	970
Golfing Wench	2	F	5	1	2	0	36,430
Golly Gree	2	F	1	0	0	0	1,195
Golly Miss Molly	3	F	2	0	0	0	700

Horse	Age	Sex	Sts	1st	2d	3d	Won
Gollyitssunny	3	G	10	1	0	2	10,650
Golo	5	M	2	0	0	0	90
Golytely	2	F	4	0	0	0	2,850
Gomer	4	C	3	0	0	0	660
Gomiago	3	F	13	0	2	2	12,800
Gomissdoeny	3	F	6	0	0	0	1,038
Gomka	8	G	14	1	1	2	6,836
Gonandunit	6	M	8	1	1	1	11,010
Gondolieri (CHI)	5	G	3	0	1	0	26,000
Gondolier's Song	8	G	4	0	0	0	0
Gone an Done It	2	G	1	0	0	0	0
Gone Awry	5	M	16	0	1	1	2,972
Gone Bad	2	G	1	0	0	1	935
Gone Ballistic	4	G	6	1	0	0	15,880
Gone Bayou	3	G	6	1	0	0	2,590
Gone By	3	F	3	0	1	1	7,940
Gone Cattin	4	G	16	2	3	4	31,813
Gone Courting	8	G	5	2	0	0	13,699
Gone Crusading	4	G	2	0	0	0	720
Gone Dancing	3	G	2	0	0	0	0
Gone Dee	4	G	11	2	2	2	7,827
Gone Exclusive	4	F	3	1	0	0	21,600
Gone First	4	F	6	1	0	0	4,320
Gone Fishin	8	H	7	0	0	0	3,294
Gone for Christmas	4	F	1	0	0	0	360
Gone for Good	3	F	1	0	0	0	170
Gone for the Roses	4	F	6	1	2	1	13,705
Gone Golfing	3	F	9	1	4	0	40,055
Gone Hunting	6	G	16	0	3	5	11,497
Gone Impressive	3	F	2	0	0	0	360
Gone in a Whisper	3	F	2	0	0	1	904
Gone Mad	3	G	11	0	3	1	8,985
Gone Musical	5	M	1	0	0	0	450
Gone Off	5	G	6	2	0	0	11,625
Gone Party Hoppin	3	F	7	1	1	0	9,918
Gone Southwest	3	F	12	2	4	1	15,769
Gone to a Change	2	C	5	1	0	0	4,650
Gone to Be King	3	G	5	1	0	1	31,768
Gone to Boston	7	M	1	0	0	0	0
Gone to Church	2	F	1	1	0	0	11,520
Gone to College	2	F	2	0	0	0	2,500
Gone to Dixie	4	G	5	0	0	0	329
Gone to Maui	2	G	2	0	0	1	1,065
Gone to Paris	3	F	12	3	2	1	58,730
Gone to Party	4	F	9	0	3	1	30,635
Gone to War	4	G	6	0	1	2	17,996
Gone Western	2	F	9	1	2	1	46,243
Gone Whirlin	3	F	7	0	1	1	5,559
Gone Wish'in	3	G	13	3	0	1	20,407
Gone With the Win	5	G	9	0	1	1	9,785
Gonetorule	4	F	8	2	1	1	70,770
Gonetothedoctor	4	F	11	0	3	1	25,392
Gonetothelake	4	F	10	2	3	0	24,735
Gong	3	G	8	0	2	0	17,940
Gonna Be a Runner	3	C	3	0	0	0	405
Gonna Be Grand	4	G	8	2	1	1	11,406
Gonna Blow	2	G	3	0	1	0	4,830
Gonna Do	4	F	12	0	4	6	34,950
Gonna Gidder	4	G	5	1	0	0	4,772
Gonnabeapartofit	4	F	16	2	2	5	53,933
Gonnabeatchabald	4	G	6	0	0	0	576
Gonnabreakeven	2	F	1	0	0	0	180
Gonner	6	H	1	0	0	0	0
Goo Bye	4	F	6	0	1	0	6,128
Good and Crafty	2	F	5	0	0	2	7,100
Good and Fast	2	C	8	3	2	2	36,079
Good and Gone	4	F	9	1	0	2	18,405
Good and Hot	3	F	6	1	0	0	9,426
Good and Pesky	10	G	11	2	1	1	3,760
Good and Rough	2	F	2	0	0	0	780
Good Answer	7	H	5	0	0	0	1,598
Good as Gold	2	F	5	1	0	1	47,411
Good as Her Word	3	F	11	3	1	4	92,837
Good as Silver	3	F	13	7	1	2	108,916
Good Better Best	5	G	5	0	0	0	1,110
Good Bidness	4	F	3	1	0	0	4,669
Good Blend	4	G	2	0	0	0	91
Good Boot	5	G	9	1	0	2	4,270
Good Boy Duke	10	G	4	0	0	0	0
Good Boy Gone Bad	2	G	2	0	0	1	2,524
Good Boy Yankee	4	G	8	1	2	2	9,108
Good Campagner	3	C	17	2	1	3	28,731
Good Charlotte	3	F	9	1	2	3	18,867
Good Company	7	G	12	0	2	0	10,410
Good Conduct Medal	4	G	11	0	0	1	1,401
Good Coochie	6	M	4	1	0	0	4,754
Good Cop Bad Cop	6	G	2	0	0	0	800
Good Day Sir	5	M	4	3	1	0	21,275
Good Eater	3	F	5	0	0	0	7,500
Good Edition	2	F	3	1	1	0	35,550
Good Effort	3	F	9	1	0	0	2,225
Good Expectation	4	G	9	1	0	2	8,945
Good Faith	3	G	4	1	0	1	5,272
Good Faith Gesture	5	G	5	0	0	0	792
Good Fella (ARG)	6	H	4	2	2	0	21,725
Good for Me	4	G	7	0	0	2	1,624
Good for Us	3	F	4	0	0	2	4,389
Good for You	5	G	13	2	1	4	11,242
Good Future	5	G	18	1	2	1	21,505
Good Glory	4	F	3	0	0	1	1,005
Good Going	4	C	3	0	0	0	260
Good Gold	4	C	8	1	0	1	43,300
Good Golly James	6	G	6	0	0	0	962
Good Gracious Ned	3	G	9	1	2	0	28,392
Good Grades	6	M	7	0	0	0	828
Good Grief	3	G	3	0	0	1	4,060
Good Humor Gal	3	F	3	0	2	0	12,000
Good Humor Man	4	C	8	0	3	2	18,440
Good Humored	2	F	4	0	1	1	11,967
Good I Dear	5	M	5	1	0	0	6,228
Good Job	3	C	6	2	1	1	59,350
Good Knight Story	4	F	11	1	1	1	11,146
Good Listener	3	F	2	0	0	0	115
Good Looker	3	F	2	0	0	0	0
Good Lookin'	3	F	1	0	0	0	320
Good Lookin Devil	5	G	14	1	1	2	10,509
Good Lookin Joe	3	G	7	0	0	1	1,841
Good Lord Laurie	2	F	1	0	0	0	400
Good Luck Strikes	3	G	3	0	0	0	0
Good Man Sam	9	G	10	2	2	0	46,635
Good Medicine	4	F	9	1	3	0	11,438
Good Meeting	6	G	6	0	0	0	6,436
Good Morning Glory	3	F	1	0	0	0	0
Good Morning Irene	2	F	9	2	3	1	34,090
Good Morning Pete	2	G	1	0	0	0	325
Good N High	3	G	3	0	1	0	3,400
Good Night	8	G	4	1	0	1	12,860
Good Night Savanna	2	F	2	0	0	0	1,710
Good Night Shirt	3	G	8	2	0	1	33,280
Good O Bunny	2	F	7	0	1	1	4,440
Good O Dolly	3	F	3	0	0	0	445
Good O Valentine	4	F	19	0	2	1	11,415
Good Old Days	5	H	2	0	0	0	381
Good Old Sprite	5	G	9	1	0	2	2,816
Good Ole Storm	8	G	12	0	0	3	1,694
Good Power	3	G	2	0	0	0	0
Good Print	8	G	2	0	0	0	114
Good Reward	3	C	8	3	1	2	444,353
Good Riddance	4	F	4	0	0	0	1,710
Good Student (ARG)	4	F	5	1	1	1	101,640
Good Terms	5	G	7	0	0	1	2,735
Good Time Gal	4	F	10	1	0	0	3,014
Good Tip	3	C	10	2	1	1	31,450
Good to Fly	2	F	1	0	0	0	0
Goodbar	9	G	11	0	0	2	12,940
Goodbye	3	C	2	0	0	0	3,280
Goodbye Beautiful	3	F	10	2	1	1	28,375
Goodbye Ben Beau	3	G	7	2	0	0	11,496
Goodbye Big Cat	4	G	7	1	3	0	21,843
Goodbye Blues	2	F	5	0	2	1	14,510
Goodbye Cammie	4	F	11	0	3	3	13,136
Goodbye Credit	5	G	6	0	0	0	0
Goodbye Earl	4	C	2	0	0	0	299
Goodbye Heaven	4	G	16	0	4	5	9,218
Goodbye Honey Two	3	F	7	2	1	1	31,377
Goodbye I'm Gone	6	G	10	1	1	1	13,220
Goodbye Mr Goodbye	6	G	12	1	2	4	38,744
Goodbye My Lovely	2	F	2	0	0	0	135

Horse	Age	Sex	Sts	1st	2d	3d	Won
Goodbye Odds	2	F	7	0	0	0	1,263
Goodbye Past	4	F	14	1	2	0	8,693
Goodbye Rose	3	F	12	2	2	0	27,423
Goodbyesisterdisco	5	M	14	1	3	1	7,910
Goodbygolddiggers	12	G	9	1	1	0	3,510
Goodbywish	3	C	3	0	0	0	620
Goodgoodgood	4	G	6	0	0	0	551
Goodie Good Girl	2	F	1	0	0	0	105
Goodies Galore	3	F	7	1	2	2	31,725
Goodin	3	G	15	2	1	1	54,847
Goodland Park	3	F	4	0	0	0	295
Goodlookingdaim	4	F	11	3	0	2	22,411
Goodluck Road	5	G	10	1	1	0	7,870
Goodmorningjudge	9	M	2	0	0	0	0
Goodmorninsunshine	4	F	5	1	1	1	9,525
Goodnews Bay	5	G	11	2	1	1	44,780
Goodnight Trail	7	G	4	1	1	1	6,395
Goodnuff	5	G	9	0	1	1	4,647
Gooduldsouthernboy	2	C	2	0	1	0	1,900
Goodonya	4	F	2	0	1	0	5,540
Goodsprings	3	F	4	0	1	0	5,145
Goodtime Jess	2	F	4	1	1	0	5,920
Goodtime Rocket	7	G	11	1	2	2	9,945
Goodtimes At Home	2	G	2	0	1	1	12,300
Goodtogonow	5	G	11	0	1	0	2,755
Goodtoknow	5	M	4	0	0	1	1,264
Goody Good	4	G	5	2	0	0	5,590
Goofball	2	G	3	0	2	0	4,360
Goofy C	3	C	9	3	0	1	18,528
Goofy Maloofy	2	F	2	0	0	0	1,150
Goombah	6	G	8	0	0	0	0
Goonwithitjones	8	G	15	0	2	2	6,544
Goose At Fifty	2	F	10	0	0	0	4,340
Goose Boy	3	G	4	0	0	0	226
Goose Dinner	4	F	7	1	1	1	11,800
Goosey Gander	7	M	1	0	0	0	400
Goosey Moose	3	G	9	3	2	1	150,600
Goosie Goosie	4	G	15	1	0	1	33,516
Goost	6	G	4	1	0	1	7,443
Gopher Bowl	3	G	21	2	7	3	33,960
Gopher This One	3	G	13	2	2	2	39,093
Gorbash	2	C	2	0	0	0	1,520
Gordon of Eden	5	G	15	1	1	1	7,068
Gordonzy	6	G	2	0	0	0	0
Gordy McCorkell	4	G	13	1	0	1	5,031
Gordy's Our Man	9	G	2	0	0	0	225
Gordys Sweet Jordy	2	F	2	1	1	0	6,758
Gore Road	3	C	2	0	0	0	95
Gorgeous Gabby	5	M	2	0	0	1	1,371
Gorgeous Guest	4	F	8	1	0	0	3,739
Gorgeous N Greedy	5	M	13	2	1	2	13,400
Gorgeous Pirate	5	M	6	1	0	2	9,918
Gorge's Redbuttons	3	F	3	0	1	1	2,700
Gorilla Dancer	2	G	2	0	0	0	0
Gorin	3	G	16	2	3	6	22,423
Goryb	3	F	3	1	0	0	6,802
Gorylla (BRZ)	7	H	4	0	0	0	10,000
Goseemama	3	G	3	0	0	0	835
Goshakiradance	2	F	3	1	0	0	7,175
Goshin's Lad	5	H	2	0	0	0	767
Gospodin	3	G	8	1	0	1	19,760
Goss the Man	4	G	11	2	0	1	17,100
Got a Beep	4	G	14	2	1	4	81,762
Got a Ticket	6	G	8	0	0	1	1,124
Got Beer	4	G	10	0	3	2	11,138
Got Brass	5	G	13	2	2	2	21,345
Got Em	3	C	2	0	0	1	2,145
Got Game	7	G	12	1	4	0	6,372
Got Gear	3	F	7	1	1	2	20,834
Got Koko	5	M	1	0	0	1	30,000
Got Mercedes	5	M	11	1	4	2	20,166
Got Milk	8	G	1	0	0	0	210
Got Moxie	3	G	13	1	5	0	12,299
Got My Geht	3	G	12	1	2	1	29,290
Got Myself a Gun	2	C	6	1	2	1	22,700
Got Pizazz	3	F	12	1	1	3	27,944
Got Rhythm	2	C	1	0	0	0	50
Got That Swing	9	G	2	0	0	0	115
Got the Advanatage	4	G	5	0	0	0	0
Got the Gold	4	C	1	0	0	0	738
Got the Goods	3	C	13	1	2	1	52,772
Got the Message	5	G	10	1	3	2	34,320
Got the Rhythm	4	C	4	1	1	0	13,400
Got to Be Magic	3	F	5	0	1	0	1,562
Got to Be Me	4	F	7	1	0	0	10,846
Got to Go Tiger	2	G	1	0	0	0	0
Got You Slew	7	M	14	1	2	1	15,817
Gotabeanureyev	2	G	3	0	1	0	1,730
Gotaghostofachance	3	G	7	4	1	1	120,600
Gotaloveitbaby	5	M	10	1	1	1	9,200
Gotcha Covered	4	F	10	1	1	1	9,071
Gotcha Goin Mecee	5	G	9	3	4	1	27,510
Gotcha Thinking	7	G	4	0	2	0	1,916
Gotemdiggin	6	H	2	0	0	0	90
Got'er Covered	3	G	13	1	4	1	13,621
Gotham Limited	5	H	12	3	0	2	37,321
Gothenburg	9	G	7	1	0	2	4,356
Gotheronawhim	3	F	2	0	0	0	0
Gothic	3	G	15	2	3	4	26,754
Gothic's Design	4	G	13	0	1	0	4,424
Gotitall	3	F	5	0	1	0	2,436
Gotoit	6	G	6	0	0	3	5,085
Gott Nickolette	5	M	5	0	0	0	284
Gotta Attack	2	F	3	0	0	0	1,312
Gotta Ballado	6	G	16	6	4	1	45,516
Gotta Be a Fox	4	F	7	0	0	0	690
Gotta Be a Rose	3	F	17	3	2	0	16,618
Gotta Be a Star	6	M	10	0	0	1	1,760
Gotta Beat Em All	4	G	13	2	1	3	14,472
Gotta Gamble	2	G	1	0	0	0	105
Gotta Get It	5	G	12	0	2	0	9,030
Gotta Get Movin	6	H	8	0	2	0	1,044
Gotta Git Gone	4	G	4	0	0	0	375
Gotta Go Gal	2	F	5	2	1	1	23,450
Gotta Go Go	3	G	6	1	0	0	14,540
Gotta Go to Work	6	G	5	0	0	3	13,925
Gotta Have Asingle	3	G	6	0	0	1	2,255
Gotta Have Fun	4	C	9	0	5	1	18,055
Gotta Have Magic	3	G	19	1	1	2	18,455
Gotta Jiboo	5	M	15	3	2	5	46,267
Gotta Lotta Speed	3	G	24	1	4	5	18,104
Gotta Pay the Lady	4	F	1	0	0	0	270
Gotta Ridan	8	M	16	1	2	5	10,812
Gotta Rush	2	F	4	2	0	2	61,556
Gotta Scoot	4	F	5	0	0	1	1,017
Gottabe Awesome	3	G	5	0	0	1	4,526
Gottabeachboy	4	C	11	0	1	1	35,465
Gottagetherefirst	3	G	16	4	1	1	22,415
Gottago Joe	2	G	3	1	0	0	3,748
Gottahavemilk	2	F	10	3	2	1	32,315
Gottahavit	3	F	1	0	0	0	0
Gottalottagas	8	M	8	2	1	0	16,070
Gottalovefaith	5	H	7	0	3	0	10,605
Gottaluvme	4	F	3	0	0	0	320
Gottawad	3	F	16	0	3	3	8,575
Gotthard	7	G	12	3	2	0	37,830
Gotthemoneyhoney	3	F	14	3	3	3	16,920
Gottherushon	3	G	1	1	0	0	1,200
Gottobadandy	7	M	7	0	0	0	619
Gouglyearly	3	G	9	0	0	0	1,095
Gouldings Green	3	C	3	1	0	0	19,560
Gourami's Notion	3	G	7	0	0	1	986
Gourmet Soup	3	F	3	0	0	0	0
Govans	7	G	16	1	2	1	6,455
Govenor Gray	2	C	8	0	0	1	2,825
Govenors Beele Boy	3	G	9	1	1	0	3,320
Govenors Diplomat	11	G	7	0	0	2	1,661
Govenors Mist	4	F	8	0	2	0	3,408
Govenors Trixie	4	F	14	1	2	0	6,109
Govern Game	6	G	6	0	0	1	1,651
Government News	3	G	8	0	2	0	1,393
Governor Arnold	2	C	3	1	0	0	10,600
Governor Bennett	4	C	11	2	1	1	64,320
Governor Brown	4	C	6	1	2	3	60,190
Governor Hickel	5	H	2	0	0	0	540
Governor Jeb	5	G	13	2	2	2	14,703

Horse	Age	Sex	Sts	1st	2d	3d	Won
Governor Joe	7	G	5	0	0	0	230
Governor Lee	3	G	8	1	2	0	25,940
Governor of Spain	3	G	11	3	1	4	50,565
Governor Roy	4	G	12	1	2	0	14,061
Governor Vasquez	4	C	10	2	0	5	25,560
Governors Gold	3	C	1	0	0	0	0
Governor's Palace	4	F	1	0	0	0	0
Governor's Pride	7	G	10	3	1	1	56,750
Gov's Ace	3	C	11	1	1	0	6,884
Gower	2	C	5	1	2	0	24,840
Gowhereyouwannago	5	H	7	0	1	1	3,298
Gowithfate	3	F	5	0	2	0	12,000
Gowrie House	4	G	9	3	0	1	15,406
Grab Bag	5	M	2	0	0	1	3,850
Grab N Gears	6	H	1	0	0	0	140
Grab Some Grass	3	G	9	0	2	4	19,980
Grab the Buck	5	M	4	0	0	0	1,365
Grab the Cat	2	F	7	1	0	4	18,435
Grab the Check	2	C	6	0	4	0	16,010
Grab the Jack	4	F	1	0	0	0	0
Grace and Style	5	M	7	0	1	3	26,270
Grace Bay	4	F	7	1	1	4	52,344
Grace Course	5	H	2	0	1	0	9,000
Grace Elizabeth	3	F	8	0	1	1	2,833
Grace for You	5	M	3	0	0	0	5,719
Grace Line	3	F	4	0	2	0	6,656
Grace of Windsor	4	F	11	3	3	1	26,535
Grace the Stage	4	F	3	1	1	1	8,200
Graceful Ballet	5	M	14	1	0	2	6,601
Graceful by Nature	4	F	8	0	1	0	4,200
Graceful Devil	6	G	4	0	0	0	735
Graceful Gal	6	M	8	1	1	2	36,695
Graceful Nancy	2	F	3	1	0	0	38,250
Graceful Pro	3	F	6	1	0	1	31,439
Graceful Rain	4	F	4	0	0	0	390
Graceful Stepper	5	M	3	1	0	1	16,610
Graceful Verse	4	F	6	1	0	0	14,430
Gracefully (IRE)	3	F	2	0	0	0	8,338
Gracefully Done	3	F	6	0	0	0	4,598
Gracewithapproval	4	F	17	3	4	1	40,335
Gracie Terrace	3	C	2	0	0	0	1,640
Gracie's Dancer	6	H	8	0	1	2	14,960
Gracie's Prospect	7	M	5	0	0	1	1,300
Gracies Trick	4	F	2	0	1	0	1,700
Gracile	3	F	11	2	1	3	44,782
Gracility	5	M	5	1	0	1	38,905
Gracinha	3	F	1	0	0	0	2,580
Gracious Brevity	7	M	6	0	2	1	7,854
Gracious Gift	6	M	1	0	0	0	0
Gracious Girl	3	F	5	3	0	0	19,372
Gracious Goodness	4	F	2	0	0	0	279
Gracious Halo	3	F	6	1	4	0	32,176
Gracious Humor	4	G	11	2	2	2	99,040
Gracious Megan	7	M	13	1	2	2	21,400
Gracious Peggy	3	F	12	4	2	2	37,704
Gracy Rules	5	M	4	0	0	0	215
Gracy's World	3	G	5	0	0	0	870
Grad School	3	G	13	0	2	2	5,809
Grada a Annie	4	F	3	0	2	0	5,210
Grade One	8	G	15	0	1	5	10,389
Graded by Results	3	C	3	0	1	0	9,772
Gradepoint	3	C	3	2	0	0	108,000
Grader Blade	5	G	8	0	0	3	3,383
Grades Gold	4	G	16	5	2	3	64,175
Grades of Honor	4	F	5	0	1	0	2,370
Graduate Course	3	F	7	1	1	1	21,310
Graduate of Honor	4	F	1	0	0	0	250
Grady	9	G	14	1	2	3	22,695
Grady N	3	C	7	1	2	1	16,920
Grady's Boy	3	C	6	1	0	2	5,675
Graeme's Gal	4	F	12	1	1	1	7,704
Graflinger	3	F	1	0	0	0	0
Grafton	4	G	8	2	1	3	105,900
Grafton Square	3	C	5	0	1	1	9,380
Graham	3	G	2	0	0	0	260
Graham Cracker	3	C	7	0	1	1	18,320
Graham Isle	3	G	1	0	0	0	0
Graham's Surprise	5	G	4	0	0	0	351
Grain of Salt	3	F	10	1	1	0	10,000
Gramar Love	4	F	17	4	4	2	28,341
Gramercy Park	3	C	3	1	0	0	17,780
Grames Rd. Kid	2	C	2	0	0	0	328
Gramma Jo's Pride	4	F	6	2	0	0	28,649
Grammy Award	5	M	2	1	0	0	4,095
Grammy's Delight	5	M	2	0	0	0	504
Grampa Howie	3	C	10	0	2	0	3,604
Gramps	3	C	10	0	1	0	3,672
Gram's Addiction	4	G	17	3	2	0	41,410
Gram's Delight	4	F	3	2	1	0	18,000
Gram's Folly	6	G	14	5	1	4	82,040
Gram's Sparkle	5	G	3	0	0	0	1,025
Gran Amiga (ARG)	5	M	13	5	1	0	51,830
Gran Cesare (ARG)	5	H	13	2	2	2	111,067
Gran Chaco	4	G	9	0	1	1	3,870
Gran City	2	C	9	1	1	0	7,765
Gran Duke	3	G	4	0	0	0	275
Gran Lady Jade	3	F	1	0	0	0	0
Gran Prospect	3	C	11	1	1	1	34,295
Gran Slam Slew	3	G	3	0	1	0	2,830
Granada Boulevard	2	F	3	0	0	0	910
Granat	4	F	4	1	2	0	10,699
Granbury	6	G	7	0	0	0	1,789
Granburys Brigade	3	C	5	0	0	0	126
Granby	4	C	3	1	0	0	14,430
Grancentral Pkwy.	3	C	5	1	2	1	47,000
Grand	8	G	3	0	0	0	218
Grand (IRE)	4	C	5	1	0	1	28,180
Grand and Fancy	9	G	20	2	1	1	9,187
Grand and Great	4	C	8	2	1	2	11,478
Grand and Warren	2	G	7	1	0	0	6,190
Grand Appeal	2	F	2	0	0	0	0
Grand Appearance	6	G	3	0	0	1	1,570
Grand Appointment	6	H	4	1	2	0	53,160
Grand Awakening	4	G	5	1	1	0	20,640
Grand Bank	3	C	5	2	1	1	20,240
Grand Canyon	7	G	19	3	6	2	11,970
Grand Cap D	3	F	9	0	0	0	2,850
Grand Caro Lynn	5	M	6	0	2	2	8,163
Grand Circus Shark	4	G	8	0	3	1	10,026
Grand Coat	3	F	6	0	0	0	607
Grand Commemorate	4	G	10	2	1	2	9,202
Grand Concourse	2	G	1	0	1	0	2,120
Grand Council	3	G	14	1	3	3	39,680
Grand Desire	5	M	3	0	0	0	459
Grand Destiny	4	F	3	1	0	1	29,750
Grand End Sweep	8	G	14	3	4	1	97,616
Grand Flash	4	G	4	0	0	0	700
Grand Gala	3	F	1	0	0	0	430
Grand Gamble	5	M	8	1	1	0	8,946
Grand Gent	3	G	4	0	0	0	280
Grand Heritage	3	C	9	2	0	3	95,716
Grand Illusion	3	F	8	1	3	1	37,730
Grand Image	3	F	6	0	0	1	1,550
Grand Island	5	G	8	1	0	1	3,416
Grand Kat	4	G	4	1	0	2	12,840
Grand Kids	4	G	22	3	1	1	53,767
Grand Legend	4	G	16	4	3	3	29,809
Grand Lucenci	4	C	12	0	2	4	23,265
Grand Man	3	G	8	3	2	1	27,434
Grand Marshall	2	C	1	0	0	0	0
Grand Miesque	2	C	1	0	0	0	0
Grand Mister	10	G	11	1	4	2	7,278
Grand Model	4	F	4	2	0	1	37,438
Grand Mystery	5	M	6	0	0	0	678
Grand Nikesha	4	F	2	0	0	0	120
Grand O Mary	3	F	3	0	0	0	569
Grand Piano	3	F	13	3	2	0	49,530
Grand Player	4	G	20	1	5	1	13,197
Grand Portege	2	F	1	0	1	0	9,400
Grand Prairie	3	G	1	0	0	0	0
Grand Prayer	3	F	11	3	3	1	127,170
Grand Prize Winner	4	F	3	0	1	0	1,740
Grand Rapids Miss	3	F	7	2	1	1	34,718
Grand Red	3	G	11	2	2	0	46,910
Grand Reserve	2	C	1	0	0	1	2,100
Grand Review	4	F	4	0	0	0	1,380
Grand Reward	3	C	11	1	2	2	76,692
Grand Runner	4	G	12	2	2	1	4,760

Horse	Age	Sex	Sts	1st	2d	3d	Won
Grand Scheme	4	F	3	1	1	0	6,840
Grand Score	3	C	5	0	2	1	24,220
Grand Sequoia	5	M	16	3	2	3	28,685
Grand Skieur	4	G	20	1	1	2	9,849
Grand Slam Jake	4	G	9	0	1	0	6,410
Grand Song	3	G	4	0	0	0	451
Grand Sorcerer	4	G	20	3	1	2	20,565
Grand Steal	4	G	4	2	0	0	44,340
Grand Storm	3	F	5	1	0	1	11,690
Grand Strand	6	M	7	0	1	4	1,390
Grand Tam	3	F	1	0	0	0	87
Grand Victor	4	G	7	1	3	0	24,040
Grand View Girls	3	F	5	0	1	1	8,560
Grand Warrior	3	C	6	0	1	2	21,275
Grandaughter	3	F	9	1	1	1	23,261
Granddaddy King	4	G	7	0	0	0	225
Grande Blue Streak	4	G	12	0	0	2	3,990
Grande Cache	5	G	3	0	0	0	82
Grande Diablo	2	C	4	1	1	1	30,277
Grande Game	3	F	1	0	0	0	320
Grande Jete	4	F	16	2	3	3	40,780
Grande Paranoid	5	M	9	1	2	0	4,466
Grande Premio	4	G	4	0	0	0	434
Grander Blue Mar	2	F	2	0	0	0	2,040
Grande's Grandslam	3	C	9	2	2	1	74,882
Grandiflora	3	G	5	3	0	0	18,918
Grandiosity	3	F	3	0	1	0	6,000
Grandiser (AUS)	6	G	2	0	0	0	10,818
Grandma Helen	4	F	1	0	0	0	0
Grandma Nena	4	F	12	0	4	1	13,724
Grandma Sandy	4	F	8	0	1	2	5,045
Grandma's Ltd	5	M	9	0	1	1	5,632
Grandma's Money	5	M	5	0	0	0	1,591
Grandmasterflash	3	G	1	0	0	0	0
Grandpa Chan	4	G	12	1	3	1	15,712
Grandpa Hillis	11	G	1	0	0	0	0
Grandpa P. D.	8	G	1	0	0	0	0
Grandpa Said Yes	4	G	7	0	0	0	352
Grandpa Two	7	G	11	2	1	1	13,716
Grandpa's Courage	2	G	2	0	0	1	2,680
Grandpa's Dreams	4	G	12	1	1	1	12,258
Grandpawroteyes	4	G	7	1	2	0	1,588
Grandson of Slew	3	C	3	1	0	0	14,100
Grandson Zach	4	G	2	0	2	0	4,160
Grandstand Girl	10	M	11	1	0	1	4,657
Grandstand Parade	3	F	4	2	0	1	18,290
Grandtech	6	H	2	0	1	0	380
Grange	5	G	13	3	2	2	28,138
Grangeville	9	G	6	0	3	0	19,100
Granique	2	C	2	0	1	0	12,540
Granita	3	F	5	0	1	0	5,322
Granite Head	4	C	11	3	2	3	93,710
Granite Peak	6	H	7	1	1	0	4,594
Granite Ridge	5	G	14	3	0	2	17,848
Granja Vivo	5	M	12	3	4	2	50,680
Granny Canny	3	F	4	2	0	1	16,540
Granny Gail	3	F	12	2	1	1	14,765
Granny Jo	4	F	4	0	0	1	455
Granny Sure Shot	5	M	15	2	1	3	23,538
Granny's Annie	3	F	9	0	2	0	5,572
Granny's Dream	3	F	4	0	0	0	0
Granny's Gal	3	F	11	1	0	0	6,061
Granny's Gold	4	G	4	0	0	1	450
Granny's Gun	6	G	9	0	0	0	620
Granny's Hope	6	M	10	0	1	1	2,354
Granny's Mountain	3	G	2	1	0	0	5,180
Granny's Pride	3	F	9	1	3	2	47,540
Grannys Rosie	5	M	10	0	4	0	4,159
Granny's Wild	3	F	10	1	0	0	4,572
Granpas Last Fling	3	F	4	0	1	0	520
Grant	5	G	3	0	0	0	303
Grant Marty a Wish	5	M	7	3	0	1	87,533
Grantcor	6	M	3	0	1	0	2,660
Grantley	3	C	3	0	0	1	975
Grantmeatrophy	4	F	13	1	0	1	36,699
Grants Farm	2	C	1	0	0	0	0
Grant's Our Boy	8	G	11	0	1	1	4,227
Grant's Vic	5	G	5	0	0	0	0
Grape Hall	3	F	1	0	0	0	0
Grapeshot	10	G	3	1	0	0	13,820
Grapevine	6	G	6	0	2	0	4,150
Graphic Avenue	5	H	4	0	0	0	1,542
Grasias Sam	6	G	12	0	0	2	1,609
Grasp It All	4	F	10	0	4	1	7,410
Grasp the Concept	2	C	1	0	1	0	11,400
Grass Shack Two	2	F	1	0	0	0	0
Grasshopper Flats	6	G	3	1	1	0	7,075
Grassy Butte	5	M	10	0	0	0	5,117
Grassy Strip	2	F	4	0	1	0	9,250
Grat	2	F	4	1	1	0	37,515
Gratefully	4	F	8	1	3	0	10,548
Gratiaen	7	H	1	0	0	0	220
Gratis	5	G	3	0	1	1	15,100
Gratitude Attack	4	G	10	4	1	0	93,731
Gratteau	9	G	2	0	0	0	0
Gravano	6	G	12	1	2	0	14,220
Gravel Gertie	5	M	21	3	4	1	48,492
Gravellona T	5	M	9	0	0	1	2,750
Graven	5	H	13	2	4	3	11,760
Graver	6	G	6	0	0	2	1,070
Gravitate	5	H	12	1	0	1	8,195
Gravitating Comet	4	G	8	0	2	1	5,917
Gray Aggie	5	M	5	1	0	0	7,821
Gray Aras	8	G	9	0	4	1	16,691
Gray Black N White	3	G	7	1	2	1	34,760
Gray Fever	3	F	13	1	2	1	22,589
Gray Forum	5	G	9	0	2	0	3,456
Gray Fox	3	G	7	0	0	1	350
Gray Going	3	C	1	0	0	0	0
Gray Heat	4	G	12	0	6	1	15,270
Gray in Time	3	G	11	2	1	1	13,495
Gray Is Great	4	G	6	0	0	1	2,795
Gray Is the Way	5	M	15	0	1	3	8,823
Gray Jag	4	G	15	1	1	4	45,168
Gray Justice	3	G	1	0	0	0	78
Gray Line	7	G	8	0	0	1	1,200
Gray Magic	3	G	4	0	0	0	1,100
Gray Mike	3	G	5	1	0	0	5,922
Gray Millie	4	F	7	0	2	2	4,657
Gray Oaks Day	5	M	12	0	1	3	4,161
Gray Package	5	H	12	0	2	3	5,532
Gray Premier	5	G	6	0	0	0	474
Gray Ryder	5	M	7	1	2	0	23,055
Gray Token	3	C	1	0	0	1	2,650
Grayboo	5	G	6	0	0	0	501
Graybull	3	C	18	1	3	2	20,125
Graydon Grey	3	G	2	0	0	0	800
Graydonna	4	F	12	0	1	1	7,748
Grayglen	4	G	10	4	1	1	35,369
Graylee Rose	3	F	13	1	0	3	10,613
Graymaster	3	C	6	0	0	0	1,050
Graypast	3	F	9	1	2	2	16,554
Grayross Gal	4	F	10	2	1	1	17,390
Grayross Sweetpea	2	F	1	0	0	0	0
Gray's Classi Boy	3	G	7	0	0	1	1,022
Gray's Surprise	4	F	1	0	0	0	156
Gray's Tee	3	C	1	0	0	0	35
Grayson Lear	3	G	9	0	3	1	13,380
Graystone Bobbie	4	C	5	1	1	3	2,420
Graysyoureyesonme	8	M	9	0	0	4	3,036
Graze	7	G	6	1	0	1	29,265
Grazie Bocelli	5	G	6	0	0	0	525
Graziella	4	F	3	0	1	0	8,408
Greased Lightnin'	4	C	3	0	0	1	1,569
Greasy and Slick	9	H	3	0	0	0	345
Great Advantage	5	G	15	3	1	1	17,837
Great Alarm	5	G	10	0	0	1	1,716
Great Alie	3	G	3	0	0	0	483
Great Ambition	3	C	1	0	0	0	0
Great Auntee	4	F	13	0	1	4	54,688
Great Awakening	4	G	1	0	0	0	0
Great Bet	7	H	7	0	1	0	933
Great Big Bag	7	H	1	0	0	0	0
Great Bloom	6	G	6	2	0	4	70,830
Great Charisma	3	C	9	0	0	1	2,200
Great Chinggis	3	C	8	1	0	1	9,926
Great Choice	4	F	11	3	2	2	24,596
Great Commander	4	G	6	4	0	0	82,530

Horse	Age	Sex	Sts	1st	2d	3d	Won
Great Dame	2	F	5	0	2	1	23,012
Great Dancer (CHI)	4	F	3	1	1	0	42,720
Great Debate	3	F	2	0	0	1	1,700
Great Dreamer	5	G	2	0	0	0	660
Great Feeling	3	G	4	0	0	0	826
Great Flyer	4	G	10	1	0	2	5,222
Great Form	3	F	4	1	1	1	18,640
Great Fortune	3	C	4	0	1	0	703
Great Future	7	G	2	0	0	0	165
Great Game	3	F	2	0	0	0	690
Great Heir	3	F	4	1	0	1	11,857
Great Honoree	4	G	11	1	1	1	14,200
Great Illusion	4	G	4	0	0	0	765
Great Intentions	2	F	1	1	0	0	27,000
Great Kisser	4	F	13	3	0	3	10,409
Great Lady B	4	F	6	1	0	0	4,200
Great Lady K	2	F	4	0	3	0	26,650
Great Niginsky	2	C	1	0	0	0	106
Great Notion	4	C	2	0	0	0	748
Great Plains	3	G	9	2	4	2	32,453
Great Power	2	G	14	1	2	0	36,479
Great Pyramid (IRE)	4	C	4	0	0	0	138
Great Quest	5	G	2	0	0	0	100
Great Recording	4	G	11	1	0	0	3,202
Great Return	4	F	6	2	1	1	22,716
Great Romancer	3	G	6	1	0	1	6,693
Great Samson	3	G	6	2	0	0	9,464
Great Sandy	3	C	10	0	4	1	4,302
Great Senaria	5	M	6	0	0	0	612
Great Sham	3	G	5	1	1	1	7,620
Great South Bay	2	G	2	0	0	0	1,348
Great Stuff	4	G	2	0	0	0	270
Great Time	3	C	2	0	1	0	2,900
Great Trilogy	6	G	9	1	1	0	5,574
Great Victory	3	G	5	1	0	2	24,430
Great Warrior	6	G	7	2	2	1	32,386
Great Waters	4	G	9	1	0	1	6,860
Great White Father	6	G	7	2	2	1	23,830
Great White North	3	F	14	3	3	3	72,980
Great Win	3	G	9	1	2	1	22,677
Great Year	8	G	4	0	0	0	1,020
Great Zotti	4	G	3	0	0	0	0
Greatdayinthelake	2	C	4	1	0	1	23,570
Greater Good	2	C	5	3	0	1	226,275
Greater Justice	8	G	10	2	2	1	4,815
Greatlengths U S A	2	C	4	0	0	0	2,370
Greattobeloved	4	F	10	2	2	0	113,840
Grecian Court	5	G	5	0	0	0	750
Grecian Lover	2	F	4	0	0	1	5,550
Grecian Note	4	G	14	2	2	2	17,371
Grecian Wings	2	F	2	0	0	0	655
Gree Lee Dee	4	F	1	1	0	0	7,482
Greed'n'glory	4	G	8	0	0	2	5,156
Greedy Executive	3	C	18	3	1	4	26,011
Greedy Raja	3	F	1	0	0	1	1,485
Greek Authority	8	G	2	0	1	0	2,385
Greek Echo	6	G	11	1	1	1	6,222
Greek Hero	11	G	3	1	0	1	18,100
Greek Legend	5	M	2	0	0	0	0
Greek Power	3	G	8	0	0	0	1,975
Greek Pride	5	G	6	0	0	0	870
Greek Speaker	4	F	10	1	1	0	4,193
Greek Stripes	5	M	6	0	0	1	638
Greek Sun	3	C	4	2	1	0	270,802
Greek Temper	3	G	15	1	7	1	17,622
Greek Tranquility	3	F	2	0	1	0	4,200
Greeley's Best	5	G	8	0	2	2	9,525
Greeleyschoice	3	F	15	3	6	1	32,368
Greeleytime	5	G	3	0	0	0	428
Greelite	4	G	6	4	0	0	45,655
Green Beer	3	G	1	0	0	0	120
Green Beret	8	G	4	0	1	0	7,105
Green Briar Rose	4	F	7	0	1	2	30,080
Green Crystal	5	H	1	0	0	0	44
Green Dancer Road	3	F	16	0	1	0	3,639
Green Dancersreply	3	C	1	0	0	0	840
Green Dragon	8	M	1	0	0	0	0
Green Earrings	3	F	4	0	1	0	1,551
Green Eyes	3	F	1	0	0	0	400
Green Fiddler	6	G	12	0	0	1	894
Green Flair	3	G	15	4	1	1	18,709
Green Gingham Girl	5	M	3	0	1	0	4,250
Green Groom (FR)	5	H	2	0	0	0	1,630
Green Ice	3	F	9	1	1	0	8,241
Green Jade	3	F	14	2	1	4	20,950
Green Jeans	5	M	3	0	0	0	2,628
Green Jewel	3	F	3	0	0	2	13,167
Green Kuntry	5	G	3	0	0	0	148
Green Line (GB)	5	G	8	0	1	2	33,490
Green Line Edition	3	G	4	0	1	0	7,270
Green Links	7	H	4	0	0	0	203
Green Music Stop	4	F	13	1	0	3	8,498
Green Power	5	G	12	0	3	1	8,556
Green Queen (IRE)	3	F	6	1	1	1	41,960
Green Riches	6	G	3	0	2	0	13,800
Green Ridge	3	F	18	2	1	2	29,685
Green Speed	5	M	15	2	5	1	18,546
Green Team	5	G	9	2	3	1	212,625
Green Thunder	5	G	3	0	0	0	989
Greenback Gal	4	F	20	2	6	2	63,910
Greenbaypacker	7	G	5	2	1	0	20,480
Greenberg	3	F	3	1	0	0	13,200
Greene County	2	C	3	0	0	1	3,450
Greene for Todd	2	F	3	1	0	0	5,773
Greengetsthetrick	2	G	1	0	0	0	880
Greenie	3	G	7	4	1	0	87,812
Greenjay	2	C	4	1	1	0	26,970
Greenland	6	H	14	2	1	0	22,659
Greenlee	4	F	3	0	1	0	3,972
Greenlight Express	4	G	6	1	1	1	4,140
Greenspan Speaks	3	C	9	0	0	2	2,645
Greenstandingseam	3	G	9	2	0	0	14,539
Greenway Diamond	4	G	12	0	2	4	16,020
Greeting Card	4	F	12	1	1	0	5,044
Gregariously	3	C	3	1	1	0	17,320
Greggie's Star	4	G	13	1	2	0	7,668
Gregg's Mistake	4	F	5	1	1	0	4,796
Greg's Deck	4	C	15	1	2	1	13,538
Greg's Gold	3	G	6	2	2	0	62,448
Greg's Syrah	4	G	10	3	1	1	63,235
Greg's Turk	10	G	12	1	2	1	9,145
Gregson	3	C	5	1	1	1	44,850
Grendel	4	G	8	1	2	1	42,820
Grenfield	9	M	1	0	0	0	32
Grenyitas	3	F	5	0	0	0	645
Greta's Joy	3	F	10	2	0	4	13,140
Gretchen's Star	9	G	8	2	3	1	103,025
Grey Beard	5	H	13	1	3	0	82,093
Grey Bouquet	4	F	13	3	1	0	48,430
Grey Charm	7	G	2	0	0	0	0
Grey Charmbracelet	3	F	2	0	0	0	0
Grey Diamonds	3	F	8	2	0	2	15,811
Grey Factor	4	F	2	0	0	0	470
Grey Foot	3	F	5	1	0	0	8,625
Grey Gallant	2	F	3	0	1	1	2,786
Grey Gatita	5	M	1	0	0	0	170
Grey Goose Kid	2	C	4	1	0	1	26,650
Grey Houdini	2	C	3	0	0	0	220
Grey Memo	7	H	4	0	0	0	3,624
Grey Minstrel	2	F	5	0	0	1	4,600
Grey Misty	3	G	10	2	1	1	49,400
Grey Muse	3	G	4	0	0	0	284
Grey Pilgrim	3	G	9	0	0	0	2,070
Grey Polluck	2	C	1	0	0	0	0
Grey Punches	2	F	2	0	0	0	0
Grey Reagle	4	G	6	0	2	1	2,829
Grey Ruby	4	F	4	0	1	1	6,385
Grey Sea's Shining	7	M	5	0	0	0	517
Grey Secret	2	C	1	0	0	0	165
Grey Traffic	3	F	5	2	2	0	106,100
Greygoose Rox	3	F	5	1	1	2	4,984
Greygoosegal	3	F	4	0	0	1	5,602
Greyhame	5	G	8	2	1	0	17,190
Greylock	3	C	9	1	1	2	33,403
Greymon	3	G	8	2	1	0	24,440
Grey's Majesty	7	H	9	1	1	3	10,150
Greystoke	3	C	5	0	0	0	844
Greystone Three	3	F	7	0	1	0	2,306

Horse	Age	Sex	Sts	1st	2d	3d	Won
Greyt Scott	5	G	9	1	1	0	4,500
Grid North	6	H	5	0	1	1	1,400
Gridlock	2	C	2	0	0	0	410
Griever Canyon	5	G	5	0	0	0	1,051
Griffin's Cow Girl	4	F	11	0	1	1	4,535
Griffin's Wake	3	G	11	1	2	2	23,668
Grifter	6	H	9	3	2	1	89,300
Grifton	4	G	1	0	1	0	3,000
Grigia	4	F	3	0	2	0	3,570
Grillberger	4	G	16	1	1	2	11,790
Grillhouse	7	G	11	5	2	2	78,075
Grimm	5	G	4	0	0	2	15,180
Grimsley	2	C	2	0	0	0	780
Grin	5	H	7	2	3	0	38,050
Grin and Frown	4	C	4	1	2	1	36,500
Grin and Picture	6	G	5	0	0	0	267
Grin and Smile	4	F	13	3	0	1	28,889
Grinamic	4	F	11	1	2	5	20,991
Grinanbearit	8	G	4	0	0	0	112
Grinch	3	F	9	2	2	1	83,530
Grind	6	G	6	0	0	0	732
Grind the Blues	4	G	12	0	2	2	6,684
Grindavik	4	F	5	1	0	2	30,228
Grinding It Out	4	C	7	1	1	1	24,920
Grindrock	8	G	9	0	2	0	5,363
Grindstone Cowgirl	3	F	14	2	4	3	20,250
Grindstone Gold	3	C	16	3	3	0	41,090
Grindtime	4	F	3	1	0	0	28,950
Gringa Hug	4	F	9	2	1	0	13,926
Gringa Negrita	3	F	2	1	0	0	3,900
Gringo Cox	3	G	1	0	0	0	0
Gringo Dancer	3	F	6	0	0	0	0
Gringo Joe	7	G	7	1	0	1	3,650
Gringo Legend	4	G	3	0	1	0	1,342
Grinnin Bear	6	G	2	0	0	0	0
Gris Souris	3	F	13	1	2	2	32,677
Grit and Glory	4	F	12	1	2	1	13,529
Grit and Steel	3	F	6	1	0	0	5,156
Gritty Kitty	3	F	15	3	2	0	16,102
Grizzly	2	G	2	0	1	0	2,565
Grizzly Gulch	4	G	8	1	0	0	3,566
Grog	7	G	8	2	1	0	13,212
Grommet	3	F	13	1	3	0	11,408
Groom a Fire	6	G	9	1	0	1	4,942
Groom Me a Star	4	C	6	0	3	0	6,062
Groom of the Year	4	C	3	0	0	0	370
Groom On the Run	5	G	7	0	0	0	1,530
Groomed Prince	2	G	1	0	0	0	0
Groomeroma	4	F	16	4	7	1	71,370
Groom's Choice	3	F	9	1	0	1	6,790
Groom's Gray Ghost	3	C	5	0	0	0	233
Groom's Kiss	4	F	16	1	1	3	33,200
Grooms Moka	3	F	8	1	3	0	16,225
Groom's Point	4	G	11	0	3	3	12,233
Grooms Trouble	2	C	7	1	0	1	20,930
Groove Jet	2	C	1	0	0	0	230
Groovewiththebean	5	G	1	0	0	0	0
Groovin Gary	4	C	9	1	0	1	7,181
Groovin Goose	2	F	2	0	0	0	175
Groovin P	3	F	4	0	0	1	1,430
Groovy Bandit	3	G	13	2	3	3	31,790
Groovy Chief	4	G	8	3	1	0	18,945
Groovy Crown	2	F	5	0	0	1	10,316
Groovy Dresser	3	F	5	0	1	0	1,320
Groovy Duck	4	G	1	0	0	0	132
Groovy Fortune	3	C	7	1	1	1	18,240
Groovy Hero	5	M	10	1	0	0	3,841
Groovy Kat	4	G	14	2	2	3	12,411
Groovy Kinda Love	4	F	1	0	0	0	0
Groovy Knight	4	G	8	0	4	2	6,360
Groovy Little Me	2	F	1	0	0	0	70
Groovy Me	2	C	2	0	1	0	5,300
Groovy Rockette	4	F	5	0	0	2	1,387
Groovy Weekend	2	C	2	0	0	0	574
Groovy Zone	4	G	7	0	0	0	1,424
Groovy's Rare Moon	4	F	3	0	0	2	870
Groovy's Rose	3	F	3	0	0	2	900
Gross Margin	4	G	6	0	3	0	13,780
Grossman	5	G	5	2	0	0	31,020

Horse	Age	Sex	Sts	1st	2d	3d	Won
Ground Assault	6	G	17	2	3	1	15,890
Ground Attack	5	G	4	0	1	0	350
Ground Breaking	3	G	1	0	0	0	0
Ground Control	2	C	2	0	0	0	1,230
Ground Forces	5	G	4	0	0	0	720
Ground Game	2	C	2	0	1	0	5,600
Ground Hero	4	G	10	2	1	1	49,370
Ground Storm	8	H	8	2	2	1	112,415
Ground Velocity	4	F	5	0	0	0	1,407
Ground Zero Hero	4	G	12	3	2	2	15,690
Groundshakers	2	C	1	0	0	0	3,060
Group Venture	2	F	2	0	0	0	0
Grove Crane	4	C	12	0	3	1	5,250
Grove Creek	5	M	4	0	0	1	1,070
Growing Demands	2	G	2	0	0	0	535
Growing Gains	4	F	8	1	2	1	31,834
Growing Wild	2	C	2	0	0	0	512
Growth Stock	6	M	1	0	0	0	1,200
Grrrgarious	5	G	9	0	0	2	16,270
Grubby Soldier	4	G	9	2	0	1	14,315
Gruff	3	C	3	2	0	0	38,100
Grugly	2	C	5	0	1	2	6,690
Grumman	4	G	7	1	2	1	52,941
Grumpy Sis	3	F	6	1	1	0	11,895
Grumpy's Gal	5	M	10	0	4	2	10,480
Gruveebit	3	F	11	1	1	2	10,732
Gruvianna	4	F	9	0	1	2	4,610
Gryffindor	4	G	8	2	1	2	56,907
Gryphon Red	4	G	2	0	0	0	122
Gtm Boy	2	C	1	0	0	0	0
Guacho (BRZ)	5	H	2	0	0	0	450
Guadalupes Tailor	6	G	4	0	0	0	159
Guaitil	4	G	6	0	0	0	1,255
Guana (FR)	5	M	4	0	0	1	7,028
Guapazo (ARG)	6	H	9	1	2	0	35,520
Guapita	3	F	14	1	1	1	8,355
Guarani's Daughter	3	F	8	1	0	1	4,829
Guarani's Princess	3	F	5	1	1	0	5,140
Guaranteed Again	3	G	6	2	1	0	15,860
Guaranteed Sweep	4	C	8	1	0	4	36,700
Guaranteed Victory	2	F	2	0	0	0	3,340
Guaranteeddelivery	6	G	14	1	0	1	7,418
Guard Cat	6	H	2	0	0	0	295
Guard Force	3	G	5	1	0	2	18,910
Guardian	4	C	3	0	0	0	1,500
Guardian Angel	5	M	16	1	4	0	26,864
Guardianofthegate	8	G	7	1	0	3	19,832
Guardrail	3	G	2	0	0	0	0
Guardsman	7	G	16	3	0	3	12,776
Guaritta	4	G	7	1	1	3	13,760
Guatagaloop	2	G	3	0	0	0	1,203
Guaymas Sky	4	C	16	2	1	2	8,102
Guelph	3	F	5	0	0	0	1,680
Guerdon	7	G	11	0	1	2	10,936
Guerrero	4	G	8	3	3	1	80,600
Guess I'm Lucky	3	C	5	0	1	0	4,270
Guess Its True	2	F	3	0	0	0	584
Guess Who Iscoming	3	G	5	0	0	0	318
Guest Table	3	F	6	1	0	2	2,250
Guestbook	7	M	15	1	2	4	15,125
Guestchance	6	G	2	0	0	0	163
Guestelaw	5	G	15	0	1	2	4,119
Guffaw	2	G	8	1	0	1	18,205
Guida	5	M	2	0	0	0	1,260
Guidance Up	3	G	11	0	0	3	14,602
Guide	3	F	8	1	2	1	50,280
Guidebook	4	F	6	3	1	0	72,590
Guiding Angel	4	G	15	1	2	2	12,532
Guiding Force	7	G	2	0	0	0	534
Guiding Star	2	F	2	0	0	0	435
Guido	3	G	2	0	0	0	126
Guilded Fantasy	8	G	5	1	0	1	1,705
Guildhall	2	C	3	0	1	0	4,362
Guilty One	6	G	13	0	2	0	4,813
Guilty Party	3	F	5	0	0	0	364
Guilty Verdict	3	F	8	0	0	0	624
Guiltyascaanbe	4	C	8	1	0	3	24,957
Guiltybysupiscion	6	M	9	3	5	0	22,925
Guineaman	3	G	10	1	3	2	39,987

Horse	Age	Sex	Sts	1st	2d	3d	Won
Guiness On Tap	9	G	9	1	1	2	7,627
Guitar	7	M	2	0	0	0	1,920
Gulch Approval	4	G	11	3	1	1	192,698
Gulcharama	3	C	2	0	0	0	160
Gulchie (GB)	6	R	6	0	0	0	6,240
Gulchrunssweet	4	G	11	2	0	1	41,322
Gulch's Sensation	6	H	4	0	1	1	8,000
Gulf Developer	10	G	16	3	2	4	28,291
Gulf News	5	H	2	0	0	0	1,250
Gulf of Gdansk	3	F	13	1	2	1	36,800
Gully Washer	2	C	3	1	0	0	15,900
Gumba	2	C	4	0	0	0	2,780
Gumbo Love	4	F	5	1	1	0	30,075
Gumby Girl	5	M	12	2	2	1	21,640
Gummy	4	F	9	0	0	0	234
Gummy Delight	7	M	6	0	0	0	780
Gump Can Run	4	G	8	0	0	2	1,029
Gumpy Toro	7	G	4	0	1	1	1,768
Gumshoe	7	G	5	0	1	2	8,501
Gun Barrel	9	G	12	2	1	1	9,733
Gun Barrel City	6	G	11	1	1	1	13,459
Gun Barrel Dan	2	C	4	0	0	0	0
Gun Boat	4	G	3	0	0	1	1,044
Gun Case	3	G	7	1	1	3	35,470
Gun Hill	8	G	9	0	2	1	7,173
Gun Is Set	6	G	10	3	1	1	14,468
Gun Point	3	G	2	0	0	0	600
Gun Runner	7	G	11	3	1	0	15,110
Gun Salute	2	C	4	2	1	0	57,794
Gun Silencer	5	H	3	1	0	0	3,402
Gun Swinger	6	G	4	1	1	1	1,620
Gun Town	3	G	9	1	3	1	34,240
Gunduwarrior	4	G	9	1	0	1	6,180
Gunnar G	2	C	2	0	2	0	4,926
Gunner Up	7	G	4	0	0	0	900
Gunnery	5	G	11	0	1	1	2,649
Gunning For	3	G	11	4	0	2	138,135
Guns for Gaze	4	C	1	0	0	0	0
Guns of Freedom	2	C	2	1	0	0	6,600
Gunstock	2	G	5	0	1	1	2,505
Guppie's Secret	5	G	17	5	4	1	67,499
Gurnzi	3	F	9	0	2	2	4,912
Gurza	3	G	9	1	1	1	9,905
Gus Again	7	G	6	4	1	0	46,410
Gus's Tribute	3	G	19	1	1	1	18,121
Gussie's Secret	3	F	5	2	0	0	23,460
Gusso	2	G	2	1	0	0	11,473
Gussy Griffin	5	H	6	0	0	0	280
Gusty Spirit	4	C	7	0	0	0	0
Gut Wrench	3	G	6	0	0	0	1,200
Guts and Glory	4	G	5	1	0	0	10,140
Gutsy Guy	4	C	2	0	1	0	3,150
Guy Getaway	3	G	13	1	3	3	63,820
Guypowder Valley	5	G	1	0	0	0	0
Guy's Gift	3	G	1	0	0	0	0
Gwaihir (IRE)	3	C	13	1	0	1	58,158
Gwanaboa Vale	3	G	10	0	0	2	6,805
Gwen's Dancer	3	G	1	0	0	0	0
Gwen's Pick	3	F	7	1	1	1	11,039
Gwynedd	2	F	3	0	0	0	0
Gygistar	5	G	12	1	1	3	295,320
Gym Kid	3	F	8	0	1	1	13,895
Gymnast	2	F	8	0	0	0	2,070
Gymnastic Girl	3	F	2	0	0	0	122
Gymnist Jack	4	F	7	1	2	1	13,025
Gyp Express	3	C	1	0	0	0	0
Gypsen Moon	5	G	9	0	1	1	6,601
Gypsey Honey	6	M	10	0	2	2	3,128
Gypsiesinthepalace	8	G	7	3	0	0	21,138
Gypsy Breeze	3	F	10	2	1	4	28,470
Gypsy Chief	3	C	3	0	0	0	480
Gypsy Dot	4	F	12	0	1	0	8,197
Gypsy Eyes	3	F	4	1	0	0	12,076
Gypsy Jazz	4	G	5	2	1	0	15,730
Gypsy John	8	G	7	0	0	0	1,723
Gypsy June	7	M	6	0	1	3	2,000
Gypsy Music	6	M	8	1	0	0	2,827
Gypsy Pole E Style	5	M	7	1	1	2	26,987
Gypsy Road	6	G	10	1	2	1	17,335
Gypsy Romance	7	M	7	1	2	0	22,644
Gypsy Shu	3	F	4	0	0	0	138
Gypsy Witch	4	F	7	1	1	3	15,208
Gypsy's Favour	3	F	9	1	0	0	8,984
Gyrene	5	M	8	1	1	3	58,398
Gyrfalcon (GB)	6	H	12	0	0	3	10,850
H and M's Prospect	4	G	13	1	2	4	16,142
H C Express	3	C	1	1	0	0	14,340
H G's Jack	4	C	6	2	1	1	10,790
H M Slew	7	G	2	0	0	0	180
H Potter	3	G	10	3	0	1	24,908
H R H Louis	3	C	2	0	0	0	0
H R Turn to Jones	2	C	1	0	0	0	384
H. B. Dancer	3	F	1	0	0	0	0
H. Hammer G.	9	G	3	0	0	0	0
H. Hour	3	C	4	0	0	0	0
H. M. S. Hollywood	4	G	13	2	2	3	20,561
H. M. S. Jackson	7	G	4	0	0	1	2,840
H. M. S. Majestic	3	G	9	3	2	1	37,315
H. R. Boss Lady	3	F	7	0	0	0	3,748
H. R. H. Doodle	4	F	6	1	2	1	17,402
Ha Ha April Fools	7	M	12	2	1	1	9,642
Ha Ha's Knight	5	H	7	1	0	0	3,164
Haaken	3	C	5	1	0	1	8,335
Haam	3	G	5	0	0	0	1,194
Haasil (IRE)	6	H	6	1	1	0	18,320
Habaneros	5	G	5	3	1	0	122,800
Habayeb	4	C	4	0	0	1	2,035
Habibi	5	M	2	0	0	0	0
Habiboo	3	F	10	3	0	3	115,520
Habitual Criminal	4	C	15	0	3	1	8,328
Hacan (ARG)	6	H	19	6	2	2	49,180
Hacienda Del Mar	4	F	7	1	1	1	34,362
Hackamans Dream	3	C	4	1	2	0	2,255
Hackle	8	G	8	0	0	0	478
Hacksaw Jane	5	M	7	1	1	1	15,407
Hacoda	6	G	14	3	3	3	29,841
Had a Great Run	5	G	16	2	4	3	19,080
Had a Kitten	3	F	10	0	0	0	754
Had to Be You	4	F	12	1	2	1	13,484
Hadalittle	8	G	14	1	2	4	8,093
Hadaya	2	G	2	0	1	0	4,600
Hadenough	6	M	10	5	1	1	53,927
Hades' Fire	4	G	3	0	0	0	0
Hadif Alley	2	F	6	1	1	0	8,835
Hadif Dancer	2	C	9	1	1	1	10,670
Hadif Declares	3	G	12	1	3	1	11,150
Hadif Princess	2	F	1	0	0	0	0
Hadif Runner	2	F	9	1	3	0	20,350
Hadif Time Machine	5	H	5	1	0	1	4,733
Hadifly	6	H	7	1	1	0	7,436
Hadifpatti	3	F	10	2	1	4	13,380
Hadifs Shoelace	5	H	1	0	0	0	0
Hadifson	4	G	10	2	2	0	17,188
Haditude	3	F	9	2	1	2	31,250
Hadivana	3	F	12	4	1	1	16,012
Hadley Hill	4	G	12	2	0	0	9,486
Hadley's Victory	4	G	11	2	2	1	24,170
Hadtoomuch	4	G	17	1	2	3	12,485
Haeley's Glitter	2	F	2	0	0	1	2,765
Hafez	6	G	11	0	3	3	4,185
Hafta Conquer	5	G	8	1	1	1	6,482
Hafta Hava Hat	5	M	2	1	1	0	4,400
Hagerstown	4	F	5	0	1	2	18,880
Haggs Castle	6	G	3	0	0	0	2,767
Hai Ichiban	3	G	1	0	0	0	300
Haiaccept	3	C	10	1	1	1	27,407
Hail Boppie	7	G	6	0	0	1	2,629
Hail Cesar	3	G	5	0	0	0	0
Hail Devongate	4	F	1	0	0	1	900
Hail Hillary	4	F	9	4	1	0	131,010
Hail Holy King (IRE)	3	G	20	2	4	4	19,679
Hail I'm Good	5	M	10	2	2	0	2,471
Hail Lively One	8	G	5	1	1	0	6,660
Hail Luthier	5	G	5	0	0	1	926
Hail Mary Bishop	3	F	7	0	0	1	940
Hail Patton	4	G	4	1	0	2	10,040
Hail Rene	2	G	8	0	0	0	3,280
Hail to Bag	5	G	15	3	2	3	31,741

Horse	Age	Sex	Sts	1st	2d	3d	Won
Hail to Don	3	G	12	1	3	3	17,439
Hail to Humor	2	F	2	0	2	0	10,000
Hail to Love	3	C	10	0	4	0	20,510
Hail to Prospector	4	F	9	1	1	1	6,795
Hail to Smokester	3	C	6	0	0	2	3,709
Hail to the Cat	2	C	3	1	1	0	13,120
Hail to the Queen	2	F	2	0	0	0	630
Hail to the World	2	C	1	0	0	0	135
Hail to Wild Again	6	H	2	0	0	0	619
Hailey	3	F	1	0	0	1	977
Hailey B	4	F	11	0	2	3	16,310
Haileys Bucks	5	H	2	0	0	0	0
Haileys Count	3	F	5	0	1	0	1,787
Hailey's Gone West	2	F	2	0	0	1	1,110
Haileys Hero	2	C	4	0	0	0	270
Haillye's A. T. M.	4	G	8	1	0	1	9,318
Haillye's Brother	3	G	18	3	5	1	27,307
Hailraiser	8	G	9	0	0	0	580
Hails Rockette	2	F	1	0	0	0	140
Hail's Stormy Love	6	M	1	0	0	0	79
Hailthelight	3	C	2	0	0	0	0
Haimish	8	G	4	0	0	1	520
Hainesome Gal	2	F	7	1	1	1	27,330
Haint Dancin	2	C	2	1	0	0	7,015
Haint Going There	3	G	2	0	0	0	128
Haint I Swell	2	G	4	0	0	0	1,613
Haint It Hot	3	G	7	1	1	1	14,685
Haint Misbehavin'	4	F	1	0	0	0	125
Haint No Stopin Me	3	F	6	2	1	0	6,832
Haint You Grand	3	G	16	4	1	4	77,660
Hair Jordan	4	G	12	2	2	3	10,348
Hairy Stimets	6	G	1	0	0	0	0
Haiti Lady	3	F	15	1	3	2	23,013
Haitian Heat	6	M	8	0	0	2	2,886
Haitian Hit	5	G	12	1	3	0	41,376
Haitian Morality	4	G	10	2	4	0	55,500
Haitian Plantation	6	G	4	0	0	0	373
Haitian Princess	6	M	9	1	0	2	8,784
Haitianreiteration	5	M	4	0	2	1	12,229
Hajji Baba	5	G	8	0	1	1	3,150
Hajji Babe	4	F	1	0	0	1	3,000
Hajji's Aloha	2	C	1	0	0	0	300
Haka Girl	2	F	1	1	0	0	30,600
Hakahana	4	C	4	0	0	0	1,271
Hakai's Miracle	2	G	2	0	0	1	1,148
Halawa Moon	2	G	6	2	0	0	21,450
Halawellfin Hala (GB)	5	G	7	3	2	1	105,587
Halcyon Bay	4	G	15	1	2	6	52,500
Hale Haven	2	F	1	0	0	0	145
Hale Ole	6	M	15	2	2	1	3,605
Hale the Bold	9	G	3	0	0	0	0
Haleakala Sunrise	3	F	6	1	1	1	39,260
Haley Mac	3	F	1	0	0	0	120
Haley's Buddy	4	G	7	0	2	2	12,445
Haley's Classic	5	M	8	0	1	1	22,348
Haley's Sharp	3	F	12	4	1	3	26,240
Half a Bag	4	C	13	4	3	3	52,677
Half a Biscuit	3	C	1	0	0	0	200
Half a Case	4	G	2	0	0	1	960
Half a Dollar Maid	3	F	1	0	0	0	300
Half a Glance	2	F	3	0	0	2	4,006
Half a Nip	3	G	2	0	0	0	300
Half a Pat	4	F	2	0	0	0	0
Half a Storm	2	F	3	1	1	0	26,500
Half a Zillion	3	C	3	0	0	0	1,200
Half Diamond	4	G	8	2	3	1	19,160
Half Feline	2	F	4	1	1	0	12,100
Half Hearted	4	F	10	0	4	0	4,604
Half Heaven	2	F	2	1	0	0	25,332
Half Merit	2	F	3	0	0	2	2,750
Half Moon	5	M	2	0	0	0	1,566
Half Moon Romance	8	H	3	0	0	0	231
Half Net	3	G	2	0	1	0	4,200
Half Off	5	M	19	1	4	2	7,508
Half Penny	4	F	2	1	0	0	1,980
Half Pint Boxer	2	G	6	1	1	1	14,329
Half Pint to Go	6	M	5	2	0	1	17,170
Half Splendor	2	C	1	0	0	0	840
Half Windsor	2	G	1	0	0	0	0

Horse	Age	Sex	Sts	1st	2d	3d	Won
Halfa (ARG)	5	M	1	0	0	0	400
Halfbridled	3	F	2	0	2	0	110,000
Halfpint	3	F	1	0	0	1	1,200
Halfway Home	4	G	19	2	1	0	13,858
Halfway to Heaven	6	M	18	1	0	7	44,791
Haliburton Eva	2	F	6	2	1	0	56,454
Haliburton Honey	4	F	9	3	1	1	97,892
Haliburton Sky	4	G	4	1	0	0	36,588
Haliburton Storm	3	G	11	0	0	1	5,567
Haliburton Wild	4	G	15	1	3	1	13,887
Haliburtonhighland	2	F	3	0	0	1	6,270
Halissee's Son	4	G	2	1	0	0	8,361
Hall Dancer	2	G	4	1	2	0	14,713
Hall Lass	4	C	9	1	0	2	10,391
Hall of Excellence	5	G	2	1	1	0	6,270
Hallas	7	M	9	2	2	2	8,063
Hallelujahnpraise	3	F	5	0	0	1	861
Hallie Cat	5	M	9	0	0	2	3,490
Hallie Laredo	3	F	5	0	0	1	1,568
Hallie Lyn	2	F	2	0	0	0	357
Hallie's Danzigjet	8	M	3	0	1	0	1,177
Hall'nhalo	3	G	4	1	1	0	8,509
Hallo Bert	8	G	9	3	0	0	10,331
Hallowed Halls	10	G	3	0	0	1	4,000
Halloween Fun	4	F	9	2	1	0	24,295
Hallshill Road	7	G	5	3	0	0	30,911
Halltheway	7	G	15	5	1	2	40,265
Hallucinogin	7	H	1	0	0	0	44
Halo Alo	5	H	2	0	0	0	120
Halo Avenue	3	F	5	0	1	3	13,137
Halo Brite	5	G	11	4	2	2	42,650
Halo Can You Go	5	M	2	1	1	0	10,640
Halo Cat	6	G	6	3	0	1	72,685
Halo Cinderella	3	F	5	2	1	0	17,530
Halo Colddeck	4	G	19	1	2	3	6,561
Halo Crossing	2	G	2	0	0	0	0
Halo Dancer	5	G	1	0	0	0	110
Halo Dare	6	G	7	0	0	0	0
Halo de Angeles	2	F	1	0	0	0	250
Halo de Oro	2	C	3	0	0	0	0
Halo Dixie Land	4	F	2	0	0	0	0
Halo Enclosed	8	G	12	3	1	3	30,760
Halo Flamingo	3	G	12	2	4	4	32,640
Halo for Mary	3	G	13	1	1	3	20,335
Halo Friday	3	G	5	1	1	1	12,185
Halo Goodbye	3	G	16	3	2	2	69,550
Halo Hallo	3	C	2	0	0	0	85
Halo Halo Halo	4	F	12	3	1	1	36,337
Halo Halo Star	3	F	4	0	0	0	870
Halo Heaven	4	G	8	0	1	1	12,670
Halo Hit	2	F	2	1	1	0	19,000
Halo Homewrecker	4	C	6	0	1	1	18,216
Halo Hunter (ARG)	6	G	9	5	1	2	40,465
Halo Huny	3	F	9	1	0	0	4,050
Halo Jamerica	2	F	11	2	1	3	48,335
Halo Jesse	3	F	5	1	2	0	13,942
Halo Jet	2	G	4	0	0	1	1,980
Halo Keely	3	F	7	0	4	0	5,000
Halo Kris	7	G	12	2	1	1	45,145
Halo Lad	2	G	2	1	0	1	13,930
Halo Light	4	F	9	2	0	2	16,232
Halo Malone	4	G	11	3	2	2	84,140
Halo Moon	5	M	1	0	0	0	250
Halo Mr Big	2	C	4	0	0	0	0
Halo Nell	7	H	5	1	0	1	6,885
Halo of Freedom	3	F	7	0	0	0	1,609
Halo of Silver	4	F	10	2	1	2	17,286
Halo of Truth	6	M	12	0	2	1	8,621
Halo Okie	2	C	3	1	2	0	10,080
Halo Rube	3	G	1	0	0	0	240
Halo Sassy	2	F	1	0	0	0	0
Halo Seeya	6	M	3	0	0	0	330
Halo Skywalker	2	F	4	0	0	0	735
Halo Special	4	F	5	0	1	2	4,363
Halo Springs	6	M	9	0	0	0	1,346
Halo Sue	4	F	7	0	0	0	3,054
Halo Sun	3	F	2	0	0	1	2,500
Halo Tyra	5	M	3	0	0	1	3,370
Halo Whitley	2	F	2	0	0	0	600

Horse	Age	Sex	Sts	1st	2d	3d	Won
Halo World	9	G	4	0	0	1	1,434
Halodramatic	3	F	5	0	2	0	15,010
Halographic	3	G	3	1	0	0	21,072
Halonator	3	F	7	1	2	2	10,817
Halory Clanton	3	F	9	1	1	1	3,790
Halory Hunted	3	G	15	2	6	3	41,133
Halory Leigh	4	F	10	3	1	1	434,634
Halory Lewis	3	F	15	2	1	1	12,760
Halory Too	4	F	5	1	0	1	4,946
Halory's Habit	3	F	11	3	3	2	44,650
Halory's Secret	4	F	7	0	0	0	768
Halo's Alarm	4	G	5	2	1	0	9,925
Halo's Appeal	4	G	3	1	1	0	29,440
Halo's Bid	4	F	7	1	0	2	35,000
Halo's Creek	3	F	3	0	0	0	0
Halo's Echo	5	M	7	2	2	1	6,829
Halo's Effort	3	F	8	2	1	0	15,194
Halos Festive	3	G	14	2	2	3	14,665
Halos for Hibiscus	4	C	8	0	1	0	7,211
Halo's Gem	4	F	10	0	0	2	3,610
Halo's Heartbreak	6	M	10	1	0	2	5,784
Halo's Honour	5	G	7	0	0	0	132
Halo's Investment	3	C	14	3	1	2	25,200
Halos Mercedes	3	F	6	0	0	0	450
Halo's Morpheus	3	G	10	2	0	0	13,292
Halo's Patriot	3	C	1	0	0	0	0
Halo's Pleasure	4	F	18	2	4	0	18,057
Halos Promise Land	4	F	4	0	1	0	1,348
Halo's Regent	4	G	18	4	0	2	29,575
Halo's Secret	6	G	2	0	0	0	110
Halo's Shadow	6	H	7	2	1	0	11,177
Halo's Song	4	F	14	2	3	1	13,148
Halo's Sugar	5	M	3	0	1	0	1,540
Halo's Sunset	3	F	3	0	0	2	883
Halo's Tiger	5	G	6	2	0	1	47,510
Halos Tresses	3	F	3	0	0	0	906
Halo's Wildcat	3	F	10	2	2	0	39,002
Halosnglory	3	G	6	0	0	0	2,144
Halover	8	G	7	0	0	0	629
Hal's Gal	3	F	9	0	1	1	2,141
Hal's Image	2	C	11	1	1	3	56,040
Halu Kour's Lady	4	F	4	0	0	1	560
Halve It All	4	C	7	1	1	1	9,240
Halvsies	5	M	1	1	0	0	894
Ham Sandwich	7	H	2	0	0	0	217
Hamaaly	4	G	19	2	4	2	25,200
Hamanjiz	5	G	18	1	2	1	11,970
Hama's	3	F	9	3	1	0	33,836
Hamburger Chef	3	C	15	2	4	2	24,260
Hamel	2	G	1	0	0	0	140
Hamel the Camel	3	C	4	0	1	1	2,435
Hamering Heart	4	F	3	0	0	0	0
Hamilton Island	7	G	6	4	1	1	13,049
Haminahaminahamina	4	G	2	0	0	0	161
Hamlet	4	F	7	2	2	0	20,020
Hamlet of Ribot	4	G	1	0	0	0	57
Hamm and Beans	3	F	7	1	0	0	3,096
Hammer Down Hank	3	C	7	2	0	0	18,635
Hammer It	3	G	8	1	0	0	6,476
Hammer Start	3	G	3	0	0	0	625
Hammerin	4	C	13	4	1	3	32,459
Hammerlane	3	G	3	0	0	1	938
Hammerlock Ridge	7	H	6	0	0	0	856
Hammerstone	2	G	1	0	0	0	0
Hamp's Champ	3	C	12	1	1	1	18,657
Hampton Express	4	F	6	0	2	0	1,710
Ham's Our Man	4	G	5	1	0	1	10,549
Ham'shotrod	2	C	4	0	2	0	6,700
Hana Highway	6	G	1	0	0	0	270
Hanalei Bay	2	F	6	1	0	1	32,540
Hananiah	5	H	4	0	0	1	1,333
Hancock Park	4	G	1	0	0	0	85
Handful of Marbles	5	M	6	1	1	1	10,073
Handlebar Hank	2	C	10	0	2	3	76,848
Handpainted	4	F	6	2	0	2	119,596
Hands in Pockets	2	G	2	0	0	0	0
Hands On	3	G	9	1	1	4	54,080
Hands to the Side	6	G	3	0	0	0	0
Handsomchamp	2	C	2	2	0	0	9,938
Handsome Change	3	G	6	0	2	1	7,350
Handsome Darby	7	G	8	1	0	0	7,764
Handsome Face	4	G	7	0	1	0	5,615
Handsome George	5	G	12	0	1	1	15,880
Handsome Henry	5	G	16	0	1	5	4,747
Handsome Hunk	5	H	10	1	1	2	16,920
Handsome Jack	6	G	8	0	0	0	2,313
Handsome Jim	5	G	1	0	0	0	0
Handsome Jolly Jim	9	G	15	1	1	0	8,907
Handsome Juan	3	C	2	1	0	0	600
Handsome Michael K	2	C	1	0	0	0	400
Handsome Pancho	3	G	6	0	0	0	1,590
Handsome Smile	6	G	13	2	1	1	52,085
Handsome Tabby	4	C	3	1	1	0	10,940
Handsome Tour	3	G	1	0	0	0	75
Handsome Twister	3	G	11	0	1	1	1,977
Handsome Will Do	6	G	3	0	0	0	0
Handy Nutcracker	5	M	3	0	0	0	124
Handy Prospect	2	C	1	0	0	0	345
Handyman Bill	5	G	2	0	0	1	8,550
Handzz Up	4	G	6	0	0	1	1,160
Hang On Brenda	5	M	2	0	0	0	0
Hang On Wheatly	3	F	4	1	0	0	5,703
Hang Up Call	4	F	4	3	0	0	25,528
Hangar	4	C	13	0	1	3	3,596
Hangin' by a Tread	5	M	16	0	2	0	2,764
Hanging Chads	2	F	2	1	1	0	36,000
Hanging Jury	3	C	16	1	2	3	11,193
Hanging Out	3	G	6	0	1	1	3,325
Hanging Sparkles	4	C	1	0	0	0	0
Hangmans Comin	3	G	3	0	0	0	184
Hangonslewpyhangon	8	G	8	1	0	1	14,166
Hangontight	5	G	9	0	3	0	5,752
Hangtime	4	G	11	0	0	0	6,095
Hangwiththehaves	3	F	10	1	0	1	15,110
Hank Man	2	G	1	0	0	0	78
Hank's Chance	4	G	6	0	0	0	803
Hank's Rib	5	G	7	5	0	0	76,800
Hanky	5	H	11	2	3	1	38,765
Hanlan	6	G	10	1	0	0	36,477
Hanna Jibe	3	F	12	1	4	3	19,280
Hanna Rules	3	F	8	0	0	0	0
Hannaboy	4	G	13	2	1	3	9,987
Hannah D	6	M	3	0	0	1	1,102
Hannah L	3	F	14	0	4	5	6,651
Hannah On Stage	4	F	11	4	0	0	13,438
Hannah Susanna	3	F	4	0	0	0	480
Hannah the Wrecker	5	M	17	2	2	5	19,975
Hannah's Grace	4	F	9	0	0	1	1,300
Hannah's Hero	8	G	3	1	0	0	2,520
Hannah's Royalrock	4	F	4	0	1	1	8,019
Hannah's Runner	2	G	3	0	0	0	0
Hannahtized	2	F	6	0	0	0	570
Hanna's Fury	2	F	4	1	0	0	16,736
Hanna's Gamble	4	F	13	5	0	3	30,455
Hanna's K C	6	M	4	0	0	0	2,274
Hanna's Kat	4	C	3	0	0	0	996
Hanna's Luck	3	G	11	2	0	1	46,842
Hannel	3	C	3	0	2	0	18,640
Hannibal Kitten	3	F	1	0	0	0	42
Hannibal Lad (GB)	8	G	2	0	0	1	5,400
Hanoi	3	G	2	0	0	0	342
Hanover Hollywood	7	G	2	0	0	0	281
Hanover Storm	3	C	5	0	2	0	5,570
Hanover Wharf	6	M	5	1	3	1	22,560
Hansbury	6	G	20	2	4	1	10,848
Hanselina	4	F	6	2	1	1	65,939
Hansello	2	G	2	0	0	0	145
Hansome Jim	3	C	8	1	1	0	5,947
Hapes County Son	7	G	4	0	0	0	476
Hapes Jr.	6	G	15	1	3	2	6,849
Hapid Ralo	2	F	2	0	1	0	1,854
Hapnin	3	F	6	0	0	0	541
Happee Kisser	6	G	1	0	0	0	0
Happiness	5	G	11	1	2	0	15,819
Happinessisapuppy	2	F	4	0	0	0	1,283
Happony	5	M	4	1	1	0	5,080
Happy Acres	7	H	2	0	0	0	83
Happy and Hasty	4	G	1	0	1	0	5,000

Horse	Age	Sex	Sts	1st	2d	3d	Won
Happy Anna	4	F	5	0	0	1	6,367
Happy Apple	6	M	8	1	2	1	12,715
Happy As	4	F	12	1	2	1	19,505
Happy as a Lark	3	G	3	0	0	0	0
Happy At Last	4	F	6	1	0	0	1,485
Happy Bert	2	C	4	0	0	0	541
Happy Camper	4	F	2	0	0	0	103
Happy Coyote	7	G	13	0	0	1	2,372
Happy Cruiser	4	F	2	0	0	0	312
Happy Day	3	F	5	0	0	1	971
Happy Endings Too	3	F	9	1	1	2	40,760
Happy Face	5	M	2	1	0	0	28,140
Happy Flag	5	G	2	0	0	1	600
Happy Gabby	2	F	2	0	0	1	1,540
Happy Go Glare	4	G	5	0	1	1	4,900
Happy Hobby	3	F	1	0	0	0	400
Happy Hour	2	G	7	0	1	0	3,881
Happy Jackie	5	M	12	4	0	0	28,590
Happy Jazz	3	F	9	1	1	1	9,627
Happy Kitty	3	F	1	0	1	0	5,300
Happy Lassie	2	F	3	0	0	0	671
Happy Legs	4	G	9	0	1	2	2,794
Happy Lil	5	M	8	2	0	0	4,621
Happy Menocal	5	G	4	0	0	0	193
Happy Numbers	4	F	1	1	0	0	8,400
Happy Pass	3	F	2	0	0	0	177
Happy Retreat	5	G	9	2	2	2	51,936
Happy Rivergo	5	G	10	2	1	1	14,012
Happy Roman	5	M	12	1	0	4	7,214
Happy Sport	7	G	12	0	2	1	4,454
Happy Taps	2	F	3	0	0	0	502
Happy Ticket	3	F	7	7	0	0	247,260
Happy to Say	4	F	5	1	0	0	3,600
Happy to Smokem	4	G	7	0	2	0	4,807
Happy Tobe Free	3	F	1	0	0	0	60
Happy Trails	4	C	6	2	0	1	63,856
Happy Yodeler	3	C	13	3	1	3	37,290
Happybirthdaygirl	2	F	1	0	0	1	5,610
Happyfrolicinganna	3	F	5	0	0	0	800
Happygolarky	4	F	5	1	0	0	2,732
Hapsirishpub	4	G	8	3	0	0	9,368
Harangue	3	G	4	1	1	0	11,555
Harbo	3	C	11	2	1	1	16,276
Harbor At Night	3	F	7	1	0	1	6,110
Harbor Blues	4	F	9	1	1	4	58,580
Harbor Chief	4	F	8	1	0	2	9,635
Harbor Court	4	F	15	2	5	2	39,647
Harbor Craft	3	G	10	1	2	1	35,220
Harbor Girl	3	F	6	0	2	1	15,280
Harbor Haven	5	H	3	1	1	0	4,020
Harbor House	3	F	4	0	0	1	3,750
Harbor Lady	4	F	2	0	0	0	0
Harbor Mist	6	G	4	0	0	0	336
Harbor Morn	3	C	1	0	0	0	70
Harbor Music	3	G	1	0	0	0	0
Harbor of Grace	8	G	7	4	0	1	33,829
Harbor Pass	5	G	1	0	0	0	0
Harbor Princess	4	F	7	0	2	1	10,540
Harbor Sail	4	F	4	1	0	0	11,070
Harbor the Dream	5	G	5	0	0	0	392
Harbor the Gold	3	C	4	1	1	0	26,750
Harbor Worker	3	G	4	1	1	1	17,480
Harboringfugitives	3	G	2	0	0	0	324
Harbour Axe	3	C	16	6	1	0	10,027
Harbour Belle	3	F	13	3	3	2	33,528
Harbour Buoy	3	F	6	1	0	1	15,501
Harbour Crossing	7	G	3	0	0	0	1,970
Harbour Gate	3	G	6	1	1	0	31,755
Harbour Ice	6	G	10	1	0	1	14,715
Harbour Melody	2	F	3	0	0	0	426
Harbour Sunset	11	H	1	0	0	0	50
Harbour Tide	2	C	7	1	1	2	10,120
Harbour Town	2	G	4	1	0	0	12,140
Harbro	6	G	8	1	3	0	6,151
Hard Break Dancer	5	G	18	0	3	2	7,622
Hard Buck (BRZ)	5	H	6	1	3	0	840,526
Hard Card	4	G	5	3	1	0	32,516
Hard Coal	4	G	10	0	0	1	2,847
Hard Currency	8	H	9	2	1	0	31,368

Horse	Age	Sex	Sts	1st	2d	3d	Won
Hard Dance	4	G	3	0	0	0	1,035
Hard Dancing Lady	5	M	1	0	0	0	72
Hard Decision	2	C	6	1	3	0	27,600
Hard Edge	5	G	13	2	1	1	115,110
Hard Four Mac	2	C	4	0	0	0	1,392
Hard Gal B	4	F	11	1	2	1	20,690
Hard Head	3	G	8	0	1	2	22,570
Hard Hearted Julio	4	G	1	0	0	0	0
Hard Held	8	G	8	1	3	0	8,612
Hard Hitter	6	G	4	3	0	0	6,822
Hard Hitting Hatt	5	G	1	0	0	0	84
Hard Knocks	3	G	5	0	0	0	1,950
Hard Luck Eilsel	2	C	2	0	0	0	0
Hard of Hearing	3	G	5	0	0	0	1,062
Hard Quality	4	C	4	0	0	0	1,424
Hard Rock Bottom	3	G	3	0	0	0	420
Hard Runnin Hannah	4	F	3	0	0	0	0
Hard Talent	2	C	2	0	0	0	175
Hard Times	5	G	4	0	0	2	5,660
Hard to B Superman	2	C	1	0	0	0	460
Hard to Call	5	M	2	0	0	0	642
Hard to Come By	5	M	13	1	1	0	6,999
Hard to Stop	3	F	5	0	0	0	98
Hardad	3	G	11	0	2	0	6,240
Hardaround	3	G	13	1	3	0	10,855
Harderthanpride	4	F	11	1	0	2	21,026
Hardhearted Hannah	3	F	9	0	2	2	5,745
Hardie's Ringer	4	G	3	0	1	1	640
Hardluck Hannah	4	F	2	0	0	0	125
Hardly a Harley	2	G	3	0	1	0	4,600
Hardly a Lady	4	F	1	0	0	0	77
Hardly an Angel	3	F	11	1	0	1	9,272
Hardmoney	2	F	3	0	0	0	950
Hardmoney Road	2	C	1	0	0	0	300
Hardridinheartache	4	G	4	0	0	0	334
Hardtobethebest	3	C	6	0	3	1	13,990
Hardtolite	3	C	2	0	0	0	380
Hardware	3	G	11	1	2	1	11,233
Hardy Child	4	G	23	0	1	4	5,778
Hare Raising	12	G	2	0	0	0	0
Hares	7	G	7	0	0	2	1,915
Hare's Love	6	G	19	2	0	3	29,205
Hargett	3	C	12	1	2	1	7,172
Hark the Sound (GB)	5	M	4	0	1	0	6,000
Harkey Malarky	2	C	1	1	0	0	7,200
Harlan Ave.	5	H	3	0	0	0	230
Harlanswitch	3	C	7	3	1	0	15,115
Harleigh David	5	G	3	0	0	0	352
Harlem Angel	2	F	2	0	0	0	1,720
Harlem Wolf	2	C	2	0	0	0	0
Harley Country	4	F	13	1	1	1	7,833
Harley Girl	4	F	8	3	1	2	20,485
Harley Queen	4	F	11	1	1	1	6,372
Harley Quinn	7	H	6	1	0	0	20,658
Harley's Game	2	C	1	0	0	0	0
Harley's Road	3	G	6	0	0	3	8,861
Harley's Star	4	F	9	0	0	0	740
Harleys Turn	6	G	4	0	0	0	180
Harlington	2	C	1	1	0	0	27,600
Harlon's Gold	5	G	1	0	0	0	0
Harmonic Harriet	6	M	5	1	0	1	1,155
Harmonist	4	F	1	0	0	0	1,800
Harmony Hall	5	H	7	1	2	1	25,860
Harmony Holler	6	M	3	0	0	0	218
Harmony Light	3	F	14	3	4	1	27,942
Harmony Lodge	6	M	6	1	3	1	176,000
Harmony Park	4	G	7	4	2	1	32,428
Harmony River	2	F	2	0	0	1	1,380
Harmony's Prospect	3	G	5	0	0	0	2,360
Harnsberger	3	C	3	0	0	1	4,945
Harold's Halo	2	G	4	0	1	2	8,750
Harold's Nickel	9	G	4	0	0	0	225
Harpers Content	4	F	4	1	0	0	3,889
Harpers Crown	4	G	14	2	1	1	21,474
Harperstown Wish	8	G	2	0	0	0	0
Harpist	3	F	11	3	0	1	33,311
Harpoon	3	C	16	5	1	1	53,595
Harriet	7	M	5	0	0	0	765
Harriett Elaine	6	M	11	0	0	1	6,742

Horse	Age	Sex	Sts	1st	2d	3d	Won
Harriett's Gem	2	F	4	0	0	1	3,520
Harriman's Bid	4	G	3	2	0	1	6,826
Harrimans Image	10	G	1	0	0	0	0
Harrington	3	G	8	0	0	0	1,331
Harrington Sound	8	H	2	0	0	0	420
Harri's Playmate	4	F	12	2	0	0	8,602
Harrisburg Mike	3	C	1	0	0	0	0
Harrison's Halo	3	G	4	0	1	0	4,640
Harrogate Hills	5	M	5	2	3	0	38,010
Harry Bailey	3	G	5	0	1	0	5,240
Harry Got Happy	4	G	14	2	0	2	27,332
Harry Has Horns	2	G	2	0	0	0	0
Harry n' Zeke	2	G	2	0	0	0	1,800
Harry Pietsch	5	G	1	0	0	0	0
Harry the Barber	4	C	6	2	1	0	11,757
Harry the Prince	6	G	9	3	0	1	34,413
Harry the Rock	3	G	8	0	4	1	41,148
Harry the Wizard	3	G	10	2	0	1	41,375
Harry's Act	5	G	5	1	2	0	4,625
Harry's Firebolt	3	G	7	1	1	1	5,130
Harrys Girl	3	F	7	0	0	0	320
Harry's Legecy	3	C	2	0	0	0	0
Harry's Nimbus	3	G	14	2	2	1	20,083
Harry's Rainbow	6	G	9	0	0	0	717
Harrys Trumpet	4	G	1	0	0	0	0
Harry's Whirl	4	G	1	0	0	0	0
Harsha's Budget	4	F	8	0	2	0	6,860
Hartford	2	G	3	0	0	0	161
Hartland Xpress	5	M	9	0	0	2	2,130
Hartney Oak	5	M	8	2	1	1	13,705
Hart's Are Green	5	M	4	0	0	0	923
Harts Gap	5	M	10	1	2	3	51,210
Harts Time	5	M	8	2	0	0	18,709
Hartshorne	4	G	14	2	0	3	13,692
Hartwell	8	G	8	0	0	1	2,450
Harvard Avenue	3	G	6	0	1	3	126,400
Harvard Bound	2	C	5	0	2	0	12,400
Harvard Thunder	2	G	2	0	0	0	0
Harvard Yard	3	G	2	0	0	0	85
Harve de Grace	4	F	3	1	0	0	12,990
Harvest Festival	4	G	15	5	5	2	52,645
Harvest Singing	4	F	11	3	1	2	39,964
Harvey Bengal	6	G	8	2	1	2	17,365
Harvey Girl	4	F	1	0	0	0	1,700
Harvey's Delight	3	F	11	2	2	0	5,373
Harveys Hammerback	3	G	10	0	1	2	6,250
Harveys Hot Summer	3	F	1	0	0	0	0
Harveys Rosebud	3	F	5	0	1	0	2,500
Harveyslittlething	4	F	5	0	0	1	1,428
Harveywallbanger	2	C	3	0	0	0	380
Harvick	4	C	5	1	1	0	7,150
Harwell	7	G	4	0	0	0	0
Harwood	5	G	11	0	2	2	7,351
Hasit	4	G	12	1	2	1	9,730
Haskin's Hope	3	C	2	0	0	0	0
Haslam	4	C	5	1	0	1	6,630
Hassayampa	2	F	4	2	0	1	63,209
Hasse	5	G	1	0	0	0	0
Hassledontheborder	5	G	7	2	3	1	50,366
Hasslefree	3	C	10	0	1	3	93,530
Hasta La Quista	3	F	6	2	0	0	35,275
Hastego	3	G	19	3	4	2	55,880
Hastings Rocks	5	G	2	0	0	1	2,580
Hastmakeswast	5	M	2	0	0	0	140
Hasty	3	F	11	2	3	1	39,155
Hasty Decorated	7	G	3	0	0	0	456
Hasty Dreams	5	M	12	3	2	1	30,381
Hasty Hedia	2	F	2	0	0	0	170
Hasty Helen	3	F	8	0	0	1	1,544
Hasty Kiss	6	M	15	2	4	0	54,131
Hasty Kris	7	G	9	1	1	2	116,016
Hasty Money	7	G	1	0	0	0	100
Hasty Satan	6	M	2	0	1	0	594
Hasty Star	5	G	11	0	1	1	5,015
Hasty Vik	3	G	13	2	0	0	9,473
Hasty's Devil	3	G	2	1	0	0	13,060
Hat Creek	3	F	6	4	2	0	157,804
Hatch (GB)	3	C	11	2	2	2	28,408
Hatchets Last Wish	7	G	14	1	2	2	9,043
Hatchetsflyingirl	3	F	12	1	4	2	16,494
Hate Mail	3	G	21	2	1	3	13,866
Hatenot	7	M	4	0	0	2	7,202
Hatif (BRZ)	5	H	6	1	2	0	61,800
Hatpin	2	F	1	1	0	0	35,280
Hats Back	4	G	3	0	0	0	112
Hats Off to Thee	2	F	3	0	2	0	6,655
Hattie's Love	4	G	9	1	3	1	14,420
Hatton Cross	4	G	7	2	1	0	25,055
Hatzic Lake	4	G	8	1	2	2	27,590
Haughty Lady	4	F	5	1	2	2	20,900
Haughty Time	9	G	2	0	0	0	91
Haul Away Joe	3	C	7	1	0	0	19,170
Haunted Forrest	5	G	13	4	0	3	13,300
Haunted House	2	C	1	0	0	1	2,860
Haunted River	5	M	5	1	0	2	8,220
Haunting Memory	2	F	10	0	1	4	7,350
Hauntingly Wild	4	F	1	0	0	0	79
Haute Gold	2	G	5	0	0	0	425
Haute Move	4	G	5	0	0	1	1,500
Haute Stuff	3	F	1	0	0	0	50
Hava Peer	8	M	9	0	2	2	14,861
Havana	7	H	7	1	0	3	35,703
Havana Anna	3	F	12	1	3	2	13,426
Havana Perfecto	8	G	1	0	0	0	0
Havana Storm	3	C	1	0	0	0	708
Havaneclair	6	G	12	1	0	1	6,778
Havasu Canyon	6	H	6	0	0	1	4,892
Have a Great Day	5	M	4	1	2	1	49,400
Have a Herat	4	F	11	2	4	2	24,170
Have Concern	3	C	4	0	0	0	523
Have No Fear	5	G	13	3	3	2	19,487
Haveitourway	6	G	6	0	0	0	0
Have'n a Lark	2	F	3	1	0	2	13,133
Haven's Rook	5	H	1	0	0	0	0
Haveslewsafun	5	M	1	0	0	0	0
Havespeedwiltravel	3	G	3	0	0	0	214
Haveyouheard	5	M	8	1	0	3	13,230
Havin' a Fun Run	2	C	2	0	0	1	3,245
Havin a Good Time	2	F	1	0	0	0	0
Hav'n a Tizzy Fit	2	G	4	1	1	0	10,188
Havocry	6	G	2	0	0	0	260
Havouimet	4	F	4	0	0	0	423
Havre Winds	6	G	13	2	1	1	7,262
Hawa Mahal	3	F	4	0	0	1	9,000
Hawaian Lord (CHI)	9	G	13	1	0	0	5,532
Hawaii Prospector	2	F	2	0	0	0	215
Hawaiian Attitude	7	M	9	0	1	1	3,551
Hawaiian Honour	3	F	2	0	0	0	264
Hawaiian Lullaby	5	M	12	1	0	2	4,100
Hawaiian Snickers	4	G	6	1	3	0	15,435
Hawaiian Storm	5	G	11	0	0	0	1,251
Hawaiian Symphony	5	G	14	1	2	1	5,057
Hawaiin Frolic	3	F	10	1	1	1	15,750
Hawaiin Gold	3	G	12	3	0	2	28,484
Hawg	6	G	4	0	0	0	958
Hawk City Lord	4	G	14	2	1	0	20,310
Hawk de Gold	2	G	4	1	2	0	14,470
Hawk in Flight	3	R	2	0	0	0	0
Hawk Lake	5	G	1	0	0	0	0
Hawk Royal	5	G	3	0	0	0	80
Hawk Speed	3	C	3	0	1	0	2,800
Hawkahontas	9	M	2	0	0	0	402
Hawkaway	6	G	9	0	0	0	560
Hawkeye (IRE)	6	H	3	0	0	0	3,720
Hawkeye Judy	2	F	7	0	0	2	3,832
Hawkeye Pierce	4	C	1	0	0	0	0
Hawkeyed	5	G	13	1	0	0	5,077
Hawking	3	C	5	1	0	2	21,200
Hawkins Little Guy	5	G	8	0	0	1	1,376
Hawkish	3	G	8	2	1	2	32,350
Hawkmoon	4	G	3	0	0	0	40
Hawk's Feather	8	G	5	0	0	0	840
Hawks Mill	3	G	2	0	0	0	495
Hawks Slugger	9	G	6	2	0	2	3,697
Hawk's Top Gun	5	H	5	0	0	1	338
Hawksbill	4	C	3	1	1	0	46,100
Hawksters Champ	4	G	8	1	0	3	6,182
Hawkwatch	8	G	6	0	2	1	19,320

Horse	Age	Sex	Sts	1st	2d	3d	Won
Hawley Lake	5	M	8	2	1	1	21,655
Hawthorne Devil	4	G	5	1	2	0	15,893
Hawthorne Lane	5	M	2	0	0	0	880
Hay Allison	4	F	8	2	1	1	36,220
Hay Amy	3	F	8	1	1	4	12,395
Hay Bailey	3	G	11	2	6	1	72,555
Hay Big Guy	7	H	1	0	1	0	1,700
Hay Cheryl	3	F	4	1	1	1	9,120
Hay Costa	4	F	9	1	1	0	23,465
Hay Daisy	3	F	8	2	2	2	23,563
Hay Dream Catcher	6	M	3	0	0	0	566
Hay Fat Mama	3	F	5	0	0	1	1,650
Hay Getoutofmyway	5	G	7	2	0	1	28,600
Hay Ho Diamond	2	F	1	0	0	0	0
Hay Jarred	2	G	6	1	0	1	37,492
Hay Lauren	3	F	2	0	0	0	6,900
Hay Low Halo	6	G	4	1	0	0	3,480
Hay Madison	3	F	8	2	2	2	54,960
Hay Matt	4	G	11	1	1	2	11,797
Hay Mr. Brassman	4	G	11	2	1	0	33,863
Hay Princess	5	M	8	5	2	0	36,790
Hay Shea	4	F	1	0	0	0	0
Hay Syd	2	G	4	0	1	1	2,950
Hay Ticket	3	G	2	0	0	0	690
Hay Worthy	5	M	1	0	0	0	150
Hayato	3	G	1	0	0	1	2,280
Haybug	3	G	10	1	1	1	17,455
Hayden Storm	7	G	12	3	0	0	5,608
Hayden's Law	5	H	11	1	0	0	5,788
Hayden's Princess	4	F	5	1	0	1	3,565
Hayes Road	4	G	14	3	3	1	31,380
Hayfield	3	C	5	2	1	0	18,734
Hayhilary	3	F	5	0	0	0	0
Haylee Moore	8	M	4	0	0	0	452
Hayley Match Me Up	4	G	9	0	0	0	0
Haystack	4	G	7	1	0	0	4,096
Haytaxi	7	G	14	0	1	3	5,587
Haytown Hill	5	G	9	1	1	2	7,409
Haz Majec	4	G	9	0	1	1	3,136
Hazaam's Appeal	4	F	11	1	1	0	9,710
Hazagrand	5	M	10	2	1	2	15,231
Hazel Dip	4	F	2	0	0	0	157
Hazelldell	5	M	2	0	0	0	590
Hazel's Shoes	4	F	4	0	0	0	113
Hazelwood	3	F	9	1	3	1	34,670
Haziness	2	C	11	2	1	4	23,440
Hazoom	4	G	11	2	4	0	15,758
Hazor	4	F	8	1	2	0	14,853
Hazy Best	3	G	1	0	0	0	70
Hazy Mirage	4	F	2	0	0	0	0
Hazyview (GB)	3	C	9	4	2	1	142,839
Hazzari	3	C	11	6	0	2	22,870
He Aint No Bull	2	C	2	0	0	0	240
He Be Irish	9	G	17	3	3	1	25,335
He Be Pretty	4	G	8	0	2	1	3,021
He Better Win	4	G	7	0	0	0	0
He Da Sheik	3	G	5	0	0	0	195
He Devil	2	C	6	0	5	0	25,680
He Did It	4	G	3	1	0	0	26,776
He Did It His Way	6	G	7	2	0	1	26,908
He Does	4	G	3	0	1	0	4,300
He Flies	6	G	8	2	1	1	58,246
He Got the Number	3	C	4	1	0	1	18,430
He Ha	4	G	5	0	0	0	205
He Has No Taste	10	G	4	0	0	1	703
He Is a Clown	5	G	5	0	0	0	699
He Is Indeed	8	G	6	1	1	0	2,248
He Loves Me	3	F	10	5	0	1	295,000
He Rose Again	3	C	15	3	2	1	36,750
He Rules	3	G	6	0	1	0	8,480
He Shall Reign	4	F	5	0	0	0	350
He Told Coe	5	G	17	0	1	5	5,814
He Will	2	C	4	0	0	0	360
He Won Laughin	5	H	10	1	0	0	10,011
He Won't Hesitate	4	C	12	0	1	0	1,914
He Won't Tell	3	G	2	0	0	0	210
Head Cat	4	G	1	0	0	0	41
Head Chief	6	G	15	1	1	1	11,100
Head Fake	7	G	3	0	0	0	150
Head for the Hills	4	G	4	0	0	0	341
Head for the Shed	2	F	1	0	0	0	1,680
Head In	7	G	9	1	0	0	6,844
Head of the Class	4	C	3	0	0	0	450
Head of the House	3	C	8	2	2	0	90,720
Head of the Rapids	2	C	2	0	1	0	4,600
Head Office	5	G	8	0	0	0	120
Head Over Heels	5	M	15	2	1	2	9,286
Head Sweeper	7	G	5	1	1	1	3,840
Head Tax	3	G	8	2	0	0	11,244
Head Turner	5	M	13	0	4	2	9,892
Headbanger	3	C	11	2	1	1	17,845
Headed Forthefront	3	G	8	0	0	0	620
Headedtothedance	3	F	10	1	0	2	11,140
Headingforaruckus	8	G	7	0	0	0	484
Headline	4	G	13	2	1	3	28,345
Headline News	4	C	3	1	0	0	6,760
Heads I Win	3	G	5	0	0	0	1,407
Heads Or Tails Hal	5	M	7	1	1	1	1,546
Healthy Addiction	3	F	5	2	2	0	77,992
Hear Come Peanut	4	G	12	1	2	3	15,748
Hear Me Clearly	5	M	6	0	1	0	2,605
Hear Me Roar	6	M	5	0	0	2	2,085
Hear My Song	4	F	9	0	0	1	2,919
Hear No Evil	4	C	10	0	3	1	182,500
Hear Us Roar	2	F	3	3	0	0	128,680
Heart Be Gone	3	F	6	2	0	0	10,231
Heart Flash	8	G	12	0	5	0	7,590
Heart in Hand	7	M	3	0	0	0	450
Heart Lite Special	7	M	3	0	0	0	986
Heart N Solo	3	F	7	0	3	2	22,287
Heart of a Fighter	3	F	1	0	0	0	220
Heart of a Hero	3	G	10	0	1	2	9,480
Heart of a Leader	3	G	3	1	1	1	41,380
Heart of Jules	3	C	11	3	1	0	58,920
Heart of Kings	7	G	12	2	3	1	15,120
Heart of Stone	7	H	3	0	0	0	202
Heart of Texas	3	C	4	0	0	0	0
Heart Ofa Champion	4	F	10	1	1	1	20,515
Heart Ridge	5	M	9	0	0	3	1,554
Heart Stormin On	6	M	8	1	2	0	4,962
Heart to Heart	2	F	5	2	0	0	21,820
Heart Warrior	3	G	1	0	0	1	2,140
Heartbreak Girl	2	F	3	0	1	2	11,471
Heartbreaker	3	F	3	0	1	0	10,840
Heartbreaker Heff	5	M	11	3	1	1	17,800
Heartfelt Honor	4	G	10	0	4	2	16,609
Heartful Hero	2	F	7	1	3	1	40,670
Heartful of Storm	3	F	13	1	2	4	21,818
Heartland Queen	3	F	12	0	0	1	1,980
Heartless	7	G	17	3	2	2	24,790
Heartontheloose	12	M	8	0	1	2	2,279
Hearts and Letters	6	H	1	0	0	0	0
Heart's Cry	9	G	14	2	5	4	28,715
Hearts Flashy Fire	3	C	10	1	1	1	14,350
Hearts in Motion	3	G	13	0	1	1	2,629
Hearts of Jones	3	F	8	4	2	0	24,480
Hearts Up	4	F	3	0	1	0	1,389
Heart's Wild Fire	2	G	5	1	0	1	33,110
Heartstopper	4	G	8	1	2	0	5,028
Heat	4	G	17	1	4	3	16,169
Heat Expectations	4	F	10	1	1	1	7,542
Heat of Dixie	7	G	7	0	2	1	6,022
Heat Resistant	2	G	7	1	0	2	14,070
Heat Rises	3	F	21	2	1	1	5,067
Heat Seeker	6	G	6	0	0	0	1,379
Heatcus	4	C	12	0	2	3	14,970
Heated Chase	2	F	7	1	0	2	12,155
Heather Ann	7	M	8	1	0	1	18,765
Heather Fire Dance	5	G	9	0	0	1	705
Heather Hurry Up	5	M	15	2	0	2	13,931
Heather Lad	6	H	3	0	0	0	550
Heather Light	7	M	3	0	0	2	7,850
Heather On	9	M	2	0	0	0	44
Heather On a Roll	3	F	15	2	7	1	27,128
Heather Ridge	4	F	1	0	0	0	400
Heathering Hights	3	F	3	0	0	1	1,000
Heatherinthemist	3	F	2	0	0	0	0
Heather's Announce	3	F	5	0	0	1	1,317

Horse	Age	Sex	Sts	1st	2d	3d	Won
Heather's Best	8	G	10	1	2	1	8,366
Heathers Blue Moon	2	F	7	1	0	1	8,560
Heathers Key	3	F	4	0	0	0	515
Heather's Lady	3	F	9	1	2	2	20,782
Heather's Lil' Boy	3	G	13	1	0	2	4,606
Heather's Prized	4	G	7	1	1	0	8,288
Heathers Warrior	3	G	8	2	1	0	13,865
Heathersspacecadet	3	G	13	1	2	2	9,688
Heathrow	3	G	8	1	1	1	56,277
Heath's Big Heart	3	C	11	2	0	1	7,874
Heath's Big Shot	8	G	12	1	0	2	2,919
Heath's Golden Boy	5	G	4	2	0	0	7,810
Heath's Hideaway	3	G	10	2	0	0	27,000
Heath's Jet	5	G	6	1	1	1	31,726
Heath's Lady	3	F	3	0	0	0	750
Heatmoney	4	G	9	1	1	0	15,525
Heaven	7	G	5	1	0	1	4,810
Heaven Blessed	5	M	9	1	2	0	8,422
Heaven Connection	5	G	16	0	3	1	4,055
Heaven Only Knows	4	F	7	0	0	3	7,271
Heavenandearth	2	C	2	1	0	0	19,150
Heavenish	4	F	1	0	0	0	285
Heavenly Account	3	F	2	1	0	0	6,540
Heavenly Anna	2	F	2	0	1	0	3,055
Heavenly Bound	3	F	13	3	1	3	68,820
Heavenly Cast	3	F	7	1	0	0	9,857
Heavenly Flash	3	G	9	0	2	1	21,689
Heavenly Funds	3	F	1	0	0	0	0
Heavenly Gold	2	G	9	1	1	0	7,785
Heavenly Helen	3	F	1	0	0	0	0
Heavenly Helper	3	F	6	1	0	0	3,281
Heavenly Hit	6	G	4	1	1	0	3,320
Heavenly Hope	7	M	5	0	0	1	772
Heavenly Host	3	F	3	0	0	0	3,250
Heavenly Humor	3	F	4	2	0	1	73,415
Heavenly Hymn	3	G	3	0	0	0	204
Heavenly Image	4	F	10	1	2	0	6,437
Heavenly Jet	4	F	9	2	0	1	31,534
Heavenly Justice	3	F	4	0	0	0	690
Heavenly Kevin	4	C	9	0	0	1	15,706
Heavenly Kisses	5	M	10	1	3	1	17,170
Heavenly Lynn	4	F	10	1	2	2	10,191
Heavenly Meeting	4	F	4	2	0	1	37,590
Heavenly Miss	4	F	3	0	0	0	680
Heavenly Monster	3	F	6	0	0	1	7,751
Heavenly Performer	7	G	11	1	0	1	3,614
Heavenly Place	2	F	1	0	0	0	400
Heavenly Powder	3	F	15	1	5	1	34,715
Heavenly Power	3	F	4	0	0	0	850
Heavenly Prince	8	G	1	0	0	0	0
Heavenly Prospect	3	F	3	0	0	0	985
Heavenly Reward To	3	F	15	3	3	3	26,040
Heavenly Rose	5	M	15	2	2	2	58,325
Heavenly Scandal	3	F	1	0	0	0	240
Heavenly Search	6	H	1	0	0	0	600
Heavenly Shades	4	F	5	2	1	0	7,778
Heavenly Star	3	F	13	1	0	2	5,355
Heavenly Trick	4	F	9	2	0	1	33,770
Heavenly Vibes	2	F	6	0	0	2	3,754
Heavenly View	4	F	6	1	3	2	15,200
Heavenlyoportunity	3	F	10	1	0	2	5,093
Heaven's Border	3	F	3	1	1	0	19,470
Heaven's Boy	2	G	3	0	0	0	0
Heaven's Cat	3	G	8	1	0	2	23,140
Heaven's Gain	4	F	5	0	0	0	2,913
Heaven's Highway	3	F	3	0	0	0	0
Heaven's Hostage	4	G	5	0	0	0	1,011
Heaven's Mirror	5	M	3	0	1	1	1,598
Heaven's Mist	6	M	14	0	1	7	17,125
Heaven's Notebook	3	F	6	2	1	2	24,860
Heaven's Prospect	8	M	10	1	5	0	16,870
Heaven's Reply	2	F	7	0	1	3	10,240
Heaven's Sake	5	M	2	0	0	0	0
Heaven's Slam	2	F	3	1	0	0	10,545
Heavens Throne	10	G	14	2	3	3	23,125
Heaven's Thunder	3	F	9	2	3	0	30,322
Heaventy Crown	3	F	2	0	0	0	484
Heavy Chimes	6	G	11	1	0	0	3,209
Heavy Cream	4	F	2	0	0	0	0
Heavy Cruiser	3	G	13	2	3	4	15,818
Heavy Duty Cutie	3	F	1	0	0	0	114
Heavy On the Roses	3	G	6	1	0	1	5,875
Heavy Traffic	3	C	1	0	0	0	780
Heavy Waters	3	F	4	1	0	0	9,040
Hebe a Genius	3	G	8	1	2	1	9,834
Heberts Impact	5	G	13	3	4	1	22,435
Hebe's Express	2	C	5	1	2	2	22,800
Hecamefromaclaim	3	C	5	2	0	0	32,060
Hecandance	4	C	2	0	0	0	108
Hecandigit	5	H	13	2	2	0	75,520
Heck Ofalotof Cash	2	G	3	1	1	0	6,426
Heckle	3	C	4	1	1	0	45,417
Heckofanactofollow	4	C	10	0	2	4	15,585
Hectic	4	G	8	0	0	0	152
Hector Louis	2	G	5	1	0	1	13,554
Hedge Your Bet	2	C	6	0	1	3	21,480
Hedging	2	F	4	2	1	0	28,500
Hediditright	4	G	8	3	0	3	24,595
Hedonism	3	G	12	2	2	3	20,762
Hedstartminer	5	H	6	1	3	1	11,630
Hedwig	5	M	4	0	0	0	0
Hee Hee	3	F	5	0	0	0	189
Heebie Jeebies	4	F	13	3	2	2	32,274
Heed Her Call	4	F	4	0	0	0	480
Heed My Decision	2	F	2	0	0	0	0
Heel Dust	10	G	4	0	0	0	774
Heezelusive	5	G	1	0	0	0	312
Heffelfinger	5	G	11	1	1	1	11,488
Heffs Lil Doll	3	F	1	0	0	0	420
Hefner Road	10	G	5	0	0	0	120
Hefty Taxes	6	M	4	0	0	0	1,115
Hegira	6	M	5	0	2	1	8,800
Hego Looking	7	H	3	0	1	1	6,427
Heidi Cat	3	F	8	2	0	0	14,940
Heidi Do	3	F	2	0	0	0	0
Heidi J. D.'s Boy	4	G	8	0	0	2	3,645
Heidi Marie	4	F	6	1	1	2	5,855
Heidi One	3	F	3	0	1	1	1,980
Heidi Sparkles	7	M	4	0	0	1	1,017
Heidi's Affair	4	F	5	0	0	0	503
Heidi's Even Keel	5	M	1	0	0	0	0
Heidi's Nel	4	F	7	1	1	1	13,992
Heidi's Rose	3	F	1	0	0	1	825
Heidi's Salt Lake	5	M	2	0	2	0	6,625
Heighchai	2	F	2	0	0	1	2,440
Height of Summer	3	G	14	2	5	4	60,205
Height Roller	9	M	12	1	1	1	5,108
Heightenedawarenes	8	G	13	1	2	3	4,640
Heightenedinterest	6	G	1	0	0	0	0
Heir D' Twine	5	G	14	2	3	5	67,300
Heir to Spare	7	G	4	1	2	0	9,660
Heir To The Throne (IRE)	3	C	3	0	0	0	3,756
Heir Today (IRE)	3	F	2	0	0	0	2,880
Heirtothecaptain	4	C	1	0	0	0	0
Heka	4	G	6	0	0	0	323
Hela Prospect	5	G	5	0	1	1	3,769
Helabhai	8	G	1	0	0	0	39
Helaine's Honour	4	F	3	0	1	0	3,750
Heldatbay	4	F	16	1	2	3	14,782
Heldinhighesteem	4	F	18	2	4	1	32,183
Helen Anna	3	F	2	0	0	0	1,275
Helen Darlin	4	F	6	0	1	0	3,894
Helen Gone	3	F	7	0	0	0	616
Helen O	5	M	9	0	0	2	2,835
Helen On Wheels	3	F	1	0	0	0	0
Helene's Dream	2	C	1	0	0	0	118
Helenico (ARG)	7	H	8	1	1	1	30,920
Helen's Eyes	3	F	13	0	3	4	6,939
Helen's Girl	5	M	6	0	0	1	801
Helen's Legacy	4	F	3	2	0	1	22,900
Helen's Magic	3	C	4	0	0	0	0
Helen's Shadow	6	M	16	0	3	5	20,680
Helen's Startax	3	F	7	2	1	2	58,810
Helensinterrogator	4	G	9	0	0	0	405
Helga	2	F	3	0	0	1	2,750
Hell Cat	4	C	5	0	0	0	1,110
Hell N High Water	3	F	2	0	1	0	3,266
Hell Roaring Creek	3	C	4	0	1	0	11,510

Horse	Age	Sex	Sts	1st	2d	3d	Won
Hellacious Curve	4	F	9	1	0	2	5,145
Hellcat Pilot	6	G	14	3	1	3	27,269
Heller	7	G	13	5	1	5	42,768
Hellish	4	F	10	0	2	0	3,668
Hello All	2	F	2	0	0	0	0
Hello Anna	3	F	5	0	0	0	0
Hello Archer	3	C	2	0	0	0	940
Hello Carolyn	5	M	5	0	0	0	1,055
Hello Concerto	2	G	6	1	0	0	7,215
Hello Crypto	7	M	5	0	2	2	4,650
Hello Dear	3	F	8	0	1	1	2,490
Hello Dixie	4	F	10	2	0	1	24,098
Hello Dyna	2	F	1	0	0	0	400
Hello Fame	4	G	6	1	1	1	22,020
Hello Funny	2	F	6	0	0	1	5,325
Hello Gitana	3	F	14	1	3	0	34,482
Hello Goodbye Cat	3	F	7	0	0	1	1,762
Hello Hatti	4	F	1	0	0	0	665
Hello Heaven	3	F	11	0	0	1	2,376
Hello Jerry	2	G	2	0	1	0	10,200
Hello John	5	G	15	2	4	1	21,740
Hello Joker	4	G	5	0	0	0	305
Hello Judy	5	M	14	2	1	2	16,900
Hello Karakorum	4	F	4	1	0	1	30,416
Hello Lila	9	M	10	0	0	0	2,659
Hello Lilly	4	F	11	1	4	1	7,419
Hello Lonelyness	5	M	16	3	1	4	26,325
Hello Lucky	2	F	7	3	0	2	142,140
Hello Matilda	4	F	3	0	0	0	1,530
Hello McMinnville	6	M	8	0	0	1	872
Hello Miami	3	F	9	2	3	3	28,890
Hello Mo	2	C	1	0	0	0	0
Hello Moto	3	C	5	0	0	0	323
Hello My Friend	4	F	12	1	0	3	21,004
Hello Out There	2	G	5	0	2	1	17,191
Hello Pepper	5	M	10	1	1	1	6,577
Hello Rosie	2	F	2	0	0	0	690
Hello Saratoga	6	G	7	0	0	1	2,120
Hello Sparky	2	G	6	0	1	1	3,675
Hello Sunshine	3	F	12	1	0	1	14,242
Hello There	2	F	2	0	0	2	1,440
Hello Trouble	3	G	9	1	3	0	13,135
Hello Victory	3	G	9	1	0	2	6,245
Helltunerider	4	F	15	1	2	3	20,654
Helms Deep (GB)	4	C	3	1	0	0	38,580
Helm's Lady	3	F	2	0	0	0	350
Helm's Press	2	C	1	0	0	0	400
Helms Princess	3	F	3	0	0	0	192
Helms the Man	5	H	8	0	0	0	308
Helmsman's Hellion	4	G	8	0	0	0	1,157
Help the Pilot	6	G	1	0	0	0	0
Helpfindacure	4	F	6	0	0	0	469
Helpful Hint	5	M	4	0	0	0	338
Helpisontheway	4	G	6	0	0	1	3,120
Helvetia	5	M	5	0	0	0	573
Heman Erickson	7	G	1	0	0	0	0
Hemandan	11	G	11	3	2	1	10,336
Hemet Thought	6	G	8	0	2	2	77,996
Hemi Inside	2	C	3	0	1	2	5,985
Hemisphere	3	C	9	1	1	0	19,440
Hemlock	4	F	11	0	0	1	2,800
Hemmingsway	7	G	13	3	3	4	39,322
Hemps Lady	3	F	2	0	0	0	162
Hen Cat	3	C	6	0	1	0	6,178
Henares (CHI)	10	G	3	0	1	0	3,844
Henbane Man	9	G	2	0	0	0	0
Henbane's Cat	4	G	16	5	5	0	35,966
Hence the Howl	5	H	3	0	1	0	1,200
Hendrix	3	C	9	1	1	2	66,430
Heneresa	4	C	14	4	2	1	87,011
Hennas Prospector	3	F	2	0	0	0	0
Hennessey's Gold	3	F	9	0	2	0	12,740
Hennessy Bay	3	G	6	1	0	0	9,942
Hennessyalater	3	F	7	1	0	2	4,590
Hennessy's Best	5	G	13	1	0	1	11,945
Hennie's Song	4	F	2	0	0	0	0
Henora W	7	M	1	0	0	0	0
Henri Martin (GB)	4	G	7	1	0	1	5,106
Henry Hawk	5	G	1	0	0	0	0
Henry Higgins	4	G	18	3	2	2	27,500
Henry J	8	G	17	1	2	3	6,963
Henry Lee Moro	6	G	2	0	1	0	1,220
Henry O	3	G	15	2	1	2	14,233
Henry Robinson	7	G	8	0	0	0	726
Henry the Fish	3	G	4	2	0	0	6,684
Henry's Court	2	C	2	1	0	0	39,476
Henry's Pride	3	G	3	0	0	0	0
Hepdaboyout	3	G	4	0	0	0	60
Hephzi Bah	3	G	13	0	4	3	13,582
Heptagone	6	G	9	2	0	2	18,541
Her Alibi	4	F	1	0	0	0	0
Her and Him	3	F	2	0	0	0	70
Her Badness	3	F	3	1	1	1	18,537
Her Brilliancy	5	M	8	1	1	0	7,083
Her Emminence	4	F	10	1	1	1	14,028
Her Excellence	2	F	5	0	0	0	3,610
Her Eyes	3	F	10	1	1	1	3,940
Her First Maki	6	G	3	0	0	1	4,075
Her Fling	4	F	11	0	1	1	5,060
Her Highness	5	M	8	2	1	0	7,722
Her Honour	4	F	4	0	0	1	1,435
Her Majesty Sara	7	M	11	0	1	0	1,690
Her Mission	3	F	9	0	1	1	7,445
Her Name Was Maud	5	M	17	0	3	5	11,452
Her Name's Ruby	2	F	1	0	0	0	0
Her Place	4	F	9	0	4	2	12,550
Her Rules	2	F	8	0	0	1	1,690
Her Song	2	F	8	2	2	2	29,290
Herald Angel	3	F	2	0	0	0	285
Herald Harold	4	C	1	0	0	0	0
Herb Avore	5	G	9	0	2	1	3,127
Herb E.	5	G	9	3	0	0	5,147
Herbe Vert (BRZ)	8	G	1	0	1	0	950
Herb's Birthday	7	G	19	1	0	6	8,018
Herbs Spirit	5	G	7	4	1	1	66,179
Herculano	8	G	1	0	0	0	40
Herculated	4	G	6	3	1	0	233,200
Herculeon Warrior	3	G	8	1	2	0	64,328
Hercules On Top	2	C	3	0	0	0	1,447
Here Comes Atitude	4	G	5	0	0	0	0
Here Comes Baby	5	G	16	6	0	3	40,888
Here Comes Bailey	3	G	2	0	0	0	510
Here Comes Baldy	3	G	3	0	0	0	330
Here Comes Billy	5	G	4	0	1	0	2,740
Here Comes Blaze	3	G	2	0	0	0	298
Here Comes Bragg	3	C	10	3	1	1	24,950
Here Comes Bullet	4	F	4	1	2	0	5,230
Here Comes Bully	3	G	14	2	2	3	18,726
Here Comes Cherry	6	M	13	2	0	3	46,300
Here Comes Chuck	3	G	8	1	1	1	9,371
Here Comes Country	7	G	15	3	2	2	48,952
Here Comes Deano	3	G	9	0	0	0	1,024
Here Comes Doon	3	G	3	0	0	1	1,785
Here Comes Freda	5	M	1	0	0	0	105
Here Comes Hannah	3	F	6	2	0	1	7,496
Here Comes Jake	4	C	6	2	0	0	19,110
Here Comes Jewel	3	C	7	1	1	0	14,630
Here Comes Jewels	4	F	8	0	1	1	2,927
Here Comes Justice	4	F	9	0	0	0	420
Here Comes Kari	5	M	8	0	2	0	2,881
Here Comes Lucinda	5	M	1	0	0	0	651
Here Comes Magic	6	G	8	0	2	3	7,285
Here Comes Maygen	4	F	2	1	0	0	1,692
Here Comes Money	4	G	6	0	1	0	1,931
Here Comes My Guy	6	H	3	1	1	0	8,663
Here Comes Penny	2	F	2	0	1	0	2,310
Here Comes Rocket	7	H	10	1	3	1	13,519
Here Comes Rootie	5	M	12	2	1	0	13,285
Here Comes Rusty	4	G	7	0	2	1	14,240
Here Comes Tee Pro	5	G	6	2	2	0	18,808
Here Comes the Dr.	4	G	7	1	0	1	10,018
Here Comes the Man	2	C	1	0	0	0	1,150
Here Comes Tiger	4	G	7	0	0	1	1,902
Here Comes Turner	6	G	11	0	1	1	9,429
Here Comes Wanda	2	F	1	0	0	0	75
Here He Goes	3	G	8	0	2	1	6,550
Here Is Lew	3	F	1	0	0	0	40
Here Me Out	6	G	8	3	0	0	28,001

Horse	Age	Sex	Sts	1st	2d	3d	Won
Here 'n' Sassy	4	F	5	1	0	1	13,680
Here N There	2	F	2	1	0	1	7,339
Hereafter	4	F	10	4	1	2	70,002
Herecomedacash	4	G	10	1	4	2	12,328
Herecomes Unc	4	G	23	2	4	4	18,766
Herecomesashley	3	G	5	0	0	0	663
Herecomesawinner	4	G	13	0	1	4	6,425
Herecomesbrice	4	C	5	1	1	1	11,013
Herecomesdabossnow	5	G	3	0	0	0	233
Herecomesdickeyjoe	3	G	6	0	0	0	1,092
Herecomesjl	2	G	3	0	0	0	0
Herecomespatton	4	C	9	2	0	2	11,341
Herecomesthebrat	7	G	12	0	4	2	4,750
Herecomesthemannow	4	G	8	3	1	0	71,548
Herecomethegirls	7	M	1	0	0	0	130
Herecomsthchoochoo	3	G	7	0	1	1	4,920
Heres a Memory	3	F	4	0	1	0	1,698
Here's Boom Boom	6	G	4	0	0	0	0
Here's Brittany	3	F	2	0	0	0	822
Here's Carrie	4	F	7	0	3	3	22,620
Here's Corey Now	3	F	1	0	0	0	52
Here's Hogan	3	F	13	1	3	5	13,801
Here's Hope	4	C	2	0	1	0	2,695
Heres Johnny	4	G	15	2	1	1	6,797
Here's Taylor	2	F	2	0	1	0	2,932
Here's the Pitch	7	G	14	1	0	2	15,867
Here's the Power	4	G	5	0	2	0	11,935
Here's to Andrew	4	G	6	3	0	2	34,002
Here's Ya Mama	7	M	11	2	4	2	33,618
Here's Ya Souvenir	3	G	13	0	3	2	42,580
Here's Your Ticket	4	C	6	0	0	0	1,325
Here's Zealous	7	H	6	2	1	2	63,600
Hereslookingatyou	4	G	13	1	3	1	28,735
Heresyour Chickey	7	M	1	0	0	0	45
Here'syourapproval	2	C	1	0	0	0	155
Herethegrassgrow	2	C	2	0	0	0	85
Herewego Champ	7	H	1	0	0	0	70
Herewegoagain	8	G	4	1	2	0	9,291
Hergesheimer	7	G	11	1	1	0	8,827
Hergun	2	F	2	0	0	1	1,125
Hermanita	4	F	8	0	0	0	946
Hermans Honor	5	M	2	0	0	0	0
Hermione Granger	4	F	17	0	4	4	11,920
Hermione's Magic	3	F	6	2	1	0	70,084
Hermitage (CHI)	5	H	2	0	0	1	4,340
Hermosa Point	4	F	14	1	2	3	15,955
Hermosilla	12	G	11	2	3	1	5,449
Hero for Her	3	F	9	2	1	1	25,590
Hero Number Zero	3	G	5	1	0	0	5,432
Hero Through Time	5	H	7	1	1	1	5,281
Hero Wood	5	H	3	0	0	0	149
Heroes Gift	3	C	9	2	2	0	18,522
Heroic Deed	3	G	11	1	1	4	45,314
Heroic Firefighter	4	G	9	2	0	1	11,178
Heroic Moment	3	C	11	1	1	1	48,150
Heroic Sight	6	G	15	7	1	3	145,370
Heroic Sovereign	2	G	2	0	0	0	770
Heroic Spirit	4	G	13	1	3	2	19,495
Heroofthegame	8	G	3	1	0	0	23,870
Heros Among Us	3	C	2	0	0	0	1,020
Hero's Glow	5	G	7	2	0	1	47,475
Hero's Hollywood	3	G	4	0	2	0	3,104
Hero's Hour	3	G	11	1	0	2	11,669
Hero's Pleasure	4	C	13	0	2	3	15,562
Hero's Taps	4	F	9	1	0	1	10,070
Hero's Task	3	G	6	1	0	0	17,396
Hero's Tribute	6	H	2	0	0	0	3,400
Hero's Warning	3	G	5	0	0	0	240
Herpotofgold	4	F	20	7	4	1	40,492
Herr Apparant	3	C	3	0	0	1	2,806
Herr Line	3	G	8	2	2	0	26,190
Herr Roesch	7	G	7	0	0	0	1,345
Herr Ruby	5	M	12	2	1	1	23,279
Herrera's Gown	3	F	5	1	0	0	9,140
Hers Funny	6	M	16	1	0	2	7,845
Her's Ok	5	M	3	1	0	0	1,330
Hershea Bard	6	G	1	0	0	0	64
Hertemptingthought	6	M	5	0	0	1	984
Herve	4	G	8	0	2	2	21,606
Hervy	8	H	1	0	0	0	0
Herwayorthehighway	3	F	10	2	1	0	9,158
He's a Bandit	9	G	2	0	0	0	47
He's a Boat	8	G	5	1	2	0	4,132
He's a Bobcat	3	G	8	3	1	2	26,289
He's a Brat	5	G	12	2	5	1	48,300
He's a Bulldog	2	G	8	1	0	0	3,840
He's a Copper King	7	G	6	0	0	0	762
He's a Doozie	5	G	3	0	0	0	70
He's a Dreamer	6	G	7	0	2	2	9,900
He's a Fine Deal	6	G	4	1	0	2	8,514
He's a Hunk	4	G	10	2	2	3	58,760
He's a Jones	3	C	11	1	1	0	11,608
He's a Knockout	6	G	11	2	1	1	42,977
He's a Lover	3	G	8	1	0	1	5,271
He's a Mystery	4	G	14	5	3	1	97,460
He's a Pleaser	2	G	1	0	0	0	0
He's a Ready Round	3	C	2	0	0	0	0
He's a Ringer	6	G	9	2	2	1	10,970
He's a She	3	F	12	1	1	4	25,811
Hes a Slew Tu	7	G	6	0	0	1	460
He's a Smokejumper	4	G	5	1	0	1	2,606
He's a Top Trek	3	G	7	0	2	1	1,206
He's About to Pop	2	G	3	2	1	0	15,540
He's Acool Breeze	4	G	4	0	0	0	105
He's Awesome	4	G	5	1	0	0	9,979
He's Back	5	H	7	1	1	0	6,800
He's Bold	2	G	3	0	0	1	1,273
He's Crafty	5	H	7	1	3	1	58,378
He's Deeliteful	3	C	8	0	0	1	1,240
He's Enchanted	3	G	12	1	1	0	13,777
He's Expensive	6	G	6	0	0	0	770
He's Fantastic	2	C	1	0	0	0	0
He's Fit	3	G	14	2	1	3	36,290
He's Game	5	G	10	0	0	0	0
He's Gone	6	G	9	1	1	1	12,640
He's Good to Go	3	G	9	3	0	2	27,058
He's Got Charm	3	G	15	0	3	1	5,891
He's Got the Goods	6	G	15	3	0	1	18,792
He's Hammered	4	G	10	3	1	2	84,686
He's Hurr Cuelee's	2	G	1	0	0	1	3,553
He's Impressive	3	C	14	4	0	2	28,500
He's in the House	3	G	1	1	0	0	11,970
He's Lookin Good	2	G	6	1	2	2	18,955
He's Mine	3	C	3	0	1	1	15,330
He's Mine Tooo	7	H	4	0	1	0	1,075
He's My Dancer	2	C	3	1	0	0	13,800
He's My Idol	4	C	7	1	1	1	16,390
He's My Man	3	C	8	4	0	0	34,525
He's My Secret	2	G	2	0	0	0	700
He's No Angel	3	C	2	0	1	0	4,260
He's No Flower	3	G	7	0	0	1	3,009
He's No Saint	4	C	1	0	0	0	2,300
He's of Royalty	3	C	3	0	1	0	4,000
He's On His Toes	4	C	2	0	0	0	122
He's Real	2	G	3	0	0	2	3,563
He's Real Special	3	G	5	1	1	0	15,600
He's Royal Dee	2	G	2	0	0	0	900
He's So Good	4	G	10	1	0	1	5,497
He's So Handsome	5	G	14	1	1	1	11,356
He's So Regal	2	G	3	1	0	1	16,974
He's Souper	3	C	13	3	1	1	28,009
He's the Last	3	C	11	0	0	1	2,130
He's the Master	5	G	18	1	2	0	11,353
He's the Rage	3	C	3	0	1	0	25,800
He's Tricky	3	G	11	3	1	0	20,600
He's Vivid	4	C	8	1	0	0	4,469
He's What I Need	2	G	2	0	0	0	280
Hesa Angel	4	C	15	5	1	0	42,768
Hesa Bad Cat	4	G	6	2	3	0	68,447
Hesa Big Star	2	C	6	1	0	3	24,380
Hesa Blumin Affair	3	G	11	1	2	2	11,139
Hesa Cadillac	8	H	1	0	0	0	0
Hesa Devin	4	C	10	1	1	2	12,894
Hesa Fortune Pro	2	C	1	0	0	0	0
Hesa Jeb	4	G	10	1	0	1	4,970
He'sa Littleturkey	5	G	7	3	0	1	8,207
Hesabullet	4	G	16	3	2	3	21,821
Hesabully	2	G	3	1	0	0	14,620

Horse	Age	Sex	Sts	1st	2d	3d	Won
Hesachaser	2	G	1	0	1	0	2,185
He'sachicmagnet	5	G	15	4	0	2	24,245
Hesacleverwolf	5	H	1	0	0	0	94
He'safineprospect	3	G	3	0	0	0	675
Hesalittlerunaway	3	G	12	2	0	3	10,190
Hesanawsumcat	3	G	11	0	0	2	555
He'sapleasantdream	4	G	14	1	1	2	11,446
Hesarunaway	4	G	4	0	0	0	522
Hesasurgeon	4	G	1	0	0	0	0
Hesatexashand	7	H	6	1	0	1	2,729
Hesaves	3	G	7	0	0	1	1,300
Hesbullievable	5	G	9	1	1	2	20,870
Hesgoddago	3	G	13	2	1	2	15,060
Hesgotattitude	3	G	2	2	0	0	27,360
He'sgotitgoinon	2	G	5	0	0	0	1,900
Hesgottabeadandy	4	G	6	0	3	1	4,457
He'sgottalottaluck	3	G	2	0	0	0	320
Heshimu	6	G	10	1	0	0	9,061
He'smydream	3	G	6	0	0	0	640
Hesneasternclassic	2	G	3	0	0	0	3,500
He'snogamble	3	C	7	0	0	0	428
Hesperus	3	F	12	1	2	3	13,515
He'ssuchabadboy	3	G	5	0	2	0	8,765
Hester W.	2	C	2	0	0	0	206
Hestillmovesstones	4	C	10	0	2	0	8,125
Hestosmartforyou	6	G	1	0	0	0	80
Hexawa	3	C	11	1	0	3	4,975
Hexerei	4	C	4	1	0	2	860
Hexham	4	F	9	0	0	2	3,663
Hey Baby Hey	4	F	5	0	1	1	3,807
Hey Bajagaloop	4	G	8	1	3	0	11,285
Hey Billy	9	H	4	1	0	0	985
Hey Boss	7	G	7	1	0	2	3,722
Hey Brother	5	G	8	1	1	1	7,364
Hey Bub	5	G	14	2	2	1	12,317
Hey Bubbah	4	G	9	2	0	0	18,232
Hey Bud	9	G	4	0	0	0	100
Hey Budman	4	G	3	0	0	0	183
Hey Buster	4	G	14	1	2	3	14,350
Hey Cap	3	G	5	1	0	0	6,900
Hey Chub	4	C	10	2	6	1	126,327
Hey Cowboy	4	C	3	1	0	0	5,550
Hey Diddle Diddle	6	G	14	1	2	1	4,766
Hey Doll	2	F	1	0	0	0	450
Hey Fabulous	5	M	3	2	0	0	15,445
Hey Freddie	4	G	6	0	0	2	1,560
Hey Georgia	3	F	2	0	0	0	182
Hey Hey	8	M	12	1	3	1	5,960
Hey Hey Vinny	7	G	1	0	0	0	336
Hey Holly	4	F	5	0	2	1	5,970
Hey Ink	3	F	9	1	1	0	1,920
Hey It's Richard	4	G	7	0	3	1	10,963
Hey Little Lady	6	M	7	1	0	0	7,192
Hey Lynn	3	F	13	1	1	2	11,433
Hey Ma	3	F	2	1	0	1	13,200
Hey Mikey	3	G	12	3	1	1	24,314
Hey Mister B	5	M	14	0	3	2	8,331
Hey Mr. Banjo	4	G	6	1	0	2	10,115
Hey Nonnie	4	G	4	0	0	0	566
Hey Poquita	4	C	2	0	0	0	970
Hey Ricky	4	C	5	0	0	0	1,123
Hey Rita	4	F	9	0	3	1	23,070
Hey Robbie	3	F	7	2	3	2	14,075
Hey Roug	5	M	2	0	0	0	0
Hey Rube	3	G	9	3	1	3	64,254
Hey Sailor	5	G	2	0	0	0	160
Hey Stretch	5	G	17	3	1	1	37,430
Hey There Joe	3	C	5	0	1	0	6,070
Hey Wajadoin	3	C	1	0	0	0	76
Hey Woody	6	H	1	0	1	0	4,200
Hey Ya	2	F	2	0	0	0	105
Hey Ya Handsome	5	G	1	0	0	0	0
Heyahohowdy	5	M	8	1	4	1	186,067
Heybaby	4	F	10	1	0	0	5,440
Heybabyletsboogie	2	F	5	0	0	1	3,930
Heyharrywhere'stom	2	G	3	1	0	1	7,190
Heyhowhatdoyouknow	6	M	6	2	2	0	50,358
Heyiamaroseprince	3	G	7	1	1	0	1,785
Heyshe'satrader	5	M	2	1	0	0	1,500
Hez a Bear	4	G	9	0	1	1	7,109
Hez Comin Thru	6	H	12	3	2	3	33,292
Hez Scott	12	G	8	1	0	2	1,191
Heza Cartwheel	2	G	2	0	1	0	2,700
Heza Clever	5	G	2	0	0	0	84
Heza Dashin Devil	4	G	5	0	0	0	764
Heza Felon	3	G	2	0	0	0	0
Heza Firecracker	2	C	1	0	0	0	65
Heza Gladiator	4	G	7	1	1	0	5,786
Heza Good Guy	4	G	7	1	1	1	27,170
Heza Hottie	5	G	3	1	0	0	1,610
Heza Leader	3	C	3	0	0	1	1,110
Heza Mama's Boy	3	G	12	0	3	4	11,640
Heza Mountain Man	3	G	5	0	1	0	11,170
Heza Pappy Slew	6	G	10	1	0	1	8,414
Heza Roany	6	G	7	0	2	0	3,880
Heza Sallisaw Kid	3	G	6	2	1	0	6,460
Heza Silver Man	3	G	1	0	0	0	105
Heza Smokin' Gun	2	C	4	0	0	0	440
Heza Spazz	3	G	6	0	5	0	3,765
Heza Storm	2	C	2	1	0	0	20,025
Heza Tell a Tune	5	G	3	0	0	0	332
Heza Wild Guy	3	G	7	3	0	0	28,853
Hezabon	5	H	3	0	0	0	258
Hezacat Number One	3	G	6	1	1	0	8,170
Hezacharmer	5	H	1	0	0	0	0
Hezadevilndisquise	5	G	2	0	0	0	80
Hezafasttrick	3	G	9	1	1	1	6,808
Hezafreedomtoo	4	C	4	0	0	0	0
Hezafreespirit	5	G	6	0	0	4	8,225
Hezajewel	4	C	4	1	0	0	4,165
Hezallheart	3	G	8	0	0	0	125
Hezamanontherun	3	G	10	1	1	3	15,344
Heze Hummer	5	G	13	0	0	0	1,331
Hezfreetofly	2	C	1	0	0	1	2,040
Hi Andre	4	G	2	0	0	0	0
Hi Boy	6	H	2	0	0	0	160
Hi Carson	3	G	10	0	1	1	7,672
Hi Cole	2	C	2	0	0	1	1,155
Hi de Ho Miss	7	M	1	0	0	0	0
Hi Desert	3	G	6	0	1	1	1,529
Hi Diddley Eye Di	4	F	3	1	0	0	8,022
Hi Dollar Haul	7	M	11	1	0	0	3,767
Hi Energy Slew	3	F	11	4	0	1	56,760
Hi Five Raven	3	F	7	1	2	1	39,570
Hi Flo	3	F	4	1	0	0	7,800
Hi Friend Kiss	4	F	15	0	2	3	10,014
Hi Goodbye	3	F	1	0	0	0	200
Hi Ho Aggie	2	F	1	0	0	0	0
Hi Layton	3	C	3	0	0	0	0
Hi Mounts Diamond	5	M	8	0	1	0	1,538
Hi Neighbor	4	F	7	1	2	2	31,375
Hi Red	7	H	5	0	0	0	366
Hi Sailor	4	G	5	1	0	0	2,213
Hi Tail	3	C	3	0	0	0	184
Hi Teck Man	3	C	4	2	0	1	298,875
Hi Tide Harry	2	G	2	0	0	1	2,018
Hi Time Scott	4	G	24	2	3	0	20,092
Hi Time Taylor	4	G	11	0	1	1	3,985
Hi Valerie	2	F	1	0	0	0	0
Hiawatha	5	M	1	0	0	0	0
Hiball Jack	5	G	12	0	2	1	7,685
Hibernate	3	G	10	2	1	2	19,280
Hibritesocialite	2	F	3	0	0	0	0
Hic Cup	5	G	19	3	2	3	15,955
Hickey Lane	11	G	2	0	0	1	1,060
Hickory Dick Doc	6	G	10	2	1	0	21,587
Hickory Doc	4	G	11	0	1	1	5,185
Hickory Flat	3	F	1	0	0	0	0
Hickory Hawk	3	G	18	3	1	2	27,200
Hickory Hills	3	G	13	0	0	0	1,067
Hickory Pete	3	C	11	3	0	2	86,140
Hickory Victory	4	F	4	0	0	0	283
Hickorys Barbidoll	3	F	3	0	0	0	215
Hickorys Hooknanny	6	G	3	0	0	0	245
Hicks	2	F	3	0	0	0	255
Hidalgo	3	C	1	0	0	0	220
Hidden	5	M	12	1	3	1	28,160
Hidden Account	5	G	7	1	2	0	22,290

Horse	Age	Sex	Sts	1st	2d	3d	Won
Hidden Agenda	3	F	2	0	1	0	5,689
Hidden Beauty	3	F	12	3	2	2	50,360
Hidden Candy	2	F	5	1	0	2	8,669
Hidden Code	8	G	18	1	0	1	4,031
Hidden Curves	3	F	7	0	0	0	8,143
Hidden Danger	4	G	7	1	0	1	27,374
Hidden Eight	4	G	8	2	1	2	2,705
Hidden Fantasy	2	C	3	1	0	0	7,950
Hidden Gold Dawn	2	F	1	0	0	0	0
Hidden Halo	6	M	11	1	4	0	17,765
Hidden Image	3	F	4	1	1	1	19,400
Hidden Key	4	G	2	1	0	0	19,500
Hidden Magic	2	F	2	0	0	0	0
Hidden Opportunity	3	G	1	0	0	0	1,320
Hidden Paradise	4	F	4	0	0	0	3,762
Hidden Path	5	G	5	0	0	0	845
Hidden Peak	2	C	1	0	0	0	145
Hidden Penny	4	G	11	0	0	1	3,335
Hidden Ransom	4	F	10	1	2	1	70,327
Hidden Zone	3	C	1	0	0	0	90
Hide and Chic	2	F	3	1	0	0	19,348
Hide and Peek	6	G	6	1	3	0	27,580
Hide N Watch	3	F	2	2	0	0	18,340
Hide Song	4	G	15	2	1	3	14,873
Hide the Chianti	6	M	5	1	0	0	4,290
Hideaway Cafe	5	H	14	4	2	2	76,625
Hideaway Dancer	3	F	1	0	0	0	412
Hierarchy	3	F	3	0	0	0	1,675
Hierarchy Rules	4	G	10	1	0	0	13,205
Hieratic	6	G	8	0	3	1	3,810
High Above	8	G	3	1	0	0	3,798
High Above It	4	C	7	1	1	0	6,412
High Alarm	3	G	6	0	0	1	1,290
High Alert	5	G	5	1	0	1	19,330
High and Low Vixen	6	H	4	1	0	1	16,860
High as the Sky	6	G	8	2	0	1	42,167
High At Last	4	G	1	0	0	0	40
High Ball	9	G	1	0	0	0	40
High Bird	3	G	5	0	3	0	9,647
High Blitz	4	G	8	3	0	2	121,463
High Bluebook	5	G	8	3	2	1	14,453
High Bluff	2	G	2	1	0	0	8,874
High Bo	3	F	11	1	3	1	27,740
High Bounty	6	H	2	0	0	0	100
High Bride	3	F	2	0	0	0	600
High Button Shoes	2	F	2	1	0	0	43,695
High Byars	4	G	7	1	0	2	16,960
High Cascade	6	H	6	0	1	1	7,870
High Caste	3	F	1	1	0	0	19,200
High Chieftain	7	G	11	1	5	2	14,678
High Class Lad	3	G	8	1	1	1	6,078
High Class Trash	4	G	8	0	0	0	2,843
High Commanchero	3	G	1	0	0	0	140
High Commissioner	6	H	5	0	0	1	3,880
High Con	5	G	10	0	0	1	2,824
High Concept	3	G	4	0	0	0	1,600
High Court (BRZ)	4	F	6	1	2	1	125,410
High Court Justice	6	G	13	3	3	1	16,684
High Dangig	3	G	15	1	1	0	7,546
High Descent	4	C	1	1	0	0	36,000
High Diva	5	M	6	3	0	0	23,950
High Dollar Gal	5	M	1	0	0	0	0
High Excess	3	C	9	0	0	0	849
High Expectations	2	C	3	0	1	1	8,060
High Fashion	3	F	1	0	0	0	118
High Fish	2	C	2	0	0	0	180
High Flag	3	G	2	0	1	0	2,060
High Fleet	3	C	4	1	0	0	4,513
High Fly	2	C	2	2	0	0	25,800
High Flying Bid	6	G	15	1	1	0	16,226
High Flying Spy	2	F	4	1	0	1	1,005
High Flying Star	3	F	4	0	0	0	195
High Forest	4	G	11	3	1	0	28,980
High Gate	2	C	3	0	1	0	1,895
High Gear	3	C	15	2	1	1	14,520
High Grade Silver	3	G	7	0	3	2	46,407
High Gun Ryder	10	G	11	2	1	2	8,939
High Hearted	4	C	5	0	0	0	720
High Heels N Deals	2	F	6	0	1	0	3,636
High Hi	2	C	1	0	0	0	126
High Honor	7	G	10	0	3	1	7,442
High Hopes Irish	7	M	1	0	0	0	1,692
High Hopes Star	4	G	7	1	0	2	32,649
High Humidity	5	M	1	0	1	0	5,700
High Jackpot	4	F	2	0	0	0	392
High Lance	4	F	7	0	0	2	640
High Liability	3	F	15	2	6	2	31,355
High Limit	2	C	2	2	0	0	42,000
High Marion	3	C	13	2	0	0	36,570
High Marks	3	C	13	2	5	1	23,180
High N Wild	2	C	2	0	0	1	524
High Octane	2	C	2	0	0	0	2,280
High Octave	4	G	11	2	0	0	10,455
High On Gin	2	F	2	0	0	0	500
High On Life	4	F	1	0	0	0	110
High On Luck	3	F	11	3	2	1	37,910
High On Madison	5	G	17	4	2	3	48,301
High On the Roost	8	G	8	0	0	0	0
High On the Throne	5	G	8	1	1	1	6,044
High On Wishes	3	G	13	3	3	1	35,357
High Peaks	3	F	9	3	2	2	114,501
High Pioneer	3	F	7	2	1	1	30,835
High Post	6	M	1	0	0	0	260
High Potential	5	M	1	0	0	1	1,812
High Powered Mack	8	G	7	2	1	1	6,185
High Priced	4	G	14	3	3	2	52,217
High Prince	2	C	3	0	0	1	1,595
High Princess	5	M	9	1	1	0	21,270
High Profit	2	C	2	0	0	0	140
High Purr	5	G	13	1	4	1	20,630
High Rank	4	G	15	2	0	3	15,151
High Ratings	3	F	12	1	1	4	30,922
High Rhode	6	M	4	0	0	0	368
High Rise Pro	2	F	3	0	0	0	360
High Riser	8	G	12	3	0	4	7,547
High River Hank	4	G	6	3	2	1	6,179
High Scorer	2	C	2	1	0	0	30,000
High Seattle Sky	3	G	8	0	0	2	4,096
High Service Ave	5	G	1	0	0	0	178
High Sheriff	7	G	6	1	1	0	10,180
High Shooter	5	G	7	0	0	0	1,330
High Sierra	3	G	8	0	0	2	2,280
High Silver	3	F	8	2	1	1	30,667
High Six Figures	6	M	11	1	2	1	16,610
High Smoke	6	G	6	0	2	0	2,116
High Speed Access	3	F	9	3	2	1	98,637
High Speed Pursuit	4	F	10	2	1	1	12,294
High Speed Travel	7	G	8	1	1	2	65,005
High Stakes Holdem	2	C	3	1	0	2	36,140
High Standards	2	G	1	1	0	0	13,200
High Steppin Steph	3	F	2	0	0	0	780
High Storada	6	G	8	1	1	3	6,110
High Street Market	4	F	6	1	1	0	3,732
High Strike	2	F	3	0	0	0	385
High Strike Zone	4	G	9	4	2	2	98,710
High Style Gent	2	G	5	0	0	0	2,520
High Supreme	5	G	2	0	0	0	0
High Sweep	4	G	14	4	1	1	24,620
High Taxes	14	G	2	0	0	0	0
High Tech Racing	4	G	7	2	0	1	11,458
High Terror	7	G	2	0	0	0	126
High Thunder	5	H	8	3	2	1	47,295
High Tone Diamond	3	F	9	0	0	0	1,760
High Tracks (BRZ)	7	G	2	1	0	1	17,250
High Volt Jolt	4	G	5	1	2	0	57,000
High Vote Count	4	F	11	1	2	2	14,542
High Wall	5	G	10	2	1	0	22,086
High Watermark	4	G	6	1	0	1	5,810
High Wire	4	F	5	1	2	2	13,790
High Wire Act	8	G	6	1	1	2	7,369
High Wire Glory	5	G	15	1	5	5	47,653
High Wire Man	7	G	1	0	0	0	0
High Zone	2	F	5	2	0	1	41,605
Highboom	3	G	2	0	1	0	2,128
Highcastle	3	G	16	1	0	4	14,375
Highdown	4	C	7	1	3	0	20,790
Higher and Higher	2	C	1	0	0	1	1,260
Higher Desire	12	G	4	0	1	0	2,750

Horse	Age	Sex	Sts	1st	2d	3d	Won
Higher Gear	5	M	11	0	1	0	2,340
Higher Ground	3	F	10	1	4	0	48,539
Higher Impact	9	G	2	1	0	0	2,460
Higher Standard	6	G	2	0	0	0	225
Higher Up	2	G	8	0	1	1	9,306
Higher World	2	F	4	2	1	0	213,210
Highest Appraisal	7	G	2	0	1	0	420
Highest Authority	4	F	3	0	0	0	397
Highest Grade	2	C	5	0	0	0	1,560
Highest Honoree	3	F	3	2	0	0	60,540
Highest Offer	4	F	8	1	2	1	19,895
Highest Value	4	G	14	1	1	2	25,520
Highgain	7	G	2	0	0	0	706
Highgate Park	3	F	4	1	1	0	40,609
Highgrove	2	C	4	1	0	0	36,808
Highhopesemilyluck	5	M	3	0	0	1	4,627
Highking	2	F	2	1	1	0	13,705
Highland Alibhai	3	G	7	0	0	2	3,603
Highland Baron	6	H	1	0	0	0	0
Highland Brim	3	F	9	1	0	3	8,037
Highland Crossing	4	G	10	3	1	0	18,833
Highland Dash	3	G	2	0	0	0	50
Highland Facts	5	M	6	1	1	1	26,780
Highland Gardens	8	G	4	1	0	0	4,288
Highland Hope	4	F	1	0	0	0	126
Highland Jabo	5	M	10	1	0	0	4,235
Highland Leader	9	G	13	3	3	2	52,288
Highland Lore	3	F	10	1	1	3	12,289
Highland Ocean	5	G	10	1	0	2	6,878
Highland Presence	4	G	10	1	0	3	52,369
Highland Reality	2	F	1	0	0	0	0
Highland Rim	5	G	4	1	0	1	7,775
Highland Road	9	G	10	4	1	2	21,003
Highland Sail	4	F	9	1	0	1	3,812
Highland Skies	3	F	5	1	0	0	7,661
Highland Skirt	5	M	15	2	1	2	20,160
Highland Spy	8	G	18	2	3	2	13,151
Highland Talker	3	F	3	0	0	0	0
Highland Thunder	5	G	7	0	0	0	1,780
Highland Turn	5	G	6	1	0	1	47,828
Highland Warrior	2	C	6	1	0	0	51,948
Highland Way	4	F	3	0	1	0	2,881
Highland Wayfarer	3	G	7	2	0	1	10,087
Highland Willows	2	F	5	1	0	0	24,354
Highlandflowergirl	5	M	16	1	2	3	11,101
Highlited	4	G	10	1	0	3	15,891
Highly Arrogant	3	F	19	3	2	4	84,040
Highly Justified	4	G	16	1	0	2	11,076
Highly Rated	4	G	6	0	0	1	1,225
Highly Suspect	5	G	11	5	4	0	35,705
Highly Tempting	5	G	12	1	6	1	44,815
Highly Threatened	3	G	11	2	0	0	7,150
Highnest	3	F	9	4	0	1	36,984
Highpockets Crane	6	G	7	0	0	1	791
Highpoint Princess	3	F	5	1	0	2	8,430
Highrunner	5	G	4	0	1	1	980
Highsideofthebay	3	G	2	0	0	0	0
Highwater Express	6	G	2	0	0	0	0
Highway Hero	3	C	10	1	0	0	11,767
Highway Home	11	G	1	0	0	0	75
Highway One O One	6	G	12	0	1	2	4,434
Highway Prospector	7	G	10	2	4	0	131,360
Highway West	6	G	4	1	1	1	24,160
Highwayman	2	G	3	0	1	0	2,685
Hija de Plata	7	M	1	0	0	0	630
Hilary Hunter	4	F	11	1	2	2	16,560
Hilbys Halo	3	F	3	0	0	0	0
Hilda Browne	5	M	16	2	2	1	22,728
Hilda's Prayers	6	G	2	0	0	0	227
Hildy's Struggle	3	F	8	1	0	0	5,958
Hilga	5	M	3	0	0	1	1,050
Hiljo's Joe	3	C	4	1	0	1	6,340
Hiljo's Rumbler	4	F	6	0	0	1	4,155
Hill Billy Grandma	4	F	6	0	1	0	4,629
Hill Cat	4	F	1	0	0	1	1,010
Hill Climb	4	G	12	0	0	2	2,806
Hill Hero	7	G	1	0	0	1	640
Hill Man	8	H	2	0	0	0	37
Hill of a Time	3	C	1	0	0	0	120
Hill Road Dancer	3	G	8	1	1	1	10,361
Hill Road Reality	3	F	8	1	2	2	14,552
Hill Station	4	G	7	0	0	1	2,600
Hill Top Man	4	G	4	0	0	0	2,227
Hillary Doc	8	M	10	0	0	0	2,250
Hillary Hickup	4	F	5	1	0	0	6,446
Hillary's Fantasy	5	M	13	1	4	3	13,959
Hillbilly Bandit	2	C	6	1	0	2	19,180
Hillbilly Bob	2	G	5	0	0	0	2,776
Hillbilly Junction	3	G	4	1	1	0	7,127
Hillbilly King	3	C	2	0	0	0	720
Hillbilly Prince	7	G	7	1	0	0	8,254
Hillbilly Princess	3	F	5	2	0	2	9,076
Hillbilly Shoes	6	G	5	0	0	0	1,242
Hill's Pride	4	G	7	0	1	1	6,880
Hillsboro Beach	2	C	4	1	0	0	14,768
Hillsboro Kid	6	G	2	0	0	0	0
Hillsdale	3	F	2	0	0	1	1,150
Hillside Dreamer	3	C	3	1	0	0	14,050
Hillside Way	3	F	11	1	5	1	17,093
Hilltown Lad	3	G	5	0	0	1	2,571
Hillview Cat	3	F	6	0	1	0	1,296
Hil's Baldski	3	F	8	0	1	1	1,860
Hilton Paradise	2	C	1	0	0	0	2,250
Hiltons Revenge	4	F	5	0	0	1	3,730
Hilty	5	G	12	1	2	0	17,055
Him	6	G	6	1	0	1	2,988
Him and I	2	G	6	1	1	0	17,700
Himalayan	4	F	1	0	0	0	586
Himdidit	3	G	7	0	0	0	525
Hindsight	5	M	9	1	2	1	24,485
Hinoon	5	G	8	1	0	0	3,495
Hint of Glory	5	H	5	0	0	2	2,810
Hip Holster	5	G	10	0	1	2	4,213
Hip Hop	3	G	11	1	1	2	29,538
Hip Hop Gold	7	G	4	0	0	0	1,000
Hip Hop Sis	3	F	7	2	0	2	15,830
Hip Hub Hero	2	C	8	0	3	1	12,480
Hipica Flash	4	G	7	2	0	0	9,063
Hippocrates	3	C	6	1	0	2	49,058
Hippogator	4	F	14	2	3	2	148,500
Hippy	3	G	6	1	1	0	4,557
Hippy Hippy Red	3	G	9	0	1	0	12,618
Hippy Hollow	7	G	3	0	0	0	0
Hips and Haws	4	F	15	3	4	4	48,859
Hirapour (IRE)	8	G	4	2	2	0	199,625
His Bimbette	3	F	2	0	1	0	2,600
His Class	4	G	4	0	0	0	1,330
His Decision	3	G	1	0	0	0	0
His Excellent Z.	7	H	7	1	1	3	2,705
His Excelsior	3	G	5	1	0	1	5,824
His Honor	10	G	3	0	0	1	1,140
His Majestys Boots	2	C	3	0	0	0	419
His Money	4	G	10	3	2	3	33,082
His Reverence	5	G	19	2	5	2	28,508
His Smoothness	3	C	7	0	2	1	110,475
His Testimony	7	H	3	0	0	0	0
His Way	3	G	10	3	3	1	33,453
Hispaniola	3	F	3	0	0	0	540
Hiss	3	G	6	0	0	0	1,421
Hisses N Kisses	4	F	7	1	1	0	2,628
Historic Countess	3	G	4	1	0	0	19,320
Historic Event	2	G	1	0	0	0	400
Historic Glo	3	F	1	0	0	0	0
Historic Native	4	G	3	0	0	1	4,556
Historic Road	3	G	1	0	0	0	0
Historic Speech	5	G	1	0	1	0	1,900
Historic Treasure	4	F	3	0	0	0	0
Historical	5	M	1	0	0	0	63
Historical Event	3	F	5	0	0	0	657
Historickristabell	3	F	3	0	0	0	0
Historic's Star	3	F	2	0	0	2	5,830
Historics Surprise	3	F	2	1	0	0	8,820
History Buff	3	G	7	2	1	1	19,619
History Forbes	3	G	5	1	1	0	20,390
History Lesson	2	C	1	0	0	0	0
Historyinthemaking	2	F	5	0	2	1	5,660
Hit and Run	5	H	6	0	0	1	2,220
Hit by Surprise	3	F	2	0	0	0	0

Horse	Age	Sex	Sts	1st	2d	3d	Won
Hit Em Low	10	G	5	0	0	0	0
Hit It	5	M	7	1	0	2	16,840
Hit It Here Cafe	3	F	3	0	0	1	2,093
Hit Lady	2	F	2	0	1	1	4,410
Hit Me	3	G	8	1	2	1	5,687
Hit 'n Giggle	2	F	9	2	0	0	34,195
Hit Now	5	G	16	1	2	3	51,455
Hit the Big Time	7	G	3	0	0	0	556
Hit the Brakes	3	F	8	1	5	2	22,097
Hit the Hardwood	7	G	5	0	0	1	932
Hit the Hay	3	F	3	0	0	0	37
Hit the Lights	5	G	4	0	1	2	12,410
Hit the Pedal	2	F	1	0	0	1	2,475
Hit the Press	7	M	4	0	0	2	4,021
Hit the Road Babe	6	M	7	1	0	1	12,078
Hit the Silk	8	H	1	0	0	0	400
Hit the Throttle	6	G	8	2	0	0	74,346
Hitaway Jay	7	G	7	0	1	0	1,040
Hitch Hike	3	G	7	0	0	1	858
Hitchcock's Best	4	G	2	0	0	0	0
Hitchin' Post	6	H	4	0	1	1	11,035
Hitchinpost Louie	2	G	6	1	3	0	11,286
Hitmaker	2	G	4	0	0	1	1,510
Hitower's Pride	5	G	6	0	1	1	3,975
Hittheflagstick	2	F	2	0	0	1	2,775
Hitthegroundrunnin	3	G	7	0	0	2	10,900
Hittherhode	3	G	17	1	4	3	12,489
Hitting Home	4	C	13	4	1	1	59,300
Hittinonallfour	5	G	6	0	0	1	2,290
Hiwaytwentyone	5	G	3	0	0	0	0
Hizzoner	5	G	10	1	0	2	34,835
Ho Ho Ho	3	C	5	2	0	0	34,440
Ho Joy	3	F	7	1	0	1	18,360
Hoagies Lil Angel	7	M	5	0	2	1	2,646
Hoax (IRE)	5	G	2	0	0	0	700
Hobbs	4	C	4	0	0	0	420
Hobby Cat	2	G	8	2	1	2	17,770
Hobert	8	G	4	1	0	0	5,640
Hobie Hobson	4	F	2	0	0	0	0
Hobin	6	G	3	1	0	0	3,855
Hobkirk Hill	3	G	8	1	0	0	4,870
Hobo Traveler	7	G	1	1	0	0	4,284
Hochs in Socks	6	M	8	3	0	1	25,322
Hockadaisy Four	6	M	4	2	0	0	6,718
Hockey Jock	3	C	4	2	1	0	45,700
Hodaruki	4	G	12	2	0	1	5,989
Hoddam	3	F	12	1	1	4	16,106
Hode's Benthere	4	G	5	0	0	0	0
Hog Heaven	7	G	10	1	1	1	8,199
Hog Run Creek	4	G	16	4	4	2	22,000
Hogan's Hero	9	G	5	0	2	2	2,819
Hogan's Spirit	4	G	8	0	2	2	28,504
Hogo Pogo	3	C	4	0	0	0	0
Hogum	6	M	1	0	0	0	200
Hogwarts	3	C	6	1	0	1	7,950
Hoh Buzzard (IRE)	4	F	2	0	0	0	10,000
Hoh Hoh Hoh	3	F	3	1	1	0	12,720
Hoh Steamer (IRE)	8	G	1	0	0	0	500
Hoho Tow	3	G	11	4	1	1	41,100
Hoist Away	2	G	1	0	0	0	180
Hoist My Colors	3	F	3	0	0	0	0
Hoist the Cat	3	G	4	0	0	0	440
Hoist the Gold	5	G	5	0	0	0	340
Hoity Toity	6	M	4	0	2	1	15,570
Hoke	7	G	2	0	0	0	292
Hola C Bright	4	G	10	3	0	5	31,244
Hold a Moonbeam	3	F	2	1	0	0	29,500
Hold Hard	3	G	19	4	3	2	50,254
Hold Me Close	3	F	2	0	0	1	2,042
Hold Me Together	10	G	5	0	1	0	1,873
Hold My Mail	3	C	9	2	1	0	9,032
Hold On a Sec	6	G	12	3	3	1	20,232
Hold On Heather	2	F	5	1	0	0	4,770
Hold On Kari	2	F	1	0	0	0	85
Hold On Sugar	4	F	9	1	2	1	28,712
Hold On to the Key	5	M	3	0	0	0	195
Hold That Bull	3	G	4	1	0	0	17,040
Hold That Glitter	5	G	2	2	0	0	30,856
Hold That Smile	4	C	10	0	4	1	10,387
Hold the Cash	5	G	13	0	0	0	450
Hold the Flight	7	G	8	1	1	1	4,872
Hold the Game	2	F	7	2	2	1	72,575
Hold the Gold	5	M	7	2	3	1	7,373
Hold the Lime	5	M	9	0	1	2	8,311
Hold the Salt	2	C	1	0	0	0	1,025
Hold Your Boots	4	C	9	1	0	1	4,505
Hold Your Goodbye	3	G	4	0	1	0	3,280
Hold Your Honor	2	C	3	0	0	1	2,620
Hold Your Thought	4	G	14	5	2	4	88,168
Holdamearound	4	F	8	0	0	1	4,477
Holdemplayer	5	G	4	0	0	0	954
Holden Champagne	3	F	5	1	0	1	32,376
Holden On	4	G	5	0	0	3	3,000
Holden Prosper	4	G	1	0	0	0	39
Holdeverything	3	G	3	0	0	1	3,185
Holdin all Cards	12	G	4	0	0	1	1,794
Holding Serve	2	G	1	0	0	0	300
Holding the Bag	3	C	5	0	0	1	954
Holdmedaddy	3	F	16	4	5	1	45,660
Holdthehelm	5	G	13	1	1	3	44,210
Hole in the Glass	5	G	11	0	1	2	7,403
Hole in the Head	2	C	4	1	3	0	27,565
Hole Ponche	4	F	10	1	1	4	11,455
Hole Shot	2	G	4	0	0	0	555
Holes in My Shoes	6	G	3	0	0	0	400
Holidaisy	2	F	6	1	1	1	25,473
Holiday Coins	4	G	15	2	2	2	10,299
Holiday Doc	7	G	6	0	0	0	3,079
Holiday Doll	5	M	16	0	0	5	4,242
Holiday Event	2	F	3	0	0	0	1,574
Holiday Flight	7	G	9	0	0	0	2,413
Holiday Gold	2	F	2	0	0	0	2,740
Holiday Lady	4	F	5	1	1	1	45,940
Holiday Music	9	G	1	1	0	0	18,600
Holiday Peak	4	C	11	2	3	2	32,840
Holiday Prospect	3	G	6	1	0	0	6,700
Holiday Runner	4	F	2	0	1	0	10,000
Holiest Punch	6	H	5	0	1	2	10,951
Holland Polland	4	F	8	1	1	2	32,671
Holley's Ticket	5	M	10	0	1	0	2,010
Hollisler	3	C	3	0	1	0	516
Hollister Slew	6	H	5	0	2	1	1,587
Hollor Back	4	G	9	0	1	4	11,390
Hollow Memories	5	G	13	2	1	1	14,557
Hollow Sky	2	F	1	0	0	0	1,410
Hollowfill	3	G	6	2	1	0	16,400
Holly Arts	4	F	11	1	1	3	6,640
Holly Cat	3	F	8	1	2	1	25,880
Holly Day Groom	5	G	13	0	0	2	2,482
Holly Day Trend	6	G	19	4	4	1	32,956
Holly Drive	3	F	5	1	0	0	18,060
Holly High	6	M	1	0	0	0	0
Holly Hill Flirt	5	M	4	0	1	0	2,795
Holly Holy I	3	F	8	2	3	0	12,266
Holly Park	4	F	5	1	0	1	8,613
Holly Rae	3	F	12	0	3	4	21,712
Holly's Champ	3	F	3	0	0	0	176
Holly's It	3	F	3	1	0	0	13,900
Holly's Loot	6	G	12	4	3	0	21,700
Hollywhirl	2	F	6	1	1	3	9,787
Hollywood and Wine	3	F	5	2	0	0	52,653
Hollywood Beach	3	F	1	0	0	0	182
Hollywood Breeze's	4	G	9	0	0	0	180
Hollywood Buzz	6	G	7	1	0	5	3,915
Hollywood Chaos	3	F	7	2	2	0	14,593
Hollywood D. A.	3	G	6	1	0	1	5,159
Hollywood Dropout	4	G	6	1	0	0	12,245
Hollywood Ending	6	M	15	4	4	1	197,174
Hollywood Fever	3	F	11	4	4	1	96,352
Hollywood Gone	2	F	5	2	2	0	35,497
Hollywood Honey	4	F	5	0	0	1	6,640
Hollywood Hustle	2	F	3	0	1	0	2,698
Hollywood Hustler	3	G	5	0	2	0	6,064
Hollywood Jam	3	C	3	0	1	0	1,860
Hollywood King	3	G	7	0	0	4	2,028
Hollywood Lawyer	7	G	9	2	0	1	2,318
Hollywood Matinee	3	F	4	0	0	0	360
Hollywood N Divine	2	F	4	1	1	1	17,709

Horse	Age	Sex	Sts	1st	2d	3d	Won
Hollywood Paragon	4	F	2	0	0	0	208
Hollywood Payday	2	C	11	0	4	1	11,342
Hollywood Princess	4	F	1	0	0	0	460
Hollywood Reversal	8	M	5	3	0	1	24,350
Hollywood Robber	3	G	11	1	0	2	8,093
Hollywood Shame	4	F	1	0	0	0	235
Hollywood Story	3	F	7	1	1	2	287,105
Hollywood Sunset	5	H	5	0	0	0	288
Hollywood Warrior	5	G	7	0	1	2	3,324
Hollywood Wonder	3	F	4	1	1	0	36,276
Hollywoodsetright	3	F	7	0	1	1	7,860
Holmdel	8	G	2	0	0	1	484
Holme Abroad	4	F	8	0	3	2	7,802
Holmeonthewire	5	M	8	0	0	1	2,010
Holy Area	4	G	15	1	4	1	10,753
Holy Astra	3	F	5	1	0	0	7,953
Holy Bee	2	C	4	0	0	0	895
Holy Bird	5	M	9	1	3	1	9,340
Holy Bubbette	4	F	4	2	0	0	108,000
Holy Bullet	2	G	5	1	1	0	18,880
Holy Bully	3	G	8	1	1	0	10,683
Holy Burrito	5	G	2	0	0	0	0
Holy Class	3	F	2	1	0	0	8,400
Holy Conflict	7	G	11	1	1	1	38,520
Holy Cow	4	G	10	1	0	1	5,739
Holy Decree	6	G	2	0	1	0	1,594
Holy Dough	5	M	2	0	0	0	0
Holy Envoy	2	F	1	0	0	0	230
Holy Gal	2	F	2	0	0	0	0
Holy Gate	5	H	5	0	0	1	1,053
Holy Gem	6	G	8	2	2	2	32,892
Holy Gin	2	G	6	1	1	1	10,628
Holy Glider	10	G	4	0	0	0	210
Holy Ground	2	C	1	1	0	0	12,300
Holy Hearthrob	3	C	3	1	0	0	6,143
Holy Holly	2	F	1	0	0	0	0
Holy Innocents	7	G	4	0	1	2	5,786
Holy Jo	7	G	13	2	3	1	10,024
Holy Kate	3	F	4	0	0	2	9,540
Holy Liason	4	F	7	2	0	1	15,585
Holy Mackerel	3	F	1	0	0	0	50
Holy Man	4	G	3	0	0	0	0
Holy Meadowstar	2	C	2	0	0	0	425
Holy Moly Oley	4	F	11	2	5	4	42,283
Holy 'n Brilliant	4	G	7	0	0	0	0
Holy Panache	4	G	9	1	2	2	59,543
Holy Peak	3	C	2	0	0	0	1,350
Holy Play	3	G	14	1	2	2	15,721
Holy Prize	7	G	5	0	0	0	72
Holy Prospect	3	C	5	0	0	0	3,020
Holy R. N.	3	F	10	1	1	1	22,758
Holy Relic	3	G	1	0	0	0	250
Holy Request	5	M	23	3	4	5	50,820
Holy Rocket	2	C	1	1	0	0	22,200
Holy Roller	4	F	11	1	0	4	37,240
Holy Run	5	G	12	4	1	2	34,586
Holy Secret	3	F	4	2	1	0	28,784
Holy Silver	2	F	3	0	1	0	10,129
Holy Spark	4	F	4	0	1	1	15,332
Holy Sudan	3	G	9	2	0	1	27,952
Holy Tamale	2	F	5	0	0	0	2,835
Holy to Us	4	F	14	1	0	4	14,620
Holy Toro	4	C	12	1	1	2	7,845
Holy Triumph	5	H	13	0	1	2	29,394
Holy Vision	4	F	20	1	1	3	9,970
Holy Wars	8	G	10	0	2	1	3,269
Holy Wood	3	G	9	1	1	1	10,255
Holyday	4	G	5	0	1	1	480
Hombre Rapido	7	G	5	0	0	3	59,250
Home a Winner	10	G	16	6	2	1	33,112
Home Brew	7	G	4	0	0	0	0
Home by Nine	2	F	3	0	0	0	1,020
Home Court	3	F	3	1	0	2	46,675
Home Dance	3	F	9	0	0	0	2,830
Home Deed	6	M	20	7	2	6	84,705
Home Early	9	G	13	2	0	1	7,118
Home Hill	4	F	12	1	1	2	16,613
Home Ice	2	F	5	1	1	2	64,359
Home James	4	G	8	1	1	1	4,960

Horse	Age	Sex	Sts	1st	2d	3d	Won
Home Made Soup	4	G	6	0	0	3	10,025
Home of Stars	4	G	9	4	2	2	149,006
Home Place	4	F	12	1	2	1	8,321
Home Run Hitter	4	F	4	1	0	0	24,750
Home Silver	7	H	5	1	1	1	28,334
Home Stead	6	G	17	0	0	4	5,515
Home Tour	3	F	9	1	2	2	38,520
Home Town Touch	6	G	1	0	0	0	114
Homebuyer	3	C	5	2	0	1	13,455
Homecoming King	6	G	9	1	3	0	7,787
Homecoming Meeting	3	F	3	0	0	0	1,200
Homecooking Ruby	6	G	12	0	2	0	9,108
Homeedontunome	3	F	3	0	0	0	700
Homegrown Queen	2	F	4	2	1	0	25,490
Homeland	3	C	2	0	0	0	960
Homeland (FR)	6	G	1	0	0	0	400
Homeland Defense	4	C	1	0	0	0	0
Homeland Security	3	G	9	1	1	0	7,986
Homeless Annie	3	F	3	0	0	1	388
Homemade Sin	4	G	6	1	0	0	3,209
Homemaker	3	F	6	2	1	1	64,368
Homeonthenet	4	G	10	3	0	1	21,493
Homeontherange	2	C	2	1	0	0	12,010
Homer Lee	7	G	5	0	0	1	1,493
Homer O	4	C	7	1	1	0	5,095
Homers White Sox	5	M	6	2	1	1	10,590
Homesick	6	G	13	1	1	2	13,690
Homeside	7	H	3	0	1	0	1,340
Homestead Ala	4	F	2	0	0	0	0
Hometown	5	G	4	1	0	0	1,654
Hometown Band	5	G	5	1	0	0	2,790
Hometown Bully	2	G	4	0	1	0	7,716
Hometown Charm	5	M	9	1	2	1	4,381
Hometrader	2	C	8	0	0	3	4,520
Homey's Sister	4	F	8	0	0	0	1,940
Homie	4	C	2	0	1	0	2,228
Homoginize	5	M	5	1	0	0	14,865
Honacode	5	G	4	0	0	0	600
Honah's Special	4	C	5	0	0	0	250
Honary Star	3	G	3	0	0	0	420
Honcho Poncho	5	G	14	0	1	5	8,770
Hondo County	3	C	5	0	0	0	682
Hondo Creek	5	M	2	0	0	0	1,380
Hondo Lane	3	G	1	0	0	0	96
Hondo Ruler	4	G	11	1	1	2	2,461
Honeagle	4	G	4	0	1	1	14,240
Honece Hokte	3	F	18	2	8	2	33,354
Honest Answer	4	F	1	0	0	0	3,600
Honest Art	7	G	3	0	0	0	0
Honest Bid	4	G	1	0	0	0	235
Honest Bob	2	G	6	0	0	1	5,892
Honest Chance	3	G	10	1	4	3	56,570
Honest Girl	4	F	3	0	0	0	0
Honest Glory	3	F	1	0	0	0	65
Honest Grade	4	F	1	0	0	0	0
Honest Groom	7	G	6	0	2	1	1,366
Honest Ice Age	5	M	14	1	2	2	16,021
Honest Illusions	3	G	10	0	0	1	2,113
Honest Jennifer	2	F	1	0	0	0	135
Honest Miss Bates	5	M	3	0	0	0	630
Honest n' Fit	8	M	4	0	0	1	832
Honest Oaks	5	H	6	0	1	1	1,875
Honest Ridge	7	G	22	1	7	2	5,732
Honest Sparkler	6	G	5	1	1	0	8,452
Honest to Ghazi	4	G	20	3	3	2	18,656
Honest Trader	2	C	6	0	0	2	6,395
Honest Tune	2	C	7	1	0	0	16,328
Honest Victor	3	C	3	0	0	0	570
Honest Wish	5	M	4	0	0	1	1,088
Honestly Agitated	6	H	4	2	0	2	8,236
Honey and King	6	G	7	0	1	0	2,060
Honey Baby	4	F	5	0	0	1	1,894
Honey Badgett	2	G	7	0	0	1	7,820
Honey Bye Bye	3	F	3	0	0	0	176
Honey Date	3	F	8	1	1	2	19,239
Honey Don't Belate	7	M	15	3	5	5	47,826
Honey Flower	4	F	4	0	0	0	0
Honey Fritters	3	F	7	0	2	0	10,644
Honey Gal	2	F	3	0	1	1	5,060

Horse	Age	Sex	Sts	1st	2d	3d	Won
Honey Girl	2	F	2	0	0	0	235
Honey Green	4	F	11	2	0	3	95,569
Honey Hit	3	C	8	4	3	1	88,787
Honey Hunt	5	G	22	0	1	3	7,082
Honey Hunter	5	M	11	2	2	2	21,607
Honey Im Charging	8	G	6	1	0	0	6,900
Honey in the Rock	4	F	6	0	0	0	396
Honey Island	3	F	4	1	1	0	18,005
Honey Jade	3	F	8	0	0	0	1,393
Honey Jet	3	F	7	0	1	1	1,050
Honey Mill	4	F	5	0	0	0	591
Honey Mustard Girl	6	M	1	0	1	0	2,100
Honey Oats	2	F	1	0	1	0	3,591
Honey of a Reason	10	H	1	0	0	0	129
Honey Rascal	4	F	19	3	6	2	38,243
Honey Ryder	3	F	8	2	0	4	97,750
Honey Sisaroo	5	G	4	0	0	0	170
Honey Suckle Rose	2	F	1	0	0	0	0
Honeycomb Gus	2	F	2	1	0	1	12,330
Honeyfoot Can Do	2	F	1	0	0	0	104
Honeymoon Babe (IRE)	4	F	8	0	1	0	1,400
Honeymoon Blues	4	F	6	0	1	3	10,320
Honeymoon Stitch	6	M	3	1	0	0	1,175
Honeymooner	5	M	9	0	1	0	12,240
Honeypenny	5	M	9	1	0	2	62,232
Honey's Emblem	3	F	4	0	0	0	0
Honey's Fancy	4	F	9	0	0	1	881
Honey's Music	6	M	7	2	0	1	5,497
Honey's Rainbow	2	F	2	0	0	2	3,230
Honey's Sky	3	F	7	1	0	1	14,700
Honey's Son	6	G	15	3	0	3	17,566
Honeysbestchoice	4	G	11	1	0	0	9,015
Honeyscat	2	F	2	0	0	0	507
Hong Kong Dancer	3	F	6	2	0	2	120,083
Hongkong	2	C	4	1	1	0	21,260
Hongkong Charley	7	M	2	0	0	0	2,360
Honies Badge	2	F	6	1	1	0	8,260
Honk N Look	4	F	2	0	0	0	642
Honky Tonk Dance	5	G	8	1	2	1	38,163
Honky Tonk Dancer	4	G	4	0	1	0	2,350
Honky Tonk Pat	2	F	9	3	2	2	63,958
Honolua Storm	3	C	10	3	0	2	161,157
Honolulu Lad	3	G	20	1	2	1	8,880
Honor and Grace	3	C	10	2	0	1	8,673
Honor and Obey	3	G	5	0	0	0	281
Honor and Valor	3	G	12	1	1	0	6,892
Honor Babe	2	C	2	0	0	0	230
Honor Bestowed	4	F	5	0	1	0	7,180
Honor Birthday	2	F	2	0	0	0	810
Honor Class	4	F	10	2	1	1	20,215
Honor Game	3	F	3	2	0	0	10,915
Honor Gulch	2	C	4	0	0	4	9,250
Honor Held High	2	C	2	0	0	0	1,800
Honor in Battle	6	H	5	1	0	0	6,964
Honor in War	5	H	7	0	1	2	159,261
Honor Issue	5	G	6	1	0	1	4,463
Honor Ma	3	G	10	0	0	1	2,602
Honor Maker	4	G	14	5	1	1	17,498
Honor Me	6	G	6	1	1	1	37,540
Honor Me Too	3	G	6	0	2	0	2,600
Honor My Grades	2	G	4	1	0	0	15,786
Honor Performer	3	F	3	0	0	1	818
Honor Play	5	G	12	2	1	2	11,068
Honor Point	3	F	12	2	2	0	106,960
Honor Prayer	3	G	7	1	0	0	22,650
Honor Pursuit	4	G	10	2	0	1	20,070
Honor R Share	3	F	15	2	1	3	14,325
Honor Ruhls	6	H	4	1	0	0	2,942
Honor Student	3	F	7	1	2	2	27,540
Honor the Chief	5	G	14	3	0	2	9,750
Honor the Dr.	3	F	4	0	0	0	1,090
Honor the Flag	2	F	2	2	0	0	30,600
Honor the General	5	M	13	2	3	2	36,080
Honor the Legend	2	C	4	0	0	0	409
Honor the Prince	5	G	4	0	0	0	245
Honor This Coyote	3	C	11	0	1	0	4,871
Honor Thy Spirit	5	M	17	2	5	4	13,777
Honor Times	3	G	9	1	2	1	12,860
Honora Helen	3	F	8	2	1	3	14,470
Honorable Book	4	F	3	0	1	1	7,170
Honorable Buck	3	G	16	4	4	1	119,975
Honorable Cat	5	M	13	2	4	1	117,721
Honorable Class	2	G	5	2	0	1	40,725
Honorable Coach	2	C	2	0	0	0	1,100
Honorable Dancer	3	F	9	1	1	1	11,055
Honorable Decision	5	G	8	0	0	1	3,214
Honorable Eagle	4	G	5	0	0	0	0
Honorable Feelings	4	F	9	1	0	1	12,810
Honorable Gal	4	F	10	1	1	3	14,245
Honorable Gold	4	G	1	0	0	0	110
Honorable Halo	4	F	7	2	0	1	18,370
Honorable Intent	6	G	11	3	1	2	5,547
Honorable King	4	G	9	0	2	2	6,020
Honorable Knight	4	G	9	1	2	2	13,975
Honorable Life	2	C	1	0	0	0	370
Honorable Man	5	G	7	4	2	1	81,830
Honorable Mark	3	G	10	0	1	2	5,583
Honorable Path	2	F	3	1	0	1	14,532
Honorable Peace	5	M	1	0	0	1	3,300
Honorable Pic	7	H	3	1	1	0	29,400
Honorable Prince	3	G	12	0	0	1	2,062
Honorable Tam	3	G	7	1	0	2	37,581
Honorable War	4	G	3	0	0	0	0
Honorable Wish	3	G	13	0	0	1	3,113
Honorable World	4	F	14	4	2	3	31,980
Honoramongthieves	4	C	6	2	0	2	26,010
Honorary Doctor	3	G	3	1	0	0	37,128
Honorary Man	4	G	3	0	0	0	3,925
Honored Code	2	C	5	1	0	1	13,510
Honored Star	2	C	1	1	0	0	14,200
Honoree Dancer	3	G	4	0	0	1	1,470
Honorett	2	F	2	0	0	0	2,410
Honoriffic	3	F	3	1	1	0	5,800
Honorifico (ARG)	10	H	1	0	0	0	61
Honoring Carolyn	2	F	6	1	0	2	17,245
Honoring Opal	3	F	3	0	1	0	3,800
Honorlee	4	F	8	2	1	0	31,570
Honornpride	4	G	4	2	0	0	7,080
Honorvan	5	G	6	0	1	0	1,480
Honorville	5	M	6	1	1	1	22,010
Hono's Baby	2	F	2	0	1	0	2,290
Honour and Fame	6	G	4	1	0	0	2,620
Honour Brett	4	G	5	2	0	0	26,449
Honour Emblem	2	C	2	1	0	0	8,100
Honour Mission	3	G	9	2	1	0	22,941
Honour Sid	3	F	6	1	2	0	12,895
Honour Star	3	G	16	0	5	4	27,118
Honour Thy Country	3	G	7	0	0	1	6,141
Honour Thy Father	2	C	3	0	1	0	4,000
Honour Topper	2	C	3	1	0	0	6,915
Honourable Asset	3	F	6	2	2	1	70,095
Hoo Gets the Gold	4	G	5	3	0	0	18,599
Hoo Knows	7	G	6	0	0	0	608
Hooch	3	G	7	1	0	0	1,980
Hooched Desdemona	3	F	4	2	0	0	14,829
Hoochy Koochy Girl	3	F	1	0	0	0	205
Hoochy Woman	4	F	1	0	0	1	430
Hoof Beats	4	F	9	0	2	1	14,372
Hoofin' It	2	G	7	1	1	0	10,815
Hook	5	G	6	2	3	0	21,540
Hook Call (BRZ)	9	G	11	7	0	2	78,120
Hook Shot	6	M	8	0	0	1	1,500
Hookahey	5	G	1	0	0	0	192
Hooked a West	6	G	5	2	1	0	8,786
Hooked On Mackee	5	H	3	0	1	0	566
Hooked On Niners	5	M	7	0	3	2	62,400
Hookedonjoy	3	F	4	1	0	0	22,380
Hooking Thefeeling	6	G	9	0	2	1	3,094
Hookshank	3	C	1	0	1	0	4,700
Hooky	2	F	3	0	0	0	2,300
Hoolie Blue	4	G	4	1	1	0	9,542
Hoolie Is Irish	3	F	1	0	0	0	0
Hoolie Unexpected	4	C	8	1	0	1	16,533
Hooliea	5	G	15	1	0	2	14,397
Hooliehoo	3	C	13	2	1	1	20,971
Hoolies Best	6	H	9	0	0	0	1,803
Hooloomooloo	3	G	1	1	0	0	8,400
Hooper's Battle	5	M	1	0	0	0	0

Horse	Age	Sex	Sts	1st	2d	3d	Won
Hoopers Open Forum	3	F	2	0	0	0	0
Hoopers Wishes	3	G	4	0	0	0	0
Hoop's Hope	2	C	4	0	1	0	2,970
Hooptheereitis	2	F	3	1	0	0	8,650
Hoosick Falls	2	F	4	1	2	0	41,454
Hoosier Daize	3	C	2	0	0	0	233
Hoosier Dealer	3	G	2	0	0	0	73
Hoosier Hotty	3	F	8	0	2	1	8,720
Hoosier Paw	4	G	1	0	0	0	40
Hoosier Redneck	3	C	6	0	0	0	990
Hoosier Time	5	M	8	0	0	0	439
Hoosier Waterlily	3	F	12	0	1	3	4,720
Hoosier Wildcat	3	F	12	0	0	2	3,598
Hoosierville	4	G	6	0	0	0	814
Hoosyateach	4	F	9	3	1	0	12,559
Hoosyer Kharma	3	F	10	0	4	0	12,514
Hoot N Dasher	3	F	2	0	0	0	1,300
Hoot N Homer	3	F	11	1	1	1	2,585
Hooten Newton	4	G	5	1	0	0	13,040
Hootend	6	G	6	0	0	3	3,430
Hooterville	9	H	1	0	0	0	39
Hootiehoot	4	G	4	2	1	0	6,568
Hoots Harri	4	G	15	2	3	3	36,165
Hoovergetthekeys	6	G	7	0	1	2	17,760
Hooves of Fire	3	G	3	0	0	2	4,800
Hop Hornbeam	6	G	3	0	0	0	0
Hop On It	3	F	4	0	0	0	800
Hop Queen	4	F	2	0	0	0	0
Hope and a Prayer	7	M	10	0	0	0	330
Hope and Faith	2	F	2	0	0	0	1,285
Hope Avenue	3	F	3	0	0	0	243
Hope Diamond Babe	2	F	1	0	0	0	0
Hope Faithncharity	4	F	4	1	1	0	8,360
Hope for a Buck	7	G	5	0	0	0	643
Hope for Love	4	F	1	0	0	0	1,350
Hope for Peace	2	C	6	1	0	0	5,658
Hope I'm Lucky	5	G	5	0	0	0	750
Hope Is Forever	4	G	11	0	1	1	3,156
Hope N Again	5	G	5	1	1	0	7,867
Hope of Nations	2	F	4	0	0	0	173
Hope On the Run	2	G	1	0	0	1	6,270
Hope Onthe Horizon	3	C	1	0	0	0	60
Hope Reigns	4	F	1	0	0	0	0
Hope Revival	7	M	9	1	3	0	15,568
Hope Right	2	F	2	0	0	0	0
Hope Rises	4	F	5	2	0	0	108,455
Hope River	2	F	13	0	0	2	13,565
Hope She's Special	2	F	2	1	1	0	12,800
Hope Springs Up	4	F	15	0	2	5	9,345
Hope to Pass	3	F	1	0	0	0	0
Hope to Prosper	6	G	5	0	1	0	1,700
Hope Victory	4	F	1	0	0	0	56
Hope Wish and Luck	2	F	1	0	0	0	1,988
Hope You Dance	5	M	6	0	0	1	840
Hopeforthecat	4	F	3	0	0	0	280
Hopefortheroses	3	C	11	0	1	0	10,180
Hopeful (NZ)	5	M	2	0	0	0	800
Hopeful Claim	5	G	5	1	1	0	2,150
Hopeful Coed	3	F	5	0	0	0	545
Hopeful Heart	4	F	10	1	0	0	18,835
Hopeful Joy	2	F	1	0	0	0	0
Hopeful Season	4	F	8	1	0	0	6,011
Hopeful Start	3	G	4	0	0	1	1,017
Hopeisfleeting	5	M	15	0	1	0	5,495
Hopelessly Devoted	3	F	14	6	4	0	499,260
Hopelessly Wild	2	C	1	0	0	0	0
Hoper	2	F	3	1	1	0	47,954
Hopes and Promises	3	F	2	1	0	0	7,175
Hope's Diamond	4	F	14	2	2	2	61,187
Hope's Intention	3	G	13	0	2	4	15,450
Hope's Triumph	3	F	2	0	0	0	1,260
Hope's Wild Vision	3	F	2	0	0	0	760
Hopethevictorious	7	M	2	0	0	0	155
Hopetobeastar	4	G	14	0	1	2	1,619
Hopeton County	5	G	11	0	1	1	4,395
Hopi Lane	5	H	7	0	0	0	889
Hoppin' John	3	G	11	1	0	3	10,047
Hoppy's Goldmine	10	G	10	1	0	3	5,482
Hopso (IRE)	5	G	16	5	1	3	36,798
Hoptuit Bud	10	G	3	0	0	1	3,840
Horatio	5	G	6	1	0	1	13,052
Horizon Affair	4	F	10	2	0	1	14,520
Horizon Coast	4	G	12	3	2	0	17,799
Horizon Weekend	3	G	2	0	0	0	554
Horn	2	C	1	0	0	0	0
Hornby	4	G	2	0	0	0	354
Hornet	7	H	4	0	0	0	562
Hornshope	3	C	13	3	2	1	109,206
Horrible Evening	6	G	8	1	0	2	36,447
Horrify	5	M	8	1	3	0	3,150
Horse Hill	4	C	7	1	3	0	31,006
Horse Nut	3	G	8	0	0	0	1,932
Horse of Course	4	G	2	0	0	0	88
Horse Spirit	2	G	4	0	0	0	330
Horse Words	3	C	2	0	0	0	0
Horsefollowclosely	4	F	6	0	0	0	492
Horsesanddivorces	4	C	2	0	1	1	2,600
Horseshoe Tear	4	C	2	0	0	0	0
Horsewithsixnames	3	G	3	1	0	0	7,657
Hortense (CHI)	4	F	5	0	1	3	26,000
Hosco	3	C	7	1	1	0	101,386
Hoss Nuts R We	5	M	4	0	0	0	0
Hoss of Fire	4	G	1	0	0	0	0
Host	4	C	8	3	1	1	107,430
Host (CHI)	4	C	6	2	2	2	204,480
Hostess Mine	5	M	15	2	1	1	10,239
Hostile Driver	6	G	4	0	0	0	0
Hostile Jet	7	G	3	1	0	1	5,420
Hostile Miss	5	M	6	1	0	0	7,410
Hostile Witness	2	C	7	2	1	2	59,530
Hostility	4	F	12	4	3	1	118,430
Hot	4	G	7	1	1	0	14,360
Hot and Cold	2	F	6	1	2	0	15,100
Hot and Sinful	5	M	14	2	3	3	18,030
Hot as a Pistol	5	M	13	1	3	1	19,708
Hot Attraction	2	F	2	1	1	0	28,000
Hot Body	4	F	7	0	0	2	1,404
Hot Boots	2	C	3	0	0	0	240
Hot Burn	8	H	1	0	0	0	138
Hot C N Broken G	4	G	4	1	0	0	4,513
Hot Chase	2	F	1	0	0	0	828
Hot Chili Boy	3	G	3	0	0	0	344
Hot Chipotle	3	F	10	2	2	1	32,261
Hot Chocolate	4	G	10	1	1	3	6,157
Hot Chocolate Mr.	3	G	8	0	1	0	6,000
Hot Commodity	3	G	10	0	4	1	7,490
Hot Conquest	4	G	12	1	1	0	5,346
Hot Contest	5	G	5	1	1	0	13,780
Hot Cookie	4	G	12	1	0	1	8,430
Hot Cowboy	6	G	12	0	0	0	1,189
Hot Dancer	4	F	1	0	0	0	180
Hot Desert	3	F	9	1	0	1	24,751
Hot Dish	3	F	6	1	0	1	11,127
Hot Dog	3	C	7	0	0	1	2,795
Hot Dog Queen	4	F	2	0	1	0	1,220
Hot Doggee	4	G	1	0	0	0	0
Hot Fashion	2	F	1	0	0	0	0
Hot Fast N Loose	4	F	14	1	3	1	19,265
Hot Finance	3	G	12	0	3	0	19,270
Hot for Love	6	M	1	0	0	0	0
Hot for You	4	G	3	0	0	0	0
Hot Fudge Bundy	3	C	5	0	1	1	5,680
Hot Fudge Sundae	2	F	1	0	0	1	3,240
Hot Golden Jet	4	F	5	0	1	1	19,290
Hot Grip	4	G	1	0	0	0	400
Hot Hand	4	C	11	0	0	4	15,714
Hot Head	6	G	7	0	2	0	13,309
Hot Honey	5	M	2	0	0	0	0
Hot House	4	F	4	1	0	1	4,050
Hot Hula Hula	6	M	12	2	1	2	7,694
Hot Ice	3	F	6	0	1	0	3,820
Hot Jelly Jam	4	F	13	2	2	1	22,489
Hot Josh	4	G	3	1	0	1	18,880
Hot Jungle Love	5	M	11	2	1	0	11,003
Hot Justice	4	G	8	0	0	0	726
Hot Kisses	3	F	3	0	1	0	4,255
Hot Line	3	F	3	0	0	0	590
Hot Little Majic	4	F	11	2	2	2	4,275

Horse	Age	Sex	Sts	1st	2d	3d	Won
Hot Little Redhead	2	F	4	0	0	0	1,530
Hot Lookn Doll	3	F	4	0	0	0	1,038
Hot Mail	3	F	3	0	1	1	10,880
Hot Malibu Moon	3	F	1	0	0	0	1,150
Hot Market	6	G	11	3	2	1	58,520
Hot Meatball Red	5	G	3	0	0	0	0
Hot Melody	2	G	1	0	0	0	400
Hot Message	3	C	1	0	0	0	0
Hot N Go	3	G	19	2	1	3	15,585
Hot Nose	2	F	1	0	0	0	300
Hot Nuggets	4	G	20	2	6	2	18,987
Hot Pepper Hill	8	G	7	2	3	1	120,751
Hot Plan	3	G	4	1	0	1	7,163
Hot Potato	6	H	7	0	1	1	11,120
Hot Quaker	4	G	7	1	0	0	3,791
Hot Red Candi	5	M	8	0	0	0	1,360
Hot Red Halo	5	M	3	0	0	0	0
Hot Redhead	3	F	4	1	0	0	8,430
Hot Riff	6	G	9	2	0	1	12,790
Hot Rod Bob	3	G	1	0	0	0	0
Hot Rod Cookie	2	F	5	1	0	0	8,780
Hot Rod Express	3	G	7	0	1	1	1,581
Hot Rod Joy	6	M	10	0	0	0	450
Hot Rod Lincoln	3	G	12	4	0	2	24,065
Hot Rodin	4	G	15	2	0	3	37,197
Hot Rox Diamond	4	C	1	0	0	0	530
Hot Sarah	4	F	5	0	0	0	1,340
Hot Saucy	4	F	2	1	0	1	1,488
Hot Sea	4	F	13	2	1	2	23,728
Hot Shooter	5	G	8	2	0	1	9,925
Hot Shot Bob	4	G	17	2	3	0	28,045
Hot Shot Dancer	3	C	1	0	0	0	0
Hot Shot Diamond	5	M	1	0	0	0	0
Hot Shot Luke	2	C	1	0	0	0	0
Hot Shot Spirit	3	G	12	1	5	1	16,351
Hot Singe	4	C	7	0	0	0	1,705
Hot Sky	2	C	1	0	0	0	720
Hot Slot	5	H	5	1	0	0	11,886
Hot Song	4	G	13	2	0	1	8,205
Hot Soup	5	G	6	0	1	1	11,027
Hot Spice	2	F	7	1	2	0	19,157
Hot Steel	3	G	12	1	3	1	42,726
Hot Stop (ARG)	6	H	3	0	0	0	0
Hot Storm	2	F	5	2	0	0	45,850
Hot Talk	3	G	7	2	1	0	28,928
Hot Tam	4	F	9	0	0	3	1,968
Hot Tap	3	F	1	0	0	0	0
Hot Tin Pan	2	G	2	0	0	0	798
Hot Tizzy	2	C	3	0	0	1	8,856
Hot to Spot	4	G	7	1	0	2	6,665
Hot to Tango	5	M	9	1	1	0	11,420
Hot Trick	3	F	6	0	0	1	511
Hot Video	9	G	7	2	1	2	3,594
Hot War	5	H	3	0	0	0	0
Hot Weather	6	G	3	0	1	1	2,520
Hot Weekend	3	F	10	1	3	1	39,080
Hotcey Totcey	6	M	3	0	0	0	130
Hotdiggitydoggedly	5	G	4	0	1	0	1,564
Hotel Del	3	G	9	1	1	2	5,166
Hotel Hall (IRE)	6	G	8	1	3	0	95,040
Hotenuforyoo	2	C	4	0	1	0	9,948
Hotlikepepper	2	C	2	0	0	0	0
Hotrod Jones	4	G	9	0	0	1	2,206
Hots Is Hot	4	C	2	0	0	1	1,540
Hotshot Salesman	2	C	2	0	1	0	3,845
Hotsie's Buckaroo	9	G	4	0	0	0	4,725
Hotspur	7	G	1	1	0	0	18,000
Hotstufanthensome	4	G	10	5	2	0	143,200
Hotsy Act	6	M	11	1	3	0	16,605
Hottentot	5	M	7	1	0	0	21,390
Hotter Than Hot	5	G	11	3	0	2	24,997
Hottie	4	F	10	2	4	1	21,300
Hottie Girl	4	F	14	0	2	1	11,077
Hottothetouch	2	C	4	0	1	1	13,667
Houdini's Trick	3	F	8	2	0	2	4,150
Houghton Regrets	3	C	2	0	1	0	4,829
Hound Deer	8	G	2	0	0	0	0
Hound of Silence	4	G	11	1	1	1	8,220
Hounded	2	C	2	0	0	0	0
Hour Cee Dee	9	G	5	0	1	0	1,580
Hour of Justice	4	F	5	3	0	2	243,953
Hour Outlaw	3	C	3	1	2	0	23,800
Hour Pocket Change	5	G	6	0	0	0	0
Hour Power	6	M	3	0	0	1	1,165
Hour Special Lady	3	F	4	0	0	0	0
Hour Storm	2	F	2	0	0	0	0
Hourglass Figure	4	F	14	0	3	4	16,765
Hourly Storm	6	H	15	2	3	2	72,209
Hourmissremy	4	F	10	2	0	0	20,675
Hourtimetocashin	3	G	2	0	0	0	0
Hourytwokprospect	4	G	1	0	0	0	0
House Alarm	2	G	2	0	0	1	1,100
House Dance	5	G	3	1	0	1	4,751
House Hunting	5	M	13	2	3	0	10,519
House Key	3	G	11	2	2	0	75,430
House Money	5	G	12	3	2	0	15,187
House of Danzing	2	F	2	0	1	0	9,940
House of Fortune	3	F	7	3	2	0	364,875
House of Gems	3	F	10	1	2	3	15,148
House of Magic	2	G	3	0	0	0	0
House of Sensation	3	G	13	2	1	1	31,494
House of Sport	4	C	1	0	0	0	70
House On the Beach	8	G	6	1	2	2	11,790
House Party	4	F	3	1	1	0	80,000
House Wine	5	H	7	1	1	0	7,500
Housebird	5	M	8	0	2	1	4,292
Houseofroyalhearts	2	C	1	1	0	0	19,200
Houston Astro	4	G	14	2	2	1	20,489
Houston Cargo	3	C	1	0	0	1	660
Houston Hustler	6	M	12	1	1	1	14,622
Houston Lights Up	4	G	6	1	0	0	2,761
Houston Pro	6	M	1	0	0	0	61
Houston Shuffle	3	G	3	0	1	0	2,800
Houston Texas	7	G	21	2	3	4	10,696
Houston to Marilyn	5	G	17	1	2	7	12,510
Houston's Arrived	4	G	4	0	0	0	800
Houston's Deal	3	F	19	1	3	3	7,964
Houston's Hope	5	G	5	0	4	0	2,380
Houston's Prayer	4	G	8	2	2	1	83,470
Houston's Touch	5	H	4	1	1	0	5,270
Houstonwehavaruner	3	F	1	0	0	0	400
Hover	5	G	1	0	0	0	0
How About Dattt	3	F	2	1	0	0	19,520
How About It	5	M	4	0	0	1	6,740
How Awesome	2	G	4	1	0	0	3,822
How Bout Jose	7	H	1	0	0	1	6,825
How Bout Now	5	H	1	0	0	0	154
How Clever Trevor	5	G	6	0	0	0	374
How Do You Do	3	G	14	2	3	1	17,912
How Fancy	3	F	16	1	0	1	10,106
How Funny (AUS)	4	F	4	0	0	0	4,400
How Good Is That	3	C	10	1	2	3	22,817
How High	3	F	8	0	0	2	2,119
How Little We Know	4	G	13	1	2	4	25,288
How Long	3	C	3	1	0	0	26,887
How Lou Doin'	3	G	1	0	1	0	3,800
How Many	3	G	2	0	0	1	1,520
How Now	9	G	6	0	1	1	1,591
How Say You	3	C	12	6	1	1	47,775
How Sweet I Am	4	F	1	0	0	0	0
How Ya Doing	4	F	3	1	0	0	10,074
Howabouthat	3	C	1	0	0	0	0
Howamidoin	3	F	10	1	0	1	4,543
Howard B.	3	G	3	0	2	1	16,040
Howard Way	7	G	21	2	2	3	10,222
Howard's Crossing (FR)	6	H	3	0	0	1	1,900
Howard's Fool	2	C	2	0	0	1	1,074
Howdidhedoit	4	G	16	1	3	4	15,195
Howies Hungry	6	G	14	0	3	2	6,033
Howl At the Moon	3	F	6	2	1	0	37,100
Howlin Wolf	10	G	12	0	2	3	2,429
Howtoo	5	G	8	0	1	0	2,859
Howyagettinon	2	F	1	0	1	0	2,034
Howyalikedemapples	3	G	4	0	0	0	810
Howyouknow	5	H	1	0	0	0	0
Howyoulikemenow Tc	5	M	8	0	0	1	12,459
Hoy	3	G	1	0	0	0	137
Hoyt	3	G	14	0	2	3	9,420

Horse	Age	Sex	Sts	1st	2d	3d	Won
Hristoforos	6	H	10	0	0	2	13,734
Hs Suave Dancer	5	M	10	0	1	0	2,289
Huanaco	3	C	2	0	0	0	0
Huatusco	2	F	1	0	0	0	160
Hub City Al	4	G	11	0	0	1	1,733
Hubba Hubba Hubba	5	G	7	0	0	0	472
Hubble the Charmer	3	C	13	0	1	1	3,955
Hubs First Bull	4	G	12	1	4	1	5,141
Hubs Ghost	3	C	5	0	0	1	694
Hucklebear	4	G	8	1	0	0	7,356
Huckleberry Blue	2	F	2	1	1	0	6,525
Huckleberry Prize	5	G	13	2	0	3	8,821
Huckleberry's Gal	3	F	15	5	3	1	63,355
Huck's Comet	4	G	1	0	0	0	0
Hudson Bay (IRE)	5	G	2	0	0	0	425
Hudson Street	5	G	15	2	3	2	21,425
Hudson Valley	2	F	2	0	1	0	10,250
Huelee's Fuzzy Man	7	H	5	0	0	0	390
Hue's Power Man	4	C	3	1	0	0	9,698
Hueyduiandlouie	2	G	6	0	0	1	4,312
Huff n' Puff	3	G	2	0	0	0	653
Huffle Shuffle	5	G	8	1	0	3	5,832
Hufflepuff	3	F	3	0	0	0	1,200
Huffs Champagne	3	F	3	1	1	1	22,830
Huffs Express	3	C	6	0	0	1	1,337
Huff's Gnome	5	G	6	0	0	0	707
Huff's Lady	6	M	3	0	0	1	1,637
Huffs Littleman	4	G	1	0	0	0	42
Hug Me Hug Me	3	F	11	3	2	0	67,560
Hug Me Royal	3	F	3	0	0	0	195
Hug the Road	7	H	4	0	1	1	845
Hugger	4	G	6	1	0	0	4,700
Huggins	3	F	6	1	0	0	5,490
Huggy Boy	6	G	10	2	0	1	9,467
Hugh Betcha	4	G	5	0	0	0	208
Hughes	8	H	4	0	0	0	492
Hugh's Barricade	3	G	4	1	0	1	2,730
Hugh's Mansion	6	G	8	2	0	0	27,640
Hug'm and Hope	2	F	5	1	0	0	4,926
Hugo Tee	3	G	2	1	0	0	13,100
Hugs for Terry	5	M	8	0	0	0	1,320
Hugs Legacy	8	G	3	1	1	0	3,552
Huh	3	G	8	1	3	0	11,195
Huka's Diamond	5	G	12	2	0	3	29,030
Huki's Last Knight	7	M	2	0	0	0	192
Hula Boola	5	M	1	0	0	0	0
Hula Hottie	4	F	13	4	3	4	21,017
Hula Kat	4	F	5	0	2	1	4,794
Hulagal	4	C	2	0	0	0	125
Hulamore	3	F	7	0	0	0	2,540
Huleo's Quest	11	G	4	0	0	0	220
Hull Bay	6	G	2	0	0	0	237
Humaita (GER)	4	F	9	4	2	0	281,440
Humberto	8	G	13	3	1	1	28,525
Humble Billie	5	M	6	1	0	1	25,715
Humble Chris	3	G	12	3	2	2	35,165
Humble Deputy	2	C	1	1	0	0	7,200
Humble Earl	4	G	9	1	0	4	13,085
Humble Felix	3	G	4	0	0	0	0
Humble Gena	3	F	1	0	0	0	0
Humble Hero	4	G	17	3	1	3	31,229
Humble Kathy	4	F	8	0	4	1	9,420
Humble Kelly	2	F	3	0	1	0	4,700
Humble Lane	3	F	14	0	3	1	19,300
Humble Lightning	4	G	6	0	0	1	4,460
Humble Madeline	3	F	11	0	2	2	7,050
Humble Roannie	5	M	5	1	2	0	20,602
Humble Traveler	2	C	1	0	0	0	0
Humblest	4	G	3	0	0	0	1,800
Humblevictor	2	C	3	0	0	1	3,585
Humdalila	4	F	7	0	1	0	4,864
Hummel	4	F	11	3	2	2	57,635
Hummer's Echo	5	G	10	0	2	0	1,473
Humming Breeze	3	F	6	1	0	0	2,780
Humming Cat	4	C	1	0	0	0	0
Humor At Last	2	C	3	2	1	0	92,805
Humor Me Molly	3	F	11	4	1	2	109,946
Humor the Rumor	5	G	2	0	0	0	0
Humoresque	5	M	10	0	2	0	2,250
Humoristic	3	F	11	4	1	1	95,260
Humorous Leader	4	C	8	0	2	2	7,460
Humorous Miss	3	F	11	4	1	1	102,275
Humorous Tune	3	F	3	1	0	0	17,280
Humorous Type	3	F	12	2	0	2	30,570
Humorously	3	C	6	2	1	1	136,700
Humphreys	5	M	15	3	3	2	22,000
Humptys Alibi	5	G	1	1	0	0	8,164
Humptys Horsepower	4	G	12	2	1	0	3,208
Humus	2	C	4	0	2	0	4,575
Hunan Princess	3	F	8	0	0	0	4,184
Hunca Munca	3	F	15	5	3	3	96,170
Hunch No Trump	2	F	1	0	0	0	700
Hunch Play	5	G	10	0	0	2	2,560
Hunch Punch	4	F	8	3	0	0	9,445
Hundred Bagger	5	M	6	0	0	1	1,566
Hundred Centigrade	2	G	4	0	0	0	0
Hunforgun	5	G	11	1	1	1	23,636
Hungarian Banker	2	C	3	0	0	2	2,800
Hungarian Dancer	8	G	2	0	0	0	120
Hungarian Princess	3	F	4	2	0	0	14,830
Hungarian Slew	3	G	5	0	0	1	2,611
Hungry Shane	4	G	12	2	2	0	10,914
Hunkahunkamango	5	G	10	1	2	0	4,952
Hunkerdown	4	G	7	0	0	0	610
Hunky Dory	3	F	1	1	0	0	5,830
Hunky Hill	5	G	11	0	0	1	804
Hunny On Ice	2	F	2	0	0	0	950
Hunt for Glory	3	G	9	2	3	2	8,898
Hunt for Heaven	2	C	2	0	0	0	2,940
Hunt for Joy	4	F	15	1	0	2	6,452
Hunt for Love	4	G	16	3	1	2	24,315
Hunt for Oz	4	C	8	1	0	2	12,045
Hunt for Paws	3	F	15	1	1	4	19,597
Hunt the Rainbow	3	G	7	0	1	1	23,819
Hunter B.	6	H	2	0	0	0	1,600
Hunter Cat	4	G	14	1	2	1	21,746
Hunter Down	3	F	14	2	3	4	50,099
Hunter in the Sky	5	H	18	4	3	4	27,270
Hunter Jay	4	G	12	2	3	1	57,414
Hunter Jo	4	G	14	3	3	4	74,898
Hunter Jr.	3	G	11	0	3	0	4,106
Hunter Lady	4	F	15	1	1	1	5,991
Hunter Royal	4	G	11	2	1	5	17,726
Hunter S.	3	G	3	0	0	0	0
Hunter Todd	6	G	12	5	0	1	69,609
Hunter's Delight	2	G	6	0	1	1	8,695
Hunters Event	4	G	19	1	0	4	7,308
Hunter's Faith	5	M	9	0	3	2	7,990
Hunters Halo	6	G	13	5	4	1	86,739
Hunter's Hope	3	F	1	0	0	0	0
Hunter's Mark	4	F	1	0	0	0	0
Hunter's Pride	3	F	12	3	1	0	30,980
Hunter's Prize	4	G	13	1	1	3	25,600
Hunters Rae	3	F	13	1	1	3	26,748
Hunters Saloon	4	F	1	1	0	0	5,555
Hunter's Storm	2	C	5	1	0	1	6,130
Hunter's Sunrise	5	M	1	0	0	0	130
Hunter's Tale	4	G	15	1	1	3	53,983
Hunter's West	4	F	7	0	1	1	1,943
Hunterwood Point	4	G	10	0	0	0	999
Huntin for Bear	3	G	6	1	0	2	14,670
Huntin Gene	2	G	4	0	0	0	2,410
Hunting Around	4	F	4	0	1	2	3,700
Hunting Course	8	G	10	1	1	0	8,683
Hunting for Action	4	F	9	1	1	0	20,004
Hunting Freedom	4	F	7	0	0	0	347
Hunting Gold	4	G	18	0	1	1	4,861
Hunting Hill	2	G	1	0	0	0	164
Hunting Hillbilly	3	G	13	3	0	3	71,810
Hunting in Gerarda	3	C	8	1	0	0	5,395
Hunting Roses	4	F	8	1	2	0	13,820
Hunting the Dance	4	G	9	0	0	0	561
Hunting the Gold	6	G	11	1	1	2	63,138
Huntingmoneyhoney	3	F	18	3	4	1	22,399
Huntingthetruth	4	F	11	5	2	1	178,771
Huntington Hill	4	F	3	0	0	0	660
Huntington Viking	7	G	6	0	0	1	956
Huntley's Creek	2	G	2	0	0	0	800

Horse	Age	Sex	Sts	1st	2d	3d	Won
Huntmaster	6	G	5	0	1	0	3,804
Huon Kid	3	G	16	3	0	5	29,318
Hup Two	3	G	11	1	3	2	22,730
Huricane Bally	3	F	9	1	1	1	7,393
Hurly Girly	4	F	4	0	2	1	1,435
Hurricane Alan	5	G	8	1	1	1	4,515
Hurricane Ally	4	F	4	0	0	0	318
Hurricane Annie	2	F	5	0	2	1	24,250
Hurricane Bay	3	F	8	1	3	1	26,520
Hurricane Bill	3	G	10	1	1	2	11,870
Hurricane Blaine	2	C	1	0	0	0	400
Hurricane Cash	2	C	1	0	0	0	184
Hurricane Charlie	4	G	15	2	0	2	17,616
Hurricane Cheyann	5	M	4	0	0	1	208
Hurricane Devin	4	C	6	0	1	1	3,522
Hurricane Erica	3	F	9	0	3	1	30,921
Hurricane Esthel	2	F	2	0	0	0	636
Hurricane Fly	3	F	1	0	0	1	1,070
Hurricane Fool	4	G	13	1	2	2	18,985
Hurricane Fury	4	G	2	0	0	0	420
Hurricane Gilbert	5	M	1	0	0	0	0
Hurricane Halo	3	F	4	0	0	0	662
Hurricane Hannah	3	F	5	2	1	2	70,800
Hurricane Henry	2	G	5	1	0	0	8,524
Hurricane Hunter	3	G	13	3	2	3	42,790
Hurricane Isabel	2	F	3	0	0	0	165
Hurricane Lilly	4	F	2	0	0	0	319
Hurricane Malone	2	G	3	0	1	0	9,450
Hurricane Marco	2	G	4	0	0	0	930
Hurricane Merle	7	G	3	0	0	0	1,740
Hurricane Mia	2	C	11	1	1	1	26,380
Hurricane Mike	5	G	11	2	3	0	21,910
Hurricane Moe	3	G	1	0	0	0	954
Hurricane Natalie	3	F	9	1	0	1	6,784
Hurricane Ray	3	C	1	0	0	0	0
Hurricane Rib	2	C	3	1	0	0	6,134
Hurricane Robb	8	G	2	0	0	0	110
Hurricane Rose	5	M	8	0	1	2	30,749
Hurricane Route	4	G	4	1	1	1	26,400
Hurricane Shannan	2	F	2	0	0	1	1,155
Hurricane Smoke	5	G	5	1	0	1	13,100
Hurricane Sue	7	M	4	1	0	0	6,950
Hurricane Whiz	3	F	7	2	1	1	55,199
Hurrikane Kane	4	C	5	1	1	0	7,260
Hurry Hard	2	G	1	0	0	0	3,420
Hurry Home	4	F	4	0	0	1	4,890
Hurry Howard	7	G	6	0	1	2	8,502
Hurry Me Home	7	G	9	0	0	2	3,250
Hurry On Reality	7	H	5	0	0	0	587
Hurry to Finish	5	G	11	4	1	2	12,916
Hurry Up Sunny	7	G	5	0	0	0	1,190
Hurry Up Victory	3	C	2	0	0	0	750
Hurt So Good	2	G	1	0	0	0	300
Hush a Bye Baby	4	F	3	0	0	0	525
Hush Lillie	2	F	1	0	0	1	2,640
Hush Now	3	F	1	0	0	0	40
Hush Tyler	3	C	8	2	0	1	13,800
Hush U Dreamer	4	F	8	3	0	2	70,205
Hushaby Babe	4	F	6	2	1	2	48,665
Hushaling	7	M	6	0	0	0	705
Hushlee	4	G	9	0	1	1	3,074
Hushnlisten	3	G	8	1	2	1	14,006
Hushood	4	C	4	0	0	2	8,280
Hush's Gold	2	F	4	2	2	0	82,905
Husker Valley	4	F	13	1	1	3	6,716
Hussar	4	C	7	2	1	0	14,764
Hussy	4	F	3	0	0	0	855
Hustings	2	C	1	0	0	0	274
Hut Maid	5	M	1	0	0	0	55
Hutches Boy	4	G	8	0	2	1	14,700
Hutchison Station	4	C	2	1	0	0	6,100
Huttutrefo	4	G	8	3	1	0	35,436
Huxley Hero	4	G	5	0	1	1	24,566
Hwy Twenty Seven	3	G	1	0	0	0	155
Hy Angel	4	F	5	0	0	0	314
Hy Karate	4	C	8	1	0	0	2,279
Hy Maureen	3	F	16	3	4	1	15,773
Hy Ms. La Pete	3	F	3	0	0	0	0
Hy Nick	6	G	11	4	4	0	16,093
Hya Doon	2	G	7	0	4	1	42,280
Hyacinth	3	F	5	0	0	0	1,051
Hyak	4	G	5	1	1	1	17,220
Hyannis	3	F	4	1	2	0	9,100
Hybernian Stream	3	F	4	2	0	0	32,530
Hybla Two	4	G	2	0	0	0	605
Hycet Lady	2	F	3	0	0	0	275
Hyder	7	G	9	3	0	1	71,774
Hydration	5	M	2	0	1	0	2,769
Hydrogen	5	H	6	0	1	2	60,610
Hydrophobia	5	G	6	0	0	0	1,503
Hyjab	3	C	1	0	0	0	200
Hy'm the Danzigkid	3	G	6	0	1	1	648
Hymies Jet	9	G	7	1	2	1	9,076
Hymn of Love (IRE)	4	F	3	1	0	0	20,218
Hymns of Glory	3	G	5	1	1	2	8,553
Hyper Dancer	3	F	1	0	0	0	70
Hypercat	4	C	1	0	0	0	0
Hyperjack	7	H	1	0	0	0	0
Hypersonic Boy	7	G	10	1	0	0	1,496
Hypertension	3	C	1	1	0	0	34,200
Hypnos	4	G	3	1	1	0	9,830
Hypnotic	5	H	11	2	1	0	8,009
Hypnotist	4	G	6	0	0	0	1,956
Hypothetical Bet	2	G	1	0	0	0	0
Hysanslew	5	M	1	0	0	0	117
I Accept	3	F	10	0	0	2	4,729
I Ain't Pokeyman	5	M	12	0	2	3	11,910
I Ain't Skeered	4	G	9	0	0	0	930
I Ain't Talkin	6	G	8	0	1	0	2,493
I Ain't Your Honey	6	M	1	0	0	0	145
I Am	2	C	8	0	0	3	15,770
I Am (NZ)	8	G	3	0	1	1	5,950
I Am a Cut Above	3	G	7	0	0	0	465
I Am a Don	3	G	3	0	1	0	3,570
I Am a Livermore	3	C	13	0	1	4	6,785
I Am a True Cat	3	C	6	0	2	1	7,546
I Am Big Enough	3	F	3	0	0	0	210
I Am Bubba	5	G	3	0	0	0	0
I Am Excessive	4	F	12	0	2	3	10,106
I Am Fast	2	F	5	1	1	0	14,140
I Am Gorgeous	4	F	6	0	0	3	17,821
I Am Impressed	5	H	15	3	2	0	15,363
I Am Kodack Moment	3	C	4	0	0	0	472
I Am Morgan	3	F	9	1	2	0	2,653
I Am Rhythm	3	G	3	0	0	0	0
I Am Said I	4	G	7	0	0	1	1,307
I Am Sam I Am	4	G	8	0	0	1	1,706
I Am Smoking	3	G	4	0	0	0	623
I Am Special	3	G	1	0	0	0	110
I Am Speechless	4	F	10	1	2	2	14,485
I Am the Champion	4	G	9	1	0	2	10,487
I Am the Count	4	G	10	1	1	2	22,845
I Am the Mail Man	6	G	6	0	1	0	3,850
I Am the Phantom	7	G	8	0	2	3	1,915
I Am the Road Man	3	G	1	0	0	0	0
I Am This Guy	9	G	2	0	0	2	400
I and I	7	G	2	0	0	0	1,283
I B Bad	4	G	4	1	0	0	27,195
I B Masterpiece	2	C	2	0	0	0	410
I B Right Back	4	F	15	2	6	3	36,110
I Be a Q. T.	4	F	12	0	1	2	3,725
I Been Swingin'	2	F	3	0	0	0	0
I Believe in U Too	3	G	5	1	0	2	4,662
I Believeitsmyturn	3	F	9	1	1	2	11,105
I Belong to Winloc	5	M	12	1	1	1	11,373
I C Jane	3	F	2	0	0	0	0
I C U Looking	5	H	4	0	1	1	5,505
I Call Front	4	G	6	0	0	0	400
I Came to Play	5	M	12	2	2	2	4,856
I Can Cook	4	G	2	0	0	0	800
I Can Fan Fan	5	M	7	1	1	1	49,098
I Can Still See U	5	G	14	0	2	6	8,464
I Can Yodele	2	F	3	1	0	0	28,380
I Can't Believe It	4	G	10	1	0	2	9,790
I Cant Refuse	3	G	11	3	5	2	62,474
I Captain	5	G	9	0	1	0	1,453
I D Queen	4	F	1	0	0	0	275
I Dalee	6	M	2	0	0	0	325

Horse	Age	Sex	Sts	1st	2d	3d	Won
I Dare Billy	3	F	11	3	2	2	41,682
I Dare You Dixie	3	C	4	0	2	0	619
I Did It Ordway	3	C	11	1	2	3	16,248
I Dig	2	C	1	0	0	0	0
I Dig U	4	F	13	2	1	5	32,803
I Don't Care	8	G	7	1	3	1	5,967
I Doubledogdareya	2	C	1	0	0	0	339
I Dr. Joe	7	G	11	2	1	0	25,770
I Dream of Jeanne	4	F	8	3	3	2	21,140
I Feel Good	6	H	2	0	0	1	1,910
I Feel Sure	3	G	2	0	0	0	486
I Follow You	3	F	14	3	0	2	39,190
I Fooled You	3	F	9	1	2	0	18,055
I Give Up	2	F	3	1	0	1	7,932
I Go Solo	2	G	1	0	1	0	2,300
I Got	3	F	6	1	0	1	5,975
I Got Silver	8	M	2	0	0	0	520
I Got Your Number	3	F	5	1	0	2	24,370
I Grow On You	7	M	5	1	0	0	4,047
I Had to Laugh	5	M	10	2	2	0	31,140
I Have No Manners	5	G	11	0	1	0	2,977
I Have Wings	4	F	9	0	1	1	4,303
I Hear a Synphony	3	F	16	3	3	2	21,159
I Hear That	5	M	13	2	2	2	21,453
I Hear Voices	4	F	8	0	0	1	838
I Heard You	6	G	7	0	0	1	2,406
I Hit the Jackpot	5	G	1	0	0	0	146
I Imagine	2	F	1	0	0	0	0
I Just Met a Girl	5	M	12	5	2	1	31,431
I Knew It	4	G	12	2	1	1	11,635
I Know Broadway	6	G	1	0	0	0	0
I Know I Can	3	G	4	0	0	0	0
I Know My Bodie	9	G	9	1	2	0	3,926
I Know You	5	M	18	1	1	4	13,712
I Know You Can	6	H	8	2	1	1	28,360
I Like Cake	3	F	10	1	0	1	6,245
I Like Spike	7	G	8	1	0	0	3,298
I Like Sushi	2	G	3	0	0	0	305
I Like You Tooo	6	H	6	0	3	0	7,736
I Live for This	2	C	1	0	0	0	2,250
I Love a Tru Saint	3	C	9	1	1	2	11,716
I Love Billy	4	F	4	0	0	0	410
I Love Chocolate	4	G	12	2	3	1	34,994
I Love Eskimos	3	F	4	0	0	0	705
I Love Lisa	5	M	11	4	4	1	71,690
I Love Racing	4	G	16	6	5	2	80,206
I Love the Organ	3	F	13	4	3	1	102,825
I Love to Say Yes	2	F	2	0	0	0	460
I Love to Win	4	F	8	1	2	0	24,759
I Love Uptown	4	F	1	0	0	0	0
I Love Vegas	2	C	4	1	0	1	6,672
I Luv This Country	5	G	3	0	0	1	1,498
I M Aking	4	G	12	1	3	3	18,303
I M Gold Bound	2	C	4	0	0	0	0
I M Polish Pride	4	F	8	2	1	0	18,480
I M Rudy D	4	G	1	0	0	0	93
I Made It	2	G	1	0	0	0	110
I Match Too	6	M	12	4	1	0	33,196
I Mena Business	2	C	5	1	0	1	9,110
I Met Somebody	7	M	7	1	0	0	28,715
I Miss You	4	F	2	0	0	0	0
I Need to Run	3	G	1	0	0	0	750
I Nita Rose	3	F	5	0	0	0	720
I Not Slow	4	F	6	0	0	1	1,536
I Nv Slew	2	G	7	0	2	2	10,445
I P O Dude	6	G	18	5	4	1	32,657
I P O Pat	5	M	3	1	1	0	23,010
I Pay the Bills	4	C	6	0	0	0	255
I Prefer Ladies	4	G	10	0	0	1	822
I Reckon It's Gold	3	F	12	0	0	0	760
I Remember You	5	M	11	1	2	1	19,280
I Rob Banks	3	G	1	0	0	0	180
I Say	3	F	2	0	0	0	855
I See the Cat	3	G	17	0	2	5	6,903
I Shot the Deputy	4	F	4	0	0	0	0
I Siyah Dancing	5	M	4	0	0	0	0
I Sub Fur You	4	F	6	0	0	1	1,098
I Tell You	8	H	13	0	0	1	4,884
I Ten West	4	F	9	1	1	0	7,592
I Testify	4	G	12	4	2	1	87,173
I the Messiah	5	G	4	0	0	1	463
I Thee Wed	4	G	8	4	0	2	314,337
I Think I Can	3	F	4	1	3	0	8,020
I Think I Can Fly	8	G	4	0	0	0	348
I Think I Cannes	7	G	11	1	1	3	11,460
I Think I Know	3	G	3	0	0	0	280
I Thought I Could	5	G	1	1	0	0	3,600
I Thought U Knew	3	G	3	0	0	2	3,450
I Time	2	F	2	0	0	0	3,528
I Useto Have Money	3	F	2	0	0	0	0
I Wanna Go Go	5	M	2	0	0	0	285
I Wanna Too	3	G	4	1	0	0	2,738
I Wanta Be Alone	5	G	3	0	0	0	240
I Will	3	G	13	2	0	2	13,956
I Will Honour You	2	F	2	0	0	2	5,125
I Will Survive	5	M	9	2	1	0	41,150
I Wish I Slew	5	G	6	0	0	0	811
I Wish I Was	4	F	14	1	1	0	7,624
I Won't Apollogize	4	G	6	2	1	1	6,185
I Wood Be a Winner	9	G	3	0	0	0	0
I. B. D. Chief	4	G	6	0	0	0	2,207
I. B. Deone	7	G	2	0	0	0	175
I. B. Quick	9	G	3	0	0	0	651
I. C. Secrets	5	M	11	1	2	2	13,210
I. C. Tony	5	H	2	0	0	0	258
I. L. C. U. Later	4	G	10	2	1	1	43,160
I. L. Fool U.	3	G	4	0	0	0	170
I. R. Wood	5	G	12	1	1	2	32,720
Iaco (ARG)	7	H	1	0	0	0	0
Iaintnosweetie	2	F	4	0	0	1	850
I'am a Red Sox Fan	3	G	8	1	1	1	7,479
Iam All Pumped Up	5	M	1	0	0	0	0
I'am Listening	4	G	12	0	0	1	5,382
Iam Nobodys Fool	5	M	5	1	1	0	8,162
Iam T. N. T.	7	M	4	0	0	3	4,511
Iam the Tax Man	2	C	2	0	0	0	800
Iamatowertoo	3	C	7	0	1	3	8,488
Iamlouie Sister	3	F	9	1	1	1	6,050
Iampunchcuptoo	2	F	3	0	0	0	449
Iams Bound	4	G	14	3	1	2	22,141
Ian's Blessing	3	G	4	0	0	0	610
Ian's Rocket	6	G	8	1	3	0	44,900
Ibe Guilty	2	G	2	0	0	1	3,914
Ibelieveinmiracles	5	M	11	0	0	0	1,067
Iberian	3	G	8	0	0	1	3,088
Ibero Grace (ARG)	5	H	9	2	1	0	61,400
Ibis's Heart	4	C	9	0	1	0	1,818
Ibred	3	F	7	2	1	1	10,180
Icandoitmyself	2	F	6	0	2	1	3,778
Icanhaul	4	F	4	0	2	1	12,480
Icanmove	3	G	12	3	3	4	84,390
Icanpunch	4	F	11	2	3	1	18,157
Icanscat	4	G	11	1	2	2	6,427
Icanseeclearly	6	M	18	5	2	2	31,790
Icanseeclearlynow	5	G	8	2	0	1	19,810
Icanseethesky	5	M	4	0	0	0	338
Icantgoforthat	5	M	10	1	0	1	79,516
Ican'thearyou	9	G	9	0	2	3	8,870
Icantmember	6	G	11	0	0	4	5,820
Icarus in Flight	6	G	1	0	0	0	0
Ice and Vice	6	M	3	1	0	1	6,537
Ice Bound	5	M	4	1	0	0	4,098
Ice Bullet	11	G	3	0	1	1	3,700
Ice Capades	2	F	1	0	0	0	468
Ice Carnival	5	M	9	1	1	2	18,205
Ice Chief	3	C	1	0	0	0	168
Ice Cold Alley	4	F	6	3	0	1	15,920
Ice Cream Maiden	5	M	10	1	0	0	3,792
Ice Cream Social	6	M	4	0	0	0	1,097
Ice Cream Sunny	4	F	2	0	0	0	532
Ice Diplomat	4	G	13	0	3	2	6,726
Ice Dude	5	G	12	1	0	0	3,469
Ice Forest	5	M	9	2	2	2	57,210
Ice Girl	4	F	10	2	0	1	64,590
Ice Glider	6	M	10	1	5	0	34,660
Ice Goddess	6	M	2	0	0	0	110
Ice Gold Dancer	3	C	4	0	1	0	3,560
Ice Gypsy	3	F	12	1	2	3	5,008

Horse	Age	Sex	Sts	1st	2d	3d	Won
Ice Hunter	2	C	1	0	0	0	306
Ice in the House	4	G	2	0	0	0	0
Ice Is Nice	3	G	2	0	0	0	0
Ice It	4	F	3	0	0	1	1,504
Ice It Honey	3	F	9	1	1	3	29,680
Ice Jules	2	F	1	0	0	0	0
Ice King	5	G	14	0	0	0	1,344
Ice Kit	4	F	7	1	2	0	2,870
Ice Legend	3	G	3	1	0	0	24,410
Ice Lemon and Rum	3	C	5	1	0	0	11,860
Ice n' Gold	4	F	11	3	2	1	58,430
Ice On the Bezzal	3	G	13	0	3	1	8,994
Ice On the Line	2	G	3	0	0	0	1,000
Ice Out There	10	G	16	4	0	3	5,683
Ice Parade	4	G	4	2	0	1	7,865
Ice Pellet	5	M	10	3	1	1	30,493
Ice Performance	3	G	2	0	0	0	0
Ice Prince (GB)	6	G	6	1	1	1	17,787
Ice Quest	3	F	5	0	0	0	698
Ice Skating	2	G	7	2	1	0	24,255
Ice Storm Patty	2	F	2	0	0	2	2,655
Ice the Dice	6	G	9	0	1	1	4,539
Ice Water	9	G	12	1	0	2	20,899
Ice Wynnd Fire	3	G	5	1	1	2	121,000
Iceanwater	4	G	11	1	1	1	19,240
Iceberg Wayne	5	G	13	1	3	1	16,325
Iced Out	2	C	3	1	1	0	38,038
Icee Cheaspeake	5	M	2	0	0	2	16,848
Icee Wee	4	G	2	0	0	0	0
Ice'em	3	F	5	0	0	0	2,150
Iceirez	12	G	1	0	0	0	0
Icekimo	6	G	18	1	4	2	12,393
Icelandic Conquest	2	G	5	1	2	1	20,566
Iceman Miss	3	F	17	0	2	3	21,000
Iceman Runneth	3	C	4	0	0	1	1,470
Iceplosion	4	G	11	0	3	0	24,150
Ice's Valentine	3	G	3	0	0	0	186
Iceshack	4	F	4	0	0	0	762
Iceslide	3	G	5	1	0	1	8,050
Icey Kisses	3	F	1	0	0	0	105
Ich Liebe Dich	3	G	5	1	1	0	15,026
Ichi Riki	3	G	2	0	0	0	1,180
Ichiban Duc	4	G	9	2	1	1	15,750
Ichigo	4	G	10	3	0	4	69,985
Ichiros Gold	3	G	9	2	2	1	12,603
Icicle Angel	7	M	10	1	0	0	11,515
Icicle Charlie	3	C	9	2	0	0	56,907
Icicle Ridge	3	F	2	2	0	0	10,010
Icicle Toes	2	F	3	0	0	0	335
Icky Tick	2	F	4	0	1	0	3,450
Iconic	2	G	1	0	0	0	340
Iconoclastic	2	C	1	0	0	0	235
Icrossmyhart	4	F	2	0	1	0	2,960
Icy Atlantic	3	C	9	3	3	1	216,720
Icy Avenue	5	M	2	1	0	0	42,120
Icy Badgett	3	C	1	0	0	0	0
Icy Banker	3	C	18	2	2	4	22,180
Icy Calm	6	M	9	5	0	1	30,818
Icy Cat	3	F	6	2	1	2	54,572
Icy Choice	5	M	15	1	3	5	95,012
Icy Glare	7	H	2	0	0	0	0
Icy Interlude	5	M	6	1	1	1	7,857
Icy King	2	C	1	0	0	1	1,000
Icy Lane	3	F	3	2	1	0	105,870
Icy Mocha	2	F	3	0	0	1	3,400
Icy Reception	3	G	2	0	0	0	0
Icy Sensation	3	F	5	1	0	1	2,619
Icy Sparks	3	F	5	1	1	1	3,097
Icy Tobin	4	G	12	3	1	1	44,200
Icy Venom	4	G	9	1	0	1	8,140
Icy Victory	4	G	10	4	0	0	6,647
Icy Witness	4	G	9	1	0	0	6,385
Icyroundtable	4	F	6	0	0	2	2,325
I'd Be First	4	F	14	2	2	3	10,906
Ida Can	3	F	2	0	1	0	6,200
Ida Hadit	7	G	8	2	0	2	6,700
Ida Red	3	F	1	0	0	0	0
Idabetabuck	2	G	3	1	0	0	4,875
Idadidit	5	M	3	0	1	0	18,760
Idahill Tootsie	6	M	5	0	0	2	1,376
Idalea Bailey	5	M	1	0	0	0	0
Idalou	5	M	2	0	0	0	130
Idaoak	4	G	1	0	0	0	0
Idapink	4	F	6	1	2	1	19,070
Idareya	3	C	4	0	0	0	120
Ida's Boy	3	G	10	1	1	1	4,664
Ida's Girl	4	F	10	0	2	2	7,295
Ida's Heart	4	F	6	0	2	1	4,717
Ida's Lil Brother	4	G	19	4	3	2	66,595
Ide and Seek	5	G	8	0	0	0	774
Ide B Blue	4	F	4	1	0	0	1,660
Ide Be a Lady	3	F	9	1	1	0	35,020
Ide Be Brave	3	G	14	2	3	4	16,213
Ide Be Gone	4	G	9	2	2	1	134,700
Ide Be Good	3	C	1	0	0	0	0
Ide Be O for Ten	5	G	17	0	1	3	11,522
Ide Be Proud	3	F	17	0	5	3	16,779
Ide Be Spencers	5	H	4	0	1	1	9,100
Ide Bet It All	5	M	5	0	0	0	534
Ide Boogie	4	F	10	4	3	2	42,415
Ide Got Style	3	C	14	1	1	3	57,018
Ide Rather	5	G	5	1	1	1	30,630
Ide Rathr B Jumpin	3	G	8	0	0	0	1,054
Ide Rejoice	3	G	3	0	1	1	10,460
Idea Man	4	G	9	1	2	0	14,511
Ideal Cut	6	G	5	1	2	0	8,550
Ideal Scenario	3	F	5	0	0	0	2,935
Idealism	4	G	10	2	3	1	27,565
Idealist	8	M	2	0	0	0	390
Idealize	3	G	8	1	0	2	9,270
Ideate	6	M	2	0	0	0	920
Idebewinner	5	G	3	1	0	1	11,250
Idel Zack	5	G	13	0	4	2	6,818
Ident	8	G	14	1	2	4	10,628
Identic	5	H	9	1	1	1	14,820
Identity Theft	3	G	8	1	0	2	10,055
Ideology	5	M	4	0	0	1	1,459
Ideratherbegamblin	3	G	13	2	1	1	17,600
Ides Pride	3	F	12	0	1	3	4,932
Ideway	5	G	6	0	0	2	2,180
Ididdidi (NZ)	6	G	2	0	0	0	1,050
Idle Dreamer	3	C	3	0	0	0	240
Idle Ide	4	G	7	1	1	0	11,395
Idle Ire	4	F	3	0	1	0	1,000
Idle Joan	4	F	7	0	0	0	225
Idle Luck	6	M	8	0	0	1	1,278
Idle Rumor	3	G	2	0	0	0	320
Idle Salute	6	H	1	0	0	0	50
Idle Spur	6	M	2	0	0	0	164
Idle Storm	4	F	5	0	0	1	1,145
Idle Waves	6	G	11	0	1	1	3,340
Id'lly Divine	7	G	6	0	3	0	6,551
Idol Gina	4	G	16	1	2	5	45,140
Idontneedone	6	G	10	1	1	1	9,373
Idon'twanto	3	F	4	0	0	0	583
Idratherbedancing	4	F	12	2	0	1	14,179
Idyll Dancer	5	H	4	0	0	0	0
If I Had It All	4	G	15	2	3	1	5,134
If I Had Wings	4	G	5	0	0	0	610
If I Were You	5	G	12	2	0	2	23,631
If Ida	6	G	6	0	0	1	1,577
If I'm Spared	3	C	4	1	0	0	13,763
If It's Meant to B	2	F	3	0	1	0	10,414
If Its Our Destiny	3	F	12	1	0	4	22,813
If Nine Was Six	4	F	10	0	5	1	31,110
If Not Me Who	4	F	2	0	0	0	486
If Not Why Not	8	G	6	1	1	3	8,566
If Six Was Nine	4	F	3	0	0	0	610
If You Believe	4	F	2	0	0	0	261
If You Please	5	G	20	1	0	3	11,401
If You're Lucky	3	F	9	1	0	1	17,308
Ifeelmisty	5	M	22	1	3	2	32,737
Iffy	5	M	9	1	4	2	40,035
Iffy Account	7	G	8	1	1	4	16,805
Ifineedyaillcallya	8	G	8	0	1	3	16,246
Ifitstobeitsuptome	7	G	10	3	2	2	19,653
Iflookscouldkill	3	F	9	5	2	0	113,350
Ifs and Buts	4	G	10	1	1	3	25,448

Horse	Age	Sex	Sts	1st	2d	3d	Won
Ifufeelfroggyleap	4	F	9	1	2	1	21,327
Ifyouknowwhatimean	5	M	5	0	0	2	2,982
Ifyouprefersilver	5	M	2	0	0	0	1,080
Ifyouseekyouscore	3	F	6	1	0	0	7,285
Ifyouvegotthemoney	5	G	5	0	0	0	1,266
Igetitfrommydaddy	3	C	3	0	1	0	4,385
Iglesias (BRZ)	4	C	12	3	3	3	63,940
Iglo Alpir	5	M	13	0	1	3	4,896
Igloo Annie	4	F	8	1	0	3	17,910
Ignitable	4	G	6	1	1	0	9,177
Ignition	4	C	2	1	1	0	27,880
Ignition Switch	4	G	4	0	0	0	680
Ignitro	4	G	5	1	0	2	27,170
Igor	3	G	4	0	0	0	2,050
Igor (ARG)	5	H	6	2	2	0	18,775
Igor's Girl	3	F	2	0	0	0	160
Igot It Goinon	4	C	10	1	0	0	4,740
Igothips	4	F	1	0	0	0	0
Ihaveadate	3	F	6	2	1	0	129,079
Ihaveseenthelight	4	C	5	0	0	0	879
Ihearyah	3	F	11	1	1	1	7,150
Ihopetobeawinner	4	F	19	1	0	2	4,154
Ikari Caroline	3	F	7	2	1	1	19,947
Ike Time	5	G	7	0	3	0	5,653
Ike'n Dunk	7	G	2	0	0	0	80
Ikes Air Day	3	G	8	0	0	2	3,932
Iknowtheprogram	3	C	12	1	0	5	19,910
Il Barone (IRE)	4	C	3	0	0	0	0
Il Capriccio	3	C	2	1	0	0	15,250
Il Est Renard	5	G	16	1	2	2	8,139
Il Meglio (BRZ)	4	G	6	1	1	0	40,540
Il Vostro Nemico	3	G	1	0	0	0	0
Ile de Ciel	8	M	12	1	0	3	8,136
Ile de Dixie Inn	5	M	11	0	0	1	3,468
Ile de Hunter	3	C	4	1	0	0	5,970
Ile de Linda	5	M	14	2	1	1	23,653
Ileana	8	M	8	3	0	0	8,318
Ile'd Irish Rose	3	F	13	1	0	2	15,131
Ilene's Dream	6	M	3	0	0	1	375
Ilha Grande	5	M	1	0	0	0	0
Iliad's Classic	6	M	2	0	0	0	0
I'll Be Watching	4	G	2	0	0	0	800
Ill Buy Dinner	4	C	1	0	0	0	1,200
I'll Decide	2	F	2	1	0	0	13,680
I'll Lead	4	F	5	0	0	0	475
Ill Naab the Win	3	G	10	4	2	0	18,280
I'll Pay My Way	4	F	11	1	3	1	10,408
I'll Play High	7	G	3	0	0	0	76
I'll Prey for You	2	C	2	0	2	0	17,200
I'll Say	4	C	9	0	0	1	5,172
I'll Survive	3	F	16	1	0	0	9,260
Illalwaysbethere	2	G	3	0	1	0	1,939
I'llcallyouback	3	F	19	1	5	2	14,577
I'lldrinktothat	3	G	14	3	6	2	39,470
Illegal	4	G	9	1	3	0	23,843
Illegal Hunter	5	G	8	1	0	0	9,712
Illegal Smile	7	G	15	2	1	1	19,265
Illegel to Hunt	3	G	5	0	0	0	0
I'llfindmywayhome	3	G	4	0	0	0	311
Illicit Encounter	3	F	9	0	0	0	924
Illini Boogy Queen	3	F	10	2	2	1	7,628
Illini Queen	4	F	15	1	3	4	49,850
Illinois Moonshine	5	H	1	0	0	0	0
I'llliteyourfire	3	G	4	0	0	0	760
I'llruinya	5	G	13	0	1	2	10,569
I'lltellyounolies	2	G	8	2	2	2	34,167
Illucination	3	F	8	1	0	0	18,141
Illuminate the Way	3	C	12	1	4	3	9,362
Illuminated Gold	3	F	4	0	0	0	300
Illusion Confusion	7	M	5	0	0	0	314
Illusionary	6	G	6	0	0	0	2,955
Illusionary Magic	3	C	11	1	4	1	33,922
Illusionist	2	C	1	1	0	0	9,690
Illusionoseduction	4	F	1	0	0	0	0
Illusive Force	4	G	10	2	3	2	137,217
Illusive Guy	4	G	13	2	1	3	86,578
Illusive Moves	3	F	1	0	0	0	107
Illusive Play	5	M	6	0	0	1	932
Illusive Trick	5	M	9	0	0	0	1,224
Illustrate	3	F	1	0	0	0	980
Illustrious Kiss	2	C	3	0	0	1	4,989
Illustrious Legend	7	G	1	1	0	0	2,750
Ilovegold	5	G	3	0	0	0	224
Ilya Balos	3	G	11	1	0	2	25,250
I'm a Babe	3	F	5	1	2	1	16,399
Im a Brazen Gal	5	M	4	0	0	0	120
I'm a Bully Too	6	G	2	0	0	0	152
I'm a Cheetah	2	F	4	1	1	1	70,105
I'm a City Girl	6	M	11	1	4	0	28,541
I'm a Cool Bull	3	G	6	1	1	1	9,518
I'm a Cool Chic	2	F	1	0	0	0	104
I'm a Crafty Gal	5	M	4	0	0	0	753
I'm a Cutie	4	F	8	0	1	1	5,435
I'm a Devil Due	2	F	3	0	0	0	210
Im a Dixie Girl	2	F	9	3	1	1	150,200
I'm a Dominator	6	G	1	0	0	0	0
I'm a Fair One Too	3	C	11	0	2	1	5,576
I'm a Fast Cat	4	F	4	0	0	0	420
I'm a Frisky Devil	3	F	1	0	0	1	486
I'm a Gem	4	G	13	3	7	0	25,383
I'm a Georgeff	3	C	4	0	0	0	210
Im a Gladiater	3	C	4	0	0	0	306
I'm a Goer	4	G	3	0	0	0	340
Im a Gold Payoff	3	F	14	3	2	1	18,564
I'm a Hottie	4	F	8	1	0	1	16,500
I'm a Hussy	4	F	6	0	0	0	891
I'm a Kipper	2	C	2	0	0	0	0
I'm a Kipper Too	2	G	5	0	0	0	510
I'm a Kuduza Too	3	F	8	2	2	0	7,398
I'm a Lil Princess	6	M	1	0	0	0	0
I'm a Lover	6	G	1	0	0	0	0
I'm a Lucky Gal	3	F	3	0	0	1	645
I'm a Monster Too	4	F	10	1	1	1	4,287
I'm a Party Hawk	3	F	2	0	0	0	708
I'm a Prankster	2	G	1	0	0	0	300
Im a Regal One	5	M	3	0	0	1	1,162
I'm a Riper	2	G	2	1	0	0	34,200
I'm a Rocket Man	5	G	8	0	0	1	1,220
I'm a Royal Pain	3	F	8	2	2	1	17,775
I'm a Sassy Al	5	G	4	0	0	0	0
I'm a Shadee Lady	5	M	6	0	2	1	3,898
I'm a Smart Alyk	5	G	16	2	4	1	24,771
I'm a Soccer Boy	4	G	2	0	0	1	3,900
I'm a Son of a Gun	7	G	1	0	1	0	2,240
I'm a Spiderman	4	G	5	1	0	1	4,875
I'm a Steamroller	3	G	14	2	2	3	23,415
I'm a Swinging Gal	4	F	8	0	0	0	435
I'm a Thunder Cat	3	G	11	2	1	0	16,738
I'm a Tigress	3	F	2	0	0	0	800
Im a Timex	7	G	3	0	1	0	505
I'm a Treasure	4	F	5	0	0	0	741
I'm a Wild Child	3	C	2	1	1	0	5,395
I'm Alarming	3	G	12	2	2	0	30,700
I'm All About Me	2	G	3	0	1	0	2,500
I'm All Attitude	3	C	3	0	0	0	2,250
I'm All Gussied Up	3	F	17	1	2	1	29,410
I'm All Yours	7	G	1	0	0	0	400
I'm Already There	3	C	11	4	1	1	24,671
I'm an Awesome Cat	4	G	15	4	2	2	22,822
I'm Angela	4	F	14	0	1	2	8,930
I'm Awesome	3	G	1	0	0	0	0
I'm Awesome Again	3	G	11	2	0	1	45,645
I'm Big Trouble	3	C	3	0	0	0	0
Im Bobby Sox	8	G	4	0	1	1	1,953
I'm Canadian	4	G	1	0	0	0	0
I'm Catisfied	4	F	3	0	0	0	206
I'm Charismatic	3	G	9	1	2	1	38,070
I'm Classified	3	F	1	0	0	0	240
I'm Confederate	4	G	14	7	1	1	42,128
I'm Connected	4	F	1	1	0	0	8,400
I'm D One	4	G	16	1	3	2	4,245
I'm Dancing	3	F	8	1	0	1	8,620
I'm Due	5	M	12	0	2	2	3,637
I'm Easy Money	2	G	1	0	0	0	0
I'm Exclusive	3	F	11	2	1	0	20,303
I'm Expensive	7	M	1	0	0	0	0
I'm Fast Too	4	G	4	1	1	2	22,502
Im Five	7	H	14	2	0	3	19,549

Horse	Age	Sex	Sts	1st	2d	3d	Won
I'm for Joey	8	G	8	1	0	1	6,775
I'm Free	6	G	13	1	3	1	24,034
I'm Free At Last	3	G	2	0	0	0	800
I'm Frisky Too	2	C	2	0	0	1	2,225
I'm From Texas	5	M	10	2	2	3	16,005
Im Great Too	3	F	14	1	6	3	24,109
I'm Handsom	3	G	2	1	0	0	3,690
I'm Hit Sarge	6	G	6	0	2	0	7,280
I'm Home Wrecker	7	M	4	2	0	0	4,514
I'm Homebound	5	M	7	1	1	2	1,533
I'm Howlin	7	H	4	0	0	0	562
I'm in Orbit	4	F	5	0	0	0	642
Im in the Soup	3	G	12	1	1	3	5,877
I'm Indy Red	3	G	5	0	0	0	234
Im Insatiable	2	G	1	0	0	0	870
I'm Irritable Two	3	F	3	0	0	0	260
I'm Jackie's Boy	3	G	9	1	1	2	16,433
I'm John's Problem	4	G	2	0	1	0	4,320
I'm Just a Peach	7	M	3	0	0	0	433
I'm Just Sayin	2	F	7	1	1	1	11,730
I'm Late	3	G	5	2	0	1	25,060
I'm Listed	5	M	12	0	0	3	4,714
I'm Lovin It	4	F	8	2	1	2	13,458
I'm Lucky	2	F	4	0	3	0	13,300
I'm Majestic	6	G	13	2	3	5	60,935
I'm Nelson Black	4	G	6	1	1	0	27,905
I'm No Angel	2	G	2	0	0	0	1,143
Im No Lady	2	F	5	0	0	0	1,386
I'm No Louie	6	G	2	2	0	0	13,200
I'm No Preppy	4	G	10	2	2	1	37,334
I'm No Rose	3	F	1	1	0	0	1,500
I'm Not Acting	4	G	8	1	2	1	17,499
I'm Not Bluffin	6	G	8	0	1	1	10,730
I'm Not Easy	4	F	6	1	2	0	4,790
I'm Not Posty	5	G	14	2	2	1	41,472
I'm Not Signing	5	M	9	1	1	4	8,805
I'm Oliver	3	G	3	0	1	0	880
Im On Stilts	5	G	3	0	0	0	0
I'm On T. V.	2	F	2	1	0	0	16,638
I'm One Tuff Cat	4	G	10	1	1	2	7,862
I'm Perfect	3	F	1	0	0	0	260
I'm Precious	3	F	5	0	0	1	889
I'm Rais'n Nell	4	F	1	0	0	0	0
I'm Real	4	G	10	2	1	2	17,558
Im Really Shining	2	F	6	1	0	0	7,035
I'm Rial	3	G	2	0	0	0	517
I'm Royalty	8	M	1	0	0	0	150
I'm Seeing Spots	4	F	6	0	1	0	1,646
I'm Seeing Stars	3	F	6	1	1	0	7,890
I'm Silver Due	7	G	14	0	1	3	12,852
I'm Sky High	2	C	7	2	1	0	35,511
Im Smart Too	8	M	4	0	0	0	1,413
I'm Smitten	4	F	5	0	0	0	690
I'm So Cool	6	G	5	0	0	1	2,900
I'm So Sexy	3	F	3	0	1	1	5,385
I'm So Silly	5	G	5	0	3	0	2,798
I'm So Special	9	M	7	0	0	0	324
I'm So Theatrical	6	G	10	0	0	1	2,628
I'm Speechless	4	G	10	0	2	4	38,477
I'm Squirley	10	M	3	0	0	0	120
I'm Steppen Out	2	F	2	0	0	0	420
I'm Suave Two	4	G	3	0	0	0	375
I'm Sure Fancy	2	C	10	1	2	1	40,389
I'm Tellin' Ya Now	5	M	6	1	0	2	9,776
Im Tezzing	3	F	3	0	1	1	3,415
I'm the Business (NZ)	7	M	5	1	1	1	17,825
Im the Game	3	G	5	1	2	1	15,645
I'm the Tiger	4	G	6	3	2	0	187,580
Im the Voice	3	F	10	2	2	2	47,704
Im too Much	3	F	1	0	0	1	1,590
I'm Tricky	2	G	2	0	0	0	120
I'm Trouble	2	F	1	0	0	0	70
I'm Tryon	7	G	3	0	0	0	228
I'm Ugly But Fast	3	F	8	0	1	1	2,563
I'm Waiting	2	F	4	0	0	1	3,345
I'm Willing	4	G	2	0	0	0	125
I'm With Norman	6	M	1	0	1	0	2,800
I'm Yer Hucklebery	6	G	4	2	0	1	4,302
I'm Your Captain	2	F	3	0	1	1	7,285
I'm Your Man	7	G	10	0	0	2	2,488
I'ma a Fax	4	G	7	0	3	1	22,511
I'ma Attitude	2	G	2	0	0	0	0
Ima Bender Boo	3	F	10	3	0	2	37,550
I'ma Butterfly	5	M	2	0	0	0	250
Ima Cartwheel	3	F	9	1	0	1	8,960
Ima Champ	4	F	5	3	1	0	4,220
Ima Charmer	4	G	7	0	0	0	0
Ima Chukker	3	G	7	2	2	1	23,882
Im'a Consultant	3	C	8	2	0	0	10,092
Ima Deer	5	M	3	0	0	0	509
Ima Dream Catcher	4	G	1	0	0	0	80
Ima Fugitive Too	4	G	5	0	0	0	0
Ima Gentleman	4	C	2	0	0	0	354
Ima Gold Nick	5	G	5	0	1	2	995
Ima Grand Gal	8	M	4	0	0	0	70
Ima Gun of a Son	3	G	6	2	0	0	3,865
Ima Handyman	3	C	4	0	0	0	195
Ima Hogg	2	F	3	1	1	0	36,431
Ima Hotrod Lincoln	2	C	1	0	0	0	775
Ima Jazzy Miss	2	F	2	0	1	0	2,040
I'ma Joy	4	F	4	0	0	0	1,130
I'ma Kanu	3	F	1	0	1	0	2,800
Ima Koukla	9	M	11	1	3	0	8,122
I'ma Lamarche	2	C	2	0	0	1	3,755
Ima Lil Lady	3	F	5	0	1	0	2,270
Ima Little Rose	3	F	5	0	0	0	347
Ima Little Waki	2	C	1	0	0	0	155
Ima Looker	3	F	7	0	1	1	9,760
Ima Mia	3	F	5	1	1	0	5,270
Ima Mile High Guy	5	G	10	0	1	1	2,638
I'ma Miracle	4	F	11	1	1	0	12,662
Ima Oakie Too	5	G	1	0	1	0	380
Ima Personal Flag	10	H	7	3	2	0	17,858
I'ma Piano Man	2	C	3	0	0	0	1,590
Ima Picture	3	F	5	0	0	1	1,350
I'ma Reck	3	G	3	0	0	0	1,358
Ima Red Runner	2	C	4	0	0	0	630
Ima Reel Bimbo	3	F	7	2	0	1	11,420
I'ma Rose	5	M	8	2	0	1	28,221
I'ma Saint	7	G	8	0	0	0	248
Ima Smarty Boy	4	G	8	2	1	0	25,616
Ima Snow Man	7	H	5	0	0	0	760
Ima Special Belle	2	F	5	0	1	1	2,722
Ima Special Secret	3	F	4	0	0	1	2,138
Ima Sugar Plum	3	F	1	1	0	0	3,600
Ima Surprise	3	F	7	1	0	1	4,422
Ima Texas Gambler	2	F	3	0	0	1	1,539
Ima Valentine	9	M	7	1	0	1	4,422
I'ma Wild One	4	F	7	0	0	0	2,900
Ima Yankee Rookie	2	F	1	0	0	0	120
Ima Zuit Suit Riot	6	G	13	1	1	2	9,755
Imablazinbeauty	4	F	16	3	2	4	19,380
I'mabletoo	7	G	9	0	2	3	3,985
Imaburnindaylight	5	H	11	3	1	2	26,792
Imachadancer	2	C	2	0	0	0	810
I'machickeytoo	3	F	8	0	1	0	3,048
Imaclassy Lassie	4	F	10	2	0	1	5,980
Imacountintime	6	G	15	0	1	0	3,218
I'macountrygal	3	F	4	0	0	0	0
I'macraftychoice	3	G	10	2	0	2	14,765
Imadeitmom	4	F	14	1	3	3	13,681
Imafavoritetrick	3	G	8	2	1	1	60,560
I'mafloridaormsby	3	G	2	0	0	0	165
Imagallantirishman	3	G	9	0	0	0	781
I'magambler	2	G	2	1	1	0	27,400
Image	6	G	12	2	1	2	48,210
Image in Flight	3	G	1	1	0	0	8,400
Image of a Cat	6	G	17	4	3	0	23,496
Image of a Halo	5	M	9	3	3	2	39,230
Image of Affirmed	11	G	4	2	0	0	17,010
Image of Approval	5	G	15	2	2	2	24,670
Image of the King	2	C	3	0	0	0	205
Image Power	3	F	6	0	0	0	3,138
Imagebylamplight	3	F	4	0	1	2	4,510
Imageofhope	5	G	5	0	0	0	963
Imagery	4	G	7	0	2	2	14,332
Images Echo	4	F	9	0	0	0	977
Imaghost	3	C	1	0	0	1	2,310

Horse	Age	Sex	Sts	1st	2d	3d	Won
Imaginary Image	3	F	3	0	0	0	1,986
Imaginary Man	4	C	6	1	0	0	4,004
Imagine Me	6	H	7	1	0	1	2,072
Imagine Me Now	3	F	16	1	2	3	14,200
Imagine the Ruckus	2	F	2	1	0	0	42,360
Imagine What	4	G	9	1	2	0	12,065
Imagineering	4	G	9	1	1	1	7,899
Imagoldseeker	3	F	12	5	1	1	157,500
Imagoodguysgirl	2	F	6	0	0	2	3,380
Imahoneytoo	3	F	10	3	3	2	61,770
I'mallrightjack	5	G	12	0	1	0	4,675
I'mallwilly	5	G	6	0	2	0	14,963
Imaluckymemorie	2	G	9	1	1	0	7,578
Imaminister	8	G	7	2	2	1	4,360
Imamyto	3	F	7	1	3	1	18,104
I'maprettyjudge	4	F	2	0	0	0	411
Imararegal	2	F	3	0	1	0	5,755
Imarealfancydehere	4	G	11	0	3	0	17,093
Imari (JPN)	3	F	4	0	0	0	5,620
Imarock	3	G	10	2	0	3	15,672
I'maseriviortoo	3	G	9	0	0	1	2,382
Imasgoodasu	3	G	14	3	2	1	27,913
Imaspeedygirl	5	M	5	0	0	0	280
Imasweetie	3	F	9	0	0	0	8,990
Imaswingertwo	6	M	2	0	0	0	129
Imatickytoo	3	F	5	1	1	1	6,020
I'mavikingprincess	3	F	4	0	0	1	5,500
Imawahoogirl	6	M	1	0	0	0	0
Imawarrior	4	C	1	0	0	0	0
Imayodelonggal	2	F	7	1	1	1	13,348
Imbali	2	F	3	1	0	0	4,925
I'mbethtoo	3	F	4	2	1	1	67,425
Imbrachium	5	M	11	1	0	3	16,965
Imdabossau	3	G	14	3	1	2	49,490
Imezru	3	F	5	0	0	1	2,195
Imgunabeinpictures	5	M	8	1	1	0	13,620
Imitate	4	G	9	1	1	0	23,470
Imma Sara	4	F	9	1	0	2	5,630
I'mmeanonthegreen	3	G	17	5	2	3	59,072
Immediate Chance	6	M	4	0	1	2	5,060
Immediate Danger	2	G	1	0	0	0	205
Immediately	3	C	4	0	0	0	1,593
Immense	3	C	2	0	0	1	6,500
Immigrant Road	3	G	9	0	2	5	2,160
Immortal Charm	4	F	16	1	3	2	30,987
Immortal Lock	3	G	16	2	2	0	11,743
Immsowaat Naamoo	5	G	5	0	0	0	336
Immune to Gloom	3	F	1	0	0	0	1,260
Immunity Idol	4	G	5	0	2	1	8,355
Imnojoehernandez	6	M	1	0	0	0	0
Imnxcelentdriveray	5	G	4	0	1	0	6,200
Impact Survivor	3	C	14	2	2	1	33,605
Impala	7	H	4	0	2	0	4,187
Impatient Michael	7	H	2	0	0	0	0
Impavid	6	G	13	1	0	0	6,484
Impeachthepro	7	G	7	2	1	3	61,830
Impecable Foe	3	F	1	0	1	0	5,040
Imperatriz Rafaela (BRZ)	6	M	2	0	0	0	2,400
Imperial Alydeed	3	G	11	1	4	2	129,201
Imperial Chariot (BRZ)	7	H	7	2	0	1	9,081
Imperial Classic	5	G	4	0	1	1	3,652
Imperial Commander	4	C	6	0	3	0	32,188
Imperial Danseur	2	F	2	0	0	0	260
Imperial Gem	2	F	3	0	0	0	1,060
Imperial Gold (NZ)	7	G	9	1	0	1	38,000
Imperial Grace	4	F	11	2	0	1	25,062
Imperial Hope	3	F	1	0	0	0	0
Imperial Hunter	4	F	23	2	5	1	26,253
Imperial Ice	5	M	6	0	0	2	1,770
Imperial Image	3	F	4	0	0	0	433
Imperial Innocence	4	F	4	1	0	0	2,870
Imperial King	7	G	9	0	1	1	6,192
Imperial Lady	7	M	6	0	0	0	174
Imperial Measure (GB)	6	G	6	0	0	0	4,840
Imperial Mistress	6	M	3	0	0	0	0
Imperial Orphan	6	C	10	1	1	0	10,925
Imperial Red	3	F	4	0	0	1	1,268
Imperial Ruler	3	G	7	0	0	1	3,139
Imperial Sky	2	G	7	1	1	0	14,150
Imperial Star	4	G	8	1	2	1	9,310
Imperial Sunrise	4	G	1	0	0	0	0
Imperial Sunshine	4	F	5	0	1	0	3,217
Imperial Theatre (IRE)	5	H	3	0	0	0	1,280
Imperial Wager	6	M	21	4	3	4	29,645
Imperial Wells	4	C	4	1	1	0	4,220
Imperial Wind	11	G	7	0	2	0	2,080
Imperialism	3	C	9	2	1	2	542,000
Impertinent Music	7	M	13	1	2	2	9,527
Impetuous Bell	4	F	9	1	1	2	7,180
Impetuous Fling	4	F	1	0	0	0	1,521
Impetuous Leader	4	G	15	0	4	1	13,164
Impetuous Sea	3	F	8	1	0	0	9,340
Impetus	4	F	1	0	0	0	0
Impish Bull	2	G	11	1	1	1	8,148
Impishly Devine	4	F	7	1	1	1	2,902
Implicit	4	G	5	2	0	1	41,060
Important Terms	3	G	3	0	0	0	420
Imposing	7	G	5	0	0	1	1,667
Impossible Dream	10	G	4	0	0	0	0
Imppy	9	M	1	0	0	0	0
Impress Me	7	M	6	0	0	0	1,116
Impress the Lady	5	M	3	0	0	0	406
Impressaria	3	F	2	0	0	0	0
Impressionable One	4	F	14	2	1	3	10,229
Impressive Crown	3	G	2	0	0	0	975
Impressive General	5	G	1	0	0	0	0
Impressive Note	4	F	6	0	0	0	0
Impressive Star	4	F	8	2	2	2	26,300
Imprint of Zignew	2	C	2	0	0	0	500
Imprinted	3	G	5	0	0	0	0
Imprints in Gold	6	G	9	2	2	0	49,820
Improbable Dream	3	G	17	2	7	2	67,279
Impropriety	3	G	9	0	3	1	15,457
Improving Time	5	G	11	0	1	3	4,185
Improvised	4	F	8	6	1	0	92,057
Impulse	3	F	2	0	0	0	600
Impulsive Bachelor	9	G	9	1	2	2	5,060
Impulsive Gal	3	F	11	2	1	2	28,010
Imreadyimready	2	C	3	0	0	1	3,755
I'mroyallymecke'd	3	C	7	0	1	1	5,350
Imski	3	F	5	0	1	0	2,995
I'mspectaculartoo	2	F	2	0	1	0	3,600
I'mthedeal	3	C	6	0	0	2	4,633
I'mtoogoodtobetrue	2	F	3	2	1	0	81,441
In a Dither	5	G	5	0	1	0	893
In a Fit of Pique	2	C	2	0	0	2	4,262
In a Flash	6	G	3	0	0	0	333
In a Run	6	G	2	0	0	1	737
In a Safe Place	3	F	11	0	0	2	3,029
In a Zone	7	G	8	0	0	0	4,250
In Accord	6	M	3	1	0	0	9,227
In Addy Case	3	F	6	1	1	0	27,685
In All Her Glory	3	F	1	0	0	0	1,185
In Barb's Honor	6	G	3	0	0	1	984
In Before Dawn	3	F	2	0	0	0	0
In Bocca Al Lupo	3	G	9	2	0	0	12,950
In C C's Honor	10	G	14	6	2	0	49,948
In Case of Love	3	F	5	1	1	0	7,140
In Case of Slots	3	G	12	1	1	0	9,400
In Case of Thunder	4	G	3	1	1	0	19,500
In Case of Wind	4	F	12	1	2	1	19,960
In Case You Forgot	4	C	6	1	2	1	12,430
In Case You Win	6	G	6	0	3	0	13,050
In Charm's Way	3	F	9	0	0	1	3,110
In Control	2	C	2	0	0	1	3,570
In Da Mix	4	F	7	0	0	0	833
In Dancing Order	6	M	11	1	1	2	8,317
In Deed a Fashion	7	M	10	0	0	2	2,041
In Disguise	3	G	12	1	0	4	5,560
In Don's Court	2	C	5	0	0	0	1,570
In Every Port	5	G	9	1	0	0	10,440
In Excess Success	4	G	1	0	0	0	0
In First Space	3	G	3	0	0	0	0
In Flying Colors	5	M	17	1	3	2	15,945
In Focus	4	F	21	2	5	7	30,291
In Frank's Honor	8	H	1	0	0	0	260
In Front	4	F	11	0	1	1	4,368
In Front by Two	10	G	1	0	0	0	303

Horse	Age	Sex	Sts	1st	2d	3d	Won
In Gold We Trust	4	F	8	3	1	1	5,825
In Hand	4	G	10	3	1	0	136,517
In Harm's Way	4	C	3	0	0	0	120
In High Form	4	F	2	1	1	0	28,800
In Hot Pursuit	5	G	1	0	0	0	150
In Joe's Honor	3	C	2	0	0	0	400
In Kent's Memory	5	G	2	0	0	0	280
In Ky's Image	3	F	3	0	0	0	116
In Limbo	3	F	3	0	0	0	0
In Love	4	F	7	3	1	2	68,630
In Love Again	4	F	2	0	0	0	2,241
In Love With Loot	4	F	11	1	3	2	13,770
In Memoriam	7	G	10	2	1	0	26,288
In Memory of Marge	3	F	3	0	0	1	1,080
In Millie's Honor	4	F	11	3	0	2	26,418
In My Prime	6	G	8	0	0	0	1,437
In My Time	4	F	8	0	0	2	12,728
In My View	3	G	7	2	1	1	16,060
In Need of Reign	5	G	15	0	3	1	23,710
In Order	3	G	2	0	2	0	4,506
In Pectore	2	C	3	0	0	1	6,080
In Position	3	F	1	1	0	0	1,500
In Print	4	G	13	2	4	2	15,575
In Rare Form	3	G	6	0	1	1	14,226
In Rome	3	F	3	0	0	0	1,429
In Root	3	G	9	0	0	1	2,312
In Season	7	G	7	0	1	0	9,625
In Spyt of My Ex	7	M	15	0	2	3	5,796
In Stitches	8	H	11	0	1	3	8,250
In Suzanne's Honor	2	F	1	0	1	0	2,790
In Sync	7	H	4	0	3	0	7,068
In the Beat	7	M	4	0	0	0	132
In The Box (BRZ)	7	M	4	1	1	0	13,400
In the Clear	5	H	1	0	0	0	0
In the Clutch	4	G	3	0	1	1	14,680
In the Crease	3	F	11	0	2	4	12,260
In the Cups	5	G	9	2	1	0	27,790
In the Game	5	H	5	0	0	0	1,343
In the Gold	2	F	4	1	1	1	83,062
In the Gray	4	F	12	1	3	3	31,160
In the Hall	3	G	6	0	4	0	8,792
In the Park	3	F	4	0	1	1	9,780
In the Pocket	4	G	15	3	1	1	39,801
In the Shadows	4	F	4	0	0	0	209
In the Show	5	M	3	0	0	0	132
In the Teepee	6	G	11	0	2	3	10,660
In the Weeds	3	G	7	3	0	0	48,148
In the Wildzone	6	H	4	0	0	0	450
In This Corner	5	M	5	0	0	0	193
In too Deep	5	M	5	2	0	0	27,410
In Top Form	3	F	2	0	0	0	0
In Trouble Again	3	G	14	0	0	1	2,820
In Tune	4	F	5	1	0	0	8,260
In Two Notes	4	F	5	0	0	1	2,650
In Unison	4	F	8	1	1	2	4,810
In Vys'eyes	4	F	6	0	1	0	3,569
In Washington	4	F	7	0	0	1	2,640
In Your Hands	5	M	5	1	0	0	8,160
In Your Prayers	3	F	7	2	0	0	10,030
Inajamsam	3	G	8	1	0	2	11,736
Inanewyorksecond	2	G	1	0	0	0	400
Inapinch	4	F	18	4	1	2	46,638
Inarush	4	G	7	2	1	1	28,887
Inaugirl	3	F	3	0	0	0	435
Inaugural Address	5	G	7	0	1	1	15,469
Inaugural Warrior	4	G	8	1	0	0	3,804
Inbound Felony	4	C	2	0	0	0	1,310
Inca Colony	9	G	2	1	0	0	6,750
Inca Halo	5	G	24	2	4	3	19,681
Inca Prince	3	G	14	2	3	1	29,750
Inca Storm	3	F	2	0	0	0	320
Incarcerated	3	G	6	0	0	3	7,590
Incase Shebets	5	M	9	0	0	0	910
Incaseyouraminer	3	G	16	1	0	1	14,025
Incaseyourkidding	3	G	7	1	0	1	9,623
Incatotus	8	G	3	0	0	0	0
Incendio	6	G	6	0	1	2	3,226
Incitatus	8	G	1	0	0	0	195
Incitatus (BAR)	11	H	1	0	0	0	0
Inciting Prince	6	G	12	0	0	1	2,135
Inclement Weather	4	G	1	0	0	0	336
Incognito	3	G	3	0	0	0	411
Income	2	G	3	0	1	0	5,200
Income Statement	7	G	12	0	1	2	2,926
Incomplete	3	G	22	2	3	0	27,495
Incontestable	3	F	2	1	0	0	6,760
Incorporatetime	2	C	1	0	0	0	118
Incorrigible	5	G	2	1	0	0	3,600
Incredible Act	4	F	13	3	4	1	34,700
Incredible Notion	5	M	6	1	2	0	4,215
Incredible Rail	4	G	1	0	0	0	0
Incredible Speed	3	G	2	0	1	0	8,568
Incredible Story	4	F	3	1	0	0	7,800
Incredible Tale	3	G	9	0	1	2	5,503
Incredible Wings	3	G	3	1	0	0	6,375
Incredible You	3	F	2	1	0	0	1,372
Incrediblee	3	G	15	1	4	1	34,736
Inda Caton	2	C	4	1	1	0	7,400
Indebted	2	F	2	0	0	0	1,260
Indecent	4	G	5	0	0	1	3,614
Indeed	5	G	3	0	0	1	940
Indefensible	3	F	10	2	1	1	45,430
Indelible Image	3	F	12	2	2	3	74,636
Indelibull Rose	4	F	9	1	1	1	13,430
Independent Cuss	4	G	5	1	0	0	3,855
Independent Gal	4	F	5	1	1	1	13,476
Independent Lad	3	G	8	1	2	0	9,088
Indestructible	2	C	2	0	0	0	2,430
India Halo (ARG)	4	F	2	0	1	0	2,354
India Star	3	F	2	1	1	0	3,360
India Sun	3	C	8	1	0	0	18,486
Indiaman	3	C	3	1	0	0	10,188
Indian Ally	9	H	1	0	0	0	210
Indian Angel	2	F	2	0	1	0	6,780
Indian Attack	3	F	6	1	0	1	21,470
Indian Avenue	6	G	1	0	0	0	184
Indian Bank	7	G	11	2	3	0	8,830
Indian Beauty	3	F	7	1	0	0	22,683
Indian Blanket	4	F	3	0	0	0	0
Indian Card	5	G	3	0	0	1	4,604
Indian Charmer	4	F	1	0	0	0	69
Indian City	5	H	3	0	0	0	50
Indian Colony	2	C	1	0	0	0	300
Indian Country	3	C	4	3	0	1	83,160
Indian Dan	6	G	5	1	1	0	14,727
Indian Day	2	C	2	0	0	0	1,280
Indian Dreamer	4	F	2	0	0	0	900
Indian Dreamin	2	C	2	1	0	0	11,800
Indian Erin	3	F	4	0	1	0	5,390
Indian Express	4	C	1	1	0	0	12,900
Indian Game	3	C	14	0	2	2	14,914
Indian Ground	5	H	5	2	0	0	24,814
Indian Hemp	6	G	7	0	1	0	760
Indian Island	3	F	8	1	2	1	29,460
Indian Jewel	3	F	7	1	1	1	30,600
Indian Keepsake	3	G	4	2	0	0	31,780
Indian Lotus (ARG)	5	H	4	0	0	0	2,970
Indian Mist	3	F	3	0	1	0	2,200
Indian Moonlight	4	F	4	0	0	1	2,400
Indian Music	5	M	1	0	0	0	0
Indian Pink	2	F	3	0	2	0	10,900
Indian Plume (GB)	8	G	1	0	0	0	360
Indian Point	4	F	8	1	3	0	11,050
Indian Prospector	3	C	10	1	3	1	44,000
Indian Reef	2	G	6	0	0	0	4,520
Indian Renegade	4	C	6	0	0	1	1,162
Indian Run	4	G	5	1	2	1	11,733
Indian Starlet	4	F	1	0	0	0	0
Indian Sully	4	C	2	0	1	1	3,920
Indian Summer Girl	3	F	3	0	1	1	3,475
Indian Sunrise	4	F	10	0	0	2	2,122
Indian Tango	3	F	5	0	0	2	3,060
Indian Trouble	8	G	4	0	0	0	549
Indian Village	3	G	12	3	3	1	44,191
Indian War Dance	3	C	5	2	0	1	77,910
Indian Weaver	2	G	5	1	3	0	41,595
Indian Willow	4	F	8	1	2	2	20,414
Indiana Affair	7	G	14	1	0	0	5,580

Horse	Age	Sex	Sts	1st	2d	3d	Won
Indiana Charlie	3	G	15	2	2	1	19,089
Indiana Classic	3	G	3	0	0	0	378
Indiana Dad	7	M	2	0	0	0	237
Indiana Express	4	C	4	0	0	0	717
Indiana Gold	2	C	4	0	1	0	4,185
Indiana Outlaw	3	G	6	0	0	1	1,010
Indiana Pirate	2	G	3	0	0	0	300
Indiana Susie	7	M	5	0	1	0	1,917
Indianazona	6	G	10	1	2	0	5,808
Indians Melody	3	F	9	1	0	5	6,037
Indian'sarecoming	4	F	2	0	0	1	707
Indiansong	3	F	5	2	2	0	35,090
Indiantown Jones	5	G	3	0	0	1	2,573
Indies (GB)	3	C	3	0	0	0	1,800
Indigestion	2	C	8	1	1	0	8,330
Indigo Flyer	3	G	8	2	2	1	49,580
Indigo Girl	2	F	5	3	1	1	82,827
Indigo Myth	7	G	1	0	0	0	0
Indika	3	F	2	0	0	0	0
Indio Helix (ARG)	6	G	8	0	0	0	2,560
Indio Memo	3	G	2	0	0	0	110
Indirect Kick	5	G	8	0	0	0	1,600
Indispensable	10	G	10	1	1	4	42,969
Indisputable	10	G	2	0	0	0	0
Individual Knight	2	G	3	1	0	1	6,700
Individual Star	4	F	4	0	0	1	1,020
Individualy Missy	3	F	6	1	0	1	4,597
Indivisible	5	H	3	0	1	0	9,650
Indixie	6	G	8	5	0	1	82,570
Indlovkazi	2	F	2	0	0	1	805
Indochina	3	F	10	2	2	0	19,685
Indolent	3	C	1	0	0	0	0
Indomable	12	G	6	0	0	2	1,080
Inducement	3	C	7	2	1	1	64,861
Induction Day	7	G	14	2	2	0	9,751
Indy Annie	7	M	1	0	0	0	45
Indy Buff	3	F	4	0	0	0	266
Indy Charmer	3	F	8	2	0	1	55,430
Indy Dancer	4	C	4	0	0	1	15,080
Indy Empire	2	G	3	0	0	0	1,075
Indy Energy	5	G	16	2	4	1	21,539
Indy Five Hundred	4	F	2	0	0	0	5,260
Indy Future	3	F	8	1	2	0	53,247
Indy Go Sky	4	F	3	0	0	0	0
Indy Groove	4	F	10	3	2	1	160,545
Indy Lady	6	M	2	0	0	0	105
Indy Lea	3	F	8	0	0	0	624
Indy Lead	6	H	7	0	1	2	28,950
Indy Lindy	2	F	4	1	0	1	5,600
Indy Love	4	G	15	2	4	1	37,240
Indy Lu	3	C	6	0	0	0	479
Indy Magic	6	M	7	0	3	1	11,130
Indy Minstrel	3	C	5	0	0	0	1,400
Indy Moon	2	C	3	1	0	0	30,080
Indy Pleaser	2	C	1	0	0	0	280
Indy Red	4	G	16	2	0	4	18,944
Indy Rock	4	G	1	0	0	0	70
Indy Snow (GB)	3	C	6	1	0	1	20,768
Indy Storm	2	C	1	1	0	0	11,400
Indy Thunder	4	C	6	1	1	1	12,565
Indy Undies	3	F	2	0	0	0	120
Indy Zone	4	C	1	0	0	0	125
Indydar's Race Car	3	F	5	2	1	0	12,160
Indygal	3	F	3	1	0	0	29,660
Indygo	4	F	1	0	0	0	40
Indy's Anna	5	M	3	0	0	0	320
Indy's Sensation	2	F	1	0	1	0	5,520
Indy's Treasure	4	G	12	1	2	3	24,295
Indyshotshot	2	G	8	1	2	0	3,635
Inesperado (FR)	5	H	6	1	4	1	135,270
Inevercmollyalone	3	F	3	0	0	0	86
Inevitability	3	G	2	0	1	0	2,660
Inevitably True	2	G	3	1	2	0	41,000
Inexcessive Drive	2	F	2	1	0	0	5,332
Inexcessivelyroyal	3	F	1	0	0	0	79
Infantry	7	G	7	0	0	0	1,959
Infantry Liz	7	M	5	0	1	0	570
Infantry Man	5	G	5	0	0	0	1,710
Infield Bound	3	C	5	1	1	0	27,420
Infiltrator	7	H	12	5	2	3	53,320
Infinate Star	4	G	1	0	0	0	0
Infinite Faith	6	G	9	2	1	4	76,480
Infinite Glory	3	G	8	4	1	0	108,404
Infinite Justice	4	G	2	0	0	1	3,925
Infinite Miracle	4	G	10	0	0	1	4,182
Infinite North	4	G	21	0	3	3	13,285
Infinite Series	6	M	7	2	1	0	3,856
Inflict	3	C	4	0	0	0	150
Infomercial	3	F	9	0	0	2	4,990
Inform	3	C	3	1	0	0	13,580
Informacion	5	M	12	2	0	5	45,529
Infra Red Rose	3	F	8	0	0	0	2,532
Infused	2	F	1	0	0	0	750
Ingenious (IRE)	8	G	8	0	0	3	3,300
Ingenius	9	G	6	1	0	1	10,230
Ingenuity	3	G	2	0	0	0	0
Ingles	4	C	10	5	2	1	67,235
Ingleside	4	F	5	0	1	1	3,625
Ingram Mountain	3	F	8	1	0	0	6,240
Inherent Gem	5	M	14	0	1	1	5,371
Inherimage	4	F	1	0	0	0	515
Inherit the Brass	4	F	8	2	1	0	16,401
Inheritress	2	F	5	1	2	0	22,300
Inhonorofjohnnie	3	F	14	1	1	2	13,993
Inis	5	M	8	1	2	1	29,630
Inish Glora	6	M	5	3	2	0	433,730
Initforthekandy	2	F	2	0	0	0	1,195
Initial Approach	3	F	3	1	0	0	22,427
Initially	2	G	7	1	0	0	6,395
Initiate	2	F	1	0	0	0	0
Injian Silk	2	F	2	0	1	0	2,200
Injusta	2	F	4	0	1	0	3,035
Injustice	3	F	12	5	2	0	111,520
Ink Grimsley	3	C	19	0	2	4	7,570
Ink Jet	6	G	2	0	1	0	2,500
Ink the Deal	2	G	3	0	0	0	531
Inklet	2	C	1	0	0	0	0
Inky Racer	8	G	5	0	0	0	196
Inlet	3	F	7	1	2	1	24,680
Inlet Moon	3	F	4	1	0	1	28,010
Inmate	3	C	17	4	3	2	33,298
Inner City Chic	3	G	4	2	0	0	12,545
Inner Harbour	7	H	1	0	0	1	3,850
Inner Spirit	4	F	3	0	0	0	570
Inner Thoughts	4	F	2	0	0	0	975
Inner Wisdom	3	F	1	0	0	0	0
Innerlifeofobjects	4	F	7	0	0	1	5,560
Innis North	2	F	2	0	0	0	137
Innisbrook	2	C	2	0	0	1	1,965
Innisfree Love	5	M	3	0	0	0	231
Innisfree Petite	5	M	9	0	1	2	3,855
Innit (IRE)	6	M	1	0	0	0	4,252
Innocent Deception	2	G	1	0	1	0	3,600
Innocent Gent	5	G	14	2	0	2	15,206
Innocent Man	4	G	3	0	1	0	6,090
Innocent Remark	6	M	16	2	2	2	17,029
Innocent Steph	4	F	2	0	0	0	42
Innocent Within	5	G	5	0	1	0	987
Innseattle	3	F	6	1	1	0	39,288
Inod	5	G	9	1	0	2	12,326
Inox (ARG)	6	M	10	5	2	0	84,474
Inquiring Picture	3	F	15	3	0	1	17,700
Inquisitive Flirt	3	F	17	2	7	4	36,138
Inrightclassitime	2	F	8	2	1	2	43,130
Insane	4	G	6	1	0	0	9,572
Insanity Defense	4	C	15	2	3	2	56,953
Inside Lane	3	G	2	0	0	2	5,599
Inside Pitch	4	G	8	0	1	1	13,773
Inside Tip	4	G	9	0	1	1	4,315
Inside Trader	5	G	4	0	0	0	469
Insideoftrouble	2	C	2	0	0	0	400
Insilver	3	G	8	1	1	1	25,080
Inspirational Kris	4	F	11	1	2	1	33,333
Inspire	4	F	17	3	1	2	18,311
Inspired Act	3	F	3	0	0	1	1,812
Inspired Angel	3	F	3	0	0	1	4,200
Inspired Magic	3	F	13	2	5	2	82,988
Inspired Purpose	4	G	4	0	0	0	215

Horse	Age	Sex	Sts	1st	2d	3d	Won
Inspired Ruckus	2	F	6	0	0	0	1,634
Inspired Verse Won	5	M	2	0	0	0	188
Inspiring	2	F	2	2	0	0	115,800
Inspiring Alf	3	G	17	2	2	4	21,934
Inspiring Miss	3	F	5	1	1	0	8,200
Inspiteofitall	6	G	12	0	0	2	3,827
Instant Catch	3	C	8	1	2	1	8,325
Instant Coffee	3	F	10	1	1	2	22,490
Instant Equity	5	G	10	1	0	0	2,507
Instant Glow	3	G	10	1	1	1	17,189
Instant Karma	6	H	4	0	1	1	1,693
Instant Mocha	5	G	7	0	2	0	7,792
Instant Punch	6	G	2	0	0	0	126
Instant Reward	8	M	5	0	1	1	2,758
Instantly	4	G	8	1	1	4	17,347
Instantpersonality	2	C	2	0	0	0	680
Instead of Red	3	G	12	1	2	2	23,517
Instigator One	4	G	2	0	0	0	0
Instinctif (ARG)	4	G	4	0	0	0	420
Instinctively	2	C	1	0	0	0	400
Instrument Flight	3	F	14	0	3	2	6,420
Insufficient Funds	4	F	7	0	1	1	3,830
Insumiso	3	G	15	2	1	3	11,884
Insurance Scam	8	M	4	1	0	0	1,540
Intact	5	G	11	1	1	0	11,729
Integer	4	G	10	3	0	1	28,960
Integral	4	G	2	0	1	0	1,900
Integrity	7	G	4	0	0	0	1,035
Integrity's Prize	7	M	10	0	0	1	2,832
Intelligence	4	G	10	2	0	0	23,100
Intelligent Male	4	G	7	5	0	0	176,984
Intemperate	4	C	7	1	0	1	14,001
Intemporal (ARG)	6	H	1	0	0	0	0
Intense Desire	3	F	4	1	2	0	42,894
Intense Flight	3	G	2	0	0	0	0
Intense Moment	3	C	8	2	0	1	29,980
Intense Motion	3	G	19	1	2	3	11,149
Intense Paces	5	M	1	0	0	0	0
Intense Strike	7	G	13	2	1	0	10,933
Intense Thunder	4	F	11	2	2	1	27,894
Intensive	2	C	4	0	1	1	6,222
Intensive Dancer	4	G	14	5	3	0	90,590
Intensive Invader	5	G	9	0	0	1	1,185
Intent of a Lady	3	F	1	0	0	0	280
Intentional Winner	10	G	10	1	1	1	12,156
Intentions	3	F	4	1	0	1	14,770
Inter Galactic	3	F	9	2	1	1	68,420
Interbell (ARG)	6	H	2	0	0	0	598
Interceptor (GB)	4	C	5	1	0	2	43,960
Intercontinental (GB)	4	F	6	4	1	0	592,386
Interdigital	6	G	8	0	0	0	630
Interested	4	F	7	1	0	0	7,085
Interesting Man	3	G	1	0	0	1	780
Interesting Talk	4	F	3	0	0	0	270
Interior Decorator	6	M	6	0	0	1	1,264
Interline	2	C	4	1	0	1	32,650
Interloper	4	C	1	0	0	1	2,090
Interlude	5	M	12	2	0	0	15,602
Intern	8	G	8	1	0	2	32,295
Internal Revenue	5	G	18	3	1	2	26,630
International City	5	M	14	3	2	2	33,469
Internet Boy (ARG)	5	G	8	2	1	3	43,500
Internet Bubble	4	G	14	3	1	2	19,140
Internet Charlie	3	G	3	0	1	0	6,500
Internet Craze	3	F	2	0	0	0	953
Interpatation	2	G	4	0	1	0	13,279
Interpelador (ARG)	6	G	3	1	0	0	3,500
Intersection	3	G	8	0	0	1	2,448
Interspace	4	G	2	0	0	0	150
Intertwining	6	G	3	0	1	0	2,045
Intervene	4	G	8	0	0	1	5,825
Interventor (BRZ)	4	G	4	0	0	2	5,220
Interview the Wind	2	C	3	0	0	0	1,370
Interwoven	4	C	6	2	2	0	54,779
Inthefastlanejerod	5	H	9	0	2	1	18,037
Inthejailhousenow	4	F	2	1	0	0	13,680
Inthenavynow	3	R	7	2	1	1	10,090
Intheslickoftime	5	G	4	0	0	0	910
Inthetide	5	M	9	0	0	1	2,207
Inthreequartertime	3	G	1	0	0	0	0
Inti Raymi	6	G	9	3	1	0	22,536
Inticing Dancer	7	M	14	1	2	6	11,505
Intimate Music	6	M	9	3	0	2	37,080
Intimate Portrait	2	F	1	0	0	0	485
Intimately	3	F	8	1	1	1	44,540
Intimidating	2	C	1	0	0	0	1,881
Intimidator	3	C	7	1	2	1	46,637
Into the Mystic	4	F	1	0	0	0	105
Into the Sunset	5	M	1	0	0	0	0
Intonation	3	F	11	2	1	0	12,695
Intore	5	G	12	1	0	2	18,536
Intothefuture	7	G	14	1	0	0	4,556
Intoxicatedwildcat	4	G	6	1	1	1	4,142
Intoxicating Air	4	G	3	0	0	0	137
Intoxication	4	F	6	0	1	1	1,355
Intoyourblues	6	M	9	1	2	0	68,533
Intractabie	4	F	9	2	3	0	65,196
Intraffic	3	F	1	0	0	0	0
Intrepid Gem	4	F	5	1	1	1	8,450
Intrepid John	3	G	10	4	0	1	31,700
Intrepid Queen	3	F	6	1	0	0	17,858
Intriguing Lady	2	F	3	0	1	0	10,630
Intrinsic Danielle	4	G	9	0	0	3	7,570
Intrinsic Worth	3	C	6	3	0	0	80,450
Introspect	4	C	8	1	0	2	43,890
Intrueflight	3	F	8	1	1	1	32,090
Intrusa	2	F	5	0	0	0	0
Intrusive Lad	2	G	8	1	0	0	10,442
Intuit	4	G	11	3	2	0	117,890
Intuitional	3	F	6	1	0	0	25,855
Intuitive Miss	5	M	18	6	3	1	27,440
Intuitive Storm	4	F	2	0	0	0	425
Inuksuk	4	G	13	1	4	3	25,137
Invader	4	F	10	0	1	2	21,879
Invaderfromtheeast	4	G	12	2	2	3	14,049
Invader's Justice	3	G	8	1	0	0	17,071
Invalid Password	4	G	8	1	0	2	12,281
Invalidate	3	F	16	1	1	4	29,165
Invest the Money	4	F	6	0	2	2	4,440
Investigate	4	C	1	0	0	0	320
Investingold	3	C	2	0	0	0	1,340
Investor's Dream (BRZ)	6	H	3	0	0	0	3,240
Invincible Native	8	M	7	0	0	1	1,539
Invisible Cat	3	G	3	1	0	0	10,032
Involvement	4	C	4	1	1	0	20,180
Inwood	9	G	1	0	0	0	110
Inwood Home	4	G	22	2	6	6	19,910
Iny Belle	5	M	1	0	0	0	660
Inyanga	3	G	1	0	0	0	85
Iodine	7	H	1	0	0	0	85
Iolanda	2	F	1	1	0	0	16,200
Iona Royal Bandit	5	H	1	0	0	0	0
Ionia	4	F	1	0	0	0	1,120
Ionian Prince	3	G	7	1	0	0	6,460
Ionosphere	4	G	8	1	0	0	2,760
Iosilver	3	G	10	2	0	2	41,000
Ioskeha	4	G	12	3	3	0	38,708
Iota	5	M	6	1	0	0	11,380
Iowa Alice	3	F	9	1	0	1	10,710
Iowa Rocks	3	G	13	0	0	1	5,940
Iowa Special	2	C	3	0	0	0	715
Iowa's Image	5	M	10	3	4	0	103,080
Iowa's Melanie	2	F	5	1	0	0	22,341
Iowna Acre	3	G	1	0	0	0	93
Ioya Forever	5	M	5	0	1	0	10,408
Ipapa Itsit	5	H	3	1	1	0	8,422
Ipi'ko	5	H	8	2	1	1	14,262
Iplanonbeboppin	3	F	5	0	1	2	7,810
Iquitos	3	G	9	1	1	2	10,575
Iquitos (ARG)	4	G	4	1	1	0	16,143
Ireland's Eye	4	C	10	1	2	0	12,045
Irena Point	3	F	7	1	0	0	10,950
Irenes' Song	3	C	8	1	0	0	25,810
Irestmycase	4	G	7	3	2	1	20,740
Ireza	2	F	4	1	0	0	13,585
Irgee	6	G	3	0	0	0	162
Irgunette	5	M	8	1	1	1	21,950
Irgunette (AUS)	5	M	3	0	1	1	37,160

Horse	Age	Sex	Sts	1st	2d	3d	Won
Irguns Star	2	F	4	1	0	2	8,400
Irgun's Trial	6	M	8	2	1	2	23,253
Irgy McGuerty	2	F	3	0	0	0	865
Iridian	2	F	2	0	0	0	2,250
Iridium	7	G	9	1	1	0	9,163
Irie Justice	6	G	11	3	2	1	41,926
Irie Sensation	4	G	9	1	1	1	9,674
Irina	6	M	1	0	0	0	309
Iris Fancy	4	F	1	0	0	0	60
Iris Road	7	G	2	0	0	0	136
Irish A. C.	4	F	6	2	2	0	20,338
Irish Accent	3	F	7	0	0	0	5,460
Irish Account	5	G	7	2	2	3	9,662
Irish Acres	3	F	12	3	2	0	20,106
Irish Actor	4	G	12	1	1	0	18,045
Irish All the Way	3	G	17	2	2	1	11,157
Irish Ann	5	M	8	1	1	1	14,380
Irish Baroness	3	F	7	0	1	1	3,759
Irish Blass	2	C	2	0	0	0	1,266
Irish Bob	4	G	7	3	1	0	7,363
Irish Breakfast	5	M	2	0	1	0	1,140
Irish Breeze	3	G	8	0	0	0	1,370
Irish Bulldog	2	C	5	0	0	1	8,700
Irish Buster	3	C	3	0	0	0	204
Irish Chance	2	F	7	0	0	0	1,884
Irish Chrome	4	G	11	2	1	0	8,343
Irish Class	2	F	8	2	0	1	30,840
Irish Classic	3	F	3	0	0	0	355
Irish Coin	3	F	4	0	0	0	3,760
Irish Colonial	5	H	9	1	0	5	148,150
Irish Colony	4	G	16	4	4	4	202,310
Irish Court	2	C	5	0	1	0	5,100
Irish Cream Taffy	7	G	2	0	2	0	5,400
Irish Crown	3	F	6	1	1	1	7,818
Irish Custom	4	G	2	0	0	0	0
Irish Dave	3	G	14	1	0	1	32,289
Irish Dawn	7	G	5	0	1	0	800
Irish Day	4	F	1	0	0	0	0
Irish Decision	5	H	11	3	2	1	29,250
Irish Decor	8	H	12	1	4	1	16,234
Irish Deputy	4	C	1	0	0	0	400
Irish Diva	2	F	2	0	1	0	5,200
Irish Dodger	2	G	1	0	1	0	7,365
Irish Dove	4	F	12	0	2	1	8,713
Irish Duke	4	C	3	0	1	0	2,040
Irish Eh	5	G	10	1	3	0	27,623
Irish Embassy	3	G	3	0	0	0	0
Irish Emblem	3	G	20	3	5	5	21,990
Irish Emily	4	F	5	1	1	0	5,017
Irish Family	2	G	7	1	2	2	12,990
Irish Femme	4	F	8	4	1	0	80,845
Irish Flyer	6	M	7	2	2	1	24,816
Irish Fortune	4	F	6	1	0	1	9,210
Irish Freckles	3	F	8	0	0	0	2,380
Irish Frolic	3	F	12	1	2	2	16,308
Irish Frost	2	C	1	0	0	0	1,590
Irish Gale	3	C	5	2	1	0	10,578
Irish Gambit	3	G	9	1	4	1	72,924
Irish Gambler	4	C	4	0	2	1	15,960
Irish Gato	3	G	18	5	2	7	56,040
Irish Ginger	6	M	12	1	2	2	14,861
Irish Glen	4	C	2	1	0	0	3,900
Irish Glory	5	M	8	1	1	0	28,400
Irish Hadif	2	G	2	0	0	0	210
Irish Honor	3	G	7	0	1	1	9,820
Irish I'd Run	3	G	3	0	0	0	340
Irish Ides	3	F	13	0	3	3	23,547
Irish Immigrant	2	C	5	0	2	1	21,997
Irish Imp	4	F	13	2	0	4	14,730
Irish Intellect	3	G	8	1	3	1	37,230
Irish Intrigue	5	M	6	2	1	0	10,907
Irish Ivana	2	F	3	0	0	0	170
Irish Jinks	7	G	2	0	0	0	285
Irish Katie	7	M	1	0	0	0	0
Irish King	5	G	11	4	1	0	26,094
Irish Laddie	3	G	12	3	0	2	73,740
Irish Lake	9	G	16	0	0	0	1,449
Irish Laughter	4	G	11	0	1	1	8,114
Irish Legacy	5	G	14	2	2	4	24,046

Horse	Age	Sex	Sts	1st	2d	3d	Won
Irish Legend	9	G	14	1	3	4	7,557
Irish Line	5	M	5	1	0	1	7,796
Irish Love	10	G	12	1	4	0	6,365
Irish Luck Is Me	3	G	3	0	0	0	0
Irish Lucky	2	C	5	0	1	1	5,760
Irish Mafia	2	F	8	0	1	2	23,100
Irish Magic	5	M	12	0	5	3	15,975
Irish Meadow	2	F	3	1	0	0	13,800
Irish Melody	3	F	9	3	1	1	88,595
Irish Mick	5	G	12	1	1	2	5,601
Irish Milligan	5	G	14	3	1	2	31,577
Irish Mountain	4	G	11	2	1	4	18,249
Irish 'n Stride	4	C	13	2	1	1	32,530
Irish Nature	2	F	8	0	0	2	8,640
Irish Nip	8	G	14	3	1	3	31,930
Irish of Dobbin	4	F	15	2	3	2	22,459
Irish Opinion	7	G	6	1	1	1	25,605
Irish Pagan	4	F	8	0	0	1	1,265
Irish Pal	6	G	17	6	0	2	21,220
Irish Patti	3	F	3	0	0	0	835
Irish Pidgeon	7	G	6	0	0	0	560
Irish Playmate	5	M	4	0	0	0	0
Irish Pleasure	6	G	6	0	1	2	13,661
Irish Power	5	H	1	0	0	0	0
Irish Prediction	4	F	7	0	0	0	100
Irish Prince (NZ)	5	G	9	1	3	3	36,060
Irish Princess	5	M	3	0	0	0	433
Irish Pudding	3	F	6	0	0	0	642
Irish Punch	5	M	8	0	3	0	6,172
Irish Quality	3	C	4	1	1	2	39,320
Irish Rail	5	M	9	0	0	1	5,932
Irish Ransom	3	F	6	0	0	1	8,892
Irish Rebel	6	G	9	1	2	0	6,098
Irish Red	3	C	10	1	2	1	27,265
Irish Relic	3	C	5	0	4	0	8,615
Irish Rogue	6	G	10	5	1	2	52,602
Irish Rope	5	G	6	2	1	0	7,489
Irish Ruckus	3	G	12	2	4	1	25,327
Irish Scholar	4	C	5	0	0	0	1,831
Irish Shots	6	H	5	0	0	1	305
Irish Silence	10	G	2	0	0	0	570
Irish Sovereign	4	F	6	2	1	2	86,752
Irish Spin	4	F	10	1	1	1	30,450
Irish Star	2	F	4	0	2	0	4,636
Irish Statesman	4	G	2	0	0	1	772
Irish Storm	5	G	18	2	5	3	18,550
Irish Strike	2	C	2	0	0	0	950
Irish Sweep	5	G	12	1	0	1	11,720
Irish Terry	5	G	1	0	0	0	0
Irish Thriller	2	F	7	1	2	0	18,875
Irish Tizzy	2	C	4	1	0	1	7,120
Irish Treasure	4	G	7	0	0	0	0
Irish Tribute	5	G	6	1	1	1	9,606
Irish Ty	3	G	11	1	6	2	82,500
Irish Victory	4	G	11	3	3	0	13,625
Irish Viking	5	G	15	1	3	1	9,857
Irish Voyage	3	G	6	1	0	2	36,517
Irish Wager	5	G	10	2	3	1	92,671
Irish Warning	4	G	5	0	0	3	9,550
Irish Warrior	6	H	4	1	0	0	96,654
Irish Wind	3	G	22	2	3	5	28,535
Irish Wit	3	F	15	0	2	5	11,540
Irish Zippin Zel	4	G	2	0	0	0	0
Irisheyesareflying	8	H	2	0	0	0	0
Irishforgold	2	F	5	1	0	0	5,225
Irishrunaway	2	C	1	0	0	0	0
Irishskysarsmiling	3	G	2	0	1	0	3,500
Irishtown	3	C	2	0	1	0	5,750
Iroc Street Jive	4	G	1	0	1	0	326
Irockdasauce	3	G	4	0	0	0	2,922
Irocksilver	5	G	1	1	0	0	4,920
Iron Ace	3	G	9	1	1	1	7,484
Iron Action	5	G	7	1	0	0	5,485
Iron Bison	3	G	5	0	0	0	2,335
Iron Boy	3	G	6	3	0	1	34,780
Iron Cart	3	F	2	0	0	0	0
Iron City Jack	3	G	6	1	0	0	11,000
Iron Clad Proof	6	M	14	0	7	1	14,160
Iron Class	2	F	1	0	0	0	0

Horse	Age	Sex	Sts	1st	2d	3d	Won
Iron Cloud	6	G	12	1	2	3	8,116
Iron County Xmas	10	G	3	3	0	0	18,000
Iron Dragon	3	G	15	1	1	3	24,291
Iron Eagle	6	H	7	1	2	0	1,748
Iron Expectations	3	C	13	0	1	1	8,520
Iron Fantasy	10	G	9	1	1	0	10,989
Iron Flight	3	F	7	3	2	0	98,180
Iron Gene	2	G	2	0	0	0	250
Iron General	4	G	11	2	2	1	12,842
Iron Halo (ARG)	5	H	5	2	1	0	104,000
Iron Head	6	G	6	0	0	0	158
Iron Hill	4	G	12	2	2	1	31,814
Iron Hold	3	G	10	0	0	1	1,092
Iron Jaw	4	G	8	0	0	0	464
Iron King	6	G	1	0	0	0	40
Iron Madonna	4	F	7	0	0	0	513
Iron Maiden Too	4	F	10	1	1	3	5,088
Iron Mans Holiday	2	F	5	1	1	0	10,500
Iron Mike (NZ)	7	G	9	0	0	3	2,610
Iron Mountain	3	G	6	0	1	0	921
Iron Pepper	4	F	3	0	1	0	3,200
Iron Power	4	F	7	0	0	0	944
Iron Rae	3	G	13	1	3	1	10,524
Iron Rogue	3	G	5	1	0	1	24,000
Iron Royality	4	G	1	1	0	0	9,126
Iron Tabby	2	F	2	0	0	0	255
Iron Tiger	4	C	5	3	0	0	36,958
Iron Top	5	G	17	2	4	3	56,305
Iron Wall	2	C	5	1	1	0	25,140
Irongray	4	G	4	0	1	0	1,017
Ironman Dehere	6	H	5	0	0	2	2,270
Ironstone Road	2	C	5	2	0	3	35,890
Ironton	4	C	8	1	1	1	41,424
Irony	4	G	9	0	1	2	9,610
Irrawaddy	4	C	4	0	0	0	1,030
Irrepressible Joy	5	M	10	3	1	0	17,861
Irrepressiblespeed	3	F	9	5	1	1	114,534
Irresistible Jewel	3	F	4	0	0	1	1,430
Irrestible Force	6	G	15	1	1	3	7,953
Irrevocable	3	F	1	0	0	0	205
Irule	4	G	8	0	0	0	923
Irunwithwind	3	F	1	0	0	0	0
Irvington (IRE)	6	H	3	1	0	1	6,010
I's a Fact	3	F	5	0	3	1	22,060
Is a Gay Time	3	F	6	2	1	2	8,750
Is and Will Be	4	F	4	0	0	0	130
Is Faaaast	5	M	4	0	2	1	9,198
Is It Bold	8	G	15	1	2	0	6,407
Is It Gold	4	F	13	2	3	3	14,352
Is It On the Green	2	F	1	0	0	0	450
Is It Peggy Or Sue	5	M	9	0	1	3	7,829
Is It Soup Yet	4	G	10	2	2	1	35,953
Is It True Mex	8	G	13	4	3	3	107,255
Is Kylie Good	4	F	3	0	0	0	1,669
Is That You	5	M	11	4	1	1	96,380
Is This Heaven	4	F	6	3	0	1	19,944
Is To	4	C	5	0	0	0	330
Isaac's Dream	3	F	2	0	0	0	800
Isabel Isabel	4	F	9	0	2	0	4,544
Isabella Beancie	2	F	2	0	0	0	0
Isabella Victoria	8	M	4	0	0	1	602
Isabella's Crown (JPN)	3	F	9	1	1	3	29,890
Isabell's Shoes	2	F	5	0	3	2	32,700
Isabel's Dance	3	F	2	0	0	0	280
Isabel's Pride	5	M	14	2	2	2	16,121
Isaiah	5	G	10	4	2	1	22,184
Isaidit	2	G	2	0	0	0	70
Isawthelight	5	M	10	1	0	1	12,315
Isbon	3	G	14	2	3	4	60,300
Iseeyoubaby	4	G	3	0	1	0	1,364
Isernia	2	F	3	0	0	0	595
Ishi Naru	3	G	1	0	0	0	0
Ishio	7	H	4	0	0	0	300
Ishkoodah	4	G	10	1	2	3	9,947
Ishudbdone	3	G	7	0	0	1	3,117
Ishwar	6	G	13	0	0	1	4,378
Isit Still Legal	4	F	12	1	1	2	23,038
Isitdustybackthere	3	C	19	3	7	1	58,253
Isitever	8	G	12	2	1	2	9,867

Horse	Age	Sex	Sts	1st	2d	3d	Won
Isla	4	F	1	0	0	0	545
Isla Vista	2	C	3	1	0	0	6,725
Islamorada	4	F	1	0	0	0	140
Island Allure	2	F	2	0	0	0	3,420
Island Banking	14	G	1	0	0	0	120
Island Brite	3	F	3	1	0	0	4,800
Island Caper	11	G	11	1	0	1	6,119
Island Chancellor	2	G	5	1	1	0	16,390
Island Charm	3	C	9	1	3	0	58,067
Island Chief	3	G	13	0	1	1	2,477
Island Code	4	G	7	2	1	1	10,551
Island Dan	6	G	7	3	0	1	20,887
Island Delight	5	M	11	1	3	0	10,880
Island Deva	4	F	12	1	1	1	4,740
Island Dynamo	5	G	1	0	0	0	73
Island Escape	2	F	5	1	1	1	43,500
Island Express	6	H	7	2	0	1	9,446
Island Fashion	4	F	7	2	1	0	615,000
Island Getaway	8	M	5	1	2	0	20,073
Island Glimmer	3	F	2	0	0	0	153
Island Gray	2	G	2	0	0	0	210
Island Intruder	2	C	2	0	0	0	1,465
Island Lad	2	G	7	0	0	1	1,965
Island Light (GB)	6	G	4	0	0	0	4,000
Island Mac	3	G	9	1	2	0	18,180
Island Melody	4	F	19	0	2	3	26,600
Island Miss	2	F	2	1	0	0	9,770
Island Music	6	M	11	1	0	0	5,160
Island Myth	2	F	2	0	0	0	360
Island N Abreeze	6	G	9	4	1	1	26,131
Island Oak	5	G	9	0	0	1	1,109
Island Paradise	3	G	4	0	0	1	2,792
Island Party	3	F	13	2	2	1	12,276
Island Peak	3	C	7	2	0	3	28,640
Island Prince	4	C	13	1	2	4	9,921
Island Princess	4	F	1	0	0	0	93
Island Rebel	3	G	4	2	1	0	14,840
Island Red	2	C	5	1	0	0	11,120
Island Reversal	2	F	4	0	0	0	4,740
Island Saga	3	F	15	2	1	4	41,445
Island Sand	3	F	7	2	2	1	391,937
Island Skipper	5	H	9	1	4	2	52,060
Island Sunshine	6	M	2	0	0	0	0
Island Twist	4	G	7	0	0	0	580
Island Winds	2	G	1	0	0	0	2,940
Islander	9	H	9	2	1	2	48,560
Islands Sucess	3	G	5	1	0	0	12,296
Isle Be True	5	M	12	1	2	5	17,353
Isle Dream	4	F	6	1	1	0	2,100
Isle of Blitz	7	H	4	0	2	0	2,150
Isle of Capri	4	F	10	2	0	2	9,634
Isle of Chios	3	G	8	1	0	1	19,170
Isle of Hope	3	F	1	0	0	0	135
Isle of Mirth	3	G	12	2	2	1	45,889
Isle of Silver	2	C	2	1	0	1	19,880
Isle of Tunes	5	M	14	2	2	3	44,190
Isle of Wind	3	G	8	1	0	1	8,968
Isle Run for You	4	G	11	3	1	3	17,024
Isle Scamum	11	M	7	0	1	0	504
Islebeready	5	G	3	0	1	2	830
Isledustyou	3	G	7	0	4	1	4,967
Isleemailyou	6	G	8	0	1	0	7,695
Islemissyou	5	M	11	1	0	0	8,571
Islendingur	4	C	6	1	1	0	29,268
Isleplunder	9	G	2	0	2	0	3,600
Isleshine	3	F	4	1	0	2	8,340
Isletrickyou	3	G	7	0	0	1	700
Isnt It Rich	2	C	2	0	2	0	5,400
Isn't It True	4	F	15	2	2	2	21,463
Isn't She Great	6	M	11	0	1	1	3,884
Isn't True	4	G	3	1	0	0	10,550
Isolato	2	C	3	0	1	0	3,555
Ispeakasiplease	6	G	8	0	1	0	1,650
Isstat a Trump	6	M	2	0	0	0	123
Issues Storm	3	F	4	1	1	1	11,060
Istanbelle	5	M	9	0	1	1	2,399
Istanbull	5	G	6	1	0	1	5,515
Istillloveya	6	M	1	0	0	0	0
It Ain't My Fault	4	C	9	0	0	0	278

Horse	Age	Sex	Sts	1st	2d	3d	Won
It Happens	3	F	3	0	0	0	300
It Is	8	G	1	0	0	0	0
It Is Asis	3	G	7	1	0	2	11,476
It Is Private	6	M	3	0	0	0	630
It Is the Dr	2	C	3	0	0	0	0
It Is True	3	C	8	1	0	1	10,824
It Is What It Is	6	G	5	1	1	1	29,440
It Pays to Be Nice	3	F	4	0	0	0	0
It Takestwototango	3	F	1	0	0	0	0
It Was Meant To Be (GB)	5	M	10	3	0	0	65,975
Itakanrun	5	G	9	0	0	0	787
Itaka's Brianna	3	F	4	2	0	0	19,221
Italian Accent	3	F	3	0	1	0	6,460
Italian Bar Road	5	G	13	2	2	1	28,238
Italian Cart	2	G	2	0	0	0	1,380
Italian Dish	3	F	1	0	0	0	460
Italian Diva	5	M	8	1	0	1	6,896
Italian Doctor C	2	G	6	1	3	1	21,025
Italian Dreams	4	F	11	1	0	2	31,960
Italian Law	3	F	9	3	0	3	77,313
Italian Riviera	3	F	8	1	2	1	28,860
Italian Skier	3	C	3	0	0	1	1,600
Italian Slew	6	M	3	0	0	0	1,002
Italian Stogie	5	G	10	0	0	1	4,101
Italian Sunset	6	G	8	2	2	0	34,235
Italian Wine	5	M	6	1	0	1	7,477
Italiana	4	F	3	0	0	0	585
Italydar	4	G	10	3	2	0	24,830
Itawtisawaputtytat	3	F	4	0	2	0	20,670
Itchetucknee	4	C	12	1	3	0	21,533
Itchy	2	C	1	0	0	0	480
Itchy Numbers	3	G	8	0	1	0	2,145
Itchy Palm Slew	2	C	4	0	0	0	0
Itchy Richie	2	G	1	0	1	0	2,940
Itchy Toes	2	F	4	1	0	1	9,210
Iteration	2	F	1	0	0	0	0
Ithinkican Abraham	5	G	9	0	2	2	2,992
Ithoughiwasacowboy	4	C	1	0	0	1	220
Itmustbesummer	2	F	1	0	0	0	164
Itron's Girl	3	F	11	0	1	2	3,818
It's a Bell	2	F	3	0	0	0	1,200
Its a Blumin Storm	3	G	3	0	0	0	280
It's a Boy	5	G	4	0	0	1	2,552
It's a Cuban Thing	6	M	13	1	2	0	8,462
It's a Ego Thing	2	G	2	1	1	0	34,713
It's a Fact Jack	3	C	4	1	0	0	5,550
It's a Gala	3	G	9	0	2	1	12,180
It's a Given	2	G	4	0	0	0	3,840
It's a Halo	2	C	4	0	0	0	595
It's a Homer	3	G	12	2	1	1	7,679
Its a Jet	4	F	11	1	2	1	10,102
It's a Lady's Car	3	F	1	0	0	0	164
Its a Ladys Game	4	F	3	0	0	1	1,180
It's a Lock	3	G	8	3	3	0	27,768
It's a New Moon	6	G	6	0	0	1	560
It's a Party	3	F	3	0	0	0	145
It's a Perfect Day	3	G	13	1	6	2	75,380
It's a Problem	6	H	9	1	4	1	17,140
It's a Rainbow	2	F	2	0	0	1	1,874
It's a Shortcut	3	G	13	2	3	3	25,766
It's a Storm	6	M	6	0	0	2	2,566
It's a Sweep	8	G	4	0	0	0	250
It's a Trap	3	C	8	0	1	3	8,195
It's a Waki Fact	7	G	13	0	4	2	26,348
It's About Me	2	F	2	1	0	1	16,110
It's About Silver	5	M	7	0	1	2	16,253
It's Ali's Time	2	F	2	0	1	1	4,504
It's all a Blurr	11	G	6	1	2	1	5,143
Its All About Gold	3	G	16	5	1	2	48,989
It's All About Me	5	M	6	0	0	0	115
It's All About Yo	2	F	1	0	0	0	750
It's All About You	4	F	20	3	2	3	21,253
It's All Attitude	4	G	9	0	0	0	6,440
Its All From Above	4	C	5	0	0	0	1,560
Its All Good Babe	2	G	3	1	0	0	6,478
It's All Jake	4	G	4	0	1	0	1,888
It's All Lies	4	F	9	0	1	0	4,660
It's Always Boldly	9	G	11	1	1	2	10,572
Its Always Now	3	F	3	0	0	0	564
It's Always True	6	G	12	1	2	3	8,455
Its Alwayssomthing	4	G	1	0	0	0	0
It's an Emerald	4	F	15	3	1	1	9,805
It's Awesome Baby	3	C	9	0	2	1	14,762
It's Bingo Bettie	4	F	6	0	0	0	1,298
It's Boldly's Baby	8	G	3	0	0	0	0
It's Break Time	2	G	4	1	1	1	15,170
It's Brite's Turn	5	G	16	1	4	3	27,677
It's Bubbles	4	F	6	0	0	0	1,047
It's Chilly	4	F	15	2	6	1	49,440
Its Ctmarie C	5	M	11	1	0	0	3,740
Its Foxy	6	G	7	0	0	0	455
It's Friday	5	G	4	0	0	0	0
Its Gold	3	F	2	0	0	0	235
It's Groovy	5	G	18	2	5	0	15,769
It's Hamer Time	3	G	6	0	0	0	0
It's Heidi's Dance	4	F	3	0	0	2	12,380
Its Her Class	9	M	5	0	0	0	119
It's Himself	3	G	4	1	0	0	5,820
Its His Time	2	G	4	2	0	0	59,311
It's Houston Time	4	G	3	0	0	0	183
It's in the Kiss	2	G	6	1	0	2	13,020
It's in the Mail	3	G	8	2	0	1	22,695
It's in the Stars	3	F	8	1	0	3	9,695
Its Inevitable	4	F	5	2	1	0	11,720
Its Jim Not Jimmy	4	G	1	0	0	0	132
It's Just a Game	4	G	10	2	3	0	59,853
It's Just Business	3	G	10	2	0	0	10,775
It's Just Mac	2	G	1	0	0	0	300
It's Kobe	4	G	13	4	1	1	38,283
Its Late September	2	F	2	0	0	0	100
It's Link Time	6	G	6	0	1	0	1,782
It's Lucky	3	G	9	2	3	0	72,016
It's Me Megan	2	F	3	0	2	0	7,361
It's Mello Time	5	M	5	1	0	0	5,850
Its Michael	7	G	12	0	2	2	5,454
It's Millers Time	2	C	5	0	2	0	4,664
It's My Buck	3	G	16	1	5	1	11,862
Its My Decision	3	F	1	0	0	0	0
Its My Option	3	F	11	3	2	0	24,737
Its My Pleasure	5	M	9	1	0	3	24,130
It's My Secret	6	M	9	1	3	1	16,763
Its My Tyme	4	G	10	1	1	2	16,447
It's No Joke	2	C	1	0	0	0	0
It's Not So	2	C	1	0	0	0	300
It's Ok	4	G	7	0	0	1	2,125
It's Quite Unusual	3	G	4	1	0	0	15,300
It's Rocketman	2	G	2	0	1	0	3,642
It's So Simple	6	H	14	5	0	4	108,260
It's Spooky	4	F	9	1	0	3	43,180
It's Stevie's Time	5	M	4	1	1	1	35,600
It's the Custom	3	G	12	2	1	1	23,945
It's Time to Smile	2	C	7	2	1	1	34,430
It's Triple George	6	G	14	4	0	5	46,618
Its True Atlast	2	C	3	1	0	0	12,500
Its True Its True	2	F	3	1	0	0	9,030
Its Tuesday	3	F	8	3	1	0	13,221
It's Valentino	3	C	1	0	0	0	77
It's Vodka Talking	2	F	1	0	0	1	1,920
Its Your Time	3	G	1	0	0	0	0
Itsa Blue Pill	4	F	4	1	0	0	1,540
Itsa Risky Maurena	3	F	1	0	0	0	101
Itsa Rizzi	3	C	19	4	2	0	20,572
Itsa Sign	4	G	1	0	0	1	1,000
Itsacakewalk	3	C	8	1	2	0	48,001
Itsaconcern	3	F	5	0	0	0	150
Itsadream	3	G	12	2	1	0	12,950
Itsagalthing	3	F	9	2	0	2	14,690
Itsahotcat	3	G	7	2	2	0	16,118
It'sallaboutmebaby	3	F	14	1	2	3	25,106
Itsallatrick	2	F	2	0	0	1	5,963
Itsallrelative	2	G	5	2	0	0	7,922
Itsalluptoyou	3	C	10	0	1	1	5,610
It'samazing	3	F	9	1	1	0	11,379
Itsanewday	3	G	18	2	4	2	18,484
Itsaninetyniner	2	G	7	3	0	1	17,328
Itsaprospector	3	G	8	2	1	1	35,885
Itsa's Ali	6	M	7	2	1	1	16,970
Itsasgoodasitgets	8	G	5	3	0	1	18,000

Horse	Age	Sex	Sts	1st	2d	3d	Won
Itsatrick	2	G	6	0	0	0	1,850
Itsawonderfulife	3	C	10	1	0	1	38,848
Itsawonderfulworld	4	G	2	0	0	0	0
Itsayatesthing	3	F	11	3	3	1	86,170
It'schemistrybaby	2	F	1	0	0	0	0
It'sdanzatime	3	F	9	1	0	1	6,660
Itsfuntobeme	3	C	7	1	2	0	11,518
Itsgointobeafight	9	G	1	0	0	0	0
Itshardtobehumble	6	G	13	0	1	0	3,092
It'slonelyatthetop	3	F	7	0	1	0	4,772
Itsmybag	4	F	3	0	0	0	1,762
Itsnowonder	7	M	14	1	0	4	11,774
Itspartofthegame	3	F	7	1	0	3	9,719
Itsthe Realthing	6	G	3	1	0	0	3,076
Itstimeforchange	2	F	2	0	0	0	3,180
Itstufftobegood	3	G	2	1	0	1	5,120
Itsurturn	7	G	5	2	1	0	12,699
Itsyourbid	8	G	6	0	1	0	3,054
Itty Bitty Bit	5	M	1	0	0	0	0
Itty Bitty Girl	5	M	11	0	2	4	10,162
Ittybittybeau	4	F	12	5	1	1	37,579
Ittybittygritty	4	F	11	1	3	3	12,466
Ituna	3	F	12	3	1	1	58,510
Itybittyboo	6	G	6	2	0	0	3,000
Itz a Ritz	2	F	4	0	0	0	900
It'z All Mine	2	F	1	0	0	0	980
Itzallgoodbaby	3	C	6	1	1	0	12,477
Iv in the Heather	5	M	10	0	0	1	1,176
Ivan	3	G	5	0	0	0	0
Ivan Jay Perry	8	G	11	3	1	1	120,327
Ivan Motley	5	H	17	2	4	3	25,196
Ivan the Gray	3	G	1	0	0	0	189
Ivanavinalot	4	F	2	0	0	0	6,000
Ivans in a Tiz	3	G	10	2	0	0	10,266
Ivan's Song	4	G	7	0	0	1	2,846
Ivar	6	H	14	1	1	1	6,977
Ivars Big Peaceful	7	G	16	2	3	1	9,171
Ivars Blues	5	G	8	1	1	0	20,500
Ivars Ms Mayhem	4	F	11	3	2	2	42,080
I've Been Crowned	6	G	10	1	2	0	4,660
I've Been Spared	4	F	5	1	0	1	5,903
Ive Been There	9	G	7	0	0	2	669
I've Decided	7	G	5	0	0	0	388
I've Got a Dream	6	H	6	0	0	1	435
I've Got Rhythm	3	G	18	1	3	6	14,384
I've Got Speed	2	G	8	3	0	2	37,520
I've Got the Power	4	F	14	1	2	2	7,557
Ive Got the Rhythm	4	G	18	3	2	3	15,479
I've Got the Time	5	H	8	4	0	1	34,650
I've Got to Win	3	F	8	3	1	1	40,615
I've Had It	9	G	5	0	0	2	792
I'vegothemusicinme	3	F	1	0	0	0	620
Ivgotmymojoworkin	3	G	5	1	0	1	10,097
Ivorget	4	F	16	2	1	0	14,409
Ivorgorian	12	G	5	1	2	0	8,400
Ivor's Motel	5	G	6	0	1	2	1,960
Ivor's Secret	7	G	4	0	1	1	1,266
Ivory	4	G	3	0	0	0	83
Ivory Coast	3	G	5	1	0	1	25,520
Ivory Tower (ARG)	6	M	1	0	0	0	3,600
Ivy League Miss	2	F	3	0	1	0	7,320
Ivy Step	3	F	3	0	0	0	510
Iwannabeacowboy	3	G	6	1	1	1	23,632
Iwantabeinpictures	6	H	2	0	0	0	132
Iwantabelovedbyyou	5	M	1	0	0	0	250
Iwanttotalkaboutme	4	F	7	0	1	1	2,132
Iwill Believe It	3	G	1	0	0	0	0
Iwin	5	G	7	0	0	0	2,666
Iwo Hero	4	G	16	2	2	3	21,673
Iwontell	5	H	2	0	0	1	462
Iwontstopdancing	6	M	8	1	3	1	18,935
Iwoodificould	6	H	7	3	0	1	52,050
Iyieldtonoone	2	F	1	0	0	1	2,640
Iz Hoolio	5	G	7	0	0	0	529
Iz Smilin Andhappy	2	C	4	0	0	0	694
Iza Big Star	3	G	5	0	2	0	18,970
Iza Bon Fire	3	F	14	3	1	4	10,921
Iza Chili Bean	5	G	18	1	1	2	16,610
Iza Doozy	5	H	3	0	0	0	475
Iza General	2	C	2	0	0	0	800
Iza Gentleman	2	G	6	0	1	0	5,600
Iza Legend	3	F	6	1	0	2	46,326
Iza Lucky Guy	5	G	15	0	6	1	8,766
Iza Reckless	2	F	5	1	0	0	7,088
Iza Redhead	10	G	8	0	1	2	9,580
Iza Righteous Dude	4	G	12	1	8	1	34,070
Iza Tornado	6	G	2	0	0	0	593
Iza Twister	8	G	15	3	3	3	6,874
Iza's Turn to Star	3	F	6	1	3	1	13,533
Izora	3	F	6	0	0	0	0
Iztla	3	F	10	6	0	0	33,017
Izy With It	4	G	7	1	1	0	3,955
Izzda	2	F	1	0	0	0	644
Izzies Rose	3	F	15	3	2	1	30,957
Izzy Zipper	5	G	13	3	2	1	18,842
J Aled Rudolph	6	G	5	1	0	0	2,994
J and J Ruler	5	M	8	0	0	2	1,320
J B Chief	4	C	2	0	0	0	0
J B Escalation	5	G	8	4	1	0	18,259
J B McQuity	4	G	9	0	0	0	945
J B Zero	5	G	3	0	1	0	2,558
J B's Crown	5	G	15	0	3	1	3,648
J B's Final Tour	2	G	3	0	0	0	75
J B's Girl	4	F	11	1	2	1	11,253
J B's Jessica	4	F	13	0	0	2	1,704
J B's Melanie	3	F	10	4	2	1	39,880
J B's Money	4	F	8	3	0	0	29,640
J B's Star	5	G	5	0	0	0	150
J B's Victoria	3	F	14	2	4	2	62,004
J B's Wolf	4	F	3	0	0	0	356
J C and Me	2	G	3	0	0	0	1,760
J C Steel	5	G	7	0	4	0	1,725
J C Three	2	C	2	0	0	0	660
J C's Classic Con	4	G	4	1	1	0	8,840
J D Dreamer	7	G	12	1	1	1	9,006
J D Man	4	G	9	1	0	2	14,037
J D's Dasher	4	G	7	1	2	0	8,828
J D's Date	2	G	1	0	0	0	0
J D's Deelites	2	F	2	0	0	1	1,905
J H Cheyenne	4	G	4	1	1	0	7,300
J H Dustin	2	C	1	0	0	0	77
J H Sovereign Hour	3	C	13	1	0	0	7,930
J J Jake	3	G	2	1	0	0	22,600
J J Mystique	5	G	12	2	2	1	43,562
J J R Prideandjoy	4	F	11	0	0	1	3,350
J J S Laddie	11	G	12	2	4	2	10,726
J J Silver Blush	6	M	2	0	0	0	530
J J Thedotcom Man	6	G	18	1	5	3	5,025
J J Wantsthefront	5	G	10	4	0	1	26,380
J J Wish	3	G	10	3	2	3	71,300
J J Zar	4	F	8	1	1	1	7,442
J Jacqueline	3	F	8	0	0	2	8,060
J J's Diamond	3	F	4	0	1	2	6,800
J J's Prospect	4	G	8	0	1	2	7,785
J J's Secret	2	F	4	0	0	1	938
J J's Son	3	G	11	2	4	1	13,324
J L Jet Stream	3	G	6	1	1	0	11,786
J Loves J	3	F	16	1	0	5	7,965
J Man's Deelite	3	F	9	2	0	2	11,070
J M's Mad Groom	5	G	16	3	3	2	19,169
J N B N Me	3	F	14	2	0	3	17,751
J N J's Executive	3	G	9	0	1	1	6,651
J P Honey	4	F	12	1	2	2	9,389
J P Jewel	2	F	5	1	1	0	42,994
J P Norcatco	3	G	11	1	0	1	10,585
J P Patches	4	G	4	0	0	1	1,255
J P Peterson	4	G	10	1	1	2	13,037
J Ramsey Rib	4	G	10	1	0	1	8,860
J Ride	4	G	11	3	3	2	20,755
J Silverheels	2	G	4	0	0	2	5,720
J Star	3	F	6	1	1	1	16,160
J T S Taz	3	G	3	0	0	0	300
J T Tower	3	C	11	3	3	2	10,912
J Town	3	C	5	2	1	1	112,680
J T's Beau	2	C	2	0	0	0	800
J T's Lemoon	5	M	9	1	1	3	16,630
J T's Princes	3	F	9	2	0	1	8,503
J V Bennett	11	G	9	4	1	0	54,558

Horse	Age	Sex	Sts	1st	2d	3d	Won
J W Black	6	G	1	0	0	0	120
J W Dollar	6	G	3	0	0	0	169
J W Dude	4	G	6	1	2	0	6,890
J W Jet	7	G	11	0	2	4	10,442
J W's Baby Girl	3	F	1	0	0	0	0
J W's Ruckus	3	G	5	0	0	0	546
J W's Wish	6	G	1	0	0	0	0
J. A. First Call	4	G	6	0	0	2	942
J. B. Jr.	4	G	2	0	0	0	0
J. B. the Vet	4	G	14	1	2	2	11,257
J. B.'s Annie	5	M	16	2	3	1	90,480
J. B.'s Ghost	9	H	2	1	0	0	5,700
J. B.'s Isis	6	G	2	1	0	0	7,620
J. B.'s Six Pack	8	H	2	0	0	0	185
J. B.'s Victory	2	G	7	0	1	1	12,010
J. Brookfield	3	G	5	1	1	0	18,122
J. C. Blue	4	F	8	0	0	0	255
J. C.s Joy	6	M	5	0	0	0	381
J. C.'s Sideoats	8	M	10	1	2	2	10,875
J. D. Belle	3	C	14	2	3	1	27,155
J. D. Cat	3	C	9	0	0	0	4,069
J. D. for Shur	7	H	4	2	1	0	5,176
J. D. 'n Coke	3	G	18	1	4	2	14,814
J. D. Safari	2	F	2	1	0	1	10,141
J. D. Tyler	5	H	2	0	0	2	2,110
J. D.'s Blue Bayou	2	G	7	2	1	1	43,550
J. D.'s Easter	6	H	4	0	2	0	729
J. D.'s Harley	3	F	8	0	1	1	6,593
J. D.'s Holdin' On	6	G	10	2	1	1	11,897
J. G. Jet	2	C	3	0	1	0	7,007
J. G.'s Jazz	3	C	11	0	2	1	15,760
J. Gordon	4	C	12	1	2	1	10,740
J. H. Diamond Head	3	G	2	0	0	0	135
J. Harmon	7	H	6	0	0	0	2,865
J. J. Cant Wag	3	C	2	0	1	0	760
J. J. Dancer	2	C	1	0	0	0	230
J. J. Maroun	2	C	4	0	0	0	1,680
J. J. Nat	3	G	15	2	2	1	12,602
J. J. Night	4	G	5	0	0	0	269
J. J. Sun Shine	5	G	13	3	1	2	8,131
J. J.'s Joy	5	G	14	2	4	2	57,611
J. J.'s Legacy	3	C	2	1	0	0	14,620
J. J.'s Twister	3	F	3	0	0	0	209
J. J.'s Voyage	3	C	4	0	0	0	1,180
J. J.'s Weekend	3	G	11	0	1	3	4,336
J. Jay	5	M	3	0	0	0	390
J. L. A. Slew	6	G	9	0	2	1	1,520
J. Leigh	3	F	3	0	0	0	110
J. M. Judge	4	G	9	1	1	1	6,456
J. O. Prado	2	C	7	0	1	1	5,282
J. P. 's Barbie	4	F	9	2	0	2	32,388
J. P. Sands	3	G	7	0	2	0	3,555
J. P. Transport	3	C	4	0	0	0	392
J. P.'s Magic	4	G	4	0	1	2	5,103
J. Q. Adams	7	H	4	0	0	1	1,102
J. R. Belongs	4	G	7	0	1	1	8,580
J. R. Coin	3	G	4	0	0	0	0
J. R. Hatfield	7	M	9	0	4	1	14,755
J. R. Honor	6	G	16	6	2	2	35,417
J. R. Jazz	12	G	1	1	0	0	1,200
J. R.'s Star	4	F	2	0	0	0	76
J. R.'s Town	7	G	7	1	1	1	7,102
J. S. Online	5	M	15	1	1	0	12,368
J. T.'s Song	7	G	14	3	5	0	30,045
J. T.'s Star	3	C	1	0	0	0	0
J. W.'s Synplay	5	M	3	0	0	0	166
Jab Jab Pow	3	G	6	1	1	1	10,110
Jabalski Princess	4	F	11	0	4	0	13,225
Jabberinjo	5	G	6	0	0	0	132
Jabibti (PER)	5	M	4	1	1	1	23,630
Jablunkov Pass	3	G	10	1	0	2	19,757
Jab's Lovin' Coin	2	F	9	0	0	0	3,549
Jabtotheright	5	M	7	0	0	0	450
Jac Four Girls	6	G	13	2	3	1	5,264
Jac Tee Ess	4	G	6	1	0	0	6,105
Jachovia	2	G	6	0	1	2	12,030
Jacira (FR)	5	M	7	4	1	0	85,727
Jaciro	4	F	10	2	2	3	65,171
Jack	10	G	15	0	0	2	1,702

Horse	Age	Sex	Sts	1st	2d	3d	Won
Jack and Emma	5	G	7	1	0	3	12,037
Jack At the Bank	10	G	1	0	0	0	65
Jack Black and Ice	4	C	9	1	1	1	17,468
Jack Brown	2	G	3	0	1	1	3,818
Jack Coleman	8	G	8	0	0	0	524
Jack Diamondfield	6	G	4	0	0	0	0
Jack Dugan	7	G	11	5	3	1	16,152
Jack in a Jug	3	G	4	0	1	1	7,115
Jack in the Black	4	G	13	1	2	2	9,556
Jack Knife Judy	3	F	2	0	0	0	120
Jack Moore	4	G	9	0	0	1	2,475
Jack O Lindy	2	G	2	0	0	0	1,085
Jack of Clubs	3	C	7	0	2	3	23,684
Jack of My Heart	4	G	10	1	1	1	35,060
Jack of Slades	6	G	11	0	1	3	14,195
Jack Star	5	G	2	0	0	0	0
Jack the Cat	4	G	2	0	0	0	0
Jack the Jackal	4	C	2	0	0	0	405
Jack the Stick	3	C	5	0	0	0	326
Jack to a King	6	H	3	0	0	0	1,125
Jacka B Boop	3	G	11	1	0	1	5,462
Jackberun	4	G	6	1	2	1	18,741
Jackdaw	3	C	6	1	1	0	26,347
Jackety Jack	4	G	12	1	2	2	59,385
Jackie Jan	4	F	5	2	2	0	40,238
Jackie Jo	2	F	5	0	4	1	8,895
Jackie M.	3	F	9	1	1	1	14,127
Jackie O's Diamond	3	F	5	0	0	0	1,245
Jackielee	3	F	5	1	0	0	5,824
Jackiemyboy	3	G	2	0	0	0	45
Jackie's Bidawalk	5	M	1	0	0	0	405
Jackies Bold Move	3	F	3	0	1	0	1,160
Jackie's Cariad	2	C	2	0	0	0	0
Jackies Dream	2	F	1	0	0	0	118
Jackies Gunner	9	G	9	1	1	1	8,243
Jackie's Hope	4	F	16	7	1	1	79,037
Jackie's Way	9	G	1	0	0	0	0
Jacki's Lil Wacki	11	M	8	2	0	2	4,070
Jacki's Story	5	G	2	0	0	0	0
Jacki's Tuition	5	M	1	0	0	0	0
Jacklin	2	F	5	1	0	2	19,660
Jacknows	2	C	8	1	2	0	42,112
Jackoranda	3	F	20	1	4	0	19,310
Jackpot	6	H	3	1	1	0	189,120
Jackpot Belle	3	F	4	1	1	1	18,480
Jackpot Party	3	F	8	1	0	1	14,205
Jackrabbit Slim	7	G	8	1	2	3	8,810
Jacks Bigwheel	4	C	6	0	1	1	1,240
Jacks Cat	4	F	7	1	2	0	8,953
Jack's Concielo	5	G	6	2	2	0	12,131
Jack's Crafty Lady	3	F	1	0	0	0	95
Jacks Express	2	G	2	0	0	0	282
Jack's Jet	4	G	4	0	1	1	14,545
Jack's Lady	2	F	1	0	1	0	4,000
Jacks Legal Eagle	5	G	2	0	0	0	150
Jack's Magee	5	G	18	3	3	4	19,103
Jacks N Ladies	3	G	3	0	2	0	7,820
Jack's Olympio	7	G	3	0	0	0	228
Jack's Own Time	5	G	5	2	0	0	21,810
Jacks Romeo	5	G	8	0	0	1	5,564
Jack's Silver	5	H	8	1	0	1	49,752
Jacks to Win	6	G	3	0	0	0	100
Jack's Touch	3	F	12	0	1	4	12,155
Jacks Trait	7	G	4	0	0	0	223
Jackson Hole	7	G	13	2	1	1	7,171
Jackson Point	8	G	16	2	1	4	16,192
Jackson Run	4	G	9	2	0	0	50,920
Jackson Spur	7	G	7	1	2	0	5,321
Jacksonian	2	C	1	0	0	0	205
Jackson's Delight	3	F	14	1	1	1	8,835
Jacktown	2	C	3	0	1	1	9,810
Jackyscraftychance	5	G	13	0	1	2	27,351
Jaclini	5	G	7	0	0	0	2,234
Jacob and Julian	4	C	4	0	1	1	8,755
Jacob the Great	3	G	13	1	1	1	10,758
Jacob V and G A	2	C	1	0	0	0	0
Jacob's Arch	3	C	3	1	0	2	31,600
Jacob's Bunny	3	F	1	0	0	0	125
Jacobs Caller	3	G	8	1	1	0	23,640

Horse	Age	Sex	Sts	1st	2d	3d	Won
Jacobs Deal	5	G	10	0	2	1	4,285
Jacob's Pep	2	C	2	0	0	0	552
Jacob's Pride	7	G	5	0	0	0	385
Jacob's Prospect	5	G	9	1	0	2	24,654
Jacobs Smile	4	F	11	3	1	3	54,930
Jacobs Spirit	2	G	2	0	0	1	3,080
Jacob's Trust	6	G	11	0	0	2	2,109
Jacque La Rock	2	G	7	0	0	0	585
Jacqueline K	4	F	5	1	2	0	19,110
Jacquelyn T.	6	M	9	0	1	1	5,220
Jacques Boy	5	G	9	1	2	2	10,158
Jacquie Rose	5	M	7	0	0	0	2,349
Jacquiere	3	G	5	0	1	1	5,120
Jacquie's Delight	6	H	1	0	0	0	0
Jacqui's Promise	4	F	6	2	0	0	54,176
Jac's Choice	2	G	3	1	0	0	5,166
Jacy's Trick	2	C	3	1	0	0	9,255
Jada Bug	5	M	2	0	0	0	120
Jada Jing	3	F	14	2	1	3	15,000
Jade Air	4	F	3	0	0	0	0
Jade Arador	2	F	3	0	1	0	2,280
Jade Arrow	4	G	9	3	0	3	33,365
Jade Dancer	3	F	11	2	0	4	22,145
Jade Devil	2	G	6	0	0	2	2,440
Jade Digger	5	G	3	0	0	0	396
Jade Dragon	3	F	13	1	2	1	12,171
Jade Express	5	M	7	1	0	1	1,675
Jade Forest	4	C	3	0	1	1	12,940
Jade Fox	4	F	1	0	0	0	0
Jade Green	6	G	8	1	2	0	22,700
Jade Halo	5	G	6	0	1	0	2,707
Jade Heist	3	G	5	0	0	0	0
Jade Legend	3	F	2	1	0	0	6,110
Jade Mountain	3	G	10	0	2	2	31,522
Jade Myth	3	F	7	0	0	0	2,715
Jade of the Nile	4	C	2	1	0	1	770
Jade Palace	4	F	6	2	0	2	27,660
Jade Peony	6	M	12	3	2	2	41,135
Jade Trader	6	H	8	0	1	0	1,543
Jadebquick	4	F	9	2	1	1	36,032
Jaded Heart	2	F	2	0	0	1	1,952
Jaded Heat	4	G	9	4	1	1	31,630
Jaded Impulse	3	F	8	1	0	3	15,980
Jaded Kim	3	F	1	1	0	0	8,100
Jaded Lane	3	F	9	1	0	0	9,445
Jaded Money	9	G	10	0	1	2	4,829
Jaded Runner	6	M	4	0	2	0	9,416
Jaded Slew	9	G	3	1	0	0	5,020
Jadeite Lady	2	F	1	0	0	0	125
Jadelicious	3	F	4	0	0	0	1,500
Jade's Ace	6	M	9	4	1	0	25,511
Jade's in Uproar	3	F	5	1	2	0	7,200
Jade's Jewel	3	G	11	1	1	1	20,358
Jadester	4	F	3	0	0	1	5,280
Jaffa	6	G	14	1	2	2	2,607
Jaftica	4	G	8	0	0	0	1,963
Jag Man	3	C	5	0	0	0	2,300
Jagged Ice	5	G	6	4	1	0	37,425
Jagger	8	H	2	0	0	0	100
Jaggered Dreams	3	F	11	0	2	0	6,433
Jaglander	3	C	3	2	0	0	55,286
Jaguar Cielo	4	F	5	0	0	1	7,540
Jaguar City	4	F	7	3	3	0	112,170
Jaguar Friend	3	C	6	1	2	0	56,332
Jaguar Groom	5	H	2	0	0	0	0
Jaguar Hope	6	G	11	3	3	1	13,770
Jaguar Jack	5	G	17	1	6	1	8,564
Jaguar Jade	6	G	11	0	1	1	2,653
Jaguar Jet	2	G	2	0	0	0	1,272
Jaguar Joe	4	G	9	4	1	2	40,925
Jaguar Lord	6	M	11	1	2	0	6,944
Jaguar Pass	6	H	2	0	0	0	0
Jaguar Princess	2	F	1	1	0	0	6,000
Jaguar Prospect	10	H	3	1	1	0	5,720
Jaha (FR)	5	G	8	1	0	0	5,932
Jahamour (NZ)	6	H	3	0	0	0	2,000
Jahar	3	G	11	0	1	1	6,855
Jahman	4	G	10	0	1	2	3,299
Jahuan	3	C	18	1	4	1	27,460
J'ai Deux Amours	2	F	5	0	2	0	6,545
Jaida's Jenney	3	F	3	0	0	0	210
Jaime Jack	6	G	7	1	0	0	6,907
Jaime's Joy	5	M	10	0	2	0	5,496
Jaime's Monster	2	G	3	0	0	0	1,370
Jaime's Pearl	3	F	1	0	0	0	0
Jak D	5	G	2	0	0	0	153
Jakarta Jade (IRE)	4	F	2	0	0	0	4,720
Jakarta Star	5	H	3	0	0	0	206
Jake	5	G	7	1	3	1	20,285
Jake Can't Wait	2	G	1	0	0	0	400
Jake Gonna Win	6	H	3	0	0	0	138
Jake Jacoby	5	G	2	0	0	0	606
Jake Leader	5	H	2	0	0	0	130
Jake Skate	4	C	10	3	4	2	139,320
Jake Storm	3	G	11	2	4	1	31,002
Jake the Flake	8	G	11	2	1	2	60,922
Jake W.	8	G	5	0	0	0	222
Jakeman	4	G	6	0	1	1	2,167
Jakes Corner	6	G	16	4	5	2	26,755
Jake's Fever	3	C	4	0	0	1	5,600
Jakes Fire	8	G	2	0	0	0	64
Jake's Flash	4	F	4	0	0	0	387
Jake's Guy	7	G	3	0	0	0	0
Jake's No Angel	2	C	7	1	0	1	12,390
Jake's Vali	2	F	1	0	0	0	0
Jakester (GB)	4	C	3	0	0	0	0
Jakey D	6	G	14	2	4	1	26,175
Jakeybabes	4	G	2	0	0	0	0
Jaki's Magic	6	G	6	1	1	3	38,320
Jaklin's Last Kin	7	G	2	1	0	0	2,994
Jakob Teddy	3	G	13	1	3	1	12,860
Jakota Moon	6	M	5	0	0	1	936
Jalaab (IRE)	9	H	9	0	1	1	6,079
Jalapeno	6	G	7	0	0	0	777
Jalyn	3	F	5	0	0	0	790
Jam Feu	7	G	16	1	3	3	23,610
Jam for the Lamb	5	G	15	3	4	1	51,126
Jam Won	3	F	14	1	3	6	15,259
Jamaari Girl	5	M	1	0	0	0	0
Jamaica Bay	2	C	2	0	0	0	4,850
Jamaica Joe	3	G	13	3	4	1	30,746
Jamaican Fun	4	G	14	0	4	2	5,466
Jamaican Justice	5	G	21	2	2	3	19,955
Jamaican Me Nuts	5	G	6	3	1	0	41,870
Jamaican Smoke	4	G	10	1	1	2	13,645
Jambalar	4	G	11	1	2	4	133,914
Jambalaya	2	G	1	0	0	1	6,270
Jambeau	5	G	2	1	1	0	10,120
Jamboree	8	G	7	0	0	0	448
James	4	G	8	1	3	0	29,830
James B.	4	G	9	0	2	2	9,873
James Clarence	8	G	13	2	4	1	18,020
James Creek	4	G	16	1	0	4	6,582
James Creek Lass	3	F	5	0	1	0	3,356
James Jr	3	G	3	0	0	0	1,200
James Logan	8	G	8	5	1	1	54,302
James Madison	5	H	6	1	0	2	5,803
James Riley	3	C	10	1	0	1	6,224
James's Highlander	5	H	2	1	0	0	3,720
Jamessonjimmyjames	5	G	7	0	0	1	2,385
Jamestown Flash	3	G	4	0	1	0	4,025
Jamestown Romance	3	F	16	1	1	5	21,484
Jami Pari	8	M	10	1	2	0	5,429
Jamian	3	C	20	1	4	4	56,411
Jamican Blue	4	G	5	0	0	2	11,313
Jamie Jamie	3	G	6	1	0	0	2,520
Jamie N Jill's Way	3	F	7	1	0	4	10,235
Jamie T. James	6	M	1	0	0	0	0
Jamie's Bad Boy	5	G	12	2	0	1	17,174
Jamie's College	7	H	6	2	2	1	19,280
Jamie's Image	8	G	11	0	3	3	5,360
Jamies Jet	3	G	3	1	1	1	37,600
Jamie's Leader	13	G	6	0	0	0	0
Jamie's Melody	6	G	9	1	0	1	6,257
Jamie's Tuition	4	G	13	2	2	0	20,920
Jamilah	4	F	4	1	1	0	7,440
Jamin Jolie	2	F	5	1	1	1	20,700
Jaming Jammer	4	G	12	3	3	1	14,012

Horse	Age	Sex	Sts	1st	2d	3d	Won
Jaming the Blues	5	G	9	2	1	0	32,430
Jamirach	3	F	1	0	0	0	115
Jammer	5	G	12	0	0	0	617
Jammin Gears	2	C	1	0	1	0	7,000
Jammin J J	3	G	7	1	2	0	17,420
Jammin Syd	3	C	3	0	0	0	480
Jamocas B Lady	3	F	1	0	0	0	118
Jamoke	6	G	2	0	0	0	0
Jamuga	5	G	2	0	0	0	180
Jamye's Mugabucks	10	G	11	2	2	1	8,451
Jan Darling	3	F	3	0	0	1	2,450
Jan Luck	7	M	1	0	0	1	484
Jana o' Gaill	7	M	5	1	1	0	3,375
Jana Rae	3	F	1	0	0	0	82
Janayen	4	F	2	0	0	0	0
Jancy Girl	5	M	19	4	1	1	14,239
Jandemar	3	C	7	2	0	1	16,150
Jane B. A.	4	F	10	1	2	1	46,285
Jane Daniels	6	M	6	1	2	0	9,630
Jane Jane Jane	4	F	10	0	1	4	5,740
Janeian (NZ)	6	M	6	2	2	0	177,820
Jane's Big Boot	4	G	1	0	0	1	1,210
Jane's Daisy	2	F	1	0	0	0	0
Jane's Halo	3	F	8	1	4	0	22,910
Jane's Luck	3	G	5	3	0	0	79,680
Jane's Rose	3	F	2	0	0	0	120
Jane's Secret	4	F	10	2	4	1	64,560
Jane's Speed	5	M	4	0	0	0	1,380
Janet Auto Win	3	F	6	0	0	0	210
Janet's Halftime	2	F	4	0	2	0	20,145
Janet's Ruff Cut	3	F	3	0	0	0	0
Janet's Tete	3	F	3	0	0	1	1,833
Janey Girl	8	M	2	1	0	0	4,785
Jangled	5	G	6	0	0	1	537
Janice's Victor	6	G	6	1	0	1	934
Janies Enjoyment	7	M	7	1	2	1	6,550
Janines Secret	9	M	3	0	0	0	450
Janitor George	3	G	3	0	0	0	0
Jankin	6	G	7	0	3	0	2,640
Jannan Jewel	6	M	10	0	1	2	3,565
Janna's Flier	4	G	8	1	0	1	9,948
Janna's Gold	3	F	10	2	4	1	46,835
Jannath	2	F	1	0	0	0	688
Janon	5	M	6	1	1	0	22,400
Jan's Au Lait	3	F	3	0	0	1	1,830
Jan's Bouquet	3	F	3	0	0	0	0
Jans Brother	4	G	4	0	0	0	0
Jans Joy	3	C	3	0	0	0	350
Jan's Texas Boy	5	G	12	1	2	2	13,450
January's Girl	3	F	8	0	1	0	2,529
Janzig	4	G	3	0	0	0	294
Janzig Affair	4	G	13	1	1	2	13,450
Janzig Warrior	4	C	18	2	5	5	24,803
Japanese Whisper (UAE)	3	F	1	1	0	0	5,520
Jar Jar	3	G	4	0	0	0	470
Jaramar Rain	5	M	6	0	0	4	27,030
Jaramillo	2	C	4	0	0	2	3,048
Jarawara (PER)	6	M	3	0	0	0	0
Jared's Atv	3	G	1	0	0	0	75
Jared's Pride	5	G	19	3	2	3	17,749
Jared's Prospect	6	G	7	0	1	0	1,862
Jared's Roadshow	3	G	13	2	0	1	9,260
Jared's Shaddow	5	G	7	0	0	0	0
Jared's Twilight	5	M	7	1	1	3	7,340
Jarett's Devil	4	F	6	1	1	1	11,396
Jarf	8	H	10	1	2	1	44,140
Jarilynbob	2	F	2	0	0	0	0
Jarrett	5	G	11	2	4	1	19,650
Jas Minister	4	F	4	0	0	0	0
Jasarett	3	F	3	0	0	0	60
Jasmine Taj	2	F	4	0	0	1	696
Jasmine's Gem	2	F	3	1	1	1	32,293
Jason's Five K Run	3	G	8	1	1	0	6,737
Jason's Halo	6	G	2	0	0	0	140
Jason's Love	5	G	3	0	0	0	950
Jason's Miracle	6	G	16	2	2	5	39,496
Jasper Park	5	G	5	1	0	0	3,940
Jasper's Secret	3	G	8	1	3	1	8,607
Jatoba	5	G	7	0	2	1	7,090
Jatt	2	F	1	0	1	0	5,300
Java Bar	2	F	1	0	0	0	400
Java Jake	5	G	8	1	0	2	14,331
Java Jasmine	5	M	18	2	1	3	9,906
Java Jolene	2	F	5	2	0	0	23,986
Java Soup	4	G	18	4	1	4	51,280
Java Time	10	G	7	1	0	2	11,921
Java to Go	10	G	1	0	0	0	400
Java Warrior	2	C	6	1	2	1	37,450
Java Wit	5	M	8	1	2	3	28,630
Java's Mate	3	G	7	0	2	2	6,505
Javelina	2	F	2	1	1	0	36,270
Javens Prodigy	4	G	11	0	4	1	13,840
Javier	3	G	5	0	1	0	3,570
Jaw Breaker Babe	3	F	6	1	0	0	5,670
Jaworski	6	G	5	0	0	0	1,602
Jax's Cadillac	6	M	7	1	0	1	1,628
Jay Black	4	G	6	1	1	1	20,557
Jay Bodean	2	C	4	1	0	0	19,335
Jay Charlie D.	2	C	7	0	3	0	8,742
Jay Eye Bee	2	F	1	0	0	0	0
Jay Tee's Gem	4	G	12	1	4	2	23,266
Jayar	4	C	3	0	1	1	15,050
Jaybo	4	C	10	1	1	1	27,585
Jaycat	3	G	9	3	0	1	24,198
Jaycejace	4	G	2	0	0	0	165
Jaygar Dancer	3	G	11	2	3	1	40,383
Jayhawk Janet	4	F	13	3	2	3	64,607
Jayhawker	4	G	4	0	0	0	0
Jaylo J G	4	F	16	1	0	5	11,887
Jaymi the Cat	2	F	12	0	2	2	12,847
Jay's Buddy Bob	5	G	11	0	1	2	15,145
Jay's Holly	4	F	2	0	0	0	114
Jay's Impact	3	F	13	4	1	4	22,460
Jay's Misty City	3	F	9	1	1	0	13,345
Jay's Shawklit	5	M	9	1	4	0	18,335
Jay's Suave	2	C	11	3	2	4	47,190
Jay's Will	3	F	9	2	0	0	59,062
Jay's Wish	4	G	10	2	2	1	91,890
Jayua	4	C	3	0	1	0	3,035
Jayveebee	3	F	2	0	0	0	88
Jazatar	6	M	8	0	2	1	2,585
Jazlyn Slew	5	M	1	0	0	0	0
Jazz Am	2	F	5	0	0	2	3,630
Jazz and Cocktails	3	G	10	1	2	1	14,560
Jazz Beat	5	G	13	0	1	1	7,760
Jazz Bouquet	3	F	6	0	0	1	4,480
Jazz Combo	3	F	8	1	2	2	13,659
Jazz Drive	8	G	2	0	0	0	237
Jazz Jazz Jazz	5	M	2	0	1	0	900
Jazz Legend	3	F	8	3	2	0	88,990
Jazz Music	4	F	12	2	1	1	10,492
Jazz Parade	7	G	2	0	0	0	924
Jazz Society	2	F	2	0	0	0	568
Jazz Styling	8	G	3	0	0	0	204
Jazz' Torrent	2	F	4	0	0	0	1,400
Jazz Ya	4	F	4	1	0	1	39,748
Jazzabell	4	F	12	1	4	2	18,497
Jazzalaya	2	G	1	0	0	0	205
Jazzamatassle	3	F	14	3	3	3	31,026
Jazzaroo	7	G	5	2	0	0	2,062
Jazzbit	5	G	6	2	0	0	10,803
Jazzer Queen	7	M	9	2	1	0	24,370
Jazzie Moon	4	F	3	0	0	1	520
Jazzin Bayou	3	G	12	2	2	0	15,480
Jazzin Julie	5	M	5	1	0	1	2,451
Jazzin With Jazzy	5	M	8	2	0	2	8,349
Jazzinarounnightly	3	G	6	2	0	3	31,366
Jazzing	3	C	5	0	3	1	15,290
Jazzing Jack	5	H	7	0	1	2	5,915
Jazzing Jadie	3	F	5	0	0	2	1,615
Jazzing Northern	3	G	9	1	1	2	2,087
Jazzing Ralph	4	G	1	0	0	0	0
Jazzitupgeorge	3	G	7	2	3	1	35,430
Jazzman (PER)	3	G	4	0	1	0	1,050
Jazzman Brian	9	G	12	0	1	2	2,674
Jazz'n Off	3	F	1	0	0	0	0
Jazznwithcandy	3	F	2	0	0	0	2,500
Jazzring	3	F	12	1	4	3	11,415

Horse	Age	Sex	Sts	1st	2d	3d	Won
Jazzy Al	4	G	16	3	2	1	15,013
Jazzy Artist	3	G	2	0	0	0	1,291
Jazzy Discovery	4	F	1	0	0	0	164
Jazzy Double	4	F	3	0	0	0	0
Jazzy Executive	6	M	2	0	0	0	0
Jazzy Express	3	F	6	1	3	1	15,581
Jazzy Gallop	2	C	8	0	2	2	17,900
Jazzy Gem	3	F	11	3	0	3	25,668
Jazzy J J	2	F	4	1	0	0	52,295
Jazzy Jay	3	G	7	2	1	1	32,560
Jazzy Jet	3	G	2	0	0	0	292
Jazzy Jizzy	5	M	2	0	0	0	0
Jazzy Letters	3	G	13	1	2	2	7,885
Jazzy Mac	9	G	8	0	2	0	5,198
Jazzy Man	3	G	11	1	1	1	4,424
Jazzy Melody	3	F	14	2	1	4	13,246
Jazzy Miss	4	F	4	1	1	0	5,993
Jazzy Place	5	G	11	0	0	1	1,848
Jc's Gold	6	M	1	0	0	0	0
Jd's Lookin Snappy	5	M	18	1	4	4	21,098
Jd's Marmel	4	G	14	2	3	4	26,824
Je Dis Command	2	C	5	1	0	1	14,905
Jealous Lover	6	M	4	0	1	0	3,573
Jean Brady	5	M	9	1	1	1	22,830
Jean de Actress	4	F	12	1	3	1	21,480
Jean N Joan	2	F	2	0	0	0	0
Jean Wayne	5	G	2	0	1	0	500
Jeanie Sue	5	M	5	0	2	0	12,564
Jeanie's Gold	4	F	16	2	2	5	45,333
Jeanies Pistol	5	M	9	0	2	1	4,177
Jeanies Rob	8	H	4	1	0	2	10,960
Jeanne's Honor	2	F	3	0	0	1	6,205
Jeanne's Jet	7	M	12	0	0	0	2,442
Jeanne's Lastdance	3	F	5	0	1	1	3,460
Jeannie Light	8	M	2	0	0	0	0
Jeans Deed	2	G	1	0	0	0	0
Jean's Hat Spray	3	F	7	0	0	0	0
Jean's Lucky One	6	M	11	0	0	1	1,100
Jeans Premier	4	F	10	1	1	2	8,309
Jeblar's Turn	5	H	6	0	0	0	327
Jeblette	6	M	6	0	0	0	780
Jebs Angel	6	M	13	0	4	1	16,444
Jeb's Crowner	5	G	2	0	0	0	0
Jeb's Honor	8	G	8	3	0	0	29,207
Jebs Lil Charmer	3	F	3	0	0	0	272
Jeb's Secret	5	M	12	1	0	2	11,226
Jeb's Song	4	F	9	2	0	2	16,602
Jeb's Strategy	6	G	9	2	2	0	18,329
Jebsroyaldiplomat	2	C	3	0	0	0	0
Jebsstar	5	G	8	2	2	3	23,832
Jebsy	2	F	9	1	1	3	29,960
Jedare	2	F	8	1	0	1	11,070
Jedi Warrior	4	C	4	0	0	0	0
Jeekee	2	F	1	0	0	0	0
Jeep Tour	4	G	1	0	0	0	0
Jeepis Missed	5	G	7	2	1	2	79,466
Jeeter	5	G	14	3	2	2	21,400
Jeet's Devise	5	G	14	3	2	3	15,191
Jeeves	6	G	12	0	1	2	15,538
Jefe	4	G	5	0	0	1	2,685
Jefe de Jefes	4	C	15	3	2	2	36,470
Jefesito	5	G	4	0	1	0	4,396
Jeff John	4	G	4	0	0	0	0
Jefferson K.	3	G	8	1	4	1	11,965
Jeffersons Annie	2	F	1	0	0	0	0
Jeffery	4	C	1	0	0	0	0
Jeffries Bay	3	C	8	4	1	0	93,978
Jeff's Chance	5	G	5	0	0	0	195
Jeff's Woodman	4	G	1	0	0	0	0
Jehosaphat	3	C	7	1	0	3	3,590
Jekyll and Hyde	7	H	6	3	1	0	7,225
Jellaba's Song	6	M	5	0	2	1	4,443
Jelly Baby (GB)	3	F	5	3	0	0	23,237
Jelly Bean Gene	5	G	9	1	0	2	4,450
Jelly Fish	8	M	2	0	0	1	2,780
Jelly Roll Horton	5	G	4	0	0	0	1,200
Jelly Roll Journey	4	F	14	3	1	2	20,448
Jelly Roll Rock	6	H	3	0	0	0	445
Jelly Roll Romp	7	H	9	0	1	0	6,064
Jellybean Jackie	7	M	1	0	0	0	0
Jellyvision	4	C	2	0	0	0	1,411
Jem Finch	3	C	3	0	0	0	485
Jemma	3	F	21	1	1	1	9,778
Jemmotts Lane	4	F	1	0	0	0	220
Jemsek	8	G	4	0	0	1	2,405
Jena's Hope	7	M	1	0	0	0	510
Jenger's Finest	3	F	6	0	2	0	6,965
Jenkim	2	C	1	0	0	0	161
Jenkins' Ferry	4	C	9	1	3	2	21,385
Jenn in the Chase	3	F	6	0	1	2	3,748
Jenna's Devil	3	F	5	2	1	1	24,914
Jenna's Dream News	4	F	3	1	2	0	15,896
Jenna's Promise	5	H	16	4	5	0	47,532
Jenna's Thunder	3	F	1	0	0	0	425
Jennaslilprincess	5	M	19	1	2	6	59,246
Jennaslollipop	4	F	7	0	0	2	1,521
Jennasluvspoppy	2	F	8	0	0	2	8,170
Jennie Jean	3	F	10	1	1	0	7,386
Jennie R.	3	F	5	2	2	0	48,800
Jennies Song	2	F	3	1	2	0	9,790
Jennifer Rose	3	F	6	0	1	0	19,092
Jennifer's Baby	9	G	1	0	0	0	61
Jennifer's Crown	5	M	10	0	0	2	1,514
Jennifers Dance	3	F	9	1	3	2	27,250
Jennifer's Hope	3	F	10	1	0	1	4,964
Jennifers Star	2	F	1	0	0	0	0
Jenn's Girl	3	F	7	0	0	0	1,275
Jenn's Jet	4	F	5	0	0	0	225
Jenny Bean Girl	2	F	3	0	0	0	3,150
Jenny Bet Her Boot	4	F	4	1	1	1	9,700
Jenny Joy	2	F	1	0	1	0	7,400
Jenny Tudor (GB)	2	F	10	2	2	2	31,684
Jennys Badboy	9	G	5	0	0	0	519
Jenny's Diamond	5	M	3	0	0	0	477
Jenny's Gold	6	G	10	6	2	0	35,815
Jenny's Good Girl	2	F	1	1	0	0	13,800
Jenny's Princess	5	M	9	3	0	1	39,423
Jenny's Prospector	4	F	8	1	0	0	27,735
Jenny'sbluecookie	7	G	4	0	0	1	430
Jenora	4	F	2	1	0	0	3,084
Jen's All Aboard	3	G	4	0	0	0	390
Jen's Diamond Girl	7	M	6	1	0	0	4,157
Jen's Secret	5	M	6	0	0	1	715
Jen's Spell	4	F	3	1	0	0	10,560
Jeopardize	4	F	9	0	1	1	5,784
Je'pardo	10	G	2	0	0	0	0
Jepbobjimjude	3	C	4	0	0	0	420
Jer Bear	3	G	6	1	0	1	15,260
Jer Dandy	3	C	1	0	0	0	0
Jeramiah John	3	G	14	1	2	2	15,170
Jerardi	3	C	11	3	1	1	52,350
Jeremiah's Judge	5	G	1	0	0	0	0
Jeremiah's Story	8	G	12	1	1	0	7,332
Jeremy Fleet Feet	4	G	1	0	0	0	0
Jeremys Hero	3	G	4	1	1	0	9,147
Jeremy's Quest	6	M	1	0	0	0	400
Jeri Ruckus	3	G	2	0	0	0	0
Jeri West	2	F	3	0	0	0	0
Jericas Princess	2	F	8	2	0	1	20,095
Jericho Jed	3	G	11	1	1	0	7,159
Jerrad's Desire	7	G	2	0	0	0	82
Jerrannama	5	M	2	0	0	0	105
Jerri Lynn	3	F	13	0	3	2	50,340
Jerry At the Barr	3	F	3	0	0	0	264
Jerry Boy	3	G	7	0	1	0	7,135
Jerry Jeff	5	G	2	0	0	0	0
Jerry Wayne	3	C	6	2	1	0	11,474
Jerry's Final	2	G	3	0	0	0	320
Jerry's Gift	6	M	10	0	0	0	1,375
Jersey Boy	4	C	3	1	0	1	24,480
Jersey Breeze	5	M	3	1	0	0	4,755
Jersey City Sue	3	F	4	0	0	1	1,780
Jersey Gia	3	F	10	3	2	3	115,656
Jersey Giant	5	G	4	0	0	0	13,700
Jersey Jack	6	G	8	0	0	0	1,290
Jersey John	4	G	10	1	2	2	4,878
Jersey Mambo	3	F	2	0	0	1	4,070
Jersey Monster	2	G	4	0	0	0	1,580

Horse	Age	Sex	Sts	1st	2d	3d	Won
Jersey Muscle	4	G	6	0	0	0	1,050
Jersey Peach	2	C	2	1	0	0	28,060
Jersey Storm	5	G	9	2	2	1	48,230
Jersey Tomato	6	M	11	3	4	2	34,852
Jersey Transit	7	G	3	0	0	0	0
Jersey's Cooley	3	G	1	0	0	0	0
Jerseys Finest	3	F	1	0	0	0	460
Jerzee Gal	3	F	2	0	1	0	7,040
Jerzee Heat	2	F	8	0	3	1	38,352
Jerzy Red	5	G	7	0	0	0	150
Jess Do It	4	G	4	1	0	1	3,360
Jessamine Jake	7	G	24	5	5	2	25,716
Jessando	2	C	3	0	0	0	1,775
Jesse Gee	8	G	10	4	2	2	10,980
Jesse Lee	8	G	18	0	1	1	2,255
Jesse Time	4	G	5	1	0	0	2,613
Jesse's Gal	3	F	4	0	0	3	1,953
Jesse's Gift	7	G	5	0	0	0	0
Jesse's Gone West	4	G	4	0	0	0	1,755
Jesses Scandel	8	H	1	0	0	1	1,260
Jesse's Trump	4	G	8	0	0	0	1,862
Jessica	3	F	4	0	0	1	1,874
Jessica Cat	3	F	1	1	0	0	2,400
Jessica Miss	8	M	1	0	0	0	0
Jessica Proud	2	F	2	0	0	0	300
Jessica Slew	4	F	3	0	0	0	252
Jessica's Angel	3	F	5	0	0	1	1,800
Jessica's Best	4	G	12	5	0	2	27,972
Jessica's Pride	4	F	12	1	0	3	12,780
Jessica's Way	4	F	7	0	0	2	3,430
Jessicasbestfriend	3	F	3	0	1	1	6,200
Jessie C.	6	M	5	1	0	0	7,074
Jessie Guest	4	F	13	1	2	1	26,203
Jessie Jones	3	F	2	0	0	0	0
Jessie Rose	6	M	4	0	0	0	627
Jessie Sue	3	F	2	0	0	1	2,260
Jessiebdancing	3	F	4	0	0	1	1,764
Jessie's Chance	3	F	4	0	1	1	7,760
Jessie's Dream	2	F	6	0	0	2	1,701
Jessie's Jewel	5	M	3	0	0	0	177
Jessie's Jig	7	G	9	1	2	0	7,034
Jessie's Joy	3	F	10	0	4	0	15,260
Jessie's Prayer	4	F	12	0	3	3	8,242
Jess'll Do	3	F	5	0	0	0	526
Jesstiflyer	2	F	1	0	0	0	0
Jest a Bag	7	G	8	0	0	1	997
Jest a Buzz	3	F	2	0	0	1	806
Jest a Zeal	3	F	14	2	1	0	24,029
Jest Unreal	3	F	12	2	1	1	25,616
Jestakick	9	G	12	1	1	1	7,294
Jestalover	5	M	1	0	0	0	110
Jester	6	M	12	0	1	3	26,564
Jester Flying	3	G	5	0	0	1	2,717
Jester Rahab	5	M	9	2	2	1	93,170
Jester's Pet	6	G	2	0	0	0	80
Jesters Reply	3	G	8	1	1	1	5,352
Jestics Favorite	3	F	3	0	1	0	1,652
Jestin in Control	7	G	6	0	0	0	345
Jestina	5	M	8	2	2	1	3,835
Jesty	3	F	8	1	2	1	15,240
Jet Alert	4	C	2	0	0	0	1,436
Jet Away	6	G	5	0	0	0	461
Jet Black Cadi	4	G	14	2	0	2	56,478
Jet Black Jack	3	G	14	3	0	1	20,158
Jet Black Magic	3	F	9	0	2	3	11,849
Jet Car	4	F	4	0	1	1	6,160
Jet City Woman	4	F	12	1	0	4	10,393
Jet Drive	6	H	7	2	1	1	11,728
Jet Engine	2	F	5	0	0	2	4,262
Jet Fighter	4	G	11	0	5	3	9,112
Jet G Pride	5	M	9	1	2	4	26,890
Jet G Star	3	C	19	1	3	4	15,882
Jet G Sun	3	G	10	0	0	1	1,537
Jet It Out Sissy	3	F	2	0	0	0	177
Jet La Rail	7	G	1	0	0	0	0
Jet Legacy	5	G	15	1	0	5	11,371
Jet Line	8	M	6	2	1	0	16,960
Jet Love	4	G	3	1	0	0	8,850
Jet n' Expectation	4	F	11	2	4	1	24,420
Jet Pass	4	G	15	2	1	1	21,787
Jet Phone	3	C	3	0	0	0	1,560
Jet Prospector	3	G	7	3	2	0	94,737
Jet Quest	6	G	3	0	0	0	0
Jet Set Bride	2	F	6	0	1	0	1,610
Jet Set Jazz	5	M	7	1	1	1	14,525
Jet Set Joan	2	F	2	0	0	0	430
Jet Set Joey G	4	G	2	0	0	0	225
Jet Set Johnny	2	G	1	0	0	0	1,560
Jet Set Vet	5	G	4	1	0	1	7,285
Jet Setting T	3	F	2	0	0	0	330
Jet Ski	9	G	13	2	2	2	8,865
Jet Support	3	F	4	0	0	0	748
Jet to Rome	3	F	3	0	0	0	154
Jet Wash	2	G	4	1	1	1	32,708
Jet West	3	C	4	2	1	1	71,993
Jet Zone	2	F	6	2	0	0	10,500
Jetabud	5	G	14	2	0	2	10,840
Jetalito	5	G	7	1	0	1	8,870
Jethro's Fling	7	G	4	1	0	0	4,350
Jetico	3	C	4	0	0	1	2,230
Jetinto Houston	5	M	7	1	1	0	73,464
Jetmeg	3	F	5	0	0	0	2,598
Jet'n Jeanie	3	F	7	1	0	0	6,580
Jetrocket	2	C	1	0	0	0	0
Jet's Account	5	M	10	0	1	0	1,331
Jet's Bonus	3	F	10	2	2	2	30,065
Jets Fan	4	G	6	2	0	0	61,655
Jet's Historic	3	F	1	0	0	0	0
Jet's Role	2	C	2	0	0	0	323
Jet's Victory	2	F	2	0	0	1	2,800
Jetson	5	G	15	2	0	1	26,000
Jetster	3	F	7	1	1	0	17,220
Jett Stream	6	G	5	0	2	0	1,260
Jetta Way Groom	2	C	10	1	2	1	17,745
Jettalyn	6	M	8	0	0	1	6,681
Jettapower	6	G	3	0	0	0	127
Jetta's Golden Boy	5	H	10	4	2	2	34,187
Jettias	8	G	7	0	0	1	480
Jetticus	3	C	5	1	0	0	16,061
Jettin Bear	4	C	4	0	0	1	1,360
Jettin Cat	2	G	6	1	0	0	4,060
Jettin Fever	3	F	9	0	1	0	1,599
Jettin High	2	C	2	1	0	0	9,465
Jettin in the Sand	2	C	1	0	0	0	105
Jettin Suzy	3	F	6	0	1	1	1,553
Jettin to Heaven	3	G	1	0	0	0	400
Jettin Tyler	2	C	2	0	0	0	369
Jettin'for Roobels	4	F	4	0	0	0	553
Jever Gal	3	F	7	2	0	1	8,512
Jewel Alarm	5	M	20	3	4	2	28,745
Jewel Beauty	4	C	3	0	0	1	797
Jewel Case	5	M	2	0	0	0	122
Jewel Creek	4	F	6	1	0	1	4,585
Jewel Hunter	3	F	8	0	1	0	1,950
Jewel in Town	3	C	7	0	0	0	0
Jewel of a Gal	3	F	3	0	0	0	223
Jewel of Asia	6	M	9	1	1	0	5,996
Jewel of Nahuel	5	M	4	1	0	0	770
Jewel of the Cat	3	F	7	0	0	0	640
Jewel of the Night	2	F	2	0	0	0	800
Jewel of the Sky	3	F	2	1	0	0	11,412
Jewel of the Year	3	F	7	3	3	1	97,028
Jewel Queen	3	F	9	1	1	1	21,704
Jewel Stick	9	M	8	0	0	0	360
Jewel Thief Jimmy	7	G	10	0	1	1	5,288
Jewelette	3	F	12	1	2	3	9,569
Jewelite	4	G	10	0	3	1	4,813
Jewell Dare	2	F	1	0	0	0	0
Jewell's Eleven	2	F	2	0	1	1	5,090
Jewelofthecrypt	3	F	12	1	1	2	8,081
Jewels Again	5	M	9	5	0	4	30,347
Jewel's Dream	4	F	13	3	0	1	21,849
Jewels for a Lady	4	F	3	1	2	0	16,772
Jewel's Haven	6	M	3	0	0	0	616
Jewel's Melody	3	F	1	1	0	0	4,620
Jewels Rocket	4	G	12	2	2	2	25,536
Jewels Royal	2	F	3	0	0	0	0
Jezabel Cant Spell	6	M	14	2	2	2	15,663

Horse	Age	Sex	Sts	1st	2d	3d	Won
Jezabel's Magic	10	M	6	0	0	0	508
Jhecho	5	G	1	0	1	0	1,160
Jiba	3	G	1	0	0	0	0
Jibarita	3	F	8	1	4	0	18,555
Jibber Jabber	3	F	18	2	3	6	30,098
Jiffy Native	3	G	17	2	2	4	33,598
Jiffy Wish	7	M	8	0	2	2	11,300
Jiffyjimmygee	4	G	5	1	1	1	22,501
Jiggee Jade	2	F	3	1	0	0	4,550
Jiggs	3	G	10	0	2	1	4,294
Jiggy Man	6	G	21	1	0	3	13,753
Jigsaw	3	G	6	0	0	0	1,333
Jila (IRE)	9	H	9	3	1	3	25,050
Jill of Slades	3	F	8	0	0	0	1,350
Jill Rabbit	5	M	16	1	3	3	28,610
Jill Regs Winner	4	F	5	0	1	2	5,666
Jill Robin L	2	F	8	1	2	0	49,500
Jill the Shill	4	F	1	0	0	0	0
Jillian Grey	4	F	1	0	0	0	294
Jilliansscoundrel	3	F	4	0	0	0	0
Jills Accent	3	F	4	0	0	0	450
Jill's Cat	2	F	7	1	2	1	26,165
Jills Classy	2	F	3	1	1	0	18,339
Jill's Ego	4	F	12	0	2	1	11,271
Jill's Joy	3	F	5	0	0	0	0
Jill's Jumpshot	5	H	13	1	2	0	8,146
Jill's Last Hero	6	M	1	0	0	0	0
Jill's My Doll	3	F	14	1	1	1	9,750
Jill's Pot of Gold	3	G	12	0	0	2	4,377
Jill's Sky	2	F	1	0	0	0	2,580
Jilluke	2	C	1	0	0	0	55
Jilly Billie	4	F	9	0	3	1	1,094
Jiltaluck	5	G	4	0	0	1	811
Jilted Heart	3	C	3	1	0	0	10,415
Jilted Lass	4	F	1	0	0	0	265
Jilted Love	5	M	12	1	1	1	13,717
Jim Abel	3	G	16	3	1	5	23,083
Jim Cat	6	H	2	1	0	0	2,520
Jim the Gent	3	G	13	1	0	5	13,730
Jim Thirds Bolero	5	G	6	2	1	2	48,980
Jimbo Don	7	G	6	1	2	0	8,214
Jimbo's King	2	G	3	0	0	0	880
Jimenez	4	G	9	2	0	1	10,876
Jimie Son	7	H	8	1	2	1	13,799
Jimini C. Dues	13	G	10	0	1	0	2,930
Jimmeys Gone	3	C	8	0	0	1	1,266
Jimmie J	5	H	5	0	1	0	7,696
Jimmielee	5	G	11	0	1	0	6,170
Jimmies Pleasures	6	G	4	0	0	0	365
Jimmy Bond	3	G	3	0	0	0	2,450
Jimmy Cracked Corn	3	G	9	3	2	3	91,595
Jimmy Dimi	3	F	12	0	0	3	4,859
Jimmy Dunne's Boy	3	G	9	1	0	2	14,095
Jimmy Dunnes World	5	G	3	0	0	0	770
Jimmy Easter	5	G	13	2	0	4	63,383
Jimmy Jingles	3	C	10	1	0	0	6,571
Jimmy Jones	7	G	14	8	2	0	59,253
Jimmy Lapa	5	H	4	0	0	1	692
Jimmy Mack	3	G	14	3	2	1	14,826
Jimmy Moon	3	C	4	0	2	2	13,485
Jimmy O	4	G	7	1	1	0	24,554
Jimmy of Paraqua	3	C	9	0	0	0	985
Jimmy One Punch	3	G	3	1	1	1	13,580
Jimmy the Dreamer	2	G	5	0	0	0	10,020
Jimmy the Hat	2	C	5	0	0	0	3,480
Jimmy the K	2	C	5	1	0	0	13,321
Jimmy Z	7	G	5	0	0	1	3,430
Jimmyboy	5	G	3	0	0	0	923
Jimmy's Account	4	G	11	1	1	1	4,166
Jimmy's Appeal	5	M	14	1	2	1	6,638
Jimmy's Best	6	G	10	1	1	2	6,327
Jimmy's Boy	4	C	10	4	2	0	76,626
Jimmy's Instinct	3	G	9	3	0	1	120,326
Jimmy's Memory	4	G	8	0	0	2	1,362
Jimmy's Move	4	F	5	0	0	0	388
Jimmy's Pennybank	4	F	5	0	0	0	552
Jimmy's Prize	6	G	4	0	1	0	8,890
Jimmy's Saber	4	G	12	1	1	1	22,690
Jim's Account	12	G	8	0	1	2	2,540
Jim's Basque	4	G	11	1	0	1	27,590
Jim's Conquista	4	F	4	0	0	0	558
Jim's Drive	4	C	3	0	0	0	1,560
Jim's Giuseppe	2	F	1	0	0	0	1,110
Jim's Golden Crown	2	C	1	0	0	0	70
Jims Lil Lady	3	F	1	0	1	0	4,050
Jim's Lisa Nor	7	M	9	0	0	3	3,037
Jim's Pal	3	G	13	1	1	2	16,982
Jim's Prize	2	C	2	0	0	0	0
Jim's Relaunch	7	G	11	1	5	3	19,543
Jim's Remember Me	6	G	7	0	0	0	520
Jim's Rusty Gem	4	G	6	1	2	2	20,125
Jim's Smokin Pinot	2	C	3	0	2	0	19,650
Jim's Super Bonus	3	G	18	1	2	1	6,921
Jimsjessy	3	F	4	0	0	0	0
Jingle Bells	2	C	1	0	0	0	250
Jinglejanglejingle	2	F	3	0	0	2	1,575
Jinglethatbell	4	G	3	0	0	1	282
Jini's Jet	6	G	14	3	2	5	95,150
Jink	4	G	15	2	2	0	34,430
Jink Williams	4	G	7	2	1	0	16,860
Jinks Gold	9	G	5	0	0	0	239
Jinny's Gold	3	F	9	2	1	3	155,744
Jinx's Boy	3	G	5	0	0	0	276
Jipapibaquigrafo	4	C	2	0	2	0	23,200
Jiroga Lite	5	M	8	1	1	1	21,500
Jiroga Winds	3	G	13	2	1	3	7,844
Jit	5	G	6	0	0	0	630
Jitter	4	G	7	2	1	0	20,480
Jitterbug	4	G	3	1	1	1	2,700
Jitterbug Jake	3	G	6	1	0	1	8,305
Jitterbug Jan	5	M	7	1	1	0	11,975
Jitterbug Joy	3	F	10	3	2	3	36,733
Jive At Five	6	G	7	0	1	0	4,425
Jive Cat	3	F	3	0	0	0	255
Jj's Greypinstripe	7	H	3	1	0	1	10,750
Jj's Smokin City	3	G	5	0	0	0	0
Jk's Dreamer	3	F	6	1	0	0	6,738
Jlynnwhiz	2	F	3	0	0	0	172
Jm Mexicanhatdance	3	F	3	0	0	0	0
Jm She's a Tee's	3	F	1	0	1	0	2,210
Jo Anna's Book	3	F	6	0	0	2	8,640
Jo Be Fantastic	3	F	3	0	0	1	2,520
Jo Cosmo	2	C	4	0	2	0	4,410
Jo de Lune	8	M	2	0	0	0	474
Jo Dee Who	3	C	6	2	3	1	36,001
Jo Jo	3	F	7	0	0	2	2,343
Jo Jo Dancer	5	H	9	0	1	3	20,750
Jo Jo Gun	2	C	2	1	0	0	9,600
Jo Jo Peaches	4	F	6	3	1	2	17,100
Jo Jo's Boy	6	G	9	0	0	1	2,290
Jo Jo's Time	3	C	8	2	0	1	11,560
Jo Leather	2	F	2	0	0	1	2,601
Jo Me the Money	4	F	13	3	1	2	57,400
Jo Moe	3	F	10	1	3	1	20,410
Jo Nitro	3	C	5	0	2	0	1,145
Jo Right Side	3	G	7	1	0	0	3,159
Jo Seppe	3	F	1	0	0	0	0
Jo the Boss	4	F	10	2	0	0	12,444
Jo Z D	6	M	2	0	0	0	153
Joa	5	G	10	2	2	3	33,580
Joan	4	F	8	2	1	0	9,805
Joan and Mary	3	F	11	2	1	2	19,100
Joan Joan Joan	3	F	11	1	0	3	15,669
Joanair	4	F	9	0	1	2	2,270
Joanie B Good	4	F	6	0	0	1	1,434
Joanie B.	5	M	15	1	1	0	8,960
Joanie's Hero	5	M	13	0	1	1	5,678
Joanie's Hit	3	F	10	1	3	0	8,892
Joanie's Jett	6	M	9	0	0	5	10,946
Joanies No Phony	7	G	14	3	0	1	21,878
Joanie's Smile	4	F	5	1	1	1	19,400
Joann Jr	3	F	14	7	0	1	100,000
Joanna's Tuition	5	M	9	1	1	0	6,690
Joanne Lacy	5	M	11	1	1	1	10,696
Joannesprincesscat	5	M	2	0	0	0	144
Joanns Downtown	2	F	4	0	1	1	4,338
Joann's Joy	5	M	12	3	1	1	37,283
Joans Charm	5	M	13	1	0	2	4,690

Horse	Age	Sex	Sts	1st	2d	3d	Won
Joan's Gray Beauty	4	F	7	0	1	1	7,940
Joans Rhetoric	2	F	1	0	0	0	450
Jocasta	3	F	8	0	1	0	6,397
Jocelyn Hollow	3	G	13	0	0	1	3,091
Jockey No Boy	3	C	12	4	1	1	28,994
Jockey's Dream (BRZ)	5	H	2	0	1	1	19,200
Jockeys Limo	5	G	8	0	0	0	659
Jocy's Coyote	6	M	2	0	0	0	150
Jodawn	6	G	3	0	0	0	376
Jodi H	4	F	4	0	0	1	1,021
Jodilynnkey	3	F	2	1	0	0	10,080
Jodi's Wings	6	M	14	1	3	2	31,640
Jody Jet	3	F	6	0	0	0	295
Jodydale	3	F	1	1	0	0	10,800
Jodys Deelite	4	F	1	0	0	0	3,600
Joe At Six	8	G	5	1	2	0	41,800
Joe Can't Quit	5	G	3	0	0	0	0
Joe Cat	5	H	10	0	1	2	8,289
Joe Dancer Too	4	G	10	4	1	1	15,336
Joe Domino	2	G	3	0	1	0	4,080
Joe Fraser	4	C	5	0	0	0	0
Joe G.	2	C	4	0	0	0	315
Joe Holiday	6	G	1	0	0	0	0
Joe Holster	8	G	13	2	0	2	6,264
Joe Java	6	G	13	1	0	1	6,597
Joe Kellys Tune	5	G	2	0	0	0	280
Joe Move	4	C	8	1	2	1	30,780
Joe N Judge	8	H	3	0	0	0	0
Joe On the Aisle	2	G	5	2	0	0	19,060
Joe Pag	4	C	11	3	2	0	45,313
Joe Pat	5	G	9	1	1	2	11,258
Joe Perfect	2	G	2	0	0	0	75
Joe Six Pack	3	G	4	0	0	1	19,890
Joe Snell	5	G	5	0	0	1	1,254
Joe T Bailey	6	G	12	1	3	2	10,804
Joe Tourist	4	G	1	0	0	0	0
Joe Two Lips	7	H	14	1	3	0	31,123
Joe W.	2	C	1	0	0	0	900
Joe What	4	G	9	2	3	0	25,450
Joeaustin	3	G	4	0	0	0	168
Joecephus	2	C	2	0	2	0	8,200
Joecollegehavinfun	2	C	1	0	0	0	105
Joel's Delight	3	G	3	0	0	1	6,270
Joeronohmoe	4	F	6	1	1	1	10,818
Joes Bad Girl Ed	6	M	1	0	0	0	61
Joe's Big Boy	5	G	11	0	0	1	1,240
Joe's Boy Adam	6	G	3	0	1	0	4,260
Joes Charmer	3	G	9	1	3	1	9,418
Joe's Command	4	G	14	3	1	1	38,175
Joe's Crown Chip	4	C	1	0	0	0	0
Joe's Josy	2	F	6	1	1	1	20,985
Joes Lover	2	F	4	0	0	0	1,500
Joes Lucky Girl	4	F	4	0	1	1	4,956
Joes Lucky Nail	5	M	4	0	0	0	61
Joe's My Faja	2	F	7	0	1	1	4,475
Joes Native Star	7	H	8	1	2	2	2,079
Joe's Sara	2	F	8	1	2	1	8,545
Joe's Son Joey	6	H	1	1	0	0	22,800
Joe's Tribute	4	C	1	0	0	0	0
Joes Wicked Aly	7	G	4	0	0	0	0
Joe'sdancing Angel	3	G	13	2	0	2	21,727
Joesfullofit	2	C	6	0	2	0	5,175
Joethehorse	3	G	3	0	0	1	1,725
Joetta	4	F	8	1	0	1	4,435
Joey Blueeyes	4	G	12	1	2	2	44,447
Joey Bota Bing	4	G	8	2	1	0	13,076
Joey Boy	3	G	8	1	0	0	8,053
Joey G	3	G	21	1	1	0	10,917
Joey P.	2	G	2	2	0	0	57,240
Joey Two Miles	2	F	1	0	0	0	400
Joey's Cat	2	C	12	1	1	2	17,485
Joeys Great Esteem	5	H	3	0	0	0	0
Joey's L	3	G	2	1	0	0	11,300
Joey's Law	8	G	10	0	3	1	9,087
Jogalongsong	3	C	2	0	0	0	416
Joggy Told	6	H	14	0	0	3	1,714
Jogo Antigo (BRZ)	7	G	14	1	0	0	3,508
John	9	G	5	0	0	1	735
John Alan	6	G	3	0	0	0	920
John and Niko	4	G	8	2	1	2	22,500
John Bobby	5	G	4	0	0	1	700
John Brown	3	C	4	0	0	0	350
John Calvin	4	G	19	1	3	5	28,890
John Coffee	3	G	15	2	3	3	44,285
John Crainer	5	G	9	1	0	0	6,860
John David	3	C	22	2	2	5	30,020
John Glen	4	G	10	1	0	1	5,834
John Grove	4	G	7	2	0	0	35,427
John Little	6	G	13	1	2	1	37,248
John Morgan	4	G	14	2	0	1	27,374
John N Tom	6	G	1	0	0	0	300
John Paul	7	G	11	0	1	2	6,892
John Paul Too	7	H	4	0	1	0	5,960
John R	4	G	4	0	0	0	2,400
John Ross	7	G	5	1	0	1	2,926
John the Broker	7	G	9	4	1	3	28,114
John the Diceman	3	G	16	2	1	2	19,405
John the Farrier	2	G	3	0	1	1	3,804
John the Mail Man	3	G	3	1	1	0	16,000
John Thomas	5	G	3	0	0	0	192
John Who	3	G	6	1	0	2	2,670
John William	3	C	11	0	3	0	7,985
Johnathan	4	G	8	3	1	1	69,159
Johnato	4	G	13	3	0	5	45,177
Johnduffswood	5	G	14	0	0	3	3,050
Johnnie Five O	3	G	8	2	0	0	11,293
Johnnie On the Run	4	G	12	3	4	1	44,618
Johnnie Thirty	5	M	1	0	0	0	0
Johnnie Thirty Six	5	M	8	0	3	2	23,903
Johnnie Thirtyfive	5	H	5	0	1	1	9,200
Johnnie's Crowner	5	G	10	1	1	2	5,783
Johnnies Wagon	6	G	9	6	0	0	26,275
Johnniethirtythree	5	H	1	0	0	0	0
Johnny	8	G	1	0	0	0	0
Johnny Acres	2	C	2	0	0	0	3,570
Johnny Avenger	5	H	7	1	0	1	2,919
Johnny Bought Me	3	C	5	0	0	0	2,700
Johnny Box	4	C	2	1	0	0	26,910
Johnny Boy	3	G	17	2	4	1	35,701
Johnny Bright	7	G	9	1	4	0	10,266
Johnny Cake Road	4	G	9	0	0	0	139
Johnny Corvette	4	G	4	1	1	1	25,280
Johnny Fitz	4	G	4	0	0	0	1,684
Johnny High Brite	2	G	4	1	1	1	45,362
Johnny Hollywood	5	G	8	0	3	2	43,536
Johnny Ice	2	G	1	0	0	0	2,100
Johnny Law	5	G	10	0	0	1	1,504
Johnny Loves Jazz	4	G	6	0	0	0	1,875
Johnny Mac	3	G	3	0	0	0	225
Johnny Magic	4	C	12	0	4	2	68,464
Johnny McArthy	2	C	1	0	0	0	300
Johnny Ola	4	G	5	1	1	0	24,608
Johnny One Note	6	G	7	2	0	1	16,285
Johnny One Sock	4	G	15	2	1	2	19,810
Johnny Q	3	G	2	0	1	0	2,185
Johnny Red Kerr	4	C	4	0	1	2	23,940
Johnny Show	7	G	9	1	0	2	16,678
Johnny too Good	3	G	7	1	0	2	5,267
Johnny Tornado	3	G	9	0	0	1	7,419
Johnny Turk Band	6	M	3	0	0	0	960
Johnny Two Fingers	5	G	8	3	2	2	33,086
Johnnycake	3	G	3	0	0	0	0
Johnnynmotion	7	G	9	0	1	0	3,471
Johnnyou	3	G	11	1	3	3	22,892
Johnny's Cache	4	G	13	3	1	1	23,923
Johnny's Chance	4	F	19	0	0	2	6,290
Johnny's Lil Girl	4	F	6	1	0	3	11,137
Johnny's Nickle	7	M	9	0	0	1	1,459
John's Castle	6	H	4	0	0	0	340
Johns Cowboy	5	G	5	0	1	0	1,148
John's Dixie Chic	2	F	1	0	0	0	0
John's Ensign	4	G	10	0	0	0	785
Johns Hot Water	5	H	10	3	1	2	26,002
John's Interview	3	C	12	2	3	1	94,299
John's Jet	4	C	7	1	0	1	33,802
John's Joker	2	C	6	0	0	2	8,103
John's Joy	4	G	9	1	0	1	35,390
John's Kinda Girl	3	F	8	1	1	2	69,313

Horse	Age	Sex	Sts	1st	2d	3d	Won
John's Magic	2	F	3	1	1	0	3,877
John's Marq	5	G	7	0	0	0	2,745
John's Mecke	3	C	8	2	1	1	45,220
Johns Order	6	G	7	0	0	0	460
Johns Place	2	F	3	2	0	1	34,160
John's Prince	4	C	3	0	0	0	0
John's Proof	5	G	8	0	1	1	1,677
John's Rockfleet	8	G	7	0	0	0	600
John's Royal Treat	6	G	12	1	1	0	4,552
Johns Rush	4	G	6	2	1	1	32,580
Johns Tofasttopass	4	G	6	2	1	1	22,140
John's Wise	6	G	8	3	0	0	58,206
John'sbirthdaygirl	6	M	8	2	0	1	17,228
Johnthegoodhusband	5	G	2	0	0	0	0
Join the Crusade	2	F	6	1	2	2	30,000
Joint Custody	5	G	2	0	1	0	2,580
Joint Decision	7	G	9	3	1	1	14,358
Jointed Glances	4	C	3	0	0	1	1,045
Jojo Dadogfacedboy	3	G	9	2	0	2	27,458
Jojo Marie	3	F	11	1	6	0	44,770
Jojo's Reality	4	C	1	0	0	0	105
Jojo's Sword	3	C	22	0	0	0	480
Jojustice	7	G	10	1	4	1	4,477
Jokeisover	5	M	22	4	3	4	25,606
Joker's Big Gun	5	G	5	2	0	1	2,677
Jokers Wild Card	2	G	3	0	0	0	3,382
Jokesonme	8	M	2	0	0	0	239
Joking Around	5	G	25	0	1	1	9,528
Jok'n Victory	4	F	6	0	0	0	913
Jol	4	G	10	0	1	1	8,096
Jolaris	4	F	4	1	0	0	3,780
Jolene's Turn	4	F	12	1	2	2	13,385
Jolie	5	M	8	0	4	1	14,699
Jolie Ben Fabie	3	G	11	1	2	1	81,100
Jolie Good	4	F	16	5	3	1	42,588
Jolie Jet	5	M	6	0	0	0	220
Jolie Louise	3	F	7	1	1	2	24,700
Jolie Miss Jolie	4	F	1	0	0	0	68
Jolie Rafaela (BRZ)	5	M	4	0	2	1	29,520
Jolie Raja	6	G	1	1	0	0	6,380
Jolie Sunrise	2	F	1	0	0	0	0
Jolie's Gift	3	G	12	5	3	0	32,750
Jolie's Hunter	2	C	1	0	0	0	0
Jolie's Leader	4	F	10	0	1	4	10,912
Jolie's Reward	4	F	8	1	2	0	6,811
Jolie's Thunder	6	G	12	2	2	3	26,235
Jolies Tom Cat	2	G	4	1	1	0	16,080
Jolie's Victory	3	G	4	1	0	0	6,750
Jollie Prince	5	G	5	1	0	0	10,320
Jollies Fortune	3	G	4	0	0	0	480
Jollie's Gold Wand	4	F	1	0	0	0	0
Jolly D	4	G	12	1	0	0	4,595
Jolly Friar	4	G	3	0	0	0	488
Jolly Good Fellow	5	G	14	1	1	1	4,903
Jolly Lady	5	M	6	0	1	1	6,005
Jolly Ol' Nick	3	G	13	1	4	5	12,137
Jolly Sammy	9	G	6	1	0	0	4,473
Jolly Wally	3	C	8	0	0	0	240
Jolly's Music	5	M	10	1	5	1	19,998
Joltin Joe	5	G	9	0	0	1	1,750
Joltin Vince	4	G	2	0	1	0	2,637
Joma	3	C	9	0	0	2	11,310
Jomarkel	2	F	3	0	1	0	8,169
Jomarsmutchkin	4	G	8	0	0	4	1,384
Jon Ali	3	G	9	2	2	3	13,904
Jon Boy	5	G	3	0	0	0	0
Jon Caymen	4	G	2	0	0	0	37
Jon Michael	8	G	15	0	1	0	2,525
Jonah	4	G	12	1	1	0	9,690
Jonah Magic	3	G	7	2	1	0	18,637
Jonathan Quick	2	C	2	0	0	0	1,650
Jonathons Gal	5	M	6	0	0	0	1,260
Jonequest	3	G	1	0	0	0	0
Jones Arena	2	G	1	0	0	0	0
Jones Reserve	7	G	15	2	2	3	25,325
Jones Tale	4	C	4	0	2	2	28,760
Jonesboro	2	C	5	0	2	1	23,325
Joni's Rose	4	F	9	0	1	2	21,296
Jonker	11	G	13	2	1	2	12,458
Jonnygetachex	3	C	8	3	1	3	135,773
Jono's Gone Fish'n	2	G	5	0	0	0	4,050
Jonquiere	5	G	6	1	0	1	10,342
Jonquil's Hope	4	F	7	1	1	0	6,229
Jon's Raindrop	6	G	2	0	0	0	0
Jonsdremingagain	5	G	13	1	1	1	5,525
Jonsey Rabbit	2	G	2	1	0	0	16,560
Jonstar (NZ)	6	G	5	1	1	2	27,460
Joopy Doopy	7	G	4	0	0	1	1,410
Jordan Creek	2	G	3	0	2	0	8,512
Jordana	4	F	5	1	0	1	6,680
Jordan's Big Rig	5	G	15	4	1	3	22,902
Jordan's Double	4	F	1	0	0	0	0
Jordan's Party	4	G	6	0	0	2	2,828
Jordan's Tractor	4	C	9	2	1	0	16,680
Jordi Moi	6	G	11	1	3	2	18,730
Jordin Foo Da Ya	6	M	5	0	0	0	930
Jordo	3	F	4	1	0	0	4,800
Jordy B	5	M	13	2	0	0	11,885
Jordyn Macoma	5	M	3	2	1	0	67,400
Jordyns Justice	4	F	2	0	0	0	960
Jordy's Pride	3	G	9	0	1	1	3,010
Jorgie Stover	6	G	6	1	1	0	64,000
Jorja's Suite	4	F	4	1	0	0	2,869
Joronimo's Smoke	4	C	1	0	0	0	0
Jo's Bro	3	G	7	0	3	1	8,300
Jo's Dancing Boy	4	G	8	2	0	2	10,372
Jo's Dancing Girl	4	F	9	1	0	0	5,266
Jo's Dream Beam	3	G	2	0	0	0	230
Jo's Eddie	6	G	10	2	3	1	20,294
Jo's Gold	2	F	4	0	0	0	460
Jo's Prospector	8	G	7	2	1	1	7,579
Jo's Sunshine	2	F	2	1	0	1	28,700
Jose	3	C	4	1	0	1	31,040
Jose Can You See	5	G	12	1	1	2	9,412
Jose Gaspar	5	H	1	1	0	0	10,960
Josefa Star (ARG)	4	F	8	0	1	2	13,208
Josefina Verde	4	F	8	0	0	1	1,715
Joseph Anthony	4	G	11	1	0	3	11,112
Joseph B	5	G	17	0	0	1	5,265
Joseph George	7	G	9	1	3	2	3,190
Joseph G's Gal	4	F	10	0	0	0	903
Josephine's Peak	4	F	7	0	3	1	8,323
Joseph's Aarival	4	G	13	0	3	4	17,740
Joses Wild Event	3	F	1	0	0	0	0
Josey Hawk	5	G	1	0	0	0	76
Josey Hill	5	F	3	0	0	0	0
Josey's Trick	6	G	14	2	1	3	10,490
Josh Daniel	3	C	3	0	0	0	315
Josh On a Roll	6	H	5	0	0	0	1,425
Joshledo	3	G	8	1	0	0	5,046
Josh's Apple	7	G	3	0	1	0	7,560
Josh's Lady	3	F	6	0	0	2	2,655
Josh's Madelyn	3	F	9	6	1	0	245,172
Josh's Prince	2	C	3	0	0	0	0
Joshua Jude	3	G	16	4	4	1	52,665
Joshua Lightheart	3	G	14	3	1	2	59,475
Joshua Storm	4	G	3	0	0	0	378
Joshua's Jaybird	5	G	17	2	1	3	15,582
Joshua's Jet	6	G	9	2	0	2	70,626
Joshuas Symphony	4	G	17	0	0	0	2,030
Josie Bells	3	F	6	1	0	0	5,070
Josie G.	3	F	8	1	2	0	60,500
Josie's Diamond	2	F	2	0	0	0	257
Josie's Luckycharm	6	M	7	0	0	0	0
Josie's Peak	4	F	15	1	4	4	14,262
Josie'scountrygirl	2	F	8	1	2	0	13,529
Josie'slil'actress	4	F	23	0	0	0	2,181
Jostlin Kate	5	M	3	0	0	0	0
Josy Girl	2	F	1	0	0	0	0
Jour de Chance	3	G	4	0	1	0	5,370
Journal Star	3	F	6	1	2	0	10,800
Journey	5	G	7	2	0	1	7,006
Journey Fever	3	F	5	0	0	0	26,571
Journeys Quest	3	G	2	0	0	0	800
Joursanvault (FR)	3	C	10	1	2	0	85,693
Joust	4	G	8	1	2	0	10,810
Joven	3	G	9	1	0	1	10,560
Joveona	3	F	12	0	2	3	5,550

Horse	Age	Sex	Sts	1st	2d	3d	Won
Jovi Slew	3	C	5	2	0	0	4,668
Jovial Belle	4	F	13	1	0	1	5,038
Jovial Forecast	8	G	7	2	0	1	12,772
Jovial Groom	5	G	13	2	1	2	9,890
Jovial Jem	3	F	11	2	2	2	14,374
Jovial Joshua	3	G	6	2	0	0	10,372
Jovial Lady	5	M	7	2	1	0	24,760
Jovial Pro	3	G	5	0	0	1	1,748
Jovially	3	F	10	1	1	1	34,360
Jovialness	4	F	10	0	0	1	14,020
Jovite	2	F	1	0	0	0	0
Jovite's Angel	3	F	7	0	1	0	2,000
Joxer	5	G	7	0	0	1	2,490
Joy Before Dawn	2	F	1	0	0	0	0
Joy Dayjur	3	F	3	0	0	0	0
Joy Knight	4	F	4	0	0	0	225
Joy N Spirit	5	M	5	1	1	0	7,442
Joy of Brandy	6	M	5	2	0	2	13,416
Joy of It All	4	F	1	0	0	0	900
Joy of Life	3	F	6	0	0	1	2,572
Joy of the Game	3	F	3	2	0	1	16,155
Joya	4	F	9	0	0	0	1,494
Joya de Saros	8	G	1	0	0	0	0
Joybelle	4	F	8	2	1	3	39,530
Joyce Ann	5	M	12	2	2	1	60,120
Joyce's Top	4	F	7	1	0	0	5,720
Joyeux Niner	4	G	1	0	0	0	192
Joyeux Occasion	4	G	5	0	1	1	2,028
Joyeux Ruler	2	F	2	0	1	0	4,932
Joyful Ballad	4	F	9	2	0	4	56,410
Joyful Chaos	3	F	9	1	2	2	55,478
Joyful Encounter	3	F	1	0	0	0	0
Joyful Flyer	2	G	2	0	0	1	2,302
Joyful Jackie	2	F	4	0	0	0	3,260
Joyful Kay	3	F	5	0	0	0	912
Joyful Summer	4	F	7	1	0	0	20,070
Joyful Time	2	F	2	0	1	0	5,850
Joyful Tune	6	G	6	2	3	0	61,420
Joyful Whirl	3	F	4	0	0	1	1,595
Joyjet	3	G	2	0	1	0	4,680
Joyjoyjoy	3	F	5	0	1	2	15,810
Joyote	3	F	11	0	3	1	4,692
Joyous Appeal	4	F	15	0	5	4	45,185
Joyous Bride	4	F	7	0	1	0	3,847
Joyous Song	2	F	8	3	1	3	110,982
Joyride	3	G	8	0	0	2	13,996
Joys Last One	3	C	1	0	0	0	0
Joy's Little Toy	6	G	12	1	2	0	6,743
Joy's Toy	7	M	9	0	3	3	4,238
Joys World	4	F	14	3	2	1	41,580
Jr Madeitpossible	3	G	15	2	2	2	24,205
Jr. Cat	4	G	2	0	1	0	1,920
Jr. Conquistador	6	G	3	0	0	0	620
Jr.'s Freedom	3	F	4	1	1	1	24,360
Jr.'s Wager	3	G	3	1	0	1	3,680
Jr's Bonus	9	G	10	0	1	1	4,403
Jr's Legacy	5	G	10	0	3	2	5,922
Jr's Scotty	3	G	12	1	2	0	10,134
Jr's Shadow Dancer	5	G	16	2	2	5	15,106
Jrsoutofcontrol	6	G	9	1	1	1	18,706
J's Boy Wonder	3	C	4	0	0	0	0
J's Cool Breeze	2	G	4	0	0	1	1,180
J's Graysyn Lady	2	F	4	0	0	0	2,450
J's Happy Holiday	5	M	4	0	0	2	1,584
J's Jule	4	F	6	1	0	0	13,030
J's Magic Jet	8	G	3	0	0	0	800
J's Sea Angel	3	G	12	2	0	2	12,995
J's Sorite Rizzi	2	F	6	1	0	1	10,730
J's Wild Slew	5	G	18	3	0	3	31,614
Ju Ju Beast	2	C	1	0	0	0	0
Juan	6	G	6	0	0	1	5,400
Juan Dixon	4	G	6	2	0	2	15,180
Juan Jose (CHI)	5	G	3	0	0	0	306
Juan to Dance	9	G	1	0	0	0	160
Juan Valdez	9	G	11	1	2	1	23,710
Juana	4	F	1	0	0	0	0
Juanita Bonita	2	F	1	0	0	0	66
Juan's Bouncer	4	G	19	1	2	3	9,185
Juan's Pepe	7	G	1	0	0	0	0

Horse	Age	Sex	Sts	1st	2d	3d	Won
Juan's Tortilla	4	G	10	2	1	2	12,711
Jubalani	6	G	10	2	0	0	21,728
Jubilation	4	G	9	0	0	0	1,579
Jubilee	2	F	3	0	1	1	14,360
Jubilee's Jasmine	4	F	9	1	1	2	4,790
Jubileetwothousand	4	G	11	2	1	0	18,280
Jubileo	7	G	1	0	1	0	7,140
Juby's Juice	3	G	3	0	0	0	105
Juddy's Storm	3	G	6	0	0	0	1,125
Judes	3	F	6	1	3	0	10,499
Jude's Boy	3	C	1	0	0	0	105
Jude's Slewd	4	G	3	0	0	2	925
Judge a Buck	4	F	2	0	0	0	0
Judge Advocate	4	G	11	2	1	1	8,254
Judge Al Cretella	3	G	6	0	0	0	5,040
Judge Amy	4	F	8	2	1	2	24,871
Judge B Bourg	7	G	1	0	0	0	0
Judge Ballad	6	G	6	1	0	0	5,100
Judge Beautiful	6	M	4	0	0	0	600
Judge Becker	5	G	12	3	2	2	13,791
Judge Ben	4	C	12	2	1	2	14,752
Judge Brandy	4	F	8	1	1	0	12,844
Judge Champs	8	H	1	0	0	0	0
Judge Chris	6	H	9	0	1	1	14,230
Judge Cielo	4	G	16	2	5	2	27,220
Judge Dery	2	G	4	1	0	0	10,200
Judge E. C.	3	G	10	0	1	4	6,777
Judge Fred	2	C	3	0	0	0	0
Judge G A	5	G	9	0	2	2	1,926
Judge Gallivan	2	G	2	0	1	0	7,400
Judge Gap	2	C	2	0	0	0	355
Judge Glitter	6	G	2	0	1	1	1,118
Judge Goldilocks	5	G	16	1	0	1	13,302
Judge Harper	4	C	15	3	2	2	50,270
Judge J B	3	F	10	1	1	0	8,191
Judge Jason	4	G	7	0	0	1	940
Judge Judy	9	M	6	1	0	0	6,842
Judge Laurenas	7	M	1	0	1	0	1,482
Judge Louie	5	G	7	1	1	1	10,203
Judge Marquesa	5	M	13	1	2	3	10,319
Judge Me Ladies	7	G	5	0	0	1	880
Judge Nancy	5	M	8	0	0	1	2,750
Judge of Character	5	H	3	1	0	0	9,887
Judge of Honor	2	F	1	0	0	1	2,040
Judge Ordway	3	G	2	0	0	0	135
Judge Peeweater	3	C	5	0	2	0	14,880
Judge Perkins	3	G	12	0	0	0	0
Judge Pritty	3	F	14	1	3	2	14,326
Judge Ray	5	G	15	0	2	2	6,452
Judge Relic Kelic	7	M	14	1	4	1	18,084
Judge Rocks	6	G	9	0	0	3	2,367
Judge Ruckus	4	G	10	1	3	1	22,860
Judge Sophie	4	F	12	2	4	1	21,436
Judge Spada	6	G	11	3	2	2	30,182
Judge Tyme	8	H	6	1	2	2	1,506
Judge With Charm	4	F	10	1	2	1	8,399
Judgemeister	4	G	14	2	6	0	22,518
Judgement Maker	3	C	5	1	0	0	7,456
Judgemental	5	M	6	0	0	1	841
Judge's Appeal	4	F	1	0	0	0	1,550
Judge's Case	7	G	11	0	2	1	25,952
Judges Decision	4	G	15	0	5	1	12,556
Judge's Delight	5	M	9	1	2	0	4,974
Judge's Halo	5	G	11	2	0	1	10,528
Judge's Pegasus	3	F	20	2	5	3	73,240
Judge's Treasure	4	G	1	0	0	0	0
Judging Dreams	3	G	3	0	1	1	2,568
Judging Lady	4	F	3	0	0	1	2,417
Judgmatic	4	C	11	2	1	1	8,827
Judicial Inquest	4	C	3	0	0	0	1,002
Judi's Blue Shoes	2	F	1	0	0	0	145
Judith Ann	6	M	17	1	3	1	12,691
Judith Come Home	7	G	10	2	2	0	22,503
Judith's Car	7	G	23	2	2	1	9,946
Judith's Creek	2	F	7	0	0	1	7,318
Judith's Deed	4	G	7	1	1	2	36,484
Judiths Formal	2	G	5	0	1	2	4,630
Judith's Jester	6	G	17	1	1	2	10,340
Judiths Minister	3	G	1	0	0	0	115

Horse	Age	Sex	Sts	1st	2d	3d	Won
Judith's Mission	4	G	20	0	5	3	10,912
Judith's Pirate	3	G	2	0	0	0	573
Judith's Reason	2	G	5	0	0	0	6,213
Judith's Road	6	M	3	2	0	0	10,261
Judiths Rumour	4	F	4	1	0	0	6,864
Judith's Secret	3	F	3	0	0	0	77
Judiths Wild Rush	3	C	8	1	0	2	122,356
Judo	3	C	12	1	4	2	19,235
Judy in Disguise	5	M	8	3	1	1	16,535
Judy Jetson	6	M	3	0	1	0	5,400
Judy Soda	3	F	11	2	2	1	112,749
Judy Would	4	F	5	0	1	0	1,006
Judy's Bet	3	F	2	0	0	0	300
Judy's Gem	2	F	1	0	0	0	0
Judy's Valentine	4	F	11	2	0	3	22,749
Juel's Jackpot	3	G	2	1	0	0	2,280
Jugoon's Crusader	3	F	1	0	0	0	112
Juicy Fruits	4	F	18	2	1	4	37,215
Juistino	3	F	1	0	0	0	0
Jujuba	5	G	6	2	0	2	12,902
Jukebox Joanne	3	F	2	0	0	1	1,190
Juldean	3	F	5	0	0	0	1,318
Jule Bandit	5	G	14	1	2	2	21,110
Jules At Four	4	F	14	2	3	3	23,161
Jules Best	2	F	8	2	0	2	50,307
Jules for A. J.	3	F	5	1	0	2	28,500
Jules Gem	4	F	1	0	0	0	0
Jules Halo	3	C	14	4	1	1	30,465
Jule's Jewel	5	G	12	1	1	0	6,467
Jule's Outburst	2	C	3	0	0	0	780
Jules Pride	5	G	7	1	1	0	5,569
Jules Rules	4	F	9	0	0	2	5,759
Jules Secret	3	C	6	1	0	1	6,270
Jules the Man	5	G	4	0	0	0	322
Julesburg	5	G	13	0	1	1	6,493
Juley's Diamond	3	F	3	0	0	0	1,740
Julia Faith	3	F	10	0	1	0	3,115
Julia Singing Bear	4	F	8	2	1	1	52,140
Julia Smyth	6	M	10	1	0	4	11,597
Julian's Commander	3	C	4	0	0	0	1,532
Julian's Special	6	H	2	0	0	0	0
Julias Gem	4	F	7	0	1	0	2,005
Julia's Javelin	5	H	2	0	0	0	292
Julia's Legacy	3	F	6	1	1	2	11,360
Julia's School Boy	3	C	2	0	0	0	159
Julia's Signal	3	G	6	1	0	1	6,396
Julie Ann Can	4	F	13	0	0	3	2,098
Julie Truly	3	F	4	1	0	2	13,510
Julieboolee	5	H	5	0	0	0	0
Julienne	3	F	1	0	0	0	105
Julie's Bronzie	4	F	7	1	1	1	14,415
Julie's Charmer	3	F	4	0	1	0	4,050
Julies Delight	3	F	1	0	0	0	0
Julie's Emerald	2	F	5	0	0	1	2,568
Julie's Fast Cat	4	F	9	2	0	3	7,995
Julies Flying Now	5	M	10	1	1	3	17,165
Julie's Go Baby Go	4	F	17	2	5	1	36,972
Julie's Halo	3	F	4	0	0	0	203
Julies Journey	4	F	2	0	0	0	500
Julie's Luck	4	F	15	1	4	0	19,179
Julies Opportunity	2	F	2	0	1	0	4,600
Julie's Petticoat	3	F	7	0	0	1	2,424
Julie's Prize	4	F	7	2	1	1	127,594
Julie's Rib	3	F	4	0	0	0	471
Julie's Songndance	3	F	6	1	0	0	5,740
Julie's Turn	5	M	1	0	0	0	0
Juliesugardaddy	2	C	1	0	0	1	5,280
Juliet (BRZ)	3	F	1	0	0	0	400
Julietas Bolger	8	G	3	2	0	1	9,640
Juliet's Kiss	3	F	10	4	3	2	165,572
Juliette (IRE)	4	F	5	0	0	2	12,332
Juli's Dancer	2	F	6	0	2	2	29,240
Juli's Jacket	3	F	1	0	0	0	0
Juli's War	3	F	7	0	1	0	1,895
Julius T	5	G	19	2	2	5	33,140
Julviya	4	F	4	0	0	0	0
July Child	4	C	9	1	3	0	49,435
Jumangi (CHI)	8	G	9	0	1	1	4,458
Jumbalayan	3	F	7	2	0	1	13,039
Jumie	6	M	1	0	1	0	965
Jumish	6	G	2	0	0	0	0
Jump for Joyeux	4	G	13	3	2	0	52,060
Jumper	2	G	2	1	1	0	8,565
Jumpin Dumplin	6	M	1	0	0	0	0
Jumpin Jackson	2	C	3	0	1	0	1,386
Jumpin Jayrod	5	H	2	1	1	0	1,050
Jumpin Jazz Man	3	G	11	2	2	3	24,290
Jumpin Joe	3	C	4	0	1	0	2,120
Jumping Jasper	5	G	1	0	0	0	40
Jumpingjupiter	4	G	11	1	3	3	28,557
Jumpscatrun	7	G	8	0	0	0	794
Jumpstarter	4	C	9	4	2	2	99,070
Jumron Won	6	G	9	1	0	1	12,796
Jumrunner	2	G	1	0	0	0	215
Junaguska	2	G	2	0	0	1	2,002
Junction Jimmy	2	C	2	0	0	0	480
June Bug Baby	4	F	8	1	2	3	19,978
June Lady	6	M	4	0	0	1	1,958
June Memories	6	M	3	0	0	0	329
June Springs	6	M	9	4	1	1	26,747
June the Tiger	2	C	3	1	0	0	31,094
Juneau	2	F	1	0	0	0	230
Junes Fair Decor	7	M	8	0	0	1	1,457
Jungfrau	3	F	1	1	0	0	15,600
Jungle Drums	6	M	5	0	1	0	1,843
Jungle Jaguar	2	C	3	0	0	2	1,270
Jungle Majesty	5	G	11	2	3	0	4,807
Jungle Prince	3	G	8	1	2	3	69,282
Jungle Queen	3	F	3	1	0	0	19,946
Jungle Red	3	G	5	0	0	1	2,690
Jungle Surfer	3	F	2	0	0	0	366
Jungle Tigre	3	G	7	0	1	1	3,869
Junior Banker	6	H	4	0	0	0	79
Junior Bunk	3	C	11	0	3	2	15,260
Junior Delaney	5	G	10	2	0	0	14,189
Junior Deputy	6	G	1	0	0	0	810
Junior in School	3	C	1	0	0	0	92
Junior Prom	8	G	19	2	2	5	27,053
Junior Ruler	3	G	6	0	0	1	933
Juniper Breeze	4	F	4	0	1	0	580
Juniper Jen	3	F	1	0	0	0	400
Juniper Kris	4	G	10	2	1	0	43,730
Junk Gypsie	3	F	1	0	0	1	1,320
Junkanoo	12	G	5	2	0	1	6,003
Junket	8	G	10	2	2	3	35,501
Junqueman John	3	C	1	0	0	0	0
Jupiter and Mars	3	G	15	2	0	1	28,032
Jupiter Gentlemen	4	G	4	0	2	2	8,880
Juramento	5	G	18	3	1	3	53,463
Juroar	4	F	4	0	1	1	7,920
Jury	6	G	10	2	0	0	26,410
Jus Another Doggie	3	F	10	1	1	1	13,302
Jus Jak	2	G	3	0	0	0	1,380
Jus Luk's Azzaro	2	F	1	0	0	1	984
Jus Ol Bob	3	G	1	0	0	0	400
Juscauz	4	F	13	3	4	5	43,585
Jusk Ask'em	2	C	2	0	0	1	273
Juskeeprollinalong	5	G	15	3	4	1	42,530
Jusred	4	F	2	0	0	1	800
Jussila	4	F	9	2	2	1	6,705
Just a Babe	4	F	9	0	4	0	9,255
Just a Berry	6	M	4	0	0	0	466
Just a Champion	4	G	10	0	2	2	8,978
Just a Chip	4	G	7	0	1	2	7,440
Just a Dance	5	G	4	0	0	0	169
Just a Dancer	4	F	9	1	2	1	5,033
Just a Eclipse	10	G	2	0	1	0	707
Just a Flash	5	G	4	0	0	0	276
Just a Fool	5	G	2	0	0	0	570
Just a Kate	2	F	3	1	0	0	12,680
Just a Kitty	4	F	15	2	1	2	20,031
Just a Lady	5	M	2	1	0	0	6,710
Just a Lil Royal	6	M	9	0	2	0	5,006
Just a Little Jet	2	F	2	0	1	1	11,100
Just a Little Jo	8	G	16	0	2	5	14,318
Just a Little Kip	2	F	3	0	2	0	7,200
Just a Nugget	5	G	3	0	0	1	1,305
Just a Patton	4	F	8	0	2	0	5,916

Horse	Age	Sex	Sts	1st	2d	3d	Won
Just a Pistol	4	F	12	2	2	2	14,087
Just a Promise	3	G	5	0	0	0	184
Just a Qtpi	3	F	3	0	0	0	0
Just a Rumor	6	G	2	0	0	0	165
Just a Scat Cat	2	C	7	1	0	0	16,774
Just a Sheila	5	M	6	2	0	0	5,500
Just a Sip	4	F	7	1	0	0	2,134
Just a Song	5	M	4	1	1	1	5,360
Just a Timemachine	5	G	5	0	0	0	96
Just a True Man	4	G	9	2	0	1	8,742
Just a Whim	3	C	13	2	1	3	25,762
Just Add Rum	2	C	6	1	1	1	16,400
Just Add Water	3	G	9	1	4	2	32,513
Just Alike	3	G	11	0	2	1	9,560
Just Allen	6	G	5	1	0	0	11,731
Just an Act	6	G	10	1	1	1	13,005
Just Another Fact	3	F	10	1	2	3	28,062
Just as Ready	2	C	1	0	0	0	205
Just At Night	4	F	2	0	0	0	0
Just Bagin It	4	G	13	1	0	0	9,949
Just Begone	3	F	7	0	1	2	2,413
Just Bill	7	G	7	0	0	1	1,390
Just Bill Me	4	F	1	0	0	0	0
Just Bloomed	4	F	6	1	0	0	1,700
Just by a Nose	3	C	3	0	0	0	0
Just Calamity	3	F	2	0	0	0	0
Just Call Me Babe	4	F	4	0	0	0	219
Just Call Me Irish	6	M	14	0	2	0	3,021
Just Call Me Jay	7	M	4	0	0	1	277
Just Call Me King	4	G	4	0	0	0	1,290
Just Call Me Max	5	G	5	0	0	0	345
Just Call Me Roma	3	F	4	0	0	0	150
Just Call Me Sal	3	G	11	1	0	1	3,116
Just Call Me Vicky	2	F	7	0	1	1	5,549
Just Cash	3	G	13	2	1	1	15,132
Just Dancer	5	G	4	0	0	0	256
Just Dancing	5	G	1	0	1	0	1,040
Just Devious	4	C	13	2	5	2	49,989
Just Ducky Too	3	G	8	1	2	0	24,150
Just Dusty	3	F	11	2	1	3	7,640
Just Email Me	6	M	10	1	2	1	7,788
Just Emma	5	M	10	1	1	2	27,907
Just Fab Dad	6	M	13	1	2	3	3,319
Just Fine	2	F	4	0	0	1	1,255
Just Flight	5	H	1	0	0	0	0
Just Fly Away	9	G	3	0	0	0	421
Just for Dad	5	G	6	0	1	0	1,914
Just for Dave	5	G	4	0	0	0	1,800
Just for Deb	3	G	7	0	1	1	10,035
Just for Flo	8	M	1	0	0	0	52
Just for Jack	4	F	2	0	0	0	0
Just for Jean	4	F	6	0	1	1	25,372
Just for John	6	G	4	0	0	0	180
Just for Love	6	G	21	2	1	3	13,014
Just Forget It	4	C	5	0	0	0	317
Just Forty Five	7	G	1	0	0	0	0
Just Four Austin	5	G	7	1	2	1	21,002
Just Free	8	G	5	0	1	0	1,550
Just Fun	5	M	1	0	0	1	2,930
Just Gabi	4	F	8	1	2	1	53,550
Just Ginger	3	F	4	0	1	1	5,200
Just Glitter	4	G	1	0	0	0	62
Just Glorious	4	F	12	0	1	0	2,041
Just Gold	7	M	9	1	2	0	7,851
Just Gossip	5	G	9	1	0	3	35,880
Just in Case Jimmy	3	G	11	3	0	1	272,825
Just in Fun	2	C	2	0	0	1	6,150
Just in Lines	3	C	1	0	0	0	0
Just J	5	M	2	1	0	0	3,120
Just Jack	7	G	1	0	0	0	510
Just Jackie	5	M	16	4	6	1	41,670
Just Jazzy	3	F	4	1	1	0	7,122
Just Jenn	2	F	2	0	0	0	350
Just Jesy	5	G	6	1	0	2	3,529
Just Jettin Holme	4	G	14	2	3	1	21,527
Just Jill	3	F	12	3	1	1	44,517
Just Joe Bridled	3	G	5	0	1	0	508
Just Jokin Jay	11	G	4	0	0	0	240
Just Justin	6	H	5	1	0	0	4,824

Horse	Age	Sex	Sts	1st	2d	3d	Won
Just Justinian	5	G	10	0	1	1	2,284
Just Kidding	3	G	9	1	0	1	26,230
Just L	2	G	3	0	0	1	2,570
Just Le Facts	5	H	4	0	0	2	9,010
Just Leave	3	F	1	0	0	0	0
Just Leaveit to Me	2	C	4	0	1	1	7,000
Just Leaving	2	F	4	0	0	0	0
Just Like Bobbyjoe	6	G	3	0	0	0	0
Just Like Bonds	3	C	2	1	0	0	7,620
Just Like Bossy	9	M	2	0	1	1	1,200
Just Like Celia	2	F	1	0	0	0	0
Just Like Dan	4	G	2	0	0	0	0
Just Like Elise	3	F	5	1	2	0	11,707
Just Like Gold	6	M	6	1	0	0	9,515
Just Like Mike	4	G	7	1	0	1	17,610
Just Like Prime	8	G	7	0	1	0	4,059
Just Like Royalty	7	M	2	0	0	0	0
Just Like Sis	2	F	3	0	0	0	608
Just Like That (FR)	4	F	2	1	1	0	39,600
Just Like You	5	M	14	1	1	4	15,574
Just Lisa Ann	2	F	6	0	2	0	2,460
Just Mark	2	G	3	0	0	0	1,200
Just Me	3	G	7	1	1	0	16,976
Just Michel	4	F	5	2	0	0	34,950
Just Murphy (IRE)	6	G	2	0	0	0	2,000
Just My Bill	4	C	4	0	0	1	1,045
Just Name Me	4	C	6	0	0	0	498
Just Not Enough	3	F	4	0	0	0	1,710
Just On Looks	7	G	11	1	4	4	10,171
Just One	5	G	9	0	1	1	2,033
Just One Bid	3	F	11	2	2	2	22,529
Just One Kiss	6	M	2	1	0	0	5,002
Just One More R	3	F	3	1	0	0	3,120
Just One Rose	6	M	2	0	0	0	291
Just Outrageous	5	G	2	0	1	0	2,100
Just Outta Here	3	F	5	1	1	0	10,050
Just Parkin	4	C	1	0	0	0	0
Just Plain Bill	4	G	8	3	0	0	22,261
Just Plain Jessie	3	F	12	2	4	1	32,048
Just Plain Lucky	3	F	10	2	1	2	14,099
Just Plain Vanilla	3	F	3	0	0	1	6,740
Just Proclaim	4	G	10	1	1	2	26,980
Just Push Play	4	F	8	1	2	3	2,854
Just Rich Enough	3	G	3	1	0	1	7,827
Just Sampson	7	G	5	1	0	0	5,728
Just Say Boo	3	G	10	0	4	3	44,200
Just Say Go	3	G	3	0	0	0	0
Just Say the Word	4	C	7	0	2	0	17,370
Just Scotty	4	G	8	2	0	1	3,978
Just See James	3	G	6	3	1	0	66,820
Just Shawklit	2	C	5	1	0	0	16,200
Just Sing	4	G	6	2	1	1	16,085
Just So Ya No	3	F	7	1	0	1	3,036
Just Southernbelle	3	F	3	0	0	0	0
Just Sow Wild	4	G	14	0	3	2	12,687
Just Speak Up	3	G	6	4	0	0	14,442
Just Speechy	5	M	6	0	0	1	2,236
Just Spoof N	7	G	11	0	2	3	14,827
Just Starting	2	F	1	1	0	0	7,800
Just Steve	3	G	1	0	0	0	398
Just Swell	4	C	2	0	0	0	0
Just Tap Once	3	F	2	0	0	0	0
Just the Cat	2	C	1	0	0	0	314
Just Thinkin	3	G	7	0	0	3	4,696
Just Thunder	2	C	5	1	0	1	13,380
Just to Demanding	3	G	6	0	0	0	1,152
Just too Salty	5	H	5	0	0	1	878
Just Triple	6	M	8	1	0	2	13,732
Just Trouble	2	G	1	0	0	0	0
Just Tucker	3	C	9	2	0	3	15,551
Just Us Honey	3	G	8	0	2	0	4,564
Just Validation	2	F	8	3	0	0	30,900
Just Waltz	4	C	8	0	2	2	6,370
Just Watch Me	4	G	9	3	3	2	114,776
Just Western	6	G	12	0	2	1	3,292
Just Wonder (GB)	4	C	4	0	1	1	58,818
Just Wyatt	9	G	3	0	0	0	82
Just You and Me	4	C	3	0	0	0	225
Justa	6	M	2	0	0	0	118

Horse	Age	Sex	Sts	1st	2d	3d	Won
Justa Bigboned Gal	4	F	5	0	0	1	437
Justa Brat	3	F	3	0	0	0	355
Justa Duck Snort	5	G	9	1	3	1	3,735
Justa Farm Girl	3	F	2	0	0	0	529
Justa Good Old Boy	3	G	8	0	0	0	1,030
Justa Gray	5	G	10	2	1	2	34,834
Justa Jammer	4	G	5	0	0	2	2,620
Justa Lil Awesome	3	F	1	0	0	0	0
Justa Little Star	3	F	6	0	0	1	2,550
Justa Monster	2	C	2	0	0	1	5,850
Justa Music Man	3	G	6	2	0	0	10,746
Justa Old Love	2	F	3	0	0	0	0
Justa Quick Silver	7	H	1	0	0	0	0
Justa Red Bird	2	C	8	2	1	0	26,780
Justa Right	5	G	2	0	1	0	313
Justa Slewzy	3	F	3	0	0	0	156
Justa Smirk	9	G	4	2	0	0	6,819
Justa Survivor	4	G	2	0	0	0	546
Justa Toad	3	F	6	1	0	0	1,795
Justa Vacation	7	M	4	0	0	0	0
Justa Valay Girl	4	F	10	0	2	0	1,668
Justabigsissy	4	F	9	1	1	0	7,565
Justabud	4	C	1	0	1	0	2,760
Justabull	6	M	3	0	0	0	510
Justadavida	3	F	5	1	1	0	12,441
Justafirecracker	3	G	1	0	0	0	0
Justaframeofmind	4	F	6	0	0	0	750
Justagallop	6	G	2	0	0	0	500
Justagesture	3	G	6	0	0	1	4,530
Justahaulin	2	C	4	0	0	0	750
Justajack	3	G	6	0	0	0	2,065
Justalilbitsmarter	3	C	5	0	0	0	213
Justalilcajun	3	G	1	0	0	0	0
Justalittle Crazy	5	H	14	1	0	1	7,294
Justalittleglitch	3	G	1	0	0	0	400
Justalittlemagic	4	G	6	0	0	1	10,096
Justalittlemore	3	F	3	1	0	1	7,230
Justamemento	3	F	3	1	0	1	17,861
Justamoment	3	C	12	1	3	1	15,102
Justanick	7	G	7	0	3	1	1,720
Justanotheractor	3	G	14	0	5	6	18,983
Justanothercruiser	4	G	2	0	0	0	0
Justaperfectscore	5	G	7	1	0	0	5,778
Justart	3	F	8	0	3	1	6,808
Justas Returns	5	G	8	0	0	0	742
Justaspringfling	3	F	1	0	0	0	0
Justastorm	5	G	1	0	0	0	340
Justatan	2	C	2	0	0	0	0
Justavalay	7	M	9	2	0	2	13,297
Justcallme Magic	3	G	10	0	0	0	996
Justcallmecasey	13	G	1	0	0	1	2,000
Justcallmesassy	4	F	7	0	0	1	700
Juste Smile	5	M	2	2	0	0	20,790
Justforgetaboutit	8	G	6	0	0	0	1,138
Justice B	4	G	8	1	0	1	8,436
Justice Bites	6	G	11	2	1	2	43,107
Justice for Auston	5	G	8	2	4	0	93,300
Justice Is Blind	2	F	3	1	0	0	5,290
Justice Mark	7	G	10	1	2	1	9,190
Justice Minister	7	H	1	0	0	0	3,360
Justice Paul	5	G	16	0	0	0	1,999
Justice Rules	5	G	9	1	0	2	8,024
Justice Wanted	2	G	4	2	1	0	54,634
Justicetopgun	5	G	12	0	0	0	834
Justiciero	2	C	5	0	0	1	2,002
Justifiable Cause	5	H	4	1	2	0	5,468
Justifiable Xpense	3	G	12	0	0	2	3,405
Justifiably	2	G	6	1	1	1	13,839
Justification	7	G	6	0	2	1	31,420
Justified Attack	5	G	6	0	0	1	5,015
Justified Devil	4	F	3	0	1	0	2,147
Justin Charge	6	G	2	0	0	0	295
Justin Itforfun	5	G	9	0	0	0	1,078
Justin Ray	5	G	5	0	0	1	1,236
Justin's Altoide	3	F	4	0	0	0	700
Justin's Big Boy	4	G	9	1	0	0	3,045
Justins Gold	2	F	1	0	0	0	105
Justin's Knight	3	G	4	0	0	0	0
Justintime G	2	C	1	0	0	0	0

Horse	Age	Sex	Sts	1st	2d	3d	Won
Justjake	6	H	3	0	0	0	253
Justlikedawg	4	C	7	2	3	0	95,410
Justlikejessejames	4	C	11	2	1	2	25,922
Justloadthewagon	6	G	6	0	0	0	344
Justly Royal	4	F	9	1	4	2	51,470
Justmakrya	5	M	6	0	0	0	360
Justnowayofknowin'	6	G	16	5	3	1	51,084
Justntime	5	H	2	0	0	0	0
Justonemoreround	3	G	11	2	0	4	24,075
Justoneofdaboyz	5	G	7	0	2	0	6,350
Justplainrita	3	F	4	0	0	0	1,002
Justslewme	6	G	14	1	4	4	5,808
Justus Hill	3	C	2	1	0	1	7,620
Justwhatineeded	4	F	3	0	1	1	3,280
Jut	3	C	11	1	0	3	13,895
Juuust Special	4	F	2	0	0	0	287
Juvee	4	G	6	1	0	1	3,254
Juvenile Court	3	F	8	3	0	1	30,150
Juventus	3	C	4	1	0	0	15,360
Jux	6	G	5	0	0	0	3,500
Juya	4	C	4	0	0	1	1,723
K B E S Delight	3	F	5	0	0	1	500
K Bo Sam	5	G	7	1	1	0	3,882
K Brown	4	F	11	1	2	3	66,270
K C Jazz	6	G	13	2	1	2	9,820
K C's Charm	4	F	7	2	3	1	19,587
K C's Sunshine Bay	4	G	15	2	0	1	26,980
K D Forum	3	F	6	0	0	1	7,304
K D Implosion	4	F	7	1	1	1	6,991
K D King	2	G	5	0	0	3	9,740
K D Magic	4	C	6	0	3	0	13,000
K D Power	5	M	4	0	0	0	927
K D Prospector	4	F	4	0	0	0	700
K Derrick	4	C	1	0	0	0	0
K G Lady	6	M	6	0	3	0	7,363
K Girl	2	F	3	0	0	1	3,307
K Hawk	4	G	2	0	1	0	416
K J's Girl	3	F	6	2	0	0	52,000
K J's Prospect	4	G	1	0	0	0	0
K J's Rose	6	M	13	0	0	2	4,050
K K Avey	4	G	1	0	1	0	2,800
K K Matty K	2	G	3	0	0	0	2,403
K K Robert	4	G	6	1	1	1	6,292
K L Ryder	2	F	7	0	1	0	2,835
K Mac	6	G	4	0	1	0	4,964
K O Gorgeous	4	F	1	0	0	0	0
K O Love	4	C	1	0	0	1	8,250
K O River Crossing	3	G	14	1	1	3	13,238
K Patrick	5	H	8	0	0	0	0
K P's Crystal	2	F	2	0	0	0	0
K P's Kandy	4	F	5	1	1	2	16,615
K S Gambler	5	G	4	0	0	0	434
K Squared	5	M	9	1	0	1	8,835
K T M Sparkler	3	F	4	0	0	0	1,150
K T Wantsafastone	4	C	8	4	1	1	5,987
K. C. Forty Niner	2	C	2	0	0	0	184
K. C. Genius	5	M	3	0	0	0	1,137
K. C. Road	3	G	12	4	1	2	32,134
K. C.'s Boy	5	G	16	1	2	4	19,340
K. D. Day	2	F	1	0	0	0	0
K. D. Tam	6	M	1	0	0	0	0
K. D.'s Shady Lady	2	F	6	1	3	1	77,320
K. J.'s Gold	4	C	10	1	3	1	23,920
K. K.'s Kiss	4	F	17	2	5	1	31,097
K. K.'s Pride	4	F	3	0	0	0	0
K. Money	3	F	7	0	1	1	4,790
K. O. Boots	8	G	7	1	2	0	3,035
K. O. Bride	4	F	2	0	0	0	800
K. O. Frankie	3	G	1	0	0	0	0
K. O. Peace	4	F	2	0	0	2	1,050
K. O. Phyllis	3	F	10	2	2	1	46,750
K. O. Power	4	G	12	1	1	3	27,230
K. P. Esquire	4	C	1	0	0	0	154
K. P. Express	4	G	12	2	0	1	10,851
K. R.'s Regent	2	C	5	1	0	1	39,327
Ka Blui	5	G	3	0	0	1	3,621
Ka Bre	2	F	7	0	1	0	4,124
Ka Poi Kai	3	G	7	0	0	3	15,630
Kabars Stay	5	M	1	0	0	0	0

Horse	Age	Sex	Sts	1st	2d	3d	Won
Kabeeb	4	F	9	0	0	1	14,761
Kabul	4	F	11	3	2	1	189,417
Kabylia (IRE)	6	M	1	0	0	0	1,120
Kaceys Dancer	8	H	15	4	2	2	19,266
Kaceysexpelled	3	F	3	0	0	0	0
Kachamandi (CHI)	7	G	3	0	0	0	960
Kachina Dream	2	F	6	2	0	0	49,780
Kachina Girl	3	F	8	1	0	1	9,524
Kadancer	5	M	4	0	0	0	114
Kadelyna Crown	3	F	2	0	0	0	0
Kadiddlehopper	9	G	4	0	0	1	921
Kadillac Kole	6	H	4	0	0	0	248
Kady Bee	5	M	2	0	0	0	0
Kae Jazz	6	H	1	1	0	0	1,140
Kaeli's Glance	2	F	8	0	1	2	4,775
Kafaf's Ship	3	G	4	1	2	0	5,140
Kagan's Corner	7	G	13	0	2	1	10,836
Kagels Fleetman	4	C	6	0	1	0	2,980
Kahala	5	M	15	2	1	3	11,035
Kahlo	3	F	1	0	0	0	176
Kahlua Hummer	4	G	12	1	3	0	12,738
Kahok	2	G	8	1	1	3	30,921
Kahula	3	F	5	1	0	0	6,936
Kahuna Nine	2	C	2	0	0	1	2,550
Kai Kai	2	F	3	0	2	0	8,701
Kai Kwan Do	3	G	1	0	0	0	84
Kaibo (GB)	8	H	2	0	0	0	214
Kaili's a Princess	3	F	3	1	0	1	14,685
Kailua Breeze	5	M	1	0	0	0	77
Kailua Whirl	4	G	3	1	0	0	8,124
Kain's Dancer	4	G	11	2	2	1	24,938
Kain's Deed	3	F	14	2	0	3	29,828
Kain's Nijinsky	7	G	2	0	0	0	156
Kaiser Road	2	G	8	0	2	2	13,059
Kaiser So Say	8	G	7	1	1	0	9,846
Kaiser Soze	2	C	5	0	2	0	5,700
Kait Can't Wait	4	F	8	1	0	0	11,471
Kaitlin's Boy	4	G	8	0	1	0	6,910
Kaitlyn's Angel	5	G	2	0	0	0	0
Kajen Lojo	3	C	13	0	1	1	4,461
Kajie Won	3	F	7	0	0	1	2,252
Kakapo	3	G	7	0	2	2	11,659
Kalahari Cat	4	F	9	1	4	3	69,560
Kalahari Gold	2	F	8	0	0	1	2,639
Kalamari Sunset	3	F	6	0	0	0	0
Kalamazoo	6	H	2	1	0	0	11,040
Kalani Girl (IRE)	3	F	3	0	0	1	6,400
Kale	6	M	3	0	0	0	114
Kaleen E	3	F	1	0	0	0	0
Kalen	4	F	13	0	4	2	16,570
Kalens Jet	4	G	5	0	0	1	2,945
Kale's Out of Cash	2	G	2	0	0	1	984
Kalfaari	7	G	1	0	0	1	3,418
Kaliga	10	G	2	0	0	0	246
Kalijah	2	C	2	0	0	0	210
Kalik	7	G	5	0	0	0	293
Kalimas (GER)	7	H	5	0	0	1	1,388
Kalim's Song	7	M	6	1	1	0	3,555
Kali's Cat	5	G	5	0	0	0	1,225
Kali's Sunshine	3	F	9	0	1	0	1,768
Kalish	4	F	6	0	0	1	2,226
Kalizar	4	G	4	1	1	0	2,505
Kalki's Pride	4	F	14	1	4	4	29,341
Kallie Bird	6	M	7	3	1	2	50,100
Kalolo	5	G	11	0	0	0	1,255
Kalookan Code	3	F	6	1	0	1	5,238
Kalookan Lady	3	F	5	0	0	0	3,410
Kalookan Lass	3	F	2	1	0	0	27,860
Kalowana Sunrise	7	M	1	0	0	0	0
Kalsem	8	G	15	2	0	5	14,458
Kalt Cafe	4	F	2	0	0	0	1,344
Kalu	6	H	1	0	0	0	146
Kalua's Back	5	M	10	2	1	2	3,317
Kalyptic	2	C	5	1	1	1	75,407
Kama'aina Girl	3	F	4	0	0	1	4,160
Kamalani	3	F	2	0	0	0	0
Kamchatka	3	F	13	2	0	0	9,722
Kamerooney	3	F	3	0	0	0	158
Kami Dee	3	F	13	3	0	4	18,102
Kami's Wish	4	F	6	0	2	0	2,064
Kamoya	4	G	7	0	2	0	3,220
Kamsack	5	H	3	1	0	0	58,579
Kan Have Fun	3	F	6	1	0	0	10,570
Kan Two	4	F	6	0	3	1	2,210
Kana Bell	2	F	9	0	4	1	17,425
Kanafa	4	F	2	0	0	0	381
Kanani Roy	5	G	9	1	1	2	9,155
Kanata Ridge	5	G	10	0	3	2	11,837
Kanati	4	G	9	1	1	3	21,420
Kandahar	4	G	6	1	0	1	4,394
Kandaroo	5	G	4	0	0	0	187
Kandinsky	2	C	4	0	0	0	3,545
Kandoolie	4	F	19	1	1	1	6,722
Kandula	4	C	4	1	0	0	18,060
Kaneohe Bay	2	F	1	0	0	0	0
Kangaroo Jack	3	C	8	0	1	2	4,955
Kanilla	3	F	3	0	0	0	0
Kannapolis	3	G	7	0	0	0	969
Kano Doble	5	G	12	1	1	0	6,894
Kanoa One	5	M	10	2	0	1	22,540
Kansas City Boy	2	C	5	1	2	0	52,765
Kansas City Scion	3	C	4	1	0	0	9,435
Kansas Justice	3	G	5	0	1	0	1,360
Kansas Pioneer	5	G	12	1	2	1	12,094
Kansi La	6	G	12	1	0	1	2,663
Kansun	3	C	5	0	0	1	1,770
Kan't Stop Jeter	3	C	3	0	0	0	378
Kant Touch	3	F	1	0	0	0	0
Kanuceeit	3	F	3	0	0	0	159
Kanu's Malagra	2	F	3	0	0	1	3,565
Kanwiaco	3	C	2	0	0	0	155
Kanyon Koyote	3	G	1	0	0	0	300
Kaough	7	H	9	0	1	2	4,750
Kapellmister	3	C	12	1	3	1	16,034
Kapodious	2	C	2	0	0	0	0
Kaptnwice	2	G	4	0	2	0	8,990
Kara Jean	7	M	1	0	0	0	144
Karabez	8	G	6	0	1	1	5,288
Karakorum Blues	6	G	10	0	0	0	851
Karakorum Cat	5	H	8	3	0	0	22,306
Karakorum Conquest	6	M	8	0	0	2	2,447
Karakorum Crusader	6	M	9	1	2	1	13,590
Karakorum Dixie	4	G	9	7	1	1	69,200
Karakorum Keepsake	3	C	3	2	0	0	51,690
Karakorum Munk	7	G	17	1	2	4	12,491
Karakorum Patriot	4	G	15	2	5	3	106,996
Karakorum Rock	3	C	5	0	0	0	1,101
Karakorum Splendor	2	F	5	2	1	0	124,072
Karakorum Tsunami	3	F	9	1	3	1	5,965
Karakorum Tuxedo	3	C	13	2	1	3	66,301
Karakorum's Appeal	5	G	11	2	2	2	70,755
Karakorum's Jodi	2	F	2	0	0	0	282
Karakorums R Wild	5	G	14	3	1	3	19,350
Karakorumseashanty	4	F	7	0	0	0	1,207
Karama Dif	2	C	7	1	1	3	14,415
Karama Trapp	5	G	12	0	0	0	1,951
Karaman (FR)	5	H	2	0	0	0	780
Karamanduka	4	G	6	1	1	1	15,790
Karamel Kay	3	F	1	0	0	0	155
Karaoke Joe	2	C	8	0	2	0	6,005
Kararun	5	M	14	2	2	1	22,096
Kara's Cat	2	F	3	0	0	0	360
Kara's Tee	2	F	4	1	0	0	9,070
Karat Tales	4	F	9	1	0	2	6,094
Karate	3	C	6	0	2	0	9,540
Karate Chris	4	G	17	1	6	4	14,294
Karazan	6	M	12	1	0	2	22,329
Karbobway	2	G	4	1	1	0	22,520
Kardiac Kid	5	G	9	2	1	1	26,232
Kardinale	3	G	5	0	2	1	12,640
Karelian	2	C	2	1	0	0	12,750
Karen B.	3	F	1	0	0	0	120
Karen Calling	2	F	1	0	0	0	50
Karen J.	3	F	9	2	0	3	21,997
Karen Sue's Cat	2	F	3	0	1	0	5,161
Karenkeel	7	M	2	0	0	0	0
Karen's Dinner	3	F	11	0	0	1	1,681
Karen's Lullaby	8	M	1	0	0	0	0

Horse	Age	Sex	Sts	1st	2d	3d	Won
Karen's Red Rose	3	F	2	0	0	0	205
Karen's Star	5	M	6	0	1	2	12,210
Karenz's Brother	5	G	2	0	0	0	600
Kari the Basket	3	F	5	0	0	0	0
Karilocco	4	G	3	0	0	0	233
Karin's Girl	3	F	12	1	3	1	12,620
Kari's Crown	4	C	1	0	0	0	460
Karis Makaw	3	F	5	2	2	1	45,623
Karison	4	G	7	0	0	1	1,570
Karlan's Buddy	3	G	4	0	0	2	1,360
Karleigh	2	F	2	1	0	0	13,800
Karletta Belle	9	M	2	0	0	0	0
Karley's Melody	6	M	12	2	1	3	11,438
Karlique	4	F	6	0	1	0	3,272
Karlyn's Coast	4	C	3	0	0	0	0
Karly's Harley	8	G	1	0	0	0	0
Karma Charma	3	C	1	0	0	0	0
Karmetory	4	G	2	1	0	1	3,400
Karms Echo	4	G	17	2	1	1	24,192
Karn	2	G	3	0	2	0	3,600
Karosel Dancer	6	M	7	2	0	1	7,003
Karra Kul	9	G	2	0	0	0	1,710
Karratha (MEX)	7	H	8	1	2	1	8,745
Karroo	4	F	9	2	2	3	32,721
Karta	6	M	3	0	0	0	190
Kary G	2	G	2	0	0	1	5,000
Karyn	2	F	2	0	0	0	162
Kaschmir	5	M	10	2	2	1	20,201
Kaseh	3	C	1	0	0	0	2,500
Kash Klip	2	F	4	2	0	0	47,800
Kashua	6	M	11	0	0	1	4,482
Kashubian	2	C	3	0	0	1	3,640
Kasino Dealer	4	F	5	0	1	1	3,190
Kaskazi	3	F	5	1	0	0	30,367
Kasparov	5	H	11	3	1	1	75,203
Kassoula's Best	4	C	5	0	1	0	1,832
Kassydee	2	F	5	0	0	0	384
Kastile	5	M	9	1	0	0	7,402
Kastria	3	F	6	0	0	1	2,750
Kasztanka	3	F	4	1	1	1	22,620
Kat Came Back	2	F	2	0	0	1	2,094
Kat Dancer	6	G	9	1	1	1	13,009
Kat Jammer	2	C	2	0	0	1	450
Kat Kool	3	G	8	4	1	1	80,764
Kat Merlot	2	F	2	0	0	1	1,504
Kata Tjuta	3	F	7	1	1	1	19,222
Katablastic	4	C	7	0	2	1	21,844
Katahaula Myst	4	G	3	0	0	0	0
Kataloo	6	M	1	0	0	0	0
Katalystic	3	C	12	2	0	1	18,276
Katana (NZ)	4	F	1	0	1	0	9,600
Katana Girl	5	M	8	0	0	0	1,065
Katano	2	C	1	0	0	0	65
Katawin	4	G	8	0	0	0	1,420
Katcherintherye	4	G	4	0	0	0	0
Katdillac	4	F	14	1	0	3	17,708
Katdogawn (GB)	4	F	9	1	3	2	264,158
Kate a Roo	3	F	5	1	0	1	18,460
Kate Fuegos	4	F	3	0	0	0	120
Kate Regal	6	M	1	0	0	0	0
Kate Siberian	3	F	4	0	0	0	1,240
Kate Winslet	3	F	9	3	0	0	83,991
Katee Jean	4	F	10	0	0	1	1,175
Katee Kris	4	F	10	1	3	1	36,017
Katelyn Rose Deane	5	M	7	1	0	0	7,280
Katelyne Legs	2	F	2	0	0	0	1,140
Katelyn's Rose	3	F	5	0	1	2	850
Katelyn's Star	3	F	12	1	3	3	38,938
Kate'n Amy	6	M	3	1	0	0	2,884
Kateri	4	F	2	1	1	0	18,060
Kate's Cat	5	M	1	0	0	0	66
Kate's Friend	6	H	12	1	1	0	11,527
Kate's Genius	3	C	7	0	1	0	10,062
Kate's Interview	4	F	9	1	2	3	12,993
Kate's Mucho Grand	2	C	7	0	0	0	1,149
Kates Night Out	4	F	3	1	0	0	7,288
Kate's Pal	3	G	10	1	0	0	6,184
Kate's Rocket	4	G	4	0	0	0	0
Kate's Storm	2	C	2	1	0	0	6,000
Katespreciousred	5	M	1	0	0	0	0
Katestormedthebird	3	F	4	2	0	0	41,900
Katherine Bug	4	F	1	0	0	1	1,190
Katherine Shannon	3	F	2	0	0	0	45
Katherine Z.	3	F	4	0	0	1	4,050
Kathern's Cat	2	F	5	2	1	0	79,603
Kathir	7	H	6	3	2	0	160,398
Kathryn Janeway	3	F	1	0	0	0	63
Kathryn Mc	2	F	3	0	0	0	306
Kathryn the Granny	5	M	11	2	0	1	10,744
Kathryns Birthday	2	F	3	1	0	0	18,368
Kathryn's Ego	9	G	10	1	5	0	7,709
Kathy Ann	4	F	5	0	0	0	259
Kathy Girl	3	F	4	1	0	2	4,060
Kathy Lee G.	4	F	9	1	0	0	14,051
Kathy Lynn	3	F	11	2	2	1	15,212
Kathy Shaboom	3	F	4	0	0	1	1,619
Kathy Shoppinspree	9	G	5	0	0	0	483
Kathy's Lil Cat	2	F	5	1	1	0	29,639
Kathythetraina	6	M	2	0	0	0	1,610
Katie Confidential	2	F	6	0	1	0	5,660
Katie First	3	F	12	0	3	2	10,453
Katie Jane	3	F	6	1	0	0	10,355
Katie Jo	3	F	8	2	3	3	8,707
Katie Kosmos	6	M	6	0	0	0	1,350
Katie Kreitz	5	M	13	1	3	0	33,480
Katie La Rue	3	F	3	0	0	0	388
Katie Lang	4	F	10	1	0	1	13,071
Katie Last	3	F	11	3	2	1	61,176
Katie Meadow Slou	2	F	1	0	0	1	2,564
Katie O Wise	3	F	2	0	0	0	273
Katies Danza	4	F	21	3	4	2	55,764
Katie's Giggle	3	F	4	0	0	0	0
Katie's Kalling	4	F	7	1	1	1	23,640
Katie's Magic	5	M	16	0	1	2	4,088
Katie's Miracle	4	F	12	3	2	0	15,886
Katies Success	6	M	1	0	0	0	0
Katie's Town	3	F	6	0	0	1	2,388
Katiesboy	3	G	13	1	0	1	4,973
Kativo	3	G	1	0	0	0	0
Katlin's Rocket	3	F	11	4	2	0	119,355
Katoclysmic Wave	2	C	1	0	0	0	348
Kato's World	6	M	18	5	5	4	30,266
Katotrick	4	F	15	2	2	5	25,930
Katrina Nipper	4	F	9	0	2	0	4,181
Kat's Fairy Tale	2	F	1	0	0	0	2,050
Kat's Malagra Fool	3	F	10	0	2	2	16,600
Katskan	3	C	7	1	5	0	14,880
Katsu	3	G	8	1	3	0	12,417
Katty Du	3	F	11	1	4	2	8,415
Katuna Terms	7	M	6	0	0	0	4,994
Katy Katers	4	F	12	1	3	2	48,130
Katy Smiles	2	F	2	1	1	0	11,200
Katy's Quick	3	F	7	0	0	2	3,305
Katz Got Rhythm	5	H	11	0	0	0	1,809
Katzanova	3	C	3	1	0	1	24,015
Katze Frau	2	F	3	0	0	0	2,175
Katzen	5	M	7	1	0	1	42,350
Kaufy Mate	3	C	4	2	0	0	215,000
Kavita Nadira	3	F	7	0	0	2	3,664
Kavon's Gold	5	M	1	0	0	0	61
Kaw Liga Sioux	4	G	6	0	1	0	8,800
Kawartha Lakes	4	G	4	0	0	0	614
Kay Colleen	6	M	4	0	0	0	0
Kay Max	3	G	1	0	0	0	780
Kayandeesdream	5	H	7	1	0	0	2,682
Kaya's Kali	3	F	1	0	0	0	0
Kaydara	3	F	1	0	0	0	780
Kaye Bear	7	M	9	0	0	0	1,156
Kaykattiva	2	F	3	0	0	0	1,230
Kaylan's Rose	4	F	4	1	0	1	27,466
Kayla's Diamond	3	F	1	0	0	0	1,440
Kaylas Scatcat	3	F	8	1	2	1	18,010
Kaylazoo	5	M	3	0	0	0	332
Kaylee Bailey	5	M	10	4	0	0	33,783
Kayleigh Karat	9	M	8	0	0	0	450
Kayleighbelle	2	F	1	0	0	1	5,280
Kayley's Crossing	2	C	1	0	0	0	0
Kaylie Kay	5	M	2	0	0	0	0

Horse	Age	Sex	Sts	1st	2d	3d	Won
Kaylynn's Memory	3	F	4	0	0	0	940
Kayo Too	4	F	13	2	0	3	10,579
Kayotic	5	G	3	0	0	0	450
Kayraque	6	G	9	1	2	0	7,208
Kayrawan's Girl	4	F	7	1	2	0	11,401
Kay's Daughter	4	F	9	0	1	0	6,653
Kay's Ok	2	F	4	0	0	1	1,951
Kays Way	4	F	11	2	4	2	9,871
Kaysome	3	F	7	1	1	1	13,255
Kaytimkris	3	G	16	0	4	0	4,429
Kaze Ninja	3	C	6	0	1	1	4,850
Kazliv	8	H	7	0	0	0	0
Kazoo	6	H	6	1	2	0	54,920
Kazu Hero	4	G	6	1	0	0	7,065
Kazziano	2	F	4	0	0	0	2,236
Kcdrew	4	F	5	0	0	0	1,072
Keaheys Woman	4	F	4	1	0	0	6,000
Kearney's Special	5	G	4	0	0	0	0
Keats and Yeats	10	G	4	0	2	1	3,975
Kebo Valley	8	H	4	0	1	0	2,550
Kedington	5	G	7	0	1	1	24,784
Kee Kaw	2	C	7	1	0	2	20,910
Keeatah	2	F	3	1	0	0	9,954
Keekee Manzotti	5	G	9	0	0	0	566
Keelhauled	3	C	11	0	1	3	5,798
Keelyn	7	M	11	1	2	2	8,252
Keen and Bold	2	F	5	0	1	1	3,740
Keen Cat	2	G	7	0	1	1	3,683
Keen Decision	7	G	4	0	0	0	433
Keen Hope	5	M	12	1	5	3	24,780
Keen Intelligence	4	G	18	2	4	3	22,660
Keen Isabella	2	F	3	0	0	0	600
Keen Lassie	2	F	3	0	0	0	406
Keen Perception	4	F	10	3	0	2	40,510
Keen Scent	5	M	3	0	0	0	790
Keenan	3	G	15	3	3	2	36,570
Keene Lady	4	F	10	3	3	2	19,472
Keene Othello	6	G	11	0	0	0	711
Keenebridge Fun	4	G	2	0	0	0	285
Keep Abreast	3	F	4	0	0	0	1,600
Keep Choken	2	F	2	1	1	0	6,880
Keep Cool	4	G	10	3	2	2	112,190
Keep Crusing	3	G	12	3	0	1	28,420
Keep 'Em Honest	5	M	1	0	0	0	210
Keep 'Em Rolling	4	F	7	1	0	1	10,030
Keep 'Em Up There	3	G	9	0	0	1	8,471
Keep Hope Alive	4	G	9	1	0	1	6,568
Keep It At Par	5	G	8	0	0	2	2,616
Keep It Country	4	F	8	1	0	0	11,120
Keep It Holy	7	G	2	0	0	0	870
Keep It Karakorum	5	G	8	0	0	0	483
Keep It Personal	3	C	15	2	2	2	16,033
Keep It Quiet	3	F	1	0	0	0	0
Keep It Real	3	F	2	0	0	0	130
Keep It Simple Guy	4	G	14	1	2	3	11,515
Keep It Strait	10	G	13	2	1	1	17,415
Keep Moving	5	G	10	0	0	0	803
Keep On Ponching	3	F	12	1	0	1	7,800
Keep On Punching	3	C	6	0	1	1	19,540
Keep On Rockin	6	M	11	1	0	2	5,334
Keep On Turkin	3	G	12	3	2	0	13,145
Keep Our Secret	3	G	12	1	0	3	8,588
Keep Sam in Cheq	2	G	4	1	1	0	15,340
Keep Shining	5	M	7	0	0	1	2,130
Keep the Cash	4	F	6	2	1	2	10,166
Keep the Feeling	3	F	9	1	1	2	43,455
Keep The Silver (GB)	5	G	11	1	0	1	4,802
Keep Thgrey Going	6	M	1	0	0	0	0
Keep This Cat	3	F	8	1	2	0	28,751
Keepairinyourtires	2	F	1	0	1	0	2,300
Keeper of Dreams	2	F	5	0	0	0	986
Keeper of the Bell	5	G	10	0	0	2	3,090
Keeperkool	3	F	6	0	0	1	328
Keeperofthelight	4	C	3	0	0	0	645
Keepin It Real	6	G	6	2	0	1	12,772
Keeping Cool	4	F	10	1	2	1	11,210
Keeping Faith	4	F	3	1	0	0	9,126
Keeping Quiet	3	C	10	1	1	1	42,470
Keeping the Gold	4	F	2	0	0	0	3,600
Keeping Watch (IRE)	3	F	8	1	1	1	22,232
Keepingthepeace	4	C	8	0	0	0	1,947
Keepitinthebag	4	G	9	1	2	0	23,690
Keepnupwidajones'	4	F	4	0	0	0	0
Keeponbelieving	2	G	8	1	2	0	19,515
Keeponthesunniside	4	F	5	1	1	0	8,440
Keepswooinshoes	2	F	4	0	0	0	4,340
Keepthefaith	3	G	4	0	1	1	6,570
Keepthescore	2	F	3	0	0	0	0
Keepurmuninupocket	7	M	11	1	0	0	9,197
Keepyoureyeonme	5	M	16	1	1	3	8,394
Keepyourhandsdown	5	G	5	0	1	0	3,875
Keepyourwitsaboutu	3	F	6	1	2	0	17,065
Keesler	3	F	8	3	1	1	95,130
Keet Brown	3	C	11	2	0	0	19,540
Keetoowah	2	F	3	0	0	0	3,040
Keezar	4	G	15	2	2	0	10,363
Keffa	2	F	2	0	0	1	4,988
Keg Kicker	5	G	12	1	0	0	3,822
K'ehleyr	3	F	7	1	5	0	74,200
Keiai Mahha	4	G	12	0	3	1	8,587
Keiai Sakura	4	F	11	2	0	1	72,158
Keikik	4	F	13	3	4	2	37,998
Keith Can Score	3	G	11	1	0	1	17,790
Keith's Town	2	F	1	0	0	1	2,035
Kel Kel	3	F	11	1	1	1	29,292
Kel Lex Edition	4	F	10	1	0	1	9,513
Kela	6	H	9	3	1	0	710,212
Kelam	2	F	1	0	0	0	0
Kelchinko	6	G	5	0	0	0	374
Keleb Ridge	9	G	2	0	0	0	112
Keles	5	M	3	0	0	0	150
Kell	3	G	6	2	0	1	50,086
Kell Belle	3	F	2	0	0	0	788
Kellans Night	4	G	8	0	1	0	842
Kellera	3	F	7	1	0	0	4,739
Kellerin	3	F	1	0	0	0	170
Kelleys Island	5	G	8	0	0	3	1,939
Kelley's Mischief	4	F	2	0	2	0	2,200
Kelleys Star	5	M	5	0	0	0	0
Kelli Likes Soccer	4	F	10	2	0	2	16,895
Kellie's Ghost	6	G	4	0	1	0	2,182
Kelli's Good Boy	3	G	6	0	0	0	870
Kelli's Good Pick	9	M	1	0	0	0	0
Kelli's Law	3	F	13	4	3	1	43,195
Kelli's Song	5	M	8	1	1	1	45,120
Kelly Bay	5	M	12	0	5	0	5,130
Kelly Bear	4	F	16	4	3	2	32,111
Kelly G's Cat	2	C	1	0	0	0	1,230
Kelly Is a Honey	4	F	14	3	2	4	11,060
Kelly Kelly Kelly	2	C	2	0	0	0	790
Kelly West	4	F	5	1	1	1	17,667
Kelly With a K	3	G	12	1	2	3	30,480
Kellynette	4	F	7	2	1	0	16,920
Kelly's Ash	3	F	3	0	0	0	0
Kelly's Chance	3	G	7	0	1	0	2,275
Kelly's Chief	2	C	1	0	0	0	780
Kelly's Concerto	4	C	13	1	2	3	9,286
Kelly's Desire	7	M	1	0	0	0	0
Kelly's Dream	4	F	9	1	1	1	8,295
Kelly's Fuego	6	G	2	0	0	1	470
Kellys Guest	3	F	9	4	1	0	71,890
Kelly's Hat	4	F	11	3	2	2	19,273
Kelly's K. C.	6	G	3	0	0	1	2,159
Kelly's Lake	3	F	2	0	1	1	7,100
Kelly's Landing	3	G	2	2	0	0	53,771
Kelly's Loot	4	G	9	0	2	1	5,282
Kelly's Princess	2	F	7	2	2	1	88,711
Kelly's Tea Time	3	F	2	0	0	0	93
Kelp	3	G	5	1	2	1	30,816
Kels Four Winds	4	G	13	1	3	2	7,163
Kels On the Attack	10	G	8	0	2	0	2,910
Kelsey	2	F	1	0	0	0	0
Kelsey Park	6	M	7	1	2	0	7,420
Kelsey's Cracker	4	F	2	1	1	0	6,000
Kelsi Marie	3	F	2	0	0	1	825
Kelsie Dawn	6	M	6	0	0	0	625
Kelsie Nelson	7	M	9	0	0	0	630
Kelsies Boy	3	C	2	0	0	0	70

Horse	Age	Sex	Sts	1st	2d	3d	Won
Kelsy's Charm	6	M	8	0	0	0	1,599
Keltic Blues	4	F	6	1	0	0	6,766
Keltic Dancer	4	G	18	2	1	6	37,180
Kelt's J Boy	4	G	19	1	1	2	14,478
Kemerton	6	G	10	0	2	3	11,265
Kemo Sabe	4	G	14	2	6	4	41,959
Kemo Sabe Ben	2	C	1	0	0	0	400
Kemp	3	G	7	2	0	1	41,360
Kemper	2	C	4	0	0	0	0
Kem's Song	5	M	1	0	0	0	0
Ken	5	H	3	0	0	0	183
Kenai River	3	C	13	2	4	1	34,640
Kenala	6	G	7	1	0	1	6,112
Kendall Point	7	G	8	1	2	1	7,776
Kendi Lou	5	M	11	3	4	2	83,975
Kendra's Undone	2	F	3	0	1	1	2,332
Kenickie	4	G	8	0	1	0	1,719
Kenjay	7	G	8	0	2	2	3,319
Kenmarita (FR)	4	F	12	0	2	2	19,292
Kennedy Sun	5	H	4	0	1	1	1,992
Kennedys Passage	2	G	2	0	0	0	420
Kennel Up	3	C	13	2	3	1	98,909
Kenner	3	G	3	0	0	0	1,580
Kenneth	11	G	18	0	1	1	3,024
Kenneth's Cat	2	G	5	2	1	0	26,640
Kennett Pike	5	H	2	0	1	0	1,640
Kennewick	5	G	13	2	1	2	28,251
Kennileeanme	4	F	12	1	2	1	13,094
Kenny B Quick	3	G	13	1	1	0	10,495
Kenny C	5	G	8	2	0	0	4,224
Kenny D	3	G	3	0	0	1	1,780
Kenny Hawk	5	H	2	0	0	0	900
Kenny K	6	G	5	0	0	2	3,317
Kenny Run	3	G	10	2	2	1	42,380
Kenny's Crossing	6	G	9	2	1	1	18,330
Kenny's Lad	3	G	7	0	1	2	3,765
Ken's Cat	2	C	3	0	0	1	2,382
Kens Dancer	6	H	14	7	1	0	38,566
Ken's Sister	2	F	6	1	0	1	12,272
Kensington Park	7	G	8	2	0	2	4,767
Kent Hall	4	F	12	5	1	1	58,870
Kent Ridge	3	C	9	2	1	2	112,685
Kenta Kun	3	G	5	3	1	1	57,250
Kenter	2	C	5	0	1	1	9,480
Kenton	3	G	7	1	2	0	33,522
Kents Account	4	G	4	0	0	1	2,486
Kentucky Bay	6	G	9	1	2	2	20,975
Kentucky Breakdown	4	G	11	1	2	0	9,355
Kentucky Cat	5	M	10	1	0	2	11,270
Kentucky Champ	3	C	13	1	2	1	32,585
Kentucky Charm	10	G	5	0	0	0	0
Kentucky Frost	3	F	8	0	0	1	1,470
Kentucky Gamble	3	F	13	2	2	1	14,320
Kentucky J B	6	G	7	3	2	0	60,630
Kentucky Joe	3	G	4	0	0	1	975
Kentucky Kris	3	C	12	1	4	1	23,862
Kentucky Lad	3	G	9	1	0	0	26,967
Kentucky Lake	9	G	14	1	0	1	3,325
Kentucky Look	2	F	4	0	0	0	660
Kentucky Mike	3	C	4	0	0	0	506
Kentucky Pride	4	C	12	1	4	2	64,116
Kentucky Ridge	2	F	7	0	1	0	2,150
Kentucky Ruckus	5	M	8	1	0	0	9,387
Kentucky Squall	6	G	10	1	1	0	11,095
Kentucky Strike	8	M	4	0	0	0	0
Kentucky Swagger	2	C	1	0	0	0	145
Kentucky Trust	5	G	12	4	3	2	26,750
Kentucky Wind	3	C	12	2	2	2	14,494
Kentucky Woman	4	F	13	1	1	2	18,670
Kenward	3	G	10	2	2	1	17,078
Kenya	4	C	6	0	0	0	1,092
Kenyan	4	F	2	0	1	0	900
Kenyawin	6	H	3	0	0	1	1,938
Kenza	2	F	4	1	0	2	37,080
Kenzie Girl	6	M	1	0	0	1	2,640
Keo Silver	3	F	6	0	0	0	555
Keoki Native	10	G	22	1	2	7	4,821
Keoni	6	G	6	0	0	0	1,290
Keosnative	3	F	9	4	1	2	20,670
Keppoch	3	C	7	1	0	0	13,531
Kept Promise	2	F	2	0	0	1	3,280
Kept the Ace	3	G	7	0	0	0	1,094
Keptherhuntinghard	4	F	18	1	2	2	8,290
Kera's Kitty Cat	2	F	3	1	0	0	16,680
Keratonic	7	G	1	0	0	0	0
Kered	2	C	3	0	0	0	250
Kermit's Choice	9	G	3	1	0	1	3,329
Kern	2	C	1	0	0	0	300
Kernal K	7	G	13	2	0	3	29,410
Kernville	2	G	5	0	0	2	1,498
Kerosene King	3	G	19	1	2	3	12,039
Kerosene Prospect	3	F	10	4	2	1	23,353
Keroson	3	G	7	0	1	2	7,000
Kerri Berri Red	3	F	7	1	1	1	4,075
Kerriada	2	F	4	0	0	1	1,699
Kerricat	3	F	9	4	3	0	41,344
Kerriokayjo	3	F	6	1	0	0	7,236
Kerri's Acre	2	F	3	0	0	0	0
Kerrobert	2	C	2	1	0	0	45,870
Kerry Wil	2	G	2	0	0	0	2,166
Kerrygold (FR)	8	H	7	0	2	0	2,081
Kes Kat	8	G	13	2	1	3	16,780
Kesia	3	F	5	0	0	1	680
Kesslars Pet	3	G	6	0	0	0	0
Ketch a Hello	4	F	4	0	0	1	21,642
Ketchikan Miss	4	F	2	0	0	0	157
Ketchmewhereyoucan	2	F	7	2	1	1	50,650
Keteky Kemoky	4	F	6	4	0	1	37,050
Kettal Creek	3	F	13	1	3	4	42,547
Kettle Island	3	G	1	0	0	0	135
Kettle Man	7	H	2	0	0	0	0
Kevin the Legend	3	G	7	1	1	2	22,670
Kevins Cherokee	9	M	1	0	0	0	135
Kevin's Decision	4	F	5	2	1	0	94,304
Kevins Nightmare	4	F	11	1	2	0	11,022
Kevin's Secret	4	G	2	1	0	1	5,080
Kevin's Way	5	G	18	0	4	2	7,941
Kevmava	5	M	4	0	0	0	159
Kewanee	5	M	8	2	0	3	11,575
Kewanee Secret	4	F	4	0	2	0	4,738
Kewarra	3	G	4	0	0	0	2,446
Kewen	4	G	9	0	3	2	53,220
Key Alfaari	3	F	5	1	0	0	14,624
Key Causeway	2	F	3	0	0	0	3,680
Key Dance	3	G	7	1	0	1	5,881
Key Decision	4	G	9	1	2	2	12,618
Key Definition	4	F	3	0	0	0	905
Key Deputy	4	C	6	2	2	0	78,177
Key Devine	2	C	2	0	0	0	185
Key Document	6	G	13	2	2	2	17,335
Key Idea	4	C	6	1	0	0	11,053
Key Issues	2	C	4	1	0	0	12,040
Key Moesaabe Kid	2	C	3	0	0	0	0
Key On Richie	7	G	4	0	0	0	1,590
Key Prosecutor	3	G	3	0	0	0	600
Key Race	3	G	4	0	0	1	1,985
Key Rate	4	F	6	1	0	0	6,537
Key Reality	7	M	10	1	2	0	11,075
Key Royalty	4	F	3	0	0	0	395
Key Runner	6	G	14	1	2	3	4,196
Key Solution	5	G	14	1	4	1	19,868
Key Sparkle	3	F	14	1	1	2	7,755
Key Squall	3	F	1	0	0	0	0
Key Storm	4	F	14	4	2	1	69,640
Key Sunday	3	G	4	1	1	0	7,209
Key to Angeline	3	F	4	0	0	0	1,911
Key to Barley	3	G	2	0	0	0	0
Key to Broadway	7	M	3	0	0	0	746
Key to Love	4	F	11	0	3	3	51,080
Key to My Fantasy	4	G	3	0	0	0	0
Key to Paris	5	G	5	0	0	1	5,254
Key to Profits	4	G	3	1	0	0	4,170
Key to the Bomb	4	G	20	2	4	2	22,748
Key to the Cat	3	F	13	2	4	3	109,706
Key to the Champ	6	G	2	0	0	0	0
Key to the Defense	3	C	1	0	0	0	88
Key to the Palace	3	F	1	0	0	0	400
Key to the Point	4	G	9	0	5	1	11,781

Horse	Age	Sex	Sts	1st	2d	3d	Won
Key to the Punch	3	G	10	0	1	2	2,104
Key to the Storm	4	F	2	0	0	1	752
Key to the Track	3	C	3	0	0	0	168
Key West Sunset	4	G	12	1	1	2	11,340
Key Wi Miss	6	M	4	0	0	1	7,000
Keyano	10	G	4	0	0	1	935
Keybar	3	F	2	0	0	0	500
Keyboard	4	G	7	3	1	0	34,747
Keymar Express	6	G	4	0	0	0	3,825
Keynote Speaker	4	G	6	0	0	0	347
Keyper of Thestorm	4	F	3	0	0	1	1,625
Keyron	6	G	7	0	1	1	5,635
Keys a Don Juan	3	G	10	1	3	2	14,973
Keys in My Pocket	3	G	1	0	0	0	0
Keys to Heaven	3	F	2	0	0	0	0
Keys to the Heart	5	M	7	1	2	0	100,800
Keysaflirt	4	G	1	0	0	0	300
Keysister	5	G	13	1	1	2	20,930
Keystone Malibu	2	F	2	0	1	0	9,100
Keystone Mountain	2	C	1	0	0	1	2,860
Keystone Point	3	C	5	2	0	0	65,580
Keyth's Karma	4	G	12	3	0	0	29,100
Keytothepenthouse	7	G	14	4	1	2	48,914
Kfar Daniel (FR)	2	C	4	1	1	1	40,617
Khaki Lee	3	F	16	1	1	2	12,194
Khalil's Mill	5	M	2	0	0	0	368
Kham Beau	6	M	8	0	0	1	7,942
Khamadee Uv Erruz	5	H	7	1	0	0	5,009
Khan	8	H	1	0	0	0	0
Kharkov Lady	4	F	2	0	0	0	225
Khe Sanh	3	F	5	0	0	1	2,420
Kherson	5	G	10	2	0	0	7,378
Khid Lat	4	F	3	0	0	0	0
Khronus	3	G	13	3	1	2	34,493
Khumbaba	4	G	4	0	0	0	0
Khyber Kelly	3	C	9	1	4	3	22,520
Kiana (PER)	5	M	1	0	0	0	1,300
Kiana's Star	4	F	10	3	1	3	17,373
Kiara Tiara	4	F	3	0	0	0	935
Kiati	5	M	5	0	0	1	5,443
Kiawah	4	C	7	1	1	1	15,901
Kiawah Island	2	C	1	0	0	1	2,760
Kick Boxer (FR)	7	G	1	1	0	0	3,900
Kick In	4	C	3	0	0	0	937
Kick It in Gear	10	G	8	1	3	1	5,480
Kick Sand	7	G	1	0	0	0	0
Kick the Can	2	F	5	0	1	1	3,500
Kickaboom	5	M	5	0	0	0	692
Kickapoo Kid	3	G	17	0	1	3	4,502
Kickback	9	G	10	3	0	0	23,272
Kickboard	3	C	12	2	2	0	58,274
Kickem Dalton	5	G	7	0	0	1	4,135
Kicken Kris	4	C	6	2	0	1	727,000
Kicken Time	8	M	8	1	0	0	2,050
Kickenthecat	3	F	1	0	0	0	256
Kickety Katy	8	M	3	0	0	0	330
Kickin Free	5	M	11	0	0	0	1,267
Kickin Kountry	4	G	14	1	2	6	24,760
Kickin Stars	3	F	2	0	0	0	0
Kickingbird	3	G	5	0	0	0	875
Kickit Baboom	4	F	3	0	0	0	0
Kickitupanotch	5	G	12	1	2	5	13,065
Kickn Chickn	4	F	4	0	1	0	1,387
Kick'n Kacie	4	F	8	0	0	0	932
Kicks and Flicks	3	G	6	1	3	1	22,320
Kicks Are for Kids	3	C	23	0	2	4	12,014
Kickserve	5	G	5	1	0	0	5,775
Kid a Lot	8	H	13	2	0	2	14,239
Kid Amour	4	G	5	0	0	0	0
Kid Attitude	3	G	12	1	1	2	30,261
Kid Ballado	6	H	3	1	0	0	4,500
Kid Buttons	3	G	4	2	0	0	60,876
Kid Carrots	4	F	11	1	5	2	39,129
Kid Chocolate	8	G	8	0	1	0	2,340
Kid Colonel	2	C	3	0	0	0	368
Kid Condo	3	G	6	1	0	0	2,574
Kid Copper	6	G	10	1	2	1	19,547
Kid Courageous	7	G	16	3	1	1	12,949
Kid Cum Laude	3	G	8	0	1	1	2,550

Horse	Age	Sex	Sts	1st	2d	3d	Won
Kid Dempsey	3	G	1	0	0	0	300
Kid Diamond	4	G	9	1	0	0	7,693
Kid Fireman	5	G	7	3	0	0	4,730
Kid Friday	6	H	5	0	1	1	1,755
Kid Garson	3	G	9	1	2	0	11,489
Kid Grindstone	2	C	1	0	0	0	0
Kid Halo	4	C	15	2	7	1	34,310
Kid Joshua	7	G	6	1	0	0	2,852
Kid Kaelin	4	G	7	0	0	2	6,950
Kid Katowice	6	G	4	0	0	0	504
Kid Matt	4	G	7	1	3	0	7,584
Kid Maverick	4	G	5	1	2	0	2,040
Kid Miraglia	7	G	12	0	1	0	1,909
Kid Quixote	3	C	11	3	2	1	36,870
Kid Ralston	3	G	7	2	1	1	31,222
Kid Red	3	G	7	1	0	0	35,280
Kid Rich	5	G	13	3	5	3	35,292
Kid Rigo	6	G	9	1	2	0	35,512
Kid Rio	4	G	11	1	0	2	7,538
Kid Royal	3	C	9	4	1	1	96,260
Kid Ruckus	5	G	10	0	3	0	2,545
Kid Russell	4	G	17	6	1	1	33,352
Kid Semoran	4	C	2	0	0	0	145
Kid Slew	7	G	7	1	0	1	2,165
Kid Smokey	3	G	12	3	3	1	41,356
Kid Stogie	2	C	1	0	0	1	2,093
Kid Sugar	7	G	16	1	4	1	9,266
Kid Trump	6	H	1	0	0	0	0
Kid Try On	9	G	8	1	0	3	4,943
Kid Tuaca	3	G	15	1	5	3	72,860
Kidd Play	4	C	5	0	3	0	13,400
Kidder Kit	2	F	2	0	0	0	1,051
Kiddle Mischief	4	G	1	0	0	0	0
Kiddo	5	H	7	1	2	2	10,979
Kiddville	10	G	11	2	1	0	16,308
Kideeakey	2	F	7	0	0	2	9,145
Kidisa's Honor	2	F	6	0	0	2	10,640
Kidkillam	5	H	2	0	0	0	110
Kidney Bean	4	G	10	0	0	2	795
Kidontheblock	5	G	2	0	0	0	968
Kids Gem	5	G	2	0	0	0	180
Kids Got Skills	3	G	2	0	0	0	415
Kids Ridge	4	G	12	2	4	3	58,955
Kids Spirit	3	C	6	0	0	0	918
Kiechlin	4	C	1	0	0	0	135
Kiitos	3	F	5	1	1	1	34,882
Kiki B	2	F	5	1	0	0	28,862
Kikika's Gold	3	G	9	1	1	1	12,705
Kikuyu	3	F	11	1	1	2	17,223
Kilbride Rd	2	C	1	0	0	1	1,650
Kilcullen	4	G	7	1	1	0	12,975
Kildare Dancer	5	G	13	2	2	4	22,826
Kiley Slew	3	F	9	0	2	1	11,530
Kilgarten	4	G	8	0	2	0	13,114
Kilgorie	3	G	9	0	0	0	998
Kilgowan	3	C	6	2	0	0	140,522
Kili	5	G	5	0	0	0	1,312
Kilkea Castle	4	C	7	2	2	1	77,466
Kill Joy	2	F	5	0	1	2	4,783
Killarney Gold	4	G	4	0	0	0	1,000
Killarney Kutie	4	F	13	2	1	1	36,100
Killenaule	2	C	9	4	3	2	198,540
Killer Angel	6	H	13	2	4	1	55,980
Killer App	4	F	10	1	0	3	11,950
Killer Creek	6	G	1	0	0	0	0
Killer Kyle	6	H	8	1	2	0	9,751
Killian's Chin	3	C	11	3	0	1	14,326
Killing Frost	3	F	14	3	0	1	32,275
Killing M Softly	3	F	9	1	3	0	35,620
Kiln	6	G	7	0	1	0	2,434
Kilo S S	4	C	6	1	0	2	15,370
Kilronan Castle	3	G	8	2	1	1	10,440
Kilt Lilt	4	F	6	1	2	0	16,290
Kiltee	6	M	3	0	0	0	0
Kim	8	M	9	1	3	2	13,455
Kim Baker	2	F	5	1	1	2	25,240
Kim Loves Bucky	7	G	2	0	0	0	11,996
Kim N Kes	4	F	2	0	0	0	270
Kim Possible	3	F	10	2	2	2	30,583

Horse	Age	Sex	Sts	1st	2d	3d	Won
Kim the Brat	4	F	2	0	0	0	680
Kimandani	5	G	4	0	0	0	122
Kimberley Regiment	4	G	5	1	1	2	18,669
Kimberleywithaneeh	4	G	8	0	0	3	2,057
Kimberly'sprincess	4	F	1	0	0	0	0
Kimbow Slew	5	M	2	0	0	0	282
Kimi Anne	3	F	2	0	1	1	9,275
Kimis Delight	4	F	7	2	0	2	8,464
Kimmy's Kid	3	F	8	1	0	1	14,700
Kimon	4	G	7	0	2	1	14,350
Kimry Moor	5	M	17	2	2	4	17,046
Kim's Angel	3	G	12	1	2	0	8,542
Kim's Attitude	3	F	5	1	1	2	10,470
Kims Career	2	F	2	0	0	0	140
Kim's Gem	3	G	7	3	0	0	69,550
Kim's Grace	2	F	3	0	0	0	1,200
Kim's Luck	3	F	2	0	0	0	0
Kim's Lucky Star	3	G	2	0	0	0	0
Kim'sgoldenmoment	2	F	3	0	0	0	329
Kimster	5	M	10	0	3	2	19,450
Kin Roar	3	G	13	1	0	1	9,408
Kina Blessed	6	M	5	1	1	1	5,200
Kina Flashy	6	M	3	0	0	1	163
Kind Connection	5	M	8	1	1	0	3,580
Kind Lena	3	F	6	1	1	0	18,220
Kind Sir	4	G	1	0	0	0	0
Kind Slew	5	G	16	5	2	2	36,180
Kinda Gotta Wanna	5	G	10	2	0	2	6,596
Kindand Generous	6	G	5	0	0	0	37
Kinderhook	4	C	5	0	1	0	3,153
Kinderscout	3	G	3	0	0	0	0
Kindling	2	F	1	0	0	0	145
Kindofanact	4	G	9	1	1	3	12,110
Kindon	5	M	6	2	2	2	6,880
Kindred Glow	4	F	4	2	0	2	4,875
Kinematics	4	F	5	2	2	1	32,400
Kiner's Korner	5	G	12	1	0	1	6,600
Kinesthesia	4	F	10	1	2	2	19,327
Kinetic Rush	5	G	18	3	1	3	36,351
King Abba	3	G	9	2	2	3	9,913
King Abed	3	F	11	1	0	0	3,677
King Adam	3	G	4	1	0	0	9,240
King Aha	3	C	12	1	2	2	9,905
King Alexander	5	G	8	1	0	0	8,226
King and Queen	4	G	9	0	1	1	665
King and the Beger	4	G	6	0	0	0	0
King Beano	4	C	1	0	0	0	220
King Biscuit	4	G	10	1	0	0	5,080
King Bishops Ruby	8	M	7	0	0	0	406
King Bling	2	C	1	0	0	0	450
King Caesar	6	G	4	0	0	0	200
King Carson	4	G	7	0	0	0	480
King Cassia	4	G	14	2	1	2	46,810
King Cephus	5	G	1	0	0	0	107
King Cha Cha	3	C	7	2	0	0	32,460
King Cielo	6	H	10	1	0	2	26,280
King City	9	G	9	1	1	1	17,474
King City Lady	3	F	2	0	0	0	0
King Cole	3	G	2	0	0	0	0
King Con	3	C	5	0	0	0	2,100
King Crafty	8	G	2	0	0	0	225
King Creole	3	G	5	1	0	1	20,150
King Dale	5	G	4	0	0	0	152
King David's Son	3	C	7	2	2	0	39,145
King De	3	C	11	1	0	3	14,210
King Decor	6	H	10	1	0	0	12,623
King Diablo	10	G	10	0	1	0	1,335
King Dynamite	2	C	1	0	0	0	400
King Ed	4	G	9	0	0	0	400
King Finesse	9	H	5	0	0	0	1,926
King Fortunate	2	G	4	0	2	1	13,980
King Fox	4	G	7	0	0	0	120
King Freddie	2	G	1	1	0	0	11,700
King Gamini	3	G	2	0	0	0	166
King George W.	4	G	14	2	0	4	81,702
King Grader	6	G	13	2	1	4	19,335
King Harvest	3	G	9	1	3	0	11,920
King Hill Rhythm	3	G	3	1	0	1	1,831
King Hope	5	G	11	1	0	1	4,160
King in Jeans	3	C	7	0	0	0	860
King Jedi	3	C	3	0	0	1	200
King Jeremy	7	G	11	1	2	2	27,403
King Justin	3	G	7	3	1	1	42,128
King Karl	3	C	10	0	1	3	6,901
King Kev	2	G	5	0	1	0	2,613
King Kevin	7	G	12	0	1	0	2,291
King Knocker	5	G	5	1	2	0	15,560
King Kohota	4	C	4	0	1	1	2,460
King Kong Daddy	4	C	1	0	0	0	90
King Ky	4	G	7	2	2	1	19,787
King Lear	4	G	6	0	1	1	5,150
King Magic	4	C	5	1	1	0	35,840
King Matthew	4	C	19	2	6	2	38,715
King Maximus	3	G	2	0	1	0	7,840
King Maxwell	4	G	7	1	1	0	2,250
King Me	9	G	13	4	1	0	37,336
King Miles	3	C	7	2	0	0	15,500
King Mobay	2	C	7	1	1	1	18,032
King Muloon	4	G	7	2	0	0	6,795
King Mustang	2	C	2	0	0	0	580
King Newt	11	G	12	5	5	1	40,390
King O ' the Igloo	7	G	13	3	2	1	18,270
King of Adventure	7	G	6	1	3	1	3,527
King of Carnival	5	G	9	0	1	0	1,750
King of Cash	4	G	4	0	0	0	0
King of Cashmere	4	C	1	0	0	0	0
King of Chicago	4	R	10	2	1	1	23,620
King of Decor	3	C	4	0	2	0	16,020
King of Destiny	4	G	2	0	0	0	280
King of Diamonds	8	G	6	1	1	2	4,740
King of Dust	3	G	13	1	2	1	10,717
King of Gold	4	G	13	0	0	3	12,041
King of Happiness	5	H	8	2	1	2	161,802
King of Jazz	2	G	1	0	0	1	3,850
King of Knights	8	G	15	1	1	3	19,044
King of Mardi Gras	3	C	16	3	0	2	52,887
King of Mountain	3	G	6	3	1	1	57,374
King of Nastar	3	G	1	0	0	0	0
King of Nasty	7	G	11	2	1	4	28,200
King of Nubia	5	G	15	3	1	1	10,654
King of Prussia	4	G	6	0	1	2	4,094
King of Rohan	2	C	1	0	0	0	400
King of Rulers	4	G	7	0	2	0	8,112
King of Siam	4	C	10	2	1	1	84,654
King of Spain	7	G	15	0	0	6	5,178
King of Speed	5	G	14	2	2	1	68,463
King of Tarts	3	G	10	1	0	2	11,638
King of the Blues	5	G	1	0	0	0	0
King of the Brass	4	G	6	0	1	1	2,130
King of the Cats	4	F	18	3	4	3	23,136
King of the Derby	3	G	3	0	0	0	400
King of the Mount	5	H	20	4	1	1	27,994
King of the Night	4	G	12	1	0	0	9,174
King of the Park	2	G	1	0	1	0	1,482
King of the Stars	3	G	8	1	1	0	11,730
King of the Valley	3	C	8	1	1	0	10,255
King of the World	4	G	7	0	0	1	3,795
King of the Yukon	4	G	7	1	2	0	2,180
King of Thieves	8	G	4	0	0	0	884
King of Thunder	8	G	7	0	0	0	2,190
King of Victory	2	G	1	0	0	0	400
King Ofthestreet	5	G	16	0	1	1	6,239
King Oro	8	G	5	0	0	0	678
King Palm	3	C	4	0	2	1	23,480
King Quin	4	G	16	0	1	2	3,380
King Richard	6	H	7	1	1	0	37,300
King Robyn	4	G	4	1	0	1	47,132
King Rodeo	3	G	6	1	0	0	7,572
King Rolando	3	G	3	0	0	0	195
King Royal	4	G	5	0	0	1	1,626
King Royale	5	H	4	0	1	0	3,000
King Ruler	6	G	10	3	1	1	11,101
King Sadler	3	C	14	0	1	5	7,209
King Simpatia (BRZ)	4	C	8	3	3	0	59,690
King Slayer (GB)	9	H	5	0	1	0	3,805
King Steven	4	C	4	1	2	0	27,210
King Sweep	5	H	13	1	0	3	12,730
King Troy	4	G	5	0	1	2	3,840

Horse	Age	Sex	Sts	1st	2d	3d	Won
King True	3	F	11	2	0	1	21,720
King Tukk	2	G	2	0	0	0	1,470
King Vic	6	G	14	2	1	2	9,420
King Victor	3	G	6	1	1	2	10,823
King William	3	G	1	0	1	0	1,400
King Wonderful	5	G	6	1	3	0	26,455
King Zonic	5	H	7	1	0	3	27,710
King Zotti	6	H	4	0	0	0	0
Kinga	4	G	8	0	0	1	1,546
Kingboro's Sword	2	F	4	0	0	0	300
Kingdom Come (IRE)	3	C	9	2	1	2	62,365
Kingidashi	4	G	11	1	0	0	7,020
Kingmenow	4	G	2	0	1	0	5,040
Kingnambi	3	G	5	0	2	2	2,776
Kingofthecourt	3	G	6	2	1	0	26,900
Kingofthemountain	6	G	1	0	0	0	400
Kingoftherawbar	6	G	11	3	2	1	15,132
Kings and Quinns	4	G	6	2	0	0	27,159
King's Banker	2	F	1	0	0	0	750
Kings Bay Boy	4	C	4	0	0	1	692
King's Beauty	3	F	10	3	0	1	17,170
King's Bid	3	G	9	0	2	2	3,962
King's Bridge	2	C	1	0	0	0	0
Kings Caboose	2	F	4	0	0	0	340
Kings Category	3	G	10	0	2	1	11,688
King's Charmer	3	F	7	1	1	2	47,440
King's Choice	2	C	2	0	0	1	4,350
King's Cloak	8	G	1	0	0	0	113
King's Cobrina	3	F	3	0	0	0	0
Kings Commotion	3	G	2	0	0	0	323
King's Conclusion	4	G	19	3	3	3	22,455
King's Coronation	3	C	6	1	2	1	64,450
Kings Course	4	C	1	0	0	0	300
King's Crossing	4	G	2	0	0	0	150
King's Decree	4	G	3	2	0	0	13,920
King's Deputy	5	G	10	2	1	0	14,241
King's Drama (IRE)	4	G	7	2	0	1	184,600
Kings Empress	4	F	5	1	0	0	28,274
King's Fancy	4	F	13	1	0	3	18,400
King's Friend	4	C	8	0	1	1	2,735
Kings Groom	3	G	12	1	1	3	8,901
King's Honor	8	G	9	3	0	0	4,122
Kings Kin	11	G	4	1	0	0	891
King's Lassie	3	F	10	2	0	0	12,509
Kings Lil Star	5	H	4	0	0	0	1,023
King's Mill	3	C	8	0	0	0	1,421
Kings Miner	6	G	5	2	0	1	15,010
Kings of the Ring	4	G	13	1	2	1	37,712
King's Option	3	C	1	0	0	0	0
Kings Own	6	G	8	0	1	2	9,190
Kings Plan	4	G	7	3	0	2	10,240
Kings Pride	4	F	8	2	1	0	17,925
Kings Reception	6	G	7	1	1	1	15,179
Kings Request	3	F	7	0	0	2	1,200
Kings Risk	6	H	1	1	0	0	4,284
King's River	3	G	6	1	1	0	21,295
Kings Sequence	5	G	12	0	1	1	2,806
King's Tale	5	G	12	0	0	2	4,371
King's Taxes	6	G	11	1	0	0	8,748
Kings Temper	4	C	11	1	1	3	14,354
King's Thrill	3	F	7	3	3	1	64,472
Kings Tudor	2	F	1	0	0	0	0
King's Tune	4	G	11	1	0	0	4,379
Kings Up	9	R	7	0	0	2	3,058
King's Verse	7	G	5	0	1	0	3,680
Kingsbury	4	G	2	0	0	0	300
Kingsgeneralissimo	2	G	2	0	0	0	110
Kingsize Performer	3	G	3	0	0	2	3,660
Kingsport	6	G	12	2	0	3	16,923
Kingstown	4	F	11	1	1	0	10,720
Kingstyle	8	G	7	1	0	0	5,456
Kingswoman	2	F	9	2	0	0	12,430
Kingwilliamstown	2	G	3	0	0	1	2,965
Kinjet	4	G	12	1	3	2	21,386
Kinkennie	9	G	5	0	2	0	4,750
Kinky Cowgirl	5	M	10	2	2	1	10,493
Kinky Pinky	3	F	2	0	0	0	312
Kinnelon	5	M	5	2	0	1	23,145
Kinscem	5	M	6	0	0	0	0
Kinship	4	C	5	0	4	0	14,800
Kinslo Pride	3	F	5	1	1	1	8,235
Kinsman Valor	4	G	12	1	2	0	7,610
Kinston	6	G	7	0	0	1	914
Kintoadancer	2	F	2	0	0	0	233
Kintu	3	G	6	0	0	0	7,140
Kinuseo Falls	4	F	2	0	0	0	470
Kinworth	4	G	9	4	3	0	38,381
Kinz	7	G	4	0	0	0	0
Kiosk	4	F	8	2	4	0	45,278
Kiowa Chief	4	G	7	1	1	1	6,989
Kiowa Kandy	4	F	10	0	0	1	2,678
Kiowa King	6	H	3	0	0	0	420
Kiowa Prince	3	C	2	1	0	0	24,818
Kiowa Scout	2	F	2	0	0	1	1,500
Kip	3	G	9	0	2	0	5,150
Kip Along Molly	5	M	1	0	0	0	77
Kip E Ah	3	G	7	2	0	1	10,356
Kip Smile	2	F	6	1	1	1	41,856
Kip to My Lu	4	F	18	2	2	2	22,494
Kipbo	2	F	2	0	0	0	348
Kiplingette	2	F	1	0	0	0	280
Kiplings Arrow	2	F	3	0	2	0	3,050
Kipling's Kiss	2	F	1	0	0	0	105
Kiplings Moon	2	F	2	1	0	0	6,850
Kipling's Tower	2	C	1	0	0	0	0
Kipper Bay	4	G	1	0	0	0	125
Kipper Chemo	4	G	3	0	0	0	412
Kipper Kiwi	3	F	2	0	0	0	0
Kipper Ville	3	G	9	0	0	2	11,640
Kippered Rue	5	H	1	0	0	0	69
Kipperella	8	M	8	0	0	2	2,173
Kipper's an Angel	5	G	16	9	2	2	100,790
Kippers N Brew	2	F	2	0	0	0	750
Kipper's Night	3	C	2	1	1	0	29,800
Kipper's Tune	3	C	15	0	2	3	6,658
Kip's Contender	2	C	1	0	0	0	250
Kip's Wild	3	G	6	1	0	0	5,508
Kipski	9	G	8	0	0	0	165
Kipur	3	C	7	0	1	1	4,537
Kiralik (GB)	4	F	5	0	0	0	1,960
Kirby Mac	3	G	13	3	2	0	38,691
Kirby's Brogue	4	G	15	0	0	2	3,494
Kirby's Fuse	4	F	6	0	1	0	11,776
Kiri Camp	3	C	10	1	4	0	25,880
Kiri Jana	4	F	8	0	1	2	9,987
Kiri Te	3	F	3	0	0	0	0
Kirianna	4	F	1	0	0	0	64
Kirimbai	2	G	2	0	0	0	0
Kiri's Beauty	3	F	1	0	0	0	160
Kiris Fee	3	G	4	0	0	2	2,575
Kiri's Princess	5	M	6	0	0	0	449
Kirison	5	G	10	0	1	0	1,439
Kirk Best	7	G	11	0	1	1	3,109
Kirkendahl	2	C	2	2	0	0	43,200
Kirkland Jct	5	G	10	3	3	1	20,270
Kirksboy	7	G	5	0	1	0	1,342
Kirkwood Kelly	5	M	1	0	0	0	235
Kirlan	4	F	9	1	2	0	34,495
Kirra's Toy	4	G	2	0	0	1	3,500
Kirschwasser	5	G	13	2	4	2	23,395
Kirtle (GB)	5	M	5	1	0	1	40,680
Kirtons	7	G	7	2	1	1	12,324
Kisatche	4	C	6	1	2	1	11,801
Kisco Light	3	G	12	2	1	2	24,370
Kisha's Quest	2	F	6	0	0	1	1,860
Kishore	4	G	13	0	1	1	4,780
Kismetoo	5	M	6	0	0	0	378
Kiss	4	G	6	1	1	0	29,950
Kiss A' Jule	5	M	2	0	0	0	122
Kiss a Miss	6	M	2	0	0	1	5,950
Kiss a Native	7	G	10	2	1	1	54,205
Kiss an Angel	5	G	5	0	1	0	4,851
Kiss an Optimist	3	G	10	1	2	2	29,040
Kiss And Fly (IRE)	4	F	3	0	0	1	8,680
Kiss and Go	2	F	6	1	3	0	21,970
Kiss Control	4	F	1	0	0	0	50
Kiss for Cody	3	F	3	2	0	1	14,320
Kiss for Julie	4	F	15	4	2	2	37,518

Horse	Age	Sex	Sts	1st	2d	3d	Won
Kiss Kiss Kiss	3	F	6	2	1	1	38,620
Kiss Me Again	3	G	12	1	0	4	21,460
Kiss Me Goodbye	7	G	8	4	0	1	17,399
Kiss Me Jim	5	G	7	0	0	0	796
Kiss Me Katie	4	F	9	4	1	0	105,296
Kiss Me Matt	2	G	5	0	0	0	3,040
Kiss Me Patrick	4	C	4	0	0	0	1,123
Kiss Me Twice	5	M	6	1	2	0	40,531
Kiss My Annie	3	F	4	0	0	0	0
Kiss My Cash	3	G	5	1	3	0	6,720
Kiss My Judge	4	G	20	1	2	3	20,865
Kiss My Sister	3	F	14	0	1	0	3,204
Kiss 'n a Smile	3	F	2	0	1	0	1,596
Kiss N Hush	4	G	7	0	0	0	720
Kiss Nana Goodbye	5	M	5	0	0	0	0
Kiss of Fury	7	H	4	0	0	0	314
Kiss of Lion (ARG)	9	H	10	2	1	2	20,013
Kiss of Truth	3	C	15	3	1	2	18,184
Kiss On the Cheek	3	F	10	1	0	0	5,815
Kiss Roam Me O	5	G	18	4	1	0	24,736
Kiss Tam	2	C	1	0	0	0	400
Kiss the Baby	4	F	7	0	0	0	535
Kiss the Blarney	4	G	11	3	1	1	17,580
Kiss the Editor	4	G	3	0	0	0	543
Kiss the Flame	2	C	1	0	0	0	400
Kiss the Groom	3	C	12	1	3	3	40,929
Kiss the Justice	4	G	8	0	0	1	2,457
Kiss the Lips	3	F	12	1	2	0	55,796
Kiss to Storm Cat	2	F	3	0	0	0	924
Kissalyssa	4	F	10	3	1	1	59,320
Kissame	6	M	8	4	1	1	20,444
Kissane	11	H	10	1	3	0	9,850
Kisscozzen	3	F	4	1	0	0	5,456
Kissed by a Prince	4	F	8	3	0	2	170,497
Kiss'em Kate	3	F	12	2	2	0	20,267
Kissen Capote	4	F	7	1	2	0	14,960
Kisses	5	M	1	0	0	0	0
Kisses for Bertie	2	F	9	3	1	1	31,134
Kisses for Kara	4	F	13	3	2	1	32,578
Kisses in Clover	5	M	17	0	4	1	9,656
Kissim All	4	G	6	1	0	0	7,000
Kissin Angie	4	F	14	2	0	1	17,612
Kissin Ashley	5	M	10	0	1	2	5,014
Kissin Beauty	5	M	9	0	0	1	4,985
Kissin Concern	5	M	5	0	0	0	1,668
Kissin Conquest	2	C	1	0	0	0	1,500
Kissin Cowboy	3	G	9	3	0	0	16,249
Kissin Game	5	M	1	0	0	0	78
Kissin in the Caar	3	G	13	1	1	0	6,073
Kissin It Away	6	M	8	4	1	1	29,065
Kissin' Jack	4	C	7	1	0	4	29,790
Kissin List	3	F	16	1	2	0	11,181
Kissin Miss	4	F	3	0	1	0	1,950
Kissin My Friends	3	F	2	0	0	0	0
Kissin Paster	4	G	8	2	1	2	20,275
Kissin Saint	4	C	8	2	1	1	88,045
Kissin Sally Falls	2	F	2	0	0	0	0
Kissin Sharp	3	F	14	5	1	2	72,040
Kissin Summer	6	M	13	2	4	2	31,566
Kissin the Boys	3	F	5	0	1	1	7,400
Kissin the Breeze	2	F	3	0	0	0	410
Kissin Ty	3	G	16	2	2	5	77,189
Kissin Zak	4	G	14	2	1	2	17,156
Kissinette	4	F	2	1	1	0	12,200
Kissing Cowgirl	4	F	1	0	0	0	650
Kissing Girl (ARG)	7	M	11	1	4	1	65,860
Kissing Time	6	M	3	0	0	0	33
Kissinique	2	F	2	0	0	0	0
Kissinleaf	5	M	18	3	1	2	53,328
Kissintobeclever	3	F	8	1	0	1	11,370
Kiss'm All Bye	4	G	18	0	1	2	3,764
Kissmecrazy	3	F	1	0	0	0	210
Kissmekissmequick	3	F	12	1	2	0	11,392
Kissmelikeumeanit	3	F	9	3	0	0	24,420
Kiss'n Dyna	3	F	10	0	0	4	19,680
Kissntheboysgoodby	2	F	1	0	0	1	700
Kissonthespot	4	F	13	1	5	1	17,352
Kisssastar	4	F	9	0	2	0	7,260
Kissthestargoodby	2	F	1	0	0	0	400
Kissthissky	6	G	12	1	1	1	11,010
Kissville	3	C	2	0	0	0	0
Kissy Kat	4	F	1	0	0	0	580
Kissy Kiss	4	F	2	0	0	0	670
Kistler	5	M	3	1	0	1	7,510
Kit Kat Creek	2	G	6	1	2	1	10,540
Kit Kat Kayla	3	F	7	1	1	2	24,111
Kit Katter	3	F	11	3	2	3	27,513
Kita's Flyer	7	M	16	2	1	4	23,857
Kitava	3	F	8	0	1	5	11,392
Kitchen Bouquet	7	M	11	0	0	1	3,523
Kite	3	G	8	0	2	2	19,650
Kite Hawk	2	C	5	1	0	0	17,550
Kite With Wings	4	G	15	1	4	2	14,263
Kith	5	G	4	0	2	1	5,930
Kit's Comet	3	F	9	1	1	0	8,913
Kitten Jones	2	F	2	1	1	0	8,780
Kitten On the Keys	6	M	12	0	1	2	5,395
Kitten's Baby Boy	9	G	2	1	0	0	4,125
Kitten's Joy	3	C	8	6	2	0	1,625,796
Kittens Tiger	3	G	1	0	0	0	300
Kitti Lake	3	F	11	1	2	1	15,104
Kittiwood	7	M	5	0	0	0	360
Kittle Camp Girl	4	F	5	0	0	0	293
Kittoman	5	G	5	0	0	0	800
Kitty and Boo	2	F	4	1	0	0	17,045
Kitty Carnes	4	F	3	0	0	0	109
Kitty Carson	4	F	3	0	1	0	6,783
Kitty Cat Creek	4	F	11	1	4	1	25,955
Kitty Coast	3	F	12	1	3	0	33,412
Kitty Connection	3	G	5	1	1	0	36,480
Kitty Conveyor	4	F	3	0	0	1	1,501
Kitty in a Tree	2	F	1	0	1	0	3,740
Kitty Kiernan	4	F	4	0	1	0	3,157
Kitty Kitty Cat	3	C	15	2	3	2	12,423
Kitty Knight	4	F	7	2	1	1	87,030
Kitty Red	3	F	2	0	0	0	210
Kitty Senor	2	C	6	1	1	0	9,102
Kitty Zip	2	G	5	0	0	1	4,580
Kittybangbang	3	F	10	0	0	0	697
Kittys Katalist	3	G	6	1	2	1	16,371
Kitty's Legend	4	F	8	1	3	1	62,763
Kitty's Mission	5	M	13	3	2	1	63,900
Kittys Mom	2	F	1	0	0	0	125
Kittys Sister	2	F	4	0	0	0	345
Kivi	4	F	4	0	0	2	10,660
Kiwi Dancer	3	G	8	0	0	0	1,064
Kiwi Gold	4	F	10	1	5	1	22,920
Kiwi's Collection	3	G	2	0	0	0	0
Kizka	2	F	1	1	0	0	26,400
Kiznitti	7	M	7	1	2	1	18,645
Kizzy Kazoo	5	M	10	0	0	0	4,192
Kj's Project	2	C	5	0	3	0	7,700
Kj's Wedding Photo	2	F	1	0	0	0	0
Klamathfallsasleep	2	G	1	0	1	0	3,800
Klassic Kick	2	F	2	0	0	0	253
Klassic Pride	9	G	5	0	0	1	1,542
Klassikbud	4	G	1	0	0	0	89
Klassy Katlyn	3	F	5	0	0	1	6,080
Klassy Kira	4	F	2	0	0	0	0
Klassy Kruzer	3	C	2	1	0	0	8,400
Klassy Lake	2	F	6	2	0	0	14,630
Klassy Woman	4	F	6	0	0	1	3,055
Klem	5	G	7	1	1	0	2,083
Kleven's Alibi	2	F	9	5	2	1	50,757
Klever Belle	3	F	5	0	0	0	1,600
Klimie	4	F	7	0	1	1	2,745
Klondike Trail	8	G	2	0	0	0	0
Klubber Lang	4	G	7	1	1	0	4,239
Klueless Keith	3	C	1	0	0	0	0
Kneel	4	F	8	2	0	0	36,976
Knickers	3	G	6	1	0	0	9,970
Knight Affair	9	G	12	0	1	0	4,124
Knight Deb	3	F	4	0	0	0	50
Knight Dragon	2	C	5	0	0	1	2,628
Knight Forturne	6	M	6	1	2	1	2,037
Knight Gallery	3	G	4	1	0	0	1,267
Knight Game	5	H	7	0	2	0	3,760
Knight Howl	6	G	5	0	0	0	612

Horse	Age	Sex	Sts	1st	2d	3d	Won
Knight in Silver	4	G	7	1	2	0	11,111
Knight Invasion	7	G	8	3	4	0	16,628
Knight Mistress	8	M	1	0	0	0	61
Knight of Cups	4	F	7	3	0	1	18,823
Knight of Darkness	3	C	10	5	0	4	152,785
Knight of Day	4	G	2	0	0	0	56
Knight of Sin	3	G	2	0	0	0	0
Knight of the Mt.	4	C	3	0	0	0	0
Knight Templar	6	G	2	0	0	0	240
Knight Villain	9	G	1	0	0	0	0
Knight Zone	4	F	2	0	0	0	0
Knightatthecasino	4	G	12	1	0	2	4,283
Knightly Ease	4	G	5	3	2	0	135,880
Knightly Signal	5	M	8	1	3	1	11,271
Knightly Swinger	4	G	13	3	2	2	10,530
Knightnsilverarmor	3	G	12	1	3	1	23,272
Knight's Agenda	5	G	8	5	0	1	39,444
Knight's Are Wild	3	G	15	3	2	2	20,415
Knight's Covenant	2	G	4	0	2	1	9,820
Knight's Gumbo	7	G	5	1	4	0	15,696
Knight's Mischief	3	G	3	0	0	3	2,040
Knights Princess	3	F	1	0	0	0	730
Knightsbridge Road	4	G	11	1	1	0	23,053
Knightsound	3	G	9	0	1	2	17,442
Knines Dream	9	G	16	7	4	0	34,294
Knob Hill	3	C	13	0	3	0	8,856
Knobby N Mert	5	H	4	0	2	0	3,300
Knock Again	7	G	11	2	1	4	18,080
Knock It Off	5	M	14	2	1	2	26,716
Knock N See	2	F	9	0	0	1	11,683
Knock Out Chick	5	M	1	0	0	0	0
Knock Out Prospect	5	M	12	1	2	3	22,260
Knockabout	10	G	3	0	0	0	240
Knock'emback	3	C	3	0	0	0	205
Knockin Boots	3	F	15	1	5	0	25,545
Knockknock Knockin	4	F	6	1	0	1	20,913
Knocklong Curaheen	5	M	3	0	0	0	0
Knockout Blow	8	G	7	0	2	0	1,400
Knockout Jab	2	C	1	1	0	0	15,900
Knockout Kid	7	G	14	3	0	2	32,386
Knockout Slew	2	F	2	0	0	0	220
Knockout Speed	5	M	1	0	0	0	0
Knockout the Truth	7	G	4	0	0	0	0
Knockout's Image	2	C	2	0	0	0	1,920
Knockwood	6	G	8	0	1	0	1,372
Knoll Lake	6	M	2	0	0	1	2,170
Knot Indy Mood	2	F	2	0	0	0	155
Knothead	3	C	3	0	0	0	0
Knotting Hill	5	M	2	1	0	0	2,709
Knotty Behaviour	4	G	8	0	2	1	40,554
Knotty Knickles	5	M	5	1	1	2	24,969
Knotty Knows	6	M	4	0	0	0	919
Knottybutnice	6	M	11	0	2	2	4,553
Know How	6	G	8	1	0	0	11,476
Know Sumthin	7	H	3	0	0	0	1,500
Know the Judge	2	G	4	0	0	0	1,520
Know What	4	F	4	0	0	0	360
Knowmee	7	G	9	0	1	2	7,284
Known Back Home	3	C	2	1	1	0	28,680
Known Rhythm	6	G	9	0	1	1	2,114
Known Tender	7	G	5	1	0	1	35,843
Known Touch	4	F	3	1	0	0	17,033
Known Wonder	4	F	2	0	0	0	505
Knows No Boundary	7	G	9	1	2	2	15,953
Knowwhatimean	3	C	11	4	3	2	55,700
Knox	3	C	9	2	3	1	120,921
Knox City	10	G	2	0	0	0	1,010
Knuckleball	5	G	16	3	7	3	32,252
Knucklehead	5	M	13	3	1	3	26,392
Kobari Time	6	M	1	0	0	0	0
Kobasa Kid	4	G	2	0	0	0	0
Kobella Bean	3	F	4	0	0	0	1,030
Kobemon	5	M	2	0	0	0	80
Kobra Kirsten	3	F	3	1	1	0	19,710
Kodan	7	G	11	1	2	2	10,356
Kodangel	2	G	4	1	2	1	19,450
Kodema	5	G	10	2	1	4	154,160
Kodon	4	G	13	2	0	2	6,752
Kofi	4	G	6	0	0	0	2,120

Horse	Age	Sex	Sts	1st	2d	3d	Won
Kohar	2	F	7	1	1	1	55,525
Kohuna Grande	7	G	5	0	0	3	11,640
Kohut	2	C	5	1	2	1	44,020
Koka Kola Kween	5	M	2	0	0	0	600
Kokand Kid	4	G	2	0	0	0	0
Kokand Rum	4	F	4	0	0	1	2,955
Kokandahotdog	4	F	6	0	2	1	7,480
Kokando	3	C	5	0	0	0	1,680
Kokeshi	4	F	5	1	0	1	14,821
Kokie Grand	6	M	7	1	1	0	8,037
Kokinaras	8	G	1	0	0	0	0
Koko Chico	4	G	13	0	3	5	16,377
Kokomo Jo	10	M	3	0	0	0	86
Kolby'slittletuffy	3	C	2	0	0	0	0
Koleta Bend	2	F	6	0	3	0	14,127
Kolika	3	F	1	0	0	0	0
Kolinor	7	G	2	0	0	0	642
Kolob	7	G	9	5	1	0	55,990
Koloft	4	G	9	0	1	0	6,660
Koloszar	3	G	1	0	0	0	320
Koluctoo's Man	7	G	7	0	0	1	674
Kom Kim Lass	2	F	2	1	1	0	21,160
Komax	6	G	8	0	2	0	29,839
Komba	9	G	12	2	2	1	17,641
Kompressor Jack	4	G	7	1	3	0	31,771
Kon Tiki	4	C	4	2	0	1	55,900
Kona Bay	3	G	9	1	5	0	19,203
Kona Beau	5	G	14	2	5	0	17,061
Kona Breeze	5	M	3	0	0	1	2,535
Kona Brick	5	G	3	0	0	1	614
Kona Coast	8	G	7	2	1	1	11,582
Kona Kokand	5	G	5	0	1	2	9,900
Kona Run	3	G	11	1	1	1	17,805
Kondoa Way	5	G	8	1	0	1	11,070
Konyak	6	G	12	2	1	1	10,584
Konza	3	F	8	1	4	0	40,670
Konza Prairie	3	G	2	0	0	0	600
Koo Bear	4	G	8	1	2	1	37,842
Koobalotchee	7	G	5	0	0	0	0
Kooka Munga	4	F	5	1	0	0	5,272
Kookaburra	4	G	7	0	0	2	15,084
Kookie Krusher	3	F	7	1	2	1	18,849
Kool and Bold	5	G	7	0	0	0	1,035
Kool Body	5	G	8	0	1	0	2,636
Kool Carma	3	F	4	1	0	1	18,520
Kool Daddy D. J.	4	G	6	0	0	0	370
Kool Humor	4	G	3	0	0	1	3,630
Kool Jazkey	9	G	10	1	1	1	6,903
Kool K. J.	4	F	7	1	1	3	36,147
Kool Kaleb	4	C	4	1	0	1	3,130
Kool Kat Karin	5	M	2	0	0	0	0
Kool Kool	5	G	3	0	0	2	5,630
Kool Smoke	4	G	14	1	3	4	22,521
Kool Suggestion	3	G	14	3	1	4	93,606
Kool Valley	3	F	1	0	0	1	1,590
Kool West Wins	4	G	6	0	0	0	813
Koola	6	G	12	3	3	2	23,146
Koolau Summer	3	F	5	0	0	1	342
Koop's Krown	3	G	5	1	0	0	12,675
Koorachee	5	H	5	1	1	1	17,711
Kootenai	3	F	4	0	0	1	6,510
Kootsopothee	6	M	11	1	3	0	17,710
Koovey	8	G	8	0	1	2	3,400
Kop Kat	5	M	3	0	0	0	218
Kopper Kilgoar	2	C	2	1	0	1	17,900
Koral Star	4	G	8	0	1	1	4,255
Korbyn Gold	3	G	7	2	1	1	64,413
Korilin	2	F	1	0	0	0	164
Kory B	3	G	11	1	2	1	5,315
Kosade	4	F	4	1	0	0	15,970
Kossu (IRE)	4	G	5	1	0	0	12,378
Kostaki	5	G	4	0	0	0	0
Kostroma Pass	4	F	9	0	0	0	2,250
Kota	2	F	7	2	2	3	139,450
Kotumaslep	4	G	6	1	2	1	16,075
Kotuspeeding	6	H	8	0	2	2	15,294
Kountry Grammer	3	G	12	1	3	3	18,730
Kountry Pride	3	C	2	0	0	0	185
Kouri Jill	4	F	14	1	4	1	59,675

Horse	Age	Sex	Sts	1st	2d	3d	Won
Kovale	3	F	7	3	3	0	36,300
Kowboy J. J.	6	M	4	1	1	0	1,292
Kowboy Ronda	7	M	1	1	0	0	935
Koy's Lil Rob	3	G	4	0	0	0	0
Kozy Polly	3	F	5	1	0	0	9,938
Krafty Kaper	3	F	12	1	3	1	26,515
Krafty Kimberlee	2	F	1	0	0	0	400
Krakowviak	4	F	8	1	2	1	19,565
Kranky Karol	3	F	4	1	2	0	17,440
Krasnaya	4	F	13	2	2	4	84,110
Kravets	2	C	1	0	0	0	205
Kraz	4	G	10	1	0	2	15,255
Krazycajun	4	G	1	0	0	1	420
Kreb's Princess	3	F	8	0	0	0	1,714
Kreeker	3	F	13	2	3	1	22,187
Kreems View	5	M	10	3	1	1	36,014
Krewman	4	G	4	1	0	0	5,820
Krews Star	4	F	4	0	2	1	1,174
Krigeorj's Gold	11	G	4	1	0	0	10,320
Kris Creek	2	F	4	0	0	3	2,965
Kris Fever	2	F	1	0	0	0	1,560
Kris Havingfunnow	6	H	2	0	0	0	1,800
Kris Miss Spirit	6	M	1	0	0	0	0
Kris S Niece	7	M	6	1	0	1	3,005
Kris Star	4	F	3	0	0	0	3,168
Kris Taly	5	G	2	0	0	0	69
Kris Taylor	5	G	16	2	1	2	52,425
Kris Xpress	3	F	3	0	0	1	1,155
Krisacia	6	M	9	2	0	1	33,130
Krisbluebayou	3	F	12	1	2	5	13,969
Krisco Kid	6	G	21	2	1	6	21,059
Krises Bells	2	G	4	1	0	3	25,385
Krisherra	3	C	5	2	0	0	44,980
Krismas	4	F	5	0	0	0	3,040
Krismenow	3	F	2	0	0	0	217
Kris's Call	4	G	4	2	0	0	4,576
Kris's Dancer	5	G	12	2	2	1	41,829
Kriss Is School	4	G	12	2	0	2	38,220
Kris's Show	3	G	3	1	0	0	2,700
Kris's Valentine	3	F	5	0	0	3	6,679
Krissbequick	3	G	11	0	2	1	13,860
Kris'sbest	6	M	3	0	0	0	275
Kris'stalwart	2	F	2	0	0	0	330
Krissy Blue Eyes	3	F	11	0	0	1	3,263
Krissy C.	2	F	2	0	0	0	4,200
Kristans Afleet	3	F	5	1	0	0	5,254
Kristas Comet	4	F	12	3	1	2	17,977
Krista's Night	4	F	7	0	0	0	597
Kristen Kristen	2	F	4	0	2	0	15,425
Kristen's Tuition	3	F	5	1	0	0	4,771
Kristen's Way	4	F	7	0	0	2	2,142
Kristenshadenough	4	F	7	0	0	1	923
Kristin R	3	F	3	0	1	0	1,168
Kristina K	5	M	11	2	0	1	10,453
Kristina S.	2	F	5	0	0	0	2,605
Kristina's Faith	2	F	1	0	0	0	860
Kristina's Wish	4	F	15	5	2	3	88,926
Kristine's King	4	G	13	3	1	3	88,540
Kristin's Charm	2	F	7	1	1	2	47,850
Kristi's Pleasure	7	M	9	1	0	3	5,746
Kristof	4	G	14	1	3	1	8,914
Kristofferson	4	C	8	3	1	1	65,800
Kristy Beethoven	3	F	7	1	1	2	46,390
Kristy Dale	4	F	11	4	1	0	52,705
Kristylynnsregency	3	C	1	0	0	0	0
Kristy's Act	4	F	14	0	0	0	1,590
Kristys Blaze	2	F	3	0	0	0	0
Kristy's Day	5	G	2	0	0	0	70
Kristy's Dream	4	F	10	2	2	1	28,400
Kristys Excellent	5	G	12	1	2	1	10,496
Kristys Expensive	3	F	6	1	0	1	4,195
Kristys Golden Boy	4	G	7	1	0	0	3,540
Kristys Goldengirl	3	F	3	0	0	0	150
Kristys Majestic	5	M	3	1	1	0	4,480
Kristys Mill	2	F	2	0	0	0	0
Kristys Sunny	4	G	14	1	0	2	9,957
Kriswen	3	F	3	0	0	2	2,280
Kritikos	3	G	16	1	3	0	15,805
Krovitz	2	G	5	2	1	1	36,295
Kruel Intention	2	G	2	1	1	0	45,600
Krum de La Krum	2	F	3	1	0	1	8,520
Kruncher	2	G	2	0	1	0	6,922
Krupa	3	C	12	4	0	1	58,060
Krusin Kristen	7	M	6	0	0	1	490
Krypto Cajun	4	F	1	0	0	0	0
Kryskaly	4	F	7	3	0	0	15,455
Krystals Kipper	6	G	7	2	0	0	7,103
Krystal's Surprise	2	G	2	1	1	0	4,875
Krystina Can Dance	4	F	1	0	0	0	0
Krystina's Day	4	F	14	3	3	2	27,888
Krz Deed	2	G	1	0	0	0	1,710
Krz Ruckus	7	G	9	4	1	1	219,351
Krz Time	3	F	6	2	2	0	95,860
K's Baby	3	F	10	2	0	0	8,310
K's Big Bird	5	G	1	0	0	0	69
K's Boy Marco	3	G	8	0	2	1	6,700
K's Charismatic	3	C	7	0	0	1	4,263
K's Commando	7	G	4	0	1	0	1,070
K's Fine Gal	4	F	13	1	0	4	4,706
K's Gold	3	F	12	1	2	2	12,289
K's Party	3	G	9	0	0	0	883
Kuanyan	4	F	9	2	2	2	85,132
Kubala's Keepsake	4	F	12	3	3	2	54,905
Kuch	4	C	7	2	1	2	72,236
Kuhl 'n' Clever	3	G	5	3	1	1	48,095
Kukicha	4	F	2	1	0	0	12,420
Kukku	3	F	14	0	0	0	3,066
Kuko Baluco	6	G	7	0	0	2	2,256
Kulik	3	F	3	1	0	0	7,358
Kumonover Soldier	2	C	4	1	0	1	8,580
Kupolee	3	F	7	0	1	2	4,961
Kurlicue (IRE)	3	F	8	1	1	0	57,740
Kurt	4	G	2	0	0	0	0
Kutenai	3	G	5	0	1	1	12,205
Kutlana Gold	2	F	3	1	2	0	8,520
Kwaito	4	F	2	0	0	1	3,366
Kwame	3	G	15	0	5	4	22,420
Kwik Start	5	M	3	0	0	0	0
Kwondo	2	C	1	1	0	0	27,000
Ky Deputy	3	G	9	3	2	0	87,665
Kya Jo	3	F	8	2	3	3	20,400
Kyle Anne	3	F	1	1	0	0	4,980
Kylea's Lady Erisa	2	F	2	0	0	0	0
Kylee's Fatcat	3	G	10	1	0	0	4,573
Kylee's Reality	3	F	4	1	1	0	7,740
Kylemore Abbey	5	H	14	2	3	2	69,448
Kylers Midge	5	M	11	3	3	1	89,990
Kyles a Brat	3	G	9	3	0	0	17,276
Kyle's Bluebird	4	F	14	1	6	1	13,615
Kyle's Darlin	2	F	2	1	0	1	17,400
Kyles Friday	4	G	1	0	0	0	525
Kyle's Hunter	2	G	4	0	0	0	300
Kyle's Joker	3	G	3	0	0	0	252
Kyles Keeper	4	G	4	0	0	1	587
Kyle's King	3	G	11	1	0	1	17,987
Kyle's Lad	2	C	1	0	0	0	60
Kyle's My Dad	5	M	8	0	0	1	1,519
Kyle's Reprized	5	G	1	0	0	0	0
Kyle's Secret	4	C	6	0	0	0	2,406
Kyle's Squaw	5	M	4	0	0	0	0
Kyle's Surfer Girl	2	F	3	0	0	1	3,080
Kyle's T. L. C.	4	F	8	1	2	0	10,123
Kylie	3	F	2	0	0	0	700
Kylie Bear	3	G	4	0	0	1	1,337
Kylie's Legacy	5	M	13	1	0	3	8,523
Kylor Creek	6	M	13	1	1	2	14,023
Kyra's Kin	3	F	8	1	0	2	10,510
Kyrenia	5	M	3	0	0	0	1,132
Kyungbokung	5	G	6	0	1	1	13,185
L and K's Dream	5	G	7	0	0	1	732
L B's Raising Star	3	C	16	2	2	1	26,060
L C Mystery	3	F	3	0	0	0	2,255
L C Wheelofortune	5	M	3	0	0	0	528
L Caitlin Eades	4	F	13	2	3	1	61,135
L D Country Road	3	G	7	2	0	1	2,043
L Diamond	6	M	10	2	1	2	4,239
L D's Hello Mom	4	F	10	0	0	1	2,996
L' esprit Charles	4	G	5	0	0	0	1,098

Horse	Age	Sex	Sts	1st	2d	3d	Won
L G Sweeny	6	G	10	2	1	2	11,203
L G's Gold	4	F	9	1	1	2	12,811
L J S Express	3	G	8	1	1	0	8,376
L J's Anabell	4	F	9	1	0	0	5,929
L J's Runaway	3	G	10	1	1	1	13,120
L L Prospect	3	F	6	0	0	0	1,208
L L Southern Cross	3	F	7	1	2	0	7,344
L M Curiser	4	F	15	1	2	3	11,608
L N B Intimidator	4	G	1	0	0	0	0
L P Teddy Bear	3	C	6	0	0	0	76
L P's Legacy	2	G	1	0	0	0	0
L S Gypsyannio	3	F	10	2	0	0	15,540
L S Matt's Dusty	6	G	4	0	0	0	309
L S Pacho Passo	3	G	2	0	0	0	555
L S Peppelady	2	F	1	0	0	0	0
L S Piannomagic	4	G	12	2	1	2	17,559
L T L Smokie	3	F	7	1	1	2	10,236
L Z Zulu	8	G	3	0	0	0	400
L. A. Cobra	4	C	2	0	0	1	650
L. A. Fitz	7	G	19	2	3	4	20,083
L. A. Jade	6	M	16	5	0	3	31,065
L. A. Legacy	3	G	1	0	0	0	0
L. A. Tootie	3	F	1	0	0	0	400
L. A. Woman	3	F	6	0	0	0	477
L. B. Long Gone	10	G	2	0	0	0	0
L. B. Won Kenobi	4	G	13	3	0	2	16,087
L. D. Crowe	6	G	9	0	0	1	2,560
L. E. Weber	4	G	8	2	2	0	7,286
L. J. Johnson	4	G	13	3	2	3	20,616
L. K. Brewster	2	C	2	0	0	0	1,080
L. L. Cat	6	G	11	2	1	1	12,720
L. L. Moody	2	G	1	0	0	0	1,140
L. L. S. Cat	3	F	7	1	2	0	6,116
L. S. Gotcha	5	G	3	0	0	0	495
La Abella Starrose	2	F	1	0	0	0	450
La Actress	2	F	1	0	0	0	137
La Aspera (ARG)	4	F	9	1	2	2	47,550
La Bala de Plata	3	G	5	0	1	1	5,245
La Balladar	2	F	4	0	1	2	18,615
La Ballerine	5	M	10	1	1	1	14,395
La Baquera	3	F	11	2	3	2	6,575
La Bella	4	F	11	0	1	3	12,465
La Bella Donna	7	M	2	0	0	1	1,060
La Bella Grata	5	M	3	0	1	1	10,500
La Bella Reina	4	F	9	0	1	0	17,740
La Bella Vista	3	F	3	0	1	1	12,718
La Belle Fleur	4	F	9	3	0	1	48,035
La Belle Frenchie	5	M	12	2	3	2	32,445
La Belle Simone (IRE)	5	M	1	0	0	0	0
La Blue Goose	3	F	4	0	1	0	2,283
La Bonte Creek	4	F	14	1	3	5	17,535
La Boom	3	F	2	0	0	1	980
La Brie Quette	5	M	7	0	0	0	1,920
La Brieanna	3	F	13	3	4	2	47,465
La Campanella (IRE)	4	F	4	0	0	0	300
La Candida	4	F	6	1	1	1	16,777
La Canoa Ranchaa	6	G	16	1	2	2	10,595
La Cerca	3	F	1	0	0	0	0
La Cerentola	2	F	2	1	0	1	6,605
La Chaiym	7	G	5	0	0	0	490
La Cheetah	4	F	4	1	1	0	22,470
La Cheryl	4	F	10	2	3	2	24,992
La Chica	3	F	9	0	2	1	3,554
La Chica Sexy	3	F	7	0	0	0	0
La Chola	3	F	7	0	1	2	10,440
La Chunk	5	G	15	0	4	2	23,887
La Cielo	2	G	1	0	0	0	140
La Cochinada	3	G	2	0	0	0	1,218
La Court	5	M	8	0	0	1	1,484
La Cubana	2	F	4	0	0	0	800
La Dame Amour	3	F	2	0	0	0	515
La Danielle	3	F	3	1	1	0	36,100
La Divina	3	F	2	0	0	0	285
La Dolce Vita	2	F	2	0	0	0	1,580
La Duncan (ARG)	5	M	5	1	0	0	7,975
La Escondida	2	F	1	0	0	0	155
La Famiglia	2	F	7	1	0	1	8,577
La Fast Cat	4	G	12	1	1	3	14,115
La Femme Bandita	3	F	4	1	1	0	18,100
La Femme Galante	4	F	1	0	0	1	7,500
La Fever	3	F	10	3	0	2	22,430
La Fino Vino	3	F	7	2	0	3	11,555
La Flairre	3	F	3	0	0	0	1,170
La Flashing Column	4	F	4	0	0	0	0
La Fleet	4	F	7	0	0	0	319
La Fontaine	6	H	16	1	2	1	7,757
La Fortuna	4	F	3	0	0	0	100
La Fosa	2	G	6	0	0	0	1,195
La Galga	4	F	5	0	0	1	1,385
La Gata Loca	3	F	15	1	1	0	7,568
La Gato Mio	5	M	9	1	0	2	1,919
La Gazelle	3	F	1	0	0	0	0
La Geri	4	F	4	1	0	0	4,218
La Gloire	5	M	11	2	1	0	9,648
La Gran Domenique	2	F	2	1	0	0	34,200
La Gran Marley	2	F	4	0	0	0	0
La Grande Ballade (GB)	7	M	2	0	0	0	450
La Grande Erreur	4	F	7	0	0	0	653
La Grande Mamma	3	F	5	1	1	0	65,380
La Grange	4	G	15	1	6	2	16,467
La Hermosa	6	M	13	1	1	1	8,720
La Hot Slew	4	G	5	0	0	0	0
La Irish Charm	4	F	5	0	1	1	6,081
La Isavela	3	F	2	0	0	0	192
La Jefa	3	F	7	0	1	2	23,490
La Joconde	4	F	8	2	1	0	20,162
La Jolie Madame	5	M	13	2	0	1	19,594
La La Boom	2	C	1	0	0	0	195
La Ladina	4	F	1	0	0	0	0
La La's Passion	6	H	11	1	0	1	10,488
La Libellule	4	F	3	0	1	0	3,139
La Lobo	3	F	17	1	3	2	11,901
La Luna de Oro	3	F	9	3	2	0	55,130
La Luz	3	F	6	1	0	0	30,213
La Luz Del Sol	7	M	7	0	0	1	1,614
La Maitresse (IRE)	2	F	7	1	1	2	31,392
La Maquina	6	G	13	2	4	2	31,490
La Mariah	5	M	1	0	0	0	615
La Memo	3	F	1	0	1	0	1,080
La Migra	9	G	1	0	0	1	450
La Minuta (CHI)	4	F	7	0	4	1	46,237
La Naturaleza	3	F	7	0	0	1	1,146
La Nina Dancer	6	M	1	0	0	0	151
La Ola	3	F	8	2	0	1	10,925
La Paramour	5	M	1	0	0	0	0
La Parita	3	F	8	3	1	1	20,511
La Pascale (GB)	5	M	2	0	0	0	0
La Patriotte	3	F	1	0	0	0	0
La Patroncita	4	F	7	0	0	2	1,574
La Perfecta (CHI)	5	M	12	1	1	0	31,072
La Petite Greek	3	F	3	0	0	0	75
La Petite Justice	4	F	4	0	2	1	25,088
La Petite Sheet	4	F	16	2	0	4	24,918
La Pique Dame	4	F	2	0	0	0	0
La Pirata de Luci	9	G	3	0	0	0	0
La Pistola	2	F	1	0	0	0	410
La Pointe	3	F	1	0	0	0	0
La Prada	5	M	8	0	2	2	7,129
La Prado	5	G	5	0	0	0	1,590
La Prairie	3	F	1	0	0	0	105
La Princesse Jolie	6	M	3	0	0	1	5,360
La Pro	5	M	8	1	1	0	40,135
La Reason	4	F	11	3	0	2	331,080
La Rein	3	F	11	1	1	1	20,201
La Reina	3	F	5	1	1	0	85,922
La Reine Victoria	3	F	6	0	4	0	33,802
La Reine's Terms	9	H	4	1	1	1	46,825
La Rizzitin	2	F	2	0	0	0	190
La Roverina	4	F	15	0	1	0	7,447
La Rubia Peligrosa	4	F	1	0	0	0	400
La Sabana	5	M	16	1	0	3	6,628
La Salle Glory	3	F	13	3	3	1	158,592
La Sanchita	3	F	10	0	2	3	13,755
La Scala	4	F	6	1	1	0	46,840
La Sentella	4	F	3	0	1	0	1,550
La Skipper	5	G	3	1	0	0	3,649
La Sola Nina	2	F	2	0	0	0	2,545
La Sorpresa (ARG)	7	M	9	3	2	0	105,820

Horse	Age	Sex	Sts	1st	2d	3d	Won
La Storm	6	H	2	0	0	0	230
La Tache	3	F	7	3	1	1	81,330
La Taj	13	G	2	0	0	0	96
La Tapatia	3	F	5	0	0	0	339
La Tequilera	2	F	8	3	0	0	26,315
La Tienda de Memo	2	F	5	0	0	1	5,180
La Tina	4	F	6	0	0	0	4,631
La Tinker	4	F	6	0	0	0	720
La Tour (CHI)	5	M	3	0	0	2	57,126
La Trillium	4	F	4	3	0	0	103,710
La Truffe Grise	5	M	9	2	1	2	11,483
La Tulipe	5	M	1	0	1	0	4,280
La Var	3	C	4	0	0	0	300
La Vedette	3	F	1	0	0	1	3,200
La Vie Cielo	5	H	13	3	2	4	14,907
La Vitesse	8	M	5	3	0	1	44,403
La Walk	5	G	7	0	0	2	5,006
La Wapa	3	F	4	0	0	0	0
La Wolfie	2	F	2	0	0	0	445
La Yucca	3	F	2	0	0	0	0
La Zorra	3	F	9	1	1	3	7,299
La Zuli	5	M	4	0	1	0	5,700
Laabity Bluebelle	2	F	3	0	2	0	3,340
Laabity's Gal	4	F	1	0	0	0	45
Lababa	3	G	9	1	1	1	5,241
Labamta Babe	5	G	2	1	0	1	41,760
Labeeb Lucky Girl	3	F	1	0	0	0	0
Labeeby	3	F	5	1	0	0	5,758
Labellebuttons	6	M	4	0	0	0	1,630
Labellum	5	M	9	1	0	1	6,888
Laberb	4	F	2	0	0	1	715
Labido	6	G	8	1	4	1	12,419
Labirinto	6	G	2	0	1	0	44,000
Laborcita	3	F	9	1	1	1	7,305
Labyrinth	5	M	1	0	0	0	210
Lac a Rock	4	G	6	1	0	1	10,880
Lac de Mere	6	M	6	2	0	1	16,741
Lac de Time	5	M	17	2	5	3	21,490
Lac Fontaine	4	G	7	1	1	0	9,061
Lac Grape	3	G	13	1	3	1	20,790
Lac Helene	3	F	2	0	0	0	0
Lac Indy	5	G	17	4	1	1	22,364
Lac Laronge	4	G	5	1	2	1	50,300
Lac Lucky	4	G	9	0	1	2	3,385
Lac of Mission	6	G	10	0	0	1	3,246
Laccabue	3	G	7	0	1	1	6,140
Lace and Lightning	6	M	1	0	0	0	350
Lace Castelli	3	F	17	0	7	3	26,124
Lace Knighty	3	F	10	1	1	2	9,329
Lace Manzotti	4	G	4	0	2	0	4,887
Lace N Leather	8	M	1	0	0	0	88
Laced Up	5	M	18	2	3	1	28,552
Lacenter Flash	4	G	3	1	0	0	5,640
Lacer	5	G	9	0	2	3	26,580
Lacewood	3	F	1	0	0	0	0
Lacey A	5	M	9	1	1	1	11,944
Lacey Dawn	3	F	11	4	2	1	46,530
Lacey Oakley	4	F	17	5	2	5	34,302
Lacharme	6	M	9	1	0	1	8,100
Lachine	2	F	6	1	0	0	27,768
Lacing Up	7	G	6	1	1	1	14,280
Lack of Money	8	M	10	1	2	1	13,106
Lackapasser	8	H	4	0	0	0	200
Lacosta	2	C	1	0	0	0	400
Lacrystal Classic	5	M	4	0	0	1	8,400
Lacy by Design	3	F	6	1	1	2	14,068
Lacy Dawn Bee	3	F	2	0	0	0	215
Lacy Gray	3	F	1	0	0	0	0
Lacy Lou	6	M	10	1	0	2	7,693
Lacy Rose	4	F	1	0	0	0	0
Laddies Kidd	3	C	12	0	1	1	3,160
Laddy	5	G	10	1	1	3	22,928
Laden in Lace	2	F	1	0	0	0	0
Ladies Bad Girl	4	F	4	0	0	0	0
Ladies Dance	3	F	7	0	1	0	2,500
Ladies Over Jacks	3	G	5	0	1	1	1,712
Ladies Precept	4	F	2	0	0	0	0
Laditude	3	C	3	0	1	0	10,400
Ladle	4	G	11	0	2	2	6,380
Ladoma	4	F	10	3	1	1	53,630
Lador Vador	5	G	3	0	0	0	450
Lado's Champ	6	G	7	0	0	0	296
Lad's Sunshine	3	G	5	0	1	0	6,840
Lads Sweet Run	3	C	4	0	1	2	3,910
Lady	5	M	6	0	0	0	1,055
Lady Aani	4	F	4	1	1	0	13,670
Lady Abadabba Due	4	F	4	0	0	0	1,140
Lady Abby	3	F	14	1	1	1	10,253
Lady Aberdeen	3	F	6	0	0	2	5,911
Lady Accountant	3	F	7	1	1	1	8,254
Lady Actor	2	F	3	1	1	0	31,860
Lady Adare	5	M	7	0	1	0	10,220
Lady Aflair	3	F	5	1	0	1	21,058
Lady Afleet	3	F	6	0	0	0	1,050
Lady Alissa	3	F	5	1	0	0	2,035
Lady Allie	3	F	1	0	0	0	1,788
Lady Aly	4	F	27	3	3	8	19,077
Lady Ana L	2	F	9	3	2	0	66,820
Lady Anet	4	F	13	1	1	1	2,919
Lady Ann	3	F	3	0	0	0	540
Lady Anna J	3	F	4	1	0	1	8,960
Lady Annaliese (NZ)	5	M	1	1	0	0	42,525
Lady Archer	3	F	8	1	3	0	21,052
Lady At the Helm	3	F	2	0	0	0	2,360
Lady Athena	3	F	6	0	1	0	3,857
Lady Au Rouge	2	F	1	0	0	0	0
Lady Bank	3	F	7	0	0	2	3,277
Lady Bartok	2	F	4	0	0	1	3,140
Lady Bat	4	F	2	0	0	0	0
Lady Bay	3	F	5	0	0	0	647
Lady Be Fast	2	F	5	0	2	0	3,762
Lady Beaver	5	M	6	0	1	2	1,896
Lady Beelzebub	3	F	9	5	0	1	78,550
Lady Begone	3	F	1	0	0	0	235
Lady Bella	2	F	3	0	0	0	11,320
Lady Belle	4	F	11	0	0	2	4,735
Lady Benchmark	4	F	8	2	2	3	10,470
Lady Benton	3	F	7	2	2	2	11,500
Lady Bernadett	2	F	1	0	0	0	195
Lady Bertrando	2	F	7	3	1	1	81,822
Lady Bi Bi	5	M	2	0	0	0	3,000
Lady Bianconi	3	F	7	0	1	0	2,388
Lady Blue Sky	2	F	1	0	0	0	475
Lady Board Member	4	F	7	0	2	0	4,474
Lady Boots	6	M	6	3	2	0	40,710
Lady Boswell	3	F	5	1	1	0	7,425
Lady Bradford	6	M	14	2	2	1	21,585
Lady Buccaneer	5	M	10	3	0	0	14,746
Lady Builder	5	M	13	3	0	1	23,625
Lady Button Eyes	6	M	3	0	1	0	4,485
Lady by Habit	9	M	9	2	1	4	10,944
Lady C	3	F	6	1	2	0	8,810
Lady Canaveral	2	F	1	0	0	0	161
Lady Caren	7	M	6	1	0	1	6,407
Lady Carmen	2	F	3	1	0	0	31,520
Lady Carol	2	F	4	0	0	1	2,690
Lady Cassandra	5	M	13	3	2	2	24,567
Lady Castlewood	4	F	9	1	2	1	8,749
Lady Caton	3	F	6	0	1	3	8,730
Lady Cavalier	3	F	2	0	0	1	5,558
Lady Ceil	3	F	14	1	0	2	6,292
Lady Chatfield	3	F	8	1	0	1	15,225
Lady Chatterly	3	F	1	0	0	0	120
Lady Chelsea	6	M	1	0	0	0	40
Lady Cherokee	2	F	3	0	0	0	690
Lady Chestnut	3	F	6	1	0	0	4,170
Lady Cheyne	4	F	7	2	1	1	54,130
Lady Christine	5	M	13	1	2	2	46,413
Lady Continental	5	M	6	1	1	1	14,450
Lady Conveyor	4	F	14	1	0	0	4,779
Lady Cora	4	F	3	1	1	0	9,100
Lady Crafty Dancer	8	M	18	2	1	1	11,397
Lady Daisy	7	M	4	0	1	0	1,950
Lady Danielle	2	F	3	0	0	0	0
Lady Danish	3	F	10	0	2	1	25,862
Lady de Fox	8	M	1	0	0	0	102
Lady Dealer	6	M	4	0	0	0	4,640
Lady Deals	8	M	3	0	0	0	336

Horse	Age	Sex	Sts	1st	2d	3d	Won
Lady Deane	7	M	1	0	0	0	0
Lady Deanna	3	F	5	0	1	1	13,087
Lady Della Rayne	4	F	11	2	4	1	11,433
Lady Delphinus	4	F	19	1	2	4	8,194
Lady Demidoff	8	M	14	0	1	1	2,232
Lady Dodger	8	M	5	0	0	1	332
Lady Doms Tiara	3	F	5	0	0	1	1,360
Lady Doodles	4	F	2	0	0	0	839
Lady Dop	2	F	5	0	0	0	630
Lady d'Or	3	F	20	1	4	3	14,478
Lady Drama	5	M	18	1	5	1	16,233
Lady Dumaani	3	F	8	1	2	0	11,730
Lady Dynasty	2	F	5	1	0	1	35,398
Lady Elaine	2	F	1	0	0	0	118
Lady Electric	2	F	2	0	0	0	275
Lady Emancipator	3	F	2	0	0	0	0
Lady Emerald	4	F	1	0	0	0	0
Lady Etain	4	F	2	0	0	0	0
Lady Exclusive	5	M	1	0	0	0	235
Lady Fabulous	4	F	14	1	0	3	14,971
Lady Fannie	4	F	13	2	3	2	17,005
Lady Fay Kay	2	F	2	0	0	0	160
Lady Fencer	2	F	2	0	0	0	137
Lady Fenwick	5	M	8	1	2	4	52,190
Lady Firebird	3	F	3	1	0	0	13,856
Lady From Lima	3	F	10	1	0	1	11,259
Lady Fury	7	M	5	1	1	2	6,886
Lady Gelaine	4	F	8	1	0	2	20,931
Lady Gemstone	2	F	2	0	0	0	1,680
Lady General	4	F	13	1	3	4	77,065
Lady Giggles	4	F	3	0	0	1	1,705
Lady Gina Rosa	6	M	2	0	0	0	390
Lady Glade	2	F	2	1	1	0	41,340
Lady Glaze	3	F	4	0	0	0	440
Lady Gold Slew	3	F	2	0	0	0	800
Lady Golda	7	M	4	0	0	0	200
Lady Gourami	5	M	3	0	1	0	2,485
Lady Grace	6	M	10	1	2	0	30,214
Lady Greystoke	4	F	10	0	2	2	12,601
Lady Gwen	4	F	6	1	2	1	42,550
Lady H	2	F	1	1	0	0	27,000
Lady Halos	3	F	5	0	0	0	940
Lady Harlow	5	M	5	2	0	1	13,350
Lady Hazaam	6	M	9	0	0	0	1,721
Lady Heart Break	4	F	3	0	0	0	298
Lady Helma	4	F	5	1	0	2	32,835
Lady High Indy	3	F	8	2	0	1	11,055
Lady Hillary	2	F	1	0	0	0	1,025
Lady Hoya	2	F	5	0	0	0	636
Lady Hurricane	8	M	4	0	0	0	344
Lady Husky	6	M	3	0	0	0	310
Lady Ide	4	F	8	1	1	1	8,800
Lady in Lights	4	F	4	1	0	0	6,102
Lady in Pink	2	F	7	3	2	1	69,010
Lady in Pinstripes	2	F	2	0	0	0	0
Lady in the Sun	5	M	9	2	0	0	20,717
Lady Ingrain	5	G	3	0	0	0	0
Lady Intimidator	5	M	4	1	0	0	3,260
Lady Irene	3	F	18	3	4	0	34,560
Lady Is a Scamp	3	F	10	0	0	3	5,831
Lady Itron	3	F	13	1	0	1	4,790
Lady J's Partner	3	F	7	0	1	2	10,300
Lady Justine	5	M	4	0	0	0	1,651
Lady Keswick	5	M	2	1	0	0	4,650
Lady Kilkeelan	3	F	12	1	2	5	14,340
Lady Krew	4	F	13	2	0	1	17,140
Lady Kyoto	7	M	2	0	0	0	283
Lady L J	3	F	3	0	0	0	250
Lady La	3	F	8	3	1	1	31,842
Lady La Rue	10	M	4	0	0	0	173
Lady Laabity	4	F	1	0	0	0	0
Lady Lana	3	F	3	0	0	0	0
Lady Lanceolot	4	F	3	0	0	0	0
Lady Lankford	2	F	2	0	1	0	2,940
Lady Larae	5	M	2	0	0	0	0
Lady Larrupin	3	F	13	4	2	0	40,667
Lady Latifa	3	F	13	2	5	3	16,934
Lady Laura G	3	F	10	3	3	0	30,880
Lady Laverne	3	F	3	1	0	2	32,875
Lady Le Quesne (IRE)	2	F	7	2	1	0	20,105
Lady Legend	2	F	6	1	1	0	7,125
Lady Leslie	3	F	13	1	1	0	7,580
Lady Libby	4	F	10	3	2	2	136,276
Lady Liberty	5	M	9	1	0	1	55,446
Lady Lileah	5	M	9	0	0	3	6,000
Lady Lilith	8	M	3	1	0	2	1,504
Lady Linda	6	M	7	1	1	2	67,454
Lady Livey Bodgit	3	F	12	0	1	2	5,843
Lady Livingston	3	F	12	1	2	3	30,740
Lady Lola	2	F	6	1	0	0	10,271
Lady Lombardia	3	F	15	2	0	1	7,296
Lady Longford	5	M	4	0	0	0	160
Lady Loot	4	F	10	6	1	0	76,020
Lady Lover	5	G	10	1	3	0	12,979
Lady Lu	5	M	4	0	0	0	184
Lady Lucky Play	3	F	3	0	1	1	9,300
Lady Luluann	4	F	10	1	3	1	11,502
Lady Lydia	4	F	10	4	0	4	65,200
Lady Lyndsey	3	F	5	0	0	0	0
Lady Lynx	4	F	4	2	1	0	31,814
Lady Lyra	2	F	3	0	0	0	491
Lady Lyra Lee	7	M	1	0	1	0	4,700
Lady Mallory	4	F	10	1	1	1	44,050
Lady Manila	3	F	1	0	0	0	0
Lady Manners	3	F	3	1	0	0	23,910
Lady Margot	4	F	3	0	0	0	1,485
Lady Markey	2	F	6	0	2	1	18,056
Lady Marquise (NZ)	5	M	4	0	0	0	1,600
Lady Mary Florence	2	F	2	1	0	0	11,520
Lady Matt	4	F	2	0	0	0	0
Lady Matty	3	F	10	3	0	2	35,000
Lady Max	3	F	10	2	0	0	14,280
Lady Mayflower	3	F	12	0	4	2	6,175
Lady Miriam	3	F	9	1	2	3	10,387
Lady Monica	3	F	1	0	0	0	0
Lady Monopoly	6	M	3	0	0	0	366
Lady Mountbatten	4	F	7	1	1	0	3,833
Lady Navigator	6	M	13	5	1	1	44,265
Lady Nelson	5	M	4	1	0	1	31,594
Lady Niknar	3	F	2	0	0	0	138
Lady of Color	3	F	4	0	0	0	0
Lady of Crimson	2	F	3	0	0	0	540
Lady of Dover	5	M	3	1	0	0	5,430
Lady of Gold	3	F	4	0	0	1	1,405
Lady of Ice	3	F	12	0	3	2	15,240
Lady of Kildare	3	F	1	0	0	0	400
Lady of Long Ago	2	F	2	0	0	1	2,110
Lady of Praise	4	F	7	0	2	1	8,745
Lady of Prestige	6	M	19	1	4	4	20,459
Lady of Quality	4	F	3	0	0	0	660
Lady of Reign	8	M	7	0	0	1	806
Lady of Savoya	5	M	5	0	0	0	126
Lady of Spain	2	F	1	0	0	0	0
Lady of Style	2	F	1	0	0	0	400
Lady of the Future	6	M	8	2	2	1	160,141
Lady of the Hunt	4	F	8	1	0	0	7,070
Lady of the Press	7	M	12	1	1	1	22,070
Lady of the West	5	M	7	2	0	1	6,902
Lady of Valor	4	F	10	1	1	0	2,359
Lady Offense	3	F	16	3	2	3	43,859
Lady On the Prowl	5	M	14	3	0	4	43,320
Lady On Tour	6	M	11	1	4	2	16,239
Lady Overture	5	M	7	1	0	3	4,892
Lady Page	3	F	1	0	0	0	0
Lady Pamela	3	F	5	0	0	1	6,420
Lady Pan Jammer (IRE)	4	F	9	1	2	0	12,410
Lady Partee	3	F	3	1	0	0	7,020
Lady Patton	4	F	2	0	0	0	164
Lady Penelope	4	F	1	0	0	0	75
Lady Perla	2	F	4	1	0	0	15,610
Lady Peyton	4	F	4	0	1	1	3,190
Lady Pharlet	4	F	2	0	0	0	147
Lady Picasso	3	F	7	0	0	0	1,580
Lady Pilot	3	F	2	0	0	1	680
Lady Pinebourne	5	M	1	0	0	0	0
Lady Prantlack	4	F	2	0	0	0	720
Lady President	5	M	9	0	0	0	1,246
Lady Raiderette	2	F	3	1	2	0	12,670

Horse	Age	Sex	Sts	1st	2d	3d	Won
Lady Rancher	3	F	8	0	0	1	1,449
Lady Rhinestone	2	F	2	0	0	0	3,498
Lady Rhonda Kaye	4	F	8	0	0	1	2,970
Lady Riss	3	F	9	4	2	0	68,036
Lady Rose Winalot	6	M	1	0	0	0	36
Lady Royale	7	M	6	0	0	0	848
Lady Ruhlmann	6	M	9	2	1	0	7,252
Lady Rundell	3	F	7	0	1	0	4,360
Lady Sabrina	4	F	17	3	3	3	162,160
Lady Sanchez	2	F	1	0	0	0	192
Lady Satin	3	F	6	2	1	1	20,075
Lady Saw	3	F	7	0	2	2	5,480
Lady Sax	3	F	1	1	0	0	11,400
Lady Scruff	4	F	17	0	2	2	6,116
Lady Seaberry	4	F	14	3	2	4	39,870
Lady Shaheen	3	F	2	0	0	0	0
Lady Shark	3	F	11	1	1	3	17,117
Lady Sharon	4	F	12	1	2	1	15,318
Lady She Is	2	F	2	0	1	1	6,355
Lady Shelby	4	F	8	2	3	2	8,071
Lady Shelley	4	F	8	2	1	1	24,293
Lady Showtime	7	M	17	5	5	3	32,148
Lady Silver	3	F	13	1	4	1	16,724
Lady Silverrod	2	F	7	1	2	0	25,980
Lady Siobhan	3	F	15	1	0	0	19,485
Lady Siphonica	2	F	5	1	0	0	31,401
Lady Soldier	2	F	4	1	0	0	15,345
Lady Sonya	5	M	12	1	2	1	54,535
Lady Sophisticate	4	F	14	4	0	1	42,728
Lady Spirit	2	F	3	1	1	0	11,332
Lady Spotswood	3	F	6	0	0	1	1,629
Lady Squirtle	5	M	2	0	1	0	1,430
Lady Stalwood	7	M	12	0	1	1	3,105
Lady Star Lite	3	F	8	0	0	2	1,763
Lady Stars	4	F	13	2	2	4	78,375
Lady Strasburg	2	F	1	0	0	0	0
Lady Struck Gold	3	F	1	0	0	0	2,100
Lady Sunshine	2	F	1	0	0	0	85
Lady T	5	M	24	3	1	5	21,831
Lady Taat	6	M	2	0	0	0	0
Lady Tak	4	F	7	4	1	1	439,412
Lady Tara	3	F	6	0	0	0	1,175
Lady Tech	4	F	12	3	1	3	37,894
Lady Texas	2	F	1	0	0	0	0
Lady Thatcher (CHI)	5	M	9	1	2	2	72,040
Lady Topper	2	F	4	0	0	0	1,600
Lady Tour	4	F	9	2	2	0	13,735
Lady True	2	F	4	0	1	0	2,440
Lady Truffles	2	F	5	1	3	0	113,905
Lady Tunafish	2	F	3	0	0	1	1,917
Lady Two Socks	4	F	11	0	5	1	5,517
Lady V Eight	3	F	12	1	1	1	8,670
Lady Val	6	M	4	1	0	0	4,216
Lady Veronica	4	F	12	2	0	2	17,920
Lady Victoria	4	F	13	2	0	1	18,585
Lady Viking	4	F	2	0	0	0	239
Lady Wallenda	5	M	14	0	0	3	8,356
Lady Wardley	3	F	5	1	1	0	8,180
Lady Watral Irene	3	F	10	0	0	3	3,004
Lady Weave	2	F	6	1	0	0	5,286
Lady What Luck	2	F	2	0	0	0	450
Lady Whimsy	7	M	14	2	0	1	11,646
Lady Whipper	2	F	4	0	0	0	130
Lady Whippet	3	F	2	0	0	0	0
Lady Wildcat	4	F	1	0	0	0	0
Lady Will Power	4	F	2	0	0	0	148
Lady Willow	3	F	7	0	0	0	360
Lady Wings	5	M	2	0	0	0	217
Lady With a Kick	3	F	6	1	1	1	12,971
Lady Woodman	2	F	2	0	1	0	5,600
Lady Zone	3	F	3	0	0	0	232
Lady Zoom Zoom	6	M	2	0	0	0	0
Ladybird Brown	3	F	5	1	0	0	2,848
Ladybug Red	2	F	1	0	0	0	66
Ladybug's Davin	2	C	3	0	0	0	0
Ladydoctorsfortune	2	F	12	0	0	2	5,130
Ladye Langfuhr	4	F	17	3	2	1	18,839
Ladyecho	4	F	8	1	1	2	46,193
Ladyformal	3	F	10	3	1	3	22,443
Ladyfromdixieland	6	M	9	4	0	3	22,005
Ladyinareddress	3	F	11	2	0	3	98,197
Ladyinastorm	3	F	5	0	0	3	6,200
Ladyinblue	2	F	1	0	0	0	135
Ladykenita	7	M	2	0	0	0	0
Ladymour	2	F	8	1	1	1	15,141
Ladyneator	3	G	2	0	0	0	0
Ladyneversatisfied	2	F	2	0	0	0	795
Ladyonalert	3	F	11	1	1	0	11,414
Ladyonthewire	7	M	2	0	0	0	112
Lady's a Pistol	3	F	5	0	1	0	6,620
Lady's Advantage	3	F	7	0	2	0	6,531
Lady's Caper	2	F	4	0	0	0	2,160
Lady's Don't Tell	3	F	3	0	1	0	2,440
Lady's Event	3	G	3	1	0	1	13,750
Lady's Fame	4	F	1	0	0	0	0
Lady's Hat	5	M	4	0	1	0	2,233
Ladys Image	2	F	6	0	0	1	3,750
Lady's Imp	2	F	2	0	0	0	0
Lady's Jewel	6	M	4	0	0	0	684
Lady's Kiss	4	F	1	0	0	0	135
Lady's Last Punch	2	F	2	0	1	0	4,870
Lady's Lil' Missy	3	F	12	1	2	0	6,753
Lady's Lil' Ringer	6	G	2	0	0	0	0
Lady's Mantle (IRE)	4	F	2	0	0	0	0
Lady's Mark	5	M	4	0	0	0	501
Lady's Memo	3	C	2	0	0	1	2,980
Lady's Red Rose	2	F	4	0	1	1	8,688
Lady's Room	3	F	11	1	2	0	53,675
Lady's Rose	4	F	11	0	1	2	4,690
Lady'sgoldenmemory	4	F	10	2	4	3	26,108
Ladysgotthelooks	3	F	2	1	0	0	7,610
Ladyslewmood	5	M	9	0	1	0	1,890
Ladyvictoriaatto	3	F	3	1	0	0	9,282
Lafleur	5	H	8	5	1	1	16,260
Lafouche Magnum	7	H	1	0	0	0	0
Lago Maggiore	3	C	10	1	3	1	9,518
Lagoda	2	F	2	0	0	0	0
Laguna Madre	2	F	2	0	1	0	5,400
Laguna Pointe	2	F	2	1	0	0	16,825
Lahaina	3	F	13	1	1	0	7,428
Lahdeanah	3	F	1	0	0	0	840
Lahinch	5	G	10	0	3	3	22,220
Laidlow	4	C	5	0	2	1	30,040
Laines Motel	4	G	2	0	0	0	540
Laird Angus	4	C	11	0	1	1	4,653
Laitee Legs	5	M	6	0	0	0	866
Lake Avenue	2	C	1	0	0	0	654
Lake Champlain	2	F	3	0	1	0	6,790
Lake Cide Boy	2	G	2	0	0	0	129
Lake Classic	3	C	10	3	4	1	29,095
Lake Como Girl	3	F	5	2	0	1	33,620
Lake Cumberland	5	H	4	1	0	0	7,330
Lake Danzig	4	G	11	1	1	2	6,365
Lake G P	2	C	4	1	0	0	8,243
Lake Garda	8	G	9	0	0	1	3,377
Lake George Fire	2	F	4	1	0	1	5,377
Lake Hamilton	8	G	9	0	3	1	3,380
Lake John	2	C	10	0	1	2	7,600
Lake Kinneret	4	F	4	0	0	1	4,960
Lake Kiowa	3	G	8	1	1	0	12,200
Lake Merced	3	F	1	1	0	0	8,400
Lake of Bays	5	G	12	0	1	6	16,535
Lake of Gold	3	F	2	0	1	0	4,725
Lake Point	5	G	3	0	0	1	1,540
Lake Ponche	3	G	5	0	1	0	2,040
Lake Ray	4	G	11	3	1	0	11,670
Lake Shore Girl	2	F	2	0	1	0	3,920
Lake Silver	6	G	11	1	0	3	11,153
Lake Skimmer	4	G	7	2	1	1	45,234
Lake Station	4	F	7	1	2	2	14,074
Lake Tearie	2	F	1	0	0	0	0
Lake Vista	4	G	4	0	0	0	450
Lake West	4	F	1	0	0	0	110
Lakefield	5	G	6	1	0	1	50,635
Lakeman	3	C	4	0	0	0	900
Laker Cheerleader	4	F	14	3	1	1	66,910
Laker Girl	5	M	5	1	1	2	17,200
Lakerette	4	F	9	2	1	2	22,485

Horse	Age	Sex	Sts	1st	2d	3d	Won
Lakeshore	3	F	14	2	4	3	31,570
Lakeshore Bliss	3	F	7	0	1	2	2,369
Lakeside Bella	2	F	5	0	0	1	5,655
Lakeside Gentry	6	G	2	0	0	0	1,170
Lakeside Trail	5	G	8	1	0	3	33,620
Lakeside Villa	3	G	3	0	0	0	0
Lakesville	4	F	8	4	2	1	41,240
Laketon	4	G	9	1	0	2	18,845
Lakeville Rush	2	G	2	1	1	0	49,020
Lakevillestar	4	G	5	0	0	1	1,946
Lakota	5	G	15	1	0	5	14,021
Lakota Creek	5	G	10	1	1	1	11,906
Lakota Road	5	M	6	0	0	0	775
Lakota Spirit	4	F	12	1	3	3	30,630
Lalene	4	F	2	0	0	0	0
Lali's Cat	3	G	11	2	1	1	8,650
Lalo	3	G	12	1	1	3	12,029
Lamarche's Oro	4	G	7	0	0	2	2,144
Lamartinique	5	G	12	1	0	3	4,753
Lambere	4	G	4	1	1	1	10,105
Lambert Point	3	F	2	0	0	0	0
Lambeth Walk	3	F	4	0	0	1	4,310
Lambourne	9	G	2	0	0	0	72
Lambrose	2	G	5	1	2	0	13,264
Lamerie (IRE)	8	G	14	0	5	1	17,019
Lametta Light	4	F	16	1	0	0	6,571
Lamina Bluestreak	3	C	4	0	1	1	4,750
Lampsas County	8	M	1	0	0	0	0
Lana Mae	6	M	6	0	2	1	2,683
Lanahan	6	G	10	2	0	1	9,909
Lanatoo of Ascot	4	F	3	0	0	0	398
Lance's Lil Jade	3	F	1	0	0	0	0
Lance's Turn	5	H	1	0	0	0	0
Lancette's Wager	6	M	13	1	2	2	12,665
Land Baron	3	G	2	0	2	0	10,080
Land Bearer	4	G	7	0	0	0	456
Land Corrupter	4	F	6	1	2	0	7,286
Land Grab	4	C	7	2	0	0	19,590
Land of Dreams	3	F	6	0	1	3	21,420
Land Tax	6	M	8	0	2	0	15,260
Land the Limit	4	F	10	1	2	0	16,010
Landa	2	F	3	0	0	2	1,608
Landana	4	C	5	0	0	0	1,425
Landers	2	F	1	0	0	0	0
Landing Gear	3	F	13	1	1	1	11,526
Landler	5	G	4	1	0	1	22,630
Landlord	5	G	1	0	0	0	0
Landmark	2	F	3	1	0	1	23,546
Landofmilknhoney	7	G	17	2	1	3	10,653
Landofthebrave	3	G	9	0	1	0	5,223
Landon	5	G	8	0	1	0	6,375
Landon's Lane	3	G	4	0	0	1	1,380
Landry	4	G	14	2	1	1	29,140
Landsdowne	3	G	9	1	1	1	19,340
Lane Throne	4	F	7	0	1	0	1,768
Langano	6	M	9	0	1	1	21,220
Langburg	3	G	10	1	2	3	89,650
Langfleur	4	G	5	2	0	0	75,770
Langfuhr's Allure	4	G	13	0	0	0	1,879
Langfuhr's Magic	3	F	9	1	1	2	30,306
Langfuhr's Wildcat	2	F	1	0	0	0	50
Languissa	4	F	2	1	0	0	5,100
Lanita G	3	F	2	0	0	0	700
Lanlicia	3	F	9	2	2	2	51,345
Lansil Field	4	G	4	1	0	2	6,370
Lanslide Lerblance	2	C	1	0	0	1	715
Lantern Court	2	F	4	1	2	0	27,770
Lanton	3	F	1	0	1	0	1,080
Lap of Honour	3	C	2	0	0	1	2,400
Lapidus	4	G	3	0	0	0	1,339
Lapis	4	F	4	0	0	1	7,650
Lapis Lace	2	F	4	0	0	0	1,305
Laplace	2	G	4	1	0	1	10,690
Laquick	5	G	2	1	0	0	4,750
Laquiera	3	F	6	0	0	0	80
Lara's Badboy	2	C	4	1	0	1	10,695
Lara's Love	3	F	6	0	0	0	270
Larceny N Tended	3	G	5	1	0	1	5,990
Laredo Lad	3	C	6	0	2	0	4,840
Laredo Lil	4	F	13	4	3	1	65,305
Larella Lin	6	M	3	0	0	0	428
Larens Bid	4	F	6	0	1	1	2,817
Largeandincharge	8	H	13	1	1	1	22,425
L'Argento	2	C	3	0	1	1	12,700
Larger Than Life	4	F	7	2	2	1	67,840
Largus	5	G	3	0	0	0	0
Lark's Halo	4	F	2	0	0	0	0
Larkwood	5	M	15	1	1	3	4,473
Larron	7	G	10	5	5	0	10,530
Larrupin Gal	3	F	3	1	2	0	24,750
Larrupin's Music	4	G	7	1	1	2	11,045
Larry and Pete	3	C	10	2	1	2	16,417
Larry B	4	G	4	1	0	1	36,845
Larry King	4	C	1	0	0	1	5,520
Larry the Longshot	7	G	9	4	3	1	17,812
Larrygene	5	G	2	0	0	0	114
Larry's Last Code	3	G	8	0	0	0	862
Larry's Signature	3	F	4	1	1	0	4,176
Larrys Sister Lari	9	M	5	0	1	0	930
Larry's Smile	3	F	11	1	3	2	64,068
Larson E Whipsnade	4	G	9	1	2	1	20,324
Las Brisas Girl	4	F	7	1	1	1	32,000
Las Devious	5	G	7	0	0	1	3,123
Las Vegas Dancer	2	F	4	0	3	1	14,800
Las Vegas Hangover	3	G	3	0	0	0	400
Laser Cat	5	M	8	0	0	1	2,667
Laser Con	6	G	5	0	0	1	2,780
Laser Gun	7	G	2	0	0	0	0
Laser Jet	3	G	3	0	0	0	510
Laser Lad	2	C	2	0	1	0	5,750
Laser Lite	5	G	6	3	0	0	17,293
Laser Loop	10	G	9	1	0	0	4,104
Laser Shot	2	C	4	1	0	0	10,560
Laser Tag	4	F	4	1	1	0	6,000
Laserblast	6	G	13	1	3	0	10,648
Lashburn	4	C	1	0	0	0	0
Lasik	3	F	5	2	2	0	72,090
Laskeek Bay	3	G	9	2	2	2	32,575
Lasmoke	4	G	12	0	0	0	2,145
Lass Lil' Sunrise	2	F	3	0	1	1	7,840
Lass Nekia	2	F	4	0	0	0	2,300
Lass of Aughrim	3	F	7	0	1	3	1,994
Lasserre	6	G	12	2	1	2	10,602
Lassie Mackee	4	F	9	2	1	2	10,560
Lasso the Sun	3	F	10	1	5	2	8,788
Last Affirmed	3	C	4	1	1	1	9,800
Last Angel	2	F	2	1	0	0	8,415
Last Answer	4	G	9	1	5	1	146,120
Last Baby	4	F	3	0	0	0	0
Last Call Buddy	2	C	3	0	0	0	395
Last Call Lover	11	G	7	1	2	1	4,324
Last Caper	4	G	11	3	0	1	4,095
Last Chance Flame	4	G	9	2	1	0	7,251
Last Chance Girl	2	F	2	0	0	0	1,080
Last Chancecharger	5	G	6	0	0	0	384
Last Class	3	G	1	0	0	0	400
Last Crown	3	F	8	0	1	0	8,978
Last Dance Lady	2	F	5	0	0	1	5,444
Last Danz	2	F	5	1	1	1	19,098
Last Day of Winter	6	M	6	0	2	1	2,702
Last Dime	2	C	2	0	0	0	0
Last Drum	5	G	15	1	3	2	17,220
Last Expression	9	G	9	1	0	2	3,659
Last Fantasy	2	F	6	1	2	0	8,010
Last Foal	2	C	2	0	0	0	1,080
Last Friday	2	C	4	0	0	3	2,770
Last Frontier	3	C	8	3	0	1	59,330
Last Goodbye	4	F	6	0	0	0	1,191
Last Intention	5	G	7	1	1	4	68,829
Last Khal	5	G	17	1	6	3	17,454
Last Light	2	F	1	0	0	0	44
Last Little Slew	3	G	4	0	0	0	289
Last Minute Detail	3	C	9	2	0	0	76,086
Last Monarch	3	G	13	0	2	1	4,419
Last Native	3	C	3	1	0	0	6,460
Last O Locks	4	G	5	0	0	0	375
Last Oasis	2	F	1	1	0	0	13,800
Last One Standing	7	H	13	2	1	4	8,522

RECORDS OF HORSES

Horse	Age	Sex	Sts	1st	2d	3d	Won
Last One Up	6	G	9	0	0	0	924
Last Outpost	2	G	5	1	0	1	7,110
Last Palace	5	H	1	0	0	0	360
Last Parade (ARG)	8	G	2	0	0	0	300
Last Party	3	F	3	1	0	0	10,403
Last Pax	7	G	10	1	0	0	4,464
Last Peak	7	G	3	0	0	2	440
Last Place	3	C	7	1	1	1	8,626
Last President	4	C	8	0	3	1	10,440
Last Puff	5	M	14	1	1	6	63,810
Last Reality	3	G	5	1	1	0	8,300
Last Rebel	9	G	2	0	0	0	486
Last Recourse	4	G	14	0	1	2	5,111
Last Rose	2	F	3	0	0	0	1,335
Last S A	3	F	5	1	0	0	7,071
Last Samurai	2	C	1	0	0	0	129
Last Second Shot	3	G	12	1	3	4	13,013
Last Serenade	5	M	5	1	2	2	8,171
Last Shoot Out	5	M	2	0	0	0	600
Last Slew	5	G	11	3	3	0	34,592
Last Song	3	F	11	3	1	2	254,253
Last Stand	5	G	7	0	1	1	14,185
Last Supper	7	M	1	0	0	0	44
Last Thoughts	2	F	3	0	1	0	5,276
Last Time in Town	3	G	7	0	3	1	41,980
Last Toots	2	F	1	0	0	0	1,140
Last Trap	4	C	3	0	0	2	1,095
Last Trial	3	C	4	0	0	0	996
Last Trick	8	G	7	1	0	0	12,503
Last Trust	4	C	16	1	3	3	15,809
Last Two Dollars	5	G	4	0	1	0	1,539
Last Verse	4	F	2	0	0	0	510
Last Waltz	3	F	5	1	0	1	38,275
Lastcallforbrandy	3	G	1	0	0	0	300
Lastcallforparis	6	G	4	1	0	1	7,460
Lastcallforwhiskey	3	G	6	0	0	0	842
Lastcallglenchek	2	C	1	0	0	0	0
Lastchancetoanswer	4	F	7	0	0	1	456
Lastchancetodance	3	F	15	2	4	2	21,451
Lasting Code	5	M	6	1	2	1	42,180
Lasting Image	4	G	7	2	1	0	36,100
Lasting Influence	2	G	2	1	1	0	2,550
Lasting Kiss	4	F	9	3	2	3	17,100
Lasting Punch	3	F	4	0	0	0	300
Lasting Tribute	6	H	8	1	0	3	46,535
Lastlee Ridge	3	G	13	1	0	2	4,741
Lastoftheline	5	G	1	0	0	0	0
Lastonehappy	3	F	12	1	2	1	10,722
Lasttorun	4	G	18	3	1	3	14,531
Lataskra	2	F	6	0	1	0	2,955
Latched On	4	G	7	1	1	1	8,450
Latchme	4	F	2	0	0	0	0
Late Again	9	G	8	0	0	0	3,200
Late Breaking News	2	F	2	1	0	0	13,860
Late Carson	8	G	12	0	3	0	8,228
Late Expectations	3	G	23	6	1	6	111,661
Late Knight Lizzie	2	F	2	0	0	0	0
Late Knight Train	2	G	1	0	0	0	0
Late Night Dancer	3	F	5	0	0	1	693
Late Night Leader	3	C	4	1	0	0	7,645
Late Night Lover	2	G	9	2	1	3	61,220
Late Night Out (GB)	9	G	9	2	1	2	38,645
Late Nite Cat	5	G	5	0	1	1	2,280
Late Not Lost	4	G	10	0	1	1	1,704
Late Performer	3	C	2	0	0	0	400
Late Survivor	4	G	8	1	1	1	18,144
Late to the Dance	5	G	10	1	0	3	10,597
Latenight Frannie	6	M	12	0	1	0	3,070
Latenite Special	3	F	9	5	1	1	142,463
Latenite Trick	4	G	16	2	4	1	64,765
Latent Image	3	G	12	2	1	0	17,065
Lateral Twenty	5	M	5	0	0	2	579
Latest Edition	3	G	17	2	3	3	23,405
Latest Technology	4	F	10	4	1	1	31,905
Latexo	4	G	16	2	1	3	14,703
Latifundiario (BRZ)	4	G	10	2	3	0	27,540
Latigo	3	G	4	0	0	0	450
Latin Beauty	6	M	3	0	0	1	1,099
Latin Devil	3	G	1	0	0	0	400

Horse	Age	Sex	Sts	1st	2d	3d	Won
Latin Express	4	G	2	0	0	0	0
Latin Gentleman	2	C	6	0	1	0	2,215
Latin Heart	2	F	1	0	0	0	400
Latin King	2	C	2	0	0	0	675
Latin Louisa	3	F	7	4	1	0	15,630
Latin Love Bug	9	G	10	0	0	1	3,022
Latin Moon	3	C	7	0	0	0	4,280
Latin Music	3	G	4	0	1	1	1,601
Latin Ruhlette	2	F	3	0	0	0	770
Latin Storm	4	F	6	0	2	0	5,460
Latin Technology	6	G	5	1	0	1	10,978
Latino (PER)	5	H	7	1	0	0	28,115
Latino Mix	2	G	7	0	0	1	1,214
Latronica	5	M	2	0	0	1	1,800
Latta Luck	3	F	10	1	0	0	4,189
Latter Day Ace	8	G	12	1	3	1	12,413
Lau Mor's Glitter	3	F	7	0	2	0	5,255
Laudatory	3	G	8	0	0	0	780
Laugh a Little	3	G	11	1	2	0	15,260
Laugh Again	3	C	6	0	0	1	935
Laugh Last	3	F	6	0	0	2	6,640
Laughinanadrinkin	8	G	6	0	0	1	300
Laughing	4	F	9	1	1	1	12,149
Laughing Academy	4	G	10	2	4	0	28,200
Laughing Luke	4	C	14	4	2	3	91,050
Laughs and Giggles	2	F	10	1	0	1	14,355
Launch a Deacon	4	G	8	1	1	1	10,196
Launch Alert	3	F	5	3	1	0	26,700
Launch Into Space	4	G	2	0	0	0	300
Launch Ready	4	G	6	2	0	0	7,812
Launch Spot	4	G	6	1	0	0	6,180
Launchetta	2	F	1	0	0	0	66
Laundering Money	4	F	7	1	0	0	5,558
Laundred Money	3	C	9	1	1	1	6,690
Laura Lynn	4	F	1	0	0	0	45
Laura N the Girls	4	F	5	2	0	0	13,631
Laura Raj	3	F	2	0	0	0	470
Laurabelle	5	M	1	0	0	0	28
Laurabobsteve	3	G	17	1	5	1	10,125
Lauraelise	5	M	15	1	1	5	16,452
Lauraelises Sister	4	F	16	2	4	2	53,770
Lauras Bright Eyes	5	M	15	0	2	1	4,216
Laura's Choice	2	C	1	0	0	0	810
Laura's Holiday	2	F	6	1	0	2	12,230
Laura's Jewel	2	F	3	1	1	0	30,430
Laura's Lucky Boy	3	C	9	3	2	1	246,730
Laura's Moment	4	G	7	1	1	2	10,078
Laura's Prospect	3	F	8	1	0	0	10,535
Laura's Testamony	6	M	3	0	0	0	0
Laura'sluckycharm	6	M	11	0	2	3	4,960
Laurceilo	4	F	12	1	0	2	9,428
Laureada	3	F	5	1	0	0	4,152
Laurel Street	4	F	2	0	0	0	154
Lauren Lynn	4	F	6	2	0	1	40,721
Lauren Michelle	2	F	6	0	0	0	3,030
Lauren N Blaine	8	G	6	0	0	0	394
Lauren Rose	3	F	3	1	0	1	4,331
Lauren Won	3	F	8	4	2	0	35,940
Lauren's Approval	4	G	5	0	0	0	314
Lauren's Baby	4	G	10	0	1	3	5,520
Lauren's Charm	2	F	7	0	2	3	31,203
Lauren's Dream	2	F	5	0	0	1	3,278
Lauren's Halo	4	F	6	1	2	1	9,990
Lauren's Hot Dance	8	M	3	1	0	1	8,160
Laurens Lacotte	4	F	1	0	0	0	0
Lauren's On Fire	3	F	4	1	0	0	6,750
Lauren's Partygirl	3	F	2	0	0	0	323
Lauren's Peak	3	F	4	1	0	0	16,740
Lauren's Tour	6	M	15	4	3	3	34,595
Lauren's Wish	2	F	1	0	0	0	118
Laurier	3	G	9	0	0	0	1,817
Laurie's Smile	3	G	17	1	0	4	13,864
Laurita Tsunami	4	F	7	0	2	2	2,725
Lava Lil	5	M	12	1	0	3	17,220
Lava Man	3	G	13	3	6	1	230,008
Lavaca	6	G	13	2	5	2	29,272
Laveen	5	M	4	1	0	0	3,210
Lavender Baby	5	M	12	4	1	0	88,560
Lavender Bob	4	C	4	0	0	2	2,123

Horse	Age	Sex	Sts	1st	2d	3d	Won
Lavender Lace	3	F	11	1	4	1	20,010
Lavender Lady	7	M	5	0	0	0	364
Lavender Lass	4	F	14	2	5	1	119,010
Lavender Sea	3	F	7	0	0	1	1,550
Lavender's Lad	6	H	8	0	3	0	28,388
Laventille	4	G	4	1	0	1	2,972
Laverluck	2	G	2	0	0	0	50
Laville	3	F	4	0	1	2	16,800
Lavishing Ruby	2	F	1	0	0	0	55
Law Partners	5	G	12	0	2	2	2,149
Law Review	7	H	4	0	0	3	6,020
Lawabidingcitizen	2	F	2	0	0	0	780
Lawbook	4	G	9	1	2	2	40,300
Lawful Nice	3	F	9	1	3	2	55,750
Lawn Mower	5	H	8	0	2	0	1,770
Lawn Party	2	F	1	0	0	0	400
Lawrenson	5	G	3	1	2	0	17,095
Lawtonite	7	G	3	0	0	0	107
Lawyer Lauren	4	F	13	1	3	2	23,460
Lawzem Gain	3	C	14	1	0	3	12,250
Lay Down Shelly	3	F	1	0	0	1	465
Lay It On Me (GB)	3	C	5	1	0	0	15,900
Layn the Smackdown	4	G	14	2	0	1	19,663
Layton's Trick	2	C	1	0	0	0	450
Layton's Warbonnet	5	M	8	0	2	0	3,626
Lazar	8	G	3	1	0	0	5,085
Lazer Speed	5	H	7	0	0	0	817
Lazer's Alymagic	7	M	3	1	1	1	5,770
Lazy Sahana	6	M	8	0	2	0	13,490
Lazzeri	3	C	1	0	0	0	2,580
L'Brown One	9	G	21	0	0	3	2,954
L'Bruiser	4	C	1	0	0	0	0
Le Amber	3	F	4	0	0	1	866
Le Beaucet	8	G	3	0	0	0	624
Le Berthon	2	F	1	0	0	0	0
Le Bon Ton Rulette	2	F	2	0	0	1	1,450
Le Boss	4	C	2	1	0	0	3,960
Le Boulevard	8	G	13	0	1	2	5,268
Le Bourget	6	H	3	0	0	1	4,677
Le Cinquieme Essai	5	G	6	3	2	1	237,004
Le Cocq	6	G	1	0	0	0	0
Le Dancer (GER)	8	G	5	1	0	0	1,846
Le Deputy	5	H	9	0	0	1	5,380
Le Feuvre Road	4	G	6	1	0	1	7,628
Le George	5	G	10	1	2	1	13,331
Le Grand Belle	3	F	7	2	0	0	33,870
Le Grand Fromage	8	G	5	0	0	0	521
Le Grande Run	3	G	3	0	0	1	1,037
Le Jester	4	G	11	4	2	2	60,480
Le Jeux Sont Fait	3	G	15	3	3	3	41,135
Le Kat	2	G	2	0	0	0	190
Le Matin	5	G	3	0	0	0	1,180
Le Monde	6	H	10	2	1	2	17,430
Le Nard	6	G	13	3	2	1	10,557
Le Notre	4	G	7	1	2	2	31,020
Le Numerous	6	G	12	0	0	1	7,977
Le Parrain (ARG)	4	C	5	0	1	2	17,890
Le Peu Roi	4	G	10	2	3	1	6,300
Le Renard Subtil	5	G	5	1	1	0	13,640
Le Rock	3	G	8	1	0	2	34,619
Le Sovereign	7	H	4	1	0	0	2,686
Le Twister	7	M	4	0	0	0	154
Le Vainqueur	6	G	5	0	0	0	0
Le Vie de Le Moose	3	G	11	0	3	0	3,328
Lead by Example	5	H	6	1	2	0	65,340
Lead for Speed	2	G	7	3	3	1	40,160
Lead Hound	4	G	10	1	2	2	16,448
Lead On McDuff	2	G	3	1	0	0	8,592
Lead Story	5	M	3	1	0	2	235,740
Lead the Jack	3	G	6	1	0	0	11,126
Lead the Parade	4	F	7	1	3	0	16,503
Lead Wolf	3	C	3	1	0	0	3,600
Leader Begone	2	C	2	0	0	0	548
Leader of the Pact	3	C	4	0	1	1	6,290
Leader Out West	7	G	6	0	1	0	4,400
Leaderofmylife	3	F	4	0	0	1	1,100
Leader's Choice	4	G	10	1	0	2	4,770
Leading Brave	4	G	9	1	0	2	9,289
Leading Colors	7	H	6	0	0	1	1,029
Leading Genius	4	F	6	0	1	0	1,160
Leading Lady Lisa	5	M	3	0	0	0	0
Leading Lioness	3	F	4	0	0	0	3,000
Leading Off	3	C	6	3	1	0	71,465
Leading Prospect	5	M	15	1	2	1	7,856
Leading Role	6	M	6	0	0	1	11,435
Leading Ruler	7	G	2	0	0	0	224
Leading Runner	6	G	7	1	0	0	5,505
Leading the Parade	3	C	7	1	0	2	38,292
Leading the Tour	3	F	1	0	0	0	135
Leading Toad	4	G	4	1	2	0	2,680
Leadingwithmynose	7	H	1	0	0	0	0
Leaf Town Boy	3	C	5	0	0	1	3,885
Leaf Treader	3	C	7	0	0	0	2,850
Leafoutofyourbook	3	C	19	4	3	3	43,581
Leafy's Comet	3	G	3	0	0	0	0
Leagueofhisown	4	C	13	3	1	5	78,815
Leah's Dolly	2	F	2	0	0	1	3,400
Leah's Legend	3	F	6	2	1	1	13,078
Leah's Look	6	M	6	1	0	1	9,548
Lean On Pete	3	G	9	2	0	1	4,825
Leanin Ontheaxe	2	C	1	0	0	0	0
Leap	7	G	2	0	0	0	420
Leap for Joy	5	M	9	2	1	2	18,742
Leap the Creek	3	C	10	1	1	2	10,540
Leapin Leprechaun	3	C	3	0	2	0	1,800
Leaping Leroy	7	G	2	1	0	1	1,074
Leaping Lord	4	G	10	0	4	0	10,746
Leaping Plum	13	G	1	0	0	0	536
Leapshin	6	G	12	1	2	3	15,100
Lear Force	2	C	9	1	0	0	11,520
Lear Jet Set	2	F	7	1	1	0	20,760
Lear Jetta	3	F	3	0	0	1	770
Lear Note	3	G	7	0	0	0	860
Lear Vision	4	F	5	0	0	2	2,742
Learbo	2	G	1	0	0	0	600
Learctic	4	G	1	0	0	0	0
Learn	3	G	4	0	0	0	300
Learnin Experience	5	M	13	1	2	2	7,826
Lea's Mag	5	M	7	1	0	0	2,689
Lea's Peak	2	F	5	0	0	0	4,080
Lea's Ruler	3	C	3	0	0	0	186
Lea's Siebe	5	G	10	1	0	2	5,231
Lease the Legand	6	G	4	0	0	1	1,070
Leasea Katera	8	M	2	0	0	0	0
Leaseholders Dream	4	F	1	0	1	0	6,000
Leathal Sting	5	G	15	3	1	2	16,156
Leather Helmet	3	G	9	0	2	2	7,492
Leather Liver	4	G	1	0	0	0	0
Leather N Lace	4	G	12	2	0	1	32,763
Leather Tough	5	G	9	2	1	1	14,878
Leathertuskadero	4	F	4	0	0	0	1,736
Leave It	5	G	9	0	0	1	1,737
Leave It Alone	3	F	9	4	1	2	30,455
Leave It to Betsy	6	M	7	0	0	0	777
Leave It to Eva	2	F	2	0	0	0	1,325
Leave It to Me	3	F	9	2	1	0	13,468
Leave Laughing	4	G	14	2	1	1	8,210
Leave Me Alone	2	F	1	0	0	0	400
Leave No Trace	11	G	1	0	0	0	0
Leave To Appeal (IRE)	4	F	13	0	2	4	36,753
Leaveiton	3	G	9	1	3	1	7,494
Leaveminthedust	4	F	3	0	1	1	13,360
Leavethestudio	6	G	9	0	1	3	9,575
Leavin Indy	4	G	9	0	0	0	1,054
Leavin the Scene	3	G	2	0	1	0	4,582
Leaving a Legend	3	G	3	1	1	0	9,600
Leaving On My Mind	2	G	13	5	2	3	299,873
Leaving Texas	6	G	23	4	2	1	19,242
Leavingemwet	5	G	1	0	0	0	0
Leavingonajetplane	4	G	4	2	1	0	19,580
Leavn Ona Jetplane	4	F	10	4	0	1	66,740
Leavuwithasmile	3	G	5	0	1	1	9,802
Lebam	4	G	4	1	0	2	1,536
Lebite	3	C	9	1	4	1	29,266
Lebo Barker N Rita	3	C	8	1	1	1	10,470
Lebontempsroulet	7	G	4	0	1	1	9,050
Lecielisfreezing	3	C	1	0	0	0	400
Lector	4	G	11	0	0	5	7,455

Horse	Age	Sex	Sts	1st	2d	3d	Won
Lecture Hall	4	G	3	0	0	0	189
Led by the Light	4	G	12	3	1	2	34,151
Ledbury	7	G	6	0	0	0	1,459
Lee Gage	4	F	20	8	3	2	44,500
Lee Lee	2	F	1	1	0	0	9,000
Lee Lee Anna	4	F	14	2	1	2	9,894
Lee Lee's Model T	6	M	8	0	0	0	133
Lee Road Glory	2	C	1	0	0	0	0
Lee Roy Boy	4	G	2	0	0	0	0
Leeaferd	9	G	9	1	0	0	4,703
Leebearski	6	M	5	0	1	0	9,174
Leedle Dee	3	F	10	1	4	0	70,581
Leeds Creek	3	G	9	2	0	0	30,140
Leegans Last	3	G	1	0	0	0	228
Leenie's Devil	2	F	6	1	0	1	6,435
Leenmealone	8	G	12	1	2	4	8,860
Lee's Best	3	G	6	0	0	0	0
Lee's Prospector	5	M	7	2	0	1	27,982
Lee's Receivable	3	G	3	0	0	0	1,680
Lee's Say So	2	C	3	0	0	1	3,825
Lees'dancer	3	G	5	0	1	0	2,828
Leestown Affair	2	F	8	0	0	3	12,435
Leestown Boy	3	G	16	1	2	0	11,262
Leestown Cajun	3	C	3	0	1	1	5,290
Leestown Code	3	G	5	1	0	1	4,200
Leestown Flirt	2	F	3	0	0	0	525
Leestown Road	2	F	5	2	1	2	38,608
Leestown Star	3	C	1	0	0	0	480
Leestown Wish	3	F	1	0	0	0	405
Leetariat	4	C	8	1	0	4	5,621
Leevia	4	F	4	0	0	0	114
Lefa Theda	7	M	11	3	0	2	11,068
Le'femme Agenda	5	M	4	1	0	0	7,350
L'Effaceur	7	G	2	2	0	0	28,200
Leffy's Launch	6	M	1	0	0	0	50
Lefors	3	G	7	0	1	1	17,457
Left Coast	4	G	18	1	3	3	9,597
Left Early	8	G	12	1	0	1	10,864
Left Hook	5	G	13	1	2	2	29,108
Left of Center	4	F	1	0	0	0	0
Left Right Left	7	M	16	0	1	4	4,850
Left Swiftly	2	F	3	1	0	1	7,884
Left to Me	3	F	1	0	0	0	0
Lefty Marciana	7	G	6	1	0	3	6,547
Leftyloosey	3	F	2	0	0	0	345
Lefty's Lady	3	F	3	0	1	2	12,940
Legacy Fighter	4	G	9	4	2	0	54,390
Legacy Lass	3	F	3	0	0	0	588
Legacy of Honor	3	G	4	0	0	0	0
Legacy Ridge	5	M	7	0	0	1	720
Legacy's Honor	3	G	11	3	1	2	50,705
Legacy's Star	4	G	14	1	1	1	7,581
Legal Control	2	C	6	3	1	1	95,782
Legal Document	4	F	1	0	0	0	400
Legal Eagle	3	C	3	0	1	0	2,855
Legal Edition	4	F	14	0	3	5	10,430
Legal Emigrant	4	F	9	2	1	2	16,470
L'Egal Ethics	4	F	15	2	0	3	13,546
Legal Force	2	G	3	0	0	1	1,255
Legal Games	4	G	5	2	0	0	9,196
Legal Jargon	5	G	7	0	0	1	844
Legal Jousting (IRE)	7	H	1	0	0	0	0
Legal Linda	4	F	4	0	0	0	378
Legal Logic	4	G	11	2	6	0	129,280
Legal Question	3	G	4	0	2	1	14,670
Legal Starlet	5	M	14	2	2	0	13,016
Legal Tactics	4	F	3	0	0	0	540
Legal Terms	3	G	2	0	0	0	1,941
Legal Testamony	2	F	5	0	1	0	2,375
Legal Thief	7	G	14	6	1	3	29,199
Legal Trap	5	G	1	0	0	0	0
Legal Vices	3	G	2	0	0	0	115
Legalize	4	G	3	1	0	1	9,230
Legally Blonde	4	F	9	1	0	1	6,252
Legally Insane	4	F	9	1	3	3	34,005
Legalopinion	6	M	1	0	0	0	0
Legend	2	F	3	1	2	0	20,210
Legend Glory (BRZ)	4	C	1	0	0	1	1,210
Legend Has It	6	H	10	2	4	2	12,290
Legend Man	3	G	4	0	0	1	1,300
Legend of Gold	5	G	18	2	4	3	34,990
Legend of the West	3	F	8	0	3	0	6,040
Legend to Be	3	G	14	1	1	0	4,604
Legendary Dream	6	M	11	2	1	2	7,597
Legendary Halo	4	F	2	0	0	0	100
Legendary Journey	3	F	6	2	0	2	39,804
Legendary Kiss	3	G	7	0	0	1	4,460
Legendary Lad	4	G	8	3	1	1	30,900
Legendary Lass	3	F	7	1	3	1	31,910
Legendary Legs	5	G	7	1	0	0	1,752
Legendary Pacer	2	C	1	0	0	0	460
Legendary Peach	6	M	9	1	0	2	11,413
Legendary Prince	4	G	17	2	5	3	37,930
Legendary Queen	3	F	15	2	5	5	83,206
Legendary Run	5	H	4	1	0	0	4,845
Legendary Smile	2	F	2	0	0	0	280
Legendary Squire	3	C	4	1	0	0	27,874
Legendary Star	3	G	4	0	0	1	3,600
Legendary Traitors	3	G	10	2	1	1	34,680
Legendary Weave	6	H	4	0	1	0	15,495
Legendaryleah	3	F	18	0	2	3	7,712
Legendinhisownmind	3	G	1	0	0	0	400
Legend's Bullet	4	G	7	0	0	1	4,010
Legend's Run	2	G	3	1	0	0	4,690
Legend's Silver	3	G	6	1	1	0	13,940
Leggo My Echo	3	G	20	2	4	4	48,065
Leggy Note	3	C	2	0	0	0	0
Legislady	2	F	2	0	1	0	10,825
Legislator	5	G	2	2	0	0	40,800
Legislature	5	G	6	4	1	0	73,704
Legitimada (ARG)	7	M	16	2	2	3	39,057
Legolas	2	C	1	0	0	0	0
Legs d'Or	2	F	3	0	0	0	1,560
Legs Legs Legs	3	G	4	1	0	0	2,970
Legs O'Neal	4	F	9	1	2	2	63,167
Lehigh Grad	4	G	9	1	2	4	60,296
Lei Diavalo	2	F	5	0	0	2	3,402
Leianne's Pet Peve	4	F	6	0	1	0	2,149
Leida Irene	4	F	2	0	0	0	170
Leif Erikson	3	C	5	1	1	1	11,150
Leigh Gold	8	M	6	2	1	0	14,919
Leigh Wells	2	F	1	0	0	0	96
Leitrim Lakes (IRE)	4	G	5	0	0	0	2,175
Leiu of Payment	4	G	3	0	0	0	50
Lejos	3	G	11	1	2	2	13,870
Leme Boogie	4	F	2	0	0	0	800
Lemon Angel	6	G	9	4	1	1	5,568
Lemon Bar	2	C	2	1	1	0	24,680
Lemon Creek	7	G	2	0	0	0	0
Lemon Drop King	2	C	2	1	0	1	16,300
Lemon Drop's Love	2	F	1	0	0	0	2,050
Lemon Lady	2	F	4	0	0	0	3,254
Lemon Shake Up	2	F	1	0	0	0	135
Lemon Sky	2	C	4	0	2	0	9,135
Lemonade Stand (GB)	2	F	1	0	0	0	0
Lemonaids Hot Jazz	3	F	4	0	0	0	100
Lena Light	4	F	7	1	0	1	13,975
Lenado Girl	3	F	3	0	0	0	0
Lenarose	4	F	6	1	1	1	8,130
Lenarue	2	F	2	1	0	0	8,100
Lenatareese	3	F	8	3	1	1	149,138
Lenawest	2	F	9	0	2	2	18,966
Lendy	8	G	4	0	0	0	166
Lenient Policy	6	G	1	0	0	1	770
Lenio Valli	3	C	3	0	0	0	159
L'Enjoleurs Tremor	6	M	5	0	0	0	1,004
Lennon	5	G	4	1	2	0	18,195
Lennoxwood	3	G	6	0	1	2	23,120
Lenny	2	C	5	1	2	1	23,000
Lenny From Dal Rae	3	C	3	0	0	1	9,960
Lenny the Lender	8	G	7	0	2	0	93,288
Lennyfromalibu	5	G	6	2	2	1	172,639
Lenny's Halo	5	M	17	2	2	4	29,806
Lens Last Astro	5	G	7	3	0	0	16,448
Lensfield	3	G	3	0	0	0	845
Lens's Irish Lass	4	F	4	0	0	0	332
Lentil	5	M	12	2	3	3	91,565
Lento	4	G	19	2	2	5	18,878

Horse	Age	Sex	Sts	1st	2d	3d	Won
Leo and Mike	6	G	7	0	0	1	5,694
Leo Getz	2	C	4	0	0	1	8,190
Leon County	3	G	6	1	2	1	10,216
Leona May	4	F	12	1	1	2	6,493
Leonard's Legacy	3	C	9	2	3	0	13,333
Leonard's Shaker	3	C	4	0	0	1	1,007
Leonard's Winner	2	F	1	0	1	0	1,500
Leona's Dr.	4	F	13	2	5	2	27,840
Leona's Knight	2	F	9	3	0	2	126,400
Leona's Lies	5	M	3	0	1	1	21,750
Leon's Best	2	C	3	1	1	1	24,685
Leon's Bull	2	C	7	6	0	0	101,714
Leon's Deed	4	F	9	2	0	2	49,580
Leopard Hunt	3	F	3	1	0	0	21,600
Leopard Lady	4	F	12	1	2	4	15,804
Leo's Act	5	G	11	1	3	3	35,274
Leo's Baroness	4	F	7	2	1	1	29,450
Leo's Blue Moon	5	G	3	0	0	0	0
Leo's Clever Trick	5	G	10	0	0	1	988
Leo's County Kat	2	G	6	1	1	2	17,872
Leo's Devil	6	G	2	0	0	0	0
Leo's Golden Tap	4	F	5	0	0	1	1,375
Leo's Last Hurrahy	4	G	4	0	0	0	1,500
Leo's Last Love	5	M	6	0	0	1	1,995
Leo's Legacy	3	G	8	2	1	2	21,180
Leo's Memory	3	G	2	0	0	0	635
Leo's Native Ruler	4	G	3	0	0	0	0
Leo's Sassy Girl	4	F	4	1	0	0	3,360
Leos the Man	4	G	6	0	0	0	625
Leo's Twister	4	G	13	0	2	2	5,192
Leo's Way	3	C	10	2	2	2	22,860
Leprechaun Kid	5	G	7	2	0	3	94,680
Leriaville	4	F	11	2	0	5	21,390
Lerma Time	2	C	4	0	2	2	14,260
Leroidesanimaux (BRZ)	4	C	6	5	0	0	436,860
Leron	2	C	4	0	0	0	1,667
Leroy J.	3	G	4	0	0	0	400
Leroy Spuds	5	H	5	0	0	0	1,857
Leru	5	H	2	0	0	0	311
Les Affaire	2	G	1	0	0	0	78
Les Be Quick	4	C	6	0	0	1	1,318
Les Crime	4	G	7	1	1	0	4,028
Les Gentil Hommes	6	G	5	0	0	1	1,632
Les Rendezvous	3	F	2	0	0	1	2,200
Leslie's Gold	10	H	5	0	0	1	1,480
Leslie's Last	3	F	6	1	2	0	17,574
Leslie's Love	7	M	10	5	4	0	189,800
Leslie's Runner	3	G	6	0	1	1	5,732
Les's Last Chance	6	G	3	0	0	0	220
Les's Legacy	3	G	9	2	1	2	19,670
Less Talk	2	C	3	1	0	0	6,300
Lessons Are Extra	4	C	12	0	3	2	19,830
Lessur	3	G	17	3	2	2	25,530
Lest We Forget	4	G	2	2	0	0	58,200
Lester N Earl	4	G	11	0	0	2	1,737
Lester's Halo	2	C	1	0	0	0	0
Let George Do It	6	G	18	2	2	4	6,886
Let Her Ride	4	F	3	0	0	1	750
Let Her Rip	6	M	11	1	2	1	7,380
Let Him Rip	6	G	12	0	2	2	23,603
Let It Be Known	3	G	3	0	0	0	170
Let It Ride Tony	4	C	1	0	0	0	0
Let It Roar	4	F	3	1	1	1	20,560
Let It Settle	4	C	1	0	0	0	160
Let It Slide	6	G	17	3	3	1	23,422
Let It Thunder	5	G	5	2	0	2	59,341
Let Me Be Frank	2	G	10	2	1	0	22,320
Let Me Dream	9	G	1	0	0	0	80
Let Me Drive	3	G	3	1	0	1	17,448
Let Ourfreedomring	3	F	3	0	0	0	86
Let Salt Fly	5	M	6	0	0	1	1,662
Let the Day Begin	4	F	12	0	1	0	3,272
Let the Fuhr Fly	3	C	9	1	0	1	10,810
Let the Sun Shine	4	G	2	0	0	0	540
Let Us Confide	3	C	6	0	0	0	1,105
Let Us Rejoice	3	G	8	2	3	2	44,580
Letart Island	4	G	13	2	2	1	50,164
Let'em Wander	3	F	6	0	0	2	8,560
Lethal Agenda	6	H	3	0	0	0	0

Horse	Age	Sex	Sts	1st	2d	3d	Won
Lethal Grande	5	G	15	6	3	2	111,367
Lethal Litigator	3	C	1	0	0	0	0
Lethal Lover	5	M	5	2	0	0	9,183
Lethal Temper	5	M	2	0	0	0	790
Lethal Weapon (ARG)	6	H	6	1	1	1	15,000
Lethegoodtimesroll	3	G	3	0	0	0	1,220
Lethimrun	5	G	6	1	2	2	22,400
Lethimthinkhesboss	3	G	8	1	4	1	67,500
Letigre	4	G	9	2	2	2	23,262
Letmeseeyourid	7	H	5	0	1	0	5,667
Letmewreckem	4	G	1	0	0	0	0
Letra de Cambio (BRZ)	4	F	9	2	2	1	99,920
Letrado (ARG)	7	G	10	0	1	1	12,310
Lets All Smoke	4	G	11	0	2	1	3,402
Let's Behave	6	G	15	1	7	1	44,880
Lets Believe C F	8	G	4	0	0	0	189
Let's Belly Up	3	G	8	2	0	1	9,572
Let's Boogie	6	M	3	0	0	0	417
Let's Coast	3	F	3	1	0	2	19,530
Let's Contend	5	M	4	1	0	0	13,610
Let's Dance Nance	5	G	15	1	4	1	23,664
Let's Face It	5	G	6	2	1	0	21,400
Let's Get Lucky	5	G	12	0	3	0	6,170
Let's Get Personal	4	F	13	3	1	3	31,031
Let's Go Race	5	M	10	1	1	0	9,182
Let's Go Rusty	7	G	3	0	0	0	5,460
Let's Go to Dodge	10	G	4	0	0	0	520
Let's Go to Town	4	F	5	1	0	0	5,247
Let's Hang Out	4	F	3	0	0	0	290
Lets Jet Girl	2	F	4	0	0	0	903
Lets Just Do It	4	F	8	3	2	1	107,905
Let's Make Life	7	G	11	1	3	4	18,597
Let's Mombo	4	F	8	0	1	2	19,456
Let's Party	5	G	14	0	1	1	2,897
Let's Party Honey	3	F	6	0	0	0	873
Lets Pay Cash	5	G	7	0	2	1	4,428
Let's Play	4	F	10	3	1	1	17,315
Lets Playit by Ear	5	G	11	0	3	2	23,807
Let's Rap	4	G	5	0	0	0	338
Let's Roll Cart	3	G	3	0	0	0	0
Lets Roll Esteem	2	G	2	0	0	0	0
Let's Roll Girl	2	F	2	0	0	1	1,540
Let's Roll Guys	3	G	10	3	1	0	28,727
Let's Roll Lady	3	F	15	2	2	4	58,618
Let's Smoke 'Em	3	F	6	1	1	0	7,078
Lets Talk About Me	4	F	6	0	0	0	3,750
Let's Tour	4	F	2	0	1	0	6,080
Letsgostreaking	3	G	13	0	0	0	1,365
Let'shavefun	4	F	17	2	5	1	52,170
Letsimpress (IRE)	3	F	10	2	0	0	21,174
Letsmoveon	5	M	11	2	0	1	35,359
Letsrollem	7	G	6	1	0	0	4,860
Letsrunfellows	2	F	2	0	0	0	76
Letter From Hoolie	4	F	8	1	0	1	5,830
Letter of Credit	4	C	12	3	1	1	46,675
Letterman's Humor	2	C	4	0	0	0	905
Letters	4	G	6	1	0	1	31,160
Letters Lady	9	M	1	0	0	0	0
Lettertotheeditor	4	F	10	2	2	1	23,530
Lettet Rumble	7	G	10	2	2	2	12,932
Letthecowboydance	9	G	8	1	2	0	7,402
Letthefreedomroar	4	F	10	0	1	2	16,130
Lettherebejustice	3	G	15	3	3	2	143,901
Lettingo	6	M	2	0	0	0	621
Lettuce Be a Devil	3	C	3	0	1	0	6,400
Lettuce Besplendid	5	G	5	0	0	0	0
Lettuce Pray	4	C	12	3	3	3	22,558
Lettuce Prevail	4	C	4	1	0	0	5,344
Lettucerace	4	F	10	2	2	1	5,942
Letussoupriseyou	3	F	8	2	3	2	53,270
Levada	3	F	9	0	2	0	14,619
Level Bid	5	M	18	1	1	3	18,960
Level Lady	4	F	2	0	0	0	0
Level Playingfield	3	C	13	3	4	3	106,250
Level Three	7	H	13	5	2	2	52,365
Levendis	5	G	11	1	3	2	73,819
Lever Trick	6	H	2	0	0	0	144
Leverage	2	G	7	0	0	1	22,507
Levin Brand	2	C	4	0	0	0	533

Horse	Age	Sex	Sts	1st	2d	3d	Won
Lew S.	6	G	3	0	1	0	2,860
Lewis Nelson	3	C	1	0	0	0	0
Lex	3	G	16	0	4	4	34,679
Lexa's Song	3	C	6	0	0	1	6,065
Lexatonic	4	F	6	1	1	0	3,720
Lexey	2	F	5	0	0	0	1,110
Lexi Las Missi	3	F	3	0	0	0	0
Lexi Star	2	F	1	0	0	0	720
Lexie Jane	3	F	10	1	1	2	9,539
Lexie's Charm	6	M	6	0	0	1	1,152
Lexiesride	6	M	12	3	0	2	22,141
Lexikatt	2	C	2	0	0	0	210
Lexiloush	5	M	5	0	1	2	22,800
Lexington Lass	2	F	6	0	0	0	1,930
Lexingtonroad	2	F	5	1	2	0	18,871
Lexi's Habit	5	M	14	2	4	2	17,125
Lexi's Moon	4	F	9	2	1	1	18,525
Lexster	5	M	10	1	0	1	3,632
Lexy May	4	F	3	0	0	0	0
Lexys Party	3	F	8	0	0	0	675
Lexy's Taxiano	2	C	3	0	1	0	5,420
Leyenda	7	M	6	0	0	1	1,597
Leys a Leader	3	F	5	0	0	0	165
Leyte	4	F	5	1	0	0	7,355
L'Grand Dancer	4	F	4	0	0	0	833
L'Homme	6	G	8	0	0	0	3,030
Li Musica	4	F	3	0	1	0	2,085
Liam E	4	G	5	2	1	0	12,952
Liam of Cashel	4	G	6	0	0	1	7,427
Liam's Gladiator	4	G	13	0	0	1	6,943
Liane's Miss	5	M	2	0	0	0	1,292
Liars Poker	2	C	2	0	0	0	750
Libasus	2	C	1	0	0	1	1,210
Libby La Vita Loca	4	F	12	1	2	0	11,352
Libby's Big Cloud	3	C	3	0	0	0	325
Libby's Dreams	6	M	3	0	0	0	762
Libby's Frolic	2	C	1	0	0	0	205
Libby's Town	3	F	4	0	0	0	460
Libby's Tune	2	F	3	0	0	0	565
Libbyslittlelibber	6	M	2	0	0	0	546
Libera (GER)	8	M	1	0	0	0	0
Liberal Media	5	G	15	2	4	0	20,133
Liberated	3	C	9	1	1	1	19,227
Liberated Look See	5	M	5	1	2	1	14,738
Liberatedbyforce	3	C	1	0	0	0	1,764
Liberation	5	G	12	1	3	1	20,695
Libertino	3	C	2	0	0	0	800
Liberty Bellah	2	F	6	2	0	0	11,900
Liberty Coin	3	G	3	0	0	0	770
Liberty County	6	M	1	0	0	0	0
Liberty Creek	5	G	4	0	0	1	1,877
Liberty Force	3	G	14	1	0	3	8,080
Liberty Girl	5	M	6	1	0	1	9,184
Liberty Hill	10	G	5	0	0	0	250
Liberty Lake	5	G	1	1	0	0	2,820
Liberty Mill	2	F	4	1	0	2	13,960
Liberty Miss	4	F	2	0	0	0	373
Liberty N Justice	3	F	4	0	0	0	0
Liberty Nation	4	G	13	1	0	2	6,260
Liberty Pike	5	H	12	1	2	0	9,515
Liberty Place	5	G	8	1	2	0	7,973
Liberty Quest	4	G	15	2	5	1	42,400
Liberty Rose	3	F	2	0	0	0	675
Liberty Son	4	C	4	2	0	0	40,357
Liberty's Cowgirl	3	F	1	0	0	0	195
Liberty's Torch	3	F	5	0	1	0	4,910
Libertyville	4	G	9	1	0	1	13,365
Libertywithjustice	3	F	8	2	1	0	89,622
Libito Point	6	H	10	0	0	0	3,293
Liblo the Mighty	5	M	8	1	1	1	12,920
Libor	4	G	4	0	0	1	1,918
Librisong	3	G	9	0	2	0	3,860
Lica Devilwind	5	M	12	0	0	0	2,441
Licari	3	C	6	2	1	2	78,365
License Free	3	F	5	0	0	1	4,380
License to Run	7	G	19	1	7	4	28,425
License To Run (BRZ)	4	C	1	0	0	1	30,000
License to Soar	4	G	2	0	0	0	325
License to Speed	5	M	9	0	2	1	21,678
License to Tour	4	G	12	3	1	3	31,535
Licenseapproved	4	F	19	0	3	3	9,156
Lickety Slick	3	F	8	1	0	0	11,115
Lickity Zickity	3	F	4	0	0	0	0
Licky's Minute	3	G	3	0	1	1	3,720
Licorice Lad	6	G	7	0	1	1	949
Lido (IRE)	9	G	6	0	0	0	1,024
Lieing Lary	6	G	3	0	0	1	3,040
Liepers Fork	3	C	12	3	3	1	57,144
Lies	3	F	9	0	3	0	7,410
Lieutenant Arch	4	C	12	1	4	5	14,300
Lieutenant Danz	2	C	4	2	0	1	36,080
Lieutenant Loreta	3	F	12	0	1	2	4,920
Lieutenant Tilly	6	G	5	1	0	0	1,740
Life	5	G	3	0	0	0	0
Life After	3	G	12	0	0	3	13,110
Life At Sea	6	G	5	1	2	0	8,314
Life of Luxury	3	F	3	1	0	0	10,290
Life Promise	5	G	3	0	0	0	545
Life Savior	4	F	13	2	3	2	66,830
Life Sayver	7	G	18	3	2	1	48,414
Life Thefirstright	3	F	3	0	0	0	1,125
Lifebythedrop	5	M	12	2	2	0	32,406
Lifeinthebigciti	4	G	9	2	0	0	27,618
Lifeisjustabeach	2	F	3	0	2	0	14,314
Lifeisjustforlivin	3	G	3	0	0	0	5,646
Lifelong Dream	3	C	3	0	0	0	1,046
Life's a Dream	3	F	1	0	0	0	0
Lifes Crown	6	G	16	5	3	3	27,026
Life's So Sweet	2	F	2	0	1	0	4,760
Lifestream	2	G	2	1	0	0	13,000
Lifestyle	4	C	4	2	0	0	49,500
Lifewithoutyou	3	F	7	1	0	0	6,815
Liffey Scent	3	G	6	1	0	1	7,195
Lift Up	6	G	7	4	1	0	48,060
Lifted Pride	3	F	5	0	0	1	3,190
Lifted Rose	3	F	10	1	1	0	6,674
Lifticet	4	G	3	1	0	0	6,930
Lifting Fog	5	G	4	0	0	1	1,171
Lifting the Veil	4	F	8	1	2	1	43,212
Ligan's Cross	4	C	4	0	0	0	171
Ligans Miss L C	3	F	1	0	0	0	135
Ligan's Star	5	H	3	0	0	0	0
Light a Candle	5	M	14	3	1	1	21,240
Light a Fire	4	F	2	0	0	0	330
Light Agenda	3	F	6	0	2	1	4,874
Light and Shadows	6	G	2	0	0	0	65
Light Artillery	4	G	9	0	0	0	694
Light Buster	5	G	4	0	0	0	388
Light Craft	7	H	12	1	3	0	8,504
Light Dancer	6	M	3	0	0	0	1,080
Light Deelites	3	F	9	1	1	0	11,197
Light Duty	5	G	4	0	1	1	6,040
Light Fandango	3	G	3	0	0	0	480
Light Fingered (IRE)	8	H	12	0	1	1	2,672
Light Fling	6	M	9	1	3	2	58,062
Light From Above	2	F	1	0	0	0	0
Light Given	3	F	10	1	1	1	15,860
Light Hearted Lass	4	F	2	0	0	1	1,500
Light Jig (GB)	4	F	7	4	1	0	494,800
Light Lou	2	C	3	0	0	0	270
Light Night	5	H	2	0	0	0	0
Light of Evening	8	M	2	0	0	0	1,097
Light of Faith	3	F	8	0	1	2	2,978
Light of Gold	2	G	1	0	0	0	0
Light of Justice	6	G	2	0	0	0	840
Light of Life	4	G	1	0	0	0	300
Light of Sky	5	M	13	0	0	0	3,050
Light of the Party	2	C	5	1	2	0	8,387
Light On Her Toes	3	F	18	0	6	3	8,862
Light On Track	7	H	9	0	1	2	1,575
Light Reflections	5	M	9	3	0	2	58,750
Light Sand	3	G	5	0	0	0	800
Light the Dawn	4	C	6	0	1	0	2,134
Light the Path	5	M	14	1	1	3	16,757
Light the Star	3	G	9	1	2	0	5,436
Light the Way Home	2	C	2	0	0	0	800
Light Tiger	5	H	2	0	1	0	1,448
Light Tones	3	F	12	4	1	1	33,723

Horse	Age	Sex	Sts	1st	2d	3d	Won
Light Unto My Path	4	F	5	1	0	0	9,710
Light Up the Board	4	G	10	1	0	0	7,507
Light Up the House	6	G	10	0	3	0	8,538
Light Up the Phone	4	G	1	0	0	0	50
Light Up the Tower	4	G	4	0	0	2	1,088
Light Up Themoment	3	F	12	0	0	1	2,928
Light Up Your Life	4	F	5	2	0	0	12,365
Lightacaper	2	G	2	1	0	1	7,050
Lightening	4	F	1	0	0	0	1,650
Lightening Ball	8	G	7	2	1	0	38,399
Lightening Dehere	5	H	7	0	1	1	7,990
Lightening Dot T.	3	F	1	0	0	0	0
Lightening Limit	5	G	9	0	0	1	2,440
Lighter Than Air	2	F	2	0	0	0	550
Lighthouse Jim	2	C	4	1	0	0	18,990
Lighthouse Lil	5	M	3	2	0	1	80,230
Lightin' Storm	6	M	7	1	0	1	3,100
Lighting Bug	7	G	6	1	1	1	7,042
Lighting Jay	5	G	9	0	6	1	6,196
Lighting Kwik	5	G	3	0	0	0	0
Lighting Ocean	3	C	6	1	1	0	12,000
Lightlively	3	F	11	2	5	1	54,550
Lightness	3	G	12	4	1	1	39,430
Lightnin Mac	7	H	1	0	0	0	0
Lightnin Mike	5	G	3	0	0	0	398
Lightning At Sea	3	C	3	0	1	0	3,381
Lightning Attitude	5	M	17	2	0	4	10,970
Lightning Bay	4	F	10	0	1	1	2,221
Lightning Cat	4	G	6	2	0	1	28,969
Lightning Charger	4	G	9	1	1	1	4,048
Lightning Draw	8	G	7	0	0	2	3,311
Lightning Echo	4	G	9	4	0	1	25,073
Lightning Fast	2	C	3	0	1	0	5,940
Lightning Force	2	G	3	0	0	2	3,370
Lightning Fox	5	M	2	0	0	0	107
Lightning Hit	4	G	5	0	0	0	0
Lightning Lydia	3	F	7	1	0	3	14,090
Lightning Lyla	3	F	10	1	2	3	43,204
Lightning Quick	7	G	10	1	2	0	5,412
Lightning Stripes	6	G	12	3	0	2	95,320
Lightning Struck	4	C	4	0	0	0	2,280
Lightning Tab	4	G	11	0	1	2	3,514
Lightning Trick	3	F	5	0	1	0	10,648
Lightning Twice	3	G	4	0	0	0	1,600
Lightning Weststar	5	G	6	0	0	0	338
Lightninginabottle	7	H	1	0	0	0	0
Lightning's Kiss	7	M	3	0	0	1	825
Lightningsbigboy	3	C	6	1	0	1	5,540
Lights of Santa Fe	4	G	1	0	0	0	0
Lights On	5	M	6	0	0	0	13,370
Lights On Broadway	7	G	10	0	2	4	51,220
Lights Out Angel	2	F	4	1	1	0	14,750
Lights Out Toney	3	G	5	1	1	1	14,900
Lightsnatcher	2	C	8	0	4	2	8,420
Lightsolovincounty	2	C	4	0	0	0	555
Lightspeedlioness	2	F	1	0	0	0	0
Lightspeedtoendor	6	H	7	0	1	0	1,251
Lignite	4	G	7	1	1	0	6,282
Like a Breeze	3	F	6	2	0	0	32,280
Like a Moth	3	F	1	0	0	0	0
Like a Princess	2	F	1	0	0	0	0
Like a Rock	3	G	6	0	0	0	1,720
Like a Star	2	C	4	0	0	0	705
Like a Tiger	3	G	3	0	0	0	4,340
Like a Woman	2	F	1	0	0	0	400
Like Down Town	3	F	1	0	0	0	0
Like Flying	5	M	14	6	1	1	25,275
Like Gold	2	F	1	0	0	0	0
Like Magic	5	M	2	0	1	0	7,160
Like Poison	3	F	1	0	0	0	0
Like Silent	3	C	2	0	0	0	110
Like This	3	F	13	1	3	2	28,740
Like to Do	3	F	3	0	0	1	2,540
Likeable Irish	11	G	4	1	0	1	4,640
Likely Excuse	3	G	2	0	0	0	113
Likely Lover	3	G	11	3	1	1	23,699
Likely Prospect	4	F	7	1	1	1	21,880
Likely Suspect	3	F	1	0	0	0	110
Lil Badger	5	G	4	0	2	0	5,250
Lil Barhop	8	M	8	0	0	3	5,746
Lil Berta	6	M	2	0	0	0	117
Lil Big Man	4	G	8	0	0	0	857
Lil Bit Bull	4	C	4	2	0	0	28,812
Lil Bit Glamorous	7	M	2	0	0	0	100
Lil' Bit Gone	3	C	12	1	2	1	13,750
Lil Bit O Fastness	4	F	11	3	3	3	19,410
Lil Bit o' Magic	4	F	2	0	0	0	0
Lil' Bit of Pucker	4	F	7	0	1	0	4,250
Lil Bit of Rouge	3	F	9	1	0	3	20,856
Lil Bit Spacey	6	M	7	0	2	3	9,619
Lil Bit Stormy	2	C	3	0	0	0	0
Lil Bit Tricky	2	G	4	1	1	0	13,077
Lil Blue Sky	2	F	3	0	0	0	932
Lil Bonit	3	F	14	0	2	1	12,900
Lil Bow	3	C	5	0	0	0	786
Lil' Bro Eddie	3	G	5	0	0	1	5,012
Lil Brother Slew	5	G	8	0	0	2	2,064
Lil' Casino	8	G	3	0	0	0	256
Lil Charlie Too	8	G	11	1	2	2	18,560
Lil Chuckie	3	G	7	0	0	0	715
Lil' Cloud	2	F	7	1	1	3	10,080
Lil Cowboy	3	G	1	0	0	0	0
Lil Cream Puff	2	F	7	2	3	1	55,471
Lil Danslet	4	F	3	0	2	1	5,100
Lil Diamond	3	F	1	0	0	0	0
Lil Dickens	4	F	11	2	0	1	6,404
Lil' Duck	3	G	7	0	0	0	655
Lil E. Tee for Hob	2	F	3	0	2	0	1,600
Lil Easy	3	F	7	1	1	1	24,860
Lil E's Express	3	G	15	2	5	3	27,267
Lil Eskimo	4	F	7	0	0	0	1,393
Lil Eva	4	F	9	4	2	0	17,254
Lil Eva Rose	3	F	1	0	0	0	2,583
Lil Fanciface	4	F	7	2	0	1	9,504
Lil Forrest	4	G	11	2	1	0	10,623
Lil Fortune	3	F	8	1	0	1	21,520
Lil G Man	6	G	2	1	1	0	28,400
Lil Gary Too	3	C	13	0	4	4	40,460
Lil General	5	G	15	2	1	2	9,908
Lil Ginny	3	F	9	1	0	1	3,848
Lil Good Bye	3	F	5	0	2	0	4,340
Lil Good Friday	2	F	3	0	0	0	0
Lil Gorgeous	3	C	10	1	0	0	5,400
Lil Gunner	3	G	4	0	0	0	127
Lil Hanna	3	F	2	1	0	0	6,210
Lil Hustler	4	G	1	0	0	0	423
Lil Instigator	3	F	4	0	0	0	1,590
Lil' Iodine	3	F	17	1	4	3	15,367
Lil Irish Eyes	6	M	9	0	2	0	8,252
Lil Jerry	5	G	9	0	1	3	4,632
Lil' Joe	5	G	11	0	1	1	7,686
Lil Joe Hossrite	8	G	3	0	1	0	1,950
Lil Josey	2	F	4	0	0	0	0
Lil Kitten	5	M	7	0	0	0	1,005
Li'l Larry B	5	G	19	3	1	1	20,198
Lil Lisa Can	3	F	9	1	1	2	7,520
Lil Lucia	6	M	4	0	1	1	2,496
Lil Luis	2	C	1	0	0	0	0
Li'l Lulu	6	M	2	0	0	0	100
Lil Man	3	G	11	3	1	2	12,376
Lil Mike	5	G	5	1	0	0	6,000
Lil Miller	11	G	1	0	0	0	0
Lil Mis Awad	2	F	2	0	0	0	0
Lil Miss Best	4	F	5	0	1	0	1,850
Lil Miss Casey	3	F	5	0	2	1	5,430
Lil Miss Devi	6	M	11	0	1	4	10,576
Lil Miss Gabi	9	M	7	0	0	1	1,521
Lil Miss Georgie	4	F	1	0	0	0	0
Lil Miss Obnoxious	6	M	1	0	0	0	750
Lil Miss Okie	4	F	2	0	0	0	0
Lil Miss Piggy	2	F	5	0	0	1	5,842
Lil Miss Sophie	6	M	14	1	2	4	18,232
Lil' Mo' Rhythm	4	F	4	1	1	0	17,280
Lil Ms. K K D	4	F	8	0	0	2	3,996
Lil Nash Rambler	4	G	8	1	1	0	7,880
Lil Native Wulf	3	G	6	1	0	0	7,000
Lil' Nickii	5	M	6	1	0	1	7,533
Lil Nugget	2	F	2	0	1	0	3,163

Horse	Age	Sex	Sts	1st	2d	3d	Won
Li'l Orphan Arnie	5	G	4	0	0	0	348
Lil Personalitee	7	G	12	1	3	2	25,476
Lil Pistol	3	F	8	1	0	1	9,150
Lil Princess Tee	4	F	12	1	0	2	4,257
Lil Purple Willie	4	F	7	0	0	0	450
Lil Red	3	C	8	0	2	2	7,830
Lil Red Flyer	3	G	11	4	2	2	56,500
Lil Red Rendezvous	5	M	21	0	0	6	5,861
Lil Rhett's Vet	4	F	6	2	0	3	15,930
Lil Rich Girl	2	F	5	1	1	1	6,900
Lil Rosa	3	F	2	0	0	1	910
Lil Rosalie	5	M	1	0	0	0	0
Lil Sister	4	F	4	0	0	1	2,358
Lil Sister's Lad	6	H	6	0	0	1	446
L'Il Sister's Wild	3	F	5	2	1	0	7,944
Lil Snowbird	4	C	4	0	0	0	0
Lil Soldier	2	F	3	0	0	0	800
Lil Spark	3	G	6	0	0	0	815
Lil Star	5	M	6	0	1	1	1,485
Lil Stevie	3	G	1	0	0	0	316
Lil Sugarman	5	H	10	1	0	1	2,360
Lil Suzie Cinnamon	4	F	11	0	1	2	2,366
Lil Sweet Tee	3	F	12	1	0	1	10,302
Lil Taste	3	F	14	1	2	5	9,278
Lil Thomas Too	6	G	17	5	3	3	100,738
Lil Tree	2	C	1	1	0	0	6,000
Lil Wanda Woman	3	F	2	0	0	0	0
Lil Whooter	5	M	3	0	0	0	0
Lil' Yiper	3	G	11	1	3	1	15,172
Lila Hope	3	F	3	1	0	0	24,480
Lila Kay's Rose	3	F	5	3	0	0	47,385
Lila Mae	3	F	5	1	0	1	3,612
Lila Paige	3	F	12	2	3	2	89,313
Lilah	7	M	6	3	0	1	75,740
Lilbirdietoldmeso	2	F	2	0	0	0	0
Li'lbito'fudge	3	G	12	1	0	1	20,770
Li'lbito'sunshine	2	F	2	0	0	0	0
Lilfreddyfastfeet	3	G	4	0	0	0	975
Liliana L	4	F	16	0	5	4	28,252
Liliano	6	G	6	1	2	0	10,700
Lilias Trotter	4	F	4	0	0	1	3,500
Lilkilngirl	3	F	14	4	1	2	43,787
Lill Trina	2	F	9	0	1	2	6,088
Lillian West	5	M	5	1	0	2	1,661
Lillian's Valley	5	M	15	1	2	1	9,243
Lillie Kay	3	F	4	1	0	1	3,700
Lillie Ridge	2	F	2	0	0	0	155
Lillison	3	G	8	0	0	0	845
Lilly A	5	M	2	0	0	0	1,380
Lilly Be Nice	4	F	14	1	1	0	7,220
Lilly Li Lo	2	F	6	0	0	0	1,440
Lilly the Kid	3	F	11	2	0	2	16,371
Lillyflower	5	M	6	0	1	0	1,485
Lillylar	3	F	11	1	2	1	3,730
Lilly'softhefield	3	F	9	1	3	3	18,075
Lil'manfromambler	3	G	2	0	0	0	0
Lilmisshonkytonk	3	F	6	0	0	2	1,592
Lilnome	4	F	6	2	1	0	11,347
Li'lpollock'sluck	3	C	2	0	0	0	648
Lil'redheadeddevil	5	M	9	2	1	0	5,900
Lil's Angel	3	F	10	0	0	1	944
Lil's Chloe	3	F	1	0	1	0	1,920
Lil's Date	4	F	3	0	0	1	1,613
Lil's Golden Boy	5	G	12	1	3	2	3,990
Lil's Golden Crown	2	F	2	0	0	0	1,220
Lil's Honor	2	F	1	1	0	0	20,400
Lil's Lady	2	F	1	0	0	0	0
Lil's Landing	2	F	6	1	1	1	16,317
Lil's Sunnie Girl	4	F	5	1	0	0	14,346
Lilsisterlightning	7	M	6	1	2	1	26,717
Lilstarshines	3	F	3	0	2	1	10,138
Lilsurgarnspice	3	F	2	1	0	0	2,200
Lilt	5	H	3	0	0	2	2,354
Lily Baba	3	F	6	0	1	0	2,345
Lily Bea Squash	3	F	4	0	0	0	246
Lily Langfuhr	3	F	12	2	1	2	12,144
Lily Martini	4	F	9	2	0	1	21,279
Lily of Seattle	3	F	4	0	0	0	0
Lily of the Valley	4	F	12	5	1	1	79,320
Lily Red Honey	9	M	13	0	2	1	6,633
Lily Vanilly	5	M	21	1	5	4	30,721
Lily Von Stupp	4	F	6	0	1	0	1,771
Lily's Big Boy	8	H	8	0	2	1	1,846
Lily's Lad	7	G	1	1	0	0	34,560
Lily's Prospect	5	M	4	0	0	0	462
Lilzachdawrangler	5	H	7	1	2	3	5,728
Limantour	3	F	1	0	0	0	0
Limehouse	3	C	5	2	0	1	367,000
Limelight Dancer	3	F	9	0	1	1	3,429
Limero (ARG)	5	H	16	2	4	3	120,972
Limestone	8	G	9	1	4	0	21,815
Limited Access	3	G	18	1	1	0	4,152
Limited Entry	2	F	3	1	1	0	52,780
Limited Number	7	G	8	0	0	2	5,830
Limitless Lady	2	F	2	1	0	0	25,420
Limo and Lunch	6	M	11	2	1	1	36,885
Limone Forte	4	G	10	2	0	1	47,505
Lincoln Abbey	8	M	5	0	0	1	2,201
Lincoln Center	5	G	4	0	0	0	210
Lincoln Hall	6	H	3	0	0	0	166
Lincoln Lodge	6	G	4	0	0	0	1,115
Lincoln Parish	5	G	11	1	3	0	12,868
Linda Belinda	3	F	5	1	0	0	32,790
Linda D's Roomy	4	F	3	0	0	0	510
Linda Eder	5	M	8	0	0	0	2,620
Linda O	4	F	15	1	6	4	12,339
Lindal Lake	3	G	3	0	0	1	847
Lindamademedoit	4	F	6	0	0	0	1,272
Linda's Future	3	F	4	2	0	1	35,206
Linda's Gold	5	M	11	2	0	1	7,231
Linda's Lad	6	G	14	2	3	1	19,918
Linda's Lass	3	F	10	0	0	1	1,820
Linda's Miracle	5	M	2	0	0	0	630
Linda's Prince	3	G	7	0	0	0	660
Linda's Vixen	4	F	9	3	2	1	15,734
Lindasladyluck	4	F	11	3	2	3	19,973
Linden Hill	8	G	13	2	1	0	16,880
Linden Lane	3	G	6	1	0	0	31,535
Linden T	4	G	10	1	0	0	6,426
Linder Blue	7	G	12	2	1	4	13,512
Lindero	3	G	11	0	4	1	54,520
Lindholm	6	G	3	0	0	1	883
Lindsay Jean	6	M	1	0	0	0	0
Lindsay O	3	F	1	0	0	0	95
Lindsey Creek	3	F	5	0	0	0	439
Lindsey Paige	2	F	1	0	0	0	170
Lindsey's Dove	4	F	9	3	0	1	40,561
Lindsey's Pride	5	M	1	0	0	1	1,100
Lindstrom	2	C	6	1	0	1	18,957
Lindt	6	G	14	1	2	0	9,502
Lindz's Dancer	2	F	5	1	0	1	5,300
Line Buster	3	F	1	0	0	0	213
Line Error	5	M	2	0	0	2	2,240
Line Memory	2	F	1	0	0	0	150
Line of Defense	7	G	5	0	0	2	9,746
Line of Departure	3	C	1	0	0	1	5,520
Line of Scrimmage	3	C	16	1	4	1	35,256
Line of Thought	2	G	9	0	2	3	16,815
Linear Accelerator	3	F	6	1	0	1	7,025
Linear Lights	4	G	14	3	2	1	22,712
Lineation	5	H	14	1	2	0	7,644
Linefighter	4	F	10	0	6	3	17,272
Lines of Love	4	F	4	0	0	0	960
Lineupforthemoney	3	G	2	0	0	0	156
Lineuponthelevee	4	F	9	0	1	1	7,135
Lingard Cat	7	G	12	1	1	4	20,980
Lingard Diamond	5	M	13	2	0	1	8,800
Lingerie	3	F	8	2	1	1	24,190
Linglestown	2	G	2	1	0	0	10,500
Lingo	3	F	11	3	1	0	24,556
Linilee	7	M	11	1	1	0	3,249
Linjack's Legacy	4	F	6	1	0	0	9,926
Link Teegather	4	G	10	1	2	1	10,840
Link to Jimmy	8	G	4	0	0	0	1,180
Link to Ordway	4	G	6	0	0	0	1,470
Link to Tour	5	G	2	0	1	1	1,820
Link Up	5	G	5	0	0	0	165
Linkoman	7	G	18	0	3	3	22,068

Horse	Age	Sex	Sts	1st	2d	3d	Won
Linmeabuck	3	F	2	1	0	0	9,600
Linnie Belle	3	F	13	2	1	2	31,876
Lino's Lady	4	F	8	2	1	0	15,988
Lin's Forty Niner	4	F	12	4	0	0	13,921
Linus	7	G	4	0	0	2	2,948
Linwin	7	M	8	0	1	1	6,315
Lion Andthe Lamb	3	G	2	0	0	0	2,253
Lion Around	3	G	15	3	3	4	85,915
Lion Cat	2	C	3	0	1	0	10,180
Lion From Zion	6	H	4	0	0	0	430
Lion Heart	3	C	7	2	3	0	1,080,000
Lion in the Sky	2	G	3	0	2	0	2,220
Lion King's Roar	4	G	5	0	2	0	9,352
Lion Lad	3	G	15	1	2	3	33,800
Lion Leader	3	C	15	1	2	0	24,994
Lion On the Siphon	3	F	9	1	0	0	7,528
Lion Spirit	2	G	3	0	0	0	1,200
Lion Tamer	4	C	9	5	1	0	592,380
Lionardo	3	G	2	0	0	0	0
Lionel Jefferson	2	C	1	0	0	0	0
Lionels Image	4	F	2	1	0	0	10,829
Lionel's Lucky Hat	4	F	1	1	0	0	15,000
Lioness Diarie's	2	F	2	0	0	0	800
Lionized	2	C	2	0	0	1	900
Lionred	2	F	5	1	0	0	15,710
Lion's Return	2	G	1	0	0	0	80
Lionstigoronbears	4	C	7	0	1	1	3,763
Lip Gloss	2	F	3	0	1	1	5,710
Lip Vice	4	F	3	0	0	0	0
Lipa	5	M	4	0	1	0	3,386
Lipan	3	C	7	1	2	0	95,140
Lips Like Sugar	2	F	1	0	0	0	400
Lipsmackingood	2	C	1	0	0	1	1,760
Lipstick Lies	4	F	7	3	2	0	34,886
Lipstick Liz	2	F	5	1	0	0	5,580
Lipstick Sammy	3	F	2	0	0	0	130
Lipsy Lake	3	G	5	0	0	0	620
Liquid Asset	6	G	8	1	2	1	1,858
Liquid Ice	7	H	5	0	0	0	780
Liquid Lightning	4	G	8	0	1	0	2,647
Liquid Louie	2	G	2	0	1	0	4,815
Liquid Romance	2	C	5	0	2	0	17,745
Liquid Sage	3	G	9	1	1	2	21,232
Liquidated Damages	3	F	13	0	0	3	3,134
Liquor Cabinet (IRE)	3	C	4	1	3	0	49,000
Lira Lira	3	F	6	1	1	0	3,766
Lisa Rae	3	F	15	3	5	2	31,625
Lisa the Great	2	F	2	0	0	0	400
Lisaized	2	F	6	2	0	1	60,470
Lisa's Approval	6	M	11	1	2	1	15,988
Lisa's Baby	6	M	5	1	0	0	4,985
Lisa's Buck	2	G	11	0	1	4	9,825
Lisa's Cat	2	F	3	1	0	0	34,594
Lisa's Deelites	5	M	13	2	0	1	20,037
Lisa's Friends	3	F	15	2	6	0	32,355
Lisa's Gold	3	F	3	0	0	1	4,540
Lisa's J	3	F	5	1	0	0	9,171
Lisa's Rainbow	3	F	8	0	0	0	1,766
Lisa's Royal Guy	5	G	6	0	2	1	10,490
Lisa's Secret	3	F	3	0	0	0	0
Lisasfriendlylover	3	F	8	2	0	1	16,225
Lisa'sgoldenangel	5	M	8	0	0	0	1,680
Lisboa (MEX)	7	M	12	2	4	1	10,443
Lisdoonvarna	3	C	5	0	1	1	11,558
Lisduff	5	M	3	1	0	1	4,615
Liska (IRE)	4	F	1	0	0	0	0
Liska's Lyric	4	F	8	2	2	0	17,620
Lismore	2	G	3	1	2	0	19,980
Lismore Knight	4	C	4	0	0	0	6,642
Lissa's Lad	3	G	11	2	3	2	21,826
Lissau	3	C	7	0	1	1	9,627
Listen Indy	4	C	7	0	2	2	41,300
Listen to Us	2	C	6	0	1	2	19,320
Listening Fr Wings	5	M	14	2	2	0	44,270
Listening Springs	3	F	7	0	0	0	4,860
Listo	3	F	1	0	0	0	135
Lit D' Or	6	M	7	1	1	0	11,669
Lit de Arch	2	C	1	0	0	0	0
Lit de Beurre	5	G	17	0	1	2	6,864

Horse	Age	Sex	Sts	1st	2d	3d	Won
Lit de Cam	5	M	5	1	1	0	8,255
Lit de Danseur	6	G	9	2	2	0	10,053
Lit de Jimmy	3	F	8	1	0	1	31,334
Lit de Lace	6	G	13	2	2	2	14,850
Lit de Matrix	3	G	4	0	0	0	2,330
Lit Up	3	F	12	1	2	1	19,290
Lita's Gold	4	F	15	1	3	3	5,423
Lita's Request	2	F	3	1	1	1	13,352
Litchfield Lad	4	C	3	0	0	0	1,155
Lite and Misty	3	F	12	3	2	1	35,140
Lite de Lite	3	F	1	0	0	0	0
Lite Man	2	G	2	1	0	0	13,600
Lite Medley	6	M	6	0	0	1	2,316
Lite O My Life	3	F	4	0	2	0	3,057
Lite On Her Feet	4	F	6	0	0	0	0
Lite On My Feet	5	M	6	1	2	2	30,045
Lite Onthe Spirits	6	G	1	0	0	0	0
Lite Ridge	4	C	8	0	0	0	1,837
Lite Source	6	G	19	2	3	2	11,250
Lite the Cab	2	G	1	0	0	0	164
Lite the Point	3	G	11	0	0	3	19,530
Lite Toast	6	G	14	3	4	1	15,341
Lite Um Up Sunni	3	F	2	0	2	0	6,500
Lite Up	6	G	12	1	4	1	53,725
Lite Write	2	F	3	2	0	1	19,730
Litefingered Louie	3	G	4	0	0	1	2,216
Litelucky	4	F	1	0	0	0	300
Lite'm Up Rose	3	F	7	0	0	2	1,813
Literacy	4	F	13	2	1	3	128,028
Literally Pretty	2	F	2	0	0	0	2,340
Literally Quick	2	G	4	0	0	1	5,065
Literary	3	F	9	1	1	2	27,431
Literary Light	5	M	8	0	0	2	19,397
Literary Row	5	G	5	1	2	1	47,243
Literossi	3	G	4	0	0	1	2,588
Litethefusegladis	3	F	7	1	0	1	14,640
Litethelucky	3	F	8	2	3	0	21,553
Liteupthetoteboard	3	F	9	0	0	2	1,335
Lithian's Legacy	5	M	3	0	0	0	865
Lithium	4	G	9	2	1	0	17,575
Lithium (AUS)	11	G	2	0	0	0	74
Litigant Cat	4	F	5	0	0	1	946
Litigasion	6	H	4	0	2	0	4,935
Litigator	5	M	3	1	0	0	17,350
Lit'l Deuce Coupe	2	F	9	1	0	0	21,080
Lit'l Nancy's Girl	6	M	9	0	0	0	515
Lit'l Red Corvette	4	C	14	0	2	1	7,244
Litlbity Dot	5	M	2	0	0	0	100
Litter the Glitter	4	F	7	3	1	1	29,825
Little Abner	4	G	13	3	1	4	35,108
Little Affair	2	G	1	0	0	0	585
Little Amante	3	G	2	0	0	0	0
Little Andrea	3	F	3	2	1	0	54,400
Little Anna	6	M	7	0	0	1	1,260
Little Anns Secret	3	F	11	0	2	1	3,536
Little Anthony	4	C	4	0	0	0	402
Little Beau Pip	3	C	7	0	0	0	424
Little Bella	2	F	1	0	0	0	400
Little Belle Starr	2	F	2	0	1	0	2,800
Little Bentley	3	C	4	1	1	1	53,175
Little Bertrando	2	G	2	0	0	0	800
Little Betty Girl	5	M	11	2	0	1	31,850
Little Bid Man	3	G	12	0	1	5	6,058
Little Big Foot	3	G	2	0	0	1	276
Little Big Heart	2	C	3	0	1	1	1,576
Little Big Hoss	3	G	1	0	0	0	40
Little Big Moon	2	C	3	0	0	1	5,520
Little Big Pistol	4	G	4	0	0	0	0
Little Big Tye	3	C	1	0	0	0	0
Little Billy Bob	4	G	2	0	0	0	205
Little Biscuit	3	F	2	0	0	0	300
Little Bit Absent	3	G	10	0	1	4	7,495
Little Bit Catty	4	F	6	0	0	2	1,245
Little Bit Foolish	2	G	2	0	0	0	435
Little Bit Lucky	2	C	1	0	0	0	0
Little Bit of El	4	F	7	0	1	2	1,490
Little Bit of Evil	2	C	10	1	2	1	19,525
Little Bit Red	4	F	4	0	0	1	3,740
Little Bit Rosy	2	F	2	0	0	0	85

Horse	Age	Sex	Sts	1st	2d	3d	Won
Little Bit Sandy	3	G	17	2	2	4	10,862
Little Bit Stormy	3	G	11	1	0	3	7,499
Little Bit Western	4	F	4	0	0	0	1,100
Little Blast	2	G	7	1	2	0	7,345
Little Blazin Sis	4	F	1	0	0	0	78
Little Blessing	3	F	3	0	0	0	237
Little Blue Fly	3	G	10	0	0	0	357
Little Bo Leap	4	G	3	1	0	0	11,136
Little Bodgit	3	F	7	0	0	2	4,730
Little Bog	2	F	1	0	0	0	230
Little Bold Anne	6	M	9	1	2	1	9,432
Little Bold Sweep	6	G	3	0	1	0	880
Little Bonnet	4	F	4	0	0	2	10,590
Little Boy Lost	5	G	6	0	1	1	6,208
Little Brava	2	F	5	0	1	1	1,612
Little Brave	2	G	8	1	0	1	27,094
Little Brick Lane	6	G	12	1	0	1	8,011
Little Brown Brick	8	M	14	0	0	0	1,571
Little Bum	2	C	12	0	1	0	2,536
Little Bumbleberry	4	F	1	0	0	0	0
Little Burner	4	F	16	2	4	0	27,969
Little Buttercup	4	F	8	1	3	2	77,100
Little Caroline (IRE)	3	F	4	0	0	1	6,700
Little Catfish	2	F	2	0	0	0	0
Little Celebrity	4	F	7	1	0	1	10,501
Little Charmer	4	F	1	0	0	0	0
Little Chubby Guy	4	G	6	1	0	0	8,400
Little Cindy Lou	5	M	17	2	4	0	10,318
Little Compassion	4	F	3	0	1	0	2,555
Little Compton	4	F	12	2	6	1	16,425
Little Concern	4	G	10	0	2	1	5,923
Little Corrie	4	F	7	0	1	0	7,965
Little Cowgirl	2	F	1	1	0	0	2,880
Little Cutie	3	F	8	0	4	0	10,307
Little Dancer	4	F	2	0	0	0	99
Little de Flight	2	F	5	0	0	1	2,965
Little Delight	9	M	2	0	0	0	0
Little Devil	4	G	7	0	0	1	1,332
Little Dickerson	4	G	15	0	0	2	2,139
Little Diva	4	F	2	0	1	0	5,600
Little Dix Bay	4	C	1	0	0	0	1,380
Little Doc	8	H	2	1	0	0	5,355
Little Doctor	6	G	16	0	1	3	3,568
Little Dom	3	G	8	0	0	1	2,080
Little Dovefeather	3	G	5	0	3	1	25,300
Little Ed	3	F	4	0	0	0	265
Little Edgar	3	G	6	0	0	3	4,968
Little Elf	3	F	6	1	0	1	6,300
Little Elmer	3	G	6	1	0	0	3,585
Little Emmy	3	F	11	2	3	1	16,234
Little Esther	4	F	7	2	0	0	26,360
Little Fireman	8	G	9	4	0	2	7,064
Little Flag	3	G	6	0	0	1	1,107
Little Floss	4	G	16	3	5	3	42,895
Little Forest	5	M	8	1	0	0	5,275
Little Foxy Baby	3	F	11	1	1	2	40,862
Little Frankie R	5	G	13	2	2	1	12,657
Little Friend	3	F	9	0	0	2	1,803
Little Gabby	5	M	6	1	1	2	29,380
Little Geezer	5	G	9	1	1	3	8,363
Little Ghazi	8	G	4	1	0	2	38,400
Little Gladiator	2	G	3	0	0	0	4,500
Little Go	3	C	8	0	0	2	2,526
Little Gold Devil	4	F	1	0	0	0	0
Little Gossip	3	F	9	0	0	0	1,770
Little Grapette	5	M	4	0	0	0	696
Little Grey Tinner	4	C	5	0	2	0	3,810
Little Grizz	3	G	6	1	0	1	16,026
Little Gusher	3	F	11	1	1	2	10,646
Little Habibi	4	F	12	1	3	1	15,237
Little Hank	4	G	4	1	0	0	5,173
Little Happy	5	G	5	1	1	1	45,745
Little Hardy	3	F	5	1	0	0	1,937
Little Hawk	6	G	11	0	0	1	792
Little Hawk Rock	4	G	10	3	0	3	24,173
Little Henry Steel	2	C	3	0	1	0	3,255
Little Hi	4	G	13	2	1	3	11,663
Little Honcho	8	G	1	0	0	0	40
Little Hoppy	11	G	6	0	0	0	282
Little Hotfoot	5	M	1	0	0	0	315
Little Hussy	2	F	3	2	0	1	74,043
Little I	4	G	4	0	0	0	945
Little Irish	3	F	2	0	0	0	0
Little Irish Girl	7	M	6	0	0	0	375
Little Isabelle	2	F	1	0	0	0	0
Little Itch	9	M	8	1	0	0	4,104
Little Jackie	4	G	11	3	1	1	6,553
Little Jackson	10	G	15	0	2	1	7,230
Little Jag	4	G	10	2	0	0	7,233
Little Jermaine	3	F	4	0	0	0	1,110
Little Jim (ARG)	4	C	5	1	1	2	393,510
Little Jo Jo	3	C	1	0	0	0	95
Little Joe Lewis	7	G	3	0	0	0	0
Little Joe Tubb	5	G	11	0	1	1	3,590
Little John John	4	G	9	2	2	0	8,259
Little Jordo	2	C	2	0	0	0	200
Little Josie	3	F	8	0	1	2	11,220
Little Julie	4	F	15	0	3	3	17,580
Little Kisatchie	4	G	16	1	1	1	12,310
Little Kitty Cat	4	F	3	0	0	0	750
Little Kleo	3	G	3	0	0	0	0
Little Kostroma	4	F	8	1	1	0	8,400
Little Lady Run	2	F	3	1	1	0	9,646
Little Lady T	4	F	15	1	1	3	10,308
Little Laney	4	F	12	3	2	0	31,129
Little Lea	4	F	5	0	0	0	742
Little Leader	3	F	4	1	0	0	5,085
Little Lee	8	G	3	1	0	0	2,929
Little Leopold	4	G	18	0	0	2	12,051
Little Less Talk	7	G	9	0	0	2	5,667
Little Lighty	8	M	7	0	0	1	2,602
Little Lil	6	M	2	0	0	0	113
Little Lori Lee	4	F	2	0	0	0	0
Little Lost Girl	4	F	15	2	0	1	11,175
Little Lucifer	2	F	2	1	0	0	15,410
Little M B	3	F	2	0	0	0	210
Little Mack Truck	4	G	17	1	2	3	15,987
Little Mama	3	F	1	0	0	0	40
Little Maricat	3	C	7	0	1	2	4,450
Little Marshall	5	H	10	3	1	2	21,429
Little Martha	4	F	6	0	0	2	8,480
Little Match Girl	6	M	10	2	1	2	10,625
Little Matth Man	3	C	7	2	1	1	139,661
Little Me Too	6	H	10	2	2	0	25,090
Little Memory	3	F	3	0	0	0	622
Little Mis General	4	F	12	2	2	1	37,850
Little Miss Alice	3	F	1	0	0	0	420
Little Miss Amanda	3	F	10	0	4	2	41,078
Little Miss Bravo	2	F	2	0	0	0	208
Little Miss Catey	5	M	5	0	0	0	530
Little Miss Deb	4	F	1	1	0	0	19,500
Little Miss Genius	3	F	10	5	0	0	70,125
Little Miss Kelsey	2	F	2	0	0	0	0
Little Miss Leap	4	F	8	2	2	1	23,101
Little Miss Lil	3	F	9	2	1	3	61,200
Little Miss Mary	4	F	11	1	1	2	11,765
Little Miss Nickel	11	M	6	1	1	2	4,972
Little Miss Pamela	4	F	4	0	1	1	17,594
Little Miss Priss	7	M	2	0	0	0	82
Little Miss Ruckus	3	F	3	0	0	0	0
Little Miss Sarah	3	F	4	1	2	0	27,060
Little Miss Uppity	2	F	1	0	0	0	184
Little Missile	2	F	3	0	0	0	615
Little Mitch	2	C	4	0	0	0	1,000
Little Mocha	3	G	8	1	0	0	8,063
Little Money Down	2	F	2	1	0	0	25,950
Little More	4	G	11	3	0	2	26,319
Little More Gun	4	G	6	0	0	0	280
Little Muffin	5	M	10	0	1	5	3,666
Little Nanc	2	F	3	0	0	0	720
Little Nell	3	F	3	0	0	0	0
Little Nicky Regs	3	G	12	4	4	1	101,488
Little Nooster Too	2	F	7	1	1	2	23,580
Little Oneal	5	G	5	0	0	0	0
Little Orphan Kris	3	F	4	1	0	1	11,319
Little Patriot	2	F	5	0	0	1	1,132
Little Piri	3	F	2	1	0	0	6,271
Little Pistol	2	G	7	0	0	0	902

Horse	Age	Sex	Sts	1st	2d	3d	Won
Little Polish Wolf	4	F	12	3	2	0	26,259
Little Poopsie	3	F	6	1	1	0	11,090
Little Pursuit	5	M	9	2	2	0	12,068
Little Quill	6	M	8	1	1	3	5,762
Little Reba's Rib	2	F	2	0	0	0	368
Little Rebel	4	G	14	2	0	1	6,346
Little Red Alfa	2	F	2	0	0	0	600
Little Red Bishop	3	F	2	0	0	0	0
Little Red Cobbley	3	F	5	0	1	0	5,570
Little Red Crimson	5	M	17	2	3	1	13,419
Little Red Devil	6	G	4	2	1	0	7,444
Little Red Ferrari	4	F	14	0	2	3	13,893
Little Red Rocket	3	G	11	3	4	2	90,044
Little Red Train	5	G	1	0	0	0	0
Little Ribs	4	G	5	0	0	1	1,998
Little Rich	6	G	8	3	0	1	14,627
Little Rich Girl	4	F	8	1	4	1	23,026
Little River Bank	2	C	3	0	0	1	5,005
Little Rock Lover	5	M	12	0	2	3	8,778
Little Roger	2	C	1	0	0	0	420
Little Rosa Lynn	5	M	4	1	0	0	4,066
Little Rose Queen	6	M	8	0	0	0	672
Little Rut	4	G	11	2	1	1	28,330
Little Ruthie	7	M	8	0	2	1	9,470
Little Sandy	7	G	5	1	1	1	16,980
Little Scholar	4	F	1	0	0	0	164
Little Season	2	C	2	0	0	0	120
Little She's Grand	2	C	3	0	0	0	363
Little Shon	5	M	11	3	2	2	25,390
Little Shyster	3	G	5	1	0	2	8,485
Little Silent Star	3	F	3	0	0	0	0
Little Skater	4	G	5	0	0	0	0
Little Slew	3	G	1	0	0	0	0
Little Slewie	6	G	6	0	3	0	7,310
Little Smarty	6	G	3	1	2	0	4,000
Little Smokey	3	G	10	2	1	0	11,795
Little Snorkie	4	F	7	0	2	2	7,420
Little Soldiergirl	3	F	11	2	2	1	25,514
Little Starburst	4	F	4	0	0	0	225
Little Stormy	4	G	6	0	0	1	686
Little Sun	5	H	2	0	0	0	60
Little Surfer	7	M	14	0	2	0	4,162
Little Surfer Gal	3	F	10	0	0	2	2,044
Little Swimmer	4	C	5	3	0	0	24,480
Little Switz	3	F	7	1	0	0	8,929
Little Tara	4	F	11	5	1	0	24,120
Little Tigress	2	F	3	0	0	0	1,095
Little Town	4	C	9	1	3	1	15,404
Little Tracey	3	F	14	1	4	2	10,718
Little Treasure (FR)	5	M	1	0	0	0	0
Little Tune	10	G	5	0	0	0	0
Little Ugly	4	F	9	1	1	2	5,288
Little Val	3	F	1	0	0	0	0
Little Velvet	5	G	5	1	1	0	7,168
Little Vernon	3	G	8	0	0	1	3,905
Little Villa	2	F	1	0	0	0	0
Little Villain	11	G	6	0	0	1	850
Little Villainess	5	M	12	0	1	3	7,184
Little Vixen	5	M	13	2	1	2	19,014
Little White Dove	3	F	2	1	0	0	4,500
Little White Lie	3	F	3	1	0	0	15,600
Little Wing	6	M	14	2	2	1	17,988
Little Wink	4	G	8	0	2	0	9,381
Little Wishes	3	G	13	2	0	1	11,975
Little Wolfie	3	F	5	0	0	0	0
Little Won Slew	2	F	1	0	0	0	78
Little Yeoman	5	M	12	3	2	3	20,125
Littlebit Onery	5	G	12	1	1	2	9,587
Littlebitaglitter	3	G	9	0	1	1	9,180
Littlebitakris	3	G	16	1	2	3	29,335
Littlebitastuff	2	F	2	0	2	0	7,380
Littlebitfrosty	2	C	3	0	1	0	4,600
Littlebitoenergy	3	F	5	0	0	0	0
Littlebitofme	2	F	5	0	0	1	1,870
Littlebitofzip	2	C	7	1	1	2	85,328
Littlebitsaintly	2	F	9	1	3	0	22,140
Littlebitstellar	2	F	4	0	0	0	347
Littlebullsbullet	4	F	11	0	2	1	3,376
Littlecooper	2	F	7	0	1	0	4,200
Littledrummergirl	9	M	1	1	0	0	4,290
Littlefield	11	G	10	0	1	1	943
Littleladiesman	4	G	14	2	3	1	18,523
Littlemagbrother	3	G	16	3	2	4	19,593
Littleman Wonsong	3	C	5	0	0	0	324
Littlemiss Susy Q	2	F	1	0	0	0	124
Littlemisscourtney	2	F	3	1	0	0	13,900
Littlemissmeaghan	6	M	3	0	0	0	150
Littlemorgusto	4	F	11	0	1	0	3,203
Littlemowine	5	M	1	0	0	0	0
Littleone Joe	6	G	9	0	0	2	1,480
Littlepieceofpie	4	F	4	0	0	0	645
Littleriverqueen	6	M	15	0	5	1	19,620
Liturgy	4	C	3	1	0	0	7,200
Livae	5	M	8	1	2	1	12,290
Live and Learn	6	M	2	0	0	0	212
Live Backwards	5	M	13	2	1	4	13,034
Live Connection	2	G	5	0	0	0	502
Live Doppler	6	M	12	1	1	2	22,189
Live for Today	4	G	2	0	0	0	286
Live Free Or Die	5	M	2	0	1	0	4,000
Live in the Dash	2	F	3	0	1	0	5,240
Live Larrupin	3	G	1	0	0	0	0
Live Prospect	2	C	3	0	0	0	280
Live the Dream	6	H	6	0	0	0	1,309
Live the Life	3	G	10	1	0	1	10,140
Live to Die	3	F	3	0	0	1	4,507
Live Well	3	F	8	1	0	0	28,986
Live Wire Lucy	3	F	8	0	0	1	3,740
Live Wire Sally	3	F	1	0	0	0	600
Liveinthepresent	2	C	2	0	0	0	145
Lively Art	5	M	4	0	0	2	3,971
Lively Cat	2	F	1	0	0	0	75
Lively Classic	3	F	6	1	0	1	18,946
Lively Classicals	4	G	3	1	0	0	20,937
Lively Dancer	7	M	2	0	0	0	0
Lively Exit	2	C	6	1	0	3	15,000
Lively Frolic	3	C	1	0	0	0	75
Lively Heather	3	F	17	2	2	3	14,656
Lively Kisser	5	H	18	4	3	3	25,024
Lively Larry	7	G	5	0	0	0	449
Lively Leslie	2	F	4	1	1	1	9,502
Lively Lew	6	M	3	0	0	0	0
Lively Liz	6	M	3	0	0	1	480
Lively Man	4	C	4	0	0	0	354
Lively Minister	8	G	11	2	0	2	39,650
Lively Moment	4	F	12	3	1	0	35,880
Lively Number	3	F	3	0	0	1	1,100
Lively Okie	3	F	1	0	0	1	740
Lively Pistol	4	G	8	0	0	1	967
Lively Sweep	2	C	1	0	0	0	1,350
Lively Swing	3	F	6	1	1	1	24,648
Lively Thunder	2	C	3	0	1	0	3,055
Liven On a Prayer	3	F	11	1	1	3	15,976
Livermore Dream	3	F	10	1	0	0	9,576
Liverpool Lad	3	G	7	2	1	1	38,985
Livestock Auction	3	F	6	0	0	1	1,650
Livewell Laughofen	2	G	2	0	1	0	6,860
Livin' On the Edge	4	F	11	2	1	1	16,890
Livin Without Fear	3	G	2	0	0	0	96
Living a Dream	7	G	7	2	1	3	41,695
Living Bade	4	F	10	0	2	1	1,650
Living Fully	3	F	3	1	0	0	5,595
Living Lavida Lisa	4	F	8	1	2	1	29,293
Living On Margin	4	F	8	0	0	0	1,520
Living Single	4	G	14	3	4	1	53,745
Living Stone	2	F	1	0	0	0	0
Living Street	3	C	5	1	0	0	1,200
Livingwill	4	C	3	0	0	0	0
Livins Legacey	3	F	4	1	1	0	3,480
Livonia	2	F	2	0	0	0	1,155
Liz Gayheart	3	F	16	3	6	3	31,875
Liz On Polk Street	3	F	6	3	1	1	77,480
Lizard Head	4	F	4	1	2	1	9,630
Lizard King	2	C	2	0	1	0	1,215
Lizawatha	4	F	6	1	1	0	3,325
Liz's Bandit	3	C	9	1	0	1	9,115
Liz's Crazy Cat	5	H	2	0	0	0	170
Lizs Fashion Trick	9	G	4	0	0	0	184

Horse	Age	Sex	Sts	1st	2d	3d	Won
Liz's Rib	5	M	6	0	3	0	7,179
Liz's Secret	6	M	6	0	0	0	120
Liz's Top Cat	6	G	1	0	0	0	48
Lizzie Lane	3	F	5	0	0	1	2,925
Lizzie P.	3	F	3	0	0	0	0
Lizzie Tradd	3	F	3	0	0	0	550
Lizzy Ridge	3	F	9	1	3	0	17,012
Lizzy's Gold	4	F	6	2	0	0	28,830
Llama Jet	4	G	8	0	0	0	0
Llanmihangel	4	F	4	0	0	1	3,689
Llaves	5	G	6	1	0	0	2,520
Llegaste a Mi	5	M	13	1	0	0	6,415
Lloyd T	5	G	1	0	0	0	40
Lloydminster	3	G	9	2	2	2	56,647
Lloyd's Ego	4	G	12	1	1	2	11,707
Lloydtown	5	G	3	0	0	0	1,873
Ll's Big Boy	5	G	11	1	1	1	8,312
L'Natural High	7	G	3	0	0	0	1,300
Lo Life Avenger	5	G	21	2	1	2	10,503
Load a Chronic	4	G	13	1	0	1	23,248
Loaded Brush	6	G	3	0	0	1	3,520
Loaded Dice	2	F	7	0	2	1	5,340
Loaded Mischief	5	M	9	0	1	2	8,927
Loaded Six String	3	G	6	2	0	1	22,520
Loaded Soda	3	G	16	1	1	4	32,146
Loaded Springs	5	G	4	0	0	0	193
Load'eminthedark	5	M	7	1	1	0	7,393
Load'im Up	2	C	2	0	0	0	260
Loadofwyatt	3	F	6	0	1	0	2,594
Loafer	4	G	8	0	0	0	510
Loan Me a Fen	5	G	5	0	1	1	12,195
Loan Me the Money	3	F	14	3	2	2	18,712
Loanlover	3	G	7	2	0	0	6,185
Lobato	4	G	15	4	1	1	26,666
Lobbyist	6	M	3	0	1	0	2,320
Lobo Joe	2	G	3	1	1	0	5,769
Lobscouse	2	G	4	0	0	0	1,344
Lobster Ontuesdays	2	F	1	0	0	0	400
Lobsterathepalms	3	F	3	1	1	0	15,400
Local Bum	6	G	1	0	0	0	45
Local Calling	7	H	1	0	0	0	158
Local Case	4	G	17	4	3	1	76,441
Local Knowledge	9	G	7	2	0	0	13,688
Local Law	4	F	10	3	1	0	27,598
Local Nobility	7	M	5	0	0	0	835
Local Stranger	5	G	5	0	0	0	0
Local Ties	7	G	7	0	0	1	510
Local Treasure	6	G	10	3	0	4	25,125
Local Yokel	3	C	7	2	0	1	28,030
Loch Nessie	2	F	8	2	2	0	42,467
Lock in the Money	7	G	3	0	0	0	189
Lock Tender	5	G	11	4	0	2	21,474
Lockdown	4	G	10	1	2	0	24,892
Locket	4	F	7	3	0	0	24,300
Locketa	2	F	8	0	1	2	5,291
Lockjaws Grandson	8	G	6	1	0	0	3,720
Lockpicker	4	G	9	2	1	0	26,841
Loco Laura	3	F	8	1	0	1	7,955
Loco Sombrero	4	G	6	0	0	0	363
Loco Tavares	6	H	10	1	1	3	11,751
Locomotive Springs	3	F	1	0	0	0	110
Locomotor	5	G	10	0	0	0	960
Locust Bloom	3	F	4	0	0	1	1,171
Lode a Trouble	4	G	15	3	1	1	11,220
Lode Amighty	4	G	4	1	1	0	11,650
Lode of Lilacs	3	F	4	0	0	0	674
Loded Arrow	12	G	2	0	1	0	2,007
Loden Speed	4	G	2	0	1	1	6,120
Lodes of Class	5	M	1	0	0	0	60
Lodesofmagic	4	G	9	0	0	2	2,801
Lodi Renagade	6	M	3	0	0	0	750
Lodo	2	F	2	0	1	0	6,318
Lodovico	4	G	8	1	0	0	10,290
Lods	3	C	9	1	1	2	44,565
Lofgren	2	F	2	0	0	1	5,550
Lofty Aspirations	3	G	2	0	0	0	154
Lofty Call	4	G	4	0	1	1	13,096
Lofty Flare	5	M	11	2	5	1	14,039
Log On	4	G	8	0	1	0	6,581

Horse	Age	Sex	Sts	1st	2d	3d	Won
Logan Field	5	G	10	1	1	0	9,494
Logan Rye	5	G	15	0	3	1	6,431
Logan Township	2	G	3	0	0	0	2,700
Logans Dancer	4	G	4	0	0	0	448
Logan's Draw	2	C	5	1	1	1	22,860
Logan's Girl	6	M	9	4	0	2	33,117
Logansport	3	C	9	1	2	2	16,264
Logger	5	H	13	1	1	0	11,938
Logical Art Form	3	F	4	1	0	0	25,306
Logical Choice	7	G	2	0	0	0	93
Logically Speaking	5	G	6	0	1	0	5,155
Logician	4	G	6	1	0	0	32,160
Logistic Queen	3	F	1	0	0	0	0
Loglor	4	G	5	0	0	0	439
Logold	6	M	8	2	0	2	12,092
L'Ohio	6	M	13	2	0	0	7,173
Loirinha	3	F	2	0	0	0	400
L'Oiseau d'Argent	5	G	9	4	1	1	142,960
Lojo	5	M	7	0	0	1	19,320
Lokari	4	G	5	1	0	0	6,015
Loki	10	G	10	1	0	1	3,190
Lokoya	3	F	4	0	0	1	8,339
Lola Darling	5	M	6	0	1	0	17,876
Lola Fastfeet	3	F	1	0	0	0	0
Lola's Fortune	5	M	21	1	3	4	14,014
Lolly Madonna	3	F	2	0	0	0	0
Lollypop Kid	5	M	6	2	0	1	9,360
Loma Del Rio	2	F	3	0	0	0	629
Lonche	5	G	15	1	6	3	37,375
London	3	G	7	0	2	2	28,950
London Lord	6	G	9	2	1	2	18,991
London Miss	3	F	6	0	0	0	1,089
Lone Arrow	3	C	8	0	1	2	37,073
Lone Heartwood	3	G	9	1	1	0	9,356
Lone Link	2	G	6	2	0	1	27,152
Lone Mountain	15	G	2	0	0	0	225
Lone Prairie	2	G	1	0	0	0	400
Lone Ranger	6	G	9	0	0	0	1,576
Lone Ryder	6	G	7	1	0	0	3,630
Lone Spat	4	C	6	0	2	1	2,461
Lone Star Deputy	4	C	10	2	1	2	16,053
Lone Star Dixie	4	F	7	1	1	1	14,190
Lone Star Dream	8	M	2	0	0	0	384
Lone Star Miss	3	F	16	1	0	2	7,800
Lone Traveler	6	G	16	7	1	2	119,362
Lone Tree	2	F	2	0	0	0	118
Lonely Angel	4	F	4	0	0	0	0
Lonely Dream	5	M	3	0	0	0	0
Lonely Groom	4	C	8	1	0	0	18,890
Lonely Hearts Club	6	M	4	2	0	0	10,660
Lonely Huntress	5	M	5	0	0	0	510
Lonely Rabbit	5	G	4	0	0	0	599
Lonely Reality	4	G	10	2	1	0	15,286
Loner Special	5	G	6	0	0	1	2,306
Lonesome Bay	4	G	7	0	0	2	3,755
Lonesome Dakota	4	G	7	0	1	1	2,642
Lonesome Knight	4	F	17	2	7	4	52,208
Lonesome Lad	7	H	7	1	0	0	8,172
Lonesome Launch	2	G	1	0	0	0	0
Lonesome Leo	2	C	3	1	0	0	9,261
Lonesome Lianna	4	F	8	1	0	0	7,990
Lonesome Quest	10	G	16	0	2	4	7,123
Lonesome River	6	M	17	4	3	4	33,190
Lonesome Too	3	F	3	0	0	0	1,862
Lonesome Wind	4	F	10	0	2	1	9,869
Lonesomenumberone	3	G	3	1	0	0	7,626
Lonesomeprospector	3	C	13	1	0	0	9,426
Lonestar Lover	4	G	13	2	1	2	12,839
Lonestar Rocket	2	F	1	0	0	1	825
Long Bay Dancer	5	G	16	1	2	4	14,925
Long Chance	3	G	4	0	0	1	7,341
Long Chun	5	M	16	1	2	0	46,780
Long For	4	F	9	0	0	0	1,713
Long for You	5	M	7	0	1	1	3,668
Long Gone Con	6	G	1	0	0	0	0
Long John	2	G	3	1	0	0	14,710
Long Kesh	4	G	14	1	4	2	11,520
Long Knife	3	G	5	0	0	1	2,760
Long Lane	2	F	2	0	0	0	1,590

Horse	Age	Sex	Sts	1st	2d	3d	Won
Long Leg Lou	6	M	3	0	0	0	5,655
Long Legged Larry	2	C	1	0	0	0	0
Long Legged Lucy	8	M	11	0	2	1	3,697
Long Legged Lydia	6	M	13	1	1	1	11,673
Long Legs	6	H	5	0	0	0	0
Long Live the King	3	G	10	2	1	2	6,287
Long May She Run	4	F	2	0	1	0	2,000
Long On Pride	5	G	7	0	2	1	2,913
Long Pond	3	C	3	2	0	0	63,540
Long Range	4	C	9	3	1	2	47,108
Long Range Missile	3	C	3	3	0	0	85,200
Long Rifle	5	G	6	2	0	0	6,757
Long Since Past	3	G	10	0	0	1	7,814
Long Star	5	H	11	6	1	1	67,904
Long Term Success	5	G	13	6	5	2	177,750
Long Term Wish	4	F	1	0	0	0	0
Long Trail	6	M	16	5	4	1	24,826
Longbranch Saloon	3	G	8	2	1	0	21,260
Longer Walk	2	G	5	2	1	1	41,183
Longfield Spud	4	C	12	1	4	2	100,730
Longford Arms	5	H	9	0	0	0	3,590
Longgonetrevorsean	3	C	5	0	0	0	4,160
Longhorn Blues	4	C	5	1	0	1	7,480
Longlivethestar	5	G	13	4	2	1	93,841
Longonot	6	G	7	4	2	0	52,180
Longrunonbroadway	3	G	17	1	1	3	14,526
Longship	4	G	9	2	0	5	106,998
Longshoreman	4	G	11	0	2	1	5,070
Longstreet	5	G	8	1	0	1	4,033
Longtown	4	G	10	1	0	2	4,700
Longview Belle	3	F	7	1	1	2	5,057
Longview Legend	9	G	21	2	6	2	13,527
Longwood Lady	4	F	5	0	1	1	5,360
Loni	3	F	1	0	0	0	0
Lonikens	4	G	12	4	1	2	21,979
Loni's Appeal	2	F	1	0	0	0	860
Lonnies Song	4	F	7	1	1	0	4,150
Loocracy	2	G	4	0	1	1	4,935
Look Again	3	F	7	0	1	2	11,980
Look Ahead	4	F	7	1	0	1	10,586
Look At Al	7	G	17	1	2	1	9,560
Look At Brook	3	F	1	0	0	1	4,191
Look At Her	3	F	9	1	2	0	14,845
Look At Me Go Now	2	G	5	0	1	2	8,863
Look At the Board	6	G	8	0	2	1	3,844
Look At You	7	G	13	2	1	1	12,792
Look N See	5	M	11	1	1	3	5,484
Look of Royalty	4	F	1	1	0	0	4,704
Look Out Evan	4	G	7	3	0	2	56,223
Look Out Joe	5	G	5	0	0	1	1,816
Look Out Now	5	M	9	0	0	0	1,148
Look Out Point	8	G	2	0	0	0	0
Look Quick	5	G	10	3	2	0	43,650
Look to Heaven	4	F	9	0	0	2	9,869
Look to Luke	6	G	4	0	0	0	427
Look to the Day	10	M	6	1	0	2	13,645
Look to the Stars	2	F	2	0	0	0	1,590
Look Who	4	F	12	3	1	2	26,282
Lookatthoselegs	3	F	5	1	0	0	15,600
Lookie There	4	G	1	0	0	0	0
Lookin' Brass	7	G	2	0	0	0	112
Lookin for Biscuit	2	C	9	1	2	1	23,195
Lookin for Love	7	G	4	0	1	0	3,343
Lookin' Proud	2	C	5	2	0	0	14,883
Lookin Semoran	2	F	3	1	1	0	13,210
Lookin So Right	6	H	9	2	0	1	5,641
Lookin' Swell	3	F	2	0	1	0	8,337
Lookin Tricky	2	F	3	1	0	0	5,400
Lookineasy	3	G	2	0	0	1	680
Lookinforagoodtime	5	M	7	1	1	0	4,805
Looking Cool	6	M	5	0	0	0	1,215
Looking for a Way	7	M	6	4	1	1	12,231
Looking for Glory	2	C	1	0	0	0	370
Looking for Loot	2	F	4	1	1	0	14,380
Looking Grand	4	C	1	0	0	0	600
Looking Twice	2	F	2	0	0	0	1,394
Looking Wealthy	5	G	13	1	4	2	7,520
Lookingforpleasure	3	F	10	1	2	3	8,672
Lookn At the Wire	5	G	3	2	0	1	13,500
Lookn Boldn Brassy	3	F	18	0	3	4	36,252
Lookn East	6	G	8	1	0	3	38,940
Lookn Mighty Fine	7	M	1	0	0	0	440
Look'n Smile	4	F	12	2	5	2	6,860
Looknsexy	5	M	1	0	0	0	0
Lookout for Ruth	5	M	8	1	1	3	4,470
Lookout Heights	4	F	9	0	1	0	4,380
Lookout Sue	6	M	17	0	0	4	4,200
Lookout Yall	3	G	3	0	0	0	190
Looks Bold	6	H	8	0	0	0	2,575
Looks Expensive	5	G	11	1	1	2	23,602
Looks Good	3	G	11	0	0	5	4,166
Looks Lika Fish	4	G	15	2	2	3	23,160
Looks Like Awinner	3	F	11	1	3	0	6,531
Looks Right	3	F	7	1	1	1	5,190
Looksgood Doinwell	2	F	1	0	0	0	0
Looksgoodonpaper	10	G	8	3	0	0	9,598
Lookslikesademon	4	C	10	0	0	1	2,863
Lookstoogood	2	F	5	1	1	0	17,950
Looming	3	C	2	0	0	0	320
Looney	4	F	11	2	0	0	7,175
Looney Lionel	4	G	20	0	4	2	18,180
Loony Chick	5	M	3	0	0	0	410
Looped	3	G	1	0	0	0	137
Loosahatchie	4	C	4	1	0	0	3,029
Loose Cannons	5	G	2	0	0	0	635
Loose Diamonds	4	F	1	0	0	0	63
Loose Fun	4	F	1	0	0	0	0
Loose Knight	10	G	15	2	3	5	11,947
Loose Rhythm	5	H	13	0	2	2	3,075
Loose Strider	2	F	1	0	0	0	0
Loose Talk	2	F	2	0	0	0	145
Loosecannonondeck	5	M	4	1	0	1	10,112
Looseonthegoose	4	C	3	0	0	3	3,050
Loosin Screws	4	G	13	2	1	1	8,947
Loot	4	G	4	1	0	0	5,070
Loot Tooten Trudy	2	F	6	1	2	1	44,336
Lootshoot Attitude	3	G	7	1	1	2	27,519
Loquacious Lover	2	G	6	0	1	1	14,260
Loramateal	2	F	2	1	0	0	28,430
Lora's Dream (BRZ)	4	F	14	1	4	1	24,410
Lora's Gamble	3	G	14	0	2	2	2,905
Lord Abounding	5	H	6	0	1	0	7,094
Lord Aferd	5	G	6	1	0	1	3,375
Lord Albert	3	G	8	3	0	1	43,687
Lord Albion	6	G	19	7	4	0	50,038
Lord Ale	6	G	13	2	2	0	8,472
Lord Alexander	4	G	11	3	3	1	69,988
Lord and Lady B	2	F	3	0	0	0	479
Lord Aragorn	3	C	11	0	1	1	2,167
Lord Ardilaun	3	C	5	0	0	0	3,585
Lord At Play	5	G	6	1	0	1	7,637
Lord Baltimore	3	C	10	1	3	1	18,852
Lord Bancho	3	G	7	2	1	1	16,005
Lord Beckett	5	G	6	0	0	0	1,148
Lord Billy	3	F	10	2	3	0	73,605
Lord Buckley	7	H	13	1	0	4	13,026
Lord Burleigh	5	G	14	2	3	2	37,142
Lord Carl	4	C	3	1	0	0	5,187
Lord Carmen	3	C	10	3	2	1	95,880
Lord Charles	3	G	11	1	1	0	13,915
Lord Chivas	4	G	6	1	1	1	16,688
Lord de Ville	5	G	13	4	2	2	52,117
Lord Don	11	G	2	0	0	1	825
Lord Emulous	4	G	5	0	2	2	5,560
Lord Exitor	5	G	4	1	0	0	5,534
Lord Farquaad	3	G	10	1	0	0	8,561
Lord Fhazio	5	G	11	3	3	1	93,595
Lord Foxcroft	4	G	8	1	0	0	9,481
Lord Gandolph	4	C	4	0	1	0	1,598
Lord Gladwin Jazz	6	G	2	0	0	0	0
Lord Gold	6	G	18	4	3	4	26,385
Lord Harmony	5	G	7	0	0	0	402
Lord Herbert	4	C	4	0	0	0	0
Lord Herby	4	G	2	0	0	0	102
Lord Imajones	5	M	4	1	2	1	82,486
Lord Jim (ARG)	7	H	2	0	0	0	1,120
Lord Jones	4	G	11	3	2	0	35,530
Lord Justin	3	G	4	0	0	0	315

Horse	Age	Sex	Sts	1st	2d	3d	Won
Lord Keller	3	G	4	0	0	0	426
Lord Kenmer	5	G	8	0	3	1	8,574
Lord Kenneth	9	G	1	1	0	0	12,000
Lord Kins Spirit	6	G	12	3	1	1	16,930
Lord Knows	8	G	7	2	2	0	7,020
Lord Kokopelli	4	G	9	1	0	1	13,260
Lord Langfuhr	4	C	15	6	5	1	231,328
Lord Larupin	3	G	8	1	1	2	13,795
Lord Leta	5	H	1	0	0	0	0
Lord Lionel	4	G	2	0	1	0	1,400
Lord Lloyd Outlaw	6	G	15	4	2	0	39,948
Lord Louis	4	G	4	1	0	0	22,180
Lord Luck	3	G	5	1	0	1	8,450
Lord Mac Lean	10	H	2	0	0	0	90
Lord Macho	2	G	3	0	0	1	8,200
Lord Mendelson	7	H	2	0	0	0	0
Lord Nelson	7	G	5	3	2	0	116,528
Lord North	4	C	1	0	0	0	340
Lord of Ewhurst	6	G	9	1	1	0	8,085
Lord of Moray	7	H	3	1	0	0	3,812
Lord of Speed	8	G	2	0	0	0	135
Lord of the Cats	3	C	12	1	1	2	29,310
Lord of the Game	3	C	1	1	0	0	6,300
Lord of the Music	3	G	5	0	0	0	743
Lord of the Storm	6	H	8	2	1	3	8,959
Lord of the Street	5	G	16	4	1	2	29,510
Lord of the Sun	4	G	22	3	5	4	20,294
Lord of the Track	2	C	2	1	0	0	14,100
Lord of the Wild	2	G	3	0	0	0	1,313
Lord Ofthe Thunder	5	H	5	1	1	1	56,554
Lord Pacal (IRE)	7	G	13	0	3	2	22,695
Lord Penny (ARG)	5	G	1	0	0	0	300
Lord Rainman	6	H	4	0	0	0	210
Lord Raja	3	G	6	0	1	1	2,161
Lord Rambo	4	C	4	0	0	0	490
Lord Ravenal	8	G	17	2	2	4	34,290
Lord Robyn	2	G	7	3	0	0	44,380
Lord Salvatore	2	C	4	1	1	2	43,040
Lord Samarai	3	G	9	2	4	1	164,980
Lord Sheryar	3	G	11	1	2	3	57,778
Lord She's Fast	3	F	4	0	0	1	2,260
Lord Shogun	5	G	7	0	1	0	11,295
Lord Sprite	3	C	1	0	0	0	0
Lord Starson	2	C	6	0	0	0	2,170
Lord Stephano	10	G	9	0	1	1	2,728
Lord Stonewood	4	G	6	0	0	1	2,856
Lord Sunday	5	G	12	0	0	0	1,024
Lord Vilzak	3	G	13	1	2	2	7,035
Lord Wallace	9	H	1	0	0	0	138
Lord Wimsey	3	C	1	0	0	0	630
Lord Zada	11	G	1	0	0	0	7,969
Lordhesasmoken	8	G	2	0	0	0	0
Lord's Idol	5	G	3	0	0	1	1,620
Lord's Katie	5	M	3	0	1	0	4,450
Lords Ransom	6	G	16	1	1	3	8,299
Lord's Salida	6	M	8	1	0	0	3,510
Lords Table	4	C	8	4	1	1	20,818
Lordslegacy	2	F	6	1	0	1	31,056
Lordy Lordy Lordy	4	G	7	0	2	0	12,440
Loreen	3	F	2	0	0	0	0
Lorelie's Legacy	5	M	1	0	0	0	0
Loren V.	2	G	2	1	0	0	12,400
Lorena Maria	4	F	11	2	0	3	12,550
Lorena's Prospect	3	G	4	0	0	1	2,310
Lorenchik	3	G	8	2	2	1	13,022
Lorenzon	3	C	4	1	0	2	11,348
Lorenzo's Star	4	C	1	0	0	0	0
Loretta Lane	4	F	2	0	0	0	170
Loretta's Angel	2	F	5	1	2	0	17,410
Lori Blue Chip	4	F	19	1	0	2	9,910
Lori M'love	5	M	14	2	2	3	40,640
Lori N Lynn	4	F	16	2	1	4	13,848
Lori Sue	3	F	13	2	3	0	29,784
Lorilyn Is a Lady	4	F	11	3	0	0	17,235
Lorna Gail	4	F	1	0	1	0	2,500
Lorna's Ruby	2	F	6	1	2	0	11,610
Lorraine's Secret	6	G	14	0	2	3	9,205
Lorrainesvalentine	6	M	2	0	0	0	309
Los Solano (GB)	7	G	8	1	2	2	55,580
Losin' My Mine	3	C	1	0	0	0	0
Losin Suzin	3	F	1	0	0	1	4,200
Lost Again	10	G	12	2	3	3	9,169
Lost Agenda	6	G	2	0	0	1	2,290
Lost All Control	6	M	11	2	2	2	30,282
Lost and Bound	4	F	13	2	1	1	36,370
Lost Appeal	6	M	3	0	0	0	31,000
Lost Bride	3	F	12	6	0	1	133,785
Lost Brigade	3	G	8	0	0	1	4,250
Lost Caper	5	G	1	0	0	0	186
Lost Cherokee	3	C	5	1	0	3	43,755
Lost City	5	G	5	0	0	0	270
Lost Composer	4	F	17	1	4	3	9,822
Lost Connection	4	G	8	0	0	0	607
Lost Creek	3	F	5	0	1	0	4,950
Lost Dance	4	F	16	3	0	3	17,568
Lost Dove	3	F	4	0	0	0	480
Lost Fact	5	M	7	0	0	2	3,505
Lost Flamingo	3	F	13	1	1	1	22,615
Lost Furlough	4	F	12	1	0	1	7,161
Lost Girl	3	F	3	0	0	0	0
Lost Her At Dawn	4	G	13	2	4	1	27,195
Lost Her Rank	5	M	11	3	2	2	25,005
Lost Her Tune	2	F	6	0	0	1	2,310
Lost in Love	7	G	5	2	0	1	8,456
Lost in the Fog	2	C	2	2	0	0	44,575
Lost in the Music	4	F	18	2	3	1	17,430
Lost in the Rush	4	F	12	4	1	1	21,830
Lost in the Woods	5	G	9	0	0	1	12,820
Lost in Transit	3	G	10	1	1	3	34,215
Lost Jewels	2	C	7	0	0	2	9,800
Lost Kincsen	4	C	3	0	0	0	377
Lost Liberty	6	G	4	0	0	0	209
Lost Market	4	C	11	0	2	2	9,646
Lost My Behrens	2	C	1	0	0	0	0
Lost My Mojo	3	G	2	0	0	0	139
Lost My Thong	4	F	5	0	1	1	843
Lost Navigator	4	C	10	1	1	0	8,733
Lost Nekia	3	G	3	0	0	0	475
Lost Obsession	2	C	1	0	0	0	105
Lost Patrol	3	G	2	0	0	0	420
Lost Picture	3	G	11	1	2	1	5,100
Lost Pride	5	M	3	0	0	0	500
Lost Question	2	F	4	0	1	1	5,325
Lost Rainbow	3	C	8	0	1	1	7,400
Lost Recital Iron	8	M	4	0	1	1	1,610
Lost Reservation	4	C	9	0	0	2	6,809
Lost Rivers Mojo	3	C	10	3	0	0	58,700
Lost Rivers Rocket	6	G	9	1	0	1	2,369
Lost Romance	4	F	11	2	3	3	17,821
Lost Tear	4	F	2	0	0	0	0
Lost the Signal	2	F	5	0	0	0	600
Lost Time	4	F	16	2	5	4	18,804
Lost Victoria	2	F	3	0	0	1	1,670
Lost Wine	7	M	4	0	0	0	523
Lostcor	5	G	9	3	1	3	11,815
Lostintheshuffle	5	G	8	2	1	1	10,112
Lostriversprospect	4	F	12	1	0	4	7,197
Lot a Smoke	4	F	7	1	1	0	15,420
Lot Angel	5	H	7	0	0	0	0
Lot o' Arctic	4	C	3	0	0	0	190
Lot o' Avalanche	4	C	4	0	0	0	590
Lot o' Bug	2	G	3	1	0	0	11,970
Lot o' Charmin	7	M	5	0	0	1	938
Lot o' Friend	3	F	1	0	0	0	0
Lot O Razzledazzle	6	G	6	1	1	1	3,720
Lot o' Rim Fire	6	G	12	0	0	4	2,249
Lot o' Sun	4	C	4	0	0	0	340
Lot of Hope	5	M	13	0	2	3	7,503
Lot One (IRE)	3	C	3	0	0	2	9,520
Lota Clearance	2	C	4	0	0	1	3,540
Lota Prince	4	G	13	2	4	3	58,858
Lota Spunk	5	G	7	0	0	0	452
Lothar	5	G	7	1	1	1	30,380
Lots Due	4	F	6	0	0	0	0
Lots O Power	5	G	6	0	0	0	584
Lots of Cash	7	G	10	0	2	0	2,910
Lots of Chrome	7	G	9	1	0	1	3,144
Lots of Glow	3	F	6	1	0	0	8,598

Horse	Age	Sex	Sts	1st	2d	3d	Won
Lots of Hope (BRZ)	4	F	2	0	2	0	42,600
Lots of Night	5	M	8	0	0	1	889
Lots of Speed	6	G	1	0	0	0	186
Lot's of Time	2	G	2	0	0	0	270
Lotsa Change	3	G	3	0	1	0	4,190
Lotsa Class	4	F	4	1	0	0	6,932
Lotsa Macho	3	G	5	1	1	0	8,762
Lotsa Mojoe	2	C	2	1	0	0	16,918
Lotsa Seasons	4	F	3	0	0	0	1,000
Lotsa Yes	2	F	3	0	0	2	4,295
Lotsalivin	5	M	1	0	0	0	0
Lotsathunder	3	C	2	0	0	0	95
Lott	5	H	10	2	1	2	62,780
Lotta Dust	7	G	11	1	4	2	9,024
Lotta Fever	2	F	1	0	0	0	0
Lotta Glitter	9	M	2	1	0	0	5,100
Lotta Hot	5	G	1	0	0	0	0
Lotta Kim	3	F	1	1	0	0	60,000
Lotta Leader	4	F	1	0	0	0	0
Lotta Light	3	F	13	2	2	2	35,970
Lotta Loot	2	C	10	1	3	2	40,356
Lotta Lucky	8	G	3	0	0	0	310
Lotta Moxee	4	G	8	1	1	2	7,146
Lotta Run	4	F	4	0	2	1	2,236
Lotta Slew	8	G	9	2	1	2	5,053
Lottaballado	8	G	6	0	0	0	186
Lottanoise	5	G	8	0	0	0	600
Lottery Luck	4	F	13	2	2	2	22,573
Lotus Creek	3	F	6	1	0	0	4,365
Lotzakrugerand	4	G	4	0	0	0	0
Lou Doc	4	F	12	2	3	2	8,502
Lou Genius	2	F	1	0	0	0	400
Loucamania (BRZ)	4	F	3	1	1	0	31,600
Loucille's Risk	4	F	7	2	2	2	17,327
Loud and Silent	5	G	11	1	1	1	19,619
Loud Enough	2	C	1	0	0	0	78
Loud Forum	3	G	13	4	2	3	16,309
Loudoun Currency	3	F	2	0	0	0	700
Loudy	4	F	4	0	0	0	768
Loue Loui	5	G	14	4	3	2	13,226
Louey Vill	3	F	16	1	3	1	14,855
Loughbeg Rambler (GB)	9	G	1	0	0	1	1,000
Loughran	4	G	12	0	0	2	3,850
Louie Downtown	3	G	8	1	3	3	54,009
Louie Gold	4	G	11	1	0	0	7,265
Louie La Dew	7	H	1	0	0	0	254
Louie Na'ssal	3	G	4	0	0	0	2,680
Louie Slew	3	G	5	0	1	0	3,741
Louie the Slew	4	C	5	1	0	2	37,840
Louie Tune	4	G	13	2	0	0	6,087
Louiecandoit	3	G	6	1	1	0	19,179
Louie's Lady	3	F	2	0	0	0	0
Louie's Luck	3	C	3	0	0	0	1,185
Louies Princess	3	F	6	1	1	0	7,825
Louie's Ransom	3	C	5	2	0	0	11,758
Louie's Refund	4	F	3	0	0	0	430
Louie's Wizard	3	F	2	0	0	0	103
Louies Word	3	G	11	1	4	2	17,500
Louis Arthur	7	H	2	0	0	0	0
Louis Le Grand	2	G	2	0	0	1	1,800
Louis Que	3	G	15	3	1	1	37,660
Louis Quinze	5	G	4	0	0	0	525
Louis' Star	2	F	6	1	2	0	10,874
Louisa	3	F	7	1	1	1	10,590
Louise's Fantasy	2	F	1	0	0	0	0
Louise's Gold	2	F	8	0	0	1	2,075
Louisiana Anna	4	F	1	0	0	0	0
Louisiana Brun	3	G	12	0	0	1	3,790
Louisiana Champ	2	C	4	0	0	0	630
Louisiana Cotton	4	G	3	0	0	0	0
Louisiana Hot Sauz	3	F	1	0	0	0	0
Louisiana Joe	2	C	1	0	0	0	0
Louisiana Rebel	3	C	3	0	0	1	1,100
Louisiana Rocket	2	C	2	0	0	0	630
Louisiana Sky	3	F	2	1	0	0	15,083
Louisiana Storm	7	G	6	0	0	0	1,310
Loula	3	F	4	0	1	0	14,820
Loumel Boy	4	G	5	0	0	1	640
Loup de Loup	4	G	8	1	1	0	16,260
Loup Longshanks	4	C	13	1	1	3	12,345
Loup Masque (FR)	5	G	5	0	1	0	2,835
Loup's Lady Love	4	F	8	2	2	0	14,550
L'Ouragan	3	F	2	0	0	0	1,680
Lou's Derby Wish	3	F	7	1	0	2	10,350
Lou's Expectation	5	G	7	0	0	1	10,780
Lou's Reality	6	M	5	0	0	0	3,120
Lous Spirit	4	F	1	0	0	0	0
Lou's Tricky Lady	3	F	5	0	0	1	680
Louvain (IRE)	2	F	6	2	2	2	87,143
Lovable Dom	3	C	10	0	2	6	19,248
Lovable Kristy	3	F	9	1	1	3	13,875
Lovable Rogue	3	C	5	2	1	0	28,140
Lovat	4	G	8	0	2	0	4,787
Love a Bull	6	M	4	0	0	0	1,046
Love a Lot	3	G	3	1	0	0	20,124
Love and Glory	3	F	6	1	1	0	21,784
Love and Honor	4	C	10	0	0	5	10,500
Love and Kris's	3	F	6	1	2	0	44,452
Love Antics	3	C	2	0	0	1	3,840
Love Attack	3	C	13	0	2	3	7,440
Love Bandit	5	G	4	0	1	1	2,359
Love Bench	2	F	3	0	0	0	900
Love Bridge	3	G	13	2	4	4	39,685
Love Broker	3	F	3	0	0	0	0
Love Chat	4	C	1	0	0	0	0
Love City	4	G	11	1	2	1	26,030
Love Dance	6	G	2	1	0	0	4,725
Love Em N Leave Em	3	F	9	4	2	1	52,880
Love Emblem	4	F	1	0	0	0	0
Love Fest	2	F	1	1	0	0	14,795
Love Flight	7	G	8	2	1	2	8,556
Love for Ali	4	F	12	5	2	1	87,687
Love for Lucy	4	F	7	0	0	0	19,080
Love Fuze	4	G	3	0	0	0	925
Love Game	3	C	13	4	1	2	60,635
Love Gem	2	F	1	0	0	0	75
Love Happy	6	G	2	1	0	0	20,550
Love Hill Lady	3	F	3	0	0	1	1,864
Love Hunt	3	F	3	0	0	0	270
Love Hurts	3	F	2	0	0	0	0
Love in an Instant	3	C	2	0	1	0	8,720
Love in Brazil (BRZ)	5	M	2	0	0	0	800
Love in the Mornin	4	F	2	0	0	0	0
Love in Your Eyes	4	F	14	2	4	1	25,840
Love Is the Answer	2	F	9	1	2	1	18,090
Love Is the Hub	6	G	1	0	0	0	0
Love Jet	4	F	7	0	1	0	880
Love Johnny	4	F	11	1	1	2	5,123
Love Lac	2	G	1	0	0	0	0
Love Lane (IRE)	7	G	6	0	2	0	7,760
Love Less	6	G	13	1	3	3	39,922
Love Love	3	G	11	1	0	1	16,440
Love Match	4	F	6	2	0	3	45,910
Love Me Always	3	F	1	0	0	0	75
Love Me Leave Me	4	C	10	0	1	2	16,220
Love Me Now	3	F	9	1	2	5	15,655
Love Me R Leave Me	5	G	12	1	0	4	8,280
Love Me Twice	3	F	1	0	0	0	480
Love Mountain	4	G	6	0	1	1	21,105
Love My Mountain	5	G	12	0	2	0	13,615
Love N On the Run	7	M	4	0	0	0	183
Love Never Fails	2	C	3	1	1	0	14,840
Love Not War	6	M	11	1	4	1	37,180
Love of Money	3	C	5	3	1	0	491,500
Love On Tap	2	F	1	0	0	0	0
Love On the Run	3	G	3	2	0	1	79,456
Love Or Money	3	F	5	0	0	2	7,920
Love Our Kinzie	2	C	3	0	0	0	1,200
Love Power	3	F	13	2	0	1	48,895
Love Rush	4	F	10	0	2	2	6,778
Love Sam	4	C	16	1	3	3	37,391
Love Shuffle	9	G	11	2	1	2	30,100
Love Sting	4	F	11	0	1	0	26,099
Love Struck	4	F	10	0	0	3	5,094
Love That Amber	5	M	4	1	0	0	6,860
Love That Bob	2	G	2	0	0	0	2,883
Love That Duck	10	G	8	1	1	0	6,408
Love That Hill	3	F	4	0	0	1	8,500

Horse	Age	Sex	Sts	1st	2d	3d	Won
Love That Man	5	G	12	5	2	1	87,967
Love That Moon	5	G	8	1	0	3	59,350
Love That Music	4	G	7	1	2	1	32,870
Love That Punch	5	G	11	1	2	2	20,045
Love That Song	3	G	3	1	0	0	17,000
Love That Touch	2	F	3	0	0	0	225
Love the City	2	G	2	1	1	0	15,600
Love the Dawn	2	F	1	0	1	0	5,040
Love the Light	4	G	11	2	1	1	16,610
Love the Princess	4	F	2	0	1	0	2,785
Love Thunder	2	F	2	0	0	0	0
Love Tinks	6	M	6	2	1	0	38,369
Love to Mel	6	M	3	1	0	1	2,072
Love to Tango	7	G	7	2	2	1	69,090
Love Tops All	4	G	6	1	1	1	15,200
Love Unlimited	6	M	1	0	0	0	0
Love Us Gold Jet	4	F	3	0	0	0	0
Love Won	3	C	6	0	1	3	11,585
Love Ya	2	F	1	1	0	0	9,360
Love You Charlie	7	G	11	0	0	0	0
Love You Dolly	3	F	4	0	0	0	250
Love You Honey	3	F	2	1	0	0	14,670
Love You Madly	4	F	10	2	2	1	73,185
Love You Mean It	3	G	2	0	0	0	0
Love You More	5	M	7	4	0	1	5,521
Love Your Whit	4	G	9	1	1	1	29,325
Loveamericanstile	8	G	6	0	0	0	1,757
Lovefromafar	3	G	8	1	1	2	13,259
Lovehermadly	7	M	11	3	2	1	17,640
Loveland	3	F	8	2	2	0	28,680
Lovely Afternoon	3	F	6	2	1	0	86,959
Lovely American	4	F	9	2	2	0	14,453
Lovely Ashley	2	F	1	0	0	0	500
Lovely Bonita	5	M	15	3	3	1	40,903
Lovely Breeze	4	F	4	1	0	0	15,425
Lovely Candles	4	F	10	1	1	2	41,390
Lovely Discovery	4	F	10	0	0	0	981
Lovely Fortune	4	F	17	2	1	1	20,493
Lovely Gena	2	F	7	0	0	0	2,365
Lovely Honor	3	F	9	1	2	2	11,615
Lovely Image	3	F	4	0	0	1	475
Lovely Irish Lady	3	F	3	0	0	0	339
Lovely Isabelle	3	F	14	1	0	1	38,964
Lovely Lauren	5	M	7	0	0	0	595
Lovely Leah	3	F	9	1	1	0	15,645
Lovely Legal	2	F	2	1	0	0	20,349
Lovely Leitrim	3	F	5	0	2	2	24,718
Lovely Living	2	F	7	0	2	0	5,073
Lovely Lola	3	F	7	1	0	1	53,926
Lovely Louisia	3	F	18	2	6	3	38,887
Lovely Meadow	2	F	1	1	0	0	9,676
Lovely n' Elegant	5	M	5	0	0	0	845
Lovely Orphan	3	F	4	0	0	1	829
Lovely Prince	4	G	1	0	1	0	2,070
Lovely Prospect	2	F	1	0	0	0	420
Lovely Queen	5	M	9	1	1	2	9,125
Lovely R R	3	F	7	1	1	0	18,460
Lovely Rafaela	3	F	6	1	1	0	125,535
Lovely Regina	3	F	3	0	0	0	1,260
Lovely Risk	3	F	6	0	0	0	485
Lovely Rose B.	4	F	5	2	1	0	23,010
Lovely Secret	4	G	5	2	0	0	8,430
Lovely Senorita	2	F	1	0	0	0	118
Lovely Sight	3	F	15	3	2	3	69,030
Lovely Slew	4	G	7	1	2	1	5,274
Lovely Stone	2	F	1	0	1	0	7,800
Lovely Syn	7	M	2	0	0	0	0
Lovely Ticket	6	M	3	0	0	2	6,810
Lovely Venture	3	F	1	0	0	0	0
Lovely Verse	5	M	5	1	0	0	5,610
Lovem and Leavem	3	F	3	0	0	0	418
Lov'emnrun	3	F	10	2	0	0	36,540
Lovenia	4	F	2	0	0	0	0
Lover Come Back	4	F	9	0	1	0	9,540
Lover Gal	2	F	3	0	0	0	0
Lover Iam	3	G	12	2	2	1	20,091
Lover Marshal (ARG)	5	G	8	1	3	1	22,105
Lover of Mine	3	C	4	1	0	1	5,334
Loverboy Rebel	6	G	6	0	1	0	1,644
Lovergirl	5	M	5	1	1	0	2,175
Loverineveryport	7	G	4	0	0	1	4,250
Loverlikeno Other	3	C	3	1	0	0	6,110
Lovers Bend	3	F	7	1	0	0	11,330
Lover's Lady	7	M	9	1	1	2	6,183
Lovers Son	7	G	11	4	2	1	19,555
Lover's Star	2	G	3	0	1	1	13,457
Loves a Fight	7	M	7	1	2	0	5,169
Loves Badge	2	F	6	0	0	0	696
Love's Conquest	2	G	2	2	0	0	20,601
Love's Illusion	2	F	3	0	0	0	190
Love's Sensation	3	F	2	1	1	0	24,960
Love's Strong Hart	3	C	2	0	0	0	3,600
Love's Tune	2	C	4	0	0	1	2,390
Lovesmegold	4	F	6	0	1	1	8,685
Lovethatchocolate	5	M	8	2	1	0	7,738
Lovethatdazzle	2	F	3	0	2	0	8,400
Lovethatlegend	3	F	2	0	0	1	9,066
Lovetheprospect	3	F	13	1	2	2	11,753
Lovetotalk	7	G	4	0	1	0	880
Lovetrando	5	G	17	3	3	3	21,833
Loveuplaindealing	5	M	2	0	0	0	97
Lovey Lovey Lovey	10	M	2	0	0	0	396
Lovie Dovie Linda	3	F	14	0	0	0	2,689
Lovin Glory	2	F	3	1	0	0	16,075
Lovin' Life	3	G	5	0	0	0	5,220
Lovin Lucille	3	F	1	0	0	0	345
Lovin Pappa	8	G	2	0	0	0	327
Lovin the Sunshine	3	F	19	2	1	2	23,596
Loving (BRZ)	8	G	10	5	1	1	214,400
Loving Angel	3	F	3	1	0	0	28,015
Loving Cup (JPN)	4	G	4	1	1	0	33,200
Loving Feeling	4	F	10	1	4	2	43,866
Loving It	2	G	8	2	0	2	66,882
Loving Lucy	3	F	4	0	1	0	7,880
Loving Thoughts	2	F	2	0	1	0	7,770
Loving Tribute	4	G	5	1	0	0	3,073
Loving Twist	3	F	5	0	0	0	240
Loving Type (ARG)	5	H	5	0	1	2	11,300
Lovingly	3	F	5	0	1	1	10,725
Lovingraina	6	M	2	0	0	2	1,221
Lov'nue	7	M	3	0	0	0	0
Low Bolly	3	C	3	1	0	0	15,060
Low Boy	3	G	7	0	1	0	1,412
Low Byars	3	F	6	1	1	1	9,820
Low Cay	3	G	8	0	2	0	8,505
Low Flyin' Jones	3	G	9	0	1	2	5,417
Low Key Affair	4	F	8	0	2	2	31,972
Low Note	3	G	8	0	0	0	2,480
Low Priced	3	C	4	1	1	0	4,128
Low Visibility	4	F	3	0	0	0	400
Lowcountry	2	F	4	0	0	1	8,485
Lowdowndirtydog	6	H	8	1	3	3	24,899
Lowell's Legacy	3	C	8	0	0	2	10,226
Lower Shore	2	G	8	0	1	1	9,360
Lower Town Sue	3	F	1	0	0	0	0
Lox and Kippers	2	C	2	0	1	0	5,290
Loyal Deer	3	G	2	0	0	0	150
Loyal Deputy	4	C	7	1	0	2	15,850
Loyal Lil	3	F	1	0	0	0	300
Loyal Royal	3	G	16	0	2	1	31,800
Loyalton	2	C	4	1	1	1	33,588
Ls Believeinmagic	3	F	16	3	3	1	53,830
Ls Storming Gypsy	4	G	9	2	2	1	16,442
Lt Selecto	2	C	2	0	0	0	422
Lt. Dan Flag	3	G	2	0	0	0	0
Lt. Gold	3	G	4	0	0	0	396
Lt. Lucky	4	G	9	1	2	0	1,892
Lt. Regent	4	F	5	3	0	0	17,600
Lt. Sampson	3	G	7	3	3	1	76,050
L'Tl Brassy	3	C	5	0	0	0	482
Ltn. Larry	3	G	9	2	1	0	10,417
L'Trump	3	C	1	0	0	0	69
Lu Las Absence	3	C	3	0	0	1	1,062
Lu Lu Ra Ra	4	C	9	1	1	2	6,434
Lubie Lubie Doo	3	F	2	0	0	0	0
Lubnan	3	C	5	0	0	1	4,305
Lubomir	3	C	3	0	1	0	7,644
Luby Blue	3	F	5	1	0	0	4,148

Horse	Age	Sex	Sts	1st	2d	3d	Won
Luca Laabity	6	G	2	0	0	1	1,300
Luca Luca	4	C	6	1	0	1	8,520
Lucado	2	C	2	0	0	1	1,155
Lucas Creek	7	G	3	0	0	0	150
Lucas Pond	3	F	12	1	3	1	22,104
Lucayan Beauty (IRE)	3	F	7	1	1	0	40,367
Lucayan Indian (IRE)	9	G	12	2	1	2	31,448
Lucayan Rodeo	3	F	2	0	0	0	300
Lucayan's Gamble	3	G	2	0	0	0	434
Lucerita	3	F	1	0	0	0	0
Lucha	2	F	5	0	0	0	170
Luci Fina	4	F	8	1	0	1	6,215
Lucid	6	M	8	1	2	0	21,560
Lucid Interval	5	G	4	0	0	0	243
Lucie's Bay	3	F	3	1	2	0	21,888
Lucifer's Fever	4	G	2	0	0	0	0
Lucifer's Lady	4	F	8	2	1	0	3,125
Lucifer's Stone	3	F	6	4	1	0	357,147
Lucinda's Flight	6	M	12	0	0	0	2,295
Luck and Fame	2	F	2	1	0	0	17,958
Luck Arrives	8	G	15	2	2	3	24,011
Luck Baby	3	F	5	1	2	0	22,200
Luck Down South	4	G	1	0	0	0	210
Luck Liz	4	F	9	0	1	0	2,890
Luck My Way	3	F	6	1	3	1	6,090
Luck of Jake	5	G	15	2	2	1	26,268
Luck of the Royal	4	G	3	0	2	0	4,195
Luck Out	5	G	10	0	1	4	15,400
Luck Stone	3	G	2	0	0	1	1,861
Luckbealadytonight	3	F	3	1	1	0	41,000
Luckie May Breeze	2	F	4	1	0	0	15,756
Luckie Thirteenth	6	M	2	0	0	0	104
Luckierthanuthink	3	F	8	1	1	0	51,941
Luckiestofthelucky	12	G	16	2	2	2	9,165
Luckisalady	2	F	3	0	0	1	2,860
Luckman Park	8	G	1	0	0	0	0
Luckoftheknight	7	H	1	0	0	0	0
Luck's Wager	6	G	4	2	0	0	8,001
Lucky Acres	4	G	6	2	0	0	12,232
Lucky Alarm	2	C	3	2	0	0	25,260
Lucky Alda	3	F	3	0	0	0	560
Lucky All the Way	8	M	6	0	0	1	1,170
Lucky Amigo	4	G	5	0	2	0	3,514
Lucky and Happy	9	G	1	0	0	0	80
Lucky and Proud	7	G	1	0	0	0	50
Lucky Autum	4	F	10	2	3	0	17,852
Lucky Baldwin	6	G	14	3	0	2	41,194
Lucky Bartender	3	G	3	0	1	0	2,110
Lucky Basket	5	M	4	2	1	0	3,853
Lucky Bid	2	C	8	1	2	0	54,540
Lucky Bluff	6	G	6	1	0	0	3,075
Lucky Bob	4	G	11	3	3	1	16,648
Lucky Bohemian	8	G	15	3	4	1	29,240
Lucky Bounty	5	H	7	1	0	3	2,266
Lucky Bridle	2	F	2	0	0	0	2,580
Lucky Bucker	2	C	3	0	1	1	3,940
Lucky Buckley	4	G	15	3	3	3	23,142
Lucky Buck's Baby	2	F	3	1	0	0	9,555
Lucky Cerscent	5	M	1	0	0	0	0
Lucky Chap	4	C	5	0	1	0	11,265
Lucky Charleen	4	F	8	2	0	0	11,040
Lucky Charm's Jet	6	G	6	1	0	0	6,547
Lucky Chip	6	G	14	1	3	1	33,200
Lucky Cielo	2	C	5	0	0	2	21,894
Lucky Clue	4	G	7	1	0	0	16,600
Lucky Colleen	2	F	8	1	2	1	27,170
Lucky Comstock	5	G	13	1	3	1	8,366
Lucky Creation	3	C	7	3	1	0	88,932
Lucky Creek	6	G	6	0	0	1	1,144
Lucky Currency	10	M	1	0	0	0	0
Lucky Cutie	3	F	11	1	5	1	24,152
Lucky Dame	2	F	4	0	1	0	1,940
Lucky Darling	3	F	2	0	0	0	1,590
Lucky Date	7	M	3	0	1	1	5,200
Lucky Dazzler	4	F	8	1	1	1	33,493
Lucky Direction	3	G	3	0	0	0	100
Lucky Dream	3	G	11	0	0	0	549
Lucky Drummer	3	G	15	1	1	4	22,960
Lucky Duck	3	G	11	1	0	2	15,950
Lucky Ducky	2	C	3	0	1	0	3,000
Lucky Dunant	6	G	3	1	0	1	1,081
Lucky Eleven	4	F	14	4	1	2	70,484
Lucky Emerald	3	F	3	0	0	0	1,253
Lucky Ending	5	M	1	0	0	1	1,105
Lucky Explosion	3	G	9	2	4	0	37,570
Lucky Feather	2	F	2	0	0	1	730
Lucky Ferdinand	5	H	13	2	2	2	40,786
Lucky Fern	3	F	4	1	0	1	43,956
Lucky Fib	4	F	12	3	0	2	20,699
Lucky Folly	6	M	8	1	1	0	5,828
Lucky Frolic	2	G	8	2	0	2	60,620
Lucky Gamble	3	C	10	4	2	3	136,784
Lucky Gambler	3	F	12	3	2	2	55,030
Lucky Geisha	2	F	8	1	1	2	17,125
Lucky Genia	3	F	2	0	0	0	578
Lucky Gentleman	2	G	5	0	0	0	1,170
Lucky Ghost	3	G	1	1	0	0	8,775
Lucky Gift	4	C	6	3	1	1	26,358
Lucky Guy	3	G	8	3	3	0	65,988
Lucky Haley	2	F	1	1	0	0	10,650
Lucky Heidi	4	F	9	1	0	1	3,490
Lucky Hooch	5	H	6	2	0	0	13,200
Lucky in Love	5	M	9	2	0	4	120,684
Lucky in the Lead	3	F	10	3	2	1	11,670
Lucky Irish Jewell	6	M	5	0	0	0	180
Lucky J. H.	2	C	5	1	1	1	56,335
Lucky Jack	2	G	1	0	0	0	960
Lucky Jen	2	F	3	1	0	1	16,685
Lucky Jennifer	4	F	1	0	0	0	0
Lucky Jill	3	F	4	1	1	1	6,735
Lucky Jim R	5	G	19	2	2	1	23,265
Lucky John T	3	C	13	1	1	1	4,164
Lucky Jump	2	F	4	0	0	0	0
Lucky June	5	M	5	0	3	0	3,396
Lucky Kaye	4	F	11	2	1	4	10,400
Lucky Kelly	3	F	11	0	5	2	16,380
Lucky Kentucky	3	F	7	0	1	2	4,045
Lucky Knight	3	G	3	0	0	0	310
Lucky Koo	3	F	11	1	4	2	18,479
Lucky Krew's	4	G	6	1	0	0	2,195
Lucky Lacotte	6	G	2	0	0	0	210
Lucky Lady Liz	4	F	3	0	0	0	170
Lucky Lady Slew	4	F	1	0	0	0	0
Lucky Laredo	4	G	1	0	0	1	1,350
Lucky Larue	4	G	12	2	4	1	27,880
Lucky Last Magic	4	F	18	2	3	1	10,699
Lucky Lazarus	4	G	15	1	1	1	8,898
Lucky Lemon	4	F	3	1	1	1	6,899
Lucky Leo	3	G	6	0	1	2	16,300
Lucky Les and Jess	3	C	1	0	0	0	105
Lucky Lief	4	C	9	1	2	1	25,104
Lucky Li'l Imp	4	F	4	0	0	0	210
Lucky Lily	4	F	8	1	2	2	13,588
Lucky Lisa	4	F	6	1	0	1	7,756
Lucky Lloyd	6	G	6	0	0	0	839
Lucky Lou	2	F	5	1	0	0	14,290
Lucky Louise	4	F	5	1	1	1	8,377
Lucky Luciano	4	G	8	1	1	0	2,795
Lucky Lucky Me	4	G	8	0	0	2	1,886
Lucky Lure	3	G	4	0	0	1	7,000
Lucky M	5	M	11	5	0	2	81,590
Lucky Magus	4	G	1	0	0	0	270
Lucky Memento	3	G	5	0	1	0	7,070
Lucky Millennium	4	F	14	0	0	3	7,043
Lucky Miss Coyote	2	F	1	0	0	0	130
Lucky Miss Lark	5	M	10	2	3	0	4,593
Lucky Mister K	6	H	1	0	0	0	60
Lucky Mount	3	G	11	0	2	3	6,812
Lucky Mudd	6	G	5	0	1	2	6,415
Lucky Mussell	3	F	8	0	2	1	3,513
Lucky n' Foxy	5	M	2	0	0	0	132
Lucky Nell	3	F	5	0	0	0	399
Lucky November	3	F	6	0	0	0	136
Lucky Obed	2	F	2	1	0	0	7,925
Lucky O'Kelly	3	G	3	0	0	0	1,000
Lucky Old Sun	6	G	1	0	0	0	2,380
Lucky Ole'	6	M	4	0	0	0	822
Lucky Ole Roan	3	G	13	1	2	2	19,110

Horse	Age	Sex	Sts	1st	2d	3d	Won
Lucky One	2	F	3	0	0	0	3,250
Lucky Patriot	6	G	6	1	2	1	13,920
Lucky Patty	3	F	9	1	1	2	5,210
Lucky Paul	3	G	14	1	5	1	31,440
Lucky Paws	9	M	7	1	2	2	26,520
Lucky Pete	2	G	2	0	0	0	1,938
Lucky Pioneer	6	G	5	1	1	0	3,680
Lucky Pip Squeak	3	C	12	1	0	3	12,495
Lucky Poet	4	F	10	1	2	1	16,657
Lucky Pollock	6	G	10	1	0	1	4,255
Lucky Pops	2	C	5	0	2	0	2,910
Lucky Prince	6	G	9	1	2	2	8,798
Lucky Prize	9	G	7	1	0	0	2,353
Lucky Proud	2	C	9	1	0	2	14,520
Lucky Pulpit	3	C	7	0	1	2	47,454
Lucky Punch	6	G	19	1	5	4	26,476
Lucky Quaker	3	G	5	0	0	0	439
Lucky Quixote	4	C	11	1	2	1	31,457
Lucky Ransom	2	C	1	0	0	0	161
Lucky Remruck	6	G	11	3	0	3	15,225
Lucky Ride	6	H	9	3	0	3	28,678
Lucky Roberta	3	F	6	0	1	1	10,426
Lucky Rocket	2	G	3	0	0	0	56
Lucky Ruckus	4	F	10	0	2	3	11,560
Lucky Ryan	3	G	5	1	0	0	7,200
Lucky Ryder	6	H	1	0	0	0	122
Lucky S. Lorenti	2	C	1	0	0	0	103
Lucky Sabre	4	F	5	1	0	1	30,003
Lucky Sam	6	H	14	4	1	0	33,718
Lucky Sand	5	G	1	0	0	0	46
Lucky Sandman	9	G	9	0	0	1	3,509
Lucky Scribe	5	G	10	0	1	1	5,150
Lucky Sherman	2	G	6	1	1	0	24,780
Lucky Shot	3	C	2	0	0	1	935
Lucky Sister	3	F	2	0	0	0	0
Lucky Sixes	3	G	9	0	1	1	3,639
Lucky Slam	3	C	6	2	1	0	39,552
Lucky Slevin	2	F	3	1	0	0	12,810
Lucky Snoop	3	F	4	0	0	0	0
Lucky So to Speak	2	F	1	0	0	0	105
Lucky Spike	2	G	6	0	0	1	4,820
Lucky Spin	3	G	7	0	1	0	2,945
Lucky Spirit	5	M	7	0	1	1	20,832
Lucky Star Baby	7	M	5	0	0	1	1,370
Lucky Streak	4	F	10	1	2	0	5,919
Lucky Strike King	4	G	9	1	0	1	2,983
Lucky Style	2	F	5	1	0	1	7,940
Lucky Sunshine	4	F	5	1	0	0	9,909
Lucky Swimmer	3	G	4	0	0	0	0
Lucky Tec	6	G	14	3	1	3	130,569
Lucky Tee	3	G	9	2	0	0	18,066
Lucky They Call Me	5	G	7	2	0	0	12,729
Lucky Third Time	6	G	3	0	0	0	0
Lucky Ticket	4	G	13	2	2	0	31,302
Lucky Tie	3	C	8	1	2	3	3,510
Lucky to Be Ours	4	G	1	0	0	0	76
Lucky to Cope	2	C	1	0	0	0	115
Lucky Tom	4	G	5	0	0	0	4,200
Lucky Tomoli	2	F	1	1	0	0	34,200
Lucky Triple	3	F	4	0	0	0	1,590
Lucky Tunnel	3	F	12	1	1	1	37,630
Lucky Turk	4	F	6	1	1	1	32,125
Lucky Twosome	5	G	2	0	0	0	420
Lucky Valid	5	M	11	3	3	3	51,310
Lucky Victor	3	F	4	0	1	0	2,757
Lucky Whizelli	3	G	10	1	3	1	15,970
Lucky Willy	2	C	3	0	0	0	745
Lucky Win	2	C	1	1	0	0	9,180
Lucky Wink	2	F	6	0	3	2	31,580
Lucky Wish	4	F	14	2	4	2	42,815
Luckyandsmart	2	G	3	1	0	1	19,198
Luckyanunoit	3	F	12	1	0	4	13,696
Luckyemilycharm	3	F	4	0	1	0	2,816
Luckylicious	3	F	6	1	0	1	5,382
Luckymata	4	C	14	6	2	3	62,605
Luckynfast	4	C	7	0	0	0	437
Luckynquick	3	G	9	0	0	0	1,530
Lucky's Adam	2	C	6	0	0	3	14,275
Lucky's Magic	6	M	11	1	1	2	9,016
Luckytogetataste	3	G	7	1	1	1	17,040
Luckyustoo	5	G	2	1	0	0	2,520
Lucy Belle	3	F	1	0	1	0	1,080
Lucy Belle B B	4	F	3	0	0	0	1,428
Lucy Can Matach	5	M	6	1	0	0	9,171
Lucy Darling	5	M	16	0	2	5	11,686
Lucy Does the Hula	7	M	4	1	1	1	3,441
Lucy Glen	5	M	8	0	0	1	4,509
Lucy I'm Home	4	G	9	2	2	2	55,060
Lucy Jr.	2	F	1	0	1	0	4,420
Lucy Liberty	3	F	13	3	2	2	30,249
Lucy Loup	3	F	6	2	2	0	27,160
Lucy Lu Wee	4	F	11	2	2	2	14,817
Lucy Whitesocks	3	F	1	0	0	1	4,100
Lucyoso	6	M	14	0	0	0	1,676
Lucy's Got Rocks	5	M	10	1	0	0	3,269
Lucy's Love	3	G	6	0	0	2	1,210
Lucy's Ride	4	F	7	1	0	2	7,272
Ludicrous Speed	5	G	3	0	1	0	6,365
Ludmig	2	G	6	0	1	2	9,977
Ludovicus	8	G	9	4	0	1	67,768
Ludwig's Mimi	2	F	4	0	0	0	0
Luewoodorbit	3	F	1	0	0	1	630
Luft	6	G	6	0	2	3	3,416
Luga	3	G	15	2	0	3	53,370
Luger	5	H	14	1	1	1	12,527
Luhan	3	F	4	2	0	0	25,020
Luhuk's Lady	2	F	5	0	1	1	4,260
Luis Alfonzo	4	C	1	0	0	0	125
Luisa's Angel	3	F	1	0	0	0	0
Luisathebeachhouse	3	F	9	3	4	1	62,700
Lujan	3	C	3	0	0	0	320
Lujuria	3	F	6	2	0	0	12,529
Lukanberry	3	C	3	0	1	0	945
Lukanela	5	M	3	0	0	1	1,050
Luke	4	C	9	1	1	1	7,725
Luke At Me Now	4	F	2	0	0	0	0
Luke Hill	5	H	14	1	4	2	21,442
Luke in My Pocket	4	G	5	2	1	0	91,030
Lukelynn	3	G	9	2	3	1	83,522
Luken Boss	4	G	9	2	0	2	8,448
Luke's Finest	3	F	8	1	1	1	25,120
Luke's Flash	3	G	6	0	0	0	4,184
Luke's Halo	4	C	6	1	1	0	22,540
Lukes Rapid Dash	4	G	10	1	2	0	14,277
Luke's Way	9	G	5	1	0	1	4,860
Lukey D.	2	G	4	0	0	0	592
Lukfata Cowboy	4	C	5	1	0	0	6,705
Lukfata Louis	4	C	14	5	2	4	52,654
Lulabell	4	F	5	1	0	1	6,930
Lulie	3	F	4	2	2	0	20,980
Lullaby League	5	M	2	0	0	1	1,750
Lulo	4	F	1	0	0	0	85
Lulu Lady	3	F	4	1	0	0	8,860
Lulu Lemon	3	F	1	0	0	0	214
Lulu Rose	5	M	9	0	0	0	1,290
Lulua	3	F	3	2	0	0	35,640
Lulu's Chance	4	F	7	1	1	0	8,862
Lulu's Dream	5	M	13	2	0	1	18,105
Lulu's Love	7	M	3	0	0	0	0
Lulu's Luck	3	C	13	1	1	5	20,595
Lulu's Wad	3	F	2	0	0	0	220
Lulu's Way	8	M	12	0	0	1	1,457
Lulu'sgotasecret	2	F	1	0	0	0	50
Lum Reek	2	G	1	0	0	0	0
Lumbre	2	C	2	1	0	1	9,310
Lumiere Sprout (ARG)	6	G	7	1	1	1	29,820
Luminescense	3	G	4	0	0	1	5,415
Luminescing	3	F	4	1	0	1	29,368
Luminism	8	G	5	0	2	0	5,130
Luminosity	3	F	12	1	2	2	25,460
Luminous Lady	2	F	5	0	0	0	1,698
Lumpy	5	H	6	0	0	1	1,024
Lumpy Rutherford	6	G	9	1	2	0	14,363
Luna Gail Echo	4	G	7	0	0	0	572
Luna Joe	6	G	7	3	2	1	35,810
Luna La Estrellas	2	F	1	0	0	0	570
Luna Mundial (ARG)	7	M	3	0	1	0	3,230
Lunar Attack	4	F	5	1	0	0	5,600

Horse	Age	Sex	Sts	1st	2d	3d	Won
Lunar Bay	3	F	1	1	0	0	15,000
Lunar Bounty	5	G	13	6	3	1	50,455
Lunar Colony	4	F	1	0	1	0	6,000
Lunar Dreams	3	F	10	1	2	0	23,680
Lunar Flight	2	F	6	2	0	1	112,620
Lunar Girl	3	F	1	0	0	0	240
Lunar Lad	3	G	9	2	0	1	26,671
Lunar Lion	3	G	4	3	0	1	50,729
Lunar Myth	3	F	1	0	0	0	77
Lunar Orbit	7	M	1	0	0	0	0
Lunar Perigee	4	G	13	2	2	1	55,081
Lunar Pie	3	F	5	1	0	3	15,670
Lunar Power	3	G	9	1	1	1	13,019
Lunar Prospect	5	G	5	1	0	1	6,911
Lunar Rendezvous	3	F	5	1	1	3	23,430
Lunar Ruler	2	F	2	0	0	0	288
Lunar Secret	6	G	4	0	0	0	274
Lunar Storms	3	F	13	1	4	2	15,715
Lunar Sway	2	C	2	0	0	0	387
Lunarpal	2	C	5	4	0	0	284,677
Lunar's Prissy	3	F	9	2	2	0	39,710
Lunaskra	6	G	2	0	0	0	360
Lunatic Fringe	5	M	1	0	0	0	55
Lunch At T's	3	G	12	1	0	0	18,200
Lunch Basket	4	F	2	0	0	0	0
Lunch Bunch	4	G	5	0	0	2	14,120
Lundy's Liability (BRZ)	4	C	5	2	1	0	1,542,500
Lundzman	2	G	4	1	0	1	28,890
Lune d'Argent	5	M	15	0	4	1	8,795
Lunelle's Pride	5	M	9	2	2	2	11,496
Lunes Grito	3	F	15	2	5	4	58,159
Luneta Drive	5	M	1	0	0	0	107
Lunge	3	F	9	4	1	3	73,262
Lupa	5	M	8	0	0	0	1,040
Lupe Blossom	3	F	9	0	0	1	2,234
Lupe's Love	3	F	7	1	2	0	8,435
Lure of Gold	3	F	7	0	0	0	3,167
Lure of the Links	4	G	7	2	1	1	19,325
Lure the Chief	4	G	9	0	0	1	5,342
Lured of the Rings	3	G	1	1	0	0	25,800
Lu's Choice	2	C	3	1	0	0	5,362
Lu's Luck	9	M	5	0	1	0	695
Lu's Reality Point	3	G	11	1	1	3	8,541
Lusby	4	F	9	2	0	3	37,820
Lush	8	H	18	1	4	2	12,522
Lusi Pond	3	F	14	2	2	2	67,384
Lust for Green	5	M	4	0	0	0	994
Lustrous Runner	10	G	3	0	1	0	4,796
Lusty Kelly	3	F	3	0	1	0	2,425
Lusty Latin	5	G	10	3	1	2	182,040
Lute Oatson	2	G	1	0	1	0	1,900
Lutece	5	M	9	2	2	0	11,375
Luther	4	G	10	4	0	0	99,420
Luther Jr	4	G	5	1	2	0	17,700
Luther Wayne	4	G	21	1	3	0	12,504
Lutherville Luke	3	G	2	0	0	0	0
Luthier's Vendetta	4	C	5	1	0	0	5,964
Lutyens	3	C	1	0	0	1	4,680
Lutz Exchange	4	G	10	1	2	0	7,915
Luv Dat Gal	4	F	11	1	0	1	4,706
Luv Er Again	7	M	11	0	2	1	2,964
Luv That Bertie	2	F	4	1	0	0	7,200
Luv U Me	7	M	5	0	0	2	1,975
Luv Ya Big	3	F	7	2	2	1	27,876
Luvagoodjoke	4	G	11	1	1	3	10,258
Luvbnme	4	C	7	0	5	0	6,542
Luvin' Bucks	4	F	5	0	0	0	434
Luvin to Win	2	F	1	0	0	0	110
Luvinbillyiseasy	7	G	1	0	0	1	671
Luvnluk	4	G	12	0	1	0	5,183
Luvole'	5	M	4	0	1	0	3,600
Luv's Gold	4	F	10	0	0	1	1,830
Luvthat' Jackie	3	F	10	0	0	1	2,380
Luvthedance	4	F	12	0	4	1	7,255
Luvtowatchimgroove	4	C	5	0	0	1	1,881
Luvvalips	2	F	3	0	0	0	460
Luvwillkeepusalive	3	F	11	2	2	0	15,100
Luvya Dubya	3	G	3	0	1	0	4,500
Luvyoudad	4	G	8	1	2	0	9,355
Lux	3	F	1	0	0	0	0
Luxana	5	M	1	0	0	0	392
Luxor	5	G	8	0	1	1	1,637
Luxulyan	6	G	6	1	1	1	5,640
Luxurious Cat	4	F	14	4	1	0	12,476
Luxury Flight	3	F	4	1	1	0	32,768
Luxury Leader	10	G	10	2	0	0	6,679
Luxury Line	4	G	4	0	0	0	316
Luxury Madness	5	G	5	0	0	0	792
Luz de Esperanza	8	G	3	0	0	0	500
Luz Lane	5	G	3	0	0	0	2,552
Luzern	4	C	3	2	0	0	29,433
Lycense to Win	2	C	5	1	0	1	31,313
Lycius Darlin	3	F	14	1	1	2	8,716
Lycius Life	3	F	6	1	1	0	24,015
Lycius Two	3	G	19	1	4	5	33,182
Lycka	7	H	1	0	1	0	2,142
Lyde Award	3	G	14	0	1	1	5,757
Lydgate	4	C	8	1	2	0	100,069
Lydia A	6	M	13	5	2	1	34,290
Lydia Rosa	4	F	2	0	0	0	0
Lydian Mode	4	G	3	0	0	0	186
Lydia's Legacy	4	G	8	1	1	3	12,460
Lydiaswild	5	M	5	0	0	0	483
Lydio	9	G	9	0	0	0	974
Lyin Goddess	3	F	8	1	3	1	56,630
Lying Blue Eyes	4	C	5	0	1	0	1,878
Lying Eyes	7	M	2	0	0	0	0
Lying to Fly	2	G	9	1	1	1	10,389
Lyka Flash	3	F	7	0	0	0	603
Lyka Speedy	3	G	11	3	0	2	12,326
Lyles Station	5	G	16	3	0	1	9,832
Lymarie's Hunter	4	G	9	2	2	1	10,102
Lymical	8	G	8	0	1	2	7,746
Lynda Dee	9	M	7	3	1	0	13,799
Lynda Lucky	4	F	6	0	1	1	6,199
Lynda's Dream	3	F	9	3	2	1	18,792
Lyndee Jo	4	F	14	2	1	1	11,788
Lyndee's Pearl	2	F	11	0	1	2	28,160
Lynhurst	4	G	3	0	0	0	180
Lynn's Bay Breeze	3	G	10	0	2	2	2,648
Lynn's Halo	4	G	10	0	0	1	3,213
Lynn's Song	3	F	12	0	0	2	10,687
Lynn's Tour	7	G	16	0	0	1	1,796
Lyn's Trinity	5	M	7	0	0	3	4,365
Lyons Point	3	C	8	0	1	0	3,398
Lyphard Cat	4	G	2	0	0	0	346
Lyphiano	7	G	15	3	1	2	13,931
Lypin Rivers	4	G	10	1	2	1	2,640
Lyra	2	F	1	0	0	0	900
Lyracist	8	H	10	1	3	3	105,470
Lyre o' Gold	2	G	4	0	0	0	0
Lyre's Peak	5	H	5	1	0	0	9,610
Lyric	5	M	14	1	5	2	20,285
Lyrical Grace	2	F	2	0	1	0	6,900
Lyrical Moment	3	F	4	0	0	0	480
Lyrical Myth	2	F	1	0	0	0	0
Lytle Creek	7	G	8	4	2	1	57,765
M and M Gold	3	C	6	0	0	0	0
M B Little John	3	G	9	1	2	0	2,995
M B Sea	5	H	4	0	0	1	7,510
M C Squared	8	G	1	0	0	0	0
M D Twenty Twenty	3	C	12	2	3	1	42,178
M D's Moondancer	5	G	14	0	1	4	8,139
M G On Tap	3	F	1	0	0	0	0
M J Forum	2	C	7	1	0	2	9,775
M J Hamer	3	G	9	0	1	2	7,090
M J in the Morning	5	M	12	3	5	1	20,997
M J Jungle Jayne	3	F	3	0	0	0	0
M J's Gal	2	F	1	1	0	0	9,600
M Js Shady Dawn	5	M	1	0	0	0	315
M K Beck	2	F	5	2	3	0	31,170
M K Le Grand	3	F	3	0	0	0	0
M K Victor	3	G	2	0	0	0	1,919
M L's Star	3	G	7	0	0	0	1,999
M One a One	2	G	1	0	0	0	56
M R Ducks	3	G	3	0	0	0	256
M Town	3	G	5	0	0	1	4,982
M. A. Fox	3	F	8	1	4	1	93,372

Horse	Age	Sex	Sts	1st	2d	3d	Won
M. B. Kate	3	F	4	0	1	0	4,520
M. C. Halo	3	F	4	0	0	0	522
M. C.'s Pride	6	M	4	0	0	0	990
M. G. Ransom	4	G	8	1	0	2	5,410
M. H. Spirit	4	G	1	0	0	0	51
M. J. Express	2	F	1	0	0	0	92
M. J. Point	2	F	4	1	1	0	8,635
M. Jay Hawk	3	G	15	1	5	0	9,297
M. P. Cat	3	C	3	1	1	0	37,200
M. R. Books	4	G	12	1	0	3	18,097
M. S. Balkhair	5	G	7	0	4	1	20,280
Ma Come Pretendi	3	F	5	1	0	0	8,938
Ma Femme	6	M	7	0	1	0	14,969
Ma Home Cat	2	F	1	0	0	1	1,890
Ma Ma Lois	5	M	4	0	0	0	0
Ma Moutski	4	F	2	0	0	0	423
Ma Noblesse (ARG)	5	M	5	0	0	1	5,880
Ma Peche	4	F	8	2	1	1	42,980
Ma Shaz Amio	3	F	2	0	0	0	104
Ma Tuohey	6	M	12	0	0	0	3,090
Maastricht	3	C	3	0	0	0	1,800
Mabelino	4	F	1	0	0	0	810
Mabel's Town	3	F	2	0	0	0	149
Mabilis Lady	5	M	8	0	0	0	768
Mabrooka Haviva	3	F	3	1	1	0	7,785
Mac Daddy	3	G	11	2	3	2	26,372
Mac Justice	6	G	15	3	2	4	33,520
Mac Lady	5	M	7	1	1	1	23,645
Mac Ler	4	C	4	0	0	0	140
Mac Rhapsody (GB)	2	F	3	0	1	1	26,541
Mac the Twister	4	G	4	0	0	0	486
Macaneo (ARG)	7	G	9	0	6	1	48,240
Macann's Promise	3	F	5	0	0	0	3,488
Macao	3	C	5	0	1	1	17,610
Macaquerie	7	G	13	2	0	1	15,867
Macarita	4	F	9	1	2	1	2,458
Maca's Last	10	G	7	0	1	0	1,185
Macatawa Bay	5	G	9	1	2	0	17,770
Macauley Gold	4	G	5	1	1	0	7,700
Macaw (IRE)	5	G	6	1	0	0	37,642
Macbird	4	G	1	0	0	0	67
Macbrae	3	G	6	0	1	0	3,060
Macchiato (FR)	4	C	4	0	1	1	12,520
Macdashi	4	F	8	1	1	0	27,428
Macdavid	6	G	7	0	0	0	526
Macduff	3	G	11	0	2	1	9,557
Macgillicuddy	5	G	2	0	0	0	0
Mach Ones Girl	3	F	12	2	2	4	17,981
Mach Speed	3	C	1	0	0	0	0
Mach Ten	3	G	8	1	1	0	5,540
Mach Twee	3	C	4	1	0	1	17,860
Mach Two	5	H	1	1	0	0	4,620
Machaera	3	C	8	1	1	2	24,336
Machine to Tower	8	G	13	2	2	2	23,413
Machinegunmoutandy	4	C	14	4	2	2	32,505
Macho Bean	5	G	5	0	1	1	2,815
Macho Boss	5	G	4	0	2	0	3,090
Macho Gato	3	C	1	0	0	0	74
Macho Image	4	C	4	0	1	0	2,856
Macho Irish	3	G	15	1	2	0	9,139
Macho Miller	3	C	5	4	0	1	68,579
Macho Mo	2	G	2	0	0	1	1,231
Macho Moon	3	C	10	1	0	0	3,323
Macho Nacho	3	G	3	0	0	0	800
Macho Pancho	3	G	8	0	0	0	576
Macho Rullah	3	C	2	0	0	0	0
Mach's Crown	2	G	4	0	0	0	788
Mack Dee Knife	2	C	5	0	1	1	4,814
Mackay Man	5	G	5	3	1	0	2,904
Mackee's Wish	5	G	8	0	0	2	2,834
Mackelwane	5	H	1	0	0	0	400
Mackenzie Elaine	7	M	2	0	0	0	104
Mackenzie Mist	4	F	15	2	2	4	13,776
Mackenzie Nicole	2	F	3	1	1	0	17,460
Mackenzie's Rock	2	C	1	0	0	0	225
Mackenzies Snow	2	F	5	0	0	2	1,960
Mackinac	4	C	8	1	0	1	20,962
Mackinaw City	4	G	2	0	0	0	0
Mackinaw Island	3	F	8	2	0	2	21,410
Mackintosh	4	G	2	0	0	0	0
Macklenin	2	C	3	0	0	0	4,218
Macks Mardi Graw	4	G	1	0	0	0	0
Macks Pleasure	5	G	3	0	0	0	558
Mack's World	6	M	1	1	0	0	6,000
Macochee Gold	2	F	4	0	1	0	2,490
Macon County	5	G	4	0	2	1	9,580
Macon Dale	4	F	19	1	2	1	17,960
Macon's Magic	4	G	9	0	0	2	3,602
Macrogold	6	M	9	2	1	3	12,143
Mac's First Dance	3	F	3	0	0	0	312
Mac's Flier	4	C	6	0	0	0	1,800
Mac's Golden Lad	4	G	15	2	2	2	20,358
Mac's Hope	4	C	3	0	0	0	285
Mac's Mark	8	G	16	2	1	1	18,995
Macs Sailing Slew	3	G	2	0	0	1	1,260
Mactaceous	2	G	4	0	2	0	6,878
Mactaquac	13	G	2	0	0	0	0
Macward	8	G	4	2	2	0	78,480
Macy B.	5	M	7	0	0	0	2,088
Macy's Boy	4	G	18	2	2	3	22,131
Macy's Grey	2	C	2	0	0	0	112
Mad About Julie	5	M	3	0	0	0	1,847
Mad Adam	2	C	4	2	0	0	19,876
Mad Anthony	5	H	11	0	1	3	18,910
Mad Banshee	3	F	5	0	0	0	0
Mad Dash Manastash	3	G	8	0	2	1	7,528
Mad Donna	4	F	3	0	1	2	3,380
Mad Joe Rielly	3	G	7	1	2	0	9,815
Mad Kipper	6	G	13	3	0	2	14,260
Mad Mac	5	G	8	1	0	1	18,354
Mad Man Max	4	G	6	1	1	2	6,220
Mad Native	4	G	10	3	0	1	33,750
Mad Neil	5	M	5	0	0	0	144
Mad River	8	G	5	0	0	0	500
Mad Salad	4	G	2	0	0	0	74
Mad Season	7	G	12	0	1	3	7,505
Madaboutloot	4	F	16	4	3	0	16,636
Madagascar (ARG)	7	G	3	0	0	0	500
Madalee	3	G	19	1	6	0	19,895
Madam Adam	2	F	4	1	2	0	9,275
Madam Bahri	3	F	1	0	0	0	580
Madam General	4	F	8	1	3	2	74,440
Madam Hertfield	4	F	8	1	4	1	46,710
Madam Hooch	2	F	2	0	0	0	714
Madam Kipper	5	M	7	0	1	4	6,191
Madam Mariko	5	M	7	1	0	0	7,033
Madam Mud	5	M	1	0	0	0	0
Madam P.	4	F	7	0	2	1	13,060
Madam Speaker	4	F	4	0	0	0	5,200
Madam Toolighsboy	3	C	14	1	1	6	28,248
Madam Vogue	3	F	7	0	0	0	384
Madam Whozit	5	M	1	0	0	0	202
Madame Currie	3	F	1	0	0	0	0
Madame Express	5	M	7	3	1	1	15,240
Madame Galore	3	F	5	0	0	0	0
Madame Glamour	5	M	8	2	1	1	28,847
Madame Janette	4	F	8	1	0	1	6,697
Madame Midway	7	M	8	0	1	0	1,870
Madame Pietra	7	M	1	0	0	0	0
Madame Rose	3	F	9	2	0	0	11,550
Madame Rouge	3	F	2	0	0	0	293
Madame Royale	2	F	1	1	0	0	15,000
Madame Stein	5	M	1	0	0	0	40
Madame Sutterfly	4	F	1	0	0	0	0
Madammazel	2	F	1	0	0	0	78
Madamne Q	5	M	8	0	2	1	10,430
Madam's Playboy	2	C	3	0	0	0	0
Madam's Prospect	5	H	2	0	0	0	218
Madcap Escapade	3	F	5	4	0	1	536,400
Madd Maddi	3	F	4	1	0	1	4,230
Maddalena	2	F	1	1	0	0	22,320
Maddashfordinner	3	F	13	3	0	0	24,025
Maddening Cat	3	F	1	0	0	0	0
Maddie H.	4	F	10	0	0	1	1,691
Maddie Irgun	4	F	3	0	0	0	120
Maddie K	5	M	15	1	0	2	4,249
Maddie Miller	3	F	9	0	0	0	2,424
Maddie Rose	5	M	19	2	2	3	14,509

Horse	Age	Sex	Sts	1st	2d	3d	Won
Maddies Blues	4	G	7	3	0	1	14,530
Maddie's Charm	4	F	5	0	0	0	1,725
Maddy Moo	4	F	5	0	0	0	450
Maddy Q	4	F	10	2	0	0	8,844
Maddycakes	4	F	5	0	0	2	962
Maddy's Bobcat	3	G	13	1	0	0	18,600
Maddy's Hero	3	G	9	1	0	3	10,656
Maddy's Lion	2	C	3	1	0	1	35,379
Maddy's Mark	3	F	1	0	0	0	123
Maddy's Partner	4	F	11	2	1	1	14,885
Made Cents	4	G	7	3	1	2	21,442
Made for Taylor	4	C	6	0	1	1	5,030
Made in America	3	F	6	1	1	2	9,290
Made in Marakesh	5	M	1	0	0	0	81
Made Ja Look	5	M	9	0	0	0	1,733
Made Man	2	C	4	0	0	0	1,418
Made Nice	4	G	6	1	0	0	9,364
Made the Basket	4	G	8	0	2	1	3,913
Madeira Mist (IRE)	5	M	8	3	2	2	195,520
Madeittothemoon	7	G	11	0	4	0	7,852
Madeleine's Jade	7	G	6	0	3	0	9,385
Madeline's Fury	2	F	1	0	0	0	135
Madeline's Manor	3	F	4	0	0	0	0
Madera Canyon	6	M	6	2	0	0	23,835
Madge's Prize	3	F	17	3	3	3	40,085
Madigan	5	G	12	3	1	1	14,904
Madi's Magic	6	M	12	2	5	1	10,138
Madison Colony	3	G	2	0	0	0	0
Madison Davis	6	M	7	1	2	1	17,328
Madison Dollie	2	F	6	1	1	2	48,440
Madison Gold	2	F	5	0	0	0	630
Madison Kitty	2	F	1	0	0	0	400
Madison Meadows	3	F	5	2	1	0	25,438
Madison Mill	4	F	4	0	0	1	625
Madison P.	4	F	6	1	1	1	5,557
Madison Ridge	4	F	5	0	0	0	522
Madison's Big Step	6	M	11	0	1	1	3,487
Madison's Music	3	F	8	3	1	1	63,115
Madison's Pleasure	6	M	11	0	1	3	4,301
Madison's Wish	3	F	5	1	1	0	33,850
Madlyn Elise	3	F	10	1	0	2	17,780
Madonna Lily	3	F	2	0	0	0	455
Madringa	4	F	9	2	1	1	81,715
Madrone	3	F	6	1	1	2	41,310
Madson	2	G	3	0	0	0	0
Maduro Haze	2	C	6	0	0	0	511
Mae and Ree	4	F	8	0	1	1	8,442
Mae Be Kate	5	M	11	3	0	0	34,735
Mae East	3	F	2	0	0	0	0
Mae Forces	4	F	11	0	0	0	916
Mae Hap	4	F	10	1	2	1	35,960
Mae Rules	3	F	9	1	1	1	22,239
Maeken Dust	2	C	4	1	0	0	3,737
Maelo	3	G	4	0	0	0	0
Maelstrom	2	F	5	0	1	0	4,140
Mae's Choice	7	M	4	0	2	0	2,380
Maes Gift	2	F	3	0	1	0	3,240
Mae's Mon	5	M	10	0	0	2	10,763
Maestria	4	F	4	0	1	0	4,400
Maestro's Debut	7	G	9	1	2	0	19,070
Mafia Wife	7	M	3	0	0	0	0
Maga Secret	5	G	5	0	0	0	609
Magally Coyote	3	F	4	0	0	0	664
Magarita Mama	2	F	6	1	0	1	6,940
Magarita Midnight	6	M	4	1	0	0	16,440
Maga's Smile	2	C	3	0	1	0	6,230
Magazine	3	G	15	1	4	2	41,840
Magcargo	4	G	3	0	1	0	4,710
Magdalena G. R.	3	F	2	0	0	0	120
Magdaleno	3	C	2	0	0	0	400
Magdelena May	3	G	9	3	1	0	23,712
Magee	5	G	7	2	1	0	23,572
Magestic Doll	4	F	3	0	0	0	1,016
Maggie B B	5	M	3	0	0	0	0
Maggie Brown	3	F	3	0	0	0	708
Maggie Cat	4	F	1	0	0	0	0
Maggie Dee	2	F	3	0	0	0	131
Maggie High	2	F	1	0	0	0	0
Maggie Iam	4	F	6	0	0	0	735
Maggie Jane	7	M	1	0	0	0	0
Maggie McGee	4	F	12	2	0	1	5,420
Maggie Mooster	5	M	2	0	0	0	616
Maggie Morris	3	F	10	2	2	2	20,075
Maggie My Love	3	F	2	0	0	1	1,650
Maggie My Memory	4	F	13	1	0	2	2,822
Maggie O'Mali	2	F	1	0	0	0	1,590
Maggiemakemyday	3	F	4	0	0	0	625
Maggie's Co Ed	5	M	4	0	3	0	6,363
Maggie's Dream	6	M	10	0	4	0	10,540
Maggie's Hat	2	F	4	0	0	0	1,020
Maggies Jeopardy	3	F	12	1	3	2	8,015
Maggie's Mist	3	F	6	2	1	1	16,940
Maggie's Revenge	4	F	6	0	0	0	481
Maggie's Song	5	M	7	0	1	0	1,860
Maggies Storm	3	F	2	0	1	0	3,200
Magi Island	5	M	2	0	0	1	640
Magic	3	F	14	3	3	3	49,405
Magic Alphabet	2	C	7	0	1	2	9,525
Magic At Last	5	M	3	0	1	1	3,150
Magic At Midnight	5	M	6	1	0	1	9,165
Magic Bag	2	C	6	1	2	0	31,510
Magic Bandit	3	G	1	0	0	0	70
Magic Berti	2	C	3	0	1	0	3,600
Magic Bid	5	C	8	0	1	0	2,979
Magic Breeze	4	F	14	2	1	2	16,631
Magic Carbo	8	G	4	0	0	0	155
Magic Cash	4	F	2	0	0	0	0
Magic Catillac	3	F	6	0	0	0	525
Magic Charm	3	F	6	0	0	0	458
Magic City Lass	3	G	2	0	0	1	998
Magic Conqueror	3	G	13	2	3	2	22,243
Magic Copy	5	G	14	1	0	4	3,022
Magic Crystals	5	M	2	0	0	0	0
Magic Cure	2	F	3	0	0	0	1,605
Magic Cutlass	4	G	1	0	0	0	400
Magic Doe	9	G	9	1	2	1	58,975
Magic Ending	6	G	8	1	0	1	7,975
Magic Feather (AUS)	8	G	6	0	0	0	690
Magic Fighter	6	G	10	0	0	0	375
Magic Flare	7	M	11	0	0	2	2,113
Magic Flight	2	C	8	0	2	1	8,358
Magic for Six	2	C	6	1	1	1	31,932
Magic Forum	5	G	12	1	2	3	12,953
Magic Guy	2	C	1	0	0	0	155
Magic Horn (FR)	6	G	4	0	1	0	7,200
Magic in the City	3	F	9	0	1	0	6,960
Magic Ink	4	F	2	0	0	0	222
Magic Island	4	G	3	1	0	0	2,520
Magic Jack	4	C	1	0	0	1	3,630
Magic Jade	3	G	11	1	1	2	29,440
Magic Jake	4	G	11	2	1	1	40,135
Magic Jester	3	G	1	0	0	0	0
Magic Key	6	G	13	0	0	1	1,530
Magic Kipper	3	G	7	1	3	1	16,298
Magic Lantern	5	G	10	1	1	1	16,250
Magic Line	3	F	16	3	3	4	37,540
Magic Love	4	F	5	0	1	0	3,485
Magic Madam	6	M	3	1	1	0	14,400
Magic Malady	5	M	5	0	0	1	610
Magic Mark	3	G	5	0	1	0	5,140
Magic Marty	2	F	3	0	0	0	165
Magic Mary	5	M	12	1	0	1	6,636
Magic Masque (NZ)	5	M	10	2	1	1	14,578
Magic Mecke	4	C	3	0	0	0	40,000
Magic Michael	7	H	4	1	1	0	1,389
Magic Midas	6	M	7	0	0	2	2,881
Magic Miles	7	G	12	0	1	0	1,513
Magic Million	4	F	5	1	1	0	4,140
Magic Mischief	2	G	3	1	0	0	3,480
Magic Mountain	3	C	1	0	0	0	1,020
Magic Muse	3	F	3	1	0	0	4,240
Magic of Spring	3	F	12	1	5	0	35,392
Magic of Stars	11	H	1	0	0	0	80
Magic On Call	3	G	3	0	0	0	40
Magic On Ice	8	G	5	0	1	1	4,113
Magic Peak	5	M	1	0	0	1	4,940
Magic Prospector	4	G	1	0	0	0	0
Magic Rain Dance	4	F	8	1	0	2	5,848

Horse	Age	Sex	Sts	1st	2d	3d	Won
Magic Reign	3	F	11	0	1	0	4,416
Magic Rose	2	F	5	1	1	2	12,120
Magic Rover	6	M	9	1	0	1	3,385
Magic Ruby	4	C	1	0	0	0	0
Magic Secret	4	F	7	0	2	2	10,605
Magic Seranade	2	C	7	0	0	2	4,992
Magic Smoke	4	F	2	0	0	1	3,840
Magic Sparkles	4	F	4	1	0	0	1,270
Magic Speed	2	C	5	1	2	0	46,730
Magic Squall	8	G	6	0	0	1	1,047
Magic Streak	2	F	4	1	2	0	27,400
Magic Strike	4	F	7	1	1	0	5,526
Magic Talker	2	C	5	1	2	0	15,433
Magic Thorne	2	C	4	1	0	0	10,200
Magic Thursday	6	M	3	0	0	1	4,000
Magic Token	3	G	10	0	1	2	6,030
Magic Trial	4	G	14	4	3	1	18,639
Magic Trump	5	M	12	3	0	3	26,746
Magic Twinkle	2	F	3	0	0	0	1,170
Magic Uno	2	F	6	1	1	0	12,930
Magic Valay	5	M	5	0	0	0	0
Magic Valley	3	G	13	1	0	5	10,531
Magic Waltz	2	F	3	0	0	0	930
Magic Weapon	5	M	11	3	0	5	37,786
Magic Wish	5	M	1	0	0	0	0
Magic Wizard	3	G	11	2	0	0	12,560
Magic Yard	3	F	1	0	0	0	0
Magical Blaze	3	F	3	0	0	0	0
Magical Broad	2	F	5	0	3	1	19,200
Magical Dust	3	G	11	2	3	1	60,560
Magical Dynasty	4	G	1	1	0	0	9,600
Magical Gem	3	C	7	0	0	4	11,760
Magical Illusion	3	F	6	3	0	1	141,220
Magical Intrigue	2	F	6	1	1	0	11,229
Magical John	2	G	4	1	1	0	8,167
Magical Madness	7	G	6	0	3	0	4,395
Magical Marlin	3	F	11	2	1	1	36,270
Magical Maxine	2	F	2	1	1	0	8,286
Magical Miss	5	M	4	0	2	1	7,300
Magical Monday	5	M	8	5	0	0	25,282
Magical Moon	3	F	8	1	0	0	4,800
Magical Odds	3	C	1	0	0	0	95
Magical Rascal	5	H	4	0	0	2	2,413
Magical Rush	4	G	14	1	2	4	28,773
Magical Serenade	3	F	3	0	0	0	1,780
Magical Silver	3	G	14	2	0	2	16,008
Magical Story	2	F	1	0	1	0	3,700
Magical Valentine	3	G	16	1	3	3	13,344
Magicalparisbreeze	3	F	11	2	0	2	30,948
Magicians Hattrick	3	F	7	0	0	1	6,209
Magicjakenjohn	3	C	8	3	1	1	29,965
Magicleigh	5	M	12	2	2	3	26,848
Magic's Delight	4	F	3	0	1	0	3,841
Magill's Boy	3	C	5	0	0	0	650
Magi's Mira	11	G	4	0	0	0	105
Magisterium	2	G	1	1	0	0	20,580
Magistretti	4	C	7	1	2	0	782,981
Magloire's Order	3	G	2	0	0	0	0
Magna Charta	2	C	4	0	0	0	290
Magna Cum Laude	4	F	5	0	0	0	1,560
Magna Doll	2	F	2	0	0	0	0
Magna Graduate	2	C	5	2	1	1	76,832
Magna Kat	6	H	6	0	0	1	1,920
Magna Tice	2	G	8	2	1	0	22,647
Magna's Turn	2	F	1	0	0	0	525
Magnata	2	C	8	0	2	0	10,395
Magnetar	4	F	1	0	0	0	0
Magnetic Blondi	3	F	4	0	0	2	946
Magnetic Glo	6	H	2	1	0	0	852
Magnetic Hill (IRE)	6	G	2	0	0	0	235
Magnetic Image	5	G	12	2	1	2	16,609
Magnetic Mel	6	G	10	3	4	0	30,077
Magnettic Affair	4	F	10	1	3	2	27,090
Magnificent	4	F	5	0	0	0	1,590
Magnificent Fly	7	G	9	0	0	0	1,466
Magnificent Matty	5	M	6	1	0	2	7,310
Magnificent Sunset	4	F	7	1	0	3	10,436
Magnificent Val	5	M	7	4	3	0	156,800
Magnified Paradise	3	G	4	0	0	0	264
Magnitude	3	G	3	0	1	0	7,200
Magnitude of One	2	F	1	0	0	0	180
Magnitudo	3	G	3	0	0	0	0
Magnolia Belle	2	F	3	1	0	1	17,750
Magnolia Fields	3	F	7	0	0	0	935
Magnolia Gold	3	F	10	1	2	1	25,731
Magnolia Hall	6	M	5	1	0	1	12,520
Magnolia Lane	4	G	2	0	0	0	142
Magnolia Light	2	F	8	1	1	1	14,940
Magnolia Mae	4	F	5	1	1	0	13,260
Magnolia Park	5	G	7	0	0	1	3,323
Magnolia Ridge	3	F	1	0	0	0	110
Magnum Force	3	G	1	0	0	0	0
Magnum Jazz	3	C	3	0	0	0	680
Magnum Mac	8	G	8	0	1	1	1,632
Mago	2	C	2	0	0	0	1,950
Mago Ilusion	2	G	4	0	0	1	6,822
Magoffin	6	G	16	1	2	1	22,601
Magooch	3	F	8	1	0	1	31,440
Magoo's Magic	2	C	4	2	1	0	70,358
Magruff	4	G	3	0	0	0	140
Magtown Missile	3	C	11	2	4	1	36,245
Magus D' Or	6	G	6	1	1	1	18,820
Magus Wheat	2	C	2	1	0	0	19,200
Maha Rushey	5	G	7	2	0	0	2,450
Mahabarat	7	G	7	2	1	2	3,451
Mahagony Chip	3	G	11	0	3	2	17,042
Mahal	6	G	12	2	1	0	20,343
Mahalo	3	F	4	2	1	1	32,635
Mahane Dan	7	G	3	0	0	1	1,770
Maharishi	2	C	1	0	0	0	300
Mahebo	4	F	5	1	0	2	19,699
Mahera's Angel	8	M	9	2	0	1	3,698
Mahican	3	G	10	3	2	2	66,150
Mahiyah	4	F	11	1	4	2	7,028
Mahogany Blaze	4	G	1	0	0	0	37
Mahogany Midnight	3	C	5	1	1	0	4,400
Mahogany Mink	6	M	2	0	0	0	122
Mahoney	3	G	4	1	0	0	6,840
Mahoning King	3	G	7	1	1	1	13,530
Mahoning Queen	2	F	4	0	2	0	11,000
Mahzouz	3	C	11	3	2	3	136,280
Mai Purple	3	F	7	0	1	1	3,500
Maid for Fun	3	F	1	0	0	0	0
Maid for Speed	2	F	8	1	4	1	33,390
Maid Guinevere	2	F	5	0	1	2	11,080
Maid in China	2	F	3	3	0	0	64,500
Maid in Monroe	3	F	8	2	1	1	9,260
Maid in the Moon	7	M	3	1	0	0	5,720
Maid of Honor	5	M	6	2	0	2	37,930
Maid of Money	4	F	5	1	0	0	12,675
Maid to Run	5	M	6	0	0	0	0
Maiden of Honor	2	F	7	1	1	2	21,900
Maiden Tour	3	F	6	2	1	1	36,555
Maiden Tower (GB)	4	F	1	0	0	0	3,000
Maidens Prayer	3	F	6	1	1	0	42,574
Maidez	3	F	11	1	4	0	65,994
Maidintheshade	3	F	9	2	1	2	46,435
Maid's Folly	5	M	3	0	1	0	1,020
Mail Call	6	G	7	1	2	0	28,455
Mail Car Johnny	2	G	6	0	2	0	6,020
Mail Carrier	6	G	18	4	1	5	9,225
Mail Time	3	C	10	3	1	2	25,110
Maillol (IRE)	2	C	2	0	0	1	6,800
Maimara (ARG)	5	M	7	3	1	0	27,200
Main Card	6	H	2	0	0	0	965
Main Day	6	G	14	0	0	0	1,257
Main Gunner	7	H	7	0	1	0	605
Main Point	2	C	6	0	0	1	8,825
Main Position	4	G	5	0	0	1	606
Main Stream	3	F	4	1	0	0	27,210
Main Street Exit	3	F	5	1	2	1	12,641
Maine Song	5	M	14	2	0	1	34,649
Mainly Henry	5	G	13	2	3	0	16,004
Mainly Irish	4	F	6	1	0	1	3,830
Maintenancemandan	4	G	9	0	1	2	1,436
Maipo	11	G	1	0	0	0	0
Maise and Blue	2	F	3	0	0	0	125
Maisie's Son	3	C	7	0	2	2	19,200

Horse	Age	Sex	Sts	1st	2d	3d	Won
Maita (FR)	5	M	13	1	3	1	10,342
Maitake Gem	5	G	13	0	1	0	1,550
Majesterial	3	C	2	0	0	0	135
Majesterical	5	G	16	1	4	2	21,286
Majestic Alliance	4	F	3	0	0	1	1,765
Majestic Ante	2	C	2	0	0	0	1,215
Majestic Asprey	8	G	4	0	0	0	163
Majestic Cat	7	G	5	0	0	0	310
Majestic Catherine	4	F	11	2	1	1	13,998
Majestic Ceeson	4	F	3	0	0	1	1,000
Majestic Cherokee	3	C	2	0	0	0	0
Majestic Cloud	9	G	2	0	0	0	0
Majestic Commander	4	G	6	2	1	1	64,760
Majestic Cookie	3	C	1	0	0	0	160
Majestic Country	5	G	10	1	0	2	8,711
Majestic Deputy	3	G	9	2	1	1	33,231
Majestic Dinner	7	G	8	1	0	1	30,001
Majestic Fan	6	G	13	1	0	0	3,634
Majestic Girl	5	M	5	0	0	1	2,080
Majestic Glitter	4	F	8	4	0	1	11,100
Majestic Homebuilt	5	H	12	1	3	2	17,960
Majestic Indian	2	G	5	0	0	0	5,820
Majestic Irish	9	H	11	4	1	0	24,990
Majestic Joey	2	G	15	1	2	3	12,383
Majestic Kris	4	C	7	4	1	2	45,164
Majestic Lake	3	C	1	0	0	1	4,500
Majestic Legs	5	M	6	0	0	0	468
Majestic Majesty	10	G	3	0	0	1	735
Majestic Mermaid	4	F	8	0	0	0	621
Majestic Miesque	5	G	7	2	0	0	21,001
Majestic Mike	6	G	14	2	2	5	12,642
Majestic Mommy	4	F	2	1	0	0	7,930
Majestic Orchid	3	F	6	1	0	0	4,411
Majestic Proposal	3	C	4	0	0	0	1,595
Majestic Sir	5	G	14	3	3	3	59,260
Majestic Slewville	2	F	2	0	1	1	6,210
Majestic Smoke	4	F	1	0	0	1	1,644
Majestic Song	5	G	8	0	0	0	4,187
Majestic Storm	2	F	5	0	1	1	6,316
Majestic Sundance	3	G	3	0	0	0	255
Majestic Taylor	2	F	3	0	0	0	3,270
Majestic Thief	5	G	7	1	1	2	54,720
Majestic Tour	3	C	1	0	0	0	0
Majestic Tower	4	G	1	0	0	0	78
Majestic Trick	4	G	3	1	1	0	6,200
Majestic Willie	5	G	6	1	0	2	3,990
Majestic Zeal	2	C	4	1	1	0	21,580
Majestically	2	F	3	2	0	0	64,415
Majestico	2	G	1	0	0	0	273
Majestics View	3	F	6	0	1	1	3,255
Majesty Bay	4	G	5	1	1	0	3,749
Majesty Cat	3	G	7	1	0	0	3,242
Majesty Hill	4	G	2	0	0	0	800
Majesty Mesa	3	G	7	1	0	2	3,433
Majesty Ridge	2	G	2	1	0	0	10,000
Majesty's Fling	7	G	7	0	2	0	4,200
Majesty's Girl	5	M	12	0	2	2	7,219
Majesty's Gold	5	G	5	0	0	1	885
Majesty's Lass	6	M	10	3	1	1	53,848
Majesty's Rolls	6	M	5	0	0	0	365
Majesty's Word	3	F	4	1	0	1	9,075
Maji Kay	4	F	2	0	0	0	600
Majic Clover	2	F	4	1	1	0	5,352
Majic Deal	7	M	6	0	1	1	2,480
Majik Beauty	2	F	2	0	0	0	304
Majo	4	F	16	2	5	1	15,536
Major Alliance	3	C	9	1	4	1	20,589
Major Aloha	6	M	7	0	1	0	1,080
Major Ascot	2	C	5	0	2	0	9,870
Major Barker	4	G	5	0	0	0	552
Major Bay	6	G	11	0	2	1	10,905
Major Blast	3	C	5	1	2	1	23,410
Major Blues	5	G	9	0	2	1	5,730
Major Bo	2	C	3	0	0	0	721
Major Bodgit	4	G	3	0	0	1	525
Major Brass	5	G	6	0	0	0	160
Major Brat Angela	6	M	15	1	2	3	5,947
Major Brick House	2	C	1	0	0	0	135
Major Chrome	3	F	5	0	0	0	1,360

Horse	Age	Sex	Sts	1st	2d	3d	Won
Major City	6	H	16	1	3	3	12,221
Major Contender	3	C	6	0	0	0	720
Major Crisis	5	G	6	0	1	1	2,623
Major Damage	4	G	7	0	0	0	295
Major Dan D.	5	G	2	0	0	0	100
Major Dependent	5	G	9	1	1	1	14,727
Major Dundee	4	G	13	1	1	2	6,736
Major Express	7	G	13	2	0	4	7,817
Major Fitpitcher	3	C	3	0	0	0	386
Major Focus	5	G	8	2	1	0	12,285
Major Forbes	8	G	7	0	0	1	2,910
Major Frank	5	G	1	0	0	0	0
Major Gold	2	G	2	0	0	0	0
Major Guide	5	M	14	0	0	1	1,956
Major Hero	8	G	3	1	1	0	15,300
Major Horn	3	G	10	1	1	3	13,503
Major Idea	4	F	2	0	0	0	3,000
Major Interval	7	G	13	1	4	0	10,229
Major Jonathan	3	C	1	0	0	1	4,100
Major Knight	3	G	5	1	0	1	1,549
Major League	2	C	8	2	3	0	97,100
Major Leaguer	4	C	8	1	2	0	39,017
Major Lightspeed	4	G	2	0	0	0	157
Major Look	3	C	7	1	3	0	19,460
Major Magua	10	G	1	0	0	0	450
Major McLean	2	C	1	0	0	0	0
Major Meadow	3	G	11	0	1	1	5,050
Major Mecke	5	G	10	0	2	0	18,260
Major Melissa	3	F	4	0	0	1	1,138
Major Mill	8	G	1	0	0	0	400
Major Mitch	2	G	7	0	2	2	7,490
Major Mo	3	G	3	0	1	0	1,638
Major Moon	3	F	1	0	0	0	315
Major News	3	C	13	1	2	1	29,253
Major Oak	5	G	6	0	0	0	594
Major Omansky	8	G	5	1	1	0	24,640
Major Parker	3	G	6	0	0	0	2,598
Major Player	3	C	4	0	0	1	3,520
Major Price	3	G	11	2	0	0	18,519
Major Prospector	3	C	2	0	1	0	1,958
Major Ray	3	G	7	1	1	2	6,764
Major Rhythm	5	G	8	3	0	2	147,318
Major Storm	5	H	1	0	0	0	2,150
Major Success	3	C	2	1	0	1	33,360
Major T Rex	4	C	5	1	0	0	1,443
Major Tanner	3	G	5	1	1	1	23,630
Major Yukon	3	C	9	1	2	0	7,440
Major Zee	11	G	5	3	0	0	69,640
Majoressy	3	F	3	0	1	0	5,800
Majors Special	9	G	4	0	0	0	300
Mak Macy Mo	3	F	1	0	0	1	2,860
Maka Me Super	4	G	4	0	2	0	3,840
Makaha	6	G	2	1	0	0	3,396
Makalapua	2	G	4	2	1	0	30,000
Makarumba	4	G	6	1	1	1	39,329
Make a Bee Line	3	C	2	0	0	0	840
Make a Statement	4	F	1	0	0	0	780
Make It Cash	6	G	7	0	2	0	4,803
Make It Fast	4	C	7	1	0	0	2,818
Make It Final	4	G	4	0	1	0	3,100
Make It Payday	3	F	6	0	0	0	787
Make It So Cutie	4	F	6	2	2	2	10,420
Make It Thrilling	3	F	14	0	2	3	7,852
Make Joe's Day	4	G	6	1	1	0	5,920
Make Lemonade	5	G	4	0	0	0	375
Make Love	6	M	9	0	1	1	3,880
Make Me a Champ	13	G	3	1	0	0	22,150
Make Mike's Day	6	G	14	1	3	2	19,275
Make Mine a Makers	4	F	2	0	0	0	80
Make Mine Silver	2	C	2	0	0	0	0
Make Mine Violets	3	F	2	1	0	0	11,480
Make My Day Jur	4	G	2	0	1	0	12,000
Make My Heart Sing	3	F	8	1	1	1	25,717
Make My Millenium	6	G	5	2	2	0	36,400
Make Smart	8	G	4	0	1	0	3,225
Make the Bend	5	H	2	0	0	0	550
Make the Deal	5	G	10	1	3	1	21,551
Make the Deposit	5	M	3	1	0	2	4,770
Make Your Move	5	G	10	1	1	1	11,114

Horse	Age	Sex	Sts	1st	2d	3d	Won
Make Your Own	6	G	5	1	0	1	11,500
Make'er Roll	3	F	9	1	5	1	10,569
Makem Hagar	9	G	4	0	1	1	6,222
Makemeanoffer	4	G	7	0	0	1	1,289
Makemineagoldmine	3	G	6	1	1	2	7,200
Makemquitngohome	3	F	3	1	0	1	6,922
Makena North	4	C	2	1	0	0	4,575
Makers At Midnight	3	C	3	0	1	0	12,350
Makes a Fist	6	M	6	0	2	0	2,938
Makes More Sense	9	H	1	0	0	0	0
Makes Sense to Me	4	F	7	0	1	0	3,300
Makeshift	3	G	3	0	1	1	8,000
Makesyourheadspin	2	C	5	2	0	1	6,305
Makeup Artist	4	F	5	0	1	1	29,194
Makeup Girl	3	F	3	0	0	0	460
Makewayforbighoss	9	G	7	4	2	0	5,079
Makewayforwendy	4	F	1	0	0	0	340
Makin Headlines	4	C	10	2	0	0	17,922
Makin Sunrise	2	F	2	0	0	0	336
Makin Trouble	4	C	7	0	1	2	3,915
Makin Violets	2	F	4	0	0	0	552
Making Believe	2	F	2	1	0	0	8,100
Making My Move	6	G	7	1	0	2	13,900
Making Nauts	4	G	3	0	0	0	243
Making Waves	4	G	5	0	1	1	3,400
Makingthegrade	4	F	9	0	0	0	962
Makinmehappy	2	F	5	0	0	0	0
Maki's Pleasure	4	G	2	0	0	0	225
Makoo	6	M	11	0	0	0	758
Makowish	2	G	2	0	0	1	1,725
Maktub (ITY)	5	H	7	0	3	0	194,275
Malachite	4	G	13	0	1	0	2,560
Maladyscat	5	M	5	1	2	1	8,062
Malagambo	3	C	9	0	3	0	7,248
Malagash	6	G	1	0	0	0	0
Malagra's Encore	3	G	14	1	2	4	18,284
Malagra's Gem	4	G	6	1	1	0	8,577
Malagrasmillennium	6	H	2	0	0	0	0
Malagreaux	3	G	9	1	2	1	27,430
Malalco	5	G	9	3	2	1	16,782
Malalucy	3	F	10	3	0	0	43,373
Malanato	2	C	7	4	1	1	99,020
Malawi Bay	3	F	11	3	2	1	20,150
Malawi Maid	3	F	10	1	0	1	5,485
Malaysia (GB)	3	F	3	0	0	0	5,520
Malcolm Miss	5	M	13	0	6	1	10,563
Malcolmsmile	4	G	23	1	3	6	18,654
Maldaki	4	G	4	0	0	0	415
Maldives	3	F	1	0	0	0	0
Male Vision	3	G	9	2	2	2	36,514
Maleficio	3	G	13	1	1	0	7,750
Malesian Cat	4	F	2	0	0	0	90
Malfoy	3	F	9	0	0	0	1,398
Malheur	2	C	4	1	1	1	42,988
Malibu Al	3	G	3	0	1	0	7,440
Malibu Baby	3	G	15	1	3	0	29,200
Malibu Barbi	3	F	6	0	1	0	1,620
Malibu Baybreeze	3	C	2	0	0	0	600
Malibu Beau	2	C	4	0	0	0	1,250
Malibu Gal	2	F	3	0	0	1	6,287
Malibu Jack	6	G	8	1	2	0	10,158
Malibu Kat	3	F	5	1	0	0	17,495
Malibu Man	4	G	6	1	1	2	21,810
Malibu Maybe	2	C	1	0	0	0	0
Malibu Miss	3	F	7	1	1	1	12,030
Malibu Momma	4	F	1	1	0	0	5,775
Malibu Moonbeam	3	F	1	0	1	0	5,040
Malibu Moonshine	2	C	6	3	0	0	65,280
Malibu Punch	3	F	8	2	2	0	34,110
Malibu Society	3	G	2	0	0	0	0
Malibu Sun	2	F	2	1	0	0	17,820
Malibu Sunset	2	C	2	1	0	0	9,000
Malibu Trick	3	F	1	0	0	0	0
Maliciousintention	3	G	12	3	2	3	31,598
Malifino	3	G	16	1	2	3	27,345
Malign	3	F	4	0	0	0	298
Malik Silver	7	H	10	0	3	0	5,355
Malikah	5	M	5	1	1	0	2,176
Malika's Gold	2	F	4	2	0	0	74,400

Horse	Age	Sex	Sts	1st	2d	3d	Won
Malindi	3	F	3	0	1	0	3,265
Mall (CHI)	7	G	6	1	1	2	24,000
Mallard	6	G	6	0	1	1	1,856
Mallory's Charger	7	M	2	0	0	0	276
Mallory's Star	6	M	3	0	0	0	1,089
Malmaison	5	G	13	0	2	3	33,760
Malmas	2	F	1	0	1	0	5,600
Malmo Match	6	H	3	1	0	1	9,500
Malmo's Tough Boy	4	G	10	1	1	0	5,326
Malo	5	M	10	4	3	0	84,155
Malo Halo	9	M	11	0	0	2	4,380
Maloboy	2	C	1	0	1	0	3,300
Malocchio	3	G	5	0	0	1	2,079
Malone	5	G	3	0	0	1	935
Maloya's Sun	5	G	10	0	2	0	1,315
Maltese Baby	4	F	4	0	2	0	10,550
Mama Kin	3	F	4	0	0	0	1,133
Mama Tried	7	M	3	0	0	0	0
Mamacafe	5	M	20	4	3	6	28,367
Mamaison Star	4	G	7	2	4	0	27,793
Mamaleen	7	M	4	0	0	1	11,486
Mamaroni	2	C	2	0	0	0	150
Mama's Advice	4	F	10	0	1	0	5,566
Mama's Copy	3	F	3	0	0	0	2,242
Mama's Gotta Go	5	M	9	1	4	1	20,267
Mama's Joy	4	G	20	5	2	2	72,940
Mama's Lil' Mon	2	G	4	1	0	1	9,255
Mama's Lucky Star	3	G	4	0	0	1	1,100
Mama's Magic	3	F	14	1	1	4	15,995
Mama'sgoldsong	6	M	2	0	0	0	0
Mamatuks	6	M	13	1	0	1	4,723
Mamba King	4	G	6	0	1	0	10,548
Mambo Bell	3	F	8	2	2	2	81,284
Mambo Dancer (CHI)	5	G	7	1	1	0	39,820
Mambo Jewel	3	F	7	2	0	1	15,903
Mambo Man	5	G	7	0	3	0	6,599
Mambo Mia	4	F	7	0	0	1	1,158
Mambo Moon	3	G	8	0	0	2	8,231
Mambo Music	3	F	4	0	1	0	2,747
Mambo Slew	3	F	8	2	2	0	183,820
Mambo Til Midnite	5	G	3	0	1	0	3,060
Mambo Train	3	C	5	1	0	0	92,688
Mamboaire	4	G	7	1	2	2	43,780
Mamboalot	4	F	3	1	0	0	19,200
Mambolero	7	G	3	0	0	0	539
Mambo's Delight	8	G	17	1	1	4	7,982
Mame	5	M	1	0	0	0	0
Mamie Jamie	4	F	6	0	1	0	2,185
Mamie Mom	3	F	11	1	1	2	9,732
Mamma Maria	2	F	1	0	0	0	0
Mammy	3	F	2	0	0	0	60
Mamone	5	G	6	1	2	0	11,525
Mamonia Gold	2	F	5	1	0	1	20,760
Mamosa	4	F	16	1	1	2	24,565
Man Among Men	4	C	1	1	0	0	38,776
Man Apart	2	C	3	0	1	0	5,322
Man At Arms	2	C	1	0	0	1	1,800
Man From Artemus	5	G	2	0	0	0	1,000
Man From Wicklow	7	G	3	0	0	0	0
Man in the Moon	2	G	1	0	1	0	3,200
Man o' Rhythm	7	G	12	3	1	3	64,590
Man o' Roar	4	G	8	1	1	0	13,113
Man of Conquest	3	C	16	3	0	1	42,583
Man of Danger	2	G	2	1	0	0	20,400
Man of Few Words	3	C	9	1	0	0	19,940
Man of Means	8	G	15	0	1	1	2,838
Man of Mystery	5	H	4	1	0	0	2,760
Man O'Mystery	7	G	6	0	1	0	3,600
Man On a Mission	3	C	4	1	0	0	16,062
Man On a String	2	G	2	1	1	0	31,340
Man On the Go	9	G	5	1	0	0	6,605
Man Overboard	10	G	3	0	0	0	342
Man the Shipp	10	G	5	0	0	1	1,457
Man Well	4	G	8	2	0	0	7,823
Mana Torpedoes	7	G	12	0	0	1	1,464
Manabozho (AUS)	6	G	7	1	1	0	16,530
Manalapan Academy	6	G	1	0	0	0	0
Mananan McLir	5	H	7	1	0	1	48,200
Manassas	4	G	26	2	0	5	27,140

Horse	Age	Sex	Sts	1st	2d	3d	Won
Manassas Two	2	C	2	0	0	0	0
Manastash Nation	5	G	12	0	2	1	5,376
Manastash's Doll	7	M	6	0	0	0	550
Manaus	4	G	8	0	0	0	5,937
Manay K.	4	F	5	0	0	0	208
Manchac Man	6	G	4	0	0	0	480
Manchenee	4	F	8	0	0	0	809
Manchineel	4	G	10	1	1	0	6,280
Manchurian	4	C	2	1	0	0	32,640
Mandalay Man	2	G	1	0	0	0	0
Mandango	8	H	4	0	0	0	660
Manda's Apple	4	F	15	2	3	0	21,410
Manda's Wheel	2	G	11	0	1	2	8,069
Mandela (GER)	4	F	3	1	0	1	66,600
Mandella	6	M	7	0	2	1	4,997
Mandera Ridge	2	F	6	0	3	2	9,880
Manderin Magic	3	F	2	0	0	0	951
Mandi Tambi	2	F	8	2	2	1	51,113
Mandinga	2	F	1	0	0	0	0
Mandisa	5	M	14	0	0	1	1,614
Manduilovekentucky	2	G	1	0	0	0	400
Mandy Belle	4	F	2	0	0	0	154
Mandy G	7	M	7	1	1	1	10,980
Mandyhubbymike	3	G	10	3	0	3	38,460
Mandylynn	5	M	1	0	0	0	0
Mandy's Magic	3	F	11	1	0	0	3,727
Mandy's Man	4	G	4	0	1	2	8,805
Mandys Prize	3	F	9	2	2	0	10,007
Mane Explosion	8	G	4	0	0	2	548
Mane Mission	10	G	5	1	0	0	1,800
Maneater	5	M	6	0	0	1	966
Manele	4	C	4	0	0	2	2,760
Maneuverable	4	G	6	0	0	0	9,600
Manfromcolorado	4	C	10	2	4	0	12,566
Mangazo (ARG)	5	G	8	0	1	0	4,593
Mangetakk	2	G	1	0	0	0	140
Mangiaracina	2	C	1	0	0	0	129
Mango Escapade	4	F	14	2	1	4	93,370
Mango Lassie	3	F	8	2	1	0	35,430
Mangusta	6	G	5	2	1	0	14,765
Manhandler	2	F	1	0	0	0	205
Manhattan Alice	6	M	3	0	0	0	0
Manhattan Appeal	2	F	4	2	0	1	30,040
Manhattan Beach	3	C	17	4	4	1	42,518
Manhattan Days	4	C	6	1	0	0	5,366
Manhattan Express	4	G	15	0	1	1	29,224
Manhattan Miner	4	F	11	0	3	3	27,606
Manhattan Moment	4	F	8	2	0	3	15,900
Manhattan Nights	4	G	15	2	2	0	31,180
Manhattan's Mo	3	F	7	2	0	2	15,670
Manhatten Punch	3	F	3	0	0	0	0
Manhunt	4	F	10	0	1	3	8,062
Manicomio Tom (ARG)	7	G	10	1	1	3	11,329
Manifest Mary	3	F	8	0	0	3	3,767
Manila Bay	2	F	2	0	0	0	710
Manila Fudge	2	F	1	0	0	0	840
Manila Light	8	G	1	0	0	0	0
Manila Summer	6	G	8	1	0	1	4,630
Manila Vanilli	4	F	9	1	1	1	10,618
Maninyalife	5	G	1	0	0	0	75
Manipulator	3	C	4	1	0	1	35,310
Manipulator (IRE)	3	C	1	0	0	0	0
Maniqui	3	C	9	0	2	0	12,770
Manish	2	G	2	0	0	0	1,710
Manito Gentleman	5	G	4	1	0	0	1,540
Manitoba Storm	3	F	2	0	1	0	1,350
Manitowish	7	G	8	1	2	1	61,804
Manitoy	3	C	10	2	1	1	29,750
Manjrekar	3	G	6	0	1	0	2,965
Manly Jack (NZ)	6	G	9	0	1	0	4,900
Manly Valentine	9	G	5	0	0	2	3,043
Mannered	12	G	9	1	0	0	3,840
Manners Choice	3	C	3	0	0	0	240
Mannie's Mistake	6	G	16	2	2	2	21,309
Manniwaki	2	F	2	0	0	0	200
Mannszville	2	C	3	0	0	0	249
Mannymissedagain	5	H	2	0	0	0	220
Manofglory	7	G	7	1	1	0	50,584
Manofthecloth	5	G	4	0	1	1	3,555

Horse	Age	Sex	Sts	1st	2d	3d	Won
Manofthehour	3	G	1	0	0	0	400
Manonthemove	5	G	7	0	1	1	5,125
Manor House	3	C	1	0	0	0	0
Manor Springs	6	M	2	0	0	0	125
Manosh	3	C	2	0	0	0	800
Manowasso	4	C	5	0	0	0	688
Man's Candy	8	M	1	0	0	0	0
Man's Gold	4	F	2	0	0	0	150
Mansilver	5	G	3	1	1	0	9,106
Mansita	3	F	3	0	0	0	465
Mansmind	2	C	3	0	0	1	6,971
Manstone	6	M	14	0	1	4	5,245
Mantin Riggs	2	C	2	0	0	0	184
Mantles Fantasy	2	F	2	0	0	1	990
Mantova Run	2	F	6	1	1	0	22,600
Mantra	5	M	1	0	0	0	169
Mantua	3	F	11	0	1	0	4,840
Manulamu	4	G	19	0	2	3	8,930
Manwhataqueen	4	F	4	0	1	1	3,100
Many Cats	2	F	6	0	1	1	4,960
Many Many Bows	3	F	13	4	5	0	89,720
Many Many Joys	2	F	7	0	1	3	9,220
Many Ministers	6	G	8	2	0	2	7,211
Many of Win's	2	F	3	0	1	1	3,750
Many Times Over	10	M	8	1	0	0	4,761
Manzanola	11	G	4	0	0	0	259
Manzee Blue	5	M	9	1	2	2	43,712
Manzotti Queen	4	F	2	0	0	0	372
Manzotti's Guest	4	C	3	0	0	0	1,410
Mapani	3	F	5	0	0	0	1,150
Mapeb	7	H	5	1	0	1	8,492
Maple	3	F	2	0	0	0	740
Maple Creek Magic	4	F	6	1	0	0	4,457
Maple Hill	5	G	3	0	0	0	340
Maple Meadow	3	F	2	0	0	0	316
Maple Park Road	4	F	14	1	2	2	5,562
Maple Syrple	3	F	4	0	0	0	4,632
Maplestreet Memory	4	F	8	0	2	3	4,467
Mapp Hill	5	G	9	1	0	2	26,540
Maps Marketing	4	G	10	3	0	2	8,643
Mapuchita	5	M	5	1	1	1	10,664
Mar Cielo	3	F	3	0	0	0	0
Mar Rojo	5	H	7	3	1	0	12,500
Mara Queen	5	M	5	1	0	0	4,106
Marais des Cygne	4	F	11	1	1	0	10,658
Maramec	3	G	4	2	1	0	23,200
Maranella	4	F	12	2	3	1	10,229
Maranilla (IRE)	5	G	3	0	0	0	2,340
Marathon Man	4	C	5	0	0	0	760
Marauder Thunder	3	G	7	1	0	2	4,760
Maravich	7	G	3	0	0	0	195
Marazdotz	8	M	3	0	0	0	120
Marbella Girl	3	F	8	2	2	1	33,660
Marbleous Kiss	3	F	11	1	3	2	20,325
Marbury	4	G	12	1	2	1	26,100
Marc Medown	2	C	7	0	2	0	6,370
Marceau	6	G	5	0	0	0	225
Marcelia (GB)	3	F	7	0	0	0	1,420
March Bloom	6	M	12	0	0	1	1,475
March Brown	5	H	2	0	1	1	6,750
March Dancer	2	C	1	0	0	1	3,600
March Hare	5	M	10	2	2	0	7,846
March of Ides	4	G	7	2	1	0	7,823
March Snowflake	5	M	8	1	1	1	2,893
March to the Bank	5	M	1	0	0	0	0
March With Me	2	G	6	2	0	0	92,050
Marchand	3	C	2	0	0	0	250
Marchand Volant (FR)	6	G	8	0	1	1	2,190
Marche Bay	2	F	4	0	0	1	945
Marchella	2	F	6	0	1	0	5,196
Marching	3	F	1	0	0	0	320
Marching Band	4	C	6	1	0	1	14,694
Marching Orders	5	G	9	1	2	1	26,860
Marching Rhythm	4	F	12	1	3	4	46,360
Marchonin	2	F	2	0	0	0	1,530
Marcie's Band	2	C	4	0	0	1	1,544
Marcies Choice Ice	5	G	14	1	1	3	9,642
Marco Be Good	2	G	2	0	0	0	0
Marco Cat	4	F	2	0	0	0	392

Horse	Age	Sex	Sts	1st	2d	3d	Won
Marco Mac	5	G	3	0	0	0	270
Marco Mania	3	F	1	0	0	0	0
Marco Pleasure	4	G	9	1	0	1	9,150
Marco Ridge	4	G	6	0	0	1	1,198
Marco T	6	G	7	2	3	0	12,070
Marcola	4	G	5	1	1	0	7,610
Marco's Word	6	G	12	4	0	3	120,230
Marc's Candy	5	G	3	0	0	0	460
Marc's Rainbow	4	F	2	0	0	0	2,228
Marcus Ibis	9	G	3	0	0	0	0
Marcutio	5	G	2	0	0	0	600
Marcy's Dancer	4	F	8	0	0	2	5,496
Marcys Emperor	7	G	6	0	3	0	7,416
Marcy's Hope	4	F	14	1	2	2	9,725
Marcy's Oscar	3	G	6	0	0	0	518
Marcy's Red	7	G	8	1	2	0	6,782
Mardi Gras Cat	5	M	1	0	0	0	0
Mardi Gras Marie	6	M	6	0	0	0	443
Mardi Gras Sauce	6	G	7	0	1	2	6,859
Mardigrascolors	4	G	5	0	0	1	1,017
Mardo Kayo	2	G	3	0	0	1	1,600
Mare Donna	4	F	11	1	3	2	18,231
Maren Approved	3	F	11	2	2	2	59,730
Maresha	5	M	7	0	0	1	13,554
Marfalous Star	7	G	1	0	0	0	40
Marfa's Lady Rhome	5	M	4	1	0	0	3,660
Marfa's Prospect	4	G	7	1	1	0	5,695
Marfa's Ridge	4	G	2	0	1	1	5,275
Marfa's Taxes	7	M	14	3	3	1	67,644
Marfin Dancer	5	M	1	0	0	0	0
Margaret Anne	3	F	9	1	0	2	42,440
Margaret's Fancy (IRE)	4	F	3	0	1	0	1,368
Margaretscheckbook	2	F	5	0	0	0	890
Margarita Maggie	3	F	5	1	1	1	19,080
Margaritafill	4	F	12	2	2	3	5,308
Margaritalosflores	2	C	2	0	0	0	800
Marge S	2	F	2	0	0	0	1,310
Margeds Dandy	6	G	7	1	1	2	18,300
Margeds Delight	4	F	4	0	0	2	3,647
Marge's Bid	4	F	23	3	0	5	24,695
Marges Stage	3	F	14	1	0	2	6,808
Margie Ann's Pride	3	F	2	0	0	0	0
Margie B	5	M	4	0	0	1	660
Margie Golden	3	F	4	0	0	0	142
Margie Good	4	F	2	0	0	0	247
Margie's Apeel	5	M	3	0	0	0	0
Margie's Echo	3	F	4	0	0	0	1,670
Margin Call	3	G	15	0	1	3	4,801
Margin Drive	4	F	3	0	0	1	790
Margin of Victory	2	C	1	0	0	0	795
Margo Duke	3	F	5	2	0	0	11,523
Margold	3	F	4	1	0	0	6,232
Margo's Boy	3	G	1	0	0	0	525
Margo's Pleasure	2	F	2	0	0	0	535
Margos Rib	3	F	12	1	0	3	6,752
Marhaba	3	F	3	0	0	0	800
Maria	7	M	12	1	0	3	17,196
Maria Clarissa	3	F	5	0	0	2	15,193
Maria Elena's King	5	G	2	0	0	0	158
Maria Farina	4	F	13	0	1	1	3,387
Maria Ferrante	5	M	5	1	0	1	1,194
Maria Is Business	8	M	8	0	0	0	1,972
Maria Kay	5	M	12	3	2	2	10,223
Maria Laya	3	F	4	0	0	1	1,800
Maria Lo Riena	3	F	5	0	1	2	2,000
Maria Pistola	3	F	14	3	4	4	14,324
Mariachi	2	G	9	0	0	0	2,700
Mariah Carrie	4	F	5	1	1	0	2,468
Mariah Prince	4	G	5	1	0	0	5,235
Mariah's Bullet	3	F	15	2	1	7	40,455
Mariah's Joy	3	F	6	0	0	1	3,025
Mariakel	4	F	11	1	3	2	76,558
Marian Centre	2	C	2	0	0	0	0
Marian's Muse	5	M	8	0	0	0	1,143
Maria's Best	3	F	2	0	0	0	240
Maria's Class	2	F	4	0	0	0	780
Marias Ecliptical	4	G	6	1	0	0	21,862
Maria's Halo	4	F	3	0	1	1	3,500
Maria's Image	4	F	22	5	4	6	126,380
Maria's Magic	3	F	20	5	3	1	28,031
Maria's Malo	2	G	5	0	0	0	860
Maria's Mojo	4	F	14	2	1	1	19,361
Maria's Posada	2	F	8	1	2	0	28,893
Maria's Pride	3	F	10	2	5	2	61,797
Maria's Reprized	2	F	4	0	0	4	3,950
Maria's Sunshine	6	M	12	2	0	1	14,339
Mariatom	10	G	14	2	2	0	12,111
Mariaworth	6	M	7	2	0	3	38,685
Maricopa	2	F	1	0	0	0	150
Maries Can of Gold	6	M	1	0	0	0	0
Marie's Eye Deal	2	F	1	0	0	0	0
Marie's Girl	5	M	5	0	1	0	737
Marie's Rose	3	F	6	2	0	3	84,486
Marie's Sunshine	3	F	5	0	0	0	588
Marie's Valentine	2	F	10	0	0	0	2,470
Marietta's Charm	5	M	3	0	0	0	0
Mariflor	3	F	15	0	0	2	3,566
Marigot Red	5	G	7	1	1	2	18,370
Marilyn My Marilyn	6	M	7	0	4	1	10,020
Marima	4	F	7	2	1	0	92,294
Marimar Light	2	F	1	0	0	0	125
Marimba Cat	2	G	3	0	0	0	0
Marina de Chavon	3	F	9	2	0	1	58,950
Marina Light	2	F	7	0	2	3	13,660
Marina Minister	4	G	17	2	6	2	102,975
Marina Mon	4	G	17	2	1	0	6,387
Marinara	4	G	11	1	0	2	10,946
Marine	8	G	4	0	0	0	0
Marine (GB)	6	G	7	1	2	0	14,105
Marine Drive	7	G	9	0	3	2	9,243
Marine Gunny	5	G	8	1	1	2	6,675
Marine Landing	6	G	11	1	1	1	13,707
Marine Matt	3	C	13	4	3	2	44,025
Marine Plt.	7	G	3	0	0	0	0
Marine Point	3	G	3	0	0	0	225
Marine Salute	5	H	1	0	0	0	72
Marine Seal	2	C	2	0	0	1	4,320
Marine Sgt Major	5	G	5	0	2	0	3,553
Marineland	3	F	18	0	1	0	3,640
Mariner's Knot	4	C	3	0	0	0	0
Marino Feliz (CHI)	6	G	2	0	0	1	1,870
Marino Marini	4	C	5	0	2	1	87,025
Marion Co Cat	5	G	9	0	2	0	2,784
Marionette	5	M	4	2	0	1	67,340
Marion's Man	4	G	16	1	5	5	64,750
Mario's Mirage	4	F	3	0	2	0	11,120
Mario's Music	4	C	1	0	0	0	0
Mariquita's Secret	8	M	11	3	0	0	26,700
Mari's Pride	4	F	1	0	0	0	42
Mari's Quest	2	C	2	1	0	0	11,728
Marisa Go	7	M	7	0	1	0	20,387
Marisleysis	4	F	8	0	2	2	6,230
Maristen	2	F	2	0	0	0	125
Marius	3	C	8	0	1	2	7,700
Marjan	4	G	13	2	4	2	18,929
Marjorie V.	3	F	8	3	1	0	8,906
Marjorymorningstar	4	F	4	0	1	1	9,194
Mark	8	G	5	0	0	0	165
Mark Aim Fire	4	F	7	2	2	0	22,130
Mark de Triomphe	7	G	7	1	0	0	14,840
Mark Me Gone	2	C	1	0	0	0	0
Mark of Courage	4	G	3	1	0	1	16,920
Mark of Diablo	3	C	4	2	0	1	42,330
Mark of Perfection	5	M	10	2	1	2	23,448
Mark of Texas	3	F	12	0	3	2	6,384
Mark of the Dragon	4	G	11	1	2	2	14,830
Mark of Victory	2	G	8	1	1	0	16,780
Mark One	5	G	10	3	3	1	378,988
Mark Out Rythm	3	G	10	1	1	0	5,835
Mark Pepn G	4	G	14	1	3	1	25,225
Mark the Ransom	2	F	1	0	0	0	1,260
Mark the Shade	5	G	16	3	1	3	26,509
Mark the Shark	5	G	4	1	0	0	7,200
Mark This Date	2	C	2	0	0	2	1,870
Mark This Rose	2	F	3	0	0	0	1,000
Mark Twelve	5	G	12	3	4	0	55,260
Mark U With Class	6	M	4	0	0	2	1,897
Markdown	3	C	8	2	0	2	11,640

Horse	Age	Sex	Sts	1st	2d	3d	Won
Marked Ace	7	G	7	0	0	0	346
Marked Bills	3	C	5	1	0	0	21,070
Marked Distinction	2	C	2	0	1	1	3,085
Marked Express	3	F	2	0	0	0	360
Marked for Cash	4	G	6	0	0	0	315
Marked for Gold	5	G	3	0	0	0	225
Marked for Promise	6	G	10	2	1	3	8,576
Marked for Ransom	4	G	10	3	0	0	15,437
Marked for Sucess	5	M	4	1	1	0	7,736
Marked Leader	4	F	2	0	1	0	1,200
Marked Native	7	G	17	2	2	1	14,155
Marked Outlaw	4	G	1	0	0	0	0
Marked Prince	4	C	10	2	0	0	11,226
Marked Private	4	G	12	1	3	0	7,995
Marked Quality	2	C	3	0	0	0	528
Marked Secret	3	F	9	1	0	0	6,264
Marked Silver	6	M	8	2	1	2	18,740
Marked to Run	3	G	14	0	6	1	13,160
Marked Widow	2	F	4	0	0	0	0
Marked Wish	7	H	11	1	4	4	10,628
Markedwithattitude	3	F	2	0	0	0	0
Markee Girl	5	M	3	0	0	0	128
Markervilleexpress	4	G	10	1	2	2	10,589
Market Advance	7	G	5	0	0	0	540
Market Affair	3	G	3	0	0	3	2,310
Market Arcade	4	C	3	0	0	0	980
Market Basket	2	G	2	1	0	0	6,825
Market Bottom	4	F	9	0	0	2	865
Market Bridge	3	F	10	1	1	1	8,545
Market Factors	4	F	10	3	2	2	16,267
Market Forecast	7	H	4	0	0	2	2,905
Market Garden	4	F	16	4	4	5	246,658
Market Guru	4	F	15	2	0	3	41,046
Market High	5	G	5	2	1	0	15,100
Market Hunter	5	G	7	0	0	0	476
Market Madam	3	F	2	0	0	0	0
Market Master	10	G	6	3	2	0	10,639
Market Meltdown	7	G	5	0	0	0	132
Market Power	4	F	3	1	0	0	6,765
Market Research	2	F	7	0	1	2	12,000
Market Secret	4	F	1	0	0	0	82
Market Street	4	C	1	0	0	0	0
Marketable	2	F	5	2	0	2	40,874
Market's Best	5	M	6	1	0	1	11,242
Marketsfinest	3	F	14	0	1	4	14,249
Markofexcess	2	G	4	2	0	0	23,400
Mark's Mad At Me	3	G	5	1	0	1	22,028
Mark's Mane Man	8	G	25	3	4	5	19,879
Marks Mark	10	G	8	2	3	0	12,743
Mark's Miner	6	G	2	0	0	0	480
Mark's Mission	6	M	7	0	0	1	3,020
Mark's Reward	4	F	5	0	0	0	348
Mark's Spirit	4	G	18	1	2	2	18,180
Marks Tree Two	5	G	7	0	0	0	664
Mark's Untouchable	3	G	9	1	0	1	13,885
Mark's Way	3	G	5	0	0	0	1,640
Marktwentyfive	6	G	12	0	0	1	1,784
Markye Royal	4	C	9	0	0	0	1,411
Marky's Man	8	G	15	1	2	0	6,404
Marla Bay	3	F	10	1	1	4	39,570
Marla Gold	3	F	6	0	0	1	3,555
Marla T	4	F	8	3	1	1	13,750
Marland	5	G	9	0	1	1	2,934
Marlarky	6	G	9	0	1	2	2,074
Marlene Plus	3	F	2	0	0	1	1,350
Marlene's Machine	3	G	11	0	2	1	4,292
Marley Hart	4	F	9	1	1	2	19,140
Marley's Revenge	3	G	10	3	0	3	86,955
Marlig	3	C	1	0	0	0	0
Marlin Bay	2	F	9	0	3	2	14,180
Marlin Dance	4	F	6	0	0	0	0
Marlin Monroe	4	C	3	0	0	0	1,200
Marlin 'n Motion	4	G	6	0	0	0	189
Marlindsey	2	F	4	0	0	0	2,710
Marlins Dancer	3	F	3	1	0	0	10,300
Marlin's Memory	3	G	3	0	0	0	0
Marlin's Nurse	5	M	3	0	0	0	675
Marlin's Rose	4	F	5	0	0	1	3,345
Marlin's Ruler	6	G	7	2	0	1	7,375
Marliz	4	F	9	1	1	5	14,180
Marllyn's Girl	3	F	1	0	0	0	0
Marlotta	3	F	9	3	2	0	31,427
Marlukin	6	G	13	1	3	1	30,165
Marlwood	8	G	1	0	0	0	63
Marmie's Promise	2	F	1	0	0	0	0
Marnesia Boy	2	C	5	1	0	0	21,280
Marnesia Light	4	F	8	1	0	1	29,020
Marnie's Heirloom	3	F	9	1	0	2	32,199
Marnie's Wish	5	M	6	1	1	1	3,460
Marnita	4	F	2	0	2	0	9,520
Marq Time	3	G	16	2	2	3	20,499
Marq Tribute	5	H	2	0	0	0	294
Marqita	3	F	1	0	0	0	250
Marquee	3	F	2	0	1	0	1,530
Marquee Affair	3	G	8	1	0	1	7,860
Marquee Bill	2	C	1	0	0	0	0
Marquee Kelly	5	M	1	0	0	0	300
Marquee Mark	5	G	10	1	0	2	8,043
Marquee's Starlett	3	F	3	0	0	0	0
Marque's Account	2	C	1	0	0	0	180
Marquet First	4	F	8	3	1	2	31,913
Marquet Gold	3	C	11	1	0	2	12,076
Marquet Legend	3	G	13	2	0	2	25,500
Marquet Rate	4	F	18	4	2	2	57,990
Marquet Rent	5	M	9	2	1	1	54,880
Marquet Star	3	C	1	0	0	0	75
Marquetarian	3	G	6	2	2	0	11,884
Marquetheat	4	F	1	0	0	0	360
Marquethi	7	H	2	0	0	0	138
Marquetry Ridge	7	G	5	0	1	0	3,604
Marquetryinmotion	3	F	16	3	3	3	23,221
Marquetrys Crown	3	F	12	1	1	1	9,103
Marquetta	2	F	8	0	0	2	9,496
Marquette	8	H	1	0	0	0	700
Marquis Du Lac	4	G	7	0	1	0	1,366
Marrakech Gold	5	M	1	0	1	0	9,400
Marriage License	3	G	14	1	1	1	7,922
Marrow Stone Point	3	F	8	1	1	3	6,113
Marry Me Moncec	4	G	4	0	0	0	540
Marsh	4	G	13	2	3	0	50,740
Marsh Harbour	4	G	15	0	0	2	5,389
Marshal Dilom (ARG)	5	G	4	0	0	0	125
Marshall Greeley	7	G	8	2	1	0	27,388
Marshall Matt	3	C	8	3	0	0	23,115
Marshall Rooster (GB)	5	G	8	0	0	2	18,084
Marshall's Pride	3	G	3	0	0	0	4,040
Marshmallow	2	F	3	0	0	1	1,685
Marshman	7	G	9	3	1	0	17,091
Marshmello Heart	2	G	1	0	0	0	300
Marshon	3	C	2	1	0	1	33,245
Martel	7	G	8	2	1	1	7,770
Martha Martha	3	F	6	1	0	0	17,199
Martha Sue	3	F	4	0	0	0	225
Marthamountainmama	4	F	8	1	2	2	85,282
Marthas Little Boy	3	G	1	0	0	0	400
Martial Jerry	6	G	12	0	3	2	5,227
Martika Tianna	3	F	3	0	0	0	1,900
Martin County	4	G	6	0	0	1	663
Martin L K	4	G	9	0	1	0	1,598
Martinblestme	4	C	4	0	1	1	8,840
Martine	3	F	5	0	1	2	3,024
Martini Bay	5	G	8	0	0	2	1,531
Martini Cat	2	F	1	0	0	0	1,480
Martini Classic	4	G	15	1	0	3	37,035
Martini Justice	4	G	10	1	2	0	28,942
Martini Lunch	4	G	5	0	0	0	1,110
Martini Man	2	G	4	0	2	0	5,780
Martini to Go	4	F	3	0	0	0	112
Martini's Trick	2	G	3	0	0	0	0
Martinisbymoonlite	3	G	5	1	2	0	23,186
Martino's Gold	4	G	10	3	3	1	50,090
Marty's Advantage	2	C	1	0	0	1	1,755
Martys Expectation	2	F	8	1	2	3	29,305
Marty's Joia	2	F	1	0	0	0	135
Marty's Legend	4	G	11	0	1	4	3,430
Marty's Lucky Coin	5	M	2	0	0	1	1,350
Marty's Power	3	G	1	0	0	0	0
Marty's Valentine	2	C	1	0	0	0	71

Horse	Age	Sex	Sts	1st	2d	3d	Won
Marty's Zee	7	M	8	2	0	1	64,502
Marva Jean	4	F	9	0	2	2	23,481
Marvel M.	2	F	5	0	1	0	3,960
Marvelous Cat	3	F	12	2	0	0	39,158
Marvelous Grace	2	F	5	0	0	0	556
Marvelous Match	4	G	3	0	0	0	217
Marvelous Monster	4	F	15	4	1	3	46,575
Marvelous Mover	7	G	7	0	1	1	4,328
Marvin	4	G	14	0	2	0	14,424
Marvy's Gal	4	F	13	1	2	3	28,941
Marwood	4	F	11	6	2	0	197,400
Marxie	3	F	5	2	1	0	40,200
Mary Alex	2	F	5	1	1	1	34,406
Mary Alice	3	F	1	0	0	0	0
Mary Amelia	3	F	3	0	0	1	570
Mary Ann	5	M	13	2	2	2	49,440
Mary Anne's Love	3	F	5	1	1	3	26,850
Mary Ann'smoment	2	F	3	1	1	0	5,480
Mary B Sharp	3	F	3	0	0	0	0
Mary Boyd	5	M	1	0	0	0	414
Mary Can Fly	6	M	9	1	1	0	7,267
Mary Carlisle	5	M	15	2	3	4	53,446
Mary Cassatt	4	F	2	0	0	0	2,018
Mary Charged It	4	F	6	0	0	1	865
Mary Donnelly	3	F	1	0	0	0	300
Mary En Tete	3	F	9	0	1	2	4,135
Mary Gertrude Root	4	F	12	0	2	3	4,737
Mary Goodnight	4	F	2	0	0	0	4,600
Mary Leta's Halo	4	F	4	1	1	1	6,760
Mary Lou Two	2	F	3	0	0	0	0
Mary Murphy	4	F	5	3	0	0	105,000
Mary Sue	3	F	10	1	2	2	15,185
Mary Swan	3	F	11	3	3	1	53,657
Mary Swanson	3	F	12	2	4	2	45,920
Mary Thomas	7	M	2	0	0	0	171
Maryfield	3	F	2	1	0	0	19,581
Marykaysandpit	2	F	2	0	0	0	0
Maryland Monroe	3	F	3	1	0	0	5,250
Marylebone	3	F	3	0	2	0	24,800
Maryneill	3	F	4	0	1	1	7,000
Maryon's Angel	7	M	10	1	2	1	14,073
Mary's Boy	4	C	3	0	0	0	246
Marys Cool Million	3	F	18	1	1	4	10,410
Mary's Empress	4	F	10	1	3	0	19,899
Marys Firey Man	3	C	1	0	0	0	0
Mary's Got Magic	4	F	14	2	1	6	23,087
Mary's Legacy	2	F	1	0	0	0	217
Mary's Lord	5	G	13	1	2	3	10,777
Mary's Love (ARG)	4	F	3	0	0	1	5,650
Marys Mon	5	G	17	2	0	1	6,683
Marys Monster	2	F	1	0	0	0	0
Mary's Nickle	6	M	6	0	2	1	20,616
Mary's Prospector	4	F	10	0	0	0	1,575
Mary's Rose	3	F	5	1	0	0	3,040
Mary's Special	3	F	3	1	0	0	8,640
Mary's Wild Flower	9	M	8	0	0	0	1,972
Mary's Wulf	3	C	2	0	0	0	0
Marzi	5	M	6	1	0	0	4,663
Marzipan	5	M	4	0	0	2	2,256
Masakado Kid	6	G	18	2	2	7	19,905
Masarin (CHI)	4	C	1	0	0	0	400
Masbut (CHI)	4	C	5	0	0	0	800
Mascalzone	3	C	7	0	1	0	4,590
Mascaradehalloween	3	F	8	0	0	0	0
Mashed Potatoes	3	G	10	1	0	3	7,839
Mashiko	4	G	9	1	2	0	22,395
Mashonthegas	4	G	6	1	0	1	7,225
Masked Angel	2	F	3	0	1	0	1,650
Masked Ball	3	F	3	0	0	0	1,672
Masked Miracle	6	G	6	0	0	0	140
Masked Warrior	3	G	8	0	0	2	1,517
Maskra's Hombre	6	G	14	0	0	0	1,612
Mason County	5	G	16	2	7	2	15,853
Mason S.	3	G	1	0	0	0	126
Mason's Entry	4	C	4	1	1	0	12,837
Maspesos	5	G	10	2	1	0	6,597
Masque of Slew	3	G	2	0	0	0	0
Masqued Monarch	2	F	6	1	0	2	20,598
Masquerade Parade	3	F	7	0	1	0	2,680

Horse	Age	Sex	Sts	1st	2d	3d	Won
Mass Attack	4	C	2	0	0	0	209
Mass Media	3	C	5	3	0	0	137,750
Mass Pallet	2	G	2	0	0	0	135
Mass Rock	3	F	4	0	0	0	0
Massacre	3	C	3	0	1	1	12,050
Massasoit	2	C	1	0	0	1	3,740
Massasuta	4	G	11	2	0	3	15,405
Masseuse	2	F	3	0	0	1	6,650
Massiah Street	5	G	4	0	0	1	1,241
Massive	4	C	2	0	1	1	7,146
Massoud	4	G	4	2	0	0	34,510
Massoun (IRE)	4	C	2	0	0	0	1,840
Master Barry	2	C	2	0	0	0	0
Master Ben	3	G	16	2	3	1	19,405
Master Boy	4	C	16	1	3	3	18,362
Master Caine	4	G	8	0	2	3	3,632
Master Carver	4	G	19	2	1	2	19,044
Master Chris	2	G	1	0	0	0	0
Master Concerto	4	G	9	3	0	0	47,380
Master David	3	C	8	1	1	2	244,640
Master de Amour	3	C	8	0	0	0	733
Master Designer	3	G	11	1	1	3	15,494
Master Fly	3	G	12	4	4	2	37,090
Master Harry	6	G	7	0	1	2	1,880
Master Heat	3	G	7	2	0	1	36,602
Master in Law	3	C	8	0	0	0	660
Master Is Ready	4	G	17	4	4	2	62,710
Master Jobie	6	G	13	1	2	2	42,561
Master Jon	7	G	7	2	0	0	51,840
Master Jubal	3	C	6	1	0	0	4,021
Master Key	4	G	3	0	0	0	935
Master Lover	3	G	3	0	1	0	1,950
Master Mechanic	7	G	4	0	0	0	220
Master of the Sea	5	G	16	2	2	3	31,953
Master of Thyme	4	C	7	2	0	2	8,609
Master Painter	3	G	13	3	1	2	32,617
Master Perfect	4	G	6	0	0	1	7,200
Master Plumber	5	G	1	0	0	0	63
Master Poet	4	C	1	0	0	0	54
Master Princess	4	F	2	0	0	0	260
Master Rasper	6	G	6	0	0	1	2,940
Master Report	4	G	6	1	0	1	7,785
Master Romano	5	G	6	1	0	1	3,834
Master Salty	5	G	10	1	1	1	3,245
Master Sandfield	5	H	1	0	0	0	300
Master Sleet	4	G	16	2	1	1	14,236
Master Swinger	11	G	16	2	4	0	10,986
Master the Game	4	G	6	0	1	1	6,056
Master William	3	C	6	0	1	1	18,127
Mastercraft	2	G	2	0	1	0	3,663
Masterful Ballet	3	F	2	0	0	0	150
Masterful Harry	4	C	2	1	0	0	5,680
Masterful Lullaby	6	M	1	0	0	0	0
Masterfully's Game	4	G	7	0	1	3	3,860
Master's Music	2	F	4	0	0	0	699
Mastersdoubleeagle	4	F	3	1	1	0	7,480
Matanzas Creek	5	H	6	2	0	0	7,156
Match Break	5	G	2	0	0	0	160
Match Chic	6	M	14	1	2	1	6,865
Match Race	2	C	9	0	0	1	4,800
Matchbaby	5	M	11	2	3	3	23,559
Matchbox Patti	4	F	5	1	1	1	6,269
Matched	5	H	12	3	5	2	32,880
Matched Prospect	5	G	15	2	4	2	18,078
Matching Colors	6	G	13	2	4	5	25,190
Matching Sox	3	F	3	0	0	0	1,077
Matchless	10	H	3	1	0	0	9,000
Matchless Hunter	8	G	7	1	0	1	5,501
Matchstriker	2	C	4	1	1	1	11,720
Materna	5	M	9	0	0	2	6,211
Mathematical	3	G	4	1	0	0	5,873
Mathewlovestoparty	2	G	2	0	0	0	0
Mathews Bridge	4	G	4	0	0	0	1,125
Mathews Gold	3	G	5	1	1	0	50,856
Matimeyev	4	F	4	0	1	0	2,700
Matin de Soleil	5	G	17	2	2	4	17,615
Matinee Marvel	5	M	3	0	0	0	610
Matinicus Rock	3	C	10	3	1	0	23,340
Matlock (IRE)	6	G	8	1	2	0	11,328

Horse	Age	Sex	Sts	1st	2d	3d	Won
Matos Gold	7	G	1	0	0	0	50
Matos Land	5	G	5	0	2	0	2,116
Matriculate	8	G	11	2	1	1	16,945
Matso	3	G	5	0	0	0	484
Matsue	4	F	8	0	1	1	9,440
Matsui	3	G	7	2	2	1	71,903
Matt Blanc (IRE)	3	C	5	0	0	0	6,587
Matt Daddy	2	C	2	0	0	2	7,370
Matt E. Cat	5	M	1	0	0	0	400
Matt the Mighty	4	G	2	1	0	0	12,400
Matt the Vet	2	G	5	1	0	0	5,238
Mattei's Smokin'	5	M	9	0	0	0	508
Matter of Fax	4	C	11	1	2	0	12,160
Matter of Honour (NZ)	8	G	3	0	0	0	720
Matter of Justice	7	M	12	1	4	0	13,031
Matter of Reality	4	F	10	1	1	3	10,549
Matterdor	8	G	3	0	0	0	323
Matters Not	10	G	2	0	0	0	0
Matthew Lee	6	G	7	0	0	1	2,900
Matthew's Blessing	3	G	11	1	1	4	31,000
Matthews Dignity	2	G	2	0	0	0	585
Matthew's Majesty	5	G	14	2	3	1	12,699
Matthew's Moon	7	M	3	0	0	0	0
Matthew's Prospect	6	G	5	1	0	1	11,166
Mattie D's Ben	3	G	9	1	1	2	9,263
Mattie Cakes	2	F	7	1	2	0	22,880
Mattie Silks	4	F	6	2	1	0	14,066
Matties Baba	6	M	9	0	0	1	1,925
Mattie's Luck	3	F	5	2	1	0	11,500
Mattie's Partyline	5	H	1	0	0	0	0
Mattie's Star	6	M	5	1	1	0	1,779
Matt's a Giant	2	C	2	0	0	0	1,440
Matts Cool D J	7	G	4	1	0	0	1,668
Matts Deeds	4	G	4	1	0	0	7,320
Matt's Ghost	3	G	8	0	0	0	453
Matt's Memo	2	C	5	2	1	1	43,080
Matt's Music	4	C	1	0	0	0	0
Matts On Broadway	6	G	4	0	0	0	47
Matts Pic	4	G	18	3	3	1	22,975
Matt's Star	3	C	4	0	0	0	277
Matt's Terms	3	G	15	1	2	5	7,832
Mattssutterrun	3	G	15	2	2	3	23,145
Matty D	8	G	7	1	1	0	10,288
Matty Fine	4	F	20	4	5	1	34,326
Matty Matty Boo	3	G	2	0	0	0	150
Matty R G	4	C	9	1	0	2	11,311
Matty's Encore	4	C	2	0	0	0	225
Matty's Gem	4	G	13	2	4	1	20,083
Matty's Princess	2	F	2	0	0	0	0
Matty's Song	3	G	9	2	3	0	64,586
Matuka	2	F	3	0	1	0	2,745
Matza's Chili	4	G	7	1	1	1	5,306
Matzo Ball	3	F	13	1	1	2	7,235
Matzoh Toga	3	C	10	2	1	0	43,240
Matzsayo	5	G	9	1	2	0	15,980
Maucho Magic	2	G	1	0	0	0	735
Maud Gonne	5	M	2	0	0	1	4,730
Maudel	6	M	8	0	3	1	2,452
Maudie K	7	M	7	0	0	1	1,204
Maudy	4	F	7	0	0	1	3,940
Maui Money	6	M	7	3	0	0	41,720
Mauk Eight	4	C	6	0	2	1	9,873
Mauk Four	4	C	5	1	1	0	17,540
Mauk Me	3	G	9	2	1	1	22,810
Mauk Place	3	F	8	2	1	2	37,359
Maukey	6	G	1	0	0	0	0
Maurice	5	G	11	0	1	1	4,502
Maurice Champagne	5	G	3	0	0	0	168
Maurice Jolie	4	C	10	2	2	0	8,094
Maurice Le Cheval	3	C	11	0	1	1	11,972
Mauritania	7	G	6	1	0	2	34,080
Maurkara	3	F	3	0	0	0	0
Mav Cat	4	C	10	2	3	0	23,375
Mav Man	2	C	3	0	1	0	5,750
Mavelous Marva	3	F	3	0	2	0	2,912
Maverick	3	C	3	0	0	0	970
Maveriki	4	G	4	1	0	0	1,976
Mavoreen	4	F	7	2	0	2	59,400
Maw Irish Hope	8	M	11	2	2	1	24,625

Horse	Age	Sex	Sts	1st	2d	3d	Won
Mawasasport	7	M	7	0	0	0	315
Max a Million	4	C	7	1	0	1	19,349
Max Brand	4	G	4	0	1	2	2,856
Max Factor	7	G	8	2	1	2	12,682
Max Fast Flight	5	G	1	0	0	0	0
Max Force	4	C	17	0	2	4	14,981
Max Forever	4	C	5	2	0	1	72,470
Max Jones	6	G	5	0	0	1	1,350
Max Mercury	4	G	3	0	0	1	1,632
Max O Max	7	H	13	3	3	4	25,647
Max Patch	6	H	7	1	0	3	19,270
Max Power (AUS)	7	G	10	3	0	1	44,000
Max Two	2	G	3	0	0	0	190
Max West	4	G	14	1	1	2	20,110
Maxamax	4	C	8	0	0	3	4,300
Maxi Max	2	C	1	0	0	1	2,860
Maxi Tune	9	G	3	0	1	0	6,500
Maxian	6	G	6	1	2	1	9,622
Maxibid	10	M	1	0	0	0	112
Maxie Match	2	F	2	0	1	0	3,280
Maxim Gold	5	G	5	0	0	0	518
Maximiliano (BRZ)	8	G	3	0	1	0	2,299
Maximillions	6	G	6	1	2	0	1,747
Maximize	2	G	1	0	0	0	230
Maximum Appeal	4	F	9	2	3	2	45,400
Maximum Degree	5	M	13	0	0	0	657
Maximum Exposure	4	G	16	2	3	3	6,416
Maximum Heat	2	C	1	0	0	0	400
Maximum Impact	6	G	9	1	0	1	3,914
Maximum Reward	5	G	18	3	2	3	31,122
Maximum Voltage	4	G	11	1	1	2	5,194
Maximus	4	G	18	0	1	3	5,440
Maximus C	2	C	3	1	0	1	45,250
Maximus Cash	5	G	9	1	1	1	7,370
Maxinkuckee	3	C	7	2	1	1	35,522
Max's Ace	5	G	14	2	1	0	11,684
Max's Baby	4	C	3	0	0	0	1,100
Max's Beauty	3	F	2	0	0	0	200
Max's Buddy	5	H	7	1	0	2	35,328
Max's Cat	4	C	5	0	3	0	13,025
Maxs Girl	4	F	6	1	2	0	20,460
Max's Missile	2	C	3	1	1	0	18,700
Maxs Position	2	G	4	1	1	1	10,914
Max's Quip	2	F	3	0	1	0	3,000
Max's Sway	3	G	14	3	0	2	17,068
Max's Sweetheart	3	F	3	0	0	0	340
Max's Tale	4	G	2	0	0	0	0
Max's Wish	5	G	7	0	0	0	200
Maxwell	3	G	4	3	0	0	49,980
Maxwell Terrace	3	C	4	1	2	0	39,000
Maxwell Turner	5	H	4	0	0	1	490
Maxwelsilverhammer	4	G	8	0	2	0	6,600
May Be Mabel	4	F	7	0	0	0	459
May Boy	4	G	10	1	3	1	16,785
May Day Warrior	4	C	2	0	0	1	800
May Expectations	5	G	10	1	2	3	39,608
May Gator	5	M	13	3	3	2	201,115
May H Berry	3	F	6	0	0	0	0
May Magic	3	G	1	0	0	0	0
May Nard	6	H	16	1	3	2	12,324
May Paul	5	G	5	0	0	1	2,467
May Snow	5	M	12	0	1	0	3,166
Maya	5	M	1	0	0	0	360
Maya Rose	2	F	2	1	0	0	5,387
Mayan Milagra	2	F	1	0	0	0	161
Maybe Blue Sky	2	F	3	2	1	0	24,270
Maybe Brandon	6	G	1	0	0	0	0
Maybe Cora	3	F	8	1	0	1	18,942
Maybe Doc	6	G	13	0	0	1	1,714
Maybe Friday	4	G	6	0	1	0	3,463
Maybe I Will	3	G	6	0	2	2	6,196
Maybe Jack	11	G	9	2	4	1	25,070
Maybe Lin	5	M	4	0	0	1	2,737
Maybe Me	9	M	11	0	1	2	6,360
Maybe Midnight	4	C	2	0	0	0	800
Maybe Rocco	4	G	3	0	0	0	904
Maybe Satisfied	2	C	3	0	0	0	2,280
Maybe Special (GB)	8	G	4	0	0	0	252
Maybefirst	2	C	2	0	0	0	781

Horse	Age	Sex	Sts	1st	2d	3d	Won
Maybemissamerica	3	F	2	0	0	0	195
Maybetheone	7	M	6	1	0	0	3,800
Maybird	3	F	5	1	0	0	4,956
Maybry's Boy	5	H	10	1	0	2	47,715
Maydeuce	3	F	4	0	1	1	3,980
Mayfield	3	F	3	2	0	0	58,253
Mayhall	4	G	9	1	1	2	16,070
Mayihavethisdance	5	M	7	0	2	2	6,144
Maymont	3	F	15	3	1	3	23,259
Maynard G	3	G	6	1	0	0	3,240
Mayne Attire	5	M	10	2	3	2	31,420
Mayne Stating	4	F	12	2	1	1	18,251
Mayneunderfire	6	G	7	0	4	0	22,789
Mayo On the Side	5	M	12	2	2	3	405,241
Mayo Post	4	G	9	0	0	2	14,375
Mayor Daley	3	G	11	1	0	1	8,710
Mayor Murphy	5	G	13	4	0	2	22,658
Mayor Steve	9	G	13	2	3	1	21,240
Maypole Dance	7	M	1	0	0	0	400
May's Moon	2	F	2	0	1	0	1,500
May's Pride	4	F	13	3	4	2	93,875
Maysville	2	F	2	2	0	0	24,450
Maysville Slew	8	G	14	3	2	0	208,440
Maytown	3	G	4	1	2	0	45,315
Maywood's Brianna	3	F	5	2	0	0	10,934
Maywood's Charlie	3	G	3	0	0	0	280
Maywood's Jack	4	G	5	1	0	1	6,429
Maywood's Jill	4	F	6	1	2	1	32,493
Maywood's Quick	2	G	2	0	0	0	280
Mazaage	2	C	5	0	1	2	8,965
Mazel Dancer	3	F	5	0	0	1	3,630
Mazel Dazel	2	C	1	0	0	0	145
Mazel Pic	3	F	14	4	2	1	52,110
Mazel Power	2	G	2	0	0	1	2,100
Mazel Tov	3	F	6	1	0	2	25,511
Mazel Tov Betty	3	F	4	0	0	1	5,070
Mazel Trickxy	3	F	2	0	0	0	0
Mazella	3	F	12	1	3	2	77,143
Mazelman	2	C	3	1	1	0	21,247
Mazengah	4	C	4	0	1	0	18,074
Mazoolian Ghost	5	H	7	3	0	0	38,840
Mazurka Danzer	3	C	13	3	3	1	65,413
Mazza	2	C	2	0	0	0	0
Mc Act	5	M	1	0	0	0	0
Mc Henry Co. Kid	6	G	10	1	1	1	9,356
Mc Meese	4	F	5	0	0	0	664
Mc Perfect Martini	2	C	3	0	0	0	436
Mc Quix	5	G	12	0	1	3	4,080
McAllister Creek	5	G	9	1	1	0	6,492
McBeal	6	M	3	0	0	0	0
McCain	3	G	4	0	0	0	402
McCann's Mojave	4	C	4	2	1	0	177,140
McCaslin	5	H	6	0	4	1	5,176
McClellan Country	3	G	5	1	0	1	2,843
McCreary	6	G	18	3	3	4	33,160
McDab	7	G	4	0	0	0	1,840
McDermitt Star	3	F	2	0	0	0	0
McDetramax	3	C	4	0	0	0	576
McDevitt	4	F	3	0	0	0	204
McDrake's Elf	5	H	8	0	0	1	1,861
McD's Wright	4	F	8	1	3	0	2,593
McDynamo	7	G	2	1	0	0	101,250
McFadden Creek	5	G	12	3	1	1	19,885
McFarland	3	C	7	1	0	1	9,655
McGeever	4	G	8	1	0	2	7,678
McGlitch	7	G	10	1	3	2	12,122
McGruddy's Tap	7	G	12	2	0	0	7,146
McGuerty Creek	5	M	14	2	2	3	12,241
McIvor	4	G	8	1	2	2	4,983
McKee's Gallery	4	G	3	1	0	0	37,375
McKenna Falls	3	F	8	1	3	0	12,410
McKennan	3	G	3	0	1	1	4,505
McKenzie's Moment	3	G	1	0	0	0	0
McKinley Rhodes	7	G	6	1	0	1	3,418
McKinna G	3	G	11	3	1	3	17,473
McKinney	6	M	1	0	0	1	3,500
McLinda Deree	3	F	6	1	2	1	8,319
McLord	2	C	3	0	0	0	780
McManus	5	G	13	1	2	1	67,884
McMaster	4	G	12	0	4	0	12,185
McMazel	3	G	11	1	2	1	10,970
McNabbadabadoo	2	F	2	0	0	0	0
McNasty	3	G	1	0	1	0	7,000
McNeal's Princess	3	F	8	0	1	0	3,350
McNellis	6	G	18	5	2	2	67,893
McSlew	2	F	5	1	1	0	6,105
McStorm	4	G	1	0	0	0	165
McTown	3	C	2	0	0	0	0
McWest	5	M	9	0	2	0	1,700
Mdme Allbright	3	F	2	0	0	0	255
Me a Green	5	M	5	0	0	1	652
Me a Mocha	2	G	2	0	0	0	0
Me and Marie	3	F	12	1	1	1	11,308
Me and Mr. North	3	C	5	0	1	1	4,677
Me and Mr. Z	6	G	7	0	2	3	14,700
Me and Thee	6	H	6	0	0	0	1,035
Me Coordinated	6	M	8	1	1	0	4,188
Me Darlin Duke	3	G	4	1	1	1	12,740
Me Darlin Kevin	3	G	4	0	0	0	0
Me Darlin Marty	5	G	4	0	0	0	506
Me Ed	3	C	4	0	0	0	2,238
Me Get It	4	F	14	2	0	1	9,161
Me Gotta Go	6	M	11	2	0	3	32,414
Me Gusta Bailar	3	C	4	1	1	1	8,690
Me I'm Amelia	6	M	2	0	0	0	608
Me in Shades	4	F	9	2	1	0	48,880
Me Inc.	3	F	5	0	0	2	6,268
Me Jane	5	M	2	0	0	0	0
Me Me Anna	6	M	7	3	2	0	36,197
Me Moe N Joe	3	G	2	0	0	1	680
Me Moe You Curly	3	F	1	0	0	0	2,580
Me My Mine	4	G	9	1	1	1	39,703
Me No Toad	5	G	11	4	2	3	18,955
Me O Me O My	3	F	2	0	0	2	1,440
Me Pay Bills	3	C	7	0	0	0	535
Me Shell	3	F	8	1	0	0	8,400
Me Son	2	C	6	1	0	1	12,705
Me Tricky	4	C	9	2	0	1	16,215
Mea Domina	3	F	6	2	3	0	116,600
Meadaaar	7	H	8	0	0	0	1,201
Meadow Aire	5	G	6	1	0	0	1,425
Meadow Belle	4	F	9	0	2	1	26,359
Meadow Blush	2	F	3	0	0	0	1,012
Meadow Bride	2	F	4	2	1	0	105,345
Meadow Crafty	3	F	6	1	0	0	10,165
Meadow Darling	2	F	1	0	0	0	2,270
Meadow Dee	5	G	1	0	0	0	0
Meadow Fox	3	F	5	2	2	0	67,000
Meadow Fun	3	G	13	1	1	4	20,145
Meadow Ghost	5	G	8	0	0	2	4,030
Meadow Kitten	2	F	5	0	1	1	8,600
Meadow Larking	3	C	3	0	0	0	640
Meadow Love	5	M	17	3	3	1	21,157
Meadow Minister	4	C	6	2	0	0	67,758
Meadow Monarch	5	H	2	0	0	0	0
Meadow Mountain	5	M	10	1	3	4	17,222
Meadow Muse	3	F	6	1	1	0	13,335
Meadow Punch	2	C	1	0	0	0	0
Meadow Quail	2	G	3	0	0	1	1,468
Meadow Robin	11	G	4	0	0	0	0
Meadow Rue	4	G	10	1	1	1	4,538
Meadow Slew	5	G	13	0	1	1	1,589
Meadow Slipper	3	F	5	1	0	1	12,192
Meadow Snowbird	4	F	2	0	0	1	660
Meadow Soldier	3	C	14	2	5	1	42,880
Meadow Vespers	2	C	1	0	0	0	164
Meadowcrest Kid	6	G	10	0	0	1	1,078
Meadowfella	4	G	10	1	0	1	4,545
Meadowlake John	4	G	12	1	1	1	25,566
Meadowlake Lodge	3	G	9	3	0	0	49,840
Meadowminer	6	H	8	1	2	1	33,790
Meama	4	F	7	3	1	1	29,230
Mean and Lean	5	G	7	1	0	0	4,108
Mean and Nasty	4	G	4	0	0	0	1,380
Mean Barbara Jean	2	F	1	0	0	0	450
Mean Beverly Jean	3	F	5	1	1	0	6,375
Mean Bone	2	F	4	0	1	1	4,595
Mean Flyer	6	H	2	0	1	0	295

Horse	Age	Sex	Sts	1st	2d	3d	Won
Mean G. I.	4	C	16	1	4	2	18,680
Mean Irene	3	F	7	0	0	0	959
Mean Jean Ipock	5	M	3	1	0	0	2,460
Mean Kisser	3	G	15	4	2	1	25,825
Mean Minister	3	G	1	0	0	0	0
Mean Streets	4	G	10	1	2	1	15,040
Mean U Gene	3	G	7	1	0	1	21,831
Meandpaul	2	C	1	0	1	0	5,300
Meanest Hombre	3	G	4	0	0	1	5,770
Meaningless	6	G	16	4	2	0	24,090
Means to Win	3	G	12	2	2	1	36,219
Meanwhile	4	C	10	3	0	2	20,492
Meany Me	2	F	4	0	0	0	0
Meara's Rollick	3	F	2	0	0	0	180
Meauxjo	4	G	10	2	0	1	19,927
Meccajelso	8	G	3	0	0	0	504
Mech Runner	3	F	4	1	0	1	16,420
Mechanic	2	G	1	1	0	0	14,500
Mechanic Man	6	G	7	0	0	1	1,841
Mechlin	6	M	2	0	0	0	0
Meckanical	5	G	14	1	3	0	10,876
Meckarenda	6	M	22	1	0	2	14,427
Mecke Change	3	G	8	0	0	0	0
Mecke Man	6	G	7	0	0	1	2,611
Mecke Me Proud	2	F	7	1	1	2	10,675
Mecke Mex	4	F	8	0	1	0	2,840
Mecke My Day	2	C	11	1	0	1	18,510
Meckeme	6	G	5	2	1	1	30,050
Meckenized	5	G	10	1	2	3	13,990
Mecke's Dancer	5	G	11	0	1	1	2,758
Mecke's Money	5	G	17	1	4	1	22,801
Mecke's Presence	3	F	11	2	1	0	35,450
Mecke's Princess	5	M	13	1	4	1	37,550
Mecke's Queen	2	F	2	0	1	0	4,000
Medaglia d'Oro	5	H	2	1	1	0	1,500,000
Medal of Freedom	3	F	3	1	0	1	30,715
Medal Play (ARG)	7	G	1	0	1	0	7,220
Medallia de Plata	3	C	8	3	0	0	14,925
Medallist	3	C	10	4	1	1	291,375
Medea	9	M	7	0	1	1	2,269
Medevil Wine	3	G	14	1	2	4	3,468
Media Alert	2	F	5	0	2	2	28,580
Media Critic	3	C	5	0	1	1	6,062
Media Event	3	G	5	1	1	1	22,657
Media Mogul (GB)	6	G	4	1	1	0	4,050
Media Rare	5	G	6	0	1	3	2,080
Media Saint	3	G	7	2	0	0	25,683
Medical First	5	G	11	1	3	2	20,331
Medicine Eyes	3	G	9	2	0	1	36,298
Medieval Jazz	4	F	10	0	3	2	7,140
Medieval Mistress	4	F	6	0	0	0	1,060
Medieval Parade	3	G	6	1	0	2	3,590
Medieval Salute	4	F	7	0	0	1	9,088
Medieval Touch	4	F	2	0	1	0	4,830
Medieval Trick	5	G	15	1	4	1	29,230
Medina Ridge	7	G	15	1	1	3	9,401
Medio Creek	8	G	9	0	2	1	3,201
Medioluna Mistress	4	F	14	2	3	2	29,010
Meditate	6	M	8	0	1	1	2,900
Medium Rare	8	G	7	1	2	2	27,848
Medjugorje Vision	6	M	1	0	0	0	38
Medlin Road	5	G	10	3	1	2	39,810
Meega	4	F	5	1	0	0	8,520
Meeho	3	G	1	0	0	0	0
Meercat	3	F	17	1	1	0	6,124
Meerkahn	4	G	9	0	0	1	3,069
Meeshiano	2	F	5	1	1	1	28,420
Meet At Eleven (IRE)	5	G	5	0	1	0	3,950
Meet in Miami	6	M	9	1	2	0	19,404
Meet in Seattle	8	M	3	0	0	0	220
Meet Me At Mary's	3	F	6	1	2	1	5,583
Meet Me At Midnite	4	F	3	0	0	0	6,140
Meet Me At Nine	3	F	7	1	0	0	17,780
Meet Me in Dixie	7	H	3	0	1	0	2,800
Meet Me in Sedona	3	F	2	0	0	0	175
Meet Mom in Heaven	3	F	2	0	0	0	0
Meet My Buddy	2	C	3	0	0	1	4,425
Meet My Kid	3	F	7	1	1	1	9,555
Meet the Challange	8	G	7	1	1	1	6,624

Horse	Age	Sex	Sts	1st	2d	3d	Won
Meet the Slew	4	G	8	1	0	0	6,480
Meeting by Design	3	G	5	0	0	1	3,720
Meeting Ended	2	G	6	0	0	0	3,088
Meeting of Minds	6	M	2	0	0	1	2,925
Meeting's Lovely	4	F	1	0	0	0	300
Meetmeatthefence	2	C	1	0	0	0	0
Meetmeatthegate	4	F	6	1	1	2	16,866
Meetmeatthegrill	3	G	4	1	0	0	11,400
Mefistofele	6	G	5	0	0	0	720
Meg Pie Baby	7	M	12	3	1	2	10,309
Mega Gift	7	G	1	0	0	1	3,000
Mega Hit	4	C	9	0	2	3	15,953
Mega Hot	2	C	1	0	0	0	0
Mega Mill	4	G	11	0	0	0	1,629
Mega Moose	2	G	2	0	0	0	480
Mega Victory	2	F	5	0	2	0	8,080
Megabyte	2	C	6	1	1	1	44,880
Megacles	7	H	6	1	1	0	10,970
Megaddim	3	G	6	3	0	2	25,287
Megafleet	3	F	2	0	2	0	7,585
Megagate	3	F	4	0	0	0	0
Megahertz (GB)	5	M	6	2	2	0	322,500
Megan Popz	3	F	9	1	1	1	37,605
Megan's Appeal	3	F	8	0	1	0	16,154
Megan's Cracker	6	M	7	0	0	0	1,550
Megan's Field	8	H	3	0	0	0	0
Megan's Halo	4	F	7	1	1	2	20,410
Megan's Lady	5	M	5	1	1	1	15,320
Megan's Man	4	G	12	4	3	2	37,495
Megans Molly	4	F	3	0	0	1	920
Megan's Music	3	F	1	0	0	0	65
Megan's Princess	2	F	7	0	0	1	1,305
Megans Rainbow	4	F	17	1	0	2	7,448
Megan's Way	3	F	5	1	1	0	12,260
Megantic	6	H	5	2	0	1	122,640
Megaphone	2	F	3	0	1	0	7,160
Megara	4	F	2	1	0	1	5,765
Megascape	2	F	5	3	0	1	161,740
Megatrend	3	G	7	1	1	2	41,588
Megawattie	2	F	2	0	1	1	8,060
Megec Blis (IRE)	3	F	7	2	1	2	54,557
Megga Gee	4	G	10	0	0	1	7,610
Meggy Girl	2	F	3	1	0	0	5,767
Megmeister	3	F	7	1	2	0	10,175
Megoman	4	C	7	0	0	1	14,407
Megoodytwoshoes	6	G	7	1	0	2	6,094
Meg's Cat	3	F	2	0	0	0	161
Meg's Operator	3	F	12	0	1	1	7,840
Mei Sing Star	4	G	11	1	3	2	15,600
Mein Love	3	F	10	2	0	0	16,540
Mejestic Creek	4	G	9	0	1	1	1,185
Mejor	8	M	7	1	1	0	9,271
Mekena South	6	G	10	1	2	1	18,545
Mel Mar	4	F	4	0	0	0	1,167
Mel Marie Ann	6	M	9	2	0	0	9,227
Meladrie	5	M	6	3	2	0	21,222
Melancholy	4	F	9	0	1	2	13,260
Melanie's Smile	4	G	9	1	0	2	2,790
Melanyhasthepapers	3	C	7	1	1	3	56,820
Melba	3	F	11	2	1	3	11,562
Melba Jewel	3	F	8	1	2	0	19,850
Melcapwalker	5	G	12	5	1	1	46,067
Mele Kalikimaka	4	C	5	0	0	0	742
Meleium	5	M	8	0	1	1	4,540
Melhor Ainda	2	F	2	2	0	0	76,920
Melind's Adam	6	M	1	0	0	0	0
Melissa Christine	5	M	13	0	1	3	5,820
Melissa Lee	5	M	9	1	1	1	14,827
Melissa Rocks	2	F	6	1	0	3	13,650
Melissa's Comet	2	C	6	2	1	0	39,890
Melissa's Glitter	4	F	5	0	0	0	384
Melissa's Luv Song	3	F	10	2	2	2	31,630
Melissa's Melody	2	F	7	2	2	1	65,829
Melissa's Miss	3	F	13	0	1	1	5,435
Melissa's Moment	7	M	1	0	0	0	0
Melissa's Star	2	F	1	0	0	0	118
Melissa's Success	7	M	4	1	2	1	6,740
Mellaluka	4	F	8	0	0	0	3,345
Mellon Brook Road	3	G	6	1	0	0	9,250

Horse	Age	Sex	Sts	1st	2d	3d	Won
Mellow Cielo	3	G	6	1	0	0	18,011
Mellow Marci	6	M	5	0	1	0	3,616
Mellow Mind	4	F	1	0	0	0	150
Mellowes	6	H	4	3	1	0	80,283
Melodar	4	F	7	0	0	1	3,143
Melodeeman	4	G	14	2	3	0	84,847
Melodioso	4	F	1	0	0	0	0
Melody Light	3	F	3	0	0	0	460
Melody Maiden	3	F	4	0	2	0	15,500
Melody of Colors	5	M	10	3	3	2	137,820
Melody of Joy	4	F	8	2	0	0	5,730
Melody Ruth	4	F	11	4	3	0	37,035
Melodyformorgan	5	M	7	1	4	1	10,420
Melody's Slasher	3	F	16	5	2	2	35,534
Melon Patch	3	C	3	0	0	0	0
Melora	3	F	12	2	1	1	12,062
Melrose Gambler	3	G	3	0	0	0	108
Melrose Miss	4	F	2	0	0	0	320
Melrose Nanny	5	M	10	2	1	0	33,803
Melrose Orphan	5	G	9	0	0	1	888
Melrose Traveler	4	F	8	0	2	2	5,831
Mels Humor	2	F	3	0	0	0	1,185
Mel's Marque	7	H	11	2	0	0	15,438
Mels Reign	4	G	3	1	0	0	10,020
Melting	11	G	1	0	0	0	0
Melting Point	4	F	2	0	0	0	198
Mema's Money	3	F	18	1	1	4	12,380
Membership Coffee	3	F	3	0	1	1	15,020
Memberwhen	4	F	18	2	2	5	19,318
Memo	4	C	14	2	1	2	50,761
Memo Bay	2	F	2	0	0	0	132
Memo House	4	G	7	1	3	1	17,835
Memo Image	5	G	14	4	3	0	17,420
Memo Lady	3	F	1	0	0	0	1,140
Memo Miss	3	F	2	2	0	0	12,950
Memo Queen	4	F	7	0	0	3	6,854
Memo to Babe	4	F	1	0	0	0	1,140
Memo to Cameron	4	G	2	0	0	0	385
Memo to Dixie	7	G	9	1	1	0	6,592
Memo to Eve	7	M	11	1	0	1	4,940
Memo to Id	3	F	4	1	1	0	12,642
Memo to Me	5	G	9	0	1	1	4,338
Memo to Russ	4	G	7	2	2	2	27,120
Memofromjessica	3	G	3	0	0	0	1,260
Memofromthelady	5	G	7	2	1	2	16,962
Memogram	4	F	12	2	2	4	69,342
Memonte	5	G	4	0	0	0	420
Memorable Gent	5	G	11	2	1	0	25,932
Memorable Night	2	F	5	0	0	3	10,330
Memorandum	3	F	4	1	0	0	6,520
Memorette	2	F	6	2	1	1	158,325
Memorial Bridge	3	C	6	1	0	2	16,646
Memories of Pa	2	F	6	1	2	0	29,685
Memorly	3	F	2	0	0	0	800
Memorolph	3	G	6	1	1	0	8,734
Memory Hill	8	G	10	1	3	0	5,372
Memory Lane	4	G	8	0	0	2	7,399
Memory Man	3	G	5	1	2	0	28,280
Memphis	6	G	2	1	0	0	8,250
Memphis Kat	4	F	6	0	0	0	325
Memphis Lady	4	F	2	0	0	0	0
Men Only	2	C	3	0	1	0	11,640
Menacing Prestige	2	C	4	0	0	0	605
Menasha	3	C	8	1	0	3	12,564
Mendham	6	H	5	2	2	0	18,920
Mendham Beauty	3	F	13	1	4	1	13,415
Mending Fences	2	C	3	0	1	0	3,000
Mendocino Rose	3	F	2	1	0	1	14,835
Menifeeque	3	F	9	1	2	1	81,520
Menorquin	3	G	13	0	1	1	2,921
Men's Exclusive	11	G	1	0	0	0	3,198
Mensa	6	M	2	0	0	0	194
Mensa Frenchie	5	M	8	1	1	0	6,625
Mensa Madam	6	M	1	0	0	0	135
Mensa Mom	3	F	4	0	1	0	5,500
Ment to Be Clever	4	F	1	0	0	0	0
Mental Floss	3	F	7	0	1	0	8,590
Mentir Pas	5	M	2	0	0	0	0
Menti's Claim	3	F	5	0	0	0	1,302
Mentow	3	F	7	2	1	1	22,369
Menuhin (GB)	4	G	8	0	0	1	13,345
Meow Meow	3	F	9	0	0	0	491
Mer Belle	4	F	10	1	0	1	13,890
Mer de Corail (IRE)	5	M	3	0	1	0	26,535
Mercato Nero	5	H	2	0	0	1	995
Merce Honey	5	M	7	1	1	1	6,659
Mercedees Red	4	F	8	1	3	1	12,893
Mercedes Dancer	3	F	2	0	1	0	5,640
Mercedes Dream	3	G	7	1	0	1	16,512
Mercedes High	3	C	11	0	1	3	3,275
Mercedes Mirage	3	F	7	1	0	1	14,576
Mercedes Mystery	4	F	3	0	0	1	4,530
Mercedes Salute	2	G	2	0	0	0	0
Mercedes Son	10	G	6	0	0	0	1,515
Mercenary	6	H	13	3	2	3	50,490
Mercer	6	M	16	0	4	2	14,683
Mercer Kid	2	C	5	0	0	1	5,658
Mercercountyqueen	4	F	8	1	3	0	7,238
Mercerized	4	G	7	0	1	0	4,620
Mercer's Cool Cat	4	G	10	1	1	4	6,064
Mercer's Launch	5	M	8	4	1	1	77,680
Mercers Run	4	F	4	0	0	0	500
Merchandise	3	C	9	1	2	0	18,590
Merchant Banker	3	G	10	2	0	1	11,291
Merchant Prince	2	C	1	0	0	0	400
Merci Beaucoup	2	C	1	0	0	0	375
Merci Bouquet	4	F	2	0	0	0	0
Merci Melody	6	M	1	0	0	0	0
Merciless	4	F	16	1	4	3	19,511
Merc's Melissa	4	F	17	1	0	2	7,223
Mercuryontherise	3	F	3	1	0	0	5,430
Mercy Matters	3	F	7	1	2	1	33,286
Mercy Mercy Mercy	2	G	9	0	0	1	3,434
Mercy Ridge	7	G	15	1	0	2	14,871
Mercywhataleader	8	G	12	0	2	2	2,898
Mere Legend	11	G	3	1	0	0	4,003
Mere Magic	3	F	3	0	0	0	671
Mere Sheba	5	M	4	0	0	0	320
Meredith Ann	3	F	3	0	0	0	150
Meregold	5	M	6	1	0	2	4,715
Merely Money	9	M	13	0	1	3	2,701
Merenguero	7	G	9	0	0	3	4,912
Merger of Equals	2	F	2	0	0	0	1,740
Merger Talk	2	F	5	2	0	0	15,240
Meri Michele	7	M	2	0	0	0	223
Meridian Brookie	5	M	4	0	0	0	0
Meridian Champ	4	G	3	1	2	0	3,195
Meridian Doc	4	G	2	0	0	0	250
Meridian Madness	5	M	1	0	0	0	206
Meridian Road	3	F	1	1	0	0	6,199
Meridiana (GER)	4	F	5	3	0	1	231,308
Merilark and Barb	2	F	3	0	0	1	450
Merimac Light	2	F	3	0	1	0	3,240
Meriray Dawn	6	M	6	2	2	0	17,658
Merits Ruler	7	G	10	1	1	0	4,110
Merkaban	8	G	7	0	0	0	487
Merlins Apprentice	2	G	1	0	0	1	2,460
Merlin's Moon	6	G	8	0	0	1	13,294
Merrie Woode	7	M	3	0	0	0	330
Merrigoldround	4	F	8	2	1	1	4,560
Merrill Gold	2	F	3	0	0	0	1,040
Merrimanista	2	C	1	1	0	0	15,000
Merry Grey	5	M	8	2	0	0	23,661
Merry Kippy	5	G	14	1	0	2	8,573
Merry Lift	3	F	8	1	2	0	8,652
Merry Mary	3	F	10	0	0	2	26,525
Merry Me in Spring	3	F	6	4	2	0	124,700
Merry Minster	4	F	13	2	3	3	15,513
Merry Mist	4	F	2	1	0	0	3,720
Merry Sizzle	3	G	8	1	2	0	12,010
Merry Whistler	3	C	1	0	0	0	400
Merryhadalilwolf	9	G	19	2	1	3	8,846
Merryland Missy	4	F	2	1	0	1	59,400
Merryvale	3	F	3	1	0	0	27,000
Mersadees' Lady	3	F	8	0	0	0	2,418
Mert	2	F	5	0	0	0	270
Mertie M.	2	F	3	1	0	2	20,675
Mertz's Lil Nelson	4	F	14	2	1	2	11,198

Horse	Age	Sex	Sts	1st	2d	3d	Won
Merychippus	4	F	1	0	0	0	0
Mesa Beauty	4	F	8	2	2	0	42,500
Mesa Me	3	F	4	1	0	0	6,653
Mesa Queen	2	F	3	0	0	0	900
Mesa Ridge	3	F	12	2	3	1	26,151
Mesmerizing	4	F	4	1	0	1	51,380
Mesne Process	6	H	2	0	0	0	255
Mesofast	4	C	2	0	0	0	1,500
Mesolithic	5	G	21	1	3	2	18,185
Mesquite M	3	F	5	2	1	1	10,097
Message Red	5	M	1	0	0	0	732
Messageinabottle	4	G	9	0	0	0	75
Messenger Springs	4	G	12	1	3	2	12,530
Messerschmitt	3	G	7	2	0	2	19,000
Messinroundwithjd	3	G	7	3	1	0	9,157
Messomania	5	G	6	0	0	0	368
Mestizio	6	G	1	0	0	0	0
Met At Dinner	3	G	4	0	0	1	2,663
Met in Seattle	2	G	4	0	3	0	17,253
Met'a Flew Z.	5	G	7	0	0	1	1,458
Metal Master	5	G	13	5	2	3	102,122
Metal Vendor	5	G	9	1	1	2	4,274
Metalian	3	F	14	1	1	2	9,962
Metallic Grit	2	C	2	0	0	0	2,255
Metallic Miss	3	F	2	1	0	1	11,450
Metallic Moon	3	C	7	1	2	1	47,624
Metalurgist	2	G	3	0	2	0	21,373
Metatron	5	G	9	3	1	1	75,800
Metcalfe	3	C	6	1	1	0	29,250
Meteor Impact	4	G	12	1	6	1	94,012
Meteor Star	5	M	3	0	0	0	0
Meteor Storm (GB)	5	H	6	3	0	1	529,800
Meteoric Man	2	C	5	0	0	0	455
Meteoric Rise	8	G	6	1	1	1	8,020
Meter	2	C	1	0	0	1	1,550
Meter's Legend	3	G	7	2	0	1	28,400
Metfield Jr	7	H	3	0	0	0	65
Metfield Runner	4	G	2	0	0	0	122
Metfleet	7	G	14	2	2	2	12,034
Method Actor	4	G	8	1	0	0	7,897
Methodist (IRE)	7	G	6	4	0	0	29,135
Methuen	3	C	2	0	0	0	800
Metoometoo	3	G	6	0	0	0	124
Metro Cat	2	C	2	2	0	0	19,800
Metro Tango	6	G	13	1	0	3	13,348
Metro Time	6	G	12	1	0	2	18,633
Metronome	4	G	7	1	1	1	6,852
Metts Reward	3	G	12	3	2	0	21,250
Metzo Soprano	4	F	11	0	0	0	1,998
Mewannaplay	3	F	8	1	3	1	7,000
Mexican Connection	7	M	11	2	0	1	9,247
Mexican Daisy (BRZ)	5	M	1	0	0	0	400
Mexican Gypsy	4	F	3	1	0	0	5,440
Mexican Moonlight	4	F	12	1	3	1	77,500
Mexican Playboy	5	G	9	0	0	1	2,616
Mexican Riviera	4	F	5	1	0	1	8,859
Mexican Sailor	3	C	1	0	0	0	0
Mexican Student	5	H	9	0	0	0	1,514
Mexican Sunset	3	F	11	2	1	3	10,551
Mexico Joe	4	G	2	0	0	0	142
Mezmer Eyes	4	F	18	2	4	4	25,063
Mezzogiorno	3	C	11	3	1	1	36,062
Mfazi	2	G	3	0	0	1	605
Mheara Maskey	2	F	2	0	0	0	274
Mi Aloha	4	F	12	1	0	1	5,256
Mi Amante	3	G	6	1	0	0	11,820
Mi Angelica	8	M	3	0	0	0	0
Mi Bienvenida	5	M	4	0	0	0	211
Mi Brujo	5	H	6	0	2	3	10,985
Mi Caramelo	3	F	8	0	0	0	128
Mi' Deserai	5	M	3	0	0	0	418
Mi d'Or	5	M	4	0	0	0	1,600
Mi Estilo	2	G	5	0	0	0	2,090
Mi Gotto Poppa	2	F	2	0	0	0	1,065
Mi Jillian	4	F	18	5	3	1	48,015
Mi Karmee	4	F	3	1	0	2	11,710
Mi Miracle	4	F	1	0	0	0	0
Mi Narrow	10	G	7	1	1	1	7,424
Mi Pais	4	G	12	1	0	2	7,532
Mi Pa's Bo Zac	2	G	3	0	0	0	0
Mi Pequeno Amigo	6	H	2	0	0	0	0
Mi Pet Rock	2	F	4	1	0	0	4,429
Mi Pingo (ARG)	6	H	3	0	0	0	1,450
Mi Quick	7	G	9	3	0	2	38,380
Mi Rio	4	G	2	0	0	0	698
Mi Select Work	3	F	2	0	0	0	0
Mi Serenade	7	G	7	1	1	1	4,794
Mi Tapitia	2	F	4	0	0	0	708
Mi Tough	3	G	8	0	0	0	549
Mia Baquero	3	F	2	0	0	0	0
Mia Casa Grande	3	F	4	0	0	0	1,560
Mia Charlie Zee	3	G	1	0	0	0	0
Mia Friend	3	C	6	0	0	1	1,371
Mia Frilly Tudor	9	G	10	0	1	1	2,616
Mia Justice	4	G	10	0	0	2	3,035
Mia Puncher	4	F	7	0	0	1	7,340
Mia Rebecca	4	F	18	2	2	2	14,435
Mia Villa	5	M	7	0	0	3	2,815
Miacomet	2	G	7	2	2	0	16,425
Miami Blue	3	F	1	0	0	0	125
Miami Gear	5	G	4	0	0	1	2,288
Miami Mike	3	G	17	1	1	3	18,230
Miami Miracle	3	G	1	0	0	0	325
Miami Princess	2	F	5	2	1	0	20,850
Miami Star	3	G	20	1	1	4	22,191
Miami Sunrise	2	G	1	0	0	0	190
Miamineedsahalo	3	G	6	1	1	0	8,660
Miamundo	3	F	1	0	0	0	0
Mi'an Mar	4	F	6	1	1	1	24,726
Mia's John D.	6	H	5	0	0	1	4,202
Mia's Momento	3	F	8	2	1	1	17,842
Mic Cup	6	H	3	0	0	1	260
Mic Mac	5	G	6	1	1	0	11,068
Mic N Ali	5	M	10	1	1	1	4,192
Micado	6	G	22	1	1	4	4,187
Micapeakmoonshine	4	G	2	0	1	0	800
Micasa	2	F	1	0	0	0	100
Micayla's Peach	6	M	11	1	2	1	10,093
Miccosukee	4	F	1	0	1	0	1,700
Michael	7	G	13	2	1	0	14,346
Michael Jay	3	G	4	0	0	0	1,020
Michael Motorcycle	2	G	3	1	0	1	8,525
Michael O	7	G	6	0	2	0	5,128
Michael Slew	3	G	3	0	1	0	800
Michael With Wings	4	G	4	0	1	0	3,645
Michaelistheone	2	G	3	1	0	0	11,200
Michaelmyboy	4	C	9	0	0	0	620
Michaels Magic	3	G	3	1	0	0	3,720
Michael's Pride	7	H	6	1	1	2	27,110
Michael's Queen	6	M	3	0	0	0	590
Michael's Scarlet	2	F	1	0	0	0	0
Michael's Temper	5	H	6	0	1	0	3,245
Michael's Will	4	C	14	3	1	1	15,321
Michael's Wolf	6	G	2	0	0	0	180
Michel With One L	5	M	11	2	2	2	13,497
Michele Marieschi (GB)	7	G	4	0	0	1	3,500
Michelle's Diamond	4	F	11	1	1	1	8,530
Michelles First	3	F	5	1	1	1	11,880
Michelle's Honour	2	F	4	1	0	0	12,720
Michelle's Soup	3	F	10	1	1	0	14,445
Michel's Angel	2	F	1	0	0	0	125
Michener	8	G	10	3	1	1	59,626
Michou Hill	3	G	10	2	0	3	15,885
Micjorgan	5	M	4	0	0	2	2,200
Mick	4	G	4	0	1	0	1,965
Mick and Bubba	3	G	19	1	5	4	14,403
Mick Mouse	4	G	5	0	0	1	6,970
Micka Anthony	3	G	6	1	0	0	9,743
Mickala	5	M	16	1	4	0	26,515
Mickey the Groom	6	G	4	1	0	0	7,459
Mickey the Muse	2	C	1	0	0	0	0
Mickey's Bankroll	7	G	3	0	0	0	152
Mickey's Hope	2	G	3	0	0	0	3,420
Mickey's Magic	4	G	17	1	1	2	9,710
Mickey's Malarkey	6	G	13	1	2	3	37,215
Mickey's Mirage	3	C	7	1	0	0	16,810
Mickey's Pride	2	G	3	0	0	0	0
Mickey's Queenmary	3	F	14	2	3	2	15,929

Horse	Age	Sex	Sts	1st	2d	3d	Won
Mickey's Reality	7	H	7	0	0	0	1,022
Micki Michelle	3	F	9	2	1	1	28,480
Mick's Rolexx	2	F	2	0	0	0	600
Micmaceuse	5	M	13	3	3	2	26,435
Micotti Lake	2	G	1	0	0	0	140
Microbodgit	3	F	17	5	2	0	28,877
Micropunch	4	F	4	0	1	0	1,350
Mid River	4	G	8	0	1	3	14,270
Midafternoon	4	G	7	0	1	2	17,682
Midas Eyes	4	C	5	2	1	0	258,600
Midas Gold	2	C	1	0	0	0	287
Midday	4	G	5	0	0	0	351
Midday Madness	5	G	13	1	0	2	8,900
Midday Son (NZ)	9	G	2	0	0	0	0
Middle Bay	4	G	5	3	1	0	110,630
Middlesex County	3	G	1	1	0	0	25,200
Middleweight	4	G	2	1	0	0	15,000
Middleworth Bay	8	G	5	0	0	0	880
Midknight Broker	3	G	7	0	1	0	5,028
Midknight Flight	6	G	7	0	4	0	4,682
Midknightmass	7	G	8	0	1	1	1,550
Midlothian	5	G	16	3	2	4	14,142
Midnight Arrival	3	G	8	3	1	1	59,193
Midnight Charlie	4	G	10	1	2	2	19,880
Midnight Charmer	5	M	10	0	0	3	8,890
Midnight Cognac	6	H	6	0	1	0	3,570
Midnight Cruiser	6	G	6	0	0	0	600
Midnight Delight	4	F	6	3	1	0	74,220
Midnight Delivery	7	M	14	1	2	4	10,994
Midnight Deposit	2	C	2	1	0	0	3,780
Midnight Echo	3	C	9	0	0	1	3,484
Midnight Explosion	3	C	7	1	3	0	26,655
Midnight Express	3	C	8	2	1	2	92,176
Midnight Frolic	4	C	2	0	1	0	2,450
Midnight Gift	7	G	7	2	0	2	8,978
Midnight Goddess	3	F	11	1	3	2	15,406
Midnight Guy	3	G	2	0	0	0	0
Midnight Interview	4	G	10	0	1	1	3,895
Midnight Jigalo	5	H	4	1	0	1	14,350
Midnight Judge	5	M	10	2	2	0	44,090
Midnight Manner	5	H	11	0	2	1	4,470
Midnight Marauder	3	C	2	0	0	0	90
Midnight Miner	8	G	6	2	1	0	16,699
Midnight Miss	2	F	3	1	1	0	34,960
Midnight Motion	3	F	8	2	0	2	7,907
Midnight Music	6	M	2	0	0	0	615
Midnight Okie	3	G	3	0	0	0	110
Midnight Pass	3	C	5	1	0	1	10,100
Midnight Rider	11	G	4	1	0	2	1,232
Midnight Rodeo	4	G	8	1	2	0	5,360
Midnight Run	4	F	2	0	0	0	0
Midnight Runner	2	F	2	0	0	0	0
Midnight Sam	4	G	4	0	0	0	503
Midnight Secret	7	G	14	1	7	3	36,428
Midnight Show	3	F	4	0	0	1	1,300
Midnight Silk	9	M	11	0	2	2	4,785
Midnight Sky	4	F	9	1	0	2	5,996
Midnight Starter	4	G	1	0	0	0	64
Midnight Storm	2	F	6	0	0	0	2,400
Midnight Summit	4	G	13	1	1	1	42,192
Midnight Testamony	3	F	1	0	0	0	375
Midnight Velvet	3	F	7	0	4	1	22,460
Midnight Venture (GB)	6	G	7	0	2	0	1,244
Midnightvictory	4	F	6	2	0	1	20,462
Midnite Black	5	M	6	2	1	0	2,937
Midnite Coach	5	G	12	3	3	1	29,687
Midnite Edition	7	M	8	1	2	1	7,132
Midnite Gambler	4	G	12	1	2	0	5,105
Midnite Jo Boy	5	G	8	0	0	3	3,266
Midnite Mel	3	F	3	1	0	0	15,180
Midnite Orchid	6	M	1	0	0	0	0
Midnite Prospector	3	G	9	2	0	1	36,234
Midnite Rumble	5	G	13	1	3	1	11,421
Midnite Temptor	6	H	9	1	0	3	3,880
Midterm Habit	4	F	8	0	0	3	4,875
Midtown Miss	2	F	7	2	3	0	51,230
Midwatch	5	G	8	1	3	1	32,910
Midway Girl	5	M	7	1	2	1	19,037
Midway Road	4	C	8	4	1	0	372,015
Midwest Mania	3	F	6	0	0	0	719
Midwife	3	F	6	3	0	1	70,900
Miercoles Noche	3	G	5	0	0	1	1,148
Miesqued Man	4	C	9	1	0	3	23,105
Miesque's Abrojo	6	M	2	0	0	0	193
Miesque's Approval	5	H	9	1	2	1	62,613
Miesque's Daughter	5	M	9	0	0	1	4,060
Miesque's Prospect	6	G	3	1	0	0	3,965
Miesques Testimony	5	M	1	0	0	0	60
Miffed	3	C	8	1	3	1	55,002
Miflin	2	F	8	4	1	1	49,160
Might E Man	3	C	5	2	0	3	17,000
Might Pass	5	G	16	1	0	0	4,578
Might Tonight	4	F	14	1	3	1	8,373
Mightbeachamp	5	M	1	0	0	0	0
Mightbeastar	3	F	8	1	1	0	22,640
Mightiest Titan	4	G	5	0	1	0	5,660
Mighty Amanda	5	M	13	1	2	3	14,885
Mighty Aphrodite	5	M	3	0	0	0	201
Mighty Awesome	3	G	7	0	2	1	18,278
Mighty Beau	5	G	8	1	1	1	107,240
Mighty Berto	3	G	8	1	2	1	13,310
Mighty Bodacious	3	G	2	0	0	0	0
Mighty Brew	3	F	5	0	0	0	1,178
Mighty Brite	3	G	8	0	0	0	2,060
Mighty Confide	4	G	2	0	0	0	525
Mighty David	5	G	15	5	3	1	135,640
Mighty Dawn	6	M	13	2	6	1	20,596
Mighty Fast	2	C	2	0	0	0	845
Mighty Fine Mike	6	G	11	2	4	1	14,200
Mighty Fortress	4	G	11	2	0	5	39,418
Mighty G.	4	C	4	1	0	1	21,573
Mighty Gulch	5	H	6	2	2	0	70,700
Mighty Haggard	3	G	9	0	0	3	2,588
Mighty Husker	2	F	3	0	0	0	1,560
Mighty Jazz	7	G	5	2	1	0	16,470
Mighty John	4	C	4	1	0	0	3,940
Mighty Little	4	F	4	0	0	0	378
Mighty Many	2	F	5	1	1	2	23,770
Mighty Match	5	G	3	0	0	0	157
Mighty Maxwell	10	G	1	0	0	0	0
Mighty Mercer	3	G	12	1	0	3	9,468
Mighty Merlin	4	G	13	2	2	1	23,852
Mighty Midas	2	C	6	0	0	2	3,895
Mighty Military	3	G	12	3	1	3	117,512
Mighty Mill	3	G	3	0	0	0	535
Mighty Mini	3	F	2	0	0	0	480
Mighty Minoru	7	M	1	1	0	0	1,650
Mighty Mistral	3	C	1	0	0	0	0
Mighty Morgan	3	G	4	0	0	0	2,680
Mighty Mute	6	G	2	0	0	0	100
Mighty Mutt	6	M	5	0	1	1	672
Mighty Mysterious	3	G	3	1	0	0	9,200
Mighty Native	4	G	6	1	1	0	4,845
Mighty Nice Bet	8	G	8	0	1	0	3,033
Mighty Nome	3	G	6	1	2	1	22,310
Mighty Oak	4	G	7	2	0	0	73,500
Mighty Ohara	6	G	10	2	2	0	10,698
Mighty O'Malley	2	C	4	1	0	0	3,300
Mighty Patient	3	G	15	2	3	2	22,996
Mighty Patriot	6	M	10	5	2	1	53,425
Mighty Picture Too	5	M	5	1	0	0	5,645
Mighty Proud	5	G	12	0	0	1	8,690
Mighty Quinn	5	H	2	0	0	0	281
Mighty Red Thunder	6	H	10	0	0	0	302
Mighty Rich	3	F	2	0	0	0	0
Mighty Rick	6	H	2	1	1	0	1,420
Mighty Roar	3	C	11	1	2	3	40,300
Mighty Ruckus	3	F	5	0	0	0	317
Mighty Sarah	5	M	11	1	2	2	8,479
Mighty Sedona	3	C	2	0	0	0	0
Mighty Silent	4	F	1	0	0	0	60
Mighty Skiff	4	C	1	0	0	0	93
Mighty Tricky	8	H	1	0	0	0	0
Mighty Try	6	M	2	0	1	0	1,434
Mighty Warrior	4	C	13	1	4	2	6,972
Mighty Wes	3	G	4	0	0	0	0
Mighty Wild	2	F	5	0	0	0	1,089
Mighty Wild Dude	2	G	5	0	0	0	1,100

Horse	Age	Sex	Sts	1st	2d	3d	Won
Mighty Wind	9	G	14	0	1	2	2,433
Mightyouious	3	G	5	0	0	2	660
Migrating Son	5	G	1	0	0	0	75
Migrating South	5	G	11	1	1	1	6,598
Migrating Zeal	4	F	6	0	0	0	1,161
Miguel Cervantes	4	C	3	0	0	0	910
Migwaki	8	G	10	8	0	1	46,276
Mija Flor	4	F	6	0	1	1	1,923
Mikango	4	G	9	0	0	1	11,180
Mikarenee	3	F	5	0	0	0	367
Mikay as Lady	3	F	8	2	0	0	10,582
Mike and Leo	6	G	1	0	0	0	300
Mike Ashley	6	G	4	0	1	0	1,800
Mike B's Bird	3	F	18	3	1	0	12,799
Mike Ken Bar	4	G	4	0	0	0	240
Mike 'n Doc	4	G	1	0	0	0	1,200
Mike Pollio	4	G	8	0	0	0	716
Mike the Mudder	4	G	6	0	1	1	5,775
Mike the Navy Man	3	G	7	2	1	0	40,850
Mike the Tiger	5	G	11	1	2	2	10,750
Mike There	7	G	4	0	0	0	1,279
Mikerto	7	G	12	2	0	1	6,587
Mike's Classic	5	G	5	3	0	1	111,200
Mike's Folly	2	G	7	1	2	1	26,920
Mike's Grand Baby	4	F	2	0	0	0	120
Mike's Greenfields	3	G	15	1	2	3	56,871
Mike's Last Chance	5	M	15	0	2	3	15,157
Mike's Malagra	6	G	1	0	0	0	0
Mike's Missile	2	C	2	0	0	0	1,380
Mikes Mom Pat	3	F	3	0	0	0	0
Mike's Pastry	8	G	5	0	2	0	5,075
Mike's Revenge	3	G	6	0	0	2	2,437
Mike's Warrior	6	G	9	0	1	2	3,180
Mikes Westwaypride	4	C	1	0	0	0	140
Mikethegeneral	2	C	8	1	1	1	46,474
Mikethemoondog	3	G	2	0	0	0	330
Mikethespike	4	G	22	2	1	3	23,109
Mikey Donuts	2	G	4	0	0	0	1,642
Mikey Likes It	4	G	3	0	0	0	387
Mikeymon	4	G	6	1	0	0	11,629
Mikey's Magic	2	C	1	0	0	0	0
Mikey's Money	4	C	3	0	0	0	0
Miki Bleu Eyes	6	G	6	1	1	1	21,628
Miki Triki	2	F	2	0	0	0	360
Miksang	3	F	4	0	0	0	0
Milady Can Fly	7	M	8	1	1	2	2,338
Milady Dee	5	M	10	0	2	0	4,986
Milady Tudor	4	F	3	0	1	0	3,540
Miladys a Prospect	7	M	12	1	1	1	17,133
Milady's Angel	4	C	14	3	1	0	19,506
Miladys Farewell	3	F	23	2	0	3	14,328
Milady's Honor	6	M	12	2	2	3	15,234
Milagro Del Paso	5	G	16	2	4	2	21,749
Mila's Gold	5	M	15	1	3	1	2,518
Mild Expense	5	G	5	0	0	0	180
Mild Manor Bill	5	G	10	1	1	1	7,325
Mild Ride	4	G	5	0	1	1	1,730
Mildred's Max	2	C	3	0	0	0	383
Mile	6	G	8	2	0	2	33,803
Mile End Monster	2	F	4	0	0	1	3,260
Milenia (FR)	4	F	1	0	1	0	7,200
Miles Ahead	7	G	7	2	0	1	34,800
Miles for Mickey	5	G	9	1	0	1	4,012
Miles of Aisles	4	F	3	0	0	0	1,414
Miles of Glory	6	M	13	3	3	3	47,510
Milestone	8	G	2	0	0	0	0
Milestone Victory	3	C	3	0	0	0	6,600
Miliblade	4	F	6	0	1	1	4,093
Milicia	6	M	4	0	1	0	2,405
Militaristic	2	C	4	1	1	2	24,870
Military Academy	5	G	12	5	1	1	31,820
Military Affair	3	F	8	3	0	0	12,024
Military Code	2	F	1	0	1	0	5,040
Military Dream	2	F	3	0	0	0	0
Military Lady	3	F	2	0	0	0	125
Military Lass	3	F	11	3	1	0	45,670
Military Man	5	G	7	1	1	0	15,900
Military Mission	3	F	14	1	1	3	16,990
Military Mystery	3	F	4	0	0	0	1,083
Military Presence	3	C	10	0	0	2	4,486
Military Rhythm	3	G	3	1	1	0	13,260
Military Road	3	G	7	0	0	1	5,050
Military Singer	3	G	8	2	2	0	24,873
Military Zone	3	G	10	0	1	1	8,110
Milk Man	5	G	11	2	2	0	18,520
Milk Money	9	G	1	0	0	0	0
Milk River	3	F	3	0	0	1	3,710
Milk River Ridge	5	G	5	1	1	1	4,290
Milk Wood (GB)	9	G	3	1	0	0	7,800
Milky Bar (CHI)	8	G	13	2	0	0	32,260
Milky Way Guy	6	G	14	7	2	1	115,600
Mill Creek	3	F	3	0	0	0	225
Mill Grief	4	G	14	2	0	2	12,112
Mill Kapp	4	G	9	1	1	1	9,773
Mill Street Blues	4	G	11	1	1	2	6,233
Mille Feville	5	M	9	0	0	3	48,894
Mille Lacs	2	F	3	1	0	0	40,165
Millenaire (BRZ)	5	H	2	0	0	0	1,100
Millenium Babe	3	F	2	0	0	0	0
Millenium Beauty	3	F	5	1	2	2	12,855
Millenium Meridian	5	G	1	0	0	0	0
Millenium Nugget	3	G	6	1	1	1	12,910
Millenium Star	6	G	10	0	1	2	5,460
Millennial Meeting	5	M	4	0	0	1	583
Millennialdominion	6	G	3	0	0	0	170
Millennium Cat	5	G	22	2	5	2	32,899
Millennium Dragon (GB)	5	H	8	1	5	0	302,520
Millennium Dream (CHI)	4	G	13	1	2	1	23,476
Millennium Fox	4	G	9	1	2	1	49,152
Millennium Ghost	4	C	2	0	0	0	542
Millennium Glory	5	H	8	0	2	1	5,938
Millennium Icon	2	G	2	0	0	0	126
Millennium Magic (GB)	6	M	1	0	0	0	115
Millennium Moon	4	G	12	0	0	1	1,616
Millennium Music	4	F	12	1	0	2	7,468
Millennium Mystery	3	C	2	1	0	0	7,500
Millennium Song	6	H	11	4	3	1	71,287
Millennium Storm	4	G	16	4	2	1	54,864
Millennium Sun	5	M	2	0	0	0	72
Millenniummillions	4	G	9	1	3	1	17,930
Millennuim Harvest	6	G	8	0	0	1	588
Miller Proof	2	F	1	0	0	1	860
Millers Tavern	5	H	4	1	0	0	8,400
Millersfourdeuces	2	C	2	0	1	1	5,931
Millesime	3	F	17	2	4	1	11,731
Millfleet	3	G	12	3	1	4	253,371
Millhopper	5	G	7	0	0	1	1,555
Millibar	2	F	1	1	0	0	8,100
Millibrook	2	G	7	2	1	1	34,491
Millie On Air	2	F	3	0	1	0	3,625
Millies Motion	7	M	5	0	0	0	312
Milliesmotherhen	2	F	2	0	0	0	0
Milligram	5	M	2	0	0	1	3,750
Milling	2	F	4	0	0	0	510
Millington Road	6	G	2	0	0	0	332
Million Coins	4	F	2	0	0	0	265
Million Dollar Day	3	F	2	0	0	0	0
Millionaire Rob	4	G	3	0	0	0	448
Millionaire's Row	7	H	2	0	0	0	319
Milliondollarlady	4	F	7	0	1	0	1,820
Millionheiress	6	M	9	1	0	0	5,018
Millionsluckyseven	2	G	8	0	0	0	461
Millonaria	3	F	17	0	1	2	7,120
Milltown Road	2	G	1	0	0	1	900
Millwood	5	G	7	1	0	0	18,998
Milly Galore	3	F	2	0	0	2	5,720
Milly La Foret B B	2	F	2	0	0	1	1,800
Milo	7	G	6	0	2	0	2,576
Milo Man	5	G	13	1	3	4	8,502
Milo's Beau	3	C	8	0	0	0	225
Milsean	4	F	8	0	0	3	1,969
Mimis Classic	3	F	3	0	0	0	142
Mimi's Kleven	4	G	5	0	0	2	4,485
Mimi's Pride	2	G	4	1	1	1	30,593
Mimi's Seven	4	F	4	0	2	1	13,260
Mim's Cat	5	G	3	0	0	0	208
Mimsy's Music	4	F	4	0	1	0	1,940
Minaka	2	C	2	0	0	0	235

Horse	Age	Sex	Sts	1st	2d	3d	Won
Minamala (IRE)	5	M	2	0	0	0	0
Minaville	5	G	14	1	3	3	18,795
Minco Missle	4	G	1	0	1	0	800
Minco Smoke	2	C	1	0	0	0	0
Mind Deals	4	C	7	0	0	1	2,428
Mind If I Wink	3	F	6	1	2	0	11,620
Mind Reader	5	M	10	1	1	2	26,761
Mind Your Business	4	G	8	0	0	2	2,180
Minden Hills	3	F	10	2	1	2	30,383
Minden Mist	4	F	10	1	1	0	8,955
Mindful	4	F	5	0	1	0	1,982
Mindful Tactician	4	C	10	4	0	1	13,792
Minds in Motion	4	F	1	0	0	0	0
Minds Locked (GB)	5	G	1	0	0	0	0
Mindsweeper	3	G	16	2	3	2	20,198
Mindys Deputy	3	G	1	0	0	0	75
Mindy's Island	3	G	13	1	2	2	14,571
Mindy's Time	3	F	4	0	1	0	2,932
Mindy's Token	5	M	3	1	2	0	8,064
Mine Alone	3	F	1	0	0	1	1,485
Mine for Keeps	5	M	3	0	0	1	1,023
Mine the Gold	4	G	4	0	0	3	8,620
Mine to Fly	4	F	9	3	2	0	17,270
Mine Valentine	3	F	12	1	1	1	10,520
Mineisremarqable	3	F	7	1	1	1	20,060
Mineisthehunter	5	G	5	0	1	1	2,640
Miner Distraction	4	F	5	1	1	0	7,850
Miner Moss	4	G	14	4	1	0	43,807
Miner Note	5	G	1	0	0	0	0
Miner Prospect	4	F	5	2	0	0	23,335
Minera	2	F	7	0	0	1	5,420
Mineral Point	3	C	2	1	0	0	11,400
Mineral Springs	3	G	3	0	0	0	250
Minergram	4	F	11	2	2	2	26,118
Miners Americanson	4	C	9	0	1	0	3,366
Miner's Bunny	2	C	2	0	0	0	240
Miner's Crown	6	M	6	0	0	0	120
Miner's Double	4	F	12	2	0	2	12,662
Miners Gamble	8	G	6	1	0	3	31,514
Miners Luck	2	C	2	0	0	1	1,495
Miner's Marquessa	5	M	9	1	0	1	5,255
Miner's Mint	4	F	15	2	1	3	39,425
Miner's Pack	3	C	3	0	0	0	2,640
Miners Patch	4	F	3	1	0	0	6,720
Miner's Road	4	G	5	0	0	1	1,493
Miners Sin	5	G	11	3	1	2	26,063
Miner's Song	8	M	14	0	1	1	2,224
Miner's Star	4	F	9	2	1	2	12,663
Miner's Surprise	4	G	14	8	1	0	24,646
Miner's Trick	8	G	17	5	5	3	46,085
Miner's Wish	8	G	6	3	0	1	9,144
Minersdixigirl	3	F	1	0	0	0	280
Minerva Leader	6	M	7	2	1	2	11,008
Minerva Lights	4	F	7	0	0	0	881
Minerva Newsleader	3	G	1	0	0	0	132
Minerveeni	5	G	9	1	1	3	38,140
Miney's Awesome	4	F	6	1	2	0	32,731
Mingarry	3	F	4	0	0	0	62
Minge Cove	3	F	7	2	0	0	80,324
Mingo	4	G	8	1	4	2	17,388
Mingo Mohawk	2	G	6	2	1	1	73,788
Mingun	4	C	3	0	0	1	30,212
Mini Affair	3	F	8	1	0	0	4,980
Mini Brush	4	F	6	1	1	1	31,140
Mini Marauder	5	G	8	0	0	2	2,945
Mini Me	5	M	12	5	1	1	14,751
Mini Mini	2	F	3	0	0	0	0
Mini Mink	4	F	11	1	2	2	29,115
Mini Skirt	3	F	4	0	1	0	9,980
Minifever	3	F	13	3	1	0	37,920
Minii'pokaa	6	G	2	0	0	0	0
Minimart	2	G	4	1	0	0	5,897
Minimuffin	5	M	1	0	0	0	104
Minimum Security	2	F	1	0	0	0	1,200
Mining for Fun	6	G	12	3	3	1	54,390
Mining for Pearls	5	M	3	0	0	0	620
Mining for Silver	3	C	5	0	0	1	2,380
Mining Lad	2	C	3	0	0	0	550
Mining Plan	5	M	11	1	3	2	6,646
Mining Shaft	3	G	6	2	1	2	41,600
Mining Silver	4	F	1	0	0	0	160
Mininsky	2	F	1	0	0	0	0
Minister Al	2	G	2	0	0	0	540
Minister Blair	3	C	6	0	4	0	41,140
Minister Eric	3	C	6	1	1	2	54,851
Minister Lady	5	M	9	2	1	3	22,660
Minister Mike	3	C	1	0	0	0	0
Minister of Note	5	G	10	1	0	0	14,419
Minister Princess	4	F	9	0	1	0	2,786
Minister Thatcher	5	M	1	0	0	0	2,940
Ministercoordinate	5	G	2	0	0	0	181
Ministerofdefense	3	C	4	0	0	0	596
Ministeroftrucks	4	F	5	0	1	2	7,378
Minister's Baby	6	M	1	0	0	0	1,800
Ministers Bullet	4	F	1	0	0	0	0
Minister's Chance	2	F	2	0	0	0	233
Minister's Gift	2	C	3	0	0	0	610
Ministers Music	3	F	3	0	0	1	4,800
Ministers Pic	2	C	3	0	1	1	6,250
Minister's Sin	6	M	4	0	0	0	0
Ministers Wild Cat	4	C	9	1	2	1	73,072
Ministry of Love	3	C	7	0	0	2	5,807
Mink n' Diamonds	2	F	7	0	3	2	29,597
Minks Star Twister	2	F	1	0	0	1	1,540
Minnamana	3	G	12	3	2	1	94,117
Minnawave	4	F	2	0	0	0	248
Minneapolis Man	5	G	15	1	1	2	7,471
Minnesota Mackee	6	G	13	5	4	0	16,995
Minnesota Pitch	5	H	5	1	0	0	13,147
Minnesota Prospect	5	M	5	1	0	0	6,000
Minnesota Shuffle	7	G	8	1	0	1	7,670
Minni Sangue	5	M	5	1	1	1	37,632
Minnie Bucks	3	F	1	0	0	1	1,719
Minnie Con	3	F	4	0	0	0	0
Minnie Jinnie	4	F	1	0	1	0	900
Minnie Miesque	3	F	8	1	0	1	4,500
Minnie the Moocher	3	F	7	2	2	1	59,700
Minnies Adam Ant	6	G	4	0	0	0	1,700
Minnie's Meadow	3	F	11	1	0	1	28,239
Minnie's Mickey	4	F	6	0	1	3	11,355
Minnie's Premier	6	M	4	0	0	0	749
Minnow Bucket	5	M	5	0	0	1	1,620
Minny's Niece	4	F	2	1	0	0	20,900
Minor Wisdom	8	G	9	2	1	0	24,162
Minor's Gold	6	M	8	0	1	3	33,660
Minoruego	5	M	2	0	0	0	0
Minotaur	5	G	15	3	1	1	30,285
Minstrel Beat	4	G	20	0	4	1	9,025
Minstrel Bud	5	H	7	0	1	1	4,127
Minstrel Got Gold	5	M	5	0	0	0	360
Minstrel Miss	4	F	13	3	1	3	59,549
Minstrel Show	2	F	3	0	1	0	8,845
Minstrel Star	2	F	4	0	0	0	779
Minstrel's Dream	5	M	1	0	0	0	0
Minstrel's Melody	4	G	9	0	0	2	6,620
Mint Condition	3	F	9	2	2	0	16,690
Mint de Gear	2	G	5	0	0	2	2,090
Mint Landing	2	F	3	1	0	1	14,484
Mint' Luck	4	F	7	1	1	1	15,689
Mint Money	5	G	1	0	0	0	0
Mint Prospector	5	G	1	0	0	0	0
Mint Royale	7	G	10	1	2	1	5,090
Mint to Kiss	5	M	11	3	0	4	71,097
Mint Valley Joe	6	G	3	0	0	0	150
Mintage	6	M	2	0	0	0	77
Minted Age	6	G	4	0	0	1	1,298
Minttopull	2	G	3	0	0	1	2,305
Minturn	2	G	4	1	0	0	12,140
Minuano	3	F	11	0	0	0	954
Minus Three	5	G	8	3	2	1	28,863
Minute Jones	2	C	1	0	0	0	166
Minute of Fame	2	C	2	0	0	1	5,240
Minutes Ahead	5	M	4	0	0	0	675
Mira Wind	2	F	1	0	0	0	235
Mirabell	3	F	1	0	0	0	0
Miracat	3	C	2	0	0	1	594
Miracle Alley	2	G	6	0	0	4	22,258
Miracle Boy	3	C	8	1	0	2	8,808

Horse	Age	Sex	Sts	1st	2d	3d	Won
Miracle Flight	5	G	19	2	1	2	8,461
Miracle Girl	3	F	2	0	0	1	648
Miracle Maid	2	F	8	0	0	3	8,550
Miracle Maker	2	C	1	1	0	0	25,800
Miracle Man	2	C	1	1	0	0	28,430
Miracle Mary	2	F	1	0	0	0	750
Miracle Mets	7	G	8	2	1	1	6,620
Miracle Monster	2	G	6	1	0	1	7,273
Miracle Pro	3	F	6	2	0	0	10,774
Miracle Runner	3	F	10	5	2	0	107,040
Miracle Tap	3	F	12	1	4	3	35,431
Miracle Whirl	5	G	13	1	0	4	8,412
Miracolo	4	F	8	0	0	2	2,094
Miracolo Won	4	C	1	0	0	0	114
Miraculous Journey	4	G	1	0	0	0	0
Mirado	3	G	5	0	0	0	405
Miramichi Magic	5	G	6	2	1	2	28,104
Miranda's Among Us	5	M	3	0	1	1	2,950
Miranda's Moon	6	M	8	0	0	0	670
Miranda's Wine	6	G	4	0	0	0	448
Mirando	3	F	6	1	0	2	6,488
Mirando City	3	G	7	1	0	1	5,120
Mirarova	4	F	6	0	0	0	315
Miriam L.	2	F	4	0	1	1	5,155
Mirific (IRE)	5	G	3	0	0	0	600
Mirka	4	F	3	0	0	0	50
Mirobolant	5	M	8	4	1	0	14,567
Miroslava	8	M	12	2	1	0	17,446
Mirror's Edge	3	G	1	0	0	0	420
Mis L. S.	6	M	3	0	0	0	183
Miscataway	3	F	4	2	1	0	18,480
Mischief Boy	5	G	1	0	0	0	122
Mischieviously	4	F	4	0	1	1	16,230
Mischievous Lover	4	G	12	3	2	0	58,470
Mischievous Merlin	4	G	8	2	1	2	26,204
Mischievous Sam	2	C	1	0	0	0	0
Mischievous Star	3	F	7	2	0	1	6,060
Miscommunicate	3	F	4	0	0	0	816
Misensor	5	H	5	0	0	0	417
Misguided Left	3	G	10	2	1	1	65,905
Misinformer	2	F	3	0	1	0	10,385
Miskip	2	F	3	0	0	1	4,250
Mismeridia	4	F	9	2	1	2	4,450
Miss Abby	6	M	6	1	1	1	6,935
Miss Aberdeen	3	F	3	0	0	1	3,095
Miss Adams	3	F	11	2	1	2	28,963
Miss Addie Downs	4	F	1	0	0	0	217
Miss Adelaide	2	F	2	0	0	1	6,270
Miss Adriana	2	F	1	0	0	0	235
Miss Air Won	4	F	11	3	0	3	15,155
Miss Alamo	5	M	5	1	0	3	4,512
Miss Albeit	3	F	6	0	1	0	1,110
Miss Alexis	5	M	1	0	0	0	0
Miss Alezzotti	4	F	7	0	1	1	2,455
Miss Alice's Boy	6	G	8	0	0	0	0
Miss All That	3	F	7	2	0	0	33,055
Miss Allocation	2	F	4	1	0	0	12,680
Miss Alyetta	6	M	2	0	0	0	1,480
Miss Alyssa	3	F	10	2	0	1	18,369
Miss Amber	2	F	9	1	1	0	7,291
Miss American Pie	3	F	8	1	3	0	13,580
Miss Angel	2	F	10	1	1	3	32,141
Miss Angel Face	4	F	1	0	0	0	0
Miss Angelia	2	F	1	0	0	0	0
Miss Angeline	2	F	5	1	2	0	23,000
Miss Anna Banana	4	F	2	0	0	0	375
Miss Anna Maria	2	F	2	0	0	1	3,278
Miss Anna May	3	F	3	0	0	1	863
Miss Appropriation	3	F	12	1	1	1	8,530
Miss Area Code	6	M	5	1	0	2	6,800
Miss Ash	3	F	8	0	1	1	3,748
Miss Ashland	3	F	9	0	0	0	0
Miss Ashley	5	G	14	4	1	3	25,766
Miss Attack	3	F	7	1	2	1	23,213
Miss Attorney	3	F	3	0	0	0	0
Miss Avalanche	4	F	9	1	1	3	8,761
Miss Awana	4	F	3	1	2	0	8,360
Miss Baba	4	F	9	2	1	2	70,258
Miss Baldesweiler	2	F	1	1	0	0	9,600
Miss Baloo	5	M	5	1	0	0	11,225
Miss Barbara Ray	4	F	13	1	3	3	32,587
Miss Barbie Slew	4	F	9	0	0	1	1,050
Miss Barner	6	M	16	2	1	3	27,128
Miss Battisti	4	F	8	2	1	0	56,350
Miss Battleaxe	3	F	8	2	0	1	18,340
Miss Beag	4	F	2	0	0	0	200
Miss Bearcat	5	M	2	0	0	0	133
Miss Beaulieu	3	F	10	0	1	2	4,743
Miss Belga Bound	3	F	4	1	1	1	23,985
Miss Believe It	5	M	8	0	0	0	1,350
Miss Beraven	5	M	4	0	0	0	810
Miss Bergdorf	3	F	4	0	0	0	1,870
Miss Bernstein	2	F	1	0	1	0	2,565
Miss Bethovens Boy	3	G	6	0	1	2	10,040
Miss Betty	3	F	10	1	1	1	20,100
Miss Betty B.	4	F	4	0	0	0	210
Miss Biggie	3	F	6	0	0	0	936
Miss Bingo Bettie	4	F	8	1	0	1	25,050
Miss Bionic	4	F	14	0	2	0	3,903
Miss Bleus Clues	3	F	9	1	2	0	38,305
Miss Bling Bling	3	F	4	1	0	0	5,283
Miss Bliss	2	F	6	1	1	1	9,824
Miss Blockbuster	3	F	7	0	0	1	2,100
Miss Bobbie Quick	2	F	6	1	0	2	24,136
Miss Bobby Ann	3	F	8	0	0	1	1,910
Miss Bold Peach	3	F	4	0	0	0	480
Miss Bonn Bonn	4	F	11	1	0	3	28,622
Miss Bossy Pants	2	F	3	0	0	0	430
Miss Boundary	4	F	5	0	0	0	1,311
Miss Bradford Co	3	F	14	4	2	3	62,260
Miss Brassy	4	F	18	1	3	6	17,981
Miss Braveheart	4	F	3	0	0	0	139
Miss Briartic	6	M	9	1	3	0	19,185
Miss Bridget Jones	4	F	2	0	0	0	1,020
Miss Briteness	3	F	14	2	1	4	26,227
Miss B's Lucky	3	C	8	3	0	3	16,820
Miss B's Rythum	3	F	9	0	1	3	6,801
Miss Buona Sera	5	M	12	3	3	2	33,868
Miss Butinsky	3	F	1	0	0	0	0
Miss C Continental	2	F	3	0	2	0	17,708
Miss C J	2	F	2	1	0	0	5,364
Miss C. B.	4	F	1	0	0	0	0
Miss Cajun Kitty	2	F	3	1	1	0	21,510
Miss Cajyn	4	F	10	1	4	1	18,160
Miss Calculation	3	F	9	1	0	2	7,179
Miss Candelaria	3	F	2	0	0	0	155
Miss Carrera	4	F	4	1	1	0	33,920
Miss Cash	4	F	11	2	1	2	37,432
Miss Cassie Jean	2	F	13	1	4	1	18,340
Miss Cat Ballou	5	M	11	3	3	1	22,260
Miss Cat Tail	3	F	4	0	0	0	570
Miss Catalina	3	F	3	0	0	0	503
Miss Catillac	3	F	1	1	0	0	12,900
Miss Cecilia	3	F	13	3	0	0	18,272
Miss Centerville	4	F	16	2	4	2	18,076
Miss Chacha Dancer	8	M	10	4	0	1	40,489
Miss Chaffee	5	M	16	0	1	5	9,720
Miss Chalice	3	F	16	1	0	5	17,930
Miss Chance	4	F	3	0	0	0	240
Miss Change	4	F	9	2	0	2	14,681
Miss Chapin	3	F	1	1	0	0	30,600
Miss Charlie Mac	11	M	3	0	0	0	209
Miss Charm Avenger	7	M	7	0	1	2	5,155
Miss Chartres	3	F	8	2	0	0	14,355
Miss Chatty	3	F	8	1	3	0	25,480
Miss Cheektowaga	3	F	2	0	0	0	180
Miss Cherokee Sue	4	F	13	0	4	2	11,118
Miss Chestervalley	2	F	1	0	0	0	480
Miss Chief Woody	7	M	9	1	0	1	9,976
Miss Chihuahua	3	F	3	0	0	0	320
Miss Chloe	3	F	7	0	3	1	6,586
Miss Chris	7	M	5	2	1	0	7,005
Miss Circle	5	M	18	1	0	1	7,000
Miss Clara Tess	5	M	7	2	2	0	27,170
Miss Classic Cut	2	F	4	0	0	0	0
Miss Classified	2	F	3	0	2	0	11,240
Miss Cody	7	M	1	0	0	0	269
Miss Combo	4	F	7	2	0	0	4,777

Horse	Age	Sex	Sts	1st	2d	3d	Won
Miss Concerto	3	F	8	1	1	2	42,640
Miss Confusion	4	F	8	2	1	3	72,150
Miss Congeniality	6	M	9	3	1	2	5,636
Miss Connie Sue	3	F	16	3	1	1	43,572
Miss Cool Soup	2	F	2	0	0	0	0
Miss Copley Hall	2	F	1	0	1	0	7,400
Miss Corey	7	M	3	0	0	0	0
Miss Coronado	3	F	5	2	0	0	137,045
Miss Costello	4	F	13	2	0	2	41,663
Miss Cotton Tail	3	F	9	1	3	0	24,200
Miss Crafty	3	F	4	1	1	0	5,440
Miss Crafty Lady	3	F	10	1	2	1	18,118
Miss Crafty Pal	3	F	10	1	2	2	29,450
Miss Crane	5	M	6	0	0	3	6,510
Miss Cree	5	M	9	0	2	0	4,105
Miss Crissy	4	F	5	0	0	1	20,667
Miss Croft	2	F	4	3	0	1	34,400
Miss Cyprus	4	F	16	3	1	0	46,500
Miss D Flawless	3	F	14	1	1	1	25,014
Miss D' Or	7	M	4	0	1	0	4,880
Miss D. Falcon	5	M	4	0	0	0	297
Miss Dakota	4	F	4	0	1	0	2,720
Miss Dan Pat	6	M	6	0	0	3	1,702
Miss Dazzling	6	M	10	0	0	4	2,257
Miss Debut	3	F	1	0	0	1	6,270
Miss Dee Sean	6	M	7	2	0	0	11,080
Miss Deed	3	F	10	1	0	0	9,888
Miss Defrere	3	F	2	0	0	0	1,090
Miss Del Mar	3	F	6	1	0	1	26,240
Miss Delia	4	F	10	0	1	1	12,275
Miss Denali	3	F	10	1	3	0	14,870
Miss Denouncer	3	F	4	1	0	0	18,480
Miss Denver Mint	5	M	12	2	0	1	9,477
Miss Deputy Dawg	2	F	1	0	0	0	0
Miss Derbyship	6	M	6	1	0	0	2,812
Miss Dewali	2	F	1	0	0	0	140
Miss Diablo's Cav	5	M	3	0	0	0	612
Miss Diamondlegs	2	F	2	0	0	0	2,670
Miss Diplomat	5	M	3	0	0	0	600
Miss Discover	3	F	3	0	0	0	1,539
Miss Dixie Brass	8	M	3	0	0	0	123
Miss Dixie Dreamer	4	F	3	0	0	0	1,960
Miss Dixie Star	4	F	8	0	0	3	2,810
Miss Dixie Wynner	3	F	9	0	1	1	4,565
Miss Doggedly	5	M	9	0	2	1	9,519
Miss Domuch (IRE)	6	M	1	0	0	0	0
Miss Dorothy	2	F	3	0	3	0	34,200
Miss Double Dots	4	F	6	2	1	2	65,000
Miss Dragon	4	F	8	2	1	2	23,720
Miss Ducketts	6	M	5	1	1	0	2,070
Miss Dumaine	4	F	7	3	3	0	41,800
Miss Durocell	3	F	2	0	0	0	0
Miss Dustski	4	F	6	0	0	0	264
Miss Dyna	2	F	3	1	1	0	15,660
Miss Eagle Pass	3	F	3	0	0	0	0
Miss Easy	3	F	1	0	0	0	95
Miss Echotoyou	3	F	7	1	0	1	7,330
Miss Elegance	6	M	7	1	0	0	2,752
Miss Elegant	4	F	4	0	0	0	2,505
Miss Eliana	2	F	2	0	0	0	800
Miss Ella B.	3	F	1	0	0	0	501
Miss Ellie J	4	F	9	1	0	3	12,482
Miss Elsie	3	F	3	2	1	0	47,800
Miss Eltish	5	M	5	1	0	0	8,408
Miss Elusive	3	F	11	2	1	1	53,710
Miss Elvia	4	F	5	0	0	0	0
Miss Emma S	4	F	3	0	0	0	0
Miss E's Report	5	M	5	0	0	0	593
Miss Event	3	F	11	1	1	1	14,190
Miss Excavate	2	F	8	1	1	4	29,179
Miss Excellent	5	M	2	0	0	0	0
Miss Expectations	3	F	12	3	0	2	36,300
Miss Eye Appeal	4	F	2	0	0	0	0
Miss Eyra	3	F	1	0	0	0	780
Miss F D N Y	4	F	2	1	0	0	8,615
Miss Fairfield	3	F	6	2	1	2	23,800
Miss Fanny	3	F	2	0	1	1	8,220
Miss Fasliyev	2	F	1	0	0	0	750
Miss Fatih	5	M	4	0	0	0	200
Miss Feather River	5	M	7	1	0	1	5,148
Miss Feature	7	M	15	3	2	2	12,432
Miss Fifty Two	2	F	4	0	1	1	4,120
Miss Filibuster	4	F	6	2	1	0	80,736
Miss Fire Water	9	M	1	0	0	0	85
Miss Fixed Income	4	F	15	2	2	5	44,412
Miss Flagship	6	M	1	0	0	0	107
Miss Flit N Flot	3	F	8	2	2	0	28,385
Miss Flor (FR)	4	F	6	0	1	1	20,845
Miss Fortunate	4	F	9	2	2	3	190,165
Miss Foxcroft	6	M	16	4	5	2	27,243
Miss Foxly	5	M	2	0	0	0	91
Miss Foxy Slew	4	F	2	0	0	0	330
Miss Freedom	4	F	4	2	0	1	11,402
Miss French	5	M	6	0	2	3	21,485
Miss Frenchie	6	M	9	2	2	0	23,491
Miss Friendly	4	F	15	0	3	2	4,350
Miss Friendship	7	M	4	0	0	0	500
Miss Fudge	7	M	11	3	0	3	31,286
Miss Fuzzi Diamond	3	F	12	0	0	4	9,735
Miss G Force	3	F	7	0	0	1	3,545
Miss Garrett	4	F	5	0	0	0	546
Miss Gazelle	3	F	1	1	0	0	7,920
Miss Genevieve	3	F	1	0	0	0	0
Miss Geniality	2	F	2	0	1	1	4,340
Miss Georgia	3	F	5	2	0	2	31,230
Miss Ginalie	3	F	13	2	1	1	16,223
Miss Gina's Bag	5	M	10	0	0	2	2,162
Miss Glen Rose	3	F	2	0	0	1	1,658
Miss Gloria	3	F	7	0	1	0	3,654
Miss Glowing Groom	2	F	5	0	0	0	888
Miss Gneiss	3	F	2	0	0	0	0
Miss Gold Ore	5	M	2	0	0	0	642
Miss Golden Girl	3	F	6	0	1	1	2,625
Miss Goodie	2	F	1	0	1	0	4,620
Miss Goose Creek	7	M	3	0	0	0	126
Miss Goosebumps	5	M	13	0	2	2	31,905
Miss Got Rox	5	M	6	1	1	1	2,752
Miss Gracie	4	F	5	0	1	2	10,883
Miss Gray Goose	5	M	7	2	1	2	12,430
Miss Greeny	2	F	3	1	1	0	33,660
Miss Gretchen	5	M	7	0	1	1	878
Miss Grindstone	5	M	8	5	0	2	271,985
Miss Groom	5	M	2	0	0	0	555
Miss Guts	5	M	6	0	2	0	8,140
Miss Hamma	5	M	5	0	2	1	27,156
Miss Happy	3	F	5	0	2	2	10,210
Miss Happy Hour	4	F	6	2	0	0	9,796
Miss Hawfield	3	F	7	1	0	0	15,060
Miss Helen Wheels	3	F	2	0	0	0	145
Miss Hellie	5	M	6	0	1	1	46,448
Miss Hennessy	5	M	7	0	1	0	2,252
Miss Hester	4	F	9	3	1	1	45,869
Miss High Brow	3	F	3	1	0	0	20,898
Miss Hilton	2	F	11	1	0	1	10,325
Miss Hit Run	3	F	1	0	0	0	95
Miss Hobbs America	2	F	1	0	0	0	0
Miss Holy Moly	3	F	8	1	1	1	32,478
Miss Holy Toledo	5	M	13	1	0	4	7,543
Miss Honey Money	4	F	1	1	0	0	12,960
Miss Honeybee	6	M	3	0	0	0	405
Miss Hot Hoofs	5	M	12	1	1	1	4,895
Miss Hotsy Totsy	7	M	9	2	2	0	12,066
Miss Hottie	3	F	5	0	1	1	3,881
Miss Icicle	6	M	9	0	0	1	10,368
Miss Ida Belle	6	M	13	2	1	4	24,141
Miss Imagination	5	M	10	2	3	1	30,295
Miss Imagine That	3	F	10	1	1	2	9,941
Miss Independent	4	F	10	3	0	0	33,849
Miss Indian	5	M	6	0	1	0	1,164
Miss Infidelity	3	C	5	0	1	0	3,080
Miss Intrepid	3	F	4	0	0	0	450
Miss Irma	3	F	7	0	0	0	1,425
Miss Issy	3	F	2	1	0	0	14,340
Miss Jangle	4	F	10	1	0	1	9,266
Miss January	2	F	2	1	1	0	50,800
Miss Jazzy	6	M	7	2	2	0	30,820
Miss Jeannie G.	4	F	10	0	1	1	4,351
Miss Jekyll	3	F	7	0	0	0	0

Horse	Age	Sex	Sts	1st	2d	3d	Won
Miss Jesy's Town	2	F	1	0	0	0	0
Miss Jet Note	4	F	10	0	0	0	1,040
Miss Jibarita	3	F	6	1	0	1	9,275
Miss Johnson	3	F	7	1	0	0	5,089
Miss Jordan	2	F	6	0	1	0	6,727
Miss Judged Me	3	F	12	0	1	0	3,838
Miss Julian	7	M	7	0	1	0	4,788
Miss Julie Anna	4	F	2	1	0	0	15,060
Miss Jumron	3	F	5	0	0	1	1,885
Miss Kajun Punch	2	F	2	0	0	0	0
Miss Karry Thenews	4	F	7	0	0	1	5,178
Miss Katarina	4	F	1	0	0	0	0
Miss Kelsey	4	F	13	0	2	2	3,703
Miss Kenai	3	F	7	0	1	0	5,615
Miss Kentucky	5	M	1	0	0	0	0
Miss Kipper Kitty	6	M	6	4	1	0	23,600
Miss Kitty Hawk	5	M	3	1	0	0	39,308
Miss Kittys Motel	4	F	4	0	1	0	972
Miss Kleven	4	F	6	0	0	2	12,586
Miss Know It All	2	F	9	2	0	2	45,451
Miss Laabity	3	F	12	2	1	0	8,174
Miss Lacy Shea	5	M	13	2	2	0	18,771
Miss Lady Randolph	5	M	18	3	0	3	21,557
Miss Lady's Lawyer	3	C	2	0	0	0	480
Miss Lakefield	2	F	1	1	0	0	24,600
Miss Larsha	3	F	3	1	0	0	7,920
Miss Laurel Canyon	4	F	6	1	1	1	4,674
Miss Leatherwood	4	F	8	0	0	0	1,087
Miss Legend	4	F	14	1	2	5	36,320
Miss Lexy	3	F	7	1	1	0	11,380
Miss Lickity Split	4	F	3	0	0	0	235
Miss Lil'	4	F	10	2	1	1	15,930
Miss Lily	3	F	8	1	0	0	25,692
Miss Lily Bee	5	M	3	0	0	0	882
Miss Lily Langfuhr	3	F	7	1	3	1	33,130
Miss Lionel	4	F	5	0	0	2	3,674
Miss Lisa	3	F	1	0	0	0	50
Miss Listo	4	F	1	0	0	0	1,400
Miss Lit de Justic	4	F	2	0	0	0	0
Miss Lizzie	3	F	2	0	0	0	161
Miss Lizzie Tish	4	F	10	1	1	3	11,280
Miss Loganville	4	F	12	1	2	1	12,363
Miss Lonestar	3	F	11	2	0	2	30,334
Miss Longevity	7	M	19	0	1	2	2,900
Miss Loren (ARG)	6	M	7	1	1	2	288,032
Miss Low Cut	5	M	6	0	1	0	1,475
Miss Lucky Buck	2	F	3	0	0	1	2,645
Miss Lucky Molar	4	F	2	0	1	0	840
Miss Lucky Strike	6	M	15	1	3	4	22,122
Miss Luminaire	3	F	2	0	0	0	0
Miss Luttie Huck	3	F	6	0	0	0	0
Miss Machisma	3	F	21	2	2	0	16,665
Miss Maddilynn	4	F	5	0	0	0	850
Miss Magnolia	3	F	4	1	1	1	8,260
Miss Malaga	6	M	2	0	0	0	240
Miss Malthus	3	F	8	2	1	0	8,681
Miss Marcy	6	M	6	1	0	0	6,740
Miss Maria	5	M	8	2	0	3	10,601
Miss Mark	3	F	10	1	1	0	20,620
Miss Marker	5	M	1	0	0	0	40
Miss Marna	4	F	4	0	0	0	1,106
Miss Marni	5	M	1	0	0	0	300
Miss Maronie	3	F	18	2	3	5	47,100
Miss Marvic	3	F	10	5	2	0	29,776
Miss Mary Apples	4	F	4	0	0	0	1,020
Miss Mary Kyle	2	F	3	0	0	0	0
Miss Masten	3	F	8	1	0	0	4,780
Miss Matched	2	F	3	1	1	0	72,200
Miss Mattie Mu Mu	6	M	7	0	0	0	481
Miss Matty Mac	2	F	1	0	1	0	1,900
Miss Maudette	5	M	11	1	1	0	18,227
Miss Me Baby	2	F	3	0	1	1	8,020
Miss Meanie	3	F	6	0	0	1	2,267
Miss Mecke	5	M	1	0	0	0	0
Miss Megabucks	2	F	2	0	0	0	0
Miss Meister	3	F	4	1	0	0	8,440
Miss Memento	3	F	3	1	2	0	24,400
Miss Memories	7	M	2	0	0	0	98
Miss Merit	2	F	5	0	0	0	2,340
Miss Merry Oaks	4	F	1	0	0	0	0
Miss Metfield	3	F	10	1	1	1	6,879
Miss Metropolitan	3	F	10	1	0	1	5,900
Miss Michelle	6	M	11	0	2	3	10,992
Miss Midas	3	F	7	0	1	0	10,435
Miss Midnight Fire	3	F	9	0	2	1	5,250
Miss Miesque	5	M	2	1	0	1	6,960
Miss Misbehavin'	9	M	17	0	0	4	11,887
Miss Mischief	3	F	2	1	0	0	4,939
Miss Misfit	3	F	10	2	0	0	20,585
Miss Mizzou	3	F	7	1	0	0	2,836
Miss Mollie M	3	F	9	0	0	1	1,367
Miss Monty	4	F	2	0	0	0	270
Miss Moolah	3	F	3	1	1	0	13,946
Miss Moon	5	M	14	0	0	3	12,150
Miss Moonraker	5	M	7	1	0	1	11,573
Miss Morning Line	3	F	3	0	1	0	2,750
Miss Mosby	3	F	6	0	0	1	3,850
Miss Moses	3	F	10	3	2	2	102,870
Miss Move Over	3	F	13	2	1	2	14,226
Miss Mt Laurel	3	F	5	0	1	1	5,250
Miss Mudville	5	M	9	1	2	0	5,273
Miss Mulie	3	F	8	3	1	0	19,785
Miss Muriel	4	F	7	0	1	0	9,911
Miss Musical Coin	7	M	12	1	2	0	5,228
Miss My Way	2	F	3	1	1	0	12,000
Miss Mystical Mon	4	F	3	1	0	0	2,670
Miss N Control	3	F	1	0	0	0	2,300
Miss Naab	5	M	3	2	1	0	12,960
Miss Nashwan (IRE)	4	F	5	2	0	1	74,090
Miss Nasty Top	7	M	9	2	1	3	7,010
Miss Necole	4	F	1	0	0	0	0
Miss Nelson Bid	4	F	1	0	0	0	0
Miss Nena	7	M	13	0	2	3	4,484
Miss New Orleans	4	F	9	0	0	1	484
Miss New York	6	M	11	1	2	0	42,640
Miss Nickels	5	M	7	0	0	1	3,860
Miss Nikki Y	3	F	13	3	0	1	23,555
Miss Nite Gold	6	M	6	0	0	0	720
Miss Norma Jean	3	F	3	0	0	0	3,090
Miss Nosy Rosy	2	F	2	0	1	1	3,967
Miss Noteworthy	3	F	7	5	1	0	95,435
Miss Oatie May	2	F	1	0	0	0	0
Miss Obedient	4	F	6	0	0	0	334
Miss O'Brannigan	8	M	12	0	0	0	520
Miss Ondatop	5	M	10	0	4	0	2,633
Miss One Two Three	4	F	2	0	1	0	1,040
Miss Ooh La La	3	F	11	3	1	1	40,460
Miss Ooh Wee	2	F	1	0	0	0	0
Miss Outlaw Biker	3	F	14	1	1	0	13,135
Miss Outrageous	3	F	11	3	0	0	66,000
Miss Overstep	2	F	1	0	0	0	100
Miss P G A	4	F	11	1	1	1	8,056
Miss Pagan Glare	4	F	1	0	0	0	0
Miss Paranoid	3	F	7	1	1	3	20,095
Miss Park Place	3	F	16	3	2	2	87,322
Miss Partee	4	F	2	0	0	0	0
Miss Patti	3	F	9	1	0	2	9,350
Miss Payton	5	M	7	1	0	0	6,841
Miss Pennie's Case	6	G	11	0	1	2	5,235
Miss Penny Fortune	4	F	5	1	1	0	25,990
Miss Pennypincher	5	M	6	1	2	0	8,925
Miss Perfect Me	3	F	2	0	0	0	635
Miss Perkinsville	4	F	9	1	1	3	13,969
Miss Photogenic	6	M	1	0	0	0	0
Miss Pistol Town	2	F	6	1	0	0	9,675
Miss Pixie	7	M	3	0	2	0	12,340
Miss Pompei	4	F	2	0	0	0	108
Miss Positive	2	F	2	0	0	0	740
Miss Precocity	3	F	9	2	0	1	14,280
Miss Prestissimo	5	M	3	0	0	0	180
Miss Primandproper	5	M	1	0	0	0	90
Miss Prissy Won	2	F	1	0	0	0	0
Miss Private	3	F	3	0	0	0	280
Miss Pro American	3	F	5	1	2	1	9,960
Miss Proper Too	4	F	10	0	1	2	6,325
Miss Proper West	4	F	10	1	2	2	24,478
Miss Prospect	3	F	13	2	0	3	16,786
Miss Ptarmigan	5	M	11	3	0	1	22,603

Horse	Age	Sex	Sts	1st	2d	3d	Won
Miss Purtenance	5	M	12	2	2	0	8,651
Miss Quackers	3	F	5	0	1	0	3,315
Miss Quick City	4	F	2	1	0	0	9,240
Miss Quiz	4	F	3	0	0	1	820
Miss Rachel Marie	4	F	1	0	0	1	2,596
Miss Rainbow	5	M	4	0	1	0	362
Miss Rainier	2	F	2	1	0	0	14,695
Miss Rajas Tactics	4	F	3	0	0	0	0
Miss Rancho Vista	3	F	4	1	0	1	4,484
Miss Rather	2	F	4	0	0	1	1,540
Miss Red Rose	4	F	2	0	0	0	570
Miss Reiko	3	F	2	0	0	1	2,460
Miss Rich	3	F	4	1	1	0	1,660
Miss Ricki Racer	3	F	12	1	2	1	6,625
Miss Riley	5	M	6	1	0	0	3,074
Miss Rita	7	M	9	1	1	2	4,442
Miss Roberson	4	F	10	5	1	2	102,658
Miss Roberts	5	M	5	0	0	1	735
Miss Robynhood	3	F	2	0	0	0	209
Miss Rocket Jag	2	F	5	1	0	1	9,780
Miss Rocket Jet	4	F	9	2	0	1	21,049
Miss Rodeo	4	F	2	0	0	0	2,610
Miss Romeo	5	M	7	0	3	0	4,371
Miss Royal Dancer	7	M	7	0	0	0	1,234
Miss Ruby Jo	4	F	3	0	0	1	1,430
Miss Rudi	6	M	6	0	0	0	505
Miss Rue Du Lac	3	F	17	4	5	2	21,646
Miss Ruffles	3	F	7	2	1	1	11,400
Miss Saga	4	F	1	0	0	0	50
Miss Sanata	5	M	13	1	1	1	31,290
Miss Sand Bar	3	F	1	0	0	1	5,640
Miss Sandi Storm	2	F	8	1	1	1	13,770
Miss Sandy	5	M	14	2	0	3	9,163
Miss Sandy Ray	3	F	1	0	0	0	0
Miss Santa Ana	6	M	1	0	0	0	0
Miss Santa Anita	4	F	7	1	1	1	60,655
Miss Sarah C	3	F	5	0	0	2	4,250
Miss Sassy	5	M	8	0	0	2	1,901
Miss Secret Ryder	4	F	1	0	0	0	498
Miss Semoran	3	F	15	1	4	2	10,645
Miss Sentry	4	F	3	0	0	0	0
Miss Seven Eleven	3	F	8	2	1	2	3,962
Miss Shahmeka	4	F	4	0	0	0	0
Miss Shares	6	M	10	0	3	2	3,801
Miss Shawnie	3	F	10	2	1	1	23,965
Miss Shiloh	3	F	7	3	1	1	15,832
Miss Sig	5	M	7	1	0	1	8,748
Miss Silver Jab	3	F	2	0	0	0	0
Miss Silvia	3	F	6	0	0	0	700
Miss Skyline	4	F	3	0	0	0	88
Miss Slew	4	F	7	0	0	1	2,087
Miss Smart Alec	3	F	14	2	1	3	16,759
Miss Smart Strike	4	F	6	3	1	0	47,585
Miss Socks	8	M	4	0	0	0	0
Miss Soldier	3	F	4	0	0	0	2,110
Miss Song	4	F	9	0	3	1	14,535
Miss Spain	5	M	10	1	3	2	24,910
Miss Speed Dial	4	F	2	0	0	0	0
Miss Spender	5	M	6	0	4	0	12,880
Miss Spiff to You	4	F	3	0	0	0	67
Miss Spires	2	F	1	0	0	0	235
Miss Spitfire	3	F	11	1	2	1	5,457
Miss Splash	6	M	4	1	0	0	10,580
Miss Sport Trac	5	M	5	0	0	0	379
Miss Spragg	5	M	6	1	1	2	28,184
Miss Stack	3	F	2	1	0	0	5,560
Miss Starlight	2	F	8	1	1	0	6,520
Miss Steppin On	5	M	3	0	0	0	490
Miss Stipends	3	F	12	0	2	0	5,408
Miss Storm Song	6	M	4	3	0	0	24,420
Miss Stormy	3	F	1	0	0	0	0
Miss Stovall	4	F	13	2	3	2	13,172
Miss Sugar	5	M	7	2	2	1	18,964
Miss Sugar Booger	4	F	4	1	0	0	3,829
Miss Sultry Song	3	F	12	1	1	3	8,832
Miss Summer	5	M	5	0	0	0	304
Miss Sun	3	F	2	0	0	0	120
Miss Super Pet	3	F	8	2	1	1	18,455
Miss Superoyale	3	F	1	0	0	0	0
Miss Supertime	6	M	12	0	0	0	568
Miss Susan	4	F	14	3	3	1	16,575
Miss Susie Roo	6	M	3	0	0	0	253
Miss Swain	3	F	1	0	0	0	0
Miss Sweep	6	M	3	0	0	0	4,200
Miss Sweet Time	4	F	10	3	1	2	62,880
Miss Sweetness	3	F	3	0	0	0	224
Miss Swiss Appeal	6	M	13	2	2	2	11,090
Miss Swisse	2	F	2	0	0	0	1,535
Miss T K O	4	F	3	0	1	0	2,016
Miss T. Luck	3	F	4	0	0	0	405
Miss T. V. G.	3	F	12	3	4	2	48,969
Miss Taat	5	M	12	1	1	0	5,044
Miss Tacky Trump	5	M	11	3	1	4	37,334
Miss Tact	4	F	5	1	1	1	8,210
Miss Talbot Road	3	F	9	1	1	1	4,977
Miss Tale Cat	4	F	10	2	4	0	33,810
Miss Tall Hammer	3	F	6	1	0	1	19,930
Miss Tamster	3	F	2	0	0	0	0
Miss Tarzan	3	F	8	0	1	1	3,305
Miss Tay Tay	4	F	4	0	1	1	2,117
Miss Temptor	4	F	8	2	2	2	7,727
Miss Tester	5	M	13	2	3	2	12,932
Miss Testified	3	F	5	0	0	0	891
Miss Texas	2	F	1	0	0	0	0
Miss Texas Star	3	F	11	1	2	0	6,662
Miss Thalia	2	F	5	0	0	1	2,060
Miss the Kiss	4	F	5	0	0	0	400
Miss Thirtyfour D	4	F	10	1	4	1	66,020
Miss Thunder	3	F	1	0	0	0	64
Miss Thunderella	2	F	2	0	0	0	330
Miss Tiburon	3	F	9	2	1	1	15,350
Miss Tiki Regent	5	M	7	0	0	0	668
Miss Timberlake	4	F	10	0	2	1	2,427
Miss Time	6	M	10	0	1	1	6,194
Miss Tina	5	M	1	0	0	0	0
Miss Tipbrand	9	M	3	0	0	0	192
Miss Torcher	6	M	2	1	0	0	2,990
Miss Towaoc	3	F	8	0	0	1	3,058
Miss Trapp	7	M	8	0	0	1	1,050
Miss Tricky	2	F	2	0	0	0	140
Miss Tricky Love	4	F	4	1	0	0	7,300
Miss Triple Turn	4	F	6	1	1	1	5,677
Miss Trixie	4	F	5	0	3	1	13,660
Miss Tropics	5	M	5	2	0	0	22,910
Miss Trouble	3	F	10	2	1	1	39,240
Miss Tuffet	2	F	6	1	0	1	11,050
Miss Twelve	4	F	9	3	1	2	21,315
Miss Twiggy	4	F	4	0	0	0	0
Miss Two Bagger	8	M	8	1	0	0	2,760
Miss Uppity	4	F	11	0	1	2	2,986
Miss Vegas (IRE)	3	F	3	2	1	0	161,160
Miss Venturous	2	F	5	3	0	0	67,961
Miss Vice Regent	4	F	11	0	1	2	4,860
Miss Victory	5	M	14	4	3	1	32,662
Miss Victory Lady	4	F	1	0	0	0	0
Miss Way West	5	M	2	0	0	0	160
Miss Weiser	4	F	9	1	0	3	17,220
Miss Wellspring	3	F	10	4	1	0	122,510
Miss Westchester	4	F	2	0	0	0	420
Miss Whirlybird	3	F	11	2	1	0	24,670
Miss Whitney	5	M	14	2	0	1	11,608
Miss Wicked Witch	2	F	3	0	1	1	3,678
Miss Willie	5	M	4	1	0	0	9,300
Miss Winetime	3	F	8	1	0	2	5,690
Miss Wiserequest	4	F	7	0	1	0	2,661
Miss With Attitude	3	F	16	3	2	1	12,256
Miss Woo	4	F	5	3	0	0	21,535
Miss Woodrow	2	F	1	0	0	0	0
Miss Woodville	4	F	11	5	1	0	55,910
Miss World's Pride	5	M	1	0	0	0	105
Miss Ya Madly	4	F	8	0	1	0	4,250
Miss Yakity	4	F	2	0	0	0	112
Miss You Dearly	5	M	15	0	5	1	12,327
Miss Zebulon	4	F	12	1	1	3	26,251
Miss Zelda	3	F	10	1	2	2	17,646
Miss Zippy	4	F	2	0	0	0	545
Missagility	5	M	10	1	1	2	8,240
Missbehavin Ihaint	2	F	7	1	0	1	9,820

Horse	Age	Sex	Sts	1st	2d	3d	Won
Missbehaviour	7	M	6	0	0	0	2,111
Missbigmama	4	F	6	0	0	0	1,320
Missblowtheshow	3	F	3	0	0	1	2,250
Misschristmasvaley	7	M	9	0	0	0	70
Missdavilynn	4	F	1	0	0	0	0
Missed	8	G	7	0	1	2	1,640
Missed Approach	3	F	12	0	2	3	5,738
Missed Connection	3	F	12	1	2	0	31,430
Missed Signal	6	G	7	0	0	0	460
Missed Summer	3	C	2	0	0	0	800
Missed the Call	3	G	17	3	4	4	70,224
Misseditbythatmuch	3	G	4	0	0	0	5,130
Missice	3	F	9	4	1	2	69,500
Missile Bay	2	F	7	1	1	3	42,570
Missile Control	2	C	3	1	0	0	13,450
Missile Strike	2	F	4	0	0	1	9,318
Missile Tone	2	F	6	1	0	0	5,545
Missileer	6	G	1	0	0	0	0
Missilery	3	G	6	0	2	1	3,531
Missin At Midnight	5	G	2	0	0	0	165
Missin You	4	G	2	0	0	0	150
Missing Assignment	4	C	12	3	0	5	42,890
Missing Jackie	3	F	10	2	3	0	19,192
Missing Night	3	G	1	0	0	1	855
Missing Position	4	F	3	0	0	0	0
Missing Sefa	2	F	11	1	1	2	18,659
Missing Silks	4	G	11	4	1	0	23,205
Missing Tab	4	F	5	0	1	0	1,475
Missing Verse	5	M	1	0	0	0	0
Missing Woman	3	F	8	0	1	3	14,226
Missingrbueno	2	F	5	1	3	0	47,129
Mission Apollo	5	G	11	2	4	1	12,866
Mission Commander	4	G	12	1	2	3	4,757
Mission Creek	4	F	5	0	0	0	300
Mission for Bag	2	F	7	1	1	0	24,338
Mission of Love	4	F	1	1	0	0	4,200
Mission Showers	5	M	10	1	2	2	16,246
Mission Slew	8	H	5	0	0	0	280
Mission Terrace	2	F	2	1	0	0	5,525
Missionary Groom	8	H	1	0	0	0	0
Missionary Lady	6	M	17	3	3	2	30,986
Missionary Monk	9	G	6	0	0	0	1,020
Mississaugas Magic	4	F	12	4	1	1	20,521
Mississippi Money	6	G	7	0	0	0	1,179
Mississippi Rain	3	G	9	4	2	0	69,700
Mississippi River	4	G	11	0	4	1	22,833
Missle Do	4	F	14	1	2	5	35,310
Missle Long	8	H	4	0	0	0	0
Misslevalay	3	F	5	0	0	0	1,240
Missmaybe	3	F	6	3	0	1	71,010
Missmayday	3	F	4	0	0	1	460
Missme	5	G	14	3	1	3	166,995
Missoni	3	F	6	0	1	4	8,635
Missouri Sunrise	4	G	1	0	0	0	0
Misspent	7	M	5	0	1	0	2,830
Missprincessashley	5	M	14	1	1	2	8,497
Missquickchick	2	F	1	1	0	0	16,560
Missstormyatlantic	4	F	13	2	3	1	38,422
Missteasious	4	F	8	1	1	0	6,697
Missthewire	5	M	15	2	5	3	53,450
Missvalley	3	F	11	1	3	2	19,781
Missy Baquero	3	F	12	0	3	1	3,650
Missy Can Do	4	F	8	4	1	2	32,068
Missy Cat	2	F	4	1	0	0	9,510
Missy Girl	4	F	12	0	0	1	1,339
Missy Llama	3	F	11	1	3	0	13,783
Missy Mae	2	F	5	0	0	0	2,340
Missy Meanor	3	F	3	0	0	0	225
Missy One Forum	4	F	2	0	0	0	1,165
Missy Reality	3	F	1	0	0	0	0
Missy Snow	2	F	3	0	1	1	4,950
Missy Turtle	6	M	7	0	1	2	14,590
Missy Two Shoes	3	F	2	0	0	0	136
Missy Won	3	F	16	1	4	3	16,112
Missy Woo Woo	2	F	1	0	0	0	118
Missy's Fan	3	F	2	0	0	1	2,200
Missy's Joy	4	F	2	0	1	1	4,200
Missy's Queen	2	F	2	0	1	0	3,245
Missy's Shadow	4	F	2	0	0	0	1,050
Missy's Thunder	3	F	3	0	1	0	9,750
Mist Me	4	F	11	1	1	2	4,376
Mist of the Empire	4	F	12	0	4	1	12,907
Mist Some Spots	3	G	1	0	0	0	0
Mist Walker	4	G	5	1	2	0	10,620
Mista Mayberry	4	F	11	1	2	2	37,300
Mistacall	2	F	1	0	0	0	0
Mistakates Mystery	6	M	7	0	0	0	553
Mistaken Identity	3	G	6	0	0	1	870
Mistda	3	F	6	3	1	0	116,996
Mistee Meenor	6	M	5	1	0	0	1,700
Mister Ajax	4	G	12	1	2	3	48,490
Mister Alfalfa	2	G	2	0	0	0	390
Mister Allen	5	G	13	1	2	2	26,388
Mister Approval	6	G	9	1	0	2	8,237
Mister Atlantic	3	C	13	3	3	3	95,250
Mister Bel	2	G	3	0	0	0	1,200
Mister Bingbangboo	4	G	2	0	1	0	9,000
Mister Blister	4	C	3	0	1	0	8,400
Mister Blues	7	H	1	0	0	0	0
Mister Boots	6	H	4	0	0	0	546
Mister Bravo	5	G	5	1	1	0	14,649
Mister Budster	3	G	3	0	2	0	6,400
Mister Charmin	2	C	4	0	0	0	1,210
Mister Cisco	6	G	1	0	0	0	0
Mister Continental	8	G	11	0	0	0	1,001
Mister Coop	5	G	7	0	1	1	40,124
Mister Cosmi (GB)	5	G	2	0	0	1	5,520
Mister Cy	8	G	5	1	0	0	7,813
Mister Deux	4	C	4	1	0	0	21,120
Mister Diz	6	G	2	0	0	0	288
Mister Doeny	4	G	8	2	3	1	17,580
Mister Dv	3	C	11	0	1	1	5,880
Mister E. K.	3	C	5	1	0	0	18,856
Mister Eight	6	G	8	0	1	0	6,260
Mister Emdee	3	C	1	0	0	0	0
Mister Excess	5	G	7	0	2	1	11,841
Mister Fizz	5	G	12	1	2	1	17,500
Mister Flowers	4	C	13	3	2	1	30,380
Mister Fotis	3	C	11	3	1	2	124,640
Mister Four	5	G	1	0	0	0	240
Mister Fox	4	G	13	3	2	2	26,028
Mister French	5	G	8	1	2	3	35,885
Mister Freud	8	G	6	1	0	2	14,487
Mister Goodie	5	G	9	1	2	0	6,572
Mister Goyo	2	G	5	0	0	2	3,780
Mister Handsome	10	G	5	0	0	0	569
Mister Hennessy	5	G	8	2	1	0	59,609
Mister Hobbles	3	C	4	0	0	0	0
Mister Hollstep	5	G	7	1	1	1	12,181
Mister Ingapomppe	3	G	3	0	0	0	0
Mister Jerald	5	G	12	1	1	0	7,130
Mister Jin Dandy	3	G	7	0	0	0	482
Mister M. E.	4	G	10	0	0	2	1,953
Mister Ma	5	G	2	0	0	0	0
Mister Mallard	2	C	1	0	0	0	0
Mister Mambo	3	G	4	0	0	1	6,920
Mister Mane Man	4	G	2	0	1	0	5,650
Mister Matthew	8	G	1	0	0	0	0
Mister Meaner	4	C	5	0	0	1	6,465
Mister Melvin	3	G	20	2	1	3	10,936
Mister Mighty Mac	10	G	6	2	0	2	9,225
Mister Misty	4	G	9	1	1	0	7,709
Mister Mo	7	G	9	0	1	1	1,942
Mister Mordecai	3	G	6	0	1	1	2,911
Mister Motif	3	G	5	0	0	0	127
Mister Mud	7	G	1	0	0	0	40
Mister Nick	4	G	2	0	0	0	0
Mister Party	5	G	7	2	0	1	19,002
Mister Quality	3	C	6	0	0	0	1,326
Mister Retsina	3	C	5	0	0	0	199
Mister Riley	4	G	22	7	5	7	78,700
Mister Ripley	5	G	9	1	0	3	2,460
Mister Slew	4	G	2	1	0	0	23,040
Mister Slick	5	G	9	0	0	1	3,227
Mister Slippery	4	C	4	0	0	0	265
Mister Stip	4	G	13	5	3	2	91,905
Mister Sultry	3	G	8	0	1	3	18,514
Mister Syn	5	G	4	0	0	2	965

Horse	Age	Sex	Sts	1st	2d	3d	Won
Mister Tornado	2	G	2	0	0	0	1,500
Mister Utopia	2	C	1	0	0	0	0
Mister Utterly	2	C	5	0	0	0	1,340
Mister Velocity	5	G	13	1	1	2	6,037
Mister Vine	6	G	2	0	0	1	1,384
Mister Vinson	6	G	1	0	0	0	210
Mister Volare	7	H	11	4	0	0	49,112
Mister Weinke	4	G	25	3	0	4	27,712
Mister Wilson	4	G	13	1	1	1	6,878
Misti Light	4	F	13	1	5	2	15,675
Misti Stephi	5	M	9	0	0	1	3,920
Mistic Ring	4	F	2	0	0	0	0
Mistical Fastness	4	C	5	0	1	0	13,363
Mistical Jaz	5	M	7	1	1	1	9,360
Mistical Magic	5	M	3	0	0	0	1,242
Mistico Cigano (BRZ)	4	C	6	0	1	0	9,300
Mistiff	4	F	5	2	1	0	22,976
Misting	5	M	2	0	0	0	132
Mistletoad	4	F	8	1	1	1	2,855
Mistoffelees	3	G	10	1	4	1	40,780
Mistpelled	7	M	6	1	0	3	7,069
Mistraction	2	F	1	0	0	0	184
Mistress Hemming	3	F	3	0	0	0	2,288
Mistress in Red	3	F	6	2	0	2	17,435
Mistress Raj	3	F	2	0	0	0	160
Mistress Vermont	4	F	8	1	2	0	10,345
Mistrick	3	F	5	1	1	1	7,540
Misty Account	3	F	4	0	0	0	190
Misty Appeal	3	G	13	2	4	2	69,530
Misty Approval	4	G	6	1	0	1	18,234
Misty Brown Eyes	3	F	3	0	0	0	180
Misty County	3	C	3	0	0	0	750
Misty Creek	4	F	5	0	0	1	2,220
Misty Digs It	2	F	2	0	0	0	330
Misty Dreamer	2	F	2	0	0	0	900
Misty Escar	4	F	3	1	0	0	5,235
Misty Expectation	5	M	4	0	1	1	23,106
Misty Fling	2	F	5	0	1	0	2,189
Misty for Mitch	3	F	1	0	0	0	0
Misty Forum	5	G	9	2	1	0	9,852
Misty Ghost	7	M	8	0	0	1	1,380
Misty Glo	3	F	13	5	1	1	99,527
Misty Heights (GB)	3	F	7	1	1	1	84,481
Misty Kilarny	7	G	4	0	0	0	331
Misty Lane	2	F	2	0	0	0	1,120
Misty Leader	4	F	16	5	3	4	19,093
Misty Light Air	3	F	6	1	0	1	20,080
Misty Mae Rose	3	F	9	2	1	3	15,218
Misty Maggie	3	F	11	3	2	2	47,300
Misty Malibu	3	F	10	0	4	2	27,376
Misty North	4	F	3	0	0	0	765
Misty Reign	4	F	10	0	2	3	7,935
Misty Riches	6	G	13	3	2	1	17,940
Misty River	4	F	8	2	2	2	13,373
Misty Sabin	2	F	1	0	0	0	700
Misty Season	3	F	4	0	0	0	184
Misty Segula	3	F	4	0	0	0	1,410
Misty Sixes	6	M	8	3	3	1	246,074
Misty Son	4	G	4	1	0	0	978
Misty Spectacular	3	F	2	0	0	0	450
Misty Storm	2	F	2	0	0	0	255
Misty Tab	2	F	2	0	0	0	792
Misty Tokenoflove	4	F	5	1	0	0	5,464
Misty Trick	3	F	3	1	0	0	4,000
Misty Wager	5	G	5	1	0	1	5,320
Misty Wave Dancer	3	F	1	0	0	0	0
Misty Wonder	3	C	16	4	1	2	58,905
Mistyandsuave	4	G	4	0	0	1	864
Mistys Blue Knight	4	G	5	0	0	0	150
Misty's Chance	4	G	7	0	0	0	375
Mistys Dark Angel	4	F	7	0	0	0	2,557
Misty'sgoldentouch	3	C	2	0	0	0	400
Miswaki Babe	3	F	10	0	0	3	6,030
Miswaki Baby	3	F	8	0	2	0	1,880
Miswaki Lady	3	F	5	0	0	1	4,500
Miswaki Mac	4	G	13	2	1	2	18,879
Miswaki Sparkle	3	G	2	0	0	0	120
Miswes	4	F	10	2	3	1	58,100
Misyodl	4	F	9	1	2	0	4,515
Mitchaman	7	G	13	3	3	3	21,158
Mitchell County Hi	8	H	5	1	0	1	2,928
Mitchell's Delight	3	G	15	2	3	0	10,864
Mitchells Folly	3	F	7	0	1	2	3,844
Mitchel's Reprized	4	G	1	1	0	0	4,800
Mitey Nice	7	M	2	0	0	0	122
Mith America	4	F	12	2	1	2	8,604
Mithaal	3	C	9	2	0	0	51,500
Mito Way	10	G	2	0	0	0	0
Mitote Maya	4	F	10	2	1	1	30,607
Mittens	4	F	8	4	1	1	54,235
Mittens Mambo	4	F	2	1	0	0	7,940
Mitternacht	3	G	1	0	0	0	180
Mitty's Main Man	5	G	14	0	0	0	715
Mitzies Lil Fun	3	G	18	2	1	0	12,585
Mitzi's Oates	7	M	10	2	1	2	25,917
Mix It Up	4	C	16	4	3	4	65,040
Mix Together	3	G	5	0	1	0	5,205
Mixed Message	3	G	1	0	0	0	1,980
Mixed Reviews	2	F	1	0	0	0	400
Mixed Signals	4	F	2	0	0	0	140
Mixed Sprouts	4	F	2	0	0	0	0
Mixed Up	5	G	8	4	0	1	74,456
Mixer	4	G	8	0	3	1	4,817
Mixer Man	2	C	5	0	1	1	5,240
Mixie's Hoolie	5	M	3	0	0	0	285
Miya Kiya	4	F	11	2	2	0	13,368
Miz Bluestone	5	M	12	2	1	3	21,501
Miz Flashy Power	5	M	8	0	2	0	4,712
Miz Heather	6	M	12	3	3	0	14,307
Miz Landy	5	M	1	1	0	0	18,230
Miz Lynne Kelly	5	M	12	3	0	2	27,036
Miz Mitzie	3	F	9	1	3	0	29,423
Miz Moody Blues	3	F	9	3	4	0	17,760
Miz Revenge	4	F	5	0	0	0	490
Miz Roadway	3	F	12	1	3	1	30,640
Miz Roxie	3	F	4	0	0	0	1,553
Miz Smoke'um	3	F	7	1	0	2	9,010
Mize	3	C	10	1	0	1	3,930
Mizmar	2	F	1	0	0	0	0
Mizter Bubbles	3	G	6	1	0	1	15,360
Mizz Joclyne	5	M	3	0	1	0	1,160
Mizzou	3	C	5	0	1	0	1,052
Mjahe	5	H	2	0	0	0	365
Mlle. Rumble	5	M	21	0	5	1	10,709
Mme. Espionage	3	F	3	2	0	0	58,922
Mo Cash	4	F	10	0	1	0	2,345
Mo Fun Forus	5	M	17	3	3	0	30,865
Mo Gater	4	G	4	0	0	1	3,625
Mo Mon	6	H	2	0	0	0	4,950
Mo Moses	3	G	8	0	0	0	2,061
Mo Spirit	2	G	3	0	0	0	610
Mo Steely	4	G	11	0	0	2	6,975
Mo Thunder	3	F	8	0	0	0	480
Mo Town Brown	3	C	11	2	1	1	15,595
Mo Town Gold	4	G	7	1	2	1	8,395
Moab	3	G	5	0	0	2	9,285
Mobeka	5	M	12	1	2	1	14,690
Mobettadancer	4	G	2	0	0	0	0
Mobil	4	C	8	3	2	0	440,213
Mobil One (BRZ)	6	H	13	4	3	2	42,110
Mobile Express	2	F	2	1	1	0	10,325
Moby	5	G	10	0	1	1	1,574
Moccasin Meadows	5	M	5	0	1	1	2,380
Mocha Chocolate	3	F	7	1	0	2	8,981
Mocha Gold	8	G	2	0	0	0	0
Mocha Ice	4	G	12	3	2	2	37,950
Mocha Jet	6	G	7	0	1	0	4,063
Mocha Lite	5	M	7	1	0	1	6,374
Mocha Mania	3	F	12	1	2	0	13,988
Mocha Queen	3	F	10	4	2	1	146,648
Mochablend	3	C	2	0	0	0	1,440
Mocha's Ego	3	C	16	4	0	3	35,884
Mocita	2	F	4	2	1	0	21,510
Mockaskin	6	G	2	0	0	0	107
Mode of the World	5	M	11	2	1	5	8,916
Model Cee	3	C	1	0	0	0	400
Model City	3	C	11	1	0	3	8,286
Model Home	4	G	6	1	0	0	27,870

Horse	Age	Sex	Sts	1st	2d	3d	Won
Modeling Margot	6	M	2	0	0	0	80
Modem Down	3	F	9	3	0	0	13,439
Modena Bay (NZ)	6	M	4	1	1	0	37,480
Moderation	3	F	9	0	1	0	6,810
Modern Design	4	F	10	1	2	1	8,502
Modern Marvel	4	F	15	3	0	0	31,480
Modest Guy	2	C	3	1	1	1	19,130
Modest Line	3	G	7	0	2	1	2,734
Modest Lover	5	G	8	0	2	2	4,754
Modest Mo	4	C	12	4	0	1	33,303
Modista	3	F	12	1	1	1	15,076
Modoc	3	G	10	2	4	0	10,934
Modocken	4	F	15	1	0	1	4,367
Modred	5	H	15	3	2	1	26,499
Modus Viblairski	6	M	7	1	0	1	5,976
Moe B Dick	7	G	9	2	3	2	68,258
Moe Boots	6	G	20	2	3	6	11,079
Moe Dandy	3	C	3	0	0	0	238
Moe Dickstein	5	G	12	2	3	1	22,750
Moe Greene	7	G	10	2	2	3	15,102
Moel	4	F	17	0	5	4	38,694
Moe's Hoedown	5	M	9	3	1	0	43,135
Moe's Mon	5	G	6	1	1	2	13,500
Moette	5	M	17	5	6	2	13,402
Mogador	4	C	8	3	4	0	134,820
Mogambo Lawyer	3	F	7	0	1	1	4,755
Mohamed's Dream	2	C	2	0	0	0	2,460
Mohegan Warrior	3	G	9	2	3	2	37,350
Mohigan Hill	4	G	12	1	0	4	18,240
Moi Ciel	8	H	12	2	3	0	7,900
Moi's Boy	7	G	12	3	1	1	16,690
Mojita	3	F	7	0	0	1	1,040
Mojo Mundo	2	G	5	1	2	1	46,662
Mojo Risin	6	G	5	0	2	2	3,118
Mojodajo	2	C	6	2	0	1	20,060
Mojoe	8	G	10	0	1	2	7,117
Mokyska	3	C	9	1	0	1	7,670
Molalla Cat	2	F	4	0	0	1	450
Molinaro Beau	2	G	3	0	2	0	22,800
Molinaro Deer	4	F	5	0	1	1	4,642
Molinaro First Las	4	F	9	0	3	1	19,313
Molinaro Magic	3	C	2	0	0	0	0
Molinaro Native	2	G	3	0	1	0	4,240
Molino Rojo	5	G	17	3	2	4	13,984
Molino Rosso (CHI)	6	G	7	1	0	1	29,940
Mollie McLash	6	M	9	0	1	2	11,322
Mollie Stone	2	F	6	0	0	4	5,720
Mollies Follies	3	F	3	1	0	0	5,415
Molly Beddard	5	M	13	0	0	0	816
Molly Jo	3	F	6	0	1	1	2,939
Molly M	5	M	5	0	0	0	832
Molly n' McKenna	3	F	16	2	2	0	8,250
Molly O'Grady	8	M	8	1	1	2	2,758
Molly Rochelle	4	F	14	1	0	0	2,408
Mollyputthepeaches	3	F	2	0	0	0	1,185
Molly's Charm	3	F	7	1	0	0	2,589
Molly's Gem	3	F	3	1	0	0	5,339
Molly's Gun Moll	3	F	15	2	0	4	23,775
Molly's Miracle	2	F	1	0	0	0	316
Molly's Runaway	3	F	14	3	1	3	42,931
Molly's Wisdom	5	H	4	0	0	0	1,908
Moloch	5	G	10	0	0	1	1,321
Molokai Connection	6	G	8	2	0	0	8,608
Molokai Express	5	H	2	0	1	0	800
Moloko	5	M	1	0	0	0	380
Molotov	4	G	4	1	0	0	9,230
Molto Bene	5	G	4	0	0	0	1,141
Molto Veloce	3	F	4	0	0	1	5,100
Molto Vita	4	F	8	3	2	0	220,730
Mom	4	F	6	1	0	1	2,753
Mom Liked You Best	4	F	7	0	0	2	5,819
Momaless	6	M	13	0	0	1	3,306
Mombay	5	M	9	0	0	2	2,524
Mombo	6	G	1	0	0	0	0
Mombo Loco	4	C	12	0	3	0	30,648
Mombo Star	5	G	7	0	0	2	4,668
Momemo	4	G	2	0	0	0	0
Moment of Attack	6	G	5	0	1	0	456
Moment of Ecstacy	8	G	12	1	0	2	4,990

Horse	Age	Sex	Sts	1st	2d	3d	Won
Moment of Honour	3	F	3	1	0	0	13,509
Moment of Peace	3	F	11	2	2	2	118,471
Moment of Silence	3	F	1	0	0	0	0
Moment of Song	3	G	15	3	5	2	32,980
Moment to Enjoy	3	C	3	0	0	0	1,640
Moment's Champ	4	G	1	0	0	0	225
Momentum	6	H	1	0	0	0	0
Momma Jean	5	M	15	1	2	4	13,242
Momma Said Yes	3	F	5	1	0	0	3,826
Momma's Eyes	2	F	2	0	0	0	720
Momma's Image	3	F	10	1	0	0	24,644
Mommas Last Dollar	4	F	11	1	2	1	10,290
Momma's Money	3	F	12	0	2	1	6,283
Mommie's Luke	3	C	6	0	0	1	1,630
Mommygotagirl	3	F	6	0	0	1	2,132
Momocha	2	F	1	0	0	0	0
Momoney Moe	5	G	9	6	0	0	94,950
Mom's an Angel	4	G	4	0	1	0	4,265
Mom's Angel	5	G	4	1	0	0	2,760
Mom's Bright Star	4	F	8	1	0	2	6,508
Mom's Grandeur	3	F	6	0	1	1	10,140
Mom's Jule	2	C	2	0	0	0	150
Mom's Real Quiet	3	F	9	2	1	1	20,695
Mom's Recruit	6	G	6	0	0	0	270
Moms Thunder	4	C	4	0	0	0	0
Mom's Treasure	2	C	2	0	0	0	262
Momskitchen	4	G	2	0	1	0	2,100
Momsmercedes	9	G	15	1	0	0	5,793
Momsnibblingcoyote	4	C	5	1	0	0	10,367
Mon Ami Amy	5	M	6	1	2	3	38,311
Mon Armour	3	F	10	3	1	0	20,825
Mon Belle	2	F	1	1	0	0	15,625
Mon Cabo	4	F	17	1	0	2	9,495
Mon Dieux	3	C	1	0	0	0	260
Mon Ile	5	G	6	0	0	0	2,928
Mon Miel	2	F	2	0	2	0	9,000
Mon Ogon	2	G	9	1	2	1	12,795
Mon Ouimet	5	G	9	0	2	1	7,486
Mon Over Miami	2	G	1	0	0	1	4,100
Mon Petit Shoe	4	F	2	0	0	0	150
Mon Repos	3	G	5	1	1	0	4,640
Mon Spirit	3	F	4	1	0	1	4,975
Mon Sweet's Crypto	4	F	1	0	0	0	44
Mon T. Hauls	5	G	12	1	2	6	4,636
Mon Treego Bay	4	G	9	1	2	5	18,395
Mon Tresor	4	F	8	0	1	1	3,471
Mona Corrine	5	M	5	0	0	0	497
Mona Lady	4	F	9	2	0	0	17,182
Mona Lisa (GB)	2	F	4	0	1	0	23,539
Mona Lisa Lady	5	M	3	0	0	1	1,891
Mona Rose	4	F	8	4	0	0	319,439
Mona the Snake	5	M	8	0	0	2	5,278
Monacas Baby	2	F	4	1	2	1	12,793
Monanore	5	G	8	2	0	1	7,055
Monarch Hunter	3	C	2	0	0	1	1,449
Monarchian	2	G	7	1	2	1	27,740
Monarchoftheglen	5	G	6	0	2	1	10,926
Monarch's Mon	5	G	13	0	2	2	3,925
Monaree	4	F	1	0	0	0	0
Monarquica	5	M	7	0	1	0	4,487
Monashee	2	F	3	1	0	0	12,180
Monastic	4	F	3	1	1	0	23,969
Mondamin	9	G	7	0	0	0	675
Monday Nite Mac	8	G	16	0	1	4	13,481
Monday Thru Friday	4	C	6	0	3	1	1,970
Monday's Bet	3	G	4	0	0	0	1,379
Monday's Moon	2	C	1	0	0	0	2,580
Mondeville (FR)	5	G	1	0	0	0	0
Monet	9	H	7	0	1	1	10,090
Moneta Cat	3	G	9	2	1	0	10,259
Monetary Dancer	3	G	15	2	0	3	27,700
Monetary Lady	6	M	3	0	0	0	197
Monetary Madness	4	F	3	0	0	0	189
Monetary Monarch	2	C	2	1	0	0	10,260
Monetary Star	4	C	5	1	0	0	12,913
Money Baby	9	M	9	0	0	1	4,106
Money Box	4	F	3	0	1	0	2,184
Money Buck	4	G	2	0	0	0	0
Money Business	3	G	1	0	0	0	300

Horse	Age	Sex	Sts	1st	2d	3d	Won
Money Call	3	G	7	0	0	1	1,709
Money Champ	3	C	4	0	0	0	275
Money for Honey	2	F	1	1	0	0	3,900
Money for Maggie	2	G	8	2	1	0	25,545
Money From Heaven	2	F	1	1	0	0	2,700
Money Helps	2	F	6	0	3	0	29,845
Money Inda Pocket	2	F	1	1	0	0	15,900
Money Inthe Basket	4	G	14	0	2	1	3,607
Money Is Boss	4	G	6	0	3	0	7,025
Money Is Due	8	G	7	0	0	0	1,837
Money Is Power	5	M	6	0	0	0	610
Money Is the Key	3	C	3	1	0	0	12,313
Money Magnet	7	H	9	0	0	1	1,550
Money Management	6	G	5	0	0	1	580
Money Marquet	4	G	10	1	2	1	21,610
Money Mover	4	F	7	0	1	1	5,780
Money Never Sleeps	3	F	2	0	0	0	0
Money On the Table	5	G	5	0	0	1	777
Money Power	3	C	2	0	0	0	225
Money Set	5	G	18	3	2	0	31,870
Money Shot	6	G	14	1	5	2	42,637
Money Spender	3	C	8	0	1	0	4,549
Money Stretcher	6	M	12	0	1	0	2,730
Money Talks	2	G	2	0	0	1	700
Money Trust	3	F	6	2	1	0	22,441
Moneybackguarantee	2	F	9	2	0	2	13,229
Moneycat	4	G	8	2	0	0	3,658
Moneyed	4	G	3	0	0	0	800
Moneyrun Up	3	G	10	1	3	2	14,509
Money's Star	6	H	13	0	0	0	4,670
Moneytrain (GER)	5	G	2	2	0	0	21,000
Moneyville	3	G	9	2	1	2	8,276
Moneywaster	5	G	1	0	1	0	1,800
Mongeon's Thief	6	M	6	0	1	0	1,597
Mongol Sky	4	G	16	1	1	2	6,992
Mongo's Review	3	G	5	0	0	0	698
Monica Sue	5	M	1	0	0	0	0
Monica's Halo	4	F	13	1	0	3	11,432
Monica's Jet	2	F	3	0	0	0	230
Monie Monie	3	F	13	0	0	0	1,043
Monika's Courage	3	F	2	0	0	0	1,306
Monique	5	M	10	1	2	1	9,708
Monique's Gold	5	M	11	2	1	3	33,035
Monkey Hill	3	C	6	2	2	0	48,625
Monkey Junior	4	C	12	2	2	0	39,050
Monkey Man	4	G	4	0	1	0	1,950
Monkey Puzzle	8	G	10	1	0	1	38,397
Monkeys Uncle	5	G	6	1	0	1	7,695
Monkton Miss	4	F	6	0	2	1	13,347
Mono Ridge	3	G	9	1	1	1	36,509
Monocular	3	G	7	2	2	1	55,188
Monologue	7	H	13	0	2	3	5,871
Monopoly Money	3	C	5	2	0	0	21,600
Monopoly Pricing	2	C	3	1	0	1	32,050
Monorail	4	G	1	0	0	0	0
Monroe Doctrine (IRE)	7	G	10	0	0	0	726
Mons Meg	3	F	7	0	0	0	845
Monserati	7	G	1	0	0	0	0
Monsieur	5	G	7	0	0	1	1,430
Monsieur Boulanger (GB)	4	C	8	1	1	1	41,980
Monsignor	5	G	18	0	0	3	4,635
Monsignor Paul	6	G	1	0	0	0	110
Monsoon Sky	3	G	6	1	1	1	10,100
Monster Affair	2	C	10	1	1	2	27,770
Monster Ballad	4	G	6	0	0	1	2,485
Monster Be Gone	5	G	2	0	1	0	4,130
Monster Binge	4	F	9	1	4	1	21,930
Monster Chaser	2	G	8	3	4	0	138,280
Monster Jack	4	C	7	0	0	0	1,880
Monster Love	2	F	3	1	1	0	15,440
Monster Mac	3	G	5	1	1	0	7,052
Monster McKilts	5	G	14	1	0	3	6,848
Monster Move	4	G	8	1	1	0	27,730
Monster Sink	2	F	2	0	0	1	2,640
Monster Zone	2	C	5	1	2	1	14,795
Monsterinmyroom	2	C	1	0	0	0	450
Monsterous	3	C	3	0	0	1	1,730
Monsterous Mitch	6	G	10	1	3	2	20,755
Mont Devil	3	C	4	1	0	0	37,566
Mont d'Or	3	F	9	1	2	0	16,085
Mont Saint Michel (CHI)	6	G	5	1	1	0	46,960
Mont Tendre	2	C	1	0	0	0	45
Montana Banana	4	F	6	1	0	0	18,020
Montana Breeze	5	G	4	0	0	0	72
Montana Cowboy	4	G	1	0	0	0	0
Montana Deputy	3	G	10	2	3	1	85,260
Montana Ma	4	F	3	0	0	0	0
Montana Mist	3	F	3	0	0	0	1,065
Montana Moon	3	G	16	2	0	1	24,271
Montana Rush	5	G	6	0	0	1	2,368
Montana Skipper	3	C	9	2	1	0	20,210
Montana Snow	8	G	1	0	0	0	113
Montana Springs	3	G	7	0	1	0	4,741
Montanaro	6	G	7	0	0	1	2,095
Montaraz	4	F	4	0	0	1	4,760
Montavonni	3	C	1	0	0	0	370
Montbretia	4	C	2	0	1	0	7,800
Montbrook Music	2	F	3	1	0	0	5,330
Montbrook's Miss	3	F	7	0	0	0	550
Monte Bianco (IRE)	3	G	5	0	1	0	12,400
Monte D.	3	C	2	0	0	0	410
Monte Real	4	G	3	0	0	0	2,080
Monte Vista	6	G	6	0	1	2	6,290
Montecastillo (IRE)	7	G	5	1	2	0	38,795
Montefiore	4	F	1	0	0	0	192
Montenapoleone	5	H	11	0	2	0	13,100
Montero	2	F	5	1	1	1	24,440
Monteslitleshadow	5	M	5	0	0	0	404
Montessa	3	F	6	0	2	1	6,450
Montezuma's Gold	8	G	1	0	0	0	0
Montford Ridge	3	G	7	0	3	0	14,430
Monthster Man	5	G	10	4	1	2	6,497
Monti's Lad	2	C	4	2	0	0	49,800
Montisi	2	G	1	0	0	0	0
Montmorenci	5	G	14	0	6	2	26,390
Montoro	6	G	9	0	2	1	4,685
Montpar	3	F	2	0	1	1	5,360
Montpicabo	3	C	3	1	0	0	13,680
Montreal Forum	2	G	1	0	0	0	0
Montreal Irish	2	G	4	0	0	0	305
Montreal Princess	4	F	9	0	0	0	1,065
Montreal Tootie	3	F	7	1	0	1	13,935
Montreal's Best	6	M	6	1	3	0	10,125
Montrosecountyline	5	H	9	0	0	1	252
Montsmoke	3	F	10	0	5	0	26,390
Montstar	3	C	6	1	0	0	9,700
Monty Man	4	C	12	4	2	0	69,420
Monty's Copy	3	F	2	0	0	2	2,310
Monument	6	G	3	0	0	0	240
Monument Valley	7	M	5	1	0	0	13,238
Monumental Factor	3	G	8	0	0	0	774
Mony's Sister	3	F	3	1	1	1	12,640
Mooch	3	F	3	0	0	0	120
Moochie Magnum	3	F	7	1	2	1	47,213
Moochie Too	5	M	5	1	1	1	14,346
Mood Indigo	2	F	2	0	0	0	600
Mood Swinger	5	H	8	0	0	0	710
Moody Box	4	G	9	1	1	0	7,086
Moody Bruce	2	C	6	1	0	0	10,095
Moody Bu	3	F	1	0	0	0	0
Moody Creek	3	G	3	0	0	0	900
Moody Mama	3	F	7	1	0	1	5,684
Moody Seas	3	F	6	1	0	0	5,965
Moody Slew	4	G	11	2	1	1	14,269
Moody Woman	2	F	5	0	0	0	1,560
Moogedy	5	M	10	3	0	2	60,727
Mooji Moo	5	M	5	1	2	0	203,500
Moolah Basket	2	G	2	0	0	0	488
Moomtazz	6	H	5	0	1	0	13,280
Moon Bay Dancer	3	F	10	1	1	1	23,207
Moon Bee	5	G	4	0	1	0	540
Moon Bird	6	M	9	1	1	0	18,747
Moon Boots	3	G	16	1	2	2	14,486
Moon Dancing	5	M	4	0	0	0	0
Moon Dolly (GB)	3	F	10	1	3	2	33,580
Moon Dove	3	F	1	0	0	0	0
Moon Duster	2	G	1	0	0	0	85
Moon Face	4	F	5	0	0	0	315

Horse	Age	Sex	Sts	1st	2d	3d	Won
Moon Feather	3	F	14	2	1	2	56,570
Moon in the Night	4	F	1	0	0	0	0
Moon Light Win'd	5	G	7	0	0	0	548
Moon Lust	3	F	1	0	0	0	0
Moon Maid	2	F	1	1	0	0	3,960
Moon Maven	3	F	3	0	1	0	10,280
Moon Mission	4	G	15	1	3	1	40,480
Moon Mullins	4	G	8	0	1	4	7,730
Moon Over Miami	3	G	3	0	0	0	1,650
Moon Over Miannie	8	M	2	0	0	0	0
Moon Over My Angie	5	M	7	0	1	0	1,315
Moon Rise Darling	4	F	5	0	2	1	2,650
Moon Shine Time	4	F	8	3	1	0	55,101
Moon Shot Margie	3	F	6	1	0	0	6,240
Moon Snow	4	G	3	1	1	0	2,175
Moon Star Cat	4	C	3	0	0	0	111
Moon Symph	5	G	4	0	0	0	812
Moon Tap	4	F	1	0	0	0	0
Moon Tip	5	G	8	1	4	1	17,203
Moon Walk	5	H	2	0	1	0	1,785
Moon Warrior	3	C	12	1	3	1	42,090
Moon Witch	3	F	9	1	2	4	5,466
Moona Lisa	3	F	4	1	0	0	26,578
Moondance	4	C	2	0	0	0	450
Moondowner	3	G	15	1	0	3	3,515
Moonlet Minister	5	M	2	0	0	0	452
Moonlight	3	F	6	0	2	1	27,600
Moonlight and Lace	5	M	3	0	0	2	1,755
Moonlight Breeze	4	F	8	0	2	0	1,199
Moonlight Bunny	2	F	5	0	0	1	1,375
Moonlight Cocktail	3	F	4	1	1	0	13,150
Moonlight Crest	3	F	2	0	0	0	125
Moonlight Cruise	3	F	9	2	1	4	84,680
Moonlight Duel	3	G	6	1	1	0	27,045
Moonlight Frost	2	F	7	1	2	2	27,871
Moonlight Lady	4	F	5	0	4	0	14,929
Moonlight Martini	3	F	1	0	1	0	1,134
Moonlight Melody	3	F	13	1	2	1	10,110
Moonlight Milagro	4	C	6	1	0	0	6,311
Moonlight Mistress	3	F	4	1	1	0	7,380
Moonlight Myth	3	G	1	0	0	0	340
Moonlight Sonata	4	F	7	1	0	2	25,243
Moonlight Storm	4	G	10	4	0	0	34,323
Moonlightdust	2	G	1	0	0	0	0
Moonlightmargarita	3	F	1	0	0	0	74
Moonlit Atlantic	2	F	3	3	0	0	50,700
Moonlit Lady	3	F	5	1	1	2	9,765
Moonlit Maddie	6	M	5	1	1	1	36,266
Moonlit Moment	7	G	4	0	0	1	2,140
Moonlit Romance	4	F	11	3	2	2	54,860
Moonlit Sand	5	H	5	0	0	0	1,483
Moonlite and Wine	3	F	8	0	0	1	2,035
Moonlite Walk	4	F	10	1	2	1	58,404
Moonluck	5	G	13	2	2	2	23,226
Moonmon	5	G	4	0	0	1	2,024
Moonover Imacomin	5	G	2	0	0	0	201
Moonray	9	G	5	1	0	0	3,656
Moonridge Bay	4	C	5	0	0	2	3,225
Moonroper	4	G	2	0	1	0	2,353
Moonrush	4	G	1	0	0	0	0
Moon's So Friendly	7	M	10	1	1	2	6,494
Moonshadow Gold	5	G	11	3	3	0	45,454
Moonshine Hall	4	C	4	0	1	1	19,814
Moonshine Justice	2	C	4	3	0	0	283,914
Moonshine Man	2	C	2	1	0	0	16,200
Moonshine Mary	5	M	3	0	0	0	562
Moonshine Ray	3	G	2	0	0	0	0
Moonshine Ridge	6	G	8	0	1	1	4,954
Moonshine Runner	5	G	7	0	0	0	715
Moonshineofthrills	2	G	1	0	0	0	0
Moonstar	3	F	1	0	0	0	160
Moonstone Bay	4	F	5	0	0	0	6,700
Moonstruck	6	H	2	0	0	0	0
Moonstruck Agenda	3	G	17	0	9	0	22,815
Moonyeane	3	F	8	0	1	0	680
Moorea	2	C	1	0	0	0	400
Moorebella	3	F	11	2	3	2	59,470
Mooring Sand	5	G	9	2	1	1	24,783
Moorish Prince	8	G	4	0	0	0	2,040
Moose Mason	4	G	1	0	0	0	73
Moosehead Jr	4	G	6	0	1	0	933
Moosup Valley	4	G	16	1	4	3	27,041
Mopac	3	C	7	1	1	0	22,260
Mopac Express	6	G	4	1	0	0	4,735
Mopbuckmolly	4	F	6	0	1	0	510
Mor Or Less	2	C	8	1	0	3	15,485
Morada Bay	2	F	3	1	0	0	13,400
Moradeno	3	C	6	1	0	0	5,767
Moralap	2	F	2	0	0	0	400
Moraluna	4	F	8	1	0	1	22,330
Mordedor	7	G	12	1	0	3	15,521
More Action	3	F	2	0	1	1	3,950
More Bands	4	G	4	0	0	0	0
More Bourb	3	C	8	3	0	1	53,220
More Crafty	6	H	7	2	0	1	65,450
More Dances	3	G	2	0	0	0	37
More Daylight	4	G	3	0	2	0	21,790
More Fun to Run	3	C	4	0	0	0	0
More Gold to Tell	3	G	2	0	0	0	0
More Heart	4	G	7	1	1	0	3,566
More Heck	4	G	7	0	3	0	23,296
More Hot Gossip	5	M	6	1	1	0	25,204
More Influence	6	G	13	4	2	3	37,970
More Mischief	4	C	6	0	1	0	510
More Modern	6	G	11	1	0	2	41,520
More Monkey Time	2	F	2	0	0	0	950
More Moonlight	2	F	5	2	0	1	72,880
More No	6	M	2	0	0	1	1,538
More of This	4	F	2	0	0	0	0
More Ore	2	C	3	1	0	0	23,952
More Red	5	G	5	0	1	2	3,363
More Shenanigans	3	F	8	1	1	0	9,373
More Smoke	2	C	3	2	1	0	34,595
More Speed	5	G	5	0	0	1	2,095
More Tell	8	G	2	0	0	0	336
More Than Golden	5	M	12	4	4	1	30,245
More Than Honor	3	F	2	0	0	0	248
More Than Odd	4	G	10	1	3	2	9,369
More Than Perfect	2	F	7	1	0	0	17,880
More Than Promised	2	F	4	2	1	0	38,000
More Than Somewhat	2	C	1	0	1	0	9,000
More Than Tricky	2	C	5	0	1	2	8,520
More Than Wild	2	C	6	2	2	1	56,890
More Tricks	4	F	4	0	0	0	1,030
Morerunawaybride	4	F	5	0	1	1	2,325
Morespeedplease	3	G	3	0	0	0	200
Morethanacceptable	4	G	5	0	0	0	286
Morethanastar	5	G	15	2	0	2	38,525
Morethanmoney	4	C	3	0	1	0	5,000
Morethanrisque	5	G	10	1	3	2	23,830
Moreto	3	C	5	1	0	1	19,262
Morfar	8	G	5	2	0	1	7,560
Morgan Canyon	5	G	10	2	1	1	9,864
Morgan City	3	F	8	0	0	2	4,480
Morgan Divy	4	F	11	0	3	5	18,631
Morgan Looker	4	G	12	1	1	2	6,765
Morgan Ridge	3	F	10	1	1	3	7,077
Morgana	3	F	5	1	1	0	12,263
Morganite	7	H	1	0	0	0	750
Morgannes Hun	3	G	3	0	0	0	225
Morgan's Charm	3	F	2	1	0	0	4,237
Morgans Creek	5	H	3	0	1	0	6,250
Morgan's Crusader	2	F	1	0	0	0	0
Morgan's Pride	4	G	2	0	0	0	0
Morgnec Voodoo	6	G	8	0	0	0	0
Morica	6	M	8	0	2	0	4,250
Morine's Victory	3	C	6	1	0	3	34,660
Morisqueta	7	M	4	1	0	1	3,040
Morley	3	C	9	1	0	3	18,752
Morna's Girl (FR)	4	F	8	0	1	1	21,498
Morning Beauty	4	F	5	1	0	0	5,317
Morning Breeze	6	M	11	2	3	4	11,308
Morning Domingo	4	F	11	2	0	3	9,572
Morning Escapade	3	F	5	1	0	1	5,326
Morning Fever	4	G	6	3	0	0	11,650
Morning Gallop	2	F	4	0	2	1	23,050
Morning Gift	3	G	13	0	2	1	16,770
Morning Gold	2	C	1	0	0	0	1,560

Horse	Age	Sex	Sts	1st	2d	3d	Won
Morning Lover	2	F	3	0	0	0	0
Morning Maneuver	4	G	7	2	0	1	19,549
Morning Merry	4	G	4	1	0	0	23,160
Morning of Truth	2	G	3	0	0	0	365
Morning Payne	2	C	3	0	0	0	0
Morning Salute	3	G	9	0	3	0	10,005
Morning Sky	4	F	12	1	2	1	26,655
Morning Star Pike	5	H	16	1	0	3	5,604
Morning Surf	6	M	4	0	0	0	380
Morning Tune	3	G	10	1	1	3	39,681
Morning Walk	5	M	6	0	0	0	285
Morning Watch	4	G	10	2	1	2	73,280
Morning Wine	6	G	5	0	3	1	3,115
Morning's Image	5	G	7	0	1	1	14,940
Mornings Minion (GB)	7	G	5	0	2	1	6,950
Morningstar Stella	3	F	2	0	0	0	134
Moro Grande	9	G	2	0	1	0	3,591
Moro Platino	4	G	10	1	3	1	13,370
Morocco	7	H	1	0	0	0	0
Moros Destiny	2	C	6	1	0	4	22,100
Moros Fantastic	2	F	2	1	0	0	8,100
Moros Jo Jo	2	F	1	0	0	1	1,550
Moro's Sugar	4	G	11	1	0	0	5,569
Morosino	8	H	1	0	0	0	0
Morph	3	C	5	0	2	0	21,272
Morrow	7	G	9	0	3	2	5,243
Mort	8	G	5	1	0	2	9,532
Mortal	2	F	1	0	0	0	0
Mortgage Man	5	G	13	1	2	3	49,282
Mortgage the House	2	F	7	1	1	1	20,775
Morton's Girl	2	F	1	0	0	0	1,020
Mortonsville	3	C	2	0	0	0	293
Mortrump	3	G	5	3	0	0	33,526
Morts Pleasure	4	F	5	0	0	0	452
Morty's Legacy	4	F	11	1	1	2	19,880
Mos Eisley	7	G	7	1	1	1	4,198
Mo's Lucky Charm	3	F	3	1	1	0	7,281
Mosby's Ranger	3	G	1	0	0	0	420
Moscola	9	G	13	0	2	2	3,395
Mosconi (IRE)	10	G	6	1	1	1	1,484
Moscow Ballet (IRE)	3	C	5	1	0	1	91,444
Moscow Blues	5	H	4	1	1	0	1,667
Moscow Burning	4	F	11	2	4	2	627,970
Moscow Caper	4	C	2	0	0	0	900
Moscow Flite	5	G	8	0	0	0	150
Moscow Kitty	4	F	6	1	2	0	4,820
Moscow Mattie	3	F	2	0	0	0	645
Moscow Moment	3	C	3	0	0	0	3,600
Moscow Spy	3	F	2	0	0	0	0
Moscow Tech	4	F	6	0	0	1	901
Moscow Theatre	5	G	7	0	1	2	1,689
Moscow Time	6	M	13	2	0	3	9,560
Moscows Quick Trip	6	G	5	0	1	1	1,030
Moses Jerome	4	G	23	2	2	2	44,480
Moses's Music	3	C	1	0	0	0	42
Moshe (ARG)	11	G	1	1	0	0	6,000
Mosman Bay	3	C	7	2	3	1	85,137
Moss Boss	5	G	10	0	0	4	5,183
Moss Rose	3	F	8	2	1	1	70,750
Mossant	3	G	11	1	1	3	28,914
Mossel Bay	2	C	2	0	0	0	425
Most	4	F	12	2	4	2	28,860
Most Charismatic	3	F	8	0	0	0	615
Most Charming	3	F	5	0	0	0	1,390
Most Feared	4	G	1	0	0	0	0
Most of All	8	M	2	0	0	1	1,320
Most Valued Player	3	G	2	0	0	0	86
Most Wonderful	2	G	1	0	0	0	112
Mostest	3	G	6	0	0	0	5,020
Mostly	3	C	2	0	0	0	3,460
Mostly Devious	3	F	15	3	1	2	32,960
Mostly Ghostly	3	G	2	0	0	1	2,507
Mostly Glory	5	M	15	2	2	4	8,567
Mostly Red	5	G	12	0	2	2	15,684
Mostly Sunny	3	F	6	0	0	0	0
Mostly Tizzy	7	G	4	0	3	1	3,220
Motel Affair	4	G	6	2	0	1	46,300
Motel Boogie	5	G	6	0	0	0	1,938
Motel Gossip	5	M	5	0	1	2	8,403
Motel Mischef	7	M	11	1	2	4	7,400
Motel Mystery	5	H	5	1	0	0	3,227
Motel Shot	8	M	10	1	1	1	4,374
Motel Staff	7	G	9	4	1	0	104,801
Motel Tricks	3	F	13	1	0	0	9,585
Mother	2	F	1	0	1	0	7,000
Mother May I	3	F	3	0	2	0	10,080
Mother Molly Boo	4	F	16	5	4	1	35,951
Mother Superior	2	F	5	0	0	1	3,600
Mothers Day Bandit	3	G	12	1	2	2	7,590
Mother's Dayruckus	6	H	1	0	0	0	890
Mothers Gift	3	F	8	0	1	1	1,270
Mother's Halo	5	G	9	0	2	0	5,010
Mothers Message	9	M	1	0	0	0	46
Mother's Sacrifice	3	F	11	2	5	1	53,099
Motion Approved	3	C	2	0	0	1	1,308
Motion Granted	3	F	3	1	0	0	2,700
Motion Study	5	G	7	0	0	0	763
Motion to Suppress	12	G	5	1	0	1	2,993
Motionoftheocean	2	F	2	0	0	0	220
Motives	5	H	4	0	1	0	9,532
Motivo	3	C	7	1	1	1	21,600
Motivus	3	C	5	0	1	1	14,244
Motley Slew	4	G	9	0	0	0	640
Motocilla	5	M	1	0	0	0	42
Motor City Babe	3	F	1	0	0	0	0
Motor City Slew	5	G	7	0	0	0	460
Motor Home	2	C	6	0	0	1	13,889
Motorin	4	F	3	0	0	0	0
Motto	9	H	6	1	3	0	55,860
Moujoudh (IRE)	4	C	4	0	0	0	2,940
Moulin de Mougins (IRE)	3	G	8	0	0	1	5,050
Mount Alto	4	G	3	0	0	0	226
Mount Angel	4	F	5	0	1	0	1,536
Mount Baker	2	G	2	0	0	0	0
Mount Everest	6	G	6	2	1	0	29,940
Mount Gay Run	3	G	10	0	0	0	1,691
Mount Intrepid	7	G	12	3	2	2	73,860
Mount Rose	9	M	1	0	0	0	75
Mount Suribachi	4	C	15	1	1	3	23,270
Mount Temple	6	G	5	0	0	0	1,070
Mount Tora Bora	4	C	17	3	4	2	20,415
Mount Vesuvio	6	G	3	1	0	0	5,100
Mount Zao	3	G	2	1	0	0	14,500
Mountain Beacon	5	G	9	1	2	2	43,620
Mountain Burgundy	5	G	1	0	0	0	0
Mountain Call	3	G	3	0	0	0	1,106
Mountain Cheif	5	G	6	0	0	1	1,051
Mountain Cougar	2	G	2	0	0	0	0
Mountain Creek	4	C	9	2	1	1	35,480
Mountain Dancer	7	G	2	0	1	0	1,160
Mountain Duty	3	F	4	0	1	0	530
Mountain Eagle	6	G	16	1	0	4	22,337
Mountain Falls	6	G	7	0	1	3	1,088
Mountain Forum	5	H	1	0	0	0	0
Mountain Fox	4	G	4	1	0	1	15,678
Mountain Fury	4	G	8	2	0	0	13,550
Mountain General	6	G	11	1	4	0	120,348
Mountain Gold	3	C	2	1	1	0	19,600
Mountain Halo	4	G	6	1	0	0	4,479
Mountain Hearted	4	G	10	0	0	2	3,009
Mountain Hunter	4	G	2	0	0	0	0
Mountain Jamboree	6	G	12	2	1	1	9,749
Mountain Lake	6	G	2	0	0	0	225
Mountain Magician	2	G	7	2	0	1	29,447
Mountain Mambo	2	F	4	1	0	1	33,795
Mountain Marmalade	3	F	2	0	0	0	0
Mountain Meeting	2	F	3	1	0	0	5,114
Mountain Minister	4	G	11	1	0	0	6,155
Mountain Miss	4	F	11	1	3	0	13,310
Mountain Music	4	F	7	1	1	1	23,194
Mountain Mustang	3	G	8	3	1	1	44,450
Mountain of Faith	4	G	6	1	1	0	9,442
Mountain of Light	4	F	9	1	3	1	6,560
Mountain Park	4	G	12	1	4	2	29,637
Mountain Pride	5	H	17	2	4	1	35,420
Mountain Pullet	4	F	3	0	0	0	0
Mountain Rage	5	G	3	0	0	1	5,160
Mountain Rainfall	2	G	2	1	0	0	7,004

Horse	Age	Sex	Sts	1st	2d	3d	Won
Mountain Ridge	3	C	5	1	1	0	13,160
Mountain Ruler	5	G	8	1	2	1	5,266
Mountain Scout	2	C	2	1	1	0	18,400
Mountain Search	3	G	7	2	2	0	7,562
Mountain Shadows	5	G	3	0	0	0	470
Mountain Slewpy	3	G	13	0	1	2	6,340
Mountain Stroll	3	G	9	3	0	2	76,062
Mountain Top	9	G	1	0	0	0	1,260
Mountain Top (GB)	3	G	8	0	1	1	9,547
Mountain Trapper	3	G	2	0	0	1	820
Mountain Trek	4	F	4	1	1	1	13,820
Mountain Village	3	G	9	1	0	2	6,090
Mountain Wave	3	F	15	2	3	1	12,678
Mountains of Love	3	F	14	1	1	3	18,426
Mounty Python	3	C	2	0	0	0	213
Mour Run	2	C	8	0	2	1	6,156
Mournful Defense	7	G	3	0	0	0	330
Mouse Hunter	3	F	9	1	0	2	1,701
Mouthadasouth	5	G	1	0	0	0	0
Moutin Blue's	5	M	10	0	0	1	4,428
Movant	3	F	6	1	2	1	85,460
Move On Slew	4	F	7	0	2	1	2,230
Move Outa My Way	4	F	7	1	2	0	6,492
Move Those Chains	5	H	10	0	1	0	15,198
Move to Strike	3	G	9	3	0	0	91,685
Move to the Music	3	F	16	1	4	1	12,832
Move West	3	C	3	0	0	0	1,850
Movealittlecloser	5	M	15	1	1	2	5,359
Moveinday	4	G	7	0	0	0	3,475
Moveitonover	5	G	5	1	0	0	3,840
Moveoverhollywood	3	G	4	0	0	1	1,201
Moveoverredrover	3	G	7	1	0	1	8,480
Mover Anda Shaker	6	G	10	1	0	1	3,413
Moves Ghostly	3	F	9	0	0	1	2,844
Movie Review	7	G	8	1	0	0	3,049
Movin N Crusin	3	G	2	0	0	0	360
Movin South	4	F	13	2	0	1	15,694
Movin to the Music	7	G	1	0	1	0	625
Movinanagroovin	11	G	6	0	1	1	1,569
Moving Danzig	4	G	13	1	0	2	7,905
Moving Experience (IRE)	7	M	9	1	2	0	17,705
Moving Fever	4	F	7	3	2	0	55,820
Moving Ghost	2	C	1	0	0	0	0
Moving Right Along	2	C	1	0	0	0	300
Movingmichael	4	C	11	1	0	1	26,005
Moving's Gold	9	G	11	0	2	2	24,225
Movinit	3	G	5	0	0	0	84
Movinlikawinner	3	F	15	3	1	3	23,574
Mowdow	2	C	10	3	1	3	45,390
Moxie Man	9	G	6	2	0	1	2,772
Moyamba	13	G	6	3	1	0	4,329
Moyanna (IRE)	4	F	10	3	0	2	59,910
Moyne Abbey	2	F	2	0	0	0	264
Moyo Simba	5	G	13	0	1	1	2,700
Mozelle's Angel	2	F	2	0	0	0	800
Mr Ammo	9	G	7	2	4	1	16,253
Mr B Following Me	3	C	3	0	0	0	0
Mr Bassett	5	G	5	1	0	1	24,990
Mr Big Time	5	G	14	3	3	2	55,660
Mr Binnion	3	G	10	2	1	1	39,390
Mr Bishop	4	C	15	0	0	3	14,250
Mr Blumin	6	G	5	0	0	1	1,521
Mr Bobanna Zarb	3	G	11	1	0	0	8,558
Mr Bombastic (GER)	5	G	2	1	0	1	7,000
Mr Boom Bostic	4	G	12	5	3	0	48,700
Mr Bulldog	8	G	1	0	0	0	0
Mr Cartwheel	7	G	15	1	2	3	9,032
Mr Charlie D	2	G	2	1	1	0	33,020
Mr Clearwater	5	G	5	2	1	0	6,318
Mr Clever	4	G	4	1	0	1	1,692
Mr Clever Socks	6	G	16	0	4	3	6,875
Mr Divine	9	G	11	1	1	2	4,878
Mr Don	4	G	10	0	2	3	17,303
Mr Dovic	4	G	4	0	0	0	0
Mr Easy E	2	G	5	0	1	1	8,820
Mr Fiji	5	G	12	1	3	1	10,749
Mr Forestrey	2	C	5	1	0	0	9,443
Mr Freckles	6	G	8	1	3	0	25,387
Mr Frosty	2	G	2	0	0	0	0
Mr Fuddy Duddy	9	G	2	0	0	0	85
Mr G	9	G	2	0	0	0	0
Mr Gator	6	G	4	0	0	0	0
Mr Gemeni Cricket	7	G	1	0	0	0	50
Mr Gigi (IRE)	5	H	1	1	0	0	21,600
Mr Gil	3	C	4	0	0	0	2,477
Mr Good Deal	4	G	1	0	0	0	49
Mr Graydon	5	G	4	0	0	0	0
Mr Halfnhalf	3	G	1	0	0	0	510
Mr Hay	4	G	10	3	0	2	34,850
Mr Hayes	3	G	5	0	0	0	0
Mr Henderson	5	H	3	0	0	1	295
Mr Higgs	4	C	1	0	0	0	0
Mr Hilarious	6	H	1	0	0	0	32
Mr Humanity	3	G	10	1	0	0	4,726
Mr Humvee	9	G	3	0	0	0	0
Mr I. Imagination	3	G	2	0	0	0	800
Mr Irish	3	G	9	0	0	0	297
Mr J. R.	5	G	8	0	0	0	435
Mr Jaw Talk	3	C	12	1	1	3	10,218
Mr Jetset	6	G	5	0	0	0	1,370
Mr Joe B	4	C	12	1	4	2	36,550
Mr Lion	5	G	22	0	4	3	26,640
Mr Mag	5	G	17	8	3	1	65,356
Mr Magic	2	G	7	2	0	1	9,606
Mr Major	8	G	11	2	0	3	23,900
Mr Manzie	2	G	4	0	0	1	3,608
Mr McClelland	9	G	8	1	0	2	3,714
Mr Mombo	4	G	1	0	0	0	0
Mr Moose	2	G	3	0	0	0	400
Mr Motion	5	G	2	0	0	0	800
Mr Mt Vernon	8	G	5	0	2	1	1,400
Mr Muddy Moose	3	G	9	0	0	2	980
Mr Mutter	3	G	1	0	0	0	1,150
Mr Natural Ability	3	G	6	0	0	0	555
Mr Nineball	6	G	12	1	2	2	19,851
Mr Northernclassic	3	C	6	0	0	1	1,870
Mr Notebook	6	G	12	3	4	0	42,742
Mr O'Brien (IRE)	5	G	9	3	1	1	514,050
Mr Oliver	4	G	2	0	0	0	0
Mr Patsy Kelly	6	H	10	0	1	2	4,151
Mr Penrose	2	C	7	1	1	0	12,520
Mr Pie	3	G	4	0	3	0	4,500
Mr Playboy	3	G	9	2	1	0	49,600
Mr Pop's Andreas	5	G	17	2	2	1	22,365
Mr Proper	4	G	3	0	0	0	575
Mr Ringold	5	G	1	0	0	0	125
Mr Riviter	3	G	5	0	0	0	0
Mr Rock Star	3	G	3	0	0	0	1,212
Mr Rocket	4	C	1	0	0	0	990
Mr Salty	4	C	3	0	0	0	330
Mr Salty Jones	4	G	18	1	1	1	6,848
Mr See Saw	3	G	7	0	0	4	6,285
Mr Shaanshu	4	C	5	0	2	0	5,385
Mr Shawkee	2	G	8	1	2	1	21,090
Mr Short Cut	7	G	5	1	1	1	4,511
Mr Silly	3	C	14	2	1	3	17,300
Mr Siphon	5	G	12	2	1	3	23,224
Mr Smeadleysmearch	3	G	5	0	1	1	8,560
Mr Song and Dance	5	G	13	1	1	1	21,830
Mr Spark	7	G	9	4	0	1	19,341
Mr Sparkles Gem	5	H	4	0	0	0	3,375
Mr Sparrow Tan	5	H	3	0	0	1	300
Mr Superior	4	G	13	1	2	1	8,619
Mr Superior Knight	9	G	6	0	0	0	572
Mr Sword	2	C	1	0	0	0	1,350
Mr Tack	2	C	5	0	1	1	6,890
Mr Tap Star	4	C	6	2	2	1	18,031
Mr Term	4	C	6	1	3	0	10,745
Mr Tickety Boo	4	G	16	1	4	2	25,200
Mr Toad (IRE)	5	G	6	0	1	0	2,540
Mr T's Song	3	G	1	0	0	0	0
Mr Twix	4	G	12	2	3	2	31,372
Mr Watsonsdream	7	G	10	3	2	1	17,458
Mr Wensleydale (GB)	5	G	12	2	2	2	22,493
Mr W's Daughter	3	F	4	1	0	0	5,873
Mr Zanetti	4	C	1	0	0	0	50
Mr Zipper	6	G	1	0	0	0	85
Mr Zooha	7	G	10	1	0	2	5,066

Horse	Age	Sex	Sts	1st	2d	3d	Won
Mr Z's	6	G	8	2	1	0	16,781
Mr. Acavano	7	G	6	0	1	1	3,300
Mr. Ace	5	G	5	0	0	0	0
Mr. Alybro	4	G	8	3	0	2	17,716
Mr. Amano	4	G	13	6	2	1	150,670
Mr. Angel	6	H	4	0	0	0	341
Mr. Antman	2	G	12	1	1	2	22,055
Mr. Archibald	5	H	4	1	2	1	72,700
Mr. Artax	2	C	4	1	0	0	14,895
Mr. Babu	3	C	4	0	0	0	1,537
Mr. Bad News	6	G	16	4	4	2	55,702
Mr. Bardak	2	C	1	0	0	0	860
Mr. Barracuda	2	C	4	1	1	0	22,935
Mr. Barricade	4	G	13	0	0	3	1,776
Mr. Bartlett	5	G	3	1	0	1	5,855
Mr. Baskets	6	H	8	2	3	0	14,535
Mr. Beecher	6	H	2	0	0	0	0
Mr. Believable	4	C	8	2	1	2	23,525
Mr. Ben	4	G	9	0	1	0	1,775
Mr. Benray	4	G	14	1	0	2	14,230
Mr. Benson	3	G	9	0	1	1	3,093
Mr. Benton	5	G	8	1	1	3	13,709
Mr. Bigbird	5	H	4	0	0	0	311
Mr. Bigglesworth	7	G	5	0	1	0	3,556
Mr. Bird	4	G	9	3	0	1	12,605
Mr. Black Creek	6	H	1	0	0	0	0
Mr. Blackie	5	G	7	0	1	0	4,140
Mr. Bo Ally Ray	5	G	1	0	0	0	0
Mr. Bo Jo	5	G	8	0	0	0	561
Mr. Boaster	10	G	5	0	1	0	615
Mr. Bocephus	5	G	12	1	0	3	5,210
Mr. Bondsman	2	G	6	3	2	0	92,184
Mr. Bones	3	C	2	0	0	0	420
Mr. Boombastic	2	C	2	0	0	0	0
Mr. Boomer	2	C	5	1	1	1	16,984
Mr. Boone	6	G	4	0	0	0	197
Mr. Bosco	5	G	2	0	1	0	2,795
Mr. Brad	8	G	2	0	0	0	36
Mr. Brave Heart	3	G	9	2	0	1	22,002
Mr. Brook	8	G	4	0	0	0	170
Mr. B's Diamond	3	G	7	1	4	1	23,750
Mr. Bubbly	4	G	14	5	1	0	50,510
Mr. Bubby	3	G	12	2	2	1	17,308
Mr. Bullseye	2	C	7	0	2	1	12,666
Mr. Bullshipper	2	C	5	0	1	2	11,040
Mr. C Note	3	G	4	1	0	2	22,960
Mr. Campbell Sir	5	H	1	0	0	0	254
Mr. Cara	4	G	8	0	1	0	3,796
Mr. Carpe Diem	3	C	17	2	5	3	25,181
Mr. Cash City	5	G	14	1	2	3	11,572
Mr. Cat	4	G	20	3	2	2	24,231
Mr. Center Storm	3	C	3	0	0	0	0
Mr. Charisma	2	C	2	1	0	0	6,600
Mr. Charming	3	G	13	2	0	3	7,426
Mr. Ching	4	C	7	0	3	1	39,462
Mr. Chipping	6	G	2	0	0	0	121
Mr. Chisum	4	G	5	1	1	0	17,418
Mr. Chris Kringle	4	G	4	0	1	0	742
Mr. Chubbs	7	H	2	0	0	0	222
Mr. Classy	3	G	7	0	0	1	2,480
Mr. Classy Action	3	G	8	2	1	1	23,430
Mr. Cliveden	2	G	2	0	0	0	1,530
Mr. Cold Call	2	C	4	1	0	0	33,698
Mr. Cold Comfort	2	C	8	1	2	1	19,740
Mr. Colin P.	4	G	10	1	0	1	4,250
Mr. Concerto	4	G	1	0	0	0	81
Mr. Congeniality	2	G	1	1	0	0	24,600
Mr. Crabapple	2	C	5	2	1	0	31,600
Mr. Crimson	5	G	5	0	0	2	5,235
Mr. Cub	4	G	2	0	0	0	0
Mr. D Man	3	G	5	0	1	0	5,850
Mr. Damille	6	H	6	1	0	0	3,294
Mr. de Falls	8	H	8	0	0	2	2,649
Mr. Decatur	4	C	9	0	0	1	5,619
Mr. Deep Pockets	4	G	14	3	2	5	11,292
Mr. Deputy	3	G	4	0	0	0	1,500
Mr. Determined	5	H	7	0	1	3	60,927
Mr. Devious	3	G	8	3	4	1	104,575
Mr. Digger	3	C	11	1	1	0	23,560
Mr. Dino	3	C	4	0	0	0	300
Mr. Diplomat	5	G	8	1	1	0	15,050
Mr. Dutton	6	G	8	0	1	4	3,380
Mr. E Cat	4	C	1	0	0	0	53
Mr. Eddie R	3	G	9	1	1	2	13,284
Mr. Eldorado	4	G	7	1	0	0	5,850
Mr. Elusive	4	G	6	0	1	0	6,105
Mr. Endeavour	5	G	3	0	0	0	180
Mr. Epperson	9	G	7	0	1	2	37,720
Mr. Ethanol	2	C	2	0	1	0	4,500
Mr. Excavate	3	C	12	2	0	1	31,330
Mr. Excellent	2	C	5	3	1	0	81,700
Mr. Excitement	8	G	10	2	0	2	15,412
Mr. Fater	7	G	1	1	0	0	6,000
Mr. Fit	2	G	7	0	2	0	10,340
Mr. Fix	5	G	14	1	4	1	7,050
Mr. Fixed Income	3	C	11	2	2	1	17,928
Mr. Flakes	3	G	6	0	1	1	3,180
Mr. Fleet Feet	5	H	3	0	0	1	1,310
Mr. Fondue	2	C	9	4	1	2	99,028
Mr. Fools Gold	8	G	8	0	5	1	5,156
Mr. Fourth of July	2	C	1	0	0	0	129
Mr. Fran Man	4	C	13	3	1	3	37,257
Mr. Frog	5	G	10	0	2	4	12,098
Mr. Frost	4	G	18	3	2	1	25,067
Mr. Frostburg	3	G	8	0	0	1	1,680
Mr. Fun	3	G	4	0	0	1	1,150
Mr. Garry C.	7	G	8	1	1	3	8,044
Mr. Gentle Ben	4	G	6	0	0	0	789
Mr. Gladiator	4	C	11	0	0	1	3,264
Mr. Glassware	8	H	4	0	0	2	1,151
Mr. Gleason	3	C	4	0	2	1	13,260
Mr. Glendale	4	G	4	1	1	0	14,712
Mr. Gold Flight	5	G	4	0	0	0	270
Mr. Gold Invader	3	G	1	0	0	0	195
Mr. Got Rocks	3	G	4	1	0	0	9,720
Mr. Gray Buck	2	C	3	1	0	0	17,430
Mr. Greedy	5	G	6	1	0	3	10,079
Mr. Gretzky (NZ)	8	G	3	0	0	0	450
Mr. Gung Ho	8	G	7	1	1	0	6,615
Mr. Guyana	8	G	10	0	0	1	5,369
Mr. Habitant	2	G	3	0	0	0	1,120
Mr. Hadley	6	G	4	0	0	0	263
Mr. Happy Hour	5	G	10	2	0	2	8,809
Mr. Hawthorn	2	C	2	1	0	0	8,790
Mr. Headliner	4	G	1	0	0	0	0
Mr. Heartache	2	G	10	0	1	2	10,670
Mr. Heartbreaker	2	C	3	0	0	2	9,800
Mr. Hemmingway	4	G	14	4	0	2	12,188
Mr. Henry Two U	2	G	2	0	1	0	5,300
Mr. Hobo Joe	7	G	3	0	0	0	495
Mr. Hockey	4	G	8	0	0	0	427
Mr. Hooch	3	G	10	1	3	0	25,403
Mr. Image	3	G	1	0	0	0	0
Mr. Insanity	9	G	1	0	0	0	200
Mr. Irish Love	3	G	7	3	0	1	12,754
Mr. J. T. L.	3	C	11	1	2	0	52,444
Mr. Jazz Man	4	C	1	0	0	0	254
Mr. Jerome	3	G	12	1	1	3	28,365
Mr. Jess	5	G	2	0	1	0	2,885
Mr. Jester	3	C	8	1	2	0	54,600
Mr. Jetson	2	G	7	1	1	1	9,579
Mr. Jimmy Gimmie	4	G	6	1	1	0	9,720
Mr. Joe Lee	3	G	6	0	0	0	1,025
Mr. Kenny H	3	G	12	4	2	1	60,298
Mr. Kimbo	4	G	7	0	2	2	10,215
Mr. King Pin	5	G	10	1	2	2	27,480
Mr. King Rex	4	G	1	0	0	0	0
Mr. Kipp	5	H	1	0	0	0	0
Mr. Kody	8	G	8	2	0	2	6,970
Mr. Krisley	6	G	7	0	0	2	29,552
Mr. Kuck	7	G	15	5	2	2	60,430
Mr. L.	4	G	4	2	0	0	40,488
Mr. L. C.	6	H	7	1	2	0	4,321
Mr. L. D.	5	G	13	1	0	0	3,512
Mr. Lee	3	C	15	3	2	3	16,666
Mr. Lefty James	7	G	9	1	2	1	5,380
Mr. Liberty	7	G	15	4	7	1	26,131
Mr. Liberty Bells	3	G	7	1	2	0	2,611

Horse	Age	Sex	Sts	1st	2d	3d	Won
Mr. Light (ARG)	5	H	8	2	2	1	74,830
Mr. Lincoln	3	G	6	1	0	1	6,110
Mr. Lion King	3	C	12	1	1	2	13,247
Mr. Livingston	7	H	4	1	0	0	21,460
Mr. Lover	6	G	12	1	3	1	22,190
Mr. Lucky Numbers	8	G	14	3	8	2	42,658
Mr. Lump	8	G	12	0	1	1	5,964
Mr. Luxury	2	G	3	1	0	0	9,000
Mr. M. G.	4	G	8	1	1	1	2,470
Mr. Mabee	3	C	4	1	2	0	45,260
Mr. Machine	4	G	10	1	4	2	8,280
Mr. Macphisto	5	G	13	0	3	1	4,243
Mr. Maestre	2	C	3	0	1	1	7,300
Mr. Maggie	3	G	2	0	0	0	771
Mr. Magic Jet	2	C	2	0	0	0	1,900
Mr. Magic Man	6	H	1	0	0	0	0
Mr. Makah	4	G	9	2	1	3	83,421
Mr. Malaprop	2	C	3	0	0	1	5,442
Mr. Marbelous	4	G	5	1	0	0	6,725
Mr. Marfa	8	G	7	0	0	0	645
Mr. Marquet Maker	2	C	3	0	0	0	236
Mr. Masquerade	5	G	1	0	0	0	0
Mr. Match	6	G	17	1	4	4	16,569
Mr. Mauk	3	G	3	0	0	0	2,010
Mr. Mayday	3	G	2	0	0	0	0
Mr. McCabe	6	G	10	0	1	2	15,090
Mr. McZu	3	C	2	0	0	0	0
Mr. Megan	4	G	10	1	1	0	42,960
Mr. Melcap	5	G	16	8	3	0	24,478
Mr. Meridian	2	C	1	0	0	0	580
Mr. Merrick	4	G	11	1	2	1	10,070
Mr. Merry	3	G	14	2	2	5	23,125
Mr. Meso	4	C	8	1	1	1	23,560
Mr. Mingo	4	G	10	2	2	0	49,545
Mr. Mini	3	G	11	0	0	0	1,024
Mr. Mink	4	G	8	4	1	0	53,550
Mr. Missionary	7	G	9	0	0	1	1,378
Mr. Mister	8	H	5	0	0	0	505
Mr. Monsoon	3	C	9	0	0	1	3,194
Mr. Monster	4	G	6	0	0	0	0
Mr. Moody Blue	6	G	18	2	1	3	8,739
Mr. Moonshine Time	2	C	2	1	0	1	11,090
Mr. Morley	2	G	1	0	0	0	300
Mr. Moses	4	G	7	0	0	1	825
Mr. Motown	2	C	3	0	1	1	4,300
Mr. Moze	12	G	7	0	0	0	228
Mr. Mulgrew	3	G	4	0	0	0	138
Mr. Mytee Mouse	4	G	3	0	0	0	770
Mr. Nancho (ARG)	4	C	1	0	1	0	10,200
Mr. New Freedom	3	G	5	0	1	0	2,204
Mr. Nifty	6	G	27	0	1	5	3,337
Mr. Nighttime	3	C	10	1	1	3	26,562
Mr. Niner	4	G	3	1	1	0	36,083
Mr. Novak	5	G	12	1	3	1	11,306
Mr. O. E.	3	C	6	0	0	0	224
Mr. O'Bryan	3	C	1	0	0	0	0
Mr. October	4	G	13	4	2	3	23,894
Mr. One Putt	2	G	7	0	0	0	2,000
Mr. Oneninehundred	3	G	7	1	2	1	27,355
Mr. Otis	5	G	14	4	2	0	13,275
Mr. Outside	4	G	10	2	1	1	5,928
Mr. P D Q	2	C	2	0	0	0	0
Mr. P T	6	G	6	0	0	0	653
Mr. Pablo	3	G	1	0	0	0	0
Mr. Paranoide	6	G	1	0	0	0	300
Mr. Parks	4	C	1	0	0	0	0
Mr. Pat	5	H	12	2	4	2	52,480
Mr. Patience	3	G	8	0	0	1	1,544
Mr. Pay Day	2	C	4	0	0	0	3,600
Mr. Peacemaker	5	G	5	1	0	1	19,737
Mr. Pee Vee	3	C	4	3	0	0	81,260
Mr. Pentel	7	H	10	0	0	1	3,306
Mr. Peppers	4	G	9	0	0	1	864
Mr. Perpetuity	7	G	11	5	2	1	175,887
Mr. Persistency	4	G	13	1	0	4	12,342
Mr. Phantom Slew	3	G	9	1	1	0	5,549
Mr. Piano Man	3	G	14	1	1	1	14,542
Mr. Pickled Gap	10	G	1	0	0	0	40
Mr. Picou	3	C	1	0	1	0	1,890
Mr. Pleasentfar (BRZ)	7	H	9	0	1	2	12,255
Mr. Plum	5	G	17	2	3	3	9,088
Mr. Popeye	5	G	9	2	0	0	11,485
Mr. Postmaster	8	G	3	0	0	0	440
Mr. Potter	5	G	5	0	1	1	5,016
Mr. Power Ball	3	G	6	0	2	1	2,408
Mr. President Sir	3	G	3	0	0	0	1,215
Mr. Presley	4	C	5	0	2	0	16,260
Mr. Punkindo	5	H	5	1	0	0	4,800
Mr. Quasar	3	G	10	1	0	2	5,555
Mr. Question	3	G	7	0	0	0	2,520
Mr. Quick	4	G	21	1	1	3	11,174
Mr. Quickly	5	G	8	1	0	0	5,817
Mr. Quist	12	G	7	0	0	0	242
Mr. Quizzical	12	G	5	0	1	1	1,662
Mr. Rainmaker	2	C	1	0	0	0	120
Mr. Rajiv	5	G	15	1	5	2	24,894
Mr. Ranger	10	G	5	1	1	0	4,060
Mr. Reed	8	G	5	0	0	0	510
Mr. Reins	4	G	3	0	0	0	675
Mr. Resale	4	G	12	0	1	2	3,428
Mr. Review	5	H	1	0	0	0	0
Mr. Riddler	8	G	2	0	0	0	0
Mr. Ridge	4	C	5	0	1	1	2,247
Mr. Rob	4	C	1	0	0	0	0
Mr. Rocket Man	5	G	12	4	2	0	39,642
Mr. Rocky T	4	G	2	0	0	0	261
Mr. Romeo	4	C	4	1	1	0	25,800
Mr. Ron	4	C	4	1	0	0	7,200
Mr. Royal Twist	5	G	3	0	0	0	261
Mr. Rumson	5	G	11	2	1	3	31,954
Mr. Ruska	4	G	3	1	0	0	9,870
Mr. Sam	3	G	11	2	0	3	50,245
Mr. Samson	4	G	13	4	2	1	47,970
Mr. San Miguel	5	G	6	1	2	0	5,180
Mr. Sandstorm	6	G	1	0	0	0	240
Mr. Saratoga	5	H	8	2	1	1	19,385
Mr. Sass	4	G	15	1	2	2	8,932
Mr. Scott Man	6	G	1	0	0	0	0
Mr. Seafarer	8	G	7	0	0	3	3,198
Mr. Secret Claim	5	H	1	0	0	0	0
Mr. Seldon	4	G	4	0	0	0	0
Mr. Sezwho	10	H	9	0	3	0	7,100
Mr. Shock and Awe	2	G	1	0	0	0	0
Mr. Shoplifter	5	H	3	0	1	0	3,690
Mr. Shu	2	C	2	0	0	0	0
Mr. Simmie	3	C	7	0	1	1	1,660
Mr. Simon to You	4	G	6	3	1	1	19,245
Mr. Smarty	2	G	4	0	2	0	2,860
Mr. Smiley	3	C	5	0	0	2	7,440
Mr. Smoke	4	G	13	1	3	2	14,403
Mr. Snap	3	G	4	0	0	0	0
Mr. Snippington	2	C	7	1	2	1	42,660
Mr. Speaks	6	G	11	3	1	2	22,850
Mr. Spectacular	4	G	7	1	2	0	6,628
Mr. Spiderman	3	C	5	1	1	0	7,090
Mr. Splash	2	G	2	0	0	0	4,200
Mr. Spock	3	C	7	0	1	2	23,525
Mr. Spoons	2	C	1	0	0	0	0
Mr. Steadfast	4	G	4	0	0	0	235
Mr. Steve	8	G	1	0	0	0	0
Mr. Stone	4	C	4	0	1	1	2,599
Mr. Storm Dancer	5	H	3	0	0	0	1,110
Mr. Stress	6	G	13	3	4	4	48,220
Mr. Sulu	6	G	8	4	0	1	140,456
Mr. Sun	4	G	14	3	1	3	24,706
Mr. Sundancer	9	G	9	0	0	2	3,904
Mr. T Cup	3	G	8	1	0	1	2,036
Mr. T. K.	7	G	7	3	1	1	14,712
Mr. Takur	2	C	4	0	1	0	827
Mr. Talisman	8	G	13	0	3	2	2,119
Mr. Tammany	7	H	11	1	1	2	8,283
Mr. Tap	4	C	4	0	0	0	301
Mr. Technique	4	C	2	0	1	0	7,500
Mr. Thermaltech	3	G	8	1	2	0	16,807
Mr. Tiago	3	C	1	0	0	0	180
Mr. Tiff	5	G	1	0	0	0	400
Mr. Tigger	3	C	2	0	0	0	142
Mr. Time Count	2	G	5	0	0	0	1,900

Horse	Age	Sex	Sts	1st	2d	3d	Won
Mr. Tipsy	6	H	13	0	4	2	25,450
Mr. Tobin	4	G	1	0	0	0	65
Mr. Touchy	5	G	6	0	0	0	536
Mr. Trash Talk	3	G	5	0	0	1	962
Mr. Travertino (ARG)	5	H	3	0	0	0	2,250
Mr. Tricky	3	G	10	0	1	2	7,065
Mr. Trieste	3	C	11	4	2	3	90,532
Mr. Trouble	5	G	9	0	0	1	6,355
Mr. Troublemaker	4	G	2	0	0	0	150
Mr. Truthful	4	G	15	4	1	4	48,290
Mr. Two Step	4	G	1	0	0	0	0
Mr. V.	5	G	6	2	1	0	69,149
Mr. V. I. P.	3	C	3	2	0	0	5,460
Mr. Value	5	G	1	0	1	0	5,600
Mr. Vanhoose	4	G	9	1	1	0	8,942
Mr. Wakette	8	G	6	0	0	0	992
Mr. Whitestone	4	G	9	3	2	3	135,460
Mr. Will	5	G	12	0	3	3	5,138
Mr. Williamson	5	G	4	0	0	1	3,188
Mr. Willie Joe	3	C	13	0	1	2	13,320
Mr. Windfall	3	G	7	2	0	0	14,267
Mr. Windy	5	G	3	0	0	0	318
Mr. Winterbourne	6	G	2	0	0	0	1,620
Mr. Wister	4	G	2	0	0	0	800
Mr. Wonderful Man	9	G	5	0	0	0	237
Mr. Word	3	G	11	1	1	1	5,665
Mr. Yano	4	C	11	0	0	2	2,802
Mr. Yatooma	4	G	6	1	1	0	7,655
Mr. Yippy Kippy	2	C	1	0	0	0	140
Mr. Zach Man	4	G	12	2	2	3	34,933
Mralwaysatisfied	3	G	12	4	3	0	81,990
Mramerica	4	C	12	0	0	3	2,090
Mrs Bigshot	5	M	6	0	0	0	1,107
Mrs Mary C	4	F	1	0	0	0	0
Mrs. Bailey	3	F	2	0	1	0	5,000
Mrs. Bassett	3	F	9	1	0	1	11,899
Mrs. Beerman	3	F	8	2	1	0	37,690
Mrs. Brown Angel	3	F	5	0	1	1	1,760
Mrs. Burns	6	M	12	1	2	2	32,283
Mrs. Cavendish	3	F	2	0	0	0	231
Mrs. Charles	3	F	9	1	1	1	17,422
Mrs. Clay	4	F	9	0	1	3	3,583
Mrs. Cook	4	F	2	0	0	0	86
Mrs. Costanza	4	F	3	0	0	0	0
Mrs. Debbie M	2	F	4	1	0	1	20,855
Mrs. Doyle	4	F	11	2	3	2	42,600
Mrs. Frosty	6	M	11	0	3	0	6,613
Mrs. Karakorum	4	F	1	0	0	0	164
Mrs. M	5	M	9	1	3	3	113,427
Mrs. Mac	7	M	5	0	0	1	5,983
Mrs. Mackey	3	F	6	0	3	2	11,174
Mrs. Mistofelees	3	F	7	0	1	0	12,299
Mrs. Muir	2	F	1	0	0	0	180
Mrs. Navarone	4	G	8	0	1	0	2,320
Mrs. Obvious	4	F	11	0	2	0	4,533
Mrs. Piggle Wiggle	9	M	12	1	3	0	15,356
Mrs. Ripley	2	F	2	0	0	0	240
Mrs. Robinson	3	F	5	0	0	1	1,870
Mrs. Root	2	F	1	1	0	0	6,600
Mrs. Rosalie C.	5	M	4	0	0	0	525
Mrs. Smith	3	F	19	0	1	1	9,615
Mrs. Smooth Moves	4	F	17	2	1	1	15,266
Mrs. Soprano	5	M	3	0	0	0	609
Mrs. Strauss	3	F	8	0	4	1	6,305
Mrs. True	2	F	2	0	0	0	370
Mrs. Vanderbilt	3	F	11	2	2	1	47,901
Mrs. Witchworth	6	M	1	0	0	0	64
Mrscoppolaskitchen	5	M	2	0	1	0	3,600
Mrsjefferson	2	F	1	0	0	1	2,332
Ms Afterglow	5	M	4	0	0	2	1,374
Ms Akins Outlaw	6	M	2	0	0	2	480
Ms Alberta	2	F	1	0	0	0	294
Ms Alex D	6	M	4	0	0	0	260
Ms Allen Oops	4	F	10	2	1	0	9,431
Ms Alleygirl	4	F	1	0	0	0	0
Ms Ally Allen	4	F	12	0	0	0	725
Ms American Champ	2	F	2	0	0	1	1,485
Ms Bessie	3	F	10	2	1	3	38,785
Ms Blue Speedy	5	M	6	1	0	2	6,519

Horse	Age	Sex	Sts	1st	2d	3d	Won
Ms Carissa	6	M	3	0	0	0	70
Ms Claudia	2	F	4	0	2	1	4,422
Ms Cow Island	3	F	10	0	0	0	863
Ms Deanor	5	M	4	0	0	0	771
Ms Deep Cover	2	F	1	0	0	1	2,750
Ms Flash of Light	6	M	3	0	0	0	558
Ms Forty Second St	2	F	8	1	1	1	25,500
Ms Freddie Bright	4	F	11	2	3	1	17,939
Ms Gal Friday	2	F	2	0	0	0	300
Ms Glamour Girl	3	F	1	0	0	0	0
Ms Go Dream Go	3	F	8	2	1	1	11,377
Ms Goda	6	M	15	1	2	3	7,991
Ms Grey Dancer	3	F	2	1	0	0	9,000
Ms Halo	3	F	9	0	0	0	600
Ms Hayseed	6	M	3	0	0	0	202
Ms Hischool	2	F	1	0	0	0	0
Ms Homer Point	2	F	1	0	1	0	8,400
Ms Hop Holmes	3	F	8	1	1	1	9,603
Ms Hush Money	3	F	5	0	0	0	1,434
Ms Ida Dealer	6	M	5	0	0	3	2,485
Ms Infinity Slew	8	M	3	0	0	0	340
Ms Jamie	3	F	2	0	0	0	0
Ms Jessi	5	M	2	0	0	0	0
Ms Kit Cat	3	F	2	0	0	2	1,950
Ms Kitty Bag	4	F	6	1	3	0	3,620
Ms Knight Lane	5	M	4	0	3	0	14,105
Ms Lady Palace	3	F	4	2	2	0	8,730
Ms Litigator	2	F	6	1	0	1	37,272
Ms Maggie Sue	5	M	13	0	3	4	8,869
Ms Majestic Lady	4	F	14	4	2	2	18,875
Ms Maryann N	3	F	9	4	0	2	69,910
Ms Mintons Excess	3	G	12	2	5	1	76,423
Ms Montana Pat	2	F	2	0	0	0	560
Ms Moves	4	F	2	0	0	0	907
Ms Nancy S	3	F	13	2	0	0	24,490
Ms Powful	4	F	9	1	1	2	32,450
Ms Prime Minister	4	F	2	0	0	0	0
Ms Regina	3	F	4	1	0	0	7,011
Ms Seneca Rock	2	F	5	3	0	1	47,140
Ms Sensational	2	F	3	0	0	0	682
Ms Shawcolat	5	M	9	3	0	2	31,980
Ms Storming Angel	3	F	7	1	0	0	28,320
Ms Technology	4	F	15	2	0	2	17,317
Ms Temprana	2	F	2	1	1	0	20,000
Ms Tish	5	M	5	1	0	0	6,146
Ms Tom Cat	4	F	6	1	0	1	6,119
Ms Touriffic	2	F	8	2	2	0	26,840
Ms Zoom Zoom	4	F	3	0	1	1	3,525
Ms. Amours	5	M	11	1	2	3	5,980
Ms. April Fool Day	3	F	5	1	1	2	7,205
Ms. April Foolish	5	M	1	0	0	0	0
Ms. Avis	3	F	11	2	2	3	43,480
Ms. Bag	5	M	7	4	1	1	58,441
Ms. Banker	3	F	7	0	3	2	17,880
Ms. Bella	7	M	11	0	0	1	1,242
Ms. Bluebird	4	F	5	1	0	0	13,270
Ms. Bonita	5	M	4	0	1	1	9,109
Ms. Brow	6	M	6	1	0	0	3,723
Ms. Carpetbagger	3	F	7	0	0	2	1,394
Ms. Chantilly Lace	4	F	4	0	0	0	1,105
Ms. Compadre	3	F	3	0	0	0	181
Ms. Dahill	2	F	3	0	0	2	4,500
Ms. Dazzler	2	F	5	1	0	1	11,600
Ms. Deandra	2	F	3	1	0	0	10,910
Ms. Dixie Time	3	F	3	0	0	1	1,487
Ms. Dottie J	3	F	11	1	1	2	6,585
Ms. Dowden	5	M	7	0	2	1	14,990
Ms. Elenie	4	F	9	1	0	0	6,017
Ms. Era	5	M	7	0	0	0	992
Ms. Executive City	3	F	8	0	1	2	11,392
Ms. Foolish Dancer	5	M	6	0	1	0	7,124
Ms. Foxy Roxy	4	F	9	3	1	0	14,465
Ms. Free Glory	3	F	8	1	0	0	3,900
Ms. Grizz	3	F	1	0	0	0	1,680
Ms. Inez	4	F	15	1	1	4	6,822
Ms. Inxs	3	F	7	1	2	0	10,290
Ms. Justice	5	M	10	0	0	1	1,570
Ms. K. L. Cat	4	F	10	2	3	2	18,405
Ms. Kinsey	4	F	7	0	2	1	12,384

Horse	Age	Sex	Sts	1st	2d	3d	Won
Ms. Lydonia	3	F	9	3	2	2	88,896
Ms. Mac N Cheese	3	F	5	0	0	1	1,470
Ms. Mary Marie	5	M	8	1	0	1	6,183
Ms. Matching	3	F	8	0	0	1	1,729
Ms. Monica	3	F	2	0	0	0	165
Ms. Morgane	3	F	5	0	0	0	729
Ms. Pie	5	M	8	1	0	1	6,920
Ms. Prenup	6	M	1	0	0	0	50
Ms. Purr	3	F	4	1	0	2	37,225
Ms. Real Thang	3	F	13	2	2	0	23,175
Ms. Remarkable	4	F	6	0	0	0	880
Ms. Rubirosa	4	F	18	1	3	3	21,587
Ms. Russian Cat	4	F	9	0	0	0	1,147
Ms. Sadira	7	M	2	0	1	0	2,850
Ms. Sarah Vye	2	F	9	1	2	1	21,022
Ms. Saskatoon	4	F	7	0	0	2	900
Ms. Sassy Lady	3	F	8	0	0	0	368
Ms. Sharoan	3	F	1	0	0	0	675
Ms. Sofia Ann	3	F	6	1	0	1	23,478
Ms. Speedo	4	F	16	1	2	1	17,915
Ms. Tahoe Ridge	3	F	8	3	1	0	11,046
Ms. Tiger Beat	2	F	1	0	1	0	4,600
Ms. Toni K	2	F	14	1	2	1	8,826
Ms. Top Pay	4	F	10	1	1	2	18,360
Ms. Tophamhat	4	F	5	1	0	0	3,179
Ms. Trick Or Treat	3	F	10	3	0	2	88,422
Ms. Via's Citation	8	M	3	0	0	1	1,068
Ms. Whiz	5	M	12	0	2	0	4,264
Ms. Will a Way	4	F	6	1	3	0	50,721
Ms. Winfrey	5	M	3	0	0	2	3,037
Ms. Wolf	5	M	8	1	0	1	10,204
Ms. Zipoy	7	M	8	0	1	0	1,685
Ms.playgirl	2	F	9	1	1	3	29,375
Msbaileyscream	6	M	12	4	1	3	185,301
Mt Dylan	5	G	2	0	0	0	214
Mt Money	2	G	5	1	0	1	9,035
Mt Pockets	3	G	7	1	1	0	21,550
Mt Waverly	5	H	1	0	0	0	960
Mt. Adamas	3	C	5	0	0	0	1,020
Mt. Carson	4	C	5	1	0	0	34,470
Mt. Classic	3	C	8	0	1	1	5,989
Mt. Grande	3	C	4	0	1	0	5,030
Mt. Ida	2	F	2	0	0	0	580
Mt. Katmai	3	F	4	0	0	0	1,410
Mt. Kenya	5	G	12	3	2	1	22,261
Mt. Livermate	2	F	3	0	1	0	6,213
Mt. Logan	4	G	17	1	1	1	14,264
Mt. Majesty	3	G	5	1	1	0	35,249
Mt. Margaret	5	M	9	1	0	1	9,686
Mt. Moran	5	G	8	4	0	0	74,550
Mt. Ouray	7	G	12	1	2	0	23,564
Mt. Palomar	2	G	6	1	2	0	16,735
Mt. Pauliano	3	G	13	3	1	3	21,137
Mt. Rainer	6	G	2	0	1	0	2,132
Mt. Rhodes	2	C	5	0	0	1	2,938
Mt. Rumanov	3	F	4	0	1	0	1,572
Mt. Silver	3	C	7	1	1	2	22,480
Mt. Sinai	2	C	5	0	0	0	443
Mt. St. Patty	4	F	13	1	2	1	11,141
Mt. St. Simon	3	C	1	0	0	0	400
Mt. Sterling Mary	2	F	1	0	1	0	2,900
Mt. Swoosh	4	F	2	0	0	0	280
Mt. Triumph	3	G	8	1	1	0	19,182
Mt. Troodos	4	C	8	0	0	0	1,166
Mt. Vernon News	6	G	2	0	0	0	0
Mt. Vernon Rd	3	C	6	2	0	1	17,652
Mt. Vista	5	G	13	3	3	2	17,101
Mt. Washington	3	G	12	0	6	2	35,470
Mtn of Expectation	3	C	1	0	0	0	0
Mubeen (IRE)	4	C	7	1	2	2	129,422
Mubtaker	7	H	3	1	0	0	215,103
Mucciacciaro	4	F	14	2	3	3	18,805
Mucci's Market	5	G	8	1	0	0	8,320
Much	3	F	12	0	1	1	11,720
Much Ransom	3	G	7	0	0	1	1,594
Much Respect	4	C	12	3	3	2	83,180
Mucha Muchacha	2	F	3	0	0	0	1,803
Mucha Prisa	4	F	11	0	1	1	7,760
Muchacha Bonita	2	F	6	0	1	1	6,900
Muchcat	4	G	9	1	2	0	4,550
Muchmusic	3	F	13	2	0	4	19,806
Mucho Bold	4	G	7	1	0	1	10,110
Mucho Bravada	3	C	4	0	1	1	6,260
Mucho Daniero	8	G	2	0	0	0	167
Mucho Gusto Man	4	G	4	0	0	0	381
Mucho Mite	4	G	6	0	1	1	2,638
Mucho Rapido	5	H	9	3	1	1	64,098
Mucho Salt	3	G	6	1	0	0	9,032
Muchtolegittoquit	3	G	6	1	1	3	13,520
Muckety Muck	2	C	1	0	0	0	125
Mud Axe Trouble	4	G	6	0	0	0	0
Mud Cat	3	C	4	0	0	0	370
Mud Flat	3	G	3	0	2	0	4,133
Mud Light	3	G	1	1	0	0	26,400
Mud Man	3	C	7	1	4	0	14,690
Mud Puppie	4	G	13	1	0	3	6,304
Mud Run	3	G	2	0	0	0	0
Mud Shark	4	G	11	2	1	2	87,780
Mud Slingin' Cat	5	M	5	0	0	0	554
Mud Warrior	10	G	5	0	0	0	221
Mudalloverme	4	F	6	0	0	2	5,035
Muddy Halo	2	F	6	2	1	1	33,860
Muddy Miss	3	F	5	1	2	0	6,755
Muddy Monarch	3	G	3	0	0	1	1,116
Muddy Woman	2	F	1	0	0	0	0
Muddypuddles	3	C	2	0	0	0	0
Mudslide	3	G	12	0	2	1	8,401
Mudslide Slim	7	H	5	0	1	0	5,134
Muevete	3	F	12	5	0	2	15,346
Mufasa's Legacy	4	G	3	0	0	0	270
Muffled Lady	2	F	4	0	0	0	210
Mug of Love	4	G	11	2	1	1	47,000
Mugee	3	C	10	4	0	1	20,156
Muggy	4	G	9	4	0	4	31,415
Muguet	3	F	6	0	4	0	35,340
Muhtabid	6	G	13	4	1	4	34,823
Muir Beach	3	F	16	7	5	1	228,710
Muir Eireann	7	M	6	1	0	0	9,710
Mujica	2	G	3	1	0	0	4,725
Mukaabed	7	H	12	1	3	3	30,702
Mukhtaser	4	C	3	0	0	0	2,887
Mukilteo Smoke	6	M	3	0	1	0	950
Mulahen (GB)	9	G	8	1	2	0	41,406
Mulberry Man	3	G	9	3	1	1	24,110
Mulch	3	G	13	1	0	0	7,706
Muley Tune	2	G	5	1	2	1	9,535
Mulhockaway	3	G	6	0	0	0	574
Mulkl	2	C	3	0	0	0	1,200
Mullen	6	G	6	0	0	2	5,920
Mulligan	2	G	5	0	2	1	7,225
Mulligan the Great	5	G	3	0	0	1	14,042
Mulligan's Rose	5	M	3	0	0	0	170
Mullingar	3	F	4	1	0	0	14,640
Multi Deed	3	G	11	2	0	4	52,946
Multiple Choice	6	G	14	1	4	1	123,008
Multiplication	3	C	4	2	1	0	102,740
Mumble Jumble	4	G	8	1	5	1	76,947
Mumbles	3	G	11	2	3	1	88,218
Mum's Gold	5	M	6	1	2	2	29,070
Muncaster Mill	3	G	7	0	0	0	980
Munchies	6	M	10	0	0	0	1,095
Munchkin	4	F	3	1	1	0	41,090
Muncy	3	G	7	0	0	0	1,102
Mundo of Sea	6	M	5	0	0	0	486
Mundos Magic	5	M	5	0	1	0	1,420
Munificence	2	C	2	2	0	0	24,900
Muntaqim	3	G	3	0	0	0	795
Murachi	4	G	4	0	0	0	803
Murani	2	F	2	0	0	1	7,980
Murano	5	G	8	1	0	0	43,200
Murder Creek	9	G	2	0	0	1	1,500
Murdock	7	G	13	0	1	2	6,915
Murky Waters	2	F	3	0	0	2	6,864
Murmadon	4	G	4	0	0	0	0
Murmuring Sea	6	G	6	0	0	0	760
Murohce	4	F	4	0	0	2	2,980
Murphy	6	G	4	0	1	0	3,150
Murphy Style	2	F	6	1	2	0	44,774

Horse	Age	Sex	Sts	1st	2d	3d	Won
Murphy's Bonus	2	G	2	0	0	0	161
Murphy's Cat	3	C	1	0	0	0	37
Murphys Photo	4	F	1	0	0	0	90
Murphy's Road	4	G	6	0	0	0	1,000
Murray's Dream	4	G	5	0	0	0	930
Murray's Mazal	4	G	14	2	3	4	43,640
Murrough	4	G	5	0	0	0	700
Musaa Ed	5	H	10	2	1	1	28,405
Musaranho (BRZ)	6	G	7	0	0	1	2,040
Musashi	7	G	16	3	1	3	20,870
Muschi	9	M	3	0	0	0	1,980
Muscle Beach	3	G	7	1	1	0	5,460
Muscle Magic	2	F	2	0	1	0	3,870
Muscle Up	6	M	3	0	1	1	3,745
Muscovy	7	G	11	1	3	2	10,092
Musetta's Waltz	3	F	11	1	1	0	30,904
Musgrove Mill	5	G	17	0	2	2	8,768
Musha Cay	2	C	5	1	1	1	26,120
Music Bythe Sea	5	H	11	1	1	1	14,547
Music City Girl	3	F	10	1	1	1	8,440
Music Daze	8	G	1	0	0	0	50
Music in the Air	6	M	6	1	1	0	6,179
Music Land	3	G	5	1	1	0	3,164
Music Lesson	5	G	10	0	0	1	7,747
Music Machine	3	F	1	0	0	0	87
Music Miss	4	F	5	3	1	1	30,440
Music Ringing	6	M	1	0	0	0	0
Music to My Heart	5	M	3	0	0	1	3,900
Music to Your Ears	5	G	5	1	0	1	6,300
Music Way	4	F	5	2	0	0	49,583
Musical Beat	3	C	3	1	0	0	14,950
Musical Beauty	5	M	18	2	1	5	22,638
Musical Chairs	6	H	3	0	0	1	2,768
Musical Chimes	4	F	7	2	1	0	438,300
Musical Ending	7	G	1	0	0	0	0
Musical Factor	2	F	6	2	2	0	72,311
Musical Finale	2	F	2	0	0	0	3,280
Musical Groom	3	G	7	0	0	1	10,628
Musical Illusions	3	F	9	0	0	1	2,210
Musical Lass	2	F	4	0	0	0	600
Musical Link	5	M	5	0	0	1	867
Musical Lionel	3	G	11	1	1	0	10,738
Musical Magic	5	G	3	0	0	0	250
Musical Native	3	G	5	1	0	1	30,741
Musical Pirouette	4	F	5	0	0	0	860
Musical Rebel	4	F	8	1	1	2	21,142
Musical Review	5	M	2	0	0	0	400
Musical Spin	4	F	11	0	0	1	1,415
Musical Type	2	C	3	0	1	1	5,660
Musical Valentine	5	H	2	0	0	0	0
Musical Vision	3	C	16	1	3	2	41,950
Musical Wisdom	4	G	7	0	0	1	2,944
Musically	3	F	2	0	0	0	0
Musicdemi	2	F	2	0	0	1	4,316
Musician's Pride	3	C	6	3	2	0	63,100
Music's Day	4	F	8	0	0	3	1,700
Music's Edge	3	G	7	0	0	0	330
Musique Toujours	4	G	6	2	1	1	100,540
Muskador	3	C	13	1	3	1	9,834
Musket Drill	5	G	2	0	0	0	0
Muskiki	4	G	3	1	0	0	2,147
Muskogee	5	G	13	3	2	1	11,555
Muskrat Ramble	6	H	7	1	0	1	5,100
Must Approve	4	F	5	2	0	1	27,395
Must Be Da Money	5	G	8	1	0	1	9,130
Must Be Platinum	2	C	5	1	0	0	5,375
Must Be St. Nick	8	G	4	0	0	0	999
Must Win Soon	3	C	8	2	2	0	56,752
Musta Been Dreamin	6	M	2	1	0	0	4,062
Mustafa	5	G	10	3	1	1	13,076
Mustanfar	3	C	11	3	3	1	394,716
Mustang Gal	3	F	5	1	0	0	5,415
Mustang Jock	4	C	11	2	2	2	27,872
Mustang Ranch	3	C	3	0	1	0	8,657
Mustang Slew	3	F	1	0	0	0	105
Mustard	7	G	10	1	1	3	3,118
Mustbeamarlin	3	G	8	1	0	0	10,954
Mustbinthefrontrow	4	C	9	2	1	1	13,412
Mutachi	3	G	15	1	3	5	62,730
Mutakki	3	F	1	0	0	0	0
Mutakolette	3	F	2	0	0	0	0
Mutalahef	2	C	1	0	1	0	9,200
Mutamayyaz	8	H	7	1	2	1	30,600
Mutawaged	5	H	12	2	1	0	23,060
Mutch Bigger Boots	5	G	7	0	0	2	1,666
Mute Gingrich	6	G	5	0	0	1	2,054
Muted	7	H	6	1	1	0	22,413
Mutesa Blitz	4	F	2	0	0	0	0
Mutt Cats Winner	5	G	5	0	0	1	842
Muttface Alison	5	M	8	0	1	4	14,445
Muttface Brad	4	G	17	2	0	5	24,829
Mutual Affair	3	F	8	2	0	1	48,330
Mutual Selection	10	G	1	0	0	0	50
Muy Bien Chris	7	G	6	0	0	1	737
Muy Pronto	4	G	11	2	1	0	3,977
My Account	5	G	9	1	2	2	9,284
My Ace	2	F	4	0	2	1	10,138
My Adam Apple	6	M	8	0	0	1	6,806
My Adell	4	F	1	0	0	0	673
My Adversary	3	F	1	0	0	0	0
My Aeneas	3	G	7	1	0	1	11,214
My Allegiance	3	F	4	0	0	1	5,870
My Alley Cat	4	F	7	0	1	1	2,291
My Amandari	3	F	3	0	0	0	3,320
My American Man	9	G	6	0	0	0	609
My Amore	4	F	7	1	0	0	3,951
My Angela	6	M	11	3	3	3	33,601
My Angelina	6	M	3	0	0	0	0
My Antonia	5	M	4	2	0	0	19,780
My Argentina	4	C	10	0	0	1	1,219
My Auntie Roxannie	3	F	3	0	0	0	496
My Authority	4	G	13	1	0	4	24,646
My Baby B	3	F	1	0	0	0	443
My Baby Girl	8	M	4	0	0	0	87
My Bae Bae	2	F	3	0	0	0	870
My Ballet	2	G	1	0	0	0	2,300
My Barbara Jane	4	F	7	0	2	0	13,570
My Beau Forever	4	G	3	0	0	0	0
My Bee Bee	2	F	10	1	0	0	8,654
My Bee Bop Baby	5	M	6	1	0	0	8,371
My Bert	2	F	1	0	0	0	230
My Best Diamond	5	G	7	0	1	0	3,559
My Best Girl	3	F	5	2	0	0	12,542
My Best Prospect	3	C	3	0	0	0	1,485
My Best Wish	3	G	8	0	1	1	8,070
My Big Dream	4	F	2	0	0	0	600
My Birthday Boy	5	G	9	1	0	3	13,902
My Blaze Son	4	G	12	1	2	2	14,406
My Blue Baby	3	F	7	0	0	1	1,410
My Blue Moon	4	F	6	1	3	1	2,885
My Blue Scooter	4	F	17	4	1	5	14,212
My Bluey	7	G	6	0	0	0	1,530
My Boot Straps	3	F	9	2	2	1	17,230
My Boston Gal	4	F	6	1	2	1	89,710
My Boy Billy	6	G	6	0	0	0	631
My Boy Danny	4	C	4	1	0	0	5,892
My Boy George	5	G	13	2	2	2	12,940
My Boy Joey	2	G	7	1	2	2	22,560
My Boy Kyle	4	G	7	2	0	2	15,685
My Boy Leroy	4	G	10	1	1	0	4,376
My Boy Roy	3	G	6	0	2	3	10,070
My Boy Tanner	4	C	5	1	1	1	10,972
My Brass Band	2	C	4	1	0	2	8,881
My Bright Light	3	F	14	1	6	3	60,500
My Bright Stone	2	F	6	1	0	2	12,675
My Broker	3	F	4	0	0	0	0
My Brother	4	C	9	1	1	1	8,781
My Brother Bill	4	G	15	2	2	3	27,140
My Brother Joey	4	G	1	1	0	0	3,120
My Brothers Pals	8	G	2	0	0	0	153
My Buba Boy	6	G	18	2	5	1	22,798
My Bud	3	C	2	0	0	0	0
My Buddy	2	G	2	1	0	1	9,493
My Buddy Badger	10	G	7	1	1	0	4,060
My Buddy Boy	5	G	3	0	0	0	412
My Buddy Duddie	4	C	1	0	0	0	215
My Buddy Frank	2	C	3	1	1	0	17,100
My Buddy Harold	3	G	14	1	1	1	38,269

Horse	Age	Sex	Sts	1st	2d	3d	Won
My Buddy Joe	4	G	5	0	0	0	0
My Buddy Joe Green	3	G	4	1	0	0	4,100
My Buddy My Pal	3	C	13	3	2	0	24,976
My Buddy Richie	2	C	10	3	1	2	47,790
My Buddy Rob	7	G	15	2	4	2	10,739
My Buddy Sid	4	G	7	0	0	0	770
My Bulls Eye	2	G	4	0	0	0	1,440
My Burning Passion	2	C	2	0	0	2	4,095
My Canonero	6	G	5	1	0	0	15,766
My Captain	5	G	5	0	2	0	28,585
My Carlsbad Cousin	4	G	9	0	0	2	1,918
My Carol Grand	6	G	1	0	0	0	105
My Carol June	5	M	4	0	0	0	1,590
My Cash Time	3	G	8	1	1	1	21,422
My Cat's Meow	3	F	2	0	0	0	0
My Cat's Seeking	4	F	2	0	0	0	67
My Champ	5	G	5	0	0	0	0
My Chance to Dance	5	M	5	1	2	0	6,982
My Chanel	5	M	1	0	0	1	3,110
My Charlie Brown	3	C	1	1	0	0	15,840
My Charmian	3	F	9	2	2	2	71,363
My Cher	3	F	9	0	1	1	7,080
My Chick Dana	3	F	5	0	0	0	450
My Chosin Choi	2	F	3	0	0	0	0
My Classic Girl	2	F	1	0	0	0	96
My Classic Lady	2	F	4	0	0	0	660
My Classy Miss	6	M	3	0	0	0	70
My Colonial Rose	3	F	15	4	1	2	23,933
My Constant Star	9	G	8	0	1	0	3,060
My Countess (ARG)	5	M	9	5	0	1	49,370
My Country Boy	4	C	2	0	1	0	1,770
My Cousin Andy	3	C	1	0	0	0	1,238
My Cousin Joey	6	G	14	2	1	1	8,040
My Cousin Matt	5	G	8	1	0	2	208,200
My Cowboy	4	G	9	2	1	3	56,885
My Crazy Redhead	4	F	13	0	2	6	33,720
My Creed	3	G	11	4	1	4	140,790
My Cupid	3	G	5	0	1	1	5,380
My Cuz Al	8	G	8	0	1	2	1,980
My Dad's Bad	8	G	14	3	1	0	26,566
My Dancin Girl	6	M	10	0	0	2	16,120
My Dancing Gun	3	C	7	0	0	0	0
My Date	4	F	16	1	2	1	6,546
My Dear Jazz	4	C	6	1	2	0	15,470
My Dear Lady (ARG)	4	F	4	1	0	2	14,256
My Dear Rose	4	F	7	0	1	2	7,984
My Decision	4	G	12	0	0	1	4,947
My Deer Marti	4	F	1	0	0	0	105
My Desert Lady	2	F	2	1	1	0	16,454
My Devious Lady	5	M	11	1	2	3	6,220
My Diamond Lady	7	M	14	2	2	3	8,772
My Diane	5	M	6	0	0	1	1,616
My Doc	3	C	1	0	0	0	0
My Dr Anne T L C	4	F	4	0	0	0	445
My Dragonfly	2	C	1	0	0	0	75
My Dream	4	G	6	1	1	2	8,090
My Dream Cat	6	G	3	0	1	0	1,325
My Dreamer	5	G	16	3	1	1	16,921
My Dreaming	3	G	17	3	1	5	50,972
My Dreams Are	2	F	1	0	0	0	660
My Duke	2	C	4	1	0	0	9,915
My Duty	4	G	6	0	0	2	3,600
My Earthly Angel	2	F	2	0	0	0	0
My Easy Charm	3	F	9	2	0	1	27,029
My Emblem	3	F	2	0	0	0	0
My Emy My Amy	2	F	5	0	0	0	1,186
My Excavate	3	C	7	1	0	0	8,918
My Explosive Star	6	G	13	0	2	1	8,780
My Extolled Honor	6	G	6	1	0	0	8,370
My Fair Angel	5	M	2	0	0	0	205
My Fair Knight	3	G	8	0	2	3	44,677
My Fair Princess	2	F	2	1	1	0	18,800
My Favorite Gal	3	F	14	3	1	2	26,082
My Favorite Girl	4	F	14	1	2	0	7,266
My Favorite Lady	3	F	11	3	2	1	22,213
My Favorite Lord	4	C	17	1	2	3	11,481
My Favorite Miss	2	F	6	1	0	1	13,762
My Favorite Sport	2	F	2	1	0	0	10,575
My Fire Within	3	F	2	0	0	0	130
My First Client	4	G	1	0	0	0	0
My First Dance	2	G	1	0	0	0	300
My First Roan	7	G	12	1	1	2	7,280
My First Wife	4	F	11	2	2	1	25,047
My Forbidden Past	5	M	1	0	0	0	235
My Foriel	3	G	8	1	0	1	9,295
My Foriels On	2	F	7	1	3	1	38,380
My Forum	5	G	11	1	2	2	6,743
My Fox Point	3	C	4	0	0	0	0
My Freedom	4	F	2	0	0	1	774
My Friend Ben	6	G	10	0	3	1	7,471
My Friend Bert	2	C	3	0	0	0	925
My Friend Bruce	3	C	3	1	0	0	6,670
My Friend Dave	4	G	6	2	0	1	5,740
My Friend Deke	3	G	1	1	0	0	16,400
My Friend Don	5	G	8	3	0	0	23,517
My Friend Forever	3	G	14	1	3	0	22,952
My Friend Frank	4	G	7	1	1	2	3,537
My Friend George	2	C	5	1	0	0	6,785
My Friend Henry	5	G	15	1	2	3	4,864
My Friend Irma	2	F	2	0	0	2	4,235
My Friend Lumpy	7	G	1	0	0	1	825
My Friend Tuff	3	C	4	0	1	0	2,320
My Fuzz	7	M	4	0	1	1	3,505
My Gabrielle	5	M	1	0	1	0	4,960
My Gal Friday	3	F	14	3	0	3	13,367
My Gal Jeanie	3	F	14	2	3	1	9,456
My Gal Tossed Me	3	G	9	0	1	0	3,098
My Gal's Gold	3	F	6	1	0	0	7,545
My Gamblin Lady	5	M	3	0	0	0	159
My Ganesh	4	C	2	0	0	0	47
My Gift of Joy	5	G	5	2	0	0	8,100
My Girl Adam	2	F	4	1	0	0	9,129
My Girl Alish	2	F	2	0	0	1	4,940
My Girl Karli	5	M	4	0	0	0	230
My Girl Kelly	2	F	1	0	0	0	0
My Girl Melissa	3	F	11	1	3	2	21,186
My Girl Natalie	5	M	14	1	1	2	60,565
My Girl Nessa	5	M	11	1	0	2	7,185
My Girl Quigly	9	M	13	1	3	1	10,943
My Girl Z	7	M	3	0	0	0	0
My Girls Holme Now	5	M	2	0	0	0	215
My Goal	3	F	10	1	4	2	18,270
My Golden Karot	4	F	4	1	0	1	4,570
My Golden Tripp	3	F	8	0	3	2	24,480
My Good Trick	5	G	4	0	1	0	11,740
My Green Machine	6	M	1	0	0	0	72
My Guru	3	C	3	1	1	1	22,370
My Guy Ty	3	C	10	0	1	3	6,825
My Happy Dream	4	G	2	0	0	1	1,173
My Heart	3	F	13	2	2	1	42,620
My Hearts Desire	5	G	3	1	0	0	12,048
My Heat	3	C	3	0	0	0	105
My Hero	3	G	9	0	1	3	13,804
My Hidden Storm	3	F	5	1	0	3	24,900
My High Roller	3	C	3	0	0	1	562
My Hobby	2	F	3	2	0	0	20,000
My Honey Bunny	4	F	12	2	4	1	76,044
My Husband	3	G	11	4	0	1	111,434
My Ice Skater	2	G	1	0	0	0	0
My Imperial Gal	2	F	3	1	0	0	12,720
My Imperial Gold	3	F	1	1	0	0	12,600
My Imperial Jet	3	F	11	1	1	1	24,730
My Intrigue	5	M	7	1	1	0	7,412
My Irish Dawn	4	F	7	0	3	1	6,816
My Irish Doll	3	F	10	2	1	0	11,055
My Irish Prince	3	G	1	0	0	0	0
My Ish Kee	3	F	11	2	2	2	59,150
My Jeff's Mombo	10	G	5	3	1	0	24,520
My Jewel	4	F	10	1	1	0	1,648
My Joy Forever	3	F	2	0	0	0	0
My Khan	5	G	8	0	0	0	831
My Kimberlee Anne	5	M	12	2	2	2	8,212
My Kind of Day	6	G	5	1	0	0	6,172
My Kind of Gal	3	F	12	0	0	1	5,875
My Kind of Girl	8	M	4	0	0	0	336
My Kind of Town	6	G	14	4	3	2	112,200
My Kinda Gold	9	G	5	1	0	0	11,027
My Kinda Town	3	G	6	2	2	0	70,060

Horse	Age	Sex	Sts	1st	2d	3d	Won
My Kip	2	F	6	1	2	1	32,350
My Kitty Cat	3	F	2	0	0	1	3,520
My Kona Girl	7	M	4	0	0	0	0
My Lady Cruella	4	F	14	1	0	5	13,963
My Lady O'War	3	F	4	0	1	0	4,455
My Lady Pearl	2	F	3	0	2	1	6,730
My Lady's Denaskra	4	F	8	1	2	0	12,095
My Last Bat	3	F	6	0	0	0	1,285
My Last Chance (ARG)	6	H	7	2	0	1	46,400
My Last Dollar	2	F	1	0	0	0	107
My Laura Dear	7	M	3	0	0	0	0
My Lawyer John	3	G	12	1	5	3	27,856
My Lee Lee	6	M	9	0	2	1	16,759
My Legal Alien	5	H	3	0	0	0	1,063
My Leos Lad	3	C	5	1	1	1	10,185
My Lil Cup o' Tee	9	G	12	0	0	1	6,030
My Lil Lu	3	F	3	0	1	0	1,036
My Limit	3	F	12	6	0	0	101,660
My Lipstick	3	G	6	0	1	2	4,215
My Little Charm	3	F	5	1	2	1	19,340
My Little Connor	3	G	8	0	2	2	12,330
My Little Fortune	2	F	8	1	1	2	13,425
My Little Gracie	4	F	4	0	1	1	10,257
My Little Heiress	4	G	3	0	0	0	1,125
My Little Man Greg	3	C	6	0	1	1	4,087
My Little Queen	2	F	2	0	0	1	1,298
My Little Ribot	2	C	2	0	0	0	410
My Little Val	6	M	14	1	6	1	9,395
My Lord	5	G	5	3	1	0	48,540
My Lord's Majesty	5	G	16	2	3	3	20,770
My Lordship	3	F	5	2	0	2	149,267
My Lou Lou's Red	3	F	3	0	0	0	0
My Love Marty Wood	6	M	8	1	2	1	9,712
My Lovely Bride	2	F	5	0	0	1	2,910
My Lovely Lady	3	F	10	0	1	0	2,998
My Lovely Louise	3	F	3	0	0	0	0
My Lucky Bill	2	C	2	1	0	0	6,290
My Lucky Ensign	4	F	5	0	1	0	3,190
My Lucky Grub	3	C	3	0	0	0	0
My Lucky Mercury	3	C	3	0	1	1	10,200
My Lucky Song	3	F	3	0	1	0	3,005
My Lucky Strike	5	G	12	1	2	2	105,396
My Lunatic Dancer	5	G	5	0	0	1	825
My Lyndsey Joy	4	F	8	1	0	0	3,480
My Mad Money	6	M	2	0	0	0	114
My Madeline	5	M	6	0	0	0	582
My Magic Indian	6	G	13	0	0	0	1,253
My Magic King	4	G	4	0	1	1	5,660
My Main Mon	3	G	6	1	1	2	21,163
My Maine Girl	2	F	2	0	1	1	8,060
My Man	7	G	9	0	0	2	3,449
My Man Alex	4	G	7	0	0	1	8,680
My Man Elliott	2	G	2	0	0	0	0
My Man Galloper	3	G	13	0	5	3	16,170
My Man George	4	G	15	7	3	1	155,369
My Man Gus	5	G	8	2	1	1	17,660
My Man Hats	3	G	4	0	0	0	400
My Man Mason	3	C	3	0	0	0	270
My Man Maybe	7	G	2	0	0	0	137
My Man Nick	4	G	3	0	0	0	0
My Man Roy	2	C	5	0	0	1	5,320
My Man Ryan	5	H	13	1	5	3	73,000
My Mariah	3	F	6	3	1	0	14,529
My Maseratti	5	M	6	0	1	0	5,672
My Master (ARG)	5	H	11	1	4	3	85,460
My Mechanicalmouse	3	G	2	0	0	0	0
My Mega Man	3	C	10	2	2	1	24,384
My Meow	6	M	13	3	1	1	50,040
My Miracle Man	5	G	22	2	4	1	17,090
My Misdemeanor	3	F	5	0	1	2	2,892
My Miss Emily	4	F	13	3	4	0	105,087
My Miss Storm Cat	2	F	2	1	0	1	38,616
My Misty Princess	4	F	9	2	1	1	91,830
My Moo	9	G	6	0	0	0	210
My More Love	6	M	2	1	0	0	1,140
My Muchacha	2	F	5	0	1	1	9,582
My Mug Shot	5	M	11	2	2	2	49,280
My My Secret	6	M	9	2	1	1	12,133
My Mystery Man	4	G	7	0	1	1	15,070
My Mystery Mission	2	F	4	1	1	0	23,648
My Name Be Mrs.	8	M	7	3	1	3	14,530
My Name Is Al	4	G	9	3	1	0	15,782
My Name Is Francis	7	G	11	2	0	1	16,677
My Name Is Royal	7	M	20	2	1	2	9,210
My Names Nicole	3	F	11	3	3	2	51,795
My Native Prince	3	C	12	0	0	2	3,135
My New Car	5	M	2	0	0	0	420
My New Love	6	G	4	3	0	1	16,620
My New Nickel	7	M	11	3	0	5	10,243
My Night Light	2	F	5	0	0	0	301
My Nin	4	F	3	2	0	1	31,170
My Nina Rose	3	F	14	1	2	1	52,781
My Niner	4	C	7	2	1	1	29,317
My Numbers	6	M	10	0	1	0	3,233
My Obvious Choice	4	G	2	0	0	0	0
My Onomatopoeia	3	G	12	3	4	0	76,560
My Other Buddy	5	G	3	0	0	0	705
My Outlet	3	F	5	1	1	1	22,740
My Oval Office	4	F	9	0	2	0	5,257
My Own Terms	11	G	3	0	0	0	120
My P J's Pride	2	F	2	0	1	0	2,900
My Pal Al	7	G	10	0	0	0	3,105
My Pal Lana	4	F	9	3	2	0	220,075
My Pal Ryan	9	G	18	1	3	0	6,752
My Pal William	3	G	11	0	1	0	11,268
My Parade	2	C	7	2	1	1	137,050
My Patriot Lady	3	F	7	1	0	2	23,660
My Peanut	3	F	5	0	0	0	410
My Pembroke	5	M	5	1	1	0	13,140
My Peppermintpatty	2	F	9	1	1	1	23,940
My Petticoat	4	F	10	0	2	4	6,897
My Philly	2	F	3	1	0	1	11,800
My Phone	4	C	2	1	0	0	2,970
My Pick to Klick	4	C	4	1	1	0	6,975
My Picture	3	F	4	1	0	1	12,841
My Pink Panther	2	G	6	1	1	2	9,392
My Pistol	5	M	9	1	2	1	7,500
My Plan	4	G	7	1	0	1	7,756
My Pleasant	3	G	11	1	1	1	11,600
My Pleasant Brenda	3	F	5	0	0	0	612
My Pocket	2	C	7	0	1	0	8,075
My Pods Steve	4	G	10	2	2	1	23,795
My Poker Player	4	G	10	4	1	0	141,660
My Pop J. T. Sr	6	G	10	3	0	0	16,768
My Poppy Bert	7	G	4	0	0	0	165
My Portfolio	5	H	2	0	0	0	175
My Position	3	F	4	0	0	0	361
My Precious Indian	3	F	8	0	1	0	9,516
My Pretty Woman	5	M	7	0	1	1	12,291
My Prince	8	G	14	0	1	5	4,598
My Prince Cat	3	G	3	1	0	1	6,090
My Princess Hailey	4	F	4	0	0	1	1,760
My Princessprosper	3	F	5	0	3	0	6,600
My Private Leader	2	F	4	0	0	0	790
My Problem	8	G	3	0	2	1	4,405
My Proximo	3	G	9	0	1	0	3,210
My Queen Burns	7	M	5	2	1	1	18,695
My Queen Michele	2	F	7	1	1	2	14,603
My Queenie	6	M	1	0	0	0	0
My Rahy	3	C	10	2	2	2	18,377
My Ranger	5	G	12	0	2	0	8,920
My Rare Prince	5	H	2	0	0	1	1,075
My Real Quiet Lady	6	M	11	3	2	1	147,757
My Red Sea	2	C	4	0	2	0	4,285
My Redneck	4	G	10	2	0	0	6,961
My Replica	2	G	1	0	0	0	324
My Request	7	G	12	3	3	2	115,049
My Retribution	3	G	1	0	0	0	0
My Retsina's Star	3	F	3	0	0	0	274
My Ro	4	F	4	2	0	0	44,400
My Romanella	5	M	8	1	1	0	4,300
My Romeo	4	C	5	0	0	0	1,380
My Royal Gift	3	F	5	0	0	0	1,150
My Royal Irish Pal	7	G	1	0	0	0	0
My Rozen Doll	3	F	2	0	0	0	0
My Ruby Charm (NZ)	8	M	9	2	2	2	28,210
My Salute to You	4	G	14	1	0	3	15,783
My Secret Brush	5	G	17	1	0	3	12,654

Horse	Age	Sex	Sts	1st	2d	3d	Won
My Secret Fantasy	3	G	7	1	1	1	7,450
My Secret Spot	4	G	5	0	0	2	3,557
My Secretary	4	F	12	1	1	2	8,905
My Signals Busy	5	G	1	0	0	0	225
My Silly Self	2	F	3	0	0	0	1,065
My Silver Dollar	6	G	7	2	2	0	4,530
My Simba	2	C	2	1	0	0	17,460
My Sir Rah	6	G	3	0	0	0	0
My Sissy Missy	3	F	11	0	2	1	6,164
My Sister Frances	3	F	5	0	0	0	785
My Sisters Girl	3	F	4	0	2	1	25,715
My Skippy Bear	3	F	5	0	0	0	535
My Sky	4	F	4	2	1	0	39,390
My Slews Princess	4	F	8	2	0	0	5,508
My Smokey Mike	5	G	13	2	0	2	8,359
My Snookie's Boy	3	C	12	4	3	1	312,766
My Snuggle Bunnie	5	M	2	0	0	0	250
My Son Jordan	3	C	10	1	2	0	10,810
My Soul to Keep	3	F	3	0	0	0	156
My Special Gift	4	F	6	0	0	0	2,063
My Spot	5	M	10	1	0	2	12,905
My Stallone	2	G	3	1	0	1	7,065
My Stars	5	M	2	0	1	0	1,400
My Statue	4	F	9	4	2	0	33,290
My Step	4	G	11	0	2	0	6,914
My Storada	3	G	1	0	0	0	400
My Storm	4	G	6	1	1	0	1,880
My Stray Cat	6	M	1	0	0	0	70
My Sunny Deelite	3	F	8	0	1	0	5,072
My Sunny Halo	5	H	7	1	0	0	3,480
My Super Lovely	4	F	3	0	0	1	1,720
My Super Man	3	C	3	1	0	0	15,240
My Super Style	4	G	5	0	0	1	955
My Survivor	2	C	1	0	0	0	0
My Sweet Amour	2	F	2	0	0	0	0
My Sweet Deputy	2	F	4	0	0	0	779
My Sweet Elizabeth	3	F	2	0	1	0	2,880
My Sweet Heart	4	F	2	0	0	0	1,050
My Sweet Leah	3	F	5	0	0	0	255
My Sweet Lucy	6	M	11	1	1	2	13,003
My Sweet Sandy	7	M	10	0	0	1	1,089
My Sweet Sug	4	F	4	1	1	0	20,565
My Sweet Vicki	3	F	3	0	1	1	6,160
My Sweetcon	3	F	9	1	1	0	5,675
My T Moody	2	F	4	0	0	0	1,180
My T Sharp	4	G	5	0	0	1	2,717
My Tabitha	2	F	3	0	0	0	201
My Taboo Diamond	5	H	2	1	1	0	6,060
My Terms	4	F	11	1	0	0	7,785
My Texas Tim	3	C	5	0	1	1	5,205
My Thirty Six	2	G	6	1	0	1	11,995
My Three Sisters	2	F	6	2	1	1	49,900
My Time Machine	6	G	3	0	0	0	1,130
My Time Now	3	F	13	2	2	2	102,020
My Tina	3	F	5	0	2	0	8,400
My Tony Boy	9	G	5	0	0	0	180
My True Identity	3	F	15	1	4	2	33,400
My Trusty Cat	4	F	10	3	3	0	311,290
My Turbeau Cat	3	F	7	1	0	1	21,862
My Turf Hero	5	H	4	2	1	0	15,041
My Turn to Dance	2	G	4	1	0	0	11,154
My Two Sons	6	G	18	4	4	2	23,741
My Two Timin Lover	3	C	2	0	0	0	0
My Typhoon (IRE)	2	F	2	1	0	0	31,710
My Unbridled	3	C	3	0	1	0	5,541
My Uncle Dave	4	G	1	0	0	0	0
My Uncle Ted	4	G	2	0	0	0	0
My Vengeance	4	F	1	0	0	0	286
My Very Own Muggle	4	F	2	0	0	0	480
My Vintage Port	3	F	9	2	1	4	383,302
My Wild Rhoda	4	F	10	1	0	2	57,680
My Wingman	3	G	7	0	0	0	6,874
My Woman	2	F	3	0	0	0	1,448
My Wonderful	5	G	11	1	3	2	14,178
My World	4	G	5	1	1	1	4,419
Myamar	4	G	6	0	0	0	1,025
Myangeljoey	2	C	2	0	0	0	1,040
Mybabyalert	2	C	5	0	0	0	1,280
Mybigfatluv	3	G	10	2	4	1	10,446

Horse	Age	Sex	Sts	1st	2d	3d	Won
Myboybruno	3	G	13	2	3	1	38,070
Mybrowneyedgal	2	F	2	0	0	1	1,540
Mycareer	4	C	5	0	0	1	1,329
Mychampion	4	C	8	0	1	1	6,048
Mycoco	3	F	6	0	0	0	699
Mydak	5	H	10	1	1	4	24,467
Myella	7	M	9	2	0	3	20,872
Myfavorite Star	6	G	8	0	0	2	6,162
Myfavoritehigh	8	M	3	1	0	1	3,348
Myfavoritepassion	3	F	8	2	3	1	66,842
Myfavoritesoldier	3	F	10	2	0	1	34,020
Myfirst	3	C	2	0	0	0	85
Myfirst 'n Lastluv	9	M	1	0	0	0	0
Myfriend Mac	8	G	7	0	0	1	669
Myfriendlaurie	5	M	4	1	0	0	2,946
Myfriendlilly	4	F	11	2	1	2	25,387
Mygalsal	3	F	2	1	0	0	6,570
Myheartsinaruckus	5	M	6	0	0	0	471
Myintention	2	F	3	0	0	0	0
Mykingcameback	2	G	8	0	0	2	3,895
Mykonos	2	R	1	0	0	0	118
Myladyeve	3	F	15	2	2	2	38,694
Myladys Flying	3	F	5	0	0	0	1,072
Mylilfellow	4	G	12	3	4	0	28,425
Myluke	3	G	7	0	1	3	4,995
Mymich	4	F	13	3	3	1	132,952
Mymomisaprincess	9	G	6	0	0	2	632
Mymommadonetoldme	6	G	8	0	4	2	11,990
Mynameischase	5	H	6	0	0	0	576
Mynameissuzie	3	F	2	0	0	0	183
Mynavigator	3	G	7	1	0	1	39,960
Mynchasa	5	M	1	0	0	0	0
Myofficewife	4	F	3	0	1	0	6,740
Myownworld	4	F	15	4	1	4	50,145
Mypleasantreality	6	M	3	0	0	0	189
Myra Gulch	4	F	5	1	0	1	7,598
Myrene	2	F	3	1	0	0	15,083
Myrna	4	F	4	0	0	0	126
Myroan	7	H	4	2	1	0	7,170
Myrtle's Brat	4	F	12	1	2	3	9,045
Myrtle's Ex Ray	6	G	11	0	2	2	4,637
Mysia Sue	4	F	16	1	1	2	20,002
Mysterfire	4	C	5	0	0	0	875
Mysterieuse Etoile	4	F	11	2	1	2	47,910
Mysterious Cat	6	H	6	2	1	2	28,320
Mysterious Dream	3	F	1	0	0	0	1,230
Mysterious Fame	3	G	6	0	0	0	2,021
Mysterious Knight	3	G	4	0	0	0	114
Mysterious Light	2	F	6	0	2	0	6,880
Mysterious Man	5	G	12	3	1	3	46,124
Mysterious Mist	11	G	9	0	1	2	2,430
Mysterious Peace	3	F	7	1	0	4	18,140
Mysterious Phoenix	3	F	6	0	1	1	5,360
Mysterious Seasons	4	G	10	2	3	2	19,726
Mysterious Sword	4	G	8	1	0	0	4,460
Mysterious Times	2	F	4	0	1	1	8,510
Mysterious Truth	3	F	3	0	2	0	9,540
Mysterious Victory	2	C	1	0	0	0	400
Mysterious Woody	4	C	2	0	0	0	211
Mysteriousness	2	F	7	0	1	0	2,850
Mystery Bay	3	F	1	0	0	0	0
Mystery Blues	4	F	1	0	0	1	1,470
Mystery Coast	4	F	5	2	1	0	3,375
Mystery Comet	2	F	1	0	0	0	164
Mystery Dancer	11	G	6	0	0	0	242
Mystery Dreams	5	G	11	1	2	0	6,673
Mystery Duck	2	G	3	0	0	0	300
Mystery Flick	2	F	2	0	0	0	145
Mystery Giver	6	G	6	2	1	1	470,390
Mystery Grey	7	G	14	2	4	0	8,356
Mystery Itself	4	F	9	2	3	0	104,606
Mystery Maiden	4	F	2	0	0	1	2,990
Mystery Mission	3	C	7	2	1	1	11,485
Mystery Money	3	C	4	0	1	0	7,100
Mystery Mountain	3	F	7	1	0	1	37,640
Mystery Rama	7	G	14	2	1	0	9,531
Mystery Tax	6	M	12	2	1	2	9,192
Mystery Vert	3	G	13	4	1	1	20,011
Mystery Water	2	G	3	0	0	0	415

Horse	Age	Sex	Sts	1st	2d	3d	Won
Mystery Yield	2	F	2	0	0	0	125
Mystery's Jules	3	F	12	5	1	0	126,590
Mystic Aferd	3	G	1	0	1	0	350
Mystic Appeal	5	G	12	5	2	1	61,927
Mystic Blue	3	G	1	0	0	0	235
Mystic Buck	4	G	15	1	0	3	8,637
Mystic Cat	6	M	2	0	0	0	86
Mystic Crown	5	M	3	0	0	0	312
Mystic Dash	4	G	9	0	1	1	32,570
Mystic Dreamer	4	F	1	0	0	0	0
Mystic Gal	5	M	13	0	2	1	4,600
Mystic Guy	3	G	3	0	0	0	221
Mystic Hawk	4	G	9	0	1	0	11,445
Mystic Illahee	2	F	3	0	0	0	0
Mystic Jazz	4	F	8	1	0	1	10,419
Mystic Jet	5	G	11	1	2	2	8,593
Mystic Journey	3	F	1	0	0	0	0
Mystic Man (ARG)	6	G	5	1	2	0	3,708
Mystic Markita	3	F	13	1	2	3	8,993
Mystic Melissa	5	M	9	0	4	0	18,927
Mystic Night	6	H	3	3	0	0	20,700
Mystic Notion	6	M	5	0	0	0	9,000
Mystic Pidgeon	3	F	3	0	0	0	0
Mystic Pine	4	F	10	1	3	0	11,030
Mystic Rainbow	4	F	4	0	1	1	7,330
Mystic River	8	G	16	1	2	5	9,528
Mystic Runner	3	C	8	1	2	4	55,270
Mystic Salse (GB)	5	H	11	1	3	0	30,940
Mystic Skye	3	G	3	0	1	0	1,100
Mystic Speed	3	C	2	0	0	0	0
Mystic Sword	5	H	5	1	0	0	4,620
Mystical Allure	5	M	13	3	3	2	33,200
Mystical Beauty	4	F	13	0	3	1	19,325
Mystical Caper	2	F	4	0	0	1	4,040
Mystical Charge	5	G	8	1	1	2	15,721
Mystical Delite	3	F	1	1	0	0	22,800
Mystical Dixie	2	F	7	1	1	1	11,679
Mystical Doll	4	F	7	0	0	0	1,035
Mystical Elusion	2	F	2	0	0	0	0
Mystical Empire	7	G	4	2	0	0	3,764
Mystical Ghazi	5	M	10	1	1	0	7,073
Mystical Jolie	3	F	1	0	0	0	0
Mystical Michael	4	G	3	0	0	0	0
Mystical Presence	3	F	1	0	0	0	468
Mystical Ridge	4	F	10	1	1	3	6,789
Mystical Sea	3	F	5	0	2	1	22,714
Mystical Susan	4	F	2	0	0	0	0
Mystical Time	3	F	4	0	0	1	3,030
Mysticize	6	G	6	0	2	1	7,640
Mystic's Fortune	6	G	13	3	2	2	36,570
Mystic's Karma	6	G	9	3	3	1	14,482
Mystified	3	F	4	0	0	2	11,360
Mystique Flight	10	M	1	0	0	0	225
Mystique Monster	2	C	4	0	0	1	1,845
Mystique Moon	3	F	9	0	1	2	9,750
Mysto's	2	C	2	0	2	0	12,400
Mysweethearts Gone	3	G	14	5	3	2	74,556
Mysweetjoy	7	M	10	2	1	1	9,482
Mytax	2	F	2	0	0	0	255
Mytee Maggee Magee	4	F	6	1	0	0	27,904
Mytee N Blue	3	G	15	2	3	4	14,795
Mythic	3	F	9	3	1	3	60,500
Mythic Hero	4	G	5	1	1	0	11,121
Mythical	3	F	2	0	0	0	0
Mythical Conquest	2	C	4	0	0	0	2,715
Mythical Flyer	7	G	3	2	0	0	19,200
Mythical Mirage	8	M	3	0	0	0	0
Mythical Muse	3	F	3	0	0	0	2,145
Mythical Rebel	4	G	5	0	0	2	915
Mythical Road	3	G	7	1	2	1	12,030
Mythical Time	3	F	4	1	1	1	35,254
Mythical Trick	4	F	3	0	0	1	965
Mythique	5	G	11	4	0	2	33,080
Myths and Legends	8	M	3	1	0	0	1,200
Mytic Out	4	F	3	0	0	0	760
Myturntopick	7	G	17	1	0	1	16,260
Myway Home	6	M	2	0	0	0	285
Myway West	6	M	2	0	1	0	9,204
Mywayforever	7	H	3	0	0	0	255
Mywifetheshrink	3	F	8	1	2	2	58,738
Myyellowrose	2	F	6	1	1	0	6,260
Mz Nanc B	5	M	7	0	2	0	10,070
Mz. Attebery	3	F	3	0	0	0	1,200
Mz. Bach's Victor	3	G	2	0	0	0	0
Mz. Winjum	2	F	5	1	1	1	28,860
N' Bearaly	4	C	3	0	0	0	412
N' Bearsohmy	2	F	2	0	0	0	410
N C Cuisine	3	F	4	0	0	0	173
N D N Storm	3	C	1	0	1	0	1,040
N J Devil	5	G	7	0	1	1	22,013
N Lou of Roses	5	G	1	0	0	0	840
N Rawlens Honor	4	G	6	0	0	0	470
N Square	4	F	11	0	2	1	16,843
N Y Biscuit	2	G	6	0	0	0	2,075
N Y Remembered	4	G	3	1	1	0	24,900
N Y Rodeo	3	F	5	0	0	0	1,935
N. J. Norquestor	5	G	8	1	1	1	47,920
N. L.'s Dream	7	G	15	2	1	0	10,833
N. Y. Senorita	4	F	1	0	0	0	0
N. Y. Sharpy	8	G	1	0	0	0	0
Na Hila	4	G	4	1	0	1	9,550
Naab the Magic	6	M	4	0	0	0	196
Naab the Rose	4	F	6	3	0	0	19,502
Naaba Trip	3	G	12	3	1	2	29,131
Nab a Copy	3	G	9	0	2	2	4,746
Nabatean	5	G	11	2	3	3	12,774
Nabby Lake	7	M	3	0	0	0	192
Nabethian	6	M	7	3	1	1	32,372
Nabisco Cat	6	G	2	0	0	0	0
Nacascolo	3	G	6	0	1	4	14,425
Nachen	4	F	8	1	0	2	17,192
Nacious Gold	8	H	16	0	0	2	3,164
Nada Bada	2	F	5	0	2	0	8,610
Nada Mais	4	F	8	0	1	1	4,753
Nadasha	2	F	2	0	0	0	400
Nadeszhda (GB)	4	F	4	2	1	0	44,807
Nadine's Cape	4	F	2	0	0	0	0
Nadira	4	F	14	3	1	3	27,011
Nae Only	3	F	4	0	1	0	5,721
Naev	4	C	3	0	0	0	120
Nafka's Chance	7	M	9	2	3	0	12,568
Nagem Nagem Nagem	3	F	8	1	0	2	24,937
Nah Nah Nah	4	G	7	3	0	0	39,240
Nahaab	6	G	11	0	0	1	1,320
Nahane (IRE)	3	G	3	0	0	0	900
Nahanni Butte	4	F	6	0	1	2	2,211
Nahar	7	M	6	0	0	0	225
Nahdu's Tune	4	F	3	0	1	1	3,193
Naif	4	C	3	0	0	0	184
Nailbird	9	G	9	0	0	1	3,003
Nairobi	4	G	5	0	1	0	4,160
Najah	2	G	5	1	1	1	12,768
Najibes Acre	3	F	8	1	3	1	50,600
Najjm	7	G	6	0	1	1	24,838
Nakayama Jazz	3	G	6	2	0	1	11,108
Nakayama Kun	4	C	8	2	0	3	49,299
Naked Again	2	C	3	0	1	0	2,800
Naked Ambition	9	M	2	0	0	0	0
Nakeeb	4	C	4	1	1	1	25,870
Nakerra Choice	5	M	4	0	0	0	0
Nakiewah	3	F	12	1	1	1	7,949
Nakini	2	C	1	0	0	0	400
Nale	7	G	4	0	0	0	258
Nalee's Classic	10	G	3	1	0	0	960
Nalees Girl	3	F	4	0	0	0	0
Nalees Law	5	G	8	0	0	0	1,980
Naletha Gray	4	F	10	1	1	0	12,670
N'all That Jazz	7	G	1	0	0	0	0
Name Appeal	8	G	7	2	1	1	10,135
Name the Prince	4	G	7	0	1	0	1,597
Name Your Price	3	G	8	0	0	0	1,080
Nameitafterme	2	G	2	0	0	0	210
Nameless	8	M	3	1	0	0	5,390
Nameless Soldier	3	G	11	1	2	1	13,200
Nameless Superstar	2	F	1	0	0	0	155
Namequest	8	G	8	4	0	0	119,230
Nami	7	G	15	1	3	3	7,010
Nana Barb	3	F	12	2	0	1	28,144

Horse	Age	Sex	Sts	1st	2d	3d	Won
Nana Lou's Boy	5	G	9	1	2	0	7,153
Nanacandypride	5	H	3	1	1	0	15,250
Nanalala	4	F	10	2	1	1	7,370
Nanaletpride	5	M	10	0	2	1	6,185
Nanandalscontender	4	C	1	0	0	0	150
Nanarae	3	F	9	0	1	0	7,970
Nana's Boy	6	G	14	3	2	1	37,917
Nana's Delight	6	M	1	0	0	0	138
Nana's House	5	M	6	0	0	0	589
Nana's Lady	2	F	7	0	2	0	3,808
Nana's Suprise	6	G	1	0	0	0	190
Nancibegood	3	F	16	3	2	3	35,190
Nanci's Zoomstick	5	M	9	1	0	0	3,387
Nancy Dollygirl	3	F	1	0	0	0	653
Nancy Jo	5	M	4	0	1	0	2,160
Nancy McWin	4	F	8	1	1	1	31,153
Nancy N Waco	4	F	5	2	0	1	13,954
Nancys Blazen Lady	6	M	6	0	0	2	2,175
Nancy's Change	3	F	14	0	0	0	1,359
Nancys Golden Star	4	F	2	0	1	0	1,860
Nancy's Jewel	3	F	1	0	0	0	1,800
Nancy's Joker	6	G	13	4	3	1	28,360
Nancy's Lil Magic	3	C	3	0	0	0	0
Nancys Magic Brush	4	F	12	1	1	3	8,290
Nancy's Slave	5	G	10	1	1	1	24,098
Nancy's Spirit	5	M	18	1	9	1	33,395
Nanden	5	M	6	0	0	1	5,100
Nandu	3	F	9	1	0	2	28,480
Naner	7	G	2	0	0	0	540
Nangie Cristina	3	F	3	0	0	0	0
Nani's Princess	3	F	13	4	1	0	24,162
Nanjing	4	F	2	0	0	0	184
Nankoweap	6	M	9	0	3	2	12,060
Nannie's Sword	5	M	3	0	1	1	12,160
Nanny Goat	4	F	4	0	0	0	6,020
Nanny Lover	4	F	19	4	2	3	19,904
Nannycam	4	F	8	2	1	0	88,256
Nanny's Ransom	3	C	16	3	2	1	48,620
Nanny'slastchance	2	F	1	0	0	0	480
Nano's Groovy	4	G	14	1	2	0	13,677
Nan's Lil Poopsie	5	M	7	2	0	0	16,516
Nan's Note	2	C	1	0	0	0	1,560
Nan's Rose	6	M	17	3	4	5	28,035
Nantucketeer	6	H	8	2	2	0	31,733
Nanys Lullaby	3	C	4	1	0	1	8,280
Naomi's Hope	2	F	2	0	0	1	4,264
Nap for Sycamore	6	G	2	0	0	0	0
Napa Spring	8	G	17	2	0	2	3,969
Napeequa Warrior	3	G	1	0	0	0	0
Naperville	7	M	12	1	1	1	19,636
Napili	3	F	9	0	3	2	9,962
Napili Bay	2	F	8	0	2	4	11,455
Napoleon Solo	4	G	10	0	0	0	5,821
Napster	4	G	8	0	1	0	10,074
Napzak	3	G	14	1	1	2	22,446
Naragansett	3	G	2	0	0	0	258
Naraingang (BRZ)	6	H	3	0	0	0	5,010
Narayan	4	G	6	1	0	1	5,305
Narcissistic Girl	4	F	5	0	1	0	2,360
Narrow River	13	G	2	0	1	0	11,700
Nascar Natalie	2	F	5	0	0	1	1,155
Nasdaq Jack	5	H	12	0	0	1	6,230
Nasdek Mayhem	5	G	7	1	0	3	26,555
Nasema's Slam	2	F	1	0	1	0	9,000
Nasheba Dancer	9	M	16	4	7	2	28,620
Nasheet	2	C	4	0	0	0	2,730
Nashinda	3	F	3	1	1	0	84,937
Nashly and I	2	G	2	0	0	0	1,440
Nashly's Groom	4	G	5	0	2	0	13,070
Nash's Valay	3	F	6	1	2	1	34,460
Nashua's Asset	6	G	10	1	3	3	10,595
Nashua's Launch	4	C	5	1	0	0	8,450
Nashville	9	G	3	2	0	0	13,618
Nashville Native	4	F	5	0	0	0	497
Nashvillessurprise	3	C	1	0	0	0	75
Nashwan Rose (GB)	5	M	1	0	0	0	0
Naskra's Cat	4	G	5	1	1	0	7,885
Naskra's Star Lily	5	M	5	0	3	0	4,471
Naso	2	C	5	0	1	0	3,388
Nasser	5	H	3	0	0	0	0
Nassuas Ruler	4	G	2	1	0	0	1,650
Nasty	5	G	10	1	0	2	6,933
Nasty and Crafty	6	M	3	0	0	0	383
Nasty Bird	6	G	6	1	0	0	5,631
Nasty Business	5	G	14	0	3	1	11,015
Nasty Butch	3	G	7	2	0	1	16,825
Nasty Canasta	2	G	2	1	0	0	8,164
Nasty Ice	6	M	1	0	0	0	73
Nasty Jab	3	G	15	2	3	4	12,407
Nasty Nemisis	2	F	4	0	0	0	1,270
Nasty Rose	4	F	1	0	0	0	0
Nasty Secret	5	M	14	1	2	3	6,876
Nasty Traitor	3	G	11	1	0	1	30,597
Nasty Weather	3	F	2	0	0	0	0
Nasty Wildcat	3	G	2	0	0	1	4,592
Nasty Won	5	H	1	0	0	0	0
Nastyattitude	2	G	7	1	1	1	14,008
Nastylittlecritter	2	F	4	0	3	0	7,080
Nasty's Progeny	6	G	6	0	0	0	1,547
Nat and Julie	5	M	3	0	1	0	6,950
Nat D Z	4	F	2	0	0	0	0
Nat Plays No Trump	6	G	16	4	3	1	22,920
Natalia	4	F	13	1	3	0	9,334
Natalia's Secret	3	F	4	0	1	0	1,035
Natalie Beach (ARG)	4	F	4	2	0	1	49,962
Natalie Jane (IRE)	2	F	5	1	0	2	16,500
Natalies Commander	3	F	10	0	4	2	7,640
Natalie's Gift	4	F	1	0	0	0	300
Natalie's Honey	2	F	2	0	0	0	600
Natalies Interview	5	H	5	1	0	0	10,710
Natasha Md	2	F	6	0	0	0	800
Natasha Pumpkin	6	M	8	0	1	1	7,609
Natasha's Reno	5	M	17	2	1	3	19,050
Natchez Trace	6	G	7	2	1	0	16,382
Nate Jr	11	G	5	1	0	1	2,310
Nate's Castle	3	F	1	0	0	0	0
Nates Colony	7	G	7	0	0	3	12,338
Nate's Rib	5	G	2	0	0	0	380
Nathan	3	G	6	1	0	1	13,586
Nathans Candy	4	G	2	0	0	0	33
Nathan's Way	5	G	10	1	1	3	6,820
National Anthem (GB)	8	H	3	0	0	0	4,200
National City	8	G	15	0	6	2	8,787
National Emblem	3	C	2	0	0	0	420
National Forrest	3	C	2	0	0	0	0
National Honors	3	C	2	0	0	0	375
National Legend	3	C	13	1	1	2	41,170
National Park (CHI)	5	H	1	0	1	0	13,000
National Park (GB)	5	G	2	0	0	0	0
National Pastime	4	F	8	2	0	0	34,497
National Pride (GB)	4	C	5	1	1	0	38,152
Nationalistic (IRE)	6	G	7	3	1	1	60,560
Native Aly	3	F	9	1	1	2	37,150
Native Annie	3	F	9	4	0	1	187,050
Native Approval	3	G	9	2	1	2	36,300
Native as Well	4	G	3	0	1	0	1,210
Native Badger	8	G	3	0	0	0	110
Native Badgett	2	C	1	0	0	0	85
Native Belief	3	G	9	1	1	0	11,279
Native Belle	2	F	1	0	0	1	1,485
Native Blanket	2	G	2	0	0	0	239
Native Brick	5	M	12	2	1	0	40,204
Native Bull	4	G	9	1	1	0	26,455
Native Caller	3	G	6	0	1	0	3,185
Native Clipit	6	G	7	0	1	2	1,900
Native Coast	9	G	5	1	0	0	15,880
Native Dasher	2	F	3	0	0	1	1,995
Native Dolly	2	F	1	0	0	0	0
Native Energy	6	G	18	0	2	0	5,365
Native Excellar	3	G	3	0	0	0	360
Native Fever	3	F	10	1	0	1	18,239
Native Flag	4	G	2	0	0	0	113
Native Flagship	11	G	8	0	1	0	1,133
Native Gambler	6	G	14	3	2	2	11,505
Native Genius	4	C	3	0	0	0	1,064
Native Glide	7	G	1	0	0	0	0
Native Hawk	4	G	7	2	1	1	82,288
Native Heartbeat	4	F	14	1	2	5	50,038

Horse	Age	Sex	Sts	1st	2d	3d	Won
Native Heir	6	G	8	2	1	1	67,275
Native Hope	5	H	2	0	0	0	0
Native Ice	6	G	11	2	1	1	19,870
Native Image	7	G	8	0	0	2	2,468
Native Jaja Ruler	4	F	8	0	0	0	408
Native Joy	6	M	4	1	0	0	5,920
Native Judge	4	G	12	0	1	3	19,385
Native King	3	C	6	1	0	2	9,190
Native Kiowa	2	F	4	0	0	0	765
Native Love	6	G	9	3	2	1	13,252
Native Malagra	3	G	1	0	0	0	1,932
Native Mark	5	G	4	0	0	0	3,540
Native Millu	3	F	12	1	3	1	13,280
Native Mint	3	C	6	0	0	2	3,937
Native Miss	3	F	7	2	0	1	22,670
Native New Yorker	5	H	2	0	1	0	2,295
Native of Eden	7	G	10	0	2	6	8,323
Native of Paris	4	F	9	1	2	2	10,248
Native of Zignew	4	F	13	2	2	3	14,324
Native Plum	3	F	9	0	1	1	6,768
Native Prospect	3	F	11	0	3	4	49,661
Native Queen	2	F	1	0	0	0	1,800
Native Quest	2	F	4	0	0	0	769
Native Red Fox	4	G	13	1	0	2	4,817
Native Rhythm	6	H	6	0	0	1	2,602
Native River	2	C	7	0	3	0	5,828
Native Ruck	6	G	13	3	3	2	31,311
Native Shore	2	C	3	0	1	1	6,980
Native Soldier	3	C	10	2	1	1	20,030
Native Spirit	4	F	12	2	2	2	23,538
Native Stone	4	G	11	1	2	1	11,634
Native Survivor	2	F	2	0	0	0	520
Native Texan	4	G	8	1	1	0	15,100
Native Topper	2	G	3	0	0	0	0
Native Tourist	4	G	1	0	0	0	0
Native Trinket	5	M	5	1	1	1	10,420
Native Two Stepper	8	G	4	1	0	0	3,850
Native Valor	3	G	5	0	1	0	1,834
Native Vice	3	F	4	1	1	0	4,224
Native Vitality	5	H	10	1	2	0	15,950
Native Wager	6	M	10	2	1	1	32,935
Native Waimea	5	M	1	0	0	0	0
Native Will	6	M	5	1	0	0	2,880
Native Wind	3	F	9	1	2	0	8,808
Native Zeal	3	F	14	1	0	4	18,384
Nato	4	G	17	0	4	5	19,491
Natomas Baby	4	F	3	0	0	0	160
Natonea	2	F	1	1	0	0	6,000
Natraski	4	G	1	0	0	0	100
Natrona	5	M	3	0	0	0	1,302
Nat's Flash	5	M	5	0	0	0	283
Nat's Fox	4	G	14	3	4	4	40,881
Nat's Golden Girl	3	F	3	0	0	0	166
Nat's Wildcat	2	C	10	2	2	0	27,290
Nattandyahoo	3	G	11	2	1	1	25,222
Nattie Nu	3	F	10	1	1	3	33,240
Nattitude	4	F	7	2	1	1	55,635
Natural Actress	4	F	1	0	0	1	2,000
Natural Advantage	3	G	9	2	3	0	20,256
Natural Balance	4	C	17	2	3	2	16,315
Natural Beauty	2	F	1	0	0	0	370
Natural Boy	2	C	4	1	1	0	13,635
Natural Cat	4	G	12	2	4	1	21,743
Natural Charmer	2	F	5	0	1	0	11,460
Natural Enemy	5	H	9	0	1	3	15,965
Natural Glory	3	F	6	1	1	2	10,480
Natural Glow	3	F	3	0	1	0	7,500
Natural Image	4	F	7	1	0	0	21,900
Natural Nine	4	F	11	2	0	4	26,717
Natural Pear	3	F	6	0	0	2	3,096
Natural Phenomenon	2	C	3	0	1	0	8,200
Natural Ridge	10	G	10	2	2	1	10,569
Natural Route	3	F	4	0	0	1	4,840
Natural Spring	3	C	1	0	0	0	0
Natural Stone	5	G	11	0	0	3	7,235
Natural Style	7	H	14	2	2	6	38,882
Natural Touch	3	G	11	1	2	3	27,132
Natural View	4	G	1	0	0	0	0
Natural Wonder	6	G	1	0	0	0	80

Horse	Age	Sex	Sts	1st	2d	3d	Won
Nature	7	H	4	1	0	2	21,472
Nature Boy Wonder	4	G	8	0	0	1	650
Nature Coast	6	M	9	0	1	2	5,232
Nature Star	4	F	10	1	2	2	14,344
Naturelle's Way	3	F	14	1	4	3	40,280
Natures Candy	5	G	12	3	4	0	19,794
Nature's Gold	3	F	1	0	0	0	0
Nature's Pick	6	G	3	0	0	0	1,566
Nature's Power	8	G	11	0	3	4	14,502
Nature's Verdict	3	C	4	0	0	0	1,170
Naughte' Tom T	7	G	1	0	0	0	0
Naughty Butterfly	5	M	5	0	0	0	367
Naughty Dreadlocks	5	M	1	0	0	0	82
Naughty E	6	H	18	2	1	4	17,480
Naughty Girl Slew	3	F	4	0	2	0	4,648
Naughty Kiss	3	G	2	0	0	0	1,360
Naughty Knight	2	C	8	1	1	2	8,115
Naughty Lady L	6	M	6	0	1	0	1,360
Naughty Laura	3	F	8	2	1	2	44,670
Naughty Nacho	7	G	16	3	5	3	12,409
Naughty Nae	3	F	1	0	0	1	4,300
Naughty Nannette	3	F	2	0	0	0	0
Naughty Natalia	2	F	4	0	0	0	1,900
Naughty New Yorker	2	C	6	2	2	1	110,195
Naughty Prince	5	G	18	3	2	3	32,550
Naughty Princess	3	F	6	0	0	0	3,184
Naughty So and So	3	F	8	0	1	0	1,054
Naughty to Spare	3	F	1	0	0	0	1,250
Naughty Tony	4	G	6	1	0	3	8,950
Naughtyasabaroness	3	F	2	0	0	0	42
Nauiti Nine	4	F	2	1	0	0	8,250
Nault	4	F	1	0	0	0	900
Naut	3	G	11	1	0	2	5,924
Nautical Allegro	7	G	12	1	2	0	18,530
Nautical But Nice	4	F	12	4	1	2	38,920
Nautical Miss	5	M	10	1	0	1	4,242
Nautical Prince	7	G	16	2	4	2	11,289
Nautico (ARG)	7	H	4	0	0	0	1,200
Nautilus	6	H	3	0	0	0	2,170
Nauvoo	3	F	5	1	0	0	15,140
Navagatior	6	G	2	0	0	0	447
Navaja (NZ)	4	F	8	2	1	0	82,720
Navajo Angel	5	M	3	1	0	0	1,362
Navajo Breeze	3	F	5	1	2	1	25,136
Navajo Princess	3	F	8	1	3	2	57,687
Navajo Red	4	G	10	1	2	0	26,780
Naval Command	2	C	1	0	0	0	0
Naval Salute	2	G	3	0	0	0	1,940
Naval Tech	4	F	6	1	1	0	9,192
Navarena	5	M	2	0	0	0	272
Navarita	3	F	4	0	0	0	720
Navastar	5	M	5	0	0	1	714
Navel (BRZ)	7	H	4	1	0	1	6,010
Nave's Prime Time	6	G	5	0	0	1	486
Navesink	6	H	1	0	0	0	0
Navesink River	3	C	7	2	0	1	89,295
Navesink Sunset	2	C	2	0	0	0	790
Navesink Tide	4	C	5	3	1	0	18,440
Navesink View	5	G	4	1	0	1	10,500
Navihawk	5	G	3	0	0	0	753
Navona	4	F	7	0	0	0	648
Navy Bird	4	C	5	1	0	0	4,940
Navy Brat	3	F	10	1	0	2	25,320
Navy Class	6	G	2	0	0	0	93
Navy Clipper	3	F	9	1	6	0	21,730
Navy Flag	3	G	7	1	1	0	12,500
Navy Girl	3	F	3	1	0	0	8,280
Navy Holiday	3	F	2	0	0	0	0
Navy Hymn	3	G	3	0	0	0	1,577
Navy J	4	G	5	0	0	1	752
Navy Seal	10	G	5	1	0	1	4,680
Navy Silks	2	F	2	1	0	0	13,455
Navy Yard	3	F	2	0	0	1	1,076
Nawras	2	G	1	0	0	0	0
Nayla	3	F	6	1	1	1	4,050
Nazareth	2	G	9	0	0	0	4,292
Nazda Jet	2	C	4	0	0	0	2,548
Nazeer	3	G	14	2	4	4	41,680
Nazgul	3	C	2	0	0	0	257

Horse	Age	Sex	Sts	1st	2d	3d	Won
Nazirali (IRE)	7	G	2	0	1	0	12,320
Nazone	4	G	7	1	1	0	20,287
Neal S	4	G	5	0	0	0	665
Neal's Rodeo	5	G	8	0	0	0	4,257
Nealville	7	H	4	0	0	0	690
Near the Lake	3	F	1	0	1	0	11,760
Near to You	4	F	4	1	0	0	6,460
Near Victory	3	C	2	0	0	0	445
Nearandfar	5	G	2	1	1	0	2,100
Nearctica	3	F	7	0	0	3	18,863
Nearly Forever	3	F	6	4	0	0	27,275
Nearly Lucky	4	G	3	0	0	0	150
Nearlymissthealarm	7	M	7	1	0	0	8,040
Neartic Ice	7	H	3	0	0	0	2,016
Neartic Rose	3	F	4	0	0	0	120
Neat and Sweet	6	M	8	1	3	1	9,591
Neatbanker	6	G	4	0	2	0	3,763
Neauxdeck	6	G	5	0	0	0	0
Neblina	4	F	10	1	2	1	87,784
Nebraska Moon	3	G	8	5	3	0	115,460
Nebraska Tornado	4	F	5	0	0	2	96,804
Nebrasska	8	G	1	0	0	0	0
Nebuchadnezzar	4	C	4	1	1	0	20,590
Nebulizer	3	G	12	1	1	1	11,113
Nebulous	3	C	4	1	0	0	16,561
Necessaire	4	G	5	2	0	0	28,685
Necessary	2	C	5	1	1	0	13,000
Necessary Noise	9	G	4	0	0	0	0
Necklace (GB)	3	F	5	0	0	1	123,439
Nectarian	3	F	5	1	0	2	37,320
Ned Pepper	3	G	2	0	0	0	0
Neda Wina	4	G	4	1	1	0	5,495
Nedra's Girl	5	M	8	1	0	1	8,760
Need a Light	3	F	1	0	0	0	86
Need a Phone	3	F	17	4	2	3	25,895
Need a Rade	5	M	1	0	0	0	0
Need Lots of Luck	4	F	5	0	0	0	392
Need to Please	2	C	4	1	1	0	21,130
Needarunner	3	G	12	1	1	1	7,328
Needham's Point	6	G	10	2	3	2	13,487
Needs to Be Tops	5	G	5	1	0	1	2,172
Needwood Blade (GB)	6	H	7	1	0	0	68,426
Neeka	5	M	3	1	1	1	5,980
Neelam	4	F	14	1	2	2	11,619
Neely	2	F	5	1	0	0	5,060
Neenamusha	4	G	18	2	3	5	18,219
Neent	4	F	11	2	1	3	11,641
Neequoia	3	F	2	0	0	0	122
Neeranjanie	2	F	6	0	1	1	8,180
Nefertiri	5	M	17	2	2	2	13,839
Negativette	4	F	8	1	0	0	9,071
Negev Class	6	G	2	0	0	0	160
Negev Dream	3	F	1	0	0	0	0
Negev Lady	8	M	6	0	3	2	4,855
Negotiation	4	G	7	0	0	2	8,388
Negotiator (JPN)	3	C	2	0	0	0	11,409
Negremundo	3	G	8	0	1	0	1,380
Neigh Highs	3	F	8	2	1	2	24,825
Neighbora	5	M	7	1	2	2	57,780
Neighborhood Bully	7	G	11	2	1	3	5,647
Neilan	2	C	1	0	0	0	205
Neil's Advice	4	G	12	0	3	3	11,134
Neil's Poor Boy	4	G	1	0	0	0	0
Neily Bop	3	F	5	0	0	0	805
Neiman	5	G	4	1	0	1	7,721
Neither We Do	9	G	9	1	1	1	5,760
Neki	8	G	5	1	0	1	9,400
Nekoda Gold	2	C	1	0	0	0	0
Nel Cat	2	F	2	1	0	0	15,600
Nelda Crypto	3	F	15	1	5	1	20,517
Nella Fantasia	3	F	6	0	0	0	1,150
Nellaluna	4	F	16	1	2	1	12,543
Nellie B Quick	2	F	4	0	0	1	1,730
Nellie L	4	F	15	1	1	1	23,410
Nellie Magee	4	F	4	1	1	0	8,331
Nellie Road	4	F	2	0	0	0	0
Nell's Angel	5	M	2	0	0	0	77
Nelly's Reef	4	F	7	1	0	1	3,730
Nellys Star	2	F	2	0	0	0	0
Nelly's Town	4	F	12	0	0	1	1,846
Nelson Street	6	G	1	0	0	0	126
Nelson's Foxy Lady	5	M	13	2	0	3	7,380
Nelson's Hawk	5	G	6	0	0	0	390
Nelson's Knight	3	F	7	0	1	1	4,860
Nelson's Magic	7	G	1	0	0	1	836
Nelsons Martini	4	F	11	1	1	1	26,584
Nelson's Pride	4	F	5	0	0	2	3,016
Nelsonstreetnancy	4	F	5	0	0	0	265
Nem Nem Shoa	3	F	2	0	0	0	0
Nemo's Lucky Fin	3	G	1	1	0	0	9,600
Nenantena	4	F	5	1	1	0	15,070
Neo Babe	2	F	2	0	0	0	1,230
Neo Brae	3	F	5	0	2	1	13,830
Neon Avenue	3	F	3	0	1	1	4,585
Neon Bright	3	F	1	0	0	0	0
Neon Jet	3	C	6	1	0	1	31,796
Neon Leon	3	G	8	2	1	1	38,925
Neon Magic	4	C	14	3	1	4	54,930
Neon Playboy	4	G	5	0	0	0	142
Neon Queen	6	M	7	2	1	0	37,380
Neon Rainbow	4	C	4	0	0	0	0
Neon Shadow	10	G	5	0	1	1	12,740
Neoshe	4	G	6	0	0	0	579
Nepal's Wickedwind	6	M	12	1	0	1	26,110
Nephele	2	F	5	1	0	0	14,130
Nephrite's Best	5	H	1	0	0	0	100
Nepotism	3	F	15	2	3	1	56,162
Neruda	12	G	7	0	3	0	13,800
Nerv E Go	6	G	8	1	0	3	4,056
Nerve Ending	3	G	7	1	0	2	18,065
Nerveinthecurve	5	H	8	1	1	0	10,275
Neshama	4	F	3	0	0	0	144
Neshoba County	3	C	3	0	0	1	965
Nessarose	2	F	5	1	3	1	36,270
Nessy's Girl	3	F	3	0	0	1	706
Nestasko	2	G	3	1	0	0	16,520
Nestle Is Quick	3	C	12	1	0	0	4,893
Nestorius	4	G	3	0	0	0	178
Net Force	4	G	1	0	0	0	134
Net Man	3	G	7	0	0	0	5,227
Net Threat	3	C	10	1	1	2	15,186
Netcong	5	H	9	1	0	1	20,370
Nettap	7	G	10	0	0	1	1,955
Netta's Poetry	6	M	13	2	2	2	9,902
Nettie Gay	2	F	1	0	0	0	0
Nettie's Pick	2	F	4	1	0	0	3,480
Nettleton	6	G	14	1	6	2	8,760
Nettso	6	M	3	0	0	0	106
Nettys Drum	6	G	14	1	1	1	5,106
Netty's Knockout	2	F	5	1	1	0	35,612
Network	2	C	1	0	0	0	230
Neucha Tel (ARG)	7	M	3	0	0	1	2,340
Neuf de Carreau	4	G	6	1	1	2	53,520
Neuf de Coeur	4	G	8	1	2	2	28,270
Neuf La Banque (PER)	6	M	3	1	1	0	10,265
Neumanns Cat	3	F	3	0	0	1	2,536
Neurotic	3	F	13	1	1	2	6,472
Neutral Bruce	3	G	10	0	0	0	5,058
Neutral Corner	4	F	8	1	0	3	20,471
Neutron	3	G	2	0	0	0	560
Neva Cloudy	4	C	2	0	0	0	305
Neva Fay	6	M	1	0	0	0	38
Nevada Miss	4	F	4	0	2	0	17,460
Nevada Mix	3	G	11	0	2	1	6,475
Nevada Smith	11	G	5	0	1	1	523
Nevada Strip	7	H	8	0	2	0	3,793
Nevada Sunrise	3	F	8	1	1	2	38,440
Nevaeh	3	F	11	0	3	0	37,842
Nevasayneva	6	H	4	1	1	0	3,580
Nevasca	4	F	3	0	0	1	8,778
Never At Dusk	2	C	2	0	0	0	800
Never Been Caught	5	M	5	3	1	1	10,130
Never Blink	4	G	21	3	2	3	13,654
Never Blue	5	M	8	0	1	1	8,215
Never Close	9	M	13	0	2	3	4,120
Never Delay	5	M	7	0	3	1	16,140
Never Ending	3	F	9	0	0	0	156
Never Ending Lunch	4	G	5	0	0	0	1,590

Horse	Age	Sex	Sts	1st	2d	3d	Won
Never Ending Tale	3	C	8	1	0	0	8,673
Never Enough Time	3	C	2	0	0	0	600
Never Ever Late	3	F	6	0	2	2	7,825
Never Ever Naughty	2	F	2	0	0	0	550
Never Fail	4	F	7	0	0	1	9,510
Never Give In	5	G	6	4	0	1	52,550
Never Gone	2	F	3	0	0	0	1,415
Never High	6	M	10	0	0	0	420
Never Late	5	G	1	0	0	0	0
Never Late Early	2	F	3	0	0	0	810
Never Left	4	F	3	1	0	1	14,940
Never Look Back	3	F	6	0	1	1	7,909
Never Met Napoleon	2	F	4	0	1	2	6,720
Never Out of Roses	6	M	2	0	0	0	400
Never Over	5	M	8	0	1	0	1,972
Never Panic	5	G	4	1	0	1	3,084
Never Pete	4	G	14	5	0	1	21,182
Never Plan Ahead	5	G	6	0	0	0	155
Never Rest	4	G	6	1	0	2	11,124
Never Satisfied	4	F	15	1	1	4	14,139
Never Say Nunca	6	G	2	0	0	0	800
Never Skeered	3	F	2	0	0	0	546
Never Skip	4	G	11	2	0	2	16,316
Never Stop	6	G	8	0	0	2	6,725
Never Surrender	3	G	7	2	2	0	58,770
Never Sweat	6	G	3	0	0	0	222
Never Take Risk	4	G	11	2	0	1	9,468
Never Tap Twice	3	C	8	2	1	2	17,746
Never Tomorrow	2	C	3	1	0	0	11,680
Never too Clever	3	G	5	0	0	0	2,935
Never Under	4	F	3	0	0	0	260
Neverasecret	3	F	3	0	0	0	280
Neverbroke	4	G	12	3	3	1	36,116
Neverdid	3	F	3	0	0	1	2,986
Neverdivorceshelly	2	F	7	0	1	1	5,470
Neverhadadinner	3	G	5	1	0	1	17,980
Neverlostforwords	4	F	2	0	0	0	690
Nevermore	4	F	8	3	1	1	153,324
Neversoeasy	3	F	10	1	0	2	14,820
Nevets	7	G	5	4	1	0	6,241
Nevetsderf	4	C	4	0	0	1	2,840
Neville	4	G	17	2	1	2	13,103
Neville's Gold	3	G	2	0	0	0	175
Nevoso	5	G	1	0	0	0	0
Nevr a Dull Moment	3	G	5	2	0	0	19,800
Nevsky Prospekt	2	C	1	0	0	0	0
New Advantage	7	H	11	1	2	1	31,515
New Age	3	C	4	0	1	0	7,988
New Alpha	4	F	2	0	0	0	0
New Car Cavier	2	C	1	0	0	0	96
New Castle Lady	3	F	8	3	2	1	113,974
New Cloud	2	G	5	0	2	0	17,300
New Course	3	G	11	2	1	1	39,700
New Cut Road	3	G	3	0	0	0	111
New Diligence	4	F	12	1	2	1	35,658
New Dreams (BRZ)	5	M	9	2	0	1	72,232
New Economy	6	M	1	0	0	0	3,750
New Element	3	G	16	2	2	1	31,614
New Evidence	5	G	10	0	0	0	806
New Hey	3	C	7	1	3	0	3,741
New Jersey Phil	3	C	16	4	1	3	46,405
New Judge	6	G	2	0	0	0	100
New Kid in Town	4	G	8	1	1	1	12,241
New Kinda Walk	3	F	7	1	2	2	5,272
New Lebanon	5	M	6	0	1	1	2,601
New Limits	3	C	5	0	0	0	1,620
New Meadows	3	F	6	0	1	2	12,005
New Miracle	8	M	8	1	2	0	4,639
New Moon Rising	3	F	12	2	1	1	7,375
New Opportunity	2	C	6	1	0	2	10,297
New Opposition	3	F	11	3	2	1	52,627
New Paradigm	6	G	17	2	3	2	19,561
New Pembroke	4	G	7	2	0	0	18,275
New Prince	4	G	2	0	0	0	0
New Program	6	G	11	3	3	1	26,972
New Release	4	F	4	1	1	1	6,261
New River Star	4	F	5	0	0	0	416
New Rule	2	C	2	2	0	0	22,200
New Science	3	C	12	2	4	2	52,370
New Shoes	4	C	5	1	0	0	10,800
New Step	2	C	4	0	4	0	11,600
New Storm	3	F	8	2	0	2	39,780
New Topper	2	C	3	1	0	0	27,669
New Town	2	C	1	0	0	0	0
New Water	4	F	11	1	1	1	39,840
New Wind Blowin'	3	F	2	0	0	0	2,880
New Years Eve Gala	5	M	2	0	0	2	7,000
New York Barb	3	F	2	0	0	0	2,286
New York Cat	3	C	2	1	0	0	26,700
New York Dancer	3	G	1	0	0	0	0
New York Dream	2	F	3	1	1	0	33,074
New York Driver	3	F	3	0	0	0	2,355
New York Fay	7	M	2	0	0	0	140
New York Gold	4	F	11	4	2	3	56,219
New York Harbor	3	G	3	0	0	1	2,970
New York Hero	4	C	15	1	1	5	111,651
New York Jessica	4	F	5	0	0	0	734
New York Judith	2	F	4	1	0	0	21,321
New York New York	8	H	2	0	0	0	0
New York P D	4	G	14	1	3	3	23,928
New York Prospect	4	C	11	3	1	2	28,215
New York Tycoon	2	G	5	1	2	1	13,075
New Yorks Finest	3	G	1	0	0	0	0
New York's Rudy	4	G	14	4	1	2	86,900
Newark	4	G	9	4	2	2	95,204
Newbury	2	C	6	1	2	1	72,234
Newer Technology	7	G	8	0	1	0	3,960
Newfoundland	4	C	9	2	3	1	523,750
Newgate	9	H	8	1	0	2	7,943
Newhouse	3	G	7	0	0	0	256
Newlymintedpenny	3	F	4	1	1	0	29,840
Newport Green	3	C	2	0	1	0	8,800
Newport Road	2	G	1	0	0	1	1,764
Newport Trick	2	F	7	0	1	2	7,570
Newpys Naked Nogin	2	G	3	0	0	0	0
News Alert	3	C	3	0	1	0	3,000
News Report	4	G	8	0	2	2	20,740
News Reporter	3	G	9	0	1	0	3,245
News Travels Fast	3	G	7	1	0	0	11,460
Newsboy	4	G	18	2	3	2	23,742
Newsbreak	4	G	9	1	0	0	10,410
Newsman	4	G	15	2	1	0	17,926
Newsprint	2	C	1	0	0	0	300
Newsqueen	4	F	1	0	0	0	0
Newt Bunyard	6	M	5	1	0	1	3,755
Newton John	2	C	1	0	0	0	400
Newton's Halo	6	M	1	0	0	0	0
Newton's Princess	3	F	5	1	0	0	4,252
Newtonspearl	3	F	12	1	2	0	5,545
Newtown Pike	3	G	3	0	0	0	201
Newtrial	6	G	7	0	0	1	1,048
Newt's Big Boy	9	G	15	4	5	4	25,338
Newwaystodream	3	F	2	0	0	0	800
Newyearresolution	3	F	5	1	0	2	12,662
Newyorkssweetheart	5	M	5	0	0	0	1,241
Newzig	5	M	4	1	1	0	7,026
Nex Onecomin	3	F	7	0	1	1	7,625
Next Account	3	G	11	0	0	2	3,780
Next Bandit	3	C	10	0	3	0	24,820
Next Cat	2	F	5	1	0	0	8,550
Next Dove	2	C	2	0	0	0	900
Next Dove Hunt	3	F	8	2	1	1	14,165
Next News	4	G	13	4	2	3	18,633
Next Payday	4	G	6	0	0	0	1,343
Next September	5	G	2	0	0	0	288
Next Step	3	C	1	0	0	0	0
Next Summer	7	G	4	0	0	0	164
Nextiger	4	C	6	2	0	0	10,834
Nextofkin	3	F	4	0	2	0	2,065
Nextquestionplease	5	G	7	0	0	0	460
Nextquestor	4	G	15	4	2	2	43,570
Nezarb	2	C	5	2	0	0	28,548
Nezzarina	3	F	3	0	1	0	4,070
Ni Jinxed	5	G	5	0	1	1	2,144
Niadhas	3	C	5	1	0	0	32,610
Nibbles and Noble	5	G	1	0	0	0	94
Niblett	5	G	7	3	0	0	21,020
Niblick	5	M	2	0	0	0	1,010

Horse	Age	Sex	Sts	1st	2d	3d	Won
Nica Ray	2	G	6	0	0	0	1,697
Nicandro	2	C	1	1	0	0	14,500
Nicarata	4	F	2	0	1	0	890
Nicasio	6	G	7	1	2	1	10,435
Niccola	5	G	13	1	3	2	6,440
Nice Affair	4	F	5	1	0	0	2,400
Nice and Ready	4	G	5	0	0	0	176
Nice Baby	7	M	12	0	0	0	2,735
Nice Boy	5	H	11	1	1	0	16,180
Nice Canter	4	F	7	1	3	1	39,910
Nice Cat	4	G	8	2	2	4	8,441
Nice Choice	4	G	9	1	4	1	23,380
Nice Fish	6	M	13	0	3	3	9,869
Nice Fit	4	G	12	2	1	0	13,817
Nice Ice Rush	3	C	7	0	0	1	7,481
Nice Kipper	4	F	13	1	3	0	34,260
Nice Legs Nahla	5	M	4	0	0	1	1,860
Nice Little Girl	5	M	4	0	1	0	1,785
Nice N Heavenly	2	F	2	0	1	1	4,085
Nice N Nasty	5	G	12	1	1	2	19,043
Nice N Wild	2	F	1	0	0	0	0
Nice Performer	3	F	10	1	0	0	4,150
Nice Philly	2	F	5	0	2	0	10,244
Nice 'sawful	5	H	4	1	0	0	2,606
Nice Thag	4	F	3	0	0	0	165
Nice Try	3	C	10	0	0	1	2,350
Nicebutnaughty	3	F	1	0	0	0	0
Nicecountryamerica	3	F	3	1	0	0	3,858
Nicelittlepackage	3	F	11	4	4	1	36,805
Nicely	3	G	11	1	1	1	19,997
Nicely Accepted	4	F	14	4	1	6	63,055
Nicely Toasted	4	G	9	0	1	1	9,030
Nichol Express	3	C	6	0	0	0	1,120
Nicholas D	5	G	4	0	0	2	2,222
Nicholas Rocco M	4	G	8	0	0	2	2,987
Nicholella	7	M	8	0	2	1	7,700
Nichole's Delight	5	M	7	2	0	3	25,662
Nicholle's Devil	5	G	3	0	0	0	0
Nici's Gold	3	F	7	0	0	1	1,140
Nick (CHI)	7	H	6	0	2	0	4,808
Nick Berryman	9	G	14	4	2	2	17,510
Nick Missed	3	G	9	2	2	2	32,571
Nick Mitchell	5	H	6	0	1	0	4,690
Nick N Court	5	G	17	1	4	4	19,392
Nick of Gold	10	G	3	0	0	0	200
Nick of Time	6	G	5	0	1	0	1,497
Nick Oz	5	G	6	0	0	2	1,237
Nick the Noodge	3	G	6	1	0	2	37,407
Nick the Vest	4	G	13	2	1	1	54,484
Nickabod	6	M	6	0	0	0	765
Nickel	7	G	16	1	0	3	4,131
Nickel Bred	3	G	10	1	1	0	9,510
Nickel Ice	4	F	7	0	0	0	988
Nickel Silver	2	G	7	1	0	0	32,216
Nickers and Bits	2	F	1	0	0	0	155
Nickie's Affair	5	G	1	1	0	0	4,712
Nickinthecity	4	F	8	1	0	1	6,985
Nicki's Wish	3	F	4	2	1	0	38,745
Nicklas T.	6	G	11	0	0	1	1,327
Nickle Oakie	7	G	16	2	3	3	24,292
Nickle Seats	5	G	9	1	0	0	4,035
Nickles Wild	3	F	2	0	0	0	0
Nickname	3	F	18	2	3	2	30,380
Nickneye	4	F	2	0	0	1	1,820
Nickotea	3	G	3	1	0	0	2,668
Nick's Delight	5	G	7	3	2	0	75,352
Nick's Fancy	4	F	7	0	1	4	984
Nick's Folly	4	F	10	0	0	0	1,250
Nick's Gladiator	3	G	8	0	2	1	2,090
Nick's Ligan	5	G	11	2	3	1	34,562
Nicks Nights	3	F	11	1	5	2	21,859
Nick's Noactor	6	G	20	1	3	2	26,677
Nicky Jolene	4	F	5	1	0	2	15,528
Nicky Santoro	2	F	1	0	1	0	9,800
Nicky the Cat	2	C	2	0	0	1	1,680
Nicky's Wee Luv	3	F	2	0	0	0	0
Nicky's World	4	G	7	0	0	1	1,490
Niclie	4	F	9	4	2	1	140,670
Nicmick	8	G	20	1	1	3	8,993
Nicobar (GB)	7	H	4	0	0	1	12,040
Nicoise	3	F	4	0	0	1	5,592
Nicol n' Dime Me	7	G	9	1	1	2	16,880
Nicole	7	M	15	0	2	2	3,771
Nicole and Ben	3	F	4	0	1	1	39,860
Nicole Kathryn	4	F	2	0	0	1	4,830
Nicole M	5	M	10	0	1	2	3,000
Nicole Miss	3	F	10	0	1	1	5,486
Nicoleismyagent	3	F	9	1	1	1	15,550
Nicole's Apollo	5	G	9	1	0	1	9,790
Nicole's Dream	4	F	10	4	3	0	176,621
Nicole's Pursuit	5	M	3	0	0	0	860
Nicolo Pace	6	G	14	0	2	2	4,774
Nicolov (FR)	4	G	1	0	0	0	0
Nicosia	4	C	11	1	0	0	14,584
Nicoyana	6	M	6	0	0	1	1,619
Nics Eclipse	7	G	4	0	0	0	355
Nieges Que Te Amo	4	C	19	1	3	5	17,860
Niesen	5	M	9	0	0	0	1,304
Nietzsche	4	G	4	2	1	0	35,360
Nifty Buttons	3	F	5	0	0	0	0
Nifty Gal	2	F	1	0	1	0	3,440
Nifty Lady	3	F	3	0	1	0	12,560
Nifty One	3	G	13	2	1	3	11,791
Nifty Susie	5	M	3	0	0	0	0
Nigel	4	G	5	1	0	0	6,364
Nigel No Mates (NZ)	5	G	9	0	0	0	6,120
Nigh Tor	2	G	2	0	0	0	540
Night Accomplice	4	F	7	0	0	0	278
Night Ballet	6	M	17	0	2	4	9,362
Night Bokbel (IRE)	5	H	8	1	3	1	58,283
Night Caller	8	H	11	2	1	4	54,850
Night Charger	3	G	7	1	2	0	9,985
Night Crier	6	G	15	2	1	3	4,246
Night Dash	2	G	7	2	1	1	22,505
Night Doctor (IRE)	5	G	1	0	0	0	500
Night Fight	2	C	1	0	0	0	0
Night Flash	4	F	13	0	0	1	2,261
Night for Bells	5	M	5	0	1	0	604
Night Games (GB)	4	F	6	1	3	1	70,840
Night Gig	2	G	4	1	1	2	9,000
Night Heron	3	F	10	3	2	1	58,270
Night Howl	6	G	4	1	0	0	2,794
Night Life (FR)	7	H	2	0	0	1	12,600
Night Magick	2	C	1	0	0	0	154
Night of Delight	8	M	7	1	0	3	13,960
Night Orchid	2	F	2	0	0	0	0
Night Passion (GB)	5	G	10	2	1	0	14,205
Night Patrol	8	G	6	0	0	1	28,390
Night Plan	6	M	3	0	0	0	159
Night Rhythms	5	G	2	0	0	0	0
Night Rock	2	G	3	0	0	1	2,760
Night Run	7	G	15	0	2	4	6,431
Night Sky	3	G	3	1	0	0	43,320
Night Splendor	3	C	4	0	0	0	0
Night Terror	2	G	3	1	0	0	16,860
Night Train Lane	4	G	11	1	2	2	10,310
Night Tripper	2	C	3	0	2	0	11,000
Night Wing	2	C	2	1	0	1	10,700
Nightattheoscars	5	G	3	0	0	0	1,335
Nighthunter	4	G	11	1	2	2	25,708
Nighthunter Two	3	F	2	0	0	0	0
Nightingale	5	M	11	1	1	0	6,652
Nightingale Mill	3	G	10	1	1	5	17,995
Nightlifeatbigblue	3	C	8	0	0	2	29,065
Nightly Appeal	7	G	8	0	2	0	23,413
Nightly Delusions	4	G	12	2	0	1	6,809
Nightmare Affair	3	C	17	2	5	5	110,390
Night's Revenge	3	G	4	0	0	0	720
Nightsnwhitesatin	4	C	5	1	1	0	14,320
Nighttimeinthecity	3	F	18	3	4	2	39,990
Nighty	5	M	7	0	0	1	2,651
Nihilator	3	C	7	1	0	1	25,553
Niigon	3	C	9	2	2	1	864,610
Nijinsky's Dancer	7	H	5	1	1	1	2,000
Nijinsky's Pride	5	G	8	0	1	2	4,925
Nijinsky's Sword	2	F	1	0	0	0	400
Nik the Stick	4	G	10	1	0	0	4,688
Nikawa	10	G	7	0	1	0	1,476

Horse	Age	Sex	Sts	1st	2d	3d	Won
Nike's Friend	3	F	3	0	0	0	1,293
Nikey Missile	2	C	6	0	3	1	99,240
Nikie Your Honor	6	G	7	2	2	0	38,118
Nikinipo (BRZ)	4	C	1	0	0	0	400
Nikken Won	5	M	9	0	0	3	1,472
Nikki's Growl	4	F	15	3	3	1	57,474
Nikki's Joy	3	F	7	1	0	0	16,943
Nikki's Prospect	3	F	4	0	1	1	2,620
Nikki's Secert	2	F	2	0	1	0	3,073
Nikobe	5	G	16	1	5	1	32,215
Nile Princess	4	F	7	0	1	0	1,286
Nile Pyramids	3	C	4	0	0	0	977
Nilegionaire	5	G	3	0	0	0	278
Nilini	3	F	8	3	0	0	65,201
Nilla	2	F	3	1	0	0	8,400
Nilly Style	3	F	12	0	1	1	5,050
Nimble	12	G	2	0	0	0	380
Nimble Shank	3	F	8	0	0	1	2,569
Nimble Wit	2	C	10	0	2	4	37,473
Nimmer	4	F	10	5	0	0	52,333
Nimrod Lake	3	G	7	2	0	2	16,706
Nina Lyn	4	F	7	0	0	0	0
Nina Marie	5	M	9	1	3	2	28,398
Ninadivina	2	F	9	3	0	1	86,174
Nina's Limelight	3	F	3	0	0	0	120
Nina's Love	2	F	2	0	0	0	0
Nina's Taxing	5	M	14	4	3	0	30,108
Ninavalentina	4	F	1	0	0	0	50
Nindawayma	6	M	13	2	1	2	16,999
Nine Ballads	3	C	4	0	0	1	3,743
Nine Bucks	3	F	1	0	0	0	550
Nine Card	4	G	3	0	0	0	450
Nine Cats	2	F	7	1	0	0	4,910
Nine Chimes	4	G	6	1	0	1	24,000
Nine Factors	7	H	7	1	1	2	8,225
Nine for Nine	3	G	11	2	1	1	8,955
Nine Iron	12	G	7	1	4	2	11,674
Nine K Enigma	3	G	4	0	0	1	1,065
Nine Moons	9	G	7	0	0	0	522
Nine Notes	5	G	15	0	5	1	30,580
Nine o' Mine	3	F	3	1	1	0	13,600
Nine of Cups	7	M	7	0	0	0	150
Nine of Hearts	3	F	3	0	0	0	550
Nine One Won	3	G	7	0	1	2	2,265
Nine Pines	4	F	1	0	0	0	0
Nine to Midnight	2	F	1	0	0	0	609
Nine Tu Tu's	5	M	9	3	1	1	49,130
Ninebanks	6	G	5	2	1	0	122,550
Nineleventurbo	6	G	7	1	2	2	35,650
Ninelinebind	3	C	3	0	0	1	1,415
Nineninefine	4	F	13	3	2	4	39,267
Nineo'clockhigh	4	G	7	0	0	0	437
Nineofus	4	G	6	0	0	0	1,050
Niner Link	3	C	4	0	0	0	300
Niner's Echo	6	G	6	1	2	0	37,559
Niners Gold Money	5	M	4	0	0	0	965
Niners Roar	3	G	2	0	0	0	800
Nine's Appealagain	6	G	9	0	0	0	1,295
Nineteen Candles	6	M	5	0	0	1	1,365
Ninetenthsofthelaw	5	G	10	4	1	1	59,513
Ninety Day Note	4	G	20	1	6	3	17,731
Ninety Day Wonder	4	G	3	0	0	0	308
Ninety Fine	2	G	4	1	1	0	17,200
Ninety Mile Island	5	M	6	1	1	2	4,125
Ninety Nine Jack	5	G	12	7	3	0	173,821
Ninety Nine Mack	5	G	8	0	2	0	20,988
Ninety Nine Proof	5	G	8	1	1	1	11,087
Ninety Second K O	3	G	3	0	0	0	0
Ninetynine	3	F	2	0	0	0	800
Ninja Barbie	4	F	1	0	0	0	105
Ninnescah	2	F	1	0	0	0	110
Nino Alegre	5	H	5	1	0	0	17,241
Nino Cat	3	C	3	0	0	0	225
Nino Dorado	6	G	9	0	2	2	5,057
Nintyfiver	9	G	11	1	4	1	7,776
Niota	3	F	1	0	0	0	0
Nip'n'tuck	10	G	9	0	0	1	1,450
Nippa Way	11	G	6	0	1	2	4,050
Nipper Nelly	4	F	5	0	0	1	1,920
Nippers	3	F	2	2	0	0	35,000
Nippert	4	C	15	2	3	2	8,869
Nipstick	4	C	7	0	0	0	855
Nipsy's Classic	3	F	1	0	0	0	0
Nirav	4	C	13	2	3	1	59,020
Nirvana Blue	9	M	3	0	1	0	424
Nishani	3	F	9	2	2	2	54,412
Nishe's Shadow	3	F	2	0	0	0	0
Nismat	3	F	20	2	1	4	22,297
Nister Bere (FR)	3	C	1	0	0	1	6,960
Nita Chiquita	2	F	4	2	1	0	44,230
Nita Wins Too	4	F	12	0	0	1	4,196
Nita's Notebook	7	G	8	1	3	1	7,492
Nita'sgotitgoinon	3	F	5	0	1	1	11,290
Nite Deelites	6	G	1	0	0	0	0
Nite Gaze	8	M	1	1	0	0	8,220
Nite Jazz	3	F	13	0	0	1	5,575
Nite of the Prom	5	G	3	0	0	0	200
Nite Owl Nick	3	C	1	0	0	1	1,650
Nite to Shine	2	G	6	0	1	0	3,403
Nite Tower	5	G	12	1	2	2	12,254
Nitranna	9	M	9	1	0	0	5,180
Nitro Attorney	3	G	6	0	0	1	2,702
Nitro Chip	3	G	7	2	0	3	99,420
Nitro Light	3	C	6	0	0	0	346
Nitro Oxide	2	C	1	0	0	0	0
Nitroisnick	5	G	2	0	0	0	86
Nitsa D	5	M	3	0	0	0	0
Nitschke	6	G	13	0	0	0	1,005
Nittany Express	3	G	11	3	3	2	61,773
Nitty Gritty	2	F	2	0	0	1	920
Nives	2	F	4	0	1	1	18,370
Nivlac's Easy Jett	6	G	2	0	0	1	730
Nix of Time	8	G	10	2	1	0	6,862
Nj's Joey	2	G	2	0	0	0	264
Nkosi Reigns	3	G	6	3	1	1	63,180
Nlotsabutter	4	F	9	1	1	2	22,067
No Affair	2	F	4	1	1	0	20,000
No Agenda	5	G	2	0	1	0	1,660
No Aggravation	3	G	3	0	0	0	1,260
No Alibis	6	G	1	0	0	0	600
No Allegiance	2	C	4	1	0	0	25,182
No Anchovies	8	M	12	0	1	1	1,887
No Approval Needed	4	G	9	0	2	0	3,134
No Arizona	3	C	10	0	0	3	9,850
No Ayne	2	F	2	0	0	0	270
No Bad Habits	10	H	6	1	1	1	7,422
No Badge	2	F	2	0	0	0	248
No Beans	3	F	6	0	0	0	4,579
No Betta Cat	4	F	1	0	0	0	120
No Better Chance	3	F	6	1	2	0	16,000
No Bettor Love	7	M	4	0	0	0	750
No Bias	4	F	8	1	2	2	16,995
No Blues	4	F	3	1	0	0	4,530
No Boots	4	G	11	1	1	1	10,709
No Borders	2	F	3	0	0	0	1,128
No Britches	6	G	2	0	0	0	100
No Bull	2	F	2	0	1	0	6,010
No Bull Baby	2	F	6	2	1	0	129,720
No Cal Bread	8	G	3	0	1	1	3,220
No Cal Bread Bro	7	G	9	0	2	1	6,428
No Cash	2	F	3	0	1	0	13,655
No Chance to Ski	4	C	9	1	1	0	7,639
No Cheating	7	M	10	0	2	3	21,639
No Comparison	4	F	5	1	0	0	3,183
No Comprende	6	G	2	0	0	1	12,000
No Concern	3	F	1	0	0	0	0
No Cover Charge	6	G	9	0	0	2	2,901
No Coward	4	F	13	1	2	2	9,991
No Crime Committed	4	G	15	0	1	0	6,322
No Dancing Here	3	C	13	1	2	3	11,165
No Day But Today	3	G	4	0	0	0	708
No Deposit	5	H	1	0	0	0	0
No Dispute	4	F	3	1	0	1	6,035
No Dress Code	4	F	3	1	1	0	15,536
No Dumb Jokes	4	G	10	0	1	1	1,864
No Factor	3	G	4	0	0	0	176
No Fast Moves	6	G	5	0	1	1	7,600
No Fear	3	G	18	5	4	2	38,332

Horse	Age	Sex	Sts	1st	2d	3d	Won
No Fears No Tears	4	F	9	0	4	0	19,554
No Fences	2	F	5	1	0	1	15,773
No Fishing	3	C	7	0	1	0	3,740
No Garden Variety	4	F	11	3	2	3	33,505
No Gin On Sunday	2	F	2	0	0	2	2,170
No Giveaway	3	G	5	3	2	0	35,163
No Given In	3	G	13	2	0	3	14,580
No Gray On Me	4	F	3	1	0	0	4,820
No Greater Coyote	2	C	1	0	0	0	93
No Guts No Glory	5	G	4	0	0	0	246
No Happy Love	3	G	9	1	0	1	7,872
No Help Needed	2	F	2	0	1	0	1,961
No Hobby	2	G	1	0	0	0	0
No Holds Barred	3	F	9	2	1	0	5,723
No Homework	4	G	9	1	1	0	7,216
No Huddle	4	G	10	2	2	2	23,495
No I Can't	6	G	13	3	3	2	38,438
No Inclusions	7	M	5	1	0	0	3,919
No Issues	4	G	3	1	0	0	8,900
No Its False	3	F	14	1	0	1	3,751
No Its Not	6	G	5	3	0	0	39,450
No Jacket Required	7	G	6	0	1	0	4,640
No Jazz	4	F	5	0	0	0	448
No Kelp Weed	5	M	9	3	2	0	23,109
No Kiss for Tipsy	4	F	1	1	0	0	3,713
No Kowtowing	4	F	12	1	1	2	12,150
No Laugh n' Kathy	10	G	2	0	0	1	1,080
No Lies Please	4	F	3	0	0	0	501
No Little Case	2	F	4	0	0	0	405
No Lo Creo	3	F	3	1	0	0	3,906
No Logo	2	F	6	1	0	2	43,561
No Looking Back	5	G	11	2	2	2	9,004
No Luck in Reno	10	G	1	0	0	0	0
No Magic	10	G	6	2	0	0	7,567
No Manners Nelson	3	G	8	0	0	1	1,530
No Man's Island	8	M	4	0	0	0	0
No Matches	4	G	8	2	1	0	16,703
No Matter Who	5	G	11	1	0	2	20,235
No Matt's My Kid	4	F	11	0	1	1	3,930
No Minimum	3	F	11	3	2	1	22,238
No Mistaken Pappa	4	C	2	0	0	0	300
No Moon	5	G	9	1	0	1	3,970
No Mor Dough	6	G	9	0	0	2	3,760
No More Allen's	5	H	4	0	0	1	2,460
No More Blues	3	F	7	1	0	1	24,760
No More Chads	5	G	12	2	2	6	76,700
No More Doubt	5	M	3	0	0	0	180
No More Jewels	3	G	3	0	0	0	325
No More Politics	2	C	2	2	0	0	23,400
No More Tax	3	F	8	0	2	0	12,114
No More Tricks	2	F	1	1	0	0	5,225
No More Twist	5	G	3	0	0	0	486
No More Two Call	4	F	14	0	0	0	0
No More War	3	F	4	1	0	0	5,608
No Music	5	G	6	0	1	0	6,738
No Mystery Here	5	M	8	0	0	1	3,495
No Nap Time	3	F	6	0	4	0	5,920
No Net Needed	5	G	17	2	0	1	11,540
No New Projects	3	G	4	0	1	0	2,890
No Nice	4	G	13	1	0	3	11,240
No Night (GB)	8	G	14	2	3	3	36,965
No No Angel	5	M	8	1	0	2	23,180
No No Chica	3	F	5	1	0	1	6,990
No No Cielo	3	F	12	0	2	3	16,157
No No Nicotine	3	F	8	1	4	1	9,386
No No Rene	4	F	9	1	1	1	12,960
No No Romeo	5	G	8	0	0	2	4,742
No Numbers	4	G	14	2	1	2	23,760
No One Like Me	2	F	1	0	0	0	400
No Ordinary Cat	3	F	4	0	0	0	530
No Other Like You	4	F	6	1	1	2	39,910
No Paige	5	M	5	0	0	0	899
No Pajamas	3	G	8	2	1	0	30,962
No Pardon	4	F	6	0	3	1	3,712
No Parole	5	G	7	1	0	3	57,278
No Pass Port	4	F	5	2	0	0	9,815
No Passing Zone	2	C	3	1	0	2	24,664
No Peso No Dance	5	M	3	1	0	0	6,200
No Phone Swabbe	7	G	10	0	0	1	992
No Picnic	5	G	5	1	0	0	7,043
No Place Like It	3	G	6	3	1	1	150,400
No Pouting	3	F	16	2	3	1	26,803
No Pressure	5	G	8	2	1	2	35,570
No Problem	4	G	8	2	0	3	4,218
No Proof	2	C	3	0	0	0	220
No Questions Asked	3	G	7	2	2	0	19,900
No Quit	2	F	3	0	0	0	75
No Regular Cat	3	G	12	2	2	1	10,982
No Response	3	G	9	1	0	2	6,675
No Restraint	5	G	3	0	1	1	3,360
No Retreating	3	G	2	0	0	0	217
No Return	3	F	9	0	1	0	883
No Risk Involved	3	F	2	0	0	1	1,100
No Saint	2	C	2	0	0	0	600
No Secrets Here	4	F	15	5	5	0	137,810
No See At Sodom G	3	F	1	0	0	0	0
No Shades	4	G	16	0	2	1	5,231
No Shame	3	F	13	4	3	0	48,300
No Shouting	2	C	4	0	2	1	23,820
No Show Jim	6	H	4	0	0	1	5,812
No Sleep	2	F	6	1	1	3	18,900
No Sleep in April	4	C	1	0	0	0	0
No Socks Doc	6	H	1	0	0	0	400
No Solution	3	C	11	2	4	0	28,965
No Sox Fox	2	G	2	0	1	1	3,153
No Spin	4	F	2	0	0	0	105
No Stop in Me	5	G	24	3	5	3	19,488
No Stop Lights	3	G	7	1	1	0	9,356
No Strings	4	G	16	6	1	1	47,995
No Surgeon	4	G	12	2	3	3	27,732
No Surrender	2	G	4	1	1	0	27,040
No Sweat Kristine	6	M	8	0	1	3	5,429
No Tan Lines	6	M	2	0	0	0	432
No Tax	3	C	4	0	1	2	11,910
No Term Limit	3	G	9	1	3	2	32,411
No Theatrics	2	C	1	0	0	1	3,080
No Ticky No Shirt	2	F	4	1	0	0	9,960
No Time Flat	5	G	8	2	0	0	17,662
No Time Soon	5	H	3	0	0	0	0
No Time to Lose	3	F	5	0	0	3	5,960
No Time to Ponder	4	G	10	1	2	1	11,717
No Tolerance	3	G	10	4	2	2	71,050
No Toro	5	H	11	5	4	0	79,620
No Touch Very Hot	2	F	2	0	0	0	212
No Traitor	4	G	8	0	0	0	500
No Trespass	5	M	4	0	1	0	860
No Trouble	5	H	3	0	0	2	2,090
No Trump	3	G	8	1	1	2	6,190
No Turbulence	5	M	3	0	0	2	8,200
No Turk	4	G	1	0	0	0	0
No Vacancy	7	H	5	0	0	0	644
No Way Johnny Ray	5	G	2	0	0	0	105
No Way Jose	7	G	7	0	0	0	0
No Way No How	2	F	4	1	0	1	31,453
No Whining	3	F	2	0	0	1	4,708
No Whistle	4	F	9	0	2	0	3,272
No White Flags	6	G	8	0	0	0	4,261
No Ya Aint I Am	2	F	3	0	0	0	0
No You Don't	4	F	4	0	0	0	386
Noaccount Mind	3	F	5	0	0	0	722
Noactoreverlast	6	M	2	0	0	0	0
Noadlah	4	G	11	3	1	0	15,911
Noaffairforgeorge	2	F	6	1	0	0	17,060
Noah A.	3	C	4	1	1	0	8,588
Noah Jake	3	G	13	1	1	0	37,180
Noahs Ark (IRE)	3	F	7	1	3	1	103,987
Noah's Chance	5	G	18	2	4	2	16,527
Noah's Courage	3	C	3	0	0	0	190
Noah's Secret	5	G	12	0	3	2	4,269
Noano	7	G	1	0	0	0	0
Noas Little Buddy	3	G	3	0	0	1	486
Noa's Toy	4	F	19	3	7	0	49,627
Noazzin	5	G	8	3	2	0	23,400
Nobilissime (GB)	5	M	1	0	0	0	400
Noble Ack	6	G	9	1	1	3	2,572
Noble Adversary	6	G	8	0	3	1	15,257
Noble and Just	5	G	9	0	0	1	1,250
Noble Ann	6	M	9	0	0	0	824

Horse	Age	Sex	Sts	1st	2d	3d	Won
Noble Ballet	3	F	14	0	2	2	14,775
Noble Bob	3	C	4	1	0	1	10,660
Noble Carr	4	G	9	1	3	2	33,570
Noble Causeway	2	C	2	0	1	0	10,380
Noble Champion	3	G	2	0	0	0	0
Noble Crown	7	G	16	5	5	2	27,754
Noble Dane	3	G	11	3	0	2	33,346
Noble de Fence	2	C	3	0	0	1	1,320
Noble Decision	5	G	6	2	1	1	33,406
Noble Delight	4	F	8	1	1	2	10,430
Noble Deputy	3	G	9	1	3	0	10,128
Noble Design	2	F	2	0	0	1	945
Noble Endeavor	4	F	8	2	3	0	3,949
Noble Evansville	2	C	1	0	0	0	0
Noble Fighter	3	C	3	0	0	0	413
Noble Genius	3	F	4	0	0	0	335
Noble Gent	5	G	5	0	0	0	283
Noble Halo	3	G	5	0	0	0	132
Noble Image	2	F	5	0	3	0	5,475
Noble Indian Maid	3	F	1	0	0	0	0
Noble Jazz	2	F	3	1	1	1	14,350
Noble Kinsman	6	G	9	2	2	1	42,114
Noble Kitty	3	F	1	0	0	0	92
Noble Love	2	F	3	0	0	0	1,080
Noble Masterpiece	5	H	8	1	0	1	25,921
Noble Maxx	2	G	2	0	0	0	160
Noble Minister	4	C	4	0	0	0	1,056
Noble Monarch	4	G	11	2	1	0	17,217
Noble Pass	6	G	5	0	0	2	2,191
Noble Place	4	F	6	3	1	1	33,963
Noble Plan	4	F	4	1	1	2	17,920
Noble Profile	2	C	4	0	1	0	5,100
Noble Ruler	7	G	8	2	0	2	41,200
Noble Runner	5	G	3	1	1	0	9,672
Noble Scarlet	6	M	2	0	0	0	0
Noble Season	5	G	4	2	0	0	5,060
Noble Silence	4	C	3	0	0	0	1,040
Noble Southerner	2	C	7	1	0	0	6,105
Noble Spread	6	M	5	0	0	0	1,155
Noble Steed	3	G	6	0	0	2	1,392
Noble Stella (GER)	3	F	6	2	1	1	53,828
Noble Topcat	2	G	3	0	0	0	514
Noble Warrior	7	G	7	1	0	0	2,688
Noble Wish	6	M	12	2	3	4	64,398
Noble Witness	5	H	2	0	0	0	300
Noble Words	4	G	2	1	0	0	2,440
Noblest	5	G	8	1	2	1	23,170
Noblest Yet	3	F	2	0	0	0	266
Nobody Can	7	G	2	0	0	1	764
Nobody Knows	8	G	17	2	5	1	12,558
Nobody Picked Five	8	G	6	1	1	0	10,436
Nobody Say Nobody	8	G	8	0	1	0	1,998
Nobodyknowsbut Ed	6	G	11	0	2	2	14,955
Nobodys Listening	6	H	12	2	1	1	44,600
Nobodywantmetilnow	3	C	2	0	0	0	840
Nobu Special	3	G	10	0	2	3	9,410
Noches De Rosa (CHI)	6	M	7	1	1	1	256,600
Nocona Gold	3	C	7	2	1	1	24,525
Nocturnal Visitor	7	H	4	0	0	0	565
Nodaker	3	C	1	0	0	0	39
Nodoubletouch	2	C	2	0	0	0	1,400
Nodoubtadude	8	G	6	0	0	0	381
Noeasyjob	8	G	7	3	0	2	35,238
Noexuse	3	G	5	1	1	0	14,355
Nofair Warning	4	F	2	0	0	0	305
Noggin Dude	2	C	4	0	1	1	11,680
Nogotahalo	5	G	3	0	2	1	14,320
Nohasslatdcastle	2	C	1	0	0	0	120
Noifsnoandsnobuts	2	G	5	1	2	1	19,500
Noi'manangel	5	M	10	1	0	2	5,889
Noinbetweeners	6	G	12	1	0	3	16,394
Noir Et Rouge	4	C	17	3	3	3	54,720
Noise Maker	3	C	13	1	2	1	19,778
Noisette	4	F	7	2	3	0	147,764
Noite	4	F	11	0	5	2	60,642
Nokoma	5	G	13	2	1	2	11,488
Nolan's Cat	2	C	1	0	0	1	2,390
Nolan's Impact	2	G	5	0	0	0	850
Noles	5	H	10	0	1	2	12,765

Horse	Age	Sex	Sts	1st	2d	3d	Won
Nolichucky Jack	4	G	4	0	0	0	228
Nolimitholdem	2	G	2	0	0	0	0
Nolimosforyou	4	C	11	2	4	1	78,810
Nolovefortrucks	5	G	17	0	5	5	27,100
Nomadic Actor	4	G	19	2	2	2	42,786
Nominee	4	G	1	1	0	0	2,800
Nomissen Target	4	G	10	2	3	1	29,386
Nomisstaken Kris	5	G	9	1	0	3	13,025
Nomistakeaboutit	3	F	9	1	1	2	61,806
Nomonynomonynomony	3	C	12	0	3	4	30,040
Nomorebills	4	C	6	3	2	0	73,605
Nomoreseconds	7	H	3	0	0	1	1,900
Nomoreskoal	7	G	14	3	3	1	17,443
Non Stop Action	4	G	3	0	2	1	762
Non Stop Scott	6	G	7	0	1	3	5,674
Nona Nona	4	F	21	1	3	2	3,425
Nonami	4	C	10	2	1	1	28,917
None But the Brave	3	C	2	0	0	0	0
None for the Road	2	F	1	0	0	0	230
Nonno Guido	5	G	4	0	1	0	1,416
Nonothillary	3	F	1	0	0	0	130
Nonour	4	F	10	5	2	0	68,740
Nonsuch Bay	5	M	8	1	2	3	119,100
Noo Noo	5	M	3	0	0	0	0
Noodles	5	G	17	1	2	2	7,345
Noodlette	4	F	11	2	1	0	16,893
Nooligan	3	C	12	2	2	2	90,740
Noon Affair	7	G	16	2	0	3	25,551
Noon Doll Three	3	F	8	0	1	0	4,528
Noon Star	3	G	6	0	1	0	3,264
Noon Time Dancer	4	F	4	1	1	0	6,090
Noon Win	2	F	5	3	1	0	74,140
Noonday Idol	2	F	7	0	0	2	4,760
Noonday Sun	12	G	1	0	0	0	40
Noontime	3	F	9	2	0	1	15,750
Noontime Bell	3	C	4	0	0	0	234
Noordinarylove	4	F	1	0	0	0	0
Nopaynenogain	5	G	18	0	1	4	2,527
Nopex (BRZ)	4	C	1	0	0	0	1,800
Noproblemfor Dino	2	G	3	0	0	1	2,530
Norainonthisparty	2	G	6	1	0	3	38,380
Nordan's Image	6	G	6	3	0	1	26,323
Nordansa	3	F	5	0	2	1	3,770
Nordic Hope	6	M	8	1	2	0	10,120
Nordic Lass	4	F	16	1	3	6	28,682
Nordic Mist	4	G	6	1	0	3	11,310
Nordique	4	F	2	0	0	0	300
Noreena the Great	7	M	7	0	0	0	1,190
Noreign	3	F	17	0	1	2	7,995
Norestforthewicked	3	F	5	0	1	1	1,120
Norfield	2	C	1	0	0	0	1,380
Norfolk Knight	5	G	13	4	0	4	338,923
Norfolk Reed (IRE)	7	G	10	1	2	0	6,692
Norhtern Blues	2	C	1	0	0	0	828
Norjet	5	G	4	0	0	0	3,490
Norlina	5	H	4	0	0	0	0
Norlos	9	G	5	1	1	1	7,050
Norman Creek	5	G	7	0	1	1	5,032
Norman One	5	G	4	0	1	1	3,492
Normandy Beach	8	G	12	4	2	1	76,260
Normandy Gold	6	G	12	3	1	0	31,486
Normandy Princess	3	F	7	1	0	0	8,300
Norma's Quiet Kash	5	H	8	0	0	0	2,340
Norma's Way	3	F	9	0	0	1	4,399
Norm's Nephew	2	C	1	0	1	0	3,520
Noromeo	5	M	3	0	0	0	214
Norris Cut	7	G	2	0	0	0	0
Nors' Proud Birdie	4	G	17	1	2	5	34,480
Norshade	3	F	7	0	1	1	9,350
North	5	G	4	1	2	0	5,962
North and South	8	G	19	3	2	1	16,141
North Broad	4	C	6	2	2	2	65,561
North Broadway	6	G	9	0	0	1	1,347
North Brooklyn	5	H	9	1	0	3	17,006
North by Six	4	F	2	0	1	0	6,900
North by West	6	G	11	0	1	0	885
North Cascade	7	G	1	0	0	0	0
North Cork	3	F	9	2	2	1	22,050
North Creek Slew	4	C	3	0	0	0	0

Horse	Age	Sex	Sts	1st	2d	3d	Won
North Decoder	4	F	3	0	0	0	255
North Duck	8	H	9	1	0	2	6,911
North East Bound	8	G	5	0	0	1	6,080
North Flare	7	G	14	3	2	3	21,875
North Flash	3	C	2	0	0	1	2,860
North Hills	7	G	3	0	0	0	165
North Image	3	G	2	1	0	0	5,681
North Jersey Girl	4	F	1	0	0	0	266
North Man	5	G	9	0	0	0	4,093
North Mill	4	G	6	0	0	1	3,022
North of Dixie	5	G	9	2	1	4	22,758
North of Nine	3	G	9	2	1	1	10,276
North of Rio	4	F	11	4	1	2	26,384
North Park	2	G	3	0	0	2	4,318
North Place	3	C	8	0	0	2	5,452
North Pole Star	3	C	3	0	0	0	249
North Ponche	5	G	4	0	0	0	309
North Potomac	2	C	3	0	1	0	6,930
North Rim	2	F	1	0	0	0	1,150
North Salem	10	H	11	0	1	1	5,669
North Stardom	2	G	3	0	1	0	2,790
North Tide	7	G	13	2	3	0	18,056
North Upper Street	3	F	4	0	0	0	3,740
North West Bay	3	F	18	3	2	3	24,520
North Win	5	G	2	0	0	0	74
Northcountry Chief	2	G	7	0	0	2	6,685
Northdrop	4	C	12	4	3	0	21,350
Northeast Blizzard	2	G	6	0	0	0	3,062
Northeast Winds	6	M	8	1	1	3	13,793
Northend	6	G	16	3	2	4	31,685
Northend of Boston	6	G	3	0	0	0	540
Northern Ace	6	G	9	2	3	1	19,562
Northern Acre	5	M	13	3	1	1	18,570
Northern Affair	4	G	9	1	3	0	34,720
Northern Aid	4	C	2	0	0	0	84
Northern Air	4	C	9	1	0	3	32,239
Northern Alert	5	G	11	1	4	2	36,700
Northern Apple	5	G	2	0	0	0	390
Northern Arrow	6	M	6	0	0	0	188
Northern Autumn	11	G	10	3	2	1	4,077
Northern Babe	2	F	8	2	0	3	62,933
Northern Ballad	3	C	9	1	1	0	25,780
Northern Baquero	3	G	14	2	1	1	10,781
Northern Baucis	7	G	12	1	0	1	3,568
Northern Bishop	5	M	8	2	1	0	19,822
Northern Blaze	7	M	9	0	0	0	270
Northern Boots	4	G	4	0	0	0	0
Northern Buck	3	C	5	0	2	1	9,475
Northern Candy	3	C	7	1	2	0	35,250
Northern Cheyenne	6	G	8	0	0	2	905
Northern Colony	6	G	12	0	4	1	4,692
Northern Computur	6	M	2	0	0	0	0
Northern Concorde	2	C	5	1	1	0	32,450
Northern Cross	7	M	5	0	0	0	888
Northern Damascus	6	G	2	0	0	0	0
Northern Dandy	3	G	11	2	0	3	10,582
Northern Deluxe	6	M	2	0	0	0	500
Northern Deputy	3	F	2	0	1	0	2,720
Northern Discover	4	G	6	2	0	1	27,320
Northern Dove	3	F	1	0	0	0	80
Northern Du	7	G	6	0	3	1	1,072
Northern Duck	7	G	1	0	0	0	120
Northern Example	3	G	2	0	0	0	0
Northern Excursion	3	F	7	2	0	1	19,700
Northern Executive	4	G	9	1	3	1	32,934
Northern Exposure	4	F	1	0	0	0	340
Northern Fantasy	8	G	5	1	1	2	23,940
Northern Frolic	3	F	8	0	1	1	6,614
Northern Gale	4	F	2	0	0	1	1,500
Northern Game	4	G	15	4	2	0	39,213
Northern Gent	2	C	2	0	0	1	3,850
Northern Gift	7	G	4	0	0	0	206
Northern Girl	6	M	1	0	0	0	0
Northern Gold	6	G	8	0	0	0	1,539
Northern Groom	3	G	8	0	0	0	3,528
Northern Heat	3	C	10	2	1	2	9,851
Northern Heights	3	F	9	1	2	2	9,008
Northern Honey	4	F	10	1	0	0	2,756
Northern Hope	6	G	7	0	2	0	3,604
Northern Indian	4	G	13	3	3	1	18,384
Northern Joe	3	G	1	1	0	0	35,280
Northern Knight	11	G	5	0	0	0	0
Northern Lane	2	F	2	1	0	1	18,460
Northern Leopard	6	G	3	0	0	0	300
Northern Master	4	C	7	1	2	1	3,983
Northern Mischief	2	F	5	1	0	1	77,260
Northern Mission	3	F	15	1	2	1	8,852
Northern Most Star	5	M	7	0	1	1	3,860
Northern Neechitoo	7	M	9	2	3	2	66,798
Northern Nile	4	F	3	0	0	0	300
Northern Pleasure	3	F	6	1	0	0	5,883
Northern Power	3	G	3	0	0	1	1,632
Northern Quest	4	F	5	0	0	0	1,300
Northern Rain	4	F	10	1	3	2	12,508
Northern Request	5	G	8	1	0	1	3,563
Northern Rex	10	G	4	0	0	0	320
Northern Ricky	8	G	2	1	0	1	1,532
Northern Riviera	7	M	7	0	1	2	3,519
Northern Rock (JPN)	6	G	5	0	1	1	25,680
Northern Root	10	G	13	1	1	0	5,873
Northern Run	5	G	6	1	1	1	21,100
Northern Satan	5	G	11	2	2	0	7,635
Northern Scene	3	G	9	4	0	4	85,430
Northern Scout	3	G	3	0	0	0	136
Northern Sioux	9	G	14	1	2	3	17,245
Northern Sleet	7	G	5	0	1	0	2,581
Northern Son	7	G	12	0	0	3	7,359
Northern Sorceress	3	F	3	1	2	0	63,100
Northern Spark	3	G	8	0	0	0	1,723
Northern Sparkles	2	C	4	0	0	0	405
Northern Squall	3	G	3	1	0	1	10,220
Northern Stag	3	C	5	0	2	2	25,110
Northern Starr Bac	2	G	1	0	0	0	0
Northern Stealth	3	C	2	0	1	1	9,000
Northern Storm	2	C	3	0	0	0	470
Northern Stride	3	G	3	0	0	0	0
Northern Sword	4	F	1	0	0	0	0
Northern Tales	2	F	1	0	0	0	450
Northern Thinking	8	H	4	0	0	2	2,250
Northern Thrill	4	G	25	3	3	3	17,070
Northern Thriller	4	G	5	0	0	0	400
Northern Tide	8	G	12	2	3	3	31,738
Northern Traveler	2	F	1	0	0	0	0
Northern Trelawny	5	M	13	2	1	0	14,237
Northern Turnstone	6	M	2	0	0	0	650
Northern Tuscanny	8	M	1	0	0	0	132
Northern Tyrant	2	G	3	0	0	0	1,240
Northern Victor	3	G	8	1	2	0	2,578
Northern Wager	6	G	4	0	1	0	900
Northern Won	5	G	7	1	2	0	7,610
Northern Wood	6	M	4	0	0	0	3,575
Northern Yukon	6	M	5	0	0	0	0
Northernprospector	11	G	6	1	2	0	6,638
Northgate Dancer	3	G	8	1	0	0	6,540
Northglen	6	M	14	1	1	3	25,285
Northlander	4	C	14	5	0	3	35,499
Northlands Fancy	3	F	2	0	0	0	105
Northland's Gift	6	G	18	3	3	3	24,701
Northrnimprovement	2	G	5	2	0	1	28,520
Northshore Road	3	G	4	0	0	0	560
Northtobaghdad	3	C	12	1	3	3	98,837
Northtown Will	2	G	6	1	2	0	30,262
Northwest Attitude	3	G	12	2	0	2	36,374
Northwest Hill	6	G	13	1	3	3	53,800
Northwest Native	3	F	4	0	1	0	1,800
Northwester	5	G	1	0	0	0	1,452
Norton Peak	3	F	7	3	1	1	25,540
Norton Street	7	G	11	2	0	2	12,455
Nortouch	5	G	6	3	1	0	74,090
Norway Hope	5	M	9	0	1	2	6,109
Norwellian	2	F	2	1	0	0	9,730
Nor'wester	3	F	9	0	1	3	28,220
Nose The Trade (GB)	6	G	7	1	2	2	125,400
Nose to It	3	C	5	0	0	0	4,715
Nosecondchance	2	F	3	0	2	1	11,500
Nosetothe	6	H	6	0	0	1	1,778
Nosey Rosey	2	F	2	1	0	0	8,028
Nosey Shirley	4	F	11	1	4	1	8,740

Horse	Age	Sex	Sts	1st	2d	3d	Won
Nosho	13	G	6	0	0	0	337
Nosotros Dos	6	G	15	1	3	0	4,665
Nospots	2	F	3	1	1	0	10,190
Nossenko	3	F	10	1	1	1	19,889
Nostalgiaonmymind	10	G	4	0	0	0	280
Nosupeforyou	6	G	13	2	5	2	96,626
Nosy Tanikely	3	F	8	1	1	1	38,340
Not a Bad Boy	3	G	12	1	0	0	9,240
Not a Dollar Off	5	G	11	2	1	1	2,847
Not a Frown	7	M	13	1	3	2	11,603
Not a Question	4	G	13	1	2	3	6,839
Not a Rookie	4	F	3	0	0	0	221
Not Acceptable	6	H	2	0	0	0	0
Not Acclaim	3	G	6	2	0	1	20,170
Not Accountable	5	G	3	0	0	0	638
Not Again Dan	3	G	4	0	1	1	18,228
Not an Illusion	5	M	8	0	2	1	3,500
Not Another One	3	F	10	0	0	2	1,533
Not Any Man	4	G	12	1	2	2	10,510
Not Behavin	3	F	1	0	0	0	0
Not Curable	3	F	8	0	0	0	1,854
Not Dasher	6	G	1	0	0	0	0
Not Enough Dancing	2	F	5	0	0	0	1,800
Not Exactly	3	C	8	1	0	1	5,123
Not for Charlie	6	G	4	1	0	0	3,196
Not for Me	6	G	2	1	0	0	10,102
Not for Nana	6	M	3	0	0	0	0
Not for Profit	4	G	14	1	3	2	16,533
Not for Sam	6	H	6	3	3	0	120,400
Not Half Bad	4	F	3	0	0	0	50
Not Happening	7	G	16	3	2	4	17,524
Not Impossible	6	M	13	1	2	2	14,976
Not in Vain	3	C	6	1	0	1	6,680
Not Missing a Key	2	F	2	0	0	0	280
Not Much	5	G	9	0	4	1	12,308
Not Offensive	3	F	5	0	1	2	12,480
Not On My Watch	3	C	6	1	1	0	8,155
Not Phone (ARG)	6	H	2	1	1	0	34,400
Not So Friendly	3	G	2	0	0	0	245
Not So Gray	2	C	5	0	0	0	368
Not So Quiet	4	G	12	2	2	1	9,610
Not So Slow Joe	3	C	13	3	2	0	29,580
Not So Wicked	4	F	8	1	0	0	6,130
Not Such an Angel	3	G	2	0	0	0	800
Not to Blame	3	F	7	0	1	0	5,350
Not too Nasty	3	F	1	0	0	0	0
Not too Sweet	4	G	15	2	3	2	27,175
Not Yet a Lady	3	F	7	0	0	2	1,563
Not Yet But Maybe	3	F	9	0	1	1	4,118
Not You Me	4	G	17	1	1	3	18,663
Notable Act	3	G	11	3	0	2	49,705
Notable Knight	4	C	7	1	0	0	9,579
Notable Max	4	G	7	0	0	0	2,400
Notable Okie	4	G	9	0	5	1	36,432
Notable Secrets	5	G	5	0	0	1	2,430
Notable Sweep	4	C	9	1	1	2	14,682
Notable Weave	6	G	10	0	0	1	1,424
Notably Frosty	8	G	18	2	3	3	65,065
Notably Mystic	4	F	5	1	2	2	31,720
Notably Slew	4	F	1	0	0	0	105
Notacheapsong	4	C	8	1	1	2	17,132
Notanother Kildew	3	G	2	2	0	0	6,120
Notaphoney	3	F	11	0	2	0	1,992
Notarized	2	C	2	0	1	0	10,200
Notastorm	4	G	8	2	2	0	12,610
Notate	5	G	16	2	1	6	9,747
Notatfirst	4	G	10	1	2	2	10,783
Notavaca	4	C	1	0	0	0	0
Note Appeal	3	G	9	1	0	0	9,290
Note d'Or	4	F	3	0	0	0	180
Note Taker	5	M	2	0	0	0	1,400
Note Whitney	2	C	9	1	1	2	21,165
Noteable	9	M	12	1	2	0	15,625
Noted	3	F	7	1	0	1	5,715
Notes and Quotes	6	M	7	0	1	0	6,261
Note's Princess	2	F	1	0	0	0	205
Noteworthy	4	G	7	2	5	0	32,630
Notfartogo	3	F	5	0	1	1	3,945
Notgonagetemtoday	2	C	2	0	1	0	3,150
Nothankyouplease	3	G	5	0	1	0	3,625
Nothin But Time	5	G	15	2	0	0	21,012
Nothinbutagoodtime	4	F	10	2	1	0	16,070
Nothinbutbadnews	10	G	17	3	5	2	22,357
Nothinbutfastnred	6	M	1	1	0	0	2,700
Nothing	3	C	8	0	0	1	4,325
Nothing But Cat	2	G	3	0	2	1	15,980
Nothing But Klass	3	F	1	0	0	0	0
Nothing But Luck	6	G	2	0	0	0	100
Nothing But Truth	3	G	7	1	0	0	14,860
Nothing Fancy	3	F	19	1	3	3	19,905
Nothing Flat	5	G	3	0	1	1	19,203
Nothing Left	5	G	11	0	2	3	6,500
Nothing Less	3	F	9	2	3	2	25,900
Nothing to Lose	4	C	9	2	3	1	643,200
Nothing Trendy	6	G	4	0	0	3	2,163
Nothinglefttogive	6	G	1	0	0	0	46
Nothingupmysleeve	3	F	4	0	1	0	2,600
Nothinlac'n	3	G	14	3	0	4	23,960
Nothintoit	2	F	2	0	0	0	535
Notice the Magic	7	G	3	0	1	0	10,654
Notimetoquit	3	F	18	3	4	5	69,120
Notinsane	3	F	10	1	0	1	32,200
Notinthecontract	3	G	9	0	0	4	16,840
Notion	8	G	9	0	0	1	1,104
Notis Otis	2	C	5	4	1	0	162,622
Notjustanothertune	5	G	15	2	2	1	11,216
Notjustanytiz	3	F	2	1	0	0	8,391
Notloc	3	G	3	1	0	0	5,470
Notmyfault	4	F	7	0	0	0	9,375
Notnot Slewsthere	3	G	5	1	1	0	6,796
Notone	2	C	6	0	1	1	7,867
Notonetoquit	3	C	12	2	2	1	38,216
Notorious Bandito	5	G	12	1	2	2	18,036
Notorious One	3	G	10	3	1	0	20,318
Notorious Rogue	3	C	11	0	3	1	37,170
Notquietforlong	3	C	7	0	1	2	3,995
Notreallykissable	3	F	3	0	0	1	606
Notreatsforyou	2	F	5	0	0	1	8,890
Notrestraintable	4	F	9	2	1	3	54,492
Notsosaintly	8	G	2	0	0	0	110
Notting Hill (BRZ)	5	M	8	1	1	1	109,656
Nottinghill Gate	7	G	8	0	0	0	1,501
Nottoworry	3	C	2	1	0	0	32,640
Nott's Gold	4	G	9	1	1	0	22,293
Notus	5	G	4	2	0	0	3,805
Nouf	5	G	6	0	2	1	2,699
Nouveau Cool	3	C	5	1	2	0	13,145
Nouveau Riche	6	G	4	1	1	0	6,378
Nova Blanca	4	F	3	0	0	0	900
Nova Creek	3	G	2	0	1	0	1,968
Nova Ice	3	G	5	1	1	1	3,190
Nova River	2	G	1	0	0	0	0
Nova Scotia Norma	2	F	2	1	0	1	3,921
Nova Sin	8	G	9	1	0	3	15,482
Novalotta Gold	3	F	6	0	1	0	1,935
Nova's Star	3	G	4	0	0	0	330
Novel	2	F	4	1	1	2	26,760
Novel Idea	3	G	6	1	0	0	14,791
Novel Robin	6	M	4	0	0	0	654
Novel T Dreamer	4	G	8	0	0	0	6,087
Novelado (CHI)	6	G	16	0	3	3	16,760
Novelista	3	F	13	2	1	1	30,832
Novelty Sue	5	M	5	0	0	0	390
November Payne	6	G	12	2	2	1	8,866
November Rose	5	M	3	0	1	0	2,020
November's Fury	3	G	5	0	0	2	2,164
Novice	4	F	1	0	0	0	0
Novice Prince	7	G	15	0	0	1	3,171
Novus Scofus	9	G	18	2	2	1	8,361
Novwar	6	G	1	0	0	1	920
Now Dats a Storm	2	F	1	0	0	0	713
Now Im Cookin	6	G	1	0	0	0	0
Now My Precious	3	F	2	0	1	0	6,400
Now Navajo	8	G	6	0	2	1	2,632
Now Now	4	F	10	0	0	0	256
Now Playing	6	G	8	1	1	0	27,560
Nowsthechime	3	F	4	0	0	1	868
Nowthen Miss	2	F	1	0	0	0	560

Horse	Age	Sex	Sts	1st	2d	3d	Won
Nowucmenowudon't	5	G	5	0	1	2	2,427
Nowush	8	G	2	1	0	0	6,000
Nowyerbarkin	3	F	3	0	0	0	2,588
Nowyouseeit	5	G	8	2	1	2	22,989
Noyac (IRE)	3	F	11	0	2	1	31,235
Noyana	5	M	12	3	1	1	11,052
Noyes Place	2	G	3	1	0	1	11,775
Nsynctoo	6	G	3	0	0	1	2,040
Nu Cat	5	G	8	1	0	0	11,038
Nu Chance to Dance	4	G	4	2	2	0	12,581
Nu Inspector	5	G	5	0	0	1	676
Nu Lady's Man	2	G	4	0	1	1	4,600
Nu Partner	3	C	5	0	0	0	150
Nu Rage	3	G	6	0	0	0	950
Nu Rays Arabella	2	F	4	1	2	0	24,463
Nuangola	6	G	4	0	1	1	3,563
Nucay's Noodles	2	G	1	0	0	0	0
Nudubya	4	G	2	0	0	0	0
Nuestro Oro	3	F	5	0	0	0	711
Nueva Cat	2	F	1	1	0	0	8,400
Nuevo	5	M	8	2	1	2	8,204
Nugget Field	3	C	3	0	0	0	1,350
Nugget Point	3	F	1	0	0	0	0
Nugget'o Gold	5	M	6	1	2	0	30,567
Nugrayontheblock	5	G	7	1	1	1	27,479
Nuit	4	F	4	0	1	2	4,200
Nukeladen	3	G	11	2	3	0	23,315
Nukes On the Loose	3	G	2	0	0	0	174
Nukidd	3	G	4	1	0	1	6,540
Nule Secundus	3	F	4	0	0	1	1,086
Numattic	4	G	6	2	1	0	11,177
Number	3	C	6	1	0	0	9,620
Number Juan	3	C	9	2	0	1	69,680
Number One Blonde	2	F	1	0	0	0	1,500
Number One Dancer	3	C	3	0	0	0	0
Number One Hammer	6	G	12	0	0	0	2,128
Number One Pegasus	5	G	8	0	1	1	4,705
Number One Sheikh	7	G	12	2	1	2	41,250
Number One Trick	3	G	12	4	1	1	22,680
Number Twentythree	5	H	4	0	0	0	0
Number Two Hammer	3	G	12	2	0	0	8,324
Numbers Don't Lie	2	F	5	0	0	0	2,499
Numbers Talk	2	G	3	0	1	1	2,750
Numeral One	2	C	1	0	0	1	1,296
Numeral Royale	2	C	2	0	1	1	6,880
Numerian	7	G	5	1	0	0	9,366
Numerically	3	F	10	2	1	2	21,030
Numero	6	G	4	0	0	0	353
Numerous Attack	4	G	6	0	0	0	365
Numerous Content	3	C	8	1	2	1	7,600
Numerous Dancer	4	G	13	2	2	2	26,031
Numerous Kidz	5	M	10	0	1	3	11,727
Numerous Lady	4	F	11	1	4	3	29,947
Numerous Luck	2	C	7	0	1	0	17,778
Numerous Moves	3	F	3	0	0	0	1,520
Numerous Rages	3	G	2	0	0	0	0
Numerous Squares	3	G	9	0	4	2	11,924
Numerousasthestars	4	F	10	2	3	1	95,978
Numerus Reasons	3	F	6	0	0	0	1,357
Nun On the Run	7	M	5	0	0	0	350
Nun too Nice	2	F	6	1	0	2	13,930
Nunsense	4	F	4	0	0	0	512
Nunziata	5	M	18	1	4	5	24,827
Nureyevictory	4	F	3	0	0	0	0
Nureyev's Halo	5	G	10	0	2	2	5,200
Nurey's Thunder	6	G	2	0	0	0	1,760
Nurse Alice	2	F	4	1	1	0	7,286
Nurse Betty	3	F	9	2	3	0	45,934
Nurse Culkin	3	F	7	2	3	2	83,560
Nurse Dora	5	M	9	0	2	0	3,665
Nurse Laura	7	M	3	0	0	1	794
Nurse Margurita	7	M	13	0	0	1	2,502
Nurse Robin	5	M	12	2	1	1	11,080
Nurse Rose	4	F	4	0	0	0	0
Nurse Type	5	M	5	0	0	0	160
Nushka	2	F	2	0	0	0	3,420
Nut Lovin	3	F	8	1	1	0	19,550
Nuth N Smart	3	G	2	0	0	0	0
Nuther Gold Mine	4	G	9	1	1	0	8,610
Nuther Mexican Bob	3	C	10	2	1	0	10,485
Nuthin But Kuntry	7	G	4	0	0	0	206
Nutter Bold Ivor	10	G	1	0	0	0	0
Nutty	3	F	2	0	0	0	195
Nuttyboom	4	G	10	2	2	2	47,340
Nyanza	2	F	2	0	0	0	365
Nycity	4	G	1	0	0	0	0
Nykee	3	F	10	1	0	1	17,305
Nylo	4	G	6	0	0	1	2,360
Nyoka	3	G	1	0	0	0	0
Nypuddles	5	M	12	1	3	1	25,097
Nyramba (GB)	3	F	8	0	2	1	63,669
Nystar	4	F	8	2	0	0	15,543
Nystateofmind	6	H	3	0	0	0	550
Nytone	5	H	1	0	0	0	123
Nyuk Nyuk Nyuk	3	G	7	1	1	2	130,434
O' Actor	4	G	11	1	0	0	8,097
O and A	4	F	6	2	0	2	36,018
O B Girl One	5	M	8	0	2	1	2,702
O' classic One	5	G	6	0	0	0	80
O Darlin Boy	5	G	8	1	1	2	10,089
O D's Accelerator	3	G	17	1	3	4	6,911
O Golly Gee	10	G	12	0	0	3	3,012
O Howrude	5	M	8	3	1	1	55,464
O I Runaway	3	C	6	1	1	0	20,985
O K Caracey	5	G	13	2	0	0	23,963
O K Elsa	4	F	1	0	0	0	140
O K Kate	4	F	1	0	0	0	250
O K Okie	3	G	6	0	0	0	1,845
O K Pard	4	C	9	2	2	0	12,417
O K to Love	4	F	4	0	1	0	6,060
O K Topless	2	F	8	1	4	3	30,614
O K With Me	7	G	9	1	0	1	9,662
O Kudsai	4	F	15	2	3	3	15,221
O Linda Lu	5	M	16	0	2	3	6,950
O Lo	7	M	12	2	1	3	25,680
O Loretta	2	F	6	1	0	0	10,340
O My Maria	4	F	6	1	0	0	19,260
O My Peggy Slew	2	F	1	0	0	0	420
O Nectar	4	F	9	3	2	1	47,160
O' Ole Smokes	4	G	8	1	3	1	20,818
O' Ririn	6	M	20	1	3	4	12,308
O' Ryan	2	G	5	1	0	0	6,661
O Sequoyah	5	G	18	1	2	0	11,264
O So Magic	2	F	2	0	0	1	1,685
O Two O Two O Two	2	F	5	1	0	0	4,268
O U Bet	5	M	9	1	2	1	38,036
O Zone Layer	3	C	3	1	0	0	36,960
O. B. Quiet	7	G	7	1	0	3	19,548
O. E.'s Mark	2	C	1	0	0	0	0
O. K. by Machalda	4	F	3	0	0	0	0
O. K. Corral	4	F	6	0	1	0	5,000
O. K. Mikie	3	G	6	1	1	0	114,425
O. K. to Go	4	G	5	0	3	1	15,435
Oak Forest	2	C	4	0	1	0	6,760
Oak Hall	8	G	1	1	0	0	12,150
Oak Hill	4	C	4	0	0	2	7,330
Oak Mills	4	F	1	0	0	0	60
Oak Run	7	M	9	0	0	1	3,281
Oakcrest Dancer	4	F	3	0	0	0	540
Oakfield	3	F	3	0	0	0	0
Oakgrove	3	F	8	3	1	0	15,874
Oakies Little Star	4	F	1	0	0	0	43
Oakland Boy	5	H	6	0	0	0	611
Oakland Hills	3	F	3	0	0	0	0
Oaks Fever	3	F	1	0	0	0	0
Oaks Victoria	2	F	2	0	0	0	2,160
Oakton	4	F	2	0	0	1	832
Oarsman	5	G	1	0	0	0	80
Oath of Office	4	C	14	3	4	0	47,040
Oatka Apollos Gold	5	H	7	0	0	1	1,646
Oatka Dans Reign	3	C	11	1	2	1	11,015
Oatka Idas Destiny	5	M	9	3	3	2	54,389
Oatka Little Girl	6	M	10	0	0	1	1,447
Oatka Magic Trick	5	H	13	1	0	2	6,944
Oatka Trail Faith	4	F	14	0	0	8	6,869
Oatsville	3	F	4	0	0	0	244
Oba Oba	2	F	3	0	0	0	315
Obeah Man	9	G	3	0	0	0	339

Horse	Age	Sex	Sts	1st	2d	3d	Won
Obermutten	3	G	12	2	2	0	20,748
Oberon's Girl	2	F	1	0	0	0	230
Oberwald	4	G	17	5	1	6	84,936
Obey the Queen	4	F	4	1	0	0	3,858
Obeya	6	M	2	0	0	0	158
Obill	7	G	5	0	0	1	1,710
Object of Desire	3	F	5	0	0	0	487
Object of Virtue	4	F	1	0	0	0	163
O'Blaney	4	F	13	1	1	4	33,560
Oblat	3	C	2	0	1	0	3,600
Obligate	3	F	4	0	0	0	420
Obligation North	5	M	4	1	1	0	10,380
Obliquity	4	G	7	2	0	1	98,751
Oblivious	3	F	4	2	0	1	37,880
Oblong	5	G	1	0	0	0	85
Obnoxious Angel	3	F	2	0	0	0	200
O'Bradovich	4	G	13	1	4	2	31,000
Obrien	4	F	15	1	4	1	12,920
O'Britt	3	F	4	0	0	0	589
O'Bryan's Luck	6	G	11	1	0	4	12,469
Ob'sbaby B	4	G	8	2	1	1	20,130
Obscene Prospect	3	F	12	1	0	2	8,530
Observe	4	F	2	0	0	0	0
Obsessedtoimpress	5	G	2	0	0	0	0
Obsidian	2	C	3	0	0	1	2,850
Obstacle	5	H	3	1	0	1	13,748
Obstinate	4	F	17	4	3	4	38,943
Obtained	3	G	9	2	0	0	9,825
Obtuse	3	G	2	0	0	0	1,400
Obvious Vision	3	G	10	2	1	1	19,750
Obviously	2	F	5	1	1	0	42,550
Ocala Bandit	3	G	4	1	0	0	3,953
Ocala Cat	3	C	2	0	0	0	420
Ocala Eagle	8	H	7	2	0	1	5,701
Ocala Outlaw	3	C	21	1	1	1	7,550
Ocala Quaker	3	F	2	0	0	0	640
Ocala Rose	3	F	9	1	1	2	19,437
Ocala Saint	2	F	2	0	0	0	510
Ocala Story	6	G	4	0	0	2	2,858
Ocala True	5	M	2	0	0	1	935
Ocala's Appeal	5	G	1	0	1	0	1,920
Ocalasecret	5	G	6	0	0	1	619
O'Calaway	4	G	16	2	2	2	13,251
Ocali Flash	7	G	5	1	1	0	16,401
Ocaso (PER)	5	G	3	0	1	0	1,156
Occatilla	7	M	21	1	2	4	19,807
Occult	4	C	17	1	3	2	33,090
Occupied	4	G	17	4	4	2	7,950
Ocean Anne	3	F	1	1	0	0	4,510
Ocean Beams	2	F	1	0	0	0	0
Ocean Bun	4	C	6	1	0	0	6,458
Ocean City	3	C	10	1	2	1	30,920
Ocean Commotion	5	G	6	1	0	0	4,050
Ocean Cove	4	G	3	0	0	2	1,326
Ocean Drive	4	F	11	4	3	3	505,900
Ocean Effect	4	F	5	0	2	0	6,760
Ocean Fox	4	F	10	1	1	2	8,559
Ocean Front	7	G	11	1	1	1	11,720
Ocean Gate	6	M	7	1	0	1	8,493
Ocean Glory	2	F	1	0	0	0	0
Ocean Grand	2	G	3	0	0	0	1,788
Ocean Intrigue	5	G	5	1	0	1	7,996
Ocean King	3	G	12	2	2	1	27,832
Ocean Lane	2	F	3	1	0	0	15,670
Ocean Locater	9	G	3	0	0	0	0
Ocean Miss	5	M	15	1	1	2	4,756
Ocean Park	4	C	4	0	0	0	293
Ocean Pointe	6	G	1	0	0	0	178
Ocean Quest	5	G	8	0	3	3	10,165
Ocean Reef	2	C	7	0	0	1	4,550
Ocean Silk	4	F	12	2	2	3	138,330
Ocean Squall	11	G	3	0	0	0	785
Ocean Symphony	3	G	5	2	0	3	40,350
Ocean Wave	2	C	4	0	1	0	3,571
Oceana Flyer	8	M	1	0	0	0	0
Oceana Miss	3	F	9	1	0	1	3,550
Oceania	3	F	1	0	0	0	600
Oceanic	4	G	16	3	3	2	38,610
Oceano	3	C	10	2	1	2	53,800
Oceans of Love	5	M	6	0	0	0	495
Oceans Reality	4	F	4	0	1	0	4,200
Oceanus (BRZ)	5	H	3	1	0	0	25,560
Ocelot	4	F	7	0	3	1	6,719
Och Tamale	3	G	8	3	1	0	67,540
Ocho	3	F	7	0	0	1	840
Ocho Negro	3	C	3	0	0	0	0
Ochoco Kitten	6	M	3	0	1	1	1,050
Ocoonita	3	F	6	1	0	2	16,278
Ocotillo	3	C	11	1	4	0	46,960
Octagon	4	F	9	2	0	0	50,610
Octibbeha	4	F	1	0	0	0	0
October Blues	5	G	10	0	2	2	8,680
October Dreamer	6	M	11	2	2	2	8,780
October Eve	2	F	2	0	0	0	975
October Glory (IRE)	3	F	8	2	0	1	51,030
October Optimist	6	M	11	2	4	2	27,070
October Storm	4	G	6	1	1	0	10,756
October Winds	3	F	2	0	0	0	1,555
Oda Mar	5	G	1	0	0	0	64
Odbeaslewpy	8	G	5	1	1	2	4,726
Odd Number	4	F	1	0	0	0	140
Odd Ree Jay	3	F	5	0	0	0	340
Odd Testamony	5	G	7	1	0	2	9,108
Odd You Should Ask	4	C	1	0	0	0	95
Odds Maker	3	C	2	0	0	0	220
Odds On	3	C	2	1	0	0	29,400
Oddsonjack	9	G	7	0	1	0	3,016
Ode to New York	4	G	8	1	0	0	11,374
Odelien	6	G	16	1	2	1	16,217
Odie	5	G	1	0	0	0	60
Odin Lad	3	G	5	0	2	0	5,678
Odyle a Genius	4	G	3	0	0	0	466
Oedy's Riches	6	M	1	0	0	0	153
Oeil de Tempete	3	G	8	0	0	1	3,840
O'Ell	4	F	16	0	6	0	10,513
Of a Lifetime	2	F	1	0	1	0	7,000
Of All Times	3	G	6	0	0	0	5,122
Of Gold	3	F	10	0	0	3	1,299
Of Good Repute	2	C	1	0	0	0	115
Of Legal Age	4	F	9	2	1	2	55,150
Ofcenterditchdiggr	3	F	12	1	3	2	9,909
Off by Three	2	F	3	0	0	1	2,500
Off My Case	3	F	3	0	1	0	1,170
Off N Annie	4	F	9	1	1	1	19,817
Off On a Tangent	3	F	9	3	2	2	89,690
Off Shore Prospect	5	H	17	3	2	2	25,173
Off the Chain	3	G	14	3	1	0	17,350
Off the Glass	5	G	10	4	0	2	75,210
Off the Richter	2	F	1	0	0	0	700
Off the Screen	6	G	10	0	0	2	1,919
Off the Wagon	3	C	4	0	0	0	455
Off to the Opera	5	M	9	2	3	2	37,635
Off Track Firstcat	4	F	8	1	0	1	5,661
Offensive	8	G	16	2	0	2	9,096
Offensively	3	F	6	0	0	0	0
Offhand	5	H	12	1	0	1	3,011
Office At Night	3	F	8	3	0	0	31,108
Office Attire	3	F	2	0	0	0	0
Office Ghost	4	C	9	1	1	1	25,200
Officer Nasty	4	G	9	1	0	2	3,957
Officer One	2	C	1	0	0	1	4,950
Officer's Mess	3	G	1	0	0	0	0
Officer's Sword	6	G	11	2	2	3	31,770
Official Account	3	F	11	5	1	1	69,875
Offlee Wild	4	C	4	2	1	0	335,640
Offshore News	3	F	5	1	2	0	14,700
Offspring	6	G	15	3	1	1	26,488
Offthebench	3	F	13	2	4	3	19,830
O'Fire Holler	8	G	2	0	0	0	235
Ogaadeen	3	F	6	1	0	0	8,320
Ogato Voador	3	G	7	1	2	1	6,167
Ogeechee	3	F	7	1	1	2	10,835
Oggi	4	F	14	1	2	5	47,848
Ogilia (GB)	7	M	1	0	0	0	0
Oglala Sue	6	M	6	0	0	1	10,850
Ogle	6	M	15	0	3	1	11,180
Ogotasecret	4	G	6	1	1	0	6,007
O'Greedy	3	G	10	2	1	4	13,265

Horse	Age	Sex	Sts	1st	2d	3d	Won
Ogygian's Rose	3	F	4	1	1	1	6,740
Ogymadi	4	F	1	0	0	0	984
Oh Absolut	3	C	6	0	0	0	1,049
Oh Be Joyful	3	F	3	0	0	1	420
Oh Boy Oh Boy	4	G	8	1	1	2	7,584
Oh by Golly Olly	4	G	3	0	0	0	197
Oh Captain	4	G	10	0	1	0	1,953
Oh Carolina	4	F	10	0	0	0	5,412
Oh Dad	2	C	1	0	0	0	0
Oh Daddy	2	C	1	0	0	0	105
Oh Dazzle Me	3	F	1	0	0	0	0
Oh Derek	4	G	13	2	3	4	20,606
Oh Domino	2	C	1	0	0	0	150
Oh Ess Who	3	G	3	0	0	0	37
Oh Gordon Look	4	G	4	0	1	0	3,293
Oh Gracie	9	H	8	4	1	1	38,697
Oh I Do	3	G	8	0	1	0	9,151
Oh I See	2	F	4	0	2	1	11,180
Oh Kay Girl	4	F	10	1	0	0	21,798
Oh Keanna	3	F	11	1	1	1	6,202
Oh Mar	8	H	3	1	0	0	11,680
Oh Mr. Chequer	3	C	7	0	1	1	3,490
Oh My Coyote	3	C	2	0	0	0	275
Oh My Gosh Magali	4	C	2	0	0	0	0
Oh My Harlan	4	C	8	0	0	0	1,863
Oh My Heck	3	F	2	1	0	0	2,472
Oh My Honor	4	F	2	1	0	0	5,400
Oh My Lordie	6	M	10	1	2	3	13,010
Oh My Love	6	M	5	0	0	0	905
Oh My Surprise	3	F	8	1	1	2	64,953
Oh No Apolo	4	G	5	0	2	1	7,580
Oh No Seven Out	3	G	4	0	0	0	190
Oh Oleg	3	G	12	2	0	3	35,326
Oh Peggy Sue	2	F	7	0	0	1	4,170
Oh Pine	4	F	13	1	1	5	63,394
Oh Rio	3	F	9	2	0	2	15,230
Oh Sable	5	M	7	0	1	1	11,070
Oh Say Glory	5	G	17	1	5	2	12,300
Oh Say Vicki	7	M	4	1	1	0	38,040
Oh Say's Pleasure	4	F	3	0	0	0	0
Oh So Easy	4	F	9	3	3	0	120,196
Oh So Gold	2	F	1	0	0	1	1,980
Oh So Sultry	4	G	9	2	3	1	46,791
Oh So Wonderful	5	M	3	1	0	0	10,865
Oh Take (BRZ)	6	G	9	0	0	0	1,662
Oh Travis	6	G	2	0	0	0	325
Oh Tri Avalli	3	G	6	0	1	0	4,834
Oh What a Cat	4	G	5	0	1	0	1,342
Oh What a Dream	2	C	1	0	0	0	0
Oh What a Storm	3	C	2	0	0	0	1,200
Oh Wow	3	G	6	0	2	2	6,255
Ohbedawn	4	F	1	0	0	0	0
Ohbeegeewhyen	3	F	8	1	0	0	33,067
Ohboyohboyohboy	2	F	3	0	0	0	650
Ohhh Hello Numan	6	G	7	2	2	1	14,025
Ohigottago	2	F	4	0	0	1	2,487
Ohio	4	G	6	1	2	0	10,067
Ohio Bob	4	G	1	0	0	0	0
Ohio Don	3	G	10	0	0	2	2,372
Ohio Rose	3	F	13	0	1	2	6,368
Ohlmeyer	3	G	4	0	0	0	4,469
Ohlund	2	C	1	0	0	0	0
Ohmychief	4	F	1	0	0	0	120
Ohmyfuzzy	4	G	8	1	2	0	9,789
Ohni	4	G	16	2	3	3	18,450
Ohpoos	5	M	5	2	1	0	15,018
Ohsoamerican	6	M	12	1	3	1	10,116
Ohso'slilamerican	2	C	1	0	0	0	150
Ohtobeastar	3	F	6	0	0	0	2,815
Ohwhataparade	3	G	8	0	3	2	14,694
Oil Man	10	G	16	2	1	5	5,313
Oiltemp	7	H	2	0	0	0	105
Ojeta	6	M	7	0	0	0	264
Ojibway	3	G	13	5	3	3	156,685
Ok Express	4	F	14	2	4	2	19,140
Ok Girl	3	F	5	1	0	1	1,182
Ok Let's Go	2	G	5	1	1	1	35,835
Ok Monsoon	3	G	9	1	1	0	17,860
Ok Thunderbird	4	F	9	0	0	0	450
Ok Travler	3	G	4	0	1	0	2,775
Okahumpka (GB)	3	C	9	0	2	2	5,375
Okanogan Anna	3	F	1	0	0	0	0
Okay Olay	5	G	11	2	2	2	5,875
Okay Oonay	3	F	2	0	0	0	135
Okay Renee	4	F	6	0	0	1	3,495
Okaya	3	F	9	2	2	1	29,208
Okeechobee Lady	4	F	17	2	7	3	24,194
Okey Dokey Doc	4	F	9	1	0	3	11,970
Okie	2	F	4	0	0	1	1,735
Okie City Cowgirl	4	F	6	1	0	0	1,748
Okie Commotion	4	G	6	0	1	1	5,695
Okie Dokie Kookie	3	F	12	3	0	2	39,525
Okie Dozer	2	C	5	2	0	0	47,799
Okie Dream	2	G	7	1	0	1	6,035
Okie I Am	8	G	9	1	1	2	12,335
Okie Nicole	2	F	5	2	0	1	34,190
Okie Quit Drinkin'	5	G	5	0	0	1	856
Okie Riddler	3	G	1	0	0	0	0
Okie Style	3	G	3	1	0	0	17,500
Okie Thunder	4	G	7	1	1	2	11,580
Okie Twister	2	C	2	0	0	0	105
Okie Wildcat	3	G	8	1	0	0	4,161
Okiegolucky	3	G	4	0	0	1	4,250
Oklahoma	5	G	13	0	2	0	1,076
Oklahoma by Storm	3	F	2	0	0	1	300
Oklahoma Natural	3	C	7	1	1	2	12,509
Oklahoma Option	7	G	5	0	1	1	1,682
Oklahoma Rose	4	F	11	2	0	1	6,563
Oklahoma Spirit	6	G	9	0	0	1	1,238
Oklahoma Star	5	M	3	1	0	0	12,055
Oklahoma Way	8	G	13	0	0	3	2,622
Oklahoma Wind	2	F	2	0	0	0	210
Oklahomalegend	3	C	1	0	0	0	120
Okolona	2	C	4	1	0	0	6,900
Ol Buddy	4	C	2	0	0	0	0
Ol Fifty	3	G	10	1	1	3	40,917
Ol' Glory	4	G	3	0	0	0	0
Ol Mike	5	G	11	1	1	3	5,048
Ol' Mine Road	3	G	16	1	0	4	12,859
Ol' Scarecrow	2	C	5	1	1	0	22,508
Ol' Stewball	3	G	5	0	0	0	336
Ola Amor	5	M	16	2	1	1	16,994
Ola Docura	3	F	9	1	1	2	24,117
Ola Flake	3	F	9	1	0	2	6,586
Ola Mae Belle	3	F	1	0	1	0	2,700
Olafs Prospect	4	F	1	0	0	0	65
Olanda	3	F	4	1	1	0	49,188
Olan's Boy	6	H	1	0	0	0	0
Old Black Coyote	7	G	14	0	1	3	5,990
Old Chapel Mission	2	F	4	0	0	0	168
Old Chenin	4	C	2	0	0	0	330
Old Chinese Copy	3	F	11	3	1	1	102,420
Old Coin	5	G	6	2	0	0	8,850
Old Court's Cat	5	M	6	1	2	2	25,880
Old Coyote	3	G	8	3	0	1	7,800
Old Crow	4	G	3	0	0	1	8,800
Old Deuteronomy	3	C	5	1	1	0	48,255
Old Dixie Home	4	F	10	1	0	1	18,555
Old Duke Puffer	7	G	14	5	1	2	72,455
Old Fashion Girl	3	F	6	3	2	0	84,016
Old Forest	6	G	8	1	0	0	3,644
Old Forester	3	C	7	3	3	1	111,600
Old Friends	6	G	7	1	0	1	6,036
Old Gold	3	G	5	1	2	1	32,550
Old Happy	7	G	9	1	4	1	21,087
Old Indian Sign	10	G	7	1	0	2	3,840
Old Ironsides	3	C	11	2	2	1	43,400
Old Joe E	4	G	3	0	0	0	158
Old Lee	3	G	12	2	4	1	151,705
Old Liar	3	C	1	0	0	0	170
Old Lodge	8	G	7	0	0	2	4,300
Old Man Boots	3	G	3	1	1	0	38,200
Old Man's Delite	8	G	16	2	4	4	18,546
Old Mizzou	7	G	10	4	3	2	30,310
Old Mother Goose	4	F	10	2	1	4	66,580
Old Oak Tree	5	G	7	1	0	0	1,066
Old Salt	5	H	2	0	0	0	383
Old Salty	3	G	10	1	0	1	5,830

Horse	Age	Sex	Sts	1st	2d	3d	Won
Old School	4	G	1	0	1	0	1,500
Old Scotch	5	G	15	0	1	1	7,065
Old Scudder	3	G	16	3	2	1	26,700
Old Shanachie	10	G	8	1	1	1	14,720
Old Snively	7	G	15	2	1	0	8,357
Old Spanish Trail	2	F	2	0	0	0	0
Old Sport	3	G	8	1	1	2	11,298
Old Spring	3	C	11	1	2	0	13,060
Old Suede	4	C	2	0	0	0	128
Old Sugar Shoes	3	G	3	0	0	0	1,650
Old Tavern	6	G	4	1	0	0	7,868
Old Time High	4	G	9	1	0	0	952
Old Time Savings	3	C	1	0	0	0	0
Old Time Stories	5	M	9	1	2	3	8,100
Old Twisted Coyote	3	C	11	0	2	0	6,336
Old Vice	3	G	7	0	1	2	4,094
Old Warrior	4	G	23	2	3	4	30,316
Older and Wiser	3	G	17	1	2	2	17,568
Older Whiskey	4	G	13	2	1	0	13,287
Oldfields	8	G	6	2	0	1	15,060
Oldies But Goodies	3	F	1	0	0	0	0
Old'nred	4	G	4	0	1	0	2,070
Ole Bad Man	9	G	7	1	0	0	9,558
Ole Bin	3	C	2	0	0	0	324
Ole Blue Boy	5	G	2	0	0	0	0
Ole Charlie	2	C	2	0	0	0	720
Ole Cheryl	4	F	7	1	1	1	23,390
Ole Dixie	3	C	5	0	0	0	520
Ole Don	4	G	21	5	7	5	45,530
Ole Faunty	5	G	5	2	1	0	214,240
Ole Flat Top	3	G	6	1	1	0	8,770
Ole Miss Twist	4	F	9	1	1	1	21,026
Ole Plugg	3	G	11	1	0	3	4,481
Ole Rebel	5	H	12	5	2	1	178,500
Ole Rivers	5	H	2	0	0	0	0
Ole' Takeover	5	G	18	1	2	3	8,892
Olechunkofcoal	10	G	6	0	0	0	0
Ole'elena	4	F	1	0	0	0	0
O'Lee's Story	4	F	12	2	4	1	38,503
O'Lees Wish	5	M	12	3	2	0	12,482
Olen	3	C	3	0	0	0	0
Olen's Deal	2	G	4	0	1	1	2,750
Oleo Med Girl	3	F	11	1	2	1	10,824
Ole's Lightening	3	G	11	0	2	0	2,920
Olga S	3	F	7	0	0	1	1,785
Oligarca	3	G	8	0	0	0	1,283
Olive Gold	4	F	3	0	0	0	0
Oliver Biscuit	3	G	4	1	0	0	17,325
Oliver Mellors	6	G	14	1	1	2	15,321
Oliver Street	3	C	11	2	1	1	66,585
Oliver Woodman	3	G	9	1	1	0	18,506
Olivers Crossing	4	G	9	2	1	1	52,340
Olivers Success	3	C	14	3	0	4	34,210
Olivia Jo	5	M	2	0	0	0	230
Olivia's Account	5	G	7	0	0	1	1,522
Olivia's Amour	4	F	10	4	2	1	25,805
Olivia's Dollar	5	M	9	2	0	2	35,485
Olivia's Notebook	4	F	14	3	3	5	65,020
Olivias Strawberry	2	F	1	0	0	0	92
Ollie Eupe	5	G	2	0	0	0	0
Olly Blast	3	G	10	4	0	1	27,977
Olmita	4	F	5	0	0	1	1,680
Olmodavor	5	H	6	1	2	1	367,000
Olmos Creek	4	G	12	1	1	3	11,962
Olviopol	4	F	2	0	1	1	7,290
Olympia Fields	2	C	4	1	2	0	81,082
Olympia Prince	5	H	10	0	2	1	5,820
Olympian	7	G	6	3	1	0	85,680
Olympian Torch	3	G	13	0	0	1	4,500
Olympic Advice	4	F	8	2	2	1	65,120
Olympic Bluff	4	C	6	0	0	0	2,151
Olympic Bon	4	C	1	0	0	0	0
Olympic Bonfire	3	F	9	0	2	1	8,555
Olympic City	2	C	2	0	1	0	9,225
Olympic Contender	4	C	12	1	1	2	10,538
Olympic Emblem	3	F	6	2	1	0	35,340
Olympic Flag	2	C	1	0	1	0	4,800
Olympic Gal	3	F	12	0	0	1	5,806
Olympic Hero	2	C	1	0	0	0	34
Olympic Image	3	F	7	0	0	1	2,795
Olympic Junction	4	G	12	0	2	1	3,110
Olympic Light	6	G	4	0	2	2	7,600
Olympic Linda	3	F	2	0	0	0	800
Olympic Miler	2	G	3	0	0	0	6,455
Olympic Miracle	5	G	4	0	0	0	522
Olympic Moment	4	G	6	1	0	0	6,408
Olympic Night	5	M	1	0	0	0	0
Olympic Power	3	G	9	1	0	2	12,162
Olympic Skier	4	F	12	2	2	3	19,677
Olympic Success	7	G	9	0	1	5	13,070
Olympic Tryst	3	F	8	0	0	1	1,228
Olympic U S A	2	G	3	0	0	0	415
Olympic Year	3	F	2	0	0	1	6,195
Olympio Girl	3	F	4	1	0	0	2,644
Olympionikes	3	G	5	0	0	1	1,770
Olympio's Dream	4	F	6	1	0	1	4,170
Olympio's Pride	3	G	10	2	2	1	10,488
Olympio's Song	3	C	1	0	0	0	400
Olympus Glory	3	F	5	0	0	0	1,605
Oly's Oak	2	C	3	0	2	1	20,720
Oly's Oasis	2	F	4	0	1	1	5,245
Oly's Opening	2	F	5	0	0	1	4,165
Oma Rosa	2	F	1	0	0	0	400
Omaggio	3	C	7	0	0	1	11,696
Omaha Brave	3	C	11	2	3	4	48,020
Omaha Envy	4	F	13	3	0	2	15,285
Omali's Action	4	F	15	1	0	1	9,730
Omali's Player	3	G	17	1	2	5	8,168
O'Malley	5	G	18	1	3	3	33,251
Omanhene	4	C	4	0	0	0	710
O'Mariah	6	M	4	2	0	1	15,345
Omega Code	4	C	3	0	0	0	727
Omen	8	G	5	0	0	1	370
Omen Way	9	G	13	2	1	3	16,478
Omens Lil Angel	2	F	1	0	0	0	0
Ometsz (IRE)	3	F	7	3	1	0	65,652
Omeya (CHI)	4	F	6	2	0	1	44,350
O'Mighty Roolah	4	G	4	0	0	0	0
Ominous	4	C	9	0	3	2	33,805
Omit the Dividend	6	G	2	0	0	0	540
Omni	3	G	6	0	0	0	439
Omnia Vincit Amor	3	F	2	0	0	1	1,772
On a Cruise	3	F	7	1	0	1	9,300
On a Curve	4	G	13	1	1	1	10,155
On a Dark Knight	4	G	6	1	1	2	1,609
On a Dream	3	F	11	0	3	2	14,210
On a Rise	3	G	7	0	0	0	728
On Account of Me	3	F	5	1	0	0	58,730
On American Ground	3	F	10	0	2	0	4,114
On Andy's Birthday	2	F	4	0	1	1	1,740
On Approach	3	G	4	0	0	2	3,542
On April's Dawn	4	F	3	0	0	0	0
On Cat's Feet	4	F	4	1	0	0	2,998
On Command	4	F	14	3	1	2	14,065
On Easy Street	6	G	3	0	0	0	369
On El Bon	6	G	15	3	2	5	9,508
On Exhibit	4	G	13	1	2	1	20,729
On Going Girl	3	F	7	0	0	0	224
On High	4	F	4	1	0	1	13,821
On Leave	3	G	7	0	1	1	1,730
On Liberty	10	G	14	4	4	1	45,090
On Location	3	F	4	0	0	1	3,140
On London Time	2	F	5	2	0	1	31,440
On Manoeuvres	2	F	3	1	0	0	6,709
On My Birthday	4	G	7	0	1	1	4,472
On My Case	4	C	14	1	0	2	10,494
On My Mind	3	F	2	0	0	0	740
On My Wall	4	F	2	0	0	1	1,155
On Nike's Wings	3	F	3	0	0	0	319
On On On On On On	3	G	12	1	0	0	3,480
On One's	3	C	3	0	0	0	0
On Patrol	3	C	3	1	0	0	5,844
On Point	7	G	2	0	0	0	600
On Prospect Street	3	F	1	0	0	1	2,300
On Rush	4	F	9	0	0	2	1,826
On Rye	6	H	5	0	0	1	7,342
On Silent Wings	3	F	3	0	0	1	5,341
On Silver Wings	4	F	7	0	4	1	13,440

Horse	Age	Sex	Sts	1st	2d	3d	Won
On the Acorn (GB)	3	C	10	2	0	3	94,280
On the Alert	6	M	5	0	0	0	354
On the Ave	3	G	8	3	2	0	32,871
On the Balance	2	C	2	0	0	0	453
On the Bay	6	G	7	0	1	4	8,235
On the Beam	4	G	2	0	0	0	2,520
On the Bill Daily	4	C	7	0	3	1	2,720
On the Bus	4	F	7	3	1	1	171,220
On the Course	4	G	9	5	0	1	133,195
On the Deck	5	M	2	0	0	0	345
On the Defensive	3	F	9	2	0	1	15,226
On the Down Lo	3	C	1	0	0	0	50
On the Edge	2	F	2	0	0	0	282
On the Expressway	5	M	10	0	1	0	3,667
On the Fan	7	G	16	3	0	7	51,482
On the Game	6	H	13	2	3	2	68,632
On the Go	3	F	6	0	0	0	790
On the Main Line	4	G	9	1	0	2	7,126
On the Mantle	2	F	3	2	0	0	17,280
On the Porch	2	C	3	1	0	1	32,490
On the Prowl	2	C	1	1	0	0	22,200
On the Q Tea	4	F	3	0	0	0	0
On the Reservation	3	G	8	1	1	2	19,125
On the Right Side	3	G	6	1	1	1	13,480
On the River	2	C	2	0	1	1	12,300
On the Severn	4	G	17	1	2	4	8,054
On the Tee	8	G	11	3	1	1	13,314
On the Tour	9	G	9	0	0	0	0
On the Waves (BRZ)	3	C	1	0	0	0	0
On the Way Out	2	F	5	1	1	2	14,635
On Thin Ice	3	G	7	4	0	1	55,710
On Time Jo	3	G	6	0	1	0	1,320
On to Boston	2	G	3	0	0	0	807
On to Richmond	6	G	6	1	3	0	42,393
On Ulises Island	4	F	6	0	0	0	994
On View	5	M	2	0	0	0	840
On Wild Ground	2	F	2	1	0	0	4,566
On Wisconsin	3	C	3	0	0	0	480
Ona	7	M	3	0	0	0	0
Ona Rampage	3	F	10	0	4	4	49,444
Onasilverplatter	6	H	4	1	0	0	4,444
Onastar	5	G	7	0	0	2	1,049
Onawingandaprayer	7	G	3	0	0	0	0
Once a Canuck	3	F	5	0	1	2	5,186
Once a Promise	3	F	11	1	0	0	5,310
Once in France	2	C	3	0	0	1	3,450
Once Is Not Enough	3	F	4	0	0	0	660
Once It Happens	7	G	7	1	0	1	3,679
Once Rich	6	G	8	0	0	0	2,815
Oncearoundtwice	3	C	9	1	1	2	42,100
Onceinafullmoon	8	G	12	0	0	0	542
Onda	3	F	3	0	0	0	1,270
Onda Calida	3	F	10	1	1	1	18,611
Onda Ray	4	F	12	2	3	4	23,575
Ondro	9	G	1	0	0	0	40
One Allie Cat	2	F	3	0	1	0	5,000
One and Done	4	G	15	3	6	1	69,794
One and Only	3	F	8	1	1	1	20,617
One and Only You	4	F	9	1	0	0	9,495
One Axe Falls	2	C	2	0	0	0	0
One Bad Dude	7	G	8	2	3	0	19,220
One Bad Sister	3	F	12	2	5	0	31,042
One Bell	6	G	2	0	0	0	0
One Bell Boy	5	G	15	4	3	4	40,880
One Below Zero	4	G	8	0	0	0	1,220
One Blue Tech	4	F	2	0	0	1	2,280
One Call Close	7	G	8	1	1	1	8,220
One Chance Fancy	3	F	7	0	1	3	5,661
One Charming Devil	3	F	9	0	3	2	28,963
One Classy Echo	4	C	5	0	0	0	0
One Colony	4	C	14	1	3	3	44,756
One Crazy Lady	3	F	9	1	1	1	14,970
One El of a Lady	2	F	2	1	0	0	10,320
One Excessive Lady	3	F	1	0	0	0	480
One Eye	3	G	5	0	0	0	385
One Eyed Bandit	4	F	9	1	0	0	5,172
One Eyed Gambler	3	G	4	0	1	1	2,681
One Eyed Jackie	5	M	10	1	2	2	30,575
One Eyed Joker	6	G	8	1	3	1	50,560

Horse	Age	Sex	Sts	1st	2d	3d	Won
One Eyed Peak	4	G	8	2	0	0	5,249
One Eyed Willing	4	G	11	2	0	1	25,420
One Eyes Wild	3	G	4	0	0	1	1,466
One Fast Cowgirl	2	F	3	1	1	1	14,929
One Fein Dad	2	C	4	0	0	2	12,640
One Fine Affair	2	G	3	1	0	0	19,276
One Fine Lover	4	F	6	2	0	0	33,720
One Fine Shweetie	5	M	14	1	4	6	96,531
One Fit	2	F	6	1	3	0	11,960
One Fit Baby	2	F	2	2	0	0	47,400
One Flew Over	4	F	8	2	1	1	27,808
One for Carmen	2	C	1	0	0	1	6,270
One for Katie	4	F	10	1	2	2	74,136
One for My Baby	6	G	5	0	0	1	6,360
One for Rose	5	M	8	4	2	0	489,832
One for Seattle	5	G	10	1	3	2	9,683
One for Wanda	5	M	5	0	2	1	4,192
One for You	3	F	10	1	0	0	11,471
One Forty Four	5	H	11	3	3	3	16,395
One Fourteen	2	F	10	2	2	1	33,220
One Foxy Knight	4	F	2	1	0	0	890
One Fun Cat	3	F	6	1	2	0	13,492
One Fun Stun Gun	3	G	9	0	1	0	1,489
One Game Bag	2	C	3	0	0	0	0
One Genius	3	F	16	1	2	3	17,112
One Giant Leap	4	G	8	1	0	0	2,880
One Good Eye	3	G	7	0	0	1	1,857
One Good Gal	2	F	2	0	0	0	309
One Good Man	2	C	1	0	0	0	360
One Good Soldier	4	G	8	2	2	0	39,789
One Green Eye	3	F	15	0	3	0	8,553
One Green Peach	3	F	5	0	0	1	4,200
One Heart	3	C	2	0	0	0	1,274
One Honest Heart	6	G	1	0	0	0	40
One Hot Girl	4	F	6	0	1	0	1,950
One Hot Knight	10	G	11	2	1	2	7,051
One Hot Pilot	5	G	12	1	4	1	8,783
One Iron	4	G	8	1	0	0	7,278
One Jazzy Lover	4	C	10	2	1	1	10,935
One Judge Trend	6	G	4	1	0	1	13,805
One Knight	5	G	8	0	1	1	3,844
One Kool Babe	4	F	11	1	2	0	4,447
One Lake	2	F	4	0	0	1	1,212
One Last Trick	8	G	5	0	0	0	449
One Last Victory	3	G	15	1	2	3	30,425
One Last Whirl	2	F	2	0	0	0	410
One Leveler	4	G	7	0	0	0	828
One Little Word	9	G	12	1	0	0	4,067
One Lively Time	2	F	1	0	0	0	0
One Look	4	F	19	3	5	3	22,226
One Lucky Day	7	M	11	0	0	1	1,963
One Lucky Gal	2	F	10	0	1	0	4,081
One Lucky Storm	3	F	12	2	0	2	27,580
One Lucky Strike	10	G	1	0	0	0	88
One Manz Fortune	7	G	1	0	0	0	0
One Mean Queen	2	F	3	0	0	1	5,604
One Mile Limit	7	M	11	1	2	2	14,280
One Misse (NZ)	6	M	4	0	1	0	1,555
One Missy Gal	3	F	11	1	2	1	12,695
One Momento	4	C	5	1	1	1	20,460
One Mon Melody	2	G	4	0	0	0	1,104
One More (NZ)	8	G	3	0	0	1	1,000
One More Bragg	4	G	15	0	0	0	1,706
One More Cookie	4	F	5	0	0	1	4,675
One More Mecke	5	G	2	0	0	0	185
One More Moondance	4	F	18	5	4	2	55,941
One More Once	10	G	3	0	0	0	0
One More Run	4	C	4	0	0	0	145
One More Shot	3	F	7	1	0	1	10,945
One More Storm	5	G	7	0	1	1	4,117
One More Turn	2	F	2	0	0	1	4,000
One More Whirl	4	G	10	3	2	1	55,655
One More Win	3	G	12	2	0	2	19,070
One N Three	5	H	3	0	0	0	4,296
One Naughty Fool	7	M	2	0	0	0	130
One Neat Trick	3	F	4	0	1	0	4,440
One Nice Cat	4	C	12	1	1	3	55,015
One Objective	5	G	19	1	1	3	8,605
One O'Clock	2	F	2	1	0	0	11,610

Horse	Age	Sex	Sts	1st	2d	3d	Won
One o'Clock Road	3	C	3	0	0	0	0
One of the Lonely	5	G	7	1	1	2	12,763
One Only Knows	4	F	9	4	0	0	150,508
One Other Than	3	F	7	2	1	1	35,230
One Perfect Fit	4	F	10	2	1	2	50,884
One Perfect Sailor	3	F	8	1	1	0	7,210
One Pit Wonder	3	C	8	1	2	1	8,940
One Precious Gem	3	F	3	0	0	0	0
One Red Hot Mama	3	F	1	0	0	0	0
One River Dolly	3	F	15	1	0	2	9,435
One Salty Sister	2	F	5	1	0	0	46,500
One Sea	4	G	8	1	1	0	15,490
One Sharp Sword	4	G	14	3	2	3	47,810
One Silent Love	3	F	7	1	3	2	20,550
One Silent Wonder	7	G	9	1	1	3	11,221
One Silver Lady	6	M	1	0	0	0	61
One Sixty	3	F	3	0	3	0	19,840
One Smart Bet	6	H	4	0	0	1	2,143
One Smart Cat	3	G	10	0	0	2	7,555
One Smart Chick	5	M	6	0	1	2	7,080
One Smart Deputy	2	C	2	0	1	0	7,400
One Smart Lady	3	F	4	1	1	0	21,050
One Smooth Ride	2	C	5	2	0	1	107,753
One Sock Becky	3	F	5	0	0	0	1,260
One Special Bob	5	G	15	1	2	2	14,573
One Special Hoss	2	G	5	3	0	1	69,288
One Special Judge	6	G	15	3	2	3	20,810
One Special One	4	G	4	0	1	0	2,781
One Stab	2	C	1	0	0	0	0
One Star General	3	G	16	1	5	2	18,044
One Step Away	4	G	9	0	2	0	3,908
One Stop Shopping	4	G	7	2	0	4	9,824
One Stormy Mama	2	F	4	0	1	1	13,130
One Stormy Night	4	C	8	0	0	0	652
One Sweet Dash	4	F	9	3	0	1	12,710
One Sweet Day	3	F	16	1	2	2	17,529
One Talented Pro	4	C	8	0	0	1	10,399
One Tall King	4	G	10	0	2	2	4,652
One to Celebrate	3	C	5	2	0	0	80,960
One to Love	3	F	1	0	0	1	1,408
One to Want	3	F	1	0	0	0	0
One Tough Deputy	2	C	8	1	1	4	20,117
One Tough Dude	3	C	14	3	2	2	104,819
One Tough Girl	2	F	2	0	0	0	370
One Tough Note	5	H	4	0	0	2	3,890
One Tough Raiser	4	C	8	1	2	1	35,242
One Tough Somethin	7	G	8	0	1	2	5,060
One Trick Ata Time	5	G	7	0	1	3	7,963
One Troy Ounce	6	G	3	1	0	0	4,040
One Tuff Chick	3	F	16	1	5	2	15,440
One Tuff Fox	5	H	4	0	1	0	7,040
One Tuff Oak	5	H	5	1	1	0	1,381
One Tuft Woeman	2	F	2	2	0	0	7,700
One Two May	3	G	9	1	3	1	21,885
One Two Ponche	6	M	6	0	0	0	306
One Two Punch	4	F	14	2	2	2	60,000
One Upman	7	G	16	3	1	1	34,760
One Way Out	2	C	4	1	1	0	16,273
One Way Wonder	3	F	3	0	0	0	700
One Wild Cat	4	G	7	0	0	0	1,377
Oneatmanale's	3	F	2	1	0	0	3,540
Onebadshark	4	C	9	3	1	1	118,072
Onebigbag	4	G	11	4	0	1	132,188
Onecoast Twocoast	3	F	8	0	1	1	2,719
Onedancewithslew	4	F	1	0	0	0	0
Oneexcessivenite	4	F	1	0	0	0	0
Oneeyedparrot	2	G	2	0	0	0	160
Oneforthegriffer	7	G	1	1	0	0	2,940
Onefortheroad	2	G	6	1	1	1	8,702
Onefourtwentyfour	7	G	4	0	0	0	1,117
Oneguiltymoon	3	F	1	0	0	0	0
Onehorsyoutside	8	H	10	0	1	0	882
Onehotprincess	3	F	14	0	0	0	768
Onehundredproofwin	4	F	9	1	1	2	18,700
Onekissisplenty	3	G	9	2	3	1	13,244
Onelittlemoccasin	3	F	5	0	0	0	1,028
Onelivelylady	2	F	1	0	0	1	693
Onella	4	F	8	1	0	0	7,977
Oneluckygirl	3	F	17	1	1	2	11,925
Oneminute	5	M	14	1	1	1	13,710
Onemorefashion	4	F	11	2	1	0	52,630
Onemorewithclass	3	G	9	1	1	1	6,440
Oneofacat	3	F	7	2	0	1	75,395
Oneofthebirdboys	4	G	9	1	1	2	15,451
Oneofthegirls	5	M	14	0	1	2	7,510
Oneofus	5	G	12	1	1	0	7,160
One's Wild	3	C	10	1	1	2	8,510
Onesassyluckylady	4	F	8	2	0	2	8,370
Onestep	5	M	11	2	0	3	34,030
Onethindime	3	F	15	4	2	1	34,735
Onetwomanyfavors	3	F	6	1	0	2	12,921
Oneverycoolcat	3	C	2	0	0	1	10,380
Oneway Only	3	F	8	0	0	0	622
Onewaytoheaven	3	F	5	2	1	0	10,205
Oneyed Cat	3	F	5	0	0	0	705
Ongoing Star	3	F	1	1	0	0	7,680
Ongoing Storm	6	G	12	0	1	3	6,976
Onhighalert	4	F	11	1	3	2	26,973
Oniomaniac	3	F	13	3	4	1	28,800
Onion Soup	4	G	6	0	0	1	930
Online	2	C	1	0	0	0	276
Online Class	4	G	12	0	2	3	4,596
Online Degree	2	G	6	1	1	2	10,791
Online Intime	8	G	12	1	4	0	25,696
Only a Day Away	3	F	9	0	2	1	4,736
Only At Night	5	M	6	1	1	0	48,125
Only by Grace	2	F	3	0	0	0	1,485
Only Fools Rush In	4	G	11	3	0	1	33,764
Only for Money	6	M	3	0	1	0	6,080
Only Heaven Can	3	G	5	1	0	0	4,650
Only Imagine	2	F	5	0	2	1	18,605
Only in America	5	M	12	0	1	1	3,327
Only in Dreams	4	G	7	2	2	1	13,788
Only in Philly	2	F	2	1	0	1	24,140
Only in Reno	2	C	1	0	1	0	8,800
Only Joe	5	G	10	3	2	0	19,997
Only Joking	5	G	12	1	1	0	15,540
Only Kings	4	G	17	1	2	2	7,411
Only Love	5	M	5	0	0	0	600
Only Money	3	G	10	0	0	0	3,518
Only Now	3	G	7	1	1	1	7,942
Only On	4	G	11	0	0	0	1,975
Only On Broadway	5	M	8	2	1	2	13,816
Only One King	4	G	14	3	4	1	47,042
Only One Regal	3	F	12	1	1	1	6,467
Only Oralee	3	F	1	1	0	0	9,680
Only Poe Knows	6	G	9	0	1	1	2,715
Only Seventeen	3	F	3	0	0	0	513
Only Son	3	C	6	2	1	0	32,525
Only the Best	4	G	6	1	1	1	41,950
Only Thrill	4	F	7	0	1	4	5,921
Only Time	5	G	14	3	3	0	25,390
Only Wings	5	M	7	0	1	0	1,420
Only Yesterday	4	F	4	0	0	0	410
Only You	6	G	9	1	1	0	14,973
Only You and I	4	F	9	0	1	1	1,629
Onlyamatteroftime	3	C	5	1	0	0	13,440
Onlycook Half Ofit	5	G	5	2	2	0	32,900
Onlyificould	2	F	2	0	0	0	2,700
Onlynurimagination	5	G	13	4	5	0	63,949
Onmygrounds	2	C	2	0	0	0	0
Onmyownterms	3	F	17	2	4	3	31,220
Onmywaytoheaven	4	F	3	0	0	0	1,149
Onrichardsaccount	5	G	10	2	4	1	13,170
Onry Wonway	4	F	13	2	3	1	36,570
Ontario Road	4	G	7	1	1	1	19,472
Ontario Star	4	C	1	0	0	0	330
Onthebrightcide	4	F	1	0	0	0	209
Onthedeanslist	5	H	2	0	0	0	1,120
Ontheflipside	5	H	2	0	0	0	139
Onthemarquet	5	G	8	1	0	0	3,526
Ontheqt	3	F	3	1	0	1	128,575
Ontheroadagain	2	G	3	0	0	0	2,000
Ontherocksnosalt	2	F	1	0	0	0	145
Onthewingsofadove	4	F	12	1	0	0	6,211
Ontodaysagenda	3	C	2	0	0	0	406
Onyx King	4	C	5	0	0	0	1,195
Onyx Star	2	F	4	2	0	1	26,110

Horse	Age	Sex	Sts	1st	2d	3d	Won
Onyxntrue	7	G	14	2	5	5	13,756
Oobi	2	F	3	1	0	0	10,632
Oobitwa	4	G	2	0	0	1	3,750
Oodles of Noodles	2	F	1	0	0	0	184
Oogie	3	F	3	0	1	0	950
Ooh Man	4	G	9	1	1	1	14,965
Oola Boola	6	M	16	1	3	1	11,384
Oompa Loompa	3	G	3	1	0	0	5,460
Oonagh	4	F	1	1	0	0	19,200
Oop's the Red	4	G	10	1	2	0	12,220
Oopsie	3	G	2	0	0	0	0
Ootah	5	G	9	2	0	2	16,275
Opa Ryno	2	C	1	0	0	0	145
Opalene	4	F	6	0	3	1	1,560
Opal's Ghost	6	M	8	0	1	1	4,719
Opal's Song	6	M	7	0	3	1	5,398
O'Parker	2	G	7	1	0	1	16,500
O'Patty Glo	2	F	1	0	1	0	289
Opelika	3	F	2	0	0	1	3,100
Open Call	6	M	8	1	0	2	6,600
Open Cat	4	F	2	0	0	0	300
Open Chronicle	5	G	8	0	1	1	7,320
Open Concert	5	G	11	0	5	0	136,457
Open Deeds	5	G	9	3	1	1	40,719
Open Fairway	3	F	1	0	0	0	0
Open Flirt	3	F	3	0	0	1	4,534
Open for Love	6	H	2	1	0	0	2,520
Open Hearted	5	M	13	2	0	1	28,437
Open Hunt	3	G	15	1	2	2	25,935
Open Invitation	5	G	15	1	4	2	9,544
Open Journey	3	C	5	0	0	3	7,270
Open Late	4	G	3	0	0	2	7,470
Open Letter	5	M	6	2	1	2	6,604
Open Line's Dream	3	C	10	1	0	3	9,351
Open Lock	3	C	11	3	3	1	135,357
Open Manner	4	F	3	0	0	0	205
Open Meeting	2	F	4	0	2	0	8,400
Open Motel	2	C	4	0	0	0	600
Open Name	4	F	6	1	1	1	4,835
Open Now	3	G	10	0	1	1	4,653
Open Promise	5	M	9	5	1	0	100,830
Open Ribbon	3	F	3	1	0	0	4,245
Open Rocket	3	G	11	0	0	4	3,592
Open Scent	5	M	11	0	1	0	2,256
Open Session	5	M	3	0	0	0	976
Open Terms	3	F	6	1	0	0	14,570
Open the Bridge	4	F	3	0	0	0	192
Open to Appeal	2	F	1	0	1	0	1,615
Open Water	4	G	8	0	0	1	1,595
Open Your Eyes	3	F	9	3	1	0	36,050
Opening Account	4	F	2	0	0	0	170
Opening Act (ARG)	6	G	3	1	1	0	18,450
Opening Day	3	F	1	0	0	0	0
Opening Pace	4	C	1	0	0	0	330
Opening Soon	5	M	9	1	2	0	13,677
Opening Wager	2	G	10	2	2	1	39,742
Opening Word	9	G	8	0	0	0	1,468
Openly	3	F	13	1	0	1	17,474
Opennshutcase	4	G	5	0	0	0	1,456
Opeongo	4	C	2	0	0	0	336
Opera Box	3	C	6	1	0	1	27,740
Opera Song	3	F	3	0	0	0	764
Operatic	4	G	7	2	0	1	40,245
Operation Freedom	4	G	7	1	0	2	4,281
Operation Gloria	4	F	11	1	1	1	11,830
Ophir City Gal	2	F	1	0	0	0	75
Opie	6	G	15	2	4	2	13,259
Opie's Bonus	4	G	1	0	0	0	0
Opie's Secret	3	C	3	0	1	0	470
Opine	9	G	8	0	3	1	16,081
Opportunist	3	F	3	0	0	0	247
Opportunity Bay	4	F	3	0	0	0	146
Opportunity Curve	2	F	1	0	0	1	4,160
Oppose	2	C	2	1	0	0	1,767
Opposing Force	5	H	12	0	2	4	4,827
Opprtunity Blue's	7	M	11	1	1	2	7,467
Opry Music	3	G	10	2	2	1	16,230
Ops Mirage	3	F	14	1	3	1	14,690
Ops Overlord	3	G	9	1	0	1	6,739
Ops Run	4	F	17	1	0	1	9,748
Ops So Lootly	2	F	2	0	0	0	1,920
Opsail	4	G	2	0	0	0	180
Opt	7	M	12	1	1	1	4,990
Optimal	8	G	14	1	3	2	9,902
Optimistic Math	4	G	1	0	0	0	210
Optimistic Roll	4	F	1	0	0	0	67
Optimistic Ruler	3	G	2	0	0	0	0
Optimize	4	F	1	0	0	0	340
Optimo	3	G	11	1	4	0	24,595
Optimystic John	3	C	3	0	0	0	680
Optomistic Cat	3	F	8	1	1	0	11,270
Opulent Fan	3	F	5	0	2	1	2,375
Opus Creek	9	G	8	1	0	0	5,464
Opus Won	7	H	8	1	1	3	20,150
Or O' Rosheen	5	M	7	0	2	2	7,742
Ora	6	M	1	0	0	0	0
O'Raaaily	4	F	7	0	0	0	833
Oraboy	3	G	2	0	0	0	0
Oracat	3	F	10	1	2	1	14,060
Oracle of Omaha	2	C	2	0	0	1	5,890
Orange 'Em	5	G	15	3	2	1	33,448
Orange Power	3	C	8	1	1	0	9,050
Orange Starburst	4	G	8	1	0	1	8,090
Orange Tangerine	2	F	2	1	1	0	11,400
Orange U Tricky	9	G	7	0	1	1	2,727
Orangeberry	4	F	12	0	3	2	17,589
Orangeville Rise	3	G	7	1	0	0	2,860
Orangina	3	F	4	0	0	1	1,782
Oration	7	G	13	1	2	3	49,260
Oratorical	3	G	9	1	1	1	7,068
Orbea	4	G	3	0	1	1	2,093
Orbited	5	M	9	1	0	0	8,905
Orbiting	5	M	1	0	0	0	0
Orbit'roundthegold	2	F	4	0	0	1	1,360
Orbit's Dancer	6	G	2	0	0	1	1,320
Orbits World	2	C	7	0	2	2	33,870
Orbit'slastdance	6	G	5	0	0	0	0
Orchard Park	5	H	5	0	0	0	3,810
Orchard Street	6	G	3	0	0	0	852
Orchestral	3	F	5	1	0	0	8,092
Orchid Island	3	F	3	0	0	0	584
Orchid Thief	3	G	12	1	1	1	35,720
Orchid's Son	6	G	2	0	0	0	0
Orchid's Song	4	F	5	0	1	0	3,769
Orchids Spirit	4	G	12	1	1	1	21,168
Ordain	2	C	1	0	0	0	360
Ordained Magic	4	F	4	0	0	2	8,400
Order Chief	6	G	8	0	1	0	2,243
Order Me First	3	C	4	1	1	0	1,965
Orderly Prince	9	G	2	0	0	0	0
Ordinal	3	G	9	1	0	1	8,049
Ordinary Luck	4	G	12	2	3	5	15,943
Ordinary Miracle	4	F	12	1	0	1	5,735
Ordvou	4	G	8	0	0	0	635
Ordwillow	2	F	2	0	0	0	894
Ore Dazzler	2	C	5	0	0	0	0
Ore Mine	6	G	13	3	3	2	40,072
Ore 'n Hatch	5	G	10	3	0	1	5,853
Ore Rush	4	G	2	0	0	0	0
Oreanda	3	F	5	0	1	1	15,860
Oregon Gus	5	G	6	0	0	1	682
Oregon Miracle	4	G	5	1	0	0	2,095
Oregon Native Sun	5	G	9	3	1	1	5,013
Oreo Hunter	5	G	16	1	3	1	11,370
Orestes	4	G	14	3	2	3	19,434
Orestida	3	F	8	1	3	1	72,883
Orezza	2	F	1	0	0	0	2,160
Orfun Ann E.	5	M	10	1	2	3	9,859
Organ Grinder	3	C	8	4	2	2	414,813
Organica	3	F	2	0	0	0	0
Organizer	2	C	2	0	2	0	16,600
Organizing Chaos	3	G	10	0	3	2	21,291
Oriana's Magic	5	M	9	1	2	2	28,525
Orieal	3	F	11	0	1	1	10,800
Oriental Doll	3	F	9	2	2	0	109,880
Oriental Glitter	2	F	6	1	1	1	25,905
Orientalspringhope	8	M	13	0	1	5	38,325
Original Cast	7	G	1	0	0	0	0

Horse	Age	Sex	Sts	1st	2d	3d	Won
Original Gold	4	F	4	3	1	0	163,020
Original One	8	G	2	0	0	0	194
Original Prankster	3	G	10	0	2	2	4,896
Original Prospect	8	G	4	0	0	0	0
Original Song	4	F	1	0	0	0	3,882
Origines	3	C	8	3	1	1	25,364
Orimack	3	G	5	0	0	0	420
Orion Red	4	G	8	0	1	2	3,035
Orions Cross	2	G	2	1	0	0	9,420
Orion's Jade	5	G	12	2	3	2	98,920
Orion's Light	6	M	2	0	0	0	0
Oriska	4	F	3	1	0	0	4,300
Orison	2	C	2	0	0	1	4,330
Oritani	3	C	1	0	1	0	4,940
O'Rival	6	M	12	1	1	3	6,792
Orka	5	H	14	2	2	2	49,867
Orkan	4	F	9	0	1	3	29,969
Orlando's Dream	5	G	6	0	0	1	712
Orlean	3	C	3	1	1	0	22,400
Orlik	3	C	12	1	4	0	44,720
Orlop	2	C	6	1	1	2	35,720
Ormonte K.	7	M	4	0	0	0	123
Ormsbys Treasure	4	F	6	1	2	1	38,100
Ornery Angel	4	F	2	0	0	0	96
Ornery B. J.	5	G	7	0	0	1	2,690
Oro Bravo	2	G	6	1	1	1	9,326
Oro Caliente	4	F	7	0	0	1	2,352
Oro Classic	2	F	4	1	0	1	9,340
Oro de Ole'	3	G	2	0	1	0	5,900
Oro de Oro	4	C	5	0	1	0	9,930
Oro Desert	4	G	9	1	4	0	66,375
Oro Grand	3	G	14	2	0	2	48,200
Oro Mountain	4	C	7	2	2	0	18,990
Oro Tunnel	3	G	3	0	0	0	640
Orofino Prize	3	F	16	2	4	1	14,747
Oromancer	3	G	10	0	1	3	17,891
Oros	8	H	10	1	0	4	8,030
Oro's Delight	3	C	10	2	3	1	29,275
Oro's Sugar	3	F	11	3	2	4	41,390
Orozco	3	C	7	1	0	2	8,850
Orphan Brigade	3	G	13	4	1	3	102,210
Orphan Cartwright	7	G	9	3	4	1	82,150
Orphan Child	4	C	8	2	1	1	22,850
Orphan Lover	5	M	10	1	1	1	22,705
Orphan Tinka	4	F	8	0	0	1	1,760
Orphaned	9	G	4	0	0	0	0
Orphan's Wager	5	M	13	2	1	0	28,900
Orphie	5	G	6	0	0	0	832
Orpington	3	G	9	3	1	0	63,820
Orsay	3	C	4	1	2	0	58,508
Ortiz	3	G	7	1	0	0	14,320
Orville N Wilbur's	9	H	2	0	0	0	242
Orwick	4	G	8	2	3	1	69,845
Osage Indian	9	G	1	0	0	1	1,630
Osceola	7	M	11	3	0	3	9,671
Osceola Warrior	3	G	11	0	0	1	2,150
Oscoda	5	G	9	1	2	0	6,172
Oseaya	4	F	11	0	0	1	2,059
Osgoode Hall	3	F	4	0	0	2	8,541
Osho	5	M	4	0	0	0	585
Osikan	5	G	8	0	1	0	1,022
Oskar	5	G	3	1	0	0	8,060
Oskar Fox	3	G	3	0	0	0	0
Osmanbek	9	G	13	1	1	4	27,131
Oso Gothic	4	F	1	0	0	0	0
Oso Naughty	5	M	4	0	0	0	100
Oso Tricky	2	C	5	3	1	0	114,711
Ossabaw	4	F	11	0	2	0	4,644
Oswayo	5	G	12	1	2	2	37,490
Oswego	2	F	3	1	0	0	8,610
Otan	4	G	12	1	1	1	7,244
Othellos Fellow	3	G	5	0	0	0	302
Other Than That	3	G	2	1	0	0	9,255
Otherwise Engaged	5	M	3	0	0	2	2,125
Otis Township	3	G	12	1	2	1	10,894
Otisshoulderroll	5	G	6	0	0	0	512
Otro Paleface	2	G	4	0	0	0	570
Ott	5	M	1	0	0	0	0
Ottawa Chief	3	C	4	0	0	0	1,508
Otter	3	C	14	3	0	1	16,329
Otter Bay	4	G	4	0	0	0	370
Otter Be Running	3	F	17	1	0	3	12,732
Otto Be Lee	7	G	4	0	0	0	285
Ott's Last Haul	3	G	5	2	1	0	25,840
Ou Wee	4	F	1	0	0	0	390
Ouagadougou	4	G	16	3	2	5	97,984
Oudachances	3	C	1	0	0	0	34
Ought a Bring Cash	5	G	14	1	0	2	7,836
Oughta Be Illegal	2	F	2	1	0	0	1,140
Oughta Ben Brown	4	G	13	1	3	2	6,470
Oui Ma Cherie	3	F	9	0	1	2	7,961
Oui Marie	2	F	7	1	1	1	12,301
Oui Oui Cherokee	4	F	7	1	0	0	17,325
Ouija Board (GB)	3	F	5	4	0	1	1,659,958
Ouilala	3	F	4	0	0	0	520
Our Advantage	3	F	9	0	0	1	4,180
Our Angel Charlie	4	G	3	0	0	0	130
Our Approval	4	G	7	1	2	0	16,660
Our Aunt Kathleen	4	F	14	1	3	1	8,962
Our Award	7	M	10	2	2	2	24,244
Our Basket	4	C	7	0	0	2	1,827
Our Best Man	7	G	16	3	2	4	56,015
Our Best Woods	4	C	2	0	0	1	500
Our Bobby V.	4	G	7	0	2	2	37,630
Our Boy Barney	3	G	9	0	0	0	1,560
Our Boy Champ	9	G	1	0	0	1	1,000
Our Boy Zach	5	G	3	0	0	0	180
Our Breadwinner	5	M	12	1	1	2	28,236
Our Buck	5	H	5	0	1	0	3,416
Our Buddy	7	G	1	0	0	0	0
Our Cat	3	C	4	0	0	0	5,040
Our Celeste	2	F	5	0	2	1	6,000
Our Chances Are	3	F	1	0	0	0	0
Our Chef	9	H	2	0	0	0	0
Our Chequer Flag	5	M	4	1	1	1	9,427
Our Cherokee	4	G	14	3	1	2	7,726
Our Colors	6	G	1	0	0	0	50
Our Concern	2	F	3	1	1	1	7,565
Our County	4	C	1	0	0	0	0
Our Cousin Rex	4	G	13	1	1	3	31,745
Our Daily Bread	5	G	10	3	0	2	23,523
Our Dear Jade	5	M	5	0	1	0	1,590
Our Decision	4	C	4	0	0	0	2,835
Our Deer Lady	2	F	3	1	1	0	37,350
Our Deputy's Lady	2	F	2	0	0	0	240
Our Diamond Girl	3	F	3	0	0	0	285
Our Dreamcatcher	10	G	2	0	0	0	0
Our Eleanor	4	F	10	0	0	0	880
Our Emerald	4	F	18	5	2	3	51,747
Our Emmy	3	F	2	0	0	0	800
Our Exploit	3	F	8	2	3	1	69,850
Our Fantasy Cat	3	G	1	0	0	0	0
Our Ferrari	4	G	12	1	2	1	7,388
Our Finale	4	C	14	2	0	6	53,550
Our First Flight	3	G	17	3	2	0	24,595
Our First Furrari	6	G	1	0	0	0	0
Our Fling (NZ)	6	M	9	0	0	3	31,620
Our Forest Delight	5	G	8	1	0	1	3,614
Our Free Bee	2	F	4	2	0	1	31,900
Our Freya	4	F	11	2	0	2	36,688
Our Friend Jimmy	2	G	4	1	0	1	7,927
Our Friend Perk	4	G	9	1	2	1	11,515
Our Friend Timmy	2	C	5	1	0	1	37,420
Our Friend Vern	3	C	12	2	1	2	19,672
Our Friend's Girl	3	F	5	1	0	1	23,640
Our Gal Fatale	5	M	8	3	0	2	18,280
Our Gal Friday	6	M	3	0	0	0	309
Our Gal Irish	4	F	14	0	3	4	13,257
Our Gal Val	3	F	5	0	0	0	930
Our Game	9	G	1	0	0	0	0
Our Gang	3	G	12	0	2	0	17,862
Our Georgia Mae	3	F	7	0	0	0	0
Our Golden Boy	4	G	4	0	0	1	936
Our Golden Dollar	2	F	4	1	0	0	14,870
Our Golden Gal	3	F	13	1	1	5	10,530
Our Golden Nick	3	F	7	1	0	2	7,255
Our Golden Pond	3	F	8	4	0	0	20,590
Our Guy	5	G	1	0	0	0	0

Horse	Age	Sex	Sts	1st	2d	3d	Won
Our Heiress	4	F	2	0	0	1	1,430
Our Here Tiz	7	M	3	0	0	1	6,800
Our Houdini	4	G	2	0	0	0	635
Our Illusion	2	F	2	0	0	0	0
Our Jillian	2	F	4	0	2	1	6,750
Our Jock Julio	5	G	9	0	0	1	1,279
Our Josephina	4	F	10	3	2	2	179,414
Our Joy	3	F	6	0	2	1	10,952
Our Judy R	4	F	3	0	0	1	1,424
Our Karma	3	C	1	0	0	0	164
Our Kathrine	3	F	8	1	0	1	18,205
Our Knockout	5	M	2	0	0	0	450
Our Lady Katie	5	M	1	0	0	1	1,400
Our Lady Megan	4	F	9	1	2	1	10,534
Our Last Dance	2	F	6	1	0	0	14,472
Our Last Hero	2	C	5	0	0	0	2,025
Our Last Novel	5	G	7	3	1	0	69,220
Our Last Turn	2	G	1	0	0	1	1,404
Our Laura Bell	3	F	8	2	2	1	12,720
Our Leader	7	G	6	1	1	0	11,650
Our Leading Lady	2	F	4	1	0	0	8,190
Our Legal Eagle	14	G	1	0	0	0	72
Our Legend	6	M	19	2	5	0	17,788
Our Lil Affair	6	H	15	3	2	0	13,325
Our Lil Moe Joe	5	G	4	0	0	1	1,360
Our Lilly	4	F	7	1	0	1	10,904
Our Little Lucy	4	F	14	5	2	1	67,651
Our Little Runaway	4	C	4	0	0	0	396
Our Louie	5	G	1	0	0	1	3,850
Our Love	4	F	4	2	0	2	51,170
Our Luc	4	C	9	0	2	1	20,456
Our Luck Will Turn	5	M	3	0	0	0	180
Our Lucky Bonnie	9	M	5	0	1	1	882
Our Lucky Bucky	3	G	11	2	0	1	13,010
Our Lucky Kiss	4	F	1	0	0	0	0
Our Lucky Number	6	G	7	0	0	0	205
Our Lucky Penny	3	C	6	1	1	0	15,020
Our Magistrate	6	G	13	5	2	2	58,970
Our Majestic Cat	6	M	2	0	0	0	1,026
Our Majestic Queen	3	F	2	0	0	0	293
Our Mango	5	M	13	2	2	2	163,992
Our March Hare	4	C	7	0	1	1	7,260
Our Mariah	4	F	5	0	3	0	37,400
Our Martini	3	F	1	0	0	0	75
Our Megabucks	5	G	2	0	0	0	0
Our Memento	3	C	3	0	0	0	910
Our Mimi	5	M	8	1	1	1	21,970
Our Miss Jones	2	F	6	1	2	1	45,310
Our Miss M	4	F	2	0	0	1	1,925
Our Mistake	3	G	18	1	4	2	41,280
Our Moment	4	C	18	0	5	4	13,529
Our Monstarr	3	F	8	2	0	2	9,522
Our Mud Pie	9	G	11	3	1	1	3,960
Our New Recruit	5	H	5	2	0	1	1,265,795
Our Niner	4	G	11	3	2	1	41,000
Our Olivia	3	F	4	0	0	1	1,762
Our Party Man	5	G	7	1	2	1	6,304
Our Peace Lady	4	F	1	0	0	0	0
Our Pee Jay	5	M	7	0	1	2	2,803
Our Perfect Storm	2	F	7	0	0	0	1,145
Our Point to Point	4	G	3	0	0	1	3,360
Our Pop	5	H	9	0	2	1	10,060
Our Preciousmoment	6	M	9	0	0	3	15,950
Our Problem	4	G	9	1	0	1	5,028
Our Queen Rules	3	F	14	0	3	2	35,534
Our Quest	2	F	3	0	1	0	5,200
Our Remy	3	C	5	2	0	1	38,630
Our Resolution	5	G	2	0	0	0	0
Our Revival	4	F	10	6	1	0	44,370
Our Rite of Spring	3	F	8	3	2	0	114,290
Our Rose	2	F	8	0	0	1	6,994
Our Royal Dancer	4	F	6	4	1	0	136,100
Our Royal Image	3	F	14	2	1	3	24,478
Our Royal Lady	2	F	2	1	1	0	24,650
Our Ruby	3	G	13	0	1	3	5,091
Our Runnin Buddy	2	G	3	0	1	0	1,582
Our Saint Ed	4	G	1	0	0	0	0
Our Shade	2	G	1	0	0	0	0
Our Shadow	2	C	7	1	0	0	7,625
Our Sharky	5	G	4	1	1	1	8,645
Our Shining Star	5	M	14	0	0	4	5,724
Our Sister Gina	7	M	5	0	1	0	2,780
Our Sleep Robber	6	G	1	0	0	0	0
Our Slewshan	2	F	1	0	0	0	0
Our Son Rob	3	G	4	0	0	0	1,740
Our Song	5	G	7	4	0	1	40,638
Our Sonny Boy	2	G	5	0	0	1	1,290
Our Southern Pearl	3	F	5	1	0	0	14,920
Our Spike	2	G	3	0	0	0	100
Our Spirits	2	C	1	0	0	0	0
Our Star Slew	3	F	3	0	0	1	550
Our Star Witness	2	F	7	0	0	1	3,573
Our Sweet Emotion	6	M	1	0	0	0	52
Our Sweet Nadine	7	M	6	0	0	0	289
Our Tanner Girl	5	M	6	1	0	1	1,553
Our Three O Seven	4	G	7	1	2	2	7,396
Our Time to Shine	3	F	4	1	1	0	20,430
Our Tomatoe Queen	3	F	14	2	2	0	11,578
Our Top Gun	5	G	3	1	0	0	24,968
Our Trick	3	C	1	0	0	0	800
Our Trump	3	F	1	0	0	0	145
Our Tune	4	F	10	4	1	0	116,799
Our Valentine	4	F	17	2	3	3	22,265
Our Valentino	3	G	3	1	1	0	23,000
Our Whizbang	3	G	11	1	0	3	10,122
Our Wildcat	5	G	9	2	1	1	100,478
Our Wildest Moment	2	F	2	0	0	0	800
Ourboymatt	4	C	8	0	1	3	2,062
Ourenay	7	G	10	1	2	2	7,955
Ourfirstbabyfund	3	F	11	0	0	1	2,172
Ouririshcoin	4	F	7	0	3	0	2,407
Ourlittledannyboy	7	H	4	2	1	0	6,149
Ourninelives	3	C	6	2	0	0	29,985
Ourpennyfromheaven	4	C	6	0	1	0	1,600
Ours to Keep	2	F	1	1	0	0	19,380
Ourwhistlebritches	4	F	7	1	0	2	8,173
Ousted	3	G	1	0	0	0	40
Out At Home	4	F	7	3	1	0	54,309
Out Cattin'	2	G	3	0	0	0	0
Out Control (CHI)	6	G	5	0	0	1	845
Out for a Spin	3	G	9	2	1	2	48,550
Out for Justice	2	G	2	0	0	0	378
Out for Sin	2	C	4	0	0	0	730
Out From Africa	2	C	2	1	1	0	55,000
Out Late	4	G	3	0	0	1	2,250
Out of Coal	3	G	6	0	1	2	19,480
Out of Cut	6	G	4	0	0	0	308
Out of Daylight	2	F	2	0	0	1	1,540
Out of Dough	6	M	7	1	1	0	17,970
Out of Fashion	8	G	5	1	1	0	31,140
Out of Focus	3	F	4	1	0	0	18,390
Out of Hearts	3	F	11	1	2	0	20,337
Out of Here	5	G	10	3	1	2	23,829
Out of Jacks	4	G	12	3	3	0	63,204
Out of Jail	3	C	7	0	0	1	6,160
Out of Kilter	3	C	8	0	0	1	2,075
Out of Kindness	4	G	9	0	2	2	5,442
Out of Line	2	F	8	1	2	1	12,205
Out of M and M's	4	G	9	0	2	0	2,453
Out of Milk	4	F	9	0	3	0	5,634
Out of My Way	7	G	4	1	0	1	61,979
Out of Pocket	4	F	4	1	1	0	19,120
Out of Pride	5	M	14	9	2	1	105,837
Out of Riches	7	H	1	0	0	0	0
Out of Sort's	4	F	12	2	1	2	47,614
Out of the Bag	5	M	7	2	0	2	13,670
Out of the Gloom	5	G	13	0	4	2	6,738
Out of the Red	2	C	5	0	1	0	3,360
Out of the Will	4	F	10	2	0	1	82,398
Out of Tune	3	F	11	1	1	1	26,980
Out On Bail	5	G	5	0	0	0	670
Out Shinin'	3	F	7	0	0	1	858
Out There	4	G	11	2	1	1	41,975
Out to Get Ya	5	G	5	0	0	0	200
Out Well	6	M	12	2	0	1	26,646
Out With It	7	M	6	2	0	1	14,498
Outa My Way	5	G	13	2	0	1	10,144
Outathechute	5	H	2	0	1	0	13,400

Horse	Age	Sex	Sts	1st	2d	3d	Won
Outatime	9	G	9	2	1	1	14,526
Outback Annie	4	F	1	0	0	0	105
Outcashem	3	G	10	2	2	1	46,340
Outcome	3	G	5	1	1	1	26,100
Outdo	10	G	7	1	0	0	5,840
Outdone	5	M	8	2	0	3	35,874
Outer Bounds	4	G	9	0	3	1	26,870
Outer Marker	3	C	1	0	0	0	320
Outer Reef	4	C	5	0	0	0	2,466
Outer Zone	4	G	5	0	1	1	10,096
Outfield Shift	3	C	9	0	0	1	4,770
Outfielder	3	C	11	1	0	3	8,329
Outfit	3	F	8	0	0	1	1,755
Outflankem	4	G	12	1	1	2	11,763
Outflanker's Token	3	G	7	1	1	1	22,429
Outflankerslass	3	F	2	0	0	0	0
Outfoxme	2	F	1	0	0	0	3,420
Outlandish One	4	G	8	0	0	1	2,690
Outlandishlady	5	M	12	0	4	1	8,721
Outlaw Bag	6	G	5	2	0	0	15,360
Outlaw Cat	2	F	4	1	1	0	24,095
Outlaw Cowboy	3	G	7	3	1	0	25,650
Outlaw Gulch	5	G	4	0	0	0	228
Outlaw Kid	3	C	7	2	0	0	45,979
Outlaw Quick	4	G	9	2	0	0	4,658
Outlook	2	F	3	0	1	0	7,280
Outofmoneyhoney	5	M	2	0	0	0	154
Outofnowhere	6	M	2	0	0	1	1,034
Outofthe Blue Slew	4	G	10	1	2	4	47,620
Outofthegate	3	F	8	1	0	2	15,225
Outoftheordinary	3	F	14	3	0	3	32,816
Outofthisworld	5	G	19	2	4	2	7,136
Outraged	3	C	3	0	0	0	800
Outrageous Queen	3	F	11	3	2	0	79,615
Outrider	6	H	9	1	1	2	6,133
Outright Buck	3	F	13	4	5	0	152,300
Outright Forum	5	G	5	0	0	0	819
Outright Stormy	4	C	13	0	6	2	46,150
Outright Wager	6	M	10	0	3	2	20,190
Outside Flanker	3	G	3	0	0	0	0
Outskier	3	G	13	0	0	3	18,045
Outskirts	4	F	5	0	0	0	0
Outsmart	4	G	14	1	1	4	14,115
Outstand	2	F	1	1	0	0	34,200
Outstander	5	H	7	1	1	0	36,510
Outstanding Bill	3	G	4	1	2	1	11,550
Outstanding Miss	2	F	7	1	0	1	5,860
Outstrip	2	F	1	0	0	0	0
Outta Bags	2	C	2	0	0	0	375
Outta Here	4	C	6	0	0	3	23,680
Outta Here Blue	3	G	4	0	0	0	0
Outta Luck	5	M	15	4	4	2	56,870
Outta the Blue	4	G	15	1	3	1	14,990
Outta the House	3	F	6	1	1	1	23,540
Outta the Way	3	F	16	4	1	3	28,404
Outwit	4	G	13	3	2	1	43,935
Oval Odyssey	3	F	13	3	2	2	32,755
Ovation	5	G	6	3	2	0	15,042
Over Budget	6	G	12	4	1	1	42,482
Over Concerned	5	M	8	1	3	0	12,345
Over Dee Fence	3	F	2	0	0	0	161
Over Expectations	4	G	2	0	0	0	255
Over Spicy	8	G	3	0	0	0	120
Over Sunset	5	G	11	0	1	2	4,785
Over the Threshold	2	F	4	1	0	0	5,510
Over There	5	G	15	3	2	4	17,316
Overact	3	F	6	1	0	2	86,566
Overbite	8	G	4	1	0	0	2,987
Overclocked	4	G	9	0	3	0	7,587
Overcome	5	H	2	0	0	0	86
Overcrowded	5	M	8	1	3	2	20,688
Overdone	7	G	19	3	4	1	19,775
Overdue Number	2	F	1	0	0	0	2,100
Overflight	4	G	2	0	0	0	880
Overflowing	3	F	3	1	0	0	20,700
Overhandright	4	G	10	2	0	0	28,410
Overkill	3	C	10	2	1	0	60,120
Overland Express	3	G	2	0	0	1	860
Overland Road	3	G	8	2	1	1	53,191
Overload Warning	5	G	20	1	2	3	11,871
Overly	5	G	9	0	1	1	3,856
Overnight Angel	6	M	10	2	0	2	11,706
Overnight Delivery	5	M	11	0	4	0	17,624
Overnight News	4	G	6	0	0	1	1,702
Overnight Storm	5	G	6	0	0	1	324
Overnightintheslew	2	F	4	0	0	1	1,985
Overnightsensation	3	F	1	0	1	0	7,000
Over'nout	11	G	10	3	1	0	33,970
Overocks	2	F	3	0	0	1	2,390
Overpass	4	G	11	3	1	4	85,385
Overprint	7	H	5	4	0	1	8,237
Overreaction	3	F	4	1	0	0	19,938
Overt Action	5	G	3	2	0	1	3,060
Overtime Ali	6	G	9	0	1	1	2,213
Overtime Bid	3	F	5	0	1	1	4,039
Overtimeangie Baby	3	F	16	1	2	1	19,819
Overton Cruiser	2	C	3	1	1	1	26,080
Overtone	6	G	13	0	0	2	2,643
Overwhelming Cher	6	M	5	0	0	0	455
Overzealous	4	G	5	0	0	0	558
Ovfour	2	C	2	0	0	0	0
Ovies Dream (PER)	4	F	4	0	0	0	800
Ovo	4	C	4	0	0	0	1,090
O'Well Hatch	3	G	7	0	0	0	1,233
Owenahincha	2	F	2	0	0	0	3,420
Owens County	5	G	11	0	0	2	1,710
Owen's Way	9	G	4	0	0	0	362
Owned Exclusively	7	G	6	1	1	3	12,196
Owns the Place	3	C	8	1	1	3	46,210
Owyee	6	M	3	0	1	0	1,116
Ox Bow	10	G	2	0	0	0	600
Oxana Mae	4	F	2	0	0	0	86
Oxanna	4	F	7	0	0	1	700
Oxbridge	3	C	2	0	0	1	3,000
Oxford Grad	4	F	12	0	1	2	5,158
Oxford Joy	2	F	3	1	0	0	10,920
Oxford Tea Party	7	G	1	0	0	1	5,500
Oxford's Legacy	2	C	1	0	0	0	0
Oxsana Royale	4	F	6	0	1	1	2,346
Oxymoron	4	C	9	0	3	1	8,165
Oyagi	5	H	11	2	1	2	14,414
Oye Yoye Yoye	6	G	1	0	0	0	152
Oyster Cove	5	G	3	0	0	0	0
Oz	3	C	1	0	1	0	8,600
Oz the Almighty	8	G	2	0	0	0	336
Oza	6	G	12	1	2	5	54,738
Ozark	6	G	14	0	1	2	3,000
Ozark Princess	4	F	20	1	6	2	10,002
Ozark Rose	3	F	8	3	0	1	11,883
Ozette Legend	3	F	4	1	0	0	9,075
Ozilda's Karen	6	M	9	2	0	3	38,440
Ozilda's Nancy Lee	4	F	16	3	2	2	38,790
Ozilda's Ronny	5	G	19	2	3	0	24,952
Ozone Al	6	G	7	0	0	0	670
Ozoned	3	G	6	2	1	0	23,528
Ozzie Cat	4	C	2	1	0	0	25,800
Ozzie Mozzie	4	G	2	0	0	0	95
Ozzie's J J	3	G	13	3	3	1	67,970
P D Vic	4	G	4	1	0	0	8,174
P Day	9	G	3	0	1	1	4,155
P F Classic	4	F	3	0	0	0	0
P F Don D	3	C	5	1	1	1	23,330
P J Prado	4	F	3	0	0	0	0
P J's Choice	5	M	9	1	0	4	2,650
P J's Kid	6	M	13	1	0	2	9,274
P J's Snowstorm	4	G	4	0	0	0	484
P M's Crown	3	F	4	0	0	2	3,129
P R Royal Princess	3	F	8	2	1	1	9,317
P Ridge	5	H	9	1	1	0	7,892
P Ridge's Keivyn	4	G	10	1	0	2	7,694
P S It's American	3	F	6	0	2	1	12,150
P Town John	3	G	3	0	0	0	7,128
P. A. McGuerty	3	G	3	1	1	0	8,424
P. A. Pistol	4	G	17	1	0	3	8,556
P. A.'s Candy	5	M	11	1	1	3	4,252
P. C. Bad Girl	9	M	8	1	0	0	4,950
P. C. Pete	2	C	6	1	0	0	5,844
P. C. Valentine	2	F	3	0	0	0	306

Horse	Age	Sex	Sts	1st	2d	3d	Won
P. D. Bucky	3	G	10	0	0	0	1,575
P. J. Steve	2	G	2	0	1	0	4,590
P. J.'s Eskimo	4	F	1	0	0	0	146
P. J.'s Faith	3	F	1	0	0	0	135
P. J.'s Paulie Boy	6	H	12	2	2	5	152,317
P. Kerney	3	C	6	2	0	0	48,820
P. L. Gold	2	C	4	0	0	0	3,120
P. M.'s Snacks	6	G	15	0	2	5	7,098
P. S. Saros	5	M	5	0	0	1	1,560
P. T. Squirt	2	F	2	0	0	1	2,860
P. T.'s Captain	2	C	7	0	0	0	410
Pa Pa Da	3	G	11	2	2	3	130,040
Pablo Diablo	3	G	12	3	2	2	14,678
Pablo's Flash	2	C	2	0	0	0	134
Pac for Arkansas	4	F	5	0	0	0	293
Pac N Iron	4	G	5	0	1	1	3,172
Pac the Cooler	2	F	5	0	0	0	1,525
Pacalac	3	C	7	0	1	0	3,373
Pace Like Fire	2	C	2	0	0	0	0
Pacer	5	H	9	2	1	0	45,498
Pacesetter	3	G	15	2	1	1	18,740
Pacewaster	11	G	2	0	0	0	130
Pachamama	2	F	4	0	3	1	12,900
Pachara (GB)	5	G	1	0	0	0	700
Pachaug	3	C	9	0	1	1	4,509
Pache's Forum	5	H	10	1	0	0	8,196
Pachiro	3	G	6	1	0	1	16,040
Pacific Armada	4	G	3	0	1	0	2,750
Pacific Blue	8	M	3	0	0	0	0
Pacific Crest	4	G	3	0	0	1	420
Pacific Island	3	F	8	2	2	1	78,536
Pacific Journey	4	F	10	1	0	1	5,522
Pacific Palisades	6	G	12	0	4	0	10,256
Pacific Plate	8	G	3	0	0	1	1,537
Pacific Sunset	4	F	9	0	0	3	15,610
Pacifico	4	G	14	2	0	2	14,920
Pacify	6	M	6	0	0	1	1,155
Pacify Me	4	G	2	0	0	0	480
Pack and Drift	9	G	7	0	0	0	951
Pack the Tack	4	G	11	2	2	3	13,295
Package Store	6	H	1	0	0	0	245
Packaged Deal	2	F	2	0	0	0	0
Packen Rhythm	5	H	4	0	0	0	357
Packin Glacken	4	C	15	1	0	1	17,315
Packy	2	C	1	1	0	0	7,673
Paco El Prado	7	G	9	2	3	1	31,427
Paco Loco	6	H	1	0	0	0	0
Pad the Wallet	3	F	4	1	1	1	21,600
Paddington	3	C	5	0	0	1	17,540
Paddle's Big Boy	4	G	11	3	2	0	10,304
Paddle's Big Girl	3	F	11	3	2	1	30,862
Paddy Drew	6	M	8	1	1	1	7,301
Paddy Gorie	7	G	13	2	1	2	12,148
Paddy Swazzie	4	G	5	1	1	0	1,754
Paddy's Daisy	2	F	6	4	0	0	186,336
Paddy's Dasher	4	F	10	2	0	3	11,352
Paddy's Spy	9	G	11	2	1	1	41,024
Paderewski	4	G	2	0	0	0	230
Padgett	4	G	10	3	0	1	27,671
Padirac	6	G	5	0	1	0	3,532
Padishah	2	C	6	0	1	1	13,143
Padlock	5	G	8	3	1	0	56,877
Padre	4	G	12	0	3	1	3,482
Padre Murphy	7	G	12	4	2	1	11,205
Padre Pete	8	G	6	0	0	0	443
Padua's Gift	2	G	6	0	1	0	5,440
Paducah	6	G	10	2	1	0	8,086
Pady's Party	3	G	6	1	0	2	17,124
Paegent Winner	2	F	1	0	0	0	0
Paesano	4	G	8	0	0	0	1,124
Paga (ARG)	7	M	3	0	0	0	920
Pagan Place	6	H	4	1	0	0	17,907
Pagan's Gold	2	C	2	0	1	0	2,200
Page Hunting	6	G	14	1	4	3	14,517
Page Me Later	4	F	12	1	5	2	57,437
Page the Way	3	F	7	0	0	0	565
Page Two	10	G	10	1	2	1	13,605
Pager	5	H	9	2	2	2	26,645
Paggy	10	M	6	1	0	0	[illegible]
Paging	6	G	15	5	2	2	96,809
Paging Beauty	3	F	10	2	2	2	26,340
Paging Dr. Gober	4	G	2	0	0	0	470
Paging Maggie	5	M	7	0	0	0	1,573
Pagliacci (GB)	6	G	13	2	3	2	23,410
Pagosa Springs	3	F	3	0	0	1	6,040
Pah	5	G	5	1	0	1	25,200
Pahsimeroi Smoke	5	H	10	2	0	2	3,455
Paid the Toll	3	G	3	0	0	0	0
Paid Vacation	3	G	7	3	0	1	11,913
Paigaroo	4	F	2	0	0	0	510
Paige	4	F	14	0	4	3	6,469
Paige Is a Lode	3	F	1	0	0	0	0
Paige Kevin Kahuna	5	H	6	1	0	1	7,477
Paige Moro	4	F	14	1	3	2	22,613
Paige the Doc	3	G	10	1	0	0	5,158
Paigeboy	4	G	2	0	0	0	0
Paiges Aly Birdie	3	F	20	1	1	1	7,602
Paiges Pebble	4	F	15	4	3	1	23,050
Paige's Recital	4	F	3	0	0	0	371
Paige's Turn	3	F	4	0	0	0	0
Pain and Glory	2	C	4	0	2	0	17,025
Pain 'n Temptation	3	F	10	1	1	0	27,520
Painless	3	F	10	0	2	0	5,546
Paint Ballado	3	G	11	0	2	1	24,447
Paint It Black	4	F	9	2	1	4	79,840
Paint Me Quick	4	F	6	1	1	0	5,742
Paint My Dreams	2	F	5	0	0	1	5,314
Paint the Wind	9	M	7	0	0	2	1,464
Paintball	4	F	6	1	0	0	20,940
Painted Bridle	4	G	2	0	0	0	226
Painted Dancer	4	G	8	1	0	1	6,840
Painted Pistol	7	G	19	4	3	2	36,635
Painted Smile	2	F	4	0	0	0	2,500
Painter	5	M	8	1	5	0	14,842
Painter Gabe	2	C	10	2	2	1	33,070
Painter's Creek	3	G	11	3	1	3	27,906
Painter's Sword	3	G	8	2	1	1	20,180
Paintmeapicture	3	G	4	0	1	3	6,475
Paiota Falls	3	F	5	4	1	0	177,354
Pair of Wings	4	F	3	0	0	0	1,260
Paisley Braes	7	M	5	0	0	1	3,844
Paisley Park	4	F	10	3	1	1	102,590
Pajama Party Girl	3	F	3	0	0	1	2,631
Pajaro	5	G	7	2	1	0	13,710
Pak Yer Tack	3	G	8	1	1	1	4,115
Pakawalup	2	C	3	0	0	0	1,116
Pakenham	5	G	7	1	1	0	2,435
Pal Joey	9	G	14	1	1	0	6,562
Pal McCartney	5	G	4	0	0	0	0
Pala Cielo	6	M	1	0	0	0	0
Palabras de Amor	2	F	2	0	0	0	588
Palace Creek	3	G	10	2	0	0	8,772
Palace de Lady	3	F	4	0	0	0	105
Palace Dove	4	F	6	0	0	1	798
Palace Heroine	8	M	3	0	0	0	511
Palace Intrigue	2	F	1	0	0	0	1,290
Palace of Dreams	6	M	8	1	0	1	10,445
Palace Rose	3	F	10	2	1	2	43,780
Palace Royale (IRE)	8	M	1	0	0	0	0
Palace Uprising	4	F	10	1	1	1	48,980
Palace Wildcat	3	F	6	0	1	1	11,753
Palaceoffinearts	3	F	11	1	3	1	14,821
Palacios Appeal	2	C	5	1	2	0	37,000
Paladdie	6	G	5	1	1	0	16,594
Paladin Power	6	G	15	0	4	2	28,482
Paladin Run	4	G	10	1	2	2	6,296
Palaestra	3	F	5	1	0	1	39,995
Palanca	2	C	1	0	1	0	800
Palatinate	3	G	1	0	0	0	217
Palatine	4	G	13	1	4	3	35,258
Palazzo One	3	G	13	0	0	1	3,750
Pale Moonlight	2	F	1	0	0	0	205
Pale One	3	G	6	0	1	1	8,680
Pale Peach	2	F	3	0	1	0	2,500
Pale Satin	2	F	[illegible]	1	0	1	31,050
Paley Jr	8	H	2	0	0	1	233
Pal[illegible] (CHI)	9	H	1	0	0	0	75
Palique (URU)	[illegible]	H	3	1	0	0	30,480

Horse	Age	Sex	Sts	1st	2d	3d	Won
Palisade Princess	3	F	5	3	0	0	14,075
Palisades Sunset	4	F	4	0	2	0	4,700
Palistar	2	C	5	1	0	2	31,636
Palladian	2	G	5	1	1	0	18,100
Palladio	2	C	3	1	0	0	44,802
Palm Avenue	2	F	4	1	0	1	42,180
Palm Beach Bud	3	C	6	1	2	1	32,375
Palm Chilly	3	F	2	0	0	0	147
Palm Island	3	F	2	0	0	0	175
Palmeiro	6	G	1	0	0	1	4,200
Palmerton	5	G	8	2	1	1	48,400
Palmetto Dunes	4	F	5	0	0	0	288
Palo Pinto	2	C	2	0	0	0	390
Paloma Parilla	5	G	7	4	0	0	32,003
Paloo	2	C	3	1	0	1	8,580
Palooka	3	C	8	1	2	1	13,270
Palpen	3	C	10	1	0	2	20,427
Pals Forever	3	C	9	1	2	1	27,355
Pal's Last Memory	6	M	11	1	0	0	14,146
Pals Pride	5	G	4	0	0	1	4,650
Paluxy	7	G	1	0	0	0	0
Pam and Gayla	4	F	19	0	1	0	2,516
Pamela's Gold	3	F	2	1	0	0	12,360
Pamela's Parade	2	F	5	1	0	1	14,576
Pamjet	2	C	3	1	0	0	11,490
Pammie's Trump	3	C	1	0	0	1	2,090
Pammy's Grand	5	M	14	0	1	5	7,934
Pampa Kid	2	C	2	0	0	0	1,600
Pampered	4	F	8	2	1	2	69,196
Pampered Pasha	3	C	6	0	0	1	2,768
Pampered Princess	4	F	11	4	3	1	138,000
Pam's Ectropy	3	F	12	1	0	1	8,287
Pam's Gale	3	F	9	2	2	0	33,545
Pam's Girl	4	F	12	0	3	5	19,210
Pam's Grey Girl	3	F	7	0	1	0	7,020
Pam's Parade	2	F	2	0	0	0	1,375
Pam's Ruckus	3	F	13	2	2	1	51,865
Pam's Thunder	3	F	9	0	0	0	5,200
Pam's Wildcat	3	C	7	1	0	2	20,370
Pam'ssummerwind	4	F	3	0	0	1	1,885
Pan Adam	6	G	19	0	2	2	5,316
Pan Out	4	F	10	0	1	0	1,630
Pana Cat	2	F	5	1	1	2	21,800
Pana Code	2	C	2	0	1	0	3,300
Pana Girl	5	M	6	1	0	2	6,170
Panagis	3	C	6	0	0	0	2,033
Panama Ana	2	F	8	1	1	1	34,459
Panama Lane	2	G	3	0	0	2	14,982
Panamacircle	2	F	1	0	0	0	126
Panasofskee	5	M	4	0	1	0	4,621
Panchita Villa	6	M	16	4	2	1	23,159
Pancho	2	G	8	2	1	2	13,360
Pancho Del Norte	5	G	5	0	0	0	320
Pancho Del Sol	3	G	3	0	0	0	1,200
Pancho Gem	2	G	2	0	0	0	0
Pancho Pequeno	2	C	4	0	0	2	1,870
Pancho Pete	9	G	3	0	1	0	2,445
Pancho Tam	2	G	3	2	0	1	16,000
Pancho's Alibi	5	G	14	0	1	4	6,220
Pancho's Cat	2	G	6	0	0	0	1,140
Pancho's Flight	5	H	3	0	0	0	0
Pancho's Gold	3	G	13	2	2	3	17,795
Panchos Irish Gal	2	F	3	0	0	0	0
Pancho's Karma	4	C	7	0	0	0	296
Pancho's Pride	4	F	11	0	3	2	13,169
Pancho's Temptress	3	F	4	0	1	0	2,055
Pancho's Tribute	2	C	5	0	2	0	4,000
Panchromatic	6	G	2	0	0	0	175
Panda Bears Dancer	3	F	3	0	0	0	320
Pandora's Secret	3	F	4	1	0	1	67,185
Pandorasconnection	4	F	5	1	1	1	36,452
Panfi	4	G	15	1	5	3	17,315
Pangaea	3	F	1	0	0	0	0
Pangle Store	6	H	1	0	0	0	0
Pangress	7	M	11	0	2	1	3,882
Paniemoniam	3	F	5	0	0	0	1,740
Panina	3	F	9	2	2	0	70,828
Paniolo Gold	7	H	5	0	0	1	1,110
Paniolo Road	6	G	12	1	5	3	9,214

Horse	Age	Sex	Sts	1st	2d	3d	Won
Panjshair	3	F	5	0	3	0	17,250
Panning	4	G	14	3	1	1	22,595
Panning for News	5	M	6	3	1	0	4,509
Panorama Ama	5	M	4	1	0	1	4,195
Panorama Drive	8	G	14	2	3	1	9,368
Panorama Valley	2	F	4	3	0	0	74,760
Panorama Village	4	F	4	0	1	0	2,813
Panoramic	4	C	3	1	1	0	40,340
Pan's Forum	5	G	4	0	0	1	3,138
Pansy Garden	5	M	10	0	4	2	9,940
Pansy Pence	2	F	1	0	0	0	1,185
Panta Ellinas	7	G	10	2	1	1	14,582
Pantages	4	G	7	1	0	0	7,658
Pantera	3	F	3	0	0	1	2,005
Panther Creek	5	H	1	0	0	0	43
Panther Pond	6	G	3	0	0	1	2,807
Panther Street	4	G	3	0	0	0	0
Pants N Kisses	4	G	11	1	1	3	50,516
Panuco	2	C	1	0	0	1	2,750
Panzano	2	G	1	0	0	0	400
Panzon	9	G	7	0	0	0	416
Paoli	5	G	12	3	4	0	49,420
Papa Dancer	2	F	2	1	0	0	10,800
Papa Fuse	3	C	4	1	0	2	21,760
Papa Luke	7	G	8	1	0	0	4,256
Papa M and M	6	H	15	2	2	1	49,493
Papa Sal	3	C	7	2	0	2	48,840
Papa Sids Girl	3	F	14	0	5	2	48,582
Papa to Kinzie	3	F	3	1	0	2	56,484
Papago	8	G	10	1	1	3	7,836
Papalito	4	G	6	1	1	2	15,772
Paparazzi	5	G	7	4	0	1	56,520
Paparazzi Miss	3	F	7	0	1	0	2,686
Papa's a Prince	4	C	5	0	0	0	77
Papa's Delight	4	G	1	0	0	0	2,640
Papa's Got Gin	7	G	12	2	0	2	11,329
Papa's Nicholas	2	G	1	0	0	1	1,600
Papa's Pickpocket	3	F	14	3	2	1	25,860
Papas Pistol	3	G	13	1	4	1	8,756
Papa's Preston	4	G	2	0	0	0	0
Papa's Prize	2	C	4	0	0	0	2,131
Papa's Pumpkin	6	M	4	0	0	0	425
Papas Yeehaw	3	F	8	0	0	0	1,476
Pape	5	G	8	1	1	0	17,460
Papeete	3	F	5	1	1	1	5,470
Paper Bag	4	F	13	2	2	3	26,053
Paper Clip	4	F	7	0	1	0	2,534
Paper Copy	4	G	11	1	1	3	14,350
Paper Kite	4	G	3	0	0	0	420
Paper Man	3	C	7	1	0	0	22,750
Paper Mountain	4	F	6	0	0	1	3,120
Paper Road	3	C	5	0	0	0	285
Paper Storm	4	G	2	0	0	0	174
Paperjam	4	F	9	0	1	0	7,790
Papi Chullo	2	C	1	0	0	0	2,500
Papi Macho Man	4	G	1	0	0	0	0
Papier Mache	6	M	13	3	3	3	61,248
Papiillon	4	F	13	1	2	0	8,070
Papillon Dreams	5	M	3	0	0	1	1,758
Papillon Rouge (CHI)	4	F	3	0	0	0	3,620
Papola Pride	2	F	1	0	1	0	1,900
Pappa Carlos	5	G	5	0	0	0	729
Pappa Joe	6	H	4	0	1	0	3,160
Pappa Sureshot	5	H	12	0	0	1	1,774
Papparratzi	3	F	6	1	0	0	11,632
Pappa's Dennis	6	G	7	0	0	2	1,716
Pappa's Luck	6	G	20	1	1	2	15,016
Pappasphlesas	2	C	2	0	0	2	5,360
Pappaw's Big Boy	4	G	1	0	0	0	0
Pappolino	6	G	19	0	1	1	3,974
Pappy's Boo	3	C	2	0	0	0	0
Pappys Legacy	4	C	2	0	0	0	182
Papua	5	H	8	1	1	3	104,654
Par a Mutual	4	G	13	2	0	3	8,824
Par Avon	7	M	8	1	0	1	2,072
Par de Deux	4	F	6	0	0	0	2,400
Par Golfer	6	M	9	2	0	1	23,833
Par Shooter	3	G	10	1	1	2	6,747
Para Alquilar	6	G	10	4	1	2	30,308

Horse	Age	Sex	Sts	1st	2d	3d	Won
Para Belle	4	F	1	0	0	1	450
Para Usted	6	G	11	1	1	1	8,780
Parachute	3	C	6	0	0	1	3,234
Parade Away	3	C	2	0	0	0	0
Parade Band	3	G	6	2	0	1	22,417
Parade King	3	G	1	0	0	0	187
Parade of Lights	4	F	4	0	0	0	494
Parade of Music	5	G	10	3	0	3	65,102
Parade Out Front	4	G	7	1	2	0	35,967
Parade Suit	3	G	8	0	2	1	5,825
Parade Trick	2	F	6	0	1	2	4,505
Paradiddle Joe	2	C	3	0	0	0	532
Parading Tomisue	3	F	5	1	1	0	43,020
Paradise Cove	2	C	1	0	0	0	400
Paradise Dancer	4	C	11	1	3	4	75,160
Paradise Girl	4	F	4	0	0	0	0
Paradise Heights	4	G	17	2	9	1	41,694
Paradise Peak	3	C	8	1	3	0	62,705
Paradise Theater	2	C	2	0	0	0	1,230
Paradise Wild	3	F	12	4	2	2	47,383
Paradise's Boss	4	G	7	4	1	0	116,400
Parado	5	G	5	1	2	1	11,045
Parador	3	F	6	1	1	4	9,150
Paradox Valley	3	G	3	0	0	0	88
Paragon John	4	G	4	0	0	0	0
Paragon Queen	2	F	7	1	4	0	85,540
Paragraph	3	G	8	0	3	1	7,680
Parajacks	2	C	4	0	0	0	3,120
Paralegal	7	M	4	0	0	0	1,030
Paralink	7	M	10	0	0	2	2,877
Parallax	4	G	6	0	0	0	4,350
Paramount Pepper	2	C	1	0	0	0	44
Paranoia	2	F	5	0	1	0	2,828
Paranoide Paul	5	G	5	1	0	0	3,578
Parapet	3	F	3	0	0	2	1,020
Parasail	4	G	4	1	1	0	51,740
Parasevens	5	G	1	0	0	0	61
Parched	2	F	1	0	0	0	118
Pard E	3	G	5	0	0	0	1,040
Pardon Me Girls	4	G	7	1	2	3	20,490
Parducci Jr.	6	G	3	0	1	0	995
Parducci Ridge	5	G	13	2	6	2	7,745
Pareepassoo	5	M	3	0	1	0	9,270
Parfect Dancer	4	G	10	1	0	1	14,218
Parfumeur (FR)	4	G	11	1	2	3	52,100
Parfy's Legacy	5	H	8	2	4	1	34,740
Parham's Music	7	H	3	0	0	0	3,375
Parhelion (GER)	4	C	7	1	1	0	34,302
Pariente Barbara	11	M	4	0	0	0	490
Parigi	4	G	1	0	0	0	0
Parioli's Legacy	3	F	1	0	0	0	795
Paris Academy	8	G	4	0	2	1	1,920
Paris Adventure	4	G	9	1	1	0	29,800
Paris Amie	3	F	5	0	0	0	479
Paris Gold	3	C	4	1	1	1	10,500
Paris Legend	4	F	11	1	0	1	12,004
Paris Mountain	3	G	1	0	0	0	0
Paris Navy	4	C	6	0	0	1	770
Paris Next Year	3	F	8	3	1	0	32,800
Paris Passport	2	G	1	0	0	0	114
Paris Past	4	F	7	2	1	1	19,714
Paris Pride	2	F	4	0	1	0	4,030
Paris Sunrise	4	G	3	0	1	0	11,450
Parish Princess	3	F	15	2	0	2	21,115
Parisian	3	G	9	2	0	1	11,807
Parisian Affair	3	F	6	1	0	0	24,060
Parisian Brass	2	F	2	0	0	0	0
Parisian Deputy	4	F	14	1	2	2	50,434
Parisian Lord	6	G	12	1	1	3	28,613
Parisian Slew	3	G	9	2	1	1	7,942
Parisian Trip	6	M	11	4	4	1	75,830
Parisiana	2	F	1	0	0	0	207
Parisienne Regime	4	F	3	0	0	0	164
Parisky	7	G	11	1	0	0	8,809
Park Avenue Ball	2	C	5	3	1	0	278,600
Park City Playboy	6	G	5	3	1	0	16,890
Park City Red	5	G	5	0	0	1	1,778
Park Falls	4	G	16	0	2	4	6,066
Park Jet	5	G	8	2	2	1	3,883
Park Ranger	3	C	1	0	0	0	135
Park Ridge	3	G	6	0	0	0	1,159
Park the Car	4	G	10	3	1	1	41,370
Park West	4	C	9	2	0	1	12,785
Parkcityutah	2	G	5	1	1	0	15,260
Parkdale	3	F	5	1	1	1	9,644
Parker P	5	G	13	0	0	2	4,179
Parker Run	3	G	7	2	0	0	34,368
Parker Valley	2	C	3	0	2	0	12,820
Parkers Chapel	6	H	14	4	1	0	20,352
Parkers Mill	3	C	12	2	3	1	84,241
Parkers Peace	3	G	9	3	1	0	21,000
Parker's Pet	4	G	11	3	2	2	33,080
Parker's Prince	3	G	6	0	2	0	5,896
Parker's Way West	4	G	10	0	0	2	8,352
Parklane Beloved	3	F	3	0	0	0	121
Parklane Best	4	F	4	0	1	0	1,715
Parklane Bite Over	5	M	9	1	0	2	3,759
Parklane Cargo	3	F	6	1	0	0	3,238
Parklane Naney	2	F	1	0	0	0	56
Parklane Oak	3	F	8	0	1	0	1,476
Parklane Patty	3	F	3	0	0	0	124
Parklane Profit	2	F	1	0	0	0	105
Parklane Saphire	2	C	1	0	0	0	105
Parklane Silver	2	F	3	0	0	0	210
Parklane Thriller	3	F	6	1	3	1	7,569
Parklane Toccata	4	F	6	0	1	0	2,620
Parksville	4	G	16	1	2	4	5,395
Parkway Express	6	G	7	0	0	0	853
Parlay Guy	5	G	8	1	1	1	6,840
Parlay Pride	4	G	10	1	1	2	10,185
Parlay Voo Van	3	F	9	2	0	0	5,509
Parlay Your Talent	3	F	4	0	1	0	1,315
Parlay's Charm	5	M	7	0	1	0	1,902
Parlay's Dee	5	M	11	1	2	1	11,018
Parlay's Prospect	4	G	11	2	1	4	62,976
Parliament Hill	7	G	10	2	1	0	10,389
Parnell Square	4	C	3	0	1	1	14,450
Paros Brass	2	C	1	0	0	0	0
Parose	10	G	8	2	2	1	114,385
Parrott	3	G	14	2	1	6	24,002
Parrott Bay	7	G	15	3	2	2	155,802
Par's Biscuit	3	F	4	0	3	0	14,000
Parsaver	4	F	8	1	0	2	7,855
Parsippany	5	M	16	2	2	2	32,772
Parsons Prospect	5	H	4	0	0	0	485
Part of a Bet	7	G	4	0	0	0	529
Part of the Plan	4	F	2	1	0	0	14,750
Partager Valay	5	G	6	1	2	0	1,683
Partee Jr.	3	G	11	0	1	2	4,125
Parterre	7	G	7	2	1	3	21,577
Parthenon	3	C	9	2	2	1	30,890
Parthenope	3	F	7	1	0	1	6,443
Particle Stream	3	F	7	1	1	1	18,752
Parting	4	F	2	1	0	0	21,000
Parting for Home	4	F	3	0	0	0	276
Partition	3	C	5	1	2	0	35,390
Partner's Bite	4	G	9	1	0	4	9,945
Partners Due	2	F	6	1	2	0	54,750
Partner's Halo	2	G	2	0	0	1	3,120
Partners No More	3	C	6	0	1	0	2,055
Partner's Pearl	4	F	7	1	0	1	11,930
Party Airs	5	G	3	0	0	1	7,388
Party Angel	2	F	2	0	0	1	1,530
Party At Lamptons	2	F	4	0	0	1	950
Party At Shu's	4	G	6	0	0	0	378
Party At the Bar	8	G	6	1	3	1	2,830
Party Believer	7	G	9	2	2	1	17,539
Party Boy	5	G	4	0	1	0	2,120
Party by Pyrite	6	M	6	1	0	0	2,040
Party Case	3	F	5	0	0	1	1,327
Party Date	4	F	1	0	0	0	81
Party Down	4	F	3	1	1	0	27,900
Party Dreams	3	F	5	1	3	0	12,940
Party Fever	2	F	5	1	1	1	27,410
Party Games	3	F	8	3	3	0	30,200
Party Girl Jo	4	F	6	1	0	0	7,365

Horse	Age	Sex	Sts				
Party Hostess	3	F	16	3	0	3	14,472
Party in the Park	4	F	9	4	3	1	6,951
Party Island	6	M	11	0	1	2	3,144
Party Maker	2	F	2	1	1	0	49,826
Party Miss	4	F	13	1	1	1	16,020
Party of Eight	3	F	3	0	1	0	3,900
Party of Six	3	F	4	2	0	2	21,117
Party On	4	G	1	0	0	0	180
Party Pirate	8	M	12	2	3	1	87,080
Party Plans	4	C	10	2	1	3	29,670
Party Queen	5	M	5	0	0	1	8,060
Party Regent	2	F	7	0	0	0	1,700
Party Request	5	G	3	0	0	0	240
Party Shu	6	M	8	0	1	5	10,850
Party Slew	2	C	1	0	0	0	155
Party Speech	4	G	15	0	1	1	2,695
Party Til Ya Whirl	2	G	1	0	0	0	140
Party Tip	2	F	6	2	0	0	17,980
Party to Party	5	M	9	0	3	1	16,370
Partying	5	M	3	0	0	0	800
Partyongarth	4	F	3	1	0	0	3,128
Partytime (IRE)	5	M	1	0	0	0	0
Partywithavengence	4	G	16	2	4	2	24,345
Partyz On	3	C	9	0	0	0	2,575
Parytime	8	G	10	1	1	1	13,245
Pas de Cat	2	C	3	0	0	1	605
Pas de Fantasy	3	F	1	0	0	0	0
Pas de Memoires (IRE)	9	G	1	0	0	0	0
Pa's Princess Mi	3	F	3	0	0	0	0
Pasado Manana	3	G	2	0	0	0	0
Pascagoula	7	G	8	1	1	0	3,361
Pasco Fiasco	5	G	5	0	0	0	395
Paseana's Girl (ARG)	4	F	2	0	0	1	5,640
Pasing Monique	4	F	4	0	0	0	0
Pasketty	4	G	6	2	1	2	64,610
Pasomonte Paul	7	G	11	1	2	3	11,270
Pasotex	10	G	9	0	0	1	1,356
Pasport	7	G	12	0	1	5	13,992
Pass a Buck	3	F	5	0	0	0	1,120
Pass a Star	4	G	14	1	0	3	6,433
Pass Bye	6	M	13	1	2	6	27,369
Pass Go Collect	4	C	3	0	0	0	372
Pass Interference	3	F	16	1	4	4	12,477
Pass It On	2	C	2	0	0	0	0
Pass Me the Salt	3	F	8	2	5	0	74,650
Pass Muster	3	G	9	0	2	2	16,110
Pass Play	3	G	10	3	1	2	84,823
Pass Rush	5	H	2	0	0	0	0
Pass the Biscuits	3	G	10	3	2	2	19,780
Pass the Buckshot	6	G	8	1	1	0	6,001
Pass the Class	3	C	10	0	0	0	1,379
Pass the Hat	5	G	8	0	3	1	20,883
Pass the Jewell	6	G	1	0	0	0	0
Pass the Luck	5	M	12	1	6	5	14,860
Pass the Native	3	G	1	0	0	0	0
Pass the Pepper	5	M	7	0	2	2	26,232
Pass the Puck	3	G	15	3	1	4	39,770
Pass the Reality	7	G	2	0	0	0	102
Pass the Sugar	3	F	2	0	0	0	0
Pass the Sun	8	G	10	1	6	2	9,862
Pass the Sunset	2	C	7	0	0	0	195
Pass Them Quick	3	G	9	3	1	1	5,384
Passability	3	G	3	0	0	0	1,045
Passage to Ararat	7	G	1	0	0	0	0
Passageway	2	F	4	1	2	0	47,641
Passaic	3	F	8	1	1	1	51,080
Passante	5	G	11	0	0	0	1,452
Passed Over	2	C	6	0	0	0	3,494
Passem All	8	M	12	0	5	2	6,382
Passem Easy	4	G	3	0	0	0	114
Passerine	3	F	6	0	0	0	3,567
Passing Approval	3	G	8	0	0	0	0
Passing Hero	6	G	5	2	1	0	8,689
Passing Pleasure	3	F	1	0	0	0	145
Passing Proudly	5	M	10	1	2	1	3,896
Passing Reign	3	G	9	0	0	0	242
Passing Ships	6	G	12	2	2	5	41,862
Passing Shot	5	M	6	1	1	2	185,460
Passing South	3	F	4	0	0	0	161

Horse	Age	Sex	Sts	1st	2d	3d	Won
Passing Storm	4	G	5	2	1	0	14,137
Passing Velocity	4	F	3	0	0	0	298
Passing Way	3	F	9	2	0	1	7,045
Passion Caper	4	F	12	2	2	2	14,100
Passion Cat	3	F	8	1	0	2	9,863
Passion Fever	2	F	8	1	3	1	15,665
Passion for Words	3	F	6	2	0	2	34,920
Passion Wheel	4	C	2	0	0	0	0
Passionate Bird	5	M	14	3	2	2	132,079
Passionate Bride	5	M	2	0	1	0	2,805
Passionate Caper	5	M	15	0	1	3	6,037
Passionate Dancer	2	F	1	0	0	1	4,700
Passionate Flight	3	F	2	0	0	0	75
Passionate John	4	G	1	0	0	0	300
Passionate Kiss	3	F	8	1	1	2	5,804
Passionate Lad	6	G	1	0	0	0	0
Passionate Soldier	5	G	3	1	0	0	10,837
Passionate Talk	5	M	6	0	1	1	2,498
Passionate Trick	7	M	1	0	0	0	0
Passionforall	4	G	17	1	2	1	14,573
Passionforanna	4	F	16	2	4	1	13,028
Passionforcashin	6	G	3	0	0	1	9,412
Passionforluck	3	F	16	1	3	2	16,978
Passion's Destiny	3	F	8	0	1	2	22,380
Passions Roar	3	F	6	1	0	0	8,792
Passive	5	G	4	2	0	0	22,000
Passive Resistance	4	C	4	0	2	1	19,130
Passmeby	9	M	2	0	0	0	0
Passover Broadway	2	C	7	2	2	1	27,560
Past Due	2	F	3	0	1	0	9,762
Past Due Account	7	G	4	0	0	1	2,693
Past Tence	6	H	1	0	0	0	0
Past the Wire	3	G	2	0	0	0	600
Past Time	7	G	12	2	1	1	11,765
Pasta	3	G	11	3	2	3	30,230
Pasta Due	4	F	5	1	0	1	5,635
Pasta Fazool	4	F	2	0	0	1	1,430
Pasta's Dream	3	F	11	0	1	3	12,980
Pastel	2	F	2	0	0	0	170
Pastel Colour	4	F	7	1	1	0	22,862
Pastel Light	2	F	8	3	3	1	30,490
Paster's Baby	5	G	8	0	0	0	2,489
Pastor Clarissa	2	F	1	0	0	0	0
Pasture Boy	4	G	13	1	1	0	15,155
Pat	5	M	6	1	0	0	9,050
Pat a Stake	9	H	7	0	0	0	1,140
Pat for Joy	3	G	9	0	0	0	1,077
Pat Speedy	3	F	6	0	0	2	5,450
Pat the Cat	3	G	5	0	0	0	460
Pat the Winner	4	G	9	1	2	0	35,730
Patacon	4	C	1	0	0	0	340
Patagonia Tango	2	F	5	0	1	2	16,380
Patapsco	3	G	3	1	0	0	4,907
Patch Conway	5	G	9	0	0	1	2,370
Patch N Ryder	6	M	3	0	0	1	1,179
Patches of Speed	2	F	4	2	1	1	38,110
Patches Park	2	G	1	0	0	0	71
Patchtomatch	3	C	7	1	0	1	3,310
Patchy Valentine	8	M	1	1	0	0	4,284
Patent	7	G	13	1	2	1	16,970
Path	4	C	1	0	0	0	360
Path of Thunder	3	F	7	3	3	0	106,700
Patience Pays	2	F	4	1	0	1	29,830
Pati's Princessa	3	F	2	1	0	0	4,440
Patito Feo	5	G	5	0	0	0	1,190
Patrician Power	11	G	4	0	0	0	600
Patricia's Song	3	F	2	0	0	0	0
Patrick O'Lion	2	G	10	1	0	1	10,378
Patrickanddibble	3	G	5	0	0	0	293
Patrick's Echo	8	G	13	3	2	1	22,255
Patrick's Exit	8	G	4	0	0	0	556
Patrick's Promise	3	C	3	0	0	0	66
Patrick's Slew	7	G	2	0	0	1	1,980
Patrick's Talent	5	G	10	1	0	3	27,415
Patrick's Tribute	3	G	8	1	0	0	7,444
Patriot Act	2	C	4	0	2	1	114,885
Patriot Breeze	3	F	2	0	0	0	130
Patriot Halo	3	C	2	0	0	0	0
Patriot Jet	3	F	10	2	1	1	17,569

Horse	Age	Sex	Sts	1st	2d	3d	Won
Patriot Noise	4	C	3	1	1	0	7,425
Patriot One	4	G	16	2	4	2	28,385
Patriot Runner	3	G	12	2	6	0	30,027
Patriot Saint	3	C	6	0	0	0	550
Patriot Spirit	4	C	7	3	0	1	30,987
Patriot Station	3	C	2	0	0	0	754
Patriota	3	G	4	0	0	0	0
Patriotforpeace	4	F	4	0	0	0	4,240
Patriotic Diva	4	F	6	1	1	1	24,840
Patriotic Emblem	3	C	8	0	1	0	1,938
Patriotic Fever	3	F	7	0	1	1	3,213
Patriotic Flame	4	G	6	0	1	2	18,540
Patriotic Jet	3	C	3	0	0	0	330
Patriotic Legend	4	C	11	3	1	1	40,177
Patriotic Princess	4	F	7	0	0	0	5,038
Patriotic Wac	4	F	9	1	0	1	9,143
Patriots Image	3	F	8	0	2	3	25,940
Patriots Light	3	C	7	0	1	1	3,330
Patriot's Pass	3	C	6	2	2	1	83,660
Patriot's Path	4	G	5	0	0	0	874
Patriots Peak	4	G	13	1	5	2	18,300
Patriot's Song	5	H	2	0	0	0	1,612
Patrol	5	H	2	0	0	0	2,400
Patron Hombre	2	C	1	0	0	0	0
Pat's Approval	6	G	2	0	0	0	152
Pat's Blast O.	6	G	4	0	0	0	924
Pat's Boy	2	G	1	0	0	0	400
Pat's Cat	2	C	3	0	0	0	3,755
Pat's Cowgirl	6	M	6	2	1	0	12,090
Pat's Creek	5	G	11	2	4	1	3,765
Pat's Expectation	5	G	14	0	2	1	54,307
Pats Pearl	2	F	1	0	0	0	1,200
Pats Picture	6	G	7	0	0	0	290
Pat's Possibility	5	M	5	0	2	1	13,610
Pat's Sexy Boots	3	G	14	0	0	5	4,603
Patsy	3	F	8	0	0	1	1,729
Patsy Won't Tell	6	M	2	0	0	0	312
Patsys Act	3	F	5	1	0	0	8,500
Patsys Cookin'	3	G	8	2	1	1	19,066
Patsy's Picture	4	F	2	0	0	0	400
Patsys Rigatoni	3	C	3	0	0	0	44
Patsy's Shadow	3	G	7	1	2	0	9,755
Patti Poole	5	M	3	0	0	0	100
Pattiano	4	F	10	1	0	4	55,576
Patti's Classy	2	F	4	0	0	0	553
Patti's Clown	3	F	5	1	1	0	8,573
Patti's Pro	6	G	16	1	6	1	9,341
Patti'sinparis	4	F	7	1	1	1	17,695
Pattison	8	G	2	0	0	0	125
Patton Leather	4	F	4	0	0	0	1,200
Patton of Gold	6	H	5	0	0	3	13,232
Patton On Speed	3	G	9	2	1	1	16,598
Patton Pending	6	G	12	2	0	3	32,185
Patton Poser	6	G	15	3	3	2	28,073
Pattons Charge	5	H	7	0	1	1	9,010
Pattons Cold War	5	H	4	0	0	0	174
Patton's Comment	4	F	1	0	0	0	0
Pattons Girl	4	F	11	1	1	1	5,998
Patton's Prince	6	G	12	2	1	2	10,707
Pattons Rosebud	2	F	3	1	0	0	7,710
Pattons Success	4	F	2	0	0	0	380
Patton's Victory	6	G	10	1	1	0	39,810
Patton's War	4	G	4	0	0	0	250
Pattons Warrior	4	G	6	0	0	0	233
Patty Cakes	6	M	7	2	0	1	43,629
Patty Girl	2	F	2	1	0	1	36,012
Patty Perfect	4	F	8	0	0	1	1,043
Patty Quake	5	G	6	1	0	0	4,917
Patty Seattle	2	F	3	1	0	0	14,810
Patty Takesthecake	5	M	3	0	0	0	413
Patty Wack	3	F	9	1	1	2	7,014
Patty's Hope	2	F	5	1	1	0	6,568
Patty's Picnic	5	G	3	0	0	0	131
Patuxent Citi	4	F	6	0	0	1	3,325
Patuxent River	7	G	10	0	0	1	2,200
Patuxent Ruby	5	M	3	0	0	0	0
Patuxent Valley	4	F	11	0	5	0	11,006
Patuxent Wind	3	G	10	0	1	0	660
Paudash Lake	3	G	12	2	3	1	66,153
Paugus Bay	6	M	6	1	0	2	23,904
Paul B. Jones	3	C	5	1	0	2	19,650
Paul H.	4	G	7	1	2	2	11,656
Paul the Speierman	3	G	11	1	1	1	8,784
Paula	6	M	21	2	6	1	18,989
Paula Jean Style	2	F	1	0	0	0	420
Paula Mae Fly	5	M	6	0	1	0	1,057
Paula Move	2	F	1	0	0	0	0
Paula O	3	F	7	2	1	2	36,958
Paula Smith	5	M	7	2	1	0	50,685
Paula's Approval	4	F	5	0	1	1	6,220
Paula's Pride	4	C	10	0	1	3	10,985
Paula's Star	3	F	12	1	2	3	11,060
Paulas Victory	7	M	2	0	0	0	192
Pauline's Angel	3	G	5	0	0	0	0
Pauline's Princess	2	F	9	0	0	1	5,565
Paulnpaul	3	G	3	0	0	1	1,990
Paul's Approval	2	C	2	0	0	0	1,088
Paul's Bonus	3	G	1	0	0	0	135
Paul's Dream	6	M	14	0	3	2	29,730
Paul's Gerth	3	G	2	0	0	0	135
Paul's Girl	3	F	3	0	0	2	8,382
Paul's Lil Mate	3	F	11	2	4	2	16,634
Paul's Past	5	G	9	0	0	0	930
Paul's Paula	4	F	18	4	1	6	32,514
Paul's Pretty Peg	2	F	5	0	0	0	880
Pauls So Lucky	2	G	8	0	1	2	3,605
Paulshomemadewine	6	G	9	1	1	1	18,485
Pauper's Pocket	3	G	6	1	1	1	15,650
Pause for Applause	3	F	2	0	0	0	320
Paver and Roller	2	F	3	0	0	0	3,360
Pavia	3	F	2	0	0	0	360
Pavillon	7	G	11	0	2	1	2,400
Pavla (FR)	5	M	4	0	0	0	1,100
Pavlina	3	F	3	0	1	0	3,617
Pavlovsk	5	G	2	0	0	2	7,920
Pavo	2	C	5	2	0	2	71,190
Pavones	3	F	2	0	0	0	275
Paw Paw's Pride	7	G	14	0	2	2	8,740
Paw Paw's Primo	3	C	16	2	0	4	10,740
Pawhuska	10	G	8	1	0	3	3,036
Pawley's Island	5	G	9	3	2	0	38,060
Pawling	5	G	9	0	3	0	4,646
Pawn Shop Pistol	5	G	16	1	2	0	9,477
Pawned	2	F	1	0	0	0	0
Pawyne Princess	3	F	7	3	2	1	117,230
Pax Americana	3	G	2	0	0	0	0
Paxil	8	G	12	2	1	2	7,160
Paxton	8	G	20	0	2	2	4,232
Pay Attention	3	C	13	2	1	4	130,747
Pay Check	4	G	11	1	2	1	10,072
Pay Daze	4	G	8	1	1	1	11,814
Pay Per Win	6	G	6	4	0	2	99,300
Pay Phone	3	G	1	0	0	0	0
Pay Ransom	7	G	4	0	0	1	1,700
Pay Something	4	F	8	0	0	0	2,345
Pay the Deputy	7	M	5	0	0	0	690
Pay the Devil	3	C	13	3	0	1	23,832
Pay the Fox	3	G	8	3	2	2	101,540
Pay the Lady	4	F	4	1	0	0	3,180
Pay the Piper	2	F	5	0	1	0	8,584
Pay the Preacher	6	G	8	3	0	2	135,580
Pay the Ransom	4	G	13	1	3	4	25,433
Pay the Secretary	5	M	10	0	0	0	657
Pay the Victor	2	C	3	0	0	1	2,500
Pay the Vid	3	C	4	0	0	0	605
Pay Up T C	5	G	3	0	0	1	178
Pay Ya Later	3	F	11	0	2	3	9,912
Payable On Demand	3	F	10	1	0	4	20,585
Payasito	5	G	17	5	5	1	71,564
Payday Chrome	2	C	5	1	1	1	15,394
Payday Friday	3	G	6	1	1	0	9,741
Payday's Queenie	3	F	4	0	1	1	6,276
Payinforcollege	2	C	1	0	1	0	440
Paying Penance	2	F	8	0	0	1	5,425
Payme	3	F	2	0	0	0	0
Payment in Full	5	H	8	0	0	1	2,264
Payment in Kind	2	C	2	1	0	0	12,630
Paynes Mill	3	C	4	0	1	1	15,276

Horse	Age	Sex	Sts	1st	2d	3d	Won
Payoff	3	C	4	0	0	0	2,450
Payroll Deposit	8	H	4	0	0	0	0
Paythedevilatdawn	4	G	12	1	3	0	6,194
Paz Ciudadana (CHI)	4	F	3	2	0	0	62,580
Pazhalsta	6	G	4	0	2	1	7,775
P'burg	8	G	12	1	2	0	3,417
Pe de Vento	2	F	7	0	0	2	2,330
Pe Quente	3	G	13	1	2	1	15,235
Peabody Jo	3	F	10	2	0	1	6,592
Peabodys Coaltrain	3	G	6	1	2	1	28,600
Peace	4	F	5	1	0	0	7,101
Peace Ambassador	2	C	2	0	0	1	3,100
Peace and Joy	5	G	10	3	0	1	51,033
Peace Bro	8	G	11	1	0	0	4,755
Peace Calling	4	F	10	2	1	0	3,513
Peace Dancer	3	G	10	2	0	2	23,970
Peace Dove	2	C	4	1	0	0	7,450
Peace Emblem	3	C	11	1	1	1	44,456
Peace Flag	4	F	3	1	0	0	8,374
Peace Lady	5	M	7	2	0	1	24,420
Peace Now	9	G	1	0	0	0	65
Peace Offering	2	F	5	1	0	1	23,600
Peace Pledge	4	F	9	1	1	1	37,620
Peace Rock	4	G	12	2	3	1	37,160
Peace Rose	3	F	8	0	1	2	6,420
Peace Rules	4	C	6	3	0	0	1,024,288
Peace Symbol	3	F	10	1	2	0	34,140
Peace Talk	3	F	3	0	0	0	700
Peacefally (IRE)	5	M	1	0	1	0	6,480
Peaceful City	4	F	13	2	2	3	29,950
Peaceful Morn	3	F	11	2	0	2	20,530
Peaceful Place	5	M	8	1	1	1	29,720
Peaceful Presence	3	F	3	0	0	1	1,400
Peaceful Queen	3	F	4	0	1	0	1,934
Peaceful Time	4	F	2	0	0	0	0
Peaceful Wager	6	M	4	1	1	0	8,212
Peaceful Warrior	3	F	5	1	1	1	7,032
Peacefull Sammy	2	C	3	1	2	0	6,725
Peacefully Accept	5	M	2	0	1	0	1,680
Peach Valley	4	F	9	3	2	0	17,474
Peaches a Flying	3	F	1	0	0	0	0
Peaches for Free	3	F	2	0	0	0	120
Peaches N Schemes	4	F	10	2	2	2	11,263
Peachesnchampagne	3	F	3	0	0	0	141
Peachy Miss	6	M	4	0	0	0	112
Peachy Perfect	3	F	7	1	1	1	3,911
Peacock Sally	3	F	8	0	0	1	8,320
Peacomb Hen	9	M	10	4	2	0	80,957
Peak a Boo Mt.	3	F	5	1	0	0	3,720
Peak a Bootrando	3	C	3	1	1	0	12,860
Peak Above	4	F	10	1	3	1	22,885
Peak Ahead	2	G	5	0	0	0	1,717
Peak Dancer	7	H	1	0	0	0	0
Peak Experience	2	C	1	0	0	0	450
Peak in Time	2	F	1	0	0	0	0
Peak Interest	9	G	12	2	0	3	6,820
Peak of Luck	3	C	8	1	1	0	4,675
Peak Performance	3	G	18	0	5	2	10,793
Peak Performer	3	C	8	2	2	2	13,850
Peak Prospector	3	C	10	1	0	1	14,702
Peak Time	4	F	2	0	0	0	0
Peak Value Al	2	C	1	0	0	0	0
Peakabbu Boy	5	G	8	1	0	1	13,960
Peakaboo Peak	4	F	8	1	0	1	25,080
Peakabooheather	3	F	12	2	0	1	12,318
Peakforthecash	2	F	1	0	0	1	3,553
Peaks	6	G	5	0	0	2	2,805
Peak's Foolish Gal	3	F	3	1	0	0	6,511
Peaks Jewell	4	F	14	0	2	5	10,785
Peaks Or Valleys	6	M	4	0	0	0	1,386
Peaktopeak	2	C	6	0	2	1	23,270
Peal Out	5	M	10	2	2	1	7,812
Peameal	2	F	6	0	0	1	1,552
Peanut Buddy	4	G	10	2	1	1	17,581
Peanut Butter Kid	5	G	9	3	1	3	6,356
Peanut Butter Man	6	G	7	0	0	1	2,320
Peanut Vendor	2	G	3	0	0	0	298
Peanutbutter Blitz	4	G	11	2	2	0	10,551
Peanutbutternjilly	4	F	8	2	0	1	15,673
Peanut's Ride	5	M	3	0	0	0	100
Peanutthetiger	3	G	2	0	0	0	37
Pearce's Fantasy	3	F	5	1	0	0	5,483
Pearl District	3	F	7	1	2	2	9,495
Pearl E.	4	F	2	0	0	0	348
Pearl Hunt	5	M	6	2	0	0	23,400
Pearls and Gold	3	F	9	3	2	1	19,465
Pearls and Jeans	3	F	5	0	0	1	6,115
Pearl's Hickey	5	M	4	0	0	1	2,630
Pearls O'Plenty	2	F	1	0	0	0	594
Pearls Shadow	3	F	5	1	1	0	3,486
Peasynq's	4	G	17	1	3	0	9,182
Peatterly	9	G	2	0	0	0	0
Peavys Time	4	G	9	3	1	1	12,730
Pebbett	4	F	11	3	2	3	41,806
Peccadillo	3	F	13	2	0	2	16,435
Pecks Bad Girl	4	F	2	0	1	0	1,300
Pecola	3	F	4	1	0	0	4,236
Peco's Girl (IRE)	3	F	10	1	2	1	24,350
Pedal Me Pretty	6	M	1	0	0	0	0
Pedaltothemetal	6	G	13	2	2	2	18,311
Pedro	6	G	9	0	1	0	5,030
Pee Wee Bee	6	G	4	0	0	0	378
Pee Wee Duncan	5	H	1	0	0	0	40
Pee Wees Kris S.	4	C	1	0	0	0	0
Peef	4	G	8	1	1	1	58,104
Peek a Blue Kiss	4	F	8	0	0	0	1,130
Peek a Boo Sara	6	M	2	0	0	0	3,696
Peek N Tell	3	F	6	1	2	1	7,050
Peekaboo Cash	6	M	9	1	0	0	3,063
Peekaboo Cat	3	F	5	0	0	0	1,560
Peekaboo Sez	3	F	11	2	3	0	37,375
Peekaboo Tommy	6	G	10	0	4	2	5,754
Peekachoo	5	H	8	2	1	0	3,238
Peekskill	5	G	8	1	0	2	35,555
Peelin Out	2	F	2	0	0	0	300
Peep and Turn	2	C	1	0	0	0	0
Peeping Tom	7	G	8	2	0	2	147,531
Peeps	3	F	6	0	1	0	1,512
Peepsight	5	G	12	4	2	2	19,774
Peer	3	F	4	1	0	1	26,270
Peering Over	8	M	7	1	2	1	11,920
Peerless Note	3	F	4	0	0	0	140
Peerless Price	4	G	1	0	0	0	0
Peerless Tee	3	C	5	3	0	0	29,940
Peetie Pistol	3	C	1	0	0	0	0
Peetiethepieman	2	G	5	0	0	0	1,680
Peg O My Heart	3	F	1	0	1	0	2,600
Pegalee	5	M	6	1	0	0	9,905
Pegaso (PER)	5	H	2	0	0	0	1,500
Pegasus Cyberspace	4	G	6	1	0	1	6,937
Pegasus Kris	3	C	11	0	1	1	3,827
Pegasus Nick	2	G	1	0	0	0	112
Pegasus Superstar	5	G	6	0	0	0	750
Pegasuseternldancr	5	M	4	0	0	0	522
Pegasusgoldendancr	5	M	4	0	0	0	585
Peggem	2	G	2	0	2	0	7,400
Peggy G. R.	2	F	4	0	0	0	180
Peggy Jo's Pride	4	C	18	1	5	3	13,177
Peggy's Aly	4	F	3	0	0	0	305
Peggy's Approval	3	F	11	0	2	0	3,680
Peggy's Beau	8	G	20	0	5	3	7,654
Peggy's Dream Boy	5	G	11	1	2	0	5,669
Peggys Favorite	2	G	6	0	4	1	12,412
Peggys' Girl	3	F	16	6	1	1	18,347
Peggys Mukora	5	G	14	1	2	3	33,857
Peggys Orchid	5	M	7	1	0	0	16,800
Peggy's Promise	3	G	5	2	0	1	48,980
Peggy's Ruby	2	F	4	1	1	1	9,370
Peggys Run	5	M	3	0	0	0	750
Peggy's Secret	6	M	3	0	0	0	201
Pegs Halo	6	G	14	0	2	2	7,495
Peg's Princess	5	M	11	1	4	0	7,935
Peg's Thunder	2	G	3	0	0	0	175
Pegylation	6	G	12	2	1	1	26,030
Pekani	3	F	1	0	0	0	1,250
Pelagos (FR)	9	H	3	0	0	0	12,500
Pele El Dorado	3	C	7	0	1	0	3,540
Pelham Bay	2	F	7	3	0	2	126,777

Horse	Age	Sex	Sts	1st	2d	3d	Won
Pelican Beach	6	G	4	2	1	0	30,300
Pelican Island	4	F	2	1	0	0	15,900
Pelican Lane	6	G	8	0	0	0	1,438
Pelican Pete	4	G	6	1	2	1	21,707
Pelicus Affair	2	F	2	0	0	0	225
Peligroso	6	G	11	0	3	2	11,625
Pelirrojo	5	G	5	0	0	0	1,800
Pell Mell	6	G	17	3	3	1	24,690
Pellegrino (BRZ)	5	H	9	3	2	2	260,060
Pelli	4	G	18	2	3	3	15,817
Pelly Pinecone	2	G	3	1	0	0	7,673
Pelted	2	G	5	0	0	0	0
Pelusa	2	F	2	0	0	0	520
Pem Bro	4	G	3	0	0	0	202
Pemaquid Point	5	G	6	1	0	0	7,138
Pembroke Dancer	7	G	10	3	0	2	8,558
Pembroke Hall	7	G	5	4	1	0	60,600
Pembroke Palace	6	M	2	0	0	0	1,080
Pembroke Rd.	7	G	14	2	4	3	10,007
Pem's Hostess	4	F	5	0	0	1	5,886
Pen Eyes	2	C	4	0	2	0	6,860
Pen Up Lady	5	M	11	3	2	3	41,857
Penalty Declined	4	G	13	1	1	1	3,756
Penalty Peat	4	G	12	3	1	2	14,395
Penance Hall	7	M	8	0	1	0	1,841
Penaty Flag	7	G	14	0	1	1	2,777
Penguin Cafe	3	F	3	0	0	0	0
Peniforyourthought	5	M	9	0	2	2	1,496
Peninsula Player	3	F	8	2	3	1	13,235
Penitang	4	G	4	0	0	0	915
Penitent	4	G	9	2	0	0	22,807
Penn Pacific	3	C	3	2	0	1	41,400
Pennant Contender	2	C	2	0	0	2	8,700
Pennant Dancer	3	F	11	2	4	1	27,045
Penne Dancer (IRE)	5	G	4	0	0	0	320
Pennington Gap	4	F	14	1	5	1	24,616
Penny Ante	3	F	10	2	2	2	53,144
Penny Belle	2	F	1	0	0	0	720
Penny Bid	4	F	7	3	0	2	8,874
Penny Dream	4	F	9	3	2	1	105,270
Penny On the Post	4	C	7	1	0	1	25,712
Penny One	6	M	2	0	0	0	480
Penny Poker	3	G	9	0	1	2	10,430
Penny Racer	2	G	2	0	0	0	0
Penny Sixpence	3	F	10	2	1	0	11,555
Penny Special	5	M	1	0	0	0	82
Penny Wisher	3	C	1	0	0	0	84
Pennyjo	2	F	4	1	0	0	9,240
Pennyrile	2	F	2	1	0	1	10,306
Pennyroyal	3	F	1	0	1	0	3,200
Penny's Best Shot	3	G	4	0	0	0	439
Penny's Flyer	7	M	11	1	2	3	10,759
Penny's Fortune	3	F	9	3	2	0	141,609
Penny's Hero	4	F	7	2	2	0	16,912
Penny's Odyssey	6	G	6	0	1	1	4,000
Penny's Turn	3	F	11	1	1	2	16,391
Penobscot Bay	4	C	6	0	2	2	19,440
Penryn Ghost	5	M	4	0	0	0	226
Pensglitter	7	H	10	5	3	0	44,098
Penshiel	7	G	17	2	1	3	13,633
Pensive Pam	2	F	8	0	1	0	3,430
Pent Up Fantasy	5	M	7	1	2	3	17,392
Pent Up Speed	4	G	9	4	2	0	44,789
Pentakato	10	G	10	1	0	4	10,365
Pentathlon	5	G	18	2	2	4	29,823
Pentavirate	4	G	10	1	2	2	11,967
Pentelic	3	F	2	1	0	0	4,870
Pentelicus Dance (ECU)	3	F	11	0	3	1	22,405
Pentelipiano	7	G	13	0	1	1	9,677
Pentelly Lil	6	M	4	0	0	0	293
Pentera	4	F	12	0	0	1	7,763
Penthium	6	G	11	2	3	2	23,599
Penthouse Prince	4	G	8	0	3	2	23,528
Penthouse Promise	4	C	6	0	0	0	4,600
Pentimento	5	G	10	0	0	1	15,675
Pents Bride	3	F	10	1	3	1	19,790
Pentupeskimo	5	M	7	0	0	1	1,840
Pepay's Steve	2	C	2	0	0	0	300
Pepe Le Moco	3	G	11	1	0	1	4,513
Pepe Pocastuercas	3	G	9	0	2	2	6,859
Pepesqueez	5	M	17	4	0	2	29,325
Pepita Raquel	2	F	2	0	1	0	6,000
Pepper Cove	3	C	19	1	2	1	17,295
Pepper Dan	3	G	7	2	0	1	9,670
Pepper Lang	2	F	9	0	0	2	2,920
Pepper Pack	4	C	9	1	1	0	7,254
Pepper Red	5	G	1	0	0	0	61
Pepper Rossi	4	F	3	0	0	0	1,440
Pepper Shaker	5	H	7	3	1	1	79,580
Pepper Taffy	8	M	13	2	2	1	12,673
Pepper Trail	3	G	6	4	0	0	64,400
Pepperberry	2	C	2	0	0	0	565
Peppered Cat	4	C	6	1	2	1	19,660
Peppermint Bay	9	M	2	0	0	0	234
Peppermint Flash	3	F	8	2	1	0	7,600
Peppermint Gift	3	F	15	3	2	3	21,202
Peppermint Lilly	2	F	4	1	2	1	53,970
Peppermint Love	4	G	7	1	1	3	27,848
Peppermint Pearl	3	F	1	0	0	0	134
Peppermint Speedy	4	G	7	0	0	2	2,902
Peppermint Swirl	2	F	2	0	0	0	0
Pepper's Reality	5	G	4	0	0	1	333
Peppy	4	F	1	0	0	0	75
Peppy Candy	3	F	10	1	1	1	35,400
Peppy Mint	5	G	9	1	0	0	3,024
Peppy Shalter	4	F	4	0	0	1	6,720
Peppy's Present	8	G	2	0	1	0	2,800
Peptide	7	G	14	1	0	4	3,285
Pepto Kid	3	G	9	0	0	0	285
Per Curiam	2	C	4	1	1	1	39,965
Per Diem	5	M	3	0	0	0	188
Per Se	2	F	3	0	1	0	8,718
Peraea	3	F	1	0	0	0	0
Perceptive Friend	3	G	6	1	0	0	17,760
Perch	3	F	6	0	0	0	2,610
Percipitate	4	G	7	1	0	0	4,110
Percy	5	G	17	2	2	3	12,401
Percy Marie	3	F	6	0	0	1	526
Perdaro	4	G	5	0	1	1	6,806
Perdition'sredwing	4	G	7	0	0	3	4,560
Peregrine Falcon	3	G	3	0	0	0	785
Perennial Favorite	3	F	11	2	1	2	29,180
Pereskia	4	F	5	0	0	0	850
Perfect Action	3	F	3	0	0	0	1,968
Perfect Again	3	G	10	0	1	1	3,223
Perfect and Regal	4	C	4	1	0	0	4,415
Perfect Attitude	4	F	2	0	0	0	0
Perfect Beau	4	G	20	1	2	3	15,505
Perfect Bet	3	G	15	3	1	1	40,980
Perfect Blue	4	F	1	0	0	0	430
Perfect Business	5	M	11	0	1	4	11,455
Perfect Call	3	G	5	0	0	2	6,700
Perfect Charm	3	F	4	0	1	0	5,050
Perfect Circle	2	C	2	0	0	0	1,320
Perfect Colony	3	F	7	1	2	1	25,714
Perfect Colours	3	F	15	0	1	1	4,620
Perfect Commander	5	G	12	2	2	1	10,328
Perfect Connection	2	F	5	1	1	0	30,850
Perfect Cut	4	C	7	1	0	1	33,372
Perfect Darling	3	F	18	3	2	2	17,913
Perfect Date	2	F	8	0	0	1	1,470
Perfect Dear	4	F	13	2	2	1	44,550
Perfect Design	5	M	3	0	0	0	2,520
Perfect Diamond	7	M	12	2	1	0	13,085
Perfect Doll	2	F	1	1	0	0	11,400
Perfect Double	3	F	14	1	0	2	6,191
Perfect Drift	5	G	9	0	5	2	947,595
Perfect Energy	5	M	11	0	3	0	39,055
Perfect Fantasy	5	G	12	2	3	1	20,141
Perfect Fit	4	G	14	5	2	1	48,925
Perfect Flame	5	M	3	1	0	0	1,680
Perfect Friend	4	G	17	1	1	5	25,645
Perfect Gal	2	F	6	0	1	2	4,920
Perfect Game	4	G	19	0	1	0	1,979
Perfect Hero	3	C	1	0	0	0	250
Perfect High	3	G	21	1	1	4	12,207
Perfect Ice	5	G	9	1	0	1	3,596
Perfect Illusion	3	F	8	1	0	2	10,234

Horse	Age	Sex	Sts	1st	2d	3d	Won
Perfect Impulse	2	F	7	0	0	0	4,475
Perfect Judgment	5	G	5	0	0	0	3,162
Perfect Justice	3	G	13	2	3	1	24,843
Perfect Lad	2	G	4	0	0	0	4,765
Perfect Legacy	3	G	7	0	0	0	0
Perfect Light	4	F	1	0	0	0	266
Perfect Lil	5	M	2	0	0	0	0
Perfect Look	3	F	9	2	1	2	78,705
Perfect Lore	3	G	2	0	1	0	5,200
Perfect Miss	4	F	1	0	0	0	0
Perfect Miss D	3	F	1	0	0	0	235
Perfect Mode	3	C	4	0	1	1	18,940
Perfect Moon	3	G	7	1	2	0	110,069
Perfect Nustorm	2	G	3	0	2	0	13,740
Perfect One	6	M	1	0	0	0	100
Perfect Paradise	4	F	15	2	2	1	21,742
Perfect Partner	4	F	5	0	0	0	1,103
Perfect Party (ARG)	5	G	7	1	3	0	29,120
Perfect Peggy	2	F	3	1	0	0	7,760
Perfect Performer	6	G	1	0	0	0	46
Perfect Pita	3	F	8	1	3	1	5,090
Perfect Plan	5	M	5	1	1	1	15,407
Perfect Pose	2	G	2	0	0	1	1,404
Perfect Preception	2	F	2	1	0	0	4,550
Perfect Present	4	F	1	0	0	0	56
Perfect Pretense	5	G	11	4	2	0	32,863
Perfect Ride	5	H	5	3	0	0	78,651
Perfect Sail	3	C	2	0	0	0	780
Perfect Sand	3	C	9	1	3	2	13,240
Perfect Score	8	H	6	0	1	0	3,740
Perfect Sight	3	F	1	0	0	0	124
Perfect Sleeper	7	G	7	3	0	0	7,880
Perfect Soul (IRE)	6	H	6	1	2	0	391,549
Perfect Speed	5	G	7	0	0	1	1,218
Perfect Story	4	F	2	0	0	0	380
Perfect Stride	4	G	12	2	3	2	13,472
Perfect Summer	5	M	2	0	0	0	276
Perfect Sunset	5	M	2	0	0	0	0
Perfect Take	3	C	5	0	0	1	8,705
Perfect Ten	6	M	8	1	0	1	5,240
Perfect Timing	4	F	5	0	0	1	8,730
Perfect Turn	2	F	5	0	0	1	4,205
Perfect Two	2	C	3	1	0	0	9,570
Perfect Vermont	5	M	1	0	0	0	0
Perfect Wisdom	5	G	15	1	1	3	10,879
Perfect World	4	F	3	0	1	1	17,120
Perfectdeal	3	G	3	0	0	0	278
Perfectly Agitated	5	M	2	0	0	0	0
Perfectly Catty	4	F	6	1	1	2	11,370
Perfectly Charming	3	F	8	0	0	0	968
Perfectly Chilled	5	M	11	1	0	1	13,531
Perfectly Free	5	M	13	1	6	1	13,551
Perfectly Legal	2	C	5	0	1	2	8,750
Perfectly Penny	5	M	5	0	0	0	0
Perfectly Perfect	3	F	5	0	0	0	1,715
Perfectly Quiet	2	F	6	1	2	1	31,681
Perfectly Stunning	5	M	1	0	0	0	380
Perfectly Theresa	3	F	14	0	2	2	7,795
Perfecto	3	G	3	0	0	1	982
Perfecto Westo	4	G	6	3	0	1	27,860
Perfectpurrfection	4	G	9	2	3	2	17,621
Perfectstormtoo	3	C	6	1	0	1	7,776
Perfellia	5	M	6	1	1	1	9,610
Performance Report	4	G	14	1	4	1	16,029
Performer Inflight	3	F	12	3	0	3	23,835
Performing Cristi	3	F	5	0	0	0	37
Perhaps Magic	4	F	11	2	1	1	10,191
Perhaps Peace	2	C	1	0	0	0	692
Pericles	3	C	10	0	4	1	32,255
Perignon (CHI)	6	G	4	0	0	1	5,900
Perilad	6	G	9	0	0	2	2,627
Perilous Night	3	F	14	3	2	4	100,120
Perimeter	4	C	7	1	1	1	24,610
Periodicals	5	G	4	1	0	0	4,936
Periquita	3	F	3	0	1	1	5,735
Periscope	6	G	10	2	0	2	32,756
Perked in the West	4	G	6	0	0	1	500
Perkins Echo	6	G	6	0	0	0	385
Perks First Knight	4	G	1	0	0	0	0

Horse	Age	Sex	Sts	1st	2d	3d	Won
Perky Pirate	6	G	7	2	0	0	9,290
Perkymon	5	G	4	0	1	1	665
Perls Best Yet	4	F	6	0	0	0	200
Permanence	3	G	6	0	1	0	2,283
Permission	2	F	3	0	0	0	800
Permissiontopass	4	G	5	0	0	0	186
Pero Dinero	9	G	13	2	1	2	3,785
Perocity	5	M	2	0	0	0	960
Perogi Pete	6	G	7	0	0	1	300
Perpetual Peace	3	C	6	1	2	0	44,675
Perpetual Spirit	4	G	6	0	1	0	7,245
Perr Sabin	6	G	11	0	3	2	10,703
Perry Road Joy	3	F	8	0	2	1	1,632
Perry T.	7	G	9	0	0	0	300
Perry's Option	2	G	3	0	1	1	1,211
Perry's Orphan	3	G	1	0	0	1	221
Persecutor	4	G	5	1	1	1	11,059
Persee Joe	5	G	5	0	0	0	1,560
Persevering	4	F	10	3	0	3	22,004
Persh	7	G	8	0	0	2	1,886
Persian Beauty	6	M	1	0	0	0	0
Persian Harmony	8	H	2	1	1	0	3,760
Persian Princess	3	F	19	2	8	2	43,258
Persian Reign	5	G	6	0	1	1	2,975
Persian Tower	4	F	4	0	0	0	312
Persian's Surprise	3	F	5	2	0	1	16,033
Persistance Pays	4	F	9	2	4	1	19,690
Persistancepaysoff	3	G	8	1	2	2	10,048
Persistent	2	C	1	1	0	0	9,600
Persistent Storm	3	C	2	0	0	0	800
Persky (ARG)	7	M	4	0	1	0	4,597
Persnickety Pride	2	F	10	0	1	3	8,080
Persnickity Gal	4	F	3	0	1	1	8,680
Persona Non Grata	3	G	9	0	0	1	1,015
Personable Pete	6	G	11	0	1	3	21,236
Personal Bag	4	G	1	0	0	0	0
Personal Beau	8	G	5	2	2	1	46,371
Personal Best (NZ)	7	G	2	0	0	0	300
Personal Case	4	G	11	0	0	4	11,338
Personal Cide	3	G	20	3	4	1	36,813
Personal Clearance	5	H	13	0	4	1	20,800
Personal Dinner	3	C	11	0	1	1	3,260
Personal Dream	6	M	11	1	4	2	13,810
Personal Flyer	3	C	12	0	1	1	3,827
Personal Gain	5	G	3	0	0	0	180
Personal Grades	3	F	4	0	0	1	648
Personal Half Mast	4	F	11	2	2	1	15,070
Personal Hit	3	F	5	0	1	0	6,000
Personal Journey	7	H	6	0	0	1	2,395
Personal Legend	4	F	8	3	2	1	224,330
Personal Lord	3	G	3	0	0	0	575
Personal Magic	5	G	6	0	0	0	981
Personal Memories	5	M	6	0	0	0	290
Personal Moon	9	G	12	2	1	3	11,090
Personal Notebook	2	F	7	1	0	0	7,314
Personal Odyssey	2	F	1	0	0	0	0
Personal Plan	4	G	3	1	0	1	6,538
Personal Prince	4	C	2	0	0	0	2,294
Personal Revenge	3	G	10	1	1	0	7,829
Personal Reward	5	H	6	1	1	1	10,518
Personal Rush	3	C	8	4	0	1	1,165,761
Personal Services	4	F	2	0	0	0	0
Personal Star	2	C	4	0	0	0	412
Personal Stash	6	G	8	1	3	1	16,284
Personal Touch	4	C	10	3	2	2	128,286
Personal Tower	4	F	8	0	0	1	3,740
Personal Vendetta	7	G	3	0	0	1	1,307
Personal Wish	7	G	1	0	0	0	0
Perspective	7	G	1	0	0	0	110
Perspicacious (ARG)	5	H	9	2	1	1	44,110
Perspicacity	3	F	2	0	0	0	170
Persuade	4	F	12	2	0	1	8,878
Persuaggle	3	C	9	2	1	0	55,322
Persuasion Girl	3	F	1	0	0	0	0
Persuasive Luck	3	F	3	0	0	0	0
Pert Pacho	5	G	3	0	0	0	0
Pert Reply	4	G	20	0	3	3	11,762
Pertain	4	F	7	1	4	2	15,320
Perty Gerty	4	F	12	0	5	3	33,216

Horse	Age	Sex	Sts	1st	2d	3d	Won
Perty Late	4	F	6	3	1	0	5,427
Perty Number	6	M	13	4	4	1	50,796
Peru B Ruby	2	F	2	0	0	0	2,000
Peruvian Heartbeat	2	F	3	0	0	0	935
Peruvian Rose	3	F	1	0	0	0	675
Pervader	5	G	6	0	1	0	1,034
Pervasive Force	3	G	4	0	1	0	5,100
Pervomaysk	3	F	4	0	0	1	2,697
Pescadito	2	G	2	1	0	0	12,835
Pesci	4	F	5	1	1	2	95,001
Pesheli	4	F	3	0	0	0	225
Peski Bride	2	F	1	1	0	0	6,000
Pesky	8	G	9	0	0	5	3,660
Pesky Angel	3	F	6	0	0	0	174
Pesky Pete	6	G	14	1	3	1	8,398
Peso Por Beso	3	C	3	0	0	0	1,960
Pessoa's Pick	5	G	3	0	2	0	5,682
Pesto	5	G	3	0	0	0	626
Pesto Perfetto	5	G	10	0	2	0	5,388
Pesto Sauce	3	G	2	0	0	0	0
Pet Bob (ARG)	7	G	6	0	1	1	4,290
Pet Deposit	7	G	4	1	0	1	13,000
Pet Wildcat	4	F	2	0	0	0	0
Pet Your Cat	4	F	14	1	4	0	10,133
Petaluma Baby	3	F	3	0	0	1	2,090
Petdinkle's Boy	2	C	7	0	0	0	1,199
Pete Attraction	7	H	7	0	0	0	150
Pete On the Fiddle	3	G	2	0	0	0	142
Pete Power	4	G	2	0	0	0	0
Pete Shure	6	G	18	0	3	2	6,608
Peter and James	2	G	2	0	1	0	2,120
Peter Habit	7	G	12	1	1	2	4,051
Peter N G Schwartz	3	G	2	0	0	0	0
Peter Peter Peter	4	G	18	2	4	5	20,950
Peter Punkin Eater	6	G	15	0	2	2	5,010
Peter Spats	5	G	10	2	2	2	6,285
Peter the Greek	2	G	8	1	0	2	10,925
Peter the Rock	3	C	5	2	0	0	34,048
Peterhoot	3	C	2	0	0	0	70
Peter's Ballad	8	G	3	0	0	1	2,025
Peters Catch	3	G	5	1	1	0	12,588
Peter's Jewel	5	M	10	2	1	2	12,483
Peter's Pleasure	4	G	2	0	0	0	144
Peter's Pond	9	G	13	1	1	2	9,848
Peter's Posada	3	G	2	0	2	0	10,800
Peter's Puddles	3	C	3	3	0	0	79,200
Peter's Quest	9	G	11	1	0	2	5,922
Petes Braggin	5	H	3	0	0	0	0
Pete's Cat	5	H	3	0	0	0	0
Pete's Dolly	3	F	10	3	2	1	23,913
Pete's Flair	8	M	1	0	0	0	0
Petes Hick Chick	3	F	5	0	2	0	16,194
Pete's Honey	2	F	7	1	1	0	8,327
Pete's Lady	4	F	6	1	1	0	2,632
Pete's Legacy	4	G	1	0	0	0	50
Pete's Nina	5	G	8	1	0	1	7,245
Pete's Panacea	7	G	6	0	0	1	1,411
Pete's Revenge	8	G	2	0	0	0	113
Pete's Skianno	8	G	14	1	3	1	18,496
Pete's Surprise	4	F	8	1	4	1	59,963
Petes Way	7	G	3	0	0	1	790
Pete's Wop Job	3	F	3	0	0	0	1,940
Petesamassbred	3	C	7	1	0	2	12,390
Petesicle	4	C	2	0	0	0	868
Peteski's Charm	7	H	1	0	0	1	15,085
Peteski's Rosita	4	F	8	0	0	0	2,733
Petey Foster	3	C	10	2	1	1	21,609
Petie B	4	F	3	0	0	0	188
Petie Boy	4	G	8	2	0	2	17,775
Petion Pat	4	G	11	1	1	1	20,803
Petionce	2	G	1	0	0	0	0
Petion's Shadow	2	C	1	0	0	0	100
Petion's Star	3	F	1	0	0	0	55
Petionville Indeed	4	F	4	0	1	0	14,560
Petionville Lady	3	F	10	1	2	2	16,497
Petite Cuille're	5	M	7	0	0	0	250
Petite Diablo	6	M	5	1	0	1	21,407
Petite Fatale	2	F	1	0	0	0	0
Petite Histoire (IRE)	4	F	6	0	0	0	1,100

Horse	Age	Sex	Sts	1st	2d	3d	Won
Petite Magon Rouge	3	F	9	0	0	0	840
Petite Mermaid	4	F	14	0	1	4	12,306
Petite Motion	3	F	8	1	1	2	12,143
Petite n' Classy	5	M	10	2	1	2	39,083
Petite Power	4	F	2	0	0	0	535
Petite Rose	2	F	2	0	0	0	800
Petite Tout	3	F	5	2	0	0	16,245
Petrina Above	9	M	11	2	2	2	100,320
Petro	3	C	2	0	0	0	0
Petro Pete	6	G	7	3	2	0	9,114
Petrolia	6	G	9	2	0	1	8,404
Petrus	2	G	3	1	1	0	30,000
Petsy Deville	3	F	11	0	2	1	5,125
Petty Bandit	5	G	10	3	3	3	12,358
Petty County	3	G	3	0	0	0	80
Petty Giraffe	5	G	2	0	0	0	92
Petty's Way	5	G	14	1	3	5	5,868
Petunia Man	4	C	4	0	0	0	0
Pevny	2	C	3	1	0	1	18,950
Pews Pond	5	M	9	0	1	1	4,571
Peycass	4	F	2	0	0	0	0
Peyton Creek	2	F	2	0	0	0	0
Peytons Pleasure	6	M	16	0	1	3	7,989
Pfenning	6	M	1	0	0	0	0
Pfilerup	4	F	2	0	0	0	0
Phabulosomomento	3	C	3	0	0	0	176
Phaedra	5	M	2	1	0	0	6,360
Phaedra (IRE)	4	F	7	2	1	0	64,340
Phantastic Secret	3	G	15	0	2	4	17,568
Phantom Cat	3	G	5	0	0	1	2,507
Phantom Chief	4	G	4	1	0	0	8,602
Phantom Flyer	3	G	7	2	2	1	39,629
Phantom Fox	5	G	10	0	0	1	4,275
Phantom Raider	4	G	5	1	0	0	10,187
Phantom Ranch	5	M	7	0	0	0	462
Phantom Stampede	3	C	2	1	0	0	5,100
Phantom Storm	5	M	6	1	4	0	8,500
Phantom Wind	3	F	5	1	0	1	109,266
Phantom's Magic	4	F	7	0	0	0	1,249
Phar Away Day	3	G	1	0	0	0	0
Phar From Blonde	3	F	10	1	0	0	3,016
Phar From the Riot	2	G	7	0	0	0	2,513
Phar to Win	2	G	1	0	0	1	4,200
Pharahrah	6	G	7	2	2	1	7,368
Pharaoh's Cat	5	H	10	1	0	1	8,950
Pharaway Wedding	3	F	11	2	0	1	12,745
Pharisdee	2	G	1	0	0	0	235
Pharos Legacy	4	G	11	2	1	2	16,715
Phat	6	M	10	1	1	2	13,015
Phat Daddy	5	G	4	0	0	1	774
Pheasant Run	5	M	1	0	0	0	0
Pheiffer	6	M	10	2	3	2	101,870
Pheisty Phoebe	4	F	15	0	2	1	20,555
Phenomanal Star	2	F	2	0	0	0	2,400
Phenomenal Knight	7	G	2	0	0	0	535
Pheonia	4	F	3	0	0	0	0
Phi Beta Doc	8	G	4	0	0	0	1,280
Phig Newton	3	F	12	1	1	0	3,442
Phighter	5	G	2	0	0	0	0
Phil a Glass	4	G	9	1	1	0	3,772
Phil the Bank	4	G	3	0	1	0	1,737
Phil Therich	2	G	2	0	0	0	360
Philadelphia Jim	4	C	6	2	1	1	74,600
Philandering	2	C	6	0	0	1	2,332
Philantha	7	M	4	0	1	1	4,500
Philanthropist	3	C	6	2	1	1	71,850
Philbert	3	G	10	3	2	1	38,945
Philip's Guest	2	G	2	0	0	0	150
Philistine	9	G	9	4	1	0	5,358
Phillies Dream	5	M	11	5	3	1	73,980
Philly Girl	5	M	6	0	0	0	415
Philmo	5	M	5	0	1	0	1,703
Philosophy	2	C	3	0	0	1	4,997
Phil's Cookie	4	F	13	2	0	1	27,466
Phil's Courage	3	G	10	0	2	1	4,120
Phils Mistake	7	G	16	1	0	3	8,111
Phil's Pill	3	F	8	2	0	1	32,950
Philymena	3	F	3	0	0	1	1,435
Phish	5	H	4	1	0	1	24,980

Horse	Age	Sex	Sts	1st	2d	3d	Won
Phoenicia	4	F	5	1	2	0	10,600
Phoenix Gold	2	G	7	0	2	3	10,705
Phoenix Jim	2	G	4	1	0	1	9,740
Phoenix River	6	G	2	0	0	0	0
Phone Affair	2	F	2	0	0	0	1,230
Phone Ahead	4	G	12	2	1	4	11,842
Phone Alone	7	G	5	1	0	0	4,794
Phone an M. D.	4	G	3	0	2	0	5,840
Phone Back	2	C	1	0	0	0	400
Phone Date	2	C	1	0	0	0	87
Phone Favorite	3	F	4	0	1	0	765
Phone First	6	G	11	2	0	1	15,462
Phone Flash	5	H	8	1	2	0	10,340
Phone Good News	4	G	3	0	0	0	195
Phone in Goodbye	3	G	2	1	0	0	4,235
Phone in the Money	2	C	1	1	0	0	15,600
Phone Joan	3	F	15	3	2	1	19,129
Phone Junky	2	C	2	0	0	0	172
Phone Kisses	3	G	12	2	1	2	10,368
Phone Me a Favor	4	F	9	3	3	1	36,200
Phone of the Huk	2	F	1	0	0	0	375
Phone Prank	2	G	2	0	1	0	2,120
Phone Prospector	8	G	8	2	0	0	16,632
Phone Ruler	6	H	6	2	1	1	18,720
Phone Scrambler	5	G	16	2	4	2	7,917
Phone Tech	4	G	1	0	0	0	0
Phone the Diva	4	F	14	6	1	1	59,057
Phone the Nurse	6	M	8	0	0	0	675
Phone the Wizard	5	G	13	0	0	1	1,108
Phoneavenger	5	H	1	0	0	0	0
Phonecall Freddie	4	G	8	0	0	2	2,508
Phoneforchampagne	5	H	12	2	0	2	36,190
Phonetastic	3	F	12	2	0	1	26,320
Phonethedragon	3	G	4	0	0	0	575
Phoney Rainbows	3	F	3	0	0	0	0
Photo Baba	4	G	10	0	2	0	3,335
Photo Delay	4	F	7	1	0	0	3,832
Photo Flash	4	C	6	0	2	2	27,520
Photo for Show	4	F	10	1	0	3	5,735
Photo Image	2	F	1	0	0	0	480
Photo Radar	3	G	6	0	0	0	300
Photo Shop	4	C	9	0	0	3	3,946
Photobound	3	F	4	0	0	0	1,200
Photographic	3	F	7	1	0	2	20,120
Photon Torpedo	3	G	3	0	0	0	0
Phrase's Wildcat	4	C	15	1	0	0	3,441
Phyllis Sassy Girl	2	F	1	1	0	0	13,800
Phyls Jr	3	G	6	1	0	2	11,615
Phyl's Storm Cloud	4	G	13	1	5	2	14,160
Phylupthecup	4	F	3	0	0	0	1,380
Physical	6	G	9	0	2	0	3,593
Physical Fit	3	F	4	1	0	0	6,930
Pi Phi Pearl	3	F	5	2	1	0	11,337
Pia Gold	5	G	3	0	0	0	905
Piana Anna	3	F	9	0	1	1	3,159
Piano Bar	2	F	2	0	0	1	2,640
Piano Chimes	5	M	3	0	0	0	2,230
Piano Girl	2	F	2	0	0	0	355
Piano Music	3	G	10	1	4	2	31,840
Piano Tunner	3	F	11	4	2	2	86,551
Pianopiano	4	G	13	1	0	1	11,227
Pia's Courage	5	M	11	0	3	2	7,533
Pias Moonlite	2	F	5	1	0	0	18,400
Piave	3	F	1	0	0	0	0
Piazzola (NZ)	5	G	10	0	1	1	7,810
Pic Em Hof	4	F	10	0	2	1	8,652
Pic N Paint	3	G	10	2	0	0	2,878
Pic Pocket	6	G	11	0	0	3	4,521
Picabo Sioux	3	F	3	0	0	0	865
Picadilly Bay	3	C	9	2	2	0	106,538
Picador Kat	3	G	8	2	4	0	27,333
Picadouble	4	F	1	0	0	0	75
Picata	2	F	3	1	0	1	10,050
Picawinner	3	G	2	0	0	0	150
Piccahoney	4	C	6	1	2	0	8,050
Piccolo Honey	5	M	10	3	3	2	80,440
Piccolo Player (GB)	6	G	5	0	1	0	1,840
Pichi Richi	4	F	5	0	1	2	2,219
Pick a Fight	4	G	7	1	0	3	7,485
Pick a Name	3	C	2	0	0	1	864
Pick a Winner Max	4	G	11	0	1	1	1,840
Pick Me Buzz	5	G	5	0	0	1	594
Pick of the Day	6	M	6	1	1	2	7,124
Pick of the Pack	3	F	8	1	1	1	65,452
Pick Pocket Buck	3	G	11	2	1	1	16,670
Pick the Best	9	G	11	1	3	0	6,136
Pick the Ravens	3	F	6	0	1	1	3,400
Pick Three Tommy C	2	C	2	1	0	0	14,220
Pick Up Six	2	F	6	0	0	0	615
Pick Up the Beat	4	G	9	1	3	0	11,615
Pick Your Passion	7	G	6	0	0	0	1,284
Picked Clean	4	F	13	1	2	2	13,619
Pick'em	4	C	1	0	0	0	15,000
Picketts Gold	3	C	9	0	0	3	5,745
Pickety Witch	4	F	10	1	1	2	9,755
Picki	4	F	14	3	2	2	24,839
Pickin Laurel	2	F	1	0	0	0	2,300
Pickin On Pearl	3	F	1	0	0	0	67
Pickinupthedayroll	5	G	3	0	0	0	80
Pickled Bay	5	G	10	2	0	4	7,441
Pickled Pepper	4	G	16	2	0	1	9,641
Pickpocket Express	3	G	6	0	0	0	481
Pick's Ruby Rose	3	F	4	0	0	0	900
Pickthekey	4	G	12	1	1	1	5,076
Pickup the Marbles	6	G	9	2	3	2	16,513
Picky Picky Picky	5	G	10	0	1	1	1,717
Picnic Point P S	3	G	10	1	4	0	13,956
Picnic Theme	6	M	9	2	0	2	84,748
Pico Central (BRZ)	5	H	7	5	0	2	1,139,000
Pico D J Alex	4	G	9	0	1	0	5,800
Pico D. J. Nick	4	C	2	0	0	1	1,050
Picollo	4	G	2	0	0	0	750
Pico's Fame	3	G	2	0	0	0	887
Pics Fancypants	3	F	2	0	0	0	104
Pic's Legend	7	G	10	3	1	4	44,008
Pic's Rate	6	H	6	0	1	1	1,733
Picts	9	G	7	2	0	0	5,311
Picture Book	7	H	11	1	0	0	6,274
Picture Gallery	6	M	10	2	3	1	51,940
Picture Line	3	F	10	1	1	1	9,405
Picture Me Single	4	C	2	0	0	0	0
Picture Please	3	F	16	2	2	1	16,470
Picture Que	4	F	13	1	1	1	8,112
Picture That	2	F	3	0	0	1	6,335
Picture the Answer	4	F	7	3	3	1	14,070
Picture This	6	M	11	0	1	1	4,350
Picture This Tux	5	M	14	1	2	3	12,625
Picturesofmemories	7	M	13	0	1	0	10,429
Pie Corner	4	G	4	0	0	0	5,052
Pie N Burger	6	G	10	3	4	1	241,200
Pie O My	3	F	2	1	1	0	14,960
Piece of Change	3	G	3	1	0	0	11,070
Pieceofperfection	5	M	1	0	0	0	213
Pieces of April	5	M	12	0	0	6	4,721
Piedmont Express	4	F	7	1	0	1	20,030
Piedra Peak Lad	7	G	10	6	0	1	85,776
Pieman	4	G	14	0	1	1	1,926
Pierced Navel	4	F	4	0	1	1	2,912
Pierhead	4	C	10	2	1	1	58,884
Pierian Spring	3	F	6	0	1	1	13,952
Pierre	4	G	6	1	0	1	6,732
Pierre Legrand	3	C	7	2	2	1	46,840
Pierre's Wish	3	C	6	0	0	0	164
Piersixer	4	F	9	2	1	1	93,998
Pie's Lil Brother	5	G	6	1	0	1	41,950
Pies Prospect	3	C	14	4	1	2	473,865
Pietra's Girl	6	M	8	1	1	1	4,766
Piety	2	C	2	0	1	0	9,425
Piggy Bank	5	M	3	0	0	1	704
Piggyback Cart	2	G	1	0	0	0	135
Pikachew	3	C	9	1	2	1	15,370
Pike Place Gold	4	C	7	2	0	1	39,460
Pikecity Baileys	4	C	14	0	1	1	4,017
Pikester	5	G	13	1	2	2	14,135
Pikeville	6	G	3	1	0	0	7,965
Piknmupnputnmdown	3	F	3	0	0	0	168
Pilfer	3	F	7	2	1	0	109,200
Pilgrim County	3	C	17	1	4	5	21,960

Horse	Age	Sex	Sts	1st	2d	3d	Won
Pillar to Post	5	G	16	1	1	1	9,153
Pillar's Starbuck	5	G	10	3	0	1	11,867
Pillow Talk	5	M	10	0	0	1	9,490
Pillowtop	3	F	5	0	1	2	3,961
Pilot Point	3	C	2	0	0	1	1,944
Pilot View	4	G	10	0	0	1	1,631
Pilot's Boy	11	G	1	0	0	0	0
Pilsner	7	G	13	1	2	2	9,448
Pilsung	2	C	1	0	0	0	0
Pilu Russu	4	F	5	0	0	0	254
Pima Cotton	2	F	1	0	0	0	0
Pimento	7	M	13	2	3	1	33,503
Pimpernick	3	G	6	1	0	0	17,280
Pin and Peck	6	M	6	1	1	2	8,490
Pin Curl Peg	4	F	3	0	0	0	1,830
Pin Drop	3	C	1	0	1	0	3,800
Pin Emerald	5	M	3	0	1	2	1,846
Pin Jig	3	G	4	0	0	1	4,680
Pin Okie O	6	G	6	2	0	2	10,933
Pin Swappin	2	C	4	0	0	1	1,620
Pin Up Gal	3	F	3	0	0	0	181
Pin Up Pat	5	M	6	1	3	0	2,790
Pinball	4	G	2	0	0	1	987
Pinball Rich	4	G	4	1	1	0	7,798
Pincay	3	C	11	1	0	0	32,488
Pinch Hill	6	M	12	0	1	0	2,110
Pinch of Reality	9	M	1	0	0	0	57
Pinch the Clown	2	G	1	0	0	0	200
Pincher Creek	2	F	5	1	0	0	15,600
Pinchme	4	G	14	1	1	3	26,199
Pindar	3	F	4	0	1	1	7,335
Pindaric	2	F	3	1	1	1	17,520
Pine Bar	3	G	5	0	0	0	0
Pine Bend	4	G	4	0	1	1	4,427
Pine Breeze	4	C	9	1	1	2	19,050
Pine Brook	4	G	14	6	3	0	71,399
Pine Cay	2	G	1	0	0	0	1,440
Pine Club	2	C	11	1	2	2	17,815
Pine Creek	4	G	7	1	0	1	7,005
Pine for Badgett	3	G	5	0	0	4	4,726
Pine for Tate	4	G	7	1	2	1	14,746
Pine Hill	4	F	6	0	1	0	1,466
Pine Knot	3	G	4	0	0	0	400
Pine Love	3	C	8	1	0	0	10,650
Pine Thymeprincess	6	M	6	1	0	1	13,468
Pine Valley	6	M	6	4	0	0	19,140
Pineapple	4	G	2	0	0	0	170
Pineapple Paul	6	G	2	0	0	0	250
Pinecall	3	F	15	1	0	2	7,980
Pinecrest Inn	3	G	4	1	1	0	4,205
Pinedale Star	5	G	10	1	0	2	38,211
Pineingmyheartaway	6	M	5	1	0	0	8,564
Piney Beat	3	F	2	0	0	0	0
Piney Bubbles	2	F	2	0	0	1	1,935
Piney Creek Duck	6	H	6	0	2	1	4,200
Pinga	5	M	11	2	3	1	20,708
Piniante	5	M	12	2	2	1	16,566
Pining	2	F	1	0	0	0	0
Pining for You	4	G	7	1	0	1	18,840
Pinion	2	C	6	0	1	0	5,050
Pink Camellia	4	F	5	0	0	0	625
Pink Carnation	4	F	13	1	3	2	4,588
Pink Champagne	3	F	9	0	1	0	13,257
Pink Duck	6	H	4	0	1	1	10,090
Pink Dusty	3	F	9	1	1	0	26,415
Pink Jade	5	M	7	0	0	0	3,888
Pink Lemonade	3	F	4	0	1	1	2,710
Pink Meow	4	F	9	1	2	3	13,845
Pink Moon	2	F	1	0	0	0	400
Pink N Crafty	3	F	5	1	0	1	6,875
Pink Note	4	F	4	0	0	0	298
Pink Power	3	G	3	0	0	0	150
Pink Storm	3	F	13	1	1	0	6,685
Pinkey Ring	3	G	3	0	0	0	135
Pinkhair (FR)	5	H	7	0	0	0	8,120
Pinkie Dare	2	F	1	0	0	1	1,600
Pinkies Valentine	3	F	4	1	1	0	21,800
Pinkmingo	2	F	2	0	0	0	160
Pinksicle	2	F	5	0	0	1	1,320

Horse	Age	Sex	Sts	1st	2d	3d	Won
Pink'ster	3	F	2	0	0	0	230
Pinky Floyd	5	G	4	0	0	0	1,757
Pinky Pizwaanski	6	G	6	0	0	0	9,780
Pinlochle	3	F	4	0	0	2	11,000
Pino Alto	3	C	8	0	2	0	5,371
Pino Doll	6	M	6	0	2	2	3,172
Pinson	4	G	8	1	0	2	4,230
Pint o' Stout	7	G	12	3	1	4	18,188
Pint Thief	2	F	4	0	0	0	6,110
Pintail	4	F	2	0	0	0	960
Pinwinee Whiskey	4	F	9	1	0	2	20,255
Pioneer Boy	6	G	1	0	0	0	1,170
Pioneer Duke	3	C	1	0	0	0	0
Pioneer Empire	3	C	12	1	1	5	51,255
Pioneer Inn	6	M	9	0	0	2	7,570
Pioneer Miss	3	F	2	0	0	2	7,480
Pioneer Pass	6	G	23	3	4	2	11,040
Pioneer Pete	5	G	13	5	3	2	52,945
Pioneer Rose	2	F	6	1	0	0	5,133
Pioneer Time	3	F	12	1	3	2	14,115
Pioneeress	3	F	1	0	0	0	500
Pioneerman	3	G	12	1	2	1	49,995
Pioneer's Gold	3	C	13	2	0	0	14,534
Piority	4	F	9	0	1	2	4,575
Piotrus' Baby	4	G	8	0	1	1	19,980
Pip	2	G	5	1	2	0	26,438
Pipe Bomb	5	G	7	1	0	1	9,520
Pipe in Spector	2	G	3	0	0	0	0
Pipe Smoker	2	G	4	1	0	1	5,790
Pipeline	7	G	9	1	1	2	39,870
Piper Anne	3	F	12	0	0	0	0
Piper Two	3	F	6	0	1	1	7,730
Piperdown	3	G	4	0	1	0	520
Pipers Honour	2	F	2	0	0	0	3,591
Piper's Revenge	4	F	6	0	0	0	0
Pipers Trick	4	F	3	0	0	0	4,200
Pipes Dreamcatcher	4	G	4	0	0	1	1,350
Pipes of Pan	2	C	1	0	0	0	0
Pipestone	3	C	1	0	0	0	0
Pipewrench	2	G	1	0	0	0	140
Pipila	4	G	7	0	2	0	1,935
Pippy Dance	4	G	10	2	4	0	5,430
Pip's Angel	6	M	9	1	1	1	11,700
Piranha	10	G	8	0	0	1	1,806
Piranhurst	9	G	10	2	1	3	25,005
Pirate Afleet	3	G	3	0	0	0	402
Pirate Drake	2	C	4	0	0	0	512
Pirate Expectation	5	G	15	0	4	4	14,362
Pirate King	3	C	3	2	0	0	21,099
Pirate Liason	3	C	5	0	0	1	3,378
Pirate Ship	4	G	10	2	0	4	15,860
Pirates Band	5	G	8	2	1	1	8,790
Pirates Bite	2	C	3	1	0	0	18,030
Pirate's Fleet	7	G	12	3	1	2	14,523
Pirate's Gem	8	M	6	0	0	0	471
Pirate's Gold	6	H	3	1	0	0	10,200
Pirate's Gold Star	2	C	2	0	0	0	200
Pirate's Hostage	11	G	10	0	3	1	3,399
Pirate's Stash	8	G	5	0	1	0	1,288
Pirate's Storm	2	G	2	0	0	0	800
Pirates Taboo	3	G	12	2	3	1	24,230
Pirate's Wench	6	G	9	0	1	0	2,799
Pirkey	8	M	12	3	2	5	13,985
Pirouetting	2	F	1	0	0	0	0
Pisces	7	H	10	0	0	3	19,618
Piscolo	4	G	9	0	0	0	150
Pisgah	3	C	4	1	2	0	41,572
Pisgah Flash	3	G	3	0	0	0	0
Pistareen	6	H	10	0	0	2	2,961
Pistol Avenue	4	G	13	0	3	2	14,051
Pistol Nui	5	H	9	1	1	0	13,059
Pistol Place	4	G	15	0	0	2	5,811
Pistol Power	8	M	4	0	0	0	500
Pistol Whip	2	C	6	1	1	1	14,300
Pistol Wind	2	F	3	0	0	2	4,960
Pistol's Baby Doll	5	M	9	1	0	1	4,783
Pistols Flower	2	F	5	0	0	1	2,920
Pistols Gold	2	G	1	0	0	0	77
Pistol's Legacy	3	F	9	1	1	0	6,420

Horse	Age	Sex	Sts	1st	2d	3d	Won
Pistols's Wildcard	3	C	10	1	1	0	18,396
Piston	5	H	2	0	0	0	355
Piston Broke	4	G	13	1	2	0	5,161
Pitch a Penny	4	F	6	1	0	1	14,692
Pitch and Toss	2	C	3	0	1	0	4,450
Pitchacurve	3	F	10	1	1	2	37,560
Pitchin' Kalim	7	G	2	0	0	0	104
Pitchingthedream	4	F	3	0	0	0	620
Piton	5	G	2	0	1	0	2,940
Pit's Zagor	5	M	7	0	0	0	620
Pittsburgh City	4	C	4	1	2	0	49,480
Pittsburgh Kid	6	G	10	0	0	2	11,070
Pittsburgh Star	7	G	8	2	1	1	30,686
Pitty Pat	2	F	1	0	0	0	0
Pitufa	4	F	10	1	0	1	5,920
Pius Aeneus	2	G	3	1	0	1	9,510
Pivotal Pete	3	C	9	0	0	1	6,580
Pivotal Run	3	G	13	2	1	3	15,978
Pixel	4	F	14	1	1	2	12,174
Pixie Dust	2	F	1	1	0	0	9,000
Pixie Piper	2	F	1	0	0	0	0
Pixie Poo	3	F	10	3	1	1	13,892
Pixie Trick	2	F	7	0	1	1	3,388
Pixie's Pride	2	F	4	0	0	1	2,090
Pizza Boy	4	G	1	0	0	0	65
Pizza Port	4	F	6	1	0	0	5,275
Pj's Halo	6	M	2	0	0	0	0
Pj'salarm	7	G	12	2	0	4	12,710
Pk's Gal	4	F	9	2	0	0	45,773
Placable	4	F	1	0	1	0	1,920
Place All Bets	4	G	9	1	0	1	24,675
Place Cowboy (IRE)	3	C	7	1	2	0	19,941
Place to Hide	4	F	4	0	0	0	1,100
Placer Creek	3	F	4	0	0	1	3,937
Placid Delight	3	F	8	2	4	1	46,412
Placid Lake	2	F	3	0	1	1	6,670
Placid River	4	C	12	2	1	2	32,934
Placid Star	3	F	7	6	1	0	258,100
Placido	4	G	5	0	1	0	6,790
Plaefare Lad	8	G	3	0	0	1	1,275
Plaid	3	F	11	2	3	2	66,615
Plain Brown Suit	8	G	13	0	4	3	10,466
Plain Clothes	5	G	3	0	0	0	1,500
Plain Jack	4	G	6	1	1	0	8,720
Plain Jane Meadows	4	F	1	0	0	0	0
Plain Ol' Rocky	3	G	8	0	1	1	6,020
Plain Ole John	4	G	8	1	0	0	3,290
Plain O'Pete	4	C	2	0	0	0	0
Plainoleabe	5	G	2	0	0	0	150
Plait	4	F	2	0	0	0	532
Plamor Princess	3	F	7	2	0	1	22,383
Plan of Attack	2	F	6	0	1	3	12,635
Plan On Me	3	F	3	0	1	1	2,310
Planca's Secret	5	G	9	0	0	0	626
Planet Kind	3	F	12	2	2	0	17,752
Planet Ruler	6	G	11	1	2	3	5,652
Planet Valor	2	C	2	0	1	0	6,460
Planets Aligned	3	G	3	1	0	0	25,578
Planning Surprises	2	F	5	0	2	0	22,600
Plans to Travel	4	F	3	0	2	1	2,585
Plant the Seed	4	G	10	1	1	2	9,904
Plantation Acres	3	C	11	2	1	2	19,041
Plantation Girl	9	M	3	0	0	0	0
Plantation Rose	4	F	15	2	3	2	13,514
Planter	2	C	4	0	0	1	3,410
Plantodance	4	G	3	0	0	0	1,200
Plaster de Lane	4	F	2	0	0	0	0
Plastic Payoff	7	M	3	0	1	2	4,726
Plata	3	F	4	3	1	0	58,320
Plate Tectonics	5	G	1	0	0	0	0
Platinum Ballet	3	F	12	2	4	2	88,760
Platinum Case	3	C	16	1	2	2	56,006
Platinum Charge	3	C	4	0	0	0	700
Platinum Credit	3	F	2	0	0	0	800
Platinum Crown	2	C	2	0	1	0	3,090
Platinum Duke (GB)	5	G	2	0	0	0	1,390
Platinum Edition	4	G	5	2	0	1	21,900
Platinum Halo	8	G	10	0	0	0	917
Platinum Hawk	5	M	4	0	1	0	3,975
Platinum Heights	3	F	4	1	1	0	29,800
Platinum Hope	4	F	2	0	0	0	513
Platinum Key	4	F	4	0	0	1	1,390
Platinum Medallion	2	G	2	0	0	1	6,270
Platinum Perfect	3	F	2	2	0	0	45,000
Platinum Priced	3	G	11	1	0	0	16,010
Platinum Prince	3	G	11	1	0	4	5,584
Platinum Princess	3	F	3	0	2	1	24,440
Platinum Record	3	F	6	0	0	0	1,250
Platinum Rose	5	M	7	1	0	2	7,340
Platinum Rush	3	F	3	0	0	1	1,840
Platinum Score	4	G	11	3	1	3	77,930
Platinum Setting	8	G	4	0	1	2	9,810
Platinum Shoes	5	M	10	1	0	0	4,200
Platinum Sky	4	F	11	1	2	3	19,250
Platinum Upgrade	3	G	6	1	2	0	21,580
Platinum Wildcard	3	F	9	0	0	0	315
Platitude	4	C	12	3	2	3	70,930
Platium Prospect	4	G	3	0	0	0	235
Platonia	5	G	4	0	0	0	0
Platte County	3	G	16	3	0	5	13,720
Platte Vally Girl	3	F	5	0	0	0	418
Plausible	5	G	4	0	0	2	2,525
Play	5	G	10	1	0	0	5,210
Play Action	6	G	1	0	0	0	0
Play All Night	3	C	2	0	0	0	3,060
Play Approval	6	G	15	4	4	3	43,886
Play Around Sam	3	G	6	0	2	1	3,680
Play At Wrigley	3	G	9	0	1	1	2,672
Play Bingo	3	C	8	5	0	1	172,230
Play Bold Fox	3	C	5	0	0	0	0
Play by Play	3	C	2	0	0	0	470
Play Creole	3	G	4	0	1	0	6,560
Play Fast Ken	2	G	3	0	0	1	1,245
Play for Dixie	5	M	10	0	0	2	2,197
Play for Saratoga	5	G	12	1	1	1	10,491
Play Hookie	3	F	4	0	0	0	600
Play in the Sand	4	F	3	0	0	0	287
Play It Forward	3	G	2	1	0	0	4,412
Play It Kerry	6	M	8	1	0	0	3,274
Play It Out	5	G	8	0	1	1	14,086
Play It Softly	3	G	8	1	1	0	9,009
Play Me a Tune	4	F	6	0	0	2	8,000
Play My Music	5	M	7	0	1	0	2,020
Play N Fare	5	M	12	1	4	2	21,868
Play of the Game	3	G	5	0	0	0	757
Play On Cart	3	G	17	3	2	0	24,198
Play Pad	7	G	13	2	2	1	8,350
Play Pretend	3	F	2	0	0	0	600
Play School	3	F	1	0	0	0	320
Play the Circle	3	G	6	0	0	0	460
Play the Over	3	C	4	0	0	1	3,570
Play the Twist	3	G	12	2	1	1	12,212
Play Three Duces	2	F	3	0	0	0	0
Play to the Max	2	C	6	0	0	0	460
Play With Fire	2	F	5	1	0	2	107,000
Play With Me	7	G	1	0	0	0	0
Play Your Bluff	4	G	5	0	0	0	756
Playa Azul	5	G	14	0	1	0	7,517
Playa Maya	4	F	3	2	0	1	45,941
Playboy Hope	6	M	16	0	0	1	1,179
Playboy Jai	6	G	1	0	0	0	95
Playboy Pete	5	G	1	0	0	0	0
Playboy Slew	4	C	7	1	2	1	25,768
Playboy Type	2	C	2	0	0	0	225
Playcodered	5	G	8	2	0	1	9,946
Played a Fool	3	G	2	0	2	0	2,940
Player Again	2	C	1	0	0	0	230
Player Piano	2	G	2	0	0	0	0
Playero	11	H	4	0	0	0	0
Player's Hillary	8	M	1	0	0	0	110
Playersfirstchoice	5	M	4	1	0	0	4,580
Playful	5	M	10	3	0	2	38,960
Playful Billy Bob	4	C	8	0	0	1	2,106
Playful Cat	3	C	9	0	0	0	2,612
Playful Dancer	5	M	5	0	1	1	3,140
Playful Illusion	3	F	8	1	0	3	8,111
Playful Prince	4	G	13	2	2	0	10,150
Playful Sara	6	M	13	1	1	2	3,933

Horse	Age	Sex	Sts	1st	2d	3d	Won
Playful Trick	2	C	3	1	0	0	10,190
Playful Witness	3	F	2	0	0	0	193
Playfuljazz	3	G	1	0	0	0	0
Playgirl	4	F	10	1	1	0	26,900
Playgirl Talk	2	F	1	0	0	0	0
Playgirls Beau	4	G	15	0	2	2	3,664
Playground Legend	4	G	9	2	0	1	14,452
Playhurt	3	G	11	1	1	1	23,414
Playin' All Day	4	G	3	1	0	0	11,418
Playin' With Magic	4	G	13	1	1	2	7,927
Playing Footsie	4	F	10	3	1	0	58,164
Playing Lit	5	G	11	1	3	0	8,480
Playing 'r Song	2	F	1	0	1	0	3,800
Playing the Game	5	H	2	0	0	0	0
Playitagain Leo	5	M	5	0	0	0	1,008
Playitagainforme	3	F	1	0	0	0	300
Playmaker	3	F	12	2	3	0	23,610
Playmera	7	M	7	0	1	0	7,164
Playoftheday	4	G	12	1	1	0	6,713
Playsamongthestars	3	F	6	0	0	1	6,101
Playsomethingfast	2	G	6	0	3	0	13,890
Playville	2	F	3	2	1	0	9,080
Playwithyourmoney	4	G	11	1	3	0	6,565
Plaza Suite	5	M	4	1	0	0	8,494
Plazas Lil Pistol	8	G	4	0	1	0	1,430
Plazas Lil Waki	6	G	2	0	1	0	2,090
Pleas Deal	4	F	12	1	4	3	18,078
Pleasant Amigo	6	G	6	0	1	0	953
Pleasant Angel	8	M	7	0	0	0	646
Pleasant Bend	4	G	14	4	1	4	111,094
Pleasant Challenge	4	G	18	0	1	4	6,598
Pleasant Chap	4	G	8	1	1	2	16,801
Pleasant Cloud	6	M	4	0	1	0	3,260
Pleasant Company	5	G	12	4	3	1	82,118
Pleasant Crossing	3	F	9	2	1	2	18,504
Pleasant Deed	6	M	10	1	1	1	7,853
Pleasant Drive	9	H	6	0	0	0	1,177
Pleasant Emily	3	F	12	2	2	0	61,928
Pleasant Feeling	10	G	8	3	1	1	21,438
Pleasant Ghost	4	F	2	0	0	0	3,200
Pleasant Glory	3	F	11	3	1	3	42,000
Pleasant Gulch	4	F	7	3	2	1	24,759
Pleasant Hall	5	G	11	1	1	4	39,590
Pleasant High	2	C	3	0	0	0	271
Pleasant Home	3	F	4	2	0	1	61,650
Pleasant Honor	3	G	5	0	0	1	5,720
Pleasant Hope	5	M	7	1	0	0	11,985
Pleasant Italian	8	G	16	3	3	2	22,842
Pleasant Lady	5	M	6	0	1	0	2,719
Pleasant Laughter	2	F	2	0	0	1	4,900
Pleasant Living	5	M	10	1	3	1	21,222
Pleasant Magic	3	C	5	0	0	1	6,802
Pleasant Mate	3	F	5	0	0	1	6,130
Pleasant Mistress	5	M	3	0	0	0	0
Pleasant Note	6	M	6	0	0	1	4,140
Pleasant Parcel	8	H	6	4	1	0	46,250
Pleasant Passage	4	F	6	0	0	0	1,090
Pleasant Pastures	5	M	6	0	0	0	4,170
Pleasant Patter	2	C	9	2	1	2	18,431
Pleasant Pick	5	G	13	1	1	0	13,561
Pleasant Punch	3	F	6	1	1	0	10,980
Pleasant Reward	3	C	4	0	0	0	300
Pleasant Risk	3	C	10	1	2	2	18,986
Pleasant Saga	3	F	6	0	1	0	4,260
Pleasant Sands	4	F	9	1	3	0	36,460
Pleasant Signal	5	H	5	1	0	1	14,475
Pleasant Skip	3	F	15	1	0	2	14,325
Pleasant Star	10	G	20	1	6	2	12,116
Pleasant State	9	M	10	1	1	3	21,729
Pleasant Success	6	G	15	0	0	0	1,257
Pleasant Tapper	4	F	6	0	1	0	1,940
Pleasant Thunder	2	F	6	1	1	1	9,713
Pleasant Trick	4	G	15	3	2	3	50,749
Pleasant Villa	4	F	2	0	0	1	2,210
Pleasant Way	3	F	3	1	0	0	11,430
Pleasant Willy	4	G	9	0	0	1	1,090
Pleasant Wolf	5	M	1	0	0	0	220
Pleasant Yukon	4	C	12	0	2	3	9,266
Pleasantdotcom	7	G	11	1	1	1	4,223
Pleasantly Dazling	2	F	3	0	0	0	250
Pleasantly Perfect	6	H	5	3	1	1	4,840,000
Pleasanton	5	M	13	0	4	1	9,577
Please Believeit	4	F	7	0	1	1	4,913
Please Bill	4	G	16	1	0	1	8,574
Please Call Home	3	F	8	2	0	0	30,575
Please Dear Please	4	F	4	0	0	1	1,770
Please Lord	3	F	6	1	3	0	32,895
Please Louie	3	G	6	1	0	1	15,205
Please Pay Artax	3	C	11	2	0	1	26,427
Please Release Me	4	G	13	3	0	3	25,690
Please Repete	6	G	10	0	1	3	4,500
Please Smile	3	G	10	1	1	0	25,726
Please Take Me Out	3	F	4	1	0	0	36,700
Please Tell	3	F	9	0	0	2	2,533
Please the Crowd	2	G	3	0	0	0	1,710
Please the Mind	4	G	6	1	1	1	7,930
Please to See Me	3	G	3	0	0	0	0
Please U Me	6	M	1	0	0	0	0
Pleaser	8	M	3	1	0	0	8,340
Pleasing Amy	2	F	5	0	1	2	4,115
Pleasing Louise	4	F	2	0	0	0	158
Pleasing Memories	3	C	1	0	0	0	0
Pleasing Punch	4	F	11	3	2	2	9,996
Pleasingagentleman	4	F	9	1	0	1	13,046
Pleasurable Steel	3	G	4	0	0	0	195
Pleasure	2	F	3	0	1	1	3,601
Pleasure Fair	3	F	7	2	2	0	32,324
Pleasure Honor	3	G	10	1	3	2	43,820
Pleasure Hunt	3	F	3	0	0	0	315
Pleasure J	10	M	3	0	0	0	263
Pleasure Pro	4	F	11	3	1	0	14,030
Pleasure Rocket	4	G	8	1	0	0	3,390
Pleasure Tree	4	G	4	0	0	1	440
Pleasureindancing	4	F	10	1	1	3	19,810
Pleasureinnumbers	6	G	12	2	1	0	13,935
Pleasures all Mine	10	G	5	2	0	0	2,085
Pleasuretobeatyou	7	M	4	0	0	1	2,050
Pledge for Allen	2	F	2	1	0	0	11,970
Pledge of Peace	4	F	6	1	0	0	8,840
Plenilunio	3	G	7	1	1	1	14,365
Plenty	3	F	6	2	2	1	100,450
Plenty Easy	4	F	4	2	0	0	9,075
Plenty Lucky	5	G	7	1	2	0	13,372
Plenty of Heat	3	C	12	3	0	0	89,340
Plenty of Jacks	4	G	14	3	3	1	12,295
Plenty of Sass	4	G	10	4	2	1	9,699
Plenty of Sweets	5	G	5	0	0	2	4,550
Plenty of Talk	5	M	7	3	0	2	6,687
Plenty Potentate	4	C	4	0	0	1	1,320
Plenty Story	4	F	7	1	1	0	3,191
Plinking	4	F	7	0	2	0	8,320
Plino	8	G	8	4	1	1	43,366
Plisky Steel	5	M	2	0	0	0	80
Plot Plan	7	G	9	1	3	0	21,355
Pluck's Doggie	6	G	13	0	1	0	3,156
Plucky Broad	5	M	1	0	0	0	0
Plucky Discovery	8	M	12	2	1	2	19,850
Plug	5	G	5	0	1	0	5,460
Plum Broke	3	C	1	0	0	0	300
Plum Crazy	3	F	3	0	0	1	548
Plum Good Day	6	H	1	0	0	0	0
Plum Gorgeous	2	F	1	0	0	0	135
Plum Great	3	G	11	0	6	2	10,010
Plum Puzzled	4	G	6	3	1	0	4,895
Plum Red	3	G	16	0	3	5	33,670
Plum Sober	3	G	9	1	2	2	47,692
Plum Wonder	3	F	17	3	1	3	33,635
Plumb	6	G	3	0	0	0	432
Plumb Salty	3	G	9	0	0	2	3,520
Plume	4	F	5	0	0	1	935
Plumeria	3	F	10	2	0	3	12,870
Plumgodlike	3	F	7	0	0	0	313
Plumlake Lady	3	F	7	3	2	1	71,265
Plummery	3	C	6	0	1	1	10,495
Plumnellie	5	M	6	1	0	2	7,994
Plumpish	2	F	6	0	2	0	9,995
Plumwood	2	C	2	0	0	0	260
Plunge	8	G	9	0	0	0	442

RECORDS OF HORSES

Horse	Age	Sex	Sts	1st	2d	3d	Won
Plunge Right In	2	F	3	0	0	0	1,380
Plunkit	2	C	2	0	0	0	800
Plus Iron	4	F	1	0	0	0	0
Plus Tax	3	F	1	0	0	0	0
Plus Three	4	F	18	2	3	4	36,295
Plush	6	M	2	0	0	0	0
Plush Treasure	2	F	6	0	0	0	3,585
Plush Velvet	2	F	1	0	0	0	300
Ply	3	C	12	1	1	0	25,075
Pnutbutterandjolie	5	M	8	3	1	0	31,060
Pocahaba	5	M	10	1	4	1	66,637
Pocazzone	2	C	4	0	0	1	3,230
Pocket Breaker	4	G	3	0	0	0	0
Pocket Fullof Hope	7	G	7	0	0	0	1,319
Pocket Phones Baby	7	M	2	0	0	0	80
Pocket Road	3	G	13	3	0	1	9,700
Pocket Treys	3	G	3	0	0	0	486
Pocketbook Passion	2	F	1	0	0	0	0
Pocketful O Mach Z	4	F	7	0	0	0	738
Pocketfullofpesos	4	F	4	1	0	0	43,810
Pockets	6	G	13	1	1	1	7,784
Poco	5	G	20	4	1	4	29,431
Poco Bueno	2	C	5	1	1	0	26,740
Poco Dinero	3	F	19	1	3	4	12,012
Poco Doc	4	F	9	2	1	2	31,202
Poco Oro	3	C	6	0	0	1	816
Poco Rey	6	G	11	1	1	1	10,625
Pocomoonshine	2	G	1	0	0	0	600
Pocono Delight	3	F	5	0	0	0	399
Pocopson Man	3	C	1	0	1	0	2,200
Pocus Hocus	6	M	5	1	1	0	120,552
Podden	9	H	1	0	0	0	75
Poe Lighten	4	G	4	0	0	0	0
Poet	4	C	10	0	2	2	36,711
Poetic Honor	3	F	14	3	1	1	30,485
Poetic Romance	4	F	6	2	0	2	62,370
Poetry in Motion	2	F	2	0	2	0	10,000
Poets and Angels	3	F	7	1	0	1	25,700
Poet's Pen	4	F	3	0	0	1	616
Pogolotti Hill	6	G	3	0	0	1	6,112
Pogowin	3	F	3	0	0	0	650
Pogue Mahone	5	M	14	0	0	0	934
Pohave	6	G	8	3	3	2	450,740
Point After	3	F	3	0	0	1	1,300
Point Blank	6	G	15	1	1	3	12,835
Point Breeze	3	G	2	0	0	0	1,140
Point Clear	4	F	1	0	0	0	360
Point Click	5	G	18	4	6	2	28,545
Point Dume	3	G	8	1	1	2	44,965
Point Fear	3	C	2	0	0	0	205
Point Five	9	G	15	2	2	0	26,123
Point Grey	4	G	12	0	2	1	8,366
Point Hidden	3	G	5	1	1	2	41,353
Point High	5	G	1	0	0	0	63
Point Info	4	F	12	0	5	4	30,430
Point Lily	4	F	13	5	2	0	108,430
Point Luck	2	G	1	0	0	0	2,583
Point of America	7	G	10	3	1	0	46,760
Point of Flight	3	G	10	1	0	2	49,231
Point Prince	5	G	2	0	0	2	8,000
Point Reyes	2	F	5	3	0	2	41,915
Point Storm	8	G	10	0	1	0	2,043
Point Sunshine	4	F	3	0	0	0	390
Point Taken	4	G	15	1	2	3	13,736
Pointe Birds	4	G	5	1	0	0	33,442
Pointe Milou	4	F	2	0	0	0	0
Pointe Taken	3	F	9	0	3	2	6,681
Pointed	10	G	6	1	1	1	1,537
Pointed Stone	4	C	3	0	0	0	0
Pointforli	2	F	5	2	0	1	33,040
Pointin West	3	G	12	2	1	3	24,043
Points On	4	F	3	0	1	0	6,825
Points West	4	F	11	3	3	3	125,630
Pointsman	2	C	2	1	1	0	18,800
Poise	5	M	9	3	1	1	41,123
Poison Cake	3	C	5	2	0	0	13,260
Poison Ivah	5	M	11	0	1	3	2,774
Poison Ivy (FR)	5	M	3	0	0	0	0
Poison Letters	4	F	1	0	0	0	0

Horse	Age	Sex	Sts	1st	2d	3d	Won
Poison Man Jack	3	C	12	1	1	2	14,814
Poison Oak	3	G	11	1	0	5	10,331
Poison Oak Camp	5	M	17	1	1	0	7,091
Poka Dot Princess	4	F	14	3	2	2	33,028
Pokeemom	4	F	2	0	0	0	366
Pokemon Jo	4	G	10	0	0	2	5,187
Poker Brad	6	G	6	2	2	0	87,745
Poker Call	4	G	1	0	0	0	190
Poker Dice	5	G	16	2	1	2	15,123
Poker Game	3	C	4	0	2	1	15,010
Poker Joe	2	C	4	0	1	2	17,630
Poker Little Devil	4	G	1	0	0	0	0
Poker Little Sugar	8	M	3	0	0	0	0
Poker Mad	2	G	3	1	0	0	7,115
Poker Money	3	F	2	1	0	0	27,400
Poker Playing Mom	2	F	5	0	1	0	2,385
Poker Rules	3	C	2	0	0	1	5,280
Pokerfaced	4	F	11	5	1	0	88,290
Pokey Aaron	4	G	10	3	1	2	21,498
Pokey Hontas	6	M	7	0	0	0	1,081
Pokey Pine	3	C	11	1	3	3	35,850
Poks Destiny	4	F	2	0	0	0	0
Polack	3	G	2	0	0	0	390
Polar Barron	8	G	7	2	2	0	24,680
Polar Bear	4	F	2	1	0	0	15,970
Polar Explorer	3	F	7	2	0	0	11,953
Polar Gem	2	C	2	0	0	0	0
Polar Miss	5	M	3	0	1	1	2,975
Polar Phlox	3	F	13	3	2	1	28,175
Polar Prospector	6	M	7	1	0	1	8,852
Polar Ray	6	H	2	2	0	0	8,760
Polar Snow	4	F	1	0	0	0	120
Polar Sparkel	3	F	9	0	0	1	5,473
Polaris	3	G	2	0	0	0	0
Polarmetry	6	M	7	0	0	1	807
Pole to Pole	4	C	10	2	3	0	28,980
Polemico (ARG)	4	G	5	0	0	0	2,560
Pole's Dancer	5	G	10	1	2	5	10,570
Pole's Fancy	4	F	12	0	1	1	2,456
Police Alert	5	G	3	2	0	0	11,414
Policy Cat	3	F	9	2	1	2	25,573
Polish Account	4	F	1	0	0	0	0
Polish Affair	3	F	3	2	0	0	27,120
Polish Baby	4	F	3	2	0	0	15,442
Polish Broad	4	F	1	0	0	0	0
Polish C	2	G	6	0	0	2	1,628
Polish Crown	3	F	5	1	1	0	37,150
Polish Dee	6	M	7	0	0	0	657
Polish Desire	4	G	12	2	1	3	16,170
Polish Dream	4	C	2	0	0	0	0
Polish Flower	3	F	1	0	0	0	0
Polish Grove	2	F	1	0	0	0	0
Polish Ham	4	G	1	0	0	0	0
Polish Influence	3	G	11	3	0	0	15,255
Polish Jewel	4	G	7	0	1	2	11,514
Polish Jig	4	F	10	0	3	0	9,222
Polish Magic	6	G	9	2	1	0	15,070
Polish Mary	3	F	13	1	0	5	22,860
Polish Memory	5	G	17	2	1	2	18,155
Polish Moe	8	G	7	1	0	1	6,042
Polish Music	7	G	7	0	0	1	7,100
Polish Nana	4	F	8	0	0	1	8,100
Polish Navigator	3	C	7	0	0	1	8,058
Polish Outlaw	6	H	9	1	0	3	10,710
Polish Pianist	8	G	15	3	1	2	27,856
Polish Pistol	5	G	1	0	0	0	288
Polish Police	7	G	8	0	0	1	1,225
Polish Posh	4	C	1	0	0	0	123
Polish Pride	6	G	6	2	1	1	64,300
Polish Prince	2	C	1	0	0	0	135
Polish Promise	3	G	8	3	2	0	27,440
Polish Prospect	3	F	1	0	0	0	720
Polish Rifle	3	C	6	1	2	0	60,100
Polish Rogue	4	G	7	0	0	1	917
Polish Slew	3	G	7	0	1	0	1,189
Polish Slip	3	G	14	2	3	2	19,870
Polish Snoop	6	M	1	0	0	0	73
Polish Summer (GB)	7	H	7	2	0	0	1,316,120
Polish Times	7	G	10	3	3	1	104,400

Horse	Age	Sex	Sts	1st	2d	3d	Won
Polish Trick	3	C	4	1	0	1	11,650
Polish Trouble	2	F	1	0	0	0	50
Polish Turn	3	C	1	0	0	0	0
Polish Unity	5	H	3	0	0	2	6,670
Polish Virtues	4	F	1	0	0	0	0
Polish Zone	4	G	1	0	0	0	0
Polished Gem	3	G	5	0	0	1	4,585
Polished Steel	5	G	3	0	0	0	0
Polished Stone	5	M	2	0	0	0	731
Polishgoer	4	F	1	0	0	0	0
Polishoffthebrandy	5	M	1	0	0	0	0
Polite Future	3	F	8	0	3	0	14,614
Political Attack	5	G	2	0	1	0	30,000
Political Choice	3	C	4	1	0	1	15,294
Political Freedom	4	G	5	0	0	1	2,614
Political Hostage	2	F	2	1	0	0	19,440
Political Prize	3	F	4	2	0	0	13,820
Political Pull	5	G	13	0	2	3	14,457
Political Rhetoric	5	G	12	0	2	5	40,140
Political Risk	4	C	3	1	1	1	29,120
Political Savvy	3	F	8	1	3	1	37,765
Political Spin	2	G	1	0	0	0	115
Political Storm	6	G	2	0	1	0	1,740
Political Triumph	5	G	3	0	0	0	1,026
Political Weapon	3	C	5	0	0	1	6,110
Politicallycorrect	4	C	10	0	0	2	1,637
Politix	3	F	5	1	0	2	10,715
Polka Coyote	10	G	11	0	0	0	788
Polka Lady	5	M	2	0	0	0	200
Polka With Me	4	F	7	2	2	0	12,740
Polkadot	2	F	1	0	0	0	1,150
Pollard's Vision	3	C	11	4	4	1	1,022,020
Pollica	10	M	3	0	0	0	915
Pollock	5	G	9	1	0	1	10,215
Pollock Flash	3	F	5	0	0	0	780
Polly B.	5	M	12	1	1	0	6,283
Polly Everafter	4	F	4	0	1	1	7,130
Polly Lynch	2	F	2	0	0	0	0
Polly Peabody	3	F	5	0	0	1	2,125
Polly Rout	4	F	6	1	2	0	4,675
Polly T.	7	M	1	0	0	0	73
Pollys Accelerator	3	F	11	2	1	2	20,325
Polly's Folly	4	F	9	0	1	1	9,520
Polly's Persuasion	4	F	2	0	0	0	0
Polly's Pistol	3	G	14	0	2	6	10,360
Polly's Princess	4	F	16	1	3	2	11,168
Polo Bender	3	G	2	0	2	0	4,730
Polo Grounds	3	C	4	2	0	0	55,338
Polo Party	4	G	9	0	4	2	1,925
Polo Ridge	4	F	3	0	0	0	3,800
Polonia	4	F	4	2	0	1	55,850
Poltical Party	3	G	16	0	2	2	5,622
Poly Is	4	C	1	0	0	0	100
Poly Pop a Top	4	F	6	1	0	0	6,654
Poly Von	3	F	3	0	0	0	270
Polyanna	3	F	6	0	0	0	530
Polygreen (FR)	5	M	3	0	1	0	22,138
Polympics	5	H	1	0	0	0	780
Polys Banner	2	G	3	0	0	0	0
Poly's Loose	6	G	13	0	0	1	1,614
Pomeranze (IRE)	3	F	13	2	1	2	36,187
Pomeroy	3	C	5	2	2	0	296,250
Pomme de Terre	4	G	7	1	0	0	3,792
Pomona Lisa	7	M	1	0	0	0	50
Pompamento	4	F	12	4	2	1	86,910
Pompano Beach	6	G	4	0	1	0	1,466
Pompeii the Great	5	G	6	0	0	0	407
Ponche de Leona	5	M	10	1	1	1	30,200
Ponche Line	3	C	9	2	0	2	19,661
Ponches Glory	4	G	17	1	5	3	14,457
Ponche's Image	6	G	14	0	2	2	4,938
Ponches Prospect	4	G	3	0	0	0	0
Ponche's Solo	2	C	7	1	0	2	10,540
Poncho Duck	10	G	2	0	0	1	1,517
Ponchos Sol	4	F	3	0	0	0	0
Ponderosa	5	M	1	0	1	0	3,680
Ponette	3	F	6	1	0	1	15,460
Poni Lee	4	F	4	0	0	1	780
Ponoka	3	G	7	2	1	1	24,874
Ponopaan	5	H	9	0	2	2	17,292
Ponsonby	10	G	1	0	0	0	800
Ponta Das Canas	2	F	2	0	0	0	3,040
Pontanal	5	G	3	0	0	0	0
Pontchartrain	8	G	18	1	3	1	11,780
Ponticiello (CHI)	6	H	10	1	1	1	23,290
Pontiff	3	G	2	0	0	0	1,348
Pontius	3	G	5	1	2	0	9,480
Pontook	3	F	3	1	0	0	8,400
Pontoosuc	2	F	2	0	0	0	840
Pony Corner	3	G	6	0	2	0	9,870
Pony Pal	4	F	4	1	0	0	8,030
Poof Be Gone	7	M	4	0	0	0	934
Poofadini	5	G	9	0	0	2	7,390
Pool Boy	3	G	5	2	2	1	33,493
Pool Music (GB)	9	G	1	0	0	0	0
Poolhall	3	G	14	0	1	1	6,967
Poolman	9	G	8	0	0	1	2,610
Poor Iggy	2	C	6	3	1	1	90,344
Poor Me	3	G	1	0	0	0	690
Poor Paul	3	G	6	1	0	0	6,527
Poor Pilgrim	8	G	7	1	1	0	8,992
Poor Pitiful Pearl	3	F	1	0	0	0	54
Poorboys Playboy	2	G	4	0	0	0	2,076
Pop On Top	3	C	14	2	2	3	37,440
Pop Pop's Fuse	4	C	7	0	2	1	13,968
Pop Pop's Hope	3	F	8	0	1	0	14,005
Pop Pop's Jimmy	3	G	15	1	1	5	15,996
Pop Princess	4	F	7	2	1	1	90,700
Pop Rocks	7	G	2	0	0	0	3,460
Pop the Cork	6	G	13	2	3	3	12,462
Pop the Latch	3	F	10	1	3	2	17,358
Pop the Question	2	C	4	2	0	0	45,000
Pop Top	3	F	10	2	2	2	12,695
Pop Tucker	3	C	2	0	0	0	0
Popacap	4	G	15	3	2	2	65,339
Popaluna	2	F	5	1	0	2	11,275
Popcorn	4	G	16	2	1	2	23,685
Popcorn Deelites	6	G	10	5	2	0	17,332
Popcorn Lady	3	F	14	0	6	4	12,895
Popcorn Mike	4	F	2	0	0	0	800
Popescu (BRZ)	7	G	5	3	1	0	4,932
Popgun	5	G	10	0	0	1	2,195
Popoki	3	G	3	0	0	1	4,500
Popozinha	3	F	9	1	2	0	26,475
Poppa Corky	7	G	6	1	0	0	8,676
Poppa's Favorites	9	G	10	0	1	0	5,872
Poppa's Hoarse	2	C	2	0	0	0	810
Poppa's Little Man	5	H	10	0	1	3	6,629
Poppa's Misty	5	M	2	0	0	0	800
Popped Corn	8	G	10	3	1	2	29,856
Poppees Demon	3	C	3	0	0	0	0
Poppie's Plan	6	G	1	0	0	0	0
Poppins Popper	5	M	6	1	1	1	16,774
Poppo's Song	3	F	7	1	0	0	26,770
Poppy Hills	4	F	9	2	2	2	15,242
Poppy Seed	4	F	4	1	0	0	10,200
Poppycop	4	F	8	0	0	0	168
Poppy's Ashleigh	2	F	4	0	0	1	7,240
Poppy's Courage	5	G	13	2	0	2	45,355
Poppys Grey Cat	4	F	9	1	2	1	5,191
Poppy's Image	4	G	3	0	0	1	4,940
Poppy's Joy	2	F	2	1	0	0	9,024
Pop's Angel	4	F	5	0	0	0	263
Pops' Bo Boy	11	G	2	0	0	0	600
Pop's Boy	2	C	4	0	2	1	11,700
Pop's Carlee	2	F	7	0	0	0	0
Pop's Nativecolors	3	C	7	0	0	1	1,350
Pop's Pick	3	G	6	1	3	0	21,678
Pops Pleasure	4	G	13	0	0	1	1,085
Pops Return	2	C	6	1	1	1	32,522
Pop's Storm	3	F	2	0	0	0	0
Popsaweasel	3	G	3	0	0	0	670
Popsicle Pete	8	G	12	0	2	1	9,613
Popsy	6	M	3	1	0	0	7,940
Popular Blues	5	M	14	1	5	2	21,828
Popular Decision	2	F	2	0	1	1	2,270
Popular Delusions	2	F	2	0	0	0	1,530
Popular Gigalo	10	G	3	0	0	0	4,950

Horse	Age	Sex	Sts	1st	2d	3d	Won
Popular Groom	4	C	2	0	0	0	360
Popular Host	10	G	13	1	3	1	10,012
Popular Kat	7	H	8	0	2	1	2,829
Popular Prospect	2	C	2	0	0	0	185
Popularize	4	G	9	1	1	2	20,670
Poquito Blanco	4	F	11	1	2	1	23,934
Poquito Blue	4	G	4	0	0	0	645
Por Favor	3	C	12	2	1	2	53,240
Por Lucky	6	G	4	0	0	1	1,104
Por Maracaibo	5	M	16	0	0	2	2,844
Poras	4	F	3	2	0	0	11,100
Porcelin Masque	2	F	1	0	0	0	0
Porches	4	F	7	1	0	2	7,386
Porfirio Cadena	4	G	8	0	0	2	5,120
Porky	5	G	7	0	1	0	7,165
Port Au Prince	5	G	10	2	0	0	14,090
Port Chester	2	C	5	0	0	0	5,189
Port Gibson	3	G	14	1	0	1	4,858
Port Henry	6	G	18	2	4	4	50,625
Port Hueneme	4	G	6	2	0	1	23,400
Port Ilse	2	C	8	1	2	0	23,808
Port n' A' Storm	4	G	10	1	1	1	4,446
Port of Texas	2	F	1	0	0	0	70
Port of Trieste	3	F	9	0	1	0	3,700
Port St. Charles	3	C	1	0	0	0	205
Port Town	2	C	2	2	0	0	25,800
Portan	5	G	5	0	1	0	1,744
Portia Picnic	3	G	5	1	2	0	9,555
Portlandate	4	G	8	2	0	0	51,626
Portlandia	2	F	1	0	0	0	288
Portly Princess	4	F	12	1	1	5	30,590
Portobello Belle	5	M	10	1	2	0	21,141
Portofino Creek	4	G	12	3	1	2	17,141
Portraitofcamelot	4	G	2	0	0	0	906
Portsea	2	F	3	1	1	0	31,730
Portside	6	H	5	0	0	0	900
Portwood	7	G	16	0	0	3	2,882
Pose for Photo	3	F	1	0	0	0	55
Posh Excess	2	F	2	0	0	0	688
Posh Party	2	F	2	1	0	0	12,775
Posh Pet	3	F	1	0	1	0	1,615
Positive (IRE)	5	G	14	0	1	4	6,541
Positive Climb	4	F	6	2	0	0	19,545
Positive Gold	3	G	7	0	2	2	26,363
Positive Pete	7	G	9	1	0	1	3,430
Positive Prize	2	G	5	4	0	1	106,663
Positive Spirit	5	M	6	2	1	0	16,449
Positively	8	H	5	1	0	0	3,842
Positively Better	2	F	1	0	0	0	135
Positively Wild	4	F	10	0	1	1	27,450
Positron	2	F	9	0	1	0	3,138
Possess (GB)	3	C	6	0	2	2	24,010
Possibilitarian	2	C	1	0	0	0	0
Possibility	4	F	5	0	0	2	14,928
Possible Punch	4	F	2	1	0	0	6,555
Possibly Silver	3	F	1	0	0	0	125
Possuletta Sue	5	M	13	0	0	5	15,250
Possum Deats	3	C	1	0	0	0	176
Post Chaplain	7	G	20	2	2	5	12,785
Post Hostess	8	M	4	0	1	1	814
Post Iron	3	G	4	1	0	1	11,492
Post Its Awesome	4	G	8	3	2	0	23,798
Post Master	4	G	1	0	1	0	1,045
Post Op	3	F	14	2	2	3	38,757
Post Pattern	4	G	12	1	3	0	38,260
Post Position	3	G	6	0	0	0	1,110
Post Road	6	H	4	0	0	0	601
Post Toasty	5	M	14	3	2	0	10,896
Postal Link	3	C	4	0	0	0	0
Poster Boy	4	G	12	0	0	1	2,031
Postnuptial	3	C	10	3	1	2	61,470
Postulant	3	F	8	1	0	1	24,110
Posture	4	G	9	0	3	1	19,200
Pot Limit	5	G	9	2	2	1	17,562
Potato Lad	5	G	9	0	2	0	16,992
Potentially	3	G	11	3	1	0	25,132
Potion	3	F	13	2	3	1	57,155
Potnia	3	F	11	1	0	3	39,600
Potomac Chase	3	C	12	2	0	2	63,250
Potomac Falls	4	G	5	0	1	0	10,080
Potomac Way	7	H	3	0	0	0	302
Potra Fabulous (ARG)	5	M	6	1	1	0	60,984
Potri Burn (ARG)	7	H	13	2	1	3	18,495
Potri Cacho (ARG)	6	G	14	5	4	2	72,855
Potri Jealous (ARG)	6	H	1	0	0	0	400
Potri Llama (ARG)	6	M	12	2	1	3	35,240
Potri Mambo	4	F	1	0	0	0	2,580
Potri Marshal (ARG)	5	G	24	0	3	2	7,006
Potri Star (ARG)	6	M	9	0	1	0	11,231
Potrilord (ARG)	7	H	2	0	0	0	2,760
Potrisunrise (ARG)	7	G	13	5	0	1	108,660
Potrithreat (ARG)	7	M	10	0	3	2	5,472
Potroast and Gravy	3	G	11	1	2	1	12,985
Potshot	2	C	3	1	0	1	19,660
Pottawatamie	4	F	13	3	3	2	22,505
Potter	5	G	12	0	0	1	875
Potter's Field	3	G	8	0	0	1	1,038
Pottersville	5	G	11	4	3	1	52,660
Potus	6	G	5	0	0	3	4,975
Pouilly Fuisse	3	F	6	1	0	0	20,328
Pouncer	3	F	2	0	0	0	0
Pound the Mound	3	C	15	0	0	2	4,736
Poundcake	4	G	14	3	4	2	53,985
Pounding	7	G	11	0	3	2	27,346
Poundmaker	2	C	5	0	0	1	14,252
Pour Elise	2	F	2	0	0	0	1,155
Pour It On	3	F	9	1	1	3	65,840
Pour La Paix	2	F	1	0	0	0	2,350
Pour Lil Devil	5	G	6	0	0	0	907
Pour the Wine	3	G	5	0	1	0	5,220
Pouring Rain	6	M	10	1	4	1	18,827
Pourmeadouble	2	F	4	1	0	0	11,355
Pout	3	F	4	0	0	0	1,401
Pow Wow Louise	4	F	8	1	0	3	36,673
Powder Bank	2	C	2	1	0	1	1,584
Powder Keg	5	G	3	0	0	0	180
Powder Puff Girl	2	F	4	0	0	0	455
Powder River Cat	2	C	4	0	1	1	4,400
Powder Your Nose	6	M	3	0	0	0	399
Powdered Wig	4	F	13	4	2	3	70,650
Powderet	4	F	4	1	2	0	6,305
Powderhouse Pete	3	G	4	0	0	0	710
Powders Wish	4	F	10	1	1	2	17,531
Powell Creek	4	C	15	0	2	2	14,595
Power	3	G	7	1	0	0	18,180
Power and Achase	6	G	15	4	1	2	24,175
Power and Panache	8	G	16	0	0	1	1,690
Power and Peace	9	H	1	0	0	0	0
Power Appeal	7	G	7	0	1	1	1,200
Power Away	4	G	4	0	0	1	866
Power Blue	3	G	3	0	0	0	0
Power Boost	6	G	1	0	0	0	202
Power Boy	4	G	10	3	1	2	100,780
Power Brew	3	G	5	1	1	0	11,920
Power by Jules	3	G	7	2	3	1	50,460
Power Connection	5	G	14	3	0	1	17,620
Power Crossing	3	F	8	0	0	0	2,870
Power Curtain	5	M	14	1	3	2	3,957
Power Dance	3	F	6	1	0	2	8,728
Power Dot	4	F	12	1	0	2	8,522
Power Failure	6	H	9	3	3	2	14,308
Power Flame	10	G	7	1	0	2	5,986
Power Flash	3	F	3	0	1	0	2,000
Power for Trey	4	G	4	1	0	0	7,200
Power Glide	6	G	12	3	3	0	32,260
Power Happy	4	G	7	0	0	0	102
Power Hawk	4	G	12	4	1	1	27,259
Power in Prayer	3	C	3	1	1	0	21,200
Power Jaws	5	G	1	0	0	0	0
Power Jr.	5	H	9	2	2	2	17,679
Power Knock	3	G	19	2	2	1	23,494
Power Launch	3	C	12	1	1	1	6,952
Power Link	2	G	2	1	0	0	24,805
Power Lion	4	G	5	0	0	0	0
Power Mission	3	G	1	0	0	0	0
Power Music	7	G	14	4	2	0	29,359
Power N Motion	4	G	9	1	0	2	4,538
Power Nap	5	G	1	0	0	0	192

Horse	Age	Sex	Sts	1st	2d	3d	Won
Power of Dreams	4	F	8	2	1	2	36,955
Power of Elprado	7	G	7	1	1	1	6,994
Power of Esteem	3	F	3	0	1	0	500
Power of Faith	5	M	13	1	0	3	19,209
Power of Flirting	3	F	1	0	0	0	235
Power of Glory	5	M	12	1	2	0	10,017
Power of Hope	5	M	10	0	3	1	11,930
Power of Jane	5	M	2	0	0	0	0
Power of Lady	4	F	3	1	1	0	8,100
Power of Lite	3	C	9	3	1	2	40,200
Power of Surprise	3	G	16	5	5	1	81,750
Power of Thunder	2	F	5	0	0	0	0
Power Overseer	2	G	1	0	0	0	0
Power Perfect	7	M	7	3	1	1	63,360
Power Phan	7	M	1	0	1	0	5,592
Power Pic	5	G	2	1	1	0	11,815
Power Power	9	H	4	0	0	0	720
Power Promise	4	F	2	1	0	0	3,426
Power Regent	3	G	1	0	0	0	0
Power Sander	3	G	10	0	1	6	11,780
Power Seeker	3	C	1	0	0	0	0
Power Serge	6	M	8	0	2	2	8,490
Power Shower	3	F	12	3	2	4	30,542
Power Soldier	2	C	1	0	1	0	2,660
Power Sox	2	F	1	0	0	0	0
Power Star	3	G	1	0	0	0	0
Power Strategy	8	G	8	1	2	1	4,765
Power Strokin	3	G	12	2	1	2	13,966
Power Tap	3	G	3	0	0	0	800
Power Teapot	5	H	3	0	0	0	400
Power Through	3	C	7	1	0	0	16,200
Power to Burn	7	M	3	0	0	0	3,276
Power to Fly	3	F	3	0	1	0	1,900
Power Tower	3	F	5	1	2	2	30,940
Power Tripper	3	G	6	2	1	0	74,108
Power Wave	2	C	5	4	0	0	73,539
Power Wheels	5	G	10	2	2	0	6,654
Power Wing	10	G	7	1	1	3	11,225
Powerchess	7	H	9	0	3	0	11,324
Powered High	4	G	11	1	0	3	15,426
Powerful Appeal	7	H	6	0	0	1	4,853
Powerful Mind	4	G	7	1	1	1	10,735
Powerful Miss	4	F	2	0	0	0	860
Powerful Potion	5	M	1	0	0	0	98
Powerful Sister	3	F	7	0	3	0	31,400
Powerful Touch	4	G	8	4	1	1	147,719
Powerfulallegation	4	F	7	0	0	0	675
Powermetoglory	2	C	1	0	0	1	4,680
Powerofappointment	3	F	7	0	1	1	1,860
Powerofataka	5	M	1	0	0	0	0
Poweroyal	4	G	2	1	0	0	28,440
Power's First Lady	2	F	2	0	0	0	0
Powers Magical	3	F	2	0	0	0	0
Powerscourt (GB)	4	C	9	1	2	2	903,837
Powershot	3	G	15	1	2	2	20,830
Poydras	4	F	2	0	1	0	6,460
Practical Paul	6	G	1	0	0	0	0
Practical Stan	5	G	11	3	4	0	45,556
Practicly	3	G	7	0	0	0	786
Prado Lady	4	F	6	1	1	0	15,280
Prado Maximus	4	C	5	1	0	0	18,440
Prado Power	7	G	17	4	3	4	50,860
Prado Wells	9	G	4	0	0	0	691
Prado's Lass	4	F	11	1	1	0	16,800
Prado's Picture	4	F	4	3	0	0	19,120
Prag	4	F	14	2	0	2	11,848
Pragmatico (ARG)	6	G	7	2	0	1	72,300
Pragmatic's First	2	G	1	0	0	0	0
Pragmatist	5	G	20	1	4	2	17,571
Prague	2	F	6	0	1	0	9,286
Praia Da Pipa	2	F	1	0	0	0	1,185
Praire Katydid	3	F	5	1	1	0	15,184
Praire Storm	2	F	5	0	3	0	12,300
Prairie Blaze	4	G	3	0	0	0	375
Prairie Boogie	5	M	1	0	0	0	0
Prairie Butterbean	5	H	1	0	0	0	0
Prairie Chief	4	C	8	3	0	0	17,700
Prairie Commander	3	G	6	0	0	0	1,480
Prairie d'Ane	3	C	7	2	0	1	11,050

Horse	Age	Sex	Sts	1st	2d	3d	Won
Prairie Doctor	5	M	3	0	0	1	375
Prairie Drifter	2	G	2	0	0	0	60
Prairie Eagle	3	F	2	0	0	0	0
Prairie Heat	2	F	2	0	0	1	3,430
Prairie King	3	G	7	1	1	1	75,565
Prairie Lady	6	M	13	1	1	2	5,888
Prairie Lites	2	G	3	0	1	1	10,760
Prairie Mist	3	F	1	0	0	0	37
Prairie Predator	5	G	7	0	2	1	22,236
Prairie Ruckus	4	F	4	0	0	2	1,496
Prairie Slam	4	C	1	1	0	0	8,700
Prairie Socialite	3	F	9	1	0	2	7,171
Prairie Swinger	7	G	11	2	1	4	10,323
Prairie Twilight	2	F	2	0	0	0	2,280
Prairie Wildfire	3	F	2	0	0	1	3,867
Prairieburg	3	G	1	0	0	0	0
Praise Be	2	G	2	1	0	0	9,310
Praise From Dixie	8	G	11	1	1	5	32,784
Praise Handel	3	C	6	0	0	0	57
Praise the Prince (NZ)	9	G	2	1	0	0	50,911
Praiseyethelord	4	C	6	0	0	1	755
Prall Street	3	F	3	2	0	1	54,700
Pranna	4	G	15	1	0	3	7,645
Pratti	5	G	13	2	4	0	23,186
Pray for Aces	4	F	4	1	1	0	40,520
Pray for Peace	3	F	1	0	0	0	0
Pray for Success	3	F	7	0	0	0	580
Prayer Bell	3	G	13	2	6	1	47,340
Prayer Card	5	G	3	0	0	1	1,508
Prayer Chain	4	F	5	2	1	0	21,860
Prayer Meeting	6	G	2	0	0	0	0
Prayer Service	2	G	2	0	0	0	2,550
Prayer Warrior	4	G	4	0	1	1	5,115
Preach by Day	2	C	2	0	0	0	1,560
Preach It	3	F	12	1	2	1	54,479
Preach the Blues	3	G	5	0	0	1	4,900
Preach to Pat	2	G	7	0	0	0	0
Preacher Bob	4	G	5	1	1	0	18,950
Preacher George	4	C	5	0	0	1	1,550
Preacher Jim	7	G	7	0	0	0	304
Preachers Daughter	3	F	2	0	0	0	148
Preacher's Prize	3	G	2	0	0	1	4,237
Preacher's Tale	2	F	3	0	2	0	17,323
Preacher's Wife	2	F	4	0	0	0	840
Preachinatthebar	3	C	7	1	0	1	177,268
Preaching	4	F	1	0	0	0	130
Precioso Viva	3	C	13	0	2	3	22,410
Precious Bag	3	F	6	1	1	0	43,720
Precious Coco	3	F	13	4	2	2	33,062
Precious Heights	4	F	12	1	3	3	10,369
Precious Interview	3	F	3	0	0	0	750
Precious Little	3	F	4	0	0	0	570
Precious Luck	4	G	8	2	0	1	14,475
Precious Mistress	4	F	11	3	2	1	34,532
Precious Prado	5	M	9	0	0	0	666
Precious Sands	3	G	9	2	0	2	18,650
Precious Sea	6	M	11	1	0	3	7,076
Precipitory's Bid	3	F	8	2	2	0	41,517
Precis	3	C	5	0	2	2	28,000
Precise Accusation	2	F	2	0	0	0	322
Precise Control	2	C	3	0	0	1	1,680
Precise Direction (IRE)	9	G	7	0	0	3	4,100
Precise Motion	2	C	2	1	0	0	24,805
Precise Star	2	C	1	0	1	0	3,690
Precise Victor	5	G	14	0	2	3	6,556
Precision Perfect	2	C	8	1	1	3	47,976
Precision Strike	2	C	2	0	0	0	630
Precocious	3	F	6	1	1	1	22,314
Precocious Aggie	2	F	4	0	2	0	8,200
Precocious Builder	3	C	8	1	0	3	15,390
Precocious Bunny	3	F	17	2	5	2	25,506
Precocious Kat	3	F	10	2	0	3	46,150
Precocious Monster	3	G	15	3	4	1	18,475
Precocious Notion	5	M	7	0	0	2	1,286
Precocious One	2	F	9	1	1	1	11,295
Precocious Rene	2	F	1	0	0	0	205
Precocious Star	2	C	1	0	0	0	85
Precocity Hoosier	3	G	7	2	1	0	10,415
Precocity J B	3	C	1	0	0	0	181

RECORDS OF HORSES

Horse	Age	Sex	Sts	1st	2d	3d	Won
Precocity Princess	3	F	6	1	0	0	7,856
Precocity's Genius	2	F	1	0	0	0	650
Precosious Willy	3	F	7	0	0	0	2,052
Predatory Pidgeon	5	H	1	0	0	0	0
Predawn Raid	5	G	8	2	0	0	30,970
Predict This Storm	6	G	4	0	0	0	264
Predictable Dancer	3	F	4	1	0	0	4,979
Predif	4	F	10	1	1	1	2,156
Predominater	5	G	1	0	0	0	0
Preeminence (JPN)	7	M	1	0	0	0	5,000
Preemptive Strike	6	G	6	3	2	0	130,688
Preemptor	2	G	6	0	1	2	16,620
Prefer Beeshee	5	G	1	0	0	0	105
Prefer Blondes	4	F	3	0	1	0	1,071
Prefer Free	3	F	1	0	0	0	37
Prefer Me	3	F	1	0	0	0	0
Preference's Gold	7	G	11	1	1	0	9,735
Preferred	7	G	11	3	2	1	22,819
Preferred Guest	6	G	3	1	2	0	18,300
Preferred Lady	4	F	9	1	2	1	8,251
Preflight	3	C	11	1	4	2	24,557
Prejm	6	M	4	1	0	0	12,393
Prejuzgada (ARG)	6	M	21	0	0	0	2,100
Prelude to Puddles	3	F	2	0	2	0	14,800
Prember	4	G	5	0	0	0	0
Premier Comic	2	C	1	0	1	0	3,400
Premier Court	2	C	6	1	1	1	22,072
Premier Girl	3	F	8	2	1	1	25,040
Premier Gold	3	G	11	1	1	1	8,195
Premier Hunting	3	G	8	2	0	0	8,714
Premier Mistress	3	F	10	1	1	0	5,990
Premier Performer	5	H	8	2	2	0	88,440
Premier Player	8	G	1	0	0	0	0
Premier Princess	5	M	15	0	1	3	18,179
Premier Promise	8	M	3	0	0	0	200
Premier Report	6	G	1	0	0	0	485
Premier Rocket	4	C	2	0	0	0	0
Premier Shot	7	H	7	1	0	1	8,205
Premier Soldier	3	G	8	0	1	0	5,910
Premier Tea	3	F	12	2	4	1	17,370
Premier Token	4	G	8	0	2	1	4,438
Premier Zak	2	G	4	1	0	0	6,600
Premiere Dancer	8	G	12	1	1	3	8,716
Premiering	5	M	5	1	1	0	10,920
Premiers Secret	2	F	3	0	0	0	875
Premiership Bid	3	C	8	0	1	1	1,624
Preminger	2	G	2	0	0	0	1,348
Premium Blend	5	G	6	1	0	2	11,429
Premium Brew	7	G	3	0	0	1	2,242
Premium Delight	5	G	1	0	0	0	217
Premium Point	4	G	3	0	2	0	3,076
Premium Port	3	G	11	1	1	2	9,457
Premium Position	5	M	7	2	1	1	34,930
Premium Saltine	5	G	6	1	0	0	22,020
Premium Tap	2	C	3	1	0	0	28,530
Premo Copy	5	M	2	0	1	1	12,250
Preneer	4	G	5	1	2	0	20,370
Prep School	3	G	11	2	2	1	66,312
Prepancy	3	G	10	0	3	1	10,245
Preppy Music	5	M	8	2	0	0	10,065
Prep's Peak	4	F	4	0	0	1	1,140
Prepster	3	C	6	1	0	2	34,237
Prepstress	3	F	4	0	0	0	145
Prerequisite	4	G	6	0	1	0	4,814
Prescapade	3	F	2	0	0	0	1,230
Prescision Winner	6	G	27	1	1	5	15,823
Prescott Road	3	C	4	1	1	0	5,893
Prescriptionneeded	2	G	3	1	1	0	20,775
Presence	4	C	2	0	0	0	350
Present	3	F	5	0	0	0	0
Present Danger	3	F	10	2	1	5	75,680
Present Image	3	C	6	0	0	3	792
Presentable	2	G	3	0	0	0	1,200
Presentation	4	F	5	1	0	0	12,735
Presenter	4	G	17	1	3	3	31,410
Presenting Milady	3	F	9	1	3	1	22,790
Presently Gone	4	G	11	3	3	2	45,195
Preservation Hall	3	F	2	0	0	1	3,840
President Alley	2	G	5	0	0	1	2,649
President Butler	5	H	4	1	0	1	6,320
President Hoosier	3	C	10	4	3	0	34,680
President Shrub	4	G	1	0	0	0	0
Presidential Fling	7	H	7	1	0	0	10,970
Presidential Lady	5	M	4	0	0	0	610
Presidential Perk	3	F	6	0	0	2	3,988
Presidential Rose	4	F	5	0	0	0	458
Presidentialaffair	5	G	8	3	4	0	285,040
President's Decree	10	G	12	2	2	1	21,677
President's Lady	3	F	6	0	0	0	735
President's Woman	2	F	4	0	0	0	1,210
Presley	2	F	2	0	0	0	0
Press Agent	3	G	2	0	0	0	410
Press All Bets	4	G	22	0	3	4	11,434
Press Beyond	6	M	13	3	4	0	32,855
Press Box	7	G	12	4	1	1	53,074
Press for Luck	3	F	1	0	0	0	135
Press Go	5	M	7	2	1	1	17,705
Press Kit	5	M	4	0	0	0	525
Press Me Card	3	G	3	0	0	0	495
Press My Bet	4	G	6	0	2	0	10,470
Press Power	5	M	10	2	0	0	29,694
Press Row	2	F	2	1	0	1	7,815
Press Scandal	3	F	6	1	0	1	9,650
Press the Bet	4	F	9	1	0	3	5,651
Pressed	2	C	2	0	0	0	0
Pressing On	3	F	8	0	0	0	2,100
Pressure King	7	G	3	0	0	1	4,500
Pressure Tester	7	G	8	1	3	0	22,168
Prestigiosa	3	F	4	1	0	0	13,560
Presto Cavallo	4	C	7	2	0	1	23,845
Presto Fast	5	G	10	0	2	3	8,284
Presto Jr	4	G	6	0	0	0	482
Presto Ridge	5	G	11	2	4	2	17,656
Preston Boy	4	G	9	0	0	0	3,200
Preston Royal	8	G	3	0	0	0	114
Preston T	4	G	7	0	1	2	2,297
Presumption	3	G	5	1	0	0	30,180
Pretence (IRE)	4	C	1	0	0	0	380
Pretenciosa	4	F	9	0	1	0	4,010
Pretentions	6	G	12	1	0	2	18,447
Pretentious	6	M	5	0	2	2	6,540
Pretentious Tiger	4	G	13	1	0	2	4,243
Pretoius	4	G	12	1	3	0	3,516
Pretolay	5	G	13	0	2	4	13,075
Pretty Ambitious	6	M	9	2	3	0	30,794
Pretty and Wild	2	F	1	0	0	0	0
Pretty Bad Boy	5	G	15	1	2	1	15,704
Pretty Blue Eyes	3	F	12	1	0	0	4,690
Pretty Bold	2	F	4	0	1	0	3,594
Pretty Bonnie	3	F	5	1	1	0	11,600
Pretty Boy Pete	9	G	8	1	1	1	5,063
Pretty Briches	6	G	5	1	1	0	4,614
Pretty Caddy Slew	4	F	8	1	1	0	2,785
Pretty Cagey	4	G	15	3	0	4	45,420
Pretty Cat	3	F	9	1	0	0	8,393
Pretty Charmeleon	4	F	4	0	0	0	184
Pretty Classy	4	F	6	0	1	0	6,700
Pretty Coed	7	M	16	0	0	2	2,660
Pretty Cozzene	5	M	13	2	4	1	22,562
Pretty Cute	4	F	7	0	0	0	848
Pretty Deeliteful	4	F	14	2	4	1	58,190
Pretty Deputy	3	F	9	1	1	1	15,290
Pretty Determined	6	M	5	0	1	2	4,310
Pretty Ditty	4	F	6	1	1	0	8,075
Pretty Excessive	3	F	8	0	0	3	6,398
Pretty Exciting To	5	M	19	3	1	2	14,390
Pretty Explosive	3	F	12	0	1	3	14,144
Pretty Fast Groom	4	F	6	3	0	0	14,151
Pretty French Girl	3	F	3	0	2	0	4,400
Pretty Fur	4	F	14	0	1	3	4,286
Pretty Galore	4	F	11	3	1	1	34,303
Pretty Girl Sherry	2	F	5	1	0	0	6,825
Pretty Girl Slew	3	F	3	1	0	0	8,400
Pretty Good Guy	2	G	1	0	0	0	105
Pretty Gritty	4	F	10	1	0	0	6,295
Pretty Honoree	3	F	9	0	0	1	3,961
Pretty Ironic	6	M	4	0	1	1	630
Pretty Jane	3	F	10	3	2	1	82,309

Horse	Age	Sex	Sts	1st	2d	3d	Won
Pretty Kool Dude	5	H	10	0	1	1	2,696
Pretty Littleangel	5	M	13	1	1	0	8,194
Pretty Majestic	5	M	2	0	0	0	0
Pretty Meadow	4	F	4	2	0	0	31,680
Pretty Miah	4	F	16	0	3	2	12,590
Pretty Miss	3	F	2	0	0	0	192
Pretty Partisan	2	F	3	2	1	0	59,200
Pretty Pattys Girl	3	F	2	0	0	0	0
Pretty Poema	2	F	3	0	0	1	1,325
Pretty Possible	3	F	2	1	0	0	30,000
Pretty Prune	3	C	1	0	0	0	0
Pretty Quiet Run	3	G	3	0	2	0	20,956
Pretty Rocky	6	M	7	0	0	1	2,824
Pretty Sly	5	G	6	1	0	1	6,090
Pretty Sneaky	4	G	1	0	0	0	0
Pretty Suave	2	F	3	0	1	0	2,800
Pretty Swanky	4	G	9	3	2	1	19,488
Pretty Toni	4	F	6	3	1	0	23,380
Pretty Wild	4	C	7	4	3	0	160,880
Pretty Wild Again	3	C	1	0	0	0	340
Pretty Willie	6	G	7	1	0	0	2,650
Prettyatclosintime	2	F	3	1	1	1	52,178
Prettypinkshoelace	3	F	5	0	0	1	3,566
Pretty's Last Aria	3	F	5	0	0	0	0
Pretty's Zagor	6	G	15	0	3	3	7,205
Pretzelstix	2	F	2	0	0	0	0
Prevalent	3	F	2	1	0	0	28,180
Prever	5	H	2	0	0	0	218
Preview the Storm	3	G	8	1	0	1	6,670
Previous Balance	4	F	15	1	0	1	6,842
Previous Selection	3	F	14	3	3	0	89,570
Prey of the Cat	3	F	9	0	3	0	10,559
Price Discovery	4	F	5	0	0	1	2,320
Price Gesser	3	G	13	2	1	4	9,853
Price of Champagne	7	G	7	1	1	1	24,660
Price of Glory	4	G	1	0	0	0	137
Price of Honour	4	G	3	1	0	0	19,298
Price of Passion	4	F	9	3	1	2	46,262
Priced Smartly	3	F	5	1	0	0	5,419
Priced to Go	5	G	10	0	0	3	6,199
Pricedale Kid	6	G	7	3	0	1	16,300
Priceless Darlin	5	M	9	1	0	0	7,044
Priceless Details	4	G	15	0	1	1	3,720
Priceless Fact	4	G	12	2	3	3	68,126
Priceless Jet	4	F	1	0	0	0	206
Priceless Legend	4	G	11	2	2	1	34,534
Priceless Quality	4	F	4	2	0	0	40,590
Pricey Tab	5	M	7	3	1	0	38,208
Prickly Pirate	4	G	13	3	4	0	18,603
Pride and Promise	5	G	20	2	4	3	19,772
Pride City	4	F	6	1	0	1	11,305
Pride of Cats	6	G	3	0	0	0	600
Pride Of Dublin (NZ)	6	G	7	1	2	1	17,650
Pride of New York	3	C	2	2	0	0	51,000
Pride of the Cats	2	C	4	0	0	1	1,504
Pride of the Fox	7	G	16	4	2	2	25,020
Pride of the Group	7	G	7	0	1	0	1,353
Prideful	8	M	6	0	0	0	1,218
Prideland	2	C	3	1	0	2	40,700
Prideofthecoombe	7	G	4	0	1	0	4,648
Prideov Fappiano	6	G	14	0	1	1	7,928
Pride's Reward	5	G	4	0	0	0	420
Prieska	3	F	3	1	0	0	22,374
Priest River	3	G	14	3	6	1	38,055
Prima Beauty	4	F	6	0	0	0	2,040
Prima Dama	4	F	11	1	0	1	5,860
Prima Dancer	2	F	3	0	0	0	420
Prima Nocti	6	G	4	0	0	1	1,074
Prima Princess	4	F	5	2	1	0	25,413
Primal Effort	4	C	7	1	2	1	12,034
Primal Passion	5	M	14	1	2	1	11,750
Primal Storm	2	C	4	2	0	1	102,798
Primal Wizard	3	C	14	1	2	6	44,330
Primary Colors	5	M	7	1	1	1	36,125
Primary Purpose	3	G	12	1	0	1	10,040
Primary Suspect	3	C	6	3	1	1	105,058
Prima's Gold	3	F	12	2	0	3	8,583
Prime	2	C	2	0	1	0	11,250
Prime Commander	6	M	9	1	2	1	14,046
Prime Deposit	4	G	14	1	2	3	12,461
Prime Event	3	G	14	2	3	1	21,630
Prime Explodent	4	C	1	0	0	0	0
Prime Gypsy	5	M	8	0	1	3	6,825
Prime Jewel	5	M	10	2	0	3	34,920
Prime Mover	4	C	11	0	0	3	2,970
Prime Pine	7	H	1	0	0	0	0
Prime Quality	4	G	10	0	3	2	10,144
Prime Queen	6	M	9	2	1	0	37,210
Prime Risk	5	M	1	0	0	0	0
Prime Star	5	H	4	1	0	0	4,761
Prime Step	6	M	7	1	2	2	28,140
Prime the Pump	4	G	8	1	1	0	13,128
Prime Time Action	3	G	9	0	1	3	18,730
Prime Time Billy	5	G	20	2	2	3	14,868
Prime Time Event	5	H	2	0	0	0	860
Prime Time King	5	G	4	0	0	0	726
Prime Time Man	7	G	5	1	0	0	3,855
Prime Time Phil	4	G	5	2	0	0	48,300
Prime Time Suzi	4	F	1	0	0	0	0
Prime Time T. V.	2	C	2	1	0	0	15,965
Prime Wisdom	5	M	3	1	0	0	9,092
Primecat	3	G	6	2	1	0	5,084
Primegold	3	C	6	0	0	0	1,200
Primer Cord	6	H	4	1	0	1	5,463
Primera Vision	3	F	1	0	0	0	140
Primerica	6	G	3	1	0	0	26,950
Primetime Girl	5	M	7	3	1	0	25,634
Primetimevalentine	5	M	6	0	1	2	36,529
Primitive Gold	2	F	4	1	0	1	17,550
Primitive Man	2	C	2	0	0	1	6,300
Primm	3	G	17	3	2	2	60,510
Primo Camino	6	H	3	0	0	0	0
Primo Cat	4	F	1	0	0	0	0
Primo Nova	4	G	5	3	0	0	89,450
Primo Primo	4	G	7	1	1	0	14,175
Primoliniator	7	G	11	1	1	2	2,827
Primordial Prince	7	G	13	3	1	0	25,387
Primos	5	G	6	0	1	0	920
Prince a Price	3	G	6	0	1	0	2,365
Prince Alexander	7	G	9	0	0	0	996
Prince Allmouth	5	G	11	0	0	0	0
Prince Alphie	4	C	5	1	1	0	82,566
Prince Ante	6	G	21	2	3	2	36,592
Prince Appeal	4	C	10	1	2	2	14,580
Prince Arch	3	C	9	4	3	1	405,946
Prince Ashby	5	G	6	0	2	0	3,543
Prince Awesome	3	C	1	0	0	0	0
Prince Ballet	3	G	15	2	0	5	13,541
Prince Benjamin	4	C	7	1	2	1	48,150
Prince Blake	2	G	2	0	0	1	1,230
Prince Cash	5	G	11	4	2	1	14,029
Prince de Reve (ARG)	8	H	3	0	1	0	2,940
Prince Decor	5	G	9	1	1	1	9,489
Prince Dixie	4	G	4	0	0	0	518
Prince Dumaani	5	G	2	0	2	0	13,000
Prince Falkor	5	G	2	0	0	0	95
Prince Fashion (ARG)	7	G	5	0	0	0	0
Prince Georgi	4	G	6	2	1	0	46,950
Prince Hadif	6	H	11	1	2	3	12,001
Prince Halo	3	C	15	2	3	3	29,940
Prince Handsome	4	G	4	0	0	0	310
Prince Harold	3	C	12	2	3	1	50,790
Prince Harper	11	G	9	0	0	0	225
Prince Harry L.	4	G	5	0	0	1	2,442
Prince Hennessy	6	H	9	2	1	0	11,550
Prince in Command	4	C	2	0	0	0	430
Prince Joe (ARG)	11	H	16	4	2	2	23,125
Prince Johnathan	4	G	2	0	0	0	2,000
Prince Joseph	3	C	11	5	2	3	154,592
Prince Julep	7	G	7	0	1	0	4,765
Prince Keono	2	C	5	1	0	0	8,640
Prince Kisty	5	G	5	0	1	0	4,458
Prince Know It All	4	G	10	1	0	0	7,201
Prince Livermore	3	G	5	1	1	1	13,830
Prince Louis	3	C	2	0	0	0	542
Prince Malagra	4	G	15	2	1	3	21,397
Prince Manila	7	H	1	0	0	0	0
Prince Marty	4	G	20	1	0	0	8,170

Horse	Age	Sex	Sts	1st	2d	3d	Won
Prince Monty	8	G	2	0	1	0	13,372
Prince Noah	4	G	4	0	0	0	0
Prince Nuntea	3	G	4	0	0	0	293
Prince o' Dreams	4	G	10	0	0	1	1,415
Prince of a Deal	5	G	14	0	4	2	24,928
Prince of Badness	3	C	10	1	1	1	16,280
Prince of China	2	C	5	1	2	0	17,965
Prince of Clover	5	H	6	1	0	4	4,780
Prince of Culpeper	3	C	1	0	0	0	0
Prince of Destiny	5	G	4	0	0	0	0
Prince of Dreams	3	G	11	0	2	1	22,172
Prince of Gold	2	C	2	0	0	0	1,140
Prince of Joy	3	C	14	2	1	1	13,417
Prince of Luck	4	C	3	1	0	0	9,840
Prince of New York	3	C	2	0	0	0	0
Prince of Rhodes	4	C	8	1	3	1	16,089
Prince of Storms	3	G	1	0	0	0	0
Prince of the Sea	3	G	4	0	0	0	114
Prince Ofthe World	5	H	6	0	0	0	644
Prince Parliament	2	G	3	2	0	0	29,700
Prince Paster	3	C	6	0	1	0	7,960
Prince Peapa	2	G	6	0	1	0	5,318
Prince Prado	4	C	9	3	1	1	122,263
Prince Quiet	3	G	16	1	4	0	9,823
Prince Rahy	2	C	3	0	0	0	626
Prince Ransome	2	C	3	0	0	0	235
Prince Reed	4	G	7	2	1	3	16,780
Prince Rio	6	H	4	0	0	0	0
Prince Silverrod	3	C	8	2	1	1	25,850
Prince Skif	11	G	7	0	0	0	437
Prince Slavic	5	G	20	3	2	5	32,775
Prince Slew	6	G	9	2	1	4	104,000
Prince Snowbound	2	G	7	2	0	1	16,957
Prince Sparkles	8	G	9	0	4	1	11,577
Prince Stanley Jr.	10	H	1	0	0	0	0
Prince Stately	4	G	13	1	1	2	4,244
Prince T.	2	C	3	1	1	1	25,480
Prince Tab	7	G	12	3	1	3	15,816
Prince Tara (IRE)	3	G	11	0	0	1	6,006
Prince Ty	4	C	3	0	0	0	315
Prince Tyree	6	G	1	0	0	0	41
Prince Uppity	5	H	6	0	0	0	1,268
Prince Versailles	4	G	3	0	0	0	0
Prince Vitality	5	G	9	0	0	0	249
Prince Wadleigh	2	C	2	0	0	0	0
Prince War Cloud	7	H	3	0	0	0	0
Prince Warner	3	C	2	1	1	0	10,192
Prince Wells	3	G	14	1	1	0	10,608
Prince Will	3	C	13	0	3	2	6,638
Prince Wolfie	4	G	8	0	1	0	1,134
Prince Wynn	5	G	14	1	4	1	21,799
Prince Zignew	4	G	11	2	3	2	40,525
Princely Flag	10	G	13	2	3	1	15,610
Princely Heat	7	G	7	1	0	0	4,883
Princely Reality	3	G	4	0	0	0	0
Princely Soldier	3	C	6	1	1	2	13,540
Princeofthestage	3	C	8	0	0	1	3,640
Princeofyork	3	G	5	0	0	0	314
Princes Mildred	2	F	1	0	0	0	105
Princes of Maine	5	H	2	0	0	0	0
Princesa Dos	2	F	1	1	0	0	3,240
Princess A. P.	4	F	6	0	2	0	19,981
Princess Account	3	F	8	2	2	2	29,510
Princess Alecia	4	F	8	0	0	0	940
Princess Alex	3	F	3	1	0	2	21,548
Princess Alina (IRE)	3	F	9	0	0	0	3,275
Princess Allison	3	F	5	0	1	1	4,632
Princess Alueta	6	M	9	1	1	1	6,015
Princess Anelda	2	F	1	0	0	0	500
Princess Appleby	3	F	7	1	0	0	12,354
Princess Atta	5	M	12	0	4	1	21,471
Princess Avalon	4	F	5	1	0	1	20,255
Princess Azure	3	F	4	0	0	0	610
Princess B.	4	F	4	0	2	0	13,720
Princess Bagheria	8	M	8	0	1	0	1,920
Princess Bahri	4	F	2	0	0	0	84
Princess Bammer	3	F	1	0	0	0	0
Princess Bandiera	8	M	8	0	0	0	5,246
Princess Barrow	3	F	4	0	0	0	335
Princess Basque	4	F	9	0	0	0	642
Princess Betty	2	F	1	0	0	1	6,270
Princess Birdeye	4	F	8	3	2	1	53,020
Princess Brenda	4	F	15	1	1	1	20,206
Princess Briartic	7	M	10	2	2	1	7,158
Princess Britt	7	M	4	0	1	0	2,936
Princess Brooke	3	F	7	0	2	1	7,750
Princess Butterfly	3	F	1	0	0	1	3,080
Princess Cara	3	F	5	1	0	0	4,500
Princess Con	3	F	2	0	0	0	2,800
Princess Condo	6	M	6	0	0	0	1,190
Princess Cooney	2	F	2	0	0	0	1,359
Princess Dee	2	F	7	1	1	1	10,198
Princess Di Forevr	3	F	6	0	0	0	3,120
Princess Dixie	5	M	2	0	1	0	17,442
Princess Dixton	5	M	1	0	0	0	500
Princess Doc	4	F	3	0	0	0	0
Princess Doeny	5	M	3	0	0	1	5,353
Princess Doodlebug	4	F	6	1	0	1	13,003
Princess Dot	3	F	8	0	0	0	0
Princess Dream	4	F	8	0	1	2	7,715
Princess E	5	M	5	2	1	0	21,300
Princess Edwina	4	F	4	2	0	0	53,160
Princess El	6	M	7	0	0	1	1,906
Princess Ellagrace	3	F	7	0	0	1	3,150
Princess Empress	3	F	7	1	0	3	6,800
Princess Estella	4	F	6	0	0	0	0
Princess Fairy	5	M	13	0	1	4	7,295
Princess Falina	3	F	3	0	0	0	1,740
Princess Fiona	3	F	14	2	1	3	10,495
Princess Forever	5	M	9	1	0	1	14,004
Princess Ginny	3	F	10	1	1	3	8,152
Princess Godiva	2	F	2	0	0	0	2,580
Princess Grandslam	2	F	3	1	1	1	14,880
Princess Hanna	6	M	5	0	0	1	1,292
Princess Hazel	3	F	2	0	0	0	1,025
Princess Heidi	6	M	11	3	1	4	31,705
Princess Helma	4	F	2	0	0	0	275
Princess Isabella	3	F	4	0	0	2	1,290
Princess Itron	3	F	11	1	2	1	17,085
Princess Jade	5	M	1	0	0	0	534
Princess Jan Jan	3	F	6	0	0	0	0
Princess Jasmine	3	F	6	0	0	0	3,130
Princess Jeb	4	F	2	0	0	0	142
Princess Jess	4	F	2	0	0	0	1,045
Princess Jillian	3	F	4	0	0	0	300
Princess Jones	2	F	2	0	0	0	0
Princess Joy	3	F	6	0	0	1	1,239
Princess Justice	4	F	2	0	0	0	0
Princess K K	4	F	19	2	1	4	27,290
Princess Katrina	5	M	7	1	0	1	2,430
Princess Krista	7	M	6	0	0	0	490
Princess Lana	2	F	6	1	2	2	34,690
Princess League	2	F	3	0	0	0	160
Princess Leal	8	M	5	1	0	0	6,745
Princess Lianna	3	F	6	2	0	0	50,994
Princess Liberty	4	F	21	1	7	3	12,906
Princess Looney	4	F	6	2	1	1	26,160
Princess Loosewire	2	F	1	0	1	0	5,300
Princess Lorna	4	F	17	0	1	6	12,215
Princess Love	4	F	7	0	1	0	5,970
Princess M	3	F	2	0	0	0	122
Princess Maddy	3	F	3	0	0	0	0
Princess Majesty	5	M	7	1	0	1	1,447
Princess Malice	3	F	14	1	1	2	19,098
Princess Marlin	4	F	6	1	0	1	18,490
Princess Medusa	2	F	2	0	0	0	600
Princess Modiste	5	M	16	3	1	2	31,975
Princess Ms. Fit	4	F	15	1	2	2	5,642
Princess Muldoon	4	F	11	2	1	2	11,624
Princess Nahuel	4	F	1	0	0	0	140
Princess Naomi	2	F	3	0	0	0	75
Princess of Ghosts	3	F	8	2	1	2	23,632
Princess of Holme	5	M	13	0	6	1	18,795
Princess of the Mt	3	F	4	0	0	0	278
Princess of York	7	M	11	1	2	0	14,495
Princess Paige	3	F	5	0	0	1	1,985
Princess Pancho	5	M	14	4	2	3	37,801
Princess Paster	4	F	10	2	1	4	52,864

Horse	Age	Sex	Sts	1st	2d	3d	Won
Princess Pater	8	M	2	0	0	1	1,126
Princess Payton	5	M	7	0	0	0	863
Princess Peak	7	M	16	0	1	0	7,200
Princess Pegasus	2	F	4	0	0	0	4,250
Princess Pelona	4	F	8	2	0	1	61,531
Princess Pollyanna	2	F	1	0	0	0	130
Princess Potoula	2	F	4	0	0	0	1,066
Princess Pump Iron	4	F	13	0	1	0	2,175
Princess Purrsalot	2	F	4	0	1	1	5,200
Princess Quista	8	M	1	0	0	0	61
Princess Razyana	4	F	8	0	1	0	5,430
Princess Rene	7	M	3	0	0	1	848
Princess Riley	2	F	2	0	0	0	800
Princess Roney	5	M	17	2	1	4	19,703
Princess Sequoia	3	F	5	0	0	2	11,480
Princess Sheila	3	F	7	1	2	2	23,585
Princess Slew	5	M	4	1	0	1	9,582
Princess Splendor	4	F	7	1	0	3	13,360
Princess Stephanie	3	F	1	0	0	0	340
Princess Teresa	2	F	4	0	1	1	4,760
Princess Terlingua	6	M	10	2	0	1	32,339
Princess Tia	5	M	6	1	1	1	4,370
Princess Tiara	5	M	1	0	0	0	0
Princess Tiffany	4	F	4	1	0	0	15,180
Princess Tish	3	F	8	1	1	0	22,975
Princess Toast	3	F	1	0	0	0	0
Princess Tooka	4	F	4	0	0	0	387
Princess V.	4	F	5	1	0	0	39,350
Princess Waki	5	M	8	3	2	0	13,232
Princess Wendy	3	F	8	0	1	2	14,060
Princess Zaboo	4	F	12	2	1	0	14,205
Princess Zosia	2	F	6	0	1	2	3,660
Princessa Mia	2	F	1	0	0	1	500
Princessaconcuervo	6	M	5	0	1	0	13,287
Princessca	3	F	6	0	0	1	5,865
Princesscassandra	4	F	2	0	0	0	413
Princesscopy	5	M	6	0	0	0	0
Princessdi's Folly	7	H	1	0	0	0	94
Princessgwenivere	6	M	5	0	0	0	1,052
Princessinwaiting	3	F	14	1	0	1	7,058
Princessmoneycrown	3	F	1	0	0	0	235
Princessofkalithea	5	M	11	0	2	1	6,210
Princessofthebayou	5	M	12	1	0	1	8,832
Princessonthebayou	4	F	5	1	0	1	11,876
Princess's Bay	3	F	4	0	0	0	1,588
Princeton Affair	6	G	4	0	0	1	1,240
Princeton Avenue	5	G	11	0	2	1	6,644
Princeton Star	5	G	13	2	2	3	20,674
Princhipesa (PER)	5	M	23	1	0	0	3,540
Principal Ray	6	G	17	0	0	0	1,218
Principal Rules	2	G	1	0	0	0	105
Prindello	6	M	1	0	0	0	0
Priness Mighty	2	F	2	0	0	0	141
Prineville	7	G	8	3	1	1	13,840
Print Out	4	G	8	0	6	0	9,457
Printed Tongue	4	F	4	0	0	0	910
Printemps	2	F	4	0	0	1	4,560
Printer's Princess	5	M	14	3	4	2	20,357
Printer's Son	3	G	16	3	1	5	27,175
Prior Lake Lady	3	F	7	0	0	0	6,130
Priority Bag	3	G	13	3	1	1	39,190
Priority Call	3	F	10	1	1	2	6,295
Priority Male	7	G	8	0	4	2	15,460
Priscilla's Chance	6	M	17	1	2	3	17,752
Priscilla's Flag	3	F	17	2	1	7	122,180
Prismatic	5	M	1	1	0	0	34,320
Prison Boy	6	G	2	0	0	0	2,204
Prison Caper	2	C	6	0	3	0	15,114
Prison of Love	3	F	9	1	0	2	12,799
Prisoner of War	5	G	2	0	0	0	119
Prissy	7	M	14	0	2	4	6,322
Prissy Britches	3	F	3	0	0	0	0
Prissy Christy	4	F	1	0	0	0	105
Prissy Girl Eve	2	F	5	0	0	1	3,388
Prissy Is as Does	2	F	1	0	0	0	795
Prissy Linda	6	M	8	1	2	0	10,056
Prissy Pants	4	F	12	3	1	2	15,700
Prissy's Prince	4	G	10	2	3	0	34,475
Privacy Act	3	C	11	3	3	1	21,900
Privano's First	8	G	15	1	1	4	26,104
Privat Gold (ARG)	7	H	9	1	0	0	8,290
Private	6	G	3	0	0	0	180
Private Access	3	C	4	0	2	0	0
Private Alert	3	G	5	0	0	0	1,810
Private Ambition	4	G	6	1	0	0	4,268
Private American	3	C	17	6	3	3	58,280
Private Attack	5	H	1	0	0	0	500
Private Aviator	5	G	18	1	1	10	57,560
Private Bail	7	G	10	0	0	0	619
Private Balcony	3	F	4	1	1	1	19,668
Private Bean	5	G	3	0	1	0	3,780
Private Bond	4	C	3	0	0	0	0
Private Boot	3	F	16	4	4	2	111,220
Private Bound	7	G	9	2	2	1	37,100
Private Buck	6	H	3	0	0	1	1,050
Private Buddy	3	G	6	0	1	0	489
Private Canyon	5	G	8	0	0	0	3,230
Private Cat	6	G	1	0	0	0	1,225
Private Change	7	G	16	3	2	4	17,088
Private Chef	4	G	1	0	0	1	5,040
Private Christmas	5	M	1	0	0	0	485
Private City	4	C	9	1	0	1	44,760
Private Club	5	G	6	0	0	1	710
Private Coin	3	G	11	0	2	1	4,988
Private Connection	3	G	15	2	3	3	32,125
Private Conquest	4	G	7	1	0	0	6,045
Private Courage	4	F	2	0	0	0	305
Private Divinail	5	G	1	0	0	0	0
Private Emblem	5	H	4	1	0	0	80,049
Private Event	3	C	13	1	3	2	15,650
Private Gamble	3	F	7	0	1	2	9,325
Private Games	2	G	2	0	0	0	620
Private Gayla	3	F	10	3	2	0	35,530
Private Gift	2	F	3	0	0	2	10,470
Private Gold	4	C	2	0	0	0	380
Private Ground	3	G	3	1	0	0	4,440
Private Harbor	3	G	13	1	1	2	25,675
Private Horde	5	H	10	2	3	0	134,440
Private Indeed	3	F	10	2	4	1	54,100
Private Irish	5	H	11	2	1	1	23,860
Private Isle	3	G	12	1	2	2	16,277
Private Issue	3	G	12	1	4	1	39,139
Private J D	3	G	6	1	0	0	5,870
Private Jackie	4	F	3	0	0	0	600
Private Jet	4	C	4	0	0	0	0
Private Jet North	2	F	8	0	0	0	2,561
Private Joke	3	F	8	2	2	2	70,870
Private Lap	5	H	8	2	2	0	141,620
Private Lass	4	F	2	0	0	0	0
Private Lear	3	G	18	2	0	4	23,035
Private Memory	5	M	10	0	1	0	3,327
Private Navy	4	F	7	1	0	0	5,190
Private Night	2	C	2	1	1	0	1,425
Private Oasis	6	G	9	0	0	2	15,650
Private O'Leary	3	G	8	0	0	1	1,500
Private Opening	5	G	14	3	5	2	100,170
Private Operator	3	F	11	0	3	5	11,382
Private Opinion	3	F	5	2	1	0	57,256
Private Pass	6	G	5	0	0	2	2,765
Private Petetion	5	G	12	0	2	2	6,390
Private Placement	3	F	9	0	0	1	3,803
Private Pleasure	4	G	9	0	2	1	6,937
Private Polynesian	3	F	5	0	0	0	150
Private Port	5	M	10	0	1	2	20,256
Private Power	9	G	7	2	1	1	24,180
Private Practice	5	H	12	2	2	3	29,315
Private Prescott	4	G	5	0	0	0	410
Private Promise	3	C	3	1	0	0	15,050
Private Proposal	3	F	6	1	0	1	12,210
Private Ransom	5	G	1	0	0	0	0
Private Reigns	4	F	12	4	2	1	19,646
Private Retreat	4	G	10	1	0	0	8,372
Private Robyn	3	F	1	0	0	0	140
Private Ryan	7	G	9	1	1	1	19,537
Private Scandal	4	C	10	2	4	0	109,443
Private Signal	5	G	3	0	0	0	157
Private Skier	3	C	1	0	0	0	130
Private Slip	10	G	8	2	0	1	30,210

Horse	Age	Sex	Sts	1st	2d	3d	Won
Private Son	6	H	1	0	0	0	105
Private Summer	3	G	11	2	2	3	37,305
Private Table	3	G	2	1	0	0	12,600
Private Thrill	3	G	7	1	0	0	4,251
Private Tommy	7	G	3	0	0	0	132
Private Tour	2	G	5	0	0	1	3,605
Private Tribute	8	G	9	0	2	1	1,158
Private Tricks	3	F	4	0	0	1	1,760
Private Twist	5	M	3	0	0	0	0
Private War	4	C	1	1	0	0	28,800
Privateer	2	G	3	1	0	0	8,164
Privateer (ARG)	6	H	19	6	3	4	43,884
Privatelife	3	C	2	0	0	0	140
Privates Chance	3	G	13	1	2	3	14,822
Privy	5	M	14	0	2	4	17,018
Prize and Honor	4	F	14	0	3	4	31,266
Prize d'Or	3	F	7	0	0	2	2,000
Prize Editor	5	H	2	0	0	0	280
Prize Giving (GB)	11	G	5	0	1	2	5,020
Prize Maker	2	G	3	0	0	0	505
Prize of Texas	6	G	1	0	0	0	150
Prize Performer	10	M	8	0	1	0	3,602
Prize Rose	4	F	7	2	1	2	43,404
Prize Runner	3	F	10	0	1	1	10,388
Prize Statue	4	G	1	0	0	0	0
Prize Story	4	G	9	3	2	4	55,580
Prize Weaver	4	G	7	4	2	1	41,623
Prized Amberpro	7	M	4	1	2	0	41,700
Prized Art	4	G	22	1	2	5	8,731
Prized Cat	3	C	11	1	3	2	59,720
Prized Gem	6	G	4	0	0	1	6,880
Prized Halo	3	C	5	1	2	0	11,035
Prized King	5	G	6	0	1	1	1,656
Prized Match	8	G	9	3	0	2	27,552
Prized Max	9	G	15	1	2	0	7,298
Prized Pilot	3	C	8	0	0	1	562
Prized Pistol	5	G	4	0	1	0	2,192
Prized Porsche	5	M	2	0	0	0	0
Prized Possession	3	C	9	2	1	1	25,040
Prized Verdict	2	C	2	0	0	0	480
Pro Band	3	C	4	0	2	1	18,546
Pro Fighter	8	H	5	0	0	1	1,324
Pro Forty	6	G	9	0	2	1	4,084
Pro Love Ruhls	4	F	9	2	0	2	29,238
Pro Occident	3	F	1	0	0	0	2,443
Pro On the Run	6	H	1	0	0	0	72
Pro Prado	3	C	6	1	0	3	163,530
Pro Preferred	3	C	4	0	0	0	400
Pro Prospect	4	G	3	0	0	0	160
Pro Scout	5	G	9	1	0	2	13,490
Pro Shopper	5	G	2	0	0	1	1,716
Pro Time	3	G	9	1	0	1	11,240
Pro Zackory	9	G	4	0	0	0	120
Proactive	4	F	11	1	1	4	15,629
Probability	6	G	4	0	0	0	101
Probable Cause	9	G	4	0	0	0	204
Probable Payoff	3	F	8	2	2	0	35,045
Probably a Blitz	6	G	4	0	0	0	648
Probably N Cahoots	7	G	4	0	1	0	1,234
Probably Purrfect	2	F	5	0	0	0	1,864
Probably's Devil	7	G	5	0	1	0	1,036
Probition	5	H	14	1	2	3	17,275
Problem Solver	5	H	3	0	0	1	1,547
Proceed	6	G	2	0	0	0	70
Proceed With Care (GB)	6	G	3	0	0	0	780
Processor	2	G	4	2	0	0	38,680
Prochonic	3	F	4	0	1	1	11,642
Procitee Slew	3	G	7	0	1	0	4,092
Proclaimer	4	G	4	0	0	1	1,119
Procreate	6	G	7	2	1	2	45,720
Procyon	5	M	8	0	0	1	2,595
Prodice Kid	6	G	5	1	2	1	2,669
Prodigious	7	G	4	1	0	1	12,437
Prodigus (BRZ)	5	H	5	0	0	1	5,530
Producer	6	G	16	6	0	3	57,285
Produckson	7	G	6	1	0	0	2,008
Prof. McGonagall	4	F	7	2	0	3	79,400
Professional	4	F	7	0	1	0	3,985
Professor Biggs	3	G	9	1	3	0	58,095
Professor Higgins	5	G	3	2	0	0	38,435
Professor Jones	4	C	7	2	1	1	30,714
Professor Maxwell	5	G	8	0	1	2	13,344
Proffy Sonn	3	C	4	0	0	0	0
Proficient	4	G	4	0	0	1	1,006
Profigliano	10	G	10	0	2	0	4,949
Profit Zone	2	F	4	0	2	0	11,960
Profound	3	C	6	3	1	0	61,590
Profusion	5	M	1	0	0	0	2,208
Programmed Appeal	7	G	6	3	1	1	9,570
Progresive World	3	G	9	0	0	0	702
Prohibido Olividar	3	F	14	2	0	5	48,840
Prohibitionist	3	C	1	0	0	0	0
Project Hope	6	H	1	0	0	0	0
Projectsis	5	M	6	0	0	0	469
Prolific Appeal	2	C	1	0	0	0	0
Prolly	2	F	3	0	1	1	14,670
Prolon	9	G	4	1	0	1	3,140
Prom Date	4	F	4	1	0	0	26,040
Prom King	4	G	5	1	1	1	7,012
Prom Kiss	3	F	2	0	0	1	1,400
Promenade Again	4	F	9	1	3	2	26,390
Promenade Girl	2	F	1	1	0	0	12,000
Promenade On In	5	M	2	0	0	0	0
Promenade Road	4	F	11	1	2	2	41,923
Prominence	3	C	5	0	3	0	26,600
Prominent Winds	2	C	3	0	0	1	1,725
Promiscuity	2	F	3	0	0	1	7,980
Promise Her Damoon	3	G	22	3	4	1	16,202
Promise Her Jules	4	F	2	0	0	0	179
Promise Mountain	6	G	5	2	0	1	10,492
Promise of War	8	G	11	4	4	3	98,080
Promise One	2	F	4	0	1	1	10,842
Promise the Banker	3	F	4	1	1	0	31,164
Promised Call	4	F	16	4	4	3	32,466
Promised Prayer	2	F	2	0	0	0	235
Promised Run	4	F	4	0	0	0	352
Promised Tour	3	F	7	1	1	0	15,340
Promises	6	G	6	1	1	0	7,184
Promising Reality	5	H	6	2	0	1	4,565
Promising Storm	2	C	6	0	1	1	7,313
Promising Theatre	3	F	3	0	0	0	225
Promo Leader	8	H	2	0	0	0	79
Promontory	2	C	1	1	0	0	35,280
Promote Business	3	F	4	0	1	1	10,560
Promptly	4	F	3	0	0	0	0
Promulgate	2	G	2	0	0	1	1,815
Prone	2	F	3	0	1	0	7,730
Pronounced	3	G	5	0	1	0	6,500
Pronouncement	3	F	2	0	0	0	0
Pronto Dash	2	C	3	1	0	1	17,750
Pronto One	4	G	10	1	1	2	12,820
Pronto Paco	3	G	17	1	2	1	8,928
Pronto Pegasus	3	F	5	0	0	0	498
Pronto Porshe	4	F	2	0	0	0	225
Prop Five	2	C	2	0	0	1	6,280
Proper Beau	9	G	1	0	0	0	61
Proper Boy	3	G	3	0	0	0	0
Proper Bull	2	C	1	1	0	0	5,280
Proper Card	5	G	6	1	0	1	24,270
Proper Carson	2	C	3	1	0	1	32,970
Proper Conquest	7	G	5	1	1	0	9,820
Proper Critic	5	H	2	0	0	0	0
Proper Dancer	3	F	5	1	1	0	15,580
Proper Decree	2	G	3	0	0	1	1,045
Proper Direction	4	G	13	3	0	2	19,249
Proper Donn	3	C	1	0	0	0	250
Proper Ensign	3	F	10	0	1	3	4,361
Proper Etiquette	6	M	10	1	1	2	3,735
Proper Fantasy	6	G	4	0	0	1	1,379
Proper Gun	5	M	19	2	0	3	12,729
Proper Joe	6	G	11	1	1	1	13,519
Proper Man	7	H	8	2	2	1	20,020
Proper Manners	3	F	4	1	0	0	10,020
Proper Mariner	5	G	10	0	1	0	2,048
Proper Moonshine	8	G	6	1	0	0	4,278
Proper Music	5	M	7	0	1	1	2,176
Proper Name	6	M	11	0	0	2	3,952
Proper Notion	3	C	4	0	0	0	0

Horse	Age	Sex	Sts	1st	2d	3d	Won
Proper Oyl	4	G	9	3	1	0	20,287
Proper Paradise	7	M	10	3	1	0	20,575
Proper Plum	10	G	11	1	1	1	4,225
Proper Prado	3	C	6	1	3	0	70,180
Proper Prince	3	G	3	0	0	0	0
Proper Prospect	5	H	10	2	1	3	47,026
Proper Prospector	3	F	11	0	2	2	7,965
Proper Runner	3	C	4	0	0	0	0
Proper Sandi	6	M	5	0	0	0	580
Proper Sky	3	G	7	1	0	1	5,240
Proper Sunday	6	G	15	1	2	4	21,294
Proper Toffee	3	G	5	0	0	0	165
Proper Top	4	F	4	1	0	0	5,722
Proper Wildcat	2	F	4	1	0	2	17,240
Properandsmelly	5	M	5	1	0	0	1,267
Proper's Peak	9	G	4	0	0	1	480
Prophetic Call	4	G	13	0	1	2	2,322
Prophet's Town	3	G	15	1	2	4	13,190
Propitious	5	G	6	0	0	1	3,235
Proposed	2	F	2	0	0	1	15,000
Proposing	3	F	1	1	0	0	10,920
Propperie	5	M	3	0	0	0	772
Proprietor	5	G	4	1	1	0	3,900
Propulsion Power	6	G	5	0	0	0	0
Prory	12	G	2	0	0	1	1,090
Proscenium	3	G	8	0	0	0	1,720
Prosecuter	4	G	3	0	0	0	150
Prosecution Rests	4	G	9	0	1	1	3,054
Prospect Clever	4	G	3	0	0	0	82
Prospect Crossing	4	G	21	2	5	2	21,165
Prospect Ends Well	4	F	8	0	0	0	3,880
Prospect for J R	6	G	14	3	3	3	16,500
Prospect Gold	4	G	10	1	2	3	57,031
Prospect Green	6	G	8	1	2	3	35,820
Prospect Heights	8	G	8	0	0	1	1,153
Prospect Kid	6	G	7	2	1	1	20,110
Prospect Lane	6	G	6	0	1	0	2,000
Prospect Mark	6	G	6	2	1	1	17,605
Prospect Mesa	3	C	4	0	0	0	509
Prospect of Flight	3	G	2	1	0	0	4,944
Prospect Ofa Rhyme	3	F	2	0	0	0	360
Prospect Valley	5	G	5	0	0	0	496
Prospect Weaver	4	C	1	0	0	0	0
Prospectforme	5	M	14	1	2	3	11,876
Prospectinforgold	3	G	9	0	1	2	4,169
Prospecting Agenda	3	C	8	0	0	0	701
Prospecting Dixie	5	M	10	0	1	4	12,941
Prospecting Eppie	2	G	2	0	0	0	0
Prospecting Possum	2	F	5	0	1	1	6,895
Prospecting Silver	3	F	2	0	0	0	0
Prospective Flight	4	F	5	1	0	1	9,980
Prospective Gal	7	M	12	0	0	1	11,082
Prospective Glow	5	M	6	2	2	1	40,040
Prospective Hit	4	G	11	3	0	0	30,773
Prospective Income	6	M	4	0	0	0	278
Prospective Kiss	3	G	10	1	3	2	42,570
Prospective Miss	3	F	12	1	2	2	29,320
Prospective Saint	3	F	7	2	1	0	87,393
Prospective Slew	4	F	12	1	2	2	20,415
Prospective Titan	4	C	7	0	0	1	5,281
Prospective Wish	6	H	12	2	4	0	14,509
Prospectivereverie	2	F	1	0	0	0	0
Prospector Cat	4	G	5	2	0	1	8,767
Prospector Irish	4	G	8	0	0	0	761
Prospector Jack	2	G	1	0	0	0	0
Prospector Jewel	5	H	1	0	0	0	96
Prospector Mattie	2	F	5	0	0	0	1,440
Prospector Nick	10	G	9	0	1	1	8,807
Prospector Nugget	6	G	7	2	0	0	26,250
Prospector Sarah	3	F	6	0	0	0	80
Prospector Who	5	G	16	5	3	2	57,271
Prospector's Bride	2	F	2	1	0	0	19,740
Prospector's Creek	8	M	7	2	1	1	17,907
Prospector's Dream	4	G	1	0	1	0	5,000
Prospector's Gala	3	C	2	0	0	0	292
Prospector's Green	7	G	13	0	2	1	2,826
Prospectors Legacy	3	G	9	1	0	1	8,110
Prospectors Link	5	G	9	2	0	0	8,597
Prospectors Lover	3	F	6	1	1	0	13,140
Prospectors Penny	3	C	9	0	3	0	6,997
Prospectors Prince	2	G	1	0	0	0	370
Prospector's Road	3	C	6	1	0	2	21,955
Prospectors Shadow	3	C	5	1	0	0	7,749
Prospectors Silver	4	G	10	1	3	0	12,540
Prospector's Smile	4	G	11	1	1	0	9,474
Prospector's Son	3	G	2	0	0	0	800
Prospectors Spirit	2	F	6	0	1	1	4,410
Prospectors Strike	5	G	12	2	0	1	24,121
Prospector's Trick	4	C	1	0	0	0	870
Prospector's Way	4	G	18	2	6	3	23,626
Prospectors Wealth	3	F	9	1	1	2	18,869
Prospector's Whim	4	F	7	2	0	1	6,685
Prospector'shimmer	3	G	5	1	0	3	5,910
Prospect's Destiny	4	C	12	1	4	4	32,125
Prospects Gold	6	M	2	0	0	0	0
Prospect's Legacy	5	G	4	0	1	0	1,856
Prospects of War	4	G	9	1	0	1	7,961
Prospects Pleasure	5	M	1	0	0	0	0
Prospects Turn	3	G	6	1	0	1	5,559
Prosperine	2	F	4	0	0	0	334
Prosperity Rose	5	M	11	2	4	2	10,331
Prosperous Move	2	F	10	0	0	3	5,788
Prosperous Night	11	G	3	0	0	2	650
Prosperous Queen	2	F	4	2	0	1	26,050
Prosperous Way	4	C	14	2	3	0	30,090
Prosperous Winter	3	F	5	0	0	0	2,064
Prospice	5	G	7	0	0	0	619
Pro'sprodigy	4	G	13	4	4	3	53,296
Prostar	7	M	5	1	2	1	8,280
Protect	7	G	11	2	0	2	8,152
Protectorate	5	G	3	0	0	0	183
Protege's Lover	4	C	5	0	0	1	3,120
Proud Abby	3	F	9	2	3	2	29,457
Proud Accolade	2	C	5	3	0	0	364,130
Proud Affair	2	F	3	0	0	3	12,210
Proud Allen	2	C	1	0	0	0	480
Proud Alvin	5	G	16	0	0	3	11,280
Proud American	4	F	9	0	1	0	7,894
Proud and Bold	4	G	7	1	1	2	34,440
Proud and Fast	7	M	10	0	3	2	5,539
Proud and Royal	4	G	6	0	0	0	540
Proud and Steady	5	G	10	1	1	0	10,240
Proud Andrew	7	G	12	3	0	4	24,485
Proud Beauty (IRE)	4	F	8	2	0	1	59,920
Proud Bella	3	F	6	2	2	1	24,233
Proud Benny	3	C	5	0	2	2	16,080
Proud Black Star	4	G	11	1	0	3	6,146
Proud Cardenal	4	C	7	2	1	2	65,420
Proud Carmela	4	F	7	2	1	0	19,050
Proud Champ	3	C	10	2	2	1	16,716
Proud Charm	2	C	2	0	0	0	1,680
Proud Cherokee	2	G	3	0	0	1	1,347
Proud Chief	2	G	2	0	0	0	800
Proud Comic	2	C	3	2	0	0	21,300
Proud Decision	3	G	14	2	3	1	27,710
Proud Delivery	2	F	2	0	0	0	486
Proud Deputy	4	G	2	0	0	1	825
Proud Diligence	2	C	3	0	0	0	3,240
Proud Dinero	4	F	16	0	3	4	4,762
Proud Edition	5	H	1	0	0	0	0
Proud Ellen	2	F	12	1	1	2	11,349
Proud Era	5	G	4	0	0	0	250
Proud Falstaff	8	G	7	2	0	1	6,712
Proud Friendly	6	G	6	0	1	1	4,951
Proud Gaby	2	F	2	0	0	0	800
Proud Gal	4	F	3	1	0	1	20,390
Proud General	2	C	8	1	2	3	31,240
Proud Gideon	2	G	7	1	0	0	10,750
Proud Hart	7	M	6	0	0	0	0
Proud Hope	3	G	3	1	0	2	40,200
Proud Joe	2	C	2	0	0	0	800
Proud John	4	G	7	0	1	1	9,930
Proud Jolle	4	C	10	1	0	0	4,395
Proud Journey	2	C	3	0	0	0	2,310
Proud Lady	4	F	13	1	1	2	39,362
Proud Lil Girl	3	F	9	1	1	1	6,345
Proud Majesty	3	G	1	0	0	0	48
Proud Man	6	H	5	1	0	1	313,334

Horse	Age	Sex	Sts	1st	2d	3d	Won
Proud Megan	5	M	9	0	2	2	9,245
Proud Memories	4	G	20	1	0	5	9,779
Proud Michael	3	C	5	0	2	1	12,740
Proud Misty	2	F	6	0	0	1	3,573
Proud Mombo	6	M	4	0	0	0	298
Proud Mr	4	G	2	0	0	0	93
Proud Mutesa	5	G	4	0	0	0	344
Proud N Perfect	4	F	10	5	1	0	57,180
Proud Nicole	4	F	11	1	3	4	83,604
Proud Night	4	C	8	0	2	3	14,290
Proud of Pyrite	5	G	19	4	5	1	31,636
Proud Okie	4	C	1	0	0	0	0
Proud Partner	5	G	10	2	3	0	64,040
Proud Patrolman	6	G	19	4	5	4	37,011
Proud Peacock	7	G	17	2	1	6	14,627
Proud Phantom	5	M	12	2	2	2	17,269
Proud Phil	3	G	1	1	0	0	7,800
Proud Pioneer	6	M	5	0	0	0	282
Proud Pixie	4	F	11	0	3	1	7,816
Proud Polina	5	M	7	2	2	3	45,500
Proud Polly	5	M	8	1	5	1	10,680
Proud Prince	5	G	3	0	0	0	328
Proud Princely	4	G	4	3	1	0	12,060
Proud Prize	8	G	1	0	0	0	51
Proud Punch	5	G	16	2	2	3	42,558
Proud Retreat	2	F	1	0	0	0	400
Proud Ringer	2	G	8	1	1	2	21,280
Proud Son	3	G	6	2	1	0	32,288
Proud Statesman	3	G	10	1	2	0	20,415
Proud Storm	4	G	4	0	0	1	922
Proud Suave	3	C	11	0	0	2	3,840
Proud Sunrise	4	G	12	2	1	1	14,737
Proud Tammie	7	M	2	0	0	0	250
Proud Tears	4	F	12	7	1	0	122,555
Proud Texan	3	G	2	1	1	0	12,320
Proud Thunder	4	C	1	0	0	0	140
Proud to Be	4	G	4	0	2	0	4,677
Proud to Be Me	2	G	6	0	0	0	1,220
Proud to Be True	3	G	10	1	1	0	15,170
Proud to Dance	3	F	11	2	1	0	13,900
Proud Token	3	F	11	2	1	1	7,948
Proud Tower Too	2	C	4	1	2	1	59,800
Proudest Queen	3	F	6	0	1	2	14,630
Proudest Sam	5	H	3	0	0	0	132
Proudest Woman	6	M	6	0	1	1	1,510
Proudly Dance	2	C	9	2	2	0	20,200
Proudly We Hailed	4	G	12	0	0	0	1,915
Proudsoldier	4	G	2	0	0	0	40
Proudtobe American	2	G	2	0	0	0	750
Proudtobeahalfterm	7	G	18	1	5	1	9,277
Proudtobecanadian	4	G	1	0	0	0	0
Prough Joe	2	C	7	0	0	0	665
Provable	5	G	14	4	2	1	28,042
Proved Them Wrong	4	F	3	0	1	0	4,230
Proven Brand	4	G	14	0	1	1	3,787
Proven Cat	3	F	6	1	2	0	25,750
Proven Cure	10	G	7	1	1	1	43,954
Proven Form	4	F	5	0	1	1	6,910
Proven Honor	4	F	17	5	3	1	40,990
Proven Promise	4	F	11	2	2	0	28,540
Proven Solution	5	G	2	0	1	0	2,560
Proven to Rule	2	G	1	0	0	0	70
Provenance	7	G	11	0	2	1	7,016
Providence	4	F	1	0	0	0	696
Providential Force	3	G	7	1	1	2	9,728
Provincetown	4	G	6	2	0	1	107,922
Provincial	4	F	9	2	3	1	85,890
Provisional	5	G	8	1	1	0	12,609
Provo Punch	4	G	1	0	0	0	0
Provobay	4	F	4	1	1	0	15,000
Provocateur	4	G	12	1	3	1	15,643
Prowling	5	G	12	2	2	2	16,035
Prowling Wolf	3	G	11	1	1	1	33,591
Proximos	5	G	10	3	1	2	115,196
Proxy Fight	3	C	12	1	2	3	15,720
Pru	6	G	13	1	0	1	3,686
Prudencia	3	F	5	0	0	3	19,351
Prudhoe Bay	4	C	5	0	0	0	797
Prunerdential	3	G	4	1	2	0	15,654
Pruner's Speed	4	G	5	1	1	1	6,060
Prune's Interest	4	F	8	1	1	2	37,440
Pruney	5	G	6	0	0	0	460
Prussian Prince	2	C	2	1	0	0	22,354
P's Song	7	M	3	0	0	0	182
Psota	4	G	5	0	0	0	123
Psych	3	F	4	0	2	2	25,270
Psychedelia	3	F	5	0	1	1	16,441
Psychic Hotline	4	G	2	0	0	0	762
Psychic Star	3	C	8	1	1	0	14,935
Psychlotropic	3	F	6	0	0	1	6,784
Psycho Sister	3	F	12	0	1	2	4,967
Psychogallantry	8	M	16	0	0	3	2,622
Psyco Gator	3	F	11	2	4	1	46,540
Pt. Pleasant	3	F	16	1	3	2	22,813
Ptah	4	G	8	1	2	0	29,730
Ptichka	4	F	2	0	0	1	2,060
Pt's Grey Eagle	3	G	7	2	3	0	184,340
Pt's Mostnotorious	3	G	9	2	0	0	18,901
Pub Lic D Fender	4	C	7	0	0	0	1,192
Pubelo Run	6	G	5	0	0	1	1,715
Public Address	5	H	9	0	2	1	9,140
Public Defender	3	C	2	0	0	0	0
Public Domain	5	G	10	5	2	2	31,016
Public Enemy	5	F	7	0	1	0	1,099
Public Officer	3	C	1	0	0	0	0
Public Official	4	C	12	1	3	2	44,880
Public Support	6	G	2	0	0	0	159
Publication	5	G	2	0	1	1	52,180
Publisher's Phil	4	G	3	1	1	0	10,980
Puchungo (PER)	8	G	14	5	2	3	38,200
Puck	5	H	4	0	0	0	240
Pucker	4	F	10	1	1	1	63,336
Pucker Power	5	M	6	2	2	1	24,020
Puckerupbuttercup	4	F	10	1	1	1	3,475
Pud	4	G	10	3	2	0	88,957
Puddle Time	7	H	16	0	1	3	9,319
Puddles Pleasure	5	M	17	2	2	3	20,789
Puddles Reflection	4	F	5	0	0	1	1,251
Pueblo de Spain	3	G	6	0	0	1	8,460
Puerto Banus	5	H	6	1	0	0	139,000
Puerto Legenda	2	F	3	0	0	0	325
Puerto Positiro	2	G	2	0	0	0	600
Puerto Romeral (CHI)	7	G	14	2	3	2	20,258
Puerto Vallarta	2	F	1	0	0	1	6,468
Puff Carmen	4	F	1	0	0	0	3,528
Puffer	5	G	7	0	1	2	25,868
Puffing Billy	2	C	1	0	0	0	0
Puffy Shirt	4	F	3	2	0	0	39,000
Puget Sound	4	C	7	1	4	0	63,785
Puggy's Last Love	4	C	10	4	1	0	61,997
Pugliese (URU)	4	C	11	0	1	1	9,640
Pug's Pistol	7	G	7	1	0	0	3,034
Pug's Pride	7	G	9	1	1	1	4,292
Pulchritude	3	F	6	0	1	1	6,485
Puledro	2	G	3	0	0	1	3,940
Pulitzer	6	G	4	2	0	0	9,600
Pull Me Out Poppy	3	F	1	0	0	0	0
Pull My Chain	4	C	4	2	0	0	62,850
Pull Over Please	5	H	10	3	3	1	24,590
Pull the Lever	4	F	15	3	3	2	19,547
Pulling for Ted	2	G	3	0	1	0	3,000
Pulpit Affair	4	F	10	0	1	1	4,020
Pulpit Harbor	7	M	14	5	2	1	41,148
Pulpit Talk	4	G	3	2	1	0	68,272
Pulpit's Edge	3	C	15	1	1	2	51,428
Pulteney's Thunder	6	M	1	0	0	0	225
Pulverizingassault	8	M	1	0	0	0	0
Puma	7	H	7	2	1	1	26,958
Puma (IRE)	4	G	6	1	2	0	52,500
Puma's Pride	4	F	11	0	1	1	20,870
Pumkin Cat	2	F	3	0	0	1	4,357
Pump Slew	6	M	1	0	0	0	156
Pumpkin Center	3	F	6	1	0	1	5,270
Pumpkin Love	2	F	6	0	0	0	707
Pumpkin Pie to Go	10	M	8	0	0	0	765
Pumpkin Roll	4	F	8	0	1	1	9,108
Pumpkin Soup	4	F	3	1	0	0	4,750
Pumpkin's Glow	4	F	8	1	0	1	13,740

Horse	Age	Sex	Sts	1st	2d	3d	Won
Pun Intended	4	G	6	0	0	1	2,075
Punch	5	G	10	1	1	2	37,665
Punch and Beauty	3	F	8	2	0	0	48,120
Punch Appeal	2	F	9	6	0	1	389,840
Punch Bag	3	G	12	1	5	1	47,285
Punch D Lites Out	4	C	4	1	0	0	15,712
Punch Drunk	5	G	18	1	2	3	7,563
Punch Drunk Dancer	2	F	1	0	0	0	1,897
Punch Taylor	4	F	8	0	0	0	4,011
Punch the Moon	3	G	13	0	2	4	11,100
Punch the Odds	2	G	3	2	0	0	70,241
Puncheon Run	6	G	8	0	0	0	1,970
Puncher	8	G	7	1	2	0	5,757
Punches Treat	3	F	1	0	0	0	110
Punchin' Gal	4	F	8	0	3	2	18,780
Punchmeoutabuck	2	F	1	0	1	0	3,700
Punchout	2	F	4	0	0	0	900
Punchski	4	G	13	3	3	1	41,810
Punchullah	4	G	2	0	0	0	3,120
Punchum	6	M	1	0	0	0	0
Punchy Victory	4	G	12	1	0	1	6,733
Punctilious (GB)	3	F	6	2	2	1	534,199
Punctual Stan	3	G	8	1	1	2	20,678
Pungent	9	G	10	0	0	2	2,160
Punguista (ARG)	6	G	14	2	3	2	11,439
Punitive	3	G	15	3	3	4	69,825
Punjaboo	4	G	4	0	0	0	887
Punk	7	G	10	0	2	1	6,775
Punk Alley	4	F	5	0	0	0	1,306
Punkin Head	6	H	6	0	1	1	9,910
Punny Guy	4	G	13	2	2	0	13,790
Punta Punta	8	M	8	1	1	2	9,060
Punxsutawney	4	F	4	1	0	0	6,023
Puny	8	M	6	0	2	1	4,520
Puppeteer (GB)	4	C	8	1	2	0	114,891
Puppy Love	6	M	2	0	0	0	566
Purdy Tricky	6	G	12	2	2	1	15,141
Purdy Zippy	6	M	16	2	0	1	8,856
Pure	3	G	14	2	5	3	70,510
Pure Amazement	5	G	8	2	3	0	8,584
Pure American	3	G	7	1	2	0	45,860
Pure Bey	3	F	5	1	1	0	38,500
Pure Chance	3	F	1	0	0	0	0
Pure D' Dash	3	C	3	0	0	0	453
Pure Desire	2	F	4	0	1	0	3,710
Pure Energy	3	F	3	1	0	0	15,180
Pure Finess	5	M	1	0	0	0	225
Pure Fun	4	G	9	0	1	1	3,291
Pure Gossip	4	F	13	1	1	2	7,687
Pure Harley	3	F	1	0	0	0	0
Pure Harmony	7	H	11	0	1	0	3,338
Pure Heart	5	G	9	2	3	1	28,723
Pure Hollywood	3	F	16	2	2	3	13,077
Pure Independence	5	M	1	0	0	0	300
Pure Offence	2	F	9	0	0	2	8,872
Pure Premium	2	F	1	0	0	0	400
Pure Pride	3	G	12	0	1	0	10,920
Pure Quality	3	F	5	0	1	0	1,810
Pure Salt	4	G	12	1	0	1	9,182
Pure Satisfaction	3	F	6	0	0	3	6,328
Pure Sweep	4	F	1	0	0	0	233
Pure Talent	3	F	1	0	0	0	300
Pure Wild	5	M	1	0	0	0	0
Purely	5	M	7	0	1	2	6,049
Purely Classic	4	C	1	0	1	0	6,480
Purely Magical	2	G	4	1	1	1	22,750
Purely Special	3	G	10	0	0	1	3,883
Purge	3	C	8	3	1	0	562,734
Purify	3	G	13	1	3	1	16,035
Purist	4	C	9	0	0	1	2,574
Purple and Gold	3	G	9	0	1	0	7,485
Purple Ballarina	3	F	3	0	0	0	1,035
Purple Emblem	3	F	3	0	1	0	2,249
Purple Heart	2	F	1	0	0	0	0
Purple Hills	5	M	2	0	0	0	480
Purple Jewel	2	C	7	0	2	1	5,885
Purple Madame	5	M	7	0	0	0	1,403
Purple Meadow	3	F	13	1	1	3	17,260
Purple Mt. Majesty	2	G	1	0	0	0	300
Purple Passage	2	C	4	0	3	0	37,980
Purple Puppy	3	G	2	0	0	0	600
Purple S Shamrock	2	C	4	0	2	0	7,120
Purple Sand	7	G	7	0	2	3	27,856
Purple Sky Dancer	4	F	4	0	0	0	235
Purple Squall	8	G	6	0	0	0	323
Purple Thistle	3	F	9	2	1	1	32,030
Purple Toi	3	F	15	1	1	2	25,960
Purple Violets	7	M	9	1	0	1	6,559
Purple Wand	4	G	8	1	2	0	5,421
Purple Wonder	5	M	15	2	2	1	15,667
Purpleshade Jewel	6	M	4	0	0	0	1,120
Purplest	6	G	8	1	2	3	45,290
Purrcat	4	G	15	5	3	4	29,440
Purrfect Toss	3	F	3	0	0	0	1,200
Purring Along	7	G	4	0	0	0	495
Pursecatcher	5	M	10	3	2	0	36,788
Pursenatcher	3	F	2	0	0	1	4,080
Push My Luck	4	F	7	1	1	2	26,720
Push On Past	2	F	2	0	0	0	3,420
Push Play	4	G	8	1	1	0	18,165
Push Pull Or Tow	3	C	2	0	0	0	280
Push Push Push	3	C	2	0	0	0	0
Push to the Top	3	G	9	0	0	0	4,915
Pushed	4	G	13	2	1	4	55,616
Pushin Perfect	2	F	1	0	0	0	0
Pushthelight	3	G	1	0	0	0	184
Pushy Little Broad	3	F	2	0	0	0	0
Pussycat Doll	2	F	3	1	0	1	32,920
Pussycat Pussycat	2	F	3	0	0	1	8,607
Put in Bay	4	G	8	0	0	0	1,134
Put It Out	4	G	13	3	4	2	26,656
Put Me In	4	F	9	5	1	1	261,222
Put On Trial	2	G	3	0	0	1	950
Put Out the Fuse	2	C	1	0	0	0	0
Put the Heat On	3	F	13	2	1	1	30,144
Put Up Your Dukes	3	G	10	1	2	0	19,070
Putt Putt Dan	7	G	5	0	0	0	346
Puttinonthedog	9	G	1	1	0	0	1,550
Puxa Saco	4	F	6	1	1	0	76,350
Puzzle	3	F	2	1	1	0	33,600
Puzzle Girl	4	F	14	0	1	1	3,009
Puzzlement	5	H	2	1	0	0	90,000
Pvt. First Class	7	G	5	0	1	0	1,289
Pvt. Holtzman	3	F	5	2	0	0	6,090
Pvt. Lynch	3	C	3	0	1	0	9,400
Pvt. Tucker	2	G	1	0	0	0	0
Pyaar's King	6	G	2	0	0	0	113
Pye King	2	C	7	1	1	1	13,630
Pyramid Girl	3	F	4	1	1	0	13,360
Pyramid Passage	3	F	16	1	3	2	8,588
Pyramid Performer	3	C	10	0	3	1	20,383
Pyramid Queen	2	F	5	0	1	1	5,340
Pyramid Star	4	F	7	0	1	1	3,149
Pyramid's Gal	2	F	4	0	0	0	310
Pyramyst	2	F	3	1	0	1	16,150
Pyrite Alena	3	F	13	1	3	1	25,647
Pyrite Alone	3	F	5	0	0	0	737
Pyrite Angel	7	G	18	5	1	1	22,482
Pyrite Bonds	2	F	6	2	1	0	29,375
Pyrite Dance	4	F	4	0	0	0	1,283
Pyrite Dash	4	G	19	6	3	0	43,708
Pyrite Gun	3	F	17	2	1	2	13,555
Pyrite in Flight	10	G	3	0	1	0	3,240
Pyrite Lady	5	M	8	1	2	4	25,405
Pyrite Mac	6	G	1	0	0	0	146
Pyrite Menu	5	M	1	0	0	0	109
Pyrite Monarch	4	F	13	2	1	2	13,663
Pyrite Or Bust	5	M	13	2	1	2	27,884
Pyrite Pansy	3	F	6	1	1	0	10,550
Pyrite Queen	2	F	4	1	0	1	17,280
Pyrite Rain	3	F	9	1	1	0	20,700
Pyrite Run	4	G	9	0	1	1	7,510
Pyrite Search	4	C	3	1	0	0	17,400
Pyrite Select	4	F	7	0	0	2	3,374
Pyrite Soup	4	F	12	2	0	2	11,569
Pyrite Springs	2	C	6	1	1	2	18,400
Pyrite Valentine	3	G	8	1	0	0	2,706
Pyrite Who	4	F	2	0	0	0	270

Horse	Age	Sex	Sts	1st	2d	3d	Won
Pyrite Wild	2	F	6	0	1	2	6,450
Pyrite's Passion	10	G	2	0	0	0	84
Pyroclastic Flow	2	F	2	0	0	0	190
Pyromania	4	G	1	0	0	0	235
Q Clearance	3	F	1	0	0	0	0
Q Commercial Jette	7	H	4	1	2	0	16,125
Q Mark	3	G	10	1	2	1	10,835
Q One for Two	8	G	9	3	1	0	34,250
Q P Cruiser	2	C	4	0	0	1	1,460
Q Risk	4	G	8	1	1	1	8,844
Q Royal Blew by U	3	F	1	0	0	0	114
Q. V. C. Karma	3	F	8	3	1	2	24,305
Qadar	2	C	1	0	0	0	150
Quachita	3	G	14	2	1	1	10,363
Quacked Bag	4	F	6	2	0	1	39,888
Quackers Appeal	3	G	13	4	4	0	72,315
Quad Bypass	3	G	9	0	1	2	8,097
Quadrant	2	C	1	0	0	0	2,040
Quadratic Equation	5	M	2	0	0	0	122
Quaffalino	4	F	15	0	0	1	1,511
Quail's Gate	6	M	7	1	1	0	4,660
Quaker Change	3	F	9	1	4	3	19,925
Quakerism	3	G	17	2	2	4	23,820
Quakers Surprise	3	G	8	1	2	4	31,856
Quakersbluelady	2	F	4	0	1	1	5,950
Qualified Opinion	2	C	2	2	0	0	50,400
Quality Armor	3	C	6	0	0	1	6,180
Quality Hero	4	G	7	0	5	0	10,615
Qualls Road	5	G	7	1	0	2	2,635
Quanaco	3	G	16	3	4	0	75,600
Quanah County	3	F	2	0	0	2	12,120
Quantico Joe	3	G	14	2	1	1	49,520
Quantis	5	G	8	4	0	0	44,700
Quantum Link	6	H	10	1	1	1	6,112
Quantum Merit	5	G	3	3	0	0	280,585
Quapaw Charlie	3	C	2	0	0	0	0
Quaremba	7	H	4	0	2	2	3,450
Quarryville	4	G	15	2	2	3	13,327
Quarter Crown	2	F	3	0	0	0	900
Quarter Irish	2	F	4	1	0	2	21,441
Quarter Pole	2	G	1	0	1	0	2,190
Quarter Pounder	4	C	2	0	0	1	2,301
Quarter Time	4	G	13	1	1	3	16,060
Quarter Ton of Fun	5	H	3	0	0	0	3,000
Quarterback Draw	5	H	11	0	1	2	3,933
Quarterelven	4	F	11	3	3	0	25,850
Quartern	2	F	2	1	0	0	3,033
Quartez	3	G	13	2	1	3	25,011
Quartz	3	G	4	0	0	3	7,135
Quassapaug	5	H	10	0	2	1	21,559
Quatra	2	F	1	0	0	0	0
Quatrain	5	M	5	1	1	2	58,360
Quatre Dix Neuf	5	G	15	3	1	4	62,459
Quatro Blanco	3	G	3	1	0	0	25,565
Quattro Latro	4	C	4	1	0	0	19,500
Quayle	3	G	9	0	0	1	12,089
Qube Tuff	6	M	6	0	0	0	522
Qudsiya Begum	4	F	5	0	0	0	343
Que Bonita	5	M	4	0	1	1	7,541
Que Borges (ARG)	5	G	16	2	2	1	33,420
Que Candy (ARG)	6	H	16	3	1	0	70,470
Que Cherie	3	F	3	0	0	1	900
Que Chulo	3	C	3	0	0	0	0
Que Diablito	4	C	9	1	3	4	21,485
Que Facil Corazon	6	M	1	0	0	0	0
Que Guapo	4	G	4	0	0	0	980
Que Leo	3	C	3	0	0	0	0
Que Puntual (ARG)	4	F	1	1	0	0	13,800
Queansco	2	F	5	2	1	1	69,250
Quebelick	4	F	9	1	3	3	32,495
Quechee Gorge	6	M	8	0	1	2	2,560
Quecreek	4	F	7	1	1	1	8,100
Queechy Lake	2	F	3	1	0	0	10,134
Queen Abadad	2	F	2	0	0	0	360
Queen Adalida	5	M	2	0	0	0	0
Queen Alexis	4	F	9	0	3	1	3,092
Queen Allayah	3	F	9	0	0	1	1,599
Queen an E	4	F	3	0	0	1	2,420
Queen Anns Revenge	3	F	3	0	0	0	403
Queen At Heart	5	M	5	1	1	1	11,766
Queen Awad	4	F	7	1	0	0	9,315
Queen Cajun	2	F	4	0	1	0	3,135
Queen Chelsey	5	M	5	0	0	1	750
Queen Clu	3	F	1	0	0	0	250
Queen Colleen	2	F	2	0	0	0	1,925
Queen Creek	7	M	3	0	0	0	2,400
Queen Daisy	5	M	5	0	0	1	2,106
Queen De	6	M	12	0	3	3	6,076
Queen de La Mint	3	F	11	0	1	2	7,162
Queen Ding	6	M	1	0	0	0	0
Queen Diva	4	F	4	1	0	0	3,600
Queen Geraldine	3	F	8	2	1	2	34,450
Queen Gloria	3	F	12	2	1	2	10,558
Queen Guinevere	5	M	6	0	1	0	1,583
Queen Halo	4	F	5	2	1	1	10,380
Queen Hypolita	2	F	6	1	3	0	39,300
Queen Irish	3	F	16	1	1	3	34,754
Queen Isabel	4	F	1	0	0	0	640
Queen Jadwiga	2	F	7	0	0	0	510
Queen Jimmy	6	M	10	1	2	3	21,808
Queen Kelly	4	F	9	3	1	2	28,100
Queen Kennelot	3	F	1	0	0	0	0
Queen Mamba	3	F	3	0	0	0	292
Queen Mary Jean	4	F	6	0	0	0	424
Queen Merlot	4	F	6	0	4	1	8,660
Queen Morgan	5	M	12	1	2	1	9,153
Queen Nel	4	F	1	0	0	0	0
Queen Noor	3	F	7	1	2	2	14,703
Queen Nova	5	M	10	1	0	2	13,634
Queen of America	4	F	2	0	0	0	2,510
Queen of Battle	2	F	3	0	0	1	7,410
Queen of Cash	5	M	6	0	0	3	2,018
Queen of Cool	3	F	4	0	0	0	4,495
Queen of Denial	4	F	9	0	0	1	3,568
Queen of Dunollie	4	F	12	0	1	1	3,530
Queen of Mecca	7	M	10	4	2	0	71,860
Queen of My Castle	4	F	4	0	0	0	372
Queen of Naples	3	F	8	0	0	0	1,082
Queen of Nostalgia	7	M	1	0	0	0	0
Queen of Paris	5	M	1	0	0	0	0
Queen of Runners	5	M	5	0	0	0	0
Queen of Saratoga	5	M	16	2	2	3	42,780
Queen of Slew	4	F	2	1	0	0	5,888
Queen of Slots	3	F	3	0	1	0	13,010
Queen of Soul	3	F	12	2	0	1	35,160
Queen of the Hunt	2	F	3	0	0	1	2,225
Queen of the Isle	5	M	13	5	2	0	31,696
Queen of the Mt.	3	F	6	0	1	2	11,379
Queen of the Road	4	F	9	1	2	2	23,500
Queen of the Turf	2	F	3	0	0	1	6,897
Queen of the Zone	5	M	10	1	0	1	7,106
Queen of Wands	4	F	7	2	2	0	17,958
Queen On Tour	7	M	8	1	1	4	10,930
Queen o'The Ship	2	F	4	1	1	0	18,150
Queen Pauline	4	F	3	0	0	0	895
Queen Red	3	F	6	0	0	0	224
Queen Sandy	4	C	9	2	1	1	15,093
Queen Sheba	4	F	3	1	1	1	15,880
Queen Speech	5	M	2	0	0	0	1,452
Queen Supreme	3	F	4	0	1	0	9,000
Queen Tango	5	M	8	3	5	0	10,692
Queen Teen	6	M	7	1	0	2	8,933
Queen Trigger	3	F	1	1	0	0	5,400
Queen Triton	3	F	4	0	0	0	0
Queen Twilla	3	F	6	0	0	0	0
Queen Twining	5	M	6	0	0	0	1,528
Queena Corrina	5	M	7	2	3	1	78,950
Queenhanna's Home	3	F	3	0	0	0	0
Queenie Dee's Jet	2	F	1	0	0	0	300
Queenies Girl	6	M	3	0	0	0	578
Queenieshoudini	2	G	1	0	0	0	80
Queenledo	2	F	5	2	1	0	39,148
Queenly Image	3	F	16	0	0	2	13,140
Queenly Luck	2	F	3	0	0	0	0
Queenmab'sdaughter	2	F	6	2	2	1	40,786
Queenofluv	3	F	3	1	0	0	18,260
Queenofmountain	5	M	14	0	1	1	21,520
Queenoftheballet	5	M	6	0	0	0	2,077

Horse	Age	Sex	Sts	1st	2d	3d	Won
Queenofthemeadow	2	F	3	0	0	0	432
Queenofthetinkers	2	F	9	0	0	1	9,000
Queenofthevilla	2	F	2	0	0	0	0
Queen's Account	5	G	16	1	2	2	9,887
Queens Are Wild	3	F	10	2	0	0	21,656
Queen's Bouquet	4	F	10	1	1	2	27,565
Queen's Caper	5	M	6	0	0	0	552
Queen's Colony	11	G	15	0	2	2	4,797
Queen's Counsel	3	C	9	2	1	1	19,740
Queens Fort	3	F	5	0	0	1	2,632
Queen's Gambit	3	F	1	0	0	0	450
Queen's Hero	2	G	3	2	0	0	24,720
Queens High	4	F	9	1	1	1	6,067
Queen's Hollywood	4	F	17	5	1	2	17,610
Queen's Jewel	4	C	5	0	0	0	375
Queen's Jungle Bee	6	G	4	0	1	0	794
Queen's Kiss	5	M	17	1	3	0	30,260
Queen's Last Hart	5	G	10	2	0	1	13,789
Queens Over Jacks	2	F	9	3	0	2	25,530
Queens Plaza	2	F	4	2	0	0	89,327
Queen's Quay	3	C	1	0	0	0	501
Queen's Route	3	F	1	0	0	0	0
Queen's Secret	5	M	1	0	0	0	288
Queen's Son	5	G	16	1	1	2	15,625
Queen's Temper	3	F	2	0	0	0	554
Queen's Treasure	4	F	15	0	1	1	4,092
Queen's Tribute	3	F	6	0	0	1	1,209
Queen's Triomphe	5	M	2	0	0	0	3,288
Queens Village	6	M	8	3	3	0	15,358
Queen's Wager	5	M	11	3	3	1	38,003
Queenscliff	5	M	11	1	1	0	4,166
Queenston Heights	2	G	4	0	0	0	1,728
Queenstown	4	F	2	0	1	0	3,600
Queensway Quay (GB)	4	G	9	0	0	0	300
Quem Se Atreve (BRZ)	4	C	7	0	0	0	6,026
Quench Wench	3	F	6	0	1	1	6,383
Querida Mia	2	F	5	0	0	2	1,954
Quero Quero	4	F	7	1	3	1	167,170
Quest	5	H	3	0	0	0	11,252
Quest Dancer	7	M	2	0	0	0	125
Quest for a Buck	4	G	9	1	0	2	3,150
Quest for Fun	7	M	1	0	0	0	139
Quest for Nirvana	2	G	8	1	0	0	14,750
Quest for Silver	8	G	4	0	0	0	480
Quest for Speed	6	H	6	1	0	1	2,495
Quest for Truth	4	F	10	2	1	2	51,900
Quest Master	9	G	5	2	0	1	5,480
Quest of Fate	6	H	7	2	0	2	63,480
Quest Star	5	H	10	2	0	0	238,035
Questa Gold	4	C	3	0	0	0	480
Questador	5	G	7	1	0	0	12,294
Questfortheroses	4	C	2	0	0	0	0
Questing Knight	5	G	14	4	1	2	94,760
Question (ARG)	5	H	7	0	0	0	8,948
Question Authority	4	G	2	0	0	0	0
Question of Gold	10	G	2	0	0	0	0
Questionable Miss	6	M	9	0	0	2	1,020
Questionable Past	3	F	5	1	0	0	40,116
Questionable Road	4	G	8	2	1	2	5,238
Questionable World	2	C	3	1	1	0	27,635
Quick Action	3	C	11	2	2	1	133,140
Quick Advice	3	F	13	2	3	1	50,588
Quick American	4	C	15	0	2	2	10,590
Quick and Crafty	3	C	6	1	1	1	24,680
Quick Apalachee	8	G	16	0	3	3	4,902
Quick as a Cat	3	F	2	0	0	0	690
Quick as a Fox	4	F	2	0	0	0	0
Quick Ball Run	5	G	1	0	0	0	0
Quick Blend	2	C	4	1	1	1	25,550
Quick Buy	3	F	4	0	0	1	2,095
Quick Chill	4	G	10	0	5	3	11,395
Quick Claim	5	G	16	4	2	0	49,190
Quick Corsage	5	M	13	2	2	1	8,965
Quick Course	3	C	4	1	0	1	7,774
Quick Cover	3	F	3	2	0	0	28,360
Quick Cure	3	F	8	1	1	3	6,013
Quick Dash	4	C	3	0	0	0	99
Quick Departure	2	C	3	0	0	0	0
Quick Divide	3	G	14	4	3	0	75,114

Horse	Age	Sex	Sts	1st	2d	3d	Won
Quick Draw Annie	4	F	9	1	0	1	17,623
Quick Dude	3	C	10	2	2	0	25,011
Quick Frost	4	F	1	0	0	0	0
Quick Fuse	5	M	13	2	2	4	27,308
Quick Ice	3	C	3	0	0	1	1,155
Quick in Deed	2	C	3	1	1	1	75,229
Quick Interview	6	M	5	0	0	1	1,110
Quick Lad	2	C	11	0	2	1	13,040
Quick Lass	2	F	5	0	2	0	13,633
Quick Lil Lady	2	F	4	1	0	0	8,820
Quick Line	8	G	1	0	0	1	1,000
Quick Links	3	C	3	0	0	0	0
Quick Look	3	G	12	1	2	0	24,783
Quick Mason	3	C	9	2	1	0	7,017
Quick Mick	3	F	8	0	3	2	13,752
Quick Mustard	4	F	7	1	1	2	10,114
Quick N Fancy	4	F	3	1	0	0	8,340
Quick N Quite	4	F	1	0	0	0	0
Quick N Sassy	4	F	2	0	0	0	0
Quick N Sweet	5	M	10	4	2	0	16,370
Quick Nip	5	M	9	2	0	0	22,820
Quick Princess	3	F	3	0	0	0	0
Quick Print	6	H	7	1	0	2	24,306
Quick Proposal	5	G	1	0	0	0	0
Quick Punch	8	G	11	2	1	2	44,009
Quick Queen	2	F	10	1	1	2	49,090
Quick Quick	5	G	7	0	0	0	661
Quick Release	4	G	16	0	1	2	1,550
Quick Rib	6	H	13	1	1	0	7,169
Quick Runner	2	G	10	3	0	1	29,320
Quick Salvo	3	G	2	1	0	0	9,600
Quick Save	6	M	6	0	1	1	1,646
Quick Shot Annie	3	F	7	1	0	2	7,768
Quick Silver Dream	3	F	5	0	0	0	2,477
Quick Smile	3	F	4	0	0	2	2,070
Quick Smoke	4	F	9	3	1	3	74,400
Quick Solution	3	C	4	1	0	0	8,815
Quick Squeeze	2	F	2	0	1	0	11,400
Quick Storm	4	G	10	2	3	0	21,669
Quick Struggle	3	G	19	2	3	1	17,612
Quick Study	3	C	4	0	1	1	7,233
Quick Suggestion	3	G	3	0	0	1	2,758
Quick Switch	5	G	2	0	0	0	100
Quick Takur	2	C	3	1	0	0	1,780
Quick Talker	5	H	19	2	5	2	53,218
Quick Temper	3	F	11	1	4	1	87,675
Quick Thinking	2	G	2	0	0	0	800
Quick Thunder	4	G	3	0	0	0	492
Quick Ticket	3	G	11	1	1	2	20,000
Quick to Belong	2	G	1	0	0	0	0
Quick to Sin	7	G	10	0	4	1	3,931
Quick Trend	3	G	13	6	0	2	36,249
Quick Tune	5	G	11	1	2	1	19,736
Quick Vision	3	G	8	0	2	0	3,649
Quick Wings	3	F	7	0	0	1	1,290
Quickdancin' Roger	4	G	7	4	0	1	35,606
Quicker Kelly	6	M	6	0	0	1	3,560
Quickerthanyoureye	5	G	9	0	2	1	8,149
Quickest of All	3	F	15	2	3	4	46,499
Quickest Way	4	F	16	0	0	3	5,225
Quickie O'Brien	2	G	2	0	0	0	280
Quickrunningriver	7	G	3	0	0	0	1,012
Quick's Affair	7	H	7	1	0	1	5,816
Quickset	2	C	2	0	0	0	705
Quicksideup	6	M	11	0	2	0	4,090
Quicksilverexpress	5	G	9	1	1	1	20,479
Quickwitch	5	M	11	0	0	1	1,507
Quickzotti	6	G	2	0	0	0	0
Quidditch Player	4	G	6	1	1	1	27,216
Quidditch Star	3	G	7	0	2	0	6,498
Quien Pregunto	5	G	3	0	0	2	427
Quiero Ganar	2	F	3	0	0	0	107
Quiero Saber de Ti	4	G	16	2	2	2	16,705
Quies	3	F	6	1	1	1	43,900
Quiet Authority	3	F	3	0	0	0	93
Quiet Cash	3	C	5	1	0	1	35,071
Quiet Casper	5	G	21	1	3	2	9,400
Quiet Celerity	3	F	7	1	2	0	24,260
Quiet Challenge	4	G	4	1	0	0	29,029

Horse	Age	Sex	Sts	1st	2d	3d	Won
Quiet Charisma	4	G	9	1	1	1	11,480
Quiet Charm	5	M	14	0	3	3	20,645
Quiet Classic	3	F	5	0	0	0	361
Quiet Colony	5	G	3	1	0	0	31,920
Quiet Command	4	C	5	0	1	1	5,430
Quiet Companion	5	M	1	0	0	0	702
Quiet Confidence	3	G	18	3	1	3	21,601
Quiet Courage	5	M	2	0	0	0	113
Quiet Cover	2	G	2	0	0	1	3,240
Quiet Creek	3	C	8	0	0	1	5,359
Quiet Delight	5	M	1	0	1	0	12,000
Quiet Desperation	5	G	14	5	0	2	171,560
Quiet Dinner	5	M	13	3	2	1	14,197
Quiet Edition	3	F	1	0	0	0	164
Quiet Express	2	G	3	0	2	0	14,631
Quiet Flyer	2	F	7	1	0	1	13,840
Quiet Ghost	3	F	4	0	0	0	1,340
Quiet Gratitude	8	G	5	0	0	0	3,720
Quiet Hero	3	C	2	2	0	0	40,800
Quiet Honor	2	F	1	1	0	0	23,400
Quiet Journey	3	C	2	0	0	1	7,920
Quiet Julia	4	F	1	0	0	0	700
Quiet Kiss	3	F	1	0	0	0	0
Quiet Manner	2	F	4	1	0	0	16,560
Quiet Master (CHI)	7	G	13	2	1	1	15,024
Quiet Mike	7	G	11	1	2	2	41,950
Quiet Minister	4	F	2	0	0	1	1,260
Quiet Money	2	C	4	1	0	0	15,420
Quiet Motion	7	G	14	1	1	1	5,364
Quiet Motivator	3	F	10	2	2	1	38,864
Quiet N Low	3	F	3	0	0	0	91
Quiet One	8	H	16	3	3	0	42,597
Quiet Optimism	2	F	9	2	1	1	50,416
Quiet Period	2	C	1	0	0	0	150
Quiet Pursuit	3	G	5	2	1	0	6,211
Quiet Qudible	7	H	4	0	0	0	314
Quiet R. N.	5	M	1	0	0	0	400
Quiet Reflection	7	G	14	3	3	0	30,578
Quiet Retaliation	2	C	4	0	0	0	2,843
Quiet Reward	4	F	6	1	1	0	25,866
Quiet Rhapsody	7	G	5	0	0	1	1,925
Quiet Rose	4	F	6	0	0	3	8,553
Quiet Ruckus	3	G	10	1	3	2	12,682
Quiet Ruler	6	G	10	0	0	1	10,243
Quiet Rumor	2	F	5	1	0	0	13,220
Quiet Shot	4	G	9	1	0	0	3,325
Quiet Soul	4	G	12	1	1	5	19,861
Quiet Sting	3	F	11	4	0	0	38,886
Quiet Strategy	8	G	4	1	0	0	6,952
Quiet Stripe	4	C	2	0	0	0	0
Quiet Syns	8	H	7	4	2	1	22,137
Quiet Taurus	2	G	3	0	0	0	399
Quiet Tipper	4	G	12	4	3	1	38,200
Quiet Virginian	3	C	9	0	1	0	8,652
Quiet Winner	3	G	17	2	2	2	12,855
Quiet Winter Sky	3	F	2	0	1	0	5,000
Quiet Woodman	8	G	11	0	0	1	3,279
Quiet Word	4	F	3	0	0	0	604
Quietly Quick	4	G	11	0	1	3	31,490
Quietly Rated	7	G	11	1	2	1	5,265
Quigley	4	C	8	4	3	0	130,300
Quilceda	3	F	13	3	2	3	13,389
Quilimanque (CHI)	6	G	7	2	1	0	67,340
Quill Play	4	F	3	1	0	0	8,400
Quillota	3	C	8	2	0	0	27,852
Quilo (CHI)	7	G	4	1	2	0	21,500
Quincy Kid	6	H	5	0	0	0	720
Quincy Light	4	F	9	0	0	0	496
Quincy's Quiz	4	F	4	0	0	0	400
Quinessential	7	G	10	0	0	2	2,163
Quinn	4	F	4	0	0	0	0
Quinn's Gold	2	F	4	0	1	1	3,805
Quins Thunder	2	G	1	0	0	0	66
Quintana Roo	3	G	5	0	0	1	624
Quintanskashticket	3	G	2	0	0	0	0
Quintara	3	F	13	2	0	1	30,705
Quintmor	6	G	11	0	2	1	3,126
Quintons Gold Rush	3	C	9	3	0	0	322,235
Quinton's Quest	5	G	3	0	1	1	1,800
Quintons Relaunch	2	G	5	2	0	0	12,014
Quisty	3	F	21	2	2	2	24,310
Quit Dodging	7	G	4	0	0	0	171
Quit It	2	C	2	0	0	0	2,325
Quit Smoking	4	G	2	0	0	0	535
Quitclaim	4	G	15	0	0	0	1,215
Quite a Dancer	4	F	7	0	0	1	1,012
Quite a Decision	3	F	9	2	2	0	23,914
Quite a Lot a Go	8	M	1	0	0	0	0
Quite a Night	2	C	1	1	0	0	12,720
Quite a Party	3	F	14	3	2	3	19,498
Quite a Ruckus	2	F	4	1	1	0	110,653
Quite a Victory	2	F	2	0	0	0	151
Quite an Angel	4	F	10	2	1	2	14,845
Quite an Evening	6	M	10	1	2	0	32,416
Quite Bold	5	G	3	1	0	2	6,641
Quite by Chance	5	M	14	2	2	3	17,807
Quite Careless	6	G	6	0	1	1	5,066
Quite Continental	3	G	7	0	0	0	4,000
Quite Exclusive	6	M	17	1	0	1	6,336
Quite George	2	C	1	0	0	0	95
Quite Precise	2	F	1	0	0	0	0
Quite Rightly	6	G	9	0	3	2	17,750
Quite Spender	6	M	3	0	0	0	0
Quite the Guy	3	G	8	1	3	2	19,810
Quite Unique	3	F	4	0	0	1	3,010
Quiteaguy	3	G	11	1	1	1	19,906
Quiten Boy	4	G	9	2	0	1	37,304
Quitman	2	C	1	0	0	0	0
Quiver Forever	4	F	7	0	1	0	4,884
Quiver Ridge	3	G	16	2	0	0	11,663
Quivering Crimson	3	F	7	0	1	1	5,160
Quiverlynn	2	F	4	0	2	0	7,182
Quixote's Hope	8	M	3	0	1	0	4,110
Quixote's Prince	7	G	4	0	2	0	6,700
Quixote's Quest	2	F	6	1	0	0	8,270
Quixotes's Best	4	C	1	0	1	0	1,350
Quixstar	6	H	6	0	0	1	1,138
Quiz the Maid	3	F	8	5	1	0	26,200
Quiz the Wizard	4	G	5	0	1	0	986
Quizzle	4	F	3	1	0	0	19,890
Quoit	3	G	8	1	0	0	7,870
Quoit a Girl	3	F	5	0	0	0	460
Quoit a Hero	3	C	3	0	0	1	4,340
Quoit a Journey	3	G	3	0	0	0	2,220
Quoit Alarming	6	M	13	4	2	2	58,203
Quoit Amber	3	F	5	0	1	2	3,474
Quoit Friskie	3	F	2	0	0	0	0
Quoit Jordan	3	G	9	1	0	0	7,920
Quoit Quick	5	M	4	1	0	0	21,230
Quoit Rich	3	G	2	0	0	0	920
Quote Me Later	4	G	14	5	4	2	103,617
Quote This	4	C	5	2	1	0	48,653
Quotidian	3	G	10	1	0	4	20,690
Quppy	6	M	15	2	2	2	83,000
Qureall	2	C	2	1	0	0	19,800
R a Wynn R	4	C	3	0	0	0	105
R Aly	8	G	5	0	0	0	0
R and B's Gi Jane	3	F	1	0	0	0	0
R and R Express	2	G	2	0	0	0	280
R B J's Blaze	4	G	6	2	1	0	42,380
R B Women	3	F	15	2	2	3	23,134
R Big Daddy	3	G	6	1	2	2	11,760
R Blossoms Awesome	3	F	4	0	1	0	1,515
R Bone Crusher	6	H	4	1	0	0	906
R Bonnie Cat	4	F	6	0	0	0	307
R B's Boy	5	H	15	1	3	3	52,807
R B's Lewis	2	C	4	0	0	1	8,836
R Bull	4	C	5	1	2	0	8,252
R C Brinker	8	G	1	0	0	0	50
R C Caro Dancer	2	F	5	0	1	0	3,530
R C Executioner	3	G	9	0	0	0	1,515
R C Gangster	5	M	1	0	0	1	2,505
R C Nasty Rob	2	G	3	0	0	0	404
R C Proud Seattle	2	G	3	0	0	0	408
R C Style	7	G	2	0	0	0	184
R C U Later Elaine	3	F	5	2	1	1	11,975
R Champ	3	G	7	2	0	1	14,935
R Choni Star	5	M	5	0	0	0	304

Horse	Age	Sex	Sts	1st	2d	3d	Won
R Coastocoast	5	G	11	0	1	0	4,290
R Contessa	2	F	1	1	0	0	5,400
R Cs Slew	6	G	2	0	0	0	372
R C's Star Power	6	G	9	1	2	1	2,058
R Double Diamond	4	G	12	0	1	2	4,156
R Easy Money	5	H	4	0	1	0	699
R Elway	5	G	4	1	0	0	3,788
R Fallsheba	7	G	1	0	0	0	0
R Fast Lady	2	F	3	0	1	1	11,600
R G Smoocher	2	G	2	0	0	0	615
R Grand Mohawk	5	G	3	0	0	0	147
R J Formula	3	F	4	0	0	0	445
R J Jackie Jo	3	F	1	0	0	0	140
R J Jiggs	3	F	3	0	0	0	195
R Jet	2	C	3	0	0	0	840
R J's Game	7	G	6	2	2	1	25,974
R J's Irish Power	2	G	1	0	0	0	0
R Keeper	4	C	3	0	0	0	710
R K's Boy	3	G	2	0	0	1	1,680
R Lady Deputy	4	F	10	1	1	2	25,636
R Lady Joy	2	F	2	0	0	1	6,300
R Last Norquestor	6	M	4	0	1	1	3,150
R Last Rabbit	3	C	2	0	0	0	460
R Lil Cat	2	C	3	0	0	0	421
R Lil Rose	5	M	7	0	0	0	1,555
R Little Ruckus	2	F	2	1	0	0	39,232
R Lucero	5	G	16	2	2	0	15,970
R Lucinda	2	F	5	2	1	0	50,392
R Maestro	3	C	13	2	1	5	34,115
R McLennen	6	G	8	4	0	0	52,575
R Meadow Luck	6	H	4	0	0	0	2,280
R Mister Forli	4	G	6	1	1	0	9,940
R Nanee	5	M	9	2	1	2	17,550
R Niele	2	F	2	0	0	0	0
R Nurse C	5	M	4	0	0	0	1,172
R Obsession	3	F	10	4	2	0	148,800
R Pocketsfull	4	G	4	1	1	0	7,680
R Princess Hailey	3	F	5	1	1	2	11,939
R P's Lady	5	M	2	0	0	0	390
R Queen Bees	4	F	1	0	0	0	45
R Raggedy Ann	4	F	8	0	0	0	2,005
R Reagan	3	G	3	0	0	0	768
R Ruby Rae	8	M	5	0	2	1	1,675
R S Express	5	G	17	4	3	1	33,740
R Saltina	3	F	1	0	0	0	0
R Soc O Choc Quah	5	M	5	0	1	0	2,847
R Stylish Cat	4	C	2	0	0	0	100
R Super Chief	4	G	6	0	3	2	7,960
R Suzie Q	2	F	5	1	1	1	21,109
R Team	5	G	1	0	0	0	0
R Terminator	5	H	5	0	0	0	80
'R Testadura	9	G	6	0	1	1	1,284
R Three	5	G	13	0	2	1	3,740
R T's Magic	5	G	12	3	1	2	29,910
R U Joshin Me	3	C	5	1	1	0	17,300
R U Mad Or Fappy	4	F	8	0	3	2	9,985
R U Ready Carmen	5	M	7	4	2	0	7,400
R U Sure	2	C	2	0	0	0	1,525
R V Dealer	6	G	11	0	0	0	461
R V Reina	4	F	4	0	0	0	189
R Valid Girl	4	F	1	0	0	0	80
R W Jett	2	G	2	0	0	2	3,763
R W Road Rage Rudy	3	F	1	0	0	0	400
R We Proud	5	G	6	0	0	0	2,680
R Zippee's Dream	3	G	7	1	0	1	3,566
R. A. F. Captain	6	G	4	1	1	1	8,835
R and R.	2	F	1	0	0	0	0
R. Associate	4	G	12	2	0	1	51,875
R. B Spirit	8	G	2	0	0	0	0
R. Baggio	6	G	6	1	2	0	61,085
R. Bob	4	C	3	1	1	0	16,239
R. C. Slocum	3	C	4	1	0	0	15,000
R. C.'s Dandy	4	G	7	1	0	2	3,720
R. Cash Back	4	G	13	3	5	1	35,771
R. Corizon de Leon	4	C	5	0	0	1	2,475
R. C's L. A. Jazz	3	F	1	0	0	0	795
R. D.'s Girl	5	M	11	0	4	4	13,855
R. Dixie Chick	6	M	1	0	0	0	83
R. Double Click	7	M	19	3	7	0	49,760

Horse	Age	Sex	Sts	1st	2d	3d	Won
R. E. Prince	5	G	11	0	1	2	8,287
R. Encounter	10	G	12	2	0	2	44,136
R. Faithful	5	G	19	0	2	2	4,864
R. G. Campbell	3	G	13	1	3	2	19,009
R. G. Georgeanne	5	M	11	0	0	0	674
R. G. Slewmeister	5	M	2	0	0	0	150
R. H Exterminator	3	F	16	2	0	3	7,431
R. J.'s Quest	3	C	6	0	0	1	1,298
R. Little Redhead	7	G	9	4	2	0	35,062
R. M.'s Lina	3	F	11	2	1	1	12,686
R. Retsina	3	G	6	0	0	0	943
R. S. Bucks	6	G	8	0	0	1	972
R. Synful Way	2	F	6	0	0	3	4,460
R. T. Gulch	6	G	11	3	1	2	43,145
Ra Der Dean	4	C	15	1	4	2	22,010
Ra Devil	4	G	15	1	3	4	10,288
Ra Ra Ricky	8	G	7	0	0	0	203
Ra Ra Superstar	4	C	5	1	2	1	49,500
Rabbit Ears Too	2	G	6	1	0	0	13,480
Rabbit Run Tootsie	5	M	5	2	0	1	15,875
Rabbit Too	3	C	13	1	3	0	26,831
Rabbit's Wish	3	G	4	0	0	0	510
Race Day	2	F	5	0	0	0	2,538
Race for Glory	3	C	6	0	0	0	3,920
Race for Stace	5	G	2	0	0	0	208
Race for the Green	3	G	1	0	0	0	44
Race On Green	6	H	9	0	1	1	15,670
Race the Dawn	7	G	5	0	0	0	0
Race to the Moon	3	C	1	0	0	0	750
Race With a Plum	5	G	15	3	4	0	56,020
Racee Rhonda	4	F	2	0	0	0	470
Raceforgrace	4	F	10	2	0	0	5,936
Racer Babe	4	G	2	0	0	0	585
Raceready	2	R	4	0	0	1	2,640
Racer's Edge	2	G	4	0	0	3	7,500
Racetrack Charlie	7	H	9	1	1	1	24,558
Racetrack Ruler	5	G	19	1	0	0	7,176
Racey Casey	3	F	7	1	0	0	6,789
Racey Dreamer	5	G	4	4	0	0	112,500
Racey Leo	5	G	17	2	3	3	18,773
Racey Renee	4	F	6	1	1	0	4,150
Racey Stacey	9	M	10	6	2	1	30,015
Rach Three	6	G	12	0	3	2	20,150
Rachael's Runner	2	C	1	0	0	0	0
Rachele R's Angel	2	F	2	0	0	0	222
Rachel's Boots	3	F	8	2	1	0	9,947
Rachel's Choice	3	F	5	0	0	1	3,118
Rachel's Gold	7	M	1	0	0	0	40
Rachel's Mt. Star	6	G	8	0	0	1	960
Rachels Rocket	3	G	2	0	0	0	150
Rachel's Sister	3	F	2	0	0	0	198
Racie Jaycie	4	F	5	1	0	1	4,952
Racie's Runaway	4	F	8	2	0	0	21,720
Racin Colors	3	F	6	1	1	1	22,177
Racing Deelite	4	C	4	1	0	0	5,273
Racing Free	6	G	8	1	1	0	14,159
Racing Luck	3	F	12	3	3	1	65,275
Racing Nut	5	G	12	3	3	1	30,432
Racing Rebel	3	G	14	4	3	2	50,170
Racing Ruby	5	M	3	0	0	0	70
Racing Rudy	3	G	3	0	0	1	1,100
Racing Sundown	5	M	8	2	1	1	60,932
Racing Thoughts	3	G	5	1	1	0	15,907
Racing Tiger	2	F	4	1	0	0	5,085
Racing Valay	2	F	5	1	0	0	12,320
Racingtothemoon	2	F	1	0	0	0	400
Racingwithdestiny	3	G	4	2	0	0	30,600
Rack Em Up	6	G	9	1	3	2	25,999
Rackelmylove	2	F	7	0	0	1	1,790
Racquet Man	5	H	12	1	1	1	10,732
Racy Cat	3	F	9	1	1	0	2,453
Raczyna	3	F	13	4	1	0	20,546
Rad	3	F	3	0	0	0	496
Radar Contact	8	G	3	0	0	0	722
Radar Screen	3	C	1	0	1	0	1,674
Radar Trap	8	H	15	1	1	5	10,909
Radar Zone	2	C	2	0	0	0	0
Rader	2	C	1	0	0	0	98
Radha	3	F	17	1	0	2	19,975

Horse	Age	Sex	Sts	1st	2d	3d	Won
Radiant Avie	2	F	4	1	0	2	25,450
Radiant Cat	3	C	7	2	0	2	72,032
Radiant Diamonds	3	C	6	1	0	2	14,851
Radiant Gold	2	C	3	1	0	1	8,920
Radiant Lilly	5	M	3	0	0	1	1,205
Radiant Nancy	6	M	7	1	1	0	12,030
Radiant Runaway	6	G	5	0	0	2	1,686
Radiantly	4	F	2	0	1	0	4,165
Radiatin' Sunshine	5	M	1	0	0	0	40
Radical Activist	6	G	9	0	1	1	11,925
Radical Banker	2	G	3	1	0	0	15,090
Radical Bubba	6	G	5	0	0	0	0
Radical Cat	3	G	5	0	0	0	570
Radical Charmer	3	C	5	1	0	1	1,067
Radical Lake	5	M	1	0	0	0	0
Radical Rage	6	H	6	1	0	2	3,758
Radical Reality	6	G	11	0	1	0	1,858
Radical Right	2	G	7	1	2	3	83,146
Radio Caroline	3	F	4	0	0	0	1,100
Radio Station Man	2	C	2	1	0	0	11,800
Radio Twist	3	C	6	0	0	0	365
Radioactive Power	3	G	5	0	0	1	1,514
Radon	5	M	14	3	2	2	54,645
Rae Hunter	3	F	11	0	0	1	7,108
Raeanne's Request	2	F	2	1	0	0	6,674
Raedon Princess	4	F	2	0	0	0	255
Raes Irish Queen	6	M	1	0	0	0	40
Rae's Totts	4	G	13	3	3	2	76,720
Raewanda	4	F	13	0	1	3	12,095
Raf and Ready	2	F	4	0	1	2	16,918
Raf Raf Rafael	2	C	1	0	0	0	230
Rafa	4	F	11	1	3	1	32,490
Raff	5	G	3	0	1	1	2,347
Raffie's Dream	4	F	8	2	0	1	71,802
Raffie's Passion	4	F	8	1	0	2	18,235
Raffie's Storm	4	F	6	0	1	0	13,310
Raffit	4	C	1	0	0	0	292
Raffle Ticket	5	G	13	1	2	1	7,366
Rafgaar	4	G	8	0	3	1	7,360
Rafinesque	6	G	7	1	0	0	3,173
Raf's Society Girl	3	F	7	2	0	1	23,329
Rafter Cat	3	F	12	1	2	0	9,530
Rafting	3	C	1	0	0	0	150
Rag King	7	G	11	2	2	0	28,840
Rag Sheet	3	C	2	0	0	0	336
Rag Time Dancer	3	G	9	1	0	1	12,080
Rag Time Dolly	6	M	3	0	0	0	0
Ragazzo	6	H	2	0	0	0	216
Rage in Warrior	4	G	1	0	0	0	0
Rageously	4	C	18	3	4	3	40,040
Raggamuffin	7	G	6	1	1	0	5,832
Ragged Blaze	4	G	10	0	2	2	7,390
Raggidy Rowe	2	G	8	1	1	1	5,188
Ragin' Raja	8	G	5	0	0	0	0
Ragin' Raven	9	G	8	2	1	3	19,425
Ragin Seas	3	G	2	0	0	0	0
Raging Blade	10	G	3	1	0	1	8,852
Raging Dancer	3	F	4	0	0	0	410
Raging Duff	2	G	3	0	0	0	0
Raging Glory	2	F	3	1	1	0	15,540
Raging Passion	3	G	13	1	4	0	7,943
Raging Rapids	3	F	4	2	0	1	35,380
Raging Redhead	4	F	15	2	2	2	49,650
Raging Riley	4	G	4	0	2	1	9,700
Raging River	7	G	9	2	1	0	6,148
Raging Roman	7	G	3	0	0	0	250
Raging Ruby	3	F	10	1	1	1	15,220
Raging Slavic	2	C	4	0	1	0	4,470
Raging Springs	6	H	4	1	1	1	4,700
Raging Tiger	2	C	7	0	1	1	5,170
Raging Wind	2	G	1	0	0	1	900
Ragingbluewater	3	G	3	0	0	1	2,663
Ragroid	4	F	15	2	4	2	22,125
Ragtime Brass	4	F	1	1	0	0	4,275
Ragtime Fun	4	G	2	0	0	1	2,440
Ragtime Gunner	6	G	2	0	0	1	687
Ragtime Hope	2	F	8	1	1	1	37,905
Ragtime Miss	6	M	8	1	0	1	7,202
Ragtime Request	3	G	5	1	0	0	21,770

Horse	Age	Sex	Sts	1st	2d	3d	Won
Ragtime Ruthie	7	M	9	1	0	0	1,840
Ragtime Special	4	G	2	0	0	0	114
Ragtime Tale	4	G	11	1	1	1	15,248
Ragul	5	G	13	2	0	5	22,610
Rah Rah Party	6	G	13	4	2	2	16,058
Rahrah Bertie	3	F	2	0	1	0	1,685
Rahy Cat	6	G	16	2	1	0	43,666
Rahy Dolly	3	F	3	0	0	0	3,000
Rahy Pavo	4	G	14	1	3	0	24,900
Rahy Rhythm	7	G	9	0	0	1	6,140
Rahyinsky	5	H	17	2	2	2	17,620
Rahyonrahy	4	C	7	0	0	0	2,300
Rahys' Appeal	2	F	4	1	1	0	38,206
Rahy's Bachelor	2	C	3	0	0	0	0
Rahy's Chance	4	G	8	1	1	3	40,748
Rahy's Gold	4	C	13	2	2	3	47,250
Rahy's Secret	6	H	10	0	2	1	24,740
Rahy's Song	4	F	10	1	1	2	16,455
Raid	3	C	4	0	0	0	114
Raid the Parade	3	G	5	0	2	1	12,821
Raider Nation	4	G	1	1	0	0	12,100
Raiderette	2	F	3	1	0	2	19,483
Rail Hunter	5	G	7	1	0	0	4,843
Rail Me	4	F	1	0	0	0	81
Rail Rose	4	C	12	1	2	2	43,230
Rail Spike	2	C	4	0	0	1	2,525
Rail Thief	2	G	4	0	0	0	726
Railed	6	G	2	0	0	0	104
Railroad	2	G	7	3	2	0	69,902
Railroad Man Jim	3	G	8	1	1	2	18,850
Railroad Mills	5	G	9	1	0	3	10,292
Railroad Red	3	C	5	1	0	0	10,435
Railroader (GB)	7	G	6	1	1	0	11,220
Railway	6	G	18	0	1	2	4,176
Rain Cat	5	M	11	1	3	2	26,065
Rain Drummer	4	G	7	2	1	1	38,472
Rain Kissed	2	C	2	0	0	1	1,250
Rain Song	3	F	2	1	0	0	11,582
Rain Spinner	3	G	3	0	0	0	320
Rainbow Acorn	5	M	16	4	4	0	48,915
Rainbow Bay	3	C	1	0	0	0	0
Rainbow Blues	5	G	11	1	0	1	11,220
Rainbow Bold	4	G	5	0	0	0	256
Rainbow Boy	4	G	14	3	1	1	26,229
Rainbow City	3	C	2	0	0	0	330
Rainbow Flyer	4	G	4	0	0	0	380
Rainbow Knight	5	G	4	0	0	0	947
Rainbow Lake	5	H	13	3	1	1	15,057
Rainbow of Music	3	F	2	0	1	0	2,125
Rainbow Pete	3	G	7	1	1	2	17,164
Rainbow Reality	2	C	6	0	0	2	3,826
Rainbow Rhapsody	3	F	3	0	0	0	289
Rainbow Robber	4	G	9	0	2	1	2,570
Rainbow Rose	4	F	10	2	1	1	15,102
Rainbow Runner	3	F	10	1	0	0	4,857
Rainbow Sand	3	F	1	0	0	0	1,050
Rainbow Springs	3	C	8	1	0	1	6,668
Rainbow Style (IRE)	7	G	5	0	1	0	3,262
Rainbow Swirl	3	G	2	0	0	0	0
Rainbow Trail	5	M	4	0	0	0	200
Rainbow Valley	6	G	6	1	1	0	4,130
Rainbow Wrangler	3	G	4	0	0	0	170
Rainbowhuntress	3	F	1	0	0	0	0
Rainbow's End	4	F	1	0	0	0	0
Rainbows for Luck	3	G	6	2	1	1	138,873
Rainbows Forever	4	F	12	1	3	1	24,394
Rainbow's Glo	4	F	12	0	3	0	6,930
Rainbowsgold	9	M	4	1	1	0	1,292
Rainier Express	4	G	8	0	1	0	3,995
Rainin Panchos	2	F	5	0	0	0	300
Rainman's Request	5	G	8	1	1	0	13,300
Rainy Bengal	4	G	13	2	2	4	15,948
Rainy Day	3	G	6	1	1	0	5,914
Rainy Day Blues	7	G	9	0	0	0	671
Rainy Day Jay	7	G	5	2	0	0	12,955
Rainy Day Lady	4	F	1	0	0	0	210
Rainy Day Romance	4	F	16	2	1	4	19,896
Rainy Isles	2	F	1	0	0	0	800
Rainy Parade	5	G	19	3	4	3	41,655

Horse	Age	Sex	Sts	1st	2d	3d	Won
Raise a Booger	5	G	5	0	1	2	10,663
Raise a Dan	6	M	4	0	0	0	104
Raise a Dance	2	F	2	0	0	0	0
Raise a Daughter	6	M	7	4	0	0	6,842
Raise a Demon	5	H	2	0	0	0	0
Raise a Dream	3	G	5	0	0	1	300
Raise a Fortier	3	C	4	1	0	2	11,504
Raise a Glass	3	C	5	1	1	1	34,046
Raise a Heart	5	H	4	0	0	0	0
Raise a Linkage	4	C	9	0	0	1	5,251
Raise a Looker	10	G	5	0	0	0	281
Raise a Mad Chief	4	C	2	0	0	0	0
Raise a Marfa	4	C	2	0	0	0	0
Raise a Miesque	4	G	16	3	4	1	74,475
Raise a Royal	4	C	5	0	0	2	1,320
Raise a Ruckus	7	G	4	0	0	1	650
Raise a Screen	5	H	9	2	1	0	17,538
Raise a Storm	9	G	5	1	0	0	2,273
Raise A Storm (IRE)	7	G	11	2	2	4	76,810
Raise Afleet	3	F	3	1	0	1	10,485
Raise an Emblem	4	G	6	5	0	0	75,540
Raise an Ovation	2	F	6	1	0	0	4,623
Raise Devil	5	M	10	2	1	2	63,250
Raise Her Flag	5	M	12	1	0	1	20,937
Raise Him Up	3	F	1	0	0	0	0
Raise Irish Lady	5	M	2	0	0	0	0
Raise My First	3	C	1	0	0	0	0
Raise Ole Glory	2	C	4	1	0	2	37,670
Raise the Bar	3	G	6	0	0	1	6,380
Raise the Capital	5	G	9	2	0	1	16,648
Raise the Heat	4	G	12	6	2	2	91,213
Raise the Level	4	F	6	0	0	0	1,430
Raise the Stakes	6	G	9	2	1	1	24,357
Raise the Stripes	4	C	3	0	1	0	8,910
Raise You Six	7	H	5	0	0	0	633
Raise Your Ante	8	G	3	0	2	0	3,935
Raised Eyebrows	5	M	12	1	3	1	9,480
Raised Right	4	C	2	1	0	0	16,800
Raised Southern	5	M	15	2	4	2	10,955
Raisedonchampagne	3	F	7	1	2	2	11,580
Raisedtobeahawk	3	G	5	0	0	0	882
Raiser'n Class	6	M	2	0	0	0	1,080
Raisin Cat	3	F	4	0	0	0	386
Raisin Dust	5	M	13	0	0	0	1,275
Raisin Slew	6	G	11	1	0	2	8,088
Raising Kane	5	G	7	1	0	1	4,656
Raising Keene	3	F	8	2	1	0	29,400
Raising O. S.	6	G	6	0	0	0	1,718
Raising Rainbows	3	F	6	0	1	0	4,935
Raising Ransom	6	G	18	2	0	4	11,862
Raising Salem	6	M	14	1	1	2	5,526
Raising the Banner	6	G	4	0	0	1	3,582
Rais'n Rampage	6	G	1	0	0	0	0
Raizata	4	F	6	0	0	0	1,283
Raizer Light	4	G	7	1	0	0	3,435
Raja Brown	2	C	4	0	0	2	10,290
Raja Hindustan	4	C	10	1	0	2	17,254
Raja's Connection	10	M	8	0	0	0	0
Raja's Jet	5	G	5	1	1	1	9,800
Raja's Pearl	5	M	2	0	0	0	40
Raja's Rhythm	8	M	10	0	0	0	707
Raja's Slate	2	G	2	0	0	0	566
Rajing Bull	8	G	7	1	1	0	5,580
Rakeen Lake	6	M	9	0	0	0	2,652
Rakeen's Reward	5	G	16	0	6	1	34,758
Rake's Progress	3	C	2	0	0	0	400
Rakhmones	5	G	12	0	1	1	1,500
Rakien	5	H	11	4	2	0	27,722
Rakin N the Cash	4	C	4	0	0	0	184
Raking in the Gold	3	F	9	1	1	2	15,435
Rakish Ryan	6	G	10	3	1	1	28,274
Rakoon	6	G	5	0	0	0	1,230
Raku	5	G	10	1	1	3	5,600
Raleigh Bay	3	F	1	0	0	0	250
Raleigh Express	2	G	10	1	2	3	28,610
Ralitsa	2	F	10	0	3	2	6,840
Ralla	3	F	9	2	0	3	81,206
Rally Cap	3	F	8	2	4	0	15,915
Rally Hill	4	C	2	0	0	1	860
Rally Mode	5	G	12	2	3	4	26,967
Rallyroundtheflag	4	F	3	0	0	0	478
Ralph Is Smart	4	G	4	0	0	0	0
Ralphie	3	G	6	1	1	1	27,596
Ralph's Launch	5	H	2	0	0	0	0
Ralph's Sweep	3	C	4	0	0	0	0
Rama Lassie	3	F	6	0	0	2	6,679
Ramazutti	2	C	2	0	0	0	266
Rambler	5	G	3	0	0	0	258
Ramblette	5	M	3	1	0	0	1,820
Ramblin' Blue	5	M	7	2	0	0	12,128
Ramblin Bob	3	G	8	2	1	0	34,653
Ramblin Gypsy	5	M	15	4	1	2	43,466
Rambling Along	4	F	4	1	0	0	6,102
Rambling Free	3	G	3	1	0	1	7,666
Rambling Rasberry	5	H	3	0	0	0	0
Rambling Rod	7	G	4	1	0	1	1,350
Rambling Ryan	9	G	4	2	0	0	1,870
Rambling Willy	3	G	10	1	2	1	9,590
Rambo Slew	2	C	2	0	0	0	0
Rambolina	4	F	3	0	0	0	338
Rambo's Gold	6	G	3	0	0	0	120
Rambunctious Reg	4	G	8	0	0	0	838
Rambunctious Ryan	3	G	13	1	1	1	15,069
Ramekin	5	M	9	3	1	2	6,000
Rameses	5	G	4	0	0	0	189
Ramianu	6	H	5	1	0	0	6,748
Ramillus	4	G	4	0	0	0	900
Ramiro	5	G	15	2	3	1	13,750
Ramito	11	G	5	0	0	0	400
Rammers Best	3	F	8	3	1	1	34,190
Ramona C	3	F	8	1	0	1	14,030
Rampaging Alf	7	G	1	0	0	0	0
Rampant	3	G	1	0	0	0	0
Rampoldi	5	G	11	5	3	0	80,252
Ran a Ground	9	G	4	0	0	0	258
Ran D Scott	6	G	5	1	1	1	9,620
Ran for the Dough	4	F	10	2	3	1	101,520
Ran South	5	H	13	0	1	2	8,764
Ranata's Gold	4	G	3	0	0	0	235
Ranch House Ruckus	3	G	10	1	3	2	28,062
Ranchipur	4	F	15	1	2	4	9,694
Rancid Billy	6	G	12	1	2	1	2,425
Rancocas Mist	7	M	5	0	0	1	2,075
Rancour	7	G	2	0	0	0	0
Randamm	3	F	6	0	2	0	18,908
Randaroo	4	F	3	2	0	1	181,365
Randell G	4	G	16	4	2	2	15,760
Randi Brandy	3	F	10	4	1	1	25,821
Randi's Ceremony	3	F	4	0	0	0	221
Randi's Man	12	G	1	0	0	0	372
Randlord	4	C	8	0	0	1	3,564
Randolph Attheloop	7	G	14	1	2	4	21,447
Randolph Leader	3	G	6	1	1	0	12,474
Random Chance	3	F	1	0	0	0	0
Random Choice	2	G	8	1	0	1	26,748
Random Genes	3	G	4	0	0	0	305
Random Gold	3	G	8	1	2	2	22,928
Random Illusions	4	F	5	1	1	0	5,946
Random Memo	3	G	4	1	1	1	42,250
Random Passage	3	F	8	1	0	2	10,645
Random Thoughts	4	F	12	2	1	2	29,069
Randy Andy	10	G	13	1	2	0	8,594
Randy's Best Man	3	C	15	2	5	2	26,980
Randy's Ruler	3	G	8	0	1	1	1,809
Raneem	6	G	10	2	0	1	40,687
Ranelagh	4	G	4	0	1	0	3,740
Rangeley Rebel	6	G	1	0	0	0	0
Ranger Annie	5	M	1	0	0	0	64
Ranger B.	3	C	11	2	2	4	16,534
Ranger Chance	4	G	14	1	5	3	44,555
Ranger One	3	G	3	1	0	1	17,020
Ranger's G Man	3	G	9	0	0	1	1,296
Rangers Gone West	4	F	8	0	0	2	1,692
Ranglen Jack	4	G	10	0	1	1	6,132
Rani Ran	3	F	2	0	0	0	462
Ranlata	5	M	8	1	0	0	3,160
Raniraj	7	G	6	0	0	0	150
Ranjan	3	G	5	0	1	0	3,780

Horse	Age	Sex	Sts	1st	2d	3d	Won
Ransom C. B.	2	G	5	0	1	0	3,640
Ransom Demanded	2	C	4	1	1	1	25,560
Ransom Paid	4	C	3	0	0	0	1,151
Ransom the Krooner	4	G	1	0	1	0	4,780
Ransom the Redhead	3	F	8	1	0	0	6,336
Ransom the Royalty	5	G	12	1	0	1	8,485
Ransome Money	4	G	5	1	0	0	7,080
Ransome Road	5	G	9	4	1	3	16,248
Ransom's Fire	6	G	9	1	0	0	5,473
Ranswan	9	H	1	0	0	0	0
Rantnrave	6	M	4	1	0	1	7,998
Rao Man	5	G	9	0	1	1	2,117
Rao Raja	2	G	1	0	0	0	0
Rap	5	H	12	1	3	2	19,345
Rap a Newe	4	F	3	0	0	0	152
Rapadash (IRE)	5	G	13	1	4	0	21,575
Raphaelite	3	C	2	1	1	0	11,520
Raphael's Finest	2	F	5	1	0	2	12,100
Rapid	7	M	9	1	3	0	9,276
Rapid Audition	6	M	3	0	1	0	1,780
Rapid Baby	4	G	8	4	2	0	16,505
Rapid Bob	4	G	2	1	0	0	6,675
Rapid Cam	3	F	9	0	2	0	3,731
Rapid Dan	3	G	5	0	0	0	280
Rapid Dance	2	G	2	1	0	0	3,120
Rapid Flow	2	F	4	1	0	0	10,340
Rapid Fred	5	H	4	1	1	1	3,850
Rapid L N L	2	F	3	0	0	0	280
Rapid Lady	3	F	18	1	1	2	6,660
Rapid Lee	4	G	10	1	1	3	7,552
Rapid Proof	4	G	6	1	2	2	52,811
Rapid Raj	5	G	8	2	0	3	40,820
Rapid Recovery	3	F	3	0	0	0	275
Rapid Red	4	G	14	3	2	2	25,568
Rapid Regal	6	G	17	0	3	0	5,207
Rapid Revalation	3	F	12	4	2	0	41,194
Rapid Rhythm	2	C	1	0	0	0	300
Rapid Rickey	3	C	4	1	1	1	37,774
Rapid Rob	3	G	10	3	0	0	43,860
Rapid Roger	10	G	7	1	1	1	11,685
Rapid Rose	5	M	3	0	0	0	0
Rapid Rotation	5	H	5	0	2	2	7,524
Rapid Royal	2	C	9	1	1	0	10,750
Rapid Runaway	3	F	4	1	1	0	18,676
Rapid Rush	3	F	10	1	2	3	6,889
Rapid Slew	5	H	4	0	0	0	227
Rapid Vali	6	G	8	0	1	1	1,672
Rapid Wolf	4	G	17	1	0	1	3,815
Rapide	5	G	16	3	3	2	23,712
Rapidough	9	G	8	1	1	1	31,367
Rapidrunstheriver	7	M	13	0	1	1	7,790
Rapier Dance	4	G	3	0	0	0	2,035
Rappahannock	4	C	12	1	1	3	15,290
Rappatap	3	C	13	2	0	3	12,698
Rappel	4	C	6	1	2	0	38,580
Raptor Speed	3	F	4	0	0	0	2,034
Rapture's Report	5	M	6	0	0	1	1,300
Rare Affair	7	M	12	0	0	2	2,456
Rare an Windy	3	G	14	2	3	5	33,079
Rare and Sixy	4	F	4	2	0	0	9,990
Rare Antique	5	M	14	0	0	0	3,572
Rare Approach	4	F	14	0	2	5	8,365
Rare Bianconi	2	F	2	0	0	0	0
Rare Bull	2	G	5	0	1	1	7,154
Rare Bush	4	G	3	0	0	1	2,020
Rare Business	8	G	4	0	0	0	228
Rare Call	3	C	12	2	2	2	52,875
Rare Catch	10	G	3	1	0	0	897
Rare Cougar	2	C	8	0	1	1	4,059
Rare Cure	6	G	10	2	3	0	124,800
Rare Deputy	5	H	16	2	5	1	26,384
Rare Discernment	3	F	11	2	4	0	17,545
Rare Echo	6	G	3	0	0	0	70
Rare Edition	8	M	6	0	1	1	1,000
Rare Expectations	3	F	3	1	1	1	13,815
Rare Fool	3	G	10	1	3	1	13,246
Rare Friends	5	G	5	2	3	0	102,860
Rare Gift	3	F	8	2	1	4	161,220
Rare Glitter	3	F	12	1	2	1	21,897
Rare Glorious	6	G	7	1	1	3	4,748
Rare Gold	4	F	4	1	1	1	42,900
Rare Honor	4	F	13	2	1	2	14,949
Rare Irish Mist	3	F	1	0	0	0	0
Rare Jewel	7	G	9	3	0	0	20,522
Rare Joey	2	G	3	0	0	0	894
Rare Kiss	3	F	7	1	1	1	7,977
Rare Magic	2	F	2	0	0	0	0
Rare Mark	6	G	1	0	0	0	0
Rare Master	6	M	12	0	0	1	1,743
Rare Miswaki	3	F	8	1	1	2	14,470
Rare N Pretty	3	F	8	0	1	0	5,297
Rare Native	8	G	13	1	0	4	8,441
Rare Overture	3	F	7	1	2	2	12,866
Rare Paradigm	8	G	7	0	1	0	3,575
Rare Pass	5	M	8	1	3	1	9,810
Rare Passion	2	F	2	0	0	0	3,153
Rare Performance	3	F	3	0	0	0	575
Rare Rachel	5	M	9	0	1	1	3,195
Rare Remark	3	G	5	0	1	1	5,688
Rare Request	3	G	13	2	4	3	54,185
Rare Stone	5	H	2	0	0	0	150
Rare Storm	3	C	3	0	0	0	373
Rare Strudel	4	F	11	1	0	1	3,322
Rare Sweetheart	4	F	8	0	2	3	7,290
Rare Tex	2	G	2	2	0	0	9,000
Rare Thro	2	F	3	0	0	0	460
Rare Time Machine	5	M	7	1	3	1	14,779
Rare Tower	4	G	16	2	1	1	18,898
Rare Treasure	3	F	7	0	2	1	12,225
Rare Value	2	G	3	1	0	1	13,708
Rare Will	4	G	11	2	1	0	21,500
Rare Wisdome	7	G	2	0	0	0	610
Rarely Caught	3	F	10	2	2	1	20,655
Rareness	4	G	6	0	0	1	2,165
Raresean	3	F	2	0	0	1	470
Rarest Love	5	H	16	3	1	5	24,926
Rarified	4	C	2	0	0	0	0
Raring to Go	6	M	1	0	0	0	300
Ras Tafari	3	G	5	1	0	0	4,953
Rasby	9	G	13	2	1	1	22,807
Rascal	2	G	1	0	0	0	0
Rascal Russ	10	G	5	0	0	1	2,310
Rascal's Lynnie	5	M	3	0	1	1	6,800
Rase a Fraser	6	M	8	0	0	1	1,086
Rasha	8	G	10	1	0	3	1,504
Rashard Lamar	4	G	2	1	0	0	14,220
Rasm	2	C	3	0	0	1	3,500
Rasor D	8	G	12	0	0	2	5,172
Raspberry Beret	3	F	9	1	0	1	15,940
Raspberry Wine	2	F	1	0	1	0	5,600
Rasta Dancer	3	F	2	0	2	0	7,140
Rasty	5	G	16	4	5	1	27,475
Rat Like Cunning	3	G	14	4	1	1	71,357
Ratafee	3	F	4	0	0	1	290
Rate Above	5	G	3	0	1	0	1,962
Rate Base	8	G	5	1	0	0	11,690
Rate Increase	3	F	2	0	0	1	1,840
Rate Me Ninety Six	2	C	1	0	0	0	135
Rated Up Blue	4	F	8	0	0	0	292
Rathdrum	5	G	1	0	0	0	34
Rather B Pennyless	3	C	14	3	2	1	40,175
Rather Be Rare	4	F	4	1	0	1	3,976
Rather Bee Good	3	F	3	0	0	0	3,485
Rather Have Rubies	3	F	9	2	1	1	78,440
Rather Risky	4	F	13	1	1	0	6,714
Rathleen	4	F	5	0	3	0	35,743
Rating Agency	3	G	6	1	1	1	39,398
Rationalexuberance	2	C	2	0	1	0	8,380
Rattata	4	G	10	0	0	1	1,445
Rattle and Hum	5	G	1	0	0	0	0
Rattle N Snap	3	G	6	0	1	0	2,200
Rattle On Son	5	G	13	3	1	4	18,480
Rattletrap Moment	5	G	5	0	0	0	486
Rattling Count	8	G	7	0	0	0	1,118
Raunchy Cat	4	F	4	1	1	0	3,200
Ravadon	3	C	1	0	0	0	0
Ravalli Girl	4	F	11	1	1	1	44,855
Ravaro (BRZ)	9	G	9	1	1	3	38,594

Horse	Age	Sex	Sts	1st	2d	3d	Won
Rave a Pok	5	M	3	0	0	0	0
Rave Party	3	C	4	2	0	0	34,440
Rave Up	4	G	6	1	0	0	4,260
Raven Cliff Falls	3	C	6	1	1	0	12,467
Raven Hill	6	G	3	0	0	0	258
Raven Ruhl	6	G	8	2	0	1	10,605
Ravens Desire	3	F	2	0	0	0	0
Raven's End	3	F	11	0	0	1	4,505
Ravens Reef	3	G	3	0	0	1	990
Ravidashinal	3	F	3	0	0	1	3,305
Ravine Rose	4	F	2	0	0	1	2,750
Raving Rocket	2	C	4	2	1	0	40,400
Raving Willie	5	H	9	0	2	0	6,680
Ravinia Girl	5	M	11	1	0	0	3,800
Ravishing Russian	3	F	5	1	0	0	4,365
Ravishly	3	F	3	0	0	0	2,177
Raw Courage	4	G	3	0	0	0	252
Raw Data	3	G	4	0	0	2	4,960
Raw Energy	3	C	3	0	0	0	1,560
Raw General	3	G	8	1	1	0	35,307
Raw Imagination	8	G	2	0	0	0	420
Raw Power	4	C	9	1	2	1	62,810
Raw Roy	4	G	11	0	1	2	4,405
Raw Talent	6	G	7	3	1	1	9,046
Raw Win	2	G	7	0	0	0	1,196
Rawlpindi Express	4	G	4	0	0	2	2,163
Rawston	5	G	8	2	4	0	6,155
Ray Boy	6	G	2	0	0	1	440
Ray Smiley	5	G	2	0	1	0	880
Rayco Steel	4	F	15	1	0	0	3,420
Raylene	4	F	9	4	2	2	210,134
Raymond Springs	5	G	15	2	1	3	33,973
Raymond's Dream	6	M	3	1	0	1	30,600
Rayo de Plata	6	G	8	0	1	0	10,063
Rayo de Sol	3	F	1	0	0	0	0
Rayo Island	5	G	9	0	0	0	1,136
Rayon	4	C	5	1	0	1	34,476
Raypour (IRE)	7	G	4	0	2	0	2,024
Rays a Ruler	7	G	35	1	1	7	36,575
Rays Derby Toy	2	C	3	0	0	0	1,120
Ray's Ego	5	H	2	0	0	0	195
Ray's Gray Gear	4	F	2	0	0	0	421
Rays Impulse	2	F	1	0	0	0	0
Rays Last Word	3	F	6	0	2	0	7,190
Ray's Right Again	2	G	5	0	0	0	900
Ray's Treasure	6	G	2	1	1	0	3,200
Rayvo's Beau	3	C	2	0	0	1	5,308
Ray'z of Gold	8	G	4	0	0	0	296
Rayzi Zu	7	G	5	0	0	0	543
Razacat	4	F	8	1	2	1	14,705
Razamataza	3	C	6	1	0	1	8,037
Razari	2	C	1	1	0	0	22,860
Razcal	2	G	1	0	0	0	910
Razen Glory	4	F	3	1	0	0	7,543
Razen Hazen	3	G	7	0	2	2	36,279
Razik	9	G	2	2	0	0	35,400
Razodiazo	6	G	4	0	0	0	200
Razoo Eighty Two	5	M	3	0	0	0	250
Razor	2	C	4	2	0	1	50,520
Razor Barb	4	F	11	3	2	4	64,653
Razor Blade	4	G	3	0	0	0	0
Razor Stubble	5	M	3	0	0	0	2,280
Razor's Terror	3	F	3	2	0	1	16,800
Razyana's Avenu	4	F	1	0	0	0	0
Razz Beret	6	G	8	0	0	0	491
Razzaam	5	M	1	0	0	0	0
Razzact	6	G	2	0	0	0	190
Razzle Dazzle Guy	3	G	20	2	4	2	24,748
Rb's Glitter	3	C	4	0	1	0	17,861
Rbslewd	6	G	10	0	0	0	487
Rchrystlsapistol	5	M	10	3	2	1	13,342
Re Gal E Tee	3	F	1	0	0	0	0
Re Quest Approval	4	F	13	3	2	0	25,149
Reach for Ameri	8	G	3	0	0	0	132
Reach for the Top	5	M	2	1	0	0	2,936
Reaching Up	4	F	5	3	0	0	62,311
Reactionary	5	G	11	4	0	1	17,800
Read Me My Rights	5	M	11	2	1	1	66,680
Read the Cards	7	M	8	1	1	1	5,255
Read the Footnotes	3	C	3	1	0	0	210,000
Readaboutme	4	F	14	3	1	3	15,335
Readers Eskimo	7	G	16	1	3	4	18,331
Readersbestbuilder	3	G	7	1	0	0	13,920
Readiness	2	F	4	1	0	0	4,940
Reading	3	F	3	1	2	0	12,800
Readon	2	G	2	0	0	0	0
Ready and Tough	3	F	6	1	0	2	22,230
Ready At Noon	4	F	1	0	0	0	0
Ready Falls	5	M	7	2	1	0	31,888
Ready Fire Aim	4	F	3	0	0	0	877
Ready for Glory	4	G	12	1	1	2	9,692
Ready for Island	8	H	1	0	0	0	163
Ready for Love	5	G	12	5	0	0	32,800
Ready for More	6	G	1	0	0	0	40
Ready for Regent	2	G	4	0	0	1	2,563
Ready for Takeoff	3	C	5	0	0	0	1,185
Ready Gold	3	C	5	0	1	1	2,810
Ready Hike	7	G	8	1	1	1	11,019
Ready Money	5	G	7	0	1	0	3,056
Ready 'n Gone	5	G	9	2	0	1	14,129
Ready Prospect	3	G	14	3	1	4	36,455
Ready Ready Runrun	2	G	3	0	1	2	5,400
Ready Ruler	2	C	7	2	2	2	114,470
Ready This Time	4	F	2	0	0	0	0
Ready to Flee	2	C	4	0	1	0	5,215
Ready to Flirt	3	G	2	0	0	0	1,300
Ready to Live	2	F	7	2	3	0	79,500
Ready to Rage	3	C	9	1	3	3	25,993
Ready to Roll (IRE)	9	G	6	1	0	0	6,921
Ready to Snap	2	F	2	1	0	0	7,095
Ready to Swing	2	C	2	0	0	0	0
Ready Won	3	G	15	1	0	2	23,458
Readyfortheweekend	2	F	4	1	0	0	15,000
Readygogo	3	F	1	0	0	0	0
Ready's Gal	2	F	3	2	1	0	155,200
Reagally Light	4	F	3	0	0	0	250
Reagan Ct.	4	G	5	0	0	0	652
Real Addiction	5	G	2	0	0	0	0
Real Assets	5	M	19	1	2	5	28,805
Real Bashful	4	G	1	0	0	0	66
Real Bear	4	F	2	0	1	0	5,540
Real Beauty	4	F	8	0	0	1	1,683
Real Big Rita	4	F	3	0	0	0	261
Real Blonde	4	F	5	0	1	1	24,640
Real Boy (AUS)	8	G	2	0	0	0	236
Real Bull	3	C	4	0	0	0	539
Real Cause	5	M	4	2	0	1	23,360
Real Classic	3	G	4	0	0	1	2,800
Real Collateral	3	C	1	0	0	0	375
Real Contender	3	C	1	0	0	0	0
Real Creek	5	G	12	4	4	0	52,675
Real Dandy	2	C	7	1	4	0	57,385
Real Deal	3	F	3	1	0	0	15,600
Real Desire	4	F	8	0	3	1	5,126
Real Dignity	4	G	9	1	2	2	6,901
Real Dreamy	3	G	4	2	1	0	88,860
Real Echo	4	G	8	5	2	0	128,100
Real Edge	2	F	1	0	0	0	0
Real Encounter	7	G	12	0	1	3	3,470
Real Endurance	3	F	1	0	0	0	129
Real Excessive	3	F	13	1	0	1	5,088
Real Fappi	6	H	9	1	2	0	22,942
Real Forum	5	G	6	1	0	0	7,620
Real Frosty	6	G	15	2	0	1	12,275
Real Gallant	6	G	1	0	0	0	0
Real George	4	C	6	0	0	0	637
Real Golden	5	G	8	0	0	2	12,494
Real Good	3	G	16	3	0	2	14,691
Real Good Deal	3	F	9	3	0	1	33,444
Real Hot	4	G	13	2	0	1	6,974
Real Intrusion	8	M	7	0	2	2	8,089
Real Irish	3	C	11	0	0	0	210
Real Isis	2	F	1	0	0	0	0
Real Kayla Dan	4	G	2	0	0	1	1,216
Real Lady's Man	4	G	14	1	2	2	8,108
Real Leader	4	G	8	0	0	0	447
Real Life	5	G	7	3	1	3	39,560
Real Mama	7	M	3	0	0	0	930

Horse	Age	Sex	Sts	1st	2d	3d	Won
Real Man	3	G	3	0	0	0	0
Real Memories	2	F	7	0	1	0	6,220
Real Monarch	4	G	16	2	2	1	18,076
Real Note	3	C	8	1	3	0	5,672
Real Nucay	4	G	4	0	0	0	451
Real Paranoide	6	M	11	4	1	2	71,200
Real Picknick	3	F	2	0	0	0	280
Real Priceless	3	F	1	0	0	0	0
Real Queen	3	F	7	0	0	2	4,180
Real Quick Sand	3	F	3	0	0	0	0
Real Quiet Cat	3	C	6	0	0	1	3,455
Real Quiet Guy	2	G	2	0	0	0	0
Real Quiet Heath	3	G	12	3	0	3	25,140
Real Rhythm	5	G	13	0	2	4	6,363
Real Ringer	9	G	14	0	3	4	3,972
Real Royal	3	C	3	0	1	0	5,886
Real Salty	4	G	7	3	1	0	12,885
Real Saucy	4	G	8	2	0	2	22,417
Real Skippy	4	C	8	1	1	2	7,700
Real Soon	3	G	9	0	1	0	2,250
Real Souvenir	3	G	11	1	0	3	10,194
Real Special	7	G	15	7	4	1	85,529
Real Spitfire	2	F	6	1	1	0	20,485
Real Stack	4	F	12	0	0	1	2,475
Real Sterling	4	F	9	3	0	0	14,265
Real Stuff	3	F	10	0	1	1	3,118
Real Sweet Deal	3	C	1	0	1	0	8,800
Real Swell	3	G	10	3	1	1	24,401
Real Tears	5	G	12	1	0	2	8,240
Real Terms	7	G	5	0	0	0	344
Real Tickled	3	F	2	0	0	0	348
Real Tomcat	4	G	16	3	0	2	10,669
Real Town Guy	3	C	24	1	4	3	23,015
Real Trooper	3	G	11	3	2	4	94,865
Real True Spirit	6	G	5	2	1	1	4,968
Real Vain	2	F	4	1	0	0	15,827
Real Valid	3	C	7	1	0	0	4,918
Real Whisper	6	G	4	0	0	0	591
Real Wildcat	4	G	4	0	0	0	660
Real Women	8	M	4	0	0	0	2,204
Real Zealot	4	F	9	0	0	2	2,564
Realacarr	5	H	16	1	3	2	24,550
Realbean	2	G	1	0	0	0	780
Realignment	5	G	14	4	0	1	18,153
Realism	3	C	10	1	2	3	11,778
Realities Runamuck	4	G	10	0	1	1	2,792
Reality Affirmed	3	F	8	0	1	0	2,840
Reality Belle	2	F	3	2	1	0	5,954
Reality Cat	4	G	5	0	1	1	3,710
Reality Check	6	G	5	1	0	0	10,390
Reality Day	3	C	1	0	0	0	125
Reality Doll	6	M	2	0	1	0	1,740
Reality Lady	7	M	10	0	0	0	625
Reality Makin	3	F	10	0	0	0	1,762
Reality Mine	3	G	3	2	1	0	26,220
Reality Mountain	3	G	5	1	0	3	13,515
Reality Quest	3	C	9	2	0	2	21,510
Reality Rox	2	F	1	0	0	0	0
Reality Sets In	8	G	4	0	0	1	2,875
Reality Step	3	F	12	1	3	2	19,965
Reality Ticket	3	G	1	0	0	0	0
Realityiscountry	4	F	13	4	1	3	33,625
Reality's Affair	6	M	11	5	0	2	42,313
Reality's Gem	9	G	12	1	0	0	6,414
Reality's Pine	9	H	3	0	0	1	825
Really a Prince	3	G	16	2	2	1	34,916
Really American	3	F	12	2	3	0	81,432
Really Bad News	4	G	11	1	0	1	10,699
Really Big	6	G	1	0	0	0	0
Really Big Boy	2	C	1	0	1	0	5,200
Really Crafty	11	G	11	0	1	0	1,496
Really Fabulous	3	G	6	0	0	0	678
Really Free	6	G	11	3	2	2	16,273
Really Good Whisky	5	G	11	0	1	3	5,643
Really Irish	7	G	12	2	1	2	16,740
Really Kissed	6	M	4	0	0	0	220
Really Ladylike	4	F	8	4	0	1	11,042
Really No Saint	6	G	10	2	0	1	6,780
Really Orr Not	9	G	5	0	1	0	1,042
Really Perky	3	F	8	2	0	1	9,748
Really Radical	9	M	7	1	1	0	1,125
Really Ready	9	G	8	2	1	1	7,548
Really Royal	5	M	12	2	3	0	92,900
Really Sharp	4	C	8	0	2	1	9,012
Really Silver	5	M	2	0	0	0	0
Really Something	5	M	14	2	0	0	11,949
Really Sumptin	6	G	1	0	0	0	73
Really Suspect	4	G	5	0	2	1	9,780
Really Tough	4	G	10	4	2	0	25,000
Really Traveling	7	G	8	3	0	1	37,010
Really Tricky	3	G	7	0	0	2	5,740
Really Unique	3	G	3	0	1	0	560
Really Who	4	G	8	1	1	2	24,240
Reallyahotnumber	5	G	2	0	0	0	620
Realriskybusiness	4	C	5	0	1	0	4,500
Reanna's Pride	5	M	3	0	0	0	180
Reap the Wind	4	G	11	1	0	1	8,984
Reaping Tirade	5	G	2	0	0	0	0
Reappear	2	F	1	0	0	0	0
Reapply	3	C	2	0	0	0	607
Reason for Justice	5	M	4	0	0	0	368
Reason This	4	G	7	1	0	0	7,590
Reason to Be Astar	10	M	20	1	1	1	5,292
Reason to Buck	4	F	6	1	1	1	1,998
Reason to Jett	4	G	9	1	0	0	8,739
Reason to Squall	7	G	2	1	0	0	10,230
Reason to Storm	4	G	9	1	3	1	10,180
Reason to Talk	5	M	8	0	0	2	17,183
Reason to Win	6	G	10	2	2	0	29,315
Reason Unknown	5	G	10	0	0	1	2,240
Reasonable Avenue	3	F	6	1	1	0	12,660
Reasonable Cat	4	G	6	2	0	0	11,613
Reasonable Code	4	F	11	3	2	3	36,008
Reasonable Diane	6	M	15	3	0	3	10,727
Reasonable Embrace	3	G	4	0	0	0	814
Reasonable Fee	2	C	1	0	0	0	0
Reasonable Tempt	3	F	7	2	0	0	9,299
Reasonably Brite	3	F	8	3	1	2	71,260
Reasonforrejection	6	M	5	0	0	1	913
Reasontofly	5	M	6	0	1	0	4,860
Reatta Pass	5	M	9	2	1	1	47,340
Reaveling Nuthin	4	G	5	0	0	0	970
Reba's Gold	7	H	3	0	0	0	22,500
Reba's Rebel	5	G	2	1	1	0	3,200
Rebbeca Gold	4	F	12	1	0	3	2,347
Rebecca G Dianne	4	F	3	1	0	0	9,504
Rebecca Rose	3	F	1	0	0	0	0
Rebecca's Charm	5	M	3	0	2	1	23,050
Rebel	4	F	2	0	1	1	4,740
Rebel Army	2	C	2	2	0	0	37,080
Rebel Cotton	7	H	1	0	0	0	180
Rebel Gal	3	F	9	2	0	2	13,280
Rebel Genes	5	G	5	0	2	2	2,485
Rebel Grey	5	G	7	0	0	0	633
Rebel Lil	3	F	5	0	1	0	8,100
Rebel Proud	4	G	5	1	0	0	3,180
Rebel Rage	5	G	6	0	2	0	9,848
Rebel Rex	8	G	1	0	0	0	70
Rebel Roots	4	G	11	2	1	2	6,888
Rebel Rose	3	F	10	3	2	1	62,500
Rebel Slew	3	F	14	2	1	0	34,410
Rebel Song	4	G	18	2	3	3	42,059
Rebel Winner	4	C	3	0	0	0	0
Rebelano	5	M	3	0	0	1	1,573
Rebelcat	3	G	9	1	3	1	12,034
Rebelette	4	F	4	2	1	0	14,588
Rebelious Peace	5	G	7	0	0	1	1,053
Rebellious Crook	3	G	3	0	0	0	0
Rebelous Zone	6	G	14	0	0	5	7,395
Rebel's Mission	5	G	17	1	2	3	20,349
Rebel's Question	3	F	3	0	0	0	3,840
Rebel's Revenge	4	G	6	1	0	0	10,983
Rebelscause	4	F	3	0	0	0	270
Rebelwithoutacause	3	G	4	0	0	0	237
Rebolero	5	M	14	3	1	2	10,917
Rebonah	4	F	5	0	1	1	5,584
Rebound Boy	12	G	3	0	1	0	880
Rebridled	10	G	2	0	0	0	0

Horse	Age	Sex	Sts	1st	2d	3d	Won
Rebridled Dreams	4	F	9	0	0	0	10,567
Rebs Agenda	3	F	8	1	1	0	8,125
Reb's Gold	11	G	6	0	0	0	668
Rebuffed	9	G	10	3	3	0	38,494
Recall	9	H	1	0	0	0	0
Received Your Fax	3	G	1	0	0	0	324
Receivership	4	F	3	1	1	1	41,100
Recency	6	G	3	0	0	0	183
Recess in Heaven	6	M	14	0	1	1	4,767
Reche Diamant	5	M	2	0	0	0	940
Recherche	4	F	3	0	0	0	1,550
Rechonic	3	G	12	1	0	1	11,427
Reciprocate	4	C	1	0	0	0	0
Reckless Affair	5	G	8	1	2	1	20,170
Reckless Babe	4	F	9	0	0	1	1,316
Reckless Ghost	4	G	7	0	1	2	11,747
Reckless Hero	3	C	7	2	1	2	83,496
Reckless Innocent	3	F	6	0	3	0	6,335
Reckless Ways	3	G	10	2	2	0	83,826
Recky	4	F	5	0	1	1	5,860
Recognize Her	4	F	7	1	0	1	10,621
Recognize Me	8	M	22	0	3	0	7,015
Recollection	4	C	2	0	0	0	680
Recommend	2	C	3	0	0	0	476
Reconnection	4	G	16	2	3	0	20,258
Reconsider Me	4	F	3	0	0	0	0
Record Assembly	4	G	13	1	2	4	46,605
Record Avenger	3	F	14	3	2	2	17,451
Record Level	12	G	8	0	2	1	7,465
Record Pick	10	G	1	0	0	0	0
Record Smashed	3	C	3	0	3	0	16,580
Record Tide	4	C	5	1	1	0	33,084
Record Toast	3	F	12	0	0	4	4,665
Recordado (ARG)	5	H	6	1	0	0	30,940
Recorded Time	4	F	9	0	0	1	6,025
Rectify	2	C	2	0	0	0	1,210
Rectory Hill	3	C	8	0	4	1	35,046
Recycle Mike	3	G	15	1	2	4	10,925
Red Ambush	3	F	5	0	0	0	845
Red and Free	4	F	1	0	0	0	103
Red and Royal	3	G	18	2	6	2	36,904
Red Antics	6	G	2	0	0	0	520
Red At Morn	4	G	18	1	2	2	10,482
Red At the Helm	4	F	12	1	3	2	16,628
Red At the Wire	7	G	11	0	1	1	1,376
Red Attraction	3	F	2	0	0	1	752
Red Azalea	4	F	6	0	1	0	2,380
Red Badge	8	G	16	1	2	3	10,762
Red Bails	6	G	19	1	7	6	22,564
Red Band	3	G	8	0	1	4	13,517
Red Band Run	3	F	2	0	0	0	1,450
Red Bird Lover	2	C	2	0	0	0	0
Red Birds Big Hart	2	C	7	1	0	2	8,196
Red Bird's Meister	3	G	2	1	1	0	10,400
Red Blast	3	G	6	0	0	0	177
Red Blaze	3	F	1	0	1	0	5,000
Red Boa	2	F	5	1	1	0	20,133
Red Booom	4	F	14	3	3	2	64,000
Red Boots	3	F	6	0	2	0	3,170
Red Box	6	G	6	0	0	0	579
Red Briar	3	G	6	0	2	2	13,666
Red Briar (IRE)	5	G	7	0	1	0	4,716
Red Brick Avenue	5	M	20	2	5	2	22,177
Red Cell	4	F	10	1	1	3	53,480
Red Chief	3	G	3	0	0	0	315
Red Cielo	6	G	12	1	4	1	14,342
Red Clay Coins	10	G	1	0	0	0	73
Red Cloud	4	G	5	1	0	0	1,607
Red Coconut	3	G	8	1	0	0	11,040
Red Craft	3	C	2	0	0	0	90
Red Creek	3	G	4	1	0	2	5,468
Red Cross	3	F	9	1	2	1	22,660
Red Crusader	3	G	13	3	2	2	57,390
Red Detonator	4	F	1	0	0	0	160
Red Dice	4	F	11	1	3	4	21,400
Red Dirt Darlin	4	F	6	0	1	1	2,786
Red Dirt Roughneck	9	G	13	0	0	1	1,050
Red Down South	4	G	10	1	1	1	38,981
Red Dragon	9	G	9	0	2	3	13,950
Red Duchess	4	F	8	0	3	0	17,620
Red Dynamite	3	F	14	1	3	4	8,379
Red Dynamo	5	G	15	1	1	3	12,735
Red Eagle	6	G	4	0	0	0	420
Red Earthquake	3	C	12	2	1	2	48,190
Red Emerald	4	F	8	2	1	1	12,147
Red Escapade	2	F	4	0	0	0	0
Red Exit	7	G	12	1	1	2	7,711
Red Eye	8	G	11	4	3	0	37,407
Red Eye Bull	2	C	2	0	0	0	675
Red Eye Radio	2	C	2	0	0	1	1,725
Red Eyed Jet	2	G	6	0	0	0	2,385
Red Film (GB)	5	M	5	0	0	0	1,410
Red Flag Ahead	6	M	7	0	0	1	3,250
Red Foe	4	G	14	0	0	1	2,840
Red Forli	6	M	7	1	1	3	2,120
Red Fox Fire	4	F	5	1	1	1	6,373
Red Fox Tail	7	G	12	0	3	3	5,312
Red Fred	7	G	7	0	0	2	1,000
Red Gulch	3	G	9	1	2	1	21,340
Red Gunner	3	C	4	0	0	1	2,660
Red Gypsy	2	F	1	0	0	0	0
Red Hair Lady	3	F	12	1	3	3	27,106
Red Handed Robin	2	F	4	1	2	0	43,150
Red Hat	3	G	5	0	1	0	1,000
Red Hawkeye	5	G	10	0	2	3	26,193
Red Haze	3	C	2	0	1	0	8,568
Red Headed Jimmy	3	G	5	0	0	0	619
Red Headed Romeo	5	G	6	0	1	0	1,398
Red Heads Bay	6	G	12	3	3	3	6,167
Red Hogan	3	C	9	0	0	0	0
Red Hot Affair	3	F	12	3	1	1	28,561
Red Hot Angel	7	M	11	1	4	1	4,888
Red Hot Cat	3	G	8	2	1	0	19,522
Red Hot Chiquita	5	M	4	1	1	0	7,540
Red Hot Chocolate	3	C	1	0	0	0	0
Red Hot Desert	2	G	6	0	0	3	3,414
Red Hot Dollar	4	F	15	2	1	2	16,278
Red Hot Fay	2	F	1	0	0	0	95
Red Hot Flyer	8	G	2	0	0	0	363
Red Hot Fox	5	G	6	2	0	2	5,760
Red Hot Helen	4	F	9	2	2	1	26,515
Red Hot Hound	4	G	2	1	0	0	3,226
Red Hot Kitty	4	F	3	0	0	2	4,108
Red Hot Luke	8	G	4	0	0	0	153
Red Hot Margaret	3	F	2	0	0	0	199
Red Hot Peppers	3	F	1	0	0	0	0
Red Hot Pistol	6	G	4	0	0	1	596
Red Hot Prospect	4	G	9	0	0	0	369
Red Hot Rocket	6	G	5	0	0	1	1,360
Red Hot Secret	4	G	14	2	4	2	55,039
Red Hot Spot	5	G	6	1	2	0	43,120
Red Hot Star	4	F	11	0	3	4	18,410
Red Hot Tequila	3	F	7	2	1	0	21,570
Red Hot to Handle	3	F	5	0	0	1	1,543
Red Hot Wish	5	G	8	0	0	1	4,698
Red I Am	3	C	13	1	0	1	4,106
Red I Ransom	4	C	6	0	0	1	1,286
Red Ide	4	F	10	1	1	2	10,889
Red Idol	2	F	2	0	0	0	210
Red in the Morning	5	M	3	1	0	1	4,901
Red Jamie	3	F	4	1	0	0	9,510
Red Jeans	2	F	3	0	0	0	1,170
Red Jeans to Dance	3	F	6	0	1	0	4,120
Red Jenny	4	F	3	0	0	0	422
Red Knuckles	2	C	6	0	0	0	3,990
Red Label	5	G	10	1	1	1	6,309
Red Lava	3	C	8	1	1	1	13,280
Red Leave Rose	4	F	16	1	3	1	12,071
Red Legend	3	G	12	1	2	3	34,940
Red Lifesaver	3	F	10	3	2	1	57,944
Red Lightning	6	G	5	0	0	0	3,300
Red Line Seven	4	G	12	5	1	0	24,062
Red Link	4	G	7	0	0	0	720
Red Lipstick	3	F	1	0	0	0	0
Red M and M	3	C	3	0	0	1	2,622
Red Magic	2	G	3	0	1	0	6,040
Red Malone	3	C	2	0	0	2	5,000
Red Man Walking	4	G	2	0	0	0	156

Horse	Age	Sex	Sts	1st	2d	3d	Won
Red Meena	5	H	5	0	0	0	1,214
Red Mercedes	5	M	6	0	0	0	1,726
Red Miah	6	G	12	2	4	1	15,346
Red Millenium	2	F	4	0	0	0	150
Red Mimi	6	M	4	1	0	0	8,970
Red Mints	4	G	9	2	1	1	17,111
Red Moment	4	G	1	0	0	0	400
Red Moon Rising	4	F	12	2	0	5	16,685
Red Mountain	7	G	2	0	0	1	2,940
Red Mountain Garth	9	G	14	2	2	1	7,552
Red Neck Lady	4	F	10	1	4	2	33,070
Red Nile	2	F	6	1	0	0	10,485
Red October	2	G	4	0	0	0	765
Red Onion	5	H	2	0	0	0	0
Red Opal (IRE)	5	M	3	1	0	0	27,520
Red Orange Cat	3	F	2	0	0	0	900
Red Panda	8	G	1	0	0	0	0
Red Parka Mary	6	M	5	2	0	0	5,410
Red Penny	3	F	14	0	0	0	3,161
Red Pepper Martini	3	C	10	1	1	3	10,365
Red Phase	2	G	1	0	0	0	75
Red Phenomon	4	G	19	3	4	4	16,746
Red Plaid	6	M	9	1	1	1	7,632
Red Point	3	G	13	1	0	0	8,710
Red Pop	4	F	8	1	2	0	9,336
Red Popsicle	2	F	3	1	0	0	8,400
Red Power	6	G	5	0	2	0	8,480
Red Press	8	G	3	0	0	1	1,820
Red Queen	2	F	2	0	0	1	4,700
Red Quest	5	H	11	1	3	3	18,713
Red Rabbit Run	2	G	7	0	1	1	5,050
Red Rage	4	F	14	1	1	0	10,530
Red Rapala	5	G	4	0	0	0	303
Red Rascal	2	C	2	1	0	1	8,520
Red Ravine	3	G	10	1	0	2	6,402
Red Regent	3	G	6	1	0	0	4,886
Red Reigning	5	G	11	0	3	4	10,170
Red Rhino	5	G	6	0	0	0	690
Red Ribbons	4	G	17	5	4	2	74,450
Red Riding Wood	4	F	17	2	1	3	10,734
Red Rioja (IRE)	5	M	1	1	0	0	55,000
Red Ripper	4	G	3	0	0	0	370
Red River Aggie	4	G	4	0	2	0	16,520
Red River Girl	3	F	2	0	0	0	200
Red River Rally	6	G	4	0	0	0	0
Red River Red	6	G	2	0	0	1	440
Red River Ridge	7	G	15	2	0	1	5,984
Red River Rock	8	G	11	1	0	2	2,792
Red River Ruby	3	F	2	0	0	0	324
Red River Showdown	7	M	1	0	0	0	0
Red River Storm	4	G	10	1	0	0	11,085
Red River Valley	9	G	9	0	1	0	3,733
Red River Wine	6	G	6	1	1	0	2,200
Red Roan Dancer	5	G	6	1	2	2	11,506
Red Rock Creek	3	C	1	0	0	0	417
Red Rock Native	3	G	11	1	2	3	30,722
Red Rock Ridge	11	G	11	0	0	2	2,057
Red Rocko	2	G	3	0	0	0	300
Red Rosalyn	6	M	13	0	1	1	3,312
Red Rose Jake	4	G	9	0	0	0	1,132
Red Ruffle	2	F	5	0	2	0	9,485
Red Ryder Band	9	G	8	1	2	2	4,300
Red Said	8	G	4	0	0	1	195
Red Sea (GB)	8	G	2	0	1	0	6,080
Red Seattle	8	G	13	6	1	3	29,940
Red Sherry	5	M	4	0	0	1	1,325
Red Shift	7	G	13	1	0	1	6,431
Red Six	2	C	3	0	0	0	563
Red Sky Guy	5	G	10	0	2	2	4,848
Red Sky's	8	H	2	0	0	1	8,824
Red Snoony	3	F	15	2	0	3	67,863
Red Soldier	4	G	15	4	5	1	92,300
Red Spark	4	G	13	3	1	4	30,470
Red Sprinkles	4	F	18	0	3	4	12,420
Red Squall Coming	3	C	1	0	0	0	0
Red Square	3	G	19	1	1	3	6,149
Red Stick	7	G	8	2	1	1	11,572
Red Streak	3	G	19	0	3	5	10,740
Red Strider	7	G	13	2	1	2	14,157

Horse	Age	Sex	Sts	1st	2d	3d	Won
Red Sunday Racer	4	G	11	1	1	0	6,037
Red Sundown	7	G	10	2	2	0	17,286
Red Sunset	2	F	1	0	0	0	0
Red T K's Star	3	C	18	1	2	4	12,240
Red Tag Clearance	4	F	20	3	4	3	19,302
Red Tag Special	4	G	8	1	2	0	4,383
Red Tequila	2	C	1	0	0	0	155
Red Threat	6	G	1	0	0	0	41
Red Tie Lady	3	F	10	2	3	0	14,245
Red Token	3	G	16	2	2	2	10,710
Red Top (IRE)	3	F	9	2	4	1	58,812
Red Torrent	4	F	3	0	0	0	174
Red Treasure	2	C	3	1	0	0	12,800
Red Truck	3	C	8	1	0	5	21,196
Red Two	9	M	4	0	0	0	489
Red Valhalla	5	G	15	0	3	1	8,496
Red Vein	2	F	2	2	0	0	8,388
Red Velvet Cake	3	G	10	2	2	1	53,014
Red Vines and Wine	2	F	7	0	0	1	4,043
Red Vintage (GB)	5	G	12	1	1	2	52,575
Red Wader	5	H	3	0	0	0	576
Red Wajir	3	G	6	0	0	0	345
Red Wand	4	G	11	2	1	1	10,338
Red Warrior	4	C	3	1	0	0	29,260
Red Watch	3	G	1	0	0	0	60
Red Water	4	C	7	0	1	0	4,050
Red Whisperer	7	H	4	0	1	0	1,416
Red Will Win	3	F	10	0	1	2	5,815
Red Willy	4	G	14	2	2	4	15,260
Red Wing Evan	5	H	3	2	0	0	31,430
Red Wing Son	4	C	1	0	0	0	90
Red Wolf	10	G	5	0	0	0	472
Red Wrecker	3	G	3	0	0	0	0
Red Your Mind	3	R	2	0	0	0	730
Red Zac	5	G	11	3	2	0	41,935
Red Zinger	4	F	3	2	0	1	17,385
Redas Skydancer	7	G	10	0	1	0	9,525
Redaspen	2	F	5	1	3	1	34,177
Redbird	4	F	4	1	0	1	3,352
Redbirds Magic Cat	2	F	1	0	0	0	405
Redbone	5	H	4	0	0	0	0
Redcarpettreatment	5	M	10	1	0	1	17,793
Redclouds At Night	2	F	9	0	0	0	455
Redcuda	4	G	7	1	0	1	8,516
Redd N Hot	5	G	14	3	2	2	14,038
Reddick	9	G	16	3	4	1	20,623
Redding Woods	6	G	9	2	2	0	39,099
Reddy Be a Groom	4	G	2	0	0	0	0
Reddy for Rubys	2	F	3	1	0	1	80,234
Redee Robyn	2	F	4	0	0	0	993
Redeeming Light	2	F	1	0	0	0	140
Redefined	3	C	7	1	0	2	36,160
Redemption Song	2	G	4	1	0	0	15,900
Redeyed Charmer	3	F	5	2	2	0	42,927
Redflex	4	G	14	1	3	3	8,620
Redford	3	G	7	0	1	1	3,725
Redhanded	9	G	5	0	0	0	310
Redhot Dy No Mite	4	F	9	1	2	3	8,400
Redhot Hadif	5	G	6	0	0	0	585
Redhot Roxie	2	F	1	0	0	0	0
Redhy	3	G	2	0	0	0	800
Redi Hot	5	G	18	1	1	4	9,295
Rediculousforever	3	F	7	0	0	0	733
Redinal	4	G	6	1	2	1	2,134
Rediskia	3	F	7	0	2	0	3,420
Redlipsnfingertips	2	F	4	0	1	1	4,566
Redly	6	G	12	3	2	1	23,866
Redmarina	3	F	6	0	0	1	2,777
Redmeansgo	3	F	9	2	2	1	40,360
Rednaround	2	F	1	1	0	0	21,600
Redneck Tune	3	F	3	0	0	0	0
Redon	4	C	6	0	2	1	12,020
Redoubled Miss	5	M	12	2	4	0	216,890
Redoys Move	7	G	7	2	2	0	3,066
Redraw	5	G	13	2	0	2	27,175
Red's Account	3	G	14	2	5	1	14,486
Red's Bokay	4	F	11	0	1	0	1,877
Reds Fling	2	F	4	1	1	0	4,866
Reds Glory	5	G	10	1	0	1	3,664

Horse	Age	Sex	Sts	1st	2d	3d	Won
Reds Gone	5	G	6	0	2	1	3,402
Red's Honor	6	H	5	3	0	0	60,570
Reds Pal	4	G	6	2	0	0	14,135
Red's Place	6	G	6	1	1	2	27,230
Red's Rainbow	4	F	3	0	0	0	1,520
Red's Red	5	G	16	4	2	2	40,267
Red's Rollin	5	G	15	3	1	2	13,326
Red's Silver Girl	3	F	1	0	0	0	0
Red's the Rage	4	G	14	4	1	1	32,863
Redserge	5	G	2	0	0	0	0
Redskin Warrior	3	C	3	1	0	0	58,095
Redstar Dancer	5	G	10	3	3	1	13,497
Reduit (GB)	6	H	2	0	0	0	1,990
Redwana	3	G	1	0	0	0	105
Redwhitenblumin	3	G	3	1	0	2	15,408
Redwinesipper	4	C	13	2	2	2	18,736
Redwood Creek	3	C	4	1	1	1	6,480
Redwood Hallzie	4	F	3	0	0	0	192
Redwood Knot	7	M	1	0	0	0	0
Redyornothereicom	3	C	19	5	4	2	46,602
Reeanita	7	M	10	3	2	2	5,141
Reece and Heather	4	F	13	1	2	2	9,709
Reece's Mark	2	F	1	0	0	0	1,680
Reed and Me	5	M	9	0	0	1	1,334
Reed Paige Won	4	F	4	0	0	1	450
Reedastraffer	3	C	1	0	0	0	653
Reedenlist	3	F	6	0	1	0	3,015
Reeds Ghost	2	G	2	0	0	1	1,310
Reeds Rich	3	G	1	0	0	1	770
Reef	4	F	7	1	2	0	49,980
Reef Diver (GB)	6	G	8	0	1	1	14,280
Reef Treat	3	F	13	3	2	1	19,219
Reefs Sis (GB)	5	M	4	0	0	0	3,337
Reel Conviction	4	F	16	1	0	0	14,523
Reel Deco	3	F	8	1	3	3	12,062
Reel d'Hiver	3	F	7	1	0	1	6,185
Reel Double	3	C	2	0	0	0	440
Reel 'Em In	6	G	4	3	0	1	85,200
Reel Fast Marco	4	G	7	1	0	1	32,990
Reel Icon	3	G	8	1	1	0	6,347
Reel Lass	5	M	2	0	1	0	2,560
Reel On Buddy	2	C	5	0	1	1	4,650
Reel Pepi	7	M	6	0	0	2	1,838
Reel Shiney Chrome	3	F	3	0	0	0	247
Reel Sooner Magic	2	F	1	0	0	0	105
Reel Spiffy	9	M	7	2	1	1	8,598
Reel Trade	4	C	4	0	0	1	2,450
Reelsweetdancer	2	F	1	0	0	0	140
Reem	5	G	1	0	0	0	0
Reenergize	4	F	10	1	2	1	9,637
Reeves Park	2	F	2	0	0	0	337
Reeves Relic	7	G	7	1	0	1	4,348
Refax	4	F	10	0	0	1	5,730
Referral	6	G	3	1	0	0	6,616
Refine	9	G	15	1	0	1	3,638
Refined Grace	2	F	1	0	0	0	0
Refined'n'smart	4	F	10	1	2	2	23,259
Refiners Fire	4	F	10	0	0	0	1,157
Refinery Road	3	G	6	1	0	1	11,800
Reflect Back	8	G	5	0	0	0	415
Reflect the Queen	2	F	1	0	0	0	135
Reflected Lite	3	F	11	1	0	1	12,355
Reflecting Colors	6	G	3	0	1	1	9,644
Reflection Bay	7	M	6	0	0	1	1,666
Reflective Halo	3	G	8	0	0	1	2,491
Reflector	4	G	8	1	0	3	22,020
Refocus	4	G	9	0	1	2	4,660
Reforest	3	F	4	2	1	0	127,715
Reformer	3	G	11	0	1	4	16,180
Refreshing Caron	3	F	9	0	1	1	4,058
Refreshing Time	3	G	8	2	2	1	43,640
Refusal	3	G	4	0	0	0	800
Refuse	3	G	3	1	0	2	7,430
Refuse to Bend	3	G	9	2	0	1	99,002
Refusilo Sur (ARG)	9	H	2	0	0	0	0
Regal Ability	5	G	11	2	0	1	39,582
Regal Aly	3	F	6	0	1	0	7,207
Regal Amy	6	M	11	1	2	0	7,334
Regal and Cool	3	F	6	0	1	2	5,540
Regal Angel	3	F	9	1	1	2	16,051
Regal Annie	6	M	3	0	0	0	269
Regal Appeal	8	G	7	0	1	0	3,200
Regal Approach	2	F	6	1	1	1	26,082
Regal At Last	5	M	1	0	0	0	0
Regal Avenger	2	F	1	1	0	0	14,500
Regal Award	2	G	1	0	0	0	204
Regal Ballerina	3	F	5	0	0	0	5,823
Regal Bear	4	C	1	0	0	0	360
Regal Beginning	5	G	18	1	6	5	15,926
Regal Ben	3	G	4	0	0	0	312
Regal Bev	5	M	9	2	0	1	19,677
Regal Blues	5	M	7	0	0	0	2,692
Regal Boot	2	F	4	0	0	0	1,980
Regal Buck	3	G	15	0	2	3	5,209
Regal by Design	9	G	10	1	3	0	6,992
Regal C Note	3	G	5	1	1	2	19,971
Regal Cache	7	H	2	1	1	0	1,640
Regal Candy	4	F	2	0	1	0	1,967
Regal Caper	3	C	5	1	1	0	20,710
Regal Case	3	F	7	1	0	0	12,711
Regal Champ	3	G	10	1	2	0	24,667
Regal Chance	3	F	10	1	0	1	7,616
Regal Colours	4	G	9	0	2	3	3,245
Regal Cruiser	4	G	5	0	0	0	1,260
Regal Dancer	4	F	2	0	0	1	538
Regal Daniell	2	F	1	0	0	0	0
Regal Destiny	3	G	9	0	1	1	3,490
Regal Di	2	F	2	0	0	0	0
Regal Dinner	4	C	3	1	0	0	7,115
Regal Disclosure	5	G	18	5	2	0	45,337
Regal Dixie	4	G	2	0	0	0	0
Regal Dr. Stuart	5	G	9	0	0	1	933
Regal Drive	7	G	21	1	6	2	10,809
Regal Edition	6	G	12	3	1	1	9,018
Regal Emblem	5	M	1	0	0	0	0
Regal Explosion	7	G	1	0	0	0	546
Regal Fan	4	G	4	1	1	1	1,972
Regal Flip	9	M	5	0	0	0	491
Regal Grace	3	F	8	2	1	2	33,163
Regal Gray	3	F	3	1	0	0	4,620
Regal Heir	5	M	10	2	1	3	44,590
Regal Heiress	7	M	3	0	0	0	120
Regal Heritage	3	G	1	0	0	0	235
Regal Hit	4	G	12	3	3	1	8,636
Regal Honey	4	F	8	0	0	1	1,080
Regal Honey Man	5	G	4	1	0	1	7,756
Regal Jem	3	F	8	2	2	0	9,900
Regal Julle	5	M	4	0	2	0	3,405
Regal Justice	7	H	13	2	4	1	26,738
Regal Kawana	3	G	4	0	0	0	1,122
Regal Knight	6	G	1	0	0	0	0
Regal Laddie	3	G	10	2	2	1	17,132
Regal Lancer	5	H	4	0	0	0	165
Regal Legacy	5	G	10	2	0	0	15,483
Regal Lexie	5	M	8	2	1	2	33,110
Regal Magnolialass	2	F	1	0	0	0	120
Regal Maxim	3	G	7	1	2	1	12,097
Regal Meg	4	F	2	0	0	0	1,020
Regal Melody	3	F	3	0	0	1	680
Regal Miracle	5	M	15	1	2	3	27,884
Regal Miss	3	F	18	0	4	4	26,940
Regal Mission	2	F	6	1	0	2	24,347
Regal Mister	6	G	12	1	3	2	28,165
Regal Model	3	C	18	0	0	0	10,920
Regal Monarch	6	G	7	0	1	3	11,886
Regal 'n Bold	4	F	9	1	2	1	77,414
Regal 'n Valiant	3	G	15	3	5	1	33,300
Regal Okie	2	G	6	0	1	3	9,848
Regal One	3	F	4	0	0	1	2,387
Regal Pacific	2	C	2	0	0	2	2,474
Regal Pan	2	C	1	0	0	0	400
Regal Pegasus	3	F	6	1	1	0	1,723
Regal Perrot	5	G	16	2	0	0	5,032
Regal Pro	4	C	3	0	1	0	8,486
Regal Promise	3	F	4	0	0	0	375
Regal Punch	4	G	4	1	1	0	5,816
Regal Pusher	2	F	3	0	2	0	9,512
Regal Rae Rae	5	M	5	0	0	0	0

Horse	Age	Sex	Sts	1st	2d	3d	Won
Regal Raider	3	G	8	3	1	0	31,842
Regal Rally	2	F	3	1	1	0	10,756
Regal Randy	5	G	7	3	1	1	29,006
Regal Rebel	5	G	4	0	2	0	8,328
Regal Red	3	F	5	5	0	0	140,313
Regal Reproach	5	G	12	2	3	2	49,002
Regal Resolve	3	G	13	1	4	2	18,171
Regal Revolt	6	G	3	0	0	0	0
Regal Road	5	H	5	2	0	0	20,290
Regal Romeo	6	H	13	3	2	2	32,573
Regal Roots	4	F	4	1	0	0	5,007
Regal Roulette	3	F	8	1	1	2	6,450
Regal Sanction	5	H	3	1	0	1	45,075
Regal Sen	4	F	11	2	2	2	26,186
Regal Shivers	6	H	4	1	0	0	5,394
Regal Sierra	4	F	9	1	3	1	10,743
Regal Siphon	4	G	2	0	0	0	86
Regal Slam	4	C	6	1	2	1	17,265
Regal Spirit	4	G	6	0	1	0	1,631
Regal Stoic	2	F	3	0	1	0	4,760
Regal Sum	3	F	10	1	2	0	17,996
Regal Sunrise	3	F	9	0	0	0	1,525
Regal Sweets	6	G	15	0	2	3	13,732
Regal Tour	6	G	10	0	1	3	4,515
Regal Treasure	7	G	18	1	0	2	6,414
Regal Valley	3	C	4	1	0	1	39,284
Regal Vicky	3	F	6	2	1	0	20,521
Regal Victory	5	G	7	0	2	1	3,715
Regal Watch	4	G	17	7	2	5	82,415
Regal Wings	4	F	14	0	2	2	14,113
Regala Di Trieste	2	F	2	1	1	0	23,200
Regalaftershock	3	C	8	0	0	0	6,430
Regale	4	F	11	4	1	1	76,565
Regalesque	2	G	2	0	0	0	1,140
Regaletta	2	F	1	0	0	0	300
Regalev	2	C	1	0	0	0	118
Regallino Prospect	3	G	1	0	0	0	0
Regallino Storm	4	F	8	0	0	1	2,712
Regally Real	5	H	3	1	1	1	6,480
Regal's Big Girl	3	F	2	1	0	0	5,635
Regal's Flirt	3	F	5	0	1	0	6,272
Regardlessly	2	C	6	1	0	0	14,715
Regatta Princess	3	F	5	1	0	0	5,168
Regency Bay	4	G	9	0	1	1	9,834
Regency West	2	F	2	0	0	0	700
Regency's Honor	5	G	14	1	1	0	8,244
Regent Commander	4	G	1	0	0	0	0
Regent Regent	3	G	10	3	1	0	17,413
Regent Ryan	4	C	3	0	0	0	0
Regent Times	4	G	11	0	0	1	2,224
Regent's Hope	4	C	4	1	1	0	27,000
Regent's Moment	2	F	6	2	0	2	15,790
Regentzee	2	F	2	0	0	0	0
Reggae Beat	4	F	5	0	0	0	972
Reggae Boy	3	G	2	0	0	0	0
Reggae Citi	4	F	4	1	1	1	7,219
Reggae Lady	3	F	3	1	1	0	6,800
Reggae Rhythm	4	G	3	0	0	0	0
Reggie for Three	3	C	8	2	1	1	71,374
Reggie Wins Big	4	G	9	2	0	0	10,621
Reggie's Magic	4	C	4	0	1	1	3,660
Reggie's Winner	6	G	11	4	3	0	61,862
Regime Change	3	G	13	2	0	1	7,122
Regimental	8	G	4	0	0	3	9,934
Regimental Flag	8	G	14	1	1	0	7,440
Regina Reason	4	G	4	0	0	0	450
Regina's Mon	3	G	11	1	2	4	8,469
Regio	2	G	4	0	2	0	6,011
Region of Merit	4	C	10	0	5	0	49,080
Regis Final Answer	4	G	9	1	0	1	8,885
Regulate	3	G	7	1	1	2	27,953
Rehaan's Finale	5	G	2	0	0	0	360
Rehabilitated	5	G	8	0	0	3	2,374
Rehocracy	4	F	1	0	0	0	1,800
Reid's Mess	3	C	10	1	0	1	9,292
Reign Dancer	9	G	1	0	0	0	41
Reign Girl	8	M	5	0	1	1	2,325
Reign of Class	10	M	3	2	0	0	6,470
Reign the Alarm	3	G	11	0	0	0	600
Reigning Count	2	G	6	0	2	0	5,512
Reigning Devil	3	F	4	0	0	0	250
Reigning Glory	3	F	9	0	0	1	1,771
Reigning Gold	3	G	13	0	0	2	2,509
Reigning Justice	4	G	5	2	0	0	1,810
Reigning Star	3	C	2	0	0	0	110
Reigning Storm	4	G	12	1	0	2	20,840
Reigningflare	3	C	1	0	0	0	0
Reign's World	3	C	8	1	1	3	21,370
Reignsofire	3	F	6	3	1	0	6,840
Reima Rose	6	M	12	3	0	1	42,562
Reimburse Me	3	F	1	0	0	0	0
Rein Man	6	G	9	1	4	0	8,060
Reina Xochilt	2	F	3	0	1	1	11,640
Reine de Chateau	5	M	3	0	0	1	5,438
Reine des Neiges	5	M	3	0	0	0	3,765
Reinforced	4	G	10	1	1	0	4,755
Reining Hearts	3	F	11	1	2	0	7,715
Reinvigorate	4	G	8	0	2	3	20,298
Reito Peito	3	F	14	2	1	2	41,570
Rejected Video	4	G	3	0	0	0	0
Rejection	5	G	9	0	2	1	4,161
Rejjie's Thunder	3	G	9	0	0	0	1,036
Rejuvenator	4	F	4	0	1	1	3,027
Rejuvinated	2	C	1	0	0	0	145
Rekha	3	F	5	2	0	2	17,200
Relapse	5	G	3	0	0	0	211
Relate	3	C	4	0	1	1	6,274
Related Issues	4	F	14	4	0	5	50,008
Related Trump	8	G	5	0	1	1	5,879
Relative Strength	6	G	11	1	0	0	14,562
Relato Del Gato	3	C	5	1	1	0	15,380
Relaunch Gal	7	M	3	2	0	0	23,400
Relaunch Star	6	G	9	1	0	0	52,872
Relaunch the Fever	4	F	5	0	0	0	612
Relaunchy Bid	4	G	5	0	0	0	1,389
Relaxed	3	F	3	1	0	0	10,058
Relaxing Green	4	F	13	1	5	5	61,895
Relay Runner	4	F	3	0	0	0	212
Release the Power	5	G	5	0	0	0	398
Relentless Luv	2	F	1	1	0	0	8,400
Relentless Passion	3	G	5	1	1	0	6,995
Relentless Red	3	G	6	1	1	0	24,550
Relentless Seller	5	G	8	0	3	0	14,960
Relevant Flyer	4	F	1	0	0	0	0
Relevant One	8	M	2	0	0	0	108
Relicon	4	F	7	1	1	1	31,530
Religious	4	F	13	0	0	1	2,393
Reluctant Groom	6	G	7	0	0	0	2,475
Rely On Me	3	F	10	1	0	1	9,285
Remagen Bridge	6	G	17	1	2	2	14,860
Remark Get Set Go	3	G	4	0	0	0	0
Remarkable Affair	5	G	7	0	0	1	350
Remarkable Appeal	5	M	8	0	1	5	4,661
Remarkable Silver	5	G	3	0	0	0	329
Remarkably	3	F	11	1	5	0	17,430
Remarkably Special	2	F	4	1	0	0	8,061
Remarqable Tale	3	F	5	1	2	2	44,250
Remarqable You	4	F	8	1	0	1	7,615
Rembecca	3	F	1	0	0	0	186
Rembo's Victoriana	5	M	10	1	0	2	13,484
Remeber	10	H	6	0	1	0	912
Remember Brian	5	M	13	1	4	1	13,884
Remember Doc	4	G	5	0	1	0	2,300
Remember Red	3	G	10	2	1	0	39,611
Remember Sam	3	G	2	0	0	0	0
Remember Sheikh	7	G	3	0	0	0	217
Remember the Groom	4	G	10	0	0	4	5,832
Remember the Mane	6	M	1	0	0	0	61
Remember the Party	5	G	10	2	1	2	17,080
Rememberin Eleanor	3	F	2	0	1	1	6,095
Remembering Beau	4	G	6	0	0	0	803
Remembering Dillon	2	C	1	0	0	0	450
Rememberthecowgirl	4	F	15	2	3	5	21,425
Remembrance Day	3	F	3	0	0	0	282
Remembrances	3	F	4	0	0	1	21,012
Remi Larue	4	F	2	0	0	0	86
Remiewaterbluz	5	M	15	5	1	2	95,280
Remind	4	C	6	1	2	0	75,871

Horse	Age	Sex	Sts	1st	2d	3d	Won
Remington Katrina	4	F	13	0	0	1	1,456
Reminiscing	3	F	1	0	0	0	107
Remi's Rocket	4	F	14	4	2	4	65,910
Remission	7	M	4	0	0	0	340
Remix	3	C	7	1	1	1	13,555
Remo	4	G	6	0	1	3	25,400
Remonte	4	G	9	1	1	1	49,440
Remote Control	3	G	15	2	5	3	29,355
Remuneration	2	C	3	1	1	0	36,600
Rena Jean	4	F	6	0	2	0	1,146
Renaca	4	G	6	0	1	1	3,045
Renade	4	F	17	1	0	1	8,520
Renaissance Lady	3	F	3	0	2	0	20,200
Renamed	3	F	14	2	4	3	100,322
Renard Bleu	3	G	1	1	0	0	19,200
Renato	9	G	13	1	0	0	2,420
Renature	4	F	7	1	1	2	7,734
Rendezvous Point	3	F	4	1	0	0	17,442
Rendies Coast	4	G	11	0	0	0	2,283
Rendies Summer	2	G	9	0	3	0	15,000
Renee's Approval	5	M	17	2	0	4	30,672
Renee's Cat	3	F	6	2	1	0	21,706
Renegade Force	7	G	7	0	0	0	200
Renegade Rogue	6	G	14	3	2	5	52,670
Renegade Ruler	3	G	7	0	0	0	0
Rene's Kickig Boot	4	F	1	0	0	0	0
Rene's Last	4	G	11	1	0	2	3,101
Rene's Luck	2	F	5	0	1	0	2,370
Rene's Prime Time	4	F	4	2	2	0	18,320
Rene's Soldier	3	C	3	0	0	1	5,010
Renewed Passion	4	F	3	0	0	0	286
Renga	2	C	3	1	0	0	21,540
Reniesmanychances	3	F	6	0	0	0	770
Renig	3	C	10	1	0	0	7,624
Rennae N Nicole	7	M	7	0	0	0	628
Rennaissance Man	5	G	9	1	2	0	6,462
Reno Bob	2	C	8	2	1	3	52,678
Reno Bound	7	G	5	2	1	0	6,595
Reno Haines	3	G	12	1	1	3	16,710
Reno Rumble	10	G	3	0	0	1	3,542
Renoir Red	8	G	9	0	2	1	4,359
Renowned Dreamer	3	F	1	0	0	0	0
Rent a Prince	3	G	12	2	2	3	53,187
Renton Benny	4	G	11	1	1	1	5,534
Rents Due	2	F	5	1	2	0	50,716
Rentway	5	H	12	0	1	2	9,677
Rentz	2	G	4	0	0	1	1,736
Renumbered	5	G	4	1	0	1	10,924
Reore	8	G	11	0	1	3	4,320
Repartment	4	C	3	1	2	0	13,860
Repay the Diamonds	2	C	2	0	0	0	0
Repeat After Me	5	M	11	3	2	3	13,540
Repeat Edition	2	F	3	0	1	1	14,480
Repeat Step One	2	G	1	0	1	0	2,415
Repeated Blues	5	H	7	1	0	2	1,925
Repeatedly	5	M	10	1	1	0	4,054
Repeater Trooper	3	G	4	0	0	0	1,380
Repecci	5	G	6	0	0	0	237
Repent Again	3	G	8	1	0	0	6,128
Repete	5	G	3	0	0	0	390
Repido's Rascal	3	F	3	0	0	0	1,155
Replacement	3	C	1	0	0	0	400
Repletions Victory	4	F	8	2	3	0	12,942
Replica	3	G	7	1	1	1	5,650
Replication	4	G	6	2	1	1	35,410
Replinka	8	M	10	2	3	1	42,290
Reply N Aces	4	F	10	2	3	1	16,760
Report	4	F	5	0	0	0	447
Report a Highfire	3	F	17	1	1	2	14,720
Report for Joy	3	F	12	1	3	0	18,020
Report On Class	3	G	14	1	4	2	15,336
Report On Time	4	F	6	2	0	2	21,250
Report Stage	6	G	5	0	0	0	300
Report to All	5	G	12	0	1	2	10,659
Reporter	9	G	5	1	0	0	8,050
Reportorial	7	G	4	0	1	0	1,860
Repository	6	M	3	0	0	0	7,805
Reprehensible	6	G	1	0	0	0	0
Reprized Angel	3	F	10	2	3	0	32,610
Reprized Doctor	5	G	10	2	0	0	8,732
Reprized Rebel	7	G	5	0	0	0	673
Reprized Strike	2	C	6	1	2	1	33,970
Reprizedrullah	5	G	7	0	0	0	2,070
Reproof	8	G	2	0	0	0	654
Reptile	6	M	1	0	0	0	0
Republican Hawk	3	G	1	0	0	0	0
Republican Lady	4	F	16	1	1	0	15,955
Repulse Bay	3	C	3	0	0	0	1,200
Repunzel's Knight	6	H	4	0	2	0	3,225
Reputare Two Win	4	G	2	0	0	0	174
Reputed Deeds	3	F	7	0	1	1	19,040
Request	6	G	6	0	0	0	0
Request All	4	F	14	0	3	2	6,234
Request Denied	3	F	9	0	3	2	38,010
Request for Parole	5	H	10	3	2	0	757,100
Request Granted	5	G	1	0	0	0	195
Request the Glory	4	G	15	2	3	1	10,731
Request the Magic	5	M	11	1	1	2	5,438
Requesto	5	G	12	1	2	1	13,657
Reride	4	G	3	0	0	2	7,933
Rerun	5	G	14	1	1	1	12,730
Res Les Spirit	3	G	3	0	0	0	260
Res Nullius	8	G	9	1	0	0	4,194
Resash	3	G	10	1	2	1	38,894
Rescigno	3	G	6	0	0	0	4,057
Rescue Five	4	F	6	4	0	1	20,025
Rescue One	4	C	17	2	0	2	10,989
Rescuedfrompreskit	4	C	7	1	1	0	18,305
Researched (IRE)	5	G	2	0	0	0	0
Reservations Only	5	H	5	3	1	0	60,530
Reserve Colonel	3	G	12	1	2	2	9,141
Resident Rogue	5	G	16	3	1	2	20,655
Residual	4	F	10	4	1	0	25,400
Resignation	7	G	9	0	0	0	523
Resigned	5	M	6	2	1	1	27,630
Resist Temptation	2	F	2	0	0	2	3,157
Resistant	6	G	9	2	0	3	10,076
Resisting	4	G	5	1	1	0	9,542
Resolution	2	F	2	0	1	0	9,900
Resolve	6	G	2	0	0	0	1,610
Resounding Echo	5	G	6	0	0	0	680
Respect the Game	7	G	9	1	2	3	14,988
Respectabeau	3	G	11	1	2	1	36,420
Respectable Gal	4	F	17	1	3	5	20,745
Respectable Man	10	G	6	1	0	1	7,810
Respectful Tutu	6	M	6	0	0	1	585
Respectmyauthorita	5	M	2	2	0	0	33,540
Resplendence	4	G	14	2	2	3	52,325
Resplendency	3	F	4	2	1	1	121,080
Respond	2	F	1	0	1	0	2,900
Response	3	C	1	0	0	0	145
Response Time	3	G	7	1	0	1	8,209
Rest Stop	2	F	1	0	0	1	800
Restage	5	G	5	3	0	1	101,185
Restigouche	3	C	8	0	1	3	24,944
Resting Easy	9	M	11	1	0	1	9,922
Restitution	5	H	16	4	0	1	16,998
Restive	4	G	3	0	0	0	240
Restless Amanda	3	F	5	1	1	1	17,619
Restless Audition	3	G	2	0	0	0	220
Restless Fever	5	M	15	0	4	3	9,524
Restless Flyer	5	G	3	0	0	0	0
Restless Halo	4	F	10	1	3	0	56,529
Restless Joshua	6	G	2	0	0	0	0
Restless Kind	6	M	16	5	1	1	34,762
Restless Luck	5	M	13	2	2	3	22,641
Restless Mon	4	C	2	1	0	1	18,680
Restless Shadow	4	F	3	0	0	0	123
Restless Sound	6	G	14	3	2	2	29,245
Restock	3	F	3	1	1	1	14,605
Restricted Access	6	M	1	0	0	0	365
Restrictions Apply	4	C	7	2	4	1	6,738
Restrider	2	G	3	0	0	0	722
Resurgence	7	G	8	2	3	0	53,734
Resurgent	2	G	1	0	1	0	1,720
Resurrect	4	C	6	1	0	0	5,540
Resurrected	2	C	1	0	0	0	135
Resurrected Hope	3	F	4	1	0	0	2,808

Horse	Age	Sex	Sts	1st	2d	3d	Won
Retail Sales	9	M	6	0	1	1	4,220
Retainage	2	F	5	0	2	2	28,550
Retaliation	7	G	11	1	3	0	25,852
Retaliator	5	G	8	1	1	0	7,927
Retam	4	G	7	0	1	1	11,230
Retention Bonus	3	C	10	1	0	0	3,087
Retinaculum	3	C	5	0	0	1	1,420
Retired Habit	7	G	4	2	1	0	60,880
Retirees Three	4	G	5	1	0	2	44,080
Retirement Gift	5	G	14	1	2	4	13,586
Retrial	4	F	4	0	0	0	1,990
Retribution	2	G	2	0	1	0	8,405
Retrieve the Gold	4	F	12	3	0	1	47,090
Retro Fever	7	G	12	1	0	1	4,968
Retro Red	8	G	3	0	0	1	1,260
Retroactive	4	F	3	0	0	0	3,500
Retrocession	2	G	1	0	0	0	340
Retrospect	2	C	1	0	0	0	0
Retsina Bound	3	G	3	0	0	0	215
Retsina K.	3	F	13	1	1	3	13,284
Retsina Year	7	G	2	0	0	0	100
Retsina's Ego	3	C	1	0	0	0	0
Retsina's Emblem	2	G	2	0	0	0	192
Return Flight	4	F	8	1	0	4	10,526
Return of the Mac	3	C	17	3	1	0	23,730
Return Receipt	3	C	5	0	0	0	77
Return To	5	G	14	0	0	1	1,682
Return to Reality	3	F	4	0	0	0	115
Returned All	4	F	2	0	0	0	250
Reuben	7	H	5	0	1	0	3,695
Reuben's Rocket	7	G	11	1	0	2	18,380
Reunion Star	4	F	3	0	1	0	4,474
Revalee	5	G	12	0	1	0	6,446
Revancha	4	F	24	0	2	4	11,394
Reva's Prince	4	G	2	0	0	0	579
Revcan	4	F	7	0	0	3	1,100
Reve D' Amazon	5	M	14	1	0	3	14,137
Reve d'Enfance	4	C	7	0	2	0	8,940
Reveal the Star	5	G	6	1	0	1	8,274
Revealed	2	F	1	1	0	0	21,000
Revealing Blush	3	F	10	0	3	2	13,550
Revealing Moment	3	F	4	2	1	0	5,773
Revealing Slew	4	F	10	2	1	1	8,477
Revello	6	G	9	2	1	4	152,548
Reven	3	F	3	0	0	0	5,400
Revenal	3	G	9	0	1	0	2,293
Revenante	5	M	1	0	0	0	0
Revend	2	G	3	0	0	0	285
Revenescent	6	H	4	0	0	0	1,840
Revenge Her Way	3	F	15	1	3	3	32,710
Revenged	6	G	8	1	1	2	7,780
Revengeful Rocky	2	F	2	0	0	1	1,430
Revenue	9	G	10	1	0	2	1,674
Rever	3	C	6	1	0	0	8,085
Reverberate	2	C	3	1	0	1	34,785
Revered Judge	5	G	2	0	0	0	128
Revered Soldier	5	G	12	3	0	1	51,624
Reverence	4	F	8	0	0	2	5,414
Reverend Du	2	C	5	0	0	0	226
Reverend Jim	6	G	4	1	0	2	1,620
Reverends Choice	7	H	1	0	0	0	500
Reverent American	4	G	10	2	0	2	15,029
Reverse Acquittal	5	G	8	0	0	0	1,076
Reverse Psychology	5	G	11	1	1	3	21,681
Reveur Belle	3	F	6	1	0	1	18,221
Review the List	3	G	11	2	0	2	21,610
Revington	6	G	10	4	1	1	30,124
Revitalized	2	F	1	0	0	0	0
Revival	2	G	3	0	1	1	14,100
Revival Site	2	C	3	0	0	0	75
Revived	2	G	3	1	2	0	11,300
Revo (IRE)	5	H	12	3	0	2	18,106
Revolt	3	G	3	0	0	0	654
Revolutionary	7	M	3	0	0	0	370
Revolutionary Act	4	F	11	4	0	1	100,561
Revolutionize	4	G	5	0	0	1	1,430
Revolver	5	G	8	0	1	0	3,130
Revolver Six	3	C	10	1	2	1	32,810
Revolver Two	4	G	10	0	0	1	968

Horse	Age	Sex	Sts	1st	2d	3d	Won
Revolving Door	2	F	2	1	1	0	12,618
Revved Up	6	G	1	0	0	1	6,000
Rewire	5	G	18	1	1	2	5,339
Rex of the Dance	2	F	2	0	0	0	470
Rexsonhopeprospect	3	G	20	1	2	3	13,610
Rey de Cafe	2	C	6	2	2	0	113,204
Rey Lake	2	F	1	0	0	0	700
Rey Sol	4	C	5	2	0	0	14,728
Reynolds Rae	3	F	2	0	0	0	313
Reynolds Ricci	2	F	2	0	0	0	273
Reynoldsrap	4	G	2	0	0	1	1,010
Rez Runner	3	C	8	0	0	0	1,462
Rezoom	3	F	3	0	1	0	1,500
Rhapsodic Gold	3	F	1	0	1	0	2,040
Rhapsodist	8	G	2	0	0	1	480
Rhapsody in A	3	F	9	1	2	1	15,380
Rhapsody Mood	3	F	4	1	0	0	6,433
Rhapsody Red	3	F	10	3	2	1	12,360
Rhea of Villanova	2	F	8	2	1	0	28,410
Rheaxthus	6	G	15	2	3	1	27,156
Rhema's Red Bird	2	F	1	0	0	0	0
Rhetoric Express	5	G	8	3	1	1	38,815
Rhett Henry	5	G	7	0	0	0	600
Rhinestone Rita	5	M	5	0	0	0	260
Rhino Chaser	3	G	10	0	3	2	24,400
Rhodes Leer	3	G	5	0	1	0	5,600
Rhodesian Storm	6	G	14	1	1	2	28,924
Rhodex	3	G	12	0	0	0	1,417
Rhodezone	12	G	9	0	0	1	1,809
Rhome Magic	2	F	7	2	0	3	27,900
Rhonda Del Cielo	4	F	3	0	0	0	417
Rhonda's Dealing	6	M	7	0	0	1	962
Rhonda's Number	3	F	4	0	1	0	11,800
Rhonesquarterswish	9	G	2	0	0	0	225
Rhumb Line	4	F	2	0	0	0	760
Rhumjar	4	G	8	0	1	3	26,784
Rhyd Ddu	4	G	5	0	0	1	5,236
Rhyeliz	6	M	7	0	1	0	2,565
Rhyme	8	G	8	1	0	0	3,009
Rhyme Time	3	F	3	0	0	0	198
Rhyolite	5	G	12	1	2	1	12,645
Rhythanda	3	F	3	0	0	0	1,380
Rhythm Ace	2	G	6	0	1	0	5,400
Rhythm Again	3	G	8	0	1	0	5,688
Rhythm and Bloom	6	M	4	0	1	0	2,652
Rhythm and Rules	5	G	2	0	0	0	0
Rhythm Down Below	5	M	8	1	2	1	12,508
Rhythm in My Boot	3	F	1	0	0	0	0
Rhythm in Shoes	4	F	10	1	3	2	63,316
Rhythm in the Nite	2	G	5	0	1	1	9,307
Rhythm King	3	C	5	1	0	1	31,520
Rhythm Mad (FR)	4	C	4	2	1	0	299,600
Rhythm n' Roses	4	F	14	1	1	4	14,406
Rhythm Princess	2	F	2	0	0	0	300
Rhythm Ridge	6	M	9	1	0	1	9,180
Rhythmair	6	H	6	2	0	0	7,948
Rhythmic Motion	4	G	12	2	1	2	80,952
Rhythmic River	6	M	2	0	0	0	0
Rhythmically	2	F	3	0	0	2	10,520
Rhythmics	3	F	5	0	1	1	3,585
Rhythmn Magic	5	M	10	1	2	1	14,844
Rial Jersey	5	G	1	0	0	0	252
Rialstress	5	M	8	1	1	0	5,615
Ria's Little Angel	6	M	3	0	0	2	3,130
Riata Goldrush	7	G	2	0	0	0	110
Ribatto	3	C	2	0	0	0	969
Ribbon Cane	5	M	6	4	0	0	119,160
Ribbon of Darkness	3	G	4	0	0	0	355
Ribomoon	3	G	5	0	1	0	4,880
Ribotland's Heir	3	C	4	1	0	0	6,835
Ricardo A	5	H	10	2	1	1	67,590
Ricardo Voador	2	C	1	0	0	0	400
Ricco Cat	3	G	11	0	1	0	1,990
Riccoslew	2	F	3	0	0	1	2,760
Rich and Lucky	7	M	3	0	1	0	2,695
Rich and Wild	2	F	7	1	1	2	7,190
Rich as Croesus	4	C	4	1	1	1	29,360
Rich Assertion	5	M	6	0	0	1	17,454
Rich Baroness	2	F	1	0	0	0	160

Horse	Age	Sex	Sts	1st	2d	3d	Won
Rich Bid	5	H	9	0	0	1	1,149
Rich Celebration	7	G	9	1	0	0	3,833
Rich City Girl	4	F	8	2	3	1	64,770
Rich Coins	6	H	11	0	2	2	9,474
Rich Deeds	6	H	1	0	0	0	327
Rich Desire	5	G	22	2	5	3	21,324
Rich Dixie	3	F	4	2	0	0	15,722
Rich Domino	6	M	2	0	0	0	252
Rich Dude	8	G	2	0	0	1	1,620
Rich Expression	5	M	9	0	0	0	1,486
Rich Fidler	4	G	12	2	1	1	19,670
Rich Find	3	F	11	3	1	0	84,622
Rich Flight	6	G	14	2	3	0	17,431
Rich Friends	2	F	2	0	0	0	470
Rich Girl	3	F	6	3	0	0	42,637
Rich Guarani	3	G	7	0	1	0	5,500
Rich in Dallas	9	G	4	0	2	0	3,816
Rich in Discretion	3	G	7	1	1	0	9,781
Rich in Love	5	M	1	0	0	0	630
Rich in Spirit	2	F	5	3	0	0	107,362
Rich Lad	10	G	10	2	0	0	5,967
Rich Lady Anne	3	F	3	1	1	0	35,074
Rich Machine	7	G	11	1	0	3	4,320
Rich March	6	G	21	6	3	3	46,098
Rich Max	4	C	5	1	0	2	12,210
Rich Mist	7	M	3	0	0	1	2,530
Rich Mover	4	G	9	2	1	0	6,304
Rich Musique	5	M	8	2	2	1	31,965
Rich Pal	4	C	12	2	1	2	7,352
Rich Rubies	2	F	2	1	0	1	10,120
Rich Scent	6	M	12	0	2	1	3,186
Rich Search	6	M	1	0	0	0	0
Rich Secret	6	G	10	0	1	2	7,472
Rich Silver Swan	5	G	17	3	1	1	19,885
Rich Tradition	4	C	5	1	1	0	2,436
Rich World	3	G	15	1	1	2	8,608
Richard the First	4	G	1	0	1	0	5,800
Richard's Boy	4	G	11	0	0	3	5,328
Richardsawesomstar	5	M	6	0	0	0	1,307
Richebourg	3	G	3	1	1	0	37,220
Richest Half	5	G	14	3	2	0	38,886
Richetta	3	F	8	1	2	3	105,800
Richie Cee	3	G	4	1	0	0	9,730
Richierichierich	5	H	9	3	1	4	81,980
Richie's Cat	3	F	12	1	2	1	16,109
Richie's Future	3	G	11	1	3	0	29,318
Richie's Reward	5	G	3	0	0	1	671
Richillini	6	G	2	1	0	0	3,185
Richland Holme	7	H	6	0	1	0	1,672
Richlands Music	4	F	1	0	0	0	0
Richly Inflated	7	M	7	0	0	0	871
Richly Pleasant	2	F	1	0	0	0	0
Richmeadow Monster	2	G	3	1	0	1	6,770
Richmond Rowdy	8	G	10	1	0	3	2,402
Rich'n Restless	6	M	10	2	1	3	40,628
Richochet	3	G	4	0	0	0	4,880
Richter's Emblem	5	M	14	2	3	0	38,163
Richwood Rebel	7	G	13	4	0	2	55,820
Richwood Royal	3	F	2	1	0	0	18,480
Rick and Funny	2	F	1	0	0	0	75
Rickenbacker	3	G	10	1	1	1	19,045
Rickety's Revenge	6	M	7	1	1	0	7,568
Ricki Power	8	M	1	0	0	0	0
Rickitte Tom	3	G	12	1	2	2	9,715
Rickles	3	G	8	0	1	1	4,530
Rick's Kick	6	G	6	1	2	0	2,236
Rick's Lad	3	G	8	1	0	1	8,870
Ricks Little Music	7	M	6	1	0	0	4,497
Ricky J	2	F	1	0	0	0	520
Ricky Marzo (CHI)	3	C	1	0	0	0	140
Ricky Rick	2	C	1	0	0	0	2,940
Rickyville	3	G	9	0	0	0	2,172
Rico Ends Well	6	M	9	0	2	3	17,160
Rico Suave	10	G	10	0	0	1	1,400
Ricoboy	4	G	3	0	0	0	0
Ridacin	5	G	14	1	2	2	8,621
Ridan's Mon	5	M	9	0	1	4	26,880
Riddell's Creek	8	G	4	0	0	2	10,141
Riddick's Jet	3	G	12	2	1	1	10,053
Riddle	3	C	13	2	1	3	41,029
Riddle Me This	2	F	3	0	0	0	0
Riddlesdown (IRE)	7	H	3	0	0	0	1,380
Ride and Shine	7	G	8	1	0	1	84,056
Ride 'Em Rags	8	G	12	0	1	1	9,451
Ride Her Out	3	F	1	1	0	0	18,000
Ride Now	3	F	13	3	3	1	37,803
Ride On	4	G	1	0	0	0	1,275
Ride On J T	5	G	5	1	1	0	2,480
Ride On Snow	3	F	13	1	4	2	9,879
Ride Point	3	C	6	0	2	0	6,545
Ride the Dream	3	C	3	0	0	1	2,277
Ride the Light	7	G	11	1	1	3	12,078
Ride the Rhythm	2	F	4	0	0	0	460
Ride the Wild Wind	3	F	8	2	2	1	37,350
Ride to Riches	3	G	7	0	1	0	2,226
Ride With Rythym	5	G	10	0	0	1	2,430
Rideforthebrand	2	C	1	0	0	0	0
Rideintothenight	8	G	10	2	1	1	10,498
Rideitout	3	F	2	1	0	0	14,787
Rideouts Patton	6	G	1	0	0	0	270
Ridge Court Lady	5	M	5	0	0	1	2,385
Ridge Jumper	4	G	9	2	1	1	12,353
Ridge Runner (GB)	6	G	14	1	1	2	12,096
Ridgecrest	4	F	1	0	0	0	212
Ridgefinder	6	M	7	1	0	0	5,582
Ridge's Boy	4	G	7	0	0	1	1,277
Ridgevalley	3	G	4	0	1	0	1,664
Ridgeways Charmer	5	H	8	0	1	0	3,904
Ridgewood Blue's	3	F	6	0	1	0	10,239
Ridin the Blues	5	G	2	0	0	0	128
Riding	4	F	2	0	0	0	127
Riding the Pine	4	G	2	0	1	0	1,995
Ridley (IRE)	5	H	7	0	1	1	2,620
Rienzi	4	C	1	0	0	0	0
Rifle Woman	5	M	15	2	5	5	56,462
Rift	5	G	4	1	0	0	6,003
Rig Hand	3	G	8	2	1	1	10,287
Rigel	4	C	4	0	0	0	234
Riggin Lady	7	M	7	1	0	2	6,737
Riggo	6	G	4	0	0	0	1,182
Right About Now (NZ)	8	G	3	0	0	1	1,225
Right Answer	4	F	1	0	0	1	594
Right At Home	5	M	2	1	0	0	4,980
Right Back Atcha	4	F	10	2	1	2	15,240
Right Catagory	2	C	4	0	0	0	540
Right Close	2	G	2	0	0	0	2,940
Right Direction	4	F	13	5	3	1	58,742
Right Girls Star	8	G	13	0	1	1	3,000
Right Hand Man	2	C	6	1	0	0	19,420
Right Hero	4	G	14	3	4	2	59,670
Right Lane	5	M	19	2	4	3	17,226
Right Mix	3	F	11	2	3	1	44,897
Right Nice	3	C	13	0	0	3	11,639
Right of Conquest	3	C	5	1	0	1	16,010
Right On Jeeves	5	G	13	0	0	0	847
Right On Lil	5	M	1	0	0	0	0
Right On Target	6	G	9	1	0	1	3,507
Right On the Hour	4	F	7	1	1	0	15,875
Right On the Line	4	G	2	0	0	0	266
Right On the Mark	10	G	3	0	0	1	1,455
Right Out Ro	4	F	11	2	2	2	71,048
Right Proof	4	G	8	1	0	1	41,160
Right Quick	2	C	9	0	2	1	11,205
Right Return	6	G	6	0	1	1	4,127
Right Revved	10	G	6	0	1	3	5,736
Right Stop	6	G	7	0	1	1	8,773
Right This Way	3	F	9	3	0	2	108,819
Right to Run	3	G	7	3	0	1	20,233
Right too Refuse	5	H	9	3	1	1	27,138
Right Uppercut	4	G	18	3	1	3	25,350
Right You Are	4	G	13	4	0	2	27,946
Rightbyu	5	M	12	4	0	1	22,350
Righteous Desire	6	G	10	0	1	1	1,143
Righteous Dude	3	C	9	2	0	1	10,741
Righteous Struggle	5	H	8	0	1	3	7,200
Righteous Witness	3	G	5	2	0	0	13,243
Rightie Tightie	3	G	8	0	1	0	1,993
Rights Reserved	4	G	3	0	1	0	2,797

Horse	Age	Sex	Sts	1st	2d	3d	Won
Rightside	4	C	1	0	0	0	75
Rightyoski	2	F	1	0	1	0	3,570
Rigid Spur	7	G	9	2	1	0	28,550
Rigmarole	3	F	4	0	1	0	2,415
Rigney	6	G	8	0	1	4	7,464
Riker	9	G	11	1	3	1	12,015
Rikers Island	5	G	5	0	1	0	1,470
Riki Ricardo	4	G	7	2	1	3	6,172
Rikman	2	C	2	1	0	0	16,050
Riley City	5	G	9	1	0	1	4,520
Riley Irish	5	G	7	0	2	0	653
Riley J.	4	C	1	0	0	0	0
Riley James	6	G	5	1	0	0	1,438
Riley My Boy	4	G	3	2	0	1	11,680
Riley Style	2	G	11	1	3	3	29,920
Rileys Knight	3	G	3	0	1	0	820
Riley's Life	2	G	4	0	2	1	13,200
Rileys Orbit	3	G	8	2	3	0	18,285
Rileys Ransom	4	G	1	0	0	0	0
Rileys Silver	4	F	11	2	3	1	7,809
Rileys Stuff	4	C	8	1	0	0	1,554
Rileys Turn	3	G	9	1	2	0	7,599
Rim Dancer	9	G	2	0	0	0	798
Rim the Cup	2	C	3	0	0	0	1,092
Rimfire's Thunder	6	G	14	3	3	1	34,864
Rimroc Gold	2	F	1	0	1	0	5,000
Rimrod	4	C	1	0	0	1	6,040
Rincon	3	C	3	1	0	0	12,400
Rindanica	4	C	8	2	5	0	82,490
Rine's Last Hope	3	F	1	0	0	0	78
Ring and a Prayer	2	F	4	1	0	1	28,920
Ring Bearer	4	G	13	2	1	2	25,099
Ring City	2	F	7	1	1	0	63,869
Ring for Diamonds	2	F	7	0	0	2	3,823
Ring of Friendship	4	G	10	3	3	2	80,242
Ring of Gold	3	F	9	3	0	1	8,910
Ring of Power	4	C	4	1	1	1	13,240
Ring of Reality	5	G	17	0	4	4	9,576
Ring of Stars	3	F	7	0	0	2	4,721
Ring of the Run	2	C	2	1	1	0	42,377
Ring of Thunder	5	M	1	0	0	0	110
Ring the Witness	3	G	8	0	0	4	4,519
Ring Toss	6	G	3	0	0	0	908
Ringading	4	F	3	1	0	0	11,400
Ringaring a Rosie	3	F	14	2	1	2	73,624
Ringaroundarosie	4	F	17	1	7	1	45,280
Ringaskiddy	8	G	7	0	1	3	43,520
Ringgold Gap	5	G	12	2	4	1	12,778
Ringing Echo	5	M	15	1	1	0	10,905
Ringing Rock	4	C	6	2	0	0	21,446
Ringlet	2	F	4	1	2	0	57,000
Ringo	6	H	2	0	0	0	0
Ringo Faar	2	C	3	0	0	0	488
Ringofdiamonds	3	F	7	2	0	1	13,050
Ringold	3	G	13	3	2	1	75,895
Ringo's Cat	3	F	8	1	1	2	27,384
Rings and Things	3	F	2	1	0	0	29,400
Rings Ov Jade	3	G	14	1	2	2	14,036
Ringside Alicia	7	M	1	0	0	0	0
Ringside Runner	4	C	2	0	1	0	1,200
Ringthatbellagain	5	M	7	1	0	0	17,670
Rinka Bell	5	M	12	4	2	1	27,874
Rinka Dazzle	6	M	2	0	0	0	0
Rinka Dink Swap	3	F	7	0	3	1	13,880
Rinka Jayne	3	F	9	1	1	2	8,980
Rinka Myth	4	G	2	0	0	0	0
Rinka Rainbow	3	F	6	0	0	2	3,070
Rinkadun	5	G	2	0	0	0	0
Rinkatink	5	H	4	0	0	2	2,261
Rinky Dinky Do	5	H	4	0	0	1	1,820
Rio Branco (GB)	3	F	4	1	0	0	6,676
Rio Cheep	5	G	6	0	0	0	120
Rio de Esperanza	6	G	12	3	1	4	36,735
Rio Dee Grande	7	G	2	0	0	0	0
Rio Devil	2	C	1	0	0	0	192
Rio Dorado	4	C	1	0	0	0	107
Rio Gaza Montado	3	F	8	0	0	3	4,662
Rio Gold	6	H	7	1	2	0	10,818
Rio Handfull	5	G	11	0	0	0	570
Rio Lady	3	F	11	2	2	0	19,850
Rio Listo	4	G	9	0	2	0	3,810
Rio Man	3	G	9	0	2	1	5,306
Rio Moro	2	G	2	0	0	0	300
Rio Neata	7	M	2	1	0	0	1,140
Rio Negro Gold	3	F	2	0	0	0	0
Rio Reyes	4	G	5	0	1	2	13,273
Rio River Rose	7	M	1	0	0	0	201
Rio Ruckus	3	G	10	1	1	1	16,253
Rio Sage	5	G	5	1	1	1	2,783
Riomaimah	3	F	4	0	1	0	1,500
Rio's Chase	5	G	3	0	1	0	3,145
Rio's Rocket Man	5	G	2	0	0	0	0
Rio's World	5	M	3	0	0	0	0
Riotous Miss	9	M	14	3	4	3	51,515
Riot's Rebel	3	G	1	0	0	0	0
Rip N Out	3	G	8	0	0	2	1,468
Rip n' Roar	4	G	11	2	4	1	22,953
Rip N Snort	4	G	6	0	0	0	670
Rip the Halo	4	F	3	0	0	0	375
Ripley	4	G	10	1	0	4	11,694
Rippin N Roarin	5	G	9	3	2	0	25,828
Ripple Water	2	F	1	0	0	0	500
Rippled Effect	4	F	2	1	0	0	8,240
Rippling Water	2	G	6	1	1	0	9,580
Rischio	5	G	9	1	3	2	21,500
Rise and Conquer	4	C	9	0	0	1	2,145
Rise and Smile	3	G	11	0	2	0	3,651
Rise Ball	6	G	2	0	0	0	135
Rise to Glory	9	G	3	1	0	1	3,872
Rise to Roar	4	F	12	2	1	1	14,075
Risen Creek	3	G	9	0	0	0	2,525
Risen Empress	2	F	2	1	0	0	7,500
Risen Honor	3	C	4	0	0	1	2,260
Risen Legend	4	F	5	1	2	0	12,388
Risen Warrior	8	G	19	2	4	4	39,916
Riserbee	5	G	1	0	0	0	0
Rises the Phoenix	3	C	4	0	1	1	13,660
Rising Account	6	M	8	0	0	1	1,884
Rising Agenda	5	M	1	0	0	0	46
Rising Artax	3	G	18	2	3	4	35,300
Rising Desert	2	C	3	1	0	0	5,296
Rising Fever	3	G	9	1	1	0	5,497
Rising Gold Mine	4	G	3	0	0	1	380
Rising Queen	5	M	4	0	0	1	3,420
Rising River	3	C	3	0	0	1	3,440
Rising Storm	2	G	2	1	0	0	6,245
Rising Tide	3	F	7	1	0	1	17,835
Risk and Reward	5	H	2	0	0	0	116
Risk de Carr	3	F	7	2	3	2	17,770
Risk It	5	M	8	1	0	2	3,438
Risk of Flight	3	G	11	1	5	2	32,860
Risk Reward	4	G	16	2	1	4	37,355
Riskaverse	5	M	6	1	2	0	717,472
Riskey Scheme	5	M	9	1	0	0	8,415
Risktaker	2	F	3	1	0	0	7,214
Risky Affair	3	G	10	1	5	0	7,417
Risky Agreement	2	F	2	0	0	0	0
Risky Behavior	2	G	1	0	0	1	1,680
Risky Cat	4	G	9	1	0	0	13,730
Risky Doc	5	G	7	1	0	0	2,847
Risky Endeavor	4	F	5	3	0	0	16,290
Risky Fling	3	G	14	0	1	0	1,686
Risky Fox	6	M	3	0	0	0	100
Risky Frolic	4	F	7	0	0	0	1,670
Risky Mover	4	C	2	0	0	0	0
Risky Notion	5	M	1	0	0	0	0
Risky Occupation	6	G	7	0	0	3	1,584
Risky Stretch	6	M	8	0	1	3	4,070
Risky Trick	3	C	6	0	4	0	62,565
Risky Weather	3	G	10	2	1	2	59,830
Risotto	5	M	5	0	1	0	8,160
Risque Centerfold	3	F	13	0	1	2	10,978
Risque Copy	5	M	13	5	0	3	30,914
Risque Number	4	F	3	0	0	0	0
Risque Ruby	2	F	1	1	0	0	7,288
Risque'betty	5	M	14	1	2	4	7,554
Rissa	4	F	3	0	0	0	0
Rita E	3	F	4	0	0	0	0

Horse	Age	Sex	Sts	1st	2d	3d	Won
Rit[illegible]ugerand	7	H	[illegible]	0	0	0	0
Rita's Partner	6	H	3	0	0	0	150
Rit[illegible]	6	G	7	0	0	0	755
Rita's Prayer	2	F	14	1	3	4	18,075
Rita's Rainbow	3	F	6	1	0	0	3,762
Rita's Rally	3	F	1	0	1	0	1,125
Rita's Royale	3	G	8	0	2	1	2,943
Rita's the One	4	F	17	3	2	4	22,860
Ritas Wampus Cat	2	F	1	0	0	0	0
Rite Wing	3	F	1	0	0	0	250
Riteonkey	5	G	4	0	0	1	988
Ritmo de Son	2	C	5	1	0	0	14,825
Ritta	3	F	5	4	0	0	120,696
Ritzy	2	F	4	0	0	0	6,100
Ritzy Dame	4	F	4	0	0	0	1,452
Ritzy Go Go	3	F	7	1	2	1	10,380
Ritzy Trick	2	F	6	1	0	0	10,672
Riva Tango	4	F	5	0	0	0	472
Riva Way	6	G	18	1	1	1	10,972
Rivalry	10	G	11	0	1	1	3,761
Rivas	4	G	3	1	0	2	16,878
Riva's Image	3	G	8	1	1	1	13,535
Riva's River Rat	3	C	17	1	1	3	11,666
Riva's Tribute	5	G	10	2	0	1	74,849
Rivatear	3	F	7	0	2	1	7,433
River Adventure (BRZ)	4	G	8	0	0	0	2,760
River Angel	5	M	3	0	0	0	335
River Baron	4	C	7	0	0	3	3,668
River Bed	7	G	2	0	0	0	1,600
River Belle (GB)	3	F	4	2	0	2	202,613
River Boat	11	G	3	1	0	0	14,736
River Bottom	5	G	16	0	2	1	3,921
River Cha Ching	3	G	9	1	1	0	7,025
River City Bert	4	G	1	0	0	0	0
River Cruise	4	F	8	0	2	1	30,560
River Dancer	2	G	7	0	2	0	5,085
River Date	6	M	6	1	0	2	4,698
River Delights	8	G	5	0	0	0	9,964
River Diamond	4	F	10	2	1	3	3,642
River Drive	3	F	3	0	1	1	8,200
River Eagle	4	C	4	1	1	0	5,247
River Eddy	2	F	2	0	0	0	0
River Ella	4	F	12	2	5	0	67,305
River Flower	6	M	9	1	4	1	90,720
River Getaway	4	G	12	0	2	0	6,370
River Girl's Boy	7	G	6	0	0	2	1,251
River Gossip	3	G	1	0	0	0	400
River Hills Cat	5	M	4	1	1	0	3,203
River Island	2	G	1	0	0	0	400
River Jordan	3	G	3	0	1	0	11,960
River Kenmare	2	F	3	0	1	0	4,800
River King	3	G	2	0	0	0	660
River Kwai	3	F	12	1	0	2	14,024
River Legend	3	C	6	0	0	1	4,680
River Lights	3	G	5	1	1	0	26,880
River Luck	3	F	7	0	0	2	12,718
River Maam	3	F	6	0	2	1	4,775
River Miss	5	M	2	0	0	0	0
River Monster	5	H	25	6	5	4	51,823
River Mount	5	G	1	0	0	0	136
River Mountain Rd	4	G	8	3	1	0	87,900
River Native	3	C	3	0	1	1	3,415
River Nore	2	F	2	1	0	0	35,910
River of Angels	4	F	1	0	0	0	118
River of Fire	3	F	1	0	0	0	0
River Otter	6	G	1	0	0	0	700
River Power	6	G	9	1	3	2	34,305
River Raft	3	F	8	0	2	2	6,635
River Rammer	4	G	7	0	0	1	1,820
River Raven (GB)	6	G	8	2	1	1	23,405
River Reed	5	G	15	2	2	1	8,396
River Rennen	5	G	11	1	1	1	12,327
River Retreat	3	G	9	1	3	1	16,280
River Rhapsody	5	G	3	0	0	0	381
River Rhine	2	G	3	0	0	0	518
River Rising	2	C	4	0	1	0	7,220
River Run	5	G	13	1	1	5	26,367
River Rush	6	G	1	0	0	0	460
River Smile	3	G	12	1	4	0	9,150
River Spirit	6	G	5	1	2	0	47,770
River Starlet	3	F	14	0	5	4	23,963
River Thames	3	F	2	0	0	1	3,055
River to Heaven	7	H	10	1	0	1	4,910
River Transport	2	G	2	0	0	2	3,850
River Treasures	2	G	3	0	0	0	1,200
River Walk Bob	4	G	12	3	0	2	34,371
River Walker	3	G	11	2	3	0	49,690
River West	4	G	10	0	0	0	923
River Wild	10	G	10	1	0	3	14,498
River Zuppardo	10	M	3	0	0	0	0
Riverbend Bogey	3	C	1	0	0	0	77
Riverboat Dan	11	G	2	0	0	0	80
Riverboat Party	6	G	15	1	4	3	5,125
Riverbrook	3	F	6	2	0	3	49,180
Riverbye Girl	4	F	13	1	0	1	3,642
Rivercard	4	G	19	2	4	1	20,901
Riverdance Tour	5	G	16	0	0	1	5,151
Rivergirls Runaway	3	F	6	0	0	1	1,769
Rivergirlspartyboy	4	G	8	0	1	1	2,987
Riveriarose	6	G	10	1	1	2	4,520
Riverinn	13	G	3	0	0	0	204
Riverman Council	2	G	2	0	0	0	212
Riverman Jack	2	G	2	1	0	1	5,120
Riverman Slew	4	G	5	1	0	0	3,010
Rivermaster	3	G	10	0	1	1	9,075
Riveroftheplains	3	F	7	1	0	0	3,270
Riverruns Thruit	3	G	4	0	2	1	5,445
River's Reach	3	F	6	2	1	2	35,563
Rivershade	10	G	7	0	1	3	1,710
Riverside Blues	3	C	5	1	0	0	14,390
Riverside Flight	4	C	7	0	0	1	1,330
Riverside Magic	3	F	13	0	6	1	16,250
Riverside Mystro	8	G	1	0	0	0	0
Riverside Rebel	4	G	18	1	2	4	19,312
Riverson	2	C	3	2	0	0	15,900
Riverstar	4	G	9	2	1	0	23,075
Rivets	7	G	14	1	1	5	7,984
Riviera	3	G	7	0	0	2	5,765
Riviera Dance	4	G	11	0	0	1	1,900
Riviera Mill	3	F	6	1	2	1	43,610
Rivulet	4	F	11	1	0	1	5,326
Rize	8	G	13	7	3	2	152,160
Rizmon	3	F	5	1	1	1	14,269
Rizzen to Victory	3	G	11	2	3	0	41,590
Rizzi Bea	3	F	15	3	0	2	22,740
Rizzi Dancer	3	F	9	1	0	0	5,473
Rizzi Fax	2	G	10	3	1	2	41,475
Rizzi Girl	6	M	11	1	2	3	26,082
Rizzi Lee	3	C	5	1	1	2	16,460
Rizzi Rich Step	2	F	5	0	1	0	2,474
Rizzi This	3	C	8	1	0	1	7,055
Rizzis Brass Band	3	C	14	1	1	0	22,249
Rizzi's Gossip	3	C	11	0	1	2	5,293
Rizzis Honor	3	F	7	0	0	1	7,287
Rizzizzi	4	G	12	2	1	1	22,500
Rluckyrock	2	C	8	0	2	1	3,897
Ro Ba Te Na	3	F	1	0	0	0	0
Ro Day Scious	3	C	3	0	0	1	4,170
Road Afleet	6	G	13	1	1	3	27,082
Road Builder	3	C	4	2	0	0	57,620
Road Closed	6	M	10	1	2	0	14,435
Road Express	4	G	6	0	0	0	477
Road Games	7	M	7	0	0	0	84
Road Grader	5	G	14	1	2	2	16,724
Road Hazord	4	G	6	1	0	1	7,378
Road Master	2	G	5	0	1	1	9,120
Road Not Taken	2	F	3	0	0	0	881
Road of Honor	3	F	5	0	2	1	3,353
Road of Tradition	2	C	6	0	0	3	6,940
Road Perfect	4	F	7	0	0	0	354
Road Race	3	C	6	0	1	1	8,613
Road Ruhler	5	G	12	0	1	3	5,995
Road Runner Jr.	4	G	2	0	1	0	685
Road Test	5	G	18	4	3	1	19,348
Road to Honor	3	F	4	0	1	1	3,610
Road To Justice (GB)	5	G	8	1	1	0	4,667
Road to Kisses	6	M	13	1	1	2	11,903
Road to Luck	2	G	4	0	0	0	1,913

Horse	Age	Sex	Sts	1st	2d	3d	Won
Road to Mandalay	3	F	13	2	2	3	63,508
Road to Power	4	G	11	1	2	1	12,312
Road to Recovery	3	G	12	2	1	3	16,127
Road to the Castle	3	G	10	0	1	1	7,761
Road to Town	2	F	1	0	0	0	118
Road to Trillora	10	M	2	0	0	0	0
Road to Zanzibar	3	G	12	1	3	2	8,521
Road Town	4	G	12	3	1	1	70,760
Road Wager	3	G	4	0	1	3	2,130
Roada Ghost	4	F	5	1	2	0	4,325
Roadaway	8	G	6	0	0	0	785
Roadhouse Rose	4	F	6	0	1	0	5,000
Roads West	4	G	8	0	0	2	4,391
Roadsideattraction	3	F	11	2	1	1	45,240
Roadsider	3	F	5	0	0	1	1,012
Roamin in Indiana	3	F	4	1	0	1	3,985
Roaming Annie	3	F	3	0	0	0	0
Roaming Gnome	3	C	2	1	0	0	5,040
Roan	4	F	2	0	0	0	102
Roan Chala Two	5	M	3	0	0	1	1,540
Roan Legend	2	G	1	0	0	0	400
Roanaway Bride	2	F	3	1	1	0	11,325
Roanoke Ridge	4	C	10	3	0	1	54,063
Roanoke Royale	3	F	3	1	0	0	11,760
Roanoke Snap	5	M	8	0	1	0	2,520
Roanoke's Best	4	F	14	2	5	3	51,132
Roanwiththepunches	3	C	3	0	0	1	7,140
Roar and Reign	8	G	1	0	0	0	0
Roar Away	3	G	13	2	0	4	31,220
Roar Emblem	2	G	1	0	0	0	115
Roar Emotion	4	F	11	2	2	3	328,652
Roar for More	3	C	5	1	1	1	10,630
Roar Like a Lion	3	C	8	2	1	0	12,626
Roar Madness	4	F	3	0	0	1	550
Roar of Africa	3	F	11	2	2	1	40,600
Roar of Joy	3	G	3	0	0	0	1,710
Roar of the Lion	3	G	4	0	0	0	831
Roar of the Tiger	5	H	4	1	0	1	37,850
Roar On Tour	4	G	11	5	1	2	115,738
Roar to Score	5	G	3	0	1	1	3,150
Roar With Laughter	4	C	2	1	0	1	9,800
Roarar	3	G	9	0	2	3	10,893
Roarin Brittney	3	F	6	1	3	0	15,050
Roaring Along	3	G	10	0	2	1	13,244
Roaring Beauty	3	F	8	0	4	0	13,095
Roaring Creek	3	G	7	0	0	0	458
Roaring Dori	4	G	13	3	1	2	16,052
Roaring Fever	4	C	9	1	2	3	83,649
Roaring Gale	2	F	3	0	1	1	5,090
Roaring Icon	4	F	3	0	0	0	546
Roaring Leo	2	C	2	0	0	0	360
Roaring Mike	7	G	3	0	0	0	413
Roaring Quick	3	G	5	0	0	0	1,512
Roaring Rage	6	M	1	0	0	0	0
Roaring Rapids	4	G	2	0	0	0	0
Roaring Rylee	2	F	2	0	0	0	450
Roaring Springs	3	G	7	1	1	1	12,910
Roark	5	G	1	0	0	0	0
Roarofvictory	3	G	14	4	2	1	94,156
Roaronthunder	5	G	8	0	1	2	2,270
Roarzak	5	G	11	2	2	2	26,564
Rob Bob	8	G	10	2	0	0	5,382
Rob D Fortune	2	C	6	0	0	0	700
Rob Rac	6	G	5	0	1	1	530
Rob the Banker	2	C	4	1	0	1	17,260
Rob the Gold	8	G	10	0	0	0	884
Rob the Streaker	4	G	7	1	0	1	3,873
Robador	2	C	2	0	0	1	5,214
Robbeau	2	C	6	1	3	1	62,570
Robber	5	M	13	0	0	1	2,202
Robber Baron	4	C	7	1	1	0	13,580
Robber Rascal	3	G	11	1	2	2	6,175
Robbery	3	G	6	0	0	0	475
Robbie	6	G	17	0	1	3	1,532
Robbies Hero	3	G	13	1	4	0	9,309
Robbin Lynn	5	M	13	4	2	2	32,405
Robbin Rachel	2	F	6	1	1	0	25,137
Robbin's Banner	3	G	12	1	0	0	7,455
Robby D	8	G	13	2	3	3	9,540

Horse	Age	Sex	Sts	1st	2d	3d	Won
Robert E	4	G	6	0	0	0	2,090
Robert R	4	G	2	0	0	0	0
Roberta Alwumar	5	M	13	2	3	3	39,720
Roberta Lady	3	F	5	0	0	0	0
Roberta's Matt	4	G	15	0	5	0	12,398
Roberto Rex	3	C	10	0	1	2	6,860
Roberto Royale	7	G	11	3	1	2	19,527
Roberto's Girl	3	F	11	0	0	2	8,873
Roberto's Honor	4	G	3	0	0	0	871
Roberto's Minister	7	G	3	0	0	0	120
Roberto's Pride	10	G	9	3	2	2	35,534
Roberto's Shadow	2	G	1	0	0	0	400
Roberto's Show	5	G	8	1	1	2	65,188
Roberto's Victory	6	M	11	2	3	1	11,850
Robert's Legacy	4	G	9	0	1	0	5,382
Robert's Tribute	5	G	9	2	0	0	15,500
Robertsstar Bar	3	C	3	0	0	0	0
Robin des Robyn	2	F	4	0	0	1	935
Robin des True	3	F	6	1	1	0	10,905
Robin des Tune	4	F	14	2	1	2	46,290
Robin of Trinidad	4	G	11	0	1	2	19,989
Robin Rocks	3	F	9	1	0	1	14,289
Robin Zee	5	G	13	4	0	4	54,040
Robins Beauty	5	H	10	2	0	0	18,855
Robin's Flight	3	F	9	1	1	2	11,780
Robin's Fling	5	M	8	1	0	1	9,743
Robin's Juel	5	M	10	2	0	0	7,665
Robins Shower	5	G	1	0	0	1	935
Robin's Snow	4	F	6	0	2	0	4,052
Robins Wish	4	F	8	1	1	0	3,530
Robinthestorm	4	F	6	0	0	1	1,491
Robnroy	8	G	2	0	1	0	2,332
Robo Secret	2	G	7	1	2	2	19,225
Robot	7	G	9	0	0	0	2,200
Robotica	4	F	9	2	1	1	46,067
Rob's Boy Mat	2	C	6	1	2	0	49,818
Rob's Bull	7	G	5	1	1	0	3,200
Rob's Charger	5	G	11	2	2	2	21,017
Robs Coin	3	G	3	2	0	0	13,820
Rob's Frosty	3	F	12	0	2	3	9,650
Rob's Little Boy	5	H	1	0	0	0	0
Rob's Pegasus	6	G	2	0	0	0	681
Rob's Quest	6	H	13	2	2	1	31,435
Robstown	2	C	1	0	0	0	0
Robthevet	6	G	15	1	4	2	22,696
Robustinnier	6	G	2	0	0	1	1,498
Robusto	3	G	3	1	0	0	7,456
Robyn Dancers Son	2	C	3	0	0	1	2,387
Robyn Ralph	6	G	19	1	1	5	9,238
Robyn Regal	4	C	10	1	3	3	24,054
Robyn Sings	4	F	12	2	2	1	14,906
Robyn Sweet Robyn	2	F	3	1	0	0	8,100
Robyn the Till	3	C	12	2	1	2	20,100
Robyn's Accord	2	G	6	1	1	0	36,960
Robyn's Day	3	F	6	1	1	1	9,936
Robyn's Diamond	7	M	1	0	0	0	80
Robyns Gold Charm	6	G	1	1	0	0	27,600
Robyn's Pal	3	F	10	3	0	0	20,161
Robyn's Pleasure	6	G	2	0	0	0	0
Robyn's Request	3	F	10	2	3	1	44,117
Robynthegold	4	G	14	3	2	4	80,200
Robys Case	3	C	1	0	0	0	0
Rocaco	7	G	3	1	2	0	19,160
Rocajul	6	M	2	0	0	0	656
Rocamana Castle	3	F	13	0	1	2	10,363
Rocchetto	10	G	6	0	0	0	0
Rocco Bull	2	G	3	0	0	0	191
Rochelle	5	M	5	1	1	0	9,956
Rocher's Approval	4	G	5	1	1	1	10,025
Rochester	8	G	8	0	3	1	136,450
Rochioli	3	C	3	0	0	2	8,304
Rocio Comargo	2	F	5	0	1	2	10,500
Rock a by Abby	4	F	4	0	0	1	605
Rock a Lot	5	M	11	1	0	1	6,979
Rock Again	4	C	2	1	0	1	57,329
Rock Away Doeny	6	G	4	0	0	0	0
Rock City Falls	5	M	11	0	6	1	11,200
Rock Climb	4	C	11	1	4	2	34,650
Rock Cod Johnny	5	H	5	0	1	0	3,028

Horse	Age	Sex	Sts	1st	2d	3d	Won
Rock County	4	G	7	3	1	0	34,040
Rock Creek Native	2	F	2	0	0	0	0
Rock de Stars	6	G	11	1	2	3	8,287
Rock Dee Times	3	F	6	1	2	1	19,373
Rock E. Hill	4	G	5	1	2	0	6,767
Rock Falls	4	G	8	1	0	1	5,680
Rock Fever	6	M	15	2	3	2	70,370
Rock Gap	5	G	2	1	1	0	6,042
Rock Handsome	3	C	6	0	1	1	4,490
Rock Harbor	3	G	6	1	1	1	18,300
Rock Hard Safe	2	C	2	0	2	0	12,000
Rock Hard Ten	3	C	8	4	1	1	790,380
Rock Island Rocket	6	G	11	3	2	3	13,072
Rock Island Salami	4	C	6	4	0	1	81,040
Rock Jock	6	G	17	0	1	2	3,060
Rock Layer	6	G	13	2	1	4	51,450
Rock Me Honey	4	G	7	0	0	1	1,016
Rock 'n Red Pop	3	F	11	0	1	1	4,575
Rock N Reel Cookie	3	F	8	1	1	1	7,135
Rock N Role Dancer	3	F	4	0	0	0	0
Rock N Roll Sarah	3	F	3	0	0	0	0
Rock n' Romance	3	F	9	3	2	1	10,550
Rock N Rosh	4	G	4	0	1	1	28,000
Rock of Fame	2	C	2	0	0	1	2,480
Rock of Gold	7	H	2	1	1	0	11,550
Rock On Athena	2	F	3	0	0	0	130
Rock On Red Robyn	7	M	3	1	1	1	10,252
Rock Opera	5	G	5	1	0	1	34,240
Rock Prada	3	C	7	1	0	0	5,880
Rock Salt Ronnie	2	G	1	0	1	0	2,800
Rock Seasons	4	G	3	0	2	0	850
Rock Steady Dan	3	G	12	2	2	3	29,399
Rock Tavern	4	G	11	3	0	0	14,384
Rock the Bank	6	G	10	1	2	2	9,283
Rock the Comet	8	M	7	0	0	0	192
Rock the Nation	4	G	5	1	1	0	8,430
Rock the Rainbow	2	C	2	0	1	1	13,230
Rock the Stone	5	G	7	0	0	1	3,540
Rock With the Hawk	4	G	7	0	1	0	4,700
Rockatowa	7	G	14	1	1	3	9,727
Rockbank	6	G	4	0	0	1	1,018
Rockchalk Jayhawk	6	G	10	1	3	0	46,410
Rockcide	3	F	6	0	1	0	12,630
Rock'd Em All	3	F	15	1	3	1	17,110
Rockem Sockem	3	G	7	4	2	0	110,493
Rockenelle	4	F	9	0	1	4	2,645
Rocker	5	G	1	0	0	0	0
Rocket Buster	2	F	3	0	0	1	638
Rocket Charge	4	G	10	2	1	1	9,695
Rocket Doctor	4	G	4	0	0	0	1,030
Rocket Flight	5	G	7	2	2	3	14,259
Rocket Girl	3	F	3	0	1	0	14,820
Rocket Hombre	5	G	6	2	0	0	14,367
Rocket Junior	3	G	14	3	1	2	35,470
Rocket Launcher	3	G	2	0	0	0	400
Rocket Ma'me	3	F	1	0	1	0	5,000
Rocket Power	5	M	14	1	1	1	10,080
Rocket Rhonda	5	M	5	0	0	0	0
Rocket Ricky	5	G	6	0	1	0	2,137
Rocket Ridge	3	F	11	1	0	3	33,670
Rocket Royale	4	F	9	2	2	0	27,560
Rocket Star	4	G	1	0	1	0	3,300
Rocket Wager	5	G	13	1	4	1	19,387
Rocket Whirl	3	G	2	0	0	0	925
Rocketeering	4	C	5	1	0	1	19,040
Rocketeightyeight	2	G	10	2	1	1	41,500
Rocketera	2	F	1	0	1	0	3,528
Rockets Fired	4	C	4	1	1	0	12,400
Rocket's Glow	6	M	14	0	0	1	3,551
Rocket's Jet	4	G	10	0	0	4	4,398
Rocket's Legacy	4	C	4	0	1	0	3,541
Rockette Road	4	G	4	0	0	0	252
Rockettorussia	3	C	1	0	0	0	0
Rockford	4	G	7	0	1	1	2,970
Rockhewn	3	C	11	1	2	0	33,164
Rockhills Jet Set	3	F	18	1	2	5	25,376
Rockhurst	5	G	6	1	1	1	31,395
Rockies	5	G	13	1	2	1	13,711
Rockim Gorge	5	G	10	0	1	1	1,952
Rockin' Again	3	G	9	2	2	0	70,922
Rockin' Bobby	4	G	4	0	0	1	4,930
Rockin Chair	4	G	2	0	0	0	860
Rockin Concern	3	C	8	1	0	1	19,910
Rockin Early	5	H	6	1	0	0	3,285
Rockin Eddie	2	C	5	1	0	0	7,017
Rockin' Kate	2	F	3	1	0	0	22,340
Rockin On	3	F	6	0	1	2	12,066
Rockin On Ice	5	M	9	1	0	2	25,105
Rockin On Ready	4	C	10	1	2	1	59,040
Rockin Rachel Anne	4	F	8	2	2	0	72,509
Rockin Regent	2	F	4	1	3	0	70,000
Rockin Rhythm	4	F	3	0	0	0	0
Rockin Rooster	5	H	9	0	1	1	8,156
Rockin Roy	7	M	11	2	2	1	52,548
Rockin the Ship	3	G	5	1	0	1	18,103
Rockin Therockies	4	G	6	1	0	1	3,239
Rockin Tunes	3	F	3	1	0	0	5,260
Rockin Your World	2	F	4	0	1	2	2,690
Rocking Bird	4	G	4	0	0	0	3,648
Rocking Chair Ride	6	G	12	1	0	1	3,405
Rocking Rolf	4	G	1	0	0	0	400
Rockingypsy	2	F	2	0	0	0	0
Rockin'in	2	F	2	1	0	0	9,487
Rockinmebaby	4	F	5	0	2	0	2,025
Rockland Road	3	C	1	0	0	0	0
Rockmania	5	G	9	0	0	1	1,686
Rockn' Roca	4	G	11	2	2	2	12,467
Rocknriverman	2	C	3	1	1	0	1,567
Rockonbambam	4	G	7	1	1	0	22,350
Rockport Harbor	2	C	4	4	0	0	210,300
Rockport Road	4	G	14	1	4	3	12,799
Rockroundtheclock	4	F	7	1	0	1	13,365
Rockrupertrose	6	G	13	1	1	3	11,958
Rock's El Dorado	5	M	15	1	5	1	18,561
Rocks in the Mouth	6	M	12	0	2	3	11,914
Rockscissorsfoil	5	G	6	0	0	1	2,172
Rockshaan	6	M	9	0	0	2	1,010
Rocky Bar	6	H	3	0	0	1	2,500
Rocky Creek	2	G	2	1	0	0	11,113
Rocky D' Or	7	G	7	0	0	0	478
Rocky Does	4	G	1	0	0	0	0
Rocky Gorge	9	G	1	0	0	0	0
Rocky Gulch	3	G	10	6	1	1	377,179
Rocky Harbor	6	G	6	0	0	0	436
Rocky Jo Loney	5	H	14	0	1	1	3,833
Rocky Joseph Pm	2	C	1	0	0	0	78
Rocky Lane	4	G	13	2	1	1	10,856
Rocky Moment	6	G	10	4	4	1	6,997
Rocky My Boy	6	G	7	0	0	0	1,125
Rocky Plains	3	C	6	3	2	0	56,000
Rocky Power	4	G	4	0	0	0	1,764
Rocky Rhodes	3	G	3	0	0	0	184
Rocky River	2	C	3	2	0	0	61,680
Rocky Roan	4	F	24	2	5	3	41,552
Rocky Robyn	9	G	5	2	1	0	23,540
Rocky Rose	2	F	4	0	0	1	1,995
Rocky Royal	3	G	9	0	2	0	4,534
Rocky Two	6	G	6	0	1	1	3,896
Rocky Way	3	C	2	0	0	0	410
Rocky Won	6	G	4	0	0	0	680
Rocky's Crew	6	G	4	2	1	1	14,470
Rocky's Dilemma	4	C	9	2	3	2	26,334
Rococo	3	F	4	0	0	0	490
Rod	6	H	2	0	1	0	1,540
Rode Dancer	8	G	6	0	0	0	120
Rodeo Cash	3	G	6	1	1	1	18,694
Rodeo Champ	4	G	9	3	1	0	12,568
Rodeo Dad	3	C	9	1	2	3	9,913
Rodeo Dancin	2	F	1	0	0	0	1,150
Rodeo Drive (IRE)	4	F	10	0	0	1	2,780
Rodeo Fun	3	C	11	1	2	4	87,651
Rodeo Joe Wells	5	H	1	0	0	0	0
Rodeo Licious	3	F	4	2	0	0	97,670
Rodeo Mom	2	F	2	0	0	0	126
Rodeo Pistol	4	C	12	2	1	2	29,104
Rodeo Raheem	2	G	7	3	0	2	38,825
Rodeo Ropey	3	F	11	1	2	0	27,977
Rodeo Roundball	2	C	5	1	0	0	5,585

Horse	Age	Sex	Sts	1st	2d	3d	Won
Rodeo Sass	4	F	6	1	0	2	18,409
Rodeo Shopper	3	G	5	1	2	0	25,335
Rodeo Spirit	4	G	8	0	0	1	14,138
Rodeo Star	4	F	2	1	0	0	3,960
Rodeoactive	3	C	4	2	0	0	17,653
Rodeo's Castle	3	C	3	2	1	0	10,700
Rodeo's Lady	3	F	2	0	0	0	840
Rodgers Forge	9	G	1	0	0	0	37
Rodney Bay	3	C	2	0	0	0	499
Rodney's Pi	3	C	9	1	1	0	12,785
Rodolfo (HUN)	4	C	7	0	0	0	0
Rodrigues	2	C	4	1	0	1	6,620
Rods Mistress	2	F	4	0	1	2	5,825
Rogan Slew	6	G	9	2	0	0	3,389
Roger E	5	G	5	0	0	1	4,440
Roger P	6	G	4	0	1	0	3,920
Roger That	4	C	3	1	0	0	15,900
Roger Wilco	3	C	5	1	0	2	22,524
Rogers Legacy	6	G	6	0	0	0	736
Rogue Agent	5	G	13	1	3	3	109,854
Rogue Rullah	8	G	4	0	0	0	88
Rogue Scholar	3	C	11	2	0	2	61,050
Rogue Storm	4	G	11	2	1	1	33,445
Rohan	2	C	3	0	0	0	1,350
Roho	9	G	7	0	0	0	421
Roi Charmant	3	C	5	1	2	2	68,620
Roi de Violette	3	G	6	0	1	3	17,090
Roi Roi	5	M	4	0	0	1	1,254
Roja Polo	3	G	1	0	0	0	48
Rojo de Amour	2	G	5	1	0	2	12,760
Rojo Grande	3	C	6	0	2	1	20,870
Rojo Rogue	3	G	10	4	2	1	28,674
Rojo Sol	2	F	4	0	1	1	8,060
Rojo Toro	4	C	7	0	1	2	76,600
Rokeby's Nugget	4	G	8	3	1	0	39,644
Rokeby's Wish	7	M	12	2	0	1	12,644
Rokocoko	2	G	2	1	0	0	7,740
Rolbiano	2	F	3	0	1	0	2,300
Rolen to Jasper	7	G	11	2	2	0	9,642
Rolf's Black Gold	5	G	2	0	1	0	1,820
Rolfs Royce	4	F	1	0	0	0	0
Rolickandroll	2	C	3	0	0	0	1,020
Roll All Night	7	G	10	0	0	0	180
Roll Call	5	G	13	2	3	1	19,099
Roll 'Em Again	4	G	11	1	2	0	17,370
Roll Hennessy Roll	4	C	1	0	0	0	600
Roll On	4	F	5	1	0	1	4,420
Roll On Albion	10	G	9	0	2	1	10,632
Roll On Big Ball	5	G	13	1	1	2	3,472
Roll On Partner	3	G	5	1	1	1	23,028
Roll On Retsina	3	G	3	1	0	0	6,695
Roll On Slew	2	F	9	0	0	1	6,946
Roll Over Roy	3	G	11	2	0	1	18,265
Roll the Gold	4	G	3	1	0	0	4,050
Roll the Stage	9	G	6	0	0	0	233
Roll V T R	3	F	2	0	1	1	5,000
Roll Your Own	3	G	7	2	2	2	55,445
Rolled Stocking	8	G	7	4	1	0	91,546
Roller Derby Queen	8	M	8	0	1	1	4,504
Roller Girl	3	F	14	2	2	1	30,140
Roller King	10	G	11	0	1	0	2,786
Roller Queen	3	F	1	0	0	0	0
Rollerbelle	2	F	1	0	0	0	0
Rollette	8	M	2	0	0	0	0
Rollicking Caller	3	C	12	3	0	4	105,678
Rollicking Oddrock	5	G	3	0	0	0	165
Rollicking Times	4	F	12	3	1	2	28,580
Rollin Lite	6	M	10	4	2	0	17,069
Rollin Me Out	7	G	15	5	1	1	36,273
Rollin Nelson	5	G	15	4	0	3	11,988
Rollin' Rat	3	C	4	1	1	1	10,364
Rollin Sixes	2	G	7	0	3	2	13,610
Rollin Trial	5	G	2	0	0	0	92
Rolling Benz	4	G	5	2	0	0	38,640
Rolling Blackout	4	G	7	1	2	1	8,058
Rolling Fork	5	M	2	0	0	0	672
Rolling Home	5	M	6	1	1	2	11,646
Rolling Rock Cheer	3	G	2	0	0	0	0
Rolling Storm	3	G	8	0	2	0	6,115
Rolling Watters	3	C	10	0	0	0	916
Rollmeaseven	2	C	2	0	0	0	348
Rollofthunder	3	G	7	0	1	1	11,322
Rolls Joyce	6	M	7	0	0	0	672
Rollthemnumbers	4	C	2	0	0	0	0
Rollthemsevens	4	G	7	0	0	2	2,120
Rollurownprincess	2	F	2	0	0	1	1,930
Rollwiththechanges	4	C	10	1	0	1	4,272
Rolphs Way	5	M	1	0	0	0	717
Rolyph	5	G	8	1	1	0	4,917
Roma Gold	4	F	6	0	1	1	3,075
Roma Royale	3	F	17	3	4	4	62,990
Romaca	3	F	12	0	2	2	17,600
Romaillian	3	F	14	2	1	2	10,657
Roman Accord	3	G	9	0	2	1	4,622
Roman Beauty	5	M	1	0	0	0	0
Roman Buck	5	M	9	3	2	1	28,184
Roman Candles	2	C	2	1	0	0	21,960
Roman d'Amour	6	M	16	2	2	3	16,455
Roman Empire	5	G	9	1	2	0	10,198
Roman Gladiator	4	G	15	0	0	0	1,437
Roman Governor	3	G	11	1	1	2	4,433
Roman Intellect	10	M	2	0	0	0	103
Roman Jake	2	G	3	1	1	1	47,288
Roman Leader	3	C	6	0	0	0	415
Roman Peace	5	G	3	0	2	1	15,300
Roman Rambler	7	H	2	0	0	0	280
Roman Ripples	3	F	12	1	2	0	8,128
Roman Romance	6	M	10	1	0	2	103,750
Roman Ruler	2	C	5	3	1	0	330,800
Roman Tango	3	F	3	1	0	1	16,200
Roman Thunder	8	G	1	0	0	0	70
Roman Twist	5	G	11	2	2	1	52,176
Romance Inthe Hall	6	G	8	0	0	0	0
Romanceisabonus	3	G	1	0	0	0	400
Romancer	6	G	6	0	0	1	1,510
Romancin Dixie	5	M	7	1	2	0	36,900
Romancin Lady	4	F	5	0	0	0	306
Romancing	4	F	5	0	0	0	487
Romanesque	4	F	7	1	2	1	50,530
Romanian Dancer	3	F	4	1	1	0	9,240
Romaninahurry	3	C	9	1	1	2	25,450
Romanov Star	4	F	5	0	1	0	4,784
Romantic Age (ARG)	6	M	5	2	0	1	26,090
Romantic Comedy	4	F	7	3	1	0	67,085
Romantic Gal	2	F	5	1	0	1	6,420
Romantic Love	2	F	8	0	0	1	2,890
Romantic Numbers	3	F	13	1	1	2	28,290
Romantic Rendezvoo	3	F	18	2	3	1	21,192
Romantic Reward	3	F	3	0	0	0	202
Romantic Romeo	4	G	6	1	0	1	8,190
Romantic Twist	4	F	9	3	2	3	74,070
Romantic Victory	4	F	8	0	0	0	885
Romantic Virginian	6	G	7	1	3	2	20,800
Romanzo	7	G	2	0	0	0	1,140
Romatwil	3	F	2	0	0	0	672
Romazzino	3	G	4	0	1	1	13,247
Rome Is Burning	2	G	5	1	0	0	8,620
Romeo Tango	4	G	4	1	0	0	6,375
Romeo's Bequest	2	C	1	0	0	0	900
Romeo's Chick	2	F	4	0	0	0	959
Romeo's Key	5	M	8	1	1	1	6,854
Romeo's Pistol	4	C	1	0	0	0	0
Romeos Wilson	6	H	6	1	0	2	15,618
Romin Ridge	4	G	14	1	2	2	7,185
Romney Marsh	3	G	15	2	2	3	82,085
Romo Cade	4	C	1	0	0	0	84
Romolo's Brush	5	G	14	3	1	2	46,370
Romolo's Fritzi	6	H	8	3	1	0	54,130
Romolo's Wine	3	C	8	2	0	3	31,038
Rompburger	2	C	6	2	1	0	42,600
Rompin Nelda G.	3	F	2	2	0	0	26,040
Romping Rosie	4	F	14	2	3	2	11,952
Ron	3	C	15	2	3	4	18,007
Ron Cherry	6	G	11	2	0	2	7,813
Ron E.	2	G	2	0	0	0	270
Ron Greschner	3	C	11	1	1	2	48,749
Ronald Jr.	2	G	1	0	0	1	2,280
Ronalda	9	H	3	0	0	0	560

Horse	Age	Sex	Sts	1st	2d	3d	Won
Rondeau	4	F	9	1	0	1	8,945
Rondelet	9	G	5	0	0	0	188
Rongus Hayman	13	H	1	0	0	0	0
Roni Rose	4	F	10	0	2	4	8,341
Ronicle	2	C	7	0	1	1	5,740
Ronnet	5	M	19	2	3	3	41,955
Ronnie B	5	G	3	0	0	1	886
Ronnie's Boy	5	G	8	0	3	1	3,368
Ron's Lad	6	G	18	1	0	2	8,690
Ron's Prince	5	G	12	0	1	0	8,068
Ron's Reason	5	G	9	1	2	1	6,808
Ron's Surprise	4	G	9	1	0	0	6,483
Ron's Temptor	4	G	3	1	0	0	2,387
Ron's Tornado	7	G	16	0	1	2	3,562
Rook'd	3	G	12	1	0	0	6,822
Roomanny	3	G	3	0	0	0	124
Roomtwothirtyeight	5	G	12	2	1	2	11,367
Roop Karna	6	G	2	0	0	0	0
Roop's Loop	3	F	9	0	4	1	26,270
Roosevelt Run	4	F	10	1	0	1	3,882
Rooska Warrior	4	G	7	0	0	1	1,970
Roostas Rastus	4	G	11	2	2	1	5,838
Rooster Rock	6	G	5	0	0	0	1,335
Rooster Rudy	2	C	7	3	0	1	17,940
Rooster Time	5	G	12	2	1	0	4,906
Rooster's Deputy	4	C	7	1	0	0	11,600
Roostin Houston	9	G	3	0	0	1	550
Root Beer Float	6	G	9	1	3	2	20,327
Root Boy's Revenge	4	G	11	0	2	2	4,121
Root Boy's Wonder	6	M	3	0	0	0	572
Root for Lady Jane	3	F	11	1	0	2	9,595
Root for Me Please	4	F	10	1	0	1	9,880
Root With Style	5	G	3	0	0	0	1,030
Rootytoottoot	5	M	11	0	0	1	1,337
Rooville	2	F	3	0	0	0	1,440
Roping Kidd	2	C	2	0	0	0	210
Roraima	2	F	1	0	0	0	150
Rorschach	4	C	3	0	0	0	220
Ro's Lady	2	F	1	0	0	0	0
Rosa Cielo	2	F	3	0	1	1	5,220
Rosa de Lima (PER)	5	M	4	0	0	2	3,120
Rosa Mundi	3	F	3	1	0	0	39,140
Rosa P	3	F	6	5	0	0	50,100
Rosa Vanozza	4	F	3	0	0	1	5,040
Rosalia Lass	3	F	1	0	0	0	0
Rosalino	5	M	8	1	0	0	3,330
Rosalita	5	M	16	2	3	4	20,217
Rosarita Beach	4	F	5	0	0	0	4,545
Rosary's Future	2	F	2	0	0	1	3,900
Rosa's Cove	8	M	3	0	0	0	120
Rosbrian (IRE)	9	G	5	0	0	2	10,250
Roscoe Pito	4	G	7	1	0	1	48,154
Roscommon Express	2	C	1	0	0	0	1,230
Rosco'sgal	5	M	7	0	3	0	12,554
Rose Ago	4	F	10	0	1	1	3,764
Rose Avenue	2	F	1	0	0	0	235
Rose City	2	F	1	0	0	0	2,040
Rose Country Man	3	G	10	0	1	1	7,950
Rose Creek	7	G	6	3	0	0	14,353
Rose Du Roi	3	G	10	2	3	2	38,455
Rose Esther	8	M	11	0	1	1	11,788
Rose Fever	2	F	6	0	2	2	24,430
Rose Fourteen	2	C	3	1	0	0	7,340
Rose Francais	3	F	2	0	0	0	88
Rose Hunter	3	F	8	2	1	0	37,900
Rose Leaves	5	M	10	3	1	2	17,187
Rose N Angelina	6	M	6	2	1	0	11,854
Rose Nessence	4	F	2	0	0	0	160
Rose of Athens	3	F	3	0	0	0	77
Rose of Edmore	4	F	5	0	2	0	5,391
Rose of Etbauer	3	F	18	6	2	1	64,390
Rose of Hadif	3	F	7	0	1	2	5,440
Rose of Pembroke	3	F	11	0	4	0	27,671
Rose of Romanov	3	F	5	0	1	2	15,150
Rose of Roxton	7	M	3	0	1	1	4,712
Rose of Sanantonio	2	F	1	0	0	0	110
Rose of Sophia	3	F	3	0	0	0	488
Rose of Troy	3	F	3	0	1	0	1,978
Rose Punch	4	F	6	0	0	0	1,110

Horse	Age	Sex	Sts	1st	2d	3d	Won
Rose Sea Meridian	4	F	4	1	0	0	2,746
Rose Thorn	3	F	13	1	0	0	5,801
Rose Wars	4	G	9	2	3	0	9,982
Rose Wing	3	C	2	0	0	0	0
Roseal	3	F	7	1	3	1	33,570
Roseavate	3	F	2	0	0	0	0
Rosecoloredglasses	5	G	7	2	1	1	61,750
Rosegate	2	F	5	0	1	0	9,360
Rosehanna	2	F	4	1	1	0	7,660
Rosella	4	F	7	0	0	1	3,190
Rosenball	7	G	13	2	2	1	8,215
Roses Are Right	2	F	7	1	1	1	17,725
Rose's Buddy	5	M	1	0	0	0	0
Roses Bull	2	C	1	0	0	0	0
Rose's Echo	4	F	12	0	1	1	3,931
Roses for Concorde	4	F	3	0	0	0	0
Roses for Grace	3	F	2	0	1	1	2,180
Roses for Lydia	5	M	10	2	4	1	17,420
Roses for Maria	3	F	11	1	1	1	10,505
Roses for Marti	4	F	10	1	1	0	11,925
Roses for Mom	4	F	8	0	0	2	3,357
Roses for My Lady	2	F	1	0	0	0	135
Roses for Ruby	5	M	3	0	0	1	2,146
Roses for Sandy	2	F	2	0	0	0	0
Roses From David	5	M	6	1	0	2	9,315
Roses From Dora	6	M	16	2	4	6	30,118
Rose's Head Games	5	M	2	0	0	0	405
Roses in May	4	C	6	5	1	0	1,723,277
Rose's Jet Stream	3	G	7	0	0	1	5,036
Roses N Bows	3	F	15	4	3	4	68,448
Roses Roses Roses	7	M	7	1	0	2	6,900
Rose's Secret	5	M	1	0	0	0	0
Rose's Sunshine	3	C	4	1	1	0	34,638
Rose's Thistle	2	F	6	0	4	0	3,235
Roses Wild Rush	3	F	3	0	0	0	0
Rosesan Ruby	2	F	2	0	0	1	1,449
Rose'shoneybun	5	M	1	0	0	0	303
Rosesnpearls	3	F	4	1	0	1	6,775
Rosethorn Road	3	F	5	1	0	4	23,807
Rosetide	6	G	10	0	3	1	37,085
Rosey Glow	6	M	7	0	0	0	895
Rosey Lass	4	F	5	0	0	0	335
Rosey Red	3	F	16	0	4	2	7,814
Rosey Ridan	4	F	6	0	0	2	1,098
Rosey Teresa	4	G	14	1	0	1	3,761
Rosey's Honor	3	G	11	1	2	3	12,054
Roshan	5	G	11	0	2	3	5,646
Rosharon	5	M	8	3	0	1	132,378
Roshneti	4	F	11	1	4	1	28,110
Rosie d'On	4	F	14	0	1	5	6,976
Rosie Gone West	5	G	1	0	0	0	0
Rosie in the Sky	5	M	1	0	1	0	4,000
Rosie Kate	3	F	9	1	1	2	6,558
Rosie Lee City	3	F	12	2	2	2	26,452
Rosie Lilac	5	M	3	0	0	1	2,050
Rosie My Buddie	6	M	12	2	2	3	13,820
Rosie o' Mali	5	M	2	0	0	0	430
Rosie O'Neal	5	M	1	0	0	0	0
Rosieontop	2	F	5	1	1	1	13,533
Rosies Bandita	2	F	2	0	0	0	0
Rosie's Big Boy	4	G	5	1	2	0	46,410
Rosie's Boy	5	G	13	3	4	2	19,833
Rosie's Devil	2	F	1	0	0	0	0
Rosies Dhabi Dude	5	G	11	0	2	3	18,964
Rosie's Gent	2	C	1	0	0	0	780
Rosie's Gold	4	F	7	0	0	0	1,350
Rosies Queenvalay	3	F	1	0	0	0	250
Rosie's Ransom	4	F	8	2	1	3	30,285
Rosie's Risk	5	M	6	1	2	0	8,180
Rosies Runn Oft	2	F	2	0	1	1	3,650
Rosie's Shamrock	6	H	4	0	0	0	810
Rosie's Wish	3	F	8	3	0	1	22,480
Rosieville	3	F	8	1	1	1	19,060
Rosinsky	3	G	11	0	1	0	4,378
Rosita's Power	5	M	2	0	0	0	0
Rosko	9	G	15	1	2	1	6,298
Rosmerta	5	M	6	1	0	0	15,900
Ross Court	3	G	9	0	0	0	570
Ross Is a Hoss	3	G	8	0	0	0	1,145

Horse	Age	Sex	Sts	1st	2d	3d	Won
Ross Kabeer	3	G	4	0	0	0	1,000
Ross n' Bens Girl	8	M	1	0	0	0	44
Ross Road	4	G	5	0	0	0	566
Ross to Dublin	3	G	5	0	1	0	12,000
Ross Valay	4	F	15	2	1	1	43,030
Rossignol	3	C	1	0	0	0	161
Rossiter	2	C	1	0	0	0	0
Rossman	8	G	7	1	2	1	4,360
Rostral	4	G	1	0	0	0	0
Rosy M	4	F	10	1	1	1	5,950
Rosy Pete	5	M	11	1	1	4	7,960
Rosy Ran	6	M	4	1	1	0	2,501
Rosy's Babe	4	F	2	0	0	0	149
Rosy's Legacy	6	G	1	0	0	0	88
Rotary	2	C	2	0	1	0	6,760
Rotator	2	F	4	1	0	1	9,755
Roth Ticket	3	C	10	2	1	0	27,680
Rothko	6	G	5	0	0	0	109
Rototiller	4	F	4	0	0	0	2,533
Rotten Ralph	5	G	1	0	0	0	0
Rotten Row	3	G	12	3	2	4	32,440
Rotunda Beauty	5	M	11	2	2	0	11,209
Rouen (FR)	8	G	6	0	0	1	4,690
Rouge County	3	G	11	1	0	0	4,687
Rouge d'Or	5	M	19	2	0	0	7,111
Rouge Royale	9	G	4	1	0	1	3,512
Rouge Sensation	4	G	10	2	3	0	21,677
Rouge Stone	3	F	6	0	1	2	29,688
Rough	9	G	6	1	1	0	1,270
Rough and Robust	3	F	1	0	0	0	0
Rough Clouds	6	G	12	1	0	1	8,066
Rough Day	4	G	5	1	0	0	20,100
Rough Doctor	6	G	7	0	0	1	1,050
Rough Draft	7	G	11	7	2	1	71,025
Rough Energy	8	G	1	0	0	0	0
Rough House Ruby	4	F	4	0	0	0	659
Rough Neck	3	G	7	3	2	0	17,985
Rough Player	3	G	11	3	2	1	15,608
Rough R. N.	5	M	4	0	0	0	7,466
Rough Trick	4	G	14	2	0	0	6,885
Roughjette	9	G	11	1	5	1	9,694
Rough'n It	3	C	5	0	1	0	3,770
Rough'n Rahy	3	C	5	0	0	1	2,978
Round Girl	4	F	5	0	0	0	1,660
Round Native Miss	5	M	12	1	3	1	12,236
Round Rock	6	G	12	2	1	2	16,884
Round the Bend	4	G	12	1	0	1	7,330
Round the Horn	3	F	4	0	1	0	12,394
Round Tree	4	C	3	0	0	0	428
Roundabout Again	4	F	1	0	0	0	0
Roundabout Jones	3	G	5	1	0	0	10,260
Roundball Casey	3	C	1	0	0	0	120
Rounded	3	F	3	0	0	0	181
Roundtree (IRE)	5	M	2	0	0	1	6,720
Roundtripper	3	C	12	3	0	0	21,801
Roused	3	F	4	0	0	0	1,020
Rouses Point	2	F	2	0	1	0	2,000
Rousing Again	4	F	7	3	2	0	62,660
Rousing Past	6	G	7	0	3	2	6,360
Rousing Victory	3	C	8	2	2	1	122,647
Roust About	2	G	3	1	1	1	24,290
Rout N Dixie	4	C	4	0	0	0	270
Route Forty Two	3	C	1	0	0	1	920
Routine Panic	4	F	8	1	0	1	8,712
Roux Be Wild	3	G	1	0	1	0	4,720
Rouxbee	3	F	9	2	2	1	47,380
Rovanna	4	F	6	0	0	2	2,043
Rove	2	C	1	0	1	0	8,600
Rover Ridge	5	G	2	0	0	0	774
Rovin Rose	3	F	1	0	0	0	0
Roving Angel	2	F	5	3	0	1	120,536
Roving Singer	5	G	10	0	2	1	10,061
Row Row Man	5	G	7	2	0	0	6,617
Rowan Express (GB)	4	F	6	0	0	0	7,716
Rowan Inish	3	G	8	1	1	1	6,685
Rowans Park	4	C	3	0	0	0	7,700
Rowdy	3	F	5	1	2	0	56,690
Rowdy Bear	4	G	1	0	0	0	0
Rowdy Begone	4	G	10	1	2	3	11,711

Horse	Age	Sex	Sts	1st	2d	3d	Won
Rowdy Creek	2	G	7	1	2	1	12,372
Rowdy Dinner	3	G	1	0	0	0	0
Rowdy Hode	5	G	1	0	0	0	0
Rowdy Lad	6	G	5	0	0	1	1,740
Rowdy Rose	4	F	7	0	0	1	2,042
Rowdy Run	3	G	1	0	0	0	37
Rowdy So n' So	4	G	16	1	7	0	13,568
Rowdy Sofia	4	F	1	0	0	0	116
Rowdy's Last	6	G	3	0	0	0	521
Rowdys Move	4	G	3	0	0	1	863
Rowland On Over	2	G	6	0	0	0	2,247
Rowsfashion Girl	6	M	1	0	0	0	0
Rox Solid	2	C	3	0	0	0	210
Roxade	8	G	6	0	0	0	330
Roxaedit	5	M	1	0	0	0	0
Roxanne's Dancer	2	F	2	0	1	1	6,200
Roxie Lou	4	F	7	0	0	0	253
Roxy Carr	2	F	2	0	1	0	3,516
Roxy Hadif	2	F	6	0	1	2	5,390
Roxy Rocket	2	F	1	0	0	0	330
Roxy Roller	6	M	1	0	0	0	850
Roxyette	3	F	1	0	1	0	7,030
Roy de France	2	C	5	0	0	0	410
Roy Jones	4	C	4	0	0	1	7,668
Roy Massiah	3	G	9	2	0	0	27,875
Roy Rodjers	5	H	3	0	0	0	0
Royal Act	4	G	11	1	1	1	13,875
Royal Admiral	3	C	15	3	4	1	35,395
Royal Admirer	6	G	13	1	0	0	2,052
Royal Advantage	5	M	8	1	1	1	13,502
Royal Affirmation	5	M	2	0	0	0	82
Royal Affirmed	6	H	9	2	1	0	79,804
Royal Again	4	F	13	5	4	0	95,630
Royal Aggravation	4	G	3	0	0	0	0
Royal Alchemist	4	F	1	0	0	0	0
Royal Ambassador	4	C	10	0	0	1	1,840
Royal Arsenal	3	G	6	0	0	0	1,477
Royal Assault	3	C	10	2	1	3	301,501
Royal Attitude	4	F	5	0	0	1	1,686
Royal Attraction	4	F	11	1	2	3	47,048
Royal B	2	F	4	2	0	1	14,198
Royal Babe	2	F	1	0	0	0	1,764
Royal Banker	3	F	7	1	0	0	21,322
Royal Baron	4	C	2	1	0	0	4,500
Royal Bauble	3	F	2	0	0	0	780
Royal Bean	2	F	3	1	1	0	27,481
Royal Beau	3	G	10	2	0	0	5,287
Royal Bella	2	F	4	0	0	0	210
Royal Birth	4	G	12	0	0	0	3,392
Royal Blend	2	F	2	0	0	0	435
Royal Bon Bon	5	M	19	1	5	6	17,870
Royal Bonus	5	H	12	2	1	1	12,771
Royal Box	3	F	5	0	0	3	10,350
Royal Brew	5	G	12	1	1	1	3,192
Royal Brittany	5	M	6	0	0	0	2,452
Royal Cache	2	F	5	0	0	1	4,630
Royal Call	3	F	3	0	0	0	391
Royal Canadian	2	C	2	0	0	0	280
Royal Canyon	3	F	8	1	2	1	33,700
Royal Case	3	F	6	1	1	0	8,400
Royal Cavall	4	G	10	2	0	2	22,635
Royal Ceremony	6	M	6	1	0	1	11,205
Royal Chalice	4	G	11	4	2	0	28,070
Royal Charisma	3	F	4	1	0	1	7,540
Royal Charley	4	G	5	2	0	0	12,031
Royal Choice	3	F	1	0	0	0	492
Royal Ciano	3	G	3	0	0	0	0
Royal City	3	G	8	3	0	0	15,208
Royal Classic	2	G	5	0	1	0	6,340
Royal Cliff Hanger	3	G	13	1	0	3	28,901
Royal Contessa	5	M	12	0	1	3	6,670
Royal Copenhagen (FR)	2	F	4	2	2	0	68,417
Royal Cousin	5	M	1	0	0	0	559
Royal Creek	5	G	7	0	0	1	1,575
Royal Cup	3	F	5	1	1	1	21,765
Royal D	4	G	4	0	0	0	5,814
Royal Dalliance	7	M	7	0	2	1	45,969
Royal Damsel	4	F	3	0	0	0	301
Royal Dauphin	4	C	1	0	0	0	0

Horse	Age	Sex	Sts	1st	2d	3d	Won
Royal Deal	5	G	8	2	1	1	13,410
Royal Decision	3	G	1	0	0	0	50
Royal Dilemma	3	F	8	1	1	1	8,660
Royal Discovery	2	F	2	0	0	0	0
Royal Discretion	2	G	5	0	0	1	3,978
Royal Distraction	5	M	7	3	1	1	101,974
Royal Divide	3	G	3	0	1	0	1,625
Royal Dove	4	F	9	1	4	1	47,770
Royal Drums	5	G	4	0	0	0	245
Royal Duke	4	G	10	1	1	3	13,268
Royal Embassy	2	F	1	0	0	0	0
Royal Emerald	4	G	9	2	1	1	15,412
Royal Empress	4	F	8	0	2	1	2,340
Royal Epic	2	F	5	0	2	0	21,560
Royal Falcon	4	G	9	0	2	3	18,875
Royal Fan	4	C	1	0	0	0	0
Royal Feast	4	C	6	2	1	0	46,775
Royal Flyer	2	C	8	1	2	0	19,895
Royal Footage	5	G	13	2	5	2	43,112
Royal for Sure	8	M	6	0	0	1	1,708
Royal Force	3	G	9	0	1	2	10,525
Royal Fudge	2	F	7	1	0	1	47,770
Royal Galaxy	4	F	8	1	2	2	9,580
Royal Gate	7	M	15	0	2	1	5,139
Royal Gem	5	H	2	0	0	1	7,200
Royal General	3	G	1	0	0	0	0
Royal Groove	5	G	15	5	2	2	28,860
Royal Group	7	G	11	3	2	3	36,440
Royal Grove	4	G	6	0	0	1	3,100
Royal Heir	3	C	1	0	0	0	502
Royal Highlander (IRE)	7	H	14	1	0	4	4,878
Royal Illusion	3	F	6	1	0	0	8,001
Royal Impact	5	M	12	0	4	1	15,705
Royal Infantry	4	G	7	0	1	1	2,566
Royal Intent	5	G	18	1	1	1	8,495
Royal Intro	4	F	5	0	0	0	1,416
Royal Irish	7	G	6	5	1	0	21,720
Royal Irish Lace	9	M	9	2	0	1	9,058
Royal Kiss	3	F	10	1	0	3	8,804
Royal Kleven	4	F	4	1	1	1	26,340
Royal Lace	3	F	2	1	1	0	13,030
Royal Lad	5	H	5	0	0	1	11,790
Royal Lady	4	F	9	1	1	2	19,682
Royal Lainie	3	F	10	0	0	1	2,434
Royal Lake	6	G	15	5	1	2	40,850
Royal Lear	2	C	2	1	0	0	4,645
Royal Lion	2	C	2	0	0	0	75
Royal Liverpool	3	F	8	1	1	3	73,619
Royal Lullaby	5	M	7	0	0	1	1,946
Royal Mac	7	G	6	1	0	0	1,744
Royal Magician	3	F	9	0	3	1	27,080
Royal Mahogany	3	G	1	0	0	0	910
Royal Mambo	4	G	4	0	0	0	846
Royal Man	3	C	10	0	0	1	10,495
Royal Maneggiare	3	G	1	0	0	0	0
Royal Marge	3	F	10	0	0	0	2,625
Royal Marquet	5	H	12	2	4	1	43,455
Royal Mast	4	F	3	1	1	0	30,923
Royal Master	3	G	14	4	2	1	52,235
Royal Mauriz	6	G	4	0	0	0	132
Royal Mecke	4	F	1	0	0	1	1,540
Royal Medal	3	G	8	2	0	0	18,074
Royal Messenger	5	G	14	3	3	2	35,698
Royal Millennium	4	G	8	1	1	0	6,435
Royal Miner	4	F	16	3	1	1	16,209
Royal Mischief	2	F	6	0	0	0	2,994
Royal Moment	2	C	5	1	1	2	46,180
Royal Moonshine	4	F	11	2	1	0	10,785
Royal Moro	5	G	7	1	1	0	59,120
Royal Night Out	6	G	12	2	1	3	4,586
Royal No Trump	7	M	8	2	2	0	19,863
Royal n'Sweet	4	F	4	0	0	1	1,820
Royal Obsession	4	F	1	0	0	0	0
Royal Parade	3	F	7	1	1	0	17,330
Royal Partner	2	F	1	0	0	0	450
Royal Payback	3	G	8	1	3	0	18,035
Royal Peace	4	G	4	1	1	1	19,360
Royal Peak	5	G	2	0	0	0	210
Royal Pet	3	F	14	2	2	3	48,561
Royal Peteski	6	G	15	1	1	2	21,360
Royal Photographer	3	G	4	0	1	0	10,180
Royal Place	4	C	10	2	1	2	137,696
Royal Prairie	5	M	3	0	0	0	273
Royal Prenup	4	G	9	1	2	1	11,295
Royal Price (GER)	4	C	8	3	0	2	121,840
Royal Prize	4	F	11	1	2	0	33,470
Royal Prophet	4	G	4	1	1	0	24,260
Royal Providence	4	C	12	1	0	0	6,771
Royal Quack	6	G	6	0	0	0	0
Royal Rahy	5	G	11	3	2	1	33,730
Royal Rapids	6	G	8	1	1	0	24,313
Royal Rebecca	4	F	2	0	1	0	2,640
Royal Reblar	2	G	3	1	0	1	3,280
Royal Reception	4	F	8	1	2	0	19,960
Royal Regalia	6	G	4	2	0	2	236,200
Royal Relations	2	F	1	0	0	0	0
Royal Revy	3	C	15	2	2	1	20,713
Royal Riley	2	F	3	1	0	2	14,780
Royal Robe (IRE)	4	G	9	0	2	2	23,438
Royal Robey	3	C	7	1	1	0	14,185
Royal Rocket	2	C	2	0	1	1	4,250
Royal Roman	4	G	7	0	0	1	890
Royal Rumors	3	F	2	0	0	0	0
Royal Rush	3	G	8	0	2	0	1,666
Royal Sabre	4	G	8	1	1	0	9,948
Royal Sailor	4	G	3	0	0	0	0
Royal Saint	2	C	1	0	0	0	300
Royal Sanction	2	F	3	0	0	0	2,985
Royal Sensation	3	C	5	1	1	0	24,200
Royal Severance	3	C	12	0	0	1	4,574
Royal Sharp	3	F	6	0	0	0	104
Royal Shyann	8	M	7	2	2	2	7,977
Royal Signe	6	M	3	0	1	1	658
Royal Siphon	4	G	3	2	0	0	54,600
Royal Slam	3	G	2	0	2	0	9,180
Royal Slammer	3	C	7	0	1	1	1,752
Royal Smoke	5	G	9	0	0	1	4,219
Royal Snooze	2	G	4	0	1	0	7,825
Royal Southerner	6	G	3	0	0	0	0
Royal Speech	4	F	13	1	2	2	10,325
Royal Speed	6	G	8	0	0	1	813
Royal Spin	4	G	1	0	0	0	0
Royal Spirit	7	G	7	0	1	1	5,075
Royal Splash	4	G	12	1	3	1	10,303
Royal Spy	6	H	5	0	1	2	40,992
Royal Stage	3	C	7	2	1	3	5,119
Royal Stamp	5	H	1	1	0	0	34,800
Royal Strategy	3	F	2	0	0	0	0
Royal Stripe	3	G	5	1	1	0	14,060
Royal Stroke	4	C	1	0	0	0	0
Royal Sue	3	F	14	3	1	5	18,448
Royal Sultan	2	C	6	0	3	0	30,850
Royal Sun	5	G	4	0	1	0	1,182
Royal Sweetheart	3	F	2	0	1	0	2,340
Royal Sweetpea	3	F	8	0	2	1	27,590
Royal T. K. O.	4	G	17	2	2	5	26,928
Royal T. N. T.	2	F	1	0	0	0	840
Royal Taste	3	G	18	3	0	3	22,683
Royal Teresa	4	F	13	4	2	0	99,790
Royal Thunderflash	4	C	1	0	0	0	0
Royal Ticket	3	F	4	0	0	1	921
Royal Tiff	7	M	13	0	2	5	3,435
Royal Tiny Wager	2	F	3	1	0	0	4,200
Royal Tour	3	G	20	2	2	0	10,737
Royal Town	2	G	4	1	1	1	10,656
Royal Tromp'e	3	F	3	0	0	0	2,590
Royal Twister	4	F	7	0	0	0	720
Royal Vic	3	C	3	0	0	0	0
Royal Vixen	4	F	6	3	1	0	28,645
Royal Viz	5	G	8	0	0	0	630
Royal Walk	4	C	1	0	0	0	400
Royal War	5	M	10	0	0	0	4,070
Royal Warrior	3	C	1	0	1	0	4,780
Royal Watch	6	G	10	0	1	2	6,597
Royal Wave	2	F	3	1	0	0	26,740
Royal Wheaton	3	F	3	0	0	1	649
Royal Win	5	G	13	1	1	1	16,275
Royal Wulff	7	H	5	0	0	0	0

Horse	Age	Sex	Sts	1st	2d	3d	Won
Royal Zar	4	C	11	1	0	0	7,002
Royale Regal	2	F	7	0	0	0	2,308
Royalette	4	F	15	6	1	2	41,920
Royalewitcheese	2	C	2	0	1	0	2,000
Royalist	3	C	13	1	0	0	5,980
Royally Blue	6	H	5	0	0	0	0
Royally Chosen	6	M	8	2	1	1	244,500
Royally Minted	5	M	4	0	0	3	7,920
Royally Yours	3	F	11	1	1	1	8,980
Royalmissglitter	6	M	12	3	2	3	26,640
Royalsaly	6	M	7	0	0	0	310
Royalton	5	H	2	0	0	0	960
Royaltry	4	G	12	2	1	1	7,700
Royalty Boy	3	C	7	3	1	0	115,202
Royalty Gal	3	F	2	0	1	0	11,080
Royalty Heights	3	G	1	0	0	0	347
Royalty Louis	2	C	3	0	0	0	2,991
Royalty of Iowa	4	C	10	3	2	1	71,140
Royalty Prospector	2	G	1	0	0	0	0
Royalty Rose	3	F	2	0	0	0	1,255
Royaltys R Star	2	G	1	0	0	0	140
Roycetherascal	2	G	3	0	0	0	0
Roy's Choice	5	G	2	0	0	0	700
Roy's Joy	8	G	4	0	0	0	720
Roy's Raise	4	G	10	2	1	0	21,042
Roy's Remedy	4	G	2	0	0	0	0
Roy's Ruckus	9	G	12	2	1	3	41,935
Roy's Secret	5	G	1	0	0	0	0
Roy's Trigger	4	C	4	0	0	0	960
Rozadante	4	G	13	3	3	2	25,152
Rozalyn Ruckus	4	F	4	0	0	0	1,600
Rozina	5	M	2	0	0	0	0
Rozys Account	5	M	9	0	1	1	21,203
Rt's Roan Rocket	3	F	1	0	0	0	0
Ru Ach's Caspian	3	G	4	0	0	1	866
Ruanwar	5	M	8	2	1	2	2,482
Rub Down	7	G	4	1	0	1	10,131
Rub the Ring	5	G	10	1	0	2	4,808
Ruba Dub Dub	3	G	12	3	3	4	87,488
Rubalamp	6	G	11	1	3	2	4,567
Rubano	2	G	2	0	0	0	0
Rubber Side Down	3	G	10	0	2	3	11,702
Rubby G	2	F	1	0	0	0	400
Rubelite	5	M	4	1	1	1	8,165
Ruben John	5	G	6	0	0	1	1,452
Rubi Chunt	5	M	2	0	0	1	610
Rubi Echo	3	C	9	1	3	1	59,840
Rubi Prince	3	G	7	2	0	0	26,300
Rubi Spice	2	F	7	0	1	0	6,274
Rubialedo	2	C	7	1	1	2	54,085
Rubian Ridge	7	G	4	1	0	0	10,278
Rubiano Casey	5	M	2	0	0	0	813
Rubiano Kat	5	G	2	0	0	0	150
Rubiano Lad	3	G	10	2	1	2	32,477
Rubiano Star	4	G	6	1	0	0	3,660
Rubiano's Flag	4	G	8	1	0	3	6,331
Rubianos Image	4	C	12	3	2	3	114,076
Rubiano's Music	2	G	3	1	0	0	7,125
Rubiano's Revenue	3	F	12	0	3	3	8,366
Rubiano's Wish	3	G	8	0	2	1	23,058
Rubies and Jade	6	M	7	1	0	0	4,216
Rubies N Roses	4	F	5	0	0	0	2,070
Rubiesandstars	7	M	5	0	0	0	348
Rubietta	6	M	14	2	2	2	14,620
Rubikisses	6	M	13	4	3	1	44,559
Rubino	5	H	15	3	0	3	26,500
Rubin's Girl	7	M	12	3	0	2	33,223
Rubin's Rose	5	M	8	4	2	0	36,428
Rubius	2	C	2	2	0	0	38,500
Rubix	3	G	11	2	0	2	16,069
Ruby Ballet	3	F	9	0	2	1	7,203
Ruby Be Mine	2	F	3	2	1	0	48,000
Ruby Brad	7	G	9	2	2	3	62,559
Ruby Choise	4	F	12	2	3	0	18,565
Ruby Dawn	4	F	8	2	0	2	27,735
Ruby Deere	3	F	6	0	0	0	1,590
Ruby Do	2	C	1	1	0	0	15,800
Ruby Essence	4	F	2	0	0	0	553
Ruby Falls	4	G	19	1	1	6	15,835
Ruby Fields	5	M	12	2	3	0	16,192
Ruby Glitter	4	F	10	0	1	2	11,755
Ruby Heist	2	F	4	0	0	0	1,613
Ruby Janes Girl	3	F	12	2	2	0	55,000
Ruby La Pearl	3	F	8	1	0	2	12,370
Ruby Lee Ann	2	F	6	0	1	0	2,354
Ruby Lover	9	G	5	0	0	1	2,225
Ruby Martini	2	F	1	0	0	0	330
Ruby Montani	5	M	5	0	1	0	800
Ruby Prospector	7	G	13	1	0	2	5,104
Ruby Red	4	G	3	0	0	0	132
Ruby Red Breast	2	F	1	0	0	1	780
Ruby Red Slippers	5	M	11	0	0	2	3,509
Ruby River	5	M	3	1	0	0	14,857
Ruby Ruby Doo	2	F	5	0	0	2	4,666
Ruby Slew	3	F	12	1	4	2	22,433
Ruby Summer	3	F	7	1	0	0	21,320
Ruby Tango	6	M	5	0	0	0	3,533
Ruby Tutor	9	G	10	4	2	2	14,534
Ruby Two Socks	2	F	4	0	0	0	500
Ruby Victoria	5	M	4	0	0	0	0
Ruby Wine	3	F	7	0	0	0	724
Ruby Wren	2	F	5	0	1	1	12,138
Rubyennf	3	F	3	0	1	2	2,550
Ruby's Cat Farm	2	F	2	0	0	0	198
Rubys Dove	4	F	2	1	0	0	14,740
Ruby's Princess	4	F	2	0	0	0	196
Ruby's Prize	2	F	2	0	1	0	9,525
Ruby's Pro	4	G	12	1	3	2	30,893
Ruby's Reception	4	F	3	0	0	1	8,150
Ruby's Rocker	2	F	3	0	0	0	1,350
Ruby's Rocket	4	F	10	1	3	1	29,079
Ruby's Ruby	3	F	7	2	2	1	13,938
Rucava	3	F	2	0	1	0	1,450
Rucker	3	G	7	0	0	0	1,170
Ruckus Dancer	3	G	6	0	1	2	3,332
Ruckus in Court	3	F	13	3	3	3	138,775
Ruckus in Rio	3	C	1	0	0	0	0
Ruckuslady	6	M	12	0	2	4	6,828
Rudbeckia	2	F	5	0	0	1	4,800
Rude Behavior	2	F	5	0	0	1	20,389
Rude Cat	6	G	1	0	0	1	616
Rude Jane	8	M	2	0	0	0	210
Rude Ransom	6	G	6	0	0	0	680
Rudirudy	9	G	12	3	2	2	110,990
Rudi's Leslie	3	F	13	2	3	1	58,880
Rudnick Bear	4	G	7	0	0	3	19,469
Rudolf (BRZ)	5	G	8	0	2	3	37,220
Rudster	5	G	16	0	2	1	8,001
Rudy Layne	6	G	1	0	0	0	40
Rudy Pooh Sue	4	F	12	1	2	2	37,005
Rudy S	4	G	11	0	0	0	3,270
Rudy Tuesday	4	F	3	1	0	0	1,300
Rudy's Dee Dee	2	F	1	0	0	0	0
Rudy's Finest	4	C	7	2	2	0	34,900
Rudy's Last Reward	5	G	9	2	1	2	8,711
Rudys Mint	5	G	4	0	0	0	0
Rudy's White Cloud	3	G	8	2	1	0	15,654
Rue des Reves	5	M	12	4	3	1	53,357
Rue the Limit	4	C	10	4	1	0	19,680
Rue's Rebel	9	G	12	2	3	1	31,744
Ruettiger	6	G	16	2	1	2	13,334
Ruff and Roady	4	G	5	0	1	0	2,280
Ruff Flight	5	G	6	1	0	0	7,740
Ruff House N	3	G	4	0	0	1	3,480
Ruff 'n Bold	3	F	4	0	0	0	878
Ruff N Stormy	5	G	16	3	2	1	49,960
Ruff Ruff	4	F	1	0	0	0	55
Ruff Tuff Stuff	6	G	8	4	1	1	45,576
Ruffaire	6	M	5	1	1	0	9,782
Ruffett	2	F	2	0	0	0	800
Ruffled Up	2	F	3	0	0	0	0
Ruffles and Ridges	2	G	10	3	3	1	53,820
Rufus P	2	G	4	0	0	0	2,265
Rufus the Glider	4	G	7	1	0	2	32,532
Rufus the Red	3	G	5	0	0	0	136
Rufustheroadrunner	4	G	10	4	1	2	94,860
Rugged Appeal	4	G	15	0	0	1	1,757
Rugged Cliff	6	G	5	2	2	0	18,201

Horse	Age	Sex	Sts	1st	2d	3d	Won
Rugged Russel	4	C	4	0	0	0	120
Rugged Zeal	8	G	15	0	1	0	6,048
Rugger	8	G	11	1	4	0	12,820
Ruggles Road	4	G	6	0	1	0	5,540
Rugula	2	F	2	2	0	0	32,400
Ruhl With Approval	3	F	4	0	1	0	2,232
Ruhla	6	M	10	0	0	1	993
Ruhletta	4	F	8	1	0	2	7,683
Ruhling Partner	3	F	5	0	0	0	0
Ruined the Program	2	C	3	1	0	0	10,190
Ruissec	5	M	1	0	0	0	0
Ruji	5	G	18	1	5	0	19,535
Rule Change	7	G	13	2	0	2	10,355
Rule the Court	8	G	1	0	1	0	3,040
Rule the Ice	3	F	6	2	0	1	10,963
Rulebook	5	H	5	2	0	2	990
Ruled by Numbers	2	F	3	1	0	1	27,840
Ruler Red	7	G	18	1	1	3	6,460
Ruleroftheforest	3	G	6	0	0	0	446
Ruler's Cat	2	F	2	0	0	0	410
Rules Easily	3	F	4	0	0	2	5,550
Rules of the Game	4	C	14	6	1	3	29,197
Rules of War	3	G	9	3	1	1	64,730
Ruling House	3	F	7	0	0	1	2,352
Ruling Interest	4	G	5	0	0	0	399
Ruling Miner	5	G	2	0	0	0	0
Ruling Monarch	5	G	5	0	0	0	438
Ruling Rascal (VEN)	2	C	1	1	0	0	9,920
Ruling Star	5	G	16	1	3	5	37,950
Rullahofthereust	4	C	3	0	0	0	460
Rullah's Bag	4	G	7	0	0	0	570
Rulo	4	G	2	0	0	0	0
Rum Bird	6	M	3	0	0	0	291
Rum Bobby	3	C	2	0	0	0	477
Rum Bottom	3	C	5	1	2	0	26,827
Rum Candi	5	M	10	4	1	4	77,616
Rum Jungle	5	M	18	1	1	6	11,524
Rum Rascal	2	C	1	0	0	0	140
Rum Shooter	5	G	4	2	1	0	14,420
Rum Swizzle	3	F	4	0	0	1	850
Rum Talk	4	G	9	0	2	0	6,842
Rumarico's Lord	6	H	1	0	0	0	900
Rumba Numba	3	F	7	0	1	0	14,153
Rumba Que Tumba	3	F	4	2	0	1	19,642
Rumbante (ARG)	7	M	1	0	0	0	336
Rumbeau Ruckus	2	F	5	1	2	1	26,034
Rumble	3	G	4	0	0	1	3,110
Rumble River	2	G	1	0	1	0	2,940
Rumble Strip	4	G	4	1	0	0	3,480
Rumbleinthejungle	4	G	2	0	0	0	225
Rumbleintheriver	2	C	2	0	0	0	330
Rumbling Disco	4	C	1	0	1	0	820
Rumbling Girl	4	F	10	2	1	3	44,390
Rumbling Storm	2	G	4	0	0	1	2,535
Rumbo's Starlet	6	M	10	1	2	0	4,702
Rummette	2	F	3	0	0	2	4,534
Rumor Denide	5	G	10	1	1	0	4,908
Rumor Had It	5	M	1	0	0	0	95
Rumor Has It	3	C	1	0	0	0	0
Rumor Hebert	4	F	3	0	0	0	0
Rumors Abound	2	F	1	0	1	0	1,410
Rumors Galore	3	F	10	1	0	1	4,485
Rumors Wild	2	F	6	0	0	2	3,770
Rumsfeld	4	C	1	0	0	0	0
Rumsonontheriver	7	G	4	0	0	0	260
Rumspringa	2	C	2	0	0	1	4,800
Rumway	3	G	11	1	2	0	11,888
Run Alexis Run	8	M	1	0	1	0	2,646
Run Along	4	F	12	1	0	1	11,390
Run Along Sonny	4	G	12	1	4	1	66,270
Run Aly Run	4	G	9	3	2	2	10,742
Run and Punch	3	G	5	1	1	1	10,355
Run Apache Run	3	F	5	0	0	0	585
Run Around Sue	9	M	13	1	3	2	30,103
Run At Night	4	C	7	1	2	1	26,467
Run Away Mama	3	F	8	1	3	1	6,404
Run Baron Run	3	C	10	1	0	0	30,032
Run Big	4	F	6	0	0	0	510
Run Bootic Run	4	G	6	1	1	1	4,644
Run Bullseye Run	4	G	14	0	4	3	5,442
Run Cat Run	3	F	1	0	0	0	0
Run Dancer Run	6	M	13	0	4	0	9,635
Run Dem	3	G	8	0	2	1	7,375
Run Do Run	2	C	4	2	1	0	25,780
Run Doeny Run	4	F	6	2	1	0	17,000
Run Don't Jump	3	F	4	0	0	0	240
Run Dot Run	3	F	9	2	0	0	16,358
Run Filly Run	2	F	7	0	1	1	3,155
Run for Bucky	2	F	5	0	0	0	1,908
Run for Charity	10	M	1	0	0	0	0
Run for Daisys	5	M	3	0	2	0	800
Run for Dakota	2	C	1	0	0	1	2,530
Run for Dessert	3	F	3	1	0	0	22,840
Run for Fun	4	G	5	1	0	0	16,660
Run for Joy	8	M	1	0	1	0	7,000
Run for Lillie	3	F	3	0	0	0	935
Run for Marc	6	M	1	0	1	0	1,520
Run for Michael	2	F	3	0	0	0	2,428
Run for Mom	4	G	6	0	0	2	6,788
Run for Sam	2	F	1	0	0	0	250
Run for the Money	3	G	7	0	0	0	1,250
Run for the Win	3	F	6	0	2	1	10,990
Run for Trcy	4	G	19	2	7	3	33,345
Run for You	4	G	8	2	1	3	11,160
Run Freddie Run	4	G	13	3	1	4	23,311
Run Free	4	F	9	1	2	1	9,805
Run Fun Sundial	5	G	5	0	0	0	321
Run Good	2	C	2	1	0	0	10,160
Run Halo Run	3	G	10	1	0	0	6,557
Run Honey	4	F	7	0	0	1	1,852
Run in the Park	6	G	3	1	1	0	8,600
Run Irene Run	3	F	11	3	4	1	13,235
Run Irish Cream	5	M	10	1	3	1	10,734
Run Jesse Run	5	G	6	2	1	1	11,580
Run Kaitlyn Run	3	F	1	0	0	0	1,950
Run Kaya Run	4	C	11	3	4	1	18,266
Run Kush Run	6	G	3	1	0	0	4,520
Run Like Hunter	4	G	12	4	2	2	49,892
Run Like Yamama	3	F	1	0	0	0	0
Run Lil Tooch	8	G	3	0	0	0	890
Run Little Richie	8	G	12	0	0	1	4,446
Run Little Sister	3	F	8	0	1	0	4,560
Run Looker Run	3	F	5	1	1	1	16,032
Run Lori Run	5	M	5	0	0	0	260
Run Lucky Vera	4	F	4	0	1	0	2,749
Run Matty Run	5	G	15	2	1	3	24,220
Run Maurice Run	6	G	17	2	0	3	11,385
Run Max Run	4	G	5	1	1	1	8,682
Run Me Down	4	F	1	0	1	0	6,520
Run Me Out	5	G	4	1	0	0	8,825
Run Mickey Run	4	G	11	1	2	1	5,775
Run Mikey Run	3	G	9	1	0	1	7,914
Run Mill Run	3	C	1	0	0	0	82
Run N Coke	3	C	22	4	2	3	69,300
Run N Love	3	F	10	4	0	1	59,290
Run Nicholas Run	2	G	3	1	0	0	5,940
Run of the Mill	3	G	6	0	1	1	2,257
Run On	2	G	5	1	1	2	64,173
Run Rebecca Run	4	F	5	1	0	0	31,980
Run Retsina Girl	4	F	10	1	4	0	27,224
Run Ricky Run	3	C	4	1	0	0	18,020
Run Rico	6	G	1	0	0	0	0
Run River Run	3	G	2	0	0	0	0
Run Roger Run	6	H	1	0	0	0	60
Run Runaway	2	F	1	0	0	0	800
Run Sarah Run	4	F	11	2	1	2	73,230
Run Stops	2	F	7	1	0	1	11,870
Run Sweetie	4	F	3	0	0	0	232
Run the Good Race	3	F	9	2	0	1	18,507
Run the Light	3	G	9	1	2	3	54,804
Run the Wham	2	F	1	0	0	0	120
Run Thruthe Sun	2	C	3	2	0	1	37,356
Run to Glory	4	C	18	1	2	2	56,345
Run to Me (CHI)	2	C	1	0	1	0	7,800
Run to the Border	5	G	10	5	0	2	79,467
Run to Victory	5	H	4	0	1	0	21,500
Run Tublin Run	3	F	9	1	0	1	5,531
Run Willa Run	5	M	7	2	1	0	22,674

Horse	Age	Sex	Sts	1st	2d	3d	Won
Run With Winds	7	H	4	0	0	0	258
Run You So n' So	5	G	10	2	1	1	3,186
Run Z Road	7	M	9	0	2	2	3,944
Run Zeal Run	6	G	8	3	2	1	83,640
Runagate	7	M	11	3	1	2	42,055
Runalong Slew	3	G	3	0	0	0	320
Runamucca	4	F	8	1	2	4	10,215
Runaround Jazz	4	G	7	0	1	0	2,059
Runaround Jonnie	2	G	1	0	1	0	3,600
Runaway Appeal	3	C	4	0	0	0	0
Runaway Bay	2	F	1	0	0	0	0
Runaway Blaine	4	G	3	0	0	0	0
Runaway Bob	6	H	2	0	0	0	0
Runaway Briartic	3	G	5	1	0	0	3,713
Runaway Broom	2	C	1	0	0	0	80
Runaway Cajun	2	F	1	0	0	0	1,590
Runaway Capade	8	G	11	1	1	2	6,483
Runaway Champ	5	M	9	1	0	2	6,224
Runaway Child	5	G	6	0	0	0	873
Runaway Choice	5	G	7	1	2	1	40,600
Runaway Chris	3	C	11	0	1	5	33,564
Runaway Chrissie	2	F	3	0	0	1	2,252
Runaway Chu Chu	3	F	6	2	1	1	33,717
Runaway Clara	4	F	6	0	0	2	10,038
Runaway Coach	3	F	2	1	0	0	3,806
Runaway Countess	3	F	4	0	0	0	420
Runaway Dancer	5	G	5	0	0	1	51,000
Runaway Devion	3	C	2	0	0	0	504
Runaway Doctor	7	G	2	0	0	0	88
Runaway Don	7	G	10	1	1	0	13,426
Runaway Eleanor	3	F	17	1	2	2	49,914
Runaway Emotions	2	C	1	0	0	0	0
Runaway Faye	2	F	1	0	0	0	60
Runaway Flight	3	G	6	0	2	1	5,258
Runaway Force	2	F	1	0	0	0	0
Runaway Forever	2	F	2	1	0	0	6,363
Runaway Fox	4	F	2	0	0	0	153
Runaway Frolic	3	F	8	0	0	3	4,718
Runaway Froze	7	M	3	1	1	0	18,480
Runaway Helen	5	M	10	0	1	2	2,529
Runaway Jewel	2	C	2	0	0	0	1,080
Runaway Julie	3	F	10	2	4	0	31,029
Runaway Kate	6	M	11	0	0	0	2,343
Runaway Kitten	3	F	11	2	2	0	36,975
Runaway Lark	5	G	5	0	0	0	0
Runaway Lil	6	M	7	1	1	1	9,059
Runaway Limit	5	M	5	1	0	0	2,790
Runaway Martha	6	M	12	5	0	0	67,290
Runaway Mike	7	G	1	0	0	0	41
Runaway Mistress	3	F	12	0	0	3	2,152
Runaway Mother	4	F	2	0	0	0	0
Runaway Pearl	2	F	1	0	0	0	0
Runaway Pokey	3	G	2	0	0	0	322
Runaway Rizzi	3	F	16	0	5	5	66,440
Runaway Road	4	F	5	0	1	0	3,502
Runaway Rossi	4	G	8	0	3	0	9,940
Runaway Rubi	4	F	12	0	4	2	12,061
Runaway Runaway	4	G	8	0	1	0	5,140
Runaway Russy	4	G	11	2	3	3	79,425
Runaway Set	2	F	2	0	0	1	1,890
Runaway Silver	3	F	1	0	0	0	125
Runaway Sreva	3	F	11	0	1	1	10,710
Runaway Steel	4	C	5	0	2	1	6,360
Runaway Stream	4	G	1	0	0	0	0
Runaway Style	4	G	9	2	2	3	23,950
Runaway Sunshine	2	F	1	0	0	0	3,420
Runaway Thoughts	5	G	3	1	1	0	6,060
Runaway Tiger	6	M	6	1	0	2	18,141
Runaway Train	4	R	8	2	3	2	90,225
Runaway Turk	4	G	6	0	0	4	972
Runaway Twins	5	H	7	2	0	1	22,245
Runaway Victor	8	G	11	1	3	4	73,192
Runaway Warrior	4	C	4	0	3	0	5,340
Runawayfun	6	M	8	0	2	0	20,142
Runawayskye	4	F	8	1	0	5	25,740
Runbayou	9	G	8	1	1	0	10,514
Runbeforethewind	4	F	3	0	0	0	812
Runco	5	M	2	1	0	1	11,020
Runder Thumble	7	M	12	2	4	0	15,754
Runderdancer	6	M	2	0	0	0	0
Rundle	5	G	14	5	2	1	119,432
Runestone	3	F	1	0	0	0	400
Runfaari	3	F	12	0	1	1	5,797
Rungs	2	F	2	0	0	0	0
Runingforpresident	3	G	7	2	2	1	75,624
Runingtothelimit	6	M	2	0	0	0	500
Runinthesun	4	G	1	0	0	0	90
Runlikethedickens	3	C	13	3	1	1	18,111
Runliketigerplays	3	F	7	0	0	1	1,725
Runmore Mema	7	H	3	1	0	1	13,030
Runnaway Mon	2	C	1	1	0	0	34,200
Runner Up	3	C	5	0	0	0	343
Runners Name	4	G	8	2	2	0	21,800
Runnightfoot	3	G	2	0	0	0	0
Runnigwithscissors	3	G	9	2	1	1	5,295
Runnin Aarons	4	F	5	1	1	0	14,637
Runnin Brook	4	F	1	0	0	0	70
Runnin for Morgan	2	F	2	0	0	2	2,900
Runnin Frankie	3	G	11	2	3	1	14,960
Runnin N the Wind	4	F	1	0	0	0	50
Runnin On Brave	5	G	18	0	1	3	7,106
Runnin On Class	3	G	6	1	0	0	5,030
Runnin' On Nitro	4	G	9	1	4	0	43,110
Runnin Pollock	5	M	7	0	1	0	1,000
Runnin Rehaan	7	G	12	4	1	1	7,922
Runnin Renee	4	F	9	0	2	1	2,925
Runnin Tella Fib	4	G	5	0	1	1	1,836
Runnin' the River	4	G	14	2	3	2	21,236
Runnin Ute	3	F	8	1	2	1	38,514
Runnin West	6	G	5	0	0	1	4,932
Runninforthebucks	2	C	1	0	0	0	400
Running Away	3	G	12	2	1	1	51,057
Running Bay	6	G	12	2	0	4	13,251
Running Bobcats	2	F	8	4	2	1	108,680
Running Brave	3	G	6	1	0	0	13,680
Running Charizard	4	G	4	0	0	0	0
Running Charlie	4	G	10	4	0	1	23,175
Running Count	6	G	18	2	3	1	17,780
Running Deniro	2	G	5	0	1	0	4,495
Running Edition	2	G	3	0	0	1	3,040
Running Eleven	9	G	17	1	4	2	18,385
Running Empho	4	C	1	0	0	0	0
Running Event	3	F	2	0	0	0	215
Running Facts	2	F	5	0	2	1	14,835
Running Footman	6	G	1	0	0	0	33
Running for Grace	3	G	5	0	0	0	210
Running Free	3	G	10	4	2	1	164,428
Running Furiously	4	C	5	2	0	0	37,050
Running Gary	3	C	7	0	0	1	700
Running Gator	3	G	12	2	3	1	15,681
Running Gun	5	G	1	0	0	1	2,330
Running Heel	4	F	5	0	1	1	3,150
Running Jin	2	F	2	0	1	0	5,962
Running Kitty	2	F	7	0	1	1	10,825
Running Light	10	H	1	0	0	0	0
Running Mistress	8	M	11	1	0	2	7,752
Running On End	7	H	4	0	1	0	12,470
Running Piper	4	G	2	0	0	0	186
Running Rewana	4	G	7	1	0	1	2,226
Running Rhythm	3	C	1	0	0	0	0
Running Rooney	4	G	10	4	2	0	27,137
Running Ryan	10	G	8	0	0	1	3,248
Running Saint	3	F	7	1	1	2	43,295
Running Slew	3	G	6	0	0	1	2,675
Running Smooth	5	H	2	0	0	0	0
Running Surprise	2	C	4	1	0	0	16,055
Running Tour	2	F	2	0	0	0	300
Running Water	6	G	13	0	0	1	2,731
Running Z	3	C	3	0	1	0	2,300
Running Zarb	6	G	15	1	1	5	12,789
Runningwithfire	3	C	1	0	0	0	0
Runnintothealter	3	C	4	1	2	1	25,040
Runn'n Wild	2	C	7	1	0	1	17,880
Runoverumbaby	5	G	2	0	0	0	0
Runpageone	3	C	1	0	0	0	105
Runs All Knight	3	G	12	2	2	2	13,050
Runs in the Family	3	C	4	2	1	1	69,900
Runs Like a Benz	5	M	6	0	0	1	3,443

Horse	Age	Sex	Sts	1st	2d	3d	Won
Runs Naked	4	F	8	1	2	1	23,966
Runs Neet	3	G	2	0	0	0	0
Runs With Scissors	3	G	9	3	1	1	39,900
Runsoncruz	4	F	1	0	0	0	78
Runspastum	7	H	2	0	0	0	1,180
Runstar	2	G	6	0	1	2	8,180
Runsumforme	4	G	8	1	0	1	6,177
Runswithatrick	3	F	4	0	1	0	2,037
Runtherapids	3	F	12	2	1	0	25,355
Runto the Mountain	9	H	5	1	0	0	2,856
Runway Dancer	4	F	16	1	0	3	8,601
Runway Heading	4	G	1	0	0	0	0
Runway Lollipop (ARG)	5	M	1	0	0	0	0
Runway Model	2	F	10	4	2	2	580,598
Runwiththedevil	3	G	4	1	0	1	15,860
Runz to Me	3	F	6	1	1	2	25,070
Rupert Haint	4	C	3	0	0	0	205
Rupert Herd	7	G	12	3	0	2	46,342
Rupert's Approval	7	M	7	1	0	1	6,227
Rupert's Fire	6	M	14	3	3	0	64,800
Rupert's Hard Fire	5	G	2	0	0	0	143
Rupert's Hazaam	3	C	4	0	0	1	2,040
Rupert's Kenny K.	3	C	5	0	0	0	425
Rupert's Kuetch	3	G	10	2	1	0	12,727
Rupert's Prospect	2	F	1	1	0	0	12,600
Rupert's Rose Morn	5	G	20	6	4	2	84,649
Ruperts Valid Dawn	2	G	3	2	0	0	16,435
Rupert's Win M All	4	G	2	0	0	0	161
Rupertwinswithrose	3	F	11	2	1	2	22,553
Rural Road	4	G	11	1	1	1	11,515
Rural Route One	2	F	8	1	2	0	13,023
Rural Vision	6	M	1	0	0	0	0
Rurd	5	G	9	1	3	1	15,690
Ruready	3	F	6	0	2	1	2,623
Rush Around	4	C	9	2	1	1	57,670
Rush Bay	2	C	4	1	2	1	87,755
Rush Country	3	G	8	1	3	0	60,900
Rush Creek	4	F	4	0	0	0	2,010
Rush Haint Darla	4	F	1	0	0	0	0
Rush Her	3	F	10	2	1	5	26,380
Rush Hour Mob	2	C	1	0	0	0	105
Rush Into Heaven	3	G	14	1	2	2	41,213
Rush Is Back	2	G	5	0	0	1	5,777
Rush Master	3	C	5	0	0	0	390
Rush 'n Amigo	4	G	8	0	1	0	2,068
Rush Note	3	F	6	0	0	2	4,216
Rush of Wind	4	G	15	4	3	4	19,539
Rush Queen	8	M	6	2	0	0	2,606
Rush Right by Em	5	H	1	0	1	0	6,600
Rush Street	4	G	2	0	0	0	255
Rush Street Miss	3	F	6	1	0	0	3,674
Rush to Defend	4	C	5	1	1	0	16,085
Rush to Glory	2	F	7	3	2	1	69,155
Rush to Market	3	C	1	0	0	0	0
Rush to the Wire	6	M	8	2	0	0	8,755
Rush Zone	3	F	1	0	0	0	400
Rushaway Native	3	F	1	0	0	0	0
Rushbo	2	C	4	1	1	0	17,863
Rushbuckler	4	C	4	1	0	0	8,720
Rushcliffe	4	G	1	1	0	0	7,980
Rushin' to Altar	5	H	2	0	0	0	3,900
Rushing Buck	3	G	5	0	0	1	1,053
Rushing Force	4	F	12	1	1	4	54,416
Rushing Rose	2	F	7	0	0	2	10,059
Rushing Water	4	C	16	2	1	1	33,470
Rushing Wild	3	C	6	1	0	0	9,420
Rushinline	2	F	3	1	0	1	8,380
Rushmo	5	G	5	0	0	1	5,523
Ruskin Drive	4	G	9	1	1	4	11,735
Ruslanova	3	F	9	0	3	2	21,080
Russell Cave	8	G	1	0	0	0	642
Russell Springs	5	G	3	0	0	2	1,592
Russellette	4	F	15	2	2	5	12,625
Russell's Devil	4	G	8	1	1	2	5,970
Russia	4	C	2	0	0	0	340
Russian Bear	4	G	1	0	0	0	40
Russian Bonus	4	F	10	2	3	0	33,159
Russian Elite	3	G	11	5	4	1	81,762
Russian First	3	G	6	0	0	0	124
Russian Hand	5	G	10	0	6	1	15,362
Russian Inn	5	G	10	3	2	4	11,392
Russian Kat	6	G	15	3	2	2	10,853
Russian Mystery	6	G	6	1	2	1	7,718
Russian News	4	G	3	1	1	0	24,780
Russian Note	3	F	6	0	1	0	5,020
Russian Palace	6	G	12	1	3	1	6,375
Russian Patty	2	F	2	0	0	0	215
Russian Royalty	6	G	14	2	1	3	13,717
Russian Ruler	10	G	6	0	4	1	6,712
Russian Squared	2	G	2	0	0	0	1,013
Russian Sweetiepie	7	M	9	1	4	0	60,540
Russian the Gold	6	G	7	1	2	2	5,359
Russian Tigress	6	M	5	1	1	2	9,073
Russian Wind	5	M	2	0	0	0	480
Russing	6	G	10	0	0	3	5,329
Rust Tully	3	F	5	0	1	2	6,968
Rustic	5	M	9	3	3	1	29,797
Rustic Girl	2	F	2	0	0	0	0
Rustic Kitten	4	F	10	0	1	2	9,933
Rustic Storm	2	F	1	0	0	0	0
Rustica	3	F	3	0	0	0	705
Rustling	2	F	1	0	0	0	2,040
Ruston Bearcat	6	G	10	1	0	1	7,070
Ruston Drive In	3	G	3	0	0	0	0
Ruston Rifle	7	G	6	0	0	0	315
Rustridge Brix	8	G	9	0	2	0	5,336
Rustridge Zin	7	G	2	0	0	0	104
Rustrum	4	G	7	2	1	1	84,614
Rusty Angle	4	G	5	0	0	0	0
Rusty Ben	3	G	6	0	0	2	2,848
Rusty Billy	4	G	11	0	1	1	1,918
Rusty Boy	5	G	11	2	0	2	6,104
Rusty Halo	2	F	2	0	0	0	0
Rusty Man	5	G	9	1	0	0	10,680
Rusty Nail	3	G	12	0	4	2	18,100
Rusty Nell	3	F	7	0	0	0	1,220
Rusty Prospector	3	C	7	3	3	0	39,866
Rusty Rolls	2	G	2	1	1	0	12,560
Rusty Rudder	2	G	2	0	0	0	255
Rusty Spur	6	H	1	0	0	0	0
Rusty Trawler	3	G	9	1	1	2	31,980
Rutabaga	5	G	1	0	0	0	0
Ruthie the Rocket	3	F	12	2	4	3	58,788
Ruthies Boy	3	G	3	0	0	0	0
Ruthie's Dance	3	F	12	2	2	2	25,163
Ruthless Babe	3	F	5	1	0	0	32,980
Ruthless Kitten	3	F	6	1	0	0	3,753
Ruthless Rebecca	2	F	7	1	0	0	6,525
Ruth's Grey Girl	7	M	10	0	1	1	4,485
Ruth's Route	4	F	7	0	0	1	710
Ruth's Sisu	4	F	6	1	0	0	3,155
Ruthy Red	4	F	4	1	0	1	12,923
Rutledge Academy	3	C	1	1	0	0	8,400
Rutledge Ballado	2	F	2	1	1	0	20,480
Rutledge Gold	5	G	7	1	2	0	17,565
Rutledge Man	4	C	8	1	3	0	33,065
Rutledge Protocol	3	G	10	1	2	1	21,852
Rutledge Punch	3	C	9	1	2	3	31,395
Rutledge Rebel	4	G	9	1	0	2	10,580
Rven Hi	5	M	2	0	0	0	227
Ryan Allen	3	G	5	0	0	0	485
Ryan D	5	G	10	2	1	0	5,732
Ryan Is Flying	4	G	12	1	1	1	55,664
Ryan's Bob	3	C	3	0	0	0	0
Ryan's Express	6	G	8	1	0	0	8,634
Ryan's Halo	3	F	2	0	0	0	0
Ryan's Lad	5	G	6	0	0	0	738
Ryan's Nanny	8	M	6	0	0	0	320
Ryan's Partner	6	H	12	4	4	0	31,800
Ryan's Rainbow	3	G	13	2	0	0	17,617
Ryans Super Star	4	G	2	0	0	0	235
Ryans Waqut Angel	3	F	8	0	1	2	10,944
Ryansdeputy	4	G	8	1	0	1	8,776
Ryding Newyork	6	M	11	1	0	1	7,875
Ryding Poupon	7	H	7	2	1	1	11,792
Rye	4	G	4	2	0	1	17,802
Ryjilla	4	C	8	1	1	1	2,067
Ryld	5	G	2	0	0	0	0

Horse	Age	Sex	Sts	1st	2d	3d	Won
Rylee C T	3	C	10	0	5	1	8,842
Rylie Cheyenne	3	F	10	1	1	3	25,508
Ryna Marlene	3	F	4	1	0	0	5,131
Ryndam	2	G	4	0	0	0	405
Ryno's Wish	3	C	8	0	1	2	4,810
Rythem n' Blues	3	F	9	1	1	1	5,297
Rythm River	2	C	2	1	0	0	14,023
Rythmic Story	3	G	2	0	0	0	129
S Ball	5	M	3	0	0	0	120
S Box	2	F	2	0	0	0	0
S C King	2	G	6	3	0	1	18,984
S K's Regent	3	F	9	2	1	1	26,260
S Lupe	4	G	11	1	0	1	1,272
S N J's Desire	4	F	9	1	1	2	36,206
S N R's Defense	3	F	4	0	0	0	286
S R Queenforaday	2	F	5	1	1	0	15,720
S S C Moonfleet	5	G	5	1	2	0	9,419
S S Enterprize	3	G	11	3	0	3	12,227
S S Game	3	G	5	1	0	0	3,186
S S Leggy	2	F	4	0	0	1	1,159
S S Lucky	3	F	4	0	1	0	5,176
S S Scribble	4	F	1	0	0	0	550
S S Sheba	4	F	7	0	0	1	1,634
S S Strange	2	G	5	1	0	0	15,260
S Table Dancer	4	F	10	3	2	1	13,261
S Train	8	G	1	0	0	0	0
S W Brean Rose	3	F	6	2	0	0	18,852
S W Flyer	4	G	10	3	1	0	9,680
S W Kissin Bee	3	F	5	0	1	0	2,833
S W Pocket Money	5	G	13	4	2	1	33,587
S W Ryan	2	C	1	0	0	0	0
S W Smoken Cat	4	G	9	1	2	1	17,031
S W Stephie	6	M	5	1	0	2	6,315
S W Sweet Marylane	4	F	16	2	3	4	30,123
S. C. Littlepest	3	G	4	1	0	0	1,820
S. Cherry Legacy	3	G	16	6	2	2	105,897
S. K. Boy	7	G	5	0	0	0	506
S. L. Charmer	5	M	8	1	1	1	29,966
S. L. Gamine	4	F	12	1	1	1	9,842
S. O. S. Be Good	3	G	11	1	4	3	23,019
S. S. Bounty	4	G	14	3	1	1	61,662
S. S. Finesse	8	M	12	1	1	0	10,735
S. S. Shadow	4	C	3	0	0	0	0
S. S. Spitfire	7	G	12	1	1	2	5,822
S. W. Silver Sky	7	M	10	1	0	1	3,312
Sa Ad	7	G	1	0	0	0	1,150
Sa Boogie Dancer	5	M	5	0	0	0	335
Sa Jollie	3	F	5	0	0	0	0
Sa Moken	4	F	1	0	0	0	131
Sa Passem	3	G	2	0	0	0	174
Saami	5	G	9	2	1	2	16,252
Saanich Sam	4	G	12	0	2	3	7,778
Saarland	5	H	4	0	2	0	39,550
Saay Mi Name	4	G	19	4	2	3	99,584
Saba	3	F	5	0	3	0	11,285
Sabaku	5	G	1	0	0	0	44
Sabalucious	4	G	5	0	1	1	4,280
Sabbath Day Point	3	F	1	0	1	0	4,200
Sabbatical	3	C	6	1	1	1	10,591
Sabella	4	F	6	0	0	0	653
Sabellina	3	F	9	4	1	1	183,223
Saber Rattle	2	G	3	0	0	0	480
Sabha	2	F	2	0	0	1	2,058
Sabiango (GER)	6	H	4	2	0	0	334,000
Sable n' Diamonds	5	M	2	0	0	0	206
Sable Trace	3	G	2	0	0	0	215
Sabogal	7	G	8	0	0	0	360
Sabona Sun	3	C	1	0	0	0	125
Saboya	7	M	2	0	0	0	582
Sabre Baby	3	G	12	2	3	2	82,340
Sabre Rattling	3	G	9	1	1	1	18,015
Sabre Tooth Tiger	6	G	1	0	0	1	1,680
Sabrina Slew	5	M	10	2	1	1	35,291
Sabrina's Magic	3	F	2	0	0	0	0
Sabrina's Quest	4	F	17	1	2	3	13,009
Sabrinas Spirit	6	M	1	0	0	0	559
Sabrini	3	F	11	1	1	0	9,575
Sac City	2	C	1	0	0	0	0
Sacagawea Park	2	F	3	0	0	1	900
Sacagawea's Spirit	4	F	8	1	3	2	23,200
Sacatricks	4	F	1	0	0	0	117
Saccharine	4	F	3	0	0	0	1,080
Sachem	7	G	4	0	1	0	2,000
Sacrament	2	G	3	1	0	0	9,450
Sacred Affair	5	G	10	4	2	0	56,963
Sacred Cat	3	F	4	0	0	0	0
Sacred Feather	2	F	5	1	0	0	17,011
Sacred Gem	5	M	10	0	0	3	6,704
Sacred Senor	2	G	3	2	0	0	22,687
Sacred Summit	3	G	7	1	1	1	17,875
Sacred Time	2	G	5	0	0	3	13,678
Sacred Vow	4	C	5	1	0	0	10,180
Sacred Winds	3	G	11	1	2	3	33,143
Sacrifice	3	G	12	3	2	0	11,955
Sacsahuaman (CHI)	6	G	9	1	1	2	20,275
Sad Cafe	3	F	4	0	1	1	10,700
Saddle a Dream	4	G	5	0	0	2	2,727
Saddle Mate	3	C	5	1	1	1	8,705
Saddle Oxfords	6	G	8	0	0	1	1,336
Saddle Up Janet K	5	M	3	0	0	0	532
Sadia's Slew	2	C	1	0	0	1	860
Sadie Bo	5	M	2	0	0	0	230
Sadie Mae	4	G	7	1	0	1	13,509
Sadies Lad	3	F	7	1	1	2	14,785
Sadlers Pride	5	G	9	1	1	0	12,270
Sadlers Secret	2	C	1	0	0	0	96
Saf Link	6	G	7	1	2	1	15,330
Safara	4	F	6	0	0	1	1,290
Safari	4	G	10	0	0	0	4,868
Safari Barbie	3	F	3	0	0	0	375
Safari So Good	3	F	10	2	1	1	7,286
Safe Expectation	5	H	8	1	1	0	12,147
Safe From Harm	4	G	5	0	1	0	8,198
Safe Haven	3	F	1	1	0	0	15,000
Safe in the U S A	5	H	1	0	0	0	960
Safe Passage	7	M	6	2	0	1	12,470
Safe Place	2	G	2	1	0	1	15,700
Safe Secret	6	H	1	0	0	0	250
Safe Signal	3	C	4	0	0	0	3,605
Safe Streets	3	F	7	0	0	0	510
Safe Sympathy	3	F	10	0	0	2	1,029
Safe Try	7	M	7	1	0	0	3,444
Safeforsure	3	F	5	0	0	0	870
Safely	3	F	3	0	0	0	300
Safely At Home	4	F	4	2	0	0	23,225
Safely Home	2	F	3	0	0	0	720
Safely Lit	3	F	2	0	1	0	2,034
Safely Run	2	C	4	2	1	0	39,900
Safety Lord	4	G	8	0	0	1	2,321
Safety Retreat	3	C	7	2	1	1	7,534
Saffi	3	F	6	0	0	0	5,643
Safley's Social	3	F	20	1	0	1	16,105
Saga Boy	3	C	14	1	1	4	36,590
Sagacious	4	G	2	0	0	0	891
Sage Field	2	C	4	1	1	1	14,844
Sage Fire	7	M	2	0	0	0	550
Sage Princess	2	F	3	0	0	1	5,570
Sage Road	6	G	6	1	1	1	11,531
Sage's Fifty Six	3	F	7	1	1	0	16,072
Sageworth	4	F	3	0	0	0	325
Sagi'sdream	5	G	5	0	0	0	209
Sagitta Ra	3	F	6	1	2	1	78,671
Sago	3	F	3	0	0	0	3,900
Sagreeno	10	G	12	1	1	2	5,385
Sagus's Pride	2	F	7	1	2	1	37,990
Sah Woosh	4	F	5	2	0	0	11,850
Sahab	3	G	8	1	2	2	31,350
Sahara Desert	4	G	15	0	1	3	6,916
Sahara Knight	4	F	4	1	1	1	2,925
Sahara Mist	4	F	8	0	0	3	5,723
Sahara Sands	7	M	2	0	0	0	300
Sahara Sound	3	F	7	1	1	1	31,199
Saharan Song	3	F	6	1	1	0	13,514
Saharan Sunrise	2	F	3	1	1	0	20,000
Sahm Iahm	3	G	10	1	1	3	19,734
Sahmkindawonderful	3	F	4	1	0	0	25,500
Sahoma Secret	4	G	20	4	4	2	22,345
Said Enough	9	G	10	2	1	1	9,422

Horse	Age	Sex	Sts	1st	2d	3d	Won
Said So	5	G	9	1	1	2	9,104
Saideira	2	F	3	0	0	0	1,250
Saide'strick	3	F	5	0	0	0	2,445
Saigon Express	2	C	3	0	1	1	4,528
Saigon Lieutenant	9	G	11	1	1	1	8,213
Sail Away With Me	2	F	2	0	0	0	0
Sail by the Sea	3	F	12	2	1	1	10,310
Sail Miss Gracie	5	M	7	1	2	2	10,391
Sail My Vessel	7	G	4	1	1	0	11,550
Sail On Classy	3	G	8	0	5	1	6,296
Sail On Kenta	4	C	4	0	0	1	2,075
Sail to First	3	F	2	0	0	0	0
Sailaway	4	C	8	2	3	1	98,820
Sailborrun	3	C	11	0	1	1	4,824
Saildust	7	G	14	1	1	2	5,773
Sailin Windswept	4	F	2	0	0	0	150
Sailing Blade	3	F	1	0	0	0	0
Sailing Factor	3	F	8	4	1	0	18,895
Sailing Images	4	F	3	0	0	0	405
Sailing Sain	11	G	1	0	0	0	0
Sailing Sioux	7	M	4	0	0	1	1,230
Sailing Skipper	5	G	12	0	0	0	1,058
Sailing Wind	3	F	8	0	1	1	6,660
Sailmaker	4	F	2	2	0	0	24,000
Sailontejano	3	F	5	0	0	0	228
Sailor Girl	8	M	2	0	0	0	174
Sailor Knot	3	G	15	3	2	2	79,334
Sailor Sue	2	F	4	1	1	1	11,830
Sailor's Dream	4	F	9	3	1	1	38,205
Sailor's Gold	3	F	7	2	0	1	27,380
Sailor's Lil' Lady	5	M	5	0	0	0	615
Sailor's Wave	4	F	11	2	3	1	58,385
Sails Are Up	6	M	6	0	0	0	446
Saint Afleet	3	C	4	2	0	0	173,851
Saint Appeal	5	H	2	0	0	0	0
Saint Barz	3	G	7	0	0	1	4,855
Saint Bonaventure	2	C	8	0	0	1	4,075
Saint Buddy	4	C	10	1	3	3	196,120
Saint Cali	2	C	3	1	0	0	25,320
Saint Charlie	3	C	8	0	0	3	12,212
Saint Chrisjon	3	C	3	1	0	0	18,535
Saint D. M.	4	G	15	2	0	2	21,503
Saint Damien	6	G	20	4	6	4	63,035
Saint d'Or	3	F	5	0	0	0	1,830
Saint Ernie	6	H	2	0	0	0	44
Saint Golddigger	5	G	9	2	0	4	21,213
Saint He Can't	4	G	8	0	1	0	4,460
Saint Kilian	5	G	10	2	1	1	17,871
Saint Labradro	9	G	6	0	0	0	380
Saint Liam	4	C	5	2	2	1	618,760
Saint Lorenzo	4	C	4	3	1	0	77,760
Saint Martin	3	G	9	2	1	1	105,826
Saint Mercedes	4	G	6	0	0	0	0
Saint Nick's Magic	3	G	10	2	2	1	17,120
Saint Nor Sinner	5	H	7	1	1	1	4,126
Saint Olivia	3	F	1	0	0	0	235
Saint Or Sinner	3	F	13	1	2	3	29,362
Saint Pete	4	G	2	0	0	0	45
Saint Prairie	5	M	3	0	0	0	50
Saint Ray	2	F	3	0	0	0	1,410
Saint Rocio	4	F	6	0	0	1	1,725
Saint Sabates	4	C	1	0	0	0	218
Saint Savio	2	G	2	0	0	0	239
Saint Stephen	4	C	6	1	1	1	40,040
Saint Waki	4	G	12	1	0	3	43,140
Saint Xavier	3	G	13	0	1	1	3,369
Sainted	2	F	8	1	1	1	9,868
Sainted Colony	4	G	13	1	5	2	48,125
Saintemerald	4	G	10	1	2	1	5,904
Saintlike	4	F	4	2	0	0	37,925
Saintliness	4	F	4	4	0	0	106,800
Saintly Act	6	G	2	0	0	0	560
Saintly Action	5	M	6	0	1	2	57,450
Saintly Corp.	4	G	7	1	0	0	14,252
Saintly Gambler	4	G	2	1	1	0	8,911
Saintly Look	4	C	10	1	0	3	31,470
Saintly Native	6	G	4	0	0	0	240
Saintly Persuasion	4	F	2	0	0	1	9,520
Saintly Sue	2	F	9	0	1	2	7,905
Saintly Wish	6	M	10	3	0	1	20,029
Saints a Plenty	4	F	5	1	1	1	13,785
Saints and Sages	5	M	12	0	1	3	22,210
Saint's Express	5	H	2	0	1	1	1,929
Saints Go Marching	5	G	4	0	0	1	5,915
Saint's Play	2	F	1	0	0	0	205
Saint's Shadow	3	G	11	0	2	0	8,635
Saison d'Or	7	M	4	0	0	1	1,690
Saitensohn (GER)	6	G	5	0	1	2	21,500
Sajak	2	G	2	0	1	1	4,150
Sajjan	3	G	9	2	0	1	34,802
Sajon	6	G	6	0	0	1	2,850
Sajuriana (ARG)	6	M	16	1	0	1	15,983
Sakiville	3	F	10	4	1	0	11,699
Saklad	8	M	7	0	0	1	2,885
Sakrov	3	G	12	1	1	1	8,792
Sala de Oro	3	F	3	0	0	0	3,000
Salally Bella	2	F	4	0	0	0	3,185
Salamaat	4	C	4	1	0	1	12,575
Salamanca	2	F	1	0	0	0	0
Salary Cap	2	C	2	2	0	0	25,710
Salaverry	8	G	14	5	3	1	30,142
Salcombe (GB)	4	C	4	1	2	1	49,180
Salda	3	F	1	0	0	0	0
Sale Choice	7	H	2	0	0	0	84
Sale the Atlantic	4	G	12	4	5	1	49,695
Saleek	4	C	2	0	0	0	800
Salem County	5	M	12	0	1	0	5,240
Salem School Road	2	C	3	0	1	0	7,080
Salem Sez	2	F	2	0	0	0	0
Salem Times	5	G	2	0	0	0	555
Salem Too	4	F	5	0	0	1	1,754
Salem Willow	5	M	3	0	0	0	492
Sales Call	4	C	3	0	0	0	540
Salespitch	2	F	2	0	0	0	900
Salford City (IRE)	3	C	6	1	0	1	134,424
Salic Law	3	C	6	1	2	1	51,745
Salient Spring	6	M	6	0	2	0	1,959
Salieri	3	C	1	0	0	0	0
Salim's Tip (AUS)	8	G	16	3	7	1	35,960
Salina's Gift	8	M	3	0	0	0	3,570
Salinas Regal Luck	5	M	5	0	1	1	1,960
Salinas Star	5	M	5	1	1	2	15,931
Salisbury Slew	4	F	16	3	1	2	20,065
Salish Legacy	4	F	8	0	0	1	1,355
Salish Prince	11	G	2	0	0	1	1,495
Salish Seas	3	G	1	0	0	0	0
Salish Secret	4	F	12	4	2	2	29,413
Salish Shaman	8	G	1	0	0	0	0
Salish Smoke	3	F	1	0	0	0	0
Sallie K.	4	F	4	0	0	0	1,890
Sallie Mae	5	M	2	0	0	1	1,186
Sally Beth	6	M	1	0	0	0	0
Sally Dear	4	F	14	2	2	3	17,193
Sally Forth	2	F	3	0	0	0	55
Sally Gap	3	F	5	2	1	0	17,012
Sally Seminole	6	M	5	0	0	0	111
Sally T	6	M	14	2	2	1	11,004
Sallyhooks	3	F	13	2	2	2	13,430
Sally's Boy	2	G	1	0	0	0	0
Sally's Comet	7	M	3	0	0	0	189
Sallys Creative	3	C	2	0	0	0	0
Sallys Fashion	8	M	11	0	1	3	4,358
Sally's Love	2	F	4	0	0	0	180
Sally's My Gal	5	M	6	1	2	0	4,408
Sallyshothesheriff	2	F	1	0	0	0	225
Salma	3	F	6	3	0	1	40,396
Salmo	8	H	3	0	1	1	5,300
Salomon Swagger	7	G	10	1	1	3	31,217
Salon	3	G	4	0	0	0	1,995
Saloon Girl	2	F	7	0	0	1	4,090
Salori	2	F	5	2	1	0	29,260
Sal's Mity City	3	G	5	0	0	0	1,080
Sal's Saloon	3	F	6	2	1	0	5,791
Sal's Solar Star	3	F	3	0	0	0	461
Salsa Brava	4	F	1	0	0	0	0
Salsa King	4	C	3	0	0	0	270
Salsa Queen	4	F	4	0	0	0	160
Salsa Real	4	F	13	1	2	2	10,395

Horse	Age	Sex	Sts	1st	2d	3d	Won
Salsa Sunny	3	G	11	2	3	2	3,969
Salsbury's Gate	6	G	3	1	0	0	4,515
Salt Breeze	6	M	13	4	2	3	23,307
Salt Chaser	4	F	15	2	2	2	20,220
Salt City Cruiser	3	G	4	0	0	0	161
Salt Coates	6	G	12	0	0	1	1,592
Salt Flat	4	F	5	1	0	0	11,650
Salt Flat Kid	3	G	1	1	0	0	27,600
Salt Grinder	5	G	3	2	0	0	32,395
Salt Gulch	5	H	3	0	0	0	0
Salt in My Soup	3	G	13	1	2	0	18,820
Salt Lake Express	6	H	5	0	1	0	2,070
Salt Lake Utah	2	C	1	0	0	0	312
Salt N Water	8	G	2	0	0	0	122
Salt Please	9	G	6	0	1	0	2,590
Salt Raker	4	G	5	0	1	1	8,561
Salt Run	6	G	12	0	1	2	2,849
Salt Silence	3	G	12	2	3	1	35,555
Salt Syn	2	F	2	1	0	0	14,100
Salt Wells	4	G	6	1	0	2	17,200
Salta Sapo	3	F	6	1	2	1	51,225
Saltaire Slew	6	G	14	2	2	2	7,790
Saltalot	3	G	8	1	1	2	17,212
Saltam	2	F	9	2	1	2	27,087
Saltant	3	F	7	2	0	0	7,403
Saltarina Lake (ARG)	4	F	2	0	1	1	8,960
Saltire	3	C	8	1	2	1	38,128
Saltish	3	F	5	2	1	1	38,776
Saltshaker	6	G	1	0	0	0	192
Saltster	3	F	2	0	1	0	6,450
Saltwater Runner	3	F	5	3	0	0	87,166
Saltworks	8	H	6	4	0	1	17,000
Salty Affair	6	G	14	5	1	2	91,809
Salty Beach	2	F	6	1	2	1	25,274
Salty Boo	2	F	8	0	4	2	18,280
Salty Boy	6	G	9	1	1	1	5,330
Salty Character	3	C	11	1	1	1	41,308
Salty Dancing	2	F	2	0	0	0	0
Salty Dog Destiny	3	C	2	2	0	0	16,800
Salty Dollar	2	F	7	2	1	1	25,690
Salty Expression	6	H	6	0	0	1	1,147
Salty Farma	6	M	4	1	2	0	50,000
Salty Genius	4	G	6	1	2	0	44,880
Salty Girl	3	F	8	1	1	1	9,668
Salty Humor	2	C	5	1	2	0	41,540
Salty Langfuhn	3	G	11	2	2	4	117,016
Salty Looker	8	M	13	1	3	1	3,360
Salty M.	7	H	13	2	5	1	14,751
Salty n' Foxy	5	M	6	0	1	0	3,322
Salty N Sassy	3	F	16	5	1	2	40,880
Salty O'Rourke	7	G	5	1	1	2	19,064
Salty Prince	6	G	7	1	0	1	12,985
Salty Punch	3	G	8	1	0	2	37,830
Salty Rocket	4	F	1	0	0	0	288
Salty Romance	3	F	5	1	1	0	50,760
Salty Sailor	4	G	10	3	2	2	78,550
Salty Sally	2	F	2	0	0	0	3,560
Salty Siphon	3	F	9	2	1	0	12,353
Salty Soup	4	G	6	2	1	1	17,180
Salty Spender	6	G	11	3	4	3	64,020
Salty Talk	5	M	1	0	0	0	0
Salty Treasure	7	G	3	0	0	1	620
Salty Win	8	G	9	2	1	0	5,723
Salty Would	4	G	6	0	0	1	1,295
Salty's Double	4	G	7	2	0	1	11,637
Salty's Home	6	G	8	3	0	0	26,635
Saluda	3	G	4	1	0	0	15,900
Saluki Cheerleader	2	F	5	0	0	2	4,976
Salut Belek	5	G	4	0	0	1	1,707
Salutatorian	7	G	13	1	1	1	5,742
Salute	2	F	4	1	2	1	87,326
Salute America	3	C	17	3	3	2	35,965
Salute Her	4	F	5	0	1	1	10,935
Salute Him	6	G	3	0	1	1	16,100
Salute the Count	4	G	9	1	4	1	38,710
Salute the News	4	C	7	0	1	3	14,850
Salute the Troops	3	C	2	0	0	1	4,430
Salute Them	3	C	4	0	0	0	324
Salute This	4	G	10	0	2	4	4,414
Salute to Paulie	3	F	13	1	2	2	15,452
Salutee	6	G	13	2	1	1	13,029
Salutress	3	F	4	3	0	0	56,460
Salvaje	6	G	5	0	0	0	2,490
Salvaje Raton	7	M	3	0	1	0	568
Salvester	3	F	12	1	1	4	41,890
Salvino	5	G	12	2	2	1	64,420
Salzurita (ARG)	6	M	10	2	1	1	82,040
Sam Allen	5	G	5	0	0	0	300
Sam Boo	4	G	3	0	1	0	9,644
Sam Burr	4	G	3	0	0	0	156
Sam George Hill	10	H	9	0	4	2	4,305
Sam Hill	11	G	13	0	2	4	3,421
Sam I Am a Circus	4	F	9	1	1	3	12,367
Sam McGee	6	G	12	1	0	1	5,352
Sam R.	7	G	6	2	0	2	7,225
Sam San	9	G	15	0	2	2	2,214
Sam Steele	6	G	11	0	0	0	852
Sam Sullivan	11	G	2	0	1	1	11,500
Sam Supreme	6	G	11	1	1	0	6,281
Sam the Little Man	2	C	2	0	1	0	1,429
Sam the Man	3	G	6	1	1	0	2,823
Sam the Soldier	3	G	8	1	0	0	11,260
Sam U Devil	3	G	11	3	1	0	69,122
Samahan	5	M	16	0	5	2	7,872
Samand	6	G	10	2	3	1	11,587
Samando (FR)	4	F	9	1	0	2	151,368
Samantha B.	4	F	11	3	2	2	101,741
Samantha Value	5	M	1	0	0	0	0
Samantha's Dream	4	F	5	1	1	1	4,050
Samba City	2	F	4	0	1	0	4,630
Samba in Rio	6	G	9	0	0	3	2,903
Sambucaescapade	3	G	9	1	0	0	6,897
Samburu Warrior	2	C	2	0	1	0	1,300
Same Ol' Love	2	F	3	0	0	0	2,780
Same Old Song	8	G	2	0	0	0	80
Same Old Trouble	5	G	12	1	3	4	26,794
Same Tune	5	M	2	0	0	0	105
Samee Brass	8	M	9	2	1	0	17,714
Samie Best	5	M	2	0	0	0	0
Samilark	5	H	1	0	0	0	88
Samir	3	C	14	3	2	4	59,260
Samira	9	M	6	0	0	1	3,560
Sami's Girl	3	F	2	0	0	0	340
Sami's Majic	3	C	17	3	6	2	77,935
Sami's Tango	8	G	11	0	0	1	2,576
Samjack	4	G	9	2	2	0	6,080
Samlot	7	G	10	2	0	0	35,775
Sammi Sou Lin	5	M	8	1	2	1	8,922
Sammie	4	C	11	2	1	2	13,555
Sammie C	3	C	3	0	0	0	250
Sammieso Sah	4	G	8	0	0	0	1,610
Sammimur	4	G	4	1	0	0	10,410
Sammy Fox	3	F	6	1	2	0	16,582
Sammy Moonammy	4	F	9	0	2	1	7,080
Sammy the Cat	4	G	10	1	1	2	9,231
Sammy the Champ	9	G	1	1	0	0	2,400
Sammys Lil Kister	4	G	15	3	2	0	34,342
Sammy's Ph	4	F	5	2	0	0	6,338
Samoan	5	G	4	1	0	0	4,570
Samoan Dream	3	F	8	0	0	1	1,442
Samphony	3	G	5	0	0	0	1,167
Sampo's Fool	3	F	11	0	0	1	3,688
Sampson's Son	3	C	9	2	4	1	84,302
Sam's Bad Boy	3	C	15	0	1	0	3,858
Sam's Boy	5	G	8	2	2	3	54,450
Sam's Buddy	3	G	5	0	0	1	5,037
Sam's Choice	3	G	1	0	0	0	0
Sam's Concorde	7	G	5	1	1	2	26,800
Sam's Cove	3	F	4	0	0	0	310
Sam's Dusty	5	G	6	0	1	0	1,532
Sams Evening Girl	3	F	7	1	0	0	5,445
Sams Halo	6	M	14	0	2	3	6,640
Sam's Honor	5	G	4	1	0	0	12,720
Sam's Last Call	3	G	1	0	0	0	0
Sams Lost Soldier	3	G	7	1	1	0	22,745
Sams Market	11	H	1	0	0	0	0
Sam's Prime	3	G	4	0	0	1	3,500
Sams Sahm	2	C	2	1	1	0	20,000

Horse	Age	Sex	Sts	1st	2d	3d	Won
Sam's Secret	5	G	11	1	1	1	21,009
Sams Sham Sheree	4	F	1	0	0	0	40
Sam's Sixteenth	3	F	8	1	1	2	14,725
Sam's Valentine	3	G	13	1	0	0	5,808
Sam's Weekend	3	F	6	0	0	0	257
Samson's Treasure	4	G	6	1	2	2	17,754
Samstheman	4	G	4	0	0	0	240
Samsville	4	G	24	3	1	2	5,051
Samtheshoeinman	8	G	17	1	0	2	2,892
Samurai Nanao	3	C	7	2	3	2	47,233
Samwise	3	C	9	2	1	1	59,700
San Bon Way	8	M	8	0	0	0	1,064
San Darbo	5	M	6	0	0	2	2,438
San Dare	6	M	3	0	0	0	6,000
San Diego Blowout	3	G	6	2	1	0	81,300
San Diego Stint	7	M	9	0	1	1	1,680
San Jacinto Sam	6	H	2	0	0	0	0
San Juan Del Sol	4	G	2	0	0	0	180
San Miguel Boy	3	F	8	1	0	0	12,654
San Miguel Slew	3	F	2	0	0	0	235
San Pedro	6	H	4	0	0	0	0
San Pete Slew	7	H	5	0	2	0	934
San Quentin	5	H	7	0	0	0	1,350
San Remy (IRE)	3	G	2	0	1	0	6,600
San Salvador	7	G	7	2	1	2	122,182
San Telmo	5	G	6	0	1	1	20,087
San Zhoos	3	F	9	1	0	0	3,226
Sanadel	4	F	6	0	1	1	11,990
Sancho's Secret	2	F	14	1	3	0	24,775
Sanctify	2	F	4	0	0	1	5,150
Sanctity	7	G	13	1	0	0	6,761
Sanctuary's Melody	3	C	6	0	0	0	0
Sanctuary's Omooni	4	C	5	1	1	1	34,050
Sand and Fight	4	F	10	1	3	3	6,717
Sand and Silver	3	C	5	0	0	1	1,918
Sand and Water	8	G	10	1	1	1	17,474
Sand Ballade	5	G	10	0	3	1	5,696
Sand Blaster	3	G	17	0	0	0	423
Sand Burner	4	G	14	2	3	4	48,585
Sand Cloud	5	M	2	1	1	0	6,600
Sand Commander	5	G	8	1	1	1	2,875
Sand Digger	6	G	2	0	0	0	100
Sand in Your Eyes	3	G	5	0	0	0	417
Sand Key	4	F	8	0	1	2	6,963
Sand Kicker	2	C	3	1	1	0	13,600
Sand King	3	C	12	0	2	2	18,385
Sand Lake	4	G	16	3	2	1	18,565
Sand Ridge	9	H	7	1	1	3	38,490
Sand Rush	4	G	9	2	0	1	21,011
Sand Saba	3	C	5	1	0	2	9,635
Sand Save	3	G	12	0	0	0	519
Sand Script	3	G	2	0	0	0	136
Sand Shuffler	2	F	5	0	0	0	1,665
Sand Slapper	2	C	7	0	0	0	560
Sand Slider	3	C	4	0	0	0	1,580
Sand Slough	4	G	14	2	4	3	31,875
Sand Spirit	3	G	9	2	2	1	55,043
Sand Springs	4	F	7	1	1	1	143,756
Sand Stormer	3	F	4	0	0	0	103
Sand Town	4	G	14	0	2	0	2,995
Sand Trapper	4	G	15	1	2	2	7,447
Sand Wolf	4	C	7	0	2	0	9,334
Sandalias	4	F	16	2	2	4	11,330
Sandbag	3	C	10	1	3	2	12,605
Sandbagger Jones	3	C	1	1	0	0	15,600
Sandbagger Sam	3	G	3	0	0	1	600
Sandbar Sally	3	F	6	0	1	0	3,011
Sandbox Sam	4	C	1	0	0	0	0
Sandburg's Remorse	2	C	1	0	0	0	135
Sandburr	5	G	5	1	0	1	12,365
Sanddoones	6	M	9	1	1	0	9,055
Sandee's Dynastee	6	M	10	0	0	1	1,465
Sandel Wood Fleet	6	G	12	1	1	1	11,870
Sanderling	4	F	8	1	2	3	39,000
Sanderman (CHI)	4	C	4	0	0	0	2,900
Sandersville	3	C	9	0	0	0	0
Sandestin	3	C	13	2	0	2	19,833
Sandflea	4	F	4	0	0	0	734
Sandhill Storm	7	G	5	0	0	0	108
Sandhill Swinger	6	G	9	0	0	3	1,869
Sandia One	2	G	3	0	2	1	2,540
Sandia Shadows	3	G	4	0	0	0	234
Sandia's Flicka	3	F	9	3	3	0	73,576
Sandias Peppermint	2	C	7	4	0	2	131,355
Sandifoss	3	F	6	2	0	0	25,920
Sandina	3	F	2	0	0	0	0
Sandinmyeye	4	F	14	2	0	3	11,075
Sandline Star	4	G	13	1	3	0	29,824
Sandlot Sue	3	F	20	3	1	1	25,615
Sandmandu	3	G	9	2	2	1	11,126
Sandpit Dancer	7	M	10	0	2	1	6,445
Sandpit's Delight	5	M	4	1	1	0	7,532
Sandra Therese	5	M	14	2	1	0	31,940
Sandra's Pride	7	G	4	1	0	1	7,645
Sandra's Star	5	M	1	0	0	0	0
Sandras Sweetie	6	M	12	1	0	2	6,123
Sandrican	3	G	11	1	2	0	7,101
Sandro	4	G	4	0	0	0	1,185
Sandrover	3	C	9	1	2	2	10,135
Sands Fury	5	M	7	2	0	0	15,792
Sands of Gold	9	H	1	0	0	0	0
Sands of Time	5	G	9	1	0	0	10,743
Sands Thru Time	4	C	6	1	1	2	6,980
Sandsebon	3	C	1	0	0	0	0
Sandshrew	5	M	9	3	1	3	22,098
Sandspit	5	G	11	2	1	3	21,410
Sandusky	6	H	8	1	2	1	14,256
Sandwoven (GB)	4	F	15	2	1	2	16,030
Sandy Rhythm	5	H	9	1	1	2	9,549
Sandy Ridge	4	F	9	1	1	0	13,688
Sandy Sneakers	5	M	5	0	2	0	8,800
Sandye's Halo	7	M	3	0	1	0	2,415
Sandye's Love Not	6	G	2	0	0	0	384
Sandyford	3	G	6	0	0	3	18,760
Sandyfourthofjuly	4	F	1	0	0	0	72
Sandyland	6	G	6	0	0	1	5,710
Sandylikethebeach	3	F	5	0	1	1	2,685
Sandyneck	2	C	1	0	0	0	0
Sandys Dandy	7	G	11	0	2	2	4,260
Sandy's Glory	2	F	2	0	0	1	1,540
Sandy's Lil Devil	4	G	8	0	0	1	2,439
Sanfran	2	G	2	1	0	0	5,525
Sanfran (JPN)	2	F	8	1	1	3	51,798
Sanger	5	G	11	2	2	2	55,692
Sangoma	4	F	2	0	0	0	0
Sangue too Loud	4	F	15	1	2	2	37,852
Sangue's Crown	4	F	7	0	0	0	898
Sanibel Sam	5	G	10	1	2	1	16,214
Sanibel Sunset	4	F	9	4	2	0	45,060
Sanjeev	3	C	2	0	0	0	0
Sankofa Two	4	F	11	1	4	0	9,056
Sanky Panky	4	G	8	0	3	0	24,140
Sanquinten Quail	5	M	9	0	1	1	2,642
Sans Sauce	4	F	7	1	0	1	3,278
Sans Win	3	G	8	3	1	0	20,860
Sansa	4	F	2	1	0	0	20,320
Sanshu	7	G	4	0	0	0	400
Sanskrit	11	G	6	0	3	0	3,510
Santa Ana Winds	2	R	2	0	0	0	740
Santa Croce	4	F	5	2	2	1	74,500
Santa Fe Autumn	4	F	4	3	0	0	51,630
Santa Fe Slewpy	13	G	9	0	1	0	1,911
Santa Lucia	2	F	6	0	0	1	2,288
Santa Maria Jones	3	F	5	1	0	0	2,700
Santa Rosalia	3	F	8	0	2	3	33,024
Santa Stella	3	F	5	1	0	0	4,795
Santana Strings	2	C	5	2	2	0	57,960
Santano	7	G	5	2	1	1	40,282
Santa's Go Go Bag	2	F	2	0	0	0	450
Santa's Playboy	6	G	6	0	1	1	7,050
Santaslittlehelper	3	F	5	0	0	0	2,570
Santee Light	2	C	3	0	3	0	7,840
Santenay (FR)	6	G	8	0	0	2	23,803
Santero	11	G	4	0	0	2	665
Santerra	4	F	2	0	0	0	1,908
Santiago Express	3	G	7	1	1	1	15,158
Santiago Rojo	5	M	11	0	3	1	7,705
Santiam Storm Cat	7	G	6	2	3	0	2,900

RECORDS OF HORSES

Horse	Age	Sex	Sts	1st	2d	3d	Won
Santiam Top Jazz	3	G	12	2	3	0	19,016
Santino's Honour	2	C	1	0	0	0	0
Santo Pio	3	C	4	0	0	0	3,950
Santo Tomas	8	H	2	0	0	0	0
Santor	4	C	9	1	2	1	8,041
Santos	3	G	8	1	2	1	11,555
Santuary's Mak	4	F	3	0	0	2	2,804
Sanzibar	3	G	10	0	5	2	23,510
Saphatic	3	F	11	0	0	2	1,342
Saphir Indien (GB)	5	G	5	0	0	0	1,380
Sapna	3	F	1	0	0	0	216
Sapodilla	4	F	5	0	0	1	3,832
Sapore Di Mare (ARG)	5	H	1	0	0	0	0
Sapphire Blues	5	G	9	2	2	3	20,155
Sapphire Hill	6	M	10	2	0	2	33,900
Sapphire Lady	3	F	14	2	1	4	36,775
Sapphireontherocks	5	H	10	0	3	0	10,718
Sapphires N Halos	3	F	11	2	1	4	32,949
Sappy Lil Tune	7	G	20	1	2	1	9,274
Saquache	7	H	1	0	0	0	2,220
Sara Baby	5	M	1	0	0	0	0
Sara Bell	5	M	2	0	0	0	71
Sara Blue	2	F	2	0	1	0	4,600
Sara Can	3	F	4	0	0	0	86
Sara G	4	F	3	0	0	2	2,290
Sara Is Peeking	4	F	2	0	0	0	0
Sara Katherine	3	F	12	1	5	0	12,613
Sara Lynn	5	M	15	4	3	1	24,372
Sara Margaret	4	F	1	0	1	0	5,315
Sara Raj	3	F	5	3	1	0	25,755
Sara Say	5	M	12	0	3	1	5,208
Sara Val	4	F	5	0	0	0	772
Sarabanna	2	F	1	0	0	0	140
Sarabird	3	F	7	0	3	2	21,535
Saracandu	3	F	13	2	2	1	28,720
Sarafan	7	G	8	1	3	0	198,400
Sarah Bain	5	M	2	1	0	0	10,547
Sarah Beaner	5	M	9	1	1	2	24,810
Sarah Creek	5	M	14	3	1	2	47,238
Sarah Elmire	4	F	1	0	0	0	0
Sarah Haras	2	F	2	0	2	0	5,470
Sarah Hold On	3	F	1	0	0	0	0
Sarah Jade	5	M	8	1	1	4	50,405
Sarah Oteka	5	M	7	2	0	1	5,051
Sarah's Beau	5	G	6	0	2	3	4,400
Sarah's Bid	6	G	12	2	0	5	17,616
Sarah's Caper	3	F	1	0	0	0	0
Sarah's Circusboy	3	C	6	1	1	1	5,628
Sarah's Code	4	F	8	1	1	1	9,860
Sarah's Faith	2	C	3	0	0	0	1,485
Sarah's Goldengirl	6	M	12	3	3	0	28,860
Sarah's Pleasure	5	M	4	1	0	1	11,420
Sarahs Power	3	F	1	0	0	0	37
Sarah's Pride	4	F	3	0	0	0	0
Sarah's Prism	2	F	2	1	0	0	11,761
Sarah's Prospect	2	G	1	0	0	0	1,230
Sarah's Wish	3	F	7	2	1	1	29,740
Sarahsdreamcatcher	3	F	7	1	1	1	10,529
Sarahshappytoo	3	F	4	1	1	0	14,840
Saramar	3	F	4	0	1	0	8,080
Sarann	2	F	3	1	0	0	8,660
Sara's Crusader	5	G	10	0	0	0	1,028
Sara's Dream Girl	3	F	6	0	1	0	10,232
Sara's Moonlight	2	F	1	0	0	0	0
Sara's Request	3	F	3	0	0	0	0
Sara's Sara Lee	5	M	12	0	0	2	5,518
Sara's Shadow	5	M	7	4	2	0	70,080
Sara's Silence	5	M	1	0	0	0	0
Sara's Tune	3	F	12	3	1	3	69,618
Sara's Yankee Girl	4	F	12	2	4	3	48,971
Sarasabear	5	M	3	1	0	1	5,674
Sarasota (ARG)	4	F	3	0	0	0	6,086
Sarasota Bay	2	F	3	0	1	1	2,790
Sarasota Sunset	3	F	12	0	1	1	9,975
Sarastorm	6	M	6	1	0	1	16,745
Saraswatie	3	F	8	0	1	0	5,600
Saratoga Apple	3	F	10	0	2	2	6,088
Saratoga Blues	5	G	5	0	0	0	1,436
Saratoga Bound	6	M	1	0	0	0	0
Saratoga Carnival	4	C	4	0	0	0	1,010
Saratoga Cat	5	M	1	0	1	0	12,860
Saratoga County	3	C	12	2	3	1	237,390
Saratoga Episode	3	G	7	1	0	1	29,530
Saratoga Evan	2	C	5	0	1	0	9,058
Saratoga Games	6	G	4	0	0	0	560
Saratoga Gent	3	G	14	3	1	3	38,741
Saratoga Harbor	4	G	6	1	2	2	17,650
Saratoga Heights	4	G	7	0	1	1	7,421
Saratoga Humor	4	F	6	1	1	0	40,266
Saratoga Jules	3	G	8	2	2	0	49,470
Saratoga Lake	5	G	19	2	3	5	17,694
Saratoga Law	4	G	10	3	0	0	27,120
Saratoga Rapture	7	G	12	2	4	1	12,520
Saratoga River	5	G	4	0	0	1	2,821
Saratoga Set	5	M	10	0	1	1	4,290
Saratoga Siren	3	F	1	0	0	0	645
Saratoga Spar	4	F	11	2	1	0	20,160
Saratoga Sport	11	G	16	1	1	1	3,355
Saratoga Spring	3	F	14	1	0	1	7,850
Saratoga Sugar	3	F	5	0	1	0	14,810
Saratoga Way	5	G	2	1	0	0	9,240
Saratown	2	F	3	0	0	0	300
Sarava	5	H	7	0	0	0	76,980
Sarawat	4	C	4	1	0	0	1,794
Sarcastic	4	F	4	0	0	0	600
Sarcee Annie	5	M	8	0	0	1	1,095
Sardaukar (GB)	8	G	9	2	0	1	61,545
Sardis	5	M	11	4	2	0	91,770
Saree (GB)	3	F	5	1	0	1	27,884
Sarellies Knight	8	M	4	0	1	0	2,013
Sarepta Hornet	2	C	4	0	2	0	8,250
Sarepta Sauce	8	G	13	1	0	2	8,733
Sargari (IRE)	8	G	10	3	1	1	36,832
Sargasso	3	C	4	1	0	3	31,690
Sargeant	5	G	11	0	1	0	704
Sargent Mike	2	C	1	0	0	0	0
Sargent Oates	10	G	5	0	0	0	312
Sargent Olson	5	G	9	0	0	1	1,672
Sargent Rite	3	G	3	0	0	0	1,641
Sargent Storm	2	G	3	0	1	0	2,244
Sargentchilipepper	3	G	2	1	0	0	10,350
Sariano	3	F	5	1	0	2	49,675
Saribinda	5	G	6	2	1	1	22,055
Sarie Marais	4	F	4	1	0	1	21,440
Sarina's Princess	3	F	3	0	0	1	1,289
Saris Chance	7	M	3	1	0	1	3,182
Sari's Son	10	G	5	1	0	1	3,080
Sarlos	4	C	5	0	0	0	1,177
Sarmentose	6	M	18	0	2	2	7,537
Sarmentum	5	M	1	0	1	0	2,100
Sarofs Man	3	C	2	0	0	0	84
Saron's Time	5	M	11	4	2	2	28,822
Saros Legend	2	F	1	0	0	0	400
Sarotess	4	G	12	0	5	3	13,124
Sarzana	2	F	5	0	0	1	8,474
Sasafras	3	F	9	0	0	0	2,771
Sash	4	F	19	4	2	2	36,165
Sash of Glory	6	H	3	0	0	0	0
Sasha M	3	F	4	0	0	0	632
Sashaying Slew	4	F	5	1	1	0	40,436
Saskatchewan	4	F	3	0	0	0	675
Sass Back	4	F	7	1	0	1	2,994
Sass n' Class	7	M	2	0	0	0	300
Sass Valay	5	M	1	0	0	0	0
Sassey Erin	3	F	9	1	2	1	14,920
Sassilou	5	M	7	1	2	1	2,476
Sassy Affair	4	F	3	0	0	1	3,960
Sassy Again	3	F	10	1	0	0	29,241
Sassy Alle Cat	2	F	7	1	0	2	8,015
Sassy and Blue	4	F	8	2	0	1	21,836
Sassy and Brash	4	F	1	0	0	0	0
Sassy April	8	M	7	1	0	1	17,540
Sassy Bayou Belle	4	F	2	0	0	0	0
Sassy Bear	6	M	9	1	1	1	17,985
Sassy Becky	3	F	6	2	1	0	9,240
Sassy Belle	4	F	8	2	1	0	42,900
Sassy Blonde	3	F	4	0	0	0	620
Sassy Brenda	3	F	10	1	0	2	19,191

Horse	Age	Sex	Sts	1st	2d	3d	Won
Sassy Broad	3	F	1	0	1	0	9,080
Sassy Cat Diamond	6	M	1	0	0	0	0
Sassy Cathy	4	F	16	1	1	4	16,240
Sassy Chasse	2	F	1	0	0	0	120
Sassy Chequer	4	F	8	0	1	0	2,820
Sassy Decision	4	F	6	1	0	0	7,620
Sassy Dot Com	5	M	2	0	0	1	787
Sassy Edith	8	M	7	0	0	0	320
Sassy Editor	2	F	2	0	0	0	639
Sassy Evie	4	F	2	0	0	0	435
Sassy Excess	2	F	2	0	0	0	800
Sassy Five	3	F	14	0	2	1	6,850
Sassy Gal	2	F	3	1	1	0	24,100
Sassy Hound	7	G	6	1	1	3	64,336
Sassy J K	3	F	3	2	0	0	11,640
Sassy Lear	3	F	15	2	3	4	26,561
Sassy Linda	5	M	15	0	5	3	15,280
Sassy Little Sarah	4	F	11	3	2	1	32,450
Sassy M	4	F	1	0	0	0	450
Sassy Mint	3	F	4	1	1	0	16,975
Sassy Moment	5	M	4	0	0	0	0
Sassy N Slew	4	F	2	0	0	0	0
Sassy Rebel	7	M	2	0	0	0	0
Sassy Romance	3	F	5	1	1	0	6,120
Sassy Rosa	6	M	1	0	0	0	0
Sassy Sam	6	G	9	0	0	1	1,558
Sassy Sarah Lou	3	F	6	0	0	1	1,468
Sassy Scarlet	6	M	8	0	2	2	7,316
Sassy Six	5	M	20	1	1	1	9,144
Sassy Songster	3	F	12	0	1	2	11,277
Sassy Stacy	4	F	8	0	1	1	4,295
Sassy Stephie	5	M	4	1	1	0	9,434
Sassy Sushi	2	F	2	1	0	0	2,732
Sassy Sylvia	3	F	10	0	1	2	1,263
Sassy Tap	3	F	7	0	0	2	2,312
Sassy Till Dawn	4	F	8	0	0	0	322
Sassy Tribute	4	F	14	3	3	3	21,690
Sassy Trisha	3	F	21	2	1	3	12,458
Sassy Vic	4	F	4	1	1	0	8,814
Sassy Way	3	F	7	1	3	1	9,040
Sassy Won	5	M	9	2	2	3	28,445
Sassyclassygirl	3	F	3	0	0	0	0
Sassylilskywalker	2	F	2	0	0	0	1,575
Sassy's Weekend	2	G	4	1	0	1	10,324
Sat. Nite Special	2	F	7	0	2	0	7,420
Satanic Verses	3	C	1	0	0	0	0
Sataniste	8	G	13	5	3	3	91,943
Satan's Account	4	G	4	0	0	0	237
Satans All Around	4	G	6	1	0	0	1,579
Satan's Code	6	G	11	4	2	3	102,850
Satan's Prince	8	H	4	0	0	1	913
Satan's Song	4	F	3	0	3	0	8,900
Satan's Waltz	3	F	11	1	4	3	52,060
Satantia	4	G	7	1	0	2	3,320
Satari	3	G	10	1	0	0	15,460
Satarra (GB)	7	H	5	0	0	0	208
Satawa Cat	3	G	2	0	0	0	150
Satch McNally	6	G	9	1	0	3	7,910
Sateen	3	F	10	2	2	0	9,554
Satellite Dancer	7	G	7	1	0	1	2,850
Satellite Heart	11	M	7	1	2	0	5,300
Satellite Problem	3	C	11	3	0	2	21,428
Satellite Skinner	3	G	6	1	0	0	1,762
Satiable	2	F	6	0	1	1	6,270
Satiate	4	F	13	2	2	0	84,045
Satilla Dreamer	4	F	1	0	1	0	2,166
Satin Black	4	F	12	3	2	1	17,290
Satin Concern	4	C	7	0	2	0	8,165
Satin Creek	7	G	12	3	2	2	13,939
Satin Dolly	5	M	5	0	2	0	6,915
Satin Dress	3	F	5	0	1	0	1,470
Satin Halo	2	F	3	0	0	0	1,890
Satin Heart	2	F	2	0	0	0	427
Satin Lady	4	F	11	1	1	3	4,700
Satin Mist	4	F	4	0	0	1	1,157
Satin N Silk	3	F	1	0	0	0	135
Satin Song	3	F	13	0	2	3	12,226
Satin Spike	5	M	4	2	1	0	5,200
Satin Storm	4	F	5	1	0	0	18,210
Satin Sun	2	C	7	1	2	1	12,155
Satina	5	M	1	0	0	0	180
Satine	3	F	10	0	1	2	13,732
Satine Rouge	4	F	12	3	2	1	32,005
Satiric	3	C	4	1	0	1	34,260
Satohina	3	F	3	1	0	0	26,283
Satrap	5	H	8	1	2	1	15,035
Saturday	7	G	16	3	3	5	36,082
Saturday Afternoon	2	C	3	0	1	1	8,770
Saturday Deelites	3	C	4	0	1	1	17,240
Saturday Detention	4	F	16	2	1	2	20,970
Saturday Sin	4	G	7	2	0	1	16,058
Saturdays Dancer	2	F	2	0	1	0	2,940
Saturday's Warrior	4	G	2	0	0	0	420
Saturn's Saint	4	F	20	1	1	3	8,269
Sauce	5	G	4	0	2	0	8,790
Sauce Pan	3	C	2	0	0	0	0
Sauce Pecan	6	G	13	3	1	3	47,538
Saucemakesmeflirt	4	F	2	0	0	1	1,735
Sauceonside	3	F	5	4	0	0	60,600
Saucey Tiger	2	C	12	0	6	1	44,660
Sauceyrubin	3	F	14	1	2	3	38,693
Saucon Creek	4	C	9	2	3	1	60,960
Saucon Sooz	2	F	1	0	0	0	1,440
Saucy Baby	3	F	12	0	0	1	2,125
Saucy Bid	3	F	7	1	4	1	46,920
Saucy Buck	2	G	3	0	0	0	180
Saucy Cat	7	G	11	3	1	2	50,330
Saucy Ciano	2	F	6	1	2	2	36,618
Saucy Gal	2	F	1	0	0	0	0
Saucy Niner	2	F	1	0	0	0	0
Saucy Pick	4	F	1	0	0	0	65
Saucy Secretary	2	F	4	0	0	2	2,942
Saucy Tapanga	5	M	8	1	0	0	3,086
Saucy Taste	4	G	11	0	0	1	1,412
Saucy Vinny	2	G	2	0	0	1	4,307
Saucy Viv	4	F	9	0	2	2	15,480
Saucy Viva	5	M	5	0	0	0	562
Saucy Vixen	5	M	6	0	0	0	1,358
Saucy Ways	5	M	1	0	0	0	0
Saucy's Hot Sauce	3	F	5	0	0	0	0
Saul	5	H	1	0	0	0	0
Sauntering	3	F	9	2	0	0	26,100
Saups	11	G	2	0	0	0	112
Sausage Link	5	G	8	3	0	1	19,820
Sauvage (FR)	3	F	6	2	0	0	42,634
Sauvignon	6	M	1	0	0	0	146
Sauxsoe	2	G	1	0	1	0	1,900
Savage (BRZ)	7	H	11	2	0	1	47,278
Savage Beauty	3	F	10	2	2	1	79,564
Savage Garden	7	G	18	0	0	0	537
Savage Recital	3	F	1	0	0	0	0
Savage Sage	5	M	4	0	0	0	398
Savage Sailor	4	G	1	0	0	0	130
Savage Sue	3	F	9	3	3	2	10,189
Savage Wolf	4	G	8	1	0	1	6,553
Savana D	9	M	5	0	2	0	1,760
Savanah Go	4	F	4	0	0	0	273
Savanalamar	4	F	9	1	1	2	8,325
Savanna Charm	2	F	7	0	1	1	13,520
Savanna Manna	3	F	2	1	1	0	8,190
Savannah Bluff	7	M	10	0	0	0	3,764
Savannah Branch	3	G	2	0	0	0	0
Savannah Breeze	2	G	1	0	0	0	300
Savannah Crest	6	M	11	2	1	1	22,695
Savannah Hanna	6	M	5	1	0	2	16,420
Savannah Harbor	7	H	5	0	1	0	4,008
Savannah Knight	6	G	2	0	0	0	470
Savannah Lane	2	F	2	0	0	0	1,410
Savannah Mist	4	F	4	0	0	0	360
Savannah Road	4	G	7	2	1	1	30,580
Savannah Rose	2	F	2	0	0	0	328
Savannah Rules	4	F	8	2	0	0	9,705
Savannah Thumper	4	G	10	2	3	2	37,368
Savannah Way	4	F	15	0	1	5	6,385
Savannah's Gold	3	F	6	1	0	0	5,580
Savannah's Prize	6	M	19	1	3	2	12,678
Savannah's Son	3	C	11	5	4	1	83,890
Savannah's Wish	3	G	16	2	2	2	18,744

Horse	Age	Sex	Sts	1st	2d	3d	Won
Savanna's Folley	5	M	8	3	0	1	5,890
Save a Nickel	8	H	1	0	0	0	150
Save Ground	4	G	15	2	2	1	37,845
Save My Assets	4	F	11	1	0	0	6,237
Save My Place	3	F	8	1	1	1	25,729
Save the Coins	3	F	8	0	0	0	640
Save the Deputy	4	F	2	0	0	0	182
Save the Forests	7	G	18	2	4	3	18,505
Save the Moment	4	F	6	0	0	0	1,029
Save the Profit	3	C	5	3	1	0	88,429
Save the Shield	2	C	8	0	1	1	14,510
Save This Dance	4	G	5	1	1	0	8,057
Save Time	3	C	2	0	0	0	0
Saved	3	F	15	1	2	3	11,462
Saved by the Sword	6	H	4	0	2	0	5,580
Savedbythelight	4	F	7	0	2	1	76,440
Saveeta	2	F	4	1	1	1	27,368
Savethebestforlass	2	F	4	1	1	1	21,300
Savin My Assets	2	F	3	0	0	0	1,075
Saving Ground	2	F	3	1	1	0	50,160
Savings Account	2	F	8	0	1	0	3,600
Savona Heat	4	G	2	0	0	0	800
Savona Victor	4	G	11	1	0	0	5,018
Savonarola (GB)	4	C	4	1	0	1	33,980
Savor	3	F	4	0	0	0	1,830
Savor the Moment	2	F	1	0	0	0	894
Savorthetime	5	M	8	3	2	1	167,762
Savory	3	F	10	1	1	1	23,975
Savoy Special	4	C	4	0	2	0	23,910
Savoya On Ice	5	G	11	2	7	1	30,860
Savoy's Dancer	3	C	1	0	0	0	200
Savoy's Prince	7	G	12	0	2	1	9,480
Savurtabs	5	G	7	0	0	0	168
Savvy Connection	10	G	3	0	0	0	0
Savvy Girl	4	F	16	6	0	3	60,662
Savvy Traveler	2	C	4	0	1	0	2,590
Savvys Tomas	3	G	5	1	0	1	8,205
Savy Miss	6	M	9	2	2	0	11,160
Saw Blade	3	C	5	0	1	0	992
Saw Grass Sabre	3	G	11	2	3	1	53,560
Sawadee	3	F	2	0	0	0	300
Sawdust	4	G	17	2	3	2	21,790
Sawdust Doll	5	M	6	2	3	0	8,292
Sawgrass	4	C	2	0	0	0	0
Sawko to It	4	G	15	2	2	5	19,093
Sawston Hall	4	G	5	0	0	0	825
Sawtelle Belle	3	F	3	1	0	0	5,940
Saxer	3	C	4	0	0	0	194
Saxmeamemo	6	G	12	3	4	2	7,315
Saxton's Engine	4	G	11	1	1	1	24,090
Say Amen	3	F	7	1	0	1	19,648
Say Cousin Lenny	5	G	8	1	3	0	57,340
Say Diamond Rico	3	G	5	1	0	1	21,230
Say First Bid	7	G	5	0	0	0	525
Say French Fry	2	F	1	0	0	0	230
Say Grace First Jo	8	M	10	1	3	0	8,398
Say Hey Charlie	4	G	19	4	1	5	32,017
Say Hey Willie	3	F	6	3	1	0	89,030
Say It Ain't True	4	F	2	0	0	0	145
Say It and Smile	3	F	1	0	0	0	0
Say It Both Ways	8	G	2	0	0	1	1,590
Say It in Code	4	F	9	1	2	2	18,800
Say It Isn't Sold	2	C	7	0	0	3	9,120
Say Mystic	6	M	6	0	0	1	2,180
Say No Justin	5	G	17	3	6	2	42,225
Say No Maw	5	G	4	0	0	1	5,510
Say Ole	4	G	7	0	0	1	900
Say Somethin Funny	4	F	9	1	0	1	16,587
Say The Word (IRE)	7	G	2	0	0	1	1,750
Say Uncle Kevin	2	C	3	0	0	0	0
Say Victory	5	M	5	0	0	1	1,726
Say What Nick	3	G	1	0	0	0	0
Say What You Think	4	G	3	1	0	0	6,647
Say Yeah	3	F	12	2	1	0	13,365
Say Yes	4	G	11	1	2	0	7,385
Say You Will	4	F	1	0	0	0	0
Say Your Mind	5	M	10	2	0	2	12,101
Say Zee	2	C	2	0	0	0	690
Sayabec	5	M	3	0	1	0	2,615
Saye's	2	C	6	0	1	1	3,030
Saygoodnightgrace	6	M	3	0	0	0	2,060
Sayhellowavegoodby	2	F	5	0	1	0	4,990
Sayitain'tso Joe	4	G	6	2	3	0	41,707
Sayitlikeumeanit	4	G	13	0	1	1	3,929
Sayonara to You	2	F	1	0	0	0	96
Sayonara Told	4	G	16	2	4	0	20,239
Sayrun	4	G	9	0	0	0	1,310
Saysenor	4	C	5	0	0	0	642
Sayucan Kid	6	G	6	0	0	0	438
Sayville	4	C	7	1	0	0	11,881
Sazerac Song	3	F	6	1	0	1	33,780
Sc Dazzle Me	5	M	4	2	0	0	3,789
Scabbard	3	G	4	0	0	1	2,760
Scadadel	4	F	1	1	0	0	770
Scaffold Man Two	8	G	6	2	1	2	8,760
Scaffolds Legacy	6	G	10	3	3	1	8,529
Scagnelli	9	G	10	1	0	2	31,510
Scags	4	G	8	3	2	0	20,375
Scalator	2	C	2	0	1	0	3,895
Scale the Heights	3	C	8	1	0	2	43,026
Scales Springs	5	M	1	0	0	0	0
Scalia	5	G	7	2	0	1	46,125
Scamp Along	5	M	4	1	0	1	4,980
Scandalously	7	M	7	0	0	3	4,670
Scandinavia	2	C	5	1	3	0	65,263
Scapade	4	F	1	0	0	1	60,000
Scar	2	C	1	0	0	0	0
Scare Air	4	G	9	1	0	1	8,558
Scarecrow	2	G	4	0	0	0	0
Scaredcat	3	G	9	0	2	2	8,323
Scarem	3	G	2	2	0	0	4,510
Scarface Sal	8	M	14	0	0	0	1,108
Scarla	3	F	1	0	0	0	205
Scarlet Baby	3	F	1	0	0	0	0
Scarlet Billows	4	F	7	0	2	0	22,180
Scarlet Blue	2	F	5	1	1	0	14,860
Scarlet Child	3	F	1	0	0	0	0
Scarlet Classic	4	G	4	0	1	1	12,527
Scarlet Dress	4	F	1	0	0	0	0
Scarlet Gilia	6	M	13	2	2	2	51,965
Scarlet Jeff	2	G	5	2	0	0	14,620
Scarlet Lad	6	G	10	1	2	1	14,938
Scarlet Lady Slew	5	M	3	0	0	0	0
Scarlet Letter	3	F	2	0	0	0	1,152
Scarlet Lily	3	F	4	0	0	0	707
Scarlet Miss	5	M	9	0	2	0	4,860
Scarlet Moon	3	F	2	0	0	0	0
Scarlet O'Mare	3	F	3	0	0	0	455
Scarlet Peppers	4	C	12	2	2	1	14,297
Scarlet Rascal	8	G	15	0	2	1	6,595
Scarlet Reflection	3	F	9	0	1	1	9,860
Scarlet Splash	3	F	2	1	0	0	6,615
Scarlet Storm	3	C	8	0	0	2	10,508
Scarlet Treasure	4	F	10	1	0	1	2,172
Scarlet Valentine	3	F	2	0	0	0	884
Scarlet's Magick	7	M	7	0	0	0	832
Scarlet's Tara	4	F	7	0	3	0	16,855
Scarlett Memories	3	F	10	3	2	0	71,280
Scarlett Story	3	F	9	1	1	2	6,875
Scarlett Wolf	2	F	6	1	0	3	26,450
Scarlett's Finest	2	F	7	0	1	4	16,850
Scarlett's Ghost	3	G	8	0	0	1	1,129
Scarlett'sprospect	6	M	9	0	1	0	1,495
Scary Bob	3	G	3	0	1	1	24,668
Scary Tim	6	G	1	0	0	0	325
Scaryzano	3	F	11	1	0	1	5,580
Scarzane	5	M	9	2	4	1	119,104
Scat Back	3	G	5	0	0	0	1,370
Scat Cat Jamey	4	C	9	4	0	1	29,130
Scat Em	2	G	1	0	0	0	118
Scat King	2	G	2	1	0	0	7,020
Scat Sam Man	3	C	4	1	0	0	21,387
Scataway	3	F	13	1	0	1	3,446
Scatcango	2	C	1	0	0	0	570
Scatcat's Dream	3	F	14	1	1	0	5,481
Scatin Satin	2	F	7	1	1	0	7,545
Scatina	4	F	4	0	0	0	832
Scatincat	3	F	9	1	0	1	5,229

Horse	Age	Sex	Sts	1st	2d	3d	Won
Scat's Meow	3	F	3	0	0	0	0
Scat's Mine	3	F	17	1	1	3	13,400
Scatter My Stars	4	F	2	0	0	0	0
Scatter' Um	9	G	7	0	0	1	1,903
Scattered	4	G	14	3	3	2	31,431
Scattering	5	M	12	3	0	3	27,045
Scattering Breezes	5	H	11	5	1	2	95,000
Scatterman	2	G	5	1	0	0	5,935
Scattin Mo Jo	3	C	8	0	1	0	1,674
Scattitude	3	F	2	0	0	0	240
Scattle Bud	4	C	15	4	4	1	77,311
Scene Maker	3	F	4	0	0	1	3,090
Scenic Wonder	4	G	4	0	0	2	9,115
Scenicsfinalanswer	4	G	11	1	1	3	15,295
Scent a Grade	12	G	1	0	0	0	0
Scent of a Lady	4	F	10	0	1	0	2,053
Scent of Heather	7	M	4	1	1	1	2,590
Schadenfreude	2	C	2	0	0	0	235
Schadow	8	M	18	2	4	1	14,793
Schaller Haller	5	M	13	3	2	5	21,398
Scharada	3	G	11	2	0	0	15,100
Scharoot	4	F	14	0	0	2	4,347
Schatzie Dreams	3	G	12	1	1	0	22,110
Schedule (GB)	3	F	8	2	3	0	102,240
Scheduled Event	4	C	14	2	0	1	23,374
Schematic Design	3	F	10	1	1	0	38,084
Schemba's Tune	5	G	7	0	1	0	1,312
Schemer	3	F	7	2	0	0	55,505
Schemes and Dreams	3	F	3	0	0	0	142
Schemshady	3	F	3	0	0	1	572
Scher Bold	3	F	6	3	1	0	22,840
Scheraboca's Tune	6	H	3	1	1	0	3,656
Schex Ni Der	3	F	1	0	0	0	48
Schiloh	2	C	5	1	1	0	37,915
Schisler	3	C	12	0	0	2	5,346
Schizzy	3	G	13	2	2	0	12,819
Schlegel	4	G	7	1	0	0	5,250
Schmooey	4	F	3	0	0	1	450
Schmoopy Hang On	3	G	8	0	0	0	1,915
Schnauser	5	G	2	0	0	0	50
Schneider	4	G	9	0	0	3	9,595
Schnell Schnell	3	F	1	0	0	0	0
School Bell	6	M	12	1	2	2	7,257
School Fashion	7	M	7	1	0	1	9,403
School of Thought	4	C	12	0	1	3	9,460
School Town	5	M	7	0	0	0	360
Schooling	7	G	4	0	0	0	88
Schoolmaster	4	G	14	1	3	1	15,748
Schools Out	7	G	14	0	1	3	2,758
Schooner	5	G	6	0	1	1	4,724
Schooner Bay	3	F	4	0	1	2	20,851
Schoonertown Lass	3	F	5	0	0	1	2,018
Schott	10	G	2	0	0	0	140
Schottische	4	F	6	0	2	1	2,033
Schroeder	4	G	4	0	0	1	1,890
Schu Nine to Five	8	M	5	0	1	2	843
Schultzie	2	G	2	0	0	1	2,065
Schwartzenegger	4	G	2	0	0	0	180
Schwarzwald	3	C	9	1	0	1	18,347
Schway	4	C	5	0	0	2	2,680
Schweitzer	4	C	4	0	1	1	12,570
Schymm Tyme	9	M	2	0	0	0	0
Scifi Flick	5	M	1	0	0	0	147
Scimitar	3	G	8	0	3	0	4,540
Scintilla	4	F	5	1	0	0	7,116
Scintillating	6	M	10	3	1	1	65,669
Scintillating Gal	8	M	6	1	1	2	8,155
Scioto Bootski	6	M	5	3	1	0	37,720
Scioto Scacat	3	F	6	0	0	1	1,821
Scipion	2	C	3	1	0	1	47,000
Sco Phone	3	F	7	1	0	0	3,250
Scobey	9	H	13	5	2	1	23,674
Scofflaw	6	G	3	1	0	0	2,120
Scofield Honour	2	G	7	0	0	2	5,953
Scooby Drew and Me	5	G	6	4	0	0	32,596
Scooby Who	4	G	10	1	0	1	3,402
Scoot Bootnboogie	3	F	9	2	1	1	10,684
Scoot Mary Scoot	3	F	3	1	0	0	2,640
Scoot N Boogieslew	3	F	2	1	0	0	2,120

Horse	Age	Sex	Sts	1st	2d	3d	Won
Scoot Scoot N Go	3	G	18	4	2	2	28,675
Scoota Begga	4	G	3	0	0	1	647
Scootcatscoot	5	G	1	0	0	0	50
Scootch	8	G	17	3	2	1	15,438
Scooter Boots	4	F	8	2	3	0	21,025
Scooter Pie	3	F	3	0	0	0	0
Scooter Poot	2	G	2	0	0	0	310
Scooter Rains	3	C	7	2	0	1	33,362
Scooter Roach	5	G	12	2	3	3	213,827
Scooters Knight	6	G	11	1	3	0	3,540
Scooter's Sunman	6	G	5	1	0	0	4,503
Scooterville	5	G	3	0	0	0	300
Scootin by Delmer	7	G	8	0	1	0	960
Scootin' Girl	6	M	3	0	0	0	2,448
Scootinaflash	4	F	11	1	0	1	9,328
Scootintohollywood	4	G	2	0	0	0	208
Scoots	3	F	5	0	0	0	219
Scooty	3	G	15	1	3	1	65,884
Scorched Earth	5	G	3	0	0	0	44
Scorcheroo	2	G	7	1	1	2	13,260
Score Card	4	G	4	1	0	2	1,715
Score High	3	C	9	2	1	1	97,800
Score King	3	G	11	0	2	0	6,047
Score Ronan	4	C	13	1	3	1	7,517
Score Six	4	F	6	1	1	0	25,360
Scorese Kids	3	G	13	3	1	2	28,498
Scoresearlygale	2	F	7	0	1	1	12,980
Scoring Slew	7	G	10	0	2	1	6,400
Scorpio Scorpio	4	G	7	1	0	0	4,972
Scotch Cap	6	G	4	1	1	0	12,540
Scotch Dancer	6	M	7	2	0	0	34,980
Scotch Storm	3	C	1	0	0	0	0
Scotchwater	3	C	10	3	2	1	48,325
Scotia Claim	9	M	2	0	0	0	0
Scotland Place	3	F	13	1	3	1	11,414
Scott	4	C	9	1	2	3	59,832
Scott County Jim	4	G	8	1	0	1	7,615
Scottago	4	G	6	1	0	1	16,065
Scottie	4	G	9	3	0	2	29,710
Scotties Abity	3	G	9	1	1	0	30,060
Scotties Lasey	5	M	9	1	3	0	16,065
Scottish Heritage	4	F	12	1	1	4	37,625
Scottish Mist	3	F	3	0	0	0	521
Scottish Punch	3	F	7	3	1	1	68,576
Scottish Saga	3	G	6	0	0	0	1,560
Scottish Thistle	2	F	7	2	2	0	30,950
Scottish Warrior	5	G	9	2	3	1	16,140
Scottislittle Boy	7	G	2	0	0	0	0
Scott's Cat	2	C	3	0	1	0	5,609
Scott's Doll	3	F	5	2	1	0	15,000
Scott's Gold	5	G	8	0	2	1	6,650
Scottsbluff	2	G	2	1	1	0	15,400
Scottsdale Road	2	C	2	1	0	0	25,610
Scottsezso	3	G	9	2	0	0	17,144
Scottsontherocks	4	F	4	0	0	0	1,530
Scotty Scotty	5	G	14	0	0	2	1,984
Scotty the Rock	3	G	4	0	0	0	698
Scotty Wotty	6	G	2	0	0	0	0
Scotty's Big Nite	5	H	3	0	0	1	2,506
Scout for Gold	3	G	1	0	0	0	0
Scout Me	7	G	10	1	2	0	22,335
Scout Time	3	F	8	0	1	1	2,493
Scouts Emblem	4	C	5	1	0	0	9,480
Scouts Heartbreak	4	C	5	0	0	0	420
Scouts Honor	5	G	1	0	0	0	40
Scr Top Player	5	G	4	1	0	1	5,360
Scrambling	3	F	1	0	0	0	0
Scrap Lumber	7	G	3	0	0	0	0
Scrap Man	3	G	7	0	0	0	638
Scrapbook	2	C	2	0	0	0	0
Scrapping the West	6	G	1	0	0	0	65
Scrappy T	2	G	5	1	4	0	55,800
Scratch Back	6	H	5	0	2	0	4,795
Scratch Em	3	F	5	0	0	0	100
Scratch n claw	3	F	13	0	3	2	10,463
Scratch Off	3	G	6	1	1	0	22,680
Scratch Resistant	3	G	3	1	0	0	3,956
Scratch Shopper	4	F	1	0	0	0	0
Scratch This	5	G	12	3	0	3	14,955

Horse	Age	Sex	Sts	1st	2d	3d	Won
Scratched	5	M	7	1	1	0	6,986
Scraven	4	F	1	0	0	0	75
Scream Machine	6	G	10	0	1	0	1,334
Screamer Too	2	F	3	0	0	0	980
Screamin Demon	6	H	11	3	5	3	59,304
Screamin Passion	5	G	6	1	0	0	4,203
Screamin Stacey	5	M	9	1	2	3	7,555
Screaming Shamal	3	F	4	1	0	1	29,310
Screaming Willy	6	G	3	0	1	0	846
Screaminkarmalita	3	F	1	0	0	0	105
Screen Idol	5	H	6	1	3	1	100,250
Screen Machine	4	F	12	0	1	1	5,630
Screen Pass	4	G	1	0	0	0	258
Screen Proof	4	F	11	0	1	1	5,266
Screen Start	4	C	14	4	1	2	24,612
Screen Test	5	G	3	0	0	0	774
Screw Loose Bruce	5	G	8	0	1	3	11,133
Screwy Louie	4	G	7	0	0	0	216
Scrimshaw	4	C	3	1	0	0	52,963
Script by Conrad	3	G	1	0	0	0	0
Scriptress	3	F	1	0	0	0	662
Scripture	3	C	6	1	0	0	31,270
Scrofa	3	F	9	4	0	0	146,280
Scrub Cat	4	F	6	0	0	0	749
Scrubbin Speed	2	C	1	0	0	0	0
Scrublist	4	C	2	0	0	0	0
Scrubs	4	C	7	2	1	1	73,075
Scruffy	2	C	5	1	2	0	8,887
Scrutinize	2	F	5	1	0	0	5,010
Scuba	3	G	5	1	2	0	20,800
Scuba Steve	4	G	7	1	0	2	16,079
Scuffler	11	G	2	0	0	0	140
Sculptor	5	G	4	1	0	1	8,330
Scuppernong	4	G	11	3	0	2	27,438
Scurry Z	5	M	3	0	1	0	1,646
Scutterbotch	4	F	8	1	0	1	9,902
Scuttlebuttin	4	C	14	4	2	0	38,840
Scyther	3	C	5	0	0	0	2,540
Se Me Acabo (CHI)	6	M	9	1	2	2	54,710
Se Poy Reggal	5	M	12	1	1	3	7,970
Sea Bag	5	M	13	3	4	2	28,512
Sea Battle's Tab	2	F	1	0	0	0	0
Sea Beau	4	C	9	0	0	0	2,759
Sea Bloom	4	F	7	1	1	2	29,780
Sea Carrgot	6	G	12	0	2	2	10,656
Sea Cat Run	3	G	2	0	0	1	342
Sea Charmer	3	F	2	0	0	0	0
Sea Chatter	4	F	2	0	0	1	2,400
Sea Classic	5	M	10	0	1	2	9,708
Sea Clip	3	G	9	1	0	1	10,790
Sea Cloud	5	G	11	0	0	1	12,796
Sea Coaster	3	F	3	1	0	1	12,320
Sea Daisy	9	M	1	0	0	0	342
Sea Devil	5	G	12	1	2	3	33,882
Sea Doctor	3	G	7	0	1	2	5,838
Sea Dove	2	F	6	0	2	3	12,785
Sea D's Salute	5	M	3	1	0	0	7,944
Sea Dub	5	G	9	3	0	2	104,030
Sea Echo	5	M	8	1	2	1	8,785
Sea Flasher	5	G	15	3	3	2	16,028
Sea Force	5	G	13	2	2	0	39,775
Sea Glass	3	F	4	0	3	0	14,040
Sea Grouch	4	F	4	0	0	0	971
Sea Gulch Sally	5	M	3	1	0	0	3,306
Sea Harbor	4	G	10	2	1	3	116,155
Sea Heather	2	C	5	0	1	0	7,000
Sea Idol	2	F	1	0	0	0	0
Sea Isle City	4	G	1	0	0	0	0
Sea Jessica	2	F	2	0	0	0	480
Sea Jet	2	F	2	0	1	0	3,700
Sea Jewel	4	F	10	0	0	2	26,645
Sea Kris	3	C	3	0	0	0	400
Sea Leon	6	H	12	2	2	1	53,655
Sea Life	4	F	12	2	6	0	23,616
Sea Light	5	G	4	0	0	0	0
Sea McLee	8	G	6	2	1	1	8,630
Sea Merge	3	F	13	2	1	3	25,690
Sea Mistress	4	F	10	0	0	0	3,676
Sea My Darling	4	F	3	0	0	0	346
Sea Navigator	6	H	11	2	2	2	32,485
Sea of Arches	3	F	3	0	1	0	1,401
Sea of Fire	4	F	8	2	1	1	13,445
Sea of Galilee	3	F	1	0	0	0	0
Sea of Grass	2	F	2	0	0	0	0
Sea of Hope	5	M	11	3	1	1	22,726
Sea of Intrigue	3	G	7	2	0	2	12,338
Sea of Lace	4	F	4	2	0	1	32,710
Sea of Promises	3	F	7	1	3	0	47,390
Sea of Red	4	C	2	0	0	0	0
Sea of Silver	3	C	6	0	0	1	8,540
Sea of Sin	3	C	11	1	2	2	27,295
Sea of Sweets	3	F	8	0	1	0	3,000
Sea of Tranquility	8	H	10	3	0	0	81,435
Sea Orage	2	G	3	0	0	1	2,400
Sea Pilot	2	C	1	0	0	0	0
Sea Pirate	3	G	8	1	1	0	14,380
Sea Place	4	F	4	0	0	0	630
Sea Pleasure	4	C	5	0	0	0	970
Sea Power	4	C	19	7	1	0	68,920
Sea Prairie	4	F	5	1	3	0	3,065
Sea Preacher	4	C	3	2	0	1	51,700
Sea Rock	4	G	9	1	1	1	12,360
Sea Run	7	H	6	2	1	0	15,926
Sea Scone	2	G	4	0	0	1	1,440
Sea Scout	4	C	4	0	0	1	1,410
Sea Sense	3	G	7	1	2	0	11,627
Sea Siren	2	F	3	0	0	0	0
Sea Span	5	M	8	2	1	1	72,400
Sea Squirrel	6	G	16	4	1	0	28,825
Sea Storm	7	G	12	2	1	1	27,866
Sea Surf	5	M	2	0	0	0	150
Sea Swallow	2	F	3	0	0	0	540
Sea Tac Jet	5	G	14	4	2	4	14,790
Sea Tactical	4	F	13	2	1	2	16,805
Sea Tales	3	G	7	1	1	0	21,206
Sea Tech	3	F	4	0	0	0	1,805
Sea the Truth	3	C	9	3	0	1	66,930
Sea to Damascus	2	F	4	1	2	0	15,990
Sea to See	6	G	1	0	0	0	2,160
Sea to Sky	3	G	9	0	2	2	7,125
Sea Tow	3	F	6	0	1	1	2,704
Sea Trek	3	C	9	1	2	2	8,916
Sea Trial	3	C	1	0	0	0	210
Sea Victory	6	G	6	0	0	0	293
Sea Walker	4	G	3	0	0	0	1,150
Sea Warrior	6	G	1	0	0	0	80
Sea Way Lady	6	M	7	0	1	1	7,746
Sea West	3	F	7	1	0	1	15,330
Seabound	3	G	2	0	0	0	1,938
Seacliff Dusty	3	F	14	1	1	3	16,665
Seacliffbythedoor	4	F	11	1	1	1	9,290
Seacliff's Return	3	C	13	2	5	0	25,785
Seacrumbs	2	F	7	1	0	1	18,880
Seafarer	6	G	6	0	0	0	450
Seafaring Man	5	G	4	2	1	0	37,900
Seafree	2	F	2	1	0	1	36,270
Seagate	2	F	1	0	0	1	4,100
Seagull's Lady	2	F	2	0	0	0	0
Seahorse Surprise	6	G	7	0	1	1	1,870
Seainsky	5	G	12	1	2	0	48,920
Seakeen	5	M	8	1	1	0	10,550
Seal Bay	4	F	6	1	0	1	18,930
Seal of Excellence	2	G	5	0	1	0	3,192
Seal the Deal	4	G	1	0	0	0	0
Sealed With a Kiss	5	G	8	2	1	0	20,740
Sealedwithapproval	3	F	5	1	0	1	18,500
Seamaid	4	F	6	2	2	1	26,528
Seaman First Class	3	C	4	0	0	2	5,031
Seamster	4	C	4	0	0	0	1,006
Seamus Bond	3	G	6	0	1	0	3,340
Seanic Loop	2	F	5	0	0	0	1,227
Seaninety	6	M	1	0	0	0	0
Sean's Baby	3	F	12	2	2	3	78,555
Sean's Pride	4	G	6	1	0	1	13,250
Sean's Spy	3	G	10	1	0	0	3,894
Seanster	4	G	7	0	0	0	471
Seaoflights	5	M	11	0	0	0	1,818
Seapoint	2	C	1	0	0	0	400

Horse	Age	Sex	Sts	1st	2d	3d	Won
Seaport	2	C	1	0	0	0	560
Seaquarius	4	G	7	1	0	0	27,490
Seaquay Ninty Nine	5	M	3	1	0	0	8,747
Searatic	4	C	3	0	0	0	590
Search Again	3	G	10	1	3	3	21,927
Search Engine	9	G	9	1	1	3	8,043
Search for a Buyer	4	G	17	2	2	1	8,771
Search for a Cure	4	F	5	1	1	0	38,865
Search for Blue	6	M	1	0	0	0	40
Search for Luv	8	G	9	4	0	0	15,582
Search for Steve	8	G	15	1	1	1	4,508
Search No More	8	M	8	1	1	5	10,232
Search the Church	3	F	11	2	2	1	150,406
Search the Sky	3	F	10	3	0	2	38,575
Searchfor Diamonds	5	M	20	6	0	5	83,478
Searchforthebest	3	G	12	3	1	3	31,978
Searchfortreasure	7	M	9	1	2	1	11,725
Searchin South	4	F	1	0	0	1	2,013
Searchinfodacrown	3	F	10	0	0	1	2,480
Searchon	6	M	5	0	2	0	3,384
Searchthestars	3	F	12	2	2	3	30,315
Seasarer	3	G	11	1	2	0	13,450
Seashore Paspalum	3	G	11	3	1	0	24,180
Seaside Dream	4	F	5	0	0	2	10,474
Seaside Drive	3	F	17	2	3	1	10,109
Seaside Hero	7	G	7	0	0	1	749
Seaside Sally	3	F	6	1	0	0	1,260
Seaside Salute	3	G	8	1	2	2	50,856
Seaside Tony	4	G	1	0	0	0	0
Season for Glory	4	F	15	1	2	3	20,220
Season of Love	3	F	4	0	0	1	2,024
Seasonal King	3	G	2	1	0	0	8,200
Seasoned Pro	5	M	14	2	3	5	17,296
Seasoned Salt	2	F	2	0	0	0	720
Seasons Come	6	G	6	0	1	0	1,130
Seasons of Wither	3	F	3	0	0	0	340
Seasons Promise	4	F	7	0	3	1	23,630
Season'sinthesun	2	F	5	0	0	0	621
Seatac's in Charge	3	G	2	0	0	1	2,464
Seatle Coin	3	F	1	0	0	0	50
Seatriscuit	3	F	3	0	0	0	140
Seattle Appeal	8	M	6	1	0	0	8,450
Seattle Ash	5	M	3	0	0	2	5,150
Seattle Ballet	3	F	13	1	1	2	8,544
Seattle Band	5	G	2	0	0	1	3,020
Seattle Borders	3	C	5	1	1	1	116,670
Seattle Buddy	2	C	1	0	0	0	400
Seattle by Nite	2	C	1	0	0	0	56
Seattle Cop	2	G	2	1	1	0	10,939
Seattle Cue	7	G	3	1	2	0	8,589
Seattle Current	4	G	11	1	3	2	12,987
Seattle Dancing	2	F	3	0	0	1	2,540
Seattle Fitz (ARG)	5	H	7	3	1	0	404,810
Seattle Ghost	8	G	11	3	2	0	23,335
Seattle Glo	6	M	3	0	1	0	1,545
Seattle Hawk	3	C	2	0	0	0	30
Seattle Hit	5	G	8	1	1	1	3,866
Seattle Hoofer	4	C	1	0	0	0	900
Seattle Kelly	4	F	3	1	0	1	3,940
Seattle Lake	5	M	10	5	2	1	71,070
Seattle Lottery	3	F	8	1	0	1	12,325
Seattle Majesty	5	M	12	2	1	3	15,472
Seattle Me Up	4	G	3	0	0	0	325
Seattle Minister	3	F	4	0	0	0	1,255
Seattle Missy	4	F	8	0	1	1	3,975
Seattle Native	5	G	20	1	0	1	2,638
Seattle P D	3	F	4	0	1	0	1,483
Seattle Play Boy	6	H	5	0	0	3	1,534
Seattle Quake	4	F	14	3	3	3	16,480
Seattle Queen	4	F	2	1	0	0	31,200
Seattle Rain	2	F	2	0	0	0	260
Seattle Rookie	8	G	5	0	0	1	895
Seattle Rosa	3	F	5	1	0	2	48,577
Seattle Salsa	2	F	2	1	1	0	12,201
Seattle Schifty	2	C	2	1	0	0	9,516
Seattle Shamus	5	H	2	0	0	0	3,240
Seattle Showers	2	F	1	0	0	0	205
Seattle Slewis	4	G	6	1	1	1	11,045
Seattle Smoke	4	C	3	1	0	0	8,800
Seattle Socks	2	C	1	0	0	0	0
Seattle Songster	4	F	13	2	0	3	27,580
Seattle Souvenir	3	C	2	1	0	0	23,100
Seattle Spike	7	G	1	0	0	0	69
Seattle Stardust	3	F	3	0	0	0	311
Seattle Steve	5	G	5	0	0	0	169
Seattle Sundance	3	C	4	0	0	1	1,125
Seattle Sunshine	6	G	14	2	1	2	25,367
Seattle Surprise	4	C	11	1	0	0	6,204
Seattle Theme	2	F	5	1	1	2	27,415
Seattle Thong	3	F	3	0	0	0	77
Seattle Tornado	7	M	14	1	6	1	5,885
Seattle Weekend	3	F	2	0	0	0	2,429
Seattle Willy	3	G	3	0	0	0	2,050
Seattlecity	8	G	10	4	0	1	11,683
Seattles Best Joe	2	G	5	3	1	0	99,415
Seattle's Doll	2	F	1	0	0	0	0
Seattle's Fortune	6	G	9	0	1	0	2,968
Seattlespectacular	4	C	7	1	1	2	66,122
Seau	3	F	5	1	1	0	6,610
Seaventure	4	F	18	0	1	3	7,553
Seaver	3	G	9	0	0	2	7,300
Seawolf	2	C	2	0	0	0	600
Sebastian Cove	2	G	7	1	0	0	10,450
Sebastian Light	5	G	15	2	0	4	51,020
Sebastian Sunshine	4	F	6	0	1	1	635
Sec C Beck	3	C	3	0	0	1	1,072
Sec C Cowgirl	7	M	8	0	1	2	3,584
Second Addition	8	G	3	0	0	0	349
Second Avenue	7	H	1	0	0	0	0
Second Collection	5	G	13	0	2	3	30,836
Second Date	3	F	7	1	0	3	11,285
Second Encore	2	C	3	0	0	2	6,380
Second in Command	4	C	4	1	0	0	27,000
Second Lining	7	M	13	2	0	0	15,705
Second of June	3	C	3	1	2	0	115,600
Second Performance	3	C	11	2	0	4	106,260
Second Pres	3	F	6	0	1	0	1,920
Second Shift	4	F	15	6	0	2	28,463
Second Star	6	M	2	0	0	0	97
Second Storm	4	G	1	0	0	0	103
Second Tam Around	3	F	10	0	2	1	7,163
Second Time Clever	2	G	3	0	1	0	2,115
Second Tuesday	5	H	6	1	1	0	18,200
Second Wind	3	F	6	1	0	3	36,430
Second Windy	2	F	4	1	0	0	7,170
Secondary School	5	M	2	0	1	1	13,700
Secondtariat	4	G	4	0	0	0	455
Secondvowsintheraw	5	M	6	0	1	0	4,530
Secrepine	3	G	9	2	1	1	24,159
Secret Ace	7	G	15	3	3	2	40,128
Secret Again	3	G	7	0	0	0	0
Secret Agent Tom	4	G	11	3	1	1	14,179
Secret Ambition	5	G	12	2	5	1	37,200
Secret Attraction	3	F	3	0	0	0	154
Secret Banker	5	G	13	0	3	4	11,592
Secret Bayou	5	G	8	1	0	0	7,712
Secret Bluff	4	F	13	3	1	2	23,185
Secret Boundary	6	G	6	0	3	0	4,216
Secret Brand	3	C	4	2	0	0	13,670
Secret Bullet	6	M	9	1	2	2	33,462
Secret Bundle	4	F	2	0	0	1	660
Secret Caller	6	G	11	0	5	2	4,683
Secret Caper	4	F	11	0	0	3	27,540
Secret Case	5	G	15	2	2	1	24,173
Secret Chief	8	G	2	1	0	0	4,663
Secret Command	5	G	5	2	0	0	14,310
Secret Compliance	5	M	11	6	2	2	26,731
Secret Conquest	3	F	12	1	2	6	49,789
Secret Corsage	3	F	9	1	2	1	58,780
Secret Cousin	4	G	9	0	1	1	8,230
Secret Crush	3	F	13	2	2	1	43,218
Secret Dash	5	G	16	2	0	3	34,935
Secret Delight	3	F	7	1	1	0	8,100
Secret Demon	2	F	1	0	0	0	0
Secret Deposit	4	G	8	1	1	1	5,894
Secret Dot Com	7	G	8	2	1	4	12,050
Secret Earnings	3	G	12	2	4	1	24,165
Secret Echo	5	M	1	0	0	0	235

Horse	Age	Sex	Sts	1st	2d	3d	Won
Secret Elite	3	F	2	0	0	0	372
Secret Escape	4	G	14	1	0	3	6,637
Secret Expectation	5	M	13	4	3	1	37,146
Secret Fantasy	2	F	2	0	0	0	0
Secret Fire	4	F	13	0	0	0	2,308
Secret Folly	3	C	2	0	0	0	314
Secret Forest	3	F	5	1	2	2	54,500
Secret Formula	4	G	18	0	3	4	28,028
Secret Forum	5	M	4	0	0	0	902
Secret Glow	3	F	8	0	1	0	5,120
Secret Guarantee	5	M	1	0	0	0	0
Secret Impression	9	H	3	2	0	0	42,000
Secret Isout	6	G	11	1	5	3	8,622
Secret John	3	G	7	0	0	0	347
Secret Journey	4	F	6	0	2	0	2,746
Secret Key	4	G	3	0	0	0	100
Secret Lake	5	G	8	0	0	0	467
Secret Lies	2	F	1	0	0	0	0
Secret Link	2	G	6	0	0	1	2,543
Secret Look	4	C	18	2	7	3	76,490
Secret Looker	2	C	1	0	0	0	64
Secret Luck	3	G	1	0	0	1	2,140
Secret Maker	3	G	11	0	2	1	6,936
Secret Messenger	3	C	7	0	4	2	30,805
Secret Miss	3	F	19	1	0	2	9,980
Secret Missile	2	F	4	1	0	1	17,150
Secret Motive	3	F	5	0	1	0	2,437
Secret Mover	5	M	9	1	0	0	3,831
Secret Mystique	6	M	4	0	0	0	486
Secret Naevy	6	M	6	0	0	0	620
Secret of Fappiano	3	F	7	1	1	0	5,164
Secret of Kentucky	11	G	1	0	0	0	0
Secret of Success	4	G	6	0	1	0	3,362
Secret One	5	G	13	2	2	3	14,575
Secret Package	3	F	9	1	2	0	19,120
Secret Patriot	3	F	1	0	0	0	340
Secret Pattern	2	F	2	0	0	0	500
Secret Pine	4	F	4	0	2	1	4,331
Secret Player	3	F	1	0	0	0	0
Secret Pride	5	M	3	1	1	1	8,960
Secret Prize	2	G	1	0	0	0	190
Secret Punch	3	G	17	1	3	3	23,767
Secret Quest	3	C	1	0	0	0	130
Secret Request	4	F	6	3	1	0	355,250
Secret Romance	3	F	3	0	0	2	6,384
Secret Romeo	6	H	11	1	4	2	43,510
Secret Roses	4	F	2	0	0	0	0
Secret Run	4	C	10	4	1	1	132,335
Secret Runner	4	G	4	0	0	0	617
Secret Rush	5	M	4	1	2	0	33,299
Secret Saratoga	4	F	7	1	0	1	9,555
Secret Secret Star	6	G	10	2	1	1	31,776
Secret Shopper	3	F	9	0	2	0	3,960
Secret Silence	3	F	2	0	0	0	0
Secret Smoker	5	M	2	0	0	0	1,032
Secret Society	3	F	4	0	0	1	1,347
Secret Song	5	G	12	2	3	3	24,806
Secret Sounds	7	M	15	0	3	2	9,448
Secret Sparkle	4	F	14	0	2	1	7,393
Secret Spot	5	G	19	3	3	0	32,180
Secret Spy	4	G	13	0	0	1	1,050
Secret Squall	9	G	3	0	0	0	218
Secret Stranger	2	C	3	0	0	0	1,726
Secret Sunset	3	F	4	1	0	0	4,830
Secret Sword	4	C	2	0	0	1	638
Secret Tantrum	4	G	8	2	1	3	11,553
Secret Target	3	F	6	2	1	2	11,997
Secret Tea	4	G	10	0	0	1	1,000
Secret Terms	3	F	12	1	2	1	12,639
Secret Testamony	3	G	2	0	0	0	0
Secret to Luv	3	F	3	0	0	0	230
Secret Tour	4	C	6	0	1	1	4,765
Secret Trait	5	G	3	0	0	0	432
Secret Treasure	2	F	1	0	0	0	1,230
Secret Treaties	3	C	2	0	0	0	600
Secret Troika	3	F	7	1	1	2	44,288
Secret Tunnel	2	C	4	1	1	0	19,810
Secret Union	5	G	13	0	1	0	4,127
Secret Venture	3	F	2	0	0	0	0

Horse	Age	Sex	Sts	1st	2d	3d	Won
Secret Victory	2	F	5	2	0	0	7,179
Secret Waters	5	M	4	0	0	0	288
Secret Woods	2	C	7	1	1	1	19,450
Secret Word	5	M	5	0	0	0	255
Secret World	4	F	7	1	1	0	22,880
Secret Yankee	4	F	9	0	1	0	2,044
Secret Zeal	3	G	8	2	1	0	7,200
Secretariats Fancy	4	F	8	1	1	2	8,825
Secretariats Hope	5	M	4	0	0	1	992
Secretary Hit	3	G	6	0	0	0	991
Secretary Tracker	3	G	9	2	1	1	33,525
Secretarys Booboo	8	G	10	0	0	0	1,617
Secretarythethird	3	C	1	1	0	0	6,600
Secretively	4	F	15	1	0	2	19,150
Secretly Free	3	F	5	0	0	0	2,859
Secreto's Ghost	4	G	2	0	0	0	720
Secrets Galore	2	F	6	1	2	1	60,083
Secret's in Gild	3	C	1	0	0	0	0
Secretsandlies	3	F	1	0	0	0	0
Secretstoforget	4	G	4	0	0	0	300
Secure Line	3	C	4	0	1	0	15,720
Security Code	2	C	4	2	0	0	19,725
Security Comet	3	C	15	2	3	1	16,391
Seczone	2	G	4	0	1	0	9,360
Sedargo	2	F	3	0	0	0	2,000
Sedition	6	H	1	0	0	0	150
Sedona Knight	5	M	2	0	0	0	800
Sedona Sun	2	F	4	1	0	0	6,980
Sedona Sunrise	6	M	9	0	0	0	1,255
Sedonas Creek	3	F	4	0	0	0	0
Seducer's Song	3	F	8	4	1	1	239,760
Seducing	4	F	1	0	0	0	260
Seductiva	3	F	3	0	2	0	10,080
Seductive	4	F	4	2	0	0	8,216
Seductive Account	3	F	3	0	0	0	0
Seductive Darling	3	F	3	0	0	0	67
Seductive Lady	3	F	1	0	0	0	240
Seductive View	3	G	4	0	3	0	21,200
Seductress	5	M	12	0	1	1	2,132
See Alice	2	F	6	1	0	1	12,265
See Ashleigh Run	3	F	6	1	0	0	8,170
See Clearly	4	G	2	0	0	0	261
See Da Breeze	2	F	9	0	0	0	636
See Frankie	3	G	8	1	0	0	8,690
See How She Runs	5	M	4	0	0	2	13,540
See Jack Run	2	G	4	0	1	0	8,072
See Latham	3	C	2	0	0	1	6,600
See Me Salute	4	G	6	0	0	0	700
See Me Shine	2	F	6	1	0	1	19,920
See Me Strut	7	M	8	2	2	0	36,775
See Me Through	3	F	10	2	3	1	157,041
See Morgan First	3	C	6	1	2	0	39,260
See My Dust	3	G	1	0	1	0	1,575
See My Tail Lights	5	M	2	0	0	0	1,158
See Sea Lady	7	M	9	3	4	0	5,360
See the Angel	5	M	10	3	0	2	17,849
See Tom Rowe	7	G	22	5	3	4	33,023
See What Imean	2	F	1	1	0	0	13,440
See Ya Cat	9	G	15	0	4	2	26,409
See Ya in Indy	3	F	13	0	1	3	7,940
See You At Siro's	6	G	5	0	1	0	9,800
See You in America	6	M	17	0	2	2	6,685
See You Real Soon	3	G	4	0	0	1	4,450
See You Tricky	5	M	9	0	0	3	1,873
Seedoubleyoubee	3	G	12	2	3	2	14,555
Seeds of Peace	3	F	5	0	0	2	1,760
Seeing Signs	4	G	4	0	0	0	216
Seeinsbelieven	2	F	1	1	0	0	29,395
Seeitobelieveit	4	G	16	4	1	2	32,254
Seek a Star	2	F	1	0	0	1	5,000
Seek Gold	4	G	9	2	3	1	236,780
Seek the Gold	6	M	8	1	1	2	6,560
Seek Up	6	H	7	0	0	0	1,258
Seeker	4	G	5	1	0	0	9,855
Seekin Treasure	7	G	1	0	0	0	54
Seeking Answers (IRE)	3	C	7	0	0	1	6,625
Seeking Approval	5	G	9	1	0	0	6,260
Seeking Diamonds	4	C	4	0	2	0	9,600
Seeking Fun	2	F	3	0	0	0	2,401

Horse	Age	Sex	Sts	1st	2d	3d	Won
Seeking Gold	3	C	5	0	1	1	4,790
Seeking Love	8	M	5	1	0	3	2,905
Seeking Redemption	3	G	3	1	0	0	27,055
Seeking Results	3	F	3	0	1	0	8,500
Seeking Royalty	4	G	9	0	2	0	7,000
Seeking Seattle	6	G	2	0	0	0	1,080
Seeking Slew	2	C	1	0	0	0	450
Seeking Snowdrops	4	F	2	0	0	0	112
Seeking the Ante	2	F	4	0	2	1	30,550
Seeking the Cape	2	F	1	0	0	1	2,200
Seeking the Carat	3	C	10	2	1	1	99,764
Seeking the Cat	5	H	7	1	1	1	19,975
Seeking the Glory	4	C	4	1	1	0	37,700
Seeking the Heart	3	F	7	2	1	3	87,300
Seeking the Heat	2	F	4	1	0	0	25,600
Seeking the Honey	2	F	2	1	0	0	6,320
Seeking the Lite	2	C	4	0	0	0	336
Seeking the Money	5	G	7	2	1	0	35,923
Seeking the Show	6	G	17	3	1	4	49,030
Seeking the Silver	4	F	3	0	0	0	2,900
Seeking the Touch	2	F	2	1	0	0	19,600
Seekinganacquittal	5	H	2	0	0	0	0
Seemeloadandfire	4	G	10	2	3	1	48,742
Seemone Seemone	3	F	1	0	0	0	0
Seemore Seemore	4	C	4	0	0	0	1,185
Seemslikeyesterday	6	G	19	1	1	7	12,709
Seewhatimsaying	5	M	15	1	0	2	7,080
Seeya in Dakota	4	G	8	2	2	3	5,693
Seeya Inthe Circle	3	G	10	0	1	2	2,823
Seeya Trouble	4	G	12	0	0	3	9,335
Seeyaat Redtracton	5	G	16	0	0	3	6,015
Seeyahoney	4	F	8	0	0	2	10,630
Seeyainseattle	8	G	8	1	1	2	10,431
Seeyouattheevent	3	C	9	2	0	2	47,850
Seeyoubychance	2	G	8	4	0	0	75,604
Sefapianos Miss	4	F	14	2	3	1	26,824
Sefapianos Way	4	C	11	3	2	0	18,518
Sefas Challenge	2	F	1	0	0	0	125
Sefas Occupation	2	G	5	0	2	0	4,755
Sefas Rose	7	M	2	1	1	0	9,600
Sefrou (ARG)	5	G	13	1	4	2	44,354
Segovia	4	F	10	0	1	1	8,225
Segregate	2	F	2	0	0	0	192
Segreto	5	M	4	0	0	0	1,200
Seguidilla (IRE)	3	F	6	0	1	1	2,520
Seilugram	9	G	1	0	0	0	41
Seinne (CHI)	7	H	9	0	3	1	71,082
Seismic Cat	4	C	10	1	1	0	9,200
Seize	2	C	3	2	0	0	37,650
Seize the Day	2	C	3	1	0	1	36,650
Seize the Flag	3	F	6	0	1	0	3,428
Seize the Gold	2	F	3	0	0	0	1,840
Sejm's Madness	8	G	7	1	2	0	8,780
Sejour	2	F	2	1	0	0	27,000
Sekari's Fun	4	F	6	0	0	1	1,693
Selangor (AUS)	5	G	6	0	0	0	9,000
Seldom Free	4	G	9	2	0	1	15,346
Seldom Silent	4	F	7	0	0	0	1,790
Select Decor	8	G	17	2	4	0	20,600
Selecta Tonic	2	G	1	0	0	0	70
Selection	3	G	11	0	1	1	5,728
Selective Security	9	M	3	0	0	0	0
Selective Wisdom	5	G	7	0	0	0	2,181
Self Esteem	6	G	7	0	0	2	3,461
Self Rising	5	M	3	0	0	1	5,941
Self Seeker	2	F	2	0	0	0	0
Selim Road	4	F	3	1	0	0	7,150
Selina Delight	3	F	2	1	0	0	6,105
Selina's Buttercup	5	M	6	0	2	1	6,104
Selina's Starlet	5	M	6	0	1	0	2,713
Selita's Dream	3	F	7	2	0	3	12,334
Sell 'm Short	4	G	15	4	4	4	35,515
Sell the Market	6	M	4	0	0	0	0
Sell the Rallies	3	F	5	2	1	0	37,430
Sell to Survive	4	G	9	2	1	1	52,519
Sellsey	2	F	2	0	1	0	7,400
Selu	2	F	2	1	0	0	8,100
Selva Mia	5	M	10	0	0	1	2,388
Selvatica	3	F	3	1	2	0	43,200
Selyou Rogerlou	3	F	7	0	0	1	1,593
Sem City	3	C	9	1	3	0	8,595
Semana Nautica	6	G	5	0	0	0	616
Semblance	3	C	1	0	0	0	77
Semi Annual	7	G	16	0	1	2	1,390
Semi Broke	4	F	6	1	0	2	13,993
Semi Lost	3	G	8	3	2	0	163,070
Semi Queen	2	C	6	0	1	1	16,180
Semichi	2	F	4	0	0	2	7,924
Semifinal	4	F	1	0	0	0	0
Seminary	3	C	3	0	0	0	0
Seminole Bid	3	G	15	0	0	2	5,375
Seminole Chief	9	G	2	0	0	0	0
Seminole Gal	6	M	17	3	2	5	35,195
Seminole Gale	3	F	13	2	1	2	30,922
Seminole Kid	5	G	3	0	0	0	438
Seminole Squaw	6	M	3	1	0	1	9,544
Semoran Boldness	3	C	14	2	4	1	25,940
Semoran Royalty	3	F	13	1	0	0	8,260
Semoran Street	4	G	5	0	0	0	890
Semoran's Decision	4	G	8	1	0	1	26,578
Semoran's Gem	2	C	5	1	1	1	16,820
Semoran's Score	3	C	3	0	0	0	880
Sempai	6	G	6	0	1	2	16,168
Sempre Blumin	5	G	12	3	3	1	42,930
Semtex Sally	4	F	6	1	0	0	5,428
Sen Yourita Oro	3	F	11	1	2	1	10,095
Senatepage	6	G	7	0	0	0	552
Senator Bennett	5	G	5	0	2	0	5,918
Senator Dick	4	G	12	3	1	2	16,605
Senator Jim	11	G	9	0	1	0	9,341
Senator Joe P.	4	C	14	0	2	2	9,370
Senator Matty	2	C	1	0	0	0	400
Senator Rock	5	G	13	1	2	1	10,227
Senator Ruby	6	G	16	0	0	0	840
Send a Pro	6	G	6	0	0	0	349
Send 'Em Pakin	3	F	11	0	0	1	2,235
Send for an Angel	3	F	11	1	4	1	37,870
Send It In	3	C	6	2	0	0	52,337
Send Me a Beau	4	G	13	1	4	1	6,587
Send Me a Copy	3	G	4	2	0	0	25,340
Send Me in Coach	3	C	7	4	1	0	30,820
Send My Pal	3	G	6	1	1	0	10,130
Send No Bills	4	C	4	0	0	1	934
Send the Facts	2	F	6	1	3	1	60,431
Send the Package	6	M	4	0	0	2	8,520
Send the Storm	2	C	2	0	0	0	145
Senda	5	M	15	2	0	0	20,086
Sendek	3	G	11	3	0	1	20,330
Sendem Sam	2	F	3	0	0	0	2,300
Sendero de Oro	3	C	3	1	2	0	7,400
Sending	4	C	5	0	0	0	690
Sendtheprospector	9	G	6	1	1	0	2,381
Sendy's Fortune	6	H	11	0	0	3	2,526
Senearose	4	F	8	2	0	0	9,207
Seneca Bunny	3	F	12	5	1	2	63,750
Seneca Dolly	4	F	13	0	2	2	4,802
Seneca Falls	6	M	1	0	0	0	0
Seneca Lizzy	5	M	6	1	0	0	2,767
Seneca Point	3	G	8	1	1	0	39,434
Seneca Rock	4	G	7	1	0	2	13,320
Seneca Song	3	F	12	4	2	2	65,854
Seneca Storm	2	G	1	0	0	0	0
Seneca Summer	3	G	11	1	3	3	64,240
Seneca Wave	2	G	7	0	0	1	3,395
Seneca Wind	3	F	5	0	0	0	1,702
Seneca's Rodeo	3	G	4	0	0	0	753
Seney	2	C	1	0	0	0	100
Senfully Easy	5	M	10	7	1	2	62,335
Senior Chief	2	C	1	0	0	0	0
Senior Coco	3	G	3	0	0	0	225
Senior Lender	3	F	6	1	0	0	2,878
Senior Macho	5	G	2	0	0	0	246
Senior Punch	4	G	5	0	0	2	3,430
Senja	4	F	7	0	2	1	10,929
Senopah	4	G	6	1	1	0	6,260
Senor Accord	2	C	8	0	3	1	11,230
Senor Amigo	4	C	3	0	0	0	3,360
Senor Armada	2	C	1	0	0	0	0

Horse	Age	Sex	Sts	1st	2d	3d	Won
Senor Arugas	4	G	14	3	1	5	13,340
Senor Badgett	6	G	7	0	2	1	3,185
Senor Baileys	4	G	10	0	1	1	3,734
Senor Balloo	3	C	3	0	2	0	1,440
Senor Bay	5	G	2	0	0	0	70
Senor Billy Bob	5	G	8	0	1	1	2,808
Senor Bull	10	G	4	0	0	1	1,494
Senor Carlos	7	G	12	2	2	1	16,277
Senor Chapo	7	G	9	0	3	0	2,049
Senor Charismatic	5	G	12	3	2	2	81,077
Senor Chuy	4	G	6	0	2	0	2,260
Senor Cielo	5	G	6	0	0	1	920
Senor Cielo Two	4	G	15	2	2	4	60,278
Senor Cloud	4	C	1	0	1	0	4,740
Senor Corona	3	C	4	0	0	0	0
Senor de Sol	5	G	11	1	0	2	15,090
Senor Eddie	5	G	3	0	0	0	0
Senor Fango	2	C	9	2	1	2	122,742
Senor Gator	3	C	17	1	3	1	11,063
Senor Gran	9	G	12	3	1	1	27,652
Senor Gran Day	3	C	18	4	1	2	34,005
Senor Ladd	3	G	10	5	3	0	119,750
Senor Mac	5	G	10	0	2	4	12,350
Senor Magico	6	G	4	0	0	0	0
Senor Markos	7	G	8	1	0	1	2,229
Senor Mas	8	G	6	1	1	2	4,460
Senor Moonlight	4	C	3	0	0	0	282
Senor Prado	7	G	10	3	1	2	6,100
Senor Realidad	4	G	7	2	1	1	19,045
Senor Rizzi	3	G	1	1	0	0	5,100
Senor Sal	6	G	14	2	3	2	16,056
Senor Sancho	4	C	3	0	0	0	160
Senor Santo	3	G	1	0	0	0	235
Senor Shayne	2	G	2	0	0	0	290
Senor Shine	6	G	16	2	3	0	8,027
Senor Swinger	4	C	10	4	0	1	418,178
Senor Valdez	6	G	9	0	1	1	4,073
Senora Soldar	2	F	1	0	0	0	77
Senorita American	4	F	7	0	2	3	15,885
Senorita Anna	2	F	2	0	0	0	630
Senorita Bear	3	F	6	0	1	0	2,920
Senorita Brown	8	M	7	0	1	0	1,819
Senorita Echo	5	M	12	1	0	2	10,707
Senorita Halo	2	F	1	0	0	0	0
Senorita Jazzy	3	F	14	1	0	0	11,845
Senorita Rosa	2	F	3	0	0	1	1,710
Senorita Susan	3	F	8	0	0	0	1,960
Senorita Valentina	5	M	8	1	0	0	3,185
Senorita Ziggy	6	M	5	2	1	0	51,905
Sensational Bid	5	H	10	3	1	2	27,545
Sensational Charm	5	M	1	0	0	0	40
Sensational Choice	3	C	2	0	0	0	3,400
Sensational Guy	6	G	5	1	2	0	13,800
Sensational Sabin	3	G	2	0	1	0	1,961
Sensationalplace	4	G	19	0	4	8	13,020
Sensationalsonny	4	G	14	3	0	4	9,704
Sensative Cindy	9	M	6	0	0	0	677
Sense of Reality	3	G	15	4	1	3	54,165
Sense of Style	2	F	5	3	0	0	369,000
Sensibly Chic	4	F	8	3	2	1	147,247
Sensitive Penguin	4	F	11	4	2	0	87,060
Sensitive Woman	5	M	5	0	1	0	6,030
Sensorious Kiss	3	F	9	0	0	1	1,960
Sensuous Cinnamon	4	F	14	1	1	1	21,402
Sensuous Silk	3	F	9	1	2	1	34,587
Sent Home	5	M	12	0	0	2	4,697
Sentenced	5	M	8	3	1	1	32,905
Sentimental Lad	5	G	13	1	5	1	14,461
Sentimental Miss	5	M	13	1	2	0	25,957
Sentimentalromance	8	M	1	0	0	0	540
Sentimentl Dinner	3	F	15	2	1	2	12,758
Sentosa	13	G	4	0	0	1	645
Sentry Lad	3	C	3	1	1	0	17,980
Sentsure	5	H	10	0	3	0	4,350
Senza Aglio	2	C	3	0	0	1	5,070
Seoul Wild	3	F	5	1	0	0	6,435
Separate Storm	3	F	3	0	0	0	235
Separato	3	C	13	5	3	1	181,360
Seppuku	6	G	10	0	0	1	1,088
September Circle	3	C	12	0	0	0	3,191
September Dawn	3	F	10	6	0	1	108,242
September Hero	4	C	7	1	0	1	33,367
September Jewel	4	F	18	2	2	3	15,984
September Remember	3	F	2	0	0	0	0
September Storm	4	F	7	0	0	1	1,320
September Sun	3	F	7	1	0	0	3,440
September's Pride	4	F	8	0	3	2	36,263
Septennial	6	G	8	1	0	2	2,357
Septiembre	3	G	3	0	0	0	1,200
Sequel Cat	4	G	14	5	1	1	16,144
Sequester	3	F	4	0	1	0	1,440
Sequoia Grove	2	C	3	1	1	0	19,501
Sequoian	5	G	1	0	0	0	0
Serafic Gold	4	F	3	0	0	0	258
Serai	5	M	11	4	2	0	79,770
Seraph	4	F	13	1	1	3	13,578
Seraphim	4	F	3	0	0	0	183
Serazzo	8	H	5	2	2	0	77,368
Serbia	6	M	4	0	0	0	1,090
Serena's Run	4	F	6	0	1	1	4,203
Serena's Storm	4	F	10	0	1	2	2,658
Serendipitous	3	F	7	2	2	0	67,749
Serendipity Bull	4	G	9	0	1	0	5,377
Serene Irene	2	F	1	0	0	0	400
Serene Joy	3	F	9	1	0	0	6,600
Serene Lady	5	M	17	2	2	4	11,289
Serene Place	3	F	8	1	3	2	28,983
Serene Valor	3	F	9	0	2	0	4,648
Serene Wolf	4	G	4	0	0	0	317
Serenity	5	M	2	0	0	1	1,610
Serenity's Smile	5	M	13	4	1	1	73,674
Sergeant At Arms	6	G	6	1	1	1	6,873
Sergeant Devious	4	G	5	0	0	1	1,306
Sergeant Lefty	3	C	9	1	3	0	11,305
Sergeant Mimi	7	M	1	0	0	0	40
Serial Bride	7	G	5	2	0	0	49,380
Serious Alert	4	G	13	0	5	1	17,914
Serious Bull	4	C	4	1	1	0	8,205
Serious Factor	3	F	5	0	1	1	6,952
Serious Lightning	2	G	4	1	1	0	9,145
Serious Sam	6	G	9	0	0	3	2,393
Serious Sister	7	M	5	0	1	0	1,527
Serious Smoke	4	G	17	2	0	1	10,417
Serious Susan	6	M	6	0	0	0	1,550
Seriousely Enough	2	G	6	1	2	0	11,425
Sermon On the Run	5	M	12	1	2	1	15,685
Serra Lee Trail	2	G	5	0	1	0	8,120
Serra Retreat	7	G	11	3	2	0	30,056
Servant King	5	G	11	3	1	2	14,687
Serve Again	3	F	8	1	1	1	10,776
Served	4	G	2	0	0	0	0
Serves Em Bud	9	G	1	0	0	0	37
Service	6	H	8	1	2	0	14,962
Service Man	2	F	1	0	0	0	0
Service Medal	3	F	1	0	0	0	0
Service Miss	4	F	6	1	0	1	3,756
Serving Ma Man	7	M	7	0	0	0	1,913
Serving Time	6	G	10	0	0	1	722
Set Down	10	G	1	0	0	0	108
Set for Life	4	G	6	0	0	1	1,047
Set It Up	3	F	7	0	0	1	3,595
Set On Go	3	F	4	0	0	1	1,720
Set Status	2	C	1	0	0	0	87
Set the Bar	2	C	2	0	0	1	2,680
Set to Sparkle	4	F	8	3	0	1	70,780
Setacourseforhome	4	F	7	1	2	3	16,965
Setanta	3	F	5	0	0	0	5,784
Setch	2	G	7	1	0	0	7,240
Setemup Joe	4	G	11	4	4	0	105,920
Sethina	3	F	7	0	0	1	3,370
Setmyheartonfire	4	G	1	0	0	0	0
Setthehook	5	G	7	2	3	1	42,160
Settimo Cielo	2	F	4	1	0	0	11,552
Setting Light	8	G	3	0	0	0	200
Setting the Scene	3	F	8	0	1	0	11,268
Settle Down	3	G	17	3	0	1	23,816
Settle Down Hunter	2	G	1	0	0	0	608
Settle in Seattle	3	F	5	0	0	0	1,635

Horse	Age	Sex	Sts	1st	2d	3d	Won
Settle Up	4	C	7	2	3	1	88,840
Settler	3	G	15	1	2	2	27,880
Settlers Beach	3	G	4	1	0	0	5,340
Setup Man	4	G	1	0	0	0	0
Seul Avenger	8	G	6	1	1	0	3,395
Seul Count	3	G	11	3	2	3	16,101
Seul Flight	6	M	11	3	2	2	25,882
Seuss' Delight	4	F	3	0	0	2	1,360
Sevasmoke	4	F	2	1	0	1	26,850
Seven Affairs	3	F	2	1	0	0	1,595
Seven Brides	5	M	2	0	0	0	7,422
Seven Card	7	G	6	1	0	1	8,060
Seven Charms	5	G	16	2	2	4	40,165
Seven Chimes	4	F	11	1	2	1	10,347
Seven Cities	3	F	10	1	1	1	13,446
Seven Come Eleven	3	C	9	3	2	0	134,169
Seven Day War	2	C	1	0	0	0	0
Seven December	4	F	7	2	1	0	12,445
Seven Gold Gems	5	M	14	1	1	3	33,890
Seven Hearts	5	G	9	1	1	3	8,706
Seven Heaven	5	M	13	0	2	0	5,723
Seven Is the Charm	4	F	8	0	1	1	5,843
Seven Keys	4	F	10	1	2	0	5,867
Seven Lakes	2	C	2	0	0	0	175
Seven Moons (JPN)	4	F	6	2	2	0	71,046
Seven No Tremp	7	G	15	3	2	2	9,008
Seven O	6	G	5	0	0	0	314
Seven Peaks	4	G	4	2	1	0	11,985
Seven Pines	5	M	15	0	0	2	1,716
Seven Sails	3	F	5	1	1	0	8,800
Seven Sands	4	G	4	0	0	1	797
Seven Seven Adam	4	C	3	0	0	0	375
Seven Stake	2	C	1	0	0	1	2,915
Seven Talents	4	G	12	3	2	0	47,058
Seven Thunders	3	F	7	0	0	1	1,287
Seven Times Seven	4	C	1	0	0	0	66
Seven Veils	5	M	4	1	1	0	7,230
Seven Way Shake	3	G	18	2	2	4	41,405
Seven Year Wonder	3	F	12	1	6	3	15,185
Seveneightone East	4	G	16	2	3	3	14,545
Sevenext	5	H	3	1	1	0	1,220
Sevenforbish	4	G	10	1	1	0	27,760
Sevenmiss	6	M	12	2	2	1	17,170
Sevens Rule	5	G	8	0	1	1	1,906
Sevens' Star	4	F	8	1	2	0	20,089
Sevens Wild	5	M	10	1	4	3	15,733
Sevensheaven	4	F	1	0	0	0	0
Seventeen Above	3	F	14	4	2	1	139,236
Seventh House	3	F	1	0	0	0	300
Seventh Inning	4	G	10	0	3	1	31,158
Seventhavenuegolda	2	C	8	1	2	2	16,535
Seventy Sixer	4	G	11	1	3	1	10,648
Seventyfivesouth	6	G	20	2	3	2	24,640
Seventyninestripes	5	G	9	2	2	2	18,274
Severado (BRZ)	8	G	5	1	1	0	23,470
Severe Storm	2	F	1	0	0	0	270
Severo	5	G	9	0	1	2	4,475
Severus	6	M	12	1	1	1	16,864
Seve's Honour	3	C	9	0	0	1	2,030
Sevier River	4	F	5	0	0	0	624
Seville's Minister	3	G	4	0	0	0	161
Seville's Prince	5	G	3	0	0	0	0
Seville's Trump	6	M	5	0	1	1	1,669
Sevnfordeesevn	3	G	8	3	1	0	10,090
Sew Sparkly	2	F	9	1	0	0	6,980
Seward's Folly	2	G	3	0	0	0	0
Sewards Son	4	C	1	0	0	0	0
Sewing Bag	4	C	1	0	0	0	0
Sex Machine (AUS)	7	G	5	0	0	1	4,530
Sexcetera	5	H	9	0	0	0	1,674
Sextet	3	C	9	0	0	0	12,402
Sexy Appeal	5	M	5	0	0	1	2,530
Sexy Beast	3	F	1	0	0	0	0
Sexy Boots	4	F	8	2	0	2	39,619
Sexy Ex	4	F	7	0	0	0	248
Sexy Helmsman	3	F	3	2	0	0	22,698
Sexy Mark	4	F	1	0	0	0	0
Sexy Miss	3	F	5	1	1	0	5,258
Sexy Mon	4	G	12	1	2	3	8,375
Sexy Rose	4	F	12	3	0	5	19,807
Sexy Royalty	3	C	2	1	1	0	12,000
Sexy Saint	2	F	2	0	0	0	800
Sexy Secrets	4	F	8	1	1	0	9,229
Sexy Splasher	3	F	8	1	1	0	7,925
Sexy Sunrise	5	G	2	1	0	0	4,788
Seyah Atthe Kazba	3	G	6	1	0	0	10,651
Seyalateralligator	3	G	18	4	1	4	54,674
Seyani	3	F	7	1	0	0	4,229
Seymour Moves	4	F	10	2	3	0	28,148
Sez Who's Gold	5	M	4	0	0	0	491
Sforza (FR)	5	H	3	0	0	0	3,400
Sgt. Alvarez	3	G	6	0	1	3	6,255
Sgt. Bert	3	C	9	4	2	0	93,323
Sgt. Dundee	4	G	12	0	0	3	1,903
Sgt. Kenny	2	G	2	1	1	0	9,680
Shaack	9	G	13	2	5	3	11,324
Shabak	3	C	1	0	0	0	400
Shabang Shabang	4	G	21	4	5	4	41,406
Shabango	4	F	7	2	0	0	32,505
Shabanu's Jet	3	F	3	1	0	0	4,590
Shabi Dabi	3	G	7	0	0	0	579
Shablam	7	G	5	0	2	0	2,982
Shaboom Shaboom	7	H	1	0	0	0	31
Shabozz	5	G	1	0	0	0	0
Shacane	5	G	4	1	2	0	38,100
Shack a Tee	3	G	3	1	0	0	6,569
Shack Martin	4	G	11	1	2	2	11,311
Shackelford	8	G	7	0	1	2	8,516
Shaconage	4	F	11	2	1	3	256,340
Shad	2	C	2	2	0	0	8,288
Shadar	4	G	17	1	2	3	11,787
Shaddai's Crusader	5	G	13	1	3	1	18,618
Shade Tree Lady	7	M	2	0	0	0	0
Shadeed's Image	7	G	3	0	0	0	261
Shades Creek	7	G	7	1	0	1	7,610
Shades of Autumn	4	F	8	0	1	0	4,948
Shades of Dixie	4	G	2	0	0	0	3,340
Shades of Grace	3	F	4	0	3	1	11,200
Shades of Halo	5	M	7	1	2	1	7,170
Shades of Light	3	F	3	0	0	0	0
Shades of Pale	5	M	8	0	0	0	410
Shades of Purple	4	F	3	0	0	0	225
Shades of Royal	7	G	4	1	1	0	1,440
Shades of Sunny	6	G	7	1	2	1	66,730
Shades of Time	3	F	5	2	0	0	8,248
Shadey Mike	5	H	4	1	1	0	3,432
Shadi Sand	5	G	10	3	2	1	10,658
Shadow Bay	3	F	3	0	0	0	0
Shadow Belle	3	F	2	1	0	0	9,550
Shadow Book	6	G	11	1	3	0	8,198
Shadow Boxing	5	H	1	1	0	0	2,460
Shadow Cast	3	F	12	4	1	4	267,480
Shadow Dance	2	F	9	1	0	0	6,573
Shadow Danceblaze	3	F	12	2	1	6	19,608
Shadow Government	4	F	10	0	0	0	749
Shadow Hawk	5	H	5	1	1	1	57,280
Shadow Mountain	10	G	17	1	3	3	16,514
Shadow of Illinois	4	G	6	0	2	0	26,312
Shadow of Mine	3	F	8	0	0	1	13,886
Shadow of the Moon	2	F	2	1	0	0	16,563
Shadow On the Rail	7	G	4	0	0	0	160
Shadow Play	4	F	10	1	2	1	52,415
Shadow Raider	4	G	12	3	1	1	41,953
Shadow Rider	4	G	16	0	0	3	4,478
Shadow Ruhler	4	C	7	0	0	1	1,119
Shadow Run	4	F	2	0	0	0	260
Shadow Steele	6	M	3	1	0	1	3,470
Shadow Wave	3	C	2	1	0	0	17,300
Shadowblade	4	G	15	1	3	2	14,379
Shadowflight	3	G	10	0	0	2	4,325
Shadowland	3	C	4	0	1	0	20,000
Shadowmon	2	C	3	0	1	0	1,810
Shadows Dancing	4	F	3	2	0	1	37,690
Shadow's Hope	3	F	1	0	1	0	2,160
Shadow's Image	5	G	7	0	2	1	3,591
Shadows N Dust	2	F	5	1	0	0	4,786
Shadows Unexpected	6	M	2	0	0	0	0
Shadowsoncanvas	3	G	7	2	2	0	20,096

Horse	Age	Sex	Sts	1st	2d	3d	Won
Shadowstone	3	G	13	3	0	1	25,233
Shadowtime	5	M	2	0	0	0	414
Shady Cache	2	F	1	0	1	0	1,968
Shady Caller	2	F	5	1	0	1	16,110
Shady Classic	4	F	7	1	1	1	70,472
Shady Deal	4	C	12	0	0	2	5,545
Shady Devil	3	C	10	1	1	2	44,896
Shady Hill	5	G	14	3	1	1	15,176
Shady Inspiration	7	M	12	0	1	0	2,123
Shady Justice	4	G	9	1	4	2	16,613
Shady Lady Jane	5	M	4	0	0	0	610
Shady Lane	3	F	4	2	0	0	54,160
Shady Light	3	G	12	2	1	1	11,768
Shady N Single	4	F	5	0	0	1	4,186
Shady Remark	9	G	13	4	4	0	55,915
Shady Report	4	F	11	0	0	1	1,460
Shady Strike	5	G	7	1	1	1	22,382
Shady Tree	4	F	8	0	0	1	2,860
Shady Valley	5	G	9	1	2	0	38,300
Shady Woman	4	F	12	2	5	2	89,670
Shadyrest	4	F	8	1	0	1	16,679
Shae Bay	3	F	4	1	0	0	9,527
Shafeera	5	M	10	0	0	1	2,184
Shaffle	4	G	11	1	0	1	6,480
Shagging	5	G	16	4	4	2	30,995
Shaggy Warrior	3	G	7	0	1	2	5,233
Shagraan (GB)	5	H	1	0	0	0	0
Shagtime Pauly	4	G	11	1	2	2	6,610
Shagwell	5	G	13	1	1	3	4,990
Shagwong	7	G	1	0	0	0	360
Shah Imran	6	H	5	0	0	0	452
Shah of Shahs	4	G	2	0	0	0	1,020
Shahalie Lake	4	F	14	2	1	1	15,640
Shaheen's Babe	3	F	2	0	0	0	100
Shaheens Flyer	3	F	6	2	0	0	8,857
Shaheen's Treat	3	F	7	0	0	0	824
Shahnana's West	7	G	5	0	0	0	802
Shahrahere	9	G	4	1	2	1	35,900
Shaina	3	F	3	0	1	0	1,690
Shaitan	4	G	9	3	1	2	68,760
Shaka Swift	3	G	7	0	0	1	4,979
Shaka's Warrior	5	G	2	0	0	0	270
Shake a Jar	3	G	6	0	1	0	3,820
Shake It High	6	M	9	0	3	3	4,672
Shake Me Down	3	F	12	3	2	0	65,009
Shake N Blake	3	G	6	1	0	1	5,850
Shake Off	3	F	10	2	0	2	104,763
Shake Salt	6	G	8	2	2	0	11,550
Shake the Bank	4	C	7	2	1	0	78,736
Shake the Dice	6	G	13	5	2	2	123,784
Shake the Dust	6	M	16	2	1	2	10,456
Shake Thechampagne	3	F	6	2	1	1	7,376
Shake Those Hands	7	G	11	0	1	3	2,567
Shake You Down	6	G	6	3	0	0	278,604
Shake You Up	3	C	1	0	0	0	127
Shakeel's Striker	2	G	7	0	1	1	4,080
Shakeel's Wish	3	G	13	3	0	2	16,116
Shake'em On Down	5	M	2	0	0	0	0
Shakeit Tothemoon	6	M	18	0	0	3	4,447
Shakeitlikeshakira	2	F	3	0	0	2	2,650
Shaker Heights	3	F	3	0	0	1	642
Shaker Made	5	M	3	1	0	0	3,263
Shakespeare	3	C	2	2	0	0	59,820
Shakespeare Critic	4	F	8	0	2	2	20,735
Shakespearesister (GB)	2	F	1	1	0	0	9,982
Shakesperean Story	3	C	3	1	0	0	11,766
Shakethemhatersoff	4	G	13	4	3	2	85,075
Shakey	3	G	9	3	0	3	23,180
Shakina Darling	2	F	7	1	1	0	16,735
Shakobe	3	G	3	0	0	0	0
Shakopee	3	F	6	1	2	0	39,379
Shakran (GB)	5	H	12	3	2	0	31,850
Shaky Town	4	G	5	1	1	1	26,707
Shaky Your Capote	3	G	9	0	0	0	411
Shalakee	3	C	4	0	0	0	230
Shalini	5	M	7	0	2	1	64,601
Shalita	2	F	2	0	0	0	280
Shalmarie	4	F	1	0	0	0	653
Sham Aciss	6	G	3	1	0	1	11,000
Shaman Chocolate	9	G	2	0	0	0	0
Shamarea	4	F	6	0	0	2	1,364
Shambala	8	M	4	0	0	0	1,375
Shame On the Moon	5	G	9	2	0	2	9,509
Shameless Music	3	F	2	0	1	0	5,975
Shamelessly	4	F	12	2	5	0	20,733
Shamenda	3	F	12	0	3	0	13,619
Shamethemoon	2	C	3	1	0	0	9,445
Shamiza	3	F	10	0	1	0	5,775
Shamless	4	F	10	3	1	2	14,582
Shamoiselle	3	F	1	0	0	0	338
Shamonyou	2	F	3	0	0	0	780
Shampel	3	G	10	1	1	2	61,792
Shampelicus	4	F	4	1	0	0	10,200
Shampoo Cape	7	M	4	0	1	1	570
Shamrock Affair	7	G	10	0	0	0	1,955
Shamrock Greene	3	G	8	0	1	0	4,509
Shamrock Peak	3	F	7	1	0	2	9,605
Shamrock Point	3	F	2	0	0	0	0
Shamrock Secret	4	F	1	0	0	0	0
Shamrock Shore	2	F	3	0	0	0	125
Shamrock's Appeal	4	F	17	3	5	2	23,850
Shamrock's Bay	2	C	6	0	0	0	1,784
Shamrocks Fibber	9	G	16	0	5	3	7,024
Sham's the Man	4	G	5	1	0	0	4,996
Shamus Shea	7	G	1	0	0	1	3,750
Shamuuu	3	G	15	4	6	0	126,680
Shamyl	7	G	5	1	0	2	6,916
Shanagain	4	F	3	0	0	1	3,010
Shanagolden Girl	5	M	2	0	0	0	180
Shananie's Finale	11	G	2	0	0	0	0
Shandon Chimes	4	G	7	2	1	0	9,162
Shandy	4	G	8	2	1	3	116,680
Shane B	4	G	8	0	0	0	1,750
Shane Jules	2	C	3	1	0	2	18,150
Shanena	3	F	16	2	2	3	22,866
Shanes Light	3	G	8	1	3	3	10,799
Shanes Treasure	5	G	16	3	4	2	17,052
Shanghai Joe	2	G	4	1	1	0	37,517
Shanghai Lady	4	F	11	0	0	3	12,925
Shanghied	3	C	7	4	0	1	98,433
Shania Lane	5	M	2	0	0	0	225
Shania Secret	3	F	6	0	2	1	3,952
Shania's Shadow	4	F	5	1	0	1	4,159
Shaniko	3	C	7	2	2	0	64,320
Shanna's Viper	5	G	7	1	1	0	4,761
Shannon Arms	3	G	6	0	4	1	16,036
Shannon Bobannon	3	F	3	0	0	0	0
Shannon Lee	4	F	7	1	1	2	9,150
Shannon Miracle	5	G	13	3	3	1	70,109
Shannon Select	7	M	13	5	3	2	26,681
Shannon Slew	5	G	6	1	1	0	6,920
Shannon the Cannon	6	G	16	0	1	4	14,458
Shannon's Boy	8	G	8	0	0	0	2,715
Shannon's Delight	5	M	6	1	0	0	5,185
Shannon's Dream	3	F	1	0	0	0	67
Shannons Gold	3	F	4	2	1	0	19,740
Shannon's Love	3	C	1	0	0	0	0
Shannons Valentine	4	F	6	2	0	1	15,320
Shann's Dream	3	F	1	0	0	1	1,150
Shanon O'Hara	4	F	3	0	0	0	0
Shanon's Sparkle	4	G	2	0	0	0	0
Shantac	3	F	8	2	1	2	16,808
Shantina	3	F	13	0	0	1	3,813
Shanty Hill Road	2	C	1	0	0	0	0
Shanty Town	4	G	1	0	0	0	300
Shapiro's Hero	5	G	5	0	0	0	750
Sharbayan (IRE)	6	G	4	0	1	0	13,760
Sharday's Legacy	6	M	5	0	0	1	1,849
Shardonas Sister	6	M	2	0	0	0	0
Shards of Silver	8	G	2	0	0	0	647
Share 'n Rainbows	4	F	15	1	2	2	11,048
Share the Love	2	G	3	0	0	1	2,020
Share the Magic	4	G	7	0	1	0	3,000
Share the Spirit	4	F	5	0	0	0	120
Shared View	6	G	10	2	2	3	12,066
Shareholder	4	C	10	3	0	3	61,335
Shareshten	3	F	3	0	0	0	900
Sharethetime	6	H	13	1	1	3	50,819

Horse	Age	Sex	Sts	1st	2d	3d	Won
Shari Bank	6	M	4	1	1	1	4,885
Shari Lee	3	F	13	3	0	2	10,575
Sharide	5	M	6	1	0	0	7,375
Shari's Delight	4	F	5	0	1	2	12,720
Shari's Gift	2	F	1	0	0	0	184
Shari's Gold Sole	4	F	13	2	6	0	108,241
Sharis High Cotton	4	F	5	1	0	0	6,971
Shark	2	C	3	0	1	0	10,655
Shark Bite	3	C	5	0	1	1	5,680
Shark Comin	3	F	7	0	0	0	0
Shark Eye	5	G	6	0	0	3	13,463
Shark Fin Soup	4	G	5	3	1	0	23,515
Shark Hunter	2	G	3	0	0	0	192
Shark in the Park	2	G	3	0	0	0	0
Sharkcantgetout	3	C	2	0	0	0	0
Sharkey's Gold	3	F	10	0	0	5	12,051
Sharkey's Iris	4	F	6	1	0	1	6,569
Sharkey's Treasure	3	F	8	1	0	2	4,347
Sharkey'seasterboy	3	C	4	0	0	0	266
Sharks and Lawyers	4	F	12	2	4	1	17,177
Sharky Brown	4	G	10	3	1	0	36,187
Sharky's Review	6	M	6	2	1	1	87,412
Sharlilly	3	F	2	1	1	0	20,000
Sharm	3	G	12	2	3	1	25,821
Sharon Marie	10	M	1	0	0	0	0
Sharons Art	6	M	3	0	0	0	175
Sharon's Delight	2	F	2	0	0	0	0
Sharon's Gold	3	G	3	0	0	0	0
Sharon's Liberty	3	F	1	0	0	0	67
Sharon's Riches	5	M	10	4	2	0	14,930
Sharons Scoundral	4	G	11	1	2	2	8,257
Sharon's Victory	5	G	24	1	1	0	8,767
Sharp Account	3	G	14	2	2	1	12,170
Sharp Agenda	5	M	3	0	0	0	411
Sharp Arrow	2	F	4	0	0	1	1,952
Sharp as a Fox	3	F	5	0	0	2	5,620
Sharp Breeze	4	G	7	0	0	0	0
Sharp Brunette	3	F	9	1	0	2	40,575
Sharp Chevron	3	C	1	0	0	0	435
Sharp Command	5	G	13	0	0	2	3,405
Sharp Cookie	4	F	4	0	0	0	150
Sharp Corner	8	M	1	0	0	0	0
Sharp Critic	7	G	6	1	0	0	10,170
Sharp Face	8	G	5	0	1	0	9,000
Sharp Forty Niner	6	G	2	0	0	0	630
Sharp Gold	5	G	7	0	0	3	7,945
Sharp Halo	4	F	7	0	1	1	5,335
Sharp Image	3	F	2	0	0	0	0
Sharp Insult	3	F	6	1	1	1	21,730
Sharp Jane	2	F	1	0	0	0	0
Sharp Lad	4	G	12	1	4	2	10,177
Sharp Lil Kilowatt	2	F	1	0	0	0	0
Sharp Lil Wildcard	6	M	3	0	0	0	200
Sharp Lisa	2	F	4	1	2	0	171,600
Sharp Little Boy	5	H	9	3	0	2	24,560
Sharp Looking Dude	7	G	12	3	4	0	24,480
Sharp Looking Man	5	G	4	0	1	1	2,529
Sharp Marc	4	G	6	1	2	1	60,730
Sharp Miss	4	F	11	1	1	3	27,277
Sharp N Dazzling	6	H	3	0	0	0	145
Sharp Park	5	H	3	0	0	0	192
Sharp Pirate	10	G	3	0	0	0	0
Sharp Quackie	3	G	2	0	0	0	0
Sharp Remark	4	G	2	0	0	0	136
Sharp Response	3	G	7	1	1	1	4,535
Sharp Roblar	4	G	16	1	3	4	6,839
Sharp Sailor	5	G	14	1	0	1	8,795
Sharp Shadeau	4	F	7	1	1	1	7,808
Sharp Spark	2	F	1	0	0	0	0
Sharp Spec	3	G	10	1	3	0	19,443
Sharp Spot	3	F	6	0	0	0	477
Sharp Strider	2	G	6	1	1	1	9,622
Sharp Tack	2	G	4	1	0	1	19,560
Sharp Tax Lady	5	M	8	1	0	1	2,789
Sharp Ways	4	F	9	4	2	0	51,382
Sharp Writer	2	C	7	1	2	2	37,208
Sharpbill (GB)	4	F	2	0	1	0	15,360
Sharpen	3	F	12	1	4	5	9,184
Sharpen Up Victor	3	G	11	2	2	3	46,720

Horse	Age	Sex	Sts	1st	2d	3d	Won
Sharpened Copy	3	F	3	2	0	0	27,600
Sharpenupjoe	5	G	10	3	3	1	16,718
Sharpeshifter	3	G	9	2	1	2	11,336
Sharppardo	6	G	11	0	1	1	3,320
Sharps 'n Flats	5	G	6	0	1	1	8,406
Sharpster	5	G	5	0	0	1	7,592
Shasheena	2	F	1	0	0	0	300
Shasta Joe	6	G	8	0	4	1	3,718
Shasta Lake	5	M	20	4	3	5	16,297
Shasta Storm	3	F	13	1	2	2	13,218
Shasta T	2	F	2	0	1	0	6,010
Shasta Willy	10	G	5	0	0	1	394
Shattered Crystal	6	M	1	0	0	0	152
Shattering	5	M	23	0	1	2	4,840
Shatterproof	7	M	2	0	0	0	336
Shattuck Street	4	G	9	1	4	0	13,733
Shaun Bashaun	6	M	8	1	2	1	5,711
Shauna's Song	4	F	5	0	0	0	497
Shaunavon	3	F	7	4	0	0	136,320
Shaun's Breakout	3	G	8	0	1	0	1,856
Shaved Ice	4	F	6	1	2	0	12,560
Shawhaam	4	C	3	0	0	0	1,404
Shawklit Cookie	4	F	3	2	0	0	14,415
Shawklit Liner	5	M	4	0	1	1	3,115
Shawklit Man	4	C	6	0	0	1	4,624
Shawklit Mint	5	M	1	0	0	0	816
Shawklit Obsession	3	C	5	0	1	1	5,770
Shawklit Premiere	3	F	14	0	1	5	11,243
Shawklit the Hawk	5	G	3	0	0	0	0
Shawklit's Gold	3	C	11	2	1	4	41,870
Shawklit's Pride	3	G	9	0	0	0	1,140
Shawklit's Sopo	4	F	4	1	0	0	12,690
Shawnaroba	3	G	5	0	0	0	745
Shawnee Miss	4	F	5	0	0	2	2,981
Shawnee Princess	4	F	14	1	1	2	9,882
Shawnee Sunrise	6	M	1	0	0	1	2,080
Shawnee Switch	5	H	3	0	0	0	0
Shawnee Warrior	3	C	1	0	0	0	0
Shawniki	5	G	3	0	0	0	0
Shaws Creek	5	H	6	1	1	1	73,531
Shawshank Shaun	3	G	11	2	3	3	8,168
Shawteesh	4	G	15	1	3	2	11,230
Shaye Alone	3	F	9	2	2	3	26,750
Shays B	3	F	2	0	0	0	0
Shays Diamond	3	F	1	0	0	0	0
Shazap	5	M	5	0	0	0	589
She a Tulsa Girl	4	F	10	1	3	2	33,560
She Ain't Much	3	F	5	0	2	0	3,100
She Ain't No Saint	3	F	2	0	0	0	440
She Aintnopaint	4	F	1	0	1	0	3,000
She Ama Angel	2	F	2	0	0	0	0
She B Cool	3	F	6	1	1	1	7,659
She Be Devil	4	F	2	0	0	1	552
She Be Fapiano	4	F	8	1	2	2	18,285
She Bird	2	F	2	0	0	0	800
She Can Punch	2	F	5	1	0	3	17,932
She Canget	4	F	10	1	2	1	13,486
She Caught My Eye	3	F	3	0	0	0	0
She Commands	3	F	6	0	0	1	4,723
She Dance So So	6	M	15	1	0	1	3,611
She Devil	3	F	1	0	0	0	144
She Did It Her Way	6	M	7	1	2	0	25,440
She Floor'd Me	3	F	11	1	2	0	12,672
She Go Flying	4	F	3	1	0	1	18,073
She Goes West	6	M	12	3	3	1	31,881
She Got the Edge	3	F	7	0	0	0	618
She Has Rhythm	4	F	14	2	3	3	10,521
She Has Wings	4	F	3	0	0	0	201
She Is a Wild One	4	F	1	1	0	0	11,340
She Is Raging	4	F	8	4	2	1	139,500
She Is What She Is	2	F	1	0	0	0	1,710
She Ledo Target	2	F	2	1	1	0	2,550
She Might Fool You	5	M	1	0	0	0	150
She of Lawton	9	M	8	0	0	0	424
She Packs Apunch	3	F	3	1	0	0	7,020
She Roves	3	F	11	2	1	3	29,205
She Run	2	F	4	0	0	0	1,080
She Runs Away	7	M	9	0	1	3	6,317
She Sings	2	F	5	1	0	1	31,520

Horse	Age	Sex	Sts	1st	2d	3d	Won
She Soca	3	F	1	0	0	0	653
She Wears Gold	6	M	14	1	3	1	13,903
She Who Dances	3	F	9	2	2	0	24,964
She Who Dreams	3	F	11	1	0	1	3,502
She Will Get Away	2	F	4	1	2	0	30,328
Sheaf of Gold	2	G	2	0	0	0	0
Sheain't a Lady	3	F	6	1	1	0	8,296
Shear Attitude	3	F	7	0	0	3	4,070
Shearer	4	G	4	0	0	0	163
Sheba Cat	3	F	4	0	0	0	220
Sheba Power	3	G	3	0	0	0	525
Shebakayskittycat	9	M	4	0	0	0	130
Sheba's Aly	3	G	5	0	2	1	9,490
Shebatim's Morrow	4	F	2	0	0	0	602
Shebatim's Token	3	G	3	0	0	0	0
Shebeen	2	F	1	0	0	0	132
Shebeen (GB)	4	F	9	0	3	0	34,195
Shebelongstoyou	2	F	5	1	3	0	63,940
Shecanrun	4	F	8	0	1	3	15,630
Sheckatoo	3	G	6	2	2	1	71,010
Shecky Punch	2	C	4	1	0	0	9,900
Shecky's Bell	2	F	1	0	0	0	0
Sheckys Gift	2	C	1	0	0	0	780
Shedabad (IRE)	4	G	2	0	0	0	2,378
Shedancesforallen	3	F	10	3	1	0	25,950
Shedoz Tricks	4	F	11	2	2	1	10,785
Shee Biscuit	2	F	1	0	0	0	600
Sheelin	4	F	12	1	1	2	6,068
Sheemaa	5	M	1	0	0	0	50
Sheen	9	G	19	5	4	1	12,773
Sheen Sky	2	F	1	1	0	0	6,000
Sheep Canyon	6	G	5	0	0	0	775
Sheep's Clothing	3	F	9	0	0	1	3,625
Sheer Enchantment	3	F	12	1	5	2	147,694
Sheer Excess	4	F	5	1	1	0	38,760
Sheer Luck	3	F	2	0	0	0	3,840
Sheer Numbers	3	F	7	2	2	0	36,465
Sheer One	2	C	4	2	0	0	25,200
Sheer Power	6	H	1	0	0	1	1,650
Sheer Sweetness	5	M	11	1	2	2	16,383
Sheer Tarra	3	F	12	3	1	2	25,758
Sheer Trouble	4	G	12	0	0	1	1,786
Sheer Velocity	5	M	3	0	0	0	728
Sheersox	5	G	15	1	1	4	4,008
Sheets to the Win	3	G	5	0	0	0	0
Sheez All Good	2	F	2	0	0	1	935
Sheeza Hot Doc	2	F	6	1	1	0	6,106
Sheeza Yankee	5	M	3	0	0	0	540
Sheezameadowmouse	2	F	4	0	0	0	740
Shegardi (GB)	9	G	3	0	1	0	960
Shego	3	F	10	0	1	0	1,161
Shehaz Pazzaz	9	M	13	3	1	0	22,356
Shehazaam Nice Car	3	F	4	0	0	0	1,050
Shehazzit	6	M	3	0	0	0	0
Sheho	2	F	2	1	0	1	37,500
Sheik of Wagoner	3	C	14	3	1	2	24,844
Sheikh Albequick	7	H	4	0	0	0	622
Sheikh and Awe	3	F	8	3	3	2	35,228
Sheikh Dancer	5	G	11	2	0	1	6,596
Sheikh Fever	5	G	5	2	0	1	55,120
Sheikh'nnotstirred	7	M	13	2	4	0	13,553
Sheila Defrere	3	F	16	1	6	2	31,330
Sheila's Catman	4	G	13	2	0	1	9,529
Sheilas Desire	4	F	10	2	1	2	16,314
Sheila's Destiny	2	F	7	0	0	2	5,165
Sheila's Ovation	3	F	2	0	0	0	3,762
Sheila's Secret	2	F	5	1	1	2	22,526
Sheisatomcat	4	F	2	0	0	0	80
Sheisreal	7	M	1	0	0	0	120
Sheiswildncageytoo	3	F	4	0	2	0	25,230
Shek O Prospect	5	G	3	0	0	0	0
Shelbar	7	G	10	2	4	3	27,694
Shelbiana Kitty	2	F	4	1	0	0	18,000
Shelbis Gold Mine	2	F	2	0	0	0	105
Shelby Blue	5	M	8	0	2	3	6,129
Shelby City	4	F	7	0	0	0	646
Shelby County	4	F	4	0	0	1	1,050
Shelby Madison	5	M	4	0	2	1	22,522
Shelby Slew	4	F	5	0	0	0	246
Shelby's Dancer	5	H	1	0	0	0	109
Shelby's Halo	5	M	8	0	0	1	2,775
Shelby's Request	5	M	9	2	1	3	21,923
Shelbys Storm	5	G	15	3	3	1	14,612
Shelby's too Smart	4	F	2	0	0	0	0
Sheldon's Devil	4	F	1	0	0	0	0
Sheldon's Success	4	G	10	0	1	1	5,955
Sheldts Prospect	2	G	1	0	0	0	2,500
She'll B.long Gone	7	M	1	0	0	0	160
Shell Creek	3	G	2	0	0	0	250
Shell in the Sand	3	F	6	0	0	0	322
She'll Sho Go	5	M	3	1	0	0	3,066
Shell Shock	6	G	3	0	0	0	283
Shelley's Delight	3	F	2	0	0	0	0
Shellie's Slew	2	F	1	0	0	0	400
Shellimo	4	F	5	0	0	1	2,265
Shellman Bluff	2	F	3	1	0	1	6,632
Shello's Secret	4	C	5	1	0	2	19,000
Shellseeker	3	F	10	2	4	1	59,900
Shelly Ha Ha	5	M	1	0	0	0	0
Shelly's Dot	2	F	2	0	1	1	4,575
Shelly's Lady Jane	4	F	6	2	2	0	5,941
Shelly's Lil Lady	3	F	9	0	0	0	174
Shelly's Pride	4	F	1	0	0	0	45
Shellys Terms	4	F	8	2	1	0	35,950
Shelter	7	H	1	0	0	0	0
Shelter Me Earl	6	M	7	1	0	2	7,696
Shelter Rain	6	G	16	1	2	3	17,710
Shelter's No Fool	6	G	14	2	2	1	25,830
Shemakesmesmile	3	F	3	0	0	0	352
Shemoveslikeaghost	4	F	7	4	1	0	174,774
Shenandoah Harley	2	G	4	0	1	1	16,174
Shenandoah King	3	C	10	0	0	0	814
Shenandoah Peaks	2	G	2	0	0	0	460
Shenandoah Smile	6	M	7	0	0	1	4,950
Shenanigan Cat	3	F	5	1	0	0	5,940
Shena's Emblem	3	F	2	0	0	0	0
Shenny	3	F	9	2	2	1	20,775
Shenogood	5	M	2	0	0	0	215
Shepherd's Star	4	F	1	0	0	0	130
Shepherdsville	2	C	7	0	1	1	7,567
Sher Choice	5	M	5	0	0	2	702
Sher Crafty	6	G	4	2	0	0	10,908
Sher Light	4	F	5	0	0	0	2,140
Sher Long	3	C	6	2	0	0	3,397
Sher Money	3	F	3	0	0	0	273
Sher Ridge	4	G	14	2	1	1	5,690
Sher Time	3	C	2	0	0	0	0
Sher Veil	3	G	8	0	0	1	1,488
Shera	5	M	3	0	0	0	539
Sherbrook Rye	2	G	4	1	0	0	18,180
Shergar River Road	3	C	5	1	0	0	1,614
Shergot Attitude	4	G	10	0	1	1	3,957
Sheridan Lake	5	G	4	2	0	0	12,260
Sheriff Dillon	3	G	11	1	0	2	6,545
Sheriff Joe	2	C	8	1	1	1	20,720
Sheriff Mike	3	G	5	0	0	0	0
Sheriff Reprice	7	G	12	0	4	3	10,899
Sheriff Shelly	2	F	6	0	0	4	8,850
Sheriff Sid Again	5	G	3	0	0	1	1,598
Sheril	3	F	5	0	2	0	1,926
Sheringham Lady	6	M	9	0	1	0	3,653
Sherintan's Zeal	2	F	7	1	1	0	11,040
Sherippedherpants	3	F	15	1	5	3	17,432
Sherizod	4	F	11	0	2	3	4,624
Sherm	5	G	9	2	2	0	19,837
Sherman Gal	3	F	3	0	0	0	217
Sherman Road	4	F	10	2	0	3	8,970
Sherman's March	2	C	1	0	0	0	2,940
Shermanthetank	2	C	7	0	1	2	20,546
Sherpa Guide	6	G	8	0	3	0	49,192
Sherrie Belle	2	F	4	2	0	0	36,650
Sherri's Dream	4	F	2	0	0	0	0
Sherroyal	6	G	4	3	1	0	15,007
Sherrylane	2	F	6	1	0	1	15,010
Sherrys Champ	3	F	6	3	0	0	12,270
Sherrysredsilkslip	4	F	6	1	2	0	4,505
Sherwood Forest	4	G	6	1	0	1	9,529
Sherwood Oak	7	G	11	2	2	2	12,614

Horse	Age	Sex	Sts	1st	2d	3d	Won
Sheryar Fox	3	G	6	0	0	0	1,660
Sheryar Special	6	H	6	0	2	2	14,520
Sheryl Kay	4	F	10	2	2	1	15,785
Shes a Bit Shady	3	F	8	2	1	0	10,158
She's a Bombshell	3	F	8	0	2	0	16,951
She's a Candice	7	M	10	0	1	2	4,200
Shes a Catty Kitty	3	F	4	0	0	0	288
She's a Charm	4	F	4	0	0	2	2,431
She's a Classic	5	M	2	0	0	0	0
She's a Clown	4	F	2	0	0	0	800
She's a Cool Cat	4	F	15	1	2	2	11,103
She's a Crook	4	F	12	0	2	1	4,245
She's a Dandy	4	F	4	0	1	0	2,531
She's a Deputy	4	F	17	3	4	3	50,610
She's a Deputy Too	3	F	10	0	0	1	7,025
She's a Dixieland	4	F	6	1	0	2	1,363
Shes a Freebie	5	M	15	3	4	2	40,420
She's a Hawk	3	F	3	0	0	0	38
She's a Jewel	2	F	5	2	0	1	70,600
She's a Marlin	4	F	3	0	0	0	252
Shes a Matchlite	4	F	19	0	3	1	3,851
Shes a Melody	7	M	12	2	1	1	13,881
She's a Mugs	3	F	8	3	2	0	111,187
She's a Nice Color	5	M	2	0	0	0	86
She's a Olympian	3	F	2	0	0	0	2,140
She's a Punter	4	F	5	0	3	0	14,460
She's a Quaker	3	F	1	0	0	0	92
She's a Queen	2	F	3	0	1	0	470
She's a Rebel Too	3	F	7	2	1	1	60,650
She's a Rich Girl	4	F	1	1	0	0	5,400
She's a Rosie Lion	4	F	7	0	0	0	444
She's a Sizzler	5	M	2	0	0	0	185
She's a Snake	2	F	1	0	0	0	135
She's a Sooner	3	F	3	0	0	0	156
She's a Sweet Deal	5	M	6	4	1	0	36,450
Shes a Sweet Mertz	4	F	6	0	0	1	3,108
She's a Tycoon Too	4	F	1	0	0	0	0
She's All American	4	F	3	0	0	0	0
She's All Fired Up	4	F	4	2	0	0	9,100
She's All Right	2	F	2	1	0	0	5,525
She's All Talk	2	F	5	0	0	2	12,242
She's an Open Book	3	F	6	1	0	1	8,980
She's Angelic	2	F	2	0	0	0	615
She's Bluffing	3	C	5	1	0	1	7,725
She's Booked	3	F	14	1	3	4	27,540
She's Classy Two	4	F	1	0	0	0	390
She's Conected	3	F	5	0	0	0	142
She's Cooking Now	4	F	8	1	3	1	32,850
Shes Dixies Eskimo	3	F	9	3	2	2	93,800
She's Enough	3	F	8	2	2	1	44,482
She's Exclusive	3	F	5	1	0	0	16,559
She's Exposed	3	F	11	1	5	1	8,970
She's Fancy Free	3	F	5	0	0	1	3,820
She's Fantastic	4	F	1	0	1	0	3,840
She's Fast	3	F	2	0	1	0	3,750
She's Finding Time	5	M	10	5	1	1	72,636
Shes Flashy	2	F	1	0	0	0	125
She's Flying High	4	F	12	1	1	1	8,692
She's Frosty	3	F	5	0	0	2	2,803
She's Funny	2	F	2	0	0	0	600
She's Gettin Busy	3	F	2	0	0	0	186
She's Got Appeal	3	F	4	1	0	1	36,120
She's Got Issues	4	F	6	0	2	1	2,690
She's Got It	5	M	7	0	2	0	4,019
She's Got Style	3	F	14	2	2	2	16,483
She's Gottogetaway	3	F	3	0	0	0	1,312
She's Her Image	2	F	2	0	0	0	1,550
She's Home Alone	6	M	9	0	1	0	954
Shes in Command	2	F	2	1	0	0	15,600
She's Insane	3	F	3	0	1	1	2,857
Shes Kiddin Around	4	F	1	0	0	0	0
Shes Knott Funny	2	F	1	0	0	0	1,320
She's Mine Forever	5	M	2	1	0	0	3,870
She's Misty	4	F	5	0	0	0	2,159
She's Movin On	3	F	12	2	1	1	36,972
She's My Girl	4	F	2	0	0	0	160
She's My Lady	3	F	8	1	3	2	48,634
She's My Lady Lou	3	F	2	0	0	0	0
She's Nifty	4	F	7	2	0	1	9,171
She's No Bo	5	M	16	3	6	1	30,573
She's No Princess	2	F	3	0	0	1	2,050
She's Noble	2	F	7	1	1	0	12,640
Shes Not Idol	5	M	13	1	1	2	8,059
She's Oakie Dokie	4	F	2	0	0	0	276
She's Our Demon	4	F	3	1	1	0	7,590
She's Our Favorite	3	F	15	1	1	1	15,640
She's Our Gal	2	F	3	1	1	0	12,800
Shes Out West	4	F	2	0	0	0	86
Shes Outa Bull	3	F	2	0	0	0	625
Shes R Gold Mine	3	F	12	1	0	4	14,002
She's Rapid	5	M	2	0	0	0	0
Shes Ready Buster	5	M	10	0	0	1	1,645
She's Really Cool	4	F	4	1	0	0	7,380
She's Relentless	3	F	9	2	1	1	13,420
She's Risky	6	M	10	0	0	1	990
She's Rosalie Jane	4	F	5	1	0	0	14,910
She's Royal Too	3	F	7	0	0	0	948
She's Salty	2	F	4	1	1	0	45,252
She's Shameless	7	M	10	0	0	2	4,608
She's So Cold	3	F	9	0	4	1	10,775
She's So Cute	4	F	6	2	1	0	18,610
She's So Mean	5	M	18	2	0	2	12,150
She's So Rebel	3	F	10	0	0	0	0
She's So Waki	3	F	3	0	0	0	455
She's So Witty	4	F	10	2	1	1	14,295
She's Some Fox	5	M	3	0	1	0	1,950
She's Sophia	7	M	9	0	0	0	990
She's Sterling	3	F	6	1	3	1	55,384
Shes Stone Country	4	F	9	0	0	0	810
She's Taboo	6	M	6	0	0	0	1,890
She's Taken	4	F	1	0	0	0	40
She's That Cat	2	F	3	0	0	1	4,845
She's the Answer	4	F	13	0	0	1	3,185
She's the Coach	4	F	3	0	0	0	520
She's the Fashion	4	F	10	1	1	1	27,541
She's the Future	5	M	5	2	1	0	13,070
She's the General	3	F	8	2	0	1	71,453
She's the Goods	2	F	3	0	0	0	1,400
She's the Ticket	4	F	9	3	0	3	30,410
She's Trouble	3	F	3	0	1	0	4,600
She's Valid	4	F	2	0	0	0	0
She's Vested	5	M	5	1	0	1	36,080
She's Wild	3	F	6	3	0	1	40,760
She's Zealous	4	F	2	1	1	0	59,125
Shesa Axe Too	4	F	11	1	3	4	20,390
Shesa Klassy Devil	3	F	1	0	0	0	60
Shesa Nasty Girl	4	F	10	1	1	0	10,805
Shesa Picture	4	F	2	0	0	0	0
Shesa Private I	2	F	3	2	1	0	21,480
Shesa Strodes Lady	4	F	4	0	0	0	986
Shesabrickhouse	4	F	5	1	1	1	14,566
Shesadorabull	3	F	3	0	0	0	535
Shesafamilygal	2	F	1	1	0	0	5,100
Shesafoxybay	4	F	2	0	0	0	0
Shesagoldmine	4	F	6	1	0	0	6,300
Shesagoodguysgirl	2	F	1	0	0	0	0
She'sagoodsport	2	F	2	0	0	0	346
Shesahottammle	2	F	5	1	0	1	6,578
Shesaidsheknowsya	3	F	5	3	2	0	30,778
Shesalittledandy	2	F	3	0	0	0	980
Shesamoneyburner	3	F	7	0	0	1	2,390
She'samystery Girl	3	F	5	0	0	0	4,410
Shesanactress	5	M	19	1	1	4	6,109
Shesanaturalactor	6	M	12	2	0	3	7,869
Shesanothergrump	5	M	7	0	1	1	21,094
Shesapartnerncrime	4	F	11	0	2	1	6,940
Shesarider	6	M	1	0	0	0	83
Shesarowdycrook	3	F	2	0	0	0	0
Shesasassiedancer	4	F	9	2	1	0	11,890
Shesasmokin	4	F	9	0	2	1	25,641
Shesasoprano	4	F	14	2	1	5	39,339
Shesaspaspecial	7	M	16	0	0	3	3,518
Shesasureshot	4	F	8	2	1	2	26,560
Shesatreasure	6	M	8	1	2	1	7,606
She'sautomatic	2	F	4	0	0	0	190
She'saxaviermuskie	3	F	11	1	0	1	6,702
She'sbubba'sdelite	3	F	9	1	3	2	35,915
Shescominundone	5	M	3	0	0	0	335

Horse	Age	Sex	Sts	1st	2d	3d	Won
Shesfastbutnoteasy	4	F	3	1	0	1	7,159
She'sfullofhope	5	M	11	2	3	2	19,055
She'sgettingbetter	2	F	5	1	1	0	13,990
Shesgoneagain	3	F	6	1	1	0	6,390
Shesgonecountry	2	F	3	0	0	0	1,041
Shesgonnabeastar	3	F	4	0	0	1	1,740
Sheshe Bold	4	F	6	0	0	1	1,335
Sheshe Moran	5	M	3	0	0	0	340
Sheshotthesheriff	4	F	11	2	2	1	13,264
Shesmiopie	3	F	4	1	1	0	35,074
Sheso	3	F	7	4	1	0	36,864
She'sonmymind	3	F	3	1	0	1	8,393
She'sonthemove	4	F	5	1	0	0	6,372
Shesoursnow	3	F	6	1	1	0	2,308
Shesprecocious	3	F	5	0	2	0	6,965
She'stenontop	2	F	2	0	0	0	1,348
She'sunbelieveable	3	F	4	0	0	0	0
Shewin	6	M	1	0	0	0	0
Shez a Bully	2	F	4	0	0	0	0
Shez a Dreamqueen	5	M	11	1	2	0	11,298
Shez Undeniable	3	F	4	0	0	0	530
Sheza Awesomecat	3	F	10	3	1	1	9,151
Sheza Cat Too	3	F	3	0	0	0	300
Sheza Cats Meow	3	F	10	1	2	1	10,823
Sheza Diva	3	F	6	3	1	0	63,920
Sheza Dream Chaser	6	M	7	0	0	2	1,951
Sheza Gladiator	5	M	2	1	0	1	7,020
Sheza Golden Girl	3	F	1	0	0	0	0
Sheza Lee Gal	3	F	2	0	0	0	585
Sheza Love Bird	4	F	2	0	1	0	3,000
Sheza Lucky Son'so	4	F	8	2	2	2	33,300
Sheza Match	2	F	1	1	0	0	7,260
Sheza Naughty Girl	4	F	10	0	1	3	6,466
Sheza Orphan	4	F	3	0	0	0	162
Sheza Pretty Gal	4	F	7	2	0	0	17,421
Sheza Princess	5	M	8	0	1	0	2,103
Sheza Scher Pleasu	3	F	4	1	0	0	13,800
Sheza Sharkey	3	F	13	1	1	3	13,849
Sheza Silver Spoon	3	F	2	0	0	1	2,318
Sheza Slick Chick	5	M	2	0	0	0	188
Sheza Tomboy	5	M	3	0	0	0	206
Sheza Whipper	2	F	4	0	2	0	7,250
Sheza Whiz	9	M	10	0	0	1	1,866
Sheza Wild Child	5	M	3	0	0	0	0
Sheza Wolf	8	M	2	0	0	0	222
Shezadiamond	8	M	1	0	1	0	900
Shezalilbitshady	2	F	4	0	0	1	2,250
Shezamarkedword	2	F	1	0	0	0	750
Shezarealpeach	6	M	10	1	1	3	9,715
Shezaroner	4	F	7	2	1	0	23,954
Shezsofoxy	5	M	2	0	0	0	1,440
Shezsospiritual	4	F	12	3	1	4	137,950
Shh Hush	3	F	14	3	2	1	21,411
Shhh Please	3	G	7	1	2	0	44,970
Shi Kai	4	F	6	0	0	0	495
Shi Shi Doll	3	F	7	1	2	2	17,376
Shi'ahs Devil	2	G	1	0	1	0	1,900
Shibui	5	M	6	1	0	2	13,700
Shidoobee	3	G	14	0	2	1	4,579
Shiesh Kabeeb	4	G	5	1	1	1	8,306
Shift Gears	2	G	2	0	0	0	800
Shift Key	5	G	8	2	2	0	10,940
Shift Quick	8	G	4	0	0	0	642
Shift Right	6	G	8	0	0	0	1,579
Shift Shape	9	M	15	1	3	2	28,153
Shifter B	4	G	9	0	0	0	1,066
Shifti Terms	4	G	9	0	0	0	206
Shifting Harmony	3	F	3	0	0	0	500
Shifting Storm	4	F	15	2	3	3	33,260
Shifting Trends	5	G	1	0	0	0	552
Shifty	5	M	8	1	2	0	15,470
Shifty Dae	3	C	8	0	1	1	7,340
Shifty Gear	5	G	5	0	0	0	218
Shifty Slew	8	G	4	0	0	0	303
Shifty's Favorite	5	G	9	0	0	0	0
Shikari	3	F	3	0	1	1	3,210
Shikhar	2	G	5	0	2	1	10,290
Shilee	3	F	12	0	0	0	8,751
Shilew	7	M	9	1	2	1	8,344
Shilinsky	2	C	4	1	0	1	8,520
Shillelagh	4	F	11	1	1	2	9,728
Shiloah	2	F	8	3	3	0	40,430
Shiloh Billy	6	G	17	2	4	3	36,109
Shiloh Bound	3	G	4	2	0	0	73,775
Shiloh Dawn	4	F	10	0	0	1	3,614
Shiloh Gold	3	C	2	0	0	1	3,520
Shilow	5	G	2	0	0	0	186
Shilukwa	5	G	13	3	1	1	33,596
Shimmer	2	F	1	0	1	0	8,200
Shimmer Shimmer	11	G	2	0	0	0	0
Shimmering Condido	5	G	5	0	0	0	560
Shimmering Eight	2	F	2	0	0	0	626
Shimmering Heat	3	F	5	1	2	0	9,776
Shimmering Sand	7	M	2	0	0	0	260
Shimmering Sea	5	M	1	0	0	0	90
Shimmy Doll	5	M	3	0	0	0	1,530
Shimmy Kokopop	4	F	2	0	0	0	152
Shimmy Shake	3	F	9	1	2	2	38,450
Shin Kan Sen	4	G	13	0	1	0	763
Shindigit	4	G	15	3	3	2	23,901
Shine Along	4	F	18	2	6	4	20,231
Shine for a Reason	4	F	8	1	0	0	15,140
Shine Forth	5	M	3	0	0	0	1,281
Shine Miss Comet	2	F	2	0	0	0	203
Shine Please	2	F	4	1	2	0	22,960
Shine So Bright	6	M	4	2	1	0	20,334
Shinegold	5	G	9	1	2	1	15,352
Shineing Arrow	4	F	14	1	0	3	11,916
Shinelightcaroline	3	F	5	1	1	0	5,600
Shineup the Silver	5	M	2	0	0	0	605
Shiney Souvenir	4	G	8	2	0	1	11,627
Shingen Knight	10	G	11	1	1	1	7,309
Shingen Thunder	5	G	8	0	0	0	1,067
Shinghaar	7	G	3	0	0	0	0
Shingle Creek	2	G	1	0	0	0	300
Shining Angel	3	F	10	0	2	2	14,710
Shining Bandit	3	G	6	0	1	2	2,548
Shining Beacon	4	F	6	0	0	0	3,420
Shining Beauty	2	F	10	1	1	1	8,045
Shining Belle	2	F	3	0	0	0	2,026
Shining Blade	5	H	15	1	1	0	4,628
Shining Blue Demon	2	C	1	0	0	0	0
Shining Britely	6	M	6	0	2	2	13,090
Shining Career	5	G	8	1	1	0	30,666
Shining City	3	G	5	0	0	1	675
Shining Event	2	C	1	0	0	0	6,669
Shining Forever	5	M	16	1	1	3	10,181
Shining Gem	6	M	8	2	4	0	21,554
Shining Hawk	3	C	6	0	1	0	11,190
Shining Hero	2	C	2	0	0	0	1,560
Shining Jack (GB)	6	G	1	0	0	0	1,250
Shining Jewel	4	F	4	0	0	1	7,876
Shining Nuggets	6	G	5	2	0	1	7,661
Shining Rock	4	C	5	0	1	1	9,240
Shining Slippers	4	F	3	0	0	0	447
Shining Strike	5	M	2	1	0	0	25,800
Shining Tap	4	F	4	1	0	1	5,325
Shining Tower	3	F	2	0	0	0	287
Shining Victory	3	F	8	0	0	1	4,405
Shiningofthesun	3	C	7	3	0	0	47,940
Shinivar	2	F	4	0	1	0	4,735
Shinnied Up	2	C	5	0	0	1	1,540
Shiny Dancer	3	F	5	1	2	0	14,500
Shiny Emblem	3	G	7	1	1	2	25,850
Shiny Gray Comet	3	F	7	2	0	1	10,376
Shiny Meadow	4	C	4	0	0	1	7,130
Shiny Prize	4	F	5	0	1	1	17,520
Shiny Sheet	6	M	10	2	0	1	127,912
Ship Ahoy	5	G	3	0	1	1	3,660
Ship Alert	4	C	11	2	2	1	50,690
Ship of the Line	5	H	13	1	3	2	19,287
Shipman	4	C	12	0	2	2	43,604
Shipping Dixie	5	M	2	0	0	0	0
Ships Blue	3	F	1	0	0	0	137
Ship's Captain	3	C	10	2	0	0	25,650
Ship's Silver	7	G	7	1	2	1	8,270
Shipwatch	3	C	1	0	0	0	320
Shirano	11	M	11	1	0	0	7,530

Horse	Age	Sex	Sts	1st	2d	3d	Won
Shirazberry	5	M	7	1	3	0	12,168
Shire	4	C	1	0	0	0	185
Shiree Amour	2	F	5	0	0	0	4,475
Shires Reflection	4	F	6	0	1	0	3,860
Shirley and Sallye	2	F	4	0	0	0	2,330
Shirley Belle	4	F	5	0	0	0	852
Shirley Bird	2	F	1	0	0	0	550
Shirley D Feather	5	M	12	1	1	1	4,918
Shirley Kelly	4	F	2	0	0	0	800
Shirley Lee	2	F	1	0	0	0	0
Shirley Patch	3	F	4	2	0	2	4,089
Shirleyalark	3	G	11	1	0	0	3,390
Shirleygettheloot	6	M	15	3	2	1	23,995
Shirley's Call	8	G	4	0	0	0	471
Shirleys Honor	2	F	1	0	0	0	400
Shirley's Rascal	4	F	3	1	0	0	2,880
Shirley's Star	4	G	3	0	0	0	0
Shirl's Girl	5	M	4	0	0	0	217
Shirttail Satch	4	G	5	0	0	0	1,925
Shishkbob Hay	4	F	10	0	2	4	8,579
Shiumansstar	3	G	1	0	0	0	430
Shivermetimber	8	G	10	0	1	2	7,755
Shluke	4	G	8	0	0	1	2,120
Shnozzle	3	G	3	0	0	0	0
Sho Me the Diamond	6	M	1	0	0	0	40
Shoal Water	4	G	5	2	1	1	336,414
Shoalihs Tale	4	C	8	1	1	2	32,782
Shock and All	3	F	5	0	1	0	4,867
Shock the Judge	3	G	8	2	1	2	7,415
Shock the World	3	G	15	0	0	0	1,862
Shocker D	2	F	8	0	0	0	933
Shocker's Beauty	5	M	15	1	1	2	15,658
Shocking Dancer	4	G	13	1	1	3	13,036
Shocking Dunn	2	F	5	2	0	1	40,430
Shocking Number	5	M	11	4	1	0	28,290
Shocking Speed	4	G	8	0	1	0	6,773
Shockproof	3	G	6	0	2	1	11,430
Shocktics	4	F	3	1	1	1	13,670
Shocorra	3	F	2	0	0	0	372
Shoe n' Sandy	3	F	14	0	0	1	2,972
Shoe Queen	6	M	6	0	0	2	2,302
Shoe Swap	2	G	1	0	0	0	0
Shoeco City	4	G	2	0	0	0	575
Shoes and Rice	3	F	2	0	0	0	379
Shoesdontfailmenow	3	G	8	1	4	1	14,215
Shogun Empire (GB)	2	C	6	1	0	1	11,765
Shomrim's Guard	11	G	14	0	0	0	1,069
Shondel	4	F	6	1	1	1	3,957
Shonetonian	3	F	13	4	3	0	53,528
Shons Secret	3	F	7	4	0	1	30,380
Shoo Brush	4	C	7	1	3	2	13,840
Shoo Fly Willie	8	G	9	3	2	2	44,617
Shoo Launch	7	H	3	0	0	0	515
Shoo Shoo Baby	5	M	3	0	0	2	507
Shoobie	6	G	7	0	0	0	165
Shoot (GB)	4	F	4	1	3	0	59,000
Shoot for the Loot	5	M	15	3	1	3	48,139
Shoot From the Hip	4	C	11	4	2	1	66,400
Shoot It	5	G	9	0	3	1	8,583
Shoot Out	2	G	6	1	0	0	20,755
Shoot the Basket	3	G	4	0	0	0	0
Shoot the Bugler	2	F	7	1	0	2	39,839
Shoot the Loot	5	G	16	4	4	2	11,160
Shoot the Wad	4	F	20	0	0	1	6,652
Shoot to Thrill	3	F	9	2	0	3	27,241
Shoot Yeah	3	G	12	1	3	2	14,705
Shootaloot	5	G	5	1	0	0	4,408
Shootandcharge	3	F	5	2	0	2	43,380
Shootin for Gold	4	F	8	2	1	1	10,642
Shootin' Z Bull	2	G	7	0	0	0	2,253
Shooting Range	4	F	2	0	0	0	86
Shooting Star	4	C	5	1	0	1	18,430
Shoot'nloot	3	G	13	2	0	1	11,566
Shoots n' Scores	3	F	4	0	0	1	2,339
Shoots Past	2	F	3	0	0	0	2,020
Shootski	5	G	12	0	2	3	8,324
Shop Again	2	F	6	0	1	3	23,102
Shop Hill	4	G	4	2	2	0	104,800
Shop the Block	4	F	9	0	2	3	1,408
Shop Till You Drop	5	M	1	0	0	0	900
Shoppers Shuttle	5	M	7	2	1	0	6,500
Shopping Cart Mary	3	F	1	0	0	0	0
Shopping Mary	4	F	3	0	0	1	2,200
Shore Blue	2	C	2	1	0	0	27,450
Shore Breaker	4	G	2	0	0	1	1,685
Shore Girl	4	F	10	2	0	1	13,745
Shore Lover	5	M	6	1	0	0	7,270
Shore Weave	4	F	12	2	3	2	16,223
Shoreman	7	G	8	1	1	1	11,662
Shorewalk Drive	3	F	8	1	0	0	22,867
Shorey Village	3	F	6	3	0	1	46,170
Shorhouse	3	F	6	0	0	0	3,375
Shornalee	2	F	7	0	2	2	6,380
Short a Boot	3	F	6	0	0	0	0
Short Cat	2	G	1	0	0	0	0
Short Cut	2	G	4	1	1	0	7,665
Short Fat Fanny	3	F	5	1	2	0	33,052
Short Fuse	6	G	7	0	1	1	5,540
Short Fuse Shorty	3	G	15	1	1	4	17,654
Short Hair	5	G	13	0	3	1	10,114
Short Leg Sue	2	F	4	2	0	1	26,500
Short Man Cool	3	G	5	0	1	0	2,138
Short Memory	4	G	5	1	0	0	13,428
Short Number	4	G	4	0	0	0	1,790
Short Odds	8	G	10	1	2	1	13,185
Short Putt	3	F	1	0	1	0	4,200
Short Route	2	F	5	2	1	0	106,995
Short Shadow	4	F	3	0	0	0	505
Short Squeeze	5	G	12	3	3	3	72,533
Short Stack	3	C	5	0	0	1	3,860
Short to First	3	G	7	1	1	0	16,536
Short Trip Home	3	F	1	0	0	0	0
Short War	8	G	4	0	0	0	558
Shortbranch	3	F	3	1	0	1	4,316
Shortbrush	4	C	7	0	0	1	2,647
Shortstop Sal	4	F	2	1	0	0	17,700
Shorty Balero	6	G	1	0	0	0	0
Shorty Knudtson	2	C	2	1	0	0	29,200
Shorty McGee	3	G	14	2	4	2	22,090
Shortys Brightstar	4	G	8	2	2	0	17,442
Shorty's Dream	7	G	12	1	2	2	13,090
Shortyspride	2	C	1	0	0	0	0
Shoshone	3	G	3	1	0	0	15,520
Shot for Shot	6	G	13	1	0	4	14,888
Shot Gun Carolyn	5	M	6	1	0	0	12,890
Shot Gun Catty	3	F	5	2	1	0	9,265
Shot Gun Ela	3	F	3	0	2	0	7,687
Shot Gun Favorite	4	F	5	1	0	0	27,196
Shot Gun Jerry	2	C	1	0	0	0	80
Shot Gun Norman	4	G	12	1	0	0	6,935
Shot Gun Selma	2	F	3	0	1	0	5,060
Shot Gun Terry	3	C	12	3	4	0	33,515
Shot Gun Treasure	5	G	8	0	0	0	540
Shot Gun Uss Hoga	4	F	19	2	3	2	42,980
Shot of Gin	4	C	3	0	0	0	264
Shot of Light	3	F	5	2	1	0	7,492
Shot Or Two	3	G	3	1	0	1	3,570
Shot Rock	3	C	5	1	1	0	8,293
Shot Sea	3	F	3	0	0	0	140
Shotafirewater	7	G	4	0	0	0	300
Shotgun	5	G	12	0	2	0	2,687
Shotgun Fire	6	G	11	1	0	1	21,425
Shotgun Gus	4	G	2	0	0	0	816
Shotgun Proposal	4	G	13	3	4	3	31,235
Shotgun Star	3	G	7	0	0	0	213
Shotgunannie	4	F	7	0	0	2	1,917
Shotiche Penny	3	G	11	0	0	0	1,593
Shotmo	7	H	8	1	2	0	2,554
Shots	3	C	10	1	1	3	52,635
Shots Dot	5	M	2	0	0	0	780
Shotsfired	7	G	16	1	1	0	2,050
Should Be Royalty	2	F	2	1	1	0	36,400
Should Excell	3	F	10	2	1	2	53,430
Shoulda Been Me	3	G	2	0	0	0	840
Shouldabeenjoebob	3	F	5	1	0	0	6,366
Shouldacouldawooda	2	G	8	1	0	0	5,860
Shouldbefast	3	G	8	1	3	1	17,960
Shouldbevictory	3	C	9	3	4	1	25,795

Horse	Age	Sex	Sts	1st	2d	3d	Won
Shout	3	F	16	1	1	4	31,890
Shout Approval	3	C	8	2	0	0	12,420
Shout to the North	2	F	5	2	1	0	132,292
Shouting	3	G	7	1	1	0	11,626
Show Bill	3	G	1	0	0	0	140
Show Boot	3	C	10	4	1	3	126,785
Show Bug	4	F	9	0	2	3	17,935
Show Career	3	F	1	1	0	0	6,600
Show Falcon	8	H	13	2	2	3	23,583
Show Hero	3	F	11	1	1	3	21,721
Show Killer	4	G	3	1	0	0	4,692
Show Me Gone	4	G	11	1	1	3	7,151
Show Me Tazz	7	G	6	1	0	0	9,170
Show Me the Fox	7	M	4	0	0	1	1,410
Show Me the Glory	5	G	12	2	3	3	14,363
Show Me the Green	3	G	13	3	0	0	10,780
Show Me the Light	3	F	16	1	2	2	16,600
Show Me the Love	2	F	4	0	1	1	8,400
Show Me the Moolah	7	G	2	1	0	0	7,000
Show Me the Roses	3	F	2	0	0	0	1,660
Show Me the Stash	4	C	2	1	0	0	5,974
Show Me the Town	2	F	6	1	3	0	36,943
Show Me Your Glory	3	F	8	2	1	1	73,588
Show Me Your World	7	H	8	0	0	1	8,370
Show of Force	4	G	5	0	0	0	1,704
Show Or Go	3	F	2	0	0	0	0
Show Ready	3	F	16	4	1	2	100,108
Show Stomper	2	G	1	0	1	0	3,600
Show the Judge	4	G	14	1	1	2	7,691
Show Us the Check	3	F	17	2	6	1	28,356
Show Your Temper	8	G	13	0	1	2	4,095
Showbird	3	F	4	0	0	0	3,420
Showboat Willy	3	G	14	4	0	3	68,475
Showcase Six	2	C	2	0	0	0	840
Showcased	5	G	8	0	0	0	340
Showdown	4	C	3	0	0	0	2,160
Shower Aquifer	3	F	6	1	0	0	4,410
Shower Lady	4	F	3	0	0	0	184
Shower Scene	4	F	7	1	0	3	18,350
Showhof	6	G	9	1	2	0	6,508
Showin Off	2	F	3	1	0	0	6,540
Showing the Flag	3	G	12	0	0	0	1,737
Showmeitall	5	G	13	3	4	4	67,970
Showmesomelove	3	F	11	2	0	5	71,430
Showmethebook	4	G	2	1	0	1	5,325
Showmetothevilla	4	F	9	1	0	1	16,921
Showmewhatyougot	3	C	4	0	0	0	0
Showmeyourtwist	5	H	5	2	2	0	24,762
Showpiece	4	F	2	0	0	0	900
Showplacewon	3	G	2	0	0	0	70
Showtankthemoney	3	G	3	0	1	1	4,862
Showtime	5	G	3	0	1	1	1,232
Showtime Dancer	3	F	4	0	0	1	3,015
Showtime Gal	2	F	2	0	0	0	390
Showtime Girl	5	M	14	1	0	4	8,943
Shoxy	3	G	12	2	3	2	14,178
Shrewd Dealer	4	G	2	1	0	0	5,057
Shrewd Deputy	3	C	5	1	1	1	23,880
Shrewd Maria	3	F	8	2	0	1	16,800
Shrewd Money	6	M	10	0	1	3	2,928
Shrewd Stipulation	4	C	6	2	2	0	40,120
Shrike One	3	G	9	1	3	4	25,205
Shrike Zone	3	G	5	0	2	0	4,985
Shril Bay	3	F	5	0	1	2	9,516
Shrimp Cocktail	4	G	6	1	0	0	13,840
Shrimp Tempura	5	M	19	1	1	1	29,058
Shrimpee	3	F	16	2	6	3	27,990
Shshonee	2	G	4	0	0	1	2,325
Shuailaan Jennings	7	G	6	0	0	1	1,140
Shubang	4	G	1	0	0	0	131
Shudaben Franca	4	F	5	0	3	2	16,935
Shudabinajumper	6	M	5	2	0	1	26,112
Shudahbenastar	5	M	8	0	0	0	446
Shudasold	6	G	11	1	0	1	6,480
Shuffle Board	4	G	11	4	1	3	45,926
Shuffle N Deal	4	F	2	0	0	0	263
Shuffle Pass	3	C	4	0	0	0	210
Shuffling Kid (GB)	5	G	4	0	2	0	4,240
Shuga Shaq	7	G	7	1	0	0	3,715
Shuggare	2	C	2	0	0	0	0
Shujune	4	F	11	1	3	2	6,780
Shulana	4	F	14	1	2	2	10,711
Shulina	3	F	1	0	0	0	220
Shultz	4	G	8	3	2	0	10,767
Shumka	2	F	1	0	0	0	0
Shuperman Two	3	G	8	0	0	0	0
Shure	6	G	9	0	2	0	9,525
Shureamsweet	4	F	5	0	1	2	7,527
Shush	2	F	4	1	0	0	22,200
Shuswap Road	3	F	5	1	1	0	2,355
Shut Out Time	8	G	13	1	1	2	13,090
Shut Up	5	G	16	1	2	1	11,944
Shut Up Rosemary	3	F	2	0	0	0	375
Shutter Speed	7	G	14	5	1	0	25,486
Shutterbug	3	F	1	0	0	0	0
Shuttle Lane	5	M	1	0	0	0	65
Shuttle Sam	6	G	9	2	0	0	7,836
Shuttlin	4	G	9	2	4	3	18,260
Shuya	3	G	6	0	0	0	944
Shwoodifshecould	6	M	18	1	3	2	14,627
Shy Cat	3	F	9	2	1	0	12,780
Shy Dawn	2	F	1	0	0	0	0
Shy Harbor	2	C	2	0	0	1	2,665
Shy Lady	4	F	4	0	0	1	5,298
Shy Lil	3	F	7	3	0	1	67,244
Shy Patada (ARG)	7	M	6	1	2	2	40,313
Shyanne Bay	2	F	3	0	1	2	4,730
Shybynature	8	G	3	0	0	1	2,200
Shypatriot	7	M	7	0	0	0	602
Shyrlents Dream	7	M	14	1	2	2	11,221
Shyroman	3	G	1	0	0	0	75
Si and I	8	H	3	0	0	0	122
Si Lo Tengo	4	F	1	0	0	0	0
Si Si Amiga (IRE)	3	F	6	0	0	0	8,546
Si' Si' Miranda	3	F	4	2	0	0	12,130
Si Soy	5	G	6	0	0	0	930
Si Tigre Lil	8	M	1	0	0	0	135
Si Ya Dancing	5	M	7	4	2	1	25,760
Siasconset	2	F	2	0	0	0	170
Sibercrasher	8	H	13	1	1	2	12,400
Siberian Amur	2	F	1	1	0	0	16,800
Siberian Eagle	5	G	8	2	1	2	5,697
Siberian Falstaff	4	F	6	4	0	2	26,830
Siberian Fantasy	4	F	8	1	0	2	4,360
Siberian Flash	3	C	6	0	0	0	1,647
Siberian General	3	G	12	0	1	1	5,863
Siberian Grey	3	C	1	0	0	0	0
Siberian Halo	2	G	9	1	3	0	27,205
Siberian Knight	4	G	6	0	0	0	214
Siberian Mike	2	C	3	0	0	0	3,270
Siberian Ridge	4	F	10	1	2	2	13,067
Siberian Silver	5	M	6	1	1	1	8,290
Siberian Slew	3	F	1	0	0	0	0
Siberian Snow	5	M	16	3	4	1	23,969
Siberian Tigress	5	M	2	0	0	0	180
Siberian Warrior	7	G	12	0	0	0	258
Siberian Wind	3	G	3	0	1	1	3,915
Siberiano	7	G	5	1	0	1	6,855
Siberschool	3	F	1	0	0	1	2,760
Sicilian Boy	3	C	9	1	0	4	49,970
Sicilian Princess	4	F	11	1	2	1	56,798
Sickling Greek	4	C	8	1	2	1	12,385
Sicnee	8	G	4	0	0	0	999
Sid	5	G	9	1	1	1	6,834
Sid Dithers	3	G	10	4	0	2	62,277
Sidcup	2	G	3	0	0	1	3,685
Siddartha	2	C	5	0	2	1	9,628
Side Bet	4	G	1	0	0	0	0
Sideburn (IRE)	7	G	19	2	5	4	8,189
Sidebuster B	3	C	3	1	1	1	31,400
Sidejob	3	G	11	0	1	3	2,611
Sidekick	7	G	12	1	2	0	20,546
Sideline Duchess	8	M	13	2	4	4	31,884
Sideofhappy	3	G	6	0	0	0	2,030
Sidepocketplayer	7	G	3	0	0	0	120
Sidereal	4	G	9	0	2	1	7,015
Sideshow Mel	5	G	9	0	0	1	1,382
Sidestepping	4	F	3	2	0	0	23,870

Horse	Age	Sex	Sts	1st	2d	3d	Won
Sidetrack	2	C	2	0	0	0	600
Sidetrack Bob	4	G	4	0	0	0	190
Sideways	5	M	10	3	1	2	73,508
Sideways Glance	2	G	7	1	1	0	35,030
Sidler	4	G	1	0	0	0	0
Sidney by the C	3	G	3	0	0	1	790
Sidney's Sham	2	G	2	0	0	0	290
Sidoslew	6	G	16	2	2	0	16,334
Siebetime	3	F	3	0	0	0	0
Siembra	5	M	3	0	0	0	270
Sienago	6	M	6	0	0	0	148
Sienna Belle	4	F	5	0	1	0	2,949
Sienna's Honor	3	F	11	2	2	0	16,595
Sienna's Lane	3	F	4	0	0	0	1,820
Sierra Babe	2	F	1	1	0	0	14,795
Sierra Bella	2	F	9	0	3	2	11,040
Sierra Crossing	3	G	5	1	1	0	26,400
Sierra Hotel	3	F	6	0	0	1	6,760
Sierra Kitty	4	F	1	0	0	0	88
Sierra Lady	5	M	7	0	1	1	16,480
Sierra Page	3	F	7	4	0	0	24,470
Sierra Red	4	F	7	0	2	3	3,387
Sierra Sands	3	F	4	0	0	0	105
Sierra Silver	8	G	4	0	0	0	350
Sierra Sky	6	M	1	0	0	0	34
Sierra Slew	3	F	10	1	0	3	7,861
Sierra Sun	4	G	4	1	0	1	4,680
Sierra's Athena	4	F	3	0	0	0	840
Sierra's Sweedie	4	F	4	1	1	1	8,100
Sierra's Victory	3	F	2	0	0	0	0
Sierre Nevada	6	M	8	2	5	0	17,025
Siesmic Sensation	3	G	4	0	0	0	1,723
Siesta Key	5	G	4	0	0	0	428
Siestaville	2	G	5	0	0	2	7,000
Siete de La Suerte	2	C	3	0	0	0	1,200
Siete Slew	5	G	1	0	0	0	400
Sifting Sand	4	G	3	0	0	0	100
Sig Sea	3	G	2	0	0	0	250
Sigalaspam	5	G	5	0	0	0	0
Sigfreto	6	G	10	3	0	1	74,980
Siggie	4	G	2	0	0	0	0
Sigh Lite	7	M	6	0	0	0	0
Sight to Behold	3	F	3	0	0	1	1,536
Sight to Watch	2	F	2	0	0	0	136
Sightseeing (UAE)	2	C	2	0	0	0	344
Sightseek	5	M	7	4	1	0	1,011,350
Sigint	4	C	5	1	0	1	43,160
Sign	4	G	3	1	0	0	2,604
Sign a Prenup	5	G	8	2	2	1	19,459
Sign of Greatness	5	G	11	2	2	0	18,526
Sign of Love	4	G	5	0	1	1	11,260
Sign of the Chimes	3	G	5	0	1	1	3,210
Sign the Ticket	3	G	8	0	0	1	5,980
Signal Caller	3	C	3	0	0	0	730
Signal Dance	3	C	3	0	0	0	1,602
Signal Man	4	G	4	0	0	0	336
Signal Mike	3	F	1	0	0	0	0
Signal Pat	5	G	2	0	0	0	80
Signal Red	5	M	3	0	0	0	535
Signal Ridge	4	G	4	1	1	0	19,137
Signal Starlit	5	M	1	0	0	1	1,860
Signal Tapper	5	M	7	0	0	0	1,067
Signal to Go	3	G	6	1	3	0	9,070
Signal Tower	6	G	4	0	0	0	93
Signal Won	4	G	2	1	0	1	6,600
Signals Diamond	5	G	3	1	0	0	6,489
Signature Mon	3	C	2	0	0	0	0
Signature Sunday (AUS)	4	C	7	1	0	1	28,137
Signature Sweep (AUS)	4	G	1	0	1	0	5,880
Signedingold	3	G	9	2	1	2	21,896
Significant One	3	G	6	1	0	0	6,942
Significant Risk	4	F	1	0	0	0	135
Significantly	3	G	10	1	0	0	6,889
Signing Bonus	3	G	4	0	0	0	320
Signontheline	4	C	10	1	2	2	6,875
Signora Mia	2	F	3	0	1	0	8,002
Signore William	3	C	6	0	1	3	25,050
Signs and Wonders	3	G	3	1	0	0	25,057
Sik	6	H	3	0	0	0	417
Sikorsky	4	C	4	0	0	0	375
Silas	6	G	10	1	2	4	8,726
Silber	3	F	8	0	0	2	10,700
Silecara	2	C	4	1	1	0	9,285
Silencieuse	3	F	1	0	0	0	410
Silent Annie	4	F	19	2	2	2	50,810
Silent Artist	3	G	6	0	0	0	488
Silent Attack	2	G	4	0	0	0	2,234
Silent Bayou	3	F	2	0	0	0	315
Silent Bet	3	F	4	0	0	0	0
Silent Bid	2	C	5	0	3	0	29,860
Silent Bull	3	F	1	1	0	0	14,820
Silent Charge	6	H	2	0	0	1	4,278
Silent Circle	3	F	3	2	0	0	72,240
Silent Clearance	6	G	15	1	1	1	6,340
Silent Comand	5	H	2	0	0	0	94
Silent Counter	7	M	10	2	1	1	12,663
Silent Delight	7	G	5	0	0	0	0
Silent Desert	5	G	10	2	1	0	10,929
Silent Dust	4	G	10	1	1	2	17,479
Silent Ego	5	G	14	1	3	1	9,470
Silent Embrace	4	F	8	0	0	0	1,415
Silent Exploit	2	G	6	1	1	0	20,040
Silent Fawn	3	F	1	0	0	0	90
Silent Fred	5	G	10	4	2	1	105,670
Silent Glory	6	M	2	0	0	0	0
Silent Gold	3	C	9	0	1	2	21,677
Silent Goodbye	5	H	2	0	0	0	0
Silent Hayley	3	F	4	0	0	0	425
Silent Kingdom	3	F	7	2	1	0	35,750
Silent Lane	5	G	2	1	0	0	1,493
Silent Majority	3	F	8	2	1	0	22,381
Silent Misty	5	M	3	0	0	0	0
Silent Moccasins	2	F	3	0	0	0	0
Silent Monarch	4	F	7	1	1	2	12,720
Silent Number	5	M	10	0	0	3	3,755
Silent Oath	4	F	9	1	3	2	56,530
Silent Olimpian	5	M	6	2	1	1	21,655
Silent Picture	3	C	7	2	3	1	78,000
Silent Prey	7	G	18	3	5	1	25,360
Silent Quarry	3	G	2	1	0	0	11,430
Silent Reason	5	M	14	2	4	3	27,356
Silent Reward	5	G	2	0	0	0	70
Silent Ruckus	5	M	8	1	1	0	7,818
Silent Ruler	2	C	3	0	0	0	315
Silent Run	5	G	1	0	0	0	0
Silent Sabina	3	F	4	0	1	0	1,790
Silent Sack	4	G	3	0	0	0	0
Silent Sam	7	H	8	0	0	2	3,415
Silent Sam Sparkle	7	M	1	0	0	0	0
Silent Samurai	3	G	2	1	0	0	946
Silent Scamper	6	G	9	2	4	2	22,148
Silent Scream	5	M	7	1	1	0	11,436
Silent Sea	4	F	1	0	0	0	0
Silent Senorita	3	F	10	1	2	1	15,389
Silent Shark	3	G	4	0	0	0	255
Silent Shoes	5	G	13	2	1	3	17,569
Silent Sighs	3	F	3	2	0	0	317,500
Silent Silver	2	F	8	0	0	1	2,540
Silent Siren	3	F	6	0	1	1	8,972
Silent Snow	3	G	12	3	1	3	41,363
Silent Splender	3	F	14	1	3	2	29,345
Silent Story	2	F	4	0	1	1	6,633
Silent Streaker	8	G	8	0	0	0	528
Silent Stream	7	M	7	0	4	0	41,610
Silent Strength	2	C	1	0	0	0	0
Silent Sun	2	C	2	0	0	0	150
Silent Text	5	G	17	1	3	1	6,502
Silent Thunder	8	G	6	3	1	0	42,650
Silent Treatment	5	M	5	1	0	0	1,748
Silent Type	5	G	5	2	0	0	11,310
Silent Wineo	4	G	5	0	0	0	590
Silent Wing	4	F	3	0	1	0	3,855
Silent Wish	3	F	4	0	0	0	1,195
Silent Wishes	5	M	15	2	2	3	12,803
Silent World	2	C	6	2	0	3	20,280
Silent Zipata	7	G	14	3	4	1	19,200
Silenus	5	G	5	0	0	0	871
Silet	5	M	12	0	3	0	21,110

Horse	Age	Sex	Sts	1st	2d	3d	Won
Silica	4	F	5	0	0	0	540
Silicon Alley	5	G	17	2	4	4	20,216
Silicon City	4	G	2	0	0	0	800
Silk	4	F	1	0	0	0	118
Silk Briefs	2	F	1	0	0	0	140
Silk Dove	4	F	4	0	2	0	3,000
Silk Drawers	5	M	1	0	0	0	78
Silk House	2	C	2	0	1	0	10,020
Silk Market	2	F	2	0	0	1	1,100
Silk Moonlight	4	G	3	0	0	0	0
Silk N Diamonds	4	F	3	0	0	1	1,520
Silk Notebook	3	G	1	0	0	0	75
Silk Purse	3	F	1	0	0	0	0
Silk Splendor	4	G	4	0	1	1	6,400
Silkamean	5	G	10	1	1	1	7,691
Silken Purse	4	F	7	2	0	2	53,410
Silken Victory	3	F	6	0	0	0	2,210
Silken's Eminence	7	G	1	0	0	0	0
Silkie's Diz	4	F	9	0	1	4	4,826
Silks N Roses	6	M	10	1	2	2	29,677
Silkworth	4	F	6	0	0	0	6,448
Silky Bay	2	F	3	2	0	0	32,400
Silky Bill	9	G	7	0	0	1	501
Silky Black	3	F	8	0	0	3	1,680
Silky Goose	6	M	2	0	0	0	477
Silky Kiss	3	C	10	0	2	2	7,892
Silky Longlegs	3	F	8	1	1	1	3,169
Silky Runner	2	C	1	0	0	0	0
Silky Silhouette	3	F	2	0	0	0	0
Silky Summer	4	F	14	2	4	3	58,465
Silky Tresses	3	F	10	1	2	2	76,767
Silky Zarb	7	G	3	0	0	0	3,000
Silkyence	3	F	12	2	0	3	23,686
Silkys Magic	5	M	7	2	2	0	5,590
Silliesaraoflucena	3	F	17	1	0	1	10,671
Sillio Season	6	G	2	0	0	0	100
Silly Bluff	3	G	14	1	3	1	17,340
Silly Cec	4	F	6	1	0	1	5,491
Silly Ghost	5	H	2	0	0	0	40
Silly Girl	6	M	11	2	1	1	20,290
Silly Puddy	2	F	5	0	0	0	968
Silly Savage	2	C	3	0	2	0	5,055
Silly Suzi	3	F	3	0	0	0	195
Silmaril	3	F	7	5	0	0	195,190
Silox	10	G	2	0	0	0	0
Silt	4	F	23	2	4	2	18,093
Silver Ace	7	G	7	0	1	1	3,228
Silver Alarm	9	G	12	5	1	1	39,171
Silver Albertson	4	G	4	2	0	0	35,680
Silver and Glory	2	C	2	0	0	0	0
Silver Artistry	5	G	10	0	0	0	0
Silver Astro	4	G	11	0	2	2	7,472
Silver Attack	6	G	1	0	0	0	160
Silver Award	6	H	18	4	5	4	33,057
Silver Axe	7	G	13	4	2	1	147,194
Silver B. Cash	4	G	10	1	1	0	2,206
Silver Bid	6	G	8	6	1	0	252,520
Silver Bird	3	F	6	0	4	1	165,819
Silver Birdie	2	F	3	1	0	0	6,485
Silver Biscuit	2	G	6	0	1	3	5,375
Silver Blessing	4	G	7	2	1	0	14,530
Silver Blue	3	C	7	1	0	1	31,762
Silver Bolero	3	F	10	0	0	2	5,063
Silver Bon	3	G	4	0	0	1	758
Silver Bonus	3	G	2	0	0	0	210
Silver Bow	6	G	1	0	0	0	28
Silver Box	5	M	7	0	2	1	8,748
Silver Brite	5	G	3	0	0	0	0
Silver Broker	3	G	8	2	0	2	19,620
Silver Bullet Bee	5	G	8	1	0	2	2,246
Silver Bullion	3	F	5	0	0	0	1,029
Silver Buttons	6	M	11	1	2	1	17,096
Silver Candy	3	F	10	0	1	3	13,572
Silver Castle	3	C	4	0	0	0	2,676
Silver Cavalier	4	G	4	1	0	3	13,800
Silver Certificate	3	F	7	0	0	4	5,484
Silver Chad	4	G	8	0	1	0	1,549
Silver Champ	5	M	5	1	1	0	37,120
Silver Chaser	3	F	10	2	1	0	8,816
Silver Chieftress	3	F	1	0	0	0	320
Silver Chip	6	M	11	0	1	2	3,897
Silver Clipper	5	M	6	0	0	1	4,132
Silver Concorde	2	F	3	0	0	0	420
Silver Crest	10	G	14	2	0	7	18,128
Silver Crown	3	F	7	2	1	1	72,174
Silver Cup	6	G	1	0	0	0	0
Silver Daddy	3	C	8	1	0	3	7,973
Silver Dawn	2	F	6	1	2	0	19,680
Silver Deputy Pal	5	M	7	0	3	1	19,035
Silver Diablo	4	G	10	2	0	0	20,000
Silver Diazo	4	F	2	0	1	1	490
Silver Dipper	4	C	1	0	0	0	0
Silver Dollar	3	C	1	1	0	0	14,810
Silver Dollar Day	4	G	8	0	1	2	986
Silver Dollar Girl	4	F	10	1	1	1	26,890
Silver Dollar Lady	5	M	5	0	0	1	1,467
Silver Donn	5	H	8	1	1	2	37,316
Silver Drummer	6	G	12	1	0	2	11,400
Silver Ducats	4	F	10	2	3	0	10,527
Silver Due	4	F	2	0	0	1	1,155
Silver Dynasty	5	G	18	3	0	1	13,708
Silver Eddie	3	G	8	1	1	0	4,001
Silver Edge	2	G	3	0	0	0	1,200
Silver Endeavor	5	G	8	2	0	1	9,246
Silver Fact	4	F	4	0	0	2	2,195
Silver Fillagree	3	F	3	0	0	0	161
Silver Fizz	3	F	3	0	0	1	2,520
Silver Flower	3	G	3	2	0	0	44,160
Silver Forest	2	G	2	0	0	1	1,664
Silver Fortune	3	F	8	2	0	5	39,110
Silver Fury	4	G	5	2	0	1	13,746
Silver Gem	7	G	6	1	0	1	4,932
Silver Genius	2	F	1	0	0	0	250
Silver Gent	3	G	6	0	0	0	0
Silver Ghazi Girl	5	M	3	0	0	0	0
Silver Girl	4	F	4	0	0	1	1,040
Silver Glen Lucy	4	F	8	0	0	0	990
Silver Gloss	3	F	2	2	0	0	13,500
Silver Goddess	3	F	4	0	0	0	1,440
Silver Goldnrobert	5	G	1	0	0	0	0
Silver Goose	8	G	12	0	0	0	482
Silver Greek	5	G	3	0	0	1	600
Silver Gun	4	G	9	3	0	3	99,864
Silver Gypsy	6	M	11	0	1	2	12,800
Silver Halo	3	G	2	0	1	1	3,190
Silver Hawk Lady	3	F	12	1	3	1	64,800
Silver Haze	2	C	7	2	1	1	56,105
Silver Hero	7	M	9	3	3	1	20,034
Silver Hound	6	G	4	0	0	0	208
Silver Hunt	3	F	4	0	0	0	186
Silver I. D.	3	C	1	0	0	0	0
Silver Ikon	5	H	18	3	1	2	14,808
Silver Illusion	5	H	4	0	0	0	0
Silver Impact	2	C	1	0	0	0	400
Silver Impulse	2	F	7	2	2	3	202,662
Silver Indy	3	C	6	0	1	1	18,000
Silver Influence	5	G	10	0	2	2	14,160
Silver Invitation	8	M	9	0	3	2	18,154
Silver Jet	7	G	17	3	2	5	34,532
Silver Kestrel	4	F	4	1	0	1	18,260
Silver Kitty	2	F	12	1	0	1	10,206
Silver Lace	4	F	6	2	1	0	48,150
Silver Lade	4	G	6	0	0	0	406
Silver Lake Road	2	F	5	0	1	0	2,040
Silver Lark	2	F	1	0	0	0	470
Silver Leap	3	G	6	0	1	0	6,980
Silver Lure	3	F	3	0	0	1	4,000
Silver Maestro	6	G	8	0	3	1	8,365
Silver Magic	7	M	17	0	0	2	5,547
Silver Magpie	6	M	4	1	1	1	22,800
Silver Mark	4	G	15	3	1	3	30,076
Silver Marker	3	F	5	1	0	0	7,370
Silver Masque	3	C	6	0	2	1	1,346
Silver Matt	6	G	16	1	3	3	11,602
Silver Mica	4	G	6	0	0	0	200
Silver Midnight	12	G	8	0	3	1	11,251
Silver Mine Ranch	4	C	13	3	1	0	18,420
Silver Minister	3	G	8	3	0	1	130,066

Horse	Age	Sex	Sts	1st	2d	3d	Won
Silver Miracle	3	F	9	0	0	2	6,480
Silver Money	4	G	9	2	1	2	12,579
Silver Moose	2	G	6	1	1	1	29,220
Silver Myth	3	F	4	0	0	0	225
Silver n' Irish	5	G	12	0	0	0	1,068
Silver Niner	4	F	7	0	0	0	2,520
Silver Nitric	4	G	4	0	0	0	180
Silver On Silver	8	G	10	0	3	0	9,223
Silver One	3	G	11	0	2	1	11,814
Silver Pact	7	G	8	0	0	0	378
Silver Passage	3	F	6	0	0	1	2,045
Silver Past	3	G	8	3	1	0	63,620
Silver Patriarch	6	G	6	1	0	0	16,368
Silver Peagus	4	G	13	3	1	3	39,974
Silver Peak	2	C	1	0	0	0	0
Silver Performer	4	C	4	0	1	0	5,000
Silver Phone	5	G	10	3	2	1	59,800
Silver Pines	5	H	11	1	1	1	5,652
Silver Pistol	2	C	1	0	0	0	0
Silver Pit	4	C	6	0	0	1	1,746
Silver Plata	2	F	2	1	0	0	23,550
Silver Plated	3	F	15	3	1	2	23,595
Silver Play	3	G	4	0	0	0	1,788
Silver Prince	7	G	2	0	0	1	605
Silver Rapt	3	G	13	2	1	3	53,945
Silver Request	5	M	14	0	5	2	7,286
Silver Review	5	M	13	0	4	4	9,664
Silver Riddle	5	M	2	0	0	0	198
Silver Rings	11	G	4	2	0	1	9,438
Silver Rolls	6	H	3	0	0	0	288
Silver Roses	2	F	4	0	0	0	1,317
Silver Ruckus	5	M	9	1	1	1	12,994
Silver Rush	3	F	1	0	0	0	230
Silver Sabin	2	F	4	0	0	2	1,965
Silver Saintry	3	F	9	0	2	0	2,170
Silver Sancat	3	F	6	1	2	0	15,190
Silver Sassy	2	F	2	0	2	0	4,315
Silver Satin Sash	3	F	12	1	3	2	18,815
Silver Scamp	6	G	14	2	3	4	14,782
Silver Scholar	3	F	9	1	1	0	15,625
Silver Scooter	3	G	2	0	0	0	0
Silver Screen Girl	6	M	3	0	0	1	2,782
Silver Screen Hero	3	G	6	1	0	1	16,344
Silver Sense	2	C	1	0	0	0	106
Silver Sequins	6	M	1	0	0	0	0
Silver Share	2	F	1	0	0	1	1,050
Silver Shield	4	G	4	0	0	0	2,840
Silver Shine	5	M	13	2	1	4	29,550
Silver Signature	4	G	1	0	0	0	0
Silver Silence	6	M	6	2	0	0	20,239
Silver Silk	4	F	1	0	0	0	0
Silver Singer	4	F	3	0	1	0	6,900
Silver Skater	4	G	7	1	0	0	4,484
Silver Skip	4	F	6	1	4	0	9,068
Silver Sky	6	G	10	4	2	0	29,593
Silver Sliver	9	M	7	0	0	0	1,391
Silver Snow	4	F	5	1	0	0	12,684
Silver Sonic	2	F	2	0	0	0	1,230
Silver Sonnet	5	M	2	0	0	0	1,100
Silver Soul	3	C	2	0	0	0	0
Silver Spear	6	H	13	1	4	3	60,635
Silver Spectre	3	F	5	1	1	1	25,377
Silver Spoon (NZ)	9	G	2	0	0	0	775
Silver Spoon Pete	5	G	5	0	0	0	225
Silver Spring Lane	3	F	6	0	0	0	189
Silver Squire	4	C	5	0	0	1	6,180
Silver Stage	2	F	6	2	0	1	39,060
Silver Step Lass	3	F	8	1	1	0	7,555
Silver Strand	3	F	6	1	1	0	7,793
Silver Strategy	4	G	3	0	0	0	0
Silver Strip	3	G	2	1	0	0	17,700
Silver Suds	5	H	1	0	0	0	410
Silver Sunset	6	G	8	1	1	1	5,794
Silver Swing	4	F	4	1	0	0	2,760
Silver Swinger	9	G	3	1	0	0	10,277
Silver Ta Gold	8	G	17	1	0	2	6,424
Silver Talon	4	G	4	0	0	0	433
Silver Things	3	F	5	0	0	0	60
Silver Thunder	3	G	4	1	1	1	13,430
Silver Ticket	3	G	6	2	1	2	229,100
Silver Tike	5	H	4	0	0	2	901
Silver Toes	4	F	11	0	1	0	4,713
Silver Token	4	F	5	1	0	0	15,945
Silver Touch	5	M	3	0	0	0	300
Silver Town	5	G	18	2	4	3	14,837
Silver Traffic	4	C	5	3	0	1	76,547
Silver Train	2	C	4	1	2	0	62,890
Silver Tree	4	C	10	3	2	2	328,060
Silver Tricon	5	M	6	0	1	1	8,175
Silver Trooper	9	G	5	0	0	0	121
Silver Trophy	7	H	3	0	0	0	500
Silver Tsunami	4	G	6	1	0	1	12,248
Silver Valay	6	G	6	1	0	1	5,092
Silver Vee	4	G	8	0	0	0	315
Silver Vessel	4	F	6	0	1	1	3,100
Silver Vista	2	C	5	1	2	0	32,030
Silver Wagon	3	C	3	0	1	1	50,500
Silver Wand	2	F	2	1	0	0	15,570
Silver Wapiti	3	G	4	1	1	1	5,443
Silver Warrant	3	C	3	1	0	2	30,240
Silver Wench	3	F	10	2	2	1	71,723
Silver Wheat	3	C	11	3	1	0	60,455
Silver Who	3	G	9	2	2	1	42,102
Silver Wine Punch	3	F	5	0	0	0	115
Silver Zipper	7	H	8	2	2	2	82,688
Silver Zone	5	M	2	0	0	0	0
Silverado Hit	3	F	12	3	0	0	15,048
Silverado Ridge	6	G	11	0	2	0	7,901
Silverado Trail	2	C	3	1	1	1	43,445
Silverbulletrocket	2	C	4	0	0	0	617
Silvercity Lady	3	F	9	2	2	1	45,719
Silverella Charm	9	M	3	0	0	0	720
Silverfeet	4	F	1	0	0	0	0
Silverfish	4	F	1	0	0	0	75
Silverfoot	4	G	9	4	0	1	177,593
Silverlado	3	F	3	0	0	0	900
Silverlake Special	3	G	1	0	0	0	130
Silvermin	4	G	14	2	3	1	20,435
Silversandsoftime	3	G	14	3	2	2	72,760
Silverspeed	6	M	7	1	1	0	6,480
Silvertail Road	6	G	10	2	1	2	4,127
Silvertipkiller	3	G	10	1	0	1	7,031
Silverton Bay	5	M	12	3	1	1	40,843
Silvertongue Fox	6	G	5	1	1	2	10,945
Silvertri	5	G	1	0	0	0	135
Silverturfcloud	3	G	1	0	0	0	0
Silveruler	2	F	2	0	0	0	360
Silverup	2	F	2	1	0	1	16,100
Silverwilldo	3	F	7	1	1	1	14,330
Silverwood	4	G	11	0	0	2	2,649
Silvery Crown	3	F	11	3	0	1	41,630
Silvery Mamoon	4	F	2	0	0	0	136
Silverzaam	3	G	5	0	0	0	1,077
Silvie's War	6	G	7	1	0	2	7,330
Silview	4	F	3	1	0	1	13,351
Sim Sam	3	F	8	0	3	0	6,142
Simacher	4	F	15	3	1	2	20,649
Simbad	4	G	15	2	0	5	17,790
Simcha	5	M	6	2	0	1	15,733
Simeon (GB)	5	H	7	0	1	1	35,967
Simi Go Easy	2	G	1	0	0	0	0
Simi Tango	2	F	2	0	0	0	113
Simidriller	2	C	1	0	0	0	0
Similkameen Brew	2	F	1	0	0	0	0
Similkameen Maan	4	G	15	2	3	1	22,922
Simma Down Now	3	G	4	0	0	1	817
Simmer	8	G	5	1	1	1	27,920
Simmer Down Slew	4	G	7	0	0	0	210
Simmerdown Now	4	F	11	1	3	1	3,653
Simmerette	3	F	3	0	0	0	615
Simon B Quick	3	C	2	0	0	0	184
Simon Slew	5	M	14	1	1	0	33,367
Simonas (IRE)	5	G	8	3	1	0	479,639
Simone Symphony	5	M	7	1	0	0	4,244
Simon's Birch	5	G	3	0	0	0	1,460
Simony	7	G	1	0	0	0	0
Simpatico	4	G	11	1	2	0	7,559
Simple Affair	3	F	9	0	1	2	12,048

Horse	Age	Sex	Sts	1st	2d	3d	Won
Simple Billie	3	C	3	0	0	0	186
Simple Exchange (IRE)	3	C	4	1	0	0	173,673
Simple Faith	2	C	2	0	0	0	0
Simple Forest	6	G	2	0	0	0	225
Simple Man	3	G	3	0	0	0	0
Simple Pic	6	H	14	2	0	2	12,029
Simple Search	4	G	3	0	0	0	0
Simple Touch	5	G	4	0	0	0	0
Simple Victory	3	G	3	0	0	0	150
Simply a Jet	5	M	12	1	2	0	5,582
Simply Accounting	2	F	2	1	0	0	6,199
Simply Again	2	F	5	0	3	0	53,558
Simply Aly	5	G	7	0	0	1	1,304
Simply Awesome	3	G	7	4	1	1	34,340
Simply Basic	3	F	11	1	0	2	5,424
Simply Because	2	F	1	0	0	0	400
Simply Brilliant	3	F	5	2	0	2	58,370
Simply Caldo	12	G	8	1	0	2	4,202
Simply Class	4	F	10	1	1	3	10,464
Simply Dana	3	F	1	0	0	1	4,100
Simply Fabulous	3	G	7	0	0	0	316
Simply Fancy	3	F	14	2	2	3	43,863
Simply Fred	3	G	3	0	0	0	0
Simply Golden	4	G	10	0	0	0	900
Simply Jolie	3	F	13	2	2	1	60,390
Simply Lovely	2	F	5	3	1	0	288,240
Simply Perfect	3	F	15	2	1	7	47,860
Simply Precious	5	M	8	1	2	0	60,884
Simply Regal	3	G	8	2	0	3	19,095
Simply Santa Fe	4	F	7	1	1	1	26,400
Simply Sensational	3	F	4	0	1	0	8,618
Simply Simon	3	C	4	0	0	0	1,335
Simply Sir	6	G	17	4	2	0	24,635
Simply Spiritual	2	G	2	0	0	0	800
Simply Splashing	8	M	10	2	1	1	29,226
Simply Super	2	C	6	1	0	1	18,510
Simply Superior	3	F	9	0	1	0	10,200
Simply Swiss	4	F	2	0	0	1	1,870
Simply Synful	3	F	1	0	0	0	235
Simply Tricky	4	F	14	2	0	2	10,220
Simply Victorious	3	F	17	4	6	3	41,115
Simplysammy	6	G	12	3	0	3	34,044
Simsimmer	6	M	12	0	0	0	0
Sin City Slew	3	F	9	3	0	2	23,497
Sin Killer	4	G	1	0	0	0	40
Sin 'n Grin	6	G	4	0	0	0	320
Sin Wagon	4	G	12	0	0	0	1,007
Sinaloa	4	G	3	0	0	1	2,278
Sincera	3	F	4	0	1	1	13,779
Sincere Man	2	C	2	0	0	0	395
Sincere Sensation	2	F	3	0	0	0	1,135
Sinclair	3	C	5	0	0	3	9,427
Sindbad	3	G	10	3	1	0	21,067
Sindbad the Sailor	6	G	12	3	7	1	62,688
Sindi's Success	3	F	11	4	3	2	53,417
Sine Die	5	G	12	0	3	1	21,363
Sinfonia	3	F	1	0	0	0	220
Sinful Lady	4	F	1	0	0	0	70
Sinful Obsession	3	F	1	0	0	0	0
Sinful Pleasures	7	M	4	0	0	0	2,202
Sinful Storms	5	G	5	0	0	0	1,635
Sinfulindulgence	4	F	3	0	0	1	1,045
Sing A'cord	6	M	20	0	3	2	5,764
Sing D Song	4	G	9	1	1	0	8,500
Sing Dorthy D	3	F	2	0	0	0	270
Sing High Sing Low	4	F	8	1	1	0	3,802
Sing Jubilee	7	M	5	0	2	0	5,358
Sing Me Back Home	6	G	10	1	4	1	111,521
Sing Me No Blues	2	C	1	0	0	0	0
Sing N Zing	5	G	17	0	5	4	8,874
Sing Out	4	G	10	0	0	1	3,570
Sing Softly	5	M	11	3	1	1	59,849
Sing to the Moon	3	F	10	1	1	1	11,347
Sing to the Sky	2	F	2	0	0	1	3,740
Sing Your Song	3	F	1	0	0	0	132
Singaballad	3	F	13	2	4	1	18,735
Singapore Charley	6	M	4	0	0	0	733
Singapore Deputy	4	G	10	2	0	3	26,858
Singapore Sam	2	G	3	1	0	1	9,670

Horse	Age	Sex	Sts	1st	2d	3d	Won
Singasongforme	4	G	10	1	0	2	18,215
Singgmeeasong	3	G	10	1	2	2	20,000
Singin At the Gate	3	F	16	0	6	3	22,710
Singin Devil	2	G	5	1	2	1	44,627
Singin N D Shower	9	G	19	1	2	4	16,330
Singing Dixie	5	M	1	0	0	0	0
Singing Flower	3	F	4	0	0	0	210
Singing Girl	3	F	1	1	0	0	6,840
Singing Hills	7	G	8	0	1	0	670
Singing Laur	3	F	14	1	0	3	9,600
Singing Man	7	G	7	1	1	0	7,963
Singing Memo	3	G	2	0	0	1	2,200
Singing Sam	7	G	8	0	1	1	5,652
Singing Siren	2	F	5	0	1	0	4,650
Singing Soldier	4	C	4	1	1	0	6,785
Singing Swiss	4	F	13	0	2	1	5,281
Singing Sword	5	M	5	2	1	0	20,400
Singit	3	F	12	2	5	1	72,704
Singlbarrelshotgun	3	G	12	1	0	4	28,465
Single Again	3	F	5	0	4	0	8,918
Single Charm	5	M	3	0	3	0	13,040
Single Disco	3	F	7	0	2	1	2,894
Single Don	11	G	2	0	0	0	270
Single Edge	4	G	6	2	2	0	13,473
Single Factor	3	F	9	2	2	0	10,705
Single File	3	G	10	2	2	1	28,789
Single Market	2	F	1	0	0	0	880
Single Mon	2	C	2	0	0	0	290
Single Prospect	5	M	11	1	4	0	8,311
Single Rainbow	5	H	14	2	4	3	21,000
Single Storm	3	F	2	0	0	0	110
Single Stroke	5	G	3	0	0	1	5,100
Single Track	6	G	5	0	1	1	2,197
Single Woman	3	F	8	1	1	1	26,950
Singles Last Kiss	4	G	1	0	0	0	65
Singletary	4	C	6	3	2	1	1,192,910
Singleton	6	G	4	1	0	0	8,202
Singsweetgil	5	H	4	0	0	0	0
Sinister G	3	C	8	2	1	0	342,466
Sinister Lady	3	F	4	0	2	0	18,240
Sink the Bismark	6	G	15	3	2	2	12,847
Sinking Feeling	4	F	9	1	2	5	13,280
Sinn Free	5	M	12	0	1	1	4,842
Sinnabon	2	F	1	0	0	0	170
Sinner's a Winner	4	F	10	0	1	0	3,420
Sinners Accepted	3	F	5	2	0	1	11,004
Sinners N Saints	3	C	2	0	0	0	1,436
Sinoso Baby	3	C	6	1	1	1	4,300
Sins and Riches	6	G	11	5	0	1	47,360
Sins of My Youth	8	G	6	0	0	0	154
Sintastic	3	G	13	2	2	1	20,900
Sion Hill	4	G	11	2	1	1	20,074
Sione	3	F	1	0	0	0	210
Sionna	3	F	7	1	1	0	15,720
Siora	4	F	9	1	0	0	3,174
Sioux	7	G	3	0	0	1	320
Sioux Beauty	3	F	5	1	2	0	20,650
Sioux City Sue	5	G	7	0	0	1	767
Sioux D' Or	7	H	1	0	0	0	0
Sioux Man	2	G	5	0	0	0	0
Sioux Rain Dance	4	F	1	0	0	0	57
Siouxbquick	3	F	6	1	1	1	8,543
Siouxpercookie	3	F	5	0	0	0	280
Sip One for Mom	2	F	6	1	2	1	52,600
Sip Sip	3	F	1	0	0	0	700
Sipas	4	F	11	0	0	1	876
Siphon City	2	C	2	1	0	1	35,970
Siphon Melody	2	F	1	0	0	0	2,580
Siphon Our Money	4	G	10	2	1	2	14,265
Siphon Up	4	G	4	0	0	0	1,600
Siphonal	3	F	4	0	1	0	8,005
Siphonette	3	F	12	1	1	1	30,900
Siphonizer	3	C	1	1	0	0	32,375
Siphonophora	3	F	1	0	0	0	0
Siphon's Charm	2	F	1	0	0	0	0
Siphon's Fire	4	G	10	0	0	1	4,716
Siphon's Glory	4	G	9	1	2	4	32,417
Siphon's Miss	2	F	5	0	0	0	1,065
Siphon's Star	3	G	4	0	1	0	3,800

Horse	Age	Sex	Sts	1st	2d	3d	Won
Sippin' Devil	4	F	9	1	1	1	12,151
Sippin T.	6	M	3	0	1	1	1,405
Sippy Gumbo	4	G	1	0	0	1	370
Sir Alec	2	C	1	0	0	0	184
Sir Alecron	2	C	3	0	0	0	810
Sir Alfred	6	H	12	1	2	2	17,299
Sir Allen	3	G	14	0	4	5	11,219
Sir Aly	5	G	8	1	1	3	16,471
Sir Angel	4	G	11	0	0	0	1,060
Sir Apwith Pride	3	G	8	1	0	1	5,727
Sir Augustus	3	G	7	0	1	0	2,525
Sir Austin	5	G	8	3	0	0	27,926
Sir Bay Sky	5	H	14	1	1	3	3,508
Sir Blitz	5	G	8	1	1	2	62,530
Sir Bovary	6	G	4	0	1	1	524
Sir Brian's Sword	6	G	1	0	0	1	11,000
Sir Bunny	2	C	2	1	1	0	8,490
Sir Caetano	3	G	1	0	0	0	300
Sir Cassanova	5	G	16	1	3	4	13,023
Sir Cat's Boy	3	C	4	1	1	1	8,252
Sir Ceasar	4	G	6	0	2	1	3,389
Sir Chancellor	7	G	1	0	0	0	63
Sir Cherokee	4	C	8	2	0	2	199,986
Sir Chip	2	C	2	0	0	0	145
Sir Crafty	3	G	7	0	0	1	862
Sir Creek	3	G	15	3	2	2	26,804
Sir Crypto	4	G	11	1	1	0	11,085
Sir Dayjur	4	G	14	4	3	1	48,725
Sir Debon Aire	7	G	5	1	1	1	11,914
Sir Dorset	9	G	11	3	1	2	50,160
Sir E F	7	G	5	0	0	0	1,275
Sir Ebony Knight	11	G	1	0	0	0	61
Sir Echo	13	G	7	0	1	3	22,283
Sir Elite	4	G	18	2	1	7	33,789
Sir Enchantment	9	G	13	0	2	1	4,162
Sir Excavator	3	G	4	1	1	1	14,187
Sir Fleet	5	G	7	0	0	0	393
Sir Forest	3	G	11	0	0	3	3,721
Sir Francis	4	C	3	1	0	0	3,324
Sir Gallahan	2	C	3	0	1	0	2,989
Sir Gallant	2	G	7	3	1	0	38,080
Sir Gavin	4	G	3	1	0	0	8,635
Sir Gawain	4	G	14	1	4	1	8,281
Sir George Prize	2	G	1	0	0	0	0
Sir Godfrey	3	C	5	0	0	0	570
Sir Golden	3	G	12	0	2	2	3,437
Sir Gregory	2	C	1	0	0	0	0
Sir Gulch	3	C	10	0	1	1	14,605
Sir Habit	2	C	1	0	0	0	0
Sir Hadley	7	H	4	0	1	0	3,549
Sir Halory	2	C	1	0	0	0	2,250
Sir Hercules	3	C	3	0	0	0	137
Sir Hillard Lewis	9	G	12	2	1	0	18,120
Sir Honey	7	G	10	0	2	0	3,180
Sir Howard	5	G	5	1	0	0	5,130
Sir Howard (AUS)	8	G	9	0	3	0	19,950
Sir Hurricane	5	G	2	0	0	0	135
Sir Instigator	3	G	3	0	0	0	0
Sir Itron	3	C	12	0	0	2	5,435
Sir Ivar's Invader	4	F	7	0	0	0	645
Sir Ivor's Comet	8	G	11	0	0	0	1,972
Sir Jackie	2	G	7	2	4	0	32,175
Sir James Cognac	5	G	2	0	0	0	748
Sir Jay	5	G	11	1	0	1	5,485
Sir Jimmy Lee	3	G	3	0	0	0	715
Sir Joe Kelly	6	G	16	1	0	0	18,975
Sir Johnny La B	3	G	8	1	0	2	9,460
Sir Josh	3	G	1	0	0	0	0
Sir Kix Alot	6	G	2	1	0	0	1,650
Sir Knight Shot	2	G	5	0	1	1	7,224
Sir Kokand	2	G	4	0	2	0	6,760
Sir Laff Alot	2	C	7	2	1	1	79,988
Sir Larry	3	G	9	1	3	2	10,023
Sir Lebold	3	G	6	0	0	1	1,836
Sir Leon's Dr.	5	H	9	0	0	1	3,238
Sir Libra	3	C	9	2	1	1	32,340
Sir Long Legs	3	C	8	2	2	2	11,702
Sir Louie	3	C	1	0	0	0	190
Sir Magic	6	H	2	0	0	0	0
Sir Malcolm	4	C	3	0	0	0	84
Sir Manfred	4	G	19	0	0	2	5,449
Sir Marlin	3	G	9	1	0	1	6,015
Sir Marvin	4	G	14	1	1	1	7,656
Sir Maskalot	6	G	14	2	5	5	41,495
Sir Maximus	2	C	1	0	0	1	1,485
Sir Miller	4	G	5	1	0	0	2,840
Sir Mombo	3	G	11	3	2	1	24,312
Sir Morgan	5	G	12	5	0	2	24,161
Sir Neptune	4	G	13	1	4	2	20,039
Sir Norman	5	H	5	0	0	0	125
Sir Nuke	3	G	2	0	0	0	0
Sir Oscar	3	C	5	0	0	0	12,600
Sir Otter	3	C	2	0	1	0	3,600
Sir Perfection	2	G	2	0	0	0	220
Sir Phil	5	G	11	1	1	2	5,882
Sir Prado	6	G	10	1	0	0	5,687
Sir Pucker	7	G	7	1	1	1	17,200
Sir Purdue	7	G	4	0	0	0	500
Sir Pyy	2	C	5	0	1	0	8,184
Sir Radar	7	G	6	1	3	2	8,180
Sir Ran Rap	2	C	2	0	0	0	991
Sir Ray	4	C	10	2	0	0	34,907
Sir Real	2	G	1	0	0	0	225
Sir Richards' Gold	3	G	1	0	0	0	0
Sir Rocky	3	G	2	0	2	0	5,300
Sir Rocky Slew	7	G	3	0	0	0	70
Sir Romeo	2	C	2	0	1	1	7,360
Sir Royale	4	C	7	0	1	0	3,050
Sir Royce	3	G	6	0	0	0	531
Sir Rubi	4	G	6	1	2	0	5,274
Sir Runsalot	3	G	4	0	0	0	246
Sir Sashay	4	G	3	0	0	2	14,990
Sir Sauceboat	4	C	8	0	1	1	2,815
Sir Seibert	7	G	14	1	0	1	4,873
Sir Shackleton	3	C	9	4	1	1	566,105
Sir Sin	3	G	3	1	1	0	9,110
Sir Siphon	3	C	10	0	4	4	21,070
Sir Slew	7	H	3	0	1	0	2,366
Sir Smart Lee	3	C	1	0	0	0	1,680
Sir Socrates	4	C	16	1	4	1	14,915
Sir Spike	2	C	4	0	2	1	7,795
Sir Spunky	7	G	6	0	0	0	416
Sir Stack	3	G	2	0	0	1	2,775
Sir Sunrise	3	G	4	0	0	0	550
Sir Swervalot	2	C	2	1	0	0	11,650
Sir Tapper	4	G	8	0	0	0	1,266
Sir Tiff	9	G	1	0	0	0	0
Sir Tificate	6	G	5	1	0	1	3,220
Sir Toasty	2	G	1	0	0	0	300
Sir Top	4	G	9	1	2	2	13,856
Sir Totem	2	C	5	0	0	1	1,690
Sir Traver	4	G	14	4	3	2	56,501
Sir Tricky	3	G	4	1	0	1	19,376
Sir Tulle T.	5	G	6	0	0	0	194
Sir Twister Dale	6	G	9	2	3	1	13,309
Sir Tyler T.	3	C	14	1	1	3	33,560
Sir Vincent	3	G	12	2	3	0	13,931
Sir Wagga Wagga	4	G	1	0	0	0	0
Sir Walsh	7	G	11	2	1	2	7,330
Sir Walter Rahy	4	C	4	2	0	1	61,408
Sir Walter Scott	3	C	5	0	0	0	0
Sir Warrickonbasil	4	G	8	0	0	1	3,842
Sir Way	5	G	13	3	2	2	23,410
Sir West	6	H	2	0	0	0	900
Sir Whinesalot	5	G	15	2	1	7	21,647
Sir William D.	3	C	1	0	0	0	0
Sir Willie	7	G	2	0	0	0	185
Sir Winsome	2	G	1	0	0	0	0
Sir Winzalot	2	G	2	1	0	0	15,600
Siracoque	4	F	12	3	1	0	38,620
Sirand	2	C	5	1	0	0	9,420
Sircatour	4	C	2	0	0	1	8,670
Sircharlesschnabel	4	C	7	1	0	1	33,100
Siren Lure	3	G	4	2	0	0	46,820
Siren Song	7	M	1	0	0	0	550
Siren Star	5	M	15	1	4	3	22,670
Sirena Sweet	8	M	2	0	0	0	0
Sirgun	4	G	11	0	2	1	7,963

Horse	Age	Sex	Sts	1st	2d	3d	Won
Sirocos	7	G	11	4	1	1	27,486
Sirona Gold	4	F	8	2	2	0	74,503
Sirona's Song	3	F	2	0	0	0	181
Sirpa	6	H	6	1	1	0	28,905
Sirrom Sirrom	7	M	9	1	0	0	5,620
Sirtan Code	7	G	4	0	0	1	1,500
Sirto	7	G	13	0	1	3	4,245
Sirwilliamwallace	4	G	14	1	1	6	23,654
Sis City	2	F	7	3	0	2	282,980
Sis Coin	2	F	4	1	1	0	10,400
Sis Go Kid	5	M	4	2	0	1	37,417
Sis See Play	3	F	5	0	0	0	178
Sisbug	6	M	1	0	0	0	0
Siskins	7	M	9	2	1	1	12,326
Sis's Honor	5	G	4	0	0	0	895
Sis's Knight Out	6	M	6	1	1	0	1,338
Sissay	3	F	12	2	2	3	26,656
Sissta Suzzie	5	M	1	0	0	0	675
Sissy Belle	5	M	7	0	2	2	8,008
Sissy Goblin	4	F	8	1	0	0	5,334
Sissy Jo	4	F	5	0	0	0	672
Sissy La La	4	F	2	0	0	0	0
Sissy's Devil	3	F	7	1	0	0	6,588
Sissy's Gal	6	M	9	0	0	1	1,765
Sissy's Hope	3	F	1	0	0	0	0
Sister Adiba	7	M	4	0	1	0	4,707
Sister Amorica	3	F	6	0	0	1	1,680
Sister Anet	2	F	3	1	0	0	6,420
Sister Babe	3	F	4	1	0	1	18,460
Sister Bay	2	F	1	0	0	1	4,700
Sister Bolton	4	F	5	0	1	0	2,557
Sister Brass	6	M	9	0	1	1	9,718
Sister Breeze	5	M	11	2	1	2	14,830
Sister Buck	2	F	1	0	0	0	0
Sister Carolina	3	F	9	1	0	1	20,850
Sister Char	3	F	3	0	0	0	780
Sister Concern	2	F	3	0	0	0	6,200
Sister Disco	2	F	3	1	0	0	6,360
Sister Dixie	3	F	5	0	0	2	2,420
Sister Flag	3	F	6	1	2	1	15,900
Sister Girl Blues	5	M	2	0	0	1	10,760
Sister Hadif	2	F	1	0	0	0	0
Sister Halo	4	F	12	0	0	1	1,890
Sister I'm a Poet	2	F	1	0	0	0	1,230
Sister Isabel	3	F	11	1	2	0	6,671
Sister Jackson	2	F	1	0	0	0	140
Sister Jill	2	F	2	0	0	0	1,200
Sister Keelson	2	F	3	0	0	1	2,455
Sister Lisa	3	F	17	0	1	2	7,589
Sister Mary Alice	4	F	4	0	0	0	0
Sister Mary Hugh	5	M	14	0	5	0	29,635
Sister Ponche	5	M	7	5	0	0	41,000
Sister Rosie	5	M	9	1	2	1	19,170
Sister Shark	2	F	2	0	0	0	800
Sister Soup	3	F	1	0	0	1	1,650
Sister Sox	3	F	4	0	0	0	500
Sister Star	3	F	4	2	1	0	183,710
Sister Strut	5	M	15	1	1	3	24,157
Sister Suzie Slew	4	F	14	2	1	5	18,675
Sister Swank	3	F	9	2	2	3	219,679
Sister Velma	3	F	6	1	2	1	8,820
Sister Vitalis	8	M	1	0	0	0	50
Sister Whiz	3	F	7	1	0	0	10,307
Sisterbull	9	M	9	0	1	1	2,080
Sisters Blackhawk	7	M	15	1	0	0	5,348
Sisters Catanna	3	F	1	0	0	0	0
Sisters Mister	3	G	1	0	0	0	78
Sister's Word	6	G	12	0	0	0	618
Sistine's Hope	3	F	6	0	0	2	5,306
Sisti's Pride	3	F	4	0	0	0	6,362
Sisty Anne	5	M	12	2	2	4	64,865
Sisu Ridge	6	M	10	0	0	0	428
Sisu Sarah	2	F	1	0	0	0	79
Siswasaflyer	4	F	1	0	0	0	0
Sit On Sitonya	5	M	10	1	2	1	12,170
Sita Ram	4	F	17	2	2	4	17,227
Sita's Surprise	4	G	13	1	1	2	12,560
Sitcom	4	C	3	0	0	1	5,890
Site Alarm	3	G	13	2	1	5	21,490
Sitkasam	4	G	4	0	0	0	795
Sittinonacloud	6	H	7	1	2	0	4,225
Siward	6	G	6	2	1	0	10,475
Siwel	2	F	2	0	1	1	5,140
Six Am	6	H	7	3	1	1	15,498
Six Away	4	F	6	1	2	0	10,600
Six Eights	3	G	3	0	0	1	5,358
Six G's	5	G	4	2	0	0	5,501
Six Gun	2	G	1	0	0	0	112
Six Gun Kelly	7	G	2	0	0	0	282
Six Halos	4	F	2	1	0	0	6,900
Six Hitter	5	G	8	1	1	0	6,693
Six Hour Wait	3	F	11	1	0	4	7,045
Six Hundred	4	F	12	1	3	3	6,260
Six Inch Heels	6	M	5	0	1	1	1,275
Six Jiggles	4	F	11	1	3	1	97,829
Six Meadows	3	F	3	0	0	0	2,770
Six Moon Dance	3	F	2	0	0	0	0
Six Numbers	4	C	5	0	0	0	7,345
Six Pack High	2	C	3	0	1	0	3,163
Six Pack Mike	6	H	8	1	1	1	4,705
Six Pack Sally	4	F	3	0	0	1	1,884
Six Penny Lane	5	G	3	1	0	1	4,763
Six Perfections (FR)	4	F	4	0	2	1	359,635
Six Picker Paul	2	G	5	0	0	1	4,380
Six Red Rubys	6	M	15	1	0	3	8,799
Six Ribbons	3	F	12	2	2	1	17,065
Six Rings	3	F	4	1	0	0	6,082
Six Sexy Sisters	3	F	1	0	0	0	1,428
Six Straight Trics	7	M	14	2	5	2	40,190
Six Strings Down	5	M	3	1	2	0	3,630
Six Trix	4	C	20	2	1	4	19,794
Six Winged Seraph	3	F	3	0	0	0	352
Sixbitfurcliff	3	G	7	0	2	1	3,280
Sixers Fan	3	F	8	1	3	4	68,920
Sixkiller	6	G	5	1	0	0	11,900
Sixpack Goldluster	2	F	4	0	0	0	228
Sixpackinthesand	2	F	1	0	0	0	0
Sixteen Deputies	6	M	2	0	0	0	0
Sixteentwenty	4	G	8	2	1	1	11,823
Sixth Formal	5	G	14	2	2	0	19,987
Sixth Jeneration	3	C	5	1	1	1	13,060
Sixthirtyjoe	6	G	12	4	1	3	106,476
Sixty Deelites	2	G	4	0	0	0	3,840
Sixty Minute Man	6	G	8	1	0	0	7,584
Sixty of North	5	G	9	0	0	0	506
Sixty Sixty	3	C	3	1	0	1	18,460
Sixty Stars	6	G	5	0	0	0	1,275
Sixty Two Lincoln	5	G	17	3	3	2	27,753
Size Matters	5	G	10	5	2	0	104,258
Sizzle'n' Sauce	4	F	8	0	0	0	1,940
Sizzlin Cisco	6	G	7	1	1	1	1,750
Sizzlin Hot Summer	4	G	8	3	0	2	16,063
Sizzlin Swiss	2	G	2	1	0	0	12,400
Sizzling	6	G	2	0	0	1	2,480
Sizzling Dancer	3	G	10	1	1	1	17,030
Sizzling Lady	3	F	2	2	0	0	27,930
Skagway	2	C	1	0	0	0	180
Skaha Scooter	6	G	6	1	1	1	1,940
Skake Em	6	G	16	2	3	1	38,521
Skalite	5	G	14	1	2	3	6,943
Skally Wag	3	F	2	0	0	0	335
Skary Karen	3	F	8	4	1	0	18,408
Skate Away	5	G	6	1	3	1	170,400
Skate Out	3	F	9	2	1	1	8,019
Skater Dude	5	G	7	0	1	0	748
Skating Katie	2	F	2	0	1	0	3,533
Skattle	4	F	1	0	0	0	130
Skava	5	M	4	0	0	0	305
Skedaddle Fast	4	F	1	0	0	0	160
Skeeman	6	G	9	2	1	2	41,898
Skeemo	4	F	1	0	0	0	300
Skeet	4	C	3	2	0	0	67,500
Skeeter Hawk Annie	5	M	5	1	1	0	9,290
Skeeterbuzz	4	G	9	0	3	1	4,066
Skeeter's Inkling	5	M	1	0	0	0	0
Skeetersbunny	3	F	1	0	0	0	84
Skeete's Bay	7	G	16	1	2	1	11,571
Skeptical Judge	5	H	12	2	2	4	16,684

Horse	Age	Sex	Sts	1st	2d	3d	Won
Sketch (IRE)	3	F	1	0	0	0	400
Ski Bowl	5	G	6	0	0	1	3,115
Ski Bum	7	G	8	2	0	1	39,025
Ski Hero	5	G	7	0	0	4	4,885
Ski Honey	2	F	2	0	0	1	3,484
Ski Lodge	3	C	4	0	0	2	5,290
Ski Onheir	3	C	2	1	0	0	6,600
Ski the Bugaboos	5	G	11	1	0	2	6,418
Ski Trickery	3	F	2	0	0	0	400
Skiatook	3	F	2	1	0	0	3,736
Skibiscuit	3	G	5	1	0	1	17,660
Skiddy	4	F	3	0	0	0	180
Skiding	4	C	7	1	1	0	42,855
Skidsteer	7	M	4	0	0	0	291
Skier	4	C	1	0	0	0	0
Skiers Appeal	3	F	3	1	0	0	6,730
Skier's Gift	4	G	2	1	0	0	20,760
Skies of Thunder	3	F	1	1	0	0	6,300
Skifalett	11	M	10	1	2	0	9,472
Skiff of Snow	2	G	2	0	1	0	3,528
Skiking	3	C	1	0	0	0	0
Skill	6	G	9	1	1	1	7,373
Skillet	5	G	15	1	6	0	21,610
Skillful Level	4	G	8	2	2	0	6,385
Skim Forever	5	M	17	2	3	3	28,517
Skimming Stones	3	F	7	0	0	1	2,843
Skin Deep	6	M	3	0	1	0	1,323
Skin Doctor	5	G	7	2	0	1	15,168
Skin Flint	3	C	1	0	0	0	0
Sking Joe	3	C	5	0	0	0	930
Skinner	3	G	5	0	0	0	2,802
Skinners Lane	3	G	12	1	6	1	26,052
Skinny Dugan	2	G	1	0	0	0	72
Skinnydippingtime	4	C	16	0	1	2	5,733
Skip a Bid	3	C	7	0	0	0	1,666
Skip a Dee Doo Dah	3	G	9	1	1	0	18,525
Skip a Grade	7	G	10	2	4	1	57,014
Skip a Nite	3	C	11	3	0	2	15,980
Skip a Page	6	G	6	0	0	2	7,570
Skip a Payment	5	G	9	2	3	2	8,550
Skip All Day	3	F	1	1	0	0	37,620
Skip All the Way	3	F	15	2	5	4	55,040
Skip and Go	3	G	12	4	1	1	74,967
Skip and Play	3	F	5	1	0	0	7,115
Skip and Splash	5	M	5	2	0	0	8,520
Skip Awhile	2	F	1	0	0	0	0
Skip Boldly	3	G	5	1	0	1	14,140
Skip Cat	4	C	8	2	1	0	12,182
Skip Class	4	F	4	0	0	0	316
Skip Command	3	F	11	3	1	2	73,235
Skip Court	3	G	3	0	2	0	12,176
Skip Fighter	2	C	1	0	0	0	0
Skip Irish	3	G	12	4	1	1	51,242
Skip Is Classy	3	G	10	1	0	1	16,345
Skip It	3	G	3	0	0	0	570
Skip My Turn	3	F	11	3	3	0	20,250
Skip N Bail	5	H	5	0	0	1	606
Skip n' Di	4	F	1	0	0	0	285
Skip n' Jump	3	G	12	4	0	1	70,307
Skip On Home	2	C	1	0	0	0	0
Skip On Water	4	G	2	0	0	0	258
Skip Over Clover	4	G	1	0	0	0	78
Skip Over Finish	5	G	12	1	0	2	8,967
Skip Past	3	C	7	1	0	0	18,710
Skip Poker	3	F	13	1	4	2	62,744
Skip Queen	4	F	11	2	2	0	74,248
Skip School	3	F	16	2	3	2	42,100
Skip Son	3	C	16	3	3	2	44,793
Skip Telbin	4	G	16	4	1	2	39,611
Skip the Blues	3	F	16	2	1	3	11,371
Skip the Country	5	G	8	0	1	0	2,406
Skip the Dessert	6	G	3	0	0	0	111
Skip the Fuss	4	F	4	0	1	1	3,744
Skip the Gold	2	G	3	0	0	0	1,020
Skip the Party	6	G	4	0	1	0	1,382
Skip the Phonies	2	C	3	0	0	0	1,550
Skip the Promise	3	F	9	2	3	0	32,405
Skip the Sale	5	M	3	0	0	1	1,017
Skip the Way	2	C	10	0	1	3	10,625
Skip the Wedding	2	C	12	2	1	2	31,755
Skip Til Dawn	2	F	3	0	0	0	261
Skip to Mizzou	3	G	8	2	0	1	11,567
Skip to My Lucy	4	F	7	0	1	4	10,095
Skip to Savannah	6	M	5	2	0	0	72,530
Skip to the Beat	4	G	9	2	1	1	13,132
Skip to the Blues	6	G	1	1	0	0	2,640
Skip to Victory	3	F	10	1	0	1	5,881
Skip Town	8	M	8	0	1	1	2,852
Skip Trial Miss	7	M	12	4	1	1	53,598
Skip Vigorously	4	G	10	2	2	0	67,845
Skip With Julie	4	F	4	1	0	1	11,278
Skipacruise	3	G	13	2	3	3	125,153
Skipamiss	4	F	12	4	0	2	58,610
Skipaslew	3	C	7	1	0	0	92,875
Skipastich	2	F	3	0	0	0	349
Skipbinnjustdiana	3	F	2	0	1	0	4,620
Skiperoo	4	G	11	1	2	1	31,340
Skipingo	7	G	3	0	0	0	1,000
Skipjack	6	G	5	0	0	2	1,572
Skip'n Fool	4	F	12	4	1	2	59,834
Skip'n True	5	M	4	1	0	0	5,475
Skip'or	2	C	3	0	0	0	212
Skippa Roo Magic	3	F	5	0	0	0	630
Skippadoo	3	F	14	1	4	0	52,020
Skipper	3	G	10	2	5	0	53,040
Skipper Jack	2	G	4	1	0	1	11,760
Skipperess	3	F	12	1	0	0	7,942
Skipper's Appeal	3	C	9	0	2	0	2,960
Skipper's Mate	4	F	8	1	0	2	28,320
Skipper's Spirit	5	G	6	1	3	0	5,000
Skipping Court	2	F	4	1	1	0	16,660
Skipping My Trial	3	G	5	1	1	0	13,190
Skipping School	3	F	1	0	0	0	0
Skipping Stars	4	C	3	0	0	0	0
Skipping Trail	2	G	1	0	0	0	300
Skipping Wild	2	F	3	1	0	0	14,630
Skippingtomontana	4	F	7	0	1	0	11,640
Skippo	3	G	7	0	0	2	8,886
Skippykeepswinning	3	C	8	1	0	0	6,315
Skippy's Flite	3	G	9	2	1	0	14,940
Skippy's Goldenboy	3	G	4	0	0	0	2,600
Skip's Best Girl	4	F	5	0	1	1	3,561
Skip's Last Quicky	4	F	6	0	0	1	1,093
Skip's Signal	4	G	6	0	0	0	4,018
Skip's Singer	6	M	10	2	0	1	18,090
Skip's Song	2	C	5	1	2	0	22,705
Skip's Star	5	G	3	0	0	1	1,538
Skip's Trick	3	F	10	1	1	1	16,585
Skipteaser	4	G	10	4	3	0	32,618
Skiptomloumydarlin	3	C	14	3	3	3	69,130
Skiptothegoodpart	3	G	5	1	2	0	11,369
Skirl	8	H	8	1	1	1	2,388
Skit	4	F	12	2	2	1	27,340
Skitter	3	F	1	1	0	0	15,625
Skokie Dancer	5	M	2	0	0	0	215
Skol	12	G	6	0	0	2	2,432
Skooch	3	G	9	1	0	1	5,355
Skookum	2	G	1	0	0	0	450
Skookum Flyer	6	G	2	0	1	0	1,200
Skookum Pass	4	G	9	1	1	1	10,165
Skoor	4	F	19	1	2	5	22,065
Skooter's Drone	6	G	6	0	1	0	1,020
Skorch Two	4	F	14	1	0	2	32,430
Skrate	4	F	3	1	1	0	19,620
Sku	2	G	3	0	1	0	11,500
Skukuza	4	G	5	3	1	0	90,800
Sky and Sea	10	G	1	0	0	0	0
Sky Blew	6	M	3	0	0	0	263
Sky Blue Bid	4	G	15	3	3	2	26,109
Sky Brio	3	C	8	1	1	1	38,150
Sky Burner	2	F	1	0	0	0	480
Sky Calling	3	G	1	0	0	0	402
Sky Country	6	M	7	2	0	0	3,250
Sky Crimson	2	C	1	0	0	0	0
Sky Cut	5	M	4	1	0	0	10,358
Sky Dawn	2	G	1	0	0	0	1,064
Sky Deputy	7	G	3	0	0	0	2,820
Sky Diamond	4	G	13	5	1	2	196,348

Horse	Age	Sex	Sts	1st	2d	3d	Won
Sky Diver	7	G	5	0	0	0	2,295
Sky Dreams	3	F	13	1	4	0	29,650
Sky Emerald	2	C	4	0	0	0	1,248
Sky Full of Hope	2	F	2	0	0	0	329
Sky Gal	6	M	9	1	0	1	12,335
Sky Girl	6	M	2	0	0	0	0
Sky Guy	2	G	5	1	1	0	7,645
Sky Harbor	2	G	8	1	4	1	33,093
Sky Heiress	3	F	9	1	0	1	18,416
Sky Hoof Hearted	3	G	8	0	2	1	3,492
Sky Hunter	6	G	8	0	2	2	38,133
Sky Jiving	6	M	10	0	0	0	1,053
Sky Lass	3	F	1	0	0	0	205
Sky Legacy	7	G	4	0	0	0	0
Sky Mart	6	G	14	2	4	1	23,996
Sky Masterson	5	G	2	0	0	0	150
Sky Missile	3	C	5	0	0	1	4,600
Sky Mist	7	M	4	0	0	0	0
Sky Nine	3	F	3	0	0	1	1,080
Sky of Gold	6	G	12	2	2	3	50,650
Sky Power	4	F	6	1	0	3	10,085
Sky Reality	4	F	9	1	1	1	33,200
Sky Ridge Dancer	5	M	4	0	0	1	990
Sky Sabre	3	G	8	1	1	2	9,570
Sky Strider	9	G	13	1	2	1	6,881
Sky Stutz	4	G	18	0	3	6	11,830
Sky Terrace	5	H	2	0	0	0	950
Sky Tower	6	G	17	1	3	0	7,355
Sky Tracker	3	C	12	1	1	1	9,865
Sky Trick	8	G	4	0	0	0	790
Sky Trip Jig	3	F	18	1	2	0	4,591
Sky Troll	2	G	3	0	0	0	190
Sky Wad	3	F	6	0	0	0	330
Sky Wolf	3	C	4	0	0	0	880
Sky Zap	3	C	4	1	0	1	1,965
Skybeau	3	G	6	1	0	1	9,206
Skycrossing	4	G	8	1	0	0	21,930
Skydive	3	C	3	0	1	0	3,950
Skye Boat Song	3	G	4	0	0	0	240
Skye's Lil Blazer	4	F	9	0	0	2	1,895
Skyey	4	G	9	2	1	0	21,814
Skyhyla	3	F	6	2	1	0	46,203
Skykomish Slew	11	M	2	0	0	0	224
Skyladysky	3	F	7	1	1	1	45,849
Skyladywalker	5	M	1	0	0	0	262
Skylar May	8	M	7	1	0	1	7,077
Skylar's Daddy	3	G	13	1	4	2	13,409
Skyler's Dancer	3	F	4	0	0	0	0
Skyline	6	M	15	2	0	1	9,519
Skyline Band	5	G	5	0	0	3	3,061
Skyline Gal	2	F	1	0	0	0	0
Skyline Trail	3	G	3	0	1	0	3,185
Skyliner	3	G	3	0	0	0	0
Skylist	3	F	6	1	0	0	8,100
Skyloper	2	F	3	0	1	0	9,882
Skylord	5	G	5	0	0	0	278
Skymaster	5	G	11	3	0	0	36,920
Skymeister	3	G	5	3	0	0	65,340
Skyrider	3	G	5	1	0	1	17,581
Skyrunner	7	H	9	0	1	3	5,245
Skys Bold Princess	5	M	2	0	0	0	0
Sky's Comet	5	M	7	0	2	0	8,205
Sky's Image	3	G	2	0	0	0	0
Skys Last Angel	4	C	7	1	2	1	12,060
Sky's the Tops	7	G	11	3	2	3	15,895
Skysmoke	7	G	13	1	5	0	6,595
Skyview Scanner	5	M	6	1	0	1	6,417
Skywalker Red	4	G	9	3	0	3	130,828
Skywalker Select	6	G	7	2	0	0	11,249
Skyway	3	G	3	2	0	0	29,400
Slab Granite	4	G	9	0	0	0	2,201
Slack	2	G	2	0	0	0	675
Slade	3	C	5	2	0	0	22,310
Slade Runner	3	G	6	1	2	1	9,401
Slade's Bayou	5	M	8	2	2	0	20,900
Slam Dancing	3	F	4	0	0	0	622
Slam of Royalty	2	F	1	0	0	0	0
Slam the Dee's	3	F	8	0	3	0	26,840
Slamdancer	6	M	9	0	0	0	4,320
Slamma	4	F	1	0	0	0	0
Slammeinthedust	9	M	4	0	0	1	1,540
Slammer	5	G	10	2	0	1	10,533
Slammers Last	3	G	8	0	0	0	1,793
Slammin' Lil	4	F	11	1	2	0	35,348
Slammin' Slew	5	G	3	0	0	0	0
Slammin Success	2	F	3	0	0	0	529
Slamming Babe	3	G	7	0	2	0	8,480
Slamming Nicole	3	F	3	0	1	0	4,550
Slammo	2	C	1	0	1	0	5,600
Slant	3	C	6	1	1	1	22,090
Slap Shot	2	G	5	0	0	1	4,490
Slapshot Dom	4	G	8	0	0	0	6,009
Slash Dot Com	6	G	16	4	2	1	32,852
Slash N Bash	4	G	6	1	0	0	9,815
Slashback	3	G	9	0	1	2	9,740
Slashing Storm	2	F	3	0	0	0	60
Slat Wall	7	M	2	0	0	0	152
Slate Run	4	C	6	2	0	1	54,967
Slater Mill	2	F	4	0	0	0	3,115
Slattery	2	G	1	0	0	0	205
Slaughter and Run	7	M	2	0	0	0	80
Slavic Turn	4	F	2	0	0	0	80
Slavic Wind	4	F	6	0	2	2	7,986
Slavic's Gold	3	G	7	0	3	1	10,085
Slawn Cheh	4	F	13	2	1	2	16,038
Slay Ride	3	G	12	1	2	2	18,560
Sledding Partner	3	F	1	0	0	0	0
Sledge	5	G	2	0	0	1	3,510
Sleek Cat	3	C	2	0	0	0	840
Sleek Jackal	2	C	5	0	0	0	6,578
Sleep Away	4	F	13	1	5	3	23,413
Sleep Till Noon	8	G	7	1	0	0	6,920
Sleep Time	5	M	1	0	0	0	31
Sleeping Around	7	M	16	1	4	1	7,968
Sleeping Potion	5	G	2	1	0	0	15,630
Sleepover Bandit	4	G	3	1	0	0	17,166
Sleepwiththefishes	3	F	10	0	0	0	930
Sleepy Dale	4	C	10	1	4	2	4,670
Sleepy Joe Jasper	3	G	3	0	0	1	430
Sleepy Jones	2	G	3	0	0	2	3,745
Sleepy Sky	4	G	1	0	0	0	50
Sleet Rod	3	G	2	1	1	0	8,840
Sleetwood Mac	7	G	9	3	1	2	55,045
Sleety	6	M	10	0	2	1	6,200
Sleeve Target	4	G	1	0	0	0	218
Sleezianna	4	F	4	0	0	0	160
Sleight	8	G	4	0	2	0	4,942
Sleight of Hand	4	F	5	0	1	1	4,690
Slerps M and M	5	M	8	1	0	1	6,718
Slerpy Water	4	G	2	1	0	0	2,820
Sleuce Robber	3	G	6	0	0	0	325
Sleuthing	4	G	11	2	0	1	8,056
Slew a Soldier	2	C	1	0	0	1	1,725
Slew Akoa	5	G	4	0	0	1	1,620
Slew Alta	3	F	14	0	2	2	5,826
Slew and a Half	4	G	12	3	0	2	9,701
Slew Angel	4	F	3	0	3	0	6,285
Slew Ann	7	M	4	1	0	0	6,610
Slew Buck	4	G	10	0	0	0	3,683
Slew Can Go	10	G	4	0	0	0	225
Slew Check	5	G	11	3	0	0	42,255
Slew City Babe	3	F	1	0	0	0	90
Slew City Charmer	6	H	15	2	4	3	28,153
Slew City Citadel	4	G	7	0	0	1	14,295
Slew City Express	3	G	10	1	1	2	14,001
Slew City Jay	8	G	7	0	1	2	2,090
Slew City Knight	8	G	14	3	1	2	17,837
Slew City Lily	5	M	12	1	2	1	21,256
Slew City Max	2	C	5	1	2	1	7,329
Slew City Mick	3	G	14	1	2	6	23,803
Slew City Mike	3	G	16	1	0	0	27,330
Slew Creek Suzy	3	F	11	0	1	2	3,324
Slew de Do	4	G	5	0	1	2	1,432
Slew Design	8	G	7	1	1	1	3,761
Slew d'Or	4	F	13	1	0	0	7,510
Slew Falls	4	F	6	0	0	1	930
Slew Feliou	7	M	3	0	0	0	0
Slew Gin Beauty	2	F	4	0	0	0	1,360

Horse	Age	Sex	Sts	1st	2d	3d	Won
Slew Grass	4	G	1	0	0	0	0
Slew Has a Message	6	G	4	0	0	1	1,088
Slew He	2	F	4	0	0	0	1,392
Slew Heffner	3	C	4	0	0	0	150
Slew In	3	C	1	0	0	0	110
Slew in the Face	8	G	12	2	4	2	13,373
Slew in Time	4	G	1	0	0	0	0
Slew Insured	2	C	3	0	0	0	0
Slew Is King	4	G	7	3	0	0	49,606
Slew Juice	3	F	2	0	0	0	0
Slew La La	2	F	1	0	0	1	5,167
Slew Marshal (ARG)	6	H	10	1	0	2	21,050
Slew Meadow	3	F	7	1	1	0	18,810
Slew Motion	2	F	3	2	0	1	35,050
Slew My Lover	3	F	3	0	0	0	295
Slew o' Aces	8	G	1	0	0	0	0
Slew o' Asti	6	G	15	0	0	0	1,971
Slew o' Rhythm	8	G	10	2	0	0	10,453
Slew of Ack	3	C	3	0	0	0	317
Slew of Enerchi	2	C	1	0	1	0	3,376
Slew of Jones	3	F	2	0	0	0	450
Slew of Love	2	C	3	0	0	0	1,050
Slew of Lovers	3	F	3	0	0	0	200
Slew of Memories	4	C	8	1	0	2	12,440
Slew of the Night	5	G	6	1	1	0	46,960
Slew of the West	5	G	4	0	0	0	180
Slew of the Year	3	F	9	2	0	0	11,973
Slew of Trophies	3	C	4	0	0	0	420
Slew of Wine	4	F	3	0	0	0	0
Slew On Fire	5	G	3	0	0	0	150
Slew Pointe	3	F	9	1	1	1	35,397
Slew Prized	8	M	1	0	0	0	0
Slew Proud	2	F	2	0	1	0	4,600
Slew Rabbit	2	G	2	0	0	0	595
Slew Rising	3	G	2	1	0	0	1,986
Slew River Sue	4	F	3	0	0	0	84
Slew Roots	8	G	17	1	4	0	6,793
Slew Rouge	4	G	11	2	0	2	20,535
Slew Royal	5	G	7	0	0	1	2,298
Slew Sally Slew	5	M	10	2	3	1	25,516
Slew Shaq	4	G	17	0	3	1	9,516
Slew Shine	3	C	12	1	0	5	43,302
Slew Shoes	3	F	7	2	1	0	8,716
Slew Shoo Slew	5	G	8	2	0	1	3,702
Slew Sider	4	F	2	0	0	0	42
Slew Slayer	3	G	11	2	1	3	55,605
Slew So Tru	2	C	3	0	0	0	0
Slew Squirt	2	F	2	0	0	0	439
Slew the Boys	3	G	8	0	0	1	1,012
Slew the City	5	G	11	3	2	0	14,828
Slew the Dragon	3	G	5	0	0	0	2,682
Slew the Enemy	4	G	10	0	1	3	4,749
Slew the Fools	7	G	5	0	0	0	1,054
Slew the Money	3	F	2	0	0	0	795
Slew the Monster	4	C	2	0	1	1	8,640
Slew the Storm	2	C	3	0	0	0	232
Slew Tin Tin	3	G	5	0	0	2	4,378
Slew to the Mint	5	G	4	0	0	2	2,604
Slew Valley	7	H	9	3	1	1	353,360
Slew Walker	5	G	7	0	1	0	710
Slewadaeen	5	M	8	0	0	0	674
Slewanna	6	M	8	0	1	0	5,703
Slewannavan	7	M	6	0	0	1	2,365
Slewaway	3	G	12	1	0	1	7,530
Slewbe Jet	3	C	4	0	1	2	15,750
Slewbee Dubee	2	F	1	0	0	0	1,380
Slewby Do Be Do	4	F	13	1	4	0	11,293
Slewcious	3	C	3	1	0	0	15,725
Slewd On Key	6	M	4	0	2	0	2,892
Slewdario	6	H	4	0	0	1	2,963
Slewdebaker	2	C	2	0	1	0	860
Slewdegrace	3	F	9	1	0	1	12,850
Slewdiano	7	M	21	0	1	0	1,382
Slewdiddy	2	F	4	0	0	0	1,406
Slewdledo Way	2	G	6	0	2	1	2,635
Slewdle's Promise	4	F	1	0	0	0	0
Slewdorado	8	G	3	0	1	0	800
Slew'em and Run	4	G	12	4	1	4	74,555
Slewey Armstrong	2	G	4	0	0	3	7,920
Slewgiana	4	F	4	0	1	0	5,160
Slewgun	3	F	3	0	0	0	0
Slewheart	4	F	1	0	0	0	0
Slewicide Cruise	4	G	10	4	4	0	67,250
Slewkey Slew	2	C	1	1	0	0	10,800
Slewlee Ridge	6	M	11	1	1	1	4,717
Slewlite	2	F	3	1	0	0	9,080
Slewlou	5	G	2	0	0	0	470
Slewlution	2	F	2	0	0	0	600
Slewmagoo	7	G	13	2	2	3	8,368
Slewnami	2	G	2	0	0	0	460
Slewofhonor	4	F	1	1	0	0	9,600
Slewp'a Doop	10	G	4	1	1	0	3,280
Slewpast	2	F	4	2	1	0	52,411
Slewper Sport	4	G	22	2	11	4	10,581
Slewpercat	4	G	2	1	1	0	4,240
Slewperwoman	4	F	7	1	2	1	13,010
Slewping	5	G	2	0	0	1	5,880
Slewps Goldenholly	3	F	12	1	0	0	3,246
Slewpy B Fast	4	F	5	0	1	0	1,209
Slewpy Ruckus	4	G	7	0	1	0	5,270
Slewpy Time	5	M	1	0	0	0	0
Slewpy's Charm	5	M	12	0	1	1	6,342
Slewpy's Gold	7	G	15	2	2	1	9,475
Slewpy's Storm	3	F	9	2	1	1	54,110
Slewreen	8	M	7	1	3	2	6,150
Slewrenity	4	G	4	2	1	1	20,630
Slewrue	4	F	12	3	2	1	41,210
Slew's Alibi	5	G	6	1	0	2	2,387
Slew's Bigcity Z	2	C	4	0	0	2	3,690
Slew's Bold Frank	5	G	5	0	1	0	1,462
Slew's Bronze	5	G	11	1	4	0	8,380
Slews Bullet	3	G	6	0	2	2	3,543
Slew's Carousel	5	G	9	4	1	1	52,248
Slew's Cateringtoo	4	F	8	0	0	0	338
Slews Child	5	G	5	1	1	0	15,060
Slew's Colony	3	G	6	1	0	0	7,926
Slews Date	4	G	2	0	0	0	245
Slews Deputy Doll	7	M	6	0	0	0	646
Slew's Double Ego	7	G	1	0	0	0	0
Slews' Doubledate	2	G	5	0	1	1	3,900
Slews Final Answer	5	M	6	1	1	1	57,800
Slew's Fyre	6	H	3	1	1	0	1,317
Slews Gem	4	F	7	0	2	1	3,509
Slew's Ha Ha	4	G	7	1	1	0	9,282
Slews Hope	2	F	6	0	0	0	0
Slew's House	3	G	3	0	0	0	3,860
Slews in Demand	3	F	11	2	3	3	48,318
Slews in Oz Now	2	F	5	2	0	1	13,796
Slews Inheritance	5	M	8	0	0	0	351
Slews Jackpot	7	G	2	0	0	0	80
Slew's Jewel	4	F	13	3	3	1	40,060
Slew's Miss	2	F	1	0	0	0	0
Slews Mistress	4	F	4	0	0	0	400
Slews Moment	4	F	11	2	0	1	15,180
Slews Motel	2	C	4	1	0	0	13,954
Slew's Mystery	3	F	10	1	1	5	16,689
Slews On First	5	G	8	1	0	1	2,113
Slews One	3	C	2	0	0	0	0
Slew's Prince	4	C	10	3	0	2	127,278
Slew's Prospector	5	G	5	2	0	0	26,431
Slews Resurrection	5	G	14	2	3	1	20,246
Slew's Right	9	G	12	2	2	2	4,232
Slews Running Mist	5	M	6	0	1	0	2,930
Slew's Saga	2	C	6	2	1	0	210,603
Slew's Smile	7	G	10	1	1	1	32,633
Slew's Sparkle	4	F	11	2	0	3	42,182
Slew's Sunny	4	F	6	0	1	0	1,320
Slew's Temper	4	G	20	1	3	4	11,506
Slew's Temptation	3	F	6	0	2	2	6,691
Slew's Treasure	7	M	12	0	0	0	488
Slewsbag	2	G	9	0	0	2	32,520
Slewssurelucky	3	C	4	1	0	0	5,262
Slewston	6	G	4	1	1	0	36,960
Slewsydneyslew	4	F	6	1	2	1	7,813
Slewth Slayer	5	G	4	0	0	1	1,275
Slewtheboat	5	M	9	1	2	3	17,750
Slewtown Boogie	4	F	2	0	1	0	580
Slewtown Dancer	3	F	1	0	0	0	0

Horse	Age	Sex	Sts	1st	2d	3d	Won
Slewville	3	F	6	2	1	0	112,520
Slewy's Gold	3	G	7	1	1	1	10,207
Slewz Q	5	M	4	1	0	0	7,332
Slewz U Lose	2	G	1	0	0	0	654
Slewzy Floozy	5	M	4	0	1	0	3,230
Slice of Glory	2	G	3	0	1	0	14,820
Slice of Heaven	5	M	9	0	3	0	7,963
Slicing Inscript	4	F	1	0	0	0	65
Slick Advocator	6	G	10	0	1	1	3,224
Slick as Sleet	5	G	3	0	1	0	15,088
Slick as Slew	4	C	2	1	0	1	26,295
Slick Bird	3	G	3	0	0	1	1,720
Slick Carson	2	C	2	0	0	0	655
Slick Debbie	5	M	8	0	2	1	9,274
Slick Decision	8	G	10	0	0	2	2,407
Slick Dude	3	G	6	1	1	2	5,142
Slick Kat Daddy	4	G	23	1	0	2	7,635
Slick Punch	4	F	8	1	1	1	35,480
Slick Rock	3	C	3	0	0	0	248
Slick Sand	5	G	7	6	0	0	17,980
Slick Shadow	4	G	2	0	0	0	113
Slick Speed	7	H	2	0	0	0	0
Slick Vick	6	G	5	0	0	0	540
Slick's Last Tiger	3	C	4	1	0	0	4,350
Slick's Turn	3	G	2	0	0	1	680
Slickster Nickster	6	G	5	0	0	1	990
Slickstone	2	G	1	0	0	0	55
Slide Home	2	G	2	1	0	0	32,720
Slide to Glory	6	M	8	2	2	0	46,380
Slider	6	G	4	0	1	0	10,230
Sliding Home	3	C	9	1	3	0	60,440
Slight K. O's	5	M	8	0	0	2	4,040
Slightly Danjurous	2	G	1	1	0	0	1,870
Slightly Gold	5	M	6	1	0	0	4,159
Slightly Psycho	3	C	3	0	0	0	1,740
Slightly Snowbound	3	F	10	2	0	1	11,670
Slightlymorelikely	3	F	1	0	0	0	414
Slighty Moody	3	C	6	0	0	0	651
Sligo Creek	7	G	2	1	1	0	5,496
Slim Cat	3	C	9	0	1	1	1,750
Slim Dusty	5	G	12	4	2	3	233,553
Slim Justice	2	F	7	1	3	1	43,861
Slimey Garfunkle	3	G	13	1	2	4	20,125
Slims Big Time	2	G	1	0	0	0	145
Slims Song	6	M	6	1	1	1	6,463
Sling Shot	3	C	6	0	3	0	23,900
Slingo Man	6	G	13	1	1	1	8,130
Slinkin	3	F	9	0	2	3	17,925
Slip and Slide	12	G	5	0	0	1	792
Slip Jig	3	C	11	1	1	1	25,672
Slip N Dazzle	4	F	9	2	2	2	10,113
Slipper Fun	3	F	6	0	0	0	0
Slipper Slew	6	M	9	1	0	1	14,536
Slippery Devil	2	F	1	1	0	0	6,900
Slippery Fool	4	G	9	4	0	0	20,218
Slippery Gator	5	H	12	4	3	2	77,690
Slippery Slick	3	C	6	2	0	3	63,070
Slippery Slope	3	F	1	0	0	1	570
Slippery When Bet	6	G	2	1	1	0	12,600
Slippery When Wet	3	F	10	1	0	0	5,586
Slippery Zibbity	4	F	5	1	0	1	5,633
Slippin Sam	4	G	11	0	1	0	3,748
Slippin Sly Slew	5	G	6	2	1	0	2,849
Slipshoe	5	M	5	0	0	1	4,404
Slipstich	7	M	10	1	0	1	4,602
Slitherin	3	C	7	3	1	2	53,670
Sloat Blvd	3	G	9	4	2	2	77,975
Slogan	5	G	5	1	0	0	3,990
Slot Bunny	2	F	3	0	0	1	2,332
Slot Girl	5	M	6	0	1	0	3,897
Slot Happy	6	M	10	0	2	1	7,668
Slot Machine Jean	4	F	10	0	1	0	1,716
Slots Imp	7	M	4	0	0	0	0
Slotsarun	7	H	6	0	0	0	451
Slotsfan	2	F	3	2	0	0	10,585
Slouise	3	F	4	0	0	0	0
Slouisiana Lew	5	G	2	0	0	0	0
Slow and Steady	3	F	9	3	2	1	64,000
Slow Dancer	3	G	7	0	0	0	1,200
Slow Dancin	3	F	4	1	0	0	17,825
Slow Go	5	G	3	0	0	0	0
Slow Heat	7	G	6	0	0	2	1,160
Slow Kris	3	F	5	1	0	0	10,218
Slow N Easy	3	G	7	1	0	0	33,620
Slow Signal	4	G	13	0	1	0	14,174
Slow Time	4	G	1	0	0	0	0
Slow Walkin' John	3	G	2	1	0	0	18,900
Slowwaterrunsdeep	3	G	4	0	1	0	1,017
Slumber Party	4	F	13	2	3	3	28,936
Slurred Words	2	C	1	0	0	0	205
Slush Fund	2	G	6	0	0	0	2,070
Sly Chick	5	M	12	0	0	4	4,170
Sly Doc	4	G	18	1	3	3	29,480
Sly Grin	5	G	13	0	3	0	14,935
Sly Illusion	2	G	3	1	0	1	22,933
Sly Kona	5	M	6	0	0	1	9,370
Sly Lady	5	M	3	1	2	0	39,000
Sly Moment	3	F	8	1	2	1	20,960
Sly Prospect	4	F	5	1	0	2	21,350
Sly Rascal	4	G	5	1	0	0	7,308
Sly Remark	3	G	11	3	1	2	33,204
Sly Schemes	7	G	9	2	0	0	5,088
Sly Secrets	4	F	2	1	0	0	7,325
Sly Style	5	G	11	1	0	0	14,690
Sly Times	6	G	5	0	0	0	220
Slyding Brush	3	G	9	0	1	1	4,860
Slyght Choice	5	G	6	0	0	1	1,802
Slywalker	5	G	11	2	1	1	15,356
Smack Down	3	C	7	1	0	0	3,532
Smacker	2	C	3	0	0	1	5,200
Smackincatz	5	G	7	1	1	1	7,449
Smackle	5	G	5	1	1	0	10,505
Smackovers Gold	2	G	3	0	0	0	1,110
Small Allen	3	G	8	0	4	2	20,315
Small Bat Slew (ARG)	6	G	9	0	0	1	1,771
Small But Sweet	6	M	5	0	0	2	1,136
Small Charger	4	G	3	0	0	0	120
Small Connection	3	F	4	0	0	0	100
Small Parcel Guy	2	G	8	0	0	1	10,544
Small Promises	6	M	10	1	1	0	43,057
Small Town Guy	3	C	1	0	0	0	0
Small Town Queen	4	F	5	0	1	0	2,100
Small Value	2	C	2	0	0	0	0
Smalltown Slew	3	G	8	2	2	1	60,560
Smallville	3	G	8	1	0	1	13,799
Smalnmighty	3	C	1	0	0	0	138
Smart Admiral	8	G	5	0	0	1	1,755
Smart Agenda	5	G	13	6	2	1	55,165
Smart Alert	8	H	14	2	1	1	21,236
Smart Alix	4	F	16	1	2	1	7,178
Smart Ana	5	M	10	1	2	4	30,544
Smart Appeal	4	F	13	2	2	2	21,680
Smart Babe	3	F	14	2	4	1	63,541
Smart Baby	4	F	4	1	0	0	9,000
Smart Bob	2	G	2	0	0	0	1,596
Smart Caller	3	F	11	3	1	1	18,449
Smart Camp	2	F	2	0	0	0	0
Smart Cid	7	G	6	0	1	0	2,490
Smart Colony	3	F	5	0	0	1	3,450
Smart Confidence	3	G	20	1	3	3	22,295
Smart Coup	5	G	6	0	0	1	2,987
Smart Dare	6	M	1	0	0	0	330
Smart Date	3	G	12	1	1	0	7,127
Smart Doc	6	G	6	0	2	1	7,190
Smart Emma	3	F	2	0	0	1	1,820
Smart Figure	11	G	2	0	2	0	2,780
Smart Finish	2	F	6	0	0	3	4,510
Smart Fire	3	G	7	1	2	0	5,545
Smart Flow	10	M	4	0	0	0	410
Smart Fun	3	F	2	0	1	1	4,160
Smart Gal's Halo	6	G	4	0	0	0	662
Smart Grace	5	M	11	3	1	2	58,740
Smart Growth	3	C	2	0	0	1	3,924
Smart Jenna	4	F	9	1	0	0	3,189
Smart Jet	5	M	5	0	0	0	224
Smart King	3	G	7	0	4	0	18,590
Smart Kitty	4	F	5	0	0	1	693
Smart Lacy	5	M	3	0	0	0	4,865

Horse	Age	Sex	Sts	1st	2d	3d	Won
Smart Lady Doc	3	F	4	0	0	0	473
Smart Link	3	F	11	1	1	2	16,707
Smart Lovin'	3	F	8	1	0	0	14,022
Smart Mae	3	F	11	2	1	0	25,710
Smart Mail	5	M	15	3	2	1	26,234
Smart n' Char	8	M	5	2	0	1	14,660
Smart N Classy	4	F	9	3	4	0	134,444
Smart N Plasant	3	C	9	1	0	1	16,430
Smart N Sassy	5	M	3	0	0	0	2,406
Smart N Smooth	5	M	8	2	2	1	53,200
Smart October	5	G	11	2	1	2	50,219
Smart Ole Jackie	4	F	8	0	0	1	1,009
Smart Pace	2	G	1	0	1	0	5,520
Smart Player	4	G	16	4	1	3	35,829
Smart Prospect	5	G	13	2	4	0	50,645
Smart Pursuit	6	M	8	0	2	1	4,024
Smart Rascal	2	C	1	0	0	0	0
Smart Regent	4	G	9	1	1	3	12,770
Smart Ring	8	G	6	1	3	0	5,435
Smart Sailing	4	F	3	0	0	0	0
Smart Serve	3	F	9	1	1	0	29,715
Smart Set	7	G	1	0	1	0	1,160
Smart Silvie	3	F	9	0	1	1	3,060
Smart Skater	3	F	11	3	3	1	65,348
Smart Swede	4	G	5	0	0	1	1,149
Smart Tale	4	G	12	1	2	3	10,752
Smart Tap	5	H	7	0	0	0	6,210
Smart Temper	3	F	1	0	0	0	1,342
Smart Thought	3	F	4	2	0	1	31,080
Smart too Late	7	G	1	0	0	0	0
Smart Voyager	2	F	2	1	0	0	9,900
Smart Willie	4	G	4	0	0	0	1,140
Smarte Smart	3	C	5	1	0	0	4,800
Smarten Op	2	C	1	1	0	0	8,400
Smarter Than Kris	5	H	24	2	1	6	25,608
Smartest Thing	2	F	3	1	2	0	99,020
Smartlee Away	3	F	8	2	0	2	52,160
Smartlildevil	2	G	8	0	3	2	23,298
Smartly Suited	6	H	1	0	1	0	1,800
Smarts	4	F	5	0	1	0	1,340
Smarty Jones	3	C	7	6	1	0	7,563,535
Smarty Mc	3	F	4	1	0	0	14,700
Smarty's Money	4	F	11	1	1	2	14,433
Smashed	5	M	8	2	2	0	30,212
Smashin Man	6	G	2	0	0	0	0
Smashing Brass	4	F	9	4	0	1	24,035
Smashing Pride	5	G	7	0	0	0	705
Smee	4	F	3	0	0	0	373
Smell My Smoke	3	G	9	1	0	2	7,660
Smellinlikearose	5	M	9	0	2	2	5,770
Smell's a Winner	4	F	9	2	2	2	47,292
Smells Girl	6	M	7	1	0	0	3,057
Smelly Mountain	4	C	17	4	2	2	35,256
Smila Fawin	4	F	6	0	0	0	504
Smile and Tears	2	C	1	1	0	0	29,395
Smile as I Go By	7	G	8	1	0	0	6,060
Smile Away	4	G	10	3	2	1	45,510
Smile Dinners Here	3	G	10	2	1	1	24,190
Smile for Blair	3	F	2	0	0	1	2,035
Smile Maker	3	F	5	1	1	0	32,830
Smile My Lord	6	G	9	2	0	2	19,258
Smile N Carson	3	C	8	1	2	1	18,677
Smile n Wildcat	5	G	10	2	0	2	95,240
Smile Pretty	4	F	3	0	0	0	0
Smileonme	2	F	3	0	0	1	1,540
Smiles Are Free	5	G	6	0	1	0	3,582
Smilesallaround	5	G	5	0	0	1	2,050
Smilewithpleasure	4	G	9	2	1	1	16,284
Smiley Eh	6	G	7	0	1	0	1,620
Smiley Face	4	F	3	0	0	0	434
Smileyberg	8	G	2	0	0	0	1,600
Smileytime	6	G	5	0	0	1	2,535
Smilie Kermit	3	G	10	1	1	0	15,486
Smilin' Ali	5	M	9	2	0	0	6,730
Smilin Fine	2	G	4	2	1	0	82,436
Smilin' Minster	4	F	9	5	0	1	29,480
Smilin' Sami	3	F	2	0	0	0	75
Smilin' Slew	8	G	12	1	4	1	42,398
Smilin So	2	F	3	0	0	0	180
Smilin Susan	4	F	9	0	1	4	5,742
Smilin' Tom	4	C	2	0	0	0	0
Smiling Betsy	3	F	9	0	2	2	8,150
Smiling Eyes	4	F	3	1	0	0	26,200
Smiling Girl	2	F	2	0	0	0	185
Smiling Irish Eyes	6	G	6	0	1	0	1,426
Smiling Jordan	2	C	2	1	0	0	12,720
Smiling Lord	7	G	10	3	1	0	26,166
Smiling Skip	4	G	4	0	1	0	2,120
Smiling Sky	5	M	5	3	2	0	53,920
Smiling Snoopy	4	G	5	0	0	0	735
Smilodon	2	G	3	0	0	2	7,258
Smith	4	F	3	1	0	0	8,070
Smith's Point	2	F	1	0	0	0	75
Smithtown Bay	2	G	1	0	0	1	2,079
Smithtown Road	3	C	11	2	0	1	24,130
Smitten's Baby	6	M	6	0	0	0	867
Smoggy Doggy	4	F	9	4	2	0	47,380
Smoke and Con	2	F	3	0	0	1	2,170
Smoke and Fame	5	H	5	0	0	0	4,052
Smoke and Ice	6	G	7	4	0	1	6,274
Smoke Bomb	5	M	11	2	3	1	36,380
Smoke Break	3	F	9	2	1	0	58,609
Smoke Chaser	5	M	7	3	1	2	112,352
Smoke Glack Attack	4	F	5	2	2	0	53,200
Smoke in Savoya	8	M	5	0	0	1	1,823
Smoke Magic	2	G	6	1	2	1	17,840
Smoke N Shadows	3	F	5	1	0	1	30,530
Smoke 'n Triumph	3	F	7	2	0	0	22,040
Smoke N Vote	3	G	6	1	1	0	13,000
Smoke Pit	2	F	2	0	1	0	5,420
Smoke Quest	3	G	16	1	1	1	20,420
Smoke Smoke Smoke	2	C	4	2	0	1	41,354
Smoke Stack Jack	5	G	7	3	1	1	21,890
Smoke Stacken	4	C	2	0	0	0	383
Smoke Stream	3	F	3	1	1	0	6,200
Smoke Talk	3	C	3	2	0	1	23,150
Smoke the Bandit	2	G	2	0	0	0	4,390
Smoke Till Dawn	5	G	10	5	1	0	95,678
Smoke Warning	2	C	6	1	1	1	61,275
Smoked Em	5	H	12	1	3	3	49,416
Smokegetenyoureyes	3	F	13	2	1	1	56,760
Smokegetsinmyeyes	3	F	4	0	1	1	2,200
Smokehouse	5	H	6	0	0	0	748
Smokem Flier	4	G	5	0	0	0	429
Smokemmakemehappy	3	F	2	0	0	0	315
Smoken Feathers	4	F	7	2	0	0	19,660
Smoke'n Jack	5	H	1	0	0	0	75
Smoken Pass You	4	G	12	3	0	0	6,153
Smoken Paster	3	F	4	1	1	1	14,024
Smoken Rollin	4	C	3	0	2	0	10,150
Smoken Shooter	4	G	4	2	0	0	36,540
Smoken Smoke	3	G	6	1	0	1	22,345
Smoker	4	G	7	0	0	0	1,531
Smokers Delight	5	M	7	3	3	0	9,191
Smokescreen	2	C	2	1	0	0	22,700
Smokestack	2	F	2	1	0	1	26,640
Smokestacklightnin	3	G	8	1	0	0	7,395
Smokester Horizon	3	F	12	3	5	1	22,643
Smokester's Alle	3	F	5	0	1	2	7,560
Smokester's Dance	6	G	6	0	3	1	8,446
Smokesters High	5	M	5	1	0	2	5,943
Smokester's Knight	5	G	4	0	1	1	3,210
Smokester's Pride	4	F	15	6	3	1	43,950
Smokette	4	F	12	4	4	0	45,445
Smokeumifyougotem	5	M	3	0	0	0	2,660
Smokeville	7	G	9	2	3	2	21,098
Smokey Bob	2	C	3	0	1	1	6,650
Smokey Boy	4	C	11	1	0	0	14,798
Smokey Busted	4	G	6	0	0	0	957
Smokey Day	4	F	13	1	4	2	67,470
Smokey Diamond	4	F	11	3	0	0	45,738
Smokey Diplomacy	3	F	7	2	0	2	45,980
Smokey Dreams	5	M	4	1	0	0	2,400
Smokey Glacken	3	F	5	2	2	1	150,080
Smokey Lass	3	F	2	0	0	0	330
Smokey On a Roll	6	G	11	0	0	2	2,020
Smokey Slew	3	F	2	0	0	1	293
Smokey Springs	6	G	10	0	0	1	2,706

Horse	Age	Sex	Sts	1st	2d	3d	Won
Smokey Way	12	G	6	0	0	0	450
Smokey's Jazz	3	G	11	0	1	1	11,380
Smokie	6	G	8	0	2	1	12,210
Smokieisabandit	5	H	11	4	3	1	60,717
Smokin Aces	2	F	1	0	0	0	255
Smokin Arrow	3	G	7	0	2	0	2,618
Smokin Barkies	4	G	9	1	2	1	10,026
Smokin Brave	5	G	13	0	1	0	3,024
Smokin Bugatti	2	G	2	0	0	0	0
Smokin City Sue	4	F	14	0	0	3	5,929
Smokin Deal	3	G	8	1	0	1	3,600
Smokin Devil	5	G	15	0	0	2	2,026
Smokin Dill	3	G	6	1	0	0	3,888
Smokin Dust	7	G	8	0	0	0	0
Smokin Forest	2	C	3	2	0	0	46,500
Smokin' Forty Five	3	C	6	0	1	0	2,915
Smokin Forty Won	3	C	9	0	2	3	18,519
Smokin' Greida	3	F	12	3	2	4	76,410
Smokin Hot	3	F	5	0	0	0	1,900
Smokin Image	3	G	6	0	0	0	1,013
Smokin in the Lane	3	F	2	0	0	0	1,500
Smokin Joe B.	4	G	10	0	2	3	3,241
Smokin' John	5	H	7	3	0	1	82,368
Smokin' Kelly	3	C	3	0	1	0	10,013
Smokin Mon	2	C	2	1	0	0	8,160
Smokin Nails	2	F	4	0	0	1	3,740
Smokin' On	4	G	9	2	1	3	25,210
Smokin Pirate	4	G	18	0	4	4	6,939
Smokin Pursuit	3	G	7	1	1	1	2,033
Smokin Red	4	C	9	1	1	1	15,124
Smokin' Six	5	G	3	0	0	0	0
Smokin Sylvia	2	F	5	1	1	0	35,844
Smokin Tahoe	2	F	3	0	0	1	450
Smokin Tempo	4	F	8	1	4	1	22,982
Smokin Tyme	3	F	3	0	0	1	974
Smokin' Vigor	3	F	13	1	4	1	26,240
Smokindowntheroad	5	G	9	2	0	1	14,220
Smokinemall	4	F	7	1	1	2	20,987
Smoking Angel	3	G	4	0	0	1	2,205
Smoking At Dawn	2	F	2	0	0	0	66
Smoking Attire	5	G	2	1	0	0	5,032
Smoking Bear	4	F	12	3	3	3	33,773
Smoking Ember	2	C	1	0	0	0	1,290
Smoking Hank	3	C	11	1	0	1	5,634
Smoking Hawk	5	G	19	2	5	2	10,762
Smoking Lad	3	G	12	2	2	4	20,078
Smoking Logan	3	G	7	0	1	0	2,585
Smoking Memo	3	F	4	2	0	0	11,060
Smoking Quality	3	F	7	1	0	2	19,640
Smoking Rib	2	C	2	1	0	0	6,140
Smoking Wise	2	F	4	2	0	1	53,330
Smok'n Frolic	5	M	8	1	3	1	258,220
Smokume	3	G	9	2	2	0	125,091
Smoky Knight	4	C	9	0	0	2	5,704
Smoochem	3	F	14	4	2	1	60,950
Smoochen Dancer	2	F	3	0	1	0	1,160
Smoochen Perner	4	C	2	0	0	0	676
Smoocher	3	C	5	0	0	0	12,831
Smoot Mahootie	4	G	4	0	0	0	0
Smooth	7	G	1	0	0	0	720
Smooth and Free	5	G	8	3	0	0	9,240
Smooth Approval	4	C	10	1	1	0	6,406
Smooth as Silver	4	G	12	4	4	3	128,275
Smooth Bid	2	C	5	2	2	1	77,410
Smooth Cruiser	5	G	8	1	2	1	30,732
Smooth Dorsal	4	F	3	0	0	0	585
Smooth Drummer	3	G	10	1	2	1	23,206
Smooth Gal	2	F	2	0	0	0	160
Smooth Ghost	2	C	8	0	1	2	23,165
Smooth Gold (GB)	3	C	1	0	0	0	0
Smooth Hand Luke	7	G	2	0	0	0	65
Smooth Italian	5	G	17	2	3	5	9,365
Smooth Jet	2	C	1	0	0	0	1,020
Smooth Louie	2	C	1	0	0	0	180
Smooth Lover	5	G	22	7	3	1	126,750
Smooth Maneuvers	4	F	6	3	2	0	97,410
Smooth N Easy	5	M	1	0	0	0	0
Smooth Reality	5	G	2	0	0	0	0
Smooth Rhythm	3	G	1	0	0	0	300
Smooth Rocket	2	F	3	0	1	0	3,800
Smooth Satin	3	G	2	0	1	0	1,262
Smooth Shannon	9	M	3	0	0	1	3,520
Smooth Stone	4	G	7	0	0	2	2,057
Smooth Talc	7	G	11	0	0	0	445
Smooth Talker	3	G	8	0	5	0	13,280
Smooth Talkin Jo	7	G	3	0	0	0	0
Smooth Turn	2	F	2	1	0	0	8,680
Smooth Velvet	4	F	1	0	0	0	0
Smooth Water	2	C	3	0	0	0	0
Smooth Willie R.	5	G	5	0	0	1	962
Smooth Wood	6	G	6	1	1	2	26,043
Smoothmovinangel	3	F	13	3	1	2	53,120
Smoove	2	F	3	0	1	0	10,840
Smoozie	7	M	10	2	2	3	6,435
S'more Smoke	5	M	9	2	2	1	41,722
Smorz	3	F	9	1	1	1	25,152
Smotheredwithlove	2	F	5	0	1	1	8,084
Smuggle Me Home	3	F	8	3	1	0	25,077
Smuggler	2	F	3	2	1	0	75,800
Smugglers Basin	5	H	10	1	4	3	45,200
Smuggler's Run	3	G	6	1	0	1	17,200
Smushy	3	G	10	2	0	0	12,600
Snack	2	C	6	2	2	2	47,800
Snack Attack	4	G	10	2	2	2	12,257
Snagged	8	G	2	0	0	0	202
Snake in the Grass	4	F	5	0	0	0	601
Snake Mountain	6	G	6	1	0	2	58,210
Snake Pit	4	G	2	0	0	0	0
Snake River	2	G	1	0	0	0	0
Snakes B G	3	C	2	0	0	0	346
Snakes n' Ladders	3	G	6	1	0	0	14,484
Snakes Princess	3	F	3	0	0	0	463
Snap Daddy	3	G	6	2	1	1	38,840
Snap Hook	5	G	4	3	0	1	29,120
Snap Judgement (IRE)	3	C	5	0	1	2	10,705
Snap Kat	4	F	2	0	0	0	498
Snapen Crackle	5	M	1	0	0	0	50
Snapped Up	3	C	1	0	0	0	0
Snappin Good Girl	3	F	6	0	1	1	6,005
Snappy Little Cat	3	F	9	1	2	2	19,641
Snappy Tale	4	F	5	0	0	0	1,440
Snappy Tim	4	G	6	1	3	0	31,860
Snappy Tune	3	F	9	1	0	2	15,260
Snaps Galore	9	G	1	0	0	1	290
Snatch the Cash	3	G	9	2	1	2	38,840
Snatchit	4	G	9	1	0	0	3,412
Snazzi's Yo Yo	3	C	5	0	0	0	444
Snazzy	3	F	6	0	1	3	16,010
Snazzy Abby	2	F	2	0	0	0	335
Snazzy Leon	2	C	5	0	0	0	395
Sneakalilpeak	4	C	8	2	0	1	7,789
Sneaker Mike	5	G	5	0	1	0	3,545
Sneakin Mac	8	G	3	1	0	1	991
Sneaking Upp	4	G	2	0	0	0	0
Sneaky	5	M	1	0	0	0	0
Sneaky First	4	F	5	0	1	2	3,000
Sneaky Jack	2	F	1	1	0	0	21,000
Sneaky Partner	4	F	2	0	0	0	141
Sneaky Petey	8	G	5	0	0	0	310
Sneaky Sam	10	G	6	0	1	0	1,104
Sneaky Secret	5	M	4	0	0	0	300
Sneem	5	M	4	2	0	1	9,627
Sneer	3	F	4	1	0	0	15,720
Sneezy Tab	5	H	4	0	0	0	258
Sneffels Street	4	G	8	1	1	2	7,348
Snertitude	4	G	7	0	0	0	1,053
Snickerdoo	6	M	7	0	3	2	13,479
Snicker's Mill	2	C	1	0	0	0	0
Sniffles	4	F	14	1	3	3	66,131
Snip Creek	3	F	18	0	3	1	8,750
Snipewalk	4	C	3	0	0	0	0
Snipper	6	G	7	2	0	1	2,200
Snipper Lou	2	F	10	2	1	2	84,495
Snitch	2	F	3	0	2	0	4,800
Snobby Curl	6	M	3	0	0	0	0
Snobby Princess	3	F	9	2	2	0	45,537
Snobby Secret	3	F	7	1	0	0	3,930
Snoden	2	C	1	0	1	0	8,800

Horse	Age	Sex	Sts	1st	2d	3d	Won
Snogun	6	M	1	0	1	0	4,500
Snohomish Fantasy	3	F	7	1	0	0	3,675
Snohomish High	2	G	6	1	1	1	9,195
Snohomish Loot	9	G	3	0	0	0	1,464
Snohomish Princess	3	F	2	0	0	0	0
Snoopbformarriage	8	M	10	1	1	2	19,915
Snoopster	2	C	1	0	0	0	0
Snoopy Blues	5	G	4	0	0	0	317
Snoopy Cat	5	G	7	1	1	2	50,643
Snooze Button	3	F	3	0	0	0	155
Snooze Zone	5	H	2	0	0	0	0
Snoqualmie Queen	4	F	9	0	0	1	4,860
Snoqualmie Ridge	4	F	4	1	0	1	12,390
Snoring Dan	3	G	4	0	0	0	1,833
Snorter	4	C	6	2	0	1	125,100
Snort's Sport	3	G	5	0	0	0	322
Snorzalot	4	G	13	1	1	3	44,104
Snow Big Deal	2	F	5	2	1	0	30,370
Snow Buck	8	G	6	1	1	0	3,790
Snow Bullet	3	G	5	0	0	0	330
Snow Capped	2	C	1	0	0	0	145
Snow Clock	2	F	1	0	0	0	0
Snow Country Cat	4	G	7	0	0	2	2,268
Snow Devil	3	F	1	0	0	1	1,400
Snow Eagle	3	C	8	2	0	2	49,010
Snow Fortune	8	M	8	0	0	1	1,904
Snow Glitter	2	F	1	0	0	0	205
Snow Mist	3	F	10	0	1	2	2,818
Snow More	2	C	2	0	0	0	0
Snow Mountain	4	F	12	3	3	2	41,628
Snow Nad	2	C	1	0	0	0	195
Snow On Cedars	4	G	2	0	0	0	63
Snow Punkin	2	F	1	0	0	0	120
Snow Queen	3	F	18	2	2	2	26,442
Snow Report	2	F	1	0	0	0	400
Snow Shot	4	C	3	0	2	0	3,980
Snow Shower	10	G	10	0	1	0	5,060
Snow Squall	2	C	1	0	0	0	600
Snow Sunset	4	F	5	1	1	2	5,803
Snow Time Lady	3	F	1	1	0	0	9,000
Snow Wonder M.d.	3	G	8	1	0	0	16,990
Snowball Flannagan	9	H	4	2	1	0	67,250
Snowball King	5	G	10	0	1	1	2,161
Snowballs Chance	4	G	4	3	1	0	16,660
Snowbell	3	F	1	0	0	0	0
Snowbird	3	F	7	1	2	1	14,800
Snowbird's Lady	4	F	5	0	0	0	304
Snowbound Bob	4	G	8	2	1	0	16,192
Snowbound Dream	3	G	3	0	0	0	360
Snowbound Express	4	C	3	2	0	0	3,027
Snowbound Knights	2	G	3	0	0	0	890
Snowbound Mike	3	G	5	1	3	0	7,240
Snowbound Nan	3	F	6	2	0	0	24,608
Snowbound Native	4	F	4	0	1	0	3,260
Snowbound Paul	4	G	2	0	1	0	500
Snowbound Sails	3	F	2	0	1	0	3,534
Snowbound Star	4	F	7	3	0	2	7,474
Snowbound Writer	3	G	2	0	2	0	10,260
Snowbound Zulu	3	G	1	0	0	0	0
Snowbound's Bonus	4	F	5	1	0	0	3,455
Snowbound's Ghost	4	G	6	2	0	0	7,351
Snowdance Kid	3	G	15	2	3	1	15,867
Snowdazzle	4	C	10	1	2	0	15,238
Snowdrops (GB)	4	F	6	3	2	0	140,281
Snowflakekisses	2	F	6	0	0	0	1,440
Snowman Hustle	7	G	13	1	1	0	14,832
Snowonecancatchme	5	M	4	0	0	0	208
Snowshoe Flyer	6	G	17	0	1	4	4,012
Snowy King	6	H	5	0	1	0	4,959
Snowy Night	5	G	16	1	0	3	7,134
Snowy Old Man	2	G	3	0	0	0	1,616
Snowy's Cafe	3	F	9	2	0	0	14,752
Snoze's Princess	4	F	3	0	0	0	194
Snu	2	C	6	1	0	1	5,890
Snub the Devil	3	C	9	3	1	0	81,380
Snuff	2	G	6	1	0	0	23,418
Snug as a Bug	3	C	3	0	1	0	6,130
Snug Harbour	2	F	5	1	0	1	30,300
Snuggle (NZ)	12	G	3	1	0	2	19,000

Horse	Age	Sex	Sts	1st	2d	3d	Won
Snuggle an Cuddle	4	F	8	0	0	0	522
Snuggle Up	6	M	7	0	0	0	347
Snuggy	2	C	4	0	1	1	5,125
So Alive	4	G	5	1	1	1	19,165
So Blue	3	F	1	0	0	0	550
So Can Do	8	G	5	0	0	0	735
So Catty	5	M	1	0	0	0	139
So Charmed	3	F	7	1	0	2	3,905
So Charming	3	F	2	0	0	0	625
So Colorful (GB)	2	F	2	0	1	1	3,450
So Compelling	4	C	10	2	1	1	15,895
So Coole Bidder	3	C	1	0	0	0	0
So Dapper	4	C	2	0	0	0	0
So Delicious	2	F	7	0	2	1	11,790
So Dixie	3	G	3	0	0	0	192
So Excited	5	M	2	1	0	1	5,675
So Far Go	3	G	10	3	1	1	32,291
So Gifted	3	C	5	1	0	0	17,000
So Good	3	F	10	3	3	1	51,770
So Grand	7	M	1	0	0	0	0
So Happy Together	3	F	12	3	0	5	37,955
So Help Me	3	F	3	0	0	1	1,430
So Hot	3	F	5	1	0	0	18,305
So It Is	3	F	10	1	3	3	12,942
So Long Birdie	2	C	2	1	0	0	21,400
So Long Charlie	4	G	7	1	1	3	9,858
So Many Memories	6	M	2	0	0	0	171
So Miss Jeopardy	5	M	12	2	4	2	13,831
So Much Love	8	M	1	0	0	0	0
So Much More	5	M	4	1	0	1	54,207
So Much Out There	3	F	7	0	0	0	1,200
So Much Pretty	4	F	6	3	0	1	15,810
So Nasty	5	G	5	0	0	2	2,301
So Nicely Done	5	M	4	0	1	1	5,522
So Obvious	3	G	2	0	1	0	2,128
So Phun	2	G	1	0	0	0	145
So Proud	4	F	17	1	0	3	14,365
So Rare	4	F	1	0	0	0	0
So Red	2	C	1	0	0	0	400
So Remarqueabubble	3	F	4	0	0	0	180
So Romeo	2	G	1	0	0	0	75
So Shattered	5	G	15	0	1	4	6,423
So Silent	3	F	7	1	1	0	21,630
So Silver	7	M	8	1	0	2	9,362
So Snazzy	4	C	11	1	1	5	14,275
So So Clever	5	G	4	2	0	0	3,145
So So Nice	2	F	1	0	0	0	155
So So Reel	3	F	3	0	0	0	0
So Sorry	3	F	10	2	2	3	47,600
So Still	2	F	4	0	0	1	3,240
So Sultry	3	F	8	2	1	1	40,830
So Superior	5	G	5	0	1	1	1,520
So Swanky	2	C	2	0	0	0	1,720
So Sweet a Cat	3	F	8	5	1	0	244,890
So Synful	3	F	15	4	0	1	39,015
So Tricky Mr. Ken	4	G	8	1	0	3	8,398
So Urgent	6	H	1	0	0	0	0
So Welcome	5	M	11	1	1	2	24,965
So What Bull	4	G	4	0	0	0	80
So Ya Know	2	F	1	0	1	0	6,800
So You Say	5	H	8	1	0	1	20,815
Soaked	4	G	10	2	1	2	57,829
Soap Box	2	G	2	0	0	0	636
Soaring	3	F	12	2	3	2	23,176
Soaring an Action	8	G	9	0	1	0	1,718
Soaring Away	3	C	4	0	0	1	8,742
Soaring Fantasy	2	F	1	0	0	0	0
Soaring Free	5	G	8	6	0	0	1,113,862
Soaring Games	7	H	13	1	2	0	10,933
Soaring Hawk	6	G	9	0	1	3	3,185
Soaring Jet	2	F	1	0	0	0	118
Soaring Leader	4	G	11	1	0	1	6,263
Soaring Magic	5	M	4	0	0	0	2,759
Soaring Strike	2	C	2	1	0	0	15,900
Soaring Swiftly	2	F	4	0	0	0	1,087
Soaring Wings	6	G	2	0	0	0	80
Soaringwitheagles	3	C	5	0	1	1	3,898
Sober Mac	8	G	2	0	0	0	170
Sober Moment	4	F	17	1	3	0	26,237

Horse	Age	Sex	Sts	1st	2d	3d	Won
Sobering Thought	3	F	2	0	0	0	161
Sobers Lane	4	G	14	2	1	3	30,925
Sobinka (IRE)	4	F	2	0	0	0	1,847
Sobriquet	3	F	5	0	0	1	7,736
Soccer Dan	3	G	10	2	1	3	48,313
Soccoro Sky	2	F	3	0	0	0	105
Social Account	6	G	14	3	2	2	32,805
Social Bin Woodman	3	C	12	1	2	3	11,825
Social Buffy	3	F	3	0	0	0	293
Social Delight	10	G	2	0	0	0	116
Social Deputy	2	C	1	0	0	0	0
Social Expense	8	G	10	2	1	1	7,900
Social G Man	4	G	4	0	0	1	2,143
Social Graces	4	G	4	0	3	0	3,992
Social King	3	C	11	5	3	0	109,600
Social Lies	5	G	6	1	1	1	11,642
Social Mix	5	G	12	0	1	2	6,220
Social Probation	2	C	5	2	1	0	60,900
Social Sands	4	F	16	2	0	3	14,530
Social Sarah Bell	4	F	4	0	0	0	144
Social Security	4	F	14	4	2	2	79,050
Social Top	6	M	4	0	1	0	6,566
Social Validation	2	F	4	1	0	1	9,405
Social Virtue	2	F	3	1	1	1	57,280
Socialize	4	G	2	0	0	0	103
Socially Cleared	4	F	25	2	2	4	27,884
Sociano	9	H	6	2	1	1	32,324
Socies Girl	3	F	2	0	0	0	0
Society Cat	3	F	8	3	4	0	36,020
Society Sal	4	G	9	2	3	1	18,965
Society Sam	3	C	14	2	2	1	43,672
Society Selection	3	F	9	3	3	1	929,700
Society Senorita	2	F	6	0	2	1	9,410
Society Storm	2	G	2	0	0	0	216
Society Zone	3	F	9	1	1	1	8,685
Society's Child	3	F	1	0	0	0	320
Sock Hop	7	G	2	0	0	0	144
Sock Hop Sally	3	F	9	1	2	2	15,626
Sockes	2	G	1	0	0	1	820
Sockitaway	4	G	10	3	0	3	54,215
Socko	6	G	9	3	3	1	100,734
Socks Muldoon	4	G	4	0	0	1	1,096
Socksnsneakers	3	F	7	2	0	1	17,580
Socorro County	3	F	9	3	3	2	146,249
Soda Girl	3	F	7	0	2	2	5,965
Sode'steddimou	5	G	6	1	0	0	6,525
Sodo Mojo	4	G	10	0	2	3	1,792
Soes Bandit	8	G	17	3	1	0	29,210
Soft as Velvet	4	F	9	0	2	3	4,784
Soft Expression	2	F	2	1	0	0	25,472
Soft Feeling	4	F	10	0	3	1	3,281
Soft Hit	3	F	4	0	0	1	5,934
Soft Judge	5	H	14	1	3	1	9,076
Soft Lika Rock	4	G	4	0	1	0	2,518
Soft n' Loud	4	F	15	1	2	4	24,499
Soft Rain	8	G	7	1	0	1	5,998
Softly Blowing	4	G	14	5	3	1	22,503
Softly Played	5	M	13	0	0	1	3,086
Softly Rizing	2	F	5	1	0	0	11,895
Softshoeshuffle	6	H	19	0	0	0	2,570
Software	4	F	8	0	1	2	6,545
Sogno Dolce	2	F	2	0	0	0	332
Soi	2	C	1	0	0	1	1,150
Soir de Soleil	3	C	3	0	2	0	8,000
Soitenly	4	G	9	1	2	1	28,999
Sokol Blosser	3	F	4	0	0	0	75
Sola Topee (GB)	8	G	1	0	0	0	400
Solamente	4	F	13	1	2	2	12,811
Solana Storm	6	M	7	0	0	0	1,795
Solar Fire	3	F	3	0	0	1	5,880
Solar Frost	3	G	5	0	0	2	3,355
Solar Man	4	G	4	0	0	0	540
Solar Sail	3	F	1	0	0	0	0
Solar Song	3	F	3	0	0	0	580
Solar Way	5	G	9	2	1	0	5,543
Solaratee	3	F	3	0	1	0	2,100
Sold	4	C	10	1	1	2	21,680
Sold the Gold	2	F	2	0	2	0	11,760
Soldier Bear	5	G	24	2	2	5	18,490
Soldier in Action	5	G	8	2	1	0	11,540
Soldier Lake	5	H	2	1	0	0	5,850
Soldier McGee	4	G	13	0	2	4	9,034
Soldier Nui	3	C	1	0	0	0	0
Soldier of Fame	3	G	14	3	4	3	79,425
Soldier Song	5	H	10	1	1	3	39,671
Soldierofpleasure	5	G	10	0	0	1	3,818
Soldier's Angel	4	F	16	1	6	2	34,397
Soldier's Curfew	3	C	4	0	0	1	1,100
Soldier's Cutlass	4	C	6	1	0	1	5,670
Soldier's Dream	2	F	7	1	1	0	14,915
Soldiers Fortune	7	G	10	0	0	2	8,000
Soldier's Lady	3	F	14	1	1	0	6,497
Soldiers Quest	5	G	15	1	4	2	21,650
Soldiersdon'tblush	2	G	3	0	0	0	0
Soldiersingsblues	3	F	2	0	0	0	400
Sole of the City	3	F	5	1	1	2	24,250
Sole Prospect	7	H	1	0	0	0	0
Sole Request	3	C	8	0	0	0	1,095
Soleaido	5	M	1	0	0	0	75
Soliantu	2	F	7	0	3	1	15,960
Solicitation	8	G	4	0	0	2	6,005
Solicitor	5	G	10	3	2	1	20,445
Solid Brass	9	M	1	0	0	0	0
Solid Demand	3	C	3	0	0	0	1,010
Solid Fuel	2	G	1	0	0	0	400
Solid Gold Bar	2	C	8	3	1	1	38,217
Solid Gold Cat	2	G	5	0	0	0	1,545
Solid Gold Copy	3	G	6	1	1	0	7,062
Solid Gone	8	G	2	0	0	0	0
Solid Mahogany	3	C	4	0	0	0	287
Solid Mon	3	C	1	0	0	0	0
Solid Platinum	3	F	4	1	0	2	36,900
Solid Reach	3	C	2	1	0	0	14,785
Solid Sensation	2	C	1	0	0	0	1,988
Solid Silver Star	4	G	7	1	1	0	17,625
Solid State	3	G	4	0	0	0	186
Solid Sterling	4	G	2	0	0	0	0
Solid Ten	5	M	8	2	1	0	22,314
Solid Wood	9	G	16	1	0	6	6,745
Solihull	4	G	7	0	1	3	47,130
Solina	4	F	2	0	1	0	6,620
Solingen	6	G	4	2	0	1	25,572
Solitario	6	G	5	2	0	0	63,050
Solitarius	3	F	14	3	2	4	30,585
Solitary	3	G	14	1	7	0	26,480
Solitary Code	4	G	3	0	1	0	1,890
Solitary Emerald	3	F	9	2	1	3	64,790
Solitary Ritzi	3	C	8	1	0	1	7,485
Solitary Starr	5	G	15	2	1	1	25,979
Solitary Strife	5	M	6	2	2	2	63,940
Soliton	3	C	3	0	0	0	235
Sollozo	4	G	17	2	1	3	6,432
Solly's Dolly	3	F	13	4	2	1	32,823
Solo Cat	4	G	8	1	2	0	36,595
Solo Colony	3	G	6	1	1	0	7,354
Solo Flight	3	F	5	0	0	0	950
Solo Lady	4	F	2	0	0	0	86
Solo Number	5	G	7	0	0	1	1,156
Solo Player	4	G	2	0	0	0	114
Solo Reflection	5	G	10	3	0	0	14,625
Solo Special	10	G	16	2	1	0	7,171
Solo Standard	5	G	8	3	1	0	4,670
Solo Strut	3	G	12	0	0	3	4,766
Solo Vivo	3	F	5	1	0	1	3,396
Solocoexpress	7	G	7	2	1	0	12,757
Soloing	4	F	7	0	1	2	15,150
Solomon's Decree	5	H	8	0	0	1	1,187
Solomon's Seal	6	H	2	0	0	0	1,311
Solongcache	2	G	2	0	0	0	1,540
Solorancho	2	C	2	0	0	0	550
Sol's Bag	4	G	11	1	0	2	11,438
Sombrio	5	G	1	0	0	0	740
Some Bold Style	2	C	8	0	0	3	8,720
Some Bold Thrill	2	C	4	0	0	2	8,415
Some Came Running	5	M	10	3	2	1	67,810
Some Chestnut	4	G	6	0	1	0	1,888
Some Crusader	2	C	1	0	0	0	1,150
Some Curves	5	M	12	0	1	3	14,685

Horse	Age	Sex	Sts	1st	2d	3d	Won
Some Devil You Are	3	G	4	1	0	1	8,791
Some Ghost	3	C	7	3	1	3	73,861
Some Girls Do	2	F	1	0	0	0	55
Some Image	3	G	1	0	0	0	0
Some Irish Legend	8	M	5	0	0	1	5,148
Some Kind of Tiger	4	C	7	2	0	0	63,641
Some Kinda Class	4	G	16	3	4	2	34,636
Some Kinda Dancer	8	G	11	1	1	1	5,060
Some Lucky Star	9	G	6	1	1	1	3,229
Some Nerve	2	F	4	0	1	0	1,495
Some One Free	6	G	4	2	1	0	10,994
Some Other Night	5	G	2	0	0	0	655
Some Party	3	C	3	0	1	0	3,150
Some Remark	5	G	2	1	0	0	4,788
Some Royal Gem	2	F	4	0	0	0	0
Some Runaway	8	G	15	2	0	3	18,744
Some Sweet Day	3	F	2	0	0	0	0
Somebody Smart	2	C	3	0	0	0	0
Somebodystopme	8	M	2	0	0	0	74
Someday's Queen	9	M	3	0	0	0	148
Somekinda Cheerful	3	G	11	3	2	0	18,489
Somekindalanding	5	M	2	0	0	0	0
Somekindofgrace	4	F	1	0	0	0	40
Somekindofire	6	G	10	0	0	1	1,970
Someones Coming	6	M	9	2	0	0	12,360
Someonestopme	4	F	1	0	0	0	0
Somer Wonders	9	M	5	1	2	0	8,322
Somerby	2	F	1	0	0	0	205
Somerset House	5	G	10	3	1	2	39,702
Somerset Legend	3	G	7	0	3	0	7,622
Somerset's Husband	6	G	2	0	0	0	0
Somethin About Amy	2	F	1	0	0	0	0
Somethin Brite	6	G	12	1	3	4	11,403
Somethinaboutlaura	2	F	1	0	0	0	400
Somethinfopleasure	3	F	4	0	1	1	2,443
Something Brewing	2	F	6	1	1	1	61,131
Something Celtic	3	G	5	0	0	0	0
Something Charmed	2	F	2	0	0	0	0
Something Clever	4	G	10	2	2	3	9,386
Something Crooked	6	H	4	0	0	0	231
Something Fierce	3	G	14	1	3	5	33,606
Something Fun	2	F	2	0	0	0	164
Something Funny	4	G	3	0	0	0	300
Something Gallant	5	G	6	1	0	0	9,540
Something in Red	3	F	4	0	0	0	1,150
Something Magic	6	M	2	0	0	0	652
Something Racy	4	F	1	0	0	0	0
Something Rushing	5	H	5	0	0	1	9,620
Something Smith	4	G	4	1	2	0	60,100
Something Stylish	3	F	4	1	1	1	4,778
Something Ventured	5	M	11	1	4	0	114,920
Somethingbold	4	G	11	1	0	1	4,989
Somethingdangerous	6	G	12	1	5	1	57,565
Somethingforlove	4	G	2	0	0	2	5,280
Somethingquiet	3	F	13	1	2	0	23,194
Somethingsecret	4	F	7	0	0	1	486
Sometime Thing	4	F	3	1	0	0	3,570
Sometimes Fantasy	2	F	1	0	0	0	75
Sometimes I Don't	2	F	7	1	2	1	15,200
Somewereoutthere	3	F	1	0	0	0	92
Somfas Dancer	8	G	13	2	1	3	3,610
Sommelier	6	G	5	0	0	1	2,860
Son Also Rises	6	G	3	0	0	0	217
Son of a Lue	5	G	14	3	7	0	54,568
Son of Appeal	2	C	7	1	0	2	15,465
Son of Danube	2	C	3	0	0	0	900
Son of Flag	7	H	2	0	0	0	260
Son of Flame	4	C	2	0	0	0	0
Son of Man	5	H	10	2	0	0	30,810
Son of Mariah	6	G	21	8	1	3	29,029
Son of Pete	7	G	12	3	5	2	13,556
Son of Rehaan	6	G	1	0	0	0	0
Son of Syn	5	G	10	0	2	1	9,735
Son of the North	2	G	8	1	2	3	51,193
Son Ofa Factor	5	G	11	2	3	3	12,542
Son Ofa Prospector	3	C	11	0	2	0	3,868
Son Sarria	2	F	3	0	0	1	9,690
Sonador	4	G	17	0	5	3	13,065
Sonas	2	F	1	0	0	0	0
Sonata Gold	3	F	1	0	0	0	118
Sonata St	3	F	4	0	2	1	2,279
Sonawho	2	G	4	1	1	2	48,067
Sonceore	4	G	9	0	3	1	7,650
Sondeo	6	G	6	0	0	1	3,990
Song Called	4	F	2	0	0	0	205
Song Dancer	6	H	15	6	2	1	53,321
Song Du Jour (AUS)	4	F	4	1	0	1	16,730
Song for Ashley	3	F	5	0	0	1	4,490
Song for Sasha	2	G	1	0	0	0	135
Song Forum	5	M	3	0	0	0	147
Song Hunter	3	F	8	0	0	3	3,670
Song Minister (BRZ)	7	G	6	1	0	1	14,560
Song of Beauty	3	F	6	1	0	0	5,010
Song of Hope	6	M	5	0	3	0	5,315
Song of Nora	5	M	10	1	3	1	25,110
Song of Shawky	4	G	10	0	1	0	2,795
Song of the Bull	3	G	14	3	2	3	46,065
Song of the Cat	2	C	1	0	0	0	125
Song of the Sword	3	C	10	4	2	1	258,600
Song of Tiger	3	F	5	0	0	0	214
Song of Versailles	4	F	15	2	5	1	29,385
Song Or Psalm	6	M	9	0	3	1	11,964
Song Sung Gold	3	F	7	0	1	3	26,740
Song Track	3	F	7	2	0	0	57,213
Songbrook Alice	4	F	13	0	2	1	6,431
Songfortc	3	F	3	0	0	0	1,417
Songinthedarkness	4	F	16	0	3	3	10,885
Song'n Dance	2	F	2	0	0	1	4,720
Sonhouse	7	G	2	0	0	0	105
Sonia (GER)	5	M	5	1	0	0	37,240
Sonia's Sonata	4	F	2	0	0	0	0
Sonia's Song	4	F	13	1	2	1	35,890
Sonic Blum	5	G	3	0	0	0	125
Sonic Boom Aly	3	F	4	0	0	0	732
Sonic Eagle	3	G	14	2	3	1	35,880
Sonic West	5	G	10	2	2	2	367,813
Sonic Youth (GB)	4	C	5	0	0	0	0
Sonic's Golden Boy	6	G	13	1	1	4	9,114
Sonique	5	M	2	0	0	0	258
Sonivere	4	C	4	0	1	1	22,426
Sonny and Rose	3	C	15	4	1	3	121,217
Sonny Boy Blue	7	G	13	0	4	1	6,870
Sonny Dale	4	F	7	0	0	0	415
Sonny Go West	4	G	6	0	0	0	240
Sonny the Sailor	7	G	5	0	0	0	1,365
Sonny's Biscuit	2	C	1	0	0	0	0
Sonny's Hammer	3	C	5	0	1	0	1,700
Sonny's Legacy	4	G	7	3	0	2	53,505
Sonny's Pride	6	G	8	2	2	1	5,175
Sonny's Warrior	4	G	8	0	1	2	877
Sonny's Zone	6	H	12	1	1	1	5,504
Sonofablonde	4	C	4	0	0	1	460
Sonofawac	4	G	11	0	6	1	52,450
Sonofpreacherman	3	G	11	0	1	2	3,479
Sonoita Sunset	5	M	14	3	4	2	48,940
Sonoma	3	F	3	0	0	0	960
Sonoma County	4	F	2	0	0	0	115
Sonora Cisco	5	M	9	3	2	2	9,577
Sonora Dancer	2	F	1	0	0	0	400
Sonora Girl	3	F	11	0	1	1	3,301
Sonora Lady	7	M	1	0	0	0	0
Sonora's Moon	4	F	9	0	2	1	7,245
Sonorense	6	G	4	0	3	1	2,880
Sonothemorningstar	3	G	14	3	1	1	43,767
Sonriente	3	G	8	1	1	2	36,464
Sonya's Smile	3	F	8	1	1	3	20,425
Soo	5	H	8	0	1	2	5,245
Soo Much	5	H	8	3	1	2	40,705
Soobadd	3	C	5	0	1	0	7,910
Soobee Frost	3	G	8	1	0	0	9,597
Sooey Express	2	F	8	0	1	0	5,040
Sookski	3	F	3	1	0	1	18,785
Soon Be Gone	3	F	6	0	0	0	675
Soon Soon	5	M	12	0	0	3	16,801
Soon Soon N Y	3	C	1	0	0	0	2,050
Soon to Be Family	3	F	12	0	2	3	6,071
Soon to Be King	3	C	4	0	0	0	1,013
Soon to Be Single	6	M	2	1	1	0	43,720

Horse	Age	Sex	Sts	1st	2d	3d	Won
Sooner Be Dancin'	3	F	9	1	1	1	12,657
Sooner Fever	2	F	2	0	1	0	2,415
Sooner Land	6	G	4	1	0	1	1,383
Sooner Pride	2	G	7	3	0	0	45,305
Sooner Risk	2	G	1	1	0	0	6,550
Sooner Shine	6	G	15	2	3	3	13,865
Sooner the Better	3	C	16	3	4	0	21,994
Soonerorlater	2	G	4	0	0	0	1,094
Soonersaige	4	F	2	0	0	1	1,900
Soos Maheer	3	C	11	1	1	2	24,878
Soot	4	G	7	0	0	0	2,640
Soota Two	2	F	3	0	0	1	1,402
Sootaa	5	M	3	0	0	0	0
Soothe the Soul	5	G	10	2	2	0	7,217
Sooty Boy	5	G	6	0	0	0	1,229
Sophette	3	F	2	0	0	1	1,480
Sophia Jones	3	F	3	1	1	0	8,200
Sophia Mae	2	F	9	0	0	0	300
Sophia Ofthe Hills	4	F	4	0	0	0	800
Sophia Storm	3	F	2	0	0	0	175
Sophiano	2	F	5	0	1	1	13,954
Sophias Humor	3	F	1	0	0	0	145
Sophia's Prince	5	G	8	1	4	0	86,356
Sophia's Secret	3	F	2	0	1	0	1,240
Sophie	5	M	1	0	0	0	163
Sophiecallingsara	2	F	3	0	0	0	3,420
Sophie's Bold	7	G	4	0	0	0	0
Sophie's Cat	4	F	2	0	0	0	875
Sophie's Crown	3	F	8	0	1	1	5,055
Sophie's Magic	3	F	10	0	1	1	4,623
Sophisticated Babe	3	F	2	0	0	0	500
Sophisticated Bit	2	F	5	0	2	0	5,815
Sophisticated Code	4	F	1	0	0	0	460
Sophisticated Man	9	H	6	1	0	1	8,570
Sophisticatedbluff	5	M	2	1	1	0	42,000
Sophisticatedwager	2	C	8	0	1	2	11,200
Sopwith Pup	5	G	12	3	2	1	33,600
Sor De	5	G	2	0	0	0	128
Sorbet	4	F	7	3	2	0	69,060
Sorcerer's Magic	3	C	3	0	0	0	0
Sordelo	3	G	3	1	0	0	6,810
Sordid Affair	4	F	6	0	0	0	871
Sorenstam	4	F	4	0	0	0	174
Soriano Cat	3	G	5	0	1	1	5,100
Sorority Girl	3	F	9	1	0	2	31,140
Sorority Pledge	6	M	9	0	2	2	7,633
Sorrel Cat	5	M	3	0	0	0	336
Sorrentino (ARG)	5	H	15	1	1	1	9,220
Sorrento Sara	5	M	11	4	0	3	26,857
Sorrytotellyou	4	F	14	1	0	6	31,634
Sort It Out	2	C	6	1	1	0	49,085
Sorte	4	G	5	0	2	2	3,883
Sorvel	3	G	5	0	0	0	1,440
Sosella	3	F	5	0	1	1	6,741
Sosie	3	F	10	1	2	2	12,391
Sosweet	4	F	7	0	2	2	15,295
Sothatswherewereat	2	F	13	1	4	4	17,080
Sothypann	5	M	5	1	0	1	8,003
Sotogrande	6	M	2	0	0	1	850
Soud	6	H	4	2	1	0	101,200
Soul Mate	4	F	4	1	2	0	28,000
Soul Obsession	6	H	9	5	2	0	17,090
Soul of the Cat	3	F	4	1	0	1	29,631
Soul Star	2	F	3	0	0	0	4,825
Soulard Swirl	7	G	7	1	1	1	3,920
Soulshine	2	C	2	0	0	0	255
Sounce a Silence	3	F	9	2	1	3	51,890
Sound Force	5	H	2	0	0	0	89
Sound Judgement	2	C	1	0	0	0	300
Sound of Gold	6	M	7	5	0	1	91,030
Sound of Power	5	M	13	0	2	3	2,816
Sound of Speed	4	G	9	2	0	0	5,780
Sound Prospect	2	G	6	0	1	0	825
Sound the Alert	5	G	4	0	0	0	772
Sound Wave	7	M	11	1	1	3	15,646
Soundless	2	F	7	0	1	2	10,031
Sounds Foolish	3	G	1	0	0	0	0
Sounds Great	5	G	9	0	0	0	450
Sounds Groovy	3	G	2	0	0	0	800
Sounds Impossible	2	C	3	1	2	0	36,400
Sounds Like Red	2	G	2	0	0	0	175
Sounds Real	4	G	12	1	0	1	6,634
Soup	4	G	14	2	3	2	29,161
Soup Abc	4	F	5	0	0	0	390
Soup Du Jour	2	C	1	0	0	1	2,640
Soup for Dinner	3	F	3	0	1	0	2,472
Soup n' Crackers	5	M	10	3	0	2	8,593
Soup Spoon	4	C	10	2	0	1	19,761
Soup Time	4	C	7	3	2	1	28,050
Soupolicious	3	G	9	2	1	0	16,203
Soupy	3	C	3	0	0	0	1,600
Soupy Sails	3	C	4	0	0	0	0
Sour Toreo	3	F	6	0	0	0	374
Source	6	H	14	2	3	3	65,550
Source of Passion	3	G	4	1	0	0	6,600
Source One	3	G	4	0	0	0	1,070
Sources and Uses	3	C	4	0	1	0	6,571
Sourdough Girl	3	F	3	0	0	0	66
Sourest Lady	4	F	4	0	0	0	450
Souris	4	F	11	3	2	5	166,150
South Africa	3	G	6	3	2	0	97,200
South Bay Cove	2	F	4	3	0	0	256,897
South Beach (CHI)	6	G	3	0	0	0	197
South Beach Boy	2	C	2	1	0	0	9,370
South Bound n Down	11	G	4	0	0	2	588
South Brook	3	C	1	0	0	0	320
South by Gosh	6	G	7	1	2	1	19,200
South Christian	4	G	13	1	1	4	16,192
South City	8	G	2	1	1	0	6,850
South Country	3	G	19	2	2	4	15,437
South Diamond	2	C	4	0	0	0	0
South Girl	3	F	3	0	0	0	0
South Gone West	3	C	8	3	0	1	25,640
South Haven	7	G	7	1	1	3	9,090
South Lan Tour	3	F	4	1	1	0	4,976
South Magnolia	3	F	8	0	5	0	24,934
South of Here	2	C	2	0	1	0	3,200
South Paw	3	C	5	1	0	2	24,660
South Sea Gulch	4	C	5	1	2	0	37,172
South Side	10	G	10	0	0	1	2,362
South Wing	3	F	10	3	3	1	168,862
Southack	2	C	9	0	1	3	31,480
Southaintbad	4	F	10	1	1	0	9,141
Southall	2	C	6	1	2	1	17,185
Southbound Katie	3	F	10	2	3	0	26,620
Southeaster	4	F	6	2	0	1	31,510
Souther Division	3	F	4	1	1	0	14,610
Southerly Flow	6	M	7	0	1	1	2,555
Southern	2	F	4	1	1	1	44,395
Southern Africa	2	C	5	2	1	0	67,190
Southern Alert	4	F	13	3	3	0	32,675
Southern Barfly	3	F	2	1	0	0	13,640
Southern Blaze	5	G	13	0	1	5	3,794
Southern Boy	8	G	12	1	1	1	12,977
Southern Cal	3	G	7	3	2	0	62,720
Southern Cartel	3	G	11	1	4	1	31,467
Southern Celebrity	4	C	8	1	0	3	10,144
Southern Chance	6	G	3	0	0	0	790
Southern Chips	3	G	16	3	1	1	22,455
Southern Cross Sky	6	G	10	1	1	1	4,325
Southern Delight	3	F	4	0	0	0	0
Southern Dinner	7	G	14	4	0	2	53,725
Southern Drive	3	G	6	2	0	0	14,814
Southern Eyes	3	F	2	0	0	0	1,241
Southern Fire	3	F	3	0	0	0	4,095
Southern Gamble	3	G	3	0	0	0	0
Southern Genes	10	G	2	0	0	0	80
Southern Glow	2	C	2	0	0	0	0
Southern Heat	10	M	6	0	0	1	3,345
Southern Honoree	4	G	9	0	0	1	3,617
Southern Hope	4	F	2	0	0	0	0
Southern Image	4	C	4	3	1	0	1,612,150
Southern Jewel	4	F	11	2	1	1	18,063
Southern Leader	3	C	7	0	0	0	3,405
Southern Legacy	4	C	15	6	2	1	54,500
Southern Love	5	G	8	0	0	0	0
Southern Macho	5	G	14	2	0	0	4,076
Southern Magnolia	2	F	1	1	0	0	4,200

Horse	Age	Sex	Sts	1st	2d	3d	Won
Southern Majesty	4	G	3	1	0	0	5,953
Southern Migration	3	F	4	0	1	2	14,880
Southern Militia	3	G	3	0	1	2	10,200
Southern Miss	4	F	11	3	2	0	31,240
Southern Miss Man	2	C	1	0	0	0	0
Southern Mist	4	F	4	0	0	0	0
Southern Oasis	6	M	2	0	0	0	4,563
Southern Okie	4	F	16	2	2	1	12,053
Southern Order	4	F	10	3	1	1	65,639
Southern Outlaw	3	C	3	1	0	2	63,120
Southern Pioneer	4	G	9	1	0	1	5,012
Southern Preacher	4	G	4	1	1	1	16,440
Southern Prime	5	H	6	0	0	0	874
Southern Prize	6	G	10	1	2	2	2,914
Southern Rage	4	G	7	1	1	0	11,653
Southern Rain	4	F	4	2	0	1	33,580
Southern Randy	4	G	14	2	0	0	14,265
Southern Rebel	7	G	11	0	0	1	720
Southern Regal	3	G	18	1	5	3	10,864
Southern Romp	4	F	11	1	0	3	11,735
Southern Rule	2	C	3	0	1	1	9,937
Southern Salt	3	F	2	0	0	0	465
Southern Sanction	4	G	6	1	0	0	11,418
Southern Scarlett	4	F	6	0	0	0	565
Southern Sensation	4	G	13	2	4	1	38,977
Southern Serenity	2	F	6	2	1	1	27,358
Southern Shuffle	9	G	4	0	0	0	151
Southern Smoke	4	F	3	0	0	2	3,450
Southern Snuggle	4	C	8	0	2	1	16,724
Southern Soldier	2	F	4	1	2	1	20,075
Southern Son	8	G	2	0	0	0	128
Southern Spring	3	F	11	3	4	2	54,560
Southern States	5	H	1	0	0	0	0
Southern Stepper	4	F	5	0	0	1	1,555
Southern Storm	5	H	4	0	0	0	210
Southern Straight	4	F	13	0	3	0	6,934
Southern Strategy	3	F	8	1	2	0	15,746
Southern Surprise	5	M	14	3	2	1	79,168
Southern Survivor	5	H	12	2	0	2	12,580
Southern Sweet	6	M	5	1	0	0	14,040
Southern Trial	3	G	8	1	1	0	14,150
Southern Trick	3	G	7	1	4	0	6,131
Southern Trouble	3	G	5	0	0	0	0
Southern Twilight	3	G	13	4	1	0	43,110
Southern Viking	5	M	11	0	2	4	7,579
Southern Voice	4	F	6	1	0	2	8,300
Southern Whiskers	4	G	12	0	1	3	6,107
Southern Wind	3	F	2	0	0	0	324
Southern Wolf	6	G	18	2	3	2	24,025
Southernblue	4	G	11	2	1	1	11,886
Southerncheckpoint	3	G	4	0	0	0	315
Southerndemolition	3	G	5	0	0	0	813
Southernengagement	3	F	8	2	0	1	53,305
Southernhemisphere	3	G	3	0	0	0	0
Southernsturn	4	F	3	0	0	0	0
Southlake Drive	5	G	11	4	0	0	38,117
Southside Johnny	5	G	8	0	1	2	4,495
Southside Johnny B	2	C	7	1	0	2	12,355
Southsider	2	F	2	0	0	0	0
Southspring Ginger	3	F	7	0	0	0	992
Southtown Slew	4	G	9	0	4	3	15,159
Southwest City	3	F	5	0	1	2	13,580
Souvenier Biz	4	G	7	0	2	0	37,524
Souvenir Charm	2	F	2	0	0	0	800
Souvenir Doll	3	F	4	1	2	0	25,472
Souvenir Gift	2	F	5	3	2	0	211,760
Souvenir Lake	3	F	9	0	3	1	13,258
Souvenir Sands	2	C	3	1	1	0	10,000
Souvenir Song	3	F	5	0	0	1	1,610
Souvenir's Lad	4	C	12	5	1	2	74,000
Souvenir's of Old	4	G	9	2	0	2	23,042
Sou'wester	7	G	13	0	2	4	6,341
Sovereign Attire	6	G	6	0	0	1	4,368
Sovereign Creek	4	G	9	1	2	3	11,802
Sovereign Domain	2	F	2	0	0	0	0
Sovereign Dreams	9	G	2	0	0	0	575
Sovereign Episode	9	M	11	0	1	1	1,500
Sovereign Kit (ARG)	8	H	8	2	2	1	59,225
Sovereign Luck	6	G	7	1	1	2	15,422
Sovereign Miss	4	F	6	0	0	0	644
Sovereign Power	5	H	3	1	1	1	10,850
Sovereign Reins	3	G	11	1	0	0	5,550
Sovereign Rip Torn	8	G	3	0	0	1	475
Sovereign Salute	4	C	3	0	0	0	35
Sovereign Summer	2	C	1	0	0	0	27
Sovereign Sweep	5	H	4	0	0	0	1,978
Sovereign Won	5	G	13	1	4	3	16,566
Sovereignoftheseas	4	F	2	1	0	0	27,892
Soveriegn Time	4	G	9	3	2	1	20,209
Soverign Honor	3	C	15	1	0	2	61,381
Soverign Willy	4	G	3	0	0	0	0
Soviet Doll	3	F	3	0	1	1	3,710
Soviet Gypsy	8	G	4	0	0	0	457
Soviet Party	7	G	4	0	0	0	940
Sovran Ice	6	M	18	1	2	4	11,865
Sovrano	3	G	4	0	2	0	8,740
Sowhatsyourpoint	4	G	7	0	0	2	4,821
Sox for Millie	6	G	16	1	2	3	16,762
Sox It to Me	3	F	12	2	2	2	73,262
Sox On Top	9	G	15	2	3	4	27,401
Soxie's Queen	2	F	1	0	0	0	675
Soy Chispita (ARG)	6	M	7	0	2	0	4,950
Soy Desatanudos (ARG)	5	H	7	1	1	1	24,070
Soy Famoso	4	C	12	1	2	2	36,300
Soy Taipan (ARG)	6	H	3	0	0	1	9,220
Soyabeanthere	4	G	14	0	1	1	4,575
Soyuz	8	G	6	0	1	1	3,448
Soze	4	G	11	2	0	3	16,380
Spac	4	G	12	1	1	3	13,805
Space Age	5	G	5	0	1	0	2,760
Space Cruise	2	F	1	0	0	0	2,500
Space Hero	2	C	3	0	3	0	23,400
Space Invader	4	C	4	0	0	1	13,742
Space Pants	3	G	4	1	0	0	2,880
Space Probe	4	F	6	1	0	2	23,430
Space Shot	4	C	6	1	1	0	22,785
Space Walker	6	M	5	0	1	0	2,355
Space Watch	2	C	2	0	0	0	573
Spaced Out	4	G	8	0	4	0	21,547
Spacey Czarina	7	M	8	0	3	1	7,267
Spacey Princess	3	F	17	1	2	1	10,447
Spacious	2	F	3	1	1	0	10,800
Spade	4	G	4	0	0	1	1,033
Spades Prospect	2	C	2	0	1	1	3,700
Spaghetti Mouse	2	C	3	1	1	0	18,836
Span	6	G	8	3	0	1	13,677
Spangled	4	F	3	1	1	1	36,400
Spanish Artist	4	G	22	2	1	4	51,312
Spanish Brandy	4	F	3	0	2	0	22,800
Spanish Castle	6	M	14	3	3	2	32,520
Spanish Cavalier	2	G	3	0	0	0	75
Spanish Charm	5	G	10	3	2	1	9,946
Spanish Chestnut	2	C	4	2	2	0	84,420
Spanish Cinnamon	3	G	3	0	0	0	147
Spanish Curse	4	G	10	1	0	3	5,250
Spanish Decree	5	M	11	0	4	1	132,438
Spanish Empire	4	C	9	2	1	1	155,000
Spanish Eyes	6	G	7	0	1	2	5,112
Spanish Flare	3	F	14	1	2	5	13,278
Spanish Forks	4	G	10	0	4	3	8,203
Spanish Fort	4	F	10	2	1	1	13,320
Spanish Gold	4	G	5	0	0	0	1,450
Spanish Groom	6	G	5	1	0	0	5,346
Spanish Harlem	5	G	9	0	0	0	2,092
Spanish Highway	3	G	8	2	1	2	51,096
Spanish Honor	4	G	11	2	1	5	17,579
Spanish Johnny	5	G	12	0	1	1	7,666
Spanish Lady	3	F	15	3	1	2	39,897
Spanish Lass	5	M	4	3	0	0	10,994
Spanish Mission	2	C	4	0	3	0	33,200
Spanish Monster	3	G	12	1	1	2	10,467
Spanish Pearl	3	F	7	0	3	1	8,000
Spanish Petition	3	F	3	0	0	0	3,420
Spanish Pine	2	C	1	0	0	0	0
Spanish Rioja	3	C	13	0	0	1	1,650
Spanish River	5	M	2	0	0	0	378
Spanish Sage	4	F	8	0	1	1	6,124
Spanish Secrets	3	F	13	3	2	0	27,290

Horse	Age	Sex	Sts	1st	2d	3d	Won
Spanish Slew	3	F	6	2	2	2	55,280
Spanish Souvenir	3	F	2	0	0	1	2,310
Spanish Spur (GB)	6	G	5	1	1	1	55,470
Spanish Surprise	4	F	14	2	3	1	38,520
Spanish Tunnel	5	M	1	0	0	0	300
Spanish Warrior	3	G	10	1	1	0	37,205
Spanishcreek	3	F	11	0	0	0	2,445
Spankintime	4	G	8	2	1	2	12,311
Spanks a Million	2	F	1	0	0	0	400
Spanning	2	F	4	2	1	0	41,600
Spar	11	G	6	0	0	2	1,540
Spar Dance	2	C	6	0	0	1	3,775
Spared	5	G	5	0	0	1	3,900
Sparhawk	2	G	4	0	1	1	7,022
Spark and Fire	3	F	4	0	1	0	1,575
Spark of Humor	3	C	13	3	2	1	39,301
Spark Sept (FR)	5	M	6	0	1	1	17,530
Spark Setter	8	G	7	2	1	0	10,025
Spark the Nat	5	M	12	1	2	3	7,285
Spark'en Prism	6	M	2	0	0	0	188
Sparkie Sharkey	2	G	3	0	0	1	2,790
Sparkle for Hailey	3	G	2	0	0	0	855
Sparkle Free	9	M	10	0	1	1	1,889
Sparkle Gulch	2	F	2	0	0	0	127
Sparkle Me	3	F	9	2	0	0	8,696
Sparkle N Classic	4	G	9	1	1	0	7,968
Sparkle N Gold	3	F	8	2	2	1	44,990
Sparkle Plentie	6	M	5	2	1	1	24,468
Sparkle Pretty	2	F	2	0	0	1	4,352
Sparkle Sparkle	2	G	7	1	2	1	17,440
Sparklelad	4	G	12	1	2	3	5,623
Sparkler	3	F	6	0	0	0	492
Sparkler Lode	4	C	10	1	1	0	6,260
Sparkles Bluebell	3	F	2	0	0	0	0
Sparkles Mattie	5	M	13	0	0	3	4,061
Sparkles Prospect	8	M	2	0	0	0	0
Sparkling Amber	3	F	7	2	2	1	16,106
Sparkling Ava	5	M	8	0	0	0	19,481
Sparkling Blue	4	F	7	3	1	1	53,720
Sparkling Brandy	2	F	7	1	0	0	6,280
Sparkling Buck	5	G	20	3	0	2	5,580
Sparkling Claim	4	F	9	0	0	0	1,707
Sparkling Forest	3	F	6	1	2	1	52,280
Sparkling Green	3	C	10	0	1	2	8,431
Sparkling Home	4	F	11	2	0	0	10,206
Sparkling Hope	8	G	9	1	0	0	4,869
Sparkling Humor	3	F	11	2	2	2	63,930
Sparkling Jayne	3	F	9	1	0	3	7,151
Sparkling Kaye	5	M	11	3	1	4	14,747
Sparkling Rozie	6	M	2	0	0	0	80
Sparkling Sabia	4	F	7	3	1	0	49,020
Sparkling Sherry	4	F	5	0	0	1	1,358
Sparkling Slew	3	F	1	0	0	0	75
Sparkman	3	G	7	2	0	2	51,386
Sparks	2	F	5	0	1	2	16,964
Sparks a Flyin	4	C	3	0	0	1	200
Sparks Can Fly	2	C	2	0	0	0	900
Sparky Bonus	4	G	3	0	0	0	0
Sparky Can Dance	3	F	1	0	0	0	125
Sparky Mon	5	G	1	0	0	0	0
Sparky Too	3	G	7	0	0	0	208
Sparrow Hawk	3	G	10	1	2	1	1,736
Spatter	3	G	14	2	0	0	6,836
Speak Easy	3	F	9	2	3	0	71,530
Speak in Code	11	G	6	2	0	0	3,217
Speak Mother	4	F	4	0	0	1	387
Speak No Evil	4	F	5	0	0	1	2,460
Speak of Kings	2	G	5	2	0	1	28,756
Speak of the Devil	4	F	9	3	1	0	27,593
Speak Out	4	F	12	3	4	3	75,930
Speak Out Loud	4	C	8	1	1	2	33,461
Speak Sooner	4	F	2	0	0	0	112
Speak the Language	3	F	4	0	1	0	7,480
Speakin Britt	2	G	1	0	0	0	0
Speaking Noty	3	G	5	2	0	1	6,397
Speaking Star	2	G	1	0	0	0	0
Speak'n the Blues	3	F	1	0	0	0	75
Speaks Volumes	5	M	8	2	2	1	35,937
Speakster	4	G	8	1	2	0	21,598

Horse	Age	Sex	Sts	1st	2d	3d	Won
Speaktomepal	3	G	4	0	0	1	864
Speaktomyattorney	2	F	1	0	0	0	0
Spear	2	C	5	0	1	1	7,636
Spearsmill	5	G	5	0	0	0	1,032
Spearsville	2	C	1	0	0	0	0
Spec Tater	2	G	3	1	1	1	5,114
Special Account	3	G	5	0	0	0	483
Special Agent Joe	3	G	4	1	0	0	7,200
Special American	6	M	8	0	0	3	19,555
Special Answer	4	G	13	1	4	3	34,515
Special Assessment	4	F	3	0	0	0	525
Special Ballad	5	M	14	1	4	6	28,087
Special Breeze	2	G	1	0	0	0	0
Special Case	4	F	3	0	1	0	1,850
Special Charade	2	C	3	0	0	0	2,160
Special Club	2	F	4	0	1	0	5,590
Special Code	2	C	1	0	0	0	775
Special Concern	4	G	20	5	3	1	68,655
Special D	4	F	6	0	0	0	636
Special Dancer	8	G	12	2	0	0	11,760
Special Deed	3	F	10	1	3	2	33,745
Special Diamond	3	C	4	1	0	0	8,750
Special Dimension	6	G	4	0	0	0	376
Special Dolly	8	M	7	0	1	0	2,720
Special Drummer	3	F	3	0	0	0	0
Special Engagement	4	F	1	0	0	0	46
Special Era	3	F	3	2	0	1	14,317
Special Excess	4	F	1	0	0	0	0
Special Fact	5	H	2	0	0	0	309
Special Fame	3	C	5	0	1	0	6,870
Special Forbes	4	F	12	1	1	0	2,210
Special Forces	5	G	6	0	2	1	20,660
Special General	3	G	12	2	2	0	10,425
Special Guest	4	F	6	1	0	1	7,191
Special Heather	3	F	1	0	0	0	0
Special Heff	3	G	11	0	1	2	10,620
Special Home	6	G	28	2	4	3	12,007
Special Insignia	6	M	7	2	1	2	21,949
Special Invitation	3	G	10	1	0	3	8,069
Special Jen	5	M	2	0	0	1	970
Special Jet	4	G	10	2	2	0	41,104
Special Jig	3	F	3	1	0	0	31,152
Special Judge	4	G	9	1	3	2	51,620
Special K. B.	4	F	6	0	0	0	1,638
Special Lawyer	4	F	2	0	0	0	773
Special Lessons	8	G	18	5	5	2	20,292
Special Lovin	3	F	9	0	0	0	1,611
Special Luck	2	F	2	0	1	0	1,510
Special Matter	6	G	9	2	0	2	149,920
Special Menu	3	F	8	1	5	2	53,600
Special Mercedes	2	F	2	0	0	0	280
Special Message	3	F	3	1	0	0	6,000
Special Morning	2	F	2	0	0	0	0
Special Motion	5	M	12	1	1	3	5,990
Special Offer	5	G	3	1	1	0	13,278
Special Ops	3	G	12	0	0	2	2,715
Special Pal	2	F	7	1	1	1	26,145
Special Payday	6	M	10	0	0	1	1,824
Special Queen	5	M	7	0	0	0	1,021
Special Rate	4	C	4	1	2	1	66,560
Special Report	3	F	11	2	2	4	103,705
Special Ring	7	G	3	1	0	0	240,000
Special Sands	2	C	5	0	2	1	8,390
Special Sign	7	H	1	0	0	0	160
Special Slew	9	G	6	0	0	0	290
Special Smug	3	F	1	0	0	0	0
Special Squall	7	G	8	0	1	0	1,842
Special Status	4	C	3	0	0	0	324
Special Tactics	3	F	10	1	0	6	53,265
Special Tapestry	4	F	7	0	1	1	11,420
Special Task	4	G	3	0	0	1	816
Special Terms	7	H	4	0	2	0	6,590
Special Topics	3	G	1	0	0	0	0
Special Tour	4	G	17	3	1	3	48,828
Special Truce	2	G	5	0	2	1	2,630
Special Version	3	F	15	2	4	2	18,240
Special Way	9	G	6	0	0	1	2,755
Special Wayne	5	G	1	0	0	0	0
Special Weapon	4	G	1	0	0	0	0

Horse	Age	Sex	Sts	1st	2d	3d	Won
Special Wife	6	M	1	0	0	0	168
Special Willy	6	G	13	1	0	1	3,932
Special Yankee	4	C	5	1	1	0	6,490
Specialanouncement	3	F	10	0	3	1	10,907
Specialexpectation	5	G	30	5	4	5	28,349
Speciality	4	F	2	0	0	0	660
Specialkindafan	9	M	7	0	0	0	641
Specialness	3	G	5	0	1	0	8,500
Specialty Cup	3	F	1	0	0	0	400
Specific Intent	3	C	1	0	0	0	0
Speck of Dawn	4	G	4	0	0	0	0
Speck of Money	4	G	12	2	2	3	8,789
Speck of Peace	4	F	13	1	0	1	12,856
Speckled Band	3	C	11	1	0	1	7,733
Speckled Spice	4	F	15	1	1	1	47,514
Spectactacat	2	C	2	0	0	0	156
Spectaculaireontap	6	M	1	0	0	0	1,750
Spectacular Anzi	4	F	4	0	0	1	13,832
Spectacular Baby	4	F	4	0	1	0	3,795
Spectacular Bay	2	C	8	0	2	2	20,320
Spectacular Beamer	4	F	6	0	2	1	6,032
Spectacular Boy	3	G	9	1	1	1	9,842
Spectacular Cat	6	H	2	0	1	0	3,800
Spectacular Chance	5	G	3	3	0	0	15,400
Spectacular Crisis	4	G	16	2	1	3	15,213
Spectacular Dance	3	F	3	0	1	0	3,790
Spectacular Dancer	7	G	8	0	0	1	1,835
Spectacular Dash	4	G	10	4	2	0	41,813
Spectacular Deal	7	G	12	2	0	3	24,898
Spectacular Dixie	2	G	7	0	1	2	15,318
Spectacular Editor	4	C	9	1	1	2	7,435
Spectacular Fan	4	G	11	1	2	1	5,582
Spectacular Greek	5	M	8	4	2	1	22,141
Spectacular Guest	3	F	4	0	1	1	3,108
Spectacular Light	7	G	9	1	2	0	29,350
Spectacular Lisa	4	F	3	2	0	0	94,000
Spectacular Milli	3	F	15	5	4	5	87,510
Spectacular Miss	4	F	4	1	1	1	12,691
Spectacular Moon	3	F	2	0	1	1	9,300
Spectacular Morgan	3	F	2	0	0	0	150
Spectacular Morn	5	M	6	0	0	1	1,020
Spectacular Orage	2	G	4	0	0	2	6,080
Spectacular Place	5	M	5	0	1	0	6,480
Spectacular Roy	4	C	3	0	0	0	0
Spectacular Trump	2	G	1	0	0	0	0
Spectacular Wager	3	F	7	1	1	0	7,507
Spectacular Won	3	G	6	0	0	0	756
Spectacularcee	3	F	1	0	0	1	900
Spectaculareleganz	4	F	7	2	0	0	29,210
Spectacularly Pink	6	H	9	0	0	0	739
Spectrin Seven	5	H	6	0	1	0	778
Spectrolaf	3	F	3	0	0	0	0
Speechmaker	4	C	4	0	1	1	3,660
Speed and Heart	2	C	10	0	2	2	9,130
Speed Bag	2	F	7	2	1	1	69,080
Speed Blast	3	G	14	3	5	1	22,128
Speed Broker	4	G	1	0	0	0	333
Speed Bump	3	F	5	0	1	0	2,720
Speed Demon	6	G	3	0	0	3	3,250
Speed Dreamer	7	G	7	2	1	1	4,248
Speed Duel	2	G	3	0	0	1	770
Speed Echo	5	M	2	0	0	0	120
Speed Factor	3	G	7	0	2	2	3,078
Speed Gun	6	G	7	0	1	0	5,936
Speed Hunter	5	G	12	2	2	0	39,558
Speed Minx	3	F	2	0	0	0	790
Speed N Thru	6	G	5	0	0	0	0
Speed of Funny	6	M	9	2	1	3	28,265
Speed of Light (IRE)	6	G	6	0	2	0	25,960
Speed Out Front	5	G	10	4	3	0	23,010
Speed Pocket	6	H	8	2	1	1	4,606
Speed Rules	2	C	1	0	0	0	0
Speed Secret	10	G	1	0	0	0	0
Speed Special	3	G	4	1	0	0	1,155
Speed Supreme	4	F	10	3	1	0	23,900
Speed Trap	2	C	1	0	0	0	400
Speed Victor	2	G	4	1	2	0	36,857
Speed Vike	7	H	11	0	3	2	5,220
Speed Whiz	3	G	12	1	1	4	43,591

Horse	Age	Sex	Sts	1st	2d	3d	Won
Speedalert	2	G	4	0	0	1	2,002
Speedball Tucker	6	G	20	2	1	1	13,413
Speeder	3	G	13	2	2	2	29,725
Speedfast	3	F	11	1	2	1	20,923
Speedies Nepal	2	F	1	0	0	0	0
Speeding Jim	6	H	8	1	0	1	30,210
Speedjama	3	C	5	0	1	2	17,634
Speedmovesme	3	F	8	1	1	1	5,030
Speedo Cat	3	C	2	0	0	0	150
Speedominator	3	G	3	0	1	0	4,840
Speeds the Key	4	F	17	2	2	2	33,430
Speedster	8	G	22	1	2	2	3,778
Speedstruck Seeker	6	M	8	0	0	3	8,355
Speedwell Beau	3	C	14	2	6	1	46,149
Speedy American	3	C	4	0	0	1	480
Speedy Appeal	3	F	10	3	1	0	26,780
Speedy Badger	3	F	5	0	0	0	1,599
Speedy Boy	3	C	7	1	0	1	8,767
Speedy Buster	8	M	6	0	2	0	1,901
Speedy Comet	6	G	11	2	1	2	28,278
Speedy Dancer	4	F	8	2	2	1	40,361
Speedy Deedy	2	F	3	2	1	0	62,600
Speedy Delivery	8	G	5	0	0	1	605
Speedy Diplomat	5	G	7	2	0	1	18,430
Speedy Escort	8	G	5	0	0	0	165
Speedy Falcon	3	F	5	2	0	1	209,112
Speedy Flight	5	G	1	0	0	0	545
Speedy Gazelle	4	G	8	0	0	0	745
Speedy Georgette	7	M	2	0	0	0	530
Speedy Gone Sally	2	F	6	2	2	2	71,444
Speedy Halo	3	G	11	3	0	3	22,500
Speedy Heels	7	G	6	2	0	0	5,330
Speedy Kitty	4	F	2	0	0	0	0
Speedy Little Car	6	G	6	0	0	0	521
Speedy Ordeal	3	G	8	1	2	0	9,013
Speedy Passing	3	G	5	1	1	0	17,718
Speedy Pete	3	C	11	2	1	1	23,215
Speedy Pick	6	G	7	0	2	1	9,390
Speedy Pie	7	G	10	1	0	0	4,119
Speedy Pieddy	4	G	3	0	0	0	500
Speedy Ransom	5	G	5	0	0	0	925
Speedy Reply	5	G	2	0	0	0	130
Speedy Sam	3	G	1	0	0	0	0
Speedy Sonata	3	F	8	3	2	0	108,066
Speedy Spires	2	F	5	0	0	0	2,502
Speedy Sue	2	F	1	0	0	0	155
Speedy Sunrise	3	F	10	1	3	0	52,130
Speedy Sweep	5	M	8	2	0	1	8,112
Speedy Tiffany	3	F	13	6	1	2	80,214
Speedy Tradition	6	M	3	0	0	0	1,008
Speedys Invention	4	G	4	2	0	1	2,668
Speedyslim Pickens	3	G	5	0	1	2	3,402
Speightstown	6	H	6	5	0	1	1,045,556
Spellbinder	3	C	3	1	0	1	39,000
Spellbook	4	G	2	0	0	0	1,475
Spellfire	3	F	6	1	0	0	6,420
Spelling Bee Jones	2	C	8	1	1	2	11,219
Spellmaker	4	F	6	1	0	0	26,800
Spell's Legacy	3	F	2	0	0	1	1,200
Spencer Creek Miss	5	M	2	0	0	0	77
Spencer Falls	5	G	5	0	0	1	249
Spencer's Magic	3	G	9	2	3	1	99,080
Spencers Storm	3	F	12	1	0	2	17,350
Spend a Web	6	G	9	1	0	1	21,790
Spend and Hope	5	M	7	0	0	3	1,869
Spend Spend Spend	5	G	14	3	1	3	40,800
Spending Floozie	7	M	7	0	1	0	1,755
Spending Jesy	4	F	1	0	0	1	2,227
Spendn Spree	8	M	11	2	1	2	12,759
Spendthemoneyhoney	4	F	4	0	0	1	3,950
Spensive	4	C	4	1	1	1	49,916
Spentorian	3	F	1	0	0	0	750
Spice Guy	8	H	1	0	0	0	0
Spice Is Nice	5	M	13	3	0	0	44,895
Spice Island	5	M	7	0	3	1	94,720
Spice It Up	3	F	7	1	2	0	48,200
Spice Rack	3	F	13	1	2	3	43,322
Spice the Price	5	M	7	0	2	0	1,580
Spice Twice	8	M	9	1	0	1	4,298

Horse	Age	Sex	Sts	1st	2d	3d	Won
Spiced	5	M	15	2	0	3	15,516
Spiced Tea	5	M	11	0	0	1	5,985
Spiced to Go	3	G	13	2	2	1	24,122
Spiced Wine	4	G	10	0	3	4	16,440
Spicey Game	5	M	6	0	1	0	2,167
Spicey N Hot	2	F	6	1	3	1	9,948
Spicoli	3	G	5	0	1	0	9,600
Spicy Cajun	3	F	13	2	2	3	39,025
Spicy Cocktail	2	F	1	1	0	0	25,800
Spicy Colony	2	F	12	0	1	3	11,530
Spicy Devil	6	G	2	0	0	0	0
Spicy Light	3	F	9	2	2	2	45,660
Spicy Prospector	8	G	5	2	0	0	17,490
Spicy Stuff	7	G	7	3	1	1	90,369
Spicysisters	3	F	6	2	1	1	10,046
Spider Annie	3	F	19	2	1	2	17,009
Spider Dann	7	G	12	4	2	1	27,986
Spider Dash	4	G	11	1	1	1	9,164
Spider Glide	4	C	2	0	0	0	220
Spider Joe	2	C	6	1	0	2	25,920
Spider Murphy	2	C	1	0	0	0	0
Spider the Glider	3	C	4	0	0	0	2,400
Spider Time	3	G	10	3	1	1	29,373
Spider Web	2	F	1	0	0	0	0
Spider Wire	11	G	6	0	0	0	834
Spiel Meister	3	G	6	1	0	0	12,375
Spike the Ball	4	G	7	0	0	0	520
Spike the Fever	3	C	2	1	0	1	32,970
Spiked Temp	3	C	7	1	0	1	16,720
Spikes	2	F	7	1	0	1	13,709
Spilled Honey	5	G	9	2	2	2	47,490
Spillikin (GB)	5	H	5	0	0	1	2,828
Spin Breaker	8	H	4	0	0	0	80
Spin Citi	5	H	13	3	0	0	28,390
Spin Control	4	F	5	1	0	1	34,352
Spin for Cash	4	G	5	0	0	0	314
Spin Four	3	C	1	0	0	1	1,155
Spin Ghar	4	F	15	1	1	0	11,939
Spin Jazz Baby	2	F	3	2	0	0	16,800
Spin the Lover	3	F	10	1	4	1	23,410
Spin the Wind	3	G	5	1	1	0	13,228
Spin Time	7	G	10	2	4	1	34,125
Spin Zone	5	H	1	0	1	0	8,000
Spinalong	5	M	2	0	0	0	530
Spinaway Lad	2	G	3	0	0	0	1,155
Spindini	3	C	9	2	1	0	46,566
Spinelessjellyfish	8	H	6	0	1	1	39,334
Spinnin Cookies	2	F	2	0	0	0	164
Spinnin N Grinnin	3	G	5	1	1	1	9,485
Spinning Affair	7	G	1	0	0	0	0
Spinning At Dawn	4	F	5	0	0	1	6,320
Spinning Heart	4	G	7	0	1	1	4,170
Spinning Jolie	2	F	5	1	1	1	34,490
Spinning Tales	5	H	10	1	2	2	24,990
Spinning Time	4	F	4	0	1	0	2,430
Spinning Wheel	4	C	2	0	0	0	0
Spirit Away	2	F	3	0	2	1	30,210
Spirit de Azure	5	M	12	0	1	5	26,123
Spirit Deputy	2	G	1	0	0	0	0
Spirit d'Oro	2	F	5	0	2	2	9,680
Spirit Dreamer	9	G	9	0	4	1	5,925
Spirit Gulch	3	G	13	4	2	3	79,240
Spirit in the Wind	9	G	6	0	1	1	2,040
Spirit Island	9	G	1	0	0	0	0
Spirit King	6	H	5	0	0	0	378
Spirit o' War	5	G	5	3	0	1	52,040
Spirit of a Legend	4	G	14	2	1	2	15,300
Spirit of Erin	3	F	1	0	0	0	0
Spirit of Freedom	4	G	5	0	1	1	1,640
Spirit of Jack	5	G	3	0	0	2	3,570
Spirit of Life	2	G	4	0	1	0	3,070
Spirit of Malagra	5	H	4	1	0	0	31,740
Spirit of Montreal	3	C	15	2	2	3	48,410
Spirit of Nature	4	F	3	1	0	1	34,080
Spirit of Pancho	4	G	6	1	2	1	25,860
Spirit of Splendor	2	F	2	1	0	1	31,950
Spirit of the Soul	2	F	6	2	1	0	12,940
Spirit of Tyson	2	C	6	0	1	0	1,913
Spirit of U S A	3	F	2	0	0	0	155
Spirit of Wailea	3	F	1	0	1	0	5,200
Spirit of Woody	5	G	17	2	5	4	33,432
Spirit Star	3	G	8	1	1	0	7,340
Spirit Talker	5	G	9	0	0	1	1,690
Spirit to Spare	3	F	5	4	0	0	50,938
Spirit Woman	2	F	3	0	0	0	450
Spirited	3	F	14	2	1	2	64,740
Spirited Amanda	5	M	8	0	0	1	1,835
Spirited Falcon	3	G	10	0	4	0	7,235
Spirited Game	3	F	11	3	2	2	103,982
Spirited Ghost	4	G	10	0	1	0	7,176
Spirited Maiden	5	M	4	0	2	0	27,450
Spirited Market	5	M	8	0	1	3	8,672
Spirited Moves	4	F	1	0	0	0	107
Spirited Niner	5	G	7	0	0	0	1,565
Spirited Thunder	4	C	11	2	0	0	17,879
Spirited Way	2	C	1	0	0	0	400
Spirited Wish	2	F	3	0	0	1	3,553
Spiritedtunetoo	3	F	14	1	0	1	8,713
Spirites Account	3	F	3	0	0	0	264
Spiritful King	5	G	4	0	0	0	133
Spiritofjimmiejack	2	F	2	1	0	0	6,987
Spiritofneworleans	5	H	9	0	0	2	6,215
Spiritridge	2	G	4	2	0	1	29,423
Spirits Afar	9	G	2	0	0	0	620
Spiritsinthenight	4	F	7	1	0	0	11,655
Spiritual Air (GB)	4	F	5	1	2	0	40,690
Spiritual Attack	3	G	6	0	0	0	516
Spiritual Drift	4	F	6	2	1	1	51,620
Spiritual Hand	3	F	8	1	0	0	7,170
Spiritual Sword	3	F	5	1	1	0	13,770
Spiritualawakening	3	F	7	1	0	2	3,738
Spiritualist	3	G	7	1	1	2	56,462
Spiritually	3	G	14	1	0	1	14,155
Spirosandnicholis	5	G	13	1	2	3	7,790
Spit Shine	7	G	13	3	1	2	20,670
Spite the Devil	4	G	9	3	0	1	256,922
Spiteful Love	4	F	4	0	1	0	3,220
Spitfire Man	5	G	2	0	0	0	0
Spit'n Spat	4	F	17	2	0	1	10,154
Splash Ensing	4	F	6	0	0	0	798
Splash o' Magic	5	M	3	0	0	0	0
Splash of Soda	4	G	4	0	0	0	325
Splash Pour Homme	3	F	10	0	1	0	2,085
Splash Tour	4	F	7	0	0	1	688
Splasha	4	F	2	0	0	1	5,600
Splashed	3	F	9	1	3	1	6,299
Splashed Soup	4	F	2	0	0	0	226
Splashin' Jack	4	G	9	0	3	1	5,673
Splashing Jazz	7	M	3	1	0	0	7,514
Splashing Louis	4	C	4	1	0	0	8,290
Splashing Princess	4	F	15	1	4	1	39,361
Splashing Rose	8	M	1	0	0	0	0
Splashisagamelady	4	F	12	0	0	4	2,153
Splashman	3	C	2	0	0	0	0
Splashof Panache	2	F	4	2	0	1	19,575
Splashofscarlet	2	G	8	1	2	1	30,420
Splashofwind	3	G	3	0	0	0	195
Splashy Wolf	5	M	2	0	0	0	305
Splatter	7	M	11	0	1	1	3,100
Splenda	3	F	5	2	1	0	41,278
Splendeed	7	G	3	0	0	1	5,000
Splenderinthegrass	5	M	1	0	0	0	0
Splendeur (FR)	5	M	4	0	0	0	1,040
Splendid Blended	2	F	4	3	1	0	327,400
Splendid Genius	2	F	1	0	0	0	400
Splendid High	3	C	4	1	0	1	2,840
Splendid Jaclyn	5	M	2	0	0	0	713
Splendid Journey	5	G	13	0	2	2	1,513
Splendid Mover	4	G	12	3	0	2	14,720
Splendid Nature	4	G	13	1	3	0	17,949
Splendid Prophecy	5	M	2	0	0	1	206
Splendid Prospect	4	G	11	0	0	1	3,657
Splendid Sunrise	8	M	7	3	0	1	26,521
Splendid Times	5	G	13	2	2	1	25,365
Splendid View	4	F	1	0	0	0	0
Splendid Western	5	G	14	1	0	0	19,634
Splendiferous One	4	F	8	1	0	1	22,355
Splice Girl	3	F	3	0	1	1	6,485

Horse	Age	Sex	Sts	1st	2d	3d	Won
Splinter	5	G	21	2	4	1	15,510
Splinter One	4	C	4	1	1	0	7,825
Split Aces	4	G	11	1	0	1	7,850
Split Personality	2	F	2	0	0	1	2,800
Split the Sheets	5	M	6	0	0	0	309
Splitthedifference	3	F	6	1	2	1	23,492
Spodie	4	G	4	1	2	0	5,240
Spoiled	3	F	2	0	1	0	13,102
Spoiled Cat	2	F	2	0	0	1	1,200
Spoils of Victory	3	C	12	0	2	2	15,130
Spoken Like a Pro	4	G	7	0	0	0	1,295
Sponge Bobbie	3	F	3	1	1	0	22,790
Spontaneous Dino	5	G	2	0	0	0	0
Spontaneous Wood	4	G	10	2	3	1	12,839
Spoof	8	G	11	1	0	0	3,208
Spoofin	7	G	4	0	0	1	3,658
Spookum	2	G	2	0	0	1	2,472
Spooky Girlfriend	3	F	12	1	1	1	9,650
Spooky Mulder	6	G	17	7	5	0	253,275
Spooky Tree	7	G	11	0	3	1	6,564
Spoon Fed	3	G	12	0	0	1	812
Spooners Hill	4	G	13	4	2	2	28,165
Spoonfullofsugar	11	H	3	0	1	0	2,700
Spooning	8	G	3	0	0	0	1,100
Spoonman	5	G	17	1	1	3	14,640
Sport Boy Tommy	3	G	7	2	0	0	29,840
Sport Cafe	3	F	3	0	0	0	315
Sport Coat	5	G	8	1	0	1	33,040
Sport Desk	3	C	3	0	0	0	395
Sport d'Hiver	12	G	10	3	0	3	38,740
Sport N Light	7	H	8	2	3	1	6,374
Sportin G T	9	G	1	0	0	0	300
Sportin' Lover	2	C	2	0	0	0	500
Sportin' Merle	3	G	4	0	0	0	0
Sportin Phil	5	G	15	5	2	1	38,383
Sportin' Songbird	3	F	4	0	1	0	1,075
Sportin' Times	3	G	1	0	0	0	0
Sportive Spirit	5	M	2	0	0	0	390
Sports Bettor	3	C	3	0	0	1	2,275
Sports Channel	6	G	7	0	1	0	1,080
Sports Medicine	4	C	11	0	0	0	1,345
Sports Ridge	9	G	13	0	1	2	3,919
Sports Tour	4	G	7	3	0	1	8,136
Sports Trooper	3	C	1	1	0	0	4,785
Sportscaster	3	G	14	4	1	1	50,044
Sportscenter Hero	6	G	13	2	3	1	12,512
Sportsmeister	2	C	1	0	0	0	0
Sportster	3	C	2	1	1	0	13,440
Sportstheone	5	H	2	0	0	0	0
Sporty Dude	2	G	4	0	0	1	1,466
Sporty Heroine	4	F	13	0	2	4	10,480
Sporty McGee	2	C	3	0	0	2	5,290
Sporty Sporty	3	C	4	0	0	0	550
S'posedtobealady	4	F	10	1	0	1	4,561
Spot Dot	4	G	9	0	0	1	3,924
Spot the Ferrara	3	G	2	0	0	0	225
Spotless	4	F	10	0	3	0	9,870
Spotlight (GB)	3	F	7	2	2	0	187,058
Spotlite On Macy	3	F	13	2	2	0	14,105
Spotted Eagle	2	G	2	1	0	0	3,190
Spotted Elegance	4	C	3	0	0	0	42
Spotted K B	2	G	2	0	0	0	1,020
Spotted Owl	6	H	12	2	2	3	70,930
Spotted Pearl	2	F	3	0	0	1	1,760
Spotted Star	2	F	3	0	1	0	2,400
Spray Lake	4	F	3	0	0	2	4,226
Spread Em	2	C	4	1	1	0	14,050
Spreadin Joy	3	F	10	2	0	1	16,309
Spred Satin	2	F	1	0	0	0	0
Spriggzee	4	C	6	1	1	0	34,200
Sprin Buck	9	G	2	0	0	0	303
Spring Act	3	G	12	1	5	3	23,235
Spring Aire	5	M	3	0	0	0	519
Spring Angel	5	M	3	1	0	0	9,910
Spring Breeze	4	R	6	0	0	1	2,807
Spring Cat	3	F	6	0	1	0	16,122
Spring Daisy	3	F	7	2	0	0	10,725
Spring Dip	4	G	8	2	1	2	19,350
Spring Dream	3	F	11	1	1	3	13,948
Spring Feather	6	M	11	1	1	1	7,281
Spring Feeling	4	F	12	2	1	1	15,230
Spring Festival	3	F	11	4	2	1	126,280
Spring Forward	4	G	2	0	0	0	1,260
Spring Heroine	6	M	4	1	0	1	5,605
Spring House	2	C	2	1	0	0	14,761
Spring in Paris	5	G	4	0	0	0	0
Spring Jet	7	G	20	1	0	3	9,460
Spring Kitten	5	M	8	3	1	1	77,040
Spring Power	3	F	5	0	2	1	5,998
Spring Queen	3	F	6	1	1	0	21,910
Spring Rade	3	F	2	0	0	0	3,000
Spring Reign	3	F	2	0	0	0	420
Spring Royal Pride	7	M	2	0	0	0	368
Spring Rush	4	F	4	1	0	1	19,060
Spring Scamper	4	F	2	0	1	0	2,950
Spring Season	5	M	7	3	1	2	91,283
Spring Sensation	2	F	2	0	1	0	2,574
Spring Sleet	4	G	4	1	1	0	10,918
Spring Star (FR)	5	M	1	1	0	0	66,540
Spring Station	9	G	5	0	0	1	1,511
Spring Stream	3	C	4	0	0	1	1,890
Spring Street	7	G	3	0	0	1	3,510
Spring Stroll	3	F	3	0	1	1	11,400
Spring Tide	2	F	1	0	0	0	184
Spring to Summer	8	M	2	0	0	1	1,135
Spring Training	3	G	8	1	3	2	20,260
Spring Winds	5	G	13	3	1	0	10,815
Springbrakemistake	3	F	8	1	4	0	18,100
Springerswar	4	F	5	0	0	0	290
Springfield Boy	4	C	15	0	3	2	17,838
Springhill Lucky	5	G	12	0	2	0	8,152
Springisintheair	2	F	12	0	4	0	8,500
Springledge	3	F	7	2	1	1	40,556
Springs Capp	3	F	2	0	0	0	0
Spring's Glory	3	F	4	1	2	0	24,200
Springs Goldengirl	3	F	10	2	2	2	5,038
Springs Lil Orphan	4	F	9	0	2	0	4,811
Springs N Things	4	F	1	0	0	0	0
Springsteen	5	G	4	1	1	0	10,300
Springster	3	G	8	0	1	1	9,740
Springthelatch	3	G	14	1	1	3	12,957
Springtime Flyer	4	F	13	1	1	3	10,470
Springtime Vision	2	C	3	1	0	0	14,700
Springtimeminster	4	C	2	0	0	0	0
Sprinkle of Class	3	F	3	0	0	0	195
Sprintaway	5	M	10	1	1	2	11,702
Spritely Walker	4	C	5	3	1	1	206,900
Spruce Belle	3	F	9	2	0	1	28,584
Spruce Hero	4	G	7	2	0	0	38,440
Spruce Jr	3	C	16	1	1	3	15,570
Spruce Lake	4	G	8	2	0	2	41,800
Spruce Meadows	3	G	6	0	0	1	1,217
Spruce Run	6	H	9	1	4	0	89,340
Spruce's Halo	2	F	3	0	0	0	795
Spruce's Prince	3	G	16	5	1	1	104,528
Spruce's Spirit	2	G	2	0	0	0	405
Sprucity	8	G	6	1	0	0	5,160
Spry Street	4	G	8	2	1	0	10,780
Spud Man	5	H	2	0	1	0	665
Spudville	3	G	4	0	0	0	410
Spun Gold	4	F	2	0	0	0	640
Spun Out	4	C	1	1	0	0	28,200
Spun Sugar	2	F	1	0	1	0	9,000
Spunky Becky	3	F	3	0	0	0	0
Spunky Bottoms	4	F	12	2	3	4	40,588
Spunky Boy	6	G	12	0	0	0	255
Spunky Gal	6	M	4	0	0	1	4,080
Spur Creek	5	M	4	1	0	0	9,360
Spur Man	5	G	1	0	0	0	100
Spuraway	4	G	10	1	2	2	20,200
Spurofthemorning	5	M	1	0	0	0	170
Spurred On	5	G	14	4	2	1	35,270
Spurt	3	F	8	2	0	1	36,365
Spy Drone	3	G	9	1	1	0	9,425
Spy Lass	3	F	3	0	0	0	1,380
Spy Me Not (ARG)	7	G	5	2	2	0	50,910
Spy Shark	8	G	9	0	0	0	488
Spyder Fyder	4	F	1	0	0	0	0

Horse	Age	Sex	Sts	1st	2d	3d	Won
Spyzotti	4	C	13	0	0	0	225
Squadron Commander	7	G	6	1	0	0	3,797
Squakum	2	G	10	0	2	1	15,670
Squall Alert	5	G	10	0	0	1	1,218
Squall Line	3	G	9	1	1	1	13,000
Squan Rose	5	M	5	1	0	0	5,251
Square Bob	5	G	6	0	0	1	5,334
Square Cut Gem	3	G	15	2	0	4	34,190
Square Dancing	2	F	2	1	0	0	27,600
Square Expectation	5	H	9	1	1	0	5,911
Square Wheels	4	G	1	0	0	0	0
Squared Away	5	M	5	0	0	0	0
Squash	5	M	4	0	0	0	0
Squaw Spirit	4	F	9	3	0	4	45,662
Squaw Valley	4	F	17	5	3	2	90,435
Squawk Talk	2	F	2	0	0	0	800
Squeaky Boots	4	F	5	1	0	0	3,507
Squeaky Wind	6	G	10	0	0	0	393
Squeeky P	3	F	6	1	1	0	18,400
Squeez Blossom	3	F	14	3	0	2	26,125
Squeeze Me	4	F	2	0	0	0	0
Squeeze Me Darling	4	F	11	0	0	0	2,561
Squeeze Me Now	3	F	12	1	2	1	7,811
Squeeze Play	2	F	6	1	0	1	10,416
Squire Brown	2	G	2	0	0	0	0
Squire West	13	G	7	0	0	3	936
Squirmlikeaworm	4	G	10	0	1	2	1,681
Squirt Monster	3	C	11	1	1	3	19,185
Sr. Razem	3	G	10	3	2	0	54,220
Sregor	5	G	2	0	0	0	182
Ss Proven Reserves	7	G	2	0	1	1	672
Sssh It'sa Secret	3	C	12	1	1	1	6,996
St Averil	3	C	4	1	1	0	140,000
St Ballado's Image	3	F	10	1	1	2	31,530
St Elizabeths Rose	3	F	9	1	1	0	5,884
St Francis Wood	3	F	7	1	1	0	12,910
St Hilaire Slew	4	C	6	0	0	0	735
St Johns Prospect	6	M	1	0	0	0	0
St Louie Blu	3	C	7	1	0	0	3,280
St Patti's Charm	6	M	8	1	0	2	6,146
St Regs (IRE)	3	G	9	0	1	1	17,154
St Roberto	3	G	2	0	0	0	0
St. Albert Fox	2	C	1	0	0	1	2,500
St. Amant Tsunami	3	C	5	0	0	0	0
St. Andrew's Star	5	H	1	0	0	1	462
St. Cajetan	4	G	8	1	1	0	7,020
St. Chad	4	G	9	2	3	0	4,158
St. Cielo	3	F	7	0	2	2	12,080
St. Croix	8	G	10	5	1	1	17,689
St. Davids Road	5	G	8	0	0	0	384
St. Dehere	6	H	7	1	0	1	12,077
St. Faustina	2	F	1	0	0	0	2,350
St. George	4	G	7	1	0	0	6,750
St. Hadif	7	G	6	0	0	0	604
St. Hilarion	5	G	15	1	1	1	12,170
St. Inigoes	4	G	1	0	0	0	0
St. Joe's Cat	3	G	3	0	0	1	1,700
St. John Dress	2	F	4	1	0	0	15,830
St. Jude's Star	3	F	3	0	0	0	0
St. Kilda	3	F	9	1	0	1	17,480
St. Louie Louie	3	C	2	0	0	0	0
St. Louie Red	4	G	1	0	0	0	0
St. Malachi	5	G	6	1	1	0	8,300
St. Martin's Cloak	7	G	10	1	1	1	15,885
St. o' Haint	4	G	12	2	3	1	23,484
St. Paddy's Ruckus	3	G	4	0	0	2	1,534
St. Paddys' Star	4	F	4	0	0	0	360
St. Patty's Choice	3	G	9	3	2	1	13,200
St. Patty's Smile	4	G	12	2	1	2	20,223
St. Patty's Tour	6	G	11	1	4	2	27,668
St. Rett	4	C	6	0	0	2	3,600
St. Roch	2	G	6	2	1	2	53,884
St. Salt	6	G	9	2	3	3	20,843
St. Somewhere	4	G	6	2	1	1	8,010
St. Vidas Dance	3	F	5	1	1	0	9,900
Stability	3	G	4	1	1	0	16,060
Stable Boy	4	G	4	1	1	0	7,330
Stable Secret	6	G	3	0	1	0	958
Staci Got Bowleggs	2	F	3	0	0	0	271
Stacie's Ballado	3	C	7	2	0	4	58,990
Stack Bit	4	G	4	0	0	0	81
Stack Fama	5	M	7	0	0	0	1,920
Stack First	4	F	1	0	0	0	220
Stack Lass	4	G	3	0	0	0	555
Stack Song	5	M	4	1	0	0	4,457
Stack Step	5	G	15	2	3	5	28,676
Stackal	5	M	2	0	0	0	312
Stackaly	4	F	1	0	0	0	195
Stackanothertime	6	H	4	0	0	0	3,470
Stacked	4	F	14	2	2	2	12,971
Stacked Deck	3	C	9	1	0	2	14,030
Stacker	6	G	1	0	0	0	90
Stacy Brew	3	F	3	0	0	1	4,970
Stacy's Double	4	F	10	0	1	5	6,315
Stacy's Favorite	4	F	7	1	0	0	11,985
Stacy's Guy	3	G	5	0	0	0	0
Stacy's Reserve	3	C	2	0	0	0	265
Stacy's Ridge	3	C	2	1	0	1	24,970
Stacy's Squaw	4	F	6	0	0	1	6,946
Staffhouse Road	3	G	1	0	0	0	0
Stag	7	G	11	2	1	2	13,129
Stag Dancer	2	F	2	0	0	0	247
Stag Nation	2	C	6	2	1	0	92,652
Stage Call (IRE)	5	H	8	2	1	0	77,076
Stage Classic	6	G	7	0	2	0	34,334
Stage Clearance	4	F	2	0	0	1	671
Stage Creek	5	G	4	2	0	0	1,827
Stage Door Dancer	3	C	2	0	0	0	0
Stage Door Jade	9	G	13	1	1	0	21,101
Stage Down	5	M	5	0	1	1	1,610
Stage Drama	6	G	13	2	2	3	23,308
Stage Gal	4	F	9	2	3	0	16,588
Stage Glitter	3	F	3	1	0	1	14,654
Stage Guest	3	C	2	0	0	0	330
Stage Hand General	6	G	3	1	0	0	2,840
Stage It	5	G	5	0	1	2	5,738
Stage Left	2	F	1	0	0	0	145
Stage Number	5	G	15	1	5	3	8,712
Stage Player	5	G	12	8	2	1	383,645
Stage Right	2	G	1	0	0	0	50
Stage Run	8	G	16	0	4	3	9,768
Stage Runner	5	M	8	2	1	0	5,856
Stage Shy	4	F	4	3	0	0	111,480
Stage Star Barbie	2	F	4	0	0	1	2,130
Stage Three	5	G	12	3	2	1	19,578
Stage Whisper	3	G	6	0	2	1	4,252
Stagecoach Bandit	3	G	13	1	0	2	8,580
Staged Reality	9	G	14	4	3	1	10,573
Stagedoor Casey	2	C	2	0	0	0	1,067
Staging	2	G	6	0	0	1	1,915
Stahlman's Tribute	3	G	8	0	1	1	12,550
Stainless Steel	6	M	2	1	1	0	16,040
Stake	4	F	10	2	1	0	74,051
Stalburst	4	F	6	1	1	0	11,362
Stalk the Princess	3	F	1	0	0	0	400
Stalkerazzi	3	C	10	1	1	2	43,372
Stalking Tiger	3	G	4	0	1	1	39,629
Stall Hunter	6	G	7	0	1	1	4,831
Stall Stomper	3	F	1	0	0	0	308
Stall Swapper	6	G	8	2	0	1	13,451
Stallgirl Cindy	6	M	2	0	0	0	186
Stallvik	5	H	15	1	3	2	15,165
Stalwart Bull	5	G	3	1	1	0	17,050
Stalwart Memory	3	C	3	1	1	0	37,030
Stalwart's Heir	2	G	6	1	1	1	18,760
Stamford Bridge	4	F	10	2	2	1	29,450
Stamp n' Pirate	6	G	7	1	1	0	3,021
Stan Israelite	3	C	8	1	0	2	21,120
Stan the Cameraman	5	H	6	0	1	0	1,299
Stanbery Lane	3	F	14	1	4	3	20,641
Stand Alone	5	M	1	0	0	0	1,620
Stand and Fight	4	C	3	1	1	0	13,740
Stand Aside	5	H	5	0	0	0	293
Stand by Your Flag	4	G	12	0	3	3	24,760
Stand Down	4	G	15	5	5	2	35,400
Stand Free	3	G	13	2	1	1	19,078
Stand On Top	3	F	8	1	1	1	46,914
Stand Ready	2	G	4	1	0	1	28,100

Horse	Age	Sex	Sts	1st	2d	3d	Won
Stand United	4	G	19	2	6	0	20,115
Stand Up and Cheer	4	G	12	0	1	1	3,955
Stand Up Guy	2	C	1	0	0	0	0
Standard Bearer	6	G	14	4	2	3	88,813
Standard Choice	5	G	2	0	1	0	3,388
Standard Setter	4	G	12	1	3	1	24,298
Standing Champ	3	F	3	0	0	0	624
Standing Regal	3	G	2	0	0	0	0
Standing Room Only	5	G	6	3	0	2	52,710
Standing Safe	2	F	8	1	2	1	37,409
Standing Tall	4	G	17	4	3	0	28,338
Standing Wager	6	M	7	0	0	0	439
Standinoutinacrowd	3	C	3	1	0	0	15,960
Standinsmall	5	M	2	0	0	0	0
Standoff	3	G	8	0	2	3	10,228
Standswithafist	3	F	12	2	2	3	66,900
Stanford Reunion	3	F	6	0	0	0	5,240
Stang Thirtysix	3	F	8	2	2	1	47,175
Stanislas	5	G	8	2	2	0	46,500
Stanislavsky	4	C	1	0	0	0	900
Stanley's Gift	4	G	16	1	2	3	17,635
Stans Dream	7	G	10	3	0	2	12,455
Stan's Friend	2	C	4	1	0	2	16,180
Stanton	2	C	2	0	1	0	13,140
Stanton Street	5	G	8	1	0	1	26,954
Stanzaic (AUS)	9	G	6	1	1	2	18,600
Star Advantage	8	H	6	2	0	1	5,420
Star Affair	6	G	6	0	0	1	2,317
Star Alarm	3	F	6	0	1	0	1,300
Star Aly	3	F	1	0	0	0	0
Star Amethyst	3	F	6	2	0	0	19,258
Star Anise	5	M	4	0	0	0	542
Star Armed	10	G	5	0	1	1	3,155
Star Behavior	4	G	6	0	1	0	984
Star Blazer	2	G	3	0	0	0	294
Star Blush	4	F	6	0	0	0	615
Star Born	2	G	2	0	0	0	270
Star Brightia	3	F	1	0	0	0	161
Star Captain	5	G	4	0	1	1	10,260
Star Care	3	G	6	0	0	0	1,020
Star Celebrity	3	F	7	3	1	2	101,270
Star Change	3	F	1	0	0	0	0
Star Charger	6	M	2	0	0	0	744
Star Chief	6	G	3	0	0	0	970
Star City	2	C	2	0	0	0	0
Star City Dancer	4	F	1	0	0	0	0
Star Class	6	G	11	1	2	4	11,945
Star Colony	8	G	7	0	1	2	2,163
Star Connection	10	G	3	0	0	0	376
Star Contender	5	G	4	2	1	0	10,440
Star Crest	3	F	6	2	1	0	36,457
Star Cross (ARG)	7	H	5	1	1	0	140,000
Star Cry	3	G	6	0	1	0	6,370
Star Dancing	6	M	9	0	0	1	450
Star de Bacchus	5	G	12	0	0	0	1,373
Star de Bag	3	C	3	1	0	0	10,035
Star des Pins	6	M	1	0	0	0	0
Star Diamond	3	F	5	0	0	2	4,935
Star Dynasty	2	C	3	0	0	0	0
Star Escort	4	F	8	2	3	0	12,300
Star Express	4	F	3	0	0	0	137
Star Goldminer	5	G	10	2	2	1	15,697
Star Gone West	7	H	3	0	0	0	0
Star Haven	3	C	1	0	0	0	45
Star Heiress	3	F	7	1	0	0	6,675
Star Honoree	3	G	6	1	0	0	10,550
Star in a Hurry	5	M	10	2	1	1	4,138
Star In Reality	6	G	4	0	0	0	546
Star Invader	4	G	8	0	1	1	3,626
Star Island	8	G	2	0	0	0	350
Star Jessi	3	F	12	0	2	2	7,515
Star Kelly	7	G	9	1	1	0	6,155
Star Lake Pete	9	G	5	0	1	2	2,576
Star Lashes	5	M	10	1	0	3	5,594
Star Launch	4	G	4	0	0	0	240
Star Leon	6	G	9	1	1	0	3,912
Star Light Star	7	G	7	1	0	0	3,591
Star Maid	2	F	2	0	1	0	3,215
Star Music	2	F	4	0	1	0	3,548
Star Nebula	5	G	12	0	0	0	690
Star Odyssey Ann	4	F	8	2	2	0	13,555
Star of Anziyan	3	F	13	2	1	2	51,040
Star of Atticus	4	F	7	1	1	1	45,515
Star of Brian	5	M	1	0	0	0	0
Star of Caveat	6	G	7	2	0	2	18,848
Star of Christmas	7	G	12	3	1	2	18,663
Star of Colleen L.	6	M	5	0	0	1	3,105
Star of Elttaes	6	G	5	3	1	1	16,830
Star of Eria	5	G	8	1	2	0	14,994
Star of Florida	4	C	12	2	2	2	31,065
Star of Ghazi	4	G	2	0	2	0	2,884
Star of Gold Fever	2	F	3	1	0	1	8,511
Star of Grace	4	G	7	0	0	1	4,950
Star of L A	4	F	1	0	0	0	400
Star of Love	4	G	4	2	1	0	8,900
Star of Maurice	2	F	1	0	0	0	1,590
Star of Midnight	8	M	9	0	0	1	1,175
Star of Nite	4	F	12	0	0	4	4,118
Star of Press	5	G	7	2	2	0	6,553
Star of Rangoon	2	F	4	0	0	0	672
Star of Reality	5	M	7	0	1	0	5,198
Star of Rehaan	5	G	3	1	0	0	3,300
Star of Richard	8	G	2	0	0	0	94
Star of Roanoke	4	G	19	1	2	1	13,935
Star of Rome	5	G	5	2	0	0	13,462
Star of Ruby	3	F	1	0	0	0	0
Star of Sahm	3	F	7	2	0	1	38,173
Star of Shaheen	3	G	4	1	0	0	4,426
Star of Stage	5	G	9	0	0	4	2,966
Star of Synastry	6	M	2	0	0	0	0
Star of the Draw	2	C	1	0	0	0	0
Star of the Lion	4	F	2	0	0	0	0
Star of Trieste	3	G	8	2	1	0	42,100
Star of Unite	4	G	14	4	4	1	24,955
Star On the Water	4	F	16	0	3	1	6,980
Star On Tour	7	M	11	1	2	2	9,570
Star Optimist	3	G	8	1	1	0	14,160
Star Over the Bay	6	G	9	5	1	0	493,960
Star Ox	3	F	2	0	0	0	0
Star Painter	4	G	2	0	0	0	0
Star Parade	2	F	1	0	0	0	1,250
Star Parade (ARG)	5	M	6	2	2	1	483,670
Star Passers Best	4	F	7	1	2	3	3,083
Star Phenom	3	F	1	0	0	1	1,540
Star Pleaser	2	G	5	0	0	1	1,166
Star Pyramid	3	F	1	0	0	0	0
Star Racer	2	F	5	0	1	0	3,540
Star Raider	4	C	9	1	1	1	16,044
Star Rainbow	3	F	11	2	1	2	44,710
Star Ring	5	G	1	0	0	1	250
Star Ring Jane	9	M	12	0	0	0	1,307
Star Seeker	7	H	3	0	1	0	1,100
Star Slugger	5	H	11	0	0	3	5,180
Star Soldier	3	G	13	3	2	0	39,855
Star Spangled Note	2	C	2	0	1	0	4,780
Star Splinter	6	M	8	0	2	0	9,740
Star Spy	5	H	9	2	1	3	14,258
Star Stalker	2	F	7	1	2	2	20,810
Star Stealer	6	G	13	2	1	1	14,990
Star Storm Dancer	2	F	2	0	0	0	300
Star Struck Latte	3	G	4	0	0	1	8,383
Star Survivor	7	G	5	0	0	0	360
Star Tap	5	G	3	0	0	0	1,343
Star Tax	3	C	4	0	0	0	696
Star Tel	3	G	11	4	1	1	59,480
Star Tier	4	G	2	0	0	0	510
Star Twister	9	M	12	1	0	0	6,751
Star Valley Star	2	C	1	0	0	0	335
Star Vega (GB)	4	F	6	0	0	0	10,840
Star Vision	3	G	1	0	0	0	0
Star Will Shine	3	G	8	1	1	0	8,410
Star Wizard	4	F	5	0	0	1	7,266
Star Zone	2	F	1	0	0	0	0
Starbrow	5	M	2	0	0	0	640
Starbuck Thief	5	G	8	0	0	1	794
Starbucks	9	G	2	0	0	0	0
Starburst Slew	2	F	4	0	1	1	5,507
Starcrossed Native	3	G	13	0	2	0	10,792

Horse	Age	Sex	Sts	1st	2d	3d	Won
Stardan (IRE)	6	H	4	0	0	0	5,220
Stardelbar	4	G	8	2	3	1	26,611
Stardimm	2	F	3	0	0	0	930
Stardust Special	4	F	13	0	1	1	7,895
Stare	3	F	5	0	0	0	440
Starella	5	M	7	1	2	1	7,310
Starez	7	G	6	1	0	0	7,328
Starful	5	M	3	0	0	0	169
Stargazey	4	C	13	1	1	0	6,118
Stargazingal	4	F	5	0	0	1	1,641
Stargirl	4	F	3	0	0	0	1,200
Starglow	5	M	12	1	1	1	5,372
Starhocracy	3	F	9	1	0	2	10,509
Stari	6	M	9	0	0	0	324
Starina's Stripes	4	F	13	1	3	1	10,896
Staring Maura	6	M	13	2	2	1	14,419
Starjon	5	G	8	1	2	0	21,750
Stark	3	G	5	0	1	0	6,960
Stark Change	4	G	5	0	0	0	492
Stark Cove	3	C	7	1	2	2	16,117
Starks Folley	5	G	7	0	2	1	2,800
Starla	3	F	1	0	0	0	0
Starlana	3	F	4	1	0	2	21,560
Starleena	2	F	2	1	0	0	29,400
Starlet Anna	4	F	3	1	0	0	4,397
Starlet Approval	4	F	13	1	1	2	39,553
Starlet Cat	4	F	16	2	3	4	21,826
Starlet Lady	2	F	2	1	0	0	7,310
Starlet Note	3	F	10	1	1	2	29,940
Starlet Sky	2	F	2	0	0	1	3,480
Starlet Terms	5	M	5	0	0	0	1,197
Starletera	4	F	4	0	0	1	1,500
Starlet's Tiger	3	G	7	1	0	1	3,297
Starlight Dancer	6	G	12	3	2	1	21,126
Starlight Express	3	F	3	0	1	1	8,250
Starlight Flyer	3	G	3	0	1	0	3,010
Starlight Girl	3	F	6	0	0	0	1,358
Starlight Serenade	3	G	11	1	4	3	26,190
Starlight Sonata	2	F	2	0	0	0	800
Starlightballerina	3	F	5	0	1	1	6,264
Starling	3	F	3	0	0	0	800
Starlit Lake	3	F	7	1	0	0	9,892
Starlit Night	3	G	12	2	0	0	9,043
Starlite Dust	5	M	10	1	2	1	18,845
Starlits Mission	2	C	4	2	1	0	35,695
Starlode	3	F	2	0	0	0	0
Starlord	5	M	14	5	2	2	46,792
Starnas	6	G	12	1	3	0	8,906
Starobinets	4	G	6	1	1	2	4,750
Starofmynight	6	G	11	5	2	2	31,079
Starofthevalley	4	G	3	0	0	0	0
Starook	2	C	4	0	1	0	4,050
Starp	7	G	11	1	0	2	5,695
Starr Just	7	G	9	0	1	1	1,060
Starr of Honor	6	M	6	0	1	0	1,609
Starr to Be	3	F	2	0	0	0	210
Starring Lady	4	F	6	1	0	1	4,374
Starring Maudlin	7	G	1	0	0	0	305
Starring Walter	2	C	3	0	0	0	332
Starr's Future	3	G	6	1	0	0	4,985
Starr's Image	7	M	4	0	0	0	600
Starry De	6	M	6	1	3	1	39,330
Starry Eyed Miss	3	F	6	0	3	0	3,175
Starry Halo	5	H	1	0	0	0	225
Starry Heaven	6	G	8	3	0	0	30,570
Starry Mark	5	M	4	0	0	1	2,123
Starry Task	2	F	2	0	0	0	102
Starry Wager	6	G	15	1	1	2	6,872
Stars Ablaze	3	F	11	1	3	1	35,370
Stars Above	3	G	6	1	0	2	43,020
Stars Aligned	4	G	15	1	3	5	68,337
Stars and Glitter	2	C	3	0	1	1	4,790
Stars and Spice	3	F	4	1	0	0	26,901
Stars and Stars	3	G	3	0	0	0	167
Stars Are Free	2	F	6	1	1	0	5,860
Star's Copy Cat	5	M	5	1	1	1	5,140
Stars Go Blue	4	F	13	2	2	2	48,590
Star's Gold	3	C	12	0	0	2	5,322
Stars in His Eyes	7	G	7	1	2	1	33,055
Star's Kandi Kane	3	F	10	1	1	2	21,340
Star's Last Chance	3	F	8	1	0	0	6,435
Stars Little Trick	6	M	1	1	0	0	1,640
Stars n' Amber	3	F	14	2	2	1	33,902
Stars 'n Dreams	7	G	8	3	1	0	14,779
Stars N Sparks	7	G	2	0	0	0	0
Stars of Orange	3	F	7	0	2	2	6,244
Stars of Silver	3	G	20	2	2	1	28,311
Stars On the Water	3	F	10	1	1	6	10,969
Stars Out Tonight (IRE)	7	G	3	1	0	0	8,750
Stars Royal	7	G	7	0	0	0	1,399
Starsandribbons	4	F	1	0	0	0	41
Starship	8	G	9	2	1	0	4,124
Starship Admiral	6	H	2	0	0	0	686
Starship Ally	2	F	3	0	1	0	1,680
Starship Bulletin	4	F	2	0	0	0	205
Starship Contessa	5	M	1	0	0	0	88
Starship Cowboy	3	G	6	0	0	0	1,050
Starship Dame	4	F	7	2	0	1	32,970
Starship Daydream	4	F	3	0	0	0	770
Starship Deputy	4	G	13	1	1	3	28,230
Starship Diligence	4	F	11	2	0	2	16,540
Starship Elaine	3	F	5	1	1	0	18,020
Starship Ensign	8	G	5	0	1	0	700
Starship Garnet	5	M	16	3	3	1	28,982
Starship Gold	5	M	10	0	1	0	4,059
Starship Outlaw	3	G	5	1	0	1	11,760
Starship Rainbow	5	G	15	1	2	4	14,963
Starship Smokester	4	F	5	1	1	0	18,180
Starship Splasher	5	G	6	0	0	0	2,911
Starship Stripper	3	F	7	0	0	0	1,205
Starship Sunrise	4	F	7	1	2	0	11,110
Starship Wonder	5	M	12	4	1	2	30,215
Starship Zim	2	G	4	1	2	1	15,790
Starshipenterprise	8	G	14	0	2	1	3,052
Starskra	6	G	5	0	0	0	1,240
Starsnstripessunny	4	C	1	0	0	0	0
Starspangleddancer	2	F	2	0	0	0	445
Starspell	4	G	10	4	4	1	81,495
Starstone	2	C	2	0	2	0	8,510
Starsunday	5	G	10	1	3	1	11,555
Start Sooner	6	G	8	0	1	3	6,253
Start the Concert	5	M	7	0	2	2	5,557
Start the Fight	4	G	4	0	0	1	750
Start to Dream	4	F	9	2	2	1	16,697
Startac	6	H	1	0	0	1	6,430
Started Witha Kiss	3	F	5	0	1	0	6,250
Startle	8	G	1	0	0	1	549
Starview's Rose	4	F	7	0	1	0	4,030
Stash the Boots	4	G	14	0	3	3	29,382
Stat Cat	8	G	3	0	1	1	1,408
State Champion	4	G	5	0	0	0	4,980
State Deputy	3	G	14	0	2	4	10,427
State Leader	5	G	2	1	0	0	3,240
State Mover	10	G	8	0	1	1	1,504
State of Luxury	3	F	7	1	1	1	4,140
State of Mind	4	F	4	0	0	1	1,244
State of Mine	3	G	5	1	2	0	2,845
State of the World	3	G	10	2	3	0	15,320
State Royality	9	G	10	0	0	0	0
State Street	4	G	13	0	1	1	6,955
State the Facts	8	H	8	1	0	0	4,514
State Twice	4	G	5	0	0	1	516
Stately and Sassy	9	G	2	0	0	0	80
Stately Clock	3	C	4	0	1	0	21,858
Stately Deputy	4	G	1	0	0	0	215
Stately Jack Flash	4	G	11	3	1	2	12,605
Stately Key	5	G	3	0	0	1	420
Stately Manor	4	F	7	1	0	4	11,580
Stately Pal	4	G	4	0	0	0	368
Stately'n Nicer	4	G	13	2	3	0	24,677
Stately's Choice	5	M	4	1	1	1	8,350
Statement	6	H	9	2	1	0	133,846
Statement (IRE)	4	C	3	1	0	1	13,080
States Victory	3	F	4	0	1	1	6,650
Statesman	3	G	3	1	1	0	31,200
Statesville	7	G	16	1	1	4	9,609
Statewide	3	F	4	1	1	1	13,540
Stateyourposition	10	G	2	0	0	0	120

Horse	Age	Sex	Sts	1st	2d	3d	Won
Static Rock	5	G	4	0	0	0	320
Station Master	3	G	2	0	0	0	630
Station Ten	2	C	4	1	0	1	7,356
Stat's Fool Heart	3	G	3	0	0	0	0
Statue	2	F	1	0	1	0	9,200
Status Seeker	2	F	2	0	0	0	328
Staubach	4	G	9	1	2	3	50,530
Stauch	6	H	6	1	0	0	32,910
Staunch Opponent	5	G	7	0	4	1	13,750
Staunchy Rascal	5	H	3	0	0	0	660
Staunton	4	C	15	1	3	1	17,077
Stavinsky's Gal	2	F	9	1	0	1	22,455
Stay for the Fun	3	F	5	0	1	1	6,070
Stay Forever	7	M	7	4	1	0	581,946
Stay Forever Young	3	G	12	2	1	0	13,201
Stay Informed	7	M	1	0	0	0	280
Stay Natural	3	G	11	1	3	0	14,918
Stay On Course	3	F	18	2	0	0	16,918
Stay Out Late	5	M	10	1	0	0	7,800
Stayofexecution	4	F	1	0	0	0	266
Stayton	7	G	1	0	0	0	0
Ste. Pecheresse	5	M	3	0	0	0	1,092
Steadfast and True	5	H	4	1	1	0	35,123
Steadiest	8	G	1	0	0	0	0
Steady Breeze	3	G	6	1	0	1	6,868
Steady Course	3	F	2	1	0	0	36,000
Steady Glitter	4	G	8	1	0	1	19,410
Steady Grind	4	G	6	0	0	0	1,742
Steady Intention	5	G	1	0	0	0	56
Steady Rollin	5	H	3	1	0	0	9,160
Steady Ruckus	8	G	6	0	0	0	11,619
Steady Smiler	4	G	13	2	0	1	60,232
Steady Streak	5	G	8	1	2	1	12,670
Steady Stream	3	C	16	1	5	2	29,035
Steadyasyougo	3	C	1	0	0	0	92
Steak House	2	G	2	0	1	1	9,863
Steakman	4	G	7	1	0	1	25,140
Steal a Band	4	F	18	4	6	2	45,230
Steal a Mac	4	F	8	3	1	0	28,628
Steal Astaire	5	G	8	0	0	1	1,240
Steal It	8	G	11	2	1	1	8,815
Steal My Kisses	3	F	6	0	0	0	2,218
Steal the Claim	4	F	7	0	2	1	9,240
Steal the Gold	3	F	11	3	3	1	32,670
Steal the Moment	3	G	13	0	2	2	13,670
Steal the Show	2	F	7	1	3	1	35,250
Steal the Treasure	3	G	3	0	1	0	4,280
Steal Your Thunder	2	C	2	1	1	0	28,200
Stealawayhome	2	G	2	0	0	0	660
Stealin' Gasoline	5	G	8	0	0	1	969
Stealing Heaven	5	G	1	0	0	0	0
Stealing Memories	4	F	12	2	2	3	21,875
Stealing Thunder	4	F	3	1	0	0	7,770
Stealth Fighter	4	G	8	2	1	3	34,080
Stealth Flier	3	C	13	2	1	2	39,452
Stealth Herself	2	F	4	0	0	0	825
Stealth Invader	3	G	12	1	4	0	12,371
Stealth Secret	3	G	9	3	2	2	69,340
Steam	2	F	6	0	1	0	2,038
Steam Ginny	3	F	5	2	0	0	14,270
Steam McQueen	4	G	12	1	0	1	6,150
Steam Train	3	G	9	1	1	3	17,630
Steamboat Express	2	G	5	0	0	1	2,710
Steamboat Road	9	G	7	1	2	0	11,778
Steamboat Springs	3	C	9	2	0	2	47,750
Steaming Artichoke	9	G	1	0	0	0	0
Steaminstacey	3	F	9	1	0	3	12,397
Steel a Day	3	C	8	0	0	0	1,170
Steel Belief	3	C	2	0	0	0	420
Steel Buns	2	F	2	0	1	0	5,840
Steel Butterfly	4	F	13	2	1	3	28,512
Steel Copy	3	G	10	4	1	1	12,046
Steel Curtain	4	G	1	0	0	0	360
Steel Cutlass	3	G	7	1	1	0	36,980
Steel Happy	6	H	2	0	0	0	340
Steel Lass	3	F	16	2	5	3	13,280
Steel Man	6	H	3	1	0	1	11,000
Steel Mine	3	C	6	1	0	1	8,180
Steel Nell	4	F	10	4	1	0	34,075
Steel On Target	7	G	15	5	2	2	29,270
Steel Power	3	C	2	0	0	0	165
Steel Princess (IRE)	3	F	4	2	0	0	62,172
Steel Shed	4	F	3	0	0	0	505
Steel the Roses	5	M	10	4	3	2	16,800
Steel Vice	5	G	7	1	1	0	10,838
Steel Wave	3	G	8	1	1	2	8,410
Steel Yur Lass	3	F	4	0	2	0	2,094
Steelbender	4	G	4	0	0	0	414
Steeleon Season	5	G	9	0	3	1	14,315
Steele's Run	3	C	1	0	0	0	0
Steels a First	3	G	11	1	0	2	3,206
Steel's Lad	3	C	13	2	2	3	20,239
Steely Blue Storm	3	F	12	1	1	1	7,402
Steely D	3	C	1	0	0	0	46
Steely Fox	4	F	4	0	1	1	850
Steely Look	4	F	7	2	0	1	6,612
Steely Max	4	G	6	0	0	3	2,884
Steely Rose	4	F	5	1	0	0	2,864
Steelyeyed	4	G	13	1	3	3	27,177
Steelyourluv	5	M	9	4	2	1	7,804
Steep Sheet	8	G	20	2	4	2	18,562
Steeple Hill	7	G	17	1	0	0	5,095
Steerage	3	G	1	0	0	0	300
Steerfurst	3	C	2	0	0	0	220
Steersman	5	G	15	0	3	3	16,608
Steev Skee	11	G	11	1	5	2	11,876
Steeveenix	4	F	1	0	0	0	450
Steeve's Nightmare	4	G	5	1	0	2	1,948
Steffiena	2	F	1	0	0	1	2,523
Steffie's Hope	3	F	4	0	0	0	135
Stefie's Brite	2	C	1	0	0	0	0
Stef's Inheritance	2	F	7	1	3	0	21,238
Stefs Silentknight	3	C	4	0	0	0	760
Steimaway	7	G	9	3	1	1	14,300
Stein's Parte Lady	3	F	8	1	2	1	10,820
Stelen's Story	2	G	1	0	0	0	0
Stella Come Back	3	F	13	4	1	3	23,857
Stella Marie	4	F	11	3	0	3	18,780
Stellacopter One	6	M	9	1	1	3	2,419
Stellar Annie	3	F	3	1	1	0	6,361
Stellar Jayne	3	F	13	3	2	3	992,169
Stellar Magic	2	G	2	1	0	0	18,948
Stellar Moment	3	F	11	1	2	1	14,100
Stellar One	3	F	6	0	0	1	3,531
Stellar Pattern	2	F	7	1	2	0	12,580
Stellar Prospect	6	M	8	1	0	0	8,691
Stellar Soldier	2	C	3	0	0	0	420
Stellar Win	4	F	10	2	0	4	7,924
Stellar Wisdom	3	F	4	0	0	1	2,518
Stellarada	5	M	2	0	0	0	170
Stella's Flare	4	F	3	0	0	0	0
Stellaspeed	7	M	9	2	1	2	12,212
Stellianos	6	G	11	3	1	0	52,337
Stello	4	G	5	1	0	1	23,128
Step and Go	4	F	8	1	2	0	17,030
Step Aside Please	4	F	12	0	0	0	17,394
Step in Time	4	F	3	1	0	0	6,090
Step Into the Fire	5	M	17	1	0	1	6,760
Step N Motion	9	H	3	0	0	0	0
Step of Greatness	3	C	3	0	2	1	11,180
Step Right In	2	G	3	1	1	1	17,260
Step Twice	4	G	23	1	2	3	15,609
Stepatatime	5	G	2	0	0	0	600
Stephanie's Angel	5	M	16	1	3	3	18,293
Stephano	4	G	11	1	2	0	3,398
Stephan's Angel	3	F	4	0	2	0	35,000
Stephan's Prize	9	G	14	2	0	2	14,341
Stephe Girl	8	M	15	2	0	2	17,550
Stephe Jean	2	F	2	0	0	0	642
Stephen Got Lucky	2	C	8	0	1	3	14,469
Stephen Hayes	5	G	10	1	0	1	8,133
Stephenes Baby	4	F	1	0	0	0	0
Stephene's Rocket	3	F	2	0	0	1	913
Stephen's Code	5	G	9	0	2	2	4,394
Stephen's Girl	7	M	3	0	0	0	147
Stephen's Pride	5	M	1	0	0	0	46
Stephens Punch	4	G	5	0	0	0	520
Stephentown	5	H	1	0	0	0	0

Horse	Age	Sex	Sts	1st	2d	3d	Won
Stephie's Cat	2	F	3	1	2	0	29,700
Stephof	2	G	5	0	0	2	3,282
Steph's Meadowlake	3	F	1	0	0	0	135
Steph's Tee	3	F	10	2	2	1	26,877
Stephs White Tower	2	F	7	1	0	0	9,370
Steping Fast	5	M	2	0	0	1	1,232
Stepinout	3	G	1	0	0	0	87
Stepit	4	F	11	4	0	0	59,610
Steponit Bad Boy	8	G	11	2	1	2	34,710
Steppen Up	5	M	5	1	3	1	24,662
Steppers Gold	4	C	1	0	0	0	0
Steppin	5	M	17	1	0	1	5,477
Steppin Charlie	4	G	5	0	0	0	1,700
Steppin Reb	4	G	10	1	0	0	5,270
Steppin Shoot	3	F	13	1	4	2	35,363
Steppin Steph	4	F	1	0	0	0	176
Steppy Quickly	3	F	1	0	0	0	40
Steps	2	F	4	1	1	0	6,700
Step's Magical Hat	3	F	11	0	0	1	2,406
Sterling Ace	3	G	13	2	4	1	49,069
Sterling Advocate	3	F	6	0	0	0	302
Sterling Bob	2	C	1	0	0	0	400
Sterling Cat	2	F	2	2	0	0	93,675
Sterling Copy	3	F	6	0	0	1	931
Sterling Fox	2	F	2	0	1	0	2,600
Sterling Gold	5	G	12	4	1	3	137,755
Sterling M P	7	G	16	1	2	2	3,343
Sterling Nichol	4	C	3	0	0	0	0
Sterling Prospect	4	G	11	2	3	1	39,110
Sterling Ridge	4	G	2	0	1	0	4,323
Sterling Road	3	G	11	0	1	0	3,960
Sterling Slipper	3	F	8	3	2	0	29,758
Sterling Wisdom	5	G	14	4	1	3	62,125
Sterlingprospector	2	C	2	0	1	0	9,400
Sterling's Lad	7	G	19	2	3	2	22,385
Stern Ties	5	G	9	0	1	1	2,316
Sternman	4	C	13	4	3	3	28,315
Sterns Lad	6	G	8	0	0	1	1,632
Sterny	4	C	1	0	0	0	400
Stetson	2	G	2	0	0	1	1,884
Stetson Cat	5	G	15	1	4	3	13,685
Stetter Jr	3	G	19	5	3	2	65,520
Steve	5	G	10	1	2	3	11,309
Steve V Boy	5	G	7	0	3	0	1,497
Stevebiscuit	2	C	5	0	0	1	2,875
Steve'e Gal	3	F	5	0	1	2	3,350
Steven At Dawn	2	C	1	1	0	0	12,400
Steveneedsaposse	4	C	13	1	1	0	10,584
Steven's Boy	3	G	10	1	2	1	10,184
Stevens Day	4	G	15	2	1	2	5,155
Steven's Storm	2	F	3	0	0	0	75
Steve's Choice	3	G	8	2	1	0	14,955
Steve's Escape	7	G	4	0	1	0	2,235
Steve's Rave	3	G	8	1	0	1	2,149
Steves Remark	4	C	2	0	0	1	6,825
Steves Sunny Comet	5	H	12	1	2	1	11,539
Steve's Thunder	6	G	4	1	0	1	14,025
Steve's Trial	4	G	2	1	0	0	6,930
Stevie Be Good	2	C	2	0	0	0	532
Stevie Stressor	3	G	10	2	2	0	80,606
Stevie's Comet	7	M	5	0	0	0	0
Stevies Lastdance	3	F	2	0	0	0	213
Stew Nada	5	G	15	1	0	1	6,387
Steward	4	C	8	1	1	0	4,770
Stewing Hope	5	H	3	0	1	0	1,608
Stewing Wonder	4	F	1	0	0	0	172
Stew's Stone	3	C	5	2	0	3	18,500
Stick N Stein	6	M	8	1	2	2	15,398
Stick to Roses	4	G	3	0	1	0	3,030
Sticker Shock	4	G	16	3	1	0	17,028
Stickman Phil	2	G	3	0	1	1	7,630
Sticktotheprogram	3	G	12	1	5	2	17,520
Stickupman	2	C	3	0	0	0	410
Sticky Cat	2	G	14	0	4	2	10,692
Sticky Note	5	M	2	0	1	0	2,304
Sticky Prospect	2	F	7	0	1	1	5,380
Stickytrickydeputy	4	G	15	3	1	1	15,636
Stigler's Sorrel	4	G	15	3	2	3	24,960
Stilaferd	10	G	4	1	0	0	1,515

Horse	Age	Sex	Sts	1st	2d	3d	Won
Still	5	G	7	1	2	1	4,350
Still As Sweet (IRE)	7	M	5	0	0	0	950
Still Be Smokin'	5	H	12	3	1	3	38,906
Still Crazy	3	F	8	1	0	1	5,795
Still Dancing	3	G	5	3	0	1	14,800
Still Foolin Aroun	4	C	14	3	0	2	35,421
Still Guilty	2	C	2	1	1	0	32,600
Still Mine	4	F	14	1	2	1	7,985
Still Smoldering	3	G	10	1	2	1	40,070
Still the Deal	3	C	6	0	0	0	581
Stillgotem	3	G	15	2	0	1	17,459
Stillsmokenglo	2	F	2	0	0	0	139
Stillwater Rose	3	F	8	2	1	1	15,101
Stillwell	2	C	2	1	0	0	18,600
Stiltsville	8	G	13	1	0	1	8,251
Stilwell Angel	2	G	4	1	1	1	22,500
Stina	2	F	1	0	0	0	140
Sting King	4	C	7	2	1	1	16,944
Sting Lear	4	C	8	3	2	1	76,970
Sting Man	4	C	12	0	2	1	21,096
Sting Me	2	C	3	0	1	1	4,620
Stinke Pant's	5	M	15	0	4	2	8,156
Stinky Secret	4	F	3	0	0	0	0
Stinky Twinkie	5	M	13	2	1	2	22,055
Stinson	6	H	15	3	1	3	11,977
Stir Fry	3	G	3	1	0	1	6,810
Stir the Mix	4	G	13	1	1	1	9,530
Stirrin Up a Storm	4	F	6	3	0	2	57,350
Stirring the Stew	4	F	8	1	0	1	5,014
Stitch n' Weave	8	G	10	3	2	2	5,743
Stitchery	3	G	5	1	1	1	8,567
Stock Rocket	9	G	5	0	0	1	2,217
Stock Tip	2	F	1	0	0	0	180
Stocked and Loded	4	F	7	2	0	0	7,788
Stockholder	4	C	2	0	1	1	21,800
Stockport	6	G	14	1	3	2	9,238
Stocks Are Rising	6	G	14	2	3	1	42,578
Stoic	3	F	4	0	0	0	4,060
Stoic Endeavour	4	G	9	1	0	0	6,819
Stoico	3	G	4	0	0	1	4,370
Stoke the Fire	3	F	2	0	0	0	0
Stoker	4	G	13	4	1	1	56,444
Stokosky	8	H	8	2	2	0	24,913
Stokowski	6	H	2	0	0	0	0
Stole	5	H	1	0	0	0	0
Stole My Heart	6	H	4	1	0	1	1,839
Stole One	3	F	4	1	0	1	20,600
Stolen Command	2	F	1	0	0	0	800
Stolen Gal	2	F	4	1	0	0	3,140
Stolen Gem	2	F	7	1	0	0	5,278
Stolen Groom	6	G	7	1	1	1	6,550
Stolen Halo	4	F	13	3	2	2	31,565
Stolen Hero	3	G	7	0	1	4	3,795
Stolen Honor	6	G	15	0	1	4	6,960
Stolen King	2	G	2	0	0	0	150
Stolen Purse	3	F	4	0	0	0	734
Stolen Sheena	4	F	11	1	1	2	13,192
Stolen Time	3	C	9	2	1	1	93,140
Stolencon	4	G	1	0	0	0	0
Stoli (IRE)	6	G	1	0	0	1	1,500
Stomping	4	F	7	1	1	2	53,781
Stone Age	6	G	13	4	3	0	83,599
Stone Blue	3	G	3	0	0	1	1,289
Stone Brush	5	M	2	0	0	0	280
Stone Canyon	4	C	12	4	3	0	81,174
Stone Carving	2	F	4	0	0	1	1,853
Stone Cat	4	C	2	1	0	1	17,320
Stone Cold	6	H	8	1	0	0	10,071
Stone Cold Cat	3	C	12	0	2	3	10,177
Stone Cold Courage	3	G	3	0	0	0	63
Stone Face	4	F	14	1	5	2	16,898
Stone Fleet	3	F	9	1	1	1	7,775
Stone King	4	G	7	1	0	1	9,732
Stone Ledge	5	G	9	3	1	1	29,142
Stone Legend	5	H	2	0	0	0	582
Stone Point	4	F	4	0	1	1	3,844
Stone Pony	4	G	3	0	0	0	225
Stone Prince	2	G	2	0	0	0	950
Stone Rain	3	G	4	1	1	0	37,000

Horse	Age	Sex	Sts	1st	2d	3d	Won
Stone Trick	2	C	4	0	1	1	4,500
Stonebridge Lady	5	M	5	1	2	0	43,560
Stonefeather	4	F	4	0	0	1	594
Stonefield South	2	F	3	0	1	0	4,032
Stonemason	5	G	3	0	0	1	880
Stonesoup	5	M	7	2	1	0	38,545
Stonewall Harris	3	G	8	2	2	3	44,091
Stonewall Peach	3	F	8	1	1	0	4,946
Stoneway	3	F	5	1	0	1	36,008
Stonewood	3	G	14	6	1	3	129,005
Stoney Character	4	G	8	2	0	2	8,300
Stoney Creek	5	G	20	1	4	5	25,200
Stoney Creek One	3	F	1	0	0	0	78
Stoney Rapids	3	G	3	0	0	0	0
Stoney River	4	G	4	1	1	0	10,015
Stoneyeyes	5	G	9	2	1	2	6,875
Stong	4	G	11	2	2	5	40,981
Stonington	5	M	4	1	0	0	43,296
Stooge Lover	4	F	12	3	2	1	37,684
Stoogie Smoker	8	G	5	0	1	0	1,120
Stop and Sea	4	C	1	0	0	0	146
Stop Dreaming	5	G	14	3	4	0	33,508
Stop for a Kiss	2	F	5	0	1	1	3,966
Stop Like Bell	4	G	10	2	1	1	8,346
Stop Looking	4	F	9	2	2	0	82,264
Stop Loss	4	F	8	0	1	1	2,023
Stop Seven	9	M	4	0	0	1	4,480
Stop Tapping	7	H	10	1	1	3	7,108
Stop That Dancer	4	F	4	0	0	2	7,150
Stop the Act	4	G	10	1	2	3	5,526
Stop the Bluffing	6	G	8	0	2	1	2,890
Stop the Clock	8	G	6	0	0	0	150
Stop the Nonsense	4	F	18	1	4	3	15,555
Stop the Race	2	C	1	0	0	0	2,150
Stop the Robber	3	G	10	1	2	2	16,470
Stop the Talking	7	M	9	2	1	0	89,380
Stop the Vice	8	M	3	0	0	2	3,300
Stop to Dance	5	H	2	0	0	0	114
Stopalong Cadillac	8	G	7	1	2	2	8,292
Stopyourtwining	6	M	14	0	4	1	14,797
Stored	3	C	1	0	0	0	300
Storied Cat	2	C	5	2	2	0	80,602
Storm a Brewing	2	F	1	0	0	1	4,540
Storm Assignment	3	C	4	1	0	1	9,190
Storm At Sunset	3	C	2	1	0	0	11,400
Storm B Comin	2	G	1	0	0	0	140
Storm Bandit	3	F	5	1	2	0	25,070
Storm Bank	6	G	11	2	4	1	41,050
Storm Bay	3	F	8	0	3	2	8,958
Storm Believer	3	F	3	0	0	1	1,074
Storm Bell	5	M	2	0	0	0	0
Storm Bite	4	C	1	0	0	0	0
Storm Bolt	5	H	8	1	4	0	13,925
Storm Booming	4	C	6	0	0	1	3,855
Storm Boot Gold	3	G	8	1	4	1	63,448
Storm Bowl	5	G	5	1	1	1	21,680
Storm Breaking	4	F	6	2	1	2	52,070
Storm Brigade	5	G	4	0	0	0	120
Storm Bull	3	C	9	0	2	1	14,815
Storm Capsule	4	G	3	1	1	0	22,870
Storm Cat Larry	6	G	3	0	0	1	1,150
Storm Cat's Kitten	4	F	2	0	0	0	360
Storm Cave	5	H	8	0	1	1	5,942
Storm Chronicle	6	H	12	2	2	3	27,200
Storm City Blues	3	F	9	1	3	0	41,592
Storm Clock	3	F	7	2	0	0	34,162
Storm Command	3	G	5	0	0	0	266
Storm Commander	5	H	6	1	1	0	43,200
Storm Counter	3	F	3	0	0	0	360
Storm Country	3	F	2	0	0	0	0
Storm Craft	6	H	13	1	4	1	57,871
Storm Creek Rising	2	C	5	1	3	1	65,490
Storm Crossing	3	G	13	1	4	0	46,960
Storm Cup	6	G	5	0	1	0	1,033
Storm Cyclone	2	C	5	1	0	0	13,707
Storm Damage	4	G	19	1	0	1	5,309
Storm Dancing	6	G	9	2	1	0	17,559
Storm Derby	2	C	2	0	0	0	1,600
Storm Devil	8	G	3	0	0	1	1,002
Storm Diamond	3	F	6	3	2	0	56,704
Storm Dorm	2	F	1	0	0	0	0
Storm Duck	4	C	10	1	2	0	11,900
Storm Envoy	6	G	9	0	0	0	4,148
Storm Express	4	G	9	1	1	1	22,554
Storm Flag Flying	4	F	8	3	2	3	963,248
Storm Flame	4	G	15	1	2	5	14,029
Storm Fleet	3	F	3	0	0	1	850
Storm Flite	4	F	8	1	1	0	10,910
Storm Flyer	3	G	2	0	0	1	700
Storm Forcast	2	F	6	1	0	2	15,865
Storm Forward	3	G	15	2	0	1	23,654
Storm Fox (CHI)	4	G	4	0	0	1	5,640
Storm Glory	4	F	3	0	0	0	0
Storm Guide	4	G	1	0	0	0	164
Storm Gulch	4	G	15	2	2	3	27,465
Storm Gull	3	C	3	0	0	0	556
Storm Harbor	3	G	10	1	0	1	23,356
Storm Heat	2	C	1	0	1	0	5,600
Storm Hen	4	F	8	1	3	2	55,620
Storm Hero	3	G	7	1	0	0	3,709
Storm in Augusta	3	F	3	1	1	0	8,937
Storm in My Heart	3	G	14	0	2	5	11,618
Storm in Philly	5	M	6	1	1	1	15,895
Storm in Session	4	G	7	2	1	1	10,293
Storm in Texas	4	F	1	0	0	0	0
Storm Kas	3	C	2	0	0	0	783
Storm Kingdom	3	G	9	1	1	1	20,330
Storm Lad	5	H	5	2	0	0	9,240
Storm Leaper	4	F	6	2	0	1	10,631
Storm Legacy	3	C	10	2	1	1	77,220
Storm Lord	5	G	19	3	3	2	18,340
Storm Mate	2	C	1	1	0	0	21,000
Storm Mill	3	G	1	0	0	0	0
Storm Minstrel	3	F	11	4	4	1	152,420
Storm Mistress	6	M	6	0	0	0	382
Storm Mont	4	G	6	0	0	1	3,285
Storm 'n' Hail	2	F	2	0	0	1	1,870
Storm N Lightning	2	G	6	1	1	0	37,742
Storm N Sunny	3	F	12	2	4	0	11,720
Storm 'n Z	3	G	15	3	4	2	15,767
Storm Now	5	G	5	0	1	0	3,290
Storm n'To War	3	F	7	1	4	0	26,946
Storm of Liberty	3	G	12	2	0	2	10,019
Storm of Stars	3	G	2	0	0	0	0
Storm of the West	4	F	9	2	0	0	13,408
Storm of the Year	3	C	8	1	0	2	11,497
Storm On the Lake	4	F	6	0	2	0	14,725
Storm On the Way	3	G	9	0	0	0	4,108
Storm On the Wire	3	G	1	0	0	0	0
Storm Page	4	F	10	1	0	2	6,214
Storm Passer Bye	3	G	9	2	1	1	15,875
Storm Peace	6	G	10	2	1	1	22,274
Storm Petrel	3	C	7	1	0	2	14,534
Storm Pilot	3	C	3	0	3	0	27,400
Storm Power	7	G	8	0	3	0	10,976
Storm Quest	4	G	22	3	3	2	32,855
Storm Reef	3	G	6	0	1	2	11,791
Storm River Kelly	4	C	12	4	2	0	36,505
Storm Rose	10	G	7	0	0	0	426
Storm Ruckus	4	G	4	0	0	0	709
Storm Rullah	3	G	4	1	0	0	6,116
Storm Saint	4	F	7	2	1	1	15,875
Storm Screen	3	F	5	0	0	2	1,161
Storm Shooter	5	H	13	1	2	2	16,029
Storm Signal	7	G	3	0	0	0	0
Storm Sizzle	3	G	9	2	1	0	56,937
Storm Soaring	3	C	2	0	0	0	1,670
Storm Speed	3	C	10	0	2	3	7,917
Storm Stream	3	F	5	1	2	0	37,600
Storm Strip	3	F	2	0	0	2	9,200
Storm Surge	2	C	7	4	1	0	192,770
Storm Tale	4	G	12	2	0	1	14,349
Storm Talker	9	G	5	1	0	0	2,643
Storm Tempest	5	M	5	0	0	0	125
Storm the Beach	3	G	14	5	3	1	114,132
Storm the Gate	7	G	6	1	0	0	5,173
Storm the Net	8	M	6	1	0	0	7,056
Storm Thief	2	G	2	1	1	0	33,600

RECORDS OF HORSES

Horse	Age	Sex	Sts	1st	2d	3d	Won
Storm This Picture	4	G	6	0	1	2	3,865
Storm to the Top	4	F	14	4	4	1	41,582
Storm Touch	8	G	3	1	0	1	8,460
Storm Train	3	G	5	2	1	0	26,957
Storm Trial	3	F	5	0	0	1	1,166
Storm Twist	3	G	19	2	4	3	48,190
Storm Unbridled	4	C	10	3	0	0	26,510
Storm Uprising	3	G	3	0	0	1	5,385
Storm Verse	6	G	10	1	2	1	16,340
Storm Walking	2	F	3	1	0	0	30,000
Storm Warning	2	C	4	1	1	0	44,150
Storm Watch	5	H	13	5	3	3	71,990
Storm Whirl	3	G	8	3	1	0	51,720
Storm Wish	6	G	9	1	1	3	8,989
Storm With Praise	3	C	2	0	1	0	3,200
Storm Witness	6	M	10	0	0	0	781
Storm Wolf	2	C	1	0	0	0	2,640
Stormacomin	3	F	8	1	1	2	12,610
Stormalot	7	H	7	0	2	0	2,093
Stormcastelli	3	G	7	1	0	0	6,435
Stormcaster	5	H	2	0	0	0	0
Stormcat's Atticus	3	F	2	0	0	1	780
Stormcats Grandson	3	G	15	3	0	2	21,593
Stormcatsvalentine	2	C	1	0	0	0	140
Stormcloudrising	3	F	7	2	2	1	17,715
Stormed	5	H	3	0	0	0	400
Stormen Cricket	2	F	1	0	0	0	235
Stormented	5	M	6	2	2	0	58,994
Stormhill	4	F	16	2	2	3	25,384
Stormhouse	5	G	9	1	0	1	3,859
Stormi Sounds	3	F	6	1	1	0	11,516
Stormica	4	F	7	2	2	1	99,120
Stormie Britches	8	G	12	2	1	0	15,380
Stormie Skies	8	H	1	0	0	0	0
Stormie's Peanut	3	G	10	0	2	4	6,900
Stormin	5	G	10	1	2	2	22,443
Stormin Alyse	2	F	3	1	0	0	5,272
Stormin Away	2	G	6	1	1	1	32,678
Stormin' Betty	5	M	6	0	0	0	1,445
Stormin Bleu	2	C	3	0	0	0	300
Stormin Charlotte	2	F	1	0	0	0	150
Stormin Cherokee	4	G	7	2	1	1	16,105
Stormin Chief	3	G	22	2	2	4	22,380
Stormin' Daina	3	F	15	2	3	1	44,294
Stormin Dancer	3	F	8	0	0	0	2,893
Stormin Devil	3	G	6	1	0	0	7,288
Stormin' Down	4	F	12	1	2	0	19,600
Stormin Eddie	2	G	5	1	0	2	24,350
Stormin Eishin	3	F	7	2	1	1	37,458
Stormin Fury	2	C	1	0	0	0	250
Stormin Gen. Tommy	3	G	9	1	4	1	42,240
Stormin Girl	3	F	4	0	3	0	5,313
Stormin Greek	3	G	15	1	3	2	17,932
Stormin in Seattle	2	F	3	0	0	0	0
Stormin Isabel	2	F	3	0	0	0	690
Stormin J' Cat	3	G	1	0	0	0	0
Stormin J. P.	2	C	3	0	1	0	8,730
Stormin Jacko	3	G	1	0	0	0	0
Stormin Janetrose	3	F	9	3	0	1	25,938
Stormin Jeannie	3	F	8	2	1	0	11,310
Stormin Jessica	3	F	1	0	0	0	0
Stormin Johnny	3	G	6	1	0	0	3,693
Stormin Lauren	3	F	5	0	0	1	1,320
Stormin Lil	3	F	7	1	0	2	8,746
Stormin' Lyon	3	C	4	3	1	0	90,705
Stormin Man	3	C	16	1	2	1	12,684
Stormin' Melody	2	F	2	0	0	0	535
Stormin Morn	4	C	11	1	3	1	14,765
Stormin Nikki	3	F	6	0	0	0	0
Stormin Oedy	7	H	13	0	2	3	27,650
Stormin' Oiseau	6	G	9	1	4	2	10,020
Stormin Palm Beach	4	F	2	0	1	0	2,240
Stormin Pat	3	F	2	0	1	0	3,400
Stormin Pattie	3	G	3	0	0	0	420
Stormin' Reprized	5	G	19	0	1	2	12,050
Stormin Sandy	3	G	10	1	1	0	6,978
Stormin Scooter	2	F	5	0	0	2	1,617
Stormin Sioux	3	F	7	1	2	0	13,620
Stormin Tammy	5	M	2	0	0	0	0
Stormin Tia	4	F	6	0	1	1	4,150
Stormin Time	6	G	4	0	1	0	3,575
Stormin Tony	5	G	8	1	2	1	16,699
Stormin Up Front	4	G	13	2	1	1	24,802
Stormin Vice	3	G	8	0	1	0	1,780
Storminbayoubabe	4	F	11	1	2	0	16,408
Stormindisguise	3	C	4	1	0	1	8,182
Storminess	2	F	4	1	0	1	14,320
Storming	2	C	1	0	1	0	8,200
Storming Ashley	4	F	7	2	0	1	16,254
Storming Kim	2	C	1	0	0	0	460
Storming Magic	3	F	7	0	0	0	2,906
Storming Maria	3	F	10	0	2	0	11,345
Storming Mimi	2	F	1	0	0	0	90
Storming On By	3	C	19	2	0	2	14,340
Storming On Merit	5	M	4	3	1	0	32,100
Storming Pride	2	F	1	0	0	0	400
Storming Renee	6	M	11	1	1	2	19,165
Storming Way	3	F	1	0	0	0	0
Storminoutahere	3	G	4	0	0	0	184
Storminthedesert	3	G	10	1	4	1	10,924
Storminthegap	3	G	7	0	0	1	1,259
Stormline	5	H	7	3	1	0	15,922
Storm'n J R	6	H	9	2	0	1	33,800
Storm'n Mercedes	2	F	4	0	0	0	900
Storm'n Trojan	3	C	2	0	0	0	100
Stormndownthelane	5	M	7	1	3	1	9,634
Stormoffthecoast	4	G	16	1	2	4	12,065
Stormofthecentury	6	G	2	0	0	0	0
Storm's Araging	4	G	11	1	5	1	9,025
Storm's Cooking	4	F	9	1	3	1	22,310
Storm's Darling	3	F	13	4	2	3	157,854
Storm's Finale	5	M	6	1	0	0	21,000
Storm's Lining	6	G	12	1	1	0	5,990
Storm's Path	7	H	1	0	0	0	0
Storm's Secret	6	M	14	4	3	2	43,088
Stormsabrewin	4	F	5	0	0	0	1,222
Stormtoremember	3	F	4	2	1	0	7,270
Stormtune	2	F	3	0	0	2	3,150
Stormwater	3	C	4	0	0	0	276
Stormworthy	3	G	6	0	0	0	1,225
Stormy Act	3	C	9	1	1	1	20,290
Stormy Afternoon	2	C	4	1	2	0	43,885
Stormy Alliance	2	F	1	0	0	0	0
Stormy Appeal	5	H	5	0	0	0	0
Stormy Arctic	3	F	3	2	0	1	30,680
Stormy Autumn	2	F	4	0	0	0	0
Stormy Bay	2	C	1	0	0	1	2,760
Stormy Brew	5	G	8	1	0	2	11,546
Stormy Brie	5	M	4	1	0	0	12,023
Stormy Business	2	C	8	1	4	0	25,560
Stormy But Crafty	2	C	5	2	1	0	33,700
Stormy Carol	4	F	11	1	2	1	6,087
Stormy Conquest	5	M	10	1	1	3	17,516
Stormy Crusade	2	C	3	0	1	0	2,250
Stormy Daisy	5	M	9	1	1	0	4,093
Stormy Danyelle	4	F	5	2	1	0	30,280
Stormy Dawn	3	F	1	0	0	0	0
Stormy Day	5	G	11	3	5	1	67,289
Stormy Dear	3	F	2	0	0	0	0
Stormy Debut	5	G	10	0	1	1	1,660
Stormy Do	11	G	13	5	2	3	55,060
Stormy Entrance	3	F	3	1	0	1	9,539
Stormy Fellow	3	G	12	3	2	3	60,507
Stormy Forest	3	C	3	1	0	0	17,000
Stormy Forever	5	H	2	0	0	0	142
Stormy Gambler	8	M	7	0	3	1	9,865
Stormy Grand Banks	2	F	3	1	1	0	34,890
Stormy Gulch	5	G	5	1	1	2	10,380
Stormy Heaven	2	F	1	0	0	0	0
Stormy Heroine	4	F	11	4	1	3	55,032
Stormy Hollow	4	G	9	0	0	0	725
Stormy Honor	4	F	10	0	1	3	3,318
Stormy Hostage	6	G	21	4	6	3	23,310
Stormy Idea	3	C	1	0	0	0	220
Stormy Impact	5	G	10	1	0	2	76,257
Stormy Isle	9	G	8	0	0	1	680
Stormy Jim	2	C	7	2	1	0	72,290
Stormy Kid	2	F	3	0	0	0	105

Horse	Age	Sex	Sts	1st	2d	3d	Won
Stormy Kitty	3	F	14	4	1	4	90,140
Stormy Knight	3	C	2	1	0	0	9,240
Stormy Kristine	2	F	2	0	0	0	0
Stormy La Reine	4	F	7	1	2	0	19,810
Stormy Lane	4	C	6	1	1	0	25,857
Stormy Looker	5	H	1	0	0	0	66
Stormy Lover	5	G	12	1	2	4	79,587
Stormy Luvin	4	G	2	0	0	0	169
Stormy Manners	3	G	7	0	1	3	1,216
Stormy March	5	M	4	1	1	0	2,400
Stormy Mary	5	M	7	0	0	1	1,945
Stormy Misty	3	F	15	2	2	2	33,430
Stormy Music	3	F	8	1	1	0	13,860
Stormy 'n Sly	4	F	3	0	1	0	2,725
Stormy Nantucket	3	F	1	0	0	0	780
Stormy Noche	3	F	8	0	0	0	0
Stormy Numbers	3	F	1	0	0	0	0
Stormy o' Bryan	3	G	9	2	4	1	30,360
Stormy Planet	4	G	12	0	2	3	11,704
Stormy Pleasure	6	H	14	1	0	0	5,304
Stormy Pride	4	F	5	1	1	1	8,645
Stormy Queen	2	F	10	0	2	3	8,296
Stormy Quest	3	C	7	0	1	1	8,700
Stormy Raccoon	4	F	9	1	3	2	10,188
Stormy Ray	5	G	11	2	3	2	85,280
Stormy Rockette	4	G	13	3	1	2	46,085
Stormy Roman	5	G	10	1	2	2	87,960
Stormy Rosa	3	F	8	4	1	0	79,660
Stormy Ruler	2	F	5	1	1	0	8,820
Stormy Seas	6	G	9	1	0	0	16,290
Stormy Season	3	F	11	1	2	3	48,830
Stormy Senorita	3	F	6	1	0	1	16,560
Stormy Session	3	C	3	0	0	1	660
Stormy Side	2	G	3	1	0	0	6,609
Stormy Siege	3	C	5	0	0	1	4,220
Stormy Sky	4	F	15	2	0	3	17,610
Stormy Socks	4	G	15	0	0	0	2,117
Stormy Sonata	8	G	3	0	0	1	1,620
Stormy South	3	G	14	1	3	1	9,094
Stormy Sparks	3	G	6	0	0	0	345
Stormy Sunset	5	G	6	0	0	1	600
Stormy Surprise	5	M	9	1	1	1	9,341
Stormy Terms	3	F	4	0	0	0	1,892
Stormy Thrill	2	G	6	1	1	1	27,590
Stormy Thunder	3	G	13	3	0	2	24,555
Stormy Town	3	F	2	1	0	0	2,988
Stormy Trial	3	C	16	3	2	1	24,025
Stormy Venus	2	F	1	0	0	0	0
Stormy Waters	5	G	4	0	0	0	386
Stormy Weather	2	F	4	0	0	0	690
Stormy Whitney	6	M	7	0	0	0	521
Stormy World	2	F	2	0	0	0	920
Stormybdancing	4	F	9	0	3	2	29,910
Stormys Treasure	3	G	3	1	1	0	8,520
Stormy'sback	3	C	19	1	2	1	18,295
Story Book Love	5	M	7	1	0	1	8,362
Story Grinder	4	C	6	2	0	0	20,960
Story of the Cat	3	F	5	0	0	0	0
Story Tails	4	G	6	2	0	2	3,012
Storybook Kid	6	G	5	0	1	1	24,620
Storybound	7	M	7	0	1	2	8,296
Storyville Girl	3	F	9	1	0	0	6,439
Stosky and Hutch	4	F	4	0	0	0	852
Stotz	4	G	8	0	2	0	4,519
Stoughton	3	C	1	0	0	0	320
Stoutest	3	F	1	0	0	0	0
Stove Pipe	4	G	11	2	1	0	21,580
Stower	4	G	2	0	0	0	460
Strabane Trail	2	G	1	0	0	0	0
Straight A	7	H	3	1	0	0	6,886
Straight Bid	2	F	3	1	0	1	20,510
Straight Boozer	3	F	2	0	0	0	0
Straight Exchange	4	F	12	4	0	2	27,632
Straight In	6	G	14	3	1	2	24,479
Straight Line	2	C	6	3	1	0	166,312
Straight n' Up	2	G	4	1	0	1	12,240
Straight Noble	5	M	2	0	0	0	276
Straight Paladin	2	C	1	0	1	0	5,600
Straight Path	5	G	6	0	3	0	12,650
Straight Poker	2	F	2	1	1	0	8,250
Straight Putt	4	G	3	2	0	0	15,982
Straight Star	4	G	10	1	1	0	32,030
Straight Street	7	G	1	0	0	0	0
Straightandstrong	2	G	3	0	0	1	6,540
Straighten Up	3	F	9	1	3	1	22,070
Straightforthetop	4	G	6	0	2	0	14,418
Straightlittlelady	2	F	5	2	1	1	60,184
Straightothefront	2	F	2	0	0	0	263
Strait From Texas	5	M	5	1	0	0	27,197
Straitfrommyheart	6	M	14	3	1	1	26,803
Strandhill	6	G	12	0	1	1	11,770
Strange Devil	2	F	1	0	0	0	156
Stranger	5	G	16	2	4	5	27,872
Stranger Among Us	4	G	12	3	1	1	7,236
Strap	5	G	6	2	0	0	5,460
Straphanger	5	G	9	0	0	0	3,100
Strapless Dancer	6	G	9	0	0	1	1,580
Strappado	7	G	3	0	0	0	300
Strapper Nick	4	G	1	0	0	0	0
Strata Climber	3	C	8	2	3	0	38,200
Stratagem	2	G	4	0	0	1	6,540
Strategic	6	M	2	0	0	1	420
Strategic Force	3	G	13	1	0	4	23,499
Strategic Intrigue	5	G	9	2	1	1	28,864
Strategic Storm	2	G	1	0	0	0	0
Strategic Strike	4	G	13	2	0	1	30,726
Strategically	4	G	15	5	3	1	41,291
Stratego	5	G	5	1	0	1	4,760
Strategury	4	G	13	2	2	3	24,315
Strategy	3	F	8	2	3	1	93,680
Strategy (GB)	4	F	6	0	1	0	8,751
Stratematic	5	G	8	2	1	1	49,700
Stratford On Avon	4	G	12	3	0	2	67,775
Strathcona	5	G	14	3	2	1	19,882
Stratostar	4	C	11	2	1	4	98,410
Stratton	2	F	2	0	0	2	6,490
Stratus (ARG)	6	H	1	0	0	1	5,160
Stratus (FR)	5	G	4	0	0	1	9,740
Strausberg	4	G	4	0	0	0	240
Strauss	3	G	15	1	0	2	6,497
Stravinsky's Fire	3	F	9	0	0	1	4,287
Stravinskys Honor	3	G	7	3	1	2	98,759
Straw Hat	2	C	9	1	3	2	57,345
Straw Hat Charlie	3	G	6	0	1	1	5,045
Straw Poll	3	G	5	0	0	0	1,200
Straw to Gold	5	G	5	0	0	1	1,275
Strawbailey	6	M	2	0	0	0	1,950
Strawberriesncream	3	F	1	0	1	0	2,485
Strawberry Banks	4	F	12	2	3	2	19,687
Strawberry Custard	3	F	6	2	0	0	12,240
Strawberry Gone	4	F	11	0	1	2	6,338
Strawberry Ice	5	M	15	2	3	3	18,903
Strawberry Kid	5	G	13	1	4	1	14,763
Strawberry Kwik	4	F	13	3	1	1	21,179
Strawberry Line	3	F	10	2	2	2	46,782
Strawberry Moon	7	M	2	0	0	0	40
Strawberry Patch	2	F	3	1	2	0	25,600
Strawberry Pet	3	F	3	1	1	0	9,456
Strawberry Pop	9	G	4	0	1	1	1,870
Strawberry Sky	3	F	10	2	0	2	26,070
Strawberry Soda	4	F	16	1	3	3	14,003
Strawberry Strut	3	F	5	1	1	0	7,840
Strawberry Treat	2	F	10	0	0	2	14,630
Strawberry Turn	8	M	7	0	0	2	1,012
Strawberry Twister	5	H	13	2	5	1	11,312
Strawberry Wild	2	G	10	0	2	3	6,890
Strawberryblondie	2	F	2	0	0	0	120
Strawberryfields	4	F	6	1	2	0	6,120
Stray Bullet	5	M	6	1	0	0	13,621
Stray Cat Blues	2	C	3	1	1	0	33,670
Streak a Roani	3	G	10	3	3	2	20,232
Streak of Light	2	C	2	1	0	0	17,640
Streak of Royalty	5	G	4	1	0	2	44,685
Streak of Smoke	3	C	9	1	1	0	16,138
Streak Smart	3	C	3	2	1	0	29,150
Streak Stroud	4	C	10	0	3	1	15,280
Streakednorth	4	F	6	1	2	0	15,680
Streakin and Strip	3	G	6	2	0	0	19,305

Horse	Age	Sex	Sts	1st	2d	3d	Won
Streakin Baha	3	G	7	1	0	1	1,030
Streakin Bocario	5	H	7	1	0	0	12,955
Streakin Devil	3	G	3	0	0	0	0
Streakin Monarch	4	C	4	1	0	1	4,517
Streakin Rob	5	G	6	0	0	0	284
Streakin Zulu	5	G	8	0	0	2	813
Streaking Echo	5	M	11	2	0	0	17,280
Streaking Light	3	G	13	1	2	1	23,589
Streaking Pine	2	C	2	1	1	0	15,700
Streaking Princess	3	F	3	0	0	0	1,410
Streaking Woman	8	M	16	2	0	2	13,065
Streakinjeb	4	F	8	0	0	1	1,910
Stream	5	M	5	1	0	1	11,301
Streamline	3	C	6	1	1	1	34,091
Streamline Gahl	4	F	9	1	0	1	3,010
Strech Out Front	5	H	12	0	2	2	9,902
Streebek	3	G	10	1	2	0	10,575
Street Angel	6	M	4	0	0	0	517
Street Chic	3	F	13	1	1	0	13,776
Street Eagle	2	G	1	0	1	0	960
Street Gamble	2	F	2	1	0	0	34,200
Street Life	5	G	6	1	2	0	24,280
Street of Gold	4	G	8	3	1	3	4,938
Street Smart Sue	3	F	7	1	0	0	13,547
Street Theatre	3	C	6	2	1	1	99,108
Street Warrior	2	G	3	0	0	0	610
Street Wheeling	5	M	4	0	0	0	0
Streetfight	4	G	14	2	3	2	12,480
Streetfightinman	3	G	1	0	0	0	653
Streetmusic	5	G	4	1	0	1	10,555
Streets of Fire	4	F	11	3	4	2	42,990
Streets of Silver	6	M	16	1	4	2	13,666
Stregawood	8	G	7	4	0	1	10,618
Streicher's Gold	3	C	1	0	0	1	4,500
Strekin Attraction	3	G	1	0	0	0	42
Strength and Honor	5	G	9	5	0	2	183,145
Strength Within	4	G	8	1	3	2	54,840
Stress N Deress	2	C	1	0	0	0	0
Stressless	3	F	1	0	0	0	400
Stretch	3	G	3	0	0	1	2,171
Stretch Run	3	F	12	2	2	2	14,420
Stretch Velvet	5	M	5	2	1	0	21,020
Stretchin' North	4	G	9	1	1	2	16,281
Stretchrunningcat	3	F	3	0	0	0	0
Stretchyourfaith	5	G	1	0	0	0	183
Stretta	10	G	3	0	1	0	914
Strickly a Dream	5	G	4	0	0	0	846
Strickly Jonesin	3	G	2	1	0	0	880
Strict Forum	5	M	13	0	1	2	8,966
Strictly Business	4	G	15	1	2	3	41,523
Strictly High Brow	8	M	12	1	1	2	5,114
Strictly Legit	4	F	6	2	0	1	20,510
Strictly Personal	5	M	10	0	2	4	5,762
Stride for Stride	3	G	5	0	1	1	7,131
Strident Fellow	3	C	7	1	0	2	7,825
Strider's Comet	7	G	8	1	1	1	12,633
Strider's Ormsby	3	G	13	2	3	1	60,260
Strider's Rocket	6	G	14	3	1	1	26,649
Striding Victory	3	F	4	0	0	1	935
Strike	2	C	1	0	0	0	0
Strike a Bargain	2	C	3	1	0	0	54,393
Strike a Match	5	G	12	3	1	1	15,866
Strike a Star	3	C	3	0	0	0	1,517
Strike an Image	3	F	9	3	2	2	41,872
Strike and Conquer	3	G	3	1	0	1	6,780
Strike and Run	3	F	6	1	0	1	46,029
Strike Breaker	4	G	3	0	0	0	233
Strike Commander	5	G	12	1	3	4	33,810
Strike de Ego	4	F	3	0	1	0	1,994
Strike Em Hard	3	G	11	0	1	2	75,074
Strike Fast	2	G	5	1	1	0	15,600
Strike for Richard	8	G	5	1	1	2	26,534
Strike Force One	4	G	5	1	2	1	10,743
Strike Hound	4	G	12	1	0	5	8,005
Strike Island	3	C	10	1	2	0	17,900
Strike It Big	7	G	17	0	2	6	7,896
Strike M Red	7	G	6	0	0	1	2,396
Strike Me Lucky	3	F	5	0	0	1	6,850
Strike Mission	4	C	6	1	1	0	2,410
Strike 'n a Deal	3	G	10	1	1	1	13,521
Strike n' Prospect	6	G	10	1	0	1	7,605
Strike Point	4	F	9	2	2	0	22,802
Strike Rate	4	F	11	3	1	2	95,236
Strike Reality	9	G	14	5	2	1	54,690
Strike Right	7	G	12	2	3	4	13,491
Strike Royalty	3	F	8	0	0	0	795
Strike the Brass	7	G	12	1	2	2	23,199
Strike the Chord	6	G	9	3	1	1	19,784
Strike the Fuse	3	F	5	3	0	2	21,363
Strike the Harp	3	F	6	0	0	0	2,397
Strike the Lord	3	C	15	1	0	3	9,112
Strike the Moment	3	G	6	1	1	2	19,876
Strike Three	7	G	13	0	2	5	26,390
Strike Twice	6	G	16	3	3	1	33,185
Strike Up	4	G	14	2	1	2	14,647
Strike With Pasion	5	M	3	0	0	0	183
Strike Your Colors	2	C	5	1	0	1	14,380
Strike Zone	11	G	3	0	0	0	1,860
Strikeapromise	5	M	1	0	0	0	0
Strikes Count	6	G	2	0	0	0	131
Strikethegold Lass	8	M	7	2	1	0	9,682
Striking B	5	G	14	0	1	1	2,636
Striking Cobra	3	F	10	2	2	0	56,738
Striking Flames	5	M	10	0	0	1	1,729
Striking Jaklin	4	F	5	0	0	1	1,473
Striking Jewel	4	F	3	0	0	0	380
Striking Michelle	7	M	7	1	1	1	22,761
Striking T	3	F	15	2	1	1	17,250
Striking Vision	2	C	1	0	0	0	230
Strikingly	4	G	12	1	0	1	28,546
Strikingly Proud	8	G	17	1	1	4	8,111
String Quartet	3	F	4	0	1	0	1,940
Stringtown Wonder	3	G	6	0	1	1	13,530
Strip	7	G	2	0	0	0	900
Strip Jr	2	G	3	0	0	0	540
Stripe Face	3	G	3	0	0	0	213
Striped	2	F	4	0	0	0	790
Striped Candy	4	C	10	1	0	0	2,925
Striped Money	2	C	3	0	0	0	0
Stripemoff	3	C	1	0	0	0	132
Stripes Be Gone	2	F	1	0	0	0	0
Stripling Warrior	4	G	10	2	0	0	6,257
Striptease	5	M	11	0	2	1	4,259
Strive	5	H	1	0	1	0	11,340
Stroboscope	2	C	2	0	0	0	450
Strodee	5	M	13	3	2	0	17,345
Strodes Baba	3	C	10	2	1	1	20,508
Strodes Commander	4	C	12	4	2	1	62,970
Strodes Lane	5	M	11	1	2	1	43,555
Stroganof	4	F	6	0	0	0	420
Stroke of Dawn	2	G	1	0	0	1	984
Stroke of Genius	9	M	12	1	3	1	5,690
Stroker	5	G	9	0	1	4	11,670
Stroll	4	C	5	1	1	0	348,524
Stroll On	8	G	5	0	1	0	3,527
Strollin Slew	4	F	7	0	2	2	27,060
Strolling Kris	4	F	10	2	3	1	21,200
Strong Cat	3	C	3	1	0	0	16,955
Strong Faith	3	F	13	1	4	4	41,437
Strong Hope	4	C	4	1	1	1	185,100
Strong Mark	2	F	1	0	0	0	0
Strong Reader	7	G	8	0	0	0	440
Strong Safety	4	G	2	0	0	0	800
Strong Stage	4	G	1	0	0	0	0
Strongbox	3	G	8	0	0	0	2,313
Strongestsovereign	3	G	3	0	1	0	8,540
Strongsilenttype	3	C	6	1	1	0	12,100
Strongsurgin'	5	G	1	0	0	0	70
Strongwilled Stuka	4	F	12	1	3	1	10,376
Stroud	5	G	8	0	1	3	8,240
Stroud Bay	6	H	7	0	1	1	4,754
Strout E	4	C	5	0	0	1	782
Structured	4	F	8	2	1	1	9,610
Strudel Lou	4	F	5	0	0	2	1,555
Struggler's Legend	3	C	8	1	2	2	35,104
Strugglers Tune	3	C	1	0	0	0	220
Struggler's World	5	H	4	1	0	0	6,090
Strugglingprisoner	5	M	10	0	0	0	378

Horse	Age	Sex	Sts	1st	2d	3d	Won
Strumminwithrhythm	4	F	12	2	0	2	15,595
Strut Sharply	4	G	11	0	2	4	11,461
Strut the Stage	6	H	4	1	0	1	231,063
Strut Your Stuff	3	F	3	1	1	0	36,645
Struttin'	4	F	11	1	3	3	51,491
Strychnine	6	G	7	0	0	1	3,201
Stryker's Flight	5	G	22	1	1	1	8,055
Stuart Beau Gull	3	G	1	0	0	0	69
Stuart's Avalanche	3	C	4	0	0	0	0
Stubborn	5	M	10	0	1	2	2,792
Stubborn Charm	5	G	9	0	3	3	12,867
Stubbsville	3	G	3	0	0	0	475
Stubsy	6	G	3	1	0	1	4,270
Stuck by Eddie	3	G	3	1	0	1	8,987
Stuck in Canada	4	G	12	2	3	0	18,022
Stuck in Limbo	5	M	13	0	1	1	7,316
Stuck in Vegas	4	G	10	1	1	0	12,748
Stuck On Speed	8	G	1	0	0	0	100
Stuck On Stuka	4	F	6	0	0	1	1,800
Stuck Up	7	G	1	0	0	0	312
Stud Cat	2	C	2	0	0	0	235
Stud Poker	5	G	15	1	5	2	10,839
Student Council	2	C	3	0	0	0	2,758
Studfee	2	C	1	0	0	0	0
Studio King	8	G	3	0	0	1	1,230
Studio Time	5	G	6	0	1	0	12,535
Study Hard	3	F	4	0	0	0	3,410
Stuff Enough	3	C	10	0	0	2	1,466
Stuff N Things	3	G	9	0	1	1	4,933
Stuka's Beauty	5	M	8	0	1	0	4,798
Stuka's Dancer	8	M	16	1	3	2	8,430
Stukatz	2	F	15	0	1	6	22,760
Stukcess	5	H	3	0	0	0	1,136
Stunning Image (IRE)	4	F	8	0	2	3	24,891
Stunning Stella	4	F	8	1	3	0	3,685
Stupefyin Jones	3	F	5	0	0	1	2,350
Stutterin' Bill	3	G	7	2	1	0	31,470
Stutz Dancer	4	G	1	0	0	0	0
Stutz Passion	5	M	4	1	0	0	5,325
Stydahar	5	H	1	0	0	0	0
Style Drifter	2	C	1	0	0	0	2,050
Stylin Cat	2	C	1	1	0	0	35,280
Stylin Melody	6	M	3	0	0	0	0
Stylish Account	4	G	10	0	1	2	9,246
Stylish Cat	4	G	10	0	1	1	1,815
Stylish Dave	3	G	8	0	0	1	2,828
Stylish Design	4	F	11	0	2	4	11,675
Stylish Event	3	F	12	0	1	0	3,768
Stylish Factor	3	F	12	3	3	1	52,754
Stylish Gal	2	F	2	0	0	0	1,360
Stylish Joe	4	G	17	2	5	3	43,235
Stylish Launch	3	C	4	0	0	0	890
Stylish Mission	7	M	11	1	4	2	19,628
Stylish N Adorable	3	F	5	2	1	1	30,170
Stylish Number	4	F	2	0	0	0	0
Stylish Rhythm	3	C	2	0	0	0	130
Stylish Rita	5	M	1	0	0	0	288
Stylish Sensation	7	G	11	1	1	3	2,912
Stylish Sultan	5	H	9	2	3	1	64,090
Stylish Sultana	2	F	3	0	0	0	2,960
Stylish Times	5	M	4	0	0	0	296
Stylish Val	3	F	12	3	4	1	47,513
Stylishly	3	C	4	1	0	0	18,676
Styx Crossing	5	G	8	1	2	0	11,564
Su Tiempo	8	G	14	2	3	2	10,875
Suave	3	C	11	2	2	2	448,328
Suave Act	4	G	11	0	0	1	9,450
Suave and Pretty	4	F	6	1	1	0	7,353
Suave Charmer	4	G	11	5	1	1	26,500
Suave Darling	5	M	11	0	2	0	4,950
Suave Devil	5	H	17	3	1	2	59,242
Suave Eye Am	3	G	1	0	0	0	0
Suave Gentleman	4	C	6	1	0	1	12,210
Suave Girl	3	F	17	2	4	3	41,850
Suave Guy	5	M	12	0	0	0	1,655
Suave King	5	G	11	0	3	2	6,468
Suave Knight	4	G	9	1	1	3	26,499
Suave Lad	5	G	12	5	2	2	88,040
Suave Lass	4	F	18	5	2	3	68,165
Suave Line	3	F	15	4	4	4	49,325
Suave Man	5	G	6	0	1	1	4,798
Suave Meteorite	5	G	5	0	0	0	1,387
Suave Nobleman	5	G	17	1	1	0	10,570
Suave Prince	2	G	8	0	3	3	17,675
Suave Princess	5	M	18	3	3	2	44,445
Suave Queen	5	M	6	0	2	3	31,450
Suave Rhapsody	5	G	7	1	0	2	32,550
Suave Romancer	3	G	6	1	0	2	9,931
Suave Smile	2	G	7	1	0	0	5,610
Suave Squaw	4	F	5	2	0	1	22,310
Suave Star	4	F	8	1	1	0	5,717
Suave Todd	2	G	6	0	2	1	11,450
Suavefancynfast	2	F	4	1	1	0	6,770
Suaves Lightning	5	M	8	1	0	1	7,167
Suaviter	3	F	7	1	2	0	19,540
Sub	2	G	5	1	0	1	15,365
Sub Atomic	2	F	3	0	0	0	600
Sub Call	3	C	11	1	2	0	15,537
Sub Futz Jr	2	G	1	1	0	0	15,600
Sub Launch	4	F	3	0	0	0	0
Subboo	2	F	8	1	2	0	11,696
Subjugate (AUS)	4	G	1	0	0	0	0
Sublet (FR)	5	G	7	0	1	0	18,220
Subliminator	3	G	5	3	0	1	29,157
Sublimity	3	F	11	0	0	1	1,633
Submediant	2	C	1	0	0	0	0
Subordinate Sin	3	F	10	0	1	2	5,492
Subsequently	4	G	10	2	1	2	52,682
Substantiate	2	C	5	1	2	0	29,405
Substorm	2	C	4	1	1	0	10,835
Subtle Breeze	3	F	4	0	0	1	1,156
Subtle Distinction	5	M	12	0	1	0	1,981
Subtle Glitz	4	C	9	0	0	0	5,860
Subtle Money	5	H	13	3	0	2	12,801
Subtle Saratoga	3	C	5	1	1	1	18,570
Subtle Style	4	F	11	2	2	1	13,179
Subway Sing	2	F	2	1	1	0	18,800
Succeedere	4	C	10	1	0	2	7,680
Success Out West	3	F	2	0	0	0	0
Success Rate	4	C	2	0	0	0	3,310
Success Trapp	3	G	14	3	2	0	18,038
Successful Affair	2	C	1	0	0	0	137
Successful Cat	3	F	8	2	0	1	18,030
Successful Seeking	2	C	1	0	0	0	400
Successfull Mike	6	G	1	0	0	0	111
Successfully Sweet	2	F	4	3	1	0	104,650
Successville	2	C	1	0	0	0	0
Succotash Road	4	G	5	0	0	0	348
Suceso	3	C	12	1	2	1	9,799
Such a Beezer	5	M	1	0	0	0	75
Such a Flirt	4	F	1	0	1	0	6,300
Such a Foxy Thing	4	F	10	5	1	1	18,844
Such a Lady	8	M	8	1	2	0	19,525
Such a Nutcase	2	G	3	1	1	0	18,680
Such an Alley Cat	2	F	2	0	0	0	145
Such as Life	2	C	3	0	0	1	2,990
Such Gold	6	M	2	0	0	0	0
Such Grace	3	F	7	1	1	0	36,349
Sucha Dandy	5	M	3	0	0	0	110
Suchala	4	F	6	1	1	0	6,720
Suchatouch	2	F	6	1	1	2	28,970
Suck Um Up Bro	4	G	12	2	1	2	12,787
Suckers Gold	4	F	8	3	1	1	17,430
Sudden Bluff	6	G	10	4	2	0	35,851
Sudden Fame	4	G	4	2	0	0	10,700
Sudden Flame	2	F	5	1	1	1	32,355
Sudden Flash	5	M	2	0	0	0	300
Sudden Flight	4	G	16	1	2	1	32,378
Sudden Glory	6	H	12	1	1	0	12,333
Sudden Pacho	3	C	1	0	0	0	0
Sudden Side	4	G	9	2	2	1	9,271
Sudden Sunlight	4	F	1	0	0	0	0
Sudden Upset	3	C	5	0	0	0	760
Suddenly Annie	3	F	9	1	1	1	8,296
Suddenly Beautiful	3	F	4	0	0	0	380
Suddenly Devilish	4	F	6	1	1	2	25,760
Suddenly Gone	7	M	2	1	1	0	28,020
Suddenly Sheila	5	M	5	0	1	0	960

Horse	Age	Sex	Sts	1st	2d	3d	Won
Suddenly Thrilled	3	F	9	0	0	0	1,966
Sudith	3	F	2	0	1	0	6,120
Sudjanas Finest	3	C	5	0	0	0	263
Sue C	3	F	9	0	1	0	2,090
Sue Etta	3	F	12	2	4	0	19,817
Sue Me	2	F	7	1	0	2	35,418
Sue of Gold	3	F	11	1	0	0	4,075
Suelagra	2	F	2	0	0	0	555
Suelle Son	5	G	6	0	0	0	473
Suellen	2	F	4	0	0	1	2,180
Suembul (NZ)	10	G	2	1	0	0	12,600
Sueno Del Mar	2	G	6	1	3	0	30,930
Suerte Proper	4	G	4	1	2	0	11,970
Sue's Adam Bomb	8	H	2	0	0	0	238
Sue's April Fool	10	G	2	1	0	1	6,745
Sue's Episode	6	G	6	1	2	0	11,095
Sue's Gold	4	F	6	0	1	0	1,169
Sue's Good News	4	F	9	1	1	1	57,278
Sues Hay	4	F	15	3	1	3	23,286
Sue's Hija	3	F	5	0	0	0	0
Sue's Slew	8	G	6	0	0	0	425
Sue's Trauma	4	F	9	2	1	3	52,060
Suey Suey	5	M	6	0	0	2	1,898
Suffering Servant	3	F	11	0	4	0	9,310
Sufficient	3	F	10	0	2	2	9,180
Suffire (ARG)	7	G	5	0	0	0	1,135
Sugah Sugah	5	M	12	3	1	6	37,634
Sugar Booger	2	F	1	0	0	0	0
Sugar Cane Fever	3	F	3	1	0	0	4,704
Sugar Charm	4	G	10	0	2	1	2,838
Sugar Creek Girl	3	F	7	0	2	1	11,545
Sugar Daddys Man	4	G	4	1	1	0	7,498
Sugar Date	2	F	1	0	1	0	5,600
Sugar Dipped	5	M	1	0	0	0	360
Sugar Doc	3	G	2	0	0	0	0
Sugar Dream	7	G	2	0	0	1	720
Sugar Gal	3	F	9	3	0	2	56,440
Sugar Gray	3	F	13	2	1	3	27,353
Sugar Hall	5	G	10	0	0	0	225
Sugar Hill	7	M	4	0	0	0	715
Sugar Joe	4	G	3	0	0	1	360
Sugar Lake Lass	4	F	9	2	2	5	8,947
Sugar Lips	4	F	1	0	0	0	75
Sugar Mags	7	G	8	1	2	0	18,834
Sugar Mtn.	4	F	2	0	0	1	570
Sugar Night	3	G	5	0	1	1	5,838
Sugar On Top	3	F	3	0	1	0	3,232
Sugar Pine	2	F	6	1	1	0	24,998
Sugar Plum Girl	2	F	2	0	0	1	4,805
Sugar Plum Miss	6	M	13	1	1	0	5,348
Sugar Punch	3	F	6	6	0	0	256,920
Sugar Queen	5	M	6	0	1	1	4,007
Sugar Ray Gold	6	G	9	0	0	0	685
Sugar Ray Silver	6	G	13	2	4	1	23,170
Sugar Ride	4	F	1	0	0	0	370
Sugar Shaker	5	G	10	0	1	1	2,355
Sugar Sleet	5	M	4	1	1	0	8,315
Sugar Toes	3	F	1	1	0	0	14,100
Sugar Twist	2	C	4	0	0	0	0
Sugarbaby Shirley	6	M	12	0	0	4	2,187
Sugarcane Road	2	G	1	0	0	0	205
Sugarcoat	2	C	6	0	1	0	4,226
Sugarfoot Slew	3	F	3	0	0	0	660
Sugarless	2	F	2	0	0	1	3,400
Sugarred	4	F	6	0	2	0	11,323
Sugar's Prince	6	G	2	0	0	1	854
Sugar's Reward	2	G	5	1	0	0	4,980
Sugarsway	4	G	2	0	0	0	279
Sugartime Gal	4	F	4	0	0	0	1,845
Sugartoniteinmytea	5	M	14	4	0	1	36,924
Sugartown Rose	4	F	9	2	0	1	14,461
Sugg Walker	6	M	3	0	2	1	5,415
Suit	3	F	2	0	0	0	1,707
Suitable Suitor	4	G	10	2	2	1	17,910
Sujimoto	3	C	6	3	0	0	71,403
Sukkot	7	M	16	2	4	1	22,588
Sula Mae	5	M	13	0	2	2	7,895
Sulamani (IRE)	5	H	5	2	1	1	1,611,523
Sulawesi	2	C	4	0	0	0	65
Suleiman	4	G	12	2	1	1	31,200
Sulky Sue	2	F	8	1	0	0	18,114
Sullied But Sweet	3	F	8	1	1	1	27,130
Sullivanballou	3	C	4	1	0	0	21,480
Sullivanitis	6	G	4	1	0	1	3,415
Sullivans Travels	6	G	6	0	2	1	2,695
Sully's Girl	4	F	12	1	2	0	5,483
Sully's Pale	3	C	5	0	0	0	522
Sully's Silver	3	G	19	2	1	2	43,083
Sully's Wish	2	F	1	0	0	0	840
Sultan Bey	3	C	3	1	0	0	11,600
Sultan of Spin	3	G	11	2	1	1	43,400
Sultan of Swat	6	G	7	0	2	2	3,829
Sultan Pepper	3	G	7	0	1	0	3,282
Sultano	3	C	2	0	0	0	300
Sultan's Double	4	C	1	0	0	0	0
Sultan's Gold	7	G	7	0	0	1	1,307
Sultan's Pride	8	G	16	2	3	2	17,884
Sulton's Glass	8	G	7	0	0	1	1,250
Sultry Affair	2	F	2	0	0	0	0
Sultry Ava	3	F	7	1	0	0	3,465
Sultry Bard	2	C	3	0	0	1	2,720
Sultry Breeze	5	M	1	0	0	0	75
Sultry Cat	4	G	10	1	0	1	16,200
Sultry City	2	C	2	0	0	0	1,333
Sultry Danse	4	F	10	4	2	2	44,203
Sultry Devil	2	F	2	0	0	0	1,250
Sultry Eyes	3	F	10	1	1	0	20,093
Sultry Firm	3	C	9	1	0	0	6,471
Sultry Fluff	5	M	8	1	0	1	24,026
Sultry Interval	5	M	9	0	0	0	4,770
Sultry Mood	8	G	11	1	0	2	11,063
Sultry of Gold	5	G	5	0	0	0	600
Sultry Prospect	5	M	14	1	2	5	18,605
Sultry Rendevous	4	F	3	1	0	0	15,870
Sultry Silence	4	G	9	1	1	0	12,830
Sultry Siren	3	F	14	1	4	3	21,600
Sultry Sound	5	M	4	2	1	0	21,800
Sultry Springs	2	C	3	0	0	1	1,912
Sultry Sreva	5	M	2	0	0	0	1,800
Sultry Star	6	M	6	1	0	0	8,945
Sultry Strike	3	C	6	0	0	0	495
Sultry Style	7	M	1	0	0	0	0
Sultry Sunshine	4	F	2	0	0	0	136
Sultry Wonder	4	G	1	0	0	0	600
Sultryann	3	F	11	0	2	2	12,740
Sultry's Kazam	3	G	5	0	0	1	2,786
Sulzano	4	F	2	0	0	0	0
Sum Bad Lady	4	F	1	0	0	0	0
Sum Breeze	4	F	1	0	0	0	0
Sum Eagle	4	F	11	1	2	1	10,568
Sum Emblem	4	G	12	2	3	1	23,780
Sum Fast Gal	5	M	1	0	0	0	0
Sum Gun	6	G	6	1	0	0	3,132
Sum Marval	3	C	12	2	2	1	77,507
Sum Mo Joe	3	C	4	0	0	0	0
Sum of It All	2	C	2	0	0	0	0
Sum Reward	5	H	13	3	2	4	35,106
Sum Royalty	3	F	2	0	0	0	0
Sum Trick	4	C	4	0	0	1	7,040
Sumac Sue	6	M	13	2	2	1	16,436
Sumagoom	6	H	4	0	0	1	300
Sumati (GB)	8	G	1	0	0	0	0
Sumcor	6	G	9	4	2	3	28,193
Sumerset	7	G	15	1	4	2	30,550
Sumgotitsumdontido	3	G	13	1	3	2	20,225
Suminister	8	M	9	1	0	0	7,130
Sumitas (GER)	8	H	1	0	0	0	2,520
Sumkindablonde	4	F	7	1	1	2	22,170
Summarily	6	H	1	0	0	0	120
Summer Applause	4	G	2	0	0	0	63
Summer Blend	4	F	7	0	1	0	12,333
Summer Book	3	C	9	2	2	2	51,540
Summer Break	3	G	12	1	1	3	9,216
Summer Camp	4	F	2	0	0	0	210
Summer Carnival	3	G	2	0	0	0	420
Summer Cat	4	F	3	0	0	0	217
Summer Charm	5	M	10	2	1	1	19,205
Summer Chil	2	C	3	0	0	0	1,035

Horse	Age	Sex	Sts	1st	2d	3d	Won
Summer Claim	2	C	5	1	0	1	8,259
Summer Dame	4	F	7	1	1	1	14,423
Summer Deposit	4	G	4	1	0	0	1,550
Summer Do Shine	3	F	10	1	1	0	18,363
Summer Dust	5	G	15	3	2	4	68,278
Summer Dynamite	3	G	3	0	0	0	100
Summer Evening	2	F	4	0	0	0	160
Summer Flash	3	F	9	0	1	2	16,547
Summer Fling	3	F	4	0	0	0	0
Summer Getaway	4	G	18	2	1	3	11,843
Summer Glory	3	F	4	0	1	1	4,040
Summer Guide	2	C	3	0	1	1	10,418
Summer Guy	4	G	5	2	0	1	23,695
Summer Halo	4	F	9	4	2	0	36,630
Summer Hit	9	G	9	0	0	1	1,578
Summer Hound	4	F	2	0	0	1	418
Summer Ice	3	F	4	0	0	0	906
Summer in Saratoga	2	F	2	0	0	0	238
Summer Ivey	3	G	1	0	0	0	235
Summer Jam	3	F	11	0	1	0	6,354
Summer Lake	2	F	2	0	0	0	280
Summer Lass	4	F	14	3	2	3	101,453
Summer Lea	3	F	7	2	0	0	29,660
Summer Legacy	2	G	3	1	0	0	7,729
Summer Lite	5	M	5	0	0	3	19,419
Summer Man	2	C	4	1	0	1	33,595
Summer Mis	5	M	7	2	0	2	127,779
Summer Moment	3	F	14	1	4	2	22,239
Summer Note	7	G	4	0	0	0	2,300
Summer of Seventy	3	F	2	0	0	0	0
Summer Prima	3	G	11	3	0	2	11,407
Summer Prince	9	G	17	4	3	4	9,167
Summer Pro	6	M	7	0	0	0	1,664
Summer Rainbow	3	F	9	3	2	2	92,280
Summer Raven	2	F	7	2	2	1	168,910
Summer Reality	3	F	2	0	0	0	129
Summer Ride	2	F	1	0	0	1	1,573
Summer Runner	4	F	2	0	0	0	80
Summer Sails	4	F	6	1	0	1	10,015
Summer Sauce	8	M	1	0	0	0	0
Summer Savoya	5	M	10	1	1	2	8,909
Summer Savy	3	F	1	0	0	0	0
Summer Scene	4	F	2	0	1	0	14,240
Summer Secret	4	F	3	0	0	0	100
Summer Service	4	G	5	2	1	2	131,176
Summer Shenanigans	6	M	7	0	2	2	14,192
Summer Silk	3	F	2	0	0	0	0
Summer Sirocco	3	C	1	0	0	0	156
Summer Slew	4	C	1	0	1	0	6,480
Summer Slice	3	F	3	0	0	0	685
Summer Social	4	F	2	0	0	0	712
Summer Soliel	3	F	3	1	0	0	8,320
Summer Sovereign	4	G	14	0	0	3	4,035
Summer Special	4	F	13	3	3	1	27,787
Summer Speed	5	M	2	0	0	0	103
Summer Sport	4	G	15	3	2	2	50,809
Summer Star	4	F	7	3	0	1	55,900
Summer Stepper	2	C	3	1	0	0	8,400
Summer Sting	2	F	1	0	0	0	1,800
Summer Stitch	2	F	1	0	0	0	300
Summer Stone	4	F	14	1	5	3	35,490
Summer Sunset	4	F	4	0	0	0	235
Summer Surf	8	G	14	2	1	2	12,264
Summer Symphony	3	F	8	3	1	0	180,729
Summer Tan	8	G	1	0	0	0	61
Summer Tone	4	F	13	2	1	3	14,830
Summer Trick	4	G	7	1	0	0	6,307
Summer Wind Dancer	4	F	7	2	2	1	598,905
Summer Wind Storm	4	F	3	0	0	1	3,108
Summerberry	3	F	3	0	0	0	0
Summerchance	3	F	16	2	2	2	20,791
Summerfield	5	M	1	0	0	0	0
Summerland	2	C	4	2	1	1	83,973
Summerly	2	F	3	1	0	1	53,035
Summeroffortynine	2	F	2	0	0	0	1,500
Summer's Breeze	3	C	10	2	3	2	20,300
Summer's Coming	2	F	1	0	1	0	1,720
Summer's Cool	4	F	9	2	4	0	22,275
Summer's Lad	3	G	12	1	0	2	9,560

Horse	Age	Sex	Sts	1st	2d	3d	Won
Summer's Truth	4	G	7	3	0	0	27,367
Summers Wesh	2	F	3	0	0	0	0
Summersault	2	G	2	1	0	0	7,980
Summerspark Delite	4	G	2	0	0	0	550
Summerstrick	3	F	1	0	0	0	0
Summersville	6	H	12	1	4	2	40,405
Summertide	6	M	10	4	1	0	37,220
Summertime Breeze	3	F	3	0	0	0	466
Summertime Mood	3	C	3	0	1	0	2,600
Summertime Robin	3	F	5	1	0	1	4,651
Summery Conflict	6	G	9	0	2	1	7,160
Summery Wish	3	F	9	0	3	1	10,598
Summing Stars (IRE)	6	M	4	0	2	0	5,279
Summings Affair	4	F	1	0	0	0	400
Summing's Boy	3	G	5	1	2	0	13,400
Summit Avenue	6	G	7	0	1	1	2,375
Summit Ridge	8	M	3	0	0	0	216
Summit Runner	2	F	10	2	0	2	21,621
Summon Mi Cielo	5	M	12	1	1	2	5,327
Sumter	6	G	5	0	0	0	159
Sumthinbad	3	F	11	1	2	1	31,296
Sumthing for Alex	4	G	4	0	0	0	785
Sumtimsudont	5	M	16	2	1	2	19,890
Sun and Sky	4	G	1	0	0	0	500
Sun Appeal	2	F	7	0	2	2	13,570
Sun Bay	2	F	1	0	0	1	1,450
Sun Block	4	F	4	1	2	1	31,697
Sun Bonney	5	M	10	0	0	2	1,996
Sun Brightia	4	F	6	3	1	1	80,760
Sun Cat	7	G	3	0	0	0	1,740
Sun City Annie	3	F	5	0	0	1	4,260
Sun City Bradley	4	C	2	0	1	1	21,632
Sun City Jackpot	2	G	1	0	0	0	400
Sun City Newport	3	C	1	0	0	0	50
Sun City Slew	3	G	1	0	0	0	97
Sun City Sue	3	F	1	0	0	0	107
Sun Commander	4	G	10	1	1	1	7,833
Sun de Mer	3	F	7	0	1	0	2,810
Sun King	2	C	4	1	0	2	244,850
Sun Kisses	5	M	8	3	0	2	34,037
Sun Marches On	2	G	1	0	0	0	0
Sun of a Blitzen	11	G	18	0	2	1	10,027
Sun of Mercer	4	G	11	0	0	0	1,765
Sun On the Beach	5	G	16	2	0	2	8,773
Sun Ray	3	G	9	0	2	2	4,843
Sun Sapphire	3	F	10	5	1	0	58,685
Sun Skier	3	F	9	2	0	1	70,274
Sun Son	3	G	10	2	2	1	4,386
Sun Spot Baby	4	F	11	0	0	3	4,956
Sun Stroke	3	G	18	2	2	7	44,347
Sun Tzu	8	H	12	1	2	0	16,492
Sun Valley Anna	4	F	12	4	3	2	41,125
Sunadir	3	F	12	3	2	1	144,622
Sunatra	9	M	4	0	1	1	8,385
Sunbelt	4	C	2	1	0	0	3,501
Sunbonnet	3	F	10	0	0	1	4,225
Sunbrella	4	F	1	0	0	0	65
Suncoast Parkway	3	F	5	0	3	0	27,950
Sundae Passion	4	F	1	0	0	0	0
Sundance Circle	3	G	2	0	0	0	810
Sundance Fever	4	G	2	0	0	0	80
Sundance Shamrock	2	F	6	0	2	2	12,960
Sundance Square	5	H	5	0	1	1	5,285
Sundar	5	G	6	0	1	1	12,678
Sundari	6	M	5	0	0	0	120
Sunday Afternoon	3	F	7	0	0	0	711
Sunday Cash	5	G	8	0	1	1	5,469
Sunday Champ	4	G	11	2	0	1	8,813
Sunday Demon	2	G	3	0	0	0	0
Sunday Girl	4	F	5	0	2	1	1,703
Sunday Knight	5	G	12	2	1	4	8,408
Sunday Myth	3	C	2	1	1	0	17,361
Sunday Nap	4	G	4	1	2	1	15,035
Sunday Quest	5	M	11	0	0	1	2,253
Sunday River	5	G	6	0	0	1	992
Sunday Roar	4	F	14	2	3	2	60,680
Sunday Sensation	4	F	4	1	2	0	48,220
Sunday Sins	3	G	1	0	0	0	0
Sunday Something	4	G	2	0	0	0	82

Horse	Age	Sex	Sts	1st	2d	3d	Won
Sunday Song	5	M	1	0	0	0	0
Sunday Storm	3	C	4	0	0	0	0
Sunday Suit	3	G	9	0	1	0	4,058
Sunday Thunder (JPN)	4	F	4	0	1	1	5,490
Sunday Times	3	C	5	1	0	0	35,300
Sunday Trigger	3	G	11	2	2	3	21,604
Sunday Whirl	2	F	3	1	1	0	6,825
Sunday Whisper (AUS)	5	M	1	0	0	0	2,940
Sundayblummer	4	F	9	3	0	0	12,317
Sunday's Honor	3	F	14	3	3	3	34,790
Sunday's Miracle	6	M	3	0	0	0	0
Sunder Bay	3	G	4	0	1	0	5,804
Sundial Time	2	F	2	1	0	0	14,330
Sundown Di	5	M	8	0	2	3	1,900
Sundown Meg	5	M	12	1	2	2	21,967
Sundown Surprise	3	G	4	0	0	0	0
Sundowncindy	8	M	3	1	1	0	2,125
Sundowner	2	C	3	1	0	0	16,200
Sundrenched	5	M	1	0	0	0	0
Sune	4	F	7	1	1	1	8,420
Sunette	3	F	3	0	0	1	10,680
Sungold	2	C	5	0	1	1	6,293
Sungold Beauty	3	F	5	3	0	0	31,980
Sungold Jenny	3	F	5	0	1	0	4,262
Sungold Skippy	3	F	6	0	1	0	4,970
Sunjata	2	C	3	0	0	0	585
Sunk At Sea	10	H	7	0	1	1	3,810
Sunka Smile	4	F	5	0	0	1	1,556
Sunkosi	5	H	6	0	0	0	2,010
Sunlined	5	M	19	0	3	1	8,600
Sunlit Ridge	6	M	6	2	1	1	51,500
Sunnidale Road	2	G	3	0	0	0	792
Sunnie Do It	10	M	2	0	0	0	643
Sunnie Parade	2	F	1	0	0	0	0
Sunny Approval	8	G	4	0	0	0	1,510
Sunny Blossom	4	F	3	1	0	1	22,230
Sunny Brick	5	G	9	4	0	1	68,028
Sunny Carnovali	2	F	1	0	0	0	0
Sunny Ciano	3	F	1	0	0	0	0
Sunny Ciegos	6	G	6	0	2	1	5,719
Sunny Cielo	8	G	6	0	0	0	384
Sunny Circus	5	G	2	0	0	0	246
Sunny Dawn	4	F	9	2	2	0	15,215
Sunny Disposition	2	F	3	0	0	0	2,900
Sunny Divine	4	F	11	0	3	2	5,854
Sunny Flight	2	F	7	1	3	0	20,885
Sunny Fragrance	5	M	3	0	0	0	1,691
Sunny Gal	3	F	9	0	1	4	15,380
Sunny Gold	4	G	4	0	1	1	4,025
Sunny Hexorian	2	C	1	0	0	0	0
Sunny Isles Beauty	2	F	7	1	0	0	26,700
Sunny K Looker	3	C	3	0	0	0	150
Sunny Limbo	5	G	2	0	0	0	760
Sunny Loves Sallie	5	M	9	1	0	3	8,802
Sunny Mulligan	4	G	14	0	1	2	4,210
Sunny 'n' Glory	6	G	6	0	1	2	2,182
Sunny Outcome	4	F	1	1	0	0	32,400
Sunny Promise	3	G	14	1	2	2	11,062
Sunny Report	5	G	8	1	1	3	17,514
Sunny Scarlett	5	M	3	0	0	0	0
Sunny Serenata	3	F	4	0	0	0	0
Sunny Simon	2	C	3	0	0	0	1,242
Sunny Sky (FR)	2	C	7	3	0	2	74,967
Sunny Slope Gal	5	M	11	1	2	0	7,659
Sunny Street	3	F	8	0	2	1	19,040
Sunny Stutz	9	G	7	0	0	0	1,339
Sunny Summer	3	G	5	0	0	0	270
Sunny Susie	3	F	9	2	0	3	19,028
Sunny Tejano	2	G	2	0	0	0	0
Sunny Texan	5	G	4	0	2	0	3,820
Sunny Thoughts	4	G	12	2	2	1	7,932
Sunny War	2	C	1	0	0	0	0
Sunny Zak	4	C	2	0	0	0	188
Sunnybgood	6	G	9	2	0	1	8,180
Sunnydale	6	M	1	0	0	0	0
Sunnydawn Miss	8	M	5	0	0	0	163
Sunnyridge Sam	4	G	6	1	1	0	33,546
Sunny's Appleseed	3	C	2	0	0	0	0
Sunny's Bold Halo	5	G	12	1	0	2	12,319
Sunnys Buddy	6	G	12	1	0	1	16,638
Sunny's Champion	3	F	9	0	0	1	1,890
Sunnys Coed	4	F	10	1	1	2	6,034
Sunny's Flash	3	G	2	0	0	0	0
Sunny's Last Kiss	3	F	3	0	0	0	244
Sunny's Miracle	3	F	2	0	0	0	295
Sunnys Prancer	3	G	6	0	2	1	3,314
Sunnys Siren	4	G	8	0	5	2	8,454
Sunny's Socialite	3	F	14	0	2	1	5,225
Sunny's Sonny	3	G	9	1	5	2	14,519
Sunnys Super Hero	5	G	9	1	2	1	1,855
Sunny's Talent	4	G	4	0	0	1	738
Sunny's Thor	3	G	13	3	3	3	15,475
Sunny's Thousands	5	G	2	0	0	0	324
Sunny's Tychonic	4	G	10	1	3	1	11,335
Sunnyside's Syn	2	C	4	0	0	0	996
Sunnytown	3	F	8	2	1	2	26,326
Sunofacat	5	G	13	2	0	1	45,385
Sunoke	9	G	5	0	1	0	2,720
Sunquero	3	F	15	1	2	2	3,233
Sunray Spirit	5	H	2	0	0	0	935
Sunrise At Six	2	F	2	0	1	0	9,118
Sunrise Curve	2	F	3	0	1	0	1,948
Sunrise Event	3	G	3	1	2	0	23,400
Sunrise Launch	3	G	1	0	1	0	2,600
Sunrise Miss	5	M	7	1	0	0	4,740
Sunrise Romance	4	F	2	0	0	0	84
Sunrise Royale	4	C	10	0	0	2	4,874
Sunrise Serenade	4	G	12	1	0	4	17,969
Sunrise Slew	4	F	4	1	0	1	14,410
Sunrise Storm	2	F	5	1	0	1	4,320
Sunrise Warrior	9	G	4	0	0	2	584
Sunriseontheoasis	2	F	5	1	1	0	17,905
Sunsational Julia	5	M	8	1	2	1	16,960
Sunset Badgett	3	F	4	0	0	0	470
Sunset Boy	8	G	13	0	2	1	5,775
Sunset Carson	3	G	3	0	0	0	77
Sunset Cruise	7	G	6	1	1	1	3,688
Sunset Kisses	4	F	10	4	2	1	97,800
Sunset Lane	6	M	10	0	4	1	7,170
Sunset Mystique	3	F	2	1	0	0	5,775
Sunset Over Water	2	F	1	0	0	0	0
Sunset Park	6	G	7	0	1	1	6,397
Sunset Pass	5	M	3	0	1	0	5,868
Sunset Passion	4	F	5	1	0	0	14,132
Sunset Place	5	H	4	0	1	2	25,560
Sunset Rose	3	F	6	0	0	0	0
Sunset Side	5	G	3	0	0	0	420
Sunset Trick	3	F	2	0	0	0	205
Sunset's Amber	3	F	9	0	0	1	1,355
Sunshine Adell	7	M	7	0	0	2	2,261
Sunshine Admiral	5	G	9	1	2	1	14,593
Sunshine Adrian	3	F	13	1	6	1	26,935
Sunshine Alan	3	G	15	2	2	7	43,664
Sunshine Allie	3	F	8	0	0	0	5,260
Sunshine and Storm	3	F	10	0	2	2	10,712
Sunshine Ave	4	F	4	2	0	1	6,130
Sunshine Bear	5	G	17	6	3	4	62,383
Sunshine Belle	6	M	4	0	0	0	200
Sunshine Brian	4	C	10	3	1	1	21,940
Sunshine Canyon	3	G	4	0	1	1	14,437
Sunshine Classic	7	M	13	1	2	2	19,305
Sunshine Denise	4	F	18	3	6	6	47,908
Sunshine Dreamer	5	M	13	0	6	4	54,560
Sunshine Ella	2	F	2	0	0	0	0
Sunshine Gail	2	F	6	0	1	0	2,100
Sunshine Glitter	3	F	13	0	0	0	1,660
Sunshine Jack	6	G	6	0	0	0	569
Sunshine Johanne	3	F	16	4	4	0	83,217
Sunshine Karlyn	2	F	5	0	0	1	2,428
Sunshine Lake	3	C	12	1	2	0	24,562
Sunshine Messenger (GB)	6	H	6	0	0	0	2,020
Sunshine Miss	6	M	8	0	0	0	1,060
Sunshine Mystical	5	M	2	0	0	0	84
Sunshine Natalie	2	F	4	0	1	2	12,120
Sunshine Nathan	4	G	17	0	1	1	3,399
Sunshine Numbers	2	G	2	1	0	0	10,492
Sunshine Priscilla	3	F	21	2	4	2	19,156
Sunshine Rondevou	4	F	15	1	0	3	9,243

Horse	Age	Sex	Sts	1st	2d	3d	Won
Sunshine Scott	7	G	13	1	0	2	6,330
Sunshine Service	3	F	9	1	2	1	12,284
Sunshine Stalker	2	G	2	0	2	0	10,500
Sunshine Success	4	F	5	1	0	0	5,888
Sunshine Summer	3	F	13	0	2	4	19,716
Sunshine Sweetie	4	F	7	0	0	0	281
Sunshine Valentine	6	H	4	0	1	1	2,464
Sunshine Village	4	C	5	0	2	0	9,750
Sunshinenbeer	3	G	8	0	3	2	29,620
Sunshineonme	3	F	2	1	1	0	11,200
Sunshineorshadows	4	F	13	1	0	2	10,279
Sunshines	3	G	6	0	0	0	940
Suntara	3	F	2	1	1	0	5,850
Sunup	4	F	8	1	4	1	59,490
Sunup Sundown	8	G	9	1	3	1	35,898
Sunwest	2	C	7	0	1	1	3,405
Suny's Boy	2	C	4	0	1	0	10,773
Sup a Looey	5	G	13	2	4	3	17,923
Supah Blitz	4	C	13	2	5	2	446,280
Supah Boots	3	F	1	0	0	0	440
Supah Brother	4	G	1	0	0	0	63
Supah Jackie	3	F	7	2	1	0	39,370
Supah Man	6	G	18	1	6	3	14,329
Supah Sensation	3	F	5	2	0	0	47,256
Supah Sweet	5	M	15	1	4	4	20,049
Super	4	G	10	0	0	3	5,327
Super Adam	2	C	2	0	0	0	1,242
Super Anjo	3	G	12	1	0	1	4,921
Super Atlantic	3	C	7	0	0	1	7,110
Super Be Buster	5	G	6	0	0	0	169
Super Blitz	7	G	4	1	0	2	10,745
Super Blue (CHI)	6	M	3	0	0	0	2,060
Super Bossy	2	F	6	0	0	2	7,222
Super Bowl	7	G	10	3	3	1	25,502
Super Bowl (NZ)	6	G	11	1	4	0	8,876
Super Bowl Cat	2	C	1	0	0	0	400
Super Bowl Eddy	4	G	4	2	0	1	16,971
Super Boy	4	C	1	0	0	0	0
Super Brand (SAF)	5	M	4	0	2	1	126,700
Super Cannon	2	G	7	0	1	1	3,595
Super Case	4	C	5	1	1	0	71,524
Super Cassie	2	F	3	0	0	1	880
Super Charge	5	H	9	1	4	0	7,889
Super Cherokee	3	C	16	6	1	5	59,583
Super Chili	3	C	5	0	0	0	460
Super Clearance	3	F	10	0	1	3	7,915
Super Composed	2	G	2	0	0	0	0
Super Coup	5	G	1	0	0	0	0
Super Coyote	3	G	11	1	2	1	16,041
Super Crown	6	G	3	0	1	0	3,860
Super Cruise	2	G	1	0	0	0	0
Super Don B	5	G	5	0	0	3	3,960
Super Dude	6	M	2	1	1	0	3,120
Super Duper Dude	5	G	1	0	0	0	0
Super Duty	4	G	3	0	0	0	0
Super Editor	5	G	12	0	3	3	4,093
Super Eight Track	2	G	1	0	0	1	2,860
Super Expectations	2	F	5	1	0	2	10,660
Super Fame	5	G	3	2	0	0	24,000
Super Fax	3	F	11	2	2	2	60,900
Super Flag	3	F	2	0	0	0	250
Super Flirt	3	G	12	2	0	1	20,056
Super Fly Prize	3	G	8	0	0	0	1,847
Super for Two	2	G	4	0	0	1	3,556
Super Frolic	4	C	12	4	2	1	140,450
Super Fund	4	G	8	0	1	3	10,089
Super Furray	4	F	8	0	0	0	990
Super Fuse	4	G	13	1	2	2	113,016
Super Fuzzy	6	G	1	0	0	0	0
Super G I	3	F	5	0	0	0	5,640
Super Gal	5	M	10	0	2	2	5,404
Super Gummi Girl	6	M	6	0	0	0	389
Super Heart	3	F	8	0	0	0	1,120
Super High	5	M	6	2	2	0	170,760
Super Highway (BRZ)	6	G	14	0	4	1	10,360
Super Individual	3	G	6	4	0	0	18,595
Super Issue	10	G	6	2	2	2	9,812
Super Itron	2	C	11	1	2	2	26,800
Super Jam	5	G	7	1	0	1	4,143
Super Jazz	2	F	3	0	0	0	2,160
Super Ladybug	3	F	2	1	0	0	15,600
Super Legionaire	3	F	11	1	1	4	5,945
Super Moe	4	G	1	0	0	0	0
Super Mood	4	G	13	4	1	1	20,697
Super Nationals	3	G	2	0	0	0	238
Super Natural	5	M	14	2	0	1	8,629
Super One	4	G	8	1	0	0	5,462
Super Perfect	5	M	3	0	0	0	726
Super Prince	3	G	4	0	1	0	2,685
Super Punch	5	M	7	1	2	1	14,039
Super Quin	3	C	3	0	0	0	1,110
Super Reviewer	4	G	19	2	4	3	37,130
Super Sail	4	G	9	0	2	0	893
Super Scout	3	C	13	1	0	2	20,840
Super Seasons	4	G	11	3	1	2	12,177
Super Sensation	7	G	15	4	2	4	7,947
Super Shinkansen	5	G	5	0	2	0	3,735
Super Short Silver	7	G	1	0	0	0	0
Super Size	6	G	4	0	1	1	2,775
Super Skip	4	C	4	1	1	0	7,740
Super Smart Sam	9	G	11	0	3	2	12,307
Super Soup	4	G	15	1	1	1	8,383
Super Stalker	3	G	10	2	2	0	18,256
Super Step	6	G	7	0	0	0	314
Super Streak	9	G	10	1	2	1	12,540
Super Stroke	3	G	7	0	0	1	2,138
Super Strut	4	G	10	3	3	0	145,094
Super Stutz	5	G	15	2	0	4	12,753
Super Suds	5	G	7	1	1	3	15,266
Super Super Sweet	2	F	2	0	0	0	800
Super Temp	3	G	2	0	0	0	535
Super Tinaway	3	F	4	2	0	0	9,535
Super Tired	2	F	2	0	0	1	2,232
Super Trooper	5	H	2	0	0	0	126
Super Trump	4	G	14	0	2	3	7,366
Super Tuscan	2	C	5	0	3	1	27,813
Super Val	5	G	2	0	0	0	520
Super Valu	7	M	4	0	0	0	172
Super Vet	8	G	13	0	1	1	3,558
Super Victory	3	C	1	1	0	0	8,400
Super Wager	6	M	1	0	0	0	0
Super Weekend	2	G	1	0	0	0	0
Super Will Power	3	G	4	0	0	1	1,880
Super Willy	6	G	5	2	0	0	14,175
Super Woman	2	F	2	0	0	0	420
Super Zim	3	G	6	0	0	0	693
Superbly Timed	3	G	12	1	2	0	10,005
Superconi	3	F	14	1	0	1	11,562
Superdumaan	4	F	5	1	0	0	15,600
Superfine Song	3	F	2	0	0	0	570
Superfines Luvey	6	M	1	0	0	0	0
Superfines Prado	6	G	3	0	0	0	824
Superfly Girl	3	F	6	0	1	3	13,810
Superfly T N T	6	G	14	2	3	3	29,783
Superget	8	M	7	0	2	0	3,540
Superior Cat	2	F	2	0	0	2	2,415
Superior Decision	3	G	4	0	0	0	1,720
Superior Deputy	2	F	5	1	1	2	14,334
Superior Gulch	2	F	1	0	1	0	1,980
Superior Kris	6	M	19	3	5	1	12,919
Superiority	8	G	6	1	0	1	28,380
Superior's King	3	F	3	0	0	0	315
Superlang	4	G	15	0	4	6	20,174
Superlative Gain	5	M	15	2	1	2	18,732
Superlative Star	5	M	4	0	1	1	2,883
Superlooper Louie	5	G	6	1	1	0	3,794
Superman Can	4	G	8	2	1	2	38,285
Supernatural Storm	5	H	6	3	0	0	18,693
Superpointyoumade	3	F	1	0	0	0	75
Superpower (ARG)	7	H	4	0	0	0	325
Superpowerman	2	G	3	0	0	0	0
Superson	7	G	3	0	0	0	75
Supersonic Mon	3	G	15	2	3	0	57,773
Supersonic Sun	4	G	5	1	1	1	18,500
Superstar Dancer	3	F	4	0	0	2	1,712
Superstar Prospect	3	G	10	0	1	3	7,535
Superstitches	4	G	6	1	0	0	3,000
Superstition Girl	5	M	11	0	2	2	5,285

Horse	Age	Sex	Sts	1st	2d	3d	Won
Supertramp	4	F	10	2	2	2	30,199
Supervelous	4	G	7	1	1	0	12,292
Supervisor	4	G	13	1	2	1	46,775
Supper Club	3	F	8	1	0	0	6,180
Suppertime	3	G	7	0	2	0	4,820
Supply House	6	M	5	1	2	0	5,880
Supra	4	F	5	0	0	1	2,670
Suprem Princes	2	F	4	0	0	1	1,147
Supreme Bidness	4	F	6	0	0	0	470
Supreme Cat	4	C	1	0	0	0	0
Supreme Commander	8	H	9	1	0	2	4,467
Supreme Cowboy	3	C	8	2	1	0	16,800
Supreme D. C.	4	G	9	0	0	0	1,090
Supreme Freedom	4	G	6	0	0	0	155
Supreme Judge	6	G	9	0	0	1	5,763
Supreme M. D.	4	G	7	1	0	1	5,929
Supreme Pleasures	7	M	5	0	2	0	5,440
Supreme Plop	8	G	3	0	0	1	935
Supreme Power	6	M	3	0	0	0	0
Supreme Regime	4	G	7	0	0	1	8,563
Supreme Sam	3	G	6	2	0	0	32,970
Supreme Silence	5	G	1	0	0	0	0
Supreme Sun	4	G	7	1	0	1	6,778
Supreme Tale	4	C	2	0	0	0	714
Supreme Ward	7	G	9	1	1	1	3,859
Supremo Miss	2	F	2	0	0	0	0
Supremo Secret	5	H	3	2	0	0	11,340
Suprise Package	8	G	6	1	0	0	4,415
Suprise Party	5	M	10	2	1	1	14,064
Suprisingly	7	M	10	2	3	0	6,900
Sur Dixie	4	C	15	1	3	2	18,552
Sur La Tete	6	G	7	3	1	3	209,310
Sur Sandpit	4	G	11	2	0	2	43,364
Surathalee	3	F	1	0	0	0	77
Surcon Sir	4	C	10	0	1	0	2,750
Sure a Gadabout	5	G	2	0	0	0	65
Sure as Shipp	7	G	3	0	0	0	614
Sure as Shootin	4	G	7	1	1	1	21,514
Sure Bet	4	F	9	1	0	2	13,035
Sure Cando	3	G	6	1	0	0	7,115
Sure Caper	3	G	4	0	0	0	820
Sure Daylight	5	M	1	0	0	0	0
Sure Delite	3	F	3	0	0	0	105
Sure Deposit	6	G	10	0	0	0	153
Sure Fit	3	F	3	0	0	0	0
Sure Flight	3	F	1	0	0	0	0
Sure I Will	5	G	5	2	0	2	15,300
Sure Is	5	G	2	2	0	0	9,204
Sure L C	3	F	9	1	1	2	5,381
Sure Opportunity	2	G	1	0	0	0	105
Sure Prize	3	G	10	2	2	2	80,360
Sure Reply	5	G	4	0	0	1	350
Sure Shot Kelley	6	G	3	0	0	0	108
Sure Special	9	M	7	1	1	2	7,362
Sure Sure	6	M	9	0	0	0	951
Sure Thing Eva	2	C	4	0	1	0	8,760
Sure to Please	5	G	3	0	0	0	86
Sure to Tango	4	F	10	3	4	0	12,247
Sure We Do	2	G	1	0	0	0	400
Sure You Can	5	G	14	4	4	4	100,070
Surefire Red	3	F	7	0	0	0	1,505
Surefire Success	2	C	2	0	0	0	800
Surely and Truely	4	G	6	2	1	0	15,180
Surely Jane	2	F	2	0	0	0	286
Sureshot Jennifer	4	F	6	0	0	1	1,480
Suretreat	4	C	1	0	0	0	0
Sureway	3	G	9	2	1	0	11,654
Sureyev	6	M	5	1	0	1	3,134
Surf Angel	3	F	6	1	0	0	7,150
Surf Fever	4	F	2	0	0	0	720
Surf Light	3	F	14	3	1	1	87,144
Surf Liner	4	G	1	0	0	0	56
Surf N Sand	5	M	7	2	1	0	78,710
Surface Strike	5	M	1	0	0	0	100
Surfin' Kat	3	F	10	3	0	2	6,560
Surfing Messina	2	F	1	0	0	0	140
Surfwatch	5	G	7	0	2	2	3,653
Surgeon of Choice	2	C	4	2	0	0	37,080
Surgeon's Cork	3	F	5	2	0	0	25,815
Surgical Strike	2	C	4	1	0	0	12,397
Surging River	4	C	7	2	0	1	204,907
Suri	6	M	8	0	3	1	15,240
Surifly	3	C	5	1	2	0	25,608
Surilla Slew	8	M	2	0	0	0	330
Surprise Affair	6	H	4	0	0	0	200
Surprise Agenda	7	M	6	2	0	0	13,421
Surprise Arrival	4	F	8	2	1	2	5,558
Surprise Call	3	F	10	3	3	0	26,342
Surprise Halo	6	G	6	0	2	1	34,958
Surprise Splash	4	F	8	2	0	1	13,140
Surprise Tour	4	G	14	4	3	0	36,720
Surprise Walker	3	F	4	0	0	0	444
Surprised Humor	3	F	8	3	0	1	127,788
Surpriseya	5	G	11	1	2	2	5,313
Surprized	5	G	10	3	2	4	101,027
Surrey	6	G	6	2	1	2	56,640
Surrey Down	3	F	13	1	4	2	51,794
Surrogate	3	G	4	0	0	1	1,250
Surrogate's Irish	9	G	4	0	0	0	960
Surtsey	5	M	5	1	0	0	4,785
Survik	4	G	4	0	0	0	620
Surville	8	G	10	2	0	3	11,636
Survino	2	C	2	0	0	0	320
Survita	3	F	14	1	5	2	14,750
Survivalist	2	C	2	1	0	0	28,950
Survive the Sea	3	F	7	0	0	1	4,105
Surviving Lady	2	F	4	0	0	0	1,600
Surviving Native	4	G	15	1	3	2	12,271
Surviving Speed	5	H	1	0	0	0	0
Survivor Kippy	5	G	9	2	2	1	35,254
Susan Gracey	5	M	11	0	2	3	24,033
Susan Rem	2	F	1	0	0	0	300
Susanne's Honor	2	C	1	0	0	0	2,250
Susan's Angel	3	F	12	3	4	2	338,540
Susan's Bid	3	G	11	0	0	2	2,442
Susan's Boy	3	G	13	2	3	0	15,402
Susan's Classichik	4	F	16	2	1	3	9,713
Susan's Dreamer	11	M	8	0	0	0	1,934
Susan's Song	3	F	7	2	0	0	24,605
Sushi	8	G	5	0	1	1	4,149
Sushi At Nobu's	4	F	3	0	0	0	210
Sushi for Noah	6	M	14	1	3	0	8,526
Susie Beau	3	F	2	0	1	1	2,170
Susie Joe's	4	F	4	0	1	1	10,800
Susie Polly's Slew	7	G	2	0	0	0	350
Susie Q Susie Q	2	F	2	0	2	0	7,400
Susie Star	2	F	1	0	0	0	460
Susie's Poker	5	G	16	4	3	3	47,044
Susie's Red Rolls	4	F	14	1	2	1	8,628
Susies Ruf Diamond	2	F	7	0	0	0	2,220
Susie's Way	4	F	12	1	2	3	8,994
Suspender	5	M	7	1	0	0	10,923
Suspicious	4	F	6	3	1	1	48,520
Suspicious Caper	4	F	5	0	0	3	6,080
Suspicious Cat	3	C	5	0	1	0	2,880
Suspicious Lite	2	G	6	0	0	0	2,345
Suspicious Minds	7	G	14	4	3	3	44,877
Suspicious Red	3	G	12	0	0	0	4,000
Suspicious Rio	3	F	9	2	1	1	12,422
Suspicious Town	3	F	7	0	0	1	5,800
Suspicious Ways	3	F	13	4	1	0	51,625
Sussex County	2	C	4	1	0	0	7,484
Sussieone	5	M	4	1	0	1	6,225
Susur	2	F	3	0	2	1	41,049
Susy Rae	4	F	12	0	0	1	1,652
Susy's a Dealer	3	F	2	0	0	1	980
Susys' Lil Listo	2	G	3	0	0	0	420
Sutter Butte	4	G	6	2	1	0	20,995
Sutter Hills	4	G	13	2	1	4	17,667
Sutter Street	4	G	8	2	4	0	49,035
Sutter Tom	3	C	5	0	1	0	1,016
Sutter's Galaxy	3	G	14	2	0	6	26,990
Sutter's Ruckus	6	M	2	0	1	0	3,884
Sutton's Bay	2	F	3	0	2	0	18,160
Suvorov	2	G	2	0	0	0	1,585
Suwannee Concerto	4	F	6	0	0	0	350
Suz Boy	3	G	14	2	3	3	32,330
Suzans Love Report	3	F	4	1	0	0	17,670

Horse	Age	Sex	Sts	1st	2d	3d	Won
Suzar	3	F	3	0	0	0	140
Suzie Little Carr	8	M	2	0	0	0	192
Suzie's Honor	4	F	7	1	0	0	7,695
Suzie's Monster	4	G	19	0	1	2	3,615
Suzy O'Brien	3	F	7	0	0	0	2,955
Suzy Q	2	F	2	0	1	0	2,415
Swadeshi	5	G	2	1	0	1	32,520
Swaggering	3	C	9	2	1	1	30,300
Swainbow	4	C	3	0	0	0	282
Swain's Gold	3	F	4	3	1	0	26,820
Swainsboroscrypto	3	C	7	0	1	0	2,683
Swami Sez	5	G	2	0	0	0	210
Swamp Creek	4	G	1	0	0	0	0
Swamp Doctor	8	H	1	0	0	0	41
Swamp Lake	6	G	3	0	0	0	858
Swamp Monkey	5	M	4	2	1	0	15,300
Swamp Rat	6	H	4	0	0	0	1,770
Swamp Scare	4	F	11	0	2	4	27,622
Swamp Spirit	6	M	22	5	3	7	44,008
Swamp Wolf	7	G	2	0	0	1	1,127
Swamper	3	G	5	1	1	0	8,770
Swampy	6	G	11	1	3	1	15,762
Swan	4	F	10	1	0	0	12,125
Swanky Bubbles	2	F	3	0	1	0	16,530
Swanky Song	7	G	6	2	0	2	13,273
Swans Star	3	F	4	0	0	1	1,160
Swan's Way	15	H	4	0	0	0	186
Swap Bids	5	G	10	0	1	4	5,754
Swaps Nickel	3	C	2	0	0	0	0
Swasti	4	F	6	4	0	0	77,928
Swatagold	4	F	11	2	2	1	23,427
Swatara Hope	2	F	6	1	2	1	16,333
Swavy	5	G	6	1	0	0	4,880
Sway of Passion	4	C	2	1	0	0	27,300
Swayo	13	G	2	0	0	0	0
Swayzo	4	F	9	0	1	1	2,452
Sweat Lodge	5	H	2	0	0	0	430
Sweday	4	G	15	0	1	0	4,288
Swede	2	F	3	1	1	0	18,200
Swede Flambe	5	G	17	3	0	3	29,794
Sweder Than Money	4	F	7	1	1	1	10,845
Swedish Radar	3	C	1	0	0	0	400
Swedish Sights	7	G	1	0	0	0	50
Sweeney Astray	4	G	4	0	0	0	480
Sweep and Go	5	G	1	0	0	0	0
Sweep Back	8	G	11	1	0	7	3,652
Sweep 'Em	6	G	13	2	3	1	51,305
Sweep in Philly	4	F	9	5	1	1	55,100
Sweep Left	4	G	10	1	3	0	6,217
Sweep N the Night	5	M	20	2	3	3	12,013
Sweep North	5	M	6	2	1	0	8,795
Sweep Sweep	6	G	17	0	3	3	17,760
Sweep the Shore	5	G	11	1	0	2	12,548
Sweep to My Lou	5	G	1	0	0	0	109
Sweep to Win	4	F	6	0	0	1	1,168
Sweep Up	4	F	11	2	2	2	57,000
Sweep Up the Gold	5	M	4	0	0	2	1,656
Sweepality	4	C	10	1	0	1	22,610
Sweepatatapi	4	F	14	1	4	2	25,010
Sweeper Four	6	G	13	1	1	3	8,068
Sweeping Analysis	7	G	12	0	2	4	27,320
Sweeping Cat	5	M	9	2	2	0	30,892
Sweeping Eva	6	M	6	0	0	0	974
Sweeping Motion	8	G	5	0	1	1	1,584
Sweeping On Bye	4	F	4	1	1	0	21,860
Sweeping Prospect	5	M	21	0	2	2	13,854
Sweeping Rita	6	M	5	1	2	0	11,830
Sweeping Smoke	6	G	5	1	2	0	23,220
Sweeping Views	3	F	1	0	0	0	2,940
Sweeping Vision	2	G	1	0	0	0	2,640
Sweeping Warmth	6	G	3	0	1	1	4,340
Sweeping Way	6	G	11	0	2	3	4,423
Sweepingly	5	G	6	1	2	0	12,892
Sweepit	3	F	8	1	0	0	11,628
Sweep's Choice	4	F	1	0	0	0	0
Sweeps Week	6	G	5	1	1	0	20,340
Sweet Accusation	4	F	4	0	0	0	0
Sweet Addiction	3	F	6	1	2	1	9,990
Sweet Alabama	3	F	1	0	0	0	150
Sweet Alaris	5	M	8	2	0	1	12,240
Sweet Alibi	2	F	8	0	1	2	3,395
Sweet America	4	F	4	0	0	0	450
Sweet and Classi	4	F	3	0	0	0	242
Sweet and Friendly	5	G	1	0	0	0	43
Sweet and Royal	4	F	9	2	1	0	6,690
Sweet and Wild	4	F	12	2	2	2	10,013
Sweet Anden	4	G	7	1	1	0	17,035
Sweet Andie	4	G	2	0	0	0	291
Sweet Angel Eyes	4	F	7	0	1	1	3,445
Sweet Annuity	7	M	4	0	0	0	0
Sweet Ante	6	M	15	0	2	3	8,326
Sweet Apple Annie	6	M	11	1	0	0	4,698
Sweet Apple Pie	5	M	5	0	2	0	2,166
Sweet April Slew	3	F	3	0	0	0	0
Sweet Archie	2	G	1	0	0	0	0
Sweet Artemis	2	F	3	0	0	0	0
Sweet as Candy	4	F	9	2	1	2	24,760
Sweet as Sarah	6	M	3	0	1	0	3,650
Sweet Attorney	3	F	12	2	0	1	12,105
Sweet Attraction	5	M	8	1	0	0	8,263
Sweet Baabaa	6	M	15	2	0	0	13,494
Sweet Baby	3	F	9	1	0	1	3,019
Sweet Baby Bull	3	F	6	0	0	2	3,632
Sweet Baby Jake	4	C	9	5	0	1	44,900
Sweet Baby Jane	5	M	8	0	1	0	14,730
Sweet Baby Slew	3	F	2	1	0	0	4,070
Sweet Band	5	H	1	0	0	0	0
Sweet Bay	3	F	13	1	1	1	28,022
Sweet Beau	5	G	7	1	1	1	20,026
Sweet Bernice	4	F	11	1	2	1	19,374
Sweet Bippy	4	C	1	0	0	0	0
Sweet Blessing	4	G	12	0	1	0	1,627
Sweet Bliss	5	M	5	0	0	1	2,030
Sweet Bo Belle	2	F	5	1	1	0	13,724
Sweet Bold Nred	3	F	2	1	0	0	10,610
Sweet Bump	3	F	3	0	0	0	500
Sweet But Salty	4	F	1	0	0	0	35
Sweet Bye Bye	2	F	1	0	0	0	0
Sweet Bynby	5	M	2	0	0	1	913
Sweet Candy Red	5	M	3	0	0	0	0
Sweet Cane	4	F	16	1	1	1	26,832
Sweet Caper	3	F	7	1	1	0	12,140
Sweet Caprice	5	M	2	0	0	0	105
Sweet Carol Ann	3	F	8	0	0	1	3,722
Sweet Carson	4	F	1	0	0	0	360
Sweet Catomine	2	F	4	3	1	0	799,800
Sweet Chantilly	4	F	3	0	0	0	145
Sweet Chatter	2	F	1	0	0	0	0
Sweet Chere	4	F	10	2	0	1	9,054
Sweet Chloe	3	F	3	1	1	0	16,900
Sweet Chocolate	3	G	1	0	0	0	0
Sweet Cindy Lou	3	F	6	1	0	0	7,844
Sweet Country Girl	4	F	4	0	0	0	1,390
Sweet Creek	4	F	12	5	3	2	76,378
Sweet Currency	2	F	6	0	2	0	8,000
Sweet Davia	4	F	7	0	1	4	14,520
Sweet Debbie	4	F	14	2	4	3	24,110
Sweet Dee's	2	F	1	1	0	0	21,000
Sweet Deimos (GB)	5	M	2	0	0	0	2,450
Sweet Destiny	5	M	2	0	1	0	1,294
Sweet Devil	4	C	1	0	0	1	3,840
Sweet Diamond Lu	3	F	17	0	1	2	5,355
Sweet Dignitas	3	F	2	0	0	0	44
Sweet Donna Jean	3	F	12	1	1	1	7,776
Sweet Dream Rhody	3	G	17	3	3	2	25,479
Sweet Dreamer	4	C	7	1	2	2	32,969
Sweet Dreamin Suzy	5	M	4	0	0	0	250
Sweet Dreams Baby	5	M	7	0	0	0	356
Sweet Dreamy Syn	4	F	4	0	0	0	861
Sweet Drummer	5	G	11	4	1	2	69,367
Sweet Dunes	4	F	2	0	1	0	2,660
Sweet Dynamite	4	F	4	0	3	0	28,500
Sweet Elena	2	F	1	0	0	0	195
Sweet Evil Hariet	3	F	12	5	3	0	35,800
Sweet Fever	3	F	6	0	0	0	779
Sweet Fleet	8	M	3	0	1	0	1,118
Sweet Frippery	6	M	12	3	3	3	132,166
Sweet Future	2	F	1	0	0	1	4,070

Horse	Age	Sex	Sts	1st	2d	3d	Won
Sweet Georgie Girl	3	F	14	0	1	2	7,534
Sweet Glory	3	F	3	1	0	0	4,909
Sweet Go	3	F	4	0	1	0	3,100
Sweet Grand	3	F	5	0	0	0	1,232
Sweet Guest	2	F	3	0	0	0	236
Sweet Harri	3	G	3	0	0	0	77
Sweet Heat	3	F	10	0	0	1	13,360
Sweet Hello	3	F	9	1	0	1	14,710
Sweet Hit	2	F	4	1	1	0	21,300
Sweet Home	3	F	1	0	0	0	0
Sweet Honor	2	F	3	0	0	0	420
Sweet Hours	2	F	4	0	0	1	1,911
Sweet Indulgence	3	F	1	0	0	0	400
Sweet Jan	2	F	3	0	0	0	300
Sweet Jessie	4	F	1	0	0	0	52
Sweet Jolie	5	M	9	0	1	1	2,371
Sweet Josefa	3	C	7	1	1	0	7,363
Sweet Julie	3	F	10	0	1	0	3,240
Sweet Juliet	3	F	2	0	0	1	4,374
Sweet Kaitlyn	3	F	1	0	0	0	90
Sweet Kassidy	3	F	1	1	0	0	14,250
Sweet Kendall Jo	2	F	2	0	1	0	3,600
Sweet La Knee	2	F	3	0	0	0	900
Sweet Lad	7	H	2	0	0	0	0
Sweet Lady Brier	5	M	4	0	1	0	2,642
Sweet Latvia	6	M	15	1	1	3	8,681
Sweet Laural	3	F	17	1	0	5	17,360
Sweet Lauren	4	F	1	0	0	0	0
Sweet Like Honey	7	M	10	0	0	0	1,354
Sweet Lil Lolly	3	F	4	0	1	0	11,828
Sweet Lil Prince	3	C	2	0	0	0	0
Sweet Lips	3	F	8	5	0	1	150,138
Sweet Little Avie	4	F	13	3	4	1	76,060
Sweet Little Buck	4	C	12	2	1	2	7,494
Sweet Loona	5	G	12	1	0	0	5,826
Sweet Loretta	3	F	5	0	1	1	7,860
Sweet Lucky Lady	4	F	4	0	1	1	2,036
Sweet Lucky T	3	C	6	0	0	0	660
Sweet Macaroni	2	F	7	2	1	3	67,203
Sweet Maneuver	3	F	14	1	1	2	9,564
Sweet Mary Jo	4	F	11	2	3	1	18,170
Sweet Meg	3	F	4	0	0	0	1,940
Sweet Melody	3	F	1	0	0	1	2,470
Sweet Mercy	2	F	6	1	1	0	6,980
Sweet Miracle	8	M	10	3	1	1	12,331
Sweet Miriam	5	M	15	1	2	3	8,450
Sweet Miss El	2	F	4	2	0	0	48,880
Sweet Molly Malone	2	F	6	1	0	0	19,047
Sweet Monarch	5	M	6	1	2	2	45,310
Sweet Moving D	3	G	8	1	3	0	51,212
Sweet N Brassy	7	M	5	1	1	0	2,925
Sweet N Crafty	5	M	4	0	0	0	124
Sweet n' Deed	4	F	8	2	2	0	17,108
Sweet 'n Fiesty	5	M	6	0	0	0	884
Sweet 'n Golden	6	M	3	0	0	1	1,605
Sweet Nijinsky	4	F	6	1	0	0	3,940
Sweet Nine	3	F	11	1	0	1	9,997
Sweet Nobility	2	F	1	0	0	0	0
Sweet Noelle	7	M	3	0	0	0	150
Sweet Numbers	3	F	3	0	0	1	4,960
Sweet O'Dale	5	M	12	1	0	3	6,154
Sweet Olympio	5	M	8	0	5	1	27,780
Sweet On Sixteen	3	F	3	1	0	0	26,556
Sweet On You Too	5	M	9	1	1	0	4,786
Sweet One	4	F	5	0	1	0	1,306
Sweet Parcel	5	M	8	0	0	0	1,185
Sweet Pea to Me	5	M	12	1	0	0	6,035
Sweet Peaches	4	F	14	2	5	1	44,385
Sweet Performance	7	M	10	0	1	1	2,760
Sweet Potato Puff	2	F	1	0	0	0	552
Sweet Price	2	C	1	1	0	0	11,100
Sweet Prince	5	G	4	1	0	0	8,523
Sweet Problem	3	F	10	4	2	1	249,205
Sweet Promises	4	G	7	2	3	0	37,210
Sweet Rachael	6	M	3	0	0	0	246
Sweet Rebecca N	8	M	6	3	0	1	11,605
Sweet Redemption	7	G	7	1	0	1	1,580
Sweet Remiss	5	M	6	0	1	0	3,063
Sweet Return (GB)	4	C	7	2	1	1	446,180
Sweet Rhapsody	4	F	15	0	5	3	21,428
Sweet Ride Laura	5	M	1	0	0	0	0
Sweet Road	5	G	4	1	0	0	3,241
Sweet S Cookies	3	F	5	0	0	0	434
Sweet Sailin	7	M	14	1	4	3	17,756
Sweet Salvation	2	C	7	1	0	0	5,485
Sweet Samantha	4	F	5	0	1	0	6,440
Sweet Sammy	4	G	16	2	2	1	29,327
Sweet Sandy	3	F	3	1	0	0	8,070
Sweet Science	3	F	4	2	1	1	63,482
Sweet Screamer	4	F	1	0	0	0	2,150
Sweet Send Off	3	G	14	1	2	1	13,229
Sweet Share	4	F	10	1	0	3	11,240
Sweet Siphon	5	M	3	0	0	0	50
Sweet Sir Galahad	3	C	1	1	0	0	4,800
Sweet Sister	4	F	9	1	1	1	4,073
Sweet Slewellen	4	F	11	3	2	3	20,398
Sweet Smilin Ali	3	F	4	0	0	0	102
Sweet Smoke	2	F	5	1	0	1	19,130
Sweet Solairo	2	F	7	1	4	1	133,683
Sweet Sounding	3	F	3	0	0	0	0
Sweet Southerngal	2	F	6	2	2	0	27,030
Sweet Souvenir	3	F	11	0	2	0	2,268
Sweet Spirit	3	C	4	0	0	1	1,207
Sweet Stepper	5	G	9	2	1	1	85,540
Sweet Stories	3	F	4	0	1	0	615
Sweet Storm Creek	4	F	8	0	0	3	27,021
Sweet Stuff	3	F	3	0	0	0	215
Sweet Sunday	6	H	7	0	0	0	311
Sweet Susie Q	3	F	1	0	0	0	105
Sweet Sweet	2	F	1	1	0	0	24,600
Sweet Sweet Molly	2	F	1	1	0	0	9,000
Sweet Sweet Spell	6	M	15	2	3	3	15,298
Sweet Taffy	4	F	19	4	2	6	26,131
Sweet Talk Me	4	C	11	1	0	0	5,100
Sweet Talker	2	F	5	3	1	0	99,760
Sweet Talking Girl	3	F	7	1	2	0	19,800
Sweet Teeth	3	F	14	0	3	2	15,420
Sweet Tender Lover	5	M	3	0	0	1	1,045
Sweet Thing	4	F	4	1	0	0	2,420
Sweet Tiffany	3	F	13	0	1	1	5,185
Sweet Time	5	M	10	6	0	2	90,455
Sweet Tour	2	F	11	1	3	0	12,630
Sweet Tracy	3	F	8	1	1	0	33,814
Sweet Triumph	3	F	3	0	0	0	825
Sweet Tzipora	2	F	1	1	0	0	12,600
Sweet Vision	3	F	5	1	2	1	54,700
Sweet Water Canyon	5	M	2	0	0	0	1,058
Sweet Water Cool	2	F	1	0	0	1	1,210
Sweet Willie G	3	G	1	0	0	1	480
Sweet Will's Joy	4	F	6	4	0	0	61,314
Sweet Win	3	F	8	3	0	2	162,980
Sweet Wittle Kay	3	F	5	0	0	0	2,341
Sweet Word	4	G	12	0	4	2	12,670
Sweetalyspleasure	6	M	9	0	0	1	1,425
Sweetcarolinagirl	3	F	2	0	1	1	5,600
Sweetcart	2	F	3	1	0	0	15,600
Sweetest of Sweets	4	F	21	3	1	4	20,191
Sweetest Tour	5	M	7	2	1	1	7,280
Sweeteyedjessilou	4	F	12	0	1	2	5,911
Sweetfingercharlie	4	G	14	1	2	0	10,455
Sweetgalintown	3	F	11	2	1	2	18,090
Sweetgum	3	F	6	0	0	1	12,513
Sweetheart Sami	4	F	4	0	1	0	7,680
Sweetheartswindler	3	G	12	1	1	0	13,240
Sweethrtofsigmachi	4	F	3	0	0	1	3,180
Sweetie G	4	F	16	1	0	3	13,826
Sweetie Halo	4	F	14	2	0	3	21,628
Sweetiegunzallus	5	M	7	0	1	2	4,538
Sweetiepieofmyeye	4	F	5	1	1	1	7,468
Sweetiewheatie	2	C	2	0	1	1	11,100
Sweetime First	2	F	1	0	0	0	785
Sweetjudyblueeyes	4	F	8	2	0	0	11,730
Sweetkindylynn	2	F	2	0	0	0	800
Sweetly Bold	7	M	2	0	0	0	610
Sweetly Defiant	3	F	4	0	0	0	294
Sweetness	2	F	1	0	0	0	135
Sweetness Song	5	H	1	0	0	0	0
Sweetninnocent	6	M	6	2	1	0	10,472

Horse	Age	Sex	Sts	1st	2d	3d	Won
Sweetnsassy Hannah	3	F	5	1	0	0	15,118
Sweetoldgirl	3	F	3	0	0	0	2,110
Sweets Money	3	G	6	0	0	0	340
Sweetsally	2	F	1	0	0	0	0
Sweetshew	5	M	3	1	0	0	29,400
Sweetsmellofsucces	3	F	3	0	0	1	2,550
Sweetsoutherndessa	2	F	7	3	0	1	47,600
Sweetsouthernsmile	2	C	1	0	0	0	0
Sweetsoutherntimes	2	F	5	0	0	1	1,820
Sweettrickydancer	4	F	6	0	1	4	38,960
Sweetwater Promise	5	M	5	0	0	0	3,360
Sweety Violet	2	F	7	0	0	2	6,324
Swell	2	G	6	1	0	0	28,648
Swelter	4	G	8	1	2	1	19,234
Swen	3	G	11	3	2	0	60,835
Swept Clean	6	G	6	1	2	0	20,540
Swept in Three	4	C	2	1	0	0	17,880
Swerve	3	G	16	5	2	5	42,623
Swift Admiral	5	G	5	0	0	1	1,192
Swift Appeal	3	F	7	1	2	0	8,115
Swift Attack	4	C	13	1	0	2	10,574
Swift Attraction	3	C	5	1	0	1	41,500
Swift Decision	4	F	5	1	0	0	1,508
Swift Defense	5	M	10	2	2	2	16,091
Swift for Sure	6	G	13	3	2	0	46,463
Swift Hero	5	G	9	1	1	1	4,335
Swift Illusion	5	G	8	0	1	1	5,300
Swift Intention	8	G	11	0	0	3	4,006
Swift Kato	2	G	4	0	0	1	2,325
Swift Mercedes	2	G	5	1	0	0	21,620
Swift Mover	4	C	9	2	1	0	7,824
Swift N Free	3	G	3	0	0	0	780
Swift N Tricky	4	G	2	0	0	1	1,287
Swift of Flight	4	F	9	1	1	1	48,656
Swift Place	7	M	2	0	0	0	0
Swift Prince	2	C	1	0	0	1	2,585
Swift Replica	5	G	9	2	2	0	80,750
Swift Response	3	G	7	2	0	1	29,480
Swift River	3	C	4	1	1	0	20,970
Swift Road	2	C	5	1	0	1	10,535
Swift Satan	2	C	4	1	0	0	15,900
Swift Sefa	3	F	9	3	0	2	16,295
Swift Sky	7	G	2	0	0	0	80
Swift Star	3	F	1	0	0	0	500
Swift Thunder	4	G	5	0	0	0	522
Swift Trial	6	G	3	1	0	0	4,275
Swift Wings	2	F	4	1	0	0	32,340
Swiftandsubtle	5	H	3	0	0	0	0
Swiftwatersweetpea	4	F	2	0	0	0	180
Swifty Diane	3	F	5	0	1	2	4,165
Swigerts Prince	4	G	8	0	0	3	2,467
Swim Around	3	G	6	0	4	0	11,534
Swim Boy	4	G	13	0	0	4	6,098
Swim Easy	4	C	13	7	4	0	89,045
Swim Or Sink	2	F	5	0	0	1	2,625
Swimtime	4	G	7	1	1	1	13,117
Swindler	4	G	11	2	0	3	13,476
Swing by the Bon	4	G	6	0	0	1	1,100
Swing in Satin	5	M	5	1	0	0	9,967
Swing Master	6	G	1	0	0	0	0
Swing N Run	3	G	14	2	3	3	12,792
Swing On	3	F	10	0	0	1	1,809
Swing Six	11	G	9	2	2	0	12,602
Swing Song	4	F	3	0	0	0	0
Swing the Belle	3	F	6	3	1	0	7,290
Swing the Cat (NZ)	4	F	3	1	1	1	21,840
Swing Time Girl	4	F	2	0	0	0	0
Swing With Me	3	F	4	0	2	1	12,385
Swing Your Lady	6	G	7	0	0	1	2,029
Swingcat	7	H	10	2	2	1	46,502
Swingforthefences	3	C	9	2	2	2	385,745
Swingin' Champ	3	F	1	0	0	0	0
Swingin Harry	6	G	5	1	0	0	3,183
Swingin Jeb	4	C	1	0	0	0	85
Swingin Leroy	5	G	8	2	0	1	11,811
Swingin Sue	4	F	6	0	0	0	0
Swingin Whiskey	2	G	4	1	0	1	47,532
Swinging	3	F	5	2	0	0	57,272
Swinging Gate	5	M	12	3	1	4	62,035
Swinging Ghost	3	G	7	3	0	2	95,240
Swinging Guy	5	G	11	1	1	3	7,615
Swinging Janie Gal	7	M	3	0	0	0	123
Swinging Ridge	8	G	10	2	1	0	6,472
Swinging Sammi	5	H	2	1	0	0	6,504
Swinging Siberian	2	F	3	0	0	1	4,000
Swingingintherain	3	G	15	4	0	3	27,901
Swingley Road	6	G	10	1	2	0	6,813
Swingn' Notes	3	F	6	2	0	0	56,450
Swingnlisa	8	M	8	5	1	1	5,313
Swingsville	4	F	16	4	0	1	30,617
Swingtime Miss	2	F	6	0	0	1	1,845
Swingtimes Appeal	4	F	5	0	0	1	1,165
Swirling Sky	4	F	9	0	2	0	6,335
Swirling Wind	4	F	6	0	0	0	1,650
Swirly Boy	4	G	5	1	0	0	9,273
Swished	5	M	3	0	0	0	700
Swishingonastar	5	M	2	0	0	0	0
Swiss Address	2	C	2	1	0	0	28,380
Swiss Affection	2	F	1	0	0	0	775
Swiss Alps	2	G	1	0	0	0	0
Swiss Arrival	2	F	4	0	0	1	1,755
Swiss Attire	4	F	3	0	0	2	2,276
Swiss Ballet	4	F	1	0	0	0	0
Swiss Banks Fraud	7	H	2	0	0	1	1,365
Swiss Bounty	3	G	10	1	3	4	18,209
Swiss Count	4	G	12	1	2	2	12,877
Swiss Debutante	3	F	1	0	0	0	300
Swiss Dove	4	F	20	1	0	5	12,878
Swiss Exchange	2	C	1	0	0	0	862
Swiss Gambler	6	H	15	0	3	2	7,498
Swiss Guy	4	G	2	0	0	0	0
Swiss Ice	3	G	1	0	0	0	155
Swiss Key	4	G	8	0	0	0	1,410
Swiss Lad	2	C	6	2	1	2	131,485
Swiss Ladybug	2	F	11	0	3	2	24,741
Swiss Mint	2	F	3	0	0	0	1,488
Swiss Mocha	3	G	16	1	2	4	26,071
Swiss Moon	3	C	10	2	0	2	12,770
Swiss Mr.	3	C	2	0	0	0	700
Swiss Please	2	F	5	1	0	1	49,993
Swiss Sarah	6	M	16	2	4	1	10,813
Swiss Silver	2	G	3	1	0	1	35,088
Swiss Sissy	3	F	12	1	1	3	6,195
Swiss Skeet	5	G	3	0	0	0	220
Swiss Skier	3	F	2	0	0	0	781
Swiss Splash	3	F	4	0	0	0	1,690
Swiss Steak	2	C	4	0	0	1	8,517
Swiss Sunset	2	F	1	0	1	0	3,100
Swiss Tamerlane	3	C	7	1	2	1	29,240
Swiss Valley	3	F	14	1	0	2	17,790
Swissle Stick	2	C	8	0	1	0	16,630
Switch Lanes	5	M	9	2	5	0	96,180
Switched	3	G	12	0	1	0	6,530
Switcheroo	3	F	4	1	0	2	11,151
Switchgear	4	G	1	0	0	0	225
Swither	2	F	5	1	0	2	128,826
Swoon Me Baby	3	F	4	0	0	1	4,122
Swoonsie	2	F	5	0	0	0	1,008
Swoony Girl	5	M	6	0	0	0	450
Swoop	3	C	1	0	0	0	0
Swoop and Soar	7	G	4	1	1	0	18,250
Swooshel	6	G	14	3	4	0	45,867
Sword and Stone	5	H	5	1	0	0	1,648
Sword Chief	6	H	1	0	0	1	1,960
Sword Fight	5	H	1	0	0	0	189
Sword of Honour	3	C	5	0	0	0	2,560
Sword of Iron	5	M	5	0	0	0	594
Sword of Isiss	3	F	1	0	0	0	0
Sword of Lords	3	G	9	1	0	2	12,155
Sword of Lucky	6	G	9	1	0	2	11,651
Sword of the South	7	G	17	3	0	3	9,955
Sword of War	7	H	9	0	2	0	1,854
Swordfish	6	G	5	1	1	1	33,700
Swordmaker	3	G	5	1	0	0	6,540
Swords At Dawn	4	F	2	0	0	0	0
Sword's Flyer	3	G	12	1	1	1	9,548
Sword's Pride	2	G	6	0	1	1	3,820
Swordswiped	4	G	10	0	0	1	1,355

Horse	Age	Sex	Sts	1st	2d	3d	Won
Sybelee	2	F	6	0	0	0	1,855
Syble Seattle	5	G	17	1	1	0	4,360
Sycamore Creek	6	G	15	3	1	1	44,045
Sydneyleigh	3	F	6	0	0	1	3,412
Sydney's Choice	3	F	6	0	2	3	4,680
Sydney's Dream	4	F	3	0	0	1	520
Sydney's Quincey	5	H	8	0	0	2	11,365
Syd's Pawpaw	3	C	10	4	2	1	40,815
Sydsational	2	F	5	0	0	0	3,911
Sygian	4	G	7	3	0	0	25,050
Sykes Alive	7	G	5	0	2	0	11,034
Syl's Aggravation	8	G	13	0	0	1	1,029
Sylvan Approval	4	G	6	2	0	0	9,403
Sylvester Questor	11	G	12	1	3	2	26,289
Sylvia's Hymn	8	G	7	2	1	0	15,068
Symbolic Cat	6	G	9	1	3	1	50,025
Symbolic Gesture	2	C	2	1	0	0	23,773
Symmetron	4	C	3	1	0	1	49,476
Symmetry Slew	7	M	21	1	2	5	14,985
Sympathie	3	F	6	0	0	1	982
Symphonic Melody	6	M	7	0	0	0	280
Symphony Bay	3	F	1	0	0	0	0
Symphony in C	3	F	3	1	1	0	29,390
Symphony of Fire	3	G	8	0	2	0	22,715
Symphony of Gold	4	F	3	0	0	2	2,805
Symphony Sid	4	C	4	1	2	1	30,375
Syn Begone	5	G	6	0	0	1	2,758
Syn Can Do	5	M	6	1	0	1	4,960
Syn D Syn	5	M	12	1	1	2	6,518
Syn Time	2	F	3	0	0	0	173
Synapse	7	G	2	0	0	0	308
Synaster Son	4	G	6	0	0	1	600
Synaway	6	M	11	1	4	1	15,575
Sync	2	G	5	0	0	1	3,965
Synchronistic	3	F	1	0	0	0	0
Synco Peach	4	F	8	6	1	0	202,940
Syncopated Silver	2	C	5	0	0	0	280
Syncopated Slew	5	G	10	0	3	1	5,546
Synergistic	5	M	2	0	0	0	2,835
Synergistic Effex	3	F	10	2	3	1	78,547
Synful Cajun	5	G	6	0	0	1	3,520
Synful Cat	3	F	12	1	0	0	6,260
Synful Charm	2	C	2	1	0	0	20,478
Synfull Charmer	4	F	9	4	4	1	21,670
Synhawk	3	C	4	0	0	0	1,420
Synlimit	6	G	8	1	1	1	2,698
Synner Or Saint	9	G	4	0	0	0	600
Syn's Baby Ruthe	7	M	6	0	1	0	920
Syns N Fantasies	5	G	4	0	0	1	328
Syphire Pine	6	G	7	0	1	0	2,194
Syphon Says	3	C	13	1	1	0	23,064
Syrian Applause	5	M	10	1	1	1	5,771
Syrian Sea	8	M	6	0	0	1	1,105
Syrian Smoke	3	G	1	0	0	0	400
Syringa Song	2	F	2	0	2	0	10,400
Syringa's Bodgit	4	F	11	1	2	4	25,842
T and S Dream	2	C	2	0	0	0	428
T Boozer	2	F	7	0	3	0	11,545
T Boy	6	G	10	1	4	3	6,964
T C Delaurinflash	2	C	2	1	0	0	10,800
T C Direct Gold	2	F	3	0	0	0	600
T C Goldpenny	2	G	2	0	0	0	0
T C Ice	4	F	6	0	0	0	103
T C Kiss	6	M	8	0	0	1	10,950
T C Lord Pleasant	3	G	11	0	3	3	15,421
T C Maiden	5	M	18	3	6	3	57,307
T C Rebel Rouzer	3	F	13	0	0	1	2,826
T C Road to Glory	3	F	6	0	1	1	5,590
T C Royale	2	G	3	0	0	1	1,553
T C S Desolo	4	G	4	0	0	1	1,131
T C S Vichine	5	G	3	0	0	0	230
T C's Cherry Hill	6	M	4	0	0	0	0
T Cs Connicut	2	F	3	0	0	0	1,200
T Cs Defar	2	F	3	0	0	0	0
T Cs Florida West	3	C	3	0	0	0	0
T C's Lesia De	4	G	16	0	5	4	11,024
T Cs Orbiting Miss	6	M	14	1	1	2	5,023
T C's Revenge	4	G	10	0	2	1	23,155
T C's Roldaffair	4	F	1	0	0	0	0
T C's Swingshot	4	G	11	0	3	3	8,773
T D Defrere	3	G	7	0	1	1	4,777
T D Silver	7	G	8	1	5	1	3,477
T D Tommy	5	G	6	3	1	0	55,250
T Diamond	2	F	3	0	0	0	426
T E Jones	4	F	4	1	0	0	20,680
T G's Prospect	3	G	9	2	0	1	10,370
T J Casey	5	M	9	0	1	0	1,200
T J Classy	3	F	9	1	0	1	4,965
T J 's Moon Shadow	3	G	12	1	2	2	20,230
T Jay's Victory	6	G	16	2	1	2	22,310
T J's Hoop	2	F	4	0	0	0	0
T J's Jackinthebox	4	C	4	0	0	0	340
T J's Monster	2	C	5	1	1	1	14,800
T J's Prime	4	F	18	2	2	4	11,861
T J's Token	3	F	2	0	0	0	0
T K Owe	3	G	9	1	0	3	4,705
T K's Reality	4	F	1	0	0	0	105
T M Black Storm	3	F	8	1	2	0	5,378
T M Gray Ghost	5	G	16	1	0	1	6,980
T M Rules	2	C	1	0	0	0	0
T M T Insider	5	G	7	0	3	2	7,698
T M Warrior	6	G	2	0	0	0	135
T N T Special	2	F	1	1	0	0	9,300
T O's Quarterback	9	M	7	0	0	0	219
T P Louie	6	G	13	1	4	1	33,813
T S Eliot	4	C	2	1	0	0	17,435
T Shirt	4	G	13	2	1	0	13,613
T Shirt King	11	G	3	0	0	0	192
T T Phares	6	G	3	0	0	0	235
T Time	3	C	5	1	0	2	9,515
T Tommie Too	7	G	3	1	0	1	6,630
T V Fan	2	F	4	0	1	0	9,202
T V Hunter	3	C	5	1	1	1	11,615
T. A. C. K. One	2	F	1	0	0	0	0
T. A. Thomas Alan	3	G	8	1	0	0	28,860
T. C. Lu	6	M	1	0	0	0	0
T. D. Irish	7	G	7	0	0	0	773
T. D. the Dawg	4	G	4	0	0	0	1,107
T. D. Vance	2	C	2	1	0	0	20,610
T. G.'s Babe	3	F	10	1	2	1	22,660
T. G.'s Gambler	3	G	12	2	0	1	41,645
T. H. Approval	3	C	13	3	2	2	112,840
T. H. Lear	6	G	3	0	1	0	8,960
T. J. Cruiser	5	G	10	0	2	4	2,568
T. J. Hogan	3	G	1	0	0	0	125
T. J. Hunter	6	H	1	0	0	0	72
T. J.'s Blackjack	4	G	2	0	0	0	160
T. J.'s Glory	4	G	13	1	1	0	19,505
T. J.'s Ivy	6	M	6	0	0	2	5,262
T. J.'s Knicknack	6	G	12	2	1	1	12,224
T. J.'s Trubs	4	F	1	0	0	0	460
T. Jay's Pep	7	G	10	0	0	2	965
T. K.'s Turn	6	G	12	3	0	0	10,681
T. L. Three	4	G	16	1	0	1	10,000
T. L. Time	9	G	6	2	2	1	24,900
T. M. C.'s Hubble	4	G	11	2	2	3	31,313
T. M. Frank	4	G	6	1	0	0	28,642
T. Mac	3	G	5	0	0	0	3,733
T. McClain	3	G	2	0	0	0	170
T. Minus Ten	3	G	13	1	1	4	12,518
T. S. Dailey	3	F	8	0	1	1	4,300
T. Soprano	3	C	1	0	0	1	2,880
T. T. Storm	2	G	3	0	0	0	475
T. V. Evie	2	F	1	0	0	1	840
T. V. Frost	5	G	8	0	0	0	473
T. V. Kiss	4	G	1	0	0	0	535
T. V. Matinee	2	F	4	0	1	1	8,310
T. V. Secretary	6	M	16	4	4	3	56,090
T.j.'s Idolchatter	6	G	8	0	0	0	750
Ta Keel	4	G	19	4	1	6	19,085
Ta Smalley	5	M	1	0	0	0	0
Ta Ta Baby	5	H	16	2	2	3	27,115
Ta Ta for Now	3	G	3	0	1	0	820
Ta'am Clever	4	F	15	2	2	2	12,357
Tab	7	G	22	2	1	3	26,094
Tab the Truce	5	G	7	0	1	4	3,070
Tabacchi	3	C	1	0	0	0	700
Tabacco Roots	4	G	12	1	2	2	5,715

Horse	Age	Sex	Sts	1st	2d	3d	Won
Tabernacle	6	M	8	1	0	0	5,245
Tabiana	4	F	8	0	1	0	3,660
Tabica Grill	3	G	8	1	0	1	9,735
Tabitango	4	F	3	0	0	1	900
Tabiz	8	G	5	0	1	2	1,610
Table Bay	3	G	2	0	0	0	0
Table Creek	5	G	11	1	1	2	3,798
Table Hopper	5	G	15	1	1	0	7,183
Table Me N Saros	5	G	14	4	2	1	18,435
Table Mountain	4	C	1	0	0	0	88
Table of Contents	3	F	4	1	0	3	19,560
Table of Fame	3	G	2	1	0	0	8,200
Table Talk	6	G	2	0	0	0	353
Tabledancinpyrite	5	H	10	1	0	2	4,776
Tablet	4	G	17	1	6	0	17,229
Tabloid	3	F	1	0	0	0	42
Taboose Creek	4	F	2	0	0	0	0
Tabor Boy	3	G	3	0	0	0	572
Tabor City	4	G	2	1	0	0	4,845
Tabulator	4	G	6	0	0	0	547
Tacaro's Dan D	3	G	6	1	1	0	7,140
Tacaro's Heaven	5	G	7	1	1	2	24,115
Tach Magic	3	C	3	0	0	1	384
Tache	5	M	18	1	4	1	10,589
Tachu	2	G	1	0	0	1	1,540
Tacirring	5	H	3	0	2	0	13,600
Tacit Agreement	3	C	4	1	0	0	30,518
Tacito Prospect	3	F	3	0	0	0	215
Tack on the Magic	5	G	5	1	1	0	4,240
Tack Room	4	F	2	0	0	0	297
Tack Room Lady	5	M	1	1	0	0	4,800
Tackers Girl	5	M	9	2	1	0	18,215
Tackling Stress	4	C	9	2	0	0	93,174
Tacky	3	G	11	0	1	3	24,916
Tacky Town	5	M	9	0	3	1	7,956
Tacloban	3	G	2	0	0	0	0
Taco Caliente	4	G	6	1	1	0	15,851
Taco Jones	3	G	14	0	0	0	3,960
Taco Kid	4	G	10	0	0	2	2,475
Taco Man	6	G	1	0	0	0	0
Taco Tuesday	5	G	14	1	4	5	52,539
Taco Willy	3	G	8	1	0	0	7,508
Taconic	4	G	8	4	0	0	55,650
Taconic Run	4	G	10	1	0	0	7,464
Tacos Swing	3	G	1	0	0	0	0
Tact Reigns	6	M	13	2	3	3	30,720
Tactargo	3	G	6	0	0	0	360
Tactful Touch	5	G	12	0	2	2	4,641
Tactfully	7	M	7	0	1	2	5,125
Tactfully Ann	4	F	13	2	3	2	19,736
Tactical Al	8	H	13	2	2	1	25,050
Tactical Allusion	6	G	11	1	1	2	10,985
Tactical Beauty	2	C	2	0	0	0	300
Tactical Blast	3	F	15	3	4	4	46,914
Tactical Blues	5	G	19	1	2	2	12,554
Tactical Charm	3	F	3	0	0	0	1,200
Tactical Chatter	3	C	4	0	0	0	345
Tactical de Naskra	6	G	7	2	0	0	36,061
Tactical Delight	4	C	1	0	0	0	360
Tactical Fight	3	C	3	0	0	0	790
Tactical Gamble	3	F	6	0	1	0	3,030
Tactical Go Go	3	F	1	0	0	0	0
Tactical Gold	3	C	2	0	0	1	4,480
Tactical Guy	3	C	5	1	0	0	4,410
Tactical Hugh	3	C	1	0	0	0	630
Tactical Jet	5	G	10	0	4	1	8,067
Tactical Juli	4	F	11	1	1	0	15,942
Tactical Kitty	2	F	6	0	0	0	4,050
Tactical Mover	4	F	1	0	0	0	0
Tactical Plan	6	H	1	0	0	0	0
Tactical Plus	4	F	7	1	1	2	48,830
Tactical Power	3	G	23	1	1	3	20,460
Tactical Prince	3	C	12	1	2	5	23,650
Tactical Princess	4	F	17	2	4	3	42,798
Tactical Rose	4	F	1	0	0	1	2,860
Tactical Scene	5	M	4	1	1	1	8,705
Tactical Side	7	G	20	2	2	4	77,778
Tactical Stan	4	G	7	0	0	1	6,430
Tactical Tabby	3	F	2	0	0	0	0

Horse	Age	Sex	Sts	1st	2d	3d	Won
Tactical Tango	5	G	18	1	5	0	14,091
Tactical Time	4	G	2	0	0	1	638
Tactical Tina	4	F	5	0	0	1	3,930
Tactical War	5	H	4	1	0	2	31,640
Tacticat	2	C	1	0	0	0	86
Taddy	4	F	4	0	0	1	385
Tadreeb	2	C	4	1	0	0	32,224
Tafaul	3	C	5	0	0	1	10,610
Tag Up	4	G	10	1	1	0	6,514
Tagadance	4	G	11	1	1	0	15,190
Taghkanic	4	F	3	0	1	0	19,585
Tagus	4	G	2	0	0	0	0
Tahizztheman	3	G	6	1	0	0	1,928
Tahoe Bay	4	F	11	3	1	2	18,975
Tahoe Believer	4	G	6	0	0	2	2,895
Tahoe Magic	2	G	1	0	0	0	300
Tahoe Time	3	F	3	0	0	0	0
Tahoe Trip	3	G	17	2	2	5	20,576
Tahoe's Gem	3	F	8	1	1	1	4,856
Tahquitz Pride	6	M	10	0	2	2	12,006
Taiaslew	4	G	2	1	0	1	34,000
Taiga Two	6	H	1	0	0	0	460
Tall Gate	7	H	9	0	2	3	8,490
Tail Gunner	3	F	7	0	0	1	1,210
Tail Number	5	H	5	1	1	0	9,062
Tailfromthecrypt	6	H	13	1	2	2	33,557
Tailgator	5	M	14	4	2	1	42,482
Tailor's Cut	2	C	12	1	2	1	12,635
Tails of the Crypt	5	G	5	0	0	0	6,454
Tailsneverfails	4	F	5	1	0	2	4,638
Tailwind Flyer	3	F	5	0	1	2	17,376
Taint It the Truth	5	H	13	7	0	1	100,124
Taint Saratoga	4	G	17	3	2	2	38,610
Taint So	3	G	4	2	0	0	55,118
Tainted Chimes	6	G	16	0	3	1	4,524
Tainted Facts	3	F	3	0	0	0	0
Tainted Tripp	7	M	2	0	0	0	46
Tainted Wishes	3	G	9	0	1	2	2,753
Tainwell (GB)	5	G	11	0	0	1	1,341
Taipan	5	G	12	1	0	2	21,478
Taittinger Rose	3	F	9	3	1	2	133,378
Taiwan Charley	3	C	1	0	0	0	0
Taj	5	G	6	0	2	0	5,600
Tajmarie	3	F	7	0	2	2	3,197
Tajranee Rose	4	F	2	1	0	0	1,595
Taka Time	5	M	9	1	3	0	11,949
Takatisu	2	F	1	0	0	0	390
Take a Chance	2	G	4	0	0	0	3,700
Take a Check	2	F	8	2	3	0	84,955
Take a Long Look	3	F	8	2	1	1	18,830
Take a Look	6	M	9	1	2	0	17,376
Take a Pass	2	C	3	0	0	0	0
Take a Shot	2	C	4	1	0	1	22,618
Take a Taxi	4	F	3	1	0	0	11,060
Take Account	7	G	11	1	4	1	10,456
Take Achance On Me	6	G	10	0	4	1	70,331
Take Advantage	5	G	12	1	2	3	10,421
Take Another Bow	6	G	1	0	0	0	61
Take Back Cat	5	G	7	2	2	0	11,730
Take Bazzie Out	2	F	2	1	0	0	25,830
Take Courage	3	G	2	0	0	1	1,375
Take D' Tour	3	F	5	1	2	0	20,240
Take Harry	5	G	7	0	1	1	6,222
Take Her Out	3	F	4	1	0	0	12,638
Take Holy Out	5	G	12	0	0	2	5,040
Take Issue	5	M	17	3	6	3	23,413
Take It North	5	M	2	0	0	0	206
Take Me Away	3	G	10	1	3	2	20,865
Take Me Dancer	6	H	3	0	1	2	1,000
Take Me Home Lady	5	M	3	0	0	0	350
Take Me Out Back	4	G	8	0	0	1	1,080
Take Me Out Deputy	3	F	9	1	2	0	8,070
Take Me Out John	3	C	10	1	2	4	59,189
Take Me Outahere	3	G	3	0	0	0	560
Take Me There	3	F	15	5	2	2	117,763
Take Me to Sealte	3	F	2	0	0	0	150
Take Me Up	6	G	9	3	1	3	109,995
Take My Heart	5	G	8	1	1	3	5,346
Take My Word	3	C	11	1	1	3	8,872

Horse	Age	Sex	Sts	1st	2d	3d	Won
Take Notice	3	C	3	0	0	0	110
Take Off and Run	4	F	8	0	1	2	5,396
Take Part	5	G	3	1	1	0	4,055
Take Some Time	3	G	2	0	0	0	0
Take the A Train	5	G	2	0	0	0	1,170
Take the Bait	6	G	7	0	1	0	2,090
Take the Blame	3	F	11	4	0	2	33,856
Take the City	10	M	6	0	0	0	1,124
Take the Helm	2	G	4	1	2	0	10,745
Take the Jolt	4	G	7	1	0	0	6,050
Take the Lady Out	7	M	3	0	0	0	514
Take the Plunge	3	G	6	0	1	2	27,453
Take the Prize	4	G	15	2	2	2	36,480
Take the Rate	3	F	8	1	2	1	50,207
Take the Ride	2	G	2	0	0	0	170
Take the Ship	3	F	12	1	0	4	11,240
Take the Shot	2	C	5	0	1	0	2,370
Take the Stage	5	M	9	0	0	0	2,185
Take This	5	G	6	2	0	1	6,926
Take Three	7	M	15	3	3	2	31,845
Take Two	7	H	13	1	1	0	2,170
Take Your Pick	2	C	4	1	0	0	6,810
Takea Letter Maria	3	F	7	2	0	3	10,910
Takealetter	5	M	10	0	0	2	3,553
Takealookatmenow	4	F	5	0	0	1	2,483
Takeh	3	C	9	0	1	0	13,529
Takeherturn	3	F	2	0	0	0	164
Takeit Or Leave It	4	G	16	2	0	4	14,548
Takeiteasyedye	6	M	11	3	2	1	100,257
Takelit	8	G	1	0	0	0	50
Takem	5	G	3	0	0	0	237
Takem and Leavem	4	F	1	0	0	0	168
Takemebacktotexas	4	G	7	2	1	1	25,258
Takemetofunkytown	5	M	4	0	0	0	766
Taken Back	5	M	6	1	1	1	1,810
Takenitallin	5	G	6	0	0	0	551
Takeonefortheteam	4	C	15	1	5	0	8,447
Takes a Buddy	4	C	8	2	2	1	12,265
Takes the Glory	2	G	3	0	0	0	460
Takethatwithyou	5	G	9	0	0	1	2,162
Takethefifth	3	G	10	1	1	1	10,823
Takethemoneyandrun	5	M	1	0	0	0	230
Takethemoneyhoney	3	F	16	1	2	1	10,652
Takeyourbestshot	4	G	5	0	0	1	1,680
Takin Aim	3	G	1	0	0	0	0
Takin Issue	2	C	5	1	0	3	18,662
Takin the Stage	4	F	5	2	0	1	10,078
Takin' Up Space	4	G	16	0	1	1	1,550
Takincare Ofbiz	3	G	12	1	5	0	27,501
Taking the Edge	3	F	2	0	0	0	0
Taking the Redeye	3	G	7	2	0	0	56,087
Takkat	3	F	6	1	0	1	20,200
Takki Tsunami	3	C	5	0	0	0	665
Takova	2	F	2	1	0	0	7,170
Takstar River	3	G	4	0	0	1	9,690
Talamascra	2	G	2	0	0	0	0
Talara	4	G	12	4	1	4	25,990
Talaris	3	C	10	2	4	1	79,780
Talavera Gal	3	F	6	0	2	0	7,000
Talavesa	4	F	10	1	2	1	5,234
Talbot County	3	G	4	1	1	1	11,580
Talc Boy	2	C	2	0	0	0	1,000
Talc of Dreams	12	G	19	0	1	2	3,212
Talc Powder	2	F	1	0	0	0	300
Talc's Quick Cat	4	F	18	1	2	3	10,573
Talculation	5	M	4	0	0	0	282
Tale of a Dream	4	F	7	1	1	0	67,630
Tale of Approval	2	C	4	0	0	1	3,150
Tale of the Hills	2	C	1	0	0	0	400
Tale of Woe	3	G	7	2	0	1	56,722
Tale Teller	9	H	3	0	0	0	1,400
Talega Creek	2	C	7	0	1	1	15,120
Talega de Oro	3	F	11	2	2	3	39,740
Talent King	3	G	8	1	3	1	43,760
Talented Prince	2	G	8	4	1	0	45,480
Talented Slew	3	G	1	0	0	0	780
Talented Star	3	F	3	0	0	0	0
Taleofdistinction	4	C	2	0	0	0	215
Taleofthewampuscat	3	G	13	3	2	2	63,550
Taleofthreeralphs	3	G	2	0	0	0	0
Tales of Glory	3	C	10	3	3	3	145,150
Tales of Magic	3	F	11	4	2	0	22,278
Tales to Tell	3	F	4	1	0	0	13,100
Tales Twice Told	4	F	6	0	0	0	1,860
Talespin	6	M	8	0	0	2	9,506
Taleur	6	M	3	2	0	0	28,200
Taliano	4	G	10	0	1	4	12,340
Talia's Choice	2	C	4	0	0	2	6,090
Talk About Fast	3	F	8	0	0	0	1,271
Talk About Luck	3	G	7	0	1	1	4,488
Talk Me Again (ARG)	6	M	5	0	0	1	9,920
Talk of the Block	3	C	11	1	1	1	23,412
Talk Sharply	5	G	12	0	2	0	3,879
Talk Show Tony	3	G	10	0	0	4	23,629
Talk That Talk	4	G	9	4	1	0	30,156
Talk the Walk	3	C	5	2	1	0	47,300
Talk to Cathy	5	M	11	2	3	1	9,379
Talk to Chrissy	5	M	13	3	4	1	28,406
Talk to Me	3	F	5	0	1	0	3,570
Talk to Me Baby	3	F	7	4	0	0	39,692
Talk to Me Jimmy	7	G	1	0	0	0	0
Talk Too	5	M	2	0	1	0	1,173
Talka Lotta Bull	7	G	7	2	0	1	10,350
Talkalot Amy	3	F	3	0	0	0	0
Talkin Desire	3	F	4	0	0	0	0
Talkin Fool	2	F	4	0	0	0	300
Talkin George	5	G	4	2	0	0	10,080
Talkin Money	4	F	6	1	0	1	22,080
Talkin Saratoga	5	M	3	0	0	0	300
Talkin the Talk	3	F	8	1	1	1	13,366
Talkin to an Angel	6	M	6	1	0	1	7,980
Talkin Tough	3	C	13	1	4	3	47,824
Talkin'american	3	F	12	0	0	0	960
Talking Bear	3	G	10	0	2	4	17,740
Talking Leaves	5	G	1	0	0	0	110
Talking Point	6	M	3	0	0	0	0
Talking Red	6	H	11	1	3	2	18,137
Talking Rosie	3	F	7	0	1	1	2,980
Talking to John	2	G	3	0	1	1	9,620
Talkingaboutmygirl	8	M	1	0	0	1	400
Talkmeister	8	G	6	1	1	1	8,960
Talk'n Angel	5	M	6	0	1	0	1,950
Talknoevil	3	G	15	1	6	1	34,350
Talk's Cheap	8	H	1	0	0	1	730
Tall American	8	G	6	0	0	0	695
Tall and Cool One	2	G	5	0	0	2	3,685
Tall Boy	4	G	10	1	0	1	3,600
Tall Cool One	3	G	11	1	3	0	31,600
Tall Honor	3	F	7	0	0	1	4,335
Tall in Seattle	4	F	3	0	0	0	1,140
Tall Order	4	G	4	0	0	0	576
Tall Pines	2	F	5	1	1	1	10,678
Tall Walkin Cat	3	F	11	3	1	1	21,868
Talladega Dust	3	G	14	0	1	1	2,291
Talladega Sweep	3	G	4	0	1	0	8,780
Tallahaxie Blue	5	M	10	1	0	1	2,295
Tallboys Tavern	2	C	7	0	1	1	8,740
Tallchief	4	C	4	1	1	0	4,150
Tallchief Cove	6	G	8	0	0	0	809
Tallest Timber	6	H	3	1	0	0	1,537
Tallielane	4	F	4	2	0	1	1,709
Tallow	8	G	5	2	1	0	50,400
Tallow Creek	4	C	2	0	0	0	95
Tally Belle	5	M	15	0	1	1	7,351
Tally Ho Dixie	2	F	2	0	0	0	0
Tally Slew	4	F	11	1	0	1	14,697
Tally Waki	3	G	4	0	0	2	1,720
Taloberto	3	G	8	1	3	1	19,878
Talon's Lark	6	G	2	0	0	0	505
Taltech	7	G	4	0	1	1	4,178
Talullah Mae	5	M	10	2	0	2	30,175
Tam I Am	4	F	5	0	2	0	3,900
Tam Win Tam	7	G	1	0	0	0	0
Tama	5	G	13	0	1	3	5,510
Tamaakajo	3	G	15	1	1	4	13,343
Tamahka Princess	4	F	6	0	0	0	0
Tamara	4	F	10	1	1	1	77,296
Tamara Star	2	F	2	0	0	0	800

Horse	Age	Sex	Sts	1st	2d	3d	Won
Tamarack Bay	5	M	9	1	2	2	58,460
Tamarack Creek	4	F	13	2	2	4	10,994
Tamarack Hills	5	G	10	1	1	0	15,650
Tamaram	5	G	2	0	0	0	280
Tamara's Babe	7	M	10	3	5	0	37,176
Tamaras Trend	8	M	12	1	0	2	6,434
Tamatia	5	G	12	1	0	0	7,075
Tamayo	5	M	1	0	0	0	0
Tamayrose	5	M	9	2	0	2	26,980
Tamazay	3	F	1	0	0	0	0
Tambo	3	G	10	1	0	1	12,832
Tambos Jazz Dancer	3	F	2	0	0	0	0
Tambos Sword Dance	3	F	1	0	0	0	0
Tambourine Dancer	5	M	10	2	1	4	10,318
Tamburello	4	G	2	0	0	0	1,504
Tamburello (CHI)	5	G	7	1	1	1	75,370
Tame	4	C	1	0	0	0	140
Tamerice	7	H	2	0	0	0	187
Tamerlane Sham	4	G	4	0	0	0	720
Tami Be Good	5	M	1	0	0	0	0
Taming the Tiger	2	C	1	0	0	1	2,160
Tamingo	3	G	6	2	1	1	43,823
Tamisa	3	F	9	2	3	0	39,800
Tammie's Turn	2	F	1	0	0	0	0
Tammy O	3	F	7	1	1	0	7,101
Tammy Star	5	M	8	3	2	1	11,028
Tammy's Carousel	4	F	4	2	0	2	8,110
Tammy's Surprise	4	F	5	0	0	0	246
Tammy's Tango	3	F	5	0	0	0	399
Tamono	3	F	7	1	2	0	15,960
Tamorons Blade	5	M	11	1	0	3	30,486
Tampa	6	H	1	0	0	0	0
Tampa's Big City	2	C	4	0	1	1	15,450
Tamper	4	G	7	3	1	1	33,075
Tam's Angel	4	F	2	0	0	0	402
Tam's Ice	11	G	1	0	0	0	0
Tam's Nitemare	7	G	11	3	1	5	13,850
Tam's Terms	6	G	7	2	1	1	113,950
Tam's Tune	4	G	9	4	2	2	54,000
Tamsin Tiger	4	C	2	0	0	0	82
Tamul (ARG)	6	G	9	0	1	0	2,739
Tamusky	5	H	13	0	0	1	1,979
Tamweel	4	F	10	3	3	1	348,240
Tamys Prospect	2	F	2	0	0	0	0
Tan Campante (ARG)	5	M	3	0	0	0	894
Tan Czar	8	G	21	1	0	1	4,427
Tan Stack	6	G	2	0	0	0	93
Tanaja	3	F	12	2	0	2	12,705
Tanallover	6	M	1	0	0	0	171
Tananda	9	M	6	0	0	0	1,081
Tanannie	3	F	10	0	1	2	4,425
Tandy Lakes	3	C	13	0	4	3	22,910
Tangara (NZ)	7	M	3	0	0	0	0
Tangarae Tango	6	G	5	0	0	0	780
Tangent	5	M	4	0	0	0	120
Tangerine	5	M	9	0	2	1	19,106
Tangier Sound	5	M	5	1	1	0	64,790
Tangle (IRE)	4	F	7	2	1	3	218,669
Tangled Creek	4	F	14	3	1	1	12,570
Tangled Heart	3	F	5	1	0	0	29,291
Tangled Mind	4	F	8	0	0	0	763
Tangled State	2	G	1	0	0	0	0
Tangled Up In Blue (IRE)	4	C	8	1	0	1	22,000
Tanglewood	2	G	6	1	0	2	7,905
Tanglin Road	6	G	2	0	0	0	125
Tangmalangaloo	3	G	10	2	1	1	40,520
Tango Fever	3	C	9	2	1	1	24,590
Tango for Tips	3	F	6	1	0	2	32,565
Tango Man	3	G	8	0	0	0	216
Tango Tales	3	C	5	1	2	1	44,490
Tango With Me	3	C	2	0	0	0	0
Tani Maru	2	C	6	2	1	2	72,924
Tanja's Cat	5	G	18	3	3	2	28,609
Tank Appeal	2	G	3	0	0	1	4,692
Tank Force	3	C	5	0	0	2	3,795
Tank Grrrl	6	M	5	0	1	0	3,732
Tank Two	7	H	5	1	2	1	9,752
Tankit Or Leaveit	4	G	11	0	3	3	7,613
Tankman	3	C	4	1	0	0	4,943
Tanks a Lot	2	F	2	0	0	0	1,840
Tank's Expectation	5	G	11	1	1	0	48,518
Tank's Lil Brother	5	G	12	1	1	3	25,174
Tank's Town	5	G	4	2	1	0	16,040
Tanksforthedance	2	C	1	0	1	0	3,360
Tanktown Drifter	5	H	7	0	0	1	2,640
Tanky Boy	6	G	2	0	1	0	6,600
Tanner Boy	5	G	4	0	0	0	1,100
Tanner Danner	3	G	16	3	4	4	69,695
Tanner Fire	6	G	9	1	3	1	3,189
Tanner Jon	6	H	9	0	1	1	1,293
Tanner Sea	5	M	2	0	0	0	510
Tanner Terrific	3	G	11	3	1	2	70,246
Tanner's Beach	2	G	4	0	0	0	894
Tanners Bullseye	4	G	10	1	0	1	6,538
Tanner's Isle	7	M	6	0	0	0	486
Tanoan	5	G	1	0	0	0	0
Tanqueray (CHI)	6	G	10	3	2	1	29,470
Tantallon	3	F	1	0	0	0	340
Tantivy	4	F	8	1	1	4	4,415
Tantoo	8	M	10	3	2	1	50,827
Tanwi Spring	6	M	8	2	2	1	62,776
Tanya's Beau	2	C	4	2	0	0	8,140
Tanya's Song	4	F	16	1	4	1	17,708
Tanyaswindycaller	5	G	11	2	2	2	9,218
Tanzanite Lady	3	F	5	0	0	0	3,528
Tanzer	4	C	7	1	2	0	10,698
Taoiseach	5	G	4	1	1	0	6,640
Taormina	6	G	11	1	3	2	21,610
Taos Gold	3	G	3	0	0	1	6,140
Tap an Sparks	4	F	11	1	2	2	6,757
Tap City Eddie	3	C	8	1	0	1	21,616
Tap Dancer	3	G	6	0	1	0	18,052
Tap Dancing Mauk	3	C	11	0	2	0	23,560
Tap Day	3	C	9	5	1	0	169,980
Tap Fab	2	G	3	0	0	0	0
Tap Into Fame	3	F	7	1	0	2	15,250
Tap It Out	3	G	17	2	2	0	14,219
Tap Kid	6	M	13	0	2	0	2,339
Tap Machine	4	F	14	1	1	1	10,308
Tap N Go	3	C	3	0	0	0	178
Tap N Jazz	2	C	2	0	0	0	410
Tap N Rack	4	G	2	0	0	1	6,280
Tap Tap	4	G	10	3	0	1	29,715
Tap the Keg	4	G	3	0	0	0	490
Tap the Magic	3	F	4	0	0	0	1,727
Tap the Rockies	6	H	2	0	0	0	74
Tap the Sky	5	M	9	3	0	1	9,307
Tap to Talk	3	F	14	1	1	1	13,200
Tap Trick	4	C	13	0	0	1	2,788
Tap Twice	6	G	14	3	1	3	22,745
Tap West	4	G	5	0	0	0	123
Tap Wood	4	G	10	1	0	0	6,766
Tap Zappa	3	C	13	2	2	1	31,580
Tapalong	2	C	1	0	0	0	1,025
Tapancourt	2	G	1	0	0	0	300
Tapantears	3	G	10	0	2	3	11,997
Tapas	4	F	2	0	0	0	150
Tapatina	3	F	3	0	0	0	1,990
Tapatio	3	F	1	0	0	0	0
Tapaway	5	G	2	0	0	0	225
Tapdancinblues	3	F	1	0	0	0	100
Tapio (IRE)	3	C	5	1	1	1	33,820
Tapit	3	C	4	1	0	0	477,500
Tap'n Tango	3	F	8	0	4	0	38,445
Tapnmachine	3	F	2	0	0	0	0
Tappedinto	3	F	10	0	2	0	9,920
Tapper	6	M	3	0	0	0	540
Tapper Time	2	F	2	0	0	1	1,145
Tappin E Z	2	C	1	0	0	0	62
Tappin for Gold	2	F	1	0	0	0	1,155
Tappin' Tasha	3	F	1	0	0	0	840
Tapping Tilly	10	M	1	0	0	0	0
Tapp's Fast Lass	3	F	2	0	0	0	0
Tappy	5	M	7	1	2	1	31,520
Taps for Liberty	2	F	1	0	0	0	2,340
Taps Return	3	F	2	0	2	0	5,600
Tapsomegoldfordan	2	C	2	0	1	0	4,140
Tapster	4	G	4	0	0	0	423

Horse	Age	Sex	Sts	1st	2d	3d	Won
Tapstone	5	G	4	0	0	0	488
Tapthewind	3	G	3	0	0	0	0
Taptonite	4	G	16	0	3	2	15,630
Taqarob	9	G	5	1	2	0	3,048
Taquan	2	G	4	0	0	1	3,370
Taquito	3	G	3	0	0	0	800
Tar Hill	4	C	3	0	0	0	0
Tar Pit	8	G	10	0	1	1	2,136
Tar River	2	C	4	0	0	0	1,182
Tara Jean	5	M	12	3	1	1	30,390
Tara On the Wire	4	F	12	0	0	1	2,634
Tara Two	5	M	1	0	0	1	1,050
Taradashi	4	F	3	0	1	1	3,605
Taraf	5	H	3	0	0	1	1,275
Tarakan	5	G	7	1	1	1	29,765
Taramot	6	G	4	0	0	0	0
Taramundi (UAE)	2	F	2	0	0	0	312
Taran T.	5	M	4	0	0	1	1,311
Taranaki	2	F	2	0	1	0	11,400
Tarantula Springs	4	C	13	1	1	1	7,586
Taras Foxy Lady	5	M	7	0	0	1	1,014
Tara's Harp	7	G	1	0	0	0	0
Tara's Royalty	6	M	5	0	0	0	0
Tarascon Diligence	3	C	9	3	2	0	30,850
Tarasina	4	F	4	1	1	1	12,453
Tarek	6	H	14	2	4	3	88,244
Tarfu	3	G	7	1	0	2	10,870
Targestina	3	F	5	0	0	1	3,400
Target Miss	3	F	7	0	1	3	6,306
Target Shoot	4	G	7	2	1	2	100,888
Target Stripes	4	G	2	0	0	0	280
Target West	6	H	12	1	2	5	16,736
Targetofoportunity	3	C	2	0	0	0	2,580
Target's Answer	3	F	9	0	2	0	5,051
Targets Gold	6	G	10	1	0	3	4,794
Targets Mark	3	G	1	0	0	0	0
Tarkio	4	G	4	0	0	0	410
Tarkovsky	4	G	2	1	0	0	32,300
Tarlow	3	F	4	1	2	0	42,340
Tarnish	3	F	3	0	0	1	1,485
Tarnished Sterling	3	C	8	1	1	0	7,829
Taro Tigress	2	F	2	0	0	0	450
Tarquin	2	G	3	0	0	0	1,344
Tarragona	3	F	5	1	1	0	15,465
Tarrah Trick	3	F	6	2	0	1	30,095
Tarrango	4	C	6	0	1	3	9,516
Tarratine	8	G	3	0	0	0	575
Tartan Tutu	5	M	16	1	2	5	7,404
Taryn	2	F	3	0	0	0	1,060
Taryn's Belief	3	F	14	5	1	0	46,344
Tarzan Cry (IRE)	6	H	12	2	1	0	23,723
Tas Force	2	F	3	0	0	3	5,700
Tasca	4	F	7	0	1	1	4,518
Tash Dash	3	F	1	0	0	0	320
Tasha Sangue	4	F	5	1	0	0	22,960
Tasha's Emblem	2	F	2	0	0	0	220
Tashdeed	2	C	1	0	0	0	137
Tashsawi Promise	2	F	3	0	0	0	405
Tasman Glacier	8	H	2	0	0	0	43
Tasmania Miss	4	F	13	1	1	0	11,421
Tasmanian Possum	3	G	13	1	2	0	5,993
Tasseling	2	F	3	1	0	0	7,920
Tasso Run	5	M	6	0	1	0	10,090
Tassosflash	4	G	4	0	0	0	300
Taste of Hadif	5	M	13	3	2	3	26,833
Taste of Paradise	5	H	8	2	0	1	134,095
Taste Sweet	4	F	6	0	0	1	2,040
Tasteoffreedom	2	F	7	0	0	0	362
Tasting Champagne	3	G	10	2	2	0	48,456
Tasty Caberneigh	6	G	8	0	0	1	8,720
Tasty Chardoneigh	5	H	8	0	0	2	2,035
Taswatha	4	F	3	0	0	0	595
Tata Pantoja	5	H	5	1	1	0	6,143
Tate Express	12	G	3	0	0	0	143
Tate J	5	G	16	1	0	0	3,538
Tate Man	6	G	13	2	2	3	6,023
Tater Bug	8	G	5	0	0	1	535
Tater Head	3	G	8	2	0	2	11,035
Tater Tate	7	G	2	1	0	0	700
Tates Time	3	F	1	0	0	0	0
Tate's Way	6	G	16	1	1	6	12,816
Tatiana	2	F	5	0	0	0	425
Tatiana B.	4	F	3	0	0	0	630
Tatie Dancer	4	F	5	1	0	1	10,290
Tatooma	2	F	1	1	0	0	24,600
Tattel Tale	5	M	11	0	3	1	1,242
Tattletail Charlie	4	G	18	3	1	2	16,192
Tattletale Tonya	2	F	1	0	0	0	400
Tattotail	4	G	2	0	0	0	265
Tatum Springs	3	C	5	0	0	0	1,317
Tatums Doll	6	M	5	0	0	1	880
Tauke	6	G	4	0	2	0	2,484
Taum Sauk Mountain	6	G	4	2	0	0	13,682
Taurus Gift	4	F	13	2	5	1	19,400
Tavacat	4	G	5	0	0	0	1,185
Tavern On Rush	3	F	7	2	1	1	35,975
Tavern Time	4	G	7	1	0	0	5,912
Tavo	3	G	7	1	0	2	10,503
Tavolino	6	G	3	0	0	1	1,747
Tawney Port	4	F	9	1	1	1	7,111
Tawny Rose	3	F	2	0	0	0	0
Tax	2	F	3	1	0	0	13,800
Tax Considerations	2	F	4	1	0	0	23,451
Tax Deferred	5	G	15	4	1	2	62,462
Tax Evader	3	G	2	0	0	0	1,398
Tax Exempt	3	C	5	0	2	0	10,718
Tax Refund	2	F	1	0	0	0	0
Tax Relief	9	M	4	0	0	0	0
Tax the Queen	3	F	8	3	0	2	89,456
Tax Write Off	4	G	14	1	3	0	4,400
Taxagram	2	F	3	0	0	1	7,560
Taxauditor	6	H	2	0	0	0	229
Taxed Out	4	G	11	1	0	0	4,948
Taxi Lady	4	F	1	0	0	0	182
Taxicat	4	C	12	2	0	3	51,080
Taxing Devil	6	G	8	2	1	1	3,385
Tay Laur	6	M	3	0	1	0	3,020
Tayazi	3	F	5	2	0	1	17,445
Taybe	3	F	4	1	0	1	9,128
Taygete	3	F	7	2	0	1	68,040
Tayla	3	F	1	0	0	0	95
Taylor Creek	9	M	6	0	0	3	918
Taylor D	2	F	3	0	0	1	2,040
Taylor Field	4	G	12	0	1	3	2,487
Taylor J	4	F	11	2	0	3	37,395
Taylor James	7	G	2	0	1	0	900
Taylor Maid	3	F	5	2	1	0	22,660
Taylor Man	4	G	15	1	1	4	7,540
Taylor Ridge	3	G	9	1	1	2	7,524
Taylor Ruckus	3	F	5	0	2	0	3,644
Taylor's a Trip	4	F	7	3	1	2	10,048
Taylor's Blues	4	F	1	0	0	0	273
Taylor's Brook	3	F	9	0	0	1	2,385
Taylor's Chief	3	F	10	0	2	2	7,255
Taylor's Choice	5	M	3	1	0	1	12,184
Taylor's Comedy	6	G	1	0	0	0	0
Taylor's Day	10	G	11	2	3	1	29,890
Taylor's First	2	C	3	0	0	0	0
Taylors Myth	3	F	10	0	1	1	5,173
Taylor's Niner	2	G	4	0	2	0	8,615
Taylor's Queen	5	M	4	1	2	0	26,090
Taylor's Series	3	F	11	1	3	2	31,520
Taylor's Spring	4	F	6	1	0	0	4,905
Taylor's Ticket	5	G	7	0	2	0	1,840
Taylor's Way	4	F	5	0	1	0	12,415
Taylor's Wish	2	F	1	0	0	0	2,150
Taylor's Zag	4	F	9	2	1	1	23,302
Taymadalex	4	F	11	2	5	1	18,454
Tayo's Tiger	2	C	5	1	0	1	2,515
Tayshauna Princess	3	F	1	0	1	0	2,000
Tazer	3	F	1	0	0	0	0
Tazi	3	F	14	4	2	2	26,050
Taziano	2	C	1	0	0	0	42
Tazotee	5	M	6	0	2	1	25,370
Taz's Treasure	10	G	2	1	1	0	3,525
Tazzy Oka	3	F	8	0	0	0	492
Tchefuncte	4	G	16	0	0	1	2,685
Tchepone	5	G	2	0	0	0	0

Horse	Age	Sex	Sts	1st	2d	3d	Won
Tchotchke	5	M	13	1	0	1	5,372
Tchula Miss	5	M	5	1	1	0	41,960
Tcs Express Prince	6	G	14	1	1	0	8,112
Tc's Priceless	3	G	12	1	2	0	8,414
Te Cuira Mucho	3	F	4	2	0	1	54,492
Te Jay Tejabo	5	H	13	0	3	1	13,730
Te Quiero Champ (ARG)	7	G	8	3	1	1	27,150
Te Quiero Manana	4	F	4	1	0	0	8,039
Te Veo Y Te Amo	2	C	4	0	0	0	810
Tea Basket	5	M	16	2	2	3	11,582
Tea Dancing	3	F	6	1	0	0	7,155
Tea Is Served	3	F	3	0	0	0	0
Tea Lady	4	F	5	0	0	0	3,340
Tea N Toddy	7	M	2	0	1	0	1,700
Tea Sipper	6	M	5	0	0	1	1,813
Tea Ta Pea	3	F	7	0	1	1	1,654
Tea Time Tomorrow	3	F	10	1	2	2	16,820
Tea With Bahri	3	C	2	0	0	0	0
Teachem Kelli	3	F	11	1	0	1	4,185
Teachers Nightmare	4	F	7	2	0	1	6,471
Teachers Tornado	2	F	1	0	0	0	0
Teach's Pet	3	F	1	0	0	0	0
Teagues Griz	3	C	2	0	0	0	0
Teak Totem	4	F	5	1	0	1	65,100
Teakable	3	G	8	0	0	1	1,496
Team Blue	3	F	11	1	0	1	6,677
Team Charisma	2	F	2	0	0	0	800
Team Decision	3	F	6	2	0	3	31,652
Team Player	6	G	4	0	0	0	6,070
Team Webster	5	M	4	0	0	0	0
Team Zachary	5	H	6	0	0	0	3,327
Teamup	3	C	6	0	1	0	3,540
Tease n' Delete	4	F	4	3	0	1	5,620
Tease Tish	5	M	2	0	0	0	200
Teasing Arlena	5	M	19	3	3	2	23,846
Teaspoon	3	G	1	0	0	0	0
Teazabull	4	F	10	3	1	1	13,535
Tebeloved Prospect	3	F	4	0	0	1	1,363
Tech Two	7	G	5	0	0	2	4,838
Teche Cowboy	3	G	6	1	0	1	19,688
Technical Analysis	3	F	3	1	1	0	41,055
Technical Marie	4	F	2	0	0	0	255
Technical Question	7	M	12	0	2	0	4,430
Technickle	4	G	16	1	4	2	19,903
Techno Baby	7	G	3	0	0	0	157
Technology's Girl	4	F	3	0	0	0	436
Techset	2	C	1	1	0	0	5,160
Teddy B.	3	G	4	0	0	0	610
Teddy Cat	2	F	4	0	0	1	4,731
Teddy Light	7	G	7	1	1	2	5,653
Teddy Papa	6	G	13	1	3	0	18,695
Teddy's Girl	4	F	15	3	1	1	50,830
Teddy's Payton	2	C	6	1	0	1	11,360
Teddy's Pick	6	G	11	0	0	2	3,269
Tedledo	3	G	8	0	0	3	2,517
Tedyuscung	3	G	5	0	0	0	351
Tee Bird	3	G	3	0	0	0	214
Tee Cat	6	G	3	0	0	0	1,811
Tee Cubed	3	F	3	0	0	1	8,040
Tee El	3	C	4	0	0	0	1,848
Tee Hunter	3	G	3	0	1	1	5,719
Tee It Up Cookie	3	G	13	2	4	1	29,604
Tee Lease	4	F	10	0	1	2	7,044
Tee N Herbs	3	F	1	0	0	0	0
Tee Off	3	F	5	0	0	0	900
Tee Off Time	4	F	13	0	1	2	14,389
Tee Pee Tomahawk	3	F	6	2	3	0	50,500
Tee Phone Home	3	G	5	0	2	0	5,490
Tee Punch	4	F	9	0	1	4	6,598
Tee Times Two	3	F	5	1	0	0	8,425
Tee to Green	4	G	11	2	2	3	21,836
Tee Toe El Coyote	3	F	13	1	2	2	25,012
Tee Tommy Slew	7	G	2	0	1	0	870
Tee Wee	4	F	14	1	2	0	12,555
Tee Wee's Cat	3	F	7	0	0	1	1,155
Teed Off	8	H	1	0	0	0	0
Teeintheroad	2	F	3	0	0	0	560
Teen Dancer	4	F	2	0	0	1	1,310
Teenage Temper	3	F	8	2	0	1	62,975
Teeney Bubbles	3	F	7	2	1	2	16,490
Teen's Rachael	5	M	1	0	0	0	0
Teepee Creeper	4	C	17	0	3	2	15,436
Teequa	4	F	16	3	1	0	16,890
Teerific Tee	2	F	2	1	0	0	9,900
Tee's Image	4	F	6	2	0	1	6,822
Tee's Lil Dancer	4	F	15	1	2	2	17,185
Tee's Pearl	3	F	5	2	2	0	76,200
Tee's Tempter	3	G	11	1	1	1	6,776
Teet Jr.	4	G	11	3	2	1	21,294
Teetau Marie	3	F	9	3	1	0	15,286
Teewee's Hope	4	F	4	0	0	0	3,936
Teflon Pattie T.	3	F	1	0	0	0	3,528
Tef's Bashful	4	F	2	0	0	0	321
Tef's Fair Lady	2	F	1	0	0	0	524
Tef's Scarlett	4	F	4	1	0	0	9,256
Tehema	4	F	7	0	0	0	1,979
Tejabelle	6	M	9	2	1	2	13,771
Tejabo Blues	5	G	8	1	2	1	31,376
Tejabo's Girl	8	M	3	0	0	0	120
Tejan	7	G	12	1	0	4	17,262
Tejano Baby	2	F	2	0	0	0	310
Tejano Chief	2	C	3	0	0	0	240
Tejano Couture	10	H	6	1	0	0	7,500
Tejano Dandy	3	C	7	1	0	2	12,905
Tejano Gal	4	F	2	0	0	0	361
Tejano Heath	2	G	2	0	0	0	0
Tejano Jr.	3	G	5	1	1	3	8,960
Tejano Ruler	8	G	11	3	0	4	19,105
Tejano Slew	4	G	3	0	0	0	0
Tejano the Beauty	3	G	9	0	1	1	5,968
Tejano Tom	3	G	10	1	1	2	7,139
Tejano Who	4	G	14	0	7	2	14,287
Tejano's Echo	5	M	1	1	0	0	5,100
Tejano's Legacy	3	F	5	0	0	0	0
Tejano's Sands	3	F	3	0	0	0	0
Tejano's Son	5	G	10	0	1	1	6,333
Tejas	4	C	5	1	1	0	9,819
Tejas Lady	3	F	10	0	0	0	840
Tejati	4	F	16	1	3	4	36,542
Tekki	3	G	11	2	1	1	21,191
Telefonista	4	F	2	1	0	0	4,920
Telefriend	2	F	2	0	2	0	6,000
Telegraph	8	H	4	1	0	0	6,970
Telegraph Road	6	M	11	1	3	1	23,740
Telegraph Trail	4	F	2	0	0	0	0
Telemark	5	G	15	3	0	3	28,571
Telemundo	4	C	5	1	0	2	7,595
Telephone Talker	4	C	13	1	1	2	8,516
Teleplay	5	G	5	0	0	0	345
Telepsychic	3	F	6	1	2	0	16,257
Televangelist	4	G	12	3	3	1	66,580
Tell a Calm	8	G	10	0	0	1	1,986
Tell a Type	3	C	3	0	0	1	1,684
Tell All	3	F	10	1	1	1	7,513
Tell J	5	G	9	0	1	1	3,689
Tell Laura	5	M	14	2	3	3	31,160
Tell Me Dear	3	F	3	1	0	0	5,385
Tell Me I'm Pritt	4	F	14	2	2	3	42,770
Tell Me Jason	3	G	5	0	0	0	120
Tell Me More	4	F	9	1	0	0	4,166
Tell Me More Angel	3	F	3	0	0	0	335
Tell Me Mr G	4	G	19	4	3	3	46,518
Tell Me Sweetly	5	M	13	1	2	1	9,155
Tell Me Two Times	3	F	5	0	0	0	240
Tell No One	3	F	2	0	0	1	4,440
Tell No Secrets	4	F	10	0	2	1	6,550
Tell No Tales	4	F	13	3	2	2	89,390
Tell Slick	3	G	9	1	1	2	5,913
Tell Tale	3	F	2	0	0	0	0
Tell Them Nothing	5	G	1	0	0	0	0
Tell You the Same	5	M	3	0	0	0	189
Tella Lion Tale	5	G	10	1	0	1	4,555
Tella Soldier	3	C	2	0	0	0	205
Tellek	4	G	12	2	2	1	23,835
Teller Belle	2	F	5	0	0	0	1,110
Teller Line	5	M	13	5	4	2	110,957
Tellheelikeitis	5	M	12	1	1	8	23,811
Telli Mae Win	4	F	1	0	0	0	65

Horse	Age	Sex	Sts	1st	2d	3d	Won
Telling Note	4	F	6	0	0	1	832
Tellmeimyours	3	F	7	1	1	3	2,340
Tellmeitsnotso	2	G	9	1	1	2	24,620
Tellmesecrets	2	G	1	0	0	0	600
Telly	2	F	2	0	0	0	0
Telsi	6	M	11	0	1	1	994
Temecula Wind	3	G	1	0	0	0	0
Temeritas (IRE)	4	G	11	2	3	3	29,630
Temis (CHI)	8	M	4	0	1	0	5,484
Temper Time	2	F	2	0	0	0	3,420
Temperamental Rose	4	F	3	0	0	0	480
Temperance Eagle	7	G	5	0	0	0	360
Temperance Lake	4	F	5	1	2	1	73,820
Temperant Lady	8	M	1	0	0	0	0
Temperature	2	C	1	0	0	0	400
Tempered Appeal	7	H	9	1	2	1	40,084
Tempered Steel	4	G	7	2	2	1	105,289
Temperence Night	11	G	2	0	0	0	2,500
Temperence Time	8	G	5	0	0	0	0
Tempers Rising	4	G	8	4	2	0	33,174
Tempest	3	F	1	0	0	0	0
Tempest (GB)	6	H	6	0	0	2	12,780
Tempest Gladiator	5	M	7	0	2	0	4,257
Tempest Run	4	G	1	0	0	0	74
Tempestry	3	G	10	3	0	0	29,795
Tempestuous Lady	3	F	1	0	0	0	106
Tempestuous Wind	5	H	1	0	0	0	82
Templar	5	G	3	0	0	0	602
Templar Knight	6	G	4	0	0	0	3,000
Templar Park	7	G	5	0	0	1	768
Temple Owl	9	H	3	0	0	1	2,100
Tempo Up T C	4	G	12	1	4	1	8,954
Temporary Zone	2	C	7	2	2	1	45,400
Temps Ghostly Star	3	C	5	0	0	0	774
Tempt Her	4	F	5	0	0	0	1,704
Temptable	3	F	13	3	2	1	18,971
Temptation Bound	8	G	1	0	0	0	0
Temptation Eyes	2	G	5	1	0	0	5,200
Temptation Lady	3	F	6	0	1	0	1,685
Temptatious	4	F	4	1	1	1	9,721
Tempted Spirit	2	G	1	0	0	0	0
Temptest	6	M	6	0	0	1	3,320
Tempting a Ruckus	5	G	11	1	2	1	5,361
Tempting Chance	4	G	13	2	0	1	12,047
Tempting Choice	5	M	13	3	2	3	47,550
Tempting Force	3	G	3	0	0	0	0
Tempting Heart	4	F	4	1	0	2	4,133
Tempting Note	3	F	4	0	3	0	37,865
Temptinglittlemiss	5	M	4	0	1	1	1,520
Temptor Cielo	4	F	12	4	1	2	19,621
Temptor Man	3	G	3	0	1	0	4,700
Temptors Alibi	3	G	16	2	3	2	20,481
Temptor's Darlin	4	F	5	0	0	1	626
Temptors Pearl	3	F	7	0	2	0	2,585
Temptors Prodigy	5	G	3	0	0	0	300
Temptors Prospect	3	C	10	1	0	3	18,116
Temptors Temper	4	F	11	0	2	0	4,225
Tempus Fugit	4	F	12	2	2	1	100,641
Temtor's Pride	4	G	11	0	1	3	6,715
Ten Across	4	G	15	4	5	3	25,118
Ten Across Todd	3	C	6	0	0	0	780
Ten Alarm Fire	5	G	1	0	0	1	1,430
Ten Carat Ruby	3	F	9	2	2	2	87,140
Ten Carat Slew	4	F	2	0	0	1	1,733
Ten Cent Dance	3	G	8	1	1	2	5,922
Ten Cents a Shine	4	G	4	2	1	0	60,060
Ten Connections	4	G	3	0	0	0	326
Ten Dreams	5	M	3	0	0	0	0
Ten Forty Easy	4	C	4	2	2	0	30,880
Ten Gallon Bonnet	3	F	7	2	1	0	6,410
Ten Hut	11	G	6	1	0	0	3,192
Ten Inches of Snow	4	C	8	2	0	0	13,920
Ten Kisses	4	F	4	0	0	0	3,260
Ten Mile Girl	5	M	13	2	5	2	11,625
Ten Mitchell	3	C	7	1	1	0	19,418
Ten Most Wanted	4	C	2	1	0	0	165,000
Ten Pound Bay	3	C	6	0	0	1	2,266
Ten Pound Test	8	G	15	2	3	1	30,480
Ten Queens	5	M	10	1	2	2	21,968
Ten Shades of Red	7	H	11	4	1	1	26,229
Ten Sharp	6	G	6	0	0	2	6,720
Ten Something	5	M	20	1	0	3	15,949
Ten Speed	4	F	4	0	0	0	384
Ten Times Better	3	G	9	3	1	2	53,460
Ten Times Nobility	11	H	2	0	0	0	280
Ten Treasures	3	F	10	2	1	1	68,803
Ten Wishes	3	F	8	2	0	1	20,103
Ten Years Gone	3	G	15	0	0	3	3,159
Tenace	3	G	4	0	1	1	15,760
Tenacious Affair	6	G	6	1	3	1	24,876
Tenacious Dee Time	3	F	4	0	2	0	3,000
Tenacious Gal	6	M	7	2	0	0	12,018
Tenacious Tart	4	F	18	3	3	2	29,838
Tenacious Tigress	4	F	6	0	1	0	1,220
Tenacious Tinker	4	C	7	1	0	0	1,098
Tenacious Tish	6	M	7	0	1	0	3,897
Tenafly	6	M	14	2	0	3	10,775
Tenaja Trail	5	G	7	1	0	2	10,180
Tenakee Inlet	2	G	2	0	0	0	460
Tenantry Road	4	F	7	1	0	3	8,625
Tencies Cat	3	G	5	1	2	0	16,920
Tender Duet	7	M	11	0	0	3	20,327
Tender Feelings	6	M	3	0	0	0	0
Tender Flyer	4	G	4	0	0	0	360
Tender Lover	4	G	6	0	0	0	378
Tender Offer (IRE)	7	H	12	9	0	0	24,345
Tender Rosemary	6	M	2	0	0	0	213
Tender Ship	4	G	19	3	4	2	24,478
Tender Tears	3	F	1	0	0	0	0
Tender Teen	4	F	9	2	3	2	74,000
Tender Toes	4	G	12	3	1	3	61,289
Tender Touch	6	M	8	1	0	1	19,295
Tender Trap	4	F	9	2	2	1	42,565
Tender Value	4	G	4	1	0	1	28,960
Tender Warrior	3	C	6	1	1	0	6,780
Tender Years	3	F	5	0	0	1	3,564
Tendollaryo	4	G	14	1	1	2	5,216
Tenerumi	7	G	6	0	1	0	4,120
Tenet	3	F	8	0	0	0	1,728
Tenfortynine	6	G	8	2	3	0	28,278
Tenille	3	F	5	0	0	1	7,148
Tenino	9	G	7	0	3	0	2,297
Teniqa Gold	3	F	7	0	0	1	1,525
Tenkiller	3	F	6	2	0	2	8,379
Tenkiller Tiger	3	G	5	0	0	0	416
Tennesee Burbin	4	G	12	2	0	0	33,493
Tennessee Bid	4	G	5	1	0	0	7,826
Tennessee Smith	3	C	3	0	0	1	5,960
Tennessee Tuxedo	6	G	7	3	0	0	43,499
Tennis C. Storm	3	F	10	2	0	1	13,890
Tenpins	6	H	1	0	1	0	12,000
Tensa Debut	3	F	1	0	0	0	0
Tensas Bodgit	3	F	7	0	3	0	2,909
Tensas Canyon	7	G	14	1	1	2	7,189
Tensas General	3	F	4	0	0	0	1,545
Tensas Joe	6	G	13	0	2	3	8,975
Tensas Star	2	F	2	0	0	1	2,475
Tensas Sweetheart	4	F	1	0	0	0	140
Tensas Teejay	5	M	2	0	0	0	86
Tense Wager	2	F	6	2	2	0	69,590
Tententwotwenty	4	G	13	2	0	3	68,810
Tenth Mountain Man	2	G	2	0	0	0	119
Tenth Street	3	G	7	2	2	1	38,460
Tenthirteen	4	G	7	1	1	2	49,450
Tepee Tot	3	F	3	0	0	1	2,420
Tepexpan	2	C	11	1	4	3	44,930
Tepid Lover	4	F	13	2	5	2	40,681
Teppi Terror	2	F	2	0	0	0	600
Tepu Sultan	5	G	6	0	1	0	6,833
Tequesta	3	C	3	1	0	1	25,250
Tequila Hombre	4	G	12	2	5	0	13,540
Tequila Lana	3	F	8	2	2	0	33,881
Tequila Line	3	F	15	2	1	3	17,795
Tequila Regal	4	G	8	0	0	0	335
Tequila Storm	2	C	1	0	0	0	0
Tequila Sunshine	2	F	1	0	0	0	0
Tequila Toast	6	G	5	0	0	0	300
Tequilacarmenlita	5	M	4	0	1	0	2,070

Horse	Age	Sex	Sts	1st	2d	3d	Won
Tequila's Trick	9	H	3	0	0	0	0
Tequilla Moon	4	G	8	0	1	1	4,503
Tequiza	5	M	15	1	1	0	6,054
Tera Hoya	3	G	1	0	0	0	300
Tera Kitty	8	M	1	0	0	0	0
Teralote	4	G	12	1	3	2	14,511
Teree's Sister	2	F	7	1	1	0	31,495
Teresa Ann	5	M	1	0	0	0	2,475
Teresa Belle	3	F	5	0	0	0	2,110
Teresa's Angel	5	M	4	0	2	1	9,310
Teresa's Doll	3	F	5	0	0	0	2,000
Teresa's Gold	3	G	12	0	0	2	1,710
Teresa's Pride	5	M	4	0	0	0	0
Tergesti	2	C	3	0	0	0	443
Teri Time	3	F	8	2	2	0	4,972
Teric Croy	4	G	6	0	0	0	490
Teri's Wild	3	F	13	1	1	0	10,190
Teriyaki Twist	4	F	21	4	2	2	22,263
Terlago Pete	6	G	3	0	1	2	775
Term in Office	3	C	11	1	2	2	30,128
Term Sheet	6	G	11	1	2	2	60,920
Termagnet	6	H	4	0	0	0	925
Terminal	5	G	6	1	0	1	5,153
Terminal Moraine	3	F	1	0	0	0	510
Terminar	3	G	9	1	0	1	2,721
Termination	4	G	2	1	0	0	5,800
Termination Dust	5	H	10	1	2	4	23,020
Terminkator	4	F	12	2	2	3	24,110
Term's Love	4	F	7	4	2	0	28,970
Terms of Glory	3	C	2	0	0	0	220
Tern Cool	3	G	4	0	0	0	770
Ternespowertakeoff	5	G	3	0	0	0	125
Terpsichore	4	F	8	0	2	2	20,960
Terra Caliente	2	F	2	0	0	0	0
Terra Firma	3	F	10	2	3	2	29,395
Terra Gold	3	F	5	1	1	1	5,903
Terra Kate	3	F	12	1	4	1	29,930
Terracotta Cat	5	M	4	0	0	0	346
Terraforming	9	G	7	0	1	0	772
Terra's Charm	5	M	8	0	0	1	2,212
Terras Terry	4	G	7	1	0	2	4,806
Terrell	4	C	2	2	0	0	55,800
Terre's Tree	7	M	1	0	0	0	0
Terrestrial Glow	3	F	2	0	0	0	744
Terribletwos	2	F	2	0	1	0	12,350
Terrific Beat	9	M	3	0	0	0	100
Terrific Shrimp	4	F	8	3	2	0	8,599
Terrific Speed	5	M	6	0	2	0	4,900
Terrific Storm	3	C	7	1	2	1	56,115
Terrific Tom	2	C	1	0	0	0	1,440
Terrifically	3	C	4	1	0	0	6,930
Terrified Ice	4	F	8	4	1	0	40,700
Terrifika	3	C	10	1	0	0	15,929
Terrifying (IRE)	5	G	2	0	0	0	0
Territorial	2	C	6	0	1	2	23,500
Terroplane (FR)	3	G	7	1	1	0	91,430
Terrorizer	3	C	8	1	1	1	22,070
Terry Dancer	3	C	12	2	2	1	22,975
Terry Kelly	6	G	7	1	2	0	11,000
Tesio (GB)	6	G	1	0	0	0	2,050
Tesla	4	F	8	2	1	1	14,183
Tesormo	7	G	12	0	2	3	3,360
Tesoro Gold	2	F	2	0	0	0	0
Tessarella	3	F	17	2	0	2	13,975
Tessa's Irish Boy	4	C	2	0	0	0	0
Test Dance	4	F	24	2	1	3	14,795
Test Drive	5	G	10	1	1	2	9,174
Test of Courage	4	F	7	0	0	0	3,282
Test of Time	5	G	1	0	0	1	2,035
Test the Limit	3	C	4	1	1	0	12,886
Test the Waters	5	M	6	3	1	1	177,870
Testa Lady's Event	4	F	1	0	0	0	0
Testame	7	G	14	3	2	1	20,349
Testamento	4	C	13	1	4	0	14,778
Testhaven	7	G	2	0	0	0	253
Testify	7	G	6	0	3	1	46,520
Testing Fate (IRE)	5	G	4	0	0	0	1,950
Testing the Limit	5	G	5	1	0	0	11,260
Testingonetwothree	2	C	7	0	0	4	4,605
Testy Guy	5	G	9	1	1	1	22,000
Testy Roo	8	G	4	0	0	1	617
Tete's Giggle	3	F	2	0	0	0	1,260
Tetherette	4	F	9	1	2	2	79,278
Tethra Slew	2	G	2	0	1	0	4,240
Tethra's Warrior	4	F	4	0	1	1	2,675
Teton Echo	6	G	6	0	1	1	950
Teton Forest	3	C	8	3	2	0	222,000
Teton National	3	F	2	0	0	0	400
Tetons Rising Sun	6	G	9	0	1	0	2,460
Tetrahedron	2	C	2	0	0	0	0
Tevya	4	G	5	0	0	0	188
Tewconi	3	F	3	0	0	0	0
Tewkin	6	M	15	0	2	2	8,502
Tex and the City	3	G	14	2	1	1	33,629
Tex Maring	4	G	17	2	2	4	14,291
Tex Notch	2	G	6	1	0	0	7,175
Tex Slewana	3	F	4	0	1	0	7,200
Tex Tumbleweed	2	G	1	0	0	0	140
Texan Storm	5	H	10	1	2	2	26,100
Texanasu	4	F	1	0	0	0	0
Texarkana	5	H	7	1	1	0	10,400
Texas	2	C	1	0	0	0	0
Texas Agenda	4	G	6	1	0	0	3,240
Texas Best	4	C	2	0	1	0	4,600
Texas Biscuit	3	C	8	1	2	2	10,654
Texas Bob	3	G	4	1	1	0	6,780
Texas Born	3	G	3	2	1	0	28,400
Texas Brick	3	F	2	0	0	2	2,970
Texas Brown	2	C	10	2	5	1	53,057
Texas Cat Lady	2	F	2	0	0	0	0
Texas Chili	6	G	5	0	1	0	13,725
Texas City Blast	3	F	1	0	0	0	150
Texas Code	7	G	8	0	1	0	5,635
Texas Deputy	3	C	3	0	1	0	8,400
Texas Diamond	3	G	2	0	0	1	671
Texas Dream	4	C	2	0	0	0	0
Texas Dude	3	G	10	0	3	1	9,250
Texas Dumplin	6	M	3	0	0	0	0
Texas Eagle	3	C	9	1	4	1	29,687
Texas Flash	3	G	1	0	0	0	150
Texas Gold Digger	3	F	13	3	6	1	81,090
Texas Gold Fever	2	C	2	0	0	1	1,980
Texas Govenor	3	G	3	0	0	0	991
Texas Guinan	2	F	4	0	1	0	6,210
Texas Heat	6	M	10	1	1	0	19,034
Texas Hill	4	G	13	2	0	2	31,967
Texas Holdem	4	G	3	0	0	1	594
Texas Honey	4	F	1	0	0	0	0
Texas Ice	5	M	3	0	0	0	0
Texas Legend	5	G	12	1	0	1	6,181
Texas Longneck	6	H	3	1	0	0	3,660
Texas Market	2	G	2	0	0	0	900
Texas Martini	2	C	1	0	0	0	450
Texas Miss	7	M	1	0	0	0	0
Texas Oasis	5	M	6	1	0	2	9,710
Texas Oil	10	G	11	1	0	2	2,340
Texas Orbit	5	G	6	1	2	0	1,972
Texas Pete	4	G	10	1	0	0	18,960
Texas Pioneer	5	G	15	1	3	2	26,441
Texas Prez	4	F	3	0	0	0	1,000
Texas Pro	3	C	8	1	2	2	57,087
Texas Prospector	3	F	7	0	0	1	1,315
Texas Queen	3	F	2	0	0	0	0
Texas Rainbow	6	G	1	0	0	0	73
Texas Red	3	C	7	2	0	2	38,812
Texas Shimmy	3	C	4	0	2	1	7,550
Texas Siphon	3	C	2	0	0	0	0
Texas Special	5	G	9	2	1	2	10,446
Texas Spice	2	F	2	2	0	0	15,000
Texas Spirit	2	F	4	1	1	0	8,930
Texas Style	7	G	9	1	1	1	16,850
Texas Swing	3	F	8	1	0	1	14,150
Texas Tab	4	F	6	0	0	0	0
Texas Tan	2	G	11	1	3	3	19,530
Texas Thunder	5	H	5	1	0	0	5,454
Texas Toga	4	G	7	0	1	2	7,479
Texas Tree	4	F	16	2	1	3	47,137
Texas Trouble	2	C	2	0	1	0	5,000

Horse	Age	Sex	Sts	1st	2d	3d	Won
Texas Ya Ya	2	F	2	0	0	0	390
Texas Zar	3	C	5	0	0	0	0
Texasbluedif	3	F	8	2	3	2	14,610
Texascountryboy	4	G	5	0	0	0	1,110
Texasourtexas	7	G	4	0	0	0	375
Texasquickstepper	6	M	11	3	1	0	31,319
Texastoothpick	9	G	20	2	2	3	8,511
Texcess	2	G	4	3	1	0	725,427
Texiano	3	C	7	1	0	3	15,720
Texmaman	11	H	1	0	0	0	95
Texmckay	3	G	12	2	1	1	44,345
Tex's Mistress	2	F	3	0	0	0	2,300
Textbook Tillie	3	F	9	2	1	1	27,320
Tez Tarak	7	G	19	1	7	2	17,258
Tezer Wasn't Tezin	3	G	2	1	0	0	3,000
Tezzie June	3	F	5	0	1	0	1,244
Thames	4	G	3	2	0	0	53,378
Thanasi	4	G	11	1	3	1	79,620
Thandi	5	G	7	1	1	1	3,745
Thank the Academy	3	F	6	0	2	3	30,280
Thank the Press	6	G	4	2	0	1	16,815
Thank the Stars	5	G	2	0	1	0	920
Thank You Dad	3	F	9	1	0	2	5,092
Thank You Dear	5	M	1	0	0	0	0
Thank You Mom	3	F	1	0	1	0	1,500
Thank You Montana	7	G	5	0	0	2	1,743
Thank You Sir	6	H	12	0	3	3	30,647
Thankless Child	3	F	10	1	2	2	20,660
Thanks Al	3	G	5	2	0	0	14,340
Thanks Amy	10	M	14	1	2	0	14,561
Thanks Cee	2	C	10	0	5	3	14,675
Thanks Dr. G	4	G	6	2	0	0	11,523
Thanks for Smokin	3	F	8	3	1	2	41,826
Thanks Fox	2	F	5	0	0	2	4,500
Thanks General	4	G	2	0	0	0	0
Thanks Given	3	F	6	0	0	1	3,695
Thanks Hajji	4	C	13	4	3	1	52,296
Thanks to Banks	4	F	4	0	0	0	455
Thanks to Dixon	4	F	1	0	1	0	800
Thanksforthetune	4	C	1	0	0	0	0
Thankstotanner	3	G	7	0	1	2	7,645
Thankubellagio	3	G	12	1	3	5	46,150
Thankyou Uncle	2	F	3	0	0	0	738
That	4	G	8	0	1	2	2,890
That Allen Thing	4	G	3	0	0	0	515
That and This	6	M	2	0	0	0	52
That Being Said	6	H	2	0	0	0	0
That Bum Charlie	10	G	12	2	3	1	19,030
That Close	3	F	14	2	0	1	9,743
That Cool Cat	6	G	10	1	0	2	9,295
That Darn Cat	4	G	17	4	3	3	48,600
That Deed	3	C	1	0	0	0	91
That Funny Feeling	3	G	3	0	0	0	208
That Gift	7	G	14	3	0	2	22,693
That Holme Man	11	G	8	1	1	0	6,633
That Look	4	F	3	0	0	0	1,200
That Monetary	9	G	11	1	3	1	11,754
That Prospect	3	G	8	1	1	0	22,675
That Smith Girl	5	M	17	6	3	2	32,510
That Tat	6	G	8	2	4	1	100,000
That Wild Thing	4	F	18	0	2	3	4,310
Thataintnomarlin	5	H	9	1	3	1	10,545
Thatallyougot	5	H	3	0	0	0	1,127
Thatcertainfeeling	4	G	11	0	1	0	4,652
Thatkrazykat	2	F	1	0	1	0	4,780
Thatkrazzymissphit	7	G	2	0	0	0	171
Thatledoit	3	G	3	0	0	0	1,130
That'll Work	9	G	9	0	1	1	1,746
That's a Cat	3	G	6	0	0	1	3,038
That's a Command	4	C	2	1	0	0	7,725
Thats a Match	4	F	2	0	0	0	350
Thats a Mink	2	C	1	0	1	0	3,100
Thats a Nono	9	H	7	1	0	0	5,043
That's a Secret	2	F	8	1	1	1	26,290
That's All Jazz	2	F	4	1	0	0	7,521
That's American	4	F	11	2	2	0	28,640
That's an Outrage	3	C	3	0	0	0	25,000
That's Annie	3	F	5	0	0	0	851
Thats Another Song	3	F	5	0	0	0	419
That's Creative	6	G	5	0	0	0	731
Thats Cute	6	M	7	2	0	3	23,885
Thats Dannys Buck	3	C	14	3	1	1	21,115
Thats Final	6	H	2	0	0	0	0
That's Forbidden	2	F	1	0	0	0	105
That's Holly	3	F	5	1	0	0	6,000
Thats How It Goes	5	M	3	2	1	0	18,080
Thats How It Is	2	C	8	1	0	1	9,252
That's It	2	F	2	0	0	1	2,730
That's Life	2	F	4	0	0	0	345
That's Me	5	G	5	2	0	0	25,032
That's Me Boy	3	F	8	1	5	1	26,522
That's My Babe	4	F	2	0	0	0	0
Thats My Buck	3	G	9	0	0	0	1,418
That's My Chick	3	F	8	1	2	0	10,550
Thats My Daddy	6	H	11	1	1	3	25,220
That's My Line	3	G	20	2	1	5	12,620
That's My Luck	7	G	13	0	4	1	2,993
That's My Miracle	2	F	1	0	0	0	100
Thats My Princess	2	F	1	0	0	0	0
That's My Steven	6	G	2	0	0	0	0
That's My Sunny	2	F	5	0	0	0	355
That's Nice	4	C	1	0	0	1	1,540
Thats No Bull	3	G	7	0	0	1	3,168
That's No Halo	5	G	16	2	2	2	20,090
That's Our Daisy	5	M	3	0	0	0	204
That's Our Gold	5	M	10	0	1	0	2,869
That's Our Jack	3	C	4	2	0	1	20,825
Thats Our Queen	5	M	18	1	3	5	11,639
Thats Our Secret	3	G	2	0	0	1	1,248
That's Our Tricky	5	M	9	1	0	1	32,164
That's Our Vernon	2	G	4	1	0	0	5,640
That's Outrageous	7	M	16	0	0	1	2,978
Thats Private	3	F	5	0	0	0	1,200
That's R Glory	4	F	4	0	0	0	436
That's Real Nice	2	F	2	0	0	0	400
That's Right	3	G	2	0	0	0	800
That's That Mister	4	G	15	2	4	3	49,259
That's the Berries	4	G	14	0	3	3	24,678
Thats the Problem	5	G	5	2	0	0	23,280
That's the Story	4	F	1	0	0	0	0
That's Toooo Cute	3	F	6	1	0	0	5,880
That's Tough	3	F	3	0	0	1	1,860
That's Tricky	4	C	5	0	0	0	299
Thatsadoablething	5	G	2	0	0	0	218
That'sahandfull	4	C	8	1	1	0	2,510
Thatsalliknow	3	F	11	2	3	1	18,225
Thatsallmon	5	G	5	1	0	1	4,930
Thatsmygeorgiegirl	4	F	10	3	2	3	16,576
Thatsmyway	5	M	6	0	2	1	10,458
Thatsoneroyalchic	5	M	5	0	0	0	1,245
Thatspowerfulstuff	5	G	10	1	1	1	3,799
Thatsthe Fact Jack	3	C	15	2	5	1	34,920
Thatsthebottomline	6	G	14	1	2	4	21,966
Thatsthegoodstuff	3	G	1	0	0	0	127
Thatswhatimean	2	F	3	1	1	0	37,620
Thatswhyweboughtto	3	G	7	1	2	0	43,944
Thaumaturge	4	C	11	1	2	2	32,890
Thawed	3	F	9	1	3	0	27,610
Thazwatimtalknabot	2	F	1	0	0	0	300
The Alphalion	3	G	6	0	2	2	4,410
The Animas	5	G	1	0	1	0	2,542
The Annswer	5	M	1	0	0	0	67
The Answer Is No	4	G	6	2	1	0	17,100
The Band Plays On	3	F	6	1	0	2	7,505
The Best Defense	9	M	3	0	0	0	550
The Best Dont Rest	13	G	8	0	0	0	340
The Best of Me	3	F	7	1	2	1	10,880
The Beter Man Can	2	F	4	3	0	0	101,298
The Big Blond	7	M	16	1	4	4	8,427
The Big Devil	4	C	8	1	0	1	5,572
The Big Edict	3	C	5	0	0	0	300
The Big Macaw	4	G	10	1	2	2	8,049
The Big Muddy	6	G	7	0	0	0	3,622
The Big O	6	G	15	1	0	3	8,019
The Big Ugly	4	F	11	0	1	0	2,467
The Bigger Picture	2	C	2	0	0	0	0
The Bird Is Wired	4	G	3	0	0	0	225
The Black Monk	4	G	15	2	4	3	13,848

Horse	Age	Sex	Sts	1st	2d	3d	Won
The Black Rocket	5	H	3	1	0	0	5,020
The Blank Vanman	5	H	6	2	0	0	17,460
The Blue Hole	3	F	7	0	0	1	1,625
The Boggie Man Can	4	G	1	1	0	0	7,980
The Bohemian	3	G	12	2	0	1	11,665
The Boiler	2	C	5	1	0	2	19,350
The Bold Bruiser	8	H	14	1	2	5	14,812
The Boogerman	4	G	9	1	1	0	6,709
The Boogie Man	4	G	13	3	2	1	20,725
The Boomer	5	G	9	0	0	1	1,444
The Borg Queen	4	F	11	3	2	1	87,820
The Boy Can Play	4	C	9	1	1	1	7,143
The Boyz Toy	3	G	6	0	1	0	2,158
The Breeze	7	G	2	0	0	0	76
The Bruce (NZ)	7	G	2	0	1	1	3,750
The Bull Is Blue	2	C	2	1	0	0	6,161
The Bushwhacker	5	M	6	1	0	2	6,656
The Business	4	G	3	0	0	0	0
The Butcher	4	C	8	1	2	1	8,155
The Buzz Express	3	G	7	0	0	1	4,972
The Cag	3	G	4	0	0	0	288
The Call of Duty	5	H	2	0	0	0	169
The Call Stands	3	G	4	1	1	0	14,500
The Candi Kid	7	G	6	0	1	2	5,202
The Candi Queen	5	M	2	1	0	1	52,416
The Candy Queen	5	M	1	0	0	0	100
The Capeman	3	C	2	0	0	0	257
The Capt.'s Reddie	2	G	5	0	2	1	5,100
The Cashew Queen	3	F	11	2	5	1	57,162
The Castle	4	F	8	1	1	0	11,173
The Cat and I	4	G	14	0	1	1	1,957
The Cats Back	7	G	13	1	0	2	2,596
The Cats Gone	3	C	7	0	0	1	2,848
The Cat's Joanna	3	G	10	2	2	0	26,075
The Cat's Tail	3	C	11	0	2	0	4,603
The Chancer	6	G	5	0	0	0	305
The Chauffeur	5	H	3	0	0	0	157
The Cheetah's Tale	3	C	2	0	0	2	6,400
The Chelsea Comet	3	F	8	1	1	1	38,962
The Chubster	5	G	6	0	1	0	1,266
The Clarkster	4	F	13	2	0	2	12,258
The Cliff's Edge	3	C	8	1	4	2	1,010,000
The Clock Man	3	G	4	0	0	0	380
The Clown	4	C	9	0	0	0	3,000
The Cluny Clipper	4	G	9	0	0	1	2,152
The Cobbler	5	H	3	0	0	0	0
The Cobra Special	4	G	14	1	2	1	5,374
The Coffin	6	G	7	5	0	1	32,520
The Comeback Cats	7	G	5	2	0	1	5,870
The Comus Kid	4	G	11	1	0	2	7,059
The Cooksville Kid	5	G	7	0	2	1	8,228
The Cool Grape	7	H	10	1	0	1	10,340
The Count	6	G	6	0	0	1	893
The Craftsman	4	G	19	4	2	5	43,527
The Crag	4	C	4	2	0	0	4,300
The Crystal Kid	5	G	7	0	0	2	1,440
The Dancer	8	H	4	0	0	0	255
The de Gray Flash	7	M	3	0	0	0	300
The Dempsey Look	3	F	10	2	3	0	94,355
The Denver Dream	7	G	8	0	0	1	3,560
The Deputy Is Home	6	H	7	0	2	3	35,410
The Deputy's Sunny	2	C	5	0	0	1	3,962
The Devil Herself	2	F	2	0	0	0	0
The Devil 'n Honey	6	G	7	0	0	1	763
The Docmeister	3	C	4	0	1	2	3,938
The Dream Lives	4	G	7	0	0	1	4,837
The Dream Rages On	3	G	13	1	1	0	7,422
The Dude Guy	2	G	3	0	0	0	360
The Duker	7	G	12	1	2	1	13,784
The Eden (ARG)	4	G	8	0	0	1	4,020
The Editor's Son	5	G	10	2	3	2	51,930
The Eighth Wonder	4	F	5	0	0	0	849
The Emerald Deputy	2	G	2	0	0	0	0
The Emerald King	2	G	1	0	0	1	1,725
The Emster	3	F	1	0	0	1	5,880
The End Is Clear	2	F	6	0	1	3	21,940
The Energizergirl	6	M	3	0	1	0	1,510
The Expresso Kid	2	G	2	0	0	0	0
The Falcon	5	G	5	1	0	2	34,398
The Fat Man	4	G	12	2	1	1	13,030
The Field General	5	G	11	2	0	0	7,971
The Fighting Chief	4	F	8	2	0	1	15,830
The Finagler	2	G	5	2	2	0	112,585
The Final Toy	3	F	3	0	1	1	3,270
The Fletchmeister	3	G	4	1	1	0	16,480
The Flying Victory	4	F	5	2	0	0	9,000
The Forham Flush	4	F	1	0	0	0	83
The Frac	3	G	4	2	0	1	38,200
The Friendly Ghost	4	G	8	0	2	1	17,660
The Full Molly	5	M	7	0	0	0	770
The Fuse Is Lit	4	F	12	1	1	0	7,882
The Fuzz	3	G	5	1	1	1	7,908
The Garbage Man	6	G	15	3	4	2	55,744
The General's Bank	5	G	16	0	3	0	16,470
The General's Lady	4	F	3	0	0	0	400
The Gin Game	4	F	4	0	0	0	1,640
The Gold Clove	3	G	13	2	1	2	17,466
The Golden Floss	5	G	2	1	0	1	8,204
The Golden Frog	3	G	7	0	0	0	5,227
The Gooch	5	G	15	2	2	4	16,056
The Good Old Flag	2	C	1	0	0	0	225
The Grand High Ho	5	M	11	0	4	2	21,890
The Gray Eagle	6	G	13	4	2	3	29,270
The Gray Jaklin	7	G	6	2	1	0	2,960
The Gray Mile	4	G	2	0	0	0	0
The Gray Spur	6	M	13	1	1	2	9,216
The Great Buzzenie	3	C	8	1	0	1	24,401
The Great Catsby	3	F	4	1	0	0	7,995
The Great Dimaggio	6	G	7	0	0	0	312
The Great Fizz	2	C	7	2	1	1	29,530
The Great Tyler	3	F	11	4	2	3	67,240
The Greene Man	4	G	11	1	1	0	6,861
The Gregster	4	G	5	0	0	0	693
The Grey Fella	3	C	1	0	0	0	220
The Greyling	6	G	6	1	0	1	11,100
The Griff	6	G	11	3	1	1	105,075
The Heats On	10	G	1	0	0	0	0
The Heavy	7	G	12	2	4	0	13,688
The Herc	3	C	7	0	1	0	11,267
The Hibb	5	H	4	0	0	1	744
The Hoedown Kid	7	G	2	0	1	0	560
The Invasion	9	G	9	1	0	0	2,733
The Irish Nun	6	M	13	0	2	3	5,366
The Ironworker	5	G	6	0	1	0	1,700
The Issue Is Power	12	G	15	3	1	1	37,920
The It Girl	3	F	4	1	0	0	10,100
The Jean Genie	4	G	3	1	1	0	9,375
The Jet Wave	5	G	11	0	0	2	2,792
The Jolly	3	F	4	1	0	0	11,237
The Jones Boy	5	G	5	3	0	0	27,866
The Judge Jose	5	G	10	2	1	1	13,348
The Judge Sez Who	5	H	11	0	0	2	194,563
The K O Touch	3	F	11	2	2	4	103,512
The Kandaly Kid	4	C	1	0	0	0	120
The Kaprikorn Kid	9	H	1	0	0	0	0
The King Is Alive	4	G	10	0	0	2	2,852
The King N Rob	4	G	12	3	3	0	130,200
The King's Brother	2	C	3	0	0	0	350
The Known Q	3	F	11	1	3	1	15,767
The Lady Roars	4	F	9	2	3	3	51,600
The Lady's Groom	4	C	10	2	3	2	262,520
The Lamp Is Lit	3	F	9	4	2	0	123,477
The Last Feisty	3	C	2	0	0	1	470
The Last Flower	8	H	7	1	0	3	30,630
The Last Hello	2	G	1	0	0	0	135
The Last Marine	6	H	1	0	0	0	0
The Last Set	4	F	11	4	1	0	19,366
The Last Spy	3	F	8	1	1	1	27,730
The Last Wish	2	F	1	0	0	0	0
The Latest News	2	C	1	0	0	0	230
The Law of Seattle	4	C	13	1	0	4	12,813
The Lights Are On	6	G	7	1	1	1	14,420
The Lion's Intern	5	M	15	1	1	3	8,347
The Lion's Scamper	4	F	7	0	1	1	2,232
The Little Boy	7	G	1	0	0	0	0
The Little Cat	4	G	3	1	1	0	4,720
The Littlest Angel	2	F	3	0	0	1	2,366
The Looper	4	G	11	3	4	1	107,767

Horse	Age	Sex	Sts	1st	2d	3d	Won
The Lord Is Eager	6	G	16	6	1	4	19,709
The Lord's Club	4	G	11	0	0	2	4,956
The Love King	2	G	5	0	1	0	5,770
The Madison Man	7	G	13	3	2	1	28,313
The Mailman	5	G	1	0	0	0	0
The Main Wife	2	F	2	0	1	1	12,400
The Man	4	G	9	0	3	0	12,100
The Man Himself	7	G	5	0	1	1	1,960
The Master's Word	5	G	12	0	0	1	4,228
The Menifee Affair	3	G	2	0	0	0	0
The Midnight Skier	3	G	10	0	2	1	8,710
The Mighty James	6	H	1	0	0	0	110
The Minkster	4	G	15	5	3	1	31,008
The Missing Key	6	H	3	0	0	0	925
The Mold	3	G	4	0	0	1	2,430
The Mount	3	C	4	1	0	0	12,040
The Move Man	2	G	2	0	0	0	410
The Mutt	7	G	10	1	1	1	17,060
The Name Was Gone	4	F	5	1	0	0	33,635
The Name's Bond	4	C	1	0	0	0	580
The Name's Bud	4	G	9	0	0	0	1,130
The Name's Joshua	3	G	4	0	0	0	689
The Name's Mister	3	C	4	0	0	1	1,820
The Name's Peanut	4	G	10	0	1	0	1,681
The Name'sdanzel	7	M	4	0	0	0	240
The Night Ridder	4	C	10	2	3	0	15,242
The Niner Account	6	G	15	7	4	3	133,610
The Nth Degree	3	G	11	2	3	3	56,241
The Old Hero	3	G	3	0	0	0	711
The One We Kept	3	F	4	1	0	0	16,240
The Other Me	5	H	1	0	0	0	0
The Other One	7	G	4	0	0	0	72
The Party Chairman	8	G	9	1	1	2	4,658
The Peddler	3	G	8	1	0	1	7,560
The Penny Drops	3	G	11	5	1	2	118,644
The Peoples Champ	4	G	1	0	0	0	0
The Percussionist	3	G	3	0	0	0	0
The Perkmeister	4	G	2	0	0	0	29
The Pink Tiger	5	G	2	0	0	0	0
The Plains	4	C	3	0	0	0	1,345
The Polski Prince	3	G	12	0	5	3	16,169
The Poseur	7	G	2	0	0	0	800
The Potters Hand	4	G	14	2	2	2	20,504
The Prez	5	G	3	0	0	0	455
The Pride of Dixie	3	G	5	0	2	1	5,210
The Princess House	3	F	4	0	1	1	2,938
The Principal Man	5	G	8	0	2	2	12,147
The Prodigal Son	2	G	3	0	0	0	1,011
The Pugilist	4	F	11	1	2	0	6,225
The Purple Ghost	3	G	8	0	0	0	2,720
The Purple Swarm	4	G	13	3	2	4	31,791
The Queen's Doc	3	G	15	4	5	1	50,038
The Queen's Stamp	2	F	1	0	0	1	6,270
The Quin Man	4	C	4	0	0	0	274
The Rain Is Gone	5	M	14	2	2	1	18,775
The Rather	2	C	1	0	0	0	0
The Real Boss Man	4	G	11	2	2	4	26,742
The Real Odysseus	4	C	4	1	2	0	2,500
The Rejected Stone	5	G	1	0	0	0	0
The Reminator	9	G	13	1	1	1	4,741
The Right Key	2	C	2	0	0	1	3,248
The Right Orbit	6	G	5	1	1	0	1,245
The Right Ticket	2	G	3	0	0	1	1,430
The Rizzer	3	G	11	1	2	1	14,280
The Road Boss	3	C	8	1	3	1	25,980
The Rockman	3	G	4	0	0	1	2,520
The Rodeo Express	4	F	11	3	1	2	72,605
The Rogue	6	G	13	3	3	3	48,579
The Rosiest	4	F	2	0	0	0	120
The Rum Runner	4	G	11	1	0	0	5,356
The Running Man	4	C	6	1	0	3	8,203
The Running Sioux	7	G	10	1	0	2	4,015
The Scatman Cometh	3	G	13	4	2	1	50,950
The Seahorse Two	4	G	9	0	0	2	5,498
The Seth Bomber	4	G	9	1	1	0	5,825
The Sewickley Kid	5	G	14	3	4	3	58,490
The Sharoan Plan	2	C	3	1	0	1	11,120
The Short Stuff	3	F	10	0	0	0	1,549
The Shulamite	3	F	1	0	0	0	0
The Silver Rod Kid	3	C	6	1	2	2	28,130
The Siphon King	2	C	1	0	0	0	560
The Skelligs	4	G	16	0	0	0	2,444
The Smoothe Groove	5	M	2	0	0	0	945
The Smurfster	3	G	1	0	0	0	0
The Snooty Fox	2	F	1	0	0	0	0
The Spark	10	G	7	0	1	1	3,915
The Spirit Runner	4	F	1	0	0	0	0
The Stalker	4	G	9	4	3	0	57,099
The Star of Bohrer	4	C	6	0	0	1	2,265
The State	5	H	5	0	0	0	2,921
The Station	6	G	17	2	3	4	11,612
The Stigmata	4	F	9	0	0	0	1,869
The Storm Tourns	2	C	1	1	0	0	8,100
The Storm Trackerr	5	G	2	0	0	1	561
The Straw Man	2	G	5	1	1	1	8,284
The Strider	4	C	5	0	0	0	496
The Strodebrothers	4	G	15	3	3	1	16,770
The Strong One	4	G	4	1	0	1	1,960
The Student (ARG)	5	H	8	3	1	0	34,080
The Suave Commoner	3	G	10	0	2	1	5,783
The Teacher Said	3	C	2	0	0	0	240
The Tin Man	6	G	3	0	0	1	23,400
The Toast of Troy	4	F	15	4	5	2	159,120
The Toff	11	G	2	0	0	0	0
The Tour Continues	3	F	13	1	0	2	12,820
The Trasher	3	F	3	0	0	0	208
The Truth Detector	3	F	1	0	0	0	110
The Usual	3	F	2	1	0	0	36,660
The Vegas Gal	3	F	2	0	0	0	0
The Vilzak Kid	6	G	12	0	3	1	1,504
The Warden Kenny B	5	H	3	0	0	0	84
The Warden's Prize	3	G	15	1	0	2	14,960
The Way Holme	8	G	12	1	0	3	12,675
The Way of the Cat	3	G	18	2	3	3	46,655
The Weej	3	G	15	1	2	2	7,675
The Weez	9	G	6	0	0	1	1,326
The White Sun	6	G	3	0	0	1	3,250
The Whole Picture	3	G	2	0	0	0	450
The Wicked One	5	G	4	0	0	1	1,484
The Wind Chiller	2	G	2	0	0	0	615
The Wine King	5	H	11	0	2	2	2,748
The Wiz Biz	6	G	3	0	0	0	262
The Woman in Black	6	M	4	0	0	0	1,300
The Wonder of You	5	G	14	4	3	0	64,895
The Wrong Face	3	F	2	1	0	1	20,830
The Yellow Sheet	4	F	10	3	0	1	121,114
The Zeal Deal	3	F	13	2	2	0	10,796
Theartfuldutchman	5	G	12	2	4	1	69,524
Theartofperfection	3	G	6	1	0	1	18,000
Theater R. N.	4	F	3	2	0	0	129,000
Theaterfest	9	G	1	0	0	0	60
Theatre Script	6	G	11	2	1	1	19,472
Theatre Thunder	5	G	4	0	0	1	311
Theatrical Cat	4	F	4	1	0	1	31,260
Theatrical Dancer	4	F	9	1	2	0	9,559
Theatrical Glory	2	C	1	0	0	0	1,195
Theatrical Review	3	F	5	0	1	0	7,085
Theatrikate	4	F	4	1	0	0	1,100
Thebeatgoeson	3	F	2	0	0	0	327
Thebigbrushoff	4	G	16	6	3	3	56,005
Thecatbelongstome	5	M	9	0	0	2	6,818
Thecatisinthewine	2	C	6	1	2	1	7,654
Thecatsoutofthebag	2	F	2	1	0	0	4,655
Theconfidenceman	3	C	8	1	1	1	44,120
Thedevilinme	3	F	9	2	1	1	19,556
Thedominantfemale	4	F	12	2	4	1	21,963
Thedreamcontinues	3	F	5	1	1	0	22,680
Thee Icon	2	G	6	0	2	0	5,114
Thefinestgreen	3	G	3	0	0	0	192
Theflash	3	F	5	0	0	1	4,195
Theforceofmachone	2	G	3	0	0	0	1,200
Thefull Circle	5	G	5	0	0	2	14,050
Thegamemustgoon	2	C	3	0	0	0	5,931
Thegirlsgotrhythm	6	M	5	2	1	1	8,980
Thegooddieyoung	6	G	12	2	0	1	26,570
Thegreatschapiro	4	G	5	0	0	0	1,016
Theguycanfly	3	G	1	0	0	0	0
Their Serve	3	F	8	0	0	2	6,226

Horse	Age	Sex	Sts	1st	2d	3d	Won
Theirelandexpress	4	F	3	0	0	0	411
Thekatsmeow	3	F	6	0	1	1	1,850
Thekeytolaughter	6	M	2	0	0	0	640
Thekingcandance	3	G	4	0	0	0	265
Thekingsqueen	4	F	7	0	2	1	11,783
Theladyisholy	3	F	12	2	2	5	13,560
Thelastpicturecho	3	G	7	0	0	0	455
Thelastword	3	G	17	1	4	0	12,582
Thelight Fantastic	5	M	3	0	1	0	2,715
Thelightsareon	3	G	16	3	1	3	17,216
Thelionshare	3	C	11	0	2	1	16,114
Thelittleirishman	3	G	7	1	0	0	3,510
Thelma's Beauty	3	F	1	0	0	0	690
Thelma's Tax Money	2	F	3	0	0	0	181
Thelonious	3	G	5	1	1	1	14,377
Themanfromlincoln	3	G	6	1	1	1	5,013
Themanwithebigcigr	8	G	5	1	1	2	10,218
Themoonshiner	5	G	12	2	1	1	10,657
Themus	4	F	5	1	0	2	12,170
Then She Laughs	3	F	8	3	1	1	117,140
Then Today Always	3	F	11	1	1	1	25,628
Thenameismolly	5	M	19	0	3	1	2,825
Thenardier	2	C	8	1	0	0	11,685
Theoakportduchess	5	M	1	0	0	0	290
Theodore's Devil	10	G	5	0	0	2	1,240
Theoldmanofhoy	2	G	2	0	0	0	0
Theoneilove	3	F	13	4	2	3	37,070
Theonlyword	3	F	4	1	2	1	45,100
Theoriginalmrsimon	4	G	6	0	0	0	432
Theo's Saint	4	C	6	1	1	1	12,945
Thepatriotgame	4	C	1	0	0	0	0
Thepesoman	3	C	6	1	0	0	6,000
Theprideofoklahoma	4	G	2	0	0	0	205
Theprinceofperu	6	H	2	0	0	0	810
Theprospectisababe	3	F	10	0	0	0	1,173
Thequeenismean	3	F	3	0	0	0	0
There and Back	4	F	7	1	0	0	10,008
There Goes Chris	3	G	6	1	2	0	11,050
There Goes Monty	4	C	7	1	0	0	5,383
There Goes Nick	7	G	13	2	3	3	14,707
There Goes Rocket	3	C	5	1	0	1	50,500
There Runs Hattie	5	M	11	1	1	3	86,599
There She Goes	6	M	2	0	0	0	0
There You Go Joe	3	G	5	0	1	0	2,930
Therecanbeonlyone	6	G	12	1	1	2	14,575
Theregoesmycruise	3	C	2	0	0	0	390
Thereisatigerahead	6	M	13	4	1	2	15,235
There's Hope Sir	5	H	4	0	0	0	643
Theres Nohalo Onme	4	G	12	1	1	1	15,045
Theres Our Money	5	G	11	0	2	5	8,285
Theres Trouble	6	M	8	0	0	0	637
There's Zealous	6	G	2	1	0	0	20,770
Theresa E	3	F	2	1	0	1	11,230
Theresa O	4	F	2	0	0	1	1,012
Theresa the Terror	4	F	2	0	0	0	177
Theresalwaysastory	3	F	12	2	1	2	10,755
Theresa's Storm	2	F	2	0	0	0	1,113
Theresa's Touch	3	F	7	1	0	0	6,930
Therightone	2	F	5	0	1	1	7,100
Theriverrunsgold	4	C	7	0	1	1	3,280
Therlo	7	G	10	5	0	0	16,735
Thermal Ablasion	5	M	11	4	4	1	156,316
Thermal Overload	2	C	2	0	0	0	500
Thermal Tay	4	F	8	0	0	0	1,021
Thermopylae	6	H	8	1	1	2	27,656
Thermostat	3	G	4	2	1	1	48,250
Thermostatic	5	M	10	3	2	0	103,495
Theschemeofthings	2	F	2	0	0	1	6,750
Thesmellofhoney	3	F	11	0	5	4	30,425
Thessaly	4	G	10	1	1	2	16,710
Thestormhascleared	4	F	18	1	3	2	15,428
Thesullivanfive	5	M	12	1	1	2	9,181
Thesyntaur	4	G	8	1	0	0	4,320
Thetactics Ofdance	3	F	10	1	4	0	94,795
Thetribehasspoken	3	G	11	1	2	1	6,235
Thewrightslew	3	G	1	0	0	0	0
Thewrightway	4	F	3	0	0	0	190
They Call Me Cody	6	G	9	0	0	2	8,867
Theycallmecolonel	7	G	16	4	4	0	8,464
Theyjustdontgetit	5	G	6	3	1	0	8,470
Thiamia Storm	3	F	2	0	0	0	255
Thick as Thieves	7	G	4	0	1	0	5,772
Thickett's Ticket	5	G	11	1	2	4	9,060
Thief River	5	H	3	0	1	0	556
Thievery	2	C	5	0	0	0	5,210
Thieves Tactics	7	G	2	0	0	0	129
Thimble	5	G	3	1	1	0	2,360
Thimbleful of Gold	6	M	14	1	5	1	13,093
Thimble's Legacy	4	F	11	1	1	1	7,033
Thin Air	3	F	7	0	2	2	31,377
Thin Man	4	G	8	1	2	2	6,096
Thing You Do	4	G	12	2	3	0	13,056
Things Happen	2	G	3	1	0	0	35,660
Think Big	3	G	8	1	0	1	7,460
Think Caper	4	G	10	1	0	1	8,939
Think Fast	5	M	9	2	4	1	81,419
Think Jazz	4	G	14	0	4	3	29,190
Think Pink	3	F	2	0	0	0	480
Think Tank (GB)	3	C	3	0	0	0	1,200
Think Win	3	C	1	0	0	0	0
Thinking Irish	6	G	4	0	0	0	0
Thinkinofyoulou	5	G	9	0	1	0	1,725
Thinksheshot	3	G	13	2	0	2	24,293
Third Avie	6	G	5	0	0	0	183
Third Collection	4	F	9	1	1	0	27,470
Third Cousin	4	F	16	2	1	0	16,920
Third Crusade	6	G	12	1	3	2	17,891
Third Daughter	4	F	3	1	0	0	6,975
Third Day	3	C	4	0	0	0	5,748
Third Gear	3	G	9	1	3	0	27,805
Third Half	4	G	8	3	0	1	110,820
Third Musketeer	4	C	8	2	0	0	11,355
Third Rate Romance	4	F	2	0	0	1	1,230
Third Shift Gal	3	F	17	1	2	3	6,283
Third Time	5	G	6	0	0	1	1,034
Third Try	5	M	3	0	0	0	0
Third Turn Angel	3	F	15	0	0	1	1,404
Third Wish	7	G	7	2	0	0	16,796
Thirdown Call	4	G	10	3	2	2	86,588
Thirdwind	2	F	1	0	0	0	0
Thirsty Guy's	2	G	1	0	0	0	863
Thirteen Below	3	G	3	0	0	0	0
Thirteen Colonies	4	G	7	2	0	2	35,335
Thirteen Mil	2	C	4	0	0	0	2,568
Thirteenth Hour	3	F	7	0	2	1	8,365
Thirtiethstreet	2	G	1	0	0	1	1,920
Thirty Eight Quest	9	G	4	0	0	0	305
Thirty Five Angels	4	G	3	1	0	0	14,546
Thirty One Jewels	3	F	7	0	1	0	2,092
Thirty One Jones	5	G	11	2	0	0	13,493
Thirty Six Hours	8	G	18	2	2	2	8,996
Thirty Two Skidoo	3	G	7	1	2	1	18,416
Thirtyeightcrusade	4	F	4	0	0	0	0
Thirtyfive Black	3	C	1	0	0	1	2,280
Thirtyfivthirtyfor	4	C	4	0	0	0	399
Thirtyforth N Vine	3	G	10	0	1	0	3,292
Thirtysix d'Lite	2	F	1	0	0	0	0
Thirtythree O Nine	7	G	11	0	0	2	2,557
Thiruvengadam	3	G	11	3	1	2	84,900
This Blues for You	3	G	3	0	0	0	0
This Books for You	4	G	11	2	1	2	22,699
This Cat Can	6	M	8	1	2	2	30,378
This Cat Can Run	3	C	1	0	1	0	3,135
This Cat Will Do	4	C	9	1	1	0	5,318
This Cats a Flying	8	G	18	1	0	2	13,461
This Cat's for You	4	C	1	0	0	0	276
This Chris	5	G	8	5	0	1	75,409
This Crime Pays	3	F	10	1	3	3	29,614
This Day Is Mine	5	M	7	1	0	2	4,675
This Guns for Hire	5	H	2	0	0	0	535
This Hicks Abeauty	5	G	10	1	2	0	13,563
This Is Bob	7	G	1	0	0	0	0
This Is Doc	4	G	4	0	0	2	3,928
This Is for Gran	3	F	3	0	0	0	282
This Is Fun Time	6	M	10	0	1	3	2,576
This Is Home	3	F	12	1	3	3	12,860
This Is I Know	5	G	5	1	0	0	4,120
This Is It	3	F	6	1	0	1	19,620

Horse	Age	Sex	Sts	1st	2d	3d	Won
This Is My Account	5	H	2	0	0	0	158
This Is That	3	C	5	1	0	1	14,645
This Is Trouble	6	H	15	1	5	3	8,909
This Isthe Big One	4	F	4	0	1	0	1,560
This Little Piggy	6	G	9	0	3	2	13,666
This Man's Darling	4	F	5	2	0	0	13,620
This N That	4	C	2	1	0	1	20,640
This One for Abbey	3	F	9	4	0	2	88,526
This One Won	4	G	7	0	0	1	1,334
This Slew Flew	4	F	5	0	1	0	15,032
This Train	9	M	15	0	0	3	2,867
This Tune Rocks	5	G	8	0	0	0	154
This Way Doris	2	F	1	1	0	0	16,560
This Wizard Rocks	2	G	4	1	1	1	49,780
This Won	5	G	2	0	0	0	0
Thisbirdcanfly	3	G	4	1	1	0	18,781
Thisbucksforyou	5	M	16	6	4	3	43,046
Thisbucksnoactor	8	M	14	2	2	4	31,376
Thiscatskrafty	4	G	16	1	2	2	18,673
Thisdevilcanfly	5	G	13	0	2	4	2,260
Thisgalsincharge	3	F	2	0	0	0	0
Thisgirldontlaugh	3	F	7	2	0	1	47,569
Thisisbarney	3	G	5	0	0	0	830
Thisistheman	2	G	1	1	0	0	6,199
Thisisyourday	2	F	1	0	0	0	0
Thislilgirlcanrun	5	M	11	0	0	0	3,195
Thisonesforjerry	5	M	6	0	1	1	4,021
Thisonesforjoan	4	F	7	0	1	0	2,762
Thisonesformysis	3	G	2	1	0	0	4,635
Thisonesforsam	3	G	7	1	2	0	15,920
Thisonesmine	3	F	1	0	0	0	57
Thisstrodesforyou	4	F	16	2	3	4	12,969
Thomas B. Lucky	3	G	8	2	1	1	10,215
Thomas F	4	G	7	0	0	3	3,817
Thomas the Cat	4	G	5	0	0	0	835
Thompson Gee	4	C	7	1	2	1	33,100
Thompson Rouge (IRE)	5	H	2	0	1	0	10,600
Thong	4	F	16	3	2	1	59,935
Thor Thors	13	G	3	0	0	1	6,375
Thorndale	8	G	10	0	2	1	7,931
Thorne Road	4	G	12	1	4	4	18,371
Thornhill	3	F	12	1	0	2	36,205
Thornwood	3	C	11	3	1	3	20,085
Thoroly Fast	3	F	1	0	0	0	400
Thoroughbabe	9	M	10	2	0	2	11,850
Thorp Springs	3	C	2	1	0	0	15,000
Thor's Echo	2	G	1	0	0	1	4,200
Thor's Fury	4	G	10	3	0	1	41,100
Those Littlethings	2	F	6	2	0	1	33,420
Thoughtful King	3	G	7	0	2	0	6,392
Thoughtfully	3	F	11	1	1	2	10,228
Thoughtuknew	2	G	1	0	1	0	2,300
Thourougly Blue	4	G	11	1	0	3	13,389
Thousand and One	4	F	7	0	0	0	45
Thousand Hills	2	F	4	1	0	1	7,980
Thread of Hope	3	G	14	2	3	2	16,727
Thread the Needle	8	M	17	1	0	3	9,873
Threat of Victory	5	G	5	1	0	1	8,752
Three Aces	3	G	6	2	1	0	39,810
Three Amigos	7	G	1	0	0	0	0
Three and Two	2	C	8	2	2	1	35,280
Three B Bobbi	3	F	9	1	1	2	22,490
Three Bags Full	5	G	4	0	1	0	2,925
Three Banks	4	C	2	0	0	0	242
Three Carat	4	G	1	1	0	0	15,000
Three Cats	6	H	4	0	0	1	400
Three Chances	7	G	10	0	1	0	2,994
Three Charms	2	G	2	0	0	0	590
Three Cianos	2	G	1	1	0	0	20,580
Three Coconuts	2	F	1	0	0	1	2,523
Three Counties	5	G	15	1	3	0	11,995
Three Cubits	2	C	2	0	0	0	0
Three Day Bullet	5	M	7	2	1	0	10,776
Three Doors Down	4	G	3	0	0	0	252
Three Ediths	2	F	1	0	0	0	150
Three Elevens	2	G	4	0	0	0	1,600
Three Franks	3	G	12	0	2	4	18,295
Three Gold Stars	4	F	6	1	1	3	11,108
Three Hour Nap	2	C	4	3	0	0	158,400
Three in the Bag	2	C	2	0	1	0	3,736
Three Jack	5	H	4	1	1	1	23,730
Three Ladies Man	5	G	13	2	3	2	17,800
Three Little Words	8	M	6	0	0	0	501
Three Marks	3	G	16	3	2	5	18,927
Three Mile Creek	3	F	11	0	1	3	6,724
Three Minds	2	F	2	1	0	0	9,360
Three Minute Call	4	F	9	0	1	1	6,855
Three Mysteries	3	F	14	2	3	0	39,204
Three Peaks	4	F	6	2	0	2	16,716
Three Piece Suit	3	G	8	0	3	2	8,015
Three Punch Louie	4	G	7	1	0	1	8,290
Three Ref's Girl	4	F	5	3	0	0	16,340
Three R's	5	G	8	3	1	1	13,500
Three Sheets	4	G	10	2	0	0	22,030
Three Sixes	6	G	2	0	0	0	0
Three Steps Ahead	3	G	11	2	2	0	14,835
Three Sticks	5	G	10	0	1	3	8,505
Three Taps	3	G	2	0	0	0	1,941
Three to Tango	5	G	25	4	3	5	30,551
Three Up	4	C	2	0	0	0	280
Three Valleys	3	C	3	0	1	1	67,690
Three Week Limit	3	F	15	1	1	2	7,824
Threeandoh	2	C	1	0	0	0	274
Threefingered Jack	2	C	1	0	0	0	0
Threeinone	3	C	2	0	0	0	247
Threeninetytwo	4	F	8	2	1	1	25,140
Threepeat Bald	3	F	1	0	0	0	42
Threepointer	8	G	7	1	1	1	6,900
Three's a Charm	8	M	14	2	0	3	11,288
Three's a Ruckus	3	G	12	1	2	2	10,456
Threesixtyfive	2	F	5	2	0	1	28,440
Threewitt	4	G	9	2	0	1	24,140
Thresher	2	G	6	2	1	1	60,291
Thrift Plan	5	G	10	0	5	1	13,387
Thrifty Nickel	7	H	3	0	0	0	120
Thrill After Dark	4	F	8	3	0	1	34,679
Thrill Hill	3	G	4	0	1	2	8,985
Thrill of My Life	3	F	8	0	0	0	1,526
Thrillin Discovery	9	G	13	4	3	1	40,100
Thrilling	4	F	11	0	0	1	2,735
Thrilling Request	5	M	12	4	2	2	25,442
Thrills Secret	5	M	1	0	0	0	0
Thrilly	5	M	9	0	1	0	3,692
Thrive	7	H	15	2	4	0	16,829
Throbbin Robin	7	G	12	3	1	1	34,755
Throne	4	F	5	0	0	0	1,800
Throphy Wife	6	M	4	1	1	0	2,455
Through His Kid	3	G	13	2	2	2	17,033
Through the Storm	2	C	2	2	0	0	24,000
Throw Her Down	2	F	1	0	0	0	0
Throw Me a Curve	3	G	6	2	2	0	90,360
Throw Me Roses	5	M	3	0	1	1	17,920
Throw Smoke	3	G	6	2	1	0	16,986
Throwatizzylizzy	4	F	13	2	1	2	13,476
Thrower	3	C	22	2	3	3	32,850
Throwin Heat	6	G	6	2	1	1	74,960
Thruitall	7	G	10	0	1	0	3,686
Thrust N Throttle	4	G	21	2	7	5	45,229
Thumbsupfredrick	4	G	4	1	0	0	2,610
Thumper Bumper	3	F	11	2	2	5	15,653
Thumper's Devil	2	C	3	0	0	0	1,316
Thumpers Gold	4	G	4	0	1	1	4,812
Thunder Again	2	C	2	0	0	0	0
Thunder and Glory	2	G	5	0	0	0	305
Thunder Atsunrise	5	H	9	1	1	0	8,896
Thunder Belle	2	C	1	0	0	1	1,560
Thunder Bid	5	G	6	1	1	1	9,186
Thunder Boot	5	G	7	0	1	1	13,650
Thunder Bull	6	G	10	5	1	0	55,086
Thunder Bullet	5	G	7	0	0	1	15,260
Thunder Bumpers	4	G	6	0	0	0	1,258
Thunder Buster	6	H	11	3	3	2	45,260
Thunder Charlie	3	G	7	1	1	1	6,630
Thunder Circle	2	G	6	0	0	0	960
Thunder Cloud	2	C	1	0	0	0	0
Thunder Days	5	G	2	0	0	1	2,530
Thunder Dragon (IRE)	8	G	14	2	3	3	23,545
Thunder Dream	3	C	4	1	0	0	21,930

Horse	Age	Sex	Sts	1st	2d	3d	Won
Thunder Dunder	5	G	7	2	0	0	10,690
Thunder E. O. G.	2	C	7	1	1	1	9,735
Thunder Fire	6	G	16	3	1	2	52,744
Thunder Force	5	H	2	1	0	0	11,050
Thunder Fox	3	G	5	1	3	0	35,460
Thunder Gulch Girl	3	F	11	2	4	1	15,202
Thunder Gus	5	G	2	0	0	1	1,500
Thunder Ibis	3	F	1	0	0	0	0
Thunder in the Air	3	C	1	0	0	0	0
Thunder Jake	3	G	2	1	1	0	7,200
Thunder Jam	6	M	4	1	0	1	5,148
Thunder Jammin	4	G	9	0	0	0	1,278
Thunder Jet G	3	G	4	0	0	0	154
Thunder Lady	2	F	2	0	0	1	6,300
Thunder Mab	3	C	11	1	0	3	17,770
Thunder Maker	2	C	1	0	0	1	4,200
Thunder Matt	8	G	12	1	2	1	6,362
Thunder Mission	2	C	4	0	0	1	8,650
Thunder N Bolts	3	G	6	1	1	0	9,047
Thunder n' Gold	2	C	2	0	0	0	980
Thunder Point	2	C	1	0	0	0	307
Thunder Power	2	G	1	0	0	0	0
Thunder Punch	9	G	2	0	0	1	1,275
Thunder Quest	5	G	12	1	0	1	7,770
Thunder Rain	3	G	7	1	1	0	37,475
Thunder Reason	3	F	3	0	0	0	1,680
Thunder Rider	7	G	16	5	3	2	60,077
Thunder Ridge	2	C	2	0	0	0	2,379
Thunder River	5	H	9	0	0	0	176
Thunder Road	3	F	5	0	0	0	340
Thunder Rock	5	H	5	0	0	0	0
Thunder Rocket	6	G	15	5	0	3	43,680
Thunder Rollin	5	G	3	0	0	1	468
Thunder Run	4	G	4	0	0	1	507
Thunder Rush	2	G	2	0	0	0	600
Thunder Score	4	C	4	0	0	0	295
Thunder Sky	3	F	2	0	1	1	2,215
Thunder Squall	4	C	12	4	1	1	55,381
Thunder Strikes	3	C	3	0	0	0	435
Thunder Till Dawn	5	G	7	0	1	0	812
Thunder Time	2	C	3	1	0	0	15,400
Thunder Touch	3	C	8	4	1	1	164,750
Thunder Twice	7	G	8	1	1	1	18,280
Thunder Zoot	6	G	3	0	1	1	2,315
Thunderama	6	G	1	0	0	0	0
Thundercase	4	C	4	0	0	0	510
Thunderchaser	2	C	5	1	2	0	24,475
Thunderfrog	2	C	2	1	0	0	30,145
Thundering a Salt	3	C	1	0	0	0	0
Thundering Creek	3	G	2	0	0	0	299
Thundering Verzy	3	G	14	4	3	2	65,302
Thundering West	6	G	1	0	0	0	288
Thunderingslew	2	G	2	0	0	0	600
Thunderinthchills	7	G	4	0	0	1	1,473
Thunderinthesky	5	G	9	0	0	1	850
Thundermann (AUS)	7	H	1	0	0	0	0
Thunderoll	8	G	2	0	0	1	1,010
Thunderous Summer	2	C	5	0	0	0	7,175
Thunderprince	2	C	3	1	0	1	29,594
Thunder's Echo	4	F	6	1	1	2	59,606
Thunders Luck	7	G	1	0	0	0	552
Thunders On	7	H	1	0	0	0	0
Thundershower	5	G	19	1	1	3	4,902
Thunderwood	3	G	3	0	0	0	735
Thunzarr	7	G	15	6	2	0	34,930
Thurber	4	G	7	0	1	1	1,170
Thurston	6	G	5	1	0	0	6,102
Thurston H	2	C	2	0	0	0	135
Thutmosis	4	G	10	1	1	2	6,082
Thy Madam	3	F	3	0	0	1	1,662
Thyer's (BRZ)	8	H	4	0	3	0	13,424
Ti Bossy	3	G	8	1	4	0	5,485
Ti Vee	3	C	2	0	0	0	131
Tia Maria	6	M	14	2	5	1	14,649
Tia Marquetry	5	M	15	1	2	4	16,946
Tia Pan	2	C	2	0	0	0	184
Tia Rose	2	F	3	1	0	0	17,298
Tia Sesa	6	M	3	0	0	0	131
Tiajuana Tour	4	G	8	0	1	1	4,189
Tialinga	3	F	15	3	2	2	79,145
Tiamo Mia	3	F	1	0	0	1	4,100
Tiara Gin	3	F	14	3	0	3	70,386
Tiara Time	5	M	2	0	0	0	105
Tia's Miss	3	F	13	2	0	4	46,620
Tia's Orphan Annie	9	M	1	0	0	0	0
Tia's Tiara	3	F	18	3	0	2	15,115
Tib Fib	3	G	3	1	1	1	17,470
Tibado	10	G	2	1	0	0	4,950
Tibbs	6	G	13	0	0	0	2,899
Tiber Tiger	5	G	19	5	2	2	50,220
Tiber Time	4	G	17	1	1	3	10,180
Tibor	3	G	15	1	0	2	6,211
Tiburon	4	G	1	0	0	0	0
Tic N Tin	9	G	11	2	1	2	48,794
Tic Tac Man (AUS)	4	C	7	3	1	0	117,775
Tic Tac Toe Louie	2	G	3	0	0	0	3,690
Tick Taat	5	G	11	1	0	2	8,882
Tick to the Wire	4	C	3	1	0	0	4,164
Tickel Me War	6	M	2	0	0	0	0
Ticker Tape (GB)	3	F	10	5	3	1	1,159,075
Tickers Diamonds	4	F	1	0	0	0	63
Ticker's Legacy	2	F	1	0	0	0	0
Ticket Holder	3	G	1	0	0	0	495
Ticket to Drive	4	G	2	0	0	0	257
Ticket to Freedom	7	G	9	2	1	0	48,414
Ticket to Fun	7	G	6	0	0	0	348
Ticket to Paris	5	H	13	0	3	2	12,489
Tickin' Okie	2	F	2	1	0	1	11,753
Tickle Bug	2	F	6	0	1	1	10,981
Tickle Me Malmo	6	M	8	1	0	3	3,330
Tickle Me Red	8	G	14	1	0	3	10,766
Tickle Me Too	6	M	8	0	1	1	3,832
Tickle My Toes	2	F	4	2	0	0	27,713
Tickle the Ivories	5	G	10	2	2	2	10,177
Tickled Purple	4	G	7	1	2	1	13,455
Ticklemyfancy	5	M	5	0	1	1	8,500
Tickles	5	M	1	0	0	0	300
Ticling Doc	5	H	7	0	1	0	2,318
Ticul	3	G	3	1	0	0	6,000
Tidal Wave	4	C	8	1	1	1	37,135
Tidbits	6	G	7	2	1	1	14,638
Tide City	2	F	13	0	3	3	30,047
Tide Mill	3	F	7	3	0	1	64,820
Tidy Step	6	M	7	1	1	1	19,140
Tidy Sweet	6	M	1	0	0	0	38
Tie Break	3	C	2	1	1	0	13,600
Tie Bucker	3	G	1	0	0	0	0
Tieaknotnholdon	6	G	9	1	0	3	4,498
Tied in Knots	4	G	2	0	0	0	315
Tied to the Mast	4	G	2	0	0	0	1,200
Tiedintwine	4	G	10	1	1	2	23,770
Tienneman Square	5	G	8	1	3	2	118,501
Tiercel	6	G	13	3	1	4	31,360
Tierra Del Sol	6	M	1	0	0	0	0
Tierra Dura	4	F	7	2	1	3	22,560
Tieta	5	M	6	0	0	2	6,952
Tietjen	3	G	11	2	2	0	30,661
Tifarah's Beauty	3	F	6	1	2	0	6,400
Tiffany Case	6	M	7	2	0	2	6,928
Tiffany Cut	2	F	5	0	0	0	3,930
Tiffany Gold	6	G	10	5	0	0	28,173
Tiffany Ice Queen	6	M	5	0	2	0	1,840
Tiffany Joan	3	F	10	2	0	1	9,461
Tiffany Ridge	4	F	8	2	1	1	14,892
Tiffany Rose	3	F	7	2	0	0	11,487
Tiffany Touch	2	F	4	1	1	0	35,950
Tiffany Tower	4	F	16	1	3	2	7,414
Tiffany's Award	3	F	5	0	0	1	1,749
Tiffany's Boot	3	F	5	1	0	1	11,800
Tiffany's Rodeo	3	F	11	1	1	0	40,078
Tiff's Bonzai	5	M	4	1	0	2	13,725
Tifonica (ARG)	6	M	5	0	1	0	16,698
Tifton	6	M	5	2	1	0	19,700
Tiger	3	C	2	1	0	0	24,920
Tiger Belle	2	F	3	1	0	0	16,980
Tiger Brush	4	G	8	2	1	0	23,164
Tiger Buff	2	C	1	0	0	0	134
Tiger Canyon	3	F	8	2	0	0	29,214

Horse	Age	Sex	Sts	1st	2d	3d	Won
Tiger Catress	4	F	2	1	0	0	6,980
Tiger Claw	2	G	2	0	0	1	2,915
Tiger Creek	6	G	1	0	0	0	288
Tiger Dream	3	F	6	0	0	1	4,428
Tiger Fever	2	F	1	0	1	0	6,600
Tiger Flash	3	G	16	0	3	1	4,488
Tiger Grunk Again	3	G	13	3	1	0	10,540
Tiger Heart	3	C	5	1	2	1	53,751
Tiger Hunt	3	C	1	0	0	0	3,750
Tiger Hunter	3	F	16	2	6	3	20,968
Tiger in a Tux	3	C	1	0	0	0	0
Tiger King	2	G	1	1	0	0	9,261
Tiger Lace	2	F	1	0	0	1	1,620
Tiger Lafem	3	F	2	0	0	0	284
Tiger Lee	3	C	1	0	0	0	119
Tiger Mania	6	G	16	0	1	0	2,113
Tiger Monarch	2	C	1	0	0	1	2,035
Tiger Moon	8	H	8	0	0	3	2,340
Tiger On Tour	2	G	4	1	0	1	16,392
Tiger Prince	3	G	7	1	0	0	2,796
Tiger Rose	2	F	2	0	0	0	1,920
Tiger Run	5	G	8	0	0	1	522
Tiger Select	3	G	5	0	0	0	1,344
Tiger Shrimp	4	G	15	3	5	1	140,084
Tiger Six	8	G	11	1	4	0	37,350
Tiger Slew	6	G	14	4	0	5	63,437
Tiger Tai	3	F	2	0	0	0	0
Tiger Talent	3	G	13	1	3	1	29,728
Tiger Tim	3	G	5	0	0	1	1,890
Tiger Time	5	G	4	0	0	0	210
Tiger Tower	7	G	2	0	0	0	0
Tiger Town	5	G	10	2	1	0	16,450
Tiger Walk	9	G	7	0	0	0	919
Tiger Woodman	2	C	1	0	0	0	370
Tigerline	2	C	1	0	0	1	5,000
Tigermite	5	M	10	1	4	0	12,670
Tiger's Edition	7	G	11	0	0	0	785
Tiger's Fool	4	C	1	0	0	0	145
Tiger's Halfmoon	5	M	7	0	0	1	15,060
Tiger's Reign	6	M	4	0	0	0	4,119
Tiger's Silverlady	5	M	4	0	1	1	4,602
Tigger Lilly Slew	3	F	6	0	0	2	7,250
Tight	4	G	5	0	0	0	0
Tight Cinch	2	G	1	0	0	0	0
Tight Security	4	F	12	0	1	3	5,511
Tight Spin	4	F	11	4	4	0	109,430
Tight Wager	4	G	4	1	0	1	17,306
Tight Wire	6	M	2	1	1	0	6,344
Tightasamousesear	5	M	3	0	0	1	1,080
Tighten Up	7	G	20	5	6	2	59,506
Tighten Up Todd	7	G	10	0	0	0	1,967
Tighthold	3	F	14	1	7	0	30,290
Tigi	3	F	6	0	1	1	24,918
Tigress Bythetail	4	F	5	1	0	0	22,539
Tijeras Taxi	2	C	1	0	0	0	96
Tijur	4	G	7	2	0	1	33,778
Tik Tak Doe	2	F	2	0	0	0	1,710
Tika's Best	4	F	14	4	2	1	44,345
Tiki Sweet (PER)	4	C	4	3	0	0	2,413
Tiki Tiki	3	C	13	2	3	2	30,700
Tikkanita	4	F	2	2	0	0	48,021
Tikkun (IRE)	5	G	3	0	0	1	6,800
Tildafatladysings	3	F	6	0	2	0	7,850
Tillie's Victor	8	G	5	0	2	1	5,600
Tilly Wagon	11	G	1	0	1	0	950
Tilly's Pulpit	2	F	4	0	0	0	1,305
Tiloys Little Rail	2	C	2	0	0	0	0
Tilt Luci's Odds	4	F	7	2	2	0	31,482
Tilt On Thejukebox	4	G	6	0	0	0	331
Tiltam	7	H	1	0	0	0	300
Tilthecowscomehome	2	F	6	1	0	0	13,340
Tilting Star	5	M	14	3	1	3	35,241
Timbalero	2	G	4	0	0	0	670
Timber	4	G	13	6	1	2	48,135
Timber Ack	11	G	15	3	5	1	19,146
Timber Chat	3	F	1	0	0	0	105
Timber Creek	3	G	10	2	1	3	19,178
Timber Jones	2	F	10	2	2	2	56,580
Timber Kitty	6	M	1	0	0	0	61
Timber Knot	2	C	1	0	0	0	92
Timber Legend	5	H	2	0	0	0	0
Timber Princess (BRZ)	4	F	2	1	0	0	25,520
Timbergreen	4	G	10	0	0	1	1,574
Timberwolf Power	6	G	9	3	0	2	56,846
Timbo	2	C	1	0	1	0	2,690
Timboruck	11	G	2	0	1	0	2,760
Timbos Dande	6	G	7	0	0	1	1,913
Timbucslew	3	G	9	2	1	2	18,047
Time	2	G	1	0	0	0	0
Time Chief	6	G	5	0	0	0	360
Time Chopper	6	H	9	0	2	0	3,085
Time Counter	3	G	13	1	2	0	17,166
Time Crafter	3	G	3	1	1	0	18,840
Time Digger	6	M	3	0	0	0	226
Time Eternal	5	H	9	2	0	0	10,431
Time Field	3	F	10	2	1	0	6,600
Time for a Heart	4	F	4	0	0	0	442
Time for a Prize	9	G	4	1	1	0	2,175
Time for a Tour	4	C	7	0	0	1	1,385
Time for a Win	5	M	7	1	2	1	2,408
Time for Drama	4	F	4	0	0	1	1,010
Time for Etbauer	3	F	11	3	2	3	63,835
Time for Giggles	4	F	5	0	0	0	272
Time for Karakorum	2	F	8	0	0	0	3,317
Time for Liberty	5	G	6	2	1	0	48,280
Time for Magic	3	F	13	3	3	3	47,851
Time for Minor	6	G	11	1	0	2	11,170
Time for Music	4	F	6	0	0	0	378
Time for Peaches	4	F	9	0	1	0	3,554
Time for Pride	3	G	9	1	2	1	11,790
Time for Revenge	3	G	8	0	1	0	4,936
Time for Scotty	4	G	6	0	2	0	6,540
Time for Smiles	5	M	5	0	0	0	456
Time for Tappy	4	G	1	0	0	0	76
Time for Wine	11	G	8	1	1	0	14,292
Time Fora Granslam	3	F	10	2	1	2	36,507
Time Gap	3	F	2	1	0	1	16,200
Time Gonnif	3	G	13	2	2	2	40,980
Time Heals	2	F	1	0	0	0	118
Time Honored	4	F	8	1	2	1	38,140
Time in Grade	3	F	13	1	2	1	28,565
Time in Space	3	F	5	0	0	0	1,716
Time Is Fleeting	4	G	11	0	0	0	228
Time Is Money	6	M	2	0	0	0	1,140
Time Lapse	4	G	1	0	0	0	400
Time Lock	4	F	10	1	2	1	11,422
Time Lost	3	F	9	1	2	0	29,370
Time of the Lepus	10	G	1	0	0	0	0
Time of Truth	5	G	13	0	0	1	4,480
Time of War	4	C	8	0	1	1	20,304
Time Ofthe Essence	3	F	5	0	0	0	1,565
Time On the Run	6	G	15	2	2	1	12,003
Time Out	2	C	2	1	0	0	16,800
Time Punch	5	G	13	1	4	1	28,268
Time Raider	4	G	7	0	1	0	1,934
Time Saver	2	F	5	2	0	0	80,870
Time Simon	5	H	8	0	1	1	1,650
Time to Accelerate	3	G	5	1	0	0	5,480
Time to Be On Top	2	F	1	0	0	0	2,583
Time to Be Sassy	5	G	19	9	1	1	65,420
Time to Blaze	3	F	10	1	1	1	4,265
Time to Buy	3	F	12	2	4	0	24,795
Time to Call	3	C	2	0	0	0	122
Time to Di	7	M	3	0	0	0	190
Time to Divorce	2	F	6	2	3	1	42,141
Time to Dyne	5	H	6	0	0	1	6,030
Time to Flare	7	G	10	0	1	2	4,252
Time to Get Wild	3	G	7	1	1	0	4,592
Time to Grow	3	F	2	0	0	0	99
Time to Jazz	5	M	7	2	0	1	9,029
Time to Jet	6	G	4	2	0	1	10,905
Time to Laugh	4	F	9	0	5	0	15,172
Time to Live	4	F	7	1	0	2	26,072
Time to Look	7	G	5	0	0	0	750
Time to Market	6	M	2	0	0	0	0
Time to Mine	4	G	5	0	1	0	2,098
Time to Rap	3	G	3	0	1	0	9,200
Time to Rush	4	F	15	3	4	3	42,831

Horse	Age	Sex	Sts	1st	2d	3d	Won
Time to Sing	2	C	8	2	3	1	41,160
Time to Ski	3	F	2	0	0	0	0
Time to Strike	5	G	6	0	0	2	6,160
Time to Time	8	G	13	2	3	4	10,490
Time to Weave	5	G	5	2	0	0	3,012
Timeaday	6	G	11	2	0	2	13,550
Timeaftertimeafter	3	C	8	0	2	2	19,181
Timeandahalf	3	G	14	1	1	2	7,400
Timed	4	C	8	1	0	3	8,514
Timed to a T.	8	M	4	0	0	0	650
Timeforabud	6	G	3	0	0	1	360
Timeforjewels	3	G	2	0	0	0	226
Timeform	4	G	3	0	0	0	618
Timeforwonmore	2	G	6	0	3	1	9,300
Timeintown	2	F	7	2	2	0	59,440
Timeisonourside	3	G	19	2	0	1	12,686
Timeless	6	G	3	0	0	0	0
Timeless Beauty	2	F	3	0	1	0	3,262
Timeless Dreamer	3	F	13	4	3	0	74,180
Timeless End	7	H	14	2	4	2	14,237
Timeless Event	3	C	3	0	0	0	225
Timeless Forest	2	F	1	0	0	0	0
Timeless Glory	3	F	6	0	3	0	8,870
Timeless Impulse	3	F	6	1	1	0	3,788
Timeless Luv	4	G	16	3	1	2	15,720
Timeless Music	4	F	9	0	2	1	3,137
Timeless Order	3	F	6	0	0	0	330
Timeless Passion	2	G	5	1	1	1	22,955
Timeless Poetry	3	F	18	1	4	3	9,936
Timeless Reality	3	F	2	0	0	0	0
Timeless Search	5	M	19	3	3	3	23,134
Timeless Zeal	5	G	19	0	5	3	24,062
Timeliano	4	F	3	0	0	0	263
Timely	6	M	3	0	0	0	288
Timely Action	5	H	5	0	0	5	28,240
Timely Baby	3	F	4	1	1	0	6,448
Timely Bid	2	C	1	1	0	0	13,680
Timely Call	4	G	17	1	3	3	11,229
Timely Deed	4	G	8	0	1	0	3,393
Timely Devil	7	H	9	0	0	0	225
Timely Ending	6	G	6	1	3	0	29,640
Timely Factor	6	G	13	3	1	3	98,025
Timely Half	5	G	3	0	0	0	39
Timely Impulse	2	C	1	1	0	0	13,680
Timely Jeff	4	G	8	3	1	2	92,320
Timely Minister	7	H	11	0	0	4	9,146
Timely Oak	6	G	9	0	1	2	2,778
Timely Perfection	4	F	7	0	1	0	1,342
Timely Presence	6	M	9	0	2	2	5,495
Timely Romance	4	G	6	1	0	2	7,140
Timely Silver	6	M	8	1	1	2	7,504
Timely Stitch	11	G	1	0	0	0	43
Timely Storms	3	C	11	3	2	1	22,675
Timely Tiger	3	G	7	0	0	0	1,946
Timely Toss	4	F	12	0	0	1	3,410
Timely Weave	7	G	1	0	0	1	1,425
Timely Whistle	4	G	8	2	0	2	8,900
Timely Writer	4	G	6	2	0	0	37,260
Times Thief	6	G	2	0	0	1	616
Timesafleeting	7	G	7	1	0	2	7,068
Timesarollin	4	C	20	2	3	3	16,687
Timestalker	2	F	6	0	0	0	1,605
Timetime	3	F	14	0	2	0	5,943
Timetoknowyou	5	G	19	3	4	5	25,707
Timetoshuffleoff	3	G	15	2	5	0	58,320
Timetotax	4	G	10	1	0	0	4,655
Timetoteeitup	2	C	6	0	0	2	5,870
Timetotrimthetree	5	G	3	0	0	0	105
Timing's the Key	6	G	5	1	1	0	3,320
Timmeran	5	G	12	3	1	2	32,146
Timmy M'boy	5	G	8	0	1	2	7,766
Timo	3	C	6	2	1	1	253,308
Timopocus	5	G	7	0	0	0	3,001
Timothy Mac	6	G	12	4	1	5	27,896
Timothy Murphy	5	G	1	0	0	0	550
Timpanogos	4	F	2	0	0	0	0
Tim's Crossing	7	G	3	0	0	0	4,020
Tim's Hat Trick	4	C	5	1	0	0	12,605
Tim's Last Chance	2	C	7	1	0	1	17,830
Tim's Talent	5	H	4	0	1	3	13,850
Tim's Tuition	4	G	8	1	3	1	15,382
Tin and Tonic	5	G	8	3	1	2	21,110
Tin Lips	3	F	5	2	0	2	13,390
Tin Man Commin	4	G	9	2	0	2	42,139
Tin Mine	3	F	10	1	4	0	15,030
Tin Pan Man	4	G	7	1	0	1	3,373
Tin Princess	3	F	6	0	0	0	2,535
Tin Smithen	7	G	4	1	2	1	17,170
Tin Star	6	H	2	0	0	1	440
Tin Tin	4	F	7	0	0	3	2,280
Tin Type	6	G	14	1	1	0	5,661
Tina Be Streakin	5	M	6	0	0	0	788
Tina Bull	4	F	7	2	3	2	140,025
Tina Can Do	4	F	19	5	3	5	47,767
Tina Sue	7	M	1	0	0	0	130
Tina Tango	6	M	5	0	0	0	644
Tinagoldengirl	4	F	7	2	0	3	21,185
Tinakilly	2	F	7	0	1	1	26,499
Tinalee	5	G	10	0	0	0	338
Tinarina	3	F	7	0	0	0	570
Tinas Angel	5	M	6	1	1	0	4,270
Tina's Love	3	F	4	0	0	1	5,800
Tincan	5	G	1	0	0	0	0
Tincan Too	4	F	8	0	2	1	20,140
Tindell	7	G	13	5	2	2	61,880
Tinder	3	F	17	2	4	2	31,869
Tiney Girl	7	M	8	1	0	2	6,431
Tingley City	3	F	4	0	0	0	833
Tingwithasting	3	F	2	1	0	0	63,000
Tinievlas	4	G	2	0	0	0	600
Tinker's Hope	5	M	9	2	2	1	17,273
Tinners Belle	5	M	9	0	3	2	9,026
Tinners Bucks	6	M	10	3	1	2	29,980
Tinner's Storm	4	G	13	1	6	0	12,478
Tinnian	3	G	4	0	0	0	0
Tinnitus Jazz	3	F	1	0	0	0	63
Tino Rossi	3	C	10	1	1	0	13,849
Tino Terrace	3	F	13	2	0	1	17,499
Tino's Deed	2	C	1	0	0	0	0
Tinseltown	2	C	1	0	0	0	180
Tinstack	3	G	1	0	0	0	50
Tiny Comet	4	F	8	0	0	0	608
Tiny Facts	3	F	13	1	2	3	20,065
Tiny Irish Dancer	6	M	5	0	0	0	587
Tiny Katie	5	M	2	0	0	0	77
Tiny Kisses	4	F	9	0	0	0	300
Tiny Lee	5	M	3	0	0	0	0
Tiny Patrica	3	F	7	1	2	1	12,859
Tiny Pink Pannies	7	M	7	1	0	1	8,368
Tiny Tim	5	G	13	2	4	2	18,843
Tiny Tutu	2	F	5	0	0	2	6,042
Tiny's Harper	3	G	10	1	0	1	5,835
Tio Cavito (CHI)	7	G	12	4	1	0	55,850
Tio Lupe	5	G	10	1	3	1	61,416
Tip Away	3	G	16	0	3	4	27,380
Tip City	2	C	9	2	1	3	66,050
Tip of Amnesia	2	F	4	0	0	0	420
Tip the Man	6	M	1	0	0	0	0
Tip Toe Softly	3	F	4	0	0	0	0
Tip Top	3	F	14	1	3	3	48,499
Tip Top Feet	4	G	7	1	1	1	4,726
Tip Top Topper	2	F	5	0	3	0	13,970
Tipalou Honey	4	F	17	1	1	2	9,878
Tipaza	5	M	2	0	0	0	101
Tipee Creeper	9	G	7	0	0	1	618
Tipical Pipp	6	G	9	0	1	2	11,240
Tiplersville	3	F	3	2	0	0	9,450
Tippa Tippa Tae	6	M	3	0	0	0	0
Tipper	2	C	1	1	0	0	9,690
Tipper Kelly M. D.	4	F	18	0	0	0	3,652
Tipperone	3	F	2	0	0	0	175
Tipping	3	F	10	3	2	2	31,123
Tipping Lightly	5	M	12	2	1	3	14,115
Tipping Point	5	G	8	2	0	1	10,845
Tippo	2	F	2	0	0	0	0
Tippy Won	6	G	15	0	2	2	8,727
Tippytoebyme	4	C	13	1	1	0	22,906
Tip's Red Rod	5	G	14	0	0	1	1,322

Horse	Age	Sex	Sts	1st	2d	3d	Won
Tip's Secret	3	C	8	1	0	0	9,360
Tipsoo Lake	3	G	4	0	0	0	75
Tipster	3	C	2	0	0	0	0
Tipsy Indy	3	F	8	2	2	1	16,975
Tipsy Scott	3	G	9	1	1	0	5,536
Tiptoe In	9	G	11	3	1	1	21,845
Tiptoe With Me	4	G	12	1	0	0	5,817
Tiptoes in Dreams	3	F	4	0	0	0	600
Tipton	2	C	3	0	1	0	3,844
Tipton County	5	M	2	0	0	0	660
Tiptop Slew	8	M	1	0	0	0	0
Tipyourbuddy	11	G	8	1	0	0	4,714
Tir Na Og	2	G	1	1	0	0	9,600
Tirak	5	G	3	0	0	0	2,440
Tire Biter	3	G	10	1	0	2	3,503
Tiryns	4	G	15	2	5	2	22,390
Tis a Belle	2	F	1	1	0	0	8,100
Tis a Deelite	3	F	1	0	0	0	360
Tis a Memoiry	3	F	9	0	0	1	656
Tis a Star	4	G	6	2	0	1	28,185
Tis Cafe Risque	3	F	8	4	1	0	55,010
Tis Captain Jackie	4	F	2	0	0	0	113
Tis Jacks Legacy	3	C	5	0	0	0	150
Tis Lycius	3	F	1	0	0	0	0
Tis Magical	5	G	5	1	1	1	25,590
Tis Me	5	M	7	4	0	0	27,918
Tis Ms C Four	2	F	4	0	2	0	7,535
Tis Nellie's Line	5	M	3	0	0	1	1,680
Tis Premixed	3	F	5	0	1	3	6,825
Tis So Fun	2	F	1	0	0	0	0
Tis Unanswerable	2	F	2	0	0	1	2,915
Tis Yo	4	G	2	0	0	0	315
Tisawink	3	C	7	2	2	1	52,440
Tisgem	3	G	1	0	0	0	0
Tishaboo	5	M	4	0	0	0	441
Tishimingo	3	G	3	0	0	0	356
Tisket a Tasket	3	F	6	2	2	0	55,140
Tisontoo	5	G	2	0	0	0	0
Tisourturn	5	M	13	1	2	1	19,674
Tissington	10	G	15	1	3	2	8,781
Tissowindy	3	G	3	0	0	1	1,320
Tit Tat	2	F	1	0	0	0	0
Tita Emerald	3	F	15	1	3	2	36,760
Titan Baseball	3	G	4	1	0	0	18,520
Titan Steel	7	G	5	0	1	1	2,515
Titanic Bea	3	F	15	2	4	2	19,769
Titanic Star	8	H	2	0	0	0	0
Titanica	3	F	2	0	0	0	96
Titanium	3	G	9	0	0	2	7,299
Titanium Ghost	4	G	6	1	1	0	34,742
Titanius	3	C	12	3	0	3	77,210
Tithing Secretary	6	H	3	0	1	0	1,012
Titia	6	M	13	2	3	0	62,980
Titian	6	G	4	0	3	0	6,405
Title Contender	4	G	2	1	0	0	6,160
Title Fight	2	C	2	0	0	0	0
Title for Title	7	G	11	2	1	1	22,730
Title Nine	5	M	2	0	0	0	0
Title Run	5	M	11	3	1	0	18,883
Title Shot	4	C	14	3	3	1	33,670
Titletown	6	G	3	0	0	0	96
Tito's Beau	4	C	13	1	5	2	50,565
Tiva	3	F	7	1	0	2	12,010
Tiva's Little Sis	4	F	4	1	0	1	24,800
Tiverton	2	C	1	0	0	0	225
Tivy's Beau	6	G	6	0	1	0	920
Tiz a Coup	4	G	9	0	0	1	8,216
Tiz a Dancer	3	F	11	3	2	2	81,130
Tiz a Windy Cee	3	F	4	0	1	1	10,005
Tiz Awesome	3	F	1	0	0	0	0
Tiz Bueno	2	G	3	0	0	0	3,380
Tiz One	3	F	6	0	3	1	7,424
Tiz Only Money	4	G	5	2	1	0	61,080
Tiz Royalty	4	F	11	1	2	1	66,478
Tiz Sandi	2	F	1	0	0	0	400
Tiz Shifty	3	F	2	1	0	0	11,400
Tiz Showtime	3	G	8	0	0	0	4,180
Tiz Too	3	F	9	2	1	1	13,017
Tiz Us	2	G	6	0	0	0	5,038
Tizadream	2	F	2	0	0	0	1,274
Tizafactor	2	G	3	0	0	1	975
Tizaflyin	3	G	6	1	1	1	16,500
Tizagal	6	M	8	3	1	1	52,890
Tizakitty	3	F	8	3	2	2	111,394
Tizamite	3	C	5	0	0	1	1,895
Tizatiger	4	C	8	1	0	0	4,190
Tizawinner	5	G	10	0	3	0	33,600
Tizawood	3	F	2	1	0	0	27,700
Tizbrite	2	C	1	0	0	0	400
Tizbud	5	H	2	0	0	0	11,000
Tizlight	3	C	3	0	0	0	780
Tizmania	7	G	4	0	0	0	451
Tizmanian Devil	2	C	4	1	1	2	55,280
Tizmyaly	3	F	2	0	0	0	800
Tizwar	3	G	4	1	0	1	6,475
Tizza Dude	4	G	9	3	1	0	17,285
Tizzaround	3	G	4	1	0	0	10,320
Tizznizzel	5	M	10	3	2	0	17,457
Tizzy Boy	3	G	10	2	1	2	18,800
Tizzy Lizzy	5	M	4	1	1	1	5,895
Tizzy Revenge	7	M	2	0	0	0	0
Tizzy Rizzi	2	F	7	1	0	1	26,970
Tizzy Time	3	C	1	0	0	0	0
Tlinget	3	F	4	0	0	0	0
Tm's El Dorado	2	F	3	0	0	0	0
Tnt Mill	4	F	9	1	0	1	6,598
Tnt Tower	4	G	7	0	0	0	1,175
To Be Announced	4	G	10	0	0	2	2,138
To Be King	2	C	4	2	0	0	19,301
To Be Or Not	3	G	15	3	3	3	34,810
To Cute for You	3	F	6	0	0	2	3,866
To Di for Again	6	G	16	4	4	2	67,800
To Do So	4	G	4	0	3	0	6,490
To Dream Again	4	F	10	0	4	2	26,072
To Fast Chica	4	F	1	0	0	0	50
To Go	4	C	10	1	1	0	37,503
To Hey	3	F	2	0	0	0	66
To Little Justice	5	M	13	1	3	2	13,175
To Lucky	3	F	1	0	0	0	112
To Much Moonshine	4	G	5	0	0	0	1,635
To Short to Punch	6	G	1	0	0	0	170
To Tall Dusty	3	G	11	2	1	4	25,248
To Tell the Truce	4	G	12	0	0	0	957
To the Alamo	3	F	4	1	0	0	14,540
To the Ballgame	3	G	9	3	0	0	14,770
To the Crowd	5	M	8	0	2	0	25,040
To the Highest Bid	3	F	20	1	1	0	9,426
To the Moon	5	G	6	0	0	0	248
To the Point	5	H	2	0	0	0	400
To the Queen	5	M	2	0	0	0	1,590
To the Republic	3	G	6	0	0	0	928
To the Victor	4	G	17	2	1	1	7,407
To the Whistle	3	G	8	0	0	0	950
To Wit	6	H	7	0	0	1	2,540
To Your Advantage	4	C	12	2	2	4	35,732
Toa	6	G	2	0	0	0	0
Toast and Jolly	2	G	10	2	1	0	22,857
Toast 'Em	2	G	4	1	0	1	17,820
Toast for Mr. Expo	6	G	3	1	1	1	12,820
Toast My Catch	5	H	3	0	0	0	0
Toast of Hadif	3	G	2	0	0	0	0
Toast of the Year	5	M	11	1	4	2	11,732
Toast the Ghost	2	G	3	0	0	0	1,260
Toast the Host	6	G	8	0	2	1	9,411
Toast to Monty	2	C	4	1	0	0	15,396
Toast to Tier	3	F	1	0	0	0	0
Toast to Wesley	6	G	5	0	0	1	1,408
Toasted	3	C	6	2	2	1	315,680
Toastfully	6	M	15	1	1	4	8,556
Toasttofriendship	3	F	8	4	1	0	42,382
Tobacco Bay	6	G	7	3	1	0	51,271
Tobasco Lake	4	C	3	0	0	0	0
Tobe Suave	3	C	6	2	0	3	95,742
Tobethemanbetheman	2	G	3	0	0	0	1,171
Tobi Raj	3	F	7	1	0	0	1,936
Tobicat	3	F	2	0	0	0	0
Tobie Lang	4	F	10	2	3	2	39,976
Tobin Miss	5	M	6	0	2	2	3,188

Horse	Age	Sex	Sts	1st	2d	3d	Won
Tobin's Clue	6	H	5	0	0	0	628
Tobin's Gabby	5	M	1	0	0	0	442
Tobins' Irish Lady	4	F	2	0	0	0	600
Toby's Success	4	G	2	1	0	1	30,500
Toca Araken	6	H	1	0	0	0	63
Toccet	4	C	8	0	2	0	83,597
Toccoa	3	F	3	1	0	0	8,175
Tocha	2	F	5	1	2	1	20,510
Toco Drive	5	G	7	1	1	0	2,284
Tocool for Words	5	G	13	0	0	2	2,668
Toda Rouge	4	F	3	0	0	0	260
Todays Cat	3	C	4	0	0	2	8,808
Today's Image	2	F	2	0	0	1	1,725
Today's News	2	C	1	0	0	0	400
Today's Tomorrow	8	G	1	0	0	1	1,300
Todd T. Shrupolini	3	C	1	0	0	0	1,250
Toddie C	7	M	5	0	0	0	507
Toddinator	7	G	6	0	0	0	560
Toddler	7	H	15	1	1	4	36,410
Todds Tootsie	3	F	12	1	0	0	5,501
Todds Volcano	4	G	9	2	1	0	8,456
Toddy'o	5	G	8	0	0	0	618
Tody's Jade	3	F	1	0	0	0	0
Toe Knee Nose	6	M	4	0	0	1	960
Toe the Mark	5	M	11	4	0	1	18,200
Toexpensivetoquit	3	G	5	1	1	2	5,738
Toga Cat	3	G	8	1	0	3	15,786
Toga Too	3	G	1	0	1	0	2,700
Toga's Triumph	4	F	9	1	1	2	6,553
Togs	5	M	3	0	0	0	192
Toi Fund	5	G	19	2	5	1	34,820
Toi Sailor	3	G	6	0	2	1	6,079
Toin and Boin	3	C	6	0	2	3	27,890
Toke 'n Classics	6	G	6	2	0	0	22,332
Token Dem	2	G	1	0	0	0	0
Token Taken	3	F	2	0	0	1	1,435
Token Tonko	4	G	14	0	0	1	8,296
Token Treasure	4	G	3	0	0	0	225
Token Wild One	2	C	4	0	1	0	9,540
Tokenness	4	F	2	0	0	0	0
Tokin N Jokin	3	F	5	0	0	1	3,470
Toknowmeistoloveme	4	F	13	2	2	3	15,071
Tokyo Baby	3	F	11	1	0	3	35,417
Tokyo Gold (JPN)	6	G	2	0	0	0	120
Tokyo Spy	5	M	9	3	1	2	43,353
Tokyo Storm	2	F	3	0	1	1	9,170
Toledo	5	G	4	0	0	0	799
Toledo King	3	G	13	3	3	2	11,791
Tolittletotalk	3	F	5	1	2	0	12,300
Toliver	2	C	4	1	1	1	42,250
Toll Bandit	3	C	11	2	1	2	23,317
Toll Free	3	G	16	0	0	3	6,107
Toll Mighty	12	G	2	0	0	0	72
Toll Taker	2	F	6	3	0	1	114,240
Tollgate's Account	3	G	9	1	3	0	25,950
Tolna City	3	G	5	0	0	0	484
Tolu	3	F	9	0	1	2	11,485
Toluca Exit	3	F	3	0	1	0	1,964
Tom and Roses	4	G	4	0	0	0	279
Tom Lane	4	G	10	0	0	1	3,035
Tom the River Rat	6	G	7	1	1	1	20,510
Tom the Terminator	3	C	1	0	0	0	0
Tom Who	3	G	22	2	7	2	42,640
Tomadache	8	G	7	0	0	0	345
Tomahawk	4	C	4	1	0	1	26,336
Tomahawk Chop	3	C	3	1	0	0	24,846
Tomahawk Lake	5	H	5	1	0	0	5,490
Tomahawk Walk	4	C	7	0	1	1	6,059
Tomarosa	4	F	6	1	0	1	2,228
Tomars Last Birdie	6	G	7	0	0	0	873
Tomasina Registina	8	M	2	0	0	0	130
Tomata Buster	3	G	14	2	3	2	16,633
Tomathan	3	G	1	0	1	0	1,825
Tomato Soup	3	C	8	0	2	1	7,030
Tomb Raider	5	G	7	1	0	0	5,639
Tomball One	3	G	2	0	0	0	300
Tombatim	2	F	7	0	2	1	6,009
Tomboy Lady	5	M	1	0	0	0	0
Tomboy Mine	4	F	10	2	3	1	17,612
Tomcolee	4	G	1	0	1	0	5,200
Tomencino	5	M	1	1	0	0	5,160
Tommy Boy	3	G	2	0	0	0	0
Tommy Crainer	5	G	15	2	1	3	11,613
Tommy Gun	5	G	4	0	0	0	495
Tommy Jeanne	8	G	6	0	1	2	3,710
Tommy Lees Shadow	7	G	4	0	0	1	1,688
Tommy O'Dea	4	G	6	0	2	2	12,750
Tommy Rock	5	G	16	1	4	3	16,917
Tommy T.	3	G	16	4	2	1	17,217
Tommy the Crook	3	C	7	2	0	1	31,145
Tommy the Gun	3	C	18	1	0	3	9,360
Tommy Wells	4	G	7	1	3	0	33,690
Tommyland	2	G	2	1	0	0	12,400
Tommyleecat	3	G	11	1	2	3	20,040
Tommys Jet	2	F	6	2	0	0	24,840
Tommy's Palm	3	G	5	0	1	1	7,020
Tommy's Topper	2	C	5	2	2	0	93,440
Tomo	4	C	5	0	1	0	4,520
Tomoka Bound	3	F	3	0	0	0	1,600
Tomoka Joy	3	F	8	0	0	1	1,567
Tomorrow No More	4	G	20	3	2	1	28,496
Tomorrow's Affair	3	F	2	0	0	0	300
Tomorrows Banquet	4	G	12	2	3	4	87,140
Tomorrows Champ	3	C	5	1	0	1	30,417
Tomorrow's Day	9	G	5	0	0	0	0
Tomorrows Forecast	3	G	2	0	0	0	0
Tomorrows Gold	3	C	17	3	4	4	46,407
Tomorrows Idol	3	C	4	1	1	0	28,322
Tomorrows Lady	2	F	1	0	0	0	118
Tomorrows Leader	3	G	2	1	0	0	8,080
Tomorrows Magic	3	C	7	1	0	3	39,950
Tomorrow's News	3	C	5	0	1	1	12,647
Tomorrow's Number	3	F	10	0	2	3	8,514
Tomorrows Peach	4	F	1	0	0	0	0
Tomorrows Reality	3	G	4	0	0	0	2,423
Tomorrows Trick	4	F	3	0	0	0	533
Tomorrow's Turn	2	G	6	1	3	2	19,883
Tomorrows War Cry	4	G	15	1	1	3	10,745
Tomprado	5	G	13	2	3	3	26,150
Tom's Angel	4	F	4	0	0	1	5,120
Tom's Big Cat	3	C	6	2	0	1	24,600
Tom's Birthday	8	G	2	0	0	0	82
Tom's Boomer	4	G	12	1	0	1	3,634
Tom's Crozier	4	G	3	0	0	0	204
Tom's Empire	4	C	2	0	0	0	0
Tom's First	3	F	1	0	0	0	0
Toms Girl	3	F	12	2	2	1	10,320
Tom's Memory	4	C	1	0	0	0	0
Toms Pickle	4	G	3	0	0	0	260
Toms Retta	7	M	1	0	0	0	0
Tom's Thunder	6	G	8	0	4	1	19,580
Tom's Treasure	5	M	1	0	0	0	75
Toms Tuffanuff	3	C	3	0	0	0	464
Tom'sthreetees	3	F	14	3	2	2	61,230
Tomtom Tommalice	7	G	3	0	1	1	7,704
Tomufta	5	G	11	1	1	0	2,626
Ton a Run	3	F	7	3	0	2	21,914
Tonality	2	F	11	1	1	1	10,490
Tonapah	6	G	10	1	1	1	6,693
Tonco	6	G	16	0	2	3	38,456
Toneless	4	G	8	2	2	2	47,743
Tonelli's Legacy	5	M	12	2	2	1	56,400
Tonc's Prospect	3	F	1	0	0	0	0
Tonga Boy Too	3	G	9	1	0	0	6,487
Toni Ann	7	M	11	4	0	2	28,548
Toni DeNitto	2	F	2	0	0	0	2,040
Toni Michelle	4	F	3	0	0	1	400
Toni T	4	G	12	0	0	3	17,759
Toni Tats	3	F	5	1	0	0	10,160
Toni Zamora	4	F	2	0	0	0	0
Tonic Nights	5	G	9	2	1	1	39,930
Tonight Rainbow	5	G	11	3	1	3	59,225
Tonights Prospect	3	F	6	0	0	1	1,712
Toni's Childhood	4	G	3	0	0	0	1,155
Toni's Desire	3	G	2	0	0	0	282
Tonith	3	G	10	2	1	0	19,100
Tonitruant	4	C	3	0	0	3	14,475
Tonka Boy	2	C	5	1	2	0	13,230

Horse	Age	Sex	Sts	1st	2d	3d	Won
Tonka Time	3	F	2	0	0	0	0
Tonkawa	7	G	1	0	0	0	0
Tonopah Alice	2	F	2	0	0	0	0
Tonopah Joe	4	G	15	1	3	3	10,871
Tons	5	H	12	1	0	0	8,880
Tonshi	6	H	3	0	0	0	0
Tonsilitis	3	F	4	2	0	1	24,380
Tonto Bloomberg	4	G	14	2	1	2	14,015
Tonto Gusto	9	G	8	4	0	0	38,968
Tontoboychuk	7	G	3	2	0	1	7,980
Tony Basich	8	G	13	2	3	1	34,145
Tony Blue Blazes	4	G	11	1	1	1	9,480
Tony Boy	5	G	5	0	0	0	881
Tony Curtis	4	G	14	2	0	3	31,439
Tony Montana	3	C	2	0	0	0	400
Tony N Jenny	2	F	8	1	0	0	10,760
Tony Soprano	4	C	14	2	1	2	21,450
Tony the Bear	8	G	5	0	0	0	229
Tonyanna	3	F	13	0	0	2	6,145
Tonyrony	6	G	15	1	2	3	12,867
Tony's Birthday	3	G	6	0	1	1	2,606
Tony's Flag	3	G	6	0	0	0	971
Tony's Girl	4	F	8	1	2	2	24,170
Tony's Loc	6	G	13	1	2	3	29,204
Tony's Royalty	6	G	7	1	4	1	32,695
Tony's Tiger	4	G	2	0	0	0	255
Tonys Touch	3	F	8	0	0	0	586
Tonyspal Craig	5	H	5	1	0	1	18,820
Tonz of Love	5	H	9	3	1	0	19,916
Too Be a Gem	5	G	4	1	0	0	6,264
Too Blue to B True	3	F	4	1	0	1	8,202
Too Brilliant	5	M	6	1	0	0	32,930
Too Chilly to Tell	3	G	4	0	0	0	219
Too Clever	4	F	10	1	2	1	17,696
Too Close to Call	5	H	4	2	1	0	3,200
Too Cool	2	G	3	1	0	0	5,940
Too Cute	4	F	10	2	3	1	49,207
Too Cute to Care	5	M	2	0	0	0	0
Too Excessive	5	G	3	0	0	1	1,086
Too Fast for Me	3	F	2	0	0	0	300
Too Fast to Top	4	G	12	0	1	1	7,398
Too Fine for You	5	M	8	0	0	1	3,508
Too Formal	3	F	2	0	0	0	0
Too Hard to Name	3	F	2	0	0	1	5,700
Too Hot to Tango	2	F	2	1	0	1	11,316
Too Hot to Trot	10	G	16	1	1	0	3,639
Too Irresistible	6	M	2	1	0	0	6,000
Too Lite Margarita	2	F	6	0	0	1	4,693
Too Many Bubbles	3	F	8	2	1	1	69,714
Too Many Bucks	6	G	2	0	0	1	3,326
Too Many Choices	5	M	9	2	3	1	30,675
Too Many Cocktails	2	G	3	1	0	0	7,275
Too Many Dollars	3	C	10	0	0	2	2,775
Too Many Mikes	3	G	4	0	1	1	2,573
Too Many Trains	3	G	12	2	0	3	18,336
Too Many Twos	2	F	2	0	0	0	500
Too Mean	3	G	3	0	0	2	6,400
Too Much Avail	7	G	7	1	0	0	10,520
Too Much Beans	2	C	2	0	0	0	0
Too Much Class	3	F	5	2	1	1	72,105
Too Much Moxie	4	F	8	0	0	0	509
Too Much Time	7	M	3	0	0	0	237
Too Much to Love	3	F	4	1	0	0	14,040
Too Pleasant	3	F	4	0	0	1	648
Too Real	6	G	23	2	1	6	16,222
Too Sly	2	G	5	0	0	1	1,450
Too Stripes	3	G	7	2	0	0	13,180
Too Suave	5	G	4	0	0	0	0
Too Tall	6	M	11	3	4	1	37,050
Too Telly Too	3	G	6	1	0	0	4,049
Too the Target	4	G	13	4	1	2	31,587
Too too Crafty	2	C	7	1	1	1	7,790
Too Tough to Blush	7	G	1	0	0	0	0
Too Tough to Tame	4	F	9	1	2	1	12,470
Too Tricky	2	F	6	0	1	0	5,130
Too Wet to Work	5	G	4	0	0	0	675
Too Willing	4	G	18	0	2	1	8,901
Toobroketocall	2	F	2	0	0	0	0
Toofastforyou	3	G	13	2	1	3	42,980
Toogie too Shoes	4	F	8	1	2	0	27,750
Toogies Kris	3	F	4	0	0	0	0
Toogoodforyou	4	G	6	1	0	2	7,240
Toogoodtobetrue	4	F	5	1	0	2	2,420
Toohappy	4	F	1	0	0	0	190
Tooitus	3	G	9	1	1	4	11,515
Took Out	5	M	7	1	1	1	32,710
Tooke Tooke	2	F	7	2	0	0	29,545
Tookie	5	M	5	0	1	0	800
Toolate Kasey	3	C	11	0	1	2	12,278
Tooles a Beauty	2	F	1	0	0	0	270
Toolight Bracelet	4	F	2	0	0	1	1,222
Toolight's Halo	3	C	9	0	0	0	1,175
Toolights' Music	5	G	10	2	1	3	17,283
Toolighttodance	4	F	7	1	1	0	20,215
Toolighttonight	6	H	16	0	4	3	14,624
Toolighttoquittoo	6	H	9	2	0	1	13,315
Tooluckytoquit	4	F	14	2	0	2	18,552
Toomuch Chavez	5	G	7	2	1	0	34,050
Toomuchinformation	6	G	14	2	1	4	15,527
Toomuchtrouble	4	G	3	0	0	1	1,167
Toons Tank	4	G	1	0	0	0	43
Toora Loora Mukora	3	G	12	0	1	2	15,750
Toorizziforoy	3	G	9	3	1	0	52,775
Toosixyformytoga	6	G	10	0	0	0	1,169
Toosmartsweetheart	2	F	6	1	0	2	17,780
Toosweetforwords	2	F	1	0	0	0	140
Toot Bird	3	F	4	2	1	0	17,605
Toot Toot	2	F	3	0	0	0	330
Toot Your Horn	7	H	6	1	0	0	6,353
Tootalltofall	5	M	1	0	0	0	78
Tooth Doctor	5	H	14	1	6	4	30,332
Tootie Fruity	5	M	1	0	0	0	0
Tooties Teddy	8	G	11	2	2	4	4,922
Tootoo	3	F	6	0	3	1	12,396
Toot's Lil Chic	3	F	11	2	1	3	70,523
Tootsie Rapper	6	H	11	1	2	3	8,291
Toowildtodrive	10	M	10	1	1	1	2,590
Top Account Queen	5	M	7	0	1	1	2,396
Top Appeal	2	C	2	0	0	0	140
Top Arazi	6	G	11	2	4	0	8,588
Top Bananna	4	F	10	3	0	1	17,194
Top Bet	2	F	4	0	0	3	9,390
Top Billing	3	G	3	0	0	1	540
Top Biscuit	2	C	1	0	0	0	0
Top Boot	4	G	7	2	2	0	30,358
Top Brass	6	H	9	3	1	0	26,881
Top Buck	5	H	4	1	1	0	11,200
Top Bunk	7	G	14	3	4	2	60,820
Top C Jim	8	G	3	0	0	0	349
Top Call	6	G	2	0	0	0	114
Top Cappelletti	4	F	7	4	0	0	26,224
Top Card	4	F	11	0	1	2	4,670
Top Carte	4	G	6	0	1	1	4,970
Top Case	4	G	10	2	2	0	9,477
Top Cash	4	G	4	1	0	0	3,780
Top City	2	C	1	0	1	0	3,690
Top Commander	4	G	9	4	2	0	59,560
Top Cut	4	G	9	3	2	0	30,421
Top Designer	4	G	13	1	2	1	29,200
Top Elimator	5	G	4	1	2	0	9,513
Top Encounter	3	F	9	1	2	0	11,375
Top Flight Express	3	C	3	0	0	0	0
Top Fox	4	F	12	1	4	1	10,836
Top Gate	3	G	2	1	0	0	31,945
Top Gent	3	G	3	0	1	1	3,700
Top Girl	2	F	3	0	0	0	3,045
Top Glory	3	G	12	2	2	1	50,581
Top Gump	3	F	1	0	0	0	110
Top Her	4	F	12	1	4	2	27,035
Top Hill	3	F	13	2	1	4	70,823
Top Hit	6	H	11	1	2	2	48,670
Top Hombre	5	G	6	1	0	0	2,618
Top Honours	6	G	6	0	1	0	15,440
Top Ingredients	4	F	15	1	3	3	20,270
Top Interrogator	4	G	11	0	0	3	6,435
Top Jar	3	G	2	0	0	0	0
Top Jet	2	C	2	0	0	0	168
Top Jig	4	G	9	1	0	0	3,919

Horse	Age	Sex	Sts	1st	2d	3d	Won
Top Kitty	3	F	8	0	0	1	5,447
Top Lavender	7	G	22	1	2	1	6,838
Top Local	8	G	5	0	0	1	1,099
Top Machine	3	G	4	1	1	1	7,926
Top Mile	2	G	1	0	0	0	0
Top Mint	5	G	10	2	3	1	31,610
Top Money	2	G	3	3	0	0	94,560
Top Notch Fox	3	G	3	0	0	1	3,480
Top O Morn	4	G	7	0	0	0	125
Top of Class	3	C	5	1	0	2	13,230
Top of His Game	5	G	9	2	0	4	9,357
Top of the Bill	3	C	7	1	0	1	25,625
Top of the Hour	6	G	8	1	1	1	19,785
Top of the Line	2	C	1	0	0	0	0
Top of the News	6	G	17	6	4	3	90,600
Top of the World	5	G	2	0	0	0	120
Top Ofthe Mountain	7	G	8	0	0	0	688
Top Park	6	M	2	0	0	0	160
Top Penny	4	F	7	2	2	0	34,605
Top Player	2	C	5	0	0	1	4,560
Top Plum	3	C	18	1	2	1	9,134
Top Pop	5	G	6	1	1	1	9,915
Top Prospector	5	H	4	0	1	0	1,350
Top Pumpkin	4	F	6	1	1	1	7,155
Top Punch	7	G	8	1	1	2	17,260
Top Row	3	G	13	2	1	1	20,190
Top Running	2	F	5	0	0	0	0
Top Sailor	3	G	5	1	1	1	4,400
Top Scruples	2	G	7	1	2	2	27,605
Top Secret Affair	6	G	7	1	0	3	15,500
Top Secret Code	3	G	10	0	0	0	2,363
Top Shoter	5	G	6	3	2	0	127,070
Top Smoke	3	G	3	0	1	0	1,940
Top Song	4	G	8	0	0	0	4,027
Top Spartan	6	H	4	0	0	0	371
Top Spinner (NZ)	6	M	6	2	1	0	69,509
Top Spock	2	G	1	0	0	0	821
Top Spot	2	F	2	0	0	0	2,160
Top Stage Dancer	5	M	6	0	1	0	5,376
Top Summer	8	G	4	0	0	0	402
Top Sword	3	G	8	0	1	2	9,900
Top Take	2	C	6	1	3	1	17,619
Top Target	3	C	10	2	1	3	19,512
Top Tech	2	C	1	0	0	1	1,952
Top This and That	2	C	1	0	0	0	500
Top Toad	2	G	8	1	0	1	3,787
Top Treasure	4	F	11	1	1	2	12,025
Top Up	4	G	15	1	1	2	5,293
Top Victory	3	G	3	0	1	0	2,700
Top Woman	4	F	12	1	5	4	13,473
Top Zarb	7	G	6	1	1	2	14,535
Topango	3	F	8	2	1	1	93,815
Topaz Jewel	4	F	7	0	1	0	6,435
Topeka	3	F	14	5	3	0	101,040
Topiary	3	F	5	1	0	0	35,730
Topic	3	F	2	0	0	0	420
Toppers Lil Trick	2	F	2	0	1	1	2,000
Topping	4	G	10	3	1	1	61,410
Topple	2	C	5	1	0	0	6,210
Tops Echo	2	F	4	0	2	0	6,169
Top's My Pop	5	M	12	2	1	2	5,248
Top's Rocket	3	G	3	0	0	0	905
Topsecretclearance	3	C	2	0	1	0	1,275
Topside	3	F	3	0	0	0	470
Topsoil King	4	G	4	0	0	0	4,360
Topsoil Lady	4	F	7	2	0	2	11,333
Topspin Lob	5	M	3	0	0	0	0
Topstitch	3	F	3	1	1	0	21,450
Topwynson	5	G	14	2	4	0	58,627
Toranado	3	G	4	0	0	0	495
Toratora	4	C	14	1	4	1	24,636
Torbay Girl	3	F	5	0	0	0	620
Torch Her Up	2	F	2	0	0	0	90
Torch It	4	G	13	2	2	5	15,369
Torch of Freedom	2	G	2	0	1	0	2,160
Torch Relay	4	G	5	1	1	1	17,850
Torch the Halls	6	G	16	4	2	0	83,380
Torchie	4	F	4	1	0	0	5,545
Torchlight	4	F	4	1	0	0	7,320
Tordue	4	F	10	3	4	0	65,708
Tori Cheyenne	8	M	2	0	0	0	150
Toriano Cat	3	G	11	2	1	1	14,400
Torioso	8	G	10	1	2	1	17,520
Tori's Connection	2	F	1	0	0	0	0
Tori's Falcon	3	F	5	0	0	1	6,376
Tori's Scalawag	4	F	8	0	0	1	892
Tori's Story	2	F	3	0	1	1	9,660
Tori's Thunder	5	G	10	1	0	0	14,958
Tori's Triump	5	M	5	1	1	0	9,662
Torke	7	G	9	2	1	2	10,438
Torment	6	G	2	0	0	0	0
Tormenta Del Gata	5	M	14	1	3	3	12,494
Tormentas Coast	3	F	10	1	0	0	3,625
Tornadic	8	G	3	0	0	0	0
Tornado Bait	3	F	7	0	2	2	9,688
Tornado Warning	3	F	11	2	0	1	16,579
Toronto Flash	2	C	3	0	0	1	1,960
Torontonian Rocket	2	G	1	0	0	0	70
Torpedo Man	2	G	1	0	0	0	140
Torquay	2	C	1	0	0	0	3,528
Torque Man	5	G	11	2	2	1	19,839
Torqus	3	F	3	0	0	1	1,010
Torre and Zim	4	G	12	3	0	0	34,641
Torre Dei Nolfi	10	G	10	0	1	4	5,919
Torreason	2	G	4	0	1	1	4,275
Torrent of Song	3	F	2	1	0	0	5,920
Torrental Kid	3	C	7	0	0	0	399
Torrential Lady	3	F	15	1	3	2	22,816
Torrential Run	3	G	7	1	0	0	3,731
Torrential Star	3	G	3	0	0	0	969
Torrestrella (IRE)	3	F	6	3	0	0	285,488
Torrid Joe Al	6	G	12	2	0	5	8,012
Torrid Sand	8	G	8	1	1	0	5,539
Torry	9	R	10	0	0	0	1,082
Tortellini M D	3	F	12	1	0	2	2,301
Tortilla Flat	3	C	1	0	0	0	0
Tortilla Soup	2	G	5	0	0	0	2,355
Torun	3	G	3	0	0	2	9,430
Tory's Tune	5	M	1	0	0	0	130
Tory's Victory	3	F	3	0	0	0	0
Tosayhowmuchicare	4	G	9	1	0	2	10,715
Toscani	4	G	3	3	0	0	58,800
Toscanini	3	C	11	1	0	0	5,021
Toss Both Ways	3	G	12	1	1	1	5,073
Toss It Again	6	M	1	0	0	0	235
Toss Me'the Money	6	G	5	0	0	0	268
Toss the Gold	5	M	2	1	0	0	4,965
Toss the Sauce	2	F	1	0	0	0	0
Tossed and Found	6	M	1	0	0	0	0
Tot	5	M	8	1	3	0	10,048
Total Advantage	4	G	9	0	5	0	42,190
Total Anilation	7	G	5	1	0	0	11,155
Total Anticipation	6	G	10	1	3	2	17,543
Total Appeal	3	F	10	1	0	2	7,045
Total Arrogance	4	F	9	1	1	0	8,233
Total Command	3	C	4	1	1	0	29,420
Total Commitment	4	C	2	1	0	0	9,600
Total Consent	5	G	15	1	4	3	7,542
Total Dominance	4	G	9	1	1	2	5,243
Total Expectations	2	F	4	2	0	1	13,070
Total Expressions	3	F	5	0	0	1	1,192
Total Fitness	2	F	2	0	0	0	150
Total Impact (CHI)	6	H	11	1	5	2	988,390
Total Knock Out	4	G	1	0	0	1	2,717
Total Pro	6	G	3	0	1	0	960
Total Reality	5	G	2	0	0	0	520
Total Return	3	G	9	0	0	0	1,906
Total Revenge	3	G	6	0	0	1	1,652
Total Teaser	6	G	6	0	0	0	522
Total Wager	2	C	6	1	0	0	31,125
Totalitarian	2	C	2	0	1	0	3,600
Totally Cosmic	5	M	1	0	0	0	2,400
Totally Grand	4	F	12	3	3	1	55,970
Totally Platinum	3	C	3	0	0	0	0
Totally Precious	5	M	11	3	4	2	155,620
Totally Tootsie	2	F	2	0	0	0	134
Totalwreck	3	G	9	0	0	1	2,385
Totalyseneca	9	G	2	0	2	0	1,680

Horse	Age	Sex	Sts	1st	2d	3d	Won
Tote the Note	5	M	1	0	0	0	0
Totebook	4	F	1	0	0	0	100
Totem's Aly	4	G	10	1	3	0	5,433
Tothe Chase	7	G	5	0	1	0	1,448
Totteridge	7	G	10	2	2	1	20,300
Tou Jake	5	G	6	1	0	0	9,150
Toubeeb	3	C	5	1	0	0	14,970
Touch Em All	3	C	6	0	0	0	3,451
Touch Em Baby	3	F	2	0	0	0	0
Touch for Luck	3	G	7	0	2	0	7,784
Touch Jade	4	G	2	0	0	0	640
Touch Lightly	4	F	11	1	2	2	14,441
Touch 'n' Fly (IRE)	8	H	11	1	0	1	5,568
Touch of Cash	3	G	9	2	0	1	19,725
Touch of Creme	3	F	3	0	1	1	8,500
Touch of Fame	4	G	3	0	0	0	185
Touch of Fortune	3	F	8	0	0	1	1,758
Touch of Ginger	5	M	1	0	0	0	0
Touch of Honey	11	G	5	0	0	1	1,509
Touch of l'Aiglon	4	F	8	0	1	2	2,461
Touch of Madness	3	F	1	0	0	0	130
Touch of Mahogony	5	G	18	0	0	2	7,209
Touch of Platinum	5	G	10	1	1	1	13,965
Touch of Power	7	G	11	3	1	0	13,384
Touch of Quality	3	G	17	2	3	3	17,799
Touch of Spirit	3	F	9	0	3	2	15,550
Touch of Splendor	2	F	3	0	0	1	2,390
Touch of Victory	3	F	10	3	3	1	75,400
Touch of Whimsy	3	F	3	0	0	1	4,173
Touch Platinum	4	C	2	0	0	0	2,640
Touch Silk	4	F	5	1	0	0	31,540
Touch Silver	8	G	10	1	0	1	14,766
Touch Softly	4	C	9	1	3	0	16,490
Touch the Wire	4	G	7	2	0	2	125,256
Touchabull	4	F	10	3	0	4	26,594
Touchdown Cat	3	C	9	1	1	0	9,913
Touchdown Run	4	G	16	2	4	2	21,749
Touchdown U S C	3	G	7	1	0	2	18,560
Touchdownminnesota	2	F	1	0	0	0	140
Touched an Angel	5	M	7	1	0	1	4,017
Touched by Angel	3	F	8	0	0	0	330
Touched by Madness	2	G	2	1	0	0	13,680
Touched by N Angel	7	M	15	3	5	3	6,236
Touched by Whitney	5	G	6	0	1	1	2,947
Touching Gold	4	G	10	1	0	0	11,937
Touchnow	3	F	9	2	2	0	327,283
Touchoville	9	M	8	1	1	2	6,138
Touchwood	4	F	6	2	0	1	13,070
Touchy	3	F	8	0	1	0	4,799
Touchy Broad	2	F	1	1	0	0	12,000
Touchy Remark	6	G	4	0	2	0	2,106
Touchy Situation	5	M	1	0	0	0	0
Tough and Gilded	2	C	3	0	1	0	1,945
Tough as Neatie	3	C	16	2	2	1	49,130
Tough Banker	4	G	16	3	3	3	12,586
Tough Beth	2	F	2	0	0	2	3,564
Tough Buck	7	G	12	1	0	0	3,851
Tough Buy	2	G	4	0	0	1	4,251
Tough City	5	G	8	0	0	2	1,310
Tough City Girl	3	F	9	1	3	1	61,540
Tough Cookie Baby	4	F	9	2	0	1	10,830
Tough Cozzene	4	C	7	2	0	1	17,097
Tough Crowd	6	G	8	3	1	1	15,607
Tough Exercise	5	G	2	0	0	0	186
Tough Gal	3	F	5	0	2	0	9,680
Tough Game	5	H	2	0	0	0	0
Tough Hagerdorn	6	G	2	0	0	0	100
Tough Joe	3	G	8	1	2	2	11,929
Tough Kid	3	G	10	2	1	1	22,945
Tough Old Joe	4	G	8	0	0	1	3,147
Tough Pilgrim	3	G	7	4	0	0	29,365
Tough Shot	3	G	2	0	0	1	900
Tough Time Victor	2	G	2	0	0	0	2,064
Tough to Handle	2	G	4	0	0	0	880
Tough to Repete	2	F	3	1	1	0	4,875
Tough Topic	2	C	1	0	0	0	0
Tougher 'n Most	2	C	2	0	0	1	4,218
Tougher Still	7	G	6	1	0	0	1,427
Toughgoshopping	3	F	2	0	0	0	920
Toughie Two Shoes	4	G	5	0	0	1	3,994
Toughkenamon	5	G	9	3	1	2	50,090
Toughonabankroll	4	F	10	1	4	2	66,972
Toughonetobeat	2	F	5	0	1	1	7,750
Toujours d'Amour	3	G	8	3	1	2	43,170
Tour a Lurah	4	F	8	2	1	0	16,960
Tour Argentina	5	G	4	0	1	2	5,982
Tour D' Gold	3	G	3	0	2	0	4,886
Tour D' Triomphe	6	G	10	1	1	3	9,991
Tour Dance	3	C	11	1	0	2	16,640
Tour d'Gem	3	F	1	0	0	0	140
Tour d'Star	4	F	10	0	5	0	33,886
Tour Hostess	8	M	10	2	3	1	38,790
Tour Japan	6	M	6	0	0	0	246
Tour of Glory	2	F	3	0	0	0	0
Tour of the Cat	6	G	8	2	0	0	69,200
Tour of the Rose	7	M	15	6	3	2	91,568
Tour of the Tiger	2	C	4	0	0	1	2,680
Tour On Review	2	C	4	0	1	0	7,690
Tour Sez	7	M	5	1	0	1	13,480
Tour the Hive	7	G	10	2	1	1	88,558
Tour the Line	5	G	17	2	2	2	35,347
Tour With Wells	3	G	5	0	1	0	1,948
Touring Dancer M	2	G	1	0	0	0	300
Touring England	5	H	7	1	0	0	10,130
Touring Star	5	M	4	2	0	0	14,280
Tourist Trap	8	G	12	1	0	3	6,436
Tournament Play	7	G	2	0	0	0	225
Tour's Bluff	7	G	3	0	0	1	2,530
Tour's Energy	5	M	1	0	0	0	0
Tour's Thunder	3	G	12	2	2	1	14,237
Tours Val	7	M	17	2	4	2	26,578
Tovu Tiku Teivu	5	M	3	0	0	0	158
Tow Path	4	G	5	0	0	1	1,330
Tower of Honour	5	M	8	3	3	0	94,136
Tower of the Winds	5	M	7	0	0	1	7,280
Tower Six	3	G	5	1	2	1	8,679
Towering Palace (GB)	2	F	1	0	0	0	132
Towering Pines	4	G	14	2	3	3	21,814
Tower's Rebel	6	G	13	0	0	0	1,402
Tower's Turf	5	G	10	0	0	2	1,924
Town Attire	3	F	7	0	0	1	5,100
Town Charmer	3	F	8	1	0	4	43,712
Town Flyer	8	G	7	0	0	0	150
Town Gambler	7	G	10	4	0	0	13,490
Town Ghost	7	G	16	0	1	1	2,350
Town Gossip	2	F	2	1	0	0	9,861
Town Hall	4	G	10	0	2	3	10,960
Town Honey	2	F	2	0	1	0	4,200
Town Luck	4	F	2	0	0	0	350
Town Meeting	4	G	12	0	0	1	1,093
Town Squire	3	C	6	1	0	0	10,560
Town Without Pity	3	G	8	1	0	0	11,690
Townline	3	F	8	2	0	2	36,870
Townncountry	3	G	6	1	0	1	6,425
Townsville	5	M	13	1	1	1	24,049
Toxaholic	3	G	4	0	1	1	1,747
Toxic	2	F	5	0	0	0	271
Toxic Country	5	H	7	1	1	0	2,452
Toxic Level	4	G	5	0	1	2	2,528
Toxic Tea	6	G	10	1	1	3	9,944
Toxicated Match	2	G	3	0	2	0	6,396
Toy At Sea	3	G	2	0	0	0	0
Toy for Roy	4	F	6	0	0	1	3,500
Toy Soldier (GER)	4	C	3	0	2	0	9,600
Toy Thief	2	C	2	0	0	1	3,660
Toy Tiger Jr.	6	H	9	0	0	1	2,751
Toy Tigress	3	F	1	0	1	0	5,220
Toyland	8	G	7	0	3	0	1,197
Trabajadora	2	F	2	0	0	1	1,050
Trabajo Gold	3	C	11	1	3	1	18,260
Trac Bound	3	G	4	0	0	0	800
Trace	2	C	1	0	0	0	0
Trace the Blush	5	M	12	0	0	2	1,550
Tracemark	5	G	13	2	1	1	16,400
Tracer	2	F	4	0	0	0	730
Traces of Silver	2	C	1	0	0	0	1,020
Tracethe Call	6	G	10	2	2	1	22,640
Tracey's Babe	3	F	5	1	1	1	15,581

Horse	Age	Sex	Sts	1st	2d	3d	Won
Tracey's Miner	4	F	9	1	2	2	14,679
Tracey's Tune	3	F	3	0	1	1	4,616
Traci Girl	5	M	14	3	1	3	92,437
Tracibee	2	F	2	1	1	0	22,000
Traci's Wild	5	M	2	0	0	0	0
Track Bar	4	F	1	0	0	0	0
Track Boss	7	G	8	2	2	1	15,000
Track Cat	5	G	13	1	1	2	12,577
Track City Lad	9	G	1	0	0	0	108
Track Hoe Jo	4	G	4	0	1	1	7,729
Track Key	4	F	10	0	0	0	1,830
Track Lover	6	G	8	0	0	0	588
Track Prince	5	G	12	1	0	1	5,934
Track Rumor	8	G	3	0	1	0	830
Track Side	3	F	3	0	0	0	621
Track Terror	5	M	3	0	0	0	304
Track Tramp	3	F	1	0	0	0	300
Track Writer	3	G	1	0	0	0	95
Trackem 'n' Wackem	4	G	9	3	3	0	16,856
Tracker Bob	6	H	11	2	2	1	8,542
Tracktalk (AUS)	4	F	5	1	1	0	49,840
Tracmac	4	F	9	2	1	1	10,338
Tract	3	C	3	1	1	0	19,320
Tractor Required	3	F	7	0	0	2	1,668
Tracy Arm	2	C	4	0	1	0	2,935
Tracy's Tonka Toy	4	G	9	0	2	0	33,523
Tracy's Tracton	4	F	15	0	6	2	32,170
Trade Beads	4	F	11	0	2	2	17,594
Trade for the Rent	3	G	1	0	0	0	0
Trade Marker	4	C	3	0	0	0	0
Trade N Treasure	4	F	8	2	0	0	21,015
Traded	3	C	7	0	1	0	2,290
Trader Hill	8	M	7	0	2	0	4,050
Trader West	2	C	10	0	0	2	5,330
Trader's Bluff	5	G	9	5	0	1	15,760
Tradewest	2	C	5	0	0	4	2,560
Trading Halt	3	G	16	2	5	2	16,878
Trading Hours	4	C	10	2	1	3	20,290
Traditional	5	H	9	1	2	3	45,110
Traditional Flyer	2	G	6	1	1	0	5,780
Trae Genius	6	G	13	3	2	2	20,364
Traffic Alert	3	C	12	2	1	1	28,550
Traffic Belle	4	F	6	2	0	1	11,817
Traffic Chief	4	C	3	0	0	1	7,773
Traffic Stop	3	G	5	1	0	0	9,656
Traffic Ticket	5	G	4	0	0	0	37
Traffic Update	3	C	3	2	0	0	52,228
Trafficade	2	F	2	1	1	0	4,660
Trafford Park	5	G	2	0	0	0	0
Trail	5	G	19	5	3	0	53,957
Trail Drive	2	G	6	1	0	0	6,685
Trail Maid	3	F	3	0	0	0	150
Trail Mix	3	G	2	1	0	1	30,960
Trail Rider	4	F	7	0	1	2	4,280
Trail Runner	3	G	9	1	0	1	3,208
Trail Striker	3	G	3	1	1	1	24,160
Trailer Man	7	G	7	1	1	1	7,131
Trailinthewoods	2	F	4	0	0	0	404
Trailode	3	C	6	0	0	2	532
Trailoftwocities	3	G	2	0	0	0	175
Trails End	7	G	10	2	2	2	7,608
Trails No One	2	C	1	0	0	0	400
Trailsun	3	C	3	0	0	0	149
Trained Observer	8	G	2	0	0	0	0
Traitor de l'Amour	4	G	17	3	3	4	25,765
Traitor On Line	2	C	2	0	0	1	2,640
Traitor Road	4	G	1	0	0	0	37
Tralee Gold	6	G	4	1	0	0	6,940
Tralee Rose	3	F	5	0	0	0	1,797
Trampus Too	7	G	8	1	1	2	19,355
Trance	2	F	2	0	0	0	254
Tranquil Sea	2	F	5	1	1	1	8,610
Tranquility Base	5	M	18	2	0	0	19,765
Tranquility Bay	3	F	10	1	1	2	29,820
Trans Decor	7	G	9	1	0	0	7,590
Transaction	5	M	2	0	0	0	204
Transcendent	5	G	16	7	1	1	82,394
Transcribe	3	G	12	1	1	2	10,878
Transept	3	C	4	0	2	0	21,840
Transfer	3	C	3	0	1	0	1,890
Transgress	3	G	6	2	1	2	45,450
Transin	4	C	7	1	3	0	19,434
Translation	3	F	9	2	1	0	12,826
Transmitter	3	C	1	0	0	0	0
Transparent	4	G	1	0	0	0	44
Transpire	7	G	2	0	0	0	602
Transtar	11	G	2	0	0	0	550
Tranup	4	G	1	0	0	0	0
Tranzachion	8	G	17	1	2	3	10,157
Trap	2	F	1	0	0	0	75
Trap Seattle	6	M	7	2	0	1	5,564
Trap the Genius	5	H	2	0	1	0	500
Trap the Shadow	5	G	2	0	0	0	0
Trapp Express	4	C	4	1	2	0	5,240
Trapp Rico	4	F	8	0	0	1	1,871
Trapp Trouble	5	G	3	0	0	0	124
Trapped Again	4	C	10	2	3	2	92,937
Trapped Echoes	7	H	2	0	0	0	0
Trapper Meek	8	G	5	1	2	0	6,160
Trash the Code	4	F	6	0	0	0	447
Traumatic	4	F	5	1	2	1	16,354
Trav a Long	5	G	8	1	0	0	4,788
Travail de Leroux	4	G	2	0	0	0	0
Travel Alarm	4	G	13	3	2	0	75,065
Travel Due Stay	2	C	1	0	0	0	0
Travel On	3	F	6	0	0	0	954
Travel Postcard	3	F	7	1	0	2	21,930
Travel Wise	3	G	6	0	1	0	3,243
Travelator	4	F	9	3	2	2	187,915
Traveler	4	F	8	1	1	1	26,152
Traveler Express	5	G	6	1	1	1	6,600
Traveleze	4	G	5	1	0	2	16,197
Travelin Edgar	4	G	7	0	1	0	3,360
Travelin' Soldier	3	G	4	0	0	1	1,095
Traveling Connie	4	F	7	0	0	0	937
Travelling Cache	2	C	3	0	1	0	2,378
Travelling Star	8	H	2	0	0	0	0
Travertine	3	G	10	2	2	0	16,025
Travis' Harley	2	C	1	0	0	0	0
Travis Will	5	G	7	0	0	0	3,182
Travlin' Polly	3	F	2	1	0	1	2,310
Travois	3	F	3	0	0	0	1,200
Tre of Roses	3	G	6	0	0	0	0
Treacherous Quest	5	G	5	0	0	1	1,750
Treason	4	C	12	3	3	1	28,350
Treasure Beach	5	M	4	0	1	1	9,110
Treasure Booty	3	G	4	0	3	1	5,100
Treasure Hunt	8	G	5	2	1	0	7,210
Treasure Lac	4	G	3	1	0	0	15,600
Treasure Links	2	C	1	0	0	0	118
Treasure Reef	2	C	2	0	0	0	1,110
Treasure Seeker	3	G	4	1	0	1	23,425
Treasure Song	2	F	2	0	0	0	2,255
Treasure Taker	7	H	6	0	0	0	526
Treasure Won	6	G	16	0	2	2	5,422
Treasure Zone	5	G	8	1	1	1	18,904
Treasured Covenant	4	F	8	2	0	1	11,625
Treasured Friend	3	G	9	3	1	0	57,280
Treasured Heart	3	F	5	0	0	0	1,216
Treasured Indian	5	G	13	0	2	0	4,567
Treasure's Dream	5	M	8	0	2	1	38,980
Treasury Deposit	3	F	6	1	0	0	8,835
Treat	3	C	5	1	0	0	17,365
Treat Me Doc	10	G	3	0	0	0	1,890
Treatherlikealady	6	M	2	0	0	0	932
Trebaw	4	G	9	0	0	2	2,741
Trebbiano	5	G	2	0	0	0	188
Trebia (CHI)	6	M	13	2	1	1	74,920
Trebizond (IRE)	8	G	6	0	0	0	5,200
Tree Bandit	6	M	13	1	1	1	9,027
Tree Foliage	7	G	3	0	0	0	332
Tree Legs	6	G	1	0	0	0	100
Tree Lover	3	F	9	1	2	2	19,695
Tree Shaker	3	G	4	0	1	0	1,500
Tree the Cat	4	F	1	0	0	0	0
Tree Tops Veil	2	F	5	1	2	1	10,560
Trees in Gold	3	C	3	0	0	0	960
Treetop Lover	5	G	1	0	0	0	40

RECORDS OF HORSES

Horse	Age	Sex	Sts	1st	2d	3d	Won
Treetop's Glory	3	G	8	1	1	0	10,723
Trefinity	5	H	14	1	1	3	22,800
Treford	4	G	13	2	2	3	40,812
Trego	2	G	5	1	1	0	13,560
Treink	6	M	11	1	2	1	6,854
Tremmor	6	G	2	0	0	0	827
Trempolino Trick	6	G	16	0	1	2	4,262
Trempolino's Jig	3	C	7	0	0	0	542
Trenchtown	4	G	9	1	0	0	5,045
Trendi Debut	4	F	4	0	0	0	486
Trendseeker	4	F	6	0	0	0	936
Trendy (ARG)	4	G	6	0	0	2	11,260
Trendy Copy	2	F	2	0	0	1	2,880
Trendy Intern	2	F	4	0	0	1	1,697
Trendy Native	3	F	12	3	2	3	33,320
Trennedy	2	F	1	0	0	0	70
Trentino	7	H	17	0	3	4	7,947
Trents Special	5	G	9	2	0	0	17,846
Tres Aimees's	3	G	10	1	2	1	12,389
Tres Chaud	4	F	4	2	1	1	19,530
Tres Diamantes	5	H	9	1	0	0	10,313
Tres Joses	2	F	3	0	1	0	5,000
Tres Ladies	4	F	3	0	0	0	0
Tres Linda	3	F	3	0	0	0	0
Tres Lucy	3	F	1	0	0	0	59
Tres' Mauve	6	M	8	0	0	0	422
Tres Netta Joe	2	F	3	0	0	0	1,075
Tres Petite	3	F	2	0	0	0	0
Tres Tiempo	2	G	1	0	0	0	216
Tres Touche	7	G	9	3	2	0	171,510
Tresor Du Jour	3	F	3	0	0	0	275
Tresor Du Soleil	2	G	4	1	0	1	7,260
Tresor l'Amour	3	F	3	0	0	1	1,305
Tressel	3	F	1	0	0	0	145
Trevanian	3	G	10	2	0	3	46,933
Trevite	3	G	3	1	0	1	30,660
Trevor Forever	4	G	8	0	0	0	1,640
Trevor's Lucky One	6	G	11	2	5	2	49,544
Trey Aero	6	G	9	0	2	2	3,157
Treylucey	3	F	8	1	0	1	15,414
Trey's Mighty One	3	G	12	1	2	2	21,346
Tri Chem	5	G	12	0	2	4	6,474
Tri Diplomacy	4	G	9	1	3	1	12,380
Tri for the Moon	3	F	10	2	2	3	27,550
Tri Like the Devil	2	F	1	0	0	0	0
Tri M All	5	G	3	0	0	0	123
Tri My Style	3	C	12	3	2	1	73,386
Tri n' Nickya	3	C	16	1	5	1	26,841
Tri Paw	7	G	2	0	0	0	100
Tri Phailme	3	G	16	1	1	5	12,590
Tri Some Irish	4	F	4	1	0	1	19,640
Tri This Way	4	F	12	0	4	0	11,210
Tri to Be True	5	G	18	1	3	3	28,650
Tri Tong	3	G	15	0	1	1	5,047
Tri Wagering	7	G	1	0	0	0	480
Tria	5	M	10	2	2	1	8,850
Trial and Error	6	G	3	0	0	0	0
Trial by Judge	4	F	14	2	4	1	12,820
Trial by Jury	5	H	7	0	0	0	2,200
Trial Dancer	5	M	9	1	1	2	23,474
Trial Judge	3	C	5	0	0	0	105
Trial Prep	5	H	12	3	0	3	93,649
Trianon Plaza	2	F	1	0	1	0	2,500
Tribal	3	G	4	1	0	0	4,090
Tribal Council	5	G	23	3	2	4	26,828
Tribal Gold	9	G	4	0	0	0	238
Tribal Heir	2	G	2	0	0	0	800
Tribal Leader	4	G	5	0	0	1	1,690
Tribal Prince	3	C	12	0	0	0	1,505
Tribal Quest	5	M	18	0	1	0	3,925
Tribal Trick	5	G	3	0	0	0	52
Tribal Wind	3	F	2	0	0	0	560
Tribarge	4	G	12	2	2	0	16,820
Tribe	4	G	7	0	1	2	8,160
Tribeca Dancer	3	F	2	0	0	0	0
Tribo Ka	4	F	1	0	0	0	0
Tribrook	3	F	6	0	0	0	180
Tribulator	4	C	1	0	0	0	0
Tribute Express	4	G	12	4	4	1	60,010
Tribute to America	4	G	2	0	0	0	297
Tribute to Gold	4	F	12	3	1	3	24,822
Tribute to Heroes	4	C	1	0	1	0	5,600
Tributetojimnded	5	G	11	0	2	0	8,835
Tributetothatcher	4	F	1	0	0	0	300
Tricia	3	F	4	0	0	0	770
Tricia's Account	4	F	14	0	1	1	15,662
Trick Again	4	F	12	4	2	3	101,120
Trick Bag	7	G	10	3	3	0	26,220
Trick Ballet	3	G	10	1	4	0	8,080
Trick Card	5	G	1	0	0	1	1,090
Trick Conviction	6	G	5	0	0	0	0
Trick Lantern	2	G	2	0	0	0	95
Trick Lover	2	C	4	0	0	0	969
Trick Me Not	3	C	9	0	0	0	835
Trick of the North	3	C	4	0	0	1	4,103
Trick of Time	3	G	5	0	3	1	22,440
Trick Or Trial	3	F	8	0	1	3	16,952
Trick Or Trixie	5	M	1	0	0	0	0
Trick Pony	4	F	6	0	1	1	364
Trick Question	2	F	2	1	1	0	14,120
Trick Shot Artist	3	C	1	0	0	0	1,280
Trick Shot Gal	3	F	15	1	3	5	14,832
Trick the Devil	3	F	3	0	0	0	0
Trick Your Man	3	F	11	3	0	0	26,323
Tricked Into Love	5	M	14	2	1	2	17,056
Tricked Twice	3	F	9	0	0	0	789
Trickey Jones	3	G	3	0	0	0	0
Trickey Mickey	4	G	8	3	0	2	14,075
Trickey Todd	2	C	2	0	2	0	21,639
Trickey Trevor	5	H	4	3	0	0	50,350
Trickinthepark	3	G	8	0	3	2	20,954
Trickle of Gold	2	F	5	1	0	3	42,225
Tricks and Grins	4	G	15	0	4	2	11,835
Trick's Bid	3	C	1	0	0	0	0
Trick's Lad	6	G	8	2	0	3	14,890
Tricks N Chips	3	F	4	0	0	0	381
Tricks Not Treats	3	C	11	1	5	1	38,350
Tricks of Glory	3	C	1	0	0	0	165
Tricks to Win	3	G	6	1	1	0	20,235
Tricksand	5	M	8	0	1	0	3,436
Tricksey Miss	3	F	9	1	1	2	10,374
Trickster Trio	5	G	1	0	0	0	109
Tricktor	3	F	4	0	0	0	1,220
Tricky Alex	4	G	5	1	0	1	4,800
Tricky Avenger	3	G	4	0	0	1	1,458
Tricky Bo	3	G	11	0	1	1	2,974
Tricky Cal	3	G	9	0	2	1	2,745
Tricky Caller	6	M	3	0	0	0	426
Tricky Cara	3	F	3	0	0	0	1,200
Tricky City	3	F	7	0	0	0	368
Tricky Clearance	5	G	17	2	4	2	26,155
Tricky Coletrain	3	G	3	0	0	0	125
Tricky Crystal	3	F	13	2	1	1	21,395
Tricky Dakota	5	G	7	1	2	1	9,382
Tricky Deal	4	F	1	0	0	0	44
Tricky Dee	5	M	13	3	4	0	17,898
Tricky Defense	3	G	4	1	0	1	2,315
Tricky Dennis	2	C	1	0	0	0	75
Tricky Destiny	3	F	6	0	1	1	7,000
Tricky Devil	3	C	2	2	0	0	43,915
Tricky Don	3	G	7	1	1	1	6,802
Tricky Dreams	5	G	8	1	3	3	3,697
Tricky E. Tee	7	H	6	0	1	0	3,000
Tricky Fashions	3	F	2	0	0	0	0
Tricky Flash Flood	3	C	9	1	1	0	43,676
Tricky Fun Smash	2	C	7	1	1	1	13,994
Tricky Gem	2	G	11	0	1	4	10,242
Tricky Gin	4	G	8	1	0	1	15,552
Tricky Greinette	3	F	10	1	0	1	15,410
Tricky Hearts	7	G	3	0	0	1	704
Tricky Hill Cat	2	F	1	1	0	0	6,325
Tricky Image	5	G	14	2	2	2	31,613
Tricky Intro	3	C	3	0	1	1	3,100
Tricky Katie	4	F	12	2	0	2	9,721
Tricky Linklee	6	G	4	0	0	0	317
Tricky Little Girl	3	F	14	2	1	2	65,832
Tricky Love	3	F	1	0	0	0	0
Tricky Luck	5	M	3	0	0	0	0

Horse	Age	Sex	Sts	1st	2d	3d	Won
Tricky Machine	6	G	6	2	2	1	17,731
Tricky Mackee	6	M	3	0	0	0	327
Tricky Maneuver	6	G	1	0	0	0	0
Tricky Marine	5	G	4	0	0	0	0
Tricky Mo Jo	5	M	6	1	0	0	5,797
Tricky Mocha	8	G	11	3	1	1	80,990
Tricky Nicki	7	M	3	0	0	0	0
Tricky Noble	3	F	16	1	3	4	9,459
Tricky Now	7	G	1	1	0	0	2,640
Tricky Pace	6	G	7	3	1	0	57,960
Tricky Phone	4	F	3	0	0	0	530
Tricky Pick Six	4	G	1	0	0	0	0
Tricky Princess	5	M	5	2	0	0	8,284
Tricky Purpose	4	G	13	0	0	1	1,142
Tricky Ransom	4	G	12	1	3	2	9,617
Tricky Ray	3	F	6	0	2	1	2,070
Tricky Ray Source	9	G	22	1	4	2	13,701
Tricky Ridge	2	F	4	1	1	0	23,600
Tricky Secret	2	G	4	1	0	0	13,500
Tricky Sister	5	M	3	0	0	0	0
Tricky Slew	2	G	2	1	0	0	6,300
Tricky Spring	2	F	1	0	0	0	0
Tricky Storm	5	H	8	1	2	2	40,740
Tricky Surf	4	F	10	4	0	0	60,322
Tricky Surprise	5	M	12	1	1	0	18,540
Tricky Taboo	3	C	6	2	1	0	138,026
Tricky Tactics	2	C	3	2	0	1	48,613
Tricky Thinker	2	G	2	1	1	0	12,861
Tricky Time	8	G	10	1	1	3	5,305
Tricky Touch	3	C	6	1	2	1	11,590
Tricky Toy	4	G	8	1	0	1	6,093
Tricky Toyotah	3	F	10	0	0	0	696
Tricky Transaction	4	F	6	1	2	1	19,181
Tricky Travis	6	G	12	2	2	0	41,747
Tricky Truth	4	F	8	0	1	1	6,100
Tricky Tyler	7	G	14	3	2	1	14,028
Tricky Vixen	2	F	3	0	1	2	9,990
Tricky Wars	7	M	15	2	0	2	11,268
Tricky Wekiva	2	C	2	0	0	0	0
Tricky Work	3	F	6	0	2	0	7,135
Trickygoesforgold	3	F	8	0	0	0	502
Tricky's Gal	6	M	12	0	0	3	5,440
Trickytrip	2	F	2	0	0	0	0
Tricon Gold	3	C	11	1	1	1	14,240
Tricona	4	G	2	0	1	0	758
Trident House	4	G	8	2	0	1	48,930
Trieste	4	G	4	0	0	0	550
Trieste's Destiny	2	F	1	0	0	0	0
Trieste's Honor	3	C	7	3	0	1	131,880
Trifecta	3	C	12	5	0	1	76,183
Trigala	5	M	17	0	1	2	4,037
Trigger Fish Lane	2	F	3	0	2	1	9,880
Trigonometry	3	F	1	0	0	0	662
Trihighfive	3	G	6	0	1	0	3,687
Trijonia	4	F	7	2	2	1	45,000
Trikarakorum'sway	2	G	3	0	0	0	1,117
Trikitrikitriki	3	F	10	2	3	0	22,020
Trilogy (GB)	5	H	7	0	0	0	1,735
Trim Image	5	G	5	0	0	0	1,050
Trimark Two	4	G	10	1	0	2	8,588
Trimmer Springs	2	F	1	0	0	0	400
Trimontium	5	G	4	0	1	1	8,805
Trinas Other Son	9	G	13	2	1	2	14,630
Trini Calling	2	C	5	0	0	0	1,105
Trinity Moon	4	F	6	0	0	1	5,855
Trinity River	7	G	9	1	0	1	9,905
Triny's Storm	3	F	4	0	0	0	1,327
Triomphe Spitfire	4	G	6	0	0	0	1,111
Trion Georgia	6	H	6	1	0	0	20,670
Trip Charge	9	G	14	2	1	2	26,035
Trip Report	8	G	5	0	0	0	542
Trip the Switch	2	F	1	0	0	0	235
Tripcord	6	G	12	2	1	0	11,142
Triplane	6	G	8	0	2	1	4,846
Triple a Society	6	G	5	1	2	1	5,700
Triple Act	4	F	2	1	0	0	32,520
Triple Appeal	8	M	17	2	4	2	12,399
Triple Cade	3	F	14	1	1	2	4,579
Triple Card	6	G	11	0	2	2	12,172
Triple Cash	5	G	9	0	0	0	1,537
Triple Chance	4	G	9	3	1	2	22,651
Triple Fantasy	3	F	5	2	0	0	58,743
Triple Fax	5	G	19	2	4	1	24,434
Triple Gold	5	M	6	1	0	0	8,820
Triple Gold (IRE)	5	M	1	0	0	0	1,020
Triple Great	10	G	9	1	3	0	3,001
Triple J	4	F	6	0	2	0	13,250
Triple Jacq	6	G	13	0	1	2	6,895
Triple Jim	9	G	13	4	2	2	18,220
Triple Man O	7	G	5	0	0	0	75
Triple Putt	6	G	6	0	0	0	824
Triple Schnied	2	F	5	0	0	1	7,248
Triple Shot	3	G	4	1	2	0	16,579
Triple Silence	2	F	2	0	1	0	3,575
Triple Slam	3	F	5	1	1	0	18,760
Triple Socks	3	G	8	1	1	0	8,549
Triple Speaker	3	G	11	0	0	0	1,302
Triple Spin	6	M	14	3	1	2	21,387
Triple the Speed	4	F	11	1	5	0	24,145
Triple Threat	7	M	2	1	0	0	4,500
Triple Tiara	3	F	4	1	1	0	17,930
Triple Time	6	G	6	2	1	0	6,080
Triple Tri	9	H	2	0	0	0	330
Triple V Account	2	F	1	0	0	0	235
Triple Vixen	4	F	3	0	0	0	326
Triple Witching	6	G	3	0	0	1	1,254
Triple X.	3	C	10	3	1	4	56,960
Tripp Wire	7	M	12	1	1	1	14,800
Triptips	4	C	7	1	1	2	7,683
Triptowin	6	G	2	1	0	0	4,785
Triptronic	4	G	11	1	1	0	10,765
Tri's Moment	4	F	2	0	0	0	0
Tri's Passion	4	F	3	0	1	0	8,970
Trish Blusher	5	M	5	0	0	0	724
Trisher	6	M	11	2	4	2	6,533
Trish's Cajun	4	F	7	1	0	2	12,900
Trish's Diamond	3	C	11	3	3	2	116,659
Trisis	4	F	6	1	0	0	7,075
Tristas Demon	4	G	3	0	0	0	132
Tristin's Race	5	G	6	2	1	0	12,495
Tristorm	6	M	9	0	0	2	1,601
Triton	2	C	2	0	0	0	2,300
Triton Missile	4	C	14	1	3	4	60,280
Tritsar	5	G	13	3	0	3	15,940
Triumph Arch	2	F	2	0	0	1	2,340
Triumphal Entry	3	C	10	0	0	0	5,640
Triumphant Potion	3	F	6	1	1	1	20,390
Trivia Queen	10	M	4	0	1	1	565
Trivial Amount	3	C	12	1	0	0	6,906
Trivilin	2	C	5	1	1	1	18,240
Trivium	2	C	5	0	0	0	2,270
Trix for Love	4	G	13	2	1	2	29,990
Trix Man	2	C	1	0	0	0	0
Trixie Chick	4	F	2	0	0	0	85
Trixie Lady	3	F	5	0	0	1	3,980
Trixie's Call	2	C	7	1	1	2	7,799
Trixie's Chokem	5	G	10	0	2	1	12,169
Trobien	6	G	2	0	0	0	750
Trodos	5	G	14	0	1	2	7,270
Trois Rivieres	4	F	7	0	0	1	1,080
Trois Villes	3	G	14	1	2	2	48,560
Troisieme Age (IRE)	4	F	6	1	0	0	4,822
Trojan Steele	3	C	7	1	0	0	7,851
Troll	4	G	14	1	3	3	27,650
Trollette	6	M	9	0	3	2	7,494
Trolley Belle	2	F	2	2	0	0	31,075
Tromp	3	C	7	0	2	0	19,736
Trompeta	2	F	2	1	0	0	8,899
Trompolino (CHI)	6	G	9	0	1	0	7,780
Tronare (CHI)	6	H	7	1	2	2	80,890
Trone	4	C	8	2	0	0	16,472
Trooper Blue	3	F	1	0	0	0	0
Trooper Lady	6	M	2	0	0	0	0
Trooper Red	8	G	6	2	2	0	38,640
Trooping the Color	2	C	2	0	0	0	0
Trophy Case	6	G	15	4	3	1	63,795
Trophy Dancer	2	C	4	0	0	1	2,035
Trophy Edition Too	5	M	1	0	0	0	0

Horse	Age	Sex	Sts	1st	2d	3d	Won
Trophy Lane	4	F	10	1	1	2	8,620
Trophy Maker	2	C	1	0	0	0	0
Tropic Rhythm	3	F	1	0	0	0	720
Tropic Rocket	2	C	1	0	0	0	1,155
Tropical Blossom	6	M	1	0	1	0	20,000
Tropical Exposure	5	M	10	0	0	3	3,686
Tropical Fever	5	G	13	2	1	2	19,252
Tropical Heatwave	4	G	2	0	0	0	1,090
Tropical River	2	G	3	0	1	0	2,538
Tropical Storm	4	C	3	1	0	0	29,570
Tropical Sun	8	H	1	0	0	0	0
Tropicalprediction	2	F	1	0	0	0	230
Tropickid	4	G	12	2	1	3	7,804
Trouble and Me	4	G	6	0	0	0	190
Trouble At Dawn	4	F	10	1	1	2	6,088
Trouble Bythe Hour	3	C	1	0	0	0	0
Trouble Doubled	3	C	15	1	0	0	5,728
Trouble From Davie	3	F	14	1	0	5	22,298
Trouble Growin Up	3	G	6	0	0	0	531
Trouble N Beantown	4	F	8	1	0	3	6,964
Trouble Now	3	G	8	1	4	0	20,080
Trouble With Mary	2	F	2	0	0	1	7,980
Troubled Son	7	G	17	0	1	0	3,675
Troubleinshangrila	4	F	3	0	0	1	2,670
Troubleintheturn	3	G	8	0	0	2	1,535
Trouble'n'fortune	4	G	6	0	2	0	4,977
Troublesamacon	3	F	8	0	0	0	807
Troublesome Tess	3	F	4	0	0	0	184
Troublesomeaffair	4	F	9	0	2	2	2,727
Trounce	7	G	6	1	1	2	28,100
Troupe	3	C	1	0	0	0	320
Troupe Disastor	7	H	4	0	0	1	800
Trove	4	F	7	2	2	1	19,810
Troy Ounce	3	C	15	3	3	2	36,383
Troyanna Miss	3	F	6	0	1	0	2,159
Troyix	8	G	8	0	0	0	870
Troy's Honor	4	G	10	1	1	2	15,895
Troy's Peak	4	G	7	1	0	0	4,083
Troy's Tramp	4	F	9	0	1	1	7,050
Tru Aldi	3	F	9	1	2	0	10,912
Tru Angel	3	F	12	1	4	2	16,777
Tru Attitude	3	F	5	1	1	1	20,270
Tru Bride	4	F	13	1	1	0	4,853
Tru Dazzler	5	M	12	3	1	0	12,267
Tru Flame	4	F	18	2	3	2	19,208
Tru Gal	4	F	6	3	1	1	43,686
Tru Piano	3	F	12	1	5	1	23,314
Trually Wild	3	F	4	2	0	0	23,722
Truce in Pecos	5	M	5	0	0	3	4,345
Truce N Hoedown	3	G	1	0	0	0	825
Truce Reigns	5	G	3	0	0	1	1,775
Truce Time	10	M	2	0	0	0	125
Truck	7	H	4	0	0	0	130
Truckee Groom	3	G	9	0	1	1	3,913
Truckee Pal	3	G	8	1	1	0	6,310
Truckee River	4	G	6	0	2	1	28,962
Truckee Traveler	4	C	9	0	3	0	23,850
Truckee Tudor	3	G	8	1	1	2	18,516
Truckee Warrior	4	G	11	1	2	0	33,845
Trucker's Special	5	M	17	2	2	2	28,951
Truckin On	4	G	11	1	2	0	7,212
Trucklen Man	3	G	3	0	1	0	2,570
Truckstar	3	F	12	1	2	3	28,200
Truckstop Vicki	5	M	3	0	0	0	480
Truculent Pow Wow	4	G	9	0	1	4	16,372
Truculent Secrets	2	G	1	0	0	0	0
Trudy's Knockout	2	F	6	1	1	0	13,610
Trudy's Sweet Gal	2	F	4	0	0	1	2,359
True and Faithful	3	F	4	0	0	0	3,278
True Anticipation	3	G	9	2	4	0	49,110
True Aries	4	F	15	2	3	0	11,225
True Baloo	4	G	3	1	0	0	1,335
True Bet	3	G	21	3	4	2	16,604
True Blonde Beauty	3	F	11	3	2	0	55,430
True Blue Moon	5	G	4	1	0	1	12,760
True Blue Prospect	3	G	17	2	3	1	35,080
True Blue Rebel	4	G	9	2	0	1	19,479
True Blue Sky	3	F	2	0	0	0	158
True Call	3	C	9	1	0	3	23,648

Horse	Age	Sex	Sts	1st	2d	3d	Won
True Calling	3	F	7	0	0	2	5,658
True Chance	3	G	2	1	0	0	4,170
True Charisma	3	C	6	0	0	1	1,805
True Cheers	6	G	4	0	0	0	210
True Concern	6	H	11	5	0	2	44,360
True Conquest	6	G	9	2	2	1	19,115
True Contender	3	G	1	0	0	0	0
True Crimson	4	C	10	2	2	0	73,321
True Cynara	7	M	1	0	0	0	0
True Dancer	4	G	11	5	2	1	112,831
True Dawn	5	M	7	0	0	0	2,268
True Direction	5	H	8	1	2	0	46,970
True Dreamer	4	C	3	0	0	0	1,050
True Eleven	2	C	3	0	0	0	720
True Facts	5	M	15	3	3	2	35,760
True Faith	2	C	4	0	0	0	559
True Fashion	6	M	18	0	1	2	11,682
True for Destiny	3	G	7	0	0	2	12,380
True Gem	3	F	6	2	0	1	25,870
True Genius	5	G	11	1	0	4	37,270
True Gift	4	F	9	3	3	1	26,960
True Girl	4	F	1	0	0	0	110
True Glit	3	C	3	1	0	1	3,966
True Gold	3	F	2	2	0	0	53,400
True Grey	2	C	5	1	0	1	7,975
True Honor	4	G	6	0	1	0	2,185
True Hope	4	C	10	3	1	1	37,220
True Justice	7	M	7	0	1	1	880
True Kiss	2	F	2	1	0	0	23,870
True Kitty Cat	2	F	1	0	0	0	0
True Lord	8	G	4	0	0	0	0
True Louie	3	G	3	0	0	1	850
True Love Is Gold	6	M	13	3	4	2	26,785
True Love's Secret	7	G	7	2	0	3	53,313
True Luck	3	F	9	1	0	1	6,885
True Metropolitan	2	G	3	0	0	1	2,745
True Monarch	5	H	15	4	2	1	19,565
True Passion	6	G	9	3	1	1	66,900
True Patriot	4	C	7	1	0	1	40,300
True Phenomenon	5	G	5	1	1	0	6,001
True Play	4	F	3	0	0	0	0
True Prince	5	G	5	0	0	0	305
True Red	6	G	12	0	0	5	4,683
True Rock	3	G	1	0	0	1	2,717
True Roledex	3	G	3	0	0	1	1,470
True Royalty	2	F	5	1	1	2	18,880
True Ruby	7	M	6	0	3	1	30,800
True Sailing	6	G	9	1	2	1	4,962
True Sensation	5	M	8	1	1	1	66,686
True Shrew	5	M	7	0	1	0	1,937
True Solution	5	G	13	4	1	3	39,578
True Spirit	3	F	15	3	1	2	29,190
True Statesman	3	G	2	0	0	0	155
True Stride	2	G	7	2	1	1	28,635
True Survivor	9	H	1	0	0	0	0
True Tails	2	F	4	2	1	1	51,930
True to Form	4	F	17	3	1	2	37,200
True to Slew	4	G	2	0	0	0	153
True Trick	4	C	12	2	0	2	28,930
True Verse	3	F	18	1	2	3	9,656
True Wisper	8	G	2	0	0	1	768
True Wonder	4	G	3	0	0	0	390
Trueamericanspirit	4	G	11	2	3	2	121,625
Trueborn	3	F	11	0	2	0	8,165
Truecat	3	F	4	0	0	0	4,046
Truely a Trooper	3	C	6	1	1	0	14,410
Truely Marked	3	G	9	0	1	2	4,089
Truely Perfection	4	G	16	2	2	2	9,564
Truely Ruby	3	F	5	0	1	1	14,006
Truely Unreal	3	F	7	1	3	2	46,628
Truenortherngirl	2	F	2	0	0	1	2,280
Truffle	2	F	4	0	0	0	840
Truitte	5	G	4	0	0	1	7,440
Truking East	4	C	11	0	0	3	2,262
Trukndowntheavenue	4	F	13	3	2	5	69,984
Trulips	3	F	4	0	0	0	1,201
Truly a Cat	2	F	1	0	1	0	2,790
Truly a Floozi	2	F	2	0	0	0	75
Truly a Judge	6	G	8	3	1	0	187,218

Horse	Age	Sex	Sts	1st	2d	3d	Won
Truly a Legend	5	M	3	0	2	1	12,085
Truly a Runner	8	G	11	2	2	0	21,141
Truly a Saint	3	F	10	0	2	0	7,455
Truly Appealing	3	F	17	2	1	2	14,528
Truly Awesome	6	G	12	1	0	1	5,984
Truly Buckaroo	3	G	8	1	1	0	4,649
Truly Clever	4	F	4	0	0	1	2,460
Truly Dawn	3	F	2	0	1	0	6,000
Truly Elegant	2	F	2	0	0	0	900
Truly Exclusive	6	M	12	2	0	3	5,185
Truly Fabulous	3	F	15	1	2	4	7,151
Truly False	2	C	3	0	0	1	3,260
Truly Fortunate	3	F	8	0	0	0	648
Truly Gold	4	F	7	0	0	0	560
Truly Honored	3	G	12	2	3	1	28,413
Truly Lovely	2	F	3	0	1	1	3,750
Truly Native	2	C	5	2	0	0	35,601
Truly Obliging	6	H	11	1	0	1	6,699
Truly Outspoken	3	F	1	0	0	0	140
Truly Prized	2	C	1	0	0	0	0
Truly Relentless	6	H	6	3	0	2	38,186
Truly Special	4	F	10	3	0	0	35,495
Truly Spoken	4	F	3	1	1	0	5,656
Truly Summing	4	F	6	1	0	1	3,171
Truly the Best	4	F	2	0	2	0	4,680
Trulyastarr	3	F	21	4	1	0	33,248
Trulymadlydeeply	2	C	1	0	0	0	450
Trumandancer	3	F	2	0	0	0	0
Truman's Raider	5	G	9	2	2	0	60,185
Trumanson	3	G	7	2	1	1	42,947
Trump Marina	5	G	2	0	0	0	2,560
Trumpeter Swan	4	G	1	0	0	0	286
Trumpets Delight	4	C	9	4	4	0	99,863
Trumpets of Glory	2	F	1	0	0	0	205
Trumps Clown	10	G	4	0	2	0	5,332
Trumps Native Lady	6	M	6	1	0	0	8,296
Trumpster	7	H	13	5	3	1	61,824
Trumpty Dumpty	11	G	16	0	1	2	3,541
Trunk Monkey	2	C	1	0	0	0	204
Trupon On	4	F	1	0	0	0	360
Tru's Last Ride	3	F	12	1	1	0	21,082
Trust	4	F	1	0	0	0	77
Trust a Buck	5	M	12	2	3	0	15,940
Trust Her	4	F	3	0	0	0	0
Trust Me	3	C	11	1	2	2	32,100
Trusted Rumor	3	F	3	0	0	0	330
Trustmenow	4	F	2	0	0	1	918
Trusty Hunter	4	C	1	0	0	0	154
Trusty Jett	5	H	2	0	0	0	0
Trustyourinstincts	3	G	7	1	0	0	7,379
Truth About Misty	6	M	1	0	0	0	200
Truth Buster	2	G	7	0	1	1	8,157
Truth by Ruth	3	F	6	2	0	0	25,440
Truth Endures	3	G	11	2	2	0	9,415
Truth Matters	5	G	7	1	1	2	20,678
Truth 'n Power	8	G	7	1	2	2	1,890
Truth of the Heart	7	G	7	0	0	1	1,348
Truth Serum	3	C	11	1	3	1	96,106
Truthful Dutch	3	F	4	2	2	0	41,000
Truthful Heart	3	G	7	2	3	0	24,360
Truxin	2	F	1	0	0	0	60
Truxton's Miracle	5	M	4	0	0	0	112
Try a Thing	2	F	2	0	0	0	215
Try Again	7	G	14	2	1	3	28,790
Try and Top This	2	F	4	1	0	1	4,686
Try for Par	6	G	10	2	0	1	13,198
Try Forever	2	C	3	0	0	0	0
Try Hard Gal	3	F	11	0	2	2	6,271
Try Harder	4	F	7	1	1	0	16,570
Try My Tune	5	G	4	0	0	1	620
Trying Hard	3	G	6	1	0	0	10,500
Try'nsteel	5	M	10	1	0	0	2,150
Tryst's Dancer	5	G	8	0	1	1	2,981
T's Fashion Find	3	F	2	0	0	2	1,419
T's Louise	2	G	5	0	0	0	2,460
T's Miracle	5	M	3	0	0	0	0
T's Sampson	2	C	1	0	1	0	2,550
T's So Shy	2	F	2	1	0	1	12,773
Tsar Czar	7	H	5	1	0	0	21,950
Tsigane (FR)	5	H	7	1	1	2	153,174
Tsu Tsu Oke	4	G	13	2	1	3	12,526
Tsu Tsu Won	11	M	12	3	4	1	43,908
Tsunami Surprise	4	F	3	1	1	1	5,300
Tsunami Wind	5	G	8	3	0	4	48,808
Tsu's Aplenty	4	C	7	1	2	2	28,400
Tsuzomin	3	G	5	0	1	2	9,040
Tu La Pia	4	C	5	0	1	0	717
Tu l'Homme	4	G	3	0	0	0	0
Tu Tone Brown	6	G	13	1	1	1	6,793
Tu Tone Corozon	6	G	9	0	0	1	2,377
Tuacahn	4	G	3	1	0	1	3,230
Tuamotu	7	G	6	0	1	0	615
Tub Tosser	6	G	1	0	1	0	3,200
Tubacity	4	F	7	0	2	1	28,480
Tubbs	4	G	2	0	0	0	0
Tubby Cat	7	G	7	1	0	0	4,702
Tubby Clinton	8	H	1	0	0	0	37
Tubrok	7	G	9	0	4	3	30,460
Tucan	2	C	2	1	0	0	10,929
Tucked Away	4	F	11	1	1	3	159,396
Tuckered	3	F	4	0	0	0	4,520
Tuckers Run	4	C	5	1	0	0	6,820
Tuckin Nickels	2	C	3	0	0	0	885
Tucky Bound	4	G	10	0	2	1	4,830
Tucson City	4	G	10	2	1	3	24,023
Tucson Magic	2	C	1	1	0	0	2,940
Tudeludelu	2	F	1	0	0	0	0
Tudge	4	G	8	0	0	2	4,093
Tudi Cielo	5	M	3	0	1	0	2,086
Tudif	2	C	2	1	0	0	4,200
Tudor Caper	2	C	3	0	0	1	4,489
Tudor Court	5	M	5	0	0	0	1,311
Tudor Needed	2	G	5	1	2	1	31,894
Tudor Ridge	6	G	8	2	1	0	3,804
Tudor Ruff	4	F	7	0	0	1	2,725
Tudor Tell	2	G	2	0	0	1	962
Tudor's Baby	4	F	7	1	0	0	3,355
Tudor's Honor Roll	3	F	3	0	0	0	355
Tuds	3	G	4	0	0	1	3,000
Tudy's Choice	4	G	11	2	2	1	47,854
Tuesday Prayer	3	F	8	2	1	3	79,130
Tuesdays Heatwave	5	G	10	0	0	0	2,078
Tuff Ante	4	G	6	0	0	0	0
Tuff as Iron	5	G	11	1	3	1	37,260
Tuff Broo	5	M	6	1	2	0	40,332
Tuff Coach	4	G	2	0	0	0	265
Tuff Expectations	3	C	1	0	0	0	498
Tuff Guy	4	G	7	1	0	0	5,395
Tuff Hint	5	M	5	1	0	0	6,495
Tuff Justice	2	F	6	2	1	0	46,760
Tuff Lakota	3	G	1	0	0	0	0
Tuff Lula	2	F	6	1	1	0	4,400
Tuff Man Dan	3	G	14	3	3	1	63,360
Tuff Muffin	2	F	2	0	1	0	4,660
Tuff N Pugnacious	8	H	5	0	0	0	366
Tuff Partners	3	F	11	1	3	1	34,171
Tuff Ray	4	G	12	0	0	1	3,683
Tuff Silver	2	C	2	0	0	0	280
Tuff Tiger Joe	5	G	4	0	0	0	100
Tuff Twist	7	H	1	0	0	0	0
Tuff Tyler Man	3	C	6	0	0	0	747
Tuffing	3	G	7	0	0	0	785
Tuffled	3	F	11	1	4	0	44,220
Tuffy	4	C	7	0	0	0	572
Tuffy O'Brannigan	3	G	3	0	1	0	900
Tufposition	6	G	4	0	0	0	112
Tufton Avenue	5	M	7	2	1	3	25,558
Tugluq	3	G	5	0	0	0	372
Tuie Louie	2	C	2	0	0	0	170
Tuktoyaktuk	6	M	5	0	0	1	3,963
Tukwilamina	6	M	9	1	3	0	5,835
Tulalip Bay	4	G	4	1	0	0	2,092
Tulane Grad	3	F	1	0	0	0	60
Tularosa Kid	3	G	12	1	0	2	11,091
Tuleyries	5	M	1	0	0	0	0
Tulira Castle	4	G	9	1	1	2	10,765
Tulisha	3	F	10	1	1	2	7,348
Tulla	4	F	3	0	0	0	390

Horse	Age	Sex	Sts	1st	2d	3d	Won
Tullynally	4	G	4	0	0	0	325
Tulogie	6	H	3	1	0	0	1,895
Tulsa Boy	2	G	2	0	0	0	160
Tulsa Party Doll	7	M	1	0	0	0	43
Tulsa Robery	3	C	5	1	0	3	4,790
Tulsa Stride	6	M	3	0	0	0	186
Tulsa Town	3	G	8	0	2	3	14,713
Tumble Me Right (JPN)	4	F	1	0	0	0	840
Tumble 'n Nelson	5	G	21	0	2	2	9,167
Tumble Twice	5	G	1	0	0	1	1,650
Tumbleweed Dancer	7	H	3	0	0	0	221
Tumbling Gold	6	M	5	0	0	0	331
Tumketa	4	C	9	0	0	1	1,299
Tuna Rocket	4	G	7	0	0	1	2,464
Tunangannya	6	M	7	1	2	1	7,176
Tunder Ponche	3	G	7	3	1	1	93,247
Tundras Token	3	C	11	0	0	1	3,174
Tune a Win for A B	7	M	12	2	1	3	26,187
Tune Lender	3	F	8	3	2	2	28,826
Tune of the Spirit	3	G	13	2	1	2	47,636
Tune Up the Band	4	F	8	3	1	2	53,445
Tuned In	2	F	4	2	1	1	105,500
Tunedinandturnedon	2	C	2	0	0	0	0
Tuner River	7	M	2	0	0	0	1,440
Tuner's Finest	3	F	8	2	1	0	20,809
Tunette	7	M	4	0	0	0	1,330
Tungsten	2	C	2	0	0	0	1,195
Tunie's Secret	5	M	14	0	1	1	3,444
Tunintothebeat	5	M	2	0	0	0	210
Tunk Ridge	6	M	6	0	1	0	880
Tunnel Man	3	C	6	1	0	0	7,230
Tunnel Time	3	F	18	4	2	4	46,365
Tunnel Vision	3	C	9	1	0	1	6,540
Tunnell's Chapel	6	G	1	0	0	0	0
Tunnel's Pick	2	C	2	0	0	0	0
Tunon	5	G	2	0	0	0	314
Tupelo	2	C	3	0	0	0	375
Tupie's Parlay	5	G	11	0	0	1	748
Tuppence	7	M	5	0	1	1	8,584
Tupper Lake	2	C	5	1	0	2	21,187
Turbine	4	F	4	0	0	0	1,012
Turbo Arrow	5	G	7	0	0	0	318
Turbo Bullet	6	M	11	2	2	2	15,394
Turbo Charger	9	G	13	2	1	4	28,718
Turbo Cooker	3	C	1	0	0	0	105
Turbo Jet	8	G	15	2	1	1	9,249
Turbo Kick	2	G	1	0	0	0	400
Turbo Paddy	5	M	12	0	4	1	7,230
Turbulent Flight (NZ)	7	G	2	0	0	0	0
Turbulent Thinking	4	F	13	1	0	3	38,000
Turbulent Tigress	3	F	5	1	0	2	1,710
Turbulent Trick	3	F	10	2	0	2	14,772
Turbulently	2	F	4	0	1	0	2,105
Turf Daddy	3	C	2	1	0	0	6,375
Turfanet	5	M	7	0	0	1	350
Turk Flyer	8	G	5	2	2	0	22,193
Turkastaire	2	F	6	0	2	0	11,592
Turkate	3	F	7	0	1	0	2,585
Turkatune	2	F	3	0	0	0	552
Turkcat	3	G	3	0	0	0	0
Turketta	3	F	4	0	0	0	186
Turkey Trick	3	F	2	0	0	0	2,450
Turkish Cavalry	3	G	2	2	0	0	57,000
Turkish Charmer	3	F	1	0	0	0	400
Turkish Echo	4	F	13	3	3	3	22,694
Turkish Lad	5	G	11	0	0	0	549
Turkish Lady	2	F	3	0	0	0	190
Turkish Prize	9	G	3	1	0	0	5,900
Turkish Rogue	4	F	10	1	1	2	8,345
Turkish Tart	3	F	5	1	0	0	2,940
Turkish Zaar	4	G	16	4	3	4	20,026
Turko Spirit	2	G	2	1	0	0	14,080
Turkocat	4	C	2	0	0	0	193
Turkothunder	3	F	6	0	1	0	1,292
Turkotreasure	5	M	5	1	1	1	11,090
Turkowar	6	H	5	1	0	0	4,817
Turkowon	3	F	8	0	0	0	1,269
Turk's Chum	4	G	6	0	0	0	528
Turk's Luck	4	F	11	1	1	0	11,266
Turks Passage	3	G	7	0	0	0	1,829
Turk's Pride	4	F	7	1	1	0	9,479
Turk's Ransom	2	G	5	2	0	0	80,490
Turk's Success	3	F	5	0	1	2	1,907
Turk's Traits	4	G	12	0	2	0	5,276
Turn a Profitt	5	M	4	0	0	1	2,370
Turn Across	3	C	4	0	0	0	227
Turn and Burn	2	G	1	0	0	0	460
Turn Around Tony	2	C	3	0	0	0	2,832
Turn Back the Time	6	H	6	3	0	0	86,140
Turn Him On	2	G	3	0	0	2	1,080
Turn It Down Low	5	H	3	0	0	0	0
Turn It On Simmer	4	F	3	0	0	0	270
Turn Lucky	3	C	8	1	2	1	9,978
Turn Me Loose	3	F	3	0	1	0	10,500
Turn Me On Baby	3	F	6	0	0	0	1,159
Turn of the Tide	4	C	2	0	0	0	205
Turn On	3	G	5	2	0	1	22,298
Turn On the Juice	2	F	5	0	1	0	12,025
Turn Silver Togold	7	M	10	2	3	0	13,939
Turn the Fire On	3	C	7	1	0	1	2,270
Turn the Kee	3	G	7	0	1	0	7,580
Turn the Page	2	C	2	1	0	0	8,540
Turn to Angel	10	M	9	0	0	0	466
Turn to Avie	3	F	6	1	0	0	21,580
Turn to Beat	3	G	5	0	1	1	2,251
Turn to Count	3	C	1	1	0	0	6,660
Turn to Lass	3	F	6	2	0	1	56,400
Turn to Romeo	2	F	4	0	1	2	6,300
Turn to the Prince	4	C	14	1	3	3	26,625
Turn to Victory	3	G	20	1	0	4	9,459
Turn to Zarb	6	G	14	2	5	1	38,292
Turn Your Radio On	3	C	7	1	1	0	6,501
Turnadieu	3	F	3	0	0	0	0
Turnapage	5	H	3	0	0	1	1,080
Turnberry Condo	3	G	6	1	2	2	26,655
Turncoat Jim	5	G	13	1	0	2	12,224
Turnemloose Big G	3	G	17	1	3	0	10,119
Turning Colors	9	G	3	0	0	0	819
Turning Night	3	G	2	0	0	0	500
Turnip the Bid	3	F	5	1	1	1	11,780
Turnkey Job	4	C	2	1	0	0	7,080
Turnoutthelites	6	G	5	0	0	0	168
Turnpike Johnny	4	G	14	1	4	4	46,560
Turnpike Road	9	G	5	0	0	0	284
Turntheheatup	3	C	4	0	0	1	1,685
Turnwestern	5	M	6	0	0	1	719
Turquoise Bead	5	M	12	3	0	1	97,210
Turtle Beach	4	F	3	0	1	0	3,350
Turtle Drive	3	F	7	2	2	0	42,680
Turtle Ridge	7	M	12	1	1	2	8,989
Turtle Soup	3	G	18	0	5	2	24,200
Turtle Town	2	F	1	0	0	0	0
Turue Lover	2	F	4	0	2	0	4,735
Tusayan	4	C	9	0	2	2	78,352
Tuscan Vino	3	G	5	0	0	0	109
Tuscan Wine	2	F	2	0	0	0	1,260
Tuscany Gal	2	F	2	1	0	0	10,800
Tuscany Light	4	F	14	1	2	1	40,050
Tushar	8	G	12	3	1	4	12,952
Tusin Tak	3	C	9	1	3	0	48,135
Tustin	3	F	2	0	2	0	3,600
Tutti	2	F	3	0	0	0	332
Tutti Fratelli	4	F	4	0	1	0	2,755
Tuttle Creek	2	F	5	0	2	0	8,655
Tutu's Barroom	5	M	5	0	0	0	655
Tutu's Little Star	6	M	3	0	0	0	159
Tuvala	6	M	8	0	0	1	2,467
Tux	7	G	6	0	0	0	1,859
Tux N Jeans	6	G	3	0	0	0	212
Tuxedo Gold	6	G	11	1	4	1	18,716
Tuxedo Jr.	5	G	11	1	0	5	11,278
Tuxson	4	G	12	2	4	2	19,175
Tuxtlan	4	G	6	2	2	1	4,970
Tuzinama Run	9	G	5	0	1	0	2,694
Tv Sports Director	6	G	12	1	0	2	14,340
Twample	9	G	15	3	3	3	19,371
Twanpumall	3	G	9	0	2	1	4,195
Tweal's Sword	3	F	7	1	1	2	16,600

Horse	Age	Sex	Sts	1st	2d	3d	Won
Tweed	8	M	8	2	0	2	3,342
Tween	5	M	12	1	6	2	18,490
Tweenthelines	5	G	1	0	0	0	63
Twelve Bells	4	F	3	0	1	1	5,020
Twelve Twenty-One	5	G	8	0	1	0	3,075
Twelve Volt Man	3	G	12	1	1	3	28,420
Twelveyearslater	6	M	3	0	0	1	2,212
Twenty Bubbles	5	M	1	0	0	0	60
Twenty Carats	5	M	8	1	0	0	8,722
Twenty One Cats	5	G	9	0	4	2	12,320
Twenty One Kisses	7	M	8	1	2	1	7,102
Twenty Shillings	3	G	4	0	0	0	0
Twenty Won Nights	4	G	9	1	1	0	8,896
Twentyeighttwelve	3	C	1	0	0	0	0
Twentyforkaratlady	2	F	2	0	0	0	2,740
Twentyniner	7	G	1	0	0	0	100
Twentyonthenose	5	G	10	3	2	2	5,749
Twentysecond Str.	4	G	2	0	0	0	0
Twentysevenkarat	4	F	1	0	0	0	696
Twentythreejaybird	5	H	13	3	1	2	68,747
Twentytwenty	8	H	8	0	1	0	1,203
Twice a Barron	3	F	13	1	1	0	16,675
Twice a Deelite	3	F	12	2	0	3	44,676
Twice as Bad	3	C	3	1	1	0	112,040
Twice as Fabulous	2	G	4	0	0	0	3,423
Twice as Royal	4	C	2	0	0	0	600
Twice as Sweet	6	M	3	2	0	1	30,460
Twice Bid	5	G	6	1	1	0	16,225
Twice Blue	3	C	1	0	0	0	0
Twice for Money	5	G	2	0	0	0	386
Twice Heaven	2	F	1	0	0	0	145
Twice Is Nice	5	G	2	0	0	1	2,460
Twice Onabet	4	G	13	0	2	2	32,760
Twice Removed	3	F	9	0	0	1	1,785
Twice Royal	8	G	14	0	0	0	3,651
Twice Southern	3	G	7	1	0	0	37,728
Twice the Cat	3	G	10	2	0	4	39,330
Twice the Energy	6	G	4	0	0	1	1,015
Twice the Ruckus	4	F	1	0	0	0	164
Twice the Syn	4	F	7	3	0	0	5,340
Twice Told	4	G	3	1	0	1	12,625
Twice Tricky	5	G	14	5	2	3	63,954
Twice Unbridled	2	C	5	0	0	2	11,140
Twice Vice	2	F	3	0	0	0	0
Twiceasneat	3	G	2	0	0	0	0
Twicecapade	2	F	3	0	0	0	250
Twickster	3	G	13	1	0	0	11,742
Twidle	4	F	16	1	3	1	16,782
Twigs Dotcom	5	M	11	1	0	0	11,395
Twilight Career	8	G	7	3	1	0	7,005
Twilight Code	4	F	12	2	1	0	22,800
Twilight Devil	3	F	10	1	0	2	6,116
Twilight Diamond	4	G	10	5	1	1	25,052
Twilight Gallop	3	F	12	2	3	4	93,260
Twilight Glow	5	M	11	0	3	1	19,550
Twilight Honors	3	G	12	0	3	0	8,293
Twilight Hunter	3	G	12	1	1	4	18,745
Twilight Kingdom	3	C	12	2	0	0	10,905
Twilight Ladd	5	G	4	0	0	0	234
Twilight League	2	F	2	0	0	0	2,220
Twilight Man	5	H	6	0	0	0	992
Twilight Peak	5	M	7	0	0	0	1,058
Twilight Prince	8	G	7	1	0	1	10,356
Twilight Racer	4	G	14	0	0	0	2,152
Twilight Road	7	G	9	3	3	0	246,500
Twilight Silver	4	C	1	0	0	0	0
Twilight Ticket	2	C	3	0	0	0	1,500
Twilight Time	7	H	12	4	1	0	67,810
Twilight Twilight	3	F	4	0	0	0	800
Twilight Vision	4	G	8	3	0	0	29,910
Twilight's Angie	2	F	2	1	1	0	5,103
Twilights Prayer	6	M	1	0	0	0	400
Twilite Testimoney	5	H	9	1	0	0	21,053
Twin Cat	4	F	3	0	0	0	390
Twin Dancer	2	C	2	1	0	1	12,075
Twin Meteors	7	G	9	0	3	1	23,905
Twin Oaks A. L.	5	G	6	1	0	2	10,126
Twin Pirate	4	F	12	2	1	3	11,028
Twin Stripes	5	M	13	1	2	2	10,955
Twin Talk	5	H	6	0	1	1	15,075
Twin Task	7	G	15	2	2	1	27,689
Twin Tower (PER)	5	M	10	2	1	2	35,905
Twine Flies	5	M	14	5	1	3	88,610
Twine Traveler	4	F	9	3	1	0	29,900
Twinful	2	G	5	2	1	0	31,280
Twining and Dining	4	F	4	1	0	1	27,550
Twining Glow	6	M	14	4	4	2	69,760
Twinkie Be Buggin	4	F	13	1	1	1	17,268
Twinkie Zone	3	F	7	2	0	3	67,050
Twinkle and Shine	4	F	2	0	0	0	720
Twinkle Drive	7	M	1	0	0	0	0
Twinkle Twinkle	6	M	2	0	0	1	1,760
Twinkler	4	F	2	0	0	1	4,480
Twinkling Ofan Eye	3	F	12	0	0	2	2,547
Twinwinwin	5	M	15	1	2	3	37,025
Twirlaway	3	F	9	2	0	1	41,580
Twirling	4	G	5	0	0	0	0
Twist a Twilight	2	F	6	0	0	0	1,695
Twist and Pop	5	M	10	6	3	0	167,440
Twist and Shoot	4	F	9	0	0	0	661
Twist of Clover	3	F	1	0	0	0	75
Twist the Sword	2	F	7	1	1	2	27,090
Twista Chu Chu	5	M	3	0	0	0	2,412
Twisted	6	G	7	0	0	0	1,657
Twisted Amour	4	F	8	1	0	0	3,861
Twisted Angel	3	F	3	0	0	0	0
Twisted Cat	2	F	2	0	0	1	1,375
Twisted Cord	7	M	10	2	1	1	29,746
Twisted Feather	3	F	19	3	4	2	21,199
Twisted Fortune	5	G	15	2	0	1	32,880
Twisted Humor	3	F	12	1	2	0	26,829
Twisted Kris	6	G	1	0	0	0	450
Twisted Lil Sister	4	F	1	0	0	0	0
Twisted Logic	3	F	11	2	1	0	23,906
Twisted Love	2	C	4	0	1	1	4,040
Twisted Mister	4	C	14	2	4	3	66,143
Twisted Truth	4	F	6	0	0	0	2,295
Twisted Tryst	8	G	6	0	0	0	2,240
Twisted Wit	3	G	8	3	2	0	305,223
Twistedervish	3	G	2	0	1	1	3,045
Twister Alley	3	F	7	0	2	3	16,860
Twister M	5	G	15	1	3	2	13,620
Twistin Bit	4	F	4	0	0	1	1,559
Twisting Sister	3	F	9	2	1	1	41,253
Twisting Woman	3	F	2	0	0	0	0
Twistingbythepool	7	G	21	4	2	4	40,441
Twist's Splash	3	F	4	2	0	0	9,120
Twisty	8	M	6	0	0	1	1,500
Twitterpated	5	G	3	0	0	0	470
Twittersburg	2	G	4	1	1	0	6,900
Twitty	5	M	5	0	0	0	245
Twixy	2	F	1	0	1	0	1,980
Two Air	7	M	2	0	0	0	378
Two Bay Two	3	C	2	0	0	0	0
Two Bayou	3	F	11	5	0	2	138,647
Two Beat Rhythm	3	G	3	0	0	0	0
Two Bit Kid	3	G	11	3	1	1	46,255
Two Bit Temptation	3	G	3	0	0	0	165
Two Bows	5	M	20	3	1	1	21,748
Two Buck Chuck	3	G	2	0	0	0	55
Two Buck Dreamer	4	F	2	0	0	0	97
Two Buck Luck	2	C	1	1	0	0	8,100
Two Car Lenny	2	G	1	0	0	0	240
Two Carat Diamond	3	F	2	0	0	0	530
Two Centsworth	4	G	8	2	0	1	29,320
Two Cold Beers	2	G	3	0	1	0	2,479
Two Condos	4	F	13	0	5	3	10,176
Two Dollar Ticket	3	F	2	0	0	0	0
Two Dot Slew	7	M	6	1	2	0	72,754
Two Double Shots	7	M	5	0	1	0	2,462
Two Down Automatic	3	G	9	3	2	2	175,978
Two Drink Date	4	F	1	0	0	0	110
Two Ducks in a Row	3	G	8	1	2	1	26,155
Two Edge	4	F	4	0	0	1	1,386
Two Eyed Jackie	3	F	18	1	7	1	30,415
Two Eyed Jake	3	G	11	0	4	0	3,505
Two Fer Marquetry	6	H	1	0	0	0	0
Two Fer Place	3	F	15	2	1	3	43,365

Horse	Age	Sex	Sts	1st	2d	3d	Won
Two for Hebe	9	M	7	1	0	1	2,696
Two Four	4	G	5	2	0	1	38,977
Two Four Dancer	7	M	11	2	1	2	29,000
Two Hearts	3	F	4	1	0	2	27,073
Two Hollys	3	F	14	3	1	0	76,694
Two Hope Diamonds	4	F	4	0	0	0	0
Two Hours Late	3	G	3	0	1	0	4,200
Two Hurrahs	6	M	4	0	0	0	149
Two in the Basket	7	G	7	0	1	3	928
Two Inch Minus	3	G	4	0	2	0	5,700
Two K Mambo	6	G	4	0	0	1	1,052
Two Knight's	6	H	11	1	2	1	29,650
Two Lanterns	6	G	8	1	0	1	4,792
Two Less a Day	3	F	3	0	0	0	0
Two Man Crew	2	G	2	0	0	0	780
Two Mile Hill	4	F	11	4	2	1	165,747
Two Minute Warning	4	G	7	0	0	2	4,139
Two My Son's	3	C	9	1	0	0	10,385
Two Night Stand	4	G	1	0	0	0	400
Two O Nine	7	G	13	1	1	0	6,096
Two O Seven	2	G	1	0	1	0	2,940
Two Out of Three	4	G	9	4	2	1	27,675
Two Over Prime	6	M	2	0	0	0	207
Two Punch Austie	4	C	3	0	0	0	339
Two Punch Gal	3	F	7	3	2	1	101,972
Two Punch Sonny	8	H	1	0	0	0	0
Two Queens	5	M	13	0	2	2	10,389
Two Reasons	9	G	10	1	0	2	4,310
Two Retired Tires	2	G	1	0	0	0	140
Two Rows of Gold	3	G	13	2	2	3	10,632
Two Scoops of Ice	6	G	2	0	0	0	138
Two Sharky Betty	4	F	13	1	0	1	30,340
Two Sixty Four	3	G	6	3	1	1	53,460
Two Sleeve Zack	3	G	16	0	6	1	11,223
Two Sparks	4	G	5	1	0	0	8,800
Two Stall	5	M	15	1	1	1	26,974
Two Star Story	4	G	11	1	0	2	4,501
Two Stars	4	F	12	1	0	0	4,665
Two Tequila Tom	2	G	3	0	0	0	0
Two Thirds Rule	2	G	4	0	1	0	3,868
Two Thirty Seven	4	G	15	4	1	1	44,890
Two Thumbs Up	8	G	7	1	0	2	3,882
Two Times Won	2	F	1	0	0	0	3,354
Two Timin Goldie	4	F	5	0	0	0	278
Two Timin Lover	5	G	15	1	5	2	42,802
Two Timin' Talk	3	G	7	1	2	0	11,598
Two Timing Paul	5	G	10	2	2	1	4,890
Two Timing Tyler	5	M	1	0	0	0	0
Two Timing Waltzer	4	F	13	2	2	0	12,008
Two to Get Ready	2	F	8	2	0	3	42,697
Two to Jig	5	M	11	2	1	2	30,305
Two Toed Sloth	2	F	5	0	1	1	14,815
Two Tops	4	G	1	0	0	0	288
Two Track	4	G	5	1	2	0	5,977
Two Trail Sioux	3	F	5	2	2	1	87,760
Two T's	3	G	14	1	1	3	16,300
Two Twenty Two	3	F	7	0	0	0	802
Two Under Par	3	G	1	0	0	0	994
Two Ways to Toast	4	F	7	0	1	1	2,711
Two Winner's Long	6	G	11	0	0	1	2,526
Two Wire	8	G	3	0	1	0	2,650
Two Wood	9	G	2	0	0	0	0
Two Year Waranty	4	F	19	1	1	3	31,071
Two Zip	7	M	6	1	0	0	5,460
Twoindytoo	5	M	1	0	0	0	154
Twolateinthegame	3	G	1	0	0	0	0
Twoleftfeet	2	F	2	0	0	0	315
Twooutsintheninth	2	G	4	0	0	1	6,573
Twosie's Best	2	F	3	1	1	0	22,000
Twosieshome	4	F	7	2	0	2	23,007
Twosisterslady	7	M	3	0	1	0	2,250
Twosisterslass	3	F	11	0	1	1	5,174
Twosistersmercedes	2	G	2	0	0	1	3,060
Twosteppincowgirl	3	F	9	2	2	1	17,360
Twothousandthree	3	F	3	0	0	0	250
Twotimes Terlingua	5	G	15	2	4	2	12,783
Twotiminsmokester	3	G	12	1	1	1	11,065
Ty Jo	4	C	6	0	1	1	2,141
Ty Life	3	G	5	0	0	1	520
Ty Man	8	G	5	0	0	2	1,663
Ty the Score	3	G	10	1	1	1	9,051
Tyabering	2	C	2	0	1	0	1,956
Tyaskin	11	G	7	0	2	1	7,070
Tybee	4	G	8	0	0	0	3,460
Tychonica	3	F	9	1	0	2	5,718
Tychonics Mistress	3	F	6	2	2	0	30,090
Tycoon	4	G	5	1	1	3	14,350
Tycoon (GB)	3	C	5	0	0	3	325,494
Tycoon County	3	G	12	2	3	2	28,077
Tygemini	4	G	8	1	2	2	21,732
Tyger Mam	3	F	1	0	0	0	75
Tyger River	5	M	12	2	2	3	37,572
Tyger Smiles	6	G	3	0	1	0	2,112
Tyko	2	G	1	0	0	0	164
Tyler B	4	C	11	1	0	1	4,579
Tyler County	6	G	5	1	2	1	13,247
Tyler Giboulee	2	F	5	1	0	0	6,600
Tyler Hill	2	C	3	0	0	0	361
Tyler Jay	7	H	1	0	0	0	0
Tyler Rex	6	G	17	1	4	5	35,110
Tyler Tack	3	G	10	2	1	0	12,390
Tyler Two	3	C	1	0	0	0	0
Tyler W	3	G	9	1	2	3	14,433
Tyler's Jewel	4	G	13	1	2	3	43,772
Tyler's Secret	3	C	5	0	0	0	450
Tyler's Stash	3	G	5	0	0	0	1,293
Tyler's Wolf	4	C	3	0	0	0	96
Tym Beau	3	C	10	1	1	1	18,468
Tynan	3	C	5	0	0	0	3,810
Tyne	4	F	3	0	0	0	1,180
Typhoon Aaron	2	G	3	3	0	0	19,223
Typhoon Alex	4	C	3	0	0	0	2,344
Typhoon David	3	G	12	2	1	0	22,174
Typhoon Island	3	F	5	1	0	1	18,680
Typhoon Tessie	3	F	3	3	0	0	48,600
Typical Bragg	7	M	19	4	1	1	14,040
Typical Situation	4	F	2	0	0	0	225
Typo	4	C	6	0	1	1	3,720
Tyr	2	C	2	0	0	0	880
Tyrade's Best Bet	4	F	1	0	0	0	0
Tyrebby	3	F	1	0	0	0	50
Tyrone's Terms	5	G	14	2	2	4	17,873
Tyronia	4	F	12	2	5	2	23,260
Tyro's One Shot	4	F	12	0	0	0	0
Tyrus Creek	5	G	9	0	2	0	3,287
Ty's Princess	3	F	4	0	0	0	600
Tyson's Squall	6	G	14	0	2	0	2,020
Tyvara	4	F	9	0	0	0	4,940
Tzar	3	C	5	1	0	0	28,344
U B C N Me	5	M	3	0	0	0	280
U B Ours	3	F	6	2	0	0	13,842
U B the Judge	4	G	22	1	4	6	23,728
U Betcha Joe	3	G	9	5	0	1	33,035
U Blue	4	G	11	0	0	1	1,074
U Da Gal	5	M	6	0	1	1	3,813
U Go Can	4	G	6	0	2	3	5,370
U Go Hugo	3	C	14	0	1	1	3,612
U Go North	2	F	1	0	0	0	140
U Got the Touch	3	F	7	0	1	2	14,125
U Gotta Luv Dee	2	F	2	0	0	0	0
U Hear Me	6	M	12	2	2	3	11,431
U K Champ	3	C	5	0	0	0	1,025
U K Fun	3	F	9	1	1	1	6,395
U K Kenny	2	C	2	0	0	0	239
U K Limey	6	G	6	0	1	0	2,200
U K Special One	2	F	1	0	0	0	0
U K Syn	3	G	2	0	0	0	74
U K Trick	4	F	7	1	1	1	56,241
U Madea Fortune	4	C	13	3	1	2	31,000
U Otabe Wild	6	H	6	0	2	1	3,340
U R My Sunshine	4	G	8	0	0	0	1,674
U R Smart	9	G	6	1	2	1	5,284
U R Toast	3	G	2	0	0	0	525
U S Jetta	4	F	12	1	3	1	36,040
U S S Tinosa	5	G	7	0	2	1	13,260
U U Star	6	G	7	1	1	1	8,055
U Wonder Why	7	G	6	0	0	0	482
U. B. Quiet	5	G	6	1	3	0	13,887

Horse	Age	Sex	Sts	1st	2d	3d	Won
U. R. My Hope	7	G	7	0	0	0	1,093
U. S. Blues	2	G	6	1	2	1	10,930
U. S. Gold	9	G	13	3	1	3	29,382
U. S. Indy	4	F	2	0	0	0	640
U. S. Jets	7	H	5	0	0	0	2,426
U. S. Patriot Day	3	G	8	1	1	0	2,386
U. S. S. Boxer	2	F	2	0	1	0	10,585
U. S. S. Goliath	3	G	10	2	1	3	19,784
U. S. Spirit	3	G	6	0	1	1	2,685
U'All	10	H	7	0	0	0	1,044
Uandirclever	3	C	2	0	0	0	0
Ubiquity	7	H	2	0	1	0	7,080
Uboughtwhat	2	F	1	0	0	0	675
Ucantbelieveit	2	G	3	0	1	0	1,598
Uchita	2	F	5	0	3	1	11,020
Udeman	5	G	8	1	1	0	18,080
Udinese	6	G	8	1	0	0	10,799
Udontneeditdou	3	G	3	0	0	0	0
Udustbuster	3	G	3	0	0	2	2,375
Ugosailin	3	G	2	1	0	0	3,300
Ugotadowhatugotado	3	F	5	2	3	0	68,420
Ugotta	2	C	5	1	1	0	15,510
Uhave Light	6	G	2	0	0	0	0
Uhohwhathappen	3	G	4	1	1	0	13,000
Ukrainian Dancer	2	F	2	0	0	0	440
Ulick's Mountain	4	F	1	0	0	0	235
Ulistnintome	2	C	2	0	1	1	13,640
Ulla Bloom	3	F	6	1	3	0	55,380
Ulloa	4	G	11	2	2	0	60,155
Ulltimate Gold	3	G	6	2	0	0	17,640
Ulterior Motives (GB)	7	G	9	1	3	2	67,350
Ultimate Diva	4	F	12	1	2	1	10,627
Ultimate Ego	5	G	9	3	2	1	20,300
Ultimate Hitman	5	G	1	0	1	0	3,000
Ultimate Karma	3	F	3	0	0	0	0
Ultimate Prize	5	M	9	0	0	1	2,633
Ultimate Reward	3	F	3	0	0	0	780
Ultimate Warrior	7	G	6	0	0	0	2,272
Ultimato	4	G	9	0	0	4	24,640
Ultra Chic	3	F	3	0	0	1	2,000
Ultra Cruise	4	C	4	0	1	0	1,980
Ultra Heat	4	F	2	0	0	0	1,932
Ultra Saber	3	G	5	2	2	0	5,863
Ultra Slew Fast	5	H	2	1	0	0	10,101
Ultra Special	2	G	1	0	0	0	0
Ultra Tech	2	F	3	1	0	0	14,120
Ultraglide	3	C	4	0	0	0	325
Uluckyu	2	C	3	0	0	0	100
Ulzana	2	G	5	1	1	0	11,033
Uma Norma	3	F	8	1	3	1	35,272
Umademyday	4	G	1	0	0	0	1,260
Umatilla Ridge	6	H	4	0	0	0	128
Umberto	6	H	5	0	0	1	2,130
Umbrella Girl	4	F	5	0	1	0	5,199
Umcane	4	G	5	0	0	0	573
Umfula	2	F	1	0	0	0	50
Umiak	5	M	2	0	0	0	239
Ummummgood	5	M	12	2	1	0	31,031
Umpa	4	C	12	2	1	0	12,400
Umpateedle	5	M	13	5	4	2	216,160
Umph	3	C	1	0	0	0	105
Umpy	3	F	8	2	0	1	7,374
Un Fino Vino	7	G	6	1	1	0	9,875
Un Galito (ARG)	5	G	9	0	0	1	1,330
Un Ochio	6	M	16	1	3	2	21,945
Unabashed	3	C	1	0	1	0	9,000
Unabashed Charm	3	F	2	1	0	0	28,040
Unaccountably Fast	4	C	4	0	0	0	400
Unaccountably Pink	3	F	2	0	1	0	8,200
Unaccounted Affair	6	H	2	0	0	0	240
Unaccounted Funds	2	G	4	1	0	0	2,950
Unaccounted Gift	3	F	14	2	2	2	25,015
Unacop	4	G	8	2	1	2	15,666
Unalienable Right	7	G	4	0	1	1	7,900
Unaltered	3	F	7	1	0	0	15,250
Unamedthegame	4	G	6	0	0	0	1,815
Unanimous Decision	5	G	5	0	0	0	1,822
Unannounced	3	F	15	1	2	0	8,090
Unanswered Prayer	4	F	2	0	0	0	122
Unbearable	6	H	12	1	0	1	7,315
Unbelekable	11	G	8	0	0	1	2,402
Unbelievable Run	6	M	4	0	0	1	964
Unbendablebaby	5	M	2	0	0	0	0
Unbendebell Cary	8	G	9	0	0	1	642
Unbound Account	3	G	1	0	0	0	0
Unbrakeable George	3	G	20	1	2	3	26,428
Unbridels King	4	C	7	2	1	3	103,610
Unbridled Affair	5	H	4	0	1	0	2,090
Unbridled America	4	C	12	2	1	2	93,065
Unbridled Appeal	3	F	4	0	1	1	14,700
Unbridled Approval	6	M	3	1	0	0	6,170
Unbridled Aria	3	F	5	0	0	0	1,920
Unbridled Ashley	4	F	1	0	0	0	340
Unbridled Boy	3	G	3	1	0	1	9,205
Unbridled Contessa	3	F	6	0	2	1	23,092
Unbridled Cyclone	4	F	4	0	0	0	316
Unbridled Diva	2	F	3	0	1	1	10,310
Unbridled Drive	4	G	6	1	0	0	30,652
Unbridled Echo	3	F	6	2	0	0	31,121
Unbridled Energy	2	C	1	1	0	0	15,625
Unbridled Flight	2	G	1	0	0	0	0
Unbridled Gamble	8	G	1	1	0	0	3,300
Unbridled Game	4	G	2	0	0	0	154
Unbridled Guy	4	G	1	0	0	0	0
Unbridled Idol	3	F	2	0	0	0	0
Unbridled J. J.	4	G	13	2	0	1	11,600
Unbridled Lad	4	C	7	0	2	0	5,582
Unbridled Lass	2	F	7	1	0	1	7,425
Unbridled Lil Star	3	F	4	0	0	1	1,160
Unbridled Mate	4	C	8	3	2	1	53,645
Unbridled Nan	3	F	3	0	1	0	4,780
Unbridled Passion	4	G	10	0	0	1	3,369
Unbridled Phantom	3	C	13	0	0	2	4,865
Unbridled Resolve	4	G	7	0	1	0	3,975
Unbridled Rose	3	F	8	0	2	0	9,718
Unbridled Sidney	3	F	6	2	2	0	69,020
Unbridled Skip	3	F	5	3	0	0	39,200
Unbridled Speed	5	H	8	4	1	2	7,000
Unbridled Sunn	3	F	3	1	0	0	1,195
Unbridled Sunshine	2	F	1	0	0	0	230
Unbridled Temper	3	F	3	0	0	1	6,775
Unbridled Tiara	2	F	1	0	0	0	0
Unbridled Trick	5	G	14	1	2	5	32,963
Unbridled Valay	2	F	2	0	0	0	0
Unbridled Vision	6	H	5	1	0	2	31,370
Unbridled Warrior	3	C	1	0	0	0	0
Unbridledobsession	3	F	4	1	0	1	8,615
Unbridled's Comet	4	C	2	0	0	1	6,020
Unbridled's Evie	3	F	7	2	0	1	14,115
Unbridled's Gal	4	F	3	2	0	0	4,860
Unbridled's Image	4	C	10	0	1	0	6,425
Unbridled's Lady	4	F	1	0	0	0	172
Unbridled's Legacy	2	F	3	0	0	0	2,700
Unbridled's Storm	5	H	5	0	0	0	1,704
Unbroken Spirit	5	G	6	1	4	0	19,617
Unbuckle	3	C	5	1	2	1	49,568
Unbuttoned Blouse	4	F	10	1	0	1	4,584
Uncalculated	4	C	10	1	0	2	38,264
Uncanny	4	C	5	0	1	0	8,085
Uncanny Judith	2	F	4	1	1	0	24,440
Unchain My Soul	6	H	3	0	1	0	441
Unchained Chaos	3	G	5	0	0	0	546
Unchecked Melody	3	F	5	0	0	0	1,011
Uncivil	3	C	16	4	3	1	82,110
Uncle Ack	5	G	17	2	4	2	14,122
Uncle Arthur	3	C	3	0	0	0	2,280
Uncle Bert	3	G	7	0	2	1	4,725
Uncle Bill	4	G	24	1	2	2	14,275
Uncle Brother	4	G	12	3	3	0	23,208
Uncle Bruce	4	C	8	1	4	1	62,760
Uncle Bryce	8	G	10	1	1	2	11,190
Uncle Bus	7	G	3	0	0	0	192
Uncle Camie	4	C	8	2	3	0	92,460
Uncle Cent (IRE)	3	C	1	0	0	0	0
Uncle Cliffy	5	G	4	1	0	0	1,300
Uncle Clip	3	G	6	2	0	0	28,410
Uncle Cook	6	G	18	0	2	0	3,875
Uncle Dave's Visa	5	M	1	0	0	0	0

Horse	Age	Sex	Sts	1st	2d	3d	Won
Uncle Denny	2	C	3	3	0	0	128,775
Uncle Divsie	3	C	8	1	5	1	59,720
Uncle Freddie	7	G	10	2	0	0	10,449
Uncle George	3	G	11	2	1	0	13,143
Uncle Itchy	3	C	1	0	0	0	110
Uncle Jack	4	G	13	2	1	1	42,635
Uncle Jack Casey	3	C	1	0	0	0	225
Uncle James	3	G	2	0	0	0	0
Uncle Jamie	2	C	2	0	0	0	0
Uncle Jer	6	G	2	0	0	0	356
Uncle Jet	3	C	13	1	6	2	28,256
Uncle Joe Boy	3	G	5	0	0	0	552
Uncle Joe's Dream	3	G	2	0	0	0	312
Uncle John	2	G	5	1	0	1	5,865
Uncle Johnny	5	G	10	1	3	1	12,655
Uncle Lee	4	G	13	0	5	4	17,820
Uncle Leroy	2	C	1	0	0	0	1,200
Uncle Luis	4	G	9	0	0	2	1,450
Uncle Mike	3	G	4	2	0	1	14,260
Uncle Mose	5	G	12	0	5	0	27,739
Uncle Nealy Bug	4	G	3	0	2	1	5,757
Uncle Ock	4	G	8	1	2	2	14,170
Uncle Paul	3	G	5	1	0	1	7,766
Uncle Punk	6	H	2	0	1	0	3,500
Uncle Rocco	7	H	1	0	0	0	103
Uncle Snip	4	G	13	0	1	2	5,294
Uncle Tater	2	C	1	0	0	0	0
Uncle Teds Cat	2	F	3	0	0	0	740
Uncle Vic	5	G	10	1	4	1	20,803
Uncle Vinnie	2	C	5	0	0	1	2,235
Uncle Walter	3	C	3	0	0	0	860
Uncle Wendell	5	G	11	1	1	1	4,333
Uncle Whiz	5	G	11	4	1	0	9,750
Uncle Zeff	5	G	11	2	2	1	35,905
Uncledannysbrother	4	C	6	0	1	3	9,325
Uncle's Girls	3	F	6	0	0	0	394
Unclouded	3	F	1	0	0	0	320
Uncoil	3	G	7	2	1	1	12,835
Uncommon Wisdom	3	G	10	1	1	1	7,923
Unconscious Bets	7	G	9	0	0	0	2,215
Uncontested	4	G	4	1	1	1	25,560
Uncontrollable	3	F	3	0	2	0	18,360
Uncontrolled Burn	5	H	5	0	1	0	4,528
Uncork	4	F	8	2	4	0	65,547
Uncorked	4	G	9	3	2	1	59,310
Uncross the Stars	3	G	4	0	1	1	3,995
Uncrowned	6	G	9	0	0	1	1,411
Undaunting	3	G	10	0	0	1	3,720
Undecided Now	4	F	12	4	3	2	24,864
Undeniable Leader	5	G	2	0	0	0	74
Undeniable Queen	2	F	6	1	2	2	53,422
Undeniable Victory	4	C	3	1	0	0	6,375
Under Caution	3	C	3	0	1	0	2,200
Under Control	4	F	6	0	1	2	1,770
Under Desert Skies	3	F	8	1	0	0	1,860
Under the Desk	5	G	2	0	0	0	446
Under the Hill	5	M	3	0	0	0	64
Under the O	10	M	14	0	2	1	3,079
Under the Sun	3	G	15	1	5	2	35,720
Under the Veil	4	F	4	1	1	0	3,430
Underbidder	3	G	5	1	0	0	31,600
Undercover	5	M	7	1	1	4	83,760
Undercover Agent	4	G	13	2	2	1	10,928
Undercover Brotha	3	G	5	0	2	0	3,130
Undercover Guy	5	G	12	1	1	3	5,551
Undercover Rage	4	F	2	0	0	0	128
Undercover Soldier	2	F	2	1	0	0	13,500
Underneath It All	4	F	6	1	0	0	15,550
Underpinning	4	G	11	2	2	0	13,750
Undertheinfluence	3	G	7	0	0	1	2,520
Undisclosed	3	C	8	2	0	1	21,228
Undisputed Terms	5	H	5	0	0	0	248
Undoubtable	3	F	1	0	0	0	0
Undun	5	G	4	1	0	0	3,330
Unend	7	G	6	1	0	1	5,838
Unending Grace	3	F	4	0	0	0	119
Unequal	5	M	4	0	0	0	345
Unexpected Glory	6	G	6	0	0	1	822
Unexpected Heat	4	G	1	0	0	0	147
Unexpected Present	3	F	4	0	0	0	300
Unfaced	5	G	10	1	2	0	8,827
Unfair Advantage	8	G	1	0	0	0	0
Unfaithful	4	C	12	0	0	0	900
Unfamiliar Melody	3	F	3	1	0	0	8,970
Unforgetable Mabel	4	F	11	0	1	1	2,172
Unforgetable Storm	2	F	2	0	0	0	610
Unforgetabull	6	M	14	5	3	1	79,563
Unforgettable Gal	3	F	18	5	4	2	47,855
Unforgettable Gem	5	G	3	0	0	0	85
Unforgettable Kiss	2	G	2	0	0	1	1,550
Unforgettable Max	4	C	10	1	3	1	194,889
Unforgettable One	2	F	3	1	1	0	6,765
Unforgettable Too	4	F	1	0	0	0	380
Unforgivenpreacher	5	G	3	0	0	1	1,820
Unforgottenpromise	2	G	7	2	2	0	36,880
Unfundisi	6	G	16	1	2	3	17,640
Unfurl the Flag	4	G	3	1	1	0	82,840
Ungoverned	5	H	20	2	5	3	39,210
Ungreatful	3	G	5	1	2	0	8,998
Unhedged	3	C	15	1	0	1	7,835
Unhurried	4	F	8	1	0	1	24,240
Unica Night	2	F	1	0	0	0	204
Unificada (BRZ)	5	M	3	0	0	0	1,946
Unifier	2	F	1	0	0	0	0
Unigold	4	G	1	1	0	0	18,000
Unimagined	4	G	10	0	0	2	2,050
Uninhibited Song	3	F	7	3	0	0	71,371
Uninspiring Truth	3	G	11	0	0	1	1,309
Union Address	8	M	1	0	0	0	254
Union Alert	4	G	12	2	1	1	17,030
Union Assault	3	G	10	1	2	1	42,178
Union Builder	5	G	4	0	0	0	863
Union County	2	C	1	0	0	0	132
Union Dues	5	G	14	1	2	0	10,175
Union Hall	3	G	5	0	0	0	355
Union Mills	7	H	1	1	0	0	4,380
Union Park	4	G	2	0	0	0	270
Union Place	5	H	6	1	2	0	80,980
Union Square	3	C	7	1	1	1	9,135
Union Street	4	C	4	2	0	0	7,194
Union Train	2	C	3	1	1	0	32,360
Unionboss	4	G	3	0	0	0	2,040
Unique	4	F	1	0	0	0	130
Unique Devil	5	G	17	0	5	2	10,695
Unique Dream	4	G	3	0	0	0	230
Unique Opportunity	5	M	10	1	1	2	46,200
Unique Ronique	3	G	11	1	2	0	13,960
Unique Savings	4	C	1	0	0	0	0
Unique Sky	3	F	6	0	0	0	3,762
Unique Technique	8	M	4	2	0	0	26,050
Unique Way	4	F	3	0	0	0	0
Uniquely Lucky	8	G	1	0	0	0	0
Uniqueness	3	F	7	4	2	0	39,580
Unison Moon	3	G	9	1	1	0	9,295
United	2	C	9	2	3	0	95,396
United Freedom	3	C	9	3	2	3	36,260
United Notion	3	G	7	0	4	1	23,820
United We Speak	3	C	10	3	2	1	13,680
Universal Boy	5	H	2	0	1	1	2,390
Universal Form	3	C	17	1	3	3	49,160
Unjustified	3	C	14	2	0	5	18,501
Unk	3	G	7	0	0	1	1,100
Unkept Secret	3	F	6	0	0	0	520
Unknown	3	G	1	0	0	0	60
Unknown Code	2	G	1	0	0	0	0
Unknown Dream	3	G	12	0	5	1	6,670
Unknown Jester	4	F	8	1	0	2	18,600
Unknown Parts	3	G	10	3	0	1	38,575
Unknown Variable	2	F	2	0	0	0	6,840
Unlawfulwrangler	4	G	4	0	0	0	600
Unleash the Cat	2	F	4	0	0	1	3,550
Unleash the Power	4	G	10	2	2	1	30,000
Unleashed Storm	2	C	4	0	0	0	0
Unleashedthedragon	3	C	3	0	3	0	21,090
Unleaven	2	G	5	0	0	0	0
Unlicensed	5	H	7	1	0	1	14,019
Unlimited Hope	3	F	1	0	0	0	161
Unlisted Phone	9	G	8	0	4	0	3,240

Horse	Age	Sex	Sts	1st	2d	3d	Won
Unlock the Vault	4	G	5	1	0	0	7,508
Unmannered	3	C	4	0	1	0	1,550
Unmarked Copy	2	G	1	0	0	1	1,725
Unmerciful	4	G	1	0	0	0	0
Unmoonable	3	C	1	0	0	0	0
Unnamed Soldier	7	H	12	0	2	2	3,245
Unnerving	3	C	7	1	2	1	58,330
Uno Cuatro	3	G	17	4	2	5	34,997
Uno I'm Special	3	F	3	0	0	0	116
Uno Passer	4	G	17	6	1	0	30,605
Uno Sham	3	F	2	0	0	1	1,705
Uno Zana	6	M	6	0	0	0	572
Unodatsrite	3	C	11	1	0	1	16,260
Unokia Thunder	6	G	2	0	0	0	0
Unokie	4	G	4	0	0	0	857
Unomes Flash	3	G	1	1	0	0	6,300
Unome's Wild Again	3	F	1	0	1	0	1,890
Unpeteable	7	G	6	3	0	1	31,630
Unpleasantsandy	4	F	8	1	2	0	10,470
Unployment	8	G	13	0	1	2	7,084
Unplugged	2	F	4	2	1	0	37,470
Unpredict Prospect	3	C	3	0	0	1	3,780
Unpredictable K D	5	M	3	0	0	0	0
Unprintable	10	G	1	0	0	0	0
Unpromised	3	F	5	1	2	0	10,344
Unquestioned	7	H	8	1	1	1	4,055
Unquizzible	4	F	4	0	0	0	300
Unreal	5	G	5	2	0	0	8,306
Unreal Adventure	5	M	9	1	2	1	12,795
Unreal Dancer	7	G	15	3	2	2	30,522
Unreal Dream	5	M	21	3	5	1	15,660
Unreal Fantasy	5	M	14	0	2	0	7,500
Unreal Favorite	6	H	3	1	0	1	8,300
Unreal General	5	H	15	2	1	1	45,510
Unreal Illusion	5	G	15	0	1	1	7,649
Unreal Joey	5	H	6	0	0	0	487
Unreal Muffin	4	C	12	3	2	3	83,180
Unreal Prospect	3	C	8	0	0	0	420
Unreal Rapids	5	G	5	0	0	1	1,308
Unreal Tune	5	H	2	0	0	0	0
Unreined	4	F	1	0	0	0	0
Unrelenting Desire	7	G	8	1	0	1	6,216
Unrelenting Grit	6	G	13	1	1	4	18,785
Unrepentant	4	F	12	2	2	3	43,805
Unrivalled (GB)	3	G	7	1	0	0	58,470
Unrullah Bull	7	G	18	3	3	3	28,524
Unruly Sun	6	G	11	2	1	3	8,225
Unscrupulous	2	F	1	0	0	0	0
Unseen	5	M	8	0	0	1	5,572
Unshackled	7	G	3	0	0	0	544
Unshackled Chief	3	C	3	0	0	0	560
Unshuttered	3	F	4	1	0	0	31,520
Unsolved Mistress	4	F	2	0	0	0	0
Unspeakable	7	G	7	1	0	0	5,850
Unspoken Reality	3	F	6	0	0	0	1,220
Unstable	4	G	8	1	1	0	9,120
Unswept	4	G	10	0	3	0	28,031
Unswerving	5	M	7	0	0	3	3,641
Untamed	4	G	14	2	1	0	12,291
Untamed Dancer	3	F	9	1	1	0	8,843
Untamed Heat	4	F	11	0	6	2	6,876
Unthinkable	3	F	11	1	2	2	17,844
Untimely Dancer	3	G	12	3	4	0	37,048
Untitled	2	G	5	0	2	0	14,770
Untold Courage	3	G	1	0	0	0	400
Untouchable	2	F	3	0	0	0	1,040
Untouchable Aly	5	G	6	0	0	0	455
Untouchable Blade	5	G	6	2	0	1	8,639
Untouchable Gal	2	F	4	1	0	0	8,630
Untoughable	3	G	3	0	0	0	0
Untwined	5	G	5	0	0	2	1,656
Unusual Babe	3	F	2	0	0	0	1,260
Unusual Count	3	F	1	0	0	0	0
Unusual Glory	4	G	2	0	1	1	3,615
Unusual Mist	4	G	1	1	0	0	10,200
Unusual Sonata	4	F	11	1	3	0	8,162
Unusual Spring	2	F	7	0	2	3	35,420
Unusual Sunrise	3	G	12	0	3	2	39,826
Unusual Syndrome	3	F	5	1	2	1	31,480
Unwaquoited Love	6	H	10	0	4	1	14,093
Unwavering Honour	3	F	4	0	0	1	2,941
Unwearied	4	C	4	0	1	0	7,564
Unyielding	4	G	4	0	1	1	5,545
Unzipper	2	F	11	1	1	0	13,742
Up a Creek	3	G	17	0	6	5	18,735
Up Anchor	3	C	9	1	0	1	50,050
Up and Again	3	F	6	0	0	0	2,530
Up and Alert	3	G	8	0	0	0	565
Up At Dawn	3	F	4	2	0	0	5,663
Up Front	9	G	20	2	2	3	18,099
Up Front Now	4	F	1	0	0	0	0
Up Henshaw Hill	3	G	12	1	1	0	8,100
Up Hill Survivor	6	G	12	0	2	2	21,330
Up in the Gods (IRE)	3	C	2	0	1	0	8,600
Up Jump the Devil	6	G	14	3	2	3	18,534
Up Like Thunder	2	C	4	2	1	0	99,265
Up Mim's Aly	6	G	10	0	1	2	1,890
Up 'n Blumin	3	F	4	2	1	0	14,450
Up Noble's Alley	5	G	5	0	0	1	2,860
Up On the Wire	3	G	2	0	0	0	0
Up Periscope	4	C	1	0	0	0	188
Up the Beat	3	G	6	0	0	0	810
Up the Volume	6	M	8	3	1	2	13,126
Up This Creek	4	G	14	2	1	1	16,960
Up to Date Event	3	F	15	3	3	1	66,508
Up to Date News	4	G	5	1	1	1	8,955
Up to the Stars	7	G	9	1	2	3	4,116
Up With the Flag	10	G	2	0	0	1	2,140
Upgraded	2	F	2	0	0	1	6,900
Uphere	7	G	6	0	0	1	292
Uphill Skier	4	F	5	2	0	1	104,400
Upickedafinetime	4	F	4	0	0	0	314
Upindeed	4	G	11	1	4	0	19,710
Upland	3	G	1	1	0	0	5,400
Upnotdown	5	M	6	2	0	0	6,360
Uppatuppa's Charm	3	F	13	2	1	2	41,195
Upper Class	6	M	7	0	2	1	18,028
Upper Room	2	F	1	0	0	0	0
Upper School	3	F	1	0	0	0	420
Upperco	5	G	1	0	0	0	0
Uppercut	3	C	2	0	0	1	3,105
Uppity Kitty	3	F	3	0	0	1	11,520
Upscaled	2	C	5	1	0	3	65,916
Upshot	2	F	4	1	0	0	11,970
Upsize My Fry	3	F	2	0	0	0	74
Upsman	3	G	3	0	0	0	620
Upstage	4	G	1	0	0	0	40
Upstairs Angel	3	F	2	0	0	0	230
Upswing	3	F	4	0	0	0	281
Uptake	11	G	10	1	1	1	1,352
Uptasnuff	5	G	9	0	1	3	6,959
Upton Alley	3	G	3	0	0	0	204
Uptown Bates	4	C	5	0	0	1	1,140
Uptown Groom	3	G	1	0	0	0	300
Uptown Lad	6	G	2	0	0	0	403
Uptown Moro	2	F	2	0	0	0	210
Uptown Parade	3	C	3	1	0	0	11,400
Uptown Sport	5	M	4	0	0	1	1,586
Uptown Tornado	5	M	2	1	0	0	6,540
Uptown Victor	3	G	11	1	1	3	13,295
Uptownkindofguy	2	C	6	1	1	1	5,310
Upturn	4	G	15	5	4	2	187,300
Upward Bound	4	G	8	2	2	0	12,356
Uraib (IRE)	4	F	9	3	1	1	137,440
Urban Angel	6	M	14	5	2	3	53,562
Urban Conquest	2	C	7	0	2	3	50,786
Urban King (IRE)	4	C	1	0	1	0	11,200
Urban Shocker	2	F	1	0	0	0	0
Urban Space	4	G	9	0	0	0	1,249
Urban Warrior	3	C	3	0	0	0	810
Urbane Hustle	3	F	10	1	2	1	54,314
Urbanissima	3	F	11	1	1	2	8,344
Urblockinme	4	G	7	0	0	3	6,242
Urge to Go	2	C	5	0	0	0	22,182
Urgent Envoy	3	C	1	0	0	0	400
Urgent Matter	7	G	8	1	1	0	5,183
Urgent Start	5	M	4	1	1	1	13,920
Urgent Valentine	5	M	10	1	0	4	3,218

Horse	Age	Sex	Sts	1st	2d	3d	Won
Urgently	5	G	2	0	0	0	388
Urlacher	5	G	7	1	1	2	30,209
Urn and Ashes	5	M	7	0	0	0	625
Urnotdabossame	4	F	3	1	1	0	2,955
Ursula	6	M	9	0	1	1	3,419
Ursula's Dreamer	6	G	2	0	0	0	414
Ursulita (ARG)	3	F	4	0	0	0	2,147
Us	6	G	8	1	0	0	26,088
Us Better Hurry	3	F	16	0	3	2	4,732
Us Tonight	3	F	4	0	2	0	13,500
Useable	3	F	13	2	2	4	9,332
Useppa	4	F	5	1	1	0	7,440
Usual Manner	3	F	4	1	0	1	41,050
Ut O	3	F	5	0	2	1	15,420
Utah Sky	3	C	11	1	2	2	22,783
Utellum	6	M	9	1	2	2	5,468
Utina	3	F	3	0	1	0	4,000
Utopian Splash	3	F	15	2	0	2	11,525
Uwharrie Wildcat	2	C	3	0	0	0	640
Uxi	2	C	1	0	0	0	184
V as in Victory	2	F	3	0	0	0	3,900
V Eight Rocket	5	G	8	2	1	0	31,270
V F Private Flyer	4	C	10	1	3	2	13,647
V H Ghost Rider	2	C	1	0	0	0	172
V J 's Champ	3	G	9	0	3	0	4,984
V J's Adonis	2	C	1	0	0	0	0
V J's Boy	4	G	1	0	0	0	300
V P Broadway	3	G	11	3	2	1	28,205
V R Blue	2	C	5	1	2	1	7,920
V. I. P. Kipper	4	G	20	4	2	4	24,580
Vaalthazar (PER)	5	G	3	0	0	0	174
Vaca City Flyer	3	F	9	6	2	1	116,280
Vacancy	5	H	5	1	0	1	8,400
Vacarri	6	M	16	2	0	3	15,064
Vacation Money	2	F	12	1	1	3	12,820
Vacation Ticket	2	F	5	1	0	0	4,845
Vacationland	4	G	1	0	1	0	1,180
Vaclav (ARG)	10	G	18	4	2	2	17,610
Vadahilla (FR)	4	F	5	1	1	0	40,580
Vagabond Queen	4	F	4	0	0	0	0
Vagabond Saint	3	F	9	0	0	4	16,476
Vagabond Star	5	G	7	0	2	0	1,179
Vage	3	F	9	1	3	1	46,798
Vagrant Heart	6	M	2	0	0	0	0
Vague Hint	5	H	4	0	1	2	7,620
Vaguely Amusing	3	F	7	1	0	1	8,282
Vai Via	6	H	5	1	0	1	9,573
Vail Peak	6	G	6	2	1	1	7,166
Vaillante	3	F	3	1	0	0	23,040
Vain Empress	3	F	1	0	0	0	660
Val de Mar	3	F	2	0	0	0	420
Val d'Isere	4	F	1	0	0	0	735
Val Rah	3	G	6	3	1	1	24,800
Valalta	2	F	2	0	0	0	0
Valamy	3	F	16	3	1	1	21,995
Valash	5	M	12	0	1	2	7,990
Valay Jeans	2	F	4	0	0	0	1,000
Valay Moon	3	G	3	0	0	0	1,380
Valay Pass	10	G	5	1	1	1	14,200
Valbon	3	F	3	0	0	0	726
Valdasia	4	F	8	0	1	5	7,810
Valdez's Mon	6	G	3	0	0	0	221
Valdini	2	C	2	0	0	2	9,720
Vale of Glamorgan	7	M	4	0	0	0	321
Vale of Wings (GB)	5	M	13	0	2	3	28,950
Valemes On Fire	6	G	19	2	3	1	4,798
Valen Gal	3	F	2	0	0	0	105
Valentina Rose	4	F	5	0	1	1	2,314
Valentine Dancer	4	F	3	1	0	0	287,000
Valentine Fling	3	F	9	0	2	1	2,983
Valentine Kisses	4	F	2	0	0	0	282
Valentine Lassie	7	M	6	0	0	0	472
Valentine Parade	2	G	2	1	0	0	3,190
Valentine Princess	2	F	1	0	0	0	360
Valentine Reality	3	F	4	1	1	0	9,370
Valentine Surprise	4	F	8	0	3	0	3,963
Valentine Xpress	3	G	9	0	0	3	4,926
Valentine's Chime	5	M	3	1	0	0	11,560
Valentine's Mist	3	F	9	1	0	2	32,484
Valentine's Moment	6	M	4	0	0	1	981
Valentino Bob	7	G	17	1	3	3	10,728
Valentino Man	2	C	3	0	0	1	2,710
Valenzo	4	G	3	0	2	0	8,550
Valerie Jo	4	F	3	1	0	0	8,220
Valerina	8	M	16	1	0	2	4,508
Valesia	4	F	3	0	0	0	530
Valet Girl	5	M	3	0	0	0	0
Valexi	5	M	1	0	0	0	2,375
Valiant Anna	4	F	3	1	1	0	26,420
Valiant Crusader	3	C	3	0	0	0	365
Valiant Dave	2	G	3	1	0	0	6,000
Valiant Dawn	3	G	8	3	0	1	19,328
Valiant Edge	4	C	3	1	1	0	26,700
Valiant Fighter	6	M	18	2	2	1	27,723
Valiant Gal	4	F	5	1	0	0	5,371
Valiant Glory	2	F	2	1	0	0	15,600
Valiant King	5	H	3	1	1	0	20,660
Valiant Knight	5	G	14	2	0	2	9,463
Valiant Michael	4	G	4	2	1	0	15,500
Valiant n' Wise	3	G	1	0	0	0	0
Valiant Queen	3	F	6	1	0	1	22,745
Valiant Slew	2	C	4	0	0	0	495
Valiant Splash	4	G	12	1	1	0	11,130
Valiant Storm	4	F	2	0	1	0	1,950
Valiant Style	7	H	12	1	3	5	19,859
Valiant Vera	5	M	7	1	0	0	4,121
Valid	5	G	3	0	0	0	186
Valid Acquisition	3	F	4	0	2	1	10,592
Valid Action	5	G	7	3	1	1	12,744
Valid Afleet	3	G	9	2	2	0	12,270
Valid Again	3	C	10	3	0	0	86,331
Valid Assembly	8	G	6	0	1	0	4,248
Valid Chad	4	G	14	0	1	6	8,490
Valid Charmer	2	C	2	0	0	0	1,935
Valid Chief	3	G	2	0	0	0	228
Valid Company	9	G	14	0	3	2	8,568
Valid Concern	2	C	1	0	0	0	480
Valid Dancer	3	G	19	2	6	3	30,775
Valid Desire	4	F	11	1	4	0	11,768
Valid Echo	2	G	5	0	0	0	750
Valid Excuse	4	F	7	0	0	0	930
Valid Faith	3	C	13	4	1	2	93,515
Valid Flight	6	H	2	0	0	0	240
Valid Freeze	2	F	2	0	0	0	165
Valid Fury	5	G	8	1	0	0	8,328
Valid Hero	4	G	6	1	1	0	6,433
Valid Indian	3	G	8	1	0	1	3,349
Valid Jet	5	H	15	0	4	2	8,540
Valid Magic	4	C	2	0	0	0	0
Valid Missile	3	F	1	0	0	0	75
Valid Move	3	F	5	1	0	0	38,292
Valid Oaks	4	F	2	0	0	0	0
Valid Patriot	3	G	10	0	3	4	17,177
Valid Prime	7	H	4	1	0	0	11,250
Valid Pro	4	F	1	0	0	0	143
Valid Prospect	6	G	8	1	0	2	1,636
Valid Purchase	3	F	7	1	1	1	12,075
Valid Redress	6	G	2	1	0	0	4,200
Valid Respect	4	G	21	3	2	5	15,440
Valid Roar	3	G	1	0	0	0	620
Valid Rush	3	C	1	0	0	0	1,560
Valid Sex Appeal	2	G	4	0	2	0	7,801
Valid Skip	3	F	8	0	1	3	8,000
Valid Streaker	3	G	2	0	0	0	0
Valid Sunset	3	F	4	0	0	2	2,288
Valid Ticket	6	G	6	1	0	2	5,843
Valid Tip	3	C	8	1	1	1	10,173
Valid Video	4	G	4	0	1	1	88,000
Valid Virtue	2	C	5	2	0	0	44,164
Valida	3	F	4	3	0	0	43,150
Validalia	2	F	2	1	0	1	17,585
Validate	3	C	2	0	0	0	235
Validcardealer	9	H	2	0	1	0	2,040
Valid's Beauty	3	F	10	2	1	1	24,331
Valid's Valid	2	F	1	0	0	1	2,280
Valient Phenom	6	G	1	0	0	0	0
Valienteslegacy	2	C	2	0	0	0	320
Valieo	3	F	10	1	3	2	43,670

Horse	Age	Sex	Sts	1st	2d	3d	Won
Valintine Pebbles	8	M	11	0	3	3	5,158
Valintineforvickie	4	F	3	0	0	2	1,210
Vali's Victory	2	F	3	0	1	0	4,500
Valkyre	5	M	1	0	0	0	0
Valkyrie	3	F	8	1	0	0	10,789
Vallarta	6	G	9	1	1	2	45,630
Vallelunga	3	G	4	1	0	1	8,195
Vallenato	4	G	6	1	0	0	5,690
Valley Doll	4	F	5	2	1	2	7,876
Valley Fling	2	F	4	0	1	0	4,495
Valley Haze	2	F	2	1	1	0	4,760
Valley High	5	M	3	0	0	1	1,100
Valley Mist	5	G	12	0	3	1	8,142
Valley of the Gods	4	F	7	0	1	1	26,260
Valley Parking	6	M	6	0	0	2	5,920
Valley Queen	4	F	5	1	0	0	9,062
Valley Roper	4	G	4	0	1	0	10,400
Valley Sunrise	3	F	11	1	1	2	15,902
Valley Town	3	F	11	1	2	4	16,544
Valleyman	4	C	14	0	4	3	47,729
Valleys Aly	3	F	9	1	2	1	12,771
Valley's Passion	4	G	6	2	1	1	64,400
Valliant Dancer	3	F	8	2	3	1	85,455
Vallonga (GER)	4	F	3	0	1	0	7,200
Valmer	5	M	1	0	0	0	0
Valor Jaket	3	G	13	2	2	1	32,835
Valorandappeal	3	F	3	1	2	0	7,640
Valorosa	5	M	2	0	0	0	400
Vals a Doctor	3	F	13	4	1	1	33,155
Val's Approval	3	C	3	1	1	0	10,800
Val's Girl	7	M	3	0	0	0	120
Val's Princess	5	M	3	0	0	0	531
Valtry	4	G	17	0	4	3	5,445
Valuable Asset	4	F	5	0	0	0	3,024
Valuator	3	G	17	4	2	0	8,474
Value Freedom	3	G	10	2	0	1	5,094
Value of Gold	2	G	3	0	1	0	4,876
Value of Luck	3	F	8	2	2	0	24,237
Value Plus	3	C	5	1	1	0	220,900
Value Taker	3	C	11	0	1	1	10,045
Value the Lady	3	F	1	0	0	0	0
Valuebull	6	M	8	1	1	1	7,380
Values of the Hunt	4	C	4	3	1	0	92,753
Valyah	4	F	1	0	0	0	206
Vamos Nina (CHI)	7	M	8	0	4	0	35,400
Vamp Inthe Heather	6	M	13	3	2	2	6,531
Vampira	5	M	6	5	1	0	27,175
Van	2	G	4	0	1	1	6,890
Van Hill	7	G	5	0	0	0	0
Van Houghten	4	G	12	2	3	0	30,364
Van Patten	11	G	1	0	0	0	0
Van Rouge	5	H	5	0	1	0	18,186
Van Whoa	3	F	6	0	0	0	1,453
Vanan	5	M	1	0	0	0	318
Vanastash	3	G	8	1	2	1	34,660
Vancouver	3	C	11	4	2	0	53,270
Vancouver Vice	9	G	4	0	2	0	3,250
Vandalay	2	F	1	0	0	0	78
Vandalize	3	F	5	3	0	2	34,515
Vandaniere	7	M	12	0	0	4	3,448
Vandiano	6	G	11	0	2	3	10,211
Vandulka	3	F	6	0	0	0	1,827
Vanessa Dancer	4	F	9	0	0	0	1,069
Vanessa's Gem	5	M	3	0	1	0	1,220
Vangelia	6	M	2	0	0	0	1,230
Vangelis	5	H	6	1	0	1	153,622
Vanguardia (ARG)	6	M	4	1	1	0	58,715
Vanilla Extract	7	M	14	2	3	2	14,281
Vanilla Sky	3	F	9	0	0	0	632
Vanilla Sky (IRE)	4	F	10	0	1	0	5,850
Vanilla Twist	3	F	10	3	0	3	33,916
Vanilla Whirl	2	F	3	0	1	1	7,195
Vanishing Raisin	3	C	6	0	0	1	547
Vanishing Wolf	2	F	9	1	1	0	12,225
Vanisle	2	F	8	1	2	1	15,339
Vanity Affair	4	G	11	3	0	2	80,215
Vanity Flair	4	F	4	0	0	1	7,950
Vannacide	3	F	7	2	1	2	29,223
Vanna's Honeybear	3	G	8	3	0	1	50,105

Horse	Age	Sex	Sts	1st	2d	3d	Won
Vanna's Tinkerbell	2	F	1	0	0	0	0
Vannieloona	4	F	8	1	1	1	11,825
Vantage Star	3	F	19	7	3	1	73,065
Vany's Forum	5	G	8	0	1	2	18,202
Vaquer Bill	4	C	6	0	1	0	6,200
Var	5	H	5	3	1	0	209,038
Varadero	3	C	8	1	1	1	10,595
Varadivine	6	G	9	1	0	1	3,016
Varaka	4	F	10	0	3	1	8,170
Varas Delight	3	F	2	0	0	0	180
Varda	4	F	7	0	0	1	2,090
Varian	7	G	16	2	3	4	16,377
Variversatile	5	G	16	2	5	2	17,113
Varmits Way	5	M	17	1	2	1	14,208
Varoom	3	C	3	2	0	0	29,100
Varsity Dan	4	G	8	1	0	0	8,415
Varsity O	7	G	14	1	3	5	12,104
Varsity Player	5	H	2	0	0	0	106
Va's Final Answer	4	C	5	1	0	0	4,318
Vasant	3	G	4	1	1	0	35,196
Vase	4	F	1	0	1	0	6,600
Vasilias	2	G	2	1	0	0	14,810
Vaskrissenya	8	M	10	0	0	0	2,103
Vasywait (FR)	5	H	9	1	2	0	56,123
Vatrena Raketa	6	M	8	0	0	1	2,150
Vaughn's Ghostown	3	G	3	0	0	0	2,295
Vault	5	G	5	1	0	0	9,720
Vaulted Numbers	4	F	6	1	0	0	12,710
Vaya Del Sol	4	G	11	1	0	1	8,040
Vazandar	3	C	9	3	3	2	105,306
Vecchia Cita (CHI)	4	F	10	1	5	0	52,340
Vee Vee Bar	5	G	2	1	0	0	2,700
Vee Voom (NZ)	4	F	11	0	2	1	17,040
Vega Sicilia	3	G	7	1	1	1	30,737
Vegas Alarm	10	M	3	1	0	0	6,045
Vegas Attraction	2	C	5	1	1	0	10,691
Vegas Baby	3	F	3	0	0	0	590
Vegas Bandit	3	G	6	1	0	0	6,385
Vegas Cat	3	G	3	0	0	0	225
Vegas Folly	4	F	7	0	1	0	16,240
Vegas Loafer	2	G	4	1	0	0	8,436
Vegas Pete	3	G	1	0	1	0	1,480
Vegas Rebels	8	G	11	2	1	4	10,708
Vegas Venture	4	G	11	3	0	3	116,304
Veiled Danger	5	M	3	1	0	0	2,480
Veiled Speed	2	C	4	1	2	0	64,740
Veiled Threat	4	F	2	0	0	0	640
Veiled Token	5	M	2	0	0	0	0
Vein of Silver	3	G	17	1	0	1	5,108
Velcro Kitty	3	F	1	0	0	0	1,560
Velis Et Remis	3	F	3	0	0	0	400
Velma Kelly	3	F	9	1	2	0	14,930
Velms Lil Dancer	5	M	2	0	0	0	0
Velm's Riot	4	C	12	0	0	0	2,328
Veloce	7	G	4	0	0	0	240
Velocious	3	C	8	0	0	2	6,397
Velocista	2	F	3	1	0	1	12,280
Velocity	2	G	1	0	0	0	100
Velourious	7	M	3	0	0	0	0
Velva	3	F	7	1	1	1	7,872
Velvet Cup	4	F	16	0	2	2	5,104
Velvet Hope	2	F	8	1	2	2	35,670
Velvet Naskra	3	F	4	1	0	0	8,250
Velvet Peaks	2	F	1	1	0	0	4,080
Velvet Snow	3	F	10	3	2	0	238,629
Velvet Tide	2	F	1	0	0	0	300
Velveteez	7	M	10	0	0	2	1,113
Velvetry	3	F	17	1	0	1	9,342
Velvets and Silks	4	F	10	2	2	3	31,456
Velziegellaub	4	G	10	1	0	3	8,735
Venator (FR)	6	G	3	0	0	0	1,388
Vencedora Amiga	3	F	5	1	1	0	39,800
Vencer	3	C	4	1	0	0	29,020
Vendage	2	G	6	1	1	0	20,600
Vendicator	3	C	2	1	1	0	5,280
Venerable	5	H	13	0	1	1	6,477
Venerable Account	2	C	5	1	0	0	9,250
Venerado (BRZ)	8	G	14	0	0	0	0
Veneration	4	C	6	0	1	2	8,800

Horse	Age	Sex	Sts	1st	2d	3d	Won
Venetian Bay	2	C	8	1	0	0	5,997
Vengadora	2	F	4	0	2	0	6,590
Venganza Dulce	4	G	15	2	0	5	16,950
Vengeful Baby	5	M	2	0	0	0	0
Vengeful Cathe	8	M	4	0	0	0	600
Venizia	3	G	11	1	2	0	19,804
Vennys Dollar	4	G	16	0	2	0	6,970
Vennys Public	3	G	6	1	2	1	53,788
Vent Yourself	3	F	1	1	0	0	6,900
Vente Mai	4	G	15	1	1	5	9,684
Venticello	4	G	1	0	0	0	675
Ventoso	2	G	3	1	0	0	6,600
Ventriglio	4	G	5	0	0	0	0
Venture Around	2	G	4	0	0	0	0
Venture Cat	4	C	7	0	0	0	1,920
Venture Forever	6	M	7	0	2	1	9,058
Venture the Storm	2	G	9	0	0	1	1,404
Venture to Say	4	F	9	1	1	0	18,830
Ventures Coin	3	F	1	0	0	0	0
Venturesome Beau	8	G	9	0	0	1	1,644
Venturi (GB)	3	F	2	0	2	0	45,240
Venturous	4	F	14	3	5	0	24,453
Venturous Lady	3	F	12	3	2	0	41,940
Venus	3	F	3	0	0	0	0
Venus Rising	3	F	4	0	0	1	1,630
Venus Rules	3	F	12	1	3	1	11,219
Venusian	8	M	3	0	0	1	1,270
Venys Problem	5	G	15	2	5	2	13,106
Vera Claudine	3	F	12	2	0	3	28,695
Vera's Joy	4	F	5	0	0	0	2,472
Vera's Luck	3	F	10	1	1	2	8,054
Verbal Inspiration	5	M	2	0	1	0	2,693
Verbatim's Chrome	5	G	11	1	1	1	5,331
Verbatinsintegrity	4	G	7	1	2	1	10,268
Verbena	3	F	9	1	0	2	17,185
Verdant Springs	2	C	4	0	1	2	15,540
Verdant Way	3	G	3	0	0	0	0
Verdell	3	C	3	0	2	1	14,689
Verdict's Peak	3	C	11	3	3	2	47,830
Veredus	3	C	5	1	1	1	27,680
Vergennes	9	G	3	3	0	0	15,000
Veri Light	4	F	6	2	0	0	24,925
Verily	6	G	11	0	3	2	4,864
Verkade	4	C	12	3	3	1	98,430
Verkari	4	F	3	0	0	0	0
Verle's Victory	3	G	11	1	1	1	5,098
Vermeil	3	C	4	0	1	0	12,760
Vermillion Lady	4	F	2	0	0	0	75
Vermont Appeal	3	F	4	1	0	0	5,292
Vermont Breeze	4	F	6	0	1	1	1,495
Vermont Mary	3	F	10	2	2	1	47,190
Vermont Miss	4	F	6	1	4	0	9,339
Vermont Riot	3	F	12	0	0	1	3,937
Vermont Summer	3	F	6	0	1	0	16,614
Vermont's Crown	7	G	2	0	0	1	730
Vermonts Harmoney	4	F	2	0	1	1	1,912
Vermonts Marie	4	F	1	0	0	0	0
Vermonts Poppy	4	F	11	2	2	1	13,026
Verne's Baby	2	C	1	1	0	0	34,200
Vernon Invader	9	G	5	1	0	1	17,404
Vernors	5	G	8	1	0	0	970
Vern's Boy	6	G	15	4	2	3	21,518
Vero Missy	3	F	14	0	1	0	3,819
Verolita	4	F	10	0	1	2	9,100
Veronicas' Dreamer	5	M	6	1	0	0	2,803
Verrazanno	3	G	8	1	0	1	7,585
Versaltile	6	M	15	0	0	2	3,213
Versatiles Secret	4	F	7	2	0	3	38,904
Versatility	6	G	4	2	0	0	13,788
Version	3	G	4	0	0	0	148
Vertical Ascent	4	F	3	0	0	0	1,680
Vertigo	5	G	9	1	1	1	8,766
Verve	3	F	6	0	1	2	19,600
Very Ameri	2	F	2	0	0	0	0
Very Clever	3	G	14	6	2	0	81,397
Very Concerned	4	G	7	1	3	0	25,710
Very Couraygeous	4	G	4	1	0	1	8,790
Very Dark Shades	3	F	6	1	3	0	15,026
Very Decent	4	G	5	0	0	3	6,213
Very Eloquent	4	C	7	1	1	0	14,330
Very Femme	3	F	13	2	3	3	17,370
Very Formal M. D.	3	G	5	2	0	0	35,830
Very Gifted	4	F	12	2	5	0	24,917
Very Gold	4	C	3	0	0	0	263
Very Professional	6	G	12	4	1	1	142,287
Very Vegas	3	F	11	3	3	2	195,498
Very Very	5	M	10	1	2	2	46,943
Very Vicki	6	M	3	0	1	0	2,281
Verybrightnshiney	3	F	14	1	2	5	13,260
Verzene	4	F	6	1	0	1	9,210
Verzy Man	9	G	10	1	0	0	3,761
Verzy Power	9	G	7	1	1	0	3,680
Verzy Tune	6	M	10	2	0	2	15,242
Veska's Jade	4	F	5	1	0	0	10,290
Vespers	6	M	9	1	1	4	62,034
Vespone (IRE)	4	C	7	0	4	0	240,073
Vestry	3	G	1	0	0	0	130
Vesuvius	2	F	1	0	0	0	0
Vet Pet	4	G	12	0	1	0	2,348
Vettriano (IRE)	4	G	9	0	2	0	22,254
Vevina	3	F	2	1	0	0	9,330
Vexation	3	G	7	0	0	1	4,568
Vexxed	3	F	1	0	0	0	217
Via Amalfi	3	F	1	0	0	0	0
Via Columbo	4	G	10	1	1	2	52,831
Via Condito	5	H	5	0	0	1	1,075
Via de La Suerte	3	F	4	0	0	0	1,600
Via Galactica	4	G	14	1	4	2	24,530
Via Rail	2	F	1	0	0	0	340
Via Sacra	3	F	16	1	6	1	69,483
Via Star	3	F	2	0	0	0	350
Via Tahoe	2	C	1	0	0	0	400
Via Ventriloquist	5	G	5	0	1	0	1,496
Viagra River	4	G	13	4	1	1	54,528
Vianne	4	F	11	0	2	2	11,050
Viansa Ossidiana	4	F	1	0	0	0	0
Viar	5	G	5	2	0	0	19,194
Viasec Son	7	G	18	2	1	4	25,116
Vibes	5	M	6	0	1	2	15,522
Vibod	5	G	12	6	0	0	26,340
Vibra	3	G	3	1	0	1	5,600
Vibrado (URU)	7	G	12	2	2	1	13,648
Vibrant	2	F	5	1	0	0	19,280
Vibrant Victress	2	F	2	0	0	0	305
Vibs	4	F	6	0	0	0	5,220
Vic Mason	3	G	14	0	3	2	22,044
Vicarage	2	C	4	1	0	0	34,470
Vicars Lady	2	F	5	0	2	0	5,600
Vice	2	F	2	1	0	0	10,373
Vice Is Nice	4	C	8	0	0	0	978
Vice Orr Versa	3	F	11	1	0	2	6,953
Vice Squad	6	G	16	1	2	3	33,450
Vicechairman	6	G	14	2	3	3	35,329
Vicente	2	G	2	1	1	0	24,915
Vicereine (GB)	4	F	4	0	1	1	16,438
Vicious Boy (CHI)	5	G	7	0	0	0	5,340
Vicious Crook	4	F	10	1	0	0	6,540
Vicissitude	2	C	6	2	2	0	26,000
Vicki Darling	4	F	10	2	1	0	11,922
Vicki Vallencourt	5	M	6	0	1	0	22,801
Vickies Song	2	F	1	0	0	0	1,218
Vicki's Eyes	2	F	5	1	2	1	15,700
Vicki's Reward	4	F	13	2	1	1	16,495
Vicki's Sister	3	F	2	0	0	0	136
Vick's Trick	4	G	6	0	1	1	3,810
Vicky's Stage	4	F	8	0	0	1	1,380
Vicky's Verse	4	F	7	2	0	1	20,652
Vic's Big Boy	4	C	11	0	2	3	9,940
Vic's Hope	5	G	3	0	1	0	2,175
Vic's Sweety	2	F	8	1	1	1	26,027
Victim of Love	2	C	1	1	0	0	19,380
Victoire Bataille	3	F	10	3	1	2	118,827
Victor in the Lane	2	G	3	0	0	0	0
Victor o' Hara	5	G	3	1	0	2	3,760
Victor Slew	5	G	7	0	1	2	16,400
Victor Victorious	6	G	7	0	0	0	756
Victor Watz	3	C	5	1	0	1	15,230
Victoria Anne	3	F	5	1	0	0	13,846

Horse	Age	Sex	Sts	1st	2d	3d	Won
Victoria Breeze	3	F	12	2	0	0	11,670
Victoria Brit	3	F	1	0	0	0	2,040
Victoria Lake	7	H	2	0	0	0	170
Victoria Princess	4	F	3	1	1	0	41,048
Victorian Bride	3	F	5	2	1	0	27,140
Victorian Damask	4	F	11	1	2	1	40,909
Victorian Dream	3	F	6	0	0	1	1,350
Victoria's Affair	2	F	7	0	0	4	7,681
Victoria's Garden	5	M	9	0	1	1	9,531
Victoria's Image	3	F	4	1	0	0	6,845
Victoria's Jewel	5	M	12	1	1	1	20,568
Victoria's Slew	3	F	2	0	0	0	480
Victorioso	4	C	6	1	0	0	10,157
Victorious Ami	2	F	4	1	2	0	188,600
Victorious Dancer	7	G	7	1	0	0	4,455
Victorious Halo	2	F	6	1	0	0	23,190
Victorious Hour	3	F	9	3	2	1	38,170
Victorious Kiss	3	F	1	0	0	0	1,764
Victorious Ladd	3	C	2	0	0	0	233
Victorious Market	2	C	6	0	0	1	1,162
Victorious Recall	7	G	12	3	5	1	36,057
Victorious Sky	3	F	4	0	0	0	560
Victorious Slam	3	G	6	0	0	0	1,163
Victorious Vicki	6	M	15	2	2	1	21,284
Victors Dance	2	C	6	0	1	2	6,086
Victor's Jewel	2	F	2	0	0	0	240
Victor's Quest	7	G	5	0	0	0	115
Victor's Secret	5	M	6	2	1	1	61,522
Victor's Star	3	G	13	2	0	1	9,427
Victory Alleged	3	C	5	2	2	0	75,470
Victory Avenue	4	C	3	0	0	0	2,640
Victory Beauty	3	F	5	0	0	1	2,582
Victory Boat	3	F	1	0	0	0	840
Victory Capp	6	G	2	0	0	1	930
Victory Case	5	G	3	1	0	0	11,580
Victory Circle	3	C	10	1	1	1	48,301
Victory City	4	G	20	2	3	2	11,630
Victory Cup	5	G	3	0	0	0	180
Victory Dawn	5	H	1	0	0	0	720
Victory Day	3	G	9	2	1	1	33,046
Victory Encounter	4	F	7	2	1	0	274,287
Victory for D J	4	F	12	1	2	1	16,757
Victory for Judge	5	M	5	1	0	1	16,830
Victory Girl	3	F	10	3	1	0	53,510
Victory Image	3	C	2	0	0	1	1,800
Victory in Valley	3	F	1	0	0	0	110
Victory Is Sweet	4	G	8	1	0	0	4,728
Victory Jazz	2	C	1	0	0	0	0
Victory Lad	5	H	1	0	0	0	37
Victory Lap	2	F	6	0	2	0	15,337
Victory Light	3	G	11	1	1	1	59,980
Victory Lover	2	C	3	0	0	0	55
Victory Mark	3	F	1	0	0	0	235
Victory Mis	4	F	4	0	0	0	341
Victory Moondance	3	G	16	1	3	4	32,540
Victory Number	3	G	2	0	0	0	0
Victory Peak	5	M	11	0	0	1	4,915
Victory Prospect	5	M	15	6	4	2	84,879
Victory Prospector	4	G	13	0	3	3	11,486
Victory Punch	3	F	7	0	0	0	2,115
Victory Red	5	G	2	0	0	0	50
Victory Rising	6	G	9	0	1	0	1,409
Victory Roar	6	G	11	1	2	2	15,415
Victory Rose	4	F	4	0	1	0	5,238
Victory Script	2	F	2	1	0	1	9,113
Victory Serenade	8	M	10	1	2	2	6,464
Victory Smile	4	C	9	0	0	0	2,211
Victory Snit	5	M	6	0	0	0	1,570
Victory Song	4	C	9	2	0	1	53,370
Victory Spin (GB)	8	G	5	2	0	0	31,453
Victory Spirit	3	F	8	1	0	0	38,139
Victory Star	3	G	5	0	0	0	3,882
Victory Steel	3	G	4	0	0	0	240
Victory Strike	3	G	9	3	0	0	56,237
Victory Sweep	5	G	2	0	0	0	630
Victory Tap	6	G	4	1	1	1	10,180
Victory Thrill	3	F	8	4	1	1	63,208
Victory Tour	3	F	2	1	0	0	7,654
Victory U. S. A.	3	F	5	1	1	1	263,267
Victory Venture	4	G	4	0	2	0	4,118
Victory Voodoo	2	C	1	0	0	0	0
Victory Walk	3	G	1	0	0	0	140
Victory Waltz	4	F	9	0	0	1	1,595
Victory Wanted	2	C	4	2	0	0	16,039
Victory Woman	3	F	4	1	0	1	4,605
Victory Won	5	G	8	1	2	1	10,327
Victory Zone	4	G	15	3	2	2	52,690
Victoryhanna	5	M	5	0	0	0	188
Victoryinovertime	3	C	9	0	2	1	12,021
Victory's Pride	3	G	5	1	0	1	4,937
Victory's Sister	4	F	3	0	1	0	5,865
Victorytonitehey	3	C	7	0	0	1	4,260
Video Commander	3	F	3	0	1	0	6,620
Video Man	3	C	10	1	2	2	22,471
Video Secret	6	G	4	0	0	0	210
Video's Account	5	G	10	0	3	3	5,868
Vidlocity	6	M	4	2	0	0	24,900
Vids Babie	6	M	4	2	0	0	8,485
Vid's Ego	4	G	5	0	1	0	3,083
Vids Last Chance	4	G	19	1	0	2	6,168
Vids Lil Breeze	4	F	8	2	1	1	26,885
Viejo's Pleasure	4	C	1	0	0	0	66
Vienna Circle (UAE)	3	G	4	0	1	2	19,340
Vienna Hills	3	C	3	0	0	0	2,700
Viennetta	5	M	4	2	0	0	24,001
Viento	6	H	10	1	2	0	23,030
Viento Fuerte	3	C	1	0	0	1	4,200
Vientos Shadow	2	C	1	0	0	0	156
View At Beaches	3	G	3	0	0	0	1,940
View From the Top	5	M	10	3	0	4	70,350
View Halloo	3	F	9	3	1	2	58,990
Vif	7	G	8	2	0	4	18,095
Vigilant Site	4	G	5	0	0	3	4,640
Vigneron	3	F	12	2	0	1	13,270
Vigorous Attack	6	M	13	2	2	3	17,064
Vigorous Guy	2	C	1	0	0	0	230
Vigors Regard	11	G	4	0	0	0	184
Vijeth	5	G	13	1	3	3	12,946
Viking	5	H	1	0	0	0	31
Vikings Bay (GB)	3	C	1	0	0	0	400
Vikingsholm Castle	5	G	12	0	6	0	8,992
Vikki Slew	7	M	1	0	0	0	0
Vilamoura (GB)	3	G	11	2	1	3	39,128
Vilar	7	G	4	2	0	0	12,720
Vilkee	5	M	2	0	0	0	0
Villa D Marie	3	F	1	0	0	0	137
Villa Lobos	5	G	17	2	3	2	18,656
Villa Roja	4	G	10	1	2	1	3,198
Villa Vernell	5	M	7	2	1	0	5,091
Village Affair	4	F	9	2	0	0	25,973
Village Band	4	G	7	2	1	3	61,200
Village Knight	3	G	9	2	1	0	17,520
Villa's Man	4	G	2	0	0	0	0
Villie	4	G	6	1	0	1	5,432
Vilma Bankey	4	F	10	1	0	3	7,356
Vim N Vinegar	4	F	7	1	0	0	9,660
Vimy Ridge	2	C	2	0	0	0	0
Vinalhaven	6	G	15	2	2	3	21,167
Vinamarino Storm	3	C	3	0	0	0	0
Vince the Mayor	6	G	3	0	0	0	180
Vinceformom	6	G	13	1	1	2	9,455
Vincent De Paul	6	G	9	1	2	4	10,626
Vinci	3	G	1	0	0	0	0
Vincita	2	F	6	0	0	1	13,452
Vindobona	3	F	1	0	0	0	130
Vine Grove	7	G	5	0	0	0	415
Vinemeister	5	H	12	3	0	2	110,620
Vines and Wines	7	G	3	0	0	0	770
Vinnie Babe	5	G	19	2	1	6	9,122
Vinny's Um Bots	4	G	1	0	0	0	80
Vino Classico	5	G	14	0	2	2	11,507
Vino Rossi	8	G	9	0	0	0	821
Vino Tinto	3	F	3	0	0	0	0
Vinotech	2	C	3	2	1	0	39,400
Vintage Class	7	G	10	1	1	2	19,306
Vintage Label	3	C	1	0	0	0	940
Vinters Reserve	5	G	7	0	0	0	661
Vinthea (IRE)	5	M	1	0	0	0	520

Horse	Age	Sex	Sts	1st	2d	3d	Won
Vinton	3	G	10	2	1	2	32,390
Vinziyan	3	G	8	0	0	2	8,140
Violanda	5	M	14	7	0	2	62,575
Viola's Reward	4	C	6	1	0	0	3,240
Violate	8	G	2	0	0	0	240
Violets for You	4	F	5	0	0	0	0
Violette Jolie	7	M	11	3	3	1	46,035
Violette Native	5	M	1	0	0	0	0
Vip Tourist	4	G	8	1	2	1	14,567
Viper Mad	4	F	1	0	0	0	60
Vipervapor	3	F	10	0	0	4	31,679
Virden	2	F	2	1	0	1	7,700
Virga	2	F	2	0	0	0	0
Virgin Run	2	G	7	1	1	1	14,800
Virgin Snow	6	M	11	2	2	1	17,690
Virgin Voyage	4	F	9	0	1	1	30,252
Virginia Accent	4	F	8	1	0	2	11,432
Virginia Dayre	4	F	1	0	0	0	565
Virginia Flash	5	G	13	0	3	2	31,050
Virginia Golfer	3	F	5	1	1	0	16,400
Virginia Miss	4	F	6	1	1	1	39,280
Virginia Plain	2	F	2	1	0	0	34,200
Virginia Pride	6	G	12	1	4	0	52,940
Virginia Sunset	3	F	5	1	1	0	14,920
Virginian Silver	5	M	12	1	1	2	12,905
Virginia's Jewel	5	M	4	0	0	0	105
Virgo Genius	2	C	2	0	0	0	800
Virgo Vixen	6	M	2	0	0	1	1,543
Virtual G	6	H	3	1	0	0	3,922
Virtual Love	7	M	3	0	0	0	300
Virtual Nightmare	7	G	14	0	3	3	10,859
Virtual Storm	4	F	10	1	1	4	6,627
Virtual Zone	5	G	9	2	4	1	66,250
Virtue Ohso	4	F	9	0	1	1	13,320
Virtuosa	4	F	7	1	1	0	24,920
Virtuous Image (IRE)	5	M	3	0	1	0	720
Virtuous Lady	2	F	7	1	1	3	26,010
Visa Tour	4	G	18	0	4	2	5,532
Visceral	9	G	13	1	6	0	14,855
Viscount Victor G	2	G	2	0	1	0	2,592
Visible Song	4	F	4	1	0	1	5,560
Visibly Houston	4	F	16	4	4	1	16,240
Visigoth	4	G	5	0	0	0	480
Visinand	3	G	5	2	0	0	13,530
Vision Boy	5	G	8	1	0	0	7,458
Vision in Flight	5	M	4	1	0	0	24,000
Vision in Silver (GB)	3	F	2	0	0	0	0
Vision of Beauty	3	F	4	2	2	0	103,040
Vision of Division	5	M	1	0	0	0	0
Vision of Hope	6	M	3	0	0	0	220
Vision of Sue	3	F	3	2	0	0	30,240
Visionary	2	C	2	0	0	0	3,280
Visionesque	2	F	2	0	0	0	938
Visit the Circle	9	G	2	0	0	0	0
Visitors Welcome	3	G	3	0	0	0	200
Vista Red	3	C	8	2	1	2	15,685
Vital Asset	5	M	1	0	0	0	0
Vital Sea	3	F	2	0	0	0	470
Vitali	2	C	2	0	0	0	800
Vitamin Fortified	5	G	8	2	0	1	5,684
Vite Vite Vite	9	G	7	0	0	0	203
Vitesse de Fusil	9	M	10	0	2	1	7,862
Viticus	4	G	9	1	0	1	5,305
Vitrify	7	M	5	0	0	1	976
Vitruvian	2	C	3	1	0	1	32,200
Vittori (ARG)	4	C	5	0	0	0	691
Viva Blanda	5	M	12	2	4	1	24,311
Viva Bourtai	4	F	21	3	1	4	18,235
Viva Chrissy	2	F	1	0	0	0	0
Viva Concorde	6	M	3	0	0	0	186
Viva El Gato	4	G	7	0	0	2	4,760
Viva El Vicar	2	C	2	0	0	0	0
Viva Herat	2	C	3	0	0	0	735
Viva Lavilla	6	G	2	0	0	1	420
Viva Los Vegas	4	F	5	1	2	0	12,370
Viva Pentelicus	8	G	10	3	0	1	48,320
Viva Riccio	3	G	17	1	2	3	30,450
Viva Vizcaya	5	G	11	1	1	1	11,670
Vivacity	6	M	7	0	0	1	1,459
Vivaki	5	M	7	1	2	0	13,078
Vivalariva	5	M	5	0	0	0	488
Vivalo	2	C	1	0	0	0	860
Vivara	10	G	14	1	1	4	5,542
Viva's Lode	4	G	12	1	0	2	5,012
Viva's Pride	4	F	5	0	0	0	980
Vivavista	5	M	2	0	0	1	670
Vive Bene	4	G	2	0	0	0	0
Vive La Vie	3	C	9	2	0	0	19,900
Vivian	3	F	9	0	0	2	7,820
Vivid Diamond	4	C	3	1	0	0	14,964
Vivid Flame	3	F	1	0	0	0	400
Vivid Imprint	6	G	24	0	4	3	5,892
Vivid Reality	5	M	16	2	2	3	18,985
Vivid Views	5	H	8	1	2	0	29,210
Vividly	3	F	6	1	0	0	27,480
Vivitz	3	F	16	3	2	1	39,321
Vixen	6	M	9	0	0	0	3,165
Vixen Cat	2	F	5	0	1	1	5,711
Viza Verzy	9	M	8	2	0	3	7,481
Vizually	2	F	2	0	0	1	984
Voce	2	F	2	1	0	0	10,572
Vodka	7	G	7	0	0	2	8,742
Vodka Martini	4	F	6	2	2	1	14,318
Voice Mail	4	F	4	0	0	1	3,000
Voice of Choice	5	M	3	0	0	1	913
Voice of Power	4	G	3	0	0	1	3,630
Voile Soar	3	G	7	1	1	1	19,843
Voladero	3	G	1	0	0	0	0
Volatile Vickie	3	F	12	2	4	0	104,680
Volcanic Glow	2	C	2	0	0	1	1,970
Volcanic Hill	6	G	21	1	4	7	19,260
Volcano Cat	5	H	3	0	0	0	597
Volcano Mtn	4	G	15	0	0	4	10,472
Volcraneo	2	G	3	0	0	0	378
Voldmort	5	G	14	1	1	6	10,603
Volente Deo (NZ)	5	M	6	0	3	2	38,680
Volhynia	4	F	7	0	1	1	11,620
Volkonsky	5	H	2	1	0	0	27,760
Volley Ball	5	H	14	2	0	4	35,562
Volleyball Bag	6	M	9	0	1	2	10,509
Volnay	5	G	3	0	0	0	1,540
Volobee (FR)	4	F	3	1	0	0	15,000
Voltemort	4	G	18	2	0	3	8,527
Volterromo (ARG)	6	G	5	1	0	1	15,018
Volunteer Annie	4	F	14	1	3	2	14,682
Voluntown	3	F	7	3	1	0	41,960
Von Barinkay	2	G	6	0	0	0	12,660
Von Bellinghausen	7	G	7	4	0	0	17,062
Von Braun	3	F	5	2	2	0	73,500
Von Daun	5	G	6	0	1	0	1,057
Von Groovey	11	G	1	0	0	0	90
Von Stauffenberg	7	G	10	0	2	4	5,720
Von Zella	6	M	12	1	0	2	16,150
Vondoo	2	F	1	0	0	0	0
Vontz	2	G	2	0	0	1	720
Voodini	2	F	3	0	0	0	420
Voodo Kiss	6	H	4	0	1	0	7,390
Voodoo	6	G	6	0	2	0	124,826
Voodoo Aly	4	F	1	0	0	0	0
Voodoo Fever	2	F	2	0	0	0	1,180
Voodoo Lounge	3	F	3	1	1	0	17,572
Voodoo Minister	6	H	3	0	0	0	2,040
Voodoo Tricks	5	G	16	1	2	1	10,070
Voodoo Valentine	5	M	8	0	2	0	5,173
Voodoomon	2	G	2	1	0	0	5,745
Voodoo's Sister	4	F	2	0	0	0	0
Vopo	4	F	2	1	0	0	11,910
Voronin	2	G	4	2	2	0	54,657
Vorticity	7	G	9	5	2	2	69,762
Voryias	5	H	7	1	2	2	18,430
Vosges	5	G	14	1	3	2	36,185
Vote for Me	4	F	10	3	2	2	14,936
Vote for Slim	5	G	3	0	0	0	225
Vote of Confidence	2	C	2	0	0	0	824
Vote of Honesty	10	G	3	0	0	0	112
Voteforhennessy	4	F	7	0	3	1	20,615
Voto	4	F	3	0	0	0	0
Vouch's Son	4	G	1	0	0	0	330

Horse	Age	Sex	Sts	1st	2d	3d	Won
Vous	3	F	10	0	3	2	118,315
Vow	6	H	2	0	2	0	10,500
Vowel Play	5	G	13	1	3	2	34,175
Voz De Colegiala (CHI)	5	M	6	1	0	1	59,050
Vronsky	5	H	3	2	0	1	69,120
Vroom Hilda	4	F	6	1	2	2	64,338
Vunerability	5	M	14	0	2	4	14,305
V'ville Lady	4	F	9	6	2	0	47,500
Vyask	6	G	5	1	1	2	7,144
Vye Me to the Moon	4	F	10	5	0	1	58,991
Vying for Gold	7	G	3	0	0	0	1,216
Vying for Power	2	G	1	0	0	0	0
Vying for Time	3	F	9	1	0	0	4,157
Vying Princess	5	M	6	0	0	0	3,610
Vying Road	7	G	5	0	0	1	3,768
Vying Vixen	4	F	13	4	4	3	27,320
Vy's Scandal	2	F	1	0	0	0	105
W B's Florida Cat	2	C	5	0	0	0	685
W F Rushingly	4	G	10	3	2	0	31,075
W G's Talkin to Me	7	G	3	0	0	0	0
W R Funny Face	5	G	3	0	0	0	0
W W Board	4	G	8	0	2	2	8,940
W W Country Girl	3	F	6	2	1	1	23,293
W W Robin de Hood	6	G	2	1	0	0	5,700
W Won	4	G	15	2	2	0	12,455
W. G. Native	3	G	5	0	0	0	496
W. W. Dixie	8	G	20	2	3	4	8,278
Wa Ha Jones	6	G	12	4	1	0	13,153
Wa Pete	6	G	8	0	0	2	1,098
Wa Shoe Shay	3	G	3	0	0	0	114
Wa Tal	4	G	7	1	1	0	9,004
Wa Wa Windy	2	F	2	2	0	0	45,420
Waac	6	M	9	0	0	1	2,137
Waakomim	5	G	1	0	0	0	0
Waakootsa	5	G	13	1	1	2	11,800
Waapatohs	6	H	9	1	2	1	12,295
Wabaroani	7	G	13	2	5	2	13,636
Wabbaseka Scatters	3	F	5	0	0	1	617
Wackadoo	2	G	1	0	0	0	70
Wackman	3	G	8	2	1	0	23,160
Wacko Jacko	11	G	3	0	0	0	1,035
Wacky for Love	4	C	10	0	1	4	55,190
Wacky Patty	3	F	10	2	2	3	118,600
Wacky Tune	4	F	6	0	0	0	663
Waco	2	C	2	0	0	1	4,250
Waco Dynasty	4	F	8	1	1	1	7,680
Waco Fun	2	C	2	0	1	0	2,200
Waco Halo	2	C	3	0	2	0	4,000
Waco Hap	2	C	5	1	0	2	10,945
Waco Legend	6	G	10	1	0	0	4,622
Waco Liz	3	F	8	1	2	1	12,095
Wacona	6	M	1	0	0	0	122
Waconda Lake	3	G	3	0	0	0	990
Wacos Cutie	2	F	1	0	0	0	0
Wada Dame	3	F	5	0	0	1	3,070
Wadadli	4	G	12	2	5	0	45,160
Wade and Tay	3	G	15	3	3	3	15,982
Wade Away	2	C	5	2	0	1	29,500
Wadena	3	F	8	1	0	1	51,538
Wade's Secret Boy	6	H	4	0	0	0	254
Wadjolino	4	G	3	0	0	0	183
Wadmalaw	2	F	2	1	0	0	5,220
Wadsworth	5	G	21	1	3	4	30,667
Wafer Me	4	C	4	1	1	1	5,030
Waffle Head	5	G	18	2	0	8	40,727
Waffles Ala Dim	5	G	1	0	0	0	387
Wag Alley	6	G	1	0	0	0	0
Wag Top	2	F	6	0	0	0	984
Wage a Penny	3	F	10	0	1	1	14,090
Wager and Roll	2	C	11	1	0	0	6,715
Wager for Love	4	F	12	0	1	4	8,379
Wager Quick	2	G	4	0	0	0	616
Wagering Angel	6	M	1	0	0	0	114
Waggaman Road	5	G	8	1	0	2	7,713
Waggle It Red	5	M	16	1	2	2	14,045
Wagon Clearance	3	G	11	3	0	3	20,390
Wagon Road	3	G	11	2	1	3	35,980
Wagon Trail	2	C	6	1	0	1	5,845
Wagon Train	5	G	2	0	0	0	184
Wagoneer	5	G	11	0	1	1	3,356
Wagonmaster	3	G	4	0	0	0	1,200
Wagons Ho	5	M	3	0	0	0	1,211
Wagons West	3	F	1	0	0	0	91
Wahiawa's Star	3	F	5	0	0	0	500
Wahine	4	F	5	1	0	0	6,145
Wahines Reality	13	G	11	0	1	2	1,710
Wahoo Wa	4	C	8	0	0	3	7,152
Wahran	2	C	2	1	1	0	41,150
Wahtowah Baby	3	F	7	1	0	1	9,960
Waikoloa	3	F	11	0	0	1	7,875
Wailea Warrior	4	G	8	1	2	1	13,528
Waimea	2	F	2	0	0	0	0
Waingarth	6	G	2	0	0	1	8,800
Waist Gunner John	6	H	1	0	0	0	0
Wait for Action	3	G	3	0	0	0	180
Wait It Out	2	F	3	1	0	0	27,600
Waitin for Pete	11	G	13	0	0	2	1,914
Waiting Forum	2	C	2	0	0	0	165
Waiting Time	6	M	5	1	3	0	10,095
Waitingonadream	2	F	5	0	0	0	0
Waitingonasunnyday	2	F	6	1	0	1	14,382
Waitonme	5	M	15	3	0	2	16,155
Wait'tilutisseesus	5	M	5	0	0	2	3,057
Wake At Noon	7	H	5	0	1	1	37,337
Wake of the Storm	6	G	11	0	0	2	2,248
Wake Up Maggie B B	3	F	3	1	1	0	15,880
Wake Up Mike	2	G	3	0	0	0	2,058
Wake Up Sugar	6	M	1	0	0	0	0
Wakefields	3	C	5	1	2	0	64,904
Waki Affair	3	F	9	0	0	0	3,183
Waki American	8	H	12	5	3	3	101,625
Waki Baby	4	F	2	0	2	0	9,200
Waki Bob's Babe	5	M	3	0	0	0	742
Waki Chick	2	F	2	0	0	0	230
Waki Dancer	10	H	1	1	0	0	9,900
Waki Daybreak	3	C	15	0	4	1	8,534
Waki General	5	G	1	0	0	0	0
Waki King	3	G	13	0	1	0	2,240
Waki Wac	4	F	8	0	1	1	4,499
Waki Wanda	5	M	1	0	0	0	187
Waky Matty	6	H	2	0	0	1	192
Waldo Pepper	11	G	13	0	2	1	2,622
Waldron	3	G	9	0	1	0	1,370
Walenjack's Dejavu	5	M	1	0	0	0	0
Walesa Miss C	4	F	10	2	0	1	11,730
Walesageorgia	6	G	2	0	0	1	528
Wali Esquire	12	G	3	0	0	0	0
Walk in the Snow	5	G	7	1	3	0	57,360
Walk the Talk	2	F	1	0	0	1	5,520
Walk This Way	3	G	14	2	4	1	148,800
Walk West	4	F	8	1	1	0	5,398
Walk With Cofer	2	G	2	0	0	0	0
Walk Your Talk	5	M	9	3	3	0	29,245
Walkalloveryou	3	G	1	0	0	0	105
Walker	2	G	3	2	0	0	20,540
Walker's Gal	4	F	5	0	2	0	13,660
Walkin ' Wild	3	F	5	0	1	0	3,792
Walkin' On By	3	F	11	1	1	1	14,660
Walking Around (FR)	6	G	6	0	0	1	2,860
Walking On Water	3	C	6	2	1	0	20,318
Walking Over	3	G	4	0	0	0	420
Walkington'orleans	5	H	2	0	0	0	0
Walkinonwallstreet	3	C	3	1	0	0	10,772
Walkinthewalk	4	F	7	0	0	0	2,320
Walkover Sidney	7	M	4	0	0	0	369
Walks Lik'n Angel	3	F	11	2	3	0	50,164
Walks On Fire	5	G	18	3	5	2	25,336
Walks On Water	8	G	6	0	0	0	1,433
Walkthruthevalley	7	G	4	0	1	1	2,950
Wall Magic	8	G	7	1	1	0	5,750
Wall Paper	5	M	4	0	0	1	238
Wall St Kid	2	G	6	1	0	1	3,849
Wall Street Afleet	3	G	10	1	1	1	39,076
Wall Street Rally	7	M	6	0	0	0	2,116
Wall Street Wally	2	G	2	1	0	1	21,840
Wall Street Woman	2	F	1	0	0	0	250
Wall to Wall	7	G	14	1	1	1	7,364
Wallendas Winkie	3	F	6	0	0	2	6,585

Horse	Age	Sex	Sts	1st	2d	3d	Won
Wallendiana Dancer	5	M	1	0	0	0	43
Waller	8	H	3	0	0	0	800
Waller Jr.	4	G	1	0	0	0	480
Walleye	2	F	1	0	0	0	0
Walleye Joe	3	C	1	0	0	0	65
Wallop	4	F	16	4	7	1	158,150
Walls of Jericho	4	G	5	1	1	0	55,014
Wallstreet Analyst	5	G	12	2	2	3	14,681
Wallstreet Raider	6	G	11	1	1	0	3,720
Wallstreet Scandal	2	C	4	1	2	0	106,909
Wally B	3	C	1	0	0	0	0
Wally Ballou	6	G	10	3	0	0	17,880
Wally Bear	4	G	16	0	4	4	25,509
Wally Bengal	5	G	8	2	0	1	7,803
Wally Boy	3	C	2	0	0	0	990
Wally T.	3	G	3	0	0	0	0
Wally Wall Street	7	G	3	0	0	0	227
Wally Wally	8	G	2	0	0	0	570
Wally's a Knockout	3	C	5	0	0	0	351
Wally's Banker	3	G	1	0	0	0	78
Wally's Choice	3	G	8	5	0	1	199,061
Wally's Faygo	3	G	14	2	0	0	15,925
Walnut Slew	5	G	1	0	0	0	61
Walt	7	H	7	1	2	1	2,497
Walter	2	G	5	2	2	0	33,519
Walter On My Mind	4	C	2	0	0	0	158
Walter P P K.	3	C	3	0	0	0	50
Walter Ringer	3	C	5	0	1	3	18,082
Walter William	6	G	8	0	0	2	5,470
Walt's Magic	2	G	4	0	0	0	441
Waltz King	6	G	13	1	1	1	12,766
Waltz Performer	3	G	5	0	0	0	818
Waltzaround Moscow	3	G	8	1	0	2	9,321
Waltzin' Storm	6	G	3	0	0	1	22,175
Waltzing Home	4	G	12	1	3	1	30,299
Waltz'n M. D.	11	G	4	0	0	0	41
Wam Bam Hazaam	4	G	2	0	0	0	133
Wampum Maker	3	C	5	1	1	1	9,305
Wampum Wager	3	F	12	2	2	1	6,405
Wampum Willie	3	G	4	0	0	0	300
Wampus's Halo	4	C	2	0	0	0	0
Wan Dare	3	F	1	0	0	0	0
Wan too Free	3	F	5	1	2	0	7,366
Wana Be a Bandit	3	G	3	0	0	0	395
Wanaka	3	G	13	2	6	2	102,770
Wand	4	F	12	0	3	0	5,994
Wanda Woman	5	M	2	0	0	0	0
Wandaland's Turk	5	G	8	0	0	2	5,003
Wanda's Song	3	F	5	0	0	0	1,110
Wandassilverstreak	3	F	12	0	1	3	7,528
Wander Alley	9	G	6	0	1	1	950
Wander Time	3	C	6	1	1	0	11,540
Wanderin Boy	3	C	2	1	1	0	41,390
Wandi	3	F	7	2	0	1	24,690
Wando	4	C	6	3	0	0	163,529
Wandofwands	8	M	7	1	0	0	16,900
Waniski	3	G	12	1	6	0	17,748
Wanna Be a Hero	4	G	6	0	0	0	741
Wanna Be Like Dad	4	G	10	3	4	1	51,421
Wanna Make It	4	G	12	2	3	3	13,581
Wanna Secret	2	F	9	1	1	2	18,310
Wannabe a Dancer	4	F	6	1	0	0	1,553
Wannabemean	3	F	2	0	0	0	0
Wannabeslew	3	F	2	0	0	2	931
Wannabgood	4	F	15	1	4	1	11,280
Wannagoto Court	3	G	7	1	0	0	6,780
Wannaknowme	5	M	11	2	3	3	14,890
Wannamakadollar	2	F	5	1	0	1	12,660
Want Summore	6	G	3	0	0	1	600
Wanta Fly	3	F	1	0	0	0	164
Wantabeademon	2	G	3	1	0	1	9,028
Wantagh Warrior	2	C	5	0	0	0	1,140
Wantagh Wildcat	3	G	10	3	1	1	44,358
Wantagh Won	2	G	6	0	3	0	6,092
Wantanotherwon	6	G	2	1	0	0	7,925
Wanted Man (IRE)	3	C	10	0	1	4	32,515
Wantedtobeagray	3	G	9	1	1	0	26,580
Wanting	2	F	2	0	0	0	395
Wanton Woman	4	F	12	1	2	3	14,219
Wapato Gold	4	G	6	0	0	1	3,982
Wapella	3	G	12	2	0	2	9,122
Wapitoule	2	F	4	0	0	1	8,151
Wapsi	3	G	4	1	0	0	2,440
War Academy	3	C	3	0	1	0	15,199
War Alliance	4	G	4	1	1	1	25,950
War Bandit	4	G	9	2	2	3	58,201
War Beau	4	F	10	1	0	0	35,790
War Bounty	3	G	11	3	2	3	30,548
War Brat	2	F	3	0	0	0	266
War Button	2	G	5	0	0	0	300
War Cash	3	G	7	0	2	1	3,084
War Cede	3	F	3	0	0	0	177
War Chatter	4	C	6	0	0	0	1,140
War Chest	4	G	14	1	1	1	7,110
War Council	6	G	7	2	1	0	24,450
War County Road	6	G	21	7	5	2	66,487
War Crest Dancer	5	M	4	0	0	1	1,238
War Devil	8	H	1	0	0	1	1,575
War Diamond	3	G	7	1	1	0	5,079
War Director	2	C	2	0	0	0	210
War Doctor	9	G	6	0	1	0	3,590
War Dog	3	G	14	1	1	2	12,364
War Fellow	5	G	6	2	0	0	8,127
War Fever	3	C	1	0	1	0	6,460
War Front	2	C	1	0	0	0	137
War Geisha	3	F	5	0	0	0	150
War General	5	G	6	1	1	1	31,298
War Hawk	4	C	2	0	0	0	730
War Image	3	C	5	1	1	1	18,191
War in the Sand	2	F	1	0	0	1	2,460
War Judge	6	M	13	4	2	2	32,242
War Just Begun	7	G	2	1	0	0	2,700
War Link	5	G	11	2	2	1	5,422
War Maji	5	M	7	0	1	1	3,997
War Medal	5	G	7	0	1	1	5,410
War Nose	7	M	9	0	1	0	1,838
War Paint	4	C	7	1	0	2	15,529
War Party Band	2	G	1	0	0	0	0
War Pidgeon	4	C	16	1	0	2	17,176
War Plan	2	C	1	0	1	0	3,895
War Poppy	2	C	2	0	0	1	600
War Proposal	3	F	2	1	0	0	10,075
War Reality	3	G	6	1	1	0	25,136
War Room	3	F	12	1	1	1	7,271
War Shield	3	G	3	0	0	0	0
War Special	4	F	7	1	1	0	11,047
War Spirit	2	F	1	0	0	0	450
War Storm	2	C	2	0	0	0	2,170
War Talk	9	G	1	0	0	0	400
War Tempo	2	C	1	1	0	0	29,395
War Threat	6	G	9	1	1	0	10,979
War Trace	3	C	6	3	0	0	86,420
War Trick	4	F	2	0	0	0	470
War Tunes	7	M	8	0	0	0	461
War Uprising	3	C	13	1	1	0	6,488
Waracle	4	G	1	0	0	0	0
Warak (CHI)	4	G	3	0	0	1	5,240
Warbond	3	F	3	1	0	1	23,330
Wardship	5	G	15	3	3	4	20,355
Warehouseman	4	G	1	0	0	1	400
Wares Wharf	7	G	1	0	0	0	615
Warewolveoflondon	2	G	5	1	2	1	10,965
Warhead	8	G	12	2	1	1	16,219
Warhound	6	M	4	0	0	0	0
Warison	3	F	7	3	1	2	70,850
Warlago	7	M	19	4	8	2	14,639
Warleigh	6	H	9	2	1	1	269,200
Warlike	4	F	5	0	0	0	1,194
Warlock's Crypt	5	G	6	0	0	0	300
Warm	3	C	6	0	0	0	426
Warm Breeze	3	F	5	1	1	0	4,126
Warm Courage	3	G	2	0	0	0	107
Warm Expectations	5	M	3	0	0	0	411
Warm Feelings	4	F	5	0	1	2	7,117
Warm Grace	4	C	7	0	0	0	672
Warm Snow	3	F	4	1	0	0	3,085
Warm Up	4	F	4	0	0	1	1,000
Warmest Regards	3	F	10	0	2	0	16,280

Horse	Age	Sex	Sts	1st	2d	3d	Won
Warmez Cat	3	G	4	2	0	1	28,720
Warmnfuzzyfeelin	3	F	7	0	0	2	10,041
Warn Me Again	6	G	11	1	3	2	39,554
Warned	3	G	16	2	4	4	29,387
Warners Music	4	F	11	2	0	4	10,975
Warning Light	7	M	12	1	0	3	6,439
Warning Sign	4	C	11	2	5	3	57,800
Warning Signal	4	G	1	0	1	0	8,200
Warningonthelake	3	G	2	0	1	0	3,840
Warp Speed Scottie	5	H	3	0	0	1	1,232
Warped	3	C	9	0	1	2	15,540
Warpfactorten Brag	4	G	13	2	1	0	8,494
Warplane	5	H	8	0	1	2	8,970
Warrant	10	G	3	0	0	1	3,780
Warrantee	6	G	10	0	0	1	2,685
Warren Avenue	5	G	7	1	2	2	21,768
Warren's Classic	4	C	2	0	0	0	2,070
Warrior Chief	3	G	11	2	1	2	13,928
Warrior King	2	G	4	0	1	1	3,010
Warrior Revenge	4	C	13	0	2	1	18,582
Warrior Song	2	C	1	0	0	0	1,560
Warrior Star	3	C	11	1	2	3	23,135
Warriorprince	4	C	3	0	0	0	0
Warrior's Dance	4	G	16	9	1	0	78,800
War's Last Secret	7	M	6	1	1	1	10,574
War's Prospect	3	G	9	3	1	2	136,138
Warsaw Warrior	2	C	2	0	0	1	2,510
Warship	5	G	2	0	0	0	0
Wart	7	G	3	0	0	0	1,760
Wartock	6	G	9	3	0	2	35,145
Warwhatisitgoodfor	10	G	1	0	0	0	200
Was My Case	4	C	6	2	0	0	48,200
Wasabi Cat	3	C	7	1	2	0	44,625
Wasabi Warrior	2	C	2	0	0	1	5,129
Washakie	10	G	9	1	4	0	9,479
Washington Apple	3	G	7	1	0	2	9,852
Washington Belle	3	F	4	1	0	0	15,420
Washington Boogidy	4	F	5	0	0	1	2,277
Washington King	3	C	3	0	0	0	0
Washington Moon	6	G	11	4	1	0	35,389
Washington Park	3	G	3	2	0	1	19,588
Washington Post	3	C	1	0	0	0	0
Washington Spring	6	M	2	0	0	0	0
Washington Winter	3	F	8	1	0	0	11,153
Washingtonprincess	6	M	4	0	0	0	0
Wasioto	5	M	13	3	3	2	36,920
Wasmi Springs	3	F	2	0	0	0	100
Wasn't Me	4	F	9	0	1	3	2,711
Waste of Money	4	F	12	0	0	1	3,348
Wasted Money	3	F	10	1	0	3	27,785
Wata Sunrise	4	F	8	0	4	1	4,778
Watafleet Miss	6	M	2	0	0	0	640
Watauga Waters	4	F	5	0	0	0	150
Watch and Wager	6	G	14	2	3	3	21,240
Watch Breaker	5	M	4	1	0	0	4,296
Watch Captain (NZ)	10	G	1	0	1	0	2,700
Watch Commander	4	C	11	0	2	1	10,909
Watch for Gold	3	C	8	2	3	1	39,568
Watch for Me	2	G	1	0	0	0	0
Watch Her Punch	5	M	6	0	0	0	1,460
Watch Me Angels	3	F	2	0	0	0	0
Watch Me Closely	3	F	7	1	1	2	20,982
Watch Me Dazzle	6	G	16	2	7	1	28,991
Watch Me Fire	5	G	10	2	1	2	12,510
Watch Me Fly	5	H	1	0	0	1	3,080
Watch Me Leave	4	F	17	3	0	2	12,541
Watch Me Smoke	3	G	11	2	2	2	36,008
Watch Me Sweep	4	G	15	1	2	1	7,804
Watch My Boy Run	4	G	8	1	2	2	9,721
Watch My Feet	4	C	3	0	0	0	249
Watch My Gold	8	G	6	1	1	1	5,952
Watch My Six	5	M	14	0	1	2	4,717
Watch Our Demon	2	F	2	1	0	0	1,650
Watch Out Boys	4	F	2	0	0	0	680
Watch Out for Ruby	3	F	6	0	1	0	804
Watch Out Forlefty	12	G	6	0	0	2	1,573
Watch Out World	4	F	1	0	0	0	0
Watch Over Me	3	G	5	2	2	0	69,800
Watch Primetime	4	G	7	0	2	0	3,719
Watch the Lady	4	F	1	1	0	0	8,000
Watch Ya Load	3	F	12	2	2	0	17,685
Watch Your Pennies	7	G	12	1	0	3	19,040
Watchamenot	4	C	6	0	0	0	927
Watchem Dream	2	C	3	0	0	0	1,200
Watchem Smokey	4	G	6	1	2	0	81,400
Watch'er Dance	5	M	9	0	0	0	742
Watcherstrut	4	F	13	1	2	2	50,815
Watchman's Warning	9	G	3	0	0	0	260
Watchmedothis	3	G	4	0	0	0	800
Watchmemove	4	F	15	2	3	0	12,183
Watchmon	2	C	1	0	1	0	9,000
Watchsusanrun	3	F	9	3	0	0	15,930
Watch'yo'step	2	F	2	0	1	0	5,060
Water an Lighting	5	M	8	0	1	0	2,011
Water Bank Road	5	G	8	0	0	0	504
Water Cannon	3	G	9	4	1	1	162,500
Water Czar	6	G	10	4	1	1	41,940
Water Gap	4	F	17	2	3	4	64,090
Water Hunter (GB)	7	G	4	0	0	1	4,250
Water Issues	4	F	16	3	1	3	21,478
Water Mark Blaze	3	G	3	0	0	0	345
Water Park	3	F	6	1	2	1	24,124
Water Quint	6	G	15	1	0	2	8,409
Water Ski	4	F	2	0	0	0	0
Water Sports	5	G	8	1	1	3	4,957
Waterborne	5	G	7	1	2	0	3,872
Waterbuck	7	M	13	1	1	4	10,337
Wateree	3	F	8	1	1	1	40,654
Waterkress	5	M	4	0	0	0	210
Waterloo Gin	5	G	5	1	2	0	4,182
Waterloo Run	3	G	7	0	1	1	4,839
Watermellon Run	7	G	9	2	0	0	9,166
Watermelon Summer	2	G	4	0	0	1	5,040
Watermelon Wine	5	M	8	1	1	0	39,820
Watershed	3	G	8	0	0	2	10,365
Watershed Event	3	C	8	3	0	1	79,547
Waterundrthebridge	5	H	9	4	1	2	42,524
Watkindadealisthis	8	G	3	0	2	0	2,952
Watral Bonnie Luck	5	G	1	0	0	0	105
Watral Fool Michel	5	M	6	3	1	0	24,952
Watral Swee Dixie	5	M	12	3	3	1	20,440
Watraladygenevieve	3	F	4	1	1	0	33,354
Watrals Bashfull	3	F	4	0	0	0	2,562
Watrals Cloud Nine	6	H	4	0	0	0	0
Watral's Dahlia	3	F	7	2	2	1	27,932
Watral's Doonsday	5	M	10	3	4	1	23,036
Watrals Hula Girl	4	F	11	0	0	1	1,882
Watrals Lady Hanne	5	M	12	1	3	2	65,456
Watrals Mr Manners	4	G	6	0	0	0	1,417
Watral's Nashua	4	F	13	1	2	4	21,656
Watrals Old Timer	5	G	9	0	0	1	919
Watrals Rich Brass	8	G	7	1	0	2	7,004
Watrals Rodeo Bob	8	G	13	0	1	1	8,492
Watral's Senor	3	G	5	0	1	1	8,490
Watrals Stephanie	7	M	8	0	0	1	1,733
Watrals Strike Go	5	M	14	1	6	1	42,288
Watrals Twelvbelow	9	M	5	2	0	0	13,316
Watralsoutherncure	5	G	12	2	2	2	36,429
Watterston	3	G	1	0	0	0	0
Watuga	3	G	13	1	2	1	8,929
Waupaca	4	C	8	2	1	1	91,050
Wautega Light	2	F	1	0	0	0	135
Wauwinet	3	G	13	3	2	1	36,200
Wave	6	G	1	0	0	0	0
Wave Babe	3	F	15	1	1	1	14,877
Wave Goodbye	2	F	2	0	0	0	1,200
Wave Land Slew	2	C	3	0	0	0	125
Wave Lenth	3	G	4	1	0	0	4,552
Wave That Flag	3	G	4	0	0	0	200
Wave the Blues	4	G	3	0	0	0	0
Wave the Sword	6	H	1	0	0	0	960
Wave Walker	5	G	5	1	0	0	7,635
Waveband	6	M	5	1	0	1	15,615
Wavering Banker	2	C	1	1	0	0	15,600
Wavering Buck	2	C	2	0	0	0	0
Wavering Chief	5	G	20	6	1	4	34,734
Wavering Creek	3	G	8	0	4	1	25,260
Wavering Lines	5	M	1	0	0	0	0

Horse	Age	Sex	Sts	1st	2d	3d	Won
Wavering Marci	7	M	5	1	0	1	6,089
Wavering Prince	3	G	1	0	0	0	0
Wavering Seasons	5	G	1	0	0	0	0
Wavering Truth	3	G	15	2	5	0	54,181
Waverly Girl	3	F	2	0	0	1	1,305
Waverly Naskra	7	G	2	0	0	0	519
Waves of Beauty	4	F	12	2	0	3	16,769
Waves of Glory	3	G	6	0	0	0	3,120
Waving Flags	3	F	5	1	0	2	44,350
Waving Monarch	3	G	8	2	1	0	31,682
Wavy	5	M	9	2	0	0	28,630
Wawota	4	F	8	0	0	2	10,279
Wax	4	G	4	0	0	0	0
Wax 'Em	3	G	7	0	0	1	4,585
Waxweed Flower	3	F	10	2	1	3	8,439
Waxy's Choice	4	G	7	0	0	0	585
Way Ahead of You	2	G	3	1	1	0	5,723
Way Beyond	4	F	7	3	2	1	16,770
Way Brite	4	F	15	5	3	2	34,373
Way Con Sue	3	F	4	0	0	1	2,100
Way Fast Beauty	5	M	15	1	2	1	14,070
Way Fleeter	4	F	10	2	2	0	14,841
Way Late	3	G	1	0	0	1	1,575
Way Marie	5	M	13	0	1	0	8,195
Way of the Knight	7	H	3	0	0	0	555
Way Out Sher	3	F	8	1	2	2	6,719
Way Out Story	5	G	8	2	0	2	6,887
Way Out Verdict	3	F	11	2	1	1	19,079
Way Out West	7	G	6	1	0	3	7,455
Way Over Due	4	F	4	0	0	0	210
Way Sexy	3	G	7	0	0	3	5,875
Way to Go Cat	3	G	7	1	0	2	15,017
Way to Go Dad	5	G	8	0	0	4	7,761
Way to Go Liz	3	F	4	0	0	0	675
Way to the Top	6	G	3	1	0	0	34,891
Way to Trieste	2	G	5	0	0	2	7,250
Way too Fun	4	F	1	0	0	0	140
Way too Many	3	G	1	0	0	0	0
Way too Windy	2	F	1	0	0	0	0
Way West Dolly	4	F	14	6	0	3	44,343
Way X S Ive	3	G	7	1	0	1	2,899
Wayinthebacktwo	4	F	13	0	0	2	6,118
Wayland	7	M	6	0	0	0	159
Waymore	2	C	5	0	1	2	5,840
Wayne Henry	3	G	16	5	0	1	29,804
Wayne O	6	G	1	0	0	0	0
Wayne Wo Weems	3	F	13	3	1	2	24,600
Wayne's Boy	5	G	8	0	1	1	3,115
Wayne's Choice	9	G	15	2	1	1	9,496
Wayne's Mister C	9	G	13	2	0	4	10,535
Wayne's On Line	3	F	4	0	0	0	249
Wayne's Princess	5	M	3	2	0	0	15,240
Wayne's Star	3	F	15	0	3	3	7,970
Wayneschoclatebar	6	G	17	1	0	4	12,179
Wayne'spointofview	4	C	2	0	0	0	0
Waynestro	4	C	9	1	2	1	9,094
Wayoutview	5	M	5	1	1	0	4,150
Ways to Win	3	F	10	0	1	1	2,916
Wayside House	2	C	4	0	0	0	1,200
Waytocutewaytocool	7	M	5	1	1	1	2,930
Waytoocoolcat	4	G	11	1	0	1	8,421
Waytoomuchfun	3	F	3	1	0	1	11,710
Waytopersonal	9	G	15	2	0	0	10,335
Waytotheleft	2	F	2	0	0	2	8,200
Wayuphi	4	G	11	3	0	1	28,878
Wayward	3	F	6	0	1	4	6,305
Wayward Liz	3	F	7	0	2	2	25,591
Wayward Rocket	3	F	13	3	0	4	16,294
Wayward Storm	2	G	1	0	0	0	400
Wayward Wild Goose	5	M	4	0	0	0	241
Wayward Will	3	G	17	1	3	2	26,999
Wayzata Bay	2	C	4	1	0	0	8,730
Wazza Cat	5	M	12	1	1	0	11,152
Wazzup Bonnie	3	F	11	2	3	2	23,659
We	6	H	3	0	0	0	1,140
We All Love Aleyna	3	G	14	6	1	1	188,020
We Be Cuzzins	9	G	11	3	0	1	8,563
We Be Glenoaks	6	G	11	0	1	2	2,434
We Be Movin	5	M	22	2	2	6	18,966

Horse	Age	Sex	Sts	1st	2d	3d	Won
We Both Walk	4	F	9	4	0	0	23,520
We Can Do	3	F	3	0	1	1	4,945
We Danced Anyway	4	F	12	6	1	1	45,757
We Did It My Way	3	F	7	0	0	0	2,525
We Fly Delta	4	F	1	0	0	0	0
We Got Money	3	G	13	2	5	2	42,780
We Have a Problem	4	G	4	0	0	1	4,730
We Love Rocky	2	C	6	1	0	2	26,082
We Miss You Son	3	G	8	2	0	0	2,450
We Think So	6	G	6	0	0	0	1,718
We Two	2	C	2	0	0	0	924
We Will Prevail	4	G	11	5	1	1	43,234
We Wonder Why	3	F	5	0	0	0	2,050
Weaddababyetsaboy	2	G	5	1	1	0	3,052
Wealth and Beauty	2	F	3	0	0	0	670
Wealth N Fame	3	G	3	0	0	0	0
Wealth of Gold	4	G	8	0	0	1	1,671
Wealthy Rhythm	4	F	15	1	0	1	5,835
Weanling Got Big	3	G	11	2	2	1	12,348
Weapon of Choice	3	G	14	1	1	3	13,554
Wear	4	F	9	1	2	2	35,364
Wear My Ring	2	F	3	0	0	0	1,785
Wearing Me Slick	6	G	11	0	3	0	3,188
Wears a Halo	3	G	6	1	0	0	7,541
Weary Blues	4	F	10	1	0	0	21,914
Weasel Royale	3	C	7	0	1	0	2,518
Weather Advisory	5	G	6	0	0	0	972
Weather Alert	2	F	3	0	0	0	129
Weather Eye	4	G	18	1	1	4	9,275
Weatherfield	2	F	3	1	0	0	15,786
Weatheringthestorm	6	M	19	2	2	3	12,498
Weathermans Folly	3	G	3	0	0	0	0
Weatherwise	3	F	6	0	2	2	13,425
Weave a Light On	3	F	1	0	0	0	225
Weave a Wager	3	F	11	1	0	1	8,550
Weave Dreamer	3	F	5	0	1	0	5,019
Weave It to Me	5	G	5	1	0	1	3,180
Weavemesomefreedom	5	G	9	3	2	0	7,837
Weaver	6	G	3	0	1	0	560
Weavin Millie	4	F	9	1	0	2	2,052
Web	2	F	2	0	0	0	125
Web Caster	4	F	17	0	0	1	11,635
Web Watch Too	4	G	5	1	0	0	7,290
Webejamminmon	3	C	9	1	1	2	14,014
Webers Drive In	2	F	6	1	1	1	22,443
Webpage	3	F	4	0	0	0	0
Wecandobetter	2	F	5	0	0	2	4,105
Wedad	4	F	4	0	0	0	441
Wedding Bells	5	M	1	0	0	0	0
Wedding Song	3	F	2	0	0	0	546
Wedonit	4	G	4	0	0	0	1,289
Wee Be Broke	6	M	1	0	0	0	450
Wee Biscuit	4	C	4	1	0	1	3,097
Wee Bit Wild	4	F	6	0	0	0	500
Wee Burn	5	M	7	0	0	1	6,120
Wee Dance	3	F	1	0	0	0	240
Wee David	3	C	14	3	1	1	32,951
Wee Georgie Porgie	8	G	7	1	0	0	2,474
Wee Guy	3	G	3	0	0	0	0
Wee Katie	5	M	2	0	0	0	0
Wee Okie	4	F	9	3	1	1	51,910
Wee Paws	3	G	1	0	0	0	0
Wee Robin	6	M	9	0	1	1	1,640
Wee Sister	4	F	3	0	0	0	220
Wee Wolf	2	G	2	0	0	0	0
Wee Wonder	6	G	10	3	2	2	9,493
Weebitofluck	2	F	4	0	0	1	2,765
Weedle	4	C	10	1	2	0	20,872
Weedwacker	6	G	4	0	2	1	8,480
Weekend At Larry's	2	C	2	0	1	0	4,400
Weekend Baby	4	F	11	1	1	1	5,328
Weekend Bar Talk	2	G	1	0	0	0	235
Weekend Binge	5	G	20	3	2	4	26,160
Weekend Ceilidh	3	F	5	4	0	1	69,306
Weekend Challenge	4	G	4	1	0	0	2,418
Weekend Charlie	2	G	3	0	0	0	1,200
Weekend Drummer	2	G	1	0	0	0	735
Weekend in Devon	5	M	2	0	0	0	517
Weekend Miracle	5	H	7	1	1	1	6,836

Horse	Age	Sex	Sts	1st	2d	3d	Won
Weekend Pow Wow	4	G	9	0	0	1	1,889
Weekend Pro	4	G	6	1	0	0	5,167
Weekend Ruckus	3	C	1	0	0	0	340
Weekend Rules	3	G	9	1	2	1	29,644
Weekend Special	10	G	10	1	0	2	3,499
Weekend Willie	3	G	7	0	1	1	6,412
Weekender	8	G	5	2	2	1	10,390
Weeks	3	F	6	3	2	0	55,200
Weeks Bay	6	G	3	0	0	0	344
Weepecket	7	M	10	1	2	1	26,490
Weepinbell	4	G	8	0	1	2	8,615
Weets Illusion	4	G	6	0	0	1	841
Weez Jammin	4	G	11	0	0	2	3,387
Wegota Cisco	3	G	7	1	1	2	3,832
Wegotchanow	3	G	5	0	1	0	1,740
Weho	4	F	4	0	0	0	3,500
Weigelia	3	C	12	4	3	3	447,790
Weigh the Coin	5	G	1	0	0	0	203
Weight's Bally	5	M	4	0	0	0	276
Weinerwatersoup	6	M	3	0	0	0	548
Wekiva	6	G	10	2	0	2	20,184
Wekiva Luck	5	G	19	3	1	0	16,966
Wekiva Mills	3	G	3	0	0	0	146
Wekiva Mist	3	F	11	1	5	1	50,735
Wekiva Queen	4	F	5	2	2	1	7,760
Wekiva Storm	5	M	7	0	1	2	5,326
Wekiva Sun	3	G	10	1	2	3	15,030
Wekiva Woods	6	G	4	2	1	1	9,300
Wekivakoo	2	F	1	0	0	0	0
Wekiva's Awesome	5	M	12	2	2	2	43,550
Wekiva's Slew	3	G	9	1	1	4	31,430
Welch	5	G	4	1	1	0	5,424
Welcome Aboard	5	G	12	4	1	1	22,735
Welcome Again	2	G	2	0	1	0	5,700
Welcome Channel	5	G	7	1	0	1	5,193
Welcome Home	3	F	6	2	2	1	66,560
Welcome Matt	6	H	4	1	0	0	12,416
Welcome Queen	2	F	3	1	0	1	16,990
Weld Elven (FR)	4	F	2	0	0	0	400
Welder's Flash	5	G	13	3	1	2	8,415
Weldlock	8	G	4	1	0	1	4,620
Well	4	F	2	0	0	0	210
Well At the Top (IRE)	4	F	1	0	0	1	4,200
Well Briefed	6	M	5	0	0	3	4,573
Well Coordinated	3	F	1	0	0	0	105
Well Done My Love (GER)	4	F	4	0	0	0	5,380
Well Dressed Man	3	G	5	0	0	0	0
Well Dun Ferdinand	7	G	6	1	1	2	5,200
Well Educated	5	G	5	1	1	1	9,379
Well Enough	5	G	1	0	0	0	340
Well Executed Cat	3	F	1	0	0	0	77
Well Fancied	6	G	3	2	0	0	189,070
Well Frosted	3	F	3	1	0	1	7,660
Well Go Then	5	M	12	3	3	1	61,335
Well Heeled	7	G	12	1	1	1	4,376
Well Hello Clarice	4	G	7	1	0	0	3,362
Well Known Act	6	G	9	1	3	3	16,840
Well Maid Woman	4	F	11	1	2	1	18,642
Well Mam	4	F	12	4	2	3	29,700
Well Protected	10	M	4	0	0	0	365
Well Rounded	2	F	3	0	0	0	0
We'll Sea Ya	6	M	6	0	0	0	2,905
Well Spring	3	F	3	0	1	0	9,750
Well Struck	5	H	5	0	0	1	5,580
Well Travelled	5	H	4	1	2	1	33,200
Wellbilt Carol	2	F	5	1	0	1	8,702
Wellfleet	4	G	10	1	0	0	8,761
Wellgetem	4	C	7	2	0	0	10,380
Wellgiven	3	G	12	3	2	2	108,362
Wellington Harbor	3	G	4	0	1	3	16,190
Wellpartnered	4	F	2	0	1	0	3,430
Well'sfargoexpress	4	G	10	0	1	3	11,896
Wellsona Road	3	G	9	0	2	1	3,710
Welo	8	G	4	1	1	0	3,567
Welsh Spirit	5	M	19	3	1	1	36,270
Wemisscam	4	F	8	2	1	0	9,446
Wend	3	F	1	0	0	0	450
Wendell's Shadow	3	G	20	1	4	2	12,941
Wendigo Wind	2	G	3	0	0	1	3,005
Wendlar	4	G	21	2	2	5	28,632
Wendover	6	H	2	0	0	0	450
Wendy Road	4	G	11	1	3	0	5,187
Wendy's Explosion	4	G	9	1	2	2	23,245
Wendy's Furl Sail	8	M	8	0	0	0	1,206
Wendy's On to Me	3	F	4	0	1	1	19,744
Wendy's Savior	4	F	11	4	3	1	13,145
Wendy'smaegadancer	3	F	8	2	1	2	17,825
Wenevrkindnesfails	4	C	1	0	0	0	0
Went South	8	M	12	1	2	0	2,605
Weoka	3	F	8	0	2	1	10,385
Weownitourselves (IRE)	10	M	1	0	0	0	0
Werblin	5	H	3	0	0	0	720
Were Ever We Go	3	F	7	1	0	1	8,430
Werehere	7	G	7	1	2	0	11,075
Wertz	8	H	5	0	1	2	12,970
Wes Side Story	4	G	6	1	1	2	5,880
Wescat	5	G	9	0	0	0	3,671
Weshaam Luck	2	F	7	2	1	0	66,960
Weshes Pearl	4	F	2	0	0	0	0
Weshing for Gold	5	M	14	1	2	3	20,980
Weshinwell	4	F	5	1	0	0	12,534
Wesh's Rul	2	C	3	1	0	1	20,330
Weshudaknownbetter	6	G	7	2	0	0	12,840
Wesley David	11	G	1	0	0	0	0
Wesley U.	4	G	8	1	1	1	10,048
Weslow	4	G	6	0	0	0	1,080
Wesman	4	G	9	0	0	0	4,765
Wesniak	3	G	5	0	1	1	12,602
Wessex (ARG)	5	H	5	0	0	1	3,047
Wesson Way	3	C	8	0	0	1	1,505
West Allis	4	F	7	2	1	1	5,059
West Ambler	3	F	13	0	2	2	8,082
West Beware	5	M	12	1	2	4	98,249
West Boggs Park	5	G	13	1	1	2	5,399
West Bound Dream	3	F	8	1	1	1	16,344
West by Dixie	4	G	4	1	0	0	18,600
West Coast Fun	4	F	8	1	0	1	8,900
West Coast Gee Gee	4	F	3	0	0	0	2,140
West Coast Monarch	3	F	6	0	0	0	7,607
West Coast Philly	3	F	8	0	0	0	720
West Coast Talk	5	G	14	3	1	1	16,350
West Code	7	G	4	1	0	0	5,240
West Con	4	G	1	0	0	0	0
West Cork Tour	7	M	3	0	0	0	189
West Dallas	3	C	8	1	0	0	6,330
West End Lady	3	F	12	1	1	2	29,147
West Flank	3	G	10	2	0	0	16,865
West for Gold	4	G	20	1	1	2	8,800
West Forty Six St.	4	G	1	1	0	0	6,050
West Greeley	2	F	3	0	1	1	9,160
West Jet	3	G	8	1	1	3	7,885
West Lakeshore	6	G	11	0	0	5	2,840
West Mountain	4	G	11	1	1	1	2,835
West of East Texas	4	G	4	0	0	0	870
West of McGuire	5	G	11	1	0	1	4,765
West of the Citi	3	F	2	0	0	1	3,470
West Park	2	C	1	0	0	0	230
West Philadelphia	5	M	1	0	0	0	0
West Point Gent	4	G	18	2	1	0	13,862
West Renovado (ARG)	6	H	13	0	2	3	4,940
West Ridge	5	G	14	0	2	3	4,487
West Road	4	G	11	1	1	0	9,529
West Saratoga	4	G	15	2	3	2	17,593
West Seattle	10	G	2	0	0	0	210
West Seattle Boy	5	G	11	3	2	3	18,238
West Side Cat	3	G	6	0	0	1	2,425
West Side Maria	6	M	19	3	1	1	17,247
West Texas Agenda	3	C	1	0	0	0	0
West Texas Wind	4	G	4	0	0	1	596
West to Coast	3	C	2	0	0	0	650
West Virginia	3	C	7	2	2	0	302,345
West War (ARG)	6	G	11	3	1	1	43,273
Westbound Road	7	G	6	0	1	1	6,300
Westbriar	3	G	14	0	1	2	3,983
Westcliffe	5	G	1	0	0	0	0
Westcoastwildcat	4	G	16	1	2	3	14,995
Westendvalues	4	G	17	2	0	4	20,514
Westerly Flow	6	M	13	3	0	1	39,169

Horse	Age	Sex	Sts	1st	2d	3d	Won
Westerly Gale	2	F	1	0	0	0	1,155
Western Acres	2	C	2	2	0	0	29,700
Western Act	2	G	2	1	0	0	2,880
Western Admiral	3	G	8	3	0	2	38,371
Western Algieri	3	F	3	0	0	0	510
Western Alliance	3	C	4	0	0	2	6,910
Western Apache	4	C	5	0	2	1	11,741
Western Artist	7	M	2	1	0	0	1,700
Western Attacker	3	G	2	0	0	0	0
Western Babe	2	F	1	0	0	0	0
Western Baby	2	F	1	0	0	0	0
Western Bandit	3	G	9	1	0	0	9,248
Western Beau	6	H	3	0	2	0	4,040
Western Blondy	2	F	4	1	0	0	37,170
Western Blossom	3	F	13	1	2	2	27,434
Western Book	4	G	9	1	0	1	5,678
Western Boot	6	G	5	1	0	1	5,166
Western Bulldog	2	C	1	0	0	0	120
Western Cee	4	F	5	0	0	0	932
Western Chick	3	F	2	0	0	0	0
Western Class	3	C	1	0	0	0	80
Western Classic	3	C	4	0	0	1	10,113
Western Cooking	4	C	6	0	0	0	445
Western County	3	G	9	1	2	0	10,773
Western Cove	4	G	6	1	0	1	5,014
Western Cruzer	5	M	18	1	5	1	12,665
Western Cutie	3	F	5	0	2	0	7,390
Western Dame	4	F	5	1	0	0	9,300
Western Devil	4	G	8	1	0	3	6,138
Western Doll	3	F	16	2	1	4	58,244
Western Dream	8	G	9	1	1	2	4,654
Western Drouilly	3	G	8	1	1	2	17,990
Western Drums	5	G	9	1	1	3	15,562
Western Duels	4	G	7	1	1	1	6,222
Western Edition	6	G	4	1	0	0	3,396
Western Event	3	C	3	0	0	1	8,612
Western Exposure	3	C	8	0	0	0	1,627
Western Fling	4	G	7	2	0	2	42,570
Western Fox	7	M	8	0	1	1	1,962
Western Future	4	F	1	0	0	0	0
Western Galaxy	2	C	4	1	0	1	32,695
Western Gale	4	G	2	0	0	0	492
Western Glamour	5	M	2	0	0	0	133
Western Glitter	5	M	19	0	3	4	10,759
Western Glo	4	F	3	0	0	0	165
Western Glory	7	G	11	1	1	4	5,620
Western Halo	8	G	10	1	4	1	43,410
Western Hawk	4	G	14	5	1	0	27,092
Western Hemisphere	3	F	9	3	3	1	274,465
Western Heritage	6	G	1	0	0	0	132
Western Hills	5	H	13	1	0	1	6,315
Western Honoree	4	F	14	4	0	2	28,030
Western Hussy	3	F	9	1	2	0	9,300
Western Idol	3	C	9	1	3	1	72,079
Western Jeff	3	G	1	0	0	0	0
Western Journey	3	G	6	0	0	0	3,638
Western King	5	G	8	0	0	0	282
Western Kiss	3	G	4	1	1	0	3,200
Western Legacy	5	G	6	1	0	0	7,408
Western Lily	3	F	10	1	1	0	9,838
Western Man	3	C	12	2	2	1	35,430
Western Marshall	5	G	8	1	0	2	6,151
Western Mindy	3	F	8	2	2	0	48,810
Western Miss	5	M	12	1	2	1	13,086
Western Note	4	C	11	1	1	0	10,719
Western Novel	6	H	4	1	0	0	6,600
Western Ocala	3	F	6	4	0	1	47,022
Western Place	2	F	1	0	0	1	5,000
Western Premier	5	H	12	2	0	1	12,515
Western Pride	6	H	3	0	0	0	1,360
Western Princess	2	F	3	1	0	1	34,073
Western Punch	4	F	15	1	1	3	13,505
Western Quitz	12	G	9	1	3	1	8,474
Western Rampage	3	C	11	2	2	0	32,940
Western Ransom	3	F	7	4	2	0	221,860
Western Reason	3	G	9	1	0	1	5,075
Western Resolve	5	M	3	0	0	1	583
Western Revenge	4	C	5	1	1	1	40,538
Western Ridge	3	G	13	2	3	1	52,875
Western Roar	3	G	10	4	3	1	146,995
Western Rodeo	3	G	6	0	0	1	4,910
Western Rosy	6	G	12	0	0	0	165
Western Royal	2	F	2	0	0	0	0
Western Royalty	3	C	5	2	0	1	40,945
Western Ruler	4	G	21	2	2	5	12,792
Western Runner	3	G	12	2	2	1	8,651
Western Rush	4	F	6	1	0	0	37,236
Western Sassy	6	M	7	0	0	3	1,195
Western Siam	4	G	9	3	2	1	24,150
Western Silk	7	G	11	4	3	0	25,022
Western Solo	4	G	3	1	1	0	10,590
Western Song	3	G	7	1	1	1	28,250
Western Special	6	G	2	0	1	0	1,545
Western Spur	3	C	2	0	0	0	0
Western Stage	5	G	11	3	1	3	18,620
Western Stranger	5	G	8	2	1	4	18,641
Western Sunrise	4	F	12	0	1	3	12,718
Western Swing	2	C	3	0	2	0	8,710
Western Temptress	5	M	3	0	0	0	0
Western Territory	3	C	4	0	0	1	9,330
Western Threads	2	C	1	0	0	0	55
Western Thunder	7	G	9	0	0	0	150
Western Times	3	F	12	3	1	3	80,900
Western Type	7	M	10	4	2	0	37,200
Western View	4	F	11	3	2	1	67,955
Western Willie	3	G	12	1	0	0	4,284
Western Winner	5	G	21	1	2	4	17,820
Western Wishes	4	C	2	0	0	0	0
Western Writer	2	G	6	2	0	2	40,663
Westerncard	2	C	6	0	1	0	6,175
Westerntock	4	G	10	2	5	0	10,186
Westhaven	4	F	4	1	0	2	6,752
Westlake	2	F	1	0	0	0	0
Westmoon	4	G	4	0	0	0	354
Westmoorings	2	C	3	1	0	0	24,624
Westofdixie	6	G	7	1	0	3	9,900
Weston Field	6	G	9	1	2	2	51,250
Weston Road	4	G	10	3	1	1	27,217
Westport Song	4	F	1	0	0	0	1,230
Westrika	6	M	2	0	0	0	130
Westsideclyde	2	G	2	0	0	1	3,413
Westtexasconection	7	M	4	0	0	0	0
Westview	11	G	8	0	4	3	1,759
Westward Miss	3	F	8	0	3	1	19,014
Westward Mountain	4	C	6	0	1	1	8,250
Westward Star	4	G	14	3	1	2	16,505
Westwind Brewing	2	F	3	0	1	0	2,100
Westwood Windy	7	M	4	1	0	1	22,000
Westys Tiger	3	C	6	0	0	0	780
Wet N Wild	3	F	7	0	1	0	2,560
Wet N Wild Money	3	F	3	0	1	0	6,160
Wetherly	2	C	3	1	0	0	30,260
Wetlands	4	F	2	0	1	0	1,660
We've Got a Chance	3	F	14	5	2	1	58,140
We'vegotchacovered	2	C	2	1	0	0	9,900
Wewakiwoowho	2	F	3	1	1	0	33,920
Wewantdagold	4	C	1	0	0	0	150
Weyauwega	3	F	5	1	0	0	5,272
Weybridge	2	F	11	1	0	1	22,168
Weza	3	F	6	0	1	2	5,185
Whacko	3	C	1	0	0	0	88
Whale	3	G	1	0	0	0	184
Whale of a Tale	3	C	9	0	5	1	20,320
Whaleman	3	G	8	0	1	1	4,005
Whammy Doubled	3	F	1	0	0	0	201
Whamo	4	G	3	0	2	0	11,918
Wha'pa	3	F	5	0	1	1	6,960
Wharped	4	F	3	0	0	0	1,554
Whas Hapnin	7	G	1	0	0	0	0
Whassup World	3	G	5	1	0	1	4,751
What a Blurr	2	F	2	1	0	1	10,665
What a Cat	4	F	3	0	0	1	1,279
What a Cook	3	F	3	0	0	0	242
What a Defense	3	F	2	0	0	0	146
What a Doc	3	C	3	0	0	1	3,640
What a Dr.	5	G	12	0	0	3	25,640
What a Falstaff	8	G	7	0	0	0	180
What a Filly Les	6	M	6	1	0	1	5,236

Horse	Age	Sex	Sts	1st	2d	3d	Won
What a Form	3	F	4	0	0	0	1,205
What a Game	3	F	7	1	1	2	48,832
What a Hoss	3	G	4	1	0	1	2,940
What a Joy	3	G	11	1	0	0	10,897
What a Lady	3	F	3	1	0	0	13,900
What a Larkspur	2	F	2	0	0	0	1,920
What a Luhuker	2	F	3	0	0	0	2,030
What a Payday	4	G	4	1	0	1	9,801
What a Pistol	3	G	8	0	1	1	2,593
What a Queen	6	M	3	0	1	0	1,900
What a Racket	10	G	7	1	0	1	5,245
What a Rebel	4	G	11	1	2	1	16,384
What a Rumor	4	G	9	2	2	2	10,363
What a Sensation	5	M	5	0	0	1	2,134
What a Shocker	3	G	12	2	1	3	18,210
What a Show	6	G	8	1	1	1	15,770
What a Smoke	4	F	10	3	3	0	20,296
What a Splash	4	F	12	1	4	1	7,068
What a Spot	3	C	5	1	0	0	12,792
What a Strike	8	G	5	0	0	1	1,551
What a Stunt	2	G	1	0	0	0	270
What a Sweep	5	M	3	1	0	1	6,086
What a Talent	2	F	2	1	0	0	5,219
What A View (GB)	5	G	1	0	0	0	400
What a Way	4	G	15	1	1	1	7,343
What About Bob	3	G	9	0	3	2	4,555
What About David	5	G	11	5	2	2	46,432
What About Now	7	M	4	0	0	0	156
What About Quin	4	C	4	0	0	0	0
What About Sue	4	F	5	0	0	0	0
What Am I Bid	2	F	1	1	0	0	1,650
What Chew Say	5	G	9	0	3	2	9,237
What Comes After	4	F	6	0	0	3	3,750
What D Ya Knowjoe	3	G	4	0	0	1	690
What Do I Do	3	F	6	1	2	0	16,704
What Fuhr	4	G	10	0	0	0	1,765
What Happened Was	3	G	4	1	2	0	22,524
What Her Name Is	4	F	1	0	1	0	10,080
What in the World	4	F	6	0	0	0	905
What Me	5	G	5	0	2	0	2,423
What Money	3	G	8	0	2	2	4,080
What Next Bert	3	G	7	0	2	0	6,830
What Now Wynn	2	G	1	0	0	0	1,150
What Say Lou	3	G	11	1	3	3	11,190
What The	3	G	7	1	0	0	4,620
What the Devil	2	C	3	0	1	1	6,000
What the Hail	3	F	6	0	1	0	9,337
What to Wear	3	F	5	1	1	0	32,890
What U No	7	G	2	0	0	0	80
Whata Bank Roll	2	G	5	1	0	1	8,442
Whata Bear	6	G	14	1	0	1	4,685
Whata Diamond	2	F	1	0	0	0	0
Whata Gem	5	M	13	1	2	4	43,844
Whata Lotta Fun	8	G	12	0	0	0	2,002
Whata Love	5	M	14	0	0	1	2,730
Whata Soldier	3	G	6	0	3	1	34,560
Whata Tan	4	F	1	0	0	0	530
Whata Trickster	3	G	9	2	2	0	16,409
Whatabeauty	3	F	4	0	0	0	310
Whatabigquista	3	G	11	2	3	1	24,215
Whatabull	3	F	3	0	0	0	4,770
Whatadish	7	M	8	1	2	1	4,990
Whatadude	3	G	1	0	0	0	0
Whataflirt	7	M	9	1	3	0	37,440
Whatagoodboy	5	H	15	3	1	0	19,970
Whataluckypunch	3	C	6	0	0	2	2,439
Whataman Sam	5	G	3	0	0	0	950
Whataman Whataman	4	G	5	0	2	1	7,170
Whatamate	7	G	6	1	0	0	1,925
Whatanactress	5	M	3	0	0	0	277
Whatanicesurprise	5	M	1	0	0	0	0
Whatarocket	6	M	5	1	0	1	5,550
Whatasaint	5	H	4	1	1	1	18,510
Whatashamemaryjane	5	M	14	2	1	3	11,983
Whatasteel	5	M	11	0	0	1	1,902
Whatatrophy Rack	2	F	4	0	1	0	10,797
Whataweekend	4	F	4	2	0	0	33,647
Whatdreamswillcome	7	G	10	0	0	1	2,064
Whatever I Want	4	F	10	1	3	0	24,560
Whatever Jim	4	G	3	0	0	0	520
Whateveralohawants	2	C	1	1	0	0	9,000
Whatevershewants	6	M	7	0	1	0	4,028
Whateveruwantittob	4	F	19	1	4	5	10,626
Whateveryouwant	5	G	13	4	2	1	56,584
Whatisayisgold	5	M	6	1	1	1	7,035
Whatley Creek	3	C	8	0	0	0	330
Whats Gonna	9	G	8	5	1	0	14,841
Whats in It for Me	4	G	8	1	0	0	3,175
What's It's Name	4	C	1	0	0	0	0
What's Next	5	G	5	1	0	0	2,903
What's So Funny	7	M	5	1	0	0	6,909
What's That	3	F	7	1	0	1	11,635
What's That Sound	2	C	3	0	1	0	5,800
Whats Up	2	C	1	0	0	0	96
Whats Up Doc	5	G	14	1	1	1	3,100
What's Up Dog	6	G	10	1	0	4	19,422
What's Up Dude	2	C	4	2	0	1	144,740
What's Up Lonely	2	G	5	2	2	0	85,020
Whats Up Pussycat	4	F	10	1	1	2	10,660
Whats What	4	G	9	2	0	3	28,410
Whats Your Angle	6	G	11	3	3	1	6,682
What's Your Beef	4	G	5	0	0	1	2,474
Whats Your Game	4	F	2	0	0	0	535
What's Your Hurry	2	G	8	0	1	0	5,975
What's Your Point	2	F	5	1	1	2	44,960
What's Your Wish	6	H	7	2	1	0	18,855
Whatsallthefuss	3	G	7	1	2	0	5,549
Whatsername	6	M	11	1	2	1	15,780
Whatsin	3	G	4	2	1	0	9,220
Whatsinstore	6	M	5	0	1	0	2,041
Whatsitallabout	5	G	3	0	0	0	750
Whatsmineisyours	3	F	9	2	3	0	54,256
Whatson	4	G	8	2	0	4	4,176
Whatsthecode	5	M	13	2	2	2	26,055
Whatsthegameplan	2	C	1	0	0	0	460
Whatstheline	4	F	2	0	0	1	1,132
Whatsthenameman	2	G	3	2	1	0	75,855
Whatsyourdrink	6	M	2	1	0	0	2,700
Whatsyourproblin	2	F	4	0	0	0	1,586
Whatta Big Ruckus	5	G	11	0	0	0	2,803
Whatta Brave	9	G	9	0	0	1	1,231
Whatta Hunc	6	G	2	0	0	0	0
Whatta Jinx	10	M	1	0	0	0	72
Whatuc Iswhat Uget	6	G	17	5	1	1	33,422
Whatwereyouthinkin	2	F	4	0	2	0	5,120
Whazat	4	G	12	1	2	4	14,028
Whazupbannyrooster	2	F	1	0	0	0	100
Whazuplittleman	2	C	1	0	0	0	135
Wheat Queen	5	M	13	2	1	2	10,820
Wheater	5	G	11	2	1	2	10,585
Wheatese	2	C	2	0	0	0	360
Wheatland Road	3	F	3	0	0	0	0
Wheaton Home	2	C	4	1	0	0	11,951
Wheaton One	5	G	15	4	0	2	16,210
Wheaton's Aly	5	H	8	3	2	1	101,200
Wheaton's Aly Cat	3	F	4	1	0	1	18,750
Wheatons Belle	3	F	12	2	2	0	15,450
Wheaton's Boy	6	G	10	1	1	0	4,132
Wheaton's Joy	6	M	8	0	2	1	6,253
Wheaty	3	C	17	3	5	3	50,220
Wheel a Mint	4	F	3	0	0	1	2,725
Wheelchair Willie	5	H	9	2	2	0	19,965
Wheel'ndeal'njohn	5	G	14	0	0	2	8,984
Wheels of Stars	3	F	4	0	0	0	0
Wheezer	3	F	13	1	3	1	55,450
When in Rome	3	G	10	2	0	2	65,686
When It Rains	5	M	1	0	0	0	110
When It Was	5	G	10	0	1	0	5,239
Whenever Wherever	5	G	22	0	6	4	17,181
Wheneverweremember	3	F	1	0	0	0	320
Whenthedoveflies	4	F	8	6	1	0	139,160
Whenthesmokeclears	5	G	11	0	4	2	25,881
Whenthewindblows	4	G	7	1	1	0	22,500
Where Are You	4	F	15	1	3	3	23,424
Where Da Go	2	F	1	0	0	0	118
Where Echo's End	4	G	10	3	1	3	27,330
Where Is My Daddy	4	F	6	2	0	0	42,240
Where It's At	5	G	2	0	0	0	0

Horse	Age	Sex	Sts	1st	2d	3d	Won
Where Ja Go	3	F	5	0	0	0	138
Where Magic Lives	3	G	10	1	0	0	7,859
Where There's Fire	5	G	11	2	3	1	42,403
Where We Left Off (GB)	4	F	7	4	2	0	194,480
Where Were You	3	F	8	1	1	3	20,085
Whereisspringfield	7	G	15	1	6	0	34,535
Whereisthedrummer	2	F	2	0	0	0	1,363
Where's Ashlee	8	G	5	0	0	1	671
Where's Bailey	2	F	5	3	0	0	35,200
Where's Bobby B	3	F	5	0	0	1	5,628
Wheres Bubba	3	G	7	1	0	1	3,773
Where's Charlie	5	G	17	3	4	0	28,966
Where's George	3	C	12	0	0	2	4,870
Where's Mike	3	C	5	0	0	0	564
Where's Mindy	5	M	3	0	0	0	0
Where's My Mama	3	C	1	0	0	0	0
Wheres My Papers	3	F	9	0	1	1	3,985
Where's Red	4	F	5	0	0	0	556
Where's Tammy	3	F	14	2	1	1	13,334
Where's the Bully	2	C	3	1	0	0	4,245
Where's the Cat	3	F	3	0	0	0	450
Where's the Ring	5	H	3	0	2	0	39,250
Wheresheat	4	G	6	1	1	0	4,952
Wheresmymoneyhoney	4	F	6	0	0	0	1,035
Wheresyourheadat	2	F	6	0	0	0	1,120
Whetstone	3	G	6	1	1	0	20,726
Which Witch	3	F	13	1	1	3	28,775
Whichi Coax	5	G	7	0	1	1	18,547
Whicked Wolfe	3	C	3	0	0	0	0
Whidbey	4	G	8	1	0	0	2,160
While We're Here	5	G	6	1	2	1	5,070
While You Wait	6	G	1	0	0	0	0
Whileaway	6	G	7	1	0	1	5,141
Whiletheiron'shot	5	M	4	0	0	1	11,043
Whilly (IRE)	3	C	8	3	0	1	165,528
Whilstone	3	C	2	0	0	0	274
Whimaway	2	C	3	0	0	0	768
Whimiscal Day	4	F	2	2	0	0	36,658
Whimsical Tammy	4	F	14	0	0	4	10,490
Whimsical Ways	5	M	1	0	0	0	0
Whin Truth Knocks	5	M	15	0	1	2	7,958
Whining	5	G	10	3	2	1	28,377
Whining Jacob	5	G	5	0	0	1	300
Whip	6	G	17	3	3	3	24,850
Whip Creme Cookie	4	F	5	0	0	0	617
Whip Me Baby	2	F	2	0	0	0	420
Whippee	4	G	10	0	0	0	1,223
Whipper	3	C	6	2	1	0	389,850
Whipper Will Win	6	M	8	1	1	0	8,310
Whippers Dream	2	F	3	0	0	0	150
Whipple Creek	4	G	11	2	0	2	14,289
Whirl Forever	5	H	5	0	0	0	174
Whirley	7	H	11	0	0	4	5,215
Whirley Side	4	G	7	2	4	1	29,060
Whirling Ace	8	G	3	0	0	0	70
Whirling Colors	6	G	7	1	1	1	4,456
Whirling Dervish	5	M	2	0	0	1	495
Whirling Skys	3	G	6	0	0	0	365
Whirling Willie	6	G	7	0	2	0	3,477
Whirling Zarb	2	C	3	0	0	0	1,215
Whirlonby	4	C	3	0	0	0	183
Whirlwind Charlott	3	F	9	0	2	0	33,335
Whirlwind Trip	4	F	4	0	0	2	5,800
Whirlwind Wanda	7	M	7	0	0	2	2,195
Whirly Wind	5	G	13	0	0	1	6,220
Whisk	5	G	9	4	2	1	36,982
Whiskey and Low	2	F	1	1	0	0	34,200
Whiskey Bend	3	G	8	2	0	0	22,883
Whiskey by the Bay	6	G	2	0	0	0	384
Whiskey City Jr	5	G	2	1	0	0	1,665
Whiskey Dancer	5	G	9	1	0	2	4,447
Whiskey Drive	2	G	4	2	2	0	32,437
Whiskey for Me	2	G	3	1	0	0	6,900
Whiskey Grin	4	G	12	1	2	1	12,220
Whiskey Jack	2	C	1	0	0	0	0
Whiskey Rhythm	4	G	4	0	0	0	1,134
Whiskey Road	6	G	1	0	1	0	2,140
Whiskey Sez	4	G	8	3	1	1	90,083
Whiskey Sour	4	G	2	0	1	0	3,060

Horse	Age	Sex	Sts	1st	2d	3d	Won
Whiskey Special	3	G	7	1	2	1	67,746
Whiskey Star	2	C	1	0	0	0	3,000
Whiskey Tails	2	C	1	0	0	0	0
Whiskey Wizard	5	G	8	1	0	1	24,752
Whiskey's Girl	4	F	6	0	0	2	3,660
Whisky Swish	3	F	10	0	2	2	41,421
Whisky Wise	5	G	10	1	1	0	55,096
Whisper Bay	3	F	2	1	0	0	28,920
Whisper Brightly	4	G	2	0	0	0	412
Whisper for Gold	6	G	8	0	0	0	1,010
Whisper Low	9	G	7	1	1	3	6,968
Whisper My Name	3	F	1	0	0	0	0
Whisper to Lou	3	C	5	1	0	0	7,070
Whispered Affair	3	F	2	0	0	0	600
Whispered Illusion	6	M	5	2	1	0	9,892
Whispered Warning	4	C	1	0	0	0	0
Whispered Ways	3	C	6	1	2	0	15,785
Whisperer	3	G	4	1	1	0	12,770
Whisperin Girl	4	F	11	2	2	2	17,647
Whispering Angel	7	H	9	1	3	1	8,902
Whispering Bells	4	F	10	4	1	0	21,590
Whispering Echo	3	F	8	3	1	1	45,250
Whispering Fever	4	G	13	1	4	2	30,048
Whispering Hope	4	F	9	2	0	1	10,541
Whispering Queen	3	F	3	0	0	0	516
Whispering Storm	4	G	9	0	0	1	4,830
Whispering Walter	2	G	1	0	0	0	80
Whispersinthemine	4	G	8	1	2	0	8,479
Whispertoascream	3	F	5	2	2	1	94,916
Whispher Honey	4	F	2	0	0	0	0
Whister's Student	6	M	8	0	1	1	2,610
Whistle Blower	9	G	2	0	0	0	522
Whistle Dick	4	G	15	1	2	1	13,454
Whistle Dixie	3	G	9	3	3	0	30,125
Whistle Tester	5	M	8	4	3	1	6,958
Whistler	3	G	7	0	1	4	5,943
Whistler Run	9	G	9	2	1	0	13,933
Whistlewhileyourun	2	F	2	0	1	0	3,080
Whistlin a Song	3	F	4	0	0	0	5,124
Whistlin' Hero	2	G	5	0	0	0	1,049
Whistling By	4	G	19	0	3	4	14,611
Whistling Eskimo	8	G	7	0	0	0	150
Whistling Maid	5	M	12	0	4	0	76,748
Whistling Straits	2	C	3	0	1	1	9,480
Whistl'n Jack	4	G	16	1	1	0	13,356
White Angel Light	3	G	13	2	3	4	35,505
White Aura	2	F	1	0	1	0	10,200
White Bean Soup	4	G	3	0	0	0	210
White Buck	4	G	13	2	1	1	56,397
White Cargo	4	G	7	1	0	0	14,960
White Cedar	3	C	8	2	1	2	19,890
White Diplomacy	4	G	11	2	0	2	7,365
White Dragon	3	F	14	1	2	3	42,554
White Dutch Clover	4	F	9	1	1	2	23,630
White Eagle Hall	4	C	19	2	4	1	48,400
White Empress	6	M	9	1	0	2	2,275
White Flag	6	G	12	1	0	2	7,821
White Flame	5	G	17	4	4	1	55,385
White Gold	3	F	10	2	5	1	34,500
White Hall Express	8	H	5	0	0	0	0
White Heat	3	G	10	1	2	4	32,248
White Hot (GB)	10	G	6	1	0	0	9,090
White Hot Rocket	4	F	11	2	5	1	45,813
White Ice	3	F	11	2	1	2	56,684
White Line	3	F	4	0	0	0	1,600
White Mercedes	4	C	8	1	0	1	12,957
White Mountain Boy	3	C	6	1	0	1	56,200
White O Morn	5	M	9	1	1	0	30,780
White Oak	3	F	9	0	3	2	20,750
White Pine	2	G	1	0	0	0	0
White Rino	5	G	8	0	1	3	4,054
White Rose Way	2	F	3	1	0	0	10,170
White Sage	4	F	5	0	1	1	2,812
White Scarf	5	M	14	2	2	4	58,675
White Secret	4	G	16	3	2	1	22,405
White Sox Secret	3	G	5	0	0	0	1,650
White Sox Slew	5	H	11	1	0	3	3,102
White Star	7	G	10	3	3	0	66,450
White Tie Ole	5	G	7	0	0	0	0

Horse	Age	Sex	Sts	1st	2d	3d	Won
White Tigress	4	F	3	0	0	1	1,425
White Wedding	3	F	7	0	0	1	6,500
White Wedding Day	4	F	1	0	0	0	60
Whiteglovesandcain	4	C	2	0	0	0	0
Whitehorsecantjump	5	G	23	4	2	0	18,975
Whitehouse Grounds	3	G	7	0	0	0	528
Whitehouse Texas	3	C	7	0	0	1	1,875
Whitehousetryst	5	M	8	0	0	0	908
Whitelaunch	5	G	11	0	1	2	6,327
Whitermorn	3	G	8	3	1	1	42,600
White's Bonus Time	2	C	1	0	0	0	105
Whites too Light	3	G	9	1	1	1	8,560
Whitesox Jones	2	C	4	0	0	0	0
Whitewater Wave	3	F	10	3	1	1	24,930
Whitewater Way	4	F	7	2	0	4	57,940
Whitewaterspritzer	7	G	7	2	2	0	49,735
Whitey's Wager	3	G	2	0	0	0	236
Whitmark	3	G	9	0	0	0	1,696
Whitney Willie	4	G	4	0	2	0	9,773
Whitney's Agenda	4	G	6	0	1	0	1,620
Whitney's Merlot	4	F	3	0	0	0	0
Whitney's Token	4	G	10	0	1	0	2,527
Whitney's Whip	4	F	2	0	1	0	945
Whitney's Wish	7	M	12	1	1	1	5,887
Whitney'srainmaker	4	G	1	0	0	0	214
Whitsonatthewire	3	G	12	1	4	0	15,953
Whittlin	2	C	1	1	0	0	13,440
Whitton Court (IRE)	6	G	16	0	7	0	12,233
Whitty Cait	4	G	3	0	0	0	855
Whiz Away	3	C	2	0	0	0	0
Whiz Kitty	2	F	3	0	0	0	1,380
Whizbang	3	G	3	0	0	0	3,182
Whizbyou	9	G	1	0	0	0	40
Whiztar	5	M	3	0	0	0	0
Whizter King	3	C	11	3	0	3	47,369
Who Believes	3	G	4	0	0	0	0
Who Cares Girl	7	M	6	1	0	2	11,634
Who Devil Who	6	G	11	1	2	3	7,271
Who Dis	6	M	2	0	0	0	0
Who Does	6	M	1	0	0	0	0
Who Goes There	3	C	3	0	0	0	2,210
Who Is Chris G.	3	G	12	0	1	3	22,233
Who Let the Katout	3	F	10	1	1	2	15,170
Who On First	2	F	1	0	0	0	164
Who Will Dance	4	G	1	0	0	0	400
Who Won	4	G	11	1	2	3	13,100
Who You Gonna Call	3	C	8	0	0	0	4,929
Whoa Babe	3	F	1	0	0	0	42
Whoa D	4	G	9	0	2	0	2,986
Whoa Joe	4	G	13	3	3	1	19,190
Whobabydatiz	3	F	4	0	0	0	365
Whoboo	6	G	11	0	1	0	4,342
Who'd Believe It	8	G	1	0	0	0	0
Whodatis	7	G	11	0	1	2	6,379
Whoisvendeladente	5	M	11	1	1	1	10,613
Whole Lotta Soul	3	G	8	1	0	0	8,093
Whole Nine Yards	2	C	2	0	1	0	8,780
Wholehearted	3	G	7	1	2	0	44,766
Wholelotacondition	4	F	2	0	0	1	1,043
Wholelotofimage	3	F	3	0	0	1	2,435
Wholelottabourbon	2	G	5	4	1	0	286,230
Wholesale	3	F	6	1	0	1	11,950
Wholetthebullout	4	F	3	0	0	0	960
Wholetthegirlout	3	F	4	0	0	0	519
Wholetthishorseout	4	G	14	3	1	0	25,438
Wholly John	4	G	5	1	0	1	35,940
Whoneedsafive	6	G	16	1	0	4	14,115
Whoo My Daddy	3	G	3	0	0	0	244
Whoop Dee Doo	5	G	4	0	0	0	253
Whoopi Cat	3	F	6	0	3	1	51,220
Whoop's Ah Daisy	5	M	5	1	2	1	75,000
Whoopsy Doopsy	3	F	3	0	0	0	180
Whopaho	6	G	10	2	2	3	75,664
Who's Aleyna	2	G	6	0	1	3	16,320
Who's Bluffing	4	G	16	2	1	2	57,510
Who's Bluffing Who	4	F	7	1	0	0	887
Who's Blushing	3	G	5	0	0	0	900
Who's Cozy	2	F	2	0	0	0	592
Whos Crying Now	4	G	6	1	0	0	30,000
Who's Dusty	5	H	8	1	0	0	7,137
Who's First	3	G	12	1	2	0	39,970
Who's for Doon	4	F	6	0	0	0	660
Who's Kidding Who	2	C	1	1	0	0	26,400
Who's Livin Bettor	3	G	6	2	1	1	22,692
Who's Looking Now	5	G	2	1	0	0	5,970
Whos Mad	3	C	7	0	1	1	7,744
Who's News	5	H	1	0	0	0	135
Who's Prospect	4	G	9	0	0	1	4,205
Who's Slewon Who	5	M	8	0	0	0	375
Who's Talking	9	G	12	1	0	0	6,642
Who's That Girl	4	F	12	0	1	4	6,145
Who's That There	3	F	3	0	1	0	7,202
Who's the Cowboy	2	G	7	1	4	0	75,763
Who's the Fox	4	F	14	0	2	0	5,895
Who's This	6	M	15	3	3	2	41,764
Whos Twining Who	5	G	11	2	0	1	9,422
Who's Ya Mama	6	M	7	1	1	1	41,126
Who's Yer Man	3	G	11	0	2	0	5,228
Who's Young Thing	2	F	6	0	1	1	4,445
Who's Zary Now	2	C	6	2	1	1	27,755
Who'sbetterthanme	7	M	1	0	0	0	0
Whose Career	3	C	6	2	0	0	31,788
Whosgotthejohnnie	4	G	14	3	2	5	39,094
Whosoeverbelieveth	5	M	11	1	3	2	17,285
Whosthatmaskedman	5	G	3	0	0	2	4,480
Whosthebetterhalf	5	M	17	1	0	0	11,241
Who'sthewildmannow	2	C	3	0	0	1	6,080
Whowearsshortpants	3	G	4	0	0	0	700
Whozoominwho	7	G	13	2	2	4	11,799
Why Grampy	8	G	2	0	0	0	116
Why Have a Plan	3	F	6	1	1	0	18,051
Why Indeed	10	G	7	1	2	0	2,800
Why Knott Me Too	4	F	11	1	4	2	59,564
Why Not Baby	4	G	13	0	4	0	17,640
Why Not Gold	3	C	6	0	1	2	19,134
Why Not Minot	2	C	1	0	0	0	140
Why Not Run	2	G	1	0	1	0	2,940
Why Not Whitney	4	F	19	3	0	5	34,794
Why Oh Why	3	C	9	1	1	1	44,419
Why Reply	4	G	2	1	1	0	7,640
Why So Quiet	8	H	3	0	0	0	0
Why So Wild	4	F	11	2	1	1	19,666
Why Stand Pat	3	G	10	2	3	0	8,081
Why Worry	4	G	6	0	0	0	189
Why You	3	F	6	2	1	1	81,770
Whyatch	3	G	4	0	0	0	987
Whychangethe Phone	2	C	1	0	0	0	0
Whynotthistrina	5	M	7	1	1	0	4,816
Whysettleforless	8	G	5	0	1	0	680
Whysoshy	4	F	4	1	0	0	2,708
Whytwocayman	5	M	8	2	1	0	17,239
Wibby	5	H	4	0	0	1	671
Wicca Day	4	F	1	0	0	0	400
Wice O Kat	2	F	3	1	1	1	28,201
Wicked Britches	7	G	3	0	1	1	1,350
Wicked Charms	4	F	8	2	3	0	23,152
Wicked College	3	G	5	0	0	1	5,280
Wicked Devil	3	G	2	0	0	0	0
Wicked Flynn	4	G	1	0	0	0	0
Wicked Hunt	3	C	4	1	0	0	4,851
Wicked Iron Man	2	C	2	0	0	0	500
Wicked Lass	4	F	3	0	1	1	7,410
Wicked Magic	3	G	5	0	0	0	635
Wicked Man	3	C	4	0	1	0	7,405
Wicked N Rude	3	G	11	1	0	1	11,849
Wicked Sami	4	G	4	0	1	1	3,698
Wicked Slick	3	C	19	1	1	3	13,656
Wicked Star	8	G	2	0	0	0	0
Wicked Storm	3	F	5	0	0	1	1,055
Wicked Sunrise	3	F	2	0	0	0	130
Wicked Term	3	G	1	0	0	0	0
Wicked Wanda	2	F	2	0	0	0	660
Wicked Weapon	6	G	8	1	0	0	6,419
Wicked Wild West	2	F	1	0	0	0	0
Wicked Will	6	G	10	1	1	2	20,110
Wicked Willie	4	F	20	5	1	4	30,363
Wicked Wish	3	F	4	2	1	0	72,501
Wicked Zip	3	G	16	0	1	3	10,462

Horse	Age	Sex	Sts	1st	2d	3d	Won
Wickedly Wise	3	F	3	0	2	1	16,160
Wickedsisofthewest	4	F	18	6	4	1	24,743
Wicken Fen	8	G	14	2	2	2	30,410
Wicken Rede	3	F	8	1	3	1	19,621
Wicki Up	3	C	12	1	1	3	32,255
Wicki Wicki	4	G	3	0	0	0	0
Wicklow Bound	3	G	7	1	2	0	19,050
Wicklow Echo	5	M	6	1	0	0	2,606
Wicklow Gate	5	G	10	0	0	1	2,590
Wicklow Highlands	8	H	16	6	2	1	88,110
Wicklow Hills	2	F	1	0	0	0	294
Wicklow Isle	6	G	21	1	0	3	10,949
Wicklow Lass	3	F	10	0	1	0	1,800
Wicklow Spa	4	F	8	0	0	1	1,979
Wicklow Vamp	3	F	20	2	5	3	25,447
Wicksy	4	G	8	0	0	0	1,585
Widdows' Night Out	5	M	16	2	0	4	18,100
Wide Awake	2	F	1	0	0	1	1,650
Wide Eye Bayou	7	G	11	3	3	1	54,105
Wide Out	5	G	8	2	2	0	15,485
Wide to Write	3	C	8	2	3	0	61,558
Widespread Panic	3	G	9	2	0	0	6,702
Wie Geht's	4	F	9	1	0	3	7,728
Wifely Duties	3	F	9	1	3	1	31,996
Wiggins	4	G	9	3	3	2	181,920
Wiki Wiki Magic	4	F	8	1	2	0	8,060
Wila West	4	F	9	3	2	1	119,169
Wilbur	9	G	10	2	0	2	15,185
Wilcox Ridge	3	C	6	2	0	2	50,692
Wild About Dancin	2	C	6	1	2	1	16,315
Wild About Debbie	4	F	3	0	1	0	2,787
Wild About Harry	3	G	12	2	3	1	35,970
Wild About Jon	2	C	3	0	1	0	7,378
Wild About Maddie	4	F	14	1	3	0	26,391
Wild About Mari	4	F	10	1	0	1	6,484
Wild Adam	5	H	10	2	2	2	27,862
Wild After Dark	6	G	8	1	1	2	4,745
Wild Again Now	2	G	6	0	0	0	876
Wild Alizone	2	F	9	0	3	0	17,430
Wild Aly	3	F	6	0	2	0	26,922
Wild Amber	3	F	11	1	2	3	19,415
Wild American	6	G	4	0	0	0	0
Wild Amy	3	F	7	2	2	1	30,530
Wild and Comfy	7	G	7	0	0	1	2,117
Wild and Dangerous	3	G	4	0	0	0	576
Wild and Lively	4	F	6	1	0	0	7,593
Wild and Lovely	4	F	6	0	0	0	865
Wild and Rakshes	3	F	4	1	1	0	10,600
Wild and Risque	3	G	10	2	3	2	27,294
Wild and Saucy	2	C	4	0	0	0	536
Wild and Stormy	5	G	4	1	1	0	8,469
Wild and Striking	8	G	6	0	1	1	2,232
Wild and Unreal	3	G	2	0	0	0	130
Wild and Wicked	4	C	1	0	0	0	3,240
Wild and Wise	6	G	10	1	3	1	38,855
Wild Angel	2	F	5	1	2	1	18,080
Wild Arrival	4	G	3	0	0	0	360
Wild Arrow	4	G	7	1	1	1	36,417
Wild as Elle	2	F	5	2	1	0	78,315
Wild as Ever	3	F	1	0	0	0	0
Wild Aspidistra	5	M	2	1	0	1	4,605
Wild At Times	4	F	11	0	0	2	4,840
Wild Attraction	3	F	2	0	0	0	0
Wild August	3	C	4	1	1	0	15,670
Wild Austrian	3	F	4	0	0	0	1,500
Wild Axe	6	H	4	0	0	0	0
Wild Babe	3	C	8	2	2	0	110,650
Wild Bag	4	C	11	1	0	1	15,035
Wild Bargain	6	M	10	1	1	1	13,790
Wild Bea	3	F	5	0	0	1	4,510
Wild Bell	4	F	9	2	1	1	9,796
Wild Bender	2	F	1	1	0	0	11,113
Wild Berry	3	F	7	0	1	2	22,699
Wild Bertie	3	F	9	2	2	0	32,228
Wild Bet	3	G	7	0	0	0	1,249
Wild Bill Hiccup	4	G	14	5	0	2	61,040
Wild Bill R.	6	G	12	2	0	2	27,650
Wild Blaze	6	M	13	2	2	4	29,470
Wild Bluff	2	G	3	0	0	0	2,583
Wild Boy	2	C	1	0	0	0	150
Wild Bredan	7	G	3	0	0	0	510
Wild Brush	4	G	12	1	2	2	14,851
Wild Bubbles	3	F	3	0	0	0	480
Wild Buckaroo	3	G	11	2	0	1	23,194
Wild Buddy	5	G	10	3	1	1	84,400
Wild Bulette	6	M	3	1	0	0	1,037
Wild Bull Cody	4	G	4	0	0	0	866
Wild But Free	3	F	12	1	2	4	7,537
Wild But Worth It	4	F	12	1	2	1	12,720
Wild Call	4	F	5	0	0	0	707
Wild Card Deck	4	C	11	1	4	2	73,310
Wild Card Wilda	3	F	1	0	0	0	0
Wild Caribe	3	G	6	0	0	1	4,919
Wild Carson	5	G	7	0	0	2	4,523
Wild Cat Run	8	G	2	0	0	0	0
Wild Catseye	3	F	4	1	1	0	43,670
Wild Cee	3	F	4	2	0	0	56,721
Wild Centurion	5	G	13	2	1	4	58,563
Wild Champion	3	C	10	1	2	1	15,393
Wild Charger	4	G	11	2	2	2	17,036
Wild Charisma	3	G	4	0	0	0	1,600
Wild Charm	5	M	8	1	1	3	22,310
Wild Chase	3	G	2	0	0	0	280
Wild Chat	3	F	2	0	0	0	0
Wild Chatter	5	M	7	0	0	1	754
Wild Cherry Baby	3	F	3	1	0	0	13,800
Wild Cheta	4	F	14	2	3	4	17,062
Wild Chick	2	F	2	1	0	1	37,200
Wild Child	3	F	14	2	5	1	24,601
Wild Chill	6	G	5	1	0	0	14,280
Wild Choice	8	H	1	0	0	1	1,500
Wild Cider	3	G	5	0	0	1	855
Wild City Zone	2	F	4	1	0	1	4,505
Wild Code	3	G	15	1	1	1	9,028
Wild Colonial Boy	4	G	12	0	0	0	180
Wild Connection	5	G	7	2	3	2	50,880
Wild Countess	2	F	6	0	2	0	6,600
Wild Country Baby	3	F	3	0	1	0	1,317
Wild County	3	F	11	3	4	0	12,656
Wild Cowgirl	5	M	7	1	2	0	5,925
Wild Cut	4	G	7	1	1	1	10,035
Wild Dan	9	H	11	2	2	0	25,239
Wild Dance	6	G	9	1	3	1	5,159
Wild Dare	6	G	12	2	2	2	25,166
Wild Dash	3	C	11	1	0	1	11,586
Wild Dasiz	3	F	2	0	0	0	196
Wild Data	3	F	10	1	0	0	5,565
Wild Dawg	2	C	5	1	0	0	4,530
Wild Daydreamer	3	F	12	3	2	1	23,795
Wild Deal	4	G	15	1	1	0	6,765
Wild Dealin Deputy	3	G	11	1	2	1	6,960
Wild Desert	2	C	8	2	2	1	89,636
Wild Deuce	3	G	17	4	3	3	31,166
Wild Dimension	3	G	7	0	2	0	6,670
Wild Dina	4	F	4	1	0	1	11,870
Wild Ditty	3	F	2	0	0	0	0
Wild Doctor	4	F	6	0	0	0	165
Wild Double Down	4	G	3	0	0	1	302
Wild Dream	11	G	7	2	1	1	22,081
Wild Dusty Ride	3	C	2	0	1	0	2,200
Wild Eagle	3	C	8	1	0	1	7,150
Wild Enough	4	F	11	1	2	2	7,250
Wild Era	6	G	1	0	0	0	0
Wild Eskimo	4	G	12	1	0	0	4,455
Wild Ethan	2	G	3	0	0	0	370
Wild Evasion	3	C	2	0	1	0	4,550
Wild Evening	4	C	1	0	0	0	0
Wild Eventure	3	C	2	0	0	1	12,375
Wild Executive	3	F	4	2	1	0	70,544
Wild Eye Bill	6	H	3	0	0	1	847
Wild Eye Willie	5	G	7	0	3	1	13,235
Wild Eyed Cat	5	H	2	0	0	0	0
Wild Fever	3	G	10	0	2	3	5,827
Wild Fey	2	F	4	1	1	0	5,620
Wild Fiesta	4	G	8	4	0	0	51,293
Wild Flower	4	F	10	1	0	3	6,206
Wild Flying Kite	6	M	11	3	4	3	18,242
Wild for Jeanne	3	F	2	0	0	0	0

Horse	Age	Sex	Sts	1st	2d	3d	Won
Wild for Sure	3	F	3	1	1	0	27,000
Wild Force	4	C	1	0	0	0	340
Wild Freedom	3	C	1	0	0	0	0
Wild Friar	3	G	9	1	1	0	8,630
Wild Fuss	3	G	9	1	0	0	4,764
Wild G Man	4	G	2	0	0	0	159
Wild Geese	3	C	5	0	1	3	11,700
Wild Ghost	4	G	4	0	0	0	0
Wild Girl	4	F	6	1	1	2	38,943
Wild Gladiator	5	G	13	1	0	1	8,981
Wild Glory	3	F	7	2	0	3	35,640
Wild Goose	5	G	16	0	1	1	3,674
Wild Grades	5	M	4	0	0	0	0
Wild Harbor	3	C	12	5	2	2	73,630
Wild Hawkeye	3	G	3	1	0	0	3,231
Wild Hits	6	H	1	0	0	0	0
Wild Holly	3	F	5	1	1	1	32,330
Wild Honey	3	F	6	0	1	0	3,565
Wild Horses	5	H	5	3	0	0	49,885
Wild Host	2	C	1	0	0	0	0
Wild House	2	F	2	0	0	1	4,420
Wild Houston	4	C	20	2	2	4	9,140
Wild Humor	2	F	12	0	1	4	34,620
Wild Icecapade	6	G	14	0	0	1	1,408
Wild Ike	3	G	1	0	0	0	0
Wild Image	3	G	8	1	0	1	6,161
Wild in Chino	3	C	1	0	0	0	150
Wild in the Forest	3	G	1	0	0	1	4,100
Wild in the Lane	4	C	6	0	0	0	1,355
Wild Inspiration	2	G	2	0	0	0	1,230
Wild Irish	6	M	4	0	1	2	5,068
Wild Irish Dancer	3	F	7	2	2	0	17,212
Wild Irish Dream	3	F	9	1	0	1	8,793
Wild J J	6	G	3	0	0	0	518
Wild Jake	4	C	2	0	0	0	245
Wild Jam	3	G	10	3	1	4	89,530
Wild Jet	6	H	2	0	0	2	1,911
Wild Jezabel	4	F	7	2	0	1	9,610
Wild Jim	3	C	5	1	2	0	22,140
Wild Juan	2	C	2	0	0	0	0
Wild Jungle	2	F	1	0	0	0	65
Wild Lady	3	F	6	1	0	0	13,380
Wild Landing	5	M	5	3	0	0	12,046
Wild Lies	6	G	4	0	0	0	1,745
Wild Life	3	F	1	0	0	0	480
Wild Lillian	3	F	3	0	0	0	198
Wild Linear	5	M	17	4	4	1	25,171
Wild Liz	4	F	9	1	2	1	12,932
Wild Louise	4	F	6	0	2	1	3,093
Wild Lulu	2	F	3	1	0	0	19,380
Wild Man Jack	3	G	9	3	0	1	11,370
Wild Maple	5	G	17	1	2	5	43,547
Wild Martha	6	M	2	0	0	0	300
Wild Meeting	3	F	12	2	4	0	53,915
Wild Mist	2	F	2	0	0	2	2,640
Wild Mistress	3	F	1	0	0	0	340
Wild Money Zone	4	G	7	0	2	1	5,580
Wild Mustang	2	G	1	0	0	0	420
Wild N Devious	5	M	11	4	0	2	27,740
Wild 'n Famous	4	G	4	0	0	1	1,106
Wild n' Majestic	2	F	8	0	0	1	2,095
Wild N Rowdy	3	C	1	0	0	0	375
Wild N Wooly	4	G	2	0	0	0	570
Wild Native Lady	4	F	14	0	3	1	6,550
Wild Nature (GB)	2	C	3	1	1	0	25,700
Wild On Gin	2	C	2	0	0	0	800
Wild On Rio	4	G	12	1	2	1	7,723
Wild On Salt	4	F	13	3	1	1	10,165
Wild Osceola	4	G	15	1	3	2	24,232
Wild Ovation	2	F	3	0	0	0	210
Wild Over Ian	7	G	15	2	0	3	27,780
Wild Over You	4	F	10	3	2	0	37,490
Wild Ozone	4	G	5	0	0	0	246
Wild Pal	2	C	4	0	0	0	161
Wild Patrick	3	C	7	0	1	0	1,767
Wild Patton	4	F	4	0	0	0	294
Wild Paul	3	C	8	2	2	2	19,350
Wild Percussionist	6	H	1	0	0	0	230
Wild Pharaoh	3	G	3	1	0	2	4,260
Wild Pick	2	C	1	0	0	0	55
Wild Pistola	2	F	1	0	0	0	969
Wild Plural	3	F	6	0	1	1	1,770
Wild Pocket	2	C	1	0	0	0	71
Wild Prince	3	C	6	1	1	0	6,266
Wild Pro	5	G	10	4	1	1	25,770
Wild Proposal	4	G	7	1	1	3	24,588
Wild Punch	5	M	2	0	0	0	300
Wild Quest	4	C	3	1	0	0	9,865
Wild Rascal	5	G	6	0	1	0	1,080
Wild Recall	3	F	16	0	1	2	4,217
Wild Red	4	G	3	0	0	0	855
Wild Red Bird	6	H	6	1	0	0	6,609
Wild Reflection	3	F	14	1	5	1	19,725
Wild Remarks	2	C	6	3	1	2	100,442
Wild Rezonution	3	F	12	3	1	3	59,726
Wild Rhett	6	G	4	0	0	0	439
Wild Roar	6	G	11	3	1	2	13,922
Wild Robin	2	F	2	0	0	0	1,875
Wild Rocket	6	G	8	0	2	2	5,968
Wild Romance	6	M	6	0	0	1	438
Wild Romeo	4	C	9	0	0	0	1,170
Wild Rose Princess	2	F	2	0	1	0	2,280
Wild Ruler	4	C	3	0	0	0	1,230
Wild Runner	3	G	10	1	0	2	6,919
Wild Running Thing	2	F	1	0	0	0	0
Wild Rusty	4	G	3	0	0	0	174
Wild Ruthie	5	M	2	0	0	0	80
Wild Salado Zone	3	G	6	0	0	0	900
Wild Scarlett	3	F	4	0	0	0	398
Wild Scat	2	C	3	0	0	0	0
Wild Senorita	3	F	9	2	1	2	47,775
Wild Shaman	3	G	7	1	1	2	41,480
Wild Shamir	4	G	2	0	0	0	143
Wild Shivers	2	C	4	0	2	1	10,180
Wild Sign	4	G	11	5	1	1	47,142
Wild Silky	4	F	11	1	2	0	9,715
Wild Sissy	4	F	11	2	2	2	18,376
Wild Smile	4	G	6	0	0	0	458
Wild Some More	7	H	2	0	1	1	4,225
Wild Soul	3	G	11	2	0	3	23,241
Wild South	3	G	7	2	2	0	38,780
Wild Speed	3	F	4	1	1	0	36,000
Wild Spender	3	F	1	0	0	0	0
Wild Spirit (CHI)	5	M	1	0	0	1	50,000
Wild Stories	5	G	14	1	1	7	9,059
Wild Storm (CHI)	4	F	2	0	1	0	14,100
Wild Stuff	2	C	2	0	0	0	2,040
Wild Success	5	G	6	0	0	0	41
Wild Summer	6	G	7	0	2	1	13,820
Wild Suwannee	6	M	3	0	0	0	234
Wild Tale	3	C	12	4	2	1	82,780
Wild Talker	3	G	1	0	0	0	0
Wild Taste	3	G	10	1	3	2	11,242
Wild Tears	3	F	12	3	0	3	29,330
Wild Term	4	G	13	1	0	0	11,579
Wild Thang	4	F	4	0	1	0	1,850
Wild Tiger	4	G	9	1	2	1	27,696
Wild Tijera	4	F	11	2	0	2	7,550
Wild Tip	6	M	3	1	1	0	8,940
Wild T'mater	3	G	7	2	2	1	37,339
Wild to Go	2	C	7	1	1	1	43,010
Wild Toga Nites	4	F	13	1	1	1	9,325
Wild Town	3	G	4	1	1	1	7,827
Wild Trial	2	F	2	0	0	1	2,530
Wild Trip	5	H	11	2	1	0	24,800
Wild Trumpet	5	G	12	0	4	2	44,782
Wild Tune	4	F	9	2	1	1	18,750
Wild U R	3	G	14	1	0	2	18,490
Wild Valay	4	G	1	0	0	0	0
Wild Valley	5	H	22	3	6	5	23,228
Wild Vanilla	3	F	3	0	0	1	11,768
Wild Vegas	2	F	1	0	0	0	0
Wild Vicar	2	G	5	0	0	1	7,646
Wild View	6	H	1	0	0	0	285
Wild Voyage	2	F	1	0	0	0	0
Wild Wadi	3	C	6	2	0	2	57,100
Wild Wager	3	G	7	4	0	1	34,676
Wild Wahine	3	F	1	0	0	0	0

Horse	Age	Sex	Sts	1st	2d	3d	Won
Wild Waki	2	F	7	1	1	1	10,810
Wild Warrior Woman	6	M	1	0	0	0	44
Wild Wedding	2	F	3	0	1	0	2,335
Wild Whiskey	5	H	3	0	1	0	15,700
Wild Whitney	4	G	2	0	0	1	2,900
Wild Wild West	3	G	9	3	6	0	110,030
Wild Wild Willie	3	G	4	0	0	1	4,517
Wild Wildcat	3	C	2	2	0	0	35,790
Wild Will	4	C	11	0	0	2	2,174
Wild Willard	4	G	3	2	0	0	61,074
Wild Willow	5	H	12	0	4	1	8,463
Wild Will's Wish	12	H	2	0	0	0	90
Wild Willys Philly	3	F	8	1	2	2	11,615
Wild Winner	3	F	5	1	1	0	9,160
Wild Witch	3	F	4	0	0	0	803
Wild Witchcraft	2	F	1	0	0	0	140
Wild Wojo	3	G	16	1	4	3	23,394
Wild Years	6	H	1	0	0	0	190
Wild You	4	G	6	2	0	2	21,448
Wild Zampano	5	G	10	0	0	2	10,225
Wildaboutaunty	3	F	17	1	3	4	23,901
Wildarada	4	F	7	2	1	1	13,700
Wildatbest	4	G	3	2	0	0	28,230
Wildcard Cat	3	F	8	2	2	1	74,488
Wildcat Brody	4	G	12	3	1	2	16,584
Wildcat Country	8	G	5	0	0	1	2,663
Wildcat Heir	4	C	7	4	2	0	305,860
Wildcat Lady	3	F	11	0	2	1	7,985
Wildcat Legacy	4	G	6	0	2	0	7,930
Wildcat Queen	4	F	2	0	0	0	2,395
Wildcat Shoes	3	C	10	1	3	1	116,725
Wildcat Widow	4	F	3	1	0	0	9,541
Wildcat Willy	2	G	3	0	0	1	2,839
Wildcata	4	F	4	0	0	0	2,280
Wildcharlie	2	C	1	0	0	0	0
Wildchild Bragg	5	G	13	0	0	0	797
Wilde Whirlaway	5	G	1	0	0	0	0
Wilde Wilde Honey	5	G	12	2	3	2	30,435
Wilder Than Wild	3	G	10	0	1	1	2,544
Wilderness Call	3	F	10	3	1	2	58,200
Wildest	6	G	13	0	0	1	2,872
Wildest Dream	2	C	3	0	0	0	1,417
Wildest Fantasy	3	F	4	0	0	0	450
Wildforyou	4	G	1	1	0	0	22,860
Wildintexas	2	G	3	0	0	0	4,449
Wildinthepark	3	F	9	2	0	1	17,932
Wildisthewind	6	G	12	1	2	1	13,763
Wildjack	3	F	2	0	0	0	162
Wildly	3	C	6	1	1	2	42,706
Wildly Delightful	4	F	2	0	0	0	204
Wildly Excessive	6	G	4	1	0	0	8,145
Wildly Ruth	4	F	10	2	1	4	36,727
Wildly Simple	4	F	18	4	2	3	30,056
Wildman Joey	4	C	12	0	0	1	7,155
Wild'n Free	2	F	2	1	1	0	5,250
Wildpayday	3	G	7	0	3	0	4,104
Wildridetothederby	4	F	1	0	0	0	0
Wildstella	3	F	11	1	3	1	44,581
Wildville	4	G	6	1	0	0	6,417
Wildwonderfulwoman	3	F	9	1	2	0	30,924
Wildwood Beauty	2	F	5	1	1	0	13,230
Wildwood Crest	4	F	12	3	3	0	100,680
Wildwood Firebird	3	C	4	1	1	1	9,100
Wildwood Firewood	5	M	4	0	0	1	680
Wildwood Flower	3	F	3	0	0	2	42,816
Wildwood Gabe	7	G	17	0	4	0	6,058
Wildwood Graduate	3	G	4	0	0	1	3,478
Wildwood Robin	8	G	4	0	0	0	444
Wildwood Royal	4	F	11	5	3	1	203,100
Wildwood Sam I Am	3	G	4	1	0	0	15,600
Wildwood Skier	3	G	11	0	0	0	1,206
Wildwood Sparkles	6	M	8	0	0	2	2,520
Wildwood Wildcat	3	F	2	0	0	2	5,720
Wildy Hot	4	C	1	0	0	0	65
Wildzone's Redbird	2	C	2	0	0	1	638
Wiley	3	G	7	1	2	0	14,738
Wiley Grey	5	G	11	0	1	4	3,804
Wiley Hunt	4	G	2	0	0	0	239
Wilful	3	F	8	1	3	1	19,667
Wilful Misbehaver	2	F	1	0	0	0	0
Wilgis	5	G	3	0	0	0	0
Wilhebeacrook	7	G	9	1	2	3	12,268
Wilkie	5	G	11	1	1	1	3,825
Wilko	2	C	12	3	2	5	934,074
Will	3	G	5	1	0	0	13,240
Will B Bootscouten	9	M	4	0	0	0	235
Will Be There	7	M	6	1	2	0	19,227
Will Be Wicked	5	M	7	1	1	2	3,897
Will Belong	5	H	13	0	4	1	6,113
Will Dare It	11	G	4	0	0	0	0
Will E Scat	2	G	2	1	1	0	14,400
Will Flirt	3	F	14	1	2	2	66,330
Will He Crow	3	C	4	1	0	1	150,584
Will J	3	G	1	1	0	0	4,284
Will N Spirit	3	F	5	1	0	0	2,335
Will Nine	3	G	9	0	0	0	1,945
Will On Wheels	5	G	6	2	0	2	13,431
Will Reason	5	G	1	1	0	0	2,146
Will Rein	2	G	2	0	1	0	2,069
Will the Fool Run	5	G	3	0	0	1	1,017
Will Willie Win	4	C	3	0	0	0	1,539
Willa Beauty	5	M	15	3	4	2	70,460
Willa Cather	5	M	8	1	3	1	21,802
Willard Straight	4	C	4	2	0	0	66,414
Willego	2	G	3	1	0	1	8,652
Willen	2	G	5	1	3	0	21,761
Willful Devil	3	F	2	0	0	0	105
Willful Wilhelmina	3	F	1	0	1	0	2,980
Willfulness	3	C	9	1	0	3	42,854
Willhanna	5	H	7	0	1	1	1,534
Willhebecharlie	3	G	4	1	0	1	2,380
William Riley	4	G	2	0	0	0	800
William's Cat	2	C	4	1	0	0	9,585
Williams Creek	5	G	10	1	5	0	15,141
Williams Hall	7	G	7	0	0	0	413
William's Token	5	M	1	0	0	0	0
Williamsburg Blue	4	F	7	1	0	0	1,910
Williamsport	5	M	1	0	0	0	0
Williamstown Cat	4	G	7	1	2	0	6,762
Williamstown Hall	5	G	10	1	0	3	6,820
Willie B Good	4	G	9	0	1	1	2,494
Willie B. Trouble	4	G	17	1	0	2	5,355
Willie Cruise	5	G	19	0	2	4	21,001
Willie Dunn	3	G	11	3	2	3	131,213
Willie E. M.	2	C	2	0	0	0	150
Willie Jones	2	G	6	0	0	2	3,263
Willie Or Wontie	6	G	1	0	0	0	0
Willie the Cat	5	G	8	3	0	1	63,370
Willie the Hum	3	G	4	0	0	0	725
Willie Waylon N Me	5	G	3	1	0	1	9,713
Willie Wire Wheels	5	G	4	0	0	0	0
Willie's Choice	2	C	6	2	1	0	41,920
Willie's Luv	5	M	3	0	0	0	1,800
Williewantsawin	2	C	1	0	0	0	0
Willing Coalition	3	C	3	1	0	1	18,600
Willing Consort	8	G	4	0	0	0	970
Willing Star	4	F	4	0	0	1	3,830
Willing Trick	8	G	5	0	0	0	450
Willionaire	3	C	6	2	1	0	34,713
Willitsnow	2	F	1	0	0	0	137
Willitstorm	4	F	4	0	0	0	585
Williwaw	2	G	1	0	1	0	4,588
Willo' Sweep	5	H	8	0	1	1	1,458
Willow Bend	5	M	10	0	2	0	4,068
Willow Cove	3	F	2	0	1	0	7,895
Willow Dancer	3	G	5	0	0	1	2,190
Willow Island	9	M	5	0	0	1	720
Willow Lane	3	F	5	1	0	0	4,900
Willow Makes Bail	5	M	7	0	0	3	4,300
Willow O Wisp	2	G	7	1	0	1	30,990
Willow Oak Dancer	3	C	9	1	0	0	4,260
Willow Rush	3	F	10	0	2	2	37,180
Willow Wind	5	M	12	1	3	1	20,950
Willowmemoney	3	G	2	0	0	0	0
Willows Captain	3	G	15	1	1	3	9,196
Willowtree Diamond	5	M	10	0	1	2	6,770
Willowy Wildcat	2	F	3	0	0	0	315
Will's a Player	3	C	11	2	2	3	42,795

Horse	Age	Sex	Sts	1st	2d	3d	Won
Will's Cannon	4	G	9	1	2	1	30,030
Will's Cat	4	C	8	0	0	3	7,180
Wills Commander	4	G	11	2	2	0	19,510
Wills Easy	2	F	5	0	0	2	2,486
Will's Gal	5	M	3	0	0	0	2,577
Will's Journey	4	C	5	2	0	1	62,186
Will's Little Sis	3	F	5	0	0	0	0
Will's Mistake	3	F	4	0	0	0	243
Will's War	3	C	1	0	0	0	87
Will's Wings	6	G	6	0	3	0	1,748
Will's Wish	3	G	6	2	1	0	71,973
Will's Woo Woo	3	G	15	1	2	5	34,253
Willstep	5	G	5	1	0	0	6,570
Willy At Work	6	H	3	0	0	0	324
Willy B Chic	8	G	14	0	0	1	2,619
Willy B Tackett	3	C	3	0	0	0	390
Willy Bear	5	G	5	0	0	0	0
Willy Girl	2	F	3	0	0	0	240
Willy Nilly	5	G	5	0	1	1	5,425
Willy o'the Valley	3	G	9	3	3	1	112,823
Willy Wompus	2	G	2	0	1	0	3,731
Willy Won't Gossip	5	G	15	4	2	3	17,826
Willybuck	5	G	10	0	0	2	1,854
Willys Classic	3	G	8	0	0	0	940
Willy's Way	5	G	1	0	0	0	235
Wilmaglen	3	F	16	4	3	1	13,970
Wilma's Dollie	3	F	9	0	0	2	3,510
Wilma's Star	2	C	4	0	1	1	6,975
Wilshe Amaze	4	F	1	0	0	0	0
Wilson Lake	3	G	3	0	0	0	0
Wilson's Rascal	4	G	10	0	0	1	1,191
Wilson's Slew	4	C	1	0	0	0	0
Wily Russian	4	F	5	1	0	0	4,635
Wily Walter	4	G	16	1	4	2	15,086
Wilyacrossmyvalle	6	M	2	0	0	1	1,460
Wimauma Mama	6	M	13	6	0	0	85,263
Wimberly's Bliss	3	G	14	1	1	3	24,305
Wimbledon	3	C	4	2	1	0	412,400
Wimplestiltskin	3	G	11	1	5	1	141,364
Wimpy Skippy	3	F	2	0	0	0	125
Win a Slew	5	G	3	1	0	1	1,630
Win Abba Win	2	C	9	0	0	2	5,130
Win Again	2	C	1	0	0	0	0
Win Cresent	3	G	6	1	0	1	8,773
Win for Bowman	3	F	7	1	2	0	6,685
Win for Destiny	3	F	9	1	2	3	23,920
Win for Kyran	3	G	9	0	0	0	0
Win for Roberta	4	F	2	0	0	0	0
Win Four Chory	6	M	4	0	0	0	180
Win Free	5	G	1	0	0	0	0
Win Habit	2	C	3	0	0	1	1,233
Win Island	3	F	5	0	2	2	5,368
Win Jimmy Win	3	G	5	0	0	0	735
Win Mambo	8	G	2	0	0	0	0
Win Me Over	2	C	7	2	3	2	114,434
Win Mon Win	2	C	5	0	0	0	1,871
Win My Heart	3	F	5	0	0	0	253
Win N Grin	5	G	5	0	0	2	5,120
Win N Secretary	4	C	8	0	0	1	1,265
Win Need	4	F	8	0	0	1	1,040
Win Only	6	G	1	0	0	0	0
Win Place Show	2	F	5	0	0	0	300
Win Suite	3	G	5	0	1	0	2,165
Win the Crowd	5	G	11	2	3	1	30,825
Win to the End	5	G	9	2	1	0	5,409
Win Win Situation	3	G	11	3	1	1	93,216
Win With Beck	3	C	7	2	0	1	62,980
Winabull	3	G	2	1	0	0	7,710
Winaferd	5	G	8	0	0	2	1,586
Winagain Mambo	3	G	13	3	2	2	17,888
Winalo	5	M	4	0	0	0	324
Winalot Wanda	4	F	1	0	0	0	0
Winaprize	4	C	13	1	1	1	7,074
Winatbingo	3	F	4	0	0	1	928
Winazul	5	M	10	1	1	1	8,216
Winburn	5	G	10	2	1	3	29,640
Winchendon Prince	2	G	2	0	1	0	1,785
Wincraft	2	G	5	0	0	1	2,245
Wind and Wine	2	F	5	0	3	2	16,233
Wind Dancer	2	G	2	0	0	0	1,950
Wind Factor	4	G	11	3	2	0	18,957
Wind Flow	3	F	2	2	0	0	49,800
Wind Glider	3	C	13	2	3	5	60,360
Wind Hacker	3	G	13	0	1	3	7,305
Wind in Your Face	5	G	7	0	0	3	17,900
Wind It Up Brim	3	F	4	0	0	0	300
Wind Jet	2	C	2	0	0	0	236
Wind Knot	5	M	2	0	0	0	480
Wind N Sea	5	G	8	0	0	0	2,607
Wind Princess	4	F	8	0	1	0	1,530
Wind Riddle	4	G	14	1	2	0	9,142
Wind Sand n' Stars	4	G	4	0	0	0	192
Wind Shine	2	C	5	1	0	0	6,140
Wind Spectacle	2	G	2	1	1	0	9,614
Wind Talk	3	F	2	0	0	0	280
Wind Talkin	3	G	10	1	0	0	7,789
Wind Trail	7	M	10	2	0	0	3,305
Wind Treader	5	G	5	0	0	0	396
Wind Twister	2	F	7	4	1	0	52,360
Wind Warning	4	G	6	2	1	0	26,436
Wind Water	2	G	7	2	1	2	99,920
Windcutter	5	G	1	0	0	0	75
Windemere Girl	6	M	5	0	1	0	682
Windham Chief	3	C	5	2	1	1	27,380
Windham Flash	4	G	5	2	1	0	20,560
Windinthevalley	4	F	10	0	1	5	20,513
Windiva	2	F	2	0	0	0	600
Windlass	4	F	7	0	1	1	2,635
Window B	6	H	10	4	3	3	67,620
Window Box	2	F	3	1	0	1	12,880
Window Woman	2	F	3	0	0	1	2,000
Winds of Love	6	G	12	1	1	2	10,870
Windsatilting	5	M	13	0	2	0	6,401
Windscore	4	G	4	0	1	0	6,230
Windshift	3	G	4	0	0	0	800
Windsor Boy	7	H	3	0	0	0	86
Windsor Castle	6	H	1	0	0	0	460
Windsor Dickens	4	C	6	2	1	0	23,720
Windsor Gray	2	F	2	0	0	0	0
Windsor Lodge	4	G	5	1	2	0	25,440
Windstruck	3	F	3	0	0	1	9,888
Windswept Anji	4	F	9	1	1	0	7,179
Windswept Kazi	3	F	1	0	0	0	0
Windswept Paddy	6	H	10	0	0	0	4,067
Windswept Way	4	G	10	1	0	1	5,740
Windumoni	4	F	7	3	1	1	13,500
Windward Bound	5	M	1	0	0	0	40
Windward Call	6	G	11	0	1	5	10,726
Windward Passage	5	G	9	0	0	3	14,830
Windwood West	4	G	3	0	0	0	330
Windy Camisite	4	F	1	0	0	0	0
Windy Coyote	3	G	7	0	0	0	1,050
Windy Flapper	3	F	11	1	1	2	29,924
Windy Gal	2	F	1	0	0	0	0
Windy Morning	3	F	1	0	0	0	476
Windy Night	3	F	7	1	0	1	7,801
Windy O	3	F	1	0	0	1	2,280
Windy O'Neill	5	G	7	2	0	1	20,231
Windy Seven	3	F	4	0	0	0	0
Windy Storm'n Rose	2	F	5	1	1	1	10,598
Windy Tour	3	F	8	1	0	1	7,455
Windy Way	6	M	16	2	2	4	14,871
Windy Zeal	5	G	13	2	0	2	8,564
Windy's Escapade	5	M	10	1	2	1	11,674
Windy's Halo	12	G	8	1	2	0	7,354
Windy's Pride	3	G	5	1	1	2	18,201
Wine and Spirits	3	F	11	0	0	1	22,518
Wine At Dawn	3	F	12	2	3	4	12,063
Wine At Me	3	G	13	2	0	3	14,365
Wine Card	7	G	2	0	0	0	0
Wine de Jour	4	F	1	0	0	0	450
Wine Express	5	M	6	1	0	1	6,606
Wine Maker	7	G	14	1	1	2	8,793
Wine Me 'n Dine Me	3	F	2	1	0	0	16,308
Wine N Wishes	2	F	3	1	0	0	11,700
Wine Spoken Here	3	G	11	4	2	1	70,635
Wine Spot	4	F	10	1	3	1	10,036
Wine Time	10	G	1	0	0	0	0

Horse	Age	Sex	Sts	1st	2d	3d	Won
Wineglass Steel	9	G	2	0	0	0	80
Wineing and Dining	4	G	7	3	2	0	47,040
Winendynme	3	F	4	1	0	1	73,209
Winewomenandsong	4	G	9	1	2	0	38,580
Wing Dancer	6	M	11	0	0	1	2,032
Wing Kai	2	G	3	0	0	0	1,707
Wing Man	2	C	4	0	2	1	22,650
Wing Tips	4	G	14	2	1	1	40,890
Wingback	2	G	5	1	1	1	12,218
Wingbrook	4	C	8	0	0	1	5,370
Wingding	5	H	8	0	0	0	673
Winged Sumac	4	C	6	1	2	2	15,023
Winged Wishes	2	F	1	0	0	1	4,700
Wingedlover	4	G	3	0	0	0	273
Winginit	4	F	5	0	0	0	1,840
Wingley	5	M	8	1	0	0	7,078
Wings Big Boy	9	G	10	0	1	0	8,032
Wings o' Change	4	F	20	3	6	2	38,928
Wings of an Eagle	3	C	5	1	1	1	21,210
Wings of Angels	4	F	4	0	0	0	0
Wings of Caromine	3	C	3	0	0	0	290
Wings of Flight	3	G	7	0	0	0	2,649
Wings of Hope	4	G	7	1	3	0	4,260
Wings of Jones	8	G	18	3	1	3	36,723
Wings of Oisin	6	G	4	0	1	1	2,800
Wings of Rain	2	F	2	0	1	0	5,788
Wings of Time	5	H	3	0	1	1	3,193
Wings of Wonder	2	C	1	0	0	0	0
Wings On Springs	3	G	10	2	1	0	36,754
Wings Play Tag	7	M	6	0	0	0	1,254
Wings True	5	M	12	4	1	4	41,662
Wingsforwish	4	C	12	0	1	1	2,291
Winikins	3	F	4	0	0	1	6,231
Winitall	9	G	1	0	1	0	1,770
Winitformom	3	G	11	3	1	3	19,891
Winkelberry	3	G	2	0	0	0	0
Winkey's Image	4	G	9	2	1	1	18,266
Winking	5	G	10	2	0	2	16,032
Winkle Free	4	G	23	2	5	2	17,649
Winky's Reply	5	M	3	0	0	0	120
Winlocs Articchill	3	F	6	1	0	2	12,900
Winlocs Big Wonder	5	H	1	0	0	0	0
Winlocs Glory Days	3	F	8	2	2	0	81,320
Winlocs Grama Rose	7	M	1	0	0	0	109
Winloc's Majesty	3	F	16	3	0	3	50,722
Winloc's Mickey	9	M	12	0	0	1	2,108
Winloc's Nelson	6	H	9	3	0	0	30,952
Winloc's Pilgrim	7	M	15	3	2	3	20,409
Winlocs Saint Jude	3	G	5	0	0	0	520
Winlocs Summerwind	3	F	9	1	0	1	14,726
Winloc's Sunshine	5	M	7	2	3	1	38,422
Winnamucca	3	F	7	1	1	1	9,755
Winner Bay Go	4	F	2	0	0	0	140
Winner From Mars	3	C	2	1	0	0	35,228
Winner Haven	4	F	7	0	0	1	1,029
Winner of the Day	8	G	1	0	0	0	0
Winner Season	6	M	10	0	2	1	2,843
Winner Takes All	4	F	10	0	1	2	19,660
Winneratthewindow	3	C	15	3	3	0	47,730
Winner's Code	6	G	15	4	1	2	33,276
Winner's Lad	7	G	10	3	1	1	5,758
Winner's Quest	3	F	9	0	1	2	7,705
Winners Smile	3	G	11	2	1	0	17,210
Winners Table	3	G	14	2	3	3	31,130
Winnertime Mood	2	C	5	0	0	1	1,820
Winnie Mae	3	F	5	1	1	1	13,220
Winnie the Feu	3	F	4	0	0	0	1,020
Winniedawhale	6	M	15	1	1	4	11,345
Winnie's Copy	5	G	4	0	0	1	578
Winnie's Pooh Bear	6	G	9	0	4	2	17,288
Winnie's Tash	7	M	14	0	2	2	12,021
Winniewood	5	M	18	1	1	1	4,691
Winnin Coin	6	H	10	2	1	2	8,323
Winninexpectations	2	F	2	0	0	0	666
Winning Affair	7	H	3	2	0	1	15,065
Winning Approach	5	M	6	0	0	1	2,984
Winning Blush	2	F	1	0	1	0	3,300
Winning Brief (AUS)	7	G	2	1	0	0	4,500
Winning Bye N Bye	3	C	5	2	0	1	26,188
Winning Chance	5	M	4	2	2	0	177,415
Winning Chances	4	F	4	0	0	0	278
Winning Connection	8	G	9	1	3	2	33,529
Winning Date	3	F	15	1	3	1	13,254
Winning Edge	5	M	8	1	0	3	9,513
Winning Expression	2	C	5	1	2	0	78,138
Winning Facts	2	G	3	0	0	0	0
Winning Fans	4	C	6	1	0	0	16,940
Winning Fever	4	F	14	1	1	4	32,867
Winning Fever (AUS)	10	G	4	1	0	1	7,210
Winning Flag	4	F	8	0	0	1	1,698
Winning Flames	5	G	15	2	1	3	43,335
Winning for Me	11	M	4	0	0	1	744
Winning Foursome	3	F	6	1	1	1	19,740
Winning Gal	5	M	11	0	0	2	1,480
Winning Hand	2	G	2	1	0	1	17,160
Winning Intentions	5	G	1	0	0	0	46
Winning Kiss	3	F	2	0	0	1	4,680
Winning Lure	4	G	10	1	2	2	16,920
Winning March	7	G	1	0	0	0	0
Winning Prospector	2	C	6	0	0	0	1,112
Winning Races	4	F	7	1	1	2	3,430
Winning Request	10	G	7	1	4	0	9,169
Winning Run	3	G	8	0	1	0	3,559
Winning Season	2	F	7	2	1	2	99,655
Winning Shows	5	M	15	2	1	4	13,388
Winning Stripes	4	G	6	0	0	0	10,239
Winning Sweep	7	H	21	2	3	5	14,066
Winning Talk	5	G	18	2	3	6	37,356
Winning Thoughts	3	G	6	1	1	3	16,810
Winning Tunes	5	G	11	0	3	3	7,000
Winning Wager	4	G	5	1	0	0	1,670
Winning Weave	3	F	11	1	0	4	9,951
Winning Witness	3	C	10	3	0	0	45,458
Winning Won	4	G	2	0	0	0	0
Winnow	3	F	11	1	5	3	42,960
Winnys Decree	3	G	1	0	0	0	90
Winny's Gal	2	F	1	0	0	0	0
Winona	6	M	1	0	0	0	0
Winslow	2	C	2	0	0	0	130
Winslow Arizona	4	F	12	0	0	2	2,334
Winsome	2	F	7	1	1	2	55,370
Winsome Lady	3	F	1	0	0	0	0
Winsome Miss	4	F	9	0	1	0	2,974
Winsome Silverlady	4	F	9	0	0	0	604
Winsome Wampum	5	M	10	1	4	0	17,660
Winsome Weekend	4	F	9	2	1	1	15,290
Winsome Witch	4	F	7	0	0	1	2,829
Winsomemoneyhoney	2	C	2	1	1	0	35,570
Winspear	4	G	12	1	3	5	44,251
Winston Chapel	5	G	4	0	0	1	2,940
Winston Winsome	5	G	4	0	0	0	218
Wintaplay	4	F	9	2	4	2	10,375
Winter Air	4	G	7	0	2	0	3,693
Winter Award	3	C	6	0	1	1	4,655
Winter Ball	3	F	3	1	0	0	6,860
Winter Cameo	4	F	7	2	1	1	22,535
Winter Classic	5	M	2	0	0	0	294
Winter Clouds	4	F	1	0	0	0	0
Winter Escape	7	G	24	2	4	4	17,177
Winter Games	4	G	16	1	3	1	9,303
Winter Garden	4	F	6	4	2	0	353,460
Winter Ghost	3	C	6	2	1	1	33,850
Winter Harbor	4	F	2	1	0	0	8,590
Winter Lady	9	M	12	0	1	3	3,088
Winter Rules	4	C	13	2	1	1	50,052
Winter Runner	3	F	11	1	2	2	42,568
Winter Storm Watch	6	G	4	0	0	1	480
Winter Tide	3	F	11	3	3	1	86,568
Winter Trick	4	G	7	0	3	2	22,912
Winter Warrior	3	G	2	0	0	2	2,610
Winter Whiskey	3	G	8	0	0	2	21,775
Winter Win	6	G	13	3	1	2	10,761
Winter Wonderland	10	G	5	0	0	0	435
Winterclearance	3	F	2	0	0	0	0
Winterfield	9	G	10	0	0	0	755
Winterized Star	5	M	11	1	0	1	5,793
Wintermix (FR)	5	M	2	0	0	2	5,390
Winter's Coin	4	G	10	2	1	3	29,025

Horse	Age	Sex	Sts	1st	2d	3d	Won
Winter's Quest	4	F	2	1	0	0	18,240
Winters Rainbow	3	F	20	1	2	3	13,955
Winters Thunder	5	M	6	0	0	0	746
Winterstarr	6	G	11	1	2	1	6,209
Winterstormwarning	3	C	6	0	2	0	3,200
Winthano	3	F	11	0	1	0	1,869
Winthrop Joe	7	G	7	3	1	2	20,400
Wintin	2	C	1	0	0	0	375
Wintrick	3	G	11	3	0	0	10,040
Wintry Twist	3	C	9	1	1	2	36,661
Wintuition	3	F	8	1	0	3	22,856
Winturman	4	G	2	1	0	0	3,660
Winvovers Gal	4	F	9	1	1	1	6,225
Winwonsoon	6	H	1	0	0	0	0
Winyah Bay	4	G	9	1	1	2	13,560
Wire Bound	3	G	12	4	1	0	189,000
Wire Editor	3	G	10	4	1	0	26,415
Wire It Up Baby	4	F	7	2	1	2	13,955
Wire Leader	7	G	8	2	0	0	9,965
Wire Me On Ice	2	C	3	0	0	1	2,475
Wire to Wire Waltz	4	F	1	0	0	0	0
Wire Transfer	4	G	2	0	0	1	3,340
Wire Whip	5	G	10	2	1	4	48,225
Wirebender	5	G	12	2	1	0	38,758
Wired N Ready	4	F	11	1	2	2	20,151
Wired to Win	8	G	9	2	3	2	11,847
Wiredforspeed	2	C	3	0	0	1	3,737
Wisdom Maker	3	G	3	1	0	0	6,960
Wisdomisgold	2	F	7	1	2	1	105,716
Wisdom's Mark	4	G	12	0	2	2	4,932
Wisdom's Whisper	4	G	2	0	0	0	0
Wise Affair	3	F	5	2	1	0	77,174
Wise and Clever	2	C	3	0	0	0	1,610
Wise Bid	6	G	4	0	0	0	224
Wise Briana	2	F	9	1	1	1	45,460
Wise Child	5	M	4	0	0	0	995
Wise Dancer	9	G	12	2	2	3	11,384
Wise Diplomat	2	C	6	0	0	3	18,640
Wise Ending	7	M	3	0	0	0	900
Wise Fantasy	2	F	1	0	1	0	4,200
Wise Fool	5	G	12	1	1	0	9,082
Wise Gal	3	F	8	1	0	1	8,250
Wise Gift	3	F	9	1	0	3	29,137
Wise Girl Karma	2	F	3	1	0	0	8,550
Wise Investor	2	F	5	1	1	1	46,808
Wise Kracker	6	G	10	2	0	1	8,098
Wise Money	3	F	6	0	2	2	17,250
Wise N Valid	4	F	7	0	0	1	3,760
Wise Prize	2	C	7	0	1	1	5,755
Wise Quack	4	G	14	1	5	2	24,685
Wise Remark	4	G	3	0	0	0	1,145
Wise Romance	9	M	8	0	1	1	1,822
Wise Talk	8	G	8	4	2	0	56,446
Wise Timmy	2	F	3	0	0	2	30,618
Wise Trader	4	G	3	0	0	0	100
Wise Up Awad	3	F	3	0	0	0	0
Wisecrack	2	C	7	1	3	1	31,650
Wiseguy's Out	5	G	10	2	1	0	6,855
Wisenheimer	4	G	10	1	1	2	10,205
Wisenup	5	G	9	0	3	1	11,056
Wiser'swisdom	4	G	14	1	2	0	13,086
Wish Again	3	F	4	0	0	0	0
Wish and Try	5	G	2	0	2	0	3,145
Wish Approval	3	F	14	2	4	1	17,341
Wish Boutique	3	F	16	3	1	3	14,606
Wish for Gold	3	F	10	1	4	0	63,602
Wish Mount	4	G	5	0	0	0	539
Wish 'n Wild	4	F	11	1	0	2	3,423
Wish Upon a Zar	2	F	6	0	0	0	435
Wish Us a Rainbow	2	F	1	0	0	0	0
Wishbone	3	C	2	0	0	0	440
Wishbone Kid	3	F	7	1	0	1	45,642
Wishfora Dime	2	F	4	0	0	0	685
Wishful Kris	6	H	4	1	0	0	6,559
Wishful Past	4	C	5	0	0	1	1,870
Wishful Splendor	5	M	1	1	0	0	60,000
Wishful Whitney	7	M	4	0	1	0	885
Wishgirl	5	M	17	1	2	4	11,771
Wishinforheaven	4	C	1	0	0	0	0

Horse	Age	Sex	Sts	1st	2d	3d	Won
Wishing	2	F	4	1	0	0	4,830
Wishing Dixie	3	F	1	0	0	0	130
Wishing for You	2	F	1	0	0	0	1,200
Wishing Lilly	4	F	17	0	1	2	7,264
Wishing Miss	3	F	12	2	4	0	46,110
Wishing to Win	4	F	1	0	0	0	0
Wishing Zone	4	F	2	0	0	0	218
Wishingitwas	5	H	5	1	0	2	77,680
Wishiniwasfishin	2	C	9	0	3	3	11,055
Wishinonastar	6	G	8	1	0	2	9,410
Wishi's Girl	4	F	1	0	0	0	186
Wishiwasinheaven	3	F	6	0	0	1	1,061
Wishn for Amillion	2	C	2	0	1	0	4,040
Wishy Washy Colton	4	G	4	1	0	0	4,950
Wisman Road	4	G	1	0	0	0	0
Wisperingwhitelies	4	F	10	1	4	0	18,686
Wispy Whiskers	4	G	11	2	1	1	8,958
Wistano	2	G	3	0	1	0	4,427
Wistla	4	F	6	0	0	0	1,134
Wit	9	G	1	0	0	0	0
Witch Approval	4	F	4	3	1	0	60,400
Witch Hunt	3	G	6	2	0	0	10,455
Witch Is It	2	F	1	0	0	0	121
Witch Love	6	M	4	0	0	0	0
Witch On a Stick	6	M	3	0	0	0	350
Witch Revival	4	F	6	1	0	0	32,310
Witch Tradition	5	M	7	1	0	0	6,206
Witch Ways West	2	C	2	0	1	1	12,700
Witches Above	7	M	12	0	1	0	3,242
Witches Rose	5	M	15	1	2	1	8,274
Witchesyn	4	F	7	1	2	1	5,125
Witchit	2	F	6	0	1	0	4,407
Witchonabroomstick	4	F	11	0	0	1	2,832
Witch's Spawn	4	C	4	0	0	0	401
With a Little Luck	5	M	11	2	2	3	16,500
With a Purpose	6	G	10	1	2	2	10,765
With a Song	4	F	4	1	0	0	6,119
With a Whisper	3	G	8	0	0	1	1,583
With Affection	3	F	8	3	2	1	95,480
With Anticipation	9	G	1	0	0	1	5,980
With Assurance	4	G	9	1	0	2	20,713
With Clearance	3	C	5	1	0	0	9,205
With Courage	5	G	2	1	0	0	9,000
With Delight	4	F	10	2	3	2	15,300
With Distinction	3	C	6	2	1	0	56,245
With Due Respect	2	F	5	1	2	0	17,300
With Essence	3	F	4	2	0	1	25,420
With Fun	5	M	2	0	0	1	1,500
With Glory	4	G	14	3	3	1	21,378
With His Authority	4	G	11	2	1	3	9,301
With Intensity	3	G	1	0	0	1	5,000
With Iris	7	G	8	0	2	2	24,470
With Liberty	3	F	4	0	0	0	577
With My Approval	5	M	8	0	0	0	723
With No Knickers	5	M	13	0	2	1	4,418
With Patience	5	M	9	3	2	2	178,750
With Peace	3	G	8	0	1	0	4,720
With Permission	3	F	4	0	0	0	0
With Probability	3	C	7	2	1	0	59,158
With Roses	5	G	10	2	0	2	16,015
With Sugar On Top	4	F	8	2	0	2	16,165
With the Irish	3	C	11	3	3	0	51,120
With the Works	5	M	4	1	1	0	13,720
With Winning Ways	3	F	3	0	0	0	450
With Zest	5	M	1	0	0	0	0
Withallmyrage	5	G	1	0	0	0	76
Withdrawn	3	F	4	0	2	0	5,910
Withflagsaflyin'	4	F	2	0	0	0	76
Withholding Info	6	G	2	0	0	0	4,280
Within Range	4	F	7	0	1	1	1,440
Withlin	2	F	7	1	1	1	17,015
Withmom's Image	3	F	19	4	2	4	52,685
Withorwithoutyou	4	F	6	0	0	1	13,660
Without a Doubt	5	G	8	1	5	1	69,243
Without a Ring	2	G	3	0	0	0	1,464
Without Bond	4	G	8	1	0	0	4,416
Without End	6	M	9	2	0	0	9,639
Without Objection	4	G	3	0	0	0	1,200
Without Regret	5	G	13	2	0	0	6,906

Horse	Age	Sex	Sts	1st	2d	3d	Won
Without Warning	4	G	6	0	0	0	1,310
Witness the Crown	3	F	3	0	0	0	419
Witness the Music	4	G	8	0	0	0	495
Witness the Queen	6	M	13	0	3	1	10,161
Witness the Storm	3	G	9	0	0	0	622
Witness This	3	G	7	1	1	0	53,300
Witness to a Fight	2	G	4	2	0	0	69,638
Witnessthesunrise	6	G	11	1	1	1	5,506
Witt Ante	4	G	11	4	2	2	240,600
Witten	2	F	4	2	0	0	37,921
Wittenberg Time	4	G	11	0	4	0	2,655
Wittle What	4	F	4	0	0	0	1,536
Witto Road	3	F	13	1	1	4	13,925
Witty Bill	6	G	13	2	0	0	8,435
Witty Factor	2	G	2	1	0	0	4,680
Witty Lady	3	F	8	1	2	1	20,490
Wixoe Express (IRE)	5	G	6	2	0	1	87,910
Wizard of Gold	3	C	2	1	0	0	21,180
Wizard of Oz	3	G	3	0	0	0	65
Wizard of Win	5	G	3	1	0	0	8,360
Wizard Wells	6	H	2	0	0	0	0
Wizard White	3	C	2	0	1	1	1,980
Wizardry	9	G	8	0	0	1	1,138
Wizky Boy	3	G	2	1	0	0	11,775
Wizman	3	C	1	0	1	0	8,200
Wndy's Tan	4	F	12	4	3	1	21,468
Wnrwnrchickndnr	3	F	3	0	0	0	150
Wobinann	5	M	5	0	0	0	215
Woke Up Dreamin	4	C	2	1	0	0	25,500
Wolf (ARG)	6	H	2	0	1	0	5,760
Wolf and Hawk	8	G	3	0	0	0	132
Wolf Colony	4	C	6	0	0	1	2,150
Wolf Creek	3	G	12	1	1	1	6,011
Wolf Eye	3	C	1	0	0	0	80
Wolf for Queenie	3	F	3	0	0	0	286
Wolf Gal's Print	3	G	17	4	2	2	42,110
Wolf Girl	5	M	6	1	0	0	3,214
Wolf Howl	5	G	10	1	4	0	91,576
Wolf Kitten	3	F	8	0	0	1	3,150
Wolf N Hen	3	F	5	1	0	1	10,460
Wolf Running	3	G	4	0	0	0	440
Wolf Trick	4	G	17	2	4	4	58,110
Wolfmon	3	G	8	1	3	0	5,987
Wolfnbankersclothn	3	F	7	0	1	4	15,865
Wolf's Babe	2	F	9	0	0	2	5,220
Wolf's Gem	3	C	16	2	4	2	33,015
Wolf's Honor	6	H	20	5	4	2	35,642
Wolf's Prospect	4	G	8	0	1	1	3,470
Wolfwithintegrity	7	G	5	1	1	0	43,420
Wolley	7	G	5	0	0	0	1,207
Wolly Bully	2	C	4	0	1	1	16,964
Wolverine	5	H	6	1	0	0	31,854
Wolvspa	7	G	12	1	1	1	23,030
Woman Onfasttrack	4	F	13	1	2	1	35,319
Woman's Touch	5	M	6	2	1	0	13,637
Won Arm Bandit	4	G	1	0	0	0	0
Won Away	2	C	5	2	0	0	24,000
Won Better	5	G	12	1	1	5	39,450
Won Bright Nickle	3	F	10	3	1	0	9,991
Won Buck	2	G	2	0	0	0	0
Won C C	6	G	12	0	3	2	34,662
Won Dozen Roses	4	F	12	3	1	4	59,217
Won Fancy Dancer	8	G	14	2	7	3	12,737
Won for Chopper	5	H	12	3	2	1	25,486
Won Forceful Lady	7	M	8	1	0	0	10,242
Won Handsome Devil	3	G	4	1	1	2	23,012
Won Jenelle	8	M	6	1	1	2	33,260
Won More Hill	4	G	8	0	0	2	2,071
Won On the Run	3	C	5	1	0	0	2,091
Won the Derby	10	G	6	0	1	1	1,985
Won to Run	2	F	4	0	0	1	3,827
Won to Win	3	G	9	0	0	0	1,545
Won Ton Toosie	3	F	12	1	3	2	18,828
Won Ton Win	6	M	11	0	2	3	19,005
Won Won Wonder Why	3	G	5	1	1	0	8,185
Won Wong Wing	2	G	7	0	3	0	12,250

Horse	Age	Sex	Sts	1st	2d	3d	Won
Wonbyfuzzi	3	G	2	0	0	1	900
Wondancewilldo	4	G	18	1	4	1	21,199
Wonder Again	5	M	5	2	0	1	611,767
Wonder Bull	6	M	7	0	0	2	2,635
Wonder Lady	3	F	2	0	0	0	640
Wonder Weapon	7	G	7	1	2	2	10,640
Wonder Werk's	4	C	1	0	0	0	460
Wonderbabe	2	F	2	0	0	0	250
Wonderboy	4	G	4	0	0	1	794
Wonderfella	3	G	12	1	1	0	6,938
Wonderful H. O. A.	3	C	11	0	2	2	14,780
Wonderful Heather	3	F	9	1	2	0	6,742
Wonderful Larry	8	G	6	3	1	2	12,730
Wonderful Life	4	F	6	0	1	0	989
Wonderful Me	3	C	1	0	0	0	840
Wonderful Miss	4	F	6	0	1	0	3,549
Wonderful Mom Sons	3	C	8	1	0	1	23,470
Wonderful News	3	F	7	0	1	0	4,283
Wonderful Prospect	6	H	8	1	0	2	34,012
Wonderful Victory	4	C	2	0	0	0	2,370
Wonderous Woman	4	F	5	0	0	3	10,540
Wonderstreak	10	G	5	0	2	0	4,326
Wondrous Zeal	6	G	7	1	1	1	11,965
Wonette	4	F	8	2	1	1	3,964
Wonforjodi	2	G	6	0	1	1	16,060
Wong Choy	4	C	17	2	2	1	12,644
Wonhorsepower	4	C	1	0	0	0	29
Wonone	2	C	3	2	0	0	33,615
Won't He Wonder	2	C	1	0	0	0	70
Wonton Soup	3	G	1	0	0	0	0
Wonwaygirl	5	M	2	0	0	0	160
Wood Dixie Dance	3	F	8	2	0	3	27,860
Wood Fern	3	F	2	0	0	0	3,528
Wood Kat	8	G	16	2	4	5	38,765
Wood Lily	7	M	15	2	3	2	21,910
Wood Not	3	F	16	2	1	2	37,470
Wood Pay	2	G	2	0	0	0	470
Wood Polish	6	G	1	0	0	0	0
Wood Pound	8	G	7	1	2	0	16,110
Wood Whistle	10	G	2	0	1	0	6,900
Wood You Be Mine	7	H	5	1	0	0	7,838
Wood You Leave	5	M	1	0	0	0	960
Woodbend Lass	4	F	4	0	0	0	233
Woodbine Willie	4	G	9	0	1	2	6,988
Woodbuck	5	G	7	0	0	0	1,843
Woodburner	4	G	5	0	0	1	5,400
Wooden Angel	2	F	5	0	1	2	3,910
Wooden Nickel	3	G	5	0	0	0	0
Wooden Ships	3	F	9	1	2	0	46,754
Wooden You	3	F	3	0	1	1	6,695
Woodfield	5	G	3	0	1	0	1,560
Woodford Cat	2	C	2	1	0	0	12,470
Woodford Lad	3	C	4	0	0	0	0
Woodford Princess	6	M	17	3	3	5	60,922
Woodhugh	6	G	12	1	2	4	17,560
Woodiano	2	G	2	0	0	0	353
Woodlaketrophygirl	3	F	5	0	1	1	5,759
Woodland Sprite	4	F	4	0	1	0	6,100
Woodlander	2	C	3	0	1	0	11,430
Woodlands Ruler	2	G	7	0	1	0	5,800
Woodlass	4	F	6	0	1	0	15,500
Woodlynn's Mandate	3	G	2	0	0	0	535
Woodlyon	5	G	7	3	0	0	11,829
Woodmans Smile	3	F	16	2	4	1	35,290
Woodman's Song	3	G	1	0	0	0	330
Woodman's Star	3	C	12	0	3	0	18,123
Woodmeister	3	G	17	3	2	4	57,022
Woodmont	4	G	6	1	1	1	9,300
Woodmoon	6	H	6	0	0	2	19,660
Woods	10	G	7	0	0	2	561
Wood's Belle	3	F	6	0	0	0	0
Wood's Queen	3	F	4	0	0	0	79
Woodside Parkway	8	G	14	5	2	2	27,044
Woodsie's Smokin	5	G	10	0	4	3	4,824
Woodsnwaters	6	H	11	1	4	0	10,635
Woodtown Bob	6	G	7	1	0	1	10,546

Horse	Age	Sex	Sts	1st	2d	3d	Won
Woodward Smiles	5	G	6	0	3	1	9,252
Woody Haze	6	G	8	1	0	2	25,773
Woody Two Shoes	2	C	4	1	0	1	8,287
Woody's Apache	2	C	8	1	2	3	36,990
Woody's Dancer	4	G	9	2	1	3	40,572
Woody's Deputy	2	C	1	0	0	0	690
Woody's Diamond	5	H	12	1	2	1	25,197
Woody's Dream	2	C	2	0	0	1	2,825
Woody's Harvest	3	G	1	0	0	0	145
Woody's Jet	3	G	2	0	0	0	0
Woody's Playmate	2	C	2	0	0	0	460
Woody's Prize	7	H	2	0	0	0	400
Wooey's Up One	2	C	4	0	1	0	4,280
Woof	4	F	8	1	0	2	17,690
Wooglin	6	G	22	5	3	2	60,755
Woolfwoolfbaby	5	M	6	0	3	0	2,644
Woolski	5	G	12	0	5	2	6,219
Woo's Prospect	6	G	8	2	0	1	38,575
Woostershear	7	H	8	1	0	2	12,340
Wooti Toot	5	G	17	1	1	6	20,542
Wootsie Rouge	4	F	1	0	0	0	0
Word by Word	4	C	7	2	1	1	17,118
Word Girl	2	F	5	2	1	1	51,133
Word of Gold	5	M	14	0	0	1	1,118
Wordly Dreams	3	C	5	0	0	0	390
Words and Music	8	H	2	0	0	1	3,500
Words Cant Explain	4	G	12	0	2	0	4,168
Words of Caution	3	G	11	1	2	2	21,860
Words of Love	3	F	13	3	1	1	12,505
Words of Warning	3	G	11	1	1	0	17,223
Work	3	C	12	1	0	3	18,066
Work for Boots	4	G	5	2	2	0	30,320
Work for Roses	2	F	2	0	0	0	900
Work Hard	6	G	8	3	1	0	9,376
Work With Me	3	C	10	2	5	2	143,401
Workaholic	7	G	4	0	0	0	1,494
Worker Man	4	C	12	4	1	1	55,120
Working Awesome	9	M	6	0	0	0	334
Working Class	3	G	16	2	4	1	22,419
Working Double	2	G	3	0	1	1	4,338
Worksformoney	3	F	2	0	0	0	1,960
Workum	6	G	5	2	0	1	17,330
Worland	6	G	7	3	1	2	28,370
World Bank	9	G	10	2	2	2	10,018
World Beater	9	G	4	0	0	0	222
World Best	5	G	13	2	2	2	8,074
World Champion	5	H	11	1	1	6	26,645
World Class Act	3	F	1	0	0	0	100
World Class Hoofer	4	G	10	0	0	1	4,552
World Class Smile	5	M	16	2	3	2	15,574
World Conflict	2	C	8	1	0	2	20,160
World Cruiser	3	F	1	0	0	0	0
World Diplomat	3	C	7	0	1	1	3,590
World Event	3	F	5	0	0	1	8,830
World Havoc	3	G	6	1	0	0	10,500
World Market	2	F	1	0	0	0	0
World of Peace	3	G	7	1	0	0	8,255
World of Reason	5	M	2	0	0	0	0
World of Wonder	6	G	11	1	0	1	42,089
World On Fire	2	F	2	0	0	0	0
World Premier	5	G	8	0	1	1	2,734
World Prince	5	G	6	0	0	0	779
World Stage Star	5	M	11	1	1	1	5,481
World Tour	5	G	10	2	0	1	8,536
World Toy	3	F	14	2	1	2	14,095
World Trade	5	H	1	0	0	0	0
World Vision	7	G	3	0	0	0	349
Worldliness	3	F	9	1	2	2	33,510
Worldly Endeavor	2	F	7	0	0	0	1,360
Worldly Navy	5	G	4	1	0	1	16,389
Worldly Pleasure	4	F	13	4	1	2	79,949
Worldly Prospect	3	F	3	0	0	0	194
Worldly Treasure	7	G	5	0	1	0	1,280
Worldwidetestimony	5	H	6	0	0	0	1,000
Worldwind Romance	6	G	5	4	0	0	113,866
Worldy Image	4	F	15	2	2	1	9,792

Horse	Age	Sex	Sts	1st	2d	3d	Won
Worldy Reason	4	G	8	1	5	0	11,700
Worray	2	C	6	1	0	1	19,820
Worry Free	3	G	5	1	1	1	23,850
Worth a Dime	6	M	6	1	0	0	6,510
Worth My While	4	C	2	0	0	0	77
Worth Remembering	3	F	14	2	4	2	25,640
Worth See'n	2	C	3	0	0	0	2,569
Worth Springs	6	G	7	2	1	1	18,740
Worth the Kissin	6	M	5	0	0	1	1,346
Worth Watching	4	G	5	2	0	0	6,717
Worth Winning	4	F	16	5	2	2	49,223
Worthing	4	G	5	0	0	3	6,060
Worththegamble	7	M	8	2	2	0	29,515
Worththewait	7	G	15	1	3	2	9,279
Worthy Adversary	4	G	12	1	2	0	6,874
Worthy Find	9	G	7	1	3	0	2,896
Worthy Forum	5	G	13	2	2	2	19,339
Worthy Gift	3	C	4	0	0	0	927
Worthy Present	6	G	1	0	0	0	40
Worthy Soldier	5	G	13	1	3	3	27,594
Worthy You	6	M	8	0	1	0	5,715
Wotta Peach	3	F	1	0	0	0	80
Would She	5	M	2	0	0	0	100
Would You Be Mine	4	F	16	3	5	3	62,219
Wouldja	3	G	4	1	2	0	26,190
Wouldn't We All	10	H	7	2	1	1	23,469
Woven Dream	3	F	11	1	3	1	21,115
Wow Man	7	G	2	0	0	0	213
Wrap Avalli	3	C	4	0	0	0	508
Wrapped Up in You	2	F	1	0	0	0	370
Wreathaspice	2	F	1	0	0	0	140
Wrecking Crew	6	G	9	2	3	2	9,488
Wren	4	F	1	0	0	0	320
Wrench It	4	G	25	1	0	0	23,432
Wretched Excess	3	F	15	2	3	1	69,720
Wright Dream	5	M	6	1	0	0	3,862
Wright On Huston	5	G	9	1	1	1	4,370
Wright Seeker	2	F	1	0	0	0	250
Wright Wing	3	G	16	2	2	0	10,850
Wrigley Culy	3	C	3	0	0	0	780
Wrinkle Free	8	G	13	0	4	0	3,293
Writ of Summons	3	G	10	2	0	2	10,368
Writer's Jule	3	F	10	2	0	1	23,542
Writer's Walk	2	C	1	0	1	0	11,760
Wrong Look	3	F	2	0	0	0	210
Wrong Religion	2	G	5	0	0	0	495
Wrong Spell	3	F	4	1	0	0	2,881
Wrong Target	3	G	10	3	1	1	9,711
Wrong Way David	5	M	16	0	1	3	9,065
Wry Humor	3	G	7	3	0	2	56,160
Wrzeszcz	3	G	8	4	2	1	122,969
Wucky Ray Ray	3	G	9	0	5	0	7,150
Wudantunoit	6	G	8	1	2	0	31,580
Wulfert Road	2	C	2	0	1	0	4,780
Wulpe	3	C	10	2	0	1	44,416
Wunderbar	3	G	14	3	3	0	22,471
Wundrcolthundrbolt	7	G	3	0	0	0	670
Wunnernaus	3	G	6	0	1	1	3,935
Wuzhap'nskycapt'n	2	C	3	0	0	0	0
Ww Conquistador	4	C	14	1	3	3	28,760
Wwwdotwindotcom	8	G	1	0	0	0	280
Wyatts Fancy Flyer	3	G	9	0	2	2	6,780
Wyatt's High Noon	3	F	7	0	2	2	8,866
Wyatt's Magic	6	G	2	0	1	0	2,160
Wyconda	8	G	6	1	1	0	6,360
Wye Factor	3	G	4	0	0	0	0
Wye River	4	F	12	2	3	4	65,530
Wye River Rugrat	3	F	12	3	2	2	20,520
Wye Road	2	F	2	1	0	1	7,183
Wye Valley	3	F	8	1	0	1	5,764
Wyndham Bay	9	G	8	1	2	1	1,600
Wynn Dot Comma	3	C	3	2	0	0	159,000
Wynn Seeker	5	M	11	2	1	2	11,515
Wynning Offer	3	G	17	0	3	1	6,473
Wynning Rainbow	3	F	8	2	1	0	11,249
Wynn's Final Offer	2	F	1	0	0	1	5,880

Horse	Age	Sex	Sts	1st	2d	3d	Won
Wynns Whim	3	F	10	3	1	1	19,710
Wynnsrazamatamayaz	3	G	11	2	1	4	44,960
Wyoming Wish	5	M	10	1	2	0	5,400
Wyrick	6	H	1	0	1	0	2,580
Wzup Ric	4	C	7	1	0	1	4,860
X Be Thy Name	3	G	9	0	0	0	1,740
X Box	3	G	12	5	0	1	161,599
X Deal	4	F	6	1	0	1	14,770
X Melrose Rascal	5	G	5	1	0	1	3,167
X Partner	3	G	8	1	1	0	10,335
X Rated Movie	4	G	8	1	4	3	19,579
X Streme	4	G	9	0	1	1	9,659
X to the Tee	3	F	10	2	1	2	11,075
X Tra Brassy	4	F	3	0	0	0	0
X Z Bit	4	G	1	0	0	0	288
Xalt	10	G	2	0	0	0	120
Xan Pandu	2	F	1	0	0	0	140
Xander	7	G	4	0	0	0	556
Xanpit	4	G	13	0	2	0	4,880
Xanthos	4	C	5	0	0	0	1,181
Xari	2	F	5	0	0	2	4,159
Xatra	3	C	2	0	0	0	392
Xavier Money	3	G	8	1	0	0	6,672
Xcape	4	G	8	0	3	1	15,780
Xedrun	8	H	3	0	0	0	264
Xena Peach	4	F	11	2	0	2	27,240
Xena Princess	3	F	3	0	0	0	250
Xenodon	6	H	5	1	0	1	12,590
Xenos Salotos	4	G	4	0	0	0	86
Xi'an	7	M	9	0	1	0	13,180
Xirius	3	C	9	2	0	2	97,777
Xitout	3	G	2	0	0	0	0
Xordinary Crown	2	C	5	0	0	1	4,692
Xordinary Love	4	F	10	1	1	2	23,754
Xpedite	5	H	4	0	0	0	263
Xtra Ace	3	G	11	2	2	4	59,960
Xtra Awesome	2	C	1	0	0	0	0
Xtra Crown	2	C	5	0	0	1	1,680
Xtra Dancer	3	F	6	0	0	0	567
Xtra Dash	4	F	2	0	1	0	7,540
Xtra Heart	4	F	2	0	0	0	2,820
Xtra Icee	3	G	11	3	2	0	43,575
Xtra Jack	3	C	14	2	6	3	79,135
Xtra Luck	3	C	1	0	0	0	0
Xtra Smooth	3	G	8	0	2	3	9,801
Xtra Tough	3	F	6	3	1	1	67,328
Xtrasensory (GB)	5	M	2	0	0	0	4,320
Xtreamotion	3	C	5	0	0	1	10,470
Xtreme Heat	3	F	9	0	2	1	11,570
Xtreme Monique	5	G	9	0	1	0	15,477
Xtreme Rush	6	G	3	0	0	0	0
Y B Bridled	4	G	9	1	0	0	6,762
Y Country	4	F	7	2	2	1	47,334
Y Not B Quick	3	G	4	0	0	0	270
Y Not Winter	4	F	5	0	2	2	11,587
Y Tu Mama Tambien	3	F	3	0	0	0	0
Y Two J	5	G	6	1	2	2	36,102
Y Two K Cat	4	F	5	0	0	0	0
Y Two K Compliant	6	M	1	0	0	0	0
Y. V. Five	4	C	4	0	2	2	22,680
Ya Big Lug	3	C	13	1	0	0	5,890
Ya Lajwaad	4	C	5	1	1	1	60,680
Ya Lateefah	5	M	14	3	2	0	45,271
Ya Who	5	H	6	0	0	0	360
Yabba Dabba You	2	G	6	2	1	0	23,420
Yacht Broker	2	C	14	1	4	2	13,855
Yada Boy	3	C	10	2	2	1	35,883
Yada Yada Yada	4	G	3	1	0	1	2,473
Yaelforhadif	4	F	12	1	2	2	17,870
Yaffa	5	G	11	0	0	1	2,686
Yagottaapproveher	7	M	8	1	0	0	5,679
Yah Sure	2	G	6	1	1	0	8,636
Yaheremenow	4	G	10	1	2	1	7,379
Yahoo	4	F	11	4	1	1	29,268
Yahoo Slew	2	C	1	0	0	0	0
Yahuh	3	F	2	0	0	0	198

Horse	Age	Sex	Sts	1st	2d	3d	Won
Yak Attack	2	C	1	0	0	1	3,975
Yak the Desert Rat	2	G	2	0	1	1	6,680
Yakima Canutt	5	H	7	3	1	0	26,820
Yakima River	4	G	8	2	1	1	16,377
Yakster	5	G	16	2	4	0	13,652
Yale Camp	5	M	4	0	0	0	0
Yamakenmecrazy	2	C	2	0	0	0	864
Yan Yarrow	2	F	2	0	0	0	0
Yanaguana	5	G	1	0	0	0	0
Yangtzee	6	G	12	0	1	0	4,420
Yankdoodle	3	G	5	1	0	0	3,590
Yankee Bride	2	F	4	0	1	0	3,415
Yankee Chant	3	G	3	1	0	0	12,180
Yankee Dan Dee	3	F	2	0	0	0	310
Yankee Doodle	4	C	4	0	0	2	1,776
Yankee Doodle Boy	6	H	11	2	2	2	54,930
Yankee Exchange	4	F	2	0	0	0	0
Yankee Fashion	3	F	11	2	2	2	50,060
Yankee Gator	2	C	4	1	0	1	11,935
Yankee Magic	2	C	2	0	0	0	2,255
Yankee Mon	3	C	3	1	0	1	20,790
Yankee Pirate	6	G	12	1	1	1	8,718
Yankee Road	2	C	2	1	0	1	7,760
Yankee Ruler	8	G	15	7	3	1	40,969
Yankee Skip	7	H	1	0	0	0	0
Yankee Summer	2	F	1	0	1	0	1,206
Yankee Trail	2	C	6	2	0	0	17,700
Yankee Treaty	2	C	6	1	2	1	20,051
Yankee Trial	4	G	1	0	0	0	0
Yankee Tribe	8	G	21	1	2	2	16,310
Yankee Trick	2	F	7	1	0	0	27,522
Yankee Val	2	F	5	0	2	0	13,140
Yankee Vice	3	C	11	1	0	0	16,237
Yankee Wildcat	6	G	4	2	1	0	69,420
Yankee Win	2	G	6	0	1	0	4,227
Yankee Wrangler	4	G	4	0	0	0	0
Yankeedandy Doodle	2	G	9	0	1	0	9,051
Yankele	4	C	8	2	0	0	12,330
Yank's Express	2	G	3	0	0	0	0
Yaqui River	5	M	2	1	0	0	9,160
Yarborough	2	C	1	0	0	0	75
Yard Bird	2	C	1	0	0	0	0
Yarico's Pond (IRE)	4	F	3	0	0	0	390
Yarnell	5	M	8	1	1	1	3,618
Yarnell Hill	7	M	1	0	1	0	1,500
Yarny's Star	13	G	5	1	2	0	4,972
Yarrow's Chief	3	G	3	0	0	0	565
Yashari	5	H	18	1	0	1	7,809
Yasie	3	F	9	2	3	1	36,140
Yasinister	4	G	1	0	0	0	0
Yasou Daniel	6	G	12	1	3	2	19,744
Yasou Johnny B	4	G	12	3	2	0	42,970
Yasou Niko	6	G	10	0	0	1	4,164
Yasou Ted G	6	G	9	1	0	2	5,272
Yasow Kerri	3	F	8	3	2	1	33,889
Yatsko	8	G	3	0	0	0	626
Yavapai	8	G	1	0	0	0	300
Yawl	3	C	6	1	0	0	9,864
Yawls Special	6	M	14	0	2	1	5,188
Yaz Am Smart	4	G	13	2	0	2	21,282
Yazoo	2	F	3	0	0	1	713
Yazor	4	F	1	0	0	0	740
Ye Jacobites	3	G	7	0	0	1	710
Ye of Little Faith	6	G	10	0	2	2	14,662
Ye Songs Last	5	M	10	0	0	0	795
Yea It Is	2	F	2	1	0	0	10,650
Yeager	3	C	4	1	1	0	15,600
Yeah Buddy	2	G	4	1	1	0	7,754
Yeah Zoomzoomzoom	3	F	5	0	0	0	898
Yeahbut	2	F	2	0	0	0	0
Year End Bonus	3	C	8	0	0	0	2,332
Year of Light	2	F	2	0	0	1	2,680
Year of the Cat	3	F	8	3	0	2	25,111
Year of the Fox	5	G	8	5	0	0	8,528
Yearbrook	3	F	14	4	5	0	21,612
Yearly Report	3	F	7	5	1	0	787,500

Horse	Age	Sex	Sts	1st	2d	3d	Won
Yearly Surprize	5	M	6	0	0	1	960
Yearn	3	G	13	0	0	2	2,093
Yell	4	F	6	0	2	1	157,826
Yellow Beauty	7	M	12	2	2	3	8,862
Yellow Heat	3	F	5	3	0	1	91,350
Yellow Out	2	G	6	1	0	3	13,880
Yellow Royale	3	C	6	0	0	1	1,410
Yellowstone (HUN)	4	C	7	0	0	0	560
Yellowstone Lady	5	M	13	2	2	1	43,249
Yelp	5	G	13	3	2	1	17,025
Yen	3	F	1	0	0	0	1,600
Yenom	4	F	2	0	0	0	0
Yeowzer	7	G	8	1	1	1	6,617
Yerevan Star	3	F	6	3	1	0	63,793
Yes	3	C	1	0	0	0	0
Yes Beth	2	F	2	0	0	1	4,265
Ye's Cookin	3	G	1	0	0	0	100
Yes He Is	3	C	2	0	0	0	0
Yes He's a Pistol	2	C	4	1	0	0	22,780
Yes I Can	3	G	9	2	0	0	10,880
Yes I Do	4	F	10	1	0	0	7,769
Yes I'm a Lady	2	F	2	0	0	0	270
Yes It's Gold	2	F	7	1	1	4	102,800
Yes Its You	2	F	4	0	1	1	5,740
Yes My Lady	2	F	1	0	0	0	840
Yes of Course	3	G	12	1	0	0	5,736
Yes Shes O. K.	5	M	1	0	0	0	0
Yes Uconn	6	G	7	0	1	1	2,833
Yes We Can	3	G	16	1	2	1	20,282
Yes Yes Yes	2	C	1	0	1	0	7,700
Yes You Can	2	G	13	0	1	2	6,266
Yessirgeneralsir	4	G	7	2	0	1	278,250
Yesss	6	G	13	3	4	1	30,231
Yester Morn	4	F	1	1	0	0	6,000
Yesterday (IRE)	4	F	3	0	0	0	60,018
Yesterday Evening	2	G	3	0	0	0	4,170
Yesterday's Cat	3	G	2	0	1	0	2,450
Yesterdays Jade	5	M	12	1	1	3	10,509
Yesterdays News	4	F	5	0	0	2	4,196
Yesterday's Rose	2	F	4	0	0	1	3,180
Yesterdays Wine	3	F	11	1	2	3	14,094
Yesyoudo	3	F	11	1	3	2	19,980
Yet Anothernatalie	5	M	8	5	2	1	100,330
Yetta	4	F	1	0	0	1	704
Yewwin	2	G	3	0	2	0	7,234
Yiddishas Princess	4	F	2	0	0	0	0
Yield of Dreams	2	F	3	0	0	1	5,145
Yield With Caution	2	F	2	1	0	1	10,472
Yimmy	3	C	11	1	2	0	16,125
Yingyingying	3	F	8	0	2	4	41,756
Yippee	5	G	10	1	3	2	19,953
Yo	4	G	9	0	1	2	24,571
Yo Af	3	G	10	0	1	0	2,798
Yo Betty	3	F	9	0	0	0	3,970
Yo Billie Bateman	5	M	10	2	0	0	11,998
Yo Can Do	3	G	9	3	2	0	37,000
Yo Capeesh	2	F	4	0	0	0	648
Yo Cuz	3	G	10	2	1	1	51,580
Yo Dan	5	G	3	0	0	0	375
Yo Jake Won	3	G	9	0	2	1	4,070
Yo Sal	3	F	4	1	1	1	27,480
Yo Say	4	G	11	3	3	1	70,689
Yo Sister	3	F	5	0	0	0	0
Yo Yo Man	4	G	5	2	0	1	16,723
Yo Yo Money	2	C	2	0	0	0	800
Yobaby	3	F	8	0	0	0	539
Yobubba	3	G	5	0	0	0	541
Yodeladytoo	2	F	3	1	0	1	37,624
Yodelayheehoo	4	F	3	0	0	0	545
Yodele Or Dance	3	G	6	1	0	0	3,768
Yodeler Lake	3	G	4	1	1	0	7,505
Yodelin Two	4	C	12	2	1	0	25,940
Yodeling Ann	4	F	4	0	0	2	12,000
Yodeltilyourblue	3	G	13	2	2	3	43,825
Yoga	5	H	3	1	1	0	23,490
Yoga Girl	3	F	7	2	0	0	4,866
Yogi's	3	F	8	1	1	2	37,680
Yokozuma	4	G	11	1	1	0	3,910
Yolanda	2	F	3	0	0	0	370
Yolanda B. Too	2	F	1	0	1	0	8,200
Yong Feathers	4	F	5	0	1	1	2,575
Yonkers	3	F	3	2	0	0	5,870
York Air (ARG)	6	H	1	0	0	0	0
York County	6	G	2	0	0	0	0
York Hills	6	M	4	1	1	0	9,668
Yorkshire Lad	5	G	13	3	3	1	29,297
Yorktown	7	G	6	2	0	2	9,040
Yoruba	6	G	13	0	0	0	625
Yoscha Bosche	3	C	4	0	0	0	250
Yoshida's Choice	5	G	2	0	0	0	0
You a Cat	3	G	7	2	0	0	26,980
You and Nelly	4	F	8	2	2	2	60,892
You Are a Kris	2	C	3	0	0	0	790
You Are Mine	4	C	8	0	1	3	4,479
You Are My Vice	3	F	2	1	0	0	6,300
You Are Stormy	3	F	8	0	0	1	5,380
You Beauty	2	C	1	0	0	0	400
You Been Told	3	F	3	0	0	0	0
You Bet We Win	5	M	12	0	5	4	22,120
You Can Call Me Mr	6	G	16	1	0	3	5,430
You Can Do Magic	3	F	2	0	0	0	470
You Can't Hide	3	F	8	0	3	0	16,194
You Choose	6	G	16	2	3	5	31,384
You Crack Me Up	4	G	6	2	1	0	28,300
You Da Bomb	4	G	9	0	0	0	0
You Da Mon	6	G	17	2	3	1	7,502
You Da Woman	3	F	12	3	4	0	21,374
You Dancing Devil	2	F	3	1	1	0	22,660
You Do the Math	5	G	8	0	4	0	16,410
You Don't Get It	3	G	13	0	4	1	9,850
You Essay	3	G	6	0	0	1	888
You Glitter Girl	4	F	2	0	0	0	519
You Go	2	F	2	0	0	1	2,340
You Go Roudy Wilma	5	M	1	0	0	0	300
You Got It Guy	8	G	1	0	0	0	0
You Got My Goat	4	C	2	0	0	0	71
You Heard Me Cart	2	F	10	0	1	1	33,597
You I Love	4	F	6	1	0	1	25,400
You Left Me	3	F	6	0	0	0	315
You Lovely Witch	4	F	5	0	0	1	2,035
You Lucky Devil	3	G	7	1	2	0	15,650
You Make the Call	3	C	2	0	0	0	83
You May	2	G	1	1	0	0	6,600
You Missed	4	F	7	0	0	1	934
You No Jack	4	G	9	1	0	5	22,457
You O K	4	C	4	0	1	0	3,559
You P. S.	5	M	4	0	0	0	218
You Pay the Bill	4	F	11	3	4	3	31,914
You Promised	3	F	10	3	1	2	103,359
You Rang	4	C	2	0	1	0	1,760
You Rule My World	4	G	1	0	0	0	0
You Talkin Bout Me	2	C	1	0	0	0	190
You Will Cry Devil	4	G	19	1	2	0	4,932
You Willgo Broke	2	C	2	1	0	1	22,721
Youareaggravatin'	3	C	9	0	2	3	65,867
Youaresweet	3	F	10	0	0	1	6,460
Youaretheman	3	G	7	1	1	1	22,640
Youcandpendonme	4	G	2	0	0	0	300
Youcan'ttakeme	4	F	1	0	0	1	4,606
You'd Blush Too	3	F	1	0	0	0	0
Youdrivememewild	7	G	7	0	0	2	2,185
Youfaxguero	2	C	8	0	1	0	3,200
Yougonow	3	G	7	0	2	2	25,672
Yougotmetwice	2	G	4	0	0	0	510
Yougottabe the One	3	F	12	2	5	2	12,509
Yougottabuck	7	G	3	0	0	1	461
Yougottawanna	5	G	11	5	3	1	223,008
Youhadyourchance	2	G	1	0	0	0	0
You'll Be Happy	7	M	11	0	2	2	16,664
Youmademeloveyou	3	F	3	1	0	0	17,880
Young and Handsome	4	G	1	0	0	0	91
Young and Restless	3	F	12	2	3	1	46,060

Horse	Age	Sex	Sts	1st	2d	3d	Won
Young Apprentice	2	C	2	0	0	0	840
Young Attorney	3	C	6	0	2	0	3,581
Young Bruiser	6	M	3	0	0	0	0
Young Dubliner (IRE)	15	G	3	0	1	1	11,300
Young Emotions	3	F	7	2	4	0	76,878
Young Guy	3	G	9	1	1	1	6,279
Young Knight	2	C	5	1	1	0	11,980
Young Man	3	C	3	0	0	0	1,127
Young Mistress	4	F	7	1	0	0	36,869
Young Neil	5	H	1	0	0	0	0
Young Runaway	12	H	7	2	0	0	26,088
Young Sage	3	F	13	1	2	1	24,540
Young Son	3	C	2	0	0	0	150
Young Star	5	M	1	0	0	0	3,000
Young Thunder	2	C	1	1	0	0	8,100
Young Trev	7	G	8	1	0	0	13,422
Young Trooper	4	G	13	2	1	1	10,165
Young Whiz	5	G	3	0	0	0	712
Young'nindependent	3	G	2	0	0	0	280
Youngs Neck Arod	6	H	1	0	0	0	0
Youngus	5	M	4	3	0	0	22,560
Younity	3	F	5	2	0	1	34,127
Youowemeone	4	F	4	1	0	0	3,031
Youpickedabeauty	3	F	4	1	0	1	15,410
Your Abc's	5	H	12	2	2	1	54,367
Your Add	4	G	1	0	0	0	0
Your Best Silver	3	C	7	0	0	0	188
Your Bluffing	4	G	8	1	1	0	41,455
Your Cat	4	F	7	1	1	4	31,080
Your Cousin J J	2	C	5	0	0	0	250
Your Excellence	2	C	5	3	1	1	65,654
Your First	9	G	6	0	0	0	375
Your Friend	4	G	8	1	1	0	8,676
Your Hired	2	C	2	0	1	1	7,250
Your Judgedship	6	H	1	0	0	0	0
Your Jules	5	G	7	0	3	0	9,564
Your Knightmare	3	F	12	0	1	2	3,410
Your Lion Eyes	3	G	1	0	0	0	50
Your Magical	4	C	3	1	0	0	4,082
Your My Baby	6	H	3	0	0	0	0
Your My Prize	2	C	1	0	0	0	312
Your Over	4	F	6	0	1	3	6,813
Your Private Stash	3	G	7	1	0	0	13,137
Your Regal	8	M	6	1	0	2	15,305
Your Selection	4	F	8	1	0	0	7,456
Your Welcome	5	G	5	0	1	0	5,082
Your Wiggle	6	M	1	0	0	0	125
You're a Funny Guy	4	C	9	1	2	1	8,845
You're a Monkey	3	F	6	0	2	1	9,674
You're Darn Tootin	4	G	12	2	5	3	45,143
You're Faded	4	F	5	1	0	0	4,230
You're In	4	C	2	0	0	0	0
You're Mine Now	3	G	1	0	0	0	125
You're So Lucky	5	M	8	2	0	1	8,108
You're Such a Deee	5	M	1	0	0	1	960
You're Up	3	F	2	0	1	0	9,080
Yourebarnormine	2	F	5	1	0	1	19,900
You'redusty	5	G	11	5	3	0	32,335
You'remakinmecrazy	3	G	2	1	0	0	13,237
Yourfinalanswer	5	M	11	2	1	2	49,070
Yourgonnagogirl	3	F	2	0	0	0	74
Yours At Six	3	F	3	0	1	0	6,620
Yours Forever	4	G	11	2	1	0	10,892
Yours Onli	3	C	4	1	1	0	8,600
Yoursmineours	3	F	7	3	1	2	111,000
Yoursormine	2	G	5	0	1	1	5,450
Yourspot	6	G	2	1	0	0	985
Yourstocommand	4	G	9	0	2	1	26,425
Yourway Highway	3	F	6	1	0	2	18,200
Youthful Comment	3	C	1	0	1	0	4,340
You've Got It	3	G	3	0	1	1	3,720
Youvegotmeflying	6	H	4	1	1	0	1,739
Youwantapieceame	4	G	9	0	0	2	7,109
Youwantmetowhat	2	F	1	0	0	0	412
Youwillaire	4	F	5	0	0	0	1,040
Yoyo Jabo	5	G	13	2	2	4	58,978
Yozo	4	G	8	1	0	0	16,530
Ys	5	G	1	0	0	0	0
Yu Gold	4	F	6	3	0	1	22,545
Yucca Road	7	H	1	0	0	0	141
Yucon Go	3	G	7	2	1	0	16,555
Yudothethingsudo	2	F	5	0	0	0	400
Yuge	5	G	1	0	0	0	0
Yuki No Princess	6	M	5	0	0	0	3,718
Yukon Charley	6	G	11	2	2	1	9,046
Yukon Fame	3	G	2	0	0	0	425
Yukon Loot	4	G	4	0	0	0	186
Yukon Mac	7	G	7	0	0	1	590
Yukon Strike	8	G	2	0	1	0	1,640
Yukon Tour	4	G	10	1	0	2	10,404
Yukon Wheat	2	F	6	0	0	1	2,960
Yukon's Angel	4	F	4	1	0	0	6,952
Yukon's Gambler	2	C	5	1	1	1	24,960
Yukon's Sugar	8	M	3	0	0	0	160
Yulans Gold	2	C	3	0	2	1	4,324
Yule Be Blue	6	G	9	1	0	1	5,467
Yulitemyfyr	5	M	9	1	0	1	4,050
Yuma Man	3	G	6	1	1	0	5,555
Yumeko	5	M	8	3	1	0	30,450
Yummy	4	F	5	0	0	0	326
Yummy Yummy	3	F	10	4	3	0	40,560
Yupslittlebuck	4	C	4	0	0	1	240
Yur Regressing	5	M	9	1	2	1	6,261
Yuriquest	4	G	6	1	1	0	8,385
Yvonne County	3	F	3	1	0	0	4,735
Yvonne Goes On	5	M	8	0	2	1	7,306
Yvonnevich	2	F	3	0	0	0	0
Yyyyes	3	F	10	0	1	0	7,289
Yzerman	3	G	16	3	2	1	18,615
Z Account	4	C	5	1	0	0	3,000
Z B's Carson City	5	G	15	1	0	0	5,434
Z Cliffnotez	2	F	4	0	0	0	4,620
Z Cool	7	G	9	2	0	0	6,711
Z Country	2	F	7	1	0	3	15,794
Z Crafty One	2	G	4	0	0	0	0
Z Cute One Two	4	F	4	0	0	0	1,056
Z Golden Boy	3	G	1	0	0	0	0
Z Halo's Secret	4	C	9	0	0	0	0
Z Man	7	G	6	0	0	0	240
Z Mariachi	4	C	3	0	0	0	183
Z Me Zipp	4	F	17	0	3	1	13,870
Z Minion	5	G	1	0	0	0	85
Z Regent's Secret	3	F	6	0	0	1	450
Z Roadster	2	C	1	0	0	0	840
Z Saint	2	F	1	0	0	0	140
Z Silver Cat	7	M	3	0	0	0	855
Z Storm	2	G	7	1	2	2	39,220
Z Trick Pilot	2	C	5	2	0	1	7,685
Z Woodman Princess	3	F	2	0	0	0	200
Z Z Haze	5	H	2	0	1	0	1,500
Z Z Jaber Jaws	4	F	11	0	0	1	2,175
Z Z Peacock	4	F	7	2	0	0	5,164
Z Z's Destiny	4	C	3	0	0	0	465
Z Z's Fantasy	4	G	15	3	1	2	14,175
Za Zoomer	3	G	2	0	0	0	205
Zaamwithattitude	3	C	12	1	1	3	10,825
Zabib	3	C	7	0	1	2	7,630
Zaby	4	G	5	1	0	0	10,250
Zaca	6	M	1	0	0	0	0
Zach Slim and Eddy	3	G	15	2	2	2	40,444
Zacharias	4	C	7	1	1	1	4,024
Zacharov	10	G	10	0	4	2	22,615
Zachary's Boy	6	G	1	0	0	0	0
Zachfiftyfour	6	G	6	0	0	0	510
Zachmiester	3	G	6	0	1	0	1,530
Zach's Contender	4	G	14	0	1	0	2,723
Zachs World	5	M	7	0	2	1	12,069
Zack Attack	3	G	4	0	2	0	12,000
Zack in the Box	3	G	8	0	0	0	480
Zackary's Verbatim	3	G	1	1	0	0	5,775
Zackdar	3	G	7	1	2	0	6,791
Zadar	6	G	9	6	0	0	46,333

Horse	Age	Sex	Sts	1st	2d	3d	Won
Zafonic's Song (FR)	7	H	8	1	0	1	13,048
Zafrika	3	C	6	0	0	1	969
Zagor's Deco Due	9	G	7	0	0	0	294
Zagor's Genie	5	M	4	0	0	0	611
Zagor's Sierra	4	G	13	0	0	1	4,575
Zagor's Walter's H	6	M	3	0	0	0	210
Zagor's War	4	G	11	1	0	0	10,200
Zagros	5	G	15	2	3	2	8,274
Zahalee Red	3	G	11	2	1	1	29,564
Zahdeal (NZ)	6	G	6	0	0	0	4,300
Zahira	2	F	2	0	0	0	840
Zain Lass	2	F	3	0	2	0	25,260
Zaire	3	C	6	2	2	1	31,656
Zairsaplan	4	F	9	2	1	1	19,976
Zakocity	3	C	14	3	3	3	240,967
Zak's Precocious	3	F	4	1	1	1	24,550
Zakster	4	G	2	1	0	0	2,589
Zalema	4	C	6	0	0	0	1,066
Zales Champagne	5	M	6	0	1	0	2,540
Zal's Pal	3	G	11	1	1	5	24,385
Zam Lady	4	F	8	0	0	0	1,610
Zam Zam	4	F	5	1	1	2	29,440
Zam Zama	3	F	2	0	0	0	280
Zamanda	5	M	9	1	2	0	24,595
Zamaroo	4	G	11	2	0	2	32,016
Zamboon	3	F	14	1	1	1	7,028
Zamdam	2	C	1	0	0	0	430
Zamek	7	G	5	0	0	0	344
Zamera	2	F	2	0	0	0	800
Zamina Gold	2	F	6	1	0	0	12,175
Zaminblue	2	F	3	1	0	0	12,840
Zamnation	2	C	3	0	1	0	6,440
Zamrite	2	C	1	0	0	1	2,860
Zanacator	3	G	10	0	1	0	1,780
Zanakar (FR)	5	G	2	0	0	0	470
Zanda's Bonus	3	G	10	3	3	0	44,125
Zanderman	3	G	3	0	0	0	480
Zane's Way	6	G	1	0	0	0	40
Zanny's Dancer	7	M	2	0	0	0	130
Zans Halo	2	G	2	0	0	0	0
Zanshin	5	G	4	2	2	0	12,694
Zantango	3	F	12	2	4	1	20,851
Zantanon	4	G	2	0	0	0	660
Zany Baby	9	M	7	0	0	2	1,618
Zany Northwestern	3	C	12	1	2	0	12,250
Zanzara	2	F	1	0	0	0	0
Zanziyan	2	G	1	0	0	0	400
Zapped in Time	6	G	2	0	1	0	1,488
Zar Nicolas	7	G	4	0	1	0	2,310
Zarba the Great	2	F	2	0	1	0	5,405
Zarbalina	2	F	5	1	1	0	11,020
Zarb's Crystal	7	G	1	0	0	0	0
Zarb's Cutie	4	F	14	1	2	2	14,327
Zarb's Dahar	4	G	11	7	0	1	157,835
Zarb's Destiny	3	F	6	0	0	0	1,418
Zarb's Dreamer	3	C	4	0	0	0	7,500
Zarb's Echo	9	G	7	0	1	1	6,932
Zarb's Gunner	2	C	7	1	2	0	29,830
Zarb's Hoedown	3	G	11	0	2	3	12,215
Zarb's Love	6	M	3	0	0	0	705
Zarb's Luck	7	G	7	2	2	0	106,715
Zarb's Lucky Charm	7	G	6	0	0	0	0
Zarb's Miss Belle	5	M	15	2	4	1	31,081
Zarb's Miss Cutie	3	F	10	2	2	5	44,945
Zarb's Music	4	G	7	0	1	0	7,908
Zarb's Music Man	2	C	7	1	1	3	36,615
Zarb's Pet	8	G	6	1	0	0	6,900
Zarb's Rose	2	F	2	0	0	0	750
Zarbsflight	7	M	7	0	0	1	1,947
Zarbysteppes	8	M	2	0	0	0	0
Zardoz (CHI)	7	H	7	0	1	1	8,398
Zarpa	6	G	4	0	0	0	749
Zarpen	3	F	9	1	0	1	15,910
Zarro	4	G	9	0	2	1	19,251
Zartax	2	C	1	0	0	0	0
Zat Darn Cat	5	M	1	0	1	0	8,600
Zatara	3	G	3	1	0	2	17,400
Zata's Secret	4	G	1	0	0	0	0
Zats It	2	C	3	1	0	1	18,540
Zattera	3	C	2	0	0	0	480
Zatz Right	2	F	1	0	0	1	1,355
Zavalla Dandy	7	G	13	2	2	3	72,296
Zawaaya	2	F	2	0	0	0	184
Zawzooth	5	M	6	1	0	2	67,560
Zaya (GB)	9	G	6	2	0	0	10,194
Zayed	4	G	5	0	1	2	26,400
Zayla's Fire	5	M	7	0	0	1	1,002
Zazen	2	F	1	0	0	0	105
Zcat Lady	4	F	13	1	0	1	10,266
Zdravo	5	M	6	0	0	0	675
Ze Fact	7	G	11	4	2	0	61,662
Zeal It Witha Kiss	4	G	4	0	0	0	317
Zeal Power	6	G	15	2	6	1	18,556
Zealette	2	F	10	0	2	1	7,577
Zealian	6	G	16	4	1	4	30,310
Zealous Baby	4	F	18	1	0	3	9,014
Zealous Capote	3	C	15	3	1	2	26,156
Zealous Flite	6	G	7	0	2	1	1,686
Zealous Jake	3	G	9	1	0	0	7,947
Zealous Kate	10	M	4	1	0	0	3,969
Zealous Prince	2	C	2	0	0	1	2,464
Zealous Runner	2	F	1	0	0	0	100
Zeal's Score	3	F	4	0	0	0	630
Zeal's Spirit	2	G	8	0	0	2	3,644
Zeal's Star	3	G	7	0	1	0	1,624
Zebadiah Eagle	9	G	4	0	0	0	1,016
Zebecca	5	M	3	0	0	0	120
Zebedee	5	G	6	0	0	1	550
Zebra	4	C	10	1	0	0	4,554
Zebulun	3	G	4	0	0	0	0
Zecho	3	G	1	0	0	0	0
Zede's Copy	3	G	1	0	0	0	0
Zede's Idle	3	F	7	0	2	0	9,108
Zee Best	5	M	10	2	3	1	18,403
Zee Bull	3	G	1	0	1	0	1,600
Zee Chalupa	7	H	12	4	2	4	7,724
Zee Fox	5	G	9	1	0	0	7,208
Zee Lady's Man	3	C	5	0	0	0	180
Zee Oh Six	5	G	10	2	4	0	91,940
Zee Topper	4	F	6	0	0	0	2,280
Zeeba Lily	4	F	2	0	0	0	162
Zeeflaco	4	G	8	1	0	3	10,461
Zeena	3	F	7	1	2	1	30,430
Zeepass	3	G	10	0	2	1	9,554
Zee's Top Ruler	6	H	1	0	0	0	0
Zeetop	2	C	3	0	0	0	1,400
Zeeville	3	G	10	2	0	3	8,539
Zeewitch	3	F	11	0	2	1	7,545
Zeferino	2	G	8	0	0	0	690
Zeffirelli	3	C	3	0	0	0	0
Zelig	3	C	5	1	0	0	9,364
Zellalou	2	F	3	0	0	1	3,355
Zellie	4	F	12	2	1	2	25,229
Zelna J	4	F	15	3	3	5	91,230
Zelo	3	F	13	2	3	1	30,559
Zeloma	4	F	8	0	1	0	2,899
Zen Diva	5	M	13	2	3	2	60,881
Zen Me a Runner	5	G	2	0	0	0	82
Zenaida'svalentine	3	F	11	3	2	1	21,158
Zencredable	7	G	5	0	0	3	2,799
Zend Gold	4	F	5	1	1	1	12,894
Zenia Zeal	5	M	17	0	2	1	4,021
Zen's a Zooming	4	G	17	1	0	0	5,506
Zen's Secret	4	C	3	1	0	0	3,202
Zen's Silverbuck	6	G	7	1	0	0	7,230
Zeph's Future	4	F	8	0	0	3	6,750
Zephyr's Boy	3	C	1	0	0	0	300
Zeppo	3	G	7	1	1	2	13,770
Zequilla	4	F	3	0	0	0	0
Zeria	2	F	1	0	0	0	420
Zero Absolute	3	G	7	0	0	0	728
Zero Call	2	C	2	1	0	0	21,600

Horse	Age	Sex	Sts	1st	2d	3d	Won
Zero Degrees	4	C	20	4	1	4	21,060
Zero Financing	3	G	9	2	0	1	16,784
Zero In	5	G	13	0	1	0	8,108
Zero U	4	G	6	1	1	0	7,790
Zeros Lad	3	G	4	0	0	0	111
Zerotosixty	4	C	2	0	0	0	0
Zes Tee	3	F	7	2	2	0	21,427
Zesty Diablo	6	G	18	0	1	1	5,044
Zesty Two Step	3	F	1	0	0	0	0
Zetetic	2	C	1	0	0	0	132
Zeuqram Li'l Devil	3	G	8	0	0	2	3,791
Zeuqram's Boo Boo	4	G	4	0	0	2	4,234
Zeuqram's Dondi	7	G	9	0	1	5	8,441
Zeuqram'smichael L	8	G	6	0	0	1	962
Zevon	3	G	6	1	0	0	32,900
Zi Night	3	F	4	1	0	1	28,840
Ziada	5	M	2	0	0	0	385
Ziasquatrosocks	4	F	2	0	0	0	172
Zibeline	2	F	1	0	0	0	50
Zig a Little	7	G	12	1	0	0	5,870
Zig Zag Leigh	3	F	2	0	0	0	0
Zigeuner	5	G	16	2	0	3	12,366
Zigfire	7	H	13	0	1	4	3,224
Ziggedy Bop	3	F	1	0	0	0	75
Ziggie	6	G	8	0	0	0	669
Ziggy Zaggy	4	G	16	3	1	5	48,048
Ziggy's April Fool	3	F	12	0	2	0	3,260
Ziggy's Haylo	5	G	8	3	2	1	15,688
Zignor	5	M	8	2	1	1	29,400
Zig's Quiet Lady	6	M	11	0	3	2	10,630
Zigzag Dancer	7	G	7	1	0	2	3,588
Zikos	3	G	5	0	0	2	4,080
Zilia	4	F	16	2	3	3	28,342
Zill Bear's Secret	2	F	3	1	0	0	7,725
Zillabreeze	4	F	12	4	0	0	23,769
Zimmerman	2	F	1	0	0	0	230
Zimmz Jet	3	G	4	0	1	1	4,062
Zim's Blur	3	F	4	1	1	1	5,470
Zina Cause	4	G	6	1	1	1	16,099
Zinash	6	G	1	0	0	0	642
Zindo	3	G	7	1	0	0	9,630
Zinga Deebleuz	4	F	4	0	0	2	1,736
Zinga Zing	3	F	1	0	0	0	135
Zinger Man	3	G	2	0	0	0	972
Zing's Info	2	F	4	0	0	0	2,140
Zinzee	4	F	13	2	3	1	22,045
Zip by Zak	9	G	9	1	1	0	8,935
Zip Gun	4	C	18	1	1	3	27,561
Zip N Buster	5	G	7	1	0	0	3,128
Zip N Go	4	C	9	1	1	2	20,290
Zip N Scoot	6	G	3	0	0	0	0
Zip the Bright	5	G	8	0	3	2	20,579
Zip to Moscow	3	C	2	0	0	0	0
Zip Zip Boom	3	F	11	2	4	1	30,505
Zipcody	3	G	10	1	2	1	36,215
Zipitup	2	G	3	0	0	0	510
Zipledo	7	G	1	0	0	0	0
Zipolator	8	G	10	1	0	0	4,545
Zipper Zipper De	3	C	4	1	1	0	21,540
Zipperfoot	6	M	9	1	0	0	3,654
Zipper's Down	5	M	7	0	2	1	3,297
Zippersnslippers	3	G	12	1	0	2	10,290
Zippin	5	M	1	0	0	0	0
Zippin Zane	4	G	17	4	7	1	11,901
Zippitydoodaaa	5	M	5	0	0	0	0
Zipporah	4	F	13	0	2	2	12,142
Zippy Chippy	13	G	2	0	0	0	300
Zippy Intrigue	8	G	13	0	0	0	918
Zippy Zak	2	G	2	0	0	0	0
Zipz	3	G	1	0	0	0	135
Zirconium	3	F	6	1	1	1	12,980
Zitlaly	3	F	15	2	4	2	87,912
Zitty	3	F	3	0	0	0	0
Zizook	2	F	1	0	0	0	0
Zlatka (PER)	4	F	4	0	0	1	891
Zloty	6	G	1	0	0	0	250
Zmoneygirl	5	M	5	0	0	0	420
Zodiamond	3	C	4	0	0	0	939
Zodiaque	7	M	5	2	1	0	16,660
Zoe in Red	4	F	7	0	1	0	2,165
Zoe Roe	3	G	10	0	2	2	10,555
Zoe's Ability	3	F	2	0	0	0	378
Zoe's Trick	4	F	10	2	0	1	14,965
Zoezeebear	4	F	9	1	0	0	3,709
Zoffinger	4	C	8	2	1	2	79,240
Zolinda	3	G	7	0	0	1	1,017
Zolishka	7	M	15	1	2	4	17,330
Zona De Impacto (CHI)	5	G	5	0	1	1	14,760
Zona Libre	2	C	1	0	0	0	0
Zone Blue	3	C	9	0	0	0	300
Zone Defense	4	G	6	0	0	0	242
Zone It	3	G	9	0	0	3	2,986
Zone Stopper	2	C	7	1	0	2	20,350
Zonely Money	4	C	9	1	1	0	7,230
Zoney	2	F	2	0	0	1	1,910
Zoning (GB)	7	H	3	2	0	1	33,360
Zoof	3	F	2	0	0	0	610
Zoolu Nights	4	G	12	2	1	3	39,520
Zoom in Jane	3	F	5	1	0	1	6,185
Zoom Zoom Meri	4	F	3	0	0	0	434
Zoom Zoom Rocket	3	F	1	0	0	0	0
Zoomzoomboom	3	C	2	0	0	0	1,090
Zoot	4	G	13	1	1	1	9,100
Zoot Scootin Hurli	5	M	2	0	0	0	0
Zora's Vijay	4	G	8	0	0	1	3,115
Zorba	3	C	4	0	0	0	720
Zores	5	H	13	0	3	2	20,331
Zorka	3	F	8	0	1	1	4,448
Zoro M I	2	C	1	0	0	0	55
Zoroastro	2	C	4	0	2	0	2,440
Zorro Del Sol	2	C	1	0	0	0	0
Zorubabel	7	G	12	0	0	3	1,730
Zosia's Genius	3	F	4	0	0	1	5,412
Zowie	4	G	4	0	0	0	618
Zowie Strikes	3	F	1	0	0	0	80
Z's Galore	2	C	1	0	0	0	65
Z's Snappy Miss	2	F	6	1	1	0	13,898
Z's Star	6	M	3	1	0	0	13,716
Zsats Victory	2	F	6	0	0	0	1,272
Ztag Uzauruz	3	C	1	0	1	0	1,720
Zubia	2	G	1	0	0	0	70
Zukinikiki	4	F	9	1	4	1	72,460
Zula Bay	4	C	3	0	0	0	90
Zulu	5	H	3	1	0	0	3,786
Zulu Bag	4	G	2	0	0	0	0
Zulu Dancer	2	G	1	0	0	0	412
Zulu Lulu	4	F	12	0	0	5	6,357
Zulu Secrets	2	F	6	1	0	0	8,045
Zumbafizz	3	C	16	2	1	5	22,345
Zumbi	8	G	14	0	1	1	3,086
Zumi	2	G	2	1	0	0	9,676
Zuni Gold	3	G	11	1	2	1	36,410
Zuper	9	H	1	0	0	0	0
Zuppar Mistress	4	F	1	0	0	0	0
Zuppardon Bleu	5	H	3	0	0	0	1,215
Zuppardo's Doll	3	F	2	0	0	0	0
Zuppardo's Word	2	F	2	0	0	0	0
Zur Guten	8	G	14	0	4	0	4,557
Zurich (IRE)	2	C	4	0	3	0	22,213
Zuryev	8	G	2	0	1	0	1,536
Zuzax	5	H	8	0	0	1	1,649
Zydeco Affair	4	G	1	0	0	1	3,960
Zydeco Blue	6	G	12	0	0	2	1,886
Zynastry	6	G	20	1	5	2	22,682
Zyphyr Cove	3	G	12	4	1	2	13,705
Zz Open	5	G	12	0	2	1	4,663

2004

Records of Trainers

The record of each trainer, who raced thoroughbreds in the United States and Canada during 2004, appears in this section, showing the number of starts, firsts, seconds and thirds, and the total purses earned by these horses.

RECORDS OF TRAINERS

Trainer	Sts	1st	2d	3d	Purses
Abbott, Frank	21	3	2	2	24,180
Abbruzzese, Eugenio	40	5	5	7	107,055
Abell, Joseph E.	80	4	10	7	71,740
Abels, Jason	23	0	2	3	7,366
Abernathy, Charles J.	10	2	1	1	19,247
Abraham, Tim	8	1	2	0	2,361
Abrahamson, Randy	19	1	6	5	5,512
Abrams, Barry	253	22	33	44	1,037,140
Abrams, Ronald B.	88	5	9	12	102,805
Abshire, Lonnie J.	2	0	0	0	0
Accardi, John	65	7	7	10	77,319
Achord, Clint E.	6	0	0	1	442
Ackel, Don	14	1	1	6	22,364
Ackerman, D. Kelly	97	20	16	10	217,781
Ackerman, Thomas M.	8	1	0	0	3,342
Acorn, Danny J.	24	2	3	1	30,553
Acosta, Charles	31	4	7	0	9,659
Acosta, Robert	8	1	1	0	2,083
Acquilano, James S.	256	41	37	34	430,421
Acres, Harold	5	0	0	0	507
Acuna, Louisa	41	2	2	2	19,460
Adair, George H.	2	0	0	0	0
Adamo, Anthony	351	56	41	37	1,073,430
Adams, Billy E.	88	9	14	21	115,415
Adams, David	4	0	0	0	184
Adams, Douglas S.	59	3	5	7	16,781
Adams, Harlan C.	7	0	3	0	2,440
Adams, John B.	17	0	0	1	4,536
Adams, Krystal	2	0	0	0	247
Adams, Lynn A.	39	2	0	6	15,022
Adams, Michael T.	10	0	4	0	8,804
Adams, Norman	17	4	3	2	9,228
Adams, Robert J.	14	4	1	3	40,726
Adams, Jr., John S.	45	2	3	5	78,462
Agilar, Anthony	132	16	12	24	198,067
Agosti, Thomas M.	371	71	74	43	844,762
Agrinsoni, Jose F.	63	6	4	8	60,164
Aguayo, Ramon Davilla	11	1	0	0	10,400
Aguayo, Vernon E.	39	0	5	2	27,182
Aguilar, Joe	3	0	0	0	114
Aguilar, Rodolfo	18	1	2	1	14,484
Aguilar, Rosario	70	5	10	12	84,461
Aguillard, Joseph Stanley	1	0	0	0	1,215
Aguirre, Anthony	121	13	14	23	330,500
Aguirre, Horacio	12	2	0	1	29,460
Aguirre, Juan Raul	36	4	6	2	33,594
Aguirre, Paul G.	159	29	22	28	1,532,835
Aguirre, Rey	34	5	5	2	95,385
Ahalt, Ronald S.	51	4	1	6	55,153
Aitchison, Lisa M.	58	7	6	5	88,395
Aiton, Levi	4	0	1	1	766
Aker, Tracie	27	1	6	5	8,361
Aker, Wiley	74	10	13	20	28,090
Akers, Stacey	10	0	1	2	2,320
Akers, Theresa	50	2	2	3	27,809
Akin, Steven R.	23	3	2	4	38,325
Albers, Dick	37	2	2	6	11,773
Albert, Linda L.	137	29	24	14	556,685
Albert III, Talbot J.	21	0	2	1	20,930
Albert IV, Talbot J.	12	0	0	2	7,560
Albertrani, Louis	48	2	5	5	101,792
Albertrani, Thomas	65	11	13	7	1,046,365
Alberts, Nancy H.	33	5	9	5	83,235
Albright, Amy	95	26	20	9	582,372
Albright, Dona M.	108	13	14	14	104,842
Albright, George R.	178	18	21	18	186,521
Albright, Raquel	8	1	0	0	3,602
Albright, Robert	53	6	8	7	48,075
Albright, Ruthann	6	0	2	2	4,396
Albu, Ken	128	18	11	16	207,522
Albulov, Jr., James M.	18	3	3	2	17,810
Alcala, Jorge L.	11	0	0	1	4,270
Alcock, Graham J.	1	0	0	0	0
Alcoser, Jr., Erasmo C.	2	0	0	0	0
Alcoverde, Ernesto	18	4	1	2	4,946
Aldavaz, Hermengildo G.	13	0	1	1	3,456
Aldavaz, Jaime	1	0	1	0	800
Alder, Zane G.	17	2	2	4	5,620
Alderman, Emery	12	2	3	4	9,848
Alderson, Anthony J.	48	5	5	8	48,466
Alderson, Ian	38	3	4	4	45,426
Alecci, John V.	145	42	18	18	821,203
Alejandre, Humberto	2	0	0	0	158
Alek, Joann M.	2	0	0	0	280
Aleman, Juan G.	50	4	12	8	42,747
Alessandrini, Donna	1	0	0	0	63
Alexander, Bruce F.	132	37	25	16	959,631
Alexander, Frank A.	141	16	16	21	684,839
Alexander, Henrietta	3	0	0	0	619
Alexander, L. C.	10	0	0	0	246
Alexander, Lauressa	65	16	12	13	192,420
Alexander, Peter B.	43	3	3	5	110,600
Alfano, Ronald A.	46	14	4	5	157,440
Alfir, David Jeff	48	5	5	7	58,372
Alfonso, Adolfo	21	6	3	3	95,050
Alford, Claudie M.	43	0	1	1	9,155
Alford, Troy	3	0	0	0	181
Alfstad, Allene D.	31	2	2	5	91,072
Ali, Alnaz	91	2	5	7	65,075
Ali, Andrew	4	0	0	0	0
Alire, Aniceto Mike	10	3	1	2	22,904
Allaby, Kim	8	0	0	1	2,048
Allain, Emile M.	34	0	5	5	89,710
Allard, Edward T.	348	86	51	40	1,596,655
Alleman, Joseph	15	0	1	4	13,481
Allen, Billy D.	19	0	0	1	5,895
Allen, Caroline G.	49	1	0	5	9,883
Allen, Carroll Joe	2	0	0	0	198
Allen, Daniel	25	5	4	0	90,600
Allen, Jack L.	93	7	12	12	105,166
Allen, Jeffery S.	109	6	11	14	157,479
Allen, Johnny	50	4	1	4	19,115
Allen, Mickey	3	0	0	0	325
Allen, Randy	474	44	52	44	752,782
Allen, Robert	22	1	2	2	6,953
Allen, Terry	4	1	0	0	6,355
Allen, Thomas	6	0	0	0	1,800
Allen, Truman	45	3	4	4	32,513
Allen III, A. Ferris	553	78	98	73	1,507,701
Allen, Sr., Ronald D.	314	69	44	47	756,125
Allery, Dave	8	0	3	0	1,595
Alley, Jess S.	56	8	5	12	179,177
Allinson, Vernon J.	16	3	3	4	58,280
Allison, Melinda	36	5	1	6	35,665
Allison, Norman E.	33	4	3	2	49,016
Allred, Alexa	22	1	0	2	9,463
Alonso, Enrique	215	30	26	26	688,020
Alonzo, Howard	71	18	12	5	378,753
Alonzo, Isidoro	5	0	1	0	638
Alpers, Jr., Curtis L.	14	1	2	1	18,907
Altemeier, Mark	4	0	0	0	1,493
Alter, Happy	82	5	9	11	169,225
Altieri, Lillian	25	5	1	9	182,566
Alvarado, Felimon	30	8	7	1	164,351
Alvarado, Jose L.	37	8	4	7	105,724
Alvarado, Juan	19	0	1	0	4,310
Alvey, Darrell E.	133	10	20	20	63,539
Ambrogi, Leo J.	21	2	4	2	27,128
Ambrosia, Joseph E.	62	4	6	6	78,295
Amescua, Rene	205	39	29	41	503,560
Amico, Lori	31	3	1	3	22,858
Amico, Vincent	87	13	8	17	101,153
Amodie, Tracy	72	6	2	8	60,275
Amonte, Andrew	19	1	0	3	18,145
Amonte, Jr., Frank A.	1	0	0	0	0
Amonte, Sr., Frank A.	9	0	1	0	1,426
Amoss, Thomas M.	484	140	88	68	3,616,785
Amparan, Alberto	24	1	2	1	10,228
Amshoff, Steven L.	183	17	19	26	200,768
Amthor, K. Gordon	11	0	1	2	10,283
Amundson, Jack	2	0	0	0	135
Amundson, Kelli	33	2	6	1	30,230

Trainer	Sts	1st	2d	3d	Purses
Ananas, Edwin	39	3	6	9	13,832
Andelmo, Joseph J.	40	2	3	2	27,648
Andenaes, Christine	1	0	0	1	850
Andersen, Ralph W.	51	11	5	9	98,030
Andersen, Ron L.	32	1	2	0	10,029
Anderson, Bill R.	22	1	3	4	14,335
Anderson, Bruce D.	283	42	43	48	434,313
Anderson, Bruce L.	23	4	4	2	71,785
Anderson, Bryce C.	10	1	0	0	3,157
Anderson, Carl Norman	122	16	13	16	185,595
Anderson, Carmela	13	0	0	2	4,677
Anderson, David C.	395	94	61	48	481,940
Anderson, Dawna Z.	66	4	8	11	51,560
Anderson, Dee	20	2	1	0	16,401
Anderson, Don L.	53	1	3	0	13,803
Anderson, Donald A.	11	0	3	1	4,168
Anderson, Doug L.	54	14	5	8	197,260
Anderson, Erin Lee	68	7	5	8	48,275
Anderson, Frank L.	16	1	0	2	16,700
Anderson, Gary L.	42	1	4	4	8,162
Anderson, George D.	35	5	4	5	58,580
Anderson, J. D.	14	2	1	1	11,467
Anderson, James E.	79	10	10	11	83,178
Anderson, Jann P.	43	7	6	8	133,615
Anderson, John E.	101	10	17	17	274,549
Anderson, Keith	15	2	4	2	10,043
Anderson, Kenneth Ellis	1	0	0	0	0
Anderson, Kenton	71	3	3	12	53,445
Anderson, Leonard	18	3	2	1	22,791
Anderson, Lucian H.	11	0	2	1	4,350
Anderson, Pete D.	9	0	0	5	13,640
Anderson, Rex C.	43	9	11	9	20,175
Anderson, Robert J.	96	15	18	15	420,886
Anderson, Rodney	16	1	1	2	11,796
Anderson, Roger J.	113	8	8	10	87,101
Anderson, Rosann M.	19	2	2	3	28,179
Anderson, Susan L.	59	7	11	4	55,357
Anderson, Suzanne A.	43	2	1	3	25,506
Anderson, Tim L.	48	4	1	3	29,790
Anderson, Wendy	71	15	9	8	87,805
Anderson, William D.	85	13	10	9	252,397
Anderson-Smith, Karen	13	2	3	1	22,568
Andrade, Pablo	120	25	11	10	322,886
Andreadakis, Georgia D.	1	0	0	0	510
Andreasen, Gillian	43	0	3	4	28,670
Andrews, Tom	72	5	8	6	50,770
Andros, Patricia	2	1	0	0	7,530
Andrus, Susan	4	0	0	1	2,203
Andry, Doug	18	0	4	3	10,220
Angelle, Brent	5	0	0	1	975
Angelle, Christopher	31	0	2	4	13,191
Angelle, Dale	372	90	66	45	1,180,918
Angelle, Grover J.	20	0	0	0	360
Angelle, James R.	149	12	15	17	170,587
Angelle, Joseph D.	157	7	5	14	82,873
Angelle, Keith J.	36	1	3	3	20,186
Angelle, Rene D.	23	4	2	3	62,867
Angelopoulos, George K.	15	1	4	1	18,710
Angevine, Pamela J.	100	11	17	12	162,072
Anglin, L. D.	54	1	1	1	9,760
Anguiano, Felipe O.	7	0	0	0	332
Angulo, Jose Luis	8	1	0	1	12,105
Anonychuk, Lawrence	22	2	4	2	22,790
Ansell, Laurie	15	0	2	1	2,093
Anson, Peggie	73	4	2	8	29,756
Anter, George	5	0	0	0	173
Anthony, Priscilla J.	3	0	0	1	1,485
Anthony, Sr., Alton	14	0	0	2	3,208
Anton, William	85	3	9	4	54,396
Antonuik, Jerry	28	1	3	4	21,226
Antrim, Arthur M.	21	3	1	3	80,390
Antus, Lawrence	31	0	0	0	3,051
Antwine, Michael	45	6	6	2	53,528
Anuario, Thomas A.	27	2	4	3	89,745
Applebee, David	7	0	0	0	2,777
Applegate, Elbert	31	3	2	3	6,868
Applegate, Kevin	6	0	1	2	3,865
Aquilino, Joseph	158	21	16	20	682,971
Aquino, Angela M.	58	9	10	11	56,946
Araiza, Albert P.	56	6	7	8	91,418
Araiza, Arnulfo	12	2	1	1	7,650
Araya, Rene A.	12	1	0	0	17,655
Arboleda, Arturo	38	0	9	5	20,369
Arcaro, Louis	35	4	2	2	17,109
Arceneaux, George	2	0	0	0	0
Arceneaux, Victor	153	28	21	13	419,478
Arceneaux, Jr., Edward	6	0	1	0	1,000
Arceo, Cresencio	24	3	4	6	7,337
Ardoin, Ronald	11	1	2	4	17,420
Arens, John T.	44	1	6	2	22,660
Ares, Paul S.	1	0	0	1	2,750
Argyle, Bert H.	3	1	0	0	2,472
Arias, Juan D.	22	1	1	3	16,100
Aristone, Philip T.	458	63	64	48	750,442
Armata, Ross	280	46	38	32	1,094,862
Armata, Vito	223	42	22	29	1,285,037
Armata, Jr., Ross	108	15	15	15	527,165
Armor, Randy	10	1	0	0	2,415
Armstrong, Barbara L.	8	0	1	0	4,592
Armstrong, Bryan R.	106	14	9	7	95,841
Armstrong, Busanda C.	6	1	0	1	15,000
Armstrong, C. Robert	1	0	0	0	0
Armstrong, Horace W.	5	0	0	1	1,435
Armstrong, Janet	53	15	8	10	290,024
Armstrong, Johnny G.	6	0	0	0	370
Armstrong, Shawnee	7	1	1	0	12,825
Armstrong, Sherry	8	1	1	0	4,250
Armstrong, Tim H.	18	1	0	1	3,915
Armstrong, Zachary	105	18	15	14	147,647
Arndt, Theodore	29	4	2	2	43,376
Arnett, Bob E.	140	10	11	17	119,509
Arnett, James G.	106	14	11	17	305,566
Arnett, Jon G.	380	61	62	42	583,562
Arnold, Allen	23	1	1	2	8,585
Arnold, Bart D.	2	0	0	0	0
Arnold, John S.	13	0	1	1	5,848
Arnold, Pamela A.	182	19	21	19	224,290
Arnold, Rise	6	1	1	0	5,556
Arnold, II, George R.	189	24	25	28	1,270,678
Arnold, Jr., Ralph E.	78	8	9	5	96,525
Arnold, Jr., Richard P.	142	9	15	16	111,295
Arnold, Sr., George R.	45	5	2	4	26,730
Arnouville, James C.	17	0	2	3	13,026
Aro, Charles	2	1	0	0	3,720
Aro, Michael Charles	162	15	28	19	213,906
Arpokia, Skip	4	0	0	1	618
Arrigo, Dan W.	7	1	0	0	7,470
Arriola, Thomas	17	1	0	1	7,431
Arterburn, Lonnie	65	9	9	10	329,117
Arthur, Floyd M.	101	27	8	14	365,521
Arthur, Lyle	20	4	2	2	10,078
Artis, Clony	3	0	0	1	1,540
Artwohl, Shirley	1	0	0	0	0
Artz, Deborrah J.	159	13	20	22	169,264
Arzola, Luis D.	107	7	7	14	91,424
Asbury, David W.	221	13	20	13	120,192
Asbury, Lonnie	6	0	2	0	3,548
Ashabraner, Billy G.	21	3	5	0	38,717
Ashauer, Norman	73	6	6	7	91,450
Ashbaugh, Richard E.	20	0	0	2	3,647
Ashby, Lynn A.	14	1	2	2	25,374
Asher, Kenneth E.	31	0	1	3	6,036
Asher, Paul	5	0	1	0	1,040
Ashford, Jr., H. Ray	177	36	27	24	577,518
Ashford, Sr., H. Ray	27	3	6	6	46,538
Ashlock, Kemp	5	0	0	0	160
Ashlock, Zack	22	1	2	5	6,100
Ashor, Jacob	42	6	5	1	66,050
Asmussen, Steven M.	2,293	555	361	348	14,004,202
Assimakopoulos, Charles	157	26	28	18	415,009
Assimakopoulos, John	7	2	1	2	29,860
Assinesi, Paul D.	45	2	6	7	95,650

Trainer	Sts	1st	2d	3d	Purses
Assoon, Jennifer	29	1	2	1	16,313
Astling, Joseph F.	9	1	3	1	19,630
Atala, Jose	72	13	11	10	104,540
Atencio, Bill	9	0	1	0	3,748
Ater, Richard	5	0	1	0	990
Ates, Brandon	6	1	0	0	15,233
Ates, Cheramy	98	6	9	10	61,412
Atkin, Jerry	273	35	36	36	192,901
Atkins, Michael G.	103	7	5	8	138,065
Atkinson, Gracie	10	1	2	0	12,052
Atkinson, James	4	0	0	0	434
Atkinson, Leonard L.	8	2	0	0	11,207
Attanasio, Robert T.	42	1	3	5	27,120
Attard, Kevin	43	3	5	2	141,899
Attard, Paul	76	4	8	12	161,252
Attard, Sid C.	315	76	55	38	3,844,401
Attard, Steve	190	22	23	21	976,978
Attard, Tino	156	9	9	26	489,985
Attfield, Roger L.	292	35	36	35	2,777,942
Aubrey, J. Kevin	34	8	2	3	109,464
Auger, Raymond J.	9	1	0	3	6,076
Auguillard, Joseph L.	3	0	0	0	675
Augustine, L. J.	12	0	1	1	5,630
Austin, Charles	24	1	3	2	46,543
Auten, Vern E.	34	0	1	3	23,625
Autrey, Cody	122	30	26	16	475,804
Auwarter, Edward K.	106	8	6	8	126,336
Avalon, Jr., William A.	4	0	0	0	797
Averett, Tammy	2	0	0	0	0
Averett, Jr., Gerald	80	7	11	7	109,398
Aversa, Albert P.	5	0	0	0	0
Avila, A. C.	185	14	20	23	524,484
Axmaker, Peter	166	19	15	17	125,470
Aylor, Jr., William L.	162	13	13	19	224,131
Aylor, Sr., William L.	9	0	1	0	5,369
Ayon, Francisco	12	3	4	1	7,145
Ayres, Jr., Joseph W.	15	1	2	5	18,605
Ayres, Sr., Joseph W.	78	5	7	9	67,315
Azpurua, Manuel J.	309	39	38	49	1,272,120
Azpurua, Jr., Eduardo	22	1	0	4	12,393
Azpurua, Sr., Eduardo	15	4	2	2	24,833
Baare, John	17	0	0	0	1,364
Babbington, Grace A.	1	0	0	0	285
Babbitt, Clifford	33	6	5	3	12,318
Babcock, Edward J.	191	16	18	19	182,103
Baber, W. G.	6	1	1	0	9,955
Babin, Jed	12	0	1	3	10,807
Babineaux, Theo	2	0	0	0	0
Baboolal, John H.	6	0	1	0	4,510
Baca, Leonard C.	1	0	0	0	96
Bachman, George T.	6	2	0	2	16,527
Bachmann, Charles A.	12	2	2	1	16,277
Backhaus, Levi	2	0	0	0	125
Bacon, Paula	66	10	16	6	161,924
Bacorn, Herbert L.	48	5	7	2	136,636
Baddeley, Charles W.	116	9	12	15	113,373
Bader, Mark S.	76	11	5	15	213,072
Badgett, Jr., William	115	13	16	15	536,836
Badilla, Sr., Jose G.	5	1	0	0	1,011
Badillo, Pedro Luis	1	1	0	0	12,180
Baffert, Bob	562	105	75	74	7,627,913
Bagby, Calvin E.	6	0	1	0	2,713
Bagnell, Dale	57	1	4	8	21,494
Bailes, W. Robert	180	23	25	20	358,484
Bailey, Charles E.	54	4	10	6	75,211
Bailey, Clifford	5	1	0	0	18,120
Bailey, Douglas L.	3	0	0	1	1,492
Bailey, Hugh	17	1	1	0	7,647
Bailey, Isaac Leonard	38	2	5	2	39,780
Bailey, Kelly Lynn	94	11	9	18	152,740
Bailey, Robert H.	19	2	3	3	22,565
Bailey, Wayne M.	41	6	3	7	138,869
Bailey, Jr., David L.	7	0	0	0	0
Bainum, Kelly	33	8	6	2	66,427
Bainum, Troy	311	75	54	47	761,085
Baird, Barbara A.	60	9	7	6	145,577
Baird, Bart	140	12	12	18	134,721
Baird, Caleb D.	68	3	8	3	32,228
Baird, Dale	1,109	131	158	132	2,063,884
Baird, J. Michael	373	73	61	36	961,956
Baird, John W.	402	64	41	43	900,886
Baker, Bryan R.	104	7	16	5	141,809
Baker, Carl A.	17	3	0	1	16,236
Baker, Charlton	377	93	59	58	1,325,775
Baker, D. Wayne	54	4	6	6	113,820
Baker, Dave	9	0	1	0	700
Baker, David F.	52	7	6	9	144,253
Baker, Dennis	26	3	1	5	13,300
Baker, James E.	78	6	9	9	146,187
Baker, Jeff	36	5	2	4	19,130
Baker, Kenneth E.	47	0	1	4	7,957
Baker, Larry	2	0	0	0	354
Baker, Reade	274	44	45	40	2,844,159
Baker, Terri M.	2	0	0	0	0
Baker, Theresa	2	1	0	0	700
Baker, Jr., Ceburn L.	3	0	0	0	411
Balcewicz, David M.	4	1	0	2	2,200
Balcom, Cliff	17	3	1	2	14,818
Balcom, Sharon	58	4	5	10	14,340
Balderas, Alfonso	96	9	9	6	99,112
Balderas, Damon	14	1	0	3	7,762
Balderrama, Concepcion	5	0	1	1	8,295
Baldwin, Alexander D.	12	2	4	1	26,341
Baldwin, Douglas W.	26	1	4	5	17,420
Baldwin, James	6	1	0	1	4,348
Baldwin, Patrick J.	10	1	1	0	6,013
Balker, Edward G.	3	0	0	0	690
Ball, Brad	31	9	5	7	9,836
Ball, Darla M.	20	0	0	1	3,561
Ball, Donald R.	43	2	4	5	42,765
Ball, Glen	21	4	0	2	19,451
Ball, Katherine G.	22	3	2	4	88,075
Ballhagen, LaVerne J.	47	4	3	11	38,134
Ballou, Lloyd H.	8	0	0	0	736
Balmer, Bruce B.	22	2	2	5	25,026
Balo, Jerry L.	147	37	17	14	250,815
Balsamo, Diane	47	2	0	4	39,366
Baltas, Richard	34	6	6	2	152,508
Balthazar, Jr., Andrew	72	5	2	9	78,934
Balut, Irene	3	0	0	0	309
Banach, Darwin D.	29	3	2	3	91,828
Bandel, Delmer W.	49	1	0	1	10,576
Bandiero, Anthony	13	0	0	3	6,757
Banford, Sharon	6	0	0	0	675
Bango, George A.	73	8	3	11	81,723
Banjoman, Jr., Paul	3	0	0	0	1,200
Banks, David P.	121	16	18	13	289,592
Bankson, Gay	50	1	4	6	28,827
Bankston, Earl	31	4	6	4	53,776
Bankuti, Alex	50	10	11	3	211,364
Banyots, Roger J.	13	0	0	0	2,039
Barana, Leo	25	1	1	5	16,603
Barba, Alexis	12	1	2	2	47,180
Barbalios, Varsamis	33	1	2	3	15,713
Barbanti, Phillip	8	4	0	1	34,650
Barbara, Robert	238	16	30	38	838,895
Barbaran, Horacio	18	3	3	1	28,410
Barbazon, Jr., Lester J.	3	0	1	0	2,610
Barber, Donald C.	139	17	12	16	369,807
Barber, James R.	43	2	1	4	35,926
Barber, Michael K.	126	22	26	20	236,855
Barber, Stanley L.	74	2	4	7	38,302
Barbour, Marcus Shane	11	2	2	1	24,539
Bard, Leon	6	1	1	0	7,160
Bardin, Arnold R.	49	5	3	7	56,682
Baresich, Stanley	79	7	8	10	462,090
Barger, John D.	162	9	15	17	129,380
Barker, Charles D	42	1	3	2	9,658
Barker, Edward R.	78	7	11	5	253,893
Barker, James R.	156	20	20	18	173,463
Barkley, Jeff	19	4	1	2	50,498
Barnard, R. Kenneth	5	0	0	0	512

Trainer	Sts	1st	2d	3d	Purses
Barndollar, Sheilagh	96	8	9	13	71,639
Barnes, Bart A.	37	2	8	5	36,498
Barnes, Edward C.	1	0	0	0	0
Barnes, James A.	30	10	7	4	93,109
Barnes, Stacy	10	2	0	1	3,547
Barnes, Tommy	1	0	0	0	0
Barnett, Bobby C.	407	48	45	46	1,712,929
Barnett, Robert Earl	117	9	7	11	730,071
Barney, Edward H.	37	6	4	4	151,827
Barney, Jessie	14	1	1	0	8,721
Barnhart, William D.	20	0	0	0	3,004
Barnwell, Jerry	43	2	2	4	15,693
Barocio, Librado	35	5	5	4	121,685
Barr, Bob	75	8	6	10	31,471
Barr, Donald H.	168	22	28	24	536,618
Barr, George N.	8	0	0	3	23,234
Barrera, Emilio L.	39	1	3	1	14,697
Barrera, Jr., Oscar S.	309	55	53	54	593,985
Barrier, Marguerite V.	15	1	0	0	7,507
Barrio, Sergio	41	3	1	6	12,889
Barroby, Frank E.	140	14	23	19	262,411
Barroby, Harold J.	273	36	45	38	591,592
Barron, Douglas R.	131	24	21	17	168,885
Barron, Mary Anne	102	11	23	15	94,908
Barrow, Marlene	13	1	0	0	9,583
Barrow, Paul W.	167	20	20	16	186,689
Barry, Henry M.	6	0	1	0	7,610
Barry, James	24	4	3	6	59,045
Bartels, Johan W.	3	0	0	0	1,806
Barth, Charles J.	59	8	19	9	178,865
Bartholomew, Jennifer A.	4	0	0	0	585
Bartlett, Desiree	4	0	1	0	1,429
Bartlett, William H.	110	4	9	12	74,429
Bartol, Tom W.	35	4	7	4	54,032
Barton, Dallas J.	54	11	4	6	147,834
Barton, Glenn A.	17	1	1	0	8,820
Bartscher, Gene	1	0	0	0	0
Bartscher, Henry	13	2	1	1	7,721
Bartscher, Tony	25	1	1	3	7,051
Bary, Pascal F.	2	0	0	1	184,800
Basham, J. Ryan	10	0	1	1	3,242
Bass, Fred	77	9	4	8	52,528
Bass, Tomi E.	25	1	1	2	18,605
Bassett, Rick	5	2	3	0	8,224
Bast, Jr., Gerald D.	158	5	21	15	200,049
Bastida, Ladeana	18	6	1	0	41,616
Bates, C. Louis	66	12	5	4	122,334
Bates, Charles	9	1	0	0	6,600
Bates, Larry	215	24	25	28	349,565
Bathon, Scott L.	8	1	1	0	16,640
Battaglia, Anthony J.	26	2	4	2	20,258
Bauer, Diane E.	4	0	0	0	0
Bauer, Erich	30	3	3	2	91,786
Bauerelen, Charlie	25	3	4	1	10,239
Bauman, Faith	3	0	0	0	460
Baumer, Gerald R.	6	0	2	0	4,777
Baumgartner, Maryanne	14	1	1	2	11,525
Bausch, Jim	355	35	38	35	311,776
Bay, Betty	15	0	3	4	4,394
Bayley, Cynthia K.	264	48	32	35	369,074
Bayley, Perry H.	47	5	6	4	37,314
Bazdor, Joseph F.	13	2	3	4	13,179
Baze, Robert	350	45	47	40	321,567
Bazeos, Peter	222	25	30	20	337,339
Bazley, Tom	12	1	0	2	5,467
Bazurto, Ramon B.	38	2	6	5	17,765
Beaber, Jeri A.	99	8	9	10	71,563
Beach, Anthony E.	1	0	0	0	46
Beach, Betty J.	1	0	0	0	88
Beach, Randall R.	8	0	0	0	1,631
Beach, Richard D.	11	1	0	0	7,678
Beagle, Barbara	6	1	0	1	19,033
Beakler, Daryl L.	103	10	8	7	102,296
Beall, Jennifer	19	3	4	5	60,109
Beall, Jr., John M.	30	7	2	3	58,445
Beam, Ed	28	3	1	4	166,523
Beamer, Bill	239	32	32	39	306,284
Bean, Robert A.	79	3	7	4	101,587
Beard, II, John A.	9	2	1	0	8,428
Bearden, Wayne	72	13	5	7	74,121
Beasley, Rebecca	75	2	6	6	33,550
Beattie, Dennis M.	16	0	0	2	1,962
Beattie, Ryan	68	16	7	8	125,515
Beattie, Stephanie S.	46	6	14	4	119,494
Beattie, Thomas G.	75	8	12	8	72,648
Beattie, Todd M.	352	88	66	45	1,219,926
Beaudoin, Thomas M.	3	0	0	0	33
Beaulieu, Norbert	6	1	0	0	1,200
Beavers, Donald	5	0	1	0	1,080
Becerra, Rafael	258	36	34	46	1,708,343
Becht, Elizabeth	43	3	4	4	43,352
Beck, Edward L.	19	3	4	3	58,522
Beck, Michael T.	4	0	0	0	425
Becker, Nadine A.	136	7	4	16	70,692
Becker, Steven H.	11	2	0	2	6,735
Beckner, Robert	97	12	9	16	28,996
Bedard, Alan	142	22	27	19	305,134
Beddo, Howard L.	3	0	0	0	143
Bedford, Janet	47	0	4	5	53,971
Bedinotti, Peter	4	0	0	1	1,688
Beebe, Crescent	20	3	3	1	19,878
Beech, George S.	103	4	7	11	68,193
Beekman, Jon	35	3	1	4	16,974
Beeton, Robert H.	3	0	0	0	0
Begay, Charles	8	0	3	1	2,278
Begley, Melissa	33	3	2	5	78,564
Begley, Jr., Earl P.	179	24	24	31	280,166
Begnaud, Charles	239	21	27	36	332,145
Begnaud, Louis	46	5	4	5	50,510
Behler, Frank	4	0	0	1	5,645
Behrens, Ronald P.	192	21	20	23	243,974
Behrle, Bruce D.	18	1	3	2	8,008
Beidel, Aaron C.	11	0	0	0	0
Belaire, Conrad A.	12	2	2	1	52,028
Belknap, David M.	39	3	5	4	25,801
Bell, Charles R.	81	7	7	8	56,057
Bell, David R.	217	36	22	32	2,019,903
Bell, Donovan K.	11	0	2	1	12,570
Bell, Janet E.	10	2	4	0	18,220
Bell, Ken	68	6	4	8	57,908
Bell, Michael H.	8	2	1	0	35,070
Bell, II, Thomas Ray	72	7	13	9	382,457
Bell, IV, John A.	67	3	5	4	88,381
Belland, Ronald W.	12	2	0	3	6,735
Bellard, Jerome G.	20	0	2	0	4,813
Bellard, Larry	34	1	1	3	28,624
Bellard, Ronald	46	4	2	5	73,832
Bellasis, R. P.	5	0	1	0	4,000
Bellasis, Tim	175	14	17	28	244,707
Bellini, Gilberto	27	1	0	2	14,472
Bellos, Tom	7	0	0	0	228
Bellucci, Bruno M.	257	14	23	43	153,444
Belmonte, Rocco J.	2	1	0	0	6,600
Belsito, Samuel D.	1	0	0	0	235
Beltran, Jesus G.	3	0	0	0	1,512
Belvoir, Howard	447	41	64	67	660,447
Belvoir, Vann	119	14	25	19	153,278
Bemiss, James H.	18	1	1	2	11,112
Bencivenga, Anthony J.	49	2	0	4	24,776
Bends, James P.	43	4	3	9	29,549
Bendzunas, Joseph	15	0	6	1	11,514
Benjamin, Kelly L.	64	9	11	4	55,095
Benko, Ronald V.	28	2	1	1	16,951
Benn, Gilbert	6	0	0	0	120
Bennett, Adele M.	41	6	0	2	33,514
Bennett, Dale	170	39	20	24	769,236
Bennett, David	127	20	20	11	119,735
Bennett, Donald W.	4	1	0	0	4,871
Bennett, Gerald S.	586	117	109	96	1,475,786
Bennett, Jerry T.	13	2	1	5	19,415
Bennett, Keith	200	63	31	29	505,847
Bennett, Leland	66	3	5	6	24,833

Trainer	Sts	1st	2d	3d	Purses
Bennett, Marvin	6	0	0	0	1,851
Bennett, Mary E.	7	0	2	0	4,165
Bennett, Melinda A.	3	0	0	1	990
Bennett, Michael D.	5	1	1	1	9,748
Bennett, S. Tony	51	8	4	3	178,567
Bennett, William D.	25	2	1	5	17,675
Benoit, Delano	1	0	0	0	0
Bensmiller, Twylla	18	2	4	2	18,691
Benson, Alan A.	37	1	7	6	57,745
Benson, David C.	10	0	0	1	2,377
Benson, Harry	78	13	11	7	272,884
Benson, Macdonald	93	13	13	9	1,072,838
Bentivegna, Teresa	2	0	0	0	74
Bentler, Don	89	16	8	17	88,989
Bentley, Fenneka	4	0	0	0	2,660
Bentley, Jack D.	16	0	1	1	6,312
Benton, Dicky	22	1	1	0	4,929
Benton, James C.	14	2	2	1	14,561
Benton, Raymond P.	6	0	1	0	4,000
Bera, Joseph	29	0	1	3	7,994
Berberena, Jorge	7	2	0	0	20,070
Berdejo, Victor	31	3	5	1	18,470
Berg, Harvey Lowell	77	3	6	6	44,655
Berg, Lorne E.	21	0	4	1	7,712
Berg, Roger	28	1	0	1	10,080
Bergeron, John	5	0	0	2	2,613
Bergeron, Ronald J.	2	0	0	0	0
Bergeson, Clair	8	1	3	1	3,902
Bergin, Tom	31	4	2	6	117,068
Beringer, Alessa	1	0	0	0	0
Berkeley, Christine	40	6	4	2	69,012
Berkelhammer, Barry	1	0	0	0	700
Berkley, Clifford E.	6	0	0	0	677
Berkram, Mel	126	19	21	24	66,121
Berman, Eric	4	0	0	0	750
Bernardini, Jay P.	171	28	21	20	392,138
Berndt, Joel	172	24	13	18	532,168
Bernhart, Walter J.	69	2	3	5	35,240
Bernier, Jr., Louis D.	8	1	1	0	6,789
Bernis, Glynn	235	19	24	20	327,086
Bernis, Kenward	171	32	24	17	345,404
Berns, Terry	3	0	1	0	2,170
Bernstein, David	68	10	8	6	443,751
Berntson, Brian	4	1	1	0	1,125
Berrett, Robert W.	43	7	3	3	46,884
Berringer, Peter	64	3	2	9	192,897
Berrios, Manuel	219	14	13	25	281,315
Berry, James F.	31	5	1	4	48,700
Berry, Michael J.	28	4	3	1	27,861
Berry, Pam	11	0	0	1	3,608
Berry, Tom	10	1	2	3	5,584
Berry, William C.	3	0	0	0	937
Berry, Jr., William J.	27	0	0	0	2,591
Berry, Jr., William S.	53	1	4	3	31,353
Berry, Sr., James R.	96	11	8	12	162,007
Berryman, Michael	27	3	2	3	42,645
Berthold, George C.	9	0	1	0	3,754
Bertschy, Randy L.	22	0	1	1	3,960
Betancourt, Eli	116	14	15	11	199,632
Betancourt, Frank	12	0	1	1	4,884
Bethke, Troy A.	173	18	15	25	160,040
Bethke, William H.	25	1	0	1	8,790
Bettis, Charles L.	169	18	24	16	349,942
Betts, John V.	45	7	4	6	130,698
Betts, Nancy	21	1	3	2	17,732
Bevelacqua, Leo J.	19	0	0	0	2,152
Biamonte, Ralph J.	140	24	25	16	781,775
Biancone, Patrick L.	130	29	24	19	3,397,917
Bickel, Leslie	6	0	0	4	1,740
Biddle, Glen	38	2	4	4	20,711
Biehler, Michael E.	191	36	33	32	742,635
Bieri, Guido	4	0	0	0	460
Biffle, Sr., Bobby Eugene	10	0	0	0	794
Big Hair, Gerald P.	11	2	1	0	10,699
Big Hair, Monica	45	6	9	6	41,349
Bigelow, Carl E.	61	9	4	9	149,953
Bigelow, Clayton	7	0	0	0	2,158
Bigham, Vern C.	1	0	0	0	0
Bignault, W. Paschal	67	8	8	12	154,375
Bilbrey, J. Keith	5	3	0	1	22,525
Billers, George	22	4	4	4	165,909
Billingsley, Sid M.	18	5	0	6	7,006
Billingsly, Max L.	1	0	0	0	76
bin Suroor, Saeed	9	2	1	0	1,504,632
Bindner, Chris	41	2	3	4	28,548
Bindner, Jr., Walter M.	109	18	20	12	1,138,357
Bingham, James A.	1	0	0	0	300
Bingham, Patrick	15	0	0	1	1,860
Bingham, Wesley A.	3	0	0	1	756
Binning, Michael J.	46	4	4	6	25,086
Bir, Barbara J.	6	1	0	2	25,072
Bir, Robert A.	11	0	2	2	8,272
Birch, Charles G.	10	0	1	0	2,462
Birch, David A.	14	0	1	5	29,669
Bird, Alan F.	11	1	2	4	22,929
Bird, Danny R.	2	0	0	0	352
Bird, Dennis	26	5	6	4	9,760
Bird, Richard J.	155	9	11	10	97,716
Bird Rattler, Harlan	35	3	3	6	6,978
Birdow, Oscar	7	1	0	0	2,682
Birdrattler, Joe	1	0	0	0	0
Birdrattler, Shawn	1	0	0	0	0
Bireta, Donna	223	27	18	38	553,363
Birtch, Daniel R.	3	0	0	0	460
Bischoff, Eulia R.	179	17	30	26	102,737
Bischoff, Thomas E.	10	3	0	4	15,770
Bish, Walter F.	28	2	2	2	26,105
Bishop, Jimmy R.	4	0	1	0	2,970
Bishop, Norman	13	0	2	1	5,341
Bishoprick, Stanley	2	0	1	1	1,190
Biszantz, Ralph V.	22	2	2	3	58,215
Bjarnarson, Don	52	19	5	10	40,892
Black, Casey	5	0	2	1	4,035
Black, Donald G.	19	4	7	2	10,600
Black, Joanne	5	0	0	1	646
Black, Maurice	2	0	0	0	0
Black, Ralph D.	38	1	2	4	16,495
Black, Jr., Ralph W.	217	25	23	32	268,157
Blackwood, Jim C.	5	1	0	0	4,047
Blain, Earl	13	1	0	3	5,158
Blake, Albert Edward	37	16	2	7	207,307
Blake, Arlene M.	86	5	4	12	45,341
Blake, Paul L.	13	0	1	3	7,970
Blake, Robert	1	0	0	0	110
Blake, Ronald C.	11	0	0	1	2,905
Blakeman, John David	13	0	0	1	1,366
Blanchard, Abel J.	126	18	10	13	163,975
Blanchard, Harold E.	25	1	4	3	8,100
Blanchard, Patrick A.	9	0	0	0	0
Blanchard, Torey	17	1	3	0	26,260
Blanchet, Christopher	2	0	0	0	0
Bland, Roy	110	11	9	13	59,368
Blankenship, Deborah K.	5	0	0	1	7,341
Blankenship, Donald E.	88	7	7	11	85,578
Blankenship, Donald T.	35	1	1	1	18,456
Blankenship, Hubert	54	2	8	12	26,868
Blasi, Joel E.	26	3	3	2	14,866
Blasi, Scott	12	4	1	0	67,440
Blatchford, George	20	1	1	2	5,443
Blatt, Barbara	41	0	0	3	5,091
Blazek, Melisa J.	11	0	0	2	3,314
Blea, Jr., Tony R.	8	0	0	0	1,190
Bleak, Travis D.	6	0	1	1	594
Blend, Zachary	14	1	0	3	8,895
Blengs, Vincent L.	198	22	37	20	537,962
Blevins, Billy C.	7	2	0	1	9,352
Blincoe, Thomas H.	67	9	6	5	187,360
Bliss, Darlene	10	0	0	0	471
Bliss, Richard Dean	77	8	8	7	45,555
Block, Chris M.	298	51	48	43	1,592,782
Blood, Susan	17	1	0	2	5,260
Bloomquist, Charles E.	5	1	2	0	9,160

Trainer	Sts	1st	2d	3d	Purses
Blouin, Marc A.	24	0	3	1	28,215
Bloy, Thomas H.	6	0	1	0	3,243
Blue, Don	38	7	4	4	16,531
Blue, Wayne	70	2	3	4	11,819
Blue, Jr., Harvey L.	4	0	0	0	0
Boak, Ingrid I.	15	0	0	1	3,690
Bobadilla, Jose F.	298	17	32	33	186,298
Bobier, Bob	7	0	1	2	1,640
Bodie, Dennis	20	4	3	4	14,641
Bodner, Deborah S.	33	0	3	0	36,704
Boegner, John	48	8	5	4	44,614
Boehm, Jim	73	15	16	14	152,654
Boehm, Walter	17	1	3	0	7,114
Bogart, Robert B.	24	0	3	1	7,478
Boggess, Lawrence E.	16	0	0	1	1,910
Boggs, M. Joanna	34	6	1	3	89,227
Bogue, David	8	1	0	1	11,065
Bogue, Jeff	25	1	3	2	11,537
Bogue, Mike	14	1	0	4	11,786
Bohlander, Steven	26	1	4	2	25,015
Boillard, John A.	35	2	0	5	13,134
Bolden, William	3	0	0	0	590
Bolen, Bradley C.	44	5	4	8	38,515
Boles, Jennifer	2	0	0	0	730
Bolinger, Michael R.	35	4	5	1	26,297
Bolinger, Nancy	1	0	0	0	127
Bolton, Jim	1	0	0	0	0
Bona, Steven A.	3	0	0	0	190
Bonaventura, Paul	33	6	3	6	46,152
Bond, H. James	191	34	22	23	1,279,019
Bonde, Jeff	303	47	51	46	1,333,438
Bone, Robert H.	26	0	2	5	15,990
Boniface, Kevin C.	164	18	19	18	396,169
Boniface, Kim	12	0	0	2	6,254
Boniface, Jr., John W.	50	7	5	6	69,834
Bonilla, Raymond	41	5	6	4	43,496
Bonn, Craig	28	9	6	3	27,519
Bonnell, Sandra Winn	4	2	1	0	27,826
Bonnett, Gerald	3	0	0	1	651
Bonno, Clyde A.	11	3	0	1	45,081
Booker, Johnnie A.	57	7	6	6	106,974
Booker, Jr., John A.	40	2	4	7	91,258
Bookman, Billy	5	0	0	0	900
Bookman, Clark A.	40	3	0	1	39,230
Bookman, Donald C.	12	0	0	3	3,239
Boone, Earnest J.	8	0	0	0	1,890
Bordner, Benjamin E.	1	0	0	0	95
Bordonaro, John A.	48	5	12	3	69,514
Borel, Cecil P.	30	2	5	3	65,220
Boreman, Roger D.	33	1	1	0	15,161
Borg, Joseph A.	27	1	4	5	26,088
Borgelt, Leonard C.	8	0	0	3	6,140
Borges, Israel	38	2	3	5	18,180
Boris, Robert P.	115	1	5	13	32,515
Borsk, David	14	0	2	4	25,441
Bosarge, Ronald	61	2	2	6	40,753
Bosley, Arthur M.	66	10	15	17	122,650
Bosley, John M.	2	0	0	0	390
Bosley, Louis H.	6	0	0	1	1,600
Bosley, Patricia L.	25	1	0	2	18,060
Bosley, Paul V.	69	8	8	7	141,685
Bossribs, Forest Calf	1	0	0	0	0
Botello, Carlos	23	0	2	3	6,579
Botello, John	2	0	0	0	0
Botkins, Dan	56	3	10	4	48,872
Bott, Alan	8	0	0	0	728
Bott, Sharon	34	6	3	2	64,384
Bottazzi, Patrick L.	44	6	6	6	161,090
Botty, John T.	46	16	4	2	99,845
Bouchard, Leslye G.	90	11	4	11	92,705
Boucher, Lilith E.	65	4	10	7	185,181
Boughner, Richard	6	0	0	0	939
Boulet, Joey	53	8	3	4	88,671
Boulmetis, Tanya	57	4	5	8	66,899
Bourgeois, Keith L.	711	132	104	79	1,789,609
Bourke, W. John	126	17	15	13	228,893

Trainer	Sts	1st	2d	3d	Purses
Bourne, Elige	97	15	6	8	102,717
Bourne, Lori J.	149	9	8	19	234,529
Bourne, Rex	6	0	0	0	0
Bourne, William T.	2	0	0	0	965
Bourque, Kevin	11	0	1	1	3,670
Bourque, Ricky	65	10	8	6	114,271
Bourque, Scotty	57	2	4	6	62,384
Bourque, Wilbert	11	0	2	2	12,294
Bouslaugh, Connie	46	12	6	3	89,649
Boutte, Thomas	14	0	3	3	10,859
Bowden, Richard B.	3	0	0	0	270
Bowden, Thomas R.	30	2	2	4	53,043
Bowen, Jeffrey D.	2	0	0	0	3,762
Bowers, Janet L.	34	1	5	7	61,787
Bowers, John K.	2	1	0	1	5,455
Bowers, Ray	26	1	0	1	10,848
Bowersock, Gary	7	0	0	0	224
Bowersock, Richard	58	6	5	4	80,204
Bowles, Norman W.	80	4	9	5	99,838
Bowman, Brent W.	3	0	0	0	72
Bowman, Carl	116	15	20	13	374,384
Bowman, Carl E.	49	1	4	2	25,519
Bowman, Elex D.	29	0	6	1	21,996
Bowman, Gregory H.	32	3	1	1	32,087
Bowman, Lavern A.	60	7	11	5	65,232
Bowman, Robert	53	10	7	5	40,333
Boxie, Jonathan	5	0	0	0	306
Boxie, Joseph Stanley	58	5	12	7	81,347
Boxie, Jr., Joseph Herman	39	2	1	2	38,258
Boyce, Brian L.	6	0	0	1	2,884
Boyce, Joseph S.	8	1	1	0	8,037
Boyce, Michele	257	38	38	29	985,684
Boyd, Donald L.	15	0	1	0	4,767
Boyd, Eric M.	1	1	0	0	2,310
Boyd, Renee M.	40	3	5	4	38,227
Boyd, Roy L.	10	0	0	0	2,570
Boyd, Terry L.	80	5	9	10	82,539
Boyer, Darryl L.	39	0	1	4	14,104
Boyer, Leroy W.	4	0	0	0	1,010
Boyer, Marvin	11	0	0	2	2,001
Boyer, V. Brooke	1	0	0	1	1,000
Boyett, Bobby C.	26	0	7	6	14,548
Bozell, Alan	75	10	7	11	52,256
Bozzo, Jerry	95	10	6	11	134,880
Bracciale, Jr., Vincent A.	9	0	1	0	5,530
Bracey, John	53	1	3	5	16,462
Bracken, James E.	103	9	15	9	195,265
Brackett, Joseph E.	7	0	0	1	2,879
Braddy, J. David	220	31	31	33	628,790
Braden, Derral	31	1	2	1	3,792
Braden, Patty J.	65	4	10	6	30,544
Bradfield, Thomas	11	2	3	0	5,760
Bradford, Carolyn	3	0	0	0	450
Bradford, Ronald C.	1	0	0	0	0
Bradley, William	229	24	28	21	1,027,462
Bradsen, Martin	7	1	2	0	15,215
Bradshaw, Gregg A.	20	0	0	2	2,116
Bradshaw, Linda	39	3	5	4	41,301
Bradshaw, Randy K.	4	0	0	1	2,785
Bradvica, Louis A.	52	0	0	2	20,875
Brady, Amy	2	0	1	0	650
Brady, Ronald R.	4	0	0	0	2,400
Brafford, Michelle C.	17	4	3	2	27,315
Bragg, Patricia A.	93	11	8	8	72,418
Bragg, Willard J.	6	1	0	0	3,240
Brajczewski, Jr., Eugene F.	74	7	5	6	177,325
Bramante, Bernard	27	0	2	4	7,956
Bramble, Clyde D.	18	1	1	1	13,898
Branch, Teresa Gail	22	1	3	3	16,116
Brand, Elizabeth	4	0	0	0	177
Brandenburg, John	104	15	13	15	149,218
Brandenburg, Stephen	4	0	0	0	264
Branger, David J.	3	0	0	0	0
Brannon, Ken W.	14	0	0	1	505
Branton, Bill	3	0	0	0	201
Brashear, Jr., Earl	74	3	5	5	23,576

Trainer	Sts	1st	2d	3d	Purses
Brashears, Bill	327	68	53	47	308,524
Brasher, Harry L.	20	1	0	3	5,167
Brasher, Wayne	36	3	2	3	5,601
Brasseaux, John	15	1	0	3	3,770
Brathwaite, Richard	27	1	2	1	57,731
Bratton, Charles	31	6	6	3	11,799
Bravenec, Darrell W.	26	0	0	4	7,950
Bravo, Francisco	157	18	19	19	286,156
Bray, Simon	47	4	5	4	145,514
Breaux, Samuel	392	70	60	53	1,231,147
Brecheisen, Dale	13	2	0	1	10,068
Brecheisen, Dale Lynn	33	2	1	4	10,298
Breed, Debra A.	96	5	11	10	70,748
Breeden, Ami	1	0	0	0	0
Breeden, Bobby	27	0	4	3	6,070
Breen, Kelly John	200	21	32	26	786,717
Brehm, Joel D.	8	1	1	3	11,671
Brehm, Kenneth L.	20	0	4	5	3,237
Brehm, Robert	9	2	1	2	4,300
Bremer, Dean	20	0	3	3	4,673
Bremner, Brent	9	1	0	1	20,610
Bremner, Kathy	46	2	3	4	35,219
Brenchley, Alexandra	12	0	1	1	3,230
Brenden, Jeanette	43	3	5	4	20,420
Brennan, Brian E.	24	3	2	3	68,410
Brennan, Niall J.	11	1	0	0	35,320
Brennan, Terry J.	96	20	17	11	244,342
Brennan, William	19	1	0	1	12,763
Breshears, Floyd Don	36	0	2	6	12,774
Bretthorst, William F.	49	3	2	2	66,684
Brettin, Scott	1	0	0	0	0
Breuer, Denise E.	38	6	2	5	209,176
Brewer, James R.	14	1	0	3	11,410
Brewer, Jimmy L.	3	0	0	0	0
Brewer, Robert C.	8	1	1	0	12,200
Brewster, Larry Joseph	26	0	1	4	13,256
Brewton, Colin	2	0	0	0	0
Brice, Michael	153	21	26	22	762,946
Brida, Juliane	35	2	2	4	92,452
Bridge, Donald L.	26	1	1	3	6,726
Bridges, Brandon M.	3	0	0	0	0
Brigden, Ross	1	0	1	0	1,040
Brigden, W. R.	58	10	6	7	36,986
Briggs, Donald B.	64	13	4	5	64,632
Briggs, William E.	10	2	1	2	2,502
Briggs, Jr., Asa D.	107	9	5	11	65,069
Bright, R. E.	4	2	0	0	35,776
Bright, Ronald L	2	0	0	0	190
Briley, Lonnie	107	12	13	9	154,242
Briley, Ronald	2	0	0	0	0
Brimsley, Monte	1	0	1	0	540
Brinegar, Tanya P.	2	1	1	0	3,239
Bringhurst, J. Owen	70	16	11	7	180,558
Brinkerhoff, Dan B.	4	0	2	0	4,040
Brinkley, Franklin	81	18	13	10	178,724
Brinkley, Jennifer	1	0	0	0	111
Brinkley, Melvin	44	3	4	2	22,338
Brinkman, Brett	15	2	3	1	22,489
Brinkman, Randy	11	2	0	0	6,830
Brinsfield, Brooken	54	2	2	4	19,894
Brinsley, Monte	17	2	4	5	13,756
Brinson, Clay	33	8	4	5	36,284
Bristow, Alford	2	0	0	0	650
Brito, Manuel J.	33	3	4	5	27,667
Brittingham, E. Earl	7	0	0	1	4,298
Brittle, III, Clay T.	8	0	0	0	1,076
Brittle, Jr., Clay T.	42	2	4	5	93,774
Britton, Irene	79	8	15	8	26,807
Brobst, Floyd D.	13	0	0	0	598
Brock, Jim N.	12	0	0	2	1,169
Brock, Kenneth	55	4	2	4	22,974
Brocka, Laurence	73	1	2	5	23,266
Broers, John E.	9	1	0	0	7,590
Bronson, P.	1	0	0	1	250
Bronson, Ron	3	0	0	2	564
Bronson, Vern	8	1	0	0	2,256
Brook, Joseph	41	3	3	4	52,085
Brooke, Crystal	32	3	0	2	8,666
Brooker, Melissa	5	0	1	1	2,406
Brooker, Terry W.	73	3	6	4	140,949
Brookfield, James	55	6	8	5	192,545
Brooks, Clifton D.	65	16	7	7	41,867
Brooks, Gerald E.	3	0	0	0	174
Brooks, Jim Dale	61	7	12	13	37,031
Brooks, Lanny G.	76	2	4	2	20,613
Brooks, Rex Dean	10	0	1	1	714
Brooks, Ronald R.	5	0	0	0	606
Brooks, Willie	5	0	0	0	0
Brooksher, Wesley	1	0	0	0	37
Broome, Edwin Thomas	259	49	40	36	1,167,863
Broomfield, Ian	17	0	1	1	5,925
Brothers, Donald W.	31	6	3	5	56,053
Brothers, Frank L.	83	16	9	13	908,057
Broussard, C. J.	9	0	0	0	3,549
Broussard, Joseph E.	93	16	7	14	341,830
Broussard, Kelly	43	8	8	10	221,810
Broussard, Kevin	7	1	2	1	13,107
Broussard, Mitchell	17	2	0	0	17,522
Broussard, Nathan	68	8	4	3	88,743
Broussard, Ricky John	20	3	3	2	38,226
Broussard, Jr., Vincent	18	1	0	0	17,768
Brown, Allan	34	10	6	8	47,694
Brown, Andrew C.	17	1	1	1	7,250
Brown, Barbara Jean	65	4	10	5	90,198
Brown, Barry D.	97	17	11	11	185,916
Brown, Brenda Kay	15	2	0	2	7,108
Brown, C. Wesley	33	2	4	5	16,637
Brown, Carl W.	118	6	7	5	44,475
Brown, Christine M.	3	0	0	0	350
Brown, Dickie	35	2	6	1	22,343
Brown, Donald L.	4	0	0	0	580
Brown, Dwight	75	2	5	7	36,756
Brown, Francis J.	1	0	0	0	0
Brown, Gary W.	59	10	8	11	81,793
Brown, George F.	47	5	6	2	72,981
Brown, Glenroy	63	2	9	11	36,336
Brown, Herbert Lee	14	0	0	1	2,882
Brown, James E.	8	3	0	1	46,460
Brown, James H.	9	0	0	0	3,108
Brown, James I.	44	3	3	4	42,454
Brown, James L.	1	0	1	0	6,620
Brown, James R.	125	16	14	16	342,966
Brown, Jared	121	12	9	11	78,748
Brown, Jody L.	1	0	0	0	120
Brown, Joyce C.	28	0	0	0	2,375
Brown, June M.	46	2	8	4	35,323
Brown, Keith A.	15	0	0	2	5,610
Brown, Ken S.	81	14	8	7	67,335
Brown, Kristina L.	62	1	6	6	29,554
Brown, Larry Ronald	33	3	7	3	85,215
Brown, Linda M.	7	1	2	0	32,700
Brown, Mazie	78	6	4	8	62,886
Brown, Noble D.	15	0	2	2	20,273
Brown, Rhonda	11	0	0	0	1,065
Brown, Ronald G.	62	8	5	7	72,644
Brown, Ronney W.	708	131	119	81	2,269,499
Brown, Steven R.	150	24	24	19	377,601
Brown, Susan L.	80	5	14	3	116,495
Brown, Ted E.	14	0	5	3	11,685
Brown, William G.	1	0	0	0	1,440
Brown, William R.	8	0	0	0	189
Brown, Wilson L.	145	22	24	18	332,536
Brown, Jr., Charles H.	36	3	2	2	49,438
Brown, Jr., Lewis W.	21	1	1	2	27,158
Brown, Jr., Paul H.	16	0	1	1	11,678
Brownfield, III, Claude L.	119	6	17	15	154,066
Brownlee, David R.	183	23	26	22	1,044,510
Brownlee, William Earl	120	11	17	9	113,655
Bruce, Dennis R.	27	4	1	1	26,183
Brueggemann, Roger A.	179	36	23	22	520,578
Brumbaugh, Roland J.	32	2	3	5	9,840
Brumley, Danny C.	2	0	0	0	2,670

Trainer	Sts	1st	2d	3d	Purses
Brumley, William S.	42	3	7	4	53,278
Brumlow, Glenn A.	61	8	10	3	128,602
Bruner, Jack A.	175	25	16	19	535,838
Brunson, Edward F.	3	0	0	0	810
Brunton, Robert L.	14	1	1	2	17,038
Bryant, George R.	14	1	0	1	4,948
Bryant, Jeff	14	0	0	1	1,810
Bryant, Jerry B.	9	0	0	1	1,165
Bryant, Larry W.	13	1	1	0	5,878
Bryant, Steve	9	2	0	1	66,830
Bryner, Ray	19	2	1	2	10,812
Buc, John R.	53	6	7	10	73,789
Buchanan, Allen Wayne	36	8	7	5	89,790
Buchholz, Ralph	2	0	1	1	3,000
Buchholz, Rick	5	1	1	1	7,230
Buchko, Joseph	23	1	2	4	26,855
Buck, Beverly	56	5	4	11	287,490
Buck, Larry Don	19	2	3	0	4,614
Buckingham, James B.	11	0	1	2	5,460
Buckler, Allison	91	4	6	4	53,080
Buckley, Jonathan B.	321	48	55	40	539,756
Buckley, Mark	53	9	12	9	26,085
Buckman, Gilbert L.	32	1	1	3	12,035
Buckmaster, Chad	12	1	0	1	8,942
Buckner, Don H.	5	1	0	2	5,448
Buckridge, Gloria	110	12	12	9	145,810
Budhoo, Steve	63	4	10	2	51,601
Budrewicz, Richard	43	3	3	6	21,381
Buechler, Simon J.	71	6	8	8	146,508
Buehler, Gordon R.	19	1	0	1	5,874
Buehrer, Mark W.	17	0	1	1	2,550
Buehrer, Wayne C.	39	1	2	4	18,919
Buentello, Michael	22	1	6	3	17,128
Buffalo, Blaine	50	6	7	7	32,201
Buffalo, Marvin	73	3	6	15	35,807
Bugeaud, Mike	7	0	1	1	935
Buhacevich, Rod M.	29	0	0	1	4,548
Buhrow, Jamie D.	39	1	5	3	26,690
Bukowiecki, Chris	6	0	0	0	990
Bulloch, Michael G.	17	2	1	0	17,310
Bullock, Steve	104	15	11	14	174,566
Bulmer, Valerie J.	3	0	0	1	888
Bumgardner, Jim	3	0	0	0	880
Bump, Susan	20	2	3	1	41,640
Bundy, Trevor	51	7	7	10	75,019
Bunting, Edward L.	43	3	3	3	52,488
Bunting, Kent	28	3	5	1	37,425
Bunyard, Lowell N.	77	14	10	13	30,599
Buonaiuto, John	6	0	0	0	3,200
Burbank, Nancy	18	0	3	5	3,193
Burbank, Rosa Lee	10	2	1	3	3,728
Burch, Eldwin	31	4	4	2	41,815
Burch, Sandra E.	20	1	0	2	20,260
Burden, Gene L.	22	0	1	2	6,124
Burdick, Barbara E.	44	3	3	7	46,968
Burdick, Jerome C.	3	0	0	1	2,860
Burelsmith, Jr., Emmitt B.	34	3	1	4	28,720
Burger, Burton B.	13	0	0	4	5,220
Burger, Wayne	10	0	0	1	1,445
Burgess, Daniel	23	1	2	2	11,984
Burgess, Dondra	19	1	0	2	9,081
Burke, Dennis O.	4	0	0	0	364
Burke, John G.	34	3	4	5	61,475
Burke, Ronald G.	34	0	3	5	74,553
Burke, II, Donald J.	21	3	3	4	290,230
Burkybile, Don	19	0	2	1	1,985
Burnam, Norma	14	0	0	0	1,106
Burneson, Sr., Charles	6	0	0	0	439
Burnett, Glenn	31	1	1	0	7,938
Burnie, Jennifer L.	36	2	6	3	50,289
Burnison, E. G.	7	4	1	0	87,580
Burns, Dale	138	13	14	11	68,007
Burns, Daniel T.	5	0	1	0	1,087
Burns, Eugene	3	2	0	0	2,580
Burns, Gerald L.	33	7	1	5	134,519
Burns, Jack D.	4	1	0	0	1,320
Burns, James M.	4	0	0	0	1,230
Burns, John M.	30	1	2	4	3,912
Burns, Patty A.	76	6	6	4	122,281
Burns, Tina	1	0	0	0	75
Burrell, Andrew	18	0	0	0	0
Burrell, Ron P.	36	4	6	1	34,571
Burress, Bobby G.	42	4	4	3	28,333
Burress, Dan	2	0	0	0	195
Burress, Jr., Billy B.	4	1	0	0	5,138
Burress, Sr., Billy B.	25	4	6	4	33,705
Burrington, Wallace D.	1	0	0	0	0
Burt, David K.	13	2	3	4	3,968
Burton, Jennivieve	13	1	1	1	9,360
Burton, Roger E.	15	0	0	0	1,315
Burton, Roger Mack	4	0	0	0	890
Burton, Ronald B.	4	0	1	0	362
Bush, George S.	103	6	6	9	45,939
Bush, Judith B.	8	0	1	1	2,840
Bush, Lynette A.	11	2	3	0	21,870
Bush, Thomas M.	130	26	19	13	1,006,603
Bushrod, Lawrence L.	100	8	7	11	134,850
Buskey, Michael L.	17	0	0	0	2,409
Buskey, Robert E.	18	1	4	1	20,831
Buskey, Jr., Robert Edward	9	3	2	1	28,066
Bustamante, J. Ray	16	1	2	1	9,330
Bustamante, Johnny G	123	7	9	8	68,195
Bustamante, Justo	27	0	3	0	4,011
Bustos, Jesus	53	3	4	6	36,593
Butcher, Charles L.	50	3	2	4	20,021
Butcher, Elijah	1	0	0	0	0
Bute, Wayne Lee	10	1	1	0	7,327
Butkevic, Richard	3	0	0	0	300
Butler, Bobby J.	7	2	0	0	2,450
Butler, Doug	6	1	0	0	1,636
Butler, Gerald	120	13	13	15	89,223
Butler, Gerard A.	1	0	0	0	2,000
Butler, Larry Jack	1	1	0	0	5,100
Butler, Jr., Wilbur R.	66	7	11	8	63,922
Buttieri, Stephen A.	1	1	0	0	7,620
Buttigieg, Erin	54	11	6	8	78,505
Buttigieg, Kevin	9	4	0	1	56,873
Buttigieg, Pasquale J.	4	0	0	0	199
Buttigieg, Paul M.	131	6	4	19	247,235
Butts, David H.	5	0	0	0	625
Butts, Jr., Richard P.	67	6	8	8	109,314
Buxbaum, Edward	64	7	15	16	23,721
Buxton, Ken	5	2	1	0	6,534
Buzzard, Ralph	33	2	3	3	7,100
Byler, Andrew	15	0	0	1	1,892
Byrd, Suzanne	31	4	1	2	36,594
Byrne, Hugh P.	5	0	0	0	488
Byrne, Patrick B.	112	21	17	10	703,845
Byrum, Jr., Ronnie	18	2	2	2	10,070
Bywaters, Sheila	14	1	0	2	3,480
Caballero, Lloyd	31	3	1	4	31,730
Cabello, III, Carlos	57	2	5	8	112,947
Cable, Matt L.	2	0	0	0	93
Cabral, Dan	28	1	2	5	18,147
Cabrera, Jose A.	139	3	5	13	74,624
Cacchiotti, Mary	160	13	18	23	127,321
Caddell, Teddy D.	5	1	0	0	3,448
Cadena, Jr., Emilio	5	0	1	0	2,557
Cahill, Steven F.	112	10	13	11	162,787
Caillouet, Howard J.	15	1	0	0	3,132
Cain, Carla	4	0	0	0	179
Cain, Don E.	7	0	1	0	10,665
Cain, Emmet	1	0	0	0	0
Cain, Jim	2	1	0	0	870
Cain, Lewis B.	7	0	0	0	0
Cain, S. Joseph	265	44	34	29	620,022
Caine, Robert E.	19	2	5	0	15,380
Calais, Joseph Lonzo	25	0	3	0	7,713
Calais, Richard W.	84	3	9	7	77,785
Calais, Sonny	125	6	2	7	70,147
Calais, Jr., Phillip	8	0	1	1	7,330
Calais, Sr., Phillip	14	1	0	0	33,786

Trainer	Sts	1st	2d	3d	Purses
Calas, Aldo	23	1	2	5	29,632
Calascibetta, Joseph G.	177	21	21	40	425,015
Calderon, Enrique A.	122	6	7	11	45,883
Caldwell, D. Jared	14	1	0	1	4,672
Caldwell, Delmar R.	129	11	11	11	138,885
Caldwell, Roscoe	44	0	0	1	1,939
Caldwell, Steven D.	1	0	0	0	0
Caldwell, Todd B.	1	0	1	0	300
Caldwell-Babb, Lillie	14	0	0	1	1,066
Calfrobe, Noran	14	1	1	1	4,146
Calhoun, John	38	5	2	7	270,065
Calhoun, Karl	54	5	7	8	63,641
Calhoun, W. Bret	714	148	124	93	2,733,984
Callaghan, N. A.	2	0	1	0	208,000
Callahan, Thomas D.	6	2	1	0	14,164
Callejas, Alfredo	39	4	2	5	174,496
Callis, Craig	12	2	2	2	32,965
Calton, Kurt	13	2	2	4	19,278
Calvario, Manuel	34	4	2	1	42,442
Calvin, Jerry D.	81	13	10	6	229,202
Camardo, Joey M.	254	30	36	33	318,324
Camerer, Angela K.	4	0	0	0	142
Cameron, Anne	76	6	14	8	206,714
Cameron, Brian	10	1	0	0	2,150
Cameron, Dean	4	0	0	0	112
Cameron, Gerard	1	1	0	0	3,720
Cameron, Mary	18	1	2	3	15,591
Cameron, Michael C.	20	1	0	3	12,078
Cameron, Raymond A.	4	0	0	1	5,762
Cameron-Liechty, Monique	27	1	1	1	36,818
Camilo, Juan	122	13	11	13	140,768
Camotta, Otis R.	26	0	1	1	10,356
Campanile, David	30	2	0	2	20,812
Campbell, Brian	5	0	0	1	2,940
Campbell, Charles J.	9	1	1	0	14,363
Campbell, D. Mike	210	19	17	28	207,350
Campbell, Donald Edward	68	4	18	9	146,923
Campbell, Donald J.	18	1	0	1	19,485
Campbell, Elizabeth	7	0	1	0	2,134
Campbell, Felicia	31	4	6	2	23,308
Campbell, Frederick T.	14	2	3	3	20,476
Campbell, Gilbert N.	3	0	0	0	126
Campbell, Jean	65	3	6	9	77,767
Campbell, Jim	6	0	0	0	675
Campbell, Lawrence H.	41	1	2	5	21,974
Campbell, Marshall T.	38	0	0	2	8,986
Campbell, Michael B.	96	14	19	14	276,787
Campbell, William A.	59	7	13	10	194,955
Campitelli, Francis P.	117	20	21	13	563,787
Campo, Jr., John P.	13	0	0	2	4,983
Campos, Orlando	3	0	0	0	0
Canady, Tony	6	1	0	0	2,450
Canani, Julio C.	186	42	31	22	3,364,545
Canani, Nick	133	15	16	12	553,424
Candlin, John	250	11	10	14	351,462
Canelo, Enzo F.	46	4	3	3	70,782
Canet, Julian	173	34	32	27	490,510
Cannedy, Eddy	4	0	0	0	832
Cannon, Charles	136	8	16	18	126,267
Cano, Gerardo	1	0	0	0	107
Cansler, Misty	9	1	0	3	8,026
Canterbury, Susan	1	0	0	0	170
Cantlon-Bubolz, Corleen	73	5	11	9	83,496
Cantrell, Margie	24	2	2	3	5,477
Capacchione, Frank	3	0	0	0	310
Capanas, Tamara	6	0	0	1	2,962
Capasso, Larry	40	0	3	4	7,207
Capellini, John A.	66	2	2	1	20,111
Capestro, Paula S.	272	56	44	35	902,324
Capi, Louis M.	66	3	13	8	92,200
Caple, Gary R.	185	18	18	32	207,858
Cappellucci, Dick	93	24	7	17	355,030
Cappellucci, Robert A.	73	12	7	13	163,451
Capps, Stacey	17	0	3	1	5,219
Cappuccitti, Audre	298	28	34	38	1,293,288
Capuano, Dale	649	136	93	111	2,452,257
Capuano, Gary	230	47	44	32	1,182,311
Capuano, Louis J.	44	6	8	5	104,031
Caraker, Doug	43	2	5	1	18,535
Caraman, Michael	78	6	7	9	160,372
Caramori, Eduardo C.	84	21	11	10	349,291
Carango, Anthony	54	5	9	4	83,813
Carava, Jack	325	55	48	44	1,435,136
Cardella, John	186	28	27	26	899,617
Carden, Kevin C.	64	7	9	7	62,896
Cardenas, Edward J.	6	0	0	0	180
Cardenas, Ruben	157	24	20	18	684,129
Cardinale, William	1	0	0	0	280
Cardone, Steve	25	1	1	3	16,415
Carey, Charles A.	39	7	5	6	141,505
Carey, Julia	29	2	8	0	131,897
Carey, Tom	9	0	0	2	3,365
Carle, Jeffery C.	24	3	1	2	70,066
Carlesimo, Jr., Charles J.	80	7	6	10	190,775
Carlisi, Frank	82	8	10	10	207,450
Carlisle, John C.	40	11	4	7	181,645
Carlisle, Phyllis C.	5	2	0	0	8,718
Carlisle, Jr., Raymond M.	30	4	4	3	53,986
Carlson, Johnny D.	28	2	1	5	20,918
Carlson, Marilyn A.	2	0	0	0	0
Carlson, Tony	8	0	0	0	269
Carlton, Anthony Daniel	7	0	0	1	3,960
Carlton, Laura S.	21	2	2	1	16,665
Carlton III, O. S.	70	3	4	5	35,905
Carlton, IV, O. S.	14	0	0	1	1,885
Carlyon, Ron	8	0	0	0	482
Carmichael, Jr., Ian L.	19	1	1	1	31,537
Carneal, Kenneth R.	2	0	0	0	117
Carnes, Gregg R.	33	0	8	6	63,964
Carnes, J Clay	28	3	5	3	30,022
Carney, Hugh J.	38	3	4	10	29,335
Carno, Louis R.	17	0	2	1	40,518
Carolan, George P.	20	0	1	2	7,257
Caroli, Donald	70	6	5	6	67,654
Carollo, Alphonse H.	21	2	0	2	10,366
Caron, Darrell	37	6	5	4	20,046
Caron, Luc	9	1	2	2	43,712
Carone, Anthony	22	1	2	2	18,530
Carothers, Theresa	33	5	0	2	35,930
Carpenter, David	1	0	0	0	750
Carr, Donald R.	15	0	0	0	2,837
Carr, Mairead	11	1	0	1	9,150
Carrasco, Jr., Abel	5	1	1	0	4,128
Carrelli, William	13	2	1	1	21,196
Carrete, Jesus J	13	1	0	0	4,109
Carrete, Oscar V.	10	2	1	0	12,712
Carrier, Cheryl L.	7	0	0	0	315
Carriker, Ashley	7	0	0	1	3,355
Carrillo, Cheryl	163	15	15	21	100,130
Carrillo-Dominguez, Cheryl	11	3	1	1	9,847
Carrillo-Dominguez, Gerardo	92	7	10	10	65,958
Carrizales, Edelmiro	34	1	2	2	7,584
Carroll, David M.	157	33	22	21	1,324,580
Carroll, Henry L.	97	9	20	14	304,392
Carroll, Josie	250	43	26	37	1,990,780
Carroll, Klobia S.	1	0	0	0	201
Carroll, II, Del W.	135	20	18	16	1,014,973
Carruthers, C. A.	1	0	0	1	275
Carson, Max W.	14	5	2	3	8,650
Cart, Jerry D.	131	17	19	15	308,587
Cartagena, Julio R.	220	54	30	27	812,746
Carter, Andrew B.	55	12	7	7	212,998
Carter, Carrie F.	3	0	0	0	0
Carter, Cary	107	13	14	14	208,115
Carter, Elmer	116	20	20	18	170,962
Carter, George M.	23	1	1	5	29,421
Carter, James R.	32	2	5	3	25,032
Carter, Les H.	8	0	0	0	0
Carter, Marvin Ray	4	0	0	0	438
Carter, Robert	2	0	2	0	780
Carter, Robert Lewis	22	1	1	1	19,167
Carter, Ronald P.	4	2	1	1	2,910

Trainer	Sts	1st	2d	3d	Purses
Carter, Susan C.	2	0	0	0	208
Carter, Troy	5	0	0	1	735
Cartwright, Michael	113	12	14	14	106,754
Cartwright, Ronald C.	112	25	20	18	653,396
Caruso, Thomas	13	0	0	2	3,311
Carver, David	10	2	1	2	4,239
Casado, Luis	20	1	1	2	18,785
Cascio, C. W. Bubba	178	32	30	33	707,932
Case, Owen Clark	10	0	2	1	6,733
Casella-Stark, Judy K.	1	0	0	0	0
Casey, James M.	46	3	4	8	91,122
Casey, James W.	191	26	29	24	737,307
Casey, Joe D.	31	2	1	2	21,591
Casey, John A.	68	7	6	7	204,877
Casey, Ronald B.	5	0	0	2	1,860
Casey, Stephen E.	46	2	6	5	59,509
Casey, Stephen M.	59	7	5	3	65,690
Casey, Steven A.	6	0	0	1	1,371
Cash, Edward C.	71	10	5	13	110,390
Cash, Russell J.	76	5	11	4	253,171
Casse, Mark E.	323	48	45	46	2,946,340
Casselman, Gail	21	5	0	3	206,994
Casselman, Mike	6	2	1	1	10,919
Casselman-Cox, Gail	12	3	3	1	108,268
Cassidy, James M.	157	18	19	18	2,580,222
Cassil, Wayne V.	4	0	0	1	825
Cast, Carol	6	0	0	1	542
Castaneda, Kelly	10	0	0	0	1,747
Castaneda, Marco A.	18	3	3	2	94,271
Castellanos, Armando	2	2	0	0	2,001
Castellanos, Jaime	160	24	19	18	186,832
Caster, Boyd	157	15	14	20	112,615
Castille, Carrol	133	25	26	12	359,729
Castille, Lee	14	2	0	3	14,864
Castille, Mark	26	1	1	2	17,641
Castillo, Judy	4	0	0	0	170
Castle, Jr., Edward J.	14	1	1	2	8,986
Castleberry, Chris J.	23	0	1	1	3,174
Castleberry, William J.	4	1	1	0	1,446
Casto, Bill	26	0	6	3	20,696
Castor, Donald F.	38	2	4	2	18,595
Castor, Gail A.	12	1	0	1	4,339
Castor, Shane	78	7	9	8	58,878
Castro, Jorge	6	0	0	0	1,805
Castro, Manuel S.	20	2	1	3	33,016
Castro, Rafael	35	4	4	11	40,050
Castro, Raquel A.	16	4	3	3	26,982
Caswell, Bradley S.	5	0	1	0	2,100
Catalano, Wayne M.	335	84	52	38	1,563,353
Cataldi, Sandy	2	0	0	1	1,150
Cataldi, Tony	51	11	8	12	106,643
Catanese, III, Joseph C.	58	5	6	3	147,584
Catania, Michael T.	7	0	0	0	636
Cathey, Bradley J.	4	2	0	0	12,360
Catrone, Patrick	2	0	0	0	0
Caudill, Donald	51	3	1	8	32,790
Caudill, Jesse E.	28	3	5	4	17,337
Caughron, Christopher N.	28	3	3	3	13,910
Cavanaugh, Edward J.	20	0	0	1	2,180
Cavanaugh, Perry	10	0	4	1	2,157
Cave, Hubert L.	46	0	3	3	15,589
Caylor, Harry	19	0	3	4	9,826
Cazares, Frank P.	17	2	0	0	10,035
Cazaubon, Daniel F.	4	0	0	0	0
Cecil, Ben D. A.	53	4	3	8	219,540
Cecil, Claude	59	3	3	6	33,753
Cecil, Willis J.	47	5	3	9	67,096
Ceciliano, Misael	22	2	1	1	37,210
Cedano, Heriberto	47	2	4	6	168,467
Cefalo, Alfred E.	67	7	10	6	116,255
Celestine, Charles Ray	12	0	0	1	5,330
Cenicola, Lewis A.	65	6	5	6	192,808
Cerano, Macario	5	1	0	0	12,639
Cerin, Vladimir	339	59	52	61	2,796,647
Cermack, Larry	17	1	3	1	3,885
Cerundolo, Diane	9	0	1	2	6,435
Cervantes, Juan M.	91	4	2	4	52,837
Cervantes, Sergio	4	0	1	1	2,590
Cerveny, Roxanne	7	1	2	2	9,515
Cerveny, Steve	35	2	2	4	10,730
Cesare, William J.	202	15	23	23	396,090
Cesarini, Diana L.	32	2	1	3	16,430
Cesarini, Joseph A.	134	6	9	17	79,041
Cetenich, Robert	1	0	0	0	0
Cezar, Jerry	5	0	0	0	0
Chabot, Rob	102	14	15	9	199,534
Chadborn, Jr., Kenneth K.	136	13	15	17	178,408
Chadwick, James	36	3	2	6	52,367
Chaffee, Gary W.	15	0	3	5	15,185
Chalich, Nick	53	8	4	8	21,919
Chamberlain, Garry	19	2	4	1	23,852
Chamberlin, Christopher	7	0	0	1	2,725
Chambless, Anna M.	25	1	0	5	14,972
Champagne, Carroll	19	0	0	1	2,183
Champagne, Dana L.	1	0	0	0	0
Chan, Gary P.	18	0	0	1	18,209
Chance, Linda	66	10	12	14	115,651
Chandler, J. M.	26	0	0	4	9,456
Chandler, Kevin	75	4	7	7	27,079
Chapa, Joe	5	1	1	0	4,614
Chaparro, Dubis	23	2	4	2	24,770
Chaparro, Gayla	24	1	3	1	8,373
Chapman, Debbie	3	0	1	0	4,480
Chapman, Dorothy Jean	32	1	3	8	20,838
Chapman, James K.	14	0	2	2	26,660
Chapman, James R.	15	2	5	1	23,997
Chapman, Robert K.	29	3	1	7	21,346
Chappell, Allan	3	0	0	0	580
Chappell, Ronald M.	104	4	6	13	27,247
Charalambous, Elizabeth R.	14	2	1	2	110,943
Charalambous, John	100	14	10	15	517,276
Charette, Stacy S.	1	1	0	0	1,640
Charles, Freddie	34	1	5	0	18,783
Charlton, Brent W.	54	9	9	10	131,547
Charlton, Daryn	6	0	4	0	4,475
Charlton, V. Joan	44	8	4	1	67,810
Charoo, Wellesley	73	5	10	1	108,941
Chase, David	29	3	4	4	57,061
Chase, Timothy K.	110	14	10	11	103,146
Chatlos, Jr., Donald	76	12	9	6	1,528,196
Chatters, Benard	84	16	10	7	166,972
Chatters, Maynard	28	2	5	2	63,678
Chaudoin, William C.	2	0	1	0	1,550
Chavez, Baldomero	2	2	0	0	5,640
Chavez, Benjamin	1	0	0	0	0
Chavez, Enrique	9	1	1	0	3,624
Chavez, Felix E.	95	9	6	9	151,921
Chavez, Fernando	1	0	0	0	0
Chavez, Francisco	88	5	7	11	65,847
Chavez, Jesus	80	10	5	7	106,968
Chavez, Joe R.	49	2	6	8	23,278
Chavez, Larry	5	1	1	0	6,813
Chavez, Lori	42	1	0	5	12,944
Chavis, Rellis	10	0	0	0	1,980
Chciuk, Richard	1	0	0	0	80
Cheeks, Joseph	166	29	19	18	252,338
Cheeks, Kitty R.	128	19	8	19	239,997
Cheff, Chrissy	36	3	2	6	8,005
Cheff, Kenneth R.	5	0	0	1	415
Cheff, William	11	2	3	2	4,626
Cheloha, Donald F.	41	1	4	5	35,826
Chesmore, Gayle	19	0	0	0	511
Chew, Matthew	109	6	17	13	341,075
Childers, James R.	95	7	18	14	57,126
Childress, Lucy	57	4	0	1	23,690
Chilton, Gary	9	1	0	2	5,942
Chin, Peter A.	45	2	4	4	25,105
Ching, Edylyn	8	0	2	3	14,290
Chinn, Fred J.	60	5	3	6	68,428
Chipman, Shane	1	0	0	1	500
Chleborad, Lynn	367	37	68	48	620,047
Chlomos, John E.	3	1	0	0	9,600

Trainer	Sts	1st	2d	3d	Purses
Cho, Alexander	10	0	2	3	4,104
Cho, Myung Kwon	14	2	1	1	64,660
Cholity, Steven R.	16	1	2	3	21,195
Chong, Patrick	23	2	0	1	17,465
Christensen, Al	59	6	2	6	47,001
Christensen, Warren	4	0	0	0	644
Christenson, Jackie	51	3	7	6	85,584
Christian, Billy	25	4	5	4	12,695
Christie, Clifton A.	23	0	0	2	6,459
Christmas, William G.	155	8	22	26	177,195
Christoffersen, Farrell	31	9	6	5	60,191
Christopherson, Pam	16	2	2	3	7,028
Chubb, Beverley	83	5	6	4	196,689
Chumney, Kevin K.	26	1	1	1	14,519
Chung, Victor	57	4	3	9	99,211
Churchman, Jr., John E.	20	1	3	3	18,733
Ciaio, Charles A.	21	1	3	2	13,770
Ciardullo, Jr., Richard J.	388	47	51	59	969,146
Ciardullo, Sr., Richard J.	6	1	2	0	13,832
Ciavaglia, Gilbert	109	12	13	10	172,988
Cibelli, Jane	121	8	20	17	241,618
Cifarelli, Frank	31	0	2	3	9,218
Cimini, Michael A.	16	2	3	2	17,045
Cimini, Paul	55	4	7	13	82,693
Cimini, Peter	7	1	0	0	2,300
Cioffi, Antonio	89	7	11	11	111,963
Ciresa, Martin E.	138	19	31	15	872,162
Cirian, Phil	32	4	3	4	23,206
Cirillo, John	63	2	7	7	231,691
Claflin, Marvin	30	0	1	2	6,600
Claflin, Ruth	55	1	2	1	9,888
Clagett, Christine F.	11	1	0	1	20,380
Claridge, Jimmie D.	137	20	17	12	403,751
Clark, Brad	1	0	0	0	0
Clark, Brandon	1	0	0	0	0
Clark, Clay W.	21	1	4	1	8,709
Clark, Dale T.	30	0	2	3	15,340
Clark, Derran Joseph	1	0	0	0	0
Clark, Dick R.	475	97	86	52	1,445,356
Clark, Edward T.	155	9	12	14	100,339
Clark, Harold G.	7	0	2	1	5,538
Clark, Ivan M.	29	1	2	1	6,090
Clark, Justin	9	0	1	0	1,053
Clark, Keith	36	5	1	2	29,941
Clark, Kelly D.	29	3	8	3	25,405
Clark, Kevin D.	5	0	0	0	0
Clark, Kevin G.	234	30	38	32	321,514
Clark, Kimberly G.	24	0	3	3	30,152
Clark, Kirt W.	1	0	0	0	50
Clark, Phillip	26	2	2	0	22,624
Clark, Sharon B.	6	1	2	2	30,045
Clark III, Henry S	1	0	0	0	1,500
Clark Loza, Beth A.	14	2	1	0	15,011
Clarke, Jamie	22	3	3	3	35,829
Clarken, Rebecca	11	2	3	2	9,408
Clarkston, Fred	9	0	2	0	874
Clary, Donald	6	0	0	1	660
Class, Raymond W.	28	4	4	4	79,336
Clatterbuck, Ronald P.	24	1	0	1	19,805
Clauson, Connie	15	1	5	3	21,226
Clauson, Geoffrey	11	0	0	2	2,160
Clauss, Keith	6	0	0	0	389
Clay, Gerald	5	0	0	0	195
Clay, Royce G.	5	0	1	0	3,290
Clay, Jr., Shirley W.	77	6	9	7	142,414
Clay, Sr., William E.	44	0	0	3	2,869
Clayton, W. L.	24	2	1	4	59,423
Cleary, Brian A.	29	3	4	1	53,345
Clemens, Darryl J.	10	3	0	0	36,803
Clemens, Edward R.	10	4	2	1	39,388
Clemens, James	4	0	0	0	277
Clement, Christophe	344	68	58	51	3,541,781
Clement, Linda M.	172	7	6	12	75,395
Clement, III, Roland P.	14	3	0	1	41,100
Clements, Alvin H.	47	7	2	2	50,527
Clements, Bob	2	1	0	0	2,173
Clements, Doug R.	6	0	0	1	1,438
Clements, John R.	27	2	4	8	14,770
Clemmer, Gregory P.	11	0	2	3	18,964
Clemmer, Phillip J.	28	3	1	3	18,593
Clemmons, Jim	5	3	0	0	36,958
Clemmons, John	4	0	0	0	462
Clemson, Elmer E.	25	1	5	4	23,828
Clevenger, Billy	3	0	0	0	1,500
Clevenger, Carl	12	0	2	2	3,971
Clevenger, David Lee	29	1	4	6	23,725
Clevenger, Linda	18	0	1	2	11,760
Clifton, Cheryl L.	32	0	3	2	11,278
Cline, Leon	32	8	3	6	82,905
Cline, Robert C.	148	18	25	18	171,204
Clinton, Donna	18	4	2	2	6,396
Close, Lewis P.	173	9	11	18	176,671
Cloud, James	1	0	0	0	0
Cloud, L. D.	30	0	1	2	2,149
Clouston, Edward	239	31	29	27	350,090
Clouston, III, Burley	106	14	18	10	226,307
Cloutier Jacobson, Toni	86	12	17	13	307,665
Cluley, Denis	117	22	18	19	165,130
Clum, James	104	6	15	14	57,339
Clyde, Doug	2	0	1	1	640
Clyde, Terry	194	24	23	32	368,368
Coates, Lowell F.	35	5	6	4	40,882
Coatney, Betty L.	109	12	13	14	145,768
Coatney, Charles R.	12	1	1	1	11,485
Coatrieux, Eric	71	13	9	9	1,335,774
Coats, Vernon	8	0	0	0	787
Cobb, Maurice W.	13	2	4	0	16,955
Coble, Kenneth	26	0	0	2	5,435
Cocciolone, Gus J.	16	1	0	1	6,347
Cocelli, Jr., Louis J.	4	0	0	1	3,230
Cochran, Henry S.	55	6	7	5	184,185
Cochran, Michael A.	4	0	0	0	86
Cockburn, Bay	1	0	0	0	0
Cockrell, John	7	1	0	1	7,740
Cockrill, Richard H.	31	1	0	3	20,063
Cocks, Edwin Burling	7	0	0	0	2,138
Cocks, William Brinton	3	0	0	1	1,850
Coey, Paul	21	2	3	1	12,383
Coffelt, Cliff	18	0	1	2	1,596
Coffey, Junior L.	49	10	14	9	157,597
Coffey, Marialice	131	4	7	6	76,378
Coffey, Pamela	4	0	0	0	117
Coffey, Jr., Chester	2	0	0	0	534
Coffman, Ray	1	0	0	0	90
Cogburn, Orrin	23	3	2	2	22,389
Coghlan, Judith	32	2	7	3	33,063
Cohen, Michael V.	65	5	5	10	43,852
Cohen, Stuart	54	12	7	5	62,871
Cohn, Alice G.	62	3	7	7	139,534
Colalillo, Dominic	5	3	0	0	31,440
Colbourne, Gordon C.	82	8	9	5	278,261
Cole, Bryan D.	29	4	3	5	37,447
Cole, Eddie A.	109	10	14	13	192,761
Cole, Jerry M.	113	13	17	8	117,097
Cole, Keith	19	1	1	1	7,599
Cole, Kim	32	0	5	5	14,275
Cole, Ralph W.	7	0	0	1	794
Cole, Scott	3	0	0	0	600
Cole, Terry James	70	7	9	7	51,747
Cole, III, Philip J.	26	0	3	0	5,635
Colee, Frank	38	8	8	8	64,006
Colello, Jr., George	54	7	13	3	36,838
Colello, Sr., George	82	15	12	13	103,438
Coleman, Cassandra	1	0	0	0	0
Coleman, Thomas R.	38	11	4	3	107,739
Coletti, Jr., Edward J.	286	36	33	31	918,211
Colflesh, Craig M.	26	2	2	3	18,252
Colgan, Kelly A.	22	0	4	3	29,300
Collazo, Henry	445	59	62	51	1,269,953
Collazo, Susan	11	2	0	0	5,366
Collazo, Victor O.	116	13	6	19	153,876
Collet, Robert J.	2	0	0	0	20,000

Trainer	Sts	1st	2d	3d	Purses
Collet, Rodolphe	1	0	0	0	0
Collier, Jimmy C.	49	2	7	5	33,932
Collier, Rickey L.	7	0	0	0	3,520
Collier, Robert W.	49	3	3	2	16,186
Colligan, Ronald	75	7	13	4	88,930
Collins, Charles M.	4	0	0	0	1,500
Collins, Dick	51	4	5	3	20,580
Collins, Don	69	10	3	10	107,890
Collins, Holly	27	2	0	4	36,522
Collins, Kim	1	0	0	0	80
Collins, Michael J.	193	25	23	31	234,601
Collins, William G.	17	1	2	1	26,787
Colson, Larry A.	3	0	0	0	0
Comber, Jamie	14	2	1	2	10,098
Combest, Reed M.	160	14	28	25	259,955
Combs, Don	71	8	6	9	180,208
Combs, Don J.	55	7	7	6	40,617
Combs, Leonard R.	5	0	0	1	1,820
Combs, Mark A.	3	0	0	0	0
Comer, Earl Wayne	17	1	2	2	18,973
Comer, II, Lon	1	0	0	0	0
Comi, Jr., Ralph W.	23	2	2	4	31,169
Comontofski, Sandy	60	2	5	10	42,578
Compher, Clark	15	0	0	0	1,040
Compton, James R.	196	37	30	34	173,493
Comstock, J. D.	22	1	0	2	6,589
Conaway, Jr., Charles C.	56	4	8	10	89,211
Concessi, Armand	108	13	18	18	292,731
Condilenios, Dino K.	194	37	26	22	650,697
Condon, Jean	14	0	0	2	1,097
Condon, Leslie A.	72	1	10	2	83,371
Cone, Rodney J.	186	16	18	23	192,079
Conklin, Susan	1	0	0	0	375
Conley, Alice F.	4	0	0	0	780
Conley, Cathy	3	0	0	0	220
Conley, Richard	3	0	0	0	0
Conley, Warren L.	7	1	0	0	2,592
Conlon, Bette	17	0	1	4	13,432
Conlon, Melody	28	1	7	4	95,820
Connelley, Richard L.	2	0	0	0	115
Connelly, Ed	7	4	2	1	7,470
Connelly, Marcus	1	0	0	1	375
Connelly, Robert B.	27	5	5	7	37,882
Connelly, Ronald Rex	82	7	12	10	129,304
Connelly, Teresa	78	10	5	7	137,086
Connelly, William R.	195	31	29	28	699,046
Conner, Barbara Jean	71	5	9	11	56,589
Conner, John D.	111	18	16	13	208,717
Connolly, Michael	72	8	6	14	85,174
Connor, III, James P.	93	9	9	8	239,285
Conover, Roy T.	22	0	2	0	5,656
Conrad, E. J.	13	0	1	3	13,222
Conrad, Paul	47	10	4	7	133,960
Constant, Chester	37	2	3	2	6,047
Constant, Tom	22	2	5	1	19,340
Constantine, Carol	157	5	18	12	97,099
Contessa, Gary C.	537	75	91	60	2,730,527
Conto, Kevin	2	0	0	0	0
Contreras, Javier	126	11	13	17	205,659
Contreras, Martin	26	1	1	1	18,135
Conway, Michael A.	51	10	8	3	123,473
Conyers, William F.	73	13	6	9	69,061
Cook, Brian	8	0	1	2	1,331
Cook, Carol	32	0	4	6	16,739
Cook, Chad	37	2	4	3	12,228
Cook, David D.	24	3	4	2	23,850
Cook, David K.	4	0	0	0	790
Cook, Deanna	2	0	0	0	0
Cook, Don C.	22	1	4	1	26,080
Cook, James H.	3	0	0	0	130
Cook, Jason G.	59	7	2	8	88,757
Cook, Joanie M.	32	5	2	2	54,336
Cook, lyle	6	2	0	2	3,012
Cook, Ruth A.	67	7	5	7	86,038
Cook, Thomas W.	2	0	0	0	410
Cook, Tim	6	0	1	0	620
Cooksey, Gene	4	0	0	0	444
Coombs, Jack	57	6	6	15	35,495
Coombs, Leroy G.	11	5	2	1	13,996
Cooney, Susan S.	200	8	20	20	255,528
Coonse, Tracy	60	7	7	12	53,692
Cooper, Carl J.	97	8	3	7	70,690
Cooper, Franklin D.	39	3	9	5	41,100
Cooper, Fred	1	1	0	0	1,200
Cooper, J. Curtis	26	3	2	3	17,862
Cooper, Jack	32	1	5	1	38,391
Cooper, James F.	3	0	1	1	2,700
Cooper, John D.	18	2	4	1	16,360
Cooper, John L.	18	3	3	4	19,898
Cooper, Kay Penny	2	1	0	0	192,678
Cooper, Stacey	56	9	9	3	115,644
Copeland, Jimmy	29	1	1	4	26,703
Coppola, Joseph M.	81	8	5	6	112,208
Copsey, John W.	23	3	3	5	73,775
Corbel, Emile J.	197	36	18	16	410,672
Corbel, Keith	43	6	13	8	101,623
Corbett, Brian	6	0	1	1	4,218
Corcoran, Deborah A.	2	0	0	0	1,440
Corcoran, William J.	9	0	0	1	1,820
Cordero, Angel M.	1	0	0	0	150
Cordova, Joe G.	45	4	3	6	34,152
Corley, Jr., William Hart	1	0	0	0	0
Cormier, Alvin	3	0	0	0	0
Cormier, Edward	10	0	0	0	315
Cormier, Houston	59	4	3	5	44,763
Cormier, John E.	25	1	1	3	35,518
Cormier, Jr., Donald	38	3	2	3	78,886
Cormier, Sr., Donald J.	427	28	39	49	526,313
Cornejo, Cesar	1	0	0	0	0
Cornelius, Carl W.	40	2	1	1	22,029
Cornell, Nathalie	2	0	0	0	289
Cornwell, Fred E.	1	0	0	0	218
Cornwell, Jr., James L.	51	1	1	1	22,265
Coronado, J. Guadalupe	5	0	0	0	424
Corrado, Robert	161	22	21	14	434,552
Corrales, Jose	66	7	8	8	124,093
Corrao, James	11	0	2	2	21,637
Correa, Alex A.	41	1	2	1	21,616
Correa, Jeff	41	1	1	4	43,442
Correa, Ray	45	1	2	3	10,089
Correa, Victor J.	6	0	0	1	1,391
Correas, IV, Ignacio	3	0	1	0	2,940
Corredor, Enrique	83	6	7	15	121,130
Correnti, Anthony	360	51	57	45	946,166
Correnti, Armand W.	1	0	0	0	0
Corrigan, Jimmy	59	6	5	7	65,217
Cortez, John E.	12	0	0	0	2,588
Cory, William R.	58	4	8	6	44,026
Coryat, John A.	5	0	0	0	1,225
Cosme, Pablo	6	0	0	0	1,406
Costa, Frank	168	13	21	18	559,642
Costa, Fred	14	0	1	1	2,473
Costantino, Frank S.	10	1	0	1	9,131
Costello, Lisa R.	3	0	0	0	1,127
Costew, John B.	63	8	11	9	171,460
Cote, Jr., Fred	6	0	1	1	754
Cote, Sr., Fred	4	0	1	0	484
Cotey, David	247	32	33	31	1,680,885
Cotrone, Denise	27	2	2	0	8,921
Cotter, Mary M.	4	0	1	0	8,670
Cotter, Mike	9	2	2	1	8,966
Cotto, Luis A.	27	2	1	3	11,282
Cotton, John M.	38	3	3	4	51,198
Couch, Derek	6	0	0	1	1,788
Couch, Terry N.	9	1	3	0	11,640
Couchenour, Lee	44	2	2	6	43,295
Coughlin, Daniel	74	9	11	10	58,561
Coughlin, Edward D.	10	1	1	2	6,590
County, Jr., Patrick	82	13	15	6	144,467
County, Jr., Thomas J.	44	3	2	3	59,526
Coursey, Elmer D.	1	0	1	0	1,835
Courtemanche, Candy R.	42	1	2	0	13,051

Trainer	Sts	1st	2d	3d	Purses
Courtright, Clarence	30	3	3	6	15,212
Courville, Leroy	8	0	0	0	1,259
Couse, Maggie P.	24	5	2	5	48,240
Cousins, Peter	2	0	0	0	0
Covello, Andrea A.	23	1	2	0	15,030
Covello, Frank W.	55	3	10	6	43,777
Cowan, Elmer C.	131	12	17	13	101,487
Cowan, Gary	58	0	5	6	17,878
Cowan, Jessie W.	1	0	0	0	0
Cowan, Jon M.	7	1	4	1	23,510
Cowan, Mark S.	7	1	0	2	7,882
Cowans, William D.	137	29	27	17	164,230
Cowden, James H.	11	1	2	1	1,736
Cowgar, Steve	5	1	0	1	3,420
Cowgill, Charles P.	8	0	1	0	1,134
Cox, Amalia B.	30	4	6	2	80,165
Cox, Brad H.	3	1	0	1	10,245
Cox, Gary Don	23	2	0	2	23,417
Cox, George	6	0	1	0	762
Cox, Greg D.	59	9	10	3	374,634
Cox, Jerry Edward	26	0	0	0	1,458
Cox, Jimmy	23	0	0	1	1,407
Cox, John E.	86	15	17	19	136,301
Cox, John M.	109	8	7	11	50,816
Cox, Kenneth M.	242	37	36	31	612,796
Cox, Kyle M.	1	0	0	0	270
Cox, L. Craig	313	50	49	46	695,154
Cox, Loren G.	259	28	39	19	420,310
Cox, William B.	26	0	1	0	4,343
Cox, III, William T.	28	0	4	2	8,793
Coyle, George R.	47	1	1	0	28,446
Coyle, Vernon D.	125	13	7	14	70,078
Coyote, Jason J.	131	6	8	11	96,305
Crabtree, Bobby L.	25	4	2	6	39,608
Crabtree, Cecil	4	0	0	1	1,479
Crabtree, Larry W.	55	7	8	4	54,582
Crabtree, Lynn	7	1	3	1	16,072
Craddock, Kari	139	18	17	15	219,897
Craddock, Patrick J.	10	0	1	0	2,945
Craft, Micky F.	15	0	2	0	4,699
Crago, Alan P.	18	1	3	4	19,390
Crago, Holly	15	0	0	2	2,933
Crago, Terry J.	75	2	3	5	35,479
Cragun, Blake L.	11	6	2	1	9,430
Craig, Gary	25	2	1	1	18,820
Craig, James R.	38	8	4	5	11,098
Craig, Jr., Lewis E.	79	1	6	7	53,287
Craig, Sr., Lewis E.	21	0	1	5	10,911
Craigmyle, Scott J.	202	9	19	23	183,167
Crandall, Cynthia A.	21	2	3	5	30,576
Crandall, David E.	14	0	0	0	1,340
Crane, Clovis	18	2	2	1	14,306
Cranford, Britt G.	55	5	16	9	35,052
Cranwell, James E.	84	13	11	9	145,529
Cravens, III, Ronnie E.	24	0	1	0	4,716
Crawford, Carl	2	1	0	1	6,745
Crawford, Clinton	7	1	0	0	1,579
Crawford, George	12	1	2	2	20,045
Crawford, John D.	26	0	1	0	3,244
Crawford, Matt	1	0	0	0	0
Crawford, Ray	7	0	0	0	3,561
Crayne, Jeff A.	28	1	3	3	15,445
Creager, Tommie	44	6	2	3	54,723
Crean, Robert F.	33	3	5	2	143,687
Creath, Heather	44	6	11	7	203,805
Creaton, Scott	25	3	3	4	38,018
Credeur, A. J.	47	5	3	7	39,501
Credeur, Joseph S.	1	1	0	0	8,100
Creel, Rick	17	0	1	3	9,844
Crenshaw, Bobby D.	3	0	0	0	1,270
Crescini, Joseph D.	31	3	1	3	21,825
Crete, Pierre	19	2	3	2	34,444
Crews, Nelson W.	9	1	3	2	13,844
Crider, Charlotte	79	6	3	4	47,305
Criollo, Manuel	173	22	10	16	366,240
Cripps, Kenneth	42	1	4	5	37,588

Trainer	Sts	1st	2d	3d	Purses
Crispin, Cathy	17	1	0	3	3,661
Cristel, Mark J.	188	15	22	17	418,590
Crock, Michael W.	9	1	1	2	6,783
Crocker, Alan	194	27	30	21	148,066
Crofoot, Eric	3	1	0	0	2,519
Croft, Barry N.	150	16	20	20	262,620
Croll, William E.	41	2	4	7	65,835
Cronk, Samuel F.	156	15	14	21	203,446
Cronquist, Donna	2	0	0	0	133
Crook, W. Byron	51	2	3	4	24,865
Crooked Arm, Dale D.	3	0	0	0	173
Crooks, Jeffrey S.	68	7	6	12	87,815
Crosby, Jr., Donald	1	0	0	0	122
Cross, Cathy	26	0	0	0	2,742
Cross, Edward D.	12	1	1	3	6,228
Cross, Gary W.	250	54	35	34	886,219
Cross, Judy	28	1	1	5	16,466
Cross, Jr., David C.	18	1	6	1	35,984
Crotts, Jim	19	2	2	3	3,764
Crouse, Drexel E.	50	1	3	4	28,873
Crowder, Mike	120	13	15	13	160,411
Crowe, Brian	3	1	0	0	6,940
Crowe, Chris M.	27	1	1	4	14,951
Crowe, Kenneth W.	6	0	0	0	764
Crowell, Duane E.	14	1	0	0	5,799
Crowell, Susan L.	57	5	9	2	75,722
Crowley, Joseph J.	1	0	0	0	0
Crowley, Tom	113	11	10	17	63,883
Crozier, Jeff	17	0	4	1	6,333
Crozier, Thomas A.	49	1	6	6	13,794
Cruce, Tina	3	0	0	0	475
Crumley, Jevon	62	13	6	7	100,295
Crumpler, Norman	1	0	0	0	85
Cruz, Eduardo	1	0	0	0	140
Cuadra, Victor	71	6	6	6	256,917
Cuadras, Jose	3	1	0	0	4,692
Cuccia, L. Jay	74	5	12	10	94,365
Cuccurullo, Pat	174	47	30	24	675,392
Cucinotta, Anthony	74	6	5	7	45,942
Cuevas, Ellis	17	0	2	3	16,635
Cugnini, Patrick L.	12	1	0	3	14,096
Cullen, Brian	6	0	2	0	2,236
Cullum, William H.	12	1	0	0	7,860
Culotta, Ray J.	14	2	5	1	25,025
Cumbie, Cora Lee	21	1	0	2	3,533
Cummings, David	102	8	11	20	121,114
Cummings, Ron	6	0	0	1	1,411
Cummins, Cindy M.	2	0	0	0	532
Cummins, George	59	5	10	7	82,215
Cunard, Murray	11	1	0	3	2,925
Cundiff, Roy	51	15	5	9	72,057
Cunningham, Andrea L.	17	1	1	4	7,615
Cunningham, Anthony F.	1	0	0	0	114
Cunningham, Donna	3	0	0	1	1,503
Cunningham, James P.	108	23	16	16	160,601
Cunningham, L. Richard	11	1	0	1	4,375
Cunningham, Michael W.	18	0	0	0	354
Cuprill, Charles A.	138	12	16	22	211,225
Currin, William L.	67	5	7	7	366,331
Curry, Dee	140	13	11	15	184,690
Curtis, Faron M.	3	0	0	0	254
Curtis, Hal V.	1	0	0	0	0
Curtis, James F.	14	2	4	1	24,080
Curtis, Jeffrey S	1	0	0	0	0
Curtis, Larry F.	25	3	2	0	49,052
Curtsinger, Scott	9	0	0	0	653
Cuttino, Marion L.	214	26	35	28	513,707
Czerwonka, Richard	1	0	0	0	45
Czyzewski, Joseph	1	0	0	0	0
Dagg, Larry	36	3	0	3	56,658
Daggett, Michael H.	39	4	4	3	170,802
Dahl, David	17	1	1	1	10,357
Dahle, Norm	49	11	11	6	63,758
Dahlke, John	2	0	0	1	326
Dahlke, Kyle	20	0	4	4	3,516
DAiello, George C.	1	0	0	0	260

Trainer	Sts	1st	2d	3d	Purses
Daigle, Ronnie J.	11	0	1	1	7,920
Daigle, Walter C.	51	3	2	8	40,813
Daigrepont, Vicki	14	4	0	2	46,698
Dailey, Ronald W.	57	3	4	6	25,674
Dale, Charles	1	0	0	1	500
Dale, Jack W.	32	3	2	4	15,653
D'Alessandro, Ralph	289	57	44	32	817,057
Daley, Bruce	6	0	0	1	3,280
Dalke, Ray	18	1	3	3	4,290
Dalrymple, Darcie C.	68	1	5	8	48,404
Dalton, Tim	3	0	0	0	173
Daly, Patrick J.	146	21	19	15	472,781
Dalziel, Robyn	4	0	1	0	2,283
D'Amario, Michael	165	29	29	16	383,413
Damm, Raymond C.	19	1	4	3	10,733
Damron, Patricia	2	0	1	0	1,488
Danaher, James E.	68	5	10	10	106,420
Dancer, Marvin J.	48	2	3	7	50,231
Dandy, Ronald J.	367	73	52	57	784,364
Danelson, Gary	171	29	26	31	244,527
D'Angelo, Michael T.	13	1	1	1	16,365
D'Angelo, Jr., Anthony F.	39	4	2	4	26,077
Danger, Kevin	65	6	6	10	82,369
Daniels, Connie L.	76	2	6	7	55,810
Daniels, Hugh	24	0	0	1	3,355
Daniels, Patrick B.	75	17	13	20	272,358
Danielson, Del S.	15	1	1	5	13,965
Danks, Thomas	26	3	2	4	52,851
Danley, Dennis B.	69	5	10	8	124,329
Danley, Fred I.	241	35	36	34	706,613
Danley, John L.	45	2	2	2	18,208
Danner, Douglas W.	125	16	20	21	178,856
Danner, Mark	45	6	4	4	113,365
Danylchuk, Dave A.	6	1	0	0	1,650
Dapp, Russell P.	8	0	0	1	2,443
Daria, Angelo J.	59	7	5	11	85,760
Darjean, Paul	56	4	4	5	120,180
Darnell, Cliff W.	29	5	1	3	48,915
Darrus, Thomas	8	1	0	0	6,930
Dartez, Lawrence	1	0	0	0	0
Dautreuil, Calvin D.	26	9	6	5	91,486
Davenport, Bill	1	0	0	0	84
David, Paul	4	0	0	0	0
David, Ron	62	8	11	15	48,633
David, Jr., Sam B.	198	44	32	21	984,012
Davidovich, Andrew	141	7	7	11	74,882
Davidson, Doug	24	1	2	0	12,309
Davidson, Ernie	9	2	0	0	12,720
Davidson, Gordon J.	15	0	3	1	8,755
Davidson, Milo Brent	250	24	41	24	248,001
Davidson, Nan	18	1	2	5	26,364
Davidson, Robert J.	16	0	0	0	1,350
Davies, Alberta	13	1	4	0	39,129
Davies, Deanne	27	5	3	6	119,169
Davies, Joe G.	6	2	2	2	22,350
Davies, Norman S.	64	2	7	14	56,911
Davies, Ronald	27	2	2	2	24,796
Davies, Scott	7	0	1	0	1,972
Davies, Stewart G.	21	0	0	0	2,190
Davis, Charles F.	10	0	0	0	625
Davis, Charlie	31	0	6	4	16,832
Davis, Clarence L.	1	0	0	0	0
Davis, Donna M.	26	3	0	6	29,710
Davis, Duke	5	0	0	0	650
Davis, Edgar	1	0	0	0	0
Davis, Frank	28	6	4	2	33,826
Davis, Gale	1	0	0	0	80
Davis, Gary K.	60	3	2	8	26,969
Davis, Gene	72	6	9	10	38,068
Davis, George	84	2	7	6	11,986
Davis, James A.	15	3	0	1	39,432
Davis, Joe	60	3	6	9	69,762
Davis, Joseph D.	187	30	29	20	280,595
Davis, Keith	17	1	1	4	3,006
Davis, Liane P.	72	3	6	3	57,572
Davis, Lloyd J.	1	0	0	1	324
Davis, Marvin J.	23	0	4	3	18,596
Davis, Melvin E.	1	0	0	0	61
Davis, Melvin W.	95	11	14	12	63,402
Davis, Nicole	4	0	0	0	660
Davis, Peter	29	0	2	6	11,487
Davis, Philip L.	2	0	0	1	730
Davis, Randy J.	10	0	1	1	4,545
Davis, Randy L.	13	1	1	0	3,969
Davis, Raymond L.	36	2	2	3	26,529
Davis, Rhonda B.	13	2	2	1	39,975
Davis, Ronald D.	5	2	1	0	2,227
Davis, Russell E.	125	16	19	15	307,976
Davis, Samuel G.	9	2	1	3	28,436
Davis, Scooter	358	68	47	34	773,589
Davis, Shawn H.	59	9	8	11	47,860
Davis, Steve H.	17	0	0	0	1,292
Davis, Terry	17	2	1	3	3,606
Davison, Melissa	4	2	0	1	35,380
Dawes, Gene	18	2	4	3	8,080
Day, Danny	2	0	0	0	253
Day, Diane M.	60	5	10	6	59,969
Day, James E.	127	5	13	10	524,106
Day, James M.	69	7	10	9	162,749
Day Phillips, Catherine	88	15	13	12	1,654,688
De Amelio, Gerald	27	2	2	2	20,190
De Angelis, Steven A.	1	0	1	0	1,500
de Brevedent, Bertrand	74	6	11	9	213,370
De Camillis, George E.	31	0	1	1	9,251
de Gannes, Gregory	41	7	4	3	257,983
De La Cruz, Inez	9	0	0	0	390
De La Pena, Manny F.	2	0	0	0	94
De La Torre, Jose	22	5	4	2	28,705
De Marni, Caesar	67	5	3	3	84,540
De Ridder, Karel A.	58	10	4	4	156,990
de Roualle, Jean	1	0	0	0	750
De Seroux, Laura	98	8	16	17	1,664,329
De Stefano, Jr., John M.	132	15	19	17	637,094
Deacon, Charles E.	4	1	0	0	1,185
Dean, Dana D.	4	0	0	0	300
Dean, Kathy	10	2	1	4	4,040
Dean, William L.	1	0	0	0	0
Deane, Samuel C.	7	0	2	1	5,595
Dearringer, Darrell	31	1	3	5	21,849
Dearth, Donald E.	73	5	5	17	71,540
Deaton, William E.	51	5	1	7	28,165
DeBattista, Rick	7	0	0	0	0
DeBruhl, Kevin B.	39	4	1	5	39,095
deCesare, Barbara	3	0	0	0	672
Decker, John B.	21	2	0	2	16,237
Decker, Kenneth	50	8	10	5	187,787
Decker, Scott	1	0	0	0	64
Decker, Steve	9	0	1	0	7,504
Decker, Willette	92	4	7	13	75,846
Decker, Jr., Cecil	15	0	1	1	3,195
Decoteau, Wally	11	2	2	3	3,486
Dee, Tony	43	2	1	5	61,364
Deibler, Tina L.	58	1	2	5	15,662
Deisley, Doug	7	1	0	3	4,892
Deisley, Virgil L.	26	10	1	1	30,803
Dejarlais, Joe	1	0	0	1	130
Del Castillo, Janet	77	1	3	4	50,605
Delahoussaye, Darrel	51	5	8	1	86,101
Delahoussaye, Glenn	103	15	11	9	199,414
Delahoussaye, Harold J.	84	6	7	5	65,742
Delahoussaye, J. Huey	36	3	2	5	35,169
Delahoussaye, Kenneth W.	3	0	1	0	2,420
Delahoussaye, Mickey	82	3	13	14	90,672
Delahoussaye, Minos	37	2	3	8	30,337
Delahoussaye, Tommy J.	68	2	7	8	53,582
Deland, Stuart L.	5	0	0	0	435
Delaney, Jr., Ralph J.	8	1	0	2	10,495
Delcher-Sanchez, Mauricio	2	0	0	0	0
DeLeon, Rafael	16	3	2	1	49,580
Delgado, Lucy	40	5	7	4	60,791
DelGiudice, Kris	114	11	6	15	134,847
Delhomme, Jerry	27	4	4	7	65,337

Trainer	Sts	1st	2d	3d	Purses
Delia, William	196	26	24	25	422,540
D'Elia, Jenny	33	2	3	8	26,877
DeLima, Clifford	152	19	15	18	344,585
DeLima, Jose E.	64	2	11	5	145,724
Delk, Danny	113	9	16	13	142,346
Dellagatta, Perry	6	0	0	1	974
Delnegro, Brian	10	3	1	1	6,185
Delnegro, Michael	42	1	0	4	8,046
Delong, Gary	46	4	8	9	108,598
Delong, Joseph A.	3	0	0	0	815
Delong, Sr., Robert E.	43	5	8	4	66,180
Delozier, III, Joseph W.	83	13	8	10	144,180
Delp, Grover G.	137	33	17	20	756,144
Deluca, Louis J.	5	1	1	1	11,330
Deluca, Shirley M.	13	3	2	2	24,567
DeMario, Charles A.	153	8	15	20	91,463
Demasi, Kathleen A.	544	61	66	56	1,170,534
DeMatteis, Mike	13	0	3	3	1,972
Demczyk, Virginia	136	7	6	20	130,086
Demeritte, Larry W.	65	5	7	8	81,366
DeMola, Richard	68	2	3	9	135,641
Demorest, Gary E.	135	32	23	22	475,702
Dempsey, Robert S.	37	3	6	10	65,361
Dempsey, Susanne	28	3	1	2	37,801
DeNenno, Donald	4	0	0	0	1,800
Dennehy, Donna	18	0	2	1	5,155
Dennis, Betty Lou	27	1	0	5	11,177
Dennis, David H.	7	0	0	1	900
Dennis, John D.	2	0	0	0	129
Dennis, Laura	36	0	0	6	38,150
Dennison, Dan H.	166	41	23	17	407,073
Denzik, Jr., William J.	31	5	6	4	63,445
Depalo, Vincent T.	74	4	8	7	154,183
DePaulo, Michael P.	202	29	22	24	1,279,814
Deperrio, Frank	21	2	2	4	15,800
Depew, Jim	45	3	7	7	17,070
Deroache, John	6	0	0	2	612
Deroin, Gene	162	28	20	16	114,620
Deroin, Jamie	16	1	2	2	8,339
DeRose, Frank	15	0	0	3	2,799
DeRousselle, Peter P.	173	14	18	19	232,519
Derr, Robert A.	4	0	0	1	866
DeSanctis, Jaclyn	25	1	3	2	16,373
DeSanctis, Ralph V.	47	1	3	4	44,259
Desautel, Dave	17	4	1	3	6,577
Desensi, Robert L.	21	3	2	2	35,285
Deshotel, Justin Wayne	6	1	1	0	10,043
Desjarlais, Arnold	15	3	0	2	3,877
Desormeaux, J. Keith	149	21	20	22	406,901
Desoto, II, Donald G.	6	0	0	0	0
DeSouza, Bancroft	84	12	8	3	124,529
DeSouza, Crafton	24	1	3	1	22,810
DeSouza, Easton	58	4	1	4	67,485
DeSouza, Norman	118	14	17	9	480,125
DeStasio, Richard A.	107	2	9	7	225,469
Destefano, Mario R.	49	3	4	6	37,116
Deters, Celia J.	29	3	3	3	25,981
Detiege, Clifton	9	0	1	0	2,828
DeToro, Nickolas	122	18	11	17	504,038
Detrick, Cynthia L.	4	0	0	0	465
Deutsch, Leo D.	67	3	9	4	31,013
Deverell, Siobhan	24	0	3	2	41,784
Devereux, Joseph A.	24	6	5	4	94,002
Deville, Dwayne	19	1	1	1	25,581
DeVille, Carl J.	63	5	4	4	101,116
Devooght, Dennis	11	0	0	2	3,952
Dewey, Tom	58	9	9	8	131,244
Dewitt, Randy F.	2	0	0	0	825
Deyotte, Ronald A.	16	3	1	3	39,011
Deyotte, Ryan T.	1	1	0	0	9,831
Di Marsico, Elaine	56	4	3	2	53,919
Diaz, Antonio L.	78	16	10	14	198,695
Diaz, Cindy	20	3	1	4	23,303
Diaz, Pablo F.	26	3	0	2	25,193
Dibben, H. Kathleen	59	4	7	10	91,586
Dibona, Robert S.	64	13	7	5	185,746
Dicato, Jr., Joseph A.	8	0	0	0	496
Dickey, Charles L.	76	7	12	9	145,533
Dickey, Keith C.	86	15	13	12	261,030
Dickey, William E.	5	0	0	0	0
Dickinson, Cecil D.	65	3	2	7	59,376
Dickinson, Dennis	22	2	4	3	10,635
Dickinson, Michael W.	190	39	27	31	2,036,362
Didio, Keith	39	2	3	8	41,794
Diekema, Judy E.	7	1	0	0	9,660
Dieno, Arlen	45	3	7	10	12,100
DiGiovanni, John	10	2	2	1	96,700
Dill, George	13	1	1	1	13,969
Dillion, Jimmy L.	34	4	8	4	36,565
Dillon, Jacob L.	38	3	0	2	36,968
Dillon, Michael E.	5	0	0	0	0
Dillow, Daniel E.	100	3	8	10	100,889
Dillow, John H.	185	10	16	22	244,648
Dilodovico, Damon R.	112	15	19	19	282,482
DiMarco, John	37	2	6	7	157,275
Dimas, Robert E.	2	0	0	0	0
DiMauro, Stephen L.	186	26	33	27	447,975
Dimitriou, Harry E.	12	3	3	0	100,680
Dimmett, James	11	1	3	2	13,196
DiMuro, Anthony	10	0	0	0	330
DiNatale, Judith Z.	35	6	4	3	80,567
Dini, Michael	141	11	7	14	206,108
Dinoto, Lori	77	2	10	6	61,572
Diodoro, Robertino	223	31	28	19	355,973
Dion, Andrew W.	44	1	1	1	19,755
Dioses, Antonio	1	0	0	0	510
DiPasquale, Sam	57	8	9	7	252,786
Dipetrillo, Chris P.	4	0	0	1	930
DiSanto, Glenn B.	13	0	1	0	16,309
Dittfach, Hugo	43	7	1	9	605,728
DiVito, James P.	159	27	32	15	776,453
Divitto, Debra	67	5	11	7	80,512
Dixon, Charles	4	0	0	0	704
Dixon, Eileen M.	9	0	1	0	8,265
Dixon, Lawrence P.	5	1	0	2	6,510
Dixon, Linda K.	68	2	6	5	47,772
Dixon, Tim	16	0	2	3	1,706
Dixson, Sr., Emmett M.	57	3	3	4	29,085
Dobbie, Edward R.	21	2	3	1	41,776
Dobson, Kimberly A.	73	7	9	12	184,009
Dodd, Robin	11	0	1	0	1,320
Dodds, Louis W.	31	1	1	3	21,505
Dodds, Thomas A.	20	2	3	1	13,490
Dodgen, James A.	47	10	7	5	147,276
Dodgen, Joe B.	1	0	0	1	1,000
Dodson, Cliff	29	2	2	2	12,767
Dodson, Philip	46	0	0	1	5,981
Dodson, William E.	20	0	0	0	580
Dodwell, Ed	149	14	16	25	237,122
Doege, Glenn	81	10	4	11	56,067
Doering, Mark	140	11	17	12	93,371
Doering, Ned A.	1	0	0	0	205
Dolan, John K.	61	7	8	8	306,880
Dollase, Aimee	6	1	0	3	42,204
Dollase, Craig	191	35	23	26	1,951,256
Dollase, Wallace A.	111	21	19	18	1,866,307
Dollinger-Stehr, Linda	71	0	0	10	29,599
Dolph, Darla	63	5	4	9	26,357
Dominguez, Caesar F.	91	15	6	9	349,575
Dominguez, David	9	1	2	1	18,080
Dominguez, Henry	446	85	78	70	1,568,023
Dominguez, Jose Luis	19	2	0	3	27,239
Dominguez, Luis R.	53	5	8	6	59,475
Dominguez, Roberto	12	0	3	2	6,720
Dominguez, Sandra	15	0	3	1	17,067
Domino, Carl J.	53	6	7	8	211,917
Donaghey, Dianna	7	1	1	1	10,980
Donaghey, John R.	31	1	4	3	33,750
Donaho, Anthony	3	1	0	0	5,445
Donahue, Denise M.	12	0	2	5	22,925
Donald, Ira J.	56	2	5	7	46,072
Donaldson, Billy M.	2	0	0	1	470

Trainer	Sts	1st	2d	3d	Purses
Donaleshen, Nick	18	1	1	1	2,965
Donathan, David B.	37	6	4	3	36,029
Donato, Robert A.	8	1	0	0	4,320
Donegan, D. Loring	1	0	0	0	450
Donelan, Gary	14	0	0	1	1,073
Donk, David G.	291	25	30	56	1,230,912
Donley, Jim	52	4	7	9	37,173
Donlin, Larry D.	126	16	32	7	179,680
Donlin, Jr., Larry D.	28	5	1	3	20,548
Donmoyer, Steve J.	6	0	1	0	6,290
Donovan, Patrick R.	11	1	0	0	7,007
Dorchester, Dennis	35	3	4	3	15,548
Dore, Ralph J.	37	0	4	1	18,356
Dorfman, Leonard	11	2	2	0	182,980
Dorgan, Ursula	32	0	5	0	10,340
Dorignac, Valerie	4	0	0	0	0
Dorochenko, Gennadi	95	3	9	12	79,760
Dorris, Chris	175	20	26	21	269,726
Dorris, Thomas P.	10	1	0	0	12,561
Dorris, Tom	287	21	38	32	632,015
Dorsey, Sam A.	61	3	4	2	33,291
Dortch, David L.	4	0	0	0	562
Doth, Peter	19	1	0	1	10,281
Dotolo, David	84	8	10	9	122,660
Dotson, Millard F.	79	0	4	6	23,851
Doucet, Glen	120	8	13	15	122,128
Doucet, James Roger	109	6	4	5	90,825
Douglas, Andrew	3	1	0	1	7,050
Douglas, Sue	6	0	0	0	490
Douglas, Van D.	6	0	0	0	586
Doumen, Francois	1	0	0	0	45,000
Douthall, James D.	4	2	1	0	9,080
Douvres, James	1	0	0	0	0
Dovalina, Cristoval	9	1	1	0	3,980
Dove, II, William K.	3	0	0	0	0
Dow, Mary	20	0	0	0	1,189
Dowd, John F.	131	20	17	12	417,750
Downer, Harold R.	3	0	0	0	400
Downey, Francis L.	58	4	11	7	36,505
Downey, Maureen	8	0	2	1	5,847
Downie, Lofflin	6	3	1	1	5,560
Downing, William	79	11	11	10	116,520
Downs, Lincoln	14	3	1	2	18,379
Downs, Jr., Leonard J.	65	5	5	9	80,338
Doyle, Casey	20	3	1	5	67,997
Doyle, Michael J.	250	22	24	26	885,307
Doyle, William H.	13	1	3	1	12,859
Dragoo, Larry L.	18	0	0	1	2,690
Drake, David	12	2	0	2	5,645
Drake, Robert	4	0	0	0	618
Drake, Sherren A.	8	1	1	0	5,024
Drake, Suzanne M.	12	1	3	0	56,529
Draper, Carl W.	3	0	1	0	13,010
Draper, Marlon	74	8	12	9	40,181
Draper, Otto	28	2	2	7	28,653
Dresch, Heath D.	1	0	0	0	0
Drexler, Martin	71	7	9	9	56,371
Driever, Doug	126	19	15	14	255,824
Drinkard, Elbert L.	23	2	3	0	13,082
Dronen, Sam	17	3	3	5	15,260
Dronet, James	43	2	4	7	43,335
Drummond, Robert	3	1	1	0	1,640
Drummond, S. Diana	19	2	3	1	30,631
Drumwright, John	61	4	9	7	66,875
Drury, Jr., Thomas	53	8	11	2	61,108
Dryer, Rex	35	0	0	1	3,685
Dryer, Vicki	5	0	1	0	1,878
Drysdale, Neil D.	180	37	26	22	2,630,399
Dubois, Pete	68	12	10	8	54,800
Duby, Carol M.	16	5	0	3	12,752
Ducoing, Sturges J.	18	1	3	7	24,766
Duffy, Joseph	17	2	2	0	18,490
Duffy, Patricia L.	12	2	1	1	14,075
Duffy, Jr., Arthur A.	127	16	25	26	160,434
Duffy, Sr., Arthur A.	15	3	3	1	63,022
Dugas, Rayford	11	1	0	0	6,124
Duhon, James	86	4	5	9	45,200
Duhon, Joe	215	26	19	29	383,556
Duhon, R. Paul	199	15	28	21	273,329
Duke, Caleb	16	1	2	1	18,535
Duke, David L.	44	6	5	5	20,440
Duke, Gary	22	6	5	6	15,377
Duke, Karen E.	51	1	3	5	64,806
Duke, Steven	41	3	2	6	27,368
Dukes, Harris T.	35	1	3	2	19,577
Dukes, Robert	96	2	6	7	33,855
Dullea, Francis M.	88	9	7	10	109,610
Dumas, Brian E.	2	0	0	0	300
Dumont, Marti L.	52	5	3	3	38,179
Dunaway, Keith	11	0	3	3	22,740
Dunbar, Julia	3	0	0	0	340
Dunbar, Larry	56	7	7	5	97,194
Duncan, Bill D.	135	17	15	18	105,959
Duncan, Danny F.	18	0	1	3	11,988
Duncan, H. R.	10	0	0	1	1,254
Duncan, James A.	7	0	0	2	1,220
Duncan, Jim	3	0	0	2	520
Duncan, Joseph T.	4	0	0	0	479
Duncan, Larry	13	1	1	2	4,816
Duncan, Leonard M.	102	12	14	8	256,562
Duncan, Steven L.	123	15	8	11	158,635
Duncan, Susan H.	2	0	0	0	154
Dunford, Justin	5	1	0	0	2,400
Dunham, Bernard G.	4	0	1	1	5,910
Dunham, Bob G.	44	3	1	5	127,732
Dunham, Daniel	69	6	4	10	218,720
Dunivan, Janice A.	89	5	4	9	88,331
Dunkelberger, Casey A.	78	11	8	10	136,746
Dunlap, Shon M.	3	1	1	0	1,995
Dunlap, Tom D.	5	3	0	1	4,750
Dunlavy, Terrence W.	71	7	17	14	158,275
Dunlevy, Gary R.	1	0	0	0	0
Dunlop, Edward	1	1	0	0	733,200
Dunn, Greg	7	0	2	2	1,840
Dunn, Henry Ray	40	4	4	8	93,464
Dunn, John J.	64	9	15	7	182,510
Dunn, Stephen D.	17	4	1	0	28,885
Dunne, Leonard T.	37	3	9	4	78,480
Duplechin, James H.	147	11	10	14	159,962
Duplichan, William R.	76	6	13	7	115,114
DuPont, Laurent E.	58	5	5	10	60,023
Dupps, Kristina	20	2	2	6	112,331
Dupre, Alain	2	0	0	0	39,000
Dupuis, Jean-Pierre	41	5	7	2	161,200
Dupuy, Allen C.	82	6	9	4	54,806
Dupuy, Donna L.	85	3	6	11	119,165
Dupuy, Patrick J.	4	1	1	1	30,430
Duran, Antonio	5	1	1	0	13,385
Durbin, James R.	66	3	8	5	33,707
Durbin, William R.	12	2	1	1	18,904
Duree, Dominic C.	75	6	11	11	122,322
Durham, Corliss	13	1	3	1	21,780
Durkee, H. Brooks	3	0	0	0	350
Durrett, Walter J.	115	13	15	12	156,940
Durso, Robert J.	79	7	11	9	356,366
Duschka, Steve	115	21	21	13	46,831
Dussembaev, Talgat	8	0	0	1	3,491
Dutrow, Anthony W.	249	49	53	40	1,402,416
Dutrow, Jr., Richard E.	603	166	117	87	7,576,986
Dutton, Jerry	165	16	24	30	690,102
Duty, Brian	1	0	0	0	40
Dwight II, Francis M.	8	1	1	2	8,730
Dwoskin, Angelmarie A.	8	0	0	1	4,313
Dwoskin, Steven	117	20	23	10	322,921
Dwyer, David	30	7	8	2	342,149
Dye, Heather	70	5	9	10	22,683
Dye, Steven	49	2	6	4	41,860
Dyer, Carl M.	164	15	15	21	292,241
Dyer, Debbie Holland	117	13	12	17	200,390
Dyer, John R.	7	1	0	0	8,711
Dykeman, Pamela	15	1	2	1	9,243
Eafford, James	65	2	6	3	32,283

Trainer	Sts	1st	2d	3d	Purses
Eagan, Mark	56	1	0	5	8,759
Eanes, Charles	41	1	6	6	24,615
Earle, Bill K.	45	10	7	9	18,254
Earlywine, Christopher	17	2	3	3	27,684
Easley, Pat	16	2	2	2	6,477
Eason, Ralph	31	1	1	1	10,260
Eastwood, Rae	9	0	2	0	1,879
Eaton, Charles K.	7	2	3	0	8,616
Eaton, Terri	117	2	8	10	65,149
Ebardt, Janice	76	3	5	4	52,720
Ebert, Dennis W.	82	11	7	9	234,086
Eck, Jake	16	2	3	7	4,675
Eckrosh, James J.	4	0	0	0	315
Ecoffey, Gilbert L.	135	17	28	18	115,158
Eddings, Larry R.	15	0	2	0	2,771
Edel, Pamela F.	24	2	2	2	31,352
Edelman, Don	31	4	4	4	30,789
Edelman, George	2	0	0	0	0
Edgar, Ernest E.	9	1	0	0	3,187
Edgerly, Ken	2	0	0	0	685
Edlkraut, Edward	23	2	2	2	24,262
Edwards, Dennis Scott	42	6	2	4	44,487
Edwards, F. Bart	21	5	2	3	88,047
Edwards, Michael L.	13	2	1	1	9,235
Edwards, Oliver S.	134	13	13	23	218,320
Edwards, Parke	21	3	3	2	7,682
Edwards, Roger D.	7	2	3	1	24,129
Edwards, Ruth C.	2	0	0	0	0
Edwards, Shirley A.	43	2	5	3	29,650
Edwards, Stephen	54	3	6	6	150,525
Edwards, Toby D.	13	2	2	1	27,110
Edwards, Walter L.	20	1	1	1	18,445
Edwards, William R.	7	1	0	0	4,965
Eff, Joseph A.	48	4	6	7	71,924
Egan, Robert	22	0	2	0	5,099
Ehret, Sandra	66	6	9	6	28,123
Eickerman, Gary	16	1	0	1	9,923
Eikleberry, Clifford R.	14	0	1	1	2,850
Eikleberry, Donald	47	4	8	3	66,174
Eikleberry, Kevin	161	31	22	24	381,959
Eilers, Larry J.	188	21	21	31	216,634
Einerson, Kerry	24	2	1	0	15,283
Einhorn, Raymond P.	45	2	3	5	45,750
Ekins, Chad	10	0	1	0	2,362
Ekins, Dennis	22	1	5	3	19,185
Ekins, Ronald W.	11	1	3	0	3,028
Elamri, Hassan	77	3	4	10	69,746
Eldridge, Danny Joe	1	0	0	0	2,500
Elias, Wayne	14	7	3	1	66,710
Eliott, Roger	20	4	1	4	30,528
Elison, Gary C.	22	2	5	5	11,928
Elison, Tawnja	34	7	8	5	37,146
Elison, Tim W.	64	4	9	6	35,129
Ellersick, Roger	18	1	1	1	9,610
Ellickson, James	33	1	0	3	12,224
Ellingson, Anita	18	1	1	3	5,940
Elliot, Janet E.	64	4	8	6	146,361
Elliott, Teri	6	1	0	1	6,213
Elliott, Tim	27	6	3	2	16,057
Ellis, Gerald D.	1	0	0	0	0
Ellis, Jerry	12	1	0	2	20,756
Ellis, Jon C.	4	0	0	0	0
Ellis, Kelly	6	0	0	1	288
Ellis, Larry	18	0	1	0	2,015
Ellis, Leonard E.	165	13	17	14	98,953
Ellis, Randy J.	80	3	6	8	59,365
Ellis, Robert J.	25	0	2	2	13,330
Ellis, Ronald W.	121	24	16	19	1,322,251
Ellis, Sam H.	99	9	17	12	123,506
Ellsworth, Kim R.	11	0	1	1	5,865
Ellul, John J.	3	0	0	0	1,200
Elordi, Donna R.	142	18	14	20	316,695
Elrod, Richard L.	7	0	0	0	636
Elsom, Laurie	19	1	2	1	8,405
Elston, Brent	51	1	5	3	15,965
Elter, Bradley J.	16	0	2	0	3,859
Ely, Janice L.	91	7	4	16	168,460
Embry, Gene	67	2	4	5	37,166
Emerson, Elisabeth	2	0	0	0	0
Emery, Ronald W.	44	1	2	3	22,261
Engebretson, Art C.	7	0	1	2	2,946
Engel, Rick S.	151	29	27	15	321,695
Engel, Roger F.	180	51	23	24	331,120
England, Clyde W.	85	6	8	11	22,691
England, David P.	137	20	8	17	130,592
England, Deborah	78	10	6	12	457,665
England, Phillip	76	5	2	11	164,719
England, Jr., G. Marion	6	1	1	0	11,895
Engle, Kathleen	28	3	2	2	23,698
Englehart, Chris J.	650	149	114	101	1,520,898
Englehart, Jeremiah C.	55	5	5	5	142,470
Engley, Harrison	6	1	1	0	9,758
English, Edward T.	31	3	5	3	39,769
Enlow, John A.	39	3	3	4	17,037
Enlow, Ray A.	9	3	0	3	13,983
Ennis, Dell	1	0	0	0	0
Enriquez, Gilbert	6	1	0	0	1,540
Enriquez, Jesus J.	13	5	2	0	23,807
Ensom, Jim	37	2	4	2	35,444
Entenmann, William J.	34	4	2	6	134,640
Eoff, Terry	95	17	18	10	214,075
Epley, Jr., Steve	54	6	3	13	119,746
Eppler, Marsha C.	7	1	2	1	20,810
Eppler, Mary E.	192	24	21	31	613,951
Erb, Darrin	10	0	2	0	3,422
Erb, Jim	47	9	4	4	66,572
Erb, Michael D.	6	0	1	2	9,183
Ercanbrack, Tracy	3	0	0	0	800
Erfle, Gerald	5	0	0	0	887
Erickson, Darrel L.	8	0	0	0	610
Erickson, Elwood C.	25	0	1	0	10,181
Erickson, Kathy	2	0	0	0	0
Ericson, Tiffany	38	4	4	3	40,759
Erler, Jacqueline J.	29	1	1	4	33,316
Ermineskin, Curtis	7	1	2	0	2,240
Ernst, Ann	10	1	0	0	2,072
Ersoff, Stanley M.	121	20	18	18	380,455
Ervin, Jody	30	1	0	3	8,413
Ervin, Raymond E.	23	0	2	2	6,912
Ervin, Timothy	12	0	0	0	150
Erving, Tim	1	0	0	0	0
Ervin-Mezzacappa, Jody	1	0	0	0	0
Erwin, Dennis M.	45	7	4	5	115,158
Erwin, Ted	31	1	1	1	5,641
Eshelman, Bonnie	20	0	2	0	5,844
Esner, Tommy Lynn	7	1	1	2	11,443
Esparza, Osvaldo	25	2	0	1	8,145
Espinosa, Victor M.	62	2	7	9	92,443
Espinoza, Leonard A.	97	5	4	10	22,340
Espinoza, Valentine	12	1	0	4	5,760
Esposito, Michael F.	11	1	0	0	7,070
Espy, Jim	53	2	2	5	14,985
Esquibel, Mark	19	1	1	2	11,989
Esquibel, Robert L.	9	0	0	0	1,324
Esquibel, Robert O.	1	0	0	0	0
Esquibel, Sr., Richard Dean	53	1	4	4	11,945
Essenpreis, Eddie M.	424	69	83	62	670,906
Essex, Charles	50	8	9	9	56,323
Estep, Gary D.	3	0	1	0	2,508
Estes, Michael R.	56	12	9	9	97,044
Estevez, Manuel A.	123	11	10	20	214,929
Estilette, Earl	34	3	2	3	37,630
Estvanko, Richard	124	18	17	17	152,621
Etheridge, Milton B.	15	0	0	2	4,571
Ethridge, David	1	0	0	0	69
Eubanks, Annette M.	138	14	15	22	201,717
Eurton, Peter	124	14	26	19	595,790
Evans, Bart B.	50	6	7	7	133,517
Evans, Dan	43	3	1	2	17,204
Evans, Donald J.	3	0	0	0	240
Evans, Holly	36	3	3	6	93,105
Evans, Jim J.	60	10	11	7	41,963

Trainer	Sts	1st	2d	3d	Purses
Evans, Justin	237	33	26	33	163,977
Evans, Lynda	5	0	0	0	1,246
Evans, Roy	57	2	8	4	30,811
Evans, Suzanne G.	86	11	9	11	196,200
Evans, Timothy	3	0	1	0	5,868
Evans, William	80	7	7	9	34,926
Evans, Jr., George A.	12	0	1	2	3,635
Everard, Elizabeth	4	0	0	1	1,645
Everett, Scott	113	14	12	17	282,242
Everetts, Lester P.	3	0	1	0	1,474
Everman, Joseph	9	0	0	1	1,894
Eversole, Larry	13	4	0	0	14,015
Ewell, Rodger	7	0	0	1	110
Ewing, Calvin E	3	0	0	0	0
Ewing, Kim S.	167	13	10	17	131,329
Exposito, Adolfo J.	64	4	6	5	88,109
Eyerman, Lee J.	31	1	1	8	9,232
Ezekiel, Jr., Marshall	33	1	1	1	15,302
Ezra, Daryl G.	170	15	15	20	394,130
Fabre, Andre	3	0	0	0	22,500
Fabre, Jamie	8	0	1	1	5,468
Fagan, Lawrence G.	2	0	0	0	0
Fagan, Patricia L.	19	2	0	4	15,130
Fahey, III, John	54	13	8	5	232,965
Fahy, Timothy J.	12	0	1	1	1,840
Fair, James L.	50	0	1	1	17,168
Faircloth, Richard	37	2	0	3	23,147
Faircloth, Ronnie E.	91	3	3	6	66,863
Fairlie, Scott H.	304	48	32	39	1,648,951
Falat, Stephen	22	2	2	5	15,594
Falk, George W.	4	0	0	1	1,033
Falkner, John	14	1	0	0	8,488
Falldorf, Fred J.	64	9	10	17	191,358
Falls Down, Adlai	17	4	3	2	7,721
Falzone, Victor	53	4	8	5	142,040
Fanning, Jerry M.	93	11	7	8	280,495
Fanning, Marvin E.	42	2	4	4	17,688
Faraci-Walder, Francine	12	6	2	0	77,140
Faragoza, Rene	36	1	0	2	6,322
Fargnoli, Anthony F.	8	0	1	2	5,308
Farias, Adan	20	4	2	2	26,892
Farias, Jorge	1	0	0	0	225
Fariello, Vincent	9	0	0	0	501
Farina, Juan A.	2	0	1	0	1,800
Farkosh, George	19	3	1	0	27,830
Farler, Larry	56	3	5	5	25,559
Farley, Burton	6	0	2	0	2,674
Farley, James	42	2	3	3	22,016
Farmer, Murrell K.	6	0	0	1	1,144
Farnsworth, Deloy	22	4	3	2	16,901
Farquharson, Barranet	4	0	0	0	710
Farrell, Tom	44	6	7	7	15,459
Farris, Kevin	6	0	0	0	159
Farris, Steven W.	8	0	1	1	6,683
Farris, Vod J.	2	0	0	0	780
Farro, Patricia	479	80	66	52	1,365,040
Fauchald, Philip C.	45	1	3	5	28,219
Faul, Kenneth	21	5	5	3	65,452
Faul, Leo P.	14	0	0	0	870
Faulkner, Floyd	5	1	0	0	6,105
Faulkner, Jeffrey	34	9	5	2	30,374
Faulkner, Joseph Clark	460	85	59	66	448,662
Faulkner, Rodney C.	622	96	94	66	683,836
Favre, Kevin J.	11	1	0	1	4,111
Fawcett, Russell	7	0	1	2	6,020
Fawkes, David	236	36	29	33	975,063
Feasel, Steve	3	0	0	0	379
Feathers-Murray, Amy	47	8	3	7	62,935
Fede, Pietro	53	4	6	7	45,410
Federouch, Bernadine	3	0	1	1	7,440
Fee, John J.	4	0	0	0	900
Feebeck, Thomas H.	76	4	7	7	39,206
Fehr, Alec	90	11	19	7	576,738
Feilner, II, Raymond F.	6	0	0	0	0
Feliciano, Benny R.	85	21	13	11	133,896
Feliciano, Miguel A.	305	32	32	51	574,887
Feliciano, Trudy Veinot	4	0	0	0	381
Feliciano, Jr., Benjamin M.	317	69	53	52	1,665,721
Felipe, Dan	50	5	3	7	31,830
Felix, Ray	4	1	1	1	6,125
Fenack, Wayne	21	1	2	3	9,798
Fenack, Jr., Tony	19	1	1	0	20,296
Fendelet, Pat	12	1	0	2	20,474
Fendenheim, James R.	9	1	0	3	2,061
Fenimore, Elbert	51	1	2	6	31,243
Fenimore, Floyd E.	49	9	4	7	95,166
Fennessy, Michael	76	9	12	6	180,195
Fenton, Diane	9	1	0	0	8,559
Fenwick, H. Bruce	1	0	0	0	0
Fenwick, Jr., Charles C.	2	0	0	0	0
Fergason, Debora	1	0	0	0	546
Fergason, Jim	230	53	33	31	254,149
Fergason, Rolland R.	134	21	17	23	116,847
Fergason, Terry Lee	6	1	1	0	2,362
Fergason, Vernon A.	20	6	3	2	16,640
Ferguson, Aileen D.	1	0	0	0	220
Ferguson, Chad M.	131	22	21	11	112,286
Ferguson, Crystal	5	0	0	1	500
Ferguson, Curt	46	4	9	3	28,331
Ferguson, Darl W.	8	1	0	0	7,731
Ferguson, Deas	8	0	1	1	4,719
Ferguson, Debi	34	5	2	4	20,741
Ferguson, Eric	4	0	0	0	670
Ferguson, Jimmy	20	3	0	4	10,318
Ferguson, Ron W.	3	0	2	0	2,840
Ferguson, Shauna	14	1	3	1	15,120
Ferguson, Sr., John W.	15	2	2	1	20,265
Fernandes, Vernon	50	4	4	3	71,852
Fernandez, Jose	11	1	2	0	41,911
Fernandez, Jose N.	20	0	1	4	24,915
Fernandez, Victor	23	3	0	1	13,502
Feron, Kathleen M.	24	0	3	5	51,817
Ferraioli, Joseph	3	1	0	0	4,950
Ferraro, James W.	166	15	13	10	729,105
Ferraro, M. Anthony	386	54	59	43	575,184
Ferraro, Michael S.	327	57	46	35	635,896
Ferraro, Robert G.	2	0	0	0	500
Ferreira, Fernando	150	7	10	17	93,808
Ferrell, Jory	61	8	11	8	71,702
Ferri, Elaine	37	3	2	3	32,437
Ferris, Jerrald M.	41	2	4	8	91,122
Fetherolf, John D.	8	1	0	1	3,647
Fett, Joseph E.	7	0	0	1	922
Fewell, Danny	48	6	3	6	40,732
Fiddler, Richard	3	0	0	2	364
Fields, Harry C	49	4	9	9	72,870
Fields, Kevin J.	16	1	0	1	15,569
Fiengo, Vincent J.	29	2	3	3	26,795
Fiesman, Robert	99	6	11	7	43,896
Figgins, Raymond R.	21	3	2	4	84,381
Figgins, Jr., Ollie L.	37	1	1	1	20,421
Figueroa, Carlos R.	241	26	40	29	187,976
Figueroa, Juan	4	0	1	0	546
Figueroa, Manny A.	38	5	1	6	15,480
Figueroa, Sr., Pablo C.	23	5	3	3	9,612
Figurell, Bernard J.	1	0	0	0	0
Filbey, Richard L.	41	5	5	6	49,344
Filewich, Jerry N.	15	2	4	0	23,306
Filipowski, Denise L.	10	2	1	1	13,705
Finch, M. Shawn	124	11	9	12	113,283
Finch, Sherry	3	0	0	0	0
Fincher, Leroy A.	51	14	3	4	142,490
Fincher, Todd W.	168	39	37	19	699,847
Findlay, Chuck	30	3	5	5	29,390
Fine, Larry	42	2	1	6	11,974
Fink, Jr., William J.	5	0	0	1	6,240
Finn, Sherry	24	3	2	2	19,321
Finnell, Boyd	12	2	2	2	10,623
Finucane, Richard	69	7	10	8	85,771
Fiore, Nicholas J.	1	0	0	0	0
Fires, William H.	165	14	30	16	516,492
Firestone, Kermit L.	11	0	1	1	1,736

Trainer	Sts	1st	2d	3d	Purses
Fischer, Mary Ann	53	1	5	6	18,271
Fishback, Jerry R.	4	0	0	0	1,070
Fisher, Allen	12	1	0	3	5,594
Fisher, Bill	4	1	0	1	6,225
Fisher, Dan	8	0	0	1	715
Fisher, Duane	2	0	1	0	2,925
Fisher, Jack	165	28	22	26	595,076
Fisher, John L.	12	1	0	1	18,395
Fisher, John R. S.	96	20	14	14	618,774
Fisher, Kerri L.	5	0	0	0	2,440
Fisher, Robert A.	40	1	0	3	5,943
Fisher, Steve	25	4	2	6	27,421
Fisher, Susan	173	30	30	24	469,871
Fisher, III, Janon	21	3	3	1	52,855
Fishman, Stanley	7	0	2	0	7,839
Fisichello, J. C.	18	1	0	1	4,326
Fister, John Kyle	10	0	0	0	1,740
Fittante, Ruth M.	14	1	0	0	8,748
Fitzgerald, Nancy P.	12	1	2	1	12,269
Fitzgerald, Shelley E.	50	7	4	11	206,756
Fitzpatrick, Dennis	1	0	0	0	0
Fitzpatrick, Joe	14	1	1	1	2,416
Fitzpatrick, Robert	56	7	4	3	46,121
Fix, Jr., Henry G.	23	2	1	2	46,221
Flanders, Grant	19	1	2	1	5,280
Flaugher, Robert I.	1	0	0	0	0
Fleck, Jacqueline	11	0	0	1	3,644
Flegel, Arlene	28	1	2	3	8,496
Fleischman, Ronald W.	25	1	4	1	63,065
Fleischmann, Marc L.	3	0	0	0	330
Flenner, Andreana	9	0	2	2	14,840
Fletcher, Kevin	93	8	10	14	92,104
Flint, Bernard S.	575	124	82	64	3,513,351
Flint, Steven B.	157	30	29	20	1,032,822
Flom, Amber	23	4	3	0	10,428
Flores, Gilberto M.	50	6	11	5	76,284
Flores, Jose Antonio	45	11	2	7	49,655
Flores, Manuel	43	4	6	5	23,820
Flores, Moses	2	0	0	0	0
Flores, Rafael Q.	6	0	0	0	621
Florez, Carlos	15	1	0	1	8,142
Flowers, Kenny	3	0	0	0	393
Floyd, Billie F.	61	4	1	6	49,858
Flud, Jr., Richard D.	3	0	0	0	196
Flugence, Wilson	26	0	1	2	8,690
Flynn, Ernie D.	81	7	6	11	60,480
Foggiano, Donna	56	6	3	10	46,818
Fogle, Allen	1	1	0	0	2,146
Fogle, Amanda	63	11	10	5	44,092
Fojan, Emilie	87	11	8	12	420,120
Foley, Dravo G.	51	1	6	8	75,404
Foley, Gregory D.	283	66	42	43	2,017,295
Foley, Kati Boden	3	0	0	0	1,225
Foley, Mark L.	17	2	1	2	17,924
Foley, Sean P.	98	6	14	16	65,488
Foley, Tom	12	1	1	0	12,580
Foley, Vickie L.	143	28	22	17	725,514
Foley, Jr., Robert B.	15	4	2	4	16,804
Follett, Norman C.	35	1	2	1	17,133
Fonnesbeck, Marc D.	1	0	0	0	0
Fonseca, Alfredo	29	3	1	3	37,660
Fontenot, Alfred Joseph	25	0	1	2	2,814
Fontenot, Allen	20	1	3	3	16,772
Fontenot, Brent C.	3	2	0	0	28,200
Fontenot, Steven P.	14	0	0	1	962
Fontes, Jr., Ramon	7	1	0	2	2,357
Foos, Lawrence E.	37	0	9	7	29,645
Fopp, Nikki	48	3	6	9	29,220
Forbes, John H.	181	19	19	25	565,955
Ford, Donald E.	7	0	0	0	524
Ford, James P.	19	0	2	2	5,706
Ford, Jesse	11	0	1	1	4,644
Ford, John	29	4	3	3	15,498
Ford, William R.	63	10	8	12	130,403
Ford, Jr., Don H.	16	1	1	0	9,045
Ford, Jr., Stephen F.	133	24	25	17	259,507
Forehand, Jr., Charles	19	1	5	0	9,215
Foreman, Ronald	7	0	0	0	906
Foreman, Thomas R.	38	1	5	5	26,749
Forster, David	116	20	19	13	778,141
Forster, Grant T.	260	48	37	24	784,124
Forster, Richard C.	10	2	2	2	4,096
Forston, Roy A.	30	2	3	1	15,769
Forsyth, Robert	4	1	0	0	12,397
Fortner, David	50	5	5	5	115,164
Fosdick, Stephen V.	125	20	20	7	161,988
Foss, Pat	1	0	0	0	0
Foster, Angela L.	5	0	0	1	847
Foster, Brenda	22	0	0	1	2,439
Foster, Dale	56	5	8	4	26,246
Foster, Daniel H.	39	7	0	7	75,825
Foster, James R.	18	3	1	2	25,980
Foster, Joseph M.	100	10	11	13	97,519
Foster, Lawrence L.	4	0	0	0	0
Foster, Linda L.	35	0	0	5	7,679
Foster, Robert	3	0	0	0	0
Foster, Thomas P.	8	1	0	0	14,710
Foster, Jr., Val Ray	74	7	4	13	88,335
Fournier, Mark	23	5	1	3	95,128
Fout, Paul Douglas	95	16	10	12	556,953
Fout, Paul R.	18	3	6	1	99,578
Foutch, John	7	0	0	0	183
Foutz, A. Kneale	1	0	0	0	0
Foutz, Andrew L.	3	1	0	0	4,240
Fowler, Beverly A.	28	2	7	2	28,360
Fowler, Earl	45	7	7	7	33,097
Fowler, Glenn	12	1	0	0	1,663
Fowler, Joe	7	0	0	1	1,495
Fox, Fred E.	12	1	0	0	11,020
Fox, Jamie	32	2	7	1	90,252
Fox, Larry Dale	2	0	0	0	190
Fox, Sondra	46	5	2	4	28,771
Fox, Sr., John	6	0	0	1	962
Frahm, Lindsey	4	0	2	0	2,440
Fraley, James E.	15	2	1	4	26,325
Frame, Melvin	121	11	15	12	84,584
Franchi, Yonif	4	0	0	0	1,410
Francis, Michelle	82	4	9	3	41,650
Francisco, Dan C.	12	2	0	3	11,726
Francy, Kate	72	5	7	8	92,815
Frank, Jeffrey	2	0	0	0	160
Frankel, Robert J.	491	135	94	60	15,605,911
Frankina, Guy	33	3	3	3	18,792
Franklin, Delbert	2	0	0	0	436
Franklin, Denise	5	1	2	1	18,574
Franklin, Don W.	7	0	0	0	777
Franklin, Michael W.	4	2	1	0	18,240
Franko, Daniel	211	27	23	30	417,636
Frasca, Steven J.	17	1	2	2	9,067
Frasca, Thomas C.	9	0	0	0	760
Fraser, Louise	24	4	1	3	20,706
Frasson, Armand	7	1	0	0	4,059
Fratangeli, Salvatore	13	2	2	2	49,010
Frazee, Larry	106	7	7	16	63,887
Frazier, F. C.	92	11	18	11	61,371
Frederick, Darul	25	2	0	2	10,228
Frederick, Edward Harrison	51	6	5	5	224,107
Frederick, Isaac A.	7	0	0	2	4,678
Frederick, Raymond	21	2	2	1	45,100
Frederick, Robert D.	1	0	0	0	0
Fredo, Patricia A.	11	0	0	1	3,503
Freel, Byron	18	1	1	0	5,960
Freeman, Edward R.	69	8	13	6	207,356
Freeman, Kenneth C.	28	1	3	4	9,075
Freeman, M. Wayne	48	4	6	4	78,516
Freeman, Robert J.	18	2	1	3	20,111
Freeman, Scott	3	0	0	0	1,191
Freeman, Willard C.	49	5	9	8	116,505
Freer, Karen M.	45	2	1	0	40,684
Fregara, John	18	1	2	1	35,218
Freije, Claude F.	12	1	0	0	3,950
Frenaye, Lisa A.	26	2	3	4	48,598

Trainer	Sts	1st	2d	3d	Purses
French, Neil	40	3	6	5	154,790
French, Quinton A.	31	1	5	4	15,708
French, Robert Mark	2	0	0	0	86
French, Wayne R.	13	0	0	2	4,552
Fresquez, James	15	1	0	2	27,860
Frey, Carson	124	14	16	13	168,707
Fridley, Steve	81	10	7	12	77,128
Friedberg, Jean S.	40	4	4	2	67,865
Friedman, John C.	28	2	4	6	53,375
Friedman, Lesley	43	4	4	6	51,795
Friedman, Mitchell E.	93	7	11	10	303,272
Friedman, S. Barry	2	0	0	0	0
Frierson, James	74	6	5	6	105,277
Fries, Dennis W.	4	0	0	1	2,166
Friesen, April	14	1	1	2	27,528
Friley, Willis R.	17	0	0	1	3,611
Fritz, Mario	21	0	1	1	3,577
Frock, Charles L.	245	18	32	28	317,756
Frodsham, Vincent	75	11	9	13	71,101
Fronterhouse, David L.	2	0	0	1	1,365
Frost, Leslie J.	42	3	6	5	55,133
Frost, Stephanie	8	0	0	0	1,372
Frostad, Mark R.	269	49	36	41	4,912,015
Frousiakis, George P.	103	6	10	11	67,166
Fruzzetti, Mary Ann	27	2	4	1	21,002
Fruzzetti, Richard J.	50	2	5	10	51,815
Fry, Toni	24	1	2	4	14,400
Fry, Una Marie	4	0	0	0	300
Frye, Greg	65	15	8	8	172,404
Fuchs, John W.	25	4	6	6	87,364
Fuchs, Mark J.	22	1	4	1	16,806
Fuchs, Thomas L.	12	2	0	2	22,790
Fuentes, J. Jaime	23	2	1	5	18,344
Fugate, James F.	24	1	7	3	26,965
Fujisawa, Kazuo	1	0	1	0	150,000
Fulgham, Billy W.	9	0	0	1	1,325
Fuller, Bonnie	27	0	2	3	7,469
Fuller, William George	2	0	0	0	80
Fuller-Catalano, Abigail	72	8	10	10	118,297
Fullerton, Harold W.	3	0	0	0	0
Fullerton, Pamela	2	0	0	0	250
Fulmer, Drew C.	175	9	21	24	73,783
Funk, Sidney J.	7	0	0	0	343
Funk, Stephanie	2	0	0	0	0
Fuoco, Carlo	12	1	1	0	61,763
Furbee, William	6	1	0	1	3,313
Furer, Bobby C.	8	0	0	1	1,930
Furlong, Kenyon G.	15	0	0	2	13,340
Furness, Ronald W.	25	2	1	7	13,380
Furr, Daniel R.	73	10	7	12	239,845
Furr, Mike A.	32	3	1	6	25,909
Furr, Sr., Robert W.	2	0	0	0	0
Fusco, Mark	456	72	68	70	1,018,544
Fuselier, Larry	3	0	0	0	690
Gabbard, Andrea	15	1	2	0	21,134
Gabbard, James	136	7	7	21	112,254
Gabriel, Bettye A.	46	5	3	5	57,135
Gabriel, Sondra	9	1	3	4	3,578
Gabriel, Toni	74	11	13	8	334,850
Gabriel, Jr., Leo G.	99	11	10	13	274,705
Gabrielli, Gino	45	4	9	2	38,429
Gach, Richard	3	0	0	0	2,523
Gaede, Milton M.	147	16	12	19	91,537
Gaffka, Sean B.	26	4	6	4	29,793
Gaffney, Hubert	32	4	4	5	70,776
Gaffney, Ronald	28	2	0	3	17,470
Gafka, Gregory Wade	57	4	8	9	45,842
Gagliardi, Jill	25	1	1	2	7,653
Gainer, William B.	40	1	1	2	10,048
Gaines, Carla	152	18	25	15	813,609
Gale, Bryce	40	2	3	4	16,482
Galindo, Armando G.	1	0	0	0	37
Gall, David A.	196	16	29	12	115,475
Gallagher, Alfred	7	0	0	0	0
Gallagher, Dorothy	29	1	0	1	22,863
Gallagher, Patrick	220	39	35	33	1,883,313
Gallant, Ernest J.	20	1	2	5	14,985
Gallaway, Eddie	3	0	0	0	0
Gallegos, Jose A.	148	29	16	25	482,856
Gallegos, Teri L.	37	3	0	4	20,537
Gallion, Danielle	21	3	4	0	13,375
Gallo, Joseph	8	0	0	1	1,729
Gallo, Louis P.	76	8	7	2	97,671
Galluscio, Dominic G.	305	39	41	41	1,297,843
Galvan, Jose Luis	16	1	0	0	10,554
Galvin, Derek	62	7	9	6	104,136
Gamber, Robert E.	66	5	4	4	85,522
Gamble, James E.	1	0	0	0	146
Gamble, Melvin	47	5	2	2	11,966
Gambolati, Cam M.	93	13	9	21	300,065
Gamez, Alfred	16	1	1	3	2,946
Gamez, Greg	59	3	6	8	9,576
Gamez, Ruben	1	0	1	0	293
Gammon, Kimmy L.	46	3	2	4	23,725
Gannaway, Bernard	1	0	0	0	0
Gape, John H.	12	0	0	1	1,247
Garcea, Eric	51	3	4	2	89,556
Garcia, Amalio	4	2	0	1	54,693
Garcia, Carlos A.	178	21	37	26	497,985
Garcia, Efrain T.	147	18	15	17	249,260
Garcia, Ermanio	7	1	0	0	4,089
Garcia, Evelio	47	4	2	2	41,782
Garcia, Harold	12	1	3	0	7,118
Garcia, Jackie	15	5	5	1	9,594
Garcia, Jose Iver	1	0	0	0	75
Garcia, Juan J.	263	21	25	45	1,044,666
Garcia, Mario L.	1	0	0	0	400
Garcia, Monica	15	0	0	1	1,786
Garcia, Oscar L.	5	1	0	0	4,802
Garcia, Phyllis D.	4	1	0	0	5,161
Garcia, Raul H.	3	0	1	0	1,480
Garcia, Rodolfo	196	29	27	27	752,792
Garcia, Ruben B.	19	2	3	4	22,746
Garcia, Salvador	17	0	3	2	10,749
Garcia, Sr., Randy L.	39	2	0	3	23,090
Gardipy, Ken	11	0	2	2	1,948
Gardipy, Russell	64	18	5	8	36,093
Gardipy, Jr., Tom	117	12	23	12	97,389
Garfield, Joseph	7	0	1	2	3,007
Gargasz, Donald W.	50	2	3	5	33,776
Garner, Jerry W.	6	0	0	0	403
Garner, Tim D.	166	32	21	22	229,840
Garner, William G.	10	0	0	0	1,088
Garofalo, Gregory P.	19	3	2	0	80,379
Garoffalo, Jose	162	25	26	18	436,278
Garrett, Billy R.	19	0	0	1	4,237
Garrett, Danny	9	0	0	0	2,500
Garrett, James A.	1	0	0	1	252
Garrett, Terry Wayne	2	0	0	0	105
Garrett, Ty J.	19	2	5	3	9,348
Garrette, Merle K.	7	0	1	0	3,660
Garrick, Worrell A.	33	5	6	8	146,990
Garrido, Raul	53	7	9	4	76,430
Garrigan, Alfred	10	0	3	3	6,460
Garrison, Diane	46	5	4	5	70,563
Garrison, James O.	49	4	4	5	29,744
Garrison, Mark	7	2	1	0	5,084
Garrison, Scotty D.	2	0	0	0	130
Garroutte, James R.	49	7	12	8	135,938
Garroutte, John L.	11	3	0	0	8,452
Garry, Thomas J.	65	10	10	7	77,947
Garvin, John Clark	20	5	4	2	24,930
Garvin, John Hart	27	0	1	1	4,997
Gary, Marty	17	0	0	1	2,968
Gary, Paul Brent	108	4	3	9	69,828
Garza, Roberto R.	10	0	1	0	1,099
Gass, Mark E.	6	0	0	0	161
Gass, II, Michael A.	80	4	2	9	53,790
Gass, Sr., Michael A.	127	6	4	9	54,259
Gastal, Glenn C.	1	0	0	0	0
Gaston, Jim L.	281	25	38	32	438,423
Gates, Allen L.	9	0	0	1	3,895

Trainer	Sts	1st	2d	3d	Purses
Gates, David N.	21	4	0	5	9,030
Gatis, Christos	140	36	25	17	455,382
Gatlin, Troy	9	0	0	0	693
Gaucher, Robert	4	0	1	0	2,469
Gaudet, Edmond D.	251	43	38	42	984,537
Gaussion, Sarah Frances	2	0	0	0	0
Gautreaux, Garrett	11	1	2	2	22,863
Gautreaux, Raymond	52	6	0	3	59,214
Gavin, Robert J.	11	0	1	1	2,430
Gayheart, Troy	66	6	7	7	48,234
Geary, Kenneth E.	6	0	0	0	530
Gebler, Robert E.	65	2	3	5	38,468
Geerdes-Boller, Debra	3	0	1	0	400
Geier, Greg	184	21	23	20	834,234
Geist, David W.	520	75	83	76	909,385
Gelner, John Charles	276	27	32	36	359,760
Generazio, Jr., Frank A.	186	14	18	27	517,826
Genovese, Richard L.	77	8	10	9	67,177
Gensler, Harold K.	33	1	3	1	22,446
Gentile, Victor	18	2	2	3	11,241
Gentner, Dorothy	17	2	0	4	14,753
Gentry, Craig W.	20	1	3	2	2,844
George, Bryon A.	3	0	0	0	0
George, Donald A.	14	0	0	0	600
George, Donald J.	5	2	1	0	3,950
George, Ernest	74	13	17	8	223,343
George, Gus	135	5	7	6	39,235
George, Wayne F.	37	0	0	0	3,482
George, Jr., Miles R.	6	1	3	0	8,205
Gerace, Janis L.	152	15	9	13	210,342
Gerber, Norbert	34	6	3	1	47,071
Gerhards, James A.	1	0	0	0	0
Geris, Jr., Samuel J.	23	2	2	4	38,780
Germany, Barry H.	90	9	11	12	253,295
Gerteisen, Adam	26	9	5	1	83,513
Gertz, Lisa	6	0	0	0	468
Gervais, George	100	9	8	15	27,272
Gholson, Clyde J.	13	1	2	1	34,587
Gibbs, Randy	1	0	0	0	0
Gibbs, Terrill	59	5	8	15	16,991
Gibson, Bob E.	44	3	4	6	15,517
Gibson, Claude	55	6	11	7	50,282
Gibson, Dewayne C.	54	7	6	6	117,127
Gibson, Linda G.	5	0	1	0	2,565
Gibson, Linda M.	14	0	3	1	6,045
Gibson, Mark A.	20	1	1	5	5,336
Gibson, Monte L.	9	1	1	2	3,322
Gibson, Ralph E.	6	2	0	0	28,830
Gibson, Richard D.	1	0	0	0	0
Gibson, Rod	9	0	1	0	967
Gibson, Ronald A.	18	1	3	3	29,065
Gibson, Vince	90	8	12	10	61,803
Gideon, Deborah	1	0	0	0	325
Giesbrecht, Brian	48	6	10	4	99,336
Giesbrecht, Lance B.	97	15	12	16	391,075
Giesse, Carl	70	7	3	8	118,568
Gift, Greg M.	4	1	1	0	860
Giglio, Heather A.	64	5	3	14	255,920
Gilbert, Bryon J.	63	11	13	5	197,835
Gilbert, Jack	14	2	0	1	18,902
Gilbert, Joseph A.	27	0	0	1	2,248
Gilbert, Robert	26	2	1	4	21,631
Gilbert, Timothy R.	12	2	1	1	14,945
Gilbert, III, Riley Miles	36	1	1	3	16,574
Gilbreath, C. Dwayne	4	1	1	1	6,109
Gilchrist, Greg	137	48	25	17	842,364
Giles, Chad	5	1	2	0	2,775
Giles, Troy F.	5	0	3	0	1,952
Giles, Wes	16	0	1	2	4,020
Giliforte, Jason	94	7	11	6	115,923
Giliforte, Layne S.	406	73	65	45	1,316,280
Gilker, Robert	60	8	7	13	159,728
Gilkyson, Don	144	21	21	13	314,732
Gillam, Jeremy J.	35	3	1	7	44,105
Gillerstrom, Deborah	6	0	0	0	488
Gillette, Kenneth D.	59	5	8	10	30,048
Gillette, Robin	8	0	1	0	4,523
Gilliam, James D.	1	0	0	0	45
Gillihan, Terry	181	27	32	27	442,317
Gillions, Claudia J.	57	3	4	4	66,366
Gilmour, Jim	2	0	0	0	150
Gilmour, Sue M.	92	19	13	9	47,827
Gino, Luigi	27	1	4	2	37,120
Ginter, Jr., Raymond E.	17	2	2	3	37,507
Gioitta, Patrick	45	2	2	5	17,909
Gipson, Kenneth	5	1	0	0	2,655
Girdley, Bernard L.	28	2	1	2	42,755
Girdley, James R.	60	4	8	4	53,620
Girten, Tim	103	21	13	16	296,778
Gittings, Cecil R.	10	0	0	0	894
Givens, Dennis	12	3	1	1	15,447
Gladd, Frank E.	22	3	2	1	19,164
Gladd, Paul B.	23	2	5	5	13,224
Gladd, Scott J.	4	0	0	0	232
Gladd, Wade Ray	11	3	1	3	31,800
Glass, Reg	2	0	0	0	243
Glass, Renee E.	1	0	0	0	872
Glatt, Mark	200	19	24	29	785,335
Glazier, Leslie G.	76	8	8	7	129,800
Glazier, Michael	60	4	13	5	75,986
Gleason, Kenneth	230	33	52	34	399,029
Gleason, Patrick	28	4	2	2	32,460
Gleason, Timothy Mark	433	61	64	67	689,280
Gleason, Tyrone	52	7	10	2	43,606
Gleaves, Philip A.	69	12	7	6	245,122
Glenn, Dwaine A.	82	10	8	10	92,503
Glenney, John	61	0	6	4	132,482
Glennon, Darren C.	49	3	2	3	88,202
Glessner, Gene F.	15	0	0	0	3,000
Glidden, Darrell	7	0	0	0	830
Glorioso, Ronald S.	108	22	17	15	333,603
Glossbrenner, Gloria L.	27	2	1	1	47,906
Glosson, Randle L.	2	0	0	0	82
Glyshaw, Tim	36	6	7	3	49,875
Godeaux, Oscar	24	3	2	3	44,740
Godfrey, Brenda M.	66	3	9	10	110,085
Godinez, Linda S.	4	0	0	0	613
Godsey, Claudie Marshall	34	4	8	2	27,204
Godwin, Albert	1	0	0	0	0
Goedken, Lisa	6	0	0	0	0
Goeing, Donald L.	69	11	4	7	113,817
Goforth, Richard	2	1	0	1	26,295
Gogas, Frances	66	9	5	9	100,769
Gogel, Donald Carl	25	4	3	2	49,916
Goldberg, Alan E.	200	33	31	25	1,185,591
Golden, Kenneth M.	2	0	0	0	210
Goldfine, Mickey A.	44	5	5	11	149,535
Goldman, Marilyn	4	0	0	0	1,085
Gomena, Julie	2	1	0	0	6,000
Gomes, Monte M	29	3	1	2	49,744
Gomez, Frank	248	26	39	26	611,545
Gomez, Jaime H.	13	3	2	0	12,222
Gomez, Jorge	49	2	3	0	44,141
Gomez, Pedro A.	14	3	2	3	10,491
Gomez, Rafael	19	4	1	3	47,325
Gonsalves, Robert	31	0	2	7	24,709
Gonzales, Robert S.	4	0	2	0	1,119
Gonzales, Thomas	10	1	2	3	10,700
Gonzalez, Andrea	144	11	18	36	237,005
Gonzalez, Angel	7	0	0	0	150
Gonzalez, Carlos	36	1	5	3	22,188
Gonzalez, Daniel	3	0	0	0	720
Gonzalez, Felix A.	60	8	7	3	58,563
Gonzalez, Felix L.	2	0	0	0	720
Gonzalez, J. Paco	59	7	6	10	425,120
Gonzalez, Jaime	15	3	0	2	13,743
Gonzalez, Jose A.	112	11	11	12	135,456
Gonzalez, Jose L.	54	3	2	3	40,668
Gonzalez, Jose M.	22	4	4	4	16,088
Gonzalez, Jose R.	55	10	6	6	143,228
Gonzalez, Juan M.	7	0	1	1	9,566
Gonzalez, Nicholas	149	28	18	17	745,284

Trainer	Sts	1st	2d	3d	Purses
Gonzalez, Ramon G.	101	12	13	2	137,691
Gonzalez, Ramon O.	373	66	48	48	933,141
Gonzalez, Raul A.	160	24	22	28	154,372
Gonzalez, Reina E.	101	9	10	13	131,555
Gonzalez, Richard C.	8	0	1	0	2,806
Gonzalez, Richard W.	15	0	1	1	4,741
Gonzalez, Roberto C.	1	0	0	0	85
Gonzalez, Sal	149	13	15	23	268,925
Gonzalez, Salvador G.	13	3	2	1	96,020
Gonzalez, Silvano M.	36	0	3	3	22,751
Gooch, Boyce K.	164	20	29	19	167,742
Good, Dennis F.	94	16	14	16	262,408
Goodale, Adam	12	0	1	0	4,206
Goodin, B. Mike	50	2	6	5	67,856
Goodlet, Mark D.	14	0	2	3	24,588
Goodman, Danielle	18	4	1	4	45,661
Goodman, Mary M.	20	1	1	1	10,560
Goodman, Randy J.	135	11	13	13	93,686
Goodnight, Bill R.	14	1	2	2	11,384
Goodridge, Ronald O.	266	20	31	36	462,570
Goodwin, Duane	3	0	1	2	1,100
Gordon, Anthony K.	9	0	1	1	3,581
Gordon, Cleveland G.	18	1	2	2	20,612
Gordon, Dorna M.	25	0	1	1	6,611
Gordon, George L.	31	2	1	1	19,301
Gordon, Howard R.	21	1	3	1	15,979
Gordon, Jim A.	11	2	2	1	5,278
Gordon-Watson, Alexander	2	0	0	0	160
Gore, Catherine A.	5	0	0	0	1,702
Gore, Terrel	172	14	26	18	496,453
Gorham, Michael E.	442	66	72	74	1,903,968
Gorham, Robert M.	425	71	69	57	947,343
Gorham, Jr., Robert M.	17	3	1	3	26,566
Goruk, Pat	7	0	3	3	7,320
Gosden, John H. M.	2	0	0	0	25,728
Goss, Richard T.	3	0	0	0	337
Goswell, Gerald	4	0	0	0	900
Gothard, Akiko M.	137	27	17	24	400,101
Gould, Ellen	11	1	1	2	4,376
Gourneau, David	32	8	6	3	18,941
Gourneau, Jerry	105	17	11	17	99,371
Gourneau, Jr., Larry	42	6	5	8	25,610
Goutierrez, Jr., Ned	1	0	0	0	0
Gowan, William G.	47	6	5	6	76,515
Gowdy, Donna	36	2	3	5	44,771
Goydich, George	4	1	0	0	7,048
Grace, Allan	36	13	5	4	23,474
Grace, Bryan P.	62	7	4	6	48,436
Grace, John R.	201	22	19	24	117,403
Grace, Lori	27	9	5	4	98,122
Grace, Lynn	112	4	10	12	30,665
Gracey, W. Phillip	103	4	8	12	256,783
Graci, Kimberly A.	5	0	0	1	3,453
Graci, III, Joseph J.	44	2	2	2	40,930
Gracia, Humberto	63	4	3	5	70,035
Gracida, Ruben	3	0	0	1	4,490
Graham, Barbara C.	3	0	0	1	2,610
Graham, Edward L.	15	1	1	3	11,090
Graham, George F.	33	1	1	3	16,543
Graham, Patrick J.	24	2	0	3	36,862
Graham, Robin L.	130	16	21	17	971,190
Graham, II, Clifford P.	5	0	0	0	1,507
Grams, Timothy C.	147	21	19	20	505,790
Granados, Oscar	7	1	2	0	5,423
Grande, Joseph	112	8	10	19	115,087
Granger, Bobby	117	14	10	12	166,891
Granger, Deryl	1	0	0	0	675
Granitz, Anthony J.	157	23	21	22	673,932
Grappe, Charles L.	7	1	2	0	15,315
Gravelle, Colinda M.	15	1	1	0	12,251
Graves, Russell B.	8	0	2	0	2,344
Graves, Toni	1	0	0	0	0
Graves, William K.	3	1	1	0	5,440
Graves-Keckler, Heather	14	5	0	1	7,330
Gray, Bill L.	16	0	1	1	3,558
Gray, Blair A.	9	0	0	0	406
Gray, Charles A.	5	0	0	0	372
Gray, Charles W.	67	6	7	6	66,533
Gray, Clayton	166	18	36	25	289,845
Gray, Dennis	12	2	1	4	36,900
Gray, Gary L.	30	3	3	5	16,954
Gray, Karen	3	1	0	0	9,000
Gray, Kenneth M.	24	3	2	6	49,372
Gray, Lorna M.	86	12	13	22	120,251
Gray, Robert H.	6	1	2	1	7,130
Gray, Robin A.	5	0	0	1	500
Gray, Sid J.	54	6	8	5	74,776
Grayson, Bobby Wayne	13	0	4	1	16,540
Greaves, William	21	2	2	4	55,174
Grech, Tom	7	0	1	0	3,965
Greco, Emanuel J.	25	1	3	2	68,424
Greelish, Patricia M.	10	0	2	0	6,696
Greely, C. Beau	126	8	17	15	961,643
Green, Clint	15	0	0	1	1,080
Green, Darlene	58	0	2	1	14,037
Green, Donna	65	9	4	3	141,270
Green, Elmer Jack	6	1	1	0	5,551
Green, Gerald	2	0	0	0	92
Green, Ike	16	6	4	2	47,350
Green, James D.	12	3	1	0	29,700
Green, James T.	6	0	0	0	745
Green, Lewis A.	12	0	1	0	1,724
Green, Martha C.	7	0	0	0	150
Green, Marvin D.	6	1	0	0	4,600
Green, Newcomb	27	3	2	4	124,200
Green, Raymond A.	39	5	2	6	22,625
Green, Richard D.	2	0	0	0	0
Green, Shelly	8	0	1	3	10,995
Green, Travis R.	32	2	2	5	4,179
Green, Wayne S.	22	2	1	1	53,543
Green, Woody D.	4	1	0	1	1,086
Greene, Shirley A.	18	2	5	0	75,515
Greene, Thomas M.	76	11	13	7	381,356
Greenhill, Jeffrey L.	129	17	10	12	195,074
Greenman, Dean	34	1	3	2	76,743
Greenslate, Sam	1	0	0	0	124
Greenway, Brad	3	0	0	0	0
Greenwell, Jerry Joe	35	4	2	2	49,727
Greenwood, Claire B.	17	1	0	3	14,290
Greenwood, Dale	250	33	40	35	486,780
Greer, Brandon Evan	1	0	0	0	0
Gregg, Carol A.	13	0	1	1	3,644
Gregg, Tony	38	10	1	5	39,007
Grego, Donald R.	56	5	6	6	62,939
Gregory, George E.	3	0	0	0	840
Gregory, Peter	4	0	0	0	651
Gregory, Ray W.	18	1	1	6	7,123
Gregory, Robert E.	1	0	0	0	107
Gregory, Sylvea	11	2	3	3	23,559
Gregory, Theodore C.	5	0	0	0	274
Gregory, William P.	2	0	1	0	4,300
Gregory, Sr., Kenneth	58	4	5	4	38,642
Greider, Glen E.	10	1	1	0	5,016
Greiner, Gary	33	4	2	1	16,296
Griego, Fabian	8	0	0	0	518
Griem, Robert J.	14	1	3	2	75,941
Grieve, Larry	44	4	8	7	61,779
Grieves, Kelly	98	15	13	14	187,599
Grieves, Ron	220	34	28	30	483,044
Griffin, Bill	1	0	0	0	42
Griffin, Jacqueline	47	3	3	11	47,362
Griffin, Roger W.	7	0	0	0	1,053
Griffin, Timothy L.	27	0	0	1	3,727
Griffith, Gregory A.	233	17	25	25	335,550
Griffith, Terry	26	3	1	3	45,977
Griffiths, Lenny	11	1	0	0	3,212
Griffo, Paul	7	0	0	0	637
Griggs, Dana S.	30	1	2	3	3,852
Griggs, John K.	11	0	4	0	16,200
Griggs, Kenneth F.	6	0	0	0	856
Griggs, Veronica	91	3	8	13	60,125
Grigsby, Anthony K.	26	4	2	1	47,925

Trainer	Sts	1st	2d	3d	Purses
Grijalva, Jose	49	6	8	8	30,463
Grimaldo, Jose	7	0	0	1	594
Grimes, David	200	18	28	27	110,741
Grimes, Michael H. R.	17	2	0	1	8,900
Grimm, Margaret E.	71	13	10	7	211,311
Grimm, Jr., Philip I.	29	0	0	5	36,362
Grimsley, Cindy R	10	1	1	0	25,096
Grinolds, Douglas	21	4	4	1	45,626
Grinolds, Rod	6	2	0	0	6,016
Grisham, Christie	1	0	0	0	43
Grisham, Kenneth M.	1	0	0	0	184
Grissom, Bobbie	29	5	1	5	33,956
Grissom, O. Dwain	138	18	23	14	271,026
Grizzard, Render Lee	9	0	0	1	1,889
Grobe, Nathan	15	1	0	1	4,579
Gross, George F.	105	6	16	12	161,692
Gross, James A.	2	0	0	0	0
Gross, John C.	57	4	6	6	53,970
Gross, Reid	741	77	82	82	408,058
Grove, Christopher W.	282	45	32	39	834,534
Groves, W. Fred	6	0	0	0	318
Grubb, Harold	52	2	3	6	41,634
Grubbs, Jamie L.	92	11	14	11	130,590
Grubbs, Russell	7	1	0	1	4,160
Grudzien, Jason G.	86	19	12	13	120,748
Grudziewski, Bob	8	0	0	1	4,155
Gruenemeier, Michael	70	6	7	8	36,701
Gruich, Philip P.	8	0	1	0	2,103
Grusmark, Karl M.	197	30	26	35	452,633
Gruss, Janell	8	0	0	2	2,369
Gruwell, Bessie S.	85	7	10	11	157,075
Gryczewski, Jerry L.	81	13	10	15	248,522
Gubanski, James H.	10	0	2	1	5,808
Gubanski, Mary Margaret	24	3	3	4	31,394
Guciardo, John	38	5	11	4	75,379
Guciardo, Kathleen A.	66	3	5	9	43,261
Guciardo, Robert	223	28	26	33	419,034
Guerin, Andre	46	4	2	4	24,164
Guerra, Hector	1	0	0	0	75
Guerra, Jacque	24	3	7	2	39,394
Guerra, Jr., Jimmy W.	3	0	0	0	600
Guerra, Sr., Jimmy	4	0	0	0	120
Guerrero, Angel	48	2	4	2	37,873
Guerrero, Helberth M.	26	0	0	2	3,353
Guerrero, J. Guadalupe	115	12	13	13	175,742
Guerrero, Juan Carlos	89	14	10	8	256,557
Guerrero, Wbaldo	3	0	0	0	434
Guerrieri, Dino	78	3	2	9	47,793
Guettler, Robert R.	2	0	0	0	300
Guidos, John	28	3	4	10	9,260
Guidry, Brandon	1	0	0	0	0
Guidry, Connie Mack	32	4	3	6	52,793
Guidry, Suzie	18	0	0	1	5,179
Guidry, Jr., Donald D.	1	0	0	0	450
Guilbeaux, Sr., Louis	3	0	0	0	0
Guilkey, Randall L.	3	0	0	0	0
Guillory, James	18	2	1	1	16,664
Guillory, Raymond	6	0	0	0	0
Guillory, Susan	2	0	0	0	293
Guillot, Eric J.	114	10	18	18	362,889
Guilmette, Henry	3	0	0	0	480
Guinn, M. Dooley	99	9	9	10	164,771
Guitard, David J.	28	1	1	3	30,248
Gulash, Rodger	2	0	0	1	680
Gulewich, Grace	20	2	1	1	10,508
Gulick, James M.	76	8	6	16	191,315
Gullo, Gary P.	10	3	2	2	131,816
Gumbel, Thomas O.	38	3	4	4	44,938
Gundlach, Raymond	11	0	0	0	795
Gunter, Michael C.	42	1	3	4	22,185
Gurney, Marilyn M.	31	0	2	1	6,721
Gurrola, George T.	16	0	0	3	3,832
Gustafson, Ricky J.	135	20	20	17	195,263
Gustafsson, Rolf	9	0	0	0	2,060
Guste, Eddie R.	8	0	0	1	1,947
Gutierrez, Angel	175	23	16	19	297,472
Gutierrez, Jaime	14	2	3	0	84,847
Gutierrez, Jorge	82	3	9	12	295,376
Gutierrez, Luis	148	7	13	26	127,653
Gutierrez, Rosie	17	1	0	2	8,230
Guyah, Hopeton R.	1	0	0	0	0
Gwaltney, John	2	0	0	0	270
Gwilliam, Robert	97	10	8	16	49,940
Gyarmati, Leah	112	7	8	19	275,950
Haarman, Jr., William E.	15	0	1	2	9,046
Haas, David A.	4	0	0	0	751
Haas, Robert	1	0	0	0	0
Haasl, Ron	36	2	6	4	9,150
Habeeb, Donald J.	62	5	5	11	72,306
Hacek, Louis F.	14	0	0	0	1,125
Hackett, Gary	44	4	3	7	25,898
Hackford, Cory	9	3	1	1	3,197
Hacking, A. L.	27	6	3	5	26,773
Hackney, Karen L.	41	3	4	1	19,341
Hackney, William N.	87	7	13	12	115,437
Hackworth, Jr., Robert S.	15	0	2	3	50,525
Hadfield, Bridget L.	44	3	5	2	13,167
Hadley, Sherman	2	1	0	0	600
Hadry, Charles J.	101	18	5	20	458,076
Hadwen, Mark S.	1	0	0	0	243
Haehn, Cindy Lee	284	37	49	31	358,660
Haehn, Douglas G.	13	0	0	1	1,310
Haehn, T. R.	179	7	14	17	68,010
Haffner, Randy	62	4	6	3	46,115
Hagge, Ron	6	0	0	0	231
Hagy, Titus	179	8	14	19	208,485
Hahn, III, Harold L.	195	25	23	21	505,590
Haiber, Homer H.	11	1	2	2	17,640
Haignere, Robert	6	0	0	0	363
Hair, Lea M.	2	0	0	1	687
Hairfield, William E.	39	2	7	6	67,340
Halbak, Jay	1	0	0	0	0
Halcomb, Denny R.	21	2	1	3	23,008
Hale, Anthony	2	0	0	0	320
Hale, Debra	75	4	11	11	82,813
Hale, Jimmie L.	91	10	8	11	89,851
Hale, Robert A.	208	37	32	33	768,875
Hale, William G.	4	1	0	0	4,264
Hale, Willie B.	8	0	0	0	208
Hale, Jr., Ronald T.	82	5	5	10	36,457
Haley, Gloria	23	5	2	1	79,688
Hall, Aimee D.	71	8	8	14	162,215
Hall, Carollyn J.	13	2	1	1	8,476
Hall, Carroll L.	9	1	0	1	2,880
Hall, Charlotte M.	15	0	1	2	5,219
Hall, Craig	2	0	0	0	100
Hall, Darrel V.	24	3	3	1	16,705
Hall, Dennis	86	16	15	12	162,055
Hall, Dick	23	2	1	5	16,079
Hall, Dru S.	91	14	14	16	132,066
Hall, Eldon	4	1	1	0	20,900
Hall, Gary B.	43	0	3	1	5,733
Hall, Jay	18	4	1	3	15,529
Hall, John L.	110	9	15	13	153,797
Hall, L. E.	18	4	1	0	17,488
Hall, Larry R.	97	0	7	13	27,469
Hall, Louise	9	0	0	3	1,331
Hall, Lynda	36	4	6	6	24,078
Hall, Mark E.	63	14	14	8	115,799
Hall, Peggy M.	19	0	0	3	10,023
Hall, Rachel	6	1	1	2	23,086
Hall, Randall J	14	5	2	0	30,220
Hall, Rex	1	1	0	0	1,200
Hall, Robert W.	5	1	2	0	15,777
Hall, Ronald D.	14	1	0	1	5,005
Hall, Sean	70	4	5	6	198,615
Hall, Steve L.	97	26	12	15	137,723
Hall, Susan	1	0	0	0	45
Hall, W. Monk	36	6	3	2	31,425
Hall, Wayne	2	0	0	0	124
Hall, William E.	94	8	16	10	202,206
Hall, Jr., Oscar J.	8	1	1	0	19,033

Trainer	Sts	1st	2d	3d	Purses
Hall, Sr., Oscar J.	24	1	2	5	14,134
Haller, Valerie K.	1	0	0	0	190
Hallgren, Sven	28	1	5	2	27,914
Halliday, Robert F.	6	1	0	0	5,740
Halloran, John A.	24	2	2	1	25,696
Hall-Sabol, Tamara Joan	15	0	1	1	5,243
Halpern, Edward I.	26	2	2	4	83,104
Halter, James K.	29	3	4	6	54,680
Ham, Doug	43	3	6	9	49,674
Hamblin, Leon H.	3	0	0	0	0
Hamby, Doyle	40	2	6	5	62,180
Hamby, Ronald	1	1	0	0	7,070
Hamer, Sr., William E.	135	5	13	2	57,136
Hamill, Lisa	53	2	0	3	12,130
Hamilton, A. Joseph	18	3	1	2	24,160
Hamilton, Beverly	38	11	5	3	55,104
Hamilton, Brenda S.	6	0	0	0	3,075
Hamilton, Harry W.	40	1	2	5	26,919
Hamilton, Kenny W.	3	0	0	1	369
Hamilton, William F.	39	0	6	8	49,726
Hamlin, Rachel	1	0	0	0	0
Hamlin, Shawna	18	3	2	3	6,438
Hamm, Timothy E.	322	45	52	48	818,471
Hammes, John D.	6	1	0	0	4,735
Hammett, Jody	41	7	3	1	120,516
Hammond, Jack R.	8	1	0	1	3,290
Hammond, Jerry	274	42	38	48	232,779
Hammond, Kim	567	97	81	85	784,344
Hammond, Robert J.	2	1	0	0	4,500
Hammonds, Randall D.	1	0	0	0	0
Han, Moon S.	8	2	3	1	41,740
Hanauer-Jackson, James	19	1	0	1	3,125
Hancock, David L.	38	0	0	0	0
Hancock, Jack L.	27	1	1	4	14,921
Hancock, John A.	115	7	9	13	65,259
Hancock, Kerny B.	59	4	1	9	47,767
Handy, George R.	118	24	15	13	387,212
Hanford, Gail M.	41	3	5	7	79,545
Hanford, Peggie	61	7	13	6	56,916
Hanley, Larry	41	1	2	0	17,247
Hanna, Clark	34	1	4	2	34,930
Hanna, Mark A.	153	31	25	27	298,410
Hanna, Patricia	13	0	1	2	14,389
Hannah, Don	8	0	0	3	2,510
Hansen, Andrew M.	144	12	21	23	419,237
Hansen, Dale A.	34	4	2	5	18,609
Hansen, Dean	49	3	2	5	17,556
Hansen, Gordon A.	146	4	9	14	35,155
Hansen, Kevin	29	0	0	4	6,178
Hansen, Roger W.	171	24	26	27	359,326
Hanson, Dan	2	0	1	0	350
Hanson, Deborah M.	10	1	3	0	5,873
Hanson, George H.	21	2	3	3	7,387
Hanson, Jim	45	9	8	6	23,511
Hanson, Joe	5	0	0	0	2,300
Hanson, Victor	67	10	8	5	145,662
Happel, Rudolph	3	0	0	0	402
Harasta, Steven P.	47	0	2	0	8,966
Harbort, Willie R.	39	4	4	6	47,744
Hardcastle, Billy	23	1	2	4	21,265
Harder, Tim	35	2	2	3	25,429
Hardie, Wade	47	3	13	6	57,111
Hardin, Angel	70	4	3	7	44,303
Hardin, Jerry K.	179	23	21	34	366,506
Hardy, Fred J.	37	3	4	1	33,131
Hardy, James Mort	96	6	9	14	386,669
Hardy, Rosamond	15	1	3	1	24,980
Hardy, Tim	1	0	0	0	61
Hare, Jearl Ace	99	12	9	10	113,603
Hargens, Robert C.	14	1	2	3	28,279
Hargrave, Kenneth L.	2	0	1	1	5,095
Hargus, Charley	1	0	0	0	56
Harigeorgiou, Konstantinos	116	6	4	8	55,610
Harigeoriou, Gus	1	0	0	0	495
Harknett, Alice T.	6	0	1	1	4,498
Harless, Gary E.	4	0	0	0	502
Harmon, Nicole	3	0	0	0	276
Harneck, Donald J.	4	0	0	0	290
Harner, Kathryn H.	11	1	3	1	35,368
Haroldson, Lowell	6	0	0	1	975
Harper, Charles W.	9	0	0	0	626
Harper, Jack L.	92	4	13	11	138,664
Harper, Richard L.	184	18	13	14	125,540
Harrell, James C.	52	3	10	8	11,949
Harrell, Linda Lee	36	5	7	4	44,048
Harries, James E.	19	2	3	5	34,595
Harrigan, William B.	7	1	0	1	15,636
Harrington, Glen	20	1	1	2	16,983
Harrington, Jack	4	0	0	1	2,875
Harrington, John F.	2	0	0	0	750
Harrington, Mike	186	34	22	24	864,425
Harrington, Patricia	9	0	2	3	16,280
Harris, Alva S.	3	0	0	0	177
Harris, Andrew	27	4	3	2	93,720
Harris, Bob J.	14	2	1	1	8,891
Harris, Chris Michael	81	6	4	7	34,293
Harris, Clifford V.	5	0	0	1	1,299
Harris, Clint	4	1	0	0	1,082
Harris, Dennis E.	13	1	0	0	6,600
Harris, Everton Alex	30	0	0	1	6,108
Harris, George R.	30	2	1	1	19,180
Harris, Herbert W.	31	0	0	1	8,556
Harris, Holly L.	16	0	2	2	10,121
Harris, John R.	1	1	0	0	1,980
Harris, John William	20	1	2	3	6,806
Harris, Joyce A.	29	0	3	2	8,225
Harris, Larry W.	3	0	0	0	498
Harris, Lyndel	17	1	1	1	5,988
Harris, Michael F.	5	0	0	0	420
Harris, Nancy S.	15	0	1	1	4,944
Harris, Russell M.	5	0	0	0	971
Harris, Tommy D.	14	1	1	1	25,540
Harris, Tyrone	35	2	5	1	29,890
Harris, Walter L.	29	3	2	3	20,421
Harris, William S.	20	1	4	1	10,302
Harris, II, Doyle	2	0	0	0	245
Harrisko, Dennis	21	4	2	1	23,385
Harrison, Don K.	8	1	1	0	21,800
Harrison, Glenn N.	27	1	2	1	30,766
Harrison, Ronald	2	1	0	1	6,960
Hart, Floyd	4	0	0	0	445
Hart, Quindie	4	0	0	0	371
Hart, Rodney B.	7	2	0	2	11,688
Hart-Burroughs, Lori	30	3	2	3	14,950
Hartlage, Gary G.	144	23	15	13	417,233
Hartlage, Mark G.	19	1	2	2	17,076
Hartley, Darrell	80	12	10	9	83,193
Hartley, James E.	42	7	6	5	95,202
Hartman, Alex T.	124	17	12	25	141,803
Hartman, Chris A.	104	15	14	14	184,204
Hartman, Chris J.	9	0	2	0	1,700
Hartman, Matthew T.	3	0	1	0	4,240
Hartman, Stan	134	9	6	16	43,047
Hartmann, Mary	140	17	17	12	514,191
Hartnett, Ronald W.	54	1	3	6	22,205
Hart-Perez, Debra	34	7	2	2	63,376
Hartsell, Jr., John J.	52	2	12	3	64,025
Harty, Eoin G.	136	18	17	19	834,211
Harty, Nicholas A.	4	0	1	0	510
Hartz, Douglas S.	7	0	0	2	5,230
Harvatt, Charles R.	136	17	13	20	287,577
Harvey, Edward J.	44	2	2	9	13,324
Harvey, Georgia D.	2	0	0	0	190
Harwood, Doris	125	25	20	22	197,355
Harwood, Ryland M.	58	8	10	11	29,442
Hasmatali, Daryl	32	8	1	2	136,272
Hasmatali, Roger	12	0	1	1	5,418
Hassenpflug, Chad	269	60	44	32	774,158
Hastings, W. Shannon	73	3	5	10	31,933
Hatcher, Linda	28	1	2	2	15,151
Hatcher, Nathan D.	29	1	1	0	8,634
Hatchett, James	140	16	15	14	635,115

Trainer	Sts	1st	2d	3d	Purses
Hatfield, Kevin	11	2	0	3	42,182
Hattori, Bruce	10	2	2	2	4,642
Haught, Dawn	105	10	12	9	85,151
Haughton, Donnovan	78	9	14	8	133,175
Hause, Ronald D.	1	0	0	0	96
Hauswald, M. James	59	4	6	4	42,986
Hauswald, Philip M.	59	8	9	4	308,084
Haverkamp, Charles K.	51	3	4	6	71,995
Haverty, Karen	78	17	8	13	102,930
Hawk, Lonnie G.	3	0	0	1	913
Hawkes, Darcy	165	23	21	23	224,328
Hawkes, Twyla	6	0	2	1	4,008
Hawkins, Charles R.	2	0	0	0	220
Hawkins, Douglas	2	1	0	1	3,190
Hawkins, Phillip	3	0	0	0	132
Hawkins, Scott	3	0	0	0	630
Hawley, Reba M.	19	0	4	4	6,282
Hawley, Sherri-Lee	9	2	2	0	47,339
Hawley, Wesley E.	182	28	26	27	626,635
Hawthorne, James Wesley	3	0	0	1	1,550
Hay, George H.	4	0	1	1	4,595
Haydel, Cliff	108	14	11	12	158,749
Hayden, Jean	56	0	4	9	5,970
Hayes, Breeda	5	0	1	1	19,938
Hayes, Frank Foster	13	1	1	2	13,363
Hayes, Larry W.	83	1	4	7	30,906
Hayes, Marvin	31	3	4	3	24,330
Hayes, Michael S.	29	4	4	3	34,035
Hayes, Robert D.	7	0	0	1	3,201
Hayford, Jennifer A.	62	2	6	2	46,012
Haynes, Brady	3	1	0	0	2,518
Haynes, Bruce	39	4	4	4	76,339
Haynes, Ernest M.	276	61	57	34	1,122,273
Haynes, Rodney	212	30	31	36	363,790
Hays, Danton O.	29	1	0	7	14,006
Hayworth, Dwayne	7	1	3	0	9,618
Hazel, Robert A.	9	0	1	1	1,542
Hazelton, Richard P.	291	36	34	45	1,091,075
Hazelton, Steve	21	4	0	1	50,442
Hazen, Jr., William E.	43	0	6	7	25,836
Head, Freddy	1	0	1	0	40,000
Headley, Bruce	134	22	19	20	1,232,704
Heads, Barbara	227	36	34	22	550,449
Healy, Art	3	1	0	0	2,391
Heaps, Cornell M.	25	1	0	2	7,762
Heaps, Phillip M.	1	0	0	0	0
Heard, Jr., Thomas H.	69	5	14	7	116,779
Heath, George	24	1	0	2	23,550
Heberle, Arthur H.	181	8	17	14	141,687
Hebert, Chris	38	4	6	5	51,295
Hebert, Doris	536	102	87	81	1,614,269
Hebert, Ernest	15	3	0	2	21,336
Hebert, J. Pervis	41	3	7	8	78,878
Hebert, Jeff A.	75	6	7	11	85,726
Hebert, Kitty A.	37	2	4	3	36,490
Hebert, R. Pete	59	4	6	11	77,876
Hebert, Rylan	97	12	11	15	168,851
Hecker, Donald	83	5	11	9	125,410
Heckrotte, Beverly L.	29	4	3	2	107,443
Hedary, Antoine Y.	31	0	0	3	11,265
Hedegaard, Randy	40	3	6	5	17,841
Hedge, Rick	155	24	19	18	445,133
Hedges, Dianne E.	5	0	1	0	4,008
Hedges, Tony	14	1	1	0	10,962
Hedus, William C.	101	18	15	10	172,675
Heggie, Rod	150	18	24	31	265,103
Hehn, Donald	9	0	0	1	1,264
Heidelberg, Bradley N.	10	1	3	0	32,520
Heidelberg, Lee Roy	40	2	3	3	14,826
Heidenreich, Philip J.	17	0	0	0	3,412
Heil, Nancy B.	77	4	6	10	100,630
Heim, Richard	7	0	0	0	1,005
Heinen, Miles H.	1	0	0	0	90
Heizer, Paul	2	0	0	0	335
Held, Dieter K.	47	2	2	4	58,766
Heldt, Donald C.	12	0	1	1	8,245
Heldt, Merle	34	4	5	6	41,420
Helfenstein, Alvina	7	1	0	0	6,102
Helfenstein, Dino	13	0	0	0	1,220
Hellman, Leroy	319	57	38	51	433,965
Hellwege, Steven Lane	11	1	1	0	5,246
Helmbrecht, Jo Dawn	59	4	5	4	25,044
Helmbrecht, William M.	2	0	0	0	840
Helmbrecht, William R.	212	16	19	12	306,113
Helmetag, Robert P.	75	7	11	9	187,967
Hemba, Brad	49	6	9	5	72,482
Hemby, Jack R.	44	5	0	5	50,952
Hemmer, Terrell M.	29	6	5	1	40,561
Hemmerick, Anthony J.	22	2	0	5	27,425
Hemmerick, Vivian	1	0	0	0	150
Hemmings, Glendon	78	4	9	10	83,114
Hemmingson, Brian	8	0	1	0	1,370
Hemsworth, Roy	8	0	1	0	568
Henderson, Eddy	10	2	0	1	13,916
Henderson, Frances	98	8	4	14	176,609
Henderson, Max	3	0	0	0	0
Hendricks, Dan L.	162	18	20	19	937,396
Hendricks, Franklin J.	2	1	0	0	9,120
Hendricks, Jalene	36	6	3	5	12,451
Hendrickson, David L.	111	17	7	16	333,240
Hendrickson, Lori	95	15	13	7	217,144
Hendriks, Elizabeth M.	37	6	9	5	227,795
Hendriks, Richard J.	204	37	29	37	622,050
Hendriks, Sanna N.	105	24	21	19	610,568
Hendrix, Charles	12	1	2	1	2,464
Hendrix, Coy	74	5	11	15	114,208
Hendrix, Laurie	5	0	1	1	4,315
Hendrix-Craig, Susan	9	0	0	0	1,370
Heniser, Tim	6	1	1	0	4,841
Henley, Michael R.	37	2	3	2	26,432
Hennessy, Joseph	31	0	3	1	12,046
Hennig, John K.	68	8	8	11	252,230
Hennig, Mark A.	516	72	100	66	3,957,058
Hennig, William H.	2	0	0	0	122
Hennigh, Alan W.	1	0	0	0	42
Henry, Ignatius	29	3	0	2	27,651
Henry, Neville	60	3	8	6	42,318
Henry, Royston A.	13	0	3	3	10,410
Henson, Steve	44	6	7	1	95,447
Hepton, Fred	42	7	10	3	20,015
Herber, M. Paula	45	2	10	5	17,157
Herbert, Grant H.	2	0	1	1	2,670
Herbert, Mark	8	0	2	0	2,286
Herbig, John	4	0	0	0	252
Herbst, Preston L.	172	26	20	24	467,179
Herdy, Fred J.	18	0	0	1	7,222
Herlinger, Victoria M.	31	3	2	1	24,760
Herman, Dev	63	3	8	13	13,073
Herman, Jamie	8	0	1	1	1,150
Herman, Robert	3	0	1	0	375
Herman, Sonja	14	0	3	1	8,961
Herman, Steve	4	0	0	1	405
Herman, Thomas	7	2	0	2	3,680
Herman, Vernon D.	14	2	0	1	15,631
Hernandez, Antonio B.	50	5	2	6	39,135
Hernandez, Gilberto J.	6	2	0	0	16,756
Hernandez, Janet	6	0	0	0	1,600
Hernandez, Obidio Otis	4	0	0	0	0
Hernandez, Pedro	13	1	0	0	2,599
Hernandez, Ramon M.	128	17	16	17	824,102
Hernandez, Raul F.	38	2	2	4	14,340
Hernandez, Salvador	19	0	0	3	12,480
Hernandez, Jr., Jose G.	48	2	9	3	25,453
Hernandez, Jr., Sandino R.	27	1	1	2	19,826
Herndon, Paul H.	6	0	0	0	339
Herndon, Terry	17	1	1	2	7,153
Herold, Russell J.	11	3	0	1	21,685
Herrell, Ron D.	1	0	0	0	130
Herren, Gene	16	1	0	2	3,230
Herrera, Arnold G.	9	2	1	3	7,148
Herrera, Arturo F.	32	0	1	3	5,905
Herrera, Javier	3	0	0	0	385

Trainer	Sts	1st	2d	3d	Purses
Herrick, Joe	21	2	2	1	121,595
Herrington, Paul	32	4	0	2	54,077
Hershbell, Lynnett A.	20	0	3	2	34,407
Hertler, John O.	159	13	15	20	556,985
Heskett, Theodore R.	34	1	3	4	37,178
Hesler, Ed H.	11	0	0	0	1,259
Hess, Jacob G.	9	1	3	1	20,685
Hess, Julie S.	79	9	8	8	190,156
Hess, Jr., Robert B.	183	31	25	27	885,339
Hess, Sr., Robert B.	173	26	25	37	507,951
Hester, Leanne	23	1	1	0	13,077
Heupel, Larry	3	0	0	0	268
Hewitt, Michael	15	0	1	0	1,940
Hewko, J.	17	2	5	3	9,781
Hiatt, Charles E.	62	3	5	6	16,504
Hiatt, Kathleen M.	11	0	1	0	1,080
Hiatt, Wayne D.	2	0	0	0	166
Hibdon, Mark N.	110	4	1	10	32,856
Hickey, P. Noel	133	10	17	15	189,005
Hicklin, Judi A.	210	25	30	28	376,778
Hickman, Charlie	2	0	0	0	0
Hickman, Kenneth G.	116	13	13	5	105,375
Hicks, Cyril F.	31	4	4	6	127,522
Hicks, Denette L.	25	3	1	2	27,958
Hicks, Harry	45	3	8	8	41,156
Hicks, Morris	6	3	1	0	12,960
Hicks, Robert	6	0	0	0	278
Hicks, William R.	51	4	6	6	60,391
Hieatt, Derek	7	2	0	1	5,870
Higgins, Dennis J.	3	0	0	0	696
Higgins, Hope M.	1	0	0	0	224
Higgins, Martha	4	1	2	1	1,180
Higgins, III, John J.	7	0	0	0	1,850
Higgs, Wayne	2	0	0	0	495
Hightower, James	4	1	0	1	1,670
Hignite, James	12	0	0	0	953
Hild, Glenn L.	87	4	6	6	52,357
Hiles, Rick	100	13	15	17	232,872
Hill, Bill F.	19	0	0	0	1,953
Hill, Brenda M.	85	13	16	10	171,529
Hill, David	3	0	0	0	625
Hill, Floyd	88	4	4	5	32,067
Hill, Jim	123	35	19	13	194,380
Hill, Jimmie E.	52	7	2	10	17,720
Hill, Joe	25	1	1	0	4,078
Hill, John F.	11	1	1	2	9,696
Hill, Marc	38	5	4	2	30,399
Hill, Rickey F.	2	0	0	0	195
Hille, Jack	32	4	2	3	22,071
Hille, Jim	9	1	1	1	2,225
Hille, Wayne	5	0	1	0	960
Hilliard, David L.	11	1	1	1	11,350
Hilling, James M.	37	8	6	2	123,750
Hillis, Wayne	1	0	0	0	0
Hills, Claire	1	0	0	0	0
Hills, Timothy A.	585	103	86	68	3,075,524
Hilton, Ann B.	3	1	0	0	16,776
Hilts, Nancy	3	0	0	0	2,454
Hinckson, Martin	28	3	3	2	43,644
Hindman, Ed	44	0	4	3	16,000
Hinds, Austin	44	2	7	7	176,363
Hinds, Lonnie	40	5	3	9	36,803
Hinds, Steven	16	0	1	2	5,280
Hinerdeer, James	8	0	0	1	2,525
Hines, Nicholas J.	214	24	20	27	748,578
Hinkle, Mike	35	11	3	6	35,051
Hinkle, Tom	2	0	0	0	210
Hinojos, Alvaro	2	0	0	0	249
Hinojosa, Isidro	1	1	0	0	2,880
Hinshaw, Gary D.	58	6	10	3	69,974
Hinsley, David H.	307	36	32	30	572,383
Hinton, Stacy	25	2	1	2	26,758
Hinton, William H.	11	1	3	5	19,516
Hirst, Robert E.	9	0	0	0	1,566
Hitt, Thomas W.	3	0	0	0	630
Hixon, Fred	36	3	7	5	19,724
Hjelm, Lawrence	18	0	0	0	1,744
Hjort, Donna	6	1	0	1	11,550
Hobbs, Kyle A.	10	0	1	3	9,500
Hobbs, Laura	111	9	7	17	45,559
Hobby, Steve	176	27	33	34	814,809
Hobson, Don	13	2	1	2	22,572
Hobson, Doug	6	0	4	0	3,120
Hobson, Ronnie	7	0	1	1	1,935
Hobson, Simon	24	0	2	3	15,789
Hoburg, Bill C.	11	3	1	3	4,830
Hoch, Jr., Frank B.	4	0	0	0	76
Hochsteiner, Gail	8	0	2	1	1,505
Hocker, Rodney L.	1	1	0	0	20,376
Hodge, Bobby	1	0	0	0	0
Hodge, Jerry	3	0	0	0	122
Hodge, Mary E.	72	2	2	4	15,461
Hodges, Dixie Lorena	13	5	4	2	34,101
Hodges, James E.	142	32	23	17	605,484
Hodges, Jodie	2	0	0	0	524
Hodges, Sharon E.	6	0	1	0	1,736
Hodges, Walter N.	21	1	0	9	15,693
Hodgin, R. E.	36	4	5	8	39,397
Hodgson, Barry	14	2	4	2	10,014
Hodson, Kevin D.	3	1	0	1	1,490
Hoegerl, Clif	37	2	3	3	20,894
Hoetzendorfer, Johanna	18	0	1	0	5,180
Hof, Bill	38	4	6	5	10,571
Hoff, Susan J.	12	0	3	3	16,835
Hoffman, James H.	48	5	6	7	13,692
Hoffman, Kenneth E.	35	3	2	3	121,478
Hoffman, Mark	44	6	6	3	84,894
Hoffman, Michael	12	2	1	2	7,352
Hoffner, Jeannie L.	1	0	0	0	75
Hoffpauir, Thaddeus	14	1	1	2	17,252
Hoffrogge, Todd M.	124	20	16	13	306,191
Hofmans, David E.	102	16	10	11	1,028,050
Hofmans, Grant	56	15	5	10	242,174
Hogan, Sara L.	4	0	0	1	3,725
Hogue, James L.	94	6	6	13	114,641
Hohensee, Karl M.	15	1	1	0	7,878
Hoksbergen, Allen D.	53	6	4	10	39,548
Hoksbergen, Larry A	34	4	5	5	39,736
Holas, Scott S.	58	1	4	7	27,387
Holden, Jay J.	81	8	15	11	52,269
Holden, Mark	22	0	3	0	13,468
Holder, Tedston	3	0	0	0	501
Holds, Whitney	3	0	0	0	0
Holifield, Jerry	40	3	7	6	22,603
Holland, Bobby G.	6	0	0	0	1,685
Holland, Mary	2	0	0	0	220
Holland, Troy S.	35	3	6	2	61,865
Hollar, Donald B.	59	8	9	7	161,415
Hollendorfer, Jerry	1,300	308	261	186	6,005,484
Hollett, Richard	60	11	16	8	108,287
Holley, Jr., Gerald E.	21	1	1	0	16,188
Holloway, Ashley	2	0	0	1	660
Holm, Dalyce	33	1	3	2	10,759
Holman, William	2	0	0	0	0
Holmes, Barry	85	18	17	11	162,632
Holmes, J. R.	7	0	0	2	2,090
Holmes, Lloyd S.	54	7	12	8	21,610
Holsapple, Stacey	11	0	0	3	3,380
Holst, Nicole	8	1	2	1	4,046
Holstein, Craig T.	18	2	4	3	21,946
Holt, Burlin C.	4	0	0	0	355
Holt, John T.	14	2	2	3	11,211
Holt, Larry W.	183	28	34	22	285,793
Holthus, Robert E.	364	72	54	55	2,635,551
Homeister, Sr., Rosemary	113	6	12	23	107,055
Homer, A. Lynn	77	12	18	7	29,012
Homer, Jason	165	30	19	25	112,441
Homewood, Michael	3	1	0	0	15,365
Hone, Bart G.	252	51	47	38	528,561
Honea, Tom D.	2	0	0	0	0
Hood, Jr., John R.	4	0	0	0	109
Hooper, Jeff D.	46	7	3	6	112,815

Trainer	Sts	1st	2d	3d	Purses
Hooper, Pamela	4	0	0	1	2,246
Hooper, Timothy	235	47	36	28	911,335
Hoover, Alton	6	0	2	1	2,683
Hoover, Anthony	6	1	1	3	1,939
Hoover, Cindy	72	8	8	10	25,502
Hoover, Donald Richard	2	0	0	1	250
Hoover, Gregg	18	1	4	1	10,589
Hoover, Herbert	9	1	0	2	8,460
Hop, Michael D.	48	6	8	2	16,462
Hopf, Jerry L.	16	0	1	1	3,951
Hopkins, Dennis	264	31	38	40	389,616
Hopkins, Terry L.	83	5	7	9	29,225
Hopmans, Jr., C. Cliff	146	10	14	19	752,213
Hoppel, Darryl G.	3	0	0	0	428
Horan, Jody	2	0	0	0	100
Horn, H. Ray	15	3	5	2	39,682
Horning, Jr., Lawrence E.	49	10	7	4	187,670
Hornsby, William	20	1	2	1	12,565
Horrell, Donald G.	89	6	10	10	61,959
Horrigan, John	26	1	1	4	12,335
Horst, Scot	2	0	0	1	300
Horton, Jr., Curtis	20	1	0	2	9,075
Hosang, Jr., Oliver P.	4	0	0	0	512
Hoskins, Ken	31	5	5	2	31,436
Hoskins, Steve	70	15	9	9	116,147
Hostler, Jr., Charles N.	85	3	6	2	60,450
Hough, Richard Lewis	5	0	0	0	264
Hough, Stanley M.	259	53	56	39	2,918,862
Houghton, Dove P.	12	1	4	0	22,235
Houghton, John W.	31	1	2	4	11,521
Houghton, Ronald B.	154	15	15	30	303,865
Houghton, Roy D.	139	12	17	16	190,665
Houle, William	47	8	2	1	103,450
Houliston, Milton	17	2	1	3	36,660
Hounyovi, Didier G.	1	0	0	0	0
House, Brian S.	72	17	5	10	191,025
House, Gary F.	35	4	5	2	32,571
House, R. Wayne	1	0	0	0	69
Householder, Charles F.	1	0	0	0	0
Householder, N. Eddie	218	24	21	39	539,307
Houston, James W.	8	2	1	1	24,291
Houston, Mickey D.	3	0	0	0	1,182
Houston, Wayne	37	2	2	1	20,096
Houtchens, Raymond J.	4	0	0	0	386
Howard, Bart D.	8	2	0	0	5,389
Howard, Blaine Lynn	1	0	0	0	105
Howard, Ian	50	4	11	8	330,431
Howard, Jack E.	46	4	7	4	41,728
Howard, James A.	31	0	1	1	8,680
Howard, L. Sam	53	3	3	7	10,876
Howard, Leigh Ann	12	0	3	2	34,912
Howard, Neil J.	173	37	30	26	1,938,175
Howard, Paul	3	0	0	0	0
Howard, Sam H.	2	0	0	1	630
Howard, Sam K.	3	0	0	0	787
Howard, Steve J.	56	4	3	5	50,551
Howard, Thomas	16	3	3	1	25,335
Howard, W. T.	1	0	0	0	990
Howard, William M.	16	2	2	2	19,256
Howe, Cathy	7	0	0	0	640
Howell, Ronald E.	12	0	0	0	1,683
Howland, Edith	38	3	10	2	131,040
Hrymak, Brent	19	4	5	2	38,315
Huarte, Frank	60	6	8	7	316,174
Hubley, Mark	47	1	7	5	69,958
Huckabay, Sid T.	23	0	0	0	1,741
Huddleston, Richard W.	4	1	0	0	4,685
Hudgens, Rodger	5	0	0	1	856
Hudman, John R.	3	0	0	0	0
Hudnut, Steven L.	56	2	5	4	35,521
Hudson, Howard L.	28	2	9	6	34,779
Hudson, James C.	129	21	19	12	305,993
Hudson, Jeff D.	120	11	16	10	86,369
Hudson, Randy	11	2	1	3	8,311
Huelsman, Ray	9	0	0	0	1,537
Huertas, Nirka	23	3	3	2	34,148
Huff, Darin	4	0	0	0	640
Huff, Kathleen A.	10	1	0	1	32,154
Huffman, Dean	7	0	0	1	909
Huffman, J. Kenneth	112	8	19	14	152,622
Huffman, Larry G.	17	1	0	1	10,872
Huffman, Neil C.	38	1	7	12	29,052
Huffman, Patrick	45	7	4	3	140,165
Huffman, Roy L.	38	2	2	1	8,410
Huffman, William G.	91	10	14	9	297,919
Huffman, Jr., John H.	1	0	0	0	750
Hughes, Baden H.	32	1	0	4	41,776
Hughes, Brandon	9	1	1	1	6,543
Hughes, Byron G.	76	4	16	1	113,812
Hughes, Dennis P.	136	8	19	18	74,359
Hughes, Jeff	2	0	1	0	3,072
Hughes, Judy E.	37	5	5	4	68,854
Hughes, Lawrence D.	47	5	7	7	87,518
Hughes, Mary J.	23	3	1	1	32,090
Hughes, Raymond C.	11	1	4	1	9,190
Hughes, Jr., Don E.	25	3	3	3	21,134
Hughes, Jr., Fred J.	13	0	2	1	14,792
Hughes, Jr., Richard E.	12	0	3	0	22,776
Hughes, Sr., Donald E.	95	12	13	21	177,668
Hukill, Charles P.	341	40	39	42	507,754
Hull, Mike	4	0	0	0	1,595
Hummer, Jerry	77	5	6	3	40,226
Humphrey, Shirley A.	13	1	0	4	32,585
Humphries, Gene	7	1	1	1	1,615
Humphries, Lonnie	18	1	1	4	12,988
Humphries, Thomas	1	0	0	0	50
Hundt, Robert L.	48	2	1	4	13,359
Hunkapiller, Louis	33	3	0	4	34,440
Hunsaker, Danny J.	52	5	4	6	35,738
Hunsucker, Jr., James F.	7	1	0	0	11,712
Hunt, Charley	2	1	0	0	4,542
Hunt, Donald F.	29	2	2	0	17,412
Hunt, Gary	1	0	0	0	243
Hunt, Gina L.	12	3	1	1	21,087
Hunt, Glen E.	30	2	4	4	25,904
Hunt, J. Sue	24	5	3	4	17,942
Hunt, Richard	4	0	1	1	1,735
Hunt, Vannessa	129	26	21	21	85,903
Hunt, Sr., Larry E.	43	5	4	4	107,174
Hunter, Debora	2	0	0	0	852
Hunter, Don	1	0	0	0	0
Hunter, F. E.	17	3	5	2	47,910
Hunter, Judy	28	11	8	3	36,506
Hunter, Regis A.	19	0	0	0	3,850
Hunter, Rick	33	4	9	6	11,498
Hunter, Robert L.	1	0	0	0	77
Hunter, Thomas E.	50	8	8	10	20,480
Hunter, Thomas W.	31	1	2	1	32,280
Hunter, Jr., Allan	16	1	0	1	11,932
Huntington, Dougal A.	13	1	0	1	7,890
Hurdle, Joe A.	16	1	1	3	6,729
Hurley, Dennis	116	6	4	8	19,807
Hurley, Kenneth L.	35	1	5	3	13,790
Hurley, Mary L.	59	2	4	5	19,530
Hurt, Clayton C.	304	50	59	27	436,802
Hurtado, Clemente	3	0	0	0	620
Hurtak, Daniel C.	334	54	46	53	702,855
Husak, Robert	29	3	4	4	40,988
Husbands, Andrew	1	0	0	0	91
Husbands, Anthony	23	2	3	0	28,806
Hushion, Michael E.	306	53	48	44	1,853,071
Hussey, David	47	0	1	4	15,079
Husson, Damie L.	2	0	0	0	515
Huston, Sharon T.	77	7	7	10	199,810
Hutchison, David J.	47	4	8	4	77,378
Hutchison, James A.	25	1	0	3	36,955
Hutchison-Hand, Julie P.	10	1	1	1	21,591
Huth, Bill	28	3	2	2	46,260
Hutt, Danny	2	0	0	0	154
Huval, Brian A.	101	9	14	14	138,811
Huval, Kelly	71	7	4	4	64,731
Huval, Robert Lee	1	1	0	0	7,440

Trainer	Sts	1st	2d	3d	Purses
Hyatt, Freddie	33	2	5	6	36,402
Hyde, Cody	1	0	0	0	189
Hyland, Angel	58	4	14	9	141,766
Hysell-Berryhill, Robin E.	15	1	1	2	6,522
Hyvonen, Joni M.	15	0	2	2	10,639
Iacone, Maryann	22	0	0	1	7,398
Iacovacci, Cynthia L.	53	5	10	4	40,983
Iacovacci, Sr., George A.	160	5	9	15	59,595
Iams, Wendell	8	1	1	1	18,280
Iannotti, Robert	4	0	0	0	200
Iannotti, IV, Thomas	4	1	0	1	6,350
Ibach, Clancy J.	2	0	0	0	301
Ibach, Clarence Clancy	1	0	0	0	0
Ibach, Jan	10	1	0	2	2,219
Ibarra, Jose	39	4	2	8	16,208
Iglar-Hughes, Joanna	30	2	4	5	112,702
Ilicin, Jr., Al	52	7	4	6	44,436
Imbesi, Joseph M.	2	0	0	0	1,140
Imperio, Joseph	137	10	15	16	369,285
Inabinett, Johnny	32	2	6	9	62,479
Inda, Eduardo	57	4	6	6	226,416
Indreland, R. Dean	1	0	0	0	0
Ingebritson, Mark	36	5	3	4	46,144
Ingels, Jerry	22	4	1	4	15,880
Ingenito, Angela M.	51	6	3	4	89,617
Ingram, Kevin	79	3	14	17	42,260
Ingram, Steve	24	5	0	2	28,456
Inirio, Olivo I.	60	3	6	3	40,766
Inman, Robert L.	9	2	1	1	17,478
Inman, Ronald P.	35	2	3	5	22,913
Inouye, Tak	26	3	3	7	57,517
Iorfida, Lou	7	1	0	1	16,913
Iorio, Jr., Sal	155	14	16	12	339,570
Ireland, Marty R.	17	4	4	3	14,640
Irion, C. Dale	1	0	0	0	100
Irion, Sue	120	15	17	17	103,602
Irish, Ray E.	5	1	0	0	1,475
Irwin, Alex T.	39	0	2	5	18,185
Irwin, Jim	7	0	2	0	2,200
Irwin, Ralph R.	120	16	13	14	246,343
Irwin, Robert D.	82	8	9	9	156,881
Isbell, Jr., Ron	9	2	3	1	103,150
Isburg, Jr., William	98	2	11	9	30,842
Isdell, John M.	3	0	0	0	0
Ishaq, Abdallah H.	36	7	3	1	98,095
Isom, James S.	7	0	0	0	105
Iverson, Mitchell L.	1	0	0	0	37
Ivie, Jimmy C.	1	0	0	0	83
Ivory, John C.	29	2	2	2	35,707
Iwan, Marilyn	23	0	0	1	2,571
Iwinski, Allen	506	98	69	64	3,004,795
Jablow, Michael	27	2	7	3	115,077
Jacavone, John J.	106	4	9	13	60,906
Jack, Allan	54	11	8	11	153,082
Jack, Crystal	9	1	0	0	3,874
Jacklin, Theodora S.	86	1	7	4	22,171
Jackson, Bruce C.	61	8	5	11	131,713
Jackson, Bruce L.	34	3	4	6	126,437
Jackson, Christopher J.	20	2	1	4	25,714
Jackson, Dale L.	21	2	1	1	20,225
Jackson, Darrell Z.	6	1	1	1	32,522
Jackson, Declan A.	21	1	1	5	61,780
Jackson, Elizabeth R.	5	0	2	1	12,410
Jackson, Ellen L.	82	2	2	7	50,743
Jackson, Fred L.	19	0	2	1	8,508
Jackson, Harvey	11	3	2	1	9,666
Jackson, Helmut S.	13	1	0	0	3,942
Jackson, James D.	2	0	0	0	240
Jackson, James R.	264	42	39	24	414,697
Jackson, Jeffrey D.	3	0	0	0	247
Jackson, Leroy	9	0	0	0	1,809
Jackson, Richard	1	0	0	0	0
Jackson, Richard D.	147	17	20	27	244,584
Jackson, Robert D.	46	0	2	1	2,698
Jackson, Ronald D.	39	3	3	9	24,777
Jackson, Sherry L.	29	1	4	5	39,534
Jackson, Jr., Evan	14	1	0	3	7,099
Jacobs, Daniel C.	36	2	6	1	23,129
Jacobs, Dudley	2	0	0	0	1,280
Jacobs, John D.	2	0	0	1	3,280
Jacobs, Nancy	1	0	0	0	122
Jacobs, Nita	4	2	0	0	3,789
Jacobs, Stephen	14	2	1	2	26,716
Jacobs, Jr., John F.	2	0	1	1	7,590
Jacobsen, Harvey T.	23	1	4	5	21,524
Jacot, William Joseph	21	3	2	4	46,066
Jacques, Dennis S.	105	4	7	9	39,723
Jacquot, Gene	74	14	7	13	191,249
Jaeger, Charles J.	17	1	2	0	21,638
Jaggers, Donnie	23	2	0	0	6,657
Jahns, Debi	7	0	1	1	1,518
James, Bob	1	0	0	0	0
James, Greg	24	6	2	5	77,835
James, Greg C.	122	18	26	13	233,084
James, Lorenzo	1	0	0	0	38
Jamison, O. D.	76	7	11	13	112,105
Janes, Mark	5	3	0	0	14,289
Janko, Christine K.	213	46	40	19	1,021,255
Jansen, Gail T.	26	1	0	0	10,330
Jansen, Kenny	10	1	3	1	5,347
Jansen, Kim	1	0	0	0	0
January, Elmer	128	13	8	15	101,547
Jaquillard, Arthur J.	25	2	0	3	22,839
Jaros, Ronald J.	21	2	1	1	18,573
Jarvis, Kathy	63	5	7	4	76,045
Jarvis, Michael A.	1	0	0	0	7,500
Jarvis, Pat	16	0	0	1	5,165
Jeannont, Dianne M.	84	7	7	12	92,607
Jeanotte, Bob	118	20	19	13	162,665
Jean-Pierre, Albert	3	0	0	0	370
Jeansonne, Albin	62	5	8	10	69,710
Jeffries, Donald L.	27	1	2	2	21,154
Jeffries, Patrick	30	5	2	8	38,767
Jeffries, Robert A.	36	5	4	1	45,131
Jelm, Christina R.	17	2	1	4	26,285
Jenda, Charles J.	268	36	42	48	883,014
Jenkins, Bobby A.	114	25	20	16	157,519
Jenkins, Brandon	32	5	0	3	23,597
Jenkins, Michael P.	1	0	0	0	0
Jenkins, Reed L.	95	11	6	12	87,155
Jenkins, Rodney	245	45	45	44	1,001,290
Jenkins, Suzanne H.	65	5	7	13	83,652
Jenkins, Wallace A.	27	0	0	5	12,692
Jenkins, Jr., N. W.	59	4	8	13	211,265
Jenne, Bonnie	132	13	20	14	162,161
Jennings, Dennis E.	6	1	0	1	2,721
Jennings, Ronald A.	3	0	1	2	1,010
Jensen, Cory	1	0	1	0	3,000
Jensen, Daniel M.	25	1	1	5	53,140
Jensen, Eric	10	1	2	0	4,815
Jensen, Kent	66	8	11	14	112,202
Jensen, Mark	15	1	2	3	11,951
Jensen, Megan	1	0	0	0	80
Jerkens, H. Allen	374	72	44	56	4,447,047
Jerkens, James A.	207	43	40	22	2,480,146
Jerkens, Steven T.	85	6	10	9	261,747
Jermain, Kathie C.	101	11	13	14	108,579
Jerman, Jerry	81	7	11	10	97,865
Jewell, Ron	36	5	1	4	55,702
Jimenez, Fidencio L.	72	12	5	17	67,576
Jimenez, Jose M.	3	1	0	1	7,265
Jimenez, Lisa A.	49	2	6	4	58,884
Jimenez, Sr., Guillermo	47	7	2	5	12,201
Jiminez, Lauren Sherman	56	2	5	6	59,959
Jocson, Gwen	4	0	0	1	1,715
Johns, Justin	53	9	6	8	135,534
Johnson, Andrew H.	55	9	6	6	66,682
Johnson, Brian S.	4	0	0	0	1,062
Johnson, Brian T.	9	0	0	0	3,539
Johnson, Bruce	33	1	3	3	13,361
Johnson, C. Allen	24	1	2	2	25,940
Johnson, Calistine I.	2	0	0	0	510
Johnson, Carrie L.	44	2	6	7	20,899

Trainer	Sts	1st	2d	3d	Purses
Johnson, Cecil H.	34	3	3	2	39,667
Johnson, Danny Smith	7	1	1	0	10,888
Johnson, David F.	2	0	0	0	486
Johnson, Doug	55	10	12	4	26,743
Johnson, Douglas L.	155	16	11	12	212,131
Johnson, Frank R.	4	0	0	0	647
Johnson, Frazer	67	3	1	7	63,653
Johnson, Freddie R.	61	9	12	10	222,291
Johnson, Gail	5	0	0	0	238
Johnson, Gary L.	741	83	87	79	822,439
Johnson, Gene A.	39	1	4	3	19,834
Johnson, Harry	21	4	1	3	31,663
Johnson, Heather A.	11	2	1	1	10,538
Johnson, James R.	7	0	0	0	468
Johnson, Jennifer A.	91	14	7	9	223,902
Johnson, Jerry W.	5	0	0	0	1,055
Johnson, Jill	3	0	1	1	2,071
Johnson, John Michael	34	6	4	7	41,966
Johnson, Joseph E.	84	5	16	15	129,391
Johnson, Joseph H.	89	22	15	12	646,397
Johnson, Joseph Harold	1	1	0	0	5,100
Johnson, Keith M.	61	7	5	10	41,122
Johnson, Kenneth L.	10	3	1	1	10,557
Johnson, Mark	2	0	0	0	0
Johnson, Marvin A.	300	54	29	35	278,126
Johnson, Murray W.	87	4	16	6	1,033,915
Johnson, Norman A.	39	0	0	0	5,325
Johnson, Paul E.	17	0	0	0	2,988
Johnson, Philip G.	79	11	5	13	367,337
Johnson, Rae	79	7	11	5	144,021
Johnson, Richard G.	17	1	1	1	6,534
Johnson, Robert Don	3	0	3	0	1,500
Johnson, Roscoe E.	47	4	4	8	74,706
Johnson, Sheri	22	0	0	2	2,489
Johnson, Sonny	57	5	2	5	34,088
Johnson, Sterling	2	0	0	0	0
Johnson, William D.	3	0	0	0	0
Johnson, Jr., Henry B.	79	9	12	9	132,020
Johnston, Carlton R.	39	1	1	3	16,574
Johnston, Edward J.	47	7	7	3	216,370
Johnston, Johnny	14	0	0	2	3,499
Johnston, Marilyn T.	18	1	2	1	19,854
Johnston, Marion	22	2	1	3	14,391
Johnston, Patrick	61	3	4	8	55,234
Johnston, Jr., Dean	4	0	0	0	0
Johnstone, Bruce	26	1	1	3	29,608
Joiner, Michael W.	1	0	0	0	95
Jolley, Leroy S.	31	0	1	2	29,024
Jolley, Jr, Dean F.	4	1	0	2	1,624
Jones, A. Mark	37	7	3	5	17,605
Jones, Angie	12	1	1	1	2,261
Jones, Anthony Gordon	2	0	1	0	268
Jones, Bobby G.	1	0	0	0	105
Jones, Bobby L.	6	0	0	1	360
Jones, Brian K.	32	2	3	4	21,886
Jones, Carl C.	24	0	1	4	6,535
Jones, Carol L.	15	3	1	1	19,835
Jones, Charles Franklin	17	3	5	2	17,105
Jones, Dale R.	2	0	0	1	475
Jones, Daniel T.	51	5	6	9	62,156
Jones, Daren K.	41	5	6	4	15,487
Jones, Daryl	1	0	0	0	187
Jones, Duwayne	11	0	1	1	13,565
Jones, G. E. Ted	41	3	4	7	16,675
Jones, Harold R.	18	3	4	3	10,740
Jones, J. Larry	189	35	33	26	1,167,990
Jones, Jack Craig	28	0	4	2	18,702
Jones, Jack W.	9	0	1	0	5,448
Jones, James E.	85	21	10	14	138,940
Jones, James R.	44	7	4	9	94,560
Jones, Jann K.	23	1	2	2	10,598
Jones, Jeffery S.	156	13	15	14	213,486
Jones, Jesse T.	9	2	0	0	11,865
Jones, Jimmy W.	1	0	0	0	0
Jones, John P.	1	0	0	0	0
Jones, Juanita	47	2	1	5	7,386
Jones, Laurie	124	10	10	18	24,536
Jones, Lynda	19	2	2	2	10,338
Jones, Mark A.	6	1	1	2	3,565
Jones, Mark Russell	8	0	0	0	1,116
Jones, Martin F.	176	30	26	27	1,276,513
Jones, Michael David	105	9	21	13	65,459
Jones, Michael P.	5	1	0	0	6,853
Jones, Phillip L.	4	0	0	0	460
Jones, Richard J.	37	2	2	3	27,144
Jones, Robin	12	0	1	1	2,589
Jones, Roy C.	8	1	1	1	16,017
Jones, Steve	4	0	0	0	122
Jones, Tommy Lee	41	3	4	4	54,040
Jones, Vaughan	1	0	0	0	170
Jones, Wilfred	53	6	8	6	86,700
Jones, William I.	15	0	2	3	9,901
Jones, Sr., Herbert W.	10	3	1	0	14,833
Jons, Claus	2	0	1	0	2,111
Jordan, Janice J.	2	0	0	1	1,705
Jordan, Michael B.	34	1	2	1	8,308
Jordan, Rick G.	87	8	13	10	135,438
Jordan, Roland G.	57	2	9	7	24,567
Jordan, Steven W.	10	0	0	0	822
Jordan, Terry	47	8	8	4	104,979
Jordan, Jr., Harold Z.	26	6	2	4	97,274
Jory, Ian P. D.	165	14	16	26	705,499
Joseph, Judy	3	0	0	0	620
Josephson, Jedd B.	188	27	26	28	454,935
Journet, Theo	88	8	12	10	122,045
Joy, Kevin J.	607	117	75	73	1,762,880
Joyner, Linda	1	0	0	0	0
Juarez, Clare A.	4	0	0	0	1,020
Juarez, Silvester	10	2	3	2	6,370
Judge, Phillip G.	15	0	0	1	6,360
Judice, Shelby	28	1	1	1	17,324
Jukosky, Richard H.	51	6	7	2	197,726
Julian, George H.	4	0	0	0	210
Julian, William A.	31	2	3	5	31,930
Junker, Jr., Milton H.	32	2	6	2	35,801
Jurado, Luis	6	0	0	1	811
Justice, Patricia D.	14	1	2	2	10,622
Juvonen, Erik R.	120	20	17	13	484,046
Kadar, Wendy	58	8	10	8	127,750
Kaden, David	3	0	0	0	274
Kaelberer, Kelly	66	9	11	12	34,800
Kaelin, Forrest	141	14	18	10	242,090
Kagee, Mary	10	1	1	0	2,303
Kagee, Jr., William H.	72	4	9	7	15,700
Kagel, Thomas F.	13	0	1	1	4,300
Kahlden, Lawrence A.	4	0	0	0	3,840
Kaiswatum, Joe	11	0	1	3	1,214
Kamps, Richard	106	23	19	21	361,812
Kane, Carrie	7	0	0	3	1,165
Kane, Mark D.	5	0	1	1	6,372
Kane, Stephen	21	1	0	2	6,062
Kanhai, Joseph	32	0	2	1	12,806
Kaplan, William A.	79	9	12	12	182,705
Kappel, Petra	6	0	2	0	3,540
Kappes, Steven W.	44	4	4	8	226,118
Kapusta, Victor	7	1	0	0	5,040
Karcher, Douglas W.	42	5	8	3	60,634
Kargus, Kevin C.	5	0	0	0	542
Karr, Angela	1	0	0	1	219
Kasmerski, Len	101	12	17	14	108,274
Kasparoff, James M.	14	0	3	3	47,174
Kasperski, Jr., Joseph E.	150	15	11	22	312,483
Kassen, Bonnie	52	6	7	2	77,375
Kassen, David C.	140	20	19	23	733,813
Kassen, Scott	16	2	0	0	9,689
Katryan, Abraham R.	295	32	55	46	1,895,649
Katsaros, Sam	1	0	0	0	0
Katz, Gary R.	16	0	0	1	5,970
Kauffman, Jr., Jack S.	42	3	3	1	25,913
Kaufman, Cathy	9	1	4	2	6,667
Kay, Gary A.	90	2	1	5	31,516
Kay, Robert	9	0	0	0	585
Kays, James H.	4	0	0	0	105
Kazamias, Peter	84	5	17	13	254,389

Trainer	Sts	1st	2d	3d	Purses
Kearl, Judd S.	15	1	0	0	7,575
Kee, Willie J	77	2	6	10	55,006
Keefe, Timothy L.	143	22	13	18	311,520
Keelan, Oliver P.	37	3	2	6	46,597
Keeler, Sandra	14	0	0	1	1,203
Keely, Martin	14	0	0	2	9,687
Keen, Dale L.	1	0	0	0	0
Keen, Dallas E.	139	23	19	21	672,422
Keen, Jim	189	24	30	33	85,788
Keenan, Edward J.	19	0	1	1	5,235
Keener, Dee	10	3	1	0	12,701
Kees, Barbara M.	45	4	2	4	76,256
Keeton, Toby	1	0	0	0	384
Keiffer, Luann	30	2	1	3	30,170
Keil, Steven D.	1	0	0	0	0
Keiser, Deborah	21	1	4	3	30,071
Keiser, Duane	7	1	0	3	14,083
Keiser, Michael	4	0	0	0	785
Keller, Caryn	61	7	10	11	88,580
Keller, Christopher M.	59	4	4	9	68,783
Keller, Ernie J.	219	29	24	41	402,462
Keller, Franklin V.	24	3	1	0	29,241
Keller, Robin M.	159	16	32	21	93,248
Kelley, Brent	60	12	9	17	154,667
Kelley, Gary L.	80	6	7	5	28,318
Kelley, Mark T.	5	0	0	0	775
Kellogg, Cory J.	31	3	1	4	16,470
Kelly, Cody	9	2	0	1	22,317
Kelly, David	14	1	0	1	7,501
Kelly, Dennis D.	35	4	3	3	22,803
Kelly, Donna L.	12	1	2	1	6,293
Kelly, Patrick J.	238	21	27	37	2,120,689
Kelly, Robert W.	21	4	1	3	50,600
Kelly, Suzanne F.	46	7	9	4	74,119
Kelly, Timothy James	129	16	11	20	558,035
Kendall, Connie	43	7	6	3	60,132
Kendall, Elise Wood	13	1	3	2	22,875
Kendall, Jason L.	3	1	0	1	986
Kendall, Vechel E.	14	2	0	2	10,874
Kendrick, Melvin A.	22	0	2	3	14,005
Kenneally, Eddie	137	17	21	18	493,394
Kennedy, Bill E.	83	7	12	13	55,536
Kennedy, Denise	26	2	7	3	102,885
Kennedy, John K.	28	1	0	1	13,763
Kennedy, M. Brent	71	6	6	9	79,258
Kennedy, Richard W.	40	2	3	3	34,639
Kenney, Daniel	157	19	12	18	122,143
Kenney, Martin	14	0	1	1	1,710
Kent, Justine	6	1	0	1	1,564
Kenway, Tom	1	0	0	0	0
Kenyon, Charles D.	3	0	0	0	625
Keogh, Michael	103	14	7	8	1,198,873
Keplin, Kevin	20	2	3	5	11,376
Keplin, Larry	4	2	0	0	1,620
Keplin, Steve	35	2	3	5	11,837
Kerchner, Ann E.	5	0	0	0	415
Kereluk, Edward J.	18	1	1	3	7,348
Kereluk, John	9	1	1	0	3,060
Kereluk, William S.	60	4	3	7	18,741
Kerins, Patrick J.	65	3	4	9	41,429
Kern, David	3	0	0	0	840
Kern, Jr., Berkley W.	52	4	5	10	44,022
Kerns, Perry R.	26	2	2	2	17,433
Kerr, Gordon L.	7	0	0	1	5,685
Kerr, Jessica	2	0	0	0	110
Kerr, Jim	17	1	2	0	4,685
Kerr, Wayne	50	10	4	1	82,726
Kerr, Jr., Robert W.	6	0	0	0	883
Kerr, Jr., William H.	5	0	1	0	1,245
Kerr, Sr., William H.	6	0	0	0	540
Kerrone, Don	51	2	6	10	30,290
Keshane, Dana T.	28	8	8	4	12,311
Keshane, Dana W.	7	0	2	1	916
Keshane, Elton	92	10	15	15	22,070
Keshane, Henry	12	3	1	3	5,166
Keshane, Leon	11	0	1	6	1,251
Keshane, Lindsey	2	1	0	0	906
Keshane, Norbert	7	2	2	0	3,366
Keshane, William	14	3	4	1	5,054
Kessinger, Jerry	1	0	0	0	55
Kessinger, Jr., Burk	22	0	1	2	20,078
Kestler, Larry A.	12	0	0	0	2,283
Ketcher, Henry Lee	4	0	0	1	490
Ketner, Richard	4	0	0	0	2,148
Ketring, Brenda	60	2	2	7	34,967
Kettell, James	144	8	12	9	102,214
Ketter, Greg	2	0	0	0	670
Ketterman, Debra J.	135	12	14	12	285,761
Keuer, Jan E.	10	2	1	2	15,231
Key, Tommy	40	3	4	6	25,800
Keyes, Joseph S.	4	0	0	0	370
Keyrouze, Samuel J.	404	52	47	50	431,214
Khalsa, G Dharma	17	4	3	1	28,965
Kidd, Lynda Ann	5	0	1	1	2,575
Kidder, Keith	25	3	1	1	20,492
Kielty, Donald E.	75	7	15	11	138,240
Kierans, Renee D.	1	0	0	0	0
Kieser, Charles H.	64	2	9	7	63,379
Killion, Benny	3	0	0	0	0
Kilmer, Todd R.	29	0	0	2	7,369
Kilstein, Matthew	3	1	0	0	27,690
Kimmel, John C.	281	34	32	37	2,055,898
Kinch, Bill	67	8	9	8	108,182
Kinchen, Herman L.	144	13	23	19	247,897
Kinder, David L.	25	0	3	4	5,802
Kindle, Jason	10	0	0	0	75
King, Byron H.	10	1	0	0	3,926
King, Eric	14	2	0	0	13,541
King, Gary M.	115	17	17	14	134,471
King, George A.	70	9	8	13	178,268
King, Gorden	3	0	2	0	8,020
King, Hunter L.	6	1	0	0	9,515
King, James W.	17	2	4	2	35,216
King, Kevin T.	3	0	0	0	0
King, Paul M.	5	0	1	0	336
King, Richard D.	7	0	0	0	1,290
King, Richard L.	3	0	0	1	550
King, Romeo	21	1	2	1	31,985
King, Terry Pat	16	1	1	0	5,248
King, Warren L.	77	12	5	9	111,691
King, Yolonda Y.	141	10	16	15	245,445
King, Jr., Edward E.	4	0	1	0	1,978
King, Jr., Robert J.	22	1	3	5	44,139
Kinghorne, George A.	33	0	2	3	20,052
Kingsland, Pamela	10	0	2	1	4,547
Kingsley, Jr., Archibald J.	7	3	0	0	37,605
Kingston, Robert C.	104	17	7	9	312,027
Kinmon, Ronald Keith	35	2	1	3	40,511
Kinnamon, Wendy	58	5	1	9	99,691
Kinsella, Tom M.	11	1	0	2	9,690
Kinser, Roger	3	0	0	1	1,778
Kintz, S. Matthew	132	13	19	14	238,274
Kipling, Gerry	109	15	15	22	278,953
Kirby, Frank J.	539	76	68	53	1,746,292
Kirby, James F.	1	0	0	0	925
Kirby, Kenneth M.	72	14	15	10	121,695
Kirby, Mike	32	7	5	5	61,032
Kirby, R. W.	2	0	0	0	165
Kirby, Timothy	34	3	6	6	74,392
Kirk, James C.	1	1	0	0	7,800
Kirk, Jeffrey C.	2	1	1	0	7,172
Kirk, Sherry	7	0	1	0	886
Kirk, Jr., David	7	0	0	1	766
Kirkham, Barry	28	0	1	1	16,184
Kirkpatrick, Alex	6	0	0	1	334
Kirkpatrick, Nancy L.	1	0	0	0	0
Kirkpatrick, Sylvia	3	0	0	0	55
Kirlin, Thomas	29	1	6	2	36,080
Kirn, Margo	4	0	0	0	546
Kisielewski, Eric	35	1	3	3	15,079
Kisielewski, Gina M.	12	0	0	0	3,040
Kissoon, Raphael B.	20	3	3	5	60,335
Kitchingman, Adam	94	21	12	12	521,493
Kite, Sandra M.	50	2	6	6	60,535
Kittson, Dorotha A.	30	1	1	1	3,986
Klapatch, Nancy	19	5	4	3	10,004

Trainer	Sts	1st	2d	3d	Purses
Klecka, Donald W.	12	0	0	2	1,479
Kleier, Michael	5	2	0	2	59,341
Klein, Linda	12	0	1	4	9,350
Klein, Sheila S.	2	0	0	0	537
Klenakis, Tony	165	18	16	18	95,754
Klesaris, Peter	188	18	21	18	284,029
Klesaris, Robert P.	310	45	44	43	896,047
Klesaris, Steve	482	97	95	60	3,205,571
Kline, Lynnelle M.	32	3	3	5	36,393
Kling, Barry	36	4	2	4	48,070
Kling, Guy	55	2	1	4	24,973
Klinger, Gary	1	0	0	0	60
Klokstad, Bud	230	33	35	41	569,448
Klopp, Randy L.	101	13	15	11	117,285
Kloth, David R.	10	0	0	0	1,493
Knaggs, Robert	6	0	0	0	600
Knapp, Neil	76	14	14	9	76,608
Knapp, Steve	436	50	54	65	1,507,223
Knechtel, Lianne	142	13	22	19	172,466
Knee, Lynda	95	8	15	15	164,749
Knepper, James M.	197	9	13	21	124,870
Knight, Edwin F.	2	0	0	0	0
Knight, Nathan	2	0	0	0	1,500
Knight, Robert B.	24	0	2	2	7,384
Knight, Terry	77	16	12	8	266,258
Knight, Thomas E.	2	0	0	0	235
Knighton, Judy L	5	0	1	0	2,444
Knipe, Duane	214	37	17	27	478,757
Knippenberg, Brian	10	3	2	1	13,261
Knisley, Heather	38	2	2	8	54,515
Knoblauch, Michelle	77	5	8	10	104,057
Knowles, Lucinda C.	87	3	2	4	39,826
Knowles, Robert A.	3	0	0	0	0
Knox, Martha	1	0	0	0	0
Knudsen, Don	29	6	5	1	18,507
Knudsen, Kevin	123	22	23	25	54,836
Kobza, Lee	18	0	1	0	953
Koch, Neil A.	15	2	0	0	5,874
Kocijan, Boris	64	3	5	5	101,279
Koenenn, Yancey	2	1	0	0	6,600
Koertgen, Timothy C.	36	1	6	4	32,440
Kohlheim, Mark A.	45	0	0	4	24,716
Kohnhorst, Richard B.	120	19	16	12	304,691
Kokoronis, Athanasios	27	1	2	4	16,497
Kokoski, Gerald	56	5	5	4	57,722
Kolarik, Jeanne M.	4	0	0	0	440
Kolb, Christopher L.	33	1	4	8	27,022
Kolb, Dale	3	0	0	1	190
Kolb, Gary Lee	59	5	5	6	62,388
Kolbrick, Cheryl R.	25	0	0	2	6,762
Koler, Dale	9	1	0	0	3,347
Koler, Steve	49	7	5	9	41,066
Kolibos, Ioannis E.	14	1	0	1	22,760
Koller, William C.	26	0	1	1	3,505
Kolochuk, John	14	1	1	2	8,405
Komardley, Donald D.	1	0	0	0	43
Komardley, Evans	10	0	0	0	674
Komlo, Edward C.	3	0	0	0	230
Komlo, John E.	21	2	3	4	15,903
Komlo, William R.	81	2	5	13	85,735
Kong, Winston C.	19	2	1	4	27,290
Konkoly, Andrew	370	61	67	33	477,865
Konrath, Frank L.	21	0	0	0	4,379
Konyk, Chris	2	0	0	0	305
Koonce, Roland	25	1	2	2	15,400
Kopaj, Paul	32	4	2	4	86,470
Kopp, Glenn	13	3	1	1	19,284
Kopycinski, Larry	8	0	0	2	1,874
Koriner, Brian J.	288	57	38	37	1,220,298
Korrell, Elizabeth C.	7	0	1	1	9,710
Koski, James	6	0	0	0	0
Kotenko, Robert	156	14	22	15	117,223
Kotsos, Patricia	15	1	0	1	4,165
Kountz, Richard	7	0	0	0	810
Kovach, Charles A.	32	1	1	2	8,807
Koza, Kristine M.	79	3	7	7	27,171
Kozak, Brian	2	1	1	0	1,640
Krafjack, Leonette	7	0	0	0	850
Kramp, Jerri L.	36	0	0	0	2,798
Kranz, Mark A.	43	1	1	5	36,244
Krasner, Cindy	162	21	15	22	394,005
Kravets, Bruce M.	942	164	127	114	1,363,168
Kravets, Lori	16	1	1	2	12,649
Krcmar, Zelko	29	3	5	2	58,120
Krebs, Steven	250	45	42	39	734,900
Kreiser, Gina M.	72	5	9	9	45,355
Kreiser, Timothy C.	270	78	40	38	783,038
Krieger, Heinz	13	1	1	1	5,170
Kriple, Zvi	18	1	0	2	8,677
Kriser, Roland D.	5	1	1	1	12,990
Krohn, Pete	8	0	1	2	3,321
Kromann, Lloyd N.	22	4	5	6	125,970
Krone, Bryan	101	16	14	18	60,801
Krone, Marvin J.	3	0	0	1	221
Kropius, Linda	18	2	2	2	8,220
Kruger, Wendy J.	121	9	19	15	224,557
Kruljac, J. Eric	282	57	38	39	742,199
Krummen, Paul	26	3	4	3	18,463
Kube, Harry	117	14	16	26	194,617
Kubovchik, Donald	45	4	2	4	29,999
Kudla, Edward T.	12	0	0	0	642
Kueffner, Dave	118	12	17	18	156,931
Kuhn, Marvin H.	40	2	4	6	46,065
Kuhns, Sr., Ernest E.	30	1	0	1	5,026
Kuiken, Randal	25	3	1	2	41,741
Kulow, Mark	2	0	0	0	129
Kumke, Myron D.	173	26	26	29	130,109
Kunes, Karen M.	188	23	19	26	214,767
Kuti, Ann	21	1	3	5	58,213
Kutt, C. Michael	48	4	7	8	43,099
Kutt, Donna M.	22	1	1	0	6,083
Kutz, Dean	5	0	0	2	810
Kuwik, Gregory	40	2	1	2	17,749
La Croix, David	107	12	16	14	308,673
La Mew, Brian	137	23	20	22	142,760
LaBoccetta, Frank	1	0	0	1	6,600
LaBoccetta, Jr., Frank	155	32	24	29	961,368
Laborde, Amos	259	44	44	43	531,444
LaBorde, Donald	87	8	7	16	73,426
Lacey, Jody	19	4	1	4	5,437
Lackey, Darrell D.	1	0	0	0	145
Lackey, James E.	8	0	1	0	8,033
Lacy, James	5	0	0	0	256
Laczo, Brant	65	5	6	8	24,014
Ladauceur, Harold	12	0	3	4	34,191
Ladd, Don	62	8	7	10	39,116
Ladd, Keith	5	0	1	1	1,992
Ladd, Perry R.	64	6	5	6	28,587
Ladd, Ronald	21	3	1	1	16,165
Ladner, Bernie	6	2	0	0	18,105
Ladner, Edwin Lee	22	0	4	0	16,966
Ladner, Patrick L.	47	10	3	6	129,552
Ladner, Roger Joe	4	0	0	0	0
Ladner, Terry	1	0	0	0	0
Ladner, Jr., Herman F.	15	0	1	1	6,043
Ladouceur, Jr., Doug	50	4	7	7	50,355
Lafavers, Laurie	66	10	12	13	473,599
Laffon-Parias, Carlos	1	0	0	0	1,500
LaFleur, Girard E.	49	1	7	3	31,742
Lafontaine, Bernard	9	0	1	0	3,278
Lage, Armando	612	84	62	82	1,117,136
Lagorio, William G.	66	5	5	7	57,245
Lagrone, Selwyn	40	7	6	6	60,879
Laing, Sherry	24	1	0	0	2,971
Lake, Barry K.	20	0	1	1	5,499
Lake, Charles Michael	96	9	10	18	241,672
Lake, James Y.	6	0	0	0	407
Lake, Scott A.	1,688	374	297	251	7,420,036
Lake, Jr., Charles M.	7	1	1	2	16,363
Lalman, Dennis S.	10	1	3	1	45,082
Lam, Kwong C.	14	4	3	1	78,638
Lamazor, Fredric P.	3	0	0	0	1,200
Lamb, Jodie L.	60	5	10	8	35,141
Lamb, Pam	1	0	0	0	44

Trainer	Sts	1st	2d	3d	Purses
Lamb, William F.	38	1	3	1	13,808
Lambert, Jacques A.	8	0	0	1	1,240
Lambert, Joanna	94	8	8	10	43,495
Lambert, Sr., Clifford C.	202	12	16	24	148,693
Lamm, Ludwig L.	93	7	12	15	91,685
Lamont, Warren E.	127	6	9	18	81,302
LaMonte, Joe	18	3	1	2	33,595
Lamparter, Larry C.	8	1	0	2	7,425
Lana, John	22	0	4	2	17,203
Lance, James L.	13	0	1	1	1,600
Lanchester, Earl T.	16	4	1	2	20,882
Landers, Bill	74	8	11	4	104,095
Landers, D. E.	45	1	4	1	10,268
Landers, Theodore A.	1	0	0	0	220
Landicini, Jr., Chris	187	17	24	27	340,282
Landis, Margaret A.	26	1	0	1	6,469
Landon, Donna J.	14	0	2	1	5,256
Landry, Betty F.	4	0	0	0	0
Landry, Ernest	65	3	3	9	56,535
Landry, Fred J.	78	7	5	9	76,579
Landry, Joseph C.	49	0	4	3	9,617
Landry, Kirk	1	0	1	0	3,600
Landry, Larry J.	72	1	2	4	27,992
Landry, Paul	4	0	0	0	0
Landry, Jr., Maxful	54	2	4	6	63,464
Lane, Mitch T.	92	12	18	18	207,958
Lane, Randy	20	1	9	1	43,839
Lane, Robert W.	31	3	3	1	101,752
Lane, S. Eugene	6	1	1	1	5,570
Lanerie, Gerald	76	6	6	7	77,422
Lang, Danny B.	84	2	6	8	21,496
Langemeier, John L.	24	0	3	6	18,547
Langford, Richard A.	10	1	1	0	11,001
Langley, Wilson C.	168	20	22	23	266,893
Langmaid, Michelle L.	3	0	0	0	0
Lankford, Billy	16	2	4	1	22,495
Lanning, Forrest H.	20	2	3	2	28,370
Lapp, Fredrick W.	5	1	0	0	7,056
Larkin, Nick	9	0	0	1	1,446
Larmon, Julie	41	3	7	5	32,235
Larsen, Corey L.	53	3	1	5	15,454
Larsen, Shane F.	13	3	0	3	5,053
Larson, Bill	2	0	0	1	4,000
Larson, Darlene	3	0	0	0	0
Larson, Michael	55	9	5	14	125,012
Larue, Benjie	35	1	3	5	28,854
Larue, Bobby	29	6	1	3	71,890
Larue, C. Steve	41	1	2	4	13,847
Lashmet, Diane	5	1	2	1	9,752
Lathrop, David	112	17	14	14	134,404
Latimer, Samuel	52	3	3	4	27,445
LaTour, Theodore J.	75	7	8	10	121,240
Lattimer, Gail L.	46	1	9	4	79,673
Lau, Kam Tak	6	0	1	1	1,588
Laudati, Kim	57	4	7	6	116,111
Lauer, Michael E.	185	28	23	24	553,422
Laugherty, Joe	18	2	2	5	35,530
Laurine, Frank C.	14	4	4	3	25,710
Lausten, Carl	63	10	5	7	143,903
Lautzenheiser, Sr., Robert	29	0	0	0	2,906
Lauzon, Ann	4	0	3	1	5,100
Lauzon, Richard F.	5	0	0	0	564
Lavallee, Alphonse	60	13	12	13	33,149
Lavanway, Dayson	31	3	5	2	19,031
Lavanway, William	58	13	7	6	110,310
Lavell, Richard A.	4	0	0	0	448
Lavigne, Jerry G.	5	0	0	0	644
Laviolette, Gerald	4	0	0	0	0
Laviolette, Harold J.	39	3	1	8	43,423
Lawrence, Coleman J.	11	0	0	0	1,915
Lawrence, Donald L.	6	2	0	1	3,329
Lawrence, Robert D.	83	15	12	13	102,066
Lawrence, Robert L.	41	11	7	7	19,836
Lawrence, Robert M.	3	1	0	0	2,427
Lawrence, Wray I.	110	13	12	20	258,509
Lawrence, II, James L.	116	12	14	18	244,980
Lawrence, Jr., Raymond S.	11	0	0	1	4,710
Lawson, Charles	165	20	26	29	108,296
Lawson, Richard E.	33	0	0	1	3,031
Lay, Don	1	0	0	0	254
Lay, Jordan B.	26	0	1	2	13,968
Lay, Larry	88	13	15	11	116,696
Layman, Ernest L.	34	2	1	2	17,281
Layne, Bret H.	38	2	2	2	35,931
Layton, John W.	58	14	2	8	41,007
Layton, Paul H.	4	1	0	0	4,758
Lazenby, Jerry Wayne	6	0	0	1	1,092
Lazuka, William E.	90	4	4	8	78,357
Le Blanc, Jr., John P.	96	12	14	9	500,902
Le Febre, Walleah C.	2	0	0	0	0
Le Vine, Carol Lynn	48	0	7	6	47,885
Leach, Tony W.	74	10	10	6	146,609
Leach, William F.	98	8	13	10	233,961
Leaf, Michael L.	10	0	1	3	10,109
Leaf, Raymond P.	11	0	1	2	4,770
Leaf Jr, Robert	46	6	6	4	68,419
Leaney, Patty	16	0	2	4	17,583
Least, II, Gary L.	111	4	5	17	57,598
Leatherbury, King T.	331	42	48	43	699,139
Leatherman, Blake	3	0	0	0	0
Leatherman, Nina L.	38	3	4	2	19,315
Leavitt, Clifford N.	83	13	8	10	92,364
LeBarron, Keith W.	106	19	20	13	251,902
LeBlanc, Jeanne	48	2	0	6	27,558
LeBlanc, Johnny	84	6	5	8	50,787
LeBlanc, Kirsten	1	0	0	0	164
LeBlanc, Melvin	14	0	0	3	3,194
LeBlanc, Milton	31	1	2	3	14,692
LeBlanc, Richard Paul	11	0	0	0	0
LeBlanc, Shelton J.	47	3	6	7	41,661
LeBlanc, Sr., Linton	13	0	0	0	263
Lebleu, Greg	1	0	0	0	450
Leboeuf, Anthony L.	11	0	1	2	7,271
Lebret, Tracy	33	4	5	3	6,675
Lebsock, Manuel M.	14	2	0	7	18,128
Lebsock, Jr., Paul	19	0	0	1	1,350
Lecesse, Michael A.	400	80	57	59	1,030,953
Lechthaler, Richard	3	1	0	0	3,984
Leckey, Michael	47	5	3	4	23,659
Ledet, Ernest J.	76	3	5	7	55,979
Ledezma, Sergio	294	27	35	41	454,759
Ledgess, C Dale	170	9	17	16	171,915
Ledoux, Mary V.	3	0	0	0	0
Lee, Anna	3	0	1	0	3,025
Lee, Douglas L.	4	0	0	2	2,110
Lee, James M.	2	0	0	0	293
Lee, Mark C.	80	8	9	9	142,859
Lee, Oswald	74	4	4	9	48,110
Lee, Robert Enos	53	4	9	14	34,446
Lee, Ron	5	3	0	0	35,772
Lee, Steven	39	5	3	4	71,235
Lee, Suzie M.	22	0	2	3	7,808
Leech, William H.	23	7	6	4	29,474
Leehy, Ryan	6	0	1	1	2,786
Leeson, John D.	1	0	0	0	110
Lefurgey, Calvin T.	2	1	0	0	8,899
Leger, Brent C.	71	7	8	9	71,074
Leger, Jake E.	79	10	10	12	148,555
Leggio, Frank	122	17	23	18	343,159
Leggio, Jr., Andrew	117	21	14	18	729,442
LeGrande, Cheryl A.	20	1	3	1	6,792
Lehman, Steven A.	8	2	0	1	2,085
Lehman, Thomas D.	124	9	10	7	49,056
Leifeld, Donald J.	5	2	0	0	22,650
Leingang, Devron	11	0	0	2	4,154
Leis, Victor J.	7	2	0	0	3,805
Leith, Steve	20	2	0	4	12,062
Lejeune, Callan	75	1	11	9	61,216
Lelito, Timothy L.	65	9	8	6	71,316
Lello, Tony P.	14	2	2	4	37,379
Lellouche, Elie	1	0	0	0	0
Lemaire, Sr., Alvin	4	0	0	0	0
Lemasurier, Paul	13	1	1	1	18,377
LeMieux, Linda	5	0	0	0	445
Lenz, Marillee	4	0	0	0	0
Lenzini, Michael	499	50	58	68	556,518

Trainer	Sts	1st	2d	3d	Purses
Leon, Priscilla	102	24	19	13	158,914
Leonard, Bruce	4	0	0	0	0
Leonard, Dorothy	15	2	2	1	43,106
Leonard, Kirby	7	0	0	0	0
Leonard, Robert W.	38	2	6	1	62,973
Leonard, III, George	230	35	22	30	283,410
Leonard, Jr., George	24	0	1	2	8,117
Leonardi, Hugo	173	15	23	30	132,656
Leos, Antonio R.	17	0	0	2	7,814
Lepage, Shirley L.	29	2	5	7	45,540
LePaine, Paul	11	0	0	0	2,009
Lerille, Jr., Arthur J.	27	1	1	3	27,389
Lerman, Michael	4	0	0	0	6,070
Lerman, Roy S.	58	5	6	4	169,417
Lesher, Michael D.	32	1	0	0	11,238
Leslie, Sue	117	17	10	13	517,160
Lester, Robert A.	12	3	3	2	72,968
Lester, Troy L.	3	0	0	0	253
Letarete, Tina	4	0	1	1	550
LeTarte, Carole	9	1	2	1	15,780
Letts, Albert P.	4	0	1	0	3,795
Letts, Jr., John D.	24	1	8	4	52,412
Levendis, Peter	3	0	0	0	300
Levengood, Eric C.	27	1	1	1	8,810
Levin, Stanley	17	0	0	0	1,500
Levine, Bruce N.	432	107	84	65	3,541,853
Levine, Earl	7	1	0	0	6,623
Levine, Peter	17	2	3	2	67,095
Levine, Robert L.	80	4	8	6	135,750
Levitt, Jeff	1	0	0	0	0
Levy, Larry	1	0	0	0	0
Lewellyn, Paul	94	9	5	6	197,010
Lewis, Billy G.	2	0	0	0	0
Lewis, Billy M.	2	0	0	0	500
Lewis, Carroll D.	29	0	0	2	4,112
Lewis, Craig Anthony	180	15	18	18	629,132
Lewis, Craig Chester	40	3	3	5	19,688
Lewis, Dennis	6	0	0	0	276
Lewis, Gary J.	8	0	2	0	14,030
Lewis, Gary O.	129	6	13	8	74,707
Lewis, Jehu	15	1	2	1	9,326
Lewis, Jerry D.	9	0	1	1	6,542
Lewis, Jim B.	7	1	0	2	1,596
Lewis, Joseph A.	26	4	4	6	29,113
Lewis, Kelly Maureen	2	0	0	0	175
Lewis, Kevin	226	38	37	39	391,681
Lewis, Kirk P.	6	0	0	2	1,494
Lewis, Lisa L.	141	16	22	20	629,936
Lewis, Richard I.	7	0	0	0	1,262
Lewis, Roberta M.	12	0	1	3	2,790
Lewis, Wilfred J.	25	2	3	5	72,240
Leyba, Bernie A.	20	0	0	1	2,441
Leyba, Michael A.	5	0	0	0	352
Leyba, Percy J.	2	0	0	0	87
Leyba, Ruben	7	0	0	1	1,704
Leyva, Fernando	13	0	1	0	2,116
Li, James K.	37	1	0	4	17,577
Libaud, Eric	3	0	0	0	37,500
Liebeskind, Louis R.	5	0	0	0	1,870
Liebig, Paul	13	0	0	1	2,675
Lies, Richard D.	18	1	3	1	62,968
Light, Frank D.	3	0	0	0	280
Lightfoot, Butch	11	0	2	0	2,467
Lightner, Michael	41	5	3	6	77,410
Lilly, James P.	8	1	0	1	7,890
Lima, Rolando J.	41	5	3	6	82,211
Limbaugh, James M.	52	5	4	8	20,127
Linafelter, Paul	59	16	11	6	75,068
Lind, Darlene	3	1	0	0	7,998
Lindemann, Lorita	129	5	11	10	60,756
Linder, Louis C.	2	0	0	0	0
Linder, Jr., Louis C.	61	7	14	7	110,411
Lindsay, Frederick	35	1	1	4	22,077
Lindsay, Ricky	111	7	20	9	213,072
Lindsay, Tanya	93	15	16	7	119,726
Lindsay, Sr., Wilbur	32	3	1	2	25,746
Lindsey, Chuck	13	4	3	2	11,706

Trainer	Sts	1st	2d	3d	Purses
Lindsey, Jack E.	7	1	4	1	3,170
Linet, Lucy	4	0	0	1	1,160
Lingenfelter, Thomas H.	95	15	8	9	121,387
Linn, Lauren	43	2	2	0	18,659
Linsey, Arthur T.	70	4	5	8	29,238
Lipowicz, Zenon	72	11	9	14	60,419
Listen, Robert L.	84	6	9	13	122,200
Literal, Lee Ann	14	4	2	2	6,014
Litfin, Nevada	82	6	9	7	48,760
Litt, Joshua M.	54	11	16	8	243,690
Little, James E.	9	0	1	1	2,270
Little, James H.	39	3	8	7	85,011
Little, Jeffery	8	1	0	3	10,308
Little, Larry J.	1	0	0	0	0
Little, Niel	1	0	0	0	0
Little, Pamela A.	109	8	10	13	207,186
Littlelight, Curtis	7	0	0	3	845
Liu, Raymond	52	6	9	5	87,985
Livesay, Charles	159	12	21	18	409,733
Livingston, Conna	7	1	0	0	3,092
Livingston, Jerry C.	2	0	0	0	136
Lloyd, Charles W.	82	6	11	11	142,222
Lloyd, Margo	27	3	4	3	18,769
Lloyd, Sandra	14	4	1	1	46,677
Lloyd, Scott	6	0	0	0	414
Lobo, Paulo H.	118	22	18	13	1,923,033
Lobsiger, Tanya	3	2	1	0	14,920
Lockard, Donna B.	24	4	1	3	38,565
Locke, A. W.	1	1	0	0	3,660
Locke, John G.	480	66	66	75	909,082
Locke, Royce	6	0	1	0	4,214
Locke, Tony	46	1	1	1	53,742
Lockhart, Jeffrey L.	56	9	8	5	79,197
Lockhart, Lloyd W.	53	3	7	4	81,980
Lockhart, Lori L.	295	36	27	33	356,123
Lockridge, Monica	53	6	4	5	86,490
Lockwood, George T.	31	1	3	2	26,214
Lockwood, Richard L.	23	0	1	1	9,630
Loescher, Paula	82	7	11	9	118,531
Loetscher, Clay	13	1	2	0	9,713
Lofton, Hannis E.	19	0	2	2	7,715
Loghry, John E.	56	3	4	5	18,178
Logsdon, G. K.	45	3	7	7	33,652
Logue, Jr., F. M.	60	4	8	11	129,151
Lombardo, Stephen	7	1	1	0	20,215
Londono, Jr., Odin J.	135	22	16	12	174,940
Loney, A. Radlie	36	8	3	2	546,621
Loney, Rex	8	0	0	0	664
Long, Bob	5	0	0	1	520
Long, J. Scott	50	4	4	4	41,338
Long, John Mike	2	1	0	0	1,140
Long, Marty	17	0	3	4	9,965
Long, Vaughn	34	3	6	6	25,601
Longacre, Charles	3	0	1	0	3,795
Longan, Mary Ellen	8	1	1	1	31,695
Longstaff, Tom	97	18	18	13	406,840
Looman, Dennis M.	29	0	3	4	9,971
Lopes, William	2	0	0	0	0
Lopez, Angel L.	7	1	0	1	7,260
Lopez, Antonio	2	0	2	0	11,200
Lopez, Arcadio	5	0	1	0	3,309
Lopez, Carlos Cruz	12	0	1	0	19,840
Lopez, Ceasar J.	37	10	7	5	18,953
Lopez, Daniel J.	118	21	23	14	377,235
Lopez, Harold	15	2	2	2	29,363
Lopez, Jodi	88	9	5	8	37,693
Lopez, Joe E.	38	0	10	0	27,880
Lopez, Jorge	1	0	0	0	320
Lopez, Jose A.	55	7	4	4	92,420
Lopez, Jose L.	8	1	0	6	5,026
Lopez, Juan Carlos	10	0	2	0	25,060
Lopez, Lisa L.	8	0	1	2	3,120
Lopez, Matias Atilano	5	0	0	0	900
Lopez, Narciso C.	4	0	0	0	0
Lopez, Pedro	109	7	12	11	112,871
Lopez, Robert E.	30	1	3	6	15,022
Lopez, Tracy	76	8	6	6	52,461

Trainer	Sts	1st	2d	3d	Purses
Lopez, Jr., Braulio	35	2	3	3	35,235
Lopez, Jr., Frank	67	3	6	7	78,394
Lopresti, Charles	71	6	7	13	233,939
Lorimer, Suzanne	4	0	0	0	9,774
Lorito, Mario	8	0	0	0	646
Lorts, Terry	42	2	4	2	19,718
Loseth, James Peter	128	7	8	19	110,695
Lostritto, Joseph A.	86	4	4	6	197,900
Loter, Betty	53	2	1	7	15,813
Lothringer, Roy	51	2	5	8	39,608
Lotruglio, Edward	80	4	4	6	66,027
Lott, Jesse D.	3	0	0	0	330
Lott, Woodrow C.	21	2	3	2	21,075
Lotze, Larry E.	34	1	1	2	18,868
Loudin-Smith, Lori	6	0	1	1	3,056
Lough, Thomas	3	1	0	0	10,752
Lovato, Patricia	6	0	0	1	3,720
Love, Michael	96	8	6	8	106,823
Love, Sr., Alan	66	7	9	10	94,264
Loveland, Del	29	1	3	0	20,097
Lovell, Jack	25	2	3	3	11,380
Lovell, Michelle	64	10	5	7	97,245
Lovin, Randy	5	0	0	1	2,487
Lowder, John M.	55	5	2	3	26,354
Lowe, Nick	136	22	14	24	70,379
Lowe, Santiago	20	0	1	4	1,680
Lowery, F. A.	4	0	0	0	0
Lowry, Kathleen A.	12	2	2	1	9,509
Lowry, Kerrie	3	0	0	0	0
Lowry, Sr., Autry	6	0	0	0	2,412
Lowry, Sr., Richard H.	7	0	0	0	1,558
Loy, F. Dewaine	151	26	25	20	380,639
Lozano, Adalberto	2	0	0	0	970
Lozano, Martin	298	52	44	51	719,836
Lozier, Kelly S.	75	3	8	6	63,950
Lozier, Michael	4	0	0	0	564
Luark, Monty	87	4	7	9	34,427
Lucarelli, Frank	369	60	50	51	570,508
Lucas, Angela	18	1	1	0	16,058
Lucas, Flo Ann	8	0	0	2	2,915
Lucas, Joe	139	14	13	16	218,865
Lucas, Robert J.	51	4	2	9	32,825
Lucas, Ted W.	17	1	3	4	11,411
Lucero, Lorence	72	15	12	3	234,145
Lucko, Gerry	9	0	1	0	2,359
Ludwig, James B.	32	2	2	3	30,590
Luellen, Roger D.	9	3	0	0	26,510
Luft, Kirsty-Anne	15	2	4	2	18,316
Lugovich, Richard J.	15	0	1	1	21,756
Lujan, Jorge	6	0	0	0	264
Lujan, Ramon	3	0	0	0	0
Lukas, D. Wayne	577	67	87	70	5,567,299
Lukenbill, Rick	19	4	5	2	33,568
Lumm, Roy	241	25	34	36	300,370
Lumpkin, Roy M.	10	2	0	0	5,705
Lumsden, John Rennie	2	1	1	0	10,939
Luna, Daniel G.	43	8	10	8	49,222
Lund, Valorie	196	27	39	17	251,930
Lunsford, Darrell A.	154	12	14	14	128,434
Lunsford, Kim	2	0	0	0	915
Lusk, Travis	4	1	1	0	2,540
Luther, III, Andrew T.	10	1	1	0	4,130
Lybert, Randal J.	13	0	0	0	1,313
Lykins, Frank	17	1	2	1	2,217
Lyman, Audrey	3	0	0	0	723
Lyman, Claude	29	4	4	5	9,515
Lyman, Jr., Arthur J.	23	5	5	4	19,136
Lynch, Brian A.	55	13	4	5	310,945
Lynch, Cathal A.	138	17	20	14	337,985
Lynch, Harry E.	14	0	0	0	802
Lynch, Martin	1	0	0	0	50
Lynde, John M.	124	15	9	12	87,265
Lynn, Jeffery C.	89	5	11	10	154,619
Lynn, Kevin	29	3	2	3	28,694
Lynn, Wilmer T.	11	1	1	3	35,361
Lyon, Hazel E.	9	1	2	2	13,610
Lyons, Beverly	9	0	0	2	1,372
Lyons, Christopher	4	0	0	0	2,625

Trainer	Sts	1st	2d	3d	Purses
Lyons, Henry D.	27	1	4	2	15,233
Ma, Francisco	48	9	7	4	80,408
Mabbott, Paul	28	3	1	2	28,390
MacDonald, Doug	104	19	15	23	180,113
MacDonald, Rita	15	3	3	2	11,242
MacDonald, Robert A.	66	4	13	8	104,168
Machovec, Joseph	8	2	1	0	15,194
Machowsky, Michael	154	23	25	22	2,529,347
MacIntosh, Marlene	5	0	0	0	340
Mack, Summie	19	5	2	1	21,135
Mackaben, Barry	13	0	0	1	3,255
Mackay, D. Verle	4	0	0	1	150
MacKenzie, Jason	7	0	0	0	600
MacKenzie, John P.	141	7	9	24	369,627
Mackert, Werner P.	18	0	1	4	6,960
Mackey, Wayne L.	40	1	5	3	46,226
Mackin, J. Lynn	2	0	0	1	759
MacKinnon, Bradley W.	35	5	6	6	83,002
MacKinnon, Scott A.	99	25	14	10	319,419
MacKinnon, William R.	21	0	1	1	7,238
MacLean, David L.	19	4	0	2	50,388
MacLean, Debra	36	3	3	4	44,570
Macon, Kevin	29	4	4	4	31,389
MacPherson, Craig	69	11	14	8	166,728
MacRae, Donald C.	123	36	17	17	445,498
Madden, Sr., Eddie	70	5	7	8	38,118
Maddox, Cody	6	2	0	1	14,216
Maddox, Mark	81	1	7	8	54,261
Madison, Paul	1	0	1	0	370
Madison, William A.	9	1	1	0	6,256
Madrigal, Sr., Rodrigo	233	43	37	33	708,959
Madsen, Kjeld	74	5	10	4	53,515
Maelfeyt, Bruno	96	8	7	11	25,124
Maes, Cynthia A.	65	5	6	6	49,532
Magadini, Leigh S.	34	1	5	1	11,100
Magana, Hector	141	23	17	16	481,538
Magee, J. Noel	11	1	2	2	16,555
Magee, Paul	17	2	2	1	20,272
Magee, Walter B.	70	8	6	7	164,781
Magill, Patrick J.	15	0	3	1	12,191
Magill, Ronald E.	2	0	2	0	11,160
Magnon, Jason H.	28	3	3	1	33,424
Magnon, III, Joseph Cleve	62	10	10	8	88,449
Magnuson, Lyle	12	2	2	3	6,610
Magnusson, Glenn	88	9	17	11	379,303
Magrell, Jr., Jack	52	0	5	3	13,695
Magrell, Jr., Norman C.	1	0	0	0	184
Magrell, Sr., Norman C.	28	3	6	3	43,363
Mahan, Hugh W.	33	4	4	2	36,927
Mahan, Joseph P.	101	10	10	19	180,324
Mahan, Kathy	73	8	2	9	60,202
Mahan, William H.	97	6	11	9	18,193
Maher, Tom	18	1	2	3	4,551
Mahler, Janine	5	0	0	1	715
Mahn, John W.	65	9	5	8	49,186
Mahoney, Robert	15	1	2	2	9,806
Mahorney, William	21	3	1	5	116,257
Maier, Roger L.	9	1	2	1	5,135
Majette, Jennifer	4	1	0	1	37,000
Majors, Sheridan	88	5	4	3	25,685
Maker, Michael J.	200	31	28	10	1,236,295
Maker, Rebecca	207	35	18	30	928,694
Malaterre, Blaine	1	0	0	0	0
Malaterre, Jennifer	12	1	0	2	3,307
Malcolm, Roger H.	20	2	0	2	11,347
Maldonado, Edgar S.	11	0	0	0	823
Maldonado, Jesse	1	0	0	0	184
Malek, Raja	1	0	0	0	0
Malgarini-Mawing, Tina	54	1	3	4	69,410
Malone, Thomas C.	2	0	0	0	0
Maloney, John	37	4	1	3	42,028
Mamakos, Jason	1	0	0	0	235
Manahan, Patricia	28	0	1	1	4,515
Manchio, Robert S.	32	0	1	4	9,708
Mandalfino, Paul R.	52	2	6	9	30,100
Mandella, Gary	121	15	22	18	737,511
Mandella, Richard E.	160	24	25	30	3,083,102
Manganaro, Joseph W.	4	0	0	0	410

RECORDS OF TRAINERS

Trainer	Sts	1st	2d	3d	Purses
Mangum, Kim	7	0	1	1	949
Maniatis, Arthur F.	8	0	3	0	13,660
Mankin, Stanley C.	9	1	3	1	14,544
Manley, Steve	459	79	84	64	569,917
Mann, Herbert Michael	52	4	9	4	57,122
Mann, P. Renia	14	1	2	0	5,935
Manners, Frank	5	0	0	0	0
Manning, Dennis J.	152	17	18	33	636,515
Manning, Don Louis	1	0	0	0	0
Manning, John F.	10	0	0	0	353
Manning, Kathleen A.	39	2	0	6	26,278
Manning, Richard C.	35	0	1	0	3,885
Manocchia, Diane	9	0	1	1	2,550
Mansell, Harrold Ray	11	0	1	1	4,760
Manuel, Patrick Dorville	19	1	3	0	13,039
Maragh, Collin	41	4	7	5	76,801
Marble, James L.	42	3	5	4	41,728
March, Eliza	6	0	0	0	1,380
March, Rhoda	28	2	2	5	50,396
Marcom, Jr., Roy L.	61	5	8	10	70,086
Marcoux, Wayne J.	166	19	29	22	262,800
Marechal, Merlin	53	3	10	10	63,147
Mareina, Michael	84	14	9	14	691,851
Margolis, Stephen R.	166	23	23	23	601,405
Maria, John J.	47	3	3	4	42,209
Maricle, Essie	6	0	1	1	4,127
Marinay, Joe L.	25	1	5	3	35,350
Marini, Jr., James V.	5	0	1	2	6,806
Marino, Gary	16	3	0	5	18,108
Marino, James G.	59	5	3	8	37,415
Marino, Joseph E.	49	5	8	5	59,304
Marino, Marilyn L.	59	2	2	5	35,973
Marino, Paul	1	0	0	0	66
Marino, Thomas	64	5	4	8	85,803
Markgraf, David	151	9	10	20	97,576
Markham, Richard L.	63	0	3	2	15,646
Markham, Jr., Richard L.	1	0	0	0	72
Markle, Dan L.	156	21	23	32	256,399
Marks, Brandon	5	0	1	1	13,034
Marks, Deborah J.	22	2	2	1	23,480
Marks, Garry	114	9	21	13	119,430
Marks, Stan	89	21	13	10	84,759
Marlow, Kimberly	1	0	0	0	125
Marlow, Mike	106	7	15	13	265,230
Maroun, Maureen Ann	12	0	2	2	5,065
Marquez, Alfredo	51	8	4	10	169,972
Marquez, Jose Luis	111	10	10	13	59,714
Marquez, Rey M.	16	1	3	2	12,283
Marr, Gerald E.	113	13	15	17	247,258
Marr, Joel H.	281	55	40	37	853,723
Marrotta, Patrick	14	1	4	3	84,018
Marsh, Gordon E.	100	13	16	11	96,604
Marshall, John Terry	36	10	2	3	87,770
Marshall, Larry C	1	0	0	0	552
Marshall, Michael	4	1	0	0	11,340
Marshall, Robert W.	6	0	3	2	42,000
Marshall, Roy	38	3	1	0	19,741
Martens, Robbin	42	1	1	3	10,898
Marthaller, Gerri	8	1	1	0	7,083
Martin, Albert R.	3	0	0	0	1,428
Martin, August R.	10	0	2	1	7,330
Martin, Cal E.	57	11	10	7	172,391
Martin, Carlos F.	177	20	26	25	848,580
Martin, Charles Lee	5	0	0	0	558
Martin, Charles W.	6	0	1	1	2,072
Martin, Dean	11	1	1	2	2,201
Martin, Dennis C.	13	0	1	2	3,676
Martin, Don H.	10	0	1	2	8,747
Martin, Eleanor	30	2	6	6	17,686
Martin, Gregory F.	157	31	27	14	687,660
Martin, Howard J.	5	0	0	0	263
Martin, Howard L.	4	0	0	0	0
Martin, Jack R.	37	3	3	7	23,871
Martin, John A.	4	0	0	0	710
Martin, John F.	487	125	98	64	2,153,411
Martin, John J.	1	1	0	0	1,980
Martin, John W.	51	1	1	8	25,750
Martin, Joseph R.	435	68	57	63	804,266
Martin, Kevin D.	10	1	0	2	7,248
Martin, Michael E.	28	0	0	3	9,525
Martin, Paul R.	4	1	0	0	9,815
Martin, Ramon F.	113	3	7	9	100,200
Martin, Robert B.	44	5	5	8	280,796
Martin, Robert L.	156	18	30	30	403,297
Martin, Sidney	75	10	16	8	161,258
Martin, Thomas P.	7	0	0	0	150
Martin, Timothy E.	257	17	32	31	230,511
Martin, Weston	31	5	5	4	40,921
Martin, William N.	6	1	0	0	25,298
Martin, Jr., Charles E.	6	1	0	0	9,546
Martin, Jr., Frank	80	7	9	7	91,767
Martin, Sr., Frank	96	12	9	8	310,530
Martinez, Alexander	68	12	5	12	94,284
Martinez, Danny E.	12	0	0	1	648
Martinez, Dickie	22	0	1	3	3,734
Martinez, Frankie W.	39	7	6	4	194,738
Martinez, Joey A.	153	17	13	17	112,422
Martinez, Jose A.	727	82	114	113	823,557
Martinez, Juan A.	10	1	1	1	7,680
Martinez, Kelli	129	17	12	8	95,534
Martinez, Leonard C.	16	2	2	3	22,449
Martinez, Lorenzo A.	80	5	5	10	74,824
Martinez, Pedro	216	25	36	37	277,276
Martinez, Rafael A.	27	1	7	9	56,025
Martinez, Ralph	796	230	149	133	1,408,259
Martinez, Sal M.	1	0	0	0	0
Martinez, Jr., Eleuterio	73	8	9	11	95,805
Martino, Phyllis	7	0	1	0	11,213
Martino, Ronald D.	8	0	0	0	1,495
Marton, Joseph J.	39	5	5	9	43,519
Marzolf, Clarence	1	0	0	0	0
Marzullo, Vincent	10	1	1	1	20,950
Mason, Ingrid	4	0	0	2	4,538
Mason, Larry A.	3	1	0	1	5,420
Mason, Lloyd C.	227	45	29	32	637,544
Mason, Sr., Ralph	25	1	1	1	6,637
Massengale, Ronald D.	1	0	0	0	0
Massey, Charles M.	2	0	0	0	122
Master, Bobby J.	7	1	1	2	12,026
Masters, Clay	37	3	1	3	45,205
Mastin, Bill	40	3	4	6	23,339
Mastin, Kathleen	50	2	4	4	23,704
Matelski, Ray	18	1	2	0	4,419
Mathiasen, Tony	7	4	1	0	96,500
Mathieson, Jr., R. Glen	15	3	0	0	17,261
Mathis, Andy	90	17	16	10	213,448
Matier, C. William	69	3	7	12	47,273
Matier, Sandra	18	3	1	2	21,459
Matier, William Bud	36	8	9	3	34,760
Matlock, Vance A.	29	1	3	4	10,266
Matlow, Richard P.	55	10	7	5	317,860
Matos, Gil	204	22	38	27	336,902
Matranga, Roy J.	75	8	5	16	106,236
Matt, Wendell L.	58	9	7	4	37,778
Mattarelliano, Pasquale J.	2	0	0	1	4,268
Matte, Blane	2	0	0	0	225
Matthews, Doug	100	11	10	17	263,026
Matthews, Jay	9	0	1	0	7,456
Matthews, John V.	25	1	2	3	11,080
Matthews, Larry P.	20	0	1	5	10,664
Matthews, Pat	27	4	1	3	22,659
Matthews, Randy	66	11	13	7	157,110
Matthews, Jr., Erwin H.	21	4	1	2	24,478
Matthieu, Ronald J.	105	9	19	13	143,580
Matties, Gregg M.	27	6	3	3	86,982
Mattine, Michael	117	7	11	17	288,917
Mattine, Tony	53	6	5	6	279,512
Mattingly, James E.	96	8	8	15	98,039
Mattingly, Tony G.	8	0	6	0	9,478
Mattis, Errol	11	0	0	0	2,726
Maturin, Chad	65	5	3	8	54,623
Maturin, Ronald	9	0	0	1	1,986
Matz, Michael R.	214	32	33	33	1,928,354
Mauk, Fletcher	27	1	3	3	51,106

Trainer	Sts	1st	2d	3d	Purses
Maul, Fred	17	0	0	0	738
Mavec, Kathleen E.	56	5	2	11	61,988
Maver, Eduardo	107	13	13	13	148,989
Maxey, Carl L.	16	2	1	3	9,468
Maxey, Tamara L.	1	0	0	0	0
Maxey, Tim	67	3	6	7	24,861
Maxville, Rick	1	0	0	0	114
Maxwell, Curtis	62	6	9	10	49,852
Maxwell, Paul M.	96	13	14	8	323,810
May, Eddy Lenard	89	6	14	7	27,129
May, Jean	7	0	0	0	45
May, John T.	13	0	1	1	570
Mayberry, Summer	77	6	10	15	378,738
Maybin, Robert	63	6	6	6	118,657
Mayer, Karl	25	1	2	4	11,387
Mayfield, Jerry	48	4	5	7	96,203
Mayfield, Patrick	32	1	0	1	7,378
Mayfield, Randy	175	20	29	21	272,249
Mayhugh, C. L.	9	1	0	1	3,550
Maynard, Desmond	50	0	2	0	11,811
Mayo, Larry A.	94	16	11	13	168,897
Mayo, Timothy M.	16	0	0	2	4,815
Mazerski, Thomas E.	18	0	0	1	3,570
Mazza, John F.	52	7	8	6	284,864
Mazzacco, Joseph	14	1	1	1	24,134
Mazzaro, Rebecca	17	1	2	1	8,059
McAlister, Bobbie J.	7	0	0	0	183
McAlister, Joe	132	13	20	12	138,818
McAnally, Ronald L.	249	26	41	34	2,479,531
McArdle, Paul B.	27	0	1	2	9,267
McArthur, Donna	1	1	0	0	3,685
McArthur, F. James	54	5	10	10	153,907
McArthur, James J.	20	3	5	3	77,270
McArthur, Jerry	45	4	8	6	181,022
McBride, Barbara I.	375	77	68	53	719,970
McBride, Burl D.	70	8	11	8	107,727
McBride, Susan	10	2	2	1	22,995
McCabe, Nancy	76	3	3	6	31,597
McCabe, Quinton	56	5	4	3	52,593
McCain, Doyle	2	0	0	0	0
McCall, Lee Ann	9	0	0	2	1,760
McCall, Richard H.	45	2	3	8	15,742
McCaman, Sam	12	0	0	0	1,011
McCann, Sr., Elwood D.	77	15	9	9	167,672
McCanna, Tim	286	51	43	49	643,474
McCarron, Gregg	38	7	5	2	148,400
McCarthy, Brenda	157	13	24	20	201,373
McCarthy, L Tracy	15	4	2	2	180,792
McCarthy, Michael J.	112	17	19	19	322,030
McCarthy, Sean	31	2	6	1	81,720
McCarthy, Teresa	5	0	0	0	0
McCarthy, Thomas R.	12	1	0	4	18,240
McCarthy, Timni S.	12	1	2	3	6,608
McCarthy, William E.	51	6	10	9	106,652
McCartney, Jack	13	0	0	2	5,035
McCarty, George S.	70	7	5	2	98,702
McCarty, Michael W.	6	1	1	2	12,182
McCaslin, John S.	80	28	9	9	378,591
McCauley, Michael L.	1	1	0	0	12,296
McClain, Stanley	40	4	5	6	22,636
McClanahan, Gilbert W.	16	0	0	0	1,903
McClarney, Jerry L.	82	4	8	5	67,148
McCleary, Karen Lee	71	4	9	9	38,036
McClelland, Paul G.	42	7	7	7	129,112
McClendon, Leon	1	0	0	0	0
McClure, Diana L.	49	0	3	2	14,211
McClure, Kenneth R.	179	12	13	16	152,021
McCollum, Daniel	15	2	1	2	14,830
McComb, Samuel A.	50	2	1	2	48,750
McConnell, Orland	15	1	5	1	49,379
McCooey, Jr., Thomas S.	143	12	16	27	199,926
McCord, Larry	2	0	0	0	129
McCord, II, John M.	48	7	15	5	109,392
McCormick, Earl H.	49	4	5	1	111,909
McCormick, John F.	11	0	3	1	10,360
McCormick, Merril L.	13	1	1	1	19,905
McCoy, James B.	411	34	37	42	764,977
McCracken, Mark	5	0	0	0	1,541
McCracken, Memory	16	4	2	2	6,612
McCullough, Curtis	53	8	7	8	37,801
McCullough, Donna	7	1	1	1	14,423
McCutchen, Robert B.	6	0	0	0	3,529
McDaniel, Carlos W.	23	0	0	0	4,001
McDaniel, Ted	89	11	14	10	84,022
McDaniel, Wendell L.	86	2	5	6	60,341
McDevitt, John	116	12	12	19	41,752
McDonald, Brandi-Rae	26	3	6	2	11,110
McDonald, Charles Butch	14	2	3	1	7,750
McDonald, Crystal	1	0	0	0	104
McDonald, Darrik	1	0	0	0	150
McDonald, Earl L.	24	2	2	1	39,815
McDonald, James H.	25	0	0	2	4,033
McDonald, James Scott	80	8	9	9	52,381
McDonald, Mary	19	3	2	6	39,245
McDonald, Melanie W.	39	2	2	3	31,006
McDonald, Michael K.	149	18	25	19	355,998
McDonald, William R.	26	0	2	0	8,581
McDonnell, Jim	5	0	1	1	801
McDonnell, Wayne	108	16	21	19	261,069
McDonough, Eric S.	50	3	7	1	74,725
McDonough, Steven L.	19	0	3	2	17,870
McDougall, Pam	139	33	20	24	325,759
McDougall, Wilf	28	3	0	4	11,626
McDowell, Becky	36	5	2	3	22,184
McDowell, Laurie A.	42	5	6	7	78,981
McDowell, R. James	6	2	0	1	5,316
McEachern, Michael	134	25	25	21	169,890
McElhannon, Rick	10	0	0	0	560
McEneaney, Edward	1	0	0	0	123
McEwin, Cathy A.	8	0	0	0	1,963
McFadden, Jada K.	44	4	7	8	71,140
McFadden, Pamela A.	3	0	0	0	228
McFadden, Thomas Edward	76	3	3	4	20,722
McFadden, William C.	34	4	6	3	50,451
McFall, Kathy	1	0	0	0	0
McFall, Robert E.	4	0	0	0	618
McFarlane, Dan L.	323	58	62	45	787,750
McGaffic, Sr., Robert T.	65	4	8	6	64,622
McGarry, John F.	4	0	0	0	0
McGaughey III, Claude R.	254	48	48	39	4,208,832
McGee, Gail J.	60	5	5	4	91,832
McGee, Paul J.	290	49	44	42	1,758,830
McGee, Rebecca K.	49	2	4	5	25,536
McGee, William E.	92	5	9	11	151,738
McGhee, Jr., Thomas	24	0	1	1	7,179
McGill, Harry	7	0	0	0	1,932
McGill, Mary Welby	20	1	3	3	24,159
McGill, Sylvester	32	3	2	3	40,080
McGillis, Richard	7	0	2	1	1,520
McGivern, Thomas P.	54	2	9	5	75,712
McGlasson, Gayle	17	4	0	3	26,075
McGowan, Sean	14	1	0	0	10,580
McGreevy, James L.	46	2	4	8	66,038
McGreevy, John P.	31	0	1	0	6,870
McGrew, Robert L.	4	0	0	0	0
McGuire, Dr. William J.	22	2	2	1	4,976
McGuire, James D.	46	2	4	4	18,530
McGuire, Mike	16	0	0	0	4,795
McHargue, Gladys	18	2	2	2	47,985
McIlvain, Vickie Lea	8	0	0	0	0
McIntosh, Alfred G.	6	0	2	0	8,025
McIntosh, William A.	22	1	2	3	29,872
McIvor, George D.	16	5	4	2	41,980
McKanas, Leona	136	10	10	15	150,668
McKee, John D.	319	27	27	37	501,960
McKeen, John R.	39	4	1	2	17,268
McKeever, Andrew	49	6	3	8	103,069
McKeever, Jr., Billy C.	180	14	20	18	253,317
McKeever, Jr., Robert J.	40	3	5	5	37,616
McKellar, Joseph P.	81	11	11	6	228,062
McKenzie, Michael B.	25	4	3	4	27,282
McKenzie, Robert Alexander	102	9	8	6	68,928
McKenzie, Scott A.	12	1	0	0	5,954
McKeon, John P.	11	1	1	1	7,971
McKibben, Roger	9	1	0	1	16,512
McKinnell, Freda	1	0	0	0	0

Trainer	Sts	1st	2d	3d	Purses
McKinnell, Michael	31	2	0	0	13,751
McKinney, F. Lee	54	2	5	1	51,797
McKinnon, Earl E.	16	5	3	2	22,880
McKinster, Leonard	6	0	0	1	2,180
McKlveen, Lisa R.	27	1	1	1	18,530
McKnight, Norman	200	18	25	27	798,904
McKnight, Rennie	39	2	3	6	17,807
McLaren, William	4	0	1	0	1,800
McLaughlin, Kiaran P.	462	84	81	56	5,525,744
McLean, Bill	177	18	28	34	374,237
McLean, Donald	23	5	2	4	28,392
McLean, Louise	28	1	1	2	27,360
McLean, Ryan	10	4	1	2	17,914
McLeod, S.	4	1	0	1	2,398
McMahon, Buddy	1	0	0	0	0
McMeans, Bill	37	2	3	5	16,986
McMeans, Bob	34	4	9	7	87,103
McMeans, Bobby	49	4	5	8	32,372
McMichael, Larry	6	0	0	2	2,828
McMillan, Donald	76	3	2	6	35,920
McMillen, Mike	7	1	0	0	5,253
McMinn, Nancy	8	0	0	3	8,355
McMullen, James R.	38	6	5	5	103,980
McMullen, Marilyn G.	111	7	10	15	163,051
McMullin, Stacy	24	3	0	0	32,055
McNair, Scotty	13	1	1	3	25,640
McNally, Kathy	57	6	5	11	32,170
McNeeley, Cathy	7	2	2	0	8,260
McNeely, Beverly A.	2	1	0	0	6,300
McNeil, Emanuel	30	0	2	4	16,510
McNerney, Gerald R.	11	0	2	1	2,362
McPeek, Kenneth G.	413	74	71	49	3,418,225
McPherson, Alexander F.	171	18	23	15	759,722
McPherson, Billy R	14	0	0	0	1,058
McQuade, Owen	44	3	1	4	25,314
McQueen, Richard O.	29	1	3	3	28,533
McRae, Charles	12	1	1	0	2,517
McRandal, August	2	1	0	0	3,904
McReynolds, Kenneth E.	60	20	6	10	72,087
McShane, David D.	288	34	35	37	605,130
McVay, A. M.	20	0	0	3	3,182
McVicker, Lamar	14	1	2	2	21,231
McWade, Barbara E.	19	1	0	1	17,125
McWaters, Alton D.	48	0	3	2	13,337
Meacham, Sheila	71	2	4	6	23,506
Meachum, Todd	74	12	9	10	221,945
Meade, Sherryl F.	53	8	13	9	90,648
Meador, Jeanette S.	10	0	0	0	722
Meadow, Patricia E.	2	0	0	0	570
Meadows, Bascum E.	11	1	2	1	8,789
Meairs, John M.	31	3	2	3	109,234
Meals, Lois	52	2	2	3	45,479
Meares, Francis A.	51	1	4	5	41,725
Meaux, Jamie A.	15	0	0	0	908
Meaux, Lisa Ann	3	0	0	0	0
Meaux, Patrick G.	21	5	1	2	40,939
Meaux, William	122	19	18	22	337,755
Meche, Harold	1	0	0	0	531
Medicine Horse, Jr., Cleo	46	5	6	5	14,732
Medina, Angel M.	178	9	19	25	285,137
Medina, Jose D.	1	0	0	1	935
Medina, Santiago	18	0	3	0	13,645
Medley, Joseph A.	29	2	3	5	88,385
Medrano, Marcos G.	28	3	3	3	29,613
Meehan, Elizabeth E.	62	4	5	6	72,986
Meeking, Robert A.	44	11	6	3	119,927
Meeks, Karl W.	38	3	4	4	13,861
Meese, Michael T.	37	1	1	2	10,523
Mefford, Kenneth A.	4	0	0	0	409
Megariz, Alex L.	16	2	1	0	4,434
Megariz, Eddie G.	2	0	0	0	254
Megariz, Jr., Michael	20	0	1	2	2,196
Megerle, Richard	17	1	0	3	5,534
Mehok, William L.	112	15	21	9	108,038
Meineke, Jack	6	2	1	0	4,214
Meister, William S.	20	1	3	1	24,415
Meittinis, Louis N.	78	7	7	11	309,215
Melancon, Donald	45	2	4	5	54,470
Melancon, Kathleen A.	21	1	0	0	4,621
Melancon, Louis Tom	35	2	2	2	31,237
Melancon, Maurice	13	0	0	1	2,238
Melancon, Jr., Antoine	1	0	0	0	0
Melancon, Jr., Francis	92	11	9	13	129,086
Melendy, Lisa	1	0	0	0	140
Mello, Cyndi	14	0	0	3	3,383
Mello, Ernest	41	0	2	3	13,304
Melson, Benny	95	6	12	10	56,084
Melson, Glen	8	0	0	0	222
Melton, Christopher W.	4	2	0	1	8,528
Melton, John D.	70	4	5	9	74,618
Melton, Lin	1	0	0	1	700
Melvin, Dave	20	0	0	0	1,659
Melvin, Leonard J.	4	0	0	0	0
Menard, Charlene	8	2	0	1	10,605
Menard, Dirk J.	16	0	0	0	1,156
Menard, Jr., Alton J.	25	4	5	4	52,009
Menarde, Frank J.	41	3	3	0	25,990
Mencio, Raymond E.	6	2	0	1	17,400
Mendez, Jose A.	188	19	22	22	261,915
Mendez, Manuel	9	0	0	2	3,480
Mendoza, Carmelo	251	53	32	36	391,722
Mendoza, Jesus	26	0	0	4	18,770
Menefee, Barry	8	0	2	0	3,806
Mercado, Francisco	14	1	2	1	6,991
Mercer, Thomas F.	22	0	0	0	5,249
Meredith, Derek	24	0	4	5	35,700
Meredith, Jim	3	0	0	0	556
Merola, Vito	25	2	3	4	81,237
Merrick, Joe D.	3	0	0	0	272
Merrill, Richard	3	0	0	0	0
Merriman, Jr., Wilbur L.	4	0	0	1	2,310
Merritt, Clayton A.	2	0	0	0	0
Merritt, Lester	12	2	1	4	11,522
Merritt, Lisa L.	40	6	2	3	78,656
Merryman, Ann W.	263	31	30	30	631,626
Merryman, Edwin W.	57	8	4	7	158,115
Merryman, Elizabeth M.	17	2	2	2	89,006
Mesenbrink, Jennie S.	4	0	0	0	610
Metcalf, Jr., Tommy	3	0	0	0	2,500
Methvin, Chris	1	0	0	0	0
Metoyer, Joseph Bernard	6	0	0	0	0
Metz, Jeffrey	63	4	9	4	46,376
Meyaard, Jim	145	26	18	22	121,364
Meyer, Jerome C.	33	5	10	4	223,986
Meyers, Errol	15	1	1	2	16,395
Meyers, Robert W.	1	1	0	0	1,425
Miceli, Michael	155	17	14	17	669,847
Michael, Brian	42	5	4	5	99,872
Michael, James A.	43	2	5	6	39,194
Michaels, J. R.	1	0	0	0	45
Michaels, Jr., Thomas H.	38	0	1	6	12,965
Mick, Stephen R.	108	32	21	18	445,261
Mickey, Joseph C.	25	3	3	6	21,407
Middlebrooks, Don A.	4	0	0	0	0
Middleton, G Allen	11	0	0	2	4,373
Miesse, Sr., David L.	100	11	8	12	121,060
Mikhalides, George	94	16	15	14	425,681
Mikkelson, Eric D.	75	4	11	6	38,507
Milburn, Dave	43	8	9	9	122,784
Miles, Charles L.	2	0	0	0	0
Miles, Diane	6	0	0	0	1,590
Miles, Jr., Clyde Linwood	4	0	0	1	2,142
Milian, Michael	56	5	3	3	60,418
Millar, Mac	131	14	23	19	351,372
Miller, Allan R.	41	0	2	3	9,609
Miller, Barbara J.	3	0	0	0	900
Miller, Blair A.	149	25	25	21	233,912
Miller, Craig S.	45	5	6	6	30,477
Miller, Daniel Charles	2	0	0	0	0
Miller, Danny L.	97	7	5	7	164,760
Miller, Darrin	116	18	16	12	573,353
Miller, Edward G.	24	2	0	2	43,254
Miller, Elizabeth A.	51	4	8	7	76,250
Miller, Elmer J.	87	7	11	11	180,360

Trainer	Sts	1st	2d	3d	Purses
Miller, F. Bruce	126	11	15	12	290,120
Miller, Gary M.	18	3	5	2	27,973
Miller, Gregory D.	75	11	16	9	163,682
Miller, Herbert	63	6	6	10	78,732
Miller, Irene	1	0	0	0	100
Miller, John Mark	7	1	0	3	5,002
Miller, Judith E.	8	2	1	1	8,244
Miller, Kenneth G.	25	4	1	1	32,029
Miller, Laurel M.	11	0	0	1	3,560
Miller, Marlin A.	78	6	14	7	134,464
Miller, Matthew	9	0	0	1	1,203
Miller, Patrice	4	0	0	0	1,200
Miller, Peggy	5	0	1	0	1,288
Miller, Peter	3	0	0	0	3,100
Miller, Quentin B.	70	0	13	8	92,556
Miller, Richard E.	11	0	1	3	12,252
Miller, Robert M.	131	28	21	21	224,242
Miller, Rory C.	65	4	4	8	52,604
Miller, Sandy Jean	70	1	3	8	15,362
Miller, Shirley T.	7	0	0	0	510
Miller, Thomas R.	24	4	1	8	49,305
Miller, Valerie J.	33	3	2	6	34,839
Miller, III, Norman C.	24	4	3	4	39,665
Miller, Jr., F. Bruce	39	5	5	7	68,281
Miller, Jr., Henry D.	32	2	3	1	30,425
Miller, Jr., Henry M.	107	6	9	13	80,955
Miller, Sr., Henry D.	1	0	0	0	0
Milligan, Allen	255	16	29	25	196,106
Milligan, Sherry	7	0	0	0	678
Milligan, Jr., Eddie	1	0	0	0	0
Milligan, Sr., Eddie R.	137	16	23	17	347,220
Millington, Brinnard	23	0	0	2	7,157
Million, William N.	90	13	8	13	283,687
Millonas, Don	109	2	15	12	128,087
Mills, Dennis R.	152	9	19	13	119,356
Mills, Don	14	0	0	0	3,050
Mills, Don J.	291	74	56	35	731,497
Mills, Ernie	175	5	10	16	136,152
Mills, Glendon	21	9	0	3	52,526
Mills, Philip W.	40	2	5	5	46,851
Mills, Tommy Ray	29	1	0	2	18,306
Mills, Sr., Ray C.	13	0	1	1	9,870
Milner, Kerwin E.	3	0	0	0	0
Milton, Rowena A.	64	2	5	6	51,239
Minard, Richard D.	50	9	1	7	178,538
Minnock, Wayne G.	256	42	37	34	368,428
Minogue, George	20	1	2	1	18,711
Minor, Suzanne	42	6	4	5	43,483
Minshall, Barbara J.	117	9	15	12	535,441
Minton, Jeffrey T.	3	0	1	0	9,762
Miracle, Jr., Norman D.	39	1	6	5	27,597
Miranda, Efrain	220	27	36	23	341,204
Miranda, Jimmy	14	0	1	4	9,599
Mita, Michael	48	2	2	0	32,992
Mitchell, Anne	22	5	4	3	123,534
Mitchell, Anthony	130	19	16	12	727,527
Mitchell, Billy	5	0	1	0	2,700
Mitchell, Bob	13	3	1	2	3,373
Mitchell, Chris D.	1	0	0	0	92
Mitchell, Christopher N.	94	1	10	8	78,055
Mitchell, Danny M.	11	1	0	0	3,254
Mitchell, Joan M.	10	2	1	1	59,241
Mitchell, Mike R.	391	97	67	45	3,834,120
Mitchell, Paraskevas G.	71	5	7	7	104,931
Mitchell, Patrick S.	35	3	2	5	69,940
Mitchell, Ralph H.	22	0	5	2	11,687
Mitchell, Sherman S.	37	4	2	10	64,808
Mitchell, Stephen	2	0	0	0	0
Mitchell, Suzun	15	1	0	1	12,278
Mitchell, Thomas M.	16	2	5	0	40,870
Mitzner, Robert R.	22	1	3	4	6,517
Mix, Kenneth R.	30	1	3	3	30,861
Miyadi, Steven	101	38	23	9	349,215
Miyashiro, Leanne	19	1	7	3	11,767
Mize, Raymond S.	15	0	3	0	5,213
Mobberley, Gretchen B.	116	9	9	20	117,060
Mobley, Brook	50	6	6	6	16,199
Mock, Thaddeus A.	19	2	6	3	29,920
Moehlig, Albert	10	0	0	0	1,887
Moffitt, Charles F.	10	1	0	1	4,118
Moga, Lucian V.	2	0	1	0	2,425
Moger, Jr., Ed	341	37	60	60	813,341
Mogge, Wayne D.	217	44	29	31	507,216
Mohamed, Dr. James A.	10	1	0	0	15,839
Mohr, Crystal	14	2	1	2	12,260
Molera, Manuel	1	0	0	0	0
Molinaro, Kent R.	83	20	18	12	351,833
Moloney, James J.	7	2	1	0	71,612
Monahan, II, Robert E.	58	1	6	7	29,519
Monahas, Dimitrios	108	7	11	8	75,012
Mondol, Jr., Eduardo	44	6	2	7	68,545
Mongeon, Kathy P.	124	8	8	17	154,016
Monjes, Ruben A.	62	7	3	6	105,995
Monk, Elmer	18	0	1	0	1,788
Monroe, Sherrie	81	4	7	9	141,747
Monroy, Robert A.	2	0	0	0	2,520
Monserrate, Felix O.	186	10	7	13	109,888
Monson, Micheal N.	2	0	0	1	120
Montano, Sr., Angel O.	104	18	14	11	283,929
Monteleone, Frank A.	3	0	0	0	651
Monteleone, Frank J.	76	14	11	9	328,020
Montes, Arturo	1	0	0	1	1,400
Montes, Danny S.	10	1	1	2	6,440
Montes, Jr., Johnny R.	119	16	15	14	135,287
Montet, Ralph	58	5	7	10	65,707
Montgomery, Darwin L.	44	1	3	5	41,369
Montgomery, David P.	25	0	1	1	9,389
Montgomery, Gary	44	7	6	4	139,625
Montgomery, Lori Hill	14	3	2	2	22,886
Montgomery, Sandra	16	2	0	2	20,293
Montgomery, Timothy	159	16	7	14	67,660
Montgomery, Jr., Harry B.	10	1	1	3	6,642
Montgomery, Jr., James K.	1	0	0	0	138
Montoya, Marya K.	66	8	9	12	116,009
Mooney, Bill	56	1	5	7	13,259
Mooney, Don	3	0	0	0	0
Moore, Amy	18	1	4	1	10,124
Moore, Billy R.	2	0	0	0	0
Moore, Bud	3	0	0	0	165
Moore, Chad	3	0	0	0	159
Moore, Dan	21	0	2	2	5,497
Moore, David W.	12	1	3	4	20,244
Moore, Dennis T.	222	28	31	26	217,595
Moore, Dorris L.	12	0	0	0	1,984
Moore, Jerald E.	16	3	1	1	10,245
Moore, Lance R.	2	0	0	2	946
Moore, Merel E.	60	4	8	6	25,348
Moore, Peter	4	1	1	0	12,152
Moore, Richard L.	19	0	1	1	9,250
Moore, Sr., Chester	28	2	2	2	75,975
Moorhead, Clifford W.	1	0	0	0	0
Moquett, Ron	247	32	29	35	479,346
Mora, Myra	156	12	14	23	153,280
Morales, Carlos J.	58	6	10	9	195,462
Morales, Mario	64	17	10	9	309,376
Morales, Nabu	82	5	7	7	144,153
Morales, Ricardo	269	28	21	34	317,277
Moran, Betty L.	17	0	3	2	8,921
Moran, Bill	45	8	3	10	101,459
Moran, Michael J.	39	5	4	2	93,105
Moran, Sr., Donald W.	85	6	7	7	81,886
Morano, Deborah	17	1	0	3	12,220
Morden, Lyle	89	21	8	13	201,370
Moreland, Lloyd	3	1	1	0	8,716
Moreno, Carlos	29	4	2	3	20,927
Moreno, Henry	55	2	6	8	98,900
Moreno, Tito	95	1	11	11	86,835
Moreno, Tomas D.	8	1	1	2	7,952
Morey, William E.	383	86	75	43	1,115,343
Morey, Jr., William J.	169	25	25	33	486,877
Morgan, Brian A.	46	1	1	4	55,915
Morgan, Carla L.	3	0	0	0	0
Morgan, Dan	122	20	16	14	263,536
Morgan, Evan B.	9	0	0	0	270
Morgan, James E.	198	30	28	16	268,596
Morgan, Janet L.	8	0	1	0	7,060

Trainer	Sts	1st	2d	3d	Purses
Morgan, Julie	7	0	1	1	3,455
Morgan, Kenneth A.	320	23	26	37	130,127
Morgan, Robert V.	1	0	0	0	0
Morgan, Tommie T.	355	56	40	33	637,592
Morisak, Robert W.	5	0	0	0	0
Morison, Don F.	41	1	3	5	45,243
Morreale, Jake V.	232	25	25	20	302,780
Morris, Brent	54	9	2	6	64,346
Morris, Charles J.	5	1	1	0	6,350
Morris, David	149	13	19	14	166,740
Morris, Gregg	1	0	0	0	0
Morris, Homer	20	2	5	1	41,920
Morris, John	1	0	0	0	0
Morris, Ned	2	0	0	0	875
Morris, Neil R.	95	17	15	18	458,090
Morris, Ray W.	15	2	2	0	23,399
Morris, Valerie L.	9	0	0	0	0
Morrison, E. Marie	1	0	0	0	348
Morrison, George E.	14	0	3	3	34,153
Morrison, John	77	6	10	9	252,439
Morrison, John D.	17	2	0	0	14,862
Morrison, Mike J.	75	12	5	13	108,314
Morrow, Ann L.	33	0	5	2	16,829
Morrow, T. Gail	45	0	2	2	16,285
Morse, David L.	38	3	6	6	46,144
Morse, Randy L.	191	27	33	30	588,981
Morse, Ronnie	48	6	4	10	50,248
Morse, Scott A.	16	2	0	2	16,989
Morsello, Joseph R.	31	5	0	4	26,875
Morsman, Trudi A.	7	0	0	0	2,088
Mortensen, Dale	3	1	0	1	2,633
Mortensen, Lyle	10	0	3	3	6,820
Morton, Blueford G.	4	0	1	1	2,705
Morton, Larry R.	9	0	0	0	1,466
Moscarelli, Vincent W.	87	4	3	5	84,658
Moschonas, Gerasimos	96	7	6	11	195,602
Mosco, Robert	288	49	45	34	626,001
Mosley, Jr., Marvin A.	6	0	0	0	0
Mosley, Jr., Thomas J.	2	0	0	0	130
Moss, Buford A.	10	0	0	4	3,128
Moss, Joseph A.	79	10	4	13	80,888
Moss, Ken T.	2	0	0	0	125
Moss, Thomas J.	39	9	6	7	111,796
Mostoller, Mary	24	0	3	3	5,260
Motion, H. Graham	424	81	65	43	4,358,674
Mott, William I.	680	116	106	98	5,730,530
Moulton, Susan	9	0	2	1	8,961
Mourar, Buck K.	9	0	1	0	2,375
Mourier, Franck	10	1	1	1	104,410
Mouton, Chadwick J.	31	1	0	0	10,162
Mouton, Enis	27	5	4	2	85,738
Mouton, Patrick	250	42	46	29	960,650
Mower, R. D.	39	1	5	2	8,199
Moyer, Meredith	21	1	8	6	33,135
Moyer, Steven L.	6	1	1	0	20,834
Moyers, Rodney D.	53	0	4	6	29,396
Muckey, Sally	63	5	9	10	29,698
Muela, Jose Luis	4	0	0	0	486
Mueller, Russell	57	1	4	4	66,106
Muench, David L.	96	9	10	10	183,335
Muir, Patrick	1	0	0	0	0
Mulcahy, Geoff	38	4	8	6	100,961
Mulhall, Kristin	154	23	18	18	1,883,697
Mullaney, Deryle	73	5	12	12	93,698
Mullen, Blair W.	4	0	0	0	300
Mullens, H. R. Pat	105	22	6	22	139,200
Muller, Sr., Thomas J.	107	1	12	8	45,877
Mullins, Jeff	538	140	98	65	6,910,572
Mullins, Jesse	12	0	1	3	7,485
Mullins, Leonard S.	6	1	0	1	1,544
Mullins, Michelle	6	0	1	0	12,702
Mulvey, Arthur V.	7	5	1	0	55,200
Mumaw, Benjamin T.	105	2	4	10	55,515
Munds, Sue	24	2	4	2	44,412
Munger, Don L.	61	7	8	4	27,843
Muniz, Ralph	2	0	0	0	294
Munoz, Fernando P.	4	0	0	0	1,230
Munoz, Jose Juan	35	2	2	5	4,689
Munoz, Sr., Arnold	7	1	1	0	11,000
Murillo, Ricardo A.	22	2	2	1	31,215
Murnan, G. Scott	58	6	6	12	125,527
Murphy, Alicia	14	1	0	2	26,125
Murphy, Don	96	3	10	7	17,422
Murphy, Earl C.	5	1	0	0	6,087
Murphy, James W.	159	18	24	25	503,179
Murphy, Pat	2	2	0	0	4,740
Murphy, Paul H.	175	24	32	21	616,363
Murphy, Raymond T.	6	1	0	0	15,060
Murphy, Scott R.	55	3	10	1	76,527
Murphy, Susan E.	33	6	3	1	63,728
Murphy, Timothy P.	231	18	21	27	234,372
Murphy, Tom G.	41	6	5	6	69,621
Murphy, Wayne L.	92	2	8	8	85,413
Murphy II, Thomas J.	38	0	4	5	51,199
Murr, Bill	6	1	0	0	2,405
Murray, Alex D.	54	3	5	7	54,496
Murray, D. Milton	31	3	2	1	35,153
Murray, Dave	24	4	2	6	46,431
Murray, Donna	22	4	3	4	15,427
Murray, Douglas A.	34	2	3	6	11,404
Murray, Jack	48	2	4	6	42,231
Murray, Lawrence E.	112	16	20	13	555,995
Murray, Michael E.	3	0	0	0	241
Murray, Scott M.	23	1	7	2	6,545
Murtough, Stephen B.	34	2	4	5	34,727
Murty, Wayne	21	0	0	0	2,980
Musarro, Jamie	36	6	7	3	56,178
Muse, Brian E.	3	0	0	0	152
Musgrave, Shawn	180	15	18	24	281,050
Musone, Joseph	1	0	0	0	0
Mustard, J. Douglas	23	3	5	2	22,480
Mustard, Wendell R.	11	1	1	1	7,150
Mustoe, Cindy	55	6	6	10	94,074
Muth, Charles V.	1	0	0	1	4,660
Myers, Daniel W.	29	5	5	1	72,488
Myers, John M.	14	1	0	1	17,530
Myers, Karl	59	4	6	6	52,751
Myers, Larry L.	2	1	0	0	9,555
Myers, Larry M.	60	4	5	4	73,727
Myers, Steven E.	3	0	0	0	980
Mynster, Patrick M.	27	1	0	2	13,520
Myres, Cheryl	1	0	0	0	0
Nafzger, Carl A.	358	54	52	52	2,732,948
Nafzger, Larry	16	1	1	0	11,183
Nagel, Clayton	8	0	2	4	2,435
Nagy, George	19	2	0	2	21,261
Nall, Johnnie L.	128	16	17	16	402,909
Nalley, Rhonda	26	1	7	2	48,305
Nance, Eugene C.	3	0	0	0	548
Nance, Jonathan	231	47	53	33	177,016
Nance, Michael W.	428	80	60	63	801,191
Nance, Scott	37	8	5	6	15,034
Nanez, Danette E.	46	4	7	3	70,480
Napier, William J.	87	11	14	5	167,904
Napoleon, Moses	1	0	0	0	105
Nasby, Dale R.	47	5	3	3	36,422
Nash, Bradley Gene	1	0	0	1	170
Nash, Christopher	2	0	0	0	434
Natale, Michael	132	16	22	19	245,320
Natho, Randy Lee	14	3	2	2	12,124
Nations, Keith	29	3	9	2	22,758
Naugle, Kenneth W.	13	0	1	3	1,793
Nault, Michael	73	9	5	12	63,263
Navarre, Jacqui	15	8	2	3	27,930
Navarro, Eloy G.	16	3	4	1	19,512
Navarro, Jody	2	1	0	0	2,460
Navarro, Jose	57	4	1	8	42,632
Navarro, Marcial	58	7	9	11	107,065
Naylor, Bruce	6	0	0	0	723
Nazareth, Jr., John	4	1	0	1	6,595
Nazareth, Sr., John Antonio	110	9	13	12	229,554
Neadow, Charles P.	10	0	0	0	1,192
Neal, Mike	11	0	0	0	324
Neatherlin, Mike R.	46	3	8	4	34,591

Trainer	Sts	1st	2d	3d	Purses
Neatherlin, Tommy	35	3	5	3	23,656
Necaise, Elliot C.	64	4	6	8	71,738
Necaise, Garrie	37	1	4	4	26,469
Necaise, Larry	14	0	0	0	0
Nechamkin, II, Leo S.	56	12	7	13	503,340
Needham, Jr., Bobby	127	7	11	8	57,213
Neff, Joe	1	0	0	0	800
Neff, Myles I.	66	8	9	9	185,473
Neff, Robert	13	3	1	3	28,976
Neilson, Katherine	131	13	18	15	331,306
Neilson, Sanna	1	0	1	0	1,800
Neilson, Wallace C.	117	4	15	12	119,176
Neilson, III, Louis	11	1	4	2	46,500
Nellessen, Leonard	50	3	7	3	17,752
Nelson, Amy	6	1	1	0	1,547
Nelson, Barry R.	15	2	2	2	10,400
Nelson, Harry N.	124	7	5	16	84,544
Nelson, Kathleen S.	38	1	3	8	24,752
Nelson, Mary S.	7	0	4	1	6,568
Nelson, Michael C.	9	1	2	0	9,820
Nelson, Reed H.	4	0	0	0	120
Nelson, Sam D.	11	0	0	3	2,762
Nelson, Thelma	35	0	0	0	1,795
Nemann, Fred A.	8	1	4	0	23,566
Nemann, Kris	148	21	16	20	215,202
Nemett, George S.	84	13	9	5	561,010
Nepple, Lloyd	43	1	3	3	21,627
Nesbitt, Kim	85	13	10	10	124,435
Nesky, Kenneth A.	52	2	5	8	154,478
Ness, Jamie	287	34	45	45	340,836
Ness, John	85	18	11	15	60,352
Nettles, Kenneth	54	4	4	4	76,250
Neubauer, Michaela	93	15	11	11	367,341
Neubuhr, Sam L.	2	0	0	0	0
Neumann, Robert E.	22	0	1	1	18,504
Nevin, Michael	60	3	6	8	161,030
Newby, Kevin D.	20	2	5	3	3,927
Newell, Kenneth R.	12	2	2	1	31,206
Newell, Michael	333	21	32	36	258,574
Newenhouse, Randy	6	0	1	0	1,121
Newland, George	20	1	1	0	46,499
Newlun, Ronald Colver	13	0	0	1	3,022
Newman, Gabe	65	6	2	5	28,491
Newman, Tracy L.	60	1	4	2	30,754
Newport, Kim	30	5	4	2	12,927
Newsom, Jack E.	30	3	5	4	25,512
Newsome, Clement	16	1	0	0	3,836
Newton, Charles R.	25	1	3	7	7,976
Newton, Troy	33	2	6	3	30,954
Ney, Andrew T.	179	20	21	20	275,993
Nicholas, Sr., Robert Lee	36	1	5	3	28,541
Nichols, Bessie Sue	5	0	0	0	220
Nichols, Bill	2	1	0	0	1,650
Nichols, James T.	3	0	0	0	190
Nichols, Pat	15	1	2	1	9,135
Nicholson, Craig P.	32	6	3	4	75,205
Nicholson, David	76	13	6	9	176,033
Nicholson, Junior W.	23	2	5	3	28,808
Nicholson, Jr., James E.	75	2	0	3	19,290
Nickels, Eddie	1	0	0	0	0
Nicks, Morris G.	186	43	26	20	794,107
Nicks, Ralph E.	85	18	9	12	497,576
Nicolo, John	43	7	3	5	68,470
Niehaus, Jonathan	10	0	2	3	10,660
Nielsen, David B.	30	1	1	5	20,779
Nielsen, David D.	8	3	2	1	3,900
Nielsen, John	3	0	1	0	260
Nielsen, Paul	29	8	7	2	447,826
Nielsen, Robert A.	17	2	2	4	13,985
Nieminski, Richard S.	15	1	1	3	52,290
Nikiforuk, Raymond	74	2	5	8	34,331
Nini, Janice T.	30	4	1	2	52,139
Nisser, Ernest	1	0	0	0	0
Nix, C. L.	151	16	16	17	269,960
Nix, Eugene H.	9	0	0	1	3,118
Nixon, Bobby Joe	2	0	0	0	0
Nixon, David R.	2	0	1	0	2,400
Nixon, Justin J.	158	43	34	30	1,213,172
Nixon, Lawrence	55	5	8	6	25,045
Nixon, Stephanie B.	24	2	1	2	31,134
Noble, Allen	17	1	0	1	4,014
Noble, Edward L.	23	2	3	4	57,450
Noble, James F.	3	0	1	0	3,050
Nobles, Reynaldo H.	62	6	6	5	188,998
Nocero, Rinzy	416	56	59	62	290,729
Nocero, Roggiero L.	21	0	1	3	3,436
Noe, Albert W.	1	0	0	0	0
Noel, Bob J.	130	14	17	13	283,291
Noel, Cody L.	1	0	0	0	168
Noel, Wayne L.	84	8	10	8	112,796
Nolan, Donna M.	29	1	2	0	28,840
Nolan, William J.	4	0	0	0	1,600
Noland, Kamala J.	6	0	1	0	6,642
Noland, Ronald A.	13	1	0	1	14,837
Nolen, Harold Whitey	26	2	2	3	16,005
Nolen, Kenneth	132	15	15	14	149,596
Nono, Robert	11	0	0	1	1,425
Norman, Cole	894	250	169	98	3,730,732
Normand, Dale	4	0	0	1	4,905
Norris, C. David	90	18	11	17	264,239
Norris, Mike	3	0	0	0	871
Norris, Tracy A.	1	0	0	0	0
Northam, Linda Bartels	51	6	2	5	29,099
Northrop, Jr., George	235	34	38	23	292,532
Norton, Melissa J.	13	0	0	0	1,528
Norton, Norbert E.	30	4	5	1	11,016
Norwood, Jerry L.	30	2	2	2	29,441
Noseda, Jeremy	1	1	0	0	780,000
Nosowenko, Nicholas	2	1	0	0	8,680
Noss, Jerry A.	3	0	0	0	207
Nouwens, Preston	10	1	0	0	8,527
Novak, Marshall L.	194	39	27	31	405,816
Nowak, Elizabeth	3	0	0	0	0
Ntonados, Gerasimos J.	45	0	0	1	1,370
Nuesch, Patrick F.	98	14	13	11	253,608
Nugent, Thomas E.	2	0	0	0	135
Nunez, Jesus	489	68	65	57	482,433
Nunez, Mauricio	33	2	3	4	23,133
Nunley, Randy	269	35	24	37	662,149
Nunley, Tracy L.	1	0	0	0	75
Nunn, David	8	2	0	2	18,255
Nunn, Douglas	100	10	9	18	197,038
Nunnally, Chris	3	0	0	1	420
Nunnally, James E.	24	4	0	2	21,450
Nydam, Michelle L.	51	3	2	6	51,927
O'Bannon, Cynthia E.	215	13	18	22	261,795
Obergfell, Sarina	131	17	16	14	126,553
Oberholtzer, Kevin	115	12	24	17	82,765
Oberlander, Randy	114	15	22	16	249,923
O'Brien, Agnes	2	0	0	0	420
O'Brien, Aidan P.	12	0	1	5	1,037,300
O'Brien, Charles	3	0	0	0	514
O'Brien, Colum	48	1	5	2	91,916
O'Brien, Danny	14	0	0	3	1,841
O'Brien, Debbie	40	6	7	4	38,178
O'Brien, Elmer J.	31	3	3	2	29,743
O'Brien, Gerald L.	37	2	6	5	29,879
O'Brien, Gerard P.	33	1	3	4	28,143
O'Brien, Keith	77	5	3	3	214,590
O'Brien, Lawrence	3	0	0	1	3,310
O'Brien, Leo	140	5	8	10	333,933
O'Brien, Maura C.	33	3	1	7	47,863
O'Brien, Michael Scott	16	0	2	0	1,622
O'Callaghan, Danny M.	99	15	7	9	425,199
O'Callaghan, Niall M.	177	23	19	21	796,352
O'Callaghan, Sarah	26	3	0	10	99,464
Occhiuto, Richard	38	5	4	6	24,397
Ochoa, Gerardo	2	1	0	0	3,024
O'Connell, Brian J.	19	3	0	4	31,950
O'Connell, Kathleen	537	59	74	65	1,035,666
O'Connell, Patrick A.	2	0	0	0	200
O'Connor, John	6	1	1	2	6,980
O'Connor, Stephen T.	258	40	29	43	346,573
O'Connor, II, Robert R.	46	5	3	7	93,466
O'Dea, Mike	10	1	1	0	9,019
O'Dell, Christopher G.	80	12	15	13	108,226

Trainer	Sts	1st	2d	3d	Purses
Odintz, Jeff	124	14	13	14	492,266
Odom, Robert L.	11	0	2	3	8,340
Odom, Sr., Raymond	42	5	4	6	71,325
Offield, Duane	80	8	12	15	192,576
Offolter, Joe S.	377	44	53	41	496,139
Ogg, Raymond L.	33	2	4	3	15,626
Ogus, Daniel	23	3	7	2	38,159
O'Harra, David C.	5	0	2	0	5,082
Ohlhauser, Robert F.	14	1	1	1	10,080
Okawaki, William N.	21	1	0	1	5,130
O'Keefe, Thomas	44	3	4	4	126,104
Olaivar, Benny D.	40	3	4	2	23,858
Olesiak, Jesse	156	12	17	13	65,581
Olijar, Curtis	35	9	7	4	53,020
Oliphant, Claude	17	3	2	1	15,160
Olito, Verla	16	1	1	1	7,309
Oliva, Jr., Louis M.	25	0	0	1	2,299
Olivares, Luis	268	34	42	34	682,973
Olivarez, Mario	17	0	0	2	11,060
Olivas, Cesario G.	100	6	16	14	83,973
Oliver, Barry E.	22	1	1	4	10,610
Oliver, Doug	287	31	42	46	558,755
Oliver, James D.	1	0	0	0	0
Oliver, Patricia J.	12	0	0	0	891
Oliver, Philip J.	136	12	15	17	510,854
Oliver, Vicki	107	14	8	18	426,334
Olman, Ronald R.	9	0	0	0	311
Olmos, Juan C.	142	19	12	12	231,399
Olsen, Gary	10	2	4	0	10,583
Olsen, Ron	30	2	2	4	17,114
Olson, Daryl	7	0	1	3	1,558
Olson, Kenneth	59	13	13	7	29,706
Olson, Lynn	37	1	4	3	33,064
Olson, Selmer B.	13	0	2	0	7,933
Omana, Romeo	1	0	0	0	0
Omer, Natalie	4	3	0	0	4,724
O'Neal, Bob	1	0	0	0	0
O'Neill, Doug	938	170	132	124	7,004,827
Oney, Robert L.	1	0	0	0	104
Ontiveros, Lalita	40	8	4	3	53,638
Opperman, Beach W.	8	0	1	0	1,495
O'Quinn, Earl	63	6	8	11	93,573
O'Quinn, Kristen Lee	73	1	7	9	28,688
Oran, John T.	16	3	4	0	40,546
Ordonez, Aggie	68	14	12	9	234,625
Orellana, Oscar J.	4	0	0	0	330
Orlando, Peter L.	9	1	2	1	21,115
Orm, Jerry	121	7	7	8	75,791
Orm, Mike	11	1	0	0	3,588
Orman, Jason R.	53	8	7	8	1,017,685
Ormesher, Arthur	13	0	2	1	1,367
Orona, Martin	3	0	0	0	429
Orozco, Salvador	27	3	1	2	22,023
Orr, Ike	38	4	10	4	46,126
Orr, James	30	1	4	5	22,000
Orr, Thomas Stephen	10	0	0	2	1,365
Orseno, Joseph F.	316	32	30	35	775,695
Ortega, Jr., Fernando	6	1	1	0	1,509
Ortega, Sr., Jesus Fernando	1	0	0	0	371
Ortenzi, Giovanni	14	0	1	2	5,204
Ortiz, Arthur Curly	19	0	4	3	9,584
Ortiz, Jose M.	11	0	1	1	3,610
Ortiz, Joseph	128	10	9	15	68,356
Ortiz, Juan	47	4	5	0	59,023
Ortiz, Paulino O.	17	0	1	0	14,664
Ortiz, Sr., Manuel	70	6	8	10	66,782
Osborn, Jan	14	0	2	4	3,421
Osborn, O. J.	59	10	3	5	84,487
Osborne, Linda K.	53	2	6	5	23,732
Osborne, Michael R.	145	8	13	8	148,624
Osment, Robbie J.	57	3	3	6	64,274
Otero, Robert	1	0	0	1	500
Otero-Hernandez, Jr., Antonio	1	0	0	0	240
O'Toole, James J.	16	6	3	4	33,819
Ott, Betty L.	31	0	2	5	10,840
Otteson, David L.	3	0	0	0	0
Otteson, Kenny	10	0	0	1	810
Oughton, Julia E.	22	2	4	1	43,990
Overturf, Roger	5	0	0	1	606
Oviedo, Phillip S.	86	10	16	12	137,734
Owen, Nate	18	2	0	1	19,234
Owens, Alan D.	38	7	2	6	82,110
Owens, Martin D.	144	21	13	22	219,201
Owens, Mickey	29	3	4	3	17,924
Owens, R. Kory	98	18	14	11	276,702
Owens, Steve	109	14	15	15	551,369
Owens, III, Edward	7	0	0	0	2,340
Oxman, Carol	37	2	3	7	45,173
Oyster, Charles H.	12	0	1	0	1,803
Paasch, Christopher S.	107	13	14	14	479,927
Pabon, Heriberto	16	2	0	2	33,160
Pace, Jennifer	3	0	0	1	796
Pace, Phillip Donato	12	1	0	1	6,709
Pacheco, Charles S.	1	0	0	0	0
Pacheco, Leo J.	8	0	0	0	480
Pacitti, Michael G.	60	7	6	4	67,175
Padgett, Virginia	1	0	0	0	145
Padilla, Tim P.	203	31	21	27	207,913
Padilla, Victor	1	1	0	0	2,700
Padilla, Willie C.	33	3	0	2	25,124
Paez, Carlos E.	104	17	13	17	355,563
Pafford, Jr., Walter C.	10	0	0	1	649
Page, Gary	91	14	17	11	81,968
Page, Tommy	94	9	9	9	69,331
Paige, Guy	25	0	3	2	18,617
Palacios, Luis Albert	347	70	56	55	738,228
Palagi, Kenneth C.	16	3	2	4	11,252
Palagruti, Sidney M.	12	1	4	1	18,275
Palaniuk, Brian	27	3	2	3	84,947
Palavecino, Norberto J.	2	0	0	0	0
Palecki, Henry J.	12	0	0	1	10,594
Pallanes, Alan	1	0	0	0	0
Pallanes, Art	10	0	1	2	1,725
Pallister, Kevin	7	0	0	1	5,600
Palma, Hector O.	29	1	4	4	84,266
Palman, Darrin	26	1	0	2	41,737
Palmer, Aaron	33	2	5	2	11,699
Palmer, Charles C.	17	0	1	3	4,337
Palmer, Charles Greg	33	4	10	5	24,123
Palmer, Jay H.	40	2	7	5	45,686
Palmer, Jim E.	16	2	2	3	14,047
Palmer, Lloyd L.	79	8	3	7	143,117
Palmisano, Gary	37	11	8	1	405,398
Pane, Pasquale J.	72	10	7	7	99,377
Paone, John A.	4	0	0	0	945
Papania, Robert A.	7	2	2	2	96,169
Papaprodromou, George	24	2	0	1	61,435
Papillion, Merrick	53	3	5	3	34,572
Papineau, Gloria	1	0	0	0	0
Papiska, Trever	7	0	0	0	971
Pappada, Michael C.	177	32	26	26	512,332
Paquette, Chantal L.	58	3	2	7	130,288
Paquette, Ida	134	8	18	14	163,093
Paquette, Linda	33	1	3	2	13,542
Paquette, III, Raymond J.	64	4	7	6	36,433
Parada, Tom	1	0	0	0	0
Paredes, Omar	2	1	0	0	4,200
Parente, Pat	15	1	2	2	20,232
Parga, Joe	58	3	6	6	91,590
Parisella, John	124	18	11	27	528,959
Parisi, Horacio	2	0	0	0	122
Parisi, Jr., Paul J.	58	11	9	6	259,510
Parisien, Theresa	5	0	0	0	150
Parker, Bob D.	55	6	4	7	45,513
Parker, C. C.	7	1	0	1	3,605
Parker, F. Hill	9	0	0	1	2,295
Parker, Horace M.	2	0	0	0	0
Parker, Janet K	3	1	2	0	2,260
Parker, Kathleen	8	0	1	0	2,291
Parker, Kevin	3	0	0	0	282
Parker, Linda	2	0	1	0	288
Parker, Mark	48	5	8	7	73,439
Parker, Robert W.	174	14	24	22	81,286
Parker, Jr., Elmer L.	1	0	0	0	0

Trainer	Sts	1st	2d	3d	Purses
Parkin, Gary W.	16	1	2	1	8,460
Parkinson, Ron	4	0	0	1	626
Parks, Raymond G.	25	0	3	2	13,140
Parnell, William E.	51	9	12	10	80,668
Parris, Jim L.	33	4	6	3	31,828
Parrish, Robert L.	10	0	0	0	620
Parrish, Steven G.	19	1	1	2	19,864
Parrish, Sr., George W.	15	1	2	3	19,885
Parrott, Gary D.	20	2	7	0	12,188
Parsley, Kenneth B.	48	8	9	11	685,349
Parsons, Dean	5	0	0	0	472
Partin, Jerry	1	0	0	0	0
Partington, Jerome	26	6	6	4	65,316
Partridge, Robert E.	103	12	5	10	65,417
Parum, Brandon	3	0	2	0	3,935
Paschal, Richard	5	0	0	0	400
Pascual, Maria Virginia	109	23	16	16	381,693
Pascucci, Ambrose	54	4	5	9	45,962
Passanah, Ian L.	9	1	0	0	10,970
Passero, Gino S.	19	1	0	1	19,763
Passero, Jr., Frank A.	9	3	0	1	189,316
Passley, Mark	104	11	13	16	100,177
Pastor, Jude	79	6	7	9	84,329
Paszkeicz, Alex	87	7	12	10	125,082
Pate, David E.	140	15	15	14	280,229
Paterno, Robert T.	23	3	3	3	10,245
Patrick, R. Gary	402	49	50	51	415,502
Patrick, Tom	26	1	1	4	16,778
Pattah, Shahab D.	67	2	3	4	18,641
Pattershall, Mary A.	18	4	1	2	46,638
Patterson, Alan	35	2	4	4	20,406
Patterson, Dennis M.	70	15	15	9	284,952
Patterson, Jeanne B.	31	0	1	4	5,241
Patterson, Loren	19	1	0	2	12,358
Patterson, Jr., Thomas L.	70	7	9	8	110,400
Patterson, Jr., William M.	17	0	0	1	4,201
Patti, Gale A.	34	6	4	3	94,400
Patton, Billy Joe	2	0	0	0	210
Patton, Kathy	54	6	10	5	221,310
Patton, Robert E.	6	0	0	0	675
Patton, Roderick G.	13	0	1	1	3,404
Patykewich, Alexander P.	105	14	16	14	131,108
Paul, Cecil	7	1	0	0	21,650
Paul, Wayne J.	1	0	0	0	0
Pauley, Joseph C.	3	1	0	0	3,906
Pauley, Jr., James E.	16	1	0	3	13,826
Paulson, Gary E.	2	0	1	0	4,080
Paulus, David E.	103	12	14	13	137,460
Paulus, Richard E.	47	9	5	4	160,479
Pavlick, Thomas B.	174	20	28	20	341,377
Pawlitsky, Joan M.	26	6	4	5	55,615
Payan, Ruben	1	0	0	0	143
Payne, Beverley	4	0	2	1	7,795
Payne, Curtis Beale	60	1	4	6	41,588
Payne, Danny W.	16	0	0	0	1,905
Payne, Felix G.	4	0	0	1	1,425
Payne, Jerry	22	2	0	3	19,607
Payne, Linda S.	14	0	0	1	2,171
Payton, Jackie	20	0	2	0	10,533
Payton, Recil L.	21	0	1	2	2,671
Payton, Shawn P.	3	0	0	1	1,355
Peach, Melissa L.	13	0	1	3	1,405
Peacock, Shane	135	18	22	18	228,784
Peacock, Jr., Roy M.	10	0	1	0	2,920
Pearce, Jason	25	4	3	1	36,879
Pearce, Ross R.	3	0	0	0	580
Pearce, William E.	47	5	7	4	232,653
Peardon, Josephine	15	0	1	0	1,329
Pearson, Michael A.	27	1	2	0	17,790
Pearson, Michael R.	1	0	0	0	100
Pearson, Molly J.	232	49	39	31	548,358
Pearson, Paul M.	214	26	19	35	563,684
Pearson, Randy	1	0	0	0	0
Pearson, Ronald N.	14	2	0	3	13,661
Peck, D. Scott	47	1	6	7	60,594
Peck, Tammy	8	0	0	0	1,930
Pecoraro, Anthony	256	46	41	38	595,646
Pecoraro, Antonio	28	0	0	2	10,428
Pedersen, Candy	17	2	2	5	27,675
Pedersen, Jennifer	423	44	46	59	2,015,485
Pederson, Dean	109	18	20	22	274,298
Pedigo, Randy	43	5	2	5	63,518
Peery, Ann	43	8	4	8	19,804
Peery, Chuck	152	22	24	19	493,815
Peguero, Jorge W.	26	1	0	2	12,038
Peitz, Daniel C.	94	11	14	10	391,249
Pellegrini, Ronald	34	2	5	1	24,338
Peltier, Walt	16	0	1	2	3,784
Pena, Diego	2	0	1	0	2,110
Pena, Juan	25	4	4	0	26,552
Pencheff, Dimitar I.	20	2	1	1	16,571
Pencheff, Robert	5	0	0	0	841
Pender, Jack	12	1	1	0	6,327
Pender, Michael	4	0	1	0	4,000
Penna, Jr., Angel J.	69	12	10	7	434,437
Pennella, Rhea M.	101	2	4	7	74,237
Penner, Larry	112	10	17	17	100,979
Penney, Jim	210	47	32	36	612,014
Pennington, J. Benny	11	1	0	3	4,169
Pennino, Joe	57	4	10	6	81,008
Penrod, Steven C.	44	3	4	5	103,992
Peone, Alfred M.	3	1	0	0	1,525
Percival, Mimie D.	12	1	2	1	16,800
Perdue, Edward C.	239	35	29	33	396,275
Peres, Fred	2	0	0	1	1,533
Perez, Carlos A.	1	0	0	0	135
Perez, Dagoberto L.	93	7	10	2	98,590
Perez, Joel	1	0	0	0	0
Perez, Jose	10	1	1	3	14,012
Perez, Lorenzo C.	8	0	0	0	601
Perez, Mag	31	1	1	3	20,949
Perez, Nicolas	15	0	1	2	5,525
Perez, Pedro W.	29	1	2	2	9,300
Perez, Ramon	81	5	8	13	68,771
Perez, Ricardo	99	9	15	11	129,217
Perez, Jr., Francisco	2	0	0	0	0
Periban, Jorge	37	1	10	11	42,695
Perkins, Diane L.	9	0	0	2	4,602
Perkins, Larry	7	0	0	0	166
Perkins, Lorna M.	15	1	5	3	74,254
Perkins, Ray Edward	5	0	0	1	1,540
Perkins, Jr., Benjamin W.	174	27	26	27	1,137,210
Perren, Lymon A.	1	0	0	0	0
Perrotta, Joseph M.	9	1	1	0	12,830
Perry, Don R.	8	0	2	2	5,831
Perry, Lisa C.	10	0	2	0	4,418
Perry, Reva	3	0	2	0	1,200
Perry, Stephen J.	62	7	10	8	183,944
Perry, William W.	88	11	14	8	565,040
Perry, Jr., Lawrence E.	17	4	0	4	98,047
Perry, Sr., Lyle	15	7	6	0	13,279
Persaud, Atreo	19	0	0	2	13,879
Persaud, Eddie	1	0	0	1	2,400
Person, Kenneth A.	24	4	3	2	28,948
Pessin, Neil L.	24	5	8	2	186,851
Petalino, Joseph	221	40	30	20	693,095
Peters, Dennis D.	11	1	3	2	23,000
Peters, Gary	16	3	1	3	4,910
Peters, Reginald D.	8	1	0	1	8,347
Peters, Robert G.	62	5	8	6	51,927
Peters, Virginia	27	1	2	1	13,524
Petersen, Dawn L.	30	2	0	1	55,893
Peterson, Alan	6	0	1	1	1,020
Peterson, Annette	1	0	1	0	2,200
Peterson, Douglas R.	149	11	17	23	448,224
Peterson, H. Zip	25	0	2	2	4,537
Peterson, Linda	6	2	0	0	2,721
Peterson, Raymond F.	2	0	0	0	330
Peterson, Robert R.	54	3	3	10	36,292
Peterson, Sr., Michael J.	46	0	2	1	12,265
Petro, Michael P.	260	31	41	45	915,871
Petrowski, Joan	346	46	41	39	721,237
Petrozzo, Frank C.	28	7	2	5	92,040
Petten, David W.	5	0	0	0	183
Pettine, James Miller	4	0	0	1	9,024
Pettit, William A.	155	18	15	16	259,571

Trainer	Sts	1st	2d	3d	Purses
Pew, Karl	13	2	2	2	11,460
Pfeifer, Randy	65	6	6	10	60,725
Phalin, Doug	3	0	0	0	462
Phar, Theresa	25	1	4	0	5,163
Pharis, Ron	17	4	1	0	10,030
Phelan, Bruce F.	66	20	12	8	361,194
Phelps, George	10	1	1	0	4,908
Phelps, Jr., Charles W.	103	7	11	11	228,649
Phelps, Sr., Charles W.	32	3	2	3	45,131
Phillips, Arlene	14	1	3	1	9,942
Phillips, Christine Sonya	6	0	1	0	730
Phillips, John L.	64	4	2	4	39,818
Philpott, Stephen	31	2	3	1	63,546
Phipps, Micky	2	0	0	0	95
Piantes, John	2	0	0	0	96
Picariello, Joseph	23	5	4	4	164,977
Piccioni, Gerard	6	0	0	0	2,840
Piches, John G.	5	0	0	0	1,175
Pichette, Raymond A.	2	0	0	0	584
Pickard, Jim	38	2	6	1	23,550
Pickard, Robert J.	38	2	2	7	26,623
Pickerrell, William D.	23	3	2	0	11,879
Pickett, Crystal G.	11	1	3	1	12,880
Picou, James E.	50	3	5	3	202,175
Pierce, Clayton	30	6	5	4	98,510
Pierce, Malcolm	182	23	28	23	1,273,698
Pierce, Michael Lee	27	4	7	7	24,566
Pierce, Oliver D.	1	0	0	0	0
Pierce, Raymond A.	38	0	0	1	4,208
Pierce, Robert G.	34	4	3	4	10,735
Pierce, Thomas W.	24	1	3	2	15,068
Pierce, Vickie	2	0	0	1	708
Pierce, Jr., Joseph H.	211	29	23	25	891,295
Pigeau, Christal	20	0	4	6	6,724
Pigeau, Nellie Opal	33	2	4	5	11,921
Pike, Alexis	4	0	0	0	351
Pike, Stewart	7	0	0	0	226
Piker, Robert E.	28	0	2	2	4,496
Pilmer, Ted G.	5	0	2	2	21,440
Pilon, Amanda	20	3	0	4	6,685
Pilon, Hubert	87	20	19	11	88,486
Pilotti, Angela	1	0	0	0	0
Pilotti, Larry	189	18	24	25	353,758
Pilotto, Linda	11	1	0	0	10,799
Pimental, Alfred J.	19	4	0	5	58,760
Pimental, John I.	32	0	1	0	13,514
Pinchin, Jose	149	20	20	24	457,201
Pincins, Robert J.	57	6	8	9	143,539
Pincione, Vito	95	5	13	5	69,470
Pino, Michael V.	458	108	85	72	1,992,141
Pinzon, Maria E.	163	17	26	16	239,129
Pion, Raymond	134	14	13	23	187,869
Pion, Robert A.	54	5	4	6	195,034
Pish, Danny	623	121	99	80	1,594,907
Pitnick, Brian J.	62	13	5	7	147,933
Pitrone, Christopher	16	0	3	2	23,061
Pittman, Donald M.	67	3	2	3	28,194
Pittman, Jodie Mack	30	1	0	2	12,033
Pitts, Daniel C.	54	5	13	6	46,108
Pitzer, Floyd D.	51	10	7	5	109,385
Pitzer, Jeffrey W.	40	2	5	3	38,306
Pixley, Carlis	3	0	0	0	730
Pizarro, Donna L.	18	2	2	1	39,940
Pizzurro, Antonio N.	179	2	7	13	85,652
Pizzurro, Jessica L.	21	2	1	0	32,212
Pizzurro, Peter	13	0	0	0	1,583
Plaisance, Doug	40	5	3	4	37,615
Plato, Sandy J.	30	1	1	2	9,960
Platts, Brad	6	0	1	1	2,870
Plaza, Alberto	48	1	3	4	35,940
Plaza, Mario	5	0	1	1	6,760
Pleasant, James R.	4	1	0	0	4,275
Pledge, Martha M.	4	0	0	0	132
Pledge, Robert M.	23	4	4	2	7,289
Plesa, Jr., Edward	397	56	60	51	1,830,409
Plesa, Sr., Edward	10	0	2	5	14,550
Pletcher, Todd A.	948	240	154	125	17,511,923
Pleterski, Don	51	3	2	7	154,648
Plever, Jr., Oden D.	38	3	2	4	35,885
Plummer, Bobby Lee	1	0	0	0	320
Plunkett, Quince	7	0	0	1	1,510
Poalucci, Frank J.	11	0	1	2	10,620
Podrapovic, Dragan	12	2	2	3	11,065
Poe, Albert O.	5	0	0	1	3,188
Poe, John	4	0	1	1	6,140
Pogue, William R.	103	11	16	13	142,117
Pointer, Norman R.	287	45	40	37	1,118,012
Poitra, Sylvester	3	0	0	0	70
Poitras, Dennis	14	1	3	2	4,150
Pojar, Pat G.	20	0	2	2	3,696
Pojar, Tom D.	7	0	0	0	743
Polachek, Janet	51	2	2	5	45,726
Polanco, Marcelo	245	26	26	26	1,810,533
Polese, Ralph	30	0	0	0	12,974
Polichena, Anthony J.	153	8	15	18	168,128
Polichena, Russell	84	1	3	2	27,996
Polillio, Frank	8	0	0	4	7,905
Politano, Ralph J.	87	13	11	9	121,877
Polito, Nancy	70	4	10	7	36,450
Poliziani, Daniel J.	103	16	10	6	120,212
Pollara, Frank L.	85	7	8	13	126,370
Pollard, Stephen N.	8	0	0	0	1,140
Pollari, Lark	1	0	0	0	75
Pollock, Bruce M.	35	3	3	5	135,161
Pollok, Leroy J.	1	0	0	0	0
Polsinelli, Dominic J.	88	10	9	14	208,545
Polsinello, Anthony F.	6	0	0	0	1,757
Poluch, Jr., Patrick J.	17	3	3	1	62,350
Pompay, Teresa M.	217	22	23	35	702,687
Ponte, Heather	6	1	0	0	4,850
Ponthieux, Gary	11	0	0	0	336
Poole, Jami C.	275	50	21	36	553,479
Poole, Jeffrey A.	5	0	0	0	389
Poole, Jr., Jack G.	20	1	2	1	10,958
Poole, Sr., Jack G.	55	8	6	2	128,095
Poore, Gene W.	12	0	2	2	13,290
Pope, Stuart	15	3	2	1	5,406
Pope, Sr., Robert H.	5	0	1	1	2,056
Poper, Donald E.	55	1	6	9	69,920
Popp, Dana	233	21	25	30	187,339
Portell, Neal	2	0	0	0	80
Porter, Brandon	29	4	6	2	10,031
Porter, Bryan	61	11	14	4	142,353
Porter, John E.	19	3	1	2	9,807
Porter, Ron	17	2	5	5	81,825
Porter, Steve G.	1	0	0	1	200
Posada, Laura	277	28	27	28	443,137
Poteet, Don R.	56	3	4	3	20,428
Potter, Douglas G.	115	15	12	12	255,595
Potts, Carl	19	1	0	1	7,398
Potts, Wayne	31	4	4	1	52,563
Potts, Jr., Ron G.	86	11	6	10	209,202
Potts, Sr., Ron H.	6	1	0	0	3,000
Poulos, Dee	185	18	28	21	409,431
Poulos, Luke E.	43	3	5	10	48,541
Powell, Billy H.	1	0	0	0	155
Powell, Claude A.	14	0	1	1	1,909
Powell, Dick	33	0	5	2	16,720
Powell, Gina	20	1	3	2	47,991
Powell, Joy A.	3	0	0	0	320
Powell, Leonard	10	0	1	1	67,100
Powell, Ron	255	23	22	36	211,356
Powell, Scot	1	0	0	0	0
Power, James N.	67	6	6	9	71,509
Powers, James M.	18	0	1	3	6,706
Powers, Paul E.	84	8	9	9	74,763
Powers, Paul J.	31	3	1	1	26,566
Powers, Robin	71	2	6	7	53,406
Poxon, Alfred J.	6	0	0	1	620
Poxon, Jr., Ernest	65	3	4	9	34,488
Poyadou, Bruce E.	38	1	2	6	20,865
Pozzo, Jack	14	0	2	0	8,809
Pozzobon, Vicki	7	4	0	2	7,250
Pradenas, Sergio H.	3	0	0	0	220

Trainer	Sts	1st	2d	3d	Purses
Prado, Jorge	53	2	5	3	34,896
Prainito, Frank	148	8	19	19	100,700
Prather, Jr., John Henry	20	1	0	5	15,965
Pratt, Everett	7	0	1	2	3,825
Pratt, James M.	22	1	2	1	12,945
Pratt, Laurie	28	1	2	1	8,713
Preciado, Guadalupe	602	118	102	88	2,464,075
Preciado, Ramon	274	53	43	33	816,865
Predium, Raymond	6	0	0	0	608
Preger, Mitchell C.	3	0	0	0	1,320
Pregman, Jr., John S.	100	7	5	14	413,463
Prejean, Norris	22	1	2	4	23,511
Prejean, Raymond	35	3	7	4	38,853
Premus, Ed	2	0	0	0	388
Prendergast, Gene D.	4	0	0	0	303
Prescott, Calcy Lee	1	0	0	1	3,100
Prescott, Calvin	108	8	12	8	112,067
Presswood, Phyllis L.	23	1	2	1	8,213
Preston, Dwight	1	0	0	0	550
Preston, Patrick K.	35	3	5	2	19,205
Preston, Randy L.	15	2	2	3	31,833
Preston, Stephanie	1	0	0	0	0
Pretty Weasel, Leon S.	18	1	2	2	3,183
Price, Andro Lee	1	0	0	0	80
Price, Angela	17	2	3	4	57,413
Price, Barry R.	21	2	2	4	10,299
Price, Faith A.	1	0	0	0	0
Price, Ira	10	2	1	1	3,666
Price, Kathleen A.	5	0	0	1	4,659
Price, Paul	35	0	4	3	13,225
Price, Twilla K	4	0	1	0	700
Price, Victor	11	0	1	1	2,941
Price, Jr., Harry W.	32	0	1	3	11,840
Primrose, Valerie	11	1	0	0	6,947
Pringle, Edmund	18	1	0	1	35,996
Pringle, Ned Wilkerson	31	1	5	3	13,540
Pritchard, Virgil C.	31	2	1	7	13,931
Procino, Gerald	143	16	17	22	367,472
Proctor, Thomas F.	116	24	20	14	738,382
Proehl, Arnie	1	0	0	0	120
Progno, Christopher	4	0	0	0	3,024
Progno, John	383	38	47	55	684,410
Progno, Michael I.	64	2	2	3	30,723
Proteau, Gail A.	25	0	0	1	7,587
Provost, Adrienne Leigh	1	0	0	0	150
Pruce, Ellis Y.	28	0	2	3	11,790
Pruett, Paul G.	54	4	6	3	55,147
Pruitt, Jody	110	15	22	21	139,065
Pruitt, Lise	49	10	3	4	72,449
Pruitt, Peggy E.	133	8	18	23	188,199
Pryor, Sheri B.	7	1	3	1	2,320
Pryor, Thomas J.	47	8	10	3	117,685
Puckett, Andrea L.	12	1	0	1	8,210
Puckett, Dwight E.	23	2	4	4	45,405
Puckett, Earl J.	6	0	0	0	431
Puckett, Mary	2	1	1	0	2,000
Puertas, Jerry F.	32	1	3	3	23,684
Puett, Jr., Lloyd J.	48	2	4	7	25,266
Pugh, David	57	0	4	0	23,425
Pugh, Ellis	6	4	0	1	8,237
Pugh, Penelope	8	0	0	0	1,004
Pugh, Peter D.	28	0	1	2	36,485
Puhich, Michael	105	12	15	13	403,263
Puhl, Kim A.	51	8	5	10	101,420
Puhl, Ronald W.	28	0	0	4	17,629
Pujol, Jean B.	28	3	5	2	50,574
Pullam, Daron	56	2	9	7	38,337
Pulliam, Curtis L.	28	0	3	3	14,047
Pullins, Harold	39	2	0	1	18,426
Purdy, Simon	29	2	8	2	52,815
Purdy, William R.	1	0	0	0	0
Putzier, Marvin	7	1	0	0	1,449
Puype, Mike	62	15	9	6	453,241
Quaid, Eddie	1	0	0	0	0
Qualls, Bill	1	0	0	0	120
Quaranta, Ralph S.	123	17	16	9	159,398
Quaranta, Samuel R.	40	4	6	4	61,445
Query, Marysue	19	2	0	0	24,200
Quesnelle, Cindy	30	2	3	4	35,683
Quick, Patrick J.	47	1	4	2	60,462
Quiles, John N.	39	1	2	1	65,099
Quiles, Victor	2	0	0	0	800
Quinn, Alonzo	20	1	1	2	7,922
Quinn, Jerry	8	0	4	1	15,195
Quinn, Steve	2	0	1	0	1,296
Quintana, Richard A.	1	0	0	0	0
Quintanilla, Victor	7	3	0	3	71,600
Quintanilla, Jr., Armando	33	6	5	3	74,178
Quintanilla, Sr., Armando	17	4	1	0	49,401
Quintero, Felipe A.	10	1	0	1	4,555
Quiroga, Alex	12	2	1	0	2,595
Quiroga, Jose E.	24	0	0	3	16,140
Racanelli, Mark Joseph	59	2	4	3	38,962
Racca, Curley	24	3	4	1	33,898
Radcliff, Jr., Donald L.	74	4	6	10	75,760
Radford, Kathryn l	2	1	0	0	3,720
Radis, Judy	3	1	0	0	8,820
Radosevich, Jake S.	454	71	51	67	427,159
Radosevich, Jeffrey A.	535	98	90	61	1,020,173
Radosevich, Joseph L.	101	7	17	6	135,372
Radosevich, Shelly R.	18	2	4	4	22,068
Radul, Jodie	5	1	0	0	3,600
Radulski, Susan	39	1	5	5	38,854
Rafaeli, Uri	3	0	0	0	775
Ragain, Russell B.	2	0	0	0	100
Ragland, Jr., Roy J.	48	3	6	4	31,447
Rahaim, Michael J.	5	0	0	0	1,216
Raia II, Francis	5	0	0	0	282
Rainwater, Owen L.	12	0	1	2	6,993
Rak, Kevin	6	1	3	0	9,070
Rakers, Steffanie	75	7	12	13	70,920
Raley, Jeffrey Scott	23	6	3	0	36,424
Raley, R. Scott	2	0	0	0	210
Ralph, Darcy	6	1	0	0	2,522
Rambally, Arnold	3	0	0	0	260
Ramirez, Alfonso R.	3	0	0	0	153
Ramirez, Catherine Kenney	5	0	0	0	0
Ramirez, Eduardo	1	0	0	0	0
Ramirez, Esteban	2	1	1	0	6,880
Ramirez, Frank Raul	2	0	0	1	2,140
Ramirez, Jose F.	2	0	0	0	144
Ramirez, Ricardo	3	0	1	0	2,865
Ramirez, Richard	30	1	3	3	3,649
Ramirez, Jr., Rudy R.	2	1	1	0	33,520
Ramos, Faustino F.	184	19	19	18	445,478
Ramos, Jose R.	73	13	14	10	131,995
Ramos, Victor	22	3	4	5	172,699
Rampadarat, Roopishwar	74	3	4	8	91,539
Rampellini, Ralph	4	0	0	0	318
Ramsey, Daryl	2	0	0	0	0
Randall, Casey	8	1	0	2	16,565
Randall, David A.	6	1	0	1	33,840
Randall, Noel	44	6	3	7	233,201
Randazzo, Teddy C.	185	18	14	27	122,424
Randazzo, Jr., Frank C.	279	42	39	34	282,512
Randle, Robert K.	37	0	2	1	12,020
Randolph, Amy	84	8	9	9	108,781
Randolph, Frank T	35	1	5	4	12,214
Ranford, Kathryn	41	2	4	4	154,713
Rankin, Doreen	37	0	2	1	7,191
Ransibrahmanakul, Vachari	43	8	6	4	56,254
Ranwick, Jr., Bobby	42	2	4	7	27,745
Rao, Larry	6	0	0	1	1,355
Raper, Ron	25	3	4	2	11,436
Raposa, Joseph	9	1	1	1	13,060
Rappaport, Mitchell	17	0	0	0	6,485
Rarick, Linda	9	2	1	0	2,774
Rarick, Lynn	9	1	2	0	11,584
Rarick, Todd A.	91	9	11	13	65,053
Rasmussen, S. Candy	6	1	2	1	25,860
Rasmussen, Stig T.	1	0	0	0	0
Raszewski, Joseph R.	52	5	2	9	54,637
Ratcliffe, William H.	4	0	1	1	5,099
Rathman, Elisha	131	7	17	18	91,146
Rathman, Michael L.	14	1	1	2	18,896
Ratliff, Curtis	3	0	1	0	1,012

Trainer	Sts	1st	2d	3d	Purses
Ratliff, Marlene C.	10	0	0	1	3,078
Rauf, Naseem	33	0	0	1	3,635
Raver, Nick	19	0	0	0	1,292
Raver, Ron	16	2	0	2	8,932
Rawlins, Jerry	39	5	3	2	37,669
Rawson, Fred	44	2	3	4	41,644
Rawson, Ryan	34	3	2	7	53,985
Ray, Chrissy	22	2	3	4	37,392
Ray, Dale V.	52	7	8	3	55,208
Ray, Jimmy L.	90	8	5	5	44,943
Rayburn, Greg	68	18	5	9	196,185
Raymond, Lyn L.	13	1	1	0	8,990
Raymond, Robert A.	374	47	39	36	419,724
Razo, Eusebio	112	14	20	12	217,420
Rea, Michael	61	6	5	9	58,346
Reading, John F.	140	21	17	20	147,019
Reagan, Jeffrey W.	5	1	0	0	9,010
Reagan, Norman G.	35	0	0	6	6,701
Real Bird, Mark	10	1	4	1	3,993
Reamy, Jack	1	0	0	0	50
Reavis, Michael L.	400	76	52	53	1,281,314
Reck, Christopher R.	11	0	0	0	4,010
Redden, James L.	8	0	0	0	635
Redding, Robin L.	150	13	20	14	184,520
Rednour, Jr., John	26	3	3	2	24,136
Reece, Joyce	13	1	0	1	7,508
Reed, Candace	6	0	1	1	4,575
Reed, Cynthia L.	12	0	0	0	2,771
Reed, Delores J.	10	2	1	3	3,920
Reed, Eric R.	159	37	30	20	627,664
Reed, Gene A.	13	2	1	1	23,469
Reed, Larry R.	8	0	0	1	1,526
Reed, Philip E.	36	1	1	6	9,296
Reed, Ralph E.	2	0	0	0	0
Reed, Tom	9	2	1	2	6,826
Reed, William	2	0	0	0	0
Reeder, Donald S.	484	80	76	66	1,233,717
Reeder, Lee R.	4	0	0	0	608
Reeder, Thomas C.	12	0	1	0	4,286
Reedy, Elizabeth M.	23	1	2	4	10,709
Reedy, Vincent W.	43	8	4	3	84,192
Reedy, III, Chester E.	11	1	1	1	5,953
Reese, Cynthia G.	147	31	37	17	680,202
Reese, Darlene E.	35	2	3	3	30,747
Reese, Walter C.	5	1	1	1	12,690
Reese, Wayne	2	0	0	0	74
Reese, Jr., Leonard	5	1	0	0	3,000
Reeves, Lloyd F.	10	0	0	0	606
Reffner, Tara B.	23	0	0	4	9,294
Regalbuto, Dolores M.	5	0	0	0	2,140
Regalbuto, Jr., Anthony R.	34	2	2	2	58,695
Regan, Maurice	2	0	0	0	0
Regan, Timothy	35	2	2	4	209,180
Regen, Patricia S.	7	0	0	1	3,414
Register, Alison	42	9	2	6	247,813
Reid, David R.	34	1	5	4	22,332
Reid, George W.	6	0	1	0	4,050
Reid, Ruth Ann	2	1	0	1	2,800
Reid, Sally M.	15	6	4	3	9,849
Reid, Sylvia	43	5	9	7	78,107
Reid, Jr., Robert E.	56	2	2	4	76,124
Reidhead, B. Odell	53	10	3	8	28,706
Reiff, Eugene	13	0	0	0	3,156
Reightler, Sr., Jeffery C.	64	0	2	7	31,578
Reihart, Gary D.	26	2	4	4	29,553
Reinacher, Jr., Robert J.	60	9	4	6	279,364
Reinholtz, Theodore	20	1	2	1	19,374
Reinstedler, Anthony L.	201	31	27	22	1,435,674
Reiste, Tim F.	8	0	0	0	932
Reller, Michelle	2	0	0	0	240
Remlinger, Katherine	26	0	0	2	3,270
Renfro, Ben A.	4	0	1	0	2,912
Renfroe, Lillian	23	3	1	3	13,544
Rengstorf, Tony	75	5	8	7	84,224
Renn, Carol	23	4	1	4	40,333
Rennekamp, Nick J.	47	6	4	5	89,634
Rennie, Richard	13	0	0	3	1,456
Retamoza, Glenda J.	5	0	0	0	250
Retamoza, Jr, Ernest P.	1	0	0	0	135
Retamoza, Sr., Ernest P.	86	6	4	9	75,688
Rettele, Richard R.	312	55	61	49	677,380
Retzel, Richard F.	2	0	0	0	2,170
Reveglia, Brenda	6	1	0	1	11,876
Revell, James E.	3	0	0	0	450
Reviriego, Juan	32	2	7	3	66,520
Reyes, III, Aurelio	4	0	0	0	200
Reyes-Frisby, Pedro	1	0	0	0	36
Reynolds, Joan A.	47	5	8	7	82,630
Reynolds, Larry E.	8	0	0	1	1,680
Reynolds, Patrick L.	186	25	29	29	1,078,403
Reynolds, Ryan	80	8	4	10	106,117
Rheinford, Mark	26	4	2	5	54,231
Rhodes, Les	16	0	1	0	1,393
Rhodes, Willys W.	88	5	6	12	77,860
Rhone, Bernell B.	413	52	59	45	658,802
Ribaudo, Robert	87	10	10	12	444,246
Riccardi, John	8	1	1	1	11,364
Ricciardi, Archie	68	7	3	8	63,596
Rice, Anthony	19	0	4	0	18,179
Rice, Carol A.	53	1	8	1	47,982
Rice, Craig	81	7	10	13	61,901
Rice, Don R.	231	25	19	31	376,133
Rice, Gregory A.	5	0	0	0	761
Rice, Howard	33	8	4	4	93,564
Rice, Jeffrey B.	3	0	0	0	0
Rice, Larry G.	1	0	0	0	0
Rice, Linda	288	38	40	27	1,389,239
Rice, Shawn	4	0	1	1	5,579
Rich, Eduardo L.	40	3	3	10	45,465
Richard, Earnest	20	1	3	1	13,365
Richard, John	5	0	0	0	1,390
Richard, Russell C.	43	3	3	4	43,641
Richard, Terry L.	8	1	0	0	2,279
Richards, Corale A.	319	39	39	43	780,142
Richards, Jerry Lee	15	0	0	2	6,752
Richards, Lorne	80	20	14	10	949,947
Richards, Rodney C.	1	0	0	0	0
Richards, Rodney T.	2	0	0	0	185
Richards, Stanley	4	0	0	0	331
Richardson, Deborah D.	63	10	2	10	142,962
Richardson, Donald P.	15	1	1	3	67,640
Richardson, Susan C.	1	0	0	0	80
Richardson, Susan G.	6	0	0	0	885
Richardson, Tim	8	2	1	0	8,185
Richardson, Toni	16	1	1	1	2,053
Richey, Tony J.	13	1	4	0	28,990
Richmond, Linda L.	5	0	0	1	902
Richter, Stephanie	25	1	1	3	16,181
Rickly, Stephanie	7	1	0	1	7,492
Riddle, Jackie E.	25	5	2	5	152,395
Riddle, James E.	29	0	3	2	17,662
Ridgeway, Elvy	5	0	0	1	984
Riecken, Bruce L.	102	8	11	12	96,810
Riecken, Herb	160	24	20	27	229,459
Riecken, Keith	19	0	2	3	5,513
Riegler, Patricia	50	7	5	9	97,633
Riesenbeck, Robin	4	1	0	0	5,683
Rieser, Raymond	56	4	11	4	24,419
Rife, Philip	17	0	2	0	11,428
Riffle, Ronald J.	34	1	4	1	22,568
Rigattieri, John	427	122	67	53	1,412,568
Rigby, Terrence	45	3	7	7	140,091
Rigdon, Paul R.	6	0	0	1	1,272
Riggleman, Jr., Ray	86	7	13	9	217,110
Riggs, Ronnie L.	33	0	3	5	8,139
Riggs, Jr., Clifford A.	11	1	2	3	11,841
Rigsbee, David W.	1	0	0	1	1,000
Rijos, Julio	2	0	0	0	260
Riley, Barbara	67	3	9	10	55,078
Riley, Jim	2	0	0	0	2,000
Riley, June	2	0	0	0	125
Riley, Marcie	36	3	2	6	12,255
Rindahl, James Eric	11	1	0	2	1,731
Rindahl, Patricia	2	0	0	0	332

Trainer	Sts	1st	2d	3d	Purses
Rinearson, Christina	2	0	0	0	552
Ring, Robert D.	21	4	2	3	17,999
Ringhoff, Robert	113	14	13	11	184,639
Rini, Anthony F.	123	10	14	16	112,897
Rini, Julie A.	2	0	0	0	126
Rippee, Tommy Gene	22	0	2	1	3,810
Rising, Robert E.	43	3	5	7	30,098
Rissi, Luiz	109	8	23	11	82,259
Ritchey, Timothy F.	414	86	87	55	2,991,693
Ritchie, Robert G.	3	0	0	1	931
Ritchie, Wanda	54	4	6	2	24,847
Ritschard, Troy	33	0	1	0	6,933
Ritter, Jack	30	1	3	3	8,838
Ritter, Randy	1	0	0	0	0
Ritvo, Kathy P.	65	9	5	12	132,430
Ritvo, Timothy	486	46	51	66	1,165,953
Ritz-Moffett, Lori	8	1	0	1	12,480
Rivelli, Larry	301	46	53	38	854,593
Rivera, Carlos M.	23	6	3	5	33,020
Rivera, Clemente	6	1	2	1	2,244
Rivera, Gilberto R.	218	9	22	19	149,607
Rivera, Gregorio P.	44	5	7	6	24,826
Rivera, Gregorio Q.	36	1	0	5	5,546
Rivera, Juan A.	1	0	0	0	0
Rivera, Juan R.	34	3	6	4	42,474
Rivera, Miguel A.	52	0	5	4	32,634
Rivera, Osvaldo	87	13	7	8	80,212
Rivera, Robert A.	18	0	0	1	2,551
Rivera, Tirso	35	3	6	8	55,994
Rivers, Woodrow V.	1	0	0	0	0
Riviere, Ray	13	0	0	0	0
Riviezzo, Ralph R.	229	19	23	22	225,500
Rizer, Eric A.	1	0	0	0	0
Rizer-Peterson, Keli J.	22	1	3	2	35,470
Rizo, J. Antonio	58	5	1	2	30,672
Rizo, Juan P.	39	2	5	4	86,680
Rizzo, Ella	3	0	2	0	8,815
Roadcap, Jerry E.	55	12	14	4	159,606
Roarty, Jim	15	0	0	1	2,198
Robb, John J.	386	66	63	38	1,290,425
Robb, Lawrence M	7	0	0	0	1,115
Robbins, Carlton	29	3	4	2	165,128
Robbins, Charles R.	55	7	11	9	141,206
Robbins, Jay M.	70	8	14	10	349,610
Robbins, Jerry	16	2	1	0	12,950
Robbins, Mark A.	4	0	0	0	0
Robbins, Richard	8	1	2	0	21,598
Roberson, Denis W.	30	5	3	2	67,550
Roberson, Don	309	42	36	44	570,702
Roberson, Kevin K.	12	1	0	0	6,138
Robert, Maryanne	55	7	5	7	57,926
Roberts, Brian M.	147	25	23	17	179,317
Roberts, Craig	92	12	4	14	104,785
Roberts, Garry	134	7	14	17	27,515
Roberts, Lanny	1	0	0	0	41
Roberts, Leon	30	2	1	1	10,162
Roberts, Merrill C.	40	2	2	4	34,075
Roberts, Robert W.	97	5	13	17	45,763
Roberts, Roy	3	0	0	0	0
Roberts, Rusty	2	0	0	1	1,785
Roberts, Scott Lynn	3	0	0	0	270
Roberts, Sharon	38	1	2	2	19,315
Roberts, Stanley W.	561	74	85	50	894,578
Roberts, Stephanie	2	0	0	0	0
Roberts, T. Mark	23	4	2	0	34,285
Roberts, Terry S.	22	2	2	4	11,026
Roberts, Tom C.	34	8	4	7	55,009
Roberts, Wilbert	1	0	0	0	233
Roberts, Jr., J. Doyal	4	1	0	1	7,137
Roberts, Jr., Wilfred	17	0	0	0	2,075
Roberts, Sr., Kenneth L.	11	2	3	4	26,690
Robertson, Craig W.	171	57	26	26	360,050
Robertson, David W.	64	6	9	10	85,986
Robertson, Elizabeth L.	2	0	1	0	11,700
Robertson, Hugh H.	469	100	82	71	2,133,342
Robertson, Jack	94	17	15	17	203,116
Robertson, James	20	4	6	2	24,659
Robertson, Jerri R.	121	14	14	19	134,132
Robertson, Maclean	16	3	0	2	53,335
Robertson, Nancy Lynn	10	1	3	2	20,606
Robertson, Robert M.	53	7	5	5	70,563
Robertson, William G.	2	0	0	1	904
Robideaux, Jr., Larry	295	51	38	40	1,101,264
Robillard, Joshua	190	12	17	22	182,616
Robin, Manuel	41	6	2	6	76,592
Robinson, Catherine H.	106	13	12	18	194,510
Robinson, Gayle M.	25	0	1	3	10,376
Robinson, Gerald E.	48	6	10	2	15,637
Robinson, Hershel	20	1	1	0	8,052
Robinson, Kelly	9	2	0	1	45,951
Robinson, Michael R.	2	0	0	0	195
Robinson, Owen L.	2	0	0	0	185
Robinson, Rick K.	1	0	0	0	0
Robinson, Ronnie	1	0	0	0	0
Robles, Leonso	9	0	1	3	3,172
Robson, Christopher B.	55	8	5	8	79,797
Rocco, Annie M.	23	0	3	3	7,943
Rocha, Pedro	11	0	1	2	4,093
Roche, Cathy E.	2	0	0	0	0
Rodak, Geraldine	183	12	9	17	72,944
Roden, Ralph	10	0	0	0	1,354
Rodgers, Cindy	48	13	5	6	49,999
Rodgers, Paula	23	3	1	1	10,652
Rodriguez, Armando	23	4	2	2	14,276
Rodriguez, Franklin	204	26	33	20	291,185
Rodriguez, John M.	195	22	32	27	305,867
Rodriguez, Mario R.	151	11	12	18	80,117
Rodriguez, Rudy G.	11	1	1	3	2,116
Rodriguez, Santiago C.	132	19	15	14	139,299
Rodriguez, Jr., Alcides C.	1	0	0	0	0
Roe, Donald	1	0	0	0	0
Roe, Larry	98	5	8	13	55,168
Roe, Loraine M.	8	0	0	0	925
Roe, Robert W.	92	9	10	13	52,341
Roesener, Thomas E.	3	0	0	0	0
Roessner, Robert E	3	0	0	0	275
Rofe, Jean L.	89	6	6	7	115,995
Roge, Sr., Edgar C.	4	0	0	0	600
Rogers, Allen E.	42	2	3	2	32,222
Rogers, Arlin R.	22	1	2	0	5,756
Rogers, Brittany	11	2	2	0	4,693
Rogers, Christopher	31	3	0	4	9,981
Rogers, Elizabeth M.	55	3	2	5	48,755
Rogers, Gary	149	8	10	20	90,952
Rogers, Heather	6	2	0	1	11,645
Rogers, J. Michael	150	22	19	15	437,216
Rogers, Jeff	5	0	0	1	703
Rogers, Maurice S.	14	0	0	0	2,691
Rogers, Patricia	14	2	2	1	26,680
Rogers, Ronald W.	21	0	2	5	13,983
Rogers, Jr., Ernest	17	3	2	4	40,923
Rohman, Robert	60	8	8	15	146,365
Rohner, James	144	14	24	12	257,577
Rohnke, Gustave C.	36	1	2	0	4,552
Rojas, Murray L.	67	8	5	10	60,992
Rojero, Luis C.	4	0	0	0	1,661
Rolffs, Marianne L.	9	0	1	1	2,324
Rolffs, Mikhael	64	7	12	7	58,200
Rolle, Elliston C.	26	1	3	4	52,350
Roller, Jerry	20	1	2	0	7,160
Rollheiser, Don	3	0	0	0	0
Rollins, Bradley L.	5	1	0	3	11,900
Rollins, Lyman H.	86	19	16	18	179,426
Rolon, Ezequiel M.	62	9	10	11	124,720
Romano, Richard J.	6	1	1	1	4,456
Romano, Sara	3	0	0	0	800
Romans, Dale L.	580	109	87	87	7,081,653
Rombis, Debra E.	216	24	25	19	435,499
Romeka, Steven	98	9	15	18	198,426
Romero, Adalberto G.	16	4	0	1	6,061
Romero, Dub D.	6	1	1	0	4,635
Romero, Edward L.	3	0	0	0	0
Romero, Gerald J.	136	17	22	20	365,589
Romero, Harold Lee	9	1	1	0	15,895
Romero, Jorge E.	3	0	0	0	4,266
Romero, Joseph M.	60	10	6	7	108,050

Trainer	Sts	1st	2d	3d	Purses
Romero, Lloyd J.	96	11	13	7	211,756
Romero, Markel D.	43	2	3	4	44,902
Romero, Russell L.	18	2	1	2	22,130
Romero, Terry M.	255	25	16	22	287,557
Romero, Sr., John J.	41	3	6	4	63,085
Romero, Sr., Lynn J.	16	0	2	2	10,672
Romine, Jr., Robert C.	43	2	7	4	43,987
Romo, Jr., Juan Jose	6	0	2	1	3,575
Roncone, Peter	36	2	5	3	21,844
Ronen, Assaf	3	0	0	0	3,417
Ronquillo, Ramon	45	4	7	6	33,563
Ronquillo, Roy V.	35	3	1	6	10,630
Roohms, Kathy	7	0	2	3	3,387
Rooney, Ronald G.	23	5	0	3	62,501
Root, Ben	283	39	40	46	223,518
Root, Heidi	25	1	2	3	17,405
Root, Richard R.	145	14	15	16	255,711
Root, Tina Marie	48	3	5	1	27,465
Ropar, Theresa	7	0	0	2	1,453
Ropp, Donald	71	9	6	6	53,654
Rorie, Joe D.	4	0	0	0	0
Rosado, Juan R.	92	2	6	4	33,862
Rosado, Vicki	97	3	3	8	67,773
Rosales, Richard	22	2	2	4	37,995
Rosas-Canessa, Walter	146	9	7	16	177,849
Rose, Barry R.	260	23	23	27	558,680
Rose, David J.	272	34	28	27	543,803
Rose, Donald E.	23	1	0	1	6,467
Rose, Ed	5	0	0	0	108
Rose, Michael	10	2	1	0	13,670
Rose, Ralph T.	11	1	0	1	6,484
Rosendohl, Jr., Kenneth	46	5	0	4	30,011
Rosenthal, Henry J.	26	0	2	0	5,025
Rosenwasser, Laurie	42	0	0	1	1,959
Roset, Olaf	8	0	2	1	22,788
Rosier, Charlie	57	4	2	9	39,519
Rosier, Timothy	12	1	0	1	18,160
Ross, Brian	52	8	6	5	121,090
Ross, James R.	19	5	3	5	5,611
Ross, Jill	27	1	1	1	9,821
Ross, John A.	141	19	16	15	747,396
Ross, Larry D.	75	9	9	8	650,626
Ross, Pam L.	4	1	0	0	6,920
Ross, Sharon	228	46	35	36	429,765
Ross, Wade	7	2	2	1	3,065
Rossi, Albino A.	27	6	1	4	99,435
Rottweiler, Glen P.	34	2	3	2	19,419
Roubion, Steve	30	0	0	1	2,988
Rouck, Martin L.	45	9	5	3	161,118
Rougeau, Abrin	29	2	3	3	43,407
Rouget, Jean-Claude	2	1	0	0	90,000
Roughton, Robert L.	38	11	4	1	68,867
Rounseville, Frenda D.	38	5	3	2	70,591
Rountree, Cathy	49	9	9	4	104,697
Rouse, Randolph D.	10	1	1	0	15,490
Roush, Chuck	52	7	2	2	31,727
Roussel, Michael	2	0	0	0	0
Rowan, Steve E.	95	8	4	13	80,632
Rowda, Aldo G.	75	6	10	8	46,443
Rowe, Donn A.	98	24	15	12	285,188
Rowe, Edward E.	14	0	1	0	4,770
Rowe, John I.	10	1	0	0	3,630
Rowe, Sarah L.	35	1	2	6	22,294
Rowland, Paul A.	14	3	4	0	134,888
Rowland, Tamela M.	55	3	7	4	32,495
Rowntree, Gil H.	46	2	5	4	202,594
Roybal, Gary L.	3	0	0	0	742
Royster, Jr., Archie	5	0	0	0	348
Royston, Donald R.	38	0	2	2	9,064
Rozanski, Cathleen	8	0	1	0	2,485
Rozell, Ron	8	1	0	0	10,200
Rubchinuk, Robert	66	5	5	7	46,987
Ruberto, Jr., Louis V.	76	24	19	6	339,025
Rubin, Donald	16	1	0	0	11,633
Rucker, Patsy	5	0	1	0	1,823
Rudibaugh, Larry	4	0	0	0	336
Rudibaugh, Terry	64	6	2	3	53,326
Rudis, Charles A.	37	2	5	5	20,069
Rudolph, Sherry K.	18	2	0	1	23,499
Ruffu, Gail E.	1	0	0	0	400
Rugar, Joseph	2	0	0	0	105
Ruggiero, Jr., Phillip A.	1	0	0	0	460
Ruiz, Jr., Rudy G.	14	0	0	1	1,661
Rumsey, Jack	32	2	3	3	17,423
Runco, Jeff C.	599	104	96	65	1,899,518
Runyon, David P.	28	5	5	6	24,083
Rupert, John C.	240	34	32	36	286,448
Ruppelius, Lisa	1	0	0	0	124
Rush, Bobbi Anne	7	0	0	0	1,660
Rushton, Stacey	16	3	1	0	9,955
Rushton, Temple D.	279	41	42	45	271,416
Russell, Monica	55	5	7	8	105,732
Russell, Randall R.	398	51	51	62	425,806
Russell, Roy	11	0	0	0	3,456
Russell, III, William	11	0	1	1	3,880
Russo, Frank J.	49	5	10	4	102,545
Russo, Sal	121	13	13	20	449,518
Russo, Scott	122	14	16	23	121,037
Russo, Settimo	70	3	6	10	97,702
Rust, Blake	62	7	3	8	40,365
Rust, Terri	10	1	2	0	13,712
Rutherford, Eddie H.	1	0	0	0	0
Rutherford, Ella Mae	96	6	13	10	96,850
Rutherford, Lyndel G.	70	4	6	5	12,410
Rutland, Jeffrey T.	49	8	6	9	53,386
Ryan, Anthony J.	31	0	3	3	13,077
Ryan, Chris A.	65	5	3	8	110,068
Ryan, Derek S.	203	34	26	29	593,145
Ryan, Lawrence B.	6	1	0	1	6,019
Ryan, Patricia B.	12	1	3	1	10,922
Ryan, Thomas J.	15	1	2	2	12,331
Ryan, Thomas V.	2	0	0	0	147
Rycroft, Carla	13	2	0	3	11,348
Rycroft, Clinton	4	0	0	1	660
Rycroft, Delbert	32	4	3	4	54,802
Rycroft, Kelly D.	43	3	7	5	77,624
Rycroft, Riley	56	10	8	4	142,612
Rycroft, Tim	71	8	12	10	76,562
Rycroft, Tom	13	3	3	2	10,008
Ryder, Firal	20	0	1	1	5,615
Rydowski, Steven	34	3	2	4	31,677
Ryerson, James T.	192	27	20	25	845,984
Ryno, Robert N.	28	2	3	1	16,535
Saam, Merl	2	0	1	1	1,950
Saavedra, Anthony K.	74	4	9	11	229,404
Sabia, Anthony	2	0	1	1	1,860
Sabine, Michael T.	25	1	4	1	29,300
Saccardo, George A.	86	12	5	23	153,488
Sacco, Gregory D.	141	19	27	16	523,076
Sacco, Richard W.	37	1	1	2	24,418
Saccocia, Sr., Gary	3	0	0	0	0
Sackett, Betsi	32	1	2	3	10,715
Sadler, John W.	396	65	59	58	2,976,823
Sadler, Ronald H.	18	3	3	1	119,689
Saenz, Jr., Octavio	1	0	0	0	0
Saffel, John	87	9	7	15	98,692
Sahadi, Jenine	114	18	20	15	956,874
Sailor, Christian L.	14	0	2	0	2,415
Saip, Jack	3	2	0	0	58,922
Saitz, Garry	21	6	2	2	33,072
Saland, Richard	14	1	1	1	35,449
Salazar, Anthony	87	2	2	4	24,123
Salazar, Leroy E.	3	0	1	0	1,320
Salazar, Marco P.	172	14	23	22	283,365
Salcedo, Ramon	109	9	12	5	93,338
Saldana, Jenny	1	0	0	0	0
Saldana, Ricardo	16	3	3	1	9,155
Sale, Luigi	2	0	0	1	300
Salih, Ahmad	13	2	1	3	57,515
Salim, Adel D.	26	1	1	4	17,270
Salinas, Angel C.	356	57	40	47	879,330
Salinas, Jose	17	0	0	2	2,262
Salisbury, Joyce	64	11	9	6	93,114
Sally, Greg	1	0	0	0	310

Trainer	Sts	1st	2d	3d	Purses
Salmen, Jr., Peter W.	56	6	3	13	99,645
Salter, Rick	53	4	8	3	66,180
Salvaggio, Jr., Michael W.	267	50	59	47	541,343
Salvato, John A.	72	7	10	9	76,912
Salvino, Neal	24	1	1	1	8,167
Salvino, Roger J.	35	4	2	1	50,934
Salzman, Timothy E.	313	51	47	51	950,253
Salzman, Sr., John E.	14	2	2	5	66,200
Sam, Thomas W.	189	29	19	30	559,691
Samaniego, Beatrice D.	12	3	0	2	46,844
Samaniego, Jose I.	10	2	2	0	57,400
Sammons, Ricky Dale	4	2	0	0	6,819
Sammut, Charles J.	27	4	4	5	94,792
Sampia, Gerald A.	1	0	0	0	0
Sams, William D.	23	0	1	2	9,546
Samson, Robert G.	2	0	0	0	398
Samulak, Julia A.	8	1	3	0	16,814
Sanchez, Adrian	40	3	1	6	37,596
Sanchez, Andy H.	29	1	0	1	9,822
Sanchez, Francisco	7	1	0	3	11,641
Sanchez, Osvaldo	1	0	0	0	0
Sanchez, Patrick L.	8	1	1	0	4,881
Sanchez, Roberto	5	0	0	0	2,165
Sanchez-Pinero, Angel	70	3	9	2	69,396
Sander, James	5	0	0	2	1,728
Sanders, Brent	5	2	0	2	11,040
Sanders, Cindy	76	4	2	7	46,040
Sanders, Gregg A.	20	0	1	1	3,400
Sanders, John A.	3	0	0	0	215
Sanders, M. Larry	67	2	4	11	55,183
Sanders, Marvin L.	69	12	14	4	187,949
Sanders, Melinda K.	81	0	4	7	28,208
Sanders, Nevin	23	2	4	0	14,091
Sanders, Richard A.	20	1	3	1	24,927
Sanders, Theresa	2	1	0	0	1,595
Sanderson, Garnet	26	3	4	3	7,992
Sanderson, Richard H.	12	1	2	1	34,795
Sanderson, Robert D.	61	2	8	7	30,020
Sanderson, Jr., Luther E.	14	0	1	1	4,052
Sandler, Scott	1	0	1	0	1,280
Sandoval, Gaston D.	63	9	13	10	239,394
Sandrowski, Gene J.	17	1	1	2	5,308
Sands, Barry E.	16	0	0	4	4,751
Sands, Shane	26	1	1	2	15,465
Sanelli, John A.	6	0	2	0	8,226
Santana, Felix	17	1	0	0	5,856
Santen, John D.	1	0	0	0	0
Santiago, Felix D.	1	0	0	0	77
Santillo, Thomas F.	35	2	4	4	32,783
Santmyer, Ron E.	126	19	10	19	255,099
Sapergia, Robert	3	0	0	0	120
Sarago, Joseph C.	45	4	7	7	57,461
Sargent, Wayne E.	75	6	6	4	61,166
Sarmiento, Ernesto	45	5	3	4	82,076
Sarson, Alisa Brooke	18	2	1	0	13,785
Saucedo, Rene	10	1	1	1	11,129
Sauer, Barbara J.	58	0	0	3	9,771
Sauerwein, Raymond	2	0	0	0	224
Saul, Beth	70	2	10	5	41,630
Saul, Heather	8	0	2	1	14,280
Saunders, Dale L.	280	50	44	33	696,580
Saunders, Jerry	27	2	3	3	14,733
Saunders, Leslie	33	1	4	4	29,455
Sauque, Alex	19	0	0	3	44,528
Savary, David A.	45	3	6	7	57,565
Savell, Steve	26	0	0	1	7,265
Saville, Donald P.	54	7	5	12	118,492
Savoie, Sherman	131	15	12	14	269,194
Savoy, Aaron	25	1	3	3	23,156
Savoy, John David	21	0	0	0	2,615
Savoy, John M.	9	0	0	1	2,538
Savoy, Kevin	40	3	3	4	38,702
Sawyer, Donal	5	0	0	0	636
Saxe, Richard	1	0	0	0	336
Sayler, Ardell	237	40	31	26	310,215
Sayler, James F.	75	13	5	10	56,238
Sayre, David	10	2	1	2	25,187
Sayre, Michael R.	10	2	1	1	9,948
Sayre, Ronald D.	33	0	1	5	5,415
Scace, Lynne M.	159	29	26	23	409,591
Scanlan, John F.	99	12	11	11	299,920
Scarberry, Howard	158	18	23	13	507,970
Scarborough, Kenneth	41	0	0	7	14,031
Schaber, Debbie	54	0	2	0	13,097
Schaefers, Larry	36	2	4	4	14,369
Schaffer, Kimberly A.	2	0	0	0	800
Schaffrick, Dale	36	5	3	5	20,068
Schembri, Albert	26	1	0	1	46,847
Schenk, Kathy	34	2	4	5	23,170
Schepis, Raymond J.	6	0	0	1	1,640
Scher, Carol	11	0	0	0	537
Scherbenske, Elery H.	25	3	1	5	29,667
Scherbenske, Percy E.	188	17	12	25	395,447
Scherer, Merrill R.	281	55	31	38	1,282,508
Scherer, Richard R.	221	34	32	36	976,602
Schettino, Dominick A.	148	29	17	15	913,814
Schexnider, Raymond	17	1	3	0	15,927
Schiano-Dicola, Raimondo	182	19	22	31	377,228
Schiemann, Shana A.	1	0	0	0	0
Schiesel, Leonard	40	4	4	7	19,553
Schiewe, Paul	8	0	0	0	2,400
Schildt, Andrew	29	3	6	3	15,899
Schindler, Wayne B.	3	0	0	0	112
Schlansky, Desra	5	1	1	0	18,122
Schlarbaum, Max	1	0	0	0	0
Schlender, Fred	25	1	1	6	6,614
Schlesinger, Renee A.	42	9	9	5	178,047
Schliefert, Brad	4	1	0	1	6,981
Schling, Brian L.	3	0	0	0	230
Schmechel, Vaughn	1	0	0	0	126
Schmidli, Ted M.	12	0	0	0	1,125
Schmidt, Denise	100	15	13	13	243,959
Schmidt, Robert D.	11	2	1	2	12,615
Schmidt, Stan	4	1	0	1	3,512
Schmitt, Bill C.	43	3	4	6	11,964
Schneider, Charles M.	184	23	17	27	490,627
Schneider, Geoffrey L.	9	0	1	0	7,154
Schneider, Lisa	27	3	4	5	17,036
Schnell, Don	28	3	1	4	24,827
Schnitzler, Rita A.	94	4	14	13	265,439
Schoenborn, Everett F.	10	0	0	0	5,662
Schoeneman, Jared	111	11	15	13	127,521
Schoenthal, Phil	373	61	68	40	1,204,822
Schoepf, Janis D.	62	12	9	6	25,399
Schofield, Sarah	2	0	0	0	300
Scholes, Sherry	7	1	1	2	4,435
Schooler, Fred A.	7	1	1	0	4,782
Schooley, Frank	11	0	2	0	2,006
Schooley, Harold	128	7	8	6	36,900
Schooley, Shane A.	17	0	1	0	2,505
Schosberg, Richard E.	195	29	25	31	980,470
Schrage, Joseph F.	17	5	2	6	69,890
Schreibvogel, Steve	5	1	0	0	1,239
Schriock, Bob	2	0	0	0	75
Schroeder, Peggy	4	0	0	0	400
Schroeder, Robert L.	23	3	1	3	5,901
Schu, Sally Sue	8	0	0	0	2,980
Schuetta, Regina	40	1	2	3	20,480
Schuette, Sheryl	20	0	2	1	3,408
Schuh, Tim	49	14	9	6	196,486
Schulhofer, Randy	78	6	8	12	415,308
Schultz, Art	1	0	0	0	0
Schultz, Bill	4	0	0	0	183
Schultz, Harold F.	139	11	8	12	169,311
Schultz, Robert D.	124	15	11	23	233,408
Schulz, Roland R.	26	3	3	4	23,183
Schunk, Byron	7	0	0	2	2,042
Schuster, Chris	7	0	1	1	2,385
Schutte, Joseph Michael	2	0	0	0	100
Schutz, Andreas	3	0	1	1	200,000
Schvaneveldt, Blane	12	5	0	0	18,162
Schwab, Heinz	9	0	0	1	4,600
Schwan, Emmagene K.	113	13	13	15	209,775
Schwandt, Emile	65	10	8	9	101,289
Schwartz, Jason E.	62	4	3	7	27,392
Schwartz, Richard F.	13	4	2	1	74,562

Trainer	Sts	1st	2d	3d	Purses
Schwartz, Scott M.	198	10	22	34	742,301
Schwieger, Frederick C.	6	0	0	0	3,300
Schwing, Terry A.	29	1	1	8	9,608
Schwizer, Marsha D.	2	0	0	0	1,260
Sciacca, Gary	269	14	26	38	796,172
Scicchitano, James V.	21	0	1	0	3,655
Scocca, Linda K.	57	2	1	4	25,986
Scolamieri, Sam J.	19	4	0	4	82,625
Score, Robert A.	25	1	1	1	13,396
Scott, Christine D.	36	2	3	7	20,776
Scott, George Ron	170	17	22	25	159,950
Scott, Jack R.	9	0	2	1	2,255
Scott, Joan	63	6	6	11	149,665
Scott, Kelly Lynn	46	1	6	7	64,392
Scott, Lloyd L.	69	13	6	10	249,599
Scott, Louis E.	23	1	3	6	35,345
Scott, Ronald	9	2	2	2	10,113
Scott, Russell	17	1	3	3	10,489
Scott, Steven C.	2	0	0	0	0
Scott, Jr, Larry D.	8	0	0	0	333
Scott, Jr., Alfred H.	67	3	3	4	69,896
Scott-Morrison, Marie	3	0	0	1	1,072
Scramstad, Harold	24	2	4	2	17,012
Scramstad, Kenton	18	1	2	4	9,128
Scudder, R. Mike	103	10	16	16	37,218
Scudder, Richard J.	6	2	0	1	1,799
Scully, Peter J.	58	5	11	8	75,404
Seagle, Stan	29	2	5	4	36,160
Sears, Leon B.	5	0	0	1	2,065
Sears, Michael	10	0	2	3	4,757
Seaton, Shad	64	4	5	8	32,893
Sebastien, James Roy	38	3	4	3	56,267
Sebastien, Tim	15	4	2	3	39,445
Sebreth, Odalie A.	2	0	0	0	154
Secor, Jake	65	16	16	10	258,803
Secor, John B.	46	9	3	5	62,466
Sedillo, Carlos	130	13	17	18	164,814
Sedillo, Paul	10	0	1	2	2,878
Sedillo, Tony E.	107	14	12	11	158,486
Sedlacek, Michael C.	96	9	10	8	363,349
Sedlacek, Roy	48	4	10	6	130,386
Seeger, Robert J.	397	51	64	51	941,098
Seely, W. C.	4	1	1	0	7,885
Seesequasis, Elmer	24	4	8	3	12,020
Seewald, Alan S.	195	28	39	31	813,398
Seglin, Luis E.	41	2	3	8	377,647
Segura, Elton	10	0	0	0	0
Segura, Kearney	340	50	39	39	753,155
Segura, Roy	38	0	2	3	8,430
Seifert, Janet	26	2	3	5	19,827
Sellers, Mark J.	2	0	0	0	230
Seltrecht, Judy	50	1	1	0	10,203
Selyem, Louis	30	1	1	3	14,498
Semer, John R.	269	38	31	29	448,604
Semkin, Sam	42	5	8	6	310,360
Senebald, Don	44	2	1	4	13,872
Senegal, Clayton J.	40	1	1	3	16,862
Senegal, Jeffrey	1	0	0	0	0
Senert, Richard W.	1	0	0	0	154
Sepich, Sr., Edward F.	16	0	1	3	4,622
Serna, III, Julian	25	1	2	0	19,187
Serpe, Philip M.	227	30	33	25	1,472,803
Serrano, Emilio	106	7	2	15	68,450
Serrano, Jose	15	4	1	2	61,570
Serrano, Marcos A.	1	0	1	0	1,760
Servideo, Cindy	5	0	0	0	636
Servideo, Robert	29	0	2	3	6,700
Servis, Jason	223	40	30	33	1,088,949
Servis, John C.	284	68	38	38	8,922,686
Sessa, Melanie	11	2	0	2	12,860
Settles, Holly	54	2	6	7	19,734
Severin, Barbara K.	67	4	6	9	39,483
Severinsen, Allen	77	8	11	8	122,983
Severson, Sam	6	0	1	1	795
Seward, Norma	2	0	0	0	120
Shackelford, Deby J.	14	2	1	0	22,662
Shade, Dale W.	78	6	8	6	49,752

Trainer	Sts	1st	2d	3d	Purses
Shade, Donald D.	14	0	0	1	2,900
Shafer, Jennifer	5	0	1	2	9,089
Shaffer, Bonnie	11	2	2	2	33,843
Shaffer, Charles E.	37	0	1	4	3,290
Shaffer, Jon T.	46	1	5	3	47,230
Shamsie, Paul	36	3	4	8	46,131
Shamsie, Sr., Randy	62	4	7	7	68,302
Shane, Ken	3	0	1	0	441
Shaneybrook, Sandra L.	25	1	1	1	17,670
Shankle, Sr., Ronald E.	37	4	1	3	55,461
Shankleton, Dennis	58	2	11	8	31,531
Shanley, Gary William	63	4	3	1	35,445
Shanley, Timothy	31	1	1	1	20,050
Shannon, Frank P.	153	24	26	23	379,569
Shannon, Jennifer	5	0	1	0	3,008
Shanyfelt, Douglas E.	330	32	37	31	467,816
Shanyfelt, Sr., William	69	4	3	1	17,441
Shapoff, Alan W.	26	0	2	3	36,906
Sharp, Lanny Z.	93	6	11	11	64,624
Sharp, Larry	1	1	0	0	935
Sharp, Michelle S.	65	6	2	3	75,633
Sharpe, Gary	20	3	2	2	7,072
Shartle, Tom	6	0	0	1	1,388
Shauf, Walter J.	18	1	1	2	10,737
Shaughnessy, Michael P.	19	2	1	2	17,473
Shavelson, Pam	184	26	29	22	401,589
Shaw, John E.	59	4	6	10	85,945
Shaw, Timothy J.	47	5	6	3	116,382
Shaw, Sr., Gerald L.	40	2	2	3	13,153
Shawyer, James W.	4	0	0	0	410
Shea, Timothy H.	73	15	13	12	225,413
Shears, Simon	5	2	1	0	22,353
Sheena, Kamal S.	50	4	10	6	90,601
Sheets, Jeffrey	23	4	1	1	62,685
Sheets, Toby E.	20	4	6	2	131,930
Shelley, Bill	48	3	3	6	21,886
Shelley, Kim	2	0	0	0	293
Shelley, Warren	4	0	0	0	755
Shellnutt, Roy D.	3	0	2	0	6,420
Shelton, Dan	7	0	0	0	471
Shenofsky, Ronald L.	181	22	17	31	410,743
Shenski, Shawn	6	0	0	0	500
Shepherd, Roxann C.	21	0	2	4	14,794
Shepherd, Shannon M	30	1	6	2	30,007
Shepherd, Sherri L.	111	6	6	5	95,993
Sheppard, Jonathan E.	423	58	58	70	1,821,893
Sheppard, Kevin R.	33	2	3	3	18,401
Sheppard, Lynn W.	10	0	0	0	970
Sherer, Sandra L.	9	0	0	0	240
Sherman, Art	611	152	102	84	2,353,216
Sherman-Jiminez, Lauren	1	0	0	0	0
Sherr, Michael B.	50	7	6	6	84,834
Sherron, Theresa	16	0	0	0	1,096
Sherwood, Colin G.	111	7	11	15	164,519
Sherwood, Dale E.	13	1	3	1	9,045
Shetron, Phyllis	110	11	17	15	135,761
Shevy, Michael J.	19	1	1	1	47,314
Shidaker, Duff	4	0	0	0	2,240
Shields, Patrick D.	5	0	1	0	720
Shields, Thomas C.	3	0	0	0	320
Shildt, Andy	1	0	0	0	60
Shilling, J. Edwin	122	11	16	11	151,327
Shipe, Douglas M.	9	2	3	1	12,478
Shipley, C. Larry	3	0	0	0	319
Shipp, Michael	11	1	4	2	7,509
Shipton, Jennifer	44	4	12	1	45,116
Shirk, Joann	17	2	2	1	12,658
Shirley, Luthia	5	0	0	0	1,333
Shirley, Patricia K.	109	14	19	6	220,025
Shirota, Mitch	54	6	10	10	421,850
Shirreffs, John A.	182	23	18	25	1,453,958
Shockey, Dale E.	75	5	6	9	119,723
Shockley, Herbert L.	3	1	1	0	1,960
Shopf, Arthur G.	16	0	2	0	7,565
Shorkey, Patrick	9	0	0	1	551
Short, Ricky J.	87	14	15	15	145,147
Short, Tommy C.	249	16	19	23	203,954

Trainer	Sts	1st	2d	3d	Purses
Shorter, Mike	2	0	0	0	140
Shows, Kenneth	26	3	2	4	30,216
Shreve, Michael B.	1	0	0	0	0
Shryock, John C.	48	8	5	5	55,147
Shufelt, Joseph A.	5	0	1	0	1,527
Shuldberg, Boyd	87	6	13	12	76,641
Shuler, Donald W.	32	2	1	3	19,530
Shulman, Sanford	107	18	14	6	584,411
Shultz, John W.	2	0	1	0	779
Shumake, Ray	107	16	14	14	131,483
Shuman, Joseph P.	319	33	37	39	511,111
Shuman, Mark	987	159	134	138	4,183,826
Shuster, Patricia C.	30	6	1	6	53,192
Shwora, Robert L.	1	0	0	0	0
Sibille, Ronnie	1	0	0	0	0
Sider, Alvin	80	9	6	7	204,645
Sides, Robert C.	35	3	5	2	108,552
Sienkewicz, William M.	30	2	4	6	15,420
Sierra, Cirilo M.	89	5	8	10	90,773
Sierra, Jesus	3	0	3	0	15,200
Sigler, Ronald G.	3	0	0	0	1,380
Signore, Jr., Joseph L.	11	1	0	0	16,185
Signs, Joshua	9	0	2	1	9,319
Signs, Nancy L.	11	0	2	1	21,551
Siler, Leroy	4	0	0	0	384
Silva, A. Clare	2	0	0	0	272
Silva, Fernando	55	9	5	12	80,228
Silva, Juan Pablo	93	17	14	11	54,364
Silva, Paul P.	75	5	5	7	28,642
Silvera, Arthur	73	9	7	9	364,117
Silvera, Laurie	139	14	24	23	907,104
Silvera, Mike	3	0	1	0	10,040
Silverman, Marshall W.	5	0	1	0	5,667
Silvers, Darren	55	4	3	5	41,401
Silverthorne, Rachelle	1	0	1	0	1,280
Simkins, Rosie	6	1	1	1	6,196
Simmons, Charles E.	5	0	0	0	868
Simmons, Jack R.	10	0	0	3	2,850
Simmons, Kasey B.	5	0	0	1	906
Simmons, Kory	8	1	0	1	15,298
Simms, Debra M.	15	1	0	1	8,424
Simms, Garry W.	76	18	7	14	235,838
Simms, John	253	31	35	34	625,297
Simoff, Andrew L.	75	4	9	12	128,573
Simoff, Richard A.	25	2	4	3	32,227
Simon, Charles	215	33	28	29	974,015
Simon, Ivory	16	0	2	2	2,313
Simon, Leroy	34	3	1	3	13,793
Simon, Linda	6	0	0	0	480
Simon, Lynn M.	71	7	7	7	272,012
Simon, Stuart C.	227	32	30	26	446,517
Simone, Victor	45	0	7	4	22,059
Simons, Howard F.	32	1	2	2	29,961
Simpson, Charles	1	0	0	0	0
Simpson, Deborah M.	94	14	13	17	206,770
Simpson, Gary	57	13	11	5	33,342
Simpson, Gene	5	0	0	0	414
Simpson, George E.	32	0	2	2	5,452
Simpson, Gerald R.	23	2	3	1	32,430
Simpson, Pamela P.	71	10	10	10	228,462
Simpson, Patricia A.	123	9	12	11	213,333
Simpson, Rolanda	4	1	1	0	10,105
Simpson, Willoughby	33	1	4	6	27,800
Sims, Philip A.	81	8	8	7	135,424
Sinanovic, Richard R.	5	1	0	1	3,834
Sinclair, Jodie L.	32	7	3	7	160,940
Sinclair, Paul L.	12	0	4	3	7,709
Sing, Antonio J.	21	1	0	2	11,130
Singletary, Robert A.	18	3	1	5	24,382
Singleton, Larry A.	6	0	0	0	427
Sinn, Michelle M.	57	11	7	7	145,663
Sipe, David L.	184	21	19	26	434,332
Sipes, Jerry W.	10	0	0	1	791
Sipp, Burton K.	401	52	54	44	418,260
Siravo, Florence Gemma	213	18	28	25	204,406
Siravo, Robert D.	2	0	1	0	4,800
Siravo, Jr., William	12	1	2	0	7,880
Sirianni, Louis	50	3	7	13	54,438
Sirota, Keith	118	10	14	13	256,712
Sise, Jr., Clifford W.	358	57	49	49	1,227,779
Sisko, Lisa	18	1	2	3	3,869
Sitsler, Virgil L.	13	2	2	2	7,340
Skaggs, Clayton Z.	15	0	1	2	4,400
Skaggs, Dodson H.	90	12	13	19	105,574
Skaggs, Winston R.	17	4	2	0	20,666
Skarpness, Travis	2	0	0	1	550
Skawinski, Carol A.	3	0	0	0	230
Skeen, Mark V.	11	5	0	3	19,503
Skelton, Chad T.	53	8	3	4	80,481
Skelton, Gary	1	0	0	0	354
Skelton, Thomas R.	7	0	0	0	324
Sketchley, John D.	5	1	0	1	9,505
Skiffington, Thomas J.	58	7	4	10	238,924
Skinner, Albert T.	10	0	0	4	5,960
Skinner, Diana L.	34	1	4	4	23,750
Skinner, Gary	7	0	1	0	772
Skinner, Jonna	3	0	1	1	1,250
Skinner, Teresa M.	1	1	0	0	1,100
Skultin, Jeffrey M.	7	0	1	0	1,582
Slack, James G.	5	0	2	1	3,809
Slack, Robert A.	2	0	0	0	103
Slager, Leonard M.	18	0	3	1	13,290
Slater, Brian	9	1	0	1	5,624
Slater, Ed	2	1	0	0	812
Slater, John	13	3	1	3	4,611
Slater, Lawrence	23	4	1	3	15,232
Slater, William	2	0	0	0	75
Sleeter, Gerald F.	5	0	0	1	5,338
Sleeter, Kevin G.	104	12	19	9	511,052
Slisz, Daniel J.	110	15	14	16	92,737
Slivka, Sandra L.	54	13	11	3	627,293
Sloan, Barbara	12	1	0	0	3,840
Sloan, Edna M.	1	0	0	0	0
Sloan, Harry	12	1	1	3	22,643
Slone, Charles E.	87	3	4	3	20,268
Slone, Mike	1	0	0	0	46
Slot, Sonia	57	2	2	5	22,795
Sluder, Arlie K.	8	0	0	0	392
Slysz, Margaret A.	12	1	1	1	14,760
Small, Richard W.	181	39	28	27	1,099,148
Small, Sue	1	0	0	0	675
Smallwood, Brian S	1	0	0	0	0
Smart, Leonard	2	0	0	0	0
Smellie, Vernon	1	0	0	0	0
Smith, Andrew	23	0	7	2	93,502
Smith, Angie D	12	2	0	1	25,193
Smith, Austin K.	119	12	11	17	296,974
Smith, Candice M.	23	2	4	7	68,350
Smith, Charles Edwin	2	0	0	0	310
Smith, Charlie Joe	36	1	10	4	9,823
Smith, Chester	25	2	4	5	18,740
Smith, Clay M.	4	0	0	0	210
Smith, Clyde N.	8	1	1	0	4,805
Smith, Constance A.	1	0	0	0	114
Smith, Craig	50	3	6	10	33,213
Smith, Curvin D.	25	3	3	2	45,241
Smith, Danny L.	99	13	9	6	58,195
Smith, David S.	24	1	1	3	31,054
Smith, Debbie	26	4	5	3	9,024
Smith, Dennis D.	10	1	0	1	3,549
Smith, Denny	3	0	0	1	240
Smith, Don R.	75	7	6	5	58,613
Smith, Donald F.	15	0	0	0	4,000
Smith, Donald W.	11	2	0	1	5,794
Smith, Doug R.	93	5	16	11	73,805
Smith, Earl D.	17	1	2	1	9,433
Smith, Frederic F.	43	2	4	2	34,913
Smith, Gary L.	3	1	1	0	1,785
Smith, Hallet P.	48	5	3	3	45,145
Smith, Hamilton A.	456	66	66	68	1,498,140
Smith, I. Henry	29	1	3	1	25,294
Smith, James J.	93	12	12	16	455,982
Smith, Jaqueline	95	20	21	13	49,272
Smith, Jeffrey W.	3	0	0	0	220
Smith, John C.	20	2	0	1	18,029
Smith, John H.	13	2	1	0	11,112

Trainer	Sts	1st	2d	3d	Purses
Smith, John P.	38	4	5	0	31,872
Smith, John S.	56	2	5	5	59,285
Smith, Joseph B.	12	0	3	1	7,965
Smith, Justin D.	49	0	2	3	5,612
Smith, Kenneth J.	6	0	1	0	6,180
Smith, Kenneth R.	118	11	11	11	123,247
Smith, Kenny P.	131	16	16	23	236,479
Smith, Kimberly M.	63	0	0	1	2,930
Smith, Larry D.	49	1	4	4	18,882
Smith, Larry E.	98	17	13	17	88,350
Smith, Larry O.	29	6	8	2	16,020
Smith, Laurie	53	5	6	7	84,730
Smith, Lavona	4	0	0	0	430
Smith, Lawrence M.	53	3	4	4	32,071
Smith, Marirose	10	0	1	0	3,653
Smith, Mark F.	98	4	4	7	39,001
Smith, Marlene J.	1	0	1	0	483
Smith, Martin	1	0	0	0	135
Smith, Mary C.	6	1	0	0	3,660
Smith, Norman H.	64	14	9	8	77,657
Smith, Pam L.	41	4	7	6	44,009
Smith, Paul A.	140	15	14	10	126,392
Smith, Peter G.	10	1	0	0	6,372
Smith, Richard Louis	15	0	0	1	6,209
Smith, Robert G.	19	3	2	2	31,151
Smith, Ron K.	348	68	54	44	1,026,602
Smith, Sandy C.	11	0	1	0	4,302
Smith, Stanley G.	130	11	18	18	164,366
Smith, Steve C.	5	0	0	0	552
Smith, Terrance	11	1	1	0	14,464
Smith, Thomas R.	7	2	0	2	11,711
Smith, Thomas Victor	53	4	9	5	92,238
Smith, Tim R.	10	1	0	2	3,009
Smith, Tracie L.	151	19	9	7	203,169
Smith, Troy	66	10	12	4	50,361
Smith, W. Bret	45	4	5	3	98,094
Smith, Walter	31	1	2	2	9,056
Smith, Wayne Harold	7	0	0	0	293
Smith, William F.	15	0	1	1	7,681
Smith, William J.	59	9	9	10	109,553
Smith, William Milton	11	0	0	0	2,495
Smith, Jr., A. Archie	24	2	1	6	44,370
Smith, Jr., Alvin	7	0	0	0	787
Smith, Jr., Frank	21	0	3	0	15,166
Smith, Jr., Franklin G.	179	16	26	22	297,854
Smith, Jr., Jere R.	18	4	0	3	30,335
Smith, Jr., Ralph R.	35	2	1	3	55,901
Smither, Bruce R.	11	1	0	1	17,870
Smithwick, Dorothy F.	24	2	2	1	25,600
Smithwick, Jr., D. Michael	73	5	7	11	172,425
Smithwick, Sr., D. Michael	24	0	1	3	11,990
Smock, Lori A.	297	39	34	35	399,157
Smoot, Don	1	0	0	0	47
Smullen, Sean	34	6	4	2	293,217
Smutz, Rosemary J.	60	6	4	6	111,712
Smylie, Jon J.	110	9	10	10	160,551
Smylie, Timothy J.	33	2	1	4	23,777
Snapp, Fred	16	2	1	3	16,540
Snatchko, Paul A.	84	4	8	13	76,583
Sneed, Dale	53	4	7	12	48,753
Snipes, Bruce	23	1	0	1	20,270
Snodgrass, John	2	0	0	0	190
Snow, Daryl	116	19	10	16	271,953
Snow, John	29	6	1	3	98,176
Snow, Mel	155	10	22	23	243,588
Snyder, Floyd W.	40	5	8	5	84,425
Sobol, Alan	81	11	10	11	184,663
Socks, Terry W.	11	2	3	2	70,861
Soileau, Darrel	5	1	0	0	11,730
Soileau, Diana	59	4	6	4	74,532
Soileau, J. Y.	12	1	0	1	6,871
Soileau, Lynn	5	0	0	0	1,080
Soileau, Sharon	61	2	5	2	46,181
Sola, Joseph L.	30	5	4	3	20,633
Sommer, Mack	1	0	0	0	0
Sones, Debra	40	6	5	3	143,479
Sonnier, Gerald	73	9	19	5	141,507

Trainer	Sts	1st	2d	3d	Purses
Soos, Herman	44	3	5	4	48,756
Sorensen, Mike	28	1	5	6	14,794
Sostre, Israel	71	5	4	4	47,986
Soto, Antonio	168	6	9	10	73,500
Soto, Carlos	19	2	1	2	25,166
Soto, Ignacio R.	58	2	7	4	19,027
Soto, John	25	1	3	4	12,010
Soto, Manuel	8	1	2	0	1,683
Soto, Jr., Herbert	8	0	1	0	2,622
Souder, Donald E.	203	19	28	28	429,281
Souter, Paul	4	0	0	1	1,885
Southard, Anne C.	55	5	4	3	72,755
Souto, Gerald A.	156	12	30	26	151,367
Sowers, Barbara L.	14	1	1	1	13,280
Sowers, Dennis T.	137	22	23	17	149,938
Sowers, Larry	4	0	0	0	1,165
Sowle, Donald G.	5	0	0	0	813
Sowle, Mark	6	0	0	2	1,898
Sowle, Scott	79	14	12	16	323,277
Spadaro, Stephen J.	2	0	1	0	3,500
Spady, Cindy	18	1	2	3	10,303
Spady, Harold	46	11	6	6	98,582
Spagnola, Ida	94	5	14	11	135,819
Spanabel, Harriette	70	2	5	5	16,869
Spanu, Antonio	1	0	0	1	15,000
Sparks, Brad	27	4	0	2	46,980
Sparks, J. Clay	15	3	7	0	76,595
Sparks, Jerry S.	203	22	30	27	328,638
Sparks, Ken	14	1	4	2	7,534
Spathanas, William	6	0	0	0	0
Spatz, Ronald B.	224	37	32	29	985,435
Spawr, William	287	64	57	37	1,826,342
Spaziano, Joyce M.	32	0	1	8	13,343
Speaks, Dennis	6	0	1	2	683
Spears, Louis T.	15	0	3	3	22,840
Spears, Stephen A.	88	10	12	3	201,839
Specht, Steven	203	36	25	21	764,783
Speck, Bobby C.	22	5	2	3	31,825
Speckert, Christopher	40	7	3	3	163,527
Spegal, Jon	14	1	1	2	5,454
Speizer, Rick	12	1	1	2	33,397
Spence, Debbie	26	1	1	3	10,335
Spence, James T.	19	2	1	0	13,502
Spencer, Clark	27	3	3	1	22,281
Spencer, Margaret A.	16	2	2	1	55,847
Spencer, Ray	39	4	3	7	130,297
Spencer, Robin Lee	13	2	2	2	15,202
Spencer, Sr., Rollen L.	4	0	0	0	715
Spicer, James T.	57	3	10	6	66,112
Spicknall, James I.	23	1	2	1	24,905
Spiess, Roger D.	115	6	7	4	111,213
Spiess, Shane M.	257	25	25	35	215,350
Spina, Chuck	61	3	6	4	52,091
Spinosa, Bobby	1	0	0	0	0
Spradling, Roy N.	6	1	1	0	6,885
Spraggins, Kenneth R.	48	5	4	7	74,880
Sprague, John A.	22	6	3	2	45,618
Spreen, Debbie	11	0	1	0	2,082
Springer, Frank R.	120	28	19	16	855,537
Springer, John	25	4	3	3	56,378
Sprock, Sondra	4	0	0	0	0
Sprouse, Loretta	10	0	2	1	5,708
Spurlock, John H.	48	1	3	4	22,196
Spurlock, Lee	49	5	6	5	39,742
St. Clair, David	6	1	0	2	2,620
St. John, Thomas M.	19	2	2	1	13,363
St. Lewis, Uriah	220	11	22	26	299,620
St. Louis, Clement J.	19	3	2	4	31,960
Stabenfeldt, John	16	5	3	1	9,995
Stack, Tommy	1	1	0	0	106,380
Stackwood, Carol	7	0	0	0	777
Stader, Troy	1	0	0	0	40
Stahlin, John L.	159	19	27	21	361,186
Stakes, David A.	1	0	0	0	105
Stalhiem, Kim	10	0	0	1	1,615
Stalhiem, Jr., Kenton	10	0	0	4	5,832
Stall, Jr., Albert M.	319	46	56	45	1,279,031

Trainer	Sts	1st	2d	3d	Purses
Stambaugh, Jerry A.	1	0	0	0	41
Stamps, Dusty	4	0	0	0	816
Standridge, Steven W.	130	22	12	21	370,400
Stanford, Maria	3	0	0	0	0
Stanford, Myrl	44	4	5	2	37,441
Staples, John	9	1	0	1	18,793
Stark, Stacey A.	12	1	5	1	18,691
Starkey, Billy F.	7	1	0	0	12,955
Starkey, James H.	106	6	4	4	120,117
Starks, Gilbert	7	0	0	0	1,300
Starlin, Gene	27	6	5	4	26,211
Staroscik, Larry L.	121	12	8	16	73,363
Starritt, William D.	77	3	7	16	100,319
Stauffer, Sr., Arthur F.	123	7	10	20	170,614
Stavely, Bruce	1	0	0	0	0
Steadman, Earl S.	39	0	3	3	16,165
Steele, Karen E.	59	3	3	9	95,034
Steele, Jr., Hal W.	9	0	0	0	1,692
Steer, Tom	7	0	0	0	1,743
Steeves, Robert	3	0	0	0	610
Stehr, Hank A.	51	2	3	3	71,529
Stehr, Joseph P.	43	0	4	8	43,057
Stehr, Vicki L.	11	0	0	1	6,946
Steigmann, James	3	0	0	0	0
Stein, Roger M.	65	2	5	9	174,140
Steiner, Jack	18	1	2	2	15,117
Steinhauer, J. Herman	4	0	0	1	5,998
Steinke, Kassidy	1	0	0	0	0
Steinke, Kenneth	1	0	0	0	0
Steinmeyer, Holly	6	0	0	1	1,310
Steinmiller, Brad Jay	12	1	1	1	6,252
Stelly, Frank J.	6	0	0	0	768
Stelly, Jane	1	0	0	0	0
Stelly, Levan	17	0	3	1	8,740
Stemmans, Don	57	7	4	1	48,445
Stenslie, Chris	19	2	2	9	20,284
Stephen, Peter	84	18	12	13	294,135
Stephens, David	17	0	1	0	4,193
Stephens, George A.	105	7	11	9	68,289
Stephens, John D.	5	1	0	0	8,652
Stephens, Steve W.	52	3	5	2	24,969
Stepp, Rochelle Lenee	2	0	0	0	105
Sterling, Larry J.	8	1	2	1	27,500
Sterling, Michael E.	30	6	3	4	88,201
Sterrett, Tim	2	0	0	0	197
Stetler, Don A.	30	2	5	1	55,010
Steve, Chris	2	0	0	0	212
Stevens, Byron	22	2	3	2	35,587
Stevens, Frank	20	0	2	1	5,185
Stevens, Richard	24	4	5	2	47,847
Stevens, Ron D.	45	5	5	6	27,770
Stevens, Wesley R.	7	0	0	2	1,715
Stevens, Jr., Lowell T.	63	7	8	6	88,754
Stevenson, Bryce	7	0	3	1	6,816
Stevenson, Daniel G.	22	1	2	1	34,042
Stevenson, Roger M.	116	18	28	19	64,953
Stewart, Ann D.	10	3	0	1	60,225
Stewart, Cecil	97	7	12	12	107,178
Stewart, Chad J.	33	3	2	1	33,381
Stewart, Cheryl	2	0	0	0	115
Stewart, Cody James	1	0	0	0	78
Stewart, Dallas	295	49	53	35	2,170,555
Stewart, Daryl J.	30	2	2	4	26,677
Stewart, Gene N.	25	2	4	2	24,124
Stewart, George	23	2	2	2	15,890
Stewart, James G.	15	1	1	4	6,419
Stewart, John	2	0	0	0	0
Stewart, John A.	10	1	0	1	9,530
Stewart, Thomas J.	91	3	4	15	69,963
Stewart, William J.	57	4	9	9	214,897
Sticka, Ron	38	3	4	3	80,969
Stickler, Jr., Lester J.	88	10	13	15	82,185
Stidham, Michael	369	81	58	41	2,228,860
Stidham, Susan D.	24	1	1	5	43,637
Stidman, Larry P.	4	0	0	0	251
Stifano, Raymond E.	407	72	73	55	820,064
Stigile, John	2	0	0	0	66
Still, Roxanna L.	11	0	0	0	621

Trainer	Sts	1st	2d	3d	Purses
Stillwell, Maureen	14	1	2	1	19,913
Stinebaugh, John A.	7	2	1	0	12,517
Stites, Flint W.	642	101	106	78	1,329,400
Stitzel, Marion	54	13	3	6	35,346
Stitzel, Patrick	7	2	2	2	4,550
Stivers, Brian J.	2	0	0	0	215
Stivers, Ryan	20	2	1	1	9,370
Stober, David T.	26	1	0	5	11,381
Stockwell, Buckey A.	20	5	4	2	17,228
Stodghill, Jonathan S.	70	10	9	6	120,349
Stoehr, Helmut E.	6	0	0	0	694
Stohr, Lewis	14	0	4	1	3,006
Stokalko, Carol	7	0	1	3	5,612
Stokes, Lonnie	88	30	21	12	428,846
Stokes, Rex	281	25	17	29	118,262
Stoklosa, Richard L.	70	9	8	8	316,035
Stolp, Roger	73	8	10	14	31,296
Stone, Earl L.	9	0	0	0	3,165
Stone, Edward H.	11	0	0	0	4,896
Stopherd, Edwin C	58	4	5	7	36,777
Stopko, Robert S.	11	2	0	3	36,423
Storer, Nancy	1	0	0	0	60
Storlazzi, Elena A.	1	0	0	0	1,170
Storms, Phil B.	32	6	3	4	73,171
Stortzum, Donna	97	3	7	8	25,387
Story, Chad	22	4	4	2	14,051
Story, Kent	8	2	1	1	5,301
Story, Shaun	5	0	0	0	92
Stotler, Gary L.	12	1	0	0	5,731
Stout, Estelle	12	0	0	1	1,510
Stout, Michael R.	23	2	5	3	12,941
Stout, Robert Shane	29	1	0	5	9,879
Stovall, Terry W.	18	0	0	1	2,725
Stover, Joseph	1	0	0	0	75
Stradling, Bruce	24	0	1	1	3,505
Straightnose, Calvin	21	2	1	1	10,020
Strain, Jerry	3	0	0	0	129
Strandquist, Calvin	10	0	1	0	2,162
Strange, William R.	14	0	3	2	1,761
Strauss, Jr., Robert	5	1	1	2	5,508
Streaker, William E.	17	0	0	2	6,050
Streeper, Doug G.	17	4	2	3	12,855
Streicher, Kenneth	20	1	3	0	67,372
Stricker, Shawnee	1	0	0	0	510
Stricker, Willie	12	1	1	0	11,521
Strickland, Marcus C.	18	0	2	0	2,972
Strickland, Ruddell	16	0	2	1	5,691
Strickland, Susan	2	0	0	0	0
Striegel, Shannon	6	0	0	0	513
Strode, Donald D.	2	0	0	0	180
Strode, Ronald E.	10	0	1	0	1,196
Strong, Brian A.	12	1	1	0	25,900
Strong, Dennis E.	23	0	1	1	2,580
Stroope, Larry	15	3	1	2	28,865
Stroud, Gene C.	18	4	3	1	44,222
Stroud, Richard W.	13	0	1	0	4,742
Strumecki, Albert	49	5	9	7	185,181
Stuart, Clinton C.	223	21	42	30	273,385
Stufflebean, Terry	7	0	3	3	14,080
Stump, Kathleen	3	0	0	0	0
Stumpf, Daniel P.	24	0	3	4	9,876
Sturgeon, Bobby T.	2	0	0	0	100
Sturgeon, Robert C.	102	13	7	18	173,348
Sturrock, Billy G.	52	5	2	4	60,226
Stute, Gary	106	16	16	12	497,535
Stute, Melvin F.	147	16	15	17	619,868
Stute, Warren	113	13	20	12	429,776
Stutts, Richard T.	2	0	0	0	160
Stutts, Jr., Bennie F.	53	13	5	4	218,870
Suarez, Sergio	5	0	1	1	3,320
Suckie, Henry	16	2	1	2	16,919
Suire, Lane P.	12	0	3	1	11,703
Sullivan, David J.	25	2	2	5	28,962
Sullivan, John	16	1	1	2	21,330
Sullivan, Les	7	0	0	0	1,245
Sullivan, Lynn	50	8	4	4	61,212
Sullivan, Mary	3	0	0	0	149
Sullivan, Michael	17	1	1	2	6,286

Trainer	Sts	1st	2d	3d	Purses
Sumja, Brent	96	21	6	8	296,388
Summers, Earl L.	32	0	1	3	10,819
Summers, William	11	1	2	0	10,945
Sumner, Marvin E.	7	1	0	0	4,972
Sun, Truth	9	0	0	0	486
Suter, Buddy L.	4	0	1	1	3,525
Sutherland, Dorthy	32	1	1	4	9,080
Sutherland, Robert	1	0	0	0	0
Sutherland, Jr., Paul C.	6	0	0	1	1,710
Sutton, Philip Q.	33	2	3	3	35,730
Swango, Kevin	2	0	0	0	131
Swartz, Barry R.	29	4	3	2	73,745
Swartz, Jack	8	1	2	1	12,360
Swearingen, Thomas H.	130	20	15	16	412,804
Sweatt, Arthur T.	133	4	7	17	70,266
Sweazey, Scott	45	5	7	1	24,540
Sweeney, Gary A.	5	0	0	1	1,622
Sweeney, Ronald M.	24	3	2	6	54,415
Sweitzer, Randy	70	5	3	8	38,263
Swenson, Dennis	3	0	0	0	0
Swentkowski, Kimberly B.	127	12	12	17	197,481
Swingley, Duane	83	9	7	9	87,816
Swisher, Randall	25	3	4	2	48,734
Switzer, Daniel G.	43	7	6	7	115,725
Swomley, Michael C.	1	0	0	0	0
Swope, Benjamin C.	2	0	0	1	2,300
Syed, Riaz N.	71	4	3	5	28,570
Sylvester, Suzanne	14	1	2	1	5,140
Synnefias, Dimitrios K.	256	37	27	30	432,232
Szafranski, Edward E.	2	0	0	0	0
Szeyller, Robert A.	45	7	12	6	97,303
Tabler, Greg A.	26	5	5	2	32,316
Tabor, Darold R.	26	2	3	5	49,085
Tabor, Johnny M.	52	3	3	11	41,450
Tackett, Hiram	2	0	0	0	162
Tackett, Larry	5	0	1	0	797
Tackett, Samantha	5	0	1	0	505
Tagg, Barclay	235	32	25	32	2,335,781
Tagg, Taryn	42	1	2	6	57,102
Tagliaferri, Gene	7	1	0	0	3,933
Taglianetti, James P.	55	2	5	3	54,657
Takemori, Hugo	33	1	6	7	47,563
Talbot, Sandra	8	0	0	0	785
Talley, Jeff	74	11	18	10	271,464
Talsma, Al	14	2	3	2	31,696
Tamargo, Raymond	48	9	8	4	111,826
Tamberino, Steven M.	8	0	2	1	4,535
Tamburello, Joey	56	5	7	6	86,218
Tamburino, Anthony	47	3	7	7	15,798
Tammaro, Michael A.	242	12	23	30	296,052
Tammaro, III, John J.	262	26	36	30	659,004
Tanner, Lynda R.	177	15	18	23	108,939
Tanner, Robert	93	6	8	14	85,470
Tanory, Dan	35	9	1	1	21,622
Tapia, Adam A.	8	0	0	0	514
Tapp, John Wayne	9	0	0	0	1,024
Tapscott, Carlyne	4	1	0	2	20,170
Tapscott, Jenile T.	9	0	0	0	1,972
Tarmon, David C.	2	0	1	0	4,600
Tarmon, Ronnie G.	15	0	0	0	1,502
Tarrant, Amy	78	6	12	12	273,110
Tassistro, Connie	55	8	13	6	223,167
Tatarniuk, Steve	16	2	0	1	14,342
Tate, Noral J.	39	7	6	7	238,154
Tate, Stephanie N.	17	0	2	2	9,537
Tattersall, Peter D.	5	0	0	0	454
Taulbee, Mark	5	0	0	0	918
Taulton, Gary L.	8	0	0	0	340
Taulton, Jr., Leon L.	4	1	0	0	6,180
Tauzin, Guy E.	124	12	12	15	127,515
Taylor, Aaron	57	9	5	10	88,201
Taylor, Barbara	5	0	0	1	2,261
Taylor, Brant L.	163	22	26	20	254,868
Taylor, Brent	41	6	4	5	11,573
Taylor, Bryant R.	33	2	5	4	30,807
Taylor, D. R.	1	0	0	0	150
Taylor, Daniel A.	71	3	6	6	65,605
Taylor, David M.	22	1	1	0	8,705
Taylor, Donald	196	8	15	19	168,245
Taylor, Gene C.	17	0	0	1	2,183
Taylor, Gerald E.	10	2	1	2	13,235
Taylor, Herman R.	123	10	9	11	110,240
Taylor, Jed	6	0	2	0	1,150
Taylor, Jeff	73	9	4	13	59,404
Taylor, John Brookshire	20	3	2	3	35,190
Taylor, John F.	181	10	9	18	198,179
Taylor, M. Heath	1	0	0	0	1,560
Taylor, Mark C.	18	0	1	1	3,182
Taylor, Mike D.	25	7	7	2	17,993
Taylor, Randall P.	4	0	0	0	1,209
Taylor, Robert J.	39	5	3	4	87,422
Taylor, Ronald E.	47	3	7	7	64,155
Taylor, Terry L.	1	0	0	0	390
Taylor, Tracy	8	2	1	1	25,369
Taylor, Troy	42	8	2	11	47,320
Taylor, William Duane	82	9	6	13	88,215
Taylor, William H.	90	1	10	12	19,015
Taylor, Jr., C. Thomas	2	0	0	0	146
Taylor, Jr., Ronald E.	116	15	17	10	108,625
Taylor, Jr., Roy Stanley	2	1	0	0	1,550
Teal, J. L.	20	0	1	1	6,430
Tebbutt, John	106	11	12	10	114,214
Teel, Mike R.	119	28	17	11	191,010
Teer, Quintus	5	1	0	0	13,803
Tekos, Jr., Angelo	69	16	13	11	154,524
Telford, Phillip W.	2	0	0	0	175
Tellez, Eddie	78	10	10	14	30,080
Tenhundfeld, Ronnie G.	45	2	4	8	62,322
Terpak, Evangela	5	0	0	0	468
Terracciano, Neal	48	2	5	3	82,380
Terrace, Tara	2	0	0	1	1,930
Terranova, II, John P.	99	11	12	15	543,495
Terre, Sr., Michael W.	28	4	5	1	42,833
Terrenzio, William	4	0	0	2	4,895
Terrien, Gary E.	3	0	0	0	998
Terrill, Sr, Robert	18	2	2	0	79,809
Terry, Dennis L.	6	1	0	0	7,037
Terry, Rick	168	26	22	23	335,938
Terry, Robert J.	44	3	6	5	14,286
Tesher, Howard M.	87	5	3	12	241,766
Tesoro, Vincent E.	31	2	3	6	112,232
Testerman, Valora A.	196	15	15	29	265,454
Tetrault, Mark R.	43	3	3	5	40,936
Tetreault, Scott	5	0	1	0	750
Thacker, Debbie	17	1	3	3	26,582
Thacker, Elbert	23	3	3	1	16,811
Thacker, Harry G.	9	0	1	0	4,072
Thayer, Allan G.	1	0	0	0	58
Theriot, Harold J.	95	4	14	12	87,922
Thibodeau, Pamela	51	10	13	5	101,941
Thibodeaux, Kenneth J.	9	0	0	1	1,457
Thibodeaux, Lynn	24	3	1	1	23,665
Thibodeaux, Melissa	1	0	0	0	0
Thoburn, William R.	27	1	3	1	21,084
Thomas, Alan R.	11	1	2	2	5,851
Thomas, Brian J.	20	1	0	1	10,840
Thomas, Charles M.	8	2	0	0	9,207
Thomas, Charles W.	12	0	1	0	4,185
Thomas, Deborah A.	1	0	0	0	80
Thomas, Edward	13	4	0	0	38,117
Thomas, Gary A.	60	5	8	4	151,120
Thomas, James A.	1	0	0	0	85
Thomas, Jamey R.	83	13	17	10	179,984
Thomas, John E.	17	1	1	1	5,216
Thomas, Karen	71	7	10	13	47,641
Thomas, Mark E.	121	15	13	26	137,271
Thomas, Michael W.	11	0	0	1	1,612
Thomas, Mike D.	26	8	2	0	16,616
Thomas, Monte R.	62	4	10	5	69,697
Thomas, Ray	63	7	12	10	80,554
Thomas, Sandra L.	37	1	3	5	34,658
Thomas, Susan C.	1	0	0	0	75
Thomas, Terry Mike	8	1	1	2	13,000
Thomas, Thomas J.	2	0	0	0	81

Trainer	Sts	1st	2d	3d	Purses
Thomas, Travis O.	23	1	1	3	9,649
Thomas, Jr., Philip J.	17	1	2	1	16,252
Thomas, Sr., Joe Frederick	113	31	16	18	137,318
Thomaselli, Richard	1	1	0	0	16,414
Thomason, Glen	61	8	5	8	54,039
Thomason, Sam L.	2	1	1	0	20,000
Thompson, Bill J.	19	3	4	1	27,134
Thompson, C. Edward	44	7	4	9	125,764
Thompson, Dabney S.	34	3	1	1	36,400
Thompson, Daniel	107	14	9	7	142,882
Thompson, Edward Joe	21	0	1	1	2,686
Thompson, Glenn R.	103	8	6	17	360,983
Thompson, J. Willard	280	20	31	33	666,448
Thompson, James B.	2	0	0	0	168
Thompson, James Emory	26	2	5	2	18,478
Thompson, Kevin	10	0	1	1	3,996
Thompson, Mark L.	37	3	2	4	72,720
Thompson, Michael R.	65	9	6	4	91,018
Thompson, Ron	6	0	0	0	180
Thompson, Steven	38	0	1	0	3,748
Thompson, Terri L.	15	0	0	3	8,857
Thompson, Yvette	99	7	1	7	85,570
Thompson, Jr., Harry F.	819	125	118	102	1,342,794
Thomsen, Paula	4	0	0	0	354
Thomson, Ronald	68	6	7	3	73,096
Thornbury, Jeffrey D.	142	16	22	20	423,580
Thorne, Joe	10	2	2	1	2,714
Thornton, Chris	19	1	3	0	6,850
Thornton, Eric	39	3	6	7	78,171
Thornton, James H.	4	0	0	0	0
Thornton, Mark	4	0	0	0	280
Thornton, Nancy	130	7	8	12	77,712
Thornton, Paul	29	5	5	3	42,142
Thorpe, Cindy	1	0	0	0	750
Thorson, Patrick	12	0	0	0	292
Thrasher, Amy	15	0	0	2	1,702
Three Irons, Gale	9	2	0	3	3,242
Three Irons, Melvin	3	0	0	0	0
Threewitt, Noble	11	0	0	2	15,830
Thurman, Kelly	6	1	1	0	3,982
Thurston, Harold	54	6	4	9	30,865
Thurston, Jerry A.	37	11	5	8	149,500
Tibbitts, Bobby K.	31	1	3	1	32,686
Tiller, Robert P.	282	69	48	33	3,939,642
Tillis, Jerry E.	11	0	0	0	0
Tillotta, Nancy L.	95	4	10	9	112,831
Timm, Robert H.	42	2	3	6	36,833
Tippett, Steve	74	10	12	6	108,039
Tisbert, Louis	20	2	2	0	13,145
Tobin, Edwin L	122	8	12	14	238,908
Todd, Jerry	27	1	2	0	4,823
Tofte, Vicki	4	0	0	1	1,232
Tohill, Kathy	4	0	1	0	1,679
Tohill, Val	15	0	0	0	2,665
Tolbert, Ron	4	0	2	0	5,148
Toledo, Herberto	25	3	3	2	63,235
Tolle, Bonnie	2	0	0	0	0
Tollett, Bill	116	25	16	17	224,028
Tomaselli, Anthony F.	30	4	3	3	42,995
Tomillo, Thomas F.	612	58	87	75	1,042,626
Tomlinson, Michael A.	180	27	21	26	568,254
Tompkins, Jimmie D.	5	0	0	0	261
Toner, David	57	6	3	10	54,663
Toner, James J.	112	19	5	15	1,276,282
Tool, Wayne	1	0	0	0	41
Toon, Kathy	56	5	1	9	37,204
Torelli, Stacy	196	17	16	30	244,170
Torevell, Chad	174	26	28	23	275,295
Torres, Ben	10	5	3	0	188,251
Torrez, Jerenesto	164	25	16	19	166,169
Tortora, Emanuel	410	58	55	49	1,381,375
Toscano, Jr., John T.	93	6	8	19	525,324
Touchet, Cerman	3	0	0	0	0
Touchet, Glenn	52	8	1	4	69,048
Touchet, Joseph L.	6	1	0	0	17,976
Touchet, Michael	13	0	0	0	1,469
Toups, Brent	96	4	10	10	72,636
Tourangeau, George H.	1	0	0	0	104

Trainer	Sts	1st	2d	3d	Purses
Tourangeau, Mike	118	19	23	19	38,880
Tourangeau, Russell	56	2	7	6	10,344
Tourangeau, Tom	9	1	0	4	1,404
Towne, Steve	89	14	13	10	262,130
Townsend, Donald P.	2	0	0	0	0
Townsend, Richard	19	1	0	0	9,505
Toy, Kevin	3	0	0	0	80
Toye, Joe	300	25	37	43	217,362
Tracy, Greg	134	26	21	19	311,869
Tracy, Jim	124	11	13	13	100,722
Tracy, Jr., Ray E.	323	48	47	34	573,252
Trahan, Jeff	2	0	0	0	0
Trahan, Oran	45	2	5	9	52,200
Traitz, Angela	52	5	5	2	59,105
Traitz, John	1	0	0	0	0
Trapani, Jerry	10	0	0	1	2,007
Treadway, Diane M.	18	2	2	4	18,492
Treasure, Paul	52	7	7	7	36,390
Tredway, E. Leroy	1	0	0	0	180
Treece, Charles S.	306	42	46	49	307,888
Tregoning, Marcus P.	1	0	0	0	90,000
Trejo, Amalio R.	100	10	9	9	63,644
Trela, Rosemary	39	5	8	4	74,707
Trent, Jr., Charles	15	1	0	1	9,440
Trett, Donald G.	4	1	0	0	6,035
Trevino, Senon	15	1	3	6	8,077
Trevino, Stephen C.	17	1	0	0	16,729
Triana, Alfredo	10	1	2	0	16,017
Tribert, C. Douglas	3	0	0	1	4,860
Trimmer, Richard K.	73	12	11	8	192,491
Triola, Nancy	2	2	0	0	70,080
Triola, Robert	9	0	0	1	5,413
Trione, Jr., Thomas E.	247	37	43	26	277,400
Trivigno, Michael T.	70	4	6	8	87,333
Troiani, Rico	5	0	0	0	125
Trombetta, Michael J.	180	35	27	26	768,799
Tronco, William L.	30	1	0	2	11,140
Trosclair, Jeff	68	14	12	10	389,536
Trotter, Jesse E.	13	2	1	1	19,720
Trottier, Burton	13	0	0	5	3,960
Trottier, John	6	1	1	0	1,245
Trout, C. R.	132	21	16	23	554,479
Trout, Robert G.	52	1	0	7	12,896
Troyer, Garnet H.	14	0	2	2	4,815
Troyer, Mark	1	0	0	0	635
Trudel, Yves	120	17	15	19	212,685
Truitt, Pat	34	3	4	4	14,460
Trujillo, Eddie	4	0	0	0	2,116
Trujillo, Michael F.	29	2	3	5	41,167
Trujillo, Jr, Celio	11	1	2	1	10,568
Trujillo, Jr., Carlos B.	1	0	0	0	0
Truman, Eddie	94	9	14	15	257,570
Truocchio, Robert	11	2	1	0	7,392
Truppa, Gaetano A	1	0	0	0	0
Tsagalakis, Mark D.	14	2	1	1	53,960
Tschan, April E.	6	0	1	0	12,368
Tschirgi, Brian	28	2	4	6	7,837
Tsirigotis, Tina	65	8	8	8	42,781
Tso, Sr., Justin	2	0	0	0	242
Tubbs, Scott	116	12	13	11	213,132
Tuck, Lewis L.	6	2	1	1	40,588
Tuck, Mary Lou	8	0	0	1	5,240
Tucker, Robert R.	32	0	1	3	7,085
Tuller, Fred	7	1	1	1	11,255
Tulloch, Roger A.	27	3	0	2	27,402
Tullock, Jr., Timothy J.	180	30	31	27	953,186
Tunks, Fred G.	1	0	0	0	0
Turchi, Frank	103	16	12	16	183,460
Turco, Chuck	123	19	21	14	274,595
Turetsky, Judy E.	43	5	5	8	46,431
Turlington, Stuart	13	0	1	2	4,145
Turner, Eric	29	4	1	4	7,364
Turner, Gus	51	3	9	7	52,557
Turner, Jack	6	0	1	0	1,931
Turner, Kris	160	17	22	25	185,737
Turner, Larry G.	13	2	0	2	6,095
Turner, Michael A.	26	3	4	2	62,905
Turner, Terry R.	8	0	2	0	3,231

Trainer	Sts	1st	2d	3d	Purses
Turner, Tom L.	6	0	2	1	1,241
Turner, Jr., Robert Rockwell	1	0	0	0	0
Turner, Jr., William H.	143	8	18	18	562,309
Turpin, Richaleen	158	22	22	22	145,597
Tustin, Rebecca	14	0	0	2	4,626
Tuttle, Chris	77	3	3	5	49,188
Tveit, Dwaine	12	1	2	0	3,187
Tweed, Perri	3	0	0	0	0
Twiggs, Leroy	43	3	8	8	13,279
Twileger, Gordon	12	0	4	2	6,070
Twyman, W. Noel	12	0	1	3	5,863
Tzortzakis, Emmanuel	78	13	10	15	230,496
Tzortzakis, Margarita	19	2	3	2	36,380
Uballe, Adam	9	0	0	0	0
Uballe, Daniel T.	3	0	0	0	165
Ubbink, Robert A.	2	0	0	0	840
Ubbink, Stephen P.	80	13	12	17	157,091
Uelmen, Larry R.	171	31	28	21	349,261
Ugalde, Arsenio R.	6	2	0	1	16,485
Uglow, Dan W.	19	2	2	1	19,486
Ulch, David M.	79	7	8	9	43,131
Ulmer, Cissy	2	0	0	0	0
Underdahl, Brice	27	4	7	4	17,040
Underwood, Sidney	36	2	4	4	29,810
Underwood, Terry L.	21	0	0	2	2,414
Ungles, Ken	22	1	3	3	7,884
Unwin, Bruce	5	0	0	0	848
Upham, Craig D.	8	1	0	2	8,659
Upton, Thomas M.	27	2	3	0	11,285
Urdiales, Ray	25	3	5	1	24,357
Urioste, Manuel D.	12	0	0	2	1,872
Uselton, Roy Gene	1	0	0	0	0
Utley, Ben	7	0	0	0	491
Utley, Doug	192	16	43	34	483,317
Utley, Sue	38	6	4	8	19,239
Uyeyama, Spud	24	1	1	4	12,234
Vacca, Joseph	7	0	0	0	177
Vaders, Jayne	225	41	38	39	615,587
Valdes, Aurelio P.	13	1	0	0	11,435
Valdez, Arnulfo R.	16	1	2	1	5,565
Valdez, Charlotte	1	0	0	0	0
Valdez, Ralph J.	25	0	0	1	1,530
Valdivia, Samuel E.	13	2	1	0	7,496
Valencia, Samantha Dyan	8	0	0	0	698
Valentine, Richard L.	43	4	2	10	84,613
Valenzuela, Jr., Martin	47	2	3	4	33,010
Valerio, Raymond G.	6	0	0	0	350
Vallance, Paul	20	1	0	3	11,836
Vallejo, Genaro	61	11	15	12	202,882
Vallejos, Gary J.	2	0	0	0	252
Vallejos, Tomas G.	44	2	5	3	24,259
Van Arem, Brian	15	1	0	0	51,657
Van Berg, Jack C.	125	4	8	8	166,608
Van Berg, Thomas L.	112	16	16	11	589,191
Van Deren, Lara	58	9	5	12	201,035
Van Horn, Tracy L.	2	0	0	0	900
Van Horne, Debbie	113	10	9	10	67,727
Van Loon, John	70	4	9	4	42,565
Van Overschot, Robert	155	17	25	17	524,061
Van Pelt, Charlotte M.	10	0	1	0	6,728
Van Tassell, Glade W.	23	1	1	2	1,743
Van Voorhis, Jan	13	1	0	4	12,752
Van Winkle, Brian	3	1	0	0	3,060
Van Winkle, David	310	56	56	45	764,336
Van Worp, Judson	3	0	0	0	2,910
Vanatta, Bart A.	28	1	2	8	19,761
Vanatta, James Bart	11	0	0	0	808
Vance, David R.	260	35	27	44	1,347,291
Vance, David W.	23	4	7	3	72,065
Vance, Terry W.	31	5	4	5	49,625
Vandane, Joseph	15	3	4	2	7,466
Vander-Heyden, Lance R.	4	1	1	0	6,538
Vandernat, Reinier	17	1	1	3	31,275
Vandersalm, Suzanne J.	49	3	1	5	38,811
Vandervort, Bernice E.	56	6	3	8	13,168
Vanier, Harvey L.	196	29	25	22	877,351
Vanklompenberg, Scott	18	0	2	2	3,874

Trainer	Sts	1st	2d	3d	Purses
Vannorsdel, Dana A.	7	0	1	1	878
Vanorio, Joe A.	25	0	1	1	10,069
Vardeman, Alfred	4	0	0	0	288
Vargas, Hector	2	0	0	1	1,820
Vargas, J. Buenaventura	53	3	3	7	83,908
Vargas, Nerio	48	3	3	4	52,213
Varner, Brad	8	0	0	1	1,787
Varner, Carrol	5	0	1	1	1,345
Varrelli, Joseph D.	29	0	3	3	15,275
Vasquez, Dario A.	136	5	10	22	115,787
Vasquez, Jacinto	1	0	0	0	230
Vasquez, Lona	19	0	2	2	6,083
Vasquez, Marcia	48	7	4	5	43,600
Vasquez, Ramon	52	2	3	3	38,948
Vaughn, Curt	33	5	3	3	27,249
Vaughn, Debra	43	3	1	2	66,279
Vaughn, Vicki L.	1	0	0	0	0
Vaught, Marie E.	1	0	0	0	50
Vazquez, Edwin	10	0	0	0	735
Vazquez, Gamaliel	309	55	48	32	1,415,285
Vazquez, Ivan	12	5	1	0	22,153
Veerhusen, Kim	21	6	4	3	38,480
Vega, Lorenzo	3	0	0	1	400
Vega, Richard	212	30	33	27	336,041
Vegh, Leslie L.	41	5	4	6	37,792
Veiga, Frank D.	41	2	7	1	79,775
Velasquez, Danny	47	0	4	6	63,611
Velasquez, Rigoberto	100	11	15	12	81,850
Velazquez, Alfredo	259	32	41	32	470,986
Velazquez-Rivas, Ismael	1	0	0	0	0
Velez, Javier	4	0	0	0	780
Velez, Jose E.	18	5	2	1	27,746
Velez, Roberto	53	4	8	5	44,753
Vella, Daniel J.	223	37	35	29	2,198,573
Venable, Ronald	57	3	5	6	60,419
Venham, Lyn Dee	11	0	1	2	13,360
Ver Mett, Chuck	5	0	1	1	883
Verderber, Greg	34	1	2	2	12,762
Verderosa, Lou	1	0	0	1	693
Verdesi, Alberto	5	0	0	2	4,020
Vest, Reeves R.	4	0	0	0	250
Vestal, Peter M.	93	9	8	10	428,701
Vestesen, Daniel C.	23	2	2	2	37,209
Viator, Dwight J.	47	3	6	4	56,285
Vickers, Richard T.	1	0	0	0	0
Vickers, Robert N.	3	0	0	0	0
Vickers, Traci	46	2	2	5	19,918
Vickers-Smith, Katharine L.	21	1	3	0	20,407
Vickery, Bret	7	1	1	0	9,714
Vidrine, Velton	54	6	10	5	83,558
Vienna, Cris	18	2	3	4	27,448
Vienna, Darrell	162	17	20	24	1,170,636
Vigneault, Julie	10	1	1	0	28,695
Villa, Jr., Alex	1	0	0	0	220
Villafranco, Frederico	76	18	14	10	108,572
Villalobos, Miguel A.	4	0	0	0	811
Villalobos, Sr., Rigoberto T.	18	0	0	1	4,811
Villanueva, Jesus	13	0	1	3	1,531
Villari, Barbara E.	36	2	3	1	24,760
Villarreal, Alex	1	0	0	0	540
Villarreal, Ezequiel	2	0	0	0	0
Villarreal, Reynaldo C.	15	1	0	2	9,435
Villegas, Benjamin	9	1	1	1	3,745
Villegas, Jesse	2	0	0	1	441
Villyard, Aubrey	58	16	10	7	201,950
Vilunas, John	5	0	0	0	2,757
Vincent, Sr., Dale C.	3	0	0	0	330
Vinci, Charles J.	248	20	32	38	489,945
Vineyard, Vance	49	4	4	5	33,631
Vinson, Garner H.	4	1	2	0	15,840
Vinson, Lynn	1	0	0	0	0
Violette, Jr., Richard A.	249	41	34	24	2,213,779
Viramontes, Rudolfo	3	2	0	1	6,800
Visscher, Patricia	6	1	0	0	3,385
Vitale, Francis J.	36	1	1	2	36,064
Vitali, Marcus J.	209	31	33	24	324,426
Vittur, Wilson E.	25	1	4	7	31,916

Trainer	Sts	1st	2d	3d	Purses
Vivian, David A.	103	21	18	10	757,269
Vivian, Jr., David A.	128	22	11	16	336,455
Vizcaya, James S.	5	0	0	0	344
Vlosich, Richard	1	0	0	1	900
Vojin, William J.	14	0	0	1	3,748
Volk, Scott J.	54	8	10	7	195,212
Von Hemel, Don	239	38	34	40	906,789
Von Hemel, Donnie K.	479	91	84	77	2,285,398
Von Hemel, Kelly R.	334	63	40	57	1,118,883
Von Wise, Kriston	24	1	3	3	14,363
Vosler, Durward L.	34	2	3	2	10,035
Voss, Katharine M.	60	12	7	9	245,727
Voss, Thomas H.	151	23	24	17	856,728
Voss, III, Ronald L.	87	10	5	11	115,348
Vowell, Dwayne	16	0	0	1	1,705
Voyce, Robyn	1	0	0	0	74
Vucurevich, Robert G.	23	1	2	3	13,726
Vuyosevich, Jeanne L.	29	2	1	4	60,013
Wadams, Dewight J.	54	1	5	7	18,918
Wade, Charles J.	32	5	5	4	77,268
Wade, Deanna	6	0	0	0	1,756
Wade, Garey	24	0	3	6	5,468
Wade, James E.	5	0	0	0	0
Wafer, George	31	6	6	2	31,896
Wagner, John G.	5	0	0	0	461
Wagner, Karin	12	1	1	2	18,615
Wainscott, Richard	2	1	0	0	6,710
Wainwright, John C.	169	16	23	19	268,246
Waite, Delcor D.	97	15	11	14	141,447
Waite, Dennis L.	71	3	4	3	40,220
Wakefield, Michael	19	0	1	2	4,658
Walcott, Jr., Charles A.	29	6	2	0	66,107
Walcott, Sr., Charles A.	29	4	5	2	47,905
Walden, W. Elliott	207	33	34	15	1,454,424
Walder, Peter R.	153	40	21	22	626,915
Waldie, Jack	207	10	22	22	139,770
Waldron, Bill	19	3	2	3	47,003
Wales, Dale E.	12	1	0	2	3,259
Walgren, Scott T.	9	2	0	0	3,772
Walker, Charles A.	57	0	6	13	40,188
Walker, Charles R.	40	2	2	5	18,381
Walker, Devin D.	41	3	2	4	47,176
Walker, Donald E.	13	1	0	2	14,597
Walker, Donald R.	5	0	1	0	1,580
Walker, Earl	57	2	4	8	22,668
Walker, Elmo K.	30	3	5	5	59,131
Walker, Leland R.	9	0	0	0	2,656
Walker, Lloyd E.	22	3	1	3	24,006
Walker, Paul R.	4	0	1	0	1,930
Walker, Phillip	22	1	5	6	57,355
Walker, Roger D.	26	3	2	3	47,272
Walker, Sheldon E.	34	2	4	3	19,268
Walker, Terry A.	115	8	15	14	474,378
Walker, Jr., Charles C.	330	24	33	33	162,126
Wall, John	1	0	0	0	82
Wallace, Bowen	4	0	4	0	1,262
Wallace, Ronnie	77	13	6	7	183,777
Wallace, Roy L.	28	0	3	2	27,770
Wallace, Waldyn H.	23	0	2	0	5,470
Wallack, Patrick H.	50	3	2	7	42,464
Wallis, Nathan	27	4	1	3	28,400
Walls, Joseph F.	54	1	6	12	130,613
Walls, Judy D.	17	2	2	4	21,102
Walper, Deanna	83	13	9	14	142,398
Walsh, Deirdre	3	0	0	0	360
Walsh, Edward	17	2	1	1	5,728
Walsh, Joseph	1	0	0	0	400
Walsh, Kathy	58	6	5	7	270,862
Walsh, Rachael L.	14	0	0	0	1,609
Walsh, Richard A.	10	1	0	1	3,833
Walsh, Ryan D.	105	14	11	14	131,071
Walsh, Thomas M.	33	3	1	0	90,741
Walsh, Timothy J.	56	9	10	7	198,935
Walsky, Michael S.	10	0	0	1	2,792
Walston, Lawson	28	0	1	1	5,550
Walt, Nicole L.	46	5	3	4	71,305
Waltermire, Bruce	2	0	0	0	219
Walters, David	271	31	26	23	634,670
Walters, Fred E.	3	1	0	0	3,127
Walters, Henry R.	72	17	16	6	264,510
Walters, Philip L.	1	0	0	0	0
Walton, John J.	6	0	1	1	1,545
Walton, Madeline	2	0	0	1	290
Waltz, Brian	76	10	7	18	119,266
Wames, John J.	47	4	4	8	49,441
Wansborough, Martin	22	3	4	0	110,347
Ward, Brian D.	7	0	0	0	655
Ward, Dale T.	1	0	0	0	105
Ward, Dean	2	0	1	0	2,145
Ward, Dennis	1	0	0	1	6,000
Ward, Derek	1	0	0	0	44
Ward, Douglas	3	0	0	0	153
Ward, Glenn S.	51	1	5	8	42,167
Ward, Joseph D.	10	0	1	0	3,017
Ward, Kenneth J.	12	1	4	2	8,806
Ward, Lida J.	34	1	2	5	12,236
Ward, Ronnie P.	323	26	36	44	292,319
Ward, Sonny	14	1	1	0	11,747
Ward, Wesley A.	447	75	82	68	1,975,167
Ward, Jr., John T.	100	14	16	16	667,238
Ward, Jr., Roger D.	1	0	0	0	75
Ware, Cody W.	6	0	0	0	140
Warmack, Sarah A.	3	0	1	0	2,000
Warner, Alison	2	0	0	0	174
Warner, Robert K.	34	2	1	5	31,355
Warnimont, Ralph B.	98	9	19	11	109,990
Warnke, Eugene E.	50	1	2	5	11,993
Warpool, Michael Shane	68	3	4	5	54,785
Warren, Donald	141	11	11	24	565,718
Warren, Fred G.	316	33	44	43	565,180
Warren, Ronnie G.	19	3	0	3	26,131
Warren, Tom M.	8	3	1	2	100,000
Wartchow, John	43	6	5	3	33,906
Warvell, Jim	92	11	10	13	109,094
Warwick, Candice	68	8	7	6	105,355
Washer, David J.	5	1	0	1	8,805
Washington, Adrian	17	1	1	2	6,747
Washington, Thomas H.	55	8	6	10	123,092
Wasilewski, Christine	30	3	2	8	43,920
Wasiluk, Jr., Peter	260	14	16	18	181,133
Wasserman, Richard A.	163	28	22	24	277,430
Wasson, Glen Stanley	165	12	21	14	116,330
Watermeier, Ann	52	6	2	2	56,291
Waters, Dean	12	0	0	2	6,185
Waters, Faryn	30	2	5	6	28,570
Waters, Karl S.	103	15	11	19	238,664
Watkins, Edward J.	20	1	0	1	6,490
Watkins, James M.	11	2	1	1	6,358
Watkins, Robert L.	81	9	12	8	68,598
Watkins, Shannon	67	5	4	12	84,635
Watkins, William L.	22	0	1	2	5,170
Watson, Jack R.	6	1	0	0	6,147
Watson, Janene M.	10	0	0	0	280
Watson, Kari	23	4	4	2	21,045
Watson, Robert S.	10	1	0	2	7,836
Watt, Randy	4	0	1	0	1,992
Watts, J. W.	4	0	1	1	845
Waugh, Joseph R.	39	1	6	5	31,616
Waugh, Virginia	15	0	1	0	2,880
Waunsch, Joseph J.	82	12	11	11	376,394
Waxman, Katherine	1	0	0	0	0
Wayar, Manuel J.	37	9	6	3	200,465
Weatherwax, Robert	16	3	4	3	13,628
Weaver, Billy Hoyt	6	0	0	0	218
Weaver, George	401	46	50	52	1,925,813
Weaver, Jerry	47	3	4	3	40,946
Webb, Bennie	1	1	0	0	1,815
Webb, Dale D.	4	2	1	0	19,740
Webb, Delmer L.	116	24	26	15	84,951
Webb, Edward	48	3	3	4	29,352
Webb, Lucy B.	71	12	10	7	185,010
Webb, Ronnie R.	1	0	0	0	40
Webb, Samuel E.	187	42	26	23	406,436
Webb, Stan	19	6	5	3	32,345
Webster, Alfred C.	11	1	1	2	5,125
Webster, Caroline	11	0	0	3	4,340

Trainer	Sts	1st	2d	3d	Purses
Weckerle, Kathy E.	23	4	1	1	99,123
Wedge, John	28	4	4	2	18,496
Wedge, Terry	17	2	2	0	18,216
Wedge, Jr., Les	7	0	0	1	1,729
Weeder, Tim	91	10	19	11	76,732
Weeks, Michael Lee	3	3	0	0	50,700
Weeks, Thomas C.	120	14	10	15	238,036
Weems, George	29	4	5	2	60,023
Weger, Bill R.	5	0	1	2	2,550
Wehling, Jr., John D.	1	0	0	0	0
Wehrli, Gerald R.	48	8	5	9	47,751
Weimer, Edward R.	33	3	9	6	22,979
Weimer, Jackie	7	2	0	1	6,471
Weipert, Bryan G.	33	3	7	0	72,865
Weir, George L.	72	4	8	8	43,067
Weir, Gregory H.	4	0	0	0	640
Weir, Kelly	35	6	7	5	72,790
Weiss, Frank R.	11	0	3	2	23,903
Weiss, Richard M.	1	0	0	0	140
Weissman, Michael F.	51	9	7	2	196,382
Weist, Rick	1	0	0	0	123
Welch, C. Eugene	26	0	6	3	11,274
Welch, J. Michael	78	11	10	3	218,395
Welch, Needham W.	36	5	4	8	39,647
Welch, Scott	1	0	0	0	122
Welch, Jr., William L.	74	5	10	10	89,734
Weld, Dermot K.	5	1	0	1	198,750
Wells, Darrell	41	4	2	2	18,626
Wells, David J.	67	20	4	6	238,312
Wells, Debra Ann	32	1	3	4	15,400
Wells, Donald V.	20	4	2	3	32,034
Wells, Forrest W.	1	0	0	0	720
Wells, Gordon	33	4	3	4	42,433
Wells, John Lee	12	1	0	1	16,569
Wells, Larry	194	20	25	26	132,929
Wells, Thomas C.	17	2	1	1	12,760
Wells, Tonya M.	8	0	0	1	2,864
Welsch, Lisa	6	0	2	1	2,866
Welsh, Gary	93	10	10	6	143,912
Welsh, Regina	3	2	0	0	48,000
Wenderoth, Gloria M.	24	2	2	1	50,649
Wendling, Ronald	54	2	8	5	63,592
Wendt, Chris	2	0	0	0	620
Wenzel, Tom	116	17	19	23	164,113
Wermes, Margaret	21	1	0	2	7,735
Wern, George	192	21	28	27	130,938
Werner, Robert Russell	69	8	3	8	46,034
Werner, Ronny W.	242	46	45	35	1,133,292
Werneth, Roger	48	3	1	6	60,588
Werneth, Jr., Hilton E.	19	3	3	2	35,640
Wessel, Jim	3	0	0	1	1,430
Wessels, Amy L.	7	0	0	0	562
Wessner, Gerald	2	0	1	0	5,250
Wessner, Tracy	9	0	0	0	636
West, Benjamin F.	88	5	6	5	41,860
West, David L.	57	7	10	2	39,638
West, Delmer G.	36	1	1	1	7,777
West, Gareld F.	32	1	2	1	17,362
West, Martha J.	12	0	2	0	4,300
West, Raymond P.	47	2	3	3	20,759
West, Ted	2	0	0	0	3,440
West, Ted H.	142	30	28	20	1,020,284
West, Wayne	16	1	2	0	12,528
West, Jr., Henry	88	2	6	12	39,046
West, Jr., Roy W.	31	3	2	3	27,601
Westergaard, Robert L.	6	0	1	1	3,720
Westermann, Ronald L.	76	5	8	12	48,025
Westerness, Randy	1	0	0	0	0
Weston, Charles	38	0	7	6	28,255
Weston, Susan	16	0	0	1	4,122
Wetherington, Margaret	8	0	1	1	3,827
Wethey, Floyd J.	17	2	0	3	7,634
Wever, Cynthia S.	71	9	5	6	136,529
Wever, Jr., Alston A.	13	1	0	0	16,355
Weymes, Andrew Patrick	8	1	0	1	5,187
Weymouth, Eugene E.	128	23	20	19	374,509
Whalen, Betty W.	5	1	1	0	6,465
Whalen, Henry	176	10	20	17	229,400
Wharton, Cliff	13	0	3	1	4,481
Whatley, Archie E.	51	5	0	3	59,315
Wheatley, Leo A.	54	3	5	7	20,223
Wheeler, Don	10	0	0	0	475
Wheeler, Jolynn	1	0	0	0	0
Wheeler, Larry A.	96	9	2	15	64,791
Wheeler, Tandi	117	15	11	10	164,333
Wheeler, Wilmer E.	69	0	3	6	12,581
Wherry, Bill	19	1	2	2	16,309
Whipple, Tim	33	2	3	5	18,344
Whitaker, Clarke D.	131	16	15	9	191,908
White, A. Ridgely	11	0	1	2	11,595
White, A. Timothy	45	3	4	2	71,455
White, Alan D.	82	7	4	12	62,627
White, Donald R.	85	1	2	4	37,378
White, Gary B.	33	0	9	1	6,253
White, J. V.	3	0	0	0	194
White, Jacqueline M.	27	2	2	1	12,702
White, James D.	22	3	2	3	48,385
White, James T.	15	0	1	2	4,284
White, Joe L.	2	0	0	0	0
White, Keith	1	1	0	0	1,100
White, M. Victoria	14	0	1	0	4,859
White, Mel	10	1	4	1	2,735
White, Mike	5	0	0	0	325
White, Ron E.	50	3	3	8	34,524
White, Vincent	148	10	14	14	93,553
White, Wade L.	4	0	0	0	245
White, William P.	361	73	55	50	1,667,257
White, Sr., Dale	26	1	6	1	30,954
Whited, Danny W.	164	28	17	21	289,102
Whited, David E.	112	11	12	17	172,559
Whitehouse, W. R.	107	9	11	12	78,136
Whitelaw, Michael R.	29	2	3	3	17,991
Whiteside, Charlene	24	3	4	1	7,652
Whiteside, Sr., Jim	6	0	1	2	983
Whitfield, Jeff	1	0	0	0	0
Whitford, Linda J.	8	1	0	1	2,010
Whitford, Rina	6	1	1	1	5,420
Whiting, Lynn S.	137	20	25	23	665,241
Whitlock, John R.	1	0	0	0	31
Whitmire, Larry	2	0	0	1	495
Whitner, IV, James H.	1	0	0	0	0
Whitney, Pamela	16	0	1	0	3,609
Whitson, Robert	4	0	0	1	1,175
Whitt, John H.	9	0	0	1	798
Whittingham, Michael C.	10	0	0	2	35,664
Whittle, John J.	3	0	0	0	390
Whitton, Mark	42	4	6	3	67,810
Whylie, Herold O.	84	4	5	6	45,552
Wichmann, Dean	1	0	1	0	1,248
Wicker, Lloyd C.	32	4	2	5	117,330
Wideman, Jane	6	1	1	0	8,440
Widenmaier, Melvin	21	1	1	3	19,383
Widmer, Wayne	30	3	2	1	89,827
Wieneke, Henry	1	0	0	0	80
Wiese, John	67	2	6	9	21,289
Wiest, Phil	63	13	15	15	62,040
Wiest, Rick	20	5	7	3	33,194
Wig, Janet C.	156	17	22	20	217,223
Wiggins, David A.	79	5	9	7	52,344
Wiggins, Deborah A.	4	0	1	0	5,390
Wiggins, Hal R.	279	32	39	33	852,061
Wiggins, Lon	102	8	5	6	149,597
Wigginton, Jesse N.	66	12	15	11	330,846
Wilborn, Beverly C.	17	0	6	2	8,018
Wilborn, J. Kevin	157	18	10	22	122,384
Wilcox, Bruce W.	41	2	6	3	28,477
Wilcox, Ron	7	0	0	2	2,690
Wilcox, Warren	145	11	12	14	440,877
Wilcoxson, P. J.	1	0	0	1	1,980
Wilensky, Herman	94	17	8	10	210,540
Wiley, Chuck W.	112	14	16	15	96,160
Wiley, Gerald T.	2	0	0	0	470
Wiley, Sue	32	1	3	4	8,094
Wiley, Jr., Leslie J.	46	3	3	7	38,041
Wilhelm, David L.	51	3	7	5	59,682
Wilhelm, Larry	36	4	2	3	15,398
Wilhelm, Jr, James R.	16	1	1	2	26,580
Wilhelm, Sr., James R.	28	0	0	1	4,411

Trainer	Sts	1st	2d	3d	Purses
Wilhelm-Saldana, Jennie	79	2	6	8	43,202
Wilke, Gordon	15	1	1	0	2,774
Wilkerson, Jimmy C.	2	0	0	0	204
Wilkerson, Tom	16	1	2	2	13,594
Wilkes, John T.	3	0	0	0	855
Wilkins, F. Bryan	63	3	5	11	86,834
Wilkins, Joe L.	30	4	5	3	25,275
Wilkinson, James D.	111	5	10	8	108,155
Wilkinson, Sherman	19	2	1	1	14,364
Wilkinson, Winston	43	2	3	5	39,126
Wilkinson, III, Jack R.	36	4	3	7	67,757
Willaford, Carol	12	3	1	1	14,904
Willey, Theresa J.	9	1	1	1	4,390
Williams, Andrew	49	1	7	6	42,245
Williams, Bryan H.	17	1	1	0	11,195
Williams, Charlie J.	75	8	15	15	110,215
Williams, Cheryl	14	2	1	0	33,803
Williams, David John	4	1	1	0	3,681
Williams, Edward L.	43	1	6	6	34,291
Williams, Ellen	12	1	2	1	11,078
Williams, Ernest R.	49	3	4	11	10,736
Williams, George	16	0	0	1	3,110
Williams, George E.	17	1	0	1	6,460
Williams, George L.	9	0	0	0	3,620
Williams, Gerald	3	0	1	2	1,000
Williams, Harold G.	7	1	0	1	14,510
Williams, Herbert B.	20	1	2	7	12,589
Williams, J. Alan	49	9	4	3	36,590
Williams, James L.	198	22	20	19	351,988
Williams, James Milton	18	1	2	0	8,497
Williams, Jeffrey M.	12	2	0	2	35,007
Williams, Jerry Wayne	7	0	0	0	1,440
Williams, L. A.	3	3	0	0	7,247
Williams, L. C.	3	0	0	0	210
Williams, Robert H.	35	7	4	6	162,692
Williams, Robert L.	68	5	4	9	76,595
Williams, Sandra E.	14	3	1	1	24,353
Williams, Sean	28	4	5	2	31,149
Williams, Wendy	34	1	2	4	30,823
Williams, II, Roger L.	6	0	0	1	1,411
Williams, III, Robert	16	0	0	0	450
Williams, Jr., Gary L.	21	4	3	1	89,182
Williams, Jr., Robert C.	14	0	1	3	4,215
Williams, Sr., Edward E.	7	0	0	0	777
Williamson, Brian	156	27	22	17	704,413
Williamson, Joseph P.	29	3	6	3	21,199
Williamson, Mark	5	0	0	0	372
Willis, Frank	12	1	1	1	3,346
Willis, Joe Don	20	1	2	1	4,869
Willis, Kevin	2	0	0	0	570
Willis, Mindy J.	127	10	15	22	131,080
Willis, Tracy A.	64	2	1	10	71,188
Willis, William L.	19	2	3	5	5,217
Willis, Jr., Alfred	78	5	5	6	23,788
Willits, Marvin W.	5	0	1	1	5,600
Willoughby, Mark	6	1	1	0	2,195
Willoughby, Scott L.	8	1	2	0	9,079
Wills, Daniel	82	15	11	11	257,023
Willson, Clint D.	6	0	0	1	3,570
Wilmot, William B.	25	0	2	2	20,367
Wilson, Ariane B.	51	1	1	4	25,266
Wilson, Brad V.	15	0	0	2	2,278
Wilson, Brenda	91	5	6	15	89,789
Wilson, Bruce E.	3	0	0	0	126
Wilson, C. L.	53	3	5	6	45,092
Wilson, Campbell	65	13	9	10	170,438
Wilson, Dale L.	5	0	0	0	0
Wilson, David	1	0	0	0	43
Wilson, Ed	5	1	0	2	2,965
Wilson, Frank K.	5	0	0	0	254
Wilson, Frank R.	23	5	6	2	26,681
Wilson, Fred S.	5	0	0	0	3,740
Wilson, Gene K.	112	23	22	12	42,849
Wilson, Gordon	7	0	0	0	0
Wilson, Gregory L.	76	8	14	4	115,305
Wilson, Jack B.	10	3	0	0	14,120
Wilson, James G.	6	3	0	1	14,780
Wilson, John R.	116	15	18	18	328,691
Wilson, John S.	19	0	0	0	1,575
Wilson, Larry L.	28	1	5	3	26,233
Wilson, Lorna S.	40	5	0	4	42,541
Wilson, Lynn	9	1	3	1	6,887
Wilson, Mark M.	1	0	1	0	375
Wilson, Nancy J.	6	0	0	0	688
Wilson, Peter	18	0	2	4	15,295
Wilson, R. Scott	22	5	6	1	50,776
Wilson, Raymond	53	9	8	8	21,809
Wilson, Ronald D.	10	3	0	0	6,405
Wilson, Russell	1	0	0	0	75
Wilson, Shane	233	21	29	25	387,767
Wilson, Stephen R.	11	0	1	1	7,072
Wilson, Tara	18	1	1	3	14,328
Wilson, Tony	35	2	3	5	30,319
Wilson, Wallace C.	11	4	1	0	13,370
Wilson, William	5	0	2	2	1,365
Wilson, William D.	2	0	0	0	261
Wilt, Ronald J.	154	14	13	11	261,268
Wimberley, Jessie	18	1	0	1	9,040
Wind, Charles M.	16	1	1	4	6,614
Windle, Richard L.	4	0	2	0	12,570
Winebaugh, Cheryl	58	9	6	10	103,651
Winfree, Donald R.	64	5	7	8	80,287
Winfrey, Troy B.	8	1	0	0	5,847
Winick, Randy	4	0	0	1	5,800
Winkelmann, Erika	47	2	1	3	25,817
Winney, Melvin	6	1	3	0	50,721
Winstead, Robert D.	30	7	1	5	96,122
Winters, Michelle	56	4	3	3	52,550
Wirth, Kenneth B.	148	13	15	17	217,560
Wirtzberger, Jodi L.	4	0	0	0	390
Wisdom, Lascelles	46	3	6	4	23,663
Wise, Anthony D.	24	2	4	5	36,552
Wise, Holly	13	2	2	1	39,145
Wise, Jason	34	4	6	5	25,319
Wise, Rick A.	72	10	8	10	110,914
Wise, Ron	18	4	2	4	16,360
Wiseman, Barry G.	20	1	1	0	11,675
Wiseman, Kelly L.	215	16	19	20	228,996
Wiser, Jimmy L.	118	16	12	14	109,726
Wismer, Glenn S.	80	7	7	7	123,430
Wismer, Norman P.	87	9	5	10	48,913
Wisner, Tracey J.	150	11	15	18	114,948
Wisniewski-Johnson, Mary	25	1	3	4	47,120
Withee, Henry E.	94	8	5	5	96,993
Witherow, Sandra J.	27	1	4	0	21,139
Wittensoldner, Joe	1	0	0	0	105
Witthauer, John K.	141	19	13	18	173,284
Wofford, Douglas L.	1	0	0	0	0
Wofford, William	8	0	1	1	4,736
Wohler, Andreas	1	0	1	0	300,000
Wolbert, Tyler	31	1	1	4	12,423
Wolf, Joan	18	0	2	2	12,150
Wolf, Larry	100	6	13	15	88,311
Wolfe, Clement	16	1	1	1	7,556
Wolfe, Greg	37	4	5	6	27,222
Wolfe, John R.	50	1	4	3	15,245
Wolfe, Jr., Robert A.	148	14	15	18	177,591
Wolfendale, Howard E.	283	75	62	46	1,193,210
Wolfendale, Ross B.	215	25	26	24	505,548
Wolfendale, Sue A.	26	3	0	3	27,480
Wolfendale, III, William H.	88	1	11	10	79,847
Wolferseder, John M.	17	1	0	3	37,452
Wolff, Perry	36	3	1	4	28,545
Wolfson, Martin D.	176	39	32	15	1,710,249
Wolfson, Milton W.	119	18	16	27	654,975
Wollfarth, III, Charles	21	0	1	3	12,852
Wolochuk, David	35	9	7	7	52,397
Womack, Hulon Leslie	28	2	0	5	10,064
Wonders, Jr., John	24	1	5	1	12,338
Wood, Blane	1	0	0	0	100
Wood, Darwin K.	39	3	6	2	31,634
Wood, Grant A.	1	0	0	0	0
Wood, Jerry S.	22	1	2	4	18,246
Wood, Robert C.	56	11	17	8	71,479
Wood, II, George A. G.	4	0	0	0	750
Wood, Sr., Glen R.	37	2	5	3	12,049
Woodard, Joe	316	49	43	47	421,411
Woodard, Walter H.	6	0	0	0	999

Trainer	Sts	1st	2d	3d	Purses
Woodger, Patricia	10	0	0	1	7,355
Woodhouse, Edward	6	0	2	0	2,112
Woodhouse, Martin	42	2	4	4	26,367
Woodington, Jamie	85	8	8	10	300,223
Woods, James W.	41	5	6	5	104,328
Woods, Ronald A.	8	0	0	0	0
Woods, Toni	9	0	2	0	2,616
Woodson, Jr., Charles A.	1	0	0	0	0
Woodson, Jr., Franklin R.	4	0	0	0	340
Wooldridge, Steve A.	3	0	1	0	1,994
Woolley, Tim	47	5	8	5	89,410
Woolley, Jr., Bennie L.	112	11	13	14	137,838
Woolsey, Lynn R.	4	0	1	0	5,903
Wooten, Donald A.	20	0	0	4	7,059
Wooten, Manuel	32	2	1	0	18,795
Worcester, III, Henry E.	196	27	29	19	470,968
Worcester, IV, Henry E.	37	9	7	2	151,370
Worrell-Springer, Hayden	43	1	2	1	33,022
Worsley, John E.	33	1	1	4	19,293
Wortman, Chris	12	0	0	0	0
Worton, Jack	2	0	0	0	630
Wren, Bobby C.	1	0	0	0	0
Wren, Steve	145	28	22	22	438,745
Wright, Albert	4	0	0	0	420
Wright, Charles D.	72	5	8	4	70,393
Wright, Clinton W.	3	0	0	0	128
Wright, Derilee	6	0	0	0	591
Wright, Floyd	70	4	4	7	35,562
Wright, J. Andy	1	0	0	0	0
Wright, James T.	236	52	30	26	545,682
Wright, Jeremy	38	5	3	5	14,942
Wright, John W.	5	1	0	0	4,099
Wright, Keith	19	2	2	5	6,468
Wright, Michael W.	83	11	11	10	477,975
Wright, Richard D.	81	6	13	9	85,814
Wright, Robert F.	4	0	0	0	840
Wright, Jr., Michael	50	3	4	4	72,169
Wyner, Harold	18	2	0	4	23,949
Wyness, James	4	0	0	1	871
Wynn, George A.	19	1	5	2	22,556
Wyrick, Jeff	36	1	2	3	7,836
Xerri, Louis	10	0	0	0	5,412
Yaegel, James F.	3	0	1	0	2,373
Yaegel, Thomas	146	18	20	14	92,261
Yakteen, Tim	28	5	4	5	217,720
Yamauchi, Kenji	1	0	0	0	0
Yanez, Moises R.	391	33	51	47	881,713
Yarberry, Gene M.	1	0	0	0	38
Yarberry, Laura Jan	1	0	0	0	69
Yarger, Jerry	38	1	2	1	11,232
Yates, Jim	59	6	3	6	67,963
Yates, Michael	21	4	1	2	62,572
Yates, Richard	14	3	2	2	36,703
Ybarra, Patricio G.	13	0	4	0	2,446
Ybarra, Rudy D.	12	0	1	0	1,014
Yeagley, William R.	93	2	2	8	24,523
Yearout, Judi	35	12	7	3	19,592
Yellowhair, Albert	1	0	0	0	31
Yelverton, Clement D.	10	0	2	2	5,431
Yelvington, Mel	25	3	7	2	8,330
Yerke, Gordon	10	0	2	0	913
Yetsook, George G.	48	12	9	10	424,219
Ylioja, Ken	16	1	2	2	3,400
Yon, Jeff C.	2	0	0	0	123
Yonker, Lyle A.	10	0	3	1	3,380
York, Jack William	85	5	3	5	33,299
York, Keith L.	11	1	1	0	6,802
York, Michael	143	7	11	17	48,496
Young, Brent	13	0	0	0	745
Young, Daniel J.	18	5	4	1	7,921
Young, Don A.	33	2	1	6	30,519
Young, Don D.	93	8	14	11	23,382
Young, Eugene	32	3	2	5	25,780
Young, Jack	59	6	6	7	98,477
Young, Joe D.	41	1	8	1	27,704
Young, John W.	45	0	4	6	19,698
Young, Louise	6	0	0	0	785
Young, Mary	1	0	0	0	0
Young, Nicole	5	0	0	0	180
Young, Phebe D.	44	4	4	5	37,128
Young, Phillip	10	0	0	1	3,441
Young, Robert A.	204	26	25	34	326,963
Young, Robert S.	8	0	0	2	2,620
Young, Stacy	1	0	1	0	7,000
Young, Steven W.	97	16	14	13	479,252
Young, Teresa L.	6	0	0	0	0
Young, Terry R.	46	1	6	4	41,394
Young, Timothy	1	0	0	0	0
Young, Troy	218	44	43	41	1,201,649
Younghans, William	4	0	0	0	2,837
Youngs, Frank W.	65	6	3	6	99,446
Yourchisin, Joseph E.	92	16	17	14	304,157
Yourman, Ernest E.	4	0	0	1	1,040
Yourman, Richard M.	2	0	0	0	0
Yousif, Edmond	6	0	1	0	3,569
Yovanovich, Donald	53	4	6	4	65,263
Yu, Danny	60	2	6	4	141,472
Zacco, Mario T.	23	3	2	2	96,385
Zagin, Nancy Ann	50	1	4	5	15,926
Zahl, Robert	95	15	12	7	159,073
Zajaczkowski, Cezary	7	1	0	3	19,721
Zamora, Jamie	6	0	0	0	761
Zamora, Ricardo	32	1	3	4	20,325
Zanelli, Dante	89	8	8	9	118,013
Zanelli, Sr., Dante J.	21	2	1	3	46,871
Zanette, Peter P.	4	0	1	2	10,467
Zanini, Maribeth	5	0	0	0	894
Zanni, Domenic	11	3	0	1	29,191
Zavash, Kerry	62	8	9	8	121,710
Zavitsanos, James	70	8	14	3	87,293
Zawislak, Dale	3	0	1	1	390
Zawitz, Joel	12	0	0	0	3,426
Zazueta, Hector	7	0	0	0	2,740
Zdunick, Fern	46	10	6	6	34,064
Zeek, Jeffrey	8	0	0	1	1,456
Zegowitz, Raymond W.	115	14	5	13	263,114
Zehnder, Charles D.	96	5	19	8	53,275
Zehnder, Clarence F.	63	4	13	7	44,873
Zeigler, Daniel L.	3	0	0	1	3,185
Zeigler, Larry E.	10	0	1	0	5,342
Zeis, Arthur J.	136	13	19	15	109,988
Zeis, Kevin J.	35	3	2	2	18,048
Zelasney, Emil A.	67	6	12	6	41,544
Zele, Jr., Mark	18	1	1	1	10,545
Zele, Sr., Mark	10	1	2	0	20,155
Zeltt, Scott M.	24	1	0	5	16,617
Zenon, Alvin	19	0	0	1	9,099
Zenon, Jr., Curley	84	1	4	8	38,903
Zeringue, Jr., Whitney J.	36	2	3	5	27,552
Ziadie, Kirk	130	41	16	13	845,423
Ziadie, Ralph	392	44	54	47	904,022
Ziccardi, Arnold W.	17	1	0	3	14,252
Ziegler, Peggy Sue	23	1	1	3	25,687
Zielinski, Cindy	5	0	0	1	2,150
Zielinski, Greg	90	9	11	15	101,322
Zielinski, Richard	41	3	6	3	73,319
Zilber, Maurice	1	0	0	1	12,000
Zimmer, Mark	20	1	6	4	38,457
Zimmer, Thomas L.	70	5	13	8	52,859
Zimmerman, John Charles	773	193	113	115	2,554,139
Zimmerman, Jon Phil	215	35	35	38	203,984
Zimmerman, Mary B.	25	2	5	1	65,580
Zimmerman, Tyler	2	0	0	0	420
Zimmerman, Sr., Reggie N.	10	2	1	1	14,012
Zissides, Gust	47	4	5	5	58,168
Zita, Danny	16	1	1	2	65,745
Zito, Nicholas P.	452	86	68	52	6,967,792
Zook, Donna S.	66	1	5	5	34,237
Zook, Jeff W.	1	0	0	0	64
Zook, Jimmy	176	37	22	23	635,309
Zoppi, Joseph	24	1	3	2	37,135
Zucker, Howard L.	81	11	10	18	336,160
Zureick, Frank J.	33	0	1	7	20,486
Zwiesler, Michael	100	21	18	14	426,265

2004

Records of Jockeys

The record of each jockey, who rode thoroughbreds in the United States and Canada during 2004, appears in this section, showing the year born, place of birth, number of starts, firsts, seconds and thirds, and the total purses earned by the horses ridden.

Jockey	Sts	1st	2d	3d	Purses
Abernathy, Becky	70	5	5	7	17,199
Acosta, J. D.	1,303	148	156	185	3,154,370
Acridge, Jeremy	413	36	40	37	273,826
Adam, Mathieu G.	862	67	89	107	670,985
Adams, John K.	8	0	0	1	6,687
Agilar, Trey	502	43	68	58	688,596
Agrazal, Jorge	9	0	0	1	3,207
Aguilar, Manuel	1,272	170	176	172	3,625,226
Aguirre, Silverio	1	0	0	0	1,200
Aizpuru, Xavier	67	8	11	8	185,777
Al Saffar, Ali	2	0	0	0	315
Albarado, Robby	1,309	213	223	197	10,371,173
Alcala, Natividad	130	6	17	11	62,574
Alexander, Samuel H.	16	0	0	0	987
Alferez, Jose O.	270	22	26	41	357,982
Alfred, Jr., Ricky	38	1	1	3	12,493
Allen, Charlie D.	6	0	0	0	330
Allen, Joel William	115	12	8	13	40,150
Allen, Mike	221	15	11	25	237,170
Almeida, G. F.	193	15	22	22	636,515
Almodovar, Gerald	939	139	132	110	2,372,230
Alpander, Tamay B.	115	4	7	8	37,940
Alvarado, Frank T.	981	117	163	163	2,612,235
Alvarado, Luis	74	5	3	8	63,491
Alvarado, Nazario	351	28	29	39	317,696
Alvarado, Pedro V.	533	130	85	87	2,216,447
Alvarado, Jr., Roberto	909	167	137	118	3,863,571
Amarsingh, Dilip	8	0	1	0	7,605
Amaya, Victor	18	0	0	3	2,848
Amonte, Frank	10	0	1	0	1,426
Amy, Jose	5	0	0	1	4,799
Anderson, Brett W.	49	3	7	10	10,229
Anderson, Dennis	16	0	1	0	5,782
Anderson, Devon	275	22	14	25	323,761
Anderson, Mark	397	29	31	38	158,969
Ando, Happy H.	327	21	25	36	440,851
Andrews, Maureen E.	530	28	35	52	513,280
Appleby, Jr., David L.	69	5	4	4	34,577
Aragon, Jorge	53	1	2	6	29,054
Aranda, Joel	2	0	0	0	0
Arango, Eli	1	0	0	0	83
Arango, Luis E.	496	58	47	54	709,704
Arce, Josue'	1	0	0	0	85
Arechiga, J. Efrain	12	1	1	1	7,231
Arguello, Jr., Fabio A.	367	25	34	43	431,495
Arias, Juan Carlos	1	0	0	0	50
Arias, Juan Pablo	51	3	8	3	27,672
Arnold, Allen Dean	19	3	5	0	10,093
Arreola, Abraham	71	9	6	6	63,974
Arreola, Alberto Hernandez	1	0	0	0	99
Arreola, Enrique H.	64	2	2	7	20,189
Arriaga, Antonio	2	0	0	0	302
Arriaga, Gregorio	1	0	0	0	300
Arriaga, Joy	2	0	0	0	973
Arriaga, Otto	124	7	6	17	77,840
Arroyo, E. Nelson	3	0	0	0	326
Arroyo, Wilfredo	4	0	0	0	1,645
Arroyo, Jr., Norberto	831	109	131	141	4,274,888
Arruda, Tonja A.	461	32	57	51	336,668
Ashburn, Mark	27	4	1	3	15,152
Ashlock, Zevi	18	0	1	5	2,846
Assoon, Dexter Anthony	9	0	1	0	2,105
Atkinson, Paul	218	20	20	21	608,415
Austin, Keith A.	81	7	4	11	61,366
Avant, James E.	192	26	35	19	347,714
Averill, Scott Alan	11	0	0	2	3,373
Avila, Juan	202	10	13	18	158,721
Ayala, Israel	2	0	0	0	356
Ayala, Manuel	28	0	0	1	4,191
Aylor, Natasha	1	0	0	0	0
Bacchas, Gerry	97	2	3	7	63,275
Bacon, Zack	9	1	2	1	2,672
Badamo, Joseph J.	356	67	56	48	807,304

Jockey	Sts	1st	2d	3d	Purses
Baez, Jose	288	16	13	27	166,405
Bahen, Steven Ronald	544	69	63	54	3,578,698
Bailey, Jerry D.	641	148	113	99	14,503,844
Bailey, Terri M.	30	0	0	3	7,873
Bain, Gary Wilbert	286	14	25	19	328,700
Baird, E. T.	379	46	60	37	1,031,358
Baird, Jerry	289	21	25	32	790,380
Baker, Christopher John	517	61	80	70	621,409
Balbuena, Carlos A.	14	0	0	2	2,415
Baldillez, Orlando	1	0	0	0	0
Baldillez, Roy	14	1	3	3	11,925
Balls, Jim D.	84	3	7	11	16,251
Banda, Sergio	4	0	1	0	2,080
Barajas, Jose J.	81	6	7	6	68,933
Barber, Monica	135	20	19	19	58,939
Barber, Ryan	442	59	62	48	900,295
Barber, Shawna	232	26	19	27	99,715
Bardales, Victor	9	1	1	0	9,590
Baros, Russell Anthony	1	0	0	0	0
Barria, Jesus	58	4	5	4	75,026
Barrio, Anna M.	311	40	33	36	100,024
Barrow, Nate	4	0	0	1	312
Barton, Jake	751	108	124	110	2,133,705
Bauman, James Ronald	28	3	1	5	4,664
Bautista, Alex	174	35	19	34	195,734
Bautista, Carlos A.	2	0	0	0	1,110
Bazan, Jesus	2	0	0	0	213
Baze, Gary	386	41	52	50	510,411
Baze, Michael C.	797	99	112	91	2,229,363
Baze, Russell A.	1,182	321	246	174	5,771,940
Baze, Tyler	1,399	239	187	205	10,181,132
Baze, Vicky	9	0	2	0	6,885
Beasley, Jeremy	914	128	122	98	2,343,436
Beauregard, Shannon	604	77	93	90	994,979
Bebon, Jodi	11	0	0	1	2,134
Beck, Daniel Lee	588	68	61	77	464,761
Beckner, Dale V.	257	19	28	27	806,556
Beckner, Twyla	524	84	111	85	295,062
Beckon, Chad	267	15	17	26	281,140
Beech, Clive T.	493	30	35	54	496,883
Beischer, Danielle	34	8	8	7	10,012
Beitia, Alexis O.	209	7	7	11	233,011
Bejarano, Rafael	1,922	455	355	280	12,210,087
Bell, Derek C.	678	115	102	84	1,550,470
Bello, Jose M.	289	18	28	28	170,662
Belmonte, Luis A.	760	92	107	87	792,006
Belmonte, Willie	249	32	22	26	141,954
Benavides, Daniel	545	54	57	59	431,422
Benitez, Jose	223	10	14	10	205,411
Benitez, Pedro	44	2	2	3	26,753
Benjamin, Chad	66	8	6	9	20,714
Bennett, Terry	190	8	17	12	54,073
Bennett, Tony Ray	23	5	2	3	10,023
Bentley, David	89	13	10	15	396,174
Bermudez, Jose E.	442	49	35	40	622,395
Bernal, Octavio	519	49	52	65	464,753
Berrio, Omar A.	248	15	26	33	636,097
Berry, Gina	9	0	0	1	479
Berry, Monte Clifton	1,191	234	176	162	3,180,955
Berryhill, Dale	38	4	8	5	16,372
Berryhill, Dennis P.	21	2	1	3	6,417
Betancourt, Headley	197	12	12	17	103,100
Betancourt, Jose R.	134	7	13	12	121,697
Biles, Stephen	21	1	4	0	10,410
Bilodeau, Ronald Joseph	73	13	15	15	32,272
Bird, Aaron D.	6	0	0	2	598
Birdrattler, Terrance	24	1	2	0	2,472
Birzer, Alex	1,002	127	122	143	1,662,355
Birzer, Gary A.	618	75	81	83	1,214,008
Bishop, Mike J.	188	13	16	20	41,901
Bisono, Alex	859	83	92	94	2,754,974
Bisono, Caesar V.	5	0	0	0	1,135
Black, Anthony S.	670	149	111	93	2,330,382

Jockey	Sts	1st	2d	3d	Purses
Black, Jo Anne	187	20	22	23	196,849
Black, Nikcela	56	7	4	8	16,573
Blake, Janice	340	16	37	37	309,072
Blanc, Brice	554	65	73	69	3,984,038
Blanco, Andry	16	1	2	2	12,757
Blinston, Ron Darryl	386	33	48	51	459,709
Boag, Daniel Raymond	123	19	14	17	57,559
Boag, Gary L.	192	22	23	21	245,472
Boag, Mark Allen	127	22	19	19	61,018
Bocachica, Orlando	670	105	100	92	1,188,348
Bochinski, Brian Todd	495	66	82	64	1,324,641
Bombek, John Joseph	5	0	0	0	2,375
Borel, Calvin H.	1,062	115	124	127	4,001,877
Boucher, Richard	187	8	16	25	282,207
Boudreau, Daniel	16	1	1	1	11,744
Boulanger, Gary	919	128	131	126	2,874,748
Bourdieu, Jorge Martin	676	95	102	85	1,771,807
Bourque, Coby J.	655	38	80	72	755,251
Bourque, Curt C.	236	37	21	26	588,648
Bourque, Steve J.	888	178	128	116	2,728,241
Bowen, Chris	19	4	6	3	12,416
Boxie, Patrick	668	44	56	58	550,844
Boyce, Robert	92	9	7	15	82,923
Boyd, Josh S.	141	14	20	19	174,054
Bracaloni, Natasha D.	130	11	12	16	179,963
Bracho, Agustin P.	327	27	25	30	211,099
Bracho, Jesus A.	134	6	10	15	153,691
Bracho, Jorge G.	481	69	71	65	779,982
Bracho, Richard A.	486	51	55	66	975,706
Braden, Darlene	330	28	22	34	75,028
Bradley, John R.	2	0	0	0	0
Bramblett, Jennifer	44	0	4	7	50,890
Brasser, Jen	4	0	0	1	1,100
Bravo, Joe	1,153	214	188	160	8,169,405
Brennan, Mary Jo	41	4	4	5	45,780
Bridges, Kelly	592	89	99	80	697,610
Bridgmohan, Shaun	1,265	153	178	178	7,093,424
Brimo, Julia	406	39	47	35	1,363,246
Brinkley, Darryl W.	484	41	44	45	591,963
Brinlee, Douglas Elton	56	3	10	3	27,112
Brock, Mary C.	1	0	0	0	690
Brocklebank, Gerry	20	0	1	1	5,742
Bronstad, Charlotte	110	6	8	8	46,144
Brooks, Jimmy Dean	1	0	0	0	105
Brooks, Melody	14	1	1	4	6,460
Brossette, Alvin	1	0	0	1	1,397
Brown, Bobbie Jean	22	1	1	3	3,615
Brown, David Deforest	62	11	13	9	26,099
Brown, David Eugene	20	0	2	2	10,480
Brown, Eddie	2	0	0	0	166
Brown, Gus M.	66	11	18	11	312,220
Brown, Ronald L.	71	2	2	3	25,137
Brown, Russell	135	9	11	13	87,151
Brown, Tracey M.	58	1	8	7	54,917
Bruin, James Edward	10	0	2	1	13,422
Bryan, Desmond	563	72	68	63	970,434
Bryan, Michael Wayne	3	0	0	0	356
Buckland, Mark	62	0	0	4	15,229
Buckley, Parker R.	650	104	85	75	1,070,795
Bugeaud, Laurina	154	9	20	25	57,258
Bui, Quyet E.	211	27	29	17	399,190
Burgess, Daniel	2	0	0	0	190
Burningham, Jeffery	1,109	118	123	141	1,531,111
Burress, Billy	58	3	2	2	28,938
Bush, Vernon	842	97	86	107	1,354,102
Bustamante, Ignacio	7	0	1	0	2,312
Butler, Beth S.	505	64	69	66	556,151
Butler, Dean P.	667	73	81	69	1,257,065
Butterfly, Roger	78	12	9	5	32,325
Byrne, John	263	17	21	23	195,948
Cabassa, Jr., Abad	124	9	9	17	121,918
Cabrera, Javier G.	76	4	3	4	37,752
Cadeddu, Lisa	34	4	3	4	49,276
Cadman, Zoe	12	2	1	1	42,845
Calderon, Mario Romero	16	0	3	3	10,827
Callaghan, Slade	555	73	68	69	3,772,048
Calo, Jose Luis	707	75	94	81	447,609
Calo, Samuel	12	0	1	0	4,239
Calucag, Caesar M.	171	3	18	14	74,624
Camacho, Eric	660	111	106	83	1,626,091
Camacho, Fernando	134	11	18	18	78,454
Camaque, Cesar	192	7	8	24	93,515
Camejo, Jose M.	131	5	7	9	59,665
Camejo, Omar	215	12	20	26	195,877
Caminita, Tony	461	33	42	61	321,055
Campbell, Cameron	75	11	11	10	23,573
Campbell, Danny L.	1	0	0	0	0
Campbell, David	1	0	0	0	180
Campbell, Jesse M.	970	119	146	119	3,067,883
Campbell, Joel	686	121	89	91	1,127,173
Campbell, Shannon	715	56	57	56	1,039,976
Canchano, Aldo	12	0	0	0	4,400
Candanosa, Adalberto	23	0	0	0	2,229
Canino, Carlos Alberto	14	0	0	2	3,225
Cano, Jr., Jack	96	10	10	11	43,307
Canon, Ricardo A.	13	0	2	3	6,636
Capanas, Steve	91	5	16	12	169,541
Capeles, Steve	727	48	60	67	290,756
Capizzi, Jr., John	35	3	4	1	19,096
Cappacetti, Gilbert	34	1	0	3	14,603
Caraballo, Jose C.	711	106	106	108	2,961,983
Cardenas, Daniel	2	0	0	0	92
Carkeek, Jerome	846	80	98	130	513,467
Carlos, Marino	302	17	36	31	151,731
Carlson, Neil	8	0	0	2	614
Carmouche, Kendrick	1,146	159	128	137	3,180,600
Carmouche, III, Sylvester Joseph	152	7	11	16	123,565
Carmouche, Jr., Frederick	105	4	2	5	64,212
Carmouche, Jr., Sylvester Joseph	418	29	27	35	437,423
Carpio, Rely	2	0	0	0	0
Carr, Dennis	939	170	163	150	3,215,657
Carrasco, Ronald Lewis	4	0	0	0	200
Carreno, Jorge	601	78	87	64	537,315
Carrero, Victor	616	70	66	80	1,012,225
Carrizales, Santos	158	12	14	16	73,019
Carter, Maggie	91	11	12	19	74,069
Carter, Peter D.	3	1	0	0	1,140
Carter, Phillip Gene	2	0	0	1	170
Carter, Tyrone	19	0	0	1	6,850
Carter, Jr., G. R.	41	5	7	4	88,555
Carwood, Gerry	8	0	0	2	20,965
Casebolt, Matthew	26	2	4	2	18,801
Casey, David	1	0	0	0	8,750
Cassaras, M.	10	0	2	0	1,577
Castaneda, Bonnie	299	27	41	27	412,541
Castanon, Antonio Lopez	388	42	57	45	376,260
Castanon, Jesus Lopez	1,008	142	151	131	2,579,835
Castanon, Jose German	187	13	21	19	180,525
Castellano, Javier	1,283	212	204	197	13,038,943
Castellano, Jr., Abel	1,209	201	203	180	5,077,531
Castillo, Elaine	523	63	57	58	605,623
Castillo, Freddy A.	8	0	2	0	4,485
Castillo, Kendri	19	1	0	0	7,455
Castillo, Luis A.	193	10	14	25	244,034
Castillo, Oliver	839	89	107	103	2,151,370
Castillo, Pablo J.	13	0	0	0	3,064
Castillo, Pedro C.	263	11	30	24	208,212
Castillo, Jr., Heberto	439	32	34	32	1,498,263
Caston, Antonio	1	0	0	1	800
Castro, Carlos L.	887	95	117	93	1,887,684
Castro, Eddie	1,552	270	249	226	6,109,838
Castro, Joe M.	445	76	63	84	1,447,396
Catalan, Jeff	4	0	0	0	1,600
Cayo, Denis J.	5	0	0	0	3,200
Cazares, Michael Alan	111	9	14	12	20,154
Ccamaque, Marco A.	1,298	200	196	181	1,165,398

Jockey	Sts	1st	2d	3d	Purses
Ceballos, Oscar	233	32	34	26	306,438
Cedeno, Amir	548	49	52	55	584,974
Cedeno, Lizetta M.	2	0	0	0	475
Cedeno, Osman A.	165	13	14	15	105,342
Centeno, Daniel	776	111	93	98	861,079
Chance, Jess	5	0	0	0	180
Chapa, Isaac	27	2	3	2	11,385
Chapa, Roman	956	214	148	129	3,205,914
Chaparro, Cayetano	162	22	19	12	291,431
Chapman, Kristi L.	16	3	2	2	21,525
Chappell, Sally	121	2	8	8	34,368
Charkoudian, Jordan	48	0	3	2	17,861
Charles, Maria	45	4	3	5	40,011
Chaves, Nathan J.	402	62	55	55	532,861
Chavez, Casey R.	627	43	59	55	363,299
Chavez, Jorge F.	932	119	131	109	5,286,952
Chavez, Luis D.	494	67	71	55	992,173
Chavez, Santos Noe	146	12	11	16	207,919
Chen, Men B.	204	12	16	27	233,685
Chiappe, Ricardo	2	0	0	0	360
Chickeness, Sheldon	89	18	15	15	36,527
Chin Sue, Roger Terrance	187	5	13	13	76,804
Chipperfield, Clayton	30	5	7	4	194,325
Chirinos, Roimes	292	21	35	46	309,329
Chopthonglang, Yuttakarn	2	0	0	0	0
Cisneros, Mario	40	2	5	5	43,499
Clair, Brian Thomas	2	0	0	0	178
Clark, Cory	272	28	29	39	512,402
Clark, David	429	55	42	46	2,818,626
Clark, Kerwin D.	486	72	59	43	766,622
Clark, Michael Dennis	54	2	8	3	216,661
Clark, Trevino	2	0	0	0	1,215
Clemente, Alfredo	791	98	104	84	1,171,511
Clemente, Alfredo V.	434	32	51	53	1,234,467
Clifton, Thomas	909	183	122	113	1,700,822
Cline, Vincent E.	352	10	11	30	294,058
Cloninger, Jr., Weldon T.	720	115	109	86	1,155,459
Cloutier, Rick	1	0	0	0	158
Coa, Daniel	535	48	49	66	785,148
Coa, Eibar	1,015	210	149	116	7,799,508
Coates, Jimmy Ray	247	22	27	17	309,476
Coburn, Lori A.	1	0	0	0	90
Cochran, Donald	4	0	2	2	3,450
Codilla, Alfredo	13	1	1	1	14,437
Cogburn, Kevin Leon	1,004	114	172	146	1,474,260
Cohen, David	244	27	22	29	648,179
Collazo, Jr., Jorge E.	263	13	17	34	104,938
Collazo, Sr., Jorge E.	430	24	28	40	177,496
Colledge, Cameron	211	55	37	32	133,839
Collier, Jeremy	455	42	47	52	505,839
Collier, Tuffy	182	15	11	9	133,194
Collins, Dennis Michael	699	101	109	99	629,467
Collins, Harold	6	1	1	0	2,235
Collins, Rhonda M.	133	13	12	11	104,162
Colon, Jose A.	257	11	10	16	80,761
Colon, Sammy	159	16	16	20	125,134
Compton, Perry	928	146	131	125	1,673,500
Concha, Gilbert	492	67	74	70	438,859
Condie, Kendall	27	2	1	0	16,114
Condie, Nathan R.	43	17	8	6	58,388
Conheeney, Jr., John	118	0	3	2	9,620
Conklin, Jay	253	60	50	38	247,801
Conn, Linda P.	21	0	0	1	4,792
Connelly, Brian J.	21	1	0	2	2,403
Contreras, Baltazar	262	44	30	31	263,858
Contreras, Cruz	583	84	82	74	1,618,810
Conway, Christopher L.	55	6	4	5	28,346
Cooksey, Patricia J.	23	1	0	1	17,487
Cooney, Michael	27	0	2	2	10,315
Cora, David	892	122	117	104	2,325,367
Corbett, Glenn W.	833	157	133	100	2,152,719
Cornwell, Marion	7	0	0	0	1,155
Cornwell, Richard Milton	371	42	36	45	802,448
Corrales, Max	11	0	0	1	4,280
Cortez, Alcibiades C.	666	87	76	76	1,612,286
Cosgriff, Katie Jo	108	9	9	10	26,649
Cosme, Emanuel	910	101	110	103	1,754,380
Cotrone, Jr., Frankie	319	11	30	15	107,458
Cottin, Aaron	13	0	0	1	1,390
Cotto, Pedro L.	5	0	0	1	5,345
Cotto, Jr., Pedro Luis	436	35	49	53	1,371,631
Court, Jon Kenton	771	82	117	102	4,606,598
Coversup, Joey	2	0	0	0	60
Covington, Raina	101	3	9	12	52,109
Cox, Danny W.	144	10	12	17	131,967
Cox, Roger W.	24	3	0	2	20,122
Crandall, Amanda L.	957	97	93	100	988,629
Crane, Dirk	90	13	13	15	33,168
Creary, Chris	65	2	7	7	45,209
Crispin, Joe A.	277	70	50	49	179,035
Crissup, Troy	1	0	0	0	90
Cruz, Anthony S.	235	12	24	22	113,116
Cruz, Carlos M.	433	50	63	59	755,768
Cruz, Efrain	11	0	0	2	1,878
Cruz, Hermes G.	7	0	0	0	2,130
Cruz, Janio	75	4	2	7	79,238
Cruz, Joel V.	12	0	2	4	6,380
Cruz, Jose A.	3	0	2	1	3,462
Cruz, Manoel R.	1,198	203	173	201	4,151,816
Cullum, Walter	16	0	0	1	4,230
Cunningham, Randy	43	4	7	3	19,096
Curry, Blake	4	0	0	0	1,400
Cushing, John L.	1	0	0	0	42
Cushny, Wyck	1	0	0	0	0
Cuthbertson, Alan	98	12	16	14	186,338
Da Silva, Eurico Rosa	524	49	52	60	2,149,351
Dacosta, Roderick	23	1	0	0	16,590
Daigle, Eric Thomas	30	1	4	1	13,814
Dailey, Douglas Allen	16	0	1	1	6,413
Dailey, James Ray	222	11	21	10	68,270
Dale, Ashton	3	0	0	1	1,308
Dalton, Bernard	16	1	0	3	14,250
D'Amico, Anthony J.	440	53	58	55	1,280,991
D'Amico, Duane Lee	267	63	51	38	163,215
Dangerfield, Ty	130	26	30	17	55,595
Daniel, Clarence	181	3	9	14	89,518
Daniels, Russell	12	0	1	0	1,862
Darcy, Tony	3	0	0	0	450
Darnell, Cindy	61	5	3	6	52,284
Dasilva, Axel	101	10	6	8	78,806
David, Daniel J.	114	12	6	13	353,234
Davies, Joe	1	0	0	0	0
Davila, Jose M.	243	26	25	24	282,560
Davila, Jr., John R.	722	137	112	81	1,490,318
Davila, Jr., Michael A.	597	59	68	82	753,724
Davis, Kenyatta	199	11	11	21	116,214
Davis, Layne	40	5	8	7	12,115
Day, Pat	798	172	134	105	10,882,222
DeAlba, Cesar	145	8	7	7	222,588
Deaville, Kevin	530	26	55	50	395,207
DeCarlo, Christopher P.	449	66	53	61	2,395,994
Deegan, Joseph	197	7	19	20	178,652
Dehdashti, Eamon	3	0	0	0	750
Del Valle, Angel	3	2	0	0	21,450
Deleon, Miguel	7	1	0	1	3,704
Delgadillo, Agapito	354	62	62	57	500,381
Delgado, Alberto	218	19	12	27	354,201
Delgado, Gilberto	4	0	0	0	880
Delgado, Gilberto Ramos	59	2	6	2	52,948
Delgado, Hector	38	0	0	0	2,382
Delgado, Jose H.	287	27	28	27	284,746
Delgado, Jose J.	743	86	88	79	855,796
Dell'Elce, Luca	1	0	1	0	4,200
Delorme, Larren	456	66	78	64	541,395
Demesme, Elliott	153	6	7	5	93,706
De'Oliveira, Wanderley G.	19	3	3	2	49,250

Jockey	Sts	1st	2d	3d	Purses
Deonauth, Kenneth P.	103	7	6	6	43,340
Desormeaux, Kent J.	696	109	108	104	8,729,543
Dettori, Lanfranco	13	3	1	2	2,312,900
Deveaux, Sean R.	265	18	23	23	184,459
Deyan, Carlos	57	1	1	5	20,346
Diamond, River	1	0	0	0	39
Diaz, Gadiel	9	0	0	2	3,865
Diaz, Jose	18	1	1	0	6,625
Diaz, Luis Felipe	174	22	17	19	518,035
Diaz, Mario	1	0	0	0	75
Diaz, Renzo	221	14	13	18	174,041
Diaz, Sunday	625	76	79	82	1,402,937
Diaz, Vladimir	1,030	143	161	134	1,399,696
Dickinson, Amber	135	33	18	23	141,575
Diego, Inosencio	835	71	69	77	773,916
Diego, Iram Vargas	569	48	57	56	751,573
Dieguez, Wilson Omar	945	188	135	125	1,306,281
Dionne, Monique	182	14	24	23	197,478
Dohnalova, Nadia	72	4	6	4	41,830
Doll-Carriere, Connie	61	2	3	5	10,245
Dominguez, Carlos Vicente	415	42	50	46	485,436
Dominguez, Ramon A.	1,353	383	231	216	11,506,889
Doocy, Timothy T.	1,029	187	183	143	3,259,729
Dore, Jason	16	0	1	1	4,050
Dos Ramos, Richard Anthony	364	35	33	47	2,107,596
Doser, Mary Elizabeth	721	128	133	110	1,555,537
Douglas, Rene R.	1,297	242	194	182	8,495,434
Dow, Andrew H.	55	0	2	1	4,408
Drexler, Hoogie	195	32	20	30	264,343
Drury, Gail	65	2	2	3	29,970
Dryden, Dyson	2	0	0	1	1,225
Duarte, Jr., Jorge I.	593	58	61	71	821,469
Dubon, Jeronimo Molina	4	0	1	0	3,616
Duncan, Barry Hill	1	0	0	0	0
Dunkelberger, Travis L.	895	160	128	111	3,310,367
Dupas, Gino	4	1	0	0	5,550
Duran, Francisco	870	132	126	110	2,102,356
Durigon, Joseph L.	174	5	7	6	31,508
Durkee, Brooks	32	4	5	3	69,025
Durkee, H. Brooks	2	0	0	0	0
Dussette, Albert	65	2	7	5	38,154
Duys, Dodie Cartier	381	35	35	47	608,567
Eads, Jason R.	658	72	69	85	1,126,344
Eason, Carroll Daniel	81	8	8	10	40,152
Edison, Randy B.	53	5	12	4	31,160
Edwards, Rhonda	21	0	0	1	3,923
Elliot, Gordon	3	0	0	2	8,100
Elliott, Stewart	1,363	262	211	177	14,533,061
Ellis, Philip	13	2	0	3	10,458
Elsner, Drew	111	5	16	17	28,242
Elston, David C.	141	6	7	8	76,983
Emamalie, Haniff	177	38	40	33	108,316
Emigh, Christopher A.	1,193	176	173	141	4,312,720
Endres, Jessica	281	4	9	28	83,418
Engblom, Henryk	3	0	0	2	4,325
Enriquez, Isaias D.	455	43	55	50	1,274,978
Enriquez, Juan C.	52	9	5	8	53,222
Epsteen, Joyce	52	6	1	4	11,329
Ernst, Bryan	126	11	16	13	61,974
Escalona, Gabriel Silva	1	0	0	0	235
Escobar, Edward	3	0	0	0	1,830
Escobar, Martin	940	106	121	96	1,369,401
Escobar, Victor	333	25	34	30	244,055
Eshelman, Bonnie	4	0	0	0	792
Espada, Jose E.	2	0	0	1	940
Espindola, A. Preto	23	1	0	0	5,406
Espinosa, Adrian	10	0	0	0	0
Espinosa, Luis	540	47	51	62	701,158
Espinoza, Jose L.	711	49	58	69	2,525,380
Espinoza, Leo	2	0	0	0	1,347
Espinoza, Victor	1,336	240	244	185	15,933,757
Espitia, Jorge	403	45	58	50	746,069
Espy, Kym	152	6	14	16	52,143
Essman, David Wilder	548	42	44	52	614,109
Estevez, Rafael	5	0	0	0	744
Estrada, Alex	479	36	39	37	655,790
Estrada, David	1	0	0	0	0
Estrada, Eberd	251	23	27	36	350,583
Estrada, Luis	7	0	1	0	1,965
Estrada, Jr., Salvador	90	6	6	4	66,996
Estrella, Rafael I.	280	15	18	36	242,487
Evans, Sean P.	61	8	5	5	79,738
Fagerstrom, Leslie	7	0	1	1	1,589
Faine, Craig Phillip	784	42	71	96	696,966
Falk, Jacklyn Leslie	4	0	0	0	186
Fallon, Kieren	11	4	3	0	1,226,640
Farachio, Giordano	10	0	1	0	4,060
Farina, Tony	47	6	7	7	364,873
Farrar, Jimmy	21	3	1	2	4,195
Farrell, Jaleina	152	5	10	16	78,181
Fatzer, Steven Dale	9	0	1	0	938
Faul, Ricky J.	839	110	87	103	1,488,917
Fayos, Borja	6	0	0	1	4,825
Fearon, Christopher	189	11	12	17	128,299
Feliciano, Ricardo	647	85	81	96	1,146,352
Felix, Angel	360	20	22	25	117,631
Felix, Julio E.	886	118	137	112	1,133,033
Fennell, Herman	74	3	4	13	10,115
Fenwick, III, Charles Cuthbert	5	2	0	1	24,250
Fergason, Jeff	18	1	4	3	4,548
Fernandez, Victor	183	12	14	14	479,009
Ferrer, Felix O.	14	0	0	1	4,180
Ferrer, Jose C.	408	46	45	40	1,251,854
Ferris, Heather	7	0	1	3	7,000
Fetters, Michal	58	5	2	1	40,078
Feurtado, Edmund	2	1	0	0	7,234
Fewster, Emily	68	4	4	4	49,627
Fiddler, Roy	23	2	1	5	3,262
Fiegen, Chris R.	124	14	18	17	68,237
Fierro, Jose M.	46	3	3	5	11,751
Figueroa, Jose	120	1	5	9	23,604
Figueroa, Louie Araiza	2	0	0	0	64
Figueroa, Omar	485	49	51	57	1,846,330
Fires, Earlie	345	35	42	45	993,112
Fisher, Jack	1	0	0	0	0
Fisher, Shelia	4	2	1	0	10,350
Fitzpatrick, Ashton	345	27	26	35	307,460
Fletcher, Jr., Charles A.	109	2	4	1	20,838
Flett, Gary	4	0	1	1	1,016
Flores, David Romero	874	123	102	128	8,365,977
Flores, Emilio	1,295	160	187	167	1,567,387
Flores, Fredric R.	35	0	1	1	7,265
Flores, Isaac Meza	9	0	2	1	5,651
Flores, Jeremias	515	76	70	65	732,934
Flores, Jose Luis	931	178	129	132	2,317,433
Flores, Jose M.	125	9	4	11	79,639
Flores, Laureano	221	17	19	26	242,504
Flores, Michael A.	1	0	0	0	0
Flores, Oscar	751	100	89	65	2,019,988
Flores, Pedro	9	0	0	0	915
Flores, Rico	1	0	0	0	150
Flores, Vicente	539	49	39	70	392,427
Fogel, Deborah	1	0	0	0	0
Fogelsonger, Ryan	1,065	217	174	179	4,525,877
Foley, Tom	83	16	10	14	379,885
Fong, Jr., Freddy	355	31	31	27	518,661
Fongsue, Garth W.	87	6	1	4	46,507
Fontanez, Jorge L.	51	3	6	7	14,431
Fontenot, Timothy J.	84	4	4	7	53,970
Forgar, Brian	8	0	0	5	2,365
Forgar, Eric	5	0	1	0	860
Forkhamer, Pauline	180	14	9	23	168,250
Forrest, Charles W.	452	30	46	47	670,647
Fortner, Joddie Lee	203	11	10	16	105,476
Fortuna, Jesus	114	3	5	8	43,173
Fowler-Wright, David	26	0	2	6	12,957

Jockey	Sts	1st	2d	3d	Purses
Fox, Tammy Lee	73	5	8	9	180,585
Fragoso, Pablo	1,181	164	201	180	7,167,990
Francisco, David	14	1	0	0	5,091
Fraser, Corey	475	67	63	57	2,401,102
Frates, Dean Joseph	341	28	26	37	440,882
Frazier, Don Lee	573	64	63	62	359,747
Frazier, Ricky	599	111	90	90	1,472,387
Frazzitta, Jr., Leonard J.	583	26	32	52	203,846
Freeman, Debbie A.	40	5	5	10	37,550
Freeman, Gregory	53	2	6	5	8,958
Freeman, Laura	14	0	0	0	3,085
French, Don Lee	1	0	0	0	0
Friesen, Shelley	3	1	1	1	3,790
Fritz, Julie	81	9	10	7	32,511
Fuentes, Adan	230	14	18	37	196,151
Fuentes, Alfonso S.	117	8	14	9	85,383
Fuentes, Edwin	162	6	6	13	101,168
Fuentes, Francisco Perez	369	46	51	46	1,045,101
Fuentes, Mauricio E.	27	4	1	3	67,790
Fuentes, Miguel V.	111	17	7	11	334,786
Fusilier, Casey	670	88	98	83	1,582,951
Gabriel, Ron E	172	22	17	13	182,182
Gaeta, Fernando	7	0	1	1	1,891
Galarza, Neftali	4	0	0	0	640
Gale, Michael Allen	354	61	57	62	514,148
Galindo, Luis	2	0	0	0	1,920
Gallo, Anthony	57	2	5	7	86,975
Galluccio, Joseph	4	0	0	0	0
Galvan, Mario A.	82	0	3	2	11,504
Gamez, Fernando Manuel	114	18	21	20	34,538
Gamez, Larry	3	0	0	0	259
Gann, Sandi Lee	479	83	82	65	831,793
Ganpath, Ray	124	15	8	8	476,763
Garcia, Alan	651	66	79	71	2,197,428
Garcia, Alejandro	219	14	21	17	121,133
Garcia, Bernardo	2	0	0	0	0
Garcia, Carlos	74	4	11	9	51,144
Garcia, David	601	76	76	73	597,830
Garcia, Francisco	338	23	34	36	381,720
Garcia, Francisco F.	25	2	4	2	27,867
Garcia, Jesse Jimenez	441	49	48	50	702,589
Garcia, Julio A.	417	76	54	52	1,773,518
Garcia, Luis	790	93	111	118	1,656,247
Garcia, Luis A.	64	2	6	4	104,275
Garcia, Matt S.	406	39	36	62	1,372,915
Garcia, Noe	9	0	0	0	1,045
Garcia, Oscar	1	0	0	0	0
Garcia, Jr., Ralph J.	24	7	5	2	13,003
Garcia, Jr., Randy L.	63	7	4	4	106,223
Gard, Terry Lee	200	13	33	38	51,624
Gardiner, Timothy N.	145	21	22	19	183,470
Garner, Cathleen J.	473	57	45	42	537,627
Garnett, Garfield E.	63	1	2	2	6,923
Gates, Lee	36	5	5	8	15,350
Gazader, Daniel	5	0	0	1	1,160
Gelpi, Jr., Angel	58	1	7	10	28,294
Gerardo, Ronald	2	0	0	0	450
Giacomelli, Tim	12	0	1	3	1,580
Gill, Lupe	12	0	0	1	1,603
Gillam, Diana	20	1	1	4	18,450
Giraldo, Alfreado J.	7	0	0	0	217
Glasser, Todd	420	71	51	67	1,080,517
Goad, Jr., Kenneth Ray	25	2	3	0	7,725
Goberdhan, C. Punchie	17	1	0	1	7,137
Goff, Jr., B. L.	14	0	0	0	1,664
Golibrzuch, Siggy	47	0	0	1	4,831
Gomez, Esteban Angel	826	121	130	99	823,045
Gomez, Garrett K.	261	36	46	40	1,314,941
Gomez, Hernan C.	36	0	1	4	5,217
Gomez, Javier R.	32	3	1	1	16,410
Gomez, Jocelyne C.	92	4	9	12	84,240
Gomez, Oscar	409	27	28	37	770,733
Gomez, Roger	363	16	22	26	158,952
Gondron, Ted D.	549	94	80	69	1,362,087
Gonsalves, Frank Albert	629	82	83	76	1,034,103
Gonzales, Billy Jack	3	0	0	0	0
Gonzales, II, James Julian	23	0	0	3	5,109
Gonzalez, Carlos	552	84	73	76	1,438,465
Gonzalez, Ivan R.	1,004	179	135	129	1,072,509
Gonzalez, Luis Antonio	878	144	114	103	1,372,312
Gonzalez, Roberto M.	966	163	141	139	3,469,182
Gonzalez, Jr., Angel	45	2	5	1	44,755
Gonzalez, Jr., Sal	196	20	14	15	426,292
Goodgame, Rachel	22	2	0	3	17,671
Goodwin, Nik G.	407	29	32	53	711,125
Gordon, David Joseph	47	2	6	6	44,578
Gordon, Duncan S.	181	8	15	27	38,438
Gott, Isabelle	1	1	0	0	12,600
Grabowski, John A.	566	100	94	74	1,093,348
Gracie, Chris	11	1	0	2	25,550
Grafton, Dwayne A.	70	11	7	7	292,404
Graham, James	1,066	135	116	125	2,887,325
Granda, Alejandro T.	390	23	54	47	198,885
Gray, Akili	180	5	9	14	52,059
Gray, Christina	177	10	7	15	130,689
Green, Brian D.	1	0	0	0	0
Green, Paul	22	1	3	4	7,728
Greene, Casey	194	28	27	32	70,580
Grenamyer, April J.	43	3	3	2	20,606
Griffin, Everett D.	34	1	2	5	12,236
Griffith, Christopher	454	51	63	57	1,051,606
Griffiths, Mark	12	1	0	3	20,100
Griswold, Jason	2	0	0	0	375
Grove, Larry	1	0	0	0	0
Gryder, Aaron T.	971	113	111	115	4,716,004
Grylls, Gary	2	0	0	0	540
Guajardo, Alonzo	418	36	32	49	246,321
Guce, Ramon	277	33	38	36	250,247
Guerra, Jorge A.	237	33	21	23	318,504
Guerra, Vince J.	799	71	86	88	821,391
Guerrero, Eduardo	7	0	0	0	787
Guevara, Tito	10	1	0	0	8,390
Guffey, Gary Rex	17	0	0	3	1,757
Guidry, Mark	785	120	97	93	3,900,613
Guillory, Susan	52	1	3	5	21,338
Guimard, Christopher	3	0	1	0	4,110
Gutierrez, A. L.	98	9	5	5	104,951
Gutierrez, Daniel W.	76	8	14	8	56,038
Gutierrez, Guillermo R.	361	63	62	51	443,058
Gutierrez, Jose Arturo	219	25	27	19	290,350
Gutierrez, Juan M.	806	142	137	141	904,865
Guymon, Tony F.	110	3	8	13	26,940
Hadley, Roy Mark	114	12	10	13	49,256
Hadley, Russel	5	0	0	1	970
Haire, Timothy	23	0	3	1	11,352
Hall, Jesse	105	11	12	19	39,284
Hambleton, Anne	3	0	1	1	3,700
Hamel, Richard Harvey	532	59	64	50	912,185
Hamilton, Desiree	73	1	0	1	7,070
Hamilton, Jennifer S.	6	0	0	0	1,504
Hamilton, John	9	0	1	1	2,160
Hamilton, Quincy	873	137	128	106	1,281,674
Hamilton, Steve D.	1,129	164	178	163	3,209,208
Hamilton, Travis	56	7	9	14	24,840
Hammett, Lisa	15	3	1	1	32,708
Hampshire, Jr., Josiah Francis	954	176	105	138	1,985,642
Hamrick, David	1	0	0	0	0
Hancock, Steve	35	1	4	5	4,618
Hannigan, Lyndon	640	57	49	60	447,158
Hansby, Antonio E.	29	3	2	4	77,062
Hansen, R. J.	2	0	0	0	442
Hanson, Ryan J.	9	0	0	0	971
Harding, Tyrone	347	44	33	36	656,567
Harmon, Kim	40	1	2	2	8,962
Harris, B. Buck	67	18	14	15	27,070
Harris, Michael F.	1	0	0	0	0

Jockey	Sts	1st	2d	3d	Purses
Harvell, Mike W.	97	4	5	14	43,702
Harvey, Barrington	297	14	24	34	242,921
Hastie, Robert M.	197	8	13	24	97,446
Hearn, Troy	29	0	4	2	21,250
Hebert, Amy	1	0	0	0	1,260
Hebert, Carl	289	34	43	48	152,747
Hebert, Tracy J.	761	113	100	90	1,706,146
Heiler, Stephan	181	23	24	20	319,879
Heim, Kenneth	12	0	2	1	1,372
Helton, Rita M.	178	6	12	14	192,285
Hemmings, Tara	508	35	37	61	341,150
Hemsley, Dale	432	44	40	38	578,061
Hendricks, Ken	229	32	36	32	409,719
Henry, Sr., Wesley	188	5	12	21	92,432
Henson, William	88	4	7	4	24,024
Herber, Jr., Donald D.	26	4	2	0	4,325
Heredia, Julio J.	54	3	2	4	36,326
Herman, Jeremy	22	0	1	5	2,065
Hernandez, Adrian	294	17	27	37	426,839
Hernandez, Alex M.	5	1	0	0	2,636
Hernandez, Alexander A.	214	12	7	12	86,735
Hernandez, Alfredo B.	194	4	6	7	76,556
Hernandez, Brian Joseph	618	81	74	64	1,118,260
Hernandez, Carlos Alberto	10	0	0	1	6,710
Hernandez, David C.	41	2	3	4	22,425
Hernandez, Miguel Luis Gaeta	783	100	131	111	952,430
Hernandez, Noe A.	21	1	1	2	8,270
Hernandez, Rafael Manuel	539	57	50	65	643,015
Hernandez, Rey	1	0	0	0	45
Hernandez, Jr., Brian Joseph	1,466	243	210	191	4,401,867
Herrell, James Christopher	784	81	68	90	670,673
Herrera, Jorge	12	0	1	2	2,062
Herrera, Ramiro	3	0	0	2	2,504
Hightower, Travis Wayne	508	102	67	72	897,521
Higuera, Alberto R.	772	86	98	114	654,389
Hilburn, Wendell John	162	21	12	14	149,731
Hill, Channing	293	25	31	30	343,357
Hill, Robert R.	43	0	0	1	7,665
Hills, Claire	5	0	1	0	660
Hills, Richard	1	0	0	0	90,000
Hinojosa, Thomas	2	0	0	0	0
Hiraldo, Joel	74	6	15	5	145,188
Ho, Sunny	121	3	2	10	64,014
Hobson, Simon	2	0	0	0	0
Hodsdon, Danielle	78	14	9	14	249,743
Hogbin, Leigh	2	0	0	0	0
Holassie, Raynau K.	2	0	0	0	180
Hole, Taylor M.	778	115	130	117	1,256,986
Hollick, William J.	196	9	10	18	197,286
Hollowoa, Windle Elroy	20	0	0	1	2,520
Holmes, Jade	1	0	0	0	1,065
Holmes, Mike	26	1	5	2	7,510
Holmes, Jr., Joe S.	36	2	1	2	4,919
Holmes, Sr., Joe	209	23	32	37	68,287
Holtzinger, Cara C.	1	0	0	0	0
Homeister, Jr., Rosemary B.	536	65	67	81	1,517,995
Honea, Gail	1	0	0	0	0
Hoonan, Deborah	595	81	89	81	628,796
Horner, Ellen	1	0	0	0	0
Houghton, T. D.	1,524	285	270	210	2,754,284
House, Cody	23	1	1	2	3,251
Hoverson, Chad	340	33	51	36	795,437
Howard, William E.	8	0	0	1	2,788
Howarth, Jr., Albert L.	8	0	0	2	1,240
Howell, Talbert	27	1	0	1	10,656
Hudson, Kehron	4	0	0	0	0
Hunt, Charleen	12	0	0	2	3,899
Hunt, Jimmie J.	79	9	10	4	65,217
Hunter, Michele L.	7	1	2	1	42,800
Husbands, Patrick	748	141	115	114	7,432,199
Husbands, Simon P.	349	32	36	26	1,345,475
Huston, Hugh Cade	68	9	6	5	36,327
Hutton, Greg W.	327	44	38	29	770,718
Iammarino, Michael Phillip	594	56	68	91	825,106
Ignacio, Rodolfo	166	12	15	19	198,284
Ikeda, Teppei	5	0	0	0	2,450
Irion, Heather	414	51	58	66	395,200
Isbell, Dan	5	0	0	0	435
Itschner, Christine	128	3	5	13	44,394
Jacinto, John	1,139	201	163	131	2,745,169
Jacobs, Dudley	17	1	3	3	3,828
Jaen, Abdiel	184	17	25	20	283,295
Jaime, Ricardo	677	89	93	93	1,951,946
James, Michael C.	443	39	37	47	499,819
Jara, Fernando	732	70	64	73	2,496,412
Jaramillo, Emisael	1	0	0	0	235
Jaramillo, Fernan	39	0	0	3	22,787
Jasso, Trinidad	1	0	0	0	0
Jauregui, Luis H.	210	16	15	14	519,289
Jawny, Alvaro	275	46	39	23	899,585
Jean, Patra	3	0	0	0	270
Jellison, Jill Ann	290	32	37	31	370,612
Jenkins, David C.	244	17	20	21	252,309
Jensen, Cody	1	0	0	0	435
Jerman, Jeff B.	159	10	21	17	161,655
Jessup, Timothy V.	115	10	22	18	94,944
Jimenez, Ada	13	0	0	0	4,297
Jimenez, Alex	130	19	11	19	285,357
Jimenez, Ender	403	27	41	47	339,865
Jimenez, Fabrizio M.	94	5	8	9	96,027
Jimenez, Miguel	9	0	0	0	1,499
Jimenez, Rafael S.	9	0	1	1	8,110
Jimenez, Samuel	1	0	0	1	4,100
John, Kerwin	597	50	62	76	2,053,203
Johns, Thomas Cecil	94	4	4	4	45,467
Johnson, Bobby L.	349	32	53	54	366,314
Johnson, Del M.	8	1	0	1	1,220
Johnson, Joe M.	682	58	69	77	1,257,724
Johnson, Patrick A.	84	5	8	12	100,651
Johnson, Richard	273	12	26	29	191,820
Johnson, Robert W.	375	41	47	45	626,734
Johnson, Stephanie A.	3	0	0	0	275
Johnson, Whyatt C.	5	1	0	1	13,160
Johnston, Jeff	716	90	103	71	1,170,902
Johnston, Mark T.	123	15	7	19	223,745
Jones, Buster Buck	1	0	1	0	360
Jones, Clark E.	303	25	36	26	413,002
Jones, Doug T.	237	16	21	22	103,279
Jones, Jono C.	670	91	90	83	5,978,103
Jones, Robert A.	42	3	2	2	26,753
Jordan, Jimmy	52	6	10	9	26,497
Joyce, Jonathan	40	0	0	6	20,622
Jsames, Jay	3	0	0	0	293
Juarez, Calixto	172	10	9	24	201,260
Juarez, Jr., Alfredo J.	652	119	105	83	1,645,983
Juarez, Sr., Alfredo V.	27	1	1	2	28,680
Judice, Joseph C.	765	108	108	88	1,303,800
Jurado, Enrique M.	336	53	45	35	1,046,324
Juvonen, Allison	1	0	1	0	2,340
Kabel, Todd	686	156	109	77	10,637,082
Kaenel, Kyle	235	40	28	29	276,136
Kagno, Julie	8	0	0	0	915
Karamanos, Horacio	956	135	151	144	3,166,819
Karn, David A.	125	14	9	12	40,898
Karr, Dan	76	5	16	15	23,446
Karr, Stephen Michael	228	38	31	30	85,052
Kato, Akifumi	165	7	21	17	111,137
Kaufman, Casey	446	31	34	53	325,384
Keckler, Ron W.	81	8	13	12	27,543
Keele, Shane	50	2	4	10	9,538
Keizer, Lorne	79	6	5	8	72,908
Kelsey, Zack	20	0	5	5	6,618
Kenny, Mike	34	0	1	4	9,146
Kenny-Martin, Jocelyne	491	33	50	70	289,498
Keshane, Chad	16	1	2	1	2,098
Keshane, Norbert	41	5	5	10	9,685

Jockey	Sts	1st	2d	3d	Purses
Kewin, Steve	235	13	12	16	130,716
Kimes, Curtis	888	142	125	93	1,048,944
King, Dallas	144	8	17	16	104,397
King, Diane Lynn	4	0	0	0	259
King, Jr., Edwin L.	837	90	108	120	2,894,221
Kingrey, Russell David	96	28	17	12	63,253
Kinsey, Jill E.	921	94	114	100	1,367,597
Kirlew, Lenworth G.	13	0	0	0	2,384
Kirlin, Thomas	3	0	1	0	3,000
Kistler, Dan	19	2	1	6	5,345
Klinger, C. Omar	426	36	44	54	739,200
Knight, Lester Cash	587	92	82	88	1,021,728
Knott, Rick L.	58	5	5	4	30,557
Korrell, Brian	17	1	2	1	28,225
Krasner, Samuel B.	116	21	11	9	275,847
Kravets, Justin	684	90	68	60	728,049
Kreidel, Kaymarie	325	25	40	35	616,119
Kretzer, Kerry D.	542	37	36	45	351,155
Krigger, Kevin	526	71	78	73	869,862
Krone, Julie A.	3	0	0	0	1,456
Kuntzweiler, Greta	502	36	42	49	1,319,779
Kurek, Gary	392	52	39	62	363,120
Kutz, Carl Mel	172	27	20	20	179,772
La Forge, Frank	65	9	10	11	16,392
La Sala, Jerry	338	41	29	45	719,222
Lacoursiere, Larry J.	25	1	4	1	10,640
Laimbeer, Richard	2	0	0	1	3,500
Lakeman, Andrew	13	0	0	3	13,780
Lamb, Orlando	3	0	0	0	0
Lambert, Casey T.	925	151	106	132	2,640,814
Lambeth, Denise	93	8	11	14	50,524
Lampton Jr., Mason	6	1	2	0	8,400
Lanci, Howard L.	161	5	11	16	56,687
Landeros, Benny C.	456	26	39	54	272,737
Landolt, Anna L.	2	0	0	0	0
Landry, Robert C.	529	58	66	64	4,144,957
Lanerie, Corey J.	1,096	165	179	149	3,602,925
Lapensee, Michel	303	29	39	40	402,701
Lara, Ruben	145	3	13	15	75,990
Larrosa, Gustavo	554	46	34	62	862,482
Larsen, Shaunda L.	45	6	2	3	12,920
Lasso, Yonis	62	0	3	8	12,302
Latchman, Rennie	182	22	32	31	78,676
Latham, Jeremy	50	3	6	7	10,587
Laurente, Godofredo	457	25	42	50	298,440
Lauzon, Jack M.	302	24	33	44	537,155
Lavergne, Danny J.	25	5	0	3	16,163
Laviolette, Shane	938	93	100	129	2,007,063
Laws, Nickey M.	1	0	0	1	2,277
Lawson, Mark	25	1	1	4	18,923
Leacock, Jason	400	53	52	57	468,629
Leacock, Paul	221	26	20	25	297,630
LeBlanc, Don C.	367	8	20	35	184,988
LeBlanc, Kirk Paul	648	65	80	80	1,265,382
Lee, Katie	241	18	19	23	173,457
Lee, Wing	1	0	0	0	145
Leeds, Damon	499	39	47	45	473,148
Leggett, Tad W.	65	7	10	3	93,538
Lejeune, John Keith	51	1	1	2	11,208
LeJeune, Jr., Sidney P.	813	75	85	91	952,119
Leonard, Brian Leslie	61	2	1	1	10,885
Lester, Robert Neal	511	47	54	73	577,770
Lewis, Cedric Orlando	61	1	5	4	44,971
Lewis, Jr., William R.	46	2	2	2	52,111
Leyva, Juan C.	279	22	24	19	472,606
Lezcano, Jose	415	33	35	59	981,235
Lidberg, David W.	4	3	0	0	25,781
Linares, Modesto	325	33	33	43	355,421
Lindo, Donovan	4	0	0	0	995
Lindsay, Eldridge K.	145	2	17	15	93,134
Logan, Greg	2	0	0	0	73
Long, James S.	157	8	14	13	110,535
Lopez, Adalberto Diaz	787	93	111	115	1,320,277
Lopez, Charles C.	658	107	100	104	3,990,297
Lopez, David G.	916	123	134	153	2,068,830
Lopez, James	612	67	87	67	1,301,176
Lopez, Jose E.	721	91	87	90	1,612,005
Lopez, Lorenzo Castane	801	91	87	109	571,730
Lopez, Reginaldo	1	0	0	0	0
Lopez, Uriel A.	711	56	68	74	1,048,198
Loseth, Chris	407	51	49	48	948,710
Louchart, Ronald Alan	11	5	1	2	8,455
Lovato, Anthony J.	126	9	17	10	219,643
Lovato, Jr., Frank	469	44	51	50	1,471,891
Lovelace, Austin K.	1	0	0	0	0
Lozano, Flavio	54	5	12	5	12,811
Lozano, Jose M.	116	7	6	12	69,189
Lozano, Jr., Wilfredo L.	355	32	40	39	350,252
Lozoya, Dario Acosta	10	1	2	1	5,160
Luark, Mark	333	17	21	34	119,168
Lucero, Delano	7	0	0	0	960
Luciani, Dino	461	67	54	67	3,164,150
Ludlow, Megan	65	4	5	7	16,364
Lujan, Alfonso	6	0	0	0	390
Lumpkins, Jason P.	701	90	83	97	1,840,622
Luna, Alejandro	1	0	1	0	967
Luna, Ramon	846	65	104	81	468,146
Luttrell, Michelle	60	4	7	5	118,488
Luzzi, Michael J.	781	114	111	108	4,695,488
Luzzi, Jr., John B.	203	10	13	25	246,736
Lybert, Anna Moore	5	0	0	0	768
Lydon, P. J.	54	3	3	6	51,553
Lyons, Christopher	3	0	0	0	2,250
Lyons, Edgar	154	10	10	9	90,511
Lyons, Gabe	44	3	4	8	8,796
Macias, Manuel	1	0	0	0	1,000
Macias, Jr., Guadalupe	206	8	16	17	176,516
Mackay, Nick	1	0	0	0	0
MacKay, Kelly A.	100	6	7	7	134,518
MacLaren, Jeff	27	4	1	3	49,084
Maddrix, Tim	10	0	0	2	3,000
Madeira, Carlos D.	360	67	46	50	830,985
Madrid, Nicky A.	160	9	14	16	147,782
Madrid, Sebastian O.	467	54	71	53	1,161,040
Madrid, Jr., Art	80	4	7	13	90,870
Madrigal, Jr., Rodrigo	504	59	91	65	1,273,913
Magera, Clint	348	19	28	25	289,385
Magrell, Jane M.	439	37	35	48	390,881
Mailhot, Pierre	171	4	6	12	64,088
Maldonado, John I.	60	0	2	1	7,768
Maldonado-Alicea, Edwin	826	71	79	112	869,622
Maloney, Paul	136	6	12	13	50,349
Manalad, Edgardo	2	0	0	0	0
Mancilla, Oscar G.	204	13	16	21	161,962
Mangalee, Navin	341	36	42	39	250,338
Mangold, Kevin	180	7	12	22	95,587
Mangual, Samuel	340	10	19	23	204,101
Manickram, Macelin	321	26	41	49	327,341
Maragh, Allen	48	5	5	6	88,735
Maragh, Rajiv	796	78	88	93	1,883,289
Marcano, Josue	192	10	11	15	118,731
Marchant, Timothy M.	33	3	2	4	25,465
Marcial, Alejandro	12	0	0	0	1,002
Marcial, Benjamin	800	57	64	81	934,333
Markham, Jr., Richard Leroy	141	4	12	8	86,794
Marks, Ronald J.	35	2	7	3	43,345
Marquez, Carlos W.	56	3	6	6	8,562
Marquez, Juan	9	0	0	1	714
Marquez, Jr., Carlos H.	765	119	101	94	3,508,554
Marshall, Danny	18	3	4	1	7,955
Marshall, Melissa	20	5	3	3	8,400
Martin, Christopher	156	15	17	11	379,323
Martin, Clyde W.	285	22	23	28	557,990
Martin, John	1	0	0	0	375
Martin, Jr., Eddie M.	1,300	225	190	172	5,658,957
Martinez, Armando	792	98	66	87	594,228

Jockey	Sts	1st	2d	3d	Purses
Martinez, Catalino	196	17	24	19	362,446
Martinez, Felipe F.	701	54	73	101	2,013,725
Martinez, Freddie L.	95	12	6	13	78,186
Martinez, Jaime	448	43	53	67	148,367
Martinez, Joe A.	17	1	1	3	21,912
Martinez, Luis Jeronimo	393	64	39	65	589,429
Martinez, Orlando A.	518	40	53	62	318,419
Martinez, Seth B.	674	114	114	96	1,911,756
Martinez, Willie	1,058	152	137	109	3,638,700
Martinez, Jr., Jose R.	576	46	42	62	1,243,337
Martinez, Jr., Luis J.	691	64	80	70	727,277
Martinez, Jr., Severiano	5	0	0	2	5,060
Martz, Kay Talman	32	3	4	3	11,637
Massey, Robert	89	11	10	9	295,631
Mata, Federico	889	136	112	119	1,311,037
Matteucci, Tony	468	40	43	40	334,968
Matutes, Leo	107	4	7	10	123,255
Matz, Nena	686	84	89	99	966,789
Maughn, Jamar	111	4	5	10	61,814
Mauldin, Jerry E.	29	2	6	3	10,583
Mawing, Anthony	1,174	127	147	141	3,113,379
Mawing, Leslie	754	68	94	97	1,121,441
May, Robert Houston	250	21	24	33	373,973
Mayhew, Glenmore W.	55	3	2	4	22,523
Mayo, Robert	9	0	0	0	1,130
Mayo, Timothy O.	3	0	0	0	0
Maysonett, Francisco Z.	130	11	17	18	207,574
Mayta, Jorge	19	1	2	2	6,566
McAleney, James	682	110	91	91	5,981,418
McAleney, Peter	218	44	36	21	169,167
McCarron, Matthew Otis	111	25	13	12	606,043
McClaran, W. Bill	47	6	4	6	35,048
McClellan, Charles Lyn	348	24	34	37	82,983
McCormack, Calvin	51	3	2	7	94,230
McCormick, Mark L.	195	14	27	22	220,092
McDaid, Joanne	280	14	23	30	190,406
McDaniel, Cody	1	0	0	0	140
McDonald, David A.	5	0	0	0	354
McFadden, David J.	559	56	67	58	994,665
McGowan, Mathew Carroll	511	32	46	58	675,322
McIntosh, Edgar	7	0	0	2	2,552
McIntosh, Kimberly R.	204	8	12	28	176,838
McKee, John	1,444	210	219	200	6,062,316
McKnight, James	210	25	21	23	1,339,398
McMahon, Charles Warren	25	0	3	0	15,248
McMahon, Cynthia Jean	77	13	11	8	191,703
McMillan, Kenneth McKay	87	5	5	5	91,499
McMullen, Michael Joseph	114	8	11	14	166,114
McNeece, Jerry Odell	18	2	0	3	7,138
McTurner, Teri	73	1	3	4	62,465
McWade, Richard	3	0	0	0	1,350
Meador, Michael V.	31	0	0	0	3,463
Means, Dennis M.	145	10	11	31	83,416
Meche, Donnie J.	432	59	58	53	1,446,659
Meche, Lonnie	925	199	136	119	3,417,018
Medina, Cynthia M.	109	26	18	14	187,350
Medina, Jose Angel	18	1	1	2	15,110
Medina, Luis	435	41	57	37	667,458
Medina, Jr., Rafael	185	24	15	23	205,147
Meier, Randall A.	637	70	76	82	1,569,440
Meister, William	2	0	0	0	600
Mejia, Cesar O.	119	11	3	11	150,801
Mejias, Larry	27	0	0	0	3,336
Melancon, Gerard	1,267	205	182	187	4,711,881
Melancon, Kevin Lee	61	3	3	3	45,075
Melancon, Larry	619	85	63	77	3,019,547
Melancon, Larry J.	361	28	29	41	390,787
Melancon, Paul	443	31	47	40	203,298
Melanson, Gary	221	23	22	23	174,420
Melchor, Victor W.	13	0	0	0	810
Melenciano, Valentin	130	7	12	9	58,274
Mellish, Brooke	253	32	33	38	149,127
Mello, David	939	107	128	121	1,452,290

Jockey	Sts	1st	2d	3d	Purses
Mena, Miguel	423	46	51	51	829,367
Mendez, Emmanuel	181	14	19	20	156,061
Mendez, Jose P.	28	0	5	2	8,594
Mera, Julio C.	27	1	0	2	16,219
Mercado, Pedro	611	72	98	79	1,226,873
Mercado, Victor V.	212	17	19	22	67,340
Mercieca, Marty J.	204	10	12	23	198,649
Messina, Robert	57	0	5	9	25,930
Meyers, Tommy	145	19	21	16	214,941
Meza, Nicholas	212	15	10	16	248,065
Michael, Stephen	65	3	8	7	79,304
Migliore, Richard	873	149	122	109	8,058,110
Milian, Jorge Luis	54	2	1	12	32,556
Miller, Patrice	2	0	0	0	600
Miller, Zach	28	9	2	4	93,850
Miller, Jr., F. Bruce	62	10	8	6	220,948
Mina, Marios	1	0	0	0	2,500
Mino, Oclides A.	75	7	4	9	70,632
Miranda, Alfredo	417	51	44	46	616,833
Miranda, Victor	418	55	41	47	575,119
Mitchell, Gallyn Vick	441	83	73	73	868,460
Mitchener, John D.	21	2	1	5	29,700
Miyashiro, Cliff James	223	41	38	30	174,292
Moccasin, Andrew	38	3	2	3	6,580
Moccasin, Tim	79	19	20	13	35,013
Mojica, Orlando	952	110	123	95	1,283,454
Mojica, Jr., Rafael	503	41	48	50	849,349
Molina, Tommy	483	36	49	56	815,980
Molina, Victor H.	665	105	101	91	1,791,385
Molina, Jr., Juan F.	240	19	33	26	339,332
Molinari, Edwin	404	46	46	68	581,012
Mondragon, Sergio	1	0	0	0	134
Montalvo, Carlos	469	43	46	51	985,120
Montano, Chris	174	9	19	17	138,883
Montano, Manuel	49	5	1	6	54,593
Montehermoso, Edgar	70	4	4	9	18,565
Monterrey, Pedro	15	0	0	1	2,870
Monterrey, Richard	764	101	114	87	1,910,556
Monterrey, Jr., Pedro	554	64	62	71	1,109,618
Montoute, Schemlin	27	6	1	2	96,390
Montoya, Daryl	150	14	21	19	284,039
Montoya, Jose	1	0	0	0	0
Montpellier, Constant	592	62	66	82	3,199,444
Morales, Adolfo A.	328	27	38	35	286,566
Morales, Chris	333	21	32	31	447,045
Morales, Daniel	199	17	22	27	200,904
Morales, Jose A.	12	0	0	1	1,240
Moran, Michael	136	3	11	17	191,545
Moran, Shelley Lee	476	33	40	35	232,964
Morgan, Clifton	8	0	0	2	2,710
Morgan, Luis	111	11	7	7	30,747
Morgan, Michael R.	126	14	15	11	200,063
Morris, Liz	595	47	73	58	910,421
Morris, Ryan	629	51	56	85	766,335
Mota, Alex	3	1	0	0	10,540
Mouton, Martel	8	0	0	1	2,192
Mower, Lavar	1	0	0	0	232
Mueller, Tiffany	2	0	0	0	1,000
Munar, Luis H.	409	50	56	53	669,223
Munaylla, Filmer	348	59	45	39	297,842
Munoz, Larry	196	11	17	20	93,923
Murphy, Chad K.	861	157	120	110	2,985,318
Murphy, Cyril	49	6	7	7	188,556
Murphy, Glen	18	2	3	2	43,607
Murphy, Jeff	50	3	7	5	71,858
Murphy, Tim S.	89	3	6	9	40,016
Murray, Kelly Michael	693	56	78	80	770,231
Murray, Kevin C.	107	11	14	10	50,560
Muzzi, Alessandro	1	0	0	0	90
Nakatani, Corey S.	1,080	220	194	146	12,466,557
Naupac, Alejo	38	1	2	3	21,077
Navarre, Crystal Lynn	19	2	2	1	27,475
Navarro, Dionicio	31	1	1	2	12,699

RECORDS OF JOCKEYS

Jockey	Sts	1st	2d	3d	Purses
Navarro, Victor G.	227	24	35	34	253,341
Navedo, Edwin	53	2	3	8	27,580
Neal, Tim	255	33	28	40	104,731
Nebeker, Troy	4	1	1	0	860
Ned, Hosea A.	124	4	7	8	72,227
Nelson, Diane	56	4	2	3	157,812
Nelson, Gary	27	0	1	4	3,504
Nelson, Leroy	722	82	79	102	1,379,963
Nelson, Tyler	4	0	0	0	152
Nguyen, Scotty D.	181	22	23	14	113,707
Nguyen, Tho	435	45	53	45	747,595
Nicholls, Keveh	283	21	22	33	191,498
Nichols, Jerri Elizabeth	488	61	47	64	920,240
Nicol, Jr., Paul Albert	520	88	76	81	1,291,848
Nielson, Tyler	6	0	0	0	208
Nieto, Carlos	414	63	54	42	454,289
Ning, Stan	226	17	32	30	200,678
Nixon, Keith	8	0	0	0	796
Noguez, Tony	337	62	41	35	953,473
Nolan, Paul M.	873	93	134	125	946,004
Noll, Cindy Sue	484	54	63	49	684,264
Nollar, Flip John	215	20	16	21	69,325
Nomee, Shann	3	1	1	0	1,460
Norwood, Jake K.	98	4	2	5	55,732
Not Afraid, Darnell	8	0	0	0	1,741
Nuesch, David C.	252	15	16	25	784,512
Nunez, Eduardo O.	740	86	100	95	1,801,905
Nunez, Elmer	20	0	0	3	2,733
Nunez, Rafael A.	40	10	3	3	83,902
Nunn, David G.	3	1	0	0	7,025
Nunn, Doug	2	0	1	1	2,800
Nuttall, Todd J.	189	25	29	27	75,039
Obed, Keturah E.	159	13	16	19	131,489
O'Donnell, Kristin	224	22	38	30	109,330
O'Dwyer, Mark	3	0	0	1	1,450
O'Farrill, Orlando	11	0	0	1	622
Offutt, Leigh	98	15	15	10	267,708
Olesiak, Jake	121	6	5	6	41,454
Olesiak, Jordan	297	12	7	29	145,328
Olguin, Ever Romero	276	20	29	28	282,207
Olguin, Gerry	415	44	49	44	2,325,902
Olivares, Frank	46	3	9	3	119,056
Oliver, Gary	5	0	0	0	0
Oliver, Rick	147	11	4	17	25,615
Olivero, Carlos	273	31	38	35	673,370
Olmo, Christian J.	413	50	37	52	701,989
Olmo, Jr., Eugene	39	3	4	4	56,190
Olmstead, Jason	5	1	0	0	2,699
Orantes, Faustino	5	0	0	0	1,355
Ore, Zarella	154	13	14	12	117,637
Orm, Scott	98	2	3	3	23,011
Oro, Ernesto	160	20	14	16	165,634
Ortega, Alejandro	28	1	4	2	4,418
Ortega, Aurelio	1	0	0	0	75
Ortega, Javier A.	404	43	43	55	240,726
Ortega, Juan	626	44	59	76	1,036,024
Ortega, Oscar	4	0	0	1	480
Ortiz, Felix L.	566	49	56	70	1,285,760
Ortiz, Gilbert	3	0	0	0	774
Ortiz, Jr., Ivan	262	33	30	30	130,729
Ortiz, Jr., Manuel Figueroa	107	7	11	7	71,238
Osorio, Jose David	218	20	24	14	202,764
Otero, William P.	994	172	134	151	1,351,632
Ouzts, Perry Wayne	1,454	212	191	178	1,592,472
Owens, Angela	55	7	7	12	86,290
Pabon, Jr., John C.	390	25	43	33	174,785
Packer, Berkley R.	348	73	50	57	314,193
Padilla, Juan	97	3	4	4	25,246
Pagan, Norberto	77	0	2	3	13,315
Page, Mark	75	1	3	7	23,710
Pailhes, Patrick	1	0	0	0	500
Painter, Janeen Erin	7	1	0	0	4,638
Painter, Leanne M.	725	98	108	104	1,492,727
Pallister, Kevin	2	0	0	1	3,000
Palmer, Roy Walter	14	0	0	0	4,907
Panas, Deirdre A.	117	8	12	13	129,428
Panell, Dyn	723	159	99	91	1,819,451
Papineau, Cammie	6	0	1	0	3,204
Parenti, Jr., Jerry J.	55	2	4	7	27,132
Parish, Ramon	31	0	2	0	10,237
Parker, Deshawn L.	1,606	238	270	194	3,751,116
Parker, Jim	7	0	0	1	412
Parra, Hernan	113	4	9	10	98,826
Paschal, Vince	5	0	0	1	2,500
Patin, Billy Charles	565	60	59	63	677,612
Patrick, Marty	25	1	1	4	16,778
Patterson, Jenn	2	0	1	0	2,880
Paucar, Edgar	605	80	56	75	495,684
Pavlovic, Goran	19	0	0	1	4,804
Payne, Eric R.	147	12	15	15	146,115
Payne, Larry D.	30	5	5	4	114,814
Peaker, Pamela M.	6	2	2	0	5,684
Peck, Brian Dale	305	28	34	23	1,027,766
Peck, Donna	11	0	3	3	19,560
Pedroza, Martin A.	828	139	113	103	3,731,447
Peery, Melissa	537	72	71	69	291,993
Pellegrino, Kathy	334	18	27	33	226,249
Peltroche, Elias	49	10	4	3	112,141
Peltroche, Fredy	44	3	4	3	40,890
Pena, Antonio	107	10	13	7	132,312
Penalba, Cecilio	607	73	66	68	1,302,407
Pennington, Frankie	1,154	140	155	156	1,750,364
Perdomo, Teofilo A.	207	19	25	22	204,571
Pereira, Oswald M.	1,284	159	188	156	2,569,745
Perez, Antonio	24	4	2	3	4,074
Perez, Benicio D.	1	0	0	0	0
Perez, Bonificio	71	7	7	9	65,395
Perez, Cristian Yermay	569	38	54	72	337,606
Perez, Eduardo E.	557	78	63	72	1,686,806
Perez, Edwin	864	91	117	113	1,662,407
Perez, Ezequiel	30	2	4	3	19,999
Perez, Luis A.	540	37	43	53	703,845
Perez, Melvin L.	146	13	8	17	179,594
Perez, Miguel A.	592	84	68	90	1,425,303
Perez, Nilo	380	14	23	25	389,112
Perez, Roberto A.	820	127	107	116	1,260,517
Perez, Salvador	351	20	23	24	164,702
Perez, Jr., John A.	518	40	31	41	564,287
Perkinson, CC	15	1	1	1	7,970
Perret, Craig	226	33	29	34	1,809,832
Perrodin, Elvis Joseph	550	86	77	78	2,140,481
Perry, Bryan Allen	15	0	2	0	3,570
Persaud, Randi	5	0	0	0	3,978
Peterson, Rhonda	1	0	0	0	390
Petro, Nicholas J.	243	32	42	42	912,263
Pettinger, Donald R.	474	72	54	76	1,716,614
Petty, Jody	56	9	10	9	167,444
Pezua, Julio Molina	173	11	15	17	421,502
Phillips, Michael D.	5	0	0	0	813
Phillips, Tony	19	0	1	1	7,592
Pierce, Brett Taylor	7	0	0	0	916
Pierce, Howard	5	0	0	0	86
Piermarini, Tammi	778	117	128	95	1,256,177
Pimentel, Julian	747	116	107	102	4,236,205
Pimentel, Rui M.	284	39	26	34	1,358,016
Pina, Modesto	4	0	0	0	270
Pindell, Michael Duane	233	24	32	22	673,681
Pino, Mario G.	922	156	145	144	4,300,470
Piques, David A.	151	13	6	14	203,652
Pizarro, Juan	6	0	1	0	1,775
Pizarro, Ruben	146	6	8	10	39,344
Platts, Lisa	51	5	4	2	148,512
Podobinski, Stacy M.	41	1	3	6	30,435
Poe, John	3	0	2	0	8,275
Poleo, Cesar	100	3	4	8	77,805
Polkey, Melissa	121	7	7	11	102,477

Jockey	Sts	1st	2d	3d	Purses
Pompell, Thomas L.	958	139	114	124	1,366,950
Potts, Clinton L.	872	125	128	115	2,789,972
Powers, Therese Marie	10	0	1	1	7,580
Poznansky, Neil	560	89	68	81	1,614,614
Prado, Anibal	496	35	59	62	544,097
Prado, Edgar S.	1,445	281	249	204	18,342,106
Prescott, Rodney A.	1,789	251	233	233	2,572,852
Privitera, Richard	2	0	0	0	235
Pruitt, Jerry	361	57	47	49	436,527
Puello, Franklin	2	0	1	0	3,210
Puello, Nathaniel	355	28	47	39	345,710
Puglisi, Ignacio	438	43	42	56	1,132,074
Purdome, Johanna	22	0	0	0	2,121
Quewezance, Enoch	4	0	0	0	234
Quinones, Angel R.	1,207	199	178	128	3,736,142
Quinones, Luis M.	659	56	46	66	834,414
Quinones Medina, Angel A.	1	0	0	0	0
Quinones, Jr., Esteban J.	41	0	0	2	8,141
Quinonez, Luis S.	1,140	148	165	174	2,567,843
Quong, Michael D.	336	25	21	36	338,231
Rabbitskin, Hector	18	3	5	2	4,345
Radke, Kevin	344	66	56	48	1,224,181
Raghunath, Raymond	194	9	17	18	186,591
Raish, Lisa	24	1	2	1	6,919
Rambaran, Lester L.	9	0	0	1	672
Ramgeet, Andrew R.	720	90	80	94	1,486,634
Ramirez, Antonio	93	7	9	17	36,963
Ramirez, Esgar	1	0	0	0	1,112
Ramirez, Luis	1	0	0	0	0
Ramirez, Martin Ramos	675	83	86	73	1,563,430
Ramirez, Ricky	8	1	0	1	3,402
Ramirez, Roberto	261	17	25	24	303,938
Ramirez, Victor	253	16	30	28	138,601
Ramirez, Sr., Raul	1	0	0	0	0
Ramos, Adrian B.	571	48	70	65	541,012
Ramos, Hector A.	1	1	0	0	7,800
Ramos, Hector G.	119	17	16	8	220,644
Ramos, Ramon	518	34	42	56	446,754
Ramsammy, Emile	935	94	135	116	6,009,954
Ramsay, Robert	5	0	0	0	1,400
Randle, Stephen	63	5	8	5	17,582
Raney, Leon Anderson	79	3	4	6	65,840
Ranilla, Luis	409	39	42	50	443,557
Ransom, Kent	1	0	1	0	625
Raper, Alfred R.	6	0	0	0	0
Rasmussen, Judd	17	0	1	4	2,449
Razo, Jr., Eusebio	985	160	144	116	4,301,244
Read, Christopher	26	5	3	7	199,560
Rechy, Ramon	137	8	9	11	95,422
Reeves, Jr., Robert F.	285	21	21	27	220,716
Reid, Alphonso	19	2	1	2	17,395
Remer, Jerry R.	7	0	0	0	75
Rengifo, Roger	71	4	9	4	37,591
Rennie, Chandra R.	369	28	41	27	364,912
Renteria, Steve	20	0	1	1	2,034
Repp, Kate M.	58	1	10	8	53,111
Retana, Gabriel Compos	108	16	17	15	86,248
Reyes, Mario Jose	310	25	29	39	345,146
Reyes, Octavio	28	2	4	0	10,173
Reynolds, Larry C.	488	49	67	54	1,374,944
Reynolds, Lori E.	3	0	0	0	212
Rice, Alan	5	0	0	0	0
Rice, Bacarra Lynne	59	6	8	6	38,752
Rice, Jessica	49	1	10	0	47,000
Rich, Jessica	1	0	0	0	0
Richards, Gary	2	0	0	0	1,074
Rini, Wade P.	427	28	41	47	419,795
Rios-Conde, Alexis	506	29	38	45	564,975
Riquelme, Jose	912	66	81	95	1,084,537
Riston, Joseph A.	82	10	8	11	61,736
Rivas, Carlos	189	16	20	24	209,177
Rivera, David M.	419	24	48	47	377,559
Rivera, Gilbert D.	54	4	3	4	7,039
Rivera, Gregorio A.	73	4	6	8	85,178
Rivera, Heriberto	14	3	2	0	24,134
Rivera, Hiram G.	525	64	67	63	1,141,239
Rivera, Javier	17	1	2	1	17,650
Rivera, Jorge	210	12	17	26	153,446
Rivera, Juan G.	753	78	83	84	707,298
Rivera, Luis Raul	1	0	0	0	300
Rivera, Marco A.	35	0	1	1	5,692
Rivera, II, Jose Alberto	371	27	46	43	578,614
Rivera, Jr., Jose L.	424	27	40	55	451,761
Rivera, Jr., Jose Luis	364	31	27	44	311,593
Rivera, Jr., Jose M.	246	26	26	29	90,485
Rivera, Jr., Luis Romero	565	39	50	58	924,745
Rivera, Sr., Luis D.	19	0	0	0	1,926
Robbins, Brinda	23	0	1	0	4,503
Roberts, Stephanie	2	0	0	0	0
Robertson, Alexandra	3	1	1	0	20,700
Robins, Mark	1	0	0	0	400
Robinson, Edward Keith	277	16	21	19	335,811
Robinson, Kristopher	189	30	15	24	528,856
Robinson, Rick B.	11	2	1	2	4,130
Robletto, Luis	312	56	45	43	388,439
Rocco, Joseph	545	51	76	52	1,158,689
Rocco, Jr., Joseph	468	58	58	51	969,905
Rocha, Jorge O.	138	10	15	20	136,987
Rochabrun, John	352	18	38	38	216,461
Roche, Jennie	477	65	56	47	1,021,909
Rocheleau, Serge R.	188	56	31	24	148,106
Rodriguez, Adolfo C.	212	15	18	27	147,173
Rodriguez, David	8	1	0	0	17,003
Rodriguez, Edilberto	729	92	91	95	799,658
Rodriguez, Eduardo E.	1	0	0	0	130
Rodriguez, Erick D.	823	102	112	114	2,023,780
Rodriguez, Filemon T.	727	54	56	58	745,067
Rodriguez, Gabriel A.	90	8	6	16	46,379
Rodriguez, Hector Q.	36	3	3	5	41,150
Rodriguez, J. C.	51	4	1	7	44,838
Rodriguez, Jerry Mendez	3	0	0	0	200
Rodriguez, Jesus G.	100	3	1	4	27,659
Rodriguez, Macario	835	109	123	119	1,428,888
Rodriguez, Marcelino	125	8	11	7	87,169
Rodriguez, Omar	345	21	25	23	250,272
Rodriguez, Pedro A.	725	143	96	96	1,579,076
Rodriguez, Ruben	187	15	20	23	258,048
Rodriguez, Rudy R.	22	1	2	3	32,356
Rodriguez, Victor	1	0	0	0	0
Rogers, Barbara A.	6	0	0	0	1,059
Rohena, J. M.	404	49	61	48	546,415
Rohena, Juan	23	0	1	1	6,533
Rojas, Christian	753	103	89	91	626,762
Rojas, Denis	30	0	2	5	14,225
Rojas, Fernando S.	388	52	49	49	423,305
Rojas, Johnny	10	1	0	0	14,140
Rojas, Martin	32	1	0	1	6,059
Rojas, Raul I.	131	9	10	8	252,010
Rojas, Ruben	227	17	16	17	156,206
Rojo, Omar	2	0	0	0	340
Roll, Michael	3	0	1	0	2,088
Roller, Robert Edward	10	0	2	0	1,084
Rollins, Chance J.	934	139	154	156	2,781,325
Romero, Arturo	156	11	12	15	77,077
Romero, Cheryl A.	3	0	0	0	0
Romero, Hector R.	271	26	38	34	375,653
Romero, Josh M.	667	48	56	77	699,397
Romero, Shane P.	282	19	21	21	259,641
Rosado, Roberto J.	372	28	42	38	608,506
Rosales, Arturo Garcia	123	2	7	9	20,189
Rosario, Yamil	452	28	40	64	484,939
Rosario, Jr., Hector L.	986	154	132	135	1,128,888
Rose, Jeremy	885	165	136	127	4,550,917
Rose, Kevin	1	0	0	0	0
Rosendo, Irwin J.	721	75	107	85	869,003
Rosenthal, Mark E.	568	65	62	56	1,356,647

Jockey	Sts	1st	2d	3d	Purses
Rosier, Chris R.	45	3	4	1	21,798
Roughley, Adam Wade	94	11	10	9	55,829
Rowland, Michael Francis	68	5	3	10	90,747
Rozas, Emeterio	3	0	0	1	2,300
Rozman, Albert A.	40	0	1	3	4,890
Rubio, Carlos	7	0	0	0	646
Ruhe, Schad	1	0	0	0	515
Ruis, Mick	1,054	172	136	133	3,305,019
Ruiz, Sergio	70	5	5	5	50,519
Russell, Ben	446	100	78	57	912,399
Russell, Chris	116	9	10	10	94,029
Russell, Wazzeer B.	1	0	0	0	77
Ryan, Colvin G.	41	2	1	3	29,225
Ryan, Greg	1	0	0	0	500
Sabourin, Raymond Brian	373	38	35	49	1,899,112
Saenz, Diego	256	18	30	22	177,837
Saint-Martin, Eric	68	11	12	7	515,677
Saito, Scott T.	402	37	48	61	452,837
Salazar, Francisco Ramiro	1	0	0	0	192
Salazar, Hector	132	2	6	2	35,644
Saldanha, Alessander	4	0	0	0	1,092
Salinas, Linda	2	0	0	0	0
Sam, Connie	7	1	0	2	1,855
Sampson, Kelly	1	0	0	1	1,100
Samyn, Jean-Luc	368	22	27	32	1,311,895
Sanches, Jose H.	2	0	0	0	217
Sanchez, Andre	239	10	12	20	229,292
Sanchez, Andres A.	10	2	0	0	4,016
Sanchez, Angel B.	20	1	3	1	18,340
Sanchez, Carlos	332	11	20	26	89,670
Sanchez, Jesus	918	104	92	98	2,062,597
Sanchez, Joseph	287	34	35	34	203,469
Sanchez, Kenny Angel	1	0	0	0	400
Sanchez, Marcos	6	0	0	0	920
Sanchez, Miguel A.	20	2	2	1	23,761
Sanchez, Richard A.	49	4	7	1	39,113
Sanchez, Jr., Jose A.	261	19	23	31	153,766
Sanguinetti, Anne	106	11	12	14	81,291
Santagata, Nick	954	124	140	128	2,111,271
Santana, Daniel	275	37	33	29	363,670
Santana, Jozbin Z.	750	131	108	80	2,667,243
Santana, Jr., Efrain	5	0	1	0	4,805
Santiago, Cruz	4	0	0	0	255
Santiago, Felipe R.	4	0	1	2	3,890
Santiago, Javier	642	88	72	74	4,237,653
Santiago, Joel	908	89	120	131	844,406
Santiago, Jr., Manuel A.	113	7	8	21	63,134
Santos, Bernie P.	10	0	0	0	2,898
Santos, Felipe J.	563	59	84	77	609,708
Santos, Jose A.	984	137	108	129	7,601,843
Santos, Romualdo	381	35	26	42	479,773
Sarmiento, Rigo	14	1	0	0	9,770
Sarvis, Dean A.	1,280	256	160	157	2,150,493
Savastano, Mark	1	0	0	0	68
Scantling, Vernon	302	21	21	34	168,565
Scarlett, Andy	5	0	1	0	665
Schacht, Randy	124	14	15	16	249,279
Schaefer, Gregory Allen	526	23	34	56	221,995
Scharfstein, Jillian	437	35	44	49	1,767,394
Schindler, Scot A.	96	19	12	9	63,035
Schmidt, Jennifer	352	16	35	30	175,827
Schmidt, Richard L.	2	0	1	0	467
Schneider, Joseph	136	6	5	16	164,619
Schvaneveldt, Chad Phillip	589	144	90	85	2,662,325
Schwartz, James Daniel	472	47	55	61	312,472
Scocca, Dante	79	8	7	5	129,629
Scott, Joy Marie	152	6	8	11	117,308
Sealock, Regina	167	13	10	18	223,905
Searchwell, Gilbert Rodney	76	1	5	4	29,979
Seesequasis, Danny	158	20	17	15	46,809
Seesequasis, Janice	145	9	20	22	45,598
Sellers, Shane J.	698	146	97	94	6,532,304
Sengotta, Corrine	3	0	1	1	3,091
Sensenbach, Lee	104	11	16	8	78,241
Sepulveda, Jr., Rigoberto	25	0	0	0	10,511
Serna, Fernando	100	5	9	12	108,381
Serrano, Angel	309	13	22	25	177,672
Sessions, Nick	2	0	0	2	1,430
Shamsie, Clayton P.	44	1	4	3	28,020
Sharp, Joe	202	18	37	26	188,057
Sharrol, Garnet D.	9	0	0	0	871
Sheetz, Deena	1	0	0	0	60
Shepherd, David R.	4	0	2	0	3,651
Shepherd, Justin	759	71	86	82	1,624,163
Shepler, David	24	1	0	0	5,520
Sherbino, Shawnette L.	25	1	2	2	12,601
Sherman, Casey	32	6	9	2	11,553
Shingoose, Alec	3	0	0	0	530
Shino, Ken A.	565	77	71	73	877,803
Shirley, Samuel Hubert	119	4	14	16	67,778
Sibille, Ray	43	3	4	3	78,095
Siddo, Augustus	246	9	10	16	78,991
Siebeneicher, Laura H.	14	0	0	1	5,123
Sierra, Jose Enrique	180	9	8	17	103,808
Sierra, Joseph A.	21	0	1	4	16,313
Silva, Carlos H.	733	86	75	94	2,098,110
Silva, Carlos Ignacio	221	25	32	30	347,959
Silva, Gilberto	8	1	0	0	3,970
Silva, Javier	23	0	0	0	991
Simard, Real E.	723	112	92	77	1,562,267
Simington, Donald Edward	679	69	94	86	1,120,808
Simpson, Gillespie	5	0	0	1	2,365
Simpson, Mike	43	4	5	7	16,597
Singh, Rohan R.	87	4	15	14	276,718
Singh, Ronald	12	2	1	0	11,379
Singh, Sunny	565	42	85	64	1,741,026
Skaggs, Tad Wayne	13	2	1	0	4,195
Skelly, Robert V.	267	32	28	32	684,518
Skerrett, Jeffrey	779	79	83	82	876,549
Skinner, Colin	425	43	47	55	419,753
Slater, Clayton	6	0	0	2	492
Slaughter, Dayton	150	5	7	8	120,006
Slaven, Mark	89	1	9	8	19,167
Slot, Sarah	1	0	0	0	180
Smallwood, Vickie Yolanda	209	19	25	28	205,921
Smith, Ariel	352	16	26	26	983,392
Smith, Cherell	214	6	12	16	114,296
Smith, Dewey Paul	4	1	0	0	3,660
Smith, Guy	1,008	154	129	128	2,827,674
Smith, Hugh	30	2	1	4	8,546
Smith, Jackie	194	28	32	29	129,494
Smith, Jeff	3	0	0	1	837
Smith, Kevin J.	74	3	3	7	50,124
Smith, Mike E.	692	111	112	75	7,863,942
Smith, Nate	204	22	22	26	100,148
Smith, Rodger W.	46	3	4	4	16,258
Smith, Stormy	465	30	35	54	453,449
Smith, Tammy	128	6	9	14	98,586
Smith, V. L.	378	21	24	28	387,927
Smith, Wayne	37	5	4	5	87,485
Smullen, Pat	2	1	0	0	170,000
Solberg, Howie	20	0	2	1	4,011
Solis, Alex O.	555	119	96	80	7,954,851
Solis, Horacio	2	0	0	0	150
Solomon, Nathan	436	44	46	52	362,758
Somsanith, Na	416	56	52	49	1,960,404
Sone, Joel	312	16	24	37	225,046
Soodeen, Rodney	257	8	12	17	367,605
Sorenson, Danny	290	38	32	34	1,479,067
Sorrells, Janna	259	33	38	30	163,098
Sorto, Domingo	44	0	1	4	13,085
Sosa, Jr., Peter	659	56	81	75	981,642
Soto, Daniel	79	6	1	7	59,658
Soto, Jr., John A.	173	8	10	20	338,782
Soumillon, Christophe	2	0	0	0	0
Spanabel, Kelly R.	132	3	9	14	36,743

Jockey	Sts	1st	2d	3d	Purses
Spence, Ian J.	390	14	20	26	142,863
Spencer, Jamie P.	15	0	1	5	1,015,900
Spieth, Scott	897	181	121	100	1,686,680
St. Julien, Marlon	866	94	114	77	1,494,346
Stanley, Angel Ortega	50	2	5	2	24,061
Stanley, Monica Kay	135	5	6	15	110,811
Stanton, Terry A.	868	119	96	124	1,340,242
Starke, Andrasch	2	0	1	1	200,000
Steele, Holly	4	0	1	0	1,275
Stein, Gary Raymond	118	9	8	9	92,305
Stein, Justin	40	4	6	5	49,841
Stein, Robert	14	4	5	1	9,375
Steiner, Joseph J.	152	13	15	18	464,702
Stephen, Anthony	347	44	38	43	678,456
Sterling, Jr., Larry J.	787	125	98	106	3,119,216
Sterr, Scott	291	61	57	48	263,882
Stevens, Gary L.	266	49	38	42	3,546,284
Stevens, Scott A.	862	142	144	143	1,757,294
Steward, Keenan	35	0	2	1	7,536
Stianson, Janine	184	24	26	33	120,409
Stiller, Clinton	1	0	0	0	0
Stinn, Caroline	37	8	9	7	18,785
Stokes, Joe	988	134	129	133	1,368,772
Stokes, Louis A.	659	41	49	70	288,682
Stokes, III, Rex A.	709	97	74	77	1,313,235
Stortz, Marcia	15	1	4	1	23,060
Straightnose, Les	2	0	1	0	344
Strawbridge, Stewart	7	4	1	2	25,850
Strollo, Michael	58	1	4	5	20,001
Sturniolo, Derek	3	0	0	0	0
Suarez, Gabriel	437	43	49	58	545,548
Suarez, Guillermo	22	0	1	1	3,470
Suckie, Marland C.	57	3	3	11	58,285
Sukie, Danush	472	68	75	67	684,833
Summers, Nancy Nichols	196	16	17	24	175,368
Sunseri, James Joseph	222	8	9	9	79,681
Surrency, Scott	291	24	21	23	210,911
Sutherland, Chantal	363	31	39	47	1,348,269
Swope, Benjamin C.	2	0	0	1	2,300
Take, Yutaka	5	0	1	0	152,340
Talarico, Michael V.	88	0	3	8	31,707
Talaverano, Ramiro	37	2	2	2	24,965
Talman, Katherine G.	89	3	5	6	31,559
Tatushiro, Ryuji	3	0	0	0	891
Taveras, Reino A.	91	5	13	15	21,553
Taylor, Kendra T.	1	0	0	0	300
Taylor, Larry	952	118	107	124	1,523,579
Teator, Phil	487	36	42	42	922,780
Tejera, Eguard A.	37	1	1	3	32,406
Telg, Tram	36	2	2	3	17,211
Termini, Chip M.	23	0	1	0	3,435
Terry, Dominic M.	329	28	29	33	426,629
Tervort, Jason	605	72	79	76	773,002
Thacker, Nathan	144	10	14	12	70,499
Theriot, Brian James	346	45	46	38	407,319
Theriot, Jamie	937	139	126	93	2,369,411
Thibodeaux, Ronald L.	9	1	0	0	11,490
Thomas, Charles C.	31	2	0	3	32,350
Thomas, Michael	341	9	9	28	98,164
Thomas, Todd	7	0	0	1	1,035
Thomason, William Thomas	56	10	5	2	31,543
Thompson, Junior A.	1	0	0	0	80
Thompson, Ted	15	2	0	0	22,800
Thompson, Terry J.	638	109	87	97	2,244,212
Thompson, Winston Albert	1,068	183	181	147	1,982,528
Thornton, Craig	2	1	0	0	101,250
Thornton, Timothy	505	69	63	79	1,756,059
Thorwarth, Otto	41	0	3	4	11,740
Tipa, Jorge	601	90	67	68	650,464
Todd, Jr., Frank	161	13	23	19	488,201
Tohill, Ken S.	829	194	138	127	2,824,550
Tolentino, Pablo	446	32	35	37	538,088
Toquinto, Victor	4	0	0	0	504
Torbit, Renee	285	20	32	23	122,189
Toribio, Abdiel	497	80	68	78	1,761,540
Toribio, Jr., Aurelio	784	92	96	104	2,199,798
Toro, Melvin	595	57	51	71	699,260
Torrealba, Raphael	69	6	5	12	102,565
Torres, Alfredo	183	20	15	19	49,789
Torres, Carlos	196	9	13	15	148,004
Torres, Cesar A.	209	7	13	24	203,540
Torres, Francisco C.	158	14	20	15	268,100
Torres, Gregorio	2	0	0	0	0
Torres, Jose	328	13	39	51	219,785
Torres, Raymond	398	30	49	57	872,912
Torres, Robert Valesquez	53	1	0	3	46,993
Toscano, Paul R.	456	52	42	39	1,375,523
Tourangeau, Bernie	29	6	9	3	8,032
Trader, Rodney R.	112	5	6	12	84,650
Traurig, Michael	26	1	5	0	49,655
Trejo, Luis	2	0	2	0	1,720
Trevoet, Jason	1	1	0	0	1,250
Triantafyllou, Kyriakos	74	7	11	8	87,109
Trimble, Patricia	347	33	41	50	644,614
Troilo, William D.	881	96	80	104	1,746,569
Troxell, Kristin	53	0	1	3	27,500
Truitt, Myra Suzanne	297	13	21	27	159,067
Trujillo, Elvis	534	55	75	73	1,463,099
Trujillo, Victor	38	0	2	4	12,770
Turner, Tom G.	180	25	12	23	716,040
Umana, Juan	869	99	100	111	1,564,377
Umarov, Otabek	6	1	0	1	1,496
Unsihuay, Arnaldo	399	33	37	36	590,598
Unsihuay, Esteban E.	27	2	1	0	41,240
Uriegas, Henry	3	0	0	0	126
Urieta-Moran, Victor	107	4	5	11	116,582
Uske, Shannon	126	9	11	19	465,134
Vail, James S.	95	4	6	9	82,861
Valdes, Ricardo A.	432	55	51	52	1,175,924
Valdez, Felipe	390	46	44	40	721,929
Valdez, Martin	16	0	0	1	1,090
Valdivia, Jr., Jose	761	76	98	98	5,648,352
Valenzuela, Fernando H.	109	7	5	7	154,960
Valenzuela, John Raul	96	8	7	15	88,763
Valenzuela, Patrick A.	202	45	26	39	1,864,873
Vales, Daniel I	79	4	2	10	27,070
Valles, Eric S.	265	38	36	27	336,530
Van Slyke, Amanda	7	0	0	2	660
Vanderwoude, Justin	74	17	9	7	27,826
VanderWoude, Matthew	2	0	0	0	225
Vanek, Helen Marie	382	18	37	28	413,678
VanHassel, Christopher	700	90	84	100	1,340,484
Vargas, Jorge L.	85	7	5	15	84,250
Vasquez, Richard M.	295	47	24	28	214,065
Vasquez, Rolando	25	0	1	1	6,210
Vaz, Eriluis	595	64	53	66	971,027
Vazquez, Gilberto	67	1	3	8	31,301
Vazquez, Julian J.	133	13	5	9	191,100
Vazquez, Manuel A.	96	2	7	9	50,585
Vega, Antonio	9	0	0	0	1,910
Vega, Harry	873	177	127	112	2,765,434
Vega, Jesse	6	0	0	1	1,368
Vega, Jose	1	0	0	1	671
Velasquez, Cornelio H.	1,593	240	260	241	11,098,689
Velazquez, Argelio	211	26	39	35	215,243
Velazquez, Daniel C.	410	34	51	44	549,350
Velazquez, John R.	1,327	335	222	181	22,248,661
Velazquez, Lucino	6	0	0	0	315
Velazquez, Mario	343	25	31	50	383,591
Velez, Juan J. L.	33	0	1	3	10,559
Velez, Pedro J.	88	2	3	2	38,597
Velez, Roger I.	45	2	3	5	50,440
Velez, Jr., Jose A.	517	60	86	72	2,749,866
Verenzuela, Jose L.	105	7	8	9	140,115
Vergara, Daniel P.	432	70	74	65	126,093
Vergara, Octavio	176	7	15	20	374,642

RECORDS OF JOCKEYS

Jockey	Sts	1st	2d	3d	Purses
Verge, Mario E.	49	5	1	9	69,759
Vicchrilli, Russell	276	47	54	38	409,495
Vidal, Francisco A.	186	11	19	20	90,645
Villa, Mark Anthony	148	14	16	17	163,969
Villafan, Roberto	151	17	19	10	216,736
Villa-Gomez, Huber	974	178	143	133	1,849,748
Villeneuve, Francine	391	67	55	48	1,457,356
Villicana, Heriberto	1	0	0	0	75
Vitek, Justin J.	458	32	47	52	489,003
Von Rosen, Anne	132	24	12	12	111,141
Wade, Gary	45	2	6	3	6,550
Wahlen, Kelly J.	10	1	0	2	1,846
Walcott, Rickey	702	138	114	106	1,835,637
Wales, Travis	299	54	38	44	411,422
Walker, Pedro L.	169	5	9	8	100,308
Walker, Jr., Bobby J.	510	93	73	49	1,635,833
Walker, Jr., Donald	6	0	0	0	592
Wall, Newil	119	2	7	14	28,215
Walsh, Michael P.	147	5	5	7	79,576
Walsh, Robert	85	10	18	4	281,711
Warhol, Vicki Lynn	179	14	15	17	89,897
Warner, Terry Neal	118	4	10	13	148,166
Warren, Jr., Ronald J.	928	170	145	129	3,350,617
Waterman, Blair	38	6	9	4	199,294
Watson, Hannah	1	0	0	0	750
Watson, Patrick James	115	11	6	10	151,793
Weatherly, James T.	264	10	18	17	161,574
Webb, Harla Kay	41	0	1	1	9,399
Webb, Robert	168	24	27	25	98,565
Welch, Quincy	794	173	135	124	2,274,600
Wellington, Thomas	74	14	2	7	54,332
Wells, Lindell	83	1	5	7	21,744
Wheat, Jr., Jesse R.	230	26	24	27	201,370
Whetstone, Perry S.	431	48	61	48	693,122
Whitacre, Brandon	918	141	125	113	2,414,794
Whitacre, Gordon	447	32	32	47	208,857
Whitaker, Jennifer	211	20	29	27	180,803
White, Andrew	3	0	0	0	605
White, Eddie H.	10	0	0	0	150
White, James Bo	52	10	2	8	77,212
Whiteside, Jim Bob	126	10	22	24	34,297
Whitner, IV, James H.	4	0	0	0	600
Whitney, Dana G.	1,428	267	214	196	4,184,757
Whittaker, Dale	289	35	36	38	686,337
Whittle, Stoney D.	56	1	6	4	10,426
Wiley, Henry William	7	0	1	0	1,600
Williams, Carl S.	351	31	36	42	168,889
Williams, Dorothy	7	0	0	0	1,478
Williams, Douglas A.	152	1	6	8	49,220
Williams, Dustin W.	82	10	18	10	43,795
Williams, Frank	11	0	1	2	1,538
Williams, Justin L.	216	15	16	12	145,796
Williams, Matt	162	14	27	22	50,899
Williams, Percival	16	0	0	3	6,799
Williams, Robert Dean	903	139	100	99	964,827
Williams, Sean	86	9	14	9	22,968
Wilsey, James A.	29	4	1	3	55,828
Wilson, Angelle	162	28	28	28	123,629
Wilson, Billy M.	357	11	18	20	202,461
Wilson, David	577	80	88	78	1,582,686
Wilson, Emma Jayne	31	4	3	4	80,295
Wilson, Janet Leah	181	19	20	22	98,596
Wilson, Melissa E.	20	0	1	2	6,447
Wilson, Melton	198	5	13	18	126,308
Wilson, Nicola	1	0	0	1	2,310
Wilson, Randy G.	80	1	2	3	23,129
Wilson, Randy R.	119	17	9	14	159,796
Wilson, Rick	110	24	16	11	554,820
Winants, Garet W.	6	0	1	0	2,700
Winants, Remy	9	1	4	2	25,300
Winkle, Curtis W.	20	4	0	2	12,335
Winters, Jerry L.	48	0	2	4	15,185
Winters, Perry A.	615	79	72	73	1,167,266
Wippert, Shannon	165	31	20	22	59,792
Wirth, Keith F.	9	0	0	1	2,390
Wloka, Jr., Ricardo A.	1	0	0	0	250
Womack, Wayne	6	0	1	0	1,260
Wong, Peter K.	264	34	27	27	411,950
Woodley, Carl James	884	157	142	97	2,180,834
Woodley, John B.	58	11	7	4	55,292
Woolsey, Russell W.	818	93	125	99	1,114,137
Worst, Gary L.	73	6	10	9	25,425
Wortman, Tim A.	12	0	0	0	0
Wright, Jody	52	2	3	4	19,420
Wright, Michael L.	628	30	63	57	639,342
Wright, Nicola	182	24	30	25	431,431
Wynter, Noel A.	6	0	0	1	1,917
Yang, Chin C.	775	79	91	85	1,163,415
Yaranga, Yuri	927	79	96	117	487,293
Yetsook, Sylvia Maria	5	0	0	1	965
Yoakum, Jerry Lee	15	1	0	4	7,002
Young, Paddy	66	6	7	9	142,585
Young, Scott Eugene	52	4	3	4	18,944
Younker, Marty	13	0	0	3	4,080
Zamarron, Mario	1	0	0	0	300
Zambrana, David A.	37	2	1	1	18,498
Zambrana, Eddie Joe	446	40	34	53	211,310
Zamora, Christopher G.	74	11	6	11	164,168
Zamora, Humberto	196	10	16	21	95,521
Zamora, Tomas A.	146	3	12	14	93,838
Ziegler, Michael G.	505	60	48	71	583,859
Zimmerman, Ramsey	1,295	326	227	181	2,597,941
Zuniga, Eddie	1,039	122	123	121	1,493,663
Zunino, Jose Luis	274	30	39	28	204,928

2004
RECORDS OF SIRES

The record of each sire represented by at least one winning thoroughbred or more who raced in the United States or Canada in 2004, showing his total performers, number of winning performers, the number of times they started and their total placings and earnings.

Sire	Perf	Wnrs	Sts	1st	2d	3d	Purses
A Change for April	5	3	30	6	9	1	$51,597
A Corking Limerick	5	1	30	2	6	4	29,369
A Lee Rover	4	1	28	1	2	1	10,461
A Man of Class	6	2	25	4	3	3	36,770
A P Ruler	4	1	27	1	3	5	45,951
A. P Jet	146	76	920	120	135	114	2,858,564
A. V. Eight	6	3	40	4	3	6	34,819
A.P. Indy	162	87	898	149	120	117	8,359,685
Aaron's Concorde	18	7	122	13	10	12	250,024
Aaron's Gold	10	3	49	5	6	5	115,432
Abaginone	63	31	384	52	41	45	1,004,882
Abbadabbadubai	3	2	9	2	1	1	8,612
Abel Prospect	21	10	177	18	15	22	265,115
Abity	2	1	17	1	2	3	38,025
Above Normal	14	4	91	6	10	6	81,518
Absent Russian	20	6	154	11	20	29	228,000
Abstract	27	17	175	38	23	19	197,719
Academy Award	48	18	305	26	33	41	402,827
Academyawardwinner	2	1	8	1	0	0	8,263
Acallade	9	2	50	3	4	1	24,306
Acaroid	13	5	87	9	13	11	127,783
Acatenango (GER)	4	2	10	3	2	1	540,600
Accelerator	77	39	538	52	58	62	1,031,557
Acceptable	50	24	347	36	42	59	672,241
Accoustical	5	1	21	1	1	0	16,991
Ack Ack Heir	1	1	15	3	5	1	19,146
Acquitted	5	2	29	3	4	1	16,687
Act Smart	10	4	52	6	2	4	81,900
Activado (URU)	6	1	27	2	0	4	6,117
Activist	14	7	77	14	5	10	139,393
Adams Trail	4	1	12	2	0	0	8,735
Adbass	5	3	33	5	3	4	11,461
Adcat	9	2	41	2	5	6	56,720
Adhocracy	9	6	62	10	7	5	288,912
Adios Mundo	6	1	22	1	2	1	48,618
Adonis	7	1	20	1	2	3	33,774
Advancing Ensign	2	1	8	2	1	2	3,632
Adventure Road	15	7	105	10	17	23	96,604
Advocate Training	4	1	31	2	3	1	13,020
Aegean's Bolger	7	4	53	9	3	13	37,102
Aerial Display	5	3	43	5	0	9	33,651
Aferd	12	9	78	13	10	6	64,831
Affirmed	52	21	292	34	32	39	1,108,572
Afleet	5	2	25	4	3	2	17,114
Afleetknowsasecret	5	2	41	2	5	3	31,738
Afternoon Deelites	120	56	750	101	100	84	2,113,444
Aggie Southpaw	9	3	68	5	6	6	71,967
Aggressive Chief	24	14	182	24	24	24	419,415
Ago	15	6	105	11	11	5	142,083
Agressive Hawk	4	1	16	1	0	3	13,933
Air Display	1	1	1	1	0	0	6,000
Air Forbes Won	45	28	336	48	45	53	522,385
Airdrie Apache	1	1	9	1	0	1	3,425
Akram	8	2	54	3	4	12	51,679
Akureyri Kid	2	1	18	1	1	4	15,362
Al Akbar (AUS)	1	1	12	1	2	2	11,612
Al Mamoon	11	3	56	5	4	8	48,647
Al Sabin	20	5	111	5	9	9	77,149
Alae Rouge	1	1	17	5	4	2	74,450
Alamo Road	4	3	23	4	1	4	24,547
Alamocitos	13	2	66	4	15	8	156,807
Alan's Ace	1	1	3	1	0	1	9,544
Alaskan Frost	44	17	314	32	28	39	426,642
Alfaari	59	27	403	46	57	59	738,524
Algenib (ARG)	1	1	7	1	1	1	24,070
Ali Gaziba	8	2	39	3	4	4	40,761
Ali-Royal (IRE)	4	2	17	2	2	2	85,228
Aljabr	5	3	10	5	0	0	65,945
All Done John	1	1	10	3	0	1	41,100
All Gone	63	34	594	69	82	69	1,051,911
All Storm	2	1	10	1	2	0	13,725
All Thee Power	14	7	81	15	7	15	163,175
Alladin Rib	10	5	77	9	8	9	131,024
Allawinir	1	1	19	2	2	2	50,810
Alleged Stardom	5	2	28	2	1	6	19,542
Allegedly Wild	1	1	13	1	2	2	19,305
Allen Charge	12	5	67	8	12	11	139,038
Allen's Prospect	193	103	1341	165	159	181	3,378,387
Allied Forces	29	12	193	12	17	24	221,220
Alnaab	33	16	227	33	24	37	195,539
Aloha Prospector	36	20	273	35	40	34	308,598
Aloma's Ruler	8	4	65	6	8	10	54,894
Alphabatim	1	1	3	1	1	0	7,800
Alphabet Soup	173	99	1232	181	151	140	5,099,550
Alquoz	1	1	16	3	7	1	35,960
Alster	5	2	27	2	3	2	23,492
Altazarr	4	2	36	9	4	3	146,060
Always a Classic	15	7	126	11	10	15	165,447
Always Fair	18	7	134	13	12	19	262,814
Always Silver	15	6	119	9	10	16	111,370
Alwuhush	6	3	44	7	2	6	57,273
Aly T.	3	2	40	4	5	5	30,884
Alybel	4	2	22	2	2	2	26,201
Alybenbo	3	3	27	4	6	5	30,222
Alybro	22	13	131	19	18	15	266,039
Alydarmer	1	1	6	1	0	1	3,692
Alydeed	92	44	623	73	71	72	1,426,386
Alyfoe	8	2	68	3	8	5	39,015
Alymagic	8	3	42	4	5	5	96,588
Alyone	4	2	40	3	7	4	50,742
Alyshadeed	4	2	23	4	2	3	61,987
Alysheba	22	8	152	14	17	12	185,997
Alyten	25	13	207	27	24	22	298,116
Alzao	5	3	37	12	4	4	101,218
Am all Charged Up	11	7	86	12	5	11	120,093
Amaruk	6	3	31	7	4	1	152,402
Ambessa	3	1	23	1	2	6	11,943
Ambivalent	6	4	44	6	8	6	41,658
Ameri Valay	40	21	326	33	42	31	716,554
American Artist	2	1	12	1	4	2	7,278
American Champ	15	4	78	9	5	11	68,085
American Chance	119	57	867	122	132	101	3,527,691
American Day	12	6	67	13	9	8	176,189
American General	13	4	74	7	8	6	53,579
American Pro	2	1	10	1	2	1	10,286
American Standard	24	8	135	15	18	11	371,720
American Tribute	6	1	26	2	2	3	15,658
Amerrico's Bullet	7	2	42	3	7	4	58,844
Amigo Menor (IRE)	3	2	20	2	1	2	7,330
Ample Amos	1	1	15	5	3	3	37,322
Anabaa	5	4	37	6	4	6	276,907
Ancient Oaks	6	3	38	4	4	6	19,926
Andean Chasqui	4	3	30	7	5	4	50,806
Anees	19	5	55	6	4	7	280,239
Anet	65	31	468	55	64	52	867,671
Anjiz	39	19	313	33	35	36	773,467
Announce	87	47	584	75	69	78	1,080,636
Another Freespirit	1	1	15	3	1	2	29,190
Another Reef	6	3	46	3	0	5	45,033
Anzel	1	1	12	1	0	2	4,283
Anziyan	24	11	157	22	19	22	500,489
Apala Destiny	1	1	4	1	1	0	1,965
Apalachee	9	5	83	9	14	6	79,164
Apalachee Prince	1	1	10	1	0	0	6,353
Apollo	45	28	349	53	72	46	702,603
Appeal for Justice	3	1	15	1	1	1	9,201
Appealing Guy	9	7	94	11	11	9	145,157
Appealing Skier	76	49	582	88	79	66	1,521,637
Apple Tree (FR)	1	1	4	1	0	1	6,010
Apprentice	1	1	23	1	0	0	3,540
Aquarian Prince	2	1	8	1	0	0	10,657
Arab Speaker	1	1	9	2	0	2	50,405
Araby Ace	5	1	34	1	2	6	18,837
Arazi	7	5	57	8	10	6	123,915
Arch	75	48	475	87	75	70	2,541,487
Archers Bay	56	29	293	42	41	33	1,954,905
Arctic Blitz	9	2	43	4	5	3	19,810
Arctic Nacht	1	1	2	1	0	0	8,400
Arctic Native	4	1	25	2	5	1	50,110
Ares Vallis	2	2	15	3	3	4	18,597
Armed Truce	4	2	31	4	4	2	32,001
Armidale (AUS)	1	1	5	1	1	0	49,840
Arnstadt	4	2	16	2	1	0	19,508
Art of Dawn	3	1	15	2	2	0	15,613

Sire	Perf	Wnrs	Sts	1st	2d	3d	Purses
Artax	72	37	421	52	45	57	1,730,613
Artema (IRE)	7	3	34	3	4	3	33,270
Artic Tracker	1	1	9	2	1	1	33,525
Artichoke	2	1	11	2	2	2	14,245
Artie Baby	1	1	3	1	0	0	4,003
As Time Flys By	1	1	9	1	2	0	15,044
Ascension	3	2	23	2	3	1	7,754
Ascot Knight	74	27	397	46	39	35	1,300,819
Ashdown	5	2	28	3	2	7	58,895
Asimov	5	1	27	1	0	5	4,682
Ask a Nice	1	1	14	1	1	0	7,220
Aspen Peak	1	1	12	1	0	1	11,590
Aspro	1	1	4	1	2	0	41,700
Assatis	1	1	2	1	0	0	90,000
Assembly Dancer	6	4	37	6	6	4	107,931
Assertive Joe	2	1	20	1	2	1	27,477
Astra Diamond	2	1	15	2	1	3	4,770
Astro	9	5	85	10	7	14	155,190
Astudillo (IRE)	6	3	42	4	8	6	51,605
At Full Feather	4	2	35	2	3	7	22,721
At the Flood	1	1	7	1	1	1	6,493
At the Threshold	26	7	166	17	30	19	154,827
Ataka	9	3	57	4	6	3	35,248
Atlantian	2	1	8	1	0	2	4,195
Atticus	57	27	290	44	39	45	992,374
Attribute	3	2	24	4	6	1	29,906
Au Point	5	2	52	4	8	9	72,347
Aurium	6	1	48	1	8	8	18,987
Autocracy	16	7	89	14	11	8	317,414
Avenger M.	1	1	14	1	2	2	11,221
Avenue of Flags	78	37	431	71	50	49	884,893
Avery	1	1	7	1	0	0	18,998
Avies Copy	18	6	116	12	3	4	80,445
Awad	57	18	372	28	28	39	570,191
Awesome Again	104	58	536	103	83	67	6,312,464
Awesome Blue	1	1	15	4	4	1	32,775
Awesome Cat	11	4	49	5	2	4	80,549
B. G.'s Drone	4	3	27	7	7	3	56,419
B. Hoedown	8	4	42	7	4	4	59,550
B. J.'s Lucky	4	1	16	1	0	0	6,184
B. J.'s Mark	4	1	9	3	0	1	69,345
Baatish	2	1	13	1	1	0	5,735
Baby I Lied	3	2	14	3	2	2	7,952
Baby Slewy	9	2	41	2	4	2	13,896
Back Alley	1	1	5	1	2	1	2,900
Back When	3	1	18	1	0	2	8,136
Badge	8	3	30	4	6	3	100,581
Badger Land	9	4	70	9	8	6	66,668
Bag	106	44	675	71	71	89	1,143,638
Bagdad Road	14	6	110	8	8	8	43,208
Baha Butch	1	1	8	1	1	2	7,258
Bahhare	1	1	9	1	3	2	264,158
Bahri	23	10	123	20	17	11	412,565
Bailbucks	2	2	13	2	1	1	12,540
Baldy's Dream	1	1	11	2	1	1	13,446
Ball Park (NZ)	2	1	17	1	4	2	13,368
Ball's Bluff	8	7	84	14	14	11	373,328
Ballindaggin	3	1	13	2	2	2	4,050
Ballistic Billy	6	4	52	6	6	6	108,161
Balmer Joe	1	1	9	1	2	1	11,265
Band Practice	5	2	30	2	4	2	21,443
Banjo	6	4	33	6	7	1	73,087
Bankbook	25	9	156	15	15	20	205,432
Banker's Gold	86	46	636	81	85	90	1,490,215
Banks Well	3	3	33	4	4	5	31,942
Banmyrh	5	1	22	1	0	1	11,609
Baquero	48	25	317	31	43	40	245,326
Barathea (IRE)	10	5	34	5	8	4	165,514
Barb's Relic	2	2	15	2	0	2	10,476
Barbaric Commander	1	1	8	1	1	1	2,875
Barbeau	29	17	237	36	38	30	639,510
Barberstown	17	8	147	13	14	21	214,847
Barcelona	9	4	84	8	8	9	50,527
Barkerville	47	23	368	40	39	42	927,977
Baron de Vaux	26	8	155	11	11	17	120,771
Baron O'Dublin	4	1	22	1	3	6	7,248
Barrera	11	3	67	7	9	10	41,643

Sire	Perf	Wnrs	Sts	1st	2d	3d	Purses
Barricade	30	17	187	37	29	16	292,650
Bartok (IRE)	38	15	149	24	21	15	637,730
Basic	4	3	35	3	4	4	18,924
Basic Rate	16	10	74	13	6	9	78,468
Basket Weave	87	52	568	85	72	75	713,258
Bastogne	6	4	67	8	11	8	71,986
Bates Motel	60	30	445	52	51	60	610,164
Batonnier	21	9	137	14	14	10	177,269
Batshoof (IRE)	2	1	13	2	2	1	20,087
Battle Creek	17	12	102	19	11	15	151,976
Battle Launch	13	6	67	8	8	5	121,235
Battle Wise (FR)	1	1	6	1	1	0	2,175
Bay Street Star	21	11	127	20	13	21	117,041
Bayou Hebert	21	10	149	20	16	22	388,004
Be a Prospect	1	1	2	2	0	0	7,530
Be Scenic	2	1	16	1	1	3	15,660
Beat Inflation	2	1	6	1	1	0	7,580
Beat the Feet	3	2	11	3	1	1	9,695
Beau Genius	106	57	874	114	105	103	1,645,410
Beau Monde (IRE)	5	2	32	4	0	3	26,894
Beau's Leader	1	1	11	1	3	2	17,285
Beautiful Crown	6	5	40	12	4	4	132,543
Becker	2	1	18	1	3	3	33,703
Bedivere	1	1	12	1	1	3	13,291
Beefchopper	19	10	133	15	16	17	115,292
Behrens	6	3	23	3	4	1	70,045
Belek	42	21	303	38	35	33	691,588
Believe It	44	22	332	43	26	37	586,646
Believe the Queen	2	2	7	2	0	0	13,185
Belong to Me	135	76	895	136	130	110	4,003,212
Benchmark	77	39	465	64	73	70	1,745,504
Bengal Bay	23	9	160	19	13	22	128,225
Benny the Dip	34	16	196	22	23	26	520,044
Benton Creek	66	36	441	71	65	70	712,266
Beowulf	8	1	32	1	0	0	8,193
Bermuda Cedar	6	2	13	2	1	1	24,920
Bernstein	18	11	60	17	18	6	525,467
Bert's Bubbleator	5	2	28	4	4	1	42,925
Bertrando	136	74	672	123	95	84	2,566,291
Best Jest	6	1	36	5	1	4	35,427
Best Man Out	3	1	17	1	2	1	31,798
Best of Luck	27	2	86	2	4	5	67,958
Bet the Omen	2	1	4	1	1	0	1,960
Bet Twice	2	1	16	1	2	2	3,982
Beveled	1	1	5	2	0	0	31,453
Beyond the Mint	11	8	89	11	15	12	148,722
Beyton	1	1	12	3	3	3	63,940
Bianconi	54	29	310	50	36	38	1,060,632
Bien Bien	12	5	89	5	9	9	218,951
Big Bad Jack	2	1	18	1	6	1	8,564
Big Jewel	16	7	104	19	7	9	181,093
Big Mukora	14	6	130	11	13	21	168,183
Big Pistol	30	14	225	24	26	25	290,039
Big Play	1	1	13	1	1	2	12,312
Big Sal	7	5	99	8	6	17	65,006
Big Sky Chester	5	5	27	9	4	3	95,707
Big Splash	24	10	167	13	18	15	223,677
Big Spruce	1	1	3	1	0	1	3,182
Big Sturgeon	3	1	26	1	3	3	12,580
Big Woods	7	3	33	3	3	4	24,037
Bigstone (IRE)	4	2	17	4	0	3	564,873
Billy Birden	2	1	8	1	1	0	4,061
Binalong	39	20	288	30	34	26	296,283
Bionic Light	6	1	36	1	1	7	17,185
Bionic Prospect	8	3	63	5	5	3	46,565
Bird Brown (BRZ)	2	1	8	1	0	0	3,062
Birdonthewire	64	29	392	49	56	59	1,244,302
Bishop's Choice	1	1	5	1	0	1	24,312
Black Mackee	31	16	192	31	24	32	216,844
Black Moonshine	21	14	189	22	24	31	265,243
Black Pretender	1	1	12	3	1	1	5,432
Black Tie Affair (IRE)	33	18	323	32	40	40	817,089
Blair's Cove	5	1	39	1	4	6	19,645
Blare of Trumpets	13	9	93	15	15	10	241,114
Blase	1	1	10	1	0	0	8,934
Blazing Bart	9	4	40	4	6	4	15,767
Blazing Fire	18	5	109	5	14	17	72,526

Sire	Perf	Wnrs	Sts	1st	2d	3d	Purses
Blind Man's Bluff	14	7	62	7	6	9	130,190
Blind Spot	1	1	11	2	0	2	6,104
Blotch	2	1	23	1	0	2	8,055
Blowin de Turn	5	2	21	2	3	3	27,329
Blue Buckaroo	6	3	52	5	3	4	41,244
Blue Ensign	31	7	220	9	22	25	162,857
Blue Grass Magic	7	2	47	2	6	5	37,583
Blue Jester	2	1	15	1	0	1	2,295
Blue Orca (IRE)	5	1	38	2	5	2	28,957
Bluebird	5	2	42	2	5	10	126,825
Bluffy	2	1	17	2	6	1	16,770
Blumin Affair	70	36	439	61	44	59	892,211
Blush Rambler	16	5	101	8	9	12	273,035
Blushing John	10	3	54	3	6	2	65,704
Blushing Song	6	2	42	2	5	4	12,044
Blushing Stage	4	3	48	6	3	5	46,450
Blushing Star	5	2	25	3	3	5	47,755
Boanerges	12	3	65	3	2	7	37,322
Board Member	9	5	61	7	8	5	62,154
Bob Back	1	1	7	2	1	3	218,669
Bob's Dusty	2	1	19	1	2	1	7,474
Bobby B Free	1	1	7	1	2	0	7,513
Bobby Ben	4	1	12	1	0	1	6,817
Bobrobbery	2	1	9	1	0	0	15,738
Boca Rio	6	4	40	6	11	4	28,082
Bojima	2	1	10	1	2	0	2,085
Bold and Greene	1	1	6	1	1	0	9,720
Bold Anthony	45	21	282	39	37	41	556,730
Bold Badgett	72	30	460	48	49	90	1,698,327
Bold David	3	1	44	1	2	8	15,108
Bold Ego	4	2	25	2	5	3	12,577
Bold Executive	88	45	612	82	69	74	2,800,055
Bold Jag	3	1	18	3	1	2	17,414
Bold James	2	2	20	2	2	2	9,739
Bold Lachee	6	1	44	2	2	3	37,420
Bold Laddie	11	6	70	10	12	7	154,150
Bold Merc	1	1	17	1	0	2	7,223
Bold n' Flashy	57	16	347	26	45	46	1,190,760
Bold Nix	2	1	14	2	1	0	7,042
Bold Pac Man	18	7	93	10	6	9	138,305
Bold Revenue	3	2	19	3	1	4	42,790
Bold Roberto	6	3	67	6	12	13	53,956
Bold Ruckus	12	7	95	13	9	9	384,930
Bold Run (FR)	4	2	22	4	4	4	101,071
Bold Target	1	1	4	1	0	0	2,987
Bold Testimony	4	2	15	3	0	2	4,260
Bolger	1	1	3	2	0	1	9,640
Bombardier	16	8	143	18	20	13	271,790
Bon Point (GB)	30	9	219	20	31	18	385,995
Bon Sang	1	1	6	1	3	0	56,480
Bonus Money (GB)	45	23	318	43	54	30	616,540
Bonus Time Cat	18	4	70	7	5	2	52,965
Book the Band	1	1	11	3	0	2	13,500
Boomerang	10	5	75	9	7	8	174,794
Boone's Mill	81	38	651	68	81	77	834,510
Bordagaray	2	1	25	2	0	3	12,472
Border Guard	3	2	37	5	8	4	68,267
Border Patrol	9	5	53	6	3	10	86,511
Born Wild	22	7	143	12	14	11	154,641
Borzoi	2	1	9	1	2	1	4,585
Boston Harbor	129	77	755	127	97	90	3,139,694
Botanic	8	3	45	4	5	7	51,605
Both Guns Blazing	2	1	7	1	1	1	4,824
Bound by Honor	20	8	163	19	14	22	172,945
Boundary	98	50	537	89	83	63	2,510,713
Boundary Ridge	4	2	30	3	10	5	18,826
Bounding Basque	18	9	141	13	19	17	240,538
Boundlessly	2	1	14	1	3	2	10,238
Boutinierre	12	9	128	11	21	20	49,868
Bowler's Wharf	6	2	16	2	3	1	31,710
Bowmans Express	3	2	22	2	3	1	12,237
Boyish Charm	8	3	47	3	5	10	57,653
Bramante (ARG)	1	1	5	1	0	1	2,310
Brass Minister	41	15	278	31	34	27	507,656
Bratcher's Choice	2	1	19	3	2	2	34,396
Brave Act (GB)	1	1	2	1	0	0	106,380
Brave Romane	7	1	27	3	1	2	30,944
Brave Warrior	1	1	7	1	1	0	16,530
Bravoure	5	1	22	1	0	1	4,171
Brenda's Ziggy	2	1	24	3	3	2	18,960
Brent's Danzig	6	3	58	10	9	7	96,270
Brents Colony	5	4	45	7	6	9	98,009
Brian's Time	2	2	12	3	4	0	135,440
Briartic Command	1	1	7	1	0	1	6,797
Bridlewood	4	1	20	1	3	0	25,821
Brief Ruckus	44	15	367	24	48	47	489,739
Brief Truce	5	2	23	3	0	3	16,858
Bright Launch	54	33	348	52	50	39	807,390
Brilliant Blue	2	2	11	4	1	1	26,899
Brilliant Protege	2	1	13	1	3	3	21,345
Brilliant Sandy	9	4	73	5	5	5	79,703
Bring To Light	2	1	12	1	0	1	13,975
Brisk Affair	7	1	38	1	4	6	5,960
Broad Brush	95	43	506	66	66	68	2,089,083
Broadway Beau	2	1	6	1	0	0	16,558
Broadway Bullet	4	4	59	9	6	9	106,470
Broadway's Top Gun	4	2	30	3	4	6	15,165
Brocco	13	6	114	13	16	14	105,018
Brogan	7	3	39	4	4	5	39,306
Brooklyn Nick	3	1	15	1	3	1	51,786
Brookover	1	1	8	1	0	0	4,761
Brown Arc	4	4	33	9	5	7	108,920
Brunswick	49	23	434	47	60	48	869,544
Brushed On	7	1	29	1	3	6	68,190
Brushed Silver	2	1	15	1	2	1	13,195
Buchman	1	1	17	1	2	3	10,157
Buck Aly	4	1	9	1	0	1	7,638
Buck Strider	13	4	82	5	10	8	79,863
Buck's Last Dream	2	1	16	1	3	1	8,504
Buckaroo	5	2	48	4	6	5	52,470
Buckbean	9	4	54	11	4	4	286,948
Buckfinder	6	3	68	6	4	8	31,677
Buckhar	39	18	281	31	42	29	427,705
Buckley Boy	6	3	68	4	3	8	49,428
Bucksplasher	27	14	193	18	29	18	292,578
Bucky Raj	13	6	84	10	10	9	88,814
Budd Believes	4	3	20	6	2	2	22,166
Buddy	12	7	111	10	13	24	150,265
Bugatti	1	1	11	1	0	2	11,644
Bugatti Reef (IRE)	18	6	99	10	9	11	314,796
Bugsy Too	1	1	6	1	0	0	10,452
Buie	15	8	89	11	14	15	147,656
Built for Pleasure	5	1	28	4	3	7	37,643
Bull Inthe Heather	28	12	178	23	29	26	175,205
Bull Marquetry	2	1	17	1	3	2	11,412
Bull Sluice	1	1	10	1	1	3	5,305
Bulldar	1	1	16	2	5	3	10,357
Burbank	5	2	20	3	0	2	40,570
Burn Annie	1	1	16	4	2	0	49,190
Burooj (GB)	3	2	17	2	2	4	75,793
Burts Star	1	1	8	1	0	1	16,553
Busterwaggley	10	2	72	2	5	7	32,528
Bustopher Jones	22	6	117	9	10	15	100,082
Buzz Saw	5	2	36	2	2	9	65,778
Buzzer	4	1	20	1	4	3	11,931
Byars	24	10	175	19	14	13	252,427
Cache In	6	2	24	2	3	3	24,877
Cachuma	12	4	68	5	12	6	93,125
Cadeaux Genereux (GB)	7	2	19	2	1	2	51,384
Cafe Creme	1	1	14	3	2	2	11,505
Cafe Mocha	5	4	54	9	2	4	79,878
Cahill Road	75	40	479	79	58	59	1,281,070
Cajun Cadet (GB)	1	1	10	2	1	0	80,795
Cajun Flagman	3	1	22	1	2	2	26,321
Caldiero	5	1	22	1	1	4	10,835
Call Me Cat	2	2	23	4	6	1	52,404
Call Me Nastie	1	1	10	1	2	4	6,205
Caller I. D.	93	45	655	81	87	72	1,199,148
Calumar	3	2	31	8	2	2	109,462
Cam a Rhett	3	1	31	2	3	5	29,112
Camisite (GB)	2	1	7	2	1	0	12,495
Camp Izard	4	2	40	3	5	3	26,009
Can't Be Slew	24	12	167	21	28	27	85,962
Canadian Factor	3	1	14	2	1	3	13,362

Sire	Perf	Wnrs	Sts	1st	2d	3d	Purses
Canaska Dancer (IRE)	5	2	31	3	6	2	11,651
Canaveral	46	23	290	38	38	28	581,908
Candi's Gold	60	34	449	65	57	63	1,021,351
Candid Cameron	28	16	204	32	28	30	315,840
Candy Stripes	69	36	477	61	58	45	1,980,865
Candyman Bee	7	3	50	3	9	5	39,390
Canny Lad (AUS)	1	1	7	3	1	0	72,740
Canvas	16	8	113	11	7	11	83,372
Canyon Creek (IRE)	59	25	410	40	42	40	796,788
Canyon Run	3	1	5	1	0	1	15,150
Cape Canaveral	30	11	106	18	25	12	864,072
Cape Cross (IRE)	4	2	19	2	1	3	822,095
Cape Storm	14	6	92	6	11	18	79,583
Cape Town	87	53	509	80	80	68	2,476,375
Capitalimprovement	8	4	56	6	4	3	81,612
Capitol South	7	2	38	2	3	4	22,458
Capo Maximo (ARG)	1	1	2	1	0	0	5,525
Capote	92	43	532	70	65	51	1,908,113
Capote's Promise	4	1	28	4	5	1	52,522
Capote's Prospect	23	11	185	29	17	23	321,465
Cappuccio	11	7	91	11	11	8	104,802
Captain Bodgit	111	49	815	78	115	135	1,472,039
Captain Codex	10	2	56	3	3	7	29,583
Captain Collins (IRE)	3	1	14	1	0	0	15,226
Captain James (IRE)	1	1	6	1	0	2	13,645
Captain Len	1	1	4	1	0	0	978
Captain Skiff	3	1	18	1	2	0	10,002
Capture the Gold	25	9	137	13	18	18	471,340
Car Dealer	8	2	27	2	2	5	23,556
Caracey	6	4	39	5	3	4	52,186
Carborundum	8	5	64	6	6	7	69,252
Career Kid	1	1	7	1	1	1	17,061
Carey's Boy	6	2	43	3	2	9	15,935
Cari Jill Hajji	9	6	84	10	12	9	169,582
Carlisle Bay	2	1	10	2	0	1	8,908
Carnivalay	78	41	577	70	70	78	1,352,146
Carolina Kid	12	5	88	10	11	9	68,881
Caros Love	7	3	54	3	4	3	25,968
Carotic	1	1	8	1	0	1	3,200
Carr de Naskra	44	27	353	45	62	57	715,225
Carson City	174	96	1089	161	160	120	5,577,819
Cartwright	94	50	656	92	81	73	1,529,175
Casa Dante	2	1	13	1	4	1	13,448
Cascadian	5	1	10	1	2	2	15,661
Case the Joint	4	3	46	6	4	7	52,068
Casey On Deck	6	2	35	2	2	2	25,277
Cash Deposit	14	6	53	6	7	3	40,270
Castle Guard	8	6	76	10	5	10	106,780
Castle Howard	7	1	23	1	3	5	11,353
Cat Creek Slew	12	6	80	11	13	16	92,316
Cat Doctor	8	4	56	9	9	8	72,825
Cat in Town	11	5	73	5	8	8	74,502
Cat Strike	5	1	17	1	1	1	9,816
Cat Thief	19	8	57	8	8	7	238,135
Cat's Career	103	54	743	108	78	91	1,456,434
Cat's Spats	5	2	29	5	7	1	31,668
Catastrophic	17	11	144	20	23	18	139,966
Category Five	30	16	177	24	27	26	314,745
Cathedral Bells	8	3	56	10	10	13	85,028
Cathy's Regal Son	8	2	43	2	6	6	30,561
Catienus	31	19	120	23	13	11	451,551
Catillac	16	4	76	7	4	7	115,851
Catonie Choke	4	3	15	3	3	2	27,999
Catrail	11	6	70	7	9	8	98,442
Cause for Pause	17	6	96	8	16	11	143,191
Cave Creek	4	2	29	2	5	5	12,726
Caveat	1	1	4	1	2	1	35,900
Cayeli	5	1	20	1	1	0	9,785
Cee's Tizzy	107	59	583	108	83	67	2,002,145
Ceejay	3	1	12	1	1	2	11,184
Cefis	7	2	31	4	1	2	54,748
Center Cut	2	1	24	3	0	3	21,992
Chad's by Geo.	6	2	46	2	3	3	29,592
Chaka	4	2	26	4	2	1	13,769
Champagne Fun	1	1	10	1	0	1	14,715
Champagneforashley	17	7	102	10	12	7	103,746
Chanate	28	9	99	15	12	15	174,778

Sire	Perf	Wnrs	Sts	1st	2d	3d	Purses
Change Takes Time	18	5	69	10	7	3	198,676
Chapel Creek	37	16	239	27	45	28	353,545
Character (GB)	4	1	40	2	5	6	29,287
Charging Through	8	1	51	2	7	8	46,244
Charismatic	88	39	464	58	50	53	1,683,095
Charlie Barley	11	4	63	6	10	6	116,742
Charlie Cielo	2	1	13	2	4	3	10,887
Charlie's Orphan	2	1	16	3	3	2	11,740
Chayim	1	1	1	1	0	0	9,920
Chelsea's Chance	1	1	6	1	2	0	8,810
Chelsey Cat	12	4	69	7	4	4	95,086
Chenin Blanc	32	12	171	19	13	14	270,185
Chequer	61	31	497	41	48	56	750,224
Cherokee Colony	20	8	135	16	11	13	270,424
Cherokee Fellow	3	1	23	1	2	5	4,262
Cherokee Run	163	95	1046	152	140	145	3,824,103
Cherokee Saga	3	1	23	1	2	2	17,505
Chester House	25	9	67	11	9	7	326,963
Chief Honcho	22	13	186	24	24	22	241,580
Chief of Dixieland	2	1	20	1	2	3	17,239
Chief Persuasion	1	1	7	1	1	0	36,853
Chief Prospect	8	4	85	7	11	14	92,176
Chief Protocol	5	4	38	6	4	5	51,519
Chief Seattle	24	9	74	10	9	12	304,361
Chief's Crown	10	5	96	15	17	8	83,760
Chief's Hope	1	1	14	1	0	1	8,193
Chief's Reward	15	6	89	10	4	18	54,773
Chilito	5	3	23	5	1	1	104,993
Chillon	1	1	3	1	0	0	2,745
Chime Time (GB)	1	1	3	1	0	0	3,675
Chimes Band	52	29	338	43	40	34	773,478
Chinati	5	1	28	1	4	4	17,766
Chisos	13	8	65	9	15	8	76,446
Chivalry	1	1	8	4	1	1	38,697
Choctaw Ridge	4	2	30	5	7	3	69,320
Chopin	18	12	126	22	19	13	198,361
Christmas Storm	3	1	7	1	0	0	7,009
Chromco	1	1	9	3	0	1	18,528
Chromite	14	8	124	14	13	12	61,377
Chullo (ARG)	2	1	5	1	0	1	12,047
Ciano Cat	28	11	161	24	19	18	341,350
Cien Fuegos	35	15	244	23	29	27	318,314
Cimarron Secret	24	11	154	15	16	20	182,226
Cipayo (ARG)	1	1	12	2	1	2	31,585
Circulating	24	13	134	13	17	22	126,856
Circus Surprise	11	5	69	5	10	9	107,353
Cisco Road	60	37	386	65	53	55	327,096
Citidancer	79	45	581	86	90	82	1,911,287
Citislipper	10	3	60	3	5	8	85,845
City by Night	13	4	92	4	11	7	114,949
City Nights (IRE)	8	2	40	2	8	3	39,607
Clackson (BRZ)	3	2	17	3	3	2	138,390
Claim	9	5	66	10	11	9	35,857
Claramount	41	24	330	43	42	42	557,529
Clash of Steel	9	7	71	16	7	11	51,135
Class Hero	4	1	29	2	1	0	9,193
Class Secret	3	1	17	2	0	4	46,989
Classi Envoy	5	3	38	5	1	5	26,715
Classic Account	23	11	175	23	25	16	359,569
Classic Cat	3	2	14	2	1	1	17,795
Classic Cliche (IRE)	1	1	4	1	1	2	22,400
Classified Facts	17	12	135	19	21	23	441,685
Classy Prospector	9	6	72	9	6	2	97,639
Claudius	5	1	17	2	2	1	302,692
Cleante (ARG)	1	1	9	2	1	1	10,449
Clear Course	9	5	69	8	6	10	128,062
Clever Champ	8	4	60	11	8	7	173,317
Clever Gold	4	1	21	1	0	1	6,789
Clever Leader	2	1	11	1	2	0	6,094
Clever Return	5	1	27	1	0	3	5,122
Clever Trick	99	54	726	96	90	85	1,488,281
Cliffs Place	1	1	17	1	0	1	4,330
Close Up	5	2	14	3	0	0	69,500
Cloud Cover	14	4	72	13	6	4	179,793
Coach George	1	1	13	1	3	2	30,103
Coastal Voyage	7	2	36	7	6	3	128,220
Coax Me Chad	25	10	158	12	11	12	101,579

Sire	Perf	Wnrs	Sts	1st	2d	3d	Purses
Coaxing Matt	5	1	30	2	2	2	15,406
Cobra King	77	45	546	82	67	79	1,567,522
Cock O'Hoop	1	1	3	1	0	0	3,076
Cocobuddy	1	1	6	3	1	0	6,478
Code Word R.	3	1	24	2	1	2	19,276
Codex's Reflection	4	1	34	1	1	0	6,464
Codified	5	2	50	2	7	10	38,218
Codys Key	9	2	27	4	5	0	39,308
Coeur de Lion (FR)	1	1	10	2	1	2	20,013
Cognizant	8	5	50	6	9	6	44,684
Cohiba	14	4	83	4	6	13	65,680
Cojak	1	1	10	3	0	1	16,447
Cold and Cloudy	3	1	6	1	0	0	9,793
Cold Bid	15	5	104	9	10	16	175,635
Cold Digger	4	1	18	1	0	2	16,268
Cold Hearted Man	14	6	96	11	14	13	108,874
Collateral	4	1	21	1	0	2	3,543
Collateral Attack	5	2	28	2	3	2	27,847
Collegian	5	4	40	8	7	2	73,500
Collier	3	1	15	1	0	0	4,605
Colonel Stevens	3	2	21	3	4	1	35,873
Colonial Affair	46	25	370	48	49	48	924,434
Colony Light	72	36	527	62	76	65	1,276,748
Color Bearer	3	2	10	3	3	0	18,519
Color Me Bold	1	1	6	1	1	1	1,940
Colorful Crew	4	1	20	1	6	4	17,386
Columbus Day	4	3	34	7	5	7	163,797
Colway Rally (GB)	2	2	10	3	1	0	18,002
Comanche Slew	2	1	31	1	2	4	8,765
Combat Ready	15	10	119	21	16	6	524,460
Come Bet	6	2	27	2	4	6	17,984
Come On Holme	1	1	14	2	3	1	21,527
Comeonmom	2	1	6	1	0	1	21,080
Comet Kat	4	2	39	3	3	3	22,292
Comet Shine	55	25	447	33	37	54	431,146
Comic Strip	43	17	207	26	22	30	517,807
Commanchero	18	7	72	9	7	13	118,416
Commemorate	36	11	202	20	19	20	207,816
Commendable	14	6	45	7	3	7	113,743
Commitisize	7	2	29	3	1	6	57,066
Commitment	6	2	27	3	2	5	17,780
Commodore Spurwink	2	1	14	1	2	2	6,635
Compadre	51	17	314	22	25	30	914,840
Compelling Sound	32	9	195	15	14	21	179,742
Compliance	23	12	204	17	14	19	277,621
Composer	15	9	127	17	15	12	195,187
Compton Place (GB)	2	1	10	1	2	1	49,780
Comstock Lode	51	22	371	35	46	35	356,545
Con Artist	7	4	41	5	7	8	93,042
Concern	69	38	491	60	68	52	1,015,257
Concerto	59	37	480	69	76	64	1,454,515
Concorde's Tune	73	43	525	74	68	75	1,565,361
Confederate Hero	3	1	14	1	3	3	18,730
Confide	72	29	404	48	49	49	914,879
Connecticut	17	6	81	8	6	6	89,462
Conquer	10	2	59	2	7	7	39,697
Conquista Fager	4	1	25	1	0	2	4,155
Conquistador Cielo	111	67	800	102	104	103	2,013,900
Consigliere (GB)	25	15	133	25	15	13	192,646
Constant Demand	6	4	30	5	2	2	72,903
Conte Di Savoya	32	15	264	24	32	35	347,773
Contempt	2	1	10	1	2	1	8,745
Contested Bid	5	1	20	1	3	5	42,748
Contested Colors	21	8	169	13	15	23	227,481
Continental Morn	2	1	6	1	0	1	2,352
Conveyor	42	21	316	41	34	33	552,138
Cool Groom	11	8	81	12	6	11	140,362
Cool Halo	8	3	61	6	3	6	47,945
Cool Joe	1	1	4	1	0	0	136,250
Cool Quaker	6	2	33	2	0	6	15,181
Cool Victor	8	5	57	6	7	7	111,527
Cooleen Jack (IRE)	2	2	15	2	1	2	41,244
Coordinator	55	13	280	19	31	34	201,899
Copelan	1	1	18	2	5	3	18,486
Copper Man	5	4	39	7	4	4	71,661
Cork (FR)	4	1	20	2	2	1	94,305
Cormorant	4	3	33	3	4	5	97,113
Cornish Hill	2	1	33	1	6	5	30,455
Coronado's Quest	82	38	404	59	47	57	2,700,964
Corporate Report	57	22	416	37	37	62	552,802
Corridor Key	26	9	137	11	9	12	155,310
Corslew	43	29	340	55	44	50	709,707
Corwyn	17	3	95	5	7	11	74,159
Corwyn Bay (IRE)	21	12	155	24	12	13	274,892
Cost Conscious	6	4	67	6	6	5	57,906
Count Eric	1	1	15	1	1	0	7,450
Count On Steve	2	1	10	1	0	1	10,570
Count the Time	83	49	575	90	82	80	1,313,333
Count von Count	4	1	28	1	1	1	8,269
Country Light	9	4	50	5	10	12	31,021
Country Manor	1	1	8	2	3	0	12,743
Country Pine	9	4	61	9	4	6	128,225
Country Side	4	1	13	1	0	1	6,425
Country Store	8	2	34	4	1	2	17,073
Courageous Leader	1	1	2	1	0	0	1,140
Court Procedure	2	1	11	1	1	3	6,257
Court Trial	4	1	18	2	2	1	5,391
Coverallbases	12	5	80	9	14	11	105,943
Covered Wagon	8	3	39	5	6	5	41,815
Cox's Ridge	14	8	100	13	16	9	121,667
Coz	3	2	26	6	1	1	24,910
Cozy Drive	21	6	120	7	8	11	158,819
Cozzene	88	48	517	76	60	60	2,507,742
Crafty	33	6	154	10	13	15	84,234
Crafty Dude	28	17	195	29	29	20	266,617
Crafty Friend	83	41	478	60	55	61	1,507,561
Crafty Harold	9	4	48	6	9	7	35,048
Crafty Prospector	132	81	1050	146	134	143	3,410,437
Crafty Ridan	21	13	193	17	20	26	92,076
Crater (ARG)	1	1	11	2	1	2	9,597
Crawford Special	1	1	12	5	1	1	14,751
Creamette City	3	1	21	1	1	1	6,217
Creative	2	1	5	1	0	2	12,460
Creative Act	12	3	58	3	2	4	53,660
Cresta Powered	3	2	22	2	3	4	4,477
Cresting Water	5	3	43	5	9	7	63,247
Crimcino	8	3	55	4	12	7	80,972
Crimson Guard	18	8	125	11	10	15	311,302
Crimson Slew	6	4	51	6	6	7	29,670
Critical Mass	1	1	9	1	0	3	4,498
Cromwell	6	2	31	4	3	5	98,750
Cross Canal	1	1	20	3	1	1	7,391
Crowd Pleaser	19	3	54	3	4	8	68,567
Crown Ambassador	33	19	249	32	22	28	404,159
Crown Attorney	28	8	138	13	9	19	340,274
Crowned Jewel	2	1	12	2	2	0	17,108
Crowning Decision	23	5	74	7	5	3	107,881
Crowning Season (GB)	31	14	222	16	27	38	96,662
Crowning Storm	13	2	36	2	8	3	97,897
Croydon	3	2	27	6	2	7	48,154
Cruisin' Prince	1	1	6	3	1	1	31,364
Crusader Sword	62	25	448	36	57	56	543,548
Crush	3	1	29	1	1	1	11,481
Crypto Star	33	18	220	33	15	36	502,015
Cryptoclearance	214	107	1596	161	189	210	3,107,485
Cryptoleen	7	5	53	5	5	6	66,505
Crystal Gazer	8	1	18	1	1	3	5,726
Crystal Run	3	1	18	2	2	4	9,549
Crystal Tas	2	2	22	8	4	0	43,464
Cure the Blues	38	18	271	27	30	29	523,414
Current Classic	1	1	6	1	2	2	1,506
Custom Body	3	1	20	1	3	2	26,427
Cute n Common	2	1	14	1	2	3	11,958
Cutlass Fax	10	4	67	8	9	9	102,423
Cutlass Reality	30	15	169	31	25	17	406,663
Cuzzin Jeb	7	1	30	1	0	2	8,087
Cyberspace	23	10	171	13	19	10	187,254
Cyrano de Bergerac	2	1	9	1	2	2	125,400
D'Accord	6	3	74	8	6	10	72,957
D'Hallevant	10	6	92	10	10	11	164,956
D. C. Tenacious	12	3	68	3	5	2	45,953
D. J. Cat	33	17	263	24	28	28	353,132
Da Nunz	1	1	13	1	1	3	16,935
Daddy Bish	2	1	8	1	0	0	2,133

Sire	Perf	Wnrs	Sts	1st	2d	3d	Purses
Daddy Watch	7	4	66	9	4	7	59,069
Daggers Drawn	4	2	18	3	1	2	124,530
Daily Ballot	3	2	19	3	3	3	12,262
Dakota Pride	3	1	21	1	4	2	25,730
Damone	2	1	25	1	2	6	5,987
Danasinga (AUS)	2	1	8	2	1	0	70,163
Dance At Dinner	2	1	11	1	0	2	4,447
Dance Brightly	115	70	799	118	96	108	2,364,046
Dance Centre	18	6	97	7	17	16	48,461
Dance Floor	49	23	275	42	27	27	387,673
Dance Master	7	4	25	7	5	7	383,496
Dance With Dan	3	1	16	2	1	2	7,701
Dancebel (GB)	6	2	61	2	5	5	20,624
Dancing Crown	9	5	84	8	16	9	117,169
Dancing Native	2	1	17	2	7	2	7,348
Dancing Pirate	6	3	43	6	7	1	30,416
Dancinwiththedevil	12	6	69	7	9	12	142,109
Dandy's Secret	3	2	18	5	3	2	73,712
Danehill	27	9	95	17	11	6	1,770,378
Danehill Dancer (IRE)	2	1	10	1	3	0	49,907
Danjur	34	20	164	29	30	25	322,033
Danotable	8	2	34	2	1	3	12,312
Dansil	4	1	22	1	4	4	9,700
Danski	5	1	24	1	0	2	8,483
Danton	1	1	5	1	1	0	6,568
Danzatame	24	11	197	14	19	23	395,160
Danzatore	46	15	271	17	26	29	217,384
Danzig	38	18	126	29	22	12	1,627,345
Danzig Connection	7	4	42	7	4	2	49,126
Dapper's Attache	2	1	20	1	1	1	9,923
Darby Creek Lance	11	6	97	8	6	10	102,556
Dare and Go	56	28	401	45	38	46	587,434
Dariyoun	5	2	30	4	3	4	51,435
Dark Hyacinth	2	2	17	2	7	1	47,305
Dark Mystery	5	2	26	3	1	1	7,183
Darn That Alarm	46	26	359	46	40	34	650,560
Darshaan (GB)	7	3	21	4	1	2	172,134
Dashing Lad	4	2	14	2	1	1	24,654
Dashing Writer	3	2	15	4	1	1	24,828
Daufuskie Pirate	6	1	25	2	1	1	15,269
Dave's Reality	7	3	46	4	5	8	21,689
David's Wolf	2	1	13	1	0	1	2,993
Dawn of Creation	2	1	17	3	0	1	16,631
Dawn Quixote	26	12	193	20	21	14	234,771
Daygata	10	4	77	8	9	6	140,155
Dayjur	55	31	343	51	43	35	938,184
Daylami (IRE)	3	1	8	2	0	0	50,000
Dazzling Falls	24	14	176	28	41	22	266,153
De Braak	12	1	67	2	4	7	19,369
De Guerin	15	4	77	5	10	12	90,244
De Jeau	2	2	18	3	1	3	19,406
De March	4	1	10	1	2	0	1,779
De Niro	35	18	259	36	26	35	395,053
De Sarmiento	6	2	29	2	0	4	20,733
Deadman's Curve	2	1	13	1	2	2	6,468
Deamon's Pouch	5	4	41	4	2	7	37,935
Dean Dill	3	2	15	2	1	0	8,683
Dearborn	1	1	7	1	1	3	15,266
Dee Lance	14	2	77	3	4	8	32,807
Deerhound	69	30	523	49	69	55	978,279
Defense Witness	16	5	105	7	13	6	74,880
Defensive Play	30	13	200	22	16	18	219,349
Definitive	1	1	6	1	0	0	3,285
Defrere	119	70	845	140	90	119	2,525,480
Dehere	70	37	461	63	57	79	1,393,746
Delineator	64	39	398	60	52	53	565,427
Delta Demon	2	1	15	1	1	2	5,260
Delta Wolf	4	1	11	1	1	2	3,257
Demaloot Demashoot	82	51	719	107	109	87	1,395,026
Demidoff	81	55	716	110	103	79	1,673,839
Demons Begone	72	38	476	69	62	67	814,873
Denouncer	10	5	59	10	5	6	150,204
Deodar	12	3	60	3	3	0	21,396
Departing Prints	1	1	8	2	2	0	31,733
Deploy (GB)	1	1	6	1	0	1	7,364
Deposit Ticket	78	34	526	55	67	61	827,783
Deputed Testamony	31	11	216	26	25	18	394,513
Deputy Bodman	22	11	158	21	13	21	200,732
Deputy Commander	132	63	832	101	118	111	2,674,917
Deputy Diamond	25	7	94	7	6	8	127,081
Deputy Minister	124	58	594	81	81	78	2,779,601
Deputy Regent	4	1	28	3	1	3	19,185
Derby Wish	20	7	104	10	8	10	167,357
Desert Classic	28	9	175	15	25	20	211,191
Desert Glow	1	1	10	2	2	0	10,529
Desert God	16	8	95	14	13	12	105,648
Desert King (IRE)	8	1	36	2	6	4	97,656
Desert Rival	5	2	17	3	0	4	32,368
Desert Royalty	13	7	98	11	7	13	160,078
Desert Secret (IRE)	36	14	252	25	21	28	293,207
Desert Sun (GB)	3	1	19	2	3	5	81,922
Desert Wine	24	13	189	25	32	31	217,097
Detox	16	5	58	6	6	3	30,344
Devil Begone	35	12	179	16	17	21	311,941
Devil Diamond	12	5	77	8	15	10	104,851
Devil His Due	190	100	1325	183	171	173	5,243,659
Devil On Ice	36	20	198	36	25	21	402,939
Devil Power	1	1	14	1	2	0	36,479
Devil's Bag	75	35	399	63	40	50	1,208,492
Devil's Cry	17	2	91	3	4	1	58,013
Devil's Delight	9	1	49	1	2	7	18,562
Devil's Joy	6	3	50	4	1	5	27,713
Devil's Luck	3	2	23	4	4	5	22,982
Devil's Rock	9	4	74	8	4	6	73,626
Devil's Share	9	3	47	4	3	3	26,022
Devious Course	47	29	414	50	43	46	530,354
Devon Lane	57	27	307	40	45	32	858,777
Devongate	25	13	169	17	17	16	233,186
Devonwood	15	5	46	8	8	9	153,358
Diablo	25	8	150	14	19	11	233,969
Diamond	55	32	368	62	47	48	1,166,495
Diamond for King (FR)	1	1	10	2	1	2	6,287
Diamond Sword	11	7	67	13	7	8	150,754
Diazo	21	10	132	18	19	16	248,173
Diesis (GB)	29	13	153	19	26	14	1,696,790
Diffie	1	1	8	1	1	1	11,087
Digamist	23	10	143	14	18	16	261,291
Digging In	10	3	54	5	3	11	46,029
Dignitas	29	12	191	18	24	27	207,935
Digression	6	4	52	9	10	5	124,903
Diligence	54	31	403	70	48	50	1,529,029
Din's Dancer	31	13	215	16	20	22	213,300
Diogenes	3	1	14	1	0	2	9,502
Diplomatic Jet	17	4	130	5	13	19	101,305
Direct Hit	17	7	73	11	12	4	219,481
Directed Energy	5	2	40	2	4	1	25,125
Disciple	3	1	21	2	3	2	25,662
Discover	18	7	124	13	14	17	178,298
Dispersal	9	2	50	4	3	3	39,721
Distant Relative (IRE)	1	1	10	3	0	0	65,975
Distant View	58	32	395	65	49	59	2,230,256
Distinct Reality	3	2	27	5	5	2	57,632
Distinctive Cat	86	33	509	60	80	80	961,564
Distinctive Pro	95	42	673	74	89	90	1,603,868
Distorted Humor	120	71	738	131	106	93	4,947,035
Dixi Man	2	1	10	1	3	3	10,799
Dixie Brass	113	67	844	120	121	124	2,958,921
Dixie Jazz Band	2	1	15	2	3	2	13,629
Dixie Power	17	10	123	17	18	15	220,157
Dixie Union	21	11	93	15	21	12	695,666
Dixieland Band	137	51	766	76	92	116	2,782,135
Dixieland Brass	48	24	297	36	37	55	476,244
Dixieland Heat	44	19	272	30	41	30	405,235
Dmitri	7	3	53	8	5	7	134,497
Do It Again Dan	16	4	117	11	11	12	96,132
Doc Davis	1	1	15	1	4	3	13,474
Doc Van	2	1	23	2	4	7	37,014
Doc's Leader	46	18	276	29	29	33	709,134
Doctor's Orders	2	1	16	2	5	3	22,579
Dodge	2	1	18	1	1	2	9,313
Doggedly	6	2	50	2	5	3	36,713
Doinitthehardway	1	1	10	2	4	1	13,735
Domasca Dan	14	5	94	9	12	11	722,958
Dome Mountain	5	2	22	3	2	1	23,083

Sire	Perf	Wnrs	Sts	1st	2d	3d	Purses
Dominated Debut	9	4	57	10	9	8	89,419
Don Gabriel (MEX)	1	1	9	1	0	1	5,667
Don's Choice	7	3	50	3	4	8	25,603
Don't Fool With Me	4	2	26	5	4	2	20,988
Don't Hesitate	6	1	30	1	1	0	5,836
Don't Say Halo	1	1	10	2	2	2	11,460
Doneraile Court	73	46	533	71	71	78	1,630,449
Doo You	1	1	14	1	2	1	7,985
Doppler	5	2	42	4	2	6	39,685
Dot's Silver B.	3	1	20	1	1	1	3,510
Double Cash	1	1	9	1	1	2	19,734
Double D. Slew	5	2	27	2	8	2	35,567
Double Honor	114	66	817	126	90	106	2,135,142
Double Negative	13	5	102	11	5	12	121,609
Double Niner	18	11	128	16	14	19	254,642
Double Quick	2	1	8	1	0	0	9,558
Double Reach	1	1	10	2	0	2	11,047
Double Ready	7	2	52	6	8	5	42,480
Double Sonic	5	3	50	3	5	7	41,360
Double Spark	2	1	12	1	0	0	4,869
Doug's My Doc	8	4	52	7	8	3	103,658
Dove Hunt	99	57	741	110	83	103	1,884,365
Dover Ridge	14	7	102	11	8	16	121,411
Down the Aisle	11	2	37	2	1	6	39,220
Downing	3	2	18	4	3	5	18,122
Downtown Seattle	3	1	15	2	1	4	51,743
Dr Devious (IRE)	4	1	15	4	5	2	247,248
Dr Fong	2	1	5	2	1	0	170,800
Dr. Adagio	48	25	389	47	53	39	845,652
Dr. Blum	3	1	23	1	3	1	48,340
Dr. Caton	64	28	449	52	42	41	830,467
Dr. Dalton	4	2	19	2	2	0	16,142
Dr. Danzig	6	2	33	3	4	0	34,778
Dr. Dave	3	2	31	4	8	4	20,649
Dr. Greenberg	3	2	22	4	2	4	17,064
Dr. Koch	4	2	23	2	3	5	21,930
Dr. Messina	7	2	39	2	5	8	19,696
Dr. Nureyev	5	3	29	5	4	4	36,851
Dr. Reality	5	4	39	6	10	6	63,662
Dr. Root	7	1	47	2	5	4	19,188
Dr. Secreto	1	1	5	1	0	1	1,564
Dream Trapp	2	1	12	2	1	3	4,479
Dream Valley	3	1	22	3	3	5	24,166
Dreamfield	6	5	38	6	6	3	39,637
Drouilly's Boy	1	1	12	2	0	1	13,556
Drumalis (IRE)	6	2	31	4	5	2	56,359
Dry Gulch	4	2	28	8	1	2	419,009
Dubious Connection	2	2	16	5	2	1	43,945
Duke of Paducah	1	1	12	1	6	2	30,044
Duke's Cup	6	1	35	1	4	2	15,798
Dumaani	44	21	266	34	40	21	667,018
Dunant (IRE)	4	4	28	8	7	4	31,358
Dunham's Gift	1	1	8	1	0	0	4,628
Dunsmuir	4	2	30	2	2	3	13,563
Duplicity (IRE)	3	1	24	1	5	4	10,143
Dusty Screen	40	24	327	36	28	50	579,288
Duxster	2	1	6	1	0	0	5,594
Dynaformer	141	60	785	91	87	104	5,380,967
Eagle Eyed	12	7	102	17	11	17	555,197
Early Gray (CHI)	1	1	6	1	1	2	24,000
Earth Star	6	3	41	5	2	6	47,508
Earthmover	5	2	54	2	7	7	32,288
Eastern Echo	78	43	585	77	57	59	1,039,669
Eastern Lord	2	1	5	1	0	0	4,000
Eastern Memories (IRE)	3	1	14	1	1	0	8,133
Eastern Money	2	1	10	3	0	0	11,416
Eastover Court	29	11	181	19	27	16	388,284
Easy Miner	6	3	41	6	4	4	87,190
Easy N Dirty	5	4	32	4	3	4	11,616
Easy Squeezy	5	1	22	1	0	1	10,717
Eclipso	1	1	11	3	1	0	61,735
Ecliptical	6	3	36	3	7	5	39,295
Ecstatic Ride	6	1	27	1	7	4	19,002
Edgy Diplomat	1	1	5	4	1	0	521,780
Editor's Note	106	50	791	80	109	87	1,645,305
Efisio	6	3	29	5	4	3	198,795
Egocentric	1	1	2	2	0	0	27,360
Eighty Below Zero	4	2	20	4	1	1	23,872
Eishin Storm	5	2	27	3	2	3	50,517
El Amante	24	12	134	21	14	9	332,499
El Gran Senor	8	6	61	9	8	3	253,404
El Jefe	4	1	17	1	0	2	5,750
El Mandingo	7	3	43	5	3	2	59,207
El Mayaguezano	17	5	114	8	7	5	90,938
El Meteoro (ARG)	1	1	3	1	0	0	3,344
El Prado (IRE)	173	94	1222	169	155	163	7,987,415
El Raggaas	1	1	7	1	0	1	5,770
El Sancho	4	1	27	1	5	4	41,115
El Set	1	1	9	3	2	1	13,252
El Torre	4	1	20	1	3	3	15,385
Elajjud	13	6	63	8	9	2	130,634
Electric Blue	10	3	64	3	4	9	39,869
Elegant Ease	4	1	30	2	1	0	16,713
Elegant Gold	4	1	19	1	1	0	4,287
Elegant Life	2	2	30	6	6	7	38,442
Elliodor (FR)	1	1	1	1	0	0	450,000
Elmaamul	2	2	11	3	3	2	495,360
Elnadim	3	3	10	4	1	0	117,110
Eltish	51	30	312	53	41	41	979,123
Elusive Quality	131	77	751	119	111	92	10,700,039
Emancipator	18	7	105	13	15	12	234,108
Embrace the Wind	1	1	16	1	0	3	8,451
Emerald Creme	11	9	86	15	15	11	159,032
Emerald Jig	26	13	196	23	14	28	228,983
Emigrant Peak	10	7	88	23	15	12	155,548
Eminency	4	1	19	5	2	3	27,905
Emphatic One	7	2	40	2	3	4	41,183
Empire Glory	3	1	21	2	4	1	17,161
En Tete	17	5	73	6	5	6	64,560
Encino	7	1	30	1	2	3	16,260
End Sweep	139	72	1101	134	162	154	2,516,558
Endow	3	1	17	1	5	3	18,115
Ends Well	19	8	145	12	25	18	337,556
Endured	1	1	18	2	1	1	11,397
Enemy Number One	3	1	12	1	4	0	16,137
Enough Reality	11	1	37	1	2	2	20,464
Ensign Bering	5	2	20	2	0	0	11,708
Epic Honor	23	13	194	26	28	31	335,426
Equalize	8	5	57	11	6	3	140,069
Eradicate (GB)	1	1	14	3	0	4	9,704
Erins Isle (IRE)	1	1	3	1	0	0	15,000
Eshu Be Elegua	1	1	3	1	0	0	3,786
Eskimo	34	20	259	29	27	31	483,853
Esplanade Ridge	7	2	21	3	1	2	43,406
Esteem	11	6	52	8	6	4	201,106
Estes	1	1	16	1	2	2	10,595
Etbauer	12	10	95	19	15	10	231,955
Eternal Orage	9	3	77	8	5	7	74,336
Evansville Slew	71	37	413	62	58	53	1,329,124
Even Faster	4	2	29	3	1	3	18,489
Evening Kris	28	13	168	21	17	17	630,392
Event of the Year	60	28	289	42	40	39	998,792
Evzone	1	1	15	3	3	2	27,436
Exbourne	4	2	18	2	0	0	32,813
Excavate	96	48	662	68	58	76	1,212,311
Excellent Secret	14	4	75	8	8	13	88,365
Exceller Vice	18	3	101	4	14	14	111,307
Excess Is Good	2	1	5	1	0	0	9,101
Exclusive Encore	7	3	42	4	4	4	25,644
Exclusive Energy	1	1	14	4	3	3	16,706
Exclusive Era	35	19	223	26	21	34	211,173
Exclusive Partner	2	2	16	5	5	0	35,700
Exclusive Praline	6	3	27	4	7	4	51,702
Exclusive Ribot	5	2	27	4	1	2	16,172
Exclusive Zone	5	2	34	3	1	3	25,555
Exclusivengagement	11	5	49	5	0	4	61,126
Executive Order	11	3	66	4	6	8	109,287
Exemplary Leader	15	6	97	11	11	10	132,736
Exetera	16	4	123	6	10	11	93,190
Exile King	3	2	17	8	0	3	114,294
Exit Poll	2	1	13	2	4	1	6,294
Exit to Nowhere	7	4	41	4	5	2	64,172
Exotic Eagle	10	8	62	15	10	3	108,720
Expedition Moon	4	1	14	2	2	3	7,192

Sire	Perf	Wnrs	Sts	1st	2d	3d	Purses
Expelled	39	17	222	29	16	13	510,704
Expense Account	22	8	144	14	19	20	175,010
Expensive Decision	13	8	115	16	17	18	390,053
Explodent	2	2	26	3	2	3	19,978
Exploding Prospect	2	1	15	1	2	1	52,847
Exploding Rainbow	10	4	41	4	5	3	23,567
Exploit	85	45	494	75	64	55	1,833,610
Explosive Red	90	49	730	88	73	91	1,413,113
Expressman	6	2	33	3	1	4	16,976
Exuberant	6	4	56	9	6	6	96,040
Fabulous Champ	64	31	399	50	58	59	614,299
Fabulous Dancer	1	1	5	1	0	0	1,846
Fabulous Frolic	54	19	369	23	27	49	328,501
Fact Book	3	3	25	6	2	1	79,342
Fadeyev	2	1	17	1	1	0	14,480
Fair American	28	11	181	18	28	24	197,960
Fair Decor	8	4	54	4	5	3	48,023
Fair Skies	9	5	68	8	7	8	59,502
Fairly Affirmed	4	3	31	5	2	4	29,755
Fairway Topper	3	3	28	7	4	2	25,746
Fairy King	2	1	10	1	2	0	39,745
Falkenham (GB)	4	2	31	3	4	3	21,299
Falstaff	49	18	324	35	37	32	588,279
Faltaat	12	7	87	11	10	6	265,447
Family Calling	77	40	570	69	74	79	1,117,930
Fanatic Boy (ARG)	7	5	57	11	6	4	112,155
Fancy Hoofer	1	1	12	3	3	1	61,335
Fantastic Fellow	27	15	178	22	16	15	233,076
Fantastic Robber	2	1	16	2	5	1	24,281
Fappiano Road	5	1	15	1	3	1	20,195
Far Out East	12	4	95	6	12	11	65,628
Far Out Wadleigh	6	2	43	3	5	9	127,883
Fargo	9	5	42	10	6	5	125,522
Farma Way	24	9	143	17	9	22	218,868
Fashion Find	10	3	56	5	7	10	91,750
Fashionable Enough	1	1	12	1	4	3	9,810
Fashioned Gold	3	1	20	2	4	5	17,404
Fasliyev	6	2	22	3	5	0	176,191
Fast 'n' Gold	6	3	46	6	6	9	87,922
Fast Account	14	7	114	11	19	12	120,002
Fast Ferdie	6	4	35	5	9	5	109,407
Fast Forward	6	1	31	2	3	0	22,210
Fast Gold	5	2	24	4	4	2	68,453
Fast Play	58	30	394	55	44	53	878,054
Faster Than Quick	4	1	28	1	0	5	23,487
Fastness (IRE)	40	16	243	27	35	24	578,643
Favorite Danzig	3	1	21	2	3	3	17,625
Favorite Trick	89	49	586	85	84	70	1,562,394
Faygo	19	11	154	21	22	18	342,811
Feather Ridge	2	1	18	2	0	1	6,200
Feel the Power	28	11	166	18	18	20	487,975
Feeling Gallant	7	2	34	4	1	2	25,888
Fenter	16	5	105	8	10	11	111,837
Ferdinand	3	2	32	2	8	4	22,047
Ferdinandthegreat	1	1	6	1	1	2	5,200
Ferrara	16	11	138	18	17	19	154,507
Festin (ARG)	4	1	24	1	1	1	24,502
Festive	8	5	66	10	7	10	89,448
Festive Lad	5	3	27	5	1	0	14,578
Feu d'Enfer	32	15	234	28	30	34	294,555
Fiend	2	1	11	2	1	2	85,305
Fiery Best	4	3	25	6	5	2	69,094
Fiftysevenvette	7	3	43	5	3	1	39,202
Fight Over	15	5	107	7	6	7	45,962
Fighting Affair	7	3	41	4	11	5	26,694
Fighting Fantasy	15	8	109	18	11	12	124,824
Fighting Fit	11	6	77	8	2	8	53,557
Final Act	3	3	34	3	5	8	45,821
Finally Class	4	2	12	2	0	1	13,704
Financial Matter	10	2	60	3	0	4	24,309
Fincher Branch	2	1	18	1	3	1	13,960
Finding Truth	1	1	5	1	1	0	4,060
Fine n' Majestic	8	3	79	3	7	7	57,180
Finest Hour	47	20	289	38	32	40	706,761
Fini Cassette	3	2	16	2	3	2	18,825
Finocchio	1	1	12	1	2	3	15,100
Fire Dancer	10	4	73	9	7	5	105,742

Sire	Perf	Wnrs	Sts	1st	2d	3d	Purses
Fire Maker	21	9	174	15	25	18	181,013
First Albert	2	1	5	1	0	1	3,007
First and Only	26	15	216	34	25	22	450,503
First Beginning	2	1	10	3	1	2	19,020
First One Up	1	1	14	1	3	1	18,395
First Patriot	8	3	58	7	5	6	100,787
First Trump (GB)	1	1	4	1	1	0	4,050
Fit to Fight	112	66	862	121	127	120	1,886,785
Fitzcarraldo (ARG)	3	1	10	3	1	0	405,390
Flag Down	21	9	158	13	11	20	203,457
Flagman Ahead	6	2	40	3	5	6	39,074
Flame	4	2	26	3	4	5	8,886
Flare Dancer	24	7	153	12	11	18	115,200
Fleet Sudan	11	4	62	6	10	4	45,923
Flight Forty Nine	32	15	288	28	35	32	270,429
Flirteando (ARG)	1	1	7	1	1	1	29,820
Fly a Kite (IRE)	3	2	27	2	5	2	35,953
Fly Cry	5	3	46	3	3	3	54,881
Fly So Free	76	21	414	34	39	53	508,475
Fly Till Dawn	29	14	157	23	18	10	281,597
Flying Chevron	33	23	291	39	26	37	679,138
Flying Continental	115	55	904	108	109	107	1,244,806
Flying Drone	3	1	16	1	1	0	5,591
Flying Pidgeon	26	6	224	10	14	18	201,154
Flying Spur (AUS)	2	1	13	1	1	0	33,370
Flying Victor	38	20	292	32	44	39	347,657
Flying With Eagles	18	5	74	5	9	11	68,344
Foligno	20	10	129	17	14	10	222,025
Fool the Experts	10	5	62	11	7	4	80,394
Foolish Flash	4	1	22	1	3	0	12,145
Foolish Intent	1	1	10	1	2	0	17,582
Foolish MacDuff	5	2	46	2	7	7	31,468
For Really	24	12	142	27	16	15	184,419
For Sure	6	3	36	6	6	5	47,992
Forbidden Valley	2	1	8	2	0	2	11,835
Foreign Holding	13	2	55	2	1	3	25,043
Foreign Legion	2	1	12	2	0	0	9,166
Foreign Survivor	7	3	57	7	3	10	152,380
Forest Fire	2	1	3	1	0	0	3,765
Forest Gazelle	18	9	134	12	10	15	189,808
Forest Joy	3	1	8	1	0	0	6,306
Forest Wildcat	165	89	936	130	131	116	3,538,680
Forestry	65	33	315	57	53	36	2,445,702
Forever Dancer	15	7	125	20	15	17	242,304
Forever Silver	15	9	134	17	12	14	231,592
Forever Whirl	11	6	52	10	5	6	168,015
Forli Winds	4	3	32	5	4	7	31,640
Forlitano (ARG)	1	1	1	1	0	0	6,000
Formal Dinner	137	83	1192	156	158	125	2,490,309
Formal Gold	107	69	699	125	95	90	2,707,994
Former	5	2	17	2	0	0	5,852
Fornell	1	1	9	1	1	0	3,510
Fort Chaffee	44	21	317	36	46	48	459,772
Fort Wayne	13	5	119	8	9	16	127,166
Fortunate Joe	2	1	13	1	1	3	18,105
Fortunate Move	3	1	16	3	1	0	12,693
Fortunate Prospect	102	63	909	134	126	125	2,132,040
Forty Niner	11	6	68	10	6	12	202,200
Forty Won	57	30	428	48	54	48	891,096
Forzando (GB)	5	1	18	2	1	5	62,530
Fountain of Gold	3	3	46	3	8	6	53,024
Fountain of Speed	2	1	18	2	3	1	28,305
Four Seasons (GB)	24	9	164	17	27	17	172,370
Fourstars Allstar	2	1	15	2	4	4	82,089
Foxhound	66	35	538	63	51	73	837,041
Foxtrail	41	17	219	27	30	22	1,233,873
Fraser River	29	15	225	31	28	28	479,906
Fred Astaire	26	7	141	12	13	15	195,100
Free and Equal	2	1	10	5	0	2	76,549
Free At Last	106	55	668	89	97	81	847,768
Free Colony	1	1	12	1	3	1	17,090
Free House	47	22	275	33	46	37	1,005,675
Freezing Rain	2	1	21	1	3	0	8,966
French Deputy	90	56	602	93	83	92	2,744,403
French Glory (IRE)	1	1	3	1	0	0	22,560
French Legionaire	36	14	268	20	19	30	166,388
French Magistrate	3	1	14	1	1	0	8,721

RECORDS OF SIRES

Sire	Perf	Wnrs	Sts	1st	2d	3d	Purses
French Parliament	12	6	75	10	11	10	144,933
French Seventyfive	6	1	23	1	3	3	31,219
Friendly Lover	122	56	934	98	118	118	1,788,419
Frio River	4	3	37	5	3	7	37,002
Frisco View	2	2	28	5	3	12	44,214
Friscosilverdollar	3	1	17	2	0	1	5,664
Frisk Me Now	23	10	154	18	13	21	406,892
Frosty the Snowman	18	12	146	23	16	14	450,937
Fruition	31	15	193	27	31	32	533,629
Fruitzig	4	1	14	1	1	0	6,111
Fugitive	3	1	16	2	0	1	11,271
Full Choke	12	3	57	4	10	4	80,322
Full Count	2	2	24	5	3	4	63,060
Full of Fight	2	1	13	2	1	2	12,550
Full of Tricks	11	5	94	8	8	15	76,791
Fulmar	1	1	13	1	1	0	5,873
Fumbo Jumbo	1	1	5	2	1	0	16,660
Funboy	2	1	12	1	0	2	3,667
Funontherun	7	4	51	6	8	9	73,208
Furiously	19	12	123	18	17	15	551,782
Fusaichi Accele	7	3	32	3	6	3	59,760
Fusaichi Pegasus	22	7	54	14	8	9	923,385
Future Storm	59	24	443	43	51	58	717,066
Fuzziano	14	1	105	1	6	15	44,396
Fuzzy	14	5	75	6	14	10	96,323
Gadzook	1	1	3	1	0	0	7,358
Gaelic Garden	1	1	7	3	1	2	2,740
Gala Array	1	1	6	1	0	2	4,320
Galaxy Road	2	2	19	4	0	2	38,096
Galileo (ARG)	1	1	14	3	3	3	34,510
Gallant Mel	4	3	26	5	1	1	52,125
Gallant Prospector	4	2	34	7	1	4	143,957
Gallant Rake	1	1	14	3	1	5	13,340
Gallant Step	7	2	43	2	4	6	35,405
Gallant Will	3	1	12	1	0	0	3,132
Gallantsky	1	1	14	2	3	2	20,258
Game Coin	5	2	21	3	2	2	18,723
Game Plan	88	54	544	91	101	86	1,107,468
Ganday	1	1	10	1	2	1	13,331
Garibi	2	1	8	1	2	0	4,321
Garthorn	6	2	22	2	1	1	10,287
Gate Dancer	17	7	139	11	14	18	133,350
Gato Del Sur	2	2	30	2	5	3	32,090
Gebbia	8	1	27	1	4	1	32,275
Gee Ryder	9	5	60	7	7	7	90,580
Geiger Counter	20	9	120	15	13	12	173,768
Gem Master	2	1	26	2	3	4	51,367
Gemini Dreamer	14	7	89	9	10	9	45,600
Gen Stormin'norman	4	3	14	3	4	0	48,960
General Gem	5	2	11	2	2	1	18,239
General Meeting	92	51	540	80	84	61	3,061,344
General Monash	1	1	10	2	0	0	21,174
General Royal	44	16	274	25	37	36	600,984
General Silver	5	2	35	3	6	2	49,850
Generous (IRE)	1	1	11	2	0	1	36,363
Gentle Shepherd	1	1	6	1	0	0	3,000
Gentleman Gene	3	1	18	1	2	0	19,090
Gentlemen (ARG)	70	22	336	29	38	38	651,924
Genuine Reward	12	2	70	6	8	8	84,824
Genuine Silver	2	2	27	6	2	3	56,830
George Augustus	1	1	4	1	0	0	8,620
George Green	4	3	38	4	3	1	27,027
Georgeff	5	1	25	2	0	1	6,947
Georgia Two	5	1	31	1	3	2	20,652
Geri	51	28	380	48	50	44	972,991
Get Me Out	10	3	49	3	3	6	40,866
Gettin Over	3	1	11	4	1	3	14,115
Gettysburg Address	2	1	7	1	0	0	7,584
Ghadeer (FR)	2	1	8	1	1	1	26,550
Ghazi	84	48	582	85	77	79	1,402,041
Ghost Power	23	7	159	9	15	14	87,185
Ghost Ranch	14	6	104	8	16	13	187,304
Ghostly Moves	29	8	133	18	20	29	638,023
Giant Asset	3	2	19	2	4	3	19,134
Giant's Causeway	17	2	29	2	5	1	113,805
Gift of Gib	12	7	55	12	16	3	201,231
Gilded Crusader	2	1	9	1	1	1	10,963
Gilded Time	145	77	939	134	113	142	3,070,001
Giuseppe	20	7	131	13	7	12	176,091
Give Me Your Ear	6	1	37	1	3	7	30,320
Glaring	25	7	140	10	15	18	191,267
Glazed	6	1	33	1	4	0	13,917
Glenview	10	6	71	11	6	8	68,780
Glib	1	1	8	1	0	0	3,136
Glide	9	1	67	4	10	9	133,490
Glitterman	142	78	994	146	138	123	3,329,448
Global View	1	1	15	1	1	0	3,899
Globel Sports	3	3	49	4	4	7	46,875
Glomar	9	3	44	3	7	5	69,185
Glorious Flag	3	1	27	2	1	1	12,107
Glyer	1	1	6	1	1	1	27,216
Gneiss	9	3	63	5	7	3	173,655
Go and Go (IRE)	8	1	48	2	4	7	52,268
Go for Class	1	1	3	1	0	0	1,483
Go for Gin	74	32	519	67	62	67	1,479,828
Go Gary Go	5	1	13	2	1	1	20,504
Go Step	1	1	7	2	0	0	7,378
Go West	2	1	8	1	1	0	39,400
Gogarty (IRE)	3	1	16	1	5	1	26,217
Gold Ace	1	1	5	1	0	0	7,090
Gold Alert	56	29	497	56	75	45	1,192,780
Gold Case	127	76	812	129	113	98	2,641,759
Gold Crest	2	1	10	1	2	0	6,897
Gold Decorum	2	1	12	3	1	2	24,946
Gold Fever	132	79	971	137	135	150	3,936,290
Gold Groovy	3	1	13	1	2	3	15,155
Gold Legend	78	43	558	83	85	66	1,384,923
Gold Market	12	8	74	11	9	12	141,614
Gold Meridian	55	21	323	43	36	35	276,726
Gold Pack	6	3	50	6	7	10	68,322
Gold Regent	38	24	262	39	33	36	545,439
Gold Ruler	40	17	243	33	35	32	231,763
Gold Saga	17	7	79	11	12	7	110,722
Gold Spring (ARG)	26	12	194	22	21	29	248,821
Gold Token	52	25	375	48	41	41	1,244,135
Gold Tribute	40	19	299	35	49	38	895,588
Golden Act	11	6	86	9	4	16	91,060
Golden Dodger	13	5	95	6	13	11	47,104
Golden Explosive	1	1	11	1	0	0	6,061
Golden Gear	69	33	443	51	63	49	979,767
Golden Legend	10	4	73	8	9	8	83,279
Golden Missile	24	6	66	7	7	5	332,496
Golden Soldier	3	1	8	1	0	1	3,150
Golden Voyager	9	3	39	5	1	2	174,004
Golden Whirl	2	1	29	3	1	5	9,108
Goldlust	20	5	97	6	12	12	149,174
Goldmine (FR)	3	1	12	1	2	0	5,627
Goldminers Gold	23	11	151	21	18	14	687,319
Goldwater	3	1	33	3	4	2	28,147
Goliard	30	13	203	20	21	22	203,035
Gone East	4	1	7	1	0	1	5,425
Gone for Real	13	10	111	19	11	15	395,457
Gone Hollywood	2	2	9	3	3	1	53,206
Gone West	86	45	473	80	58	55	3,179,564
Good and Tough	45	31	304	55	49	42	1,091,717
Goodbye Doeny	71	30	464	49	63	48	806,946
Goofalik	1	1	7	1	0	1	45,800
Gorky Park (FR)	5	3	41	5	5	5	66,841
Goshen Store	1	1	9	1	0	2	5,954
Gothic Revival	13	5	111	9	10	9	122,342
Gotzum	1	1	8	1	1	1	6,078
Gourami	12	3	60	4	3	5	25,679
Grace of Darby	5	3	46	8	5	9	127,753
Gracious Ghost	3	1	23	1	2	2	13,391
Gran's Halo	2	1	12	1	1	0	8,671
Grand Allegiance	1	1	5	2	0	2	11,040
Grand Circus Park	15	5	73	7	12	10	194,927
Grand Flotilla	8	3	66	5	9	10	90,294
Grand Jewel	13	8	110	20	14	7	187,813
Grand Lodge	8	2	35	4	5	5	248,510
Grand Slam	152	84	859	138	128	93	4,970,163
Grande Jette	3	3	21	4	8	1	42,779

Sire	Perf	Wnrs	Sts	1st	2d	3d	Purses
Grant Approval	1	1	15	2	2	2	24,670
Gray Slewpy	7	3	27	3	2	2	16,537
Graydon Pool	20	2	110	2	1	11	61,738
Great Above	6	2	45	3	5	4	106,849
Great Allegiance	6	6	60	7	7	5	42,008
Great Commotion	2	1	7	1	1	1	46,892
Great Gladiator	34	12	230	17	30	27	541,632
Great Ovation (IRE)	5	2	28	3	1	1	16,418
Great Prospector	4	4	24	5	4	5	21,653
Great Regent	4	2	19	2	2	2	54,850
Great View	2	2	20	3	2	1	21,446
Greek Costume	7	3	35	8	2	5	81,608
Greek God	1	1	11	1	1	3	7,818
Green Alligator	12	5	87	10	11	13	292,423
Green Dancer	55	19	329	26	35	44	771,711
Greenwood Lake	14	7	68	8	8	8	175,395
Greggie's Wheel	4	1	29	1	6	1	15,158
Gremlin Grey	6	2	47	7	8	1	49,664
Grey West	8	3	47	7	5	4	22,140
Grindstone	96	48	563	87	81	86	3,518,346
Gringo Pilot	7	3	29	5	2	1	26,955
Groom Dancer	3	1	12	1	1	1	53,335
Groom's Image	5	2	32	2	8	4	26,272
Groomstick	46	20	409	31	28	55	609,647
Groovin' Time	1	1	3	1	0	0	8,970
Groovy	25	14	189	23	22	21	281,071
Groovy Jett	7	3	45	6	6	6	48,368
Groshawk	2	2	13	4	4	3	19,950
Ground Stroke	4	1	11	1	1	1	14,898
Grub	7	3	49	5	6	7	83,974
Guadalupe Peak	4	1	32	1	4	3	16,382
Guarani	8	6	50	7	8	3	76,938
Gulch	102	61	667	95	104	107	3,949,278
Gulch It	7	2	41	3	5	2	47,712
Gulpha Gorge	1	1	11	1	0	1	8,785
Gumboy	12	4	67	5	4	10	39,239
Gunston Road	1	1	6	1	1	0	4,360
Guys From Space	2	1	6	1	1	1	17,020
H E R E S Tommy	1	1	1	1	0	0	5,160
H. E. Miller	4	1	13	4	3	3	80,034
H. J. Baker	12	5	63	7	7	4	102,118
Habitonia	3	3	32	6	5	7	39,766
Habitony	7	1	43	4	2	6	38,482
Hadif	93	60	752	102	102	106	1,127,112
Hagley's Reward	1	1	15	1	3	2	28,153
Hail Hailey	1	1	13	3	0	1	9,700
Hail the Ruckus	19	10	108	13	17	11	190,366
Hail Victorious	4	3	32	5	4	4	27,967
Haint	23	13	175	21	17	23	358,645
Half a Year	36	14	230	22	28	34	274,041
Half Term	62	28	409	39	56	58	584,449
Halissee	12	7	94	12	7	11	155,761
Halo Sunshine	5	3	33	9	4	4	218,588
Halo's Dream	6	1	43	1	5	4	21,695
Halo's Image	110	60	767	113	103	96	3,484,769
Halory Hunter	67	43	654	78	99	93	1,482,621
Halos and Horns	14	6	85	11	14	14	236,778
Hamas (IRE)	1	1	5	3	0	0	52,767
Handsome Halo (ARG)	1	1	7	2	1	1	58,380
Handy Pete	1	1	11	3	0	1	3,577
Hanging Road	4	2	38	5	5	5	45,165
Hannibal Cat	12	7	111	12	11	14	108,209
Hansel	18	7	117	13	11	16	541,230
Hapes Mill	3	1	21	1	3	2	7,425
Happy Bid	4	2	40	2	3	7	18,038
Happy Trap	21	11	110	19	12	9	130,670
Happyasalark Tomas	6	3	46	4	0	2	23,950
Harbor Man	4	4	26	5	3	4	80,610
Hard Circle	9	2	73	2	5	7	31,890
Harlan	19	10	188	21	24	23	262,349
Harmony Creek	1	1	2	1	1	0	3,760
Harperstown	12	10	101	16	10	13	137,234
Harriman	27	10	147	16	17	13	206,034
Harry	6	1	34	1	1	1	8,912
Harry the Hat	14	4	84	8	10	9	255,247
Hasten To Add	13	5	91	9	10	9	101,346

Sire	Perf	Wnrs	Sts	1st	2d	3d	Purses
Hasty Spirit	2	1	14	2	3	4	27,095
Hatchet Man	3	2	23	3	2	4	47,753
Havanace	1	1	5	1	0	1	9,210
Have Fun	13	2	52	3	6	1	86,994
Hawk Attack	9	2	41	2	5	3	58,125
Hay Halo	36	17	211	30	27	32	450,593
Haymaker	27	13	196	21	18	22	271,409
Haymarket (GB)	19	6	110	10	12	14	98,588
Hazaam	56	29	469	65	63	50	804,079
He's a Looker	20	4	96	5	6	5	66,241
He's Tops	54	33	334	50	47	42	474,062
Heather's Prospect	21	7	130	9	15	12	100,995
Heaven's Wish	11	7	92	14	12	11	119,421
Heavenly Legacy	4	3	42	5	3	9	41,025
Hector Protector	2	2	9	2	0	3	84,640
Heff	20	9	142	18	11	19	231,579
Heir to Nijinsky	2	2	14	4	1	2	28,957
Helmsman	81	47	628	94	94	83	1,947,037
Hemi Head	1	1	12	2	2	4	64,865
Henbane	11	6	104	15	13	11	116,426
Heniu	9	4	60	6	8	9	45,373
Hennessy	141	75	803	127	92	95	3,758,224
Here We Come	70	33	433	63	57	56	750,023
Hermes	8	3	34	5	4	3	33,577
Hermitage	11	5	78	7	7	10	74,861
Hernando (FR)	4	2	13	4	3	2	1,255,518
Heroicity (AUS)	3	2	15	2	1	3	39,225
Hesabull	31	15	193	26	25	25	517,052
Hestheman	6	4	43	9	6	4	58,646
Hey Rob	19	11	73	13	11	2	67,831
Heza Lawman	1	1	4	1	1	0	3,480
Hezafastgold	6	1	25	1	1	1	13,770
Hi Plains Drifter	7	2	35	3	2	10	54,870
Hickman Creek	11	3	77	5	7	6	46,860
Hickory Ridge	13	7	95	9	10	9	73,308
Hidden Prize	4	1	17	3	6	0	99,817
Hidden Tomahawk	1	1	8	2	1	2	2,705
Hidden Vice	2	1	23	1	0	2	8,846
Hierarch	2	1	13	1	0	0	13,205
High Brite	128	80	986	158	147	134	2,484,565
High Comedy	7	2	38	2	7	4	23,460
High Energy	8	2	48	4	4	1	43,893
High Occupancy	1	1	6	2	0	0	42,240
High Yield	27	8	74	11	4	13	299,331
Highest Honor (FR)	7	2	27	3	2	3	291,342
Highest Ody (FR)	2	2	21	4	2	2	61,487
Highland Blade	1	1	3	1	0	1	8,852
Highland Park	12	3	62	3	3	12	43,636
Highland Ruckus	58	27	348	43	44	47	760,435
Highly Praised	2	2	22	4	2	3	17,445
Hill Pass	3	1	28	1	0	1	7,702
Hill Street Jove	8	2	51	3	8	10	28,808
His Excellence	22	12	165	20	25	19	183,754
His Majesty	5	1	24	4	1	1	26,249
Historic	20	8	103	12	9	9	187,493
Hoedown's Day	9	1	36	1	2	3	9,349
Hold for Gold	32	22	263	38	31	38	715,355
Hold On Chris	7	3	49	5	5	7	57,135
Hollywood Knight	2	2	18	2	3	5	7,455
Hollywood Reporter	23	11	176	17	16	23	112,799
Holme On Top	3	2	28	2	4	5	27,110
Holy Bull	136	71	849	110	82	113	2,912,741
Holy Mountain	37	17	235	29	32	34	398,919
Holzmeister	30	17	178	30	24	22	438,793
Home At Last	28	21	243	33	34	28	524,373
Home Run Trot	7	6	48	8	5	9	47,751
Homebuilder	22	11	165	22	18	13	575,723
Homo Sapiens	2	1	8	2	0	1	24,530
Honest Ensign	10	4	72	7	3	2	50,172
Honeyland	13	6	111	9	13	11	81,590
Honkytonk Blaze	2	1	15	2	1	6	19,953
Honor Grades	136	63	834	115	109	100	3,018,364
Honour and Glory	167	87	916	141	120	116	3,041,134
Hooched	3	1	21	1	3	1	23,389
Hoolie	12	5	75	6	2	5	72,090
Hopeful Word	1	1	9	1	1	1	8,045

RECORDS OF SIRES

Sire	Perf	Wnrs	Sts	1st	2d	3d	Purses
Hopeville	1	1	16	2	2	4	14,871
Horatius	32	14	240	28	25	36	442,034
Horse Chestnut (SAF)	29	14	139	22	10	15	857,185
Hotoffthepress	2	1	16	1	0	4	10,488
Housebuster	36	20	294	39	39	28	591,156
Houston	41	20	309	33	37	36	441,644
Houston Sunrise	4	4	37	8	3	8	69,466
Hubble	9	5	88	8	7	10	82,471
Huckster	11	7	122	12	23	17	114,396
Huddle Up	6	4	28	6	8	7	346,281
Huff	18	9	96	13	15	14	268,857
Hula Blaze	2	1	11	2	1	0	9,802
Humble Eleven	6	2	36	2	7	3	54,152
Humming	11	5	50	7	5	5	118,111
Humpty's Hoedown	10	6	84	12	12	4	100,561
Hunter's Glory	3	1	12	2	3	3	14,178
Hunter's Phone	2	2	21	2	3	3	40,568
Hunting Hard	45	21	345	32	36	40	626,494
Hunting Horn	6	4	57	5	3	4	34,965
Hunza Court	1	1	10	2	1	1	14,578
Hurlingham	6	2	40	2	4	2	19,851
Hurontario	3	1	23	1	0	1	4,666
Hurricane Ed	3	1	29	1	3	3	13,926
Hurricane Mars	1	1	7	1	2	1	3,926
Hurricane Sam	2	1	6	2	0	0	12,856
Hurricane State	3	2	15	2	4	2	51,168
Husband	21	6	96	9	7	8	273,639
Hussonet	14	3	68	4	12	13	522,014
I Am Not a Crook	2	2	6	2	0	1	2,319
I Am the Game	4	2	21	2	1	2	22,151
I Can't Believe	42	19	299	35	35	38	650,064
I Enclose	5	3	40	6	3	6	59,792
I'll Raise You One	8	3	60	4	8	6	47,539
I'm a Lyre	2	1	10	1	0	0	9,610
I'm Reckless	3	2	16	2	2	1	28,616
I'ma Hell Raiser	43	18	290	33	40	36	508,002
Iam the Iceman	17	8	109	11	15	23	305,081
Ian's Affair	3	2	30	2	4	5	17,663
Ibero (ARG)	4	3	28	8	5	1	189,964
Ice Age	6	3	56	6	5	10	118,206
Ice Hole	5	2	29	3	1	2	34,734
Icy Glow	2	1	25	2	1	6	25,608
Icy Kevin	3	2	28	2	4	3	16,094
Idabel	36	19	297	32	36	37	458,004
Idaho's Majesty	2	2	19	2	2	3	14,568
Ide	86	52	672	88	99	84	1,694,378
Ideologico (ARG)	1	1	3	1	0	0	30,480
Ihtimam	27	15	195	28	29	26	163,314
Ikari	11	2	67	3	4	9	50,865
Il Est Gran	1	1	16	2	3	4	30,123
Ile de Jinsky	14	6	103	7	6	16	94,290
Illinois Storm	21	8	88	11	10	9	386,910
Illuminate	3	1	20	1	4	3	9,890
Ima Good Gamble	3	1	9	1	0	1	6,465
Image of Greatness	1	1	5	1	0	0	5,371
Impeachment	6	2	17	2	2	2	37,417
Imperial Ballet (IRE)	10	4	64	4	7	7	94,493
Imperial Falcon	26	9	176	13	14	20	203,136
Imperial Seal (GB)	1	1	9	1	0	1	38,000
Important Notice	1	1	12	4	1	3	106,476
In a Walk	31	11	167	18	26	16	599,961
In Case	97	50	664	81	70	65	1,299,267
In Excess (IRE)	109	60	607	109	83	62	3,913,762
In Excessive Bull	63	34	345	47	40	40	733,332
In the Ruff	1	1	6	1	0	0	3,192
In the Slammer	6	3	48	4	4	3	63,133
In the Swing	6	4	37	5	7	2	43,377
In the Zone	13	4	72	4	6	3	35,545
Inchinor (GB)	6	2	31	3	1	5	133,346
Incinderator	18	7	113	9	7	15	102,471
Incurable Optimist	18	9	131	13	14	15	517,303
Indian Charlie	95	65	663	138	105	107	3,392,633
Indian Groom	5	1	22	1	1	4	44,790
Indian Ridge (IRE)	10	5	68	8	8	10	181,591
Indian Rocket (GB)	1	1	11	1	0	3	33,670
Individual Style	18	10	90	11	11	17	97,487

Sire	Perf	Wnrs	Sts	1st	2d	3d	Purses
Indomitable Reb	3	1	18	1	1	5	11,633
Indy Mood	37	8	233	15	21	21	151,179
Inevitable Hour	2	1	10	1	3	0	9,935
Inherent Kal	8	1	63	1	2	6	20,023
Innkeeper	2	2	14	2	0	0	15,160
Insan	1	1	3	1	0	0	8,750
Insistent Beat	10	2	44	2	1	6	6,815
Inspired Prospect	25	8	217	12	21	18	292,533
Instant Pleasure	1	1	7	1	0	2	3,840
Instrument Landing	2	1	15	1	1	0	6,972
Intensity	16	8	89	13	14	7	324,503
Interco	6	1	22	1	2	3	4,297
Interprete (ARG)	9	4	36	6	3	4	146,701
Intidab	4	1	13	3	1	4	232,834
Intimidation	2	1	10	4	0	2	7,107
Introductivo	1	1	9	1	0	0	5,180
Intrusion	2	1	20	2	2	4	18,444
Iowa Best	3	1	15	1	0	1	2,270
Irgun	39	20	219	33	22	24	428,540
Irish Bear	4	1	17	2	3	2	18,281
Irish Dreamin	12	5	56	8	4	4	63,068
Irish Open	81	35	607	60	77	80	791,985
Irish River (FR)	34	19	227	31	13	26	609,551
Irish Scoundrel	1	1	7	1	2	0	9,030
Irish Sur	4	2	21	3	2	3	49,875
Irish Tower	10	5	105	7	12	7	44,158
Iron	3	2	20	3	5	4	48,354
Iron Cat	19	15	122	31	20	7	468,735
Iroquois Park	11	6	71	12	7	5	68,396
Is It True	97	57	683	106	84	96	2,047,878
Is Sveikatas	3	1	11	1	1	1	23,367
Iskandar Elakbar	20	8	134	15	19	18	451,601
Island Born	2	1	7	1	0	0	11,330
Island Whirl	40	21	247	39	26	39	568,224
Islefaxyou	67	35	525	59	55	69	829,608
Isnad	3	2	11	4	2	2	16,115
It's Always You	10	3	58	4	2	6	38,540
It's Not My Job	2	1	9	3	0	2	35,550
It's True	1	1	16	1	0	0	14,523
Itajara	1	1	18	4	2	2	17,610
Itaka	27	9	163	14	14	15	261,663
Itron	6	3	63	3	5	8	57,928
Its Acedemic	5	1	27	1	1	2	12,086
Ivor's Desert	2	1	12	1	3	3	6,249
Iz a Saros	12	6	95	8	23	11	152,962
J P Hamer	33	14	270	27	27	35	407,588
J. Burns	2	1	17	1	3	1	5,751
J. C.'s Challenge	6	3	38	3	4	2	27,621
J. L. Sullivan	3	2	32	2	6	2	24,478
J. P. Brother	1	1	8	1	0	2	4,337
J. T. Hurst	1	1	17	1	0	2	2,892
Jack Livingston	22	7	165	13	23	18	269,037
Jack n Coke	1	1	12	4	0	0	28,590
Jack Wilson	24	13	155	21	30	16	477,974
Jackson's Gap	2	1	14	2	0	0	10,273
Jacksonport	15	6	105	13	14	8	165,819
Jacodra	25	14	215	20	23	33	191,725
Jacquelyn's Groom	29	14	202	19	29	20	256,084
Jade Hunter	108	57	760	106	65	89	2,988,455
Jaggery John	6	4	42	6	3	3	34,653
Jake Is Jake	1	1	16	2	2	2	15,995
Jaklin Klugman	2	1	4	1	0	0	3,241
Jalaajel	1	1	12	1	1	1	20,568
Jambalaya Jazz	35	17	209	26	36	32	656,336
Jamiano	9	2	79	4	9	4	51,934
Jarraar	1	1	9	1	1	3	38,594
Java Gold	6	3	34	3	3	3	40,101
Java Royal	1	1	19	3	4	2	55,880
Jay Bryan	1	1	2	1	0	0	7,620
Jay Cee Slew	1	1	8	2	0	1	3,702
Jazzing Around	54	26	297	37	53	36	363,887
Jd's Determination	3	1	30	2	6	5	39,472
Jeblar	72	41	556	68	77	55	1,430,404
Jeff's Companion	6	5	51	8	6	5	47,598
Jelly Roll Blues	3	1	27	3	2	4	25,843
Jerrio	1	1	16	3	2	3	28,685

Sire	Perf	Wnrs	Sts	1st	2d	3d	Purses
Jersey City	4	1	19	1	1	1	15,125
Jessie Jet	6	2	42	2	2	6	41,496
Jestic	14	6	79	10	6	4	66,990
Jett Sett Joe	6	1	37	3	4	3	32,360
Jiltaloom	3	1	24	1	2	7	12,826
Jimmy Barnie (GB)	7	4	56	5	2	5	50,683
Jimwaki (BRZ)	3	1	20	1	2	3	33,719
Jitterbug Chief	8	4	39	4	1	2	47,224
Jo's Eleven	2	1	11	1	0	1	5,213
Joanie's Chief	5	2	38	2	3	5	22,451
Joe D	8	4	66	4	5	8	30,898
Joe Spatts	1	1	5	3	0	1	44,403
Joe the Dancer	6	1	38	3	5	2	21,318
Joe Who (BRZ)	8	4	45	4	8	3	55,177
Joey the Student	6	2	46	4	2	6	64,966
Jog My Memory	8	3	88	5	9	20	85,833
John the Magician	14	3	53	4	9	7	119,773
John Willy	2	1	12	3	1	1	18,845
Johnny's Prospect	2	1	19	2	2	1	34,314
Joker	9	6	94	7	8	7	105,367
Jolie's Halo	8	4	61	12	8	4	257,659
Jolies Appeal	3	1	19	1	1	4	13,253
Jolly Blade	6	3	38	5	2	3	20,271
Journey's End	1	1	9	2	1	0	5,409
Jovial Turn	1	1	7	2	0	1	12,772
Joy's Report	10	7	108	17	19	10	225,870
Joyeux Danseur	75	35	463	64	61	50	1,378,647
Jr. Prospect	11	3	83	5	8	8	61,453
Judge Costa	3	1	10	1	0	0	11,430
Judge Smells	32	12	242	26	21	23	350,798
Judge T C	115	62	983	113	135	131	2,719,835
Judge Vonsteubon	2	1	14	1	1	2	17,038
Jules	109	58	658	104	77	67	3,712,521
Jumron (GB)	37	12	191	16	27	29	197,135
Junction Road	1	1	2	1	1	0	1,640
Jungle Blade	3	1	13	1	2	0	13,395
Jungle Express	5	2	26	3	5	3	40,966
Just a Cat	44	19	272	28	22	29	350,263
Just a Swangin	4	1	22	1	1	1	5,744
Just a Tab	6	1	46	3	3	6	22,313
Just a Tune	11	4	86	9	10	13	133,757
Just Like Jo	4	1	38	1	3	7	33,259
Just Like That	2	1	23	1	2	1	7,033
K One King	6	1	16	3	1	5	39,830
K. O. Punch	76	37	506	78	64	80	1,298,403
Kadial (IRE)	5	2	33	2	1	1	13,008
Kahuna Jack	4	1	15	1	1	2	12,155
Kahyasi	4	1	9	2	3	1	222,445
Kalim (IRE)	2	1	8	1	1	0	3,659
Kan d'Oro	11	6	107	11	8	12	76,708
Kandaly	13	6	103	12	13	12	106,055
Kansas City	6	1	33	1	4	7	7,999
Karate Kick	5	2	20	2	0	2	15,489
Karen's Cat	6	3	17	7	1	1	109,430
Kashgar	2	1	17	2	3	2	70,598
Katahaula County	70	34	492	55	70	78	1,035,173
Katowice	52	28	400	61	49	54	586,719
Kayrawan	28	18	211	31	28	23	547,637
Keep Dreaming	22	7	165	15	24	14	237,212
Keep It Down	9	4	65	5	7	5	72,051
Kelly Kip	11	3	38	3	11	2	118,053
Kelly's Copy	1	1	13	5	0	3	30,914
Kelly's Gold	8	3	38	4	2	1	55,182
Kennedy Factor	12	4	59	5	7	8	40,002
Kentucky Cookin	6	1	24	1	1	4	8,138
Kentucky Jazz	19	12	125	20	13	14	230,891
Keos	14	7	123	15	12	9	158,446
Kept His Cool	2	1	16	1	0	1	10,577
Kerosene	13	7	109	15	13	15	234,657
Kessem Power (NZ)	7	2	16	2	1	0	18,817
Key Contender	48	21	374	33	57	52	734,450
Key Guy	1	1	14	2	0	2	17,419
Key Image	3	1	19	1	3	2	5,739
Key of Luck	1	1	11	5	1	1	102,300
Key Recognition	5	2	45	2	4	3	28,038
Key to the Carr	13	6	68	8	10	7	60,059
Key to the Flag	3	1	29	2	3	2	22,554
Key to the Mint	1	1	9	4	1	0	54,558
Khamaseen (GB)	2	1	15	1	0	1	12,951
Kicking Boot	9	3	37	4	0	5	19,665
King Alphonse	1	1	4	1	0	0	891
King Crypto	3	1	19	1	1	6	11,901
King Heir	1	1	7	1	2	0	8,828
King Mutesa	7	2	47	4	2	9	21,093
King of Cats	3	1	13	1	4	3	25,751
King of Kings (IRE)	77	26	475	46	48	55	1,191,134
King of Scat	12	6	37	8	3	6	79,732
King of Storyland	5	2	39	3	2	4	20,658
King of the Heap	8	5	80	10	2	9	120,022
King of the Hunt	3	2	14	2	1	5	24,261
King's Arrow	3	1	17	1	0	3	12,280
King's Canyon	6	2	23	4	1	5	36,381
King's Grant	12	6	86	10	17	9	195,520
King's Nest	28	11	146	17	17	13	154,723
King's Theatre (IRE)	4	4	17	7	1	2	554,230
King's Wailea	6	4	42	7	7	4	79,773
Kingmambo	75	33	386	54	56	37	1,780,330
Kings Blood (IRE)	5	2	27	2	1	2	9,027
Kings Fiction	4	2	27	2	1	1	59,310
Kingsboro	11	2	72	2	4	7	68,248
Kipling	13	2	24	2	3	2	24,753
Kipper Kelly	86	40	663	87	76	75	1,151,073
Kiri's Clown	18	4	137	4	8	20	82,706
Kiridashi	72	35	492	59	56	73	1,906,365
Kissin Kris	140	76	1049	147	125	120	2,623,396
Kitwood	6	3	34	8	5	2	95,821
Kleven	13	7	94	15	11	14	174,575
Knick Press	1	1	12	2	1	1	12,224
Knight	3	2	20	2	1	6	10,522
Knight in Savannah	26	12	139	24	29	14	261,699
Knight Skiing	10	5	55	6	12	5	26,912
Knightly Rapport	1	1	9	3	2	2	12,398
Knockadoon	13	8	94	11	17	14	240,045
Known Fact	48	25	299	44	46	50	836,738
Knyaz	1	1	7	1	0	2	11,476
Kodiack	4	3	29	4	3	6	31,372
Kokand	66	28	422	50	58	63	791,511
Kozak	3	1	16	1	1	3	13,166
Kracotowa	1	1	14	1	1	3	9,727
Kris (GB)	6	4	37	8	3	5	162,407
Kris in Me Kris	1	1	10	1	2	2	4,954
Kris S.	84	40	458	72	66	63	4,172,340
Kriskris (IRE)	4	3	33	7	2	7	23,112
Kuetch	4	2	32	5	2	0	38,825
Kunjar	1	1	7	1	0	3	2,552
Kuwaiti Brass	2	1	12	1	1	1	5,704
Ky Alta	1	1	8	2	0	2	4,070
Kyle's Our Man	34	10	217	14	26	21	190,214
L'Enjoleur	13	7	93	9	8	12	77,961
L. B. Commander	2	1	8	1	0	0	4,722
L. B. Jaklin	11	6	80	12	13	9	108,016
L. D. Bowers	2	2	24	4	2	0	18,678
L. J. Express	3	1	23	3	5	1	45,332
La Saboteur	18	12	114	18	15	13	123,086
Laabity	52	24	333	30	30	40	397,101
Labeeb (GB)	54	27	381	39	36	67	1,245,033
Lac Ouimet	99	57	725	92	80	77	1,548,974
Lacotte (IRE)	15	5	73	9	8	5	70,615
Lahib	3	3	16	5	1	5	247,268
Lahint	5	2	26	2	1	4	23,323
Lajara	5	4	38	6	2	4	13,095
Lake George	24	17	197	31	22	28	358,778
Lake Holme	9	5	38	5	4	4	71,371
Lakeshore Road	12	1	43	1	8	2	44,024
Lanburg	1	1	10	1	0	1	4,584
Land Speed Record (AUS)	1	1	8	1	3	0	60,240
Landing Zone	5	3	17	3	1	3	57,848
Langfuhr	173	95	1236	167	173	153	5,402,570
Laramie's Deputy	1	1	5	1	0	0	2,035
Larrupin'	54	30	425	52	66	57	1,097,158
Larry the Legend	33	14	156	24	23	26	270,503
Last Lion	16	3	72	3	5	8	47,093

Sire	Perf	Wnrs	Sts	1st	2d	3d	Purses
Last Tycoon (IRE)	1	1	6	1	1	1	1,484
Lasting Approval	29	14	198	29	14	28	797,880
Lasting Value	2	2	20	4	4	1	20,517
Late Act	3	1	26	2	0	2	14,560
Late Nite Louie	4	2	15	2	1	0	4,170
Latin American	54	17	344	41	38	39	593,308
Latin Dancer	1	1	4	2	0	0	12,130
Latvia	14	4	88	6	9	8	106,370
Laubali	1	1	7	1	0	0	28,115
Launch a Leader	15	10	127	12	11	21	127,260
Launching	2	2	6	2	0	1	10,188
Laxey Bay (IRE)	1	1	7	2	0	2	16,525
Lazaz	4	1	26	1	2	3	30,633
Le Ciel	10	6	83	11	6	11	133,660
Le Gosse	2	1	32	3	1	3	18,064
Le Merle Blanc	3	1	19	1	3	0	11,236
Leading Hour	2	1	6	1	1	2	10,218
Leah n Leah's Last	1	1	13	1	2	2	14,484
Lear Fan	60	28	354	36	42	39	1,302,555
Leave Seattle	8	4	75	9	5	10	54,186
Lee n Otto	2	1	14	1	2	1	16,499
Lee's Badger	3	2	26	4	3	3	53,155
Leestown	75	29	420	45	49	40	992,629
Left Banker	10	7	80	12	17	9	161,166
Legal Prospector	5	3	42	7	5	6	63,847
Lemhi Slew	1	1	10	1	0	0	5,250
Lemon Drop Kid	16	6	46	7	11	10	342,983
Lenado Road	13	5	55	5	5	5	76,929
Lens	5	2	38	2	3	8	22,045
Leo Castelli	59	28	412	42	51	44	551,476
Leonard's Lad	3	2	20	4	4	2	21,754
Lesley's Express	1	1	5	1	0	0	6,366
Let Goodtimes Roll	3	1	11	3	1	2	234,763
Let's Go Blue	8	4	50	5	6	10	58,023
Level Sands	69	30	473	61	67	50	879,435
Lexingtonian	1	1	15	2	1	3	11,035
Lieutenant Dad	2	1	11	1	2	0	11,077
Life Interest	7	3	41	4	6	6	15,217
Ligan's Gold	4	2	27	3	5	2	50,085
Light Idea	7	2	43	2	3	2	44,880
Light of Mine	8	5	53	5	3	5	78,834
Light of Morn	25	12	223	28	32	17	426,044
Light Pleasure	1	1	7	1	1	2	5,653
Light Years	3	1	17	3	0	2	61,090
Lightning Leap	19	7	115	9	11	16	59,802
Liginsky	3	2	27	6	2	9	65,440
Like a Brother	2	1	23	1	1	3	9,241
Like a Soldier	15	9	105	14	18	13	274,523
Lil E. Tee	70	35	491	57	55	46	658,586
Lil Honcho	6	4	34	6	4	3	41,070
Lil Tyler	43	22	293	36	35	46	573,142
Lil's Lad	65	36	387	53	47	59	1,069,894
Limit Out	14	9	109	14	11	18	307,518
Lindsey's Roberto	8	3	56	3	6	3	84,896
Line Dance	2	1	14	1	4	4	3,928
Line In The Sand	154	72	1272	119	145	155	1,868,655
Lines of Power	8	1	28	1	1	3	13,545
Linkage	15	4	103	8	8	9	96,142
Lion Cavern	32	11	148	16	15	16	536,840
Lion Hearted	13	9	40	12	5	7	391,917
Lit de Justice	111	62	938	117	131	104	2,965,855
Lite the Fuse	108	61	738	111	89	91	2,234,366
Literati	4	1	12	1	0	2	10,977
Little Current	1	1	11	2	0	1	11,019
Little Missouri	29	11	218	17	26	18	250,163
Little Nureyev	5	4	28	6	7	2	51,021
Littlebitlively	21	6	93	6	14	14	216,700
Live At the Half	2	1	11	3	0	1	5,929
Lived It Up	8	6	54	12	3	6	112,755
Lively One	7	3	41	4	2	3	54,746
Llama Lover	15	2	97	2	19	13	86,774
Loach	8	5	60	6	4	5	86,722
Local Artist	9	3	49	4	5	6	32,034
Local Talent	5	2	28	6	1	1	23,229
Local Time	10	2	65	5	5	5	129,997
Locochon (MEX)	1	1	14	4	4	0	29,405

Sire	Perf	Wnrs	Sts	1st	2d	3d	Purses
Lode	12	5	70	9	11	7	222,573
Lomitas (GB)	3	1	11	3	0	2	235,216
Lone Star Bar	2	1	7	1	0	0	2,480
Look Ahead	1	1	11	3	0	2	22,411
Look See	11	4	84	5	7	8	87,716
Looks Good to Me	2	2	22	3	2	3	37,493
Lord At Law	12	7	107	10	16	19	219,395
Lord At War (ARG)	22	13	173	33	23	19	1,049,938
Lord Avie	83	41	560	77	60	69	1,594,956
Lord Ballina (AUS)	1	1	2	1	0	0	17,000
Lord Byron (URU)	1	1	9	1	0	0	4,792
Lord Carlos	8	3	69	5	9	9	55,320
Lord Carson	122	61	714	97	100	99	1,804,029
Lord Charmer	7	2	32	3	5	5	21,727
Lord John	4	3	46	6	2	9	32,544
Lord of All	5	1	29	6	2	4	22,007
Lord of Men (GB)	1	1	1	1	0	0	29,400
Lord of the Apes	7	3	49	4	9	7	17,491
Lord of the Sea	1	1	15	1	2	3	5,947
Lord Parham	13	5	70	7	7	7	132,578
Lord Pleasant	8	4	67	11	8	10	149,298
Lord Rebeau	3	1	10	1	2	1	4,652
Lordhyexecutioner	9	5	51	13	9	5	225,285
Lost Code	86	39	597	68	69	70	797,370
Lost Opportunity	14	4	62	5	4	8	34,941
Lost Soldier	129	62	879	102	106	100	1,918,241
Lot o' Gold	7	3	51	8	12	6	131,867
Lot o' Rem	10	2	71	2	5	9	32,197
Loto	1	1	10	1	1	1	17,060
Louis Quatorze	142	69	863	117	89	98	2,660,975
Louisiana Slew	21	8	123	11	11	10	62,366
Loup Sauvage	38	20	234	32	26	21	428,350
Loustrous Bid	8	5	66	7	5	9	110,196
Love That Mac	5	2	30	2	1	2	14,014
Lover's Trust	6	1	34	2	2	6	34,311
Loverue	1	1	12	2	3	1	31,744
Loyal Double	11	9	94	12	17	10	126,611
Lt. Gulch	1	1	11	1	2	2	29,115
Lucayan Prince	14	2	60	5	10	11	151,237
Lucky Lionel	88	50	632	73	91	68	1,665,073
Lucky North	41	19	306	26	54	29	503,041
Lucky Point	1	1	11	2	2	3	16,500
Lucky Roberto	16	9	127	13	16	15	455,696
Lucky Sec	2	1	22	2	6	1	6,423
Lucky So n' So	22	13	142	24	27	14	287,758
Lucky South	13	6	96	8	15	15	62,418
Luhuk	21	8	105	10	8	7	254,772
Lummox	2	1	17	2	1	2	26,826
Lure	11	3	53	4	6	8	101,657
Luthier Fever	14	5	91	10	8	10	175,840
Lycius	45	23	291	30	28	38	731,615
Lyphaness	6	4	38	9	5	6	151,838
Lyphard	1	1	3	1	0	0	9,000
Lytrump	30	14	250	26	35	28	272,727
M. Double M.	2	2	19	9	1	1	94,878
M.D.'s Relampago	1	1	11	1	0	1	6,082
Mach One	6	1	34	2	2	5	26,127
Machiavellian	11	6	55	9	10	9	249,865
Mackee the Mick	3	1	18	1	2	3	3,532
Madjaristan	1	1	12	4	1	0	55,850
Mag Power	2	2	25	2	1	3	10,507
Magabird	9	3	56	4	3	4	69,930
Magesterial	2	1	7	1	1	1	1,871
Maghnatis	4	2	20	4	2	1	42,475
Magic Banner	1	1	16	1	2	5	9,528
Magic Cat	29	11	101	13	13	11	279,934
Magic Flagship	8	3	29	3	2	4	32,692
Magic Level	8	7	70	14	9	8	62,191
Magic Prospect	44	22	253	35	29	34	409,683
Magic Rascal	3	2	35	3	3	3	24,466
Magical Mile	3	1	18	2	3	0	24,311
Magloire	21	11	183	15	32	22	263,027
Magnetism	3	2	16	2	1	0	16,980
Magnificent One	4	1	28	1	3	0	10,210
Maheras	1	1	9	2	0	1	3,698
Mahogany Hall	38	15	258	23	38	34	491,734

Sire	Perf	Wnrs	Sts	1st	2d	3d	Purses
Majesterian	36	25	271	53	49	43	514,566
Majestic Light	31	11	220	19	23	29	310,673
Majestic Style	4	1	19	2	1	1	17,797
Majestic Twoeleven	5	1	34	3	3	1	36,206
Majesty's Imp	18	10	180	25	31	31	213,397
Majesty's Prince	8	2	33	2	3	4	30,939
Major Howey	2	1	21	2	0	4	9,608
Major Impact	35	17	255	29	35	30	424,978
Major Luck	2	2	10	2	2	0	28,320
Makaleha	31	13	163	20	40	23	388,622
Makhraj	14	5	82	7	9	6	51,069
Makin	13	4	60	6	4	4	147,211
Makula King	3	3	15	5	3	1	70,330
Malagra	50	23	315	35	34	35	655,605
Malek (CHI)	12	1	36	1	8	8	81,757
Malibu Moon	70	35	365	56	51	36	1,900,933
Malibu Wesley	7	2	23	2	1	5	47,382
Malmo	22	11	164	18	22	27	152,185
Maltese Flag	3	1	18	1	0	3	7,332
Malthus	9	4	66	10	7	5	55,538
Mamaison	4	2	36	4	5	3	37,798
Mambo	11	5	76	9	5	10	66,276
Man From Eldorado	16	9	118	17	12	12	81,628
Man of Heart	4	1	44	1	2	8	20,761
Manastash Ridge	16	3	122	4	12	21	127,017
Mandamus	4	2	19	3	1	1	23,260
Mane Minister	13	6	96	9	9	18	107,010
Mangaki	2	1	6	4	1	0	6,241
Manila	8	3	44	6	2	4	102,861
Manlove	24	11	171	25	19	16	668,993
Mantles Star (GB)	5	2	10	3	1	1	29,490
Many a Wish	5	2	31	3	7	6	39,417
Manzotti	43	12	264	22	23	22	365,523
Marchand de Sable	2	1	12	2	2	1	632,190
Marcie's Ensign	4	2	25	3	3	2	6,098
Marco Bay	10	5	68	11	5	12	226,858
Marco Ricci	1	1	14	1	1	4	5,542
Marfa	17	10	147	17	24	16	319,790
Maria's Mon	163	84	1026	133	126	107	2,864,607
Marine Brass	5	2	26	3	3	2	16,770
Mariner	2	1	10	2	1	1	4,983
Marju (IRE)	7	6	45	7	7	1	168,362
Mark of Esteem (IRE)	2	2	17	4	6	1	439,960
Marked Tree	99	48	632	86	85	75	1,000,041
Marlin	62	24	384	39	34	52	930,411
Marquee Star	9	4	73	7	10	5	80,564
Marquetry	148	78	1018	127	150	143	2,689,881
Marscay (AUS)	1	1	11	2	3	1	58,420
Marshua's Dancer	1	1	11	3	2	1	10,336
Masakado	2	2	36	4	3	10	31,748
Mashaallah	1	1	14	3	1	5	11,775
Maskrullah	3	1	24	4	6	4	15,815
Master Bill	51	27	450	62	69	59	1,077,922
Master Robery	1	1	5	1	0	3	4,790
Master Slew	3	1	23	2	2	1	4,538
Masterfully	7	4	71	6	9	13	60,915
Match Trick	7	5	52	7	10	8	63,546
Matchlite	46	23	343	35	46	51	586,918
Matricule	9	4	34	4	2	5	38,479
Matter of Honor	33	20	254	35	38	22	619,768
Matty G	39	25	375	51	41	51	1,381,853
Maudlin	28	18	210	30	29	22	490,762
Maximum Wager	1	1	10	2	2	1	39,742
Mazel Trick	77	38	416	65	61	48	1,855,552
Mc Gruder	4	1	33	1	1	0	15,161
McGinty (NZ)	1	1	9	2	2	2	28,210
Meacham	5	3	32	4	1	4	73,135
Meadow Flight	37	21	330	44	35	29	553,510
Meadow Monster	57	30	379	51	52	48	803,974
Meadow Prayer	6	2	15	5	0	2	168,542
Meadowlake	102	52	645	83	90	86	1,768,052
Meadowtime	2	1	14	1	5	0	26,314
Mecke	83	38	626	67	87	69	1,808,795
Medieval	8	3	30	3	2	8	75,507
Medieval Man	2	1	16	2	0	0	5,782
Medieval Rival	1	1	10	1	3	2	21,292
Medifast	7	1	26	3	0	3	16,988
Medium Cool	7	2	47	4	7	4	51,090
Meena	3	1	23	2	2	2	44,729
Melodisk	6	2	46	2	4	5	61,095
Meloy	4	1	29	4	5	6	27,522
Memo (CHI)	86	50	452	90	70	62	1,734,700
Menewa	2	1	5	1	0	0	4,819
Menifee	59	34	284	58	33	37	1,807,034
Mercedes Won	32	16	244	22	26	33	398,889
Mercer Mill	52	26	390	34	37	39	516,072
Meritable	3	2	29	2	4	5	8,543
Merrimack T. J.	2	2	19	4	3	2	24,058
Mertzon	6	3	55	4	5	8	46,140
Mesopotamia	13	3	76	3	7	12	88,356
Metfield	45	24	328	42	42	35	580,621
Mexican Bandit	10	2	49	3	1	1	24,948
Mi Cielo	41	23	367	43	54	58	675,360
Mi Selecto	19	8	81	11	8	9	176,606
Michael's Flyer	13	5	54	10	8	6	257,251
Mickey's Road	2	2	24	3	1	3	18,473
Midnight Drama	4	1	32	1	3	4	18,614
Miesque's Son	64	32	415	55	36	56	821,187
Mighty Adversary	1	1	11	2	3	1	29,890
Mighty Duke	1	1	16	1	1	1	11,373
Mighty Magee	22	10	130	15	16	18	210,965
Migrating Moon	50	27	406	47	49	65	935,231
Military	35	20	235	32	24	31	871,963
Mill Native	6	3	55	5	6	6	57,428
Millions	5	2	17	3	1	3	63,767
Milt's Overture	1	1	6	2	0	1	44,350
Mind Games (GB)	2	1	7	1	3	1	71,540
Miner	19	12	138	21	20	18	237,938
Miner's Mark	87	41	706	82	89	82	1,105,926
Miner's Path	1	1	14	1	1	3	24,305
Mineral Ice	5	3	34	3	8	6	53,551
Mining	3	1	13	1	1	2	8,239
Mining for Money	7	3	34	5	5	2	60,095
Minister's Mark	10	7	100	12	14	8	200,227
Minneapple	3	2	28	4	5	2	23,525
Minor Saint	2	1	11	2	1	1	18,266
Minstrel Alley	12	2	49	2	1	4	27,586
Minstrel Dancer	19	9	155	16	19	14	188,170
Minstrel Glory	4	1	19	2	1	2	16,497
Miracle Heights	20	10	118	13	17	22	144,036
Misnomer	1	1	7	1	0	1	30,990
Missionary Ridge (GB)	19	10	167	19	16	13	283,164
Mister Baileys (GB)	56	24	399	48	44	46	866,495
Mister Frisky	3	1	19	1	3	0	7,551
Mister Herbert	5	1	44	1	4	6	44,415
Mister Jolie	83	54	637	107	97	83	1,523,221
Mister Modesty	1	1	10	3	5	1	20,600
Mister Slippers	9	5	68	6	2	6	68,222
Mister Wonderful (GB)	6	3	44	4	5	5	53,527
Misty Wind (IRE)	9	4	67	9	10	16	66,091
Miswaki	60	34	413	65	57	57	1,912,607
Miswaki Bandit	9	3	61	4	7	11	80,110
Miswaki Gold	15	6	113	11	13	16	123,991
Mocha Express	5	2	15	2	2	2	29,863
Mogambo	1	1	6	3	1	0	4,329
Mokhieba	5	1	14	1	2	4	21,519
Mombo Gambo	3	1	19	3	2	3	28,980
Mombo Jumbo	1	1	5	3	1	0	24,520
Moment of Crisis	7	2	40	2	2	6	17,090
Mommu	1	1	2	1	0	0	6,290
Momsfurrari	8	3	43	3	4	5	29,985
Mon Capitan	3	3	22	3	4	2	33,022
Monde Bleu (GB)	2	1	24	2	3	4	12,451
Monetary Gift	21	14	172	29	25	23	250,730
Money Run	3	1	13	1	3	2	14,509
Mongol Warrior	5	3	41	3	2	4	21,400
Montbrook	126	72	838	122	107	101	2,688,969
Montreal Red	52	19	307	27	38	28	449,306
Moon Prospector	3	1	29	1	1	5	10,941
Moon Up T. C.	7	3	41	7	8	2	75,983
Moonlight Dancer	25	10	158	15	18	17	283,279
More Pleasure	2	1	15	1	1	0	5,087

RECORDS OF SIRES

Sire	Perf	Wnrs	Sts	1st	2d	3d	Purses
More Royal	3	1	17	2	1	1	16,433
More Than Ready	34	17	134	24	23	18	837,567
More to Tell	8	2	27	4	1	0	41,389
Moro	16	1	45	1	4	2	12,424
Moro Oro	24	19	185	26	24	28	371,295
Mortlock (FR)	8	3	54	4	3	7	46,410
Moscow Ballet	61	27	366	47	53	54	1,322,892
Moses Tablet	3	1	20	1	4	3	11,974
Most Welcome (GB)	3	1	28	1	2	5	58,936
Mottly Moseley	1	1	7	1	0	0	8,004
Mountain Bike (CHI)	6	2	32	5	3	4	83,667
Mountain Cat	86	41	582	80	82	61	1,244,079
Mountain of Laws	8	3	87	6	9	10	103,922
Moving Shoulder	18	7	124	10	13	10	110,747
Mr Peter P.	1	1	2	1	0	0	14,220
Mr Purple	27	13	156	15	18	16	266,488
Mr. Atty. General	3	1	16	1	1	1	4,471
Mr. Badger	6	3	51	6	9	9	50,088
Mr. Beasley	6	4	58	4	9	9	56,466
Mr. Bolg	2	1	19	3	1	3	8,353
Mr. Brilliant	8	3	66	9	7	7	101,844
Mr. Easy Money	15	6	64	21	9	9	180,209
Mr. Executioner	8	1	27	2	4	1	33,889
Mr. Explosive	9	3	97	3	4	12	38,683
Mr. Expo	10	5	37	6	8	5	43,322
Mr. Goldust	14	2	98	5	7	9	72,311
Mr. Greeley	162	83	998	123	124	135	2,839,027
Mr. Integrity	19	7	116	9	19	17	161,557
Mr. J. C.'s Mons	1	1	17	3	3	2	31,345
Mr. Krugerand	5	2	41	4	4	2	26,288
Mr. Leader	4	2	26	5	6	3	155,429
Mr. Listo	3	1	14	1	1	1	4,205
Mr. Meadow	1	1	5	1	1	1	13,476
Mr. Nasty	3	2	24	5	4	7	56,599
Mr. O. P.	13	3	51	3	3	7	17,137
Mr. Procrastinator	23	9	109	11	18	17	145,350
Mr. Prospector	26	13	124	21	12	14	703,041
Mr. Redoy	6	4	55	9	5	5	73,188
Mr. Roberts	4	1	30	1	5	2	16,969
Mr. Shawklit	35	16	206	26	22	19	378,565
Mr. Sparkles	30	10	199	17	15	29	219,541
Mr. Sutter	13	4	79	11	8	14	132,546
Mt. Livermore	144	73	971	120	159	124	2,808,984
Mt. Magazine	20	6	133	18	9	16	164,815
Mtoto	2	2	25	4	1	4	22,913
Mud Route	31	14	152	20	30	25	578,822
Mughtanim	2	1	11	1	1	2	37,643
Muhtafal	9	6	72	17	6	10	211,719
Mukaddamah	2	1	13	3	1	2	518,300
Muldoon	35	17	214	25	22	30	224,981
Multiengine	1	1	13	1	0	0	5,532
Munch n' Nosh	11	3	96	6	3	15	71,870
Muqtarib	8	3	28	4	6	4	149,932
Murrtheblurr	7	3	58	5	6	8	78,505
Music Master	7	3	35	8	4	7	102,068
Music Prince	3	3	37	4	4	6	30,145
Music Prospector	4	2	38	4	6	6	69,573
Musical Dreamer	10	5	72	8	6	6	100,822
Musical Fappi	7	5	68	7	3	13	60,197
Musique d'Enfer	4	2	15	4	1	1	123,145
Muskoka Music	2	1	12	1	0	0	5,788
Must Be War	4	1	14	1	1	0	5,375
Mustache	1	1	5	1	1	0	6,860
Mutah	10	1	53	1	4	5	29,322
Mutakddim	98	50	667	114	95	92	2,545,324
Mute Dancer	6	1	44	1	4	3	18,426
My Boy Adam	63	22	336	31	39	45	929,104
My Favorite Grub	4	1	19	1	1	1	21,732
My Friend Max	6	1	23	1	5	1	41,744
My G. P.	4	2	20	4	0	3	18,975
My Imperial Slew	5	3	37	3	4	3	62,408
My King (GER)	7	3	45	4	4	1	26,262
My Liege	6	1	18	1	2	3	17,093
My Memoirs (GB)	6	3	30	4	3	2	33,122
My Mike	21	12	131	19	9	14	201,800
My Omen	2	1	8	2	0	3	14,801

Sire	Perf	Wnrs	Sts	1st	2d	3d	Purses
My Prince Charming	14	6	110	9	6	7	116,955
Myrmidon	8	4	66	10	12	11	112,374
Mystery Storm	42	20	263	28	40	25	443,008
Naevus	63	24	426	44	44	35	455,180
Naevus Star	10	3	29	3	1	0	34,044
Nahuel	4	2	30	2	1	4	5,313
Nalees Man	1	1	16	1	6	1	24,436
Name for Norm	2	2	29	4	8	7	21,486
Nancy's Champion	2	1	11	1	0	3	4,425
Napa Valley	4	1	29	2	2	3	10,999
Nasgame	9	5	65	8	10	8	39,332
Nashwan	5	2	19	2	4	1	57,096
Nassau Square	2	1	5	1	1	0	2,140
Nasty and Bold	18	7	143	12	12	17	170,494
Nataraja	2	1	12	2	1	1	12,936
Native Factor	24	17	192	37	31	29	447,413
Native Fir	5	3	76	9	6	4	55,463
Native of Seattle	6	2	40	3	4	3	34,488
Native Prospector	25	12	136	20	18	19	221,267
Native Regent	51	28	422	50	45	44	1,005,766
Native Slew	18	5	127	10	5	11	220,079
Native Storm	11	3	49	3	6	6	58,808
Native Tactics	5	2	16	2	1	0	10,583
Naturally Nicer	1	1	13	2	3	0	24,677
Naturals Grand	7	2	43	6	2	2	44,002
Navarone	23	5	119	9	9	13	220,173
Navegante (CHI)	3	1	18	1	4	2	8,379
Navy Admiral	7	1	63	1	6	8	17,532
Near the Limit	7	2	52	4	4	8	45,107
Negative	4	2	31	3	0	3	21,867
Nelson	59	25	406	35	43	44	602,191
Nepal	14	5	83	8	10	15	178,023
Nephrite	3	1	13	2	3	1	15,007
Neptuno (ARG)	4	4	46	4	3	2	35,683
Nerud	4	2	32	3	5	5	91,109
Net Asset	9	3	39	4	5	4	50,102
Never Wavering	16	5	117	9	12	12	149,104
New Doc	1	1	4	1	2	0	9,513
New Way	15	7	81	8	12	8	77,261
Newton's Law (IRE)	20	11	118	12	13	9	112,380
Nice Krews	4	2	21	3	4	5	11,935
Nicholas	25	11	194	17	26	27	237,501
Nickel Slot	12	6	71	13	3	13	37,960
Nicolotte (GB)	5	1	24	1	5	0	44,125
Nicou Nicou	1	1	11	3	4	1	37,050
Night Above	14	7	113	10	9	16	131,267
Night Ceremony	6	1	16	1	0	1	8,327
Night Runner	12	5	74	8	5	9	45,479
Night Shift	11	3	63	5	9	8	114,836
Night Visitor	1	1	6	1	2	0	10,314
Nightofthegaelics	5	3	44	5	6	5	101,910
Nikos	1	1	8	1	0	0	9,000
Nineeleven	12	4	66	5	2	6	62,384
Niner Bush	6	3	27	5	3	0	15,752
Nines Wild	54	19	384	39	34	29	518,488
No Bondage	5	2	28	4	2	4	32,823
No Louder	4	3	36	5	2	4	47,915
No Malice	1	1	8	1	3	3	24,899
No Upper Limit	3	1	17	1	0	0	3,241
Noactor	65	39	561	59	68	77	841,948
Noble Assembly	4	2	32	4	4	9	60,133
Noble Cat	26	5	146	17	15	15	292,462
Noble Novice	5	1	24	2	3	2	23,855
Noble Savage (IRE)	3	1	23	1	0	2	9,694
Nooo Problema	6	1	32	1	4	4	14,384
Nordic Legend	1	1	7	1	2	1	40,680
Norquestor	52	26	401	54	43	46	1,106,657
North Pole	4	1	29	1	6	4	16,973
North Prospect	30	15	192	24	16	21	285,183
North Woodsman	6	2	38	5	6	3	28,511
Northern Afleet	64	45	460	75	72	70	2,829,201
Northern Andy	3	1	15	1	0	1	2,467
Northern Baby	38	12	216	22	25	39	331,033
Northern Crook	1	1	9	2	0	2	35,485
Northern Devil	6	2	36	4	10	4	31,992
Northern Flagship	7	2	59	2	9	4	26,998

Sire	Perf	Wnrs	Sts	1st	2d	3d	Purses
Northern Horizon	3	1	20	1	2	3	6,069
Northern Idol	37	21	275	33	34	35	944,378
Northern Jay	2	2	16	2	2	4	18,642
Northern Majesty	2	2	23	3	3	1	16,086
Northern No Trump	26	9	198	18	19	20	221,599
Northern Park	11	6	93	9	11	10	126,506
Northern Prospect	15	8	119	14	13	13	163,379
Northern Score	2	1	11	1	0	1	3,628
Northern Spur (IRE)	28	13	198	26	24	24	654,671
Northern Strike	2	1	13	1	3	0	56,893
Northern Symphony	11	3	91	5	3	7	39,272
Northern Trend	18	11	159	27	19	24	384,381
Northern Wolf	7	1	36	2	0	8	56,183
Northernhemisphere	5	1	43	1	1	4	19,688
Northrop	2	1	8	1	0	2	15,549
Northstar Prospect	5	2	32	3	0	4	21,735
Norway Gray	4	2	28	3	7	4	37,735
Nostalgia's Star	2	1	6	1	1	0	15,362
Not For Love	179	102	1201	195	169	137	5,439,082
Not So Fast	1	1	6	1	1	0	8,636
Not Tricky	8	6	34	8	3	4	57,300
Notable Cat	39	18	184	26	12	18	218,769
Notation	1	1	14	1	0	0	3,508
Notebook	116	69	852	122	139	107	2,300,806
Nova Scotia	4	1	21	1	1	3	18,535
Novel Nashua	4	2	44	2	2	6	33,345
Now Listen	7	4	63	4	7	9	51,822
Nowi'veseenitall	1	1	14	1	2	3	11,572
Nowork all Play	2	1	10	1	0	1	3,700
Nucay	10	5	49	8	4	4	23,796
Nugget Point (IRE)	3	2	23	6	5	3	322,430
Nuit's Dandy	1	1	14	2	5	0	17,061
Numerous	118	50	898	94	113	117	2,852,231
Nureyev	16	5	82	7	3	9	369,540
O'Brannigan	15	7	106	13	13	15	122,482
Oakmont	4	2	19	2	3	1	36,657
Obijove	1	1	13	1	1	3	8,943
Obligato	10	7	115	14	14	16	173,762
Obstructed	8	3	55	4	1	5	51,413
Ocala Slew	34	10	214	15	25	24	188,708
Ocean Crest	19	9	112	11	11	8	164,338
Ocean Falls (IRE)	1	1	14	1	2	4	19,365
Ocean Native (MEX)	4	1	11	1	1	0	12,000
Ocean Splash	7	3	65	8	5	7	115,686
Ocean Trick	3	1	9	2	1	0	14,656
October Gold	3	2	18	2	0	5	21,994
Odyle	23	8	161	15	10	12	185,363
Ogydoug	4	1	22	1	7	2	13,501
Oh Say	29	13	174	20	26	26	508,623
Ojai	1	1	11	4	1	1	25,194
Old Stories	27	14	196	19	18	30	90,582
Old Topper	19	10	76	15	20	11	498,815
Old Trieste	64	27	296	46	33	40	1,404,244
Ole'	50	19	372	35	49	56	451,030
Oliver's Twist	31	18	280	40	29	34	562,675
Olmos	8	4	40	4	1	5	30,237
Olympio	93	40	516	62	62	65	1,095,841
Omali's Buckaroo	6	3	56	3	3	8	24,775
On Report	5	1	49	1	3	8	29,520
On Target	79	43	529	81	81	74	1,082,474
On the Sauce	21	7	135	10	17	13	213,449
Once a Sailor	18	11	128	14	15	17	144,974
Once Wild	7	3	40	4	2	5	32,235
One Golf Sierra	3	3	21	5	4	1	83,360
One in a Mil	3	2	34	6	2	2	55,862
One Little Hustler	3	2	26	2	1	0	11,651
One to Envy	1	1	13	1	1	0	2,170
Onefinesilverbuck	5	2	36	3	2	8	72,398
Ongoing Mister	3	1	10	1	0	1	9,039
Onward	4	1	18	1	3	3	36,872
Open Forum	105	47	709	80	92	87	1,644,627
Opening Verse	39	16	229	27	21	19	506,839
Ops Smile	46	27	383	44	53	54	761,886
Oraibi	7	4	47	7	8	5	61,848
Orbit Dancer	11	5	74	6	6	6	45,149
Orbit's Revenge	2	1	4	1	0	0	3,660
Orbit's Scene	4	3	16	4	2	2	39,753
Orchid's Devil	19	9	90	14	17	14	326,572
Order	7	2	39	5	7	2	38,749
Ordway	43	25	351	45	47	31	836,699
Ore Grade	11	5	42	8	6	3	42,424
Organizers Cousin	6	2	38	4	1	2	42,257
Ormonte	8	2	51	3	2	2	10,389
Ormsby	29	21	254	34	32	26	818,632
Othello	25	8	140	15	6	17	301,669
Our Emblem	82	46	552	82	58	55	1,409,837
Our Gary	7	3	66	4	11	11	49,153
Our Gatsby	7	3	42	3	5	5	39,179
Our Lewis	1	1	9	1	2	1	8,344
Ourcurtaincall	11	5	53	8	3	7	24,271
Out of Place	147	75	1062	132	141	136	2,805,290
Out of the Realm	6	3	59	6	11	11	58,821
Out On the Town	2	1	13	2	0	0	9,748
Outflanker	60	38	432	72	47	54	1,115,443
Outlaw Image	1	1	10	1	2	0	6,437
Overdrawn Account	1	1	7	1	0	1	4,422
Overnight Express	4	1	16	1	3	4	28,945
Overpeer	5	2	37	2	7	3	36,643
Oxalagu (GER)	1	1	8	3	0	2	121,840
Pachinko	4	1	29	2	2	3	23,689
Pacific Waves	20	9	130	17	14	14	145,081
Pal's Memory	2	2	27	5	2	1	46,998
Palance	6	2	34	2	3	2	27,246
Palmister	10	6	62	6	11	4	78,390
Pana Brass	3	1	8	1	2	1	24,915
Pancho Press (ARG)	7	2	38	3	3	2	51,491
Pancho Villa	71	24	466	43	56	53	438,915
Pangbourne	3	1	24	3	4	3	43,882
Papa Chan	1	1	12	1	3	1	15,712
Pappa Riccio	21	7	170	9	17	21	248,869
Parade Ground	52	20	291	34	40	42	836,231
Parade Marshal	9	4	68	7	9	8	608,096
Paramount Jet	5	1	37	1	4	4	11,869
Paramour	4	2	30	2	5	4	39,012
Paranoide (ARG)	36	15	208	30	23	30	324,561
Parentheses	11	4	70	5	7	8	119,758
Parfaitement	16	4	94	6	8	12	77,483
Parlay Me	13	6	84	8	9	14	227,989
Part the Waters	3	2	12	2	2	3	22,270
Partager	1	1	6	1	2	0	1,683
Partner's Hero	94	50	692	94	87	96	1,928,686
Party Manners	49	19	362	29	35	37	508,405
Pas Seul	3	2	20	2	2	3	13,339
Paskanell	6	2	34	3	0	1	11,027
Pass Fail	4	1	37	1	1	1	6,481
Pass the Line	7	3	42	3	3	1	32,072
Paster's Caper	4	1	34	2	3	3	50,715
Patchy Groundfog	2	2	10	3	3	2	71,082
Patriot Strike	9	5	53	7	9	11	93,089
Patriotically	2	2	13	2	2	3	25,841
Patsyprospect	3	1	17	1	2	1	11,142
Patton	117	71	922	128	91	103	2,158,848
Pauliano	27	8	150	20	12	20	243,645
Pax Nobiscum	1	1	10	1	0	0	4,464
Payalon (ARG)	2	1	16	1	0	0	7,085
Payant (ARG)	4	3	36	5	8	4	152,482
Peace Arch	3	2	18	3	4	2	17,269
Peaked	1	1	4	1	0	0	1,382
Peaks and Valleys	169	94	1209	151	172	157	2,920,548
Pecos River	4	1	15	2	0	0	8,667
Peintre Celebre	7	3	18	3	0	2	496,855
Pele's Smile	3	1	22	1	1	0	12,960
Pembroke	112	64	855	139	122	96	1,790,804
Penalty Shot	2	1	21	2	3	4	27,660
Pendleton Ridge	4	2	20	2	1	3	8,887
Pentelicus	148	86	1192	166	158	146	2,305,476
Pep Up	5	3	40	3	1	8	16,728
Percifal	8	5	60	7	8	5	135,382
Perfect	22	8	130	11	22	8	205,519
Perfect Mandate	22	4	80	7	11	12	255,551
Perfect Parade	3	2	13	2	4	1	49,910
Perfect Vision	36	14	247	25	31	33	259,244

Sire	Perf	Wnrs	Sts	1st	2d	3d	Purses
Perfecting	20	9	145	14	13	18	210,205
Perforce	10	3	82	4	10	16	46,292
Perkin Warbeck	3	1	20	1	0	2	9,822
Persian Star	3	1	14	1	3	0	14,938
Personable Joe	47	25	280	40	40	35	435,733
Personage	1	1	9	3	4	0	5,360
Personal	3	1	24	1	4	1	14,728
Personal Five	4	1	31	1	2	3	9,838
Personal Flag	109	49	877	93	99	116	1,690,776
Personal Hope	18	6	121	11	17	17	189,378
Personal Matter	4	2	33	2	4	4	30,921
Perugino	7	1	12	1	0	1	42,082
Peruvian	23	12	183	19	27	23	261,456
Pesty Axe	1	1	11	2	1	1	3,760
Petardia (GB)	2	1	14	1	1	2	16,035
Peterhof	48	27	363	42	51	62	275,359
Petersburg	49	29	318	45	43	44	591,047
Peteski	42	21	339	35	48	38	551,147
Petionville	116	62	829	107	111	106	3,711,026
Petong	1	1	11	1	0	1	4,802
Petra Forbes	2	1	8	1	1	1	23,330
Petrel's Flight	5	1	22	1	1	3	19,914
Petty Crime	2	1	12	3	3	3	12,450
Peyrano (ARG)	6	3	40	5	9	3	60,323
Phantasma	5	1	42	1	0	4	6,845
Phantom Jet	12	3	71	4	3	4	45,680
Pharisien (FR)	8	1	41	1	2	1	12,045
Phil Barrera	1	1	4	2	1	0	7,540
Philadream	7	1	39	1	8	3	26,892
Phoenician	5	1	28	2	2	6	5,335
Phone Fantasy	4	2	17	2	1	1	27,492
Phone Prince	1	1	2	1	1	0	10,192
Phone Roberto	14	3	63	3	6	4	36,144
Phone Saga	14	6	88	7	11	10	237,015
Phone Trick	120	67	792	106	105	92	1,978,184
Phonetics	5	1	13	1	1	1	30,980
Photo Memory	6	2	46	2	5	5	17,658
Pic Iron	1	1	9	1	1	0	10,989
Picabo Too	1	1	5	1	0	0	8,600
Piccolino	33	14	215	27	15	17	379,178
Piccolo	4	3	22	3	5	0	77,755
Pick Up the Phone	5	3	24	4	2	3	55,345
Pillar of Wisdom	2	2	20	4	1	1	16,274
Pin Stripe	2	1	12	1	1	3	12,699
Pine Bluff	99	55	603	100	70	73	2,248,850
Pineing Patty	7	3	41	3	6	3	47,732
Pioneering	106	63	816	127	109	121	2,674,521
Pirate's Bounty	24	13	166	29	20	17	266,112
Pistol's Cowboy	2	2	14	3	1	1	17,786
Pistols and Roses	29	8	172	12	12	22	193,099
Pitch In	6	2	32	4	3	2	90,786
Pitso Cassello	2	1	9	3	0	1	5,508
Pivotal (GB)	2	2	13	3	2	0	390,926
Placid Fund	27	15	216	28	26	18	634,449
Plain Dealing	17	7	136	16	15	12	210,999
Platini	1	1	2	2	0	0	21,000
Platinum Pleasure	1	1	10	1	0	0	4,200
Play Both Ends	6	1	35	1	2	4	28,395
Play Fellow	3	1	27	2	1	3	24,175
Play the Gold	3	1	7	1	1	1	25,130
Pleasant Colony	45	23	297	39	43	42	2,728,433
Pleasant Dancer	7	2	59	3	3	11	38,837
Pleasant Line	6	4	53	7	9	2	133,405
Pleasant Tap	133	68	917	126	116	115	2,620,987
Pleasant Variety	1	1	8	2	0	2	89,761
Pleasure Bent	4	2	33	4	5	2	47,930
Plenty Chilly	8	1	49	2	1	2	26,997
Plentyofit	6	1	24	1	2	0	14,938
Pocket Book	3	3	31	3	3	4	42,525
Pocket Phone	3	1	13	1	2	0	10,720
Pok Ta Pok	28	15	149	21	11	13	234,901
Polar Falcon	5	2	28	2	6	6	74,742
Pole Position	37	18	259	29	35	36	455,417
Poles Apart	11	2	61	5	7	1	195,521
Poliglote (GB)	3	1	14	1	4	2	90,000
Polish Navy	31	14	150	24	19	12	321,567

Sire	Perf	Wnrs	Sts	1st	2d	3d	Purses
Polish Numbers	132	72	848	128	97	125	3,221,466
Polish Precedent	4	2	16	4	1	2	108,605
Polish Pro	42	16	270	25	35	36	508,875
Political Folly	3	1	13	1	1	1	12,361
Political Whit	5	3	23	3	3	3	72,486
Polka	7	1	36	2	4	2	17,586
Pollock's Luck	50	16	311	28	26	28	339,714
Polynesian Flyer	3	1	34	1	4	3	11,452
Ponche	47	26	406	48	56	64	906,659
Porto Foricos	14	4	53	7	6	8	761,947
Portoferraio (ARG)	2	1	21	6	2	2	49,180
Portroe	5	2	43	2	5	6	30,312
Positiveness	2	2	24	3	2	2	29,387
Poster Monarch	4	1	31	1	1	2	33,645
Potentiate	1	1	7	1	0	0	4,216
Potrillazo	8	4	74	14	10	11	255,113
Potrillon (ARG)	1	1	6	1	1	0	60,984
Powderityourself	4	3	37	4	9	4	44,459
Power Boat	1	1	5	1	2	0	4,132
Power by Far	4	1	11	1	0	2	12,355
Power of Mind	32	12	177	19	28	18	344,024
Power Storm	4	1	9	1	0	0	7,110
Preacherman	15	6	107	7	13	10	181,147
Precise End	27	11	98	12	20	17	689,598
Precocity	33	18	225	29	36	28	792,865
Predecessor	8	3	68	7	7	7	46,485
Prefabricate	1	1	4	1	0	0	1,650
Preferences	7	2	42	2	6	4	24,995
Premier Ministre	3	1	23	1	3	4	16,433
Premiership	58	29	429	45	43	42	500,355
Prenup	50	18	324	31	34	41	542,710
Present Value	23	8	112	10	19	17	113,102
Presently	12	3	57	3	3	8	27,099
Presidential Order	44	17	368	37	38	46	477,620
Presidents Summit	2	1	10	1	0	1	1,030
Press Card	78	43	578	88	66	70	1,422,222
Presto Lad	11	6	73	6	5	8	40,388
Prete Khale	1	1	16	2	3	2	17,884
Pride of Burkaan	3	2	11	4	1	2	52,227
Primehaul	1	1	4	1	2	0	21,500
Prince Cox	4	2	39	5	5	5	75,011
Prince Don B.	6	2	35	2	0	1	10,156
Prince of Fame	22	5	138	6	10	10	76,616
Prince of Praise	2	2	11	2	3	3	86,971
Prince of the Mt.	27	15	158	19	20	23	324,386
Prince Valid	1	1	7	1	0	1	5,998
Princely Verdict	3	2	22	2	2	1	14,304
Priolo	3	1	12	1	0	2	17,951
Privano	1	1	15	1	1	4	26,104
Private Admirer	7	3	47	8	4	5	63,030
Private Game	1	1	10	1	1	1	23,290
Private Interview	55	24	390	37	48	44	1,115,543
Private Key	24	7	151	10	13	14	153,669
Private School	27	9	197	17	16	22	209,500
Private Suspicion	3	1	23	1	0	0	17,927
Private Talk	15	5	128	12	14	20	229,855
Private Terms	89	43	709	78	78	101	1,289,020
Prized	76	40	563	75	70	75	1,978,375
Probable	5	1	25	1	4	3	10,647
Proof	7	1	45	1	8	4	33,666
Proper Reality	57	33	394	49	39	56	385,171
Prospect Bay	82	46	550	76	74	69	1,256,458
Prospect Feature	14	2	90	4	3	4	24,393
Prospect North	11	5	78	8	3	6	43,742
Prospector Jones	59	28	396	53	51	39	1,049,973
Prospector's Halo	19	9	151	11	27	15	148,515
Prospector's Music	51	30	391	51	55	51	967,145
Prospector's Pick	2	2	18	2	3	0	13,056
Prospectors Gamble	68	38	511	67	68	56	985,168
Prosper Fager	32	15	255	30	29	26	812,035
Protect Yourself	7	1	46	2	3	2	27,830
Proud and True	66	36	530	75	70	64	1,234,178
Proud Birdie	6	3	47	9	3	6	63,575
Proud Capital	3	2	16	4	1	0	18,749
Proud Irish	54	31	422	58	54	65	868,377
Proud Northern	4	2	35	4	6	3	38,909

Sire	Perf	Wnrs	Sts	1st	2d	3d	Purses
Proud Truth	24	7	163	9	14	18	175,867
Proudest Duke	6	2	42	3	3	2	20,127
Proudest Romeo	27	12	148	20	22	13	317,746
Prudent Manner (IRE)	4	1	18	1	0	2	15,025
Prune	5	3	25	3	1	3	63,815
Pug's Hart	7	4	59	5	1	6	29,989
Pulling Punches	12	1	24	1	3	1	23,775
Pulpit	98	50	528	80	72	65	3,846,835
Pulverizing	3	1	22	2	6	1	48,667
Purple Comet	12	2	75	4	7	8	78,624
Purple Mountain	1	1	13	2	3	0	29,641
Pursuit of Love	2	1	18	1	4	2	28,280
Put Em Up	5	3	27	8	3	2	14,187
Pyramid Peak	40	23	253	35	35	22	581,780
Pyrite	7	2	27	2	1	3	10,947
Quaker Hill	16	7	90	7	13	14	145,104
Quaker Ridge	28	21	227	37	39	29	583,397
Quarry	11	4	54	6	5	6	111,838
Queen's Gray Bee	11	3	45	4	5	4	29,259
Quest for Fame (GB)	14	6	76	10	4	10	124,885
Qui Native	1	1	22	1	2	7	4,821
Quick Buck	2	1	10	1	0	1	5,335
Quick Cut	33	16	205	24	20	18	380,185
Quick Speed	1	1	6	1	1	1	11,568
Quiero Dinero	2	1	8	1	1	2	30,209
Quiet American	146	83	1034	163	134	132	3,955,954
Quiet Enjoyment	24	17	171	33	27	26	425,999
Quintillion (IRE)	4	1	26	1	0	2	9,070
Quinton	3	1	21	1	3	1	13,122
Quite Special	12	5	56	8	3	7	91,337
R. Cooper	5	2	46	5	4	4	39,259
R. Payday	12	7	74	10	12	8	122,061
Raamz	2	1	10	1	0	0	4,320
Racing Rhinocerous	5	2	28	3	3	3	23,391
Radio Daze	12	5	64	6	12	3	71,518
Raffie's Majesty	24	10	150	16	17	17	392,315
Rage	16	8	140	11	21	15	240,375
Ragtime Rascal	3	1	14	5	1	1	72,976
Rahy	88	47	565	73	91	75	2,118,832
Raider	2	1	13	1	1	2	5,155
Rail	30	16	207	28	23	18	509,801
Railway Cat	11	6	64	8	9	3	98,410
Rainbow Blues (IRE)	10	2	42	3	8	5	74,682
Rainbow Corner (GB)	4	3	18	3	1	2	68,930
Rainbow Dancer (FR)	2	1	10	1	1	0	40,126
Rainbow Prospect	7	3	51	5	4	8	183,041
Rainbow Quest	3	2	19	3	1	3	125,760
Rainbows for Life	2	1	11	4	1	0	32,397
Raise a Champion	12	5	81	5	7	7	51,496
Raise a Govenor	15	4	81	4	5	5	27,333
Raise a Man	3	2	14	2	0	1	21,035
Raise a Rascal	12	6	78	14	17	8	81,640
Raise a Stanza	1	1	6	1	1	2	18,600
Raised On Stage	2	2	13	2	0	1	5,107
Raising Hill	1	1	10	3	2	1	13,342
Raj Waki	6	2	30	2	3	5	118,939
Raja's Best Boy	11	5	74	7	7	10	94,334
Raja's Revenge	7	1	51	6	6	6	198,930
Raji	10	7	74	15	7	9	88,434
Rakeen	31	15	276	29	33	29	476,042
Rambo Phil	5	2	42	3	3	5	52,042
Rampart Road	2	1	6	1	0	2	25,840
Ramplett	3	2	25	4	2	2	50,395
Ranger (FR)	10	1	61	2	6	4	16,802
Rapacity	1	1	11	1	0	3	4,320
Rare Brick	58	26	358	39	51	47	619,664
Rare Performer	3	2	19	3	1	1	12,941
Rare Red	6	4	45	6	7	6	41,011
Ravenwood	11	3	77	4	10	10	51,463
Ray's Word	21	5	178	8	18	15	106,349
Raykour (IRE)	6	2	39	2	2	7	21,208
Re Ack	1	1	24	2	5	5	12,343
Reack Boldly	8	2	35	3	1	3	24,082
Real Partner	8	3	42	5	3	4	47,725
Real Quiet	70	33	411	50	51	36	1,207,167
Real West	9	5	51	5	7	9	96,899
Realitos	3	1	15	1	0	1	8,258
Reality Road	8	4	60	6	5	9	77,896
Reality's Conquest	2	1	8	1	0	0	3,159
Really a Rainbow	7	2	33	3	1	4	23,584
Really Golden	10	5	53	11	9	7	28,929
Reavealing Gold	4	1	23	2	1	1	9,855
Rebmec	15	6	72	9	6	10	111,135
Recital Hall	2	2	18	3	3	2	15,542
Recognized	7	3	44	5	2	4	56,557
Recommended List	2	1	22	1	3	0	14,196
Record Catch	16	9	147	14	15	18	140,556
Red	31	18	186	31	34	26	318,269
Red Attack	9	4	76	5	13	16	73,424
Red Bishop	15	4	73	5	6	5	76,416
Red Castle	4	3	23	3	3	0	14,604
Red Clay Country	3	1	14	3	0	0	19,180
Red Hammer Red	1	1	6	1	1	1	32,522
Red Ransom	80	33	383	60	47	47	1,724,279
Red River Gorge	18	7	111	10	13	20	98,452
Red Scamper	8	6	90	10	15	15	106,797
Red Screen	4	1	22	1	0	2	4,922
Red Wing Bold	6	1	26	1	1	5	7,317
Reel On Reel	21	11	129	17	19	17	153,961
Regal Affair	8	1	34	2	4	1	21,581
Regal Affirmation	7	4	47	8	9	10	117,969
Regal and Royal	4	1	16	2	2	1	8,662
Regal Classic	142	73	1086	120	137	142	3,120,289
Regal Discovery	7	2	56	6	6	8	109,195
Regal Flight	1	1	8	1	0	4	10,526
Regal Groom	5	2	30	4	3	5	37,605
Regal Humor	16	5	123	6	13	11	120,516
Regal Intention	81	46	520	75	78	65	1,137,671
Regal Remark	76	49	569	83	71	84	962,085
Regal Search	34	21	296	36	35	37	391,682
Regal Song	1	1	12	2	1	1	13,881
Regalstaff	1	1	1	1	0	0	14,500
Regent Act	3	1	15	1	4	2	18,282
Rehaan	16	8	99	13	9	16	73,363
Reign Road	24	5	169	7	12	21	100,015
Reincarnate	11	2	71	2	5	8	51,414
Relagate	1	1	5	1	2	0	22,300
Relaunch	13	5	61	8	3	5	90,085
Relaunch a Tune	11	6	82	9	17	8	60,575
Relic Relic Relic	1	1	14	1	4	1	18,084
Remember Hope	3	1	31	2	5	10	30,826
Remington Slew	5	2	24	3	2	3	10,770
Reno City	1	1	10	3	2	2	5,141
Renteria	12	7	75	12	15	17	225,422
Reparations	1	1	1	1	0	0	20,580
Replant	2	1	7	1	1	0	1,270
Repletion	8	3	72	6	11	5	98,816
Repriced	61	27	402	48	51	42	828,353
Reprized	23	12	181	21	20	17	328,396
Reputed Testamony	4	1	26	2	5	2	47,365
Restless Con	7	1	23	2	4	1	76,938
Retsina Run	16	5	74	5	10	7	82,768
Reuben's Grand	5	2	36	2	5	8	57,805
Reve Dore	1	1	4	1	1	0	13,400
Reve Du	5	4	58	9	6	8	90,663
Revelrout	2	1	10	1	2	0	4,945
Reverse Mulligan	2	1	25	1	2	0	8,384
Revoque (IRE)	2	2	23	7	2	3	108,879
Rewana	7	3	32	3	2	2	10,688
Rhodes	20	6	145	8	19	14	104,405
Rhythm	54	22	343	39	33	33	674,262
Rial (ARG)	12	3	94	3	11	9	47,501
Ribot Land	3	1	15	1	0	0	7,535
Rich Doctor	2	1	7	1	1	0	1,885
Rich Man's Gold	3	1	13	1	2	1	87,970
Richter Scale	14	5	38	5	3	3	204,013
Rick's Double	3	2	14	2	3	0	4,142
Ridan Clarion	3	1	17	1	3	1	10,720
Ride the Rails	10	6	90	14	11	7	299,653
Ride the Storm	7	4	38	10	6	2	262,441
Riflery	3	3	43	5	6	12	94,888
Right Con	2	2	20	5	6	2	30,947

Sire	Perf	Wnrs	Sts	1st	2d	3d	Purses
Right Jab	11	2	45	2	3	3	47,370
Rine's Hope	9	2	54	2	6	8	42,650
Ring Proud	4	4	30	5	6	3	10,599
Ringside	22	11	139	16	20	23	203,770
Rinka Das	49	24	380	47	34	53	574,140
Rinoso	1	1	11	2	2	0	25,239
Rio Verde	19	5	99	7	12	7	180,496
Rio's Lark	13	5	83	5	10	5	28,503
Rip Entry	3	1	11	1	1	2	7,546
Ripley's Class Act	3	1	8	1	0	0	2,232
Risen Roman	5	1	22	2	2	1	22,361
Risen Star	13	5	81	5	15	7	81,160
Riva Pass	1	1	14	1	1	1	8,543
River Basin	1	1	10	1	2	1	2,640
River Flyer	21	8	120	16	18	16	194,915
River Special	20	6	122	9	9	8	239,827
River Squall	12	5	79	5	8	7	51,333
Rivergo	2	1	14	2	1	1	14,285
Riverman	5	1	51	1	5	9	17,400
Rixby	5	1	26	2	2	2	29,869
Rizzi	110	63	829	111	98	96	1,602,243
Road Rush	2	2	16	3	2	3	22,692
Road to Seattle	1	1	2	1	0	0	11,266
Roanoke	79	41	686	73	66	97	1,116,093
Roar	144	91	1132	174	173	167	3,991,395
Roaring Camp	18	3	79	4	12	5	118,522
Rob 'n Gin	5	1	14	1	3	1	44,330
Rob an Plunder	12	8	99	20	18	11	74,127
Rob's Freeze	13	6	125	13	12	17	259,341
Robannier	16	6	60	8	11	8	213,070
Robb	5	3	34	3	2	6	85,482
Robellino	8	3	45	5	3	4	108,105
Roberto Grande	2	1	14	1	3	2	26,451
Roberto Reason	1	1	6	1	0	1	3,005
Robin des Pins	30	11	199	24	19	32	318,863
Robyn Dancer	123	62	951	114	117	106	2,083,990
Rock Band	9	5	69	6	15	6	58,011
Rock Hill	5	2	30	2	1	3	17,903
Rock Point	10	1	32	1	1	3	22,488
Rockamundo	10	2	54	3	2	5	52,516
Rocky Mountain	16	7	138	9	13	6	98,019
Rod and Staff	2	1	7	1	2	1	25,380
Rodeo	80	39	501	66	45	52	1,444,428
Rodeo Road	2	2	11	2	0	2	3,412
Rodrigo de Triano	1	1	10	3	1	1	25,493
Roglee	4	1	25	2	0	3	7,808
Roi Danzig	2	1	29	4	9	2	35,645
Roi Normand	4	4	30	6	2	3	167,437
Rokeby (GB)	12	5	71	9	4	9	104,065
Roll Credits	3	2	20	2	5	4	18,109
Rollin On Over	2	2	20	2	4	3	10,983
Rolls Aly	6	3	49	7	3	7	78,788
Roman Diplomat	4	1	17	2	1	1	20,543
Roman Majesty	3	1	34	2	0	11	30,265
Romanov (IRE)	31	12	237	23	30	35	343,675
Romo	2	2	20	2	1	2	18,011
Ron's Gold	1	1	6	1	0	0	5,291
Roo Art	28	13	190	22	17	15	142,293
Root Boy	14	6	99	10	10	15	135,666
Roscius	3	2	23	7	1	1	70,957
Rosenose	1	1	7	2	2	0	7,020
Rougemont	4	2	24	3	5	2	12,704
Rouse the Louse	6	3	46	8	9	7	98,763
Rowdy Regal	3	1	30	2	4	2	8,145
Rowdy Rowdy Dee	1	1	12	1	1	1	5,750
Roxbury Park	15	4	106	6	6	16	89,267
Roy	88	58	662	96	99	95	2,546,396
Roy's Saint	1	1	7	1	0	0	1,752
Royal Academy	114	59	620	96	97	71	3,089,478
Royal Albert Hall	7	3	35	5	5	3	71,277
Royal Anthem	17	2	42	2	3	3	74,392
Royal Applause (GB)	7	3	38	7	6	2	1,260,745
Royal Blue Eyes	1	1	2	1	0	0	3,000
Royal Capote	1	1	5	1	1	0	2,070
Royal Danzig	3	1	17	2	4	0	20,746
Royal Egyptian	13	4	71	4	7	10	83,603

Sire	Perf	Wnrs	Sts	1st	2d	3d	Purses
Royal Empire	26	7	138	11	8	15	204,282
Royal Link	4	1	28	2	1	3	22,540
Royal Martial (ARG)	1	1	18	2	3	0	8,538
Royal Monarchy	3	2	24	4	0	2	21,863
Royal Pennant	10	3	67	6	7	7	54,773
Royal Quiz	16	6	87	10	14	9	73,635
Royal Regatta (IRE)	5	2	39	3	9	5	45,610
Royal Roberto	15	7	83	10	8	9	99,183
Royal Rumpus	2	2	13	2	0	2	23,763
Royal Solo (IRE)	1	1	5	2	0	1	101,640
Royale Future	9	2	40	4	8	3	61,081
Rubiano	132	67	895	111	114	126	2,663,036
Rubiyat	7	6	52	11	9	5	263,866
Ruckus Hosner	6	3	62	6	4	1	40,218
Rudy's Fantasy	1	1	9	1	0	0	8,290
Rugged Angel	1	1	7	1	2	1	7,176
Ruhlmann	29	11	214	19	21	29	231,793
Rumbo	3	1	18	1	3	1	6,637
Rumbo Al Este	1	1	11	1	3	1	10,257
Run On the Bank	3	1	27	2	7	6	18,510
Run Paul Run	5	2	38	2	3	3	23,668
Run Softly	54	27	395	37	58	45	667,722
Run Turn	3	1	23	3	2	2	47,385
Runaway Groom	161	93	1181	155	153	153	3,347,556
Runaway Macho	6	2	34	4	5	1	61,089
Running Memories	2	1	13	1	2	0	6,396
Running Stag	33	10	107	15	13	14	516,682
Rush	4	2	20	3	0	0	13,546
Russellthemussell	7	3	58	6	8	12	46,022
Russian Courage	14	5	106	5	15	8	152,488
Rustic Light	3	2	24	4	1	5	31,704
S. S. Hot Sauce	1	1	8	2	0	1	9,925
S. W. Wildcard	2	1	13	1	0	1	4,112
Sabona	19	3	117	3	11	12	87,286
Sadler Slew	7	2	44	4	2	7	45,061
Sadler's Wells	20	4	60	5	4	9	1,326,568
Safe Prospect	11	5	101	9	18	13	187,604
Safely's Mark	17	6	113	13	7	12	604,011
Sahm	25	20	189	34	22	19	511,433
Sail Me Again	15	9	126	12	29	16	146,971
Saint Ballado	156	82	879	129	121	140	6,614,013
Saithor	4	3	39	5	6	7	57,446
Salem Drive	20	5	119	7	10	20	63,729
Salse	2	1	12	1	3	0	31,065
Salt Dome	6	3	35	4	3	3	17,850
Salt Lake	147	82	867	143	124	109	2,425,995
Salty Shoes	8	5	52	9	5	5	49,220
Salutely	5	2	17	2	0	2	30,844
Samarid	2	1	9	1	2	3	5,728
Same Day Delivery	11	5	81	8	13	8	130,305
San Romano	4	3	36	5	2	5	126,080
Sanctuary	16	4	98	8	6	10	183,745
Sand Tunnel	15	8	109	11	11	16	189,466
Sandia Slew	8	4	54	9	8	9	272,082
Sandpit (BRZ)	98	55	782	85	93	92	1,461,719
Sandrigo	6	3	38	4	5	3	44,896
Sandy's Honey	1	1	14	2	1	0	31,940
Santiago Peak	4	4	39	7	3	8	59,300
Saratoga Express	7	2	33	2	3	4	37,478
Saratoga Six	44	20	354	35	43	42	557,164
Saros (GB)	9	2	51	5	5	5	31,776
Sasha's Prospect	7	3	27	6	3	1	83,155
Satan Sleeps	3	1	16	1	1	2	11,145
Satellite Signal	8	4	54	4	6	6	20,858
Satellite Sun	2	1	20	3	2	2	36,010
Saucey Avenger	2	1	17	3	3	3	24,950
Saucy Token	10	4	51	4	5	0	55,068
Savin Eyes	10	3	62	3	3	5	39,401
Savings	10	3	63	4	6	4	49,449
Saxton	6	3	41	3	4	5	70,100
Sayaret	2	2	10	2	0	3	69,050
Scarlet 'n Gray	12	3	90	5	11	10	106,294
Scarlet Ibis	28	10	195	23	25	21	318,366
Scatmandu	65	30	409	46	55	51	708,252
Scenic (IRE)	1	1	4	1	0	1	7,210
Schembechler	5	1	29	2	3	3	20,434

Sire	Perf	Wnrs	Sts	1st	2d	3d	Purses
Scherando	12	6	60	8	3	5	78,527
Schizoid	5	1	24	2	3	0	14,880
Schossberg	17	10	125	20	23	17	547,197
Score Quick	14	9	91	13	10	12	225,405
Scott's Scoundrel	7	1	15	2	1	0	15,000
Scottsville	15	7	88	11	16	8	216,516
Scroll	3	1	20	3	2	3	21,834
Sea Hero	85	47	622	80	80	78	1,498,232
Sea of Secrets	60	30	373	37	54	41	797,735
Sea Salute	57	27	419	52	50	56	988,303
Sea Twister	3	2	15	6	1	2	72,960
Sea Wall	31	15	272	19	35	37	663,858
Seacliff	27	16	200	25	22	25	346,482
Search for Gold	1	1	22	5	4	2	13,419
Seattle Battle	4	2	24	3	1	2	16,686
Seattle Bound	38	14	202	23	17	28	248,779
Seattle General	5	1	17	1	1	0	3,550
Seattle Knight	3	1	12	1	1	2	10,651
Seattle Morn	12	4	90	5	11	13	60,683
Seattle Pattern	2	2	12	2	3	2	39,995
Seattle Proud	14	6	59	7	5	6	105,244
Seattle Sleet	47	27	306	49	42	46	831,147
Seattle Slew	60	29	297	42	40	29	1,352,871
Seattle Sun	8	5	54	7	3	4	63,826
Sebrof	9	3	68	5	13	8	34,374
Second Childhood	10	4	67	8	8	8	141,840
Second Episode	1	1	14	2	3	3	38,160
Secreniner	16	3	69	4	2	6	43,243
Secret Claim	30	12	186	31	11	26	219,703
Secret Counsel	3	1	16	1	5	3	8,876
Secret Firm	5	1	17	1	1	3	17,321
Secret Hello	57	28	417	58	62	50	943,605
Secret Odds	17	6	127	13	9	17	178,329
Secret Prince	8	1	64	1	12	14	42,686
Secret Slew	1	1	9	1	0	0	2,733
Secretariats Ghost	2	1	10	1	0	2	14,460
Secretary Forli	3	2	15	3	1	1	43,680
Secretary General	1	1	3	1	0	0	2,840
Secretito	3	1	15	2	2	1	22,930
Seeker's Journey	7	2	49	2	5	13	46,663
Seeker's Reward	1	1	9	1	1	2	20,275
Seeking the Crown	14	2	75	2	8	5	69,999
Seeking the Gold	73	34	341	52	55	45	2,026,886
Sefapiano	80	46	645	89	106	70	1,465,924
Sejm	7	3	50	3	8	6	37,268
Sekari (GB)	6	4	52	5	5	7	50,398
Selkirk	4	4	24	4	5	5	158,580
Semoran	45	24	312	36	35	25	423,350
Seneca Jones	37	24	221	45	26	28	548,282
Senor Conquistador	10	5	85	9	14	6	176,892
Senor Foxfire	2	1	12	1	0	1	6,727
Senor Speedy	51	26	360	39	33	47	724,167
Senor Vermonti	3	1	10	1	0	0	9,360
Sentinel Star	2	1	20	3	5	2	26,331
Sepoy (ARG)	7	4	60	4	2	4	28,081
Septieme Ciel	19	7	114	17	10	13	200,184
Serves Em Right	6	2	38	3	4	2	31,620
Service Stripe	39	22	236	40	30	28	537,078
Seven Rivers	11	3	82	3	14	4	44,082
Seven Zero	7	4	60	8	12	9	76,121
Sewickley	7	4	63	11	9	8	211,644
Shadeed	13	5	94	7	20	7	87,204
Shadow Launcher	7	2	29	2	4	3	22,005
Shaheen	22	11	104	16	6	6	84,677
Shakeel	16	10	137	19	19	22	133,213
Sham	2	1	16	1	1	2	7,254
Shamrock Ridge	8	3	57	5	10	4	60,745
Shanekite	7	4	70	8	7	8	49,135
Shaquin	6	5	53	12	7	4	203,789
Sharkey	32	14	209	19	17	29	290,102
Sharp Frosty	46	10	310	14	27	37	274,727
Sharp Victor	32	18	218	24	35	29	517,856
Sharper One	4	2	28	3	3	6	10,686
Shawaf	2	1	10	1	3	1	24,690
Shawklit Won	4	1	31	2	2	2	19,856
Shecky Iron	2	1	7	2	2	1	71,010
Sheikh Albadou (GB)	19	11	158	27	22	21	353,461
Shelly's Charmer	4	1	30	1	0	2	5,802
Shelter Half	12	5	98	7	9	17	96,237
Shergar's Best (IRE)	20	12	154	20	18	22	129,189
Sheryar	8	5	72	8	9	9	199,201
Shinko King (IRE)	2	1	7	1	0	1	57,630
Shirttail Flying	5	4	48	7	5	3	37,465
Shortys Moovr	2	1	12	1	3	1	3,622
Shot Block	6	3	44	3	4	8	61,139
Shot Gun Scott	3	2	19	2	4	2	10,850
Shotiche	15	4	114	4	12	11	107,556
Show'em Slew	2	1	24	1	1	1	9,488
Shrike	9	1	34	1	8	5	40,831
Shuailaan	41	16	245	30	34	32	565,274
Shudanz	1	1	11	2	0	1	47,278
Shuttleman	7	1	21	2	2	2	10,687
Shy Tom	4	4	49	4	6	7	67,940
Siberian Express	4	1	53	1	12	5	37,465
Siberian Pine	24	8	155	16	10	19	179,492
Siberian Summer	85	50	572	92	64	67	2,176,034
Siebe	9	4	46	5	5	4	37,787
Sifounas	2	1	10	1	4	0	9,614
Signal	8	3	41	3	7	4	90,150
Signal Tap	76	34	593	56	72	76	1,174,077
Signoir Valery	1	1	4	2	0	1	19,642
Signoretto (FR)	2	1	15	1	0	3	16,147
Silent Generation	7	2	40	4	1	6	52,423
Silent King	17	5	100	5	9	7	67,104
Silent Landing	2	1	21	1	3	5	12,757
Silent Link	1	1	11	5	2	3	83,073
Silent Tempest	3	2	14	3	2	1	18,727
Silic (FR)	5	1	17	1	2	2	18,053
Silk Song	2	1	4	1	1	1	17,879
Silken Reality	6	2	29	3	0	2	10,294
Silver Buck	35	13	227	28	30	23	488,667
Silver Canyon	1	1	13	2	0	0	11,885
Silver Charm	75	32	368	49	55	55	1,864,055
Silver Deputy	158	85	1038	154	155	123	4,206,718
Silver Element	4	1	18	1	1	2	8,620
Silver Finder	2	2	29	2	4	3	60,337
Silver Fox	20	8	118	12	20	17	211,441
Silver Ghost	136	71	808	120	88	98	2,570,419
Silver Hawk	27	10	105	15	10	9	1,072,911
Silver Launch	9	5	45	6	1	5	35,046
Silver Music	18	6	98	9	9	10	190,301
Silver of Silver	16	8	97	16	16	13	106,498
Silver Ring (FR)	2	2	20	2	1	3	10,582
Simi Dancer	8	1	28	1	0	3	10,337
Simply Majestic	12	4	89	7	4	10	81,264
Sinceilostmybaby	11	8	79	10	8	17	81,154
Sing the Praise	1	1	8	2	1	2	5,558
Single Solo	3	1	8	1	0	1	3,198
Singspiel (IRE)	7	3	25	3	2	1	209,822
Sinndar (IRE)	1	1	1	1	0	0	45,000
Siphon (BRZ)	132	48	696	79	74	81	1,689,495
Sir Ap	20	7	138	11	14	22	150,575
Sir Cat	119	74	781	122	94	112	2,162,388
Sir Eric	17	4	132	8	13	18	113,845
Sir Fir	6	1	64	2	8	6	44,612
Sir Harry Lewis	1	1	12	2	1	0	18,120
Sir Ivor Again	1	1	5	1	2	0	8,400
Sir Leon	21	8	200	12	25	26	240,595
Sir Naskra	3	2	14	3	2	3	24,683
Sir Reed O	7	3	66	4	9	12	42,225
Sir Richard Lewis	7	3	45	4	8	7	110,215
Sir Riddle	5	1	22	1	3	3	16,901
Sir Sian	1	1	3	1	0	2	19,000
Sir Spellbinder	5	5	39	7	8	10	80,360
Sitting Appeal	3	1	14	1	0	2	1,819
Six Below	5	1	14	1	0	1	13,621
Six Fast Nickles	2	1	16	4	5	0	16,773
Six Speed	9	2	35	3	5	5	53,153
Siyah Kalem	15	5	113	13	9	14	111,808
Ski Champ	2	2	18	5	4	1	54,690
Skip Away	121	77	880	142	118	122	3,368,862
Skip Out Front	3	1	13	2	0	1	73,883

RECORDS OF SIRES

Sire	Perf	Wnrs	Sts	1st	2d	3d	Purses
Skip Trial	74	34	490	62	58	62	1,261,917
Skip West	1	1	5	2	0	0	8,520
Sky Act	2	1	7	1	1	0	3,520
Sky Classic	144	68	914	106	99	112	3,896,069
Sky Command	1	1	2	2	0	0	8,640
Sky Harbour	3	1	6	1	0	2	1,266
Sky Tracer	4	2	41	3	1	4	20,397
Sky White	17	9	120	19	17	8	201,245
Skywalker	97	48	524	77	51	63	1,489,889
Slapshot Morty	1	1	20	1	0	0	8,170
Slavic	38	12	191	21	20	25	449,270
Slerp	4	3	22	5	2	1	20,033
Slew Baby	2	1	16	3	5	1	36,986
Slew City Slew	136	72	1020	114	123	119	2,506,545
Slew Gin Fizz	35	19	147	23	15	20	459,376
Slew Mood	16	5	85	7	8	5	52,759
Slew o' Gold	19	11	150	17	13	8	249,950
Slew O'Quoit	6	1	25	1	1	2	13,246
Slew of Angels	18	5	100	9	22	13	73,501
Slew Sangue	19	12	139	15	16	17	256,087
Slew the Bride	8	2	39	3	3	2	29,422
Slew the Coup	26	9	153	13	16	16	72,886
Slew the Knight	10	4	82	8	15	4	113,620
Slew the Slewor	21	6	142	11	13	5	150,998
Slew the Surgeon	20	10	130	21	26	19	278,306
Slew You	3	1	8	1	0	0	8,598
Slew's Royalty	25	12	174	18	18	28	368,239
Slewacide	67	35	426	65	55	45	863,525
Slewacide Red	1	1	11	1	2	1	3,730
Slewdledo	141	82	806	128	110	109	1,586,607
Slewdonza	3	1	10	1	1	2	27,239
Slewly Yours	1	1	9	1	3	0	16,065
Slewpy	26	11	181	18	21	27	311,076
Slews Gold	6	2	60	2	3	7	16,751
Slewship	2	2	12	4	1	1	58,810
Slewvescent	14	4	71	6	11	7	160,766
Slewy Jet	1	1	7	1	1	1	10,207
Slice of Reality	17	10	148	14	12	20	197,041
Slick	3	1	26	1	3	7	30,197
Slick Prince	2	1	10	1	1	2	5,913
Sligh Jet	7	3	62	7	4	7	77,651
Slow Fuse	5	1	23	1	3	1	6,394
Sluggard	1	1	9	1	0	0	8,415
Smart Alec	3	1	9	1	0	0	3,840
Smart Magician	10	4	59	5	9	7	47,459
Smart Strike	128	80	791	150	109	105	6,464,274
Smarten	12	5	74	6	12	9	74,552
Smelly	7	3	51	3	5	7	55,883
Smile	2	1	8	2	0	0	7,005
Smile and Be Happy	3	2	10	2	1	1	22,659
Smilin Singin Sam	14	3	68	3	6	8	65,706
Smoke Glacken	143	95	1123	179	160	180	4,777,548
Smoke Jumper	1	1	10	2	0	2	3,455
Smokester	136	83	939	150	136	119	2,651,586
Smooth Performance	1	1	11	1	2	3	33,565
Snake Doctor	8	1	29	1	2	1	12,557
Snake Oil Man	2	1	7	2	2	1	2,632
Snow 'em	5	2	25	3	4	1	15,467
Snowbound	47	19	204	30	25	24	274,655
So Ever Clever	8	4	31	6	2	5	20,537
So La Me	5	3	27	4	3	4	48,867
So Private	6	2	34	4	2	3	57,251
Soaking Smoking	7	1	40	2	4	5	50,921
Social Diamond	3	1	13	1	0	0	10,028
Social Jokes	1	1	5	2	0	1	2,677
Society Max	30	20	226	31	24	33	326,703
Society Road	2	1	13	2	3	1	19,434
Soft Gold (BRZ)	19	13	153	24	22	27	414,076
Solar Launch	1	1	5	1	1	0	14,637
Soldier Boy	2	2	17	2	1	2	9,303
Soldier On	1	1	6	2	0	1	19,631
Solo Guy	2	2	26	3	3	0	13,611
Somekindofmiracle	2	1	6	1	0	0	2,135
Someplace Fast	3	1	18	1	0	2	3,900
Something Lucky	8	4	57	5	5	6	26,461
Son of Briartic	63	40	448	67	56	57	610,244
Son's Corona	2	1	5	1	1	1	5,745
Sonny's Solo Halo	3	2	24	4	4	1	22,601
Sounds Fabulous	7	1	55	1	6	9	17,369
South Boy (JPN)	4	1	24	1	3	3	10,871
South Pass	6	3	34	5	5	4	36,310
South Salem	5	2	26	2	2	1	30,700
Southern Forest	12	5	97	12	7	8	126,506
Southern Halo	146	68	984	127	126	123	2,858,080
Southern Rhythm	13	6	89	13	14	5	171,383
Southern Sign	12	6	76	8	14	7	40,577
Souvenir Copy	122	68	780	115	136	117	2,991,615
Sovereign Dancer	1	1	7	1	1	3	11,225
Sovereign Exchange	2	1	12	1	1	2	15,914
Sovereign Romance	3	1	17	1	3	1	14,113
Sovereignall	3	2	43	2	4	2	17,229
Space Mountain	1	1	12	3	3	2	21,480
Space Rider	2	1	21	1	2	1	13,592
Spanish Dancer (IRE)	1	1	6	1	2	2	11,506
Spanish Drummer	23	9	166	11	19	16	161,829
Spanish Drums	10	3	74	5	10	5	39,813
Sparkling Blade	3	1	8	2	2	2	23,230
Sparkling Jay	2	2	15	2	0	3	10,003
Spartan Victory	17	5	110	12	12	13	172,755
Speak	27	12	133	17	17	9	140,003
Speakerphone	1	1	2	1	1	0	34,400
Spearhead	1	1	7	1	0	2	6,737
Special Advice	5	3	45	6	4	2	32,666
Special Invention	3	1	11	2	0	2	3,333
Special Nash (IRE)	1	1	1	1	0	0	24,000
Spectacular Bid	30	12	156	16	11	12	271,237
Spectacular Round	4	1	24	2	0	2	12,943
Spectacular Son	2	1	8	1	0	0	1,856
Spectaculardynasty	5	2	52	2	2	7	26,866
Spectacularphantom	2	1	7	1	1	1	18,600
Spectrum (IRE)	10	3	51	5	4	4	122,140
Speeding Light (ARG)	3	1	23	2	3	6	14,856
Speeding Moment	7	3	35	3	2	4	44,791
Speedy Cure	11	5	69	7	6	6	56,119
Speedy Nijinsky	12	4	66	4	8	10	50,221
Speedy Valdez	1	1	8	2	2	0	21,800
Spellbound	4	3	32	4	4	3	41,848
Spellbounder	2	1	10	1	0	0	3,372
Spend a Buck	59	22	322	38	36	34	1,773,629
Spend a Franc	4	1	13	1	2	2	4,293
Spicy Monarch	1	1	13	1	3	2	11,603
Spinning World	40	20	229	33	32	35	1,056,279
Spinoza	3	1	17	1	1	2	15,002
Spirit Voices	5	2	40	2	4	4	16,375
Spiritbound	2	1	13	1	4	3	32,335
Sport Hunter	4	1	23	1	1	4	25,811
Sportful	4	1	26	1	2	2	27,841
Sports View	3	1	25	1	1	3	8,651
Spotter Bay	2	1	7	1	0	1	2,393
Sprizzo	5	2	26	3	2	4	42,120
Spruce Bouquet	11	5	75	10	4	9	192,208
Spunky Rascal	8	3	75	7	8	6	104,116
Spy Signal	14	8	127	13	13	13	177,640
Spy Wayne	1	1	13	2	2	1	10,928
Squadron Leader	14	7	118	11	14	7	192,237
Squan Lake	8	5	87	7	11	6	53,387
Sri Pekan	6	3	37	6	2	6	487,697
St. Forbes	4	3	41	5	7	3	58,796
St. Jovite	21	7	119	10	11	13	146,634
St. Valentine	4	2	30	2	4	3	18,355
Stack	50	16	312	29	32	32	988,058
Stacked Pack	1	1	11	1	0	1	6,327
Stacy's Knight	3	1	11	1	0	1	26,270
Staff Riot	5	1	27	1	2	2	9,779
Stage Colony	46	30	402	68	43	71	1,082,131
Stagecraft (GB)	5	1	31	1	4	4	285,148
Stake a Claim	7	3	31	3	2	3	26,702
Stalwars	38	18	339	33	44	36	327,372
Stalwart	30	20	239	38	27	27	361,067
Stalwart Boy	1	1	7	1	0	0	1,980
Standing On Edge	17	3	84	4	10	7	132,406
Star Choice	5	2	42	2	3	6	24,385

Sire	Perf	Wnrs	Sts	1st	2d	3d	Purses
Star de Naskra	36	14	242	22	35	35	298,717
Star Gallant	14	6	169	8	10	14	190,047
Star of Halo	4	2	22	6	3	1	32,740
Star of Ransom	2	1	8	1	0	1	8,194
Star of the Crop	17	11	136	23	22	18	327,907
Star of Valor	18	10	111	16	20	15	361,259
Star Programmer	12	2	29	2	2	3	46,398
Starbird Glacier	2	1	15	1	0	2	3,915
Starborough (GB)	2	1	6	1	2	1	52,120
Stark Ridge	11	9	74	10	12	14	163,044
State Craft	19	11	125	14	11	9	147,103
State Performer	15	8	95	10	8	12	122,100
Stately Cielo	10	2	50	3	2	11	109,315
Stately Slew	5	1	43	2	1	2	28,593
Stately Wager	12	7	87	12	7	19	56,287
Statesmanship	14	8	123	14	15	11	163,174
Stauder	11	8	84	15	10	11	134,102
Stay the Course	1	1	3	1	0	1	18,100
Steady Effort	2	2	18	2	3	3	9,390
Steady Naskra	4	1	36	2	9	3	23,714
Steel Robbing	15	5	97	12	11	10	78,077
Steinlen (GB)	7	5	68	11	14	10	178,368
Stephanotis	26	9	95	14	14	18	338,111
Stephen Got Even	22	7	76	8	6	13	314,967
Stephene Mon Amour	10	3	47	4	0	4	26,097
Stevie Ruckus	2	1	12	1	3	2	28,275
Stewing Sid	4	2	23	2	3	2	40,127
Sticks and Bricks	6	2	38	3	4	7	66,401
Stolen Gold	24	14	141	19	15	19	166,523
Stop the Fighting (IRE)	5	1	37	3	5	0	17,500
Stop the Music	19	11	162	20	18	18	169,004
Stop the Stage	11	6	76	9	13	12	58,096
Storada	8	2	28	2	4	4	14,350
Storm a Head	4	2	29	2	7	4	20,535
Storm and a Half	12	5	42	6	9	7	166,425
Storm Ashore	8	1	27	1	2	3	25,413
Storm Bird	5	3	33	4	2	4	45,017
Storm Blast	26	16	190	25	21	27	244,975
Storm Boot	174	96	1167	182	142	153	3,637,687
Storm Brewing	8	3	54	3	8	8	51,887
Storm Broker	73	38	474	54	68	60	969,482
Storm Cat	103	56	461	91	69	63	6,709,124
Storm Center	22	5	114	8	18	9	233,840
Storm Creek	159	76	1098	130	138	130	2,502,450
Storm of Angels	52	21	331	36	36	31	540,216
Storm of the Night	4	2	15	3	3	2	20,940
Stormin Fever	83	38	471	55	68	55	1,421,609
Stormy Atlantic	123	66	679	118	83	92	2,929,520
Stosky	3	2	17	3	0	4	29,362
Straight Man	33	12	105	15	18	16	413,206
Straight Polarity	1	1	9	1	1	1	7,632
Stravinsky	46	23	238	32	26	34	1,116,507
Strawberry Road (AUS)	5	1	24	1	6	1	29,146
Strawberry Sheikh	1	1	10	1	2	0	5,399
Streaker Gotchey	1	1	10	3	3	2	20,232
Strelka	4	1	44	1	3	2	19,828
Strike Gold	31	15	178	29	14	23	286,690
Strike the Anvil	11	6	88	9	7	7	108,878
Strike the Gold	33	19	287	28	38	44	451,539
Strodes Creek	50	32	448	66	68	64	1,017,087
Strolling Along	3	1	14	1	3	2	11,939
Strong Minded	7	4	37	5	6	7	19,603
Strong Performance	6	2	49	2	5	1	15,876
Struggler (GB)	37	20	273	32	34	31	728,818
Stuka	37	22	278	30	39	40	1,362,895
Stutz Blackhawk	37	14	286	31	22	26	276,679
Stutz Keys	3	2	26	4	3	5	30,676
Stylish Senor	2	1	14	2	2	1	16,407
Suave Prospect	99	56	858	119	95	113	2,142,040
Subordination	62	39	424	64	54	53	1,338,992
Successful Appeal	20	15	76	31	13	10	1,724,080
Suggest	21	11	144	21	19	26	373,414
Sultry Song	99	46	674	76	89	87	2,685,573
Sumba Wine	2	1	17	1	2	5	4,181
Summer of Storms	3	2	24	3	4	5	69,394
Summer Squall	71	38	509	71	55	58	2,074,850

Sire	Perf	Wnrs	Sts	1st	2d	3d	Purses
Summer Squire	1	1	9	1	1	1	7,484
Summing	10	3	38	3	4	2	19,269
Sumsing Sweetly	6	3	48	6	7	10	98,612
Sun Catcher	5	5	50	6	11	9	39,753
Sun Man	2	1	6	1	0	0	4,568
Sun Master	7	4	75	6	3	10	59,103
Sundance Ridge	10	4	49	7	11	7	219,010
Sunday Minister	24	11	108	16	9	14	230,770
Sunday Silence	6	2	21	3	4	3	263,908
Sundial	5	2	30	2	3	5	31,622
Sunny Feet	18	11	124	17	24	19	129,288
Sunny's Halo	92	31	576	56	71	55	699,809
Sunrise Shower	34	13	255	19	29	28	172,187
Sunset Ridge	7	2	48	3	4	7	30,386
Sunshine Forever	5	1	23	2	7	1	69,770
Sunshine Money	1	1	8	1	0	0	5,702
Super Gun	6	1	39	1	2	4	40,329
Super May	2	2	31	7	3	7	27,365
Super Native (IRE)	5	2	28	3	0	2	36,907
Super Seven	6	4	33	5	6	6	18,028
Super Special	8	4	45	9	8	3	213,813
Super Squall	2	2	13	3	0	1	26,672
Superbity	2	1	10	2	2	2	10,152
Superior Success	6	3	36	5	6	2	23,347
Supremo	54	25	352	44	38	52	688,733
Surachai	16	5	81	6	9	7	93,565
Sure Swift	2	1	12	1	1	0	3,867
Surumu (GER)	1	1	9	4	2	0	281,440
Survival	3	2	31	2	7	6	9,516
Sutter's Prospect	23	9	153	11	9	23	182,905
Swain (IRE)	31	12	124	14	10	6	457,428
Swamp King	3	2	40	7	5	12	90,656
Swear by Dixie	26	21	167	32	30	13	407,502
Swedaus	7	3	71	5	4	10	58,983
Sweetsouthernsaint	23	11	106	19	15	10	494,024
Swing and Miss	29	17	187	25	15	30	172,668
Swing Shift (GB)	8	5	83	12	6	11	88,735
Swing Till Dawn	2	2	8	3	0	2	21,395
Swingin Sway	3	2	21	3	1	5	14,442
Swiss Native	3	2	18	6	3	3	48,575
Swiss Trick	18	7	86	12	8	7	80,504
Swiss Yodeler	98	56	624	102	78	95	1,873,892
Sword Dance (IRE)	138	69	981	135	116	138	2,279,344
Sword Devil	3	1	8	2	0	0	14,100
Synastry	59	25	395	49	43	58	397,521
T. H. Bend	3	3	20	4	2	3	21,111
T. H. Fappiano	10	2	45	2	4	3	25,210
T. U. Slew	6	4	39	4	4	8	41,067
Tabasco Cat	102	57	745	102	113	92	3,362,777
Tabib	5	2	18	2	1	3	7,728
Taconic Road	11	5	91	10	8	7	95,361
Tactical Advantage	144	73	1093	129	154	156	2,240,866
Tactical Cat	55	29	328	54	45	58	1,569,377
Tagish	8	3	63	4	5	5	53,482
Tahoe City	27	13	200	19	29	24	140,897
Tail Toss	1	1	7	2	0	0	5,850
Tailings	3	2	15	6	1	1	44,437
Taj Alriyadh	11	3	67	4	8	9	35,610
Tajawa	6	3	49	7	4	3	42,293
Take Action	2	1	16	1	0	1	5,899
Take Me Out	97	58	737	105	75	91	2,043,087
Take That Step	14	10	144	12	13	13	208,763
Takur	8	3	37	5	4	5	75,732
Tale of the Cat	170	98	956	162	155	127	6,031,213
Talk Nice	3	3	34	7	5	5	96,426
Talkin Man	25	10	169	17	23	18	1,778,782
Tamarisk (IRE)	1	1	11	2	3	3	29,630
Tamayaz	85	36	677	62	69	90	1,050,070
Tammany	8	4	65	7	7	6	85,210
Tamourad	1	1	8	5	1	1	16,260
Tandem	2	1	7	1	0	1	5,362
Tank	10	2	39	2	5	10	101,665
Tank's Number	15	8	115	17	17	11	245,954
Taos Tewa Dancer	1	1	8	1	0	1	5,160
Tap N Snap	8	2	47	3	3	9	47,644
Tarakam	15	4	64	5	7	4	33,620

Sire	Perf	Wnrs	Sts	1st	2d	3d	Purses
Tarr Road	5	1	31	1	2	5	8,351
Tarsal	8	3	51	3	4	6	42,340
Tatum Canyon	7	3	57	9	8	7	48,078
Tax Collection	17	4	93	5	10	5	38,737
Taylor Road	1	1	18	1	0	2	8,690
Taylor's Special	4	1	35	1	1	6	8,311
Technology	40	18	269	32	27	30	454,284
Tejabo	43	20	362	33	34	46	863,323
Tejano	17	12	162	20	22	16	202,989
Tejano Run	51	28	409	44	68	71	1,378,199
Telemarket	2	1	25	2	2	5	43,784
Tella Fib	6	2	47	4	7	7	27,699
Temper Time	3	3	46	12	3	3	87,584
Temperence Hill	20	9	152	23	16	12	267,121
Temperence Two	3	2	24	2	1	2	15,892
Tempranero (CHI)	1	1	4	2	0	1	49,962
Temptor	35	15	268	25	27	32	246,252
Ten Gold Pots	3	3	24	4	2	3	46,892
Ten Keys	4	1	35	1	4	4	28,506
Ten Star Fleet	11	1	47	1	2	4	28,670
Tenesir	1	1	12	1	1	1	4,376
Tepee Creek	3	2	17	2	1	6	33,391
Tethra	62	27	391	44	36	58	1,305,850
Tex R. Rabbit	7	3	68	7	8	5	128,361
Texas City	33	13	227	21	35	29	317,559
Thank the Bank	3	1	30	2	2	3	36,100
That's a Nice	8	5	70	12	9	8	196,261
Thatching (IRE)	1	1	10	1	2	0	6,692
Thats a Nono	2	1	15	1	2	1	17,975
Thats Our Buck	50	19	365	39	33	35	585,281
The Cool Virginian	4	2	32	2	6	4	40,381
The Deep (IRE)	1	1	5	2	0	0	27,410
The Deputy (IRE)	16	5	57	5	6	9	89,025
The Gifted One	1	1	9	1	0	2	3,659
The Good Life	11	6	58	11	7	9	132,896
The Great Carl	1	1	4	1	2	0	2,500
The Great Shark	4	3	37	6	4	0	91,585
The Jogger	1	1	6	2	2	0	177,820
The Mad Doctor	1	1	12	2	3	0	3,901
The Name's Jimmy	42	18	287	39	24	23	539,860
The Pilot	2	1	23	1	7	4	39,582
The Prime Minister	46	23	305	37	39	35	454,081
The Red Rolls	1	1	14	1	2	1	8,628
The Silver Move	8	1	43	1	4	7	32,677
The Vid	28	19	269	34	30	28	377,967
The Wicked North	25	8	118	11	19	19	155,230
Theatre Critic (IRE)	14	4	76	4	1	5	40,510
Theatrical (IRE)	77	35	341	62	40	30	2,447,149
Thirty Six Red	3	1	22	1	1	3	9,702
This Bulls for You	2	1	14	2	1	2	47,278
This Picture	25	10	181	14	12	18	164,010
Thisjudgeisaprinc	3	3	37	11	5	4	87,760
Thisnearlywasmine	10	5	63	10	7	10	173,309
Thorn Dance	14	6	75	12	14	5	74,928
Thousand Ores	1	1	15	1	1	0	21,500
Three Coins Up	1	1	14	2	0	3	11,288
Three Torsions	3	2	24	3	2	3	26,582
Thug	3	2	30	2	4	4	41,280
Thunder Gulch	123	48	567	81	83	88	2,419,702
Thunder Puddles	16	6	104	15	12	10	321,533
Thunder Rumble	29	10	222	20	33	35	417,312
Thunder Runner	2	1	20	1	6	3	12,356
Thundering Force	1	1	10	5	1	1	214,400
Ti Valley	2	1	10	1	4	0	5,616
Tiffany Ice	23	12	125	23	10	11	104,934
Tiger Ridge	25	11	82	13	15	7	517,686
Tiger Star	2	1	20	4	3	2	17,599
Tiger Talk	7	1	40	1	4	1	12,198
Tiger Tiger	9	5	68	9	3	3	36,501
Tilt a Buck	1	1	8	1	1	0	6,697
Tilt the Odds	19	7	118	12	9	12	255,445
Tilt Up	1	1	11	1	3	5	22,561
Timber Country	4	1	10	3	3	0	623,056
Time Bandit	18	11	111	16	15	11	318,056
Timebank	19	10	128	16	19	15	154,983
Timeless Design	4	2	16	3	2	1	37,130
Timeless Native	5	4	40	8	2	2	36,297
Timeless Story	4	2	21	5	1	0	15,861
Tinners Way	65	29	455	43	63	48	537,021
Tip On Slew	5	1	38	3	3	1	8,160
Tirade	21	7	85	12	8	3	191,138
Titus Livius (FR)	2	1	6	1	0	1	31,368
Tizano (URU)	1	1	12	2	2	1	13,648
To a Wild Kris	2	1	20	1	5	2	27,622
To Freedom	8	2	46	5	6	5	81,556
To the Quick	5	3	28	4	3	3	24,869
Tobi D	1	1	8	2	1	1	3,964
Tom Cobbley	13	7	71	10	8	10	204,403
Tom Cruiser	5	5	49	8	8	8	92,695
Tommy the Hawk	1	1	1	1	0	0	2,700
Tomorrow's Slew	1	1	6	1	3	2	19,883
Tomorrows Cat	119	55	691	83	77	78	2,422,843
Tong Po	1	1	7	1	1	0	9,496
Tonga Boy	1	1	9	1	0	0	6,487
Toolighttoquit	43	25	335	39	40	55	647,758
Toooverprime (IRE)	2	1	27	1	5	3	8,076
Top Account	63	35	465	58	64	53	783,469
Top Secret Formula	6	1	37	2	6	1	63,441
Torcher	5	3	34	5	3	9	33,144
Torey Ridge	16	9	102	13	17	17	94,064
Torontonian	8	1	29	1	2	4	15,097
Torrential	56	19	366	32	32	49	553,515
Torsional	2	1	16	1	2	0	4,508
Tory Hole	6	1	36	1	2	4	26,149
Tossofthecoin	50	19	348	27	33	37	316,348
Totem and Taboo	11	5	51	6	6	3	45,069
Touch Gold	128	58	723	85	86	86	3,194,085
Touching Wood	2	1	16	1	3	1	22,550
Tough Call	13	4	84	7	7	10	108,666
Tough Knight	36	17	202	23	22	28	174,758
Tour d'Or	129	67	1017	120	138	114	1,879,527
Tower of Power	6	2	57	3	8	4	51,713
Town Caper	26	9	187	23	15	27	290,981
Track Barron	17	13	102	21	11	6	126,417
Track Rebel	19	7	105	10	14	11	132,874
Traffic Breaker	1	1	6	2	0	1	11,817
Traffic Zack	10	2	84	5	7	7	82,547
Trail City	18	10	67	16	10	9	340,730
Trail Class	1	1	17	4	3	4	18,592
Traitor	46	19	328	38	35	33	491,347
Tralos	2	1	6	1	1	1	7,091
Trancus	6	5	52	9	8	4	57,927
Trapeze Dancer	11	3	96	5	14	8	69,969
Trapp Mountain	24	7	189	11	13	16	91,120
Treasure Cove	9	2	36	2	3	1	34,420
Treasury	5	3	41	5	8	7	51,221
Tree	10	3	51	4	4	6	148,490
Treetopper	3	2	40	5	5	2	38,273
Trempolino	32	10	218	15	21	23	278,766
Trench Digger	1	1	8	1	0	2	10,886
Trenchant	2	1	12	1	2	3	28,279
Tres Hombres	3	1	5	1	0	0	5,575
Tresor du Mesnil (FR)	4	1	13	1	0	2	9,675
Tri for the Gold	14	6	120	13	18	8	257,548
Tri Line	6	2	37	3	6	3	41,616
Trick Me	17	5	91	6	6	8	68,459
Trick Question	4	2	38	3	6	4	15,084
Tricky Creek	82	44	618	74	82	83	1,051,028
Tricky Fun	34	16	219	25	31	28	385,466
Tricky Mister	6	3	52	4	6	7	97,852
Tricky Six	17	11	119	15	20	18	163,116
Tricolor	4	1	40	1	3	1	20,394
Tricon	19	8	140	13	17	15	143,353
Tricuit	5	3	54	5	6	7	49,279
Triple Sec	5	3	43	8	6	7	55,918
Trophy Hunter	13	3	77	5	2	4	65,468
Tropic Lightning	3	1	6	1	2	1	15,798
Trouble Onthe Line	9	3	54	3	1	5	20,037
Truce Maker	15	2	80	4	9	14	58,364
Truckee	35	15	217	26	31	13	458,297
Truculent Schular	18	1	90	1	4	9	51,146
True Confidence	13	1	43	1	2	4	24,561

Sire	Perf	Wnrs	Sts	1st	2d	3d	Purses
True West	1	1	13	2	2	1	17,674
Truluck	4	1	14	2	2	1	43,941
Truly Met	5	3	42	4	5	2	58,646
Truman C.	2	1	10	2	0	1	8,742
Truman's Tiffany	6	5	56	8	6	5	119,631
Trust No Lawyer	6	1	34	1	2	4	20,371
Tsunami Slew	8	3	38	3	4	2	16,964
Tuckerstown	2	2	36	2	6	7	25,498
Tuggles	1	1	9	2	0	1	7,011
Tunbridge Wells	1	1	14	1	1	0	10,608
Tunerup	5	1	38	2	8	5	30,949
Turbulant World	3	1	20	1	3	2	18,711
Turbulent Dancer	1	1	3	1	1	1	23,850
Turbulent Kris	31	19	257	24	33	49	320,562
Turkancer	1	1	5	1	0	0	4,817
Turkoman	70	30	472	53	47	54	519,487
Turkonoir	5	1	31	1	1	2	17,922
Turn West	10	4	69	7	7	9	143,575
Turnberry	2	1	7	1	0	1	1,203
Turtle Island	1	1	1	1	0	0	21,600
Tuxedo Suit	2	2	17	3	2	6	16,248
Twanger	1	1	14	2	0	3	19,549
Twilight Agenda	62	27	367	51	27	29	587,410
Twin Bridges	3	1	16	1	1	1	24,434
Twin Halo	4	1	13	1	3	0	28,055
Twin Rocket Power	2	1	9	1	0	0	7,385
Twin Spires	46	30	296	48	34	39	635,524
Twining	85	44	736	98	98	87	1,707,533
Two Bagger	1	1	8	1	0	0	2,760
Two Davids	14	3	84	5	4	10	55,642
Two Punch	132	78	919	134	101	126	2,875,021
Two Smart	6	4	36	6	4	3	88,753
Two's a Plenty	4	1	34	2	3	3	29,260
Tychonic (GB)	42	22	284	32	39	33	406,606
Tyler Wayne	6	3	32	3	3	3	31,979
U. S. Flag	10	4	61	6	3	6	63,058
Ulan	2	1	16	1	1	3	6,365
Ulises	16	5	100	11	12	8	190,035
Umrigar	4	3	27	8	2	2	205,808
Unaccounted For	112	49	723	94	90	84	1,680,609
Unbridled	104	46	467	68	68	58	3,873,111
Unbridled Desire	5	2	25	2	1	0	9,068
Unbridled Jet	26	2	84	2	11	11	133,071
Unbridled Success	5	3	26	6	0	2	30,801
Unbridled's Risk	13	7	79	10	11	12	124,656
Unbridled's Song	152	76	831	141	110	112	5,853,286
Uncas Chief	3	1	23	2	5	2	39,863
Undeniable	14	6	93	13	12	11	95,389
Under David's Wing	16	8	94	13	14	7	109,796
Unfuwain	1	1	7	1	0	0	58,470
Unite	27	12	228	25	36	34	247,411
Unome	11	6	45	9	9	5	86,670
Unpredictable	5	2	38	3	2	3	19,674
Unreal Currency	3	1	25	1	2	4	12,351
Unreal Zeal	118	69	985	114	129	112	1,653,357
Unsecured	2	2	30	2	3	1	15,874
Untold Gold	3	2	12	3	4	1	100,917
Untuttable	14	7	64	12	10	7	263,005
Unusual Heat	49	25	343	57	57	51	1,932,697
Unzipped	12	9	99	17	11	8	211,650
Upmost	3	2	23	3	5	2	22,383
Upping the Ante	21	9	201	16	22	25	484,074
Uprising	1	1	12	3	0	4	7,547
Urgent Request (IRE)	34	18	267	35	44	37	483,180
Urigo	1	1	7	2	0	3	37,894
Val d'Arno	1	1	2	1	0	0	12,600
Valanour (IRE)	2	1	7	2	2	0	272,800
Valdali (IRE)	8	3	48	6	6	7	28,955
Valeme	1	1	19	2	3	1	4,798
Valiant Lark	3	1	22	4	3	4	87,934
Valiant Nature	42	23	324	44	51	46	705,787
Valid Appeal	18	9	130	14	20	17	227,813
Valid Expectations	131	81	954	159	130	144	3,693,552
Valid Request	3	2	17	2	3	1	26,802
Valid Runner	2	1	17	4	1	2	93,515
Valid Trefaire	5	1	32	3	4	1	33,370
Valid Vengeance	9	5	70	7	14	8	122,837
Valid Victorious	6	1	35	2	2	6	39,091
Valid Wager	86	49	669	90	95	74	1,644,122
Valley Crossing	68	33	517	69	73	48	1,544,862
Valoric	2	1	17	1	2	0	21,745
Van Go	7	1	39	1	3	0	28,567
Varadavour (IRE)	3	2	22	2	0	1	10,803
Varennes	3	2	30	8	7	5	36,222
Variety Road	9	4	59	5	9	9	55,799
Vaudeville	36	17	202	35	24	23	328,894
Vendor	1	1	11	7	1	1	83,975
Ventriloquist	14	4	83	8	12	8	110,132
Verbatim Run	4	1	13	1	0	0	6,007
Verglas (IRE)	4	2	15	4	1	1	479,660
Verification	6	3	31	3	3	2	79,262
Vermont	29	12	185	20	29	16	340,304
Vernon Castle	3	1	15	1	0	1	4,340
Veronica's Sir	2	1	8	1	0	1	4,756
Vert Amande	2	1	10	1	1	2	8,785
Verzy	52	31	435	59	64	46	616,136
Vettori (IRE)	1	1	5	1	1	0	38,152
Via Lombardia (IRE)	13	5	74	9	9	5	127,669
Vicar	29	9	86	9	9	12	278,996
Vicksburg	12	4	77	8	5	9	132,343
Victor's Gent	8	2	46	3	2	5	16,206
Victorian Line	2	1	26	2	8	5	16,557
Victorious	9	7	89	17	12	8	153,491
Victory Gallop	85	49	531	81	79	91	2,784,293
Victory Speech	78	36	546	79	71	53	1,239,615
Video Ranger	9	5	71	8	7	14	99,004
Vigors	4	1	18	1	1	3	8,284
Vilzak	33	15	186	20	20	23	212,614
Vindictive Silence	3	2	22	3	2	3	16,205
Virginia Rapids	29	14	241	28	24	26	440,283
Vitello	1	1	6	2	1	0	9,047
Vittorioso	1	1	10	1	2	1	17,520
Viva Deputy	16	10	134	20	15	18	227,534
Vivid	2	2	24	6	4	5	83,035
Vixens Native	2	1	15	1	2	0	5,808
Vizard	5	3	36	4	2	5	28,638
Volksraad (GB)	3	1	11	1	5	2	85,760
Volochine (IRE)	2	1	7	1	0	0	16,100
Vouch for Me	4	1	28	3	1	2	36,122
Vying Victor	106	50	657	84	105	90	1,564,244
Wa Bert	9	7	61	8	1	7	82,031
Wabasha	2	1	16	2	5	2	13,636
Waco Connection	14	7	73	10	9	9	86,640
Wagon Limit	26	15	146	27	13	23	534,116
Wagon Master (FR)	1	1	13	2	1	1	15,024
Wajir	16	4	90	6	7	12	80,909
Wake Up Alarm	6	4	56	6	8	6	49,266
Waki Bob	8	4	47	7	2	5	78,543
Waki Warrior	24	9	165	25	14	15	191,720
Walesa	7	3	42	5	6	4	54,172
Wall Street Dancer	13	5	108	11	8	10	85,559
Wallenda	33	14	283	26	30	38	360,131
Walsingham	1	1	14	1	1	1	13,710
Walter Willy (IRE)	39	14	307	29	43	42	498,018
Waltzing Along	3	1	15	1	4	0	11,569
Wander Kind	4	1	25	1	2	3	6,627
Wanpum	8	4	75	7	11	13	44,245
Waquoit	73	37	511	60	63	67	1,319,279
War	7	2	31	2	1	2	19,052
War Chant	14	7	38	8	4	5	306,168
War Deputy	45	27	352	49	39	44	1,135,654
War Machine	4	1	20	1	4	3	17,756
War Secretary	3	1	33	1	6	1	42,169
Wardrobe Test	5	1	28	1	3	5	70,464
Warfield	6	3	45	7	13	4	23,374
Warner Jones	1	1	11	2	0	4	10,975
Warning (GB)	2	1	4	2	0	1	33,360
Warrantor	3	1	26	1	1	5	14,210
Water Bank	20	7	115	10	7	11	56,592
Water Moccasin	1	1	7	1	3	0	19,434
Wave Forever	1	1	12	2	2	0	8,651
Wavering Monarch	54	30	424	51	60	51	689,023

RECORDS OF SIRES

Sire	Perf	Wnrs	Sts	1st	2d	3d	Purses
Way West (FR)	71	41	480	71	40	54	1,116,773
Way Wild	7	1	48	3	2	6	29,206
Wayne County (IRE)	69	32	486	54	53	53	898,495
Wayne's Crane	54	22	403	36	47	54	340,371
Wee Thunder	9	4	68	5	6	6	44,349
Weekend Guest	58	33	374	63	43	49	779,753
Weiss Rennen	3	1	19	1	1	2	14,615
Wekiva Springs	130	79	956	127	120	114	2,113,529
Welbred Fred	1	1	8	2	0	2	66,882
Weldnaas	2	2	11	3	1	0	65,070
Well Decorated	50	30	416	46	58	44	552,732
Well Selected	4	1	22	1	0	2	42,459
Wertaloona	14	7	66	11	9	5	102,056
Weshaam	41	17	281	30	28	35	891,243
West Acre	43	30	279	61	41	30	983,066
West Buoyant	15	3	86	6	5	5	61,507
West by West	147	81	1237	156	146	161	3,002,281
Westbridge	1	1	11	3	1	1	43,273
Western Borders	24	11	143	13	18	11	336,574
Western Cat	38	19	298	32	27	24	659,259
Western City	3	1	9	1	0	2	3,400
Western Echo	31	18	279	37	29	26	430,452
Western Expression	20	7	60	8	9	7	384,961
Western Fame	46	28	255	42	34	35	756,286
Western Front	1	1	2	1	0	0	7,935
Western Gentleman	19	12	154	23	24	12	267,004
Western Miner	12	2	74	5	6	6	52,597
Western Playboy	27	13	194	15	22	24	312,968
Western Regent	1	1	9	1	3	1	8,474
Western Trader	5	1	31	1	1	9	15,610
Western Trick	40	15	236	24	25	35	284,600
Westminster	14	7	91	15	18	9	215,674
Whadjathink	6	3	34	9	1	4	219,237
What a Shock	5	1	29	4	3	2	35,422
What a Spell	10	4	51	9	5	7	81,937
Whatever For	2	1	9	1	1	1	16,774
Wheatly Hall	15	2	79	6	6	4	71,413
Wheaton	101	64	755	136	102	102	1,910,402
Whiskey Wisdom	77	42	528	69	65	63	2,745,065
White Mischief	1	1	9	3	2	2	35,534
White Rammer	2	1	15	3	1	1	34,967
White Spade (GB)	3	1	8	1	0	0	7,962
White Tie Tryst	4	1	35	3	3	6	25,650
Whitebrush	9	5	61	8	6	6	77,264
Whitney Tower	69	31	491	52	50	51	649,791
Whiz Along	10	7	120	12	7	12	150,347
Who's John Galt	5	2	27	3	6	4	35,048
Whosinfront	4	1	27	1	4	1	8,347
Why Change	4	1	20	1	3	1	24,407
Wild Again	111	56	762	99	111	91	3,083,844
Wild Colony	7	3	38	5	8	6	45,305
Wild Deputy	40	24	317	39	52	41	534,034
Wild Escapade	50	33	423	63	56	48	966,979
Wild Event	48	27	300	46	38	37	1,267,433
Wild Gale	4	3	35	5	4	1	116,095
Wild Gambler	2	1	8	1	1	2	27,000
Wild Gold	50	34	332	52	51	49	679,727
Wild Invader	22	12	144	22	21	16	253,215
Wild Johnny	3	2	17	2	0	1	7,362
Wild Kiss	6	1	49	1	4	4	41,733
Wild Rush	123	73	835	132	107	112	5,063,397
Wild Syn	22	9	112	16	11	9	166,736
Wild Wonder	50	21	341	34	47	42	709,774
Wild Zone	140	69	866	106	102	104	1,803,514
Wilde Rufo (GB)	4	3	34	4	4	2	50,543
Wildly Irish	1	1	8	2	0	0	10,582
Will Be Dancing	8	3	44	4	6	6	36,730
Will Cut	1	1	10	2	0	1	9,234
Will's Way	66	35	496	68	64	52	1,751,595
William Lawrence	2	1	10	1	1	1	4,215
Williamstown	74	37	561	60	63	70	1,311,405
Willing Worker	4	1	28	1	5	3	15,592
Willowy Ambassador	5	3	33	4	2	3	39,823
Win Lose Or Draw	3	1	14	1	1	4	29,418
Win M All	9	2	53	7	6	5	139,228
Wind Chill	3	3	36	7	10	6	97,058
Wind Flyer	4	3	26	4	7	4	52,966
Wind Whipper	10	5	42	5	4	3	51,896
Windsworth	1	1	1	1	0	0	5,850
Windy'slittleman	5	1	16	1	2	2	10,553
Wing Commander	4	1	35	1	0	4	12,034
Winged Love (IRE)	1	1	2	1	0	1	7,000
Winning	2	2	19	2	7	2	124,380
Winter Halo	22	9	132	17	12	11	234,175
Winthrop	21	10	116	21	10	12	209,003
Wire Me Collect	11	2	29	2	3	3	42,897
Wised Up	13	5	57	6	9	6	173,748
With Approval	147	78	952	138	104	103	3,076,229
With It	7	5	70	9	13	10	73,500
Wolf Power (SAF)	79	37	554	57	66	61	977,360
Wolf Touch	10	6	79	10	10	13	87,054
Won Song	8	1	38	1	3	2	47,169
Wood	2	2	13	2	4	1	23,654
Wood Reply	5	4	36	6	9	5	41,632
Woodland Drive	3	1	14	1	2	0	5,264
Woodman	102	27	595	36	60	60	923,319
Woody Win	7	1	25	1	1	5	10,391
Working Late	2	1	17	1	1	3	15,678
World Appeal	18	9	140	16	13	17	96,435
World Stage (IRE)	56	22	441	34	47	37	482,983
Worldly	3	1	11	1	0	1	4,961
Wrong Way Joe	3	1	16	1	2	0	3,182
Xray	11	4	81	6	16	9	164,293
Yachtie (AUS)	1	1	9	2	0	1	33,640
Yankee Fan	31	14	213	27	30	20	203,062
Yankee Victor	27	12	86	13	15	8	399,274
Yarnallton Native	1	1	5	1	2	0	4,972
Yaros	1	1	9	1	2	1	6,758
Yarrow Brae	55	29	400	51	62	57	1,082,194
Yates	3	2	10	2	0	2	20,657
Yellow Creek	1	1	24	5	5	2	25,716
Yendaka	1	1	16	5	3	3	52,235
Yes I'm Blue	4	2	31	5	4	6	61,163
Yes It's True	40	15	141	25	12	31	1,424,382
Yesterdays Hero	4	2	31	4	1	3	29,713
Yeti	4	2	35	2	6	8	25,738
Yoh May Kenta	3	2	26	3	1	4	57,875
Yoonevano	26	7	126	13	20	16	471,134
You and I	92	41	543	61	66	64	1,141,570
You Know How It Is	3	1	12	1	0	1	9,680
Youmadeyourpoint	13	5	72	12	9	6	114,521
Young Devil	9	7	62	12	9	3	177,004
Young Ralph	11	3	94	4	11	15	62,557
Young Turk	9	5	62	7	7	2	94,207
Your Majestic	2	1	16	1	1	0	12,863
Yukon Son	2	1	11	1	2	0	2,423
Z Z Cat	32	14	217	23	29	22	271,023
Zafarrancho (ARG)	17	8	141	15	12	21	221,944
Zafonic	14	6	86	12	3	9	263,529
Zagor	7	1	60	1	2	4	23,795
Zalipour	4	1	16	1	3	2	18,744
Zamboni	8	4	47	6	5	7	60,158
Zamindar	16	2	35	2	2	3	59,502
Zanferrier	2	1	13	2	4	1	21,151
Zapped	5	2	35	5	3	2	19,271
Zarbyev	70	35	503	54	63	64	1,187,828
Zayyani (IRE)	1	1	6	1	4	1	135,270
Zede	11	2	53	2	4	4	44,594
Zeeruler	13	6	102	7	9	10	62,984
Zen	2	1	16	3	1	4	123,126
Zen's Hang Up	2	1	18	1	0	0	5,506
Zieten	4	1	33	2	4	7	51,743
Ziggy's Boy	1	1	12	1	0	0	5,870
Zigiante	3	2	23	5	5	2	92,265
Zignew	15	9	121	16	16	21	197,769
Zigtrick (FR)	2	1	6	1	1	1	4,780
Zuppardo's Crown	5	1	42	2	3	8	21,650
Zuppardo's Future	9	4	53	6	9	5	96,732
Zuppardo's Prince	47	18	323	25	27	32	367,812

2004 RECORDS OF JUVENILE SIRES

The record of each juvenile sire represented by at least one winning thoroughbred or more who raced in the United States or Canada in 2004, showing his total performers, number of winning performers, the number of times they started and their total placings and earnings.

RECORDS OF JUVENILE SIRES

Juvenile Sire	Perf	Wnrs	Sts	1st	2d	3d	Purses
A. P Jet	46	16	145	20	20	13	$772,446
A.P. Indy	19	7	50	7	6	6	547,981
Abaginone	16	4	59	6	9	10	187,939
Abstract	6	2	13	2	0	2	16,695
Academy Award	10	2	29	2	5	1	49,701
Academyawardwinner	2	1	8	1	0	0	8,263
Accelerator	19	7	65	8	13	5	244,228
Acceptable	8	1	24	1	2	7	57,163
Activist	4	2	11	2	2	1	22,189
Adams Trail	3	1	7	2	0	0	8,510
Adcat	9	2	41	2	5	6	56,720
Adios Mundo	5	1	17	1	2	1	48,132
Adonis	7	1	20	1	2	3	33,774
Afternoon Deelites	31	12	110	17	19	20	600,556
Aggressive Chief	9	4	43	4	5	8	74,057
Alfaari	6	2	17	2	4	1	53,094
Aljabr	5	3	10	5	0	0	65,945
All Thee Power	3	2	10	5	0	0	80,164
Alladin Rib	1	1	3	1	0	0	6,134
Alleged Stardom	2	1	6	1	0	2	5,830
Allen Charge	3	2	6	2	1	1	29,320
Allen's Prospect	40	11	130	14	21	20	414,045
Allied Forces	7	1	25	1	1	3	29,403
Aloha Prospector	5	1	6	1	0	1	10,205
Alphabet Soup	15	4	44	5	5	6	106,744
Always Silver	4	1	20	1	0	2	10,140
Alybro	3	1	13	1	1	0	18,389
Alydeed	7	3	22	3	5	2	219,334
Alyten	1	1	5	1	0	0	6,825
Ameri Valay	5	1	22	1	2	3	25,990
American Champ	7	1	23	1	1	2	9,455
American Chance	23	7	79	13	8	11	365,335
American Tribute	1	1	5	2	0	1	6,305
Ancient Oaks	1	1	2	1	0	1	1,584
Anees	19	5	55	6	4	7	280,239
Anet	10	2	30	2	5	4	52,743
Anjiz	5	2	24	5	1	1	52,586
Announce	8	2	18	3	0	5	48,808
Anziyan	5	1	15	1	0	3	15,890
Apollo	6	3	17	3	1	1	39,159
Appealing Skier	8	5	29	7	4	5	110,632
Arch	17	5	63	6	4	10	210,536
Archers Bay	19	7	50	7	6	5	346,801
Artax	25	8	76	8	5	7	144,093
Artema (IRE)	2	1	3	1	1	0	8,286
Ascot Knight	19	2	51	2	6	5	105,145
Assembly Dancer	1	1	4	3	1	0	64,100
Atticus	6	1	7	2	0	2	31,625
Autocracy	4	1	10	1	1	2	24,815
Avenue of Flags	6	1	15	1	0	2	22,279
Awad	5	1	16	2	2	0	25,725
Awesome Again	23	9	65	10	12	6	1,100,214
Awesome Cat	3	2	10	2	0	2	31,165
B. G.'s Drone	1	1	7	1	1	2	7,799
B. Hoedown	2	1	4	1	0	0	18,540
B. J.'s Mark	4	1	9	3	0	1	69,345
Badge	8	3	30	4	6	3	100,581
Bag	14	6	44	6	9	5	145,935
Banjo	1	1	2	1	0	0	8,899
Banker's Gold	17	6	67	7	5	5	123,752
Banks Well	1	1	8	1	3	1	15,665
Baquero	16	6	54	6	10	8	64,444
Barberstown	1	1	6	1	0	0	9,675
Barkerville	5	1	15	1	0	2	33,948
Barricade	8	5	31	9	2	3	142,762
Bartok (IRE)	32	13	114	21	19	9	422,829
Basic Rate	3	1	6	2	1	0	25,915
Basket Weave	18	12	69	14	7	6	156,826
Bates Motel	3	1	15	1	1	3	15,920
Bay Street Star	4	2	13	4	1	2	34,359
Bayou Hebert	3	2	16	3	3	2	67,991
Beau Genius	11	1	17	1	0	1	19,633
Beefchopper	4	2	12	2	0	2	11,735
Behrens	6	3	23	3	4	1	70,045
Belek	3	1	9	1	1	0	22,160
Belong to Me	16	8	44	9	8	6	280,775
Benchmark	23	5	48	5	2	7	89,708
Benton Creek	8	4	35	5	3	8	49,744
Bernstein	18	11	60	17	18	6	525,467
Bertrando	21	12	73	17	5	6	311,089
Best of Luck	27	2	86	2	4	5	67,958
Bianconi	10	3	39	4	6	4	165,168
Big Sky Chester	2	2	8	4	0	0	33,638
Big Splash	5	3	24	3	4	4	75,348
Bionic Prospect	1	1	2	2	0	0	9,000
Birdonthewire	5	1	15	1	1	1	24,784
Black Mackee	4	1	13	1	4	1	10,727
Blare of Trumpets	3	3	9	3	1	0	42,618
Blazing Fire	6	3	23	3	6	2	39,843
Blind Man's Bluff	4	3	10	3	0	3	49,057
Blowin de Turn	3	2	8	2	2	1	23,834
Blumin Affair	13	7	38	10	0	4	162,875
Blushing Star	2	1	5	1	0	0	11,970
Boanerges	5	1	17	1	1	4	21,287
Bold Anthony	6	1	15	1	2	0	24,300
Bold Badgett	14	4	59	6	5	11	188,096
Bold Executive	9	2	26	4	6	1	366,015
Bold n' Flashy	18	3	57	3	6	6	144,269
Bold Pac Man	2	1	10	1	1	0	15,573
Bon Point (GB)	2	1	7	1	1	0	9,145
Bonus Time Cat	4	1	12	1	0	0	6,881
Boomerang	2	1	6	1	3	1	41,323
Boone's Mill	6	1	15	1	1	0	9,770
Born Wild	6	2	21	2	1	1	25,883
Boston Harbor	19	8	59	10	8	8	332,388
Boundary	12	4	31	7	4	6	353,237
Brave Act (GB)	1	1	2	1	0	0	106,380
Brave Romane	3	1	13	3	0	0	28,327
Bright Launch	12	5	51	5	4	4	76,078
Brilliant Blue	1	1	5	3	0	1	24,076
Broad Brush	9	1	27	1	6	4	87,588
Brushed On	7	1	29	1	3	6	68,190
Buck Strider	9	1	37	1	4	1	29,883
Buckhar	1	1	4	1	0	0	8,970
Buddy	3	2	13	2	1	0	38,941
Bugatti	1	1	11	1	0	2	11,644
Bugatti Reef (IRE)	7	1	23	1	0	0	34,950
Bull Inthe Heather	3	1	9	1	2	1	13,934
Burbank	5	2	20	3	0	2	40,570
Cache In	5	1	16	1	2	3	18,402
Cahill Road	13	5	45	6	3	8	73,734
Caller I. D.	7	2	32	2	0	2	40,950
Canaveral	8	4	35	4	4	4	40,140
Candi's Gold	3	1	8	1	3	1	119,700
Candyman Bee	1	1	6	1	1	0	10,073
Canyon Run	1	1	2	1	0	0	11,520
Cape Canaveral	30	11	106	18	25	12	864,072
Cape Town	20	12	76	16	14	10	456,305
Capitalimprovement	1	1	5	2	0	1	28,520
Capote	10	4	41	5	6	7	220,962
Capote's Prospect	8	3	20	3	1	2	37,905
Captain Bodgit	16	2	59	2	8	8	85,864
Captain Collins (IRE)	3	1	14	1	0	0	15,226
Capture the Gold	14	3	49	3	7	8	174,410
Carnivalay	5	2	14	2	1	0	31,725
Carson City	35	15	108	19	13	14	806,117
Cartwright	24	10	88	11	8	7	270,254
Cascadian	5	1	10	1	2	2	15,661
Cash Deposit	11	4	27	4	4	2	22,307
Castle Guard	1	1	10	1	0	0	8,654
Cat Doctor	2	1	10	2	1	1	32,375
Cat Strike	5	1	17	1	1	1	9,816
Cat Thief	19	8	57	8	8	7	238,135
Cat's Career	17	4	54	4	6	8	77,904
Category Five	11	4	34	4	4	8	60,730
Catienus	31	19	120	23	13	11	451,551
Catonie Choke	2	2	5	2	2	0	12,649
Catrail	6	2	10	2	1	1	23,187

Juvenile Sire	Perf	Wnrs	Sts	1st	2d	3d	Purses
Cee's Tizzy	15	7	49	8	8	4	326,067
Chanate	14	3	35	4	5	4	42,934
Chapel Creek	5	3	9	3	1	1	30,408
Charismatic	37	10	112	11	7	10	491,531
Charlie Barley	2	2	8	2	1	0	19,503
Chayim	1	1	1	1	0	0	9,920
Chelsey Cat	4	1	14	1	0	1	7,025
Chequer	5	2	16	2	2	1	39,645
Cherokee Run	29	13	101	17	8	13	530,736
Chester House	25	9	67	11	9	7	326,963
Chief Seattle	24	9	74	10	9	12	304,361
Chimes Band	11	5	30	6	3	3	103,685
Chopin	2	1	8	1	3	0	48,351
Christmas Storm	1	1	1	1	0	0	6,283
Chullo (ARG)	2	1	5	1	0	1	12,047
Ciano Cat	12	4	30	4	4	4	82,398
Cien Fuegos	5	2	24	2	5	1	70,286
Cimarron Secret	16	7	76	7	5	12	90,057
Circulating	4	3	11	3	1	2	42,555
Cisco Road	2	1	7	1	0	1	4,879
Citidancer	6	3	21	7	4	5	347,410
Claramount	5	1	9	1	0	2	20,253
Classi Envoy	2	1	5	1	0	0	10,000
Classic Cat	3	2	14	2	1	1	17,795
Classy Prospector	2	1	8	1	0	0	10,553
Clever Trick	14	6	46	6	8	5	122,206
Close Up	5	2	14	3	0	0	69,500
Cobra King	3	1	10	1	1	3	29,642
Codys Key	4	1	8	1	1	0	2,125
Cohiba	6	2	21	2	1	3	23,983
Colony Light	16	6	84	11	18	11	308,347
Colway Rally (GB)	1	1	3	1	1	0	10,756
Combat Ready	2	2	8	3	1	0	50,020
Comeonmom	2	1	6	1	0	1	21,080
Comet Shine	6	1	18	1	4	0	20,004
Comic Strip	18	5	50	6	7	5	206,174
Commendable	14	6	45	7	3	7	113,743
Commitisize	7	2	29	3	1	6	57,066
Compadre	10	5	44	5	5	3	183,823
Comstock Lode	7	1	32	2	3	2	31,303
Concern	10	3	31	3	3	3	49,685
Concerto	12	8	54	9	4	9	290,756
Concorde's Tune	18	8	79	11	10	9	307,907
Confide	12	7	45	10	6	4	171,361
Conquistador Cielo	15	5	44	6	1	6	128,193
Consigliere (GB)	4	1	11	1	2	0	9,826
Constant Demand	3	3	11	3	0	2	38,200
Conte Di Savoya	4	2	13	3	1	1	46,988
Conveyor	5	2	16	3	1	1	93,200
Coordinator	10	1	24	1	3	2	19,515
Coronado's Quest	16	5	54	8	11	4	343,170
Corslew	3	1	11	1	3	0	26,768
Corwyn Bay (IRE)	7	4	32	7	4	0	96,627
Count On Steve	2	1	10	1	0	1	10,570
Count the Time	15	6	49	7	6	3	167,625
Courageous Leader	1	1	2	1	0	0	1,140
Coverallbases	3	1	13	2	3	1	28,301
Cozzene	9	5	27	6	2	4	233,982
Crafty Dude	3	1	9	2	3	1	28,439
Crafty Friend	27	8	95	8	9	17	201,732
Crafty Prospector	13	2	39	2	4	6	48,952
Creative	2	1	5	1	0	2	12,460
Crowd Pleaser	19	3	54	3	4	8	68,567
Crown Ambassador	4	4	16	4	4	1	73,686
Crown Attorney	5	2	12	2	0	3	48,189
Crowning Season (GB)	3	1	11	1	3	1	12,224
Crowning Storm	13	2	36	2	8	3	97,897
Crusader Sword	5	1	16	1	1	1	21,252
Crypto Star	7	2	16	2	0	2	26,905
Cryptoclearance	26	6	102	6	13	16	233,632
Cutlass Fax	2	1	9	2	2	2	39,570
D. J. Cat	2	1	5	1	1	1	11,530
Dance Brightly	21	6	81	9	17	7	286,941
Dance Centre	3	1	6	1	0	0	3,590

Sire	Perf	Wnrs	Sts	1st	2d	3d	Purses
Dance Floor	9	1	16	1	2	3	24,226
Dance Master	7	4	25	7	5	7	383,496
Dancing Crown	1	1	6	1	2	0	25,140
Dancinwiththedevil	3	3	11	3	2	1	40,135
Danjur	12	7	35	12	5	6	120,297
Danton	1	1	5	1	1	0	6,568
Danzatore	10	1	40	1	4	2	35,094
Danzig	7	4	15	5	2	0	212,061
Darn That Alarm	4	2	19	2	2	0	78,124
Dashing Lad	1	1	3	1	0	1	17,750
Dashing Writer	1	1	3	1	0	0	1,650
Dawn Quixote	2	1	7	1	0	0	8,270
Dayjur	3	1	8	1	2	1	30,923
De Guerin	4	2	15	2	0	1	41,856
De Niro	4	2	12	2	0	0	19,000
Deerhound	3	1	7	1	1	0	38,250
Defrere	7	1	21	2	1	1	52,845
Delineator	11	1	25	1	4	3	43,993
Demaloot Demashoot	10	4	34	5	4	5	177,210
Demidoff	3	1	12	2	2	1	38,251
Demons Begone	11	5	37	5	5	6	50,939
Denouncer	2	1	10	1	2	0	34,342
Deodar	3	1	8	1	1	0	6,995
Deposit Ticket	7	2	35	2	2	6	36,531
Deputy Commander	19	4	60	4	11	5	202,475
Deputy Diamond	25	7	94	7	6	8	127,081
Deputy Minister	17	6	49	8	5	7	330,450
Derby Wish	4	2	18	2	1	3	47,425
Desert God	4	3	11	4	1	0	45,460
Desert Rival	2	1	9	2	0	3	27,254
Desert Wine	2	1	11	1	5	3	23,887
Devil Begone	10	2	28	2	2	4	36,458
Devil His Due	38	14	128	17	20	19	430,551
Devil On Ice	3	1	7	2	0	0	18,788
Devil Power	1	1	14	1	2	0	36,479
Devil's Bag	11	2	22	2	1	3	71,930
Devious Course	3	2	10	3	0	3	31,700
Devon Lane	12	3	25	3	2	3	37,426
Devonwood	15	5	46	8	8	9	153,358
Diamond	11	3	29	3	8	2	103,980
Diamond Sword	1	1	2	1	1	0	7,206
Digamist	2	1	5	1	0	2	17,316
Digging In	4	1	11	1	1	2	16,689
Diligence	7	4	21	5	2	3	109,700
Din's Dancer	7	1	21	1	1	2	16,105
Direct Hit	8	4	25	5	4	1	79,435
Distant View	3	1	8	1	0	0	18,455
Distinctive Pro	16	1	37	1	2	4	71,685
Distorted Humor	28	11	87	14	12	13	451,206
Dixie Brass	10	3	32	4	1	8	160,380
Dixie Union	21	11	93	15	21	12	695,666
Dixieland Band	14	5	36	6	5	6	361,835
Dixieland Brass	8	1	16	1	0	5	15,881
Dixieland Heat	12	4	39	7	5	2	92,184
Doneraile Court	21	11	81	13	14	7	423,669
Double Honor	37	20	177	30	17	26	575,537
Double Niner	1	1	5	1	0	0	5,375
Dove Hunt	7	1	22	1	3	3	38,975
Down the Aisle	11	2	37	2	1	6	39,220
Downtown Seattle	3	1	15	2	1	4	51,743
Dr. Caton	15	5	51	5	3	4	84,349
Dreamfield	3	3	17	3	4	2	25,477
Dynaformer	26	7	81	8	10	9	257,631
Eastern Echo	5	1	16	1	2	1	11,196
Eastern Memories (IRE)	2	1	13	1	1	0	8,133
Eastover Court	4	2	14	4	3	0	114,692
Editor's Note	13	4	47	4	5	5	67,944
Eishin Storm	3	1	10	1	1	1	11,694
El Amante	5	2	14	3	1	0	87,249
El Prado (IRE)	13	2	32	2	2	3	82,734
El Sancho	3	1	17	1	3	1	27,360
Elnadim	3	3	10	4	1	0	117,110
Eltish	15	5	67	8	7	6	158,390
Elusive Quality	10	3	21	4	5	2	213,303

Sire	Perf	Wnrs	Sts	1st	2d	3d	Purses
Emerald Creme	3	3	19	3	5	4	52,953
Epic Honor	7	1	29	2	2	5	29,818
Eskimo	4	2	19	3	1	4	52,416
Esplanade Ridge	2	1	5	2	0	1	29,423
Esteem	3	2	9	2	1	0	23,473
Evansville Slew	16	7	54	8	7	7	149,720
Evening Kris	2	1	8	1	2	3	53,927
Event of the Year	18	3	50	4	9	5	235,656
Excavate	13	5	47	7	5	8	183,008
Excess Is Good	2	1	5	1	0	0	9,101
Exclusive Encore	2	1	5	1	0	0	5,292
Exclusivengagement	2	1	3	1	0	0	11,070
Expelled	10	4	37	4	4	0	76,145
Expense Account	4	1	9	1	0	1	10,715
Expensive Decision	1	1	3	1	2	0	41,000
Exploit	32	10	125	13	12	14	310,082
Fabulous Champ	11	4	46	5	5	6	89,364
Fabulous Frolic	14	1	52	2	4	5	46,385
Fair American	2	1	3	1	0	0	8,552
Falstaff	6	2	31	5	3	4	206,826
Family Calling	25	11	118	13	15	25	242,885
Fargo	4	3	14	5	3	1	74,997
Fast Ferdie	3	2	11	2	5	2	54,800
Fast Play	11	2	37	2	7	6	68,681
Favorite Trick	16	7	43	8	7	8	201,656
Faygo	2	1	12	1	0	0	29,163
Fenter	3	2	13	2	1	2	25,930
Ferrara	2	1	5	1	0	0	5,516
Fiend	2	1	11	2	1	2	85,305
Fiery Best	1	1	3	1	1	0	22,000
Fighting Fantasy	2	1	4	1	1	0	11,670
Fine n' Majestic	8	3	79	3	7	7	57,180
Finest Hour	12	2	34	3	3	6	133,547
Fit to Fight	15	8	60	13	9	5	270,763
Flight Forty Nine	3	1	8	1	2	0	24,196
Fly So Free	19	2	60	2	5	10	76,930
Flying Chevron	4	2	18	2	3	3	53,117
Flying Continental	7	2	21	3	2	4	146,408
Flying Victor	8	3	40	3	9	4	54,843
Flying With Eagles	12	3	42	3	5	5	34,079
Foligno	1	1	5	1	2	0	13,230
For Really	3	1	6	2	1	1	7,979
Forest Gazelle	3	1	16	2	2	2	38,660
Forest Wildcat	28	15	101	18	13	15	547,562
Forestry	16	7	48	10	5	2	278,063
Forever Silver	2	1	11	1	0	4	36,453
Formal Dinner	15	9	66	11	11	6	180,033
Formal Gold	20	9	77	10	12	19	340,695
Fort Chaffee	2	1	8	1	3	2	30,523
Fortunate Prospect	22	12	99	17	8	9	315,093
Forty Niner	1	1	8	1	1	3	51,798
Forty Won	6	2	18	2	4	3	67,412
Foxtrail	24	8	91	15	11	12	739,773
Free At Last	22	10	72	13	7	9	131,396
Free House	11	3	44	4	11	5	104,243
French Legionaire	1	1	7	1	0	0	7,222
French Parliament	3	1	8	2	0	2	39,715
Friendly Lover	31	6	114	8	14	17	287,016
Fruition	4	1	9	2	3	2	67,246
Furiously	1	1	4	2	0	1	144,740
Fusaichi Accele	5	3	24	3	5	2	55,745
Fusaichi Pegasus	22	7	54	14	8	9	923,385
Future Storm	9	2	23	3	4	2	81,213
Game Coin	1	1	4	1	1	0	10,400
Game Plan	11	6	43	8	4	10	171,785
Gen Stormin'norman	4	3	14	3	4	0	48,960
General Gem	3	1	6	1	2	1	10,700
General Meeting	10	6	31	6	5	2	199,690
General Royal	18	5	70	6	5	9	197,520
Gentlemen (ARG)	11	2	36	2	6	3	99,274
Get Me Out	1	1	3	1	0	1	19,530
Ghazi	1	1	5	1	0	2	9,925
Ghostly Moves	12	1	38	1	7	6	71,378
Giant Asset	1	1	5	1	0	0	6,844

Juvenile Sire	Perf	Wnrs	Sts	1st	2d	3d	Purses
Giant's Causeway	17	2	29	2	5	1	113,805
Gilded Time	24	14	90	17	11	15	478,366
Glitterman	23	6	75	7	9	14	285,580
Go for Gin	18	3	45	3	2	6	48,838
Go Gary Go	5	1	13	2	1	1	20,504
Go West	2	1	8	1	1	0	39,400
Gold Alert	7	3	39	3	3	3	65,051
Gold Case	17	5	45	7	5	6	234,953
Gold Fever	14	6	46	7	7	6	156,007
Gold Market	5	4	20	5	3	3	80,172
Gold Meridian	6	2	13	2	0	2	12,081
Gold Regent	11	5	49	6	10	9	138,663
Gold Ruler	7	1	19	1	5	0	14,570
Gold Token	7	1	22	1	2	1	36,697
Gold Tribute	8	3	28	5	9	4	90,893
Golden Gear	12	4	33	6	2	7	160,682
Golden Legend	3	2	13	2	1	1	12,876
Golden Missile	24	6	66	7	7	5	332,496
Goldminers Gold	2	2	6	2	0	1	58,103
Gone for Real	1	1	4	1	1	1	39,450
Gone Hollywood	2	2	9	3	3	1	53,206
Gone West	12	6	30	7	0	3	225,192
Good and Tough	15	7	44	11	8	6	321,588
Goodbye Doeny	8	2	25	2	3	4	59,322
Gran's Halo	1	1	9	1	1	0	7,765
Grand Circus Park	6	2	22	2	3	4	53,293
Grand Slam	25	9	63	13	14	7	396,762
Great Ovation (IRE)	4	1	14	1	0	0	5,253
Greenwood Lake	14	7	68	8	8	8	175,395
Grindstone	16	3	32	3	4	5	85,316
Gringo Pilot	1	1	5	2	0	1	7,685
Groomstick	6	3	21	3	1	2	42,705
Groovy Jett	2	1	3	1	0	0	6,315
Ground Stroke	4	1	11	1	1	1	14,898
Guarani	1	1	5	1	2	1	10,965
Gulch	10	5	40	6	4	9	161,047
Guys From Space	2	1	6	1	1	1	17,020
Hadif	18	10	92	12	18	12	175,285
Haint	3	2	13	2	0	1	18,448
Half a Year	1	1	2	1	0	0	11,800
Half Term	3	1	7	1	0	1	9,170
Halo's Image	25	6	110	9	15	23	298,651
Halory Hunter	2	1	11	3	1	2	63,322
Halos and Horns	5	1	18	1	2	5	33,700
Happy Trap	2	1	4	1	0	0	6,773
Hay Halo	4	1	17	1	1	4	49,367
Haymarket (GB)	3	1	4	1	0	1	7,950
Hazaam	5	1	25	2	1	9	34,313
He's Tops	13	7	47	9	8	6	108,285
Helmsman	12	7	30	8	5	6	109,407
Here We Come	10	3	29	3	3	1	31,875
Hermes	1	1	2	1	0	0	5,525
Hesabull	11	4	43	4	5	6	97,139
High Brite	19	10	72	11	13	14	268,656
High Yield	27	8	74	11	4	13	299,331
Highland Park	4	1	13	1	1	3	10,940
Highland Ruckus	14	5	48	5	4	5	239,542
His Excellence	4	1	20	3	2	2	74,381
Hold for Gold	4	1	11	1	1	0	23,980
Holy Bull	20	7	48	7	6	3	262,235
Holy Mountain	10	2	29	3	3	1	138,118
Holzmeister	6	2	26	2	3	5	76,560
Home At Last	2	1	5	2	2	0	30,690
Homo Sapiens	2	1	8	2	0	1	24,530
Honor Grades	20	6	66	9	8	4	294,803
Honour and Glory	46	15	130	18	14	26	488,491
Horse Chestnut (SAF)	12	6	39	8	4	4	258,553
Huddle Up	1	1	1	1	0	0	21,000
Humble Eleven	2	1	2	1	0	0	7,200
Humming	6	1	11	2	1	3	73,534
Humpty's Hoedown	1	1	2	1	1	0	8,565
I'm Reckless	1	1	5	1	0	0	7,088
Iam the Iceman	4	1	9	1	1	2	67,259
Ide	6	3	21	3	3	0	60,136

Juvenile Sire	Perf	Wnrs	Sts	1st	2d	3d	Purses
Ihtimam	2	1	10	1	1	2	8,197
Illinois Storm	8	3	23	3	3	0	78,633
Ima Good Gamble	3	1	9	1	0	1	6,465
Impeachment	6	2	17	2	2	2	37,417
In Excess (IRE)	12	6	27	11	5	2	1,019,531
In Excessive Bull	26	13	96	18	13	9	277,363
Incinderator	5	1	17	1	1	3	24,582
Indian Charlie	14	8	71	13	13	14	488,045
Individual Style	7	5	31	5	5	7	57,485
Intensity	7	2	25	2	6	3	135,211
Intidab	4	1	13	3	1	4	232,834
Irgun	15	7	51	8	3	7	127,768
Irish Dreamin	1	1	4	1	0	0	7,707
Irish Open	4	1	9	1	0	1	8,475
Iron Cat	4	3	11	3	3	0	32,375
Is It True	14	4	43	4	2	5	81,119
Island Born	2	1	7	1	0	0	11,330
Island Whirl	5	2	19	2	3	3	35,715
Islefaxyou	7	3	32	3	2	3	34,600
Itron	2	1	16	1	2	2	26,800
J P Hamer	2	1	11	1	0	5	21,063
Jack Livingston	2	1	6	1	0	1	34,240
Jack Wilson	3	1	4	1	1	1	43,283
Jacquelyn's Groom	7	3	28	3	2	1	41,520
Jade Hunter	10	2	38	3	1	5	45,529
Jambalaya Jazz	7	2	20	2	3	3	87,600
Jazzing Around	6	2	13	2	3	1	27,642
Jeblar	6	2	18	2	3	3	38,090
Joe Who (BRZ)	8	4	45	4	8	3	55,177
John the Magician	9	2	19	2	3	3	19,833
Joy's Report	2	1	4	1	1	2	12,260
Joyeux Danseur	14	6	56	8	11	4	283,652
Judge T C	2	1	5	1	1	1	41,165
Jules	18	5	61	7	6	7	197,890
Just a Cat	9	4	35	5	5	2	114,388
K One King	6	1	16	3	1	5	39,830
Kahuna Jack	4	1	15	1	1	2	12,155
Kandaly	2	1	7	1	0	1	11,730
Kansas City	1	1	3	1	0	1	2,220
Karen's Cat	6	3	17	7	1	1	109,430
Katahaula County	17	5	74	7	12	21	273,396
Katowice	9	2	22	2	4	5	51,850
Kayrawan	5	3	16	3	2	1	56,712
Kelly Kip	11	3	38	3	11	2	118,053
Kennedy Factor	3	1	9	1	0	2	6,481
Kessem Power (NZ)	7	2	16	2	1	0	18,817
King of Cats	2	1	5	1	2	1	21,661
King of Kings (IRE)	12	2	46	5	5	7	254,473
King of Scat	12	6	37	8	3	6	79,732
King of the Hunt	3	2	14	2	1	5	24,261
King's Canyon	2	1	3	2	0	0	15,000
King's Nest	4	2	15	2	2	2	25,563
Kingmambo	3	1	12	2	2	1	120,232
Kings Blood (IRE)	2	1	8	1	0	0	3,730
Kingsboro	2	1	13	1	1	0	11,050
Kipling	13	2	24	2	3	2	24,753
Kipper Kelly	9	2	24	4	2	2	99,230
Kiridashi	16	5	43	7	2	3	290,745
Kissin Kris	21	4	67	4	11	12	145,010
Kleven	1	1	9	5	2	1	50,757
Knockadoon	5	3	21	3	7	3	96,971
Kodiack	1	1	4	1	2	1	19,450
Kyle's Our Man	5	2	11	2	1	2	44,674
La Saboteur	3	1	8	1	1	0	6,265
Laabity	9	4	38	4	5	3	80,360
Labeeb (GB)	5	2	11	2	0	2	22,780
Lac Ouimet	12	3	41	4	5	4	73,049
Lake George	1	1	6	1	0	0	13,480
Lake Holme	2	1	6	1	0	0	11,310
Lakeshore Road	5	1	14	1	4	0	32,489
Landing Zone	1	1	3	1	0	0	17,940
Langfuhr	19	6	69	6	15	8	199,555
Larrupin'	7	2	25	3	6	1	48,005
Larry the Legend	9	1	18	1	3	4	26,163

Sire	Perf	Wnrs	Sts	1st	2d	3d	Purses
Last Lion	7	1	22	1	3	2	26,106
Lasting Approval	5	1	18	1	1	3	25,359
Latin American	11	1	39	1	4	2	51,404
Launch a Leader	1	1	3	1	1	0	11,332
Lear Fan	6	4	24	4	2	2	70,878
Leestown	32	10	108	17	13	16	430,376
Lemon Drop Kid	16	6	46	7	11	10	342,983
Leo Castelli	1	1	6	1	1	0	6,106
Like a Soldier	4	1	13	1	0	3	16,920
Lil E. Tee	7	3	21	3	3	0	35,732
Lil Honcho	1	1	1	1	0	0	6,000
Lil Tyler	3	1	12	1	1	4	17,855
Lil's Lad	21	6	61	8	9	6	171,750
Limit Out	4	3	13	3	2	4	64,170
Line In The Sand	32	11	163	16	17	24	312,371
Lion Cavern	13	5	59	6	8	5	179,686
Lion Hearted	13	9	40	12	5	7	391,917
Lit de Justice	6	1	19	1	5	4	41,200
Lite the Fuse	26	6	63	7	8	12	377,573
Little Nureyev	1	1	5	1	2	0	8,887
Littlebitlively	21	6	93	6	14	14	216,700
Lord At Law	1	1	2	1	0	0	7,710
Lord Avie	8	4	28	7	1	6	188,699
Lord Carson	34	16	118	17	16	22	498,791
Lord Parham	2	1	2	1	0	1	18,240
Lost Soldier	20	10	88	11	10	10	223,330
Louis Quatorze	35	10	98	11	8	12	222,588
Louisiana Slew	2	1	7	1	3	1	10,395
Lucky Lionel	26	9	106	11	19	10	401,009
Lucky So n' So	1	1	2	1	0	0	15,780
Luhuk	11	1	28	1	2	1	33,487
Lycius	12	5	31	5	2	5	142,085
Maghnatis	4	2	20	4	2	1	42,475
Magic Cat	29	11	101	13	13	11	279,934
Magic Prospect	6	3	19	4	2	2	82,442
Majesterian	4	1	4	1	0	0	3,513
Makaleha	9	1	37	2	9	4	79,908
Makhraj	2	1	4	1	0	0	13,870
Makin	5	1	17	1	2	0	28,718
Makula King	3	3	15	5	3	1	70,330
Malagra	10	4	38	8	4	7	211,347
Malek (CHI)	12	1	36	1	8	8	81,757
Malibu Moon	27	9	84	18	6	8	872,112
Malibu Wesley	7	2	23	2	1	5	47,382
Mantles Star (GB)	5	2	10	3	1	1	29,490
Marco Bay	2	1	10	1	1	1	25,560
Maria's Mon	38	14	126	15	21	6	546,303
Marked Tree	12	1	27	1	1	4	17,136
Marquetry	19	5	67	6	6	7	195,162
Master Bill	7	2	26	2	5	4	53,391
Match Trick	1	1	4	1	1	0	13,077
Matchlite	10	4	31	4	5	4	96,727
Matricule	9	4	34	4	2	5	38,479
Matter of Honor	3	1	6	1	0	0	13,075
Matty G	6	1	21	1	1	2	24,623
Maximum Wager	1	1	10	2	2	1	39,742
Mazel Trick	22	6	61	8	7	3	235,600
Meadow Flight	2	1	11	1	0	2	19,533
Meadow Monster	26	13	109	19	17	17	423,620
Meadow Prayer	6	2	15	5	0	2	168,542
Meadowlake	17	5	52	5	11	4	199,701
Mecke	8	4	41	5	6	6	132,470
Memo (CHI)	10	3	32	6	5	4	274,707
Menifee	25	10	66	16	6	7	540,178
Mercedes Won	6	2	19	3	1	3	91,480
Mercer Mill	11	3	50	3	5	9	83,011
Metfield	4	2	15	2	5	4	138,594
Mexican Bandit	2	1	9	1	0	0	8,545
Mi Selecto	5	1	10	1	0	0	8,426
Michael's Flyer	1	1	6	1	1	0	5,780
Miesque's Son	11	5	40	6	5	9	123,450
Mighty Magee	10	2	33	2	1	6	69,314
Migrating Moon	3	2	25	2	3	3	39,285
Military	10	6	30	7	3	5	184,872

Sire	Perf	Wnrs	Sts	1st	2d	3d	Purses
Millions	5	2	17	3	1	3	63,767
Miner's Mark	15	3	57	3	4	6	69,934
Miracle Heights	3	1	4	1	0	0	4,950
Misnomer	1	1	7	1	0	1	30,990
Mister Jolie	9	7	45	10	5	6	174,224
Miswaki Gold	3	1	9	1	1	1	10,106
Mocha Express	5	2	15	2	2	2	29,863
Mommu	1	1	2	1	0	0	6,290
Mon Capitan	1	1	9	1	2	1	12,795
Montbrook	23	9	90	12	12	4	297,486
Moon Up T. C.	1	1	5	2	3	0	31,170
More Than Ready	34	17	134	24	23	18	837,567
Moro Oro	8	7	37	10	3	10	168,480
Moscow Ballet	8	1	16	1	1	2	26,215
Mountain Bike (CHI)	2	1	10	2	1	2	37,581
Moving Shoulder	5	1	18	1	0	5	11,492
Mr Purple	6	2	20	2	3	6	29,502
Mr. Easy Money	6	1	10	1	0	1	2,838
Mr. Greeley	17	5	49	5	6	4	142,010
Mr. Procrastinator	8	4	29	5	3	3	68,071
Mr. Shawklit	3	1	11	1	0	1	20,352
Mt. Livermore	18	6	60	6	12	10	363,303
Mud Route	15	6	70	9	12	12	339,717
Muldoon	6	2	18	2	2	2	16,588
Muqtarib	8	3	28	4	6	4	149,932
Musical Dreamer	4	1	14	2	0	1	22,123
Must Be War	2	1	5	1	0	0	3,300
Mutakddim	17	3	42	5	8	7	122,704
My Boy Adam	15	6	51	7	7	7	159,806
My Favorite Grub	2	1	7	1	0	1	13,762
My Friend Max	6	1	23	1	5	1	41,744
My Imperial Slew	2	1	7	1	0	1	16,328
My King (GER)	3	1	13	2	0	0	13,630
My Liege	1	1	1	1	0	0	6,550
My Mike	5	3	22	3	4	4	66,610
Mystery Storm	5	2	17	2	2	1	35,945
Naevus	5	2	21	2	5	3	25,500
Naevus Star	1	1	2	1	0	0	9,487
Native Factor	5	3	13	4	2	0	84,859
Native Regent	10	2	40	5	3	1	107,209
Net Asset	3	1	6	1	0	1	10,789
New Way	6	2	16	2	1	1	22,968
Newton's Law (IRE)	2	1	4	1	0	0	10,248
Noactor	8	4	28	5	6	1	163,727
Noble Cat	9	1	44	3	7	3	96,360
Northern Afleet	13	8	51	12	10	4	814,430
Northern Andy	1	1	4	1	0	1	1,005
Not For Love	16	2	43	3	6	5	108,393
Not So Fast	1	1	6	1	1	0	8,636
Not Tricky	5	3	7	3	0	1	20,155
Notable Cat	4	2	17	4	1	0	51,932
Notebook	18	7	60	8	5	9	200,908
Numerous	5	1	20	1	4	2	38,315
O'Brannigan	1	1	3	1	0	0	8,180
Old Topper	19	10	76	15	20	11	498,815
Old Trieste	30	6	82	6	8	9	225,273
On Target	7	2	22	2	3	3	90,857
On the Sauce	5	1	26	1	8	1	72,931
Once a Sailor	5	3	17	3	4	2	39,750
One Golf Sierra	1	1	5	1	2	0	36,430
Open Forum	17	6	72	7	10	12	159,501
Ops Smile	7	3	25	4	4	5	100,891
Orbit's Scene	1	1	3	1	0	0	8,400
Orchid's Devil	3	2	13	4	4	2	150,379
Ore Grade	4	2	13	2	3	1	20,464
Ormsby	2	1	11	1	2	1	52,451
Our Emblem	8	2	20	2	3	2	29,415
Out of Place	24	6	83	6	12	10	258,217
Outflanker	15	7	62	9	4	11	179,485
Overnight Express	3	1	13	1	2	3	25,225
Pana Brass	2	1	5	1	2	1	24,915
Pancho Villa	10	1	32	2	6	5	40,213
Parade Ground	22	6	84	9	12	9	345,732
Paramour	4	2	30	2	5	4	39,012

Juvenile Sire	Perf	Wnrs	Sts	1st	2d	3d	Purses
Paranoide (ARG)	7	2	25	2	4	1	28,691
Parentheses	2	1	6	1	0	1	15,036
Part the Waters	3	2	12	2	2	3	22,270
Partner's Hero	15	5	48	6	7	4	181,730
Party Manners	7	3	24	4	1	3	102,832
Patton	5	2	16	2	0	0	18,135
Peaks and Valleys	31	13	96	19	12	14	608,262
Pentelicus	16	2	52	2	11	4	70,395
Perfect Mandate	4	1	14	2	0	3	44,432
Perfect Vision	11	1	32	1	2	2	21,762
Personable Joe	5	1	23	3	6	5	118,300
Personal Flag	11	1	29	1	2	2	22,954
Peterhof	3	2	14	3	0	3	28,437
Petersburg	5	4	13	4	2	2	26,563
Petionville	26	8	97	13	10	15	950,910
Phantom Jet	2	1	9	1	1	1	14,176
Phone Fantasy	4	2	17	2	1	1	27,492
Phone Saga	2	1	15	2	2	4	137,573
Phone Trick	17	9	68	9	15	7	257,481
Phonetics	5	1	13	1	1	1	30,980
Pin Stripe	2	1	12	1	1	3	12,699
Pine Bluff	22	6	54	7	10	8	209,515
Pioneering	14	4	44	6	4	4	169,173
Placid Fund	8	3	36	4	1	5	85,746
Pleasant Tap	19	4	47	5	4	5	102,598
Pok Ta Pok	1	1	1	1	0	0	7,950
Pole Position	5	2	13	2	3	2	28,097
Polish Navy	9	2	18	2	1	1	36,553
Polish Numbers	12	6	39	7	3	8	196,235
Political Folly	3	1	13	1	1	1	12,361
Pollock's Luck	6	2	23	2	0	3	22,668
Ponche	2	1	10	1	0	2	10,920
Porto Foricos	9	2	25	3	2	4	256,098
Power by Far	4	1	11	1	0	2	12,355
Power Storm	4	1	9	1	0	0	7,110
Preacherman	4	1	14	1	0	1	13,770
Precise End	27	11	98	12	20	17	689,598
Precocity	12	4	46	6	8	2	252,948
Prefabricate	1	1	4	1	0	0	1,650
Premiership	6	2	21	2	3	1	39,308
Prenup	4	1	8	1	0	2	18,515
Presidential Order	6	1	23	2	3	4	48,369
Pride of Burkaan	1	1	2	1	0	1	9,520
Prince of Fame	3	1	6	1	0	0	7,337
Prince of the Mt.	8	4	29	4	3	2	52,938
Private School	1	1	5	1	1	0	15,720
Private Terms	7	1	17	1	0	2	10,779
Prized	8	2	19	5	2	3	131,773
Prospect Bay	8	2	18	4	3	3	77,929
Prospect North	2	1	11	1	1	1	6,372
Prospector Jones	12	1	36	1	2	4	22,559
Prospectors Gamble	4	3	11	3	1	0	70,679
Proud and True	16	3	50	3	5	7	67,184
Proud Irish	16	5	71	5	7	13	154,748
Proudest Romeo	6	2	23	4	5	4	64,570
Pulling Punches	12	1	24	1	3	1	23,775
Pulpit	23	6	54	7	11	7	374,406
Pyramid Peak	9	1	32	1	5	3	45,565
Quaker Hill	6	3	19	3	4	5	74,540
Quaker Ridge	8	7	44	10	12	5	151,914
Quarry	1	1	6	1	0	0	17,060
Quick Cut	4	1	11	1	0	0	12,620
Quiet American	15	5	41	7	6	6	252,193
Quite Special	5	1	11	1	0	0	8,619
R. Payday	1	1	5	1	1	1	15,394
Radio Daze	1	1	5	1	0	2	12,100
Rage	1	1	6	1	0	0	28,648
Rahy	11	2	29	2	4	1	83,885
Rail	4	1	15	2	5	0	38,650
Real Quiet	23	7	75	7	5	7	200,443
Real West	4	2	14	2	1	1	27,249
Reality Road	4	1	21	2	1	1	32,086
Rebmec	4	1	12	1	2	3	49,133
Red	7	5	16	7	1	1	51,788

Juvenile Sire	Perf	Wnrs	Sts	1st	2d	3d	Purses
Red Hammer Red	1	1	6	1	1	1	32,522
Reel On Reel	4	1	9	1	1	1	12,045
Regal Classic	22	3	56	3	6	4	177,769
Regal Humor	3	2	14	2	3	2	45,318
Regal Intention	26	9	87	9	15	12	179,553
Regal Remark	5	4	25	4	1	3	78,437
Regalstaff	1	1	1	1	0	0	14,500
Reincarnate	4	1	5	1	0	0	8,909
Relagate	1	1	5	1	2	0	22,300
Renteria	5	2	22	2	4	3	104,331
Reparations	1	1	1	1	0	0	20,580
Repriced	9	2	24	4	3	2	147,369
Reprized	6	1	19	1	2	5	40,852
Richter Scale	14	5	38	5	3	3	204,013
Ride the Storm	3	1	6	1	1	1	18,445
Right Jab	5	1	20	1	1	1	27,899
Rio Verde	9	4	40	4	8	4	121,756
River Flyer	2	1	8	1	2	1	33,094
River Squall	5	1	12	1	0	0	7,400
Rizzi	28	12	112	17	10	14	318,113
Roanoke	6	1	18	1	2	5	31,141
Roar	14	4	43	4	5	4	98,771
Rob 'n Gin	5	1	14	1	3	1	44,330
Robannier	3	1	8	1	2	2	46,775
Robb	5	3	34	3	2	6	85,482
Robyn Dancer	38	11	165	18	22	19	455,740
Rod and Staff	2	1	7	1	2	1	25,380
Rodeo	10	1	23	3	1	2	54,807
Royal Academy	11	6	30	6	2	4	157,387
Royal Anthem	17	2	42	2	3	3	74,392
Royal Quiz	5	3	14	3	3	2	33,594
Royal Roberto	1	1	3	1	0	2	14,780
Rubiano	31	11	108	15	15	14	464,271
Rubiyat	1	1	5	2	1	0	31,600
Runaway Groom	16	5	55	8	7	3	285,929
Running Stag	33	10	107	15	13	14	516,682
Rush	1	1	7	1	0	0	10,550
Safely's Mark	2	1	12	2	1	1	50,444
Sahm	4	2	6	2	2	0	40,656
Saint Ballado	15	5	27	5	3	1	132,053
Salt Lake	17	7	55	8	8	8	197,814
Salty Shoes	1	1	5	1	0	1	2,515
Sand Tunnel	7	1	26	1	3	1	31,029
Sandia Slew	2	1	8	4	0	3	132,215
Sandpit (BRZ)	10	2	32	2	3	1	33,489
Sasha's Prospect	7	3	27	6	3	1	83,155
Savin Eyes	3	1	12	1	2	1	17,311
Scarlet Ibis	3	1	9	2	2	0	26,483
Scatmandu	17	4	59	4	9	4	105,165
Scherando	5	2	21	2	1	1	23,808
Score Quick	3	2	21	2	2	4	47,876
Sea of Secrets	17	6	64	6	7	6	158,640
Sea Twister	3	2	15	6	1	2	72,960
Sea Wall	2	2	11	3	1	3	179,535
Seacliff	2	2	7	2	1	0	36,420
Seattle Pattern	2	2	12	2	3	2	39,995
Seattle Proud	1	1	2	1	1	0	12,201
Seattle Slew	10	4	31	6	3	0	291,723
Seattle Sun	2	1	4	1	0	0	8,720
Secreniner	7	1	22	1	0	1	10,065
Secret Claim	1	1	7	1	2	2	19,225
Secret Firm	5	1	17	1	1	3	17,321
Secret Hello	4	3	10	3	1	0	46,000
Secretary Forli	1	1	5	2	0	1	33,040
Seeking the Crown	5	1	18	1	0	2	17,340
Seeking the Gold	11	4	32	5	11	3	254,823
Sefapiano	11	2	41	2	5	4	60,717
Semoran	12	7	57	8	7	7	112,421
Seneca Jones	11	7	44	10	6	6	179,725
Senor Speedy	2	1	10	1	2	2	40,154
Service Stripe	8	2	24	3	4	1	44,573
Shaheen	6	3	14	3	0	2	26,334
Shakeel	3	1	12	1	1	1	19,680
Sharp Frosty	6	1	14	2	2	2	38,685

Sire	Perf	Wnrs	Sts	1st	2d	3d	Purses
Shawaf	2	1	10	1	3	1	24,690
Shotiche	3	1	15	1	3	1	35,712
Shuailaan	6	1	23	1	3	2	32,225
Siberian Summer	7	2	30	2	6	3	64,667
Silic (FR)	5	1	17	1	2	2	18,053
Silk Song	2	1	4	1	1	1	17,879
Silver Charm	30	10	100	13	13	16	556,645
Silver Deputy	18	7	47	9	12	9	308,746
Silver Ghost	22	8	57	10	6	7	392,942
Silver Hawk	5	2	12	2	1	0	47,310
Sinceilostmybaby	3	2	12	2	2	5	20,852
Singspiel (IRE)	1	1	3	1	1	0	25,700
Sinndar (IRE)	1	1	1	1	0	0	45,000
Siphon (BRZ)	28	6	85	7	5	13	246,835
Sir Cat	15	7	50	7	5	9	196,126
Six Below	5	1	14	1	0	1	13,621
Skip Away	22	7	74	8	6	16	239,659
Skip Trial	9	4	36	5	4	2	109,097
Sky Classic	20	4	59	6	2	5	155,730
Skywalker	24	8	72	9	14	6	185,578
Slavic	2	1	10	2	1	1	27,010
Slew City Slew	18	7	75	9	8	14	401,619
Slew Gin Fizz	34	18	138	20	13	20	353,556
Slew o' Gold	1	1	5	1	1	0	6,105
Slew the Slewor	1	1	4	1	0	0	4,755
Slew the Surgeon	7	2	24	4	3	4	80,435
Slewdledo	18	7	50	9	9	4	145,000
Slewpy	1	1	2	1	0	1	17,160
Slewship	1	1	3	1	0	0	6,900
Smart Strike	26	11	69	15	7	12	632,789
Smile and Be Happy	2	1	5	1	0	0	13,174
Smoke Glacken	22	14	90	19	13	17	519,737
Smokester	4	3	13	3	2	1	54,258
Snowbound	7	2	23	3	3	4	28,846
Son of Briartic	4	2	20	2	5	1	52,980
Son's Corona	2	1	5	1	1	1	5,745
South Pass	1	1	5	1	0	0	5,675
Southern Halo	12	5	38	11	6	3	490,571
Souvenir Copy	15	4	46	7	7	9	361,335
Spend a Buck	9	3	17	3	0	0	47,430
Spinning World	7	5	23	6	5	3	172,684
Spiritbound	1	1	4	1	1	1	16,785
Spruce Bouquet	3	1	9	1	0	0	9,443
Stake a Claim	2	1	11	1	0	1	9,733
Stalwart	6	2	19	2	3	3	36,731
Standing On Edge	5	2	22	2	6	1	80,457
Star of Valor	10	5	46	5	8	7	140,941
Star Programmer	12	2	29	2	2	3	46,398
Stark Ridge	5	3	16	3	2	0	50,620
State Craft	6	3	30	3	3	3	49,217
State Performer	1	1	4	1	1	1	13,625
Statesmanship	4	2	17	3	2	2	42,760
Stauder	1	1	7	1	0	1	8,560
Stephanotis	15	3	33	6	5	8	218,319
Stephen Got Even	22	7	76	8	6	13	314,967
Stolen Gold	6	3	22	4	1	1	36,080
Storada	2	1	5	1	2	0	6,725
Storm and a Half	12	5	42	6	9	7	166,425
Storm Blast	4	2	14	2	3	2	14,755
Storm Boot	25	7	85	9	7	8	274,642
Storm Broker	9	3	33	4	2	4	39,410
Storm Cat	18	7	56	14	7	4	1,616,329
Storm Center	2	1	11	1	2	1	40,849
Storm Creek	38	9	113	9	15	12	294,201
Storm of the Night	2	1	9	1	2	2	11,636
Stormin Fever	31	11	103	13	16	12	402,948
Stormy Atlantic	43	16	152	21	20	24	558,563
Straight Man	33	12	105	15	18	16	413,206
Stravinsky	9	5	32	6	2	4	117,008
Strike Gold	3	2	8	2	2	0	34,432
Strong Minded	1	1	3	1	1	0	1,567
Suave Prospect	19	11	116	18	13	20	364,177
Subordination	16	10	75	13	7	12	189,197
Successful Appeal	20	15	76	31	13	10	1,724,080

Sire	Perf	Wnrs	Sts	1st	2d	3d	Purses
Suggest	2	2	10	2	1	0	32,945
Sultry Song	7	2	24	3	6	4	63,398
Summer Squall	9	3	26	4	2	3	241,359
Sundance Ridge	4	1	14	1	5	2	43,305
Sunday Minister	5	3	9	3	1	0	62,788
Sunny's Halo	11	1	39	1	5	4	24,423
Super Gun	3	1	20	1	2	4	38,978
Super Special	5	1	14	1	1	1	14,510
Superior Success	4	2	16	2	1	1	10,428
Supremo	4	1	12	1	1	1	16,747
Swain (IRE)	6	3	21	3	4	2	124,430
Swear by Dixie	3	2	16	2	7	1	29,405
Sweetsouthernsaint	23	11	106	19	15	10	494,024
Swiss Trick	6	1	15	1	1	1	17,340
Swiss Yodeler	37	15	151	20	19	24	611,810
Sword Dance (IRE)	27	13	132	18	9	11	330,070
Tactical Advantage	16	2	40	4	1	6	109,419
Tactical Cat	13	3	39	3	4	5	82,975
Take Me Out	9	4	31	4	2	1	90,340
Takur	6	1	22	1	3	3	18,875
Tale of the Cat	30	14	96	21	22	8	629,414
Tejano Run	10	1	26	1	1	2	32,920
Tepee Creek	1	1	2	1	0	0	4,355
Thats Our Buck	10	2	38	2	3	7	37,800
The Deputy (IRE)	16	5	57	5	6	9	89,025
The Good Life	4	2	9	2	1	2	40,078
The Prime Minister	3	1	7	2	0	0	18,750
Theatrical (IRE)	8	4	16	4	0	2	121,925
Thunder Gulch	50	15	153	20	20	20	916,731
Tiffany Ice	4	2	10	3	0	1	9,170
Tiger Ridge	25	11	82	13	15	7	517,686
Timber Country	4	1	10	3	3	0	623,056
Time Bandit	5	1	20	2	3	3	45,997
Tomorrow's Slew	1	1	6	1	3	2	19,883
Tomorrows Cat	26	9	92	10	12	8	273,430
Toolighttoquit	6	1	18	1	3	2	27,928
Top Account	12	6	47	9	6	4	193,572
Torey Ridge	4	1	14	1	3	2	15,685
Touch Gold	31	9	83	10	8	7	372,643
Tough Knight	8	3	26	3	4	5	48,509
Tour d'Or	22	10	118	13	21	8	221,980
Town Caper	8	1	33	1	5	5	43,583
Track Barron	2	2	7	2	0	0	11,699
Trail City	8	3	24	4	5	3	115,168
Traitor	3	1	9	1	1	1	12,345
Trancus	1	1	9	1	1	2	13,605
Treasure Cove	7	1	15	1	1	0	15,777
Tree	2	1	6	1	0	1	33,410
Tresor du Mesnil (FR)	2	1	7	1	0	1	8,095
Tricky Creek	6	3	23	3	2	4	33,503
Tricky Fun	6	3	25	6	5	2	203,185
Tricky Mister	1	1	4	2	0	1	61,900
Tropic Lightning	3	1	6	1	2	1	15,798
Truckee	13	2	43	2	4	1	43,558
Truculent Schular	3	1	5	1	0	0	11,460
True Confidence	13	1	43	1	2	4	24,561
Truluck	4	1	14	2	2	1	43,941
Turbulent Kris	3	3	15	3	1	3	41,464
Turkoman	8	1	19	1	2	0	17,072
Twilight Agenda	9	2	25	2	2	2	30,118
Twin Halo	4	1	13	1	3	0	28,055
Twin Rocket Power	1	1	6	1	0	0	7,175
Twin Spires	16	8	78	11	8	7	206,056
Two Punch	14	5	43	6	3	7	189,625
Two Smart	4	2	19	3	1	3	46,339
Tychonic (GB)	5	1	16	1	4	4	28,281
Tyler Wayne	2	1	6	1	0	2	13,700
Unaccounted For	12	3	41	5	5	7	105,140
Unbridled	11	4	24	5	3	6	258,791
Unbridled Jet	26	2	84	2	11	11	133,071
Unbridled's Song	19	9	50	18	7	8	870,306
Unreal Zeal	16	4	57	4	4	4	88,595
Untold Gold	3	2	12	3	4	1	100,917
Untuttable	14	7	64	12	10	7	263,005

Juvenile Sire	Perf	Wnrs	Sts	1st	2d	3d	Purses
Valiant Nature	4	1	12	1	2	0	12,370
Valid Expectations	33	17	133	32	19	24	1,074,026
Valid Request	1	1	3	1	1	1	13,352
Valid Wager	13	7	55	9	7	7	245,865
Valley Crossing	9	2	27	2	2	1	42,505
Vaudeville	5	4	19	6	3	3	45,095
Via Lombardia (IRE)	7	1	27	1	5	4	47,715
Vicar	29	9	86	9	9	12	278,996
Victory Gallop	25	8	93	11	18	16	653,377
Victory Speech	11	2	39	2	2	2	41,524
Vilzak	8	4	18	4	2	5	49,600
Viva Deputy	3	1	8	1	0	2	19,740
Vying Victor	23	11	90	16	13	8	382,110
Wa Bert	1	1	2	2	0	0	45,420
Waco Connection	5	1	16	1	3	5	26,885
Wagon Limit	8	2	23	2	3	2	31,719
Waquoit	3	2	11	2	1	0	33,863
War Chant	14	7	38	8	4	5	306,168
Wardrobe Test	1	1	8	1	1	3	58,798
Wavering Monarch	9	4	31	4	1	4	74,114
Way West (FR)	4	2	9	2	1	0	24,328
Wayne County (IRE)	6	1	16	2	0	2	62,885
Wayne's Crane	4	1	17	1	0	0	10,938
Weekend Guest	12	6	30	9	2	5	149,477
Wekiva Springs	9	3	35	4	7	8	101,572
Welbred Fred	1	1	8	2	0	2	66,882
Well Decorated	2	1	4	1	0	1	12,745
Wertaloona	2	2	13	4	3	2	51,705
Weshaam	6	2	20	3	1	1	91,890
West Acre	6	3	17	4	1	0	77,625
Western Borders	6	2	25	2	3	1	45,495
Western Cat	10	4	44	5	6	5	107,601
Western Echo	1	1	2	1	0	0	9,750
Western Expression	20	7	60	8	9	7	384,961
Western Fame	8	6	34	8	4	6	212,315
Western Front	1	1	2	1	0	0	7,935
Western Playboy	5	2	23	2	3	3	79,515
Western Trick	8	3	34	4	7	4	114,786
Wheaton	39	21	138	33	16	18	610,032
Whiskey Wisdom	14	9	42	13	7	5	759,611
Whitney Tower	4	4	30	4	3	4	62,845
Why Change	4	1	20	1	3	1	24,407
Wild Again	7	1	29	2	3	6	77,367
Wild Deputy	4	2	18	2	4	2	30,768
Wild Escapade	7	1	19	2	2	2	49,063
Wild Event	17	9	86	15	11	10	696,800
Wild Gambler	2	1	8	1	1	2	27,000
Wild Gold	9	5	19	5	2	1	99,913
Wild Invader	6	1	18	1	1	3	16,401
Wild Rush	22	8	90	14	14	14	514,205
Wild Syn	5	3	8	3	0	0	50,111
Wild Wonder	17	4	69	4	11	8	236,180
Wild Zone	42	15	159	21	25	25	499,683
Will's Way	9	2	26	2	1	7	72,304
Williamstown	8	3	21	3	2	0	69,690
Win Lose Or Draw	2	1	10	1	1	3	27,280
Wind Whipper	10	5	42	5	4	3	51,896
Winthrop	6	1	23	3	2	0	80,398
Wire Me Collect	11	2	29	2	3	3	42,897
Wised Up	13	5	57	6	9	6	173,748
With Approval	6	2	13	3	0	0	58,406
Wolf Power (SAF)	11	4	44	4	4	7	93,930
Yankee Fan	4	3	15	5	1	0	30,099
Yankee Victor	27	12	86	13	15	8	399,274
Yarrow Brae	12	6	38	6	5	6	108,324
Yes It's True	40	15	141	25	12	31	1,424,382
Yoonevano	12	1	31	1	5	4	43,576
You and I	13	7	51	9	7	4	136,335
You Know How It Is	3	1	12	1	0	1	9,680
Z Z Cat	4	1	17	1	2	1	19,438
Zamindar	14	2	30	2	1	2	43,064
Zarbyev	15	4	61	5	5	6	120,532
Zigtrick (FR)	2	1	6	1	1	1	4,780

2004 RECORDS OF BROODMARE SIRES

The record of each broodmare sire represented by at least one winning thoroughbred or more who raced in the United States or Canada in 2004, showing his total performers, number of winning performers, the number of times they started and their total placings and earnings.

Broodmare Sire	Perf	Wnrs	Sts	1st	2d	3d	Purses
A Change for April	1	1	9	3	1	1	$44,260
A Corking Limerick	2	1	7	2	0	0	25,815
A Gypsy Says	3	1	17	1	1	1	15,102
A Native Danzig	9	4	56	7	4	10	691,379
A Sure Hit	3	2	15	2	0	3	29,796
A Title	11	3	48	4	5	6	42,623
A Toast to Junius	6	2	56	3	4	12	63,651
A-Okay	1	1	8	1	1	0	14,292
A. M. Swinger	3	2	22	4	5	2	34,782
A.P. Indy	57	27	316	35	44	37	1,200,576
Abel Prospect	8	5	61	10	6	3	103,639
Absalom	2	2	18	2	3	2	9,978
Academy Award	47	24	322	33	39	36	752,201
Acallade	8	4	47	6	3	3	85,643
Acaroid	35	13	191	17	23	21	333,809
Accipiter	19	10	135	18	16	18	249,387
Accomplished Lover	2	1	15	4	1	3	52,665
Accoustical	5	3	51	4	9	8	94,654
Accused	8	1	32	1	1	3	16,095
Ace II	2	1	17	2	1	6	8,359
Ace of Aces	5	1	19	2	0	1	22,550
Aces Might Do	1	1	10	1	0	1	7,106
Ack Ack	77	31	408	47	51	51	838,324
Ack Kerala	7	6	61	11	10	6	92,991
Acque	1	1	15	7	3	1	40,969
Adancer	1	1	6	2	2	1	11,636
Addy Boy	6	2	33	2	0	2	14,165
Admiral's Flag	4	3	44	10	4	2	72,167
Admiral's Shield	8	4	41	5	3	5	46,777
Advance Guard	3	1	11	1	3	2	18,688
Advance Man	2	1	6	1	1	1	6,245
Advertent	7	4	39	4	6	6	38,234
Advocator	37	16	257	27	22	31	438,983
Advocatum	4	1	19	4	1	2	41,727
Aegean's Bolger	3	1	12	1	1	2	21,825
Aerial Dancer	1	1	10	2	4	2	15,969
Aetolian	2	1	10	3	2	1	37,170
Aferd	30	14	183	22	31	17	323,184
Affiliate	5	2	33	3	7	3	35,733
Affirmed	225	125	1539	217	196	194	5,613,315
Afleet	153	78	989	144	119	118	3,290,637
African Sky (GB)	11	4	90	8	15	12	134,642
After Eight	2	1	9	1	1	2	5,285
Aggravatin'	8	2	53	4	4	8	107,616
Agitate	35	21	224	34	36	25	571,603
Ahira	4	3	32	3	5	5	23,420
Ahmad (ARG)	18	7	163	16	21	23	361,021
Ahonoora (GB)	10	5	42	12	5	0	1,594,271
Air Cover	3	2	32	4	3	5	72,725
Air Forbes Won	145	88	1037	150	138	127	2,524,849
Ajdal	2	1	14	1	2	2	33,827
Akarad	9	4	44	7	3	3	96,115
Akubarb	1	1	4	1	0	0	1,100
Akureyri	26	16	196	23	21	16	509,057
Al Hareb	2	1	20	4	5	1	20,466
Al Hattab	29	15	186	20	23	21	431,633
Al Mamoon	41	16	253	31	31	25	541,540
Al Mufti	1	1	15	1	5	3	8,712
Al Nasr (FR)	50	28	397	51	53	53	1,289,663
Al Sabin	1	1	6	1	0	1	13,221
Alaskan Frost	18	10	151	14	16	17	203,276
Alberta Green	1	1	12	2	4	1	11,957
Alhambra	1	1	11	3	3	1	26,972
Ali Oop	15	4	97	5	11	9	61,089
Alias Smith	5	3	40	3	4	6	62,273
Alkalde	1	1	2	2	0	0	21,000
All Bold Forbes	1	1	5	1	1	1	16,450
All for Fun	6	1	21	1	0	1	6,662
All Glory (NZ)	3	1	8	2	1	2	13,263
All Gone	1	1	1	1	0	0	7,800
All Hands	1	1	16	2	2	3	16,455
All of a Sudden	3	2	21	5	1	7	66,519
Alla Breva	6	4	50	5	9	7	84,051
Alleged	175	88	1069	144	143	121	4,862,754
Allegedly Wild	2	2	15	2	0	4	24,165
Allen's Prospect	154	85	1141	160	154	124	2,979,095
Alligator Reef	1	1	13	1	3	0	8,197
Ally Runner	2	1	10	1	0	3	17,220
Alnaab	9	5	47	6	6	4	31,449
Aloha Mood	1	1	3	2	0	0	7,790
Aloha Prospector	18	9	106	14	16	10	295,015
Aloma's Ruler	33	20	222	34	32	32	415,863
Alomado	2	1	22	1	7	2	25,502
Alphabatim	17	6	144	14	15	20	184,017
Alwasmi	31	17	181	25	17	13	556,758
Always a Cinch	1	1	12	1	3	1	15,712
Always Fair	2	1	9	1	1	0	91,430
Always Gallant	5	2	27	4	2	2	15,602
Always Run Lucky	6	2	48	2	4	6	45,243
Alwuhush	87	41	600	72	67	77	1,331,843
Aly North	3	1	28	1	1	7	23,179
Alybrave	8	2	51	3	9	7	26,850
Alydad	1	1	10	1	0	3	27,785
Alydar	175	80	1111	143	153	143	3,752,801
Alydart	4	1	21	1	1	3	5,118
Alydeed	41	23	246	39	40	24	1,355,424
Alymagic	2	1	15	1	3	0	21,165
Alysheba	111	48	751	88	102	102	2,159,666
Alzao	21	7	86	9	10	8	508,341
Am all Charged Up	2	2	13	2	1	8	39,711
Amasport	3	1	14	1	1	0	6,625
Amazing Prospect	9	5	71	8	5	9	79,627
Ambehaving	2	1	26	1	2	5	23,978
Amber Eagle	2	1	15	3	1	1	19,031
Amber Morn	2	1	10	1	0	2	14,135
Amber Pass	15	5	71	5	14	4	97,847
Amber Sioux	1	1	1	1	0	0	15,600
Amberbee	6	1	27	1	5	0	15,284
Ambernash	13	6	99	11	13	11	163,915
Ambessa	1	1	8	2	1	2	18,475
American Artist	1	1	3	1	1	1	17,739
American Chance	6	5	47	7	10	8	238,714
American History	4	1	27	2	4	6	31,771
American Legion	11	8	65	13	11	8	260,580
American Standard	45	23	385	41	48	51	778,545
Amerrico	15	9	91	11	17	6	179,141
Amerrico's Bullet	1	1	15	2	5	2	37,330
Amino	1	1	9	2	1	0	17,575
Amorelu	1	1	8	1	1	3	27,220
An Act	4	2	34	6	3	3	116,136
An Eldorado	4	1	23	1	2	3	11,971
Ancestral (IRE)	16	7	105	12	19	11	182,553
Ancient Oaks	1	1	5	1	1	3	2,420
Angle Light	17	7	102	14	11	11	115,711
Anjiz	9	3	38	3	4	5	69,484
Ankara	5	2	44	5	7	5	47,630
Annihilate 'em	9	3	74	3	7	9	45,011
Anob	2	1	15	1	1	2	5,260
Another Reef	4	1	31	1	1	6	21,117
Antheus	2	1	5	1	1	0	37,753
Anticipating	19	7	84	9	5	12	210,260
Antidiluvian	2	1	23	2	7	2	35,199
Apalachee	169	79	1112	141	143	119	2,338,088
Apollo	3	1	12	1	0	2	30,574
Apuron	1	1	11	1	0	5	10,331
Arabacus	4	2	34	6	4	3	75,773
Arabian Law	3	1	26	1	1	1	8,355
Arabian Sheik	4	2	27	2	6	1	17,702
Araby Ace	3	1	14	1	2	2	16,916
Arachnoid	1	1	12	2	1	6	19,608
Aragon	2	2	17	2	4	5	79,218
Aras an Uachtarain (IRE)	10	6	55	7	11	7	72,213
Arazi	5	3	29	4	3	4	62,968
Architect	23	13	159	16	14	22	184,201
Arctic Ace	1	1	6	3	1	1	31,364
Arctic Action	4	2	33	4	5	2	29,038
Arctic Blitz	7	3	43	5	7	5	93,175
Arctic Flash	2	1	16	1	0	2	15,000
Arctic Groom	2	2	22	4	4	7	62,685
Arctic Tern	55	33	382	55	51	39	735,233
Argante	1	1	3	1	0	0	6,600
Ariva	1	1	21	1	3	2	9,400

Broodmare Sire	Perf	Wnrs	Sts	1st	2d	3d	Purses
Arkoma	1	1	6	2	0	0	13,197
Armin	1	1	4	2	0	1	29,844
Armor	3	1	23	2	3	6	26,920
Arms and the Man	4	3	28	6	3	5	37,965
Arratos	1	1	13	2	0	3	9,288
Arrogant Boy	5	2	27	2	5	4	23,820
Arroyo	3	1	20	3	2	1	21,523
Artichoke	17	5	106	10	12	15	242,074
Artie Baby	2	1	22	1	3	1	12,728
Artistry (SAF)	1	1	4	1	0	1	17,306
Arts and Letters	38	15	268	24	34	27	292,917
As Alleged	1	1	14	4	2	3	7,333
Ascot Knight	73	37	506	65	66	62	1,751,818
Ashmore	2	2	23	5	7	2	24,177
Ask Me	7	4	50	15	9	2	176,297
Ask Muhammad	9	4	67	4	4	4	26,439
Ask Us	4	1	17	1	3	1	10,838
Aspro	11	3	56	4	5	4	73,521
Aspy	2	1	9	1	2	1	22,970
Assagai Jr.	3	1	23	1	0	8	14,811
Assault Landing	16	8	100	10	9	15	167,473
Assert (IRE)	56	21	314	36	41	39	1,293,004
Assertive Joe	1	1	2	1	1	0	6,880
Astray	2	2	24	7	1	3	32,781
At Full Feather	10	6	51	6	9	4	102,082
At the Threshold	47	27	347	48	51	54	1,325,626
Atmosphere	3	1	14	2	1	1	18,392
Attaway to Go	1	1	5	1	1	0	15,026
Au Point	17	8	84	10	10	14	84,156
Auction Ring	7	3	47	5	9	7	89,071
August Agent	4	1	22	1	0	3	6,485
*Aurelius II	2	1	6	1	0	1	2,480
Aurium	12	6	67	10	3	9	139,601
Autumn Double	1	1	10	3	2	1	4,077
Avatar	61	28	431	43	54	56	718,709
Avenger M.	7	5	50	7	5	6	93,581
Avenging Storm	1	1	8	3	1	0	19,785
Avenue of Flags	40	24	226	37	35	31	655,339
Avies Copy	17	7	119	11	5	14	182,204
Avodire	11	2	87	7	6	18	69,007
Ax the Fax	4	2	28	2	2	4	31,691
Axe T. V.	5	2	44	2	3	5	31,620
Aye's Turn	21	8	136	10	12	25	251,314
Ayman	3	1	21	1	1	1	11,340
Azirae	2	1	11	1	2	3	8,040
Aztec Red	2	2	14	2	1	4	10,656
B. in Time	3	1	11	1	1	2	16,558
Baalbek (CHI)	1	1	11	1	2	3	33,565
Babur	3	3	41	5	4	6	25,934
Baby Chile	2	2	22	2	2	3	15,312
Baby King	2	2	15	2	0	4	23,295
Baby Slewy	2	1	13	1	1	1	2,376
Back Alley	1	1	9	1	0	3	36,312
Back Bay Barrister	5	2	41	4	3	9	52,527
Backbencher	2	1	19	1	1	1	15,989
Badger Land	54	29	364	63	59	47	975,788
Baederwood	58	28	380	40	48	58	879,213
Bag	13	5	52	6	8	7	139,971
Bagdad	5	1	35	3	6	2	117,574
Bagdad Dawn	2	1	15	2	6	2	8,707
Bahamian Star	1	1	11	1	0	2	5,424
Bahri	2	1	19	1	1	1	35,415
Bailjumper	55	26	350	42	42	40	1,166,444
Baillamont	4	1	25	2	3	2	59,280
Balance of Power	5	1	19	1	4	3	25,959
Balboa Native	2	1	19	2	2	0	10,850
*Balconaje	5	2	32	2	0	5	11,235
Baldski	130	62	874	106	94	124	3,694,905
Ballacashtal	3	2	28	2	6	4	48,705
Ballad Rock	6	2	42	10	3	2	70,069
Ballydoyle	22	8	135	17	18	16	155,055
Balmerino (NZ)	2	1	11	3	1	1	79,700
Baltic Dancer	2	1	14	2	2	1	6,405
Balzac	26	11	195	15	17	30	240,614
Band Practice	22	10	172	12	31	23	218,025
Banderilla	16	10	147	17	18	33	291,860

Sire	Perf	Wnrs	Sts	1st	2d	3d	Purses
Bang Boom	3	3	15	5	0	2	25,492
Bankbook	1	1	10	2	0	2	23,970
Banker Bud	1	1	14	3	7	0	54,568
Banner Bob	10	4	65	6	11	7	129,389
Banner Sport	4	3	32	3	4	1	35,178
Banners Image	1	1	10	2	2	2	6,285
Banquet Table	19	9	136	11	19	23	148,163
Baptism (GB)	2	1	9	2	3	0	21,853
Bar Dexter	3	1	25	2	3	2	18,988
Barachois	32	16	229	26	34	24	543,627
Baranof	1	1	6	2	2	0	18,775
Barathea (IRE)	2	1	6	2	0	2	147,820
Barbaric Spirit	17	8	96	13	11	13	76,154
Barberstown	17	7	87	8	5	6	108,665
Barbizon	5	3	56	3	4	4	18,353
Barbizon Streak	1	1	10	1	2	2	5,457
Barboon	2	2	18	2	2	1	14,237
Barcas	2	1	13	1	1	1	10,520
Barcelona	6	5	46	14	10	5	175,244
Bargain Day	24	9	117	12	17	9	118,297
Baron O'Dublin	5	2	18	4	1	2	19,428
Baronius (BRZ)	3	2	23	3	4	5	333,410
Barrera	32	13	186	19	17	29	257,712
Barrydown	1	1	12	3	1	1	5,432
Bartok (IRE)	1	1	6	1	0	1	11,765
Basic Rate	3	1	14	1	2	3	5,770
Bask	5	3	47	6	8	5	39,023
Basket Weave	21	10	115	14	10	18	124,196
Bastogne	2	2	20	4	5	1	37,130
Bates Motel	137	67	1010	118	125	128	2,687,374
Batonnier	41	19	250	33	26	32	530,578
Battle Launch	11	4	69	5	5	9	62,303
Batty	3	2	21	2	1	0	19,420
Bay Express	2	2	8	2	1	1	62,592
Bayou Black	8	4	41	4	8	12	104,284
Bayou Hebert	28	16	183	29	25	14	694,548
Be a Native	15	5	91	10	9	11	384,159
Be a Prospect	31	13	169	19	21	16	222,253
Be a Rullah	15	9	134	14	10	21	181,771
Be My Chief	4	1	17	1	2	2	114,925
Be My Guest	35	18	207	25	17	30	536,987
Be Scenic	1	1	11	1	1	1	14,240
Bear Branch	3	1	22	1	2	1	13,454
Bear Hunt	4	3	20	7	4	1	309,090
Bearer Bond	5	2	35	2	4	4	33,551
Beat Inflation	24	11	163	25	18	17	250,514
Beau Buck	2	1	22	1	1	2	13,186
Beau Chemin (FR)	2	1	11	2	2	3	5,258
Beau Genius	91	42	582	80	67	71	1,956,216
Beau Groton	20	7	156	9	11	14	138,956
Beau Sovereign (NZ)	1	1	8	1	3	0	60,240
Beau's Eagle	60	30	395	53	53	56	988,114
Beaudelaire	31	12	218	22	23	20	273,325
Beautiful Music	6	5	67	8	8	7	41,390
Becker	2	2	21	4	0	3	50,820
Bedford	12	5	100	7	12	6	100,448
Beechcraft (NZ)	1	1	9	2	2	2	28,210
Bejilla	8	3	51	4	2	4	24,362
Bel Baraka (FR)	1	1	4	1	0	0	3,780
Bel Bolide	43	18	264	27	32	34	331,330
Beldale Flutter	1	1	9	1	1	1	6,345
Belek	8	3	45	5	5	6	46,391
Believe a Little	4	2	35	4	6	4	34,330
Believe It	127	66	867	104	118	112	1,551,879
Believe the Queen	27	14	193	28	17	16	522,396
Bellissimo (FR)	1	1	6	1	0	1	1,456
Bellman	1	1	13	2	3	2	24,800
Bellvoy	9	2	32	2	1	1	38,149
Bellypha (IRE)	4	1	10	1	0	1	14,145
Belong to Me	23	13	142	22	12	17	387,932
Belted Earl	11	4	34	5	2	4	30,109
Ben Fab	10	2	62	2	8	8	130,249
Bends Me Mind	7	4	63	5	5	6	53,928
Benedictor	2	1	18	2	3	2	56,012
Benefactor	2	1	5	1	0	1	13,080
Benefice	7	4	53	7	4	3	124,414

Sire	Perf	Wnrs	Sts	1st	2d	3d	Purses
Bengal Tiger	3	2	20	4	4	1	23,232
Benny Bob	7	6	73	14	7	13	131,969
Benny Q.	1	1	13	2	2	1	50,164
Bering (GB)	32	9	132	11	17	13	765,655
Berlin's Burning	1	1	15	3	3	2	23,901
Bert B. Don	2	2	20	3	2	4	70,560
Bertrando	28	14	155	21	18	21	621,490
Best Exit	2	1	14	1	2	2	13,929
Best of Both	9	4	45	7	2	7	47,661
Best of It	6	1	23	1	2	3	16,275
Best Person	3	1	11	2	0	2	11,640
Best Turn	21	8	119	14	12	17	145,217
Bet Big	62	26	465	51	42	42	774,192
Bet Twice	48	21	366	38	47	47	610,110
Better Arbitor	30	14	231	22	31	20	635,575
Better Believe Me	1	1	12	1	2	1	5,450
Beveled	4	3	28	6	3	5	210,378
Beyond the Mint	7	4	42	5	9	8	92,148
Bicker	11	2	56	2	3	7	28,956
Bidder Be Better	1	1	8	2	0	2	9,535
Bien Bien	6	2	44	3	9	7	64,322
Big Bold Sefa	15	7	97	15	9	15	160,878
Big Bronk	2	1	19	3	2	2	34,396
Big Burn	20	6	165	8	17	18	154,330
Big Chill	4	1	23	2	1	1	18,467
Big Current	1	1	5	1	0	0	3,180
Big Doug	2	1	16	2	0	1	13,697
Big Jess	5	2	32	2	2	3	22,281
Big John Taylor	5	1	37	1	3	6	13,750
Big Kohinoor	2	1	4	1	0	0	6,489
Big Leaguer	5	3	54	4	5	5	30,616
Big Mukora	8	4	71	6	9	9	136,463
Big Pistol	19	9	128	15	18	13	279,672
Big Presentation	3	1	16	1	0	1	11,121
Big Sal	7	3	30	4	6	1	86,036
Big Splash	1	1	14	4	2	1	94,156
Big Spruce	79	44	544	81	55	53	1,287,758
Big Stanley	6	2	50	4	11	3	127,750
Big Ted K.	1	1	15	2	2	2	33,430
Bikala	1	1	5	1	1	0	40,580
Billy Blue	2	1	5	1	0	0	11,136
Binalong	5	1	21	2	3	2	89,295
Bionic Light	18	11	134	19	17	16	331,482
Bionic Prospect	2	2	23	5	4	4	32,691
Bishop Family	3	1	15	1	1	1	3,538
Bishop Northcraft	1	1	17	1	0	1	16,260
Black Claret	3	1	14	2	3	1	13,821
Black Is Beautiful	3	1	14	1	2	1	7,514
Black Mackee	26	12	166	20	27	22	182,190
Black Mountain	2	2	18	4	4	4	16,480
Black Reason	1	1	14	2	0	0	9,763
Black Tie Affair (IRE)	155	83	1159	131	170	157	2,726,369
Blade	54	25	396	33	42	47	690,711
Blair's Cove	3	2	28	5	2	4	91,075
Blazing Ryder	2	2	15	2	3	3	11,795
Bless Saggy	2	1	20	1	0	2	3,536
Bletchencore (AUS)	1	1	7	1	0	2	7,272
Bletchingly (AUS)	3	1	14	3	1	2	121,898
Blew by Em	1	1	3	1	0	0	25,560
Blind Spot	5	2	31	3	1	2	28,999
Blitz Biz	1	1	1	1	0	0	1,500
Blood Royal	9	4	73	6	4	7	92,024
Blue Buckaroo	17	7	80	9	10	18	98,849
Blue Cashmere	1	1	12	2	1	2	7,694
Blue Ensign	92	45	658	85	80	79	1,097,993
Blue Grass Magic	8	5	61	10	6	15	103,928
Blue Jester	2	1	22	1	2	2	11,300
Blue Moss (URU)	1	1	11	2	1	2	9,597
Blue Quadrant	8	2	58	5	5	8	85,005
Blue Times	5	3	42	6	3	4	44,713
Bluebird	7	3	42	6	4	3	168,451
Blues Alley	2	1	10	1	1	0	8,729
Blues Parade	5	3	30	5	8	0	155,528
Blush of Fame	1	1	9	1	0	2	3,150
Blushing Groom (FR)	68	39	400	61	48	41	1,854,869
Blushing John	105	47	668	79	62	71	1,201,873

Broodmare Sire	Perf	Wnrs	Sts	1st	2d	3d	Purses
Bo Jinsky	7	4	62	6	6	5	89,698
Bob Back	1	1	9	2	2	2	87,140
Bob Mathias	3	2	24	4	5	1	60,340
Bob's Dusty	44	21	348	41	46	53	613,569
Bobby Ben	12	6	86	7	14	16	122,760
Boca Rio	18	11	101	16	12	11	204,246
Boitron (FR)	6	3	41	4	9	2	95,178
Bold Agent	10	3	65	6	7	8	81,436
Bold Arian	8	3	80	7	8	5	164,255
Bold as Blade	3	1	27	3	1	1	38,275
Bold Badgett	13	7	64	10	13	8	222,557
Bold Bidder	13	6	65	7	5	6	98,919
Bold Commander	2	1	14	1	2	0	5,405
Bold Conquest	2	1	14	3	1	3	10,626
Bold Destroyer	2	1	21	2	2	4	6,794
Bold Dun-Cee	5	4	40	8	6	7	153,271
Bold Ego	58	24	341	38	44	40	766,164
Bold Executive	39	17	242	26	30	24	1,128,687
Bold Favorite	1	1	9	1	0	0	2,725
Bold Forbes	88	51	711	82	85	82	1,196,920
Bold Forli	4	2	32	4	5	4	99,951
Bold Gun	3	2	31	7	6	7	56,671
Bold Gusto	2	2	21	3	3	4	16,716
Bold Hour	24	12	185	22	26	23	249,163
Bold Josh	16	8	143	14	21	19	238,954
Bold Kabota	1	1	12	3	0	3	25,150
Bold L. B.	7	3	59	5	4	17	91,236
Bold Laddie	54	33	336	52	40	39	614,743
Bold Legend	2	2	31	5	2	4	84,295
Bold n Bizarre	17	7	106	14	12	15	117,833
Bold n' Flashy	1	1	1	1	0	0	14,795
Bold Navy	9	2	52	2	2	7	37,675
Bold Nix	4	2	32	3	1	5	18,224
Bold Nuisance	3	2	16	3	0	1	10,978
Bold Pac Man	3	2	27	5	3	4	69,265
Bold Play	6	2	36	2	4	4	31,505
Bold Preference	2	1	14	2	1	0	4,440
Bold Rapport	3	2	15	3	0	2	10,522
Bold Reason	17	7	151	10	16	10	141,148
Bold Revenue	14	7	114	13	22	10	303,739
Bold Roberto	2	1	11	1	1	0	15,262
Bold Ruckus	229	130	1696	246	258	216	6,883,093
Bold Run (FR)	3	1	29	1	1	3	15,638
Bold Second	2	1	14	3	2	1	46,213
Bold Show	1	1	17	3	2	4	13,984
Bold Sphere	2	1	10	1	2	0	4,974
Bold Testimony	4	1	17	2	1	1	3,599
Bold Tropic (SAF)	17	9	110	19	17	10	202,556
Bold Victor	2	1	13	1	6	2	9,862
Bolductive	2	1	14	1	1	1	8,493
Boldwood	2	1	13	4	1	2	28,919
Bolger	58	23	366	39	43	41	492,369
Bolting Holme	2	1	11	2	0	3	24,405
Bombay Duck	6	3	40	8	7	8	176,781
Bonnie Tim	2	1	14	1	2	2	59,979
Bonsoir	1	1	10	5	2	0	84,474
Born Proud	1	1	12	2	1	1	14,737
Borzoi	8	4	49	5	8	6	68,349
Boss Hoss	2	2	16	3	2	3	16,939
Boss Koss	2	1	8	1	1	0	18,406
Botchery	2	2	18	2	0	2	18,248
Boulder Dam	5	2	29	4	2	6	31,501
Boundary	17	7	85	14	6	8	309,540
Bounding Basque	53	23	356	38	51	46	928,184
Bowmans Express	5	3	30	3	4	5	62,467
Boys Nite Out	13	5	61	6	9	9	127,297
Bramante (ARG)	1	1	11	5	0	1	13,912
Brambles	3	1	32	1	5	3	34,000
Brass Minister	9	3	71	8	4	11	77,973
Brave Bidder	2	1	17	2	2	0	36,895
Brave Flyer	1	1	3	1	1	0	6,350
Brave Lad	11	7	84	9	13	9	151,487
Brave Regent	8	4	47	7	4	6	72,975
Brave Salute (AUS)	1	1	5	1	0	0	7,090
Brave Scout	1	1	5	1	0	0	1,740
Brave Shot (GB)	36	20	231	31	36	40	849,044

Broodmare Sire	Perf	Wnrs	Sts	1st	2d	3d	Purses
Bravest Roman	4	1	26	2	2	3	14,346
Bravo	4	1	21	2	2	3	26,867
Brazen Brother	13	6	79	8	8	10	122,859
Breeders Bonus	9	2	40	4	4	5	66,195
Breezing On	6	3	30	6	3	2	89,696
Brent's Prince	24	11	194	17	34	25	292,282
Briar Bend	4	2	42	5	7	9	66,847
Briar Wind	4	1	14	2	0	1	15,098
Briartic	58	23	392	40	51	42	703,835
Brief Ruckus	3	1	33	2	2	3	50,159
Brief Truce	4	2	30	3	2	4	41,252
Bright Launch	1	1	4	1	0	1	17,260
Brilliant Protege	18	5	82	10	11	6	255,645
Brilliant Sandy	20	7	131	15	9	13	239,255
Bring to Reason	2	1	7	1	0	1	6,709
Broad Brush	176	100	1177	182	153	184	3,791,890
Broadway Bill	3	1	9	1	0	1	5,099
Broadway Forli	16	9	102	14	12	10	206,815
Broadway's Top Gun	2	1	17	4	4	4	23,783
Brocco	22	8	88	15	9	6	292,841
Brogan	7	3	45	5	2	6	80,943
*Broker's Tip II	2	2	15	3	2	1	44,918
Brookover	4	1	33	3	4	7	21,717
Brother Liam	2	1	20	3	1	1	18,866
Brother Machree	1	1	5	1	0	0	8,043
Brothers Three	3	2	31	3	0	0	37,792
Brown Arc	6	2	30	2	3	1	46,682
Bruni (GB)	1	1	7	1	0	0	6,841
Brush Aside	1	1	3	1	1	0	7,800
Bubble Gummo	1	1	8	1	0	0	8,063
Buck 'n Bronc	2	2	20	8	1	3	124,316
Buck Forbes	1	1	8	1	2	0	9,013
Buck Hill	1	1	2	1	0	0	7,620
Buck Island	1	1	8	1	2	0	9,088
Buck Private	7	2	51	4	5	5	40,957
Buck's Club	1	1	16	2	5	3	10,357
Buckaroo	137	61	940	117	124	114	1,901,246
Buckboard	2	1	12	2	3	1	34,562
Buckfinder	74	43	501	73	63	58	1,123,136
Buckland's Halo	1	1	6	1	0	0	3,000
Buckley Boy	22	11	135	18	20	12	835,079
Buckpasser	5	4	49	10	6	3	189,793
Bucksaw	2	1	5	1	1	0	6,771
Bucksplasher	94	49	638	74	76	67	1,256,626
Bucky Raj	2	1	7	1	0	2	4,360
Buddha King	1	1	9	1	0	3	3,880
Buddy	5	1	24	1	1	2	47,205
Buffalo Beau	2	1	10	1	2	1	6,261
Buffalo Lark	6	3	45	7	7	9	191,841
Bugle Note	2	1	13	1	0	3	2,124
Bull Shoals	1	1	1	1	0	0	7,200
Bulldar	4	2	29	5	9	1	41,270
Bupers	8	4	77	9	8	6	89,041
Burd Alane	1	1	7	2	2	1	25,157
Burning On	3	2	11	2	0	1	7,416
Bushido	3	1	21	3	1	3	10,125
Busted (GB)	3	1	17	1	2	3	61,840
Bustino (GB)	3	2	22	2	3	8	25,378
Busy Chief	2	1	7	1	0	1	2,729
C. G's Count	1	1	13	1	1	4	10,337
Cabildo	6	3	28	5	4	2	30,704
Cabin	2	1	19	1	3	0	8,742
Cabrini Green	22	15	188	26	20	25	394,672
Cabriole	5	3	37	3	6	3	23,924
Cactus Road	7	3	54	7	9	8	60,036
Cadeaux Genereux (GB)	4	1	16	3	2	3	259,930
Cadoudal (FR)	1	1	8	1	0	0	9,000
Caerleon	45	20	198	31	18	17	880,826
Caesar's Dream	2	2	12	3	4	0	12,126
Cahaba Gold	1	1	9	1	1	0	3,624
Cahill Road	46	30	273	54	28	45	1,106,621
Cajun Prince	11	5	65	15	10	16	188,825
Calender Stack	2	1	10	1	2	1	21,467
Caller I. D.	47	25	299	48	36	36	963,507
Calligraphy	1	1	11	1	1	1	10,107
Caltech	10	2	61	5	7	2	110,219

Sire	Perf	Wnrs	Sts	1st	2d	3d	Purses
Calumar	11	6	58	8	7	4	177,619
Can Can Sam	1	1	9	1	0	0	6,487
Can You Beat That	1	1	3	1	0	0	7,020
Canadian Bound	3	1	30	1	0	2	6,998
Canadian Gil	9	3	29	5	3	5	53,756
Candi's Gold	51	22	314	34	37	40	537,610
Candle Stand	3	2	34	4	4	7	51,323
Candy Command	1	1	16	1	2	2	14,045
Candy Stripes	6	3	31	9	4	4	75,978
Candyman Bee	2	2	21	5	2	0	25,450
Cane Field	2	2	10	2	0	2	14,692
Cannon Dancer	6	4	47	5	9	7	50,223
Cannon Shell	14	5	74	8	6	12	125,642
Cannonade	51	25	332	43	36	29	676,588
Cantatore	1	1	8	3	0	0	26,315
Capital Idea	6	5	55	9	4	10	173,216
Capital Punishment	3	1	17	3	3	4	10,015
Capitol South	12	5	84	7	8	10	65,895
Capote	167	83	1050	140	125	129	3,334,613
Capt. Don	6	6	47	11	10	8	141,009
Captain Cee Jay	3	1	12	2	3	0	4,941
Captain Courageous	23	14	146	26	22	15	175,358
Captain James (IRE)	4	2	31	3	1	5	60,903
Captain My Captain	2	1	26	1	1	3	9,481
Captain Valid	2	1	25	3	4	4	60,282
Caracolero	8	1	55	3	6	8	50,593
Caradja	1	1	8	1	0	1	7,615
Carborundum	12	5	69	11	5	3	64,776
Cari County	2	2	18	2	4	3	23,917
Cari Jill Hajji	3	1	16	1	1	2	10,718
Cariellor (FR)	3	2	25	3	6	2	27,570
Carload	7	4	34	12	3	5	131,676
Carmelite House	2	1	12	1	1	1	9,559
Carnivalay	85	34	577	58	57	64	1,155,128
Caro (IRE)	63	26	389	41	45	50	1,153,132
Carodanz	5	2	23	2	1	3	17,746
Carolina Ridge	2	1	13	2	4	1	7,173
Caros Love	5	3	29	3	4	4	63,269
Carr de Naskra	85	36	535	57	68	81	1,359,385
Carson City	136	76	815	146	138	101	3,679,408
Cartesian	9	4	45	4	1	4	40,582
Cartwright	4	2	27	6	4	2	59,198
Casa Dante	12	9	86	27	7	12	244,653
Cascade Chief	1	1	12	2	1	3	14,552
Case the Joint	5	1	24	1	0	3	4,766
Cash the Ticket	2	1	14	1	4	2	16,992
Cassaleria	32	15	209	30	16	33	367,906
Castle Green	1	1	6	1	0	0	5,291
Castle Guard	22	11	205	16	20	33	283,973
Castle Howard	5	4	50	7	5	10	87,538
Catalpa Lane	2	1	12	3	1	1	27,690
Catane	3	2	21	5	4	7	160,207
Cathedral Bells	7	5	40	6	5	9	67,263
Cathies's Goal	1	1	9	1	1	1	9,131
Cathy's Reject	13	3	58	4	5	6	47,195
Catrail	3	2	15	2	3	1	132,721
Caucasus	33	18	221	33	19	31	480,115
Cause Celebre	8	3	67	4	8	4	49,070
Cause for Pause	8	3	46	4	2	10	40,226
Cavalry	3	1	18	5	2	4	100,455
Cavamore	2	1	29	1	4	5	18,078
Caveat	162	84	1177	137	152	137	3,488,226
Cavo Doro (IRE)	1	1	3	1	0	1	6,010
Cawdor	2	1	14	1	0	3	14,163
Cee's Tizzy	20	11	107	21	15	15	467,002
Cefis	2	1	8	1	0	0	4,320
Centaine (AUS)	10	4	51	8	4	11	116,374
Center Cut	6	5	82	10	6	12	142,012
Central Paris	1	1	8	5	2	0	128,100
Centrust	3	2	22	6	2	5	236,524
Century Flyer	1	1	11	3	1	2	17,821
Century Prince	4	1	20	2	1	1	37,162
Certain Times	3	2	19	3	1	2	28,738
Cestare	1	1	7	1	2	0	4,321
Chaka	2	1	8	1	0	1	10,055
Chalk Hill	4	1	20	1	1	1	6,039

Sire	Perf	Wnrs	Sts	1st	2d	3d	Purses
Champagne Charlie	7	1	29	1	1	2	8,511
Champagneforashley	3	1	11	2	1	3	20,395
Chanago	2	1	21	3	0	4	52,049
Chapel Creek	14	8	77	10	15	6	153,107
Charging Falls	17	8	119	15	11	13	169,765
Charging Forbes	1	1	3	1	0	1	2,220
Charging Prince	1	1	8	3	1	2	20,485
Charles Elliott	1	1	7	2	0	1	11,036
Charlie Barley	12	4	73	7	10	10	142,051
Charming Turn	12	6	103	10	10	5	97,899
Chas Conerly	13	6	84	10	5	8	204,027
Chati	4	1	14	2	1	1	19,548
Cheer On	3	2	18	4	3	3	22,306
Cherokee Colony	52	26	374	47	48	39	916,766
Cherokee Fellow	44	29	334	53	37	27	854,240
Cherokee Run	7	1	26	2	3	5	72,070
Cherry Pop	6	1	26	1	3	1	13,348
Chic Boutique	1	1	15	4	4	0	22,706
Chicago	6	3	29	3	3	7	97,346
Chicanery Slew	2	1	6	1	1	1	11,891
Chidester	6	3	35	4	5	7	57,209
Chief Honcho	7	2	34	5	7	6	70,998
Chief Seabird	3	1	15	2	3	3	28,518
Chief Singer	9	6	40	7	4	4	460,928
Chief's Crown	145	67	839	127	95	98	3,059,997
Chieftain	27	9	162	16	25	18	299,338
Chili Pepper Pie	1	1	4	2	0	0	23,515
Chilicote	2	1	15	1	3	4	13,566
Chillon	3	1	6	1	0	0	8,067
Chimes Band	4	2	20	2	2	5	74,372
Chimineas	6	2	27	2	2	6	132,282
Chiromancy	3	1	11	1	1	3	12,626
Chisos	26	8	118	19	14	20	248,865
Chivalry	8	2	41	2	6	7	37,301
Choreographer	5	1	32	1	1	2	12,069
Christopher R.	13	9	94	15	6	8	195,393
Chromite	44	14	272	22	28	35	420,826
Chumming	9	4	59	6	12	3	109,223
Cien Fuegos	2	1	11	1	2	0	8,435
Cimmarron	2	1	5	1	0	0	12,180
Cinco Grande	3	1	11	1	2	0	10,610
Cinteelo	3	1	21	1	2	3	11,956
Cipayo (ARG)	17	5	103	16	11	9	302,311
Circle	6	2	31	7	4	3	149,343
Circle Home	11	5	81	7	2	4	78,429
Circulating	1	1	3	1	0	1	19,530
Cisco Road	4	1	10	1	0	2	6,604
Citidancer	44	28	290	54	31	31	1,636,928
City Council (IRE)	1	1	5	1	0	0	4,323
Civil Ceremony	1	1	8	1	3	0	10,048
Clackson (BRZ)	2	1	7	1	0	1	14,960
Claim	39	20	250	35	40	30	520,644
Clansman (NZ)	2	2	8	2	1	2	35,769
Claramount	9	4	46	7	3	3	63,100
Clash of Steel	1	1	4	1	0	1	5,334
Clasico (FR)	2	1	17	3	1	5	13,495
Class Chief	1	1	13	1	1	1	4,741
Classic	6	4	68	9	9	4	134,343
Classic Account	17	10	133	15	16	15	452,655
Classic Clipper	4	1	24	1	3	1	12,389
Classic Fame	2	1	23	1	0	2	9,004
Classic Go Go	44	26	323	45	43	44	911,707
Classical Ballet	4	1	17	1	3	1	18,358
Claude Monet	1	1	7	2	1	1	446,180
Clear Choice	1	1	2	1	0	0	4,500
Clear Course	1	1	9	4	1	0	105,458
Clear Sun	1	1	5	1	0	0	3,165
Clem	1	1	7	1	0	0	3,444
Clev Er Tell	10	4	75	8	13	11	160,356
Clever Allemont	5	1	17	1	1	2	7,170
Clever Champ	38	19	228	30	26	26	461,471
Clever Secret	22	5	126	8	15	16	98,091
Clever Shot	3	2	25	3	2	2	29,609
Clever Trick	307	156	2051	256	252	260	5,913,450
Cliff Flower (ARG)	1	1	11	2	3	0	18,994
Clint Maroon	5	3	39	3	6	7	63,545

Broodmare Sire	Perf	Wnrs	Sts	1st	2d	3d	Purses
Close Watch	1	1	5	1	2	1	7,360
Cloud Encounter	1	1	9	1	1	0	7,086
Cloudy Dawn	11	5	101	7	6	13	82,321
Coach's Call	3	2	15	4	1	2	20,703
Coastal	84	38	600	69	57	74	1,071,618
Coax Me Chad	14	7	98	9	10	14	107,072
Code Word R.	4	1	35	1	3	7	25,962
Codex	13	8	88	13	9	9	135,129
Cogency	8	1	58	1	3	2	9,797
Cognizant	9	3	53	5	3	8	52,871
Cojak	30	15	203	20	16	26	310,098
Cold Reality	2	1	18	1	3	2	10,470
Cold Reception	12	2	52	2	6	5	55,830
Collectible	3	1	33	2	6	3	26,888
Collier	28	11	163	24	19	17	268,884
Colonel Power	11	4	62	8	8	4	112,370
Colonel Stevens	10	5	62	6	4	7	46,088
Colonial Affair	17	8	91	8	13	10	134,405
Colony Light	15	9	127	14	16	18	278,495
Color Bearer	6	3	27	3	3	2	32,421
Color Me New	2	1	13	1	0	1	17,847
Combat Ready	7	2	29	2	2	3	74,583
Combatant	3	1	22	4	2	1	16,178
Come Rain Or Shine	2	1	18	2	0	0	10,095
*Comeram	1	1	11	4	1	0	13,370
Comet Kat	10	5	64	9	6	6	199,528
Comet Shine	5	2	36	9	6	2	181,655
Comical Clown	6	1	25	5	4	5	63,613
Commadore C.	13	8	91	13	11	22	273,429
Command Control	5	1	38	3	3	4	67,297
Command Force	2	1	20	1	2	4	21,210
Commanding Lead	2	1	21	2	3	2	38,661
Commemorate	41	19	293	34	36	30	666,157
Commissioner	9	7	107	10	22	12	101,100
Common Grounds	9	4	44	6	5	3	265,224
Compelling Sound	16	6	97	10	12	12	203,093
Compliance	49	24	368	50	38	46	649,359
Con Man	3	1	15	1	0	1	5,554
Concatinate	1	1	18	2	1	3	15,322
Concertino	1	1	10	2	2	2	19,047
Concierge	2	2	15	3	1	1	22,425
Concorde Bound	22	10	192	18	17	37	480,427
Concorde's Tune	10	5	72	6	6	3	101,421
Conduction	1	1	6	1	1	1	4,140
Conesaba	2	1	14	2	4	1	12,945
Confidant	5	4	47	4	5	5	31,780
Connaught	1	1	8	1	2	2	55,580
Conquer	1	1	12	4	2	0	17,680
Conquistador Cielo	267	137	1896	248	247	260	5,014,327
Conquistador Oro	3	2	32	3	6	8	36,296
Consigliere (GB)	7	5	33	6	2	4	59,919
Contador (ARG)	2	1	5	1	1	1	13,475
Contare	14	6	89	9	7	10	162,242
Conte Di Savoya	6	2	40	3	6	6	42,974
Conte Grande (FR)	4	1	17	1	3	0	55,267
Contempt	3	1	18	1	2	1	10,300
Contested Colors	5	1	25	4	2	6	50,195
Contorsionist	7	3	56	5	9	8	112,365
Conveyor	4	3	36	4	7	3	82,081
Convincingly	5	3	35	5	5	4	137,681
Convoy Scout	1	1	5	1	2	1	2,669
Cooky Greene	3	2	28	2	1	3	25,872
Cool	3	2	26	3	6	2	41,099
Cool Frenchy	1	1	9	1	0	0	3,294
Cool Groom	4	1	31	1	4	3	22,242
Cool Halo	12	4	58	6	7	10	76,647
Cool Hand	1	1	9	1	3	4	21,485
Cool Joe	1	1	9	1	2	2	12,297
Cool Moon	1	1	10	2	4	1	13,170
Cool Victor	21	8	141	12	23	19	557,325
Coolfin (IRE)	1	1	11	1	3	2	18,137
Copelan	175	94	1054	155	150	125	3,795,622
Cormorant	120	57	755	103	87	87	2,349,042
Cornish Music	2	2	19	4	2	4	35,116
Cornish Prince	34	14	202	20	23	22	313,140
Corporate Report	69	36	428	50	51	63	2,145,264

Broodmare Sire	Perf	Wnrs	Sts	1st	2d	3d	Purses
Corridor Key	28	10	181	14	21	25	482,431
Cortan	4	1	21	1	2	2	41,609
Corwyn Bay (IRE)	20	10	102	17	16	10	551,098
Cost Conscious	8	4	52	4	5	5	54,161
*Cougar II	42	19	311	28	30	28	413,478
Cougar's Crown	9	1	57	1	6	5	97,161
Council Rock	4	1	16	1	5	2	16,589
Count Brook	5	1	23	2	0	1	27,297
Count Eric	5	4	49	7	4	5	83,062
Count Francescui	5	4	35	5	5	1	35,902
Count Giacomo	2	1	19	2	0	2	10,366
Count My Love	4	2	20	2	2	2	16,253
Counterfeit Money	3	1	30	2	0	2	7,383
Country Boy Jim	2	1	15	3	1	2	57,634
Country Doctor	3	2	28	3	2	2	38,094
Country Light	35	16	232	27	25	25	365,618
Country Manor	3	2	14	3	1	1	54,207
Country Pine	65	37	496	71	53	73	954,220
Country Store	2	2	19	3	5	2	75,869
Coup de Chance	1	1	6	2	0	1	17,652
Coup de Kas	9	4	44	7	3	3	133,558
Courageous Sailor	2	1	7	1	0	0	2,213
Court Open	2	1	23	4	2	2	58,155
Court Ruling	7	3	31	4	4	4	25,096
Court Trial	34	18	270	28	32	40	369,628
Couvreur (IRE)	3	2	20	4	0	3	37,397
Cox's Ridge	229	119	1564	206	215	195	4,696,972
Cozzene	134	59	905	114	94	105	2,182,400
Cracklin Cool	1	1	4	1	0	0	1,668
Crafty Drone	14	8	87	12	14	17	158,478
Crafty Native	9	6	73	15	9	9	249,314
Crafty Prospector	281	154	1908	280	248	262	5,054,773
Crash Cash	1	1	8	1	2	0	20,089
Crawford Special	4	2	19	4	3	5	14,812
Creamette City	1	1	6	1	0	0	1,748
Creekarosa	7	1	40	4	2	5	35,029
Creole Dancer	12	6	77	13	11	8	156,582
Cresta Rider	18	4	84	8	6	8	101,660
Crested Wave	3	2	11	3	1	2	58,842
Crewman	3	1	23	1	1	4	28,767
Criminal Type	60	32	441	63	50	44	1,564,145
Crimson Battle	10	2	73	3	9	4	48,673
Crimson Falcon	7	3	52	3	2	6	23,991
Crimson Man	2	1	10	2	3	1	6,595
Crimson Satan	11	5	75	6	8	7	80,695
Crimson Slew	6	4	26	7	3	7	53,983
Crimsons Thrill	1	1	12	1	1	4	9,123
Critique	5	3	30	4	5	7	351,503
Crocap	1	1	7	2	0	1	9,504
Crocation	1	1	7	1	0	0	2,522
Cromwell Park (GB)	1	1	4	1	0	0	5,155
Crow (FR)	13	3	60	4	2	8	111,578
Crown Gift	2	1	7	2	1	1	68,350
Crown Pleasure	3	2	17	3	3	1	26,687
Crown Thy Good	1	1	1	1	0	0	6,000
Crowned Jewel	6	4	41	7	5	5	166,293
Crowned Prince	1	1	2	1	0	0	90,000
Crowning	3	1	12	1	2	0	20,279
Crowning Honors	5	1	47	1	3	9	14,715
Crowning Season (GB)	4	2	24	2	5	3	10,133
Crozier	8	3	54	5	8	5	27,986
Cruise On In	3	2	44	7	4	4	63,858
Crusader Sword	69	36	476	57	54	70	1,249,324
Crying to Run	1	1	9	1	1	3	38,594
Cryptoclearance	172	81	1168	138	135	125	2,715,593
Crystal Glitters	14	7	83	10	10	13	750,949
Crystal Palace	4	1	24	1	2	6	20,947
Crystal Run	5	2	26	3	6	5	52,313
Crystal Star	2	1	5	1	0	0	1,048
Crystal Water	23	8	89	11	7	10	159,531
Cuchillo	3	2	20	4	4	3	19,429
Culcita	1	1	10	1	2	0	17,582
Cullendale	4	4	42	4	9	5	46,758
Cure the Blues	235	121	1575	205	184	208	4,624,546
Currency Control	3	1	6	2	0	0	19,380
Current Hope	9	4	64	6	6	5	75,102

Sire	Perf	Wnrs	Sts	1st	2d	3d	Purses
Curtain King	4	2	48	4	6	8	56,094
Cut Throat (GB)	16	5	106	7	8	11	92,989
Cutlass	106	49	666	78	84	69	1,286,883
Cutlass Reality	40	18	220	32	14	22	518,944
Cyane	22	11	167	19	20	20	343,739
*Czar Alexander	2	1	11	1	0	4	2,938
Czaravich	46	16	313	26	40	38	429,460
D'Accord	112	59	790	104	108	105	2,022,331
D. J. Cat	1	1	5	1	1	0	21,860
Da' White Judge	5	4	46	6	6	6	100,170
Dactylographer	19	5	113	7	18	11	155,141
Dahar	54	23	374	49	33	36	913,321
Daily Dispatch	1	1	14	2	6	1	16,534
Daily Review	3	2	23	2	4	1	25,327
Damascus	97	44	599	73	77	79	1,623,591
Damascus Silver	2	2	30	4	3	4	100,317
Damister	5	3	50	5	6	3	56,378
Dance Bid	34	19	266	31	31	37	370,274
Dance Centre	6	1	37	1	5	5	18,577
Dance Furlough	4	1	27	1	1	1	8,803
Dance God	2	1	21	4	4	0	19,455
Dance in Time	20	9	139	15	15	26	199,511
Dance of Life	8	4	35	6	2	3	80,958
Dance Spell	5	1	14	1	0	2	16,970
Dancer's Image	1	1	3	1	0	0	4,800
Dancer's Profile	1	1	11	1	5	3	8,622
Dancing Again	6	3	36	3	4	5	109,362
Dancing Brave	7	3	40	5	3	3	60,069
Dancing Champ	13	5	83	8	6	10	158,511
Dancing Count	59	31	408	47	68	40	796,476
Dancing Crown	9	4	53	7	9	3	108,987
Dancing Czar	14	5	86	6	12	12	207,978
Dancing Dervish	6	3	41	3	8	4	35,797
Dancing Dissident	5	3	29	4	4	2	182,554
Dancing Groom	1	1	4	1	1	1	44,395
Dancing Moss	2	1	26	4	2	3	25,316
Dancing Pirate	1	1	12	2	1	2	11,028
Dancing Robe (GB)	1	1	10	2	1	2	20,013
Dancing School	3	1	27	1	3	4	8,412
Dancing Spree	2	2	16	4	3	0	38,038
Dandy Binge	3	2	14	2	1	1	11,710
Danebo	4	4	42	7	2	3	35,346
Danehill	19	9	116	12	11	22	232,495
Daniel Boone	6	4	52	11	10	2	138,235
Daniri (FR)	2	1	15	2	0	1	12,995
Danny's Keys	4	2	21	2	7	2	34,783
Danotable	5	3	45	6	7	4	50,624
Dansil	5	3	28	4	2	1	51,593
Danski	8	5	49	8	7	5	145,007
Dansons	18	4	120	5	10	13	143,006
Danton	6	3	32	3	7	4	81,811
Danzatore	60	30	406	46	51	45	836,265
Danzig	176	96	1061	166	164	121	6,762,695
Danzig Connection	128	68	918	131	102	115	1,989,552
Danzig Dancer	2	1	15	2	0	1	36,439
Daranstone	2	1	19	1	1	2	7,062
Darby Creek Road	52	23	364	37	39	48	427,333
Dare to Command	4	1	48	9	3	6	115,250
Daring Groom	10	3	64	5	4	7	103,015
Daring Jim	6	5	44	6	7	9	34,005
Daring March	3	2	27	5	4	2	53,536
Dark Brown (BRZ)	4	2	26	3	5	0	83,982
Dark Illusion	1	1	21	1	6	3	28,574
Darn That Alarm	46	21	312	38	42	41	1,156,375
Darshaan (GB)	21	7	110	12	5	12	301,883
Dash It Off	1	1	11	2	1	3	11,343
Dash n' Raja	3	1	21	3	3	0	17,861
Dashing Blade	2	1	6	3	0	1	235,808
Dauphin Fabuleux	24	11	200	18	22	25	369,542
Dave's Indian	1	1	12	1	1	1	11,113
Dave's Reality	6	4	26	4	5	5	51,790
David's Dream Boy	1	1	13	4	2	2	32,405
Davie Dancer	1	1	9	1	1	0	15,525
Dawn Flight	2	1	17	2	2	1	29,284
Dawn of Creation	6	1	39	1	6	4	32,599
Dawn Quixote	17	8	96	12	7	8	204,494

Sire	Perf	Wnrs	Sts	1st	2d	3d	Purses
Dawn Revival	1	1	8	2	0	0	12,420
Dayjur	57	32	354	62	42	47	1,799,823
De Braak	13	4	74	4	9	5	52,031
De Jeau	12	8	110	19	14	13	159,480
De Niro	3	2	16	4	1	2	56,938
Dearest Doctor	11	5	68	6	5	4	66,974
Debonair Roger	22	9	118	20	11	19	298,363
Debut	1	1	7	1	0	0	7,033
Decidedly	9	3	47	4	3	7	36,752
Decies II	1	1	8	1	0	2	11,546
Decimator	3	2	34	4	2	4	23,531
Deck Hand	11	5	109	14	23	12	83,898
Dee Lance	15	6	85	10	11	4	100,650
Deerhound	15	7	119	12	23	19	255,043
Defense Verdict	18	9	114	13	9	18	185,732
Defensive Play	22	9	111	12	10	16	292,275
Defiance	18	7	118	8	5	17	130,524
Defrere	5	2	35	5	4	9	55,516
Degenerate Jon	5	3	48	3	6	10	99,906
Dehere	24	11	103	13	14	9	344,260
Delaware Chief	7	4	49	11	9	5	134,343
Delayer	2	1	14	1	0	2	15,131
Delegant	1	1	15	2	6	3	36,110
Delineator	3	1	10	1	0	0	18,450
Delinsky	4	1	20	2	2	1	11,261
Delta Flag	10	1	59	1	6	4	31,875
Delta Judge	3	3	41	5	7	5	63,094
Delta Oil	3	1	12	1	2	3	10,946
Demons Begone	37	15	224	31	30	25	829,308
Deposit Ticket	26	19	196	27	30	19	510,526
Deputed Testamony	50	31	327	48	34	42	1,007,852
Deputy Minister	313	170	1933	292	256	245	9,035,408
Deputy Regent	2	1	12	1	1	1	4,365
Derby Dawning	3	1	17	3	1	2	25,500
Derby Wish	18	6	113	10	15	14	183,689
Derek (BRZ)	2	1	16	1	0	2	13,861
Desert Classic	4	2	19	4	4	1	34,923
Desert God	2	2	8	4	1	0	36,130
Desert Review	2	1	13	1	3	3	10,970
Desert Serpent	1	1	8	1	3	0	2,593
Desert Wine	108	58	656	99	68	86	1,718,578
Destroyer (SAF)	5	4	30	6	1	2	45,029
Determinant	2	1	20	2	2	2	15,168
Determined Cosmic	7	3	57	9	5	10	99,391
Devil Begone	1	1	2	1	0	0	22,620
Devil His Due	5	2	18	3	1	1	28,265
Devil On Ice	1	1	6	2	0	0	24,608
Devil's Bag	210	99	1323	169	192	175	3,648,570
Devil's Cry	5	1	11	1	0	0	8,331
Devil's Punch Bowl	4	2	28	3	3	0	18,024
Devoted Ruler	4	2	38	4	4	4	37,920
Dewan	26	12	183	20	18	16	364,717
Dewan Keys	15	11	129	16	14	15	323,618
Dewdle's Dancer	3	3	12	4	3	2	38,514
Diablo	47	28	275	45	40	40	1,163,563
Diabolo	14	1	53	1	1	6	21,644
Dial a Lad	1	1	6	1	1	0	5,916
Diamond Bag	1	1	7	1	1	0	7,963
Diamond Prospect	36	16	238	35	31	23	552,004
Diamond Shoal (GB)	19	5	96	7	14	7	162,286
Diamond Sword	9	2	50	3	4	4	68,782
Diamonds Are Trump	2	1	24	1	2	1	15,685
Diazo	2	1	12	2	1	4	18,641
Dickerson	1	1	17	1	2	3	12,396
Diesis (GB)	70	33	381	48	48	38	1,124,949
Digression	9	5	59	11	6	5	203,660
Dike	7	3	54	4	5	7	41,705
Dimaggio	33	14	219	34	18	28	430,933
Din's Dancer	8	3	53	5	3	7	51,253
Diplomat Way	24	7	131	15	11	15	156,662
Diplomatic Note	12	6	117	9	13	19	107,656
Dispersal	23	12	105	15	14	13	274,847
Distant Day	4	1	38	2	0	7	42,530
Distant Heart	2	1	12	3	3	1	5,555
Distant Land	6	2	55	4	6	10	43,305
Distant Memories	1	1	12	2	3	3	31,738

Broodmare Sire	Perf	Wnrs	Sts	1st	2d	3d	Purses
Distant Relative (IRE)	6	3	23	3	2	2	90,411
Distant Ryder	10	5	104	7	12	16	75,203
Distinctive	26	13	213	26	30	26	540,564
Distinctive Cat	1	1	8	2	3	1	41,160
Distinctive Pro	121	63	833	112	100	118	2,228,002
Distinctly North	3	3	18	6	3	1	120,020
Distinctpartner	1	1	5	1	0	0	1,700
Dixie Brass	28	12	192	19	22	19	988,613
Dixieland Band	325	182	2197	326	299	305	11,556,169
Dixieland Brass	35	14	231	24	27	30	352,136
Dixieland Heat	2	2	17	2	3	3	36,194
Dmitri	4	3	24	4	0	1	65,110
Do It Again Dan	8	5	64	9	9	12	66,791
Do Lishus	4	2	18	2	1	1	35,453
Do Tell George	2	1	14	1	0	4	8,606
Doc Scott J.	1	1	4	2	1	0	5,176
Doc Van	5	2	43	7	4	3	129,392
Doc's Leader	8	4	46	9	9	7	302,725
Docile Boy	3	1	16	2	1	3	8,218
Dock Robbery	2	2	19	3	0	3	27,478
Dock Side	2	2	34	3	6	2	16,997
*Doctor of Music	4	2	29	4	1	0	33,103
Doctor Stat	39	13	289	25	29	38	263,545
Doctor's Orders	8	2	47	7	11	7	112,497
Dodge	4	2	36	6	13	3	85,551
Dogwood Passport	10	5	81	10	15	10	136,652
Dolly's Prince	2	1	8	1	1	1	7,851
Dom Alaric (FR)	43	23	377	40	39	47	622,425
Dom Dancer	3	2	32	4	3	3	90,886
Dom Pasquini (FR)	2	1	16	1	3	4	42,630
Domasca Dan	3	2	27	5	3	4	172,186
Dominant Star	7	4	51	4	11	5	47,153
Dominated	5	3	43	3	7	6	36,893
Domineau	3	2	19	7	2	4	601,200
Dominion (GB)	10	3	47	4	8	7	95,383
Don B.	24	15	189	25	26	30	317,806
Don B. Jr.	4	1	28	3	1	4	48,985
Don F.	1	1	10	3	2	1	23,913
Don Rickles	6	4	61	5	2	4	35,083
Don Sebastian	3	2	33	4	4	7	56,137
Don's Choice	13	6	61	7	9	2	77,257
Don's Joke	6	3	33	3	2	5	35,557
Don't Forget Me	7	4	44	8	6	8	158,099
Don't Hesitate	12	3	79	5	17	9	165,416
Donut King	3	1	20	1	5	3	20,715
Doonesbear	3	2	28	5	3	2	38,451
Doonesbury	32	15	189	23	22	24	354,514
Double Hitch	4	2	18	3	1	1	30,935
Double Leader	4	1	24	8	4	3	89,720
Double Letter	2	2	5	2	1	0	2,227
Double Line	5	3	39	7	5	7	80,841
Double Negative	26	13	141	20	18	12	467,012
Double Reach	2	1	15	4	1	0	51,625
Double Ready	8	5	49	9	2	7	83,271
Double Reason	1	1	10	1	0	2	4,310
Double Schwartz (IRE)	1	1	12	2	1	2	31,448
Double Sonic	13	6	96	10	13	15	192,855
Double Zeus	35	19	283	37	26	29	681,518
Doulab	1	1	7	1	2	1	23,964
Dover Ridge	8	4	41	6	4	4	75,971
Doyoun (IRE)	5	2	26	5	4	1	56,032
Dr. Adagio	11	6	55	10	6	2	155,206
Dr. Blum	79	44	543	75	78	75	1,686,267
Dr. Bonanno	1	1	7	1	1	0	5,509
Dr. Carter	56	26	410	47	41	53	813,647
Dr. Dalton	6	1	41	2	3	6	29,990
Dr. Dan Eyes	3	2	16	2	0	2	5,534
Dr. Danzig	7	3	44	4	11	11	96,857
Dr. Do Much	5	2	40	2	2	4	26,946
Dr. Fager	4	2	15	3	1	2	43,270
Dr. Geo. Adams	13	9	81	14	7	8	198,439
Dr. Koch	5	1	32	1	4	7	23,105
Dr. McGuire	10	3	64	5	7	6	63,634
Dr. Reality	4	2	23	3	2	5	53,836
Dr. Schwartzman	12	5	71	9	9	12	269,172
Dr. Valeri	4	3	32	6	7	3	96,045

Broodmare Sire	Perf	Wnrs	Sts	1st	2d	3d	Purses
Draconic	10	7	68	13	12	5	184,255
Dramatic Desire	2	1	5	1	1	0	14,050
Dreadnought	4	2	21	3	6	5	98,063
Dressage	1	1	13	1	4	2	67,470
Droll Role	4	2	35	3	2	2	13,294
Drone	76	39	528	63	55	61	1,532,823
Drone's Reward	2	2	16	4	1	2	25,420
Drouilly (FR)	32	18	214	33	35	26	391,765
Drouilly's Boy	5	1	25	3	2	2	15,166
Drum Fire	18	11	129	16	19	21	221,169
Drumalis (IRE)	5	2	17	4	3	3	26,599
Drums of Time	4	1	16	1	2	1	58,963
Duc de Flanagan	2	1	16	2	0	1	17,798
Duck Dance	12	2	64	5	4	4	44,369
Due Diligence	2	1	20	2	2	2	50,810
Duke Mitchell	1	1	10	3	1	1	13,578
Duke Tom	5	1	33	2	2	3	35,809
*Dumpty Humpty	2	1	11	1	0	0	2,238
Dumpty's Cutter	2	1	16	3	4	3	19,974
Dunant (IRE)	2	2	4	2	0	0	6,435
Dundee Marmalade	1	1	7	4	0	1	33,829
Dunham's Gift	16	7	108	8	11	10	76,677
Duns Scotus	10	6	78	12	5	13	232,597
Durban Deep	1	1	6	1	0	0	3,285
Dust Commander	44	19	377	31	40	51	411,642
Dustin Power	2	1	29	2	6	6	81,815
Dusty Sassafras	2	1	17	1	1	3	18,732
Dusty Spy	2	1	15	2	2	1	10,928
Dynaformer	139	68	923	111	114	110	3,723,250
Dynastic	6	2	44	5	6	4	58,900
Dyno Stat	3	2	27	3	6	5	34,158
Eager Native	7	2	34	4	7	1	69,487
Easter Sun	1	1	7	1	1	1	11,965
Eastern Bazaar	5	4	37	6	6	7	103,814
Eastern Echo	78	44	522	74	73	72	1,828,237
Eastern Lord	11	3	43	6	2	8	48,211
Eastern Music	3	1	9	1	1	0	17,585
Eastover Court	3	1	20	2	5	2	24,930
Easy Goer	45	26	255	46	38	35	2,088,667
Eclipso	1	1	3	1	0	0	18,125
Ecliptical	12	7	78	12	12	5	182,609
Ecole Etage	1	1	10	1	0	4	9,975
Editorial Comment	4	1	14	2	2	1	25,153
Edsar	1	1	11	3	3	1	86,170
Effervescing	19	13	137	18	16	19	193,709
Efisio	3	1	25	2	6	4	42,261
Egg Toss	6	4	59	6	6	11	121,279
Eighty Below Zero	3	1	22	4	2	4	92,359
El Asesor (ARG)	4	2	24	2	4	2	78,413
El Baba	35	18	256	29	30	27	385,922
El Barril (CHI)	4	3	39	8	2	3	87,659
El Bravo	2	1	6	1	0	1	8,395
El Dorado Bob (GB)	6	2	28	2	8	2	24,029
El Gran Capitan (ARG)	6	3	34	5	5	2	58,353
El Gran Senor	74	37	476	61	68	52	1,703,153
El Lagarto	2	1	9	1	1	2	1,940
*El Loco	1	1	8	1	1	2	8,825
El Mandingo	3	1	23	3	3	2	29,702
El Pitirre	7	1	43	2	4	10	33,138
El Prado (IRE)	38	17	232	23	29	24	648,100
El Raggaas	32	16	202	23	16	28	541,266
El Rastro (IRE)	6	3	42	3	2	2	29,811
El Senor	5	3	35	4	3	1	32,355
El Terresto	2	2	8	3	1	0	25,295
El Tiron	3	1	33	3	9	4	51,563
El Toro	1	1	5	2	0	1	6,003
El Virtuoso (ARG)	1	1	5	2	0	1	26,090
Ela-Mana-Mou (IRE)	7	3	46	6	12	8	248,283
Elbow Grease	4	1	36	1	1	4	24,079
Eldag's Boy	1	1	11	5	2	3	83,073
Eldorado Kid	3	2	19	3	2	5	18,899
Electric Blue	6	2	30	3	2	2	35,174
Electric Flag	1	1	4	1	0	0	3,196
Eleven Stitches	5	4	39	7	6	6	48,958
Elk's Uz	2	1	11	1	0	2	6,745
Elkadi	1	1	3	1	0	0	30,480
Elmaamul	12	3	69	5	5	6	98,469
Elocutionist	54	25	378	48	35	39	751,224
Embassy	2	1	13	2	0	0	5,382
Embrace the Wind	13	8	97	13	5	9	152,786
Eminency	15	6	100	9	9	13	96,804
Emmons Corner	11	6	66	9	6	4	72,802
Empery	15	2	54	6	1	0	524,165
Empire Glory	18	10	129	15	19	16	256,771
Enchanted Hemp	3	2	22	5	8	2	24,610
Encino	44	21	325	46	49	35	782,479
Encoriva	1	1	8	1	2	0	4,383
Encourager	10	4	69	8	8	8	102,876
End Sweep	7	1	19	1	3	0	82,003
Endow	7	4	57	4	7	8	47,319
Ends Well	41	17	242	30	27	30	563,775
Enough Reality	3	1	9	1	1	0	7,740
Entitled To	2	1	17	1	3	2	35,996
Entropy	27	14	217	29	28	25	443,120
Envoy	1	1	12	2	2	4	17,981
Epic Journey	5	3	36	6	3	6	80,230
Equalize	9	5	69	10	8	8	402,620
Erimo Ciboulette	3	3	21	6	1	4	48,412
Erins Isle (IRE)	20	9	156	14	25	23	351,334
Escaped	1	1	9	1	2	2	12,618
Eskimo	74	34	528	56	71	55	869,337
Esops Foibles	2	1	16	1	3	4	13,541
Estate	3	1	13	1	0	5	5,482
Estoril	5	2	38	2	5	7	70,933
Eteelya	4	1	25	3	4	2	42,981
Eternal Prince	25	13	134	23	23	11	345,364
Euclid (IRE)	1	1	13	1	1	4	13,925
Euclidean	3	1	16	1	0	2	3,667
Evansville Slew	1	1	3	1	1	0	13,160
Evaristo (BRZ)	1	1	2	1	0	1	11,020
Even Stephen	2	1	12	1	1	1	24,207
Evening Kris	5	2	15	2	0	1	18,570
Evzone	4	1	25	1	2	5	47,836
Exalte (FR)	1	1	3	1	1	0	18,450
Exalted Rullah	2	1	11	1	0	2	4,875
Exbourne	14	4	59	5	7	7	109,460
Excavate	2	1	6	1	0	0	15,995
Exceller	48	22	347	39	44	34	486,830
Exclusive Bidder	4	1	18	1	5	1	10,962
Exclusive Canadian	1	1	8	1	3	0	51,212
Exclusive Darling	12	8	104	19	12	9	187,437
Exclusive Encore	6	2	29	2	5	3	47,339
Exclusive Enough	13	4	79	5	11	6	69,494
Exclusive Era	45	21	265	37	29	26	596,986
Exclusive Gem	12	5	69	7	15	5	126,658
Exclusive Native	35	15	244	26	33	33	353,249
Exclusive One	8	3	46	5	4	6	44,246
Exclusive Ribot	10	5	64	5	6	7	42,612
Executioner	5	2	21	3	0	2	19,659
Executive Counsel	3	1	14	1	0	0	7,817
Executive Intent	7	2	22	3	0	2	25,011
Executive Officer	2	1	15	2	2	2	6,165
Executive Order	55	30	424	63	45	52	521,178
Executive Pride (IRE)	15	8	88	16	9	14	198,327
Exemplary Leader	4	1	17	1	0	0	6,725
Exile King	6	3	61	6	7	11	60,926
Exit to Nowhere	4	1	14	2	1	1	79,460
Expediter	1	1	3	1	0	0	1,125
Expense Account	5	2	17	3	2	1	18,769
Expensive Decision	12	6	126	10	13	11	162,789
*Explode II	2	2	13	2	5	3	28,448
Exploded	3	2	24	4	2	2	60,184
Explodent	162	69	1074	108	143	96	1,939,368
Explosive Bid	39	15	285	28	28	28	412,700
Explosive Red	5	2	12	3	1	2	45,751
Explosive Wagon	18	9	134	24	15	13	236,800
Expressman	16	10	95	15	16	11	164,875
Extra Man	2	1	14	1	2	1	8,773
Extra Turn	3	2	24	2	10	4	31,608
Exuberant	78	39	554	66	71	48	799,966
Ezzoud (IRE)	1	1	16	1	0	4	8,417
Fabled Monarch	17	10	133	19	12	15	122,423

Broodmare Sire	Perf	Wnrs	Sts	1st	2d	3d	Purses
Fabuleux Dancer	10	6	66	13	5	2	214,709
Fabulous Bid	1	1	6	2	0	1	70,780
Fabulous Dancer	11	3	48	4	6	6	161,572
Fabulous Pleasure	1	1	22	1	0	2	14,427
Fabulous Reason	2	1	15	1	1	3	10,109
Face the Moment	2	1	7	1	0	1	5,023
Fain (ARG)	2	1	24	1	1	0	12,840
Fair Skies	2	1	11	1	0	4	26,718
Fair Test	2	1	17	1	1	1	9,532
Fairly Certain	2	1	20	2	2	3	17,172
Fairway Fortune	12	6	82	9	3	11	88,728
Fairway Phantom	13	4	86	7	10	8	102,244
Fairy King	16	7	116	12	18	11	376,905
Falamoun (FR)	3	2	19	6	2	6	66,978
Faliraki (IRE)	11	3	60	5	11	8	73,021
Falkenburry Road	2	2	16	3	2	3	18,825
Falstaff	38	22	230	37	34	26	663,656
Fame International	2	1	7	1	0	0	6,661
Family Doctor	29	13	218	22	27	30	471,450
Family Physician	1	1	4	2	0	1	6,731
Famous Trial	1	1	8	1	4	0	5,485
Fanaan	4	2	19	3	2	3	46,791
Fancy Tammy	2	1	12	1	1	0	5,326
Faneuil Boy	2	1	17	2	2	1	16,997
Fantasy 'n Reality	6	4	58	10	7	5	116,738
Fappiano	145	78	943	129	118	115	2,924,854
Far East Sun	3	2	36	4	2	6	43,218
Far North	132	56	863	96	100	94	1,771,203
Far Out East	101	54	772	94	112	109	1,732,523
Faraway Son	26	10	165	21	20	23	290,401
Farley (ARG)	2	1	23	6	2	2	49,180
Farma Way	77	39	519	56	55	62	1,173,375
Farnesio (ARG)	14	7	73	9	11	7	280,145
Fast	14	7	90	11	8	14	162,877
Fast 'n' Gold	9	1	31	1	1	2	52,270
Fast Account	10	4	52	7	5	5	68,567
Fast Forward	10	3	42	6	4	1	37,453
Fast Gold	58	28	396	42	52	46	678,614
Fast Hilarious	5	2	20	3	3	2	48,250
Fast Play	86	48	564	90	63	80	1,531,437
Fast Prospect	4	3	36	5	8	5	57,452
Fasten	1	1	10	1	1	0	4,755
Faster Than Sound	3	2	18	3	1	3	45,792
Father Hogan	2	1	16	1	3	3	15,131
Fatih	23	9	154	12	13	13	174,405
Favorecidian	2	2	19	2	1	4	18,538
Favorite Danzig	1	1	15	1	1	0	7,546
Fayruz	1	1	6	1	0	0	10,115
Fearless Knight	2	1	10	1	1	3	20,290
Feather Ridge	3	3	38	5	3	6	74,620
Federal Chief	1	1	10	1	1	2	9,515
Feel the Power	31	11	185	16	22	28	474,362
Feeling Gallant	2	1	20	2	1	2	18,403
Felter On the Quay	3	2	10	2	1	1	24,173
Fenter	8	7	71	13	9	7	140,765
Ferdinand	68	33	473	57	57	50	929,887
Festin (ARG)	9	4	61	4	6	8	103,702
Festival	1	1	4	1	0	0	3,085
Festive	18	9	137	10	17	11	149,281
Feu d'Enfer	10	8	81	14	16	8	194,757
Fiasco	1	1	15	3	5	1	26,010
Fichte	5	1	23	1	1	4	26,784
Fiddle Dancer Boy	5	2	27	2	3	3	14,709
Fiery Best	3	2	28	3	4	6	34,187
Fiery Sea	1	1	4	1	2	0	5,468
Fiestero (CHI)	5	2	20	2	2	1	37,273
Fiesty Fouts	5	2	30	5	1	7	81,788
Fifth Marine	20	5	79	11	6	3	126,777
Fight Over	57	27	341	41	33	39	758,889
Fighting Affair	1	1	2	1	0	0	1,595
Fighting Bill	2	1	20	2	2	4	13,409
Fighting Fit	57	24	414	38	46	52	556,666
Filiberto	10	2	61	7	6	13	188,814
Final K.	4	2	19	3	2	2	4,906
Financial Matter	2	2	14	4	3	0	55,185
Finding Truth	1	1	7	2	1	1	28,635

Broodmare Sire	Perf	Wnrs	Sts	1st	2d	3d	Purses
Fire Dancer	97	46	701	84	77	81	1,203,493
Fire Maker	6	4	47	9	6	7	134,283
First Albert	17	6	115	10	9	9	142,796
First Ambassador	3	1	13	1	4	0	15,593
First and Goal	3	1	29	1	4	3	16,489
First Dawn	5	1	34	1	2	2	16,345
First Draft Choice	4	1	20	1	4	3	24,747
First Landing	5	2	24	2	1	4	46,174
First Norman	3	1	10	1	0	1	6,105
First of the Line	2	1	13	1	0	1	6,446
First One Up	2	1	21	1	0	0	10,382
First Patriot	1	1	16	5	1	4	31,486
Fit to Fight	188	92	1294	173	164	156	3,391,358
Fitzcarraldo (ARG)	7	4	44	5	8	10	198,304
Fitzhugh	2	2	17	2	2	1	10,210
Five Star Flight	14	7	90	12	5	11	110,166
Fixture	1	1	5	1	0	0	1,441
Flag Officer	5	3	34	7	5	3	49,312
Flag Raiser	4	3	30	6	3	6	28,045
Flagman Ahead	1	1	5	1	1	0	6,796
Flaring Dancer	9	6	54	11	6	3	73,574
Flashing Gun	1	1	5	2	0	1	2,677
Flashy Image	2	1	9	1	0	3	8,411
Fleet Elite	2	2	19	3	1	2	8,278
Fleet Excuse	2	1	10	2	1	1	7,918
Fleet Mel	3	1	17	1	6	2	72,841
Fleet Nasrullah	3	1	27	6	1	4	40,212
Fleet Sudan	5	1	20	1	2	1	21,243
Fleet Swaps	12	5	90	6	8	7	51,365
Fleet Twist	16	3	123	5	16	13	95,231
Fleet Velvet	3	1	24	5	3	2	23,483
Flip Sal	11	6	78	14	11	5	183,455
Floating Reserve	2	1	22	1	1	2	18,386
Florida Sunshine	18	6	112	10	5	13	148,107
Flout	2	1	15	3	3	1	15,926
Flow Swiftly	5	2	44	2	4	3	25,848
Fluorescent Light	26	11	185	15	20	21	233,230
Fly a Kite (IRE)	3	2	21	2	1	2	15,781
Fly So Free	31	16	189	26	37	32	914,079
Fly Till Dawn	9	5	64	10	5	8	197,147
Flying Continental	16	7	80	10	9	9	296,622
Flying Granville	7	3	47	3	4	2	77,815
Flying Lark	8	5	73	9	11	5	82,650
Flying Paster	158	82	1016	124	125	141	2,566,040
Flying Pidgeon	24	9	148	14	11	13	283,472
Flying Straight	2	1	8	1	0	1	16,517
Flying Target	3	2	24	2	2	6	15,993
Flying Victor	16	9	107	23	8	12	366,219
Fobby Forbes	8	5	77	15	21	11	226,251
Fol's Native	3	1	11	2	1	0	8,558
Foligno	7	3	50	5	5	8	66,606
Folk's Pride	3	1	12	1	0	2	5,153
Follow the Drum	14	7	88	17	10	21	246,771
Fool the Experts	23	14	180	25	22	23	286,282
Foolish Pleasure	95	47	625	73	66	69	1,306,854
Foolish Tanner	1	1	10	1	2	2	6,296
Fools Dance	13	7	91	11	15	9	199,671
Fools Turn	2	1	20	1	0	1	6,032
For Love and Glory	3	1	16	1	2	3	58,910
For Real	1	1	2	1	0	0	4,944
For Really	8	5	53	12	7	5	241,236
For Sure	3	1	15	1	0	1	9,759
For The Moment	21	9	146	18	14	21	305,890
Forbidden Pleasure	3	2	19	3	2	1	34,356
Forceful Intent	1	1	11	2	1	3	18,408
Forceten	15	8	105	16	17	11	130,556
Foreign Power	6	3	62	6	8	12	48,837
Foreign Survivor	9	3	52	3	6	5	37,283
Forest Of Dean (GB)	1	1	13	2	1	2	9,584
Forever Casting	14	6	108	16	11	5	160,114
Forever Silver	10	4	73	5	6	8	160,180
Forever Sparkle	23	9	153	18	16	13	781,040
Forget the Showers	3	1	15	1	0	2	27,265
*Forli	49	24	353	37	33	42	662,143
Forli Light	4	1	16	1	0	4	25,003
Forli Road	2	1	10	3	0	0	13,230

Broodmare Sire	Perf	Wnrs	Sts	1st	2d	3d	Purses
Forli Winds	15	8	132	12	12	14	162,193
Forlion	5	1	17	2	2	1	28,871
Forlitano (ARG)	4	2	28	3	4	3	383,932
Formal Dinner	16	7	83	10	13	10	251,499
Formula One	3	1	31	1	5	1	41,720
Forsythe Boy	10	5	79	10	5	16	145,550
Fort Calgary	11	5	60	7	8	5	116,554
Fort Chaffee	3	3	18	6	5	3	139,057
Fort Prevel	11	5	77	10	15	4	92,693
Fortunate Harbor	1	1	6	1	2	1	2,037
Fortunate Moment	5	2	29	5	3	5	113,232
Fortunate Prospect	147	80	1103	139	162	126	2,923,488
Forty Niner	162	90	948	147	123	120	4,129,967
Forward Charger	1	1	16	1	4	1	35,256
Forzando (GB)	6	3	31	4	4	4	178,542
Fountain of Gold	28	17	184	32	20	30	380,824
Four Fingers	1	1	12	3	3	1	61,335
Four Seasons (GB)	2	1	7	1	3	2	19,968
Four Ten	4	2	26	2	3	3	32,568
Fourche Lafave	1	1	15	3	4	4	40,920
Foxhound	2	1	6	1	0	1	34,601
Foyt	15	5	95	8	12	9	125,020
Francis U.	1	1	10	1	1	3	18,105
Fred Astaire	76	38	509	75	57	67	1,948,309
Free At Last	12	6	64	9	2	16	120,660
Free Barb	1	1	11	1	3	0	3,540
Free State	2	2	10	3	2	1	40,505
Free Up	2	1	7	1	0	2	4,407
Freezing Rain	8	3	58	9	8	9	104,110
French Colonial	6	1	35	1	10	7	47,069
French Cut	5	3	30	3	3	7	35,649
French Deputy	5	3	21	6	4	3	159,733
French Legionaire	15	3	98	4	9	14	96,451
French Regency	1	1	8	1	2	1	23,966
French Sassafras (GB)	3	2	27	5	3	5	82,804
Friend's Choice	16	5	107	10	11	15	123,696
Friendly Lover	2	1	10	1	5	0	54,120
Friscosilverdollar	3	3	18	5	1	1	32,009
Frosty the Snowman	21	11	150	27	19	18	771,587
Frosty's Luck	1	1	14	5	2	3	38,200
Fruitzig	3	1	20	2	1	3	18,117
Fuego Seguro	6	1	43	1	5	9	33,448
Full Choke	36	16	206	21	24	27	472,904
Full Intent	9	2	56	3	4	10	39,569
Full of Drive	2	2	22	3	2	1	29,534
Full of Fools	4	1	26	6	5	3	78,599
Full of Promise	3	1	27	2	0	3	17,568
Full Out	46	28	337	44	49	54	750,401
Full Partner	19	8	114	18	14	12	294,161
Full Pocket	67	37	487	64	65	62	1,067,678
Fulmar	11	5	84	8	9	9	108,851
Funny Fellow	1	1	9	2	1	3	28,265
Furiously	2	2	18	5	3	2	96,749
Future Hope	7	3	62	6	3	6	86,897
Future Storm	21	9	123	19	14	15	229,545
Fuzzbuster	11	8	101	18	7	12	268,697
Fuzziano	7	2	58	4	7	5	81,850
Fuzzy	20	6	108	10	14	20	180,531
Fuzzy Freeze	1	1	6	1	0	3	7,455
Ga Hai	5	1	27	2	2	3	52,194
Gaelic Christian	8	3	31	4	1	1	37,503
Gaelic Dancer	5	4	44	9	11	3	33,854
Gala Array	3	2	14	2	2	3	13,463
Gala Double	9	4	67	6	10	12	74,509
Gala Harry	7	3	39	4	3	7	111,269
Gala Skipper	3	1	21	3	3	1	45,007
Galaxy Bound	1	1	11	1	4	0	8,876
Galaxy Guide	3	1	9	1	0	4	38,145
Galaxy Libra (IRE)	21	7	139	14	16	15	112,316
Galaxy Road	5	2	43	3	4	10	60,697
Gallant Best	18	9	120	21	20	18	164,486
Gallant Knave	7	1	44	1	2	3	27,685
Gallant Lad	2	2	5	3	2	0	18,780
*Gallant Man	3	2	23	4	3	1	61,827
Gallant Romeo	24	12	198	16	17	22	230,116
Gallant Serenade	1	1	5	1	2	2	8,171
Gallant Wings	2	2	24	2	0	4	21,549
Gallantsky	3	3	21	4	1	6	325,390
Gallapiat	40	15	283	29	35	30	539,519
Garda's Revenge	2	1	7	1	4	0	9,570
Garde Royale	1	1	9	2	1	2	62,365
Garthorn	31	17	241	28	27	24	749,395
Gas Energy	4	1	19	5	3	1	89,070
Gate Dancer	124	68	819	131	112	112	2,654,235
Gato Del Sol	15	6	117	10	11	16	100,393
Gay Apollo (GB)	1	1	9	2	0	1	33,640
Gay Fandango	1	1	7	1	3	0	29,120
Gay Mecene	6	3	40	3	6	5	89,481
Gay Old Blade	2	1	12	1	1	2	12,099
Geiger Counter	117	49	737	74	86	91	2,085,606
Gemini Dreamer	3	2	12	2	1	3	54,840
General (FR)	3	2	30	2	4	4	66,012
General Assembly	91	56	648	105	74	79	2,064,082
General Holme	21	13	175	26	19	20	341,296
General Meeting	33	16	177	18	34	23	537,509
General Pleasure	3	1	20	1	1	2	16,154
General Silver	4	2	23	2	2	3	30,525
Generous (IRE)	10	5	66	9	8	12	195,498
Gentle Bluffer	2	1	8	1	0	0	8,364
Gentle King	15	6	117	7	18	12	121,849
Gentleman Gene	11	1	61	4	5	8	84,762
Genuine Guy	3	1	10	1	0	1	5,251
Genuine Silver	2	2	13	2	4	3	28,824
Geology	1	1	10	1	1	0	2,359
George Lewis	2	2	10	2	1	2	14,657
George Navonod	5	4	42	8	4	8	114,851
George Royal	2	2	19	3	3	1	25,793
Georgeandthedragon	7	1	31	4	5	0	33,646
Georgeff	7	3	33	3	5	3	22,961
Getit	1	1	6	1	0	0	9,710
Ghadeer (FR)	10	6	55	11	4	7	298,896
Ghazi	12	6	63	9	4	7	228,036
*Giacometti	5	3	28	3	2	4	36,607
Giboulee	32	13	235	19	26	23	332,049
Gift of Gib	3	2	15	3	2	2	42,798
Gifted Dancer	7	1	42	2	5	2	24,580
Gilded Age	22	8	100	13	9	12	195,771
Gilded Time	54	22	291	30	31	49	603,292
Gin Tour	1	1	10	2	2	3	35,501
Ginistrelli	20	8	142	11	10	20	469,564
Girl's Castle	3	2	21	2	0	0	14,376
Giuseppe	8	5	54	6	5	9	106,772
Give It a Chance	3	1	9	1	0	1	8,870
Give Me Strength	7	4	55	4	8	5	88,633
Glaros (FR)	3	1	21	3	7	2	164,280
Glenstal	3	3	15	3	2	2	96,268
Glide	4	3	25	4	1	3	68,966
Glitterman	53	31	401	56	67	45	779,721
Globe	6	4	62	9	10	12	111,655
Glomar	2	1	18	1	1	3	17,785
Glorious Flag	5	2	32	4	3	2	31,594
Glossary	1	1	6	1	0	0	9,515
Gnome's Gold	7	6	58	8	11	6	161,106
Go and Go (IRE)	13	3	68	3	10	6	66,986
Go Exclusive Go	3	1	12	1	1	2	13,605
Go for Gin	3	2	18	3	2	2	102,412
Go for It Matt	1	1	9	3	1	1	8,441
Go Forth	1	1	13	2	2	3	20,674
Go Go Roger	2	2	21	4	2	5	39,591
Go Loom	1	1	11	1	0	1	5,860
Go Step	25	5	147	7	15	21	119,815
Goal Line Stand	2	1	5	1	0	0	6,902
Godswalk	5	1	25	1	3	2	24,822
Gold Alert	66	36	496	61	57	75	1,101,191
Gold and Myrrh	15	7	137	13	20	14	261,572
Gold Crest	44	14	277	23	33	35	419,107
Gold Cup	3	1	15	2	3	4	11,605
Gold Exchanged	8	2	56	3	1	0	24,876
Gold Legend	14	6	80	10	13	6	269,080
Gold Meridian	51	24	315	44	32	37	640,608
Gold On Green	3	1	20	1	4	0	8,342
Gold Pack	1	1	9	2	1	0	18,215

Broodmare Sire	Perf	Wnrs	Sts	1st	2d	3d	Purses
Gold Prince	4	1	14	1	2	0	2,393
Gold Ruler	2	1	15	2	4	2	14,259
Gold Seam	8	2	32	4	1	4	173,317
Gold Stage	60	29	442	56	59	43	717,082
Golden Act	87	37	568	55	74	63	1,090,200
Golden Choice	3	2	26	2	6	4	53,557
Golden Derby	5	1	41	4	3	3	19,130
*Golden Eagle II	34	19	216	30	28	35	319,689
Golden Fleece	5	3	39	6	5	6	202,659
Golden Gear	3	2	8	2	3	1	51,088
*Golden Pal II	1	1	11	2	2	3	16,500
Golden Peak	2	1	12	1	1	1	17,083
Golden Reserve	44	18	268	29	42	35	506,228
Golden Ruler	2	2	29	5	10	3	45,428
Golden Souvenir	1	1	9	1	0	1	5,667
Goldlust	21	10	124	14	21	14	311,255
Goldwater	10	5	82	8	2	7	99,878
Goliard	2	1	23	2	2	1	8,031
Gone Digging	2	1	8	2	1	3	28,625
Gone West	126	58	795	117	92	101	3,390,287
Gonzales	16	8	135	12	17	10	153,083
Gonzo's Mistake	1	1	14	1	1	1	5,106
Good Behaving	10	6	92	9	8	18	132,946
Good Bloke (ARG)	2	1	18	3	2	2	261,722
Good Counsel	8	3	44	4	6	11	68,063
Good Manners	4	1	17	1	2	3	32,555
Good Old Mort	2	2	12	2	1	0	20,310
Good Port	1	1	12	1	2	1	5,366
Good Rob	2	1	25	1	2	9	17,884
Good Tensions	1	1	7	1	0	2	6,094
Gorky	3	1	10	1	0	3	14,298
Gorytus	4	2	31	2	0	0	16,421
Gothic Revival	11	5	76	9	6	16	120,332
Gotzum	1	1	6	1	1	0	4,360
Gourami	3	2	20	2	2	3	23,153
Government Program	5	2	30	6	6	3	70,810
Gran Zar (MEX)	23	12	163	24	17	8	272,058
Granacus	2	2	21	2	2	4	28,012
Grand Allegiance	2	1	22	2	3	4	10,696
Grand Alliance	8	3	50	7	7	10	50,049
Grand Chelem (IRE)	1	1	9	2	1	1	10,449
Grand Limit	2	1	12	1	1	1	6,215
Grand Mogol (FR)	2	2	14	3	1	1	31,533
Grand Revival	14	4	72	9	5	8	76,283
Grand Rivulet	6	1	27	2	2	2	11,077
Grand Ruler	2	1	9	1	2	0	9,421
Gratification	3	2	35	3	5	7	29,915
Graustark	57	23	312	42	34	43	949,507
Graustark Dancer	3	2	26	3	2	2	27,861
Gray Dandy	1	1	18	2	6	4	20,231
Gray Slewpy	7	3	46	5	5	5	71,934
Gray's Exclusive	11	3	61	6	11	11	29,743
Great Above	152	70	980	135	147	116	2,703,321
Great Charmer	5	3	35	8	4	3	78,239
Great Deal	6	5	56	6	6	6	84,477
Great Gladiator	58	25	372	36	52	49	1,085,621
Great Mystery	3	1	18	1	1	3	19,731
Great Neck	11	8	104	13	15	13	282,896
Great Nephew (GB)	3	2	23	3	2	1	78,499
Great Prospector	6	2	41	4	2	1	17,868
Greatest of Ease	2	1	15	1	2	2	31,893
Greek Answer	10	4	62	6	13	7	135,698
Greek Prince	1	1	13	2	1	1	37,030
Greek Sky	3	1	7	1	0	2	16,251
Green Alligator	4	2	26	4	1	3	35,347
Green Dancer	198	90	1288	169	137	186	4,631,856
Green Desert	12	2	53	4	7	6	57,279
Green Forest	97	43	581	67	65	67	1,174,246
Green in Hands	2	1	22	1	0	0	6,565
Green Shoon	2	1	6	1	0	2	16,250
Greenough	6	2	32	3	6	3	73,611
Greenwood Star (GB)	3	2	14	2	2	2	11,245
Gregorian	29	15	194	24	24	28	446,280
Greinton (GB)	77	43	488	72	57	61	1,108,782
Grenfall	12	5	73	5	10	4	41,620
Grey Adorn	2	2	20	8	1	0	187,524

Broodmare Sire	Perf	Wnrs	Sts	1st	2d	3d	Purses
*Grey Dawn II	110	60	830	90	95	99	1,607,803
Grey Judgement	4	2	21	3	0	2	47,460
Grey Legion	3	1	11	1	2	1	1,705
Grey Parlor	6	2	68	3	7	10	48,535
Grits and Gravy	1	1	11	2	2	2	12,614
Groom Dancer	6	4	38	4	8	1	460,358
Groomstick	8	5	84	15	8	11	132,043
Groovy	90	48	629	92	85	80	1,729,809
Groshawk	8	2	50	7	4	8	232,031
Grosor (CHI)	1	1	6	1	1	2	24,000
Grosvenor (NZ)	1	1	1	1	0	0	42,525
Groton	16	5	101	6	7	15	74,928
Groton High	8	5	39	6	3	6	31,628
Ground Breaker	2	1	13	3	1	0	61,735
Ground Zero	2	1	11	1	2	1	20,170
Grub	11	5	64	7	8	5	288,184
Guards	3	1	23	1	2	3	7,376
Guillaume Tell	4	1	21	2	2	1	25,295
Guilty Conscience	14	6	69	9	7	6	113,674
Gulch	111	62	753	120	105	106	2,238,772
Gumboy	22	14	162	22	17	18	169,727
Gummo	18	6	126	14	16	10	163,511
Gunflint	4	2	24	2	1	4	13,516
Gustoso	8	2	60	3	4	7	44,109
H. D. Orphan	4	3	22	4	4	3	27,026
Habitat	10	1	43	1	6	3	36,281
Habitonia	16	10	123	24	18	15	392,259
*Habitony	62	27	395	39	56	36	569,921
Habitony's Ace	1	1	11	2	2	0	30,661
Hadif	23	9	136	13	18	16	161,442
Hagley	78	34	497	57	71	63	993,196
Hagley Mill	1	1	3	1	0	0	8,635
Hagley's Nest	3	2	14	4	0	1	32,478
Hagley's Reward	3	2	34	3	6	7	57,162
Hail and Sail	2	1	8	1	1	1	4,064
Hail Bold King	19	7	111	11	14	13	59,538
Hail Emperor	16	9	122	20	12	13	284,861
Hail the Pirates	23	10	169	15	21	23	683,540
Hail the Ruckus	12	5	62	11	8	9	284,090
Hail to Reason	3	1	26	2	3	6	51,276
Hajji's Treasure	2	1	17	3	4	2	17,352
Half a Year	64	35	362	59	47	46	1,816,062
Half High	3	3	28	4	3	7	51,496
Half Iced	1	1	2	1	0	0	12,600
Half Term	1	1	6	2	2	1	14,593
Hall of Fame (ARG)	1	1	18	2	4	5	20,950
Hall of Reason	7	3	43	6	9	2	54,256
Halo	258	134	1623	214	206	189	4,409,242
Halo Fire	1	1	10	1	1	1	23,290
Halo'd Moon	2	1	16	1	0	2	6,234
Halyard	7	4	44	5	3	3	47,208
Hamza	7	2	31	2	0	3	21,307
Hang Ten	1	1	5	1	1	0	23,470
Hansel	32	14	179	25	24	24	526,613
Hapgood	12	5	87	5	12	7	38,697
Happy Bid	5	1	41	1	3	6	18,754
Happy Delegate	3	2	16	4	1	1	7,305
Happy Escort	3	1	13	1	2	0	6,534
Happy Hooligan	4	1	18	1	3	1	22,272
Harasul	1	1	9	1	1	2	9,263
Harbor Prince	1	1	4	1	0	0	35,807
Hard Crush	2	1	7	1	0	2	7,686
Hard Hit	2	2	4	2	1	0	8,092
Hard Work	19	8	126	8	9	11	71,299
Hardy Hawk	2	1	12	2	1	2	33,419
Harlan	4	2	22	2	5	3	44,820
Harmony Creek	2	2	10	2	4	1	21,530
Harperstown	4	3	30	6	6	4	121,778
Harriman	4	3	28	4	2	4	77,724
Harry 'n Bill	2	1	14	2	1	1	21,963
Harry L.	4	2	22	2	7	0	28,463
Harry the Great	1	1	8	1	2	2	30,378
Harry's Cary	2	1	7	1	0	0	1,462
Harry's Secret Joy	4	2	21	4	1	5	59,821
Harvard Man	15	3	105	4	9	8	91,680
Harvest Ruler	1	1	18	1	1	3	11,068

Broodmare Sire	Perf	Wnrs	Sts	1st	2d	3d	Purses
Hasty Flyer	13	5	91	10	9	10	116,927
Hasty Groom	1	1	3	2	0	0	14,100
Hasty Judge	1	1	6	1	2	0	3,150
Hasty Runner	1	1	10	1	0	1	3,664
Hasty Spring	9	2	51	2	6	3	54,402
Hasty Tam	2	1	18	2	1	3	15,396
Hatchet Man	92	43	649	79	71	79	1,139,279
Havanace	3	2	35	4	6	5	44,317
*Hawaii	62	29	391	47	33	36	782,710
Hawaiian Sound	4	1	27	2	0	0	8,841
Hawk Attack	1	1	1	1	0	0	8,100
Hawkin's Special	50	23	300	26	25	28	396,092
Hawkster	49	23	374	44	48	45	1,484,573
Hay Halo	21	11	131	18	23	18	373,262
Haymarket (GB)	2	1	10	2	1	3	15,255
Hazaam	5	4	39	6	4	7	151,818
He Loves Me	3	1	11	1	1	0	14,420
He's a Looker	6	5	43	9	10	2	116,611
He's Bad	5	4	45	9	2	3	301,579
He's Our Native	8	3	45	7	8	10	367,108
Head Hawk	2	1	5	1	2	1	14,689
Head Over Heels (FR)	1	1	5	1	1	0	49,840
Head Scout	3	1	10	2	0	0	11,244
Hearts of Lettuce	2	2	24	2	2	5	8,102
Heavenly Plain (IRE)	6	5	47	12	13	4	161,473
Hechizado (ARG)	7	4	36	4	4	10	57,329
Hedevar the Gold	2	1	17	1	3	3	10,369
Heed My Speed	1	1	4	1	2	1	6,740
Heir to the Legacy	3	3	26	5	4	2	24,641
Hello Gorgeous	25	12	172	15	22	10	289,225
Henbane	19	12	146	19	14	13	185,007
Herat	66	35	488	84	54	61	1,213,799
Herb Water	3	2	31	3	1	2	45,298
*Herbager	3	2	27	3	2	0	28,097
Herbalist	3	1	19	3	0	1	22,026
Herculean	8	5	59	5	10	7	78,685
Here We Come	17	6	118	12	13	17	133,327
Hereditary	2	1	14	2	0	1	40,424
Hermitage	25	13	176	25	19	18	316,515
Hero's Honor	53	25	383	43	56	51	914,788
Hey O'Shea	1	1	9	2	0	3	20,872
Hey Rob	6	4	31	7	2	3	53,458
Hi Pi	2	1	17	3	1	4	60,937
Hickman Creek	7	4	47	8	6	4	58,552
Hickory Ridge	4	2	22	2	0	3	11,254
Hidden Capital	1	1	2	1	0	0	19,500
High Brite	92	46	616	79	76	62	1,198,836
High Comedy	8	7	79	11	12	11	83,765
High Counsel	16	5	72	8	6	7	110,026
High Echelon	13	7	105	8	16	14	130,535
High Energy	2	2	19	6	2	2	177,088
High Estate (IRE)	1	1	2	1	0	1	5,325
High Gold	7	2	49	3	3	1	38,577
High Honors	10	1	40	1	4	1	74,324
High Master (CHI)	1	1	12	1	1	0	31,072
High Tribute	8	2	30	3	4	6	33,391
Highest Honor (FR)	4	2	18	3	2	2	55,352
Highland Blade	68	28	496	55	57	54	852,818
Highland Drummer	6	3	39	5	9	5	117,871
Highland Park	50	25	364	40	42	44	643,328
Highland Ruckus	24	11	125	19	16	19	339,650
Highly Praised	5	2	39	2	6	5	49,046
Hilal (IRE)	3	3	17	3	2	0	27,621
His Excellency	2	2	11	2	0	1	18,243
His Majesty	152	71	1111	136	125	134	2,765,756
Historically	2	1	12	1	2	3	7,817
Hit in Haste	7	3	53	5	4	13	72,713
Hittias (GB)	2	1	11	2	0	1	29,733
Hittite Glory (GB)	2	1	20	3	4	0	52,880
Ho Choy	2	1	15	1	3	0	9,608
Hoedown's Day	18	4	93	9	4	8	134,697
Hoist the Flag	14	9	105	17	17	17	256,900
Hoist the Silver	27	17	248	28	32	35	402,745
Hold the World	2	2	10	3	0	3	26,370
Hold Your Peace	106	59	745	109	92	85	2,750,125
Hold Your Tricks	12	6	85	13	7	5	115,207

Broodmare Sire	Perf	Wnrs	Sts	1st	2d	3d	Purses
Holli Spect	2	1	9	1	1	1	11,249
Hollywood Brat	6	1	21	1	2	3	13,842
Holy Bull	37	20	178	27	30	17	792,897
Holy War	22	14	148	19	24	22	157,216
Homasassa	3	1	9	1	0	1	12,379
Home At Last	14	7	77	8	7	14	200,537
Home Run Trot	3	2	15	4	0	1	11,478
Homebuilder	50	25	343	46	40	50	802,053
Homeways	3	2	27	2	4	1	17,540
Homme de Loi	2	2	17	4	4	2	219,265
Honest Bullet	8	6	88	8	9	9	90,824
Honest Moment	9	6	101	13	16	12	336,024
Honest Pleasure	57	21	407	35	44	44	422,025
Honey Jay	76	37	568	67	68	68	867,394
Honeyland	17	11	111	21	15	15	315,175
Honor Grades	28	10	175	18	30	32	434,298
Honour and Glory	3	2	21	7	2	3	100,950
Hooched	63	34	452	60	64	46	1,047,419
Hookano (JPN)	4	1	25	1	1	2	19,741
Hopeful Venture	4	1	42	1	8	6	15,920
Hopeful Word	23	11	197	16	23	24	308,674
Horatius	95	45	569	81	75	57	1,777,998
Horse Flash (FR)	2	1	4	1	1	1	36,770
Hostage	37	19	249	32	25	25	369,186
Hot Mop Darby	1	1	1	1	0	0	2,310
Hot Oil	7	4	68	6	3	9	128,611
Hot Red Streak	1	1	20	1	2	5	7,010
Hot Words	1	1	13	3	1	6	9,040
Housebuster	95	52	556	93	67	69	2,445,409
Houston	106	51	752	77	81	96	2,071,071
How Curious	3	1	20	3	4	4	60,275
Hubble	3	2	21	3	4	2	33,240
Hubbup	1	1	9	2	0	0	10,060
Huckster	32	13	235	19	27	42	320,708
Huddle Up	6	4	58	7	9	6	34,162
Huge Success	1	1	14	1	1	2	5,773
Huguenot	5	1	25	1	2	0	7,424
Hula Blaze	10	5	58	11	7	3	104,622
Humbaba	2	1	9	1	0	2	5,883
Hunting Horn	10	6	93	13	13	10	260,331
Hurlingham	5	3	36	8	7	5	102,463
Hurok	9	1	43	1	3	1	15,328
Hurontario	8	3	35	4	6	4	42,313
Hurricane Ed	9	4	83	5	8	6	49,456
Hurry to Market	6	4	37	5	3	6	24,628
Hurry Up Blue	9	3	66	6	5	8	40,044
Husar (MEX)	2	1	9	1	1	0	19,100
Husvik	1	1	8	2	3	1	15,835
Hy Lucky Jay	2	1	19	1	2	2	6,670
Hy Swaps	1	1	19	6	2	3	40,162
Hyannis Port	10	3	46	3	5	5	50,369
Hyperborean	25	11	152	18	15	16	182,526
I Am the Game	14	9	115	20	13	11	280,948
I Enclose	20	8	114	13	13	13	209,179
I'll Be Good	1	1	11	1	4	3	23,019
I'll Raise You One	6	3	43	3	5	2	44,883
I'll Take Vanilla	1	1	9	1	0	0	8,415
I'm a Banker	2	1	5	1	1	1	41,383
I'm a Lyre	3	2	23	5	2	1	147,118
I'm Daring	2	1	21	3	2	2	18,138
I'm For More	9	3	40	3	5	2	42,818
I'm Glad (ARG)	9	7	88	13	9	10	116,254
I'ma Hell Raiser	44	19	313	33	35	43	460,453
Iades (FR)	9	5	38	6	2	4	60,206
Iam the Iceman	1	1	9	1	1	1	10,389
Ibacache (CHI)	1	1	6	1	0	0	4,157
Ice Age	29	12	181	24	26	31	576,411
Ice Cool	2	1	10	1	0	0	5,136
Ice Power	4	1	22	5	3	5	75,309
Icecapade	94	44	645	90	69	76	1,281,572
Idabel	9	5	79	13	14	7	158,143
Idaho's Majesty	5	2	28	2	6	2	9,499
Ide	1	1	3	1	1	0	7,365
If This Be So	7	3	45	3	4	5	58,714
Ile de Bourbon	3	2	14	2	4	3	55,721
Ile de Jinsky	4	1	19	1	1	1	15,638

Broodmare Sire	Perf	Wnrs	Sts	1st	2d	3d	Purses
Illiopolis	4	1	27	1	4	4	26,209
Illuminate	14	6	96	8	15	10	140,252
Illustrious	8	3	53	6	5	7	123,727
Im Maheras	3	1	17	1	2	1	9,692
Imacornishprince	2	1	19	1	0	0	4,199
Image of Greatness	28	7	176	13	14	20	151,401
Imaleader	1	1	17	1	4	2	18,385
Imapuncher	3	1	14	2	1	0	20,303
Imasmartee	3	3	13	3	1	3	72,697
Imp Society	63	28	358	38	32	39	448,933
Imperial Ballet (IRE)	1	1	4	1	0	1	16,530
Imperial Dilemma	3	1	24	2	2	7	18,961
Imperial Falcon	75	35	599	68	79	66	1,180,472
Imperial Fling	9	4	65	7	13	3	107,999
Imperial Guard	7	3	53	4	7	5	61,323
Imperial Guard (GB)	2	2	23	7	2	1	64,030
Imperial Native	5	2	42	3	4	7	87,121
Imperial Prince (IRE)	2	1	5	1	2	0	48,620
Impernade	3	3	26	3	1	3	26,917
Implement	2	1	13	4	1	1	12,046
Impressive	14	6	109	7	8	9	61,622
In all Respects	2	1	9	1	1	1	9,603
In Excess (IRE)	29	17	171	37	29	14	773,041
In Fijar	8	5	57	9	4	6	120,559
In From Dixie	3	1	19	1	1	5	12,816
In Good Tune	4	2	38	3	1	6	19,589
In Reality	86	37	577	77	67	65	1,086,720
In the Slammer	2	1	25	2	4	2	15,828
In the Swing	7	3	55	6	5	9	92,762
In the Wings (GB)	2	2	6	2	0	1	53,280
In the Woodpile	2	1	16	1	4	1	5,777
In Tissar	14	3	69	10	8	7	114,735
In Totality	5	1	17	1	3	2	11,637
In Zeal	1	1	12	5	1	1	14,751
Inca Roca	2	1	23	1	2	3	13,119
Inchwood	1	1	9	1	2	2	72,040
Incinderator	28	17	181	31	25	18	796,092
Incite	2	1	17	1	1	1	8,995
Income Tax	1	1	9	1	0	2	8,460
Incubator	2	1	13	1	0	0	10,300
Indian Detail	3	1	41	2	7	4	22,520
Indian Groom	6	2	45	4	5	12	106,106
Indian King	2	2	18	4	5	3	110,414
Indian Ridge (IRE)	2	1	4	1	0	1	843,580
Indulge	2	1	17	1	7	1	17,772
Industry Standard	5	2	27	2	7	5	18,901
Infantry (GB)	3	3	39	5	6	6	94,850
Info	5	1	38	1	6	1	15,492
Inherent Star	5	3	30	7	2	5	138,868
Inishpour (IRE)	2	1	9	1	0	1	14,545
Inland Voyager	4	3	30	4	5	3	73,238
Inspired Prospect	3	1	22	2	2	2	13,897
Instant Profit	4	1	21	1	3	2	12,451
Instant Ruler	1	1	12	2	3	1	20,016
Instead of Roses	2	1	16	2	7	2	8,740
Instrument Landing	14	4	76	6	6	13	223,402
Insubordination	5	2	24	2	2	1	13,291
Interco	37	18	271	25	35	31	308,062
Interdicto	16	8	131	13	20	12	179,334
Interprete (ARG)	4	2	23	4	5	3	191,704
Intimidation	15	4	85	7	3	10	45,362
Intrepid Hitter	3	1	19	1	1	4	22,188
Introienne	2	1	20	1	2	2	19,724
Intrusion	6	2	36	3	7	4	24,186
Inventive	1	1	8	1	0	0	3,448
Inverness Drive	46	25	297	43	46	30	529,986
Invested Power	2	2	20	2	1	3	18,739
Invincible Dooley	2	1	13	1	1	4	70,456
Iram	3	1	25	2	3	1	22,481
Irepeat	2	2	18	2	3	4	32,912
Irish Castle	26	9	163	22	20	14	301,710
Irish Conn	4	1	28	1	3	3	15,923
Irish Escapade	4	1	14	1	0	2	8,879
*Irish Faberge	2	1	9	1	2	0	13,301
Irish Heart (IRE)	1	1	6	1	0	1	8,037
Irish Open	39	11	192	16	22	19	255,288

Broodmare Sire	Perf	Wnrs	Sts	1st	2d	3d	Purses
Irish River (FR)	130	58	729	93	94	78	2,135,819
Irish Ruler	15	6	108	11	16	18	332,062
Irish Stronghold	8	3	35	5	2	6	217,761
Irish Sur	10	5	52	10	4	2	131,885
Irish Tower	154	72	1070	125	150	122	2,621,982
Iroko (GB)	1	1	9	1	2	2	54,710
Iron	33	13	228	25	28	29	388,012
Iron Constitution	32	13	231	24	28	22	631,144
Iron Courage	20	9	139	14	32	26	487,478
Iron Duke	2	1	9	1	0	0	7,173
Iron Gladiator	3	2	18	3	0	2	19,621
Iron Man	2	1	13	2	1	5	10,623
Iron Ruler	21	10	163	14	19	18	239,000
Iron Ruler (IRE)	5	1	23	3	0	5	39,990
Iron Warrior	11	3	79	9	8	7	121,938
Iroquois Indian	3	3	23	3	1	3	15,844
Iroquois Park	7	4	48	4	3	9	83,022
Is It True	9	4	37	5	4	4	91,335
Isella	2	1	9	1	4	2	17,724
Isgala	3	1	17	1	2	2	13,504
Iskandar Elakbar	6	4	36	5	2	7	177,657
Island Agent	3	3	22	6	1	1	19,457
Island Champ	1	1	9	3	1	2	22,651
Island Fling	6	2	52	2	6	8	25,694
Island Kingdom	2	1	18	1	1	2	7,548
Island Sultan	5	1	40	2	3	2	20,388
Island Whirl	94	44	692	73	89	81	1,205,941
Isle Charge	2	1	19	2	3	5	27,477
Islefaxyou	1	1	10	3	1	2	41,475
Isopropyl	1	1	4	1	0	0	26,578
It's Freezing	144	73	1022	118	142	133	1,998,442
It's the One	9	3	53	3	3	7	46,211
It's True	11	5	84	5	14	9	92,292
Itajara	2	1	4	1	0	0	14,883
Itch a Lot	1	1	5	2	1	0	17,670
Its Acedemic	3	3	31	4	3	1	45,384
Its Good	2	2	12	2	0	1	35,397
Itsallinthegame	1	1	16	4	1	4	39,715
Ivan Lendl	4	2	33	2	4	5	78,144
Ivan Phillips	10	2	47	2	1	6	45,969
Ivy's Prince	3	1	38	2	6	6	32,343
Iz a Saros	4	1	23	3	3	4	18,891
J. Burns	5	2	31	3	4	4	38,743
J. O. Tobin	39	16	244	25	20	32	284,088
J. P. Brother	2	1	13	1	1	0	8,574
J. R.'s Pet	7	2	45	2	2	7	24,732
J. T. Hurst	1	1	8	1	1	0	2,795
Jacango	9	4	52	6	6	8	72,810
Jacinton	1	1	11	1	3	4	6,817
Jack Livingston	2	1	10	2	0	2	45,451
Jack Slade	6	2	59	4	6	10	60,113
Jack Wilson	4	2	24	4	6	4	66,789
Jack's Charger	2	1	11	3	2	1	19,546
Jacodra	5	2	22	2	2	4	32,031
Jacques Who	18	11	136	16	21	25	435,559
Jade Hunter	115	64	798	116	105	83	3,018,913
Jaded Dancer	1	1	3	1	1	0	42,720
Jahafil (GB)	2	2	16	4	3	1	76,035
Jahan	4	2	17	2	0	1	14,845
Jaklin Klugman	24	12	185	23	26	24	370,598
Jalaajel	1	1	4	1	0	0	4,979
Jammed Gold	3	3	20	3	1	3	70,000
Jan's Kinsman	1	1	14	3	1	1	43,767
Jatski	3	1	14	1	1	3	6,308
Java Gold	81	42	587	74	62	83	1,472,422
Jay Bryan	1	1	13	3	1	2	28,498
Jayan	2	1	11	2	1	1	73,700
Jaycean	1	1	14	2	0	3	10,775
Jazz Singer	6	4	49	5	6	6	47,771
Jazzing Around	35	21	189	29	24	29	397,176
Jeblar	80	45	577	90	70	65	1,371,082
Jeff D.	1	1	6	2	3	0	21,540
Jeff's Companion	4	1	13	2	1	1	7,751
Jeffers West	2	1	9	1	1	0	7,946
Jeloso	7	3	54	3	5	5	44,340
Jeopardy	1	1	13	3	2	4	35,106

Broodmare Sire	Perf	Wnrs	Sts	1st	2d	3d	Purses
Jerimi Johnson	13	4	67	6	9	13	109,436
Jerry Crow	2	2	26	4	3	5	35,617
Jersey Pleasure	3	1	21	1	0	3	5,167
Jesterson	3	3	39	6	4	5	56,749
Jet d'Eay	1	1	4	2	0	1	19,642
Jet Diplomacy	3	2	23	3	7	4	61,526
Jett Sett Joe	1	1	5	1	1	0	2,355
Jig Time	18	9	164	15	18	22	171,319
Jiltaloom	1	1	16	1	1	2	10,237
Jim J.	10	1	61	3	4	10	31,771
Jimmy Plains	3	2	30	3	3	4	78,399
Jitterbug Chief	7	2	37	2	2	7	46,914
Jo Moses	1	1	14	3	3	4	74,898
Joachim	2	2	28	2	5	3	23,563
Joanie's Chief	21	10	144	19	16	25	225,270
Joduke	1	1	10	1	1	0	9,182
Joe K.'s Lester	3	1	16	1	2	2	25,484
Joe Vee	2	1	12	3	2	0	24,830
Joe's Knight Ruler	1	1	15	1	2	3	12,383
Joey Bob	8	3	42	4	5	5	55,827
Jog My Memory	1	1	10	1	1	3	25,508
John Alden	68	29	476	61	50	62	1,789,119
John Casey	9	4	57	8	5	9	72,686
John William	1	1	5	1	0	1	3,348
John's Choice	6	1	27	2	6	2	40,970
John's Gold	18	7	123	11	13	8	177,584
Johnlee n' Harold	2	1	10	1	2	0	8,181
Johnny's Prospect	4	2	19	3	2	3	75,840
Johns Bobbi	1	1	5	3	0	0	4,540
Johns Treasure	4	2	27	4	2	4	32,873
Joker's Farce	1	1	6	1	0	2	6,880
Jokester	7	4	46	8	5	5	81,136
Jolie Jo	14	6	97	8	13	6	160,600
Jolie's Halo	47	27	289	48	39	37	1,298,781
Jolly Jake (NZ)	1	1	15	1	1	1	14,500
Jolly Johu	10	6	82	7	8	9	106,018
Jon George (GB)	1	1	5	1	1	2	27,460
Jontilla	1	1	13	1	4	2	8,767
Jose Binn	6	1	32	1	2	2	10,761
Journey At Sea	20	4	127	10	14	19	153,370
Jovial Turn	3	1	21	3	3	5	151,045
Joyful Hope	1	1	7	2	0	0	2,450
Juddken	1	1	7	2	0	0	3,430
Judgable	5	1	27	1	2	1	24,410
Judge Kilday	2	1	14	2	0	1	10,524
Judge Lex	8	4	74	9	12	9	178,987
Judge Power	2	1	4	1	0	0	9,698
Judge Smells	80	43	565	65	66	59	938,664
Judger	14	7	100	11	8	7	140,680
Judy'sotherbrother	1	1	11	1	2	1	11,253
Jugah	1	1	11	2	3	1	58,420
Julio Mariner	3	1	13	2	2	0	17,173
Jump Over the Moon	9	3	51	4	3	6	33,427
Jumping Hill	3	2	20	2	4	4	15,112
Junction	6	2	39	2	6	7	41,407
June's Blazer	9	2	58	3	7	1	18,459
Jungle Blade	21	11	166	16	12	25	247,878
Jungle Boy (GB)	2	2	21	4	2	4	112,207
Jungle Express	3	2	15	3	4	2	59,421
Jungle Jove	1	1	8	2	1	1	18,830
Jungle Pocket	5	2	51	7	5	9	84,301
Jungle Savage	9	3	58	10	3	2	262,655
Just a Swangin	1	1	6	1	1	0	3,732
Just a Tab	8	3	34	4	1	4	61,352
Just Plain Tuff	1	1	11	4	3	3	7,116
Just Right Classi	2	1	13	1	0	2	11,112
Just Right Mike	9	2	51	2	7	5	27,159
Just the Time	49	31	340	49	53	45	454,199
Kadampa	1	1	10	2	1	2	4,127
Kahyasi	6	1	20	4	3	0	618,858
Kajun Native	3	2	26	4	4	6	29,113
Kaldoun (FR)	6	3	17	5	0	3	446,543
Kalim (IRE)	5	3	29	7	3	6	117,692
Kamehameha	3	1	5	1	0	1	7,048
Kansas City	3	3	24	3	5	6	10,423
Kaskaskia	3	1	19	2	2	1	32,496

Broodmare Sire	Perf	Wnrs	Sts	1st	2d	3d	Purses
Kasteel (FR)	9	3	37	5	2	6	65,960
Katahaula County	4	3	18	4	5	1	70,501
Katowice	18	12	118	21	16	15	310,713
Kazaroun	1	1	10	1	5	0	52,340
Kebrimo (IRE)	9	4	52	9	5	5	64,229
Keel	2	1	8	1	1	0	3,725
Keen (GB)	2	1	9	1	0	0	8,011
Keep It Down	5	5	37	6	5	9	86,834
*Keep It Up II	1	1	4	1	0	1	10,340
Kellsapaul (IRE)	1	1	4	1	1	1	3,760
Kelly's Might	4	1	24	1	2	0	14,234
Kemal	1	1	3	1	0	0	8,750
Ken Graf	1	1	11	2	0	1	47,278
Kendor (FR)	4	2	25	2	4	2	36,725
Kenmare (FR)	6	1	16	1	2	1	39,461
Kennedy Road	87	45	561	80	73	67	1,535,633
Kentuckian	7	1	37	1	2	2	26,911
Kentucky Cookin	2	2	19	2	1	3	29,597
Kentucky Gold	8	4	52	4	6	7	52,251
Kentucky Jazz	10	6	62	7	5	10	138,283
Kerosene	4	3	33	6	4	3	140,283
Kerriby	2	1	9	1	2	0	27,804
Kew Gardens (BRZ)	1	1	13	4	3	2	42,110
Key to Content	14	4	104	7	11	14	107,732
Key to the Carr	7	2	26	2	3	3	17,981
Key to the Kingdom	41	14	262	27	24	24	415,050
Key to the Mint	150	72	957	128	101	101	2,600,585
Key to the Moon	13	6	113	8	10	17	128,966
Kfar Tov	2	1	11	1	3	1	13,656
Khartoum	3	1	19	2	1	2	28,346
Khatango	4	1	40	4	5	7	45,235
Khyber King	2	1	10	1	1	2	17,270
Kibe	3	3	23	4	3	3	27,863
Kick	7	3	71	5	8	13	68,711
Kid Colin	2	1	13	3	1	2	17,977
Kigrandi (BRZ)	1	1	10	5	1	1	214,400
Killany River (IRE)	5	2	33	5	3	1	41,380
Kim's Trick	2	1	10	1	2	0	10,870
Kind of Hush	3	2	22	3	3	2	32,133
King Alphonse	9	3	69	3	11	15	51,162
King Cane	1	1	15	5	3	2	44,953
King Celebrity	5	2	28	6	7	1	132,408
King Concorde	4	1	14	1	2	0	6,161
King Emperor	10	6	85	7	8	12	97,408
King Jody	8	2	51	2	6	7	43,565
King Lyph	1	1	3	1	2	0	8,360
King Nerraw	2	1	22	3	6	3	42,330
King of Clubs (GB)	2	2	22	4	4	1	45,813
King of Kings	6	4	47	8	4	7	303,391
King of Macedon	2	1	15	2	1	1	18,543
King of the Castle	1	1	7	1	0	0	3,660
King of the Mint	3	2	11	4	0	0	67,210
King of the North	5	3	31	5	9	4	48,235
King of the Sea	1	1	9	3	4	0	5,360
King Pellinore	28	15	177	20	13	16	265,216
King's Bishop	14	3	71	3	3	6	79,765
King's Dusty	1	1	3	1	0	0	3,649
King's Glory (GB)	1	1	8	2	1	1	3,964
King's Nest	8	5	71	7	12	4	119,466
King's Signet	1	1	15	1	3	2	22,816
Kingdom Bay (NZ)	1	1	15	1	4	2	21,650
Kingdom Keep	1	1	8	5	1	0	14,841
Kingmambo	25	16	160	28	19	24	845,556
Kings Lake	9	1	32	3	1	2	379,607
Kinsman Hope	2	1	20	1	7	1	17,866
Kipper Kelly	22	8	176	12	15	22	241,752
Kirby Lane	3	1	29	2	1	5	23,311
Kirtling (IRE)	2	1	19	2	4	2	27,795
Kissin Kris	10	6	51	6	4	5	106,242
Kissinsky	2	1	22	1	2	0	5,839
Kitwood	3	3	23	5	5	0	42,754
Klassy Charger	1	1	7	1	0	3	6,800
Klassy Flight	2	1	15	1	1	3	20,430
Knight	23	11	139	24	14	23	279,697
Knight Counter	2	1	13	1	2	3	6,637
Knight in Savannah	6	3	39	4	6	9	67,388

Broodmare Sire	Perf	Wnrs	Sts	1st	2d	3d	Purses
Knight Skiing	5	3	25	5	6	6	19,063
Knightly Dawn	3	1	13	3	1	1	207,775
Knightly Rapport	2	2	18	4	0	4	38,175
Knightly Sport	6	4	58	7	5	8	47,801
Knights Choice	119	68	750	109	99	118	1,103,536
Knock Knock Bird	1	1	4	1	0	0	8,904
Knoll	1	1	3	1	0	0	8,400
Know Your Aces	5	4	39	6	8	1	47,121
Known Fact	137	66	824	113	128	106	2,571,695
Kodiack	8	6	45	10	9	9	92,012
Kohoutek	6	4	60	6	8	6	54,626
Kokand	12	4	52	7	6	8	156,967
Koluctoo Bay	15	7	119	12	11	15	203,939
Kona Tenor	4	1	16	1	1	1	12,385
Kreisler	3	1	8	1	0	1	15,208
Kris (GB)	24	6	134	10	12	20	778,079
Kris S.	221	118	1463	212	211	203	6,471,678
Ky Alta	3	3	22	3	2	2	17,388
Kyle's Our Man	16	8	122	20	14	9	279,633
L'Aiglon	4	2	39	3	2	7	17,861
L'Amour Rullah	5	2	53	3	8	6	99,073
L'Emigrant	37	20	290	34	27	23	790,880
L'Enjoleur	110	60	880	112	100	105	1,496,202
L'Heureux	8	7	56	9	10	4	116,833
L'Natural	38	14	242	25	32	24	294,213
L. B. Commander	4	1	28	2	6	5	15,730
L. B. Jaklin	5	2	24	3	3	3	20,770
L. D. Bowers	1	1	5	1	1	1	8,284
La Cima	2	1	18	4	2	2	18,513
La Saboteur	17	9	84	16	6	7	140,057
Lac Ouimet	39	15	269	26	41	25	387,677
Ladnesian	3	1	21	1	2	2	9,600
Ladron	3	2	22	2	3	2	18,773
Laguna Breeze	3	1	25	2	3	2	6,931
Lahib	5	2	26	4	3	6	184,817
Lanburg	2	2	27	3	1	3	23,668
Lancastrian (IRE)	2	1	12	2	1	2	14,081
Land of Eire	4	2	41	4	5	2	38,531
Landish	1	1	10	1	0	0	4,200
Lanvin	1	1	14	5	3	0	90,590
Lanyon	5	2	34	3	7	2	35,288
Laomedonte	19	4	91	6	4	11	62,573
Laramie Trail	3	2	19	2	5	4	69,338
Lark Oscillation (FR)	1	1	11	1	1	2	8,036
Lark Thor	1	1	10	1	1	2	10,270
Lashkari (GB)	1	1	5	1	0	1	31,368
Last Picture	1	1	8	1	1	2	7,146
Last Tycoon (IRE)	23	14	166	25	19	22	762,756
Lasting Value	13	6	71	8	7	10	62,369
Late Act	11	4	63	8	10	9	132,754
Latin American	4	2	20	4	1	0	40,670
Laughing Boy	2	1	14	1	1	3	42,591
Launch a Dream	1	1	15	3	1	3	23,259
Law Society	6	2	15	2	0	1	27,672
Lawmaker	12	5	84	12	11	12	80,933
Lazaz	1	1	2	1	0	0	2,200
Le Braconnier	1	1	8	1	0	2	10,234
Le Cou Cou	3	1	12	1	1	0	7,153
Le Danseur	7	3	52	5	7	7	78,738
*Le Fabuleux	23	12	183	23	30	21	449,867
Le Gosse	5	3	61	4	5	12	52,270
Le Gros Lot	1	1	11	1	0	1	8,421
Lead Astray	2	1	14	1	2	2	16,868
Leading Hour	3	2	19	3	2	0	12,909
Leading Scorer	1	1	8	1	2	1	33,700
Lear Fan	128	64	859	108	98	110	3,529,599
Leematt	8	4	54	5	5	5	55,731
Lefty	3	2	28	4	8	4	142,440
Legal Prospector	15	6	82	11	8	15	155,696
Legatee	5	2	28	5	1	0	104,008
Legend of France	1	1	3	1	0	0	15,000
Legendary Wealth	1	1	7	1	0	0	1,752
Lejoli	9	4	65	6	5	4	113,842
Lemhi Gold	29	13	188	21	23	19	258,095
Leo Castelli	45	25	305	48	42	43	603,724
Leprechauns Wish	3	2	36	5	7	5	44,574
Leroy S.	8	3	53	4	2	10	22,687
Les Aspres (FR)	9	4	56	6	11	8	67,977
Let's Go Blue	4	4	31	5	4	2	136,830
Levee Dancer	3	1	23	1	5	1	12,726
Liberty Hall	1	1	13	2	1	4	17,667
Liberty Lane	4	2	25	4	2	3	70,119
Libra's Rib	2	1	16	1	2	0	12,608
License to Steal	1	1	19	1	7	4	28,425
Lieutenant's Lark	5	1	22	1	2	1	55,691
Light Idea	16	10	123	13	16	19	311,193
Light of Morn	6	4	48	6	9	9	178,796
Lightfeet	4	4	25	5	5	4	52,016
Lightning (FR)	1	1	13	1	3	1	10,342
Lightning Leap	11	4	64	10	8	5	93,807
Lil E. Tee	22	12	116	18	16	9	276,004
Lil Fappi	10	7	68	10	14	11	266,311
Lil Tyler	9	4	70	5	12	6	85,194
Liloy (FR)	32	12	206	19	24	22	371,817
Limbo	1	1	8	2	0	1	9,280
Limit to Reason	5	2	27	2	1	1	11,354
Lin D. Charger	8	4	69	4	6	13	41,164
Linamix (FR)	4	1	11	1	0	1	40,268
Line In The Sand	20	8	120	15	16	14	238,769
Lines of Power	67	35	418	52	37	47	608,643
Lingot d'Or	4	1	20	1	0	1	4,489
Link (FR)	1	1	9	1	0	0	4,792
Linkage	79	33	546	68	80	56	1,169,736
Lion Cavern	6	2	44	3	5	9	63,122
Lion d'Or	18	7	108	10	7	15	167,012
Lion of the Desert	2	1	4	1	0	0	2,387
Liquidity	1	1	9	1	1	1	9,773
List	20	7	123	7	11	16	90,018
Lit de Justice	1	1	5	4	1	0	286,230
Lite Line	2	1	15	1	1	4	25,060
Literati	8	6	45	8	5	7	47,534
Litigator	2	2	13	4	0	3	60,875
Little Current	48	21	297	33	48	38	819,467
Little Drummer Boy	1	1	8	2	0	0	9,207
Little Miracle	2	1	14	2	2	1	7,210
Little Missouri	47	19	304	23	44	46	783,303
Little Mustard	1	1	11	1	0	0	1,865
Little Nureyev	3	1	11	1	1	2	11,974
Little Secreto	6	1	35	2	1	5	30,037
Lively One	66	29	427	46	58	49	727,963
Living Proof	3	1	13	3	0	0	10,792
Lobsang (IRE)	3	1	5	1	0	0	8,571
Local Talent	23	8	152	16	14	19	259,513
Lockjaw	12	8	88	9	10	14	75,353
Locust Bayou	1	1	12	1	2	2	13,385
Lode	10	6	56	9	10	2	199,297
Loft	13	4	107	7	17	13	103,341
Logan Elm	3	2	13	3	0	1	38,562
Logical	10	7	64	9	6	7	359,172
Lomax	6	2	36	2	7	4	20,376
Lombardi	21	7	149	13	19	16	150,463
Lomond	48	33	378	73	36	53	1,308,143
London Bells	12	4	60	5	9	6	83,098
London Company	20	8	116	14	12	14	239,687
Lone Secretariat	1	1	6	1	0	0	7,000
Longleat	3	2	20	4	4	2	105,447
Lookinforthebigone	1	1	7	1	1	1	20,280
Loom	4	1	22	1	2	8	19,709
Loose Cannon	9	3	80	7	9	11	114,338
Lord At Law	1	1	5	1	0	0	8,568
Lord At War (ARG)	108	46	574	85	77	69	1,826,609
Lord Avie	158	72	959	124	128	119	2,345,193
Lord Carlos	15	9	129	14	9	18	209,911
Lord Chilly	2	1	9	1	1	0	6,475
Lord Durham	6	3	28	6	3	3	72,126
Lord Gaylord	87	42	565	79	61	66	1,837,494
Lord Layabout	1	1	11	3	0	2	13,500
Lord Ligonier	5	3	38	7	3	6	63,235
Lord of All	18	12	147	22	13	16	181,714
Lord of the Apes	2	2	23	2	2	4	25,756
Lord of the Night	9	2	39	2	3	5	30,213
Lord of the Sea	11	7	94	12	13	8	121,943

Broodmare Sire	Perf	Wnrs	Sts	1st	2d	3d	Purses
Lord of Trillora	3	1	25	1	1	2	9,789
Lord Parham	5	2	38	2	5	4	132,427
Lord Pleasant	2	1	19	1	0	2	36,996
Lord Rebeau	22	16	199	28	29	25	304,951
Lord Trendy (IRE)	1	1	5	1	2	1	10,743
Lord Triad	1	1	16	2	1	0	16,920
Lord Vancouver	2	1	31	6	2	8	129,863
Lordly Love	4	1	30	3	7	5	103,824
Lost Code	191	105	1313	183	162	184	3,597,852
Lost Mountain	8	4	40	7	6	2	62,449
Lost Opportunity	18	9	77	10	7	8	188,021
Lot o' Gold	29	10	201	16	28	28	304,458
Lothario	4	2	38	8	6	3	148,103
Loud and Clear	2	2	13	2	0	1	13,123
Louis Le Grand	2	2	21	4	0	4	21,153
Louisiana Slew	31	12	199	21	27	22	457,255
Loustrous Bid	15	8	118	19	16	13	416,466
Love That Mac	3	1	30	2	2	3	22,497
Lover Boy Leslie	4	1	32	2	5	2	32,326
Lover's Cross	1	1	10	1	2	2	17,646
Loyal Double	3	1	16	3	1	0	38,620
Lt. Stevens	13	5	61	6	5	5	77,964
Lucence	10	5	66	8	5	1	82,755
Luckey Jin Beau	5	4	49	7	8	5	204,083
Lucky Colonel S.	5	3	51	5	5	5	39,882
Lucky Fool	1	1	11	2	0	1	13,010
Lucky Legend	5	2	34	4	2	4	25,526
Lucky North	94	43	673	97	89	70	2,291,862
Lucky So n' So	9	6	75	12	9	6	178,156
Luckylite	2	1	6	1	1	0	7,751
Lucy's Axe	7	2	39	4	2	3	45,993
Lugnaquilla (IRE)	3	1	14	1	2	2	5,846
*Lumberton	1	1	10	1	2	1	13,447
Lustra	7	4	45	6	4	3	56,807
Luthier (FR)	4	1	21	2	1	1	25,002
Lycius	8	5	42	8	4	5	225,864
Lydian (FR)	18	10	128	14	8	8	148,283
Lyllos (FR)	5	2	36	4	4	3	38,024
Lympstone	3	1	9	1	1	1	10,970
Lyphard	105	48	639	83	72	85	2,193,775
Lyphard's Ridge	26	15	150	27	18	9	454,860
Lyphard's Wish (FR)	116	46	788	78	83	89	995,034
Lypheor (GB)	37	15	202	27	12	26	573,990
Lytrump	6	4	31	6	4	4	70,751
M. Double M.	17	4	94	5	11	12	122,482
Mabel's Boy	2	1	7	1	2	2	10,295
Mac Corkle	3	1	13	2	1	1	18,010
Mac Diarmida	14	8	89	17	9	12	483,685
Mac's Imp	1	1	2	1	0	0	11,400
Macarthur Park	5	2	34	4	9	6	36,001
Machiavellian	9	2	54	2	6	5	51,470
Macho Hombre	8	5	44	8	6	8	103,339
Macs Fleet	1	1	15	3	3	2	36,383
Mad Lane	2	1	14	2	1	1	16,481
Mad Scientist	3	2	24	4	1	3	57,380
Made Up My Mind	1	1	7	1	1	1	7,808
Maelstrom Lake (IRE)	4	2	28	5	4	0	38,999
Magesterial	91	43	592	85	86	58	2,358,603
Magic Banner	7	4	63	4	15	9	124,783
Magic Level	2	1	8	2	1	0	23,581
Magic Moment II (FR)	4	3	33	3	7	6	142,044
Magic Prospect	15	7	99	11	11	8	181,736
Magic Rascal	1	1	21	5	1	1	88,535
Magical Wonder	5	1	8	1	0	1	19,859
Magloire	7	4	47	7	4	7	103,044
Maha Baba	8	3	45	4	2	7	50,988
Maheras	14	6	95	10	18	16	156,028
Mahogany	1	1	18	1	4	2	12,393
Main Debut	13	9	90	14	15	11	111,191
Main Reef	1	1	6	1	1	1	41,960
Majesterian	3	1	11	1	1	2	14,980
Majestic Honor	1	1	10	3	2	1	18,105
Majestic Kat	1	1	15	1	1	4	19,597
Majestic Light	234	114	1587	196	155	196	3,914,370
Majestic Man	3	1	17	2	2	4	11,464
Majestic Marvel	2	1	10	2	2	4	17,089

Broodmare Sire	Perf	Wnrs	Sts	1st	2d	3d	Purses
Majestic Native	3	1	23	3	1	1	20,234
Majestic Prince	11	3	41	4	4	0	46,037
Majestic Red	3	3	38	5	2	6	38,892
Majestic Regent	1	1	7	1	0	1	3,873
Majestic Shore	7	2	39	4	5	5	46,439
Majestic Style	3	1	17	3	1	1	10,871
Majestic Venture	17	10	138	28	20	8	471,931
Majesty's Prince	52	30	390	42	43	46	535,920
Major Account	3	1	25	1	3	3	11,400
Major Gundry (GB)	1	1	7	1	1	1	29,820
Major Impact	19	8	139	9	28	22	319,248
Major Moran	16	9	140	15	27	16	634,575
Malagra	37	14	210	20	25	19	421,279
Malinowski	9	2	56	3	3	6	56,251
Mamaison	24	11	135	17	11	20	498,683
Mambo	25	10	147	14	19	18	207,125
Man From Eldorado	12	3	56	7	9	7	130,666
Man of Fire	2	2	13	5	0	2	9,584
Man Tan	3	2	28	4	2	7	36,208
Manado (IRE)	3	2	18	2	3	2	47,835
Manastash Ridge	17	8	104	15	10	13	223,968
Mane Minister	31	13	192	24	24	19	490,018
Manguin	2	1	11	3	1	1	125,354
Manifesto	1	1	8	1	2	0	12,200
Manila	82	40	578	65	70	53	1,671,892
Mannerism	3	3	26	5	4	3	71,234
Manos de Piedra	4	2	35	2	9	6	888,033
Mantecon (ARG)	3	1	15	2	3	1	31,894
Manzotti	37	14	236	19	34	35	327,579
Mara Lark	4	3	23	4	3	1	36,916
Marcellini	14	8	82	15	10	8	184,779
Marfa	103	47	693	85	88	75	1,341,941
Mari's Book	82	45	555	94	75	79	3,846,576
Maria's Mon	4	2	12	2	4	0	94,416
*Mariache II	3	2	17	2	1	0	28,620
Maribeau	10	4	52	7	3	6	78,531
Marine Brass	24	11	123	16	18	14	362,523
Marine Patrol	7	1	37	3	4	4	54,040
Marju (IRE)	2	1	8	2	0	0	57,135
Mark Chip	3	1	14	2	2	3	22,275
Mark in the Sky	4	2	18	2	1	3	10,906
Mark of Nobility	13	9	94	16	9	10	241,438
Marked Tree	6	3	33	3	2	4	20,634
Market Control	4	2	17	2	1	0	14,382
Market Fever	12	3	54	5	6	4	51,165
Marks Mill	1	1	12	2	2	3	5,308
Marquetry	56	24	332	40	42	44	938,459
Marsayas	8	4	56	5	6	2	99,568
Marscay (AUS)	2	1	12	3	0	1	45,230
Marshua's Dancer	96	48	658	83	84	84	1,448,724
Martial Law	11	5	61	6	5	9	121,079
Martins Rullah	1	1	13	1	0	4	12,033
Marvin's Policy	1	1	9	2	0	0	12,615
Masked Dancer	26	11	190	21	26	30	411,764
Masked Marvel (IRE)	3	2	22	2	2	9	102,540
Masked Native	5	3	36	9	2	2	121,083
Maskos	1	1	3	1	0	0	2,948
Masqued Dancer	2	1	20	2	3	4	27,539
Master Builder	1	1	9	2	1	1	6,575
Master Christopher	4	2	39	3	6	11	142,555
Master Derby	77	36	566	55	56	72	609,430
Master Hand	7	5	46	8	9	5	48,626
Master Holmes	2	1	13	2	1	3	27,029
Master Pruner	8	1	50	2	11	3	31,215
Master Style	3	3	46	6	7	5	45,936
Master Willie (GB)	11	4	70	7	11	8	209,514
Masterful Advocate	5	1	39	1	5	3	27,420
Mat-Boy (ARG)	7	3	40	6	3	5	125,558
Match the Hatch	12	8	107	15	5	11	172,340
Matchlite	14	5	94	11	11	12	248,845
Mateor	5	1	20	1	3	1	4,131
Matsadoon	28	6	167	9	11	17	170,308
Matsadoon's Honey	1	1	6	1	1	1	11,045
Matter of Honor	11	5	69	8	12	6	237,523
*Matto Grosso II	4	3	29	5	6	2	63,027
Mau Mau (BRZ)	1	1	4	1	1	0	13,400

Broodmare Sire	Perf	Wnrs	Sts	1st	2d	3d	Purses
Maudlin	60	30	426	48	55	57	820,439
Mawsuff (GB)	3	2	28	3	3	5	51,638
Maxistar	3	3	16	3	2	3	23,845
May I Rule	4	2	29	5	6	1	135,852
McCann	5	1	20	1	1	2	14,504
McCracken	2	1	15	2	1	0	8,499
McGinty (NZ)	5	3	36	6	4	5	200,671
McKim	2	1	15	1	0	0	7,950
Me and My Troy	2	1	13	1	1	1	10,270
Me Native	1	1	10	2	1	2	16,417
Meadow Flight	3	1	16	1	0	3	10,763
Meadowlake	203	104	1208	163	164	151	3,424,222
Mecke	1	1	9	2	0	1	8,503
Medaille d'Or	25	15	165	25	23	36	447,391
Media Starguest (IRE)	5	1	26	1	1	3	22,878
Medieval Man	73	35	552	63	61	56	987,364
Medieval Victory	3	2	26	4	1	5	30,684
Megaturn	23	10	155	21	16	19	522,724
Mehmet	64	31	449	50	53	53	762,617
Meinberg	2	2	21	2	0	5	49,085
Melyno (IRE)	5	3	41	3	3	6	19,983
Memo (CHI)	6	2	21	4	5	2	64,960
Mendel	1	1	4	2	0	0	4,300
Mendez (FR)	2	1	8	1	0	0	29,670
Meneval	5	1	30	1	3	4	29,351
Menocal	5	5	61	11	10	7	134,456
Merce Cunningham	4	1	15	1	1	3	52,232
Mercedes Won	22	13	142	28	17	13	751,782
Merger	1	1	12	2	2	3	11,384
Meritable	32	13	188	25	22	22	128,893
Mertzon	30	13	204	20	23	17	202,443
Messenger of Song	31	14	182	26	24	23	229,486
Metfield	44	24	283	41	32	37	762,199
Metrogrand	4	2	34	3	3	5	53,950
Metropolis	8	3	53	3	7	5	30,857
Mexican General	2	2	22	3	3	2	17,635
Mi Cielo	8	2	37	2	7	3	34,970
Mi Selecto	18	6	135	16	22	16	292,149
Mia's Boy	4	2	36	5	2	8	56,731
Mickey McGuire	18	8	152	15	24	13	286,728
Midnight Matinee	2	1	11	1	2	0	49,950
Midnight Prospect	1	1	6	1	2	1	12,593
Midnight Tiger	1	1	12	3	3	3	63,940
Midway Circle	14	6	118	12	13	15	369,285
Midyan	6	2	32	3	4	5	227,248
Mighty Adversary	31	15	252	27	39	36	461,739
Mighty Appealing	14	9	113	28	22	9	489,807
Mighty Courageous	8	1	38	1	3	5	10,405
Mighty Crafty	1	1	5	1	2	0	4,972
Mighty Prospector	2	1	11	1	1	1	6,936
Mighty Sky	1	1	8	1	0	0	7,078
Miglietti	3	1	17	1	1	1	6,705
Mill Native	14	5	97	9	9	14	117,854
Mill Reef	5	3	26	4	2	2	74,062
Mille Balles (FR)	1	1	12	3	1	3	59,726
Millenium (GB)	1	1	12	1	3	1	10,749
Miller's Mate	2	2	10	2	3	0	54,460
Miner's Mark	22	14	160	23	18	23	475,863
Minera	2	1	25	2	5	3	42,119
Mining	138	71	836	120	104	116	2,537,422
Ministry	2	1	3	1	0	0	3,010
Minneapple	8	4	59	7	5	9	137,681
Minnesota Mac	5	4	43	10	8	5	77,821
Minshaanshu Amad	19	7	111	9	9	14	163,933
Minstrel Glory	3	2	24	3	4	5	77,130
Miracle Heights	3	2	23	4	3	5	66,784
Misrepresentation	4	3	36	6	3	2	101,054
Missionary Ridge (GB)	13	4	85	5	8	4	109,717
Mississipian	4	2	13	2	1	1	5,612
Mista Vap	1	1	13	1	2	3	32,937
Mister Frisky	9	4	59	8	12	9	145,403
Mister Jacket	2	1	9	1	0	0	1,618
Mister Modesty	3	2	30	2	5	2	31,050
Mister Pitt	1	1	14	2	3	2	17,267
Mister Slippers	2	1	19	1	2	5	22,393
Mister Wonderful (GB)	4	1	17	1	3	3	30,397
Misty Flight	3	2	18	4	4	1	43,216
Miswaki	244	128	1490	224	204	171	4,940,625
Miteas Well Laff	9	5	84	8	8	14	178,347
Mitey Mad	1	1	7	1	0	0	6,285
Mitey Prince	2	1	17	1	5	1	44,172
Mo Exception	5	4	45	7	7	3	71,118
Mo Power	1	1	13	5	1	1	78,420
Mocito Fogoso (CHI)	1	1	1	1	0	0	15,000
Mocito Guapo	6	4	49	9	8	6	272,432
Modern Prince	1	1	11	1	0	0	6,061
Mogambo	34	12	260	17	34	34	491,328
Mokhieba	7	3	47	4	7	5	195,080
Moment of Hope	37	10	202	13	29	26	261,507
Mon Classique	2	1	18	1	3	3	11,106
Monetary Gift	33	19	278	41	33	41	456,509
Money by Orleans	4	2	40	2	2	5	49,359
Moneychanger	7	2	44	6	4	4	51,582
Mongo's Image	1	1	11	2	2	0	13,368
Monopoly	1	1	14	3	3	3	34,510
Monsieur Champlain	14	6	146	13	13	22	198,330
Montagnet	1	1	10	1	0	3	6,206
Montbrook	13	7	85	18	8	6	180,738
Monteverdi (IRE)	16	6	87	8	7	9	155,833
*Montparnasse II	2	1	5	2	0	0	3,896
Moon Prospector	4	1	28	1	5	8	38,355
Moon Up T. C.	8	3	54	4	7	10	25,489
Moonsplash	9	5	60	9	9	7	44,136
More Horsepower	2	1	12	2	2	2	26,417
More Pleasure	4	2	18	3	1	5	44,182
Morning Bob	68	29	490	48	62	47	821,412
Morning Came	1	1	6	2	1	1	10,590
Morning Haze	3	2	24	2	4	3	37,173
Moro	2	1	17	4	4	1	30,512
Moscow Ballet	120	53	696	79	92	106	1,585,473
Moses Tablet	2	2	18	2	1	2	14,175
Most Welcome (GB)	1	1	5	1	0	1	8,600
Motrill	2	1	9	1	1	0	2,389
Mouktar	1	1	4	2	2	0	199,625
Mount Hagen (FR)	21	7	106	12	11	11	164,391
Mountain Cat	51	26	287	49	33	29	716,717
Mountain Express	8	1	21	1	2	1	11,598
Mountain Native	7	3	50	4	4	9	28,811
Mountdrago (ARG)	4	3	21	4	3	5	80,214
Move Off	1	1	6	1	0	1	8,660
Mr R. T. F.	2	1	19	1	2	0	3,616
Mr. Badger	6	5	34	5	11	3	38,701
Mr. Bold Tea Arr	1	1	8	1	0	0	2,760
Mr. Brilliant	4	1	17	1	3	1	20,143
Mr. Clinch	5	3	32	7	5	3	51,003
Mr. Cockatoo	9	5	91	11	16	16	190,544
Mr. Cool M.	2	1	10	1	0	0	1,427
Mr. Crimson Ruler	3	1	27	1	1	3	17,523
Mr. Dreamer	3	1	18	1	1	5	9,775
Mr. Exclusive	1	1	2	1	0	0	4,542
Mr. Free Spirit	2	1	15	1	0	1	5,151
Mr. Greeley	10	7	78	10	21	7	555,671
Mr. Howard	9	4	51	9	3	12	51,915
Mr. Inspector	5	1	33	3	6	3	33,593
Mr. Integrity	12	4	86	9	13	11	113,838
Mr. Justice	6	1	28	1	1	1	11,169
Mr. Kaskaskia	4	3	26	5	4	0	84,965
Mr. Leader	188	86	1263	148	149	171	4,117,753
Mr. Long	9	4	74	6	7	13	62,979
Mr. Nasty	2	1	22	2	6	2	38,715
Mr. O. P.	1	1	6	1	1	2	9,392
Mr. Paul	3	2	20	4	5	4	75,727
Mr. Pitty Pat	2	1	22	1	4	3	16,112
Mr. Prospector	252	131	1512	236	185	188	8,447,383
Mr. Ralph	3	1	18	3	1	3	25,672
Mr. Redoy	60	24	428	35	62	51	785,572
Mr. Sidney	2	1	11	1	0	2	2,799
Mr. Sparkles	13	7	102	11	14	19	244,760
Mr. Torsion	1	1	8	1	0	1	5,727
Mr. Ward	2	2	24	6	2	1	8,952
Mr. Washington	3	1	14	1	2	2	23,670
Mt. Livermore	209	97	1373	171	185	155	3,705,649

Broodmare Sire	Perf	Wnrs	Sts	1st	2d	3d	Purses
Mt. Magazine	4	1	20	2	0	4	14,451
Mt. Ruritania	7	5	69	12	13	12	145,866
Mtoto	4	2	25	3	6	3	42,672
Mud and Water	4	1	17	1	6	0	20,963
Mufti	4	2	21	2	3	2	59,984
Mugassas	6	4	54	6	4	1	39,966
Mugatea	16	8	112	21	13	15	279,503
Mujtahid	3	1	24	1	3	4	51,364
Mukaddamah	2	1	14	4	2	1	164,728
Mulberry (FR)	1	1	5	1	0	0	1,200
Mullineaux	4	3	36	7	1	4	41,348
Mummy's Pet (GB)	6	3	35	10	3	2	149,758
Murrtheblurr	29	15	194	27	16	23	242,888
Muscovite	10	3	55	4	5	10	57,125
Music On Ice	8	3	41	5	4	5	75,437
Music Prince	1	1	7	1	1	2	10,114
Mustard Plaster	3	2	30	3	4	7	19,281
Mutakddim	2	1	8	1	2	1	26,165
Muttering	18	9	120	17	15	19	216,075
My Boy Adam	7	1	28	2	3	3	105,243
My Favorite Moment	8	2	32	3	2	2	296,911
My Gallant	16	8	115	15	18	17	429,217
My Habitony	8	4	55	7	3	6	148,386
My Memoirs (GB)	5	2	26	3	4	1	38,310
My Old School	1	1	11	1	3	1	11,987
My Phillipe	3	2	17	2	1	1	12,700
My Prince Charming	6	4	38	6	5	6	141,820
Mystery Storm	5	2	24	2	0	2	22,689
Mythical Ruler	18	10	130	13	6	17	380,240
Nabeel Dancer	1	1	16	2	4	2	18,076
Naevus	78	37	463	63	58	66	1,007,132
Nain Bleu (FR)	14	6	95	12	9	12	676,063
Naked Sky	31	16	232	28	38	31	598,266
Nalees Man	56	15	313	26	42	33	416,684
Nalees Rialto	3	2	23	3	1	3	80,852
Nantequos	7	3	52	6	9	7	58,836
Nasgame	1	1	8	1	2	1	5,458
Nashaglo	4	1	20	1	4	1	33,326
Nashua	5	1	30	1	4	2	16,481
Nashwan	16	9	89	18	10	7	574,547
Naskra	111	44	801	78	100	98	3,871,669
Nasty and Bold	93	43	560	73	75	76	1,411,110
Nataraja	9	2	55	2	5	2	20,256
Nathan Detroit	5	2	33	3	2	2	48,705
National Zenith	11	5	70	9	9	8	123,096
Native Aid	2	1	14	1	1	0	15,190
Native Alliance	2	1	6	1	1	2	7,144
Native Bidder	2	1	9	2	0	1	12,105
Native Born	6	3	48	10	8	9	85,941
Native Charger	30	11	229	15	20	28	243,905
Native Factor	6	3	24	7	6	3	176,421
Native Horizon	1	1	8	2	3	0	18,285
Native John	3	1	18	1	3	3	32,090
Native of Kentucky	4	2	35	2	2	5	24,637
Native Orbit	3	2	24	4	1	4	8,115
Native Prospector	65	32	420	61	57	48	1,120,074
Native Royalty	64	25	380	42	38	40	655,906
Native Rythm	2	1	20	2	3	3	19,001
Native Secret	6	2	44	3	2	4	18,274
Native Slew	2	1	15	1	2	2	32,827
Native Supreme	2	2	18	5	2	3	22,736
Native Tactics	33	16	200	21	17	28	259,348
Native Uproar	26	13	206	27	37	24	596,199
Native Wizard	6	2	35	5	4	5	67,841
Natomas	4	2	14	2	2	1	53,439
Natural (NZ)	3	1	14	1	1	2	9,549
Naturals Grand	2	1	18	1	2	3	11,231
Navajo	34	17	264	32	40	29	377,612
Navajo Trail	3	1	14	1	0	3	10,803
Navarino (CHI)	2	1	6	1	1	1	6,132
Navarone	3	3	35	7	5	1	61,702
Nearctic Traveller	1	1	9	3	1	1	39,900
Nearly On Time	3	1	21	1	6	1	11,904
Neat Native	2	1	23	2	5	5	17,145
Nebos	5	1	25	1	4	0	90,622
Nelson	8	4	39	7	5	4	92,994
Nepal	23	15	182	30	24	32	676,008
Nevada Reality	3	2	22	3	4	1	27,226
Never a Lark	4	2	27	4	2	3	57,333
Never Bend	4	2	27	3	5	3	22,472
Never Down Hill	8	2	45	3	2	3	21,486
Never Return	1	1	8	2	0	0	5,508
Never Tabled	60	33	367	53	49	51	468,919
Never Wavering	2	1	11	1	1	2	8,715
New Dandy (ARG)	2	2	31	8	3	1	89,136
New Prospect	9	4	49	5	6	10	205,271
Newsprobe	2	2	22	2	3	2	21,250
Nias	10	2	72	2	12	6	62,996
Nice Catch	13	6	65	9	5	5	108,056
Nice Dancer	7	1	13	2	1	0	15,506
Nice Pirate	1	1	13	3	0	2	15,285
Nicholas	14	7	90	8	7	11	162,592
Nickel Slot	2	1	11	2	3	1	15,402
Nielbueh	1	1	19	2	6	4	13,823
Night Eagle	3	1	28	1	1	3	15,916
Night Invader	5	2	36	3	0	2	34,422
Night Mover	16	10	103	12	20	19	237,857
Night Musical	7	4	38	7	2	5	14,632
Night Shift	34	13	214	20	20	28	526,965
Night Time	3	1	15	2	2	1	5,858
Nijinsky II	129	60	820	112	113	114	3,475,440
Nijinsky Model	3	1	22	1	2	6	90,079
Nijinsky's Secret	16	6	108	8	6	5	55,550
Nijinsky's Table	2	2	10	3	3	0	28,361
Nikoli (IRE)	3	1	14	1	0	1	1,720
Nikos	6	5	45	9	4	4	121,619
Nile Delta	22	11	134	16	9	16	191,679
Niniski	8	3	41	7	3	4	85,424
Nishapour	2	1	13	1	1	2	7,280
Nisswa	1	1	9	1	0	1	6,529
No Back Talk	10	8	74	17	8	10	72,677
No Bend	4	3	30	7	0	4	30,226
No Budget	1	1	3	1	0	0	8,220
No House Call	7	2	55	2	5	9	69,844
No Louder	42	21	309	44	35	45	1,106,098
No Malice	1	1	14	5	1	0	46,344
No No Billy	2	2	19	5	4	2	21,409
No Points	9	6	66	10	9	6	159,410
No Robbery	16	9	134	20	9	13	190,792
No Sale George	20	11	141	20	26	9	451,066
Noactor	11	7	89	15	9	4	143,332
Noble Assembly	15	10	105	19	7	19	220,604
Noble Commander	1	1	6	1	1	0	2,720
Noble Dancer (GB)	10	3	69	4	11	6	64,613
Noble Fighter	1	1	7	1	1	1	256,600
Noble Lord	2	2	15	2	2	0	8,467
Noble Monk (IRE)	4	2	28	2	3	3	64,446
Noble Nashua	24	9	154	16	17	12	172,029
Noble Novice	2	1	11	3	0	1	25,683
Noble Orphan	1	1	8	2	1	1	28,115
Noble Peer	2	1	9	2	3	1	60,180
Noble Saint	5	3	35	6	4	4	100,806
Noble Table	4	1	22	3	0	1	57,661
Noble Title	4	2	29	2	2	2	30,724
Nobloys (FR)	2	1	11	1	0	2	21,936
Nobubble	1	1	8	2	3	0	8,649
Nodouble	72	31	480	55	38	48	718,194
*Noholme II	12	4	74	5	4	7	50,254
Noholme Way	5	4	44	9	10	7	143,751
Noisy When Hot	2	2	12	3	1	0	58,463
Non Combatant	2	1	13	3	2	1	10,190
Nonno (IRE)	4	1	27	6	1	4	50,242
Nonparrell	7	4	58	5	5	8	62,240
Noon Time Spender	2	1	18	1	0	0	8,992
Norbot	5	1	48	2	6	10	44,956
Norcliffe	30	16	181	24	10	22	243,469
Nordic Legend	11	7	83	9	8	6	87,906
Nordic Prince	7	4	27	10	2	3	296,309
Nordico	7	3	36	5	3	1	61,415
Norquestor	53	24	377	47	53	48	1,283,988
North Flight	3	1	14	2	1	2	32,713
North Pole	17	8	117	11	17	15	225,862

Broodmare Sire	Perf	Wnrs	Sts	1st	2d	3d	Purses
North Prospect	25	10	152	15	19	17	214,357
North Sea	12	6	103	7	9	10	115,790
North Tower	22	4	145	6	16	29	182,641
Northerly	1	1	9	1	0	4	49,970
Northern Answer	3	2	24	4	6	4	164,476
Northern Baby	130	62	884	103	121	113	2,262,377
Northern Best	2	2	24	5	3	4	21,143
Northern Dancer	43	21	315	35	44	40	868,506
Northern Fashion	7	4	58	5	6	8	684,057
Northern Flagship	52	23	314	33	37	26	442,355
Northern Fling	19	10	129	17	18	18	316,549
Northern Guest	1	1	1	1	0	0	450,000
Northern Horizon	26	14	177	21	23	24	229,522
Northern Ice	3	2	19	3	1	1	24,511
Northern Idol	1	1	10	3	1	0	28,727
Northern Jove	148	72	1079	116	122	126	2,199,639
Northern Legend	2	1	16	2	3	0	16,219
Northern Magus	9	5	50	7	3	4	84,820
Northern Majesty	7	1	46	4	4	5	28,404
Northern Monarch	2	1	16	3	2	4	64,653
Northern Mystic	7	4	52	7	6	12	94,698
Northern Native	3	2	29	3	3	1	30,194
Northern Play	2	1	7	1	1	1	12,229
Northern Prospect	90	48	631	85	70	98	1,600,401
Northern Raja	11	2	67	6	6	4	105,587
Northern Ringer	7	2	46	3	14	5	37,259
Northern Score	30	11	200	20	29	25	368,405
Northern Smartee	9	5	73	8	7	9	82,634
Northern Spell	5	3	48	4	5	7	70,163
Northern Supremo	22	10	154	16	17	14	175,345
Northern Symphony	2	1	13	2	4	1	22,165
Northern Tab	1	1	4	1	0	1	3,700
Northern Treat	2	1	20	2	3	0	26,457
Northern View (IRE)	1	1	7	2	1	1	8,598
Northern Wolf	15	7	116	8	12	13	202,816
Northfields	12	6	57	15	5	1	222,792
Northiam	9	5	71	7	11	13	103,235
Northjet (IRE)	47	21	295	33	28	34	625,968
Northrop	37	19	244	25	32	19	527,363
Northstar Prospect	1	1	14	2	4	5	17,404
Northwest Passage	4	1	32	2	10	5	31,923
Norwegian	1	1	3	1	0	0	7,390
Nostalgia	11	5	65	10	7	7	120,964
Nostalgia's Star	16	8	94	15	14	12	383,998
Nostrum	31	14	162	23	28	20	304,428
Not For Love	2	1	3	1	0	0	15,847
Notebook	85	54	566	93	78	74	2,175,524
Notna's Prince	3	2	18	3	3	1	29,410
Nova Scotia	6	3	31	4	2	2	70,589
Now Listen	2	2	19	3	2	1	50,355
Numa Pompilius	7	5	43	8	11	6	34,648
Numchuek	1	1	17	1	4	2	7,037
Numerous	6	2	25	2	2	2	110,923
Nureyev	109	59	650	98	83	79	4,615,323
O'Danny Boyle	1	1	8	1	0	0	4,740
O. K. by You	4	2	28	4	6	2	45,687
O. K. Holme	1	1	11	1	0	0	11,395
O. K. So Far	5	1	15	2	3	3	6,494
Oak Dancer (GB)	5	5	44	13	6	9	457,165
Oak Ridge (FR)	2	1	10	1	0	2	16,940
Obligato	16	8	119	12	12	13	565,160
Obraztsovy	9	6	79	9	6	5	65,618
Ocala Slew	4	3	29	4	3	2	75,135
Ocean Bar	2	2	11	2	0	1	17,180
Ocean Falls (IRE)	2	2	15	3	1	1	17,506
Ocean Trick	5	2	39	4	10	7	81,835
Off Shore Gamble	1	1	8	1	0	1	20,962
Ogygian	132	63	845	110	85	107	2,301,378
Oh My Windland	3	1	20	3	1	2	41,688
Oh Say	101	57	709	100	85	91	1,606,669
Oka Revolt	2	2	11	3	2	2	15,847
Olantengy (FR)	10	6	75	7	6	5	79,282
Old Chronicle	2	1	12	1	3	0	16,604
Old Man (FR)	3	2	23	4	1	4	29,998
Old Pueblo	1	1	10	2	0	0	10,453
Olden Times	62	25	426	44	56	49	744,526
Ole Bob Bowers	21	11	161	16	12	25	137,080
Ole'	8	5	49	12	6	3	423,705
Olympiad King	8	6	76	8	11	10	83,086
Olympian King	1	1	12	2	3	1	20,141
Olympic Native	11	5	62	9	5	10	137,755
Olympio	37	19	218	29	26	28	1,549,502
On Target	2	2	4	2	2	0	7,425
On the Sauce	13	6	96	8	11	9	109,489
On the Sly	7	4	63	6	11	7	100,376
On to Glory	85	37	665	69	79	77	1,135,046
Once Wild	34	16	230	28	12	30	397,077
One Drink	1	1	4	1	0	0	11,420
One for All	40	25	308	41	44	38	766,888
One in a Mil	6	4	35	4	1	10	16,397
One More Slew	2	2	19	3	2	0	40,143
*One Pound Sterling	2	1	9	2	2	0	27,970
Only Dreamin	2	1	12	1	2	3	31,995
Opachisco	3	1	13	3	4	1	44,644
Opening Lead	9	5	102	7	13	17	123,110
Opening Verse	52	18	343	24	39	42	596,316
Opposite Abstract	1	1	7	1	1	1	10,198
Optimism	2	1	10	1	1	1	1,828
Opus Dei (FR)	4	2	23	3	3	4	18,160
Oraibi	7	4	41	6	6	4	19,831
Orange County	2	1	9	1	1	0	3,955
Orbit Dancer	56	17	363	26	35	51	348,500
Orbit Ruler	5	3	53	5	3	5	88,880
Order	11	6	65	9	8	9	157,621
Ormonte	4	1	22	2	3	2	42,734
Orono	2	2	17	3	2	3	22,857
Osorno (ARG)	4	3	32	6	3	4	64,746
Our Blue Chip	4	2	32	4	3	7	62,243
Our Boy Kirk	2	1	23	3	0	2	17,000
Our Captain Willie	8	1	49	1	5	6	76,131
Our City	1	1	9	1	1	2	7,409
Our Escapade	1	1	20	1	4	3	12,898
Our Gary	22	8	156	17	19	25	167,740
Our Hero	8	4	48	6	5	8	59,041
Our Liberty	5	3	31	5	6	1	56,507
Our Michael	49	17	290	26	37	27	505,183
Our Native	164	82	1136	152	148	139	3,195,432
Our Recital	3	1	19	1	2	5	9,432
Out of Place	29	19	201	30	19	18	627,067
Out of the East	6	2	56	5	2	11	28,280
Out of the Way	2	1	8	1	1	0	6,160
Outward Bound	5	2	22	2	0	1	20,490
Over Arranged	6	2	34	3	3	4	80,004
Over Mountain	5	3	24	6	3	2	26,989
Over the Rainbow	6	5	62	9	5	8	122,419
Overskate	33	9	256	18	24	34	494,642
Oxford Flight	2	1	16	3	1	1	23,727
P. R. Man	1	1	3	1	0	1	8,852
P. Vik	1	1	13	2	0	0	9,473
Paavo	4	3	40	5	4	1	62,163
Pac Mania	6	3	33	3	4	5	46,550
Pachuto	13	3	74	4	5	6	76,907
Pacific Native	21	3	104	4	7	7	50,618
Paderoso	1	1	5	1	1	1	7,900
Page	3	1	22	1	2	6	12,978
Page Nijinsky	2	2	25	5	2	4	39,143
*Pago Pago	3	2	34	2	3	4	21,908
Painted Wagon	7	3	46	6	4	7	48,672
Pair of Deuces	7	4	47	4	6	5	52,183
Palace Music	72	34	449	61	49	55	1,042,167
Palacios	2	1	12	1	2	1	33,399
Palm Beach (FR)	1	1	7	1	2	1	17,650
Pancho Villa	124	62	927	106	130	128	1,816,808
Pappa Max	2	2	29	6	7	2	41,549
Pappa Riccio	26	11	180	19	24	20	252,442
Pappa Steve	6	2	50	4	10	6	134,684
Pappagallo (FR)	17	7	94	11	14	10	98,864
Pappy	4	2	21	2	3	3	25,194
Par Five	2	1	12	1	1	1	21,009
Parade Marshal	4	1	36	1	2	3	17,745
Parade of Stars	3	2	10	3	1	1	57,875
Paradise Bay (GB)	3	1	21	4	3	0	120,606

Broodmare Sire	Perf	Wnrs	Sts	1st	2d	3d	Purses
Paramount Jet	11	8	83	16	11	12	365,180
Parfaitement	34	19	281	34	38	39	735,319
Paristo	8	5	83	7	16	9	107,745
Park Regent	7	5	58	10	6	6	59,062
Partez	41	13	246	26	27	35	299,591
Partial Settlement	1	1	2	1	0	0	6,670
Partner's Hope	9	3	43	5	5	6	34,983
Pas de Cheval	4	2	28	4	3	3	27,400
Pas Seul	29	12	178	24	25	23	339,187
Paso's Ray	1	1	16	2	4	2	21,749
Pass Catcher	17	6	104	12	13	9	109,724
Pass the Glass	33	13	189	18	25	21	193,511
Pass the Line	42	17	258	26	35	28	532,296
Pass the Tab	34	13	184	22	14	18	901,507
Passing Base	1	1	15	3	3	3	23,142
Passing Zone	6	2	58	5	7	8	79,496
Patch of Sun	3	2	16	3	2	3	44,699
Paternity	3	2	17	2	2	0	12,869
Patriot's Dream	4	2	18	4	0	0	12,613
Patriotically	8	4	56	6	4	5	117,274
Patton	1	1	3	1	1	0	38,038
Paul's Stark	1	1	11	1	0	0	14,146
Pauper Prince	6	3	32	4	0	1	27,976
Pax Nobiscum	2	1	10	2	1	1	84,614
Peace Arch	5	2	43	5	4	10	25,678
Peace Corps	4	3	25	4	1	5	42,179
Peace for Peace	10	6	68	11	7	5	126,799
Peaked	5	3	35	7	2	2	37,713
Peaks and Valleys	4	3	16	4	4	2	166,390
Pellinore	1	1	15	1	1	3	4,473
Pembroke	7	2	26	2	1	4	29,643
Pencil Point (IRE)	12	8	85	14	14	7	151,064
Pentaquod	8	5	45	5	10	4	136,065
Pentelicus	94	52	586	82	71	73	1,828,557
Pep Up	5	2	31	2	5	2	25,495
Pepenador	7	2	54	3	5	7	47,188
Peppermint Schnaps	5	1	21	1	4	3	13,903
Perceive Arrogance	2	1	24	1	0	0	6,274
Peregrinator (IRE)	4	1	28	4	5	8	37,575
Perfect Parade	4	3	27	3	2	3	72,081
Perfect Tan	2	1	16	1	0	6	18,553
Perfecting	1	1	5	2	1	0	31,600
Perkin Warbeck	6	4	39	4	5	5	84,745
Perrault (GB)	28	14	186	26	24	21	284,236
Persevered	9	3	59	7	4	11	78,445
Persian Bold (IRE)	16	9	97	13	8	14	409,023
Persian Emperor	5	3	41	5	7	2	41,746
Personable Joe	1	1	3	1	0	0	7,920
Personal Flag	120	72	952	132	132	121	2,368,422
Personal Hope	35	16	219	27	31	33	591,816
Personality	7	6	72	7	12	9	127,070
Persuasive Leader	1	1	10	2	1	2	8,323
Pertsemlidis	1	1	12	1	2	0	7,217
Petardia (GB)	3	1	20	2	2	2	23,665
Peterhof	48	27	310	41	34	33	449,185
Petersburg	17	9	79	14	8	9	113,883
Petes Innate	2	1	16	2	2	3	7,920
Peteski	24	14	124	22	23	20	466,415
Petionville	1	1	2	1	0	0	6,315
Petong	8	3	47	5	4	7	180,854
Petorius (IRE)	4	2	26	4	2	7	59,841
*Petrone	20	9	124	12	15	10	99,405
Pettibone Prince	1	1	11	2	1	1	21,191
Phantom Jet	2	2	27	5	5	1	194,053
Pharisien (FR)	1	1	7	2	1	2	83,496
Pharly	9	5	58	9	11	5	318,783
Pheidas (IRE)	2	1	17	1	4	0	11,287
Philosopher	1	1	7	2	0	0	19,260
Phone Order	17	12	72	13	6	9	88,218
Phone Trick	229	119	1464	196	200	176	4,207,981
Pia Star	7	2	46	2	1	4	10,631
Pia's Promise	1	1	10	3	0	1	11,867
Piaster	6	2	33	3	6	5	25,673
Piccolino	19	11	149	20	13	18	322,915
Picturesque	7	1	34	2	2	4	55,886
Piedmont Pete	3	1	27	2	1	4	15,610

Broodmare Sire	Perf	Wnrs	Sts	1st	2d	3d	Purses
Piker	22	13	165	24	15	27	277,503
Pilgrim	39	20	266	35	35	30	798,383
Pillager	1	1	6	2	0	0	7,954
Pillar of Wisdom	1	1	11	2	3	1	38,803
Pilot Ship	11	6	80	12	8	10	185,554
Pine Bluff	56	22	328	36	46	41	820,166
Pine Circle	6	3	45	4	4	4	54,096
Pink Dust	1	1	9	1	1	3	2,419
Pipe of Peace	1	1	15	1	3	2	9,279
Pirate's Bounty	193	90	1262	160	151	164	2,390,020
Pirateer	21	11	160	19	26	19	261,524
Pirouette	4	3	31	5	3	5	78,207
Pitching Wedge	1	1	7	1	0	1	7,077
Pitso Cassello	19	8	101	16	11	15	72,065
Plain Dealing	34	11	188	17	25	20	289,656
Plastic Surgeon	5	2	39	3	5	7	53,413
Platinum King	3	2	21	2	4	2	35,222
Platoon Leader	3	3	18	4	4	1	58,530
Plaxtol	2	2	7	2	1	0	8,180
Play Fellow	74	34	542	66	61	60	971,237
Play It My Way	3	2	30	3	3	4	73,990
Play On	20	12	154	17	16	18	278,170
Play the Ace	1	1	13	1	1	1	17,524
Play the Red	2	1	10	2	0	1	5,317
Pleasant Colony	221	120	1570	213	222	229	5,271,283
Pleasant Tap	35	17	178	34	26	25	923,804
Pleasure Appeal	1	1	3	1	0	0	644
Pleasure Bent	2	1	19	2	3	5	40,007
Plenum	5	3	41	3	6	10	31,921
Plotting	4	1	11	1	0	0	6,339
Plugged Nickle	65	34	472	64	45	48	1,064,457
Pluie's Sylvester	8	3	52	6	3	4	54,159
Plum Bold	8	2	59	2	9	7	28,419
Plunk	5	2	22	2	0	1	12,754
Pocket Coin	3	2	30	3	5	3	15,182
Pocket Park	8	5	64	8	7	9	95,788
Pocketful in Vail	5	2	23	2	1	1	38,196
Point of Fact	2	2	20	3	3	2	23,073
Poison Ivory	4	2	30	3	2	7	34,458
Poker	15	6	78	13	5	4	183,117
Polar Night	1	1	7	2	2	0	24,680
Polar Palace	2	1	14	1	5	3	20,920
Pole Position	21	9	130	10	12	16	84,462
Poleax	10	6	56	8	5	10	98,646
Poles Apart	11	4	77	6	11	10	84,600
Police Car	21	10	158	15	21	25	173,713
Police Dust	6	3	42	5	3	2	73,198
Police Inspector	5	5	42	5	3	4	55,382
Policeman (FR)	4	1	33	3	1	5	31,410
Polish Mark	1	1	5	1	0	0	14,346
Polish Navy	91	47	573	79	99	67	1,606,200
Polish Numbers	68	32	411	62	53	52	1,283,258
Polish Patriot	5	2	21	3	3	5	231,565
Polish Precedent	3	2	21	2	2	2	47,324
Political Ambition	11	5	48	8	9	5	191,139
Political Coverup	2	1	18	1	0	3	6,628
Polka	1	1	11	2	1	2	29,280
Pollinize	16	7	106	9	10	16	98,994
Poly's Blade	8	3	49	5	5	6	90,509
Polynesian Flyer	5	5	47	10	9	4	68,864
Polynesian Ruler	2	1	8	1	0	0	10,576
Pondelli	2	1	16	2	1	1	9,249
Pontoise	5	3	44	5	5	4	38,588
Port Eads	2	1	10	1	0	1	6,762
Port Master	8	4	76	5	8	13	63,528
Posen	6	3	41	7	6	2	68,493
Positiveness	4	2	16	2	1	2	40,637
Posse	5	2	27	3	4	2	41,685
Poster Prince	1	1	14	2	0	0	8,326
Potrillazo	5	3	47	6	6	4	233,648
Power Break	5	1	26	2	0	4	5,992
Power of Mind	1	1	14	2	2	2	24,905
Power Ruler	3	1	12	1	5	0	16,533
*Practicante	5	3	35	3	5	7	109,413
Practitioner	12	4	69	7	6	4	65,839
Pranke (ARG)	2	1	11	1	1	2	12,937

Broodmare Sire	Perf	Wnrs	Sts	1st	2d	3d	Purses
Precious Man	2	1	4	1	0	0	2,400
Precisionist	4	2	23	4	3	3	32,726
Prefontaine	1	1	12	2	0	2	12,662
Preking	1	1	7	2	1	0	20,993
Premier Ministre	9	3	52	5	9	8	63,194
Premiership	162	83	1165	164	138	150	2,833,038
Present Value	29	18	204	30	23	25	298,095
Presidium (GB)	2	1	11	3	1	1	515,550
Press Card	9	5	52	8	8	6	187,752
Pressure	2	1	17	1	3	4	8,877
Presto Lad	15	7	103	9	14	17	91,874
Prete Khale	1	1	13	1	0	3	19,209
Pretense	19	6	131	16	14	11	215,987
Pretensor	2	1	20	1	5	4	27,380
Primo Dominie (GB)	7	5	49	6	3	6	118,796
Prince Aly	4	1	17	1	1	1	10,937
Prince Alydar	5	4	42	7	4	5	106,101
Prince Astro	12	7	59	11	2	4	89,394
Prince Card	10	3	49	3	3	6	27,149
Prince Forli	12	3	74	6	9	7	82,844
Prince Gala	5	1	14	1	0	3	5,097
Prince Hedstart	3	1	16	1	4	1	15,136
Prince John	4	1	21	1	0	1	27,029
Prince O'The Bronx	3	2	18	2	1	5	19,969
Prince of Ascot	1	1	3	1	0	0	9,840
Prince of Fame	7	4	39	7	2	8	99,770
Prince of Saron	3	2	29	6	3	3	40,689
Prince Patty	1	1	7	1	0	0	4,936
Prince Sabo	5	1	22	1	5	0	383,384
Prince Spellbound	7	5	52	7	3	4	44,118
Prince Street	5	3	22	4	4	2	81,295
Prince Valiant	1	1	12	2	1	2	31,296
Prince Valid	18	9	145	19	21	11	379,889
Princelet	2	1	14	2	1	3	9,847
Princely Native	30	12	146	18	25	17	216,465
Princely Pleasure	19	9	132	14	16	17	453,627
Princely Song	4	2	34	5	0	4	14,841
Princely Verdict	7	2	18	2	1	1	14,357
Princeteen	1	1	6	1	1	1	32,522
Private Account	228	116	1468	190	198	207	4,678,004
Private Express	9	3	56	8	9	8	215,054
Private Key	2	2	22	6	4	2	57,135
Private Talk	2	1	10	1	2	1	15,410
Private Terms	116	54	771	85	86	85	1,462,160
Private Thoughts	27	15	231	31	31	24	436,229
Privato	2	1	6	1	1	1	25,130
Prize Ring	5	2	19	3	1	0	29,407
Prized	40	21	261	31	33	33	597,987
Pro Consul	3	3	23	7	5	2	185,251
Probable	4	1	35	3	5	5	30,723
Procida	67	40	511	68	65	76	1,111,811
Proctor	4	2	29	2	2	3	16,793
Professor Blue	12	3	74	5	5	5	171,230
Project Manager (IRE)	1	1	3	1	0	0	15,000
Proliferate	1	1	12	1	0	2	6,434
Prominent	2	1	20	1	2	0	9,801
Promised City	3	1	29	4	4	5	36,648
Pron Regard	6	2	29	2	3	5	19,668
Proof	18	10	148	16	19	20	453,557
Propelled	3	3	35	4	7	10	31,636
Proper Reality	75	39	514	60	68	63	1,155,287
Properantes	15	7	90	14	6	13	139,514
Proponent	3	3	17	5	1	0	25,182
Prospect Bay	1	1	5	1	0	0	4,410
Prospect North	15	7	96	10	13	13	50,172
Prospective Star	29	16	233	32	24	36	337,806
Prospector Mo	1	1	5	1	0	2	25,072
Prospector's Bid	7	3	50	4	3	4	93,153
Prospector's Gold	15	7	100	11	9	8	203,592
Prospector's Halo	26	10	202	14	34	27	490,205
Prospector's Joy	3	3	30	4	4	7	98,575
Prospector's Music	4	2	22	2	3	2	50,940
Prospector's Pick	4	3	24	8	0	3	162,507
Prospectors Gamble	78	38	560	72	67	65	1,340,760
Prosper Fager	9	4	58	6	2	6	50,168
Prosperous	16	6	107	13	3	19	135,144
Proud Appeal	37	23	266	40	49	38	625,925
Proud Birdie	85	34	679	55	74	84	907,439
Proud Clarion	9	3	75	8	4	5	55,720
Proud Dhabi	5	1	29	1	3	3	20,021
Proud Irish	7	4	44	7	3	9	85,422
Proud Ling	3	3	19	5	2	3	33,207
Proud Northern	5	2	35	2	3	4	16,274
Proud Pocket	5	3	41	6	2	8	36,887
Proud Truth	78	45	629	78	78	77	1,269,331
Proudest Doon	1	1	16	5	4	2	44,209
Proudest Duke	8	3	48	9	6	7	145,009
Proudest Roman	37	12	251	21	38	37	466,543
Prove It	3	2	20	3	3	1	31,413
Prove Out	3	1	23	1	2	3	21,544
Proven Reserve	1	1	10	1	1	3	2,461
Providential (IRE)	13	1	49	1	8	9	31,854
Pukka Gent	8	3	43	3	0	3	22,968
Pumpkin Moonshine	11	6	79	8	12	13	83,695
Pumpkin Time	1	1	10	1	0	2	5,231
Puntivo	9	6	77	12	12	9	262,111
Pure Jest	1	1	6	2	1	1	16,670
Purely Pleasure	6	4	43	6	3	2	69,754
Purple Comet	7	3	64	7	5	5	58,381
Purple Mountain	1	1	7	5	0	2	1,139,000
Pursuit	10	5	86	12	13	8	120,614
Pyrite	7	3	48	4	7	6	92,947
Quack	71	31	426	53	51	56	1,000,908
Quack Attack	1	1	8	1	1	2	7,258
Quadrangle	4	2	38	2	5	6	30,672
Quadratic	54	21	339	36	43	46	623,838
Quebec Dancer	1	1	6	1	2	1	12,430
Queen City Lad	11	3	72	5	5	7	40,535
Queen's Splendour	6	2	55	3	12	11	149,549
Quest for Fame (GB)	6	2	23	3	3	4	67,378
Qui Native	17	8	97	12	13	12	123,010
Quick and Nervous	2	1	10	1	1	2	18,102
Quick Dance	2	1	23	2	1	2	16,902
Quick Dip	4	2	31	3	1	2	29,444
Quick Snap (GB)	1	1	8	1	2	1	5,867
Quick Style	3	1	17	1	0	3	6,715
Quicksilver	1	1	21	1	1	3	11,174
Quid Pro Quo	3	1	16	2	1	2	39,289
Quiero Dinero	2	1	16	1	1	2	9,588
Quiet American	60	28	347	54	38	45	1,962,337
Quiet Fling	8	3	48	5	4	4	44,235
Quip	3	1	20	2	5	2	23,644
Quite Special	2	1	15	1	0	0	5,090
R. B. Chesne	1	1	12	1	2	1	35,658
Raba Deal	1	1	10	2	1	3	8,439
Racconto	2	1	6	1	1	0	43,425
Racing Star	16	8	108	11	19	10	198,287
Raconteur	3	1	17	1	1	3	16,330
Radar Ahead	4	2	11	2	0	2	8,130
Raft	7	4	44	6	4	10	96,595
Ragtime Band	8	5	70	9	14	9	122,014
Rahy	164	74	890	122	130	81	3,652,309
Rail	2	1	12	1	4	2	18,479
Rainbow Corner (GB)	1	1	3	1	0	0	5,850
Rainbow Quest	30	11	134	21	13	19	1,608,527
Rainbows for Life	3	1	13	1	3	3	89,764
Rainy Lake	6	4	62	10	7	7	123,379
Raise a Bid	61	22	373	31	45	32	444,821
Raise a Champion	8	4	47	10	5	4	187,620
Raise a Cup	55	29	331	44	32	46	839,462
Raise a Digit	2	1	20	1	1	0	13,077
Raise a Man	58	22	362	38	37	47	389,081
Raise a Native	97	43	630	76	92	64	1,521,238
Raise a Pickle	2	1	9	1	0	0	2,827
Raise a Racer	12	2	53	2	2	3	37,254
Raise a Rascal	1	1	6	2	1	0	6,460
Raise a Regal	10	4	100	9	12	10	133,263
Raise an Orphan	4	2	24	5	5	5	57,078
Raise Your Glass	4	1	31	1	6	0	18,006
Raise Your Hope	1	1	11	2	1	0	13,143
Raised On Stage	5	2	27	4	5	0	74,123
Raised Socially	61	31	481	51	65	59	570,970

Broodmare Sire	Perf	Wnrs	Sts	1st	2d	3d	Purses
Raised Well	3	1	12	1	0	1	6,538
Raisor Smart	4	2	23	2	1	4	30,546
Raj Kapoor	2	1	32	1	3	0	11,479
Raja Baba	86	36	554	60	48	73	903,472
Raja Native	4	1	30	1	2	4	30,125
Raja's Best Boy	13	5	72	8	7	6	64,421
Raja's Revenge	15	8	123	14	20	20	541,328
Rajab	57	29	373	58	33	48	928,936
Ramannolie (FR)	5	1	36	2	0	3	8,457
Rambling Rector	7	2	36	5	1	5	112,479
Rambo Dancer	2	2	20	8	2	3	333,097
Rambunctious	4	1	29	2	2	1	23,109
Ramirez	12	7	63	12	7	8	168,943
Rampage	11	6	72	15	7	8	174,982
Ramparts	1	1	9	1	4	1	72,924
Ramplett	4	2	33	4	3	4	30,635
*Ramsinga	8	1	46	2	3	6	48,572
Rare Brick	52	26	406	45	48	51	624,915
Rare Performer	97	55	710	96	93	118	1,625,133
Rarerullah	9	3	54	4	7	7	92,617
Rarity	1	1	11	2	2	4	76,810
Rash Move	4	1	31	1	5	9	27,649
Ratification	3	1	12	2	0	0	52,558
Ravisher	1	1	4	1	0	1	3,130
Ray's Pegasus	2	1	17	2	2	2	16,081
Ray's Word	5	4	40	4	4	6	46,674
Raykour (IRE)	4	2	37	3	2	8	22,967
Reach for More	0	1	33	1	1	3	13,871
Reading Room	7	3	68	3	14	10	58,192
Real Courage	26	18	227	29	29	27	437,651
Real Emperor	5	2	30	7	4	2	151,268
Real Landing	4	1	29	3	5	3	86,772
Real Top Deal	4	1	19	2	4	1	18,467
Real Value	9	6	58	8	4	5	63,627
Reality and Reason	8	2	65	3	10	6	42,078
Really Awesome	6	3	40	4	5	5	76,894
Really Cooking	5	1	40	1	4	4	56,667
Really Golden	1	1	5	1	2	0	2,845
Really Secret	4	1	36	2	4	2	229,222
Reasonable Bid	6	3	36	3	2	3	33,106
Reasoric	3	3	31	4	5	3	28,430
Reb's Policy	7	3	56	3	5	6	21,809
Recaptured	2	2	21	4	3	3	25,027
Recitalist	4	1	22	1	2	4	20,081
Reckless Blade	5	4	43	5	3	6	128,823
Record Catch	2	1	15	1	2	1	12,146
Rectory	9	4	54	4	7	8	83,239
Rectus	1	1	10	1	2	1	28,225
*Recupere	3	2	25	3	3	1	34,606
Recusant	14	3	84	4	7	9	45,686
Red Alert	2	1	18	3	3	6	108,620
Red Anchor	4	2	29	3	3	5	36,969
Red Anchor (NZ)	2	1	6	2	0	0	9,815
Red Attack	40	22	259	36	28	36	513,029
Red Clay Country	5	3	42	6	5	2	133,550
Red Crescent	6	2	28	2	2	3	21,493
Red Monk	4	1	24	1	3	1	22,908
Red Ransom	130	77	833	127	104	101	2,919,416
Red Ryder	55	27	360	42	32	59	732,653
Red Tempo (NZ)	4	3	29	6	6	3	70,161
Red Wing Bold	25	12	144	15	21	17	204,109
Red's Copy	1	1	15	4	2	2	19,266
Reef Searcher	3	1	12	2	0	1	28,275
Reel On Reel	4	3	43	6	2	5	58,779
Reference Point	6	4	38	6	3	2	51,155
Reflected Glory	13	4	91	8	6	19	78,415
Refuse to Lose	1	1	3	1	0	0	4,845
Regal Affair	6	4	35	5	3	2	54,450
Regal and Royal	55	30	375	53	56	50	1,099,800
Regal Bearing (GB)	7	1	47	1	7	6	27,742
Regal Classic	152	82	1078	151	148	137	4,614,148
Regal Companion	5	4	26	4	4	3	27,863
Regal Embrace	14	8	90	9	5	15	274,875
Regal Flag	3	2	25	3	3	4	39,372
Regal Flier	2	2	24	5	3	1	27,088
Regal Humor	6	1	46	3	4	5	45,286
Regal Intention	51	24	327	44	51	39	1,243,821
Regal Remark	67	39	474	73	68	71	965,831
Regal Search	48	22	382	42	43	56	732,167
Regal Song	2	2	11	2	2	1	21,015
Regalberto	8	3	60	5	7	13	49,871
Regent's Dancer	3	2	21	5	3	1	60,359
Rehaan	3	1	15	1	1	1	6,249
Rehearing	1	1	5	1	0	0	8,408
Reign Road	6	2	30	2	1	3	24,501
Reinvested	6	4	53	8	7	8	162,562
Relaunch	323	186	2200	297	283	262	9,442,575
Relaunch a Tune	10	6	80	9	13	8	130,113
Religiously	2	1	6	1	0	0	6,003
Remedial	4	2	35	8	9	5	111,415
Reno City	6	4	37	4	4	3	81,108
Repel	1	1	4	1	0	0	9,180
Replant	9	5	64	12	11	7	571,125
Reprized	1	1	20	4	2	4	24,580
Requested Honor	1	1	4	1	0	0	2,942
Restivo	11	4	65	11	9	9	115,503
Restless Con	4	3	22	6	4	1	129,510
Restless Jet	3	2	22	6	2	4	37,737
Restless Native	16	6	87	8	9	12	111,132
Restless Run	1	1	22	1	1	4	4,187
Restless Sam	1	1	8	1	2	1	8,922
Restless Sinner	2	1	17	2	2	1	13,131
Restless Wind	2	1	12	2	0	2	14,997
Retsina Run	2	1	13	1	0	0	4,450
Returnee	7	3	50	7	8	6	86,472
Reve Dore	2	1	15	1	0	2	7,013
Reve Du	5	3	28	5	1	1	45,595
Reviewer	5	3	49	6	13	7	118,482
Rewarded	1	1	7	1	1	2	3,537
Rex (CHI)	4	1	24	3	3	1	52,508
Rex Imperator	7	2	42	2	2	4	23,633
Rex Lake	3	1	11	1	2	2	8,713
Rexson	24	11	195	21	24	25	311,633
Rexson's Hope	39	17	262	32	29	32	649,235
Rheffic	1	1	11	1	4	0	12,820
Rhinflo	6	3	35	5	4	5	94,889
Rhodes	5	1	27	1	3	7	30,251
Rhymeroni	2	1	14	1	2	3	5,042
Riad	3	3	28	7	2	1	37,862
Riboronde	1	1	16	1	0	0	4,167
Ribots Verset	2	2	31	2	6	5	40,154
Rich Cream	50	19	299	40	41	31	601,111
Richman	2	1	6	1	0	1	3,360
Ridge Fighter	4	2	40	2	6	3	35,997
Rig Up	1	1	3	1	0	0	1,483
Rigel II	1	1	4	1	2	0	21,500
Right Con	4	1	24	1	2	4	8,544
Right Honorable	1	1	8	1	2	1	10,718
Right n Ready	4	2	50	3	5	8	39,347
Right Off (ARG)	1	1	14	1	0	0	3,508
Right On Blue	5	2	34	7	6	5	57,788
Ringaro	9	5	43	8	8	2	113,710
Ringside	6	2	32	2	2	3	36,659
Rinka Das	1	1	4	1	0	0	15,610
Rinoso	15	7	82	8	20	11	81,064
Rio Carmelo (FR)	9	3	48	5	5	9	72,254
Rise Jim	6	3	45	7	3	6	91,750
Risen Star	78	39	502	69	62	68	1,440,003
Rising Market	19	8	116	11	8	7	75,312
Rising Raja	1	1	10	3	3	3	12,358
Riva Ridge	27	11	167	21	21	14	230,759
River of Kings (IRE)	4	2	27	2	8	1	15,310
River Prince	1	1	10	1	0	0	5,346
River Special	11	7	71	10	14	7	274,040
Rivergo	2	1	9	3	3	0	40,430
Riverman	118	46	688	80	76	86	1,570,322
Riverton (FR)	1	1	16	1	2	5	9,528
Rivertot (FR)	4	1	19	1	1	0	3,813
Rizzi	3	1	12	1	2	2	13,694
Road Checker	2	1	8	1	1	2	4,706
Roan Drone	1	1	7	1	2	1	2,689
Roanoke	51	21	321	25	44	31	729,156

Broodmare Sire	Perf	Wnrs	Sts	1st	2d	3d	Purses
Roanoke Island	12	3	58	6	3	5	161,378
Robellino	30	17	193	24	17	17	377,858
Roberto	79	40	506	67	68	61	1,426,933
Robin des Pins	21	12	131	19	16	15	368,762
Robin's Song	4	2	20	3	3	3	35,391
Robyn Dancer	27	13	165	20	17	17	427,899
Rock City (IRE)	1	1	15	2	1	2	16,030
Rock Dance	1	1	10	1	0	0	4,610
Rock Lives	2	1	15	2	3	3	15,238
Rock Point	6	2	39	4	1	5	44,734
Rock Royalty	6	4	38	5	5	6	92,080
Rock Talk	13	7	101	11	10	14	194,979
Rock'n Rollick	1	1	20	1	0	0	8,170
Rockport Crossing	2	1	13	1	0	1	11,223
Rockwall	5	1	27	1	0	2	10,079
Rocky Marriage	3	2	38	4	3	5	37,892
Rocky Mountain	5	2	19	2	1	0	24,190
Roderic	7	4	52	9	6	5	97,702
Rogrox	2	1	17	2	5	5	56,462
Roi Danzig	4	3	17	5	1	3	180,361
Rokeby (GB)	4	2	19	5	3	1	99,626
Rolfson	10	5	80	14	12	8	139,945
Rollick 'n Roll	2	2	13	3	0	2	35,930
Rollicking	65	25	404	44	43	60	943,233
Rollicking's Image	1	1	4	1	1	1	12,453
Rollin On Over	15	4	56	5	4	8	267,490
Rolls Aly	13	8	77	10	8	6	56,977
Roman Blood	2	1	24	1	2	3	19,378
Roman Diplomat	16	7	108	9	8	15	146,075
Roman Empire	1	1	10	2	1	1	14,578
Roman Majesty	6	4	35	4	3	5	80,423
Roman Missile	2	1	14	4	2	2	240,600
Roman Reasoning	12	4	79	5	8	7	133,492
Romantic Lead	5	1	15	1	3	2	50,990
Romeo	26	12	151	23	16	18	385,534
Roo Art	12	6	100	9	14	7	134,655
Root Boy	1	1	4	1	0	0	18,180
Rose Argent	2	1	12	2	3	2	15,105
Rose Laurel	1	1	5	1	0	1	12,590
Rouge Sang	1	1	10	2	1	1	9,482
Rougemont	9	5	40	7	2	4	78,307
Rough Pearl	2	1	9	1	1	1	5,526
Roulette Wheel	8	3	60	5	4	5	50,950
Round Reb	2	1	2	1	0	0	21,600
Round Ridge	2	1	12	1	0	1	7,181
Round Table Jr.	3	1	14	1	0	3	5,164
Roundtop	2	2	10	3	1	3	19,930
Rousillon	6	2	34	7	3	2	75,646
Rowdy Regal	1	1	7	1	2	1	12,372
Roxbury Park	10	3	67	7	8	6	71,411
Roy	23	11	118	23	17	8	605,010
Royal Academy	20	9	78	12	8	8	421,777
Royal and Regal	24	8	137	11	15	15	161,851
Royal Chocolate	10	8	72	18	11	11	276,971
Royal Design	8	3	54	4	4	5	49,863
Royal Egyptian	1	1	8	2	1	1	9,317
Royal Hierarchy	2	1	12	1	1	1	13,464
Royal Mandarin	1	1	9	2	0	1	13,026
Royal Manner	2	1	4	1	1	0	7,713
Royal Pavilion	3	1	22	3	2	0	10,896
Royal Pennant	7	2	38	4	10	4	44,605
Royal Prayer (GB)	3	1	18	4	5	3	21,692
Royal Reasoning	2	1	13	1	0	0	11,260
Royal Roberto	43	20	320	34	34	47	475,301
Royal Ski	8	4	52	8	8	10	117,188
Royal Surrender	2	2	26	5	5	1	39,315
Royal Union	2	2	26	4	5	2	33,794
Rubiano	66	26	375	42	61	58	1,300,743
Rudimentary	2	1	14	2	3	1	58,880
Ruff Mark	4	2	28	4	3	2	72,059
Ruffinal	9	3	68	5	8	13	80,948
Ruffled Feathers	2	1	13	3	5	1	20,794
Rugged Man	1	1	12	1	1	0	6,894
Ruhlmann	35	14	216	22	29	30	313,068
Ruler's Conquest	1	1	4	1	0	1	17,700
Ruler's Downfall	1	1	11	1	1	2	2,461

Broodmare Sire	Perf	Wnrs	Sts	1st	2d	3d	Purses
Ruling Eagle	2	1	11	1	0	1	5,213
Rumbo	10	4	58	6	13	6	142,705
Run Dusty Run	10	6	56	9	6	5	138,213
Run For Nurse	1	1	7	1	1	0	14,179
Run Johnny Run	4	1	15	1	0	0	4,660
Run of Luck	27	8	173	13	21	19	186,194
Run the Gantlet	21	8	144	18	16	17	294,710
Run to Daylight	1	1	3	1	0	0	4,725
Runaway Groom	183	76	1219	132	133	173	2,826,309
Runderbar	2	1	13	1	0	1	5,025
Runnett (GB)	3	1	13	1	2	0	3,688
Running Gold	4	3	23	6	3	3	90,020
Rupert's Wing	5	4	57	10	11	9	159,130
Ruritania	4	4	42	10	5	12	300,143
Russ Miron	1	1	10	1	3	1	6,097
Russian Mark	2	1	15	1	2	3	12,706
Rustic Ruler	13	6	89	11	14	11	165,398
Ruthie's Native	24	11	146	17	14	15	191,213
S. S. Hot Sauce	4	2	26	5	5	1	110,863
S. W. Wildcard	2	2	21	4	6	4	84,321
Sabona	13	6	71	11	10	16	132,926
Sadler's Wells	47	23	257	35	29	37	1,719,400
Sagace (FR)	5	1	38	2	4	6	89,186
Sail Ahoy	5	2	22	3	2	3	36,375
Sailing Along	1	1	14	2	2	5	17,037
Saint Ballado	54	30	340	45	49	40	925,187
Saint Cyrien	2	1	20	3	3	1	48,600
Saint Sever (FR)	7	3	43	6	6	6	183,341
Saint Tropez	4	2	47	3	6	7	38,673
Salem	8	6	52	12	1	6	210,026
Salem Drive	18	8	120	21	18	18	294,951
Salem End Road	2	1	10	1	2	2	32,095
Sallust	3	1	17	2	2	1	35,296
Salse	4	3	33	7	4	5	77,575
Salt Dome	1	1	5	1	0	0	4,530
Salt Lake	89	41	551	71	68	61	2,126,399
Salt Marsh	7	3	34	4	5	5	152,598
Saltville	2	1	7	1	2	0	3,802
Saltwell	2	1	23	2	2	2	13,751
Salutely	41	23	331	41	31	37	690,214
Salydar	1	1	3	1	0	0	10,930
Sam M.	1	1	12	4	1	0	55,850
Sam Ransom (VEN)	4	2	25	3	4	4	47,752
Sam the Lion	1	1	6	1	1	0	10,925
Sam's Sunny Hour	1	1	4	1	0	0	28,230
Samarid	4	2	32	8	3	6	181,412
Samba Boy	1	1	5	1	1	0	7,425
Same Direction	10	6	54	7	6	5	129,755
San Feliou (FR)	7	1	26	2	2	1	14,518
San Simon	2	1	8	1	0	1	3,770
Sanhedrin	3	2	15	2	4	0	21,996
Santiago Peak	8	3	42	4	6	4	68,487
Saratoga Six	181	93	1157	169	136	152	4,192,898
Sarawak	6	2	24	2	4	3	28,748
Saros (GB)	45	18	290	43	39	35	712,247
Sassafras (FR)	27	13	186	18	24	15	245,187
Satan	1	1	11	2	0	0	3,257
Satan's Flame	4	1	51	2	5	11	60,212
Satan's Hills	2	1	15	2	2	0	7,828
Satan's Parade	1	1	6	1	0	0	6,842
Satan's Secretary	4	2	26	3	1	2	47,318
Satan's Thunder	3	3	31	5	4	5	43,894
Sauce Boat	114	53	784	106	81	120	1,229,138
Saumarez (GB)	2	1	11	1	1	2	5,750
Saunders	3	1	13	1	1	1	7,648
Sauvage (FR)	3	2	33	7	4	4	59,073
Savings	13	4	125	11	18	10	163,197
Savona Tower	2	1	24	3	2	6	34,608
Sawbones	31	14	217	25	23	16	306,538
Say Guv	2	2	16	2	2	0	30,801
Scarlet 'n Gray	7	5	42	6	7	4	109,321
Scarlet Ibis	26	9	132	18	11	11	312,620
Schaufuss	4	1	12	1	0	1	9,000
School Hero	4	2	31	4	2	5	46,215
Score Twenty Four	3	1	24	2	4	1	27,948
Scotchman	2	2	21	3	1	6	58,634

Broodmare Sire	Perf	Wnrs	Sts	1st	2d	3d	Purses
Scottish Reel	1	1	17	2	1	3	13,633
Scout Leader	5	1	24	2	2	1	16,955
Screaming Fife	2	2	21	4	2	2	53,211
Screen King	51	22	340	42	40	33	648,245
Scroll	3	1	8	1	1	0	3,399
Sea Aglo	13	6	120	9	9	11	48,111
Sea Cadet	2	2	13	2	4	0	54,160
Sea Chimes (IRE)	2	1	13	2	1	1	60,932
Sea Hero	7	3	34	4	6	2	74,671
Sea Songster	4	1	45	3	6	5	34,282
Seafood	9	8	67	12	13	6	94,612
Seaport Mac	1	1	11	1	4	1	30,469
Search for Gold	28	17	175	28	18	19	198,360
Seaside Dancer	1	1	13	3	0	2	16,087
Seat of Power	5	3	59	9	10	8	163,974
Seattle Battle	8	3	44	9	5	7	139,395
Seattle Bound	3	1	14	1	3	1	15,889
Seattle Dancer	96	44	581	78	89	75	2,014,307
Seattle Knight	12	8	94	15	9	10	150,144
Seattle Sleet	10	6	49	10	4	7	159,826
Seattle Slew	220	98	1257	179	179	153	5,579,573
Seattle Song	85	41	523	77	56	85	1,906,699
Seattle Sun	4	1	11	1	0	0	7,258
Sebrof	1	1	4	1	0	1	7,998
Seclusive	12	3	76	7	5	8	100,075
Secret Claim	20	12	158	29	34	15	695,903
Secret Hello	33	21	229	33	41	49	853,815
Secret Prince	15	6	91	11	13	10	430,410
Secret Slew	19	12	126	17	19	12	387,753
Secretariat	199	90	1433	148	174	168	3,377,668
Secretary of War	7	2	37	3	0	5	23,170
Secreto	70	36	493	58	62	81	1,407,283
Security Council	2	1	9	1	1	1	4,286
Seeking the Gold	126	69	704	102	109	89	4,263,103
Sefapiano	5	4	34	6	5	6	141,738
Sejm	14	7	72	15	17	9	267,649
Selma's Boy	2	1	19	1	1	1	12,310
Selous Scout	2	1	12	3	0	1	17,646
Semaj	2	1	12	1	2	3	66,388
Semenenko	9	5	36	7	3	6	209,075
Semi Royal	1	1	8	1	0	0	4,714
Semipalatinsk	1	1	6	1	1	2	18,600
Senate Whip	2	1	19	2	4	2	24,660
Senator Amo	2	2	12	2	0	0	12,531
Seneca Jones	1	1	4	1	1	1	24,440
Senor Lucky	2	1	18	2	4	2	17,760
Senor Pete	5	2	34	5	3	7	127,527
Senor Speedy	10	4	81	6	11	13	72,246
Sensitive Music	4	2	16	3	0	3	32,934
Sensitive Prince	23	12	178	20	15	24	315,480
Sentimental Slew	10	6	86	8	14	11	203,336
Separate Realities	1	1	11	2	0	2	24,158
Septieme Ciel	64	30	425	55	58	46	1,419,610
Sepulveda	2	1	3	1	0	0	3,850
Serves Em Right	1	1	8	1	0	2	5,690
Set Free	11	4	64	12	4	13	125,336
Sette Bello	1	1	8	2	1	0	16,960
Settlement Day	16	7	92	14	6	6	113,011
Sevastopol	13	4	98	4	16	17	205,291
Seven Zero	1	1	12	1	1	4	16,106
Sewickley	19	11	169	17	24	19	210,711
Sexist	6	3	24	4	3	3	43,545
Sezyou	59	25	424	37	47	55	627,088
Shack	2	1	11	1	5	0	5,213
Shadeed	60	35	427	58	52	49	1,286,589
Shady Character	3	1	19	3	2	0	34,272
Shahrastani	26	12	168	18	21	19	425,999
Shahrud	1	1	16	4	0	3	5,683
Shakapour	2	1	11	3	1	1	60,880
Shalom 'N Salaam	1	1	3	1	2	0	6,725
Sham	74	28	413	42	51	47	811,830
Shamgo	6	2	49	5	5	5	117,206
Shamtastic	3	1	22	1	2	4	12,450
Shananie	41	25	297	45	42	36	703,399
Shanekite	51	23	337	32	36	34	466,080
Shantarlat	2	1	9	1	3	1	22,259

Broodmare Sire	Perf	Wnrs	Sts	1st	2d	3d	Purses
Shareef Dancer	11	7	61	10	13	8	303,825
Sharp Hoofer	4	1	12	1	1	0	9,896
Sharp Kid	4	2	21	8	1	3	25,698
Sharp Prospect	1	1	12	1	0	0	4,595
Sharp Reason	1	1	9	1	3	1	10,180
Sharp Terdankim	4	1	24	4	3	3	29,148
Sharp Victor	8	3	40	6	3	4	75,379
Sharpen Up (GB)	48	20	277	27	31	29	522,047
Sharper One	32	19	237	27	28	31	323,205
Sharrood	3	2	10	2	1	0	39,660
Shawklit Won	10	6	69	8	9	9	176,541
Shecky Greene	22	10	135	16	18	10	207,929
Sheikh Albadou (GB)	21	12	133	17	20	18	327,857
Shelly's Charmer	4	4	37	7	4	2	111,966
Shelter Half	48	25	321	39	36	34	850,298
Shenadoah River	2	1	21	2	2	2	9,035
Shergar's Best (IRE)	7	4	37	7	2	3	96,361
Shernazar (IRE)	2	1	9	1	0	1	34,200
Shifty Sheik	6	2	36	2	3	4	46,047
Shimatoree	25	11	143	18	21	15	789,875
Shining So Bright	2	1	8	2	2	2	55,270
Ship Leave	11	6	53	8	4	8	61,984
Shipmate Sam	7	4	38	5	4	5	46,031
Shipping Magnate	7	4	52	14	4	6	173,456
Shirley Heights (GB)	19	8	106	14	8	16	532,801
Shirley's Champion	3	3	27	5	4	4	36,377
Shock Wave	1	1	10	2	0	0	11,226
Short and Sharp (FR)	1	1	5	1	0	0	5,041
Shot Block	1	1	9	1	0	3	8,037
Shot Gun Scott	8	4	67	7	12	4	151,029
Shotiche	8	1	32	1	5	3	92,603
Should Fly	1	1	5	3	0	1	24,076
Show Dancer	29	16	216	24	30	29	391,477
Show'em Slew	4	2	22	2	7	1	74,431
Shuttleman	4	1	22	1	5	2	27,875
Shy Groom	1	1	1	1	0	0	26,400
Shy Guy	4	3	21	4	1	4	64,059
Shy Native	5	2	40	3	6	2	72,166
Siberian Express	20	9	150	13	19	22	276,699
Siberian Pine	3	2	23	5	1	4	45,179
Sicyos	5	4	29	5	2	3	57,548
Side Door	2	1	19	2	0	5	12,607
Sifounas	3	1	19	2	3	1	23,787
Signed Contract	4	3	36	4	4	4	36,762
Sijjaal	1	1	1	1	0	0	35,280
Silent Cal	11	4	61	9	4	4	76,475
Silent Dignity	11	5	87	7	8	4	88,191
Silent Fox	14	2	67	6	15	8	116,041
Silent King	14	6	78	9	4	9	151,521
Silent Landing	5	2	41	3	6	5	34,478
Silent Link	1	1	10	1	3	2	28,062
Silent Review	11	6	63	8	5	9	121,519
Silent Screen	121	66	819	103	74	91	1,466,555
Silent Slander	2	1	23	1	3	5	18,340
Silent Tempest	1	1	6	3	0	0	35,666
Silk Or Satin	5	1	25	1	2	0	13,720
Silky Baby	6	1	46	1	6	5	68,501
Sillery	4	1	13	2	3	0	179,348
Silver Badge	8	4	61	6	9	7	170,928
Silver Buck	137	68	1022	124	113	116	2,268,801
Silver Deputy	110	62	694	120	113	64	3,439,722
Silver Ending	2	1	12	1	5	3	55,420
Silver Ghost	102	50	647	88	71	87	1,605,595
Silver Hawk	136	61	799	94	102	97	3,369,215
Silver Nitrate	2	2	31	4	1	3	31,598
Silver Ring (FR)	5	2	34	2	3	8	18,389
Silver Series	12	2	58	6	4	3	133,691
Silver Spade	1	1	12	1	1	1	7,776
Silver Supreme	21	10	155	18	13	18	232,588
Silver Survivor	8	2	35	2	3	2	37,246
Silveyville	20	9	94	14	9	10	140,167
Simply Great	1	1	10	1	0	0	5,687
Simply Majestic	46	21	333	35	41	47	487,380
Sing Sing	8	4	65	9	11	7	119,883
Singh	6	3	40	6	5	8	210,658
Singh America	2	1	15	2	1	3	3,702

Broodmare Sire	Perf	Wnrs	Sts	1st	2d	3d	Purses
Single Lane	2	1	15	1	4	2	55,909
Singular	34	16	257	30	42	32	574,581
Sir Ack	5	4	61	4	13	5	80,637
Sir Concorde	3	2	18	2	1	1	7,832
Sir Eric	9	4	79	4	4	10	63,780
Sir Gaylord	3	1	18	2	5	3	35,294
Sir Giles	2	1	11	1	5	1	11,321
Sir Godfrey (FR)	2	2	24	2	4	1	28,942
Sir Habitat (GB)	3	1	25	1	1	3	5,126
Sir Halo	1	1	1	1	0	0	2,700
Sir Harry Lewis	25	17	180	32	26	24	551,283
Sir Ivor	75	36	565	67	58	71	1,027,095
Sir Ivor Again	21	10	157	23	15	25	259,058
Sir Jinsky	12	9	107	17	12	10	188,855
Sir Leon	7	4	47	6	7	9	124,473
Sir Naskra	8	3	42	4	6	6	61,330
Sir Optimist	1	1	16	1	0	1	15,983
Sir Paulus	6	3	31	4	3	3	16,538
Sir Raleigh	14	6	92	13	13	12	185,809
Sir Richard Lewis	11	4	38	6	3	2	117,577
Sir Session	10	7	64	11	9	10	94,046
*Sir Tristram	4	2	19	2	5	0	34,271
Sir Wiggle	2	1	9	1	0	0	9,714
Sir Wimborne	23	9	156	18	14	24	247,560
Sir Winzalot	1	1	9	2	0	2	8,781
Sir Woodley	3	1	22	2	2	1	20,477
Sirlad (IRE)	1	1	6	1	2	0	16,582
Sirtaki	2	1	12	2	4	0	12,746
Sitzmark	5	2	18	2	1	2	22,040
Six Fast Nickles	1	1	4	1	0	0	2,080
Six Speed	5	4	41	7	8	4	180,154
Siyah Kalem	55	21	342	35	43	40	540,396
Ski Champ	2	2	10	5	1	0	119,960
Ski Chief	1	1	15	4	3	4	90,353
Ski Racer	4	1	29	2	6	0	24,118
Ski Resort	8	5	61	9	8	4	86,939
Skin Head	6	2	61	5	15	7	47,793
Skip Trial	85	53	640	94	81	73	1,595,209
Sky Classic	61	31	410	45	62	41	1,176,562
Sky Command	8	2	31	2	0	3	23,980
Sky Filou (NZ)	2	1	18	4	4	2	106,601
Sky White	1	1	5	4	1	0	162,622
Skywalker	98	49	574	85	81	77	1,791,007
*Slady Castle	11	5	76	11	7	10	365,580
Slam Bunk	1	1	11	1	2	2	11,139
Slew Baby	5	3	37	5	5	2	115,932
Slew Bunny	3	1	20	1	1	3	11,666
Slew City Slew	71	40	588	75	94	75	1,381,594
Slew Dancer	2	2	27	4	4	5	89,445
Slew Express	1	1	3	1	0	0	22,427
Slew Machine	18	11	124	17	17	14	199,963
Slew Maker	2	1	12	1	0	2	20,235
Slew o' Gold	148	70	970	124	132	140	3,249,892
Slew o' the North	8	5	57	7	8	6	94,950
Slew of Angels	1	1	3	1	0	1	13,708
Slew the Bride	23	6	91	8	9	6	55,786
Slew the Coup	24	10	124	11	20	11	184,889
Slew the Knight	4	2	19	7	1	3	135,196
Slew the Slewor	5	2	50	4	4	5	72,091
Slew the Surgeon	2	2	10	2	2	1	68,740
Slew's Folly	4	1	21	1	2	0	13,767
Slew's Royalty	31	15	189	30	25	30	308,931
Slewabration	4	2	30	3	2	1	13,980
Slewacide	91	34	541	50	49	57	1,710,093
Slewbop	1	1	11	1	0	3	17,770
Slewdledo	40	21	289	40	29	54	503,794
Slewdonza	8	3	36	5	2	4	92,905
Slewpy	104	54	641	95	85	81	1,836,628
Slewvescent	1	1	6	1	0	1	6,548
Slick	7	3	50	4	4	4	47,846
Slip Anchor (GB)	6	3	42	5	6	5	60,406
Sluggard	3	3	16	4	0	3	28,139
Smart Alec	2	1	5	1	0	0	26,219
Smart Review	2	2	24	5	4	3	88,210
Smart Strike	3	3	9	4	0	3	153,100
Smart Style	9	3	42	4	6	2	126,388

Broodmare Sire	Perf	Wnrs	Sts	1st	2d	3d	Purses
Smarten	175	87	1249	155	155	154	4,316,654
Smasher	3	2	12	2	0	1	4,016
Smelly	2	2	15	5	3	0	41,400
Smile	76	41	561	83	65	54	8,828,709
Smoggy (GB)	7	5	76	10	9	8	242,878
Smoke Pole	2	2	7	2	0	0	22,345
Smoked Salmon	3	2	21	3	4	3	60,622
Smoken Tobin	1	1	10	1	3	2	6,775
Smokester	7	3	39	3	5	7	111,472
Smokey Oso	2	1	8	1	0	1	9,960
Smokin' Satan	1	1	6	1	1	2	4,972
Smoking Gun	8	1	60	2	9	7	43,158
Smoking Straw	1	1	5	1	1	0	13,677
Smooth Commander	1	1	8	1	2	1	6,650
Smooth Dancer	6	1	35	1	1	4	10,768
Smug	1	1	6	1	1	0	2,168
Smuggler (GB)	1	1	3	1	0	2	19,000
Snake Oil Man	7	3	48	3	4	5	11,089
Snar	3	1	14	3	1	1	21,999
Snohomish County	4	2	50	2	11	7	30,347
Snow Ball	1	1	7	1	0	2	4,356
Snow Chief	43	16	242	26	33	28	458,211
*Snow Knight	7	4	46	6	7	3	47,413
Snow Paramount (ARG)	1	1	4	1	2	0	11,970
Snow Satyr (ARG)	2	1	15	1	0	2	9,401
*Snow Twist	3	2	22	2	1	1	12,648
So Oh Fast	3	1	25	1	1	2	7,912
Social Diamond	9	5	59	8	6	6	139,342
Society Max	19	13	132	29	21	20	342,808
Society Scion	3	1	13	2	2	3	7,192
Solar City	38	22	316	38	34	36	560,785
Solar Launch	1	1	13	2	1	1	56,760
Soldier Boy	6	5	34	7	5	1	70,495
Solford	9	5	51	7	6	5	148,523
Solid Print	2	1	10	4	1	3	14,115
Solly	1	1	10	1	4	2	4,670
Solo Bold (ARG)	1	1	2	2	0	0	13,200
Solo Guy	3	3	22	4	1	3	14,433
Some One Frosty	2	1	15	3	1	2	42,788
Somebody's Great	1	1	12	1	0	3	12,495
Somerset	2	1	10	1	3	0	8,892
Something Lucky	22	12	135	17	21	16	479,610
Somethingfabulous	68	26	457	57	55	73	650,899
Somethingpoetic	1	1	4	2	0	0	40,488
Somethingwonderful	2	1	19	1	3	1	14,266
Son Ange	8	3	63	5	7	13	102,912
Son Excellence	8	4	70	5	6	9	108,175
Son James	3	2	23	2	2	0	15,638
Son of Bagdad	2	1	17	2	3	1	36,242
Son of Briartic	79	41	493	61	80	71	1,161,061
Son of Shaka	1	1	10	1	0	0	1,496
Song (GB)	3	2	26	2	3	2	14,301
Song of Delta	7	1	26	1	3	0	17,480
Songhay	1	1	3	1	2	0	3,630
Sonny Fleet	2	1	26	1	3	3	8,684
Sonny's Solo Halo	6	4	36	4	3	3	36,894
Sooner Slew	2	1	9	3	0	0	45,417
Soranzo	3	1	15	1	2	3	28,279
Sot More	3	1	14	1	0	5	22,643
South Pass	2	1	28	1	2	8	26,213
Southern Halo	32	19	156	34	25	13	842,659
Southern Rhythm	1	1	9	1	5	0	58,611
Southern Slugger	2	1	14	2	1	0	9,612
Southern Sultan	14	6	96	12	19	13	348,611
Sovereign	1	1	13	1	2	3	10,010
Sovereign Dancer	213	116	1552	195	191	222	4,995,786
Sovereign Dignity	5	3	37	4	4	3	54,298
Sovereign Don	14	6	100	8	13	17	101,034
Sovereignty	12	1	74	1	6	6	27,416
Soviet Lad	6	2	29	3	1	3	34,734
Soviet Star	13	7	63	9	7	7	174,711
Soy Numero Uno	29	12	186	15	19	25	260,479
Space Cup	3	2	37	4	8	11	145,392
Space Rider	2	2	23	3	3	3	43,067
Space Station	2	1	24	1	4	2	4,975
*Spaceman II	1	1	10	1	0	1	3,413

Broodmare Sire	Perf	Wnrs	Sts	1st	2d	3d	Purses
Spanish Drums	16	6	117	8	11	14	157,726
Spare Card	5	2	37	2	3	2	39,498
Sparkling Blade	1	1	4	1	1	0	12,642
Speak John	6	2	24	6	2	2	1,759,223
Special Blend	5	2	39	4	3	7	35,642
Special Lineage	11	6	59	7	13	5	81,219
Special Secret	11	2	71	2	6	7	52,262
Spectacular Bid	180	100	1160	164	145	133	4,267,865
Spectacular Turn	4	2	24	3	5	1	17,054
Speculating	1	1	3	2	0	0	12,670
Speed Play	2	2	14	2	1	0	20,313
Speeding Moment	1	1	5	2	0	0	32,060
Speedy Cure	1	1	14	2	4	4	41,680
Speedy Nijinsky	2	1	5	1	0	0	5,110
Speedy Prospect	14	3	91	6	9	6	112,730
Spellbound	8	2	36	3	1	3	30,907
Spend a Buck	130	61	778	98	100	107	2,425,094
Spicy Story	7	5	78	6	7	13	104,461
Spirit Rock	8	4	50	9	7	0	77,177
Spirited Boy	7	3	54	5	2	6	66,557
Splendid Courage	10	3	73	5	13	6	51,808
Splendid Hour	12	6	88	9	8	12	101,105
Splitting Headache	4	1	14	1	0	0	3,909
Sporran (FR)	1	1	3	1	0	0	22,560
Sport Royal	2	1	11	1	5	1	33,135
Sportful	3	3	27	5	1	7	32,535
Sportin' Life	51	13	307	20	33	29	219,194
Sports View	7	3	40	3	4	3	35,813
Spotter Bay	5	1	23	1	1	1	9,975
Spread the Rumor	25	8	151	16	21	23	290,477
Spring Double	27	15	203	24	30	28	594,562
Springhill (IRE)	4	1	25	1	4	7	32,059
Sprizzo	2	1	17	1	2	2	16,420
Spruce Baby	2	1	15	1	0	3	7,973
Spruce Bouquet	8	5	62	11	10	11	306,688
Spruce Needles	8	5	79	9	6	11	130,784
Spy Signal	12	4	68	4	0	6	31,089
Squabble	1	1	17	3	5	2	22,357
Squad Car	2	1	11	2	1	0	8,729
Squan Lake	2	1	18	3	0	3	13,481
Squire	3	2	25	3	2	4	54,386
Sr. Diplomat	7	3	76	3	8	7	64,022
Sri Pekan	1	1	2	1	0	0	29,400
St Puckle (GB)	2	1	11	1	0	1	38,775
St. Hilarion	4	1	37	1	2	5	21,708
St. Jovite	42	16	228	26	16	30	647,103
St. Petersburg	6	2	37	3	5	6	29,912
Stack	2	1	5	1	1	1	11,585
Stacked Pack	20	11	161	15	17	13	301,773
Staff Riot	7	4	37	7	2	5	39,723
Staff Writer	100	58	728	106	96	117	1,425,945
Stage Colony	3	1	17	1	2	1	11,695
Stage Door Johnny	62	34	439	53	48	57	777,670
Stage Presence	3	1	29	2	3	5	30,741
Stagtune	1	1	10	1	1	2	15,895
Stake Knife	2	2	16	2	1	2	6,642
Stalwart	173	93	1264	171	183	149	3,536,014
Stancharry	4	1	19	3	3	5	17,532
Stand Proud	2	1	13	1	1	1	3,629
Stanford	1	1	8	3	0	2	121,840
Stanstead	9	4	38	9	5	2	77,381
Star Choice	19	8	152	22	13	15	270,779
Star de Naskra	179	94	1193	164	155	156	4,783,238
Star Envoy	15	6	100	12	14	9	140,525
Star Gallant	29	14	210	26	22	19	579,500
Star of the Crop	13	5	70	15	11	7	296,060
Star Spangled	13	6	78	8	7	3	113,666
Stark Secret	1	1	9	2	1	0	13,468
Starry Night	1	1	12	2	3	0	13,931
Stars n' Stripes	3	2	23	2	0	3	18,910
State Dinner	74	29	468	51	61	39	668,436
Stately Don	34	15	200	23	39	30	949,597
Stately Native	2	1	8	1	0	2	15,370
Statoblest	2	1	12	1	3	0	52,950
Staunch Avenger	48	12	229	16	17	18	146,098
Stay the Course	6	2	34	3	5	2	25,958
Steady Beat	11	8	85	11	8	11	122,208
Steady Growth	33	14	218	21	31	19	557,107
Steel Emperor	3	3	12	4	1	2	11,796
Steel Heart	4	3	28	3	3	1	32,648
Steel Robbing	4	2	44	3	7	8	33,793
Steelinctive (GB)	5	4	33	4	6	3	70,607
Steinlen (GB)	12	7	96	14	3	17	222,044
Step Nicely	2	1	9	1	3	1	5,930
Stephen Ray	2	1	6	1	0	1	8,856
Sterling Key	2	1	10	2	0	1	8,326
Steve's Friend	5	3	48	5	8	4	102,591
Stevedore	1	1	7	1	2	2	31,375
Stick Together	3	1	23	1	2	4	11,530
Stifelius (GB)	2	2	18	4	3	3	34,393
Stiff Sentence	9	6	108	10	13	22	209,622
Stone County Kid	1	1	11	3	2	1	15,000
Stone Manor	2	1	12	1	0	0	4,954
Stonewalk	12	3	68	5	5	4	24,758
Stop the Bells	5	3	42	4	6	6	44,999
Stop the Fighting (IRE)	3	2	26	4	4	5	27,991
Stop the Music	183	83	1232	132	156	130	2,205,563
Storm a Head	1	1	16	1	2	1	12,543
Storm Bird	243	132	1531	210	207	177	6,801,246
Storm Boot	9	5	77	6	9	6	124,495
Storm Brewing	8	3	26	3	4	0	21,979
Storm Cat	221	105	1274	175	173	165	5,309,637
Stouci (GB)	1	1	1	1	0	0	24,000
Stradavinsky (IRE)	4	1	21	1	2	3	13,193
Straight Flush	4	1	27	2	2	3	8,981
Strategic Command	2	1	17	4	0	5	46,618
Stratford	3	1	26	1	0	4	15,463
Strawberry Road (AUS)	145	91	907	144	142	122	3,653,252
Strength in Unity	3	1	16	1	1	2	7,058
Strike Gold	93	41	505	68	62	59	1,444,821
Strike the Anvil	26	11	184	14	26	18	332,108
Strike the Gold	36	16	247	32	40	30	1,079,646
Strolling Along	19	8	85	14	11	10	353,163
Strong Bid	1	1	8	2	1	1	47,080
Strong Gale	2	1	6	1	1	3	23,900
Strong Performance	6	2	36	3	6	3	29,642
Struck Out	1	1	6	2	0	0	7,567
Stuka	11	8	78	15	10	8	142,114
Stutz Blackhawk	61	25	429	37	43	55	682,096
Stutz Keys	2	1	25	4	1	3	27,960
Stylish King	2	1	20	2	2	3	15,984
Su Ka Wa	1	1	7	2	0	1	15,950
Suave Dancer	2	2	14	4	1	3	265,080
Subpet	4	2	34	3	5	8	47,095
Such a Rush	1	1	6	2	0	1	4,109
Sucha Pleasure	14	5	62	6	11	8	50,303
Sultry Song	20	6	87	9	9	9	170,701
Summer Advocate	17	8	86	13	8	9	97,328
Summer Squall	75	37	510	65	70	60	1,625,731
Summer Time Guy	9	4	64	11	10	5	161,545
Summing	82	32	497	49	55	42	812,680
Sun and Shine (GB)	2	1	16	1	3	2	34,865
Sun Canyon	2	1	13	1	0	0	2,419
Sun Catcher	1	1	5	1	1	0	12,441
Sun Cross	1	1	5	1	1	0	15,654
Sun Master	9	3	55	5	7	8	49,607
Sun Power	15	5	114	6	9	12	79,592
Sun Seeker	1	1	12	2	0	3	5,185
Sun War Dancer	10	6	73	7	12	13	306,429
Sunny Clime	69	39	485	60	56	68	958,561
Sunny Feet	11	6	67	12	12	7	69,652
Sunny North	21	9	115	13	10	11	167,478
Sunny South	8	2	60	3	14	12	51,677
Sunny's Halo	166	84	1172	147	158	159	2,559,719
Sunrise Shower	3	1	7	1	1	1	5,744
Sunshine Drive	1	1	13	4	3	3	52,677
Sunshine Forever	47	20	302	33	38	33	623,433
Sunshine Today	6	1	31	1	6	0	39,404
Super Concorde	28	11	190	24	24	18	291,749
Super May	1	1	6	1	0	2	9,190
Super Moment	16	6	117	10	14	15	237,878
Super Native	3	2	20	5	4	3	64,382

RECORDS OF BROODMARE SIRES

Broodmare Sire	Perf	Wnrs	Sts	1st	2d	3d	Purses
Super Pleasure	2	1	18	2	2	3	11,707
Super Smile	1	1	10	1	1	1	32,633
Superbity	29	15	207	28	16	26	338,466
Superoyale	7	3	55	3	4	5	31,213
Superpower	1	1	12	1	1	2	52,575
Supremity	3	2	22	3	5	4	19,124
Supron	3	1	12	1	2	0	11,323
Sure Blade	3	1	10	1	0	1	12,442
Sure to Fire	3	2	21	3	1	2	7,207
Surreal	13	5	81	7	5	10	138,865
Surrey Regiment	2	1	6	1	1	0	6,628
Surumu (GER)	5	1	15	1	0	0	7,521
Sutter's Prospect	19	10	135	15	20	16	336,376
Suzanne's Star	5	1	24	1	1	3	12,851
Swap's Fire	2	2	22	2	1	7	45,298
Sweet Candy (VEN)	6	1	33	1	5	0	64,616
Sweetwater Springs	1	1	2	1	0	0	8,790
Swelegant	7	3	49	6	6	5	131,404
Swing Music	3	2	23	3	6	1	27,969
Swing the Harbor	3	1	6	1	1	0	6,525
Swing Till Dawn	56	24	350	34	38	41	542,046
Swingin Sway	5	3	27	4	8	2	63,749
Swiss Native	1	1	6	1	0	0	8,400
Switch (CHI)	1	1	8	1	3	1	18,935
Switch Partners	13	6	97	9	13	12	141,792
Swoon	13	5	82	9	9	16	124,332
Swoon Swept	1	1	13	5	1	5	42,768
Sword Dance (IRE)	52	23	345	48	34	48	752,581
Sword Dancer	1	1	4	1	0	0	3,241
Sword Devil	3	1	9	1	1	0	9,100
Synastry	54	26	270	40	32	31	535,520
Syncopate	9	3	55	4	7	2	182,185
Syntariat	5	1	34	2	3	2	18,207
Syrian Silver	1	1	12	1	1	1	13,470
Szerbusz	1	1	3	2	0	1	6,826
T. Bill Syndrome	3	2	26	3	8	4	24,483
T. Dykes	2	1	10	2	0	1	3,702
T. V. Alliance	3	2	33	2	6	2	39,455
T. V. Charger	5	3	45	4	7	5	38,580
T. V. Commercial	36	12	225	23	25	21	380,615
T. V. Lark	4	3	45	4	9	4	66,362
Tabasco Cat	9	4	44	4	5	6	223,862
Table Express	4	3	25	3	3	0	10,051
Table Play	2	1	10	1	0	2	7,940
Table Run	45	23	271	39	32	44	365,927
Tabun Bogdo	7	3	48	3	3	3	19,283
Taconeando (ARG)	2	1	17	1	2	0	13,692
Tactical Advantage	8	4	48	5	10	7	227,355
Taga	2	1	10	1	0	1	8,734
Tagish	6	3	27	5	1	2	81,509
Tai	5	1	19	2	1	2	24,987
Taj Alriyadh	22	10	125	17	13	16	465,824
Take Action	3	2	32	2	2	3	26,462
Take by Storm	4	2	36	2	3	3	9,499
Take Me Out	6	4	66	4	10	12	135,476
Take the Floor	13	4	88	8	14	7	99,912
Take the Rap	4	3	35	8	4	4	54,870
Take Your Partner (AUS)	4	1	26	1	3	4	39,153
Take Your Place	5	1	54	4	2	2	20,196
Talc	107	54	761	96	88	104	1,723,061
Talc Duster	1	1	11	1	0	3	10,540
Talent Town	6	1	31	1	2	4	31,982
Talented Native	5	3	39	5	6	6	21,284
Talinum	62	24	411	44	42	47	753,541
Talkin Man	3	2	23	2	2	1	20,355
Tall and Stately	5	1	37	3	1	2	22,370
Tally Ho the Fox	12	7	102	23	16	10	229,634
Tammany	2	2	23	3	3	6	18,927
Tampa Trouble	2	2	29	4	2	1	26,632
Tan Pronto	3	2	31	5	4	2	53,594
Tank's Prospect	75	34	510	48	50	64	1,123,410
Tanthem	28	12	210	18	27	23	252,421
Tantoul	20	13	151	20	18	24	203,088
Taos Tewa Dancer	1	1	5	1	1	1	10,598
Tap On Wood	2	2	20	3	1	3	38,588

Broodmare Sire	Perf	Wnrs	Sts	1st	2d	3d	Purses
Tap Shoes	12	5	92	10	10	12	104,251
Tapping Wood	2	1	8	1	0	0	8,090
Tarboosh	1	1	16	1	3	3	18,362
Targowice	4	3	28	8	2	6	117,601
Tariffic Prince	1	1	13	1	0	2	8,733
Tarleton Oak	9	3	50	4	4	4	53,839
Tarmoud	4	2	50	2	9	10	79,468
Tarsal	21	17	150	31	26	19	324,795
Tartar Chief	1	1	10	1	0	3	5,250
Tasso	55	29	429	39	55	44	739,306
Tasting	14	6	114	9	14	17	114,799
Tasty Victory	2	1	12	1	2	2	7,370
Tate Gallery	2	1	7	1	0	1	10,304
Taufan	12	3	73	8	10	6	160,759
Taunton	5	2	23	3	3	1	33,097
Tax Appeal	4	1	25	2	0	2	11,152
Taxachusetts	9	4	50	5	4	4	39,768
Taylor	1	1	9	1	1	3	12,110
Taylor's Falls	65	29	431	51	49	45	586,559
Taylor's Special	24	12	187	21	28	31	358,780
Technology	9	5	55	8	9	7	74,369
Tejabo	7	4	39	5	7	8	180,270
Tejano	63	32	456	64	61	61	1,163,190
Tell	20	9	129	11	13	14	123,912
Tell the Tale	8	3	61	5	7	3	50,675
Tella Fib	1	1	5	1	1	0	13,228
Temerity Prince	20	8	101	9	12	11	96,902
Temperence Hill	164	75	1117	122	115	138	1,938,017
Tempest Ways	2	1	21	1	0	3	13,102
Tempranero (CHI)	1	1	1	1	0	0	13,800
Temptor	6	2	18	4	0	4	19,372
Ten Gold Pots	28	10	203	16	26	16	252,481
Ten Keys	3	1	16	1	2	3	27,410
Tenacious Tom	3	2	12	3	1	1	21,472
Tenagain	1	1	11	2	1	1	12,720
Tender King (IRE)	2	1	17	1	3	3	48,943
Tentam	12	5	97	6	12	8	99,851
Terete	3	2	29	8	0	1	33,057
Terlago	2	1	22	4	9	4	15,414
Terresto	3	2	34	4	2	4	40,817
Tersanctus	1	1	12	2	2	2	23,538
Texas City	12	6	73	10	10	10	192,885
Texas Dancer	1	1	14	1	0	0	2,592
Text	25	8	153	11	21	14	218,700
Thaliard (GB)	1	1	6	1	0	0	7,065
Thanks to Tony	5	3	48	8	4	6	63,636
That's a Nice	23	10	152	14	16	14	238,169
Thatching (IRE)	12	7	80	14	11	12	272,421
The Astonisher	12	4	62	6	7	9	51,689
The Axe II	13	6	72	12	10	9	152,207
The Bart	14	4	66	8	8	3	71,629
The Breeze	4	1	33	2	4	6	20,582
The Captain	6	5	39	6	4	7	93,254
The Carpenter	3	1	17	1	5	4	12,992
The Cool Virginian	16	7	100	11	12	5	187,147
The Corps	2	1	22	2	0	1	13,053
The Flips Comin	1	1	6	1	2	0	25,750
The Gifted One	1	1	14	1	3	3	10,042
The Great Shark	1	1	16	5	3	3	52,235
The Hague	6	3	49	5	11	7	55,269
The Home Secretary	2	1	8	1	0	2	28,757
The Irish Lord	62	24	388	44	52	42	593,328
The Minstrel	106	50	639	81	68	80	1,847,676
The Prime Minister	22	12	164	17	14	21	276,001
The Pruner	14	4	72	9	8	4	173,392
The Real McCoy	3	1	30	2	1	6	16,774
The Reprobate	5	4	45	6	6	8	76,647
The Very Best	9	4	50	7	10	4	61,520
The Watcher	2	2	22	3	4	5	499,213
The Wicked North	5	3	38	4	8	6	131,365
The Wonder (FR)	9	3	54	4	3	9	57,798
Theatre Critic (IRE)	5	3	43	3	5	5	66,271
Theatrical (IRE)	150	67	885	115	119	104	2,591,247
Theatrical Charmer (GB)	1	1	11	1	1	2	4,433
Theurgist	1	1	15	1	4	3	13,474

Broodmare Sire	Perf	Wnrs	Sts	1st	2d	3d	Purses
Third and Lex	2	1	17	1	0	3	5,412
Third Martini	2	1	14	1	1	1	8,694
Third World	3	2	25	2	2	3	15,216
Thirty Eight Paces	63	29	421	48	45	49	719,352
Thirty Six Red	55	24	350	48	42	44	848,816
Thorn Dance	6	4	38	4	6	7	52,917
Three Bagger	3	2	27	4	3	4	24,265
Three Martinis	25	9	158	16	26	16	246,286
Thunder Cat	1	1	9	1	0	2	1,919
Thunder Gulch	12	6	70	8	15	10	276,642
Thunder O'Shay	1	1	11	3	3	0	25,850
Thunder Puddles	18	6	127	10	13	14	268,260
Tibaut Two	3	3	27	6	6	2	148,769
Tiffany Ice	26	11	141	16	25	17	330,355
Tillamook	1	1	7	2	2	1	4,360
Tilt the Odds	11	5	56	7	3	2	65,394
Tilt Top	4	3	32	3	3	1	28,812
Tilt Up	44	18	262	26	34	32	574,847
Tim Beam	1	1	12	1	5	0	12,613
Tim Plum	1	1	5	1	1	0	4,614
Tim the Tiger	9	2	54	4	6	4	90,696
Timbo	1	1	5	1	1	0	7,052
Time for a Change	161	76	979	126	116	110	2,086,343
Time to Explode	69	37	484	55	59	54	1,046,464
Time Whisper	2	1	22	2	3	6	11,149
Timebank	2	1	10	1	1	3	3,275
Timeless Moment	107	51	733	73	100	89	1,229,990
Timeless Native	72	28	405	51	48	43	848,543
Timely Albert	2	1	6	1	0	1	15,294
Timely One	8	4	59	4	11	9	139,159
Tinajero	10	4	60	6	3	2	32,758
Tinners Way	1	1	5	1	1	1	8,768
Tiny Rollick	1	1	5	2	1	0	7,492
Tip On Slew	2	1	12	3	1	2	8,043
Tisab	3	1	12	1	0	0	2,353
Titanic	11	4	99	5	12	5	159,033
To a Wild Kris	1	1	7	4	0	2	131,355
To B. Or Not	12	4	62	8	5	9	61,879
To the Quick	37	18	261	32	26	29	343,891
*Tobin Bronze	8	4	75	6	8	7	82,182
Told	8	2	50	3	5	7	33,860
Toll Key	5	3	27	3	4	2	50,120
Tolstoy	2	2	4	2	1	0	28,260
Tom Buck	20	6	109	9	11	11	48,354
Tom Cobbley	2	1	9	1	2	2	8,535
Tom Rolfe	80	29	538	53	45	72	901,793
Tom Swift	7	2	44	3	6	6	77,865
Tom Tulle	9	1	44	1	4	2	10,525
Tommy Bruce	1	1	13	3	1	2	7,040
Tong Po	11	6	112	13	17	8	206,139
Tonk	1	1	8	2	2	1	3,835
Tonkaton	12	2	49	4	3	6	60,500
Tonzarun	5	1	33	1	5	4	22,183
Toomuchholme	2	1	18	1	4	1	14,915
Toooverprime (IRE)	19	10	127	14	16	14	78,769
Top Avenger	35	14	220	20	16	25	249,373
Top Command	26	13	174	23	30	15	354,202
Top Horn	2	1	12	1	2	1	11,565
Top Rank	3	2	8	2	0	0	12,867
Top Trojan	1	1	14	3	2	2	53,180
Top Ville	9	4	60	9	14	2	197,399
Topsider	147	87	1087	148	143	125	3,418,305
Torcher	1	1	7	1	0	1	7,740
Toronto	4	3	37	3	3	5	28,907
Torquelle	2	2	6	3	1	1	18,194
Torsion	54	26	369	45	41	53	752,632
Tossofthecoin	4	1	18	1	2	1	7,224
Total Departure	4	1	25	1	0	3	37,543
Total Pleasure	1	1	16	2	1	1	14,236
Tough Assignment	10	2	63	4	2	11	65,365
Tough Critic	5	3	28	5	10	3	221,945
Tough Knight	29	13	159	22	18	31	249,535
Tour d'Or	23	9	111	16	15	18	393,675
Touring Dancer	2	1	11	1	2	1	12,174
Tout	7	1	33	2	1	2	10,058
Track Barron	82	33	603	47	60	75	832,717
Track Dance	4	1	30	1	3	1	20,510
Track Rebel	6	2	38	2	4	1	45,414
Track Reward	2	1	7	1	1	1	13,695
Traffic Breaker	3	1	26	3	4	3	19,894
Traffic Mark	6	2	41	5	2	2	42,870
Trail Dancer	2	1	9	1	0	2	9,072
Tralos	22	9	122	12	7	13	149,153
Transworld	30	11	203	21	19	24	302,707
Trapeze Dancer	2	1	14	1	0	0	6,102
Trapp Mountain	17	10	148	15	18	20	292,664
Travelling Music	12	5	75	7	8	14	120,958
Travelling Victor	39	19	223	29	31	29	524,015
Tread Lightly	1	1	10	1	0	1	4,964
Treasure Kay	4	1	21	1	4	2	36,970
Treasury Secretary	7	1	30	1	1	4	12,057
Tree of Knowledge	8	3	70	5	12	8	64,278
Trempolino	48	22	326	40	44	49	1,322,579
Trench Digger	4	2	36	3	2	5	34,467
Trenchant	2	1	18	1	2	2	28,207
Trepan	3	3	19	3	2	2	25,800
Tri Jet	108	46	623	67	74	85	1,323,997
Tri Swaps	3	2	30	3	5	2	22,019
Trial Basis	1	1	15	2	5	2	13,106
Tribal Line	1	1	7	1	2	1	2,497
Tribal Ruler	3	1	14	2	2	0	20,049
Tribal Unity	1	1	12	2	2	1	6,405
Trick Me	6	1	23	1	4	1	35,553
Tricky Creek	29	10	156	19	26	21	723,011
Tricky Fun	2	2	12	3	0	4	48,285
Tricky Six	1	1	10	1	1	1	9,940
Tridessus	16	5	77	7	6	9	107,893
Triocala	9	8	87	14	18	15	328,546
Triomphe	4	1	40	5	8	7	146,352
Triple Bend	13	2	75	5	6	6	82,487
Triple Crown	3	1	16	1	3	0	19,126
Triple Plum	1	1	12	1	2	1	21,256
Triple Schnap	3	2	26	3	0	1	30,961
Triple Sec	29	13	181	30	26	16	442,170
Triplicador (ARG)	2	1	7	1	0	0	3,920
Trojan Bronze	2	1	7	1	1	0	20,039
Tromos (GB)	1	1	4	2	1	0	127,715
Trooper Seven	8	2	43	3	3	8	34,357
Tropic Wave	2	2	30	5	3	3	110,010
Tropular	3	3	31	10	5	3	699,179
Truce Maker	8	3	54	10	2	11	172,972
True Colors	21	8	131	11	14	15	192,471
True Knight	14	6	74	7	7	11	60,010
Trulo	3	2	23	3	2	3	38,038
Truly Vain (AUS)	3	3	23	5	1	4	86,610
Trumpeteer	5	3	33	3	2	6	30,019
Trust the Kid	1	1	13	5	2	2	131,720
Truxton King	6	1	31	1	6	2	15,100
Tsuba	3	1	20	1	1	4	16,186
Tsunami Slew	89	44	615	79	53	69	1,151,623
*Tudor Black	5	2	44	3	4	4	26,457
Tudor Frank	2	1	13	4	0	0	11,944
*Tudor Grey	4	2	21	2	1	2	19,869
Tumble Lane	1	1	6	1	1	0	3,815
Tumble Lark	2	2	16	2	3	2	36,768
Tumble Wind	2	1	34	4	5	5	25,103
Tumbler	7	3	53	5	4	10	93,492
Tuneful Tip	3	2	20	3	6	1	42,831
Tunerup	80	40	551	61	75	64	1,520,887
Tunic	2	2	26	3	5	4	38,160
Turf Hero	1	1	7	1	1	1	6,624
Turfland	1	1	8	1	4	1	15,223
Turkey Shoot	31	15	185	29	19	16	544,058
Turkoman	103	45	665	81	85	75	1,827,348
Turn and Count	8	2	58	3	14	6	80,179
Turn Right	1	1	10	3	0	0	12,914
Turn to Bo	6	2	47	2	3	6	34,265
Turn to Mars	16	7	111	13	12	21	143,237
Turn to Reason	9	6	72	9	7	3	154,669
Turnberry	7	2	34	5	3	5	38,103

Broodmare Sire	Perf	Wnrs	Sts	1st	2d	3d	Purses
Turnbuckle	11	6	81	11	2	12	128,796
Turnverein	4	1	21	2	2	2	20,945
Turville (FR)	4	2	21	2	2	0	13,005
Twice Bold (IRE)	1	1	10	1	0	2	6,402
Twice Burned	14	10	100	14	13	13	98,412
Twice Elegant	1	1	2	1	0	0	3,720
Twice Worthy	6	3	42	5	10	4	125,235
Twig Moss (FR)	1	1	16	3	7	1	35,960
Twilight Agenda	29	11	211	18	20	24	243,501
Twining	9	4	41	6	5	7	95,665
Twist the Axe	2	1	18	1	2	4	9,694
Two Davids	15	7	90	16	17	16	209,726
Two Punch	144	78	1000	128	113	108	3,572,566
Two's a Plenty	12	10	106	24	15	11	653,285
Tyrant	25	13	186	21	20	15	196,835
Tyrone Terrific	5	1	28	1	8	0	30,745
U. S. Flag	33	19	229	30	22	28	583,970
Ulan	4	1	31	4	3	1	36,177
Ultimate Pleasure	2	2	20	2	1	1	7,114
Ultimate Pride	2	1	12	3	2	2	35,962
Ultramate	3	1	16	1	3	2	25,060
Ulysses	3	1	13	1	0	1	24,575
Unaccounted For	6	4	30	4	5	3	51,186
Unbridled	78	34	458	58	44	61	1,912,790
Unbridled's Song	3	1	18	1	1	2	41,583
Uncle Georger	2	1	11	2	2	3	7,997
Under Orders	2	1	17	1	3	1	9,584
Under Tack	8	5	77	7	12	17	82,029
Under the Table	3	1	24	1	3	1	13,409
Unfuwain	4	4	25	5	2	4	124,202
Unite	8	3	64	6	6	5	119,315
United Holme	4	2	27	2	5	4	31,564
Universal	2	2	15	5	0	2	24,267
Unmistaken	6	4	60	9	6	7	50,087
Uno Roberto	3	1	12	1	1	1	17,580
Unpredictable	29	13	212	20	26	25	355,277
Unreal Currency	3	1	27	1	5	3	18,990
Unreal Zeal	77	43	606	98	80	67	2,018,292
Unzipped	17	11	128	15	16	11	326,646
Upmost	14	5	92	7	8	12	230,520
Upper Bend	1	1	9	2	1	1	10,684
Upper Case	28	12	179	19	12	21	272,643
Upper Nile	43	22	304	42	45	29	736,676
Uprising	6	2	36	3	6	4	38,795
Ups	2	2	13	3	3	3	97,453
Upton	3	2	23	3	5	2	22,480
Vaal Reef	16	9	99	14	12	10	221,580
Vacarme	1	1	8	1	0	0	9,550
*Vaguely Noble	50	21	286	41	28	33	566,572
Val de l'Orne (FR)	74	33	498	54	56	60	1,061,581
Valdali (IRE)	2	1	18	1	2	1	17,547
Valdez	23	9	198	18	31	22	286,596
Valedor	2	1	9	1	1	0	37,920
Valet de Pied (FR)	5	2	38	4	5	3	65,518
Valiant Lark	2	1	9	3	3	0	36,300
Valid Appeal	302	164	1968	284	256	257	5,939,964
Valioso	3	2	32	5	8	5	84,627
Valiyar	3	2	26	4	1	5	79,741
Valley Crossing	13	4	69	5	10	10	129,418
Van Go	1	1	8	1	2	1	34,660
Vanlandingham	64	31	457	56	62	53	1,210,683
Varennes	1	1	5	2	0	1	38,977
Varick	7	3	45	4	2	7	93,094
Variety Road	16	7	96	14	11	13	140,835
Vast Empire	2	1	13	1	3	2	20,144
Vatina	1	1	5	1	0	0	5,251
Vayrann	1	1	11	1	0	3	33,670
Vegas Vic	3	1	14	1	1	2	5,273
Vencedor	15	12	118	13	9	10	182,402
Vencedor's Return	1	1	5	1	0	0	2,848
Ventriloquist	7	2	31	2	4	2	54,075
Veraneante	1	1	12	2	2	1	13,648
Verbatim	80	34	510	61	47	48	852,132
Verification	10	2	56	2	4	6	85,021
Vermont	4	3	34	11	4	3	104,217
Vernon Castle	10	5	75	7	12	6	102,696
Vertee	1	1	10	2	1	1	31,776
Verzy	12	7	91	9	16	11	132,242
Vice Lucky	1	1	8	1	2	3	3,510
Vice Regal (NZ)	4	2	30	3	8	1	100,830
Vice Regent	237	120	1623	227	205	213	5,229,968
Viceregal	1	1	6	1	1	2	14,630
Vicksburg	9	3	46	5	7	2	110,508
Victor's Gent	5	3	18	3	2	0	46,398
Victoria Park	2	1	20	1	5	0	20,782
Victorian Double	2	2	15	2	1	1	5,537
Victorian Line	3	1	29	1	2	1	18,970
Victorian Prince	14	6	111	10	17	17	246,488
Victoriate	3	1	20	1	1	6	56,283
Victorious	9	5	83	11	12	10	114,289
Victory Stride	21	6	162	7	13	22	115,614
Victory Times	1	1	11	2	3	1	11,850
Video Ranger	3	1	13	1	3	1	11,562
Vigors	140	74	1038	130	121	95	1,967,966
Villamor	21	10	150	13	18	15	181,419
Vilzak	27	12	173	18	19	18	478,001
Vindaloo	4	1	20	3	4	4	63,594
Vinnie the Viper	1	1	11	3	2	1	21,158
Vintage Proof	1	1	13	1	5	1	16,655
Violado	5	3	24	4	1	4	13,755
Virginia Boy	2	2	23	2	3	3	17,189
Visible	5	2	36	3	2	1	48,764
Visier	4	2	30	3	2	6	97,884
Vision	4	3	31	4	7	2	100,987
Vital Envoy	2	2	4	2	0	1	16,758
Vitality	1	1	12	1	5	3	9,214
Vitriolic	8	2	47	3	8	4	24,468
Vittorioso	4	1	33	2	4	4	17,259
Viva Maxi	1	1	6	1	0	0	1,585
Vodika Collins	5	1	30	5	2	2	51,035
Voom Voom	4	1	35	1	4	4	11,563
Vornorco	1	1	6	1	0	0	4,623
Vuela Vuela	1	1	11	3	2	1	61,176
Vying Victor	8	2	38	4	6	8	63,716
W. D. Jacks	12	7	77	10	10	12	129,276
Wage Raise	3	1	20	1	2	2	21,630
Waj. Jr.	2	1	16	1	3	1	7,386
Wajima	60	23	422	34	41	57	497,839
Waki Bob	2	1	4	1	0	1	7,242
Waldmeister	3	3	21	5	1	2	91,565
Walesa	7	4	40	6	8	4	85,389
Walker's	5	1	28	1	3	5	20,376
Wall Street Dancer	5	3	26	6	3	3	45,913
Wallenda	4	1	23	1	6	1	11,087
Wallet Lifter	2	1	25	1	2	7	6,238
Wander Kind	25	10	165	19	22	26	334,003
Waquoit	89	49	640	95	97	89	2,191,630
War	19	10	133	13	10	17	278,900
War Deputy	3	2	13	2	3	2	129,351
War of Words	5	1	34	3	1	4	25,650
War Secretary	1	1	3	1	0	0	8,820
Ward McAllister	5	3	38	5	4	3	36,778
Ward Off Trouble	5	5	49	5	3	1	41,699
Wardlaw	13	5	106	9	13	7	118,803
Warm Front	3	1	16	1	1	5	28,614
Warning (GB)	9	2	38	2	8	8	113,077
Warrshan	1	1	6	1	2	0	13,255
Wasa	2	1	8	1	0	0	5,585
Washington County	13	5	80	12	6	14	187,660
Wassl	4	1	18	2	3	3	52,238
Watch Your Step	1	1	16	2	2	2	9,165
Water Bank	45	28	318	46	35	38	713,590
Water Gate	1	1	12	1	3	1	10,376
Wavering Monarch	123	64	805	107	89	101	1,980,966
Wayne's Crane	34	16	236	34	22	21	382,183
Wayward Ace	3	1	25	1	1	2	35,156
Wedding Ring	5	1	23	1	3	2	16,469
Weekend Guest	4	2	21	3	4	3	37,444
Weimar	1	1	11	1	0	3	6,146
Welcome Roan	1	1	7	1	0	0	3,159

Broodmare Sire	Perf	Wnrs	Sts	1st	2d	3d	Purses
Welcome Suitor	2	1	12	2	1	2	10,578
Well Decorated	192	108	1413	180	170	175	2,857,505
Well Mannered	5	1	21	1	1	1	17,426
Well Written	2	1	12	2	0	2	6,104
Welsh Idol (GB)	1	1	4	2	0	2	4,089
Welsh Legend	4	2	22	2	0	1	35,195
Welsh Pageant (FR)	6	5	34	6	10	3	886,746
Welsh Saint	4	1	22	3	2	0	11,293
Weshaam	14	3	76	4	3	10	140,416
West Boy (BRZ)	1	1	7	1	0	0	3,679
West by West	17	12	99	18	7	8	183,961
West Coast Scout	3	3	26	3	4	4	44,897
Western Miner	1	1	16	1	0	1	14,025
Western Playboy	8	6	68	12	10	11	287,838
Western Series	3	1	17	2	1	2	35,148
Western Trick	20	6	122	14	21	10	177,373
Westheimer	13	3	113	4	9	14	64,596
Westmann Dust	3	2	26	2	0	1	9,844
Westway	1	1	6	1	0	1	4,560
Whadjathink	4	2	15	5	1	1	105,955
What a Gent	9	5	69	11	12	8	129,032
What A Guest (IRE)	3	1	18	1	1	3	28,446
What a Hoist	4	2	18	4	3	1	30,962
What a Pleasure	41	16	301	28	17	32	372,948
What a Romance	3	1	27	3	4	7	34,069
What a Shock	1	1	8	1	0	2	11,736
What a Spell	9	7	63	11	6	9	126,847
What a Spy	2	1	7	1	0	1	1,005
What a Threat	2	1	16	2	3	2	14,281
What Luck	63	33	480	57	76	66	1,101,308
What's Dat	3	1	15	1	3	4	26,108
Whatever For	1	1	5	1	0	0	3,060
Whatsyourpleasure	3	1	23	2	1	3	26,608
Wheatly Hall	8	6	68	11	13	10	112,107
Wherewithal	1	1	5	1	1	0	3,520
Whirl Cite	3	2	11	2	0	1	12,998
Whirling Saucer	1	1	11	2	2	0	9,642
Whiskey Road	5	4	41	6	7	11	201,223
White Bridle	3	1	20	1	1	2	30,985
White Clover	1	1	9	2	0	1	72,232
White Fir	8	3	56	3	9	10	37,027
*White Gloves II	1	1	7	1	0	3	13,960
White Mischief	7	2	44	3	3	5	85,758
White Rammer	10	1	46	3	3	4	28,266
White Spangles	1	1	8	1	0	2	4,428
Whitesburg	50	19	297	41	38	38	702,209
Whitney Tower	6	3	31	4	6	4	94,552
Who's Fleet	6	3	64	7	16	14	163,078
Who's for Dinner	14	8	111	19	11	17	185,704
Whodunit	1	1	11	1	0	1	5,664
Whose That Guy	1	1	13	1	1	1	6,181
Wig Out	6	1	26	1	3	8	92,237
Wild Again	247	129	1559	209	210	197	4,800,658
Wild Bill	6	2	19	2	1	2	9,248
Wild Catch	1	1	7	1	2	0	15,650
Wild Surf (IRE)	5	4	56	10	12	9	65,332
Will Hays	3	1	10	3	0	2	9,348
Will Win	15	4	91	10	12	17	163,279
Willard Scott	4	1	15	1	3	3	36,926
William Lawrence	2	1	10	1	1	1	2,612
Williamstown	3	2	15	2	1	3	56,763
Willie Pleasant	1	1	10	1	1	3	21,729
Willing Worker	4	1	25	1	0	2	8,917
Willow Hour	23	13	167	16	29	19	165,348
Win Dusty Win	1	1	23	1	0	0	3,540
Winaben	2	2	17	2	4	3	10,805
Wincoma's Torque	2	1	7	1	0	1	2,417
Wind and Wuthering	11	4	69	9	7	4	105,276
Wind Flyer	5	2	22	4	6	3	44,901
Winds of Thought	5	2	45	4	9	8	24,637
Winds of Winter	13	6	88	9	3	7	97,198
Windy Sands	4	1	23	2	5	1	15,354
Windy Tide	10	5	60	6	10	12	39,652
Wing Out	16	5	89	6	13	6	57,324
Winged T.	10	6	81	8	18	7	99,954
Winged Universe	3	2	23	3	6	1	42,085
Wingmead	3	2	20	2	3	4	14,921
Winning	1	1	5	1	1	0	18,760
Winning Hit	23	11	152	17	18	18	156,380
Winrightt	9	4	44	4	2	2	60,211
Winter Flower (ARG)	1	1	8	3	1	1	27,150
Winterset	4	2	33	7	4	3	49,099
Wise Exchange	12	7	103	11	15	11	199,278
Wise Times	16	6	123	15	15	16	299,406
Wishful Thinker	1	1	11	1	5	1	9,025
With Approval	107	48	700	82	89	89	2,349,032
With Caution	4	2	32	3	4	2	18,512
Within Hail	2	2	12	5	1	1	82,280
Witness Tree	5	2	43	3	2	5	30,590
Wolf Power (SAF)	142	66	947	119	142	106	2,142,233
Wolf Touch	2	1	6	1	0	0	3,516
Wolfgang	4	1	30	1	3	1	36,847
Wolfhound	3	3	16	4	1	0	40,632
Wolfie's Rascal	1	1	9	1	0	1	3,430
Wonder Lark	4	2	34	2	2	7	43,667
Woodman	207	122	1422	212	182	174	5,095,320
Wop Wop	1	1	4	1	0	0	9,824
Word Pirate	1	1	9	1	1	4	11,210
World Appeal	86	52	646	94	90	77	1,574,318
World Court	10	5	61	7	14	6	143,931
Worldwatch	9	3	53	6	10	10	338,353
Worthy Endevor	4	1	10	1	2	0	1,779
Wrangle	1	1	11	1	0	2	8,882
Write Off	3	1	17	2	1	2	20,593
Wronsky	4	2	14	3	2	0	50,245
Yallah Native	2	1	14	3	1	0	9,919
Yankee Fan	2	1	16	1	2	2	11,784
Yarnallton Native	3	1	12	1	1	1	5,344
Ye	7	2	29	2	2	1	26,673
Ye Ye Prince	1	1	9	1	0	0	7,088
Yes I'm Blue	6	2	37	5	2	0	121,988
Yesterdays Hero	10	8	86	11	5	10	156,759
You and I	5	3	26	3	6	1	84,180
Youmadeyourpoint	15	9	116	11	9	19	155,819
Young Bob	9	1	52	1	5	7	59,288
Young Commander	3	1	13	1	0	0	41,289
Young Devil	3	1	8	1	0	0	6,363
Young Native	1	1	13	5	2	3	27,610
Young Ralph	3	1	10	1	3	1	35,915
Youth	8	1	32	1	2	2	19,748
Yukon	67	31	441	44	56	50	1,055,170
Yukon Eagle	6	3	38	7	4	1	60,757
Zacky Do	3	1	18	3	3	2	15,320
Zafarrancho (ARG)	15	8	125	14	19	9	237,888
Zafonic	8	5	40	9	5	4	150,141
Zaizoom	8	3	75	3	11	6	41,781
Zalipour	2	1	21	3	2	0	24,142
Zamboni	18	7	115	16	16	16	343,904
Zante (IRE)	2	1	13	1	0	2	4,283
Zanthe	19	9	124	12	14	19	304,594
Zarbyev	21	10	127	17	15	16	382,660
Zen	50	24	329	43	44	48	719,350
Zevi	3	3	28	6	5	1	62,190
Ziad	21	11	128	13	18	13	239,997
Zie World	4	1	12	1	3	3	15,564
Ziggy's Boy	34	10	217	13	21	35	211,008
Zilzal	23	14	128	17	13	21	593,518
Zingalong	5	2	42	2	3	5	25,448
Zino	2	1	18	1	1	2	26,440
Zinov	11	5	84	7	10	13	124,159
Zodiac	3	2	27	3	10	2	29,493
*Zografos	4	1	29	1	2	1	13,371
Zonic	16	9	102	13	9	14	128,094
Zoning	8	1	46	1	2	2	19,551
Zoot Alors	13	6	78	11	13	12	104,304
Zulu Tom	6	2	44	3	6	9	23,531
Zuppardo's Love	2	1	15	2	3	0	59,853
Zuppardo's Prince	72	35	409	52	50	47	863,173